1990-91

Fourteenth Annual Edition

Volume I

Educational Communications, Inc.

The students listed in this regional volume attend school in the following states:

Alabama, Connecticut, Delaware, District of Columbia, Florida, Georgia, Kentucky, Maine, Maryland, Massachusetts, Mississippi, New Hampshire, New Jersey, New York, North Carolina, Ohio, Pennsylvania, Puerto Rico, Rhode Island, South Carolina, Tennessee, Vermont, Virgin Islands, Virginia and West Virginia.

Compilation of the copyrighted matter published in this volume has required considerable time, and has been carried out only at great expense. The copyrighted matter contained herein is intended for the exclusive use of our subscribers. No information contained in this volume may be key punched, entered into a computer, or reproduced in any manner for any purpose whatsoever. The use of any such information as a mailing list, either in whole or in part, is strictly forbidden unless authorized in writing by the publisher. The entire contents have been checked and cannot be copied without detection. Infringements will be prosecuted.



Educational Communications, Inc.
[illegible]
[illegible], IL [illegible]

Printed in U.S.A.
ISSN [illegible]
ISBN [illegible]
LC [illegible]

# The National Dean's List®

1990-91

## Fourteenth Annual Edition

Volume I

Educational Communications, Inc.

The students listed in this regional volume attend school in the following states:

Alabama, Connecticut, Delaware, District of Columbia, Florida, Georgia, Kentucky, Maine, Maryland, Massachusetts, Mississippi, New Hampshire, New Jersey, New York, North Carolina, Ohio, Pennsylvania, Puerto Rico, Rhode Island, South Carolina, Tennessee, Vermont, Virgin Islands, Virginia and West Virginia.


721 N. McKinley Rd.
Lake Forest, IL 60045

Printed in U.S.A.
ISBN #1-56244-019-5
ISBN #1-56244-018-7 (2 Volume Set)
LC #79-642835

ECI

# Table of Contents

PAUL C. KROUSE
*Publisher*

# Publisher's Message
## *We Need You*

Congratulations to the outstanding students being honored now in the 14th Annual Edition of THE NATIONAL DEAN'S LIST. Your academic achievements indicate that you are all gifted students who know how to get the most out of your talents, skills and abilities and how to focus on well defined objectives. Your achievements would also suggest that you are individuals with great promise and potential.

Where you direct your energies and how you define your goals in the future represent individual decisions that many of you have probably already made. Certainly for most of you, starting and advancing your careers will be a number one priority, perhaps fueled by the incentive to pay off educational loans. Some of you may be contemplating starting families of your own soon and some of you are already working to support families, a responsibility which requires considerable effort.

At this time I want to encourage you to allocate time and effort for civic responsibilities, in addition to your own individual needs and desires. Your involvement and participation in government is crucial now. As well educated, high achieving students and citizens your voices need to be heard, your views need to be known, your commitment needs to be felt.

Today, the problems we confront as a nation are varied and plentiful. Whatever your special interests may be, there is an area where you can be helpful. Our educational systems are in dire need of repair and reform, and access to the better systems is not equal for everyone. Our federal budget deficit is stifling economic growth and jobs and opportunities are shrinking, not growing, for even our best students. The debt you and your children will inherit is staggering. Social programs appear to be perpetuating an underclass and locking too many people into an existence of despair. The war on drugs is not going well and crime on our streets is rampant. Environmental concerns, healthcare costs, the homeless and the hungry represent problems which must be addressed immediately. I could go on, but you get the idea.

Our nation's problems will not magically disappear. To be sure, solving our problems will require considerable effort, sacrifice and pain. Your activism is needed, no matter what your political views or social bent. As representatives of the best and brightest our nation has produced it is important that you communicate your views to your government representatives at the local and national levels. Your participation as a group gives you influence, your vote gives you power. Use it.

Certainly many of you are already concerned and involved citizens. To you I can only say keep it up. To those of you who haven't had the time or inclination to venture beyond your individual responsibilities lately, I urge you to get involved now. We need you. Your country needs you.

# Program Highlights

This year, in two separate regional volumes we are honoring approximately 110,000 high achieving students. Most of these students were nominated by deans and registrars representing 2,400 colleges and universities.

To provide listed students with meaningful recognition among institutions and individuals concerned with achievement, the appropriate regional edition is distributed to all participating colleges and universities and made available to over 1,000 of the largest public libraries in the nation. This wide distribution enables honored students to view the book with their listing conveniently and at no cost.

Other valuable educational services for honored students include a scholarship program of twenty-five awards of $1,000 each (see current winners beginning on page XI), and the student referral service which links listed students with prospective employers and/or graduate/professional schools.

Of course, recognition in THE NATIONAL DEAN'S LIST® is not contingent on any fees whatsoever to students or schools. Legitimate honors should not cost the recipient money.

# Guest Editorials

WILLIE T. HOWARD
*Professor*
*School of Education*
*Howard University*
*Washington, D.C.*

## WILLIE T. HOWARD

Congratulations to each of you on your election to THE NATIONAL DEAN'S LIST. You are among a select group of people who epitomize the highest ideals of dedication, achievement and scholarship.

You have the opportunity to play a significant role in the future development of this nation. Many challenges await you. The future of our country will one day rest in your hands.

I hope your inclusion in THE NATIONAL DEAN'S LIST will be viewed by you as the beginning of a series of successes designed to make our world a better place for all people.

DR. CLAIRE RONDEAU BARRETT
*Associate Professor*
*School of Education*
*Seton Hall University*
*South Orange, New Jersey*

## DR. CLAIRE RONDEAU BARRETT

Congratulations to the young men and women whose names appear in the current edition of THE NATIONAL DEAN'S LIST. This honor represents not only your quest for knowledge and wisdom but the actual achievement of these high priorities. You dreamt of achieving many personal and educational goals when you entered the collegiate environment. This honor gives testimony that many of these goals have been realized. Without a doubt, they were not accomplished without a great deal of searching, diligence, courage, and perseverance on your part. May you continue to develop these admirable qualities in your milieu whether this be in furthering your education or in finding your rightful place in the professional world.

As parents, educators, and others, who love and admire you, we applaud you for your success and we entertain the hope that you will always be among those who dare to be different and who make a difference in this world of ours. We know that our destiny in many areas will depend upon your willingness to be as responsible and dedicated as you are today. "You are the hope of tomorrow" is not a worn-out cliché, but a statement that rings true in the history of mankind. It is now your turn to step forward and make our tomorrows in a free society safer, healthier, more educationally sound, and more fulfilling for both young and old. Your input will indeed make the difference in politics, education, science, business, art, and in other fields of human endeavor. You have been blessed with many gifts and have sought to develop and use them. Let us hope that for you this will be a lifelong commitment.

Tomorrow is yours — embrace it with the same enthusiasm, ideals, and sense of responsibility which you manifest today. In order to do this, live each day with an attitude of openmindedness, critical thinking, unflinching resiliency, and, most of all, humanistic interpersonal relations. As such, your life will be filled with rewards and satisfactions of significant value and untold lives will be better for having journeyed down the days with you.

JOSEPH S. DOMITRZ
*Dean*
*College of Business and Economics*
*University of Wisconsin*
*Whitewater, Wisconsin*

## JOSEPH S. DOMITRZ

Your selection for this honor is primarily based upon your academic achievement as measured by the grades you have received. This is a noteworthy accomplishment and one deserving congratulations. Success as a person or in your career, however, is more than achieving good grades. It involves a concern and a willingness to help others, a responsibility to maintain high ethical standards and a belief in doing the best that you can.

Many individuals have contributed to your current success. As you continue in your career, I encourage you to give of yourself to your community. It does not matter whether your contributions are financial or personal time. What is important is your willingness to help others to achieve their goals in life or to make your church, neighborhood or community a better place for everyone.

Best wishes for continued academic and personal success.

DR. BRUCE M. DAVIDSON
*Former Academic Dean*
*U.S. Naval Academy*
*Annapolis, Maryland*

DR. BRUCE M. DAVIDSON

The tide is in and soon the currents of events shall sweep you forward to new adventures and increased responsibilites. I am reminded of a time in history some 500 years ago when Columbus sought to find a new route to the Orient. Since the earth was flat, this idea was preposterous. In response to his appeal to the Senate of Genoa for financial backing, they appointed a committee which generated a 964 page report discouraging the venture adding,

> "We feel that you will be quite pleased with the output of the progressive, forward-looking committee of profound scholars. Incidentally, there was one additional member of the committee, a rather brash and impetuous young engineer, lately of Florence, who was sent in place of the ailing Dr. Taglatti of the University of Milan. Though he came highly recommended, he showed his immaturity and poor judgment by advocating that the voyage itself be initiated immediately. Investigation proved him to be quite eccentric (he talks of flying machines and fancies himself an artist), and he was therefor dismissed from the committee. He is the son of a Florentine notary and in case you desire to contact him, his name is Leonardo da Vinci."

Our world still abounds with skeptics. Who predicted a united Germany? Does anyone believe Europeans can agree on a common currency? Is it possible to have a two party system in Russia?

Where the human race is involved, the future is uncertain but change will surely come. Its form and impact will depend upon the vision, determination, and understanding of your generation. You hold in your hands the opportunity to lead in the ever changing world. Do not hesitate. Do not shirk your calling. It is never too soon to pick up the reins and be a part of the effort to make this world a better place for its inhabitants. Congratulations to all of you. May your future be even more successful and rewarding as you seek challenges that will allow others to share in your rewards.

MOLLIE FRANCES DeHART
*Program Director for Undergraduate Studies*
*School of Music*
*Florida State University*
*Tallahassee, Florida*

MOLLIE FRANCES DeHART

It is with pleasure that I take this opportunity to congratulate those of you selected for inclusion in THE NATIONAL DEAN'S LIST!

In the pursuit of your educational and personal goals you have faced and overcome many challenges. To be listed in THE NATIONAL DEAN'S LIST indicates that you possess academic excellence, leadership, and personal qualities for success. The ambition, discipline, and perseverance displayed will continue to be valuable assets in the pursuit of your educational and professional goals.

The achievements you have attained carry an inherent responsibility and obligation to continue utilizing your talents and attributes to the fullest potential. The colleges and universities you represent applaud your achievements and share your pride. You are encouraged to continue your quest for excellence in all future endeavors.

EMILY QUINN POU
*Former Dean*
*College of Family & Consumer Sciences*
*The University of Georgia*
*Athens, Georgia*

EMILY QUINN POU

Welcome achievers! Welcome to a fast-paced, competitive world in which you have rightfully earned an honored place. With this welcome comes a challenge: Take your best and make it better — for you, your community, your nation and, ultimately, your world.

The bright minds, able bodies and enthusiastic outlooks represented by these pages in the current edition of THE NATIONAL DEAN'S LIST convince us that the potential for tomorrow's leaders has never been greater. We are proud of you all!

DONALD O. DEWEY
*Dean*
*School of Natural & Social Sciences*
*California State University*
*Los Angeles, California*

DONALD O. DEWEY

While you must feel honored to have been nominated for inclusion in THE NATIONAL DEAN'S LIST, we who have participated in its development are likewise honored by your presence in the volume. Outstanding academic performance demonstrates a University's true role — scholarly and academic achievement. After generations of recognition for athletes, cheerleaders, student political leaders, debaters and performers of every sort, the academic world has been laggard in granting similar notice to those of you who have excelled academically.

I trust that recognition of this sort will provide the inspiration which encourages continued success both within Academe and in your careers. The true mark of a University's success is the accomplishments of its alumni. Hence, our future is in your hands.

DR. B.K. MARKS
*Vice President for Academic Affairs & Student Services*
*Sam Houston State University*
*Huntsville, Texas*

DR. B.K. MARKS

Congratulations to each individual listed in this current edition of THE NATIONAL DEAN'S LIST. Your inclusion in this prestigious listing of our nation's finest student scholars is a tribute to your commitment to academic excellence and undoubtedly means that you have given an extra measure of time and effort to your studies. You may rightfully take pride in this accomplishment, and I assure you that you are a source of pride for the faculty and administration of thc cducational institution you represent.

Continue giving your best effort to all you attempt in life. As the hope of our nation's future, you must be committed to the solution of those problems facing our nation, including drugs, health and peace. Just as every generation of Americans has faced problems and has successfully found solutions to them, so will your generation. With outstanding individuals such as you, we face the future of our nation with confidence. Continue to give your best effort and you will reap great results for yourself and for mankind.

DR. S. NORMAN FEINGOLD
*Honorary National Director*
*B'nai B'rith Career & Counseling Services*
*President*
*National Career & Counseling Services*
*Washington, D.C.*

DR. S. NORMAN FEINGOLD

Another year has quickly passed. It is again time for me to share some thoughts with a new group of talented young adults who have already achieved excellence in scholastic ability, leadership and extracurricular activities.

Congratulations on your outstanding attainments and for your inclusion in this prestigious NATIONAL DEAN'S LIST. You represent a very special group of young men and women who have so much to offer your families, society, and yourselves.

Learn how to maximize your assets and minimize your limitations as you pursue the career of your choice.

These are not easy times. In a competitive, technological society there is an acceleration of both problems and opportunities for those who wish to grab a fistful of tomorrow. The questions are eternal, but the answers change.

For young men and women who have much to offer, values may be the hidden agenda as we approach the 21st century. Who am I? Where am I going? How am I going to get there? Why? The answers to these simple questions will make the big difference as we colonize new planets, but at the same time show we can live on earth. The destiny of the United States rests on your shoulders as you accept a meaningful role as a citizen who cares and does something about it.

You are the hope of today and tomorrow.

## JULIE COLLIER-ADAMS

JULIE COLLIER-ADAMS
*Vice President, Dean of Students*
*Goucher College*
*Baltimore, Maryland*

I would like to express my sincere congratulations to the individuals who have achieved the honor of being nominated to THE NATIONAL DEAN'S LIST. To be specific, I'd like to congratulate you for the drive and perseverance you have exhibited in order to attain this prestigious accomplishment.

As you pursue your career, I hope you will approach it with the same vigor and enthusiasm that has earned you your current status. I'm sure you will carry the quality of excellence into your future endeavors, whatever they will be.

Please do not forget the words of Eleanor Roosevelt —

> "It is easier to have no ambition and just keep on the same way every day and never try to do grand or great things. It is only those who have ambition and who try that meet with difficulties and they alone feel the disappointments that come when one does not succeed in what one was meant to do. Others say 'it was meant that we should not succeed — fate has so decreed it.' They do not think of it again. But those who have ambition try again and try until they at last succeed. It is only those who ever succeed in doing anything great."

## BLAINE R. PORTER

BLAINE R. PORTER
*University Professor*
*Brigham Young University*
*Provo, Utah*

Congratulations on being selected to have your name and biographical sketch included in THE NATIONAL DEAN'S LIST. This single honor is one more milestone that recognizes your success in the pursuit of excellence. The good news is, your greatest challenges and opportunities still lie ahead of you.

For some individuals, education means power and the opportunity to rise above other people. For them it means making more money, being smarter, being better. For these individuals the task is endless and filled with the frustrations of finding others who are smarter, have more status, or making more money. The power of education is not to be better than others, but rather it is the power and/or the opportunity to help others improve their lot. It enables one to serve more effectively, more meaningfully. Those who have had the opportunity to become educated, magnify their value as they contribute to the growth and betterment of other people.

For most of you, your immediate future will probably include the pursuit of furthering your education. In the process, I invite you to carefully examine your values and how you wish to invest your life. The world in which you live is changing at an unusually fast rate and in challenging ways. Never before have young people been faced with so many opportunities to have an impact upon the world. I extend a challenge to you now to use your education for the betterment of mankind.

Your name is included on a distinguished list of outstanding scholars. You will have an opportunity to be on many "lists" in your lifetime. These lists will represent powerful statements about you. On which lists will you be included? You have already demonstrated that you have the ability to excel. The opportunity now lies before you to seek, to find and to share with others a validated, usable system of human values that we believe in and devote ourselves to because they are true.

May the joy of being in service to your fellow human beings and the inner peace that comes from being true to yourself, be yours.

## KRISTIN DAVIDSON

KRISTIN DAVIDSON
*Assistant Dean for Administration*
*School of Nursing*
*University of Pennsylvania*
*Philadelphia, Pennsylvania*

Congratulations on the academic achievement you have been recognized for by being named to THE NATIONAL DEAN'S LIST. Each year it is a pleasure to submit the names of the outstanding students from this school who are in the top ten percent of the class, to join other students nationwide in this list. While grades and percentages are only one of the indicators of future performance and success, they are a means of identifying those most likely to continue to sustain outstanding achievement in the future.

Working in an academic institution brings many fringe benefits. One of the nicest is to be involved with young men and women who are enthusiastic, serious about their careers, and willing to make an effort to be the best they can be. The studies are not easy, but the satisfaction of doing well when that is sometimes difficult, is a reward that pays all of us back many times. I hope you all will find many more honors in life after you have left the academic world.

# Educational Communications Scholarship Foundation®

We are pleased to present the twenty-five scholarship winners from THE NATIONAL DEAN'S LIST® competitive awards program. Each student received a $1,000 award. Selection was based virtually entirely on merit and academic achievement with some consideration for leadership, extracurricular involvement and need for financial aid.

Since 1968, the Foundation has been funded almost entirely by the publishing company and has distributed over $1,300,000 to qualified students entering college. For the first fourteen years of THE NATIONAL DEAN'S LIST, a total of $262,500 has been distributed.

## 1990-91 National Dean's List Scholarship Winners

Robin Marie Abdullah
Billings, MT
Eastern Montana College
Billings, MT

Isaac Alonso
Eugene, OR
University of Oregon
Eugene, OR

Daniela Irmgard Bright
Colorado Springs, CO
Colorado Tech
Colorado Springs, CO

Robert Andrew Cardona
Berrien Springs, MI
Andrews University
Berrien Springs, MI

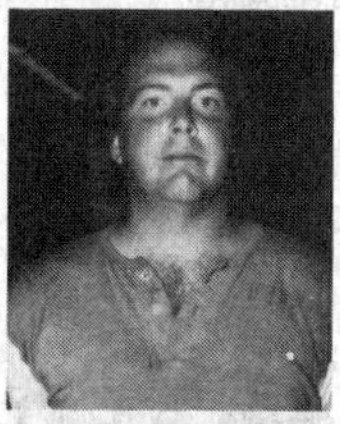

Ryan Ray Corman
Indianapolis, IN
Indiana University
Terre Haute, IN

Nadine Levy Coulton
Lauderdale Lakes, FL
University of Florida
Gainesville, FL

Karen Marie Darger
Colorado City, AZ
Mohave Community College
Kingman, AZ

Anthony Conway Dorsey
Severn, MD
Morehouse College
Atlanta, GA

Beverlin Eigner
Columbia, SC
Florida State University
Tallahassee, FL

Connie Jo Halvorson
Albert Lea, MN
University of Minnesota
Duluth, MN

Marie L. Hatton
Mobile, AL
Bishop State Community College
Mobile, AL

Neysa Gail Hess
Bayard, NM
Western New Mexico University
Silver City, NM

# 1990-91 National Dean's List Scholarship Winners

Deana Yolanda
Hopkins
Fayetteville, NC
Howard University
Washington, DC

Carmen Raquel Izcoa
Bayamon, PR
University of Puerto
Rico
Rio Piedras, PR

Penny Elizabeth
Jeffery
Mankato, KS
University of Iowa
Iowa City, IA

Lynn Marie Laitinen
Champion, MI
Wayne State
University
Detroit, MI

Theresa Ann Lams
Carsonville, MI
Western Michigan
University
Kalamazoo, MI

Carmen Iberia
Manrique
Cambridge, MA
Emerson College
Boston, MA

Mark Clifford
McFadden
Washington
Courthouse, OH
Ohio University
Chillicothe, OH

Carla Kay Newsome
Mesa, AZ
Arizona State
University
Tempe, AZ

Paula Marie
Nuernberger
Chaffee, NY
State University of
New York
Buffalo, NY

Charissa Leigh Palmer
Liberty, MO
Samford University
Birmingham, AL

Thanh Vincent Pham
Federal Way, WA
University of
Washington
Seattle, WA

Michael Alan Radake
Scheller, IL
Southern Illinois
University
Carbondale, IL

Amy Elizabeth Wright
San Diego, CA
Cornell University
Ithaca, NY

# Glossary of Abbreviations

**AB** ... Bachelor of Arts
**ACAD** ... Academic
**ACCT** ... Account (ant), (ing)
**ADM** ... Administration
**ADV** ... Advertising
**AM, AMER** ... American
**ASST** ... Assistant
**AS'N** ... Association
**ATH** ... Athletic
**AWD** ... Award

**BA** ... Bachelor of Arts
**BAE** ... Bachelor of Art Education; Arts in Education; Agricultural Engineering; Aeronautics; Aeronautical Engineering; Architectural Engineering
**BArch** ... Bachelor of Architecture
**BBA** ... Bachelor of Business Administration
**BCE** ... Bachelor of Chemical Engineering; Christian Education; Civil Engineering
**BChE** ... Bachelor of Chemical Engineering
**BD** ... Bachelor of Divinity; Board
**BE** ... Bachelor of Education; Engineering
**BEd** ... Bachelor of Education
**BEE** ... Bachelor of Electrical Engineering
**BES** ... Bachelor of Engineering Sciences; Science of Engineering
**BFA** ... Bachelor of Fine Arts
**BIE** ... Bachelor of Industrial Engineering
**BLS** ... Bachelor of Liberal Studies
**BMechEng** ... Bachelor of Mechanical Engineering
**BMus** ... Bachelor of Music
**BMusEd** ... Bachelor of Music Education
**BPharm** ... Bachelor of Pharmacy
**BPS** ... Bachelor of Professional Studies
**BRelEd** ... Bachelor of Religious Education
**BS** ... Bachelor of Science
**BSA** ... Bachelor of Science in Agriculture
**BSC** ... Bachelor of Christian Science
**BSCerE** ... Bachelor of Science in Ceramic Engineering
**BSE** ... Bachelor of Science in Education
**BSEE** ... Bachelor of Science Electrical Engineering; Elementary Education; Engineering & Economics
**BSFS** ... Bachelor of Science in Forestry Service; Foreign Service
**BSME** ... Bachelor of Science in Mechanical Engineering; Mining; Music Education
**BSN** ... Bachelor of Science in Nursing
**BT** ... Bachelor of Science in Theology; Teaching
**BUS** ... Business
**BVA** ... Bachelor of Science in Vocational Agriculture

**CNTR** ... Center
**CERT** ... Certificate
**CHMN** ... Chairman
**CO-CHMN** ... Co-Chairman
**CHEM** ... Chemistry
**COL** ... College
**COM** ... Committee
**CO** ... Company
**CORP** ... Corporation
**COUNC** ... Council
**COUNS** ... Counsel, (or), (ing)
**CTRY, CNTRY** ... Country
**CTY, CNTY** ... County

**DC** ... Doctor of Chiropractic
**DDS** ... Doctor of Dental Science
**DEPT** ... Department
**DIR** ... Director
**DIST** ... District
**DMA** ... Doctor of Municipal Administration; Musical Arts
**DMD** ... Doctor of Dental Medicine
**DPM** ... Doctor of Podiatric Medicine
**DVM** ... Doctor of Veterinary Medicine

**ED** ... Editor
**EDUC** ... Education
**ENG** ... Engineer
**ENGL** ... English
**EXEC** ... Executive

**FIN** ... Finance, (cial)
**FR** ... Freshman
**FRAT** ... Fraternity
**FRESH** ... Freshman

**GD** ... Graduate
**GOVT** ... Government
**GRAD** ... Graduate

**HON** ... Honor
**HOSP** ... Hospital

**INST** ... Institute

**JD** ... Doctor of Law
**JR** ... Junior

**LIB** ... Library (ian)
**LLB** ... Bachelor of Laws

**MA** ... Master of Arts
**MNGR** ... Manager
**MBA** ... Master of Business Administration
**MD** ... Doctor of Medicine
**MDiv** ... Master of Divinity
**ME** ... Master of Engineering; Education
**MED** ... Medical
**M, MEMB** ... Member
**MFA** ... Master of Fine Arts
**MGMT** ... Management
**MS** ... Master of Science
**MSW** ... Master of Social Work

**NATL** ... National
**NOM** ... Nominee, (ated)

**OD** ... Doctor of Optometry
**OFF** ... Office, (er)
**ORG** ... Organization

**PHARM** ... Pharmacist (ceutical)
**PhD** ... Doctor of Philosophy
**PHY ED** ... Physical Education
**PRES** ... President
**PUB** ... Public

**REP** ... Representative
**RN** ... Registered Nurse

**SAL** ... Salutatorian
**SCHL** ... Scholar
**SCHLSP** ... Scholarship
**SEC** ... Secretary
**SEN** ... Senate
**SR** ... Senior
**SERV** ... Service
**SO** ... Sophomore
**SOC** ... Society
**SOPH** ... Sophomore
**SOR** ... Sorority
**STU** ... Student

**TECH** ... Technical
**TREAS** ... Treasurer

**UNIV** ... University

**VAL** ... Valedictorian
**V-PRES** ... Vice President

# Professional Fraternities (Sororities)

ALPHA ALPHA GAMMA ............... Architecture
ALPHA BETA ALPHA ............. Library Science
ALPHA CHI SIGMA .................. Chemistry
ALPHA DELTA THETA ........ Medical Technology
ALPHA EPSILON RHO ............... Broadcasting
ALPHA ETA RHO ......................... Aviation
ALPHA KAPPA KAPPA .................. Medicine
ALPHA KAPPA PSI ........ Business and Commerce
ALPHA OMEGA ......................... Dentistry
ALPHA PSI ..................... Veterinary Medicine
ALPHA RHO CHI ...................... Architecture
ALPHA TAU ALPHA ........ Agricultural Education
ALPHA TAU DELTA ...................... Nursing
ALPHA ZETA ......................... Agriculture
ALPHA ZETA OMEGA .................. Pharmacy
ATLAS CLUB ......................... Osteopathy

BETA ALPHA PSI ..................... Accounting

DELTA KAPPA PHI ....................... Textiles
DELTA OMEGA ....................... Osteopathy
DELTA OMICRON ........................... Music
DELTA PI EPSILON ........... Business Education
DELTA PSI KAPPA .............. Physical Education
DELTA SIGMA DELTA .................. Dentistry
DELTA SIGMA PI .......... Commerce and Business Administration
DELTA SIGMA THETA .................. Pharmacy
DELTA THETA PHI .......................... Law

GAMMA ETA GAMMA ........................ Law

IOTA TAU SIGMA ..................... Osteopathy

KAPPA ALPHA MU .............. Photojournalism
KAPPA BETA PI ............................. Law
KAPPA DELTA EPSILON ............... Education
KAPPA DELTA PHI ..................... Education
KAPPA EPSILON ........................ Pharmacy
KAPPA PHI KAPPA .................... Education
KAPPA PI SIGMA .......... Commerce and Business Administration
KAPPA PSI ............................. Pharmacy
KERAMOS ................... Ceramic Engineering

LAMBDA KAPPA SIGNMA .............. Pharmacy
LAMBDA OMICRON GAMMA .......... Osteopathy

MU PHI EPSILON ........................... Music

NU BETA EPSILON ........................... Law

OMEGA DELTA ........................ Optometry
OMEGA EPSILON PHI ................. Optometry
OMEGA TAU SIGMA ........... Veterinary Medicine

PHI ALPHA DELTA ........................... Law
PHI ALPHA TAU ...................... Forensic Arts
PHI BETA ...................... Music and Speech
PHI BETA GAMMA ............................ Law
PHI BETA PI ............................. Medicine
PHI CHI ................................. Medicine
PHI CHI THETA ...... Business Administration and Economics
PHI DELTA CHI ........................ Pharmacy
PHI DELTA EPSILON .................. Medicine
PHI DELTA PHI .............................. Law
PHI EPSILON KAPPA .......... Physical Education
PHI GAMMA NU .......... Business and Economics
PHI LAMBDA KAPPA .................... Medicine
PHI MU ALPHA-SINFONIA ................. Music
PHI RHO SIGMA ......................... Medicine
PHI PSI ............................... Textile Arts
PHI SIGMA GAMMA ................... Osteopathy
PHI SIGMA PI ......................... Education
PHI THETA UPSILON .................. Optometry
PHI UPSILON OMICRON ......... Home Economics
PI LAMBDA THETA ..................... Education
PSI OMEGA ............................. Dentistry
PSI SIGMA ALPHA .................... Osteopathy

RHO PI PHI ............................ Pharmacy

SCARAB ............................. Architecture
SIGMA ALPHA IOTA ....................... Music
SIGMA DELTA CHI ..................... Journalism
SIGMA DELTA KAPPA ........................ Law
SIGMA SIGMA PHI .................... Osteopathy
SIGMA PHI DELTA ................... Engineering

TAU EPSILON RHO ........................... Law
THETA KAPPA PSI ...................... Medicine
THETA PSI ............................ Osteopathy

WOMEN IN COMMUNICATIONS ... Communications

XI PSI PHI .............................. Dentistry

ZETA PHI ETA .... Communication Arts and Science

# Women's Social Fraternities (Sororities)

ALPHA CHI OMEGA
ALPHA DELTA PI
ALPHA EPSILON
ALPHA GAMMA DELTA
ALPHA KAPPA ALPHA
ALPHA OMICRON PI
ALPHA PHI
ALPHA SIGMA ALPHA
ALPHA SIGMA TAU
ALPHA XI DELTA
CHI OMEGA
DELTA DELTA DELTA
DELTA GAMMA
DELTA PHI EPSILON
DELTA SIGMA THETA
DELTA ZETA
GAMMA PHI BETA
KAPPA ALPHA THETA
KAPPA BETA GAMMA
KAPPA DELTA
KAPPA KAPPA GAMMA
LAMBDA DELTA SIGMA
PHI MU
PHI SIGMA SIGMA
PI BETA PHI
SIGMA DELTA TAU
SIGMA GAMMA RHO
SIGMA KAPPA
SIGMA SIGMA SIGMA
THETA PHI ALPHA
ZETA PHI BETA
ZETA TAU ALPHA

# Men's Social Fraternities

ACACIA
ALPHA CHI RHO
ALPHA DELTA GAMMA
ALPHA DELTA PHI
ALPHA EPSILON
ALPHA GAMMA RHO
ALPHA GAMMA SIGMA
ALPHA KAPPA LAMBDA
ALPHA PHI ALPHA
ALPHA PHI DELTA
ALPHA SIGMA PHI
ALPHA TAU OMEGA
BETA SIGMA PSI
BETA THETA PI
CHI PHI
CHI PSI
DELTA CHI
DELTA KAPPA EPSILON
DELTA PHI
DELTA PHI KAPPA
DELTA PSI
DELTA SIGMA PHI
DELTA TAU DELTA
DELTA UPSILON
FARMHOUSE
KAPPA ALPHA ORDER
KAPPA ALPHA PSI
KAPPA ALPHA SOCIETY
KAPPA DELTA RHO
KAPPA SIGMA
LAMBDA CHI ALPHA
OMEGA PSI PHI
PHI BETA SIGMA
PHI DELTA THETA
PHI GAMMA DELTA
PHI KAPPA PSI
PHI KAPPA SIGMA
PHI KAPPA TAU
PHI KAPPA THETA
PHI LAMBDA CHI
PHI MU DELTA
PHI SIGMA EPSILON
PHI SIGMA KAPPA
PI KAPPA ALPHA
PI KAPPA PHI
PI LAMBDA PHI
PSI UPSILON
SIGMA ALPHA EPSILON
SIGMA ALPHA MU
SIGMA BETA KAPPA
SIGMA CHI
SIGMA GAMMA CHI
SIGMA NU
SIGMA PHI
SIGMA PHI EPSILON
SIGMA PI
SIGMA TAU GAMMA
TAU DELTA PHI
TAU EPSILON PHI
TAU KAPPA EPSILON
THETA CHI
THETA DELTA CHI
THETA TAU
THETA XI
TRIANGLE
ZETA BETA TAU
ZETA PSI

# Honor Societies

ALPHA CHI ............ Scholarship
ALPHA EPSILON ......... Agricultural Engineering
ALPHA EPSILON DELTA ............ Premedical
ALPHA KAPPA DELTA ............ Sociology
ALPHA KAPPA MU ............ Scholarship
ALPHA LAMBDA DELTA . Freshman Scholarship
ALPHA OMEGA ALPHA ............ Medicine
ALPHA PI MU ............ Industrial Engineering
ALPHA SIGMA MU ... Metallurgical and Materials Engineering
ALPHA SIGMA NU ............ Jesuit

BETA GAMMA SIGMA ............ Commerce
BETA KAPPA CHI . Natural Sciences and Mathematics
BETA PHI MU ............ Library Science
BETA SIGMA KAPPA ............ Optometry

CHI EPSILON ............ Civil Engineering

DELTA EPSILON SIGMA ............ Scholarship
DELTA MU DELTA ......... Business Administration
DELTA PHI DELTA ............ Art
DELTA SIGMA RHO—TAU KAPPA ALPHA Forensics

ETA KAPPA NU ............ Electrical Engineering

GAMMA SIGMA DELTA ............ Agriculture
GAMMA THETA UPSILON ............ Geography

IOTA SIGMA PI ............ Chemistry

KAPPA DELTA PI ............ Education
KAPPA GAMMA PI ............ Leadership
KAPPA MU EPSILON ............ Mathematics
KAPPA OMICRON PHI ............ Home Economics
KAPPA TAU ALPHA ......... Journalism and Mass Communications

LAMBDA IOTA TAU ............ Literature

MORTAR BOARD ............ Student Leadership

NATIONAL COLLEGIATE PLAYERS ... Dramatics

OMEGA CHI EPSILON ....... Chemical Engineering
OMICRON DELTA EPSILON ............ Economics
OMICRON DELTA KAPPA ............ Leadership
OMICRON KAPPA UPSILON ............ Dentistry
OMICRON NU ............ Home Economics
ORDER OF THE COIF ............ Law

PHI ALPHA THETA ............ History
PHI BETA KAPPA ............ Scholarship
PHI ETA SIGMA ............ Freshman Scholarship
PHI KAPPA PHI ............ Scholarship
PHI SIGMA ............ Biological Sciences
PHI SIGMA IOTA ............ Romance Languages
PHI SIGMA TAU ............ Philosophy
PHI THETA KAPPA ............ Junior College
PI DELTA PHI ............ French
PI GAMMA MU ............ Social Science
PI KAPPA LAMBDA ............ Music
PI MU EPSILON ............ Mathematics
PI OMEGA PI ............ Business Education
PI SIGMA ALPHA ............ Political Science
PI TAU DELTA ............ National Chiropractic
PI TAU SIGMA ............ Mechanical Engineering
PSI CHI ............ Psychology

RHO CHI ............ Pharmacy

SIGMA DELTA PI ............ Spanish
SIGMA EPSILON SIGMA ............ Scholarship
SIGMA GAMMA EPSILON ............ Earth Science
SIGMA GAMMA TAU ...... Aerospace Engineering
SIGMA PI SIGMA ............ Physics
SIGMA TAU DELTA ............ English
SIGMA THETA TAU ............ Nursing
SIGMA XI ............ Scientific Research

TAU BETA PI ............ Engineering
TAU SIGMA DELTA .... Architecture and Allied Arts

XI SIGMA PI ............ Forestry

# Recognition and Service Societies

ALPHA PHI GAMMA .................... Journalism
ALPHA PHI OMEGA ........................ Service
ALPHA PHI SIGMA.................... Scholarship
ALPHA PSI OMEGA ........................ Drama
ANGEL FLIGHT ........................... Air Force
ARNOLD AIR SOCIETY .................. Air Force

BETA BETA BETA.......................... Biology
BLUE KEY ..................... Student Activities

CARDINAL KEY .......................... Activities
CHI BETA PHI ............................. Science
CHI DELTA PHI ......................... Literature

DELTA PHI ALPHA ........................ German
DELTA TAU KAPPA................. Social Science

EPSILON SIGMA ALPHA ...... Leadership/Service
ETA MU PI ............................... Retailing
ETA SIGMA PHI ........................... Classics

GAMMA ALPHA .................. Graduate Science
GAMMA SIGMA EPSILON ............... Chemistry
GAMMA SIGMA GAMMA ................... Service
GAMMA SIGMA SIGMA.................... Service

INTERCOLLEGIATE KNIGHTS ............ Service
IOTA LAMBDA SIGMA......... Industrial Education
IOTA TAU TAU ................................ Law

KAPPA ETA KAPPA......... Electrical Engineering
KAPPA KAPPA PSI ............................ Band

KAPPA PI ......................................... Art

LAMBDA DELTA LAMBDA ........ Physical Science
LAMBDA SIGMA ............ Sophomore Leadership
LAMBDA TAU ................. Medical Technology

MU BETA PSI ................................. Music

NATIONAL BLOCK AND BRIDLE Animal Husbandry

PHI DELTA GAMMA ...................... Graduate
PHI LAMBDA UPSILON................... Chemistry
PHI ZETA ...................... Veterinary Medicine
PI ALPHA XI ............................ Floriculture
PI DELTA EPSILON ..................... Journalism
PI KAPPA DELTA ......................... Forensics
PI SIGMA EPSILON ........... Marketing and Sales Management

RHO EPSILON .......................... Real Estate

SCABBARD AND BLADE ................. Military
SIGMA DELTA EPSILON ........ Graduate Science
SIGMA DELTA PSI ......................... Athletics
SIGMA IOTA EPSILON................ Management
SIGMA MU SIGMA ........................... General
SIGMA PHI ALPHA................. Dental Hygiene
SIGMA ZETA.............. Science and Mathematics

TAU BETA SIGMA.............................. Band
THE NATIONAL SPURS ..................... Service
THETA ALPHA PHI ..................... Dramatics

# Sample Biographical Sketch

**Biography** **1** **WOLK, ALAN I,** **2** Harvard Univ; **3** Cambridge, MA; **4** SR; **5** BS; **6** Pres Stu Body; Golf Team; Ed Stu Newspaper; Phi Beta Kappa; President's Awd; **7** Journalism; **8** Political Reporter; **9****

**Key**
**1** Name
**2** College or University
**3** City & State of College or University
**4** Academic Year
**5** Degree Sought
**6** Accomplishments
**7** Major Field of Study
**8** Career Plans
**9** **(Student included in previous edition)

This sample is presented to familiarize the reader with the format of the biographical listings. Students are identified by name, school and school location. Home addresses are not published in order to protect the privacy and integrity of all students.

Biographies are listed in alphabetical order by surname. In those cases where surname is identical, biographees are arranged first by surname, then by first and middle name. For alphabetical arrangement, names having a space (Mc, Von, Des, etc.) or punctuation (O'Hare) are properly spelled out but treated as though there were no space or punctuation. These surnames are listed under the first character of the surname (i.e., Mc under M). The flow of data is consistent with the key numbers shown on this page, and the abbreviations most frequently used are shown in the glossary.

# STUDENT BIOGRAPHICAL SKETCHES

# A

**AARDEMA, KATHERINE G,** Va Commonwealth Univ, Richmond, VA; SR; BSN; NSNA Dir 88-; VNSA 88-; Currclm/Eval Cmte 89-; Sigma Theta Tau; Alpha Sigma Chi; VA Valor Prog 90; RA/YR Awd; Un Ldrshp/Svc Awd; Soccer Tm 86-88; Sftbl/Flag Ftgl 89-; Nrsg; Ph D Hosp Admin.

**AARON, AMMERZINE I,** Stillman Coll, Tuscaloosa, AL; SR; BA; Chrstn Stu Assoc Sec 90-; Al Educ Assoc VP 90-; Intl Assoc; Alpha Kappa Mu; Cordell Wynn Hnrs Pro; Deans Schlr; Elem Educ; Tchr.

**AARON, AVRUM,** Yeshiva Univ, New York, NY; SR; Stdnt Govt VP Jr Class 89-90; Clg Nwspr Assoc Edtr 88-90; Philantrhpy Soc Chrmn 89-; Bsktbl 88-90; Philosophy; Law.

**AARON, KELLY E,** Fl St Univ, Tallahassee, FL; JR; BA; Amer Red Cross 89-90; Gldn Ky 90-; Mrtr Bd 90-; Alpha Phi Omega V P 89-; Comm/Intl Affrs; Pblc Rltns Wrk.

**AARON, LELA N,** Walker Coll, Jasper, AL; FR; Coffe Clb Crdnl Caff 90-; Coll Sngrs 90-; Frds Dsc St 88-; Bio; Sec Educ.

**AARON, LISA D,** Walker Coll, Jasper, AL; SO; BA; Phi Theta Kappa; Acctg; CPA.

**AARSTAD, MARK P,** Wagner Coll, Staten Island, NY; FR; BA; Hstry.

**ABABIO, PATRICIA K,** Central St Univ, Wilberforce, OH; FR; BSC; Intrntl Stdnts Assc; Cmptr Info Ststms Clb; Stndrd Chrtrd Bank 80-90; Bsn Admin/Cis; Data Prcssng Mngr.

**ABAD, HILDA B,** Univ Of Miami, Coral Gables, FL; BA; Cir K Intrntl 90-; Fdng/Impctng Hngry; Prvsts Hon Roll; Acad Schlr; J F Pearson Schlrshp 90-; Dade Cty Yth Fair Schlrshp 90-; Bus; Mgmt

**ABAD, JESUSA,** Univ Of Pr Humacao Univ Coll, Humacao, PR; SR; BA; Amer Chem Soc Sec 90-; AVETA 88-90; MARC Fllwshp 89-; NHSF Award; Acad Excel 88-; Bio Med Rsrch Careers 90; Purdue Marc/Aim Pgm 90; Analytical Chem.

**ABADIA MUNOZ, MARESSA,** Inter Amer Univ Pr San Juan, Hato Rey, PR; GD; JD; Amer Bar Assn 89-; Amer Assn Univ Wmn; MENSA 90-; Law Review Assoc Dir 90-; BS Syracuse Univ 89; Law.

**ABADIE, GEORGE A,** Miami Dade Comm Coll, Miami, FL; SO; MBA; Archtctr Clb Tres 88-89; Otstndg Coach Awrd Kndl Boys Clb 90; Cert Achvmnt Coll Schlrshp Serv; Deans Lst 90-; Assoc Arts; Archtctr; Cntrctr.

**ABANGAN, JONNABEL M,** Univ Of Southern Ms, Hattiesburg, MS; FR; Hlth Prof; Med.

**ABARE, MARIA A,** Pasco Hernando Comm Coll, Dade City, FL; SO; Phi Theta Kappa; Schlrshp W Pasco Chmbr Cmmrc; AA PHCC; Ed; Spcl Ed.

**ABATE, STEVEN J,** Duquesne Univ, Pittsburgh, PA; FR; Alpha Phi Omega; Crs Cntry 90; Phrmcy.

**ABBATE, ELAINE M,** East Stroudsburg Univ, E Stroudsburg, PA; SR; BA; SG 90-; Spch Cmmnctn Assn Orgnztn Sec 90; Spch Cmmnctn Assn Of PA Pres 90-; Ambssdr 90-; Dale Snow Schlrshp 90-; SCAP Awrd; Gen Hnrs Magna Cum Laude; Cmmnctn; MA.

**ABBATE, STEVEN M,** Providence Coll, Providence, RI; JR; BS; Phi Chi 89-; Alpha Epsilon Delta 90-; CRC Chem Awd 88-89; J Joseph Hanley Awd 89-90; Analytical Chem Awd 90-; IM Hockey/Sftbl 88-89; Bio/Chem; Med.

**ABBEY, JUDITH L,** Valdosta St Coll, Valdosta, GA; JR; BED; PAGE; Alpha Chi Ntnl; Hnrs Prgrm 89-; Prsdnts Frshmn Schlr 90-; Deans Lst 89-; Erly Chldhd Edctn; Elem Edctn.

**ABBOT, CHRISTY M,** Univ Of Scranton, Scranton, PA; SO; BS; Ski Clb 89-90; Univ Sngrs 89-; Bus Clb 90-; Omega Beta Sigma 90-; US Achvmnt Acdmy 90-; Serv Orntd Stdnts 89-90; Mktg.

**ABBOT, ERIC C,** Oh Wesleyan Univ, Delaware, OH; JR; BA; Fllwszhp Chrstn Athlts 89-; By Scts Asst Sct Mstr 89-; Vrsty Ftbll Capt 88-; Phi Eta Sigma 89; Mrtr Brd; By Scts 88-; Hnrbl Mntn All Amrcn Ftbll 89; Vrsty Ftbll Capt 89-; Pltcs Govt.

**ABBOTT, ASHLEY E,** Univ Of Sc At Columbia, Columbia, SC; GD; MA; Econ Soc Pr 90-; Flyng Tm 89-90; Flyng Clb Act Chr 89-90; Omicron Delta Epsilon; Gamma Beta Phi; Chi Omega 87-89; AS Long Bch Cty Clg 90; Econ; Phd.

**ABBOTT, BRIAN L,** Memphis St Univ, Memphis, TN; FR; BA; Audit Engr Soc 90-91; ASCAP Assoc 91; Demo Prty 91; Alpha Lambda Delta 91; Flm/Music Prod; Motn Pctr Dir.

**ABBOTT JR, BRUCE A,** Marywood Coll, Scranton, PA; JR; BA; Ltry Mgzn; Nwsppr Nws Edtr 89-90; Delta Epsilon Sigma; Lambda Iota Tau; Lambda Iota Tau; Delta Epsilon Sigma; Mrywd Pres Schlr; Englsh Ltrtr; Prfsnl Wrtr/Bsns.

**ABBOTT, CHRISTINA L,** Lock Haven Univ, Lock Haven, PA; FR; Psychlgy; Exprmntl Psychlgst.

**ABBOTT, DAVID C,** Merrimack Coll, North Andover, MA; JR; BS; Entrepreneurial Network Treas 89-; Coop Edn Cncl Pres 88-; Econ Soc 90-; Omnicron Delta Epsilon; Wheelabrator Tech Inc Staff Accnt 90-; Intrnshp Ms Fin Serv Jr Acctng 89; Boston Safe Deposit-Trust Co Fnd Accnt 89; Fcin/Econ; Fin Anlst.

**ABBOTT, JEFFREY C,** Univ Of Tn At Knoxville, Knoxville, TN; FR; MBA; Exec Undergrads Prgm; Phi Eta Sigma; Alpha Lambda Delta; IM Bsktbll; Bus; Econ.

**ABBOTT, JENNIFER L,** Cornell Univ Statutory College, Ithaca, NY; JR; BS; Yrbk Bsn Mgr/Sports Ed 89-; Ambsdrs 90-; Orientation Cnslr 90; Ho-Nun-De-Kah; Alpha Gamma Delta 90-; Bsn Mgmt/Mktg.

**ABBOTT, JENNIFER L,** Univ Of Ky, Lexington, KY; FR; MBA; Tm UK Stdnt Rcrtnmnt; Stdnt Dev Cncl; Hosp Vol; Phi Eta Sigma; Alpha Lambda Delta; Delta Delta Delta Asst Pldg Trnr; Emrgng Ldr Inst; Chnclrs Schlrshp; Law.

**ABBOTT, LORI L,** Univ Of Tn At Martin, Martin, TN; JR; BA; Phi Theta Kappa JSCC V P 89-90; Soc Wrk Club; AA Jackson State Cmnty Clg 90; Soc Wrk; MSW.

**ABBOTT, MELISSA A,** Wv Univ At Parkersburg, Parkersburg, WV; JR; AD; Student Nurses Assoc VP; Phi Theta Kappa; BS Glenville State Clg 88; Nursing.

**ABBOTT, PAULA D,** Ny Univ, New York, NY; FR.

**ABBOTT, PHYLLIS,** Oh St Univ, Columbus, OH; SR; BA; Hnr Soc 88-; Phi Kappa Phi; Schlrshp Awd For Exclnc 90; Univ Hnrs Pressey Awd & Sigma Xi Sci Grant; Stu Rsrch Grant 90; Cnbslng Psych.

**ABBOTT, REBECCA M,** Liberty Univ, Lynchburg, VA; SR; BS; Yth Quest Clb Chrm 87-; Scty Hmn Rsrc Mgmt 90-; Prayer Ldr/Sprtl Lf Dir Pgm 88-; Alpha/Lmbd Dlt 88-; Hon Pgm 88-; Hghst Acad Achvmnt Awrd; Hon Schlrshp 89-; Chnclrs Schlrshp 87-89; Bus Mgmt; Human Rsrc Mgmt.

**ABBOTT, SUSAN C,** Vance Granville Comm Coll, Henderson, NC; SO; AA; Bnd Bstrs Assn Sec 89-; Music Awrd Louisburg Jr Coll 73; Corcpnt Bst Actrss Awrd 89; Athltc Bstrs 88-90; Prfssnl Sec Intl 85-88; NC Trffc Pssngr Assn; Cooper Tls Cooper Ind; E Ray Cardwell Inc; Bus Admn/Accntng; Bus Mngmnt BA.

**ABBOTT, TERRY L,** Marshall University, Huntington, WV; JR; BA; Bus Mgmt; Entrepreneur Real Est.

**ABCEDE, ELISA-MARIE V,** Coll Of Charleston, Charleston, SC; SR; BS; Lettie Pate Whitehead Schlrshp 89-; Elem Educ; Tch.

**ABDA, JANICE GERALYN,** Marywood Coll, Scranton, PA; SR; BS; Delta Sigma Epsilon; AS Lackawanna Jr Coll 88; Acctg; CPA Law.

**ABDALA, MIGUEL ANGEL,** Miami Dade Comm Coll, Miami, FL; SO; BA; Dnc/Msc.**

**ABDEL SATER, NINA K,** Bunker Hill Comm Coll, Boston, MA; SO; BS; Hnr Prog; Phar Medl; Medl Doc.

**ABDELLA, DANA L,** Old Dominion Univ, Norfolk, VA; SR; BS; Alumni Assn; Wolf Trap Asscts 90; Tau Alpha Pi 90; Alpha Chi 88; Phi Kappa Phi 90; Alumni Assn Award 90; Amer Soc Naval Engr 89-; Virginia Hstrcl Soc; Engr; Newport News Crrnt Shpbldg; Jrnymn AEM Nvl Air Rwrk Fclty 87; Mech Engr Tech; Engr.

**ABDELNABY, ASHRAF H,** East Stroudsburg Univ, E Stroudsburg, PA; SR; BS; Mgmt/Econ Clb 89-; Econ Tutr 90-; Cum Laude; IM Sccr; Mgmt/Acctg; CPA.

**ABDOU, FADI M,** Wv Univ, Morgantown, WV; JR; Chi Nu Scl Chrmn 87-88; Instt Elec Enctrncs Eng 90-; Elec Eng.

**ABDUL RAHMAN, HANIZA,** Univ Of South Al, Mobile, AL; JR; BSC; Malaysn Stdnt Assoc Comm 90-; ASSOC Of Genl Stdies IN Univ 90; Fin; Bsns.

**ABDUL-WAARITH, ZAHEERA,** Fl A & M Univ, Tallahassee, FL; FR; Phi Eta Sigma; Non-Vbl Opera Hon Soc; Comp Sci; Comp Sys Anlys.

**ABDULHALIM, SAMA M,** Memphis St Univ, Memphis, TN; FR; BBA; Bus; Finance.

**ABDULLA, ANNE-MARIE,** Lesley Coll, Cambridge, MA; JR; BSC; Educ Nwsltr Comm 90-; Dns Lst 88-; Tchng Asst Early Chldhd Educ Course 90; Educ; Tchr Early Chldhd/Spec Educ.

**ABDULLA, TAREQ Z,** Clarkson Univ, Potsdam, NY; SR; Deans Lst 90; BSC 88; BSC; Mngmnt; Mngmnt Pstn.

**ABDULLAH, A-KAREEM,** Howard Univ, Washington, DC; GD; MSW; Stu Cncl Pres 83-84; Awrd Cmmtt 83; Muslim Stu Assc 90-; Dean Lst 82-84 89-; All Amer Schlr; All Amer Soc Scntst; Alpha Phi Alpha; Legal Lnkg Grnt 83; Cncl Soc Wrk Educ; Educ Fllw 89-.**

**ABED, WIDAD J,** Va Commonwealth Univ, Richmond, VA; SR; BS; Educ; Tchr.

**ABED-RABBU, YAMILLA IVETTE,** Miami Dade Comm Coll, Miami, FL; SO; BA; Almn Rcrtmnt Pgm; Phi Theta Kappa Cmnctns; AA; Bsn; Bsn Mgmt.

**ABEDNEGO, DAVID A,** City Univ Of Ny John Jay Coll, New York, NY; JR; BS; Crbbn Clb 88-; Orgnztn Blk Stdnts 88-; Law Soc 90-; NY ST Dept Ed Intrnshp 90; Bronx Supreme Ct Intrnshp; Dns Lst 89-90; Law.**

**ABEL, CYNTHIA L,** Hilbert Coll, Hamburg, NY; FR; ASSC; Comeback Clb; Acctg; CPA.

**ABEL, JUDITH K,** Cumberland County Coll, Vineland, NJ; SO; AAS; Pltcl Clb Secr 89; Stdt Sen Secr 90; EOF Peer Cnslr 90-; Phi Theta Kappa Treas 90; Pres Lst 89-; Paralegal; Law.

**ABEL, KIMBERLY M,** Indiana Univ Of Pa, Indiana, PA; JR; Ski Clb 88-89; Anthrplgy Clb 90-; Delta Zeta 90-; IM; Anthrplgy; Grd Stds.

**ABEL, LESLIE D,** Univ Of Sc At Columbia, Columbia, SC; FR; BA; Elem Ed; Tchg.

**ABEL, PATRICIA A,** Fayetteville St Univ, Fayetteville, NC; SR; BS; Atty Gen 89-90; Natl Stdnt Bus Lg 90; Untd Natl Bank 90; Cmbrland Cnty Bus Offc 90; Trck 86-89; Basketball Schlrshp; Vllybll 89-90; Bus Admn; Slf Emplyd.

**ABELING, CHRISTIE A,** Va Commonwealth Univ, Richmond, VA; SR; BFA; Alvin Ailey Schlrshp Dance Stdnt 87; Tchr/Perfmr VA Fine Art Museum Day Art 89-; Hmeless/Devlpmntly Delayed Chldrn 88-; Summa Cum Laude Grad VCU; Outstndg Undergrad Dance Mjr Awd NDA 90-; Outstndg Perf Awd Mid-Atl Dance Oper 90; Dance/Choregrphy; Dance Indonesia/Japan.

**ABELL, KENNY J,** Univ Of Louisville, Louisville, KY; SO; MA; IEEE 90-; Assoc Computing Machinests 90-; Phi Eta Sigma 89-; Presidents Schlrshp 89; Nettelroth Schlrshp 90-; Commonwealth Schlrshp; Electrcl Engrng.

**ABELL, TIM P,** West Liberty St Coll, West Liberty, WV; JR; BA; Ftbl; RA; Elem Ed/Sci; Tch/Coach/Principal.

**ABELLA, JULIE I,** Fl International Univ, Miami, FL; FR; MBA; Busn; Cpa.

**ABELLANA, JASMIN A,** Bridgeport Engr Inst, Fairfield, CT; JR; BSEE; Fll Tm Emply Nght Stdnt 87-; AS 85-87; Elec Eng.

**ABEND, JENNIFER GWEN,** Univ Of Miami, Coral Gables, FL; JR; Japan-Amer Dlgt; Layouts/Invrvws Capt 89-; Sigma Delta Tau 88-; Dns Lst 89-; Intl Bsn/Fnce; Corp Fld.

**ABER, JENNIFER A,** Elmira Coll, Elmira, NY; SO; BA; Career Serv Asst; Dorm Cncl Rep; Stdnt Actvts Brd; Hon Schlr 90-; Pres Schlrshp 90-; Elmira Key Awd 90-; Vrsty Tennis 90; Intl Bus/Japanese; Japanese Trade Co.

**ABERCROMBIE, DANIEL R,** Tri County Tech Coll, Pendleton, SC; SO; AA; Line Foreman Electrc Coop; Indstrl Electrncs.

**ABERLE, MARILYN S,** Univ Of Sc At Aiken, Aiken, SC; FR; BA; Gamma Beta Phi; Intern Cngrssmn Derrick; Sclgy/Crmnl Jus; Law.

**ABERNATHY, MICHELE L,** Middle Tn St Univ, Murfreesboro, TN; JR; BS; Elem Ed; Fdrl Govt.

**ABERNETHY, CHRISTAL E,** Western Piedmont Comm Coll, Morganton, NC; SO; BA; Busn.

**ABERNETHY, REGINA K,** Western Piedmont Comm Coll, Morganton, NC; GD; Drg/Alchl Tchnlgy Clb; Deans Lst; 300 Hr Intrnshp Sbstnc Abuse Trtmnt Cntr; Sbstnc Abuse; Cnslr.

**ABERNETHY, TAMARA W,** Univ Of Nc At Charlotte, Charlotte, NC; SR; PA; Golden Key 89-; Phi Kappi Pi 90-; Pi Syma Alpha 90-; Poltcl Sci/Economics; Internatl Law.

**ABERRA, BETHLEHEM,** Cumberland Coll, Williamsburg, KY; SO; BS; Intl Stdnt Clb Hmcmng Prd Org 89-; PBL 90-; All Amrcn Schlrs 90-; Acctg Comp Info Systm; Mgmt Acctg.

**ABEYWICKREMA, KOSALA U,** Temple Univ, Philadelphia, PA; SO; Indust Mgmt Stdt Asst Univ Kelaniya Sri/Lanka 86-; Alpha Lambda Delta 90-; IEEE 90-; Rugby/Ftbl Univ Kelaniya Sri/Lanka 86-; Ntnl Instit Bus Mgmt 89-; BSE; Electrical Engineering.

**ABHYANKAR, JAYASHREE R,** Broward Comm Coll, Ft Lauderdale, FL; FR; BA; Phi Theta Kappa Sec; Tuitn Schlrshp; Pres Lst; Bus Admin; Law.

**ABICHANDANI, KISHORE D,** City Univ Of Ny City Coll, New York, NY; SO; BE; Economics Soc 90-; Math Clb 89-; Indo Pak Clb; Peer Academic 90-; Advsr; Dns Lst 90; Elec Eng; MS Eng MBA.

**ABICHT, EUTONIA G,** Western Piedmont Comm Coll, Morganton, NC; SO; AASC; Paralgl Assoc 89-; SGA 89-; Crmnl Justce Clb 89-90; YES Evalutr 90-; Parlgl Tech; Paralgl.

**ABIDEMI, KAREEM A,** Al A & M Univ, Normal, AL; JR; BSC; Phy/Hlth Educ; Tchng.

**ABIDI, SAFDAR A,** S U N Y At Buffalo, Buffalo, NY; GD; MARCH; Hl Intrntl Ctr Pres 84; Admsns Cmt Evltr 90; Russo/Sonder Intrnshp 89; Strctrs Crs Tchng Asstntshp 88; Archtctrl Cmnctns Tchng Asstntshp 89; BS Cvl Eng Un New Hampshire 87; Archtctr.

**ABILLA, THOMAS O,** Central St Univ, Wilberforce, OH; JR; BA; Intl Stdnt Assn 89-; Fin/Inv Clb 89-; Dns Lst 89-; GE Arcrft Eng Cinn Intern 90-; Ftbl 89-90; Sccr 90-; Fin.

**ABKOWITZ, PAMINA A,** Kent St Univ Kent Cmps, Kent, OH; SR; BA; Cncl Fmly Rltns 90-; Intrhl Cncl Hall Rep 86-87; Hillel 86-; Alpha Xi Delta Scl Chr 86-90; Intr Grk Pgmg Bd VP Scl 88-89; Deans Lst 90-; Psychlgy Rsrch Asst; Indvdl/Fmly Studies Psychlgy; Schl Psychlgst.

**ABLES, AMY E,** Univ Of West Fl, Pensacola, FL; JR; BA; Alpha Delta Pi 88-; Erly Chldhd/Elem Ed; Tchg.

**ABLORDEPPEY, SETH Y,** Univ Of Ms Main Cmps, University, MS; GD; PH D; Phi Kappa Phi; Rho Chi Soc; Sigma Xi; Grad Achvmnt Awd 90; Schlrshp Fndtn Inc Awd 90; Amer Chem Soc; BSED Univ Cape Coast Ghana 77; MSC Univ Sci Tech Ghana 80; Mdcnl Chem; Medcnl Chmst.

**ABNER, JENNIFER L,** Union Coll, Barbourville, KY; SO; BA; SGA 90-; Campus Actvts Bd 90-; Stdnt Tour Cncl 90-; Gamma Beta Phi 90-; Mst Imprvd Swmr 90-; Electd Hmcmg Ct 90; Swmming 90; Ele Educ; Tch.

**ABNER JR, THOMAS M,** Auburn Univ At Auburn, Auburn, AL; JR; Fisheries Sci; Rsrch Fish Biology Fish Gen.

**ABNEY, MONICA L,** Univ Of Southern Ms, Hattiesburg, MS; JR; BS; Sigma Nu 89-; Dnc Tm Capt 88-; Lambda Sigma Rtls Chrm 89-90; Delta Gamma VP 88-; Grt Amer Smkt Chrmn 88; Anchrsplsh Fndrsr Chrmn 89; Psychlgy; MA Soc Wrk.

**ABNEY, WADEA L,** Athens St Coll, Athens, AL; JR; BS; Yrbk Stf NE AL St Jnr Clg; Lambda Alpha Epsln; Phi Mu Dir; Crmnl Jstc/Sclgy; Jvnl Prbtn Offcr.

**ABOOD, PAUL H,** Rutgers St Un At New Brunswick, New Brunswick, NJ; SO; BA; Prog Cncl Pub Rltns Comm Vice Chp 89-; Frshmn Cncl Frshmn Dinner Comm Co Chp 89-90; Deans List 90-; Acctng; CPA.**

**ABORN, JENNIFER A,** Providence Coll, Providence, RI; FR; BA; Bd Pgmrs Chrprsn; Res Bd V P; Stdnt Life Comm 90-; Psych; Prfsnl Psychlgst.

**ABOTT, BRANDON R,** Merrimack Coll, North Andover, MA; SO; BA; Pscyh.

**ABOU GHAIDA, GHASSAN N,** Old Dominion Univ, Norfolk, VA; SO; BS; Intl Assoc Pres 89-; Phi Kappa Phi; Outstndng Soph 90-; Deans List 89-; Elec Polit Sci; Engrg.

**ABOU KHALIL, ALI K,** Hillsborough Comm Coll, Tampa, FL; JR; BS; Arbc Amer Assn Pres 90-; Phi Eta Sigma; Natl Assn Prfssnl Engrs 90-; FL Eng Scty 90-; AA 90; Eng; Comp Eng.

**ABOU-CHEDID, GHADA J,** Univ Of Sc At Columbia, Columbia, SC; JR; BS; Cath Stdnt Assn; EOPA Ldrshp Trng 89-90; Habitat For Hmnty; Phrmcy.

**ABOU-SHAKRA, SAMIA,** Notre Dame Coll, Cleveland, OH; SR; BA; DRE Youngstowns Parish St Maron; Yth Ldr Lebanon; Bnkng Studies Univ St Joseph/Lebanon 81; Engl/Catechetics; Soc Serv Adult Day Care.

**ABOUESSA, AHMED FARIS,** Hillsborough Comm Coll, Tampa, FL; SR; Acctg; Bus.

**ABRAHAM, JAMES J,** Allegheny Coll, Meadville, PA; SO; Allghny Nwmn; Lambda Sigma 90-; Alden Schlrs; Phi Kappa Psi Tres 90-; IM Bsktbl; Ecnmc/Biol; Bus.

**ABRAHAM, JERRY A,** Univ Of Akron, Akron, OH; FR; MBA; Univ Hnrs Pgm 90-; Mech Engrg; Mech Engr Auto Dsgn.

**ABRAHAM, JULIUS G,** Southern Coll Of Tech, Marietta, GA; SR; BS; Activities Brd 89-90; Inst Elec & Electronics Engnrs; Natl Soc Black Engrs V P 90-; Southern Bell Acdmc Exclnce Awe; IM Bsktbl Flag Ftbl Vlybl; Elec Engrng.

**ABRAHAM, MINI M,** East Tn St Univ, Johnson City, TN; FR; BS; Dietetics.

**ABRAHAM, PAULA O NEILL,** Rivier Coll, Nashua, NH; JR; BA; Non Trad Stdnt Clb 90-; Mddlsx Comm Coll Dns Lst 90; Stndt Cmmncmnt Spkrs 90; Chrprsn Irish Cltrl Wk Lwll 90; Lwll Flk Fstvl Fd Bth Co Orgnzr 88-; Assoc Degree Hiddlesex Comm Coll Lowell Campus 90; Erly Chldhd Educ Spec Educ; Tch Erly Intrvntn.

**ABRAHAM, SALOME,** Georgian Court Coll, Lakewood, NJ; JR; BS; Mendel Scty Secy 89-; AM Chmcl Scty 90-; Intrntnl Clb VP 89-; Grdn State Sclr 89-; Georgian Crt Clg Blgy Awrd 90; Blgy; Professor.

**ABRAHAM, SHANNON M,** Union Univ, Jackson, TN; FR; Hnrs Clb 90-; Stdnt Govt Sntr; Zeta Tau Alpha 90-; Dorm Cncl; Biol; Phys Thrpst.

**ABRAHAM, VIVEK C,** Franklin And Marshall Coll, Lancaster, PA; FR; BA; Franklin/Marshall Cmnty Orch 90-; Choral Soc Singer; Hackman Summer Rsrch Pgm Franklin/Marshall Rsrch Embrlgy 90-; Bio/Chem; Rsrch Cell Bio.

**ABRAHAMS, JOHN F,** Le Moyne Coll, Syracuse, NY; SO; BA; Intl Hse Pres 90-; Sngrs 90-; Engl; Educ.

**ABRAHAMSEN, PAUL H,** Va Commonwealth Univ, Richmond, VA; JR; BFA; Intervarsity Christian Fllwshp; Soccer Assoc Pblcty Chair; Community Church Membership Elder; QED Systems; AA 74; AAS 76; Communicating Arts Design; Profssnl Designer.

**ABRAM, OTRIAS L,** Clark Atlanta Univ, Atlanta, GA; FR; BA; Sr Clss Treas 90; Drma Clb Sec 90; Ftre Bus Ldrs Of Amer Pres 90; Beta Clb 90; Qd AAAA 90; Kappa Clb Sec 90; Jr Cvtn Sec 90; Intr Clb Cncl Pres 90; Bus Awrd Rcpnt 90; Hme Econs Awrd Rcpnt 90; BA; Bus Fnnce; Bnkng.

**ABRAMOWITZ, MARK S,** City Univ Of Ny Baruch Coll, New York, NY; SR; BBA; Fin/Ecnmcs Soc VP 89-; At/T Invstmnt Chllng 89-; Deans Lst 87-; Gldn Key 90-; Beta Gamma Sigma; Trnsfr Schlr 89-; Mis Rgnts Schlrshp 87; IM Sftbl Vlybl 87-89; Fin; Invstmnt Bnkg.

**ABRAMS, ANITA,** Piedmont Tech Coll, Greenwood, SC; FR; AD; VITA Tax Serv 90-; Pres Lst 90-; Bus/Acctg.

**ABRAMS, CAROLYN M,** Hudson Valley Comm Coll, Troy, NY; SR; Presidents Lst 89-; Cycle Cte Spec Educ; Religious Educ Teach; Early Childhd Educ; Preschool Dir.

**ABRAMS, GLEN J,** Oh St Univ, Columbus, OH; SR; BA; Mns Glee Clb 90; Sth Cmps Stdnt Assn Pres 90; Alpha Lambda Delta 88; AIDS Educ Com 89-; Arts And Scis Awrd Exclnce Schlrshp 90; Grad Asstntshp Fr Grad Sclgy; Psychlgy; Prfssr Of Sclgy.

**ABRAMS, HOLLACE D,** George Mason Univ, Fairfax, VA; SR; BS; Prof Dvlpmnt Steering Comm 89-90; Prof Dvlpmnt Plnng Com 90-; Wrtng Tchng Case Studies 90-; Bd Dir Sideburn Run Pool 90-; Fairfax Cnty Tchr; AA Cnty Clg Of Morris 86; Educ.

**ABRAMS, JASON R,** Cornell Univ Statutory College, Ithaca, NY; FR; Ag/Life Sci Ambsdr 90-; Orntn Cnslr; Tns IMS 90-; Stats; Actry.

**ABRAMS, LEONARD DOUGLAS,** Univ Of Ky, Lexington, KY; JR; BSW; Scl Wrk; LCSW.

**ABRAMS, STEPHANIE FAYE,** Fl A & M Univ, Tallahassee, FL; FR; Ntl Hnr Soc; Mrchng Bnd; Stdnt Cncl Rep 87-89; Ntl Hnr Soc 87-88; Leander L Boykin Awd 90; Bsns Ecnmcs; Ecnmcs.

**ABRAMS, VIVIAN D,** William Paterson Coll, Wayne, NJ; SR; MA; Fair Lawn Jewish Ctr 76-; Eng Teacher 79-; BA Queens Coll Flushing N Y 59; MS Queens Coll Flushing N Y 63; Sch Guidance Cnslr.

**ABRAMSKI, JUNE A,** East Stroudsburg Univ, E Stroudsburg, PA; JR; BS; Cmptr Sci; Pgmmng.

**ABRAMSON, JEREMY SCOTT,** Boston Univ, Boston, MA; JR; BS MS; Fall Orien Crdntr Srgnt Coll; Co Chrmn Hmcmng Float Sargent Coll 90-; Phys Thrpy.

**ABRAMSON, STACY L,** Wheaton Coll, Norton, MA; FR; BA; Anml Awrns 90-; Whtn Wire 90-; Fthrs Wknd Comm 90-; Dns Lst 90-; Intl Ordr Rnbw Advsr 87-.

**ABRANTE, ENID,** City Univ Of Ny Bronx Comm Col, Bronx, NY; JR; BA; AAS EDP Coll Puerto Rico 83; Accntnt.

**ABRAVANEL, LESLEY S,** Univ Of Miami, Coral Gables, FL; FR; Nwspr 90-; Alph Lmbd Dlt 90-; Nws/Edtrl Jrnlsm/Crtv Wrtng; Mag Jrnlsm.

**ABREU, DEBORA,** Georgian Court Coll, Lakewood, NJ; SR; BA; Psi Chi 89-; Deans Lst; RN; RN E Orange Gnrl Hosp Schl Nrsng 76; Psychlgy.

**ABREU, GREGORIA PADILLA,** Inter Amer Univ Pr San Juan, Hato Rey, PR; JR; BS; Hon Pgm 89-; Nurse/Bio.

**ABREU, ILEANA AURORA,** Fl International Univ, Miami, FL; JR; BA; Un Way Crisis Nrsry Vol 85-; Futr Eductrs Amer 90-; Kappa Delta Pi 90-; Un Way 85-; Deans Lst 90-; Outstndng Achvmnt Awrd 90-; Outstndng Emplyee Awrd 88-; Ldrshp Awrd 88-; Serv Awrd 88-; AA Miami Comm Coll 84; BA Fl Intl Univ; Educ; Elem Ed Tchr.

**ABREU, JOSE L,** Univ Politecnica De Pr, Hato Rey, PR; FR; Ninos Escuchas 87; Eng.

**ABREU, MARINA,** Fl International Univ, Miami, FL; SR; BS; Inst Indstrl Engrs Crntr 89-90; FL Engr Scty 87; Scty Hispanic Prfssnl Engrs 89; Alpha Pi Mu Pres 90; Alpha Omega Chi Sec 90; Omicron Delta Kappa; SHPE Ed Grant 90; Deans List 90; Engr; Industrial Engr.

**ABREU-REINO, MARIA,** Caribbean Center For Adv Stds, San Juan, PR; GD; Amer Mntl Hlth Cnslrs Asc 89-; Portico Medal 87; Dns Lst 88; BA Summa Cum Laude Univ Sacred Hrt 87; MS Summa Cum Laude 89; Clncl Psy.

**ABRIL, CARLOS R,** Univ Of Miami, Coral Gables, FL; JR; BM; CMENC Cllgte Msc Edctrs Natl Cnfrnce 89-; Univ Of Miami Sympny Orchsta; Undergrad Wdwnd Qntet; Fstiva Sympnic Orchsta; Pi Kappa Lambda; Stdnt Tchr Cyprss Elem Schl Msc 89-; Schlrshp To Stdy Salzburg Austira 90; Msc Prfrmnce Educ; Tch And Rsrch Fld Of Msc.

**ABRIL, FLOSERPIDA C,** Bloomfield Coll, Bloomfield, NJ; FR; BSN; RN.

**ABRONSON, LOUIS S,** Ny Univ, New York, NY; FR; BFA; Soc Creative Anachranisms Pres 90; Drama; Prfrmng Arts.

**ABSALOM, CATHI Y,** Averett Coll, Danville, VA; SR; BA; Averett Stndt Fndtn Sec-Treas 90; Phi Eta Sigma 88; Alpha Chi 90; Beazley Schlr 90; BSA/ACCTG/COMP Sci; Acctng.

**ABSHEAR, APRIL D,** Univ Of Ky, Lexington, KY; JR; BA; Stdnt Natl Educ Assn 90-; Kappa Kappa Gamma 90-; Educ; Tchr.

**ABSHER, DALE R,** East Tn St Univ, Johnson City, TN; GD; MD; Fmly Practice Stdnt Interest Grp 90-; Christian Medical Dntl Soc 90-; Med Stdnt Govt Assoc; AMA 90-; TMA 90-; BA Carson Neuman Coll 89; Medicine.

**ABSHER, LISA R,** Wilkes Comm Coll, Wilkesboro, NC; FR; Phi Theta Kappa; Deans Lst; Marshall; Math; Bus Mgmnt.

**ABSHIRE, CARLA R,** Univ Of Ga, Athens, GA; SR; BS; Natl Assn Educ Yng Chldrn; S Assn Chldrn Under 6; Ga Assn Yng Chldrn; Phi Upsilon Omicron Pres 90-; Golden Key; Phi Kappa Phi; Delta Gamma La Sta Univ; S Nunn Snte Intrn Prog; Clg Fam/Cnsumr Sci Deans Side 90-; V W Kilgore Schlrshp; Chld/Fam Dev; Law.**

**ABSTON, COLLEEN M,** Western Ky Univ, Bowling Green, KY; SO; BS; Phi Eta Sigma 90-; Alpha Sigma Lambda 90-; Red Cross Elem Sch PTO Sec 85-; Cub Scout Asstnt Cbmstr 89-; Elem Educ; Tchr.

**ABU-HANIEH, MUSTAFA ABBALRAHIM,** Comm Coll Algny Co Algny Cmps, Pittsburgh, PA.

**ABU-JOUDEH, MANAR M,** Saint Pauls Coll, Lawrenceville, VA; JR.

**ABUDO, HILDA E,** Inter Amer Univ Pr San German, San German, PR; SR; Art Assoc; Prof Mdlng Fontecha Acad 87; Altacostura Ydiseno 85.

**ABUIN, MARISOL,** Fordham Univ, Bronx, NY; SO; BS; Pre Law Clb 89-; Dante Socty 89-; Stdnt Govt Gen Assmbly; Beta Gamma Sigma 90-; Dns Lst 89-; Math Tutor Calculus 89-; Envrmntl Awrns Clb 90-; Acctng; Law Schl.

**ABUL JOBIAN, AHMAD N,** Univ Of Miami, Coral Gables, FL; SR; BS; Palestinian Stdnts Assoc Pres 88-; Muslim Stdnts Org Secr 88-; Arab Frndshp Clb 87-; Sigma Tau Delta 90-; Campus Sports/Recr Intl Stdnts Repr 87-90; Miami Hurricane Opinion Columnist 89-; Cncl Intl Stdnt Orgs 88-89; Rsrch Asst 89; Advrtsg Cmnctn/Greative Wrtg.

**ABUZEID, MARIA C,** Univ Of Miami, Coral Gables, FL; SR; MBA; Hnrs Stdnt Assoc 90-; Erth Alrt 90-; Fnc; Mny Mgmt.

**ACCA, LISA M,** Wagner Coll, Staten Island, NY; JR; BA; English; Law.

**ACCARDO, MICHELE,** Coll Of New Rochelle, New Rochelle, NY; SO; BA; Drama Clb 89-; Readers Theatre Asst Dir 91; Natl Clg Hons Cncl Campus Liasion 90-; Psi Chi; CODE 89-; Psych.

**ACCARDO, MICHELLE I,** Wv Univ, Morgantown, WV; FR; BSW; Scl Wrk/Gerontlgy; Spec Gerontlgy.

**ACCETTA, KATHLEEN,** Wilmington Coll, New Castle, DE; GD; MA; Psych Clb 90-; Delta Epsilon Rho 89-90; Psych; Indstrl Org.

**ACCETTA, LINDA C,** Indiana Univ Of Pa, Indiana, PA; FR; BED; Education.

**ACCLES, KRISTAN A,** Westminster Coll, New Wilmingtn, PA; SR; BA; Omicron Delta Kappa Sec 90-; Phi Alpha Theta VP 89-; Pi Sigma Pi 90-; Pres Schlrshp 87-; Schlrshp 90-; Hist/Soc; Law.

**ACCORSO-COON, MARGARET M,** Bryant Stratton Bus Inst Roch, Rochester, NY; GD; AOS; Cmptr Prgrmg; Cmptr Oper.

**ACE, CHERILLYN K,** Middle Tn St Univ, Murfreesboro, TN; SR; BBA; Stdnt Govt Sen; Tenn Intercoll St Leg; Chi Omega; Intrnd Congrsmn Brt Gordn 90; Mktg/Busn Admin; Mktg/Mgmt Pos.

**ACE, MELISSA J,** East Stroudsburg Univ, E Stroudsburg, PA; FR; BA; Cncrt Bnd 90-; Math.

**ACEBAL, JULIETA,** Boston Coll, Chestnut Hill, MA; SO; BS; Nrsng.

**ACEVEDO CARRERO, LAURA V,** Univ Of Pr At Mayaguez, Mayaguez, PR; JR.

**ACEVEDO HERNANDEZ, SOAMMY D,** Inter Amer Univ Pr San German, San German, PR; JR; BA; Spcl Edctn Assn 90-; Mu Delta Sigma Tres Fndr; Cnslng 89; Cmmnclgcl Prblms; Spcl Edctn.

**ACEVEDO MARINEZ, JOSE A,** Inter Amer Univ Pr Hato Rey, Hato Rey, PR; SO; BBA; Finance.

**ACEVEDO ROSA, GLORIE A,** Inter Amer Univ Pr Hato Rey, Hato Rey, PR; FR; Sec Scnc.

**ACEVEDO SERRANO, MANUEL I,** Univ Of Pr At Mayaguez, Mayaguez, PR; SO; BE; J A C Cath Ch V P 87-88; Youth Grp; Ind Engrng.

**ACEVEDO SOSA, ALEXIS,** Univ Politecnica De Pr, Hato Rey, PR; SO; Yth Soc Pres Nazarene Church 88-89; Bsktbl 90; Logic Prog Ladder Wkrshp; Cert UPR Rio Piedras PR; Cert Scuba Centro Hato Rey PR 88; Eng.

**ACEVEDO, BENICIA M,** Molloy Coll, Rockville Ctr, NY; JR; BA; Spnsh Clb 88-; Lit Mag Illstr 89-; Delta Epsilon Sigma 90-; Omicron Alpha Zeta 90-; Art/Engl; Comp Grphcs.

**ACEVEDO, BETTY,** Commonwealth Coll, Virginia Beach, VA; FR; MAA; Lab Asst Col Tecnico Profl 83; Med Asst Centro Voc Tecnica Destrezas 77; Med.

**ACEVEDO, DOLORES MEJER,** Inter Amer Univ Pr Hato Rey, Hato Rey, PR; SR; BA; BS Mrktng Univ Of FL 85; Elem Educ; Elem Tchr.

**ACEVEDO, JULIO G,** Inter Amer Univ Pr Hato Rey, Hato Rey, PR; FR; BA; Air Force ROTC; Bus Admn; Fin/Acctg.

**ACEVEDO, MARIA A,** Caribbean Univ, Bayamon, PR; AD; Summa Cum Laude 90; Lions Clb; Sec 61-; Acctg 90-; AS 90; Real Estate; BA-ADMIN.

**ACEVEDO, ORTENCIA,** Univ Of Pr At Rio Piedras, Rio Piedras, PR; SO; Hm Ecnmy Pgm/Smnry Ldrshp/Thtrcl Grp/Lit Actvts/Med Cdts 87-89; Mrt Awds Trng Ars Med Cdts 89; Awd Outstndng AJED Dr Ed Pres 88-89; Hgh Hnrs Awd Frst Yr Univ 89-90; Stdnt Frgn Lng 90-; DECA 89-; Hm Ecnmy Pgm 87-89; Frgn Lng; Trsm.

**ACEVEDO, SALHOM N,** City Univ Of Ny Baruch Coll, New York, NY; JR; Gold Key 90-; City Govt Intrnshp Manhattan Borough Pres Ofc; Provost Schlrshps 90; USMC; Navy Achvmnt Medal Sgt E5 Hon Dschrgd 83-87; Pol Sci; Law Sch.

**ACEVEDO, VICTOR X,** Univ Politecnica De Pr, Hato Rey, PR; FR; BEE; Elec Engr/Fire Prev; Eng.

**ACEVEDO JR, WILLIAM,** Inter Amer Univ Pr San German, San German, PR; GD; BBA; Peer Cnslng Assn Treas 89-; Natl Assn Acctnts; Acctg Dept Awrd; BBA; Acctg; Ma.

**ACEVEDO-CARDONA, EILEEN,** Bayamon Central Univ, Bayamon, PR; JR; Psych Stdnts Assn 89; Religious Assn 86.

**ACEVEDO-MARRERO, CARLOS A,** Evangelical Seminary Of P R, Hato Rey, PR; GD; MAR; Amer Acadmy Pediatrcs; Amer Brd Pediatrcs; Pediatrcn Priv Pract; MD Univ PR Schl Med 80; BA Univ PR 76; FAAP Amer Acadmy Pediatrcs 86; Relgn.

**ACEVEDO-TOLEDO, MARISOL,** Univ Of Pr At Mayaguez, Mayaguez, PR; SR; BSEE; Inst Elec/Electrncs Engrs 89-; Tau Beta Pi Pres 90-; Motorla Cmnctns Intrn 90; Eng.

**ACEVES-MANNING, BIANCA L,** Barry Univ, Miami, FL; SR; MA; Intl Clb 69-70; NADAAC 90-; NAFE 90-; Cert U M 90; BLS; Adm Hlth Svcs/Hosp Ind.

**ACHA CINTRON, LUIS R,** Univ Of Pr Medical Sciences, San Juan, PR; GD; MSA; Evaltn Rsrch Hlth Sys; Publc Hlth.

**ACHANG, JANET,** Fl International Univ, Miami, FL; SR; BA; FMA 90-; Dns Lst 90-; AA Miami Dade Comm Coll 88; Bus Admin; Fnnce.

**ACHILLES, CONNIE J G,** Middle Tn St Univ, Murfreesboro, TN; JR; BS; Tau Omicron; Kappa Delta Pi; Gamma Beta Phi; Spch Pthlgst.

**ACKAH, SAMUEL,** Howard Univ, Washington, DC; GD; PHD; Staff Stdnts Rltns Repr 76/77; Sec 76/77; Assn Grd Sclgsts Sec/V P 88-89; Alpha Kappa Delta 89; NCSSA 86/87; Acad All Amer 86/87; Intrnshp Ofc Repr John Ray 86/87; BA Unvi Cape Coast 77; MA 88; Sclgy; Prof.**

**ACKER, CINDY M,** Columbia Union Coll, Takoma Park, MD; FR; BA; Phi Eta Sigma 90-; Elem Educ; Tchr.

**ACKER, JENNIFER LYNN,** Allegheny Coll, Meadville, PA; SR; BA; Disc Jockey WARC 88; Alden Schlr 89-90; Alpha Delta Pi Asst Pldg Educ 87-; Alpha Phi Omega 87-; Exchg 89-; Sociology; Spec Educ.

**ACKER, JENNIFER R,** Brown Univ, Providence, RI; FR; BA; Band; Alpha Delta Phi; Psychology; Soc Serv.

**ACKER, PAMELA M,** Erie Comm Coll, Buffalo, NY; SR; ASSOC; Crim Just Clb 89-; Hnr Pgm Stdnt Crim Just 89-; Phi Theta Kappa 90-; Stdnt Svcs Receptnst; Dns Lst 89-; Outstndg Talent Roster 90; Crim Just; Law FBI Agent.

**ACKERMAN, ERIC D,** S U N Y Coll Of Envr Sci & For, Syracuse, NY; SO; BS; Lab Tech 83-; AAS 83; Forest Engr; Engr.

**ACKERMAN, JANE E,** Univ Of Rochester, Rochester, NY; SO; BA; Phlsophy Cncl 90-; Equestrian Clb 90-; Gymnastics Clb 88-; Phlsphy; MA Ethics.

**ACKERMAN, JASON A,** Wilmington Coll, Wilmington, OH; FR; BA; Aggies 90-91; Agriculture; Animal Sci.

**ACKERMAN, JILL L,** Kent St Univ Kent Cmps, Kent, OH; JR; BA; Beta Gamma Sigma; Golden Key; Beta Alpha Psi 90-; Acctng.

**ACKERMAN, JODIANNE,** Schenectady County Comm Coll, Schenectady, NY; JR; BA; AA Scl Sci; Scl Sci; Ed/Lang.

**ACKERMAN, MATTHEW D,** Miami Dade Comm Coll, Miami, FL; FR; AA; Sci; Psychlgy.

**ACKIE, PATRICIA E,** City Univ Of Ny Bronx Comm Col, Bronx, NY; SR; AS; Phi Theta Kappa P R Ofcr 90-; Tlntd Rstr Hon Awd 90-; Phi Theta Kappa Hon Awd 90-; US Cngrssnl Awd BEOC 88; Cert Bronx Ed Oprtnty Ctr 88; Bus Admin Mgmt.

**ACKLEH, SAMER S,** Cumberland Coll, Williamsburg, KY; JR; Tutor 90-; Lab Asst 90-; High Hnr Lst 89-; Rsrch Sci Alliance UT; IM Soccer; Physics/Math; Rsrch.

**ACKLEY, BRANDT A,** Memphis St Univ, Memphis, TN; FR; BA; Ftbl 91-.

**ACKLEY, MARGARET A,** Le Moyne Coll, Syracuse, NY; SR; MS; Psych Clb 87-; Psi Chi 90-; Beta Beta Beta 90-; Extraordnry Mnstr 88-; Int SUNY Hlth Sci Ctr Gentc Cnslng Dept 90-; Intgrl Hons Prog Le Moyne Clg Sr Rep 87-; BS; Psych.

**ACKOUREY, CHRISTINE M,** Western New England Coll, Springfield, MA; SR; BSBA; Acctng Assn Sec 89-; Intrnshp Frndlys Ice Crm Corp 90-; Acctng.

**ACOSTA ACOSTA, JULMARIE,** Inter Amer Univ Pr San German, San German, PR; FR; BA; Jr Achvmnt; Cath Yth Serv; Cmptrs; Bus Admin.

**ACOSTA FEBO, ZULMA V,** Univ Of Pr At Rio Piedras, Rio Piedras, PR; JR; BA; Acctg Stdnt Assoc 88-; Amer Mrktng Assoc 89-; Tennis Trnmnt 89; Acctg; Law.

**ACOSTA FLOER, JUAN B,** Univ Politecnica De Pr, Hato Rey, PR; SO; BA; Psi Delta Omicron Mmbr 87-; Pwr Wght Lftng Tm Scnd Pl Unv 89; ASSOC Deg Envrnmntl Tch Rgnl Clg Unv Puerto Rico Aguadilla 87-90.

**ACOSTA GARCIA, LUIS A,** Inter Amer Univ Pr San German, San German, PR; SR; BS; Natrl Hstry Soc Dr Isml Velez Pr 88-; Premed Soc Cad 88-; Inv Microbio Water; Bio Beta Beta Beta Vowel 88-; Hnr Pgm 86-90; Adelphos 85-88; Res Invest Grp 90-; Bst Frshmn Stdnt Enter Cls 87; Hnr Lst 86-; Bio; Med.

**ACOSTA MARTINEZ, VERONICA,** Univ Of Pr At Mayaguez, Mayaguez, PR; SO; MBA; Bio.

**ACOSTA RAMIREZ, DEBORAH,** Univ Of Pr At Mayaguez, Mayaguez, PR; SO; BS; Beta Beta Beta; Hon Lst; Bio; Med.

**ACOSTA SANABRIA, IRMA I,** Inter Amer Univ Pr San German, San German, PR; SR; BBS; IEEE 89-; Math; Electrnc Eng Technlgy.

**ACOSTA, ANA C,** Univ Of Miami, Coral Gables, FL; FR; BA; Circle K 90-; Hnrs Pgm 90-; Arch.

**ACOSTA, GILBERTO J,** Univ Of Miami, Coral Gables, FL; SR; Fed Cuban Stdnts Pres 88-90; Univ Ctr Brd Chr 89-90f Gov Sen 88-89; Omicron Delta Kappa 90; Hons Stdnt Assn 87-88; Cir K Intrntl 88-90; Schlrshp 87-90; BS 90; Chem; Med Dr.

**ACOSTA, JUAN C,** Fl International Univ, Miami, FL; SR; BS; Im Sprts 85-; Exercs Physlgy; Physcl Thrpy.

**ACOSTA, M MICHAEL,** Univ Of Hartford, West Hartford, CT; SO; BSBA; Interfrtrnty Cncl Sec; Theta Chi Pldg Clss VP 90-; Orttn Stdnt Advsr; Acctg; Law.**

**ACOSTA-IRAOLA, YAZMIR G,** Univ Of Pr At Mayaguez, Mayaguez, PR; FR; Chmcl Eng.

**ACOSTA-MERCADO, DIMARIS,** Univ Of Pr At Mayaguez, Mayaguez, PR; SO; BS; Assn Blgy Stdnts Chrmn Smpsm/Prpgnda 90-; Zlgcl Soc PR 90-; Assn Btny Stdnts 90-; Tri-Beta 90-; Blgy; PHO Ethlgy.

**ACQUAFREDDA, CHRISTINE L,** Dowling Coll, Oakdale Li, NY; SR; BA; Educ Clb 89-; Mntrshp Actvts 89-; Grp Ldr Ornttn 89-; Phi Theta Kappa 87-; Kappa Delta Pi; Racanelli Schlr 89-90; AAS Suffok Co Comm Col 89; Spec Elem Educ; Spec Educ Tchr.

**ACQUAVELLA, DAVID F,** S U N Y Maritime Coll, Bronx, NY; FR; BE; Navy ROTC 90-; Elect Eng; US Navy.

**ACQUAVIVA, GINA M,** Villanova Univ, Villanova, PA; FR; Kappa Kappa Gamma Class Offc; Cmmnctns.

**ACQUAVIVA, MARY K,** Anne Arundel Comm Coll, Arnold, MD; SO; BA; Summa Cum Laude; Hmnty/Sclgy Awrd; Bkkpr; Gen Stdy; Phtgrphy.

**ACREE, EARNEST J,** Al A & M Univ, Normal, AL; FR; BS; Math; Engrng.

**ACRES, CHARLES ETHAN,** Ms Gulf Coast Comm Coll, Perkinston, MS; SO; BFA; Phi Theta Kappa 89-; Hnrs Assn 89-; Pres Lst 90; Art.

**ACTON, DOROTHY G,** Wallace St Comm Coll At Selma, Selma, AL; SO; AS; Bus Admin; Bus.

**ACUNA, PATRICK F,** Columbia Union Coll, Takoma Park, MD; SR; BS; Phi Kappa Psi; Corp Acctnt DK Brdctng Bethesad MD; Busn Adminf Acctng.

**ADACHI, MISA,** Truett Mc Connell Coll, Cleveland, GA; FR; BA; Pres Clb 90-; Intrntl Relations.

**ADAIR, ELIZABETH C,** Allegheny Coll, Meadville, PA; SR; BA; Hon Com 88-; Tutor 90-; Kappa Alpha Theta Panhel 88-; Alden Schlr 87-; Pltcl Sci/Envrnmntl Sci.

**ADAIR, JAYNE A,** Longwood Coll, Farmville, VA; JR; Ambsdr Comm Serv 90-; Geist VP 90-; Kappa Delta Pi Pro Chr 90-; Alpha Sigma Alpha Chpln 90-; Ldrshp Awrd VP; High GPA 90-; Ntl Coll Educ Awrd; Otstndg Cls Recog; BS; Elem Educ; Tchr.

**ADAIR, MARIA N,** Nova Univ, Ft Lauderdale, FL; GD; MBA, BA Univ Miami 74-.

**ADAIR, MATTHEW A,** Embry Riddle Aeronautical Univ, Daytona Beach, FL; JR; BS; Prof Aviation Maint Assn 90-; Riddle Sftbl League Mgr; Aviation Tech; Cmrcl Aviation.

**ADAMCIK, TERESA M,** Immaculata Coll, Immaculata, PA; JR; BA; Comp Oprtns Spclst 86-; AD Delaware County Comm Coll 89; Bus Admin Econs.

**ADAMES, NERY E,** Univ Of Pr At Mayaguez, Mayaguez, PR; SO; BA; Clb Rotary Flwshp 87-89; Explrs Post 281 V P 85-89; Karate Green Belt 86-; Presby Flwshp Grp Pres 83-; Mayaguez Clg 89-90; Soc Sci; Law.

**ADAMI, DAVID L,** Ramapo Coll Of Nj, Mahwah, NJ; JR; BA; Hist Clb; Delta Mu Delta; Bus Admin; Acctng.

**ADAMIC, ANGELA M,** Kent St Univ Geauga Cmps, Burton Twp, OH; SO; BA; Cmrcl Arts; Ad.

**ADAMIC, META,** Va Commonwealth Univ, Richmond, VA; SR; ISC Intrntl Stdnt Union 89-; OAP 89-90; Golden Key 90; Phi Eta Simga 89; Fine Arts-Pntng; Pnt/Exhbt Wrk/Tch.

**ADAMOW, ANDREW J,** S U N Y Coll Of Tech At Frmgdl, Farmingdale, NY; SO; BT; Mach Tool Clb NY Cty Tech Coll VP 88-89; Grtr NY Soc Mfg Eng 89; Frank Zimmer Mem Awd; AAS 89; Mfg Eng Tech; Mech Eng.

**ADAMS, ALEX C,** Univ Of Al At Huntsville, Huntsville, AL; SR; BS; Eta Kappa Nu VP 89-; Tau Beta Pi 88-; Dr Wernher Von Braun Schlrshp Awd 89-90; NASA MSFC Coop Yr 88-89; Elctrcl Engrg.

**ADAMS, ALICIA M,** Al A & M Univ, Normal, AL; FR; BS; Deans Lst; Engr; Cvl.

**ADAMS, AMY C,** Middle Tn St Univ, Murfreesboro, TN; SR; SGA 86-88; Ambsdr 87-88; Hmcmng Queen 88; AS Dyersbrg St Comm Clg 88; BS Mddl TN St Univ; Elem Educ; Tchr.

**ADAMS, AMY P,** Fl St Univ, Tallahassee, FL; JR; Vars Chrldr; Deans Lst; Phi Soc; Gold Key; Beta Kappa Alpha; Phi Beta Phi.

**ADAMS, ANGELA C,** Richard Bland Coll, Petersburg, VA; SO; BA; SGA 89-; Pr Schlrshp 89-90; AA Richard Bland Clg 90-; Govt; Law.

**ADAMS, ANGELA D,** Univ Of Nc At Charlotte, Charlotte, NC; SR; BA; JC Penney; AA Wilkes Comm Coll 89; Hstry/Sec Educ; Tchr.

**ADAMS, ANGELA D,** Ms St Univ, Miss State, MS; SR; Phi Kappa Phi 90-; Sigma Ti Delta 90-; Stdnt Tchg Neshoba Central H S; BA 89-; Engl; Tch.

**ADAMS, ANITA M,** Notre Dame Coll, Cleveland, OH; SR; BA; Stdnt Govt Assn Treas 89-90; Msqrs 87-; Pi Delta Phi 88-; Phi Chi Theta Treas 90-; Intrcllg Vlybl 89; IM Vlybl Bsktbl 87-; Bus Mgmt; Real Est.

**ADAMS, ANNE M,** Memphis St Univ, Memphis, TN; SR; BPS; Bd Paralegal Stud Advsry Comm 88-; Mbr Stdnt Plng Comm Univ Coll 90-; Gamma Beta Phi 87-; Academic Schlrshp 90-; Cert 88; Legal; Law.

**ADAMS, ARLISA D,** Coll Of Charleston, Charleston, SC; FR; BA; Acctg Assoc; Cougaretts Dance Squad 90-; Stdnt Union Minority Affairs 90-; Alpha Kappa Alpha; Panhallenic Grk Cncl; Bsn Adm; CPA.

**ADAMS JR, BILLY R,** Union Coll, Barbourville, KY; SR; BS; Stdnt Govt Assn Sen 90-; Stdnt Hs Coun Sen Rep 90-; Iota Sigma Nu 90-; Ftbl 87-; Bapt Stdnt Un Flwshp Chrstn Ath 89-; Sr Asst Hlth Phys Educ 90-; Hlth Phys Educ Faclty Awd 90-; Dns Lst Top 12 Campus Men Awd 90-; Phys Educ/Scndry Educ; Tchng.

**ADAMS, CAROL D,** Allen Univ, Columbia, SC; SO; BA; Chrldr Miss Chrldr 89; Sylvia P Swinton Awrd 89-90; Deans List 89-90; Bsn Admin; Cmptr Prgrmmr.

**ADAMS, CATHY G,** Middle Tn St Univ, Murfreesboro, TN; JR; BA; Spec Ed; Tch.

**ADAMS, CHRISTOPHER J,** Trevecca Nazarene Coll, Nashville, TN; SO; Rotaract Hstrn 89-; Chr Prsdnt; Hnr Soc 89-91; Deans Lst 89-; USAA Amrcn Schlr 90-; Rotaract Hstrn Pblcty 89-; Stdnt Gvrnmnt Attrny Gnrl Atty Gnrl 90-; Prsdnts Schlrshp 89-; Sccr Tm 89-; Rlgs Stds; Fmly Cnslng.**

**ADAMS, CLINTON R,** Saint Andrews Presbytrn Coll, Laurinburg, NC; FR; BA; Chess Clb 90; Var Tennis 87; History.

**ADAMS, CRAIG T,** Oh Wesleyan Univ, Delaware, OH; SR; BA; Sigma Phi Epsilon Almni Oprtns 89-90; Intrfrat Cncl Schlrshp 90-; OH Epsln Almni Assn Schlrshp 90-; Deans Lst; Vrsty Ftbl Lttrmn 87-89; Engl/Wrtng; Tech Wrtng.

**ADAMS, DARREN CHAD,** Univ Of Cin R Walters Coll, Blue Ash, OH; SO; AAS; Rdlgc Tchnlgy; Mdcl.

**ADAMS, DAVID A,** Central St Univ, Wilberforce, OH; JR; BA; Econ Clb; Poet Prod Inc Pres 89-; IM Bsktbl Coach; Res Hl Cncl Mntr Advsr 90-; K Mart Intrnshp Asst Mgr; Bus; Econ/Mktg.

**ADAMS, DAVID R,** Northern Ky Univ, Highland Hts, KY; SR; BS; Cmptr Sci; Coll Prof.

**ADAMS, DEINNA M,** Univ Of Ga, Athens, GA; JR; BSED; NSSLHA 90-; Phi Eta Sigma 89-; Cmnctn Sci/Disordrs; Spch Lang Pathlgy.

**ADAMS, DENISE L,** Univ Of Md At Eastern Shore, Princess Anne, MD; BS; Alpha Lambda Mu 89-; Otstndng Envir Sci Stdnt 89; Blgy.

**ADAMS JR, DONALD E,** Memphis St Univ, Memphis, TN; SR; BSME; Am Soc Mech Engs; Mech Eng; Indl Mgt.

**ADAMS, DOROTHY M,** Atlantic Comm Coll, Mays Landing, NJ; SO; BA; Atlantic Co Hist Soc; Natl Edn Assoc; New Jersey Ed Assoc; Spcl Edn/Tchr Handicap.

**ADAMS, ELIZABETH A,** Niagara Univ, Niagara Univ, NY; SR; BS; Alpha Kappa Sec 89-; Univ Comm Actn Pgm 90-; Asst Mgr Marriott Stdnt Dng 88-90; Prcng Dept Intern Carborundum Abrasives Co 90; BS CIS; Mgmt; Mgmt/Human Rsrcs.

**ADAMS, ELLA KATE,** Univ Of Sc At Columbia, Columbia, SC; FR; BS; Frshmn Cncl; Preview Cmte; Alpha Lambda Delta; Epsilon Sigma Alpha; Alpha Delta Pi; Acctng.

**ADAMS, EMILY C,** Oh Univ, Athens, OH; JR; BA; IIE; Water Ski Clb 90-; Theta Tau Comm Head 90-; Co Op Pre Mix EMS Inc; Fld Hcky Varsty 88-90; Eng.

**ADAMS, ERIN A,** Duquesne Univ, Pittsburgh, PA; SO; Orientation Stf 90-; Phi Eta Sigma 89-90; Lambda Sigma 90-; Kappa Delta Epsilon 90-; Sacred Hrt Church Lector 86-; CESTA; Elem Ed; Tchg.

**ADAMS, GEORGE M,** West Liberty St Coll, West Liberty, WV; JR; BA; Order Of AHEPA 88-; USWA Fin Sec 89-; Cert Airco Techincal Inst 84; Business; Mgmnt.

**ADAMS JR, GORDON E,** Mount Olive Coll, Mount Olive, NC; SO; BAS; Unit Advsry Cncl 87-90; Drm Cncl 87-90; AF Bsc Trng Hnr Grad 86; NCO Prep Hnr Grad 90; Spcl Olympics Vol 86-90; Red Cross Dstr Svc Vol 90; AS Comm Coll Of AF 90; Microbiology; Research.**

**ADAMS, GRETCHEN M,** Bloomsburg Univ Of Pa, Bloomsburg, PA; FR; BS; Field Hcky 90; Bio.

**ADAMS, HILDA J,** Livingston Univ, Livingston, AL; SR; BS; Natl Educ Assn; Ala WMU Exec Bd 87-88; Lang Arts; Educ.

**ADAMS, JACK D,** Garrett Comm Coll, Mchenry, MD; FR; Tae Kwon Do Club Pres 90-; Math Project Standout.

**ADAMS, JAMES J,** Univ Of Va Clinch Valley Coll, Wise, VA; JR; BS; ACM 89-; Dean Lst; Asst Mngr Doug Ftns Wrld Stck Mngr 87-; Math Cmptr Infrmtn Systm; Sftwr Engnrng.

**ADAMS, JASPER M,** Denmark Tech Coll, Denmark, SC; SO; AD; Elctrncs Club Pres 90; Alpha Phi Psi Hstrn; Elctrncs Tech.

**ADAMS, JENNIFER M,** Howard Univ, Washington, DC; SR; BARCH; Wmn Arch/Plng Pres 89-90; Tau Sigma Delta; Golden Key; Arch; Prvt Prctc.

**ADAMS, JOANNE S,** City Univ Of Ny City Coll, New York, NY; SO; BA; City Clg Flwshp; Psychology; Clncl Psychlgst.

**ADAMS, JOHN A,** Medical Coll Of Ga, Augusta, GA; SR; BSN; GA Assoc Of Nursing Raising Comm 89-; Sigma Theta Tau Internatl; Collegiate Nursing Awd 90-; BA Augusta Clge 82; Nursing.

**ADAMS, JONATHAN T,** Va St Univ, Petersburg, VA; JR; Engrng Clb 89-; Applied Sci; Electrnc Engrng Tchnlgy.

**ADAMS, JOY L,** Univ Of Southern Ms, Hattiesburg, MS; JR; Hnrs Assoc Pres 88-; Egl Cnctn Awd Outstndng Srvc Awd 89-; Gldn Key 90-; Gamma Beta Phi 89-; Kappa Mu Epsilon 89-; Phi Delta Rho; Omicron Delta Kappa; NASA Goddard Spc Flght Ctr Grnt; Pres Schlr 88-; British Stds Trvl Schlrshp 90; Math; Rsrch/Dvlpmnt.

**ADAMS, JUDITH E,** Univ Of Nc At Charlotte, Charlotte, NC; JR; BA; Chld Psych.

**ADAMS, JUDY C,** Va St Univ, Petersburg, VA; JR; BS; Eng Clb 90-; BS; Elctrnc Eng Tech; Eng.**

**ADAMS, KEITH M,** Union Inst, Cincinnati, OH; SR; BA; Cmmnctns Wrkrs Of Amer VP 88-; AT/T Cmmnctns 83-; Labor Rel; Mgmg/Union Offcrshp/Arbrtrtr/Wrtr.

**ADAMS, KELLI L,** Auburn Univ At Auburn, Auburn, AL; FR; BA; Delta Zeta Acvty Chrmn; Txtls; Mgt.

**ADAMS, KELLY K,** Hillsborough Comm Coll, Tampa, FL; FR; BA; Crmnlgy; Crmnl Law.

**ADAMS, KIMBERLY A,** Univ Of Akron, Akron, OH; SR; Dns Lst 87-; BS; Elem Educ; Tchng.

**ADAMS, KIMBERLY L,** Va Commonwealth Univ, Richmond, VA; FR; BFA; Art; Cmptr Grphcs Artist.

**ADAMS, KRIS M,** Oh Univ, Athens, OH; SR; BA; Arts Society Treas; Art History; Professor Gallery Grad Schl.

**ADAMS, KRISTINA M,** Fl St Univ, Tallahassee, FL; JR; BA; Mtl Hlth Assist Psy Hospital; Psychy/Sociology; Therapy Rehbtn.

**ADAMS, LA DAWN,** Alcorn St Univ, Lorman, MS; FR; BMUS; Interfaith Gospel Choir Mscn/Tchr 90-; Cncrt Choir 90-; Hon Soc 90-; Accmpnst Msc Mjrs/Cncrt Choir 90-; Pres Schlr 90-; Music Edn; Choral Tchr/Rcrdng Artist.

**ADAMS, LAWRENCE W,** Bryant Stratton Bus Inst Roch, Rochester, NY; GD; AOS; Elctrncs; Elctrncs Tchncn.

**ADAMS, LESLIE A,** Wv Univ, Morgantown, WV; FR; BS; Hnr Pgm 90-; Elctrcl/Cmptr Engr.

**ADAMS, LISA G,** Marshall University, Huntington, WV; SO; AD; Comp Tech; Prgrmmng.**

**ADAMS, LORI A,** Ms St Univ, Miss State, MS; SO; BBA; Fnce; Fncl Cnslng Frm.

**ADAMS, LORI M,** Valdosta St Coll, Valdosta, GA; JR; BED; GA Speech/Hrng Assn 90-; Speech/Lang Pthlgy.

**ADAMS, LUTHER MORRIS,** Marshall University, Huntington, WV; FR; BA; Phi Eta Sigma 90-; Natl Hon Soc; Schlrshp; WV Natl Grd 89-; Bus Mgmt; Orthpdcs Mgmt.

**ADAMS, MARCY S,** Winthrop Coll, Rock Hill, SC; SR; BS; SNEA 85-86; PSTA 90-; Deans Lst 86-90; Winthrop Schlrshp 90-; Ele Educ; Tch.

**ADAMS, MARY KAY,** Oh St Univ At Marion, Marion, OH; FR; BA; Crisis Prgnncy Cntr Mngr/Dir 84-87; Hstry Engl; Law.

**ADAMS, MARY ROBYN,** Longwood Coll, Farmville, VA; SR; BA; Bptst Stdnt Unn Cncl Mmbr 89-; Amer Astrlia Assn 89-; Mcklnbrg Hstrcl Scty 87-; Phi Kappa Phi 90-; Lambda Iota Tau 89-; Natl Frnsc Fnls Imprmptre Spkng AFA Ancl; Chi Cmmndtn 90; GG Wade Engl Educ Schlrshp 89-; AS Southside VA Comm Coll 87; Engl; Tch Hgh Schl Engl.

**ADAMS, MELANIE,** Johnson And Wales Univ, Providence, RI; FR; MBA; Gospel Chr; Drama; Christian Stdnts Clb; Intl Food Svc Exec Assc; Deans Lst 90-; NH Schl Food Svc Schlrshp 90-; Johnson/Wales Miss Natl Teenager Schlrshp 90; Intern Caesars Intl; Hotel/Restaurant Mgt.

**ADAMS, MELISSA D,** Lexington Comm Coll, Lexington, KY; SO; BA; Eunice Beatty Schlrshp/Acad Excel 90-; Cmptr Sci; Busn/Fince.

**ADAMS, MELISSA D,** Ashland Comm Coll, Ashland, KY; FR; MBA; Dns Lst 90-; Bsn Ad/Acctg.

**ADAMS, MICHAEL L,** Tri County Tech Coll, Pendleton, SC; SO; IE; Alpha Zeta Beta; Grad With Hnrs; Am Soc For Quality Control 90; Church Asst Tchr 89-; R A Ldr; Degree IE; Cert Quality; Engrng/Human Resources.

**ADAMS, MONICA D,** Duquesne Univ, Pittsburgh, PA; SO; BA; Blck Stdnt Un Treas; Delta Sigma Theta Financl Sec; Serv Clb 90; Bus; Acctg/Law.**

**ADAMS, MONICA L,** Ms St Univ, Miss State, MS; SR; BA; Soc Adv Mgmt 89; Stndt Adv Cncl Coll Arts/Sci VP 90-; Phi Kappa Phi 90-; Soc Schlrs; Phi Alpha Theta 89-; Pres Lst 88-; Hstry; Govt/DEA/USAID.

**ADAMS, NICHOLE H,** Clark Atlanta Univ, Atlanta, GA; SR; BA; United Negro Clg Fund Pre-Alumni Cncl 88-; CAU Tour Guide 89-; Natl Blck Media Coalition V P 89-; Sigma Delta Chi Secr 88-90; NAALP 87-88; Delta Sigma Theta V P 88-; Atlantic Rec Cor Intern 88-89; Natl Blck Arts Fest Intern; Radio/TV/FILM; Entertnmnt Law.

**ADAMS, PATRICIA E,** Univ Of Nc At Charlotte, Charlotte, NC; SO; BS; Dns Lst 90; Acctg; CPA.

**ADAMS, PATRICIA M,** Univ Of Med & Dentistry Of Nj, Newark, NJ; SR; MPT; Pre Phys Thrpy Clb Univ IA 86-87; Gldn Key 90-; Phi Kappa Phi 90-; Phi Beta Kappa 90-; BS IA St Univ 90; Physical Therapy.

**ADAMS, RAMONA L,** Medical Univ Of Sc, Charleston, SC; JR; BS 87; Nrsng.

**ADAMS, REBECCA J,** Emory Univ, Atlanta, GA; SR.

**ADAMS JR, ROBERT C,** Berry Coll, Rome, GA; SO; BS; Cncrt Choir 90-; Sngrs 90-; Lambda Sigma Tres; Mu Alpha Theta Pres 90-; Music Flwshp 90-; Math; Cmptr.

**ADAMS, ROBERTA T,** Newbury Coll, Brookline, MA; FR; ASSOC; Interior Dsgn.

**ADAMS, ROBIN R,** Va St Univ, Petersburg, VA; SR; Acctg Clb 86-90; Cert Pub Acctg Clb VP 88-90; Natl Assn Blck Actnts 89-90; Phi Beta Lamda 89-90; NAACP 90; Cert Aerobic Instrctr Hd Instrctr 86-90; Acctg; CPA.

**ADAMS, ROCHELLE L,** Clark Atlanta Univ, Atlanta, GA; JR; BS; Mrktng Clb Mbr 89-; Spanish Clb Mbr 90-; Elem Students Vol Tutor 90-; Beta Psi; Bus Admin; Advertising.

**ADAMS, RODNEY E,** Morris Coll, Sumter, SC; GD; MS; Stdnt Govt Assc NAACP VP 89-90; Gospel Chr Tres Gspl Chr Pres Tres; Stdnt Natl Educ Assc Pblc Rltns 88-90; Alph Kappa Mu; BA 90; Engl; Clg Stdnt Prsnl.

**ADAMS, RODNEY WAYNE,** Columbia Union Coll, Takoma Park, MD; SR; BS; Dean Lst 90; Prison Mnstry 83-84; Stf Acctnt 89-; AA 82; Bus Admin; Finance.

**ADAMS, ROGER G,** Liberty Univ, Lynchburg, VA; SR; BS; Tae Kawn Do Clb 87-90; Sprts Admin.

**ADAMS, ROXANA R,** Middle Tn St Univ, Murfreesboro, TN; SO; BS; Indstrl Orgnztnl Sociology.

**ADAMS, SHARON YVETTE,** Ky St Univ, Frankfort, KY; SR; BS; Miss Stdnt Life 87-88; Class Pr 89-90; Gospel Ens 87-90; Deans Lst; Hon Rl; Delta Sigma Theta 89-; Allen-Bradley A Rockwell Intl Intrn 89-90; Comp Sci; Analysts.

**ADAMS, SHERRI LYNN,** Atlantic Comm Coll, Mays Landing, NJ; FR; BA; Taking General Courses At ACC Wish To Transfer To 4 Yr School & Finish Major; Radio/TV Broadcasting; TV Broadcasting.

**ADAMS, SHERRY K,** Chattahoochee Vly St Comm Coll, Phenix City, AL; FR; BA; Gamma Beta Phi; Goal Nmnee 88; Dns Lst 90-; Pres Lst 90-; Elem Educ; Tch.

**ADAMS, SHERRY S,** Radford Univ, Radford, VA; SO; BA; Phys Educ Mjrs Clb 90-; Am Alnc Hlth Phys Educ Rcrtn/Dance 89-; IM 90-; Phys Ed; Tchr.

**ADAMS, SHERYL L,** Comm Coll Algny Co Algny Cmps, Pittsburgh, PA; SO; BA; Tutor Linden Elmtry Sch; Tch Math Jr Sr Hgh Level; Mathematics.

**ADAMS, SHIRLEY S,** Phillips Jr Coll Spartanburg, Spartanburg, SC; GD; GERT; Nursng Asst.

**ADAMS, SHIRYL J,** Franklin Univ, Columbus, OH; FR; BA; Accntng Assctn 90-; Tutor 90-; Finance/Real Estate; Law.

**ADAMS, STACIE A,** Teikyo Post Univ, Waterbury, CT; SR; BS; Exc In Auditing Awd; Cert Huntington Inst Business Schl 87; Accounting; Cpa.

**ADAMS, STEPHEN B,** Abraham Baldwin Agri Coll, Tifton, GA; SO; BS; Frst/Wldlfe Clb Pres 90; AS; Wldlfe Tchncn; Cnsrvtn Law Enfrcemnt.

**ADAMS, STEVEN E,** Milligan Coll, Milligan Clg, TN; JR; BS; SGA Chf Just Trffc Ct 90-; Cir K 89-; IMS 88-; Busn Admin/Cmptr Sci; Mgmt.

**ADAMS, SUSAN H,** Georgian Court Coll, Lakewood, NJ; JR; BS; Asst Ofc Mgr Convlcnt Ctr; Bus Admn; Pharmctcl Mgt.

**ADAMS, TAMARA PAIGE,** Univ Of Tn At Knoxville, Knoxville, TN; JR; BS; Bapt Stdnt Union 88-; Executive Undergrads 90-; Gamma Beta Phi 90-; Beta Alpha Psi; Acctg; CPA.

**ADAMS, TAMMY DUNN,** Fayetteville St Univ, Fayetteville, NC; JR; BSB; Stu Amer Dntl Hygn Assoc 88-89; Deans Lst 90; Fytvl Tech Comm Coll Dntl Hygn Dept; Lab Asstnt 90-; Grtr Fytvl Dntl Assoc Grnt 89; Mnrty Prsnc Grnt 90-; Reg Dntl Hygnst 90-; ASC Dh 90; Bio; Dntl Sch.

**ADAMS, TAMMY S,** Central Pa Bus School, Summerdale, PA; FR; ASSC; Lgl Asstnt; Law/Crmnl Jstc.

**ADAMS, TANYA L,** Saint Vincents Coll & Seminary, Latrobe, PA; SO; BA; Hstry Clb Pre Law Clb 90-; Phi Alpha Theta; Hstry; Law.

**ADAMS, TEDD D,** Ky Christian Coll, Grayson, KY; SO; BA; Stdnt Govt Acad Cmtee Chrmn 89; Interdiscplnry; Engr.

**ADAMS, TONYA R,** Prestonburg Comm Coll, Prestonburg, KY; FR; BA; Bsns; Bsns Admn.

**ADAMS, TORRI LYNN,** Wilberforce Univ, Wilberforce, OH; JR; Yth Dept Mt Moriah Chgo 87; African Modern Dance Lys 86; NAACP 88-; Dns Lst 89-90; Sweetheart Kappa Alpha Psi 88-89; Indus Psych.**

**ADAMS, TRACY M,** Alcorn St Univ, Lorman, MS; JR; BS; Hnry Achvmnt Awds; Communication; Broadcasting.

**ADAMS, VANESSA L,** Tougaloo Coll, Tougaloo, MS; JR; BS; Pol Sci Clb 89-; Yng Coll Dmcrts 88-; Pre Almni Clb 90-; Phi Beta Sigma Swthrt Clb; Wa Kadzi 90; Dns Lst 87; Pol Sci; Corp Lwyr.

**ADAMS II, WALTER E,** Morehouse Coll, Atlanta, GA; SO; BA; Congrsnl Blck Intrn Assoc Parlmntrn; Pol Sci Soc Secy 90-; Atlanta Univ Ctr IL Club Parlmntrn 89-; Hons Club 89-; AFS Intrntl-Intrcltrl 89-; Congrsnl Intrnshp Sentr Paul Simon; Pol Sci; Law.

**ADAMS, WESLEY W,** Memphis St Univ, Memphis, TN; SR; BA; Young Life Ldr 87-; Dns Lst 86-; Phi Alpha Theta 89-; Jugglers Assn; Academic Schlrshp 86-; J C Penney Schlrshps 87-89; Hist; Tchr.**

**ADAMS, WILLIAM J L,** Stetson Univ, Deland, FL; SO; BS; Scty Of Physcs Stdnts 89-; Phi Eta Sigma; Sigma Pi Sigma; REU Smmr In Math At FSU; Barry Goldwater Awrd; George L Jenkins Awrd In Physics 90; Math And Physics; Prfssrshp.

**ADAMSKI, JOHN P,** Youngstown St Univ, Youngstown, OH; GD; Vars Ftbl 77-79; Amer Soc Civil Eng 89-; Amer Sod Hwy Eng 89-; Const Eng 84-; BE; Eng; Env Eng.

**ADAMSON, CHRISTINE,** Rust Coll, Holly Springs, MS; JR; BA; Pre Law Clb Pres; Intrntl Stdnt Assn Sec; Rust Coll Hnr Awds 88-; Trck Crs Cntry 88-; Mst Val Trck Crs Cntry Rnr 88-; Miss Intrntl Stdnt 90-; BA; Pol Sci; Lawyer.

**ADAMSON, DANIEL D,** S U N Y Coll Of Tech At Alfred, Alfred, NY; FR; AS; Sigma Tau Epsilon 90-; BSA Jr Asst Scout Mas 88-; Eagle Scout; Cl IMS 90-; Drafting.

**ADAMSON, JAMES M,** Spartanburg Methodist Coll, Spartanburg, SC; SO; Tutor 90-; IM 90-; Pblc Spkng Tutor 90-; Bsktbl Team Mgr 90; AA Spartanburg; Engl; Lawyer.**

**ADAMSON, KYLE F,** Univ Of Cincinnati, Cincinnati, OH; SO; BA; IEEE; Tau Alpha Pi; Elctrncs Eng.

**ADAMUS, MARISHKA BRIGIDA,** Fl A & M Univ, Tallahassee, FL; SR; BA; Caribbean Clb Assn 88-; Gldn Key; Hon Rl; Deans Lst 88-; Mdrn Bus Admin Schl Voor MAO 87; Acctg.

**ADAN, KAREN M,** Univ Of Pr At Rio Piedras, Rio Piedras, PR; SO; AIAS 89-; Dsgn; Archtctr.

**ADAY, AMANDA J,** Belmont Coll, Nashville, TN; FR; BA; Biology; Genetic Research.

**ADCOCK, ANITA M,** Univ Of Sc At Columbia, Columbia, SC; SR; Assn Personnel Admin; BS 90; Bus Grad Schl.

**ADCOCK, DAVID F,** Univ Of Sc At Columbia, Columbia, SC; FR; BA; Phlsphy; Univ Lvl Tchng.

**ADCOCK, LAURA E,** Oh Wesleyan Univ, Delaware, OH; FR; BA; Envir Wldlf Clb 90-; Phi Eta Sigma 90-; Eng; Pblshg Co.

**ADCOCK, TRACY T,** East Central Comm Coll, Decatur, MS; SO; BED; Phi Beta Lambda Treas; AA; Elem Educ.

**ADDEO, MARIA E,** Fl International Univ, Miami, FL; JR; BA; FEA Tres 89-; SGA; Phi Delta Kappa; AA Beoward Comm Clg 85-88; Elem Edctn; Elem Schl Tchr.

**ADDIE, EMMA J,** Coll Of Charleston, Charleston, SC; FR; Vrsty Swmng Tm 90-.

**ADDINGTON, DEBRA L,** Univ Of Va Clinch Valley Coll, Wise, VA; JR; BA; Beta Sigma Phi Grl Yr 87-88; Stu Mrshl 90-; AA SE Comm Coll 90; Educ K-4; Tch.

**ADDIS, ANGELIA M,** Spartanburg Methodist Coll, Spartanburg, SC; FR; Yrbk; Hist; Secndry Educ.

**ADDISON, ANTHONY F,** Univ Of Rochester, Rochester, NY; SO; BA; Med Emer 1st Resp 89-; Charles Drew Pre-Med Soc Bus Mgr 90-; Estrn Svc Wrkrs Assoc; Deans Lst; Rochester Summer Res Flwshp Awrd; Bio/Hlth/Soc; Med.

**ADDISON, ANTHONY G,** Truett Mc Connell Coll, Cleveland, GA; FR; Phi Beta Lambda 90-; Phi Theta Kappa 90-; 1st Pl Bsn Prncpls Cmptn Phi Beta Lambda St Ldrshp Conf; Alld Paper Inc; Bsn Adm; Bsn Ed.

**ADDISON, MAVIS H,** George Mason Univ, Fairfax, VA; JR; BS; Alpha Lambda Delta 90; Alpha Chi; Golden Key; Chi Omega 90; Fin.

**ADDISON, TRACY L,** Marshall University, Huntington, WV; FR; BA; Bus; Bus Mgmt.

**ADDISON, TRACY V,** Christian Brothers Univ, Memphis, TN; SR; BS; Assoc For Comptng Mach 90-; Pr Acad Schlrshp 87-; Deans Lst 87-; Comp Sci; Pgmng.

**ADDY, SANDRA B,** Valdosta St Coll, Valdosta, GA; SR; BED; UGA March Redcoat Band Percussion; Carolina Pottery Supvr 89-; Classic Grndcvrs Athens GA; Propagation Mgr Carolina Pottery 89-; Sci; Teach.

**ADEDUN, EBENEZER A,** Savannah St Coll, Savannah, GA; JR; BS; Pi Sigma Eta 89-90; AS Chem Okla City Comm Coll 85; AS Mortuary Sci Gupton Jones Coll Of Funeral Serv 90; Med Tech; Biomed Sci.

**ADEGOROYE, ADEOLA O,** Fl A & M Univ, Tallahassee, FL; SR; BED; Bus Educ Assn 89-; Gldn Key 89-; Dns Lst 89-; Hnr Rl 89-; FLA A/M Hnr Rl 89-; Bsktbl 78-84; Natl Cert Of Educ The Polytechnic Ibadan Oyo State Nigeria; Bus; Tchng.

**ADEKOYA, MICHAEL A,** City Univ Of Ny La Guard Coll, Long Island Cty, NY; SO; AS; Cmptr Clb 89-; Phi Theta Kappa 90-; Cmptr Sci; Cmptr Spclsts.

**ADELMAN, JUDD B,** Univ Of Miami, Coral Gables, FL; JR; BA; Gldn Key 90-; Zeta Beta Tau 88-; Infrat Cncl Awrd 90; Pearson Schlrshp 88; Treasure, Paideia 91-92; Pol Sci; Physician.

**ADELSPERGER, GINGER L,** Univ Of Ky, Lexington, KY; SO; BSN; Nrsng.

**ADEN, CARRIE G,** Univ Of Southern Ms, Hattiesburg, MS; SR; BS; SAA Treas 89-91; SG VP 88-89; Phi Theta Kappa 89-; Phidelta Rho 89-; Pi Tau Chi; Dns Lst 89-; Mahperd Schlrshp 89-; Jr Coll Acad Schlrshp 89-; Athltc Schlrshp 89-; Hons MDCC; Hl Fame; Ms MDCC; Pres Lst; Dns Lst 87-89; Delta Delta Delta Trnr 90-; Physcl Thrpy/Athltc Trng.

**ADEN, LEIGH M,** Univ Of Southern Ms, Hattiesburg, MS; SR; BA; Stdnt Dietetics Assc Trea 90; Stdnt Home Economics Assc 90; AM Dietetics Assc 90; AM Home Economics Assc 90; Kappa Alpha Theta Hse Mngr 85-89; Dietetics; Rgstrd Dietitian.

**ADEPOJU, ESTHER F,** Fl A & M Univ, Tallahassee, FL; SR; BSC; Gldn Key 89-; Samgo H S Ibadam-Oyo State Nigeria Hd Dept Tchnlgy 87-89; Ind/Voc Educ.

**ADEWUNMI, CATHERINE S,** Schenectady County Comm Coll, Schenectady, NY; SR; BS; Sci; Phrmcy.**

**ADEWUNMI, FELICIA O,** Univ Of The Dist Of Columbia, Washington, DC; JR; BS; Math/Cmptr Sci; Sftwre Eng.

**ADEYEMI, AKINBOKUN A,** City Univ Of Ny Bronx Comm Col, Bronx, NY; JR; BA; African Stdnts Orgnztn 90-; Fusionist Chemstry Clb 90-; Phi Theta Kappa 90-; Deans List 89-; Phi Theta Kappa 90-; Phi Theta Kappas Turoring Serv; Sccr/Tnns 89-; Otstndng Mnrty Stdnts Tlnt Board; NICAA Acdmn AM 90-; Cuny Stnt Ath Awrd Cnfr 90-; Rsrch Phrmcy.

**ADEYEMI, MOBOLAJI A,** Tuskegee Univ, Tuskegee Inst, AL; SO; BS; Tchncl Edctn; Nrsng.

**ADEYEMO, MUDASIRU A,** Southern Coll Of Tech, Marietta, GA; SR; BSC; Sigma Lambda Chi Trea 90-; Amer Inst Cnstrctrs Cnstrcts Guild; HND Rivers St Univ Nigeria 82; Cnstrctn; Eng.

**ADHIKARI, PRASANNA,** Oh Wesleyan Univ, Delaware, OH; SO; BA BS; Amtr Cncl Sci/Tchnlgy Pres 85-; Soc Physcs Stdnts VP; Cmps Pgm Bd Film Series; Phi Soc; Sigma Pi Sigma; J Diploma Prayag Sangit Samiti 88; Physcs/Eng Math.

**ADICKS, V KYLE,** Fl St Univ, Tallahassee, FL; FR; BA; IM Bsktbl Tm Capt; Phi Eta Sigma; Bus.

**ADJEI, ANTHONY KWASI,** City Univ Of Ny Baruch Coll, New York, NY; JR; BBA; Pub Acctng.

**ADJIRI, JAHARI M,** Central St Univ, Wilberforce, OH; SR; MMED; Sankofa Afrcn Jazz Bnd; Stl Bnd Menc; OSMEA; Cntrl St Choir 88-; USAA All Amer Schlr 88-; US Achvmnt Acdmy Coll Prog; Hnr Rl; Acdmc Schlrshp 88-; Music Ed Spclzg Multi Cltrl Music/Voice; Cert Music Ed 88-; BA 78-81; Cmnctns; Prod Educ Videos.**

**ADJODHA, MICHAEL E,** Univ Of Rochester, Rochester, NY; SR; BS; Wrldwd Chrch God 88-; Tau Beta Pi 89-; AICHE Awrd 89; Scty Mltry Eng Awrd 90-; Chem Eng.

**ADKINS, ANDREA M,** Wv Inst Of Tech, Montgomery, WV; FR; BA; Ambassadors; IMS 90-; Bus; Cmptr Mgmnt/Data Process.

**ADKINS, ANGELA R,** Beckley Coll, Beckley, WV; FR; AS; Bnkg/Fnc.

**ADKINS, ANNETTE,** Denmark Tech Coll, Denmark, SC; JR; BA; Human Svc.

**ADKINS, APRIL D,** Univ Of Charleston, Charleston, WV; JR; BS; Chi Beta Phi 88-; Alpha Lambda Delta 88-; Theta Kappa Pi 90-; Pres Schlr 88-; Envrnmntl Studies; Rsrch/Consrvtn.**

**ADKINS, CANDY JO,** Marshall University, Huntington, WV; SO; BBA; Acctng/Mngmnt; Prsnl/Hmn Rsrcs.

**ADKINS, CARLA A,** Marshall University, Huntington, WV; JR; BA; Multi Subjct Elem K; Tchr.

**ADKINS, CASSANDRA D,** Fl A & M Univ, Tallahassee, FL; FR; BA; Econ; Corp Law.

**ADKINS, CATHERINE L,** Univ Of Sc At Columbia, Columbia, SC; JR; BA; Class Sec 83-84; Deans List 90; Office Sec 89-; Church Yth Ldr; Chldrns Ldr; AS Tomlinson Clg 84; Early Chldhd Ed; Tch.

**ADKINS, CHARLES A,** Univ Of Md At Eastern Shore, Princess Anne, MD; SO; BA; Htl Rstrnt Mgmt Hnrs Chrmn Advrtsng Comm 90-; Hnrs Prgrm 90-; Certf Apprctn Dnnr Theatr 90-; Htl Rstrnt Mgmt; Htl.

**ADKINS, CRYSTAL G,** Marshall University, Huntington, WV; GD; MA ED; Kappa Delta Pi 89; Beta Sigma Phi 89-; Amer Assn Univ Wmn 89-; Jr Hi Algebra Tchr; BA 88; Sci Math Admn; Prin/Supt.

**ADKINS, CRYSTAL J,** Univ Of North Fl, Jacksonville, FL; SR; BS; Lgl Asst 83-; Econ; Law.**

**ADKINS II, DAVID A,** Central Fl Comm Coll, Ocala, FL; FR; Weight Lftng/Swmng 90-; Aerospace/Cmptr Eng.

**ADKINS, DEBORAH K,** Marshall University, Huntington, WV; GD; MA; WVEA 88-; Elem Tchr 88-; BA Elem Ed; Reading Ed.

**ADKINS, DENICE F,** Miami Jacobs Jr Coll Of Bus, Dayton, OH; SO; AS; Clrk Typst Dept Vtrns Affrs US Fdrl Govt 88-; Cert 87; Comp Bus Admn.

**ADKINS II, JAMES M,** Marshall University, Huntington, WV; FR; BBA; Fin; Bus.

**ADKINS, JOHNNY M,** Bristol Univ, Bristol, TN; GD; MBA; BS U TN 75; Exec Mgmt.

**ADKINS, JOY R,** Univ Of Va Clinch Valley Coll, Wise, VA; FR; Bsns; Acctg.

**ADKINS, KIMERLY D,** Ashland Comm Coll, Ashland, KY; SO; BSN; Parents Spcl Needs Assn Pres 87-; March Dimes Vol 88-90; Bio Nrsng; Pre-Med.

**ADKINS, L ALLYSON,** Marshall University, Huntington, WV; SO; MBA; Sigma Sigma Sigma; Cnslng/Rehab; Fmly Therapist.

**ADKINS, LEAH C,** Univ Of South Al, Mobile, AL; SO; Stdnt Govt Assn Rep 89-90; Vrsty Chrldng 89-90; Nwspr Stf 89-90; Bus; CPA.

**ADKINS, MARY E,** Miami Dade Comm Coll, Miami, FL; SO; AS; Cert Otstndng Acdmc Achvmnt 90-; Grad Hnrs 85; Prlgl 89-90; BA 85; Prlgl; Law.

**ADKINS, MELINDA S,** Marshall University, Huntington, WV; SO.

**ADKINS, NANCY J,** Wilmington Coll, New Castle, DE; JR; BSN; Stdnt Govt V P 88-89; Beebe Sch Nurs Treas 86-89; Vol Amer Heart Assn 87-89; Deans Lst 89-; Vldctrn Nurs 89; Wmns Aux Clb Awd 87; Stf Nurs 90-; Dip Beebe Sch Nurs 89; Nurs; Nursing Fld Tchr.

**ADKINS, RICHIE D,** Univ Of Ky, Lexington, KY; SR; BA; Caucus Clb VP 87-; Phi Beta Lambda 87-; Pi Sigma Alpha; Am Cvl Lbrts Un 89-; Musician/Bnd Mngr; Pol Sci; Law/Govt.

**ADKINS, SONYA L,** Georgetown Coll, Georgetown, KY; JR; BS; Data Proc Mgmt Assn 89-; Phi Beta Lambda 90-; Acctg/Comp Info Syst; Actnt/Comp Pgrmr.

**ADKINS, SUSAN M,** De Tech & Comm Coll At Grgtwn, Georgetown, DE; FR; BAAC; Tutor For Acctng/Sec 90-; Acctng; CPA.

**ADKISSON, RALPH G,** Davis & Elkins Coll, Elkins, WV; SR; BA; Var Ftbl Capt; Prof Muscn; Prof Landgnt Abstrctr; AA John A Logan Clg 88; Pol Sci/Hstry/Music; Muscn/Lwyr.

**ADKISSON, SCOTT M,** Tn Tech Univ, Cookeville, TN; SO; BS; Hrtcltr Jdgng Tm 90; 4h Frstry Jdgng Tm 90-; Deans Lst 89-; Otstndng Plnt Soil; Science Jr; IM Sftbl; Engnrng.

**ADLER, ANDREE A,** Waycross Coll, Waycross, GA; FR; AA; Coll Nwsppr Msc Edtr Elect; Music; Prfrmr/Music/Voice.

**ADLER, JOSHUA T,** City Univ Of Ny Baruch Coll, New York, NY; SO; Bsn; Acctnt.

**ADLER, MICHAEL B,** Cornell Univ Statutory College, Ithaca, NY; SO; BS; Kappa Delta Rho 90-; Emerg Medical Serv 90-; NY St Rgnts Schlrshp; March Bnd 90; Pre Med Studies; Doctor.

**ADLER, NICOLE L,** Fl St Univ, Tallahassee, FL; SR; Amrcn Mrktng Assoc; Gldn Key; Pi Sigma Epsilon; Intern WFSUTV; Dept Natl Rsrce; Cmmnctns.

**ADLER, SHANNON K,** Ky Wesleyan Coll, Owensboro, KY; SO; Bapt Stdnt Un Pres 90-; Parnassus Soc VP 90-; Stdnt Govt Assn Com 90-; Play All My Sons Pblcty Chmn; Psychlgy Clb 89-; Crmnl Jstce Assn; Hall Recycling Chmn 90-; Friend Friend Pgm; Behvrl Sci Cncl Rep Fr Rep 89-90; Crmnl Jstce/Psychlgy; FBI.

**ADOLPH, KIMBERLY ANN,** Fl St Univ, Tallahassee, FL; SR; BS; Future Edctrs Am 90-; Sigma Kappa Asst VP Mbrshp 87-; Intern Havana Elem Schl; Elem Ed; Tchng Schl.

**ADOMAITIS, JENNIFER L,** Duquesne Univ, Pittsburgh, PA; FR; Phi Eta Sgm; Bus/Admn; Mgmt Inf Systms.

**ADORANTE, MICHAEL F,** Bristol Univ, Bristol, TN; GD; MBA; IEEE Sec 87-; DPMA 87-; Pi Kappa Alpha; Mrkt Mgr Bus Dvlpmnt; BS 79; Cmptr Info Mgmt; Mktg.

**ADORNO, MICHAEL C,** Univ Of Pr Cayey Univ Coll, Cayey, PR; SO; BA; Bsbl/Sftbl 88-89; Acctng; MBA Law.

**ADORNO, ZAHIRA,** Univ Of Pr At Rio Piedras, Rio Piedras, PR; FR; BA; Assn De Ex-Alumnos Del Proyecto CAUSA Vcl 90-; Blgy; Med.

**ADRIANO, JENNYLYN P,** Anne Arundel Comm Coll, Arnold, MD; SO; BA; Gnrl Stds; Fshn Mrchndsr Byr.

**ADRIEN, LESLIE R,** Fl International Univ, Miami, FL; SO; BA; Biology; Med.

**ADSHEAD, R EDWARD,** Salisbury St Univ, Salisbury, MD; SR; BS; Elem Ed.

**ADUBOFOUR, SANDRA,** Bennett Coll, Greensboro, NC; FR; BA; Intl Students Assoc; English; Law.

**ADUMA, KENYETTA T,** Hampton Univ, Hampton, VA; SR; BA; Sociology Clb VP 90-; Alpha Kappa Mu 90-; Alpha Kappa Delta 90-; Track Tm 87-89; Sociology; Law.

**AELKER, JOAN M,** Defiance Coll, Defiance, OH; JR; BA; Acctg/Fin Clb Treas 89-; Alpha Chi; Math Tutor 89; Pres Host 89-90; Acctg Intrn Zeller Corp; Schlr Athlete Awd AAUW; Var Bkbl Crs Cntry 89; H Willet Asstnshp Bus Admn; Co Capt B B 90-; Acctg/Math; Acctg.

**AESCHLIMAN, GREGORY J,** Memphis St Univ, Memphis, TN; SR; BBA; Mem Rnnrs Trck Clb 88-; Pblc Acctg.

**AFANADOR, ROBERTO,** Univ Of Pr At Mayaguez, Mayaguez, PR; SO; BBA; CAUSA Alumni Assc VP 89-; Natl Hon Scty VP 88-89; Bus Admn Hon Roll; Acctg.**

**AFANESKO, SUSAN A,** Comm Coll Algny Co Algny Cmps, Pittsburgh, PA; SO; BA; Natl MS Scty; Spcl Olympics88-; Hnrs Stdnt Bradford Bus Schl 82; Sh; Shadyside Hosp Bwlng Pres 90; Awrd Outstndng Shrthnd Skills Bradford 82; Emplyd Shadyside Hosp; Cert Bradford Bus Schl 82; Lib Arts/Sci; Mrktng/Comm.

**AFFERTON, SUSAN E,** James Madison University, Harrisonburg, VA; JR; BA; Assn Educ Yng Chldrn 88-; Alpha Sigma Alpha 89-; IMS; Early Chldhd Educ; Primary Tchr.

**AFFLERBACH, LISA M,** Lansdale School Of Bus, North Wales, PA; SR; AS; Notary Public 91-; Prop/Casualty Ins Agnt; Cert 88; Bus Admin/Mgmnt; Mktng Ins Ind.

**AFZAL, JOI K,** Clark Atlanta Univ, Atlanta, GA; SO; BA; Peppermint Dream Orgnztn VP 89-; Inspiration Voices Of Faith 90; NAACP 89; Inroads Internship 90; Crowned Ms Gamma Kappa Kappa Alpha Psi; Acctng; CPA.

**AGAN, SANDRA K,** Ny Univ, New York, NY; JR; BA; Stdnt Cncl Pres 90-; Alpha Sigma Lambda; AA 90; Psych; Law.

**AGANS, SUZETTE M,** Schenectady County Comm Coll, Schenectady, NY; FR; AAS; Asstd Empr Games; Bus; Hmn Rsrc.

**AGARD, CARL L,** City Univ Of Ny Baruch Coll, New York, NY; JR; BBA; Cmptr Info Systms; Pgmr/Anlyst.

**AGATI, ANDREW,** Allegheny Coll, Meadville, PA; JR; BA; Pre Lgl Comm Co Chrmn 90-; Jdcl Bd 89-90; Radio Nwscstr 90-; Lambda Sigma 89-90; Dist Atty Intrn; Alden Schlr 88-89; Dstngshd Alden Schlr 89-90; IM Athlt 88-; Econ; Law.

**AGBENOWOSI, NEWLAND K,** Central St Univ, Wilberforce, OH; FR; BS; Flwshp Of Chrstn Stdnts Flyers Admn; Intl Stdnts Assoc 90-; Giro Club Treas 90; Water Resources Mgmt; Civil Engrng Comp Sci.

**AGEE SR, JEREMIAH,** Central Al Comm Coll, Alexander City, AL; SO; AAS; Elect; Eng.

**AGEE, LEIGH A,** James Madison University, Harrisonburg, VA; GD; Psychlgy Clb 87-90; Med Alld Hlth Soc Treas 86-89; Vol Wrk Physcl/Ocptl Thrpy 87-90; BS 90; Psychlgy; MS-OCCPTNL Thrpy.

**AGEE JR, RICHARD L,** Dyersburg St Comm Coll, Dyersburg, TN; JR; Lambda Chi Alpha.

**AGEMIAN, THOMAS,** Atlantic Comm Coll, Mays Landing, NJ; SO; Hstry/Govt Clb Rep 90-; Amer Phltlc Soc 90-; Dns Lst 89-; Audubon Soc 88-; AA; Educ; Tch Elem.

**AGLIOZZO, MARGARET J,** Georgetown Univ, Washington, DC; JR; BSN; Acad Stdnt Cncl Cls Rep 90-; Eucharistic Minister 90-; Sigma Theta Tau; Nrsng/Pre Med; Med Schl.

**AGNELLO, RAY,** Passaic County Comm Coll, Paterson, NJ; GD; ADN; Natl Stdnt Nurses Assoc 90-; LPN Bergen Pines Co Hosp Sch Of Nsg 85; Nursing Sci; Reg Prof Nurse.

**AGNER, TROY L,** Old Dominion Univ, Norfolk, VA; SR; BS; Spcl Engr Secy/Treas; Golden Key; Dip Electrncs Danville Cmnty Clg 89; Elec Engr Tech.

**AGNIHOTRI, SHIMALIYA,** George Mason Univ, Fairfax, VA; SEA; VEA; AIS; Intrnl Assn; Drama Assn; Clsscl Dnce; BS Ed; Educ; Tch.

**AGNOLI, SCOTT J,** Savannah Coll Of Art & Design, Savannah, GA; SR; Var Sccr 90; BFA; Graphic Design; Advrtsng.

**AGOHA, PAUL O,** Lincoln Univ, Lincoln Univ, PA; FR; BS; Bio; Bio-Med Tech.

**AGOSTA, MARIA ANGELICA,** Miami Dade Comm Coll, Miami, FL; SO; BA; Sci Socty Pres 89-; Stdnt Govt Assn 90-; Phi Theta Kappa Pres 88-; Stdnt Govt; Coll Boards 91 Tlnt Rstr 90-; Dns Lst 88-; AA 91; Chem Engr.

**AGOSTO DIAZ, ANTHONY,** Inter Amer Univ Pr Guayama, Guayama, PR; SR; BA; Hnr Rl Stdnt 89-90; Bsktbl/Ftbl Tm 87-88; Biology; Med Tech.

**AGOSTO, ESTHER N,** Inter Amer Univ Pr Hato Rey, Hato Rey, PR; JR; BA; Soc Work Stdnt Assoc; Vlybl; History; Soc Work.

**AGRAWAL, DEWESH,** Duke Univ, Durham, NC; SO; BS; India Assn Pr 89-; Stdnt Govt Tr 89-90; Phi Eta Sigma 89-; Chi Psi 90-; Cir K 90-; Round Table 90-; Bio/Econs, Med.**

**AGREDA, CAROL S,** Fl International Univ, Miami, FL; SO; Lrng Disabilites; Educ.

**AGUILA, MARTHA,** Saint Thomas Univ, Miami, FL; JR; BA; AA Miami Dade Comm Coll 90; Elem Ed.

**AGUILAR ALVAREZ, CARIDAD Y,** Inter Amer Univ Pr San Juan, Hato Rey, PR; SR; BBA; Honor Pgm 89-; Dn Lt Interamer Univ; AA Intl Fine Arts Clg 87; Mktg; Intl Law.

**AGUILAR ARROYO, JORGE A,** Oh Wesleyan Univ, Delaware, OH; FR; BA; Hrzns Intrntl 90-; Phi Eta Sigma; Pi Mu Epsilon; Nwmn Comm Cath Org 90-; Ftbl Tm; Intrntl Bus/Cmptr Sci; Biomed Eng.

**AGUILAR, MAURICIO E,** Howard Univ, Washington, DC; JR; BA; AA Montgomery Coll 88; Arch/Plnnng.

**AGUIRRE, DIANA S,** Miami Dade Comm Coll, Miami, FL; SO; BA; Phi Delta Kappa 90; Vllybl Tm Capt 89-90; Chem; Med.**

**AGUIRRE, GIOCONDA M,** Barry Univ, Miami, FL; SR; BS; Staff Acctnt; AA Miami Dade Comm Coll 87; Acctg; MBA CPA.

**AHERN, STEPHEN R,** Duquesne Univ, Pittsburgh, PA; SO; German Clb; Drmcrtc Clb; English; Amer Lit; Tch.

**AHLFELD, TONYA M,** Northern Ky Univ, Highland Hts, KY; SO; BA; Educ/Hstry; Lawyr.

**AHLSTROM, CHRIS T,** Nova Univ, Ft Lauderdale, FL; GD; MBA; BS Univ WY 76; CPA; Mba; BS Acctng; Acctng/Bsn Anlys.

**AHLUWALIA, ISH K,** City Univ Of Ny City Coll, New York, NY; FR; BE; Indo Pak Cltrl Socty 90-; Coll Debtng Clb 90-; Dns Lst 90-; Elec Engr; Cmptr Sci.

**AHMAD, EYAD M,** Coll Of Aeronautics, Flushing, NY; FR; AAS; Intl Stdnt Cncl 90-; Peer Cnclr 90-; Stdnt Servs; Eagle Excellence Awd 90-; Eagle Ldrshp Awd 90-; IM Ftbl/Vlybl 90-; Aeronautics Eng.

**AHMAD, YASSER M,** Bethany Coll, Bethany, WV; JR; BS; Solid State Phys Rsrch Intrn; Phys/Math; PhD Phys.

**AHMED, ESRA,** Memphis St Univ, Memphis, TN; JR; BA; Espirit Corps; MSA; Psych.

**AHMED, FAROQUE,** City Univ Of Ny La Guard Coll, Long Island Cty, NY; SR.

**AHMED, KALEEM,** Univ Of Ky, Lexington, KY; FR; BS; Eng.

**AHMED, LISA,** Georgian Court Coll, Lakewood, NJ; SR; BA; Sigma Tau Delta VP; Engl Elem Ed.

**AHMED, RIZWAN,** Univ Of Al At Huntsville, Huntsville, AL; FR; BSC; Elec Eng.

**AHMED, SYEDA N,** City Univ Of Ny La Guard Coll, Long Island Cty, NY; SO; Bngldshi Clb Laguardia CC 88-90; Alpha Beta Phi Soc 89-90; Phrmcy.

**AHMED, TAHA SEID,** Univ Of The Dist Of Columbia, Washington, DC; SR; BA; Deans Lst 87-; Schlrshp Awrd 90; Cert Kenya Acctnts/Sec Brd; Acctg.

**AHN, HANA J,** Bloomfield Coll, Bloomfield, NJ; FR; MBA; Bus Mrktng.

**AHN, STEVE J,** Emory Univ, Atlanta, GA; SR; BBA; Intrx Incrprtd Prsdnt COB 90-; Wstmnstr Prntng Co Prsdnt 85-87; Plbctns Edtr Fndr 90-; Beta Gamma Sigma; Phi Sigma Iota 87-; Alpha Epsilon Upsilon 87-; Emory Stff 87-; Korean Stdnts Assn 87-88; Intrntnl Finance; Intrntnl Trd.

**AHRENS, CHANDLER B,** Savannah Coll Of Art & Design, Savannah, GA; FR; BARCH; Arch Drftng Cntst Ntl Assn Wmn Const; 1s Pl Rgn NC SC VA; 1s Pl Cntrl VA 90; Sccr 90; Arch.

**AHRENS, SYLVIA M,** Western Ky Univ, Bowling Green, KY; SO; BA; Jrnl Edtr 90-; Ladies Club Fiction Awrd 90; Creative Writing Schlrshp; G S Co-Ldr; AAS Spencerian Bus Clg 68; Engl; Tchr.

**AHUJA, PREMNATH,** Fl International Univ, Miami, FL; SR; BS; Natl Restaurant Assn; Phi Theta Kappa; AA Miami Dade Comm Clg 89; Hosp Mgmnt; Hotel/Restaurant.

**AIELLO, ANGELO S,** D Youville Coll, Buffalo, NY; SO; BSRN; NSNA; NYSSNA; DCSNA VP 90-; Lambda Sigma Orntn 90-; Nrsng; Nrs Prctnr.

**AIELLO, TRACEE,** Westminster Choir Coll, Princeton, NJ; JR; Std Govt Asc 88-89; Cls Offcr Sec 88-90; MENC Treas 90-; Msc Educ; Tchr.

**AIKEN, CAMERON J,** Univ Of Sc At Columbia, Columbia, SC; FR; BM; Presb Stdnt Cntr Vice Mdrtr; Estmnst Presb Chncl Choir 90-; Chrch Yth Advsr; Music; Perf/Opera/Musical Theatre.

**AIKEN, JENNIFER K,** Univ Of Sc At Columbia, Columbia, SC; JR; MENC 89-; Bnds 88-; Alpha Lambda Delta 89; Gldn Key 90-; Lbrn Drctrs Asst; USC Bnd Clnc Cndctrs Sympsm 90-; Msc Edctn; Tchr.

**AIKEN, MARY LOU,** Comm Coll Of Beaver County, Monaca, PA; SR; ADN; Nrsg.

**AIKEN, SANDRA A,** Morgan St Univ, Baltimore, MD; SR; BS; Internatl Clb 89-; Med Spec U S Army 84-; AS Kingsborough Cmnty Clge 89; Med Tech; Dntstry.

**AIKEN, SHAWN R,** Univ Of Akron, Akron, OH; SO; BS; Amer Scty Cvl Eng; Univ Hnrs Prgrm; Deans Lst; Ntl Merit Schlr; Pres Hnry Schlrshp; Cvl Eng.

**AIKENS, JAMES E,** Greenville Tech Coll, Greenville, SC; SO; AS; BSA Arch Explrng Post Treas 88-; Phi Theta Kappa 89-; Comp Elect Tech; Elect Engrng.**

**AIKENS, KRISTINA N,** Radford Univ, Radford, VA; FR; BA; Lit Arts Mag Prose Edtr 90-; Amnesty Intl 90-; Alpha Lombda Delta 90-; English/Theatre; Freelance Wrtr.

**AIKERSON, DARRYL V,** Alcorn St Univ, Lorman, MS; SO; BS; Stdnt Natl Educ Assn; Racquetbl; Elem Tchr.

**AIKEY, LAURA J,** Indiana Univ Of Pa, Indiana, PA; SR; BSED; Symphny Orchstr 88; Wnd Ensmbl 88-90; Mrchg Bnd 87-89; Pi Delta Phi 89-; Alpha Xi Delta Mbrshp Chrmn 89-; Frnch Ed; Frnch Tchr.

**AINSPAN, SARA M,** Hudson Valley Comm Coll, Troy, NY; FR; AAS; Resp Care Clb 90-; Amer Assn Rsprtry Care; Resp Care Dept 90-; BA Brandels U 86; Resp Ther; BS/PRFSN Cert.

**AINSWORTH, LAURA A,** Univ Of Southern Ms, Hattiesburg, MS; SR; BA; Psi Chi 90-; Gamma Beta Phi 90-; APA; Psychlgy; MA.

**AINSWORTH, PATRICIA DAWN,** Univ Of Southern Ms, Hattiesburg, MS; GD; BSN; Stu Nrs Assoc So Miss; Extrn S Cntrl Rgnl Med Cntr 90; AS 89; RN Lcnsr; Nrsg.

**AIOSA, KATHLEEN,** Eckerd Coll, St Petersburg, FL; SR; BA; TV 87-88; Prsdntl Schlr 87-; All Amrcn Schlr; Natl Coll Scl Sci Awrd; IM Sprts 87-; Intl Bus.

**AIOSE, THERESA ANN,** Comm Coll Algny Co Algny Cmps, Pittsburgh, PA; JR; RNBSN; Med Secy/Assist 79-; Assoc Spec Bus Duffs Bus Inst 77-79; Sci; Nrsng.

**AIRAKSINEN, SARI S,** Univ Of Sc At Columbia, Columbia, SC; SR; BBA; Mktg; Bsn Mktg Rsrch.

**AIRALA, SUSANA M,** Fl International Univ, Miami, FL; SO; BA; Pre Med Soc 90-; Intrntl Clb 90-; Hospice 90-; Biology Pre Med; Med Schl.

**AKAMUNE, IDOMO CYNTHIA,** Southeastern Coll Of Hlth Sci, N Miami Beach, FL; SR; PHARM; APA Mbr 89; Kappa Epsilon Treas 90; Dns Lst 89-90; BSC Univ Benin 83; MSC Univ Benin 87; Pharm; Clncl Pharm.

**AKARD, MARY ALISON,** Belmont Coll, Nashville, TN; FR; BSN; BSU Sec Of BSU Frshmn Cncl 90-; Historic Belmont Assoc; Stdnt Auxilary; Nursing; Nurse Practitioner.

**AKBAR, CAMILE D,** City Univ Of Ny Med Evers Coll, Brooklyn, NY; JR; Jr Cls Pres; Acctg Clb 89-; Non-Profit Org Secr 88-; Dns Lst 88-; Finance; Fncl Analyst.

**AKBAS, YAVUZ,** Savannah St Coll, Savannah, GA; SR; BS; ASCE Stdnt Clb 89-; Cvl Eng Tech.

**AKE, JAMI L,** Smith Coll, Northampton, MA; JR; BA; Debate Tm; Intrshp Oxford Clg; D; Engl.

**AKEN, VICKI J,** American Univ, Washington, DC; FR; BA; Coll Dmcrts 90-; Mdl Senate 90-; Intl Stdy; Law.

**AKENHEAD, LISA M,** Oh Univ, Athens, OH; SR; BFA; Alpha Lambda Delta; Lib Stu Asst 88-; Art Hstry.

**AKERET, CHRISTOPHER D,** Atlantic Comm Coll, Mays Landing, NJ; SO; Sons Italy 90-; EANGUS 89-; Cncl Psych.

**AKERKAR, SANKET A,** Cornell Univ, Ithaca, NY; FR; BS; Orientation Cnslr; Engr Ambassador; John Mc Mullens Dean Schlr 90-; Zeta Beta Tau; Dist Svc Awd Assembly Of NY; Engr; Bus/Resrch.

**AKERS, DENISON BARRY,** Fl International Univ, Miami, FL; JR; BA; Amnsty Intl VP 89-; Peace Sco 89-90; Intl Stu Assoc 90-; Big Bro/Big Sis; Intl Rltns; Law.

**AKERS, JEFFREY L,** Univ Of Ky, Lexington, KY; SR; B; Ky Acdmy Of Stdnts Of Phrmcy Authr 90-; Amrcn Phrmcy Assn; Ky Univ Coll Of Phrmcy Phon-A-Thon Co-Org; Alpha Lambda Sigma; Kappa Psi Chrmn 90-; Rho Chi Treas; Phi Kappa Psi Athltc Chr 86-88; KASP AIDS Awarnss Comm; Clinical Phrmcy.

**AKERS JR, JOHN F,** Air Force Inst Of Tech, Wrt-Ptrsn Afb, OH; GD; MS; Tau Beta Phi 83-; Sigma Iota Epsilon; Delta Chi Treas 81-; Scty Armcn Mltry Eng 84-; AR Assoc 84-; US AF Cvl Eng 84-; BSCE WV Inst Tchnlgy 83; Eng Mgmt.

**AKERS, KRISTIE A,** Radford Univ, Radford, VA; FR; BS; Hlth Svcs; Dietetics/Nutrition.

**AKERS, LISA CHRISTINE,** Marshall University, Huntington, WV; SR; BA; Sigma Sigma Sigma Prlmntrn/Mert Chrmn 90-; Multi Sbjct K-8 Educ; Tchr.

**AKERS, MARIELLA,** Savannah Coll Of Art & Design, Savannah, GA; GD; MFA; BA Hood Ocll 89; Hstrc Prsrvtn; Envrnmntl Rsrce Mgmt.

**AKILOV, BORIS,** City Univ Of Ny Queensbrough, New York, NY; SO.

**AKIN, MICHELLE L,** Ms St Univ, Miss State, MS; FR; BS; Bapt Stu Union 90-; Flwshp Chrstn Athlts 90-; Alpha Lambda Delta; Phi Eta Sigma; Pres Lst 90-; All Amer Schlr; Var Glf Tm 90-; Pre Med.

**AKIN, PATRICIA T,** Valdosta St Coll, Valdosta, GA; FR; BED; Erly Chldhd Ed; Tchng.

**AKING, MARLENE A M,** Univ Of Miami, Coral Gables, FL; FR; BA; Englsh; Law.

**AKINPELU, EDWARD A,** Worcester St Coll, Worcester, MA; SR; BS; Sara Ella Wilson Mem Schlrshp 88-; AS Quinsigamond Comm Coll; Business; Cpa.**

**AKINS, DEBORAH L,** Univ Of Sc At Columbia, Columbia, SC; JR; BA; Carolina Bnd Twrlr 88-; Gamma Beta Phi 89-; Alpha Lambda Delta 90-; Tau Beta Sigma Cls Treas 88-; Peru Deleg 89; World Baton Chmpnshps Slvr Mdl Holland 90; Rtlng Fshn Mrchndsng.

**AKINS, NANCY J,** Tn Tech Univ, Cookeville, TN; SR; BS; Stdnt Govt Assn Supreme Ct Chf Justc 88-90; Intervar Chrstn Flwshp Pres 86-; Soc Advnmnt Fin/Econ 88-90; Mrtr Bd Hon Soc 90-; Alpha Kappa Alpha V P 89-90; Beta Gamma Sigma V P 88-90; GTE Bus Schlrshp 88-90; Otsdng Clg Bus Stdnt IM 86-; Fin; Fin/Law.

**AKINS, SHERRY E,** Memphis St Univ, Memphis, TN; JR; BBA; Nwsltr Beta Alpha Psi; Gamma Beta Psi 89-; Dns Lst 89-; Acctng/Rsk Mgmt/Ins.

**AKLE, DAVID J,** Memphis St Univ, Memphis, TN; SR; BBA; RHO Epsilon 90-; SHRM 90-; Gldn Ky; Phi Kappa Phi; Beta Gamma Sigma; Mgmt/Real Est; Bus Career.

**AKOTH, NELLY C,** Saint Thomas Univ, Miami, FL; SO; BA; Intl Stdnts Org Exec Bd 90-; Circle K Ed; Cmptr Sci/Math; Syst Analyst.

**AKOURI, GEORGE,** Fl International Univ, Miami, FL; GD; ASCE 87-; ACE 87-; NSPE 87-; Hon Scty 88-; AA Miami Dade Comm Clg 88; BS FIU FL Intrntl Univ 90.

**AKRAMI, RAMIN,** Univ Of Louisville, Louisville, KY; JR; MENG; Bahi Clb Treas 89; Deans Lst 90; IEEE 90; AS Rets Elctrnc Inst 82; Eng; Elctrcl Eng.

**AKRIDGE, KENNETH R,** Univ Of Ky, Lexington, KY; SR; BS; Thurston Strunk Schlrshp 88-; Deans Lst 86-; Elect Eng.

**AKRIDGE, TUESDI J,** Cumberland County Coll, Vineland, NJ; FR; Intrnshp Prudential Ins Co; EOF Peer Cnslr; Acctg/Lbrl Arts Bus Admin; CPA.

**AKSU, YAMAN M,** Franklin And Marshall Coll, Lancaster, PA; SO; BA; Radio 90-; Bessie Smith Soc 90-; Physics Clb 89-; Hckmn Schlr Rsrch 90-; Thrtcl Physics Rsrch 90-; Math/Cntst Mdlg 90-; Intl Sccr Tm 90-; Physics; Cmptr Engr.

**AL-AMMARI, KHALID SALEM,** Daytona Beach Comm Coll, Daytona Beach, FL; SO; MD; Soccr Tm 89-; Chem/Bio; Med.

**AL-JASSAR, MOHAMMAD K,** Univ Of Miami, Coral Gables, FL; JR; BE; Natl Unn Of Kwti Stdnts; Amer Awrd Fr Exclnce 88; AEN; Eng.**

**AL-NASSER, ABDULLAH A,** Al A & M Univ, Normal, AL; GD; BS; Techn Colg/Saudi Arabia 84-88; Mgr/Stdnt Affair 88.

**AL-NAWAL, FAWZI,** Ny Univ, New York, NY; FR; BA; Intl Stu; Mddl East/Ecnmcs.

**AL-SALEH, NATALIA B,** Palm Beach Comm Coll, Lake Worth, FL; SO; BS; Stdnts For Intl Undrstndng; AA 90; Acctg; Pub Acctg.**

**AL-SMADI, OTHMAN M,** Tn St Univ, Nashville, TN; SO.

**AL-YAQOUT, ANWAR F,** Univ Of Miami, Coral Gables, FL; JR; BA; MSO; NSAE; Phi Alpha Epsilon; USAA; NCEA; Arch/Cvl Engr.

**ALABRE, MARJORY,** City Univ Of Ny Queensbrough, New York, NY; SO; AA; Phi Theta Kappa; Lbrl Arts; Med.

**ALAIMO, JOANNE C,** S U N Y Coll At Fredonia, Fredonia, NY; SR; BM; Amrcn Chrl Drctrs Assoc 90-; Kappa Delta Pi 89-; Kappa Lambda Pi; Cum Laude; Music Ed; Tchng Music.

**ALAIMO, MARY BETH,** Elms Coll, Chicopee, MA; JR; BA; Clss Offcr Sec 90-; Cmps Mnstry 88-; Stdnt Fclty Snt 89-; Stdnt Govt Assoc; Orntn Advsr Chrprsn 89-; St Catherine Medal; Elem Educf Teaching.

**ALAIN, JOSEPH C,** Fl Baptist Theological Coll, Graceville, FL; SR; BA; Soph Cls Pres 88-89; Govt Assn; Deans Lst/Pres Lst 88-; Spkr Sr Wk; AA Bethany Bible Coll 90; Thlgy; Tchng/Pstrng.

**ALALOUF, OPHIR I,** S U N Y At Buffalo, Buffalo, NY; FR; DDS; Clss Ofcr Treas 90-; Clss Ofcr Pres; Alpha Omega 90-; B Sc Univ Toronto 90; Dntl Med.

**ALAMO, ROSANNA,** Inter Amer Univ Pr San German, San German, PR; JR; BA; Painting/Graphic Arts; Illustr.

**ALARCON, TANIA A,** City Univ Of Ny Baruch Coll, New York, NY; SO; BA; Hispanic Soc; Latin Amer Yth; Indstrl Psych.

**ALATTAR, LINA,** Middle Tn St Univ, Murfreesboro, TN; FR; BFA; The Fine Arts Comm 90-; Campus Rec 90-; Hnr Roll 90-; Vlybl/Track 90-; Art; Graphic Designer.

**ALBA, KIMBERLY A,** Coll Misericordia, Dallas, PA; JR; CMSOTA Archvs 90-; Dns Lst 90-; USAA Awd 90-; Natl Mrt Schlr Awd 90-; Hnrs Schlp 90-; Mary Fout Schlp; Natl Banking Asc 90; Rtl Mgr/Bnkng/Crdt Card Supv; AS Lzrn Cnty Comm Clg 88; Occptnl Thrpy.

**ALBANESE, ANTHONY,** Norfolk St Univ, Norfolk, VA; JR; BA; Praise Flwshp PR 90-; Art Guild 89-; Spartan Alpha Tau; Alpha Kappa Mu 90-; US Army Med Corps 84-88; Cert Acad Hlth Sci 84; Fine Art; Profsr.

**ALBANESE, KRISTIN M,** Stonehill Coll, North Easton, MA; FR; BA; RFK Soc; Aerobics; Bus/Acctg; CPA.

**ALBANESE, LAURA R,** Va Commonwealth Univ, Richmond, VA; SR; BFA; Grad Cum Laude 91; Cmctn Arts/Design.

**ALBANO, DAVID J,** Fl International Univ, Miami, FL; SR; IEEE 90-; Sigma Phi Epsilon Hsg Chr 87-; AAS Clg Aerontcs Flushing NY 84; BSEE; Elctrcl Engr.

**ALBANO, DAVID M,** Nova Univ, Ft Lauderdale, FL; GD; MBA; Ftr Tlphn Pnrs Amer; Fncl Systms Mgr; BS Math Wilkes Univ 85; BS Cmptr Sci Wilkes Univ 85; Exec Mgmt.

**ALBANO, LIDYA,** Central Fl Comm Coll, Ocala, FL; SO; AA; Math/Sci Hnrs Clb; IFAW 88; WWF 88; PETA 88; Doris Day Anml League 88; Coop Wrk Stdy Prog At Ocala; Vet Hosp Intrnshp; Deans Lst; Exec Sec To Pres In Mjr Corp 80-89; Vet Sci; DVM.

**ALBARANO, SHERYLE A,** Saint Francis Coll, Loretto, PA; SR; BSN; Stf RN Rehab Hosp Altoona PA; ADN Mt Aloysius Jr Coll Cresson PA 89; Nrsng.

**ALBAUGH, MICHAEL D,** West Liberty St Coll, West Liberty, WV; SR; Music Educ Ntl Conf 89-; Tutor 89-; Cls Rep 90-; Riesbecks Mrkts; Taught Priv Guitar Lsns; Lead Guitar; BA; Music; Theory/Cmpstn.

**ALBAUGH, TAMMY S,** West Liberty St Coll, West Liberty, WV; JR; BS; Chi Omega Sec 90-; Spch Pathology.

**ALBERS, KAREN M,** Radford Univ, Radford, VA; JR; BA; Wesley Fndtn-Mthdst Stdnt Grp Pres 88-; Holston Cnfrnce Cncl 90-; Pi Gamma Mu Pres; Circle K 89-; Lbrl Stdies; Mnstry.

**ALBERS, LUISA E,** Inter Amer Univ Pr San Juan, Hato Rey, PR; JR; BBA; Hnr Prog 89-; Bus Admin; Mktg.

**ALBERS, MICHAEL S,** Le Moyne Coll, Syracuse, NY; SR; BS; W G Egan Mem Mdl; MBA Tuition Schlrshp; Regents Schlrshp; AAS Broome Comm Coll 89; Mngmnt/Infrmtn Sys; MBA Syst Anlyst/Admn.

**ALBERS, NANCY E,** Savannah St Coll, Savannah, GA; SO; BS; Mrn Blgy Clb 90; Beta Beta Beta; Hbtt Hmnty 90; Prtr Schlrshp 90-; Mrn Blgy.

**ALBERS, PAUL J,** Univ Of Sc At Columbia, Columbia, SC; JR; BS; Sport Admn.

**ALBERSON, LANA P,** Lake Sumter Comm Coll, Leesburg, FL; FR; AA; Deans List 90-; Trustee Schlrshp 90-; Speech Pathology/Audiology.

**ALBERT, JAMES T,** Ms St Univ, Miss State, MS; GD; DVM; Delta Phi Pres 87; BA Univ Pl 87; BS 87; Vet Med; Orthpdc Srgn.

**ALBERT, MARTIN S,** Norfolk St Univ, Norfolk, VA; JR; BS; Beta Gamma Sigma; Alpha Kappa Mu Pres 90-; Kentucky Fried Chicken 84-; Acctg; CPA.

**ALBERT, MICHELLE M,** Univ Of New England, Biddeford, ME; SO; MB; Soccer 89-; Sci; Medicine.

**ALBERT, NANCY R,** Univ Of New England, Biddeford, ME; SO; BS; Jdcl Brd 90; Prkng Tckts Appls Brd Pres 90; Deans Lst 89; Beta Sigma Phi 87; USAF 85-89; Physcl Thrpy.

**ALBERT, RUTH E,** Liberty Univ, Lynchburg, VA; SO; BS; Alpha Lambda Delta 90-; Natl Hnr Socty 89-; Hlth; Phys Thrpy.

**ALBERT, THOMAS J,** Hillsborough Comm Coll, Tampa, FL; FR; AS; Elect Eng Tech.

**ALBERTI, GWENDOLYN JOYCE,** Suffolk Comm Coll Eastern Cmps, Riverhead, NY; Pi Alpha Sigma; Eucharistic Minister; Church Lector; Coord Chldrns Masses; Tchr Aide Elem Sch Tchg Asst BOCES Gifted.

**ALBERTORIO, EDWIN R,** Inter Amer Univ Pr Guayama, Guayama, PR; GD; BA; Busn Admin Clb Pres 90-; Clss VP; Dns Lst 90-; Hnr Rl 90-; Syndic Stdnt 90-; Table Tenns Vllybl 90-; Mgmt; Law.

**ALBIN, RANDI D,** Univ Of Miami, Coral Gables, FL; SR; BA; Rathskeller Advsry Brd Pblcty Chr 89-90; Ad Club 90-; Amer Mrkting Assc 87-90; Psi Chi Scty; Golden Key; WSHE Radio Prdctn Intrnshp 89; Media Dpt II Media Byng 90-; AT&T Stdnt Cmps Mgr Mrkting Int 88; Psy/Advrtsng; Advrtsng/Mrktng.

**ALBINO FIGUEROA, JANICE,** Inter Amer Univ Pr San German, San German, PR; FR; Cath Dghtrs Amer VP 89-90.

**ALBINO RIVERA, WALESKA,** Inter Amer Univ Pr San German, San German, PR; FR; BA; Math; Acctng.

**ALBINO, MICHELE M,** Felician Coll, Lodi, NJ; JR; BA; Educ Clb 91; Dns Lst 89-; Drozd Skaewinski Awd 90-; Elem Educ/Art; Tchng.

**ALBINO, NILSA J,** Inter Amer Univ Pr San German, San German, PR; SR; BA; Assn Chem Stdnts 90-; Pre-Medcl Assn-Caduceus 90-; Beta Beta Beta 90-; John W Harris Schlrshp 87-; Blgy-Biomed Sci; Med.

**ALBINUS, NIKOLAJ,** Univ Of Miami, Coral Gables, FL; SO; BA; Bus/Finance; Law.

**ALBIZZATTI, JORGE N,** Fl International Univ, Miami, FL; SR; BS; Amer Soc Civil Eng 90-; Alpha Omega Chi Chrmn 90-; Phi Sigma Kappa Pres; Deans Lst 90-; Eng; Med Schl.

**ALBRECHT, JOAN T,** East Stroudsburg Univ, E Stroudsburg, PA; SR; BA; Engl Clb VP Pr 88-; Speech Clb; Sigma Tau Delta 88-; Omicron Delta Kappa; Hons Convocation ESU; Amer Cancer Soc 81-; AA Cnty Clg Of Morms 88; Engl/Speech Cmctn; Pub Rels.

**ALBRECHT, MICHELLE L,** Daemen Coll, Amherst, NY; JR; BA; Delta Mu Delta; AAS 90; AS 90; Acctg.

**ALBRIGHT, ALISON L,** Radford Univ, Radford, VA; FR; Dance Theater Soloist 90-; Alpha Lambda Delta 90-; Ambassadors 90-; Phi Sigma Sigma 90-; Radford Schlr 90-; Dance Schlrshp 90-; Mary Blevins Schlrshp 90-; Arts Schlrshp; Publ Rel/Dance.

**ALBRIGHT, DEBBIE L,** Univ Of Tn At Martin, Martin, TN; SR; BS; Tchr.

**ALBRIGHT, JAMES,** Nova Univ, Ft Lauderdale, FL; GD; MBA; BPM 89; Mngmnt; Phd Finance.

**ALBRIGHT, JAMES A,** Salisbury St Univ, Salisbury, MD; JR; MSN; Crew Team/Stockton State 74-76; Commissioned Offcr USN 77-83; BA Stockton State Coll Pomona NJ 76; BA Wayne State UMV Detroit MI 81; Nrsng.

**ALBRIGHT, LISA S,** Savannah St Coll, Savannah, GA; SR; BA; Acdmc Awrd SSC Sftbll 86-87; Bus Admn Mgmt.

**ALBRIGHT, MARGARET R,** Converse Coll, Spartanburg, SC; SR; BA; Bapt Stdnt Un 87-; Stdnt Govt FR Treas 87-88; Crscnt Sec 88-89; Elem Ed.

**ALBRIGHT, MARK C,** Saint John Fisher Coll, Rochester, NY; SR; Hstry Clb 87-; Delta Epsilon Sigma 90-; Hstry; Prmry/Scndry Educ.

**ALBRIGHT, TRACY A,** Mount Saint Mary Coll, Newburgh, NY; JR; BA; Drama Clb 90; Intrnshp Cblvsn Of NJ Prctcm Prgn Cble Asst 90; Cmmnctn Arts; TV Prdctn.

**ALBRIGHT-WILLIS, JANET E,** Univ Of Cincinnati-Clrmnt Coll, Batavia, OH; SO; BS; Sigma Gamma Rho 80; Hons Day Prog; Vol Life Sqd Crew Chf 88-; Vlg Cncl 90-; Hosp Clncl Asst 86-; Psychlgy.

**ALBRIGHTON, JUDITH M,** Duquesne Univ, Pittsburgh, PA; JR; BED; Orntn Co Ldr; Jr Achvmnt Instr 89-90; Phi Eta Sigma 88-89; Mrtr Brd; Kappa Delta Epsilon Soc Chrmn 89-; Minnie Hyman Schlrshp 89-; Parish Grant Schlrshp; Dean Lst 88-; Elem Educ; Tch.

**ALBRIGO, PERRY M,** Fl St Univ, Tallahassee, FL; SO; BME; Mens Glee Clb 90-; Dns Lst 90-; IM Bsktbl/Sftbl 90-; Music Ed-Choral; H S Chorus Tchr.

**ALBRITTON, CLAUDIA M,** City Univ Of Ny City Coll, New York, NY; SR; PHD; Golden Key 90-; Alpha Sigma Lambda; AIDS Rsrch Prj Coord NYC Dept Hlth 89-; AAS Rockland Comm Coll 72; Apprsl Cert; Anthro; Profssr.

**ALBRITTON, CRISTA S,** Valdosta St Coll, Valdosta, GA; FR; BS; Nrsng; Rn.

**ALBURY, LISA M,** Mount Saint Mary Coll, Newburgh, NY; SR; BA; Hse Cord 90-; Stu Gvt Rep 88-; Chr 90-; Hnrs Allnc 90-; Dean Lst 90-; Hstry/Pol Sci; Intl Law.

**ALBURY, ROCHELLE A,** Emory Univ, Atlanta, GA; JR; BA; Gospel Choir 90-; Yng Adults Grp Church; Coopers/Lybrand Adm Stf 90-; Bsn/Acctg; CPA.

**ALCAZAR, CAROL M,** City Univ Of Ny Baruch Coll, New York, NY; SR; BA; Tour Guide 88; Baruch Schlr Newslttr Ed 88; Barush Schlr Advsry Rep 89; Deans Lst 87; Golden Key; Baruch Schlrshp 87; Engl; Acad.

**ALCID, MICHEL S,** Hudson Valley Comm Coll, Troy, NY; SO; AAS; Prgmr Anlyst Grdn Wy 77-; Mgmt/Info Syst.

**ALCINI, BRIAN D,** Univ Of Akron, Akron, OH; JR; BA; Internatl Bsn Clb 90-; IM Sprts 88-; Gldn Key 90-; Mktg; Sls Repr.

**ALCORN, MARY B,** Watterson Coll, Louisville, KY; JR; Watterson Cllg Prsdnts Lst; Dean Lst; Accntng; CPA.

**ALCOTT, JANENE P,** Slippery Rock Univ, Slippery Rock, PA; JR; BED; PA Assn Hlth/Phy Ed/Rec/Dance 88-; Assn Hlth/Phy Ed 88-; Lambda Sigma 89-90; Phi Epsilon Kappa Sgt At Arms 90-; Alpha Omicron Pi Treas 90-; Deans Lst; IM Capt 88-; Phy Ed; Tchng/Sprts Mgmnt.

**ALCOTT, S ROGER,** Merrimack Coll, North Andover, MA; SR; BS; Amer Soc Cvl Engrs 87-; Cvl Engr; Engr.

**ALCURE, RITA WALSH,** Fl International Univ, Miami, FL; SR; BED; Gldn Key 89-; PTA 83-; Wmns Gld 85-; Spec Ed.

**ALDER, BRENDA COLBY,** Barry Univ, Miami, FL; SR; BS; Yng Wmn Cmp Dir 90-; Clncl Microbio Intrnshp/Mt Sinai Med Cntr; Microbio; PhD.

**ALDERFER, STACEY,** Temple Univ, Philadelphia, PA; SO; BA; Elem/Spcl Ed; Tchr.

**ALDERMAN, AMY K,** Birmingham Southern Coll, Birmingham, AL; JR; BS; Archealogy Club; Phi Eta Sigma; Alpha Lambda Delta; Alpha Kappa Delta Pres 91; Alpha Epsilon Delta; Chi Omega Pres 91; Pres Stdnt Svc Org; Stdnt Alumni Assn; Tennis Team; Sclgy; Med.

**ALDERSON, TABATHA L,** Volunteer St Comm Coll, Gallatin, TN; SO; AS; English; Clg Teach.

**ALDINGER, KARLA K E,** Valdosta St Coll, Valdosta, GA; SR; BGS; Reserve Officers Assoc Lds/Spouse Secty 85; Camden Area Plyrs Commty Thtr Pbly 90; Carroll County Commty Thtr 88; Substitute Tchr Schltc Edtng; Human Resource Mgt; Public Admin.

**ALDOUS, TODD E,** S U N Y Coll Of Tech At Canton, Canton, NY; SR; AAS; Com Drug Abuse; Referee Chf/Louisvl Minor Hockey Assoc 90-; Phi Theta Kappa 90-; Amer Cncr Soc 90-; Cert Achvmnt 89-90; Acctg; CPA.

**ALDRED, JENNIFER L,** Syracuse Univ, Syracuse, NY; SO; BARCH; Arch Orgztn 89-; Pcuralist Lgue 89-; Arch.

**ALDRIAN, DOUGLAS E,** Embry Riddle Aeronautical Univ, Daytona Beach, FL; SR; BS; Omicron Delta Kappa 90-; Aircrft Ownrs/Pilots Assoc 87-; Stdnt Ct Schlrshp 90; I M Sftbl Capt 89-; Aeronautical Sci; Cmrcl Pilot.**

**ALDRICH, GEM K,** Coker Coll, Hartsville, SC; SO; FDIC 90-.

**ALDRICH, KEANE D,** Marywood Coll, Scranton, PA; JR; BA; Engl; Engl Prfssr.

**ALDRIDGE, CARLA J,** Centre Coll, Danville, KY; JR; Kappa Kappa Gamma Pres; United Med Ctr Intrn; Trk 90; Ecnmcs; Hlth Adm.**

**ALDRIDGE, CHERYL A,** Glassboro St Coll, Glassboro, NJ; SR; Psych Clb Trea 89-; Psi Chi Fndng Trea; S Jersy AIDS Allnc Buddy; AA Cumberland Co Coll 89; Psych; Cnsclng.

**ALDRIDGE, DAVID W,** Samford Univ, Birmingham, AL; SR; BS; Phi Kappa Phi 87-; Pi Kappa Lambda 89-; BM 89; Math; Comp Sci.

**ALDRIDGE, DEBORAH P,** Snead St Jr Coll, Boaz, AL; SO; BED; Phi Theta Kappa 90-; Otstndg Msc Schlr Awrd 90; Otstndg Tchr Of Yr 87; Tch Piano; Msc Educ Piano; Msc Tchr.

**ALDRIDGE, JENNIFER S,** Memphis St Univ, Memphis, TN; FR; BS; Angel Flight/Silver Wings Soc Prlmntrn 90-; Phi Eta Sigma; Tutorcore 90-; Outstndg Fr Chem Awd; Physics.

**ALDRIDGE, MELISSA G,** Union Univ, Jackson, TN; SR.

**ALDRIDGE, THERESA M,** Middle Tn St Univ, Murfreesboro, TN; FR; BS; Delta Zeta 90-; Nrsng.

**ALDRIDGE-WILLIS, CAROL L,** Cheyney Univ Of Pa, Cheyney, PA; GD; BA; Sigm Agamma Rho Sec 89-; Vllybll Capt 87-90; Chyny Rcrd Rep 88-90; Deans Lst 88-90; Natl Cncl Ngr Wmn 90-; Tstmstr Intl VP Ed 88-90; WDSD Cntry Rd Stn Intern 90; Cmmnctn Arts.

**ALDUNCIN, JUAN P,** Univ Of Miami, Coral Gables, FL; SR; BA; Japan Karate Assn; Intnrshp Amer Publsng Grp 90; Intl Finc/Mktg; Intl Busn.

**ALEA, ANA J,** Fl International Univ, Miami, FL; SO; BA; Bus; Accntng.

**ALEGER, JEAN V,** City Univ Of Ny City Coll, New York, NY; SO; BS; Haitian Stdnts Assoc 89-; ASPIRA Of NY Inc 89-; Bio Chem; Medcn.

**ALEGRE VELEZ, WANDA I,** Inter Amer Univ Pr Hato Rey, Hato Rey, PR; SO; Acctg Stdnt Assn 90-; Hnr Rl 90-; Acctg.

**ALEIDA, VELLON FIGUEROA,** Inter Amer Univ Pr Hato Rey, Hato Rey, PR; SO; BA; Pltcl Sci Stdnt Assc; Jose/Ortega Gasset Fndtn Stdnt Assc Sec; Exec Chrch Org 89; Ldrshp Yng People Assc PR 89-; Vol San Juan Dtntn Ctr; Co Prtcpnt Svnth Ldrshp Wrkshp OI Univ San German PR 89; Pltcl Sci; Intl Law/Phd.

**ALEIXO, JOAO C,** Univ Of New Haven, West Haven, CT; SR; BS; Avtn Mgmt; Cmmrcl Plt.

**ALEJANDRO CISNEROS, ROGELIO E,** Inter Amer Univ Pr Hato Rey, Hato Rey, PR; FR; BASM; Deans Lst; Airway Sci Mgmt.

**ALEJANDRO LORA, RAMON,** Univ Politecnica De Pr, Hato Rey, PR; SR; BED; US Coast Grd Rsrv-Petty Offcr 3rd Cls 87-; Cvl Engr; Eng.

**ALEJANDRO, CARMELO,** Schenectady County Comm Coll, Schenectady, NY; FR; Bowling Tm; Cul Arts/Htl Mgmt.

**ALEJANDRO, EDWIN,** Univ Politecnica De Pr, Hato Rey, PR; SO; Engnrng.**

**ALEJANDRO, EVA M,** Western New England Coll, Springfield, MA; FR; BA; Untd Mtlly Eql; Mrtl Arts Clb; Year Bk; Indstrl Orgnztnl Psychlgy.

**ALEJO, WINSTON R,** City Univ Of Ny City Coll, New York, NY; SR; BS; Presby Hosp Vol 89-90; Emrgncy Sqd 89-90; Peer Acdmc Advsr 90-; Minority Biomedl Research Prog Aide 90-; Biology; Medicine.**

**ALEMAN, HARRY E,** Univ Of Pr Ponce Tech Univ Col, Ponce, PR; SO; BA; Talent Roster Certif Achvmnt; Bsktbl 89-; Bsn Adm; Acctg.

**ALESSANDRO, MELISSA D,** Northern Ky Univ, Highland Hts, KY; FR; BA; Blgcl Soc 90-; Indr Scr 90-; Blgy; Phy Thrpy.

**ALETICH, KIMBERLY A,** Atlantic Comm Coll, Mays Landing, NJ; SO; BS; Math; CPA.

**ALEXANDER, ALEXIS T,** Morgan St Univ, Baltimore, MD; SO; Yrbk Staff 89-90; Alpha Mu Gamma 90-; Alpha Lambda Delta 90-; Iota Beta Sigma 90-; Chem/French; Med.

**ALEXANDER, ALTON M,** Al St Univ, Montgomery, AL; SR; BS; Bptst Un 90-; Ntnl Rcrtn Prk Assn 90-; PACCA 90-; Ntnl Thrptc Rcrtn Soc; Hnr Roll 89-90; Coop Hlth Mnpwr Edctn Prgrm 90; Tskegee Vtrns Affrs Mdcl Cntr; Tskegee VA Intrn; Thrptc Rcrtn; Rec Thrpst.

**ALEXANDER, AURELIA K,** Fl A & M Univ, Tallahassee, FL; SR; BS; White/Gold; Alpha Kappa Alpha 89-; Intrn Sprngfld Hosp Cntr; Intrn Tallahassee Mem Rgnl Med Cntr; Occptnl Thrpy.

**ALEXANDER, BRIAN P,** Bunker Hill Comm Coll, Boston, MA; FR; Masschsts Ntnl Grd Sldr Yr; Lbrl Arts; Scl Change.

**ALEXANDER, BRIAN S,** Radford Univ, Radford, VA; FR; BS; Brdcstrs Gld 90-; UNLV Sta Brd Oprtr; Spch; Radio/TV Prdctn.

**ALEXANDER, CHRISTINA L,** Garrett Comm Coll, Mchenry, MD; SO; AA; Bsnss Admin; Accntng.

**ALEXANDER JR, CLAUDE W,** Jackson St Univ, Jackson, MS; FR; BS; Alpha Lambda Delta 90-; Fin; Fin Cnslnt.

**ALEXANDER, CYNTHIA W,** Middle Tn St Univ, Murfreesboro, TN; SO; BBA; Gamma Beta Phi 90-; Stdnt Wrkr Accts Recvbl Dept MISU; Bus; Acctg.

**ALEXANDER II, DANIEL J,** Howard Univ, Washington, DC; SR; MD; Stdnt Assn Treas 90; St Clb Snte Sntr 90; Gldn Ky 89-; Pol Sci Hnr Scty 89-; Oprtn Rsce Ttr 90; Urbn Lgue 90-; NIA Prec 90; CBCF Cngrssnl Intrshp Intrn; Lyndn Bns Jhnsn Cngrssnl Intrnshp Intrn 90; Magna Cum Laude; BA 90; Intrntl Rltns; Intrntl Law.**

**ALEXANDER SR, DAVID H,** Miami Jacobs Jr Coll Of Bus, Dayton, OH; FR; Cert; Data Entry; Comp Engr.

**ALEXANDER, DAVID J,** Univ Of Sc At Columbia, Columbia, SC; FR; German Clb; Gamma Beta Phi; Foreign Lang Plcmnt Tst Asst; Hist; Tchng.

**ALEXANDER, DEBORAH P,** Univ Of Sc At Spartanburg, Spartanburg, SC; SO; BSN; Stu Nrsng Assn 90-; Gamma Beta Phi 90-; Nrsng Schlrs Schlrshp Awrd 89; Natl Assn Fml Exctvs 85-90; Gldn Addy Awrd 86; Nrsng; Mtrnl Chld.

**ALEXANDER, DIANE S,** Middle Tn St Univ, Murfreesboro, TN; SO; BS; Spec Educ; Tch.

**ALEXANDER, DINA M,** Univ Of Al At Birmingham, Birmingham, AL; JR; BS; AS 90-; Cert Rad; Radiology; Admin.

**ALEXANDER, EMMET DWAYNE,** Richard Bland Coll, Petersburg, VA; SR; BA; Spnsh Clb Pres 90; Econ Clb; Phi Beta Kappa; Deans Lst 89-; Rrss Rt Envrnmntl Lgstn; Stdnt Asst 90-; AA 90; Govt.

**ALEXANDER, GRANT S,** Embry Riddle Aeronautical Univ, Daytona Beach, FL; FR; BA; Aerontcl Sci; Airln Trnsprt Pilot.

**ALEXANDER, JAN-NEEN,** Central St Univ, Wilberforce, OH; SR; BS; Elctns Bd Comm Chp 88-; Mrktng Club V P 90-; Fin Club 90-; NAACP Pres 87-88; SCLC 87-; Mrktng Club V P 90-; Bank One Dayton Intern 90-; Sftbl IM Capt 90-; Mrktng Mgr.

**ALEXANDER, JERALD D,** Wilberforce Univ, Wilberforce, OH; FR; Ohio Pre-Alumni; Natl Soc Blck Engrs Treas; BEP; Elect Eng.

**ALEXANDER, JEROME,** Al St Univ, Montgomery, AL; JR; BS; Sen Stdnt Govt Chrmn 90-; Msnry 89-; Phi Eta Sigma 88-; Alpha Kappa Psi 90-; Alpha Phi Alpha Edtr Sphinx 90-; Proj Alpha 90-; Hgst Rnk Soph Cls 89-90; SWAC Acad All Amer Trck Tm 89-; Trck Fld Top Comp 89-; Comp Inf Sys/Pre Law; Law.

**ALEXANDER, JILL B,** Western New England Coll, Springfield, MA; JR; BA; Radio 90-; Yrbk 90-; Lit Mag 88-; Big Sis; Cmctns.

**ALEXANDER, KATHI J,** James Madison University, Harrisonburg, VA; SR; BS; Phi Theta Kappa 88-89; VA Tchng Schlrshp 90; Spec Educt Lrng Disabities; Tchr.

**ALEXANDER, KATROMPAS M,** Edinboro Univ Of Pa, Edinboro, PA; SO; Asn Fghtn Arts Krte Clb Blck Blt 84-; Hnr Scty 90-; Bus Admin Econs; Acads.

**ALEXANDER, KEITH A,** Life Coll, Marietta, GA; GD; DC; Intl Chrprtc Assn; Gonstead Club Motion Paplatn Clb 90-; Thompson Clb; Univ Of Fl Symph Orch Jazz Band 85-89; Sigma Alpha Mu Fndg Father 86-90; Ind Univ Med Res 84; Intrnshp Undr Dr A Strickhlm; Univ Fl Schl Med Res Asstnshp; Neurphyslgy; Chrprtc Med.

**ALEXANDER, LANDRY L,** Univ Of Miami, Coral Gables, FL; FR; BS; Natl Soc Black Engr 90-; Amer Soc Mech Engr 90-; Alpha Lambda Delta; Provost Hnr Roll 90; Dns Lst; Mech Engr; Engr/Mktg.

**ALEXANDER, LISA M,** Schenectady County Comm Coll, Schenectady, NY; FR; Spnsh Clb.

**ALEXANDER, MARK LINLEY,** Asbury Theological Sem, Wilmore, KY; SR; MDIV; Stdnt Gove Jr Cl Pres 89-90; Stdnt Body V P 90-91; Christians For Biblical Equality; J C Mc Pheeters Schlr; Susan Nall Schlrshp; G A Steinman Awd Mc Murray Coll; BA Mc Murray Coll 89; AAS Odessa Coll 80; Religion; Pastoral Ministry.**

**ALEXANDER, MARY JO,** Univ Of Tn At Chattanooga, Chattanooga, TN; SO; BSN; Deans Lst 89-; Kosmos Wmns Clb Schlrshp Awrd; Cert Chaha St Tech Comm Coll 79; Nrsng; IV Thrpst/Mgmt.

**ALEXANDER, NORMAN EVERETT,** Memphis St Univ, Memphis, TN; JR; BSEE; Eng; Elec Eng.

**ALEXANDER, PATRICIA E,** Miami Jacobs Jr Coll Of Bus, Dayton, OH; FR; Natl Hon Soc 87-; Info Sys Mgt; Analyst.

**ALEXANDER, PHILLIP VERNON,** Al St Univ, Montgomery, AL; JR; BSW; ITANI Treas; Scl Wrk V P 90-; Alpha Phi Omega Chrmn 87-88; IM Bsktbl Head Coach; Scl Wrk; Cnslr.

**ALEXANDER, REGENA FRAZIER,** Memphis St Univ, Memphis, TN; SR; BSE; Kappa Delta Pi; Savnah Jr Axlry; AS Jcksn St Comm Coll 89; Elem Ed; Tchr/Cnslr.

**ALEXANDER, REGINA D,** Memphis St Univ, Memphis, TN; JR; BA; Phi Theta Kappa 88-90; Beta Alpha Psi; Assoc Arts NW Miss Comm Clg 90; Acctng; CPA.

**ALEXANDER, RICKY N,** International Bible Coll, Florence, AL; JR; BA; Bible; Evangelist.

**ALEXANDER, ROSE M,** Univ Of Southern Ms, Hattiesburg, MS; SR; BS; Stdnt Cncl Excptnl Chldrn Pres 90; Cncl Excptnl Chldrn; Abbie Rogers Schlrshp Awd 90-; BS; Spec Educ; Teachng.

**ALEXANDER, ROSLYN M,** Walker Coll, Jasper, AL; SO; BS; Bapt Cmps Mnstrs 89-; Dw Clb 90-; Explrs Clb 89-90; Phi Theta Kappa 90-; Deans List 89-; Math; Educ.

**ALEXANDER, RYCHELLE S,** Wilberforce Univ, Wilberforce, OH; SR; MBA; Ohio Pre Alumni Assn Exec Spc; Hlth Care Admn Clb V P; Alpha Kappa Mu; Hlth Care Admin.

**ALEXANDER, SHAWN M,** Univ Of Pittsburgh At Bradford, Bradford, PA; FR; BS; Bsn Econ; Mgr Econ.

**ALEXANDER, SHAWN P,** Univ Of Sc At Columbia, Columbia, SC; FR; BS; Alpha Lambda Delta 90-; Gamma Beta Phi 90-; Acctng; CPA.

**ALEXANDER, SHAWNA R,** Johnson C Smith Univ, Charlotte, NC; JR; BS; Bkrs Educ Soc Inst 90-; Bkng/Fin; Corp Lawyer.

**ALEXANDER, SHERRIE D,** Univ Of Al At Birmingham, Birmingham, AL; JR; BFA; Phi Theta Kappa 89-90; Gldn Key 90-; Hnrs Schlrshp 90-; Prsdntl Hnrs 89-; Deans Lst 88-; Cert Cmpltn Walker Jr Coll; Art Std; Grphc Dsgnr.

**ALEXANDER, STEVE K,** Tusculum Coll, Greeneville, TN; SR; Peer Cnslr 87-; Alpha Chi; Walter T Dette Awd; Psych Awd; Dale Alexander Awd 90-; Bsbl 87-; BS; Psychology.

**ALEXANDER, TINA M,** Piedmont Tech Coll, Greenwood, SC; FR; LPN; Natl Voc Tech; Hlth Sci; Nrsng.

**ALEXANDER, TRACY L,** Lesley Coll, Cambridge, MA; GD; BS; Yrbk Stff 87; Dnc Clb 87; Commuter Clb Pres 87-90; Orntn Com 89; Commuter Affrs Rep 88-90; Emerald Key 87-; Deans Lst 90; Elem Ed; MED Reading.

**ALEXANDER, WENDY B,** Old Dominion Univ, Norfolk, VA; SR; BS ED; Phi Kappa Phi 85-; Beta Gamma Sigma 86-; Instr Fin 87-; BSBA 85; MBA 86; Ele Educ; Ele Mdl Sch Tchr.

**ALEXANDER IV, WILLIAM J,** Univ Of Sc At Columbia, Columbia, SC; SR; BSM; Bodrbuilding Club 88-90; Amer Scty Mechl Engrs 87-; Mechl Engrg; Engrg.

**ALEXANDER-KENNEDY, TONYA R,** Chattanooga St Tech Comm Coll, Chattanooga, TN; SO; BS; Phi Theta Kappa 89-; Psi Beta Pscy VP 90-; N Park Emply Mnth 88; Untd Wy Bdgt Allc; Comm Ktchn Vol Fnd Rsng 89-; Med Lab Tech 87-; AAS Cleveland St Comm Coll 87; Biol/Psych; MD PHD.

**ALFANO, CATHERINE M,** Bunker Hill Comm Coll, Boston, MA; FR; Accntng.

**ALFIERE, ROSANNE,** City Univ Of Ny Queensbrough, New York, NY; SO; BSA; Deans List 89-; Arnold Smithline/Simon Trefman Award; Hons; Ed/Soclgy; Tchng.

**ALFIERI, LUCINDA H,** Wagner Coll, Staten Island, NY; SR; BA; Sigma Tau Delta Pres 90-; Omicron Delta Kappa VP 90-; Engl.

**ALFONSO CLARO, CAROLINA I,** Fl International Univ, Miami, FL; GD; Chrch Yth Chr 86-90; Cmps Mnstry 86-90; Phi Eta Sigma 86-90; BED 90; Elem Educ/Art; Adminstrtr.

**ALFONSO, ALBERTO J,** Inter Amer Univ Pr Hato Rey, Hato Rey, PR; JR; BA; Assn Estdnts De Cntbldd 90-; Natl Assn Of Accts 90-; Univ Dns Lst 90-; Otstndng Stdnt Of AEC 90-; Acctng; Law.

**ALFONSO, CARMEN R,** Miami Dade Comm Coll Med Centr, Miami, FL; JR; BSN; Chld Dev Lab Asst 87-89; Acad Cmnty Educ Cnslr 89; Sftbl Schlrshp Tm Cpt 85-87; NIH Prog Fr AIDS Rsrch Cnslr 89-; Hsp Cnslr 89-; BA FL Intrntl Univ 89; HRS Hlth/Rehabltv Srvcs 90; Cert Amer Scty Phlbtmy Tech 90; Anatmy/Physlgy; Rsrch.

**ALFORD, BRAD G,** Piedmont Tech Coll, Greenwood, SC; HVAC; AUT Grnwd Vctnl Schl 88.

**ALFORD, CHRISTY ANN,** Ms St Univ, Miss State, MS; SR; Famous Maroon Band Flag Line 87; Alpha Gamma Delta Actves/ Pub Cmtee 88; Otsdng Clg Stdnts Amer 88; Deans Pres Lsts90.

**ALFORD, DEBRA A,** Benedict Coll, Columbia, SC; SR; BS; Pres Sr Cls 90-; Alpha Kappa Mu Hon Soc Pres 90-; Alpha Chi Hon Soc 89-; BS Benedict Clg 91; Off Sys Mgmt; Admn Off.

**ALFORD, DUNCAN E,** Univ Of Nc At Chapel Hill, Chapel Hill, NC; GD; JD; NC Law Review Stf 89-90; Phi Sigma Iota 82-85; Phi Alpha Delta 88-; Assn Jstc B B Mtchl Jr NC Sprm Crt Jdcl Clrk; Amer Bar Assn 88-; Bus Anlyst 85-87; BA Ecnmcs/ Frnch Univ VA 85; Law.

**ALFORD, GREGORY R,** Univ Of Miami, Coral Gables, FL; JR; BSCE; Amer Soc Civl Eng Pr 90-; Chi Epsilon; Civl Eng.

**ALFORD, JACKIE S,** Univ Of Al At Huntsville, Huntsville, AL; SO; BSE; Mechanical Engineering; Navy.

**ALFORD, JAY CURTIS,** Fl Coll, Temple Terrace, FL; SO; BA; Yrbk Ed 89-; Arete 89-90; Stdnt Govt Drm Rep 89-90; Phi Theta Kappa Treas 90-; Brain Bwl 89-90; Mgna Cum Laude; AA; Hstry; Tchg.

**ALFORD, JENNIFER E,** Western Carolina Univ, Cullowhee, NC; JR; BA; NC Stdnt Legsltr; Stdnt Assn Gvrnmnt Lgl Affrs; Stdnt Mrshl 90; Pi Ghamma Mu; Alpha Lambda Delta 89-; NC Inst Gvrnmnt Intrnshp Rcpnt; Dean Lst 89-; ROTC Asst Rapelling Instrctr 90; IM Sftgbl Vlybl Trck 89-; Spanish; Gvrnmnt Srvc.

**ALFORD, LORINE,** Meridian Comm Coll, Meridian, MS; FR; AD; DECA; Amrcn Poetry Assn; Htl Rstrnt Mgmt.

**ALFORD, PAMELA L,** Univ Of Ga, Athens, GA; SR; BSED; Proj LEAD Ltrcy Actn Brnch Athens Vol 89-; Erly Chldhd Ed; Tchng.

**ALFORD, SHANTI E,** Hampton Univ, Hampton, VA; JR; BA; Sr Exec Cncl; His Chsn Snds Gspl Chr Treas 89-; Stdnt Ldr 89-; Hnr Rll 90; Dns Lst 90; Sgn Lnnge Mnstry Co Coor 88-; Natl Assn Of Blck Accts 88-; Smmr Enrchmnt Educ Prog 90; Acctng; Entrprnr.**

**ALFORD, TAMARA J,** Johnson C Smith Univ, Charlotte, NC; FR; BS; Cls Treas; Dorm Treas; Alpha Swthrt; Bio; Phrmcy.

**ALFORD, TAMMI F,** Coll Of Charleston, Charleston, SC; SR; BA; SCEC 90; Alpha Delta Pi Scl Chm 87; Phlnthrpc Awd For Alpha Delta Pi; Im Sftbl Vllybll Bsktbl 87; Spcl Ed LD EH; Tchr.

**ALGEE, CRYSTAL A,** Fl A & M Univ, Tallahassee, FL; FR; MBA; WSBI Camera Oper Audtr Asst VP 90-; Acctng; Bus.

**ALGEO, DONALD W,** Univ Of New England, Biddeford, ME; SO; BS; ROTC Clr Grd NCOIC 90-; SG Vets Com Chr; Spcl Olympcs Cch 86-; Phi Beta Upsilon; Drg Awrnss 90-; Fd Pntry; ROTC Schlrshp 90-; 82nd Arbrne Infntry Sldr 87; EMT Southern Maine Voc Tech Institute 90; Phys Thrpy Hmnts; Rgstrd Phys Thrpst.

**ALGIERS, JULIE C,** Webber Coll, Babson Park, FL; SR; BS; AA Univ Wisc Whitewater 85; Cert Amer Career Training Trvl Schl 89; Mrktng; Travel.

**ALI, ALISHA G,** Broward Comm Coll, Ft Lauderdale, FL; SO; BA; Mntrs Pgm Pr Mntr 90-; Hnrs Pgm 90; Math Tutor 90; Acctng; CPA.

**ALI, DANA L,** Duquesne Univ, Pittsburgh, PA; SR; BA; AMA; Deans Lst; Mktng.

**ALI, FARIDA F,** City Univ Of Ny Baruch Coll, New York, NY; SO; BA; Acctg.

**ALI, MOHAMED R,** Univ Of Sc At Columbia, Columbia, SC; SR; BS; Hall Govt Pr 89-90; Res Hall Assn Sen 90-; AICE 89-90; Phi Beta Kappa 89-; Tau Beta Pi 89-; Omega Xi Epsilon 90-; Phi Beta Kappa Awd 88-89; Peer Condct Brd 90-; Carolina Schlr 88-; IM Indoor Outdr Soccr Tm Capt 88-; Chem Eng; Med.

**ALIBOZEK, SCOTT F,** Western New England Coll, Springfield, MA; JR; Marketing Business.

**ALIBRANDI, VINCENT J,** Univ Of Miami, Coral Gables, FL; SR; BA; Univ Miami Dept Awd Msc Sch-Percussion; BA; Msc; Prfsnl Msc.

**ALICEA MORALES, HECTOR L,** Bayamon Central Univ, Bayamon, PR; JR; BA; Psychlgy Stdnts Assn 90-; Comm Chrch Choir Ltrgy Comm Crdntr Ltrgy 90-; Dir Of King Arthur Socty 83-86; Cert High Hnr; Mdl Of Hnr 90; Math Comp 105/107; Rcvd Mdl Hnrbl Mnto For Math 105; Trophy Math 107/Cert Competion 89; Psychlgy; Mstrs Degree.

**ALICEA QUILES, MELISSA,** Inter Amer Univ Pr Hato Rey, Hato Rey, PR; JR; Englsh Ttr 87-; Cmp Cnslr Hyatt Cerromar Htl 88-; Air Traffc Cntrlr Intrnshp Fdrl Aviatn Admin ATC Trainee 89-; Mgmt Aviation; Air Traffic Cntrlr.

**ALICEA VILA, JOHANA,** Inter Amer Univ Pr Hato Rey, Hato Rey, PR; FR; Orgnzcn Shnstf 87; U S Slvtn Army 86; Estdnt D Hnr De La Unvrsd 90; Volibol 87; Intrmrcn Metro De Pr Lista De Hon Del Decano.

**ALICEA, ALBAROSA,** Univ Of Pr At Mayaguez, Mayaguez, PR; SO; Biology Stdnts Assn 90-; Beta Beta Beta 90-; Amrcn Cncr Soc Vlntr 89-; Biology; Biochemestry.

**ALICEA, DANIEL,** City Univ Of Ny Queensbrough, New York, NY; FR; AA; Engl; Law.

**ALICEA, SHEILA E,** Univ Of Pr Medical Sciences, San Juan, PR; GD; MS; Stdnt Gen Cncl UPR Mdcl Sci Sec Act 89-; Amer Adtry Scty; La Confra Christian 87-89; Ntl Stdnt Spch Lang Hrng Assc 90-; Adlgcl Evltns Eldrly People Vol 90; Dr Ramon E Betances Awd UPR Med Sci; BS Univ Puerto Rico Cayey Campus 90; Audiology; Audiologist.

**ALIHASSAN, SAMMEH M,** Embry Riddle Aeronautical Univ, Daytona Beach, FL; SO; BA; SAE; Deans Lst 90-; Chem Lab Assist 90-; Embry Riddle Speech Nite Nominee Spkr 90; Aero Eng; Eng.

**ALIOTH, LA VONNE J,** Hillsborough Comm Coll, Tampa, FL; FR; Early Chldhd Dvlpmnt; Tchr.

**ALIX, KIMBERLY J,** Hudson Valley Comm Coll, Troy, NY; FR; BED; Early Chldhd Educ.

**ALJANCIC, ANDREW J,** Muskingum Coll, New Concord, OH; SO; BA; Flwshp Chrstn Ath 90-; Kappa Mu Epsilon VP 90-; Omicron Delta Kappa; Brnz Slvr Keys 90-; Dorm Res Asst; Vrsty Ftbl 89-; Vrsty Bsbl 90; Math/Comm; Educ.

**ALKEISI, AMJAD D,** Univ Of Louisville, Louisville, KY; GD; BSEE 90; Meng E E.

**ALKEMA, ELIZABETH A,** Memphis St Univ, Memphis, TN; JR; BM; Ltr Dy St Stdnt Assoc Sec 89-; Pi Kappa Lambda; Msc Ed Natl Cnfrnc Treas 89-; Msc Ed; Elem Msc Tchr.

**ALKIRE, SARAH B,** Univ Of Cincinnati-Clrmnt Coll, Batavia, OH; SO; BA; Deans Lst 90-; Frgn Admnstrtr Mjr Law Firm; Mktg Asst Lg Cable Co; Exec Sec; Intl Affrs; Intl Law.

**ALKIRE, WILLIAM T,** Univ Of Al At Huntsville, Huntsville, AL; SR; Am Soc Mech Engs 89-; Am Soc Wght Engs; Pi Tau Sigma 90-; Phi Eta Sigma 88-; Mech Eng.

**ALKOBI, DAFNA,** City Univ Of Ny Baruch Coll, New York, NY; JR; Accounting; CPA.

**ALLAIN, JEANNETTE D,** Univ Politecnica De Pr, Hato Rey, PR; FR.

**ALLAIN, JEANNIE L,** Univ Politecnica De Pr, Hato Rey, PR; FR; Vllybll; Swmmng.

**ALLAN, ANDREW,** Oh Univ, Athens, OH; JR; BSEE; Phi Kappa Phi; Worked In Publ Utilities; Res Dsgn/Eng; Radar Site Dvlpmnt 75-89; Eng.

**ALLARD, DONNA L,** Middlesex County Coll, Edison, NJ; FR; AAS; MDA Monmouth Cty Voc 81; Dntl Hyg.

**ALLEBACH, MARK A,** Liberty Univ, Lynchburg, VA; JR; BA; Stdnt Govt Snte 89-; Stdnt Bdy Pres Cbnt Chief Of Staff; Alpha Lambda Delta 89-; Phi Sigma Tau; Cycling Team; Hstry/Phlsphy; Tchng.

**ALLEGRETTI, JEAN M,** Saint Vincents Coll & Seminary, Latrobe, PA; JR; BA BS; Physcs Clb 90-; IM Ftbl 90; Math Eng; Eng.

**ALLEN, ADRIENNE D,** Fl A & M Univ, Tallahassee, FL; FR; Pharmacy.

**ALLEN, AMBER R,** Va Union Univ, Richmond, VA; JR; BS; Cncrt Chr; French Clb; Sci Clb; Alpha Kappa Mu 90-; Beta Kappa Chi; Pres Lst 88-; Deans Lst 88-; Biology; Pharmacy.**

**ALLEN, AMY S,** Univ Of Montevallo, Montevallo, AL; JR; BA; Sigma Tau Delta 90-; Pi Kappa Phi; Pres Awrd; Engl; Ed.

**ALLEN, ANDREA M,** Middle Ga Coll, Cochran, GA; FR; BSU Jyfl Mnstrs 90-; Gamma Beta Phi 90-; Vet Med.

**ALLEN, ANGELA R,** Free Will Baptist Bible Coll, Nashville, TN; SR; BS; Chrstna Rossetti Soc Hstrn 87-; Forgn Missns Flwshp V P 89-; Stdnt Life Comm 90-; Elem Educ; Childcr.

**ALLEN, ANN H,** Wilmington Coll, New Castle, DE; JR; BS; Cvc Assn Offcr 90-; Amrcn Cmpnstn Assn; AS Wdnr Unvrsty 80; Hmn Rsrcs; Mgmnt.

**ALLEN, ARLONDA Y,** Livingston Univ, Livingston, AL; FR; Lvngstn Univ Bnd; Anglc Vc Fth 90-; Bptst Cmps Mnstrs 90-; Alpha Kappa Alpha; Comp Sci; Eng.

**ALLEN, ASHLEY G,** Livingston Univ, Livingston, AL; JR; BS; Theater; Alpha Psi Omega Pres; Biology; Educ.

**ALLEN, BILL E,** Wv Univ At Parkersburg, Parkersburg, WV; FR; BA; Lib Asst Wood Co Publ Lib 87-; Biol; Wldlf Res.

**ALLEN, BOBBIE L,** Wilberforce Univ, Wilberforce, OH; SO; BA; SG Brd Trustee Rep; Vogue Phi Vogue Pres 90-; Psych Tutor; Kappa Swthrt Pres; Var Chrldr; Pol Sci; Law.

**ALLEN, BRIAN M,** Bellarmine Coll, Louisville, KY; SR; BA; Rcylng Tm Coord 89-; HS Alumni Brd 89-F Ldrshp Ed/Dvlpmnt 89; Pres Schlrs 89-; Delta Epsilon Sigma 90-; Untd Way 89-; Camp Mnstry 90-; Ldrshp Awd 90; Allen Soc Awd Judge; Penny Golden Rule Awd 90-; Cty Spec Evnts Coord 90; Bus; Mktg Spec Evnt Prdcr.

**ALLEN, CECELE J,** Broward Comm Coll, Ft Lauderdale, FL; SO; BA; Mktg/Mgt; Bus Mgt.

**ALLEN, CHEN,** City Univ Of Ny City Coll, New York, NY; JR; BE; Tau Beta Pi; Electrcl Engrng.

**ALLEN, CYNTHIA K,** Fayetteville St Univ, Fayetteville, NC; SR; BS; Mthrs Mrch Dimes 90; Kappa Delta Pi 89-; Chnclrs Lst 89; Dns Lst 89-; US Army Vet 85-87; Cvl Srvnt 80-81 83-85; Math/Physcs; Tch.

**ALLEN, CYNTHIA L,** Sue Bennett Coll, London, KY; FR; BA; Phi Theta Kappa 90; Educ Club 90; Elem Educ; Tchr.

**ALLEN, CYNTHIA L,** Coll Of Charleston, Charleston, SC; JR; BA; Hnrs Pgm Stdnt Assn V P; Coll Rep; Hnrs Pgm 89-; Pi Sigma Alpha; Schlrshp 89-; Pol Sci; Law.

**ALLEN, DEBORAH E,** Saint Catharine Coll, St Catharine, KY; FR; CKCAC Brd Dir; St Monica Parish Cncl; NAACP Nelson Co Sec; Scl Wrk.

**ALLEN, DEBORAH V S,** Winthrop Coll, Rock Hill, SC; SR; BME; Delta Omicron Msc Dir 89-; Kappa Delta Pi 89-; MENC 89-; Natl Assoc Deaf 80-; Dilworth Chld Dev Ctr Secr 84-86; Svc Awd PTA 78-88; Dns Lst 89-; Pres Lst 90-; Outstndg Sr Awd; Amer Guild Engl Handbl Ringers 82-; Chorusters Guild 82-; Msc Ed.

**ALLEN, DENISE S,** Univ Of Cin R Walters Coll, Blue Ash, OH; SO; BA; Nrsng.

**ALLEN, DEON,** Denmark Tech Coll, Denmark, SC; SO; AS; Pres Lst 90-; Deans Lst 89-; Sci; Archtct.**

**ALLEN, DONNA B,** Hampton Univ, Hampton, VA; SO; BS; VA Pre Alumni Assn 90-; Hnr Stdnt 89-; Nrsg.

**ALLEN II, EDDIE N,** Univ Of Tn At Martin, Martin, TN; SO; BSW; Soc/Socl Wrk.

**ALLEN, ERICK M,** Central St Univ, Wilberforce, OH; FR; BS; Mfg Engr; Engr.

**ALLEN, FRANKIE B,** Univ Of Sc At Columbia, Columbia, SC; JR; BED; Cncrt Choir 90-; Msc Edctrs Natl Cnfrnc Coll Chptr Pres 90-; Outstndng Msc Stdnt Awd 90-; BA 77; Msc; Educ Admin.

**ALLEN, GINGER LEE,** Coll Of Charleston, Charleston, SC; SO; Physcl Ed Clb; AA Edison Cmmnty Coll 88; Physcl Ed; Physcl Thrpy.

**ALLEN, IVY L,** Union Coll, Barbourville, KY; FR; BA; BLTN Clb; Tchr Aide Knox Cntrl H S 87-; Englsh Scl Stds; Edctn.

**ALLEN SR, JAMES H,** Manna Bible Inst, Philadelphia, PA; FR; BED; St Matthews Bapt Church Brd Of Deacons Vice Chrmn 90-; Christian Educ.

**ALLEN, JEFFREY SCOTT,** Northeast State Tech Comm Coll, Blountville, TN; SO; AAS; Elec Tchnlgy.

**ALLEN, JEFFREY W,** Wilmington Coll, New Castle, DE; SR; BA; Bus Soc 90-; Bus; Mgmt.

**ALLEN, JENNIFER C,** Tn Tech Univ, Cookeville, TN; SO; BS; Amer Home Ec Assn; TN Home Ec Assn; TN Tech Home Ec Assn Secy; Kappa Omircron Nu Rprtr; Concert/Mrchng Bnds; Home Ec; Marriage/Fmly Therapist.

**ALLEN, JENNIFER D,** Georgetown Coll, Georgetown, KY; SO; BA; Religion.

**ALLEN, JENNIFER L,** Univ Of Louisville, Louisville, KY; SO; DPMA.

**ALLEN, JERMAINE B,** Fayetteville St Univ, Fayetteville, NC; SO; BS; Collegiate DECA Prlmntrn 90-; Stdnt Ldr 90-; Bus Edu; Tchng.

**ALLEN, JO ANN M,** Hudson Valley Comm Coll, Troy, NY; FR; BA; League Of Women Voters 89-; Hairstylist 10 Yrs; Nutrition; Registered Dietitian.

**ALLEN, JOHN M,** Birmingham Southern Coll, Birmingham, AL; SO; BA; Coll Demo Pres 89-; Alpha Phi Omega 90-; Stf Wrtr; Phi Eta Sigma 90; Alpha Lambda Delta 90; Phi Alpha Theta; Intrnshp Birmingham Pub Lbry Arch 90; Hist; Coll Tchng.

**ALLEN, JOHNETTA,** Tn St Univ, Nashville, TN; JR; BS; Stdnt Govt VP; Class VP 89-; AECOMP VP 88-; Golden Key 90-; Alpha Lambda Delta 89-; Hons Prog Pblc Rltns Dir 88-; Alpha Kappa Alpha 90-; SADD Co Chair 90-; Thomas Edward Poag Plyrs Guild Rep-At-Large 90-; Comp Sci; Corp Info Sys.

**ALLEN, JONATHAN K,** Fl A & M Univ, Tallahassee, FL; JR; BA; Std Govt Asc Dir 88-; Alpha Phi Alpha Pres 89-; St Farm Ins Co Intrn; FAMU Rttlr Prd Awd; Nphyt Yr Alpha Phi Alpha 89-90; Spec Olympcs Vol 88-; NAACP 90-; 100 Blck Men 90-; Ecnmcs; Pblc Admn.

**ALLEN, JULIA J,** Univ Of Sc At Columbia, Columbia, SC; SO; BA; Grn Pc 89-; Amnsty Intl 89-; Gamma Beta Phi; Eng; Law.

**ALLEN, KAREN E,** William Paterson Coll, Wayne, NJ; SR; BA; PTO 86-; Sftbl 82-; Mrtg Repr 87-89; Clsc Athltc Clb 90-; Math/Sec Ed; Tchr.

**ALLEN, KAREN K,** Univ Of Ga, Athens, GA; SR; MED; Inner City Minstrs 88-89; Natl Stdnt Spch Lang Hrng Assn 89-; Colorgrd 86-88; Golden Key 87-; Kappa Chi Epsilon 87-88; Chi Omega Chptr Corr 86-88; Univ Tenn Chattng Fndtnl Schlrshp 86-88; Dns Lst 86-; BSED; Spch/Lang/Path.

**ALLEN, KAREN M,** Dyersburg St Comm Coll, Dyersburg, TN; SO; BA; Acctg.

**ALLEN, KARI L,** Richard Bland Coll, Petersburg, VA; SO; BA; Eqstrn Tm 89-90; Chrldr 90; AS; Psychlgy/Ntrtn; Mtrnl Hlth Cnslr.

**ALLEN, KATHRYN C,** Univ Of Ga, Athens, GA; SR; BED; Foster Prnt Assn Clarke Cnty 88-; BFA 79; Erly Chldhd; Tchr.

**ALLEN, KEISHA L,** Johnson C Smith Univ, Charlotte, NC; SR; Book Clb Co Founder Pres 90-; Shaki Mdlng Troupe Treas 87-; Yrbk Stf 90-; Deans Lst 88-; Alpha Kappa Alpha; Intern WSOC TV; Intern WCNC TV; Intern Mngr Radio Station Campus 89-; BA; Broadcast Jrnlsm; News Reporter.

**ALLEN, KEITH W,** Wilmington Coll, New Castle, DE; BA; USMC Viet Nam Vet 66-70; US Army Dvrty Chem NCIC 78-86; Spcl Olympics Vol; MBNA Amer Corps Prsnl Bnkng Offcr In Scrty 87; AA De Tect Comm Clg 90; Crmnl Jstce; Bnkng.

**ALLEN, KELLI S,** Memphis St Univ, Memphis, TN; JR; BS; Sigma Kappa Sorority Rcrdg Sec 83-86; Bapt Minor Med Ctr Emplee; Med; Phys Thrpy.

**ALLEN, KEVIN D,** Oh Univ, Athens, OH; FR; BFA; Scty Fr Crtve Amchrnsm 90-; Actng; Thtr And Flm.

**ALLEN, KEVIN M,** Univ Of Nh Plymouth St Coll, Plymouth, NH; SO; Ftbl 89-90.

**ALLEN, KILEY L,** Radford Univ, Radford, VA; SR; BS; Alpha Lambda Delta 87-; Pi Gamma Mu 89-; Crmnl Juste; Law.

**ALLEN, KIMBERLY,** Bowie St Univ, Bowie, MD; JR; BS; Comm Clb 90-; Antl Brdcsntg Hnr Scty Pres 90-; Delta Sigma Theta 2 VP; Deans Lst 90; Comm Media Awd 90-; Broadcast Tech; Prdctn/Prgrmng.

**ALLEN, KIRSTEN E,** Fl St Univ, Tallahassee, FL; JR; BA; Almn Fndtn; Pnhllnc Nwsppr Corr; FL Pblc Rltns Assc; Phi Theta Kappa 89-; Hnrs Schlrs 90-; Nwsppr Stff 89; Kappa Delta VP 90-; Cmp Cnslr U M Yth Tm Ldr 89-; Sntnl Ambssdr 89; Trnsfr Schlrshp 90; AA FL Comm Coll 90; Pblc Rltns/Engl; Wrtr Cmmnctns.

**ALLEN, KRISTA S,** Univ Of Ky, Lexington, KY; SR; BA; Mid Schl Assoc CEC 88-; Direcotry Committee; Golden Key 88-; Deans List 88-; Delta Gamma 88-; Mid Schl & Spcl Ed; Teach.

**ALLEN, KRISTI A,** Western New England Coll, Springfield, MA; JR; BS; Mrktg; Prmtn.

**ALLEN, LA TONYA J,** Al St Univ, Montgomery, AL; SO; BA; Socty For Advncmnt Of Mgmt 90-; Pre-Law Socty; OES 90-; Cert Taylor Bus Inst 88; Finc; Real Est/Entrprnr.

**ALLEN, LAGINA M,** Sue Bennett Coll, London, KY; FR; MBA; Pep Clb 90; All Amer Schlr; Turor; Chld Psychlgst.

**ALLEN, LAWRENCE J,** Univ Of Sc At Columbia, Columbia, SC; FR; BA; Phi Eta Sigma; Acctg; Bus.

**ALLEN II, LEIGH R,** Morehouse Coll, Atlanta, GA; JR; BA; Bus Assn 89-; Pol Sci Soc 89-; Pre-Law Soc 89-; Hon Rl 90; Tutor 90-; NAACP 89-; Young Demos 89-; IM Vlybl/Bsktbl 88-; Pol Sci/Pre Law; Corp Law.

**ALLEN, LINDA J,** Schenectady County Comm Coll, Schenectady, NY; SR; AA; Erly Educ.

**ALLEN, LINDA M,** New Comm Coll Of Baltimore, Baltimore, MD; SO; AA; Hddn Jwl Awrd 90; Otstndng Srvc Rcgntn Ovrll Sprr Evltn 87-90; Prfct Attndnc 81-82; Cthlc Dghtrs Amrcs Crt 90-; By Scts Amrc Cb Sct Trp Comm Mmbr 89-; Vol Asst Chrprsn; Vol Elem Schl Ast Chrprsn Unfrm Comm 90-; Comp Info Systms.

**ALLEN, LISA D,** Univ Of Nc At Greensboro, Greensboro, NC; JR; BS; Intrvar Chrstn Fwlshp 88-90; SNCAE VP 90-; Elem Educ; Tchr.

**ALLEN, LISA L,** Toccoa Falls Coll, Toccoa Falls, GA; FR; BS; Choir 90-; Mime/Drama Tm 90-; Chldrns Chrch/Camp Chrch Tchr 90-; Erly Chldhd Ed; Tchr.

**ALLEN, LOIS J,** Montgomery Comm Coll, Troy, NC; FR; AAS; SGA 90-; Prsdnts Lst 90-; Mcrcmptr Systms Tchnlty; Cmptrs.

**ALLEN, LORI A,** Univ Of Nc At Charlotte, Charlotte, NC; FR; BA; NC Tchng Fellow 90-; Walter L Mitchell Mem Schlrshp Awd Rcpnt 90-; Engl; H S Tchr.

**ALLEN, LORI M,** S U N Y Coll At Fredonia, Fredonia, NY; SR; Kappa Delta Pi; Hon Pgm; BA; Educ; Tch.

**ALLEN, MARK T,** Newbury Coll, Brookline, MA; FR; ASSOC; TV Prdcng; Cmmnctns/Prdcng.

**ALLEN, MARSHA J,** Univ Of Nc At Greensboro, Greensboro, NC; SO; BS; Fellows Ldrshp Org 89-90; Smphonic Chorus; Intervrsty Christian Flwshp 89-; Small Grp Ldr IVCF 90-; Shoats Yth Cncl Sec 90-; Elem Ed/Speech Comm; Tchr.

**ALLEN, MARY E,** William Paterson Coll, Wayne, NJ; SO; Humanities Clb; Stdnts For Better Reg 90-; Mbr Of Hum Hons Pgm 90-; Passaic Cnty Chptr Natl Org For Women Co-Edtr Nwsltr 88-; Sec 88; Engl Lit; Tchr.

**ALLEN, MARY ELIZABETH,** Univ Of Rochester, Rochester, NY; JR; BA; Stdnt Actvts Aprptn Cmte Cntrlr 89-; Mrdn Scty Mrdn 89-; Pltcl Sci Cncl Treas 89-; Dstrct Atrny Intrnshp; Pltcl Sci; Law.

**ALLEN, MELISSA C,** City Univ Of Ny La Guard Coll, Long Island Cty, NY; MS; AAS; Physcl Thrpy.

**ALLEN, MELISSA E,** Radford Univ, Radford, VA; SR; BS; Stdnt Govt Assn Pres 88-89; Phys Ed Mjrs Clb VP 90-; Stdnt Govt Senatr 87-88; Stdnt Of Yr 89; Comm Wlkr Fn Arts Bldg 88; Jmp Rope For Hrt 89-; Sftbl 89-; AAS Patrck Henry Comm Coll 89; Phys/Hlth Ed; Tchr/Coach.

**ALLEN, MELISSA E,** Rutgers St Un At New Brunswick, New Brunswick, NJ; FR; Yrbk Staff 90-; IM Vllybl 90-; Bio; Vtrny Schl.

**ALLEN, MELISSA R,** Lexington Comm Coll, Lexington, KY; FR; Specl Educ Tchr.

**ALLEN, MELODY A,** Oh Dominican Coll, Columbus, OH; FR; BS; Auto Prcng Anlyst 85-; Cert Insurance Institute Of America 90; Elem Educ; Tch Math.

**ALLEN, MICHAEL B,** Southern Coll Of Tech, Marietta, GA; SR; BS; Inst Indstrl Eng 86-; Bathtub Rcng Assc 89-; Amer Scty Qlty Cntrl 89-; Natl Assc Corsn Eng 88-; Lmbd Chi Alph Cnclr Corspdnt 90-; Sch Orntn Ldr 87-88; Intrn Printpack Inc 90; D; Indstrl Eng; MS Eng/JD.

**ALLEN, MONIQUE R,** Saint Elizabeth Hosp Sch Nurs, Utica, NY; SR; AD; Stdnt Prsnl Cmtee 89-; BA Le Moyne Clg 81; Nurs.

**ALLEN, MYLINDA W,** Middle Tn St Univ, Murfreesboro, TN; SR; MSN; Stdnt Nrs Assc Pres 89-; Cls Stdnt Rep; Nrsng Hon Scty; Tau Omcrn 87-90; Gamma Beta Phi Hstrn 87-; Sgm Phi Epsln 87-89; Humane Scty 87; Red Crs 88; Valor Stdnt Alvin C York Vetrns Admn Med Ctr; York Spirit Awrd; BSN; Nrsng; Fmly Nrs Prctnr Cardiac Prfsnst.

**ALLEN, PAMELA L,** Fort Valley St Coll, Fort Valley, GA; SO; SGA BSU Treas 89-90; Bus Mgmt.

**ALLEN, PATRICIA L,** Chatfield Coll, Saint Martin, OH; JR; BA; Hist/Sci; Elem Educ.

**ALLEN, PAUL E,** Piedmont Coll, Demorest, GA; FR; BA; Vocal Perf; Opera.

**ALLEN, RAYLEAN,** Morgan St Univ, Baltimore, MD; SR; BA; Kappa Delta 90-; Elem Educ; Tchr.

**ALLEN, REBECCA L,** Univ Of Southern Ms, Hattiesburg, MS; SO; BS; Wesley Fndtn Chrmn 90; AED 90-; Math/Sci; Phys Thrpy.

**ALLEN, REBEKAH J,** Messiah Coll, Grantham, PA; FR; BS; Elmntry Ed; Tchng.

**ALLEN, ROGER W,** Beckley Coll, Beckley, WV; SO; BSN; Nursing.

**ALLEN, ROYCE M,** Tougaloo Coll, Tougaloo, MS; FR; Intrnshp-Jdg Denise S Owens-Hinds Co Chancery Crts Rsrchr; Engl; Law.

**ALLEN, SARAH ELIZABETH,** Colby Sawyer Coll, New London, NH; SR; JD; Clscl Vc 87-89; Mmbr Clby-Swyr Key Assn 88-89; Mmbr Alpha Chi 89-; Vlntr Hyns Hmls Shltr 87-; Law.

**ALLEN, SCOTT P,** Newbury Coll, Brookline, MA; SO; Aviation Ordnance 2 Cls Petty Ofcr 87-; US Navy; Career Navy; Business Mngmnt.

**ALLEN, SENIQUA N,** Lincoln Univ, Lincoln Univ, PA; SO; BA; Lincoln Un Hon Scty; Acctg; CPA.

**ALLEN, SHARON A,** Craven Comm Coll, New Bern, NC; GD; Csmtlgy Clb 89-; Deans Lst 90; Hi Hnrs 90; Roux Csmtlgy Cert; Csmtlgy.

**ALLEN, SHARON K,** Davis Coll, Toledo, OH; SO; Design Grp; Pres Ohio Child Cnsrvtn League Pres 84-85; Interior Design; Fine Arts.

**ALLEN, SHARON M,** Alcorn St Univ, Lorman, MS; SO; BS; NAACP 89; Bio Hnr Scty 89-90; Alpha Mu Gamma 90; Ordr Of Estrn Star 90; Food/Ntrtn; Dietician.

**ALLEN, SHONDA R,** Tougaloo Coll, Tougaloo, MS; FR; Stdnt Spprt Serv Secy 90-; CBS Schlr; History; Law.

**ALLEN, SUZZANNE R,** Boston Coll, Chestnut Hill, MA; JR; Rio Hondo Stdnt Nrs Assn Prsdnt 88-90; Rsdnc Hl Cncl Flr Rep 90-; Alpha Gamma Sigma 89-90; Alpha Sigma Nu Schl Nrsng Rep; Otstndng Stdnt Awd Rio Hondo Clg Hlth Sci Dpt 90; Nrs Edctr.

**ALLEN, TAMMY M,** Comm Coll Algny Co Algny Cmps, Pittsburgh, PA; FR; AS; Crmnlgy; Plce Offcr.

**ALLEN, TERESA L,** Wv Univ At Parkersburg, Parkersburg, WV; SO; RN; Med; Nrsg.

**ALLEN, TERRI L,** Univ Of Southern Ms, Hattiesburg, MS; JR; BS; Almni Assn 90-; Schlrshp Comm; Kappa Delta 90-; Chld Abuse Fnd Rsr; Sigma Alpha Epsilon Lttl Sis; Fndrs Day Chrmn; IM Ftbl 90; Elem Ed; Tchr.

**ALLEN, TERRY P,** Anne Arundel Comm Coll, Arnold, MD; SO; BA; Fantasy Role Players 80-; MD Army Natl Guard Cavalry Scouts Spec 89-; Kick Connection Escrima/Kali/Arnis Sch Yellow Sash; Hstry; Cmrcl Pilot.

**ALLEN, THEODORE J,** Al A & M Univ, Normal, AL; JR; BS; Alpha Rho Delta VP 89-; Oakwood Coll Chrstn Otrch Pgm 89-; Forest Serv Coop; Acctg; Bus Law.

**ALLEN, TIFFANY D,** Howard Univ, Washington, DC; SR; BS; Judcl Brd 89-; RHA 89-90; IN Clb 89-; HVFTA 90-; Kappa Omicron Nu 90-; Mrshl Flds/Daytn/Hudsn Intrn; Dns Lst 89-; Hon Rl 89-; Res Hl Schlstc Achvmnt Awds 89-; Fshn Merch; Intl Buyer/Mrktng.

**ALLEN, TIMOTHY P,** Temple Univ, Philadelphia, PA; FR; BARCH; AIAS 89-90; Grove Assoc Engr/Srvyrs Intrn 89; John Butler Davis Asc Archts 89-90; AA Hrrsbrg Area Comm Clg 90; Reg Arch.

**ALLEN, TOMEKIA R,** Tougaloo Coll, Tougaloo, MS; FR; Stdnt Spt Serv Cultural Cnctn 90-; Deans Lst 90-; Engl; Law.

**ALLEN, TONYA A,** Bowie St Univ, Bowie, MD; FR; BS; Pep Clb 90-; Rcpnt Of MD St Sntrl Schlrshp 90-; Dns Lst 90; Bus Acctng.

**ALLEN, TRACI L,** Univ Of Sc At Columbia, Columbia, SC; FR; BA; Carolina Cares 90; Stdnt Gvrnmnt Appt Commt; Alpha Delta Pi Innr Srty Rltns 90; Alpha Delta Pi Innr Srty Rltns 90; Deans List 90; Jrnlsm-Pblc Rltns; Nws Brdcrstr.

**ALLEN, TROY LAYMAN,** Univ Of Louisville, Louisville, KY; FR; Bptst Union; Industrl Engrng; Engrng.

**ALLEN, YOLANDA M,** Mary Holmes Coll, West Point, MS; SO; AA; Stdnt Govt Assoc VP 90; Phi Theta Kappa Pres 89; Bus Adm; Mrktng Mgr.

**ALLEN, YOLONDA P,** Al St Univ, Montgomery, AL; SO; Ordr Estrn Str.

**ALLEN, YUL D,** Fl Memorial Coll, Miami, FL; FR; BA; Michigan Clb V P 90-; Clg Newspaper Rep 90-; Alpha Phi Alpha Treas; Acctg.

**ALLESPACH, HEIDI H,** Fl International Univ, Miami, FL; GD; PHD; Psi Chi VP 90-; Phi Kappa Phi; Ntnl Hnrs Cncl 90-; FAAA; ADA Stdnt Afflt; Sbstnc Abuse Cnslr; BA 91; Clncl Hlth Psychlgy.

**ALLEY, ANGELA S,** Roane St Comm Coll, Harriman, TN; SO; AAS; Bptst Yng Women 87-; State Brd Rgnts Schlrshp 89-; Acctng.

**ALLEY, CHRISTINA K,** Roane St Comm Coll, Harriman, TN; SO; AAS; Bapt Yng Wmn Org 89-; Acctg.

**ALLEY, JAMES A,** Univ Of Nc At Asheville, Asheville, NC; FR; Phi Eta Sigma; Var Bsbl; Computer Science; Programmer.

**ALLEY, MICHELLE L,** Univ Of Tn At Martin, Martin, TN; SO; BFA; Spec Olympcs 90-; Art/Bus; Advtsng.

**ALLEY, VANESSA H,** Memphis St Univ, Memphis, TN; SR; BA; Spnsh Clb Pres; Gamma Beta Phi; Spnsh/Grmn; Tchg.

**ALLEYNE, DEBORAH Y,** City Univ Of Ny Med Evers Coll, Brooklyn, NY; JR; BS; Invstgtn Spclst Bankng; Bus Admn; Lecturer/Mgt.

**ALLEYNE, DELBERT C,** Hampton Univ, Hampton, VA; FR; BA; Eng Dsgn Proj Tm Grphcs Chr; Hnr Lst; Elec Eng; Elec Systms Dsgn.

**ALLEYNE, GAIL J,** Ny Univ, New York, NY; GD; BA; Urban Bnkrs; VP Kngs Vllgr Brd Of Dir Co-Op 87-89; United Negro Clg Fnd UNCF; Ecnmcs; Bsnss.

**ALLEYNE, GEORGE N,** City Univ Of Ny Med Evers Coll, Brooklyn, NY; JR; BS; Caribbn Assn Pr 90-; Acctg Clb Tr; Acctg/Cmptr Inf Syst; Acctnt.

**ALLEYNE, SHARRON D D,** Inter Amer Univ Pr San German, San German, PR; JR; BBA; Intrntl Stdnts Org 88-90; Mktg; Bus Mgmt.

**ALLGOOD, DAVID C,** Christopher Newport Coll, Newport News, VA; FR; BS; US Navy Elctrcn E-5 84-90; Physcs; Engr.

**ALLGOOD JR, JIMMY L,** Vance Granville Comm Coll, Henderson, NC; FR; AS; Phi Theta Kappa; Clge Trnsfr Schlr; Pre Engrg; Arspc/Biomed Engrg.

**ALLGOOD, KEVIN S,** Averett Coll, Danville, VA; FR; BSU 90; Phi Eta Sgm 90-; Pre Pharm; Pharmst.

**ALLIGOOD, F CARTER,** Va Commonwealth Univ, Richmond, VA; JR; BS; Stu Govt Sntr; Alumni Ambsdrs Chr Bnqut Comm 90-; Pblcty Comm Undrgrad Crclum; Gldn Key 90-; Phi Eta Sigma; Psi Chi; Psychlgy; Bus.

**ALLIGOOD, KRISTY L,** Radford Univ, Radford, VA; JR; BS; Intrnshp News Jrnl 90-91; Intrnshp NASA-LANGLEY Rsrch Nwspr; Pblc Rltns Cnsltnt.

**ALLIGOOD JR, MANFRED D,** Life Coll, Marietta, GA; SR; DC; Cum Laude 90; 12 Mo Tour Viet Nam Received 2 Prple Hrts/Brnz Str/Slfemplyd; Pursue Career In Chrprctc; BSBA East Carolina Univ NC 72; DC 90; Doctor Chrprctc.

**ALLIMAN, TANIA N,** Fl International Univ, Miami, FL; SR; BA; Crbn Stdnts Assn; Tch Intrshp Joe Hall Elem; Art; Tchng.

**ALLING, DAWN M,** Univ Of New Haven, West Haven, CT; SR; Acctg Clb 89-; Soc CPA Schlrshp Awrd; Bl Crss/Bl Shld Schlrshp; Intrnshp Bl Crss/Bl Shld 90; Acctg.

**ALLING, GREGORY D,** Castleton St Coll, Castleton, VT; SO; MBA; Rpblcn Party Cmpgn; Pres Schlrshp 89-90; Deans Lst; I M Ftbl Vybl Sftbl 89-; Bus Admn; Invstmnt/Fin.

**ALLING, MARK L,** Univ Of Pittsburgh, Pittsburgh, PA; SO; BA; Eng Chem; Eng.

**ALLINGHAM, DEBORAH LYNN,** Comm Coll Algny Co Algny Cmps, Pittsburgh, PA; SO; BA; Acctg.

**ALLISON, BELINDA K,** Snead St Jr Coll, Boaz, AL; SO; BS; Ambsdrs; Prfrmng Arts Schlrshp; Phi Theta Kappa; Outstdng Stdnt; Music Awd; Pres Lst; Dns Lst; Alabama Coll Systm Music Showcase Piano Mstr Cls; Music; Music/Math Tchr.**

**ALLISON, CAROL R,** Limestone Coll, Gaffney, SC; SR; BA; Jr Marshall 89-90; Education; Teaching.

**ALLISON, CHARLES J,** Univ Of Southern Ms, Hattiesburg, MS; SO; Shotokan Clb 89-90; Aikido Clb 90-; Bnd 89-; Choir 89-; Phi Kappa Phi; Phi Mu Alpha Sinfonia 87-; Most Outstdg Frshmn Male Awd 90; Troy Chem Outstdg Soph Polymer Sci; Barry M Goldwater Schlrshp; Polymer Sci.

**ALLISON, CHRISTY L,** Beckley Coll, Beckley, WV; SO; BA; Brownie Trp Asst Ldr 90-; Oaur Girls Camp Camp Cnslr 90; Edn; Teach.

**ALLISON III, JAMES C,** Lexington Comm Coll, Lexington, KY; FR; BA.

**ALLISON, JAMIE A,** James Madison University, Harrisonburg, VA; SR; BA; Psych/Frnch; Cnslng.

**ALLISON, JANET,** Univ Of Cincinnati, Cincinnati, OH; SR; BS; Phi Theta Kappa 83-84; Clermont Chbr Comm Cert Recog Hiring Hndcpr 90; Red Lobster Rest 84-90; Dining Rm Mgr 87-90; AAS Sinclair Commty Clg 84; Criminal Justice; Law Schl/MS.

**ALLISON, JEFFERY M,** Univ Of Akron, Akron, OH; FR; BS; Phi Eta Sigma; Alpha Lambda Delta; Pres Schlrshp 90-; Hon Pgm 90-; Deans Lst 90-; Elec Eng.

**ALLISON, KIMBERLIE D,** Ms Gulf Coast Comm Coll, Perkinston, MS; FR; BA; Coll Hon Pgm; Coll Wrk Stdy Pgm-Sec Fine Arts Dept 90-; Bus; Acctg.

**ALLISON, LISA C,** Univ Of Al At Birmingham, Birmingham, AL; SO; BS; Alpha Lambda Delta; RN Chldrns Hosp; Dpl Dgr Rgstrd Nrs; Nrsng.

**ALLISON, MICHAEL E,** Church Of God Sch Of Theology, Cleveland, TN; SO; MA; BA Lee Coll 89; Theology; Missions.

**ALLISON, TIFFANY M,** Oh St Univ At Marion, Marion, OH; SR; BS; Educ Soc; OSU M Chorus; Educ.

**ALLISON, TINA L,** Georgian Court Coll, Lakewood, NJ; SR; SGA Secy 87-; CEC 87-88; Ed Club 87-; Sigma Phi Sigma VP 88-; Phi Delta Phi 88-; Deans List 88-; Humanities/Elem Ed; Tchr.

**ALLISTON, JERRY R,** Ms Gulf Coast Comm Coll, Perkinston, MS; SO; AA; Nwsppr Editor In Chf 89-; Yrbk Editor In Chf 89-; Phi Beta Lambda VP 90-; Hnrs Prog 89-; Schlrs Bowl Statistician 89-; Recruiting 89-; SADD 90-; Lit Prog 90-; Cmmnctns; Advrtsng.

**ALLITON, VAUGHN,** Nova Univ, Ft Lauderdale, FL; GD; MBA; Jr Achvmnt Natl Alum Assoc 88-; Univ Of Mi Alum Assoc 88-; Sot Human Rsrce Mgmt 89-; Human Rsrce Assoc Of Broward Co 89-; Human Rsrce Gnrlst 88-; BA Univ Mi Ann Arbor 88; Intl Fin; Fin/Human Resources.

**ALLMAIER, MELISSA C,** Elmira Coll, Elmira, NY; JR; BSN; Nrsng Clb; Vldctrn Nrsng Schl 76; Vol At Red Cross Vol; Pbl Hlth Nrsng; AA Corning Cmmnty Clg 73; RN Dplma Arnot Ogden Mem Hosp 76; Nrsng.

**ALLMAN, BRIAN D,** Nc Agri & Tech St Univ, Greensboro, NC; JR; BS; Model Untd Ntns 90; Phi Alpha Theta; Hstry/Soc Sci; Educator.

**ALLMAN, DEBORAH D,** City Univ Of Ny City Coll, New York, NY; GD; BS; Chrch Brthrn 79-; Elem Ed.

**ALLMAN, SCOTT A,** Nova Univ, Ft Lauderdale, FL; GD; MBA; Agncy Mgr Natl Supprt Systms 90; BS OH St Univ 82; Bsns Admn.

**ALLNUTT, CHRISTINE M,** Univ Of Ga, Athens, GA; SR; BA; IM Sftbl; Recr Mjrs Clb; Alpha Lambda Delta; Phi Kappa Phi; Frshmn Wmns Hnr Soc; Golden Key; B Ed Recr Univ GA; Jrnlsm/Publ Rels.

**ALLOWAY, MATTHEW R,** Miami Univ, Oxford, OH; FR; BA; Cir K 90-; Acctng Clb 90-; Alpha Lambda Delta 90-; Phi Eta Sigma 90-; Sigma Nu 90-; Bsn Acctng.

**ALLRED, ALISON S,** Univ Of Nc At Greensboro, Greensboro, NC; JR; BS; Natl Clgt Nrsng Awd 90-; All Amer Schlr 90-F US Achiev Acad Awd 90-; Nrsng; RN.

**ALLRED, CINDY M,** Ms St Univ, Miss State, MS; JR; BA; Bptst Un Sngng Ensmbl 88-89; Bpts Un Mssn Chrprns 89-90; IM Sftbll 88-89; AAD NE MI Cmmnty Coll 90; Offc Admn; Clrcl.

**ALLRED, SHARON D,** Saint Andrews Presbytrn Coll, Laurinburg, NC; JR; BA; Chorale 90-; Gspl Msc Assn 90-; Fletcher Msc Schlrshp 90-; Deans Hon Rl 90-; Creatv Arts Schlrshp 90-; AFA Sandhls Comm Coll 87; Msc Prfrmnc/Mass Cmnctns.

**ALLRIDGE, AMY K,** Memphis St Univ, Memphis, TN; JR; BA; Art; Interior Dsgn.

**ALLS, KELLI A,** Radford Univ, Radford, VA; SR; Peopl Ethcl Trtmnt Anmls 85-; BBA 90; Sm Busn Admin.

**ALLTMONT, ELLEN B,** Univ Of Ga, Athens, GA; SR; BSED; Rcrtn Mjrs Clb Ther Rcrtn Rep 88-; Golden Key 90-; Alpha Lambda Delta 88-; Gamma Beta Phi 88-; Delta Phi Epsilon Comm Svc Phlnthrpy Chr 87-; Shphrd Spnl Cntr Intrnshp; GA Rcrtn/Pks Soc 88-; Amer Ther Rec Assn 90-91; Ther Rec.

**ALLUMS, MAURY,** Morehouse Coll, Atlanta, GA; JR; BA; Glee Clb 90-; Mus Educ; Music Tchr.

**ALLUMS, STEPHANIE,** Al A & M Univ, Normal, AL; SO; BS; Stdnt Sprt Svc 89-; Chem; Rsrch Chem.

**ALLWATERS, ALVEE O,** Atlantic Union Coll, S Lancaster, MA; JR; BS; Wmns Clb Sec 89-; Psych/Pre Law; Law.

**ALLYN, CYNTHIA L,** Comm Coll Algny Co Algny Cmps, Pittsburgh, PA; FR; Deans Lst 90-; Rdtn Thrpy Tchnlgy Intrnshp 90-; Allghny Gnrl Hosp Rdlgy File Clrk 89-; Rdtn Thrpy Tchnlgy; Sci.

**ALMAGUER, ELSA,** Miami Dade Comm Coll North, Miami, FL; JR; BED; Bus Mngr Vet Hosp 78-; AA Miami Dade Comm Coll 90; Engl Educ; Tch.

**ALMANSA, MOISES I,** Univ Politecnica De Pr, Hato Rey, PR; FR; BA; Hon Soc 90-; Tennis Tm 90-; Ba; Fnce; Busn Comm.

**ALMEIDA, JEAN E,** Univ Of Nh Plymouth St Coll, Plymouth, NH; SR; BA; Sci Soc Sec 89-; Judical Brd 89-; Pres Lst 89-; Dns Lst 90-; Stdnt Touls At PSC 90-; Tutrng Sci Undergrad Stdnts 89-90; Skiing; Scuba Divng Cert; Sftbl; Bio/Mar Bio; Mar Bio Tech.**

**ALMEIDA, JORGE E,** Nova Univ, Ft Lauderdale, FL; GD; MBA; Phi Theta Kappa 83; Alpha Chi 89; Data Prcssng Mgmt Assn Chptr 127; AAS Union Coll NJ 83; BS 89; Bus; Mgmt.

**ALMEIDA, LUCINDA,** Atlantic Comm Coll, Mays Landing, NJ; SO; BS; Nrsng; RN.

**ALMEIDA, MARITZA M,** Bayamon Central Univ, Bayamon, PR; SR; Chemistry Clb 89-90; Acdmc Cncl; Chemistry; Medicine.

**ALMEIDA, MELISSA V,** Bayamon Central Univ, Bayamon, PR; JR; Pre Med/Bio Asc 90-; Bio; Med Dctr.

**ALMEIDA, SERGIO ALTINO,** Rutgers St Un At New Brunswick, New Brunswick, NJ; FR; Pre Med Clb 90-; Blgy Clb 90-; Tae Kwon Do; Phlsphy/Blgy; Med.

**ALMENAS-PABON, BRENDA I,** Inter Amer Univ Pr Hato Rey, Hato Rey, PR; FR; BA; Stdnt Cncl Vcl/Intrn S; Cnslr; Thtr Grp 90; Ntl Hon Soc P 89-90; Ldrs Peace Coord Asst 88-; Pell Grand 90-; Chem; Sci.

**ALMENDARES, LISA M,** Hillsborough Comm Coll, Tampa, FL; SO; AA; Engl; BA Ed.

**ALMETER, KRISTEN M,** Daemen Coll, Amherst, NY; FR; BS; Bus.

**ALMODOVAR, ALVIN A,** Inter Amer Univ Pr San German, San German, PR; SR; BS; Comp Sci/Bus Admina.

**ALMOND, ANGELA G,** Richard Bland Coll, Petersburg, VA; JR; BA; AS 90; Sociology; Educ.

**ALMONTE, GISELA A,** Hudson County Comm Coll, Jersey City, NJ; SO; BED; Dns Lst 89-90; BA Elec Coll/Cmptr Prgrmng 86; Engl; Cmptrs.**

**ALMONTE, JOSE A,** City Univ Of Ny Baruch Coll, New York, NY; JR; Hispanic Soc 89-; Latin Amer Yth 89-.

**ALMONTE, MAYRA E,** Mount Saint Mary Coll, Newburgh, NY; JR; BA; Pblc Rltns Assn Pres 89-90; Stdnt Nwspr Assoc Ed 88-90; Coll Tour Guide 88-90; Deans Lst 88-; Hons Allnc 88-; Ntl Coll Stdnt Gov Awd 90; NCAA Div III Wmns Vlybl 89-; Cmnctns; Brdcst Jrnlsm.**

**ALOI, TRACI L,** Alfred Univ, Alfred, NY; SO; Stdnt Snte Bldng Sntr Rep 90-; IM Vlybl Capt 89-; Ht Dg Dy Com 90-; Sigma Chi Nu 90-; Crmc Eng Math Sci; Crmc Eng.**

**ALOIS, LOIS,** S U N Y Coll Of Tech At Frmgdl, Farmingdale, NY; SR; Good Smrtn Hosp-Acctg/Fin Dept 81-; Nrsng; RN Grtrcs.

**ALOISI, GINA M,** Lasell Coll, Newton, MA; FR; BA; Yrbk Stf Co Ed 90-; Stdnt Govt Soph Cls Rep; Vrsty Sftbl; Hnrs Lst 90-; Erly Chldhd Educ.

**ALOMENU, EVELYN E,** Central St Univ, Wilberforce, OH; FR; BSC; Cmptr Info Systs Clb; Intl Stdnts Assn; Bus Mgmt.

**ALONSO, DANAY,** Fl International Univ, Miami, FL; FR; BA; Bus; Mktg.

**ALONSO, MARLENE E,** Saint Thomas Univ, Miami, FL; SR; BA; AA Miami Dade Coll N Campus; Elem Educ; Tch.

**ALONSO, MERCY G,** Fl International Univ, Miami, FL; SR; BA; Intl Rdng Assn 90-; FEA 89-; Tspns 80-82; Phi Kappa Phi 90-; Kappa Delta Pi 90-; Elem Ed Intrnshp 89-; AS Miami Dade Comm Coll 89; Elem Ed; MA Rdng.

**ALONSO-MONFERRER, FERNANDO,** Univ Of Ms Main Cmps, University, MS; GD; MSES; Achvmnt Awd; Fulbright Schlp 89-; Erasmus Schlp 88; Iaeste Intrshp 86; Sccr 86-; BE Univ Politecnica De Catalunya 89; Elec Engr.

**ALONZO, CHRISTOPHER P,** Allegheny Coll, Meadville, PA; SO; BS; ASG Senator 89-; Curriculum Comm Repr 89-; RA; Soccer/Vlybl Capt 89-; ALLIES 90-; Econ; Sml Bsn.

**ALOS, ELBA M,** Inter Amer Univ Pr Hato Rey, Hato Rey, PR; JR; BA; Interamer Hon Soc 89-; LAPA 89-; Grad Assoc Ciencias Sec; Assoc Univ PR 77; Elem Ed/Spnsh; MBA.

**ALOZIE, CHIDI N,** City Univ Of Ny City Coll, New York, NY; SR; BS; Ngrn Stdnts Org Treas 88-90; SGA Sci Sntr 89-90; Goldn Key 89-; Cty Wmn Awrd 89; Grp Ldr Fr Orientatn; Biochem; Med Schl.

**ALPIZAR, MARY,** Fl International Univ, Miami, FL; GD; HFTA; Les Amis De Vins; BS FIU; AA Miami Dade Comm Clg 89; Hosptlty Mgt.

**ALSBROOK, BARM C,** Dyersburg St Comm Coll, Dyersburg, TN; SO; AS; Phi Theta Kappa 90-; Hstry; Tchng.

**ALSHAFIEI, SALEM A,** Al A & M Univ, Normal, AL; JR; BS; Amer Plnng Assoc 90-; AL Plnng 90-; Intl Sccr Clb 89-90; Cert Engl Univ AR 88; Urban/Reg Plnng.

**ALSINA, JENIRA GERENA,** Univ Of Pr At Rio Piedras, Rio Piedras, PR; FR.

**ALSIP, JULIE A,** Bethel Coll, Mckenzie, TN; SR; Bus Clb VP 89-; Lambda Sigma 89-; Otstndng Bus Stdnt Awrd 90-; Bob Hope Acdmc Schlrshp 89-; AS Jackson Stae Cmmnty Coll 89; BS; Acctg; CPA.

**ALSTER ARNOPP, ELEANOR,** Dowling Coll, Oakdale Li, NY; SR; BA; Phi Theta Kappa 88; Alpha Chi; AA Suffok Cnty Comm Coll 90; Spec Ed; Tch.

**ALSTER, STACEY I,** Univ Of Rochester, Rochester, NY; JR; Vrsty Sccr 88-; Hllt Fndtn 88-; Optcl Scty 89-; RA 80-; Untd Athltc Assoc 90; Optcs.

**ALSTON, CHRYSTAL A,** Norfolk St Univ, Norfolk, VA; GD; MSW; Sclgy Clb 87-90; Comm Orch 88; 1st Bapt Chrch Yng Adlt Choir; Alpha Kappa Delta 90-; Delta Epsilon Beta 87-; Amer Cancer Soc 88-90; Web Du Bois Citation 90; Hm Agd Brd Mgrs 90-; YWCA 90-; Brd Crek Cvc Leag 90; Sub Tchr Pblc Schl Sys 90-; Med Scl Wrk.

**ALSTON, DONNA M,** Nc Agri & Tech St Univ, Greensboro, NC; FR; BA; NESBE/NAACP; Engr; Elec/Comp.

**ALSTON, MARK O,** City Univ Of Ny La Guard Coll, Long Island Cty, NY; JR; PTA; Phys Thrpy Clb; Mntr; Tutor; Schlr Incntv Pgm; Hndbl Tm; BS State Un NY Stonybrook 89; Phys Thrpy.

**ALSTON, REBECCA C,** Lane Coll, Jackson, TN; SR; BA; Stdnt Crhstn Org Treas 90-; Bible Cls Choir; Order Of Eastern Stars; Sub Tchr Humboldt Schls; Dorm Dir; Cmmnctns/Cert Elem Sec Educ; Tchr.

**ALSTOTT, TANYA L,** Univ Of Nc At Asheville, Asheville, NC; SR; BA; Ecology Clb 88-89; Chnclr Collaquim 88-; Deans List 88; All Amer Schlr 90-; City Plng Dept Intrn 89; Hosp Vol; Psychlgy; Ph D MBA.

**ALSUP, TRACI L,** Middle Tn St Univ, Murfreesboro, TN; FR; BS; Aerspce; Admin.

**ALTBERGER, JASON T,** Georgetown Univ, Washington, DC; FR; Actvts Cmsn; Asst Ambsdr Pgm; Bus Admn.

**ALTEMOS, MEGAN S,** Va Commonwealth Univ, Richmond, VA; SO; BFA; Phi Eta Sigma 90-; Interior Desgn.

**ALTEN, SCOTT W,** Atlantic Comm Coll, Mays Landing, NJ; SO; BA; Lit Mag Mngng Ed 87-; Coll Stdnt Paper Stf 90-; Coll Theater Grp Actor 87-89; Engl; Teach.

**ALTENBAUGH, ERIC D,** Comm Coll Algny Co Algny Cmps, Pittsburgh, PA; SO; BS; Cmptr Sci; Systms Analyst.

**ALTHOFF, JULIANN M,** Oh Wesleyan Univ, Delaware, OH; SR; BS; Republicans Clb Pres 88-; Trap/Skeet 90-; Mortar Bd Treas 90-; Crs Cntry/Swmng/Track 87-; Pre-Med/Pre-Profl Zoology; Medicine.

**ALTHOUSE, MATTHEW J,** Oh Univ, Athens, OH; SO; BCHE; Trustees Outstndng Schlrshp 89-90; Chemical Eng.

**ALTIERI, KIMBERLY L,** Univ Of Pittsburgh, Pittsburgh, PA; JR; BS; Pitt Intnl Stdnt Org Pres 88-; Soc/Wmn Engr Fund Raising Chpsn 88-; Inst Indus Engr 89-; Mortar Bd; Gold Key 90-; Druids 89-; Kappa Delta Chpsn; Intnshp Packard Elec; Intnshp P C Rizzo/Asso Inc 90; Indus Engrg.

**ALTIERI, SANDRA M,** S U N Y Coll Of Tech At Frmgdl, Farmingdale, NY; GD; BA; Admin Optcl Firm; AS 90; Bus Admin; Mgmt Finc/Bnkng.

**ALTIZER, EVA ANN,** Northeast State Tech Comm Coll, Blountville, TN; FR; BA; Ed; Spcl Ed Tchr Cnslr.

**ALTIZER, SUZANNE D,** Radford Univ, Radford, VA; SR; BS; Erly/Mddl Educ; Teacher.

**ALTLAND, BRIAN L,** Univ Of Pittsburgh, Pittsburgh, PA; SO; BS; Amer Inst Chem Engrs; Amer Chem Soc; Lambda Sigma; Hnrs Schlrshp 89-; Arco Chem Co; Natl Merit Harsco Spons Schlrshp 89-; IM Vlybl/Ski; Chem Engr; Envir Engr.

**ALTMAN, CATHERINE C,** Univ Of Pittsburgh, Pittsburgh, PA; FR; BSN; Phi Eta Sigma; Deans Lst; Nrsg.

**ALTMAN, CHRISTINA M,** Coll Of Charleston, Charleston, SC; FR; Zeta Tau Alpha 90-; Bio; Pediatrics.

**ALTMAN, LAURIE B,** William Paterson Coll, Wayne, NJ; SR; BA; Spec Ed Clb/Cncl Excptnl Chlrn 86-; Proj LINK 87-90; Pi Lambde Tehta 88-; Kappa Delta Pi 88-; Grad Magna Cum Laude; Deans List 86-; Spec Educ; Teacher.

**ALTMAN, MICHELLE LEE,** Univ Of Akron, Akron, OH; JR; BED; Hall Govt/Rsdnc Hall Cncl Pres/Spcl Events Chair 88-90; Rsdnc Hall Prog Brd Mjr Events Comm 89-90; Natl Rsdnc Hall Sec/Treas; IM Ftbl 88-89; Elem Ed/Hist; Tch/Prncpl.

**ALTMAN, MITCHELL P,** Univ Of Sc At Coastal Carolina, Conway, SC; JR; BA; Cmptr Sci.

**ALTMAN, STACEY R,** Va Commonwealth Univ, Richmond, VA; SO; Glf Schlrshp VCCL Winthrop Coll 89-90; Winthrop Coll Glf Tm All-Cnfrnc Tm 90; VCU Glf Tm; Pltcl Sci; Law/Govt Serv.

**ALTMANN, KARL A,** Univ Of Fl, Gainesville, FL; SR; BS; Tau Epsilon Phi Comptrllr 89-90; Finance; Grad Stdies/Bus.

**ALTMANN, KYRSTEN E,** Univ Of Rochester, Rochester, NY; JR; BS; Res Life Stff Res Advsr 90-; Hall Gov 88-89; Intrnshp Asst Physcns; IM Flr Hcky/Vlybl 88-; Microbio; Physcn.

**ALTOMARE, CHRISTINA A,** Dowling Coll, Oakdale Li, NY; SR; BA; Bus Intrnshp; AS Suffolk Cnty Cmnty Clg 89; Bus/Mktg; Law.

**ALTON, JACQUELENE F,** Roane St Comm Coll, Harriman, TN; SO; ASSOC; Hlth Physics Soc; Hlth Physics Tech Martin Marietta Energy Sys; Hlth Physics.

**ALTROCK, CHRISTOPHER R,** Harding Grad School Of Relig, Memphis, TN; GD; MDIV; BA New Mexico State Univ 90; Religion; Campus Mnstry.

**ALTSCHULER, KAREN G,** Atlantic Comm Coll, Mays Landing, NJ; SO; BA; Bus Mgnt.

**ALTUG, AYKUT M,** Univ Of Pittsburgh, Pittsburgh, PA; SR; MS; Gldn Ky 89-; Dns Lst 87-; Mech Eng; Eng.

**ALVARADO PAGAN, MARIA DEL C,** Inter Amer Univ Pr Guayama, Guayama, PR; SO; MEPSE Pr Inter Amer Univ 89-90; Sec Sci Clb Pr 90-; Stdnt Cncl Sec 91-; Cmnty Svcs 87-90; Cert 87; Medals 87-; Sec Sci.

**ALVARADO VARGAS, EDDA I,** Catholic Univ Of Pr, Ponce, PR; FR; Gerontology.

**ALVARADO, DAMARIS I,** Univ Of Pr Cayey Univ Coll, Cayey, PR; SO; BA; Ftr Hlth Pro Cir 90-; Deans Hon Rl 89-; Wrk Rsrch Pgm MBRS; Ntrl Sci; Medcl Tchnlgy.

**ALVARADO, FERNANDO,** Valdosta St Coll, Valdosta, GA; JR; BS; Alpha Epsilon Delta Hstrn; Order Of Omega; Otstndng Clg Stdnts Of Amer; Kappa Alpha Plrmntrn; Biol; Med.

**ALVARADO, IVAN,** Univ Politecnica De Pr, Hato Rey, PR; SO; BA; Cvl Air Ptrl Cdt Cmndr Capt 80-85; U S Air Frc Sgt 86-90; Air Frc Achvmnt Mdl 89; Air Frc Gd Cndct Mdl 90; Exprt Mrksmnshp Sml Arms; Vet Adm Rgnl Ofc; AS Cmnty Clge Air Force 90; Math/Physcs; Cvl Engrg.

**ALVAREZ CRESPO, DIANA,** Inter Amer Univ Pr Arecibo Un, Arecibo, PR; BBA; Pgm Hnr; BA; Acctg; CPA.

**ALVAREZ DE ARKAIA, DIEGO,** Saint Thomas Univ, Miami, FL; Intrnshps Bentn Corp Rome Italy; BA.

**ALVAREZ LEBRON, MIGUEL,** Inter Amer Univ Pr Hato Rey, Hato Rey, PR; SR; BA; Bass Anglers Sprtsmn Soc; Fnce; Law.

**ALVAREZ, ALISA R,** Univ Of Miami, Coral Gables, FL; SO; BBA; Mahny Pgm Cncl Soc Chr 90-; Fllwshp Chrstn Athl 89-; Orntn Asst 90-; Alpha Lambda Delta Sec 90-; Phi Eta Sigma 90-; Hnrs Pgm 89-; Dns Lst 89-; IM Sprts 89-; Acctg.

**ALVAREZ, ANA M,** Miami Dade Comm Coll, Miami, FL; FR; Pscyh.

**ALVAREZ, ANGEL,** Univ Of Pr At Mayaguez, Mayaguez, PR; SO; Sngng Cmptition 90; Chem Eng Tech Assn 89-90; Alphbtztn Tutr 88; Chem; Eng.

**ALVAREZ, BEATRIZ MARIA,** Fl International Univ, Miami, FL; JR; Scl Wrk.

**ALVAREZ, BRIAN E,** Springfield Tech Comm Coll, Springfield, MA; SO; BS; Alpha Nu Omega 90-; Mech Tech/CAD/CAM; Aeronautical Engr.

**ALVAREZ, CELIA L,** Univ Of Miami, Coral Gables, FL; SO; BA; Engl; Sec Educ.

**ALVAREZ, DANIEL,** Glassboro St Coll, Glassboro, NJ; SO; BA; Spnsh Club 89-90; Econ Club Sec 90; Dns Lst 90; Tutor Cntr 90-; NCAA Div III 90; Natl Champs Soccer 89-90; Econ; Mgml Cnsltn.

**ALVAREZ, DENISE L,** Rutgers St Un At New Brunswick, New Brunswick, NJ; FR; BS; Cls Cncl 94 90-; New Std Ornttn Comm 90-; Off Cmps Std Asc VP 90-; Mrchng Band 90-; Acctng; CPA.

**ALVAREZ, DOROTHY,** Duquesne Univ, Pittsburgh, PA; SR; BS; Internatl Stdnt Org 88-; Political Sci Org 86-88; Amer Cancer Assoc 86; Marketing; Product Manager.

**ALVAREZ, ELMA L,** Miami Dade Comm Coll, Miami, FL; FR; AA; Outstndng Acad Cert VP; Deans Lst 90; Cmptr Sci; Progrmmng.

**ALVAREZ, ERASMO L,** Fl International Univ, Miami, FL; SR; BA; AA Miami-Dade Comm Coll 89; Exrcs Physlgy; Phys Ther.

**ALVAREZ, JOSE A,** Univ Of Pr Medical Sciences, San Juan, PR; JR; DMD; Amer Std Dntl Asc Rep 88-; Cir Premedicos Vcl 87-88; Tri Beta 87-88; BBS 88; Bio; Dentistry.

**ALVAREZ, JOSE M,** Central Fl Comm Coll, Ocala, FL; JR; BS; Amer Inst Aeronautics/Astrnts 88-; Cmptr Sci.

**ALVAREZ, JOSEPH WM,** Univ Of Miami, Coral Gables, FL; FR; BA; Alpha Lambda Delta 90-; Deans Lst; Provosts Hnr Lst; Communications; Broadcasting Producing TV.

**ALVAREZ, LEONIDES,** Miami Dade Comm Coll South, Miami, FL; SR; BA; Lrng Dis Ed; Ed.

**ALVAREZ, LIDSY DIAZ,** Univ Of Pr At Rio Piedras, Rio Piedras, PR; JR; BBA; Finance Assn 90-; Natl Coll Bus Merit Awds 90-; Finance; Law.**

**ALVAREZ, LIRIANA,** Bunker Hill Comm Coll, Boston, MA; FR.

**ALVAREZ, MARIO G,** Miami Dade Comm Coll South, Miami, FL; SO; BA; Chief Tech/Soung Eng Rflctns Prdctns 88-; Sound/Music; Own Top Live Sound/Studio Co.

**ALVAREZ, OSORIO,** Miami Dade Comm Coll, Miami, FL; GD; BSEE; Amer Inst Aerontcs Astrontcs 90-; IEEE 90-; AA; Pilot Nvl Acad Cuba; Elec Engr; Aerospce Electrnc.

**ALVAREZ, PATRICIA,** Montclair St Coll, Upr Montclair, NJ; SO; BA; Engl/Litr/Flm; Scrn Wrtng.

**ALVAREZ, PEDRO,** Inter Amer Univ Pr San German, San German, PR; FR; BA; Clb Exchng Cb Rj; Myqz Bwlrs Clb 88-; Bnkng 85-; Bus Admn.

**ALVAREZ, ROBERTA J,** Duquesne Univ, Pittsburgh, PA; JR; BS; MENC 90-; Phi Theta Kappa 83-84; Wstrn PA Sch Deaf Intern; Catholic Daughters Of Am; Mgmnt Pos Leewards Crafts 85-90; AS Comm Coll Allegheny Cnty 85; Music; Edn.

**ALVAREZ, ROSE MARIE,** Fl International Univ, Miami, FL; FR; Law.

**ALVAREZ, SANTIAGO J,** Barry Univ, Miami, FL; GD; MBA; Ecnmcs Clb 87-; Spnsh Clb 87-; Miami Rwng Clb 83-; Deans Lst; Ltl Havana Chld Care Cntr Comm Mbr 90-; Amer Cncr Soc 83-86; Amer Hrt Assoc 84-85; Yng Rpblcns Hspnc Ball Pres Bush Ingrtn 89; 1st Pl Andreas Sch Bus Mgt Smltn; BA; Ecnmcs; Fncl Mgt Career.

**ALVAREZ, SOPHIA,** Fl International Univ, Miami, FL; JR; BA; Phi Theta Kappa 88-90; MDCC Schlrshp 88-90; AA Miami Dade Comm Coll 90; Elem Ed; Tchng.

**ALVAREZ, STACEY LYNN,** Miami Dade Comm Coll North, Miami, FL; SO; BA; AA; Bus Admin; Law.

**ALVAREZ, SUSAN M,** Saint Thomas Univ, Miami, FL; SO; BA; Stu Govt Rep 90; Sch Nwspr Edtr In Chf 90; Stdy Abrd Pro Spain Stu Intl; Orntn Ldr; Yrbk Edtr Chf; Deans Lst; Delta Phi Epsilon Comm Serv Chrprsn 90; Cmnctn; Wrtr.

**ALVAREZ, VICTOR JAVIER,** Univ Politecnica De Pr, Hato Rey, PR; SR; BS; Stdnt Chptr Mech Eng Inst 90-; Water Dept City Tampa 82-88; Mech Eng.

**ALVARINO, MADELYN L,** Villanova Univ, Villanova, PA; SR; Spanish Club; Sigma Delta Pi.

**ALVERS, TRACY A,** Bowling Green St Univ At Huron, Huron, OH; SO; BSBA; Weight Club VP; Stdt Actvts Organ 90; Alpha Lambda Delta 90-; Firelands Clg Deans List 89-; IM Vlybl; Business Administration.

**ALVEY, DAVID K,** Univ Of Cincinnati-Clrmnt Coll, Batavia, OH; JR; BA; Bsn; Acctng.

**ALVIN, DAVID A,** Stetson Univ, Deland, FL; FR; BA; Amnesty Intl Death Pnlty Coord 90-; Baptist Cmps Mnstrs 90-; Coll Bow 90-; Scndry Ed/Social Sci; Teaching.

**ALWANG, CHRISTOPHER N,** Cornell Univ Statutory College, Ithaca, NY; SR; DVM; Ultmt Frisbie 87-; IM Sccr Ftbl 87-; BS; Vet Med.

**ALWORTH, GLYNIS L,** Kent St Univ Kent Cmps, Kent, OH; JR; BA; Golden Key; Sigma Tau Delta 90-; Eng/Wrtng; Childrens Librn.

**ALZERRECA-FRAMBES, JAVIER W,** Univ Of Pr At Rio Piedras, Rio Piedras, PR; SR; MBA; AIAS; Amateur Triathlete; High Degree Awd; Arch.

**ALZUGARAY, MARIA C,** Univ Of Miami, Coral Gables, FL; SR; BA; Yng Repblcns; Alpha Sigma Phi Pres 89-90; State Sntr Intern; State Attys Ofc Intern; Psychlgy; Law.**

**AMAD, RANA Z,** Univ Of Nc At Greensboro, Greensboro, NC; FR; BS; Intl Clb 90-; Aerobics 90-; Interior Design.

**AMADIO, DEAN M,** S U N Y Coll At Fredonia, Fredonia, NY; SR; MA; Cir K Pres 87-; Big Bro/Big Sis 89-; Gay Lsbn Bisxl Stu Union 90-; Psi Chi 90-; Alma Mater Soc 90-; Pscy Mrt Awrd 90; Dist Clb Pres NY Dist Cir K 90; N Cnty Cnslg Intrnshp; Psych; Cnslr Educ.

**AMADOR SANTIAGO, DORILUZ,** Univ Of Pr Medical Sciences, San Juan, PR; JR; BA; APHA Sec 90-; Yrbk Comm Edtr 89-; Chorus 89-; Pharm Hnr Soc 90-; Natl Pharm Cncl Ind; All-Amer Schlr Clgt Awd; Vlybl Tm 90-; AS Univ PR 89; Sci; Pharm.

**AMADOR, GUILLERMO A MANGUAL,** Inter Amer Univ Pr San Juan, Hato Rey, PR; JR; JURIS; ABA; Assist Fo Prof Of Lgl Rsrch 90; Wrtng/Anlysis Crse; BA Magna Cum Laude U Of PR RP Campus 85.

**AMANDOLA, JANET A,** Barry Univ, Miami, FL; SO; BA; Blood Dnr 86-89; Pttry 86-91; Oprtn Oprtn Hmfrtn Vlntr 89-; Key Clb 86-89; Peer Mnstry 86-89; SADD 86-89; CCD Instrctr 86-89; Trck Sccr 86-89; Englsh; Tchr.

**AMANN, MICHELLE L,** Saint Joseph Coll, West Hartford, CT; SO; BA; Stdnt Govt 89-; PALS 89-; SADD 89-; Cmps Mnstry 90-; Engl; Hgh Sch Tchr Nvlst.**

**AMANTIA, JACQUELIN B,** Fl St Univ, Tallahassee, FL; SR; BA; AA Tallahassee Comm Coll 89; Visual Arts; Visual Artist.

**AMARATUNGE, SADHANA S,** City Univ Of Ny La Guard Coll, Long Island Cty, NY; SR; ASSOC; Acctg Clb Pres; Acctg.

**AMARO JR, ELIAS,** City Univ Of Ny City Coll, New York, NY; SO; BS; Ch Yth Orgztn Pres 89; PRES 89-; Intervar Chrstn Flwshp 89-; Intrn Hewlett Packard 90; Motorola Intrn; Rsrcn Asst Ctr Analysis Structures CASI; Elect Engr.

**AMARO, JOHN D,** Me Maritime Academy, Castine, ME; SO; BS; Alpha Phi Omega Soc VP 89-; Marine Trnsprtn; Harbor Pilot.

**AMARO, MARIA C,** Rockland Comm Coll, Suffern, NY; FR; BED; Spnsh Clb 90-; Bllybll; Bus; Fnncng.

**AMAT, SITI HANIZAH,** Univ Of South Al, Mobile, AL; JR; BSC; Bsn Mgmt; Fin Exec.

**AMATEAU, LEIGH M,** Va Commonwealth Univ, Richmond, VA; JR; BA; Alt Student Rep Brd Of Visitors 90-; Univ Council; Amer Psychological Assn 90-; Psi Chi Pres 90-; Golden Key 90-; VA Interfaith Centr 89-; Psychology.

**AMATO, DINA M,** Fl International Univ, Miami, FL; SR; Eastern Airline Air Scts Advsr 83-89; AGBU Pub Rel 86-89; Phi Sigma Sigma Socl Chrprsn 85-88; Dns Lst 90-; Sba 90; Engl; Tchr.**

**AMATO, JOSEPH,** Univ Of Al At Birmingham, Birmingham, AL; JR; BS; Stdnt Govt IRHC Legisltr 89; Phi Sigma Pres 90-; Alpha Epsilon Delta Hstrn 90-; Omicron Delta Kappa; Autauga Med Ctr Vol 89; Chldrns Hosp AL Vol 90-; All-Amer Clgte Awd 90; Pres Hnrs 89-; Dns Lst 89-; Bio; Physician.

**AMATO, JOSEPH S,** Worcester Poly Inst, Worcester, MA; FR; MS; Jz Wrkshp 90-; Elctrcl Engrg; Engr.

**AMATO, NAOMI J,** Elms Coll, Chicopee, MA; SO; BA; SGA Co Pres 90-; Stdnt Ambsdrs 89-; Res Cncl 89-; Yrbk Copy Edtr; Stdnt Actvies Comm; Elem Educ/Psych; Tchr.

**AMATUCCI, MICHAEL,** City Univ Of Ny Baruch Coll, New York, NY; SO; BA; Bsns; Accntng.

**AMAYA, EDWARD I,** Univ Of Fl, Gainesville, FL; SR; BA; Mrchng Bnd 89-90; MENC 89-; Prfsnl Mcsn; Avtn Sht Mtl Mchnc 87-89; Msc Edctn; H S Bnd Drctr.

**AMAYA, NANCY L,** Univ Of Md At Eastern Shore, Princess Anne, MD; JR; BA; Engr Tech Soc 90; Phi Kappa Phi; Alpha Kappa Mu 88; Phi Theta Kappa 85; Airway Sci.

**AMBAS, BEATRIZ,** Fl International Univ, Miami, FL; FR; BS; Fclty Schlrs Prgm 90-; Hnrs Gprm 90-; Fclty Schlrs Prgm 90; Hnrs Prgm 90-; Math.

**AMBROISE BEAUVIOR, REGINE,** Inter Amer Univ Pr Hato Rey, Hato Rey, PR; FR; Cmptr Sys Mgmt.

**AMBROSE, ANITA F,** Wv Northern Comm Coll, Wheeling, WV; SO; AAS; Little League Bsbl Statitician; Deans Lst 90; Alternatives To Abortion Hotline; Aid Math Lab; Acctng; CPA.

**AMBROSE, DANI J,** Allegheny Coll, Meadville, PA; SO; BA; Chrs/Wmns Ens 90-; Alghny Vol/Latin Tutor; Alden Schlr 90-; Lambda Sigma; Alpha Gamma Delta Chr 90-; Std Ornttn Advsr 90-; Vlybl IMS 90-; Engl/Clsscs; Nvlst.

**AMBROSE, JULIE R,** Univ Of Nh Plymouth St Coll, Plymouth, NH; JR; BA; Alumni Assoc VP 85-; Mdvl Froum Flwshp; Pres Lst 90-; Lgl Sec 82-; AS 81; Hstry; Law.

**AMBROSE, MAUREEN A,** Bunker Hill Comm Coll, Boston, MA; FR; BA; Math/Bsns; Acctg.

**AMBROSE, MELISSA L,** Univ Of Nc At Greensboro, Greensboro, NC; SR; BS; NC Council Of Teachers 3 Math 87-89; Stdnt NC Assoc Of Ed 89-; English Lab Assistant 88-89; Intrnshp Peeler Open Schl; Assoc Of Ed Beaufort Co Cmnty Clge 89; Elem Ed; Teacher.

**AMBROZIAK, MICHAEL T,** Oh Coll Of Podiatric Med, Cleveland, OH; SO; DPM; Amercn Clg Of Foot Surgeons Stdnt Chptr 90-; Sports Medcn Club 89-; OPMSA 89-; Alpha Gamma Kappa 90-; Mens Bsktbl Team 89-; BA Miami Univ 89; BS Miami Univ 89; Podiatric Medcn.

**AMBURGEY, DEBORAH W,** Univ Of Va Clinch Valley Coll, Wise, VA; SR; AA Hzrd Comm Clg 89; BA Clnch Vly Clg; Elem Ed.

**AMEDE, KELLY,** Daytona Beach Comm Coll, Daytona Beach, FL; FR; AA; Psychology; Chld Psychlgst.

**AMEERALLY, RYHAAN,** Fl International Univ, Miami, FL; FR; Bus; Acctg.

**AMEIS, PAUL A,** S U N Y Coll Of Tech At Alfred, Alfred, NY; FR; BS; Eng Clb 90-; Dns Lst; Pres Hnrs; Chem Eng; Eng.

**AMEND, CHRISTINE L,** Duquesne Univ, Pittsburgh, PA; FR; BA; One Of My Papers Was Nom To Be Published In 1991 Workbk Of Compositions; Communications; Law.

**AMENDOLA, DOROTHY ANN,** Springfield Tech Comm Coll, Springfield, MA; SO; Bus; Court Reprtng.

**AMENDOLA, LISA ANTOINETTE,** S U N Y Coll Of A & T Morrisvl, Morrisville, NY; SR; BS; Sftbl; AAS; Envrnmnt Studies/Info/Tech.

**AMENGUAL, STEVEN,** S U N Y At Stony Brook, Stony Brook, NY; FR; Engl; Prof.

**AMENTO, GAIL R,** Hudson Valley Comm Coll, Troy, NY; SO; AS; Bus Admin.

**AMERSON, KAREN D,** Univ Of Sc At Sumter, Sumter, SC; SO; BA; AS Sumter Area Tech Coll 89; Bus; CPA.

**AMES, ELIZABETH A,** Fl International Univ, Miami, FL; SR; BA; Phi Lambda; Amer Psychlgcl Assn 89-; Spec Ed/Psychlgy; Tch.

**AMES III, STUART TOLMAN,** Mount Olive Coll, Mount Olive, NC; JR; BS; Psy Clb; Psy Hnr Soc; Ret US Coast Guard MCPO Persnl Ofcr CEA; Psych; Ed Cnslg MBS Psych.

**AMEY, KEISHA M,** City Univ Of Ny City Coll, New York, NY; SO; BA; Psy; Educ.

**AMEYAW, JOSEPH,** Cincinnati Bible Coll & Sem, Cincinnati, OH; GD; MDIV; BS Univ Ghana Legon 80; MA; Theology/Cnslng; Evnglst.

**AMEZ, SONYA B,** Central Fl Comm Coll, Ocala, FL; FR; AS; Cert Withlacoochee Voc Techl 86; Cert Withlacoochee Voc Techl 86; Nursing; Medl.

**AMICK, BRYAN M,** Univ Of Sc At Columbia, Columbia, SC; JR; BS; Mt Olivet Lthrn Church Yth Advsr 90-; Vienna Summer Stdy Schlrshp; SC Tax Comm Tax Examiner 88-; Business Adm; Law.

**AMICK, CAROLYN S,** Univ Of Sc At Columbia, Columbia, SC; SR; BAIS; Elem Educ; Tchg.

**AMICK, HEATHER B,** Univ Of Southern Ms, Hattiesburg, MS; SR; Kappa Delta Pi 90-; Kappa Mu Epsln 87-88; SEA 90-; IM Bwlng; BS; Elem Educ; Tchng.

**AMIKER, DAWN MARLENE,** Tn St Univ, Nashville, TN; SR; BS; Thomas Edwardy Poag Plyrs Gld Sec 90-; MI Clb Trvl Coor 87-88; NAACP 90-; WYHY Intern Prmtn Asst 90; Chnnl 5 Flr Dir 90; Spch Cmmnctns/Thtr; Brdcstng/Flm/Radio TV.

**AMILL ORTIZ, MARIA M,** Inter Amer Univ Pr San German, San German, PR; SR.

**AMIN, ASEDRI ONZIMA,** Casco Bay Coll, Portland, ME; FR; AS; Bus Accts; Acctng.

**AMIN, DAKSHESH S,** Clayton St Coll, Morrow, GA; JR; BA; Acctg Assc; Deans List; Acctg; CPA Bus Ownr.

**AMINA, MARY ANN N,** Savannah St Coll, Savannah, GA; JR; BA; Mass Cmmnctns Clb; Cthlc Cmps Mnstry Clb; Tnns Tm; Vol Wrk Cmps Radio Sta; Ply Yr Bst Rch Yr 88-90; Acdmc Awrd 89-90; Lwn Tnns; Mass Cmmnctns; Prdcr/Dir.

**AMIR, GALIT,** Fl St Univ, Tallahassee, FL; FR; Phi Eta Sigma; Bio Sci; Med-Pediatrics.

**AMLAW, KAREN L,** Univ Of Rochester, Rochester, NY; SR; BA; Univ Symphny Orchstra Bd Chr 88-; W Irndqt H S Nwsltr Chem Advsr/Edtr 90-; Sci-Fi Clb Hndbk Edtr Mrl Offcr 87-90; Smalley Fndtn Schlr 87-91; Bausch/Lomb Schlr 87-91; Beach Rochester Schlr 90-; UR Stdnt Stdnt Pgm Stdnt Rep 88; Psychlgy/Msc; Educ/Jrnlsm/Pblc Rltns.

**AMMAR, PATRICIA A,** Queens Coll, Charlotte, NC; SR; BA; Hnr Cncl Soph Rep 88-89; Psychlgy Clb Chrmn 89-90; Justiniam Socty Mbr 89-90; Beta Beta Beta Assoc Mbr 89-; Alpha Delta Pi Pldg Cls VP 87-88; Guard/Panhel Rep 88-89; Panhellenic Cncl VP/PRES 89-; Bell Schlr 87-; Psychlgy; Law WV Univ.

**AMMONS, BILLIE B,** Memphis St Univ, Memphis, TN; SR; BA; AAOHN Comm Chrprn Certfcn Comm; TAOHN; MAOHN; Okatorio Chorus; RN Du Pont Corp Bd Certfd By ABOHN; AD Sci Shelby State Comty Clg Cum Laude; AS 81; Publc Admn/Hlth Educ.

**AMMONS, MARY M,** Waycross Coll, Waycross, GA; SO; BA; Bus Clb 90; Bus; Mrktng.

**AMOAH-DARKO, FREDERICK L,** Capital Bible Seminary, Lanham, MD; GD; THM; Smnry Stu Cncl Msns Dir 90-; Pre Prof Trng 5th/6th Grdrs Wshngtn DC Area Tutor/Asst Prog Dir; Indr Sccr; BA 88; MDIV 90; Old Tstmnt/Hebrew; Lctr Old Tstmnt.

**AMOAKU, PATRICK K,** Central St Univ, Wilberforce, OH; SO; BSC; Econ Clb 89-; Bsn Econ; Bsn.

**AMODEO, GINA M,** Comm Coll Algny Co Algny Cmps, Pittsburgh, PA; JR; Lcns Mgr Csmtlgy 87; Hrdrsr Pittsburg Beauty Acd 77; Hlth Sci; Nrsng RN.

**AMODEO, MARY ANN,** Ny Law School, New York, NY; JD; Law Rvw 90-; Jon Ben Snow Tuition Schlrshp 89-; Starr Fndtn Schlr 90-; T V Cmrcl Coord 85-89; BA N Y Univ 85; Law.

**AMOEDO, MARISOL,** Fl International Univ, Miami, FL; JR; BA; Tchng Prvte Schls; AA Miami-Dade Comm Coll 89; Ed/Scndry Math; Tchr.

**AMOIA, THOMAS,** Manhattan Coll, Bronx, NY; SR; BS; Am Soc/Civil Engr Pres 87-; Am Concrete Inst 89-; Amnesty Intnl 87-; Ridgeway Awd; MET Sect Schlrshp 90; Rgnts Schlrshp 87-; Chi Epsilon 89-; Soup Kitch 86-; Tutor Prog 88-; CCD Tchr 89-90; Thornton-Tomasetti P C 88-90; Civil Engrng; Strctrl Dsgnr.

**AMORE, ROSANNE,** Lesley Coll, Cambridge, MA; SO; BA; City Schl Vol Cert Rcgntn 89-90; Acdmc Hon Lst 89-90; Educ; Tch.

**AMORIM, ROGER,** Columbia Union Coll, Takoma Park, MD; SO; BS; ACM Sec 89-; Delta Sigma Tau 89-; Cmptr Sci; Cmptr Prgmmng.

**AMORUSO, ADRIANNE H,** Univ Of Ri, Kingston, RI; FR; BS; Bus; Acctng.

**AMOS, AARON A,** Morehouse Coll, Atlanta, GA; FR; BA; Hlth Crrs Scty 90-; AVC TX Clb 90-; Hnr Rll Stdnt 90-; Pre Med; Peds Srgry.

**AMOS, EVELYN L,** Snead St Jr Coll, Boaz, AL; FR; Bapt Campus Ministries.

**AMOS, JENNY A,** Middle Tn St Univ, Murfreesboro, TN; SR; BSN; Alpha Omicron Pi; Nrsg Hnr Soc; Nrsg; Nrs Ansthslgy.

**AMOS, MARY K,** Univ Of Nc At Greensboro, Greensboro, NC; SO; BS; UNC-G Rsdntl Coll; Univ Symphnc Choir; Elem Ed; Tchng.

**AMOS, SALLY M,** Blue Mountain Coll, Blue Mountain, MS; JR; BED; Cmmtr Clb 90-; MAE SP 90-; BSU 90-; Elem; Tchr.

**AMOS, TANGIE NERISSA,** Ms St Univ, Miss State, MS; SR; Amer Inst Chem Engrs 87-; Panhllnc Cncl Delg 89-90; Hl Cncl Sec 88-89; Tau Beta Pi 90-; Omega Chi Epsilon; Alpha Kappa Alpha Pres 89-90; Co-Op Educ Stdnt; BS; Chem Engr; Engr.

**AMOS, WENDI A,** Carnegie Mellon Univ, Pittsburgh, PA; GD; JD; AFROTC Exec Stff 86-90; Sprng Crnvl Swpstks Rce Drvr 88-90; Stdnt Advsry Cncl 86-90; Kappa Kappa Gamma Soc Chrmn 87-89; Hmntrn Awrd 86; Amer Red Crss Brd Dir 84-; Amer Lgn Excllnce Awrd 87 89; IM 86-90; BS 90; Law; Mltry Lgl Cnsl.

**AMOS, WILLIAM B,** Wv Northern Comm Coll, Wheeling, WV; SO; BA; Comodore Home Users Group; Merit List 89-90; Working Toward Gvt Intrnshp; Pol Sci; Gvt Admnstrn.

**AMOSS, CORENE E,** Goucher Coll, Towson, MD; SO; BA; Econ & Mgmt Club; Charlotte Killman Wright Browh Schlrshp For Econ 89-; Varsity Bsktbl Field Hockey Tennis Capt 89-; Econ/Bus Mgmt; Fin/Acctng.**

**AMPELA, JOHN A,** S U N Y Coll At Fredonia, Fredonia, NY; SO; BFA; Opr Thtr Brd Bus Mgr; Jchmbr Sngrs; Vcl Jzz; Opr Scns Prdctns; Vcl Prfrmnc; Op Thtr.**

**AMPHLETT, AMY M,** S U N Y Coll Of Tech At Alfred, Alfred, NY; SO; BA; Dorm Cncl 90-; Karate Clb; Dns Lst; RA Stf 90-; Drm Cncl; RA Schlrshp 90-; Dns Lst 90-; Karate; Bwlng; Crmnl Jste/Sclgy; Law Schl.

**AMRHEIN, WENDY A,** Wv Univ, Morgantown, WV; FR; BS; Alpha Phi Omega Ambssdr 90-; Hnrs Prog 90-; Pres Schlr 90-; Indstrl Eng.

**AMRINE, SHEILA A,** Oh St Univ At Newark, Newark, OH; SR; BSED; Pi Lambda Theta; Newark Rtry Clb Schlrshp 90-; AA; Elem Ed; Tchng.

**AMUSAN, SOLOMON A,** Univ Of Sc At Columbia, Columbia, SC; JR; BAAR; Carolina Prog Union Ideas/Issues Comm 89-90; Greater Columbia Lit Cncl Tutor; US Soccer Fdrtn Referee 89-; Gldn Ky; Minority Stdnt Affairs Awd; SC Hnrs Clg; Deans Lst; Gamma Beta Phi Soc; Pres Lst; Col Bus Admin Alumni Schlr; Bus; Law/Doctoral Info Mgmt Sys.

**AMUSO, JOSEPH M,** Western New England Coll, Springfield, MA; SR; BSBA; Data Prcssng Mngmnt Assn 90-; Deans Lst 87-; Phi Theta Kappa 88-; Intrnshp Stnhm 90; Sftbl 90; AS Brkshr Comm Coll 89; Comp Info Syst; Prog Anylst.

**AMYX, TAMARA E,** Univ Of Cin R Walters Coll, Blue Ash, OH; FR; AAB; Intrnshp Marion Merrell Dow Phrmctcls; Bus; Offc Admin.

**ANABLE, MICHAEL G,** Univ Of Miami, Coral Gables, FL; JR; Univ Miami Flmmkrs Assn 90-; Motion Pic/Engl; Film.

**ANADON IRIZARY, MARCO A,** Catholic Univ Of Pr, Ponce, PR; SR; BBA; Acctg Stdnts Assoc Treas 89-90; Natl Bus Hon Soc 89-; Hon Prog 87-; Phi Delta Gamma Pres 88-90; Acctg.

**ANAGNOST, KATHRYN L,** Elmira Coll, Elmira, NY; SR; MS; Kappa Delta Pi; AS Corning Comm Coll 87; Elem Educ; Tchr.

**ANANTHAKRISHNAN, BINDIYA,** Univ Of Miami, Coral Gables, FL; SO; BS; Pres 100 89-; Orientation 90-; India Assoc Secr 89-; Provost Lst 89-; Hnrs Cncl 90-; Tau Beta Phi 90-; Literacy Corps 90-; Henry Stanford Schlr 89-; Natl Merit Schlr 89-; Biomed Engr; Md Med.

**ANASTASI, KATHLEEN M,** D Youville Coll, Buffalo, NY; SR; BS; Cmpus Mnstry Sec 87-; Booster Clb Sec 87-90; Progrmng Bd 89-; SOTA 87-; Lambda Sigma 88-89; Sr Hon Soc Treas 90-; D'youville Schorshp 90-; Deans Lst 87-90; Occptnl Thrpy; MS Pediatric Occptnl Thrpst.

**ANASTASIA, CHARLES P,** City Univ Of Ny Baruch Coll, New York, NY; SO; BBA; Italian Clb 89-; Beruch Schlr 89-; Alpha Phi Delta 90-; Acctng.

**ANASTASIA, MARIE E,** Greenville Tech Coll, Greenville, SC; SO; ASSOC; PAMA Secr/Treas 90-; Aviation Maint Tech; Aviation Maint Tech; Aerontcl Engr/Mech Engr.

**ANCHELL, BRUCE P,** Univ Of Miami, Coral Gables, FL; SR; BA; BA Univ Of FL 88; Arch.

**ANCONA, JAMES P,** Univ Of Ma At Amherst, Amherst, MA; SR; B MUS; Mrchng Bnd 87-90; Sectn Ldr/Asst Percusn Dir; Pep Bnd; Brass Choir; Five Clg Orch; Alpha Lambda Delta; Golden Key 89; Schlrshp Music Alumni 87-; Music; H S Music Educ.**

**ANCONA JR, JOHN P,** Cornell Univ Statutory College, Ithaca, NY; JR; BS; Med Asst Stu Hlth Cntr; Stu Hlth Allnc 90-; Natl Schlr 88-; Ho Hun De Kah; IM Athltc 88-; Biol Sci; Med.

**ANDERS, WENDY R,** Immaculata Coll, Immaculata, PA; SO; BA; Hatfield Quality Meats 85-89; Dietetics; Reg Dietitian/MA Doctorate.

**ANDERSCH, JENNIFER A,** Glassboro St Coll, Glassboro, NJ; FR; BA; Res Assn; Cmunctns/Radio T V Film.

**ANDERSEN, JULIE L,** Univ Of Miami, Coral Gables, FL; SO; BS; Beta Beta Beta; Bio; Vet Med.

**ANDERSEN, ROBERT D,** Univ Of Ky, Lexington, KY; JR; BA; Kappa Alpha Pres 88-; Alpha Lambda Delta; Smmr Yndrgrad Flwshp Biochem; Chem; Medcl Sch.

**ANDERSON, ALLISON R,** Tallahassee Comm Coll, Tallahassee, FL; SO; BA; Pres Lst 90; Pres Lst Tllhse Comm Coll 90-; Eng.

**ANDERSON, ALMA W,** Va Commonwealth Univ, Richmond, VA; SR; BS; Gldn Key 90-; VA Rehab Asc 70-; Natl Rehab Asc 70-; Rehab Cnslng.

**ANDERSON, AMY E,** Indiana Univ Of Pa, Indiana, PA; FR; BED; Chi Alpha Christn Flwshp 90-; Mathmtcs.

**ANDERSON, AMY R,** Union Inst, Cincinnati, OH; SR; BA; Natl Cncl Ngr Wmn Pblc Rltns Comm 90-; Rsc Cmmnty Cntr Brd Mbr 80-; Rsc Tmpl Chrch Gd Chrst Sec Brd Trsts 78-; Natl Urbn Lg 88-89; Amrcn Scty Qlty Cntrl; Bus Admn; Admn Mgmt.

**ANDERSON, ANDREW J,** Marywood Coll, Scranton, PA; JR; BS; St Tikhons Orthodox Smnry SGA Pres 89-90; FROC 86-; Alpha Gamma Sgma 86-; Prsdntl Schlrshp 90-; Lena/Fay Reynolds Mem Schlrshp 88-90; Arnold Leross Award 86; KSRA; AA Fullerton Clg 86; Cert St Tikhons Orthdx Thlgcl Smnry 90; Elem Educ; Chrch Wrk/Educ.

**ANDERSON, ANNE E,** Middle Tn St Univ, Murfreesboro, TN; JR; BA; Tau Omicron Wmns Scty 90-; Gamma Beta Phi 89-; Alpha Kappa Psi 90-; Bsn Mgmt; Hotel Mgmt.**

**ANDERSON, ARLEN G,** Univ Of Sc At Columbia, Columbia, SC; SR; BS; Phi Theta Kappa 89; Alpha Beta Gamma Treas 88-89; Beta Alpha Psi; AA Northland Cmnty Clge 89; Acctng; CPA.

**ANDERSON, BARBARA L,** Allegheny Coll, Meadville, PA; SR; BS; Collegium Musicum Hrpchrdst 87-; Math Assn Amer 89-; Piano Stdy 75-; Phi Beta Kappa 90; Lambda Sigma 88-89; Allegheny Schlr 87; Doane Schlr 87; Math/Music Junior Mjr Przs 89-90; Wmns Clb Lacrosse 87-90; Math/Music; Appld Math.

**ANDERSON, BERNADETTE R,** Fayetteville St Univ, Fayetteville, NC; SO; Early Chldhd Ed; Tchr.

**ANDERSON, BETH L,** Winthrop Coll, Rock Hill, SC; JR; BA; PLS Clb Pres; Hstry Clb; Model UN Clb Coord; Pi Sigma Alpha 90; Phi Alpha Theta Pres 90; Assist To PLS Dept Prof; Chr Of Scrty Cncl Moden UN; Law.

**ANDERSON, BEVERLEY A,** Lincoln Univ, Lincoln Univ, PA; JR; BA; Acctg Clb Senator 90-; Spnsh Clb Treas 90-; Leukemia Soc Amer Prog Coord 90; Acctg/Spnsh; Acctnt/Trnsltr.

**ANDERSON, BRANDE A,** Wilberforce Univ, Wilberforce, OH; FR; BA; Comp Sci/Math.

**ANDERSON, BRIAN M,** Washington State Comm Coll, Marietta, OH; FR; AS; Acctng; Private Accountant.

**ANDERSON II, CARL G,** Atlantic Comm Coll, Mays Landing, NJ; SO; Bus.

**ANDERSON, CARRIE M,** Univ Of Cincinnati, Cincinnati, OH; JR; BED; Elem Ed; Ma.

**ANDERSON, CATHERINE C,** Wv Univ, Morgantown, WV; SR; MSJ; Stdnt Nwspr Bus Mgr 86-88; Stdnt Un Wknd Oper Sup 84-; Amer Advrtsng Fed 84; Alpha Delta Sigma 87; Kappa Tau Alpha; Gldn Key 87; Chi Omega Rush Cnslr 83-; BSJ 87; Mountainlair Mrktnggrad Asst 88-; Natl Assc Cmps Actvts Grad Intern 90; Jrnlsm; Advrtsng/Mrktng.

**ANDERSON, CATHY L,** Univ Of Tn At Martin, Martin, TN; SO; BS; UAC Undergrad Alumni Cncl; PEP Ldr; Orntn Incmng Fr Psychlgy Clb; Deans Lst; Chi Omega Alpha Tau Omega Lil Sis Chi Omega Com Chrmn 89-; Alpha Phi Omega Pldg Cls Pres; Pom Pon Squad Capt/Choreographer 89-; Clncl Psychlgy.

**ANDERSON, CHRISTOPHER J,** S U N Y At Binghamton, Binghamton, NY; SO; BS; All-Amer Schlrs; Bsn; Mgmt.

**ANDERSON, CHRISTOPHER J,** City Univ Of Ny Baruch Coll, New York, NY; SR; Business To Business Society Dir Of Promotions; Sacred Hearts Church; Marketing.

**ANDERSON JR, CLIFTON,** Fl A & M Univ, Tallahassee, FL; JR; BA; Stu Govt Cbnt Mmbr 90-; Natl Ass Blck Accntnts; Alpha Kappa Mu Pres; White Gold; Intern The Williams Com Inc 90; Intern Eilbilly & Co; Accntng; Corp Accntng.

**ANDERSON, CRISSY L,** Shippensburg Univ, Shippensburg, PA; FR; BSBA; Cncrt Chr; Hmcmng Com; Hnrs Pgm; Hnrs Pgm Strng Com; Mrktng/Mgmt; Bnkng Ind.

**ANDERSON, CYNTHIA A,** Roane St Comm Coll, Harriman, TN; SO; AS; Gamma Beta Phi 89-; Bus Mgmnt; Cmptr.

**ANDERSON, CYNTHIA D,** Ky St Univ, Frankfort, KY; FR; Band 90-; Angel Clb 90-; Erly Elem Educ; Tchg.

**ANDERSON, DALORA E,** Commonwealth Coll, Norfolk, VA; FR; Stdnt Govt Trvl/Hosp Repr; Alpha Beta Gamma; Exclint Attndnc Awd; Aluminum Co Of Amer Admin Asst 84-88; Price Waterhouse Asst Sprvsr Wrd Proc Dept 78-; Travel/Hosp; Mngr/Yeoman.

**ANDERSON, DARLA G,** Alice Lloyd Coll, Pippa Passes, KY; FR; BS; Acdmc Tm; Hkng Cmpng Clb; Alld Hlth Scics Clb; Otstndng Frshmn; Crss Cntry Capt 90; Blgy; Med.

**ANDERSON, DARRYL,** Morris Brown Coll, Atlanta, GA; JR; BS; Crmnl Jstc Clb VP 88-90 Crmnl J 89-90; SGA Prlmntrn 90-; Kappa Alpha Psi; Bg Brthrs Mntrshp Prgm 89-90; Crmnl Jstc Ed.

**ANDERSON, DEBORAH A,** Fl International Univ, Miami, FL; FR; Medical.

**ANDERSON, DEBORAH L,** Syracuse Univ, Syracuse, NY; JR; BSW; Stdnts Cncrnbd Rp Ed 90-; Undrgrdt Scl Wrk Stdnt Orgnztn; Scl Wrk.

**ANDERSON, DEBRA A,** Univ Of Southern Ms, Hattiesburg, MS; SR; BS; Miss Utah Sta U Schlrsph Pgnt 81; H S Vocal Schlrshp 81; Schlrshp Pagent 80; Meridian Ltl Theater 87-88; Comm Chorus 87 88; Mgr Food Serv; Pre Sch Tchr; Ele Educ; Ele Tchr.

**ANDERSON, DIANA M,** Unity Coll, Unity, ME; FR; BA; Env Awrns Clb; Sftbl; Wk Farm 90-; Vol Wk Stdnt Affrs; Dns Lst; Badmntn; Vlybl; Flr Hcky; Sftbl; Outdr Rec; Tch.

**ANDERSON, DONNA M,** Albany St Coll, Albany, GA; SR; BS; SGAE 90-; Summa Cum Laude; Early Chldhd Edn; Tchr.

**ANDERSON, DORICE J,** Le Moyne Owen Coll, Memphis, TN; SR; BED.

**ANDERSON, DOUGLAS L,** Univ Of Nc At Charlotte, Charlotte, NC; JR; BS; Gldn Key; Natl Sci Fndtn Rsrch; REU Proj; USMC 85-89; Physcs; Rsrch.

**ANDERSON, ELDIN T,** Kent St Univ Stark Cmps, North Canton, OH; FR; BA; KSSEA; Educ; Tchr.

**ANDERSON, ELIZABETH J,** Bryant Stratton Bus Inst Roch, Rochester, NY; FR; AA; Bsnss Mngmnt; Bsnss.

**ANDERSON, ELIZABETH V,** Univ Of Tn At Knoxville, Knoxville, TN; GD; BS; Advtng Club Amer Advtng Fed Treas 88-; Timettes 86-87; S Eastern Panhellenic Conf PR Comm 90; Kappa Delta 87-90; Pracficum Tombras Grp 90; Advertising.

**ANDERSON, ELLEN T,** Fl St Univ, Tallahassee, FL; SR; BS; Amnsty Intrntnl Member 89; Todays Ntrtn Clb Member 89-90; Rsdnt Hsng Advsry Cncl Gov Rep 87-88; Kappa Omicron Nu 90; Gldn Key 90; Flrnc Smith Mcallister Schlrshp 89-90; FL Undgrdt Schlrs Ard 87; AA Univ W FL 88; Nrtn Food Science; Food Indstry.

**ANDERSON, ERIC SCOTT,** Wv Univ, Morgantown, WV; JR; BS; Eng; Cmptr Eng.

**ANDERSON, GERALDINE M,** Villanova Univ, Villanova, PA; SO; BA; Legal Asst; Psychlgy; Hlth Ed.

**ANDERSON, HEATHER G,** Wilmington Coll, Wilmington, OH; FR; BA; Elem Ed.

**ANDERSON, HEATHER R,** Bethany Coll, Bethany, WV; FR; BA; Soc Wrk; Soc Wrkr.

**ANDERSON, IAN E,** Ramapo Coll Of Nj, Mahwah, NJ; JR; BA; Clg Nwspr Exec Edtr 89-; Prgrssv Cltn 90-; Comm; Jrnlsm.

**ANDERSON, JACOB W,** Worcester Poly Inst, Worcester, MA; FR; BA; Shotokan Karate 90; Nuc Eng Physcs; Eng.

**ANDERSON, JAMES A,** Roane St Comm Coll, Harriman, TN; JR; BFA; AS 87; Art.

**ANDERSON, JAMES M,** Belmont Coll, Nashville, TN; SO; BA; Phlsphy.

**ANDERSON, JANNA L,** Abraham Baldwin Agri Coll, Tifton, GA; SO; AS; SHEA; GSHEA 89-; Dnc Tm 89-; Home Ec Dttcs; Rgstrd Lcnsd Dttcn.

**ANDERSON, JASON J,** Fl A & M Univ, Tallahassee, FL; FR; BS; Phi Eta Sigma; Bsns Admnstrtn; Bsns.

**ANDERSON, JENA L,** Univ Of Tn At Martin, Martin, TN; SO; BA; Stdnt Mbr Section Amer Hme Ec Assoc Local Secr/State 3rd V Chr 90-; Phi Eta Sigma; Campus Nursery Sch Vol; Soc Hnrs Seminar Stdnts; Gen Hme Ec; Chld Lf Spec.

**ANDERSON, JENNIFER L,** Kent St Univ Kent Cmps, Kent, OH; JR; BA; Peer Awrnss Stdnts Rep 90-; Dvsty Cmmt 90-; US Army Rsrv Sclst 87-; Chml Dpdncy Mbr 89-90; Otstndng Ldrshp Awrd 90-; Phlsphy/Psychlgy; Marriage Divorce Cnlng.

**ANDERSON, JENNY R,** Univ Of Sc At Columbia, Columbia, SC; FR; BA; Alpha Lambda Delta 90-; SC Hse Reps Page 91; Poli Sci/Engl; Law.

**ANDERSON JR, JESSIE B,** Tn Temple Univ, Chattanooga, TN; SO; BA; Alpha Omega Delta SBR 90-; Ftbl/Bsktb/Sftbl; Plpt Cmmnctns; Assoc Pstr.**

**ANDERSON, JIM L,** Piedmont Comm Coll, Roxboro, NC; FR; Eng.

**ANDERSON, JOETTA L,** Univ Of Miami, Coral Gables, FL; SO; BS; Coll Stdnts Christ 90-; Soc Wmn Engrs Pres 89; Tau Beta Pi 88; Intercoll Ltrng Track/Field Crs Cntry; Am Phys Therapy Assn; Reg Phys Therapist; BS Univ FL 82; BS Oregon State Univ 80; Music Eng Tech; Recording.

**ANDERSON III, JOHN H,** Atlantic Comm Coll, Mays Landing, NJ; JR; BA; Lit Mag Edit 90; Govt Clb 90; Econs Clb 90-; Dns Lst 90; Grad Wth Hnrs 90; AS Atlantic Comm Coll 90; Econs; Grad Schl.

**ANDERSON, JON H,** S U N Y Coll At Fredonia, Fredonia, NY; JR; BA; Sclgy; Indstrl/Lbr Rltns.

**ANDERSON, JOSEPH W,** Salem-Teikyo Univ, Salem, WV; FR; BA; Yrbk Photo Edtr; Cmps Nwspr Offc Mngr; Comp Sci/Eng Tech; Engr.**

**ANDERSON, JOYCE P,** Catawba Valley Comm Coll, Hickory, NC; FR; ADRN; LPN 88- LPN Burlington Co Vo Tech 84; Nrsng; BSN.

**ANDERSON, JUDITH R,** Glassboro St Coll, Glassboro, NJ; GD; Psi Iota Pi 89-; Psi Chi; EPA Conf 90-; BA; Psychology; MSW Ph D Cnslng Psych.

**ANDERSON, JULIE M,** Colby Sawyer Coll, New London, NH; FR; BFA; Art Clb 90; Stdnt Govt Rep 90; Outing Clb 90; Coffee Hse Grp 90; Fine Arts; Fshn Dsgn.

**ANDERSON, KARLENE A,** Cornell Univ, Ithaca, NY; FR; BA; Blk Bio-Med Tchncl Assoc 90; Lbry Cmmttee Of Ujamaa Rsdntl Clg 90; Cmptr Cmmttee Of Ujamaa Rsdntl Clg 90; Theatre Arts; Law.

**ANDERSON, KATHLEEN,** Fl Atlantic Univ, Boca Raton, FL, SO; BA; Acctg Stdnts Assn 90-; CPA Asst 90-; Bus/Mgmt; Law.

**ANDERSON, KATHY S,** Univ Of Ky, Lexington, KY; JR; BA; Scl Wrk.

**ANDERSON, KENNETH L,** Radford Univ, Radford, VA; SR; BS; Amrcn Crmnl Jstc Assn88-89; Phi Theta Kappa 88-89; All Amrcn Schlr 88-89; Ntnl Cllgt Mnrty Ldrshp Awd 88-90; AAS ADJU Dabney B Lancaster Comm Clg 89; Crmnl Jstc Crtf Dabney B Lancaster Comm Clg 88; Scl Wrk; Law Enfrcmnt Chld Cnslng.

**ANDERSON, KEVIN A,** Morehouse Coll, Atlanta, GA; SO; BA; Atlanta Univ Cntr Ill Clb Sgt At Arms 89-90; Hnr Rl 90-; Boys/Girls Clbs Of Metro Atlanta 90-; Swim Tm 90-; Psych/Pres Law.

**ANDERSON, KIMBERLY A,** Beckley Coll, Beckley, WV; FR; Elem Scndry Tchng; Tchng.

**ANDERSON, KIMBERLY L,** Union Coll, Barbourville, KY; SO; BA; Campus Activities Board 90; Union Clg Sngrs; Tutor; Crmnl Justc; Law.

**ANDERSON, KIMBERLY L,** Cornell Univ Statutory College, Ithaca, NY; FR; BA; Sage Chapel Chr 90-; Linguistics/Gvmt; Foreign Svc.

**ANDERSON, KIMBERLY R,** S U N Y Coll At Fredonia, Fredonia, NY; JR; BS; AMA; Am Red Cross Donor Vol 88-; Deans Lst 89-; Fac Assn Schlr All Acad Athletic Awd 90; Vlybl Capt 88-; AAS Villa Maria Coll Buffalo NY 90; Bus Admin; Mktg Rsrch.

**ANDERSON, KRISTIN D,** Le Moyne Coll, Syracuse, NY; JR; BA; Drm Cncl Pres 90; Le Myne Coll Tr Gde 89-; Le Myne Coll Fr Orntn Com 90-; Dns Lst 90; Intrnshp NY St Assmbly; IM Indr Sccr 90-; Pol Sci; Pltcs.

**ANDERSON, KYRA M,** Capital Univ, Columbus, OH; SR; BSRN; Stdnt Nrsng Affrs Com Rep 90-; Otstndng Coll Stdnts Of Amer; Sigma Theta Tau; Nrsng.

**ANDERSON, LARRY M,** Ky St Univ, Frankfort, KY; SR; BS; Cmptr Sci Clb Pres 90-; Alpha Kappa Mu 89-; Cmptr Sci.**

**ANDERSON, LAURA L,** Univ Of Southern Ms, Hattiesburg, MS; SO; BS; Stdnt Alumni Assn Hosptlty Chair; Hon Stdnt Assn Cncl Soph Rep 90-; Gamma Beta Pi 90-; Spch Cmnctns; Publ Rel.

**ANDERSON, LAUREN E,** S U N Y Coll Of Tech At Alfred, Alfred, NY; SO; BA; Sigma Tau Epsilon 89-; AAS; Spcl Educ; Tchg.

**ANDERSON, LAUREN R,** Duquesne Univ, Pittsburgh, PA; SO; SHARP 89-; Soc Prof Jrnlsts 89-; Cmnctn; Publ Rels.

**ANDERSON, LAURI J,** Merrimack Coll, North Andover, MA; SR; BA; Stdnt Intrnshp Prog 90-; Intern/Phtgrphr Peabody Museum Salem Ma 90-; Cum Laude Merrimack Coll; Modeling Degree Barbizon Mdlng Sch 84; Eng; Writer.

**ANDERSON, LAURIE C,** Marshall University, Huntington, WV; FR; BA; Engl/Hlth Ed; Tch.

**ANDERSON, LINDA D,** Temple Univ, Philadelphia, PA; JR; BA; Nrs Extern Grad Hosp; U S Army Act Duty E-K Sgt; Mbr IRR; Nrsng; Med.

**ANDERSON, LISA N,** Howard Univ, Washington, DC; JR; BA; Rsdnce Hall Gspl Choir 90; Rep 90; Free Lance Rep 90; Golden Key; Intrnshp WKYS Radio; Jrnlsm; Brdcst Jrnlst.

**ANDERSON, LORI A,** Univ Of Sc At Columbia, Columbia, SC; SR; SCEA; BA; Erly Chldhd Edctn; Tchng.

**ANDERSON, LORI J,** Univ Of Cin R Walters Coll, Blue Ash, OH; FR; ASSOC; Banking Full Time 2 Yrs; Acctng Tchnlgy.

**ANDERSON, LORI M,** Univ Of Sc At Aiken, Aiken, SC; SO; BA; Bst Bddies Ed Mjr Clb 89-; Intl Clb; Chorus; Spnsh.

**ANDERSON, LYNNETTE L,** Salisbury St Univ, Salisbury, MD; SO; MBA; Alpha Omega; Beta Beta Beta; Intern Salisbury Phys Thrpy; Biol; Physcl Thrpy.

**ANDERSON, MACHELLE P,** Fl International Univ, Miami, FL; SR; BA; Jesus People Msntrs; Lgl Sec Dade Cty State Atty Ofc 82-; AA Miami Dade Comm Clg 80; Crmnl Jstc; Law.

**ANDERSON, MARGARET ANN,** Commonwealth Coll, Virginia Beach, VA; GD; AAS; Deans Lst; Pres Lst; Mdcl Offc Mgmt.

**ANDERSON, MARGARET K,** Saint Andrews Presbytrn Coll, Laurinburg, NC; SR; BA; ECO Actn Clb; Hons Pgm 87-89; Tutr 89; Stdnt Tchng 90-; Chrldr 87-89; Engl; Tch.

**ANDERSON, MARIE E,** Univ Of Miami, Coral Gables, FL; SR; Yrbk Stf Sect Edtr 87-89; Nwspr Stf Wrtr 87-90; Phi Kappa Phi; Pi Delta Alpha Soc Fndr; Alpha Epsilon Phi Stndrds Brd; Stdnt Cnslr 89; Mgmt Intrn Mgr 90; Pres Schlrshp Brdgwater Clg 87-89; Bowmn Ashe Schlrshp 89-; Sprts; Psych/Art; Busn Mgmt.

**ANDERSON, MARK A,** Univ Of Md Baltimore Prof Schl, Baltimore, MD; JR; PHRM; Awd Exclnc Clncl Imnlgy 80; Amer Soc Clncl Pthlgsts 80-; Med Tchnlgst UMMS Baltimore MD 80-; BS Univ Maryland Baltimore 80; Phrmcy; Clncl Phrmcy.

**ANDERSON, MARK D,** Nyack Coll, Nyack, NY; SR; Journal Arts/Lit 90-; Newspaper Assoc Ed 90-; Poem Publ Nyack Clg Jrnl 90-; AA Jamestown Cmnty Clg 87; Engl; Clg Prfsr.

**ANDERSON, MARK J,** S U N Y Coll Of Tech At Canton, Canton, NY; GD; BA; PHI THETA KAPPA 90; Hon Convoctn; Bus Admin; Transfer Stu.

**ANDERSON, MARTHA E,** Univ Of Southern Ms, Hattiesburg, MS; JR; BSBA; Outstndng Colg Stdnt/Am 88; Alpha Lambda Delta 88-; Beta Gamma Sigma 90-; Golden Key 90-; Beta Alpha Psi Reptr Sec 90-; Gamma Beta Phi 89-; L Y Foote Schlrshp 88-89; Dr J J Morgan Schlrshp 89-90; Excel/Ms Schlrshp 90-; Acctng.**

**ANDERSON, MARY G,** Georgetown Coll, Georgetown, KY; SO; BS; Alpha Lambda Delta; Beta Beta Beta Sec; Blgy And Envir Sci; Rsrch Blgst Fr US Fsh Wl.

**ANDERSON, MARY R,** Indiana Univ Of Pa, Indiana, PA; JR; Actvties Brd 90; Radio Statn 90-; Alpha Epsilon Rho 90-; Phi Sigma Sigma 90-; Deans Lst 89-; Cmnctns Media.

**ANDERSON, MICHAEL B,** Ms St Univ, Miss State, MS; SR; BS; Stdnt Crrctns Assn Tres 89-; Cllg Rpblcns; Alpha Kappa Delta; Kappa Sigma Hse Mngr 89; Fdrl Law Enfrcmnt Intrn; Sclgy; Fed Law Enfrcment.

**ANDERSON, MICHAEL R,** Radford Univ, Radford, VA; SO; Sigma Alpha Epsilon; Psychlgy; I/O Psychlgy.

**ANDERSON, MIKE L,** Christopher Newport Coll, Newport News, VA; FR; BA; Honors Prog 90-; Math; Educ.

**ANDERSON, MYONGHUI Y,** Univ Of Sc At Sumter, Sumter, SC; FR; BA; Comp Sci; Pgmr.

**ANDERSON, NANCY M,** Univ Of Ga, Athens, GA; JR; BSED; Camp Crusade For Christ 90-; Flg Ftbl/Indr Soccer/Bsktbl/Tennis/Sftbl 90-; GA Rec/Park Assoc GAHPERD Rec Majs Clb Pr 90-; Golden Key 90-; Kappa Delta Pi 90-; Zeta Tau Alpha 90-; Awrd Coca-Cola Fndtn Sci Schlrshp 89-90; Therapeutic Rec.

**ANDERSON, OLGA M,** Wv Univ, Morgantown, WV; FR; Helvetia; Alpha Phi Omega; Eng; Ind Eng.

**ANDERSON, ONYA M,** Tusculum Coll, Greeneville, TN; SO; BA; Psychlgy/Bus; Clncl Psychlgy/Indl Orgnztnl.

**ANDERSON, PAIGE C,** Va Commonwealth Univ, Richmond, VA; SR; BFA; Phi Eta Sigma 88-; Cls Awd 88· Fashn Merchndsng; Buyng/Sales.

**ANDERSON, PATRICIA A,** Georgetown Univ, Washington, DC; SO; BA; Assc Stdnts Fresno Cty Clg Pres 88-90; CA Stdnt Assc Cmnty Clgs Rgnl Pres 88-90; Stdnt Fr Peace/Jstc Fndr/Pres 88-89; CA Schlrshp Fdrtn 88-; Phi Theta Kappa 90; Alpha Gamma Sigma 88-90; Intr Clb Cncl Pres 88-90; AIESEC Co Chrmn 90-; Mngmt/Mrktg; Intrntl Bus/Poli.

**ANDERSON, PATRICIA A,** Bowie St Univ, Bowie, MD; SR; BS; CEC; ECE Advsry Comm; Tchr Ed Clb; Sharon Christa Mcauliffe Mem Schlrshp 88-; Spcl Olympics Sprts Coach 88-; Erly Chld/Spcl Ed; Tchr.

**ANDERSON, PEGGY J,** Wright St Univ Lake Cmps, Celina, OH; SR; BS; PTA 88-; Educ/Bio Sci; Tchr.

**ANDERSON, PHILIP B,** Univ Of Miami, Coral Gables, FL; SO; BARCH; AIAS; Archtctr.

**ANDERSON, R SCOTT,** Marshall University, Huntington, WV; SR; BBA; Stdnt Org Alumni Rel Pres 89-; Rugby Clb 88; SOAR Ambsdr 90-; Soc Yeager Schlrs 88-; Omicron Delta Kappa Hist 90-; Order Omega 90-; Lambda Chi Alpha Pres 88-; Acctg.

**ANDERSON III, RANDALL HUDSON,** Univ Of Cincinnati-Clrmnt Coll, Batavia, OH; BS; Yaba Bwlng Capt; Indoor Soccer; Outdoor Soccer Tm Capt; All Amer Schlrs At Lrge; Chldrns Hosp Annual Crnvl Vol; Deans Lst; Ntl Cllgte Mnrty Ldrshp Awd; Yaba 300 Ring/800 Ring Hnred In Lcl News; Intrntl Fnce; MBA Bsnss Law.**

**ANDERSON, RAYMOND E,** Va St Univ, Petersburg, VA; SO; BA; Sclgy; Law.

**ANDERSON, RICARDO P,** Howard Univ, Washington, DC; JR; BA; Amercn Inst Of Arch; Intrntl Stdnts Assoc; Im Soccer; Diplma Hons Clg Of Arts Sci/Technlgy 90; Arch/Plnng.

**ANDERSON, RICHARD C,** Wv Univ, Morgantown, WV; FR; BS; Pres Hon List; Colg/Engrng Deans List; Chmcl Engrng.

**ANDERSON, ROBERT BRANTLEY,** Old Dominion Univ, Norfolk, VA; SO; BEET; Engrs Music; Intrn El Dupont 90; AS 89; Elec Engr.

**ANDERSON, ROBIN C,** Univ Of Nc At Asheville, Asheville, NC; SR; BA; Pep Bnd 87-88; Ltn/Grk Tutor 89-; Sr Clscl Lg St Sec 90-; Dns Lst 90-; Vol Tutor Stdnts Ltn Asheville Jr Hgh 90; Vol Org Jdg NC Jr Clscl Lg Cnvntn UNC CH Hgh Schl Stdnts; Prz Grk Lng Stdy; Clsc Ltn/Grk Lng/Ed; Tch Mdl/Hgh Schl Ltn.**

**ANDERSON, ROBIN D,** Alcorn St Univ, Lorman, MS; FR; Med; Phys Thrpst.

**ANDERSON, ROBIN L,** Wv Northern Comm Coll, Wheeling, WV; SO; BA; Psychlgy.

**ANDERSON, ROBIN-LI C,** Salem St Coll, Salem, MA; FR; BA; Clncl Psychlgst.

**ANDERSON, RONALD H,** S U N Y Coll Of Tech At Delhi, Delhi, NY; FR; AAS; Elctrcl Engnrng.

**ANDERSON, ROSIE M,** Lane Coll, Jackson, TN; SR; BS; Stdnt Govt Assoc 87-; Stnt Natl Educ Assoc Pres 87-88; Stdnt Free Entrps Sec 89-90; Pres List 86-87; Natl Hnr Rl; Chmbr Of Cmmrc Clrk 87; Slvtn Army 88; Shltr/Homeless 89; Flwshp TN Tech Univ; Schlrshp United Negro Clg Fund; Tnns Trnmnt; Bus Admin; Mgmnt.

**ANDERSON, ROZANNE M,** Univ Of Akron, Akron, OH; JR; BFA; Schlrshp 90-; BS Un/Fl 65; Art; MFA.

**ANDERSON, SHARON M,** Medical Coll Of Ga, Augusta, GA; JR; BSN; GANS 90-; Natl Stdnt Nrsng Assc 90-; Nrsng.

**ANDERSON, STACYE R,** Univ Of Tn At Martin, Martin, TN; SR; Stdnt Govt Assn Chf Justice 90-; Soc Hon Seminar Stdnts Pres 88-; Econ Club 88-; Phi Eta Sigma 88-; Phi Kappa Phi 89-; Phi Chi Theta Treas 88-; Outstndg Stdnt Sch Bus 90-; Summa Cum Laude; BS; Econ/Finance.

**ANDERSON, STEPHANIE D,** Univ Of Tn At Martin, Martin, TN; GD; MS; Undrgrdte Alumni Cncl 88-; Majorette Capt 89-; Kappa Alpha Treas 87-; Pres Rndtble 89-; Order Omega Sec/Treas 88-; Phi Kappa Phi 88-; Phi Eta Sigma 87; Psy/Chi Advrtsng Comm Chrmn 87-; Mu Epsilon Delta Scl Chrmn 87-; Psychology; Doctorate Pysch Prvt Pract.

**ANDERSON, STEPHANIE D,** Al St Univ, Montgomery, AL; FR; BA; Stdnt Govt 90-; Sntr Alpha 90-; Phi Eta Sigma 90-; Bsn; Corp Exec.

**ANDERSON, SUSAN K,** Univ Of Cin R Walters Coll, Blue Ash, OH; FR; BBA; Fnncl Cnsltnt.

**ANDERSON, TALITHA E,** Univ Of Tn At Martin, Martin, TN; SR; BS; Soc Wrk Clb Comm 89-; Psychlgy Clb 88-; Baptst Stdnt Un Comm 87-88; Phi Kappa Phi; Alpha Delta Mu 90-; Psi Chi 89-; Deans Lst 88-; Intrnshp; Soc Wrk; Grad Schl.

**ANDERSON, TERRANCE H,** Columbia Union Coll, Takoma Park, MD; SR; BS; SGA Sprtl VP 90-; Amer Psychlgcl Assn 90-; Psi Chi 90-; Delta Sigma Tau 89-; Big Bro Pgm Dir 85-86; Advntst Yth Vol Corps Japan 86-88; Puppet Tm 89-; A Cannon Memrl Schlrshp 90-; Cnslng Psychlgy; Occptnl Thrpy.

**ANDERSON, TERRY E,** Northeast State Tech Comm Coll, Blountville, TN; JR; AAS; Auto Serv; Bsn.

**ANDERSON, THEOPHILUS K,** Interdenominational Theo Ctr, Atlanta, GA; GD; Dip Th Trnty Coll Legon Ghana W Africa 84; Chrch Msc; Mnstry/Pastor.

**ANDERSON, TIFFANY C,** Central Al Comm Coll, Alexander City, AL; FR; BS; Deans Lst; Rdlgy.

**ANDERSON, TIFFANY L,** Ms St Univ, Miss State, MS; SR; BA; Intrschl Cncl 90-; Educ Assoc VP; NEA 90-; Kappa Delta Pi Sec 89-; Gamma Beta Phi 88-; Phi Alpha Theta 90-; Vry Spcl Arts; Pres Schlr; Scndry Educ; Tch.

**ANDERSON, TODD A,** Marshall University, Huntington, WV; JR; BS; Gamma Beta Phi 89-; Pi Mu Epsilon 89-; Upsilon Pi Epsilon 90; -; Intrnshp Ashland Oil; Cmptr Sci; Sys Analyst.

**ANDERSON, TODD A,** Oh St Univ At Marion, Marion, OH; SO; BA; Psychlgy Clb; Stdnt Alumni Coun; Stdnt Bus Soc; Bus; Law.

**ANDERSON, TRACI D,** Howard Univ, Washington, DC; SO; BA; Lbrl Arts Hnrs Assoc Grvnc Comm 89-90; Cmnty Wrkr Ls Krtz Cvc Ctr Cnslr 89-; Pblshd Melyns Pn 87; Englsh; Tchng/Frlnc Wrtng.**

**ANDERSON, TRACY L,** Indiana Univ Of Pa, Indiana, PA; JR; BA; Bg Brthrs/Bg Sistrs 89-; Ambsdrs Clb 90; Kappa Delta Pi 90-; Deans Lst 89-; Provosts Schlr 90-; Educ; Tchr.

**ANDERSON, TRAVIS B,** Morgan St Univ, Baltimore, MD; FR; BS; Soc Advncmnt Cmptr Sci Treas; Assoc Cmptng Mchnry 90-; Alpha Lambda Delta; Phi Eta Sigma; NAACP; Cmptr Sci.

**ANDERSON, TRAVIS W,** Castleton St Coll, Castleton, VT; JR; BA; Otng Clb Pres 90-; Stdnt Assn Sntr Pres Pro Tem; Phi Eta Sigma 89-; Crmnl Jstce Hstry; Law Enfrcmnt.

**ANDERSON, TRUDY S,** S U N Y Coll At Fredonia, Fredonia, NY; JR; BA; Grad JCC Hgh Hon; MADD; Sndy Schl Tchr; AS Jmstwn Comm Coll 90; Early Chldhd Educ; "'.

**ANDERSON, VICKI ANN,** Gallaudet Univ, Washington, DC; SR; Never Too Late Club Treas 89-90; Art History Museum Studies; Teacher.

**ANDERSON, VIRGINIA A,** Norfolk St Univ, Norfolk, VA; SR; BS; Alpha Kappa Mu; PTA V P 89-90; ASS Tidewater Comm Clg 70; Lrng Dsbltes/Mntl Rtrdtn; Tch/Admnstr.

**ANDERSON, WAYNE A,** City Univ Of Ny Baruch Coll, New York, NY; SO; BBA; Sigma Alpha Delta 90-; Acctnts Payable Clrk Bantam Doubleday Dell Publ Grp Inc 88-; Acctg; Intl Finance.

**ANDERSON, WAYNE C,** Samford Univ, Birmingham, AL; FR; Parents Weekend Cmmt Treas; Inner City Missions 90-; Sigma Nu Rsk Reduction 90-; Habitat Hmnty 90-; Step Sing Schlrshp; Grad Mrshll; Soccer Clb 90-; Bio; Med.

**ANDERSON, WENDE J,** Samford Univ, Birmingham, AL; SR; BMUS; Phi Kappa Phi; Pi Kappa Lambda; Delta Omicron 89-; Cncrto Aria Cmptn Wnr 88; Cncrto Aria Cmptn Fnlst; Snfrd Prfmg Arts Pro 89-; Music.

**ANDERSON, WILLIAM K,** Radford Univ, Radford, VA; JR; Mngmnt.

**ANDERSON-GALLO, MELBA M,** Miami Dade Comm Coll South, Miami, FL; GD; BA; Phi Theta Kappa 88; Untd Way Chldrn Home Soc Asst 89; AA 90; Psy/Tchng; Cnslr.

**ANDERSSON, KIMBERLY A,** Fl St Univ, Tallahassee, FL; FR; BA; Phi Eta Sigma; Zeta Tau Alpha; Cmpus Crsde; Deans Lst; Music.

**ANDERT-SCHMIDT, DARLENE M,** Nova Univ, Ft Lauderdale, FL; GD; MBA; Amer Soc Trnrs Dvlprs Bd 89-; Pilot Svc Clb; Cert Fin Mgr Designation 87; Cape Conal Jr Ftbl Assn Bd 88-89; Primary Trnr Bus Indstry Svcs; BA Bus Alverno Coll 83; BA Comm Alverno Coll 83; Bus Admin; Trnr Bus Phd.

**ANDINO, GLORIA M,** Fl International Univ, Miami, FL; SR; BS; FEA; Cmps Mnstry; Intl Rdng Asc; Kappa Delta Pi; Amoren Accion; Elem Educ; Tch.

**ANDINO, MARIA D,** Bunker Hill Comm Coll, Boston, MA; FR; Lgl Secr/Lib Arts; Law Ofc.

**ANDINO, MICHELLE M,** Univ Of Nc At Charlotte, Charlotte, NC; FR; BA; Phi Eta Sigma; History; Teaching.

**ANDJEVSKY, CYNTHIA J,** Alfred Univ, Alfred, NY; SR; BS; Vrsty Swm Capt 89-90; Deans Lst 90; Bus Admin; Mgmt.

**ANDOL, MARY J,** Ms St Univ, Miss State, MS; SR; Fed Dspst Insr Corp 83-85; 1ST TN Natl Corp 85-89; BPA 83; Frgn Lang; Tchng/Intl Bnkng Inds.

**ANDOLLO, ARACELY,** Miami Dade Comm Coll, Miami, FL; FR; AA; Civil Eng/Math.

**ANDONOVA, MONIKA L,** Columbia Union Coll, Takoma Park, MD; FR; BA; Phi Eta Sigma; Bio; Med.

**ANDRADE, ELWYN G,** City Univ Of Ny Baruch Coll, New York, NY; SR; BBA; Cmptr/Quantitv Mthds Soc Brch Coll 90-; Beta Gamma Sigma; Deans Lst 89-90; Baruch Prvst Schlrshp; City Univ NY Frgn Stu Schlrshp 89; LM Ericsson Kuwait City Kuwait Admin Asstnt 78-86; Cmptr Info Sys.

**ANDRADE, JAIME,** Univ Of Pr At Mayaguez, Mayaguez, PR; JR; Vlybl Tm 88-; Marines Corps Rsrv; Am Scty Mech Eng 90-; Natl Clgt Eng Awrds.

**ANDRE, ANN M,** William Paterson Coll, Wayne, NJ; SR; Math Clb Pres 90-.

**ANDREAUS, DOUG T,** Hillsborough Comm Coll, Tampa, FL; SO; BED; Phys Educ; Coach.

**ANDREJACK, JESSICA L,** Western New England Coll, Springfield, MA; FR; BA; Alpha Lambda Delta; Acctng; CPA.

**ANDRES, LISA M,** Fl Atlantic Univ, Boca Raton, FL; SO; BBA; Bsn; Bsn Mgmt.

**ANDRES, STEPHANIE N,** Commonwealth Coll, Virginia Beach, VA; SR; CPL; Alpha Beta Gamma; Cmmnwlth Clg Law Soc Pres 90-; Top Salesperson Real Estate 85; Denver Bd Of Rltrs 82-83; Auroka Bd Of Rltrs 85-86; Paralegal Studies; Law.

**ANDRESEN, KRISTEN M,** Cornell Univ Statutory College, Ithaca, NY; FR; BS; Eqstrn Tm 90-; Blck And Brdle Clb 90-; Alpha Epsilon Phi 90-; Anml Scis; Med.

**ANDRESS, CYNTHIA DIANE,** Univ Of South Al, Mobile, AL; SR; BA; Delta Zeta; Spinsters Young Womens Soc; Kappa Delta Pi; Kappa Delta Zeta; BA-ED; Elem Educ.

**ANDRESS, JACQUELINE LEE,** Ms St Univ, Miss State, MS; GD; Fshn Brd; Cheerleader; Pgm Cncl; Alpha Psi; Delta Gamma Actvts Chrmn 89-90; Aid To Blind; Pres Schlr; IM Sports; BS Mississippi State Univ; Bio; Vet Schl.

**ANDRESS-UDALL, SUZANNE,** George Mason Univ, Fairfax, VA; SR; BSW; Soc Wrk Stdnt Assn V P 90-; Alpha Chi 90-; Vol Award Alternative Hse Intern 89; BSW; Soc Work.

**ANDREW, LEON E,** Morehouse Coll, Atlanta, GA; SO; BA; Hon Rl 90; Morehouse Clg Big Bro 90; Mentor Prog; Psychology; Clncl Child Psychlgst.

**ANDREW, TINA M,** Oh Univ, Athens, OH; SR; BFA; Hnrs Clg Advsry Cncl 89-90; Phi Kappa Phi; Amer Ctr For Dsgn 89-90; Kappa Phi Clb 90; 3rd Cntry Schlrshp 89; Ohio Brd Of Rgnts Schlrshp 89; Art Hist; Museum Admin.

**ANDREWS, AMY L,** Ga St Univ, Atlanta, GA; MS; HPRD Clb Treas 88-90; IDEA 88-; ACSM 90-; Spec Olympics 90; AID Atlanta; Girl Sct 89; Hosp Crdlgy Intrn 90; Orthpdc Clinic Intrn 90; Stdnt Trnr 90; BS 90; Exer Sci; Med Schl.

**ANDREWS, AMY R,** Ramapo Coll Of Nj, Mahwah, NJ; JR; BA; Delta Mu Delta; Bus/Mktg.

**ANDREWS, AMY T,** Piedmont Bible Coll, Winston-Salem, NC; JR; BA; Clg Chorale/Class Sec 87-90; Chrldr/Traveling Ens Capt 87-88; Chorale/Ens Accomp; Jr Marshall 90; Music.

**ANDREWS, ANGELINE,** Paine Coll, Augusta, GA; FR; Bapt Stu Union 90-; Stu Ntl Educ Assoc 90-; Alpha Phi Alpha Frat Inc Swthrt 90-; Paine Coll Pres Schlr Awrd 90-; Vivian U Robinson Awrd 90-; Educ; Mdl Grd Math Tchr.

**ANDREWS, BRIAN J,** Niagara Univ, Niagara Univ, NY; SR; BS; Mktng Club 90; IM Sports 87-; Mktg; MBA.

**ANDREWS JR, CHARLES LAWRENCE,** Southern Coll Of Tech, Marietta, GA; SR; BS; ACM; Tau Alpha Pi; Kappa Sigma; Cmptr Sci; Bus.

**ANDREWS, DAVID J,** Newbury Coll, Brookline, MA; GD; AS; Phi Theta Kappa; Paralegal Studies; Law.

**ANDREWS, DEBRA L,** Univ Of South Al, Mobile, AL; JR; BA; Bapt Stdnt Cntr; Chi Alpha; Wmns Golf Tm 88-90; Bus; Mktg.

**ANDREWS, ELIOT H,** Ms St Univ, Miss State, MS; SR; MS; Coop Ed 90; Symphnc Bnd 86; Acad Affrs Com 89; Phi Kappa Phi 89-; Gamma Beta Phi 86-; Lambda Sigma 87; Upsilon Pi Epsilon 88-; Hnrs Prog 90; ACM 89-91; PS 85-87; Magna Cum Laude 90; Rsrch Asstshp Comp Sci; BS 90; Comp Sci; Comptng Mgmt.

**ANDREWS, GERTERLYN O,** Tuskegee Univ, Tuskegee Inst, AL; SR; BSEE; NSRE 88-89; SWE 90-; Eta Kappa Nu HKN Pres 90; Elect Eng; Rcpnt SPUR; Natl Sci Fndtn 90; JPL 88-; HBCU Flw; Acqr Phd Elect Eng.

**ANDREWS, HAROLD A,** Coll Of New Rochelle, New Rochelle, NY; SR; MDIV; Outstndg Schlstc Achvmnt Hnr 88-; Lay Spkr United Meth Church 88-; Cert Chrstn Min NY Theolgcl Semnry 89; BA; Theology; Ordnd Mnstr.

**ANDREWS, HEATHER N,** Faulkner Univ, Montgomery, AL; FR; BA; Phi Lambda Scl Clb; Elem Educ; Tchg.

**ANDREWS, JAMES M,** S U N Y Coll Of Tech At Frmgdl, Farmingdale, NY; FR; Bond; Aircrft Maint; Dutchess Cnty Bd Of Coop Educ Srvcs 90; Aircraft Engr.

**ANDREWS, JEFFREY A,** Univ Of Rochester, Rochester, NY; JR; BS BA; Yrbk Edtr 89-; Sailing Clb 88-; Delta Upsilon 89-; Ecology/Envrnmntl Biol/Pol Sci; Academia.

**ANDREWS JR, JERRY L,** Fl A & M Univ, Tallahassee, FL; FR; Mrchng/Cncrt/Pep Bnd 90-91; Bsns Mgmt.

**ANDREWS, JUDY L,** Middle Ga Coll, Cochran, GA; FR; ASN; GA Assoc Nrsng Stdnts 90-; Natl Assn Nrsng Stdnts 90-; Wmn Of Moose; Nrsng.

**ANDREWS, LINDA R,** Longwood Coll, Farmville, VA; SR; BS; Fncy Ft Clggrs Dir 87-; Clnial Sqrs Trea 87-; Phi Kappa Phi; BS Ricahrd Bland Coll Wm/Mary 88; Ed Mdl Schl Math; Tchr.

**ANDREWS, LYNNE D,** Siena Coll, Loudonville, NY; SR; BBA; Fin Club 88-89; Acctng Club 89-90; Stdnt Chapt Natl Assoc Of Acctnts 89-; 21st Century Ldrs Hnr Soc; Big Bros/Big Sis Project Challenge 90; Tax Intrn Ewrnst & Young 90-; Field Hockey Mgr 89; Acctng; CPA.

**ANDREWS, MICHELLE R,** Birmingham Southern Coll, Birmingham, AL; JR; BA; Triangle Clb 89-90; Prsdnts Srvc Orgnztn 90-; Edtr Stdnt Nwspr 90-; Alpha Lambda Delta 89-; Phi Eta Sigma 89-; Omicron Delta Kappa Mrtr Brd; Sigma Tau Delta; Zeta Tau Alpha Schlrshp Chrmn; Dana Car Srvcs Intrn 89-; Writing.

**ANDREWS, PETER A,** Westminster Coll, New Wilmingtn, PA; JR; BS; Chmstry Clb 90; Beta Beta Beta 89; Mortar Brd 90; Sigma Phi Epsilon 88; James Mem Hosp Intrnshp Assist Dr Chatuce; Im 89; Bio; Med Fld MD.

**ANDREWS, REGINA L,** Middle Ga Coll, Cochran, GA; FR; BS; Biology; Medicine.

**ANDREWS, ROBERT L,** D S Lancaster Comm Coll, Clifton Forge, VA; FR; AAS; Chess Clb 90; Phi Theta Kappa 90; Dunlap Vol Fre Dept/Rescue Sq Qtrmstr 86; Va Dept Of Frstry Lcl Frst Fre Wrdn 90; Va Dept Of Hlth EMT-D 89; Tappi Ntnl Schlrshp; Tappi Va-Crlna Schlrshp; Untd Paprwrkrs Union Lcl 884 88; Pulp/Papr Tchnlgy; NC State.

**ANDREWS, ROGENE M,** East Stroudsburg Univ, E Stroudsburg, PA; SR; BS; Intern Lhghtn Schl Dstrct; Sychlgy Stff; LA 88; Psychlgy; Cnslng.

**ANDREWS, ROSETTA L,** Fl A & M Univ, Tallahassee, FL; FR; PHARM; Fresh Cls Pharm Treas 90-; Pharm.

**ANDREWS, SARA K,** Univ Of Rio Grande, Rio Grande, OH; FR; BA; Chrc Yth Grp 87-; Hstry/Eng; Prfsr.

**ANDRIJOWYCH, KATHY A,** Univ Of Dayton, Dayton, OH; SO; BS; Amer Inst Chem Engr 89-; Campus Cnctn 90-; Soc Wmn Engrs 89-90; Coop Educ; Chem Engr; Rsrch.**

**ANDRIKOPOULOS, PANAGIOTA,** City Univ Of Ny Baruch Coll, New York, NY; GD; BBA; Fnc.

**ANDRIOLA, THOMAS J,** S U N Y Coll Of Tech At Frmgdl, Farmingdale, NY; SO; BS; Flying Clb 90-; Aerospace Flight; Comm/Military Pilot.

**ANDROUIN, GEORGE A,** Fl International Univ, Miami, FL; JR; Hosp Mgmt; Hotel Gen Mgr.

**ANDRUS, DEBORAH E,** S U N Y Coll At Postdam, Potsdam, NY; SR; MM; Crane Stdnt Assc Sec 88-; Music Edtrs Ntnl Conf 90-; Pi Kappa Lambda; Prfrmrs Cert; Dprtmntl Schlr 90-; Rocque F Dominick Awrd; BM; Music; Tchng.

**ANDRUS, LAURA R,** Radford Univ, Radford, VA; SO; BS; Native Amer Heritage Assn Sec; Explrs Boy Scouts Amer; Interdiscplnry Stdes; Tchr.

**ANDRUS JR, RICHARD C,** Christian Brothers Univ, Memphis, TN; SR; BA; Bsn Mgmt; Shoe Slsmn.

**ANDRUS, SHARON S,** Middle Tn St Univ, Murfreesboro, TN; SO; Sociology.

**ANDUJAR ALVAREZ, MIGUEL,** Inter Amer Univ Pr Hato Rey, Hato Rey, PR; SR; BA; Acctg Assoc; Acctg; CPA.

**ANDUJAR MATOS, GILBERT,** Inter Amer Univ Pr San German, San German, PR; SR; BS; IEEE 89-; Elctrnc Engr Tchnlgy; Engr.

**ANELONE, AMOUYA HILAIRE,** Southern Coll Of Tech, Marietta, GA; SR; BS; Math Tutr Minorities; Math Tutr So Tech; Cmptr Eng.

**ANGEL FONTANILLS, ENNIO,** Inter Amer Univ Pr Hato Rey, Hato Rey, PR; FR; Assoc De Acampadores 85-; En Navidades Voy A Hosp 88-89; De Personas Enf; Biology; Odontlgy.

**ANGEL, KIRK J,** Univ Of Nc At Asheville, Asheville, NC; JR; BA; Stdnt Ct Jstc 88-90; Chnclrs Colloquim 88-90; Phi Eta Sigma 88-; UNCA Hons Prog 88-; Pi Lambda Phi Pres 88-; Philsphy; Law.**

**ANGEL, ROXANNE I,** Memphis St Univ, Memphis, TN; SR; MFA; Delta Sigma Pi 88-89; Delta Gamma Soc Chrpsn 86-88; Graphic Dsgn.

**ANGELINI, FRANK J,** Villanova Univ, Villanova, PA; JR; BS; Phi Kappa Phi; Rsrch Oxford Univ Dept Exprmntl Psychlgy; Psychlgy; Clncl Psychlgy.

**ANGELL, NICOLE R,** Livingston Univ, Livingston, AL; SO; MBA; Prgms Brd 90-; Theatre Mgr 90-; Bio; Rngr/Rsch.

**ANGELL, SHANNON L,** Anne Arundel Comm Coll, Arnold, MD; FR; AA; Bus.

**ANGERAME, WENDY L,** Georgian Court Coll, Lakewood, NJ; FR; BS; Bus Admn.

**ANGERMEIER, DANIELLE M,** Wesley Coll, Dover, DE; FR; BS; Acctng Scty 90; Pmi Theta Kappa 90; Acctng.

**ANGLE, JAMES STEVEN,** Nova Univ, Ft Lauderdale, FL; GD; MBA; Dns Lst; Schlrshp Internatl Assoc Fire Chiefs 84; Internatl Scty Fire Srvc Instrctrs; Btln Chf So Trl Fr Dept Ft Myers Fl 88-; AS Broward Comm Clge 84; BS Univ Cincinnati 89; Bsn.

**ANGLIM, COLLEEN P,** S U N Y Coll Of A & T Morrisvl, Morrisville, NY; SO; BS; Educ; Tchr.

**ANGLIN, JACQUELINE E,** Howard Univ, Washington, DC; SR; BS; Rho Chi Treas 90-; Golden Key; Dip Pharm Coll Arts Sci/Tech 85; Pharm.

**ANGRABE, CATHERINE E,** Saint Francis Coll, Loretto, PA; SO; BA; Red Key Clb 89-; Psychology.

**ANGRAND, VERGNIAUD,** Atlantic Union Coll, S Lancaster, MA; SR; BA; AS La Guardia Comm Clg 87; Theolgy/Biblcl Langs; Tchr/Mnstr.

**ANGUS, DENITA L,** Marshall University, Huntington, WV; JR; Hall Advsry Cncl 88-90; Gamma Beta Phi 89-; Kappa Delta Phi 90-; Deans List 88-; Elem Ed; Tchng.

**ANGUS, L ALISON,** Va Commonwealth Univ, Richmond, VA; SO; BA; Acctng Soc 90-; Campus Crusade; Coop Educ Pgm; Pres Schlrshp 89-90; Deans Lst 89-; Acctng; CPA.

**ANGUS, LEIGH ALISON,** Va Commonwealth Univ, Richmond, VA; SO; BS; Acctg Soc 90-; Co-Op Ed; Pres Schlrshp Midway Clg 89-90; Acctg; CPA.

**ANIBA, MICHAEL A,** Widener Univ, Chester, PA; SR; BSE; IEEE; Electrcl; Eng Dsgn/Mng.

**ANICITO, KRISTINA M,** Univ Of Sc At Columbia, Columbia, SC; JR; BA; Grk Jdcl Bd; Wmn Stdnt Assn 90-; SEED Orgnztn; Delta Zeta 89-; IM 89-; Erly Chldhd Ed; Tchng.

**ANIUNOH, CELESTINE O,** Coppin St Coll, Baltimore, MD; SR; BS; Jaycees Treas 90-; Phi Beta Lambda 82-81; Christian Council Pres; Soccer Schlrshp 82-; Soccer 80-; AA Commty Clg Baltimore 81-; AA Commty Clg Baltimore 82; Mgt Sci/Scolgy; Public Admin.

**ANKER, CHERYL L,** Univ Of Miami, Coral Gables, FL; SO; BS; Hon Stdnts Assoc 89; Filmmkrs Assoc 89; Alpha Lambda Delta 89; Motion Pictures/Engl; Scrptwrtr.

**ANKNEY, JEFFREY A,** Bowling Green St Univ, Bowling Green, OH; SR; BS; Archtctrl Dsgn; Dsgnr/Drftr.

**ANNA, CATHERINE A,** Mount Aloysius Jr Coll, Cresson, PA; FR; ASSOC; Patton Sprtsmns Assoc Treas; Nrsng.

**ANNA, SHAREN M,** Niagara Univ, Niagara Univ, NY; FR; Hon Pgm; Intl Studies.

**ANNAMALAI, THENAMMAI S,** Rivier Coll, Nashua, NH; JR; BA; Rivier Clg Nwspr Staff Wrtr 88-89; Wmns Soc Stdnt Rep 89; Engl/Cmnctns; Jrnlst.

**ANNAND, CAROLYN MARIE,** Ringling School Of Art, Sarasota, FL; JR; BFA; Grphc Dsgn Advsry Comm 89-90; Rnglng Schl Of Art Rep; Pres Lst 88-; Smmr Intrnshp Sea Dog Sprtswr Grphc Artst 89-90; Wrkd As Grphc Artst For 3 Yrs; Cert St Petersburg Vocatnl Tech Inst Comm Art 82-83; Grphc Dsgn; Dsgnr.

**ANNASENZ, MARIE K,** Trenton St Coll, Trenton, NJ; JR; BA; Area Res Govt Treas 88-; Stdnt Educ Assn 88; Pi Mu Epsilon 90; Kappa Delta Pi; Hon Prog 88-; Gov Tchng Schlrs Prog 88; Math Tutor Sci Lab 90; Deans Lst 88-; Summer EOF Prog Tutor 90; Soph Math Awd 90; Math Mem Schlrshp; I M Bowlng/Sftbl; Math Educ; Tch.**

**ANNES, ELISE H,** Univ Of Rochester, Rochester, NY; SO; Wmns Vrsty Tns Tm Capt 90-; Wmns Vrsty La Crosse Tm Capt; Frshmn Cmmndtn; Sigma Delta Gau Pldg Cls Pres 90-; Pol Sci/Econ; Politics Law.

**ANNES, GABRIELLE R,** Univ Of Rochester, Rochester, NY; JR.

**ANNESE, LINDA M,** Merrimack Coll, North Andover, MA; SR; BS; Cls Cncl VP 88-; MORE 87; Deans Lst 90-; Sigma Phi Omega 88-; Best Pldg Awd 88-90; Exec Bd Pgm Awd 89-90; IM Bsktbl Sftbl/Aerobicx 88-; Bus Mgmt.

**ANNESE, MARIANNE,** Univ Of Sc At Columbia, Columbia, SC; SO; BA; Alpha Chi Omega 90-; Jrnlsm/Advtsng/Pub Rltns.

**ANNIBALE, CURTIS B,** Old Dominion Univ, Norfolk, VA; SO; BS; IM Sccr Ftbl 89-; Mech Eng; Eng.

**ANNICET, DIAHANN O,** Clark Atlanta Univ, Atlanta, GA; FR; BBA; NAACP Mem Chr 90-; Bus Admin-Fnc; Fncl Exec.

**ANNIS, NICOLE T,** Norfolk St Univ, Norfolk, VA; SR; BS; BS Mary Washington Cllg 90; Food Sci-Ntrtn; Reg Dietn.

**ANNUNZIATA, ANTHONY MICHAEL,** Manhattan Coll, Bronx, NY; BS; St Lasalle Hon Soc 90; Deans Hon List 90; Sci; Engr.

**ANORMALIZA, ALEXANDRA,** City Univ Of Ny Baruch Coll, New York, NY; JR; BED; Tchrs Tomorrow; Gldn Key 90; Bsn Ed; Tchng.

**ANORUO, GODSON C,** Coppin St Coll, Baltimore, MD; JR; BA; AA Nw Comm Clg Balto 90; Mgmt Sci/Acctg; Sys Anlyst.

**ANSARI, SALMAN A,** Univ Of Sc At Columbia, Columbia, SC; JR; BS; SGA Awds Com; SGA Hrseshoe Hist Restrtn Com; Peer Cnslr; Drg/Alch Prog 89; Tau Beta Pi 90-; Gldn Ky 89-; Phi Eta Sigma 89-; Engr Schlrshp 90-; Elec Engr.

**ANSARI, TEHZEEB,** Elmira Coll, Elmira, NY; JR; BA; Lgsltve Brd Stdnt Govt 88-; Reps Intl Clb 88-; Stdnt Nwsppr; Jdcl Brd Class Rep 89-; Acdmc Cncrn Comm Class Rep 88-89; Prsdntl Acdmc Ftnss Awd 86-87; Cncr Ptnts Aid Assn 87-88; Tchng Fllw Pltcl Sci 90-; Tchng Fellow Hindi; Rtry Exchng; Intrntnl Studies; Intrntnl Rltns.

**ANSARI, VIRGINIA M,** Comm Coll Algny Co Algny Cmps, Pittsburgh, PA; GD; MSN; Phi Theta Kappa; RN Hbg Hosp Schl Nsng 63; BS; Nrsng; MS Nrsg Admin.

**ANSELL, DEBORAH L,** Strayer Coll, Washington, DC; SR; BS; Alpha Chi; Bus Admin; Mktg.

**ANSELM, DARLENE A,** Comm Coll Algny Co Algny Cmps, Pittsburgh, PA; SO; ASSOC; RN Nrsng.

**ANSELMENT, AMY E,** Le Moyne Coll, Syracuse, NY; FR; BA; Karate Clb 90-; Chrldg 90-; Bsn.

**ANSHUS, KAY L,** Univ Of Sc At Columbia, Columbia, SC; SO; BA; Gamma Bata Phi; Bus; CPA.

**ANSLEY, JAMES R,** Ms Coll, Clinton, MS; GD; JD; Law Stdnt Bar Assoc Pres 88-; Moot Ct Brd 90-; Phi Delta Phi 88-; Vlybl Sftbl 89-; BS N Caro St Univ 84; M Ag Ed Clemson Univ 88; Law.

**ANSZELOWICZ, DANIEL A,** Dowling Coll, Oakdale Li, NY; SR; Sch Newspaper Editing; Alpha Chi 90-; Peer Tutoring Svcs Tutor; Cmptr Ctr Lab Aid; Boces Ofc Automation Intern Pgmr; IM Soccer; Cmptr Sci; Pgmr.

**ANTALIK, CHRISTINE,** Western New England Coll, Springfield, MA; SO; BS; Comm Pgrgrmmng Entrtnmnt 89-90; Peer Alcohol Resrc Tm 89-90; Alpha Lambda Delta 90-; Deans Lst 89-; Bus; Acctg.

**ANTAR, JAMAL,** Central St Univ, Wilberforce, OH; SO; BA; Yrbk Artst 90-; All Amer Schlr 89-90; Alpha Pi Alpha; Cmmrcl Art; Bus Admn.

**ANTCZAK, TERESA,** Newbury Coll, Brookline, MA; SO; BA; Clss Rep; Phi Theta Kappa; Dns Lst 88-; Law.

**ANTENUCCI, NATALIE SABINA,** Temple Univ, Philadelphia, PA; SR; BBA; Natl Assn Actnts; Phi Theta Kappa 89; Beta Gamma Sigma; Beta Alpha Psi 90-; Alpha Phi Pen/Beta Alpha Psi Edtr Templ Univ; Gross Lambers CPA Rvw Rep 90-; Natl Assn Actnts Mnscrpt Cntst Awd; AGS Mntgmry Cnty Comm Coll 89; Acctg; CPA.

**ANTHEY, ASHOK,** City Univ Of Ny Baruch Coll, New York, NY; SO.

**ANTHONY, KARLYN M,** S U N Y Coll At Postdam, Potsdam, NY; FR; BA; Intvars Chrstn Flwshp 90-; Msc Edctrs Natl Conf 90-; Chrs 90-; Phnx Clb 90-; Pres Schlrs Pgm 90-; Breaky Piano Schlp; Pres Schlr; NY St Schl Msc Asc St Conf 90; Msc Educ.

**ANTHONY, MELISSA A,** Marshall University, Huntington, WV; SR; BBA; Amer Mktg Asc Pres; Res Hl Adv Cncl Treas; Phi Eta Sigma 88-; Gamma Beta Phi 89-; Dns Lst 88-; IM Mgr 90-; Mktg.

**ANTHONY, MELISSA ANN,** Meridian Comm Coll, Meridian, MS; FR; Med Lab Tech; Med Lab Tech.

**ANTHONY, MICHAEL W,** Md Coll Of Art & Design, Silver Spring, MD; SO.

**ANTHONY, MICHELLE L,** Catawba Valley Comm Coll, Hickory, NC; SO; AASC; Gamma Beta Phi; Ed; Elem Schl Tchr.

**ANTHONY, NICOLE V,** Alcorn St Univ, Lorman, MS; FR; Dns Lst; Nrsng; Anethesist.

**ANTHONY, PATRICIA J,** Univ Of Tn At Knoxville, Knoxville, TN; FR; BS; Phi Theta Kappa 85-; Andrew Johnson Papers Ed Asst 82-; AAS Pellissippi State Tech Cmnty Clg 89; CPS Inst Certifying Secr 88; Bsn Adm.**

**ANTHONY, PERRY C,** Thomas Nelson Comm Coll, Hampton, VA; FR; BSEE; Cyprus Bnnvlnt Soc 90-; Yng Adlt Leauge 90-; Rugby; Phi Theta Kappa; Order Of Ahepa 90-; Norfolk Food Bnk; Sovran Bank C/S Career Tm; Elec Engr; Robotics/Vision Dgtl Image.

**ANTHONY IV, RAYMOND B,** Thomas Nelson Comm Coll, Hampton, VA; GD; BA; AAS; Bus.

**ANTHONY, ROBYN K,** Ms St Univ, Miss State, MS; SO; BED; Choir 89-; MS Magic Show Chr 89-; Alpha Lambda Delta; Phi Eta Sigma; IM Sftbl 90; Elem Ed; Tchr.

**ANTHONY III, WILLIAM A,** Univ Of Nc At Charlotte, Charlotte, NC; JR; BA; Hnrbly Dschrgd Vet US Navy 83-87; Pltcl Sci; Law.

**ANTIGIOVANNI, TINA M,** Univ Of New Haven, West Haven, CT; JR; BS; Clnry Clb; Eta Sigma Delta; Htl/Rstrnt Mgmt; Htl Indstry.

**ANTJAS, SOPHIA C,** Oh St Univ At Marion, Marion, OH; FR; BA; Jrnlsm/Pblc Rltns.

**ANTLE, CYNTHIA K,** Union Coll, Barbourville, KY; SR; BS; Campus Actvts Bd 88-; Flwshp Of Chrstn Athlts 90-; One Of Top 12 Campus Women 90-; Edn; Teach.

**ANTOINE, MARY J,** Univ Of Miami, Coral Gables, FL; SR; BA; Mktg Clb 90-; Intl Org; Caribbean Org; Intl Flight Attndnt 78-87; Mktg; MBA.

**ANTOINE, WAYNE ANDERSON,** Middle Tn St Univ, Murfreesboro, TN; BA; Aerospace Maint Mngmnt.

**ANTOLIK, NANCY A,** Atlantic Comm Coll, Mays Landing, NJ; FR; AAS; Prfssnl Chfs Assoc 90-; Clnry Stdnts Assoc 90-; St Agns Chrch CYO Ldr 90-; Clnry Arts Chf.

**ANTONATOS, JERRY,** City Univ Of Ny La Guard Coll, Long Island Cty, NY; JR; BA; Amer Scty Notaries 89-; Acctng; Intl Acctng.

**ANTONELLI, KAREN M,** Univ Of Fl, Gainesville, FL; JR; BSBA; Rsdnc Hall Assn Flr Rep 88-89; Bsns Admnstrtn Clg Cncl 91-; George Wshngton Shotokan Karate Clb 89-90; Phi Kappa Phi; Delta Gamma 90-; Bsns; Finance.

**ANTONELLI, LINDA E,** Neumann Coll, Aston, PA; JR; Viva 88-89; Bus Clb 89-90; PICPA 90-; NAA 90-; Acctg.

**ANTONETTI, MICHAEL,** Univ Of Pittsburgh, Pittsburgh, PA; SR; BS; Amer Soc Mech Eng; Natl Soc Prof Eng; Tau Beta Pi; Mech Eng; Eng.

**ANTONIO, GREGORY S,** S U N Y Coll At Fredonia, Fredonia, NY; SR; Jdcl Bd Chrmn 89-; SG Repr 88-89; Budget/Approp Comm 88-89; Phi Sigma Alpha 90-; Tutor 89-90; Lacrosse Capt 87-; Law.

**ANTONIO, ROBERT L,** Hampton Univ, Hampton, VA; JR; BARCH; Amer Inst Archtctrl Stdnts 89-; Filippino-Amer Stdnt Assn; Archtctr; Archtctrl Dsgn.**

**ANTONIOU, NICOLAS M,** Kent St Univ Kent Cmps, Kent, OH; SO; BBA; Bsn.

**ANTONUCCI, MARIA A,** Seton Hall Univ, South Orange, NJ; JR; BSN; Stdt Nurses Assoc 90-; Sigma Theta Tau; White Roses VP 88-; So Orange Rescue Sqd 90-; Cmps Mnstry 88-; VA Schlr 90-; Athletic Trainer Rugby Tm 90-; Nursing.

**ANTUNES, PAULA F,** Tusculum Coll, Greeneville, TN; SO; BA; SGA Dorm Pres 90-; Ambassadors Chrpn 90-; Deans List 90; Vlybl 90-; Busn Adminf Bank Mgr MBA.

**ANTZOULIDOU, ANDROULLA G,** S U N Y Coll Of Tech At Frmgdl, Farmingdale, NY; SO; BA Suny Farmingdale; Bus; Acctg.

**ANZALONE, LORIN K,** S U N Y Coll Of Tech At Delhi, Delhi, NY; SR; MBA; AS; Psych.

**ANZALONE, SCOTT J,** Westminster Coll, New Wilmingtn, PA; SR; BS; Stdnt Govt Assn Sntr 87-89; Interfrat Cncl VP 89-90; Theatre Westminster; Mortar Brd; Omicron Delta Kappa; Beta Beta Beta VP 8 7-; Alpha Sigma Phi; Alpha Phi Omega Natl Svc Frat 87-91; Intrnshp Sweden Hosp 89; BS Westminster Clg 91; Bio/Moleclr; Med.

**ANZILOTTI, PAUL,** Manhattan Coll, Bronx, NY; GD; BSME; Soc Auto Eng; Am Soc Mech Eng; Alpha Delta Phi; Mech Eng; Engrng.

**AOKI, MOTOKO,** Duquesne Univ, Pittsburgh, PA; FR; Intl Std Org; Sclgy.

**APEL, CHRISTINE E,** Georgetown Coll, Georgetown, KY; SR; BA; Bapt Stdnt Un 87-; Bapt Young Women V P 87-90; Drama Club V P 87-90; Campus Drug & Alcohol Task Force 90-; Phi Mu Otstndng Sr Of Yr Sec 88-; SCAD Intrnshp 89-90; Coll Schlrshp 87-88; L & P Gaines Schlrshp; R K Larue Schlrshp; Sociology; Soc Work.

**APEL, KRISTEN L,** Kent St Univ Kent Cmps, Kent, OH; JR; BA; Ski Clb 88-90; Alpha Lambda Delta 88; Outstndg Clg Stdnts Amer 88-90; Alpha Phi 88-; Bsn; Mktg/Mgmt.**

**APEL, TIMOTHY W,** Kent St Univ Kent Cmps, Kent, OH; GD; MBA; Beta Alpha Psi Treas 88-; Acctg Assn 88-; Natl Assn Accnts 88-; Grad Mgt Assn 90-; Delta Tau Delta Chrmn 87-90; CPA Exam 90; Intrnshp Ernst/Young; Intrnshp Deloitte/Touche; BBA 90; Schlstc Achvmnt Awd 89; Deans List 88-90; Acctg.

**APICELLA, MARK V,** Broward Comm Coll, Ft Lauderdale, FL; SO; AS; Drv/Oper/Parmdc W/Fire-Rescue Dept; AS 89; Fire Sci Tech; Fire Rscue Svc Mgmt.

**APO, ALLYSON K,** Georgetown Univ, Washington, DC; JR; BS; Intl Mgmnt.

**APOL, MARY R,** William Paterson Coll, Wayne, NJ; SR; MA; Chrstn Rfmd Chrch Plng Comm 89; Dctrs Offc 89-90; Slvtn Army Hm 86; BS Calvin Clg 78; Cnslng.

**APOLLONIO, THOMAS,** Me Maritime Academy, Castine, ME; JR; BS; Marine Eng.

**APOLONIA, MARIA M,** Seton Hall Univ, South Orange, NJ; SO; NRSG.

**APONTE DUCHESENE, INES,** Inter Amer Univ Pr San Juan, Hato Rey, PR; GD; JD; Piano Tchr; Exec Sec; BA Univ Puerto Rico 86; Hum/Music; Law.

**APONTE FIGUEORA, FELIX J,** Univ Of Pr Cayey Univ Coll, Cayey, PR; FR; BS; Bio; Med.

**APONTE OSORIO, STEVEN V,** Bayamon Tech Univ Coll, Bayamon, PR; JR; BA; Hnr Roll; AS 90; Digtl Elec; Elec Eng.

**APONTE PAGAN, JESINETTE,** Inter Amer Univ Pr Hato Rey, Hato Rey, PR; SR; BA; CIRPE Treas 87-89; Pre Schl Educ; Tchng.

**APONTE, CARMEN A,** City Univ Of Ny Hostos Coll, Bronx, NY; AA; Spcl Ed; Spcl Ed Prfssr.

**APONTE, CELIA I,** Univ Of Pr At Mayaguez, Mayaguez, PR; JR; BA; Am Inst Chem Engs 89-; Eng Hon Roll 88-; Chem Eng.

**APONTE, ILIANA,** Univ Of Pr Cayey Univ Coll, Cayey, PR; SO; Rctr Hnrs 89-; Educ Serv Pgm Hnr 89-.

**APONTE, INALVIS,** Univ Of Pr Cayey Univ Coll, Cayey, PR; FR; Acctg.

**APONTE, KIMBERLY J,** Oh Univ, Athens, OH; FR; BAS; Campus Radio Network 90; Telecmnctns; Audio Telecmnctns.

**APONTE, LEILA M,** Univ Of Pr At Mayaguez, Mayaguez, PR; GD; BS; Circle Premedic; Soc Stdnts Inds Microbiology; Pre-Medics; Medicine.**

**APONTE, LYDIA E,** Univ Of Pr At Rio Piedras, Rio Piedras, PR; JR; BA; Frnds Of Origami Cntr Of Amer; Pre Law; Law.**

**APONTE, MARTHA P,** Ny Institute Of Tech Ny City, New York, NY; JR; BA; Peer Mntr 90; Dns Hnr Rl 88-; NU Ypsilon Tau; Archtctr.**

**APONTE, VICTOR L,** Inter Amer Univ Pr Hato Rey, Hato Rey, PR; SO; BBA; Assn De Estudiantes De Contabilidad; Univ Hnr Sq 90-; Acctg.

**APONTE, VIRGEN M,** Univ Del Turabo, Gurabo, PR; GD; BA; Univ Hnrs 88-; Magna Cum Laude.

**APONTE, XAVIER F,** Univ Politecnica De Pr, Hato Rey, PR; SO; BS; Air Frc ROTC 88-; Phi Zeta Chi 89-; Impulso 90; Movimeinto Cursillo De Cristiandad 90-; Deans List 90-; Mech Engr; AF Pilot.

**APP, LAWRENCE J,** Daytona Beach Comm Coll, Daytona Beach, FL; SO; BMED; Accomp/Comp DBCC Soc 89-; Cert Of Merit In Lit 89-90; Cert Of Merit In Educ 90-; BMI Writer/Pub; Musician/Band Ldr; Music.

**APPALSAMMY, DANE L,** Middle Tn St Univ, Murfreesboro, TN; SR; BS; Assn Cmptgmchnry Cache Dir 88-; Comp Sci Intrnshp Comp Pgmr 89-; Outstndg Sr Comp Sci 90-; Comp Sci Alumni Awd 89-90; Outstndng Soph Comp Sci 88-89; Comp Sci; Comp Pgmr.

**APPELIAN, MARY ANN,** Broward Comm Coll, Ft Lauderdale, FL; GD; AS; LPN William Mc Fatter Voc Schl 90; Nrsg; Nrsg/Trvl Ntnly.

**APPELKVIST, CAROLYN M,** Fl International Univ, Miami, FL; JR; BA; Future Edctrs Amer 90-; Kappa Delta Pi 90-; AA Miami-Dade Cmnty Clg 90; Ed; Elem Sch Tchr.

**APPELROUTH, LISA B,** Va Commonwealth Univ, Richmond, VA; SR; BA; Psy; Scl Wrk.

**APPERSON, CATHY J,** Meridian Comm Coll, Meridian, MS; SO; BA; Nrsng.

**APPERSON, KAREN L,** Coll Of Charleston, Charleston, SC; JR; BS; Zeta Ta Alpha 89-90; Socilgy.

**APPIA, TRACY D,** Miami Dade Comm Coll North, Miami, FL; SO; BA; Psychlgy.

**APPLE, STACI J,** Central Pa Bus School, Summerdale, PA; FR; Trvl Clb 90-; Bwlng; Trvl Agnt.

**APPLEBY, ALISON S,** Columbia Greene Comm Coll, Hudson, NY; FR; BA; Fine Arts.

**APPLEBY, DEBORAH E,** Wellesley Coll, Wellesley, MA; FR; BA; Cmps Girl Scts 90-; Frnch/Math; Doctor.

**APPLEGATE, BARBARA A,** Georgian Court Coll, Lakewood, NJ; SR; BS; Mendel Soc 89-; Sigma Delta Mu 88-89; Soccr All St Scnd Team 90-; Schlr Athlt 89-90; Deans Lst 89-90; Soccr Capt 89-; AA Ocean Co Coll 89; Biolgy; Tchng.

**APPLEGATE, MARY R,** Va Commonwealth Univ, Richmond, VA; JR; BSN; Intrvrsty Chrstn Flwshp Large Grp Coord; Nrsng.

**APPOLD, WAYNE H,** New Comm Coll Of Baltimore, Baltimore, MD; FR; AA; Sci And Biotech Clb Treas Sec 90-; Stdnt Govt Advsry Brd Fr Clbs 90-; SHOPS Tutor 90-; Sci Lrnng Cntr 90-; Earth Sci; Scntst.

**APTT, VALERIE L,** De Tech & Comm Coll At Dover, Dover, DE; SO; AAS; Human Serv Org 90-; Intrnshp At Risk Youth Grp Ldr 90-; Human Serv; Chld Thrpst.

**APUZZO, ROSEMARY E,** Albertus Magnus Coll, New Haven, CT; SR; BA; Alpha Simga Lambda; Tau Pi Phi; AS Gen Bus Quinnipiac Coll 79; Bus/Econ; Advrtsng.

**AQUILA, LOUISE A,** Kent St Univ Kent Cmps, Kent, OH; FR; PHD; Bio Clb 90-; Alpha Epsilon Pi 90; Karate 90-; Bio; Pre-Med.

**AQUILINA, DONNA L,** Georgian Court Coll, Lakewood, NJ; SR; BS; Bsns Admn; Mrktng/Sls.

**AQUILINA, SISTER TERESA,** Spalding Univ, Louisville, KY; SR; BED; Tchr RCIA 87-88; Ldr Renew Grp In Parish 88-89; Ldr Lit Grp Parish 87-89; Vol Wrk As Catechist; Bsktbl Coach; PTA 87-89; Tchr; State Dept Of Educ 60; Engl; Elem Tchr.

**AQUINO, ADETTE A,** Univ Of Pr At Rio Piedras, Rio Piedras, PR; JR; BBA; Pblc Politc Org 87; LETA 88; Ntl Stdnt Exchng 90; Acctg; Law.

**AQUINO, MARIE J,** Duquesne Univ, Pittsburgh, PA; GD; BSBA; Chrstn Clb 88; Stdnt Acctg Assn 88-90; Beta Alpha Phi 89-90; Phi Theta Kappa 87-88; Phi Chi Theta 88-90; P Marwck Main Co Intrnshp 89-90; Deans Lst 86-90; Competitv Schlrshp 89; Bus Schl Schlrshp 89; AA Comm Coll Allegheny Co 88; Acctg; CPA.

**ARABIO, JOHN L,** Hudson Valley Comm Coll, Troy, NY; SO; BS; AS; Bus Admin.

**ARAGHI, SASAN S,** Methodist Coll, Fayetteville, NC; GD; BS; Mgmnt; Architecture Eng.

**ARAGON, MONICA G,** Univ Of Akron, Akron, OH; SO; BA; Intl Bus Club 90-; Ch Omega Prsnl Chm 89-; Mrktng/Intl Bus; Mrkt Rsrch.

**ARAI, YOSHIMASA,** Newbury Coll, Brookline, MA; FR; BA; Konan Univ Field Hcky Tm 87-90; Prz Contrbtn Field Hcky 89; BA Economics 90; Business Admin.

**ARAKAWA, TAKASHI,** Lees Coll, Jackson, KY; SO; Ed; Engl Tchr Japan.

**ARAKELIAN, CHRISTINE A,** Villanova Univ, Villanova, PA; FR; BA; Lit Mag 90-; Sesquicentennial Cmtee Undgrd Rep 90-; Piano Cmpstn Prfrmnc 90-; Hstry/Music; Music Cmpsition.

**ARAMINOWICZ, HANNA,** Medical Univ Of Sc, Charleston, SC; SR; DMD; ASDA 88-; Oral Bio Jrnl Clb 90; Omicron Kappa Upsilon; Psi Omega 90; DMD Akademia Medyczna Gdansk Poland 83; Denstry.

**ARANGALA, ADHEESHA S,** Univ Of Ky, Lexington, KY; FR; BS; Math Sci; Statistics.

**ARANOFF, RONALD J,** Yeshiva Univ, New York, NY; JR; BA; Yrbk Edtr 91-; Nwsppr Sprts Edtr 90-; Dan Lst 89-; Ramaz H S Bsktbl Head Coach 90-; IM Bsktbl Tm Capt 90-; Hstry; Law.

**ARAQUE, CELIAH A,** Fl St Univ, Tallahassee, FL; JR; BS; Golden Key 90; Phi Kappa Phi; Phi Beta Kappa; Kappa Delta 88-90; Intrntl Affairs/Spanish; BA Bsnss.

**ARATINGI, ROBERT N,** Villanova Univ, Villanova, PA; BA; Assoc Commuting Stdnts 88-90; Republicans V P 88-; Radio 90-; Phi Alpha Theta Chrmn Conv; Dns Lst 90-; Hstry; Lawyer.

**ARAUJO, LIZA MICHELLE,** Bowie St Univ, Bowie, MD; SR; BS; Psychlgy Sclgy Anthrplgy Clb; Bg Brthr Bg Sstr; Hll Cncl; Psi Chi Psychlgy VP 90-; Alpha Delta Mu; Alpha Kappa Alpha Mmbrshp Chr 90-; Alpha Kappa Alpha Mmbrshp Chr 90-; Magna Cum Laude; Rsdnt Asst Yr; Prgrmmr Yr 89-90; Asst Grdt Prgm; Psychlgy.

**ARAV, ADRIAN J,** S U N Y Coll Of Tech At Frmgdl, Farmingdale, NY; SO; Dfndrs Of Anmls 90-; Un Actn Anmls; Sftbl; Aerntcs; Pilot.

**ARAYA, GREGORY M,** Savannah Coll Of Art & Design, Savannah, GA; JR; BFA; Kinetic Intactv Sclptr 90; Illstrtn.

**ARBAUGH, ANDREW C,** Univ Of Louisville, Louisville, KY; FR; BA; Mdl Schl Bsktbl Coach; IM Bsktbl; Elec Eng.

**ARBENA, ROBIN D,** Coll Of Charleston, Charleston, SC; JR; BS; Psych Clb Co Pres 879; Felwshp Chrstn Athletes 90-; United Way 90; Pscylgy; Cnslng Industrial.

**ARBIA, LAURIE A,** Alfred Univ, Alfred, NY; FR; BA; Rescue Squad; Alpha Phi Omega; Performing Arts; Acting/Singing.

**ARBINO, AMY K,** Northern Ky Univ, Highland Hts, KY; JR; Actvts Pgmng Brd Hmcmng Cmt 89; SGA Ofc Admn 90; Norse Ldrshp Scty Pres; Kentucky State Stdnt Rep Natl Assc Cmps Actvts; Hmcmng Ct 90; SGA Rep Yr 90; SGA Exec Cncl Mbr Yr; Psychlgy/Hmn Svc; Clg Stdnt Prsnl.

**ARBOGAST, KARYN E,** Kent St Univ Stark Cmps, North Canton, OH; FR; BS; Stdnt Ambsdrs 90-; Alpha Lambda Delta 90-; Dns Lst 90-; Vlybl; Elec Engr.

**ARBOGAST, MICHELE D,** James Madison University, Harrisonburg, VA; JR; BS; Dnc Thtr VP 89-; Cntmpry Dnc Ensmbl 89-; Gldn Key 89-; Kappa Delta Pi 89-; Cntr Serv Lrng 89-; Trnsfr Trnsfr Pgm 90-; Beth Hefner Memrl Schlrshp Awd 90-; Pres/Deans Lsts 89-; Mddl Schl Educ/Tch.

**ARBOLEDA, LISBETH,** Fayetteville St Univ, Fayetteville, NC; SO; BS; Ch Jesus Chrst Ltr Day Snts Nursery Assn; Sunbeam Tchr; Chancellors Lst 89-; Excell Hispanic Studies; Cert Achvmnt; Spnsh Edn; Teach.

**ARBOLEDA, MONICA A,** City Univ Of Ny La Guard Coll, Long Island Cty, NY; SO; BA; Phi Theta Kappa Sec 88-90; Scty Hspnc Prfsnl Eng Tres 90-; Scty Wmn Eng 90-; Amer Inst Chem Eng 90-; Dlt Heta Sisterhood; Rsrch Asstnt Laguardia Comm Clg 88-90; Lab Techcn 89-90; Exxon Intrnshp; AS Laguardia Comm Clg 90; Chem Eng.

**ARCADIPANE, LISA A,** S U N Y Coll At Fredonia, Fredonia, NY; SR; BA; Phi Alpha Theta; ASS Jamestown Comm Coll 89; Soc Studies Edn; Teach.

**ARCANGELO, CHRISTINA P,** Marywood Coll, Scranton, PA; JR; Tchrs Tomorrow 90-; Prsdnts Awd Penn State 88; Deans Lst Frst Hnrs 90-; Abington Cmmnty Library Brd 75-80; Bicentennial Comm Chrmn Chldrns Actvts 76; Ntnl Assn Italian American Wmn PA Rdng Assn 90-; Elem Edctn; Tchr.

**ARCARO, GREGORY F,** Mount Saint Mary Coll, Newburgh, NY; SO; BA; Stdnt Jdcl Bd Assoc Jstc; Engl; Law.

**ARCE, RINA-ELIZABETH,** Seminole Comm Coll, Sanford, FL; FR; AA; Elem Ed.

**ARCE-ALMENA, MARIA T,** Univ Of Pr At Rio Piedras, Rio Piedras, PR; SR; BA; Prog De Estds De Hnr 88-; Ltn Amer Stds; Law And Cmmnctns.

**ARCEMENT, CHRISTOPHER B,** Univ Of Southern Ms, Hattiesburg, MS; SO; BS; Hnrs Stdnt Assn 90-; Gamma Beta Phi 89-; Phi Eta Sigma 89-; Microbiology; Med.

**ARCHACKI, PATTI,** Neumann Coll, Aston, PA; SO; BA; Stu Govt Assn Fresh Pres 89-; Educ Clb 90-; Elem Educ; Tchng.

**ARCHAMBAULT, CHRISTOPHER R,** Rutgers St Un At New Brunswick, New Brunswick, NJ; FR; BSEE; Sccr Clb 90-; Phi Eta Sigma 90-; Deans Lst 90-; Cmptr; Engr.

**ARCHAMBAULT, CLAUDE M,** Embry Riddle Aeronautical Univ, Daytona Beach, FL; JR; BS; Hitting Awd 89; Vrsty Bsebl 88-; Aircraft Eng Tech; Aeronautical Engr.

**ARCHAMBAULT, DENISE J,** Fl International Univ, Miami, FL; JR; Hosptlty Mgt; Law Sch.

**ARCHAMBAULT, LYNN M,** D Youville Coll, Buffalo, NY; SO; BS; Ed Clb 90-; Lena S Michaels Mem Awd Spec Ed 89-90; AAS Cayuga Cmnty Clg 90; Spcl Edctn; Spcl Edctn Tchr.

**ARCHER, DAVID W,** Univ Of Ky, Lexington, KY; SO; BS; Co-Op IBM; Cmptr Sci; Prgmmng.**

**ARCHER, FERNANDE R,** Bloomfield Coll, Bloomfield, NJ; JR; Exec Brd VP 89-; African Amer Assoc 88-; Fine Prfrmng Arts Clb; Vlybl 90; Soclgy; Med Soc Wkr.

**ARCHER, PAULA C,** Christopher Newport Coll, Newport News, VA; SR; BSA; Alpha Chi; Alpha Kappa Psi VP 90-; Acctng.

**ARCHER, STEVEN J,** Southern Coll Of Tech, Marietta, GA; JR; AS; Civil Engr.

**ARCHER, TIFFANY L,** Paine Coll, Augusta, GA; SO; Ntnl Ed Assc; Ed/Erly Chldhd; Tchr K/4.

**ARCHEY, RITA M,** Wv Northern Comm Coll, Wheeling, WV; SO; AAS; Slmni Assn Serv Comm 90-; Sec Sci; Med Sec.

**ARCHIBALD, ALVA M,** Fl A & M Univ, Tallahassee, FL; SO; PHD; Psychology Clb 90-; Psychology Hnr Soc 90-; Clinical Psychologist.

**ARCHIE, SHIRLECEIA C,** Stillman Coll, Tuscaloosa, AL; FR; BS; Rtract Clb 90-; Untd Negro Col Fnd Chpln Pub Mgr 90-; Ntl Assoc Advncmnt Clrd People Sec 90-; Pre Prof Sci Clb 90-; Yrbk Stf 90-; Cordell Wynn; Gamma Iota Sigma; Alpha Swthrt; Chnclrt Scl Clb; Cpstn Smmr 89; Pre Med; Pediatrcn.**

**ARCHILLA, LISA M,** Fl International Univ, Miami, FL; JR; BA; Elementary Education.

**ARCHULETA, ELAINE M,** Univ Of Sc At Columbia, Columbia, SC; JR; BA; Hall Cncl Wmns Rsdnce Ctr/New Mexico State Univ V P 89; Club Mgrs Assn Amer V P 90-; Natl Stdnt Exch Assn V P 90; Hotel/Rstrnt/Trsm Admin; Club Mgmt.

**ARCHUNG, KEITH T,** Saint Josephs Coll, Windham, ME; SO; BED; Eleme Ed; Tchng.

**ARCIA, RICHARD J,** Fl Atlantic Univ, Boca Raton, FL; SR; BA; Beta Alpha Psi Treas; VITA 88-89; BS Adm Chapman Clg 82; MBA Finance CA State Univ San Bernardino 85; Acctg.

**ARCORACI, LISA A,** S U N Y Coll At Fredonia, Fredonia, NY; SR; BS; Ed Clb; Lbrty Prtnrshp Gd90; Orgnzd Ski Trps 90-; Kappa Delta Pi 90-; Deans Lst 88-; Kappa Delta Pi 90-; Elem Ed.

**ARD, DEREK B,** Faulkner St Jr Coll, Bay Minette, AL; SO; BS; Pow Wow; Phi Theta Kappa; Eng.

**ARD-JORDAN, ANITA D,** Univ Of South Al, Mobile, AL; SR; MBS; Alpha Lambda Delta 88; Cttge Hll Bapt Chrch Chr 90; Tchr 90; Sub Tchr 90-; BS; Elem Educ; Tchng.**

**ARDEN, ELISA,** Univ Of Nc At Charlotte, Charlotte, NC; FR; BA; Phi Eta Sigma; Audvsl Comms; Flm Mkr/Prod.

**ARDO, ANDREW J,** Kent St Univ Kent Cmps, Kent, OH; SR; BA; Phi Sigma Alpha; Pol Sci/Intl Rel; Muscl Career/Law Schl.

**ARDOIN, TODD A,** Fl Atlantic Univ, Boca Raton, FL; GD; Phi Kappa Phi 90; Coral Sprgs Chmbr Commerce; Florida Detary Public; Bnk Emply 88-89; BA Louisiana State Univ 87; Acctg; Legal.

**ARDOVINO, BARBARA A,** Univ Of Al At Birmingham, Birmingham, AL; SR; BS; Deans List 87-; Pres Hon 90-; Ed; Tchng/Cnslng.

**ARDREY, PHILIP D,** Liberty Univ, Lynchburg, VA; JR; BS; Alpha Lambda Delta 88-; Acctng.

**AREAN, IVONNE G,** Fl International Univ, Miami, FL; JR; BA; Psi Chi 90-; Phi Kappa Phi 90-; Psych; Med Sch.

**AREHEART, LYNDA M,** Comm Coll Algny Co Algny Cmps, Pittsburgh, PA; SO; ASN; Phi Theta Kappa; Frnds Of Lbrry Chrmn 87-; Nrsng.

**AREHEART, MELISSA LORICK,** Univ Of Sc At Columbia, Columbia, SC; JR; BA; Mothers Before Marriage Fndr 86-; Personal Growth Grp Co-Ldr 89-; AA Midlands Tech Coll 90; Psychlgy; Cnslr Adolescents.

**AREL, MARC A,** Univ Of Miami, Coral Gables, FL; SO; BA; Psych; Medcl Schl.

**ARELLANO, BOBBIE J,** Univ Of Va Clinch Valley Coll, Wise, VA; JR; BS; AAS VI Highlands Cmnty Clg 87; Psych/Sclgy; Psych.

**ARENA, LEE ANN,** Fl International Univ, Miami, FL; JR; BS; Stdnt Dietc Assoc 90-; Broward Dietc Assoc 90-; Amer Dietc Assoc Stdnt Undrgrd Comm 90-; Phi Kappa Phi; Stdnt Hons Mntr Prog; Dietcs/Nutrn; Res.

**ARENA, MARGARET A,** Wagner Coll, Staten Island, NY; JR; BA; Concert/Pep Band; Jazz Ensemble; Woodwind Ensemble; Omicron Delta Kappa; Aletha; Epsilon Delta Omicron Soc/Rush Chair; Res Hall Cncl Exec Bd Publ Rel; Engl/Edn/Music; Tchr.

**ARENA, NICHOLAS J,** Nova Univ, Ft Lauderdale, FL; GD; Corp Spnsr Mk Wsh Fndtn Broward Chptr 89-; Mkt Sprvsr Brown Forman Bvrg Co 84-; BA Mktg Univ S Fl 83; MBA; Mgmt/Mktg; Internatl Mktg Mgmt.

**ARENADO, EDNA M,** Central Fl Comm Coll, Ocala, FL; JR; BA; Schl Vol Grace Epscpl Schl 90-; Scl Wrkr 73-78; BA Interamerican Univ Hato Rey Puerto Rico 73; Scl Work; Pharmacy.

**ARENT, HEATHER A,** Newbury Coll, Brookline, MA; FR; PAL; Fash Mrchndsng.

**ARESTA, CHRISTINE LYNN,** Fl International Univ, Miami, FL; JR; BS; Thrpy Cls 92 VP; Deans Lst; APTA; AS 88; Phys Thrpy.

**ARFSTROM, JOSEPH J,** Nova Univ, Ft Lauderdale, FL; GD; MBA; Toastmasters Beuspeakers Bureau Treas; IEEE 88-; Eta Kappa Nu 89-; Pi Mu Epsilon 89-; Coopr Ed Exem Perf Awd 90; Baseball 88-90; BSEE Univ Fl 90; Computers Commtns; Engrg.

**ARGENTO, CHRISTOPHER W,** Wv Univ, Morgantown, WV; JR; BS; Amer Inst Of Aeron/Astron 89-; Pi Mu Epsilon 90-; IM Ftbl; Aero Engr.

**ARGERSINGER, MICHELLE E,** Cornell Univ Statutory College, Ithaca, NY; SO; BS; Crnl Cthlc Comm Echrstc; Big Brthr Big Sstr Mnstr 89-; Vet Stdnts Assn; Alpha Phi Stwrd; Smmr Intrnshp Phldlphia Zoo; Pre Vet Biology; DVM.

**ARGIRO, DOMINICK P,** Dowling Coll, Oakdale Li, NY; JR; BBA; Acctg Soc 90-; Alpha Chi; Co-Op Intrnshp; Acctg; CPA.

**ARGO, MELISSA G,** Univ Of Tn At Martin, Martin, TN; FR; BED; Ldr Rsdnce Pgm 90; Girl Scouts 90; Alpha Delta Pi Spirit Chrmn 90; Dns Lst Hghst Hnrs 90; Hlth Sci; Nrsg.

**ARGOLO, RENEE O,** Memphis St Univ, Memphis, TN; SO; BBA; Mgmt Intl Bus; Bus Admn.

**ARGOTTI, LEONARD,** Comm Coll Algny Co Algny Cmps, Pittsburgh, PA; SO; ASSOC; Kappa Sigma IUP 88-89; Sci/Nclr Med; Nuc Med Tech.

**ARGYRIS, GREGORY,** S U N Y Coll Of Tech At Frmgdl, Farmingdale, NY; FR; ASSOC; Flying School Private Pilot License 85-; Aircraft Maintenance; Aviation Mgmnt.

**ARIAS BASABE, JULIO A,** Inter Amer Univ Pr Hato Rey, Hato Rey, PR; FR; Bsktbl Tm 90-; Medl Tchnlgy.

**ARIAS, JENNIFER S,** City Univ Of Ny Baruch Coll, New York, NY; SO; BBA; Inrds NYC Inc 89; Hispanic Clb 90; Mentoring Prog; Acctg Intrnshp 89-; Acctg.

**ARIDAS, CARL J,** City Univ Of Ny Baruch Coll, New York, NY; SR; BBA; Chs Clb Treas 87-; Econ/Fnce Soc 87-; Beta Gamma Sigma 90; Golden Key 89-; Omicron Delta Epsilon; Econ; Fince.

**ARIETA, GERALDINE M,** Inter Amer Univ Pr Hato Rey, Hato Rey, PR; FR; BA; Finance/Acctng/Mrktng; MBA Mrktng.

**ARIGO, MARK T,** Univ Of Pittsburgh, Pittsburgh, PA; SO; BS; Amrcn Soc Mchncl Engnrs; Lambda Sigma Rgnl Comm Chrprst 90-; Phi Eta Sigma 90-; Hnrs Deans Lst 89-; Wayne Rawley Schlrshps 89-; Intrnshps State Wrk Stdy Prgrm 90-; Mchncl Engnrng.

**ARIOLA, KELLY M,** Le Moyne Coll, Syracuse, NY; JR; BA; Mktg Club 90-; Deans List 90-; Bus/Ed; Eductnl Admnstrtr.

**ARISTIZABAL, JUAN CAMILO,** Central Fl Comm Coll, Ocala, FL; SO; Campus Dplmts 90-; Bus Admin; Stckbrkr Intl Fin Mktng.

**ARIZAGA, ROSA A,** City Univ Of Ny Baruch Coll, New York, NY; JR; BA; Deans Lst 89; Cmptr Sci; Syst Analysis.

**ARJUNE, UMAH,** City Univ Of Ny Baruch Coll, New York, NY; SR; BA; Soclgy Hnr Socty; Krim-Benjmn Prize/Excllnc In Soclgy; Endwmnt Fnd Prvst Schlrshp 89; Yrkvll Cmmn Pntry/ Soup Ktchn; Sociology.

**ARKAAH, YAABA EKUA,** Clark Atlanta Univ, Atlanta, GA; SO; BA; Trailblazer; Psychology; Social Administration.

**ARLING, KEVIN T,** Radford Univ, Radford, VA; FR; BS; Inter Rsdnc Hll Cncl Hll Rep; Wrtng Awrd Northern Essex Comm Coll 89-90; Sprts Med; Physcl Thrpy.

**ARLOTTA, CHRISTOPHER J,** Teikyo Post Univ, Waterbury, CT; SR; Student Govt Assoc Pres 90-; Class Pres 89-90; Class Pres 88-89; Red Cross Bld Dr Vltr/Coord 89-90; Commty Assoc CT Vltr Painter 88-89; Aetna Life/Casualty Intshp 90; Accounting; Sales.

**ARMALY, SHONALEE A,** Fl A & M Univ, Tallahassee, FL; JR; BA; Michigan Clb 88-89; Radio Sta; Radio Announcer Freeport Bahamas 90; Jrnlsm; Brdcstg.

**ARMAND, ISABELLE C,** City Univ Of Ny Queensbrough, New York, NY; FR; Haitien Clb 90; Math; Comp Sci.

**ARMAND, JENNIFER N,** Miami Dade Comm Coll North, Miami, FL; SO; BA; Phi Theta Kappa Sec 90; AA; Pol Sci; Law.

**ARMANINI, DAVID A,** Cornell Univ, Ithaca, NY; FR; BS; Alpha Tau Omega; Bsebl; Lightweight Ftbl 90; Envir Tech.

**ARMBRISTER, CLIVE A,** Al A & M Univ, Normal, AL; SR; BSC; Intl Stdnts Assn Tr 90-; Carribbn Stdnts Assn Pr 90-; Natl Assn Blck Acctnts; Dept Acctg Top Schlr 90-91; Acctg.

**ARMBRUSTER, BRAD A,** Winthrop Coll, Rock Hill, SC; SO; BS; Vrsty Soccer 89-; Bus; Finance.

**ARMEL, WENDY S,** Comm Coll Algny Co Algny Cmps, Pittsburgh, PA; FR; BA; Exec Sec 87-; Completion Bradford Bus Sch 87; Comp Inf Sci; Bus.

**ARMENTEROS, SUZETTE,** Fl International Univ, Miami, FL; JR; BFA; Vsl Arts/Art Educ; Vsl Artst.

**ARMENTO, LINDA L,** Comm Coll Algny Co Algny Cmps, Pittsburgh, PA; SO; BA; Bus.

**ARMENTROUT, RICHARD P,** Wv Inst Of Tech, Montgomery, WV; FR; BSEE; Vrsty; Elctrcl Engnrng; Engnrng.

**ARMES, JANA L,** Middle Tn St Univ, Murfreesboro, TN; SR; Sngls Christian Fellowshp; Pi Sigma Epsilon 88-89; BBA; Bus Admn; Fincl Svcs.**

**ARMFIELD, LORRIE A,** Univ Of Md At Eastern Shore, Princess Anne, MD; SO; BA; Stdnt Gvmt Assc 89-; NAACP; Pre-Med Assc; Natl Hnrs Scty 90-; Amer Chem Scty 90-; Delta Sigma Theta VP 90-; Natl Merit Schlr 90-; Vrsty Chrldng Tm Cptn 89-; Dept Ntrl Sci Natl Schlr 90-; Pre-Med Blgy; Med-Peds.

**ARMIENTO, KRISTA T,** Fordham Univ, Bronx, NY; SR; BS; Beta Alpha Psi 89-; Beta Gamma Sigma 89-; Magna Cum Laude; Dns Lst; Pblc Acctng; CPA.

**ARMITAGE, CLAYTON D,** S U N Y Coll Of Tech At Alfred, Alfred, NY; FR; BT; Stdnt Senate; Eng; Cvl Serv.

**ARMITAGE, KIMBERLY A,** Edinboro Univ Of Pa, Edinboro, PA; FR; BA; Physcs/Engr Clb 90-; Mrchng Band 90-; Hnrs Pgm 90-; Physcs/Co-Op Engr.

**ARMITSTEAD, CRAIG C,** Bunker Hill Comm Coll, Boston, MA; SO; AD; Clnry Arts.

**ARMOGUM, ARLETTE,** City Univ Of Ny Baruch Coll, New York, NY; SR; BBA; Comp Qnttv; Mthdst Scty; Gldn Key; Comp Info Systms.

**ARMOND, ALICIA M,** Univ Of Southern Ms, Hattiesburg, MS; FR; BS; IMS 90-; Hnrs Coll 90-; Hnrs Stdnt Assoc 90-; Comp Eng.

**ARMOUR, DAVID C,** Liberty Univ, Lynchburg, VA; FR; BS; Liberty U Intercoll Debate Novice 90-; Intrn Cnty Of Summit Bdgt/Mgmt; Dns Lst 90-; Bus; Acctng.

**ARMOUR, DAVID M,** Savannah Coll Of Art & Design, Savannah, GA; SO; BARCH; Arch.

**ARMOUR, LEWIS B,** Univ Of Nc At Charlotte, Charlotte, NC; SO; BA; Psych Clb 89-90; Nwspr Rprtr 90-; Ntl Exchng 90-; Intrdscplnry Hons Pgm 89-90; Psych; Jurnlsm.

**ARMOUR, MARGARET L,** Columbus Coll Of Art & Design, Columbus, OH; FR; BA; Exhbt Preparator/Grphc Dsgnr CA Acad Of Sci San Francisco 85-90; Cert Grphc Dsgn Pgm U C Berkeley Extnsn 90; Advrtsng Dsgn; Grphc Dsgn.

**ARMOUR, SUSAN R,** Memphis St Univ, Memphis, TN; JR; BS; Hnrs Stdnt Assoc 90; Amrcn Chmcl Scty 89-; Stdnts Actvts Cncl 89-; Beta Beta Beta 90; Chi Beta Phi Pres; Delta Gamma 89-; Bapt Mem Hosp Vol; Blgy; Med.

**ARMS, ERIC S,** Univ Of Ky, Lexington, KY; JR; BA; Chemcl Depndcy Cnslr Chrtr Ridge Hosp 86-; Chem Depdncy KY St Brd Chem Dep 89-; Cnslrs Cert; Soc Wrk; Hlth Admn.

**ARMSTEAD III, HENRY,** Tuskegee Univ, Tuskegee Inst, AL; FR; BS; SADD 90-; Manonic FAAYM 87-; Chem Eng.

**ARMSTRONG, ANNE M,** Oh St Univ, Columbus, OH; SR; Alpha Lamda Delta; Arts Sci Awrd Excllnc Schlrshp 90; Summa Cum Laude; IM Rqtbll; IM Tnns Flg Ftbll 86-89; BA 90; Engl.

**ARMSTRONG, CARLIN M,** Clark Atlanta Univ, Atlanta, GA; FR; BA; Dorm Sen VP 90-; La Face Rcrds Inc Intrnshp Asst In A/R Dept 90-; Pol Sci; Sports/Entertnmnt Lawyr.

**ARMSTRONG, CAROLYN A,** Univ Of Miami, Coral Gables, FL; SO; BA; Engl; Univ Tchng/Schlrshp.

**ARMSTRONG, CYNTHIA K,** Embry Riddle Aeronautical Univ, Daytona Beach, FL; SR; BS; Deans Lst Lycoming Coll 84-85; GTE Prdcts Corp Process Eng 86-89; BA Lycoming Coll 86; Arntcl Sci; Pro Pilot.

**ARMSTRONG, DANIEL R,** Ms St Univ, Miss State, MS; FR; BS; Hall Cncl Flr Rep; Hons Prog; Phi Eta Sigma; Alpha Lambda Delta; Gamma Beta Phi; Coop Educ Stdnt With Dow Chemicals; Chem Engr.

**ARMSTRONG, DENNIS D,** Stark Tech Coll, Canton, OH; SO; Exec Sec Chrch Jesus Christ Of Lttr Dy Snts; Deans List 89-; USMC; DAV; Athl Sprts Med Trnr; Lcnsd Ins Agnt; MDA Tlthn; AS; Sml Bus/Cmptr Prgrmmg.**

**ARMSTRONG, DONALD W,** Va Commonwealth Univ, Richmond, VA; SO; BM; Singers Choral Arts Madrigals Opera Theatre; Otstndng Artist Awds 90-; Voice Perf; Opera Singer.

**ARMSTRONG, FONDA G,** Univ Of Tn At Martin, Martin, TN; SR; BS; STEA 90-; Gamma Beta Phi 88-89; Alpha Delta Pi 87-89; Elem Edn; Elem Tchr.

**ARMSTRONG, GLORIA K,** Ms St Univ, Miss State, MS; JR; Stu Advsry Comm Psy Dept; Psi Chi; Psych; Clncl.

**ARMSTRONG, GREGORY K,** Middle Tn St Univ, Murfreesboro, TN; FR; BA; Indstrl Engr.

**ARMSTRONG, HELEN R,** Univ Of Ga, Athens, GA; SR; MED; Univ Cncl Elect Clg 89-90; Intl Assoc Bsn Cmnctrs 89-90; Bapt Stdnt Union 86-90; Phi Beta Lambda Pres 89; Delta Gamma Actvts Chr 86-90; Circle K 89; GA Ctr Continuing Ed Intern; BSED 90; Bsn Ed; Trng.

**ARMSTRONG, JUAN L,** Univ Of Pr At Rio Piedras, Rio Piedras, PR; JR; BS; Pre Med Assc; Beta Beta Beta Treas 90-; Golden Key; Univ Puerto Rico Deans Hnr Lst; Bio; Med.

**ARMSTRONG, KARRIE L,** Gulf Coast Comm Coll, Panama City, FL; FR; BA; Lit Mag 90-; Newspaper 90-; Phi Theta Kappa Exec Bd 90-; Jrnlsm/Engl; Elem Ed Tchr.

**ARMSTRONG, KATHERINE N,** Va Commonwealth Univ, Richmond, VA; SR; BFA; Kuy Kendale Intrs Intrn 90-; Friends Of Art/VA Museum Of Fine Arts; Muses Carperter Cntr For Prfrmng Arts Chrmn Sls/Promotion 88-90; Admin Asst 86-90; BA Randolph Macon Coll 86; Cert J Sargent Reynolds Comm Coll 90; Art; Intr Dsgn.

**ARMSTRONG, KATHLEEN H,** Catawba Valley Comm Coll, Hickory, NC; SR; AAS; Gamma Beta Phi 90; Gamma Beta Phi 90; Qlty Utlgtn Mgmt NC 89-; Reg Nrs Clncl Data Spec 83-; AD Sumter Area Tech Clg 83; Bsns Comp Prog.

**ARMSTRONG, KELLI L,** Marshall University, Huntington, WV; SO; BA; Mktg; Sls.

**ARMSTRONG, KENYA L,** Nc Agri & Tech St Univ, Greensboro, NC; FR; BS; Elem Educ; Tchng.

**ARMSTRONG, KERRY A,** Univ Of Nc At Asheville, Asheville, NC; SR; BA; Sclgy.

**ARMSTRONG, MARIA A,** Catholic Univ Of Pr, Ponce, PR; JR; BA; Acctg Stdnt Assn 90-; Natl Bus Hon Soc; Hon Pgm VP 90-; Ldrshp Comm Serv Pgm 90-; Acctg; CPA.

**ARMSTRONG, MASHANA L,** Hampton Univ, Hampton, VA; SO; BA; SGA 90-; Drlldng Tm 88-89; Hon Cncl 90-; Hon Lsts; Psychlgy; Indstrl Orgztnl Psychlgst.

**ARMSTRONG, MELINDA SUE,** Kent St Univ Kent Cmps, Kent, OH; FR; Bus; Mrktng/Mgmt.

**ARMSTRONG, PATRICIA A,** Morgan St Univ, Baltimore, MD; SO; BA; YWCA 90-; Pre Law Clb 90-; Peer Cnslr 90-; Promethean Kappa Tau 90-; Phi Eta Sigma 90-; Alpha Lambda Delta 90-; Gvnrs Intern; Blzrs Patch; Pltcl Sci; Lawyer/Judge.

**ARMSTRONG, R BRENTON,** Coll Of Charleston, Charleston, SC; SO; MBA; Acctg Assoc 89-; Fclty Hghly Dstngshd 89; Fclty Dstngshd; Vrsty Sccr 89-; Bus Admn.

**ARMSTRONG, STEPHANIE J,** East Tn St Univ, Johnson City, TN; SR; BA; Acctg Soc 89-; Alpha Lambda Delta 87-; Gamma Beta Phi Coord 88-; Phi Kappa Phi 90-; Beta Gamma Sigma 90-; Omicron Delta Kappa 89-; Rho Lambda 90-; Kappa Delta Treas 87-; Deans Lst; Fred C Ward Outstndng Stdnt Acctncy 90-; Fclty Awd 90-; Bus; CPA.

**ARMSTRONG, TEDRA K,** Belmont Coll, Nashville, TN; FR; BA; Acctg; CPA.

**ARMSTRONG, VERONICA G,** Norfolk St Univ, Norfolk, VA; JR; BS; Alum Va Beach Chpt 90-; NAACP 88-90; Natl Black Nurses Assoc 90-; Boys & Girls Club Vol 88-90; U S Navy Hosp Corpsman 79-; AD Tidewater Comm Coll 86-88; Nursing; U S Navy Nurse Corps Officer.

**ARMSTRONG JR, WILLIE C,** Albany St Coll, Albany, GA; SO; BS; Dept Hnrs In The Area Of Acctng 90-; US Army 89; Alld Hlth; Hlth Care Admin.

**ARNDT, KATHLEEN E,** Saint Joseph Coll, West Hartford, CT; FR; BA; Stdnt Govt Fnctnl Co-Chr Elect; Dorm Cncl Scl Rep Elect; Psych; Psych/Ph D.

**ARNDT, RAMONA E,** Univ Of Al At Huntsville, Huntsville, AL; SR; BS; Scty Wm Engrs 90-; Cncrt Chr 87-; Grmn Clb VP 89-90; Omicron Delta Kappa Treas 90-; Alpha Lambda Delta 88; Tau Beta Pi; Pr Cnslr Sr Hghs Cvnt Prsbytrn Chrch 87-90; Al Scty Prfsnl Engrs Schlrshp 90; Schlrshps; Chmcl Engrg.

**ARNER, KRISTI L,** Central Pa Bus School, Summerdale, PA; SR; AS; Dns Lst; Acctng.

**ARNESON, KRISTIN P,** Fl St Univ, Tallahassee, FL; GD; Varsity Lacrosse St Marys Clg 85; Skydiving U Fl 90; Literary Council; Linstitut Cath Paris; Sailing Club 86; BS; Poltl Sci; Law.

**ARNET, WILLA A,** D Youville Coll, Buffalo, NY; SO; BA; Blck Stdnt Union; Stdnt Nurses Assoc; Alpha Lambda Sigma; Nursing.

**ARNETT, EARL T,** Thomas Nelson Comm Coll, Hampton, VA; FR; AAS; Elect Tech; Artificial Intelligence Rsrch.

**ARNETT, GEORGIANA W,** Univ Of Cincinnati, Cincinnati, OH; SR; BM; NAJE; Jazz/Studio Guitar; Jazz.

**ARNETT, MERRY P,** Fayetteville St Univ, Fayetteville, NC; JR; BA; Stu Free Entrprs 90-; Delta Mu Delta; Bus Admin.

**ARNETT, PAMELA L,** Tn Wesleyan Coll, Athens, TN; JR; BA; Isobel Griscom Awd For Excllnce In Engl 88; Kiwanis Intrntl Acad Awd Jr 90; Vol Ombudsman Rep; Psychlgy/Human Serv; Mntl Hlth Eldr Cre.

**ARNETT, SCOTTIE D,** Volunteer St Comm Coll, Gallatin, TN; FR; BA; Mech Engnrng; Science.

**ARNETTE, LEISA M,** Western Piedmont Comm Coll, Morganton, NC; FR; CTRA; Phi Theta Kappa 91; ARC Nc 87-; Spcl Friend Vol 90-; Therptc Rec; Rsrch/Clin Rec Therapy.

**ARNEY, GORDON N,** Oh St Univ At Newark, Newark, OH; SR; BS; Chorus 90; OH Stdnt Ed Assn 90-; Pres Acad Excell Recog Dinner 90; Thomas J Evans Medallion 90; OH St Alumni Assn 81-; Coshocton Comm Choir VP 86-; ASSO 81; Ed; Elem.

**ARNOLD, ALEXIA MICHELLE,** Univ Of Miami, Coral Gables, FL; SO; BED; FCMENC Pres 90; Music Stdnt Cncl 90-; Symphony Orch 90-; Theatre Prod 90-; Phi Eta Sigma 90-; Alpha Lambda Delta 90-; Pi Kappa Lambda; Sigma Alpha Iota Rcrdng Sec 90; FCMENC Undergrad Schlrshp; Provosts Hnr Rl/Pres Lst; Music Educ/Perf; Pub Schl Tchng.

**ARNOLD, ANDREA M,** Clark Atlanta Univ, Atlanta, GA; SO; Educ; Tchr.

**ARNOLD, ANGELA K,** Univ Of Ky, Lexington, KY; FR; Actvts Bd Cinema Comm; Phi Eta Sigma; Delta Gamma; Hlth Adm.

**ARNOLD, ANGIE L,** Al A & M Univ, Normal, AL; JR; BA; Kappa Delta Pi; Natl Cllgt Bus Merit Awd 91; Spec Ed; Tchng.

**ARNOLD, ARLENE J,** Schenectady County Comm Coll, Schenectady, NY; FR; BA; Schenectady Symphny; Achvmnt Awd 90-; Msc; Prfrmnc.

**ARNOLD, BETTY P,** Bishop St Comm Coll, Mobile, AL; SO; Phi Theta Kappa 90-; Nrsg.

**ARNOLD, BRIDGET A,** Univ Of Al At Birmingham, Birmingham, AL; SO; BS; Stdnt Rcrtr 90-; Bd Stdnt Pblctns 90-; Alpha Epsilon Delta Treas 90-; Alpha Almbda Delta 90-; Intrnshp Lureleen B Wallace Tumor Inst 89; Intrnshp Cardvsclr Disease 90; Intrnshp Pdtrcs; Blgy; Med.

**ARNOLD, CAROLYN M,** Newbury Coll, Brookline, MA; SR; AS; Prnt Tchr Orgnztn Sec 90; Acctn; CPA.

**ARNOLD, CLAUDIA E,** Va Commonwealth Univ, Richmond, VA; JR; Engl Clb 86-87; Co-Edtr Lit Mag 90-; SOLD 89-90; Pblshd Srt Strs/Poems 87-; Engl/Erly Chldhd Educ; Tchr/Athr.

**ARNOLD, DAVID A,** Ms St Univ, Miss State, MS; SR; BBA; Innovative Mrktg Grp 90-; Pi Sigma Epsilon 90-; Msspi Mltry; Ofcr Cand Schl; IBM Co-Op; A A Hinds Jr Clge 87; Mktg; Grad Schl MBA Mktg.

**ARNOLD, EMILY L,** Wilberforce Univ, Wilberforce, OH; JR; BS; Vogue Phi Vogue Mdlng Treas; B E Campus Str Mgr; Bio Med Sci Clb; Alpha Kappa Mu; Hon Soc; Phi Beta Sigma Chpln; Hlth Careers Enhncmnt Prog; Sci/Engr Res Sem; Otstndng Stdnt Awd; Biol/Pre Med; Med Dr Pathlgy.

**ARNOLD, GLENN N,** Valdosta St Coll, Valdosta, GA; JR; MBA; Bainbridge Clg Stdnt Govt Assn Pres 86-89; Phi Theta Kappa 88; Alpha Gamma Epsilon 88; GA Occuptnl Award Of Ldrshp Finlst 88; Norman A Whitten Award 88; AA Bainbridge Clg 87; AAS Bainbridge Clg 89; Bus; CPA.

**ARNOLD, HILTON WARREN,** Southern Coll Of Tech, Marietta, GA; SR; MSEET; IEEE 88; Dns Lst 90; Co-Op Prof Engr 88-90; Air Force 83-87; Elctrcl Engr Tech.

**ARNOLD, JEFF A,** Univ Of Akron, Akron, OH; SR; BFA; IM Sftbl/Ftbl/Scr 87-; Natl Paperbox Awd 89; Natl Prtng Mag Qualifier; AAB 89; Graphic Dsgn; Ilstr.

**ARNOLD, JEFFREY J,** Oh Univ, Athens, OH; SR; BM; MENC 87; Wind Symph 87-90; Golden Key 90; High Hnrs; Music Ed; Teach Band Grades 5-12.**

**ARNOLD, JIMMY W,** Medical Coll Of Ga, Augusta, GA; SO; DMD; Gamma Beta Pi 87-88; Dns Lst; ASDA 89-; R N; ASN Ga Clg 76; Dentstry.

**ARNOLD, KESHA I,** Albany St Coll, Albany, GA; SR; Stdnt Gvrnmnt Assn 90-; Mgmnt Assn; Alld Hlth Clb Chrprsn Bnvlnc 89-; Phi Beta Lambda 90-; Alpha Eta; Alpha Kappa Alpha; Intrnshp HCA Palmyra Mdcl Cntr; Deans Lst 90-; BA; Alld Hlth Sci; Hlthcare Admnstrtr.

**ARNOLD, LAURA R,** Franklin And Marshall Coll, Lancaster, PA; FR; Cngrss Rep Sec; Almn Assn Sec; Ornttn Advsr; Dana Schlr; Dean Lst 90-; Classics/Anthrplgy; Pblctn/TV Prod.

**ARNOLD, MARK W,** Bethel Coll, Mckenzie, TN; FR; BA; Engl; Sec Educ.

**ARNOLD, MARY STEELE,** Middle Tn St Univ, Murfreesboro, TN; JR; Ttn Wvr 85-86; Wrk Schlrshp 90-; Pn Prfrmnc.

**ARNOLD, MELANIE B,** Univ Of Tn At Martin, Martin, TN; SR; Math Assoc Amer VP 89-; Bapt Stdnt Un Cncl Mbr 87-; Stdnt TN Educ Assoc 87-; Otstndng Stdnt Sec Educ Math 90-; BS Ed; Math; Tchr.

**ARNOLD, MICHELE M,** Old Dominion Univ, Norfolk, VA; JR; BS; IEEE 90-; Elect Eng.

**ARNOLD, MIRIAM A,** Clark Atlanta Univ, Atlanta, GA; FR; BA; Insprtnl Voices Of Faith; Hall Govt; Speech Tm; Deans List; Pol Sci; Lawyer Governor.

**ARNOLD, PATRICIA L,** William Paterson Coll, Wayne, NJ; SR; BA; Hm/Schl Assn Pres 87; Elem Ed/Engl; Tchng.

**ARNOLD, PAULA MARTIN,** Alcorn St Univ, Lorman, MS; FR; AD; Stdnt Body Org Treas 90-; MS Stdnt Nurses Assn 90-; Natl Reg Emerg Med Tech 90-; Humana Hosp Natchez EMT 90-; Nrsng RN.

**ARNOLD, PENNY L,** Rider Coll, Lawrenceville, NJ; JR; BA; Psi Chi; Baccalaureate Hnrs Pgm; Lehigh Vly Undergrad Psych Conf Poster; Psychology.**

**ARNOLD, REGINA GEORGETTE,** East Tn St Univ, Johnson City, TN; FR; BA; ETSU Art Show Hnrd Exhibit 90-; Art; Drawing/Fashion Dsgng.

**ARNOLD, SHANNON L,** Memphis St Univ, Memphis, TN; FR; BA; Communications; Video Production.

**ARNOLD, YOLANDA L,** Birmingham Southern Coll, Birmingham, AL; BA; Blck Stu Unn 87-90; Vol Yr Awrd Crisis Cntr Inc 89-90; Vol Tchr Exchng Clb 89-; BA Birmingham Southern Coll 90; Educ; PHD Educ Psych.

**ARNONE, MARGARET MARY,** D Youville Coll, Buffalo, NY; SR; BS; Yrbk Edtr Cheif 90-F Student Assoc Prog Brd Chrpn 87-90; Future Tchrs Council 89-90; Sr Hnr Scty 90-; D'youville Mdl; Student Tchr Buffalo City Schl District; Student Tchr Theodore Roosevelt Elem Schl; Ed Visually Imprd Elem Ed; Tchng Visually Imp.

**ARNOTT, AMBER L,** Daytona Beach Comm Coll, Daytona Beach, FL; FR; AS; Intr Dsgn.

**ARNOULD, ISABELLE N,** Univ Of Sc At Columbia, Columbia, SC; JR; BA; USC Swim Team 89-; Anthropology.

**ARNOULD, TERESA L,** Univ Of South Al, Mobile, AL; JR; BA; Legal Sec 80-83; AA Pensacola Jr Clg 77-79; Ele Educ; Tchr.

**ARNSTEIN, ELIZABETH M,** Saint Francis Coll, Loretto, PA; FR; BA; Key Clb 90-; Actvts Orgnzatn 90-; Drama Clb; Englsh.

**ARNUM, MICHAEL J,** Cornell Univ Statutory College, Ithaca, NY; SR; BS; Amer Coll For Life Rgnl Dir 90-; Protestant Coop Mnstry 87-; WVBR Radio News Dept; Natl Tropical Botanical Gdn Intrnshp 90; 4th Plc Oratorical Cntst 88; Horticultural Sci; Law.

**ARNWINE, ANGELA R,** Ky St Univ, Frankfort, KY; FR; ADN; LPN Central KY Voc Tech 89; Nrsng.

**AROCHA, PABLO M,** Miami Dade Comm Coll South, Miami, FL; SO; BA; He Cares Mnstries Inc Cnslng And Referl Prgrm 88-; Tlnt Roster Otstndng Minrty Coll Stdnts; US Achvmnt Acdmy; Ntnl Collgte Bus Mrt Awd; Comp Infrmtn Systms; Systms Anlysts.

**AROCHO, CARLOS A,** Univ Politecnica De Pr, Hato Rey, PR; SO; Engr.

**AROESTY, DAVID E,** Univ Of Miami, Coral Gables, FL; SR; BA; Retail Mgr Dept/Spclty Stores 86-; BBA 86; Psychlgy; Ph D.

**AROLA, TRAVIS M,** Alfred Univ, Alfred, NY; SO; BSME; Forest People 89-; Chrldng 89-90; Hnrs Pgrm 89-; Alpha Lambda Delta 89-; Presdntl Schlrshp Alfred Univ 89-; Cross Cntry 89-; Tae Kwan Do 89-; Mech Eng; Eng.

**ARONSON, GEOFFREY E,** Savannah Coll Of Art & Design, Savannah, GA; GD; MFA; Photo Grp 90; Photo Rsrc Ctr 87-; Catskill Ctr Phtgrphy 90-; BA Univ CT 90; Photo; Educ/Pblshng.

**ARORA, KANAN,** Comm Coll Algny Co Algny Cmps, Pittsburgh, PA; SO; AAS; Nutrition Club V P; MA Univ Of Rajasthan 86; B Sc Univ Of Delhi 85; Foods & Nutrition; Clinical Dietitian.

**AROSEMENA, JORGE FEDERICO,** Old Dominion Univ, Norfolk, VA; JR; BS; Armed Frcs Elect Cmmncntns Assn Schlrshp 89; Politechnical Inst Schlrshp 84-85; AAS Cum Laude Nrthrn Vl Comm Coll 90; Elect Eng Tech; MS Eng.

**AROUTIAN, LISA,** City Univ Of Ny Baruch Coll, New York, NY; JR; BBA; Admin Assist; Chief Credit Officer; Fin/Cmdts; Portfolio Mgmt.

**ARP, JULIE D,** Valdosta St Coll, Valdosta, GA; SO; BBA; Cncrt Chr 89-; Chmbr Sngrs 89-90; Alpha Lambda Delta 90; Sigma Alpha Chi; Pres Schlr 90; Fnnc.

**ARP, PATRICIA A,** Western New England Coll, Springfield, MA; SO; BS; Soc Wmn Engrs SWE 89-90; Asst WNEC Jr H Prog; Engr; Engr.

**ARRANTS III, JOHN E,** Bristol Univ, Bristol, TN; GD; BBA; Yrbk Stf Co-Ed 88; H B Arrington Acd Awd 88; Std Yr 88; Sales Rep 90; Crt Unv MI 87; Bus; Mrktg.

**ARRAS, NORMA R,** Bishop St Comm Coll, Mobile, AL; SO; BS; Phi Theta Kappa Treas 89-; Pres List 89-; Deans List 89-; Dance Tm Dir 88-; Hostess Govr Convtn 90; Dental Techn 75-; Biology; Secdy Ed.

**ARRATIA, JUAN I,** Inter Amer Univ Pr San German, San German, PR; FR; BA; Erly Admssn Pr 90-; Conf Prblms Yth P R Del 90-; Natl Hnr Soc Pr 90-; Musclr Dstrphy Assn 90-91; Pol Sci; Govt.

**ARRATOON, LYNDA E,** Ny Univ, New York, NY; JR; BSC; Dghtrs Of Brtsh Empire Treas 90; Fncl Rprtng; AAS 90; Finance.

**ARRECHEA, MARISA HAWAYEK,** Inter Amer Univ Pr Hato Rey, Hato Rey, PR; JR; Jet Ski Rider & Racer 88-; Bus Admn; Acctng.

**ARRELL, VINCENT D,** Univ Of Southern Ms, Hattiesburg, MS; JR; BS; Alumni Assn 90-; Plnng Ntwrk 90-; Gamma Theta Upsilon 90-; Gamma Beta Phi 90-; Cmmnty Rgnl Plng; Cty Plnr.

**ARRIA, ANTHONY C,** Bunker Hill Comm Coll, Boston, MA; SO; BA; Intern Medford Cmmnty; Cblvsn Edctnl Chnnl Tchrs Asst; AD; Brdcst Cmmnctns; Brdcstr.

**ARRIBAS, DAVID,** Embry Riddle Aeronautical Univ, Daytona Beach, FL; SO; BS; Precision Flight Dmnstrtn Tm 89-; Soc Commercial Aviation Techs; Summer Intrnshp Washington Intl Airport Oper Office 90; Aero Sci; Prof Pilot.

**ARRIBAS, ELSA M,** Univ Of Pr At Rio Piedras, Rio Piedras, PR; SO; MD; Hnr Roll Natl Sci Fclty 90-; Dns Lst 90-; Natural Sci; Med.

**ARRICK, AMY G,** Memphis St Univ, Memphis, TN; SO; PHARM; Cmps Crsd Chrst 89-; Actv Cncl 89-90; Bptst Std Un 90-; Gamma Beta Phi 89-; Chem; Pharmcst.

**ARRIETA, MARTHA I,** Univ Of South Fl, Tampa, FL; GD; PHD; Delta Omega 90-; E Escomel Sci Assn Pres 88; Jrnl Editor 82-; Escml Sci Assn; Outstdng Grad Dept Epdmlgy/Biostatcs 90; Fla Pblc Hlth Assn 89-; Prvn Med Assn 87-; Assoc Rsrch USF Dept Epdmlgy/Biostatcs 90-; MD San Agustin Ntl Univ 87; MPH 90; Epdmlgy/Biostatcs; Prevntv Med.

**ARRIETE, ODALYS,** Fl International Univ, Miami, FL; SR; BA; Ftr Ed Amr Treas 90-; Phi Kappa Phi 90-; Bnkng Mrktng Offcr 82-89; Elem Ed.

**ARRINGTON, BETH M,** Univ Of New England, Biddeford, ME; SR; Fr Cls VP 87-88; Am Phys Therapy Assn 89-; Campus Night Life Tm 87-88; Tour Guide Univ New England 89-; BSPT; Phys Therapy.

**ARRINGTON, DAVID M,** King Coll, Bristol, TN; SO; MBA; Deans List 90; All Am Schlr Awd; Workship; Pol Sci/Hist/Econ; Corp Intl Law.

**ARRINGTON, JANICE D,** Fayetteville St Univ, Fayetteville, NC; SO; BS; Cmptr Sci; Prgmng.

**ARRINGTON II, JOSEPH,** Clark Atlanta Univ, Atlanta, GA; SO; BA; Jazz Orch; Kappa Alpha Psi Stategus; Journalism; Law.

**ARRINGTON, LYNN Y,** Piedmont Tech Coll, Greenwood, SC; SO; BS; Phi Beta Lamba 90; Deans Lst 90; Mktg; Cmptr Sci.

**ARRINGTON, MICHAEL I,** Univ Of Southern Ms, Hattiesburg, MS; SO; Spch Cmnctn Assn 90-; Phi Eta Sigma 90; Outstndng Spnsh Stdnt Awrd; Spch Cmnctn; Prfssr.

**ARRINGTON, RUSSELL D,** Johnson C Smith Univ, Charlotte, NC; JR; BA; RA 89-; Hon Coll 88-; John Mcdonald Pub Rel Schlrshp; Cross Cntry/Track 88-; Cmnctns; Air Traffic Cntrlr.

**ARRINGTON, TONYA P,** Chattahoochee Vly St Comm Coll, Phenix City, AL; SO; BA; Gamma Beta Phi 90-; Pres Lst; Awd Excell; Soc Sci; Famly Conslr.

**ARRINGTON, TOYIA L,** Albany St Coll, Albany, GA; SR; Mrchn Gbnd; Chrldrf Brd Mgrs; NAACP 87-; Crmn Jstc Clb Treas 87-; Alpha Kappa Mu 90-Alpha Phi Sigma VP 89-; Delta Sigma Theta; GA Lgl Srvcs Intern; Crmnl Jstc Schlr; All Armcn Schlr: US Achvmnt Acdmy; Chrldng; Mrchng Bnd; BS; Crmnl Jstc; Law.

**ARRITT, TINA M,** James Madison University, Harrisonburg, VA; SR; BS; Amnesty Intl 89-90; Stdnt Edn Assoc 90-; Phi Theta Kappa 89-; Kappa Delta Pi/Golden Key 90-; AS Dabney S Lancaster Comm Coll 90; Edn; Teach.

**ARROWOOD, BARBARA G,** Greenville Tech Coll, Greenville, SC; FR; AD; Dns Lst 90-; Publc Relatns Chrmn; Comm For Med Lab Tech Blood Drv; Bannon Schlrshp/Allied Hlth 90; Ed/Dvlpmnt Prjct Schlrshp; Chldrn Chrch Actvts; Med Lab Tech; Med Tech BA.

**ARROWWOOD, JOSEPH L,** Chattahoochee Vly St Comm Coll, Phenix City, AL; SO; AS; Dean Lst 90-; Pres Lst 90-; Sci/Math; Cmptr Eng.

**ARROYO DEL RIO, FERDINAND,** Univ Of Pr At Mayaguez, Mayaguez, PR; GD; BA; AEPSIC 88-90; Hnr Stdnt 89-90; BA; Psychology; Cnslng.**

**ARROYO ESTARELLAS, GLORIBELLE,** Inter Amer Univ Pr Hato Rey, Hato Rey, PR; GD; BA; APNI Summer Camp Tutor Handcppd Chld; BA; Spcl Ed Severe Mltpl Hndcps/Doc Degree Sp Ed.

**ARROYO MUNIZ, EFRAIN,** Univ Politecnica De Pr, Hato Rey, PR; FR; Army ROTC Private; Civil Air Patrol Cadet 1 Lt 88-; Elec Eng.

**ARROYO, MARISOL,** Inter Amer Univ Pr San German, San German, PR; JR; BA; Math/Computer Sci; Engrg.

**ARROYO, SANDRA G,** City Univ Of Ny Queensbrough, New York, NY; JR; 25 89-90; PTA Bus Mgr 86-90; Para Prof; AA.

**ARROYO, TARA T,** Hudson Valley Comm Coll, Troy, NY; SR; AAS; Erly Chldhd Clb 89-; Grad Wth Hnrs; Erly Chldhd Educ.**

**ARROYO-COLOMER, JORGE A,** Univ Of Pr Humacao Univ Coll, Humacao, PR; SO; BBA; Scty Acctg 89-; Acctg; Law.

**ARROYO-COLOMER, MIGUEL A,** Univ Of Pr At Mayaguez, Mayaguez, PR; JR; BS; Amer Soc Mech Eng 90-; Mech Eng; Eng.**

**ARSEGO, SHARON E,** Saint Joseph Coll, West Hartford, CT; JR; BA; Cmps Mnstry 90-; Nwspr 90; Dorm Rep 90-; Sftbl 89-; Englsh; Wrtng Edtng.**

**ARSENAULT, JEANNE M,** Bunker Hill Comm Coll, Boston, MA; FR; Cert Erly Chldhd Dvlpmnt Educ 91; Erly Chldhd Dvlpmnt/Ed; Chld Psychlgst.

**ARSI, MELANIE,** Seton Hall Univ, South Orange, NJ; FR; BS; Bsn; Acctnt.

**ARSLAN, MAZEN,** Tallahassee Comm Coll, Tallahassee, FL; SO; BA; Risk Mgmt/Insur.

**ARTALE, CARLA S,** Pace Univ At Ny, New York, NY; FR; MBA; Bus Mgmnt.

**ARTHANARI, LENIN,** City Univ Of Ny Baruch Coll, New York, NY; JR; BBA; Ticker Bus Mgr 90-; Fnc/Econ Soc 89-; Acctg Soc 89-; Golden Key 90-; Deans Lst 89; Beta Gamma Sigma; Intrn 1st Boston Corp 90-; Fnc/Econ; Invstmnt Bnkng.

**ARTHERS, CINDY L,** Univ Of South Al, Mobile, AL; SO; BS; Kappa Delta Fnd Rsr 90-; Oper Sys Mngmnt; Bus Mngmnt.

**ARTHUR, BARBARA METCALFE,** Southern Coll Of Tech, Marietta, GA; SR; BSIET; ASIET; Indstrl Engr.

**ARTHUR, CRYSTAL G,** Sue Bennett Coll, London, KY; FR; BA; Sigma Nu; Phi Theta Kappa; Bus; Accntng.

**ARTHUR, GINGER L,** Univ Of Sc At Columbia, Columbia, SC; SO; Campus Crsde; Bapt Un; Mth/Comp Sci Clb; Gamma Beta Phi.

**ARTHUR, KONETA A,** Beckley Coll, Beckley, WV; SO; BA; Nrsng Sci; Med.

**ARTHUR, LANA D,** Wv Univ At Parkersburg, Parkersburg, WV; FR; AAS; Phi Theta Kappa; Business; Medical.

**ARTHUR, LAURA J,** Univ Of Nc At Charlotte, Charlotte, NC; FR; BA; Prgm Brd 90-; ICE 90-; Hll Cncl 90-; Phi Heta Sigma 90-; Chmstry.

**ARTHUR, MATTHEW B,** Vance Granville Comm Coll, Henderson, NC; SR; Phi Theta Kappa; Elec Engineering.

**ARTHUR, SANDRA L,** Comm Coll Algny Co Algny Cmps, Pittsburgh, PA; FR; BA; Engl; Tchr.

**ARTHUR, STEPHEN M,** Cooper Union, New York, NY; SR; BSENG; NSBE Treas 89-90; ASME 89-; Amigos; Roney Mc Nair Sci Entry Prog Instr 90-; Mech Engr.

**ARTHUR, TROY C,** Newbury Coll, Brookline, MA; FR; BA; Mgmnt; Law.

**ARTIME, CARLOS,** Barry Univ, Miami, FL; SR; BA; Phi Alpha Theta; Hist; Scndry Tchr.

**ARTIS, HATTIE P,** Alcorn St Univ, Lorman, MS; SR; Bio/Tchr.

**ARTIS, SANDRA A,** Tougaloo Coll, Tougaloo, MS; SR; BA; Sclgy Human Srvcs Clb Pres 90-; Jdcry Comm SGA Sec 89-90; Pltcl Sci Pre Law 90; Alpha Lambda Delta 87-; Alpha Kappa Delta Co Chrprsn 90-; Alpha Kappa Alpha; Ben Marcato Clb 87; Intrnshpcntrl MS Plng Dvlpmnt Dist 90; Sclgy Stdnt Yr 89-; BA; Sclgy; Law.

**ARTIS, VIVIAN L,** Saint Andrews Presbytrn Coll, Laurinburg, NC; JR; BS; St Andrws Chrl 89-; Blk Un 89-90; Beta Beta Beta; St Andrws Hon Soc 90-; Vol Brs Rehblthn Cntr Attndt 89-; Acad Tutr 90-; Achvmnt Schlrshp 89-; Soph Hon 90-; St Andrws Hon Soc; Bio Pre Med; Ncontlgst.

**ARTLIP, CHRISTINE M,** S U N Y Coll Of Tech At Alfred, Alfred, NY; SR; Bus Adm Clb; Phi Theta Kappa; Dns Lst Alfred St; Stdnt Yr Bus Adm Trnsf Alfred; Nom P B Orvis Awd; AAS Alfred State Coll; Bus.

**ARUFE, JORGE A,** Miami Dade Comm Coll, Miami, FL; SO; Cthlc Chrch Yng Adlt Grp 90; Chrstn Life Cmmty 90-; Deans List 88-; Hghst Hnrs Dstctn; Phychlgy Awrd; AA 90; Hstry; Ed.

**ARUS, EMERIC,** City Univ Of Ny Baruch Coll, New York, NY; SO; BBA; Bus.

**ARVESU, CARMEN DE PAZ,** Fl International Univ, Miami, FL; SR; BA; Dance Rep 90-; Phi Kappa Phi; Key Biscayne Theater/Drama Clb Choreogrphr; PE/DANCE Tchr New World Ctr 87-; AA Miami Dade Comm Coll; Dance/Edn; Tchr.

**ARVIZO, PENNY L,** Columbia Union Coll, Takoma Park, MD; SR; BS; Business.

**ARWOOD, ANGELA S,** Christopher Newport Coll, Newport News, VA; FR; BA; Vlybl Chrch Lge 90-; Math; Educ.

**ARWOOD, SCOTT M,** Univ Of Tn At Knoxville, Knoxville, TN; FR; Cnstrctn Spcfctn Inst 90-; Phi Eta Sigma; Alpha Lambda Delta; Engnrng.

**ARZOLA, ANTONIA,** Fl International Univ, Miami, FL; SR; BA; Phi Kappa Phi 90-; Alpha Phi Sigma 90-; Intrnshp Pub Dfndrs Offc; AA Miami Dade Comm Coll 89; Crmnl Jstc; Law.

**ARZOLA, JOANNE E,** Univ Of Pr Ponce Tech Univ Col, Ponce, PR; SO; BA; Stdnt Assn Contabilidad 90-; Hnr Roll 89-90; Accntng.

**ARZOOMANIAN, DENISE,** Seton Hall Univ, South Orange, NJ; FR; BS; Nrsng; MS.

**ASAAD, TAMER M,** Univ Of Sc At Columbia, Columbia, SC; FR; CPU; Intl Stdnts Assoc; MSA; Phrmcy.

**ASAMOAH, JOHN,** Central St Univ, Wilberforce, OH; FR; ISA; Manuf Engr; Engr.

**ASBRAND, KIMBERLY D,** Moravian Coll, Bethlehem, PA; JR; BS; Beta Beta Beta; Alpha Epsilon Pi 89; Intrnshp At St Lukes Hosp/Mhlnbrg Hosp; Spcl Olympcs; Bio; Med Rsrch.**

**ASBURY, CAROL L,** Concord Coll, Athens, WV; SR; BS; Delilah Untd Methodist Wmn Soc Prsdne Past 86-89; Kopperston Biddy Buddy Assn Spnsr 89-; AA Sthrn W VA Comm Clg; Elem Edctn Multi Sbjct; Tchng.

**ASBURY, CATHY L,** Roane St Comm Coll, Harriman, TN; SO; AAS; Deans List Pellissippi St 89-90; Deans Lst 90-; Radiology Tech.

**ASBURY JR, WESLEY L,** East Tn St Univ, Johnson City, TN; GD; MD; Cls Pres 89; Promotions Cmt 88-89; Admsns Cmt 89-; Alpha Omega Alpha Sec; Dlt Tau Delt Frtrnty 76-; Wrld Hlth Day Plng Cmt 89; Dept Enrgy Awrd Exclnc 85-88; Bio/Medcn Prsntn Awrd 89; AICHE; AMA; BS Massachusetts Inst Tech 80; Medcn.

**ASBURY, WILLIAM R,** Marshall University, Huntington, WV; JR; MBA; H C Price Schlrshp; IM Bsktbl 89; Bus; Mktg.

**ASCAR COLON, EVELYN,** Inter Amer Univ Pr Hato Rey, Hato Rey, PR; JR; Art; Mrktng.

**ASCENCIO, ARIANNE M F,** Barry Univ, Miami, FL; GD; BS; Intl Stdnt Org Sec 87-88; Haitian Clb 87-90; Acctg Assn 90-; Acctg.

**ASCHENBRENNER, LAURA M,** Marywood Coll, Scranton, PA; JR; BS; Cmps Mnstry Clowns Chrprsn 88-; Players 88-; Pugwash Liaison Offcr 89-; Delta Epsilon Sigma 90-; Kappa Delta Pi; Hnrs Prog 88-; VIA 88-; Karate Clb 89-; Elem Educ; Tchr.

**ASEFAW, SENAI,** Harvard Univ, Cambridge, MA; FR; SG; Ecnmcs.

**ASEL, TONIA M,** Slippery Rock Univ, Slippery Rock, PA; FR; BS; Jazz Bnd 90-; Mrchng Bnd 90; MENC 90-; Orch 90-; Flute Chr 90-; Dixieland Bnd 90-; Wind Ensble; Phi Eta Sigma 90-; Univ Acad Hnrs Schlrshp 90-; Music Educ; Perfrmnc.

**ASENCIO ORTIZ, ANGEL F,** Caribbean Univ, Bayamon, PR; SR; Civil Engineer.

**ASETRE, STEVE B,** Univ Of Al At Huntsville, Huntsville, AL; JR; BSE; Stdnt Govt Treas 84; Socty Amer Mil Engrs 89-90; Math; Elec Engr.

**ASH, EDDIE,** Univ Of Al At Birmingham, Birmingham, AL; SR; MD; Prehealth Clb; Alpha Epsilon Delta; Phi Sigma; Golden Key; Phi Kappa Phi; Childrens Hosp Ala Vol; Auburn U Dudley Schlrshp; UAB Johnson Schlrshp; State Medl Schlrshp; BS UAB; Medicine; Anesthesiology.

**ASHANY, EYAL D,** City Univ Of Ny Baruch Coll, New York, NY; BA; IM Vlybl 88; Mktg; Rsrch.

**ASHAR, RACHITA S,** Muskingum Coll, New Concord, OH; JR; BS; ACM; Intrntl Stdnt Org; Kappa Mu Epsilon; Mensa; Intertel; Sigma Xi; Awrded Miss CSI-87 Cmptr Soc India Upon Wnng Ntnwd Pgmng Cntst; Cmptr Sci/Math; Ph D/Neuval Ntwrks.

**ASHBAUGH, JENNIFER J,** Wright St Univ, Dayton, OH; FR; BED; Elem Ed; Tchng.

**ASHBAUGH, MARLENE ANN,** Wright St Univ Lake Cmps, Celina, OH; JR; BED; Bus Prof Amer 90-; Chrch Schl Dir; S S Tchr; Dist Adtr; Thspn Advsr; Drmtcs Dir 88-; Advrtsng Dsgn Layout 90-; Gen Infr Serv 88-; Bus Educ; Tch.

**ASHBROOK, JOHN E,** Radford Univ, Radford, VA; SR; PHD; Hnrs Prog 90-; Pi Gamma Mu 90-; BA; Hstry; Professor.**

**ASHBURN, CAROLYN JOYCE,** Fl St Univ, Tallahassee, FL; JR; MS; Cncl Excptnl Chldrn; Phi Theta Kappa 89-; AA Tllhsse Comm Coll 89; Spec Educ; Tchng Excptnl Chldrn.

**ASHBY, CLAIRE C,** Va Commonwealth Univ, Richmond, VA; SO; BA; Phi Eta Sigma Fr Hon Soc 90; Natl Coll Edn Awd; Art Hist.

**ASHBY, PENNY P,** Piedmont Comm Coll, Roxboro, NC; JR; ADN; Cert Word Proc 85; Med; Nrsg.

**ASHBY, VICKY C,** Ky St Univ, Frankfort, KY; SR; BA; Stdnt Supprt Svcs; Alpha Kappa Mu 90-; Deans List; Intrnshp US Dept Of Lbr 89-90; Publc Admn; Fedrl Govt.

**ASHCRAFT II, DAVID CLINTON,** Oh St Univ, Columbus, OH; SR; BA; Clgs Arts/Sci Exclnc Schlrshp Awd 90; Crew 88-; Hist/French; Law/Dplmcy.

**ASHCRAFT, HILLARY B,** Univ Of Southern Ms, Hattiesburg, MS; JR; Campus Choice Pres; SOS; Deans Lst; Alpha Lambda Delta; Pi Beta Sigma; Pi Beta Phi; Spch Pathology.

**ASHCRAFT, TROY K,** Northern Ky Univ, Highland Hts, KY; JR; BA; Bio Soc 90-; Bio; Med.

**ASHCROFT, BRYANT J,** Wv Univ At Parkersburg, Parkersburg, WV; FR; AAS; Phi Theta Kappa; IM Vllybl; AAS Cannock Chase Tech Coll 88; Drftng; CAD.

**ASHCROFT, JULIANN M,** Hudson Valley Comm Coll, Troy, NY; FR; PA; Tutor 87-89; Med Tech Clb 86-88; Vldctrn 90; BS Utica Clg 90; Phys Asst.

**ASHDOWN, TODD A,** Bowling Green St Univ, Bowling Green, OH; JR; BS; Intrmrl Advsry Brd Pres 88-; Intrmrl Sprts Sftbll Ftbll Bsktbll Tnns 88-; Sprt Mgmt Crrclm Stdnt Rep 90-; Phi Eta Sigma 88-; Delta Tau Delta 90; Asst BGSU Stdnt Rec Cntr Bthln Dir; Std Rep Nw Fldhs BGSU 90-; IM Sprts 88-; Sprt Mgmt.

**ASHE, PAMELA R,** Dartmouth Coll, Hanover, NH; FR; BA; Dartmouth TV 90-91; Stdents Fghtng Hngr 90-; Catholic Student Yth Grp 90-; NASA Undrgrd Fllwshp 90-; Wmn Sci Prjct Intrnshp 90-; Earth Sci; Geology.

**ASHEN, FAYGALA B,** City Univ Of Ny Baruch Coll, New York, NY; SR; MBA; Comp Clb; Beta Gamma Sigma; Gldn Ky; Ft Tryn Nrsng Hme; Ttr; Prvst Schlrshp Awrd 89; Robert Demb Fnd Schlrshp Awrd 90; Dns Lst; Comp Info Systms.

**ASHER, BARRY J,** Ga St Univ, Atlanta, GA; SR; BS ED; Alpha Epsilon Pi 84-; Assn Of Tchrs 89-; Bando Karate 90; AS De Kalb Clg 88; Midl Sch Educ; Tch.

**ASHER, KEVIN A,** Univ Of Md Baltimore Prof Schl, Baltimore, MD; GD; DDS; Soccr 84-86; BSC Howard Unv 86; Dntstry Physlgy; Rsrch.

**ASHFORD, CURTIS L,** Al St Univ, Montgomery, AL; SO; BS; Phi Eta Sigma 89-; Cmptr Sci; Cmptr Analyst.

**ASHFORD, DIANNE D,** Fl A & M Univ, Tallahassee, FL; FR; BA; Honor Rl; Math; Acctg.

**ASHLAND, BRIAN A,** Gordon Conwell Theol Sem, S Hamilton, MA; GD; MDIV; BA Univ Of Wis/Mad 88; Theolgy/Chrch Hstry; PhD/PRFSSR.

**ASHLEY, CARL P,** Univ Of Fl, Gainesville, FL; SR; Fine Arts Cncl Pres 90-; MENC; Alpha Lambda Delta 87-; Gold Key 89-; Arts Hall Fame; Pres Awd; Music Schlrshp 87-; BMME; Music Edn/Vocal.

**ASHLEY, CHADD C,** Oh Univ, Athens, OH; FR; BFA; Env Nwspr Artst 90; Alpine Clb 90; Mtn Bike Clb; Camps Cafeteria 90; IM Rqtbl 90; Art; Cinemtgrphr Art Tchr.

**ASHLEY, MICHAEL T,** Northern Ky Univ, Highland Hts, KY; JR; BA; Frgn Lngge Mrt Awrd Spnsh; Intrnatl Stds; Frgn Srvce.

**ASHLEY, ROBIN M,** Wv Wesleyan Coll, Buckhannon, WV; SO; BS; Econs Clb 89-; Intr Vrsty Smll Grp Bible Stdy 90-; Alpha Lambda Delta 90-; Amer Jr Pnt Hrse Assn WV Dir 88-; US Achvmnt Acad Awrd; Natl Cllgte Mrt Awrd; Stdnt Asst To The Acctng Dept; Dns Lst; Acctng; CPA.**

**ASHLEY, VICKIE L,** Valdosta St Coll, Valdosta, GA; SO; Academic Deans List; Cook Cnty Hstrcl Soc Adel GA Rec Sec 81-; 10 Yrs Sec/Bookkeeper & Ofc Mgmnt 81-; MCEE Math History; Teaching.

**ASHMAN, DONETTE C,** S U N Y Hlth Sci Cent Brooklyn, Brooklyn, NY; JR; BSN; Cndt AACN Crtcl Cr Nrsng Cert; Nrsng.

**ASHMORE, FRANCES AMY,** Univ Of Sc At Columbia, Columbia, SC; GD; MED; Yrbk Stf Photo Edtr 86-88; Clg Rep 86-90; Flyng Clb 89-; Kappa Delta Epsilon 89-; Amer Red Crs Water Sfty Inst 84-; Mary J Heimbrgr Mem Schlrshp 90; Dns Lst/Pres Lst 87-; Grad Asst 89-; Aqutc Stf; BA 90; Elem Educ; Phd Rdng Educ.

**ASHMORE, JENNIFER,** Western Ky Univ, Bowling Green, KY; JR; BSW; Assn Stu Soc Wrkrs VP 89-; Pre Law Clb 89-; Res Hll Govt 88-89; Phi Eta Sigma 89-; Pi Sigma Alpha VP; Coll Hghts Mrtrs Schlrshp 89-; Ky Bar Aux Schlrshp 90; Soc Wrk/Govt; Victim Advccy.

**ASHMORE, LAYNETTE S,** Ms St Univ, Miss State, MS; SR; BPA; Natl Assoc Accts 89-; Alpha Lambda Delta Phi Eta Sigma 88; Phi Kappa Phi 90; Beta Alpha Psi 90-; Gamma Beta Phi 88; Acctg; CPA.

**ASHMORE, RODNEY M,** Jackson St Univ, Jackson, MS; JR; BA; Pierian Literary Soc 90-; NAACP 90-; Sigma Tau Delta; Alpha Phi Alpha V P 90-; Eng; Law.

**ASHRAF, MOHAMMAD ADNAN,** Cumberland County Coll, Vineland, NJ; FR; BS; Cricket 89-90; Tbl Tennis 89-90; Matriculation Exam Awd; Electric Eng.

**ASHTON, CHRISTINA,** Univ Of New Haven, West Haven, CT; SR; BA; Italian Am Stdnt Assn 89-90; Day Stdnt Govt Sntr 88-90; Inter Frat Sorority Cncl Sec/Treas 89-90; Phi Sigma Treas 88-; Phi Sigma Big Bro/Big Sis 90-; Head Start Phonathon 89-90; Meals Wheels 89-; Archtctr/Grphc Dsgn.

**ASHTON, MICHAEL R,** Univ Of Scranton, Scranton, PA; FR; BS; Blgy Clb 90-; Chem Clb 90-; Spcl Jst Lbrl Arts Schlr 90-; Gavigan Rsdntl Coll; Pres Schlrshp 90; Blgy; Med.

**ASHTON, RICHARD M,** Univ Of Nc At Charlotte, Charlotte, NC; SR; BA; Architecture GPA Awd; Architecture.

**ASHTON, SHANNON C,** Middle Tn St Univ, Murfreesboro, TN; SO; BS; BS 90; Nursing; Psychiatric.

**ASHWORTH, JODY LIN,** Radford Univ, Radford, VA; SR; BS; Thrtr 86-; Natl Jr Coll Hnrs Soc Treas 83-84; Pi Gamma Mu; Prof Grtt 8-86; Radford Sngrs Madrigal Sngrs 86-88; Pol Sci; Prfssnl Actr Sngr.

**ASHWORTH, REBECCA E,** Radford Univ, Radford, VA; SO; BS; Equestrian Team Treas 90-; Deans List 90-; Cmnctns Scis/Disordrs; Spch/Lang Pahtlgst.

**ASIHENE, EVELYN A,** Mercer Univ Schl Of Pharm, Atlanta, GA; SO; PHARM; Omicron Delta Kappa Natl; BS Emory Univ 84; Pharmacy.

**ASIMAKOPOULOS, NICHOLAS,** Western New England Coll, Springfield, MA; JR; BA; Peer Advsr 90-; Orntn Grp Ldr; Stu Tchg Asstnt 90-; Deans Lst 89-; Govt; Dfns.

**ASIMOS, BARRY J,** Bapt Bible Coll & Seminary, Clarks Summit, PA; SO; BS; Plyrs Clb; Sprts Mgmt; Frnt Offc Wrk-Pro Tm.

**ASKARI, MITRA,** Fl International Univ, Miami, FL; JR; BA; Chem; Attnd Pharmcy Sch.

**ASKEW, JUANITA,** Christian Brothers Univ, Memphis, TN; JR; BA; AS State Tech Inst Memphis 88; Telecmnctns.

**ASKEW, TIMOTHY D,** Univ Of Akron, Akron, OH; SO; BA; Mscl Entrtnmnt Comm 89-90; Theatre Gld Tres Prsdnt 90-; SGA Acdmc Actn Comm 90-; Deans Lst 89-; Stdnt Advsr Dean; Homer F Allen Mmrl Awd; Paul A Daum Endwd; Theatre Actng; Actng Tchng.

**ASKEW, WILLIAM C,** Univ Of Al At Huntsville, Huntsville, AL; GD; BSE; Sigma Chi V P 74-78; Tech Wrtr USBI Co Huntsville AL 87-; BA Memphis State U 83; Mech Engr; Engr.

**ASKINS JR, HARRY W,** Draughons Jr Coll Nashville, Nashville, TN; JR; AS; Part Time Hero Scty Pres 88-; Jr Classical League 81-; Cert Training Lotus/Serv Merchnd 85-; Cert Training Multimatel-Serv Merchnd 85; Cert Training Mai Basic Four/Safety Serv 89; Cmptr Prgmr 90; Bus Data Processing; Computer Programmer.

**ASKREN, PATRICIA L,** Fl Atlantic Univ, Boca Raton, FL; JR; BBA; Phi Kappa Phi; Wilbur Wallace Jones Schlrshp 90; AA Indian River Comm Coll 90; Bus; Mgmt.

**ASLIN, SHARON B,** Norfolk St Univ, Norfolk, VA; FR; Owned/Oper Own Cleaning Bsn 84-; Phys Educ; Coach.

**ASMANN, DAVID G,** Widener Univ, Chester, PA; SO; BS; Partl Pres Schlrshp 89-; Swmmng 89-; Mech Engr.

**ASOKAN, SUHANDHINI DOLLY,** Atlantic Comm Coll, Mays Landing, NJ; SR; AAS; Mbr Phi Beta; Post Scndry Lvl Future Bus Ldrs Of Amer; NJ Assoc Pub Acctnts Schlrshp 90; State Ldrshp Conf 89-; Acctng/Finance; CPA.

**ASPHALL, GISELLE A,** Fl International Univ, Miami, FL; SO; MBA; Stdnt Asst Audiovisl Dept; Biology; Anesthelgst.

**ASPINWALL, MARIA TERESA,** George Mason Univ, Fairfax, VA; GD; MBA; APICS Pres 90; Dcsn Sci Clb 90-; Chmbr Cmmrc 90-; Latin Amer Yth Cntr Tchr; Dean Lst 90; Sml Bus Admn Awrd 90; AS Northern VA Cmmnty Coll 85; Spnsh Trnltn Cert Lima Peru 80; Bus.

**ASSALI, JAMES B,** Univ Of Miami, Coral Gables, FL; SR; BBA; Hnrs Student Assoc; Golden Key; Finance.

**ASSAVAPICHAISUK, BENJAPORN,** Coll Of New Rochelle, New Rochelle, NY; SR; BS; Bus/Intl 89-; Hsptlty Clb 88-90; Hnrs Lst 90-; Deans Lst 88-89; All Amer Schlrs 89; CC Intern 90; Chase Manhattan Bank Intern 90; Intl Catholic Org 90; Tennis/Lanphony 88-90; Bus Admin; Intl Mktng.

**ASSELIN, RENEE R,** Western New England Coll, Springfield, MA; SO; BA; Peer Tutor 89; Alpha Lambda Delta Hon Soc 89-; Acctg; CPA.

**AST, JEFFREY W,** Univ Of Cincinnati-Clrmnt Coll, Batavia, OH; SO; BA; U Of Cin Stdnt Govt 89-; Flwshp Of Christn Athlts 88-90; Morehead St Univ Bsbl 87-88; Pol Sci; Publc Svc/Govt.

**ASTACIO BURGOS, GLADYS,** Univ Of Pr Medical Sciences, San Juan, PR; GD; BA Blgy/Spnsh-UPR Rio Piedras Cmps 84; MPHE-UPR Medcl Sci Cmps; Trst Gd-Sch Trsm 90.

**ASTFALK, DEBORAH L,** Wv Northern Comm Coll, Wheeling, WV; JR; AAS; Nrsng.

**ASTI, DANIEL J,** Duquesne Univ, Pittsburgh, PA; FR; MBA; Alpha Phi Delta Treas Elect; Phrmcy.

**ASTORELLI, NANCY M,** Newbury Coll, Brookline, MA; SO; AS; Cosmetologist Shp Ownr 84-; Cert Henry O Peabody Vocational 74-75; Med; Med Tech.

**ASTORINO, AMY L,** Univ Of Sc At Columbia, Columbia, SC; JR; BAC; Univ Actvts Org 88-89; Natl Stdnt Exc Assc Com Head 90-; Alpha Xi Delta Mbrshp Chrmn 88-; Alpha Xi Delta Rep Natl Cnvntn 90; Natl Stdnt Exc Pgm; Communications; Personnel Services.

**ASU, ALOYSIUS M,** Univ Of The Dist Of Columbia, Washington, DC; GD; MBA; BBA 90; Bsn/Fin; Bnkng.

**ASUNCION, REDANTE M,** Indiana Univ Of Pa, Indiana, PA; FR; BED; Engl; Tchng/Wrtng.

**ASUNCION, VAN-JOHN A,** Embry Riddle Aeronautical Univ, Daytona Beach, FL; JR; BS; Griffas AFB Aero Clb 89-90; AFROTC Dep 157 Embry Riddle Aero Un 90-; USAF Rsrv 90-94; USAF Sgt 86-90; AA Comm Clg Ar Frc 89; Prfsnl Arntcs; Avtn.

**ASUQUO, RONKE D,** Commonwealth Coll, Virginia Beach, VA; SR; AAS; Fashn Clb; Alpha Beta Gamma; Phi Beta Lambda; Pres Lst; Dns Lst; Fash Merch; Fash Dir.

**ATANGAN, DEBBIE P,** George Mason Univ, Fairfax, VA; SO; BS; Gamma Phi Beta Rcrdng Sec; Dcsn Sci.

**ATCHISON, DEBBIE D,** Livingston Univ, Livingston, AL; SR; BS; Erly Chldhd Educ; Tch.

**ATCHLEY, JEREMY W,** Central Al Comm Coll, Alexander City, AL; FR; BA; Engl; Ed.

**ATCHLEY, MELISSA D,** Univ Of Nc At Charlotte, Charlotte, NC; FR; BA; Acctng; CPA.

**ATCHLEY, TAMBRE A,** Univ Of Miami, Coral Gables, FL; JR; BS; Drum/Bugle Corps US Nvl Acdmy Oprtns Offcr 88-90; Smmr Dtl US Nvl Acdmy 90; Marine Tchnlgcl Soc US Nvl Acdmy 89-90; Vol Unit US Nvy 88-90; Misc Vol Wrk 90-; Hosp Vol Phys Therpy 90-; Swmming US Nvl Acdmy 88-; Hlth Sci; Phys Therpst MSPT.

**ATHENS, CHRISTINE M,** Columbus Coll Of Art & Design, Columbus, OH; SO; BA; Illustration.

**ATHERLEY-DAVID, MARY M,** Fl International Univ, Miami, FL; SR; BS; Jr HS Belize CA Tchr; Bio; Tchr.

**ATHERTON, KENNA L,** Univ Of Ky, Lexington, KY; SR; BA; Hstry 89-90; Engl 89-90; Clg Bowl 89-90; Phi Alpha Theta 89-90; Kappa Delta Pi 89-90; Epsilon Delta; Scndry Educ/Engl; Tchr.

**ATHERTON, LORI L,** D Youville Coll, Buffalo, NY; SO; BA; Psychlgy.

**ATHEY, JOEL M,** Rutgers St Un At New Brunswick, New Brunswick, NJ; FR; BS; Engr Cvrng Cncl V P 90-; Phi Eta Sigma 90-; Phi Kappa Sigma V P Pldge Cls 90-; Deans Lst; Chem Engr.

**ATIENZA, KRISTEN A,** Georgian Court Coll, Lakewood, NJ; JR; BS; Amer Chem Soc 89-F Mendel Soc 89-; Intrntl Stdnts Assn 88-89; Deans Lst 89-90; Bio/Chem; Med.

**ATIENZA, MANUEL,** Newbury Coll, Brookline, MA; FR; AA; Charles Htl; Clnry Arts; Chef Clnry Fld.

**ATKINS, ALICE G,** Beckley Coll, Beckley, WV; SO; WVARNG Fmly Support Grp Sec 89-90; Paralegal Stud.

**ATKINS, ASHLEY L,** Ms Univ For Women, Columbus, MS; SR; BA; FCA 90; Nu Epsilon Delta 90-; Bsktbl 90; Prlgl; Law.

**ATKINS, ASHLEY L,** Duke Univ, Durham, NC; FR; BS; Kappa Alpha Theta 90-; Math/Frnch; Intl Bsns/Bnkng.

**ATKINS, BROADUS Z,** Univ Of Nc At Charlotte, Charlotte, NC; SR; BS; Allied Hlth Club 88-90; ROTC Squadron Cmndr 87; Phi Eta Sigma 88; Phi Kappa Phi 90; Arnold Air Soc Cmndr 88; Chem Rsrch Assist 90; Chem; Med.

**ATKINS, CARROLL STEWART,** Univ Of Sc At Columbia, Columbia, SC; SR; Alumni Assn 89-; Chi Omega 87-; A Walsh Ctr 87-90; Child Abuse Ctr 87-89; Red Crs 89-; Ford Boyd Interiors 90-; Dsgn Place 89; BA; Art Studio/Interior Dsgn.

**ATKINS, CHERIE L,** S U N Y Coll At Fredonia, Fredonia, NY; SR; BA; Stdnt Prnts In Educ 89-; Kappa Delta Pi; Soph Acad Awrd 90; Cmp St Untd Meth Chrch; Elem Educ; Tchr.

**ATKINS, DONNA M,** Volunteer St Comm Coll, Gallatin, TN; JR; BS; Gamma Beta Phi 90-; Assoc; Elem Educ; Tchr.

**ATKINS, ELLEN T,** Univ Of Miami, Coral Gables, FL; JR; BS; Deans Lst 90-; Prsdnts Hnr Roll 90-; FL Assn Fin Aid Admnstrtrs 88-; Fnncl Asst Advsr UNIV Of Miami 88-; Cmmnctns Pltcl Sci; Write.

**ATKINS, ELVONNA V,** Jackson St Univ, Jackson, MS; FR; MBA; Stdnt Govt Assoc 90-; ROTC Sgt 90-91; Alpha Lambda Delta 90-; Alpha Swthrt; Math/Pre Engr; Mechanical.

**ATKINS, HAROLD P,** Asbury Theological Sem, Wilmore, KY; JR; MDIV; AA Harford Comm Clg 71; BS Towson St Univ 73; BA Moody Bible Inst 76; Pstrl.

**ATKINS, JANET M,** Anderson Coll, Anderson, SC; FR; BA; Phi Theta Kappa 90-; Coll Bwl 90; 3.6 GPA 90-; Rlgn; Mssns.

**ATKINS, KRISTI D,** Univ Of Ky, Lexington, KY; JR; BA; Dance Ensemble Pres 89-; Zeta Tau Alpha 88-90; Elem Ed: Teach.

**ATKINS, LATISHA R,** Hampton Univ, Hampton, VA; FR; BA; Pltcl Science; Law.

**ATKINS, MONICA R,** Univ Of Al At Huntsville, Huntsville, AL; SO; BA; SWE 90-; Alpha Lambda Delta 90-; Hnr Schlr 89-; Indstrl Eng; Eng.

**ATKINS, RANDY K,** Univ Of Sc At Columbia, Columbia, SC; JR; BED; Hnrs Prog; Dean Lst 89-; PTA; Math; Tchng.

**ATKINS, ROBERT A,** Radford Univ, Radford, VA; JR; BA; Engl; Frlnc Wrtr.

**ATKINS, TIMOTHY J,** Catawba Valley Comm Coll, Hickory, NC; SR; AASC; Furniture Design/Development; Frntr Engrg.

**ATKINS JR, WALTER L,** Alcorn St Univ, Lorman, MS; FR; Army ROTC 90-; Bio; Dntstry.

**ATKINSON, JOEY G,** Ohio Valley Coll, Parkersburg, WV; JR; Sigma Timothy Clb TIE Clb SGA Soph VP 89-90; Ambsdr Msns Clb 89-90; Sigma Ath Dir 89-90; Ohio Vly Clg Rep Ft Hill Yth Camp 89; Winter Spg Banq 1st Rnnr Up Sigma Beau; IM Part 89-90; Bible; Counselor.

**ATKINSON, JOHN A,** Coll Of Charleston, Charleston, SC; JR; BA; Coll Rpblcns 90-; Pol Sci; Law.

**ATKINSON, KENNETH R,** Harding Grad School Of Relig, Memphis, TN; GD; MDIV; SG Pres 90-; W F Albright Centenary Symposium; BS Oakland Univ 82; Biblical Studies; Teach.

**ATKINSON, PAMELA D,** Ny Univ, New York, NY; FR; BA; Acctng.

**ATKINSON, PATRICIA A,** Fayetteville St Univ, Fayetteville, NC; SO; BA; RA 90-; Spc Olympc Vol 89-; IM Rec Sprt Asst 89-; Bus; Own Bus.

**ATKINSON, ROBERT C,** Univ Of Southern Ms, Hattiesburg, MS; SO; BSBA; Hnrs Student Assoc 89-; Student Eagle Club Nwsltr Edtr 90-; Gamma Beta Phi 90-; Busn; Mgt.

**ATKINSON, ROGER HALL,** Spartanburg Methodist Coll, Spartanburg, SC; FR; BA; Golf Team 90-; Deans List; Golf Team 90-; Business; Sales.

**ATKINSON, SANDRA L,** Norfolk St Univ, Norfolk, VA; SR; BA; Erly Chldhd Clb V P 90-; Stdnt Va Educ Assn 90-; Alpha Kappa Mu 90-; By Scts Amer Tidwtr Cncl 80-; St Pius X Chrch Nrflk Va 80-; Assc Deg Tidwtr Comm Clg Va Bch Va 88; Elem Educ; Tchng.**

**ATKINSON, SUSAN ANNE,** Longwood Coll, Farmville, VA; SO; BA; Psych Club; Psi Chi; Psych; Abuse Cnslr.

**ATKINSON, THOMAS D,** Villanova Univ, Villanova, PA; JR; BA; Phi Alpha Theta Pres; Pi Kappa Alpha Alumni Chrmn 90; Blue Key 90-; Vrsty Water Polo 88-; Hstry.

**ATKINSON, WANDA G,** Meridian Comm Coll, Meridian, MS; SO; BFA; Art Clb VP; US Achvmnt Acdmy; Deans Lst 90-; Hmr Cstl Art Schlrshp 90-; Cmpttn Dsgn; Hn Mnt Cmpttn Dsgn; Mst Otstndng Fine Arts Stndt; Mmbr Brd Dir 90-; Rfstrd Dntl Hygnst; RDH 81; Art.

**ATLAS JR, DAVID MARLOW,** Salisbury St Univ, Salisbury, MD; JR; BA; Bio Soc; Med Careers Clb; Omicron Delta Kappa; Beta Beta Beta; M S Vol; M D Assn Vol; Deans Lst; Margaret Brent Flwshp; Track/Cross Cntry Capt; Bio; Med.

**ATOUT, SAMER N,** City Univ Of Ny Baruch Coll, New York, NY; SR; BA; Gldn Key 90-; Deans Lst 90; Prvst Schlrshp 90; Prgrmmng Mgmt Bnkng 81-; ADCS 82; Comp Info Systms.

**ATSUMI, MADOKA,** Univ Of Akron, Akron, OH; JR; Rep Dnce Co 89-; Gldn Ky 90-; Fr Sclstc Hon 89-; Fine Appld Art/Dnce; Prof Bllet Mdrn Dnce.

**ATTAWAY, COURTNEY M,** Clemson Univ, Clemson, SC; SR; BS; SC Rec/Park Assn Pres 88-; Pi Beta Phi Chpln 87-; Am Hotel/Motel Assn Cert; John Q Hammons Inc 90; Travel/Tourism; Hotel Mgmnt.

**ATTENBERGER, RAYMOND D,** Univ Of Pittsburgh, Pittsburgh, PA; SO; BSN; Big Bro/Sis 90-; AS Comm Clg Allghny Cnty 86-89; Nrsng; Neonatal ICU.**

**ATTIPOE-KPLOANYI, EVELYN S,** City Univ Of Ny City Coll, New York, NY; SR; BS; Afrcn Stdnts Assn 89-; Sigma Theta Tau 91-; Nrsng Stdnts Clb 90-; Presby Chrcn Wmn Srvc Socty 86-; Sci; Lctr.

**ATWAH, MAHER M,** Edinboro Univ Of Pa, Edinboro, PA; SR; Stdnt Govt Assn Assist 89-90; Intl Stdnt Assn Pres 90-; Cmptr Clb V P 90-; Phi Eta Sigma; Alpha Chi Treas 90-; Pi Mu Epsilon Math Hnrs Assn Sec 89-90; Deans Lst; Hnr Schlrshp Oxford Univ; Intl Stdnts Tuition Waiver 88-; Cmptr Sci; Cmptr Expert.

**ATWATER III, FREDERICK H,** Averett Coll, Danville, VA; SO; MBS; AS; Physics; Military Aviation Pilot.

**ATWELL, HUGH C,** Univ Of Nc At Charlotte, Charlotte, NC; SR; BS; Crmnl Jstce; Law Schl.

**ATWELL, MARCIE L,** Western Ky Univ, Bowling Green, KY; SO; BA; Engl; Elem Tchr.

**ATWELL, MARY CATHERINE,** Univ Of Cin R Walters Coll, Blue Ash, OH; FR; Bus.

**ATWELL, PAMELA T,** Va Highlands Comm Coll, Abingdon, VA; SO; BA; SGA Tres 90-; Phi Theta Kappa Rgnl Sec 90-; GS Ldr 84-87; Hnrs Lst88; Deans Lst 89; Acad All Amer Tm; PTK Outstndng Mem Rgn 89-90; PTK Bierkoe Dist Mem Natl Awd 90; PTK Dist Chptr Pres 90; All Amer Schlr; Math; Scndry Ed.

**ATWELL, SHARON H,** Univ Of Nc At Charlotte, Charlotte, NC; SR; BA; Anthrpolgy Scty 90-; Psych Clb 90-; Scty Fr Hmn Rsrce Mgmt 90-; Chncllrs Lst; Dns Lst; Anthrplgy And Psych; Trvl Areas.

**ATWOOD, DAVID E,** Bridgewater Coll, Bridgewater, VA; FR; BS; Stage Band; Concert Band; BSF; BSU; IM Sftbl/Bsktbl/Ftbl; Math/Cmptr Sci; Tch.

**ATWOOD, ELIZABETH A,** Springfield Tech Comm Coll, Springfield, MA; JR; BA; Bus Club Sec 84-85; VIP Amer Red Cross Bld Dnr 89-; Beths Tax Serv Owner 90-; Sec Educ Math/Bus.

**ATWOOD, RHONDA H,** Gaston Coll, Dallas, NC; SO; Gamma Beta Phi Sec 89-; Cmptr Sci Clb; Pres Lst; Cmptr Pgmr.

**AU YEUNG, MEI HAN,** City Univ Of Ny Baruch Coll, New York, NY; SR; Beta Alpha Psi V P 90; Beta Gamma Sigma; Goldn Key; S Irvng Wenstrn Schlrshp 90; Samuel/Rae Ecknr Schlrshp 89; Barr Provst Awd 88-90; BBA; Acctg.

**AU, DICKSON T,** City Univ Of Ny Baruch Coll, New York, NY; SO; BBA; Acctg Soc; Acctg.

**AU, PETER Y T,** Columbia Univ, New York, NY; SO; BS; Snds Of China ECM 90-; Mech Engrng.**

**AUAIS, ALEXANDER,** Univ Of Miami, Coral Gables, FL; SR; BA; Alpha Sigma Phi Corresp Sec 87-89; Jcksn Mem Hosp 90-; Untd Crbl Plsy 88; Amer Hrt Assoc; Bio; Med.

**AUBAS, CHERYL B,** Va St Univ, Petersburg, VA; SR; BA; SGA Pres 89-; Phi Beta Lambda VP 87-; ROTC 87-; Kappa Delta Pi Treas 89-90; Pi Omega Pi 90-; Alpha Kappa Alpha VP 89-; Ms Future Busines Teacher 89-90; Academic Pin 89-; All Amer Schlr Awrd 89-90; Bus Educ; Bus Teacher.

**AUBE, TAMORA S,** Hudson Valley Comm Coll, Troy, NY; SR; BA; Early Chldhd Clb 89-90; Prsdnts Lst 89-; St Rose S Schlrshp 90-; Elem Ed; Tchr.

**AUBIN, JENNIFER L,** Fl St Univ, Tallahassee, FL; SR; BS; Beta Gamma Sigma; Golden Key 88-; Pi Delta Phi; Ltl Sis Minerva 88-; Finance.

**AUBLE, A GABRIEL,** Cornell Univ Statutory College, Ithaca, NY; JR; BS; Luso Brzln Assn; IM Sccr 90-; CUSLAR 89-; Yth Bureau; Lcrss Prog Hd Coach; Actvtc Cntr; JV Lacrss 88-89; Educ; Tchng/Sclgy.

**AUCONE, ALLYSON L,** Merrimack Coll, North Andover, MA; SO; BA; Soclgy.

**AUDET, RICHARD S,** Holyoke Comm Coll, Holyoke, MA; SO; BM; Clg Chorale 88-90; Msc Ensmbl 88-90; Hnrs Pgm; Phi Theta Kappa 89-; Msc Clb 89-; Hnrs Recitalist Awd Clsscl Guitar 90; Clg Hnrs Convocation Awd 89-90; Cecil Erard Msc Awd 89; AA; Msc; Msc Engr Tech.**

**AUDIA, NATALIE J,** George Mason Univ, Fairfax, VA; FR; BA; USCTA Eqstrn Natl 84-; U S St Pny Clb 84-; Intrnshp Washington Invstmnt Corp 89-; Bsn; Law.

**AUDIA, ROSE J,** Wv Univ, Morgantown, WV; SR; IIE Chrmn 88-; Alpha Pi Mu Crrspndng Secy 90-; Tutor; WV Univ Ldrshp Schlrshp; Schlrs Prog; Deans Lst; BSIE; Indstrl Engrng.

**AUDINO, CHERIE M,** Hudson Valley Comm Coll, Troy, NY; JR; BAACC; Hair Tech 83-; Acctnt 90-; AAS HVCC 87; Acctg.

**AUGUST, AMANDA A,** Atlantic Comm Coll, Mays Landing, NJ; FR.

**AUGUSTE, ELIZABETH,** Norfolk St Univ, Norfolk, VA; SR; Sclgy.

**AUGUSTIN, LEAH D,** Andover Coll, Portland, ME; GD; AS; Med Asstng; Med Ph D.

**AUGUSTINE, KIRK E,** Univ Of Louisville, Louisville, KY; FR; BEE; Elec Engr; NASA.

**AUGUSTINE, SANDRA E,** Univ Of Scranton, Scranton, PA; SO; BS; Stdnt Govt 89-90; Acctng Assn 89-90; Bus Clb 89-; Omega Beta Sigma 90-; USAA Natl Awd; Preate Awd; Pres Schlrshp; Bus; Mktg/Advrtsng.

**AUGUSTINO, DIANNE,** Niagara Univ, Niagara Univ, NY; SR; BA; Natl Tchrs Ftr 89-; Tchng Asst FR Ornttn 90; Elem Ed.

**AUGUSTUS, ASHOK J,** Manhattan Coll, Bronx, NY; SR; BE; Engrs Cncl; IEEE; Tau Beta Pi VP 88-; Eta Kappa Nu Rcrdng Sec 898-; Epsilon Sigma Pi; NY State Rgnts Schlrshp; Pres Schlrshp; Dns Lst; Elec Engr.

**AUGUSTUS, KISHORE F,** Manhattan Coll, Bronx, NY; SR; BSEE; Engrs Cncl; Cmpus Radio Sta; Tau Beta Pi Cores Sec 90-; Eta Kappa Nu Cores Sec 90-; IEEE; Epsilon Sigma Pi; Elect Engr.

**AULEN, DAVID B,** Clarkson Univ, Potsdam, NY; JR; BS; Amer Mrktng Assn VP Admn 90-; Stu Ppr Bus Mgr 90-; Invstmtn Clb Fndrsng Chrm 88-89; Alpha Kappa Psi VP Mmbrshp 89-; Kraft Gen Foods Inter 88-; Fnnc/Accntn; Oprtns/Fnncl Plnng.

**AULISIO, WENDY M,** Univ Of Scranton, Scranton, PA; SO; Deans Lst 89-; Pr Schlrshp 89-; Fin.

**AULL, M ALISON,** Univ Of Sc At Columbia, Columbia, SC; FR; BA; Bptst Stdnt Un; Pltcl Sci.

**AULT, HEATHER S,** Columbus Coll Of Art & Design, Columbus, OH; FR; BFA; Pr Lst; Color Wheels Art In Rec Ctrs; Sat Schl Art Pgm Asst 90-; Art; Graphi/Adv Design.

**AULT, SHANNON D,** Univ Of Al, Tuscaloosa, AL; SO; Crmnl Jstce Stdnt Assn 90-; Gamma Beta Phi 90-; Intl Rel; Govt Wrk.**

**AULT, YVETTE L,** Univ Of Ky, Lexington, KY; FR; BARCH; Secretary 87-; Architecture.

**AULTMAN, DOROTHY M,** Alcorn St Univ, Lorman, MS; SO; BS; Tri-Beta Treas 90; Intrfth Gspl Choir; Deans Lst; WYA; Schlrshp Acdmc; Blgy; Hlth-Rltd Pro.

**AULTMAN, FARRELL JAY,** Univ Of Al At Birmingham, Birmingham, AL; SO; BSEE; IEEE 90-; Peer Advsr 90-; Crawford/Virginia Johnson Schlrshp; Pres List; Deans List; Elec Eng.

**AULTMAN, STEPHANIE L,** Univ Of Southern Ms, Hattiesburg, MS; SR; BS; Bapt Stdnt Un Noonday Chmn 90-; Gamma Beta Phi 89-; Spch Pathology; Spch Therapist.

**AUMAN, JUDITH STONE,** Christopher Newport Coll, Newport News, VA; SR; Panhellenic Pres 66-67; Judicial Bd; Sigma Tau Delta; Kappa Delta Pi; Phi Mu V P 67; Acad Ldrshp Honorary Marshal; Prtsmth Music Stdy Clb; Prtsmth Comm Concerts Bd; PTA Pres 84-85; Officers Wives Club Pres; BA; Engl; Admin.

**AUMILLER, LESLIE A,** Anne Arundel Comm Coll, Arnold, MD; SO; BA; SOC 90-; Hlth Serv 80-; Scndry Ed.

**AURDAHL, ANITA L,** Wagner Coll, Staten Island, NY; JR; BS; Commuter Clb 88-; Alethea; Iota Delta Alpha Secy 89-; Zeta Delta Alpha Fndr 90-; Dean Freshman Awd 88; Esther/Anderw Clauson Mem Prize 89; Biol; Human Genetics.**

**AURILIO, JENNIFER R,** Georgetown Univ, Washington, DC; FR; BA; Slng Tm 90; Polo Clb 90; Bsnss Admin; Intrntl Bsnss Mngmnt.

**AUSBAND, ELIZABETH A,** Univ Of Nc At Charlotte, Charlotte, NC; FR; MBA; Campus Newspapr Assist News Ed 90; Phi Eta Sigma 90; Engl; Tchr Or Jrnlsm.

**AUSBORN, SUSAN E,** Greenville Tech Coll, Greenville, SC; GD; AA; SG 90-; Phi Theta Kappa 90-; Model UN Hd Del 90-; Fncl Industry 87-89; Pol Sci/Intl Studies; Intl Law BA.

**AUSBURN, SHANNON M,** Fl Atlantic Univ, Boca Raton, FL; FR; BA; Bus Admin; Bus Mgmt.

**AUSTILL JR, HAROLD W,** Spartanburg Methodist Coll, Spartanburg, SC; SO; AA; Crmnl Jstc Clb 89-; Day Stdnt Assc 89-; Phi Theta Kappa 90-; Psi Beta 90-; Pres Hnr List; Exc Crmnl Jstc; Crmnl Jstc; BS Law Enf.

**AUSTIN, ANN C,** Longwood Coll, Farmville, VA; FR; BA; Stdnt Ed Assn 90-; Bptst Stdnt Un 90-; Alpha Lambda Delta Sec; Dghtrs Amer Rvltn; Math; Tchr.

**AUSTIN, ANTONIO D,** Hampton Univ, Hampton, VA; FR; BA; ROTC 90-; Color Guard 90-; Ecnmcs; Law/Mltry Offcr.

**AUSTIN, ARCHIE R,** Univ Of Tn At Martin, Martin, TN; SR; Stu Govt Cngrsmn 88-89; Phi Theta Kappa; Sigma Pi VP 88-; Ftbl Schlrshp 88-; Ftbl Acdmc All Conf 89-; Ftbl Tm Capt 88-; BED; Math; Tchr.

**AUSTIN, ARTHUR C,** Univ Of Sc At Coastal Carolina, Conway, SC; SR; BA; Mktng; Corp Level Advrtsng.

**AUSTIN, CARL L,** Univ Of Nc At Charlotte, Charlotte, NC; SO; BS; Accounting.

**AUSTIN, CAROLYN G,** Columbia Union Coll, Takoma Park, MD; GD; BSOM; Mt Rona Bptst Chrch Pgm Chrprsn 90-; Mt Rona Bptst Chrch Chrl Ensmbl Pres 87-; BSOM; Org Mgmt; Mgmt Cnsltng.

**AUSTIN, CATHERINE M,** East Tn St Univ, Johnson City, TN; SR; BS; ASME 83-88; SME 90-; RI 90-; Engr.

**AUSTIN, DEBORAH D,** Univ Of Tn At Knoxville, Knoxville, TN; SR; BS; Exec Asstnt Berkline Corp; AS Lees Mc Rae Clg 72; Mktg; Mktg Mgr.

**AUSTIN, DIRK,** Nc St Univ At Raleigh, Raleigh, NC; FR; BS; Order St Patrick 90-; Alpha Lamba Delta 90-; Dean List 90-; Elctrcl Engrng.

**AUSTIN, GENIA G,** Radford Univ, Radford, VA; SR; Cath Stdnt Assn Flk Grp 89-; Phi Kappa Phi 90-; Sigma Tau Delta 90-; Cir K Intrntl 88-; Sftbl Tm Capt 87-90; BA; Engl; Ed.

**AUSTIN, HOPE M,** Wake Forest Univ, Winston-Salem, NC; FR; BA; Mrchg Bnd 90-; Bsktbl Pep Bnd Libr/Ofc Help; Pit Orch; Church Accompanist 90-; Harbinger Corps; Res Advsr; Dns Lst 90-; Engl/Msc Ed; Tch.

**AUSTIN, JEFFREY P,** Oh Univ, Athens, OH; JR; BS; IM 88-; Tau Beta Pi 90-; Varsity Bsbl 88-; Engrg; Chem Engrg.

**AUSTIN, JENNIFER L,** Nyack Coll, Nyack, NY; JR; BS; St Agathas Gospel Tm Pres 89-; Jr Cls Ofcr Acad Affairs Rep 90-; Res Asst 90-; Alpha Chi 90-; Elem Edn; Publ Sch Elem Tchr.

**AUSTIN, JULIA E,** Voorhees Coll, Denmark, SC; JR; Alpha Kappa Mu; Dean List 89-90; Cmptr Science; Prgrmmr.

**AUSTIN, KATHLEEN A,** Christopher Newport Coll, Newport News, VA; FR; BS; Cmps Actvts Bd Chrmn Spec Events; SGA Sec; BACCHUS; Williamsburg Comm Hosp Physcl Thrpy Vol; Pre-Med Blgy; Occptnl Thrpy/Physcl Thrpy.

**AUSTIN, KEITH P,** Tn Temple Univ, Chattanooga, TN; FR; BED; Science; Teacher.

**AUSTIN, KELLY S,** Ky Mountain Bible Coll, Vancleve, KY; SO; BS; Class Pr 90-; Yrbk Bus Mgr 90-; Stdnt Cncl Class Rep 90-; Drama Stdnt Dir 89-90; AA; Cnslng; Socl Wrk.

**AUSTIN, KIMBERLY S,** Draughons Jr Coll Nashville, Nashville, TN; SO; AS; Fshn Mrchndsng; Fshn.

**AUSTIN, KRISTA P,** Pellissippi St Tech Comm Coll, Knoxville, TN; FR; AA; Deans List 90; Lib Arts.

**AUSTIN, LYNETTE F,** Cincinnati Metropolitan Coll, Cincinnati, OH; SO; MAP Pres 90; Deans Lst 89-90; Grp Hlth Assn Intrnshp; MA; Med; Med Admin.

**AUSTIN, MICHELLE T,** City Univ Of Ny La Guard Coll, Long Island Cty, NY; SO; AS; Drma Clb Actr 90-; Phi Theta Kappa 90-; Sci Engl; Dttcs Jrnlsm.

**AUSTIN, SEMMING,** Univ Of Sc At Columbia, Columbia, SC; SR; BS; Delta Sigma Pi 88-; IM Sccr 89-; Business Admin; Information Systems.

**AUSTIN, STEPHANIE K,** Central St Univ, Wilberforce, OH; JR; BS; Educ Soc 90-; NAACP Coll Div 87-; Elem Ed; Educ Admin.

**AUSTIN, TAMMY L,** Beckley Coll, Beckley, WV; FR; Sci; Med.

**AUSTIN, TYRONE S,** Central St Univ, Wilberforce, OH; FR; BA, Accntng Clb 90-; ACE VP; Accntng/Rl Est; CPA Rl Est Brkr.

**AUSTIN, YOLANDA L,** Univ Of Tn At Martin, Martin, TN; GD; BS; Ldrs Rsdnc 86-87; Alpha Kappa Alpha 89-; Psychology; MA.

**AUTERA, MATTHEW J,** Life Coll, Marietta, GA; GD; DR.

**AUTH, CLIFFORD H,** Le Moyne Coll, Syracuse, NY; JR; BA; Rugby Club 89-; International House 90-; History Minior Education; Teaching.

**AUTREY, CINDY S,** Mayland Comm Coll, Spruce Pine, NC; FR; BA; Yancey Cnty Bus Drivers Assoc 89-; Mayland Cmnty Clg Deans Lst 90-; Crim Just; Juv Cnslng.

**AUTREY, JENNIFER M,** Livingston Univ, Livingston, AL; FR; BA; Bus Admin; Acctg.

**AUTREY, JOHN E,** Morehouse Coll, Atlanta, GA; FR; BS; Natl Soc Blck Engrs; Physcs/Elec Engr.

**AUTRY, LAWRENCE G,** Lincoln Univ, Lincoln Univ, PA; SO; Forencs Soc 90-; Nwspr 90-; Bus Admn/Ecnmst.

**AUTRY, LEAH G,** Saint Andrews Presbytrn Coll, Laurinburg, NC; FR; BS; Lab Asst Co-Envrnmntl Chair 90-; Suite Ldr Dorm Cncl; Hon Pgm 90-; Scotie Vlg Rtrmnt Hm Vol 90-; Deans Lst Acad Schlrshp; Bio; Genetic Eng.

**AVALLONE, PAMELA J,** Univ Of New Haven, West Haven, CT; SO; BS; Floor Repr 89; Dorm Govt Sec 90; Campus Ministry 89-90; Biology Clb 89-90; Presidents Ldrshp Scty 89-90; Ambassador 89-90; Hnrs Prog 89-; Radio Sci News Rprtr; Biology; Medical Schl.

**AVALTRONI, JEANNINE M,** City Univ Of Ny Baruch Coll, New York, NY; JR; BA; Gldn Key 90-; Dns Lst 88-; Psy Chi; Thrpst Ltl Stps YMCA 90-; Cnslnt Serv; Psy; Scl Wrk.

**AVANCENA, CHARMAINE Q,** City Univ Of Ny Baruch Coll, New York, NY; SO; MBA; Filipino Club 88-89; Hlth Sci; Physcl Thrpy.

**AVANT, DUANE P,** Univ Of Sc At Columbia, Columbia, SC; FR; BS; Eng; Chem Eng.

**AVANT, JERALINE M,** Kent St Univ Kent Cmps, Kent, OH; SR; BS; Flying Clb 87-90; Flight Instr Intern 90-; Mktg; Pilot.

**AVEARY, BRENDA D,** Lane Coll, Jackson, TN; JR; Chrm 90; Bsktbl Trck Vlybl 90; CNA 88-89; Hist/Elem Educ.

**AVENA, MARY G,** City Univ Of Ny Queensbrough, New York, NY; FR; Gold Honor Roll; Gold Medal Italian; Bsns Mgmt.

**AVENT, MELANIE D,** Georgetown Coll, Georgetown, KY; SO; BA; Chrl Lbrn 89-; Phi Mu Ordrng Chrmn; Intl Ordr Kings Dghtrs/Sons 90-; Kings Dghtrs/Sons Schlr 90; Hon Rl 89-; Psychlgy; Chld Psychlgst.

**AVERETT, LISA L,** Univ Of Ga, Athens, GA; JR; BSED; Early Chldhd Educ.

**AVERETTE, STACY M,** Livingston Univ, Livingston, AL; BA; USAF 87-90; Chem/Bio; Chmst.

**AVERILL, BRENT A,** Gordon Conwell Theol Sem, S Hamilton, MA; GD; MA; Phi Alha Theta VP 63-64; Asstshp Byingtn Schlr; Pstr 68-90; BA TX Chrstn Univ 64; D Min Wstmnstr Sem 87; Cnslng.

**AVERILL, DANIEL S,** Mount Aloysius Jr Coll, Cresson, PA; FR; ASS; Natl Hardwood Lbr Assn 88; English Hon; U S Navy 83-87; Agr Tech; Golf Crs Mgmt.

**AVERILL, JASON W,** Me Maritime Academy, Castine, ME; JR; BS; Soc Cncl/Band 88-89; NROTC 88-; Drama Clb 89-; Bagaduce Rvw 90-; Nautical Sci; Military.

**AVERILL, TOD H,** Univ Of Ct, Storrs, CT; JR; BS; Frstry Wldlf Clb 90-; Soil Wtr Cnsrvtn Soc; Alpha Zeta Chnclr; IM 90-; US Navy Nclr Mchncl Oprtr Sprvsr Brd Sbrmns 82-88; AS Unvrsty NY 90; Ntrl Rsrcs Mgmt Engnrng; Land Use Lnd Plnng.

**AVERITT IV, RICHARD G,** Savannah Coll Of Art & Design, Savannah, GA; JR; BA; Pres Cncl Pres 90; Photo Grp Pres 90; HOW 90; COOL; Local Sccr Coach; Relations Rep 88-89; Prmtn Mngmnt Asst 89; Fine Art/Phtgrphy; Prffsnl Phtgrphr.

**AVERSANO, LAURA A,** Univ Of Al At Birmingham, Birmingham, AL; SO; Alpha Lambda Delta.

**AVERY, CHRISTIANNE F,** Univ Of Nh Plymouth St Coll, Plymouth, NH; SO; BED; Colg Chorale 89-90; Plymouth Acad Supp Svcs 90; Pres List 90; Cl/46 Schlrshp 90-; Elem Ed; Tchr.

**AVERY, COLLEEN ANN,** Mount Saint Mary Coll, Newburgh, NY; JR; AA Dutchess Cmnty Clg 90; Engl; Elem/Spec Ed.

**AVERY, JASON B,** Wallace St Comm Coll At Selma, Selma, AL; FR; BA; Mrchng Bnd; Cncrt Bnd; Frshmn Frm Fnlst; Pi Lambda Phi Asst Pldg Chrmn; Pre Med; Ped Stds.

**AVERY, JEANETTE,** Univ Of Nc At Greensboro, Greensboro, NC; SO; BS; Actvts Board Rtnd Rcrtmnt Chrprsn 89-; Rsdnt Assist 90-; Stdnt Govt Dlgte 90; Alpha Lambda Delta; Alpha Kappa Delta; Spartan Spirits 89-90; Success Assist 90-; Peer Mentor 90-; Neo Black Soc 89-90; Educ/Sclgy; Tchng.

**AVERY, LAURA G,** East Carolina Univ, Greenville, NC; FR; BA; MENC Stdnt; Forum Cmmt Selection Dean 90-; Mrchng Band/Wind Enpsemble; Music; Ed.

**AVERY, LINDA L,** Owensboro Jr Coll Of Bus, Owensboro, KY; GD; BA; Bus/Prof Wmn Clb 83-; Army Rsrv 74-; Sec; Exex Sec 69; Assoc; Bus; Law.

**AVERY, R COLLEEN,** Western Piedmont Comm Coll, Morganton, NC; FR; AA SC; Med Asst Clb Pres 90-; Med Asst Schlrshp; Med Aux Schlrshp; Med Asst.

**AVICHAL, NEPABEN I,** Atlantic Comm Coll, Mays Landing, NJ; FR; AA; Comp Info Systms.

**AVIGDOR, SARA,** Tri County Tech Coll, Pendleton, SC; SR; ACT; Cmptr Tech; Cmptr Prgrmg.

**AVILA DEL RE, CAROLINA TERESA,** Immaculata Coll, Immaculata, PA; FR; Econ/Bus Admn; Mgr.

**AVILA, ALBERTO J,** Fl International Univ, Miami, FL; FR; BS; Faclty Schlr 90-; IM Soccr/Vlybl; Comp Eng; Eng.

**AVILA, CARLOS J,** American Univ Of Pr, Bayamon, PR; FR; BA; Hnr Scty; Acctng; Fncng/Mgmt.

**AVILA, EFRAIN,** Univ Politecnica De Pr, Hato Rey, PR; JR; Bsbl; Math; Engrg Elctrcl.

**AVILA, ELIZABETH,** Miami Dade Comm Coll South, Miami, FL; SO; BA; Phi Lambda Asst Tm Ldr; AA 90; Elem Ed; Tchr.

**AVILES HIDALGO, JULIO E,** Inter Amer Univ Pr Aquadilla, Aguadilla, PR; JR; Sml Bus Inst Intramercn Campus 90; Natl Hon Soc Academia Montesori 85; Track/Fld Intramercn Campus; Mktg; Publc Rltns.

**AVILES SANTIAGO, MARITZA,** Inter Amer Univ Pr Hato Rey, Hato Rey, PR; FR; Math; Acctg.

**AVILES-ROMAN, ALBERTO,** Inter Amer Univ Pr San German, San German, PR; SO; BBA; Natl Assoc Accntnts 90-; Hnr Pgm 90-; Acctg/Finance; CPA Cnsltnt/Stckbrkr.

**AVIS, LEIGH A,** Thomas Nelson Comm Coll, Hampton, VA; SO; ASSOC; Sailing Clb 90 ; Amer Qtr Horse Assn 89, Va Qtr Horse Assn 89; Bus Admn; Corp Law.

**AVITABILE, GINA M,** Newbury Coll, Brookline, MA; FR; Exprssns Fshn Clb 90-; Fshn Dsgn; Fshn Dsgnr.

**AVRAM, RARES F,** City Univ Of Ny City Coll, New York, NY; SO; BS; Deans Lst; Comp Sci; Eng.

**AVRETT, VICKIE L,** Memphis St Univ, Memphis, TN; JR; BA; AS Jackson St Comm Clg 90; Elem Educ; Tchr.

**AWAD, NOUAR,** City Univ Of Ny La Guard Coll, Long Island Cty, NY; SO; BA; Prtnrs In Coop Ed Awrd; Mntr Hnrs 90; AS; Comp Sci; Prgrmmng Anlyss.

**AWAMLEH, DIMA A,** Strayer Coll, Washington, DC; SR; BSCS; Acctg Clb 89; Alpha Chi Sec 90-; AAMR; Cmptr Info Sys; Copr Law.

**AWAN, GHULAM S,** Univ Of South Al, Mobile, AL; SO; BS; Intl Clb Pres 90; Phi Theta Kappa 89-90; AS Allen Co Comm Clg 90; Acctg; CPA.

**AWENOWICZ, PATRICK W,** Allegheny Coll, Meadville, PA; SO; BS; Vars Debate Team 90; Rsdnt Advsr; Psi Chi 90; Phi Gamma Delta; Alden Schlr 90; Intrnshp Psych Dept; Psych; Neuro Sci.

**AWGULEWITSCH, NATALIA P,** Coll Of Charleston, Charleston, SC; SR; Frnch Clb SCSU 87-88,Treas 89-90; Grmn Clb 87-88; Mntry Awds; Awd Alliance Francaise 90; Endowed Schlrshp 90-; BA; Frnch/Grmn; Lang/Lit.

**AWKWARD, LYNN D,** Va Union Univ, Richmond, VA; SR; BA; Frgn Lang Club 88-89; Minister Alliance Chrstn Ed 89-90; Stdnt Ldr 88-89; Comm Of Schlrs 88-; Alpha Phi Alpha 90-; Am Bapt Flwshp; Otstndng Stdnt Ldrshp; C Herbert Marshall Schlrshp; Phlsphy & Rel; Pastor/Grad Prof.

**AWOFISAYO, ADEMOLA O,** Howard Univ, Washington, DC; FR; BARCH; Afrcn Stdnts Assn 90-; A Tm Sccr Clb 90-; Deans Lst; J Srgnt Rynlds Comm Cog Rich VA 89-90; Archtctr; Real Est Devlpmnt.

**AXELROD, STUART MARK,** Univ Of Sc At Columbia, Columbia, SC; JR; BA; Repr Stdnt Govt Senator 90-; Stf Wrtr Paper 89-; Pres List 90-; Chandler Lst 90-; Laubach Literacy Action Tutor; Political Sci; Law.

**AXMACHER, JAMES A,** Roane St Comm Coll, Harriman, TN; SO; BS; Chem; Dr Phrmcy.

**AXON JR, JAMES W,** Birmingham Southern Coll, Birmingham, AL; FR; BA; Sigma Alpha Epsilon Bst Pldg; Intrfrtrnty Cncl; Alpha Lambda Delta; Phi Eta Sigma; Sigma Alpha Epsilon; Birmingham Mens Sltr; Kings Rnch Chldrns Hm; Dscvry Pl; Ecnmcs; Law.

**AYALA RODRIGUEZ, OLGA I,** Caribbean Center For Adv Stds, San Juan, PR; MSW Assn 90-; Cum Laude 79; Intrnshps Crbn Cntr Advncd Studies Cum Laude 89; Magna Cum Laude; 1st Hosp Pnamer Employee Yr 89; BA ED Turabo Univ 74; MA MSW Puerto Rico Univ 82; PhD 90; Psychlgy.

**AYALA, EDWIN A,** Univ Of Pr At Mayaguez, Mayaguez, PR; Eng Hnr Soc 89-; Vllybl 89-; Chem Eng.

**AYALA, EDWIN ROMMEL,** Central Fl Comm Coll, Ocala, FL; AS; Phi Theta Kappaf Clb Intrntnl; Phi Theta Kappa; BED Eswela Nrml Mixta De Olancho Honduras 87; Qlty Cntrtl Prd Mgmnt; Engnrng.

**AYALA JR, MELVIN,** Univ Politecnica De Pr, Hato Rey, PR; FR; BA; Indust Eng.

**AYALA-ROBINSON, HUGO J,** Univ Of Pr Humacao Univ Coll, Humacao, PR; SO; BA; Exemption Of Pay Of Matriculation 90; Bsnss Admin Mngmnt; Mngmnt.

**AYANDIPO, ABIMBOLA IBIDUNNI,** Tuskegee Univ, Tuskegee Inst, AL; SR; Assn African Stdnts Treas 89-; Nigerian Stdnts Assn Treas 89-; BS; Tutored Economics 90; Acctg.

**AYAZO, CLAUDIA P,** Fl St Univ, Tallahassee, FL; SR; BA; Alliance Francaise 88-90; Latin Am Soc 89-; Phi Beta Kappa 90; Pi Delta Phi 89; Phi Eta Sigma 89; Aa Belle-Winthrop Schlrshp 90; Intrnshp Fl Dept Of Comm 90-; Modern Lang; Master In Intl Affiars.

**AYCOCK, MELANIE A,** Jefferson St Comm Coll, Birmingham, AL; FR; Child Dvlpmnt; Teacher.

**AYCOCK, PAMELA G,** James Sprunt Comm Coll, Kenansville, NC; GD; SIA Grp 89-; AA 90; East Duplin Boostrs Club Athltc Prog Chrmn 87-88; Natl Assoc Of F; Emale Exec 87-; Onslow Assoc Of Ins Profsnls Pres 89-; Stdnt Of The Mo 90; Pres List 89 Who's Who Of Women Exec 89; Who's Who Amer Women 90; Who's Who Among Yng Profsnls 90; Bus Admn.**

**AYCOCK, TANYA H,** East Central Comm Coll, Decatur, MS; SO; AD; Mu Alpha Theta; Phi Theta Kappa; Gen W P Wilson Awrd 90; Kappa Kappa Iota; Math; Educ.

**AYCOCK, WENDY L,** Clemson Univ, Clemson, SC; SO; BED; Stdnt Nurses Assoc 90-; Fellowship Christian Athletes 89-; Yng Life Ldr 89-; Alpha Delta Pi 89-; Oconee Memorial Schlrshp 90-; IM Ftbl Sftbl 89-; Nursing; Community Pediatric Nurse.

**AYER, AMANDA J,** Western Ky Univ, Bowling Green, KY; SO; BS; Phi Eta Sigm 90-; Pres Schlr 89-; Rgnts Schlr Coop Stdnt 90; Chem; Tchng Scndry Lvl Indstry.**

**AYER, KIMBERLY E,** Univ Of Sc At Columbia, Columbia, SC; FR; BS; Blgy.

**AYERS HUGHES, VALERIE D,** Meridian Comm Coll, Meridian, MS; SO; Newel Chapel Church/Meridian; Work Prob Chldrn/Yng Adul; Physlgy; R N.

**AYERS, ALYSON L,** Liberty Univ, Lynchburg, VA; SR; BA; Yth Quest Clb 88-; Chi Alpha Clb 90-; Varsity Track/Field 88-; Cnslng; Lic Cnslr/MA.

**AYERS, AMANDA L,** Univ Of Montevallo, Montevallo, AL; FR; BS; Cmps Mnstrs 90-; NSSLHA 90-; SHAA 90-; Alph Lmbd Dlt Pres; IM Sftbl; Sctsh Rite Schlrshp; Pres Wrtng Awrd; Lbry Bk Rvw Awrd; Spch Lang Pthlgy.

**AYERS, CAROL A,** Ramapo Coll Of Nj, Mahwah, NJ; SR; BA; Italian Clb 90-; Sigma Tau Delta 90-; Dns Lst; AS Bergen Comm Clg 89; Engl Lit; Tchng.

**AYERS, HOPE M,** Al St Univ, Montgomery, AL; SO; BA; Golden Ambssdr Org 90-; Fresh Class Sec 89-90; Miss Bibb Graves Queen 89-90; Pltcl Sci; Law.

**AYERS, JOEL E,** Middle Tn St Univ, Murfreesboro, TN; FR; BS; Aerospace; Prof Plt.

**AYERS, JOHN M,** Hocking Tech Coll, Nelsonville, OH; SO; BS; Mid Ohio Vly Commodore Club Sec 88-; Phi Theta Kappa 89-; Assoc Of Applied Sci Drftng & Design; Ind Tech; Teach.**

**AYERS, JOSEPH E,** Schenectady County Comm Coll, Schenectady, NY; SO; BA; Pr Tr Pgm; Stdnt Afrs Comm; Sci; Engrg.

**AYERS, JOSEPH T,** Ky St Univ, Frankfort, KY; SO; BS; Ntnl Scty Blk Engrs 88-; Ntnl Tchnl Assn 90-; Alpha Phi Alpha Hstrn 89-; Deans Lst 90; Comp Sci; Rsrch/Dvlpmnt/Cnsltng.

**AYERS, LAURA A,** Univ Of Al At Huntsville, Huntsville, AL; JR; BSEE; Math Club Pres 90-; Hnr Schlr; Techni-Core Prof Inc Huntsville AL 79-; Engrg; Elec Optical.

**AYERS, LAWRENCE E,** Southern Coll Of Tech, Marietta, GA; SO; BA; Advsry Cncl Rep 89-90; Stdsnts Of Engrng Tech Pres 89-90; Tae Kwon Do Orange Belt; Assoc Athens Tech Inst 90; Assoc 90; Elctrncs Engrng Tech.

**AYERS, MICHELLE R,** Univ Of Ga, Athens, GA; SR; BED; Natl Stdnt Spch Lang Hear Assn 90-; Gold Key 90-; Cmnctn Sci/Disorders; Spch Lang Pathology.

**AYERS, SANDRA G,** Itawamba Comm Coll, Fulton, MS; SO; BS; All Amer Schlr Collgt Awd; Cmpstn New Albany Gazette 86-; Elem Ed; Tchng.

**AYERS, SANDRA G,** Queens Coll, Charlotte, NC; SO; BA; Natl Assn Acctnts 90-; Lrng Socty 90-; Global Socty 90-; Org Agnst Socl Injstc/Sfrg; Queens Schlr 89-; Dana Srhlr 89-; Stdnt Mrshl 89-; Pres Schlr Fnlst 89-; Dns Lst 89-; Indus Acctng.

**AYERS, SANDRA M,** Christopher Newport Coll, Newport News, VA; JR; BS; Religious Studies; Foreign Serv/State Dept.

**AYERS, TERESA L,** Univ Of Cin R Walters Coll, Blue Ash, OH; SO; CSI 90-; Pgm Com Nmntng Com; Hon Stdnt 90-; Intrn Amer Fin Corp; Assoc; Lgl Offc Admin.

**AYERS, TIFFANY A,** Union Univ, Jackson, TN; SO; Stdnt Fndtn Tourguide; Stdnt Govt Assoc; Dorm Cncl Sec; Stdnt Actvts Cncl Prog Cncl; Bapt Stdnt Un; Phi Beta Lambda; Sigma Zeta; Zeta Tau Alpha Rec Sec; Cir K; Betty Hellix Foellinger Schlrshp; Deans List; Comp Sci; Sys Anlst.

**AYLETT, KENNETH E,** Western New England Coll, Springfield, MA; SR; Mktg Assn 89-; Peer Tutr 89-; IM Sprts 88-; Intrnshp Carousel Stdios 90; BS; Mktg; Advtsng.

**AYLSTOCK, BRYAN F,** Univ Of North Fl, Jacksonville, FL; JR; Sccr Clb VP 88-90; Pltcl Sci Clb; Hist Clb; Phi Kappa Phi 90-; Golden Key; Stdnt Of Summer 90; Intrnshp Brdcstng; Deans List 88-; First NCAA Sccr Tm; History; Law.

**AYOTTE, ALLISON A,** Teikyo Post Univ, Waterbury, CT; SO; AS; Eqn Rsrcs Comm 90-; Eqn Stds; Thrptc Hrsbck Rdng Instrctr.

**AYOTTE, KIRK R,** Defiance Coll, Defiance, OH; SO; BA; Bsktbl; Cert LSSU 89-90; Math; Tchng.

**AYRES, CAROL L,** Ny Univ, New York, NY; FR; BA; Brass Bnd; Jazz Bnd; Ltrcy Pgm Hmls Tutor; Hmls Asst; Slvtn Army; Deans List; Engl Lit; Tchr.

**AYRES, KEITH M,** Va St Univ, Petersburg, VA; JR; BS; Vets Tutorial Clb; ROTC 89-; Eagle Scout 89-; Pres Acad Awd; Food Mgmnt/Mktng/Bus; Bus Mgmnt.

**AYRES, LISA S,** Univ Of Akron, Akron, OH; SO; BA; Prog Bd V P 89-; Hon Clb 89-90; Deans Lst 89-; Hon Prog 89-; Arts Educ; Tch.

**AYSCUE, EMILY U,** Univ Of Nc At Chapel Hill, Chapel Hill, NC; GD; JDMBA; Stdnt Bar Fndtn Pres 91-; Ordr Golden Fleece V P 87-88; Ordr Grail Valkyvies; Ordr Old Well; BA 88; Law.

**AYTES, DONNA M,** Coll Of Charleston, Charleston, SC; SR; BSED; Coll Actvts Bd 87-88; Educ Clb 90-; Elem Ed; Tchr.

**AYTON, INGRID H,** Radford Univ, Radford, VA; SO; BBA; NAACP 89-90; Univ Ambsdrs Chrprsn Schlrshp Comm 90-; Phi Beta Lambda 90-; Res Asst 90-; Mktg.

**AYUB, WASIF,** City Univ Of Ny Queensbrough, New York, NY; JR; BS; Tau Alpha Pi 89-90; Tech Hnr Soc; AAS 90; Elec Eng.

**AYUK, ATEM DIDACUS,** Tri County Tech Coll, Pendleton, SC; SO; BS; Mnyu Stdnts Dev Assn 89-; Cmrn Stdnts Assn 89-; Mnyu All Stdnts Unn VP 87; Acctng; Bus.

**AZAB, MARCOS S,** Jersey City St Coll, Jersey City, NJ; GD; BS; Cmptr Sci Clb; Cmptr Shw Cntsts BBS 88-90; Intrntl Stdnts Assoc Cltrl Gthrngs 87-90; Clg Deans Lst 88-90; Cmptr Sci; MS PHD.**

**AZCUY, BEATRIZ,** Fl International Univ, Miami, FL; SR; JD; Econ Stdnt Org 90-; Omicron Delta Epsilon 90-; Otstndng Achvmnt Awrd Econ; Econ Intl Rltns; Law.

**AZEEM, ROSHMA A,** Allegheny Coll, Meadville, PA; SO; BA; Fencing Clb Pres 89-; Allies; Alden Schlr 89-90; Psi Chi 90-; Kappa Kappa Gamma 89-; Psych/Econ; Cnslng.

**AZEVEDO, MARGARIDA T,** Univ Of Nc At Charlotte, Charlotte, NC; SO; BS; Blk Stdnt Un 89-90; Afrcn/Am Stds Clb 89-90; Acctg; CPA.

**AZI-LOVE, EMMANUEL N,** Cheyney Univ Of Pa, Cheyney, PA; JR; Pre-Law Scty 89-; Tstmstrs Clb Org Sec 89-; Blck Colgstdys Man 90-; Bsktbl 89-; Phldlpha Hmls Food Drv 90-; Law.

**AZIE, YVES N,** Univ Of The Dist Of Columbia, Washington, DC; SO; BS; Hon Stdnt Univ DC 90-; Straight A Awd Univ DC 90-; Mech Eng.

**AZIKIWE, NDIDI N,** Lincoln Univ, Lincoln Univ, PA; FR; BA; Chem Club 90-; Engr Club Secy 90-; Natl Soc Of Physcs Stdnts Secy 90-; Deans List 90-; Tennis Team; Chem; Medcn.

**AZIKIWE, NNEKA R,** Lincoln Univ, Lincoln Univ, PA; JR; BA; Intl Stu Assoc 89-; Stu Ldr Ntwrk 90-; Alpha Xi; Dns Lst 89-; Gen Chem Awrd 89-90; Nrmn Edwrd Gskns Awrd Orgnc Chem 90-; Chem; Med.

**AZIZ, DEBORAH A,** Franklin And Marshall Coll, Lancaster, PA; JR; BA; Radio Sta Prog Dir 89-; TV Sta 89-; Pi Gamma Mu; Phi Alpha Theta; Hist; Profsr.

**AZORE, PAULINE E,** Columbia Union Coll, Takoma Park, MD; GD; BS; Level 4 Stf Nurs 80-; Dip Wash Hosp Ctr Sch 79; Hlth Care Admn; Admnstr.

**AZPURUA, MONICA MEDINA,** Barry Univ, Miami, FL; SR; BA; Public Reltns Students Scty Amer Public Dir 90-; Hnr Student Univ MD Clg Park 88-89; Deans List Barry Univ U Of MD 88-; Intshp Voss Intntl Studio 89; Intshp Channel 23 Miami FL; Brdcst Comm; Anchor Wmn.

**AZULAY, JONE T,** Nova Univ, Ft Lauderdale, FL; SR; MBA; Amer Chmbr Cmrc Dir 87; Brzln Assoc Cocoa Indstry Dir 87-89; CEO Chdlr SA Cocoa Prcsg Indstry 90; BA 65; Intl Bus.

**AZZIZ-BAUMGARTNER, EDUARDO,** Univ Of Pr At Mayaguez, Mayaguez, PR; SO; BS; Engl Dept Stdnt Assoc Literary Annual Chf In Editor 89-; Assist Electrphoresis/Population Genetics Lab; Biol Stdnts Assn 89; Proj Neptune 89-; Red Cross 89-; Acad Excellence Awd Arts/Sci 90-; Biol/Pre Med; Clincial Care/Rsrch.

# B

**BA, YASMINE R,** Central St Univ, Wilberforce, OH; SO; BA; Econ Clb 90-; Intl Stdnt Orgz 89-; Economics.

**BAAH, SOPHIA M,** Hudson Valley Comm Coll, Troy, NY; FR; BA; Intrntl Stdnts Clb 90-; Afrcn Am Orgnstn 90-; Intrnl Revn Asstnt; Bsktbl Fld Hcky Tm Capt 87-88; Intrntl Rltns; Law.

**BAASE, GRETCHEN L,** Bryant Stratton Bus Inst Roch, Rochester, NY; FR; AAS; WP Sec Clb; Dns Lst 90-; Wrd Prcsng/Sec.

**BABAEI, HAMID,** Pellissippi St Tech Comm Coll, Knoxville, TN; SO; Otdr Clb 90-; Photo Freelance 83; Natl Geographic Soc 90-; Deans Lst 90-; Cert Photography 83; Mech Engr; Engr.

**BABASHAK, JAMES E,** Cornell Univ Statutory College, Ithaca, NY; SO; BS; Daily Sun Spts Brd 90-; Alpha Epsilon Delta Comm Dir 90-; Plum Islnd Anml Disease Ctr Intrnshp; Biol.

**BABATUNDE, CATHERINE A,** Comm Coll Algny Co Algny Cmps, Pittsburgh, PA; SR; AS; Stdnt Educ Assn 89-; Intl Club 89-; Gen Stds/Nrsg; Nrsg/Hlth Svc Admin.

**BABB, LISA M,** City Univ Of Ny Baruch Coll, New York, NY; SR; Dlrs/Snse Mag Phto Edtr 90-; Rliabl Dsgn Stdios Intrn; Phtgrphrs Forum Awrd 90; Ba; Bus Comm/Grphc Comm; Grphc Dsgnr.

**BABB JR, RALPH E,** Middle Ga Coll, Cochran, GA; JR; BARCH; Engrg Clb; Intrmrl Cncl 89-90; Clge Rpblcns Clb Pres 89-90; Pres Clb 89-90; Sigma Nu 90-; Archtctr.

**BABCOCK, CHRISTOPHER R,** The Kings Coll, Briarclf Mnr, NY; FR; BS; IM Ftbl Co Capt 90-; IM Bsktbl; IM Hcky; Acct; CPA.

**BABCOCK, CHRISTY N,** Middle Tn St Univ, Murfreesboro, TN; FR; BA; Gamma Eta Phi; Dean Lst 90-; Hnr Rll 90-; Psych.

**BABCOCK, DARTHA J,** Union Univ, Jackson, TN; GD; Sthrn Bptst Mssnry Sierra Leona W Africa 86-; BS 84; MED; Elem Ed; Ltrcy Coord.

**BABCOCK, DEBORAH M,** Fayetteville St Univ, Fayetteville, NC; SO; BA; Math; HS Educ.

**BABCOCK, DEBORAH M,** Univ Of Fl, Gainesville, FL; SO; MBABA; CORP 90-; Habitat Hmnty 90-; Hnrs Prgrm 90-; Rsrch Asst Pre/Natal Cociane Exposure; Psychlgy/Pre/Med; Dvlpmntl Ped.

**BABEL, TEBERRUZ,** Univ Of Southern Ms, Hattiesburg, MS; FR; Hon Stdnt Assn 90-; Deans Lst 90-; Bnkng/Fin; Bnkng.

**BABER, ANITA M,** Christian Brothers Univ, Memphis, TN; SR; BA; Sftbl Co 89; Bowling Co Team Cptn 89; Accnts Rcvl Spclst Smith/Nephew Richards Inc 89; AS State Tchnl Inst Memphis 84; Acct; CPA.

**BABER, DONOVAN M,** Gaston Coll, Dallas, NC; FR; AAS; Archtctrl Drftng/Dsgn.

**BABER, KATHRYN ANN,** Emory & Henry Coll, Emory, VA; JR; BS; Cncrt Chr 89-90; Ortr Chr 88-90; Pep Bnd 88-89; Stdnt Govt; Theta Chi Epsilon; Alpha Phi Omega 90-; Emry Hnry Schlr 88-90; Untd Mthdst Schlr 88-90; Physcs Math; Astrnt Astrphyscs Rsrch.

**BABER, MELISSA A,** Univ Of Sc At Columbia, Columbia, SC; SR; Jaycees 89-90; Dept Yth Servs 87-89; SC Sci Tchrs Assn 89-90; Order Omega 88-90; Panhellenic Delegate 88-89; Delta Zeta VP 86-90; Lambda Chi Alpha Ltl Sis Fndrsng Chrmn 88-90; Pres List; Deans List; Elem Ed/Engl; Tchng.

**BABER, TRACIE M,** Christian Brothers Univ, Memphis, TN; JR; BS; Chorale 88-89; Career Peer Coun; Academic Schlrshp; Bus Mngmnt; Mngmnt.

**BABIAK, MARY S,** S U N Y Coll At Fredonia, Fredonia, NY; SO; BA; Proj Envir; Orchesis; Engl; Ed.

**BABIAK, NATALIE A,** Medaille Coll, Buffalo, NY; JR; BED; Tch; U S Jyc E Aurora Pres 88-89; U S Jycs Kenmore VP 90-; Outstndng Brd Mbr Jcs 89; Sobiesla Blck Clb; U S Gymnstcs Fdrtn; Dir Mgr Hd Ch 84-; Elem Ed; Tchg.

**BABIC, RENEE M,** Kent St Univ Kent Cmps, Kent, OH; SR; BA; Lambda Alpha Epsilon CJST Assoc Speaker/Social 89-; Phi Alpha Delta V P 87-90; Phi Kappa Tau Secr 87-89; Order Omega 90; Alpha Phi Sigma 90; Phi Gamma Pi 89-90; Vol Portage Co Prosecutors Ofc 90; Vol Awd Stdnt Senate 90; Publ Def Ofc Washington; Crmnl Jstc; Law Enfrcmnt FBI DEA.

**BABIK, KATHLEEN M,** Indiana Univ Of Pa, Indiana, PA; GD; MBA; Cncl Exptnl Chldrn 88-90; Visitor To The Aged 87-90; SGA 86-87; Alpha Phi Omega 88-90; Sdtnt Tchng 90; Cross Cntry 87-90; Bed 90; Educ/Cnslng Serv; Spec Ed Tchr.

**BABIN, BRIAN W,** Saint Thomas Univ, Miami, FL; SR; BA; IM Sftbl MVP 89; Hockey 88-90; Miami Avena Intern; NBA Franchise Miami Heat Asst; Ath Admn; Entertainment.

**BABIN, TAMMI L,** Bay Path Coll, Longmeadow, MA; SO; AS; Theater Wrkshop Exec Comm 89-; Intl Frnd 90-; Stdnt Ambsdr 90-; Maroon Key 90-; Tour Guide 89-; Epirotiki Cruise Line Piraeus Greece Intrnshp 90; Trvl Admin.

**BABINGER, BETSY A,** Defiance Coll, Defiance, OH; FR; BA; STATUS 87-; Mgr; Bsn Mgmt.

**BABITT JR, JOHN L,** Univ Of Miami, Coral Gables, FL; JR; BA; Intrfrtrnty Cncl Trea; Rho Alpha Rsh Asst 90-; Beta Alpha Psi; Sigma Alpha Epsilon Treas 90-; Ldrshp Cert; Ldrshp Schl Del 90; IM Ftbl Sftbl; Sthstrn Intrfrtrny Cncl Del; Accntng.

**BABUSCHAK, JEFFREY MICHAEL,** Saint Francis Coll, Loretto, PA; JR; BA BS; Chmstry Clb Treas 90-; Biology Clb; Math/Cmptr Clb Red Ky Clb Cinema Clb; Kappa Mu Epsilon; Beta Beta Beta; Alpah Phi Omega Sgt Arms 88-; Vrsty Rifle 88-89; Brkhvn Natl Lab Flwshp Nuclr Chmstry 90; Argonne Natl Lab Smr Rsrch; BA BS; Biology Chmstry; Med.

**BABWAHSINGH, VIRGINIA,** Jersey City St Coll, Jersey City, NJ; SO; BA; Scndry Educ Engl; Pblshng Tchng.**

**BACA, ANTHONY K,** Ms St Univ, Miss State, MS; JR; BMIC; Bctrlgy; Eclgy.

**BACA, LISA DIANE A,** Memphis St Univ, Memphis, TN; GD; MBA; BS US Mltry Acdmy West Point 86; Acct-Bsn.

**BACCARO, LORRAINE J,** Felician Coll, Lodi, NJ; SO; BA; Fine Arts.**

**BACCUS, ALICE M,** Miami Jacobs Jr Coll Of Bus, Dayton, OH; SO; AS; Pres Lst; Info Prcssng.

**BACH, VICTORIA I,** Saint John Fisher Coll, Rochester, NY; FR; BS; Bus.

**BACHER, JAMES T,** Jefferson Comm Coll, Louisville, KY; SO; MBA; Math/Elec Engr.**

**BACHER, MICHAEL W,** S U N Y Maritime Coll, Bronx, NY; JR; Vrsty Sailing Tm 90; Meba I USYRU CBYRA; USN 80-89; Mrchnt Mrne Offcr 89; AS Me Mrtme Acad 89; AS Rgnts Clg SUNY 88; Trnsprtn Mngmnt; Mrchnts Mrne/Trnsprtn.

**BACHMAN, AARON L,** S U N Y Coll At Fredonia, Fredonia, NY; SO; BA; Wldrns Clb 89-90; Chi Alpha Mnstry 89-; Pi Mu Delta; IM Sccr/Bsktbl; Physics; Engr.

**BACHMAN, CHRISTOPHER W,** Saint Andrews Presbytrn Coll, Laurinburg, NC; SO; BSBE; St Andrews Stdnt Snte VP; Rsdnce Hall Cncl VP; St Andrews Hrng Ct Chr Of Ct; Gnrl Hnrs Assoc 89; Hnrs Soc; Adopt-A-Hwy 89; Scots-For-Yth 89-90; Gnrl Hnrs Prog 89; Soph Hnrs; Math Phlsphy; Law.

**BACHMAN, SHERRY E,** Univ Of Cin R Walters Coll, Blue Ash, OH; FR; Rad Tech.

**BACHMAN, STEVEN J,** S U N Y Coll Of Tech At Alfred, Alfred, NY; SR; Outstndg Senior; Dsgn/Drftng Tech; Eng.

**BACHURA, DEBORAH E,** Indiana Univ Of Pa, Indiana, PA; SR; BED; Cncl Excptnl Chldrn 90-; PSEA; Deans Lst 90-; Elem Ed; Tchr.

**BACIK, JENNIFER M,** Fairfield Univ, Fairfield, CT; FR; BA; Fresh Exprnc Pgm 90-; IM Vlybl 90-; Math.

**BACK, JAMIE C,** Cumberland Coll, Williamsburg, KY; SR; BS; Math Sci Clb Pres 87; Amer Chmcl Scty 87-89; Math Physics.

**BACK, LINDA J,** Ky St Univ, Frankfort, KY; SO; BA; Menifee Cnty Bd Of Educ Chrprsn 83-85; KY Schl Bd Assn 83-85; Voc Educ Rgn 9; Menifee Cnty Prnt/Tchr Assn; Big Bro/Big Sis Frnkfort Bd Of Dir 87-89; Franklin Cnty Dem Wmns Clb 87-; Ky Assn Gifted Educ 86-; Adopt A Grndprnt Prog 78-80; Pol Sci/Hstry; Law.

**BACKENSTOSE, HEATHER N,** Villanova Univ, Villanova, PA; FR; BA; Musical Theatre 90-; Glee Clb 90; Forgn Lang; Govt.

**BACKER, BRIAN S,** S U N Y At Buffalo, Buffalo, NY; SR; MS; IEEE 90-; Tau Beta Pi; Golden Key 90; U B Engr Hon Rl 87; BS Univ Buffalo; Imaging Sci; Engr.

**BACKHUS, TAMMMY L,** Ms Gulf Coast Comm Coll, Perkinston, MS; SO; BA; Stdnt Bdy Govt 88-89; Annl Stff 88-89; Bus.

**BACKUS, MARY M,** S U N Y Coll Of A & T Morrisvl, Morrisville, NY; SR; AAN; Sm Cmpnt Inspctr; Nrs Aid; Engl/Psy; Mntl Hlth Fld/Thrpst.

**BACKUS, VICTORIA M,** Saint Josephs Coll New York, Brooklyn, NY; JR; BS; ENA; Hosper Head Nurse 88-; Health Admin.

**BACO-SANCHEZ, LUIS E,** Catholic Univ Of Pr, Ponce, PR; GD; JD; Cthlc Univ Pr Law Rvw Ed Chf 90-; Am Bar Assn Lw Stdnt Div 89-; Ntnl Mdl Un Del 89-; Acdmc Ttr Crm Lw 90-; Pol Sci Stdnt Assn Bp 86-89; Ntnl Egl Sct Assn; Phi Alpha Delta 89-; Phi Sigma Alpha Vp 86-; All Amer Sclr Awrd 89-; Pol Sci/Hstry; Law.

**BACON, BECKY S,** Univ Of Akron, Akron, OH; SO; BSN; Nrsg Clb Treas; NSNA 90-; Nrsg.

**BACON, BRIDGIT L,** S U N Y Coll Of Tech At Alfred, Alfred, NY; FR; BED; Pres Hnrs Schlrs Pgrm 90-; Human Svcs; Psychology.

**BACON, CANDACE R,** Hillsborough Comm Coll, Tampa, FL; SO; Poltcl Sci; Lobbyst.

**BACON, DEBORAH S,** Coll Of William & Mary, Williamsburg, VA; FR; BS; Hall Cncl Secy 90-; Orchestra 90-; Hand Bell Choir 90-; Wesley Fndtn 90-; Math/Chemistry.

**BACON, ELAINE M,** Northern Ky Univ, Highland Hts, KY; SR; BS; Ntl Assn Accntnts 89-; Nu Kappa Alpha Brd 90-; Alpha Chi Treas 89-; Hons Lst 86-90; Outstndng Coll Bus Stdnt 90-; Fncl Exec Inst Outstndg Stdnt 90; Epsy Bailey Mem Acctg Schlrshp 90; Acctg; CPA.

**BACON, JENNIFER S,** Univ Of Sc At Columbia, Columbia, SC; JR; BA; Gay Lsbn Stu Assn Pres 90-; Stu Choice 89-90; Arnie Childs Mem Awrd; Reynolds Awrd Wrtng 90; Engl Wrtng; Wrtr/Tchr.

**BACON, KYLE R,** Howard Univ, Washington, DC; SR; BSW; Social Work SGA Pres 90-; Inroads 87-89; SW Newsletter Editor 89-90; Pi Sigma Delta 90-; Omega Psi Phi 88-; Masons Sr Warden 90; Eastern Star 90; Public Affairs Prog Intern 90; All Amer Schlr Awrd; Natl Cllgt Scl Sci Awrd; Social Work Bus Admin; Clinical Psychologist.

**BACON, LORI D,** Waycross Coll, Waycross, GA; FR; ADN; GA Assoc Nrsng Stdnts; Phi Theta Kappa 90-; Nrsng; RN.

**BACON, MARK E,** Bunker Hill Comm Coll, Boston, MA; FR; BA; Bus/Lbrl Arts.

**BACON, MATTHEW L,** Manhattan Coll, Bronx, NY; SO; BE; Cvl Eng; Eng.

**BACON, MINDY K,** Ms St Univ, Miss State, MS; JR; Vet Med.

**BACON, SHEILIA V,** Paine Coll, Augusta, GA; SR; BS; Alpha Kappa Alpha 87-; Stdnt Ntl Ed Assn Pres 90-; Amer Acad Achvmnt Isiah Washington/Stdnt Pres Schlr/Deans Lst/Schlr/Hon Roll 89-; Mnrty Schlrshp 89-; Ed; Tchr.

**BACOT, BRIAN C,** Al A & M Univ, Normal, AL; GD; PHD; Stdnt Govt; Toast Mstrs V P 89-; Stdnt Ind Clstr Parlmntrn 89-; Alpha Kappa Pr 90-; Alpha Zeta; Pres Schlrs Soc 87-; Beta Kappa Ki 89-; Cir K 87-88; Univ Tutrl 87-; Extra Tch Tutrl Pgm 89-; Res Fellwshps 88-; Otstdng Stdnt Schl; Natl Otstdng Min Std 90; Env Sci; M D.

**BACOTE, CATINA J,** Wesleyan Univ, Middletown, CT; FR; BA; Vjamma Acad Cmt; Blck Theater Clctv; Inrds; Sclgy; Law.

**BACYK, KATHLEEN M,** Springfield Tech Comm Coll, Springfield, MA; FR; AS; Surgical Tchnlgst Rep 88-90; Hnr Grad Surgical Tchnlgy 90, Palmer Drug Cncl Advsry Comm 90-; Hltn Hmn Serv Awrd Srgcl Tchnlgy 90; AS 90; Nrsng.

**BACZKOWSKI, MARK W,** Duquesne Univ, Pittsburgh, PA; SO; BS; Cls Sec 89-; Phi Delta Chi Wrthy Crrspndnt 90-; Intrn Allegheny Gen Hsp; Ftbl/Hcky; Phrmcy.

**BADAL, AMY A,** Western New England Coll, Springfield, MA; JR; BA; Peer Tutor 90-; Clg Succs Skls Stdnt Tchg Asst 89-; Stdnt Ambssdr 90-; Stdnt Assn Prgrmg Awd 90; Stdnt Assn Awd Excell; Engl; Highr Educ Admin.

**BADAR, ARIF M,** City Univ Of Ny La Guard Coll, Long Island Cty, NY; JR; BBA; Germn Clb 88-; Pakistani Crickt Tm 87-; Geothe Inst 88; Lit Soc Fndtn Inc 88; Math Lb 89; Typng Lb 89; Intrnshp At Nat Wst Bnk Plc Fin Cntrl Asst 89-90; AS W Hnrs La Guardia C C 90; Bsns Admn; Econs.

**BADDER, LORI A,** Free Will Baptist Bible Coll, Nashville, TN; SO; BS; Elizabeth Barrett Browning Socty 90-; Bus Admin.

**BADDLEY, RUSTY M,** Ms Univ For Women, Columbus, MS; JR; BA; Delta Sigma Omega T 88-89; Bus Admin CIS; Prgrmng.

**BADDOUR, ELIZABETH JOSEPH,** Capital Univ, Columbus, OH; SR; BSN; Police Athltc League Tutor; Deans List 90-; Nrsng.**

**BADE, JENNIFER B,** Radford Univ, Radford, VA; JR; BA; Psi Chi Sec; Psych; Clncl Psychlgst.

**BADEAUX, ALYCE C,** Univ Of Southern Ms, Hattiesburg, MS; JR; BA; Univ Actvies Cncl 89-; Stdnt Eagle Clb 89-; Assoc Stdnt Body Elec Comm 89-; Cath Stdnt Assoc Treas 89-; Stdnt Almni Assoc 89-; Rght To Lf 89-; Phi Kappa Phi 91; Gamma Beta Phi 91; Lambda Sigma 91; Alpha Lambda Delta 89-; Phi Eta Sigma 89-; Engl; MPH Law.

**BADEN, AMY D,** Oh Wesleyan Univ, Delaware, OH; FR; BA; Environment Wildlife Clb 90; Phi Eta Sigma; Zoology Geography.

**BADENOCK, NEVILLE O,** City Univ Of Ny Baruch Coll, New York, NY; JR; BBA; Fin/Invstmnt; Bus.

**BADER, DEBRA L,** Life Coll, Marietta, GA; GD; DC; Motion Palpation Clb Life Clg 90; Biomed Soc N Y Tech 89; Nu Ypsilon Tau N Y Tech; BS N Y Inst Tech 89; Chiropractic.

**BADER, LAWRENCE R,** Bellarmine Coll, Louisville, KY; SR; MBA; Natl Mbr Assn Cmptng Mchnry 89; Bellarmine Chptr ACM V Chrmn 87; Stdnt Repr Bellarmines Cmptr Lbs; Intrnshp Louisville Gas/Elctrc 90; KY Cert Fire Fighter 87; KY Cert First Rspndr 90; BS 91; Cmptr Engr; Sys Mgmt.

**BADER, ROBIN E,** Longwood Coll, Farmville, VA; SR; Drill Tm 87-89; Alpha Sigma Alpha Fund Rsr 88-; Intern Juvenile Det Ctr; BS; Psychology; Work With Abused Chldrn.

**BADERTSCHER, MARSHA S,** Beckley Coll, Beckley, WV; BS; Comm Chorus; Asst Cashier Brnch Mgr; Bus Educ.

**BADGER, SHARON A,** Univ Of Akron, Akron, OH; JR; MBA; Beta Gamma Sigma; Outstndng Jr; Mgmt; Mtrls/Prdctn Mgmt/Law.

**BADGETT, MELANIE D,** Marshall University, Huntington, WV; Hall Govt 88-; Orgztns Vol; Spch Lang Hrng Assn 90-; Phi Eta Sigma 89-.

**BADIAS, FRANZ,** Univ Of Sc At Columbia, Columbia, SC; JR; BS; Phi Beta Kappa; Deans Lst 87-; Pres Lst 90; Cmptr Sci; Analyst.

**BADILLO, DANIEL E,** Inter Amer Univ Pr Aquadilla, Aguadilla, PR; FR; BA; Biol; Med.

**BADILLO, ETIENNE M,** Univ Of Pr At Rio Piedras, Rio Piedras, PR; SO; BA; NCADA; Swmng; Envrmntl Dsgn; Arch.

**BADILLO, HUGO A,** Univ Of Pr At Mayaguez, Mayaguez, PR; SO; BA; Math; Engr.

**BADJATIA, NITIN,** Kent St Univ Kent Cmps, Kent, OH; SR; BBA; Amer Mrktng Assn 89-; Mrktng/Mngmnt; Intl Bus.

**BAE, KRISTIAN,** Atlantic Union Coll, S Lancaster, MA; SO; BS; Human Rel Com 90-; Hon Core 89-90; Bio; Dntstry.

**BAECHLER, CONSTANCE E,** Valdosta St Coll, Valdosta, GA; SR; BA; Lit Mag Assist Ed; Sigma Tau Delta VP; Acad Of Amer Poets Awd; Gainesville Clg Poetry Awd 90; Engl; MA PHD Wrtr Fctn.

**BAEK, PETER S,** The Johns Hopkins Univ, Baltimore, MD; FR; BS; Krn Assoc 90-; Hopkins Chrstn Fllwshp 90-; Mdcl Univ SC Rsrchr; Holpins Fncng Tm 90-; Biomdcl Eng; Med.

**BAENS, GENEVIEVE G,** Univ Of Sc At Columbia, Columbia, SC; SR; Cert Prfcncy In Germn; Goethe Inst Awrd Exclnce In Germn; BA 90; Cert Tchng; Germn; Ed.

**BAER, BARBARA A,** Valdosta St Coll, Valdosta, GA; GD; MSN; Sigma Theta Tau Coorspndg Sec 89-; Natl Assn Female Exec; Natl Clgte Nurs Awd; USAA All Amer Schlr; BSN 88; RN 59; Nurs.

**BAER, CHRISTOPHER W,** Oh Univ, Athens, OH; JR; EE; Elec Engrng.

**BAER, HAYLEY M,** Longwood Coll, Farmville, VA; SO; BS; Im Bsktbl & Sftbl 90-; Psychlgy.

**BAERGA-VARELA, FLAVIA,** Univ Of Pr At Rio Piedras, Rio Piedras, PR; SR; BBA; Acctg Assoc Repr 90-; Golden Key 90-; Bsn Merit Awds 90-; Hnr Tuition 88-; Price Waterhouse Audit Intern 90; Acctg.

**BAERNS, LORI L,** Univ Of Tn At Martin, Martin, TN; SR; BS; Stdnt Teacher Educ Assoc; Pi Kappa Alpha Rush Girl; Alpha Omicron Pi 90-; BS Educ 90; Educ; Teacher Elem Sp Ed.

**BAEZ RIOS, GILBERTO,** Univ Of Pr At Mayaguez, Mayaguez, PR; JR; BS; Leo Club 85-89; Mvmnto Jfnl Ctlco Pres 84-90; Cdr D Hnr D L Fcltd D Arts Cnecs 88-; Dplma D Hnr 88-89; Dplma D Hnr 89-90; Natl Coll Natrl Scncs Awrds 90-; Blgy; Mdcn.

**BAEZ, CAROLINE A,** Columbia Univ, New York, NY; FR; BS; Alianza Latino Amer 90-; Blgy; Med.

**BAEZ-RIVERA, EMILIO RICARDO,** Univ Of Pr At Rio Piedras, Rio Piedras, PR; SR; BA; Hnrs Prog Univ Of Puerto Rico 90-; Gldn Key; Yngr Schlr Awd 90; Hspnc Stds.

**BAFFA, LINDA K,** Lehigh Univ, Bethlehem, PA; FR; BS; SWE; CAD; Cvl Eng.

**BAGALEY III, R DAVID,** East Tn St Univ, Johnson City, TN; SO; BS; Joiner/Bld Tmbrfrm/Log Hms; Tech/Educ; Voc Educ.

**BAGBY, DENT A,** Univ Of Southern Ms, Hattiesburg, MS; SR; BS; Refrmd Univ Flwshp 86-; Miss Right Life 89-; Math Assn; Kappa Mu Epsilon; Coop Educ Prog; Math; Rsrch.

**BAGGA, AMIT,** Manhattanville Coll, Purchase, NY; SO; BA; Intrntl Club 89-; Intrcltrl House 89-; Math/Cmptr Sci Club 90-; Hons Schlr 89-; Deans List 89-; Math/Comptr Sci; Comptr Engr.

**BAGGETT, GALE E,** Ky Mountain Bible Coll, Vancleve, KY; SO; AA; Christian Serv KMBC; PTO Mt Carmel Elem VP 90; 5 Mile Cmnty Ch Active Mem 90-; Fncl Inst; Elem Edn; Elem Tchr.

**BAGGETT, MARK E,** James Madison University, Harrisonburg, VA; FR; BA; Mrchng Bnd 90-; Pep Bnd 90-; Art; Grphc Dsgn.

**BAGGETT, SANDRA M,** Univ Of Nc At Asheville, Asheville, NC; JR; BA; Prsbytrn Yth Grp 89-; Vol Autumn Care Nrsng Hm 90-; Deans List 88-89; AA Mc Dowell Tech Clg 90; Soclgy/Grntlgy; Rtrmnt/Nrsng Hm.

**BAGGETT, STEPHANIE S,** Coll Of Charleston, Charleston, SC; SR; BS; Chi Omega 88-; Blgy; Physcl Thrpy.

**BAGGOTT, LAURIE A,** Univ Of Sc At Columbia, Columbia, SC; SR; BS; Cncrt Choir 87-; Opera Wrkshp 88-; Vocal Schlrshp 87-; Pres Lst; Dean Lst 87-; Music Educ; Tchr.

**BAGINSKI, ROBIN M,** Georgian Court Coll, Lakewood, NJ; JR; BA; Pi Mu Epsilon; Math; Actrl Sci.

**BAGLEY, CHARLES E,** Fayetteville St Univ, Fayetteville, NC; SR; BA; Soc Club 90-; N C Soc Assoc 90-; Alpha Kappa Delta Pres 90-; Alpha Kappa Mu 89-; Kappa Delta Pi 90-; Deans List 87-90; Chancellors List 88-90; Intrnshp Cumberland Co Mental Hlth Ctr; U S Air Force 57-85; Soc.

**BAGLEY, JACQUELINE A,** Bunker Hill Comm Coll, Boston, MA; FR; Third Rail Rep; 02127 Rep 88; Tutor Supv S Boston/Charlestown; Engl/Cmnctns; Jrnlst.

**BAGLEY, LYNN M,** Fl International Univ, Miami, FL; JR; BA; FL Intrntnl Univ Law Assc 90; Phi Lambda 90; Sigma Sigma Sigma; Politcal Science; Law.

**BAGLEY, PAUL C,** Columbia Greene Comm Coll, Hudson, NY; FR; Auto Tech; Engr.

**BAGLINO, ANGELA,** Marywood Coll, Scranton, PA; JR; BED; PA Rdg Assoc 90-; Natl Rdg Assoc 90-; Elem Ed; Tchr.

**BAGNAL, RENEE DOUCETT,** Univ Of Sc At Columbia, Columbia, SC; SR; BA; Deans Hon Lst Slvr Mdlln 90; Assn Flght Attndnts 76-; Flght Attndnt 76-; AS U SC 90; Engl; Law.

**BAGWELL, BRAD A,** Central Fl Comm Coll, Ocala, FL; JR; BA; Phi Theta Kappa; Coop Emer One Ocala Drftsmn CADD Systm 89-91; IM Ftbl 90-91; Sci; Cvl Eng.

**BAGWELL III, EDWARD L,** Samford Univ, Birmingham, AL; GD; JD; AA S Ga Coll 87; BBA Univ Ga 89; Law.

**BAGWELL, TAMMY L,** Piedmont Coll, Demorest, GA; SO; BS; Sftbl 89-; Bsktbl Stats 90-; Math/Scndry Ed: Teach/Coach Hgh Sch Sftbl.**

**BAH, COUMBA,** Central St Univ, Wilberforce, OH; FR; BS; ISA; Moslem Assc; DEF Notre Dame Du Niger 86; Bcclurt Notre Dame Sdu Niger 89; Chmstry; Industrial Tchnlgy.

**BAHER, JENNIFER L,** Univ Of Akron, Akron, OH; SR; Am Soc Mech Engs Sec 89-; Am Inst Aerospace/Astrntcs Sec 90-; Deans List 87-88 90-; Mech Eng.

**BAHL, JENNIFER L,** Western New England Coll, Springfield, MA; SR; BA; Mktg Assoc 90-; Mktg; Adv.

**BAHNLEIN, CHERYL L,** Anne Arundel Comm Coll, Arnold, MD; SO; BA; Bus.

**BAHR, DAWN M,** Dowling Coll, Oakdale Li, NY; Suffolk Chld Dvlpmnt Ctr Little Plains Lake Grove Schl; Sagamore Wood Rd Schl BOCES; BA Sped Ed Elem Ed; Spec Educ; Tchng/Spch Thrpy.

**BAI, LICHUEN,** Columbus Coll Of Art & Design, Columbus, OH; FR; BFA; China Invntn Assn 88; China Natl Sci Tech Assn 87; BS Chengdu Univ 84; Indstrl Dsgn; Prod Dsgn.

**BAIER, DAVID B,** Cleveland Inst Of Art, Cleveland, OH; FR; Artist.

**BAIER, KATHLEEN M,** Glassboro St Coll, Glassboro, NJ; JR; BA; Pblc Rltns Stdnt Scty Am 90-; Cmnctns/Pblc Rltns; Fld Pblc Rltns.

**BAIER, SCOTT J,** Univ Of Al At Huntsville, Huntsville, AL; SO; BSEE; Bwlng Cap Photo 90-; Huntsvl Grotto Natl Skelgcl Soc 89-; Army ROTC 90; Hnrs Prog 90-; Elect Eng; US Army Res Dev.

**BAILES III, JAMES P,** Univ Of Sc At Columbia, Columbia, SC; SR; Bus Soc 89-90; Piedmont Soc 89-; Gamma Beta Phi 89-; Pres Hon Lst 87-90; Deans Lst 88-; Exec Com Union Cnty Rpblcn Prty 86-; Chrmn Com Union Cnty Rpblcn Prty; BS; Bus Admin; Bnkng/Cmmrcl Lndng.

**BAILEY, AARON M,** Memphis St Univ, Memphis, TN; SO; BSN; Sci; Nrs Anesthetist.

**BAILEY, ADELE,** Bennett Coll, Greensboro, NC; SO; BA; SNCAE Cor Sec 90-; Schlrs; Zeta Phi Beta; All Amrcn Schlr; Elem Ed.

**BAILEY, ALLEN T,** Christian Brothers Univ, Memphis, TN; SO; BA; NAMASTE Sec/Treas 90-; Hstry; Tchr.

**BAILEY, CARMELA J,** Univ Of Rochester, Rochester, NY; JR; BS; ICE Pblcity Mgr 89; Host HS Stdnts 88-; Sndy Schl Tchr 90; Mobil Chem Intrnshp; Bio Med Rsrch Fllwshp 90; Bausch/Lomb Schlr; IM Floor Hcky 89-90; Chem Engr.

**BAILEY, CHRISTOPHER GLENN,** Emmanuel Coll Schl Chrstn Min, Franklin Sprg, GA; SR; MDIV; Singers Pr 87-; IM Capt 87-; Highest Praise Quart 87-; Phi Theta Kappa 87-89; Intrnshp Assoc Pastor 90; IM Bsktbl/Tennis 87-90; AA 89; Theo/Ministry.

**BAILEY, COURTNEY,** Duke Univ, Durham, NC; FR; BA; Chpl Choir Tour Drctr 90; Habitat For Hmnty Lsn 90; Duke Rcycles Rep 90; Proj BUILD Crew Ldr 90; Ntl Cllgte Sftwre Of Duke U Press Intrnshp 90; Hstry; Tchr.

**BAILEY, CYNTHIA M,** Union Univ School Of Nursing, Memphis, TN; SO; BA; Nrsng.

**BAILEY, DAVID E,** Muskingum Coll, New Concord, OH; FR; BSBA; Amer Chem Soc 90; Beta Beta Beta 90; Deans Lst 90; 1st Yr Schlrshp Awd; Bio Hist; Rsrch/Grad Studies.

**BAILEY, DENISE M,** Coppin St Coll, Baltimore, MD; SR; BA; Ball Pres Committ Co Chrprsn 90-; Ronald E Mcnair Schlr 90; Alpha Kappa Mu; Rsrch Asst Univ CA 90; Indus Psychlgy.

**BAILEY, DIANE H,** Bryant Stratton Bus Inst Roch, Rochester, NY; SO; AA; LPN Educ Opprtnty Cntr 76; Med Lab Tech.

**BAILEY, DIANNE C,** Univ Of Southern Ms, Hattiesburg, MS; SR; BSBA; Beta Alpha Psi; AT Data Processing Jones Jr Cllg 83; BS Accounting USM; Accounting.

**BAILEY, DUSTIN L,** Univ Of Cincinnati, Cincinnati, OH; SO; BS; Wgtlftng Clb 89-; Air Force ROTC 89-; IM Vlybl; Track/Fld 89-90; Mech Eng Tech.

**BAILEY, DWIGHT L,** Wilberforce Univ, Wilberforce, OH; JR; BA; BEP 2nd Grnd Chnclr; Blck Male Cltn; VP Stdnt Govt; Free/Accptd Mason PHA; Alpha Phi Alpha VP; IM Bsktbl; Ind Psychlgy.

**BAILEY, ELIZABETH C,** Savannah Coll Of Art & Design, Savannah, GA; GD; MFA; Teach Asst Photography Savannah Coll Art/Dsgn 90-; BA Univ South 89; Cmrcl Photography Teaching.

**BAILEY, GARY C,** Free Will Baptist Bible Coll, Nashville, TN; SO; BA; Theology; Profsr.

**BAILEY, JACINTHIA C,** Bloomfield Coll, Bloomfield, NJ; SO; BSN; Nrsng.

**BAILEY, JANICE M,** Longwood Coll, Farmville, VA; SR; BS; Phi Kappi Phi; Brd Of Dir Bikes For Kids; Brd Of Dir VA Emrgncy Familys Chldrn; Social Work Supervisor Dept Of Social Services Chatham VA; BA Averett Clge 76; Bus Admnstrn; Marketing.

**BAILEY, JEFFREY E,** Marshall University, Huntington, WV; GD; MS; Tchng Asstshp 90; Rsrch Asstshp; BS Concord Coll 89; Biol; Envrmntl Cnsltng.

**BAILEY, JEFFREY W,** Liberty Univ, Lynchburg, VA; SR; BS; Cls Offcr Pres 87-88; LIGHT Mssns Mnstry Pres 88-89; Chmbr Sngrs 87-88; Natl Phlsphy Soc; Wrshp Ldr; IM 87-90; Poltcl Sci; Phlsphy/Theolgy.

**BAILEY, JENNIFER D,** Ms St Univ, Miss State, MS; FR; BA; Alpha Lambda Delta; Phi Eta Sigma 90-; Gamma Beta Phi; Frgn Lang.

**BAILEY, JENNIFER E,** Valdosta St Coll, Valdosta, GA; JR; Campus Otrch; Campus Forernrs Treas 89-90; Choir; Alpha Omicron Pi Bid Day Chair 88-; Tchrs Asst Lawrence Jr High Sch 90; Pi Clb 89-; Stdnt Totor Edn Pgm 89; IMS 88-89; Edn; Tchr.

**BAILEY, JENNIFER S,** Clayton St Coll, Morrow, GA; SO; BBA; Full Tuition Acad Schlrshp; Dns Lst 89-; Acctg; CPA.

**BAILEY, JOHN H,** Mayland Comm Coll, Spruce Pine, NC; GD; Pr Lst 90; Deans Lst; Natl Deans Lst 90-; Phi Thetta Kappa 90; Alpha Phi Kappa; Spruce Pine Jaycees 90-; Co-Op Educ; Dept Of Corrs Intrn; Crim Just; Law.

**BAILEY, KAREN A,** Winthrop Coll, Rock Hill, SC; FR; Alpha Lambda Delta.

**BAILEY, KAREN A,** Beckley Coll, Beckley, WV; FR; ASSOC; Sec Sci; Med.

**BAILEY, KATHLEEN M,** Cornell Univ Statutory College, Ithaca, NY; SR; Equstrn Tm 87-; Orntn 88-90; Acdmc Advsr 89-; TA; Var Bsktbl 88-89; Ntrl Rsrcs; Envrnmtl Plng.

**BAILEY, KAYE M,** Central Fl Comm Coll, Ocala, FL; FR; BA; Comm Schlrs; Engl; Educ.

**BAILEY, KENNETH L,** Middle Tn St Univ, Murfreesboro, TN; SO; BBA; Gamma Beta Phi; Bsns Admn; Intl Bsns.

**BAILEY, KIMBERLY L,** Radford Univ, Radford, VA; SR; BMTBA; Msc Thrpy Clb 86-90 Pres 88-89; Natl Assc Msc Thrpy 90-; Alpha Lmbd Dlt 87; Msc Edctrs Natl Cltn VP 86-88; Vry Spec Arts Fstvl 87-90; Prsr Schlrshp 89-90; Otstndng Stdnt Awrd 87-88; Msc Thrpy/Spnsh.

**BAILEY, KRISTIE A,** Queens Coll, Charlotte, NC; FR; BA; Fllwshp Of Chrstn Athletes; Im Bsktbl Vllybl; Engl/Cmmnctns.

**BAILEY, KRISTINA N,** Univ Of Sc At Spartanburg, Spartanburg, SC; FR; Gamma Beta Phi 90-; Psych; Cnslng.

**BAILEY, LA JUANA A,** Central St Univ, Wilberforce, OH; FR; BA; Acctg.

**BAILEY, LENNADENE L,** Columbia Union Coll, Takoma Park, MD; SR; BS; Tstmstrs 87-88; Afrcn Amrcn Emplys Assoc 89-; MS Assoc; AA 89; Hnrs; Bus Admn.

**BAILEY, LINDA M,** Comm Coll Algny Co Algny Cmps, Pittsburgh, PA; SO; BA; Tchng; Spch Path Audiology.

**BAILEY, LISA G,** Lindsey Wilson Coll, Columbia, KY; FR; BA; Acctg; CPA.

**BAILEY, LISA R,** Univ Of Tn At Martin, Martin, TN; SR; BS; SADD 89-; Unvn Schlrs Org Jr Rep 88-; Phi Kappa Phi 88-; Ord Omega 88-; Beta Beta Beta Pres 88-; Mu Epsilon Delta Rprtr 87-; Alpha Delta Pi VP 87-; Univ Schlrs Shlrshp 88-; Ldrs In Res Schlrshp 87-90; Biol; Med.

**BAILEY, LORA Y,** Univ Of Sc At Columbia, Columbia, SC; SR; BSN; USC Aiken 89; Nrsng; BSN.

**BAILEY, LYNN R,** Hampton Univ, Hampton, VA; JR; BS; Natl Assn Blck Acctnts 90-; Big Bro Big Sis Pgm 90-; Ill Pre Alum Assn 88-; Alpha Kappa Mu; Atlantc Richfld Co Intrnshp; Amer Inst CPA 89-; Dns Lst 88-; Acctg; Corp Lawyr.

**BAILEY, MARGARET D,** Univ Of Sc At Columbia, Columbia, SC; FR; BS; Gamma Beta Phi; Chem; Rsrch.

**BAILEY, MARK D,** Southern Coll Of Tech, Marietta, GA; SO; BS; Cmptr Sci; Sftwr Engr.

**BAILEY, MARSHALL S,** Univ Of Southern Ms, Hattiesburg, MS; JR; BS; Alpha Epsilon Delta Treas 90-; Gamma Beta Phi; Psychlgy; Dntst.

**BAILEY, MELISSA A,** Univ Of Cincinnati, Cincinnati, OH; SR; BS; Deans Lst 86-; Elem Ed; Tchr.

**BAILEY, MICHAEL S,** East Tn St Univ, Johnson City, TN; SR; BS; Chmstry; Med Dr.

**BAILEY, MORGAN C,** S U N Y Coll Of Tech At Frmgdl, Farmingdale, NY; SR; ADN; Stu Nrs Assoc Pres 90-; Crclm Comm 89-; Actvs Awrd; Trnsltr Hrg Imprd Crisis Intrvntn Htln Metro Comm 79-80; Resp Thrpst; Diploma 70; Nrsg.

**BAILEY, PAMELA E,** Wilmington Coll, New Castle, DE; JR; BS; Jaycee Wmn 87-86; Intrn-State DE Dept Labor IU; Dept Labor Mstr Dir Com 90-; Intrn-Big Bro/Big Sis DE 84; Lttr Cmmndtn Dept Labor UI 89; AAS DE Tech Comm Coll Sthrn Cmps 84; Hmn Rsrcs Mgmt; Mgmt/Law.

**BAILEY, PAMELA V,** Al St Univ, Montgomery, AL; JR; BA; Soc For The Advncmnt Of Mgt Mbr 90-; Bus Admn; Acctng.

**BAILEY, RAYMOND D,** Atlantic Comm Coll, Mays Landing, NJ; SO; BS; Prfrmg Arts Clb; Envrnmntl Sci; Spclz Rutgers Univ Cook Clg.

**BAILEY, RHONDA C,** Blue Mountain Coll, Blue Mountain, MS; JR; BED; MTAI 90-; Hairdressr 82-; Cert Costmelgy NE Comm Coll 82; Elem Ed; Tchng.

**BAILEY, RITA A,** Univ Of Southern Ms, Hattiesburg, MS; SR; BA; K C Ladies Aux Cncl 1583 90-; Cmmnctns Officer; AA Gulf Coast Comm Coll/Jeff Davis 90; Eng With Tchr Cert; Teach.

**BAILEY, ROBERT G,** East Tn St Univ, Johnson City, TN; FR; Chrch Yth Grp; Sndy Schl Asst Sprntndnt 90-; Chrch Yth Chr; Bus; Mltry.

**BAILEY, ROBIN S,** Christopher Newport Coll, Newport News, VA; GD; CPA; Local Orch; Stdnt Cnslnt 90-; Small Bus Inst; BS 90-; Acctg; CPA.

**BAILEY, RODERICK D,** Tuskegee Univ, Tuskegee Inst, AL; SR; BS; IEEE 87-89; SAM 89-; Silvr Trwl Lodge 86-; Silvr Trnl Lodg Princ Hall Masns 86-; ATIT Baskng Rdg NJ Legl Dept Intrnshp; IM Bsktbll Leag 86-; Busn Admin; Mba.

**BAILEY, RONALD J,** Clayton St Coll, Morrow, GA; SO; AAS; Acad Hon Awd 89-90; IM Golf 90-; Airlines Agent 73-89; AA Central Piedmont Cmnty Clg 70; Aircraft Mech; A/P License.

**BAILEY III, SAMUEL R,** Tn Temple Univ, Chattanooga, TN; SO; BS; Vllybl Clb Capt-Coach; Sigma Chi Pelta 90; Soccer Tm 89; Bible/Cmptrs; Mssnry.

**BAILEY, SANDRA L,** Jackson St Univ, Jackson, MS; FR; Blck PRIDE Asstnt Sec 90-; Deans Lst; Pol Sci; Law.

**BAILEY, SHARON D,** Va St Univ, Petersburg, VA; SR; BA; Vets Of St Pres 90-; Soc Advmnt Mgmt Sec 90-; Coop Clb Treas 90-; Outstndng Ofc Wkr 89-; Outstndng Rcrdng Sec 90-; Adm Syst Mgmt; Admstr.

**BAILEY, SHAWN,** Western New England Coll, Springfield, MA; FR; BA; Pltcl Sci Clb 90-; Pre Law Soc 90-; Glf 90-; Govt; Law.

**BAILEY, SHERRY M,** Wilmington Coll, New Castle, DE; FR; BA; Admin Asst To Adv Mngr Local Daily Nwspr; Elem Educ.

**BAILEY, SONIA D,** City Univ Of Ny Med Evers Coll, Brooklyn, NY; JR; BA; Cert Tchr Ed Church Teacher Coll 75.

**BAILEY, SUSAN L,** Savannah Coll Of Art & Design, Savannah, GA; SR; Graph Design Clb 88-; Magnum Cum Laude; Outstndng Graphic Design Awd; Print Intl Stdnt Cover Awd; BFA; Graphic Design/Cmrcl Art; Art Dir.

**BAILEY, SYLVIA S,** Longwood Coll, Farmville, VA; SO; BA; Hon Phi Kappa Phi Hon Soc 90-; Socl Wrk.

**BAILEY, TARA D,** Tuskegee Univ, Tuskegee Inst, AL; SR; BS; Stdnt Natl Educ Assoc 87-90; Erly Chldhd Educ.

**BAILEY, VICKY I,** Beckley Coll, Beckley, WV; SO; BA; Prlgl/Psychlgy; Tchng Scl Sci.

**BAILEY, VONDA F,** Stillman Coll, Tuscaloosa, AL; SR; BA; Chr 86-; Deans Lst 89-; Phi Beta Lambda Prlmntarn 89-90 Asst Sc 90-; Yth Chr Dir; Bus Admn.

**BAILEY, WILLIAM K,** Piedmont Tech Coll, Greenwood, SC; SO; ASSOC; Peer Advsr 90; D C Electrnc Tutor 90; Indstrl Electrncs.

**BAILEYS, JASON R,** Embry Riddle Aeronautical Univ, Daytona Beach, FL; FR; BA; AAAE 90-; Sccr Clb 90; Arntcl Sci; Prfsnl Plt.

**BAIN, ANDREW C,** Univ Of Nc At Asheville, Asheville, NC; JR; BA; Hnrs Pgm; Pol Sci; Intl Law.

**BAIN, MARK E,** Ms Gulf Coast Comm Coll, Perkinston, MS; SO; BA; Untd Wy; Engl; Advrtsg.

**BAIN, RISELLE,** Daytona Beach Comm Coll, Daytona Beach, FL; SO; BA; Hnrs Entrnc UC LA 65; Pres Lst Daytona Bch CC 90-; Sngr/Dncr/Actress Prof Flms/TV/RCRDS/STG/CNCRTS; Japan Rcrdng In Japanese; Chld Prfrmr Apprd In 12 Flms A Star Is Born W/Judy Garland; Music; Prof Perf/Tchng Music Perf/Cntrla.

**BAIN, STACIE R,** Univ Of Sc At Columbia, Columbia, SC; JR; BS; Indian Stdnt Assn VP 90-; Clb Mgrs Assn; Htl/Rstrnt/Trsm Mgmt; Rsrt Clb Mgr.

**BAIN, WILLIAM H,** Va St Univ, Petersburg, VA; GD; MBA; Yrbk Stff 88-89; Engl Soc; Cdt Lt VMI Crps 88-89; Karate Clb 87-90; BA VI Military Inst 90; Engl/Psych/Educ; Tchr.

**BAINBRIDGE, MARJORIE KAY,** Wv Northern Comm Coll, Wheeling, WV; GD; AAS; Phi Theta Kappa; Deans List 84-; Pres List 90; Accctg; CPA.

**BAINES, AMY M,** Air Force Inst Of Tech, Wrt-Ptrsn Afb, OH; GD; MBA; Capt USAF/5 Yrs Active Duty; BA Univ South Florida 83; Logistics Mngmnt; Continue AF Career.

**BAINES, ANNE L,** Thomas Nelson Comm Coll, Hampton, VA; SO; AS; PTA Pres 76-; Grmn Amer Vlkssprt Assn 87-; Jr Clrk 68-70; Comp Sci; Comp Pgmg.

**BAINES, JANIE R,** Coll Of Charleston, Charleston, SC; JR; BED; Zeta Tau Alpha 89-; Educ; Tchr.

**BAINES, MARY A,** Thomas Nelson Comm Coll, Hampton, VA; FR; AASD; Gamma Tau Pres; Xi Delta Psi; Beta Sigma Phi 83-84; Sec 72-79; Bnk Tllr 86-88; Grphc Cmmnctns; Cmmrcl Art.

**BAINS, SHELIA L,** Middle Tn St Univ, Murfreesboro, TN; FR.

**BAIONE, THOMAS E,** Univ Of Md At Eastern Shore, Princess Anne, MD; SR; BED; Jazz Band/Small Jazz Combo Basssist 89-; Concert Band/Concert Choir 89-; J B Express 86-; Good News Sound 86-; Prfrmd For U S Senate Lnchn Wshngtn D C 90; Prfrmd With Stanley Turrent & Julius La Rosa 90-; W Germany 2 Wks Tour 90; Perform & Teach Music.

**BAIRD, AMANDA G,** Union Univ, Jackson, TN; FR; BS; Schlrs Exclnc Schlp 90-; Chem; Pharm.

**BAIRD, BRIAN S,** Livingston Univ, Livingston, AL; JR; DCH Regnl Schlrshp Leon Prog 91; U S Army Natl Guard; EMT-A Lakeland Comm Clg 90; 91-A Cmbt Medic 88; Nurs; Nurs.

**BAIRD, CHRISTOPHER S,** Saint Pauls Coll, Lawrenceville, VA; FR; BA; Readers Digest Awd Acad Excellence; Spec Pres Schlrshp; Bus Mgmnt; Office Mgr.

**BAIRD, JONATHAN D,** Western Carolina Univ, Cullowhee, NC; SO; BA; Soc Crtv Anchrnsm Chrnclr 89-; Anthrplgy Clb Sec 89-; Hnrs Prog 89-; Anthropology; Fieldwork.

**BAIRD, MANDY L,** Middle Tn St Univ, Murfreesboro, TN; FR; BA; Bsn Admin; Law.

**BAIRD, TASHA A,** Univ Of Tn At Martin, Martin, TN; SO; BS; Pi Sigma Epsilon Mst Achv Pldg 90; Sec Educ/Biol; HS Tchr.

**BAISDEN, BOBBIE C,** Alice Lloyd Coll, Pippa Passes, KY; SR; BED; SGA Sr Rep 90-; Sr Clss Gov Plrlmntrn 90-; Acad Tm 88-90; Alpha Chi Pres 89-; Kappa Delta Epsilon 88-; Bapt Stdnt Union Pres 87-; Envrnmntl Awrnss Grp 90-; Judy Howard Mem Awd 88-89; Geo I Alden Awd 90-; Sftbl Mst Imprvd/Rbi 88-89; Math/Scl Stds; Tchr/Gudnc Cnslr.

**BAISDEN, BONNIE S,** Marshall University, Huntington, WV; SR; BED; Pstmstr Rlf Dngss WV 90; AA Southern WV Comm Coll 90; Elem Educ; Tchr.

**BAISDEN, BRYAN J,** Wv Univ, Morgantown, WV; FR; BS; Univ 4 H Clb 90; Deans Lst; Eng.

**BAITY, DAVID C,** Toccoa Falls Coll, Toccoa Falls, GA; SR; BA; Stdnt Cncl Rep Pres 88-89; Summr Yth Pstrat Prspct UMC; Elec Technen US Navy/Eng Firm 76-87; Pre-Smnry Stdies; Chrstn Mnstry.

**BAITZ, STEPHANIE A,** Castleton St Coll, Castleton, VT; SR; BS; Erly Educ; Tchr.

**BAJADA, FRANCES C,** City Univ Of Ny Baruch Coll, New York, NY; JR; BA; Rtl Trd Soc VP/FINANCE 90-; Goldn Key; Intrnshp Mt Sihai Hosp; Intrnshp Wash DC; Provost Awd; Psi Chi; Dean's List; Psychlgy; Law.

**BAJUS, DAWN M,** Duquesne Univ, Pittsburgh, PA; SO; BA; Natl Hnr Scty 87-89; Spnsh Hnr Scty 87-89; Bus Mrktng.

**BAJUS, KIMBERLY A,** Duquesne Univ, Pittsburgh, PA; SO; BA; Acctg.

**BAKALIS, CHRYSANTHE,** Radford Univ, Radford, VA; JR; Scl Wrk Clb Pres 88-; Spnsh Clb 88-90; Cthlc Stdnt Assn 90-; Floyd Hl Hs Cncl 88-89; Cir K Intl 88-90; Ambssdrs 90-; Intrnshp 89-; Scl Wrk; Cnslr.

**BAKAN, STEPHANIE A,** Miami Jacobs Jr Coll Of Bus, Dayton, OH; AS; Bus Admin; Own/Oper Retail Store.

**BAKER, AIMEE M,** Adelphi Univ, Garden City, NY; SR; BA; Pre Law Scty 89-; Pi Sigma Alpha 90-; Magna Cum Laude 90-; Pltcl Sci Hnrs; Political Science; Law.**

**BAKER, ALNITA B,** Al A & M Univ, Normal, AL; JR; BA; Stdnt Gov Chpln 88-89; Stdnt Drug Tsk Frc; Kappa Delta Phi; Pres Schlrf; Delta Sigma Theta 90-; Blgy/Psych; Scndry Ed Inst.

**BAKER, AMANDA H,** Norfolk St Univ, Norfolk, VA; SR; Praise Flwshp Treas 87-; Norfolk Sta Un Voice Of Inspiration Pres 87-; Kinesiotherapy Clb Mbr 88-; Otsdng Prfrmr; Miss NSU Pageant 2nd Runr Up 90-; Quality Life Awd 90; Otsdng Wmn Amer; Emplee Mo Burger King 88; Kinesiotrerapy; Phys Thrpy Doctoral Dgree.**

**BAKER, ANGIE A,** Middle Tn St Univ, Murfreesboro, TN; SR; Stdnt Ambssdr 89-90; STEA 89-90; Teachers Educ Assoc NIE 88-90; BED 90; AS 88; Elem Educ; Teacher.

**BAKER, BARBARA A,** Univ Of Pittsburgh At Bradford, Bradford, PA; SR; BA; Lit Mag; Humntes Achvmnt; Frmwrks Fictn Cntst; English; Prfsr English.

**BAKER, BETH LYNN,** Radford Univ, Radford, VA; JR; BS; Arbcs Clb 89-90; Hse Cncl Rsdnt Hls 88-90; NEA/VEA; Pre Stu Tght Dbln Elem Sch; Rsdnt Asstnt 90; IM Sftbl 89; Elem Educ; Tchr.

**BAKER, BONNIE J,** Christopher Newport Coll, Newport News, VA; JR; BA; Educ; Tchng.

**BAKER, BONNIE L,** Macon Coll, Macon, GA; FR; BS; Engl; Law.

**BAKER, BRENT D,** Univ Of Sc At Columbia, Columbia, SC; FR; BA; Arete Hon Prog; Elec Eng.

**BAKER, CAROL E,** Nc Agri & Tech St Univ, Greensboro, NC; SO; BS; Stdnt Natl Educ Assoc 90-; Wmns Cncl 89-; Fayettevl Aggie Clb 90-; Spec Educ; Tchr.

**BAKER, CHENA S,** Hampton Univ, Hampton, VA; SR; MPA; Sclgy Clb 90-; VA Pre Almn 88-; Alpha Kappa Mu 89-91; Alpha Kappa Delta; Gradtd Wth Dptmntl Hnrs; BA; Pblc Admin.**

**BAKER, CHESNEY S,** Univ Of Va Clinch Valley Coll, Wise, VA; JR; BA; Judd Lewis Soc Pres 90-; Natl Coll Hon Conf 90-; Engl Lit; Grad Sch.

**BAKER, CHRISTINA L,** S U N Y Coll At Fredonia, Fredonia, NY; JR; Kappa Delta Pi; AA Jamestown Cmnty Clg 90; Elem Ed/Spanish; Tchr.

**BAKER, CYNTHIA L,** Middle Tn St Univ, Murfreesboro, TN; SR; Summa Cum Laude; Dns Lst; AS Columbia State Cmnty Clg 89; Bsn/Acctg; CPA.

**BAKER, DAVI-LEE,** Bay Path Coll, Longmeadow, MA; BA; Soccer/Trck/Skiing; Fshn Mrchndsng; Buyer.

**BAKER, DEBORAH A,** Garrett Comm Coll, Mchenry, MD; SO; AA; Stdnt Govt Assn Pres 90-; Wldlf Clb VP 89-90; Phi Theta Kappa; Math/Sci Trnsfr; Envrnmntl Law.

**BAKER, DENISE M,** Union Univ, Jackson, TN; SR; Stdnt TN Ed Assoc 88-; Actvts Cncl Exec Cnl 89-90; Bptsts Stdnt Un 877-; Rtldg Hnry Hstry Clb 88-90; Deans Lst 90-; BS; Elem Ed; Tchr.

**BAKER, DIANE E,** Franklin And Marshall Coll, Lancaster, PA; JR; BA; Yrbk Edtr Chf 90-; Accntng Clb Exec Cmmtt 89-; Hstry Clb Pres; Pi Gamma Mu; Blck Pyrmd; FAMINE 90-; Dana Schlrs; Marshall Schlr 88-; Harry Ness & Co Intern 90-; Picpa Trstee Schlrshp 89-; Bus Admn/Accntng.

**BAKER, DINA D,** Wallace St Comm Coll At Selma, Selma, AL; SO; BA; Pres Lst/Dns Lst 89-; Erly Chldhd/Elem Ed; Tch.

**BAKER, DIXIE L,** Coll Of Charleston, Charleston, SC; FR; BA; Biol; Anesthetist.

**BAKER, DONNA C,** Methodist Coll, Fayetteville, NC; GD; Meth Clg Employee 88-; Bus Admin; Persnl Mngmnt.

**BAKER, DONNA J,** Marshall University, Huntington, WV; FR; BED; Yth Christ; Phi Eta Sigma; Hist; Tchr.

**BAKER, DONNA S,** Univ Of Va Clinch Valley Coll, Wise, VA; SR; Stu Dscplnry Brd Sec 90-; Peer Advsng Prgm 90-F Coll Rpblcns 90-; Darden Soc; Phi Upsilon Omega Sec 89-; BA Clinch Vlly Coll; Hstry/Soc Sci; Educ.

**BAKER, DOUGLAS P,** Milligan Coll, Milligan Clg, TN; JR; BABS; Scl Affrs Cmmttee 89; Acad Affrs Cmmttee Drm Rep 90; Cmptr Sub-Cmmttee 90; German Lang Tutor 89; Im Bsktbl Sftbl Ftbl Vllybl 88; Math/Eng.

**BAKER, ELIZABETH A,** Univ Of Tn At Martin, Martin, TN; SR; BSSW; Social Work Clb Sec 88; Alumni Council 90; Order Omega 90; Alpha Delta Mu 89; Chi Omega Sec 87; NASW; Serv Awrd; Infant Stimulation Prgrm Intrn; Social Work; LCSW.

**BAKER, ELIZABETH A,** Bridgewater Coll, Bridgewater, VA; SR; Res Counselor 90-; Res Hall Council 90-; Dorm V P 90-; Stdnt Counselor 88-; Campus Cntr Prog Council Prog Dir 88-89; Admissions Tour Guide 87-; Res Hall Rep 88-90; Stdnt Intrn Dis 39 Parole & Prob Ofc; Stdnt Dir Kline Campus; Sociology; Parole & Probation Ofcr.

**BAKER, ELIZABETH ANNE,** Fl St Univ, Tallahassee, FL; JR; BA; Adv Club/Panhellenic Rush Cnslr; Golden Key 90-; Kappa Alpha Theta 89-; Fl Acdmc Schlr 88-; Sor IMS 89-; Media Cmmnctns; Law.

**BAKER, GLORIA J,** Fl A & M Univ, Tallahassee, FL; FR; BA; Pres Schlrs Assn 90-; BACCHUS 90; Phi Eta Sigma; Bus Admin; Bus.

**BAKER JR, HARRY E,** Univ Of Tn At Martin, Martin, TN; FR; BS; Univ TN Martin Comp Lab Assts 90-; Area VII Spec Olympcs Com 90-; Gooch Schlrshp; Acdmc Schlrshp; IM Bsktbl Sftbl Ftbl; Math/Comp Sci; Comp Pgmg.

**BAKER, HEIDI L,** Catawba Valley Comm Coll, Hickory, NC; FR; BA; Roteract Clb Treas 90; Acctg Clb 90; Gamma Beta Phi; Acctg.

**BAKER, HELENA R,** Univ Of Cincinnati, Cincinnati, OH; JR; BED; Hnrs Schlrshp 90-; Church Elder; C S Tchr 88-; Soc Wrkr; AA 87; Sclgy; Elem Educ.

**BAKER, HENRY ALLEN,** Univ Of Va Clinch Valley Coll, Wise, VA; SR; MA; VA Ed Assn; Natl Ed Assn; Deans List 90-; BA Elem Ed 90-; Cnslng.

**BAKER, HOLLY E,** Muskingum Coll, New Concord, OH; FR; Yrbk Stff; Theta Phi Alpha; Bronze Key 91; Elem Educ.

**BAKER, JACQUELINE E,** Duquesne Univ, Pittsburgh, PA; JR; BED; NYE 88-89; Education Schlrshp 90-; Penn St Sftbll 88-90; Elem Ed; Tchr.

**BAKER, JANE W,** Univ Of Sc At Columbia, Columbia, SC; SR; BA; Delta Delta Delta Lcl Chptr Mag Edit 89; Dns Lst 87-; Cert Of Ltrry Stds Univ Of Sheffield 90; Engl; Pblshing.

**BAKER, JENNIFER J,** Averett Coll, Danville, VA; SR; BS; Alpha Chi; Phi Theta Kappa; Deans Lst; Provosts Lst; Grad Summa Cum Laude; AAS Danville Cmnty Clg 89; Acctng; CPA.

**BAKER, JESSICA O,** Eckerd Coll, St Petersburg, FL; SO; BS; Stdnt Crt Jstc; Psych Clb; Circle K; Caphe Smmr Schlr; Frd Apprntcshp; Spec Tlnt Schlrhp/Sftbl; IM Sprts Cpt; Psych; Cnslng/Univ Teach.

**BAKER, JOAN F,** Miami Dade Comm Coll, Miami, FL; SR; MSN; Amer Assc Crtcl Care Nurses 88-; Amer Assc Neuroscience Nurses 86-; Dip Kingston Jamaica 75; Nursing/Neuroscience; Clinical Nurse Spec.

**BAKER, JOLYNDA A,** Liberty Univ, Lynchburg, VA; SO; BA; Frch Clb; Alpha Lambda Delta 89; Acctng; Bsn.

**BAKER, JOSEPH J,** Hillsborough Comm Coll, Tampa, FL; FR; AA; Knights Columbus 3rd Dgr Knght 88-; Lbyst 81-82; Holy Name Soc 89-; Sr Frmn/Oprtns Mgr Nwspr Mlrm 74-; Bsn Admin; Nwspr Mgmt/BA/MBA.

**BAKER, JOSEPH P,** Mount Aloysius Jr Coll, Cresson, PA; SO; BA; Lyl Ordr Moose Govr 90-; Mgt Info Sys.

**BAKER, JOYCE O,** Broward Comm Coll, Ft Lauderdale, FL; JR; AS; Chllng Yth 90-; Phi Theta Kappa 89-; Nrsng Tchnlgy; PhD Hlth Serv Admin.

**BAKER, JUDY L,** Colby Sawyer Coll, New London, NH; SO; BA; Drama Clb Prsdnt 89-; Alpha Chi 90-; Cmmnctns; Radio Tlvsn Theatre.

**BAKER, KIMBERLEY D,** Univ Of Ky, Lexington, KY; JR; BS; RHA Cmnctns Chrmn 89-90; Crsde Fr Christ 89-; SAC 89; Phi Beta Sigma; Lambda Sigma; CAE 90; RA 90-; Spch/Lang Pthlgy.

**BAKER, KIMBERLY L,** Central Fl Comm Coll, Ocala, FL; SO.

**BAKER, KIMBERLY N,** Western Piedmont Comm Coll, Morganton, NC; SO; AA; Travel Assoc Chnclr 90-; Toured USSR 90; Phi Theta Kappa 90-; Cmnctns/Jrnlsm; Radio Brdcstng.

**BAKER, KRISTIN L,** Old Dominion Univ, Norfolk, VA; JR; BA; DECA; Deans Lst 90; Mktg Educ/Fshn.

**BAKER, KRISTY,** Itawamba Comm Coll, Fulton, MS; SO; BA; Phi Theta Kappa 90-; Pres Deans List; Acctg; CPA.

**BAKER, L MERIANNE,** Coker Coll, Hartsville, SC; SO; BA; Pgmg Bd Sec 90-; Crhstns Hlpng Others 89-; Cls Pres SGA Sntr 90-; Ambssdrs 90-; Top 10 Fresh 89-90; Top 10 Soph 90-; Math/Rlgn; Archtctr.

**BAKER, LAURA K,** The Boston Conservatory, Boston, MA; JR; BM; Exec Cncl Stdnt Gov Sec 89-; MENC Sec 89-; Sigma Alpha Iota Sec 89-; Peer Supprt Aid 90-; Music Educ; Tchr.

**BAKER, LAURA M,** Fl St Univ, Tallahassee, FL; SO; BA; AA; Eng Edn; Teach.

**BAKER, LEIGH ANN,** Brewer St Jr Coll, Fayette, AL; SO; BS; Biol Sci; Med.

**BAKER, LEMONT,** Tn St Univ, Nashville, TN; JR; BS; Peer Counselor; Natl Scty Black Engrs; Golden Key Secy; Alpha Kappa Mu; Intern Motorola Phoenix Az; IM Bsktbl; Electrcl Engrng.

**BAKER, LIAM P,** Bob Jones Univ, Greenville, SC; FR; BA; Alpha Theta Pi 90-; Bsktbl/Vlybl/Track 90-; Biology Ed; Teacher.

**BAKER, LINDA SUE,** Union Univ, Jackson, TN; SR; BS; STEA 90-91; AS Jackson State Comm Clg 90; Elem Ed; Tchng.

**BAKER, MARJORIE A,** Medaille Coll, Buffalo, NY; JR; BSED; K-6 Ed; Rdng; Tch K-6/Rdng.

**BAKER, MARSHALL S,** Duke Univ, Durham, NC; FR; BS; Partnership For Ltrcy 90-; ICF 90-; Phi Eta Sigma 90-; Chemistry; Medicine.

**BAKER, MARY R,** Univ Of Tn At Martin, Martin, TN; FR; Stdnt TN Educ Assn 90-; Peer Enabling Prog 90-; Ldrs In Res 90-; Early Chldhd Educ; Elem Tchr.

**BAKER, MELANIE K,** Notre Dame Coll, Cleveland, OH; SO; BA; English Scty Pres 89-; French Clb 90-; Activities Brd 90-; Pi Delta Phi; Communications French; Public Relations.

**BAKER, MELISSA R,** Miami Jacobs Jr Coll Of Bus, Dayton, OH; SR; AS; Clgte Sec Internatl VP 90-; Info Prcsng; Exec.

**BAKER, MIA S,** Norfolk St Univ, Norfolk, VA; FR; BA; Finance/Mktg; CEO.

**BAKER, MICHAEL E,** Va Commonwealth Univ, Richmond, VA; JR; BS; Gold Key; Acctg.

**BAKER, MICHAEL K,** Northern Ky Univ, Highland Hts, KY; FR; Commonwlth Schlrshp; Bus; Accntntng.

**BAKER, MICHELLE E,** Columbia Union Coll, Takoma Park, MD; JR; BA; Phi Eta Sigma 89-; Alpha Chi; Math/English.

**BAKER, MICHELLE M,** S U N Y Coll Of Tech At Alfred, Alfred, NY; SR; BA; Acctg Clb 89-; Hll Govt 89-90; Alfrd St Coll Tchr Yr Awrd 89; Acctg.

**BAKER, NANCY A,** Hillsborough Comm Coll, Tampa, FL; SO; BA; Govt Sen 89-; Stdnts For Schlstc Succs 90-; Phi Theta Kappa Pres 90-; Ldrshp Awd Phi Theta Kappa 90-; Blck Schlr Awd Univ FL; Hon Mntn G E Otstndng Mnrties Bsns Admn; AA; Acctg; CPA.

**BAKER, NANCY L,** Oh Univ, Athens, OH; FR; BED; Bnd 90-; Clarinet Choir 90; Educ; Tchng.

**BAKER, NATASHA L,** Univ Of Sc At Beaufort, Beaufort, SC; FR; MBA; Chrch Choir Sec 88-; Acctg.

**BAKER, NICOLE S,** Pa Coll Of Tech, Williamsport, PA; FR; ACS; Alpha Omega 90-; Advrtsg Art.

**BAKER, PAMELA B,** Univ Of Sc At Columbia, Columbia, SC; BA; Educ Clb 90; Certified Laubach Tutor; Carolina Power & Light Employee; BS Mngmnt USC Aiken 86, Elem Educ.

**BAKER, PAMELA J,** West Liberty St Coll, West Liberty, WV; SR; BA; Elem Educ.

**BAKER JR, PAUL T,** Univ Of Md At Eastern Shore, Princess Anne, MD; JR; BA; Intl Food Svc Exec Assc 90-; Hnr Scty 89-; Eta Rho Mu 89-; Dinner Thtr 89-; Ward Fndtn 89-90; Asst Prdctn Mgr 90; Hotel/Rest Mgmt/Bus.

**BAKER, PETER S,** Univ Of Cincinnati, Cincinnati, OH; FR; BA; Brdcstng Clb 90-; Alpha Lambda Delta 91; Brdcstng.

**BAKER, RAMONA,** Ny Univ, New York, NY; JR; BA; NSRA 84-; NSR 84-; Admn Med Asst 89-; AA N Y U 89; Psych; Hlth Care.

**BAKER, RANDAL J,** Nova Univ, Ft Lauderdale, FL; GD; MBA; DPMA 90-; Crisis Line Vol 89-; CAP Vol 88-; Mktg Rep; BSCS Purdue Univ 85; Bsn Mgmt.

**BAKER, REGINA J,** Central Al Comm Coll, Alexander City, AL; FR; Bus Mgmt.

**BAKER, RICHARD C,** Wv Univ, Morgantown, WV; FR; BS; Hnrs Pgm 90-; Mchncl Engrg; Engr.

**BAKER, ROBERT C,** Wv Univ, Morgantown, WV; SR; MSCE; Amer Scty Cvl Eng Vp 89-; Rcqtbl Clb 90-; Pi Kappa Alpha 88-; Ldrshp Awd 90-; Deans Acad Hnrs Lst; Pres Awd; BSCE; Geotech Eng; Cnsltnt.

**BAKER, ROBERT O,** Church Of God Sch Of Theology, Cleveland, TN; Tchng Asstnshp 90-; BA Lee Coll 89; AS Manatee Comm Coll 85; Thlgy; Smnry Prfssr.

**BAKER, RODNEY L,** Marshall University, Huntington, WV; SR; BA; All AM Schlr 90; Deans List; Mngmnt; Law.**

**BAKER, RORY L,** Fayetteville St Univ, Fayetteville, NC; FR; BS; Cross Cntry Tm 90; Phys Ed; Tchr.

**BAKER, SABRINA A,** Univ Of Al At Birmingham, Birmingham, AL; JR; BS; Jefferson State Jr Clg Alum Assn 88-; Phi Theta Kappa 84-86; Outstndng MCT Stdnt-Jefferson State Jr Clg; MLT Amer Soc Of Clin Path 85; CT Hlth/Human Svcs-Clin Tech 87; AS Jefferson State Jr Clg Birmigham 85; Comp Sci; Syst Anlyst.

**BAKER, SAMANTHA L,** Al St Univ, Montgomery, AL; SR; BS; Invstmnt Clb NABA; Lettie B Waller Schlrshp 88; Pres Schlrshp 87-; Acctng.

**BAKER, SARAH J,** Northern Ky Univ, Highland Hts, KY; GD; Deans Lst 90; BA Miami Univ 74; Elem Ed Math; Tchr.

**BAKER, SCOTT A,** Slippery Rock Univ, Slippery Rock, PA; SO; BA; IM Vllybl 90; Vrsty Sccr 90; Physcl Educ Hlth; Tchr.

**BAKER, SCOTT A,** Coll Of Charleston, Charleston, SC; SO; Bsbl 90-.

**BAKER, SCOTT M,** Daytona Beach Comm Coll, Daytona Beach, FL; FR; ADN; Natl Stdnt Nrs Assn; Nrsng.

**BAKER, SHARON L,** Westminster Coll, New Wilmingtn, PA; JR; BA; Mortar Brd; Deans List 89; Bsktbl 88-89; Sftbl Capt 90-; Elem Educ; Law.

**BAKER, SHASTA Y,** Alcorn St Univ, Lorman, MS; FR; BA; Psy; Prfssr.

**BAKER, SHEILA D,** Ga St Univ, Atlanta, GA; SR; BS; Elem Sch Practicum Intern; Stdnt Tchg; Early Chldhd Ed; Tch.

**BAKER, SHERRY J,** Fayetteville St Univ, Fayetteville, NC; SO; BA; Outstndng Coll Stdnts Amer 88-89; Early Chldhd Educ.

**BAKER, TERESA M,** Hampton Univ, Hampton, VA; FR; BA; Dance Company Treas 90-; Bio; Medicine.

**BAKER, TERRI D,** Livingston Univ, Livingston, AL; JR; BS; Cmps Outrch 88-90; Trsts Acdmc/Ldrshp Schlrshp 88-; J P Homer Schlrshp 88; IM Flag Ftbl/Sftbl 88-90; Bus Admin.**

**BAKER, TIANNA M,** Tomlinson Coll, Cleveland, TN; SO; BS; Drama Tm; Spiritual Life Com Grp Ldr 90-; Phi Theta Kappa 90-; Ch Invlvmnt; Boilermakers Schlrshp 89-90; AL Power Schlrshp; Valedictorian Schlrshp 89-90; Math; Profr.

**BAKER, TIFFANY A,** S U N Y At Buffalo, Buffalo, NY; FR; BS; Ldrshp Tsk Frce 90-; Natl Soc Prof Engrs Career Plnng Comm 90-; Amer Cncr Soc 90-; Dns Lst 90-; Amer Soc Mech Engrs 90-; Natl Soc Prof Engrs 90-; Un Carbide Linde Div; Tech Intrn Res Dev; Vllybl; Mech Engr; Engr/Law.

**BAKER, TIMOTHY C,** S U N Y Coll Of Tech At Alfred, Alfred, NY; SR; AOS; Peer Tutor Prgrm; Diesel Hvy Eqpmnt Srvc.

**BAKER, TRACY E,** Univ Of Sc At Columbia, Columbia, SC; FR; Residence Hall Gov 90-; Hall Emergng Ldrs Prgrm 90-; Gamma Beta Phi 90-; Phi Eta Sigma 90-; Kappa Psi 90-; Deans Lst 90-; Phrmcy.

**BAKER, TRACY LYNN,** Memphis St Univ, Memphis, TN; SO; BBA; Tutor Corps 89-; Peer Mntr Orgztn 89-; Gamma Beta Phi 90-; Delta Gamma 90-; Acctg.

**BAKER, WESLEY F,** Univ Of Al At Birmingham, Birmingham, AL; SR; BS; Fin Mgmt Assn V P 90-; SGA Fin Comm 90-; Inter Frat Comm Acdmc Chr 90-; Lambda Chi Alpha Acdmc Chr 87-; Asst Trader Universal Securities 90; Customer Serv Rep So Trust Bank; IM Ftbl Wrstlng Sffttttbl Water Polo 87-; Acctng/Fin.

**BAKER, WILTON D,** Morehouse Coll, Atlanta, GA; SR; BA; NAACP Glee Clb 86-90; Coll Bus Assn 89-; Fla Clb Chmn Socl Fncnts 87-; Hnr Rl; Kappa Alpha Psi; Guide Right; Jacn N Jill Of Amer Inc Pres 86-87; Asst Pres Alphagrphcs Orlando Fla 90; Bnkng/Finance; Fncl Analyst/Entrprnr.

**BAKER-HAYES, CAROL D,** Savannah St Coll, Savannah, GA; JR; BA; Tn Yth Advsr Of Hppy Hme Bapt Chrch And Mmbr LL Smlls Chr; Accnts Rcvble Clrk; Acctng Info Systms Dble Mjr; CPA.

**BAKKEGARD, JOHN I,** Birmingham Southern Coll, Birmingham, AL; SR; BS; Natl Assoc Accntnts VP 90-; Phi Eta Sigma 87-; Alpha Lambda Delta 87-; Dana Intrnshp Math Lab Asst 88-; Vrsty Scr Capt 87-; Acctg/Bsn Fnce; CPA.

**BAKO, MARGIE S,** Comm Coll Algny Co Algny Cmps, Pittsburgh, PA; FR; BA; Scndry Educ; Hstry Tchr.

**BAKO, VALERIE L,** Western Carolina Univ, Cullowhee, NC; SR; BA; Chncllrs Ambssdr 89-; Sigma Tau Delta 89-; Mrtr Bd Soc 90-; Tnns Capt 87-; NCAA Wmn Athlt Yr; Athltc Dir Acdmc Achvmnt Awd; Most Vlbl Plyr Tnns; Engl; Tch.

**BAKOS, MITCHELL J,** Cleveland St Univ, Cleveland, OH; JR; Tau Beta Pi Recrdng Secy 90-; Phi Kappa Tau VP 88-90; Varsity Tennis Team 89-; Comptr Engr.**

**BAL, REBECCA L,** Univ Of Miami, Coral Gables, FL; FR; BS; Marine Bio.

**BALA, NICOLE,** Teikyo Post Univ, Waterbury, CT; JR; BS; Assoc Of Legal Stdnts 87-89; Paralegal Club 90-; Phi Theta Kappa; Green Key Hnr Soc; AS SUNY Farmingdale 89; Gen Studies; Law.

**BALA, PRIYA,** Colgate Univ, Hamilton, NY; FR; BA; Res Life Comm Treas; Intl Rltns Cncl 90-; Amnesty Intl 90-; Deans List 90-; Alpha Chi Omega Delta Pledge Class Schlrshp Chm 90-; Red Cross 90; Legan Intrn Law Firm Knutson Colt Atty 90; Rcptnst Herrington Co Export Firm 90; Intl Rltns/Latin Am Studies; Law.

**BALAGOT, EMELINE R,** Seton Hall Univ, South Orange, NJ; JR; BSN; Seton Hall Clge Nrsg Stdnt Nrs Assoc; Alpha Phi Schrshp Chr 88-; Nrsg; Nrs.

**BALAHTSIS, DEANA,** Le Moyne Coll, Syracuse, NY; SR; Interantl Relations Club Sec 88-89; Judicial Brd 89-; Pi Gamma Mu 90-; Alpha Zigma Nu 89-; Projects N Cmnty 87-; Intrnshp Elmcrest Placement Center 90-; Natl Undergraduate Research Conf 90; Womans La Crosse Captain 88-; Law.

**BALAS, VINCENT M,** Univ Of Akron, Akron, OH; SR; Srch Prog Chrstn Yth Grp Spkr; USA Karate Fed 85-; Deans List; Andy Maluke Meml Schlrshp 90; Karate Clb 87-; BS; BA; Phys Ed/Math Ed; Ed.

**BALASARIA, NIRAJ K,** Edinboro Univ Of Pa, Edinboro, PA; SR; BS; Comp Clb Treas 89-; Intnl Stdnt Assc Sec 90-; Intl Stdnt Nwspr St Edtr 89-; Univ Hnrs Pgm 89-; Pi Mu Epsilon Sec/Treas 89-; SGA 90-; Lcl Schls India Spkr 90-; Dns List 89-; Tuition Wvr 88-; Oxford Schlrshp 90; Cmptr Tutor 89-; Comp Sci; Prgrmr.

**BALASH, REBECCA J,** Notre Dame Coll, Cleveland, OH; FR; BA; Edctn Cncl 90-; Pall Mall Englsh Soc; Lambda Sigma Soc 90-; Elem Edctn; Elem Tchr.

**BALASKA, KEVIN J,** Univ Of Sc At Columbia, Columbia, SC; SO; BA; German Clb; IM Rqtbl; Georgraphy; Research.

**BALASQUIDE VELEZ, ZULMA N,** Inter Amer Univ Pr Hato Rey, Hato Rey, PR; SR; BBA; Acctng Stdnt Assn 90-; Hnr Stdnt Assn 90-; Natl Acctng Assn 89-; Stdnt Govt; Dns Lst 90; Acctng; CPA.

**BALBIERER, MICHAEL F,** Widener Univ, Chester, PA; JR; BS; Civil Engrng; Engrng.

**BALDAUF, MARY C,** S U N Y At Stony Brook, Stony Brook, NY; GD; MD; Anatomy Tutor; Sftbl Tm Mgr/Capt 90-; Cardiac Neurological Tech 88-89; BA Harvard Univ 88; MS Univ Hlth Sci/Chgo Med Sch 90; Med.

**BALDICK, RENEE L,** Univ Of Tn At Martin, Martin, TN; SR; BS; Baptist Stdnt Union 88-; Phi Eta Sigma 87-88; Phi Kappa Phi 90-; Psych; Occup Ther.

**BALDINO, DENISE,** S U N Y Coll Of A & T Morrisvl, Morrisville, NY; SO; BS; SGA 90-; Stdnt Tchr; AS; Elem Ed; Tch.

**BALDINO, LAURA R,** Newbury Coll, Brookline, MA; FR; AA; Fash Merchndsng.

**BALDUCCI, RALPH P,** City Univ Of Ny Baruch Coll, New York, NY; SO; BSED; Tchrs Tomorrow Clb 90-; Crisis Cnslr Covenant Hs Nineline N Y C 88-; Erly Chldhd Educ; Chld Psychlgy.

**BALDWIN, ALLEN P,** Columbia Union Coll, Takoma Park, MD; SR; BS; 1st Svnth Day Chrch Asst Frst Eldr 86; Ptnt Accnt Rep Grgetwn U 88; BS; Org Mngmnt; Mnstr.

**BALDWIN, BRENDA T,** Ky St Univ, Frankfort, KY; SR; BS; Cum Laude/Dept Hon; Meth Ch Chancel Choir; KY Revenue Cabinet 85-; AAS Lexington Tech Inst 85; Bus Admin.

**BALDWIN, CHRISTOPHER S,** Univ Of Md Balt Cnty Campus, Catonsville, MD; FR; Hnr Clg 90-; Engr.

**BALDWIN, CYNTHIA J,** Univ Of South Al, Mobile, AL; SO; BS; Acctng.

**BALDWIN, GEORGIA S,** Va Commonwealth Univ, Richmond, VA; SR; BA; AAS G Sargeant Reynolds 89; Psych.

**BALDWIN, JENNIFER D,** Univ Of Cincinnati, Cincinnati, OH; JR; BS; Golden Key; Kappa Delta Pi; AS Raymond Walters Clg 90; Educ; Elem/Kndrgrtn Educ.

**BALDWIN, JEROLD C,** Morehouse Coll, Atlanta, GA; JR; BA; Harland Boys Clb; Fmly 2 Fmly; Bus Assn; SHRM; Cornnuts Intern 90-; Allied Sysco Foods Intern 89-90; E B Williams Achvmnt Awd; Mgmnt; Human Resources Mgmnt.

**BALDWIN, KAREN E,** Mobile Coll, Mobile, AL; SO; BS; Stdnt Govt Assoc V P 89-90; Clinical Psych.

**BALDWIN, LEIGH A,** Gordon Coll, Barnesville, GA; JR; BBA; Coll Rpblcns 90-; Stdnt Rcrtmnt Team 90-; Phi Theta Kappa 89-; Sigma Kappa 90-; AA 90; Acctg; CPA.

**BALDWIN, SUSAN G,** Glassboro St Coll, Glassboro, NJ; GD; BA; IM Soccer 86-87; IM Vlybl 87-88; Epsilon Theta Sigma Sec/Tr 88-90; Tutor 88-90; BA 90; Engl; Tchr.

**BALDWIN, TANYA S,** Univ Of Nc At Asheville, Asheville, NC; SR; BA; IM Vlybl Sftbl 87-; IM Bsktbl Scr 87-89; Deans Lst 88-; Mathmtcs; Sec Lvl Tchr.

**BALDWIN, TRACEY A,** Saint Josephs Coll, Windham, ME; SR; BA; Delta Omicron; Math; Clg Teach.

**BALDWIN, TRACY L,** Tn Tech Univ, Cookeville, TN; FR; BCHE; Scty Wmn Eng 90-; Circle K 90-; Stdnt Sfty Com 90-; Alpha Delta Pi Asst Tres 90-; Chemical Eng.

**BALDYGA, JAMES E,** Springfield Tech Comm Coll, Springfield, MA; JR; BA; Hstry Clb 88-89; Ski Clb VP 87-89; Psy; Clncl Psy.

**BALEGA, RUTH A,** Univ Of Pittsburgh, Pittsburgh, PA; GD; MSN; Sigma Theta Tau 85-; BSN 87; Nrsg; Admin.

**BALENTINE, KATHRYN M,** Al A & M Univ, Normal, AL; JR; BS; Huntsville Art League Gallery; AAS John C Calhoun Jr Coll 86f; Interior Dsgn.

**BALES, KAREN A,** Univ Of West Fl, Pensacola, FL; SR; Natl Assn Educ Yng Chldrn 89-; AA Pensacola Jr Coll 83; BA; Elem Ed/Early Chldhd; Educ.

**BALFOUR, DAVID L,** Va Commonwealth Univ, Richmond, VA; JR; BS; Pre-Dntl Clb 89-; Gldn Key 90-; Phi Sigma; Blgy; Dntstry.

**BALGLEY, ALLAN,** Bridgeport Engr Inst, Fairfield, CT; SO; BS; Conel IPC Lab Tech 88090; Eltrnc Info Sys Asst Engr 90-; AAS Elctrnc Tech Bramson Ort Tech Inst 87; Elec Engr.

**BALIJA, VIVEKANAND,** City Univ Of Ny Baruch Coll, New York, NY; SO; MD; Pre Med Soc 89-90; N E Brnch Ts Cltr Assoc Ed 89-90; St Johns Thtrcl Soc VP 89-90; Dns Lst; CAUSE 90-; Blgy.

**BALIKER, HEATHER K,** Hillsborough Comm Coll, Tampa, FL; SR; AS; Rdlgy Clb; Deans Lst 90-; Hnrs Grad 90-; Rdlgc Tchnlgy.**

**BALILES, PEGGY S,** Patrick Henry Comm Coll, Martinsville, VA; FR; DPMA 90-; Stdnt Sprt Srvcs 90-; Dns Lst 90-; Tutorng Awd; Appl Sci; Data Entry Oper.

**BALIN, KATHY S,** Cumberland County Coll, Vineland, NJ; SR; BA; Pol Scnc Clb Treas 89-90; SG 90-; Phi Theta Kappa 90-; Wm Marts Schlrshp 89-; Pol Scnc/Pre Law.

**BALKE, PAMELA J,** Univ Of Cin R Walters Coll, Blue Ash, OH; SO; ADN; Eastmnot Prsbytrn Wmns Assn; Music Mnstry Eastmont Prsybtrn Ch 82-; Med Asst 83-; Levy Com Retarded Handicapped Chldrn Clermont Cnty; RMA Inst Med Dntl Tech Cincinnati Ohio 83; Nrsng; BSN RN.

**BALKWILL, SEAN L,** Savannah Coll Of Art & Design, Savannah, GA; SR; BA; Illus; Animation.

**BALL, ANTHONY W,** Univ Of Cin R Walters Coll, Blue Ash, OH; FR; AAS; Phi Theta Kappa; Phi Kappa Tau Adm VP 85-87; Outstndng Achvmnt In Bio; Env Sci.

**BALL, CINDY M,** Univ Of Sc At Columbia, Columbia, SC; JR; Soc Prof Jrnlsts 90; Gamecock Television Anchor; Gamma Beta Phi; Tri Delta Philanthropy 89-; Jrnlsm; Brdcstng.

**BALL, ELIZABETH,** Newbury Coll, Brookline, MA; FR; Fshn Mrchndsng; Buyer.

**BALL, GINA C,** Marshall University, Huntington, WV; FR; MBA; Business; Mngmnt Mrktng.

**BALL, HEATHER L,** Appalachian Bible Coll, Bradley, WV; FR; Class Offcr Sec/Treas 90; Drama Tm 90; Soccer Statistician 90; 1 Yr Bible Cert 90-91; Bible; Cnstnl Law.

**BALL, JAMES E,** Univ Of Ky, Lexington, KY; SR; BSCE; Amer Socty Cvl Engrs 89-; Stdnt Athl Cncl 89-; Tau Kappa Epsilon Hstrn 89-90; Cvl Engr.

**BALL, JOHN E,** Ms St Univ, Miss State, MS; SR; Omicron Delta Kappa; Eta Kappa Nu 87-; Tau Beta Pi 87-; Phi Kappa Phi 87-; Kappa Mu Epsilon 87-; Phi Alpha Theta 87-; Gamma Alpha Epsilon Natl Sec 90-; Delta Chi Sec 87-; Marine Corps Schlrshp 87-; Hons 87-; IM Ftbl Sftbl Trck; Engr.

**BALL, KAREN M,** Univ Of West Fl, Pensacola, FL; GD; Golden Key 89-90; Kappa Delta Phi 89-90; Deans Key 89; Pr Lst 90; B S Of Amer; BA UWF 90; Elem Tchr.

**BALL, KEITH D,** Oh St Univ, Columbus, OH; SR; Soc Physcs Stdnts 89-; Fncng Clb 88-90; Romophos 88-89; Alpha Lambda Delta 87-; Phi Eta Sigma 87-; Exclnc Schlrshp Awd 90; Undrgrdt Rsrch Schlr 90-; Grdt Hnrs Dstnctn Physcs; Wtr Polo; BS; Physics; Grdt Schl Ph D/Acdmc Rsrch.

**BALL, KIMALA M,** Fort Valley St Coll, Fort Valley, GA; SR; BS; Agri-Demic Forum 87-; Alpha Kappa Mu 90-; Hnrs Convcatn 88-; Jr Hghst Avg Ag Econ; Ag; Finc.

**BALL, KIMBERLY A,** Marywood Coll, Scranton, PA; SR; BFA; Art Clb Sec 89-90; Illustrtr.

**BALL, KIMBERLY S,** Univ Of Va Clinch Valley Coll, Wise, VA; JR; BA; Baptst Stdnt Un 90-; AAS Southwest VA Cmnty Clg 90; Elem Ed; Tchng.

**BALL, KRISTIN L,** Univ Of Ga, Athens, GA; JR; BS ED; Alpha Lambda Delta; Kappa Delta Epsilon; Golden Key; Gamma Beta Phi; Kappa Delta Pi; Math; Tch.

**BALL, MEREDITH A,** Kent St Univ Kent Cmps, Kent, OH; JR; BA; Alpha Phi Sigma 90; Crmnl Jstice; Law.

**BALL, NEDRA R,** Memphis St Univ, Memphis, TN; SR; BBA; Soc For Human Resrce Mngmnt 90-; Mngmnt-Human Res.

**BALL, PENNY S,** Oh St Univ At Marion, Marion, OH; FR; Psy Club 90; Science; Allied Medicine.

**BALL, SCOTT A,** Marshall University, Huntington, WV; SR; BS; Assn Cmptng Machry Sec; Upsilon Pi Epsilon Sec 90-; Cmptr Sci.

**BALL, SHIRLEY M,** Lexington Comm Coll, Lexington, KY; BS; Bsn; Marketing.

**BALL, TERRIE L,** Kent St Univ Kent Cmps, Kent, OH; SR; BBA; AA 89; Acctg/Cmptr Sci.

**BALL-WALKER, HILARY E,** Samford Univ, Birmingham, AL; GD; Envir Law Soc 90-; Amer United Separation Church/State Treas 90-; Family Violence Ctr 89-; Firehouse Shelter 90-; Magna Cum Laude; Cordell Hull Tchg Flwshp 89-90; JD; BA Trinity Univ 86; Spnsh/Frnch; Law.

**BALLANCE, ELIZABETH A,** Univ Of Sc At Columbia, Columbia, SC; SO; BM; Symphony Chmbr Orch; Delta Omicron; Aerobics Class; Delta Omicron 90-; Full Schlrshp; Dns Lst; Music Perf.

**BALLANTINE, JENNIFER F,** Emory Univ, Atlanta, GA; GD; RN; Amer Assoc Of Critical Care Nrs Pres SW GA Chptr 90-; Practcd Profsnl Nrsng 76-; CCRN 85-; ASN Floyd Clg Rome GA 76; Nrsng; Clncl Nrs Spclst In Crtcl Care.

**BALLARD, CAROLYN T,** Winthrop Coll, Rock Hill, SC; SO; BA; Pi Sigma Alpha; Model Outstdg Delegate; E Twn Nghbrhd Assoc Pres 90-; Ebenezer PTO Sec 90-; Holiday Inn Middle Mgmt 71-87; Pltcl Sci; Foreign Serv.

**BALLARD, CHERRY K,** Union Univ, Jackson, TN; SR; BS; Alpha Chi 89-; Rutledge Honhstry Clb 89-; Sigma Zeta Sec 88-; Chem Awd 88; Biology/Chem; Med Rsrch.

**BALLARD, DA LANA E,** Fl A & M Univ, Tallahassee, FL; FR; MBA; Natl Asc Blck Acctnts; Jack/Jill Amer 90-; Natl Asc Advcmnt Clrd People 90-; Phi Eta Sigma; Bsn Admn.

**BALLARD, DARTHA M,** Dyersburg St Comm Coll, Dyersburg, TN; FR; Pi Theta Kappa V P; Gideons; Nrsg.

**BALLARD, DEBRA D,** Defiance Coll, Defiance, OH; SO; BA; Gen Motors Corp; Psych; Priv Ther.

**BALLARD, DEIRDRE B,** Univ Of Sc At Columbia, Columbia, SC; SR; BS; Stdnt Cncl Mbr 90-; Amr Allnc PE Rcrtn Hlth Dnc Mmbr 90-; Gldn Key 88-; Spcl Olympcs Vol Offcl 89-; IM 86-; Physcl Ed; Tch.

**BALLARD, DIANA H,** Mary Baldwin Coll, Staunton, VA; SR; BA; Phi Beta Kappa 89-; Sigma Tau Delta 89-; Eng/Math/Jpns; Actrl Sci.

**BALLARD, JAMES S,** Lexington Comm Coll, Lexington, KY; FR; BA; Rdgrphy; Wrk Rdlgy Dept.

**BALLARD, KRISTINA M,** Longwood Coll, Farmville, VA; SO; BA; Sigma Sigma Sigma; Bio; Med.

**BALLARD, MICKEY L,** Embry Riddle Aeronautical Univ, Daytona Beach, FL; JR; BS; Arnld Ar Scty Cmptrllr 90; Ar Frce ROTC Wng Cmmndr; Vlsia Hse Bg Bro 89-; Pne Trl Elem Ttr Big Bro; Red Crss Hmlss Prog Vol 90-; USAF Ryl AF Exchnge Prog; VICE Cmmndnts Awrd AF Fld Trng 90; IM Sprts Ftbl Rqtbl 89-; Arntcl Sci; AF Offcr Plt.

**BALLARD, POLLY R ASHER,** Antonelli Inst Of Art & Photo, Cincinnati, OH; SR; AA; PTA; Alpha Beta Kappa; Cmrcl Art.

**BALLARD, TOSHEIA N,** Bloomfield Coll, Bloomfield, NJ; FR; BA; Psyclgy.

**BALLARD, VELEANOR,** Jackson St Univ, Jackson, MS; JR; BBA; Karate Clb Sec 89-90; SGA Rep 89-90; Ecnmcs Clb; Alpha Lambda Delta 89-; Alpha Mu Gamma 90-; Alpha Chi; Schlp Rcpnt 89-; Pres Lst Schlr 89; Dns Lst Schlr 89-; Bsn Admn; Entprnr.

**BALLENGER, CANDACE L,** Hillsborough Comm Coll, Tampa, FL; FR; AS; Cmmnty Serv Coord SHARE Prog; Womens Bwlng Assoc; IBM; Amer Hosp Spply Corp; Accntng.

**BALLENGER, KEITH J,** Southern Coll Of Tech, Marietta, GA; GD; BSEET; Yllw Jckt Invstrs Clb 86-87; GA Tech Sccr Clb 85-86; Beta Theta Pi Hstrn 82-87; Amer Cncr Soc Vol 82-87; Yth Leag Sccr Coach; Chemtrac Syst Inv Rsdnt Rngd 89-; BS/IMGT GA Inst Tchnlgy 87; Mgmt Eng; Prod Eng.

**BALLENTINE, ROBIN D,** Memphis St Univ, Memphis, TN; FR; BA; Pol Scif Law.

**BALLESTER, BRIGITTE,** Univ Of Pr At Mayaguez, Mayaguez, PR; SR; Chmcl Eng Dept 88-; Spcl Hnrs Cert Chmcl Eng Dept 90; All Amer Schlr Clgte Awd; Chmcl Eng.

**BALLEW, MELISSA A,** Univ Of Nc At Asheville, Asheville, NC; JR; BA; Psychlgy Clb 90-; Alpha Kappa Delta 90-; Sclgy; Law.

**BALLIARD, LEANNE J,** Duquesne Univ, Pittsburgh, PA; FR; BA; Dance Team 90-; Busn Admin; Fincng.

**BALLIET, ERIC S,** Salisbury St Univ, Salisbury, MD; JR; BS; Alpha Omega; Beta Beta Beta; Vrsty Tennis 88-; Biology; Optometry.

**BALLIET, KRIS,** Coll Of Charleston, Charleston, SC; SR; BA; SGA Comm Chr 90-; Glgy Clb Treas 90-; Visual Arts Clb Pres 88-89; Omicron Delta Kappa 90-; Hghly Dstngshd Hnrs 90; Dstngshd Hnrs; Self Emp 74-88; Geology/Natl Sci; Env Law.

**BALLIETT, DEBORAH S,** Wilmington Coll, Wilmington, OH; SO; BA; Wilmington Clg Chorale 89-; DTS Lil Sis Sor Sec 89-; Dns Lst 89-; Vrsty Trk Ltr 90-; Psychlgy; Cnslr.**

**BALLINA, STEPHEN C,** West Chester Univ, West Chester, PA; SO; BS; Theatre Clrnt Plyr 90-; Mrchng Bnd Sec Ldr 89-90; Woodwind Ensmbl; Clrnt Choir; Univ Choral; Mstrwrks Chorus; Symphy Orch; Symphonic Band 90; Music Educ/Clarinet; Tch.

**BALLINGER, JOANNE L,** Univ Of Fl, Gainesville, FL; GD; Acad Stdnts Pharm 87-; Rho Chi 89-; Grad High Hnrs; APHA 87-; ASHP 90-; Pharm D; BS Barry Clg 76; Pharm.

**BALLOU, ANN E,** Univ Of Ky, Lexington, KY; SR; Epsilon Delta 90-; NCTE 90-; NEA 90-; BA UK; Engl Tchr.

**BALLOU, MARYLEE E,** S U N Y Coll At Postdam, Potsdam, NY; FR; BA; English; Tch.

**BALLOVERAS, GINA C,** Fl International Univ, Miami, FL; SR; Phi Lambda 90-; Sierra Clb Asstd Envrnmntl Clean Up 90-; Emplyd W Archtcts Inc Ofc Mgr; AA Miami Dade Comm Clg 89; BS; Spcl Edctn SLD EH; Law Schl.

**BALLOW, SARAH,** Cornell Univ Statutory College, Ithaca, NY; JR; BS; GAMMA Dir 90-; Sprvsry Orntn Cnslr Alchl/Drg Prog 89-; ALERT Peer Educ Ntwrk/Cornell Campus Grk Repr 90-; Mortar Brd Sec; Chi Omega 89-; Fld Hcky 88-89; Neurobiology; Medicine.

**BALOG, AMY E,** Le Moyne Coll, Syracuse, NY; JR; BA; Frhse Theatre PR Dir 88-; Radio Sta 88-89; Amnsty Intl 90-; Bsn Clb 88-89; Cmps Tours 88-89; Echrst Mnstr 88-89; Intl Hse 88-89; Prjcts Comm 88-; Bkfst Trck 90-; Engl; Scl Hmnts.

**BALOGH, MICHAEL F,** Fl St Univ, Tallahassee, FL; FR; BA; Soccer; Phi Eta Sigma; Bio; Sports Med Doctor.

**BALOGH, TINA M,** Walters St Comm Coll, Morristown, TN; SO; BA; Bus Admn.**

**BALONEK, JENNIFER S,** Univ Of Rochester, Rochester, NY; SO; NHS 89; Sigma Delta Tau 90-; Stdnt Intrn Harris Evans Fox Chesworth Law Ofc 90-; IM 89-; Engl.

**BALOUCH, THERESA A,** Univ Of Southern Ms, Hattiesburg, MS; SR; BA; AA N IA Area Cmnty Clg 83; Sec Ed/Engl; Tch MA.

**BALOUCOUNE, ROGER M,** Hudson Valley Comm Coll, Troy, NY; FR; BA; Internatl Clb; Bsn Admin; Entrprnr.

**BALOUE, DAVITA S,** Jackson St Univ, Jackson, MS; JR; BBA; Phi Beta Lambda 89-; Alpha Lambda Delta 89-; Delta Mu Delta 90-; Hnrs Coll 88-; U Of I Rsrch Pro 90; IMB Co-Op; Acctg.

**BALROOP, ANIL,** City Univ Of Ny Queensbrough, New York, NY; FR; MBA; Bus; Acctg.

**BALS, KRISTINE R,** Kent St Univ Kent Cmps, Kent, OH; FR; BA; Athl Dpt 90-.

**BALTAZAR, SUSANA M,** Elms Coll, Chicopee, MA; SR; BA; Acct/Bsn Mgmt; CPA.

**BALTZEGAR, STACY W,** Univ Of Sc At Columbia, Columbia, SC; JR; BS; Carolina Cares; Amer Scty Of Mchncl Eng; Gamma Beta Phi Treas 89; Golden Key 90; Pi Tau Sigma 89; Tau Beta Pi Tutor Coord; Mchncl Eng Intrnshp At Ethyl Corp; Trck Tm 88-90; Mchncl Eng; Eng Dsgn/Tstng.

**BAMBERG, JOHN A,** Benedict Coll, Columbia, SC; SO; BS; Soc Of Physics Stdnts 89-; Benedict Clg Hons Stdnt Assn 89-; Soph Class VP 90-; B C Dance Co/B C Cheerldr 90-; Sci/Physics; Engr.

**BAMGBOSE, OLAYINKA N,** Strayer Coll, Washington, DC; SR; BS; Hrmbe Jrrd Rep To Stdnt Snte 87; Comp Info Systms; Intl Law.

**BAMISHE, AFOLAKE A,** Howard Univ, Washington, DC; SR; BA; Amer Soc Intr Dsgnrs Treas 89-90; Fndrsr 90-; Intr Dsgn; Fclties Mgmt.

**BANBILU, AMELEWORK W,** Univ Of The Dist Of Columbia, Washington, DC; SO; BA; Nrsng.

**BANCE, MEDJINE,** City Univ Of Ny La Guard Coll, Long Island Cty, NY; JR; BA; Diplma Eco Le De Formtn De Cadres 82; Accntng; Mgmt Accntng.

**BANCROFT, SHERI L,** Memphis St Univ, Memphis, TN; SR; BEA; Classcl Ballt Co 88-89; Danc Co Ens VP 89-; Hnrs Pgm 89-; Fr Hnr Soc 89; Erly Schlrs Mbr 89-; Snd Tech Proj Motion Danc Co Publ 90-; Mst Creatv Chrgrphr Yr; Thtre/Danc; Prof Modrn Danc.

**BANDA, ANDREA A,** Syracuse Univ, Syracuse, NY; JR; BS; ASID 88-; Phi Kappa Phi; Phi Eta Sigma 89-; Kappa Omicron Nu 90-; Gldn Ky 90-; Awrd 90; Rhodes Schlr; Design Firm Intern 90; Cert Museum Fine Arts 88; Intrr Dsgn/Envrnmntl Dsgn.**

**BANDA, THABANI M,** Howard Univ, Washington, DC; SO; BARCH; Gentlmn Drew Soc Clb 89-90; Intl Camps Pals 90-; Intl Stdnts Assn Sec 90-; Phi Beta Sigma; Trck Tm 89-; Arch.

**BANDRICH, JORGE L,** Univ Of Miami, Coral Gables, FL; SO; Cmmtr Orgn Offc 89-; Ornttn Asst; FEC 89-; Bus Mngt; Law.

**BANDUKWALA, ALIBHOY,** City Univ Of Ny City Coll, New York, NY; JR; BS; Indian Clb Sec 89-90; Asme 90-; Phi Sigma Omicron 89-90; BS Univ Karachi 88; Comp Sci; Syst Analyst.

**BANDY, CAREN R,** Middle Tn St Univ, Murfreesboro, TN; JR; BA; RA 89-; Omega Phi Alpha V P 88-90; Mass Commctn/History; T V/Edctn.

**BANDY, DANNA L,** Anne Arundel Comm Coll, Arnold, MD; SO; AA; George Ebersberger Schlrshp; Wrkd Flltm In MD Rnl Admin Socty; Bus/Pub Admin; Hlth Care Mgmt.

**BANDY, FONDA R,** Univ Of Tn At Martin, Martin, TN; SR; BS; AA Wabash Vly Clg 76; Scndry Ed Engl; Mktg.

**BANDY, HELEN,** Elizabethtown Comm Coll, Elizabethtown, KY; FR; BS; Baptist Stdnt Union 90-; Phi Theta Kappa; IM Vlybl; Comp Sci.

**BANDY, JOHN D,** Univ Of Louisville, Louisville, KY; SR; ASCE; Cvl Eng.

**BANDY, MELANIE M,** Roane St Comm Coll, Harriman, TN; FR; BA; Bus.

**BANE, AMY BETH,** Marshall University, Huntington, WV; SR; BA; OURTNDA 87-89; Ntl Radio/T V News Dir Assn 87-89; Elem Ed; Tch.

**BANE, ANGELA D,** Roane St Comm Coll, Harriman, TN; FR; AAS; CSI V P 90-; Pres; Office Admn; Exec Sec.

**BANE III, DAVID C,** Bethany Coll, Bethany, WV; SR; BA; Stdnts Free Enterprise; Smart Clb Pres; Publ Rel; Omicron Delta Epsilon; Kappa Mu Epsilon; Alpha Sigma Phi Treas; Diving Tm; Econ; Finance.

**BANE, MICHELLE R,** Indiana Univ Of Pa, Indiana, PA; FR; BA; Cheerleading; Adopt A Grandparent Pgm Vol; Bio; Psychiatric/Med.

**BANE, STEVEN M,** Marshall University, Huntington, WV; JR; BA; Gamma Beta Phi Serv/Hnr Org 89-; Counseling & Rehab; Counseling Hearing Imp.

**BANE, SUSAN A,** Middle Tn St Univ, Murfreesboro, TN; SR; BA; Acctng Clb 83-84; Mrktng Clb 84-88; Scty For Advncmnt Mngmnt; Data Proc Mngmnt Assoc; Amer Mrktng Assoc; Reprtr For Bus Schl Nwsltr; Assoc For Future Accntnts; Alpha Kappa Psi 84-87; BS BA 88; Acctng; Cost Acctnt.

**BANENS, TANIA C,** Univ Of Fl, Gainesville, FL; SR; Ecnmcs Soc; Gldn Key; Omcrn Delta Epsln; Vctm Wtns Serv Vol Unit; Dns Lst 88-; BSBA; AA; Encmcs; Banking.

**BANES, DANA J,** Meridian Comm Coll, Meridian, MS; FR; Phi Theta Kappa Hstrn.

**BANFIELD, ELISE C,** Mansfield Univ, Mansfield, PA; FR; Aerobcs Instr; Dnc Tm VP; Psych Clb; Intrntl Stdnt Org; Nwspr; Lambda Sigma; Phi Sigma Pi Bro 90-; Hons Pgm; Hons Assn Sec 90-; Delta Zeta; Red Crss Phn-Thn Vlntr 90-; State Sys Highr Ed Smmr Pgm Westchester U Schlrshp; Pblc Rltns/Psych; Pro Rltns.

**BANG, JEFFREY E,** Lexington Comm Coll, Lexington, KY; SR; AAS; Dental Lab Assoc Pres; Deans Lst 89-; Phi Kappa Psi 87-; Dental Tech.

**BANGERT, CHRISTINA M,** Central Fl Comm Coll, Ocala, FL; FR; BA; Stdnt Govt Rep Treas 90-; Cmps Diplmt 90-; Vrtns Rep 90-; Civic Thtr 90-; Dnce Trp; Music; Thtr Prfrmnc.

**BANGERTER, KURT D,** Univ Of Miami, Coral Gables, FL; GD; MD; Alpha Omega Alpha 90-; Phi Beta Kappa 87-; Phi Kappa Phi 87-; Phi Eta Sigma 83-; Amer Med Assn 87-; Fla Med Assn 90-; Dade Cnty Med Assn 90-; BS Univ Utah 87; Medicine; Neurosurgery.

**BANGSTON, ELIZABETH C,** Univ Of Sc At Columbia, Columbia, SC; SO; Literacy Tutor VP 90-; Gamma Beta Phi 90-; Hnrs Assn 90-; Cmmnty Srvc Intrn; Prsdnt Lst 89; Deans Lst 89-; Hstry; Law.

**BANGURA, BERNARD ANSU,** Clark Atlanta Univ, Atlanta, GA; FR; BS; Soccer; Cmptr Sci; Eng.

**BANISTER, THELMA,** Bloomfield Coll, Bloomfield, NJ; SR; BA; Alc Mrlyn Crss Schlrshp; BA; Psychlgy.

**BANKEMPER, THERESE K,** Northern Ky Univ, Highland Hts, KY; SR; BA; Pblc Rltns Std Soc Pres 90; Comm Std Asc Pres 90-; Kntn Cnty Brthdy Intrn 90; Turway Park-Jim Beam Stakes Intrn; Scrps Hwrd Corp Comm Ofc; IM Bsktbl/Sccr/Sftbl; Jrnlsm; Pblc Rltns.

**BANKER, ANGELA M,** Troy St Univ At Dothan, Dothan, AL; SR; BA; Gamma Beta Phi Hstrn 90-; Acctg.

**BANKER, GEORGE H,** Univ Of South Al, Mobile, AL; SR; BS; SGA Sen/ATTRNY Gen; Intrfrtrnty Cncl Sec; Cmps Rec Imprvmnt Brd Fndr Pres; Mrtr Brd Hstrn; Order Omega Pres; Fnncl Mngmnt Assn VP; Phi Chi Theta Big Bro; Fab 50; Alpha Chi; EARTH VP; Betta Gamma Sigma; Kappa Alpha VP 88-; Nvl Rsrvs; Fnnc; Real Est.

**BANKHEAD JR, JESSE A,** David Lipscomb Univ, Nashville, TN; GD; MA; Mu Alpha Gamma 87; Prather Greek Medal 87; BS 87; Biblical Studies; Tchng.

**BANKO, SHERI M,** Duquesne Univ, Pittsburgh, PA; FR; BS; ASP; Phi Eta Sigma; DUV; Pharm.

**BANKOWSKI, SUSAN M,** Drew Univ, Madison, NJ; FR; BS; IM Vlybl 90; Tribeta; Bio; Med.

**BANKS, ANTHONY R,** Univ Of Miami, Coral Gables, FL; SR; CFA; Stu Govt Sec Prod 74-75; Beta Gamma Sigma 90-; Phi Kappa Phi; Gldn Key; Dep Hnrs; S Fl Fncl Anlyst Soc; Bnd Clb; Dir Mgt Info Sys Ganz Cptl Mgt 89-; BBA; AA 88; Finance; Invst Anlysis.

**BANKS, BEVERLY K,** Univ Of Nc At Asheville, Asheville, NC; SO; BS, Acctng; CPA.

**BANKS, BRANDON K,** Samford Univ, Birmingham, AL; SR; DA; A Cappella Choir 90-; Exec Grtr Cncl 90-; Chorale 88-89; Oper Wrkshp 89-90; Pi Kappa Lambda 89-; Phi Eta Sigma 88-; Ruic E Wheeler Schlrshp 89-; Pres Schlrshp 88-; Church Music; Minstr.

**BANKS, DAWN NICOLE,** Talladega Coll, Talladega, AL; FR; BS; Cmps All Str Chllnge Schl Prlmnry Capt 90; Pres Lst Awrd; Mss Fr UNCF; Sclgy Math Educ; Estblsh Afrcn Amer Cnslng.

**BANKS, DEANNA M,** Norfolk St Univ, Norfolk, VA; SO; Sprtn Alph Tau.

**BANKS, DEBRA F,** Mount Saint Mary Coll, Newburgh, NY; FR; BA; Psych; Chld Psych/Scl Svc.

**BANKS, DEMETRIAS A,** Al St Univ, Montgomery, AL; FR; BA; Clss Stdnt Gov Sec 90-; Biology; Medicine.

**BANKS, GAYLA D,** Alcorn St Univ, Lorman, MS; JR; BA; Alpha Kappa Mu Miss AKM 89-; Beta Kappa Chi 90-; Blood Drive; Biology; Med.

**BANKS, JASON C,** Columbia Union Coll, Takoma Park, MD; JR; BS; ACM 90-; Phi Eta Sigma Treas 89-; Alpha Chi; Vrsty Bsktbl 88-; Comp Sci; Pgmr.

**BANKS, JULIANNE K,** Columbia Union Coll, Takoma Park, MD; SR; Pre-Law Clb 90-; Phi Eta Sigma 88-; Alpha Chi; Bus; Admin.

**BANKS, KATHLEEN J,** Commonwealth Coll, Virginia Beach, VA; FR; MAA; RN.

**BANKS, LA SHANDRA Q,** Al St Univ, Montgomery, AL; FR; Cls/Sprts Edtr Hrnt Yrbk 90-; Phi Eta Sigma; Univ Hnrs Cnctn Hrn Std; Pres Schlr; Alpha; Cmptr Info Sys; Prgmmr/Sys Anlyst.

**BANKS, LACEY J,** Hampton Univ, Hampton, VA; FR; BA; Pres Eminant Schlr 90; Pres Eminant Schlrs Hnr Soc; Sclgy; Law.

**BANKS, LISA N,** Bloomfield Coll, Bloomfield, NJ; SO; BA; Bus Adm/Comptr Info Sys; Sys Anlyst.

**BANKS, MARY A,** Miami Jacobs Jr Coll Of Bus, Dayton, OH; SO; AD; Student Advisory Comm 90-; CPA.

**BANKS, MARY ANNE,** Univ Of Toledo, Toledo, OH; GD; JD; Stdnt Bar Assn Clss Rep 87-90; Law Review Tech Ed 88-90; Moot Ct Brd 89-90; Orde Coif 90; Phi Alpha Delta Clrk/Sec 87-90; Alpha Phi 83-90; Law Clrk Hon Jdg J L Ryan 6th Ctr US Ct Appls 90-; BSJ W VA U 87; Law; Tax.

**BANKS, MELANEE R,** Al St Univ, Montgomery, AL; SO; Phi Eta Sigma 90-; ASU Dnc Co 90-; Math; Eng.

**BANKS, MONICA C,** Lincoln Univ, Lincoln Univ, PA; SO; BA; Bus; Fnnc.

**BANKS, NICOLE,** Pellissippi St Tech Comm Coll, Knoxville, TN; SO; BS; Pub Rltns Intrn Cty Knxvl Prks/Rec Pub Rltns Spec Asst 89-90; Prlglsm; Law.

**BANKS, RUFUS A,** Nc Central Univ, Durham, NC; GD; JD; Brrstr News Jrnl Sec 90-; Crrclm Comm; BLSA 89-; St Frm Ins Co Intrn; IM Bsktbl 90-; BA Old Diminion Unv 87; Certf Inst Paralgl Trnng 88; Law.

**BANKS, SAMUEL A,** Western New England Coll, Springfield, MA; SO; Psych.

**BANKS, SUSAN F,** Bunker Hill Comm Coll, Boston, MA; SO; AS; Ofc Edn Clb VP 89-; Exec Sec Ofc Edn; BS.

**BANKS, TERETTA L,** Alcorn St Univ, Lorman, MS; SO; Pol Sci Clb; Hon Stdnts Org; Pol Sci; Law.

**BANKS, VICTORIA LYNN,** Southern Vt Coll, Bennington, VT; JR; BSN; Stdnt Nrs Assn 90-; NHNA; Smrtns Wmns Crisis Ctr; Nrsg.

**BANKSON III, MANNON G,** Auburn Univ At Auburn, Auburn, AL; FR; BS; Pharm.

**BANKSTON, AMY E,** Univ Of Southern Ms, Hattiesburg, MS; FR; BA; Stdnt Alumni Assoc 90-; Eagle Connection Stdnt Recrtmnt 90-; Stdnt Eagle Clb 90-; Lambda Sigma 90-; Alpha Lambda Delta 90-; Phi Eta Sigma; Gamma Beta Phi 90-; Pi Beta Phi Sor Pldg Cls Pres 90-; Elem Edn/Spcl Edn; Tchr.

**BANKSTON, KATHY E,** Univ Of Al At Birmingham, Birmingham, AL; SR; BA; Spply Tchr; Aerobc Instr; Erly Chldhd Educ; Erly Educ Tchr.

**BANN, ELIZABETH A,** Kent St Univ Kent Cmps, Kent, OH; GD; MBA; Am Acctg Assn; Beta Gamma Sigma; Golden Key; Beta Gamma Sigma; Asstnshp; Schlrshp Acdmc; AA 83; BBA 90; Acctg.

**BANNAN, PATRICIA M,** Univ Of De, Newark, DE; FR; BS; Dietetics Club 90-; Dietetics.

**BANNISTER, ELIZABETH BROOKS,** Converse Coll, Spartanburg, SC; FR; BA; Cmps Btfctn Comm Fr Rep; Dnc Comm Fr Rep; Alpha Lambda Delta 90-; Bowden Schlrshp 90-; Deans Lst 90-; Hstry/Engl; Grad Schl.

**BANNISTER, JANE L,** Smith Coll, Northampton, MA; SR; BA; Outing Clb Treas 88-90; SG 89-90; Career Dev Ofc 89-90; Svc Org 88-89; Deans Lst 89-90; First Grp Schlrs 89-90; Lacrosse 89-90; Tchr.

**BANNISTER, RICHARD P,** Winthrop Coll, Rock Hill, SC; SR; BFA; Artery VP 89-; Sthrn Vsns Photo Show Yrk Co Museum 90; Intrnshp George Lee Studio Grnvll SC 89; Art Prntng Schlrshp Wnnr 89; Phtgrphy; Cmmrcl.

**BANNISTER, STACY A,** S U N Y Coll Of Tech At Alfred, Alfred, NY; JR; Dnc Instr Ballet/Jazz/Tap; AA Monroe Comm Coll 90; Nrsng.

**BANOCY, JILL A,** Indiana Univ Of Pa, Indiana, PA; JR; BS; Habitat Hmnty 89-; Kappa Delta Pi 90-; Provosts Schlr 89-; Elem Ed; Tchng.

**BANOVIC, TAMARA A,** Marywood Coll, Scranton, PA; SR; BS; Cathlc Yth Org Chrldng Coach 88-89; AS Broome Cmnty Clg 89; Cmnctns Disordrs; Audiolgy.

**BANSAVAGE, LYNNE POHL,** Schenectady County Comm Coll, Schenectady, NY; SO; PTA Scotia Glenvl Schls Treas 82-86; Analytical Studies Comm; Vol Scotia Glenvl Schls 76-; Altar Guild St Andrews 90-; Niagara Mohawk Pwr Corp; John Scott Mdlng Agcy; Sunnybrook Acres Ranch Resort; Avon; Nuskin; Travel Trsm; Bus Admin.

**BANSKY, RONALD TODD,** Glassboro St Coll, Glassboro, NJ; SO; BA; Theta Chi 90-; Cmmnctns; Pblc Rel/Insrnc.

**BANU, LIGIA C,** Liberty Univ, Lynchburg, VA; SR; BA; Urban Outrch Coord 88-90; Light Clb 87-; Romanian Flwshp Grp 87-; Chi Alpha 90-; Good Smrtn Cntr 89-90; Thomas Road Bptst Chrch 87-; Div Rlgn Awd 90-; Hmnts; Tchng.

**BANYON, MAURICE L,** Univ Of Ms Main Cmps, University, MS; FR; IM Ftbl/Bsebl/Vlybl/Bsktbl; Track Ltrd.

**BANZHOF, ABIGAIL E,** Villanova Univ, Villanova, PA; SR; BA; Dnc Ens Treas 90-; Alpha Phi Frat Edctr; Sci; Vet Schl.

**BANZHOFF, HONEY H,** Hagerstown Jr Coll, Hagerstown, MD; FR; Phi Theta Kappa; Educ/Engl; Tch.

**BAO, LIN,** City Univ Of Ny La Guard Coll, Long Island Cty, NY; SO; AS; Asian Club 89-90; Alpha Theta Phi 80-; Tutoring Svc Math Tutor; Deans List 90-; Swimming/Tennis 90-; Comptr Sci; Mgr.

**BAO, XIAO YUAN,** Bloomfield Coll, Bloomfield, NJ; SO; BS; Alpha Chi; High Hnrs; Accntng; CPA.

**BAPTISTE, CHARLENE A,** Strayer Coll, Washington, DC; SO; AA; CIS.

**BAR-COHEN, YANIV,** The Johns Hopkins Univ, Baltimore, MD; FR; BS; Union Board 90-; Hosp Vol; Bio; Med.

**BARADELL, KIMBERLY S,** Meridian Comm Coll, Meridian, MS; SO; AA; Bapt Stdnt Union Pres 89; Yth Cncl Pres 89f; Bsnss Offce Tech; Bsnss Type Wrk.

**BARAGANO, MARIA D,** Boston Coll, Chestnut Hill, MA; SR; BS; Mrktng/Fnnc.**

**BARAK, AUDREY,** City Univ Of Ny Baruch Coll, New York, NY; JR; BBA; Finance.

**BARALL, ROBIN M,** Nj Inst Of Tech, Newark, NJ; JR; BS; Crr Advncmnt Pln Prog 89-; Big Sis Lil Sis 90-; Hnrs Prog 89-; Tau Beta Pi 90-; Eta Kappa Nu Rcrdng Sec 90-; Phi Eta Sigma 89-; Alpha Sigma Tau Treas 90-; Alld Sgnl Schlr 90-; Pres Schlrshp 89-; Physcs Awrd 90; Comp Eng.**

**BARAN, DARIUSZ,** William Paterson Coll, Wayne, NJ; SR; BA; Intl Stdnts Assoc Treas 88-90; Bus Stdnts Assoc 89; Pltcl Sci Clb 89; Plsh Natl Assoc 85-; Intl Mgmt Hnrs Awrd; Bus Admn.

**BARAN, STACIE A,** Univ Of Rochester, Rochester, NY; SO; BS; Gymnastics Clb 89-90; Hunger Coalition 89-; Regents Schlrshp; IM Sports 89-90; Biological Sci; Medl Schl.

**BARANOWSKI, LORI A,** Averett Coll, Danville, VA; JR; BA; ACAB Pblcty Chrmn 88-89; Sngrs 89-90; SOAR Ldr; Chi Delta Epsilon Pldg Dir 88-; Sftbl Tm; Art Educ; Tchr.

**BARANYAI, GARY M,** Hillsborough Comm Coll, Tampa, FL; FR; BBU; Blmngdl Hm Ownrs Assoc/Air Frc Srgnts Assoc PTA US Air Frc; Bus Mgmnt.

**BARATTA, FRANCES E,** Niagara Univ, Niagara Univ, NY; SO; BA; Engl/Pre-Law; Law.

**BARBA, MARLENE S,** City Univ Of Ny Baruch Coll, New York, NY; SR; MBA; BBA Bernard M Baruch Coll 90; Dean's List 90; Bus Mgmt; Hmn Rsrcs.

**BARBABELLA, SEAN P,** Univ Of Pittsburgh At Bradford, Bradford, PA; JR; BS; Blgy Clb 88-; Alpha Lambda Delta Hstrn 88-90; Beta Beta Beta Hstrn; Deans Lst 88-; Alpha Phi Omega Treas 88-; Univ Schlr 90-; Intrcllgt Cross Cntry 88-90; Blgy; Med.

**BARBANEL, ERIC W,** Univ Of Rochester, Rochester, NY; SO; BA; Humor & Satire Mag 90-; Hillel 89-; Zeta Beta Tau 90; Lab Of Cerebral Metabolism; Lacrosse 89-90; Bio; Med Sch.

**BARBARA, MARIO A,** S U N Y Coll Of Tech At Frmgdl, Farmingdale, NY; SO; AAS; Flying Clb; Aero Tech; Aviation.

**BARBAROSSA, BRENDA L,** Muskingum Coll, New Concord, OH; SR; BA; Muskingm Chrstn Fllwshp 84-87; Nwspr Stf 86-87; Dns Lst; Educ Hnry; Chi Alpha Nu Clb; Muskingum Vol 85-86; 1/2/3 Yr Awds Schlrshp 85-91; Asst Tchr Chrch Yth Grp 89-90; Elem Educ; Tchg.

**BARBEAU, MICHELLE L,** Newbury Coll, Brookline, MA; FR; AS; Fshn Dsgn.

**BARBEE, ALECIA L,** Howard Univ, Washington, DC; SR; BS; ASID Mason Prof Fld 89-; WAP 85-87; Band Feature Batn Twlr 85-87; U S Dept Just Arch Clrk Intrn 89-; Int Desgn.

**BARBEE, CHUCK W,** Univ Of Nc At Charlotte, Charlotte, NC; SR; BA; BSU Mnstry Tm Nmntg Comm 88-; Intrvar Chrstn Flwshp; IM Ftbl/Bsktbl/Sftbl 87-; Psych Clb 90-; Deans Lst 88-; IM Cert; Sch Psych.

**BARBEE, DERRICK B,** Central St Univ, Wilberforce, OH; SR; MBA; Alpha Phi Alpha Frat Inc Rec Scrtry 90; Campus Newspapr Ed 89; Page Dvrsfied Vntres Scrtry 89-90; Cntrl State Hnrs Prog 87; Ntl Assoc Of Blk Jrnlsts Sec 88-89; Alpha Phi Alpha Rec Sec 90; Jrnslm Intrnshp 90; Bsnss Admin; Bsnss.

**BARBEE, DIANNA L,** Oh St Univ, Columbus, OH; SO; BA; Intern Nature Conservandy Vol; Cmmnctns/Envrnmntl; Pblc Rel.

**BARBEE, JENNIFER L,** Kent St Univ Kent Cmps, Kent, OH; FR; BS; Hnrs Coll 90-; Med Assn; Alpha Lambda Delta; Blgy Pre Med; Med Rltd.

**BARBEE, KIMBERLY J,** Univ Of Nc At Charlotte, Charlotte, NC; FR; BS; Tchr Day Cr; Tchr Sndy Schl; Nrsng.

**BARBER, ANNIECE N,** Middle Tn St Univ, Murfreesboro, TN; SR; BBA; Yng Rep Clb 88-89; Nashvl Entrtnmt Assoc 85-87; Omicron Delta Epsilon 90-; Pi Gamma Mu 90-; Intrnshp RCA Rcrds 86-87; Econ; Law.

**BARBER, CLIFFORD A,** Ms St Univ, Miss State, MS; SR; BBA; Mrchng Concrt Pep Bnds 86-; Campus Crusd For Chrst 86-; Beta Gamma Sigma; Chrch Coll Actvties Cncl 89-; Gamma Beta Phi; Soc Logstc Engrs 89-; IM Bsktbl 90; Acdmc Schlrshp 86-90; Intrnshp Rydr Dstrbtn Rsrcs 90; Pres Schlr 89-; Transprtn; Trfc Mngmnt.

**BARBER, CYNTHIA P,** Univ Of Nc At Charlotte, Charlotte, NC; JR; BA; Math; Tch.

**BARBER, DAVID R,** Univ Of Rochester, Rochester, NY; SR; BA; NROTC Bsktbl Team Capt 88-; Schlrshp 87-; Poltcl Sci; Law.

**BARBER II, EDWARD L,** Fl A & M Univ, Tallahassee, FL; SO; PHD; Engnrng.

**BARBER, GEORGE HARTFORD,** Roane St Comm Coll, Harriman, TN; JR; BS; Avery Lodge 593 Free/Accpted Msns 3rd Degree 75; Scottish Rites Mason 32nd Degree 77; Phi Kappa Phi; Kappa Delta Pi; Magna Cum Laude 90; AS 90; Scndry Ed; PHD Ed Psy Or Schl Psy.

**BARBER, HUNTER R,** Cumberland Coll, Williamsburg, KY; SO; BS; SGA Crt Jstc 90-; Amrcn Chmcl Soc Tres; Bptst Stdnt Union Cncl 90-; Drmtry Cncl VP; Bptst Stdnt Un Bnd Raise Mny Smmr Mssns Prsdnt 89-; Hnrs Day Rcgntn 90-; IM Sccr Ftbl Vlybl Archry Sftbl Rcqtbl Sccr Tm Cpt 89-; Chmstry; Physcl Thrpy.

**BARBER, JACQUELYN L,** Univ Of Tn At Martin, Martin, TN; SO; BS; Natl Assoc Of Acctnts; Phi Eta Sigma 90-; Soc Of Hons Semnr Stdnts 89-; Alpha Kappa Psi Secy; Estes Kefauver Schlrshp; Bus Admn; Acctng/Fin.

**BARBER, MARCIA E,** Kent St Univ Kent Cmps, Kent, OH; JR; BA; Undergrad Stdnt Senate Pblcty Dir 90-; Dance Assoc 88-90; Beall Hall Hse Cncl Pblcty Coord 88-89; Phi Beta Kappa; Golden Key; Alpha Lambda Delta 88-89; Desns Lst 88-; Pres Lst 88-; Outstndng Serv Awrd; Psychology; Law.

**BARBER, PAMELA J,** Univ Of Tn At Martin, Martin, TN; SR; BS; Alpha Mu Alpha; Phi Kappa Phi Hon Cos; Alpha Kappa Psi; Schlrshp Key Awd; Top Ten Fresh; Top Ten Soph; Mktg.

**BARBER, SAMUEL W,** Univ Of Montevallo, Montevallo, AL; FR; BA; IFC Pblc Relatns Offcr 90-; Delta Chi 90-; Bus; Acctnt.

**BARBER, SARA E,** Queens Coll, Charlotte, NC; SR; BA; Natl Assoc Acctnts Treas 90-; Peer Advsr 90-; Kappa Delta VP 90-; Pres Scholar 88-; Acctg/Bus; CPA.

**BARBER, SUSAN R,** Christopher Newport Coll, Newport News, VA; JR; BA; Hist.

**BARBER, TAMMY S,** Anne Arundel Comm Coll, Arnold, MD; SO; US Dept Of Jstc Legal Intrn; Fedrl Bureau Of Prisons; Real Est License Penn State Univ Behrend Clg 87; Paralgl; Law.

**BARBER, TERESA T,** Fayetteville St Univ, Fayetteville, NC; GD; MA; Baptist Chrch; BS 90; Ed/Math; Tchr.

**BARBER, TERRY L,** Central Al Comm Coll, Alexander City, AL; FR; BA; Acctng; Bus Ed; Acctng.

**BARBER, TRICIA L,** Middle Tn St Univ, Murfreesboro, TN; SR; Gamma Beta Phi 87-88; Cum Laude 90; Clnl Dms Amrc Schlrshp 86-90; Univ Hnr Rll; Dean Slst 86-90; Jms Acdmc Sclgy Awrd 90; BS 90; Psychlgy.

**BARBER-CONDE, MARIA DE L,** Univ Of Pr Medical Sciences, San Juan, PR; GD; MS; Natl Stdnt Spch Lang Hrng Assoc 90-; Magna Cum Laude Grad 89; Deans Lst 89-; Hnr Ttn; BA Univ PR 84-89; Spch Lang Pthlgy; Spch Pthlgst.

**BARBERESI, STEVEN A,** City Univ Of Ny Baruch Coll, New York, NY; SO; BA; Italian Society Treas; Acctg.

**BARBERIO, EDWARD J,** Fl International Univ, Miami, FL; JR; BA; Martial Arts; Stdnt Hon Mntr Prog; Omega Chi; Amer Soc Pub Admnstrs; AA Miami Dade Comm Clg 90; Pub Admn; Pub Serv.

**BARBERREE, MELISSA D,** Univ Of Southern Ms, Hattiesburg, MS; JR; BS; Wind Ensemble 88-89; Symphone Bnd Concermstr 87-; Acitivites Council 87-89; Mall Assoc Publicity 87-88; Experimental Psy; Steep Therapist.

**BARBIER, MARK H,** Fl St Univ, Tallahassee, FL; SR; BA; World Affairs Prog 88-90; Hist/Ecnmcs; Frgn Serv.

**BARBIER, SHERI E,** Radford Univ, Radford, VA; JR; BS; Alpha Sigma Alpha; Art Ed; Tchr.

**BARBIERI, KARIN L,** D Youville Coll, Buffalo, NY; SO; MS; SPTA 89-; Athlete Buddy (YS Games Physically Chllngd 90; Lambda Sigma 90-; Physical Therapy; Physical Thrpst.

**BARBIERI, KIMBERLY A,** Springfield Tech Comm Coll, Springfield, MA; SO; BA; IM Sftbl/Sccr/Flr Hcky/Vlybl 90-; Engl/Cmcntns.

**BARBIERI, MARK L,** Memphis St Univ, Memphis, TN; SR; BBA; Gamma Beta Phi 87-; Phi Kappa Phi 90-; Gamma Beta Sigma 90-; Kappa Alpha Order 87-; Deans Lst 87-; Kappa Alpha 87-; Summa Cum Laude; IMS Kappa Alpha Bsktbl Sftbl Ftbl Sccr Vlybl; Fin.

**BARBO, DEAN N,** Oh St Univ, Columbus, OH; JR; BA; Forestry Forum 90-; Hon Prog 90-; Clveland Metropks Intrn; Scarlet & Gray Schlrshp; Forestry Forum Schlrshp; E Shaw Long Schlrshp; Forest Biology.

**BARBOSA, MONICA,** Univ Of Pr At Mayaguez, Mayaguez, PR; SR; Inst Of Indstrl Engr 88-; Wmn Engr Soc; Alpha Pi Mu; Tau Beta Pi; Hnr Clss Of IE Dept; Engr; Indstrl Engr.

**BARBOSA-ALVAREZ, FERNANDO,** Evangelical Seminary Of P R, Hato Rey, PR; SR; Stdnt Cncl P 89-90; Hispnc Schlr Fund Theo Ed 90-; BA U Puerto Rico Rio Piedras 87-88.

**BARBOUR, GAIL,** Memphis St Univ, Memphis, TN; JR; BS; Tchrs Aide Northeast Comm Mntl Hlth Cntr; AS Jackson State Comm Coll 83; Nutrition; Dietitician.

**BARBOUR, REBECCA S,** Patrick Henry Comm Coll, Martinsville, VA; FR.

**BARBOUR, STACEY L,** Durham Tech Comm Coll, Durham, NC; FR; CERT; Medcl Trmnlgy; Hlth Ins Agnt.

**BARBOUR-CHAUVIN, SARAH J,** Johnson St Coll, Johnson, VT; SR; BA; Org Psych Grp Prtcpnt Mgr; Pres Acdmc Lst; Rsrch Mthds Coll Srvys Part 89; Video Prod Psych Of Aprnc Dir; Indstrl/Org Psych Grp Mgr; Vol Day Care Wrkr Hlpr 90; Psych; Guidance Cnslr.

**BARBUTO, CHRISTINE M,** Newbury Coll, Brookline, MA; AD; Leg Sec.

**BARBUTO, DANIEL C,** Manhattan Coll, Bronx, NY; SO; BE; Tutor 89; Radio Prgrmmr; Elctrcl Eng.

**BARCHETT, LARRY D,** Fl A & M Univ, Tallahassee, FL; JR; BS; Army ROTC 88-; IEEE; Rl SME 86-; Alpha Kappa Mu 90; White/Gold; Engrng Hon Soc; Kappa Sigma 89-; Minority Stdnt/Yr 90; Am Legion Schlrshp Excel; Gold Cord Ldrshp Awd 88; AS Vincennes Un 88; Elec Engrng.

**BARCHITTA, ANTHONY R,** Wagner Coll, Staten Island, NY; SR; BS; Stdnts Plnt Earth 89-; Gtr Lt Ensmbl 87-; Omicron Delta Kappa 88-; Tri Beta 89-; Blgy; Dntstry.

**BARCLAY, BETTY M,** Central Fl Comm Coll, Ocala, FL; SO; BA; Phi Theta Kappa 90; Prnt Tchr Assoc Fndrsng Chr 85-86; Elem Ed; Tchr.

**BARCLAY, KRISTEN L**, Allegheny Coll, Meadville, PA; SO; BS; Chrs 89-; Wmns Ensmble 90-; Lambda Sigma 90-; ALLIES 89-; Vrsty Tnns 89-; Blgy; Physcl Thrpy.

**BARCLAY, THOM B**, Univ Of Southern Ms, Hattiesburg, MS; FR; BS; Chem; Polymer Sci.

**BARD, SHERI S**, Mount Saint Mary Coll, Newburgh, NY; FR; BA; Tennis Tm; Chris Ambrose Mem Run; Socl Psychlgst.

**BARDAK, STEVEN G**, S U N Y Coll Of Tech At Frmgdl, Farmingdale, NY; FR; BA; US Swming 89-; Archtctr; Law Enfrcemnt.

**BARDALES, KIMBERLY M**, Univ Of North Fl, Jacksonville, FL; FR; Assistant 90-; Montessori Schl; Elem/Early Childhood Ed; Tchng.

**BARDEN, CHRISTINE K**, Memphis St Univ, Memphis, TN; SR; MBA; Womns Panhellnc Cncl Rho Chi; Phi Eta Sigma 88-; Dns Lst 88-; Beta Alpha Psi; Alpha Delta Pi Reg 88-; Chrch Mbr 88-; Bdo Seidmn Intrnshp Tax Prep; IMS 88; Acctg.

**BARDESCHEWSKI, LISA A**, S U N Y Coll At Oswego, Oswego, NY; FR; BA; Jewelry Club; Art; Photogralphy.

**BARDOUN, MARTIN**, S U N Y At Buffalo, Buffalo, NY; GD; MARCH; BA 83; Archtctr.

**BARDOWELL, COLLIN E**, Newbury Coll, Brookline, MA; FR; BA; Acct; Corp Acct.

**BARDSLEY, URSULA L**, White Pines Coll, Chester, NH; FR; Stdnt Senate Frshmn Rep 90-; Phi Theta Kappa; Vlybl Trnmnt Fndrsr; Phtgrphy; Wildlife Phtgrphy.

**BARDWELL, CYNTHIA M**, Elms Coll, Chicopee, MA; JR; BSW; Scl Wrk Org 90-; Jwsh Home Aged Intrn 90-; Scl Wrk.

**BARDWELL-JONES, RACHEL F**, Old Dominion Univ, Norfolk, VA; SR; BS; SAE 90-; Sierra Clb; Mech Eng.

**BARE, CHARITY W**, Marywood Coll, Scranton, PA; FR; BS; Cncl Excptnl Chldrn 90-; Larche Asc Chr; Ski Clb 90-; Vol Actn 90-; Big Sis; Ornttn Comm; Fld Exp De Paul Schl 90-; Spec Ed/ Psy; Tchr/Chld Psy.

**BARE, SUSA E**, Univ Of Pittsburgh, Pittsburgh, PA; JR; BSN; Lthrn Unvrsty Cntr Brd Mmbr 88-; Chpl Chr 89; Cmpln Chr 89-; Lambda Sigma Srvc Chrmn 89-90; Gldn Key 90-; Alpha Tau Delta; Hnd Hnd Fstvl Hndcpd Chldrn Fcltr 88-; RA; Prvst Schlrshp 88-; Nrsngf Nrsng Care.

**BARE, URSULA M**, Anne Arundel Comm Coll, Arnold, MD; SO; AA; Math; Eng.

**BAREFIELD, BRIAN M**, Coll Of Charleston, Charleston, SC; FR; Hstry.

**BAREFIELD, MYLA D**, Duke Univ, Durham, NC; FR; BA; Black Stdnt Alliance 90-; Chronicle 90-; Southgate House Cncl Sec 90-; CHANCE Stdnt Tutor 90-; CHANCE Big Sis 90-; CHANCE Pblc Rltns Com 90-; Inroads Chicago 90-; DDB Needham Worldwide Inc Advrtsng Intrnshp 90-; Engl/Pblc Plcy; Brdcst Jrnlsm/Law.

**BAREFOOT, DEDRA L**, Univ Of Southern Ms, Hattiesburg, MS; SR; BS; Spch Dbt Tm 87-89; Gamma Beta Phi; Stu Almni Assc 90-; Tchng Asst S W TX; Spch Cmmnctns; Pblc Rltns/ Cmmnctns.

**BAREFOOT, FAYE H**, Fayetteville St Univ, Fayetteville, NC; GD; Sociology Clb Treas 89-90; Non Trad Stdnts Org 89; N C Sociological Assn; Alpha Kappa Delta 90; Alpha Kappa Mu 90; Rho Beta Chi 90; Magna Cum Laude; Chncllrs Lst 90-; Deans Lst 88-90; Meth Wmns Soc; Human Serv Coord; Soc/Psych; MBA Sociology.

**BAREFOOT, JAMES A**, Christopher Newport Coll, Newport News, VA; JR; BA; Soccer 89-; Pltcl Sci/Crmnl Juste; U S Fed Marshall.

**BAREFOOT, JEFFREY A**, Christopher Newport Coll, Newport News, VA; JR; BSGA; Crmnl Jstc; Fedrl Bureau Invstgtn.

**BARFIELD, DAWN H**, Fayetteville St Univ, Fayetteville, NC; FR; BED; Snyder Mem Bapt Ch; Sec; Elem Edn; Teach Spec Ed.

**BARFIELD, DONALYN L**, Valdosta St Coll, Valdosta, GA; SO; BS; Student GE Assoc Edtrs Secty 89-F Alpha Lambda Delta 90-; Sigma Alpha Chi; Tifton Elks Lodge Schlrshp; Valdosta State Clg Foundtn Schlrshp; :Vsc Freshmn Schlr; IM Vlybl/Sftbl 90-; Secondry Ed; Tch High Schl Level.

**BARFIELD, ELIZABETH L**, Univ Of Sc At Columbia, Columbia, SC; JR; BA; Rabbit/Cavy Club Show Dir 90-; Amer Rabbit Breeders Assoc 88-; Hall Gvt VP 86-87; RHA Natl Commtn Coord 87-88; English; Univ Profr.

**BARFIELD, KIM L**, Al St Univ, Montgomery, AL; FR; Crmnl Jstc; Law.

**BARFIELD, RACHEL L**, Alcorn St Univ, Lorman, MS; FR; BS; HSO 90-; Nrsng; RN.

**BARGA, AMY J**, Univ Of Toledo, Toledo, OH; FR; BA; Lambda Kappa Sigma; Pharm.

**BARGALLO, HECTOR S**, City Univ Of Ny City Coll, New York, NY; JR; BED; Italian Cultural Exchangew 88-89; Amer Scty Mecl Engrs 90-; Scty Automv Engrs 90-; Diploma Computerized Accouting 87-88; Mecl Engrg; Engrg.

**BARGELLINI, ANTHONY**, Manhattan School Of Music, New York, NY; SO; BM; Opera Pgm; Hohokus Comm Chrch 89-; Itln Cltrl Soc 84-85; Gamma Kappa Alpha 84; Phi Beta Kappa 85; Phi Kappa Phi 84; Alpha Mu Gamma 84; Outstndng Yngmn Amer 87; BA Fordham Univ 85; Voice; Pro Sngr.

**BARGER, GRACE L**, Memphis St Univ, Memphis, TN; SR; MA; Gamma Beta Phi Pres 83-84; Phi Kappa Phi 90-; BA; Tchr.

**BARGER, KIMBERLEY S**, Duquesne Univ, Pittsburgh, PA; FR; BS; Pharm.

**BARGER, LINDA J**, Lees Coll, Jackson, KY; FR; BA; Bsns; Acctg.

**BARGER, OLEVA R**, Univ Of Pittsburgh At Bradford, Bradford, PA; SO; MBA; Stdnt Govt 90-; Alpha Phi Omega Treas 90-; Hmn Reltns; Phy Thrpst.

**BARGER, REBECCA L**, Univ Of Nc At Asheville, Asheville, NC; JR; BFA; Phi Eta Sigma; Art; Free Lance Artist.

**BARGER, SUSAN M**, Nc Agri & Tech St Univ, Greensboro, NC; FR; BA; Tchng Asstnt 85-; Elem Ed; Tchng.

**BARGERON JR, MILLER**, Savannah St Coll, Savannah, GA; SO; BA; Acctg/Info Sys; CPA.

**BARHAM, MICAH M**, Meridian Comm Coll, Meridian, MS; JR; BA; Tennis Team 2 Player 89-90; Bldng Sci; Glazing Sub Cntr.

**BARICKMAN, JOSEPH V**, Edinboro Univ Of Pa, Edinboro, PA; SR; Univ Hon Prog 87-90; Kappa Delta Pi 88-90; Alph Chi 90-; B E D 90; Math; Educ.

**BARIE, PATRICIA A**, Duquesne Univ, Pittsburgh, PA; SR; BS; Math Council Of Western A 90; CCAC High Hnrs 89; Cmnty Vlntr Work Teaching International Students 89-; Assoc Deg Cmnty Clge Of Allegheny Cnty 89; Elem Ed; Teacher.**

**BARILE, ANGELA**, Teikyo Post Univ, Waterbury, CT; FR; BA; Fin; Intl Fin Bus.

**BARILE, KELLY**, Daemen Coll, Amherst, NY; JR; BS; Travel/ Tourism Clb Pres; Trvl/Trnsprtn Mgnt; Own Trvl Agcy.

**BARIMO, JOHN F**, Va Commonwealth Univ, Richmond, VA; JR; BS; Rcyclng Cprtv VP 89-; Rcyclng Tsk Frc Paper Cmt; Gldn Key 89-; Hon Pgm 89-; Woods Hole Flwshp; Univ Svc Awrd; IM Vlybl 90; Acstcl Scty Amer 90-; Sierra Clb 87-; MCI Telcmnctns Sr Fld Eng 83-89; Bio; Envrnmntl Txclgy/Ocngrphy.**

**BARING, ELIZABETH A**, Marymount Manhattan Coll, New York, NY; SR; MA; Cert Art Sothebys London 74; Gen Cert Educ London Univ 64; Brearley Schl Exec Asst; Antique Shws; Natl Museum Philippines Rsrch Ctlgd; Guide Philippines 79; Metropolitan Museum Art Trnsltd Ctlg 73; Manufactures Hanover Ltd Exec Asst; Art Thrpy.

**BARISHAW, SCOTT R**, Univ Of Rochester, Rochester, NY; JR; BA; Econs; Mrktng.

**BARISO, LORENE MICHELLE**, Middle Tn St Univ, Murfreesboro, TN; SR; BS; STEA; Good Frnds Awd Metro Publ Sch; Regnl Visual Arts Conf 90; Miami Dade Comm Coll Tennis Tm 75; Flight Attdnt 84-87; Profl Nanny; Profl Food/Beverage Server 80-; Elem Edn/Soc Sci; Tchr.

**BARKALOW, M KATHLEEN**, Mount Saint Mary Coll, Newburgh, NY; JR; BA; Vybl Sftbl 88-; Drma Clb 88-; Coach Awd Sftbl; English; Sec Educ.

**BARKER, ANGELA G**, Univ Of Nc At Charlotte, Charlotte, NC; SR; BA; Psychlgy Clb 90-; Jcrmnl Jstc Assoc; Rsrch Asst Psychlgy 90-; Psychlgy Crmnl Jstc.

**BARKER, BARRY I**, Univ Of Southern Ms, Hattiesburg, MS; JR; BS; Scty Physics Stdnts Pres 90-; Mrchng Bnd 88-90; Alpha Lambda Delta 88-; Gldn Key 90-; Omicron Delta Kappa 90-; Phi Kappa Phi 90-; Kappa Mu Epsilon 90-; Outstdng Phys Awd; CRC Chem Achvmnt Awd 90; Kappa Mu Epsilon Outstdng Fresh Math Awd 89; Physics/Math; Rsrch Physicist.

**BARKER, BETH N**, Radford Univ, Radford, VA; JR; BS; Stdnt Trnr 90-; Deans Lst 90; I M Soccer 88-; Sprts Med/Pre Phys Thrpy; Athl Trnr/Phys Tpy.

**BARKER, BRUCE W**, Miami Univ, Oxford, OH; FR; BA; Mrchng Bnd 90-; Math/Tch Cert; Sec Educ.

**BARKER, CAROL A**, Memphis St Univ, Memphis, TN; JR; BS; Gamma Beta Phi 88-; Golden Key 90-; Kappa Delta Pi 90-; Simga Kappa Sorority VP 89-; Ed; Tchr.

**BARKER, CASSANDRA G**, Western Ky Univ, Bowling Green, KY; SR; Beta Alpha Psi 89-; Gold Key 89-; Phi Eta Sigma 88-; J C Holland Awd 90-; Pres Schlr 88-90; Grad Summa Cum Laude; Acctg; CPA.

**BARKER, CHARLES D**, Kent St Univ Kent Cmps, Kent, OH; SO; BA; Crmnl Jstce Studies; Law.

**BARKER, DURENDA B**, Central Fl Comm Coll, Ocala, FL; FR; AS; Acctg/Med; Medical.

**BARKER JR, FORESTER**, Thomas Nelson Comm Coll, Hampton, VA; SR; BS; Vet Frgn Wrs; Rtrd Offcrs Assoc; Non Cmmssnd Offcrs Assoc; Chf Wrrnt Offcr Fr; USN; AS 90; Acctg.

**BARKER, GREGORY G**, Univ Of Tn At Martin, Martin, TN; SR; BS; Chptr Wldlf Soc 90-; NRM/WLDLF Biology.

**BARKER, HELEN M**, Univ Of Sc At Columbia, Columbia, SC; JR; Gldn Ky 90-; NASPE P E Major Yr Awd 90-; Battle Of Classes 89-90; Spec Olympics 89-90; SCAHPERD 90-; AAHPERD; Elem Educ Tchr.**

**BARKER, HOLLIE D**, Averett Coll, Danville, VA; FR; BS; Pi Eta Sigma; Ringgold Vol Fire Dept Ladies Aux Histrn 90-; Grls Vlybl; Elem Ed; Tch.

**BARKER, JONDA L**, Wv Univ At Parkersburg, Parkersburg, WV; JR; BA; Phi Beta Lambda 89-90; Bsn Admn/Acctng.

**BARKER, KATRINA J**, Univ Of Me, Orono, ME; FR; BA; Stdnt Hlpln 90-; Hist; Tchng.

**BARKER, KIMBERLY E**, Hillsborough Comm Coll, Tampa, FL; BA; FL African Amer Stdnt Assoc; NAACP; Afro-Amer Stdnt United Secr 90-; Phi Beta Lamda; Phi Theta Kappa; Intrnshp Sunbank; Mktg Bsn; Intl Mktg.

**BARKER, LISA A**, Va Commonwealth Univ, Richmond, VA; BED 90; Elem Ed; Tchr.

**BARKER, LORA B**, Univ Of Ky, Lexington, KY; SO; BA; Pol Sci; Law.

**BARKER, MELISSA A**, Univ Of Cincinnati, Cincinnati, OH; SO; BED; Scndry Engl Educ; Tchr.

**BARKER, MELISSA A**, Univ Of Ky, Lexington, KY; SR; BA; NCTM 90-; Pi Mu Epsilon 89-; Epsilon Delta 89-; Gldn Ky; Sallie E Pence Awd; Chrslr Corp Schlrshp; Educ; Math Tchr.**

**BARKER, RENEE M**, Univ Of Akron, Akron, OH; SR; BED; ACES 90-; Tch Rlgn Classes 89-; Head Pre Schl Prgrm 89-; Immclt Cncptn Chrch; YWCA Head Tchr; Rgnl Mgr Dan Howard Mtrnts; Mass Media Concentration; Elmntry Ed Tchng.

**BARKER, RONDA L**, Marshall University, Huntington, WV; SO; BA; Res Hl Advsry Cncl 89-90; IMS 89-90; Math; Bsn Mgmt.

**BARKER, TAMMY J**, Kent St Univ Geauga Cmps, Burton Twp, OH; FR; BA; GA Hsptl; Ntrtn Fd.

**BARKER, TAMMY K**, Ms Gulf Coast Comm Coll, Perkinston, MS; SO; BS; Bus Admn; Accntnt.

**BARKET, KEVIN J**, Union Coll, Barbourville, KY; JR; BA; Bsbl; AS Wabash Vlly Jr Coll 90; Bus Fin.

**BARKEY, KAREN L**, Lancaster Bible Coll, Lancaster, PA; JR; BA; Bsktbl Sftbl New Hope Spprt Grp Capt 89-; Beth Shalom Asst Hsprnt; Cnslng; Biblcl Cnslng.**

**BARKHAU, KEITH D**, Univ Of Louisville, Louisville, KY; GD; ME; Stdnt Cncl Repr 88-90; Am Scty Mech Engnrs 88-; Intrnshp KFC 88-; Honorary KY Colonel 90; Granted Patent US Patent Ofc; BS Univ Louisville 90; Mech Engr.

**BARKLEY, AUDRA A**, Central Al Comm Coll, Alexander City, AL; SO; BS; Phi Theta Kappa 89-; Schlrshp 89-; AUM Schlrshp; AS Central Ala Cmnty Clge; Envrnmntl Blgy; Envrnmntl Scntst.

**BARKLEY, CATHY R**, Memphis St Univ, Memphis, TN; SR; BA; NAEYC; TAYC Tn Assoc For Yng Chldrn; SACUS; Kappa Delta Pi; Ed Erly Chldhd; Tchr.

**BARKLEY, JESSICA W**, Univ Of Tn At Martin, Martin, TN; SO; BS; Res Hl Assoc 89-; Soc Hnr Smnr Stdnts 89-90; Stdnt Nrs Assoc Pres 89-; Alpha Omicron Pi Asst Corr Sec 89-; Otstndng Nrsng Stdnt 90-; Nursing.

**BARKMAN, JEFFREY P**, William Jennings Bryan Coll, Dayton, TN; FR; BE; Intrntl Union 90-; Im Sports 90-; Varsity Soccer 90-; Engr.

**BARKSDALE, LARRY A**, Univ Of Al At Birmingham, Birmingham, AL; SR; BS; Jeffrsn Co Shrffs Resrv Assoc 85-88; Assoc Advncmnt Med Instrmntn CBET 86-; Cert Biomed Elec Tech 83-; Alld Hlth; Biomed Engr.

**BARKSDALE, LESLIE ANN**, Longwood Coll, Farmville, VA; JR; BS; AAS Danville Comm Col 90; Educ; Elem Tchr.

**BARLETTA, CHIARINA**, Newbury Coll, Brookline, MA; FR; Hotel/Rest Mgmnt.

**BARLEY, CRISTI J**, Juniata Coll, Huntingdon, PA; FR; BA; 4 H Ldr Meth Chrch; Elem Educ/Erly Chldhd Ed; Tch.

**BARLEY, MELISSA A**, Central Fl Comm Coll, Ocala, FL; Honors Math & Science Club Pres; Outstanding Participant Award For Math & Sci Club; Biology & Sciences; Marine Biologest.

**BARLICK III, JOHN T**, Pittsburgh Tech Inst, Pittsburgh, PA; SO; AST; Vctnl Indstrl Clbs Amer 89-90; Drftng Clb Pres 89-90; PA Skls Cert 90; Cmptr/Drftng/Dsgn; Engr.

**BARLOW, ADAM GORDON**, Va Polytechnic Inst & St Univ, Blacksburg, VA; FR; BS; Res Hll Fed 90-; Karate 90; Ind Engr.

**BARLOW, AMANDA J**, Abraham Baldwin Agri Coll, Tifton, GA; SO; FFA 88-90; Rodeo Tm 88-; GA Ctlmns Assn; UGA Exprmnt Statn Intrnshp 88; Anml Sci/Agribus Mgmt.

**BARLOW, JOANNA C**, Univ Of Sc At Columbia, Columbia, SC; FR; BS; Sailing Clb 90-; Fllwshp Chrstn Athlts 90-; Biol; Phys Thrpy.

**BARLOW JR, ROBERT DAVID**, Ms St Univ, Miss State, MS; SR; MBA; Hist/Russian; Prof.

**BARLOW, ROBERT S**, Va Commonwealth Univ, Richmond, VA; SO; BS; Chstrfld Karate Inst 86-; Gldn Key 90-; Kings Dmnm Scrty Intshp; Admn Jstc; Law Enf.

**BARLOW, STEPHEN M**, Richard Bland Coll, Petersburg, VA; SO; BS; Republican Clb 88-89; Pres Lst 89-90; Deans Lst 90-; AS 90; Cmptr Sci; Analyst/Pgrmmr.

**BARNARD, BRIAN J**, Bethany Coll, Bethany, WV; JR; BS; Math Hon Soc; Phi Kappa Tau Treas 89-; Bethany Comp Sci Intrnshp; Math/Comp Sci; Grad Schl.

**BARNARD, JOSEPH E**, Bethany Coll, Bethany, WV; JR; BS; Soc Phys Stdnts Pres 88-; Phi Kappa Tau Treas 89-; REU Univ VA; Var Cross Cntry; Physcs.

**BARNES ROSICH, FERNANDO**, Catholic Univ Of Pr, Ponce, PR; SO; JD; IEEE 89-; Phi Delta Gamma; BS Fl Inst Tech 89; Math; Law.

**BARNES, ALLISON R**, Univ Of Sc At Columbia, Columbia, SC; SO; BA; Sirrine Schlr; Jrnlsm; Media Law.**

**BARNES, ANGELA M,** Fayetteville St Univ, Fayetteville, NC; SR; BS; Socology Clb; GAD 89; Soc Wrk; Soc Wrk.

**BARNES, BRIAN E,** Al A & M Univ, Normal, AL; SO; BS; Alpha Phi Alpha Hstrn; Ttr 90-; Comp Sci; Comp Anlyst.

**BARNES, CATHERINE J,** Va Highlands Comm Coll, Abingdon, VA; SO; AS; Estrn Star 81-; Phi Theta Kappa P 90-; Advsry Comm Schl Brd Spec Ed 89-; Steerng Comm Ed; Drftng/Dsgn; Eng.

**BARNES, CHARLES E,** Wv Univ, Morgantown, WV; SR; Chi Epsilon Sec Treas 89-; Cvl Eng Intrn PA DOT 89-; IM Ftbl Sftbl Vlybl 87-; BSCE; Cvl Eng; Prfssnl Cvl Eng.

**BARNES, CONNIE J,** Alcorn St Univ, Lorman, MS; SR; Alpha Kappa Mu 90-; All Amer Sclr 90-; Pres Schlr 89-; Dns Schlr 85-88; BS; Blgy; Instrcrtr.

**BARNES, DANIELLE S,** Norfolk St Univ, Norfolk, VA; SO; Spartan Alpha Tau; Dept Navy Intrn; Bus; Fin/Mktg.

**BARNES, DAVID J,** Univ Of Tn At Knoxville, Knoxville, TN; JR; BS; Recr Restoration/Childrens Outreach 90-; Intervars Chrstn Flwshp 90-; Beta Gamma Sigma; Econ; Urban Plng/Econ Dev.

**BARNES, DENISE M,** Coll Of Charleston, Charleston, SC; SR; Phi Kappa Phi; Sftbl Coach 87-; Tee Ball Mgr 87; US Naval Reserve 82-; AS Tidewater Comm Clg 86; Elem Educ; Tchr.

**BARNES, DEONNE MELISSA,** Univ Of Nc At Charlotte, Charlotte, NC; SO; Coll Demcrts 89-; Blck Stu Unn 89-90; NAACP 89-90; Hnrs Prog 89-; NC Tchng Fllws Schlrshp 89-; Nws Stff Wrtr 89-; SAFE Cnslr 90-; Natl Paideia Inst; SOAR Ornttn Cnslr 90; Engl/Pblc Rel; Tchr.

**BARNES, DONNA E,** Portland School Of Art, Portland, ME; SO; BFA; NEA MAEA; Tch K Thru 8; BA Art Educ Univ S Maine 74; Art; Painter/Sculptor.

**BARNES, DONNA M,** City Univ Of Ny Baruch Coll, New York, NY; SO; BA; Intrvrsty Chrstn Fllwshp Grp Ldr 89-; Acctg.

**BARNES, ELIZABETH R,** Itawamba Comm Coll, Fulton, MS; FR; BA; Stu Govt Sec; Fshn Tribe 90-; Indianette 90-; Deans Lst; Mus Drama Chrgrphr; Acctg; CPA.

**BARNES, GRETCHEN M,** Cornell Univ Statutory College, Ithaca, NY; SO; BS; Cltn Lf Nwslttr Ed 90-; Cmps Crsd Chrst 89-; Ltrcy Vol; Cornell Tradition Schlrshp; 2M Ice Hcky; Ag Econ; Ag Bus.

**BARNES, HAZEL HYDIE,** City Univ Of Ny City Coll, New York, NY; SR; Afrcn Dnc Drm Clb Pres 87-89; Antg Brbd Stdnt Assoc 88-; Day Stdnt Govt Sen 89-90; Apr Hnrs Acdmc Excllnc 87; Chrldr 88-89; Afrcn Stds Sclgy; Law.

**BARNES, HOLLY E,** Birmingham Southern Coll, Birmingham, AL; FR; Cnsrvncy 90-; Alpha Lambda Delta; Phi Eta Sigma; Alpha Chi Omega 90-.

**BARNES, JACQUELINE A,** City Univ Of Ny Queensbrough, New York, NY; SO; BS; Phi Theta Kappa 90-; Walter Zozulin Mem Awd Excell Orgnc Chmstry; Sondra Farber Mem Awd Excell Math; AS; Chemistry; Dentistry.

**BARNES, JAMES T,** Univ Of Al At Birmingham, Birmingham, AL; FR; BA; Alpha Lambda Delta; Sigma Nu; Philosophy; Law.

**BARNES, JEFFERY W,** Univ Of Tn At Martin, Martin, TN; FR; BS; Clgte FFA 90-; Blck/Brdle Clb 90-; Alpha Gamma Rho Pdg Treas 90; Golfhrly Intrn; Agri Bus.

**BARNES, JENNIFER D,** Johnson C Smith Univ, Charlotte, NC; SO; BS; Hmcmng Com 89; Assn Of Ftre Blck Execs 90-; Frst Bapt Chrch West Ttrl Prog; Nwrk Bth Isrl Med Hosp Vol; Bllfst Com 90; Acctng Mnr Mgmt; Corp Acct.

**BARNES, JEREDINE B,** Jackson St Univ, Jackson, MS; JR; BS; SNEA; Bapt Stdnt Union; WEB Du Bois Hons Coll; Phi Lambda Theta Sec; Elem Ed; Tchng/Cnslng.

**BARNES JR, JERRY M,** Saint Andrews Presbytrn Coll, Laurinburg, NC; JR; BA; Debate Tm Treas 89-; Scl Chr Mcklenbrg Drm 90-; Math C S Clb VP 89-; Hnr Scty; Soph Hnrs; Hnrs SAGE; Rugby Clb 89-; Math/Comp Sci; Tchng.

**BARNES, JOYCE E,** Nc Agri & Tech St Univ, Greensboro, NC; SO; BS; Guilford Co N C Assn Tchr Asst 88-89; Tchr Asst 88-; Ele Educ; Pub Schls.

**BARNES, JUDY A,** Univ Of Tn At Martin, Martin, TN; SR; MS; Wildlf Soc Pres 89-90; Gamma Beta Phi Reprtr 86-87; Outstndng Stdnt Natrl Rsrcs Mgt 88-89; Glenn Elkins Consrvtn Award 89-90; Deans List 86-88; BS 90; ASS MS Cnty Cmnty Clg 87; Wldlf/ Silvaculture Rsrcs; Consrvtn Rsrcs.

**BARNES, KAREN L,** Middle Tn St Univ, Murfreesboro, TN; JR; BBA; Tau Omicron; Gamma Beta Phi Comp Opers Sec 90-; Alpha Kappa Psi; Wmns Crs Cntry Trck Tm; Bsns; Bsns Admn.

**BARNES, KATHRYN A,** Va Commonwealth Univ, Richmond, VA; JR; BA; Mktg Intern Alfa-Laval Thermal Inc; Cmnctn Arts Dsgn; Graphic Dsgn.

**BARNES, KATRINA M,** Al A & M Univ, Normal, AL; JR; BS; Natl Soc Blck Eng 89-; Deans Lst 88-; Hnr Stdnt; Summer Intern Caterpillar Inc 90; Cmptr Sci; Eng.

**BARNES, KEITH L,** Jackson St Univ, Jackson, MS; FR; BA; Hon Coll 90-; Bptst Stdnt Union 90-; Cert Acdmc Excllnc 90-; Pres Lst Schlr 90-; Fin; Real Estate.

**BARNES, KENDRA MICHELLE,** Univ Of Nc At Charlotte, Charlotte, NC; JR; BS; Criminal Justice.

**BARNES, KIMBERLY A,** Univ Of Akron, Akron, OH; JR; BS; Delta Gamma 89-90; Elem Ed; Kdg Tchr.

**BARNES, KIMBERLY J,** Richard Bland Coll, Petersburg, VA; SO; BA; Spnsh Clb 89; Stdnts Free Entrprs Vp 89-; Phi Theta Kappa 90-; Pres Schlr 89-; Busns; Tchng Bsns Clss.

**BARNES, LARRY H,** Fl A & M Univ, Tallahassee, FL; SR; CERT; BS Univ Of MD 85; Ed; Tchng.

**BARNES, LINDA M,** Northwest Al Comm Coll, Phil Campbell, AL; SO; Cmptr Inf.

**BARNES, MARGARET E,** D Youville Coll, Buffalo, NY; SR; MS; Snr Hnr Soc 90-; Dns Lst 89-; Amer Nrs Assc Dist I 90-; Pstrs Wife/Sndy Schl Tchr/Brd Mbr Rvrsd Chrch Nzrn 86-; Stf RN 88-; RN St Lukes Hosp Schl Nrs 84; BSN 90; Nrs; Comm Hlth Nrs/Tch.

**BARNES, MARK A,** Oh Univ, Athens, OH; SR; BFA; Amer Ctr Dsgn Stdnts Dsgn Sec 88-90; Golden Key 89-90; Grphc Dsgn.**

**BARNES, MARK E,** Milligan Coll, Milligan Clg, TN; FR; BA; Fstvl Of I Act Plays; Stdnt Bible Stdy 90-; NE TN Chrstn Home Big Bros 90; Deans Lst 90-; IM Vllybl/Ftbl/Bsktbl/Sftbl 90-; Engl; H S/Clg Educ.

**BARNES, MARY H,** Limestone Coll, Gaffney, SC; FR; BS; Stdnt Sen Sec/Treas 90-; Clss Ofcr Pres; Res Asst; Hons Pgm 90-; Kappa Delta Kappa; Grk Cncl; Mktg; Advrtsng.

**BARNES, METZ L,** Faulkner Univ, Montgomery, AL; SO.

**BARNES, MICHELLE D,** Univ Of Fl, Gainesville, FL; SR; BA; Hmcmg Parade Stf; Greek Wk Stf; Alpha Lambda Delta 89-; Goldey Key 90-; Phi Kappa Phi; Beta Gamma Sigma; Phi Sigma Sigma Correspndg Sec 90-; Amer Cancer Soc 90-; Retail Intrnshp; AA 90-; Mktg.

**BARNES, MONIQUE,** Va St Univ, Petersburg, VA; JR; BA; Tidewater Pre Almn Treas 89-; Pre Law Soc 89-; Admn Jstc Clb 90-; Sclgy/Admn Jstc; Law.

**BARNES, MORIA T,** Atlantic Comm Coll, Mays Landing, NJ; GD; DR; Stanly Holms Vlg Worktm Pr 87-; Atlantc Comm Clg Gospl Chrs; Sr Achvmnt Awd; Chiroprtc.

**BARNES, PAUL M,** S U N Y Coll At Fredonia, Fredonia, NY; JR; BA; IM Ftbl 88-; Stdnt Tchr Newman Cntr 89-; Pol Sci Assoc; Pol Sci; Law Schl.

**BARNES, RHONDA J,** Catawba Valley Comm Coll, Hickory, NC; FR; AS; Gamma Beta Phi 90-; Dns Lst 90-; Bsn Admn; CPA.

**BARNES, SANDRA L,** Fayetteville St Univ, Fayetteville, NC; FR; BA; Comp Sci.

**BARNES, SANDY K,** Univ Of Sc At Columbia, Columbia, SC; FR; BM; String Prjct 89-; Sub Orchstra Dir; Msc/Grmn; Prfssr.

**BARNES, SHANDRA MAQUEL,** Univ Of Ky, Lexington, KY; SR; SAC; NEA; Early Educ BA; Early Elem Ed.

**BARNES, SHELLY M,** Hudson Valley Comm Coll, Troy, NY; JR; BA; Sr Accntng Clrk; AS 88; Accntng; CPA.

**BARNES, SHERNARD R,** Allen Univ, Columbia, SC; JR; Stdnt Govt Assn Pres 90-; Deans Lst 90-; Groove Phi Groove Pres; Most Likely Sccd 90-; Good Hskpng Higgins Hall Dorm 90-.

**BARNES, SHERRI L,** Univ Of Nc At Greensboro, Greensboro, NC; JR; BSN; ANS; Dns Lst 90-; NC Nrsng Schlr 90-; Nrsng; RN.

**BARNES, STEPHEN A,** Kent St Univ Kent Cmps, Kent, OH; SR; BS; Army Intllgnce Offcr; Rssn Lang Stds; Tchng Rssn/Grmn.

**BARNES, SUSAN S,** Broward Comm Coll, Ft Lauderdale, FL; GD; BAMBA; AA 91; Bus Admin; Law/Hlth Admin.

**BARNES, TERRI R,** Salisbury St Univ, Salisbury, MD; SO; BA; Corr Sec P R Assn Stdnt Govt 90-; Telemrktg Rep Tour Guide 90-; Var Chrldr 89-90; Librl Stds; Publ Rel; Mktg Assc.

**BARNES, THOMAS A,** Univ Of Southern Ms, Hattiesburg, MS; JR; BA; Outstndng Stdnt-Jrnslm S D Bishop State Comm Coll; Press Oper 90-; Phi Theta Kappa-S D Bishop State Comm Coll; Engl; Post-Scndry Educ.

**BARNES, TIMOTHY A,** Cincinnati Bible Coll & Sem, Cincinnati, OH; GD; Untd Mnstrs 88-; Delta Sigma Nu 85-87; Grdte Asst 89-90; Ancnt Nr East Stds Awd 88; BA 88; MA Cincinnati Chrstn Smnry 90; Theolgy; Mnstry.**

**BARNES, TOXIE A,** Commonwealth Coll, Norfolk, VA; SO; Med Club Am Assn Of Med Assts 90-; Adv Comm Hnrs Cncl 89-90; Alpha Beta Gamma; Most Likely To Succeed; Stdnt Asst Awd; Pres List; Stdnt Of Mo 89; Summa Cum Laude Grad; Med Asst.

**BARNES, TRACY LA TRESE,** Al A & M Univ, Normal, AL; FR; BA; Comp Sci; Anlyst.

**BARNES, VIVIAN J,** Univ Of Ga, Athens, GA; GD; MS; Profssnl Assc GA Edctrs; Grad Cum Laude Barry Unv; PAGE; BA Barry Unv 89; Ed; Schl Cnslng.

**BARNET, ADAM,** Fl International Univ, Miami, FL; SR; MS; Deans Lst; Art Schlrshp; BS; Psychlgy.

**BARNETT, ANGELA C,** Wallace St Comm Coll At Selma, Selma, AL; SO; BS; All Amer Schlr; Early Chldhd/Elem Educ; Tchr.

**BARNETT, BILL K,** Univ Of Tn At Martin, Martin, TN; JR; PHD; Hnrs Smnr 88-89; Mu Epsilon Delta VP Pldg Cls; Biology; Pharmacy.

**BARNETT, CHARLENE M,** Kent St Univ Kent Cmps, Kent, OH; JR; BA; Engl; Tch Coll Lvl.

**BARNETT, CHERYL L,** Miami Jacobs Jr Coll Of Bus, Dayton, OH; SO; AD; Acctg; CPA.

**BARNETT, CHRISTIAN M,** Oh St Univ At Marion, Marion, OH; SO; Ftbl Tm At Furman Univ 89; Bio; Med.

**BARNETT, DAPHNE L,** Alcorn St Univ, Lorman, MS; SO; Pryr Bnd 89-; Bapt Stdnt Un 89-; Nrsng Clb 90-; Rgstrd Nrs.

**BARNETT, DEBORA L,** Mayland Comm Coll, Spruce Pine, NC; FR; AAS; Chrch Of God Of Prophecy 80; Hon Roll 90-; Admn Ofc Technlgy; Law Ofc/Govt.

**BARNETT, DEBORAH A,** Oh Wesleyan Univ, Delaware, OH; SO; BA; Stdnt Fndtn 90; Stdnt Admsns Assist 90; Plyers/Thtr Org 90; Choral Art Soc 90; Pi Eta Sigma; Pi Society; Pi Beta Phi 90; Thtr; Thrpy/Acting.

**BARNETT, ELIZABETH A,** Ga St Univ, Atlanta, GA; GD; SGAE 89-90; Cum Laude 90; Yth Dir Midway Bptst Chrch 88-90; NEA/GAE 89-; Newton Cnty Schls Porterdale Elem Schl 90-; BSED 90; Early Chldhd Educ; Tch.

**BARNETT, GEORGE M,** Univ Of Ky, Lexington, KY; SO; BS; Pence Phys Clb 89-; Coll Schlrs Of Amer 90; Dns Lst 89-90; Physics.

**BARNETT, IFE D,** Johnson C Smith Univ, Charlotte, NC; SO; BS; Honr Roll 89-; Math; Profssr.

**BARNETT, IRENE J,** Saint Francis Coll, Loretto, PA; SO; BA; Adpt Grndprnt 89-90; Plus One Pgm 89-; Pre Law Clb; Hnrs Pgm 89-; Phi Sigma Iota; Phi Delta Kappa 90-; Career Plng/Plcmnt Intshp; Rep Jeff Coy Intshp; Pol Sci/Intl Rltns; Law.

**BARNETT, LAURA L,** Univ Of Charleston, Charleston, WV; JR; BS; Resp Care Stdnt Assn 88-; Amer Assn Resp Care 88-; Deans Lst 88-; Ordr Of Eastrn Str Str Pt Offcr 90-; Passd CRTT/RRT Exams 90; Acdmc Schlrshp 88-; AS 90; Resp Thrpy/Bus Admin.

**BARNETT, NATHAN WAYNE,** Kent St Univ Kent Cmps, Kent, OH; SR; Gamers Gld 90; Gldn Ky; Sigma Tau Delta; KSU Hnrs Clg Dist Stdnt Schlrshp 88-; Ishinryu Karate Treas 89-90; Engl; Clg Prof.

**BARNETT, ROBERT K,** Al St Univ, Montgomery, AL; SO; Tstmstrs Intrnatl 90-; Soph Cls Pres 90-; Phi Eta Sigma 89-; Gft Lf Fndtn Brd Dir 88-; Gdprnt Pgm 90-; Chmstry; Dr Int Med.

**BARNETT, ROCHELLE L,** Longwood Coll, Farmville, VA; JR; BS; Stdnt Ed Assoc 90-; Kappa Delta Pi; AS N VA Cmnty Clg 90; Elem Ed; Tchg.

**BARNETT, SHERRY D,** Univ Of Ky, Lexington, KY; JR; BA; Psi Chi 90-; Psychlgy; Clncl Psychlgst.

**BARNETT, THERESA L,** Univ Of Tn At Martin, Martin, TN; SR; Acctg Clb Union Univ; Tennis Var Union Univ; Natl Assoc Accntnts; Deans List; Zeta Tgau Alpha; Aerobics; IM Sprts Bsktbl/Vlybl/Union Univ; BS; Acctg; Pblc Acctg.

**BARNETT, TRACEY J,** Clarion Univ Of Pa, Clarion, PA; FR; BS; Symphnc Nbd/Mrchng Bnd/Mrchng Bnd; UAB Flm/Rcrtn Com; Hl Cncl-Wing Rep; French Horn Qrtet/Brss Choir; Phi Eta Sigma; Tau Beta Sigma; Math; Optmtry.

**BARNETT, TRACY L,** Union Univ, Jackson, TN; JR; BVA; Socl Wrk.

**BARNETT, WENDY A,** Mount Saint Mary Coll, Newburgh, NY; JR; BS; Cmmtr Cncl 89-90; Bus.

**BARNETT-KOLEK, URSULA C,** Va Commonwealth Univ, Richmond, VA; SR; BSN; Boy Scouts Amer 86-; Phi Kappa Phi; Goldn Key; Cancer Soc Vol 85-; RN 85-; ANA Cert Med-Surg Nrsng 90-; Boy Scouts Amer Comm Member; VA Nrs Assn 90-; Nrsng.

**BARNETTE, KRISTIN D,** Auburn Univ At Auburn, Auburn, AL; JR; Fire ROTC Pres 89-; Wom Chorus 88; Hstss Trck Tm 88; Phi Kappa Phi 91; Alpha Lambda Delta 88-; Phi Eta Sigma 88-; Ord Of Owi 88-; Chi Omega 87-; Intl Serv/Perf Grp Up With People 89-90.

**BARNETTE, TINA M,** Univ Of Va Clinch Valley Coll, Wise, VA; JR; BA; Nwspr Reporter 89; Peer Advsng Grp 90-; Darden Scty VP 90-; Phi Upsilon Omega Secy; Deans Lst 88-; Jack Holland Educ Awrd Schlrshp; Elem Educ; Tchng.

**BARNETTE, YVONNE F,** Univ Of Sc At Columbia, Columbia, SC; SR; BA; Crmnl Jstc; Law.

**BARNHARDT, JOAN B,** Univ Of Nc At Greensboro, Greensboro, NC; JR; BS; St Pauls Lthrn Church; PAGE; RN 77-; ADN Sandhls Comm Coll 77; Pblc Hlth Educ/Blgy; Admin/Tch Schl Hlth/Blgy.

**BARNHART, CHRISTY L,** Univ Of Sc At Sumter, Sumter, SC; SO; BS; NEA SCEA SEA 89-; Deans Lst 90-; Elem Ed; Tch.

**BARNHART, MARILYN L,** Hudson Valley Comm Coll, Troy, NY; SR; AAS; Intrnshp At St Anne Inst For Grls 90; Intrnshp St Cthrnes Ctr For Chldrn; NYS Dept Of Soc Serv; Human Serv; Admin In Human Serv.

**BARNHART, STEPHANIE L,** Goucher Coll, Towson, MD; SO; SAR Womens Issues Grp Dir Of Wmns Ctr 90-; Cmnty Svc Org; Sociology; Soc Wrk.

**BARNHILL, LORI A,** Valdosta St Coll, Valdosta, GA; SR; BA; Drama Clb 88-89; Sch Newspaper 89; High Score GA Regents Exam Awd 89; AS Waycross Clg 90; Hstry; Tchg.

**BARNHILL II, ROBERT J,** Univ Of Nc At Charlotte, Charlotte, NC; GD; BA; AIAS 90-; Dns Lst 90-; Chnclrs Lst 90-; Arch Smmr Intshp; Mcklnbrg Cty Pharm Asc; Phrmcst; BS 78-83; Arch; PHD Arch/Dsgn Thrpy.

**BARNHILL, WILLIAM B,** Union Coll, Barbourville, KY; SO; BS; Academic Tm Capt 89-; Cmmtr Cncl 90-; Gamma Beta Phi 90-; Chem Awd 89-; Tremco Chem Awd 90-; Chemistry; Chemical Eng.

**BARNICKEL, JOLANE L,** Univ Of South Al, Mobile, AL; JR; ECE; Early Chldhd Educ; Tchng.

**BARNISH, BRENDA D,** Western New England Coll, Springfield, MA; FR; BACH; Mngmnt Assoc 90; Mrktng; Advrtsng.

**BARNOSKI, M DENISE,** Elmira Coll, Elmira, NY; SO; BA; Theatre Dept Pub Coord; Asst Bus Mgr 90; Phi Eta Sigma 90; Theatre/Mktg; Theatre Mgmt.**

**BARNUM, MICHAEL J,** Hahnemann Univ, Philadelphia, PA; SO; MD; Alpha Delta Phi Sgt At Arms; Lange Pblshrs Awd 90-; Mubraw Hill Pblrs Awd 90; Ludwig Schlrshp 90-; BS Biomed Eng Johns Hopkins Univ 89; Med; Doctor.

**BARNWELL, IVA L,** Oh St Univ At Marion, Marion, OH; FR; BA; Educ Socty 90-; Cornfield Review An Annual Of Crtv Arts Fctn Edtr 90-; Marion Comm Bnd 90-; Engl Educ; H S Tchr/Mshnry Wrk.

**BARNWELL, JANET L,** Tusculum Coll, Greeneville, TN; FR; FCA Vllybl/Bsktbll; Full Schrshp; Vllybll/Bsktbll.**

**BARNWELL, JEFFREY ALLEN,** Coll Of Charleston, Charleston, SC; SR; BA; Stdnt Legis Hse Rep 88-; Stdnt Govt Sntr 88-; Phlsphy Clb VP 89-; Silvery Key; Omicron Delta Kappa; Campus Amnesty Crdntr 88-; Assoc Degree Johnson/Wales Coll 86-88; Phlsphy; Intl Law Anthrplgy.

**BARNWELL, JULIE L,** Oh St Univ At Marion, Marion, OH; JR; BA; Edctn Soc Pres 90-; Deans Stdnt Advsry Cncl 88-; Stdnt Alumni Cncl 88-; Griffon 89-; Chimes 89-; Golden Key 90-; Mssnry Ldr Pres 90-; Sunday School Sec 88-; Vacation Bible Schl 88-; Stdnt Ldrshp Srvc Awd 90; Elem Edctn; Tchng.

**BARNWELL, YOLANDA D,** Univ Of Sc At Columbia, Columbia, SC; SO; BA; Cmps Crsd Christ 89-; ROTC 89-; Mnrty Stdnt Awd; Cmmndnts Lst; Deans Lst; Intl Studies; Pltcl Anlyst.

**BARON, ALLISON M,** Univ Of Rochester, Rochester, NY; SO; BA; Cmpus 4 Big Str 89-90; Sigma Delta Tau Exec V P; Psychology; Psycho Thrpy.

**BARON, DARLYSE,** Seton Hall Univ, South Orange, NJ; JR; Haitian Assn Club; Nrs Extrnshp St Michaels Hosp; Nrsg.

**BARON, JUDITH A,** Hillsborough Comm Coll, Tampa, FL; SO; BA; Multiple Sclerosis Soc Tampa Chpt Vlntr 89; MS Soc 89; Gloria Phillips Outstanding Stdnt Human Serv Awd 90; Hillsborough Cmnty C Foundation Schlrshp Awd 90-; Interdisciplinary Social Sci; Therapist.

**BARON, KRISTIN M,** Elmira Coll, Elmira, NY; SO; BA; Outing Clb 89-; Intl Clb 89-; Studys Org 90-; Dance Grp 90-; Anthrplgy.

**BARON, SCOTT A,** Limestone Coll, Gaffney, SC; JR; BA; US Navy Nuclear Mchnst Mate; Bsn Admin.

**BARONE, LISA A,** Tampa Coll, Tampa, FL; SO; BBA; Prsdnts Hnr Rll 90-; Deans Lst 90-; Grl Scts USA Co Ldr 89-90; Emplyd Lgl Asst; Bus Cmmnctns.

**BARONE, PAUL F,** Hampton Univ, Hampton, VA; FR; BA; Jack Jill Amer Cor Sec 84-90; Bishops Ldrshp Proj 89-; African Std Clstr 90-; Tutor Roy Wilkins Park 89-; Comm Svc Clb 86-89; Offctng Spts 89; IM Bsktbl 90-; Bus Mngmnt; Intrntl Busmn.

**BARONE, RALPH,** S U N Y Coll Of Tech At Frmgdl, Farmingdale, NY; JR; BA; Long Island Svgs Bnk Loan Acctg/Cntrlr Dept 89-; Atndg Hofstra Univ; AC Suny Farmingdale; Acctg; Pblc Acct.

**BARONGAN, PAUL G,** Univ Of Va, Charlottesville, VA; FR; BA; Orgnztn Yng Filipino AM 90-; Madison House Hosp Vol; Vllybl; Chmstry; Med/Hlth.

**BARONI, ANTHONY X,** Duquesne Univ, Pittsburgh, PA; SR; BS; Am Pharmaceutical Assn 90-; Outstndg Coll Stdnts Am 89-; Natl Eagle Scout Assn Asst Scoutmstr 87-; Rho Chi Hon Soc 90-; Phi Lambda Sigma; Phi Delta Chi 88-; Thrift Drug Schlrshp Intern 87-; Undergrad Teach Asst Duquesne; Phrmcy; Med Sch.

**BARONI, NANCY L,** Central Fl Comm Coll, Ocala, FL; SO; BA; Intrnshp 8th St Elem Sch 88; Engl; Tchng.

**BAROODY, SAMI W,** Hellenic Coll/Holy Cross, Brookline, MA; GD; MDIV; Bk Clerk/British Bk/Middle East 86-90; BA Am Un/Beirut 86; Theology; Priesthd.

**BAROULAKIS, HARALAMBOS,** City Univ Of Ny City Coll, New York, NY; JR; BA; Golden Key 90-; Engl Lit; Tch Univ Lvl.

**BAROUSSE, PHILLIP C,** Saint Thomas Univ, Miami, FL; JR; BA; Intrntl Stdnt Orgnztn 90; Ddeans List 90; Sprts Admnstrtn Man Yr 90-; Chmpnshp Lnd/Wtr Sqd 90; David Fitzgerald Awrd; IM Bsktbl/Sftbl; AA Bus Gloucester Cty Clg 88-90; Sprts Admn.

**BARR, ALAN W,** West Liberty St Coll, West Liberty, WV; SO; BS; By Scts Amer Egl Sct Sr Ptrl Ldr 83-89; Theta Xi; Egl Sct 88; Ordr Arrw 85; Tns/Lcrs 89-; Crim Jstc; Cr Mltry.

**BARR, CHRISTIAN D,** Oh Northern Univ, Ada, OH; FR; Ftbl 90-; Mech Eng.

**BARR, CRYSTAL L,** Univ Of Sc At Columbia, Columbia, SC; JR; BS; Alpha Chi Omega 90-; Crmnl Jstce; Law.

**BARR, DEREK D,** Wv Univ, Morgantown, WV; JR; BA; Daily Athenaeum Lf Sctn Edtr 88-; Kappa Tau Alpha Natl Jrnlsm Hnrary ; WVU Hnrs Pgrm 88-90; Charleston Dly Moil Intrnshp Schlrshp 90; Spts Trvia Contest; Amer Soc Mag Edtrs Intrnshp; Presdntl Natl Mrt Schlrshp 88-; Jrnlsm.

**BARR, JULIE M,** Brescia Coll, Owensboro, KY; JR; BA; Owner Mgr Enterprise Clng Svc 88-; Bus/Mktng; Law.

**BARR II, LESSLEY H,** Northeast State Tech Comm Coll, Blountville, TN; FR; AAS; Drftng.

**BARR, MARSHA R,** Oh St Univ At Marion, Marion, OH; SO; History/Elem Educ; Teacher.

**BARR, MARY BETH,** Brescia Coll, Owensboro, KY; SR; BS; NSSLHA Tres 89-; Cmnctns Sci; Spch Lang Pthlgst.

**BARR, MELISSA J,** Springfield Tech Comm Coll, Springfield, MA; SR; AS; Graphic Arts Cl; Alpha Nu Omega 90-; Graphic Arts Tech; Cmmcl Art.

**BARR, REBECCA A,** Bridgewater Coll, Bridgewater, VA; JR; BS; Day Stdnt Org Sec 90-; Yrbk Copy Edtr 90-; Thtr 88-; Lambda Soc 89-; Brethn Stdnt Flwshp 88-89; Bst Actrs 88-89; Bio; Env Bio.

**BARR, RICHARD MARSHALL,** Valdosta St Coll, Valdosta, GA; SR; BFA; Sigma Alpha Chi 89; Alpha Chi 90-; Dns Lst 87-; Cmnctns; Corp Cmnctns.

**BARR, ROSEMARY,** Brescia Coll, Owensboro, KY; FR; BS; Stdnt Ambsdr 90-; Mth Clb 90-; Hons Prog 90-; Cir K 90-; Math; HS Tchr.

**BARR, STEPHEN A,** American Baptist Coll, Nashville, TN; BA; Prsn Missionary; Crusade Mngr; Theology; Busns.

**BARR, THELMA JEAN,** Tn Wesleyan Coll, Athens, TN; JR; BA; New Expnt Rprtr Schl Papr; Bapt Stdnt Union; Better Late Than Never Clb; SS Tchr Sr Adlt Ladies 87-90; Chrch Choir 85; Jr Class 90; 13 Yrs Offce Wrk 71-84; Offce Assist Tn Wslyn Adlt/Cont Ed 90; AA Fla Keys Cmmnty Clg 84; Engl; Tchncl Edtng Or Pblc Rltns.

**BARRAGAN, HUGO R,** Eckerd Coll, St Petersburg, FL; SR; BA; Soc Advncmnt Of Mgmt 90-; Amer Mgmt Assn 89-; Intl Stdnt Assn 87-; Lgsltv Cncl Membr 90; Res Advsrs Intrvwng Team; Deans Lst 90; Mgmt; Finance.

**BARRALL, JENNIFER A,** Barry Univ, Miami, FL; FR; BSN; Air Force Reserve ROTC Cadet 90-; First Aid Squad Vol 90-; Nrsg; ER Nrsg.

**BARRANCO FRANCOIS, DAVID G,** Univ Politecnica De Pr, Hato Rey, PR; SR; BA; Bapt Yth Socty Pres; Cvl Engr Clb; Highway; Engr.

**BARRAS, LOLA R,** Hillsborough Comm Coll, Tampa, FL; SO; BA; Bus; Fnc.

**BARRAS JR, PAUL E,** Hillsborough Comm Coll, Tampa, FL; SO; BA; Bus; MIS.

**BARREIRO, MANUEL A,** Inter Amer Univ Pr Hato Rey, Hato Rey, PR; JR; BA; Great Art Kick Boxer Prpl Belt 88-; Jordan Grp Rlgs Grp 87-; Hon Assn Acctg Stdnts 90-; Roberto Clemente Awds Wnnr 87; Cert Caribbean Tchnlgy 88-89; Acctg; CPA.

**BARREN, YOLANDA MARCHI,** Southern Junior Coll, Birmingham, AL; BA; Bsn Admin.

**BARRENTINE, MELANIE S,** Abraham Baldwin Agri Coll, Tifton, GA; SO; AGS; Choir; Mu Alpha Theta 89-; Hon Stdnt; Sci; Rsprtry Thrpy.

**BARRER, MICHELLE L K,** Fayetteville St Univ, Fayetteville, NC; SR; Alpha Kappa Mu; Phi Beta Lambda; Highest Ranking Frshmn; Deans Lst; Chnclrs Lst; Magna Cum Laude; BS 90; Acctng.

**BARRERA, CARMEN,** Fl International Univ, Miami, FL; JR; BA; AA Miami Dade Cmnty Clge 73; Elem Ed; Tchr.

**BARRERA, MARGARITA M,** Miami Dade Comm Coll South, Miami, FL; SO; MBA; Accntng/Intl Mrktng; Bus.

**BARRERAS-CIFREDO, JORGE,** Univ Of Pr At Rio Piedras, Rio Piedras, PR; JR; BBA; Acctng Stdnts Assoc 90-; Golden Key 91; Natl Coll Bus Merit Awd; All Am Schlr Coll Awd; Acctng; Law.

**BARRETO ROMAN, MARIA G,** Inter Amer Univ Pr Arecibo Un, Arecibo, PR; SR; BS; Hon Circle 86-; Bio; Med Tech.

**BARRETO YBARRA, JUAN W,** Univ Of Pr Medical Sciences, San Juan, PR; GD; MS; Stdnt Cncl 89; BA Caribbean U Clg 83-86; Envrnmntl Hlth; Law.

**BARRETO, REINA M,** Agnes Scott Coll, Decatur, GA; FR; BA; Chimo Clb Treas 90-; Hon Lst 90; Most Imprvd Plyr Awd; Tennis Tm 90-; Intl Rel; Foreign Serv.

**BARRETT, BELINDA K,** Univ Of Al At Birmingham, Birmingham, AL; JR; AS; Beta Clb; Radiography.

**BARRETT, BENITA D,** Clark Atlanta Univ, Atlanta, GA; SR; BS; Zeta Phi Beta Vp 89-90; CAV Cmptr Sci Clb 87-; Ntl Cncl Negro Wmn; Deans Lst Rcpnt 90-; Archntt Of Yr 87; Frst Plc Dade Cnty Cmptr Ltrcy 86-87; Cmptr Sci; Bnkng/Pblc Rel.

**BARRETT, CHRISTOPHER D,** Univ Of New Haven, West Haven, CT; SR; BS; Aviation Clb; Alpha Lambda Delta; Comm Pilot 90-; License/Instrmnt Rating; Air Trans Mgmnt; Prof Aviation.

**BARRETT, DAVID M,** Temple Univ, Philadelphia, PA; SR; BS; Messiah Clg Soc Eng Pres 88-; Phila Stdnt Gov Chr Prsn 90-; Amer Soc Mech Eng 90-; Spring Brk Serv Proj Asst Ldr 88-90; Teen Missns 89-90; Track Fld Power Vlybl Letter 87-; Mech Eng.

**BARRETT, DEBRA D,** Univ Of Sc At Columbia, Columbia, SC; SO; BAIS; Carolina Cares 89-90; Alpha Phi Omega 89-90; Educ/Erly Chldhd; Tchr.

**BARRETT, DENISA L,** Univ Of Tn At Martin, Martin, TN; SR; BS; Amer Diet Assoc 90-; Amer Hm Ec Assoc 89-; TN Hm Ec Assoc 89-; Phi Kappa Phi; Alpha Sigma Alpha Sec 82-84; Diet Intrnshp Vndrblt Univ Cntr; Otsdng Diet Stdnt 90-; Mgmnt Smmr Intrnshp Univ MI 90; Mplewd Baptist Chrch SS Tchr; Sprvsr 84-; Hm Ec/Dietetics.

**BARRETT, DONOVAN ROY,** Univ Of Sc At Columbia, Columbia, SC; FR; Actvts Brd; Intl Assoc; Afrcn Amrcn Stdnts; IM; Bus Mgmt; CPA.

**BARRETT, JILL M,** Thomas Nelson Comm Coll, Hampton, VA; SO; BA; USAF Cntrct Spclst 86-90; Bus Admn; Prchsng Agnt.

**BARRETT, JULIE M,** Univ Of Akron, Akron, OH; SO; BA; Stdnts Choice V P 89-90; Sec Ed/Scl Stds; Tch MA Hstry.

**BARRETT, JULIE N,** Middle Tn St Univ, Murfreesboro, TN; SR; BBA; DPMA 87-; Gamma Beta Phi 87-88; Alpha Kappa Psi 89-; Otstndng Jr Cmptr Infrm Sys 90; Cmptr Infrmtn Sys; Sys Anlyst.

**BARRETT, SARA R,** Univ Of Sc At Aiken, Aiken, SC; SO; BA; Gamma Beta Phi 89; Pol Sci/Hstry; Law.

**BARRETT, SHARON L,** Univ Of Southern Ms, Hattiesburg, MS; JR; BA; Assoc Jones Jr Coll 90; Spec Ed; Tch.

**BARRETT JR, THOMAS LEON F,** Univ Of Nc At Charlotte, Charlotte, NC; JR; BA; Cath Yth Org VP 79-85; Clifton Heights Swm Club Diving/Swmng Tm 76-82; IMS; Am Psychlgcl Soc; Coll Prep Del City Comm Coll 90; Psychlgy; Yth/Edn.

**BARRETT, TRACY D,** Waycross Coll, Waycross, GA; SO; Bus Clb; Phi Theta Kappa; Ntrl Sci/Math Awd; Frshmn Schlr; Business; Law.

**BARRETT, VALERIE V,** Fayetteville St Univ, Fayetteville, NC; FR; BS; Chnclrs List 90; Educ; Tchng.

**BARRETTA, CARMEN F,** Hudson Valley Comm Coll, Troy, NY; FR; BA; Bus; Law.

**BARRICK, DENISE M,** Youngstown St Univ, Youngstown, OH; SR; BE; ICE 88-; ANS Secr 88-89; Engr Stdnt Soc Cncl; Centurians 88-90; Outstndg Centurian Awd 89; Tau Beta Pi Pres 90-; Omega Chi Epsilon V P 90-; Research Asst USF REU Pgm 90; Dns Lst; Fdtn Schlrshp 87-; Engr; Chem Engr.

**BARRICK, PAMELA D,** Medical Coll Of Ga, Augusta, GA; JR; BSN; Ntl Assn Nrsng Stdnts 90-; GA Assn Nrsng Stds 90-; Extrnshp Pgm Egleston Chldrns Hosp; 1st Stps Pgm Vlntr Spons Amer Cncl Chld Abuse; AA Gordon Jr Coll 80; Cert Athens Tech Schl 83; Nrsn; Ped/Psych RN.

**BARRINEAU, ELIZABETH D,** Williamsburg Tech Coll, Kingstree, SC; FR; BA; Wmsb City Hstrcl Soc-Alchl/Drg Abs Treas; Cmmsn-Cub Sct Ldr-Chrch Tchr; Mssn Ldr-Yth Advsr-Grdn Clb Pres; Miss DAR; Pres Deans Lst; CP/L Schlrshp; Phi Theta Kappa Pres; Alpha Sigma Gamma Pres; Stdnt Govt VP; Vlybl; Sclgy; Wrk Sr Ctzns.

**BARRINEAU, JULIE CLARICE,** Birmingham Southern Coll, Birmingham, AL; SO; Kappa Delta Asst Pnhllnc 90-; Ed; Early Chldhd Tchr.

**BARRINGER, DANIEL K,** Cumberland County Coll, Vineland, NJ; SO; AS; Pntbl Tm Afflтn Brtpck; Pntbl Ref 2 Lt 90; Pntbl Tm Afflтn Pntbstrs 89-90; Math Sci; Rsrch/Dsgn In Aerospace Eng.

**BARRINGER, HOPE A,** Columbia Greene Comm Coll, Hudson, NY; FR; Bus Admn; Bus.

**BARRINGTON, KIM C,** Howard Univ, Washington, DC; JR; BA; Bapt Stdnt Un Choir 89; Comm News Exe Edtr 89-; Deans Lst 88-; Intrnshp Gannett Fndtn 90; Intrnshp Minneapolis Star Tribune; Jrnlsm; Tch Univ Level.

**BARRIONUEVO, RUBEN C,** Univ Of Pr Cayey Univ Coll, Cayey, PR; FR; BA; Fedl Pool Organ 89; Natl Hnr Lst Stdnt Supp Svcs; Acctg/Bus Admin; Actnt.

**BARRIOS, LUIS E,** Fl A & M Univ, Tallahassee, FL; JR; PHARM; Hillsborough Cmmnty Clg 89-90; Hnr Soc Membr; Intrnshp Wth Wlgrns Corp; AA Hillsborough Cmmnty Clg 90; Phrmcy; Phrmcst Clncl.

**BARRIOS, LUIS G,** Miami Dade Comm Coll, Miami, FL; JR; ARCH; New Age Club 90-; Architecture.

**BARRIOS, NELSON C,** City Univ Of Ny Queensbrough, New York, NY; SO; BS; Alpha Beta Gamma; AS; Bus Admn.

**BARRIOS, ROQUE,** Univ Of Pr At Mayaguez, Mayaguez, PR; SR; BBA; APICS 90-; AIESEC 90-; Phi Kappa Phi 89-; Bus Admn Coll Hnr Rll 88-; Indstrl Mgmt Fnc.**

**BARRITEAU, LISA M,** Marshall University, Huntington, WV; GD; MBA; WVEA; NEA; Kindgrtn Tchr; B S Eastern Ky Univ 80-; Ele Educ.

**BARRON, BRIAN K,** Greenville Tech Coll, Greenville, SC; FR; BS; U S Navy 84-90; Comp Engrng.

**BARRON, DIANE M,** Univ Of Miami, Coral Gables, FL; JR; Intrnshp WTVJ Chnnl 4 NBC Miami Publ Rels 90; AA Univ FL 90; Mtn Pctrs/Spnsh.

**BARRON, JAMES W,** Liberty Univ, Lynchburg, VA; JR; BS; Libty Biology Club; Christ Serv Prog Grp Ldr 90-; Deans List 90-; Ftbl 89; Biology; Research/Tch.

**BARRON, JOHN M,** Univ Of Cincinnati-Clrmnt Coll, Batavia, OH; SO; BA; Internal Sec Spclst 88-; AS; Crmnl Sci; Private Fed Law Enfrcmnt.

**BARRON, REBECCA D,** Middle Tn St Univ, Murfreesboro, TN; SO; RRA; Assoc Stdnt Body Hmcmng Dir 90-; Beta Beta Beta Biological 90-; Phi Mu Delta; Rho Lambda; Chi Omega Ch Rm Mngr 89-; Bus Admin; Reg Rec Admin.

**BARRON, ROBIN GOOGE,** Tallahassee Comm Coll, Tallahassee, FL; FR; ASN; AA No FL Jr Coll 77; BFA Thtr ; Fl Atlantic Univ 79; Phi Theta Kappa NFJC Madison FL VP 76-77; Omega Delta Epsilon NFJC Madison FL 76-77; Nrsng; Geriatric Nsg/Onclgy.

**BARRON, SHELDON D,** Columbia Union Coll, Takoma Park, MD; SR; BS; Natl Field Archery Assn Md Archery Assn Tuscarora Archers Frederick Md 82-86; Natl Rifle Assn & Baltimore Rifle Club 80-; Black Belt Club 1st Dan Blackbelt 85-; World Martial Arts Cong For Edn 85-87; Controller Comp Firm 85-90; MIS Dir; Bus; Fin Sys Mgmt.

**BARROSO GOVEO, YALIZ,** Univ Politecnica De Pr, Hato Rey, PR; FR; MBA; Mech Engr.

**BARROSO, DIANA,** Fl International Univ, Miami, FL; GD; MS; Phi Theta Kappa 88-; Psi Chi 90-; William L Mc Knight Schlrshp 86; Ntl Dns Lst 86-87; Ntl Dns Lst 89-90; Emphs Exclnc Crtfct Achvmnt 86; AA Lib Arts Miami Dade Cmnty Clge S 88; BA Psychlgy 90; Mntl Hlth Cnslng; PH D Cnslng Psychlgy.**

**BARROW, ADRIAN G,** City Univ Of Ny Ny City Tech, Brooklyn, NY; FR; BA; Lng Islnd Clnry Assc; Morgan Grnty Trst Co Clnry Intern; Les Dames D Escoffier Schlrshp Awd; Sciete Culinaire Philanthropique De Schlrshp; Hotel/Rest Mgmt; Clnry/Hosptlty Ind.

**BARROW, ANN P,** Ny Univ, New York, NY; SR; BA; Vol The Door 90; Amer Red Crs Vol 90; Trck/Fld Actvts 90; NAFE; Occup Admin Sec ; AAS Cmptr Sci Borough Of Manhattan Comm Coll 86; Psychlgy; Pub Hlth.

**BARROW, CAROL-ANN,** The Kings Coll, Briarclf Mnr, NY; FR; BA; Drug Helphine Coord 89-; Evang Explosion Clinic Socl Coord Trnr 88-; Asst Mgr 88-F; Admin Asst 89-F; Psychology/Sociology; Counsellor.

**BARROW, ROSALIND E,** Alfred Univ, Alfred, NY; SR; BS; NAA Sec 90-; MEGA Pres 89-90; Theta Theta Chi Treas 90-; Hot Dog Day Comm Mbr 88-90; Svita 90-; Bus Admin; Acctng.

**BARROWS, DIANNE C,** Commonwealth Coll, Virginia Beach, VA; SO; Acctg Clb 89-.

**BARROWS, RHONDA S,** Castleton St Coll, Castleton, VT; JR; BA; French.

**BARRY, AMY J,** Univ Of Miami, Coral Gables, FL; JR; BS; Women In Cmnctn Inc 90-; Provost Hon Roll 90; Ring Theatre Ensmbl On The Town; Brdcstng BS Theatre BA; Theatre TV.

**BARRY, BETH A,** S U N Y At Buffalo, Buffalo, NY; SO; BS; Greater Buffalo Assn Rltrs 85-; Citzns Agnst Govt Waste 90-; PTA; Real Estate Agnt 85-; Bus Admn; Law.

**BARRY, CHRISTOPHER J,** Southern Vt Coll, Bennington, VT; SO; BA; Hmnts.

**BARRY, DANIEL G,** Western New England Coll, Springfield, MA; JR; BA; Hist; Law.

**BARRY, EDWARD M,** Oh Univ, Athens, OH; JR; Coop Stdnt Gen Elect Aircraft Engines 90-; Mech Engrng.

**BARRY, JOHN HILARY,** Univ Of The Dist Of Columbia, Washington, DC; JR; Caribbean Stdnts Assn Fndrsng Comm; CERT MMED Univ W Indies 88; Mass Media Arts; Tlvsn Prod.

**BARRY, KEVIN P,** Anne Arundel Comm Coll, Arnold, MD; SO; Crmnl Jstce Assoc Pres Treas 90; Intrnshp Anne Arundel Co Plce Dept; Crmnl Jstce.

**BARRY, MAREN E,** S U N Y Coll At Fredonia, Fredonia, NY; SO; BS; Tonmeister Assn 89-; Audio Engr Soc 90-; Clg Choir 89-; Engr; Elect Engr.

**BARRY, PATRICIA A,** George Mason Univ, Fairfax, VA; SR; Ntnl Asso/Socl Wrkrs 90-; AS N Va Comm Colg 89; Socl Work.

**BARSE, DAN E,** Cumberland County Coll, Vineland, NJ; FR; MBA; Bus Admin; Mktg/Mgmt.

**BARSHINGER, TIMOTHY A,** Indiana Univ Of Pa, Indiana, PA; JR; BS; Thtr Grove Prdtns Cst/Asst Stg Mgr 90; Dns Lst 88-90; Elem Ed.

**BARSKAYA, BETYA,** Miami Dade Comm Coll, Miami, FL; AS; Russia Refugee; Tele Tech Russia; Med; Phys Thrpst Asst.

**BARSKY, CAROL LYNN,** Memphis St Univ, Memphis, TN; SR; BS; Stdnt Activ Cncl Spec Evnts Comm Dir; Stdnt Ambssdr Bd Sec 90; Desoto Yrbk People Edtr 87-89; Phi Kappa Phi V P 90-; Omicron Delta Kappa 90-; Alpha Epsilon Delta Hstrn 89; Beta Beta Beta Pres 89; Biol; Med Schl.

**BARSTOW, THOMAS R,** Memphis St Univ, Memphis, TN; SR; BA; Kappa Tau Frat Pres 71-73; Horry Cnty Rope Rescue Tm Sec 88-; Hazardous Matrls Tm 89; Internal Soc Fire Serv Instrs 87-; N Myrtle Bch Pub Sfty Off Of Yr 89; Horry/Georgetwn Co Fire Chief Assoc 89-; AAS Pol Sci 73; AAS Ophth Disp 78; Fire Admnstrn; Chief Fire Serv.

**BART, JENNIFER A,** Draughons Jr Coll Nashville, Nashville, TN; FR; AS; Pres Lst 90; Bus Mgmt.

**BART, MELINDA E,** Clark State Comm Coll, Springfield, OH; SO; AAB; Phi Theta Kappa Alpha Nu 89; OH Chld Cnsrvtn League Steppng Stones VP 81; Cmmrcl Art; Grphc Dsgn.

**BARTEE JR, HOWARD,** Tougaloo Coll, Tougaloo, MS; SO; BA; Pltcl Sci Clb: NAACP; Spnsh Clb 90-; Alpha Phi Alpha; IM; Pltcl Sci.

**BARTEL, BRENDA J,** Comm Coll Algny Co Algny Cmps, Pittsburgh, PA; FR; BS; Carnegie Mellon Univ-Anml/Lab Tchncn 86-89; Ameri-Shred Corp-Asst Offc Mngr 89-; Assoc Median Schl Alld Hlth Careers 85; Eng; Chem Eng.

**BARTER, NANCY E,** Oh Dominican Coll, Columbus, OH; JR; BA; AIB 80-; Seminar Coord 88-89; Soc Bk Chief Rep 88-; Society Bk Op Ctr Empl Month 89; Outstndg Perf Cust Serv 88; Installment Loans 89; GBD Amer Inst Bnkg 88; SUS Cert 89; CD Bsn Concentration; Bnkg.

**BARTER, STEPHANIE,** Atlantic Union Coll, S Lancaster, MA; SO; BSC; Cmps Mnstrs 90-; Hon Core 89-; Pres Schlrshp 89-90; Chem Schlrshp; Blgy Rsrch Grant; Tmblng/Gymnstcs Clb 89-90; Blgy; Med.

**BARTH, DAVID A,** Hillsborough Comm Coll, Tampa, FL; FR; BA; HELP 90-; Sr Eng Dev Tech; Cmptr Sci; Mngmnt Infor Sys.

**BARTH, JERROLD,** Univ Of New Haven, West Haven, CT; SR; BS; Laurel Bicycle Club Of New Haven Ct; Missile Tech U S Navy Sub Serv 80-86; Elec Engrng.

**BARTHELMAN, ROLYN T,** Oh Univ, Athens, OH; SO; BA; Graphic Dsng; Advrtsng.

**BARTHOLOMEW, BOBBIE RIGGS,** Union Univ, Jackson, TN; SR; STEA; Calvary Bapt Ch; Nurs Hm Vol; FFA Local Chpt Hon Mbr; FFA Alumni Lftm Mbr; Hair Stylst; AS Jackson Sta Comm Clg 88; BS; Ele Educ; Ele Educ Tchr.

**BARTHOLOMEW, MATTHEW R,** Va Commonwealth Univ, Richmond, VA; JR; BS; Stdnt Govtmnt Sntr; Phi Eta Sigma 89-; Golden Key; Kappa Delta Rho 90-; Biology; Medicine.

**BARTICK, TRACY E,** Ms St Univ, Miss State, MS; SO; DVM; SCAVMA 90-; Amer Assn Equine Prctnrs 90; Alpha Psi 90; Pres Schlr; BA Univ Pa 87; Vet Med.

**BARTLAM, LEIGH A,** Va Commonwealth Univ, Richmond, VA; JR; BS; Urban Studies Stdnt Assoc; Drs Dwyer/Austin/Bones 88-; Urban Studies/Plng.

**BARTLE, ROBERT S,** Immaculata Coll, Immaculata, PA; SR; BA; Alpha Sigma Lambda 90-; Acctng Spvsr; Acctng.

**BARTLESON, DEBORAH J,** Wilmington Coll, New Castle, DE; SR; BSN; BSN; ADN Gloucester Clg 86; Nrsng; Cont Educ MA Phd.

**BARTLETT, CHERYL A,** Univ Of Ky, Lexington, KY; SR; BSN; Gldn Ky 89-; Nrsng; Ansthetst.

**BARTLETT, CHRISTINE B,** Univ Of Montevallo, Montevallo, AL; SR; MCS Nws Grphcs 90-; Campus Lf Crha 90-; Clg Night Hmcmng Chrldr 89-; Alpha Epsilon Sho 89-; Stdnt Supprt Tutor 90-; Dns Lst 90-; Mass Comm; Brdcstng.

**BARTLETT, STEPHAN C,** Univ Of North Fl, Jacksonville, FL; SR; BA; Hmnts Awd 89-90; Chrch Msc Mnstry; Eastern Srfng Assoc 88-89; Cert Pltng Smnshp Ycht Srvyng Chapman Scl Smnshp 87; AA St Johns Rvr Cmnty Clg 90; Ntcl Hstry/Archlgy/Ed.

**BARTLEY III, GEORGE K,** Wv Northern Comm Coll, Wheeling, WV; SO; BA; I M Bkbl; Phar; Pharmst.

**BARTLEY, KELLY L,** Univ Of Sc At Columbia, Columbia, SC; FR; MBA; Deans Lst 90-; Intrnshp Sec US Attys 90-; Engl; Jrnlsm.

**BARTLEY, NANCY G,** East Tn St Univ, Johnson City, TN; MD; AMA; Military Med Assoc; Phi Rho Sigma Sec 89-90; Rsrch Technlgst Knox Tn 82-88; AA Brghm Yng U Bio 76; BA U Of Tn Knxvle Microbio 77; Med; Med Prctce.

**BARTLEY, TAMBRA KAY,** Oh St Univ At Marion, Marion, OH; SO; BA; Psych Clb; Env Clb; Dns Lst 90; Compreh Soc Stds; Sec Educ.

**BARTLEY, WANDA E,** Cumberland Coll, Williamsburg, KY; JR; BA; Bapt Stdnt Union Clwns Coor 90-; Mrchng And Pep Bnds 90; Clr Grd 90; Acad Schlrshp 88-; Dns Lst 88-; All Amer Schlr Awrd; Educ; To Tch Hndcppd Chldrn.

**BARTO JR, RICHARD W,** Clarkson Univ, Potsdam, NY; SR; BA; Amer Mktg Asc 88-; Invstmnt Clb VP 88-89; Ordr Omega 90-; Beta Gamma Sigma 89-; Phi Kappa Phi 89-; Delta Sigma Phi Pres 90-; Clrksn Acad Spprt Ctr Tutor 87-; Pres Lst; Dns Lst; Indl Mkgt/Mech Engr.

**BARTO, WILLIAM W,** S U N Y At Buffalo, Buffalo, NY; SR; BS; Phi Eta Sgm 88-; Gldn Key 90-; Sgm Nu Almn Cntct Ofcr Sntnl 89-; Intrnshp Wrld Un Games 90; Buffalo 93; Vrsty Ftbl MVP All Amer 87-89; Mgmt/Mktg; Sales.

**BARTOK, CYNTHIA J,** Univ Of Ct, Storrs, CT; FR; BS; Intrnshp Windham Comm Meml Hosp; Windham Hosp Meml Schlrshp 90-; Cycling Tm Soc Chrwm 90-; Nutrition; Rsrch Soc Wk Intrntl.

**BARTOK, RORY E,** Edinboro Univ Of Pa, Edinboro, PA; FR; BFA; Phi Eta Sigma; Art/Apld Media Arts; Grphc Dsgn/Advrtsng.

**BARTOLOMEO, SHARONE S,** City Univ Of Ny Baruch Coll, New York, NY; SR; BA; Legl Sec/Syst Admin; AAS NYC Tech Clg 81; Acctg.

**BARTON, AMANDA C,** Univ Of Sc At Columbia, Columbia, SC; SR; Academy Stdnts Phrmcy 89-; Univ Band 86-88; Rho Chi 89-; Gamma Beta Phi 87-88; Phrmcy.

**BARTON, CHERYL L,** Fl St Univ, Tallahassee, FL; SR; Phi Theta Kappa 85-86; BSN; Nrsng.

**BARTON, KAREN LISA,** Southern Coll Of Tech, Marietta, GA; JR; BA; Pi Kappa Phi 88-; Im Sftbl 90-; Ind Eng; Tech Sls.

**BARTON, KATHRYN J,** George Mason Univ, Fairfax, VA; JR; BS; Stu Educ Assn 89-90; VA Educ Assn 89-90; Erly Elem Educ; Tchr/Spec Educ.

**BARTON, LINDA I,** Roane St Comm Coll, Harriman, TN; SO; BS; Nrsng.

**BARTON, MELANIE LEA,** Kent St Univ Kent Cmps, Kent, OH; JR; BA; Peer Awrns 90-; MENSA 90-; Golden Key 90-; Natl Rsdnc Hall 90-; Zeta Iota Psi Pres 90-; Serv Awd; Outstndng Prgrmng Ldrshp Rsdnt Staff Advsr 90-; Pltcl Sci; Hstrn.

**BARTON, MICKEY L,** Univ Of Southern Ms, Hattiesburg, MS; FR; BS; GA Boys State; Church Serv Sounting Pres 81-; Little League Bsbl Coach 87-88; Carpenter Superintendant; Computer Sci.

**BARTON, RAYMOND C,** Columbia Union Coll, Takoma Park, MD; SR; BA; Delta Sigma Tau 89-; Boarder Babies Vol DC Gen Hosp 90-; Pblshd Poems Amer Poetry Anthology 89; Publshd Shrt Stry Insight Mag 90; Jrnlsm; Freelance Wrtng/Publshng.

**BARTON, SCOTT P,** Embry Riddle Aeronautical Univ, Daytona Beach, FL; FR; Army ROTC; BSA Egle Sct; Yng Mrnes Ntl Yng Mrne Of Yr; Aeronatical Sci; Mltry.

**BARTON, SUZANNE M,** Marywood Coll, Scranton, PA; JR; BA; TV News Dir 89; Radio News Dir 90; Rsdnt Cmmttee 88; Class Pres SG 90; Newspapr Cpy Ed 90; Deans Lst 88; Stdnt Ldrshp Schlr 90; Pres Schlr 88; RA 90; Amtrak Intrn 89-90; TV Intrn; Cmmnctns; Prog Syndctr.

**BARTON, TARRA L,** Winthrop Coll, Rock Hill, SC; SO; BS; Cncl For Excptnl Chldrn 90; Intrntl Clb 90; Bapt Stdnt Union 90; Alpha Lambda Delta 90; Spec Ed; Tchr.

**BARTON, TRACEY L,** Comm Coll Algny Co Algny Cmps, Pittsburgh, PA; SO; Sclgy; Thrpst.

**BARTON, WENDE A,** Univ Of Nc At Charlotte, Charlotte, NC; SR; BA; Psychlgy Clb Pres 88-; Dnc Ensmbl Sec 89-; Apt Area Cncl 89; Pshi Chi 90-; NC Assn Rsdnc Hls Trans/Hsptlty Comm 89; Gldn Key 90-; Most Outstdng Sr Psychlgy Stdnt 90-; Psychlgy; Grad Schl Clin Psychlgy.

**BARTOSEK, SONIA E,** Indiana Univ Of Pa, Indiana, PA; JR; BS; Ntl Cncl For Tchrs Of Math 90; Math Cncl Of Wstrn Pa 90; Pa State Ed Assoc 89; Kappa Mu Epsilon 90; Phi Eta Sigma 88; Cncl For Excptnl Chldrn Treas; Ntl Cllgte Math Awd 90; All Amer Schlr Awd 90; Prvst Schlr 89-90; Math; Tchr.

**BARTOSH, SHERRY L,** West Liberty St Coll, West Liberty, WV; SR; BS; Kappa Delta Row Lil Sis 88-90; Sftbl All Conf Tm 3 Yrs 86-90; Exercise Sci; Corp Fitness.

**BARTOSHEK, GREGG R,** Villanova Univ, Villanova, PA; JR; BA; Pre-Law Scty; Phi Kappa Phi; Alpha Phi Delta 89-; Eng; Law.

**BARTOSZEK JR, JOSEPH J,** Springfield Tech Comm Coll, Springfield, MA; GD; ASN; Emt Assc; Amer Acdmy Phys Asstnt; Emr Nrs Assoc; Paramedic 84-; Cert St Augustine Tech Ctr 84; Nsg; Bs Phys Asstnt.

**BARTOW, THOMAS E,** Norfolk St Univ, Norfolk, VA; SR; BS; Army ROTC 87-; Stdnt Gvmt 90-; Natl Merit Schlr 89-90; Hnr Scty 89-90; Dstngshd Mltry Stdnt 90-; Computer Sci; Programmer/Analyst.**

**BARTRAM, JANE TAYLOR,** Marshall University, Huntington, WV; SR; SGA 88-89; Returning Stdnts Orgnztn 86-88; Sigma Delta Pi Pres 89; Eng Hnr Scty 89; BA; Spanish/Eng; Tchr.

**BARTTLEY JR, HAROLD,** Fort Valley St Coll, Fort Valley, GA; SO; BS; Sci/Math; Veterinarian.

**BARTZ, EARL N,** S U N Y Coll Of Tech At Alfred, Alfred, NY; SR; AAS; Med Lab Tech Clb Pres 90-; Phi Theta Kappa; Stdnt Emply Yr Alfred State Clg; Pres Dhon Schlr 90-; Sci; Hosp Lab Techncn.

**BARTZ, KAREN A,** Niagara Univ, Niagara Univ, NY; JR; BA; Phi Theta Kappa 90; AAS 90; Acctg; Bus.

**BARUCH, DEBORAH L,** Univ Of Rochester, Rochester, NY; SR; BS; Biochemistry Soc Co-Chrmn 89-; Cinema Group 88-; TA 90-; Emergency Vol 89; Radiology Vol 90; Marshal; Tae Kwon Doe Club 87-88; Biochemistry; Medicine.

**BARUFALDI, JAMES M,** Western New England Coll, Springfield, MA; JR; BS; Elec Engrng; Law.

**BARUM, CAREY A,** Niagara Univ, Niagara Univ, NY; FR; BBA; Stdnt Advsry Cncl Bsns Ad Orntation 90-; Alpha Kappa Psi 90-; Accntng; Tax Law.

**BARYCKI, JACQUELINE A,** S U N Y Coll Of Tech At Delhi, Delhi, NY; SO; BA; Phi Theta Kappa 89-; Phi Theta Kappa Schlrshp; PTA Past Pres 87-; Girl Scts 83-; Computer Sci Info.

**BARZANA, MARIA G,** Univ Of Pr Medical Sciences, San Juan, PR; JR; SGA Phrmcy Class Secy 90-; Math Comp Recinto Univ De Cayey 89-90; Sci; Phrmcy.

**BASA, ALAN A,** Univ Of South Al, Mobile, AL; SO; BS; Alpha Lambda Delta 90-; Bnus Mgt.

**BASAME, SOLOMON B,** Paine Coll, Augusta, GA; JR; BS; Pan African Students Alliance 89-; Chemisty Club VP 90-; Alpha Kappa Mu 90-; Amer Chem Scty 90-; Upwrd Bund Tutoring Serv Tutor 89-; Resch Prog Unv Mn; Hnr Roll 89-; Chemistry; Chemical Engrg.**

**BASCON, SERGIO R,** Saint Francis Coll, Loretto, PA; FR; BA; Eng V P 90-; Math/Chem 90-; El Circulo Espanol Sec; Natl Coll Eng Awds 90-; All Amer Schlrs 90-; Deans Lst 90; Eng; Lib Arts/Eng.

**BASEL, JOSEPH W,** Manhattan Coll, Bronx, NY; JR; BS; Amer Soc Cvl Engrs 89-; N Y Water Plutn Cntrl Assoc V P 89-; Soc Amer Mltry Engrs Sec 90-; Chi Epsilon Mrshl 90-; I M Vybl Bkbl 88-; Cvl Engr; Cvl Engr.

**BASHAM, AMY L,** Radford Univ, Radford, VA; SO; BA; Educ; Tchr.

**BASHIR, NAJAF,** Univ Of Al At Huntsville, Huntsville, AL; FR; BS; Alpha Lambda Delta; Civil Eng.

**BASI, MARYROSE,** Saint John Fisher Coll, Rochester, NY; SR; BA; Admsns Vol 90-; Radio 89; Cancer Soc Intern 90; Cert Mohawk Vly Comm Coll 89; Cmnctn/Jrnlsm; Publ Rel.

**BASICH, GINA M**, Oh Univ, Athens, OH; FR; BFA; Dnce Org 90; Dance.

**BASILA, JENNIFER A**, Barry Univ, Miami, FL; FR; BA; Life Clb Sec; Circle K; Campus Ministry; Stdnt Svcs Awrd; Pr Lst.

**BASILE, COLEEN R**, Edinboro Univ Of Pa, Edinboro, PA; JR; BS; Hnrs Pgm 88-; Phi Eta Sigma 89-; Alpha Chi 90-; Beta Beta Beta 90-; Outstndg Fresh Achvmnt Chem Award; Rocky Burkhart Schlrshp; Biology; Micr Biology.

**BASILEO, NICOLE J**, Glassboro St Coll, Glassboro, NJ; SO; BA; Dance Extnsns 89-; Chrldng 90-; Engl; Law/Attorney.

**BASINGER, LORRINE R**, Univ Of Miami, Coral Gables, FL; GD; BA; Musical Enseb FL Intl Univ Primary Flautist 84-86; Muscl Ensemb Miami Dade 86-88; Phi Kappa Phi 89-; Golden Key 89-; Alpha Kappa Delta 90-; Deans List 86-90; Prov Hnr Roll 90; AA Miami Dade Commty Clg 88; AS Miami Dade Commty Clg 88; Soc/Elem Ed; Sociology.

**BASIRICO, MATTHEW G**, Univ Of Rochester, Rochester, NY; SO; BA; Wrestling Clb 88-; Sigma Alpha Mu 87-; Mount Hope Family Ctr Cnslr 90-; Psychology; Clinical Psych.

**BASKERVILLE III, CHANNING F**, Va St Univ, Petersburg, VA; JR; Kappa Delta Pi 90-; Alpha Kappa Mu; Cubmaster 89-; Soccer Assoc Coach 76-; Good Shepherd Episc Church Vestryman; VA Stdnt Ed Assoc 89-; Natl Ed Assoc 89-; VA Bnkrs Assoc 79-89; Cert Achvmnt Elem Ed; Childrens Theatre 86-89; Elem Ed.

**BASKERVILLE, FRANSHON P**, Va St Univ, Petersburg, VA; JR; Htl/Rest Clb 88-; Mrchg Bnd 88-89; Human Eclgy; Mcdonald Intrn; Qulty Inn Intrn; Htl/Rest Mgt; Htl Ownr.

**BASKERVILLE, LINDA D**, Norfolk St Univ, Norfolk, VA; SR; BA; Spartan Alpha Tau 87; Intrnshp-Hunton YMCA; Sclgy; Urban Rsrch.

**BASKERVILLE, RAVENA L**, Clark Atlanta Univ, Atlanta, GA; SO; BS; Ntl Soc Blk Eng 89-90; Miss Fresh 89-90; Hon Spgm 89-F Miss Beta Psi 90-; Kiewit Schlr; Rowland Schlr; All Amer Schlr; Pres Schlr; Outstndng Fresh Awd; Eng; Law.

**BASKIN, BRIAN S**, Univ Of Southern Ms, Hattiesburg, MS; FR; BA; Econ; Crp Law.

**BASL, BONNIE L**, Univ Of Pa, Philadelphia, PA; FR; BA; Chrstn Flwshp 90-; Hse Cncl Rep 90-; Comp Lab Mgr 90-.

**BASL, CAROL A**, Va Commonwealth Univ, Richmond, VA; JR; BS; Golden Key; Phi Eta Sigma 90-; Kappa Tau Alpha; Intrnshp Rprtr/Prdcr/Dir Fr Commonwealth Tlk Shw 90-; Mass Cmmnctns/Grmn; Brdcst Nws.

**BASLER, CHRISTINA A**, Memphis St Univ, Memphis, TN; SR; BA; Mgmt; Hmn Rsrce Mgmt.

**BASORA-CINTRON, GRACIELA E**, Inter Amer Univ Pr Hato Rey, Hato Rey, PR; SR; BED; Spec Olympics PR 90; Hnr Rl 86-; Dns Lst 86-; Hnr Prog 86-; Spec Educ; Med.

**BASOVSKY, SVETLANA**, Univ Of Rochester, Rochester, NY; JR; BA; Shotokan Krt Clb Pres 88-; Clge Dmcrts 90; Truman Schlrshp Fnlst 90; US Hs Repr Intrnshp; Econ/Pol Sci; Pblc Serv.

**BASRI, AHMAD KAMAL HASAN**, Univ Of Rochester, Rochester, NY; SO; BS; IEEE VP; Sthsd Dorm Cncl 2nd Flr Rep 90-; Trnsfr Orntn Trnsfr Peer Advsr 90-; Elect Eng; Pro Engr.

**BASS, BRENT E**, Marshall University, Huntington, WV; JR; BBA; Ntl Mngmt Assc Sec Elect 90-; Pi Kappa Alpha Pldg Cls Sec Elect; Ashland Exploration Inc Stdnt Emplymnt Prog 88-89; Bus Mngmt.

**BASS, CHRISTIE A**, Univ Of Southern Ms, Hattiesburg, MS; FR; BS; Gamma Beta Phi; Hlth Hmn Sci; Nrsng.

**BASS, DEMOND F**, Alcorn St Univ, Lorman, MS; FR; BS; Hon Orgztn 90-; Acctg; CPA.

**BASS, E BILLY**, Fl St Univ, Tallahassee, FL; SO; BA; Indpndt Prspctv Wrtr 90-; Zeta Beta Tau Pldg Educ; AA 90; Educ; Tchr.

**BASS, FAYE B**, Norfolk St Univ, Norfolk, VA; JR; MS; Spartan Alpha Tau 90-; Beth Chaverim Temple 82-; Pres 5b Enterprises 71-; Food Sci/Nutrition.

**BASS, LYNN R W**, Utica Coll Of Syracuse Univ, Utica, NY; SR; Delta Mu Delta 85-86; Slf Emplyd 90-; BS SUNY 86; Acctg.

**BASS, MONTICA A**, East Carolina Univ, Greenville, NC; BS; Music; Educator.

**BASS, NICOLE**, Univ Of Sc At Columbia, Columbia, SC; FR; MBA; SC Athl Trainrs Assc 90-; SCAPHERD 90-; Prncpls Lst 90; Deans Lst; Bsktbl 90-; Clg Hlth; Phy Educ/Athl Trng.

**BASS, WILLIAM L**, Central Al Comm Coll, Alexander City, AL; FR; BA; AA Chair; NA Area H/I; Soc Wrk; A/D Cnslr/Adm.

**BASS, ZANDRA M**, Alcorn St Univ, Lorman, MS; JR; BS; Inter Faith Gspl Choir Treas; Inter Rsdnc Cncl Bus Mgr; Bus Ed; Tch High Schl.

**BASSETT, BETSY L**, Teikyo Post Univ, Waterbury, CT; SO; Drama Club 89-90; Day Care Ctr 89-90; Family Studies; Psych.

**BASSETT, DANA M**, Univ Of Nc At Greensboro, Greensboro, NC; SR; BS; Elem Ed; Elem Tchr.

**BASSETT, JOHN C**, Univ Of New Haven, West Haven, CT; SR; BS; Outstndng Elect Eng Stdnt Awd; Elect Eng; Eng Dsgn.

**BASSETT, LYNETTE M**, Univ Of New England, Biddeford, ME; SR; Alumni Schlr 90-; Deans Lst; RA Slctn Comm 89-; Part Actvy Jr Cls; Part Univ Nw Englnd Opn Hs 90-; Org Intractnl Theater Prod Alcohol Awrns Wk; Chrprsn Prfmg Arts Clb 89; BS; Phys Thrpy.

**BASSETT, LYNNETTE R**, Bridgewater Coll, Bridgewater, VA; SR; BA; SG Hnr Cncl Jstc 88-; Phi Beta Lambda Sec 89-; Cnslnc Assoc 88-89; Lambda Scty 88-; Alpha Chi 89-; Bus Admn.

**BASSETT, ROBIN M**, Holyoke Comm Coll, Holyoke, MA; SO; BSN; Gauntlet Berkshire Cmnty Clg Ed 83; Phi Theta Kappa 83-; VISTA 87-88; Mntl Hlth Wrkr; Nrsg.

**BASSETT, SCOTT F**, Hudson Valley Comm Coll, Troy, NY; JR; BA; Hist; Teach.

**BASSFORD, MARILYN L**, Anne Arundel Comm Coll, Arnold, MD; SO; BS; Gov Marylnd Intrnshp 90; London Town Publ Hse Edgewater M D Pr 81-; Busn; Offc Mgmt.

**BASSHAM, ANDREA J**, Univ Of Ga, Athens, GA; SR; BSED; Zeta Tau Alpha 85-86; Baptist Stdnt Union 87-88; Cmmiv Big Sis 87-; Alpha Lambda Delta 86; Gold Key Natl 88; Zeta Tau Alpha 85-86; Vol Pgm 87-; Magna Cum Laude; German 90; Tchr; German.

**BASSOLINO, ROSEMARIE**, Wagner Coll, Staten Island, NY; SR; Rsdnc Hl Cncl VP 90-; Yrbk Cmt Stf Mbr 90-; Hmcmng Cmt Flt Cmt 89; BS; Alph Dlt Pi Hnry Mbr 87-; IM Sftbl Capt 87-; Bus Admn; Mgr Mktg Cpcty.

**BASTEDO, CARLEEN SHAWN**, Atlantic Comm Coll, Mays Landing, NJ; SO; ASSRN; Catholic Church 85-; Mktng Sprvsr 85-87; Nrsng.

**BASTIAN, BRIAN A**, Saint Thomas Univ, Miami, FL; JR; BA; Rtry Clb Abaco/Mrsh Hrbr/Abaco Isl/Bahamas Dir 86-88; Snr Banker 78-90; AS Bahamas Inst Bnkrs/Clg/Bahamas 84; Acctng.

**BASTIDAS, ARTURO B**, Broward Comm Coll, Ft Lauderdale, FL; GD; MS; Sr Lab Tech; Electrncs; Engr.

**BASTIN, ERIC W**, Univ Of Tn At Martin, Martin, TN; SO; BS; TN Nat Guard 90-; US Army 86-90; Engineering.

**BASU, JEET**, Univ Of Tn At Chattanooga, Chattanooga, TN; SO; BSE; Indo Cultural Exc Org VP Acad Yr; Phi Eta Sigma; Alpha Lambda Delta; Dns Lst; Natl Coll Engr Awd; All Amer Schlr; IM Bsktbl; Engr/Math; Mech Engr.

**BASWELL, DAVID C**, Central Al Comm Coll, Alexander City, AL; FR; BS; Deans Lst 89-; Outstanding Stdnt Awd 90; SGA Rep 90; Outstanding Stdnt Awd 90; Deans Lst 89-; Cert 90; Gen/Sed; Crpntry/Tchr.

**BATALIS, BRIAN J**, Univ Of Ma At Amherst, Amherst, MA; JR; BA; Mortar Brd; Deans List 89; Hon List 90; Natl Deans List 89-; Pol Sci; Govt.**

**BATATA, SARA N**, Smith Coll, Northampton, MA; JR; BA; Tutor 90; Chr 89-; Dytn Anmtn Clb 86-; Ocnc And Atmsphrc Scis Intrn 90; Frst Grp Schlr 88-; Dns Lst 88-; Physcs Rsrch Asst; Physcs; Med.

**BATCHELOR, BEVERLY R**, Univ Of Ga, Athens, GA; SO; BSED; English Educ; Teacher.

**BATCHELOR, KATHLEEN M**, City Univ Of Ny Lehman Coll, Bronx, NY; SR; BS; Golden Key 90; Pres Schlr 90; Casslar Award/Lehman Alumni Assn 90; Lehman Fndtn Schlrshp 90-; Intrnshp NY Assn For New Americans Inc; Love Gospel Assmbly/Mnstry Cmnty 89-; Lincoln Hosp Boarder Babies Vol 90; Hlth Educ/Prmtn; Cmnty/Pblc Hlth.

**BATE, MARC C**, Univ Of Miami, Coral Gables, FL; SO; BSME; Am Soc Of Am Engrs Soph Rep; Band 89-; Hnr Stdnt Assoc 89-; Mech Engrng.

**BATEMAN, DEBRA O**, Abraham Baldwin Agri Coll, Tifton, GA; SO; AA; Chpl Chr; Alpha Beta Gamma 89-; Econ Finance; BBA State Dept.

**BATER, DAVID E**, Univ Of Sc At Columbia, Columbia, SC; SR; MBA; IM Bsktbl 88-; BS In BA; Bus.

**BATES, ADRIANE L**, Middle Tn St Univ, Murfreesboro, TN; SR; BSW; Alpha Omicron Pi Treas 88-89; Lebanon Grp Hm Intern 90; Metro Child Care Ctr Intern; Soc Work; Dir Soc Servs.

**BATES, ANDREA L**, Comm Coll Algny Co Algny Cmps, Pittsburgh, PA; SO; AS; Vol Firefighter 89-; Bus Mgmnt; Mgmnt.**

**BATES III, ARCHIE P**, Christopher Newport Coll, Newport News, VA; SO; BA; Mnrty Stdnt Assn 90-; Phi Beta Sigma VP 90-; US Air Frc Vtrn 86-90; Comp Sci; Prfssr Comp Sci.

**BATES, ARLENE A**, Ramapo Coll Of Nj, Mahwah, NJ; SO; Natl Rsdnt Shll Assoc Pres; Oprtns Assts 90; NACURH 90; Natl Rsdnts Assoc Hnry Awrd; Otstndng Actvts Awrd; Otstndng Oprtns Asstnts Awrd; Deans Lst 90; Bus Admn.**

**BATES, BRAD D**, Ky Wesleyan Coll, Owensboro, KY; JR; BS; Crmnl Jstc Assoc; Deans Lstf Oak Ivy; Rsdntl Lf Stff; Rsdnt Asst; Kndll Hll Cncl; Gmortn Intern; Ky Prre Trl Srvds Agncy; Pre Trl Rls Offcer; Ftbll; Bsktbll; Vllybll; Crmnl Jstc; Fdrl Law Enfrcmnt.

**BATES, CARLISS E**, Tuskegee Univ, Tuskegee Inst, AL; SO; BS; Eng; Law.

**BATES, CAROL H**, Livingston Univ, Livingston, AL; SR; BS; Ldrshp Schlrshp; Bus Educ; Tch.

**BATES, FRANCINE L**, Univ Of Akron, Akron, OH; SO; BA; Elem Ed; Elem Tch.

**BATES, HOLLY A**, Clemson Univ, Clemson, SC; JR; BS; SC Rec Prks Assoc Educ Chr; Clmsn Univ Union Spcl Evnts Chrprsn 90-; Clmsn Univ Union Pres; Rho Phi Landa 90-; Intrshp George Williams Coll Wisc; Stevenson/Smith/Lovett Awrd Otstndg Ldrshp/Serv; Prks Rec Trsm Mgmnt; Camp Dir.

**BATES, JESSICA L**, Va Commonwealth Univ, Richmond, VA; SR; BS; Diving Tm 88-90; Spec Ed/Mental Retardation.

**BATES, KARL ROBERT**, Spalding Univ, Louisville, KY; SR; BS; Stdnts Scl Actn Pres 90-; Amnsty Intl Pres Orgnzr 90-; Itern Kntcky Yth Advcts 90-; Natl Assoc Scl Wrkrs 90-; Bus Exprnc; AA 88; Scl Wrk.

**BATES, LARANNA LYNN**, Ky Christian Coll, Grayson, KY; FR; BA; Lwr Grssy Chrch Chrst 85-90; Wstsd Chrstn Chrcn 90-; Sci Math; Physcst.

**BATES, LEE ANN MARIE**, Univ Of Southern Ms, Hattiesburg, MS; SO; BM; Pride Of Ms Mrchng Bnd 89; Phi Eta Sigma 89; Nu Phi Epsilon 90; Tau Beta Sigma Treas 89; Music Perf/Bsnss; Music Bsnss.

**BATES, LINDA M**, Draughons Jr Coll Nashville, Nashville, TN; SO; AS; Pres Lst; Dir Human Rsrceds 87-; Bus Mgmt.

**BATES, MICHAEL W**, Univ Of Tn At Martin, Martin, TN; SR; BA; Phi Theta Kappa; Gamma Beta Phi; Phi Chi Theta; Dean Lst; Hnr Rll; Ecnmcs; Law.

**BATES, PAUL J**, Univ Of Nc At Charlotte, Charlotte, NC; SR; BS; Pi Mu Epsilon 88-; MAA 89-; SSA 89-; Dstngshd Hnrs Lst Clge Charleston 87; Coop Bell Northern Rsrch Inc 90; Coop VPS Div Info Systms 89-90; Math.

**BATES, RACHEL J**, Univ Of Sc At Columbia, Columbia, SC; SO; BA; Golf 89-; Sport Admin; Golfing Bsn.

**BATES, RETA M**, Ky Wesleyan Coll, Owensboro, KY; JR; BA; Mthdst Stdnt Flwshp 87-; Mc Lean Cnty HELP Offc Pres 85-90; KY Wslyn Pres Schlrshp 88-; Islnd Untd Mthdst Chrch Schlrshp 88-; M/G Hutton Schlrshp 90-; K A Stovall Schlrshp 90-; M Christian Fndtn Schlrshp; Rlgn/Phlsphy; Ordnd Mnstr.

**BATES III, ROBERT EDWARD**, Univ Of Miami, Coral Gables, FL; FR; Mbr Crew Tm 90-; Lambda Chi Alpha 90-; 8 Man 1st State 90-; Sci/Engr; Ocean Engr.

**BATES, SHELLEY L**, Westminster Coll, New Wilmingtn, PA; JR; BA; Union Prgmrg Comm Sec 89-90; House Cncl VP 88-89; Res Hall Adv Brd Sec 88-89; Kappa Delta Phi 90-; Omicron Delta Kappa; Alpha Gamma Delta Sec 89-; Dns Lst 90-; Hnr Role 90-; Elem Educ; Tchg.

**BATES, SHELLY R**, Oh Univ, Athens, OH; SO; BFA; Pblc Rltns Phtgrphr Intrn 90; Vsl Comm.

**BATES, STEPHANIE L**, Univ Of Ky, Lexington, KY; FR; BS; Baptst Stdnt Un; Bio; Medcn.

**BATH, CHRISTOPHER W**, Pellissippi St Tech Comm Coll, Knoxville, TN; FR; BA; Acctg; Bus.

**BATH, ERIN J**, Lancaster Bible Coll, Lancaster, PA; SO; BS; New Hope Support Grp Facltr; CheerLDNG; Biblical Cnslng.

**BATHRAS, PATRICK J**, Anne Arundel Comm Coll, Arnold, MD; SO; BA; AA 90; Elem Educ; Elem Tchr.

**BATISTA TORRES, GLADYS S**, Univ Of Pr At Rio Piedras, Rio Piedras, PR; GD; MPA; Bnd 81; Taller Mscl Grp 83-84; Stu Assn Pblc Admn 90-; 1st Hgh Hnr Grad Univ PR 83; 2ND Hgh Nrs UPR 87; Angel Ramos Fndtn Schlrshp 81-82; PR Assn Physcl Thrpy 86-87; AD Univ PR 83; BS 87; Pblc Admn; Sprvsry Tsks Physcl Thrpy.

**BATISTA, NANCY A**, Fl International Univ, Miami, FL; FR; BACH; Bus Admin; Mngmnt.

**BATOR, KATHLEEN M**, Ramapo Coll Of Nj, Mahwah, NJ; SR; BS; Hmn Rsrce/Mgmt Soc Pres 90-; Yrbk Phtgrphr 87-88; Tenure Comm Stdnt Rep 90-; Delta Mu Delta 90-; Phi Alpha Delta 90-; Deans Lst 87-; Bus Mgmt/Intl Bus; Intl Law.

**BATSON, ALLYSON L**, Ms St Univ, Miss State, MS; JR; BA; Kappa Delta Pi 90-; Kappa Delta; Sigma Chi Lil Sister Alumni Rltns 90; Elem Educ; Teach/Counsel.

**BATSON, APRIL L**, Winthrop Coll, Rock Hill, SC; JR; BA; BSU Pianst 88-; Piano Tchr 88-90; Glee Clb Acmpnst 88-; Alpha Lambda Delta 88-90; Phi Kappa Phi 90-; Delta Omicron Chpln 90-; Brnx Smmr Mssnry 90; Cmp Music Dir; Wnthrop Schlr Schlrshp 88; Music/Psychlgy; Music Therpst MA.

**BATT, CHRISTINA M**, Defiance Coll, Defiance, OH; SR; BS; Gamma Omega Kappa Pres Advsr 90; Elem Educ; Masters El Educ.

**BATT, ERIK D**, S U N Y At Buffalo, Buffalo, NY; SR; BS; Alumni Assn U S Chess Fdrtn; Dns Lst 88-90; Admin Aide Mayor Elizabeth Hoffman 89; Assoc Niagara Cnty Comm Coll 89; Acctntng.

**BATT, PAUL J**, Alfred Univ, Alfred, NY; JR; BS; Amer Soc Mech Engrs 90-; Soc Auto Engrs 90-; Sigma Alpha Mu 89-; Vars Diving 88-89; Mech Engr; Engr.

**BATTE, R LEONE**, Oh Dominican Coll, Columbus, OH; SR; BED; Emplyd Franklin Cnty Bd Mntl Rtrdtn/Dvlpmnt Disabilities; Spec Educ; Tchr.

**BATTEN, BRENDA K**, Miami Jacobs Jr Coll Of Bus, Dayton, OH; SO; AD; Med Ofc Admin.

**BATTEN, SHIRLEY J**, Waycross Coll, Waycross, GA; FR; ADN; Nrsg; Hosp Admin.

**BATTEN, TONI L**, Univ Of North Fl, Jacksonville, FL; SR; BED; Phi Theta Kappa; Elem Ed; Tchg.

**BATTERSBY, KAREN R**, Georgian Court Coll, Lakewood, NJ; SO; BA; Spec Educ; Teach/Law.

**BATTISTA, FRANCES H**, Bunker Hill Comm Coll, Boston, MA; SO; BSW; Phi Theta Kappa; Steve Harper Awd; Smrvl Rcrtn Dpt; Psychiatric Srvcs; Spcl Edctn Rsdntl Shltr Prntng Teens; Hmn Servcs Scl Wrk; Lic Sw.

**BATTISTA, JOANNA**, Fl International Univ, Miami, FL; JR; BA; Pub Admin; Fedrl Gov.

**BATTISTA, MARIA,** Univ Of South Al, Mobile, AL; SO; BA; Cert Otsdng Acad Achvmnt Hon Soc Phi Kappa Phi; Bkkppr; Bus Admn; Intl Bus.

**BATTISTA, MARY K,** De Tech & Comm Coll At Dover, Dover, DE; LPN; DAFB NCD Clb 86-; Phi Beta Lambda 84; NCO Wives Clb DAFB 86-91; St Clares Rlgus Educ 82-84; Ltl Lgue Coach 81-83; Deans Lst 90-; Ct Phi Beta Lambda 84; Vol Sprt Desert Storm; Dip Acad Bus Careers 84; Nurs.

**BATTISTE, CATHLEEN A,** Glassboro St Coll, Glassboro, NJ; JR; BS; NJ PIRG 90-; Math Club; Hon Studies; Tutoring Ctr 90-; Math.

**BATTLE, BERTHA M,** Saint Petersburg Jr Coll, St Petersburg, FL; SO; AA; Fla Women In Govt 87-; AS Bus Admin Mgmt SPJC 78; Bus Admin.

**BATTLE, DEANA N,** Va St Univ, Petersburg, VA; SR; BS; Big Bro/Sis Org 88-; Bus Admin Clb 88-; Ntl Assn Advnc Clrd People 89-; Bus Mgmt; Own Htl/Mc Dnlds.

**BATTLE, KIMBERLY A,** Valdosta St Coll, Valdosta, GA; FR; Mnrty Acad Perf Awd 90-; IM Bsktbl 90-; Frnch; Lang Trnsltr.

**BATTLE-MULLICE, BRIDGET,** Savannah St Coll, Savannah, GA; JR; BA; Mass Cmnctns Clb PR Rep 90-; Nwspr Bus Mgr 90-; TV Prod Asst 90-; Mass Cmnctns; Pblc Rltns.

**BATTLES, MEGAN I,** Md Inst Coll Of Art, Baltimore, MD; GD; MFA; Glry Intrn 90; W Fergeson Schlrshp Mrt 88-89; F B Thalthiemer Schlrshp 87; Grainger Trvlng Schlrshp; BFA Md Inst; Fine Arts.

**BATTOE, ANITA K,** Eckerd Coll, St Petersburg, FL; SR; BA; Hlth Advsry Comm 90-; Psychlgy Clb 89-90; Lbrary Comm 90-; Hon Schlrshp 87-; Intrnshp Bayfrnt Med Cntr; Hmn Dvlpmnt; Law.

**BATTON, JAMES S,** Univ Of Sc At Columbia, Columbia, SC; SO; MBA; Econs; Govt.

**BATTS, LEIGH A,** Belmont Coll, Nashville, TN; JR; BS; Soph Jr And Sr Clss VP 89-; Bapt Stdnt Unn 88-; Gamma Beta Phi; Blue Key Sec; Scl Wrk; Cnslng.

**BATTS, PAULETTE M,** James Sprunt Comm Coll, Kenansville, NC; SO; BA; Stdnt Of Mnth; Dpln Cnty Fr Mgr; Comm Srvce Coor JSCC; Bus.

**BAUDISCH, JERRI M,** Univ Of Bridgeport, Bridgeport, CT; SR; Phi Kappa Phi; Pres Lst 90; BES 90; Tchr.

**BAUER, BONNIE S,** Northern Ky Univ, Highland Hts, KY; JR; BS; NAFE; Bptst Chrch Sndy Schl Dir 88-90; Psy; Cnslr.

**BAUER, CAROL P,** Univ Of De, Newark, DE; FR; BSPE; Res Stdnt Assn Flr Rep 90-; Deans Lst 90-; Track/Fld 90-; Phys Educ; Tchr.

**BAUER, CONNIE M,** Atlantic Comm Coll, Mays Landing, NJ; FR; Actng/Finance; Cpa.

**BAUER, DANA E,** Pa St Univ Allentown Cmps, Fogelsville, PA; SO; BA; Communications; Brdcst/Cable.**

**BAUER, DEREK T,** Brevard Coll, Brevard, NC; FR; BA; History; Foreign Serv/Tchng.

**BAUER, JOSEPH M,** Univ Of Rochester, Rochester, NY; SR; BA; Phi Beta Kappa; Math.

**BAUER, MARLEEN L,** Univ Of Sc At Aiken, Aiken, SC; JR; BS; Math/Comp Sci Clb Pres 88-91; USCA Pcstr Stdnt Orientatn Ldr 88-90; USCA Pep Band 88-89; Gamma Beta Phi 89-; 1SCA Stdnt Ambssdr 90-; Math/Comp Sci; Comp Prgrmng.

**BAUER, MICHAEL C,** Tn Temple Univ, Chattanooga, TN; JR; BA; Pstrl Stds; Yth Mnstr.

**BAUERLE, DOLORES DE FANTI,** Univ Of Fl, Gainesville, FL; SR; BSN; Fla Trck Clb 90-; FNA/ANA Fl Nrs Assoc/Amer Nrs Assoc; Cert Ophthlmc Asst; Cert Ophthlmc Surg Asst; Cert Jnt Cmsn Ald Hlth Prsnl Ophthmlgy; ADN Santa Fe Cmnty Clge 89; Nrsg; Nrsg Rsrch/Ed.

**BAUGESS, HEATHER E,** Oh Dominican Coll, Columbus, OH; GD; CERTI; Phi Kappa Phi 88-; Kappa Delta 85-88; Faith Untd Meth Chrch 84-; Elem Schl Sub Tchr 89-; BA Morehead St Univ 88; Lbry Sci; Tchr/Librarian.

**BAUGH, ANNIE C,** Nova Univ, Ft Lauderdale, FL; GD; MBA; South FL Divers Inc; Sr Tech Support Specist; BS 90; Bus.

**BAUGH, CRYSTAL D,** Va St Univ, Petersburg, VA; JR; Acctng Cl; Pres List Kee Busn Colg 87-88; BCA Dipl Ntnl Edctn Cen Kee Busn Colg 88; Acctng; CPA.

**BAUGH, JONI L,** Ms St Univ, Miss State, MS; SO; BA; Church Puppeteer Ldr 89-; VBS Tchr; Dns Lst U AR Little Rock 90; Pres Schlr MS State U; Am Bsn Wmns Assc Schlrshp NALR Schlrshp 89-90; Pltcl Sci; Pltcs Natl Level.

**BAUGH, KATINA,** Tougaloo Coll, Tougaloo, MS; FR; Drill Tm; Alpha Lambda Delta; Econ; Acctg.

**BAUGH, LISA M,** Middle Tn St Univ, Murfreesboro, TN; SR; Rush Cnslr 89; Orientation Asst 87-88; Alpha Delta Pi 86-; Ltl Sis 88-; IM Vlybl/Sftbl; BS; Mktg Ed.

**BAUGH, MELYSSA E,** Livingston Univ, Livingston, AL; SR; BS; Bptst Stdnt Un 87-; Lvngstn Univ Tgr Bnd 88-89; Phi Theta Kappa 87-; Alpha Sigma Tau 87-; Delta Phi Sigma VP 88-; AS Shltn St Comm Coll 87-88; Elem Educ; Tchr.

**BAUGHAN, MARY KATHERINE,** Patrick Henry Comm Coll, Martinsville, VA; SO; ASS; Cllgt Sec Intrntnl Sec 89-; Phi Theta Kappa 90-; Deans Lst 89-; Mmbr Yr Cllgt Sec Intnl 89-; Offc Systm Tchnlgy; Exec Sec.

**BAUGHER, JOHN D,** Salisbury St Univ, Salisbury, MD; SR; BA; 1986 Ntnl Chmpnshp Team 86-90; Member German Clb 86-88; Member Phi Alpha Theta 90; Mc Cormick Unsung Hero Awrd Schlrshp 85-86; Bobby Richards Memorial Awrd 90; Stdnt Tchr Patuxent Vly MS Oaklnd Mills HS Howard; History/Ed; Tch.

**BAUGHMAN, ANGELA J,** Livingston Univ, Livingston, AL; SO; BS; Cardinal Key; Mathematics; Secondary Education.

**BAUGHMAN, LAURIE MICHELLE,** Univ Of Sc At Aiken, Aiken, SC; FR; MBA; Bus; Acctg/CPA.

**BAUGHN, KYLE S,** Defiance Coll, Defiance, OH; JR; BA; Defiance Clg Chmbr Sngrs Pres 89-; Pres Hosts 90-; Tchrs Ed Loan Pgm; Eagle Sct 86; Gamma Omega Kappa 90-; Herbert S Beane Schlrshp 90; Msc Grant 89-; Vrsty Ftbl 89-; Dorothy Houck Weaner Mem Schlrshp 89-; Vrsty Wrstlng 89-; Math/Msc; Scndry Ed.

**BAUGHN, TRENTON C,** Univ Of Southern Ms, Hattiesburg, MS; SR; BS; Sigma Lamda Chi Pres; Archtctrl Eng Tech; Archtct.

**BAUKMAN, WILLIE L,** Univ Of Sc At Columbia, Columbia, SC; SO; BS; Natl Scty Blck Eng 89-; Gamma Beta Phi 90-; Alpha Lambda Delta 90-; Phi Eta Sigma 90-Intern Rnld Mcnr Prgm; Mchncl Eng; Eng.

**BAUKNIGHT, AMY L,** Univ Of Sc At Columbia, Columbia, SC; FR; BA; Business Admin; Marketing Finance.

**BAULSIR, JAMES T,** Bridgeport Engr Inst, Fairfield, CT; FR; Mgr Spcb Dsgn V Band Corp Elmsford NY; Elec Engr.

**BAUM, ANYA J,** Smith Coll, Northampton, MA; FR; BA; Coll Chr Alpha 90-; Audubon Soc Vol 90-; Govt; Envrmntl Admn.

**BAUM, WENDI C,** Memphis St Univ, Memphis, TN; JR; BS; Physcl Thrpy.

**BAUMAN, DONALD G,** Bowling Green St Univ, Bowling Green, OH; SR; BS; Instrmntn Soc Amer 2nd Fhr 88-; Soc Manuf Engr 88-; Phi Kappa Phi 89-; Intrn AT/T Bell Lab; Assoc Appld Sci 90; Elctrnc Tech; Elec Engr.

**BAUMAN, JAMES A,** Lexington Comm Coll, Lexington, KY; FR; BS; USAF Sgt 85-90; Sci; Engr.

**BAUMAN, TAMMY J,** Mt Saint Marys Coll & Seminary, Emmitsburg, MD; SO; BS; Hall Govt Sec 90-; Phi Beta Delta 89-; Admsns Asst 89-; G H Miles Hon Soc 89-; ACS; I M Vybl 90-; Bio Chem; Rsrch.

**BAUMANN, ERIC C,** Xavier Univ, Cincinnati, OH; FR; BA; Pre Med Clb 90-; Deans Lst 90-; Floor Hcky/Flg Ftbl 90-; Natural Sci; Medicine.

**BAUMANN, HEIDI M,** Univ Of Tn At Martin, Martin, TN; SO; PHARM; Chi Alpha 89-; Amer Chmcl Scty 90-; Hnrs Smnr 89-; Phi Kapp Phi Awd; Univ Schlrs; Hortons Pre-Proffessional Awd; Sftbl; Pharmacy.

**BAUMANN, KAREN L,** Endicott Coll, Beverly, MA; Bus Clb 89-; Shpmts 89-; Orient Ldr 89-; Phi Theta Kappa VP 90-; Sftbl Capt 89-; Sccr 89-F Bsktbl 89-; Law.

**BAUMANN III, RICHARD M,** Dowling Coll, Oakdale Li, NY; SR; BBA; Mngmnt; Trnsprttn Mngmnt.

**BAUMER, MARGARET MARY,** Northern Ky Univ, Highland Hts, KY; JR; BED; Soup Ktchns Vol 85-; Vol Cafeteria Local High Schl; Cook 85-; Phy Ed/Hlth; High Schl Phy Ed Tchr.

**BAUMGARNER, CHARLES D,** Pace Univ At Pleasantville, Pleasantville, NY; SR; ACS 89-; Chem Scty Vp 89-; Scitfc Scty 89-; Scitfc Scty Pres 90-; Deans Lst 90-; ACS Awd 90; Biochem Awd; Srvc Awd; BS; Biochem; Orgnc Chem.**

**BAUMGARTNER, GARY J,** Georgetown Univ, Washington, DC; JR; BBA; Acdmc Cncl 88-; Admssns Ambssdr Pgm 88-90; Stdnt Asst/Advsr 90; Deans Lst 89-; Bd Dir 90-; Assoc Cnsltng Asst; Crdt Union Mngr 90-; Intl Mgmt/Fin; Fincl Serv.

**BAUMGARTNER, THERESA,** Gallaudet Univ, Washington, DC; JR; BSW; Social Work Stdts Assoc Sec; Social Work.

**BAUMGARTNER, WENDY A,** Univ Of Pittsburgh, Pittsburgh, PA; SO; BSN; AF Rotc 89-; NSA 89-; Arnld Ar Scty Comptrllr 90-; Ar Frc Assoc 90-91; Deans Lst 90; Nrsng.

**BAUMLE, LAURA K,** Defiance Coll, Defiance, OH; FR; BS; Rstrtn Eclgy Scty; Phn Thn; Chmstry Lab Asst; Sci.

**BAUSERMAN, DIANA L,** Muskingum Coll, New Concord, OH; SO; Adlt Lrnrs Clb 90-; Sclgy Clb; Stdnt Sclgy Asst; Sclgy/Psych,Bsns; Tchng.

**BAVA, MELANIE L,** Davis & Elkins Coll, Elkins, WV; SO; BS; Stdnt Advsry Cncl Retention; Beta Alpha Beta; Mgr Retail Outlet State WV Alcohol Beverage Cntrl Commission 85-90; Mgmt-Bsn; Mgmt.

**BAVARO, PATRICE A,** Fordham Univ, Bronx, NY; SO; BA; Acctg.

**BAX, STEPHANIE L,** Niagara Univ, Niagara Univ, NY; JR; BA; Niagara Univ Plyrs 90-; Intrntl Thes Soc 83-; John F Eiklor Thtr Schlrshp 85; Acad Schlrshp 90-; Assoc Niagara Cnty Comm Coll 87; Thtre/Engl Mnr; Aspiring Actress/Tchr.

**BAXA, LOUISE M,** Valdosta St Coll, Valdosta, GA; JR; BBA; Alpha Epsln Alpha VP; VITA; Dewar Fdn Schlp 90-; Quota Clb Schlp 89; Becker Schlp; GA Soc CPA Schlp; Acctng/Fnce.

**BAXA, SARAH H,** Coll Of Charleston, Charleston, SC; SR; BS; Srrty 88; Coll Chr 89; Stdnt Cncl Fr Except Chldrn 89-; Spec Educ; Tch Emtnlly Hndcppd Lrng Dsbld Kds.

**BAXLEY, DONNA R,** Judson Coll, Marion, AL; SR; BS; Stdnt Gov Cl Rep 90-; Sci Cl 88-; J Jewett Hon Soc Pres 90-; Judson Schol Treas 88-; Beta Beta Beta Pres Pres 89-; Perry County Litcy 90-; Biol Awd 89; Chem Awd 89; Faulkner Awd; Biol; Med.

**BAXLEY, LANCE,** Central Fl Comm Coll, Ocala, FL; FR; BA; Bus Admn; Law/Accntng.

**BAXTER, KELLY R,** Livingston Univ, Livingston, AL; SO; BA; Stdnt Gvrnmnt Assn Rep 90; IM Sprts Actvty Non-Athletics Prgrms Brd Drctr Pblcty; Sigma Tau Delta; Hghst Grd Point Avrg Spieth Hall Rsdnt Asst; Englsh; Cvl Srvc.

**BAXTER, KEVIN W,** Defiance Coll, Defiance, OH; JR; BS; Comp Oper; AA Nrthwst Tech Clg 85; Comp Sci.

**BAXTER, MARIAN L,** Univ Of Tn At Knoxville, Knoxville, TN; FR; BS; Ut Mrchg Cncrt Bnds 90-; Bnd Schlrshp Flute; Spcl Educ; Deaf Ed.

**BAXTER, RONALD D,** Nova Univ, Ft Lauderdale, FL; GD; MBA; Air Frc Sgts Assoc Dvsn Pres 78-80; Sr Engrg Wrtr Allied Signal Bendix; BS 88; Mgmt.

**BAY, KRISTIN KELLI,** Lasell Coll, Newton, MA; FR; BA; Stdnt Govt Exec Sec 90-; Planning Comm Comm Mbr 90-; Vlybl Player 90; Hnrs List 90; Spec Olympics 88-; Vlybl Varsity 90; Human Serv; Psych.

**BAYATAFSHAR, MEHDI REZA,** Germanna Comm Coll, Locust Grove, VA; Poetry Awrd 90-; Math Tutr 90-; AS Tehran-Iran Univ 77; Cvl Eng.

**BAYE, KEVIN L,** S U N Y At Buffalo, Buffalo, NY; SR; BS; Amer Mrktng Assc 90-; Delta Sigma Pi Pres 90-; Bus Admn; Mrktng Mngmnt.

**BAYER, ALLISON L,** Univ Of Sc At Columbia, Columbia, SC; JR; BA; Deans List 90-; Govt/Intl Stds.

**BAYER, JILL M,** Nova Univ, Ft Lauderdale, FL; GD; MA; Soc Hmn Rsrc Mgmt Prfsnl Hmn Rsrc Assoc Broward Co 89-; Hmn Rsrc Mgr Dayton Granger Inc 89-; BA Cmnctns MI St Univ 84; Trng/Tchg.

**BAYGENTS, KATHY H,** Univ Of Southern Ms, Hattiesburg, MS; JR; BS; Crmnl Juste Assn 90; Sftbl Coach 83-; Lttr J Awd JCJC 90; AA Jones Cty Jr Clg 90; Psychology; Crmnl Psychlgst.

**BAYLES, BOBBY RAY,** Church Of God Sch Of Theology, Cleveland, TN; GD; M DIV; Soph Cls V P 81-82; Sr Cls Pres 88-89; Delta Epsilon Chi; Magna Cum Lauds 89; Chrstn Serv Awd Prison Asst Chpln 89; Louis Cross Endwd Schlrshp 90; BA E Coast Bible Clg 89; Theology; Tch.

**BAYLES, KENNETH C,** Newbury Coll, Brookline, MA; GD.

**BAYLESS, ANGELA P,** Central St Univ, Wilberforce, OH; SO; BA; Phi Mu Alpha; Hon Rctl NATS; IM Sftbl; Music; Educ.

**BAYLEY, KERRY M,** Air Force Inst Of Tech, Wrt-Ptrsn Afb, OH; GD; MSC; Sigma Iota Epsilon; Aircraft Engineering/Maintenance Mgmt/Materials Specifications; BSC Univ Melbourne 79; BE Swinburne Instit Tech 86; Logistics; Engineering/Logistics.

**BAYLIS, RANDI J,** Saint Francis Coll, Loretto, PA; SR; BA; Loretto Wrtr; Peer Tutor; Sigma Tau Delta 89-; Phi Sigma Iota Pres 89-; Theta Phi Alpha Hstrn; Hmcmng Queen; Sccr Capt 87-; Amer Stds; Grad Schl.

**BAYLIS-JONSSON, RUTHELLYN,** Univ Of Md At Eastern Shore, Princess Anne, MD; JR; BA; Kappa Delta Pi; Sub Tchr 90-; AA Allegany Comm Coll 89f; Spec Ed; Tchng.

**BAYLOCK, IRENE E,** S U N Y Coll Of Tech At Alfred, Alfred, NY; FR; AAS; Acctng Clb 90-; Acctng.

**BAYLOR, ALONZO L,** Va St Univ, Petersburg, VA; SO; VSU Drftng Clb Sed; VSU Almn Assoc.

**BAYLOSIS, ANNA MARIE EDNACO,** Old Dominion Univ, Norfolk, VA; SR; BS; AS Dgr Tidewater Comm Coll 89; Mktng Ed Trng Spec; Buyer Tlng.

**BAYNARD, JAMES D,** Brevard Coll, Brevard, NC; FR; Prcsn Ensmbl; Coll Sngrs; Cncrt Bnd; Phi Theta Kappa; Rcqtbl/Tnns; Music.

**BAYNE, MARIAN T,** Notre Dame Coll, Cleveland, OH; SR; BS; Masquers Theatrical Grp VP 90-; Campus Activities Brd Publ Chr 89-90; Amer Inst Biological Sci Tres 89-; Amer Red Cross Bloodmobile 87-; Natl Clgt Student Govt Awd; Hnrbl Mention Clg Art Show; Vlybl 88-89; Biology; Environmental Hlth.

**BAYNE, ROBERT E,** Hillsborough Comm Coll, Tampa, FL; FR; AA; Drama Clb 89-; Engl; Prof.

**BAYNHAM, SHANNON L,** Univ Of Sc At Columbia, Columbia, SC; SO; BA; FCA 89-; Rfrmd Univ Fllwshp 89-; Kappa Alpha Theta 89-; Jrnlsm.

**BAYNUM, PAULA ANN,** Northern Ky Univ, Highland Hts, KY; SR; BSW; Socl Wrk Clb 89-; Pinnacle 90-; Schlrs Amer 90-; Alpha Chi; Stdnt Schlrshp Awd 89-; Diocse Asst Coordntr Nw Bgnngs Mnstry 88-; Clncl Socl Wrk/Tchng.

**BAYRON, HECTOR J,** Inter Amer Univ Pr Hato Rey, Hato Rey, PR; SO; Cngrjs Ycht Clb 78-; PRNG 1st BN 155 FA B Btry Chf Of FDC Sctn 85; Prche Clb Treas 88-; Chmbr Of Cmmrce 85-; Natl Assn Of Msc Mrchnts 81-; Snd And Lght Tech Eng; BBA Mrktng; Law.

**BAZAN, NANCY,** Western New England Coll, Springfield, MA; JR; BSBA; Mgmnt Assoc Pres 88-; Peer Advsr 89-; Delta Mu Delta; Alpha Lamda Delta 89-; Stdnt Ambssdr 90-; Var Sftbl 88-; Var Bsktbl Co Cpt 88-; Finance.

**BAZAN-ARIAS, NORMA C,** Univ Of Pittsburgh, Pittsburgh, PA; JR; BS; Natl Soc Of Profsnl Engrs VP; Pittsbrgh Intrntl Stdnt Org Secy 90-; Engr Stdnt Cabnt Civil Engr Rep 89-; Golden Key Treas 90-; Tau Beta Pi Treas 90-; Chi Epsilon Treas; Latin Amercn Cultural Un Dancer 85-; Engr Hon Schlrshp 88-; Civil Engr; Consltng Firm.

**BAZAROV, ALEX V,** Cornell Univ Statutory College, Ithaca, NY; SO; BS; Hebrew Immigrant Aid Scty Schlrshp 89; Alpha Zeta Schlrshp 90; Entmlgy; Rsrchs Bio Chmstry.

**BAZARTE, NERISSA A,** Central Fl Comm Coll, Ocala, FL; FR; BS; DCT I 87-88; DCT Ii 88-89; Bus Admn; Cmptrs.

**BAZELAIS, DINA,** Va St Univ, Petersburg, VA; FR; BA; TAPS Assoc Plctcl Sci Stdnts; NJ Pre Almn Clb; Pltcl Sci; Law.

**BAZELEY, CHRISTOPHER C,** Oh Univ, Athens, OH; FR; BSCE; Air Frc ROTC Prjct Warrior Ofcr 90-; IM Sprts 90-; Cvl Eng; Mngmnt Eng Fld.

**BAZEMORE, CARTHENE R,** Norfolk St Univ, Norfolk, VA; SO; Premed Soc Sec 89; Band New Recruits Pres 90-; SG 89-; Spartan Alpha Tau 90-; Alpha Kappa Mu; Dozoretz Inst Schlr 89-; Gen Mills Schlrshp/Intern; Chem; Chem Eng.

**BAZEMORE, DAPHNE S,** Univ Of Nc At Chapel Hill, Chapel Hill, NC; FR; BS; BSM Gospel Choir 90-; Musical Theatre 90-; INROADS Intrnshp IBM; N C Fellows; Bus Admn; Acctg.

**BAZINET, LINDA L,** Springfield Tech Comm Coll, Springfield, MA; FR; ECE; Daycare/Fmly Lvng Clb Pres; OLSH Schl Assn VP 88-; Lgl Sec; Fulltime Mother; Early Childhood; Tchr.

**BAZYLAK, GREGORY M,** Duquesne Univ, Pittsburgh, PA; GD; Sigma Tau Gamma VP Mgmt 87-88; BS 90; Law.

**BAZYN, BRIAN J,** Univ Of Sc At Columbia, Columbia, SC; JR; BS; Acctg; CPA.

**BAZZIE, KIMBERLY A,** Wv Univ, Morgantown, WV; JR; BS; Pharm.

**BEACH, ANDREW B,** Univ Of Cin R Walters Coll, Blue Ash, OH; SO; BS; Alpha Beta Gamma; Byr Cntrct Admin Arcrft Engne Prts 85-; Mnfc Mtrls Mgmt.

**BEACH, HEIDI M,** Christopher Newport Coll, Newport News, VA; SO; BSBA; Mngmnt; Chldcr Admn.

**BEACH, SALLY A ASIP,** Ga St Univ, Atlanta, GA; GD; Stu Tch 90; BSE GA St Univ 90; Educ; Tchng.

**BEACH, STEVEN F,** Univ Of Louisville, Louisville, KY; SR; MA; Am Soc Mech Eng; Dow Chem Co Coop Intrnshp 89-; Mech Eng; Engrng.

**BEACHAM, CHRISTINE R,** Castleton St Coll, Castleton, VT; SR; BED; Polt Disc VP 88-; All Amer Schlr Clg; Kappa Delta Pi Histn Local 90-; Serv Awd 90; Pres List; Deans List 89-; MVP 90 Seanson Tns 89-90; Middlebury Recre Brd Chrmn; Brd Trusters Addison County Hlth Co 79-81.

**BEACHY, STEPHEN R,** Millersville Univ Of Pa, Millersville, PA; FR; BA; Hnrs Prgrm 90-; Accntng; Cpa.

**BEACOM, JAMES P,** Kent St Univ Kent Cmps, Kent, OH; SR; BBA; Bus; Mgmt.

**BEADLING, LEE R,** Glassboro St Coll, Glassboro, NJ; JR; BA; Jrnlsm; Publshng/Nwspr.

**BEAGLE, BRENDA J,** Richard Bland Coll, Petersburg, VA; JR; AS; Coll Lit Mag 88-; Pres Schlr 88-90; Fndtn Schlr 88-90; Psych; BS Clinical Phych.

**BEAL, BARBARA C,** Vance Granville Comm Coll, Henderson, NC; SO; AA; Phi Theta Kappa 90; Deans Lst; Acad Schlrshp 90; Erly Chldhd Ed; Day Care Opr.

**BEAL, LUCAS A,** Muskingum Coll, New Concord, OH; FR; Lambda Sigma; Outstndg Schlr 90-; Spch Dept Schlrshp; Vrsty Ftbl 90.

**BEAL, VIDA D,** Middle Tn St Univ, Murfreesboro, TN; JR; BED; Perf Grp VP 76-80; Delta Omcrn 78-80; Brdcst Msc Inc 87-; Sngwrtrs Gld 87-90; BM NE LA Unv 80; Educ; Tchr.

**BEALE, ADRIAN G,** Norfolk St Univ, Norfolk, VA; FR; MBA; NROTC 90; Active Duty Navy Spartan Alpha Tau 90; IM Ftbl/Bsktbl/Sftbl 90; Bsn Mngmnt Cmptr Info Systms; Naval Officer.

**BEALE, DAWN M,** Christian Brothers Univ, Memphis, TN; SR; BA; Wmns Assn Motivate Spirit 88-90; BACCHUS Pres 89-; Alpha Chi 90-; Psi Chi 89-; Gamma Theta Phi 89-; Peer Cnslr 88-90; Stdnt Ambassador 89-; Bldg/Grnds Com 89-90; Intrnshp Chldrns Museum Memphis 90-; Magna Cum Laude; Psychlgy; Teach.

**BEALE, HEATHER A,** Mount Aloysius Jr Coll, Cresson, PA; FR; AA; Legal Asstnt; Prlgl.

**BEALE, KEENA L,** Anne Arundel Comm Coll, Arnold, MD; FR; AA; Fldwrk Plcmnt New Life Add Cnslng; Human Serv; CAC.

**BEALL, F MORGAN,** Emory Univ, Atlanta, GA; JR; BBA; Sigma Alpha Epsln; US Marine Crps Crprl 87-89; Mktg/Sales.

**BEALL, JON T,** Ms Univ For Women, Columbus, MS; JR; BS; ACT Related Schl Schlrshp 90-; Business; Acctg.

**BEALL, MARY SUSAN,** Univ Of Sc At Columbia, Columbia, SC; JR; BA; Amer Mktng Assn 90-; Kappa Delta 88-; Schlstc Imprvmnt Awd Kappa Delta 90-; Bus Admin; Finance/Mktg.

**BEALMEAR, MARY BETH,** Brescia Coll, Owensboro, KY; SR; BA; Aacdmc Excllnc 89-; Hnr Sengl; Engl Ed; Scndry Ed Tchng Engl.

**BEAM, BARBARA N,** Univ Of South Al, Mobile, AL; JR; BED; PTA Sec 88-90; Math; Scndry Educ.

**BEAM, CHRISTIE L,** Univ Of Montevallo, Montevallo, AL; JR; Linly Heflin Schlrshp; Erly Chlhd/Elem Ed.

**BEAM II, JAMES F,** Nc St Univ At Raleigh, Raleigh, NC; FR; BS; Alpha Lambda Delta 90-; Schlrs Pgm 90-; Benjamin Franklin Schlrs Pgm 90-; Order St Patrick 90-; Textile Engr; Engr.

**BEAM, JENNIFER A,** S U N Y Coll At Fredonia, Fredonia, NY; JR; Trng 88-90; Delta Phi Epsilon 88-89; Spch Pthlgy Adlgy.

**BEAM, THEODORE E,** Asbury Theological Sem, Wilmore, KY; GD; MA; BS Oh Nthrn Un 86; M Div 90; Biblcl Studies; Pastoral Minis/Tch.

**BEAM, WILLIAM D,** Al A & M Univ, Normal, AL; JR; MET; Cert Soc Manuf Engrs 89; Engr.

**BEAMAN, RHONDA M,** City Univ Of Ny Baruch Coll, New York, NY; JR; BBA; Untd Negro Clg Fund Vol; Mktg Mgmt; Mktg Rep.**

**BEAMER, TERRI L,** Radford Univ, Radford, VA; SO; Cmnctn Dsrdrs; Spch Pthlgst.

**BEAMESDERFER, MELINDA S,** Harrisburg Area Comm Coll, Harrisburg, PA; FR; MBA; VIP Clb; Dns Lst 90-; Psy/Sclgy; Social Work/Cnslng.

**BEAMISH, ANNE M,** Coll Of Charleston, Charleston, SC; FR; BS; Biolgy; Chrprctry.

**BEAMON, GENISE R,** Tougaloo Coll, Tougaloo, MS; SO; BA; Deans Lst 89-; Alpha Kappa Alpha; Econ Bus Admin; Business.

**BEAMON, GLORIA M,** Spalding Univ, Louisville, KY; SR; BSSW; Std Scl Actn 89-; Delta Epsln Sigma 90-; Chld Prtctv Serv Intshp 90-; Work Stdy/Vol Wrk Brdghvn 89-90; Psy Pgm Crncly Mnty Ill Adlts 88-89; Comm Rcvry Ctr Cnslr Asst; AS Louisville Clg 87; Scl Wrk; MSSW.

**BEAN, ARTHUR L,** Morehouse Coll, Atlanta, GA; SO; Drama Clb; Mu Alpha Theta; Ftbl Trck; Bnkng/Fnnc.

**BEAN, C WHITNEY,** Union Univ School Of Nursing, Memphis, TN; FR; BSN; Nursing.

**BEAN, CANDACE WHITNEY,** Union Univ School Of Nursing, Memphis, TN; FR; BSN; Deans Lst 90-; Nurs.

**BEAN, KIM J,** Castleton St Coll, Castleton, VT; SR; BS; Kappa Delta Pi 90-; Hmn Scty U S 87-; AA 90; AA Adirondack Comm Clge 87; Elem Ed/Rdng Cncntrtn; Tchg.

**BEAN, LANCE E,** Edinboro Univ Of Pa, Edinboro, PA; SO; BS; Hons Prog 90-; Deans List 90-; Hons Cnvctn Cert 90-; Acctg; CPA.

**BEAN, LORNE K E,** Central St Univ, Wilberforce, OH; SR; BA; Bapt Stdnt Union Advsr 88-90; Intrfth Campus Mnstry Mnstr 88; Psi Chi; Mid Estrn Hnrs Assoc 89-91; Kettering Fndtn Rsrch Assist 89-90; Phillips Acad Intrn 90; AME Licentiate 83; Psych; Full-Time Christian Mnstry.

**BEAN, REBECCA J,** Univ Of Tn At Knoxville, Knoxville, TN; FR; BA; Promise Coll Sngng Chrch Grp; Cmps Crusd Chrst; Alpha Lambda Delta; Phi Eta Sigma; Bus Adm; Acctg.

**BEAR, ELIZABETH J,** Longwood Coll, Farmville, VA; SO; MED; Alpha Lambda Delta 89-90; Spec Educ; Tchng.

**BEAR, ELIZABETH K,** Univ Of Cin R Walters Coll, Blue Ash, OH; FR; AB; Rymnd Wltrs Stdnt Ct Jstce 90-; Phi Theta Kappa; RWC Hnrs Prog; CPA Frm; Acctng; Acctng Invstmnt.

**BEARD GLENN, FRANCES,** Ms St Univ, Miss State, MS; SR; BS; Stdnt Assn Intr Design 87-; Home Ec Clb 87-; Kappa Omicron Nu 90-; Chi Omega 87-90; Home Ec; Interior Design.

**BEARD, ALEXIS L,** Hampton Univ, Hampton, VA; FR; BS; Wmns Sen 90-; Afrcn Stdies Clstr 90-; MO Pre-Alumni Clb 90-; Hons Prog 90-; Pres Enicut Schlrs Awd 90-; Acctg; CPA.

**BEARD, CHARLES S,** Cornell Univ Statutory College, Ithaca, NY; SO; BS; Sigma Nu Alumni Rels 90-; Vars Ftbl 89-; Track; Bsn.

**BEARD, CHRISTOPHER B,** Castleton St Coll, Castleton, VT; SO; BS; SG 90-; NY St Hsptlty Trsm Assoc 88-89; Ntl Hnr Soc 87-88; Paul Francis Peroni Mem Awrd Hghst GPA Htl Mgt 89; Pres Schlr 90-; Untd Crbrl Plsy VT Schlrshp 88-; AAS 90; Bus Admin; CPA.

**BEARD, DEE DEE,** Abraham Baldwin Agri Coll, Tifton, GA; SO; BA; WOW Ldr 90; Elem Edn; Teach.

**BEARD, GAIL M,** Univ Of Southern Ms, Hattiesburg, MS; SR; BA; Elizar Pillars; Nrs Assn; BSN; ADN Meridian Jr Clg 81; Nrsg; Prctnr.

**BEARD, KENNETH A,** Western Ky Univ, Bowling Green, KY; JR; BS; Flwshp Chrstn Athletes; Campus Crsde Christ 88-; Phi Eta Sigma 89; Chem Hon Soc 89-; Big Bro Big Strs; R Nelson Schlrshp 88; Rgnts Schlrshp; Rotary Clb Schlrshp; Chem; Med.

**BEARD, PATRICK W,** Lenoir Rhyne Coll, Hickory, NC; FR; BA; Stndt Mrshl Sprg Bacca Pgrm; Furn Uphlstry 86-; Art Educ; Tch Art Mdl Hgh Lvl.

**BEARD, RACHEL S,** Univ Of Ky, Lexington, KY; JR; BS; Alpha Epsilon Delta 89-; Coll Acad Excell; Deans Lst; Coll Schlrs Amer; Vlntr Humana Hosp; Bio/Pre-Med; Dr Ped Med.

**BEARD, ROBERT M,** Univ Of Al At Huntsville, Huntsville, AL; FR; BSE; Am Inst Of Aero & Astro 90-; Alpha Lambda Delta; Hnrs Prog; Mech Engrng.

**BEARD, ROGER M,** Univ Of Nc At Charlotte, Charlotte, NC; SR; BA; Natl Merit Schlrshp 87-; Psych; Psychologist.

**BEARD, TONYA K,** Univ Of Nc At Charlotte, Charlotte, NC; SO; BSN; Assn Nrsng Stdnts 90-; Psychlgy Clb 89-90; IM Sprts 89-; Dns Lst 90; Dnc Tm 90-; Nrsng.

**BEARD, VICKI L,** Dyersburg St Comm Coll, Dyersburg, TN; SO; Stdnt Govt Sec; Stdnt Ambsdr; Jzz Choir Stdnt Dir; Music Educ; Music Dir.

**BEARDEN, ELAINE A,** Oh Wesleyan Univ, Delaware, OH; SO; Habitat Humty VP; Wesleyan Foundation; English Brd; Phi Eta Sigma; Phi Scty; Sigma Tau Delta; English.

**BEARDEN, JOAN K,** Owensboro Jr Coll Of Bus, Owensboro, KY; GD; AS; Student Govt; Amer Cancer Scty; Deans List 90; Pres List 90; Prefect Attendance 90-; AS 90-; Computer Sci; Operations/Mgt.

**BEARDEN, MARTHA J,** Tri County Tech Coll, Pendleton, SC; GD; AAS; Sec Sci.

**BEARDEN, MELISSA L,** Univ Of Al At Birmingham, Birmingham, AL; SR; BS; Blgy.

**BEARDI, MARK J,** Cornell Univ Statutory College, Ithaca, NY; FR; BS; Cornell Entrprnrs Frsh Rep; Rugby Tm; Bsns Mgmt; Law/Bsns.

**BEARDSLEE, LYNN D,** Liberty Univ, Lynchburg, VA; SR; BED; Assn Chrstn Tchrs 89-; Vars Bsktbl 88-; Big Sister 89-90; Kappa Delta Pi 90; Elem Educ; Tch.

**BEARDSLEE, PEGGY S,** Lycoming Coll, Williamsport, PA; SO; BA; Publ Forum 90-; Lycoming Schlrs Prog 89-; Fld Hcky 90-; Hstry/Pol Sci; Govt Wrk.**

**BEARDSLEY, CONNIE T,** The Johns Hopkins Univ, Baltimore, MD; JR; BSN; BA 78; Nrsng.

**BEARDSLEY, MICHAEL G,** Salisbury St Univ, Salisbury, MD; SR; BS; Med Careers Clb; Bio Clb 87-; Phi Kappa Hi; Beta Beta Beta Chr; Alpah Omega; Lcrss/Vlybl/Sftbl 87-; Bio; Med.

**BEARE, ANISSA K,** Memphis St Univ, Memphis, TN; SO; BA; Madison Cntry Congressional Art Comp 88; Natl Congressional Art Comp 88; Art Schlrshp Jackson State Omm Coll 88-90; Deans Lst 89-90; Art History.

**BEARFIELD, JONATHAN M,** S U N Y At Buffalo, Buffalo, NY; SR; BS; Alpha Phi Omega VP 88-; Eas 231 Quattro Asst 89-; IM Vlybl; BSA Scout Mstr 89-; USMC Sgt 83-88; Dsgn Engr CMC Tech; Elctrncs; Dsgn Engr.

**BEARRENTINE, MERRI C,** Valdosta St Coll, Valdosta, GA; SR; BA; BSU 87-89; Alpha Lambda Delta 87-88; Alpha Kappa Delta; Pi Gamma Mu; Schlr; Sclgy; Fam Ther.

**BEARROR, DANIELLE L,** Fl St Univ, Tallahassee, FL; JR; BA; Radio Cmptlr 90-; Dns Lst; Sigma Iota Epsilon; Ims Sftbl 89; AA 90; Mngmt; Hmn Rsrc Mngmt.

**BEASLEY, ARISTA D,** Univ Of Al At Birmingham, Birmingham, AL; SR; MS; Ambssdr 88-89; Psychlgy Clb 87-; Dbt Tm Pres 87-90; Gldn Key 89-; Pres Lst 87-; Omicron Delta Kappa VP 89-; Delta Sigma Rho-Tau Kappa Alpha 87-90; Deans Lst 87-; Alpha Tau Omega Aux 89-90; Psychlgy Hon Pgm 89-90; Passey Prz 90-; Ldrshp Awd 90-; Clncl Psychlgy; Rsrch.

**BEASLEY, CARLENE A,** The Johns Hopkins Univ, Baltimore, MD; JR; BSN; Blk Nrsng Stdnt Assn 90-; Intrnshp Johns Hopkins Hosp; Mntl Hlth Cnslr 89-; BS SDC VA Tech 89; Nrsng.

**BEASLEY, CARLOTTA M,** Germanna Comm Coll, Locust Grove, VA; SR; BS; Ada Anderson Schlrshp 85; LPN Piedmont Educ Tech Schl 86; Nrsng.

**BEASLEY, DENISE,** Maryville Coll, Maryville, TN; FR; BS; Student Prog; Alpha Lambda Delta 90-; Chrldng; Chemistry; Med.

**BEASLEY, EULICA S,** Va St Univ, Petersburg, VA; JR; BS; Acctg Clb Sec 90-; Natl Assoc Blck Acctnts 90; Acctg.

**BEASLEY, FELICIA R,** Alcorn St Univ, Lorman, MS; GD; BA; English Clb; Alpha Kappa Mu; Easter Star Fort Herron 166-A, Intrnshp WKPG Radio Sta 13-20 AM; English/Communicaiton.**

**BEASLEY, GREGORY L,** Al A & M Univ, Normal, AL; JR; BA; Bus Finance; Invstmnt Bnkng.

**BEASLEY, JUDY A,** Northwest Al Comm Coll, Phil Campbell, AL; SO; AS; Phi Theta Kappa 89-; C/S.

**BEASLEY, JULIA A,** Samford Univ, Birmingham, AL; GD; JD; Amer Jrnl Trl Advcy Assoc Rsrch Wrtng Ed 90-; Envrnmntl Law Scty; Chrstn Lgl Scty; Cordell Hull Tchng Flw Lgl Rsrch Wrtng Pgm 90-; Dns Lst 90; Chrch Mbr; BA Huntington Clge 85.

**BEASLEY, KEITH L,** Univ Of Al At Huntsville, Huntsville, AL; FR; BA; Alpha Lambda Delta; Math; Elctrcl Engr/Robotics.

**BEASLEY, LANI A,** Univ Of Ga, Athens, GA; SR; BSED; SCEC 90-; Mntl Rtrdtn; Teach.

**BEASLEY, LINDA K,** Oh Univ, Athens, OH; SR; BFA; Yearbook Photo Editor 90; Kappa Phi Club 90; Deans Scholarship 90; Photography.

**BEASLEY, MARK D,** Va Commonwealth Univ, Richmond, VA; SR; BS; Acctg Scty; Pi Lambda Phi Pres 87-; Acctg/Mrktg; CPA.**

**BEASLEY, SHERITA K,** Christopher Newport Coll, Newport News, VA; FR; BS; Deans Lst; Red Crss Cert; Sec 90-; Bio; Med.

**BEASLEY, TRACIE L,** Univ Of Sc At Coastal Carolina, Conway, SC; SO; BS; Bio/Marine Sci; Bio Tchr/Envrnmntl Ed.

**BEASLEY, WILLIAM M,** Middle Tn St Univ, Murfreesboro, TN; JR; BA; Aerospce Adm.

**BEASLEY-LEE, KIMBERLEY D,** Univ Of Southern Ms, Hattiesburg, MS; JR; BA; Bsn; Mktng.

**BEASON, BRENDA G,** Nova Univ, Ft Lauderdale, FL; GD; MBA; St Johns Comm SGA Rep Sec 85-86; Univ W FL AMA Mktg Clb 86-88; Pres Lst 85; Deans Lst 84; Delta Sigma Pi 87-; Stdnt Fac Cmmssn 85-86; Deans Cmmndtn Outstndng Serv 85-86; AS St Johns Comm 83-86; BS Univ W FL 86-88; Mktg.

**BEASON, CYNTHIA A,** Cumberland Univ, Lebanon, TN; FR; BED; Bapt Un 90-; Alpha Lambda Delta; Sftbl; Elem Educ; Tchr.

**BEATON, LISA M,** Univ Of Sc At Columbia, Columbia, SC; SO; BA; Sta; Brdcst Jrnlst.

**BEATON, LISA S,** Univ Of Ky, Lexington, KY; SO; BED; Phi Eta Sigma 90; Epsilon Delta 90; Bkkpr 89; Elem Educ.

**BEATON, PAMELA M,** George Mason Univ, Fairfax, VA; JR; BS; Cir K Clb 87-88; Creat Wrtg Clb 88-89; Stdnt Wel Comm 87-88; Goldn Key; Alpha Chi; Offcr Electn 90-; Socl Wrk; Fmly/Chld Welfr.

**BEATSON, KAREN L,** Coll Of Charleston, Charleston, SC; SO; BS; Flwshp Chrstn Athletes 90-91; Delta Delta Delta; Pharm; Doc Pharmcy.

**BEATTIE, MARSHA E,** Spartanburg Methodist Coll, Spartanburg, SC; SO; AA; IM Sftbl/Vlybl 90-; Sociology.

**BEATTIE, NANETTE L,** Providence Coll, Providence, RI; SO; Vars Vllybl 89-; Spec Educ; Educ.

**BEATTY, CATHY E,** Bowling Green St Univ At Huron, Huron, OH; SO; ASS; Deans Lst; Cmptr Prgrmng Tech.

**BEATTY, DEBORAH S,** Saint Francis Coll, Loretto, PA; SR; BS; Phy Asst Soc Pr 90-; Singrs 88-89; Hnr Soc; Delta Epsilon Sigma; Phy Asst Awd; Pres Schlrshp 87-; Phy Asst Fndtn Schlrshp 90; Phy Asst; Med.

**BEATTY, JANE R,** Methodist Coll, Fayetteville, NC; SO; AA; Chrch Asst Actvty Dir 89-; Choir; Asst Orgnst; Lib Tech; Accntng; CPA.

**BEATTY, JERRY L,** Coppin St Coll, Baltimore, MD; SR; BS; Social Science.

**BEATTY, JOYCE MICHELLE,** Winthrop Coll, Rock Hill, SC; JR; BS; Natl Ed Assn 90-; Biolgy Clb VP 90-; Beta Beta Beta 89-; Kappa Delta Pi 90 ; Epsilon Sigma Alpha 90-; Biolgy, Tch.

**BEATTY, MICHELLE R,** Duquesne Univ, Pittsburgh, PA; JR; BA; Elem Ed; Tchng.

**BEATTY, WILLIAM M,** Wv Univ, Morgantown, WV; SR; BSEE; IEEE; Golden Key 90-; Eta Kappa Nu; Tau Beta Pi 90-; Pr Awd Excel Schlrshp 90; Appntmnt U S Air Force Acad 81; Deans Lst 89-; AAS-EET Univ Of Akron OH 84; Elec Engr.

**BEATY, ELIZABETH L,** Tn Tech Univ, Cookeville, TN; FR; BS; Univ Hnrs Pgm 90-; Business.

**BEATY, TRACY S,** Univ Of Tn At Knoxville, Knoxville, TN; FR; BA; Bus; Mktg.

**BEAUCHAMP, DIANA A,** Univ Of Miami, Coral Gables, FL; JR; BS; NSAE 90-; ASCE 90-; Tau Beta Pi 90-; Chi Epsilon Sec 90-; Phi Alpha Epsilon Sec 90-; Deans Lst 90; Arch Engr Schlrshp; Bowman Ashe Schlrshp 88-; Cvl/Arch Engr; Engr.

**BEAUCHAMP, TAMMY L,** Fl St Univ, Tallahassee, FL; JR; BSN; AA 90; Nrsng.

**BEAUCHER, JENNIFER ANN,** Merrimack Coll, North Andover, MA; SO; BA; Psi Chi; Psychology.

**BEAUDET, KAREN,** Newbury Coll, Brookline, MA; SO; AS; Paralegal Stds; Law JD.

**BEAUDETTE, MICHELE J,** Memphis St Univ, Memphis, TN; SR; BA; Sgm Tau Delta; Peer Mentor Pgm; Rsdnc Hall Assc; Engl Clb; Gamma Beta Phi Hstrn; Gldn Key Mrtr Brd; Hon Stdnt Assc; IM Bsktbl Sftbl; Engl; ESL Tchng.

**BEAUDOIN, LINDA M,** Elms Coll, Chicopee, MA; JR; BED; Nwsppr Ed 89-; Slf Assssmnt Comm 90-; Ldrshp Awrd 90; Mnsgnr Fgn Awrd 89; -; Engl.

**BEAUDOIN, MICHAEL J,** Elmira Coll, Elmira, NY; SO; BA; Gold Key Ambsdrs 90-; Outing Clb 89-; Phi Eta Sigma 90-; Deans Lst 89-; Acdmc Hnr Awrd 89-; Coachs Awrd Var Bsktbl 90-; Var Bsktbl 89-; Engl; Educ.

**BEAUDOIN, NYANZA L,** Albany Coll Of Pharmacy, Albany, NY; FR; BA; Intl Cltrl Awrnss Clb 90-; Rho Pi Phi 90-; Phrmcy; Rsrch/Hosp Phrmcy.

**BEAUGEZ, SANDI J,** Univ Of West Fl, Pensacola, FL; JR; PHD; Support Grp Co Chrmn 89-; Sftbl League Co Chrmn 89-; AA Okaloosa Walton Jr Clg 90; Religion/Philo; Phd.

**BEAULIEU, JENNIFER J,** Bay Path Coll, Longmeadow, MA; JR; BAB; Maroon Key 90-; AS 90; Bus Admin; Retail Mgmr.

**BEAULIEU, LEONARD J,** Fl International Univ, Miami, FL; JR; BS; Cncl Excptnl Chldrn; Sierra Clb; Profl Assn Diving Instrs Bluemstr 79-; US Coast Guard 88-; Pol Sci; Law.

**BEAULIEU, MATTHEW J,** Univ Of New Haven, West Haven, CT; JR; BA; Architecture.

**BEAULIEU, PAMELA J,** Newbury Coll, Brookline, MA; FR; Bus Tech; Exec Sec.

**BEAUMONT, ANDREA L,** Miami Dade Comm Coll South, Miami, FL; SO; Yth Choir Grace Ch 1st Born Grp/Ldr 88-; Vol Parkway Regnl Cntr.

**BEAUMONT, JAMES H,** Morehouse Coll, Atlanta, GA; JR; BA; Pre Alumni Assoc Exec Liaison 87; Psy Assoc 88-; Psi Chi Secty; Research Assist 90-; Student Tchr; Psy; Clinical Psy.

**BEAVER, ADINA R,** Radford Univ, Radford, VA; SO; BA; Hist; Law/Teach.

**BEAVER, DENISE M,** Fl St Univ, Tallahassee, FL; FR; BA; Phi Eta Sigma 90-; Hmn Sci/Nutrtn; Dietetcs.

**BEAVER, FRANKIE L,** Norfolk St Univ, Norfolk, VA; JR; BA; Student Govt Assoc Exec Secty 90-; Student Ldrshp Prog 89-; Student Cts 90-; Alpha Kappa Mu 89-; Alpha Kappa Delta; Spartan Alpha Tau 88-89; Mayors Task Force Against Drugs 90-; WEB Dubois Outstndng Schlrshp Citation 89-; Ciriminal Justice; Clg Profr Lawyer.

**BEAVER, TINA C,** Univ Of Nc At Charlotte, Charlotte, NC; SR; BAMED; Psychlgy Clb 89-90; SCEC 90-; Phi Eta Sigma 87-; Psi Chi 89-; Golden Key 89-; Chi Omega Chrmn Comm 89-; Practicum St Marks Ctr 90; IM Sports 89-; Psychlgy/Spcl Ed; Tch Hndcpd.

**BEAVERS, LINDSEY M,** Univ Of Pittsburgh At Bradford, Bradford, PA; SR; Am Chem Soc Clb Pres 89-90; Internshp St Univ NY Lab Asst 90; BS Univ Pitt 90; Chem; Sec Educ/Pharmacy.

**BEAVERS, LYNNE M,** Univ Of Pittsburgh, Pittsburgh, PA; SR; BSW; BASW Club Treas 90-; Soc Work Conf Comm; Intrnshp Jefferson Hosp Stdnt Med Soc Worker 90-; Soc Work; Med Soc Work.

**BEAVERS, MARY J,** Owensboro Jr Coll Of Bus, Owensboro, KY; AS; Computers; Computerized Ofc Professional.

**BEAYON, MICHAEL W,** Southern Vt Coll, Bennington, VT; SO; BA; Big Bro/Big Sis Chrprsn 89-90; Prjct Dir Lcl Comm Action Agncy 86-90; Cntrl VT Pblc Serv Corp Cstmr Advsry Pnl Chrprsn 89-90; Acctg; Actnt.

**BEBBER, JULIA A,** Univ Of Nc At Charlotte, Charlotte, NC; SO; NCAE-NEA Mbr; Young Alumniu Cncl Mbr; Prospective Tchr Schlrshp 90-; Math/Teacher Cert; Teaching.

**BEBBER, TERRY L,** Catawba Valley Comm Coll, Hickory, NC; FR; BS; Coll Ttr 90-; Gamma Beta Phi 90-; Hnr Crps 90-; Chf Cmmncmnt Mrshl; Stdnt Mnth Awrd; Sci; Phrmcy.

**BEC, EDWARD,** Univ Of Miami, Coral Gables, FL; SR; BARCH; AIA 83-88 90-; CSI 88-; Intern Dev Prog 88-; Intern Archtct; BD Univ FL 88; Arch; Law.

**BECHARD, BRYAN J,** Le Moyne Coll, Syracuse, NY; FR; BS; Clb Hockey 90-; I M Bkbl 90; Deans Lst 90-; Golf Schlrshp 90-; Bus Ad/Econ; PGA Golf Clb Prfsnl.

**BECHT, RACHAEL G,** Daemen Coll, Amherst, NY; FR; BA; Business; Mngmnt Admin.

**BECHTEL, BETSY A,** Bridgewater Coll, Bridgewater, VA; SO; BA; Oratorio Choir 89-90; Concert Choir 89-90; Chorale 90; Concert Band 89-90; Brethern Stdnt Fllwshp; Stdnt Senator 90; Music Ed Ntnl Cnfce Pres 89-90; Music; Tch.

**BECHTER, GERALYN M,** Univ Of Akron, Akron, OH; SR; BA; Phi Sigma Alpha 90; Golden Key 90; Pixley Schlr 89; AA 86; Eng/Child Dvpmnt.

**BECHTLER, PATRICIA F,** Va Commonwealth Univ, Richmond, VA; GD; BS; Exclncy Frnch Awd; Summa Cum Laude; BA 89; Frnch Educ; Tchng Frnch/Spnsh.

**BECK, ALISON S,** City Univ Of Ny Baruch Coll, New York, NY; SR; Italian Scty 87-; Acctng Scty 89-; Beta Gamma Sigma 90-; Golden Key Exec VP 90; Acctng; CPA.

**BECK, AMY S,** Glassboro St Coll, Glassboro, NJ; SO; BA; Deans Lst 90-; ACC Deans Lst 89-90; Fire Co Ladies Aux 88-; Aerobic Instrctr 90-; Schl Dstrct Sub Aide 90-; Tchr Handcpd.

**BECK, ANGELA M,** Daytona Beach Comm Coll, Daytona Beach, FL; SO; AA; Smmr Cmp Cnslr; Phi Beta Kappa; Pres Acdmc Ftnss Awd 89; Lbrl Arts; Intl Law.

**BECK, BRIAN,** Savannah Coll Of Art & Design, Savannah, GA; SR; Deans Lst 87-; Sculputre Art Fstvl 88-89; Video Prod; Soccer 88-89; BA Fine Arts; Art Hist; Graphic Arts/Jewelry Dsgn; Cmrcl Art.**

**BECK, CHARLES R,** Memphis St Univ, Memphis, TN; SR; BBA; Kraft Foods Cmptr Oprtr; Mgmt/Hmn Rsrcs; Prsnl Mgr.

**BECK, DANA M,** Va Commonwealth Univ, Richmond, VA; SO; BA; Fin; Bnkng Or Bus.

**BECK, DAVID P,** Univ Of Rochester, Rochester, NY; JR; BS; Tau Beta Pi 90-; Phi Beta Kappa 90-; Acdmc All Amrcn Tnns 90-; Optcs Hnr Srsrch Prgm; Vrsty Bsktbll 88-; Vrsty Tnns 88-; Optcl Eng.

**BECK, DAWN MARIE,** Marywood Coll, Scranton, PA; SR; BS; Busn Club 89-; Computer Infor Syst; Progr.

**BECK, DEBORAH L,** Longwood Coll, Farmville, VA; SR; BS; CEC; Kappa Delta Pi V P 90; Alpha Delta Pi Schlrshp Chr 88; Spec Educ; Tch.

**BECK, DENNIS EDWARD,** Univ Of Cincinnati, Cincinnati, OH; SR; BED; Sci Educ Cncl Of Ohio; Roger Baron High Schl Alumni Assn 86-; Amer Swim Coaches Assn 90-; Boy Scts Of Amer Cmmsnr 89-; Amer Red Crs Vol Crdntr 90-; Bd Of Hlth City Of St Bernard 89-; Cmprhnsv Sci; Sci Tchr/Swim Coach.

**BECK, ELAINE S,** Western Carolina Univ, Cullowhee, NC; JR; BA; Marshals Clb 89-; Wstrn Gold 89-90; Alpha Lambda Delta 88-; Phi Alpha Theta 90-; Pi Gamma Mu 90-; Dns Lst 88-; Mc Cracken Schlrshp 89-; Hstry Schlrshp 90-; Alice Matthews Schlrshp; Swain Cnty Genealogical/Hstrcl Socty Pres 84-85; Hstry; Law/Hstry Professor.

**BECK, GLORIA N,** Fl International Univ, Miami, FL; JR; BA; Amer Mktg Assn 90-; Rotarct Clb Sec 88-89; Dns Lst 90; Career Plng Plcmnt Peer Advsr; Fla Intl Univ Crew Clb; Intl Busn/Mktg; Law Schl.

**BECK, HERMAN H,** Morehouse Coll, Atlanta, GA; JR; BA; Pltcl Sci Soc 89-; Morehse Mntrng Prog 89-; Mn Jack/Jill Amer 84-89; TEC Yth Mnstry 86-; DFL Vtr Educ; W Wilson Flw Summer Intrn; Intl Stdes; Pub Plcy/Intl Afrs.

**BECK, JENNIFER K,** Univ Of Ms Medical Center, Jackson, MS; SR; BSN; Miss Assoc Stdnt Nrs 90-; Nrsng.

**BECK JR, JOSEPH M,** Middle Ga Coll, Cochran, GA; SO; Gamma Beta Phi 90-; Engrg Awd 90-; Deans List 90-; Regents Engrg Transfer Prog 90-; BS; Mechl Engrg.

**BECK, KATHLEEN A,** Univ Of Pittsburgh, Pittsburgh, PA; SO; BS; Admin Asst 76-89; Assoc Degree Cntrl PA Bus Schl 78; Indust Eng.

**BECK, KEITH L,** Middle Ga Coll, Cochran, GA; SO; BA; Bapt Student Union; Engeer Club; Natl Scty Profl Engrs; Im; Engrg.

**BECK, KIMBERLY K,** Memphis St Univ, Memphis, TN; JR; BED; Baptist Stdnt Union 90-; Youth For Hrist Campus Life Dir 89-; Dental Asst Dr James E Sexton 86; Mgr 87-89; Elem Ed; Councelor.

**BECK, MICHAELA S,** Oh St Univ At Newark, Newark, OH; SO; BA; Acad Excell Schlrshp 89-; Bus; Acctg.

**BECKA, THERESE MARIA,** Notre Dame Coll, Cleveland, OH; SR; BED; Pi Lambda Theta; Pall Mall Engl Award; Dinning Rm Suprvsr/Bkkpr 88-; AA Lakeland Cmnty Clg 86; Engl; Tchr.

**BECKER, ADAM C,** Southern Coll Of Tech, Marietta, GA; SR; BS; Tau Alpha Pi; IEEE; Pi Kappa Phi; Dns Lst 89-; Res Tech 89-; Elec Eng Tech; Res Eng.

**BECKER, BRIAN G,** Immaculata Coll, Immaculata, PA; JR; BA; Samson Paper; Hist/Pltcs; Law.

**BECKER, CAROL J,** Pa St Univ York Cmps, York, PA; FR; Elem Ed; Teacher.

**BECKER, CHRISTINE M,** Univ Of Ga, Athens, GA; SR; Natl Cncl Tchrs Eng 89-; Ga Cncl Tchrs Eng; Dns Lst; BS Ed; Eng Ed; Tchr High Schl Eng/Thtr.

**BECKER, CYNTHIA LYNN,** Mount Saint Mary Coll, Newburgh, NY; SR; BA; Sgt US Army W Point NY 10996 87-; AAS Coll Dupage Glen Ellen IL 86; Cmptr Sci.

**BECKER, DEBORAH A,** East Tn St Univ, Johnson City, TN; JR; BS; Gamma Beta Phi 89-; Mktg.

**BECKER, DEBORAH L,** D Youville Coll, Buffalo, NY; FR; BA; Deans Lst; Sch Prog Tchr 88; Ele Educ.

**BECKER, DIANE R,** Nc Central Univ, Durham, NC; GD; MD; Amigos De Las Amer Spvr Ecuador 87-89; Kent Intrhl Cncl Rep 85-86; Kent Hse Cncl Exe Asst 85-86; Alpha Phi Sigma 87-88; Lake Cty Bar Assn Schlrshp 90; Deans Lst 90; BA Kent State Univ 89; Intl Law.

**BECKER JR, JAMES R,** Memphis St Univ, Memphis, TN; SR; BA; Gamma Beta Phi 88-; Deans List 87-; Pltcl Science Pre Law Awrd; Pltcl Science; Law.

**BECKER, JEFFREY W,** Washington State Comm Coll, Marietta, OH; SO; AAB; Phi Theta Kappa VP 90-; Data Proc; Cmptr Pgrmr.

**BECKER, JO ELLEN,** Lexington Comm Coll, Lexington, KY; FR; AD; Sci; Nrsng.

**BECKER, KRISTINE T,** Clayton St Coll, Morrow, GA; SO; BS; Stu Govt 90; Hnrs Soc 89-; Acdmc Achvmtn Awrd 90-; Math/Sci.

**BECKER, LISA ANN,** Northern Ky Univ, Highland Hts, KY; FR; BS; Biolgy Soc 90-; IM 90-; Pre Med Bio; Med.

**BECKER, MARTHA E,** Univ Of Nc At Charlotte, Charlotte, NC; SR; BA; Phi Kappa Phi; Phi Beta Delta 89-; Gldn Ky 90-; Data Proc Asst IV; AA CPCC 89; Anthrplgy; Archglst Res.

**BECKER, RACHEL L,** Univ Of Cincinnati, Cincinnati, OH; SO; BSN; Nrsng/Hlth Tribunal Rep 90-; Alpha Lambda Delta 90-; Deans Lst; Acad Schlrshps; Natl Coll Nrsng Awd; US Achvmnt Acad; Nrsng.

**BECKER, SARAH C,** Le Moyne Coll, Syracuse, NY; SO; BA; College Nwspr Staff Writer 90-; Internatl House Cmnty Serv 89-90; Phi Alpha Theta; History; Law Jrnlsm.

**BECKER, STEFAN,** George Mason Univ, Fairfax, VA; JR; BS; Stdnt Senate Chr; German Clb Pres 88-90; Intl Stdnt Assn Rep 88-90; Alpha Lambda Delta 88-; Alpha Chi 90; Gldn Key 90-; Kappa Alpha Order Sec 89-; Yth Undrstdng 87-89; Intl Stdnt Exch 87-89; Stdnt Fclty Liaison 90-; Decision Sci/MIS; Systs Analyst.

**BECKER, SUSAN E,** Middle Tn St Univ, Murfreesboro, TN; SO; BS; Psychlgy.

**BECKER, TAMMY M,** Schenectady County Comm Coll, Schenectady, NY; JR; BA; NAA 90-; Acctng.

**BECKER, THERESA L,** Gettysburg Coll, Gettysburg, PA; FR; BA; Choir 90-; Math; Actry.

**BECKER, TINA-MARIE,** Bethany Coll, Bethany, WV; SO; BA; Soc Prfsnl Jrnlsts 90-; Sftbl Ltrwnr 89-; Stdnt Nwspr Chf Cpyed; Soc Clgte Jrnlsts; Alpha Xi Delta Almn Rltns 90-; SADD Sec 89-; Intrn Bethany Admsns Ofc 90-; Cmnctns; Pblc Rltns.

**BECKER, TRACY L,** Lenoir Rhyne Coll, Hickory, NC; SR; BA; Lenoir Rhynean Nwspr Editor 90; Carnival Magazine Edtr 90; Literary Scty Sec Treas 89; Scty Profssnl Jrnlsts; Internshp Hickory Daily Record Temp Bus Edtr 90; English; Journalism.

**BECKER, WAYNE A,** Univ Of Akron, Akron, OH; JR; BA; Phi Eta Sigma 88-; Golden Key; Delta Tau Delta; Fin; Stockbroker.

**BECKER-BLOOMFIELD, SHEILA,** Memphis St Univ, Memphis, TN; SO; BA; Hebrew Tchr 88-; Pre Schl Edtr 82-88; Math; Secdy Ed.

**BECKERINK, MATTHEW R,** S U N Y Coll Of Tech At Alfred, Alfred, NY; SO; BS; AAS; Ag Sci; Dairy Hrdsmn.

**BECKERMAN, SHAWN E,** Duke Univ, Durham, NC; FR; BA; Delta Gamma 90-; Math/Econs; Intl Bus.

**BECKETT, AMY L,** Marshall University, Huntington, WV; FR; BBA; Alpha Xi Delta 90-; CPA; Acctng/Fin.

**BECKETT, CAROL L,** Univ Of Sc At Columbia, Columbia, SC; SO; BSN; US Army ROTC S 5 Stff Clr Grd Cdt 90-; USC Stdnt Nrss Assn; Gamma Beta Phi; CST Association Of Surgical Technologist 88; Nrsng; Army Nrsng.

**BECKETT, JOANNE A,** Davis Coll, Toledo, OH; SO; Deans Lst 90-; Pres Lst; Owens Tech Deans Lst 84-87; Prbtn Vol Yr 87-88; Bus Offc Mngr Dntst Offc; Admin/Sec.

**BECKETT, KELLY C,** Univ Of South Al, Mobile, AL; SO; BA; Dns Lst 89; Pres Lst 89-; Chrstn Applchn Prjct 90; Elem Educ; Tchng.

**BECKETT, RONALD A,** Univ Of Sc At Columbia, Columbia, SC; SR; Advancement Of Medical Instrumentation Assn; 13 Yr Active Duty Army Ofcr; AS St Regis Clge Denber CO 89; BA USC Clge Of Applied Prof Sciences; Interdiciplinary Studies; MBA/MHA.

**BECKFORD, ANTONIO O,** American Baptist Coll, Nashville, TN; FR; Stu Govt Sen 90-; Fresh Clss VP 90-; Phi Beta Sigma; Thlgy; Mnstr/Psychlgst.

**BECKFORD, COREY C,** S U N Y Coll Of Tech At Delhi, Delhi, NY; SO; Delhi Stdnt Snte Sntr 90-; Delhi Bus Assn Sntr 90-; Stdnt Cndct Com 90-; Pres Srch Com 90-; AAS; Mgmt Info Sys; Systms Eng.

**BECKHAM, GARY L,** S U N Y Coll Of Tech At Frmgdl, Farmingdale, NY; FR; BS; Basketball 90; Criminal Justice; Law.

**BECKHAM, JULIUS E,** Central St Univ, Wilberforce, OH; SO; BA; Mrchng Bnd 89-90; Psy Chi; Alpha Phi Alpha; Psych; Cnclng.

**BECKHAM, SHERRY L,** Univ Of Tn At Martin, Martin, TN; FR; BS; Society Hnrs Seminar Stndts 90; Ed.

**BECKHOUSE, DAVID L,** Radford Univ, Radford, VA; JR; BS; Pi Gamma Mu; Poly Sci.

**BECKLEHIMER, AMANDA L,** Belmont Coll, Nashville, TN; JR; Natl Assn Acctnts; Acctng; CPA.

**BECKLEY, ANTHONY T,** Hampton Univ, Hampton, VA; FR; BS; Natl Assn Blck Accntnts 90-; Univ Choirs 90-; Churchg Missionary 87-; Office Assistant Chrprsn Of Engl Dept 90-; IM Ftbl/Bsktbl 90-; Acctng; Mgngrl Accntnt.

**BECKLEY, DOUGLAS S,** Hudson Valley Comm Coll, Troy, NY; FR; BA; Not A Bit Dffrnce Clb 90-; Stdnt Snte Sntr 90-; Rcrtnl Thrpy.

**BECKLEY, JENNIFER L,** Dickinson Coll, Carlisle, PA; FR; BA; Inter Var Christian Flwshp 90-; Clg Musicum Bd Mbr; Clg Choir 90-; Comp Sci.

**BECKMAN, CHERYL E,** Yeshiva Univ, New York, NY; SR; BA; Deans Lst 89-90; Art/Interior Dsgn.

**BECKMAN, DIANE M,** Elmira Coll, Elmira, NY; SO; BS; RA 90-; Orntn 90-; Parents Weekend Chmn; Phi Eta Sigma; Pres Schlr 89-; Iris Ldrshp Awd; Chrldng 89-; Pol Sci; Law.

**BECKMAN, KIM A,** Univ Of Cin R Walters Coll, Blue Ash, OH; FR; Bus Anlys 80-; Bus.

**BECKNELL, VANESSA A,** Univ Of So At Coastal Carolina, Conway, SC; SR; BS; Retrng Stdnts Assoc; Bio; Cytotechnlgy.

**BECKNELL, VANESSA M,** Univ Of Sc At Columbia, Columbia, SC; SR; BS; Ret Stdnt Assoc 90-; Biology; Hlth Rltd Prof.

**BECKNER, LEE A,** Roane St Comm Coll, Harriman, TN; SO; AS; Law.

**BECKNER, LIZA E,** Methodist Coll, Fayetteville, NC; FR; BS; Cape Fear Dog Trng Clb 89-; Phi Eta Sigma 90-; Rape Crs Vol; Frat Ordr Plc; Cumberland Untd Methd Chrch; Dept Treas 90; Sclgy/Prelaw.

**BECKNER, MONICA L,** Milligan Coll, Milligan Clg, TN; JR; BA; Sigma Tau Delta 90-; Eng; Tchng/Wrtng.

**BECKSTINE, IDA M,** Piedmont Coll, Demorest, GA; FR; BS; SEEKERS 90-; Bptst Stdnt Union 90-; Chpl Chr/Annl Stff 90-; Acdmc Schlrshp 90-; Calc Awrd 90-; Dns Lst 90-; Trstees Acdmc Schlrshp 90-; Math; 2ndry Ed.

**BECKWITH, BARBARA E,** Bay Path Coll, Longmeadow, MA; SO; BA; Envir Awareness Grp; Dns Lst 90; Sub Tchr; Interior Dsgn/Chldhd Educ; Elem Schl Tch.

**BECKWITH, KARI ANNE,** Liberty Univ, Lynchburg, VA; SR; BS; Mltry Mnstry Trvlng Team 89; Camelot Nrsng Home Social Actvities 89; Letter Writing Club Servicemen; Acct; CPA.

**BECOUARN, LAURENT J P,** Anderson Coll, Anderson, SC; SO; BA; Tnns Tm; Hon Pgm; Res Asst; Hon Stdnt; Kiwanis Awd; Bus Admin.

**BECTON, BELINDA M,** Duquesne Univ, Pittsburgh, PA; SO; BA; Blck Stdnt Union Pres; Rsdnt Asstnt 90-; Stndt Advsry Cmt 90-; Phi Eta Sgm VP 90-; Lmbd Sgm 90-; Sgm Dlt Chi 90-; Girl Scts Grp Ldr Asst 90-; Hunger Clean Up; Rookie Rsdnt Asst Yr 90-; Lmbd Sgm Schlrshp; Brdcst Cmnctns; News Brdcstng TV.

**BECTON, P ANGELA,** Mount Olive Coll, Mount Olive, NC; SO; BS; Engl Socty 90-; Art Clb 87-88; Pres Lst 88-; Dns Lst 87-88; Marshall 89; AS; Educ; Prncpl Tchr.

**BEDARD, SALVATORE C,** Widener Univ, Chester, PA; SR; BS; Acctng Soc; Tnns; Acctng; CPA.

**BEDASIE, DEONAUTH S,** City Univ Of Ny La Guard Coll, Long Island Cty, NY; GD; Elec Mech Engr Tech Clb Grphc Artst 90-; BSC; Cmptr Tech/Engl; Mgmt Info Sys.**

**BEDDINGFIELD, TRACY L,** Univ Of Nc At Asheville, Asheville, NC; SR; BA; Undrdog Prdctns 86-88; Inter Vars Chrstn Fllwshp 86-88; RHA 87-90; UNCA Dns Lst 88-90; Grad Ushr 89; Sigma Delta Chi 89-; Alpha Delta Pi VP 86-; RA 88-90; Std Nwspr 89; Prof Intrnshp 89; Ims 86-88; Big Bro/Big Sis 88; Mass Cmnctns; PR/ADV/MKT Rsrch.**

**BEDEAU, DESIREE D,** Lincoln Univ, Lincoln Univ, PA; FR; BA; Intl Stdnts Assn 90-; Frnch Clb Sec 90-; Cncrt Choir Sec 90-; INROADS Intrnshp; Hstry; Tch PhD.

**BEDEKOVICH, THERESA L,** Duquesne Univ, Pittsburgh, PA; JR; BED; Educ Schlrshp 90-; Ele Educ; Tch.

**BEDELL, CRAIG E,** Hudson Valley Comm Coll, Troy, NY; FR; AAS; Phi Theta Kappa; Cmptr Sci; Cmptr Analyst.

**BEDENBAUGH, MELANIE A,** Winthrop Coll, Rock Hill, SC; JR; BS; Alpha Delta Pi Pnhllnc Dlgte; Early Chldhd Ed; Tchr.

**BEDFORD, CHRISTOPHER W,** Duquesne Univ, Pittsburgh, PA; SR; BA; Swckly Bptst Chrsh Msc Dir 89-; Deans Lst 87-; Music Prfrmnce; Bass Plyr.

**BEDFORD, JOHN L,** Univ Of Al At Birmingham, Birmingham, AL; GD; ASCE 90-; Pres Dean Lst; BS; Cvl Eng.

**BEDNAR, KAREN R,** Indiana Univ Of Pa, Indiana, PA; FR; Cncrt Dnc 90; Hall Govt; New Stdnt Assn; Nwmn Cntr Chrch Vol; Elem Ed; Rdng Speclst.

**BEDNAR, LORI L,** Duquesne Univ, Pittsburgh, PA; SO; BSN; Stdnt Nrs Assc PA Pres 89-; Phi Eta Sgm 90-; Lmbd Sgm 90-; Alph Tau Dlt 90-; Natl Clgt Nrsng Awrd 90-; Dnatl Clgt Med Prof Awrd; Nrsng; Nrsng/Matrnty Pdtrcs.

**BEDNARZ, SHARON L,** Univ Of Akron, Akron, OH; SR; BS; Golden Key 89-; Kappa Delta Pi 90-; Oh Bell 80-83; Pick-N-Pay 75-77; US Sec Svc Clk/Steno 74-75; Elem Edctn; Tch.

**BEDNER, LORAN M,** Univ Of Pittsburgh, Pittsburgh, PA; SR; BA; Pitts Womns Swm Tm 87-89; Plnd 91 Socl Wrk Conf; Topic Wrn Persn Gulf; Intrnshp Sthsd Hosp 90; Socl Serv Dept; Big E Chmpnshp Estrn Chmpnshp; BFA Schl Soc Wrk; Socl Wrk.

**BEDWELL JR, JOHN R,** Kent St Univ Kent Cmps, Kent, OH; JR; BS; House Cncl Flr Rep 90-; House Cncl Res Stff Advsr; Socty Of Physcs Stdnts; Hnrs Coll 88-; Sigma Pi Sigma; Dns Lst 88-; Pres Lst 89; IM Vlybl/Flg Ftbl Capt 89-; Phys; Graduate.

**BEE, LORINETTE R,** Al St Univ, Montgomery, AL; JR; BS; Dscndnts Mthr Africa 88; Pi Mu Epsilon Tres; Pres Schlr 88; Math; Engr.

**BEEBE, BARBARA L,** Fayetteville St Univ, Fayetteville, NC; JR; BA; Newspaper Mng Ed 90-; Dept Crmnl Jstc Schlr Awd 90; AA 90; Crmnl Jstc; Law/Jrnlsm.

**BEEBE, BRIAN ROWELL,** Univ Of Fl, Gainesville, FL; JR; BS; Amer Nuclear Soc; Hnrs; Natl Cllgt Eng Awrd; Nuclear Eng.

**BEEBE, JADA L,** Defiance Coll, Defiance, OH; JR; BS; Campus Act Bd Pres 89-90; Stdnt Sen Sgt Arms 90-; Gamma Omega Kapa Sor; Wellness; Wellness Coordntr.

**BEEBE, JANICE R,** Univ Of South Al, Mobile, AL; JR; BA; Educ; Tchr.

**BEEBE, PAULA K,** Wilmington Coll, New Castle, DE; JR; BS; Elem Ed Erly Chldhd Ed; Education.

**BEECHER, MICHELLE M,** Memphis St Univ, Memphis, TN; SR; BA; As Librl Arts Sinclr Comm Clg 79; Mktg; Advrtsng.

**BEECHUM, CARRIE B,** Stillman Coll, Tuscaloosa, AL; SO; BS; Trng Chr; Chrldr Capt; Cordell Wynn Hnrs Pgm; Alpha Kappa Alpha Mbrshp Intk Prsn; Clge Chrldr; Chmcl Engrg.

**BEEG, LAURA L,** Cornell Univ Statutory College, Ithaca, NY; SR; JD; Admn Stdnt Rep 87-91; Res Asst 88-; Dorm Govt Adv 87-; Ho Nun De Kah; Alpha Omicron Pi Sr Rep 90-; Ho Nun De Kah Tufts Serv Clbs 87-; Phln Comm 90-; Nw Engl Med Ctr Vol 89; Dns Lst 87-; James Mion Awd 87-; Acorn Soc Schlrshp 87; Biol; Env Law.

**BEER, CHRISTOPHER TODD,** Savannah Coll Of Art & Design, Savannah, GA; SO; BFA; Fine Arts; Phtgrphy.

**BEERS III, ALVA E,** Asbury Theological Sem, Wilmore, KY; GD; M DIV; Praise/Wrshp Mus Tm Ldr 88-; Theta Phi V P 90-; BM Univ S Ala 87; Tch/Pstrl Mnstr.

**BEERS, KATHALEEN A,** Bloomfield Coll, Bloomfield, NJ; JR; BS; Challenge Grnt 88-; Deans Lst 89-90; Bus Admin/Mgmnt; Bus.

**BEERS, NATHANIEL B,** Univ Of Rochester, Rochester, NY; SR; BS; Prchc Actn Com Treas 89-; Yng Dmcrts 88-; Wmns Caucus 90-; Mrdn Soc 89-; Stdnt Intrvwrs 89-; Indpndnt Rsrch Nuerosci 90-; Vrsty Swm Tm 88-; IM Inner-Tube Water Polo 88-; Neurosci; Pdtrcs Med.

**BEERS, STEPHEN C,** Alfred Univ, Alfred, NY; FR; BS; Alpha Lambda Delta 90-; IM Sftbl 90-; Ceramic Engr.

**BEERS, TIMI J,** Univ Of Cincinnati, Cincinnati, OH; JR; BA; Alpha Lambda Detla 89-; Gldn Key 90-; Spec Ed; Tch.

**BEETS, JACQUELINE R,** Middle Tn St Univ, Murfreesboro, TN; SR; BS; SGA V P 87-89; Phi Theta Kappa V P 87-; Delta Psi Omega Pres 87-; Vars Sftbl 87-89; AA Martin Methodist Clg 89; Math; Scndry Educ.

**BEEVER, EMERY J,** Marshall University, Huntington, WV; SR; BA; Socl Studies; Tch.

**BEG, MIRZA H,** Oh Wesleyan Univ, Delaware, OH; SO; BA; Assoc Sqsh Plyrs Treas; Stdnt Cntr Entrtnmnt Comm; Islmc Stdnts Scty Treas; Phi Eta Sigma; Fclty Schlr 90-; Econ.

**BEGANY, AILEEN B,** Pace Univ At Pleasantville, Pleasantville, NY; JR; Mgt; Para-Legal/Law Schl.**

**BEGGINS, DAVID PAUL,** Fl International Univ, Miami, FL; SR; BS; Intl Food Serv Exec Assn Pr 90-; SG 89-90; Phi Lambda 90-; Stdnt Of Mnth 90; AS Culinary Inst Amer 88; Cert La Varenne Ecole De Cuisine 86; Hosp Mgmt; Restrnteur Profssr.

**BEGGS, JARED T,** Niagara Univ, Niagara Univ, NY; JR; BA; Bus Mgmt; Ins Indstry.

**BEGGS, TIFFANY E,** Glassboro St Coll, Glassboro, NJ; SR; BA; Advrtsng Clb 89-; Sigma Sigma Sigma Pres 89-; Intrnshp Ambassador Advrtsng 90; Cmnctns; Advrtsng/Merch.

**BEGIN, WENDI L,** Rivier Coll, Nashua, NH; SR; BS; Stdnt Govt Exctve Brd 90; Class Pres 88-90; Mdl United Ntns Dlgte 87; Prjct Hug 90; Bddy Prog 89; Prlgl Intrnshp Wth Twn Attrny In Hdsn NH; Athletic Assoc Pres 90; Prlgl Studies; Law.

**BEGIN-JAMES, JACQUELINE S,** Clark State Comm Coll, Springfield, OH; SO; BA; SAVE Fndr/Pres 90-F Stdnt Gov Rep Lrg 90-; Phi Theta Kappa 90-; Comm Cmmtmnt Schlrshp 89-90; Faclty Schlrshp 90-; News Sun Schlrshp 90-; Peace Stds.

**BEGLEY, JOSEPH J,** Atlantic Comm Coll, Mays Landing, NJ; JR; BA; Lit; Publshg/Wrtg.

**BEGLEY, SUSAN J,** Glassboro St Coll, Glassboro, NJ; GD; BA; Advrtsng Clb 88-90 Wrtr 90-; AAF; Cntnl Data Cntr Neptune NJ Sply Str Coord 89-; IM Sftbl; Cmmnctns Lbrl Arts.

**BEGOLE, JAMES M A,** Va Commonwealth Univ, Richmond, VA; JR; BS; Mltry Srvce Mdl 89; Natl Dfnse Mdl; Army Cmmndtn Mdl 85; Non Cmmssnd Offcrs Assn 84-; Assn Of US Army 82-; Arbc Intrprtr US Army; Comp Sci Math; Comp.

**BEGUN, YELENA,** City Univ Of Ny Baruch Coll, New York, NY; SR; BBA; Beta Gamma Sigma; Acctng Scty 88-; Acctng; Law.

**BEHAN, JOSEPHINE,** Christopher Newport Coll, Newport News, VA; JR; BA; Sclgy Scl Work Clb 90-; Alpha Kappa Delta; Willow Oaks Evng Grdn Clb Sec 79-; AAS Thomas Nelson Comm Clg 89; Scl Wrk/Sclgy.

**BEHAR, ROBERT,** Fl International Univ, Miami, FL; FR; Aids Info/Educ Pro Spksprsn 90; Bus; Law.

**BEHARRY, SHARON,** City Univ Of Ny Queensbrough, New York, NY; SO; BA; Alpha Beta Gamma; Acctng.

**BEHEE, BERNETA L,** Broward Comm Coll, Ft Lauderdale, FL; SO; AS; Phi Theta Kappa 90-; Pres Lst 90-; Phi Beta Lambda Proj Chrprsn Pub Rltns 88; Delta Epsilon Chi 89-; Achvmnt Awd Phi Beta Lambda Chrprsn Pub Rltns 88-; Cert Acad Exclnc Bus Law I 89; Hair Sylst; Mgmt; Mktg.

**BEHELER, LISA M,** Cecils Coll, Asheville, NC; GD; AAS; Paralegal; Real Estates Paralegal.

**BEHNERT, ELLEN B,** Bloomfield Coll, Bloomfield, NJ; SO; BSN; Stdnt Nrs Assoc; Nrsng; Rn.

**BEHNKEN, ANNA M,** Longwood Coll, Farmville, VA; FR; BA; SGA 90-; Hall Cncl 90-; Frhmn Hall Fame 90-; Eqstrn Tm 90-; Pltcl Sci/Pre Law; Law.

**BEHR, PETER J,** Univ Of Miami, Coral Gables, FL; FR; BA; Alpha Lambda Delta; Marine Biolgy; Marine Biolgst.

**BEHR, SUSAN E,** Univ Of Rochester, Rochester, NY; JR; BS; Scty Udrgte Bilgy Students Co Chrprn 90-; Microbiology; Med.

**BEHTZ, THOMAS E,** Milligan Coll, Milligan Clg, TN; SR; BA; Bus; Mktg.

**BEHUNIAK, KATHRYN M,** Schenectady County Comm Coll, Schenectady, NY; JR; AAS; SUNY Geneseo Rugby Clb 83-86; Lgl Sec; BA/ENGL SUNY Geneseo Cum Laude 86; Prlgl Studies.

**BEICHMAN, ROBIN B,** S U N Y At Binghamton, Binghamton, NY; JR; BS; Clg Woods Comm Council Hall Rep 89; Mngmnt Deans List 88-90; Sigma Delta VP 90; High Hopes Cnslng Cntr Cnslr 89-90; Acct; CPA.

**BEICHNER, HEIDI M,** Duquesne Univ, Pittsburgh, PA; SO; BS; Acdmy Students Pharmacy 90-; Pharmacy Intern Marianne Pharmacy; Chemistry; Pharmacy.

**BEIER, KAREN M,** Middle Tn St Univ, Murfreesboro, TN; JR; BS; Psi Chi; Phi Kappa Phi 90-; Gamma Beta Phi 88-89; AS Vlntr State Comm Coll 89; Psych; Cnslng/Clncl Psych.**

**BEIERSDORFER, ELIZABETH A,** Northern Ky Univ, Highland Hts, KY; SR; BME; MENC; Natl Assn Tchrs Sing Auditions Ky Wnr 90; Reg Vet Tech 78-84; Tch Voice; AS Appld Vet Med Purdue Univ 77; Music Educ.

**BEIGELMAN, HELENE S,** Yeshiva Univ, New York, NY; GD; Grad Magnum Cum Laude Stein Coll; MA Deolphi Univ; Judaic Stds/Educ.

**BEINHOCKER, ROBERT M,** Univ Of Rochester, Rochester, NY; JR; Amnsty Intl Chrprsn 8-; Flmmkng Clb 90-; Crew Nvc Crew Coach 88-90; Hstry/Film Stu; Flm Prdctn/Dir/Scrnwrtng.

**BEINSU, PATRICIA FUH,** Univ Of The Dist Of Columbia, Washington, DC; SR; BA; Econs Clb 87-89; Acctng Clb 88-89; Acctng; Bus Fin.

**BEIRNE, TIMOTHY M,** Va Commonwealth Univ, Richmond, VA; FR; BS; Coll Bwl 90-; Phi Eta Sigma 90-; Deans Lst 90-; Prsdntl Schlr; IM 90-; Chmstry.

**BEISH, SHAWN D,** Radford Univ, Radford, VA; SO; BA; Tns/Bk Rdg/Ping Pong/Pool/Wghtlftg; IM Tns; Mrktg; Mngmtn.

**BEISWENGER, JOHN GUNNAR,** Vt Law School, S Royalton, VT; GD; JD; Vermont Law Review Hdnts Edtr 90-; Solid Waste Grp Treas 90-; BA Univ Wi/Madison 86; Law; Envi Law.

**BEITING, JIM P,** Northern Ky Univ, Highland Hts, KY; SR; MSW; Mngmnt Awd 90; Fl Tme Chem Dpndncy Cnslr 90-; BA 90; Pblc Admin/Econ; Socl Wrk.

**BEKE, SUSAN E,** Univ Of Akron, Akron, OH; JR; BA; Acct Asc; Inst Mgmt Acctnts Sec 90-; Beta Alpha Psi Dir; Acctng/Bsn; Acctnt.

**BEKIROV, IDDIL H,** Univ Of Rochester, Rochester, NY; JR; BA; Soc Undrgrad Blgy Stdnts 87-88; Blgy/Psychlgy; Med/Rsrch.

**BEL, DELPHINE C,** Va Commonwealth Univ, Richmond, VA; FR; Ntl Hon Soc 90-; Frgn Echng Stdy Amer Scndnvn Stdnt Exchng Pgm 89-90; Bus; Intrntl Mktg.

**BELAND, MICHAEL P,** Univ Of Southern Ms, Hattiesburg, MS; SO; BA; Hnrs Stdnt Assoc 89-; Stdnt Eagle Club 89-; Fencing Club 89; Phi Eta Sigma 90-; Gamma Beta Phi 90-; Phi Kappa Phi; Phi Chi Theta 90-; Beta Gamma Sigma; IM Rcqtbl Soccer Team Tennis 89-; Acctng; CPA.

**BELANGER, ELIZABETH C,** Muskingum Coll, New Concord, OH; SO; BA; Mskngm Plyrs Drmtc Soc Actvts Dir 89-; Msknqm Clg Cncrt Choir 89-; Msknqm Vly Comm Bnd 90; Lambda Sigma Zeta 90-; Phi Sigma Iowa VP 89-; FAD Soc Clb 90-; Ohio Acad Schlrshp/Pres Schlrshp 89; French; Sec Educ.

**BELANGER, JAMES P,** Andover Coll, Portland, ME; SR; Accntng; CPA.

**BELANGER, KAREN L,** Univ Of Cin R Walters Coll, Blue Ash, OH; FR; BA; English.

**BELANGER, LINDA A,** Univ Of Nh, Durham, NH; FR; Safe Wlks Escrt Svc Vol 90-; Bus.

**BELANGER, MARY K,** Univ Of South Al, Mobile, AL; SR; BA; Deans List; Presdntl Deans List; S; Erly Chldhd Ed; Cnslng.

**BELANGER, MICHELLE A,** Unity Coll, Unity, ME; SO; BS; Flr Hcky/Vlybl 90-; Cnsrvtn Lw Enfrcmnt Clb 89-; Frst Fire Clb Sqd Bss 89-; Hghst Hnrs 89-; Hgh Hnrs 90-; Peer Cnslng; Crss Cntry Runng Vrsty Pin 89-; Prk Mngmnt.

**BELAVICH, TIMOTHY G,** Niagara Univ, Niagara Univ, NY; JR; BA; SABAH 88-; Ambassadors 88-; Gaelic 88-90; Phi Sigma Iota Treas 89-; Delta Epsilon Sigma 90-; NUCAP 88-; Psych Hnrs Thesis; Dns Lst 88-; Psych/French; Psych.**

**BELBASE, EKNATH,** Oh Wesleyan Univ, Delaware, OH; Vlybl 88-90; Stdnt Brd/Math Scncs Pres 90-; Pi Mu Epsilon Pres 89-; Phi O Soc 89-; Flrnc Leas 89-90; Whlr Poetry Prz 90; Math CS.

**BELCHER, AMY L,** Lock Haven Univ, Lock Haven, PA; FR; BA; Date Rape Task Frce; Spcl Edn; Tchr.

**BELCHER, CYNDI L,** Oh St Univ At Marion, Marion, OH; SR; BS; Ed Soc Chrprsn Ways/Means Comm 87-; Dns Lst 87-; Pi Lambda Theta; Sftbl Coach 89; Praire Tour Guide 88-; Campus Schlrshps 87-; Ed Soc Schlrshp 89; Vol Girl Scouts 87-; Elem Ed; Tchr.**

**BELCHER, DARA S,** Univ Of Montevallo, Montevallo, AL; FR; BA; Frshmn Hnr Soc; Hnrs Awd; Bsn; Acctg.

**BELCHER, DEBORAH I,** Univ Of Sc At Columbia, Columbia, SC; FR; BA; Shwchoir 90-; Scndry Educ/Engl; Tchr.

**BELCHER, GREGORY D,** Bristol Univ, Bristol, TN; GD; MBA; Summa Cum Laude; Big Bro 88-; Yth Mnstry 90-; Cmptr Anlyst 88-; BA Translvn Univ 88; BA Translvn Univ 88; Cmptr Inf Syst; Cmptng/Telecomm.

**BELCHER, JOE W,** Mountain Empire Comm Coll, Big Stone Gap, VA; SR; BA; AAS; Engr.

**BELCHER, JOSEPH M,** Oh Univ-Southern Cmps, Ironton, OH; SR; BS; Dns Lst; Jrnlsm; Law.

**BELCHER, MICHAEL L,** Va Highlands Comm Coll, Abingdon, VA; AAS; Patrick Henry Band Boosters Pres; Cert VA Cmptr Coll Alexandria VA 71; Bus Mgmt; Bus Owner/Tchr.

**BELCHER, MICHELLE D,** Middle Tn St Univ, Murfreesboro, TN; JR; BSN; Res Hl Assoc Treas 89-90; Stdnt Govt Assoc Elect Ofc 88-90; Gamma Phi Beta 89-90; Nrsg; Acute Care Nrsg.

**BELCHER, SHARI J,** Tn St Univ, Nashville, TN; JR; BS; Phi Theta Kappa 89-; Golden Key; Sigma Tau Delta V P Elect; SGA V P 88-89; Lit Mag Asst Ed Elect; AA Aquinas Jr Clg 89; Engl; Chldrns Wrtr/Poet.

**BELCHER, VICKIE C,** Central Fl Comm Coll, Ocala, FL; FR; AS; Paraprfsnl Org Sec; Phi Theta Kappa 89-; Legal Courses/Law.

**BELDARRAIN-CAPUTO, YOANY,** Fl International Univ, Miami, FL; GD; MA; Kappa Delta Phi 90-; Future Edctrs Amer 88-89; AA Miami-Dade Cmnty Clg 89; BA 90; Stdnt Tchg Intern Earlington Hts Elem 90; Ed; Tchg/Ed Resrch.

**BELDEN, CHRISTINE M,** Newbury Coll, Brookline, MA; FR; Exprssns Clb; Frshmn Encrgemnt Awd; Fshn Mrchndsng Bsnss; Boutique Ownr.

**BELEN, MIGUEL A,** S U N Y At Buffalo, Buffalo, NY; FR; Latinos Unidos 90-; Drm Ptrl 90-; NSPE 90-; Eng; Cvl Eng.

**BELEN, UZZIEL E,** Univ Politecnica De Pr, Hato Rey, PR; GD; BSEE; Inst Of Elect Elctrncs Engrs 90-; Elect Engrng.

**BELESOVSKI, REBECCA,** Daemen Coll, Amherst, NY; FR; BA; Intl Rltns.

**BELESSIMO, JOSEPH A,** S U N Y Coll Of Tech At Frmgdl, Farmingdale, NY; SO; BA; Bus Admin; CPA.

**BELEW, GREGORY L,** Univ Of North Fl, Jacksonville, FL; SO; BBA; Stdnt Govt Assn Sntr; Finance/Invstmnt Soc; Delta Sigma Pi; Intrnshp CSX Tchnlgy Strtgc Plng Analyst 90; Apprntcshp Nussbaum/Sons Cmrcl Real Est; Finance/Bus; Real Est Dvlpmnt.

**BELEY, SANDRA J,** Duquesne Univ, Pittsburgh, PA; SR; BS; Mgmt Infrmtn Systm; Databs Mgmt Cmptr Orntd.

**BELIVEAU JR, JOHN B,** Villanova Univ, Villanova, PA; SR; BA; NROTC Bttln Cmmdr 87-; RA 89-91; Phi Kappa Phi; Cmps Mnstry 88-90; Rof Navl Sci Awrd; Sec Navy Dist Mdshpmn Grad; Pol Sci; Ensign U S Navy.

**BELIVEAU, LYNN M,** Springfield Tech Comm Coll, Springfield, MA; GD; Alpha Nu Omega 89-90; Lcnced RN; Hosp RN; ASN 90; Nrsng.

**BELIZAIRE, FARHESE,** Saint Thomas Univ, Miami, FL; JR; BA; Haitian Ibo Clb Treas 84-87; Ibo Clb Soccer Tm Capt 86-87; Edn; Teach.

**BELK, BELINDA ANITA,** Johnson C Smith Univ, Charlotte, NC; SO; BA; Pre-Tchng Prog Grp Ldr; Otstndng Ldrshp Awd Grp Ldr; Accting; Internal Auditor.

**BELK, DENISE A,** Univ Of Sc At Columbia, Columbia, SC; GD; PHARM; Orchestra 85-86; Acad Stdnt Phrmcy 87-90; Amer Scty Hosp Phrmcst 90-; Kappa Epsilon Chpln 86-; Prsbytrn Stdnt Ctr Sec 85-90; Greater Alumni Schlrshp 85-88; BS 90; Pharmacy.

**BELKHIRIA, NACEUR M,** Bunker Hill Comm Coll, Boston, MA; SO; BS; Oil Drilling Equip Trading; Math; Intl Bsn.

**BELKIN, MARNI B,** Univ Of Miami, Coral Gables, FL; SO; BA; Hmcmng 89; Grk Wk 89; Delta Phi Epsilon Risk Mgr 89; Hrrcnes Hlp The Hmtwn 89; Fun Day 89; Sprtsfst Grk Wk 89; Crmnl Jstce; Law.

**BELKNAP, JOHN W,** Kent St Univ Kent Cmps, Kent, OH; FR; BA; Alpha Lambda Delta; Sigma Phi Epsilon; Intrnshp Congrsmn Ralph Regula; Bsns Admn; Fin.

**BELKNAP, ROBERT W,** Kent St Univ Kent Cmps, Kent, OH; FR; BS; IM Bsktbl 90-; Alpha Lambda Delta; Sigma Phi Epsilon; Pres List 90; Zoology; Pediatrician.

**BELL, ANDREA D,** Univ Of Montevallo, Montevallo, AL; JR; BS; Bptst Cmps Mnstrs Mssns Chrmn 90; Lambda Sigma Pi; Phi Kappa Phi; Phi Beta Kappa; Pow Wow Ldrshp Scty VP 89-90; Mssnry; Citizenshp Awrd; AA Faulkner State Co 90; Sclgy; Inner Cty Mssnry.

**BELL, ANDREW C,** Northeast State Tech Comm Coll, Blountville, TN; FR; AAS; Amer Chem Soc; Chem Tech; Envir Engr.

**BELL, ANGELA M,** Radford Univ, Radford, VA; JR; BS; Panhellenic Hsng Chrmn 90-; Sigma Kappa Schlrshp Chrmn 90-; St Albins Psych Hsptl Vol; Psychology; Grad Phd Prgrms.

**BELL, ANIKA V,** Fl A & M Univ, Tallahassee, FL; FR; MBA; Class Adv Brd 90-; Res Hall Dorm Pr 90-; Phi Eta Sigma 90-; Bus Admin; Mktg.

**BELL, ANNETTE D,** Memphis St Univ, Memphis, TN; SO; MBA; Hons Stndt Assn 89-; Stndt Act Cncl; Tigern Den Comm Sec 89-90; Peer Mentor Pgm Exec Cncl 89-; Phi Eta Sigma 90-; Alpha Lambda Delta Histrn 90-; Gamma Beta Phi 90-; Pi Beta Phi; Barlett Bapt Chrch Coll/Career Cncl 90-; Acctg; Txtn.

**BELL, ANNETTE M,** Hudson Valley Comm Coll, Troy, NY; SR; AAS; Intrnshp Lwyrs Offce Gleason Dunn Walsh O'shea Fld Scrty; Deans Lst Pres Lst 90; Exec Scrtrl Sci.

**BELL, ANTHONY W,** Northern Ky Univ, Highland Hts, KY; SR; BS; Indstrl Rel Rsrch Assn 90; Indstrl Labor Rel; Personnel Labor Rel.

**BELL, BEVERLY MIMS,** Ga Coll, Milledgeville, GA; JR; BBA; Advrtsg Clb; Phi Kappa Phi; GEICO Ins Co Schlrshp; Wal-Mrt Fndtn Schlrshp 88-90; Outstdg Stdt Schlrshp 88-; Mrktg; Bsn.**

**BELL, BOBBI A,** York Coll Of Pa, York, PA; FR; MBA; Math Tutor 90-; Education/History; Coll Prof.

**BELL, CAROLYN M,** Univ Of Sc At Columbia, Columbia, SC; FR; BA; S Carolina Clg Hnrs Clg; Kappa Kappa Gamma Treas; Alumni Schlr; IM Tennis Vlybl; Gov Intl Studies.

**BELL, CHANTELE C,** Tuskegee Univ, Tuskegee Inst, AL; SO; BS; NABA 90-; SGA 90-; Acctng; CPA.

**BELL, CHARLEIGH T,** Univ Of Ga, Athens, GA; SR; BLA; GSLA 88-; Sigma Lambda Alpha; Deans Lst 89-90; Landscape Arch.

**BELL, CHARLENE Y,** Fl A & M Univ, Tallahassee, FL; FR; Phrmst.

**BELL, CHARLES A,** Va Commonwealth Univ, Richmond, VA; SO; BS; Bow Clb Pres; Nom Otsdng Stdnt; Forman Sys Engr; Cmptr Sci; Cmptr Engr.

**BELL, CHARLES L,** Middle Tn St Univ, Murfreesboro, TN; JR; BS; MTSU Flyng Raiders Flght Tm 90-; Alph Eta Rho Arspc Frat Pres; Arpsc Admn; Nvl Avtr.

**BELL, CHERYL A,** Univ Of Akron, Akron, OH; JR; BED; ACES; GTE; SW Genl Hosp; Elem Tchr.

**BELL, CHERYL L,** Tougaloo Coll, Tougaloo, MS; SO; BA; Stu Spprt Serv 89-; Spnsh Clb 90-; Math Cmptr Sci Clb 90-; Psychlgy; Chld Psychlgst.

**BELL, CHRISTINE M,** Univ Of Nh Plymouth St Coll, Plymouth, NH; JR; BA; Phi Kappa Phi; Pres List 88-; Concord Mntr Newspr Concord NH 83-; Elem Educ; Tchng.

**BELL, CONNIE J,** Tn Tech Univ, Cookeville, TN; GD; Dorm Pres 81; Golden Stab Drill Tm 78-79; BS TTU 83; Home Ec; Tchng Pstn.

**BELL, DANIEL F,** Oh St Univ, Columbus, OH; SO; BS; Wildlife Soc 90-; Top Schlr Awd 90-; Dns Lst 90-; Carpenter 85-90; Zoology; MS Ph D Zoology.

**BELL, DAWN R,** Wv Northern Comm Coll, Wheeling, WV; JR; AS; Triadelphia Vol Fire Dept Wmns Aux; Sec Wheeling Dollar Bank 89-; Sec Sci.

**BELL, DONNA M,** Univ Of Fl, Gainesville, FL; FR; BA; United Daughters Confederacy 90-; Alpha Lambda Delta 90-; Univ Habitat Hmnty 90-; News Rep/Anchor WRUF AM/FM Stdnt Intern 90-; Telecmnctns; Brdcst Jrnlsm.

**BELL, DUANE J,** Al St Univ, Montgomery, AL; FR; BA; Interstate Natl Corp Gen Clerk Intern 90-; Syst Analyst.

**BELL, ELISE B,** Bluefield Coll, Bluefield, VA; JR; BA; Bptst Stdnt Un VP 87-88; Psychlgy; Cmps Mnstry.

**BELL, ELIZABETH Y,** Coll Of Charleston, Charleston, SC; JR; BS; Org Non Tradtnl Stdnts Tr 88-; Charlstn Area Chptr Archlgcl Soc 89-; Dist Vol Yr Murray La Saine Elem 89-90; Dist Vol Yr Murray La Saine Elem 86-87; Serv Awd Murray La Saine Elem 88-89; Car Low Cntry Grl Scts 85-91; PTA 79-91; Elem Educ/Antrhplgy; Tchg/Archlgy.

**BELL, ERIK M,** Fl A & M Univ, Tallahassee, FL; FR; BS; Hlth/Phys Educ; Phys Thrpst.

**BELL, FRANK D,** Comm Coll Algny Co Algny Cmps, Pittsburgh, PA; FR; ASSOC; Emt II Trng Emer Rm; Sec Corr Admn.

**BELL, GENE A,** Tougaloo Coll, Tougaloo, MS; FR; BS; Psych; Med.

**BELL, GENEVA D,** Fayetteville St Univ, Fayetteville, NC; FR; BS; Med Tech.

**BELL, GLENDA D,** Northern Ky Univ, Highland Hts, KY; FR; BS; Blck Untd Stdnts Rec Sec; Act Prgmg Brd; Mentr Pgm; Natl Blck Wmns Org; NAACP; Prop Transfr Examnr Guilfrd Cnty Tax Dept Greensboro N C 79-90; RESL Mosly Flnt Schl Real Est Greensboro 83; Soc/Afrcn Amer Stds; Educ.

**BELL, GLORIA C,** Lincoln Univ, Lincoln Univ, PA; SO; BA; Thurgood Marshall Law Soc 90-; Ziana Fashion Clb 90-; Que Pearl Treas 89-; Actvts Comm Chrprsn 89-; Stdnt Ldr Ntwrk 89-; Track 89-90; Pol Sci; Corp Law.

**BELL, JANETTE E,** Memphis St Univ, Memphis, TN; SO; BA; Peer Mentor Prog 89-; Hnrs Stdnt Assoc 89-; Phi Eta Sigma Pres 90-; Alpha Lambda Delta 90-; Gamma Beta Phi 90-; 1st Tenn Bank Coll Intern 89-; Bus; Acctng.

**BELL, JUDY CHRISTINE,** Univ Of Southern Ms, Hattiesburg, MS; JR; BSN; SGA VP 88-89; Hrt Of Dixie 90-; Gamma Beta Phi; Nursing; Anesthetist.

**BELL, KAREN B,** Savannah St Coll, Savannah, GA; SR; BS; Psychlgy Clb Sec 90-; Nwspr Rprtr 89-; Ntl Assc Black Accnts 89-; Pi Gamma Mu 90-; Alpha Kappa Mu; Alpha Kappa Alpha Hodegos 90-; Acad Scholor Award; History; Education.

**BELL, KEVIN T,** Mayland Comm Coll, Spruce Pine, NC; FR; Eagle Scout; Crmnl Jstc; Parks/Rec Mgmt.

**BELL, KRISTINE A,** Lasell Coll, Newton, MA; FR; Chorus 90-; Drama 90-; Human Serv 90-; Red Cross Coord 90-; RA; Vllybl/Sftbl 90-; Hmn Serv; Admin.

**BELL, LEA N,** Kent St Univ Kent Cmps, Kent, OH; FR; BA; Alpha Lambda Delta; Pre Med/Psych.

**BELL, MELISSA,** Alcorn St Univ, Lorman, MS; SR; Sch Nwspr Edtr Chf 89-; Prfsnl Sec Intl; Stdnt Free Entrprs; Alpha Kappa Mu; BS; Sec Sci; Admn Asst.

**BELL, MICHAEL D,** Univ Of Montevallo, Montevallo, AL; FR; Math; Bus.

**BELL, NICHOLAS P,** Duke Univ, Durham, NC; FR; BS; Phi Eta Sigma 90-; Sigma Chi 90-; Bio; Med.

**BELL, NICHOLAS R,** Univ Of Nc At Asheville, Asheville, NC; JR; BA; Psi Chi; Psychlgy; Clncl Psychlgst.

**BELL, PARTHENIA K,** Johnson C Smith Univ, Charlotte, NC; JR; U Choir 88-; Biology; Phrmclgy.

**BELL, PATRICIA L,** Salisbury St Univ, Salisbury, MD; SR; BS; Stdnt Natl Educ Assn 89-; Phi Eta Sigma 88; Psi Chi 90-; Phi Kappa Phi 90-; Kappa Delta Pi VP 90-; Pi Kamma Mu 90-; Wicomico Cnty Wmns Clb Schlrshp 90; Dns Lst 87-; Mrylnd Distgshd Schlr Schlrshp 87-; Paul Douglas Tchrs Schlrshp 87-; Elem Educ; Tchng.

**BELL, RANDALL E,** Middle Tn St Univ, Murfreesboro, TN; JR; BS; Alpha Gamma Rho 90-; Agri Bsn.

**BELL, ROBIN D,** Clark Atlanta Univ, Atlanta, GA; FR; BA; Advrtsng Clb 90-; Clgte All Amer Schlr 90-; Dns Lst 90; Waok/Wvee V-103 Intrnshp; Mjrtte Mrchng Bnd 90-; Mass Cmnctns; Brdcst Jrnlst.

**BELL, SANDRA M,** Univ Of Ga, Athens, GA; JR; BSED; Hall Cncl 88-89; Clg Rep 87-90; Erly Chldhd Educ; Elem Tchr.

**BELL, SHERRED W,** Commonwealth Coll, Virginia Beach, VA; SR; CERT; Cmmnwlth Clg Law Scty Treas; Amer Mrktng Assoc Applchn State U 85-88; Phi Beta Lambda Applchn State U 87-88; Engl Hnr Roll Applchn State U 85; Pres Lst 90; Arlgl Intrnshp; Var Vllybl Applchn State U 84-85; BS 88; Prlgl Studies; Law.

**BELL, STEPHEN T,** Roane St Comm Coll, Harriman, TN; SO; BA; Bptst Stdnt Un 89-; Engrg.**

**BELL, SUSAN ELIZABETH,** Hillsborough Comm Coll, Tampa, FL; FR; BA; Educ; Cnslng.

**BELL, TAJUAN N,** Al St Univ, Montgomery, AL; FR; Phi Eta Sigma.

**BELL, TERESA R,** Alcorn St Univ, Lorman, MS; SO; BS; IM Bsktbl Team Co-Capt 89-90; Acctg/Bus Admin; Bus Exec.

**BELL, TIMONY A,** Univ Of Southern Ms, Hattiesburg, MS; JR; BA; Gamma Beta Phi; Soc Rehab Svcs; Cnslr.

**BELL, TRACEY D,** Ms Gulf Coast Comm Coll, Perkinston, MS; FR; BA; Phi Theta Kappa; Phi Beta Lambda; Acctg; PTA.

**BELL, TRACY C,** Univ Of The South, Sewanee, TN; FR; BABS; Soc Of Wilkins Schlrs 90-; Engl; Math.

**BELL, VICKY L,** Al St Univ, Montgomery, AL; SR; Pi Gamma Mu Pres 90-; Lambda Alpha Epsilon 90-; Cshr/Chckr Cert Food Serv Schl; BS; Crmnl Just; Jvnl Cnslr/Prbtn Offcr.

**BELL, VIOLETTE P,** Piedmont Comm Coll, Roxboro, NC; FR; ASN; NC Nrs Assoc; Phi Kappa Phi; Phi Omicron Nu; NC Nrs Schlr; Prsdnt Shnr Rll; Psychlscl Rhbltn 60-; BS E Carolina Univ 70; Nrsng; Prfssnl Nrs.

**BELL, WENDI D,** Nc St Univ At Raleigh, Raleigh, NC; FR; BA; Peer Mentor; Deans List; Inroads 88-; Intrnshp J A Jones Constrctn Co 90-; Arch.

**BELL, YVONNE M,** Univ Of Al At Birmingham, Birmingham, AL; SR; BS; Kappa Delta Pi 90-; Erly Chldhd Educ; Tchng.

**BELL-RANEY, WENDY L,** Saint Leo Coll, Saint Leo, FL; SR; BA; TX State Tchrs Assoc 90; TX Ed Assoc 90; Dns Lst 90; Paris Jr Clg Schlrshp 87; Sclgy; Tchg.

**BELLA, ALYSSA N,** Univ Of Rochester, Rochester, NY; SO; BA; Univ Glee Clb Soc Dir; Undrgrd Hstry Cncl 89-90; Tutorng Baden St Sttlmnt 89-90; Prtnrs Rdng Prog Loc Sch Chldrn 90-; IM Flr Hcky 89-; Hstry; Tchr/Admn.

**BELLAMENTE, ELLEN JENNIFER,** Georgetown Univ, Washington, DC; JR; BSBA; Big Sis Pgm 89-; Busn; Mktg.

**BELLAMY, CAROLYN W,** Abraham Baldwin Agri Coll, Tifton, GA; SO; B; Kappa Delta Pi; AS ABAC 90; Math-Lang Arts; Teaching.

**BELLAMY, GEORGIA M,** Univ Of Sc At Coastal Carolina, Conway, SC; FR; BA; Minrty Profsnl Bus Assoc; Proprty Mngmnt; English; Tch Law.

**BELLAND, SALLY A,** Comm Coll Algny Co South Cmps, West Mifflin, PA; GD; BA; Scl Work; Fmly Thrpy.

**BELLANTONI, LISA M,** Allegheny Coll, Meadville, PA; SR; BA; Soup Kitchen Vlntr 89-; IM Sprts 87-; Phi Belta Kappa; Dstnshd Alden Schlr 88-; Phlsophy.

**BELLAVE, ROBERT L,** Bryant Stratton Bus Inst Roch, Rochester, NY; GD; AOS; Tech Clb; Lab Monitor Tutoring Stdnts; Elect; Cmptr Tech.

**BELLER, REBECCAH LEE,** Fl St Univ, Tallahassee, FL; SR; BA; Seminole Fllws Prog Advsr 89; Tech Staff Wrtr 87-88; Vllybl Ims Capt 90; Golden Key 90; Gamma Beta Phi 88-89; Ordr Of Thirty/Three 88-89; Alpha Phi Omega 90; Res Schlrs 87-89; Dean Witter Intrnshp 89; Magna Cum Laude; Womens Var Vllybl Mgr 88; Cmmnctn; Law.

**BELLILE, JOYCELYN A,** Univ Of The Virgin Islands, St Thomas, VI; SR; BA; Phi Beta Lambda Treas 90-; Stdnt Govt Jr Sntr 89-90; Cls Treas 90-; Pres Clb 90-; Dns Lst; Advntst Yth Ldr/Cnslr 89-90; Red Crs First Aid Instrctr 87-88; RA 90-; Intrnshp Bus Offc; Vlybl VP 89-90; Acctng; Law.

**BELLINA, AMY J,** S U N Y Coll At Buffalo, Buffalo, NY; FR; BS; Cncrt Bnd 90-; Acdmc Hnrs Lst; Excptnl Educ; Tchg.

**BELLINGER, SARA JANE M,** Clarkson Univ, Potsdam, NY; JR; BS; Clrkson Univ Stdnt Assoc Stdnt Sen Snr Rep; Amrcn Mrktng Assoc 90-; Natl Ag Mrktng Assoc Pres 88-90; Scty Wmns Mgrs 90-; Phi Theta Kappa 89-; Phi Sigma Sigma Jdcl Brd Rep Hstrn 90-; Pr Advsr Stdnt Crdntr; Mgmt.

**BELLIZZI III, JOHN J,** Ma Inst Of Tech, Cambridge, MA; FR; SB; Hse Gov Undergrad Assc 90-; Mscl Thtr Co 90-; Stdnt Alumni Com 90-; Sclng/Rd Rcng; IM Vlybl/Sprng Wknd Olympiad; Chemistry; Medicne/Rsrch.

**BELLO, ANA MARIA,** Fl International Univ, Miami, FL; SO; BA; AMA; Phi Lambda; Mrktng; Bus.

**BELLO, BRENDA,** City Univ Of Ny City Coll, New York, NY; SO; MBA; Arch.

**BELLO, JOAQUIN P,** Saint Thomas Univ, Miami, FL; GD; Deans Lst; Crcl De Cltrl Pnamrcn; Prfssr 68; BA Spnsh 90; Ed.

**BELLO, MAGALY L,** Fl International Univ, Miami, FL; FR; BA; Deans Lst 90-; Sciz; Med Lab Sci.

**BELLOCCHI, LUKE P,** Univ Of Rochester, Rochester, NY; SR; BA; SG Prlmntrn 90-; Acad Affairs Com Chair; Deans Lst; Serv Dorm Steering Com 87-88; Escort Serv Exec 88; IM Soccer Capt 87-; Pol Sci/Psychlgy; Law.

**BELLONE, MICHELLE A,** Saint Thomas Univ, Miami, FL; SR; BA; Math Soc VP 85-87; Stdnts Global Preservation; Deans List; Trnsfr Asst Grant; Soft Ball; AS North Shore Comm Clg 90; Finance; Banking.

**BELLOTTI, STEPHANIE L,** Niagara Univ, Niagara Univ, NY; SO; ROTC-RANGE Chllng Tm; Bus; CPA.

**BELLUCCI, SUSAN J,** City Univ Of Ny Queensbrough, New York, NY; SO; AS; Phi Theta Kappa 89-; Alpha Beta Gamma 89-; GSA; St Matthews Chrch Cncl 86-88 Sndy Schl Tchr 83-; Goldberger Doll Mfg Co Inc 73-; Bsn; Mktg/Sales.

**BELLVILLE, SUSAN A,** West Liberty St Coll, West Liberty, WV; SR; BA; Newspaper 89-; Delta Sigma Pi VP 88-; Bus Admin Acctng; Auditing/Acctng.

**BELMAN, ROGER P J,** Eckerd Coll, St Petersburg, FL; SR; BA; Pltcl Sci.

**BELMONTE, NATALIE A,** Fl International Univ, Miami, FL; SR; BA; Ford Fndtn Intern 90-; Elem Ed.

**BELMORE, TIMOTHY A,** Nova Univ, Ft Lauderdale, FL; GD; MBA; PTA 90-; Soc Mktg Prof Srvs 89-90; Sprvsr Prjct Cmrcl Srvcs 80-; BA Univ Mass 75; Bsn; Mktg Engrg Serv.

**BELOIN, DONNA R,** Saint Josephs Coll, Windham, ME; FR; BSN; Sprkds 90-; Natl Stdnt Nrs Assoc 90-; Deans List 90; IM Bsktbl/Sftbl/Vlybl 90-; Nursing.

**BELOT, SUSAN V,** Springfield Tech Comm Coll, Springfield, MA; SO; AS; Brtndr; Nrs Asst; Nrsng; RN Psychtrc Nrsng.

**BELOWSKY, ALISON K,** Hillsborough Comm Coll, Tampa, FL; SO; BA; Political Sci; Law.

**BELT, TANJA C,** Christopher Newport Coll, Newport News, VA; FR; Pol Sci/Educ; Tchng.

**BELTON, DAVID,** Coppin St Coll, Baltimore, MD; SR; BS; AA Essex Comm Coll 88; Psych; Cnslng.

**BELTON, INNIS KILA KITU,** Univ Of Sc At Columbia, Columbia, SC; SO; Bus; Acctg.

**BELTON, JESSICA A,** Kent St Univ Kent Cmps, Kent, OH; FR; BSN; Gymnstcs Clb 90-; Nurs.

**BELTON, TAMMY L,** Longwood Coll, Farmville, VA; FR; BS; Bptst Stdnt Un, Psychology; Eduoation.

**BELTON, TERESA R,** Univ Of Southern Ms, Hattiesburg, MS; JR; BS; AS Mississippi Gulf Coast Cmnty Clg 84; Elem Educ; Tch.

**BELTOWSKI, DENISE L,** Saint Francis Coll, Loretto, PA; FR; BS; AS Cambria Rowe Bus Clg 80; Physcns Asstnt.

**BELTRAN, FRANCOISE E,** City Univ Of Ny La Guard Coll, Long Island Cty, NY; SO; AS; Parent Clb V P 90-; Phi Theta Kappa 90-; Cabrini Med Ctr 90; Our Lady Of Mercy Med Ctr Vol; Wic Prog Vol; Nutrition; Food Sci.

**BELTRAN, JOSE E,** Fl Inst Of Tech, Melbourne, FL; FR; Crew 90-; Aviation; Pilot.

**BELTZ, ANGELA D,** Pasco Hernando Comm Coll, Dade City, FL; FR; AA; Fashn Dsgn/Mktg; Merchdsng.

**BELTZ, BEVERLY A,** Central St Univ, Wilberforce, OH; GD; Southwestern Ohio Schl Nrs Assn; RN Chrst Hosp Schl Nrsng 55; BS Hlth Educ 90; Cert Schl Nrsng 90.

**BELTZ, KAREN E,** Salisbury St Univ, Salisbury, MD; SR; BA; Psych Clb 87-; Psi Chi Treas 89-; Phi Kappa Phi; Mental Hlth Intrnshp 90; Psych Inst Of Washington DC; Psych; Ma Soc Wrk.

**BELTZ, MARY ALLISON,** Belmont Coll, Nashville, TN; JR; BBA; Judcl Cncl Assoc Jdg; Belmont Vision Layout Edtr 90-; Gamma Beta Phi; 25 Plus Club 90-; Jr Achvmnt; Natl Assoc Of Female Exec 86-89; Amercn Mkts Assn Exec VP; Htl Bus Sls Mgr 86-90; Untd Way Admnstrtv Asst 90-; Mktg; Clg Profsr.

**BELU-JOHN, YVONNE A,** Univ Of The Dist Of Columbia, Washington, DC; SO; BA; Blgy Clb; Bio Chmstry; Med.

**BELUSIK, JOHN A,** Fl Atlantic Univ, Boca Raton, FL; JR; BA; Bus Mgmt.

**BELVIN, MICHELE L,** Christopher Newport Coll, Newport News, VA; JR; BA; Elem Ed; Tchr/Cnslr.

**BELZ, MICHAEL A,** Memphis St Univ, Memphis, TN; JR; BA; SGA Elctn Comm 90-; Pre Law Scty; Beta Gamma Sigma; Lgsltv Intern 90; Abe D Waldauer Mem Schlrshp 89-; Cert Natl Assc Securties Dlr 87; Finance; Law.

**BELZAGUY, VALERIE,** Miami Dade Comm Coll, Miami, FL; SO; AA; Switchbrd Of Miami Crises Intervntn Cnslr/Trnr 82-; James L Knight Schlrshp; Personnel Brd City Hialeah Vice Chair 88-; Mgr Whlslr Dist Importer Of Wines 78-; Business; Bus High Level Mgmnt.

**BELZEL, JENNIFER C,** Univ Of Miami, Coral Gables, FL; FR; BS; Res Clg Cncl; Alpha Lambda Delta 90-; Provosts Hon Rl 90-; Sprts Fest; Biology; Med.

**BELZER, ROBERT A,** City Univ Of Ny Baruch Coll, New York, NY; SR; BBA; Fin/Econ Scty Sec 90-; Golden Key 90-; Golden Key Schlrshp Awd 90-; Crpntr 83-; Fin; Anlyst.

**BELZILE, ETIENNE,** Cornell Univ Statutory College, Ithaca, NY; SO; BSC; Athlte In Actn 90-; Red Key 90-; Ice Hcky 89-; Nrblgy And Bhvr; Med Sci.

**BEMBENEK, JAMES A,** Ms St Univ, Miss State, MS; SO; BA; Prfssnl Glf Mgmt Clb 89-; Mrktng; Glf Prfssnl.

**BEMBO, GLADYS P,** Oh Coll Of Podiatric Med, Cleveland, OH; JR; DPM; Amer Assc Wmn Podtrsts 89-; Educ Tst Comm 88; Pi Delta; Kappa Tau Epsilon Clncl Dir 90-; BS Hofstra Univ 88; Podiatry.

**BEMBRY, REBEKAH C,** Fl St Univ, Tallahassee, FL; JR; MACC; Lady Scalphntrs; Camps Crs Chrst 90-; Lond Stdy Pgm 90; Litl Sistr Phi Kappa Psi 89-90; AA 90; Acctg.

**BEMPKINS, JENNIFER L,** Univ Of Rochester, Rochester, NY; SR; BA; Cornelius Wrght Schlrshp; Bio Psych; Pharmaceutical Co.

**BEN-GAL, IRIS Z,** Univ Of Nc At Greensboro, Greensboro, NC; SR; BA; Dns Lst 86-; Intrnshp Moser Mayer Sutphin Assoc 89-90; Int Desgn; Arch.

**BENALI, OTMANE,** Radford Univ, Radford, VA; JR; Intl Clb 89-; Kappa Mu Epsilon 90-; Kappa Delta Rho 89-; Awd Excllnc Math Schlrshp; Math/Statstcs; Prfssr.

**BENAMATI, MARCIA L,** Indiana Univ Of Pa, Indiana, PA; SR; BS; PA State Ed Assoc; Natl Educ Assoc; Deans Lst; Elem Educ; Teach.

**BENAVIDES, BRADLEY S,** Northeast State Tech Comm Coll, Blountville, TN; SO; BA; Tn Tae Kwon Do Judo Clb Blk Blt; Chmcl Sclrshp Estmn Kodk Chmcl Cmpny; Cmnstry; Chmcl Rsrch.

**BENCH, MICHELE M,** Univ Of Nc At Chapel Hill, Chapel Hill, NC; FR; BA; Spnsh.

**BENCHIMOL, SANDRA,** Yeshiva Univ, New York, NY; SR; BA; Chem Clb 87-; Sigma Delta Rho 87-88; Sphrctc Clb 87-; Vstg The Sck Soc 87-; Roth Schlrshp 90; Jzzrcs Clb; Math; Med.

**BENCIC, LINDA J,** Kent St Univ Kent Cmps, Kent, OH; GD; Alpha Lambda Delta Tr 74-75; Beta Gamma Sigma 75-76; Beta Phi Mu; Schlrshp Awd Burroughs Corp 75-76; Jamestwn Newcmrs Clb Tr 81-83; Matheson Park Schl Girl Scout Ldr VP 87-; Bank Examer State Ohio 76-79; Library Sci; Librarian.

**BENCIVENGA, ANDREA G,** Nova Univ, Ft Lauderdale, FL; GD; MBA; Deans List Barry U; Bus/Bnkng; Fnc.

**BENCIVENGA, ANTONIA D,** S U N Y Coll Of Tech At Frmgdl, Farmingdale, NY; SO; BA; Alpha Beta Gamma V P 90-; NAA 90-; NSPA; Alpha Beta Gamma; Louis J Rizzo Schlrshp 90-; Acctg; CPA.

**BENCIVENGA, MARY JO,** Georgian Court Coll, Lakewood, NJ; SO; BS; Rep Clb Camps Coord 89-90; Phi Theta Kappa 88-; Mendel Soc 90-; Amer Chem Soc 90-; Tutr 88-90; Alpha Delta Kappa Awd 89-; 89-; Pres Lst 88-; Cum Laude; Orthodx Chrstn Chrch 88-; Realtrs Act Pol 89-, Act Duty U S Navy Air Trfc Cnt 83-87; Bio/Chem Educ; Prof.

**BENCOMO-LARA, MARIA J,** Inter Amer Univ Pr Hato Rey, Hato Rey, PR; FR; BA; Bus Admin; Acctng.

**BENDA, KRISTI L,** S U N Y Coll At Fredonia, Fredonia, NY; JR; BA; Orchesis Sec 88; Tchr Ed Clb Tutoring 88; Vol At Day Care Ctr 90; Deans Lst 88; Kappa Delta Pi; Classical Ballet Schlrshp 90; Elem Ed; MS In Elem Ed.**

**BENDER, ANDREA LOUISE,** Coll Misericordia, Dallas, PA; SO; BS; CMSOTA 89-; Commuter Cncl 90-; Rsrch Cnfrnce; Occptnl Therpy.

**BENDER JR, DONALD H,** Duquesne Univ, Pittsburgh, PA; SO; BED; WLDSR Stdnt Radio 89-; Duquesne Duke Nwspr Wrtr 90-; Russian Clb 90-; Phi Eta Sigma 89-; Intgrtd Hon Prog; Sec Educ/Soc Stdes; H S Soc Stdes Tchr.

**BENDER, ELIZABETH L,** Mary Baldwin Coll, Staunton, VA; SR; BA; Jdcl Bd Flr Pres 88-89; Amnsty Intl Treas 90-; Extrcrrclr Educ Com Stdnt Rep 90-; Omicron Delta Epsilon Pres 90-; H S Tutor 89-90; Task Frc Stdnt Rep 88-89; PEG Plnng Com Stdnt Rep 89-90; Pblshd Miscellany 90-; MB Hstrcl Rvw 88-89; Ecnmcs; Coll Prfssr.

**BENDER, MARK C,** James Madison University, Harrisonburg, VA; JR; BA; Psych Clb; Psi Chi; Psych; Clnclr Soc Psych.

**BENDER, SUSAN A,** Christopher Newport Coll, Newport News, VA; SO; BA; Stdnt Orientatn Ldr; Crss Cntry/Track/Fld 89-; Hstry; Elem Tchr.

**BENDERS, STEVE,** City Univ Of Ny Baruch Coll, New York, NY; JR; BBA; Mngmnt Operations; Bsn Mngmnt

**BENDLER, DOROTHY L,** Cumberland County Coll, Vineland, NJ; SO; BA; Ed; Elem Tchr.

**BENDO, JOHN D,** S U N Y Coll Of Tech At Frmgdl, Farmingdale, NY; SO; BS; Engr Sci Soc Prspctv Engrs Pres 90-; Phi Theta Kappa 90-; Mu Alpha Theta 89-; Rnsslr Plytch Unv Phi Theta Kappa Schlrshp; Am Nclr Soc 85-; Nclr Prplsn Plnt Oper/Tech 81-88; AS; Nclr Engr; Engrng.

**BENDT-FORBES, ELIZABETH A,** Savannah Coll Of Art & Design, Savannah, GA; JR; BA; Intr Dsgn.

**BENEBY, SEVERNA A,** Benedict Coll, Columbia, SC; SO; BA; Intrntl Stdnts Assn Sec 90-; Mgmt; Bus.

**BENEDETI, GIOVANNA,** Fl Atlantic Univ, Boca Raton, FL; SR; BA; Intrnatl Clb 87; Spnsh Assn; Intrnatl Bus.

**BENEDETTI DIAZ, ANALISSA,** Fl International Univ, Miami, FL; JR; BA; Garden Clb 87-89; Fuprobeco 88-90; AS BA Panama Canal Clg 88-90; AS BDP 88-90; Bus; Mgmt Inf Systms.

**BENEDETTO, JENNIFER,** Univ Of Miami, Coral Gables, FL; FR; BS; Alpha Lamda Delta Hon Soc 90; Deans Lst 90; Elem Educ/Bio; Tchr.

**BENEDETTO, KATE S,** West Liberty St Coll, West Liberty, WV; FR.

**BENEDICT, LINDA J,** Glassboro St Coll, Glassboro, NJ; SO; BA; Res Stdnt Assoc Sec 89-90; Natl Panhellenic Conf Sec 90-; Tri Sigma Class Pres 90; Edn/Cmmnctns; Teach.

**BENEDICT, PATRICIA R,** Saint Catharine Coll, St Catharine, KY; SO; BED; Intl Clb 90-; Phi Theta Kappa Sec 90-; AA; Spec Ed; Tchng.

**BENEFIELD II, JOHN L,** Abraham Baldwin Agri Coll, Tifton, GA; SO; BSA; Walnut Grove Vol Fire Dept 87-; Agri Econ; Govt.

**BENEFIELD, SHERRY D,** Univ Of Al At Birmingham, Birmingham, AL; SR; BS; Alpha Sigma Tau 88-90; Sci; Tchng.

**BENEFIELD, THOMAS S,** Middle Tn St Univ, Murfreesboro, TN; JR; BS; Beta Beta Beta 90-; Gamma Beta Phi 88-89; Phi Mu Delta V P 90-; Pre-Med/Chem/Bio; Med.

**BENEFIELD, TRACY C,** Northwest Al Comm Coll, Phil Campbell, AL; GD; AAS; Offc Admin; Offc Wrkr.

**BENET, JOSEPH,** Oh St Univ, Columbus, OH; JR; BS; Elect Eng Bbl Stu Pres 89-; Radio Sta Disc Jcky 89-90; Eng Coop United Tele Syst; IM Flg Ftbl Vllybl Capt 88-; Elect Eng; Eng/Real Est Prt Tm.**

**BENETTI, MICHAEL E,** Niagara Univ, Niagara Univ, NY; SR; BS; IM Ftbl Bsktbl 87-; Grad Asstnshp Bio Dept; Div III Ftbl 87; Bio; Cncr Rsrch.

**BENFIELD, CRYSTAL R,** Univ Of Sc At Coastal Carolina, Conway, SC; SR; BS; Yrbk Staff 89-90; Rep Miss Coastal Carolina Pageant Hmcmng 90; Deans List 88-; Hardship Schlrshp 88-89; Psych; Neuropsych-Head Trama.

**BENFIELD, DESSALEE B,** Catawba Valley Comm Coll, Hickory, NC; FR; Surgical Technlgy; Nursing.

**BENFIELD, SANDRA ANN MICHAELS,** Winthrop Coll, Rock Hill, SC; SR; BS; Nom Outsdng Sr; Pres List; Deans List; Elem Educ; Teach.

**BENGE, KEVIN L,** Lenoir Rhyne Coll, Hickory, NC; FR; BA; Mrshl Cmmncmnt; Pres Hnr Lst 90; Sci; Eng.

**BENGSTON, ELLEN,** Glassboro St Coll, Glassboro, NJ; JR; BA; Our Living Legacy Arts Festival On AIDS; Parks & Rcrtn Org; Soc Serv W/The Dvlpmntly Disabled 89-; Psych; Rsrch & Edn.

**BENHARROCH, ESTHER,** Miami Dade Comm Coll, Miami, FL; GD; BPSY; JCC 89-90; AA Miami Dade Cmmnty Clg 90; Psychlgy; Psychlgy.

**BENIGNO JR, JAMES B,** Univ Of Southern Ms, Hattiesburg, MS; SO; BS; Sigma Phi Omicron Sec 90-; Gamma Beta Phi 89-; Sci Educ; Optometry.

**BENINCASA, CHERYL A,** Muskingum Coll, New Concord, OH; JR; Cmptrlr/MIS 79-87; Intrntl Bus; Intrntl Trade.

**BENITEZ, GISELLE,** Fl International Univ, Miami, FL; SR; BA; Phi Lambda; AA Miami Dade Comm Coll 90; Spec Educ; Tchr.

**BENITEZ, JANELYS A,** Hillsborough Comm Coll, Tampa, FL; FR; VICA Pres 89-90; Mu Alpha Theta 88-90; Natl Hon Soc 86-87; Math; CPA.

**BENITEZ, JORGE A,** East Carolina Univ, Greenville, NC; SO; Mrchng Bnd 89-; Music Quintet 90-; Running Clb 89-90; Military Policeman Natl Gd 89-; Desert Storm Vet; Music; Music Educ.

**BENITEZ, MANUEL,** Univ Of Miami, Coral Gables, FL; SR; BSEE; FL Eng Soc Pres; IEEE; Eta Kappa Nu Treas 90-; Tau Beta Pi Treas; Bowman Ashe Schlrshp; Barfield Inst Corp Jr Eng 86-; AS Miami Dade Comm Coll 85; AA 87; Cmptr Eng; Eng.

**BENJAMIN, CAROL L,** Norfolk St Univ, Norfolk, VA; SO; BA; Intrnatl Stdnt Orgnztn Asst Sec; Spartan Alpha Tau; Bus; Mgmt Comp Info Systms Systms Anlyst.

**BENJAMIN, CHRISTINA H,** Norfolk St Univ, Norfolk, VA; SO; Stdnt Intl Org 90-; Spartan Alpha Tau Hnr Socty 90-; Grphc Dsgn; Cmmnctns Dsgnr.

**BENJAMIN, DOUGLAS A,** Kent St Univ Kent Cmps, Kent, OH; JR; BA; Ambsdr Treas; Orntatn Instr 89-; Mrtr Bd; Sygma Alpha Epsilon Treas 88-; Acctg; CPA.

**BENJAMIN, JOHN M,** Univ Of Sc At Columbia, Columbia, SC; SR; Ftbl Intrmrls 87-; Sftbl Intrmrls 87-; Hstry; Sprt Admin.

**BENJAMIN, LIVINGSTON A,** Cheyney Univ Of Pa, Cheyney, PA; SR; BS; DEX-NSBL 89-; Cmmtr Stdnts Assn 90-; Richard Humphreys Schlrshp 90-; AA Roxbury Comm Clg 88; Bus Admin; MBA/JD Degree.

**BENJAMIN, MAKESSA M,** Ms St Univ, Miss State, MS; FR; Pre Law Soc 90-; Rfrmd Univ Flwshp 90-; Stdnt Sprt Svcs 90-; Acctg; Attrny Law.

**BENJAMIN, MELANIE Y,** City Univ Of Ny Baruch Coll, New York, NY; SR; BBA; Beta Gamma; Goldn Key; Sigma Iota Epsilon; Soc Humn Res Mgmt 90-; Wollmn Med Otstdng Achvmnt Mgmt; Humn Res Mgmt.

**BENJAMIN, MOSHE,** Yeshiva Univ, New York, NY; GD; JD; Hist Soc Pres 88-90; Peer Grp Soc Cnslr 89-90; Cultural Soc 88-90; Emerg Med Unit Amb Serv For Comm Fund Rsr 89-90; Deans List 87-90; BA 90; Law.

**BENJAMIN, PAUL J,** Univ Of Pittsburgh At Bradford, Bradford, PA; SO; BA; Am Studies Club Treas; Phi Kappa Epsilon Sec; Am Studies; Hi Sch Teacher.

**BENJAMIN, ROBERT S,** S U N Y Coll At Fredonia, Fredonia, NY; JR; BS; Appld Comm Asc; Scuba Dvng 89; Comm; Cnsltng.

**BENJAMIN, RUTH A,** D Youville Coll, Buffalo, NY; SO; MA; Stdnt Physcl Thrpy Assn 89-; Stdnt Assn Sntr 89-; Cmps Mnstry 89-; Physcl Thrpy; Sports Rhbltn.

**BENJAMIN, VICTORIA,** Tougaloo Coll, Tougaloo, MS; SO; BA; Elem Ed; Instructor.

**BENKERT, TIMOTHY M,** Univ Of Cincinnati, Cincinnati, OH; SO; BED; Educ Trib 90; Kappa Delta Pi; Elem Educ.

**BENKO, CHERILYN,** Columbus Coll Of Art & Design, Columbus, OH; FR; BFA; Art; Adv Dsgn.

**BENKO, MARJORIE A,** Columbia Union Coll, Takoma Park, MD; GD; BS; Cls Sec 87-88; Bus Clb 87-88; Phi Eta Sgm 86-87; Hlth Sci Dept Dstnctn 90-; Cmps Mnstrs Co Dir Collgt Advntsts Better Lvng 87-88; Vrsty Bsktbl Capt 86-89; Tnns Sftbl 90-; Hlth/Ftns Mgmt; VA Dept Hlth.

**BENKOSKI, PATRICIA J,** James Madison University, Harrisonburg, VA; SR; BS; Golden Key 90-; Phi Kappa Phi 90-; Psychlgy; Ed.

**BENLINE, JOSEPH W,** Wv Northern Comm Coll, Wheeling, WV; JR; AAS; Elect Tech.

**BENN, DORPHELIA L,** Al A & M Univ, Normal, AL; SO; BS; Pres Acad Cup; Bus Admin; Lawyer.

**BENNANE, AHMED,** The Boston Conservatory, Boston, MA; SR; BFA; SUNY Old Westbury Long Island NY Dance 87; Boston Conserv Boston MA 88-; Alvin Ailey Schl NY NY 87; Ligue Franc De L'enseighnment 69-72; Deans Listf Boston Conserv Schlrshp 90-; Jan Veen Schlrshp 90; Dance/Choregraphy; Stadium Chore.

**BENNANI, OUSSAMA,** Univ Of Sc At Columbia, Columbia, SC; FR; Intrntl Clb 90.

**BENNATAN, HADAS,** City Univ Of Ny City Coll, New York, NY; SO; BSEE; Hon Prog Lbrl Arts; Elec Eng.

**BENNECKER, ERIC V,** Univ Of Akron, Akron, OH; SR; BS; Ski Clb 87-88; Golden Key; Phi Sigma Kappa Sec 88-; Advrtsng.

**BENNER, JAY B,** Widener Univ, Chester, PA; SR; BS; IFC VP 88; Omicron Delta Epsilon 89; Order Omega 89; Theta Chi Treas 88-89; Acctg; Mgmt.

**BENNER, LA VERN K,** Univ Of Pa, Philadelphia, PA; JR; BA; Bus/Acctng; Bus Mgmnt.

**BENNER, MICHAEL J,** S U N Y At Buffalo, Buffalo, NY; SR; BSBA; Economics Clb 89-; Golden Key 90-; Economics Corp Finance.

**BENNER, TIMOTHY L,** Univ Of Nh Plymouth St Coll, Plymouth, NH; SR; BS; Plymouth St Thea 90-; Campus News Wrtr 89-; Kappa Delta Pi V P 90-; Phi Kappa Phi; Tutor/Rdng/Wrtng/Cen 90-; Plymouth Schol 90-; Pres List 89-; Undergrad Rdng/Wrtg/Fllwshp 90-; Thea Co 89-; USN Vet; Ex Chem Anal/Rdtn Safe Tech; Engld/Edctn; Tch/Engl/Drama.

**BENNETT, AMY R,** South Ga Coll, Douglas, GA; SO; BA; Stdnt Govt Pres; Bapt Stdnt Union; Stdnt Actvty Srvc Awd; AS Educ; Early Chldhd Educ; Tchr.**

**BENNETT, AMY S,** Indiana Univ Of Pa, Indiana, PA; SO; BS; Chorus 90-; Pblc Rltns Clb 90-; Chrl; Psychlgy; Educ.

**BENNETT, ANGELA D,** Univ Of Ga, Athens, GA; JR; BSED; Svc Orgnztn Tchng Asstnt 90-; Kappa Dlt Pi; Sftbl Frmn Un 88-89; Erly Chldhd Educ; Tchng.

**BENNETT, ANTHONY D,** Clarkson Univ, Potsdam, NY; JR; BS; Intl Stdnt Org 90-; Alpha Epsilon Pi Hse Mgr 89-; Dns Lst 89; Vars Soccer 89-; Mktg Mgmt; Mktg Rsrch.

**BENNETT, ASHLEE F,** Univ Of Sc At Columbia, Columbia, SC; FR; BA; Campus Coalition Literacy Adult Stdnt Tutor 90-; IM Vlybl Bsktbl 90-; French; Teaching.

**BENNETT, BARBARA L,** Alcorn St Univ, Lorman, MS; FR; BA; The ASU Gspl Choir 90; Hnr Soc Org 90-; Enlg; Scndry Educ.

**BENNETT, BETH R,** Middle Tn St Univ, Murfreesboro, TN; SO; BA; Hmn Sci; Intrr Dsgn.

**BENNETT, BRIAN C,** Wake Forest Univ, Winston-Salem, NC; FR; BA; Econ; Fin Analyst.

**BENNETT, BRIAN E,** Kent St Univ Kent Cmps, Kent, OH; SO; Msc Prfrmnce; Msc Educ/Clg Lvl.

**BENNETT, BRIAN E,** Spartanburg Methodist Coll, Spartanburg, SC; SO; BA; Psi Beta 90-; AA; Sociology.

**BENNETT, CATHERINE B,** Owensboro Comm Coll, Owensboro, KY; SO; Hmn Serv/Hmnties; Soc Wrkr.

**BENNETT, CHAD E,** S U N Y Coll Of Tech At Alfred, Alfred, NY; FR; AAS; Archtctrl Clb 90-; Stdnt Senate 90; Archtctr.

**BENNETT, CHAD E,** Univ Of Sc At Columbia, Columbia, SC; FR; BS; Chem.

**BENNETT, CHRISTOPHER D,** Life Coll, Marietta, GA; GD; BS; Phi Delta Theta 79-83; Univ TN Pwrlftng Tm 79-81; Intl Chrprctc Assoc 90-; Ntrtn/Chrprctc.

**BENNETT, DARA H,** Waycross Coll, Waycross, GA; FR; BS.

**BENNETT, DARLENE M,** Tn Tech Univ, Cookeville, TN; SR; BS; TN Tech Hm Ec Econ Assn 90-; Hm Ec Stdnt Acad Advsry Cncl 90-; Ag/Hm Ec Acad Mscndct Comm 90-; Phi Kappa Phi 90-; Kappa Omicron Nu 90-; Pi Lambda Theta; AS Roane State Comm Coll 83; Chld/Fmly Sci; Chld Life Spec.

**BENNETT, DAVID F,** Univ Of Ga, Athens, GA; SO; BLA; Diploma Data Prcsng Grffn Area Tech Schl 83; Lndscp Archtctr.

**BENNETT, DAWN M,** Boston Univ, Boston, MA; FR; BS; Choral Union 90-; Sargent Clg Deans Host; Sargent Clg Peer Counsellor; Physical/Therapy.

**BENNETT, DEBORAH A,** S U N Y Coll Of Tech At Alfred, Alfred, NY; FR; BS; Krte Clb 90-; SG 90-; Otdr Rcrtn Clb 90-; Engl; Tch.

**BENNETT, DOANE M,** Univ Of Sc At Columbia, Columbia, SC; SR; BS; Stdnt Bar Assn Aux 90-; Andrsn Coll Almni Assn 88; Psych; Scl Wrk.

**BENNETT JR, DOUGLAS R,** Bridgeport Engr Inst, Fairfield, CT; SR; BSEE; IBM 89-; Elect Engrng.

**BENNETT, ERIC C,** Glassboro St Coll, Glassboro, NJ; FR; BS; Chrstn Flwshp 90-; Deans Lst 90-; Tech Educ; Tch/Own Bus.

**BENNETT, GERALD L,** Erie Comm Coll South Cmps, Orchard Park, NY; SO; BS; Yrbk Stf Phtgrphr 89-90; ECC South Hnrs Pgm V P 89-90; Hnrs Pgm Grad; Liberty Partnershp Pgm Tutor 90-; William Major Byers Schlrshp Math; Grad Distinctn; Malcolm Pirnie Inc 90-; US Navy Vet 82-88; AS; Chem Engr; Chem Engr/Mgmt.

**BENNETT, GERALD S,** Univ Of North Fl, Jacksonville, FL; SR; BA; Gldn Key; Finance Invstmnt Soc 90-; Gldn Key; AA FCCJ; Fnncl Stmnt Analyst.

**BENNETT JR, HARRY LEE,** Southern Coll Of Tech, Marietta, GA; JR; BSEE; IEEE 90-; Elec Eng Tech.

**BENNETT, JACKIE L,** Cornell Univ Statutory College, Ithaca, NY; SO; BS; Dairy Sci Clb Treas 89-; Agway Mgmt Dev Pgm; Lightweight Ftbl Mgr 89-; Agri.

**BENNETT, JAMES D,** Univ Of Nh Plymouth St Coll, Plymouth, NH; FR; BS; Meteorolgy.

**BENNETT JR, JAMES W,** Southern Coll Of Tech, Marietta, GA; SR; BS; Comp Eng Tchnlgy; Eng.

**BENNETT, JANET K,** Daytona Beach Comm Coll, Daytona Beach, FL; RN; Saras Otrch Flwshp Pres 89-; PTA; Pool Nrs/Med/Surg 85-; LPN Sandusky Schl Nrs 73; Nrsng.

**BENNETT, JANET L,** Univ Of Akron, Akron, OH; FR; BA; Hnrs Prog 90-; Phi Eta Sigma; Bus; Hlth Serv Admn.

**BENNETT, JANICE S,** Savannah Coll Of Art & Design, Savannah, GA; JR; BA; Amer Socty Intr Dsgnrs 90-; Natl Outstdng Alumnae Sthrn Inst Dsgn 83; Intr Dsgnr; Owner Kitchen/Bath Revue 80-83; Janice Bennett Dsgns 86-88; Assoc Appl Sci Intr Dsgn; AAS Sthrn Inst Of Dsgn 78; Archtctr.

**BENNETT, JEFFREY A,** Roanoke Bible Coll, Elizabeth Cy, NC; FR; BA; Stdnt Life Com 90; Spiritual Life Com 90-; Class Pres 90-; Yth Mnstry Colonial Pl Ch Christ Hampton VA; Preach Mnstry.

**BENNETT, JENNIFER A,** Memphis St Univ, Memphis, TN; FR; BA; Phi Eta Sigma; Lambda Alpha Delta; Hon Stdnt Asso/Campus 90-; History; Law/Tchg.

**BENNETT, JENNIFER J,** Univ Of Tn At Martin, Martin, TN; JR; BED; Resident Asstnt Sr RA 90-; Stdnt Tenn Educ Assoc VP 90-; Zeta Tau Alpha Pres 89-; Univ Serv Awrd; TN Educ Assoc Don Sahli Schrlshp; Elem Educ; Teacher.

**BENNETT, JENNIFER L,** Fl St Univ, Tallahassee, FL; SR; BA; Intl Affrs Soc Pr 89-; Mrchng Flg Line; Ambssdr 89-; Phi Eta Sigma 89-; Golden Key 90; Phi Kappa Phi; Truman Schlr 89; Stdy Engl 90; Fla Dept Commerce; Bur Intl Toursm; Fla Gov Offc Budgtng Plnng; Intl Affrs; Hosp/Toursm.

**BENNETT, JENNIFER S,** Middle Tn St Univ, Murfreesboro, TN; SR; Alpha Omicron Pi Pnhlnc Dlgt Chptr Rltns 86-90; Cert Exclnc 88; Cert Recog 89; BBA 90; Bus.

**BENNETT, JOANNA T,** Anderson Coll, Anderson, SC; FR; BA; Stu Alum Cncl 90; Sci Club 90; Phi Theta Kappa; Gamma Beta Phi; Mu Beta Psi; Frshmn Marshall; Theatre Dept Rookie Of Yr 90; Theatre.

**BENNETT, JOHN A,** Mobile Coll, Mobile, AL; JR; BSN; Deans List 90-; Pres Schlr 80; Magna Cum Lauda; BS Spring Hill Coll 80; Nursing.

**BENNETT, KATINA A,** Jackson St Univ, Jackson, MS; FR; BS; Alpha Lambda Delta 90-; Math; Engrg.

**BENNETT, KEVIN J,** Univ Of Ky, Lexington, KY; SR; BS; Frm Hse Blddr Chr 88-; Cvl Eng; Engrng.

**BENNETT, KORY L,** Temple Univ, Philadelphia, PA; JR; BSE; Inst Elec/Elctrnc Eng 90-; Mnrty Eng Stdnt Assn Trea 88-; Golden Key 90-; Phi Sigma Pi 90-; Explore Comm Boy Scts Amer Post 539 90-; Intrn Indian Point III Nclr Pwr Fclty Buchanan NY 89-; Pwr Lftng Tm 90-; Elec Eng Tech.

**BENNETT, LARISSA L,** Queens Coll, Charlotte, NC; SO; BA; Natl Org Wmn Coord 90-; Org Agnst Soc Infstce/Sfrng Co-Pres 89-; NC Stdnt Lgsltr Sec 90-; Intrnshp W/Senator T Snfrd; Poltcl Sci; Tch.

**BENNETT, LAURA M,** Univ Of Nc At Asheville, Asheville, NC; SO; BA; Phi Eta Sigma 90; Env Studies; Resrce Mngmnt.

**BENNETT, M LE ANN,** Middle Tn St Univ, Murfreesboro, TN; SO; BS; Flute Ensemble 89-90; Hnr Soc 89-; Natl Hnr Soc 89-; Msc; Msc Bsn/Tchg.

**BENNETT, MARK E,** Christian Brothers Univ, Memphis, TN; JR; BA; Asstnt VP 86-; Econ/Fin; Law.

**BENNETT, MELANIE D,** Sue Bennett Coll, London, KY; SO; BA; Bus; Bus; Acctg.

**BENNETT, MELISSA M,** Hillsborough Comm Coll, Tampa, FL; FR; AA; History; Educ/Law.

**BENNETT, MELONIE L,** Portland School Of Art, Portland, ME; SR; BFA; Photo Rsrc Cntr 90-; Dns Lst 89-90; Phtgrphy Intrnshp Portland Museum Of Art 90-; Phtgrphy.

**BENNETT, MICHAEL G,** Fl A & M Univ, Tallahassee, FL; FR; BA; Phi Eta Sigma 90-; Deans Lst 90-; Physcs; Sci Rsrch/Rdlgy.

**BENNETT, NATHALIE B,** Averett Coll, Danville, VA; SR; BS Assc 91; Elem Edctn; Tchr.

**BENNETT, NICOLE J,** Va St Univ, Petersburg, VA; SO; Bus Admn Clb 89-; NAACP 90-; Big Sis 90-; NJ Pre Almn 90-; Alpha Kappa Alpha Acdmn Awrd 89; Bennett Ramsey Schlstc Awrd 89.

**BENNETT, PATRICIA A,** Sue Bennett Coll, London, KY; SO; BSN; Lang Club Activ Dir 90; Nursing.

**BENNETT, RACHEL L,** Tn Tech Univ, Cookeville, TN; FR; BS; Educ; Tchr.

**BENNETT JR, RAYMOND O,** Tn Tech Univ, Cookeville, TN; SR; BS; Ag Eng Tech Clb Pres 89-; Aggie Cntct Alumni Nwsltr Ed 89-; Delta Tau Alpha 90; Ag Fndtn Schlrshp 89-; Ag Fndtn Pblc Comm; US Army 85-88; Ag Eng.

**BENNETT II, RONNIE M,** Southern Coll Of Tech, Marietta, GA; SO; BA; Campus Crusade Mscl Dir 89-; Sigma Pi Corp Secr 89-; Cvl Engr; Engr/Coast Guard.

**BENNETT, SCOTT A,** Rochester Inst Of Tech, Rochester, NY; FR; Math Clb 90-; Comp Math; Math.

**BENNETT, SHAMRA C,** Jackson St Univ, Jackson, MS; JR; BA; Bk Proof Corr Clerk 88-; Busn Admin; Hmn Rsc Mgr.

**BENNETT, SUSAN M,** Univ Of Miami, Coral Gables, FL; FR; BA; OJU; Phtgrphy Clb; Otdr Sprts Rctnl Clb 90-; COISO; UBS; CSA; AIAS 90-; Alha Lambda Delta 90-; Hnr Stdnts Assoc 90-; LEO Sec 87-; Archtctr.

**BENNETT, SUZANNE N,** Volunteer St Comm Coll, Gallatin, TN; SO; Sddl Clb 88-.

**BENNETT, TARSHA C,** Central St Univ, Wilberforce, OH; FR; BA; Hnrs Pgm; Comm; Tlvsn/Radio Prod.

**BENNETT, TERRI M,** Providence Coll, Providence, RI; JR; BS; Stdnt Cngrss Cls Offcr 88-89; Pstrl Cncl Exec Treas 88-; Alpha Epsilon Delta 90-; Phi Sigma Tau; Deans Lst; Blgy/Hlth Serv Admin; Med.**

**BENNETT, THERESA M,** Tallahassee Comm Coll, Tallahassee, FL; SO; BA; Bkkpr 84-; Busn Cpa.

**BENNETT, TIMOTHY C,** Tn Temple Univ, Chattanooga, TN; SR; MA; BS; Math; Prfssr.

**BENNETT, TINA L,** Salisbury St Univ, Salisbury, MD; GD; Phi Kappa Phi; NASW.

**BENNETT, TISHA L,** Univ Of Tn At Martin, Martin, TN; SR; BS; Am Hom Ec Assn 87-89; Order Omega 90-; Phi Eta Sigma 88-89; Phi Kappa Phi 89-; Alpha Delta Pi VP Pledge Ed 87-; Intrnshp Lebonheur Chldrns Med Ctr Intern 90; Univ Serv Awd 90-; Awd Most Outstndg Chld Dvlpmnt Stdnt 90-; Home Ec; MA.

**BENNETT, VELMA J,** Fl A & M Univ, Tallahassee, FL; SR; BS; LAE Crmnl Jstc Assc 90-; Career Svc Emp 90-; AA Manatee Comm Coll 88; Crmnl Jstc/Econ; Corp Law/Labor Rltns Ins.

**BENNETT, WILLIAM M,** Fayetteville St Univ, Fayetteville, NC; JR; BS; Campus Crusade Chrst 90-; Flwshp Chrstn Stdnts 90-; Chnclrs Lst 90-; Deans Lst 90-; AS; Edn/Middle Grades; Chrstn Msns.

**BENNETT, WYNELL M,** Univ Of West Fl, Pensacola, FL; SR; BA; Alpha Beta Gamma 87; AS Pensacola Jr Clg 87; Mddl Schl Ed/Lit/Lang Arts; Teach/Speech Thry.

**BENNING, LORINDA A,** Villanova Univ, Villanova, PA; JR; BA; Ski Clb 89; Pi Beta Phi 89; Im Sftbl Soccer; Psychlgy; Cnclng.

**BENNINGFIELD, KEITH R,** Allegheny Coll, Meadville, PA; SO; LAW; Alden Schlr 89-; American Schlr 84-; Var Wrestling 90; IM Hockey Captn 89-; History English; Law.

**BENNINGTON, JAMES L,** Emory & Henry Coll, Emory, VA; JR; BA; CSA Rep 88-; Kerygma 88-; Cmps Chrstn Fllwshp 89-; Blue Key; Emory/Henry Schlr 89-; W C Mason Schlrshp; Thomas Moore Schlrshp 89-; Rlgn; Ordnd Mnstry.

**BENNINGTON, JUDITH L,** Northern Ky Univ, Highland Hts, KY; SR; BA; Psych Clb 89-; Pinnacle Chapt Pres; Alpha Chi 90-; Psi Chi 85-; Dns Schlrshp; Charles Baron Awd; Resrch Presented Midwestern Psych Assoc Conf; Hnrs Lst 89-; Rsrch Presented Mid-Amer Undergrad Psych Conf; N KY Adult Rdg Pgm Tutor 90-; Psych; Clncl Psych/Tchg.

**BENNIS, LESLIE C,** Union Univ School Of Nursing, Memphis, TN; FR; BSN; Deans Lst 90; Nrsng; Nrse Anesthetst.

**BENOIT, GREGORY F,** Univ Of Nh Plymouth St Coll, Plymouth, NH; SO; S; Sci Clb 89-; Plymth Schlr 90-; Pres Lst 90-; Lmnlgy Intrn Dpt Env Srv St NH; Natl Yth Sprts Cchs Asc 90-; Gnrl Prtnr Ovr/Trdn Wl Lndscp 85-90; Env Bio; Envr Prtctn/Rsch.

**BENOIT, LEEANN L,** Univ Of North Fl, Jacksonville, FL; JR; BA; Psyc Hon Soc 90-; Golden Key; AA Lake City Cmuty Clg 89; Psyc; Clincl Psycgst.

**BENOIT, MARY H,** Bryant Stratton Bus Inst Roch, Rochester, NY; GD; BA; Hnr Rl; Bus Mgmt; Mgmt Retail.

**BENOMAN, EUNESA S,** Alcorn St Univ, Lorman, MS; SO; BS; Cmptr Sci/Math Clb; Hnr Org; Cmptr Sci Math; Cmptr Anlyst.

**BENORE, GRETCHEN A,** Oh Wesleyan Univ, Delaware, OH; JR; Eng Stdnt Brd VP 90-; Chrl Art Soc 88-90; Deans List 88-; Mrtr Brd ; Phi Soc 89-; Pi Alpha Theta; Sigma Tau Delta; Eng/Hist; Sec Educ.

**BENRSTEIN, DARREN E,** Glassboro St Coll, Glassboro, NJ; SO; BA; NJRIRG Mag; Astrnmy Clb 89-; Stu Actvtc Brd 89-90; BOSPC 89-; Dean Lst 89-; Tutor; ALF CIO Schlrshp 89-; Kckbxng 89-; Cmmnctns; Law Arbtrtn.**

**BENSHAFRUT, RONNIE,** City Univ Of Ny John Jay Coll, New York, NY; SR; BS; Dns Lst 87-; Nu Gamma Sigma 88-; Lambda Alpha Epsilon 88-; Moleculr Bio; Dna Lab; Med Exam Offc N Y Cty; Forensic Sci.**

**BENSING, TRACY MICHELE,** Savannah Coll Of Art & Design, Savannah, GA; SO; BA; Grphc Dsgn/Bus; Advrtsng/Prmtnl Bus.

**BENSINGER, GITI,** Fl International Univ, Miami, FL; SO; Yavne Tchrs Coll Wmn 89-90; Bio; Med.

**BENSLEY, TRACY A,** Fl St Univ, Tallahassee, FL; SR; BS; Inst Elctrcl/Elctrncs Engrs 90-; Natl Soc Pro Engrs 88-; Eng Hon 90-; Gldn Key Natl 90-; Deans Lst 89-; Pres Schlrshp 89-; FL Undrgrad Schlr 87-; AA Pensacola Jr Coll 89; Elect Eng; Eng.

**BENSON, ANDREA M,** Morris Brown Coll, Atlanta, GA; JR; Stdnt Govt Assn Sec 89-; Stdnt Sprt Srvcs 88-; Hnr Stdnt 90-; Precious Pearls 89-; Big Brthrs/Bib Sis; Natl Blck Chld Dev Inst Inc; Early Chldhd Educ; Tchr.

**BENSON, DAWN B,** Univ Of Hartford, West Hartford, CT; JR; BA; Biology Clb VP; Deans List 90; AA Univ Of Hrtfrd 90; Biology/Physlgy/Anatomy; Med Schl.

**BENSON, DEBORAH F,** Glassboro St Coll, Glassboro, NJ; SO; BS; Acdmc Excllnc; Deans Lst; Dstrbtng Fd Clthng Aide 89-90; Blgcl Sci; Dctr.

**BENSON, DIANE,** Valley Forge Christian Coll, Phoenixville, PA; SR; Resident Asstnt 90-; Missions Comm Asst Prayer Cordntr 89-; Teen Challenge Ministry Team NYC Homeless Ministry Team; Acdmc Deans Schlrshp 88-; Tunmore Schlrslp; Summa Cum Laude; Mission Practicum Asslar W Germany 90; BSB; Bible Missions; Counselling.

**BENSON, EILEEN C,** James Madison University, Harrisonburg, VA; JR; BSN; Natl Stdnt Nrs Assoc 90-; Nrsng Hon Soc 90-; Golden Key 88-; Alpha Phi Omega 89-; Mary Waples Schlrshp; Hghst Cumltv GPA 90-; Natl Colgt Nrsng Award; Nrsng.

**BENSON, ELEANOR BLAIR,** Univ Of Sc At Columbia, Columbia, SC; JR; BA; Rape Asrnss Co Chr 90-; Peer Cndct Brd; Desk Asst 90-; Gamma Beta Phi 90-; Alpha Lambda Delta Cncl 88-89; Psi Chi; Rape Crss Ntwrk 90-; SEED; Romantic Attchmnt Rsrch 90-; Hnrs Coll 88-; Psych Rsrch.

**BENSON, KAREN L,** Univ Of Ga, Athens, GA; SR; BPHAR; Amer Chmcl Soc 87-88; ASP 89-; GPHA 89-; Lambda Kappa Sigma 89-; Phrmcy.

**BENSON, KAREN LISA,** Md Coll Of Art & Design, Silver Spring, MD; SO; BA; Orntn 90; Asst Dir Inner-Vsns Art Gllry 89-; Prtrt Artst Party Art Prod; AA Maryland Coll Art/Dsgn; Fine Arts/Pntng; Pro Artst.

**BENSON, RENEE A,** Univ Of Akron, Akron, OH; JR; Phi Eta Sigma 89-90; Alpha Lambda Delta 89-90.

**BENSON, ROBERT A,** Univ Of Ga, Athens, GA; JR; BSED; MESA; Math Educ; Tch.

**BENSON, SHERRON D,** Rust Coll, Holly Springs, MS; JR; SGA VP; Theatre Guild; Sigma Tau Delta Intl Englsh Hnr Scty Sec 90-; Alpha Kappa Mu; Gamma Sigma Sigma; Outstanding College Woman; English/Speech/Drama.

**BENSON, STACI L,** Queens Coll, Charlotte, NC; JR; BA; Hon Cncl Pres 89-; RA 89-; Adm CORE 89-; Janusian Ord 89-; Mortar Brd Pres; Phi Mu 88-; Pub Def Ofc For Mktg Cnty 90; Guardian Ad Litum Pgm 89; Bus Admin; Corp Law.

**BENSON, STEVEN M,** Hillsborough Comm Coll, Tampa, FL; FR; AA; Natl Dns Lst 90-; Tampa Bay Vo Tech Schl 89-90; Elec Eng.

**BENSON, TRACY DEWAYNE,** Univ Of Tn At Knoxville, Knoxville, TN; JR; BS; Frst AM Ntnl Bnk Knxvle 86; Fnce; Bnkng.

**BENSON, WANDA LORRAINE,** Norfolk St Univ, Norfolk, VA; JR; BA; Educ; Elem Tchr.

**BENSON, WYNETTE J,** Fl A & M Univ, Tallahassee, FL; FR; BA; Phi Eta Sigma; Acctng.

**BENT JR, WESTIN R,** City Univ Of Ny Queensbrough, New York, NY; SO; BS; Jmcn Clb 89-; Chmcl Eng.

**BENTEL, HEIDIMARIE,** Univ Of Fl, Gainesville, FL; SR; Stdnt Govt Asst Chrmn Asst Dir 87-90; Pnhllnc Cncl Rsh Cnslr 90; Blue Key 89-; Omicron Delta Kappa 89-; Beta Gamma Sigma; Delta Gamma Pres 88-89; Fndrs Awrd; Fnc.

**BENTFELD, EARLYN R,** Youngstown St Univ, Youngstown, OH; SR; BS; SHEA 90-; Golden Key 90-; Coord Prog/Dietetics 91-; Dietetics/Nutrn; Dietitian Fd Svc Mgr.**

**BENTLE, TONYA D,** Middle Tn St Univ, Murfreesboro, TN; SO; BA; Physcl Thrpst.

**BENTLEY, DANIEL M,** Univ Of Nc At Asheville, Asheville, NC; SR; BA; Psi Chi 88-; Lab Asst 88-; Edward C Tolman Awrd Fr Rsrch; BA; Psych; Indstrl Psych.

**BENTLEY, DEBORAH A,** Cornell Univ Statutory College, Ithaca, NY; FR; BS; NY State Yng Wmn Yr Prgm; Trdtn Schlr; Cmmnctns Govt.

**BENTLEY JR, JOHN V,** Marietta Coll, Marietta, OH; FR; BA; Sprtswrtr Nwspr Staff 90-; Jrnlsm/Engl; Sprts Jrnlsm.

**BENTLEY, LESLIE C,** Bennett Coll, Greensboro, NC; JR; BA; Hs Cncl Vp 89-90; Bennett Plyrs 88-89; Afrcn Amer Assmbly 89-90; Schlrs Prog; Alpha Kappa Alpha Prlmntrn 90-; Schlr 90-; Hnr Rl 88-; Deans Lst 88-; Sftbl Ptchr/Ctchr 89-90; Elem Educ; Tchr.

**BENTLEY, PAULA M,** Garrett Comm Coll, Mchenry, MD; FR; Stdnt Govt Assoc 90; Gen Studies; Law.

**BENTLEY, SARAH K,** Westminster Coll, New Wilmingtn, PA; SO; BA; Cncrt Chr 89-; Res Asst 90-; Chrstn Ed.

**BENTLEY, SHANNON K,** Bethany Coll, Bethany, WV; SO; BS; Amer Chem Soc Pres Elect; Stdnt Bd Gov; Wmn Bible Study Grp; Beta Beta Beta Treas 90-; Deans Lst; Biology; Med.

**BENTLEY, SHIRLEY E,** Pensacola Jr Coll, Pensacola, FL; SO; AA; Outstndng Mnrty Comm Coll Grad; AS; Law.

**BENTLEY, TED H,** Central Al Comm Coll, Alexander City, AL; SO; BA; Acctng; Bsn Admn.

**BENTLEY, TIM C,** Fayetteville St Univ, Fayetteville, NC; JR; MBA; Frmn Fy Hs Mvrs; Math; Eng.

**BENTLEY, WENDY M,** Univ Of Ky, Lexington, KY; JR; BA; Socl Wrk.

**BENTOLILA, ANNE P,** Univ Of Miami, Coral Gables, FL; FR; BHSC; Pre-Phys Thrpy Club 90-; Org Jewish Stdnts 90-; Hnr Stdnts Assn 90-; Alpha Lambda Delta 90-; Spec Olympics 90-; Tennis Aerobics 90-.

**BENTON, BENITA L,** Chesterfield Marlboro Coll, Cheraw, SC; FR; BA; Cmptr Prog.

**BENTON, BETTY J,** Morris Brown Coll, Atlanta, GA; JR; Provost-Vice Provost Hon Soc 89-; Golden Key; Vol Svcs West End Girls Clb; Atlanta Outrch Pgm Vol; Vlybl Capt; Bsktbl Capt.

**BENTON, GARY LAWRENCE,** Ms St Univ, Miss State, MS; SR; Phi Kappa Phi; Sigma Gamma Tau; Phi Theta Kappa 89-88; Circle Of Excllnce; MCC; Headway Awd 88; Ptrns Schlrshp; ACT Schlrshp; Univ Schlrshp; Aerospace Engnrng.

**BENTON, JULIE A,** Univ Of Ky, Lexington, KY; SR; BA; Wsly Fndtn 87-; Cmps Crsd Chrst 87-; HPER 89-; Frmhs Lttl Sstr 87-89; Dghtrs Amrcn Rvltn 88-; Cmmnty Rcrtn.

**BENTON, KATHRYN R,** Nova Univ, Ft Lauderdale, FL; GD; MBA; Alpha Chi Omega Alumni 82-; Hmownrs Assn Tr 90-; Bnkg/Factrng.

**BENTON, LEAH M,** Univ Of Ga, Athens, GA; JR; BSED; Mddl Schl Ed Clb Sec 90; Gldn Key 90; Kappa Delta Epsilon 90; Zeta Tau Alpha Fdrasr 88; Cmmnvrsty Tchrs Asst 88-89; Srty Rsh Cnclr 89; Middle Schl Ed Mth Science.

**BENTON, PATRICIA M,** Coker Coll, Hartsville, SC; JR; BS; Mrshl; Plnt Anlyst Frmrs Tlphn Coop Inc; Bsn Admin/Mgmt.

**BENTZ, CHRISTINE M,** Kent St Univ Kent Cmps, Kent, OH; SO; BA; Soccer Club Gymnastics Club Outdoor Club IM Bsktbl; Alpha Lambda Delta; Sherrie Jo Luft Memorial Awd; Acctg & Mgmnt; Continue Ed To MBA.

**BENTZ, EDUARDO K,** Daytona Beach Comm Coll, Daytona Beach, FL; SO; BA; Soc Orslvs Yth Envrmntl Sstnblty 90-; Lbrl Arts; Law Edctn.

**BENTZ, KIM L,** Univ Of Pittsburgh, Pittsburgh, PA; GD; MSN; Sigma Theta Tau 90-F Caplan Grad Stdnt Awd 90-; BSN PA State Univ 82; Nrsng; Ped Nrs Prctnr.

**BENYAK, DARIN M,** Youngstown St Univ, Youngstown, OH; SR; BE; Amrcn Scty Mchncl Eng 89-; Deans Lst 86-; Tau Beta Pi 89-; Est Oh Gs Cmpny Schlrshp; Fndtn Schlrshp 86-; Mchncl Eng.

**BENZELL, KIMBERLY B,** Providence Coll, Providence, RI; SR; BA; Clg Radio Stat Asst Gen Mgr 89-; Dancer Choreographer 88-; Pastoral Cncl Sec 88-90; Outstndng Wmn Amer; CCD Tchr 88-; WOR Talk Radio Intern 88-89; BA; Elem Spec Educ; Tchr Media Spokesperson.

**BERANEK, JENNIFER R,** Indiana Univ Of Pa, Indiana, PA; SR; BED; Pnnsylvn St Ed Assoc; Natl Ed Assoc; Deans Lst; Sigma Kappa Rcrdng Sec; Prjct Uplft; Intl Ordr Rnbw Pres; Dean Slst; IUP Chrldr Co Capt; Elem Ed.

**BERARDESCA, GIOVANNA F,** Albertus Magnus Coll, New Haven, CT; SO; BA; Stg Mgr Cmps Thrtr 90; Dir Shksprs Scns 90-; Stf Mbr Albrts Mgns Slvr Hrn; Amty Chrtbl Trst Fnd Schlrshp; Fncng Trnmnt 89; Engl; Athr/Scrnwrtr.

**BERARDI, JACQUELYN G,** James Madison University, Harrisonburg, VA; JR; BS; ARC Pres 90-; CEC VP 91-; AEYC 89-90; SEA 89-; ARC Bd Of Dir 90-; Gldn Ky 90-; Kappa Delta Pi 90-; Alpha Phi Omega 89-; Spec Educ; LD.

**BERARDINO, KATHLEEN M,** Seton Hall Univ, South Orange, NJ; SR; Kappa Delta Pi; Phi Alpha Theta; Alpha Phi Pres 90-; Ldrshp Awd; Deans Lst; Elem Educ/Hist.

**BERBACK, KRISTIN A,** S U N Y Coll At Fredonia, Fredonia, NY; JR; BS; Chem Clb 89-; Tutor 88; Env Chem Intrnshp 90; Resrch Wrk At Univ Of Buffalo 90-; IM Vlybl 89-; Sci; Genetic Engr/Chem.

**BERBERICH, JENNIFER M,** Va Commonwealth Univ, Richmond, VA; FR; Hon Prog 90-; Acctg; CPA.

**BERDANIS, DENNIS G,** Southern Coll Of Tech, Marietta, GA; SR; BSEET; IEEE 90-; Tau Alpha Pi 88-; Engr.

**BERENS, DAVID F,** Roane St Comm Coll, Harriman, TN; SO; BA; Comm Radio; Radio Brdcstng.

**BERESFORD, CHRISTOPHER L,** S U N Y Coll Of Tech At Frmgdl, Farmingdale, NY; FR; Lbrl Arts6; Law.

**BERESFORD, MARCIA N,** Hilbert Coll, Hamburg, NY; SO; AAS; Acctg Clb; VFTA; Alpha Beta Gamma; Acctg.

**BERESIK, CHRISTIAN,** Atlantic Comm Coll, Mays Landing, NJ; GD; State Cert/Sanitation; Conv Srvcs/Trvl Indstry; BS Culinary Arts Johnson/Wales Univ 87; Hsptlty Mgmt.

**BEREZANSKY, SUSAN,** Indiana Univ Of Pa, Indiana, PA; SR; BS; TV News Prdcr 90-; Wrtr Rptrt Anchr Hst Prdcr; Alpha Epsilon Rho 90-; Intrnshp WKBD 90-; Cum Laude; Cmmnctns Media; Brdcst Nws.

**BERG, ADAM T,** Castleton St Coll, Castleton, VT; SO; BCIS; Cmptr Sci/Math; Cmptr Smltns/Prgmmng.

**BERG, ALLISON L,** Univ Of Hartford, West Hartford, CT; JR; BA; Stdnt Assoc 89-; Ski Clb 89-; AA 90; Mass Commnctns.

**BERG, CATHERINE H,** Clemson Univ, Clemson, SC; SO; Stdnts For Env Awrns Sec 90-; Stdnt Nursing Assoc 90-; Deans Lst 90-; Pres Lst 89; Nursing.

**BERG, ELIZABETH M,** Methodist Coll, Fayetteville, NC; JR; BS; Stdnt Crt Chf Jstce Elect/Juror; Stdnt Govt Sen 90-; Dns Lst 90-; Spec Olymp 88-90; Sccr Capt 88-; Comms; Prod.

**BERG, EVAN B,** Univ Of Rochester, Rochester, NY; SO; Theta Chi; Pol Sci; Law Schl.

**BERG, JENNIFER L,** Hillsborough Comm Coll, Tampa, FL; SO; BA; Educ; Ele Educ.

**BERGA, CHRISTOPHER G,** Univ Of Miami, Coral Gables, FL; FR; BA; IM Vlybl Bsktbl; Vlybl Clb; Fnnce; Law.

**BERGDORF, TIMOTHY K,** Kent St Univ Kent Cmps, Kent, OH; SR; IM Vlybl Capt 87-; Gldn Key 89-; Alph Lmbd Dlt 87-; Eta Sgm Psi 87-; Phi Beta Kappa; Phi Sgm Alph; Distgnst Schlrshp Awrd 87; Schlrshp Exclnc 87-; Wash Pgm Natl Issue; Intrnshp Natl Inhldrs Assc; Deans List 87-; Pres List 87-; BA; Pol Sci; Tchr.**

**BERGE, JACKIE M,** Mount Saint Mary Coll, Newburgh, NY; SR; Girl Sct Ldr 89-; Grdn Clb Vol 90; ER Nrs Assn; Nrs Quarter 90; RN; Crtfd ER Nrs; ACLS Qualified BLS Instrctr CPR; Diploma Tacoma Gen Hosp Schl Nrsng 74; Nrsng; Master Sci Nrsng.

**BERGEN, ROBIN M,** Univ Of Va, Charlottesville, VA; SR; JD; Madison Hs Big Sblng Vol Pgm 88-; Yrbk 87; Betta Gamma Sigma 89-; Phi Etta Sigma 87-; ACC Schlr Athlete Awd; David W Thompson Acctng Schlrshp; Carmen Blough Acctng Awd; Vrsty Sftbl Cptn 87-; BS; Acctng; Law.**

**BERGENER, MARGARET SUSY,** Memphis St Univ, Memphis, TN; SR; Soc Wrk Clb Pres 90-; Stdnt Cnsl; BA; AA 86; Soc Wrk.

**BERGER, GERTRUDE M,** Marywood Coll, Scranton, PA; SR; BA; Soc Comm Stu Govt Chrmn 90-; Hnrs Prog 87-; Folk Grp Cmps Mnstry Co Charmn 87-90; Delta Epsilon Sigma 90-; Theta Apha Kappa 89-; Religious Stu; Mnstry.

**BERGER, JEFFREY J,** Univ Of Rochester, Rochester, NY; JR; Vrsty Lacrosse Ltrmn 87-; Acdmc Advsr 90-; Greek Job Smnr Com Fndr 90-; Deans List 90-; Delta Kappa Epsilon; Tutor 90-; Rochester Pblc Dfndrs Inter Ofc; IM Ftbl/Bsktbl/Sftbl Capt 87-; Psychlgy/Bio; Law.

**BERGER, JENNIFER G,** Cornell Univ Statutory College, Ithaca, NY; SR; BS; Clg Agrcltr Life Sci Ambsdr; Gldn Key 89-; Phi Kappa Phi; Gamma Sigma Delta; Pi Beta Phi Prsdnt 88-; Stdnt Advsr 89-; Cyril Crowe Awrd Otstndng Achvmnt Ag Ec; Agrcltrl Ec Bsns Mgmt; Systm Cnsltnt.

**BERGER, MARY ELLEN,** Saint Francis Coll, Loretto, PA; SO; BED; Elem Ed; Tchr.

**BERGER, MICHELE L,** Temple Univ, Philadelphia, PA; SR; BSN; Sigma Theta Tau; Nrsg.

**BERGER, PAUL R,** Fl St Univ, Tallahassee, FL; SR; BA; Fla State Univ Sailing Assn Vice Commodore 90-; Intl Affairs Socty 90-; Phi Theta Kappa 89-90; Gamma Theta Upsilon 90-; Cities In Schls Prog Tutor 89-90; Amer Prof Capt Assn 86-; AA Palm Beach Comm Coll 90; Intl Affrs/Geography; Comm Shipping.

**BERGER, WILLIAM J,** Univ Of Pittsburgh At Bradford, Bradford, PA; SO; BA; Anthrplgy Clb Advrtsg Secr; Guitar Clb Secr 90-; Lit Mag 90-; Hmn Rels; Anthrplgy/Archlgy.

**BERGER-JESUKIEWICZ, LYNDA MARIE,** George Mason Univ, Fairfax, VA; SR; BS; SEA 88-; Outsdng Stdnt Teach Evltn 90; IM Sftbl 88; Cert K-4 Cmmnwlth Of VA; Early Chldhd Educ; Teach Elem Educ.

**BERGERON, J DAVID,** Univ Of Sc At Columbia, Columbia, SC; SR; BA; Phi Eta Sigma 85; Cir K 90; Open Door Hlth/Wlns Pgm Cnslr; Lxngtn Cnty EMS 86-90; Intdsplnry Stds.

**BERGERON, JENNIFER A,** Lasell Coll, Newton, MA; SR; AS; Res Life Staff 90-; Deans List 90; Hnrs 90; Limited Intern 89-; Vars Vllybl 90; Fashion Merch; Trvl/Intl Bus.

**BERGERON, PAULA M,** Merrimack Coll, North Andover, MA; FR; BS; Big Brothers/Big Sis 90-; Spec Olympics 90-; Biology; Optometry.

**BERGERON, SARAH J,** Kent St Univ Kent Cmps, Kent, OH; FR; BA; Alpha Lambda Delta; Bus; Acctg.

**BERGERON, STACY L,** Univ Of Southern Ms, Hattiesburg, MS; SR; River Navigators 89-90; Pre Med Clb; Dns Lst 90; Psychtrc Nrsng; Psychtrc Admin.

**BERGERON, TIMOTHY N,** Western New England Coll, Springfield, MA; SO; BA; ROTC 90-; Alph Lambda Delta; Acctng; CPA US Army.

**BERGEVIN, JAMES J,** Salisbury St Univ, Salisbury, MD; JR; BA; Univ Nws Mag Dist Mngr Asst 89-90; Stdnt Radio Sta Prod Mgr 90-; WSUR Bst New Mbr Awd 90; Comm Arts; Radio/T V Brdsctng.

**BERGGREN, DAVID J,** Eckerd Coll, St Petersburg, FL; SO; BA; Immanuel Peace Cmnty 90-; Amnesty Internatl; Ford Schlr Prog; Religious Studies/Hist; Clge Prfsr-Relgn/Hist.

**BERGHOLM, DEBORAH LYN,** Rivier Coll, Nashua, NH; SR; Natl Assoc Ed Yng Chldrn Pres 89-; BA.**

**BERGIDA, RUTH,** Boston Univ, Boston, MA; JR; BSMS; B Nai Brith Hillel Fndtn Rlgs Lf Chrmn; Gldn Key Ntnl Hnr Soc 90-; Rsrch Undr Jean Berko Gleason Drctd Stdy Asst; Rhbltn Inst Chicago Prctcm; Accptnc Cmbnd BSMS Aclrtd Prgrm; Cmmnctn Dsrdrs; Comm Dstdrs Lngstcs.

**BERGIN, MATTHEW W,** Univ Of Rochester, Rochester, NY; JR; BA; Vrsty Ftbl 88-90; Coll Republicans 89; Assoc Coll Entrepreneurs 88-89; IMS 89; Deans Lst 88-; Theta Delta Chi Treas 88-; Thomastames Assoc Intrnshp; Prudential-Bache Intrnshp; Sen Alphonse Damato Intrnshp; Vrsty Ftbl 88-90; Econ; Bus Sch.

**BERGMAN, DEBBORA,** Northeastern Christian Jr Coll, Villanova, PA; SO; AA; Waitress 86-89; Psychology; Ph D Psychology.

**BERGMAN, ELIZABETH K,** Columbia Univ, New York, NY; FR; BA; Intern Riverside Symphony Admnstrtv Asst 90-; Anthrplgy; Prfsr.

**BERGMAN, KRISTINE,** Georgian Court Coll, Lakewood, NJ; SR; BS; Bus Clb 89-; Pre Law Scty 89-; Delta Mu Delta 90-; Bus/Mrktng; Law.

**BERGMAN, SUSAN L,** Roane St Comm Coll, Harriman, TN; SO; BED; Emp Of The Yr 88; Emp Of The Mo 89; Waste Mngmt; Cert Amer Hotel Motel Assoc 89; Env Scci; Waste Mngmt.

**BERGMANN, MELISSA A,** Bloomfield Coll, Bloomfield, NJ; SR; BS; Alpha Chi; Bsn Intrnshp Union Camp Corp; Bsn Admin; General Mngmnt.

**BERGOUIGNAN, DANIA M,** Fl International Univ, Miami, FL; SO; BA; Xi Delta VP 90-; History; Professor.

**BERGQUIST, JOHN M,** Samford Univ, Birmingham, AL; GD; Cumberland Law Review 90-; Moot Court Bd; Trial Advsry Bd; CLS 89-; Am Jur Book Awd Civil Proc I 89; Const Law I 90; Law.

**BERGSTRESSER, TARA L,** Va Commonwealth Univ, Richmond, VA; SO; Intern Atty John Boatwright Spclzs Crmnl Def; Aerobic Instr Sch Gym; Admin Justice/Legal Studies; Law.

**BERHALTER, KAREN L,** S U N Y Coll At Fredonia, Fredonia, NY; SO; BS; Vars Bsktbl Stats Asst 90-; Hlth Serv Admn.

**BERICK, YEHONATAN M,** Univ Of Cincinnati, Cincinnati, OH; JR; BM; Music; Violinist.

**BERIGAN, JOHN C,** Hudson Valley Comm Coll, Troy, NY; FR; BA; AS Hudson Vly Cmnty Clg 87; Bsn Finance; Invstmnt Bnkg.

**BERINGER, ALBERT F,** Portland School Of Art, Portland, ME; SR; AS; FPC Pres 78-79; US Navys Nvl Sci Awd Acdmc Achvmnts 76-77; RA 88-89; Deans Lst 89-90; BA F Pierce Coll 89; AS Strlng Inst Crftsbry VI 77; Archtctr; Eng Strctrl/Mech.

**BERIO-SUAREZ, MARIA T,** Univ Of Pr Medical Sciences, San Juan, PR; Assoc Med P R AMA FACS FACOG; Brd Cert Ob/Gyn 67; MD Tulane Univ Sch Med 49; Cert; Gyn; Med.

**BERKE, ERICH D,** Duquesne Univ, Pittsburgh, PA; JR; BABS; Union Prog Brd Chrprsn 88-; Dnc Mrthn Fin Chrmn 89-90; Sign Wvs Treas 90-; Phi Sigma Epsilon; Alpha Phi Omega Frst Vp 90-; Duquesne Univ Vol; Deans Lst 90; Crw 88-90; Fin/Poli Sci.

**BERKEBILE, JEFFREY A,** Univ Of Akron, Akron, OH; SR; BS; ACES 90-; OCIRA 90-; Deans Lst 88-90; AAS Stark Tech Coll 85; Elem Edn.**

**BERKENSTOCK, JENNIFER L,** Bucknell Univ, Lewisburg, PA; FR; Actvts Cncl Prgrm Coord; Cncrt Chrl Hstrn; Dance Tm; Vrsty Crew.

**BERKLEY, G MAREA,** Marshall University, Huntington, WV; JR; Symphonic Bnd 88-90; Theatre Actress 90-; Gamma Beta Phi; AA Valencia Comm Clg Orlando Fla 90; English; Classical Studies; Clg Professor.

**BERKLEY, SARAH B,** Philadelphia Coll Pharm & Sci, Philadelphia, PA; SR; BS; ASP Pres 87-; IPSF USA Delg 89-; AGAPE 87-; Alpha Lambda Delta VP 88-89; Rho Pi Phi Chpln 90-; Pres Schlrshp 87-; Deans Lst 87-89; Phrmcy.

**BERKLEY, STEVE W,** Univ Of Rochester, Rochester, NY; SO; BABM; Cncrt Plnng Clb 88-89; Comp Sci/Music Comp; Elec Music/Flm Scrng.

**BERKNER, BONNY M,** Univ Of Miami, Coral Gables, FL; SO; BA; Hmcmng Actv 89-90; Dsk Asst Res Hls 89-; Link Vol Serv Comm; Dns Lst; IM Sprts 90-; Geogrphy/Intl Stds; Dplmcy/Frgn Serv.**

**BERKOVICH, EVGENY,** Ny Univ, New York, NY; FR; Znst Pres 90-; Flm 90-; Chbd 90-; Premed Soc 90-; Rsn Clb 90-; Judo Tm 90-; Premed/Chmstry; Med.

**BERKSHIRE, CHAD W,** Univ Of Miami, Coral Gables, FL; SO; BBA; Dns Lst 89-90; Provosts Hnr Rl; Finance; Invstmnt Bnkng.

**BERKSHIRE, DEBRA J,** Anne Arundel Comm Coll, Arnold, MD; SO; BS; Pub Schl Systm Vol 85-; Psychlgy.

**BERLEY, WENDY CAVELLA,** Univ Of South Al, Mobile, AL; SR; BS; Blck Stdnt Un 88-; Intl Clb 90-; Abeneetoo Kuo 88-; Pres Lst 89; AS Southern Coll SDA 87; Health Ed; Educator/Coordinator Ms Pblc Hlth.

**BERLIN, KENNETH A,** Edinboro Univ Of Pa, Edinboro, PA; SO; BA; Mrchng Bnd; Jazz Bnd; Symph Bnd; Opera Wrkshp; Phi Eta Sigma; U Hons Pgm; Estock Music Schlrshp; Hons Pgm Schlrshp; Music; Scndry Ed.

**BERLIN, TERESA,** Fayetteville St Univ, Fayetteville, NC; JR; BS; Spcl Frcs Wvs 89-; Chnclrs Lst 90; Vol Comm Wrk 89-90; Elem Educ; Tchr.

**BERLINER, SUSAN N,** Central Fl Comm Coll, Ocala, FL; SO; AA; Stdnt Lbr Assist 90; Libr Sci; Lbrn.

**BERLINGERI, MARTA T,** Fl International Univ, Miami, FL; SR; Stdnt Govt Sen Comm Chp 89-; Am Mrktng Assn 89-; Cir K Intl Pres 87-; Ostndng Stdnt Awd Flu Div Of Stdnt Affairs 90-; BBA; Mrktng; Fashion Mgr.

**BERLUS, PIERRE R,** Bunker Hill Comm Coll, Boston, MA; FR; Church Scientology 90-; RESOFA; Engl/Cmptr/Math.

**BERMAN, ARI D,** Yeshiva Univ, New York, NY; SR; BA; Coll Rvw Clb Chr 90-; Phlsphy Soc VP 90-; Phlsphy; Ed.

**BERMAN, DMITRY,** City Univ Of Ny Queensbrough, New York, NY; GD; BABED; Orientation 89-90; Mentor Pgm 90; AA; Psych; Tchr.

**BERMAN, LISA M,** Fl International Univ, Miami, FL; CERT; Future Eductrs Amer VP 90-; Delta Delta Delta; Alpha Theta Chptr Pub Rel Chr 84-87; Bg Sistr/Bg Bro Broward Cnty; On Air Promtn; Comm Dir March Dimes 87-89; BA Univ Pitts 87; Elem Educ; Tchg.

**BERMAN, PAUL I,** Clarkson Univ, Potsdam, NY; FR; BS; Class Treas; Vrsty Bsbl; Acctng; Bus.

**BERMANN, TINA M S,** Univ Of Ga, Athens, GA; JR; BSED; Erly Chlhd Educ; Tchg.

**BERMUDEZ VALENTIN, LIMARIES C,** Inter Amer Univ Pr San German, San German, PR; FR; Comm Admin/Fiannce.

**BERMUDEZ, DAFNEE,** Fl International Univ, Miami, FL; SR; BS; Soc Wmn Engs Pres 90-; IEEE; MDCC Hons Schlrshp; Nautilus Trng; AA Miami Dade Comm Clg 86; Cmnctns; Elec Eng.

**BERMUDEZ, DAVID R,** Univ Of Pr At Rio Piedras, Rio Piedras, PR; JR; Gldn Key; Dns Lst 90-; $500 Awd Ntl Sci Fndtn 90; Blgy; Med.

**BERMUDEZ, ZOILA F,** Miami Dade Comm Coll South, Miami, FL; SO; BA; Educ.

**BERMUDEZ-CARRASQUILLO, ALEXIS A,** Inter Amer Univ Pr Hato Rey, Hato Rey, PR; FR; MBA; Hi Enrgy D J 89-90; Digitek D J/Highwave D J 90-; Spermercados Amigo Cashier 90-; Natl Hnr Soc V P 87-90; Math; Airway Cmptr Sci Eng.

**BERMUDEZ-FRESSE, MARIA I,** Univ Of Pr Cayey Univ Coll, Cayey, PR; FR; Chemistry Cir 90-; Ntnl Sci Tchrs Assn Area Cnvtn 90; Science; Med.

**BERNACKI, JAMES P,** Duquesne Univ, Pittsburgh, PA; SO; Acctg; Music/Acctg.

**BERNAICHE, DAWN S,** Andover Coll, Portland, ME; SO; BA; VITA; NSPA; Acctg; CPA/CMA.

**BERNARD, ALAIN M,** Morehouse Coll, Atlanta, GA; FR; BA; Glee Clb 90-; UNCF Schlrshp 90-; Wrk Stdy 90-; Sclgy; Law.

**BERNARD, BARBARA T,** Va Commonwealth Univ, Richmond, VA; SO; BS; Rsrch Asst; Blgy; Hon Pgm 90-; Blgy; Med.

**BERNARD, CHRISTINA M,** Volunteer St Comm Coll, Gallatin, TN; SO; BA; Sclgy/Crmnlgy.

**BERNARD, CHRISTINA M,** Va Commonwealth Univ, Richmond, VA; SO; BA; Natl Frshmn Hnr Soc 89-90; Hnrs Pgm 89-; Dns Schlr Awd 89-; Provost Schlrshp 89-; Acctg; CPA.

**BERNARD, DAVID A,** Meridian Comm Coll, Meridian, MS; SO; ACC; Tennis Tm; Acctg; CPA.

**BERNARD, JAN R,** Western Piedmont Comm Coll, Morganton, NC; SO; AASC; High GPA; Owner/Operator Jans Plant Care 87-; Horticultural Technologies; Degree Botany.

**BERNARD, LESLIE C,** Longwood Coll, Farmville, VA; JR; BS; Earth Clb 90-; LURE 90-; Alpha Delta Mu VP 90-; Alpha Phi Omega VP Mbrshp 89-90; Peer Advsr 90-; Stu Coordntr Give Vol Serv 90-; Scl Wrk; Med Scl Wrker.

**BERNARD, LINDA G,** Northeast State Tech Comm Coll, Blountville, TN; SO; AAS; Amercn Chem Soc 89-; Phi Theta Kappa 90-; Bethel Apsotolic Church 90-; Chem; Chem Techcn.

**BERNARD, NICOLE M,** Univ Of Rochester, Rochester, NY; SO; BA; Religion/Classics Asian Studies; Edn/Transl.

**BERNARD, REGINALD D,** Jackson St Univ, Jackson, MS; JR; BA; Econ Clb Pres 90-; Acdmc Hnrs Cncl 88-; Advsry Cncl 90-; Phi Kappa Phi Soc; Alpha Lambda Delta; Procter Gamble Dist Co 90-; Bsn; Pblc Acctg.

**BERNARD, ROSE C S,** Columbia Union Coll, Takoma Park, MD; BS; SPPCH 86-89; Yth Clb 87-; Soc Clb 89-; Dance Co 78-89; Assn Caribbean Stdnts 78; DCNA 82-; ANA 81-; MNA 81-90; PSNA 90-; ANILH 71-76; Wrld Hlth Org Haitian Rep Intl Conf Tropical Diseases 72; Stf Nrs Wash Hosp Ctr; Bus Admin; Anesthesia.

**BERNARD, SUSAN C,** Univ Of Nc At Charlotte, Charlotte, NC; JR; BA; Math Assoc Of Amer 90-; Coop Ed Microsoft Corp 90; Mgr Dominos Pizza 84-90; Math; Sftwr Sprt.

**BERNARD, TERESA S,** Kent St Univ Kent Cmps, Kent, OH; GD; MA; Kent Cncl Fmly Rel Pres 90-; Sprng Banquet Comm 90-; Grad Asst Fmly Stds; Outstdng Sr Fmly Stds; Cmbnd Baccalaureate/Mstrs Deg Prog 90-; Natl Cncl Fmly Rel 90-91; BA; Indvdl/Fmly Stds; Ph D Tch Univ Lvl.**

**BERNARDO, ELIZABETH M,** Providence Coll, Providence, RI; SO; BA; Pep Bnd 89-; Rng Cmmtt 90-; Pstrl Cncl Lctr 89-; Intl Fndtn Emply Bnfts 90-; Hmnts; Hmn Rsrc Mgmt.

**BERNATOWICZ, SHAWN P,** Saint Francis Coll, Loretto, PA; JR; BS; Educ Clb Pr 88-89; Camps Mnstry; Spec Frnds Pgm; Delta Epsilon Chi 90; Hnr Soc 90; Delta Sigma Phi Pldg Educ 88-; Knghts Colmbs Dpty Grnd Knght 88-; Dns Lst; IM Hcky/Ftbl/Bsktbl/Sftbl Capt 87-; Elem Educ; Elem Schl Tchr.

**BERNDT, DEBRA A,** Ny Univ, New York, NY; FR; MTV Ntwrks; VH1 Mrktng 88-; Mrktng; Adv/Promo.

**BERNDT, PAUL E,** Saint John Fisher Coll, Rochester, NY; SR; Pre Law Assn Pres 88-; Pol Sci Clb 90-; Phi Alpha Theta 90-; Pi Gamma Mu 90-; Intrnshp Monroe Cnty Dist Att Ofc 89; Hist/Pol Sci; Law.

**BERNEBURG, SCOTT W,** Oh Coll Of Podiatric Med, Cleveland, OH; SO; DPM; Alpha Gamma Kappa 90-; OCPM Merit Schlrshp 89-90; Magna Cum Laude 88; Katherine Robertson Mc Cartney Prize 85; BS Geneva Coll 88; Pdtry.

**BERNER, JEFFREY E,** Germanna Comm Coll, Locust Grove, VA; FR; Elec Cmptr Sci; Eng/Cons.

**BERNHARDT, CATHERINE A,** Univ Of North Fl, Jacksonville, FL; SR; BA; Gldn Key; AA 83; Elem Ed; Tchr.

**BERNHEISEL, MARILYN H,** Beaver Coll, Glenside, PA; GD; MA; SPSEA 67-71; Coll Radio Sta Pro/Pub Dir 68-71; Phi Delta Kappa; Rho Lambda Phi Mllrsvll Univ 69-71; Grad Asst 70-71; APA; AACD; NEA; PSEA; ASCD; Elem Clsrm Tchr 71-83; BSED Mlrsvil Univ 70; M Ed Mlrsvl Univ 71; Cnslng; Schl Gdnc Cnslr.

**BERNICK, TODD D,** S U N Y At Buffalo, Buffalo, NY; JR; MBA; Gldn Key 90-; Clg Mthmtcl Sci; Undrgrd Tchng Asstnt Ststcs 90; Hcky 90-; Finance Mrktng; Mrktng Exctv.

**BERNIER, MICHELE M,** Teikyo Post Univ, Waterbury, CT; SO; BA; Eng; Teaching/Journalism.

**BERNIER JR, PAUL D,** Albertus Magnus Coll, New Haven, CT; FR; BS; Peer Cnslng; CRC Press Frshmn Chem Achvmnt Awrd; Sci/Bio/Chem; Med/Rsrch.

**BERNIER, ROBERT D,** Capitol Coll, Laurel, MD; SR; BS; U S Cyclng Fed 87-; Natl Off Rd Bicy Assoc; Clg Park Bicy Clb; Alpha Chi; AA Hagerstown Jr Clg 89; Elec Eng Tech.

**BERNINI-SCHIMPF, NICOLE A,** Dowling Coll, Oakdale Li, NY; SO; BA; Psychlgy Clb; Religious Instrctn 90-; Chrst The King Chrch; Clin Psychlgy.

**BERNSTEIN, ALAN L,** Barry Univ, Miami, FL; JR; Pres Lst 90-; Broward Cnty Schls Prnt Vol Tutor 90-; Stck Brkr-Mrtge Brkr-Lcnsd Ins Agnt 84-; Bus; Law.

**BERNSTEIN, JENNIFER P,** West Chester Univ, West Chester, PA; GD; Unvrsty Cnct Choir Pres 88-89; 89-90; Symphony Orchstr Lbrn 88-89; Opera Chorus; Chorus Mbr Aworld Premiere Opera; Hnr Soloist Chral Prgrm; 2nd Pl Nats Winner; Hillary H Parry Memorial Schlrshp Excellnc Voice; Opera Performer.

**BERNSTEIN, JOSHUA E,** Univ Of Nc At Asheville, Asheville, NC; SR; BA; Stdnt Govt Senator 88-; Outing Clb 90-; Phi Eta Sigma 87-; Omicron Delta Kappa 89-; Schlrs Hon 87-; Bio; Med.

**BERNSTEIN, MARC M,** Comm Coll Algny Co Algny Cmps, Pittsburgh, PA; SO; BA; Phi Theta Kappa; AA; Educ; Teach.

**BERNSTEIN, NAUM,** Bunker Hill Comm Coll, Boston, MA; GD; Math/Cmptr Sci; Edn.

**BERNSTEIN, SARAH,** Bunker Hill Comm Coll, Boston, MA; SR; Liyterature; Liberal Arts.

**BERO, JILL C,** Oh St Univ At Newark, Newark, OH; SO; BS; SGA VP 89-; Actv Brd 90-; Phi Eta Sigma 90-; Hnr Soc Pres 89-; Rmphs Chr 90-; Alpha Lambda Delta 90-; Fclty Asstshp Zlgy/Chem 90-; Ldrshp Awd 90; Nwrk Rtry; IM Vlybl/Sftbl 89-90; AA; Agri Engr; Engr/Farming.

**BEROTH, MELANIE A,** Liberty Univ, Lynchburg, VA; SR; Yearbk 88-; Adv Clb Sec 90-; Radio Stf 87-88; Alpha Lambda Delta 88-; Prisn Fellwshp Edtrl Intrnshp 90; Journlsm; Wrtng.

**BERQUIST, BRETT S,** Bowling Green St Univ, Bowling Green, OH; SO; BA; Mens Chrs 89-; Acapella Chr 89-; Hon Rcrtmnt Cmt 89-; Alph Lmbd Dlt VP 90-; Phi Eta Sgm Tres 90-; Hon Stdnt Assc Fndrsng Chr 89-; Psi Chi 90-; Gldn Key; Un Psychlgcl Assc 90-; Bwlng Grn Rcyclng Ctr 90-; BGSU Tr Guide; BGSU Tlfnd Caller; Psychlgy; Indstrl Psychlgst.**

**BERRETTINI, CHRISTOPHER,** S U N Y Coll Of Tech At Alfred, Alfred, NY; FR; AS; Ski Clb 85-89; PAL 89; Tutr 90-; Sigma Tau Epsilon; IM Vlybl/Hcky 90-; Bldg Const; Const Engr.

**BERRETTINI, LESLIE A,** Elmira Coll, Elmira, NY; JR; BA; Kappa Dlt Pi; Elem Educ; Tchr.

**BERRINGER, MEREDITH L,** Indiana Univ Of Pa, Indiana, PA; SR; Pa State Ed Assoc 90; RAGE 90; Delta Gamma Ntl Srty Frat Awareness 89; Deans Lst 89; BS In Ed; Elem Ed; Tchr.

**BERRIOS DIAZ, ZORAYA M,** Univ Of Pr At Mayaguez, Mayaguez, PR; SO; BS; Chrs 89-90; Hnr Rl 88-; Chem Engr.

**BERRIOS LOPEZ, CAROL D,** Inter Amer Univ Pr Hato Rey, Hato Rey, PR; JR; BA; Sci; Comp Info Systms.

**BERRIOS MENDEZ, BRENDA L,** Inter Amer Univ Pr Hato Rey, Hato Rey, PR; JR; BA; Intr Amer Univ PR Hnr Rl 90-; Finance; Invstmnt Brokr.

**BERRIOS, EDGARDO,** Univ Of Pa, Philadelphia, PA; SR; BBA; Sigma Kappa Phi; Beta Alpha Psi; Pi Delta Epsilon Treas 89-; Knights Of Col 90-; Sands Hotel/Casino 80-; Mngmnt/Acctng; Law.

**BERRIOS, JOSEPH S,** Inter Amer Univ Pr Hato Rey, Hato Rey, PR; JR; BS; Soc Hspnc Prfsnl Engrs 89-; U S Nvl Inst 90-; Ofcrs Chrstn Flwshp 90-; Cert Nvl Tech Trng Ctr 87; Cmptr Sci/Math; Nvl Ofcr/Nvl Avtr/Plt Jts.

**BERRIOS, MARIA,** Inter Amer Univ Pr San Juan, Hato Rey, PR; GD; Assoc Natl Estudiaantes De Derecho 88-90; Law Schl Cls/89 Stdnt Govt Sec 88-89; Law Schl Cls/90 Pres 89-90; Phi Alpha Delta 89-90; Amer Bar Assoc Law Stdnt Dv 89-90; Law Review 89-90; Staff Asst 89-90; Juris Doctor.

**BERRIOS, SONIA I,** Inter Amer Univ Pr Hato Rey, Hato Rey, PR; JR; MBA; Stdt Cncl VP 87; Hnr Prog; Summa Cum Laude 87; ETC Metropolitan Inst Tech 87; Mthmtcs Comps; Cmptr Engr.

**BERRIOS, VIRNA I,** Univ Of Pr Cayey Univ Coll, Cayey, PR; GD; Bus Admin Clb 88-; Hnr Stdnts Lst 88-; BBA; Acctng; CPA.

**BERROA MENDEZ, MARISOL,** Inter Amer Univ Pr Hato Rey, Hato Rey, PR; FR.

**BERROCAL SANCHEZ, LIRDANICE,** Inter Amer Univ Pr Hato Rey, Hato Rey, PR; SO; Aerobics; Mrktg.

**BERROCAL, CARLOS J,** Univ Of Pr Medical Sciences, San Juan, PR; Amer Cncr Socty 87-; Zetha Phi Beta 87-89; Amer Med Socty 82-90; Flw Amer Acad Fmly Physcn 83-; PR Med Assn; PR Fmly Physician Acad; Med Dir Comm Med Ctr; Md 80-; MPH 80-; Faafp Amer Acad Fmly Physicians 84; Gerontology.

**BERROW, DAVID A,** Kent St Univ Kent Cmps, Kent, OH; JR; BA; Acctng Assoc 90-; Tutoring Comm; Golden Key; Beta Alpha Psi Pblcty Ofcr; Acctng; CPA.

**BERRY, ANN C,** Univ Of Rochester, Rochester, NY; SR; BS; Glee Clb 89-90; Soc Undrgrad Blgy Stdnts 89-90; Cert Biotchnlgy; Cell/Dvlpmntl Blgy; Medcl Tchnlgy.

**BERRY, CHARLENE K,** Oh St Univ At Marion, Marion, OH; JR; BED; Psych Clb 88-89; Deans Stdnt Advsry Cncl 88-89; Edn Soc 89-; Alpha Lambda Delta; Phi Eta Sigma 88-; Griffin Soc 90-; Engl/Soc Studies; Teach.

**BERRY, CHERLYN A,** Concordia Coll, Selma, AL; SO; BED; Dns Lst; Hstry; Law.

**BERRY, CHRIS B,** Liberty Univ, Lynchburg, VA; SO; Pre Med/Sci; Chrprctc.

**BERRY, DONALD E,** Toccoa Falls Coll, Toccoa Falls, GA; SR; MDIV; Deans List 86-90; Altr Cnslr Ebnzer Bapt Chrch 87-90; Pstr Bethel Bapt Chrch 90-; Pstrl Intrnshp Ebnzr Bapt Chrch 89; Prcher Of The Yr 89-90; BS 90; Thlgy; Pstr.

**BERRY, GEORGIA A,** Central Fl Comm Coll, Ocala, FL; FR; Phi Theta Kappa; Bus Admn; Nrsng.

**BERRY, JAMES C,** Liberty Univ, Lynchburg, VA; JR; BS; Math; Actuarial.

**BERRY, JARVIS M,** Morehouse Coll, Atlanta, GA; JR; BA; Pre Law Soc 88-; Pol Sci Club 88-; Golden Key 88-; Phi Beta Kappa; Pol Sci; Law.

**BERRY, JAUNA N,** Lesley Coll, Cambridge, MA; FR; BA; Acad Hnrs List; Educ; Teacher.

**BERRY, JENNIFER D,** Marshall University, Huntington, WV; JR; MBA; Intrnshp; Acctg; CPA.

**BERRY, JOY S,** Saint Andrews Presbytrn Coll, Laurinburg, NC; JR; BA; Blck Stdnt Un Pres 90-; Film Soc Chrtr Mbr 90-; Suplmntl Wrtng Prog Tutor 89-; English; Undergrad Tch.

**BERRY, KAREN D,** Radford Univ, Radford, VA; SO; BS; Alpha Lambda Delta 89-; Phi Sigma Pi; Humana Schlp; Dns Lst 89-; Gymnstcs Tm 89-; Psy; Chld Psy.

**BERRY, KIMBERLY D,** Al A & M Univ, Normal, AL; JR; BA; Phi Beta Lambda 90-; Acctg Clb 89-; Alpha Kappa Alpha 90-; Acctg; CPA.

**BERRY, KIMBERLY N,** Central St Univ, Wilberforce, OH; SO; Delta Sigma Theta Schlr 89; Acctg.

**BERRY, KRISTINA M,** Western Piedmont Comm Coll, Morganton, NC; FR; BS; Phi Theta Kappa 90-; English; Ele Educ.

**BERRY, LEA J,** Union Univ School Of Nursing, Memphis, TN; FR; BA.

**BERRY, LORI L,** Univ Of North Fl, Jacksonville, FL; FR; BSN; Actvy; Ballet Dncg/Prfmg; Zeta Tau Alpha; Schlrshp St Vncnts Med Cntr; Deans Lst; Nrsg; Neonatal.

**BERRY, MARK S,** Al A & M Univ, Normal, AL; SR; BS; SGA Assc Ed 90-; Ntl Scty Blck Engs 88-; IEEE 89-; Tau Alpha Pi 89-; Alpha Phi Alpha Pres 89-; Sigma Tau Epsilon 88-; Untd Wy Illtrcy Tskfrc 90; Prjct KEEP Chrmn 89-; US Nvy BDCP Schlrshp Rec 88-; Math; Eng/Scntst.

**BERRY, MARSHA D,** Northern Ky Univ, Highland Hts, KY; JR; BA; Covington Dist Ldrshp Dev Chrmn 89-; KY Conf Sec Of United Meth Women 89-90; Journalism; Hosp Pub Rels.

**BERRY, MEENU,** George Mason Univ, Fairfax, VA; SO; BS; Assoc Indian Stdnts 89-90; ROTC Schlrshp 89-90; Bus Mgmt Info Sys; Law.

**BERRY, MELANIE D,** Birmingham Southern Coll, Birmingham, AL; SR; Pres Stdnt Svc Org 90-; Quest II Prog Bd Coord 87-90; Peer Advsr 89-90; Omicron Delta Kappa 90-; Order Omega Secr 89-; Psi Chi 89-; Alpha Kappa Delta 90-; Alpha Omicron Pi Pres 87-; Australia/New Zealand Intern 90; AL Dem Party Intern 90-; Psych/Sclgy; Law.

**BERRY, MICHELLE L,** Oh St Univ At Marion, Marion, OH; FR; Deans Stdnt Advsry Cncl 90-; Poetry Ed Cornfield Review 90-; Griffin Soc 90-; Fr Ldrshp Conf 90-; Engl; Photojrnlsm.

**BERRY, PAMELA M,** Pellissippi St Tech Comm Coll, Knoxville, TN; JR; BA; Vision Vol/Pellissippi State Grp 90; Nrsg.

**BERRY, ROBERT M,** Comm Coll Algny Co Algny Cmps, Pittsburgh, PA; JR; BS; Stdnt Govt Sen 90-; Cultural Advsry Bd 90-; Bd Publications 90-; Allegheny View Asst Ed 90-; Phoenix Mag Arts Art Dir 90-; Ulcom Camera Tech 90-; Gaming Clb 90-; Outstndg Stdnt Publctns 90-; Outstndg Participtn Publctns 90-; AS; Psych; Psychobio.**

**BERRY, ROGER D,** Piedmont Tech Coll, Greenwood, SC; FR; AAS; Monsanto 67-; Elect Eng Tech; Eng.

**BERRY, SHANNON A,** Merrimack Coll, North Andover, MA; FR; BS; Big Sister; Orient; Bio; Med.

**BERRY, SHARON M,** Univ Of Md At Eastern Shore, Princess Anne, MD; SO; BA; Chrty Vol 90-; Crbbn Clb 90-; Frnch Clb 89-90; Hnrs Pgm 90-; Early Admssns 89-90; Psy; Cnslng.

**BERRY, SHAUNA L,** Ky St Univ, Frankfort, KY; SO; BS; Crmnl Jstc; Atty.

**BERRY, STACY A,** Memphis St Univ, Memphis, TN; FR; BED; Elem Edn; Jr High Tchr.

**BERRY, STACY S,** Fl St Univ, Tallahassee, FL; JR; BS; Deans Lst 90; Finance; Fncl Ofcr.

**BERRY, TAMMY M,** Univ Of West Fl, Pensacola, FL; JR; BA; AA Pensacola Jr Clg 89; Spec Ed/Lrng Dis; Tchg.

**BERRY, TY NOLAN,** Univ Of Nc At Greensboro, Greensboro, NC; JR; BA; Natl Egle Sct Assn 78-; AA Central Piedmont Comm Coll 89; Lsre Arts; Prks Mgmt.

**BERRY, VIRGINIA C,** Ky Wesleyan Coll, Owensboro, KY; GD; BA; Phi Beta Lambda; Cum Laude; AS Owensboro Cmnty Clge 89; Bsn; Mgmt.

**BERRY, WARREN L,** Thomas Nelson Comm Coll, Hampton, VA; SO; AAS; Nwprt News Shpbldg Dsgn Co-Op 90-; Drftng/Dsgn; Eng.

**BERRYANN, JILL M,** S U N Y Coll Of Tech At Delhi, Delhi, NY; Highest GPA Trvl/Tourism Mjr 89-; Brooks Pharcy Mgr Trn 87-89; New Paltz Trvl 90-; Greenwalds Trvl Serv; AAS Travel/Tourism Mgt.

**BERRYMAN, BARTLETT T,** Longwood Coll, Farmville, VA; GD; SAM 90; Alpha Lambda Delta V P 88; BSBA 90; Bsn Admin; MS/BNKNG.

**BERRYMAN, KIMBERLY L,** Ga St Univ, Atlanta, GA; SR; BED; Early Educ; Tch.

**BERSON, MARLA J,** Univ Of Nc At Charlotte, Charlotte, NC; SO; BA; AIPAC 89-; Hmecmg Comm Pgm Bd 89-; RA; Bsn/Engl; Mktg.

**BERSUDER, CYNTHIA A,** Miami Jacobs Jr Coll Of Bus, Dayton, OH; FR; English/Math; Higher Acctng.

**BERT, KARLA E,** Temple Univ, Philadelphia, PA; SR; BS; Mrchg Bnd; Coll Bnd 89-; Wrld Chrstn Flwshp 87-89; IEEE 89-; Elec Engr; Psychlgy.

**BERTAGNOLLI, AMANDA KAY,** Faulkner St Jr Coll, Bay Minette, AL; SO; BA; Humane Soc; Cvl Engr; Engr.**

**BERTE, LISA F,** Neumann Coll, Aston, PA; FR; Chrldng; Acad Excel Awd; Chrldng; Lib Arts; Tchng.

**BERTELLI, MARIA ANGELA,** City Univ Of Ny La Guard Coll, Long Island Cty, NY; FR; AAS; Xaverian Mssnry Soc Nrs 88-89; Harlem Hosp Vol; Terence Cardinal Cooke Hlth Cntr; Nrs Italy 81-82; Dipl Acctng A Meucci Tech Inst Italy 78; Dipl Nrsng 81; Physcl Thrpy Asst.

**BERTHAY WHITE, JOYCE ANN,** Ms St Univ, Miss State, MS; SR; BS; Phi Beta Lambda 90-; Bus Educ.

**BERTHELOT, DEBORAH M G,** Univ Of Montevallo, Montevallo, AL; SR; BS; Lambda Sigma Pi 90-; Deans Lst 90-; Pres Lst 90-; Hgst Hon 90-; Pres Awd; Educ/Psychology; Prfsr/Cnslr.

**BERTHINEE, ELIZABETH A,** Univ Of Akron, Akron, OH; JR; BS; AICHE 89-; Tau Beta Pi 90-; Chem Engr.

**BERTI, MONICA,** Manhattan Coll, Bronx, NY; SR; BS; Rowing Tm; Chi Epsilon Sec; Tau Beta Pi; Epsilon Sigma Pi; Pres/Rgnts Schlrshp; Civil Eng.

**BERTIG, JEANNINE L,** Duquesne Univ, Pittsburgh, PA; SO; BA; Engl Clb; Soclgy Clb; Law Soc; Tutor; Phi Eta Sigma; Deans List; SHARP; Barbor/Cicola Law Firm Intern; Stdnt Intern IN Cty Dept Hmn Serv; Engl/Crmnl Just; Law.

**BERTIN, BEVERLY J,** George Washington Univ, Washington, DC; SR; BS; Trvl/Trsm Rsrch Assc 89-; Trsm Plcy Forum Asst 90; Gldn Key 89-; Deans Lst 89-; Phi Alpha Delta 90-; St Marys Ct Intern; Pblshd Intl Enfrcmnt Law Reprtr Author 90; Inter/Edtr Oppenheimer Wolff/Donnelly 90; Intern ANA/WESTIN Hotel; Phys Fitness 89-; Tourism Adm/Mrktng; Law.**

**BERTINE, DEBORAH A,** S U N Y Coll Of Tech At Frmgdl, Farmingdale, NY; SO; AS; Dns Lst 90; Acad ExclInce Awrd 90; Envir Sci; Envirmntlst Cnsrvtnst.**

**BERTINE JR, PETER K,** Ny Univ, New York, NY; JR; BA; Law.

**BERTKE, BEVERLY N,** Brescia Coll, Owensboro, KY; SR; BA; Scl Sci Clb VP 90-; Bcclrt Cmmtt; Alpha Chi; Hnrs Cllqy; Schlrshp Brsc 89-; Tp Hnrs Prjct 90-; Blwr Hmls Cntr Brd Drctrs Pres 87-; OH Vlly Hmlss Cncl 89-; KY Cltn Hmlss 89-; Psychlgy Sclgy.

**BERTMAN, ERIK G,** Univ Of Sc At Columbia, Columbia, SC; FR; Tnns Clb; Sccr Clb; Bus; Law.

**BERTON, THOMAS S,** Dowling Coll, Oakdale Li, NY; JR; BA; Accntng Soc 90; Alpha Chi; Accntng.

**BERTONI, MICHAEL A,** Widener Univ, Chester, PA; SR; Acad Hons 87-; Dns Lst 89-; BS; Acctg.**

**BERTRAM, JANET M,** Mount Aloysius Jr Coll, Cresson, PA; FR; AS; Phi Theta Kappa; Deans Lst 90-; Magna Cum Laude; SR Magdalene O'reilly Schlrshp; Nursing.

**BERTRAND, FLORA C,** Stillman Coll, Tuscaloosa, AL; JR; BA; Deans List 87-; Stillman Schlr 87-; All Amercn Schlr; Zeta Phi Beta 90-; Phi Beta Lambda VP 90; Oakdale Elem Sch Secy 90-; AS Shelton State Cmnty Clg 88; Bus Admn; Corp Lawyr.

**BERTRANG, BONNIE VIVIAN,** Liberty Univ, Lynchburg, VA; SO; MBA; Weight Rm Super; Hstry/Engl; Law/Jrnlsm.

**BERTSCH, DIANE M,** Northern Ky Univ, Highland Hts, KY; SR; Stdnt Natl Ed Assn Treas 90-; Cncl Excptnl Chldrn; Alpha Chi 88-; G Bohn Awrd; Kappa Delta Gamma 89-; Deans Schlrshp 90-; Outstndng Stdnt; BA; Early Elem Ed; Tchng.

**BERTUCCI, KIMBERLY M,** Univ Of Southern Ms, Hattiesburg, MS; SO; BA; Mktg; Adv.

**BERUBE, DEE-ANN M,** Saint Josephs Coll, Windham, ME; SR; BSN; Stdnt Nrs Assoc 87-; IM Vlybl/Sftbl 87-; Sigma Theta Tau 90-; Delta Epsilon Sigma; Vet Admin Schlrshp Fl Tn 90-; Sister Mary Consuela White Awd Hgst GPA Nrsg Cls; Nrsg; Med/Surg Nrsg.

**BERUBE, NANCY E,** Univ Of New England, Biddeford, ME; SO; BS; Non Tradtnl Cmtr Stdnts Organ Co Pres 89-; Cmtr Rep Stdnt Sen 90; Eartsh ECO 89-90; Massabesic PATCH 87-90; Yrk Cnty Comm Act 88-; Qual Cntrl Insptr 82-87; Occptnl Thrpy Spclzng Sensory Intgrtn Chldrn.

**BERYMON, TANJANYKA L,** Al St Univ, Montgomery, AL; FR.

**BESAW, BETH A,** Defiance Coll, Defiance, OH; JR; BS; Intl Brd Cert Lact Cnsltnt 86-; Bio; Lab Rsrch.

**BESCH, JEANNE M,** Immaculata Coll, Immaculata, PA; SR; BA; Corale; Madrgls; Pop Ensmbl; Music Mnstry; Vrsty Vlybl Tm Co-Capt 89; Sftbl Tm; Outdr Clb; Ed Clb; Campus Mnstry 89-90; Wrkstdy; Rtrt Comm Chr; Vclst/Instrmntlst; Mssnries Chrty 87; Intrn In Irlnd/Italy 89; Deans Lst 90-; BA; Cert Theolgy; Music/Elem Ed; Tchr.

**BESSELLIEU, DENISE L,** Univ Of Sc At Columbia, Columbia, SC; SR; BS; Air Force ROTC Depty Cmdr 90-; Alpha Phi Omega; Air Force ROTC Schlrhsp 87-; Mnrty Acad Achvmnt Awd 87; Math/Stats; Air Force Offcr.

**BESSEMER, CRISSY A,** Oh Univ, Athens, OH; SO; BFA; Art Thrpy Org 90-; Art Thrpy; Cnslng.

**BESSER, LEE ANNE L,** Wv Univ, Morgantown, WV; FR; BA; Hons Lst 90; Jon Scott Nelson Awd; Bus/Ecnmcs; Bus Mgmt.

**BESSETTE, DALE E,** Castleton St Coll, Castleton, VT; JR; BS; Sci; Scndry Educ.

**BESSEY, DEBORAH C,** Commonwealth Coll, Norfolk, VA; SR; AAS; Alpha Beta Gamma; US Nvl Spply Bdgt Assist 80-88; Accntng; CPA.

**BEST, DANIELLE L,** Fl A & M Univ, Tallahassee, FL; SO; BS; Alliance Cultrl Dev Comm Coord; Orchesis 90-; Nwspaper; Pres Spec Schlrshp 90-; A Concrt Danc; Journlsm; Law.

**BEST, ESTHER DUNSTENE,** Univ Of The Dist Of Columbia, Washington, DC; FR; BSN; Caribbean Stu Assoc Sec 90-; Sbstnc Abs Ldrshp Tm Pr Cnslr 90-; Intl Stu Org Exec; Hnrs Pro 90-; Frnds The St Marys Chldrn Hm 87-; Crdt Asst 80-89; Tlr/Accts Super; Scl Wrk; Admin.

**BEST, LASHEECO F,** Fayetteville St Univ, Fayetteville, NC; SO; BS; AFROTC Publ Afrs Ofcr 89-; SIFE 90-; Acctg/Econ; Ofcr Aire Force.

**BEST, PATRICK S,** Univ Of Sc At Coastal Carolina, Conway, SC; JR; BS; Psychlgy Clb; Psi Chi 89-; Psychlgy.

**BEST, PEGGY ANN,** Medical Coll Of Ga, Augusta, GA; SR; Stdnt Bdy Vp 89-90; Sigma Theta Tau; Lettie Pate Whitehead Fndtn Schlrshp.

**BEST, TIMOTHY A,** S U N Y At Buffalo, Buffalo, NY; SR; BS; IEEE 87-; Univ Stdnt Alumni Brd 87-; Ski Clb 87-; Stdnt Assoc 87-; Soc Prof Engrs 87-; Schlry Aths Lst 87-; Dns Hon Lst 89-; Intrnshp Xerox Clg Educ Lrng Intrnshp 90; Dsgn Dual Mode Sensor Bvs 90; Sccr 87-90; Elec Engr; Sftwr/Comp Engr.

**BEST, VICTORIA A,** Hiwassee Coll, Madisonville, TN; FR; BS; Phi Theta Kappa; Pre-Pharm; Pharmacist.

**BESTER, CHARLES E,** Jackson St Univ, Jackson, MS; JR; BS; YMCA Bnd Bstr Clb; S Cntrl Bl; PO; Math; Instr/HS.

**BESTRYCKI JR, CHESTER M,** Marywood Coll, Scranton, PA; SR; BA; Sigma Pi Sgu 87-; Law Advsry Brd 90-; Delta Epsilon Sigma 87-; Pi Gamma Mu 90-; Sigma Pi Mu 87-; Police Offcrs Trng Crs Lackawanna Jr Clg 86; Pre Law; Law Schl.**

**BETANCOURT, DENISE,** Caribbean Center For Adv Stds, San Juan, PR; GD; Cnslr Soc 87-; Cum Laude 90; Sxl Abs Prog Trpst 89-90; Vllybl; Dnc; MS 90; BA Uni Sajrato Corazon 81; Clnc Psychlgy.

**BETANCOURT, ELIZABETH BORGES,** Caribbean Univ, Bayamon, PR; FR; Engl Spnsh Scrtrl; Exec Sec.

**BETANCOURT, JAVIER A,** Univ Of Pr At Mayaguez, Mayaguez, PR; SO; MBA; Hon Stdnt 90-; Mech Eng.

**BETANCOURT, JEANNETTE DE L,** Univ Of Pr Medical Sciences, San Juan, PR; GD; MPH; Med Techs PR 88-; ASCP 88-; Assoc Ctzns Untd Hlth Envrmnmnt Fnder90-; Cntrs Ds Cntrl Intern; Mdcl Tchnlgst; Epdmlgst; Bs Univ PR 86; MT Inter Amrc Univ; Sci; Epdmlgy Rsrch.

**BETANCOURT, JOSE A,** Univ Of South Fl, Tampa, FL; SR; BA; Best Of Coll Photogrphy 89-; AA Seminole Comm Coll Sanford FL 87; Art/Photography; Photographer.

**BETANCOURT, KARINE D,** Suffolk Comm Coll Selden Cmps, Selden, NY; SO; BA; SAM; Finance.

**BETANCOURT, MADELINE,** Duquesne Univ, Pittsburgh, PA; JR; BS; Lambda Sigma Soc 89-90; Lambda Sigma Soc 89-90; Sci; Pharmacy.

**BETANCOURT, MIGUEL A,** Inter Amer Univ Pr Hato Rey, Hato Rey, PR; FR; BS; Aerontcs; Profssnl Pilot.

**BETANCOURT, NANNETTE L SANTIAGO,** Inter Amer Univ Pr Hato Rey, Hato Rey, PR; FR; MBA; Blgy; Micro Blgy.

**BETANCOURTH, EDWIN B A,** Pace Univ At White Plains, White Plains, NY; FR; BS; Comp Srvce Clb 90; Chrch Yth Grp 90-; Math Clb Spnsh Clb 90; Fclty Awrd; Dns Lst; Tau Epsilon Pi Acad Hnrs; Fclty Mem Awrd; High Hnr Rll; MVHS Fclty Mem Awrd; Min And Bernard Barrish Awrd; PTSA Awrd; Comp Sci; Comp Prgrmmng.

**BETBEZE, PHILIP J,** Ms St Univ, Miss State, MS; SO; BA; Rugby Ftbl Clb 90-; Rsdnc Hl Cncl 3rd Flr Rep 90-; Cath Stdnts Assn 89-; Gamma Beta Phi 90-; Dns Lst 90-; IM Bsktbl/Ftbl/Sftbl Pres Bsktbl 89-; Engl/Econ; Tchr/Wrtng/Lawyer.

**BETETA, WANDA D,** Phillips Jr Coll Charlotte, Charlotte, NC; GD; BA; SGA VP 89-90; Peer Cnslr 89-90; Tutor; Pres List; Cert Heald Bus Clg 88; Bus Admn/Acctng; CPA.

**BETH, SUSAN H,** East Tn St Univ, Johnson City, TN; SR; BS; Fclty Awd Outstdng Stdnt/Offc Mgmt Dept 90-; NBEA TBEA STEA; TN Eastman Co Kingsport TN Loan Ofcr Eastman Credit Union 75-86; Bus Ed; Tch.

**BETHEA, ALBERT J,** Coppin St Coll, Baltimore, MD; JR; BS; Psychlgy Clb Ways/Means Sec 90-; Psychlgy/Sosc; Cnslr.

**BETHEA, CRAIG D,** Bloomfield Coll, Bloomfield, NJ; JR; Afrcn Hist Clb 89-; Comm Cln Up Proj 90; Bus Mgmt/Real Est; Own A Chain Of Stores.

**BETHEA, LESLIE L,** Ms St Univ, Miss State, MS; JR; BS; Stdnt Assn Sec; Act Brd 89-; Striders 89-90; Omicron Delta Kappa 90-; Mortar Bd; Order Of Omega; Pi Sigma Epsilon; Chu Omega Chpln 90-; Cres Sis Tean Cncl 90-; Support Svcs 89-; United Way Asst Chrmn; John C Stennis Schlrshp 88-90; Bus.

**BETHEA, MARY A,** D Youville Coll, Buffalo, NY; JR; BSN; Blck Union Pres 88-; Prgrmmng Board 89-; SG; St Catherines Medal Hghst Jr Hnr; EPIC Cert 90-; Nrsng; RN.

**BETHEA, SALLIE L,** Univ Of Ms Medical Center, Jackson, MS; SR; BSN; Clss Pres 90-; Miss Assn Stdnt Nrses Treas 90; Beta Beta Beta 86-89; Phi Mu VP 86-87; UMC Stdnt Nrs Yr 90-; Ms Brd Ed Hghr Lrng Schlrshp 89-; BS Millsaps Coll 89; Nrsng.

**BETHEA, TRACEY,** Benedict Coll, Columbia, SC; SR; BS; SC Ed Assc 89-90; SGA 89-90; Cncrt Chr Sec 88-89; Alpha Kappa Alpha Pres 89-90; Miss Benedict Coll 89-90; Cum Laude; Deans Lst 86-90; Early Chldhd Ed; Teach.

**BETHEA, WENDY L,** Coker Coll, Hartsville, SC; FR; BA; BACCHUS Pres 90-; Brshmn Cls Ofcr Treas 90-; Cultural Arts Comm Treas 90-; Soc Dance Comm Treas 90-; Envrnmntl Clb Treas 90-; SGA Treas 90-; Coll Un Treas 90-; Commissioners; Top 10 Frshmn Cls,Dns Lst 90-; Crew Tm; Engl Educ; Engl Tchr.

**BETHEL, ADRIAN L,** Clark Atlanta Univ, Atlanta, GA; BA; Rlgs Clb Pres 89-; Hnrs Prog Clb 88-; Tutor For Univ John Hope Homes Hsng Proj 88-90; Rlgn/Hist; Teaching.

**BETHELL, NICHELLE L,** Paine Coll, Augusta, GA; SR; BA; Sclgy Clb 88-; Yrbk Phtgrphr 89; Alpha Kappa Mu 90-F Pres Lst 90; All Amer Schlr; Chldrns Emrg Hstl; Deans Lst 90; Hon Roll 90; Pres Lst 90-; Sftbl Tm; Sclgy; Crmnlgst.

**BETHKE JR, JAMES J,** Temple Univ, Philadelphia, PA; JR; BA; Alph Lmbd Dlt; Archtctr; Msc.

**BETHUNE, JACQUELINE A,** Smith Coll, Northampton, MA; SR; Art Rsrcs Com 87-; Jr Yr Abrd 89-90; Hd Acdmc Rep Stdnt Govt 88-89; Rape Awrns Cnslr 90-; Psi Chi 90-; Phi Beta Kappa 90-; Reynolda House Flwshp 88; BA Magna Cum Laude 90; Psychlgy.

**BETHUNE JR, ROBERT E,** Newbury Coll, Brookline, MA; FR; AS; Scnnr Oprtr; Bus Mgmt; Bus.

**BETIT, DIANE HELEN,** North Central Tech Coll, Mansfield, OH; SR; ADN; Nom Natl Coll Nrsng Awd 90-; Natl Stdnt Nurses Assn 90-; Ohio Air Natl Guard 88-; USAF 86-; CCAF Comm Coll Air Force 88; RN; ICU/OPERATING Rm.

**BETTANO, MATTHEW C,** Newbury Coll, Brookline, MA; GD; Assoc Degree; Bus Mgmt.

**BETTERSON, JOHN E,** Va St Univ, Petersburg, VA; SO; Mass Comm; Engl/Mass Comm; Law.

**BETTINGER, APRIL L,** Ohio Valley Coll, Parkersburg, WV; FR; BED; Expressions 90-; Theta Soc Clb 90-; Chrldng 90-; Phys Educ.

**BETTS, CARLIE A,** Schenectady County Comm Coll, Schenectady, NY; SO; AS; Deans Lst 90-; Grl Scts Ldr 89-; YMCA 90-; Rosary Soc Chr 85-; PTA P 83-; Real Estate 88-; Cert Siena Coll 88; Bus Admin; BS Acctg.

**BETTS, CHARLES B,** Univ Of Tn At Martin, Martin, TN; SO; BA; PEP Frshmn Orntn Ldr; Phi Eta Sigma 90-; Pi Sigma Epsilon 90-; Dns Lst 89-; Kappa Alpha Order Schlrshp Chrmn 89-; Accntng; Corp Law.

**BETTS, JUNIECE D,** Clayton St Coll, Morrow, GA; SO; AS; Stdnt Amer Dental Hybienists Assoc 90-; GA Dental Assoc Stdnt Awd 90; Dental Hygiene.

**BETTS, MICHELE L,** Comm Coll Algny Co Algny Cmps, Pittsburgh, PA; FR; AS; Phi Theta Kappa; Intern Allegheny Gen Hosp Radiation Thrpy; Radiation Thrpy; MS Radiation Physics.

**BETTY, RENEE M,** Rivier Coll, Nashua, NH; SO; AA; NH Assoc Ed Yng Chldrn Secr/V P 90-; Early Chldhd Ed; BA.

**BETZ, MARGARET A,** Villanova Univ, Villanova, PA; SR; MA; Phi Kappa Phi; Phi Sigma Tau; BA; Philosophy; Teaching.

**BETZ, TRICIA L,** Marywood Coll, Scranton, PA; FR; BA; SG 90-; Vol Eldrly 90-; Fshn Clb Treas 90-; Retl/Fshn Merch; Retlng.

**BETZNER, RAYNA A,** Univ Of Pittsburgh, Pittsburgh, PA; SO; BA; Sngr In Mry Lou Wllms Msss Mlln Jazz Fstvl; Crtve Wrtng; Wrtng Sngng.**

**BEUCHERT, ELIZABETH J,** Indiana Univ Of Pa, Indiana, PA; FR; BA; Alpha Xi Delta; Sec Tchr.

**BEUKENHORST, ESTHER W,** Univ Of Tn At Martin, Martin, TN; FR; BA; English Soc 90-; Soc Creative Anach 90-; Interfaith 90; Enlgish; Law.

**BEUNIER, YVETTE R,** Saint Francis Coll, Loretto, PA; SR; BA; Math Clb 90-; Math Tutor; Kappa Mu Epsilon 89-; Delta Epsilon Sigma 90-; AA Altoona Schl Commerce 83; Math/Sec Educ; MBA.

**BEUTLER, BARBARA A,** Liberty Univ, Lynchburg, VA; SO; BS; Urbn Otrch 90-; Alpha Lambda Delta 90-; Nrsg; Msnry Nrs.

**BEUTLER, JULIE M,** Liberty Univ, Lynchburg, VA; FR; BA; Reportr/Writer Liberty Champion 90-; Frshmn Hnrs Soc; Hnrs Prog Schlr; Helper At Inner-City Mission; Englisg; Writing.

**BEVACQUA, PAUL A,** Fl St Univ, Tallahassee, FL; SR; BS; Advise; United Way Big Bend; IM Bsktbl 90; AA Tallahassee Cmnty Clg 90; Cmnctns; Pol Cmnctns.

**BEVAN, JASON S,** Coll Misericordia, Dallas, PA; FR; BS; Acctng Club 90-; Wghtlftng 89-; Deans List 90-; Acctng; CPA FBI Acdmy.

**BEVANS, MILLICENT A,** Johnson St Coll, Johnson, VT; SR; BA; Semester Abrd London 90; Robert A Ellsworth Hist Awd; Pol Sci.

**BEVELLE JR, WESLEY,** Al St Univ, Montgomery, AL; FR; BA; Bsn; Own/Manage Bsn.

**BEVER, GRANT E,** Embry Riddle Aeronautical Univ, Daytona Beach, FL; FR; BA; Scuba Clb; Nvl Aviation Clb; IM Vlybl Sftbl 90-; Aerontcl Sci; Nvl Aviatn/Pro Pilot.

**BEVERIDGE, GEORGE S,** Morehouse Coll, Atlanta, GA; JR; BS; Calif Clb; Deans Lst; Chldrns Christian Ministry Tutorial Egleston Hosp Vol; AUC Tutorial; Morehouse Sci Mntrng Prog; Los Alamos Natl Lab Intrnshp; Undergrad Minority Access To Rsrch Int; Biol; Biomed Rsrchr.

**BEVERIDGE, SCOTT T,** Univ Of Ga, Athens, GA; JR; BLA; GA Stdnts Land Arch 89-; Sigma Lambda Alpha; IM Sprts 88-; Envrnmntl Dsgn; Acrdtd Lndscp Arch.

**BEVERIDGE, SHARON Y,** Univ Of Al At Birmingham, Birmingham, AL; SO; BA; Rlgs Edr Rtrd Chldrn; Pres Hnrs; Hnr Schlr; Occptnl Thrpy.

**BEVERLY, WENDELL ROGER,** Univ Of Sc At Columbia, Columbia, SC; FR; BS; Alpha Lambda Delta 90-; Gamma Beta Phi 90-; Phrmcy.

**BEVIL, KRISTI M,** Middle Ga Coll, Cochran, GA; SO; MARCH; Eng Clb 89-; Gamma Beta Phi 90-; Dns Lst; Arch.

**BEVILACQUA, M JOAN,** Erie Comm Coll, Buffalo, NY; FR; BS; X Ray Tchnlgst; Appld Sci; Mdcl Prfsn.

**BEVINGTON, LISA M,** Univ Of Akron, Akron, OH; JR; BA; Acctng Assoc 90; Alpha Lambda Delta 89-; Deans List 88-90; Bus Edn; Teach.

**BEVINS, CONNIE L,** Univ Of Ky, Lexington, KY; GD; LBRN; Phi Beta Lambda; Alpha Lambda Delta; Phi Mu; Scott Cnty Wmns Clb 86-; Dghtrs Amrcn Rvltn Sec 80-; Scott Co Adlt Rdng Prgrm Coord 89-; MSLS 85; BS Georgetown Clg 80; Edctn; Schl Lbry.

**BEVINS, DONNA M,** Anne Arundel Comm Coll, Arnold, MD; FR.

**BEY, STEPHANIE B,** Cheyney Univ Of Pa, Cheyney, PA; SR; BS; Stdnt Newspaper Sec 89-; Natl Coun Negro Wmn Prlmnt 89-90; Ambass Corps 90; Soc Sci; Tchng.

**BEYER, BONNIE M,** Wilmington Coll, New Castle, DE; JR; Crmnl Jstc; Law.

**BEYER, GWYNN A,** Indiana Univ Of Pa, Indiana, PA; JR; BS; Sgn Lang Clb 88-; Sgn In Prfrmng Grp 89-; IM 89; Educ Hearg Imprd; Tchr.

**BEYER, KRISTEN,** Fordham Univ, Bronx, NY; JR; BS; Mngmnt Infrmtn Sys Sec 90-; Psych Clb 90-; Assn Sys Mngmnt 90-; Lab Aide; Jzz Dnc 88-89; Mngmnt Infrmtn Sys; Cmptr Prgmmr Anlyst.

**BEYER, NANCY A,** Northern Ky Univ, Highland Hts, KY; FR; ASSOC; Nrsng.

**BEYER, SARA O,** Gaston Coll, Dallas, NC; JR; BS; Deans Lst St Paul Bible Clg 76; Pr Lst Gaston Clg 90-; Big Sis Pgm; Cosmetology; Bio; Med Schl.

**BEYER, THEODORE M,** Cornell Univ Statutory College, Ithaca, NY; SO; Coop Intern Dow Corning Chmcl Corp; Dean Lst; Amer Wldrs Assn; Mech Eng.

**BEYERLE, NORA S,** Univ Of Cincinnati, Cincinnati, OH; GD; MM; Pi Kappa Lambda 90-; Bowr Vc Cmptn 1st 88; Gorno Vc Cmptn 1st 89; BM CCM 90; Vc Prfrmnc; Pro Singing.

**BEYERS, ELISA R,** Milligan Coll, Milligan Clg, TN; JR; BS; Sga 90-; Delta Kappa Sec 90-; Hart Hall Drm Cncl Pr 90-; Res Asst 90-; Comm; Publ Rel.

**BEYMAN, BRIAN J,** Univ Of Toledo, Toledo, OH; FR; MBA; Deans Lst 90-; Phi Eta Sigma 90; Pharmacy.

**BEZARES HERNANDEZ, LIANNE,** Inter Amer Univ Pr Hato Rey, Hato Rey, PR; JR; Dns Lst 89-; Hons Lst 90-; Tai-Fu Shoi Karate Do Grn Blt 87-89; Bsns Admn; Acctnt.

**BEZON, FRANCIS ROBERT,** Kent St Univ Kent Cmps, Kent, OH; SR; UCT 90-; Salem Jr Bsbl Assn Mgr 87-90; BA 90; Acctg/Bus Mgmt.

**BHAGAT, DEVANGI R,** Va Commonwealth Univ, Richmond, VA; JR; BS; Am Chem Soc Stdnt Affliates 90-; Pre-Med Clb 90-; Phi Eta Sigma 88-; Gold Key 88-; Univ Hon Pgm; Deans Lst 88-; Hon Schlrshp 89-90; ACS Undergrad Awd Analytical Chem 90-; Organic Chem Rsrch Asst 90-; Chem; Med.

**BHAKTA, NAILESH H,** Univ Of Scranton, Scranton, PA; SO; BS; Publ Acctg.

**BHANSALI, MANAN,** Georgetown Univ, Washington, DC; JR; BS; S Asian Clb 88-; Intl Rltns Club 88-; Wash AD Club Cmptn 1st Runner Up; Point Of Purchsng Advtsng Inst Stdnt Mktg Comp Wnr 90; I M Bkbl 88-; Mktg; Advtsng/Entrepreneurshp.

**BHARDE, IRFANULLAH H,** Greenville Tech Coll, Greenville, SC; FR; Math; Mech Engr.

**BHARGAVA, SANGEETA,** City Univ Of Ny Baruch Coll, New York, NY; SR; Beta Alpha Psi Pres 90-; Beta Gamma Sigma; Gldn Ky; Acctg; MBA.

**BHATIA, GURPREET S,** Univ Of Al At Huntsville, Huntsville, AL; SO; BSEE; IEEE 89-; SGA Lgltr Chr Of Intl Stdnt Comm 90-; Indian Stdnt Org 89-90; Alpha Lambda Delta 90-; Elec Engr.

**BHATIA, HONEY L,** Duquesne Univ, Pittsburgh, PA; SR; BBA; Intrnatl Stdnts Orgnztn Sec 90; Mrktng; Bus.

**BHATIA, MANISH S,** Youngstown St Univ, Youngstown, OH, SR; BE; Indian Stdnt Org V P 89-; Tau Kappa Epsilon; Elect Eng; Eng.

**BHATIA, RAJESH,** City Univ Of Ny Baruch Coll, New York, NY; JR; BBA; Acctng Soc 89; Clb India 90; Acctng.

**BHATTACHARYA, SUPRIYO,** Univ Of Md At Eastern Shore, Princess Anne, MD; SR; BSC; Eta Sigma Delta 89; Hnr Grad; Intrnshp Sands Casino Atlantic City 90; F & B Intrnshp Hotel Du Rhone Geneva Switzerland; Cert Intl Coll Of Hotel Mgmt 87; Cert St Gingolph Switzerland 88; Hotel & Rstrnt Mgmt.

**BHATTACHARYYA, SUDHIR,** City Univ Of Ny Baruch Coll, New York, NY; SO; BA; Acctg.

**BHIMANI, TARULATA P,** Univ Of Louisville, Louisville, KY; SR; Tau Beta Pi; Intnshp IBM Lexington; Deans List; Math Awd; Merit Schlrshp; J M Atherton Schlrshp; Engrng/Math/Cmptr Sci; Engrng.

**BHOJWANI, TINA V,** Georgetown Univ, Washington, DC; FR; MBA; Big Bro/Sis Prgrm; Ornttn Stff; Southern Soc 90-; Frst Hnrs 90-; DC Schl Cmmty Serv; Crss Cntry 90-; Bus Admn; Intl Bus.

**BI, HONG,** City Univ Of Ny Baruch Coll, New York, NY; SR; BBA; Gldn Ky; Fin Invstmnt; MBA.

**BIAGIARELLI, PHILIP J,** Merrimack Coll, North Andover, MA; SR; BS; Amer Soc Of Cvl Engrs Pres 89-90; Cvl Eng; Eng.

**BIALOUSZ, MELANIE M,** Radford Univ, Radford, VA; FR; Hse Cncl Rep 90-; IM Sftbl Capt; Occptnl Thrpy.

**BIALY, FRANCIS J,** Niagara Univ, Niagara Univ, NY; SO; BSW; Soc Wrk Actn Clb Pres 89-; Hnrs Pgm 89-; St Vincnt De Paul Soc Tr 90-; Socl Wrk; Admin/Soc Pol.

**BIANCA, MICHELE L,** Univ Of Sc At Columbia, Columbia, SC; FR; Chi Omega; Pre-Med.

**BIANCARDI, KENNTH J,** Daytona Beach Comm Coll, Daytona Beach, FL; SO; BA; Ar Frce Frnkfrt Germany 87-90; Rl Est Practce/Mgmt 84; Bsns; Acctg.

**BIANCHI, RANDOLPH R,** Glassboro St Coll, Glassboro, NJ; SR; BA; Stu Ecnmc Soc Pres 87-; Bureau Educ Org VP 89-; Stu Govt Assoc Econ Sntr 88-; Kappa Sigma Ntl Frat Schlrshp 90-; Peer Rfrl Orntn Stf Cnslr 90-; Pi Sigma Chi Frat Fndg Mbr Sec 88-90; Bando Clb VP 88-; Ecnmcs; Corp Exec.

**BIANCHINI, DANIELLE M,** Villanova Univ, Villanova, PA; SR; JD; Dnce Ensmble Pres 87-; Spnsh Clb VP 87-; Phi Kappa Phi; Omicron Delta Kappa VP 90-; Omicron Delta Kappa; Alpha Phi Phlnthrpy Chrprsn 87-; BA; Engl Bus; Law.

**BIAS, JENNIFER D,** Marshall University, Huntington, WV; FR; BS; Business; Comp Sci.

**BIAS, MELISSIA D,** Marshall University, Huntington, WV; JR; BA; Acctng; CPA.

**BIAS JR, WETZEL P,** Oh Univ-Southern Cmps, Ironton, OH; SR; BED; Golden Key 89-90; Phi Kappa Phi 89-90; Gamma Pi Delta 89-; Tri-State Bible Clg Tchr 89-; Whlsle Florist Slsmn 88-; Elem Ed/Hstry; Tch.**

**BIBB, RUTH ANN,** Valdosta St Coll, Valdosta, GA; JR; BS; AA N FL Jr Clge 89; Sec Ed/Math; Tch.

**BIBBO, KAREN MARIE,** Lesley Coll, Cambridge, MA; SR; BSE; Hnrs Pro 89-; Stu Tchg Plymptn Sch Wlthm; Tchr Hlpr 89; Assoc 86-89; Elem Educ; Tchr.

**BIBBY, TANYA N,** Nc Agri & Tech St Univ, Greensboro, NC; JR; BA; Psych Clb T 89-; Alpha Lambda Delta 89-; Psi Chi S 89-; Delta Sigma Theta 90-; Rsrch Asst U N C Chapel Hill; Acad Awds 88-; Bsbl Statstcn/Scrkpr 88-89; Indust Psych.**

**BIBERICA, JOYCE D,** Marymount Manhattan Coll, New York, NY; SR; DDS; Alpha Chi V P 90-; Alpha Epsilon Phi; BA; Engl; Dnstry.

**BIBLE III, CARL B,** Univ Of Cin R Walters Coll, Blue Ash, OH; SO; Bus.

**BIBLE, DENNIS R,** Roane St Comm Coll, Harriman, TN; SO; BA; US Army Ntl Grd 90-; Dns Lst 90-; Crmnl Jste; Law Enfrcmnt/Crmnl Law.

**BICE, STEPHANIE L,** Univ Of Ga, Athens, GA; JR; BSED; Chrstn Cmps Flwshp 89-; Pi Delta Phi 90-; Kappa Delta Pi 90-; Gldn Key 90-; C P Willcox Awd Excllnc Frnch; Frnch Educ; Tchng.

**BICHE, DEBRA L,** Univ Of Nh Plymouth St Coll, Plymouth, NH; JR; BS; Admssns Rep; IM Sports 88-; Psi Chi; Phi Kappa Phi; Sccr Plyr Yr 90; Plymouth Std Athlte Awd 88-; Vars Sccr 88-; Psych; Sports Psych.

**BICKEL, CHRISTOPHER S,** Univ Of Sc At Columbia, Columbia, SC; JR; BA; Deans Lst; Prfsnl Sci; Media Arts; Media.

**BICKEL, RICHARD T,** Univ Of Louisville, Louisville, KY; SR; BES; IEEE 88-; Consmr Elec Soc 90-; Elec Eng; Mgmt.

**BICKEL, TODD A,** Oh St Univ, Columbus, OH; SR; BA; Pre Law Clb 87-; IM Ath 87-; Hnr Soc 87-; Arts Sci 89-; Phi Kappa Phi 90-; Gldn Ky 90-; Summa Awd Univ Coll 88; Excel Schlrshp Awd Arts Scie 90; IM Ftbl Bsktbl Sftbl 87-; Pol Sci; Law.

**BICKELHAUPT, MICHAEL J,** Central Fl Comm Coll, Ocala, FL; JR; BA; AA CFCC 90; Htlh Rel Sci; Phys Thrpst.

**BICKERS, KRISTI L,** Clayton St Coll, Morrow, GA; FR; Phi Beta Lambda 90-; Busn.

**BICKERS, WENDI M,** Univ Of Ky, Lexington, KY; SO; BA; Epsilon Delta; Delta Delta Delta Treas 89-; Elem Educ.

**BICKERT, SANDRA L,** S U N Y Coll At Fredonia, Fredonia, NY; JR; Wilderness Clb Pres 90-; Prfmng Arts Co 89-; Undergrad Alumni Cncl 90-; Kappa Delta Pi; Kappa Delta Pi; Upper Cls Buddy; Fredonia Schlr Awd; Engl, High Sch Tchr.

**BICKHAM, DEBORAH F,** Savannah St Coll, Savannah, GA; JR; BBA; AA South College Draughons Jr Coll 84; Bus; Acctg.

**BICKLEY, MELANIE D,** Univ Of Sc At Columbia, Columbia, SC; FR; BS; Bptst Stdnt Union Com 90-; Phrmcy.

**BICKLEY, TAMMY D,** Univ Of Sc At Columbia, Columbia, SC; SO; BS; Bsnss.

**BICKNELL, MICHELE L,** Univ Of Al At Birmingham, Birmingham, AL; JR; Amer Mktg Assn 90-; Phonetician Bus Clb 89-90; Gldn Key VP; Best Of Amer Prog Comm 90-; Dns Lst 90-; Pres Lst; Mktg; Sales.

**BIDDLE, ANNIE KATHRYN,** Christian Brothers Univ, Memphis, TN; SR; BA; Blck Stdnt Assn Chrstn Bros Univ VP 87-88; Cannon Nwspr Chstn Bros Univ 86-87; Galleon Yrbk 89; Alpha Kappa Alpha Rcdng Sec 87-; Mktng Intrn Ctr Cty Comm Mmphs 87; Comm Arts.

**BIDDLE, ROBERT C,** Univ Of Rochester, Rochester, NY; SR; BA; Russian Lang Hall 90-; Russian/Pol Sci.

**BIDDLE, TRUDY A,** Juniata Coll, Huntingdon, PA; JR; BS; Bsn Info Mgmnt; Bsn Cmptr Cnsltng.

**BIDERMAN, RONALD,** Teikyo Post Univ, Waterbury, CT; SO; BS; Std Govt Asc Cmmtr Sntr; CT Trmtc Brain Injry Asc 88; Std Asst Pgm Comm; Morris Fdn Thrptc Shltr Cnslr/Intrn; S New England Tele Co Oprtr 87-; Behav Rsch.

**BIDOT, MARIA E,** Univ Of Pr Medical Sciences, San Juan, PR; GD; MSG; Alzheimer Assn 90-; Adult/Agng Dev Assn 90-; BS 80; Gerontology, Prfsr.

**BIEBER, TERRY J,** Fl Atlantic Univ, Boca Raton, FL; JR; BA; Phi Theta Kappa 89-90; Alpha Florida 90-; Phi Beta Lambda Sec 88-90; Phi Theta Kappa Schlrshp 90; Burdines Schlrshp 90; AA Edison Comm Coll 90; Acctg.

**BIEBERICH, KIMBERLY A,** Univ Of Nc At Charlotte, Charlotte, NC; SO; BA; Univ Prog Bd 90-; Alpha Delta Pi I M Chrm 90-.

**BIEGEL, ALDA E,** Columbia Greene Comm Coll, Hudson, NY; FR; AAS; VICA; Nrsng; RN.

**BIEGEL, DENNIS J,** Cooper Union, New York, NY; SO; BE; Mech Engr.

**BIEGEN, GREGORY A,** City Univ Of Ny Baruch Coll, New York, NY; JR; BBA; Golden Key; Econ; Finance.

**BIEGNER, STEPHANIE L,** Univ Of Sc At Columbia, Columbia, SC; JR; BA; Coastal Carolina Advrtsng Clb 90; Lit/Art Mag Coll Asst Ed/Art Dir 90-; Philosophy Frat 90-; Art Studio; Graphic Dsgn/Advrtsng.

**BIEHL, CHRISTOPHER M,** Kent St Univ Stark Cmps, North Canton, OH; FR; BBA; Math; Acctng.

**BIELAT, TINA MARIE,** Georgetown Univ, Washington, DC; JR; BA; Prblca Stdnt Cngrss Fndr Treas 89-; Intrntl Mrktng; Corp Law.

**BIELBY, BRETT A,** Pa St Univ Delaware Cty Cmps, Media, PA; FR; BS; Pres Sci Awd 90; Sci; Cmptr Sci.

**BIELE, VALERIE B,** Univ Of Miami, Coral Gables, FL; JR; BS; Pre Physcl Thrpy Clb; Hlth Sci.

**BIELEC, BONNIE L,** Belmont Coll, Nashville, TN; SO; BBA; WAM Pres; Music Bus; Law.

**BIELSKI, JANA D,** S U N Y At Albany, Albany, NY; FR; BA; Psychlgy/Bus; Ind Orgnztnl Psychlgy.

**BIEMER, LOUISE M,** Georgetown Univ, Washington, DC; SR; BSN; Class Cmmttee Orient 89; Acad Cncl Emer Prog About Lrng; Med Rspnse Syst Tour Guide; Nrsng/Psychlgy; Nrsng.

**BIENKO, MARY C,** S U N Y Coll At Fredonia, Fredonia, NY; JR; BA; AAS Jamestown Cmuty Clg 90; Sociology; Geriatrics.

**BIENSTOCK, ANDREA J,** Hofstra Univ, Hempstead, NY; SO; BBA; Org Of Commuter Stdnts; IM Vlybl; Business; Personnel Adm.

**BIERGANS, JAMES D,** Spalding Univ, Louisville, KY; JR; BA; Eclgy Clb Pres Fndr 88; Fcs Grp Pres 90; Psi Chi 88; Psychlgy.

**BIERLY, DENA K,** Defiance Coll, Defiance, OH; SO; BS; Wmns Bsktbl 89-; Wmsn Sftbl 90-; Ltl Sis Theta Xi 89-; Sci/Hlth; Phys Therapy.

**BIERWIRTH, JEAN P,** Crichton Coll, Memphis, TN; JR; BS; Phi Theta Kappa; Sing Small Cntry Music Shw Horn Lake Ms; Sing SHCC Southaven 1st/3rd Sun; Barber Stylist; Elementary Education; Teacher.

**BIERY, KAREN ANN,** Northern Ky Univ, Highland Hts, KY; SR; BA; Spch Clb 87-88; Psi Chi 90-; Psych; Law.

**BIEVENUE, RICHARD J,** Hudson Valley Comm Coll, Troy, NY; SO; BS; Mech Engrng.

**BIGBIE, MARC W,** Savannah St Coll, Savannah, GA; SO; BS; Nvl ROTC; Elec Eng Tdch; Nvl Avtr.

**BIGELOW, JOYCE M,** D Youville Coll, Buffalo, NY; JR; BS; Future Tchrs Cncl; Cmmtr Cncl; Cargill Schlrshp Awrd 89-90; Spcl Elmntry Ed; Tch.

**BIGELOW, MARTIN T,** Univ Of Md At College Park, College Park, MD; FR.

**BIGELOW, MARY ELLEN,** Hudson Valley Comm Coll, Troy, NY; SO; BA; Phi Theta Kappa; Hrstylst Mk Up Artst 81-; AA; Psychology; Cnslng.

**BIGELOW, RAINI S,** Univ Of Sc At Coastal Carolina, Conway, SC; SR; BA; Educ Clb 90; Kappa Delta Pi 90-; Omicron Delta Kappa 90-; D L Scurry Schlrshp 90-; Fred Denglar Schlrshp 90-; Early Chldhd Educ; Teach.

**BIGGAR, STEPHEN R,** Univ Of Rochester, Rochester, NY; JR; BS; Phi Beta Kappa; Theta Chi VP 88-; Summr Rsrch Flwshp 90-; EUREKA Rsrch Cnfrnce; Adidas Acdmc All Amer 89; Vrsty Soccer 88-89; Moleclr Genetcs; Rsrch.

**BIGGER, TERESA T,** John C Calhoun St Comm Coll, Decatur, AL; SO; AAS; Dns Lst 88-; Pres Lst 88-; NASA Co-Op Stdt 89-; AAS; Math/Drafting; Math Engr.**

**BIGGERS, APRIL SUSAN,** Univ Of Nc At Chapel Hill, Chapel Hill, NC; JD; NC Jrnl Intl Law/Cmrcl Rgltn 90-; Crmnl Lgl Clnc; BA Wake Forest Univ 88; Law; Lawyer.

**BIGGS, BRENDA J,** Wilmington Coll, New Castle, DE; SR; BS; PTK; Acctng; Acctnt.

**BIGGS, CATHERINE D,** Hudson County Comm Coll, Jersey City, NJ; JR; BS; Natl Assc Female Exec 90-; Amer Inst Prof Bkkprs 90-; Summa Cum Laude; IBC 90-; Acad Tutor 89-; Project Lit US 90-; Network Sup 90-; AAS; Computer Sci.**

**BIGGS, CHERYL ANN,** Ga St Univ, Atlanta, GA; SR; Stewart Cooper Purdue Univ Sec 87-89; Kappa Delta Pi; Golden Key; SCHOLAR 88-; Pres Plaque Acad Achvmnt; Undergrad Awd Acad Achvmnt; IM Sprts 87-89; Church Dir Song Serv; Chldrn Church; Youth Grp Assist; Vac Bible Schl 90-; Mdl Chldhd Educ; Educ.

**BIGGS, ROBERT C,** Southern Coll Of Tech, Marietta, GA; SR; Tau Alpha Pi Hon Soc 89-; Alpha Alpha Chap 89-; Mech Engr.

**BIGIO GONZALEZ, GRISELLE,** Univ Of Pr At Rio Piedras, Rio Piedras, PR; SO; BA; Accntng Stu Assc 90-; Fnnc Stu Assc 90-; AFROTC Cmptrllr 90-; Sol Isolina Ferre 88-; All Amer Awrd 90-; Natl Coll Bus Merit Awrd 90-; Trck Fld 88-89; Accntng; CPA.

**BIGIO, AIDYMAR,** Univ Of Rochester, Rochester, NY; SO; BS; Scty Hspnc/Prfsnl Eng Pres; Mech Eng.

**BIHARI, JEEVAN J,** Muskingum Coll, New Concord, OH; FR; BS; Math Awd 90-; Edinburgh Silver Awd; Schlrshp 90-; Math/Cmptr Sci.

**BIHLER, HEATHER ERIKA,** Bethany Coll, Bethany, WV; JR; BS; Std Brd Gvnrs Rep 88-89; Amer Chem Soc Rep 88-; Grmn Clb Rep; Lcrs 88-90; Tri Beta 88-; Zeta Tau Alpha 88-; Amnsty Intl 88-89; Rnbw Grls 88-; Boyd Schlp 88-; Chrldng 88-90; Bio; Large Anml Vet.

**BILBO, MELISSA F,** Univ Of Southern Ms, Hattiesburg, MS; SO; BA; Krte Clb 89-90; Gamma Beta Phi; Frnch/Soclgy; Clg Prfssr.

**BILBO, WENDY R,** William Carey Coll, Hattiesburg, MS; SO; BA; Elem Edctn; Tchr.

**BILBREY, GINA K,** Volunteer St Comm Coll, Gallatin, TN; SO; BA; Deans Lst 90-; Sls Assoc; AS; P E Hlth/Rcrtn; Tch.

**BILBROUT PIRELA, ANNIECELY,** Bayamon Central Univ, Bayamon, PR; FR; Mchdsng; Sales.

**BILES, CHARLIE B,** Univ Of Ga, Athens, GA; JR; BS ED; Pes Clb 89-; In M Ftbl Sftbl Bkbl 89-; Assoc Gordon Clg 89; Phys Educ; Tch/Coach.

**BILHEIMER, TRICIA L,** Western New England Coll, Springfield, MA; FR; BA; Deans Lst 90-; Import Acctg Clrk; Cmptr Info Sys.

**BILICKI, KRISTEN D,** Hudson Valley Comm Coll, Troy, NY; FR; BA; Bus Admin.

**BILKER, LAWRENCE A,** Univ Of Rochester, Rochester, NY; SR; BS; Yrbk Mgng Ed 87-; Optcl Scty Armc Treas 87-; Tau Beta Pi 90-; Delt Aupsilon Frtrty 90(ASA Lngly Arspc Rsrch Schlr 90; GTE Intern 89; Hrns Prgm 90-; Optcs.

**BILL, TAMI L,** Unity Coll, Unity, ME; JR; BS; Martl Arts Clb 88-89; Drama Clb 90-; Stdnt Rep Pk Mgmt Fac Srch Comm 90; Crs Cntry 89; AA; Pk Mgmt; Peace Crps.

**BILLER, ALLISON L,** Univ Of Pittsburgh, Pittsburgh, PA; SO; BSN; Delta Phi Epsln 90-; Nrs.

**BILLETT, DEBRA J,** Bridgewater Coll, Bridgewater, VA; JR; BS; Rsdnt Cnslrs 90-; Pres Schlrshp 88-; Psychlgy; Clncl Psychlgst.

**BILLI, JOSEPH C,** Hillsborough Comm Coll, Tampa, FL; FR; BED; Science Education.

**BILLING, BERNADETTE M,** Northern Ky Univ, Highland Hts, KY; FR; BA; Rsdnc Hl Cncl Cmns Repr 90-; Dns Lst 90-; Acdmc Athlt 90-; Sftbl Tm 90-; Pltcl Sci; Law/Sprm Crt.

**BILLING, SALLEY L,** Univ Of Sc At Columbia, Columbia, SC; SR; Stdnt Aslumni Assn 90-; Carolina Pgm Union 89-90; Amer Mktg Assn 89-; SC Coll 87-; Golden Key 89-; BA; Engl; Mktg.

**BILLINGS, MARY A,** Loyola Coll In Md, Baltimore, MD; JR; BBA; NAA 89-; Commuters Assoc 89-; MAPA; Beta Alpha Psi; Business Award 90; Accounting; Public Accounting.**

**BILLINGSLEY, CHRISTINE C,** Barry Univ, Miami, FL; SR; BS; Miata Clb Amer 90-; Boy Scts Amer Comm 88-; Womns Rel Soc Lds Chrch 72-; Brevard Symph Yth Orch Brd Dir Exec Sec 89-; AA Music Cabrillo Clg 80; Librl Stds; Tchg.

**BILLIONS, LESLYE A,** Lexington Comm Coll, Lexington, KY; SO; BA; Bus; Mktg.

**BILLIPS, CHARLES W,** Ashland Comm Coll, Ashland, KY; JR; BA; Asst Comptr Lab Instrctr 89; AAS 90; Pomptr Sci; Sys Anlyst.

**BILLITTIER, MARY BETH,** D Youville Coll, Buffalo, NY; SR; BS; Bsn Clb 90; AAS Erie Cmnty Clge 89; Bsn Mgmt; Rn Fmly Rstrnt.

**BILLMAN, ELIZABETH A,** Oh St Univ, Columbus, OH; JR; BS; Colour Columbs Fndtn 89-90; Scarlt Gray Schlrshp 88-89; Sam S Wrtzl Schlrshp 90-; Landscp Arch.

**BILLMAN, SHAWN L,** Univ Of Pittsburgh At Bradford, Bradford, PA; SR; Bus Clb 89-; Sigma Lambda Chi VP 89-; IM Ftbl/Bsktbl 89; AS 90-; BS; Bus Mgt.

**BILLOCH, JUAN CARLOS,** Miami Dade Comm Coll South, Miami, FL; SO; MBA; Rstrnt/Clb Mgr 88; Accntng/Bsnss; Rstrntr.

**BILLOUPS, CYNTHIA MARIE,** Tn St Univ, Nashville, TN; JR; NAACP Vol Intrn; Yrbk; Brdg Pro; Gldn Key Hnr Soc; Alpha Kappa Mu; Deans Lst; Dept Schlrshp; Lgsltv Intrn Tenn Gen Assmbly.

**BILLS, JACQUELINE D,** Tougaloo Coll, Tougaloo, MS; SO; BA; Ntl Yth Clb 87-89; Hnr Roll 87; Vol Yyth Grp 87; Adiombo Schl Intrnshp Tchr 90; Chrldr 87-88; Elem Ed; Ed Admin.**

**BILLUPS, DEBORAH J,** Birmingham Southern Coll, Birmingham, AL; GD; Dns Lst 88-90; Delta Sigma 81-; Elem Tchr; BA 82; BS 90; Bsn Admn/Elem Ed; Tch/Admn.

**BILODEAU, CRAIG A,** Savannah Coll Of Art & Design, Savannah, GA; SO; BA; Intrntl Tlvsn Assoc 89-; Intrnshp WSAV TV Savannah; Video; Entrnmnt.

**BILTZ, AMY ELIZABETH,** Anne Arundel Comm Coll, Arnold, MD; FR; AA; RN.

**BINA, JILL M,** Wv Univ At Parkersburg, Parkersburg, WV; SO; BBA; Phi Theta Kappa; Cmptr Sci; Syst Analyst.

**BINDER, JANEEN C,** Barry Univ, Miami, FL; SR; BS; Alpha Chi; Newspaper Assoc Ed 89-; Psych; Physlgcl Psych.

**BINDLEY-BEICKELMAN, ANN M,** Oh St Univ At Marion, Marion, OH; SR; BS; Ed Soc 89-; Psych Clb 84-86/89-; Stdnt Govt 84-86; Stdnt Alumni Cncl 84-86; Spnsh Clb 84-85; Drama Clb 85-86; AS 86; Cert Amer Sch Brdcstg 87; Ed; Tchg.

**BINEGAR, LAURIE J,** Washington State Comm Coll, Marietta, OH; FR; Phi Theta Kappa.

**BINEGAR, SHAWN P,** West Liberty St Coll, West Liberty, WV; SO; Hstry/Pol Sci; Law.

**BINETTI, DENISE ANN,** Hillsborough Comm Coll, Tampa, FL; SO; AA; Phi Theta Kappa 90-; Math; Eng.

**BINETTI, MARIO,** Coll Of Insurance, New York, NY; SO; BA; Tillinghast TPFC Trainee; Actrl Sci; Actuary.

**BINGHAM RICE, PRISCILLA J,** Union Coll, Barbourville, KY; FR; SGA; News Pblctn Stf; Yrbk Stf; Sprts Feature Ky Intr Press Assn; Jrnlsm.

**BINGHAM, KIMBERLY L,** Al A & M Univ, Normal, AL; SO; NAACP 89-; Chem Clb 89-; Gospel Choir 89-; Hnr Roll 89-; Dns Lst 89-; Alpha Kappa Alpha; Chem; Rsrch Chem.

**BINGHAM, MATTHEW E,** Fl St Univ, Tallahassee, FL; FR; BM; Music.

**BINGHAM, MICHAEL A,** Roane St Comm Coll, Harriman, TN; SO; Business; Secondary Ed.

**BINGHAM, PATRICIA A,** Western Ky Univ, Bowling Green, KY; SO; BA; Mddle Grd Ed.

**BINGHAM, ROBERT D,** Univ Of North Fl, Jacksonville, FL; SO; BA; Fla Undergrad Schlr 89-; Acctng; CPA.**

**BINGHAM, SAMANTHA D,** Union Coll, Barbourville, KY; SO; BA; Fnd Rsng Comm 90-; Gamma Beta Phi 90-; Fnd Rsng Comm; Acctg.

**BINGIEL, ALANA L,** Wv Northern Comm Coll, Wheeling, WV; FR; ADN; Phi Theta Kappa; Pres Lst; Nrsng; RN.

**BINGOL, A DEMIR,** Christopher Newport Coll, Newport News, VA; SR; BSBA; Phi Theta Kappa 85-; Alpha Tau Omega 82-; Intrnshp-Newport News Shpbldg/Dry Dock Co; ASBA Thomas Nelson Comm Coll 90; Mktg; Advrtsng/Pblc Rltns.

**BINKLEY, CONNIE M,** Wright St Univ, Dayton, OH; JR; BA; Wmn Cmmnctns Inc; AA 90; Orgnztnl Cmmnclts/PR.

**BINKLEY, LAURA F,** Univ Of Ga, Athens, GA; BSHE; Mrchng Bnd Cncrt Bnd 85-90; Pep Band 90-; Trombone Assoc 87-90; ADIS 88-90; Pres Citation 89; Wholesale Furniture Intrn 90; Culpepper Osborne; Furnishings & Interiors.

**BINKLEY, MICHAEL R,** Kent St Univ Kent Cmps, Kent, OH; SO; BS; Nat'l Hnr Scty 89-90; Conservation; Agribusiness.

**BINNIX, LYNN C,** Bowie St Univ, Bowie, MD; SO; BS; Poli Sci Club 90; US Captl Police Dept; Poli Sci/Pre-Law; Law.

**BINSLEY, AMY M,** Va Commonwealth Univ, Richmond, VA; SR; BA; VA Art Educ Assc 89-; Art; Art Educ.

**BINUYA, CATHERINE T,** Univ Of Sc At Columbia, Columbia, SC; SO; St Thms Mre Chr 90-; Cntr Pl Hbtt Fr Hmnty And Rrl Mssns Vol; Blgy; Pre Med To Do Wrk In Afrca Or Rsrch.

**BINZER, JILL R,** Oh St Univ, Columbus, OH; SO; Rnssnc Fstvl 87; Alpha Lambda Delta 88-89; Phi Eta Sigma 88-89; IM Vllybl 87-88; Ntrl Rsrcs Dvlpmnt.

**BIRCH, CHERYL L,** Kent St Univ Kent Cmps, Kent, OH; SO; BA; Kent Cncl Fmly Rltns 90; Hon Coll 89-; Indvdl/Fmly Stdies; Soc Wrk.

**BIRCH, MICHELLE A,** Marshall University, Huntington, WV; FR; Campus Crusade For Chrst 90-; Rsdnc Hl Assn 90-; Educ; Tchng.

**BIRCHUM, KIM A,** Western Piedmont Comm Coll, Morganton, NC; SO; AA; Phi Theta Kappa; Engl; Tchng Elem.

**BIRD, AMY D,** Marshall University, Huntington, WV; JR; BA; Mrchg Bnd 89-; Pep Bnd 88-; Gamma Beta Phi 89-; Phi Eta Sigma 90-; Sigma Tau Delta; Mst Cmps Prtcptn Buskirk Hl 90; MOVIN Prtcptn Awd; Lang Arts; Tchr.

**BIRD, DEBORAH R,** Mercer Univ Schl Of Pharm, Atlanta, GA; GD; PHARM; Cls Offcr VP 90-; APHA/SASP 88-89; Rho Chi Hstrn 90-; Phi Kappa Phi; Phi Delta Chi 90-; Merit Schlrshps 88-90; MA Chmbrs Awd 89; Minnie M Meyer Awd 90; Phrmcy.

**BIRD, LYNDA J,** Nova Univ, Ft Lauderdale, FL; GD; MBA; Paalegal; AA 88; BPS 89; Law.

**BIRD, MARLA L,** Marshall University, Huntington, WV; FR; BBA; Acctg.

**BIRD, REBECCA D,** Wv Univ, Morgantown, WV; JR; BS; Bapt Cmps Mnstrs 88-; ASP 90-; Gamma Beta Phi 89-90; SCODAE 90-; Phrmcy.

**BIRD, SANDRA J,** Anne Arundel Comm Coll, Arnold, MD; SO; BA; Discipline Comm 89-90; Legislative Intern Maryland General Assembly; AA; Hstry/Econ; Bsn Adm.

**BIRD, SCOTT E,** Univ Of Tn At Knoxville, Knoxville, TN; JR; BS; Amrcn Mrktng Assn 90-; SGA Comm Rsdnc Hall Lf 90-; Mrktng.**

**BIRD, SHEILA M,** Elmira Coll, Elmira, NY; FR; BS; Bus Admin.

**BIRD, STEVEN R,** Villanova Univ, Villanova, PA; JR.

**BIRDSELL, ROBERT J,** Villanova Univ, Villanova, PA; BA; Rugby Ftbl Clb Treas 88-90; Deans Lst 89-90; Phi Gamma Delta Exec Ofcr 90; Polacheck Co Intern; Habitat For Humanity Vol 90; Asst Ski Coach 90-; Alpine Ski Tm Capt 88-90; English Psychology; Teach.

**BIRDY, CHERYL A,** Allegheny Coll, Meadville, PA; SR; BA; Stdnt Gvrnmnt 88-89; Allies 90-; Lambda Sigma 88-89; Psi Chi 90-; Kappa Alpha Theta 88-; Psychology.

**BIRK, PAMELA D,** Winthrop Coll, Rock Hill, SC; JR; BA; Wsly/Nwmn/Wstmnstr Fndtn 90-; Mass Cmnctn; Advtsng.

**BIRKBY-MEYERS, JENNIFER G,** Garrett Comm Coll, Mchenry, MD; SO; AA; FFA Alumni 90-; Hrvst Bptst Chrch 87-; Scrtrl Intrnshp; Deans Lst 89-; Scrtrl Sci; Sec.**

**BIRKEDAL, CHRISTIAN L,** Fl St Univ, Tallahassee, FL; FR; MENSA V P; Clg Bowl; Phi Eta Sigma; IM Bsebl/Bsktbl; Biochem; Surgeon.

**BIRKHEAD, DAVID Y,** Univ Of Ky, Lexington, KY; FR.

**BIRKHIMER, RITA J,** Oh St Univ At Newark, Newark, OH; FR; Bus Acctng.

**BIRKITT, DIANE M,** Emory & Henry Coll, Emory, VA; JR; Sigma Mu; Bd Cert RN 86-; RN 90-; RN Ohio Vly Sch Nrsng 86; Eng Lit/Religion; Edn.

**BIRMINGHAM, ERIC C,** Roane St Comm Coll, Harriman, TN; SO; BA; Arnold Air Scty 90; AA; Mass Cmmnctns; Advrtsng.

**BIRMINGHAM, JASON K,** Brewer St Jr Coll, Fayette, AL; SO; BA; Phi Theta Kappa 89-; Wstrn Cvlztn Awrd 90; Bus; Law.

**BIRO, RICHARD G,** Univ Of Bridgeport, Bridgeport, CT; SR; BS; Acctng Soc Treas 87-; Deans Lst 89-; Manuscript Contest Awd; NAA Schlrshp 90; Continental Can Co Co-Op 88-89; Proj Choice Schlrshp 87-88; Acctng; CPA/LAW.**

**BIRT, ADRIENNE M,** Univ Of Sc At Columbia, Columbia, SC; FR; BA; Alpha Dleta Pi Sprtswear Chr 90-; Rollerblade Hcky 90-; Carolina Tour Guide Assn 90-; Carriage Driver/Tour Guide Charleston SC; Jrnlsm; Advrtsng.

**BIRT, CARLA C,** Fl International Univ, Miami, FL; JR; BS; Phi Eta Sigma 86-; Fnnce And Intl Bus; Get MBA.

**BIRTWELL, SUSAN E,** Neumann Coll, Aston, PA; JR; BSN; Stdnt Nurses Assn 89-; Delta Epsilon Sigma Pres; AAS Delaware Cnty Comm Coll 88; Nrsng.

**BIRZER, LISA A,** Va Highlands Comm Coll, Abingdon, VA; SO; BS; Instr/Crrclm Comm 90-; SW VA Brd Of Rltrs VP 89; Res Real Est Agnt 86-89; AA Bus Admin Lincoln Schl Of Cmmrc Lincoln NE 81; Mgmnt/Acctg.

**BISCHOF, DANIELLE L,** Barry Univ, Miami, FL; SR; BS; Acctg Assoc 90-; AS 89; Acctg.

**BISCHOFF, JULIE L,** Georgian Court Coll, Lakewood, NJ; SO; Mendel Socty 89-; Cultrl Affrs Chrprsn 89-; Res Hll Assn 89-90; Bus; Bio.

**BISCONTE, MARGARET M,** Cumberland County Coll, Vineland, NJ; SO; AA; Bus Admin; Finance/Acctng.

**BISCOTTO, ROSALIE G,** D Youville Coll, Buffalo, NY; SO; MBA; Occupational Therapy.

**BISEL, HEIDI L,** Kent St Univ Kent Cmps, Kent, OH; SO; BS; Math; Edn.

**BISEL, TAMBRA S,** Capital Univ, Columbus, OH; FR; BSN; Ambassador 90-; 94 Corp 90-; Nursing.

**BISELOW, BRENDA A,** Endicott Coll, Beverly, MA; FR; BA; Bsn Clb 90; Peer/Tutoring Prgrm; Hnrs Prgrm; Intrnshp 90; Bsn Law; Bsn Mngmnt.

**BISH, DEBORAH F,** Fl St Univ, Tallahassee, FL; SO; Wnd Orchstra 89-; Symphnc Bnd 89-; Chmbr Orchstra 89-; Sigma Alpha Iota; Music Schlrshp; Music.

**BISH, JAMES E,** Comm Coll Algny Co Algny Cmps, Pittsburgh, PA; SO; BA; Cmptrs Inf System/Bus.

**BISHARA, SUSAN L,** Univ Of Rochester, Rochester, NY; SR; BA; Mrdn Scty 89-; Drm Cncl; Pr Advsr Stdy Abrd Offd Hlth Scty Dept; Delta Gamma Cor Sec; London Hlth Sci Intern 90; Hlth Prctn 90; Cum Laude; Distrctn Hlth Scty; Cert Prsnnl Mgmt; Hlth Scty Psychlgy; Mgmt.

**BISHIP, SUSAN J,** Albertus Magnus Coll, New Haven, CT; SO; ASSOC; Ptnt Cnslng Vol 89-90; Dev Coord 89-; Soc; Soc Work.

**BISHKO, TIMOTHY M,** Becker Coll At Leicester, Leicester, MA; SO; AS; Deans Lst 89-; Intrnshp Bckr IM Dir 90-; Bsktbl 89-90; AS 89; Sprt Mngmnt; Mngmnt.

**BISHOFF, MICHAEL S,** Wv Univ, Morgantown, WV; FR; BA; Coll Mnrl Enrgy Rsrcs Lwr Dvsn Awrd; Otstndng Frshmn Awrd; Pi Epsilon Tau Awrd; Otstndng Frshmn Ptrlm Eng; Ptrlm Eng.

**BISHOP, AMY E,** Milligan Coll, Milligan Clg, TN; FR; BA; Mdrgl Prdctns 90; Engl.

**BISHOP, ANTHONY E,** Anderson Coll, Anderson, SC; FR; BA; Bsn Mngmnt; Law.

**BISHOP, BARBARA A,** Phillips Jr Coll Spartanburg, Spartanburg, SC; GD; Nrsng Asst 90; Med Admn Asst.

**BISHOP, CHELSEY A,** Kent St Univ Kent Cmps, Kent, OH; FR; BA; Alpha Lambda Delta 90-; IM; Bus.

**BISHOP, CHRISTINA K,** Univ Of Sc At Columbia, Columbia, SC; SO; BA; Equestrian Clb 89-; Exercise Sci; Nutrition.

**BISHOP, CYNTHIA E,** Pellissippi St Tech Comm Coll, Knoxville, TN; GD; Collegiate Sec Intl 89-; Phi Theta Kappa 89-; AAS IST; Cert Mgmnt.**

**BISHOP, CYNTHIA L,** Univ Of Southern Ms, Hattiesburg, MS; JR; BA; Wom Clb Sccr Tm 90-; Alumni Assoc 90-; Gamma Beta Phi; Wom Clb Sccr Tm 90-; Bnkng/Finance; Planner.

**BISHOP, DESMOND F,** City Univ Of Ny Lehman Coll, Bronx, NY; JR; BA; Golden Key 90-; Psi Chi; Peer Tutoring 89-; Writing Ctr Advsry Comm 89-; Stdnt Liaison Fclty 90; Peer Cnslng; Dns Lst 90; Pres Schlr 90; Prnt/Tchr Assn 86-; Prnt Repr Rdng Pgm 89-90; Tchrs Aide 86-89; Psych/Educ; Tchr/Spec Educ.

**BISHOP, DIANE L,** Univ Of Md At Eastern Shore, Princess Anne, MD; JR; BA; PTA; Vol Awrd Srvc PAES Elem Schl 90-; Crftsprsn Pntr Shws Sls; Art Ed; Tchng.

**BISHOP, HEIDI E,** Comm Coll Algny Co Algny Cmps, Pittsburgh, PA; SO; BS; Exercse Sci.

**BISHOP, HOPE L,** Johnson C Smith Univ, Charlotte, NC; SO; Computer Sci; Computer Syst Analyst.

**BISHOP, JAMES M,** Univ Of Sc At Columbia, Columbia, SC; JR; BA; Beta Clb 85; Ftbl Equip Mgr 88-; Sprt Admin; Gen Mgr Sprts Org.

**BISHOP, JULLIAN C,** Norfolk St Univ, Norfolk, VA; FR; BA; Naval ROTC Sqd Ldr; Alpha Tau; Pltcl Sci; Nvl Offcr/Fdrl Law Enfrcmnt.

**BISHOP, KAREN A,** Univ Of Southern Ms, Hattiesburg, MS; SR; SNASM; AA Jones Cnty Jr Clg 79; Nrsng B S.

**BISHOP, KEIL B,** Univ Of Al At Huntsville, Huntsville, AL; SR; BS; IEEE 90-; Phi Theta Kappa; Jr Chmbr Of Comm; Co-Opert Educ Stdnt; US Army Msl Commd; Elec Eng.

**BISHOP, KELLY D,** Va Commonwealth Univ, Richmond, VA; JR; BS; Pblc Rltns Stdnt Soc Amer 90-; Phi Eta Sigma 89-; Golden Key; Kappa Tau Alpha; Golden Key Schlrshp; Mass Cmnctns; Pblc Rltns.

**BISHOP, KIMBERLY J,** Memphis St Univ, Memphis, TN; JR; BS; Phi Theta Kappa Jackson State Comm Coll Jackson TN VP 89-91; AS Jackson St Comm Coll 90; Elem Educ; Tchr.

**BISHOP, LESLIE R,** Indiana Univ Of Pa, Indiana, PA; SO; BA; Natl Brdcstng Scty 90-; Mnrty Affaris Com 90-; Phi Sigma Pi 90-; Habitat Humanity Bd 90-; Communications; Advertising.

**BISHOP, LORI M,** Duquesne Univ, Pittsburgh, PA; JR; BSBA; Stdnt Govt Assn V P 89-; Cmmtr Cncl 88-; Bus Deans Advsry Bd 88-; Beta Alpha Phi Pres 90-; People To People Intl 86-; Delta Sigma Pi 90-; Beta Alpha Phi Pres 90-; Beta Pi Sigma 88-; Stdnt Alumni Rltns 88-; Finance/Intl Bus; Corp Finance.

**BISHOP, MANDY E,** Univ Of New Haven, West Haven, CT; JR; BA; Day Stdnt Govt Sen 89-; Psi Chi; Chi Kappa Rho Srrty Pres 90-; Cmmnty Clncl Psychlgy.**

**BISHOP, MARGARET M,** Western Ky Univ, Bowling Green, KY; JR; BS; Pres List; Ed K-4.

**BISHOP, MARK A,** Western Piedmont Comm Coll, Morganton, NC; FR; AASC; Ind Eng; Mgmt.

**BISHOP, PHYLLIS J,** Union Coll, Barbourville, KY; SR; Alpha Psi Omega Pres 89-; Iota Sigma Nu 89-; BS; Bus Admin/Acctg.

**BISHOP JR, R WILSON,** Univ Of Al At Huntsville, Huntsville, AL; SR; BSEE; Slvc Clb 86-87; SEDS 89; Tau Beta Pi VP 89-; Eta Kappa Nu 89-; Elec Eng.

**BISHOP, RANDALL L,** Univ Of Ky, Lexington, KY; SR; AIAS 87-88; Psi Chi 90-; Peer Asst Ldrs 90-; BA; Cnslng Psych.

**BISHOP, RHONDA C,** Spartanburg Methodist Coll, Spartanburg, SC; SO; BS; Jjr Achvmnt 90; Phi Theta Kappa 90-; ARM Spartanburg Methodist Clg 90; Fincl Mngmnt; Fincl Mgr.

**BISHOP, RITA F,** Va Commonwealth Univ, Richmond, VA; JR; BA; AS Richard Bland Coll 90; Bus.

**BISHOP, RONALD E,** Bryant Stratton Bus Inst Roch, Rochester, NY; SR; AOS; Drug Alcohol Abuse Cncl 89; Deans Lst 89; Vet Foreign Wars 79; Assoc Cmptr Prog 74-88; Cmptr Prog; Cmptr Sci.**

**BISHOP, SALLY C,** Coll Of Charleston, Charleston, SC; SO; BS; Dstngshd Hon Lst 89; Hghly Dstngshd Hon Lst 90; Blgy; Tchng.

**BISHOP, TELLIE A,** Ms St Univ, Miss State, MS; SO; BS; Fashn Bd 90-; Beta Beta Beta 90-F Gamma Beta Phi 89-; Phi Eta Sigma 89-; Alpha Lambda Delta 89-; Biolgcl Sci; MD.

**BISHOTA, FURAHA L,** Widener Univ, Chester, PA; SR; BS; Intl Stdnts Clb V P 89; Acctg Soc; Alpha Chi; Pi Gamma Mu; Acctg.**

**BISIG, VALERIA K,** Univ Of Cincinnati, Cincinnati, OH; SR; Natl Stdnt Nrss Assn 90-; Chrs 87; Bapt Stdnt Union 87; Sigma Theta Tau; Zeta Tau Alpha Mmbrshp Chr 88; BSN; Nrsng; Emer Rm.

**BISOGNA, GINA,** Georgian Court Coll, Lakewood, NJ; SO; BA; Camp Against Hunger 89; Halloween Party For Terminally Ill Childrn; Nursing Hm Vol 89-; Convocaton Awrd 89-; Engl/Soc; Law.

**BISSONNETTE, KAREN A,** Molloy Coll, Rockville Ctr, NY; JR; BA; Sierra Clb 89-; NY St Zlgcl Soc 88-; NA Amer Vet Tech Assoc 89-; AAS Suny Farmingdale 89; Blgy/Sec Ed; Tchr.**

**BISTA, DIGVIJAY,** Teikyo Post Univ, Waterbury, CT; JR; Stdnt Govt Assn Bus Sntr 90-; Stdnt Ambssdr 90-; Rsdnt Asst 90; Peer Guide; Lab Asst/Tutor 90-; Cnfrnc Aide 90; Mgt.

**BISTRANSKY, WILLIAM J,** Kent St Univ Kent Cmps, Kent, OH; SR; BA; Clg Dmcrts Pblc Rltns 89; Friends Amng Ntns Pblc Rltns 88-89; German Clb VP 88-89; Golden Key 89; Phi Beta Kappa; Morter Brd VP 90; Gvrnrs Hnrs Intrn 89; AF Assmbly; Fulbrght Fllwshp; Kayak Clb Pres 89; Intrntl Rltns German.

**BITER, ROBERT M,** Juniata Coll, Huntingdon, PA; JR; BA; Theatre 88-; Class Pres 89-; Centerboard 88-; Beta Beta Beta 90-; Scapel/Probe 88-; Haiti Wrktrip 89; RA 89-; Richard M Simpson Schlrshp 88; Whitaker Schlrshp Milton S Hershey Sch Of Med 90; Med Asst Altoona Hosp 90; Theatre; Med.

**BITET, CRAIG H,** City Univ Of Ny Queensbrough, New York, NY; BA; Perf Arts.

**BITTER, SHARI A,** Northern Ky Univ, Highland Hts, KY; SR; BA; Fr Yr Pres Schlrshp 90-; Dns Lst 89-; Ed K 8; Tch Math.

**BITTERMAN, KAREN D,** Lancaster Bible Coll, Lancaster, PA; JR; BED; Choir 89-; SGA Sec; Elem Schl Intrn; Sftbl 90; Educ; Missions/Lingstcs.

**BITTINGER, CHRISTIE A,** Wv Univ, Morgantown, WV; FR; Hll Cncl 90-; Delta Gamma 90-; Bus And Econs; Mrktng.

**BITTMAN, AMY K,** Kent St Univ Kent Cmps, Kent, OH; SO; Math Tutor Lrng Dev Ctr 90-; Acctg; CPA.

**BITTNER II, HARRY M,** Glassboro St Coll, Glassboro, NJ; JR; BA; Stdnt Gvrnmnt Mrcr Cnty Comm Clg Drctr Pblcty 89-90; AA Mrcr Cnty Comm Clg 90; Psychology.

**BITTNER, JASON D,** Schenectady County Comm Coll, Schenectady, NY; FR; BA; SGA; Hmnts/Scl Sci; Prfsnl Mscn.

**BITZER, CAROLYNN A,** Seton Hall Univ, South Orange, NJ; SO; BSN; Freshman Class Council 89-90; Seton Hall U Stdnt Ambassador 90; Tae Kwando Clb 89; Nrsng Stdnt Assoc 91; Division Vlntr Effrts 89; POW/MIA 89; Steuben Scty AM; Clg Nrsng Deans List; CNA Medical Center Princeton 90; Nrsng; RN.

**BITZER, PATRICK L,** Atlantic Union Coll, S Lancaster, MA; SO; BA; New England Yth Ensmbl 89-; Prcsn Ensmbl; Clgte Bnd 90-; Amnsty Internatl; Asst Bnd Dir 90-; Bsn/Msc; Mktg.

**BIVENS, JOYCE ANTOINETTE,** Wv Northern Comm Coll, Wheeling, WV; FR; AAS; Phi Theta Kappa; Amer Cul Fed 90-; Culnry Arts; Chef.

**BIVENS, PAMELA S,** Roane St Comm Coll, Harriman, TN; SO.

**BIVINS, CHRISTINE M,** Le Moyne Coll, Syracuse, NY; SO; BA; Ski Clb 89-; Sclgy Clb 89-; Chldrns Aids Ntwrk 90-; Admssns Tr Gde Ovrnght Hst 89-; Vol Cmps Mnstry 90-; Orttn Com 90-; Sprng Olympcs Capt 89-; Sclgy Crmnlgy Crmnl Jstce; Law Enfrcmnt.

**BIXBY, LISA A,** S U N Y Coll Of Tech At Alfred, Alfred, NY; SR; Amer Chem Assc 89-; Sgm Tau Epsln 90-; CRC Awrd.

**BIXBY, SCOTT H,** Bapt Bible Coll & Seminary, Clarks Summit, PA; SR; BS; Sr Cls V P 90-; Dorm Ofcr Soc Coord 88-; Dorm Res Advsr 89-; Msnry Apprntshp Prog 90-; Chrstn Serv Awd 90-; Interclgte Wrslng 87-90; Pstrl Stdes/Religion; Pstr/Msn.

**BIXLER, MARK A,** Univ Of Ky, Lexington, KY; JR; BARCH; Amer Inst Architecture Stdnts 90-; Athletic Cncl 90-; Golden Key 90-; Lances 90-; Presidential Schlrshp 89-; Design Studio Awrd 90-; Architecture.

**BIXLER, MEGAN K,** Allegheny Coll, Meadville, PA; SO; Allies; Kappa Alpha Theta Schlrshp Chrmn 90-; IM Vllybl 89-; Englsh Psychlgy; Law.

**BIXLER JR, RAYMOND P,** Garrett Comm Coll, Mchenry, MD; FR; AA; Vet Clb VP 90-; Stdnt Govt Assn VP; SPC Maryland Army Natl Guard Co C 121st Eng Blt Combat 90-; Bus Admin; MBA.

**BIZUB, ANNE L,** Duquesne Univ, Pittsburgh, PA; GD; MA; Technical Assistant In Metalwork/Jewelry 89-90; Fine Arts/Montclair State Clg; Phi Kappa Phi 89-; Psi Chi 89-; Hnrs Prog In Psychology 89-90; Phi Kappa Phi Schlrshp Acdmc Excellence 91; Jerome Seidman Schlr 90; BA Mt Clr Clg; Psychology; Clinical Psychology.

**BJERKHAMN, KAREN I,** Barry Univ, Miami, FL; FR; BA; Crmnl Jstc Sysm; Law.

**BJORKLUND, MADELEINE J,** Bay Path Coll, Longmeadow, MA; FR; BA; Stdnt Govt Pres 90-; Glee Clb 90-; Keynotes 90-; Travel; Medicine.

**BJORN, KRISTIN B,** Univ Of Sc At Columbia, Columbia, SC; JR; Alpha Lambda Delta Pres 88-; Gamma Beta Phi 88-; Pi Mu Epsilon 90-; Flwshp Exprnc Undergrads UTK; Math/Statistics; Statiscan.

**BJORNDAL, KRISTIE M,** Univ Of Sc At Columbia, Columbia, SC; SR; BS; Stdnt Govt Comm Membr 89-90; Gamma Beta Phi 87-; Phi Beta Kappa 90-; Beta Alpha Psi 88-; Alpha Delta Pi Asst Rsh 87-; Acctg; Law Schl.

**BLACHE, SHELLY ANN,** Norfolk St Univ, Norfolk, VA; JR; BA; Youth Group Pres 90; Kindergarten Sunday Schl Tchr 87; Christian Life Mnstrs Chr 90; Erly Chldhd Ed; Tchr.

**BLACHER, ELENA,** Univ Of Miami, Coral Gables, FL; FR; Brdcstng Hstry.

**BLACK JR, ALLEN E,** S U N Y Coll Of Tech At Delhi, Delhi, NY; FR; AOS; Phi Theta Kappa.

**BLACK, ANTHONY J,** George Mason Univ, Fairfax, VA; SR; BS; Physcl Ed.

**BLACK, BETH A,** Longwood Coll, Farmville, VA; SO; BA; Tri Hi Y 87-88; Phi Beta Lambda 90-; Bsns Admn; Priv Acct.

**BLACK, BRIAN W,** Cornell Univ Statutory College, Ithaca, NY; JR; Stu Drm Rep 88-89; Bsktbl 88-90; Anml Sci; Vet.

**BLACK, CAROLYN J,** Al A & M Univ, Normal, AL; JR; BS; Bapt Stndt Union 89-; Drug Task Force; Delta Mu Delta; Bus Admin.

**BLACK, CATHEY S,** Va Commonwealth Univ, Richmond, VA; JR; BSN; VALOR Prog; Paralgl 86-90; BS 85; Cert 89; Nrsng.

**BLACK JR, DARRELL A,** Tn Temple Univ, Chattanooga, TN; JR; BA; Stdnt Mssns Flwshp Otrch Ldr 90-; Pi Kappa Delta Athltc Dir 90-; Rlgn; Mssnry.

**BLACK, DEBORAH W,** Atlantic Comm Coll, Mays Landing, NJ; SR; AS; Sci Clb 89-; Absegami P T BTMH Millville Hsp 89-; Phy Thrpy Asst.

**BLACK, DEBRA T,** Piedmont Tech Coll, Greenwood, SC; SO; AD; Phi Theta Kappa; Crmnl Jstce; Jvnile Serv.

**BLACK, EDWARD S,** Birmingham Southern Coll, Birmingham, AL; SO; BA; Stu Govt Tres 89-; Pres Stu Serv Org; Grksng Coordntr; Alpha Lambda Delta; Pi Sigma Alpha Tres; Sigma Nu Pldg Trnr 89-; Mccy Tutrg; Prgrsv Frmr Mag Intrn Wrtg; Pol Sci; Attrny.

**BLACK, HOWARD W,** Ms St Univ, Miss State, MS; FR; BS; Mchncl Eng; Eng.

**BLACK, JENNIFER M,** Wilmington Coll, New Castle, DE; SO; Deans List 90-; Bsktbl Chrldng; Crmnl Justice; Law.

**BLACK, JOEL B,** Livingston Univ, Livingston, AL; FR; BS; Phi Eta Sigma; Sgt USMC 86-90; Bsns Admn; Econs.

**BLACK, JON C,** Teikyo Post Univ, Waterbury, CT; JR; BA; Intl Stdnt Lsn; Vrsty Sccr 88-89; Hstry Sclgy; Law.

**BLACK, KENDAL L,** Midlands Tech Coll, Columbia, SC; SR; ASSC; Mdcl Lbrtry Tchnlgy.

**BLACK, LISA J,** Univ Of Tn At Martin, Martin, TN; JR; BS; Delta Kappa Gamma Award; Dns Lst 89-90; Pre Schl Tchr 85-; Erly Chldhd Educ; Tch.

**BLACK, LORI G,** Univ Of Sc At Columbia, Columbia, SC; JR; BA; Hll Govt 88-89; Pblc Srvc Mrthn 89-; Alpha Delta Pi Bbl Stdy Crdntr 89-; Alpha Lambda Delta VP 88-89; Gamma Beta Phi 88-89; Alpha Delt Api Chpln 89-; Deans Lst 88-90; Scndry Engl Ed.

**BLACK, MARSHA A,** Pfeiffer Coll, Misenheimer, NC; FR; BA; Jazz Ensmbl Trumpet Plyr 90-; Theater Crew 90-; AWS 90-; Swim Mgr 90-; Bio; Dentist.

**BLACK, MARSHA G,** Union Coll, Barbourville, KY; JR; BA; Bapt Stdnt Union Bible Stdy Ldr 88-; Act Board 88-89; Acad Team Capt 88-; Gamma Beta Phi Sec 89-; Ronald Mcnair Post Achvmnt Prog 90-; Chem; Medicine.

**BLACK, MELANIE ELIZABETH,** Clemson Univ, Clemson, SC; JR; BS; Intrnl Trade/Germany.**

**BLACK, MICHAEL T,** Ky St Univ, Frankfort, KY; FR; BS; Math; Civil Engr.

**BLACK, MICHELLE MARIE,** Comm Coll Algny Co Algny Cmps, Pittsburgh, PA; FR; BA; Accounting; Cpa.

**BLACK, SHAWTAIN M,** Ky St Univ, Frankfort, KY; FR; English Club Pres; Deans List; English.

**BLACK, STACEY A,** Univ Of Va, Charlottesville, VA; JR; BSN; Raven 90-; Golden Key 90-; Ntnl Collgte Nrsg Acad 88-; Pi Beta Phi Rec Sec 89-; Madison Hse Vol Org 88-; Intnshp St Luke's Hosp Boise Id; IM Fld Hockey 89-; Nrsg.

**BLACK, TAMARA L,** Univ Of Ga, Athens, GA; SO; BSED; Hl Cncl PR 89-; Wsly Fndtn 89-; ZODIAC; Phi Kappa Phi; Alpha Lambda Delta 89-90; Red Crs Bld Dnr 89-; Athns Hmls Shltr Vol 89-; Phi Kappa Phi Schlrshp; Hon Cert UGA Hon Prog; Erly Chldhd Educ; Tchng.

**BLACK, TAMMY L,** Univ Of Southern Ms, Hattiesburg, MS; JR; BS; Deutsch Klub Pres 90-; Hnrs Stdnt Assoc; Gamma Beta Phi; Math German; Teaching.

**BLACK, VANESSA MAE,** New Comm Coll Of Baltimore, Baltimore, MD; GD; AA; Alpha Sigma Lambda Bdgt Ofcr 90-; Eng Aide Black/Decker Corp; Cmptr Info Sys; Prgrmmr Anlyst.

**BLACKBURN, KELLI R,** Ky St Univ, Frankfort, KY; JR; Bsns Accntng.

**BLACKBURN, LAURA A,** Univ Of Ky, Lexington, KY; SR; BA; Sigma T Delta 90-; Gldn Key 89-; Engl/Lbry Sci; Educ.

**BLACKBURN, MARY J,** Fl International Univ, Miami, FL; JR; MS; Amer Dietetic Assc 90-; Stdt Dietetic Assc 90-; Phi Kappa Phi; Aerobics/Fitness Assc Amer 87-; IDEA Fndtn 87-; Exer Safety Assc 89-; Fitness Instrctr Bptst Hosp 87-; AA Miami Dade Comm Clg 71; Dietetics/Nutrition.

**BLACKBURN, PATRICIA A,** Northern Ky Univ, Highland Hts, KY; SR; BA; Kappa Delta Pi 90-; SNEA 90-; NKCTM 89-; Alpha Chi 89-; Elem Ed; Tchr.

**BLACKBURN, SUSAN E,** Bowie St Univ, Bowie, MD; SR; BS; Kappa Delta Pi 90-; AA/ELEM Educ Prince Georges Cmnty Clg 88; Elem Educ; Tchng.

**BLACKHAM, DIANNE M,** S U N Y Coll Of Tech At Alfred, Alfred, NY; FR; AAS; Biotech Clb 90-; Grce Bible Bptst Chrch 88-; Ira Dvnport Hosp Unit Sec 84-; Ag Biotech; Gntc Eng Tech.

**BLACKLEDGE, JANE E,** Univ Of Southern Ms, Hattiesburg, MS; SR; BS; Kappa Mu Epsln Sec 88-; Asc Cmptng Mach Treas 90-; Std Eagle Clb 89-; Hnrs Clg 86-; Alpha Lambda Delta 86-87; Gamma Beta Phi 88-90; Phi Delta Rho; Cmptr Sci/Math.

**BLACKLEDGE, JOEL L,** Univ Of Southern Ms, Hattiesburg, MS; FR; BBA; Stdnt Almni Assn 90-; Stdnt Egle Clb 90-; Hnrs Coll 90-; Phi Eta Sigma 90-; Alpha Lambda Delta 90-; Gamma Beta Phi 90-; Dns Lst 90-; Acctng; Law.

**BLACKMAN, ANGELA N,** Al St Univ, Montgomery, AL; SO; BS; Sim Bsktbl 90; Acctng; CPA.

**BLACKMAN, PATRICIA C,** Vance Granville Comm Coll, Henderson, NC; FR; AA; Trnsfr Schlrs; Phi Theta Kappa; Toler Oak Hill Schl PTO Tres Exec Comm; Hsptlty Bsns 85-; Accntng; CPA.

**BLACKMAN, ROSLYN L,** Long Island Coll Hosp Of Nrsng, Brooklyn, NY; GD; AAS; L R Aprea Mem Awd; Switzer Fndtn Awd; Intl Bnkg Emplee 78-90; BA 85; Nurs.

**BLACKMAN, SHELLEY D,** Univ Of Sc At Columbia, Columbia, SC; JR; BA; Alpha Lambda Delta 89-; Gamma Beta Phi 89-; Sigma Delta Pi; Francis W Bradley Awd Rmnc Lang 91; Spnsh; Tchng.

**BLACKMON, DAVID W,** Univ Of Sc At Columbia, Columbia, SC; SR; BA; Bed 88-89; Mgnt; Real Est.

**BLACKMON IV, ROBERT C,** Morgan St Univ, Baltimore, MD; JR; BS; Chem Clb 89-; Amer Chem Soc 89-; Chem Clb Nwsltr Co-Edtr 90-; Beta Kappa Chi Edtr; Rcqtbl; Chem; Med.

**BLACKMON, SARA R,** Stillman Coll, Tuscaloosa, AL; JR; BA; Rtrct Clb Treas; Gamma Iota Sigma 88-; Delta Sigma Theta; IM Bsktbl 90; Elem Ed; Tchng.

**BLACKMOND, JANIE K,** Itawamba Comm Coll, Fulton, MS; SO; Hd Psych Dept; Awrd Phi Theta Kappa; Clncl Psych; Med.

**BLACKSIN, MELISSA S,** Emory Univ, Atlanta, GA; JR; BBA; ACE Dir Membrshp 90-; AMA 90-; Res Hall Assoc Pblcst 90-; Deans Lst; Delta Phi Epsilon Fndrsr 88-; Bus; Finance/Mgmnt.

**BLACKSON, JAMIE L,** Kent St Univ Kent Cmps, Kent, OH; SO; BA; Hse Cncl Wrght Hl Flr Rep; Hons Clg; Fine/Prof Arts; Intr Dsgn.

**BLACKSTOCK, DEBORAH L,** Christopher Newport Coll, Newport News, VA; SR; BA; Substitute Tchr; Poquoson Sch Sys Poquoson VA 87-90; Elem Edn; Teach/Admin.

**BLACKSTOCK, M JANET,** Univ Of Tn At Knoxville, Knoxville, TN; SR; BS; Beta Gamma Sigma; Tenn Veterinary Tchn Assoc Pres 88-90; Registered Veterinary Techn; AS Abraham Baldwin Agri Clg Tifton Ga 76; Business; Mngmnt.

**BLACKSTON, AMY R,** Univ Of Ky, Lexington, KY; FR; BA; Team For Stdnt Rcrtmnt 90-; Alpha Lambda Delta 90-; Alpha Gamma Delta Actvts Chrprsn 90-; Chnclrs Schlrshp 90-; Psychlgy.

**BLACKWELDER, ELIZABETH J,** Wagner Coll, Staten Island, NY; FR; WCBG Bus Mgr 90-; Deans Lst.

**BLACKWELDER, JENNIFER L,** Wallace St Comm Coll At Selma, Selma, AL; SO; BA; Business; Mrktng.

**BLACKWELL, ANTHONY J,** City Univ Of Ny City Coll, New York, NY; GD; JD; Chess Clb 87-90; Brittain Prz 90; BA 90; Ecnmcs/Mgmt Admn; Law.

**BLACKWELL, BRADLEY K,** Univ Of Ky, Lexington, KY; FR; Bus/Finance; Law.

**BLACKWELL, CANDACE C,** Univ Of Sc At Columbia, Columbia, SC; JR; BA; Erly Chldhd Ed; Tchr.

**BLACKWELL, CAROL J,** Radford Univ, Radford, VA; SR; BSN; Extrnshp Fmly Brth Cntr Comm Hosp Roanoke Valley 90; Nrsng; Obstrtcl Nrsng.

**BLACKWELL, DEBORAH L,** Univ Of Sc At Aiken, Aiken, SC; SO; BA; Educ Clb Sec 89-; Lit Pblctn Stf 89-90; Chldns Shltr; Gamma Beta Phi; Schlrshp Aiken Jr Wmn League; In St Schlrshp; Educ; Elem Tchr.

**BLACKWELL, GAIL F,** Piedmont Tech Coll, Greenwood, SC; SO; Psi Beta 90-; Pub Serv/Human Serv.

**BLACKWELL, JAMES C,** Livingston Univ, Livingston, AL; FR; Pi Kappa Phi; Lamp Key Awrd; IM Free Thrw Chmpn; BSKTBLL; Bus Acctg.

**BLACKWELL, JOHN A,** Univ Of Tn At Martin, Martin, TN; SR; BS; Stdnt Ambsdr 89-; Pi Kappa Alpha Sec 89-; Sec Educ/Biology.

**BLACKWELL, MELISSA L,** Greenville Tech Coll, Greenville, SC; SO; ASSC; Radlgc Technlgy; Radlgc Technlgy.

**BLACKWELL, MITCHELL C,** New Comm Coll Of Baltimore, Baltimore, MD; JR; AA; Phi Theta Kappa 90-; Citation Dist Schlrs 89-90; Dietcs Currclm Awd; Dietetic Tech; Caterng.

**BLACKWELL, MITZI D,** Univ Of Sc At Columbia, Columbia, SC; GD; Univ Business Scty 89-90; Deans Lst 88-90; Wofford Schlr 87; Kappa Delta 87-; Realtors Educ Fndtn Schlrshp 89-90; Wofford Clg JV Chrldr 87-88.

**BLACKWELL, MOLLY C,** Univ Of Tn At Martin, Martin, TN; SO; BS; Hon Smnr; Alpha Omicron Pi Kpr Rtl; UT Martin Stdnt Ambssdrs 89-; Chld Psychlgy.

**BLACKWELL, MONICA L,** Bennett Coll, Greensboro, NC; FR; BS; Dns Lst; Award Acad Excel; Hnrs Award; Sftbl; Bio; Pre Med.

**BLACKWELL, REBECCA T,** Middle Tn St Univ, Murfreesboro, TN; JR; BS; Dns Lst; Stdio Snger Entrtrn 83-; Otstndng Yng Wmn Of Amer 87; Pol Sci; Lgsltn Pol Actn.

**BLACKWELL, RITA GAIL,** Spartanburg Methodist Coll, Spartanburg, SC; SO; AA; Fut Bsns Ldrs Of Amer 86-88; Dist Educ Of Amer VP 87-88; Jr Achvmnt VP 86-87; Acad Awd SMC 89-90; Sprtnbrg Stl Prod Schlrshp 89-; Fut Bsns Ldrs Amer Conf Acctg Tst 87-88; Acctg; CPA.

**BLACKWELL, ROGER D,** Univ Of Sc At Columbia, Columbia, SC; JR; BS; Kappa Psi 90-; Pharm.

**BLACKWOOD, ROBIN K,** Univ Of Sc At Columbia, Columbia, SC; SR; BS; Crmnl Jstc 89-90; Gldn Key 88-; Alpha Phi Sigma 88-; USC Schlrshp 90-; Crmnl Jstc; Law.

**BLACKWOOD, TAMMY M,** Univ Of Al At Birmingham, Birmingham, AL; SO; AAS; SOTA Fndrsr Comm; AOTA; Occptnl Therpy.

**BLADE, CHRISTY S,** Anne Arundel Comm Coll, Arnold, MD; SO; BS; Chem Clb Tres 90-; US Army Russian Lngst Sgt/E5 84-88; Rsrv Stf Sgt 88-91; Sci; Med.

**BLADES, MARYLOU SPEZIALE,** Wilmington Coll, New Castle, DE; SR; BA; Sussex Co Brd Of Rltrs; Natl Assoc Of Rltrs; Behav Sci; Cnslng.

**BLAES JR, CHARLES E,** Univ Of South Al, Mobile, AL; SR; BS; SGA Spcl Projcts Comm 85-87; USM Recrtmnt Vol 87; Mortar Bd; Omicron Delta Kappa; Gamma Beta Phi 85-; Lambda Sigma Svc Chrmn 85-; Phi Chi Theta 90-; Kappa Mu Epsilon 85-; Sigma Chi Tribn 84-; Mgt Info Sys.**

**BLAIN, JASON D,** Christian Brothers Univ, Memphis, TN; FR; BS; Mech Engr.

**BLAIN, THERESA M,** Coll Of Charleston, Charleston, SC; SR; BA; Psi Sigma Alpha; Pol Sci; Law.

**BLAINE, KRISTIE C,** Kent St Univ Kent Cmps, Kent, OH; SR; BA; ASID Stdnt Chptr; Exprnc Sclptr; Deans List; Interior Dsgn; Cmrcl/Rsdntl Dsgnr.

**BLAIR, ALISA L,** Morehead St Univ, Morehead, KY; FR; BS; DECA Clb 87-88; Natl Beta Clb 88-90; Natl Hon Soc; Bus; Hotel/Restaurant Mgr.

**BLAIR, BETH L,** New England Coll Of Optometry, Boston, MA; GD; OD; Vol Optmtrc Srv Hmnty Lctr Coord 89-; Amer Optmtrc Stdnt Assoc 89-; Natl Optmtrc Stdnt Assoc Rcrdng Sec 89-90; Phi Beta Kappa 89-; Beta Sigma Kappa 90-; BA Univ NH 89; Optmtry.

**BLAIR, DWIGHT I,** Wv Univ, Morgantown, WV; JR; BS; Mrchg Bnd 88-89; Kappa Psi Pres 90-; Hnrs Lst 89-90; Acad Excell Certif 89; Phrmcy.

**BLAIR, GREGORY M,** Broward Comm Coll, Ft Lauderdale, FL; JR; BS; Phi Theta Kappa; Grad With Highest Hnrs; AA 90; Acctng.

**BLAIR, JAMES R,** Piedmont Coll, Demorest, GA; JR; BA; Psy Chi; Mnstr Untd Mthdst Chrch 89-; Psychlgy; Pstrl Cnslng.

**BLAIR, JASON D,** Salisbury St Univ, Salisbury, MD; SR; BED; Dns Lst 89-; Kappa Delta Pi 90-; Acad Dns Lst 89-; Elem Educ; Tchr.

**BLAIR, JOANN L,** Georgetown Coll, Georgetown, KY; SO; BA; Stdnt Govt 90-; Stdnt Crt Review; Newspaper Stf News Info Editor 89-; Phi Beta Lambda 89-; Math Assoc Amer 89-90; Political Sci Economics; Law.

**BLAIR, KARL M,** Bunker Hill Comm Coll, Boston, MA; SR; BA; Pathfndrs Math; Math Tutor 88-89; Ftbl Clb 88-90; Deans Lst 90-; Acdmc Achvmnt Mnrty Stdnt 90-; Otdr Edctn 85-86; Fnrl Drctr.

**BLAIR, KENNETH D,** Lincoln Memorial Univ, Harrogate, TN; GD; ASN; Eastern Ky Univ Russian Clb Pres 82-84; EKU ROTC Pershing Rfls Cmd 83-84; EKY ROTC Rngr Co Cdt Advsr 83-84; Ntl Soc Scabbard/Blade Treas 82-84; Gamma Beta Phi 82-83; USAF Tact Air Cmnd Schlstc Achvmnt 82; Appl St Univ Grad Bio; Nrsng; RN Anesthetist.

**BLAIR, MARGARITA M,** Fl International Univ, Miami, FL; SR; BA; Grdtd With Hnrs 89; Sndy Schl Tchr/Biscayne Cmnty Chrch 90-; Tchr Day Schl; AA Miami-Dade Cmnty Clg 88; AS; Educ/Elem/Erly Chldhd; Tchr.

**BLAIR, MELINDA M,** Univ Of Charleston, Charleston, WV; SO; BA; Lit Mag Sec 90-; Alpha Lambda Delta; Lang Arts Educ; Edctr.

**BLAIR, MELISSA D,** Univ Of Ky, Lexington, KY; SO; BA; Commuter Stdnt Bd 89-90; Phi Beta Lambda 90-; Award Successfully Completing Master Stdnt Prog By UK 90; Deans List; Bus Edn; Teach.

**BLAIR, MERILYN M,** Fl A & M Univ, Tallahassee, FL; SR; Chmstry Clb Sec 89; Beta Kappa Chi 90-; Prshng Kss Srv Orgn 88-89; 3m Intern 89-; Mnrty Accss Rsrch Carrs Schlr 89-; FL Undrgrd Schlr 87-90; BS; Pre Mdcnl Chmstry; Med.

**BLAIR, MOLLI K,** Sinclair Comm Coll, Dayton, OH; FR; AAS; OH Scty Rdlgc Tchnlgsts; Rdlgc Tchnlgy Clb Sec; Phi Theta Kappa; Rdlgc Tech; Rgstrd Tchnlgst.

**BLAIR, MORDENA,** Paine Coll, Augusta, GA; GD; BA; Soc Clb 88-90; Deans Lst 89-90; Alpha Kappa Alpha Asst Den Of Pldgs 89-90; Bethlehem Cmnty Ctr Tutor 87-90; Yth Dev Ctr Socl Wrks Asst 90; BA 90; Sociology.

**BLAIR, NANCY T,** Limestone Coll, Gaffney, SC; SO; BS; Schdlr Expdtr 88-; Bus Admin Mgmt; Mgmt.

**BLAIR, SONJA L,** Middle Tn St Univ, Murfreesboro, TN; FR; BBA; NAACP Press/Pub Cmtee; Intrnshp Genesco Inc; Mktg; Mktg Cmunctns Mgr.

**BLAIR, SUZANNE J,** Elms Coll, Chicopee, MA; SO; BA; Rsdnt Cncl 89-90; Birthday Clb Coord 89-; Math Cmptrs; Prgrmmr Statistician.

**BLAIR, TANYA L,** Andrew Coll, Cuthbert, GA; FR; BED; Std Govt Asc Sec/Sntr 90-; Bptst Std Un Chrstn Grwth Chrp 90-; Phi Theta Kappa 90-; Chldrns Choir Vol 90-; Pblc Elem Schl Vol; Erly Chldhd Educ; Tchng.

**BLAIR, TARA D,** Al A & M Univ, Normal, AL; SR; BS; Ben Marcato Clb Pres 90-; Alpha Kappa Mu; Beta Kappa Chi; AL Acad Sci; Marc Flw; AS Morristown Coll 88; Zoology; Vet Med.

**BLAIR, TERRY SWENSON,** Tri County Tech Coll, Pendleton, SC; SO; Intl Frnds Prog; Calhoun Coll Hon Soc; VIMM; KOBA 88-; Grl Scouts Ldr 89-90; St Mrk Un Mthdst Chrch Snday Schl Tchr 89- Choir 88-; Abndy Fndtn Schlrshp; Outstndng Grad; PTC Pub Chrmn 90-; Free Lnce Artst 90-; AS; Elem Ed.

**BLAIR, TRACEY L,** Ms St Univ, Miss State, MS; JR; BS; Edctnl Psychlgy.

**BLAIS, PETER R,** Me Maritime Academy, Castine, ME; FR; BS; Engnrng.

**BLAISDELL IV, WILLIAM B,** Niagara Univ, Niagara Univ, NY; SR; BA; Basebl Pitchrs 87-88; Mktg/Mgmt; Grad Schl/Law.

**BLAKE, CHRISTINE M,** Indiana Univ Of Pa, Indiana, PA; SR; BED; ACEI 88-90; PSEA 88-90; Deans Lst 88-; IM Vllybl 90; Elem Educ; Elem Tchr.

**BLAKE, CHRISTOPHER R,** Univ Of Al At Birmingham, Birmingham, AL; SR; BA; Golden Key; Pi Kappa Phi Sec 88-; Omicron Delta Kappa Soph Ldrshp Awd 89; Pres Lst 90; Deans Lst 89-90; IM Sprts 89-; Acctg; Corp/Pblc Acctg.

**BLAKE, DEBORAH A,** Comm Coll Algny Co Algny Cmps, Pittsburgh, PA; SO; RN; Data Entry Clrk Med Rcrds; Mail Msngr; File Clrk; Nurs Aide; Nurs; BSN.

**BLAKE, HEATHER S,** Univ Of Rochester, Rochester, NY; SR; BA; Alumni Assoc 89-; Tae Kwon Do Club Pres 87-; Dorm Cncl 87-89; Psi Chi; RA 90-; Pres Lst 87-88; Dns Lst 87-; Study Abroad London Intrn 90; IM Flr Hcky 87-88; Rochester Psychtrc Cntr Intrn 87-; BA; Psychlgy; Higher Educ Cnslng/Admin.

**BLAKE, JASON R,** Univ Of Md Univ Coll, College Park, MD; FR; BA; Spch Cmnctns/Govt; Law.

**BLAKE, JENNIFER A,** Neumann Coll, Aston, PA; FR; BA; Neumann Coll Hon Pgm 90-; A Beechwood Vol Fire Co Shfs Sec; Wrk Stdy Pstn Pr Asst; Schl Pblctn Asst Edtr; Engl; Jrnlsm.

**BLAKE, LISA A,** Fl International Univ, Miami, FL; SO; BS; Phi Lambda; Elem Educ; Teacher.

**BLAKE, MARGARET THERESE,** Ny Theological Seminary, New York, NY; GD; Task Force Wingate HS Tutor 82-84; Caribbean-Amercn Eductnl Grp Tutor 87-; Medcl Asst; AAS Borough Of Manhattan Cmnty Clg 87; Soc Sci; Hlth Care Mgt/Admn.

**BLAKE, MICHAEL S,** Franklin And Marshall Coll, Lancaster, PA; JR; BA; Frenc Club Pres 88-; Chess Clug Pres 89-; Planetarium/Astronomy Club Treas 89-90; Black Pyramid Sr Hnr Scty; Pi Gamma Mu; Student Life Intshp Prog; Managing Consult Martin Computer Ctrf Mass Under 1400 Chess Champion 90; Econ/French; Busn.

**BLAKE, PAMELA S,** Wv Northern Comm Coll, Wheeling, WV; FR; AA; Math; Early/Middle Educ.

**BLAKE, POLLY S,** Memphis St Univ, Memphis, TN; SO; BA; Peer Mntr Prog; Hnrs Stu Assn 89-; Jwsh Stu Unn 89-; Gamma Beta Phi 90-; Alpha Gamma Delta VP 89-; Rgnl Med Cntr; Jvnl Diabetes 89-; Spcl Olymp 89-; Early Schlrs Schlrshp 89-; Tutor 89-; Rsrch Asst; IM 89-; Chld Psychlgst/Law.

**BLAKE, ROBERT W,** Univ Of Akron, Akron, OH; SR; MBA; Assoc Student Govt Asst To The Crmn 89-; Golden Key 88-; Beta Gamma Sigma 90-; Beta Alpha Psi; FMA Natl Hnr Scty; Deans List 87-; Racquetbl Tourtmnt 88; Acctng; Trade Options On CBOT.

**BLAKE, ROGER A,** Widener Univ, Chester, PA; JR; Phi Theta Kappa 89-; Elec Eng.

**BLAKE, SABRINA L,** Lexington Comm Coll, Lexington, KY; SO; BS; LCC Cmnty Schlr; Deans Lst 90-; NCO PLDC Inst US Army; Cert Of Achvmnt Essay Contest; US Army NCO; US Army Combat Med Specist; Bio; Med Schl.

**BLAKE, STEPHEN D,** Univ Of Ky, Lexington, KY; FR; BS; KY Kernel Stff Wrtr 90-; Comm Affrs Comm Stdnt Gov Assn Comm Mem 90-; Coll Lvng Vlntr 90-; Blue Grss Assn Rtrd Citzns 89-; Hghst Avg Fresh Chem 90; Biotech; Scndry Ed/Pharm.

**BLAKELY, LINDORF S,** Tuskegee Univ, Tuskegee Inst, AL; JR; BA; Inrds Dallas/Ft Wrth Inc 88-; Financ Clb 88-; Alpha Kappa Mu; Delta Mu Delta; Kappa Alpha Psi Reportr; Northrn Telecom Intrnshp 88-; Bus/Financ; Law.

**BLAKELY, SUSAN L,** Wv Northern Comm Coll, Wheeling, WV; FR; BA; Island-Athltc Assn Sec 89-90; Hon Engl 90-; Scl Sci/Serv; Scl Serv.

**BLAKEMAN, EDWARD S,** Ky Christian Coll, Grayson, KY; SR; BS; VITA; Socer 87-90; Bus Admin; Profssr History.**

**BLAKEMORE, MICHAEL B,** Bowling Green St Univ, Bowling Green, OH; SO; BA; Swmmng/Trthln Trng 84-; First Frnds Chrch 75-; Co-Op Sprntdnts Asst 90-; Res Advsr; IMS; Cnstrctn Mgmt/Arch Dsgn.

**BLAKENEY, CAROLYN E,** Anne Arundel Comm Coll, Arnold, MD; SO; BA; Mgr Harstlng Salon; Hist/Econ; Law/Env Fld.

**BLAKER, GENEVA L,** Christopher Newport Coll, Newport News, VA; SR; AMA; BSBA; Mgmnt/Mktg; Fshn Retail Buyer.

**BLAKESLEE, DARREN J,** Univ Of Fl, Gainesville, FL; SR; BSN; Sigma Theta Tau; RN 87-; AS Manatee Comm Clg 87; AA Santa Fe Comm Clg 90; Nrsng.

**BLAKLEY, MARGRET A,** Univ Of Tn At Martin, Martin, TN; FR; BS; Lakeview Bapt Yth Grp 87-; Beta Beta Beta; Dns Lst; Mu Epsilon Delta; Southern Belles Svc; Biology; Med.

**BLALOCK, BAYE F,** Univ Of Southern Ms, Hattiesburg, MS; JR; BA; Cert; Co-Lin Jr Coll 83; Prlgl; Law.

**BLALOCK, CATHERINE L,** Davis & Elkins Coll, Elkins, WV; SR; BS; Stdnt Educ Assoc Sec 88-; Davis Elkins Schlrshp 89; Elem Educ; Tchr.

**BLALOCK, CHRISTINE E,** Univ Of Ga, Athens, GA; GD; MED; Cncl Excptnl Chldrn 90-; Magna Cum Laude 90; Tchr Interrelated Sp Ed; BSED 90; Spec Ed; Tchng.

**BLALOCK, JESSICA M,** Clark Atlanta Univ, Atlanta, GA; FR; Booster Club 90-; Assoc Blck Psy 90-; Ushers Various Prog 90-; Deans List 90-; Tri-M Hnrs Scty 90; NAACPF Schlrshp Assoc Blk Psy; Cert Outstndng Acad Achtmt; Psy; Clinical Psychologist.

**BLANCHARD, CARRIE A,** Hudson Valley Comm Coll, Troy, NY; SO; AAS; Pres Lst 90-; Eddy Memrl Grtrc Cntr Vol 90-; Hill Hs Adlscnt Res Fclty Intrn 89-90; Rnsslr Cty Prbtn Dept Intrn 90-; Hmn Serv; Cnslng.

**BLANCHARD, CRAIG G,** Univ Of Me At Farmington, Farmington, ME; JR; BS; Stdnt Snte Sntr 90; Frnch Clb Pres 88-90; Schl Newspapr 88-89; Alpha Pi Omega 88; Ims Capt 90; Hstry; Ed.**

**BLANCHARD, HELAINE C,** Univ Of Sc At Columbia, Columbia, SC; SR; MED; Stdnt Alumni Assoc 88-90; Psychology Club 87-88; Women Stdnts Serv Chrprsn 88-90; Mortar Brd 89-90; Psi Chi Mbrshp Rush Dir 87-90; Golden Key 89-90; Sigma Sigma Sigma; Vlntr Hugo Relief Fund 90; Vlntr Tucker Ctr For Elderly 89; Outstndg Sr Award 90; Clinical Counseling Ed Dept; Psychology Ph D.

**BLANCHARD, JEFFREY C,** Western New England Coll, Springfield, MA; SR; ACM 90-; Bwlng Clb Sec/Treas 82-; Deans Lst 89-90; BS; Comp Sci; Cnsltnt/Slf-Emply.

**BLANCHARD, LAWANDA T,** Howard Univ, Washington, DC; FR; BA; Ntl Assn Blk Jrnlsts 90-; Ga Clb 90-; Stf Rprtr Cmps Nwspr 90-; Cmps Pal; Jrnlsm; Edtr.

**BLANCHARD III, ROGER C,** George Mason Univ, Fairfax, VA; JR; BS; Intrnshp Frontier Engineering Inc Comptr Support Grp; Acctng; CPA.**

**BLANCHARD, SABRINA C,** City Univ Of Ny La Guard Coll, Long Island Cty, NY; SR; Phi Theta Kappa 90-; Bus Admn; Bus.

**BLANCHARD, TRACY L,** Kent St Univ Kent Cmps, Kent, OH; SR; BBA; Std DPMA 88-; Gldn Key 89-; Alpha Lambda Delta 88-; Delta Sigma Pi VP 88-; Pres Lst; IM Bsktbl/Vlybl; Cmptr Sci Bsn Org; Sys Anlys.

**BLANCHARD, TROY A,** Embry Riddle Aeronautical Univ, Daytona Beach, FL; FR; BA; Aviation Maintnce Tchnlgy Avionics; Avionics.

**BLANCHARD, VERNON,** Benedict Coll, Columbia, SC; GD; NAACP 87-88; Frnch Clb 88-90; Stdnt Rel Awarness Org 87-90; Ded Svcs Sprngfld; Bapt Chrch.

**BLANCHET, SCOTT C,** Univ Of Miami, Coral Gables, FL; SO; BSME; Hon Prog 89-; Deans Lst; I M; Mech; Engr.

**BLANCO RIVERA, FRANCISCO J,** Univ Of Pr Cayey Univ Coll, Cayey, PR; JR; Coll Bd Exmntn Rcgnzd Frst Stdnts In PR With Hghst Pnctuatn; Sci; Med.

**BLANCO, BARBARA M,** Saint Thomas Univ, Miami, FL; GD; MS; Cuban-Amer Ntl Fndtn Vol 88-89; Acad Advsr 87-89; Art/Lit Awd 86; Hispanic Hrtge Schlrshp 87-89; Outstndng Acad Achievemnt 88-89; Grad Hghst Hnrs 89; Tlnt Rstr Of Outstndng Mnrty Grad 90; Alpha Gamma Kappa 89; St Thomas Schlrshp 89; Psych; Doctorate.**

**BLANCO, BETTY,** Univ Of Miami, Coral Gables, FL; SR; JD; Mktng Clb 90-; Intl Finance/Mktng Clb 90-; Finance Clb 90-; Phi Theta Kappa 87-; Phi Kappa Phi 89-; Golden Key 90-; Beta Gamma Sigma 90-; Community Serv Clb 87-; Youth Co Op 88-; Pres Hnr Rl 90-; Deans Lst 87-89; Intl Finance/Mktng; Law.

**BLANCO, CARLA M,** Univ Of Pr At Mayaguez, Mayaguez, PR; SO; BA; Beta Beta Beta; Research Medl Sci 90-; Biology; MD PHD.

**BLANCO, CARMEN L RODRIGUEZ,** Catholic Univ Of Pr, Ponce, PR; GD; BED; Crclo De Pre Med 86; Cptlo Betta Betta Betta 88; B Ed UCPR 90; Quimica; Maestina En Educacion.

**BLANCO, ISABEL,** Fl International Univ, Miami, FL; SO; Unv Accntng Assn; Accntng; CPA.**

**BLANCO, MELANIE NISHEA C,** George Washington Univ, Washington, DC; JR; BS; Pre Mdcl Soc 88-; Phillippine Cltrl Soc 90-; Zoology; Physician.**

**BLAND, ALETHA J,** Univ Of Va Clinch Valley Coll, Wise, VA; JR; BS; Phi Beta Lambda; All Amer Schlr Awd; Deans List; PTA Pres; PTA VP 90; Tchr Busned Obtain MBA; AAS SW VA Commty Clg 75; Busn Admin; Busn Educ Tchr.

**BLAND, ANTOINE M,** Ky St Univ, Frankfort, KY; JR; BA; Bptst Stdnt Union 90-; Alpha Phi Alpha Treas 90-; Outstndg Jr 90-; Deans Lst; Cmnl Jstc; Law.

**BLAND, CHARLES E,** Alcorn St Univ, Lorman, MS; JR; BS; Hnrs Stu Orgn 88-; Pres Achlr 89-90; IM Bsktbl 89-90; Cmptr Sci/Math.

**BLAND, ELIZABETH M,** Allegany Comm Coll, Cumberland, MD; FR; AA; Delta Epsln Chi 90-; Retail Mgmt; Bsn.

**BLAND, KAREN D,** Southern Coll Of Tech, Marietta, GA; FR; BS; Yrbk Stf 90; Bapt Un 90; Gamma Phi Beta; Indstrl Engr Tech; Engr.

**BLAND, LASHUN R,** Al St Univ, Montgomery, AL; JR; BS; Biomed Sci Clb Pres 88-; Panhllnc Cncl; Phi Eta Sigma Com Chr 89-; Alpha Kappa Mu; Beta Kappa Chi VP; Zeta Phi Beta Treas; Jr Cvtn Sec 88; MARC Hnrs Stdnt 88-; Rsrch Intrnshp Prdue Univ; Rsrch Apprntce Fllwshp 88; Blgy; Pthlgy.

**BLAND, LOUANNE,** Ms St Univ, Miss State, MS; JR; BS; Pres Lst; Deans Lst; Elem Ed; Tchr.

**BLAND, MINDY L,** Univ Of Akron, Akron, OH; JR; BS; Golden Key; Beta Gamma Sigma; Acdmc Schlrshps; Finance; Intl Tax Accnt.

**BLAND, NEAL A,** Univ Of Charleston, Charleston, WV; FR; BA; N Of Englnd Sch Boys Soccer Cptn 88-90; Natl Champshp Winner U/Bs Soccer Cptn 89-90; Deans List 90-; All Confrnc Plyr Soccer 90-; Cert Barnsley 6th Frm Clg Englnd 89-90; Cert Barnsley 6th Form Clg Englnd 88-90; Sprts Medcn; Athltc Trainer/Prvt Clinic.

**BLANDING, DONNA S,** Norfolk St Univ, Norfolk, VA; SO; BA; NAACP; ACM; Phi Beta Lambda; Spartan Alpha Tau; Lincoln-Zane Fdtn Schlrshp; Mgmt; Cmptr Info Syst.

**BLANE, REGINA HUMPHRIES,** Madisonville Comm Coll, Madisonville, KY; SO; AA; Phi Beta Lambda Sec 90; Deans Lst 90; Drctrs Lst 72; Coord Sr Citizens Grp Mt Olive Bptst Chrch Coord 84-; Sbst Tchr Vrs Clrcl Pstns; Appld Sci Bsns Mgmt; Mstrs Elem Edctn.

**BLANEY, LORRAINE A,** Central Fl Comm Coll, Ocala, FL; SO; AA; Elem Educ; Tch.

**BLANK, ANDREW D,** Glassboro St Coll, Glassboro, NJ; SR; BA; SGA Senator 90-; Stdnt Actvts Bd Advrtsg Chr 90-; Stdnt Econ Soc V P 90-; Alpha Chi Rho Founding Father Treas 89-; Dns Lst 90; Econ; Law.

**BLANK, DEBORAH E,** Elmira Coll, Elmira, NY; JR; BS; Frshmn Clss Offcr Sec 88-89; Ski Clb Pres 90-; Ed Clb 89-; Kappa Delta Pi; Tchng Bahamas; Tnns 88-89; Elem Ed; Tchng.

**BLANK, KATHLEEN C,** Fl International Univ, Miami, FL; SR; BS; Fndlng Clb; Vol Learn/Read Vols Miami; Brd Frdrck Brtchr Dncrs; Physcl Thrpy; Physcl Thrpy.

**BLANK, MICHELLE L,** Ky Wesleyan Coll, Owensboro, KY; GD; Parnassus Soc 86-88; Sigma Kappa Fndrsng Chr 86-90; Comps Clb Fndrsng Chr 88-90; Intrnshp Audubn Area Svcs Inc Tech Wrtng; BA 90; Engl/Tech Wrtg; Law.

**BLANKENSHIP OLIVER, REGINA M,** Anne Arundel Comm Coll, Arnold, MD; GD; AA; Yrbk Edtr/Chr; Grp Rep 90-; Omicron; Acad Excellence; Church Orgs; PTA 89-; RN.

**BLANKENSHIP, ANITA J,** Marshall University, Huntington, WV; JR; BBS; Bus Info Sys.

**BLANKENSHIP, BRENDA M,** Oh St Univ At Marion, Marion, OH; JR; BEA; Dns Lst; AA; Art Educ; Tchr Art Educ.

**BLANKENSHIP, CAROLYN,** Union Coll, Barbourville, KY; FR; BA; Cmps Nwspr Copy Edtr-Photo Edtr 90-; Cmmtr Cncl 90; KIPA Nws Stry Nwspr Cntst; Jrnlsm Awd 90-; Engl/Jrnlsm Emphs/Psychlgy; Psychlgst/Jrnlst.

**BLANKENSHIP, JAMES R,** Gordon Conwell Theol Sem, S Hamilton, MA; GD; MATS; Byington Schlr 90-; Former Lawyer; BS IN Univ 83; JD Vanderbilt Univ 86; Thlgcl Studies; Professor.

**BLANKENSHIP, JEFFREY D,** Union Univ, Jackson, TN; JR; BS; Acctng Clb 88; Alpha Chi 90; Phi Beta Lambda 89; Acct; CPA.

**BLANKENSHIP, KELLY M,** Fl St Univ, Tallahassee, FL; SR; BA; Engl; Tchr.

**BLANKENSHIP, PAMELA A,** Union Univ, Jackson, TN; JR; BSBA; Phi Theta Kappa; AS Jackson State Cmnty Clg 90; Bsn; Acctg.

**BLANKENSHIP, RITA K,** Central St Univ, Wilberforce, OH; GD; BA; Ohio Schl Nrs Assn 90-; Hlth Educ; Schl Nrsng.

**BLANKENSHIP, ROBERT B,** Old Dominion Univ, Norfolk, VA; SR; BSEET; Vol Spec Eng 89-91; Gldn Key 89-91; Elect Equip Svcng Danville Comm Clg 86-88; Gen Electrc Danville Comm Clg 88-89; Math/Eng; Elect Eng.

**BLANKENSHIP, TAMMY D,** Tn Wesleyan Coll, Athens, TN; JR; Bus Clb Hiwassee Coll 87-88; Chrstn Stdnt Mvmnt Hiwassee Coll 87-89; Bapt Stdnt Un TN Wesleyan Coll 90-; Phi Theta Kappa 87-89; Alpha Chi 90-; Circle K 88-89; Dorm Cncl Sec 88-89; J H Brunner Hon Awd 89; Alumni Merit Awd 90-; Elem Edn; Teach.

**BLANKENSHIP, TODD M,** Oh Univ-Southern Cmps, Ironton, OH; SO; Hstry.

**BLANKS, BRIDGETTE L,** Rust Coll, Holly Springs, MS; JR; BA; Pre-Law Clb Treas 90-; Pre-Almni; Ltry Clb; Alpha Kappa Mu Prlmntrn; Alpha Kappa Alpha Crsspndg Sec; Crmsn Schlrs Pres 90-; Chrldr 88-; Pltcl Sci; Lwyr.

**BLANTON, BRIAN K,** Univ Of Va Clinch Valley Coll, Wise, VA; JR; BA; Peer Advsr 90-; Res Asst 90-; Pi Kappa Phi V P 90-; Acctg Firm Intrn 90-; Bsbl Tm All Dist 89-; Bus Acctg; Law.

**BLANTON, HAROLD D,** Valdosta St Coll, Valdosta, GA; SR; BA; Phi Alpha Theta Pres 89-; Pi Gamma Mu Mbr 89-; Otstndg Sr; Hghst GPA; Hstry.

**BLANTON, KATHRYN DAISY,** Univ Of Sc At Columbia, Columbia, SC; JR; BA; Psych Clb 90-; Piedmont Soc 90-; Marshall 90-; Psych.

**BLANTON, RANDALL M,** Univ Of Nc At Charlotte, Charlotte, NC; SR; BA; Bio; Ed.

**BLANTON, RENA L,** Valdosta St Coll, Valdosta, GA; JR; BED; PAGE 90-; Erly Chldhd Educ; Tchng.

**BLANTON, STANLEY B,** Tri County Tech Coll, Pendleton, SC; SR; AD; HVAC/IMT; HVAC Bsnss Of My Own.

**BLANTON, TIFFANY J,** West Liberty St Coll, West Liberty, WV; SO; AB; Cncrt Bnd; Arts And Scis; Scl Wrk.

**BLASCO, MARTIN A,** City Univ Of Ny City Coll, New York, NY; SR; BA; Stdnts Nn Intrvntn Cntrl Amrc Crbn Pres 90; Stdnts Edctnl Rghts; Magna Cum Laude; Grhm Wndhm 89; Intrfth Assmbly Hsng Hmlssnss 90; Sclgy.

**BLASHAW, WILLIAM M,** Univ Of Pittsburgh, Pittsburgh, PA; SR; BS; Eta Kappa Nu; Phi Theta Kappa; AAS W WY Coll 87; Elec Eng.

**BLASINSKY, DIANE M,** Duquesne Univ, Pittsburgh, PA; FR; Phi Eta Sigma; Pharmacy.

**BLASS, LAURA L,** Fl International Univ, Miami, FL; JR; BS; P E Mjrs Club Secty 90-; Phi Lambda; Physl Ed K-12; Tch.**

**BLATA, MOHAMED S,** Central St Univ, Wilberforce, OH; JR; BS; Mfg Engr.

**BLAUSER, MICHAEL J,** Daemen Coll, Amherst, NY; SR; BA; ECC Slt Cr Clb 86-89; Knghts St Jhn 87; Assoc Erie Cmmnty Coll 89; Cert 86; Bus; Mgmt.**

**BLAUTH, STACEY A,** Lasell Coll, Newton, MA; SO; BA; Stdnt Act Cncl 89-90; Human Serv Clb 89-; Glee Clb 90-; Comm Outrch Opp Lg 89-; Pres Awrd 90-; Intrnshp Salv Army Hmless Shltr 90; Social Wrk.

**BLAY, CHRISTINA E,** Coll Of New Rochelle, New Rochelle, NY; SR; BA; Intrntnl Clb VP 89-; Bsn Board 89-90; Ltrt Clb 90; Prsbytrn Chrch Choir 88-90; Hnrs List 89-90; Deans List 88-89; Intrnshp UN Dprtmnt Intrntnl Ecnmc Social Affrs 90; Bsn/Intrntnl Studies; Intrntnl Affr/Mngt.

**BLAY, EMMANUEL K,** City Univ Of Ny Baruch Coll, New York, NY; JR; BBA; Acctng Soc; Golden Key; Sigma Alpha Delta; Proposed Baruch Math Ctr; Accountant; Acctng.

**BLAYLOCK, CARMAN U,** Clark Atlanta Univ, Atlanta, GA; JR; BS; Dorm Rsdntl Asst Big Sis 90; Med Rcrd Admin; Rgstrd Rcrd Admin.

**BLAYLOCK, LESLIE K,** Univ Of Nc At Asheville, Asheville, NC; SR; BA; Psi Chi VP 90-; Orntn Ldr 90-; Deans Lst 89-; Psych; Tchr.

**BLEATTLER, KAREN L,** Richard Bland Coll, Petersburg, VA; SO; BA; Stdnts Free Enterprise 90-; Bus; Law.

**BLEDSOE, CAROLE R,** Central St Univ, Wilberforce, OH; SR; BA; Baptst Stdnt Un; Nwspaper; Choir; All Amercn Schlr 90; Alpha Kappa Mu Pres 88-; Alpha Kappa Alpha; Cmnctns/Jrnlsm; Law.**

**BLEDSOE, L BERNARD,** Milligan Coll, Milligan Clg, TN; FR; BS; Yrbk; Hmlss Cmtee; Biology; Med.

**BLEDSOE, LUTRINA D,** Alcorn St Univ, Lorman, MS; SR; BA; Bus Admin/Acctng; Loan Officer/Acctng.

**BLEDSOE, MARY LOUISE,** Jacksonville St Univ, Jacksonville, AL; SR; BSN; Dorothy Stearne Mem Schlrshp 90-; Chrch Muscn Dir 85-; LPN Coosa Vlly Med Cntr; LPN N F Nunnlly State Vocatnl Tech Inst 71; AA Alexndr Cty State Jr Coll 89; Nrsng.

**BLEDSOE, SHARON A,** Piedmont Tech Coll, Greenwood, SC; GD; AS; Dns Lst; Phi Theta Kappa; Cmptr Lab Asst; Cmptr Tech; Cmtpr Prgmmr.

**BLEGEN, MICHAEL L,** Cornell Univ Statutory College, Ithaca, NY; SR; BS; Alpha Phi Omega 90-; Intern Bio Field Station; IM Ftbl/Sftbl 88-90; Natural Resources; Envrmntl Policy/Mgmnt.

**BLEIDORN, CONNIE J,** Univ Of Dayton, Dayton, OH; FR; BME; Ntl Soc Prof Engrs SSC Sec/Budg Admin; Jnt Cncl Engrs VP; Amer Inst Aero/Astro Sec; Campus Cnctn 90-; Intrnshp Rsrch Inst 90-; IM Vlybl/Sftbl/Flg Ftbl 90-; Mech/Aerospc Engr.

**BLESSE, DEBRA L,** Univ Of Southern Ms, Hattiesburg, MS; SR; BS; Stdnt Cnstr Pres 89; Stdnt Eagle Club 90; Stdnt ABET Audit/Rvw Comm 89; Sigma Lambda Chi 90; Phi Kappa Phi; Golden Key Natl 89; Gamma Beta Phi; IM 84; Laborer; Punch/Out; Assist Prchsng Agnt; Engr Aide; Cnstr Engr Tech; Cnstr Prjct Mgmt.

**BLESSING, LISA A,** Rutgers St Univ At Camden, Camden, NJ; JR; BA BS; Rutgers Mrktng Clb Secy 88-; Ecnmcs Mngmnt; Graduate Schl/Ecnmcs.

**BLESSING, MICHAEL S,** Daemen Coll, Amherst, NY; JR; BS; Phys Thrpy Assoc Pres 90-; Stdnt Adv Brd 90-; Phys Thrpy.

**BLESSING JR, WALTER D,** Univ Of Sc At Columbia, Columbia, SC; FR; BA; Kappa Alpha 90-; Frshmn Schlrshp Ctn; Eng; Law/Med.

**BLEST, ANGELA C,** Immaculata Coll, Immaculata, PA; JR; BA; Commtr Rep 88-90; Commtr Cncl Chr 90-; Clss Sec; Hon Soc 88-89; Prjct Outrch Day 90-; Psychlgy.

**BLEVINS WATSON, SUZIE A,** The Johns Hopkins Univ, Baltimore, MD; SR; MS; Hon Soc; Acdmc Hon; E J Becwith Cullen Awrd; R G Merrick Awrd; Amer Nrsng Assn 89-; Sntr J D Rockefeller IV Intrnshp 90-; RN 88-; BSN; AA Nrsng Hrfrd Comm Coll 86; Hlth Plcy Nrsng.

**BLEVINS, BETTY T,** Bristol Univ, Bristol, TN; SR; BS; Bus Admin; Bus Mgmt.

**BLEVINS, KIMBERLY A,** Memphis St Univ, Memphis, TN; JR; BA; Cath Org Histrn 88-; Gamma Beta Phi 89-; Lambda Pi Eta 90-; Flm/Video Prdctn.

**BLEVINS, MARSHALL G,** Univ Of Ky, Lexington, KY; SO; Clgns Acdmc Exclnc 90-; Phi Eta Sigma 89-90; Emrgng Ldrs Smnr 89-90; Frm Hse Frtrnty 90-; Gen Chmstry Awd 90; Chmstry; Med Dr.

**BLEVINS, PAMELA R,** Roane St Comm Coll, Harriman, TN; SO; BA; Dale Carnegie Impromptu Spkng Awd 87; Dale Carnegie Spcl Achvmnt Awd 87; Brushy Frk Assc Future Vsns Brnch Sec 90; Cert Oneida Area Vo Tech Schl 83; Elgblty Spec I 79-80; Home Aide 77-78; Comp/Lab Tech 83-87; Tech Svc Mgr 87-89; Scndry Ed/English; Tchng.

**BLEVINS, SHERRY L,** Univ Of Nc At Greensboro, Greensboro, NC; SR; BM; Coll Music Ed Ntl Conf VP 88-; Mu Phi Epsilon P 88-; U Wmns Choir 89-; U Marshal 88-89; Alpha Lambda Delta 88-; Outstndng Coll Music Edctr Mem 90-; Music Ed; Pblc Schl Chrl Dir.

**BLEVINS, STEPHEN S,** Univ Of Md Baltimore Prof Schl, Baltimore, MD; GD; PHD; Grad Stu Assoc Pres 89-; Alumni Assoc 80-; Sci Soc 80-; Ntl Hnr Soc 74; Rsrch Flw Cario Plmnry Clncl Rsrch Lab 8-; BS 78; RRT 82; Phslgy; Educ Rsrch.

**BLEVINS, SUSAN R,** Ashland Comm Coll, Ashland, KY; SO; MBA; Educ.

**BLEVINS, TAMMY L,** Univ Of Akron, Akron, OH; SO; BA; Stdy Budy Pgrm Tutoring 89-; Math/Scndry Educ; Tch.

**BLEVINS, TAMMY M,** Univ Of Cin R Walters Coll, Blue Ash, OH; SO; AD; Comp Comm 90-; CST Assoc Srgcl Technlgsts 85; Nrsng.

**BLEWS, PATRICIA G,** Fl International Univ, Miami, FL; GD; Phi Soc 60-61; Phi Kappa Phi 90; Tch Dade Cty Pub Schls 84-; BS F I U 78; MS F I U 90; Ele Educ; Tch.

**BLIAMIS, CHRISTOS,** Hellenic Coll/Holy Cross, Brookline, MA; FR; BA; Ski Club Racing Dir 88-; Chess Soc 87-; Bsktbl Tm ARIS 86-; Blood Donor Soc Purple Hrt Awd 88; Police Chf Assoc Awd 89; Phtgrphy Club Awd 88; Folk Dance Assoc 86-90; Annunciation Cathedral Cnslr 87-; Rel; Byzoutive Arch.

**BLICK, GREGORY D,** Schenectady County Comm Coll, Schenectady, NY; SR; AA; Lib Arts.

**BLIDY, KRISTY R,** S U N Y Coll At Fredonia, Fredonia, NY; JR; BS; Ed Club WCVF Clg Radio/Yrbk Phtghr/Festival Chorus 89-90; Fredonia Hamburg Tchng Intshp; Elem Ed; Tchng.

**BLISH, LAURA C,** Union Coll, Barbourville, KY; SR; BS; Clg Sngrs 87-89; Iota Sigma Nu 88-; Top 12 Womn Camps 89; Bio; Optmtry/O D.

**BLISSMAN, STEPHANIE L,** Westminster Coll, New Wilmingtn, PA; SR; BA; Intrntl Cltrs Clb Pres; Pi Delta Phi Vp; Pi Sigma Pi; Slf Stdy Prog; Frnch.

**BLITZ, BRENDA M,** Bowie St Univ, Bowie, MD; SR; BS; Ed Clb 88-; CEC 90-; Deans Lst 88-; Chrst Mclff Awrd; Erly Chldhd Spcl Ed.

**BLIVEN, JENNIFER A,** Elms Coll, Chicopee, MA; SO; BA; Paralegal; Law.

**BLIZINSKI, MICHAEL A,** Hudson Valley Comm Coll, Troy, NY; FR; AS; U S Mar Crps Hon Dis 84-86; Humn Svcs; Alchlsm Cnslr.

**BLOCH, HOWARD D,** Fl Atlantic Univ, Boca Raton, FL; SR; BS; Bus.

**BLOCH, PHILIP L,** Juniata Coll, Huntingdon, PA; SO; BA; Pa Prison Soc 90-; War Reg League; Comm Contrbtn Awd 90; AA Elec Inst 77; Poli Soc.

**BLOCK, ALISA K,** Univ Of Miami, Coral Gables, FL; GD; MARCH; AIAS 89-; Schlrshp Vlgrs Local Hstrc Prsrvtn Grp 90; BA Un Ml 87; Archtr.

**BLOCK, ELISABETH N,** Lesley Coll, Cambridge, MA; JR; BED; Cls Ofcr Pblcty 88-90; Hl VP 90-; Co Ed Yrbk; Emerald Key 90-; England Intrshp; Elem Ed/Spec Ed; Tchr.

**BLOCK, JULIE W,** Beaver Coll, Glenside, PA; GD; MED; Mktg Clb Amer Univ Pres 87-88; Vol Elem Schl; Dun/Bradstreet 87-88; BA Mktng Amer Univ 88; Elem Educ; Elem Tchr.

**BLOCK, KAREN M,** Emerson Coll, Boston, MA; FR; BS; Stdnts Offrng Srvc Pres 90-; Drmtc Prdtcn 90-; Bllt Tchr; SOS 90-; Rcylng Prgms 90-; Cncr Scty 90; Deans Lst 90-; Gen Thtr; Actng Drctng.

**BLOCK, LAUREL H,** William Paterson Coll, Wayne, NJ; SR; BA; Kappa Delta Pi Histrn 90-; Alumni Schlrshp 90-; Gender Eqty 90; Rmsn Conf Prsntn; Crrclm Evltn Comm 89-; Affmtv Actn Comm 90-; Ed/Poly Sci; Crrclm Dsgn Cnslng.

**BLOCKER, HAROLD D,** Univ Of Sc At Columbia, Columbia, SC; JR; BA; Stdnt Govt Senator 89-90; Gamma Beta Phi 89-; High Hnrs 90; Deans Lst 88-; Presidents Lst 90; SC Emplymnt Sec Commssn; US Postal Serv 89-90; AA 90; Intrdscplnry Stds/Ed Psychlgy; Scl Wrk.

**BLOECHER, CHRISTA M,** Univ Of Sc At Spartanburg, Spartanburg, SC; FR; BS; Fncl Anlyst.

**BLOECKER, BARBARA A,** Mount Saint Mary Coll, Newburgh, NY; SR; BA; Alpha Chi 90-; Lrng Asst Wappngrs Cntrl Schl Dist 83-88; AA Dutchess Comm Coll 89; Scl Sci; Tchr.

**BLOESCH, CHRISTINE L,** Immaculata Coll, Immaculata, PA; SR; BA; Stdnt Gove Class Treas 87-; Cmps Mnstry Exec Comm 87-; NAA Delco Pres 87-; Coll Hnr Soc 89-; Kappa Gamma Pi 90-; Sftbl 87-89; Acctg.

**BLOMER, ANN M,** Northern Ky Univ, Highland Hts, KY; SR; BS; Amer Mktg Assn Pres 90-; E Seton Schlrshp Coll Mt St Joseph 87; Sis Chrty Schlrshp CMSJ 87; Deans Lst 89-90; CMSJ Vlybl 87-89; Mktg/Ecnmcs; Advrtsng.

**BLOMQUIST, JOHN H,** Salem-Teikyo Univ, Salem, WV; FR; BA; Hmncs Stu Assoc Chrmn Finances 90-; Nwspr Edtr 90-; Drm Cncl Rep 90-; Gamma Beta Phi Tres; Alpha Phi Omega Tres; Bus Mgt; Sys Anlyst.

**BLONDEL, ALEXANDRA M,** Fl St Univ, Tallahassee, FL; SO; BA; Phi Eta Sigma 90-; Engl; Law.

**BLOOD, ANDREA M,** Fl St Univ, Tallahassee, FL; JR; BA; Stdnt Activ Bd Sec Int Affrs 88-90; Phi Theta Kappa 88-; Ingrid Johnson Rachesky M D Awd 89; AA Gulf Coast Comm Clg 90; Biol; Optometry.

**BLOOD, JASON N,** S U N Y Coll At Fredonia, Fredonia, NY; JR; BSSS; Boy Scouts Amer Jr Asst 87-88; Natl Eagle Scout Assn 88-91; Ordr Arrow Treas 87-88; Alpha Psi Omega; Eagle Scout88-; Tech Theatre; Tech Dir.

**BLOOD, MATTHEW G,** S U N Y Coll Of Tech At Alfred, Alfred, NY; SR; AAS; Capt Cncl 89-90; Wrstlng Regn I Champ 88-90; Lndscp Desgn Nrsry Mgmt.

**BLOODWORTH, BYRON C,** Clark Atlanta Univ, Atlanta, GA; BA; Ftbl 86-90; BA Phys Educ 90; Phys Educ Tchr.

**BLOODWORTH, DAVID A,** Memphis St Univ, Memphis, TN; SR; BA; Bptst Union; Gldn Key; TV Intrn; Early Schlrs Schlrshp; Cmnctns; TV/FILM.

**BLOODWORTH, DONNA M,** Fl St Univ, Tallahassee, FL; JR; BED; Mrchg Chiefs Brd 89-90; Kappa Delta Pi 90-; Delta Zeta Crtsy Chrmn 88-; Educ; Tchg.

**BLOOM, ADA M,** Oh St Univ At Marion, Marion, OH; SR; BA; Griffin Soc; Psych Clb; Alpha Lambda Delta; Phi Eta Sigma; Mrtr Brd; Gldn Key; Phi Kappa Phi; Phoenix; Otstndg Stu Yr 90; Mothers Clb Tres VP-P; PTO; Mbr UCC Chrch; AA 89; Psychlgy.

**BLOOM, BROOKE J,** Cornell Univ Statutory College, Ithaca, NY; JR; BS; Grk Lttrs Mag Chf Phtgrphy Edtr 88-; Genetic Rsrch 90-; Ho Nun De Kah; Dean Lst; Alpha Phi Hse Clrk 88-; Hughes Schlrs Prog; 1st Wmn Vrsty Men Crew Tm 88-; Biol; Med.

**BLOOM, DAMARIS R,** Inter Amer Univ Pr Hato Rey, Hato Rey, PR; FR; BA; Blgy Sci.

**BLOOM, GREGG P,** Univ Of Miami, Coral Gables, FL; SO; BBA; Entrpshp Club 90-; Alpha Lamdba Delta 89-; Sigma Phi Espilon Ctrl 89-; Acttng; Busn.

**BLOOMER, LAURA A,** Becker Coll At Leicester, Leicester, MA; SR; AS; PETA ASPCA NWF WWF 88-; Phi Theta Kappa 89-; Subject Specific Tutoring 89-; Animal Care; Animal Psy.

**BLOOMFIELD, MARCY S,** Oh Northern Univ, Ada, OH; FR; BA; Pblc Rltns Stdnt Soc Amer 90-; Alpha Vi Delta 90-; 3H Nrthrn Bear Ambass; Pblc Rltns.

**BLOOMFIELD-SABLJAK, RENEE B,** Fl International Univ, Miami, FL; JR; BA; FEA 87-89; CEC; AA Miami Dade Comm Coll 88; Spcl Edn/Lrng Disabilites; Masters.

**BLOOMINGDALE, LAURA A,** Radford Univ, Radford, VA; SR; BED; Council For Excptnl Chldrn 86-; Stndt Ed Assoc 86-; Deans List; Bed; Special Early Education; Teaching.

**BLOSE, DOUGLAS A,** Villanova Univ, Villanova, PA; FR; BA; Bnd 90-; Mscl Thtr 90-; Hons Pgm 90-; IM Sprts 90-; Math Ed; Tchng.

**BLOSS, EDWARD D,** Elmira Coll, Elmira, NY; SR; BS; LISP 89-; Hnrs Schlr Prog; ASHA 90-; Spch And Hrng; Tchr.

**BLOUIN, CAROL A,** Saint Josephs Coll, Windham, ME; SR; BS; Currier Bus Soc 87-90; Stdnt Govt Treas 88-89; Superkids 89; IM 87-90; New Englnd Soc CPAS Schlrshp 90; Bus Admin/ Acctng; Pub Accntnt.

**BLOUNT, DAVID R,** Univ Of Al At Birmingham, Birmingham, AL; JR; BS; Pre Law Scty 90-; Delta Chi 87-; Criminal Justice; Law.

**BLOYD, MELISSA M,** Villanova Univ, Villanova, PA; SO; BA; Blue Ky Chrmn 90-; Hs Coun Wing Rep 89-90; Panhellanic Coun 90; Gamma Phi; Phi Kappa Phi; Alpha Phi Cls Pres 90-; Tutors; Dns Lst; IM Scr; Mngmnt/Bus Admin; Law.

**BLUBAUGH, DONNA L,** Kent St Univ Kent Cmps, Kent, OH; SO; Prgrsv Stdnt Ntwrk 89-; Amnsty Intrntnl Sec 89-; Schema Jrnl Maj Edtr 89-; Englsh; Phlsphy; Clg Tchng.

**BLUCK, SAMANTHA R,** Muskingum Coll, New Concord, OH; FR; Center Brd; Chamber Singer; Muskingum Choir; Dvlpmnt Phonathoner 90-; Lambda Sigma; Chi Alpha Nu: Sigma Alpha Iota Sec; English & Lrng Disabilities; Teacher.

**BLUE, GAYLE C,** Jackson St Univ, Jackson, MS; JR; BA; Bahai Faith Clb V P 88-; Hon Clg 88-; Miss Sta Atty Gen Off Intrn; Crmnl Juste; Instr/Rsrch.

**BLUE, KELLY S,** Wake Forest Univ, Winston-Salem, NC; FR; Nwspr 90-; Env Clb 90-; Dns Lst 90; Spirit Grp 90-; Comm.

**BLUETHGEN, JANE M,** S U N Y Coll Of Tech At Frmgdl, Farmingdale, NY; JR; BS; Phi Theta Kappa 88-90; Crmnl Justice 90; Forensic Sci.

**BLUM, JEFFREY MICHAEL,** Univ Of Rochester, Rochester, NY; SR; BS; All Cmps Jdcl Coun Assoc Chf Just 89-; Res Advsr 89-; Stdnt Lf Comm 88-90; IEEE; Phi Beta Kappa 90-; Tau Beta Pi; Tau Kappa Epsilon VP 88-; Univ Rchstr Wrstlng Clb; Seth H Harriet S Terry Prize; Genl Mtrs Schlr Smr Intrnshps 89-; Elec Eng; Law/Eng.

**BLUM, MELANIE JO,** Teikyo Post Univ, Waterbury, CT; GD; Adult Prob/Judicial Intrn 90-; G Fox/Co Sls Intrn 89-90; BS 90; AS Mattatuck Comm Coll 90-; Gen Stds; Socl Wrk/Crmnl Jstc.

**BLUME, CAROL A,** Univ Of Fl, Gainesville, FL; JR; BS; Delta Phi Epsilon Alumni Chrmn 88-; Gldn Ky 89-; Phi Eta Sigma 88-; Dns Lst 89-90; Alpha Lambda Delta 88-; Florence Dewey White Fndtn Schlrshp; Fin; Econ Fin.

**BLUME, HEATHER H,** Univ Of North Fl, Jacksonville, FL; BFA; Jcksnvll Cltn Vsl Arts 87-; Phi Kappa Phi 90-; Heritage Foundation Tile Making Schrl; Haystack School Of The Arts Asst; FA Flklf Prgms; Hrtg Fdtn Arts Mn; Arts Assmbly; AA FL Cmmnty Coll 89; Fine Art Pntng; MFA Crmc Tile.

**BLUME, VICKI L,** Atlantic Comm Coll, Mays Landing, NJ; SO; AAS; Casino Dealr Sprvsr Atlantic City Casinos 80-; Nrsng; Midwife.

**BLUMENFELD, ELISA B,** Yeshiva Univ, New York, NY; GD; Bus Socty VP 89; Yrbk Bus Edtr; Sy Syms Schl Of Bus Srvc Awd; IM Bsktbl; Mktg.

**BLUNDETTO, SANDRA G,** Ny Law School, New York, NY; GD; Law Rvw Nts/Cmnts Edtr 90-; Sumr Assc Leboeuf Lamb Leiby Mau Rae 90-; BBA Clg Ins 88; Law JD; JD Atty.

**BLUNT, TERRA,** Abraham Baldwin Agri Coll, Tifton, GA; FR; BSN; Chrs 90; Task Frce; Phi Theta Kappa 90-; Pres Lst; Nrsng.

**BLUVOL, IGAL,** American International Coll, Springfield, MA; JR; Poli Sci Org Pres 88-; Pnhlnc Cncl Pres 88-; Mdl Cngrs Asst Head 88-; Gldn Key 90-; Almni Asc 90-; Std Scrty Capt 88-90; Phi Zeta Epsln Pres 88-; Soccer 88-; Hstry/Poli Sci; Law.**

**BLY, LISA M,** Portland School Of Art, Portland, ME; JR; BA; Grphcs; Grphc Dsgnr.

**BLYTH, JAMES D,** Barry Univ, Miami, FL; GD; BA; Assctd Stdnt Bdy Hghlne Coll VP 70; Theta Chi Pldge Pres 71; Stdnt Bdy Mn Of Yr 70f; Cty Of Nrth Ple AK Myr 83; Pres Sfd Shpprs Inc 90-; AA Highline Coll 70; Bus.

**BLYTHE, JONATHAN M,** Western Piedmont Comm Coll, Morganton, NC; FR; Tool Mkr Apprntc; Machnst; Elec Tech.

**BOAL, SHANE G,** Oh St Univ At Newark, Newark, OH; FR; BS; Sci; Medicine.

**BOALS, JON R,** Univ Of Cincinnati, Cincinnati, OH; SO; BS; IEEE 90-; Coll Applied Sci Assoc Grad Yr; ASEET; Sci; Elec Eng.

**BOAN, DARRELL E,** Coll Of Charleston, Charleston, SC; SO; BA; Pre Law Soc 90-; Mgmt; Law.

**BOAN, DEBBIE B,** Coker Coll, Hartsville, SC; SO; BED; SS Tchr 88; Yth Choir Dir 90; Jr High Tchrs Aide 88; Elem Ed; Tchr.

**BOAN, JIMMY WAYNE,** Spartanburg Methodist Coll, Spartanburg, SC; FR; Scuba Clb; Bapt Stdnt Union; Phi Theta Kappa; Stdnt Aid On Campus; Biology; Med Dr/Engr.

**BOARD, CHRISTINA L,** Northern Ky Univ, Highland Hts, KY; GD; Theta Phi Alpha 81-; BA 86; Scndry Educ/Engl; Tchng.

**BOARD JR, DANIEL L,** Bridgewater Coll, Bridgewater, VA; JR; BS; Res Hl Cncl Pres 90-; Pres Hl 90-; Stdnt Sen; IM Athltcs 89-; Bio; Med.

**BOARMAN, HEATHER L,** Anne Arundel Comm Coll, Arnold, MD; FR; AA; Bus Pblc Admin.

**BOATEN, AFUA S,** Bennett Coll, Greensboro, NC; FR; BSC; Blgy Clb 90-; Intl Stdnts Assn 90-; Pre-Med; Med.

**BOATMAN, ROBIN LYNN,** Middle Tn St Univ, Murfreesboro, TN; JR; BSN; Stdnt Nrs Assn; Natl Hon Roll 88; Deans List 90; Nrs Extern Parkview Hosp; Nrsng; Nrsng Prctnr.

**BOATNER, AUBREY K,** Chattahoochee Vly St Comm Coll, Phenix City, AL; SO; Bsbl 89-; Acctng.

**BOATRIGHT, LESLIE JOSEPH,** Fl St Univ, Tallahassee, FL; JR; BS; Phi Theta Kappa 88-89; Math Awd Lk Cty Comm Clg 90; AA N FL Jr Clg 90; Engr; Space Prog.

**BOATWRIGHT, CHARITY D,** Ms St Univ, Miss State, MS; JR; BFA; Yrbk Sctn Ed Reveille 90-; IM Offcl 88-; Gamma Beta Phi 90-; Summer Co-Op W/Walt Disney World; Art/Graphic Dsgn; Professor.

**BOATWRIGHT, DONNA F,** Ms St Univ, Miss State, MS; SO; BA; Kappa Delta 89-90; Deans Lst 90-; Cmnctns; Rep/Pblc Rltns Mjr Corp.

**BOATWRIGHT, JUANITA,** Al A & M Univ, Normal, AL; SR; MA; Delta Sigma Theta Pres 89-90; Sigma Tau Delta 89-; Cmps Ldr Awd 89-90; NCTE Engl Tchrs 88-90; Dns Lst 86-90; NCAA Dvi II All Amer 88-90; Trck/Fld/Crs Cntry Capt 86-90; BS Engl; BS Soclgy; Engl; Supt Of Schs.

**BOATWRIGHT, MARNEY B,** Univ Of Sc At Coastal Carolina, Conway, SC; JR; BA; Marion Baptist Church Yth Ldr 86-90; GA Dir 89-; Chldrns Church Ldr 90-; Elem Educ; Tch For Blind.

**BOATWRIGHT, ROGER D,** Univ Of Sc At Columbia, Columbia, SC; FR; BS; Mrchng Bnd 90-; Blgy; Medcl.

**BOBB, DONNA I J,** Fl Atlantic Univ, Boca Raton, FL; GD; MA; Phi Theta Kappa; Admn Asst 90-; BA; Lang & Ling; Teach French German Spanish.

**BOBB, JEREMY A,** Fort Valley St Coll, Fort Valley, GA; SO; DVM; Sci Clb Rep 89-; Vet Sci Clb Rep 89-; MANRRS Treas 90-; Coll Deans Lst 89; Hon Convocation 90-; Pre-Vet Med; Vetrnrn.

**BOBBIN, DAVID E,** Me Maritime Academy, Castine, ME; FR; AD; Drama Clb Stage Engr 90-; U S Power Squadron Pilot 89-; Charter Mngmnt; Marina Mngmnt.

**BOBBITT, DONNA G,** Longwood Coll, Farmville, VA; JR; BS; Acctg Assn VP 90-; Acctg/MIS Dept-Stdnt Advsry Bd 90-; Alpha Lambda Delta 89-; Phi Kappa Phi; Phi Beta Lambda VP 88-; Alpha Delta Pi Treas 89-; VITA; Zukerman/Assoc Ltd Intrnshp; Acctg.

**BOBBITT, LORI L,** Ms St Univ, Miss State, MS; SO; BS; Sci Clb; Cncrt Chr; Phi Theta Kappa; Gamma Beta Phi; 1000 Petals Lace Schlrshp; Mdcl Tchnlgy.

**BOBBITT, MELINDA A,** Vanderbilt Univ, Nashville, TN; FR; BA; Phi Eta Sigma; Alpha Chi Omega; Acctg Intern Worthen Bnkng Corp Little Rock AR; Math.

**BOBER, NATALIE,** Atlantic Comm Coll, Mays Landing, NJ; FR; BA; Bio; Nrsg.

**BOBES, STEVEN M,** Fl International Univ, Miami, FL; GD; MPA; Pblc Admn Scty Sec/Tres 90; Intr Orgnztn Cmt 90-; Phi Kappa Phi 90; BA 90; Am Scty Pblc Admn; S FL Chptr Am Scty Pblc Admn; AA Miami Dade Comm Clg 78; Pblc Admn; Govt/ Law.

**BOBILLO, BEN M,** Saint Thomas Univ, Miami, FL; SR; BA; Pol Sci Clb; Natl Hon Soc; Delta Nu Alpha Dir 87; Good Conduct Metal U S Army 85; Lottery Dist Sls Mgr 90-; AA Miami Dade Cmnty Clg 82; Pol Sci; Law.

**BOBIS, ALLISON T,** Cornell Univ Statutory College, Ithaca, NY; SO; Pi Beta Phi Asst Rush Chrmn Elect.

**BOBISH, RANDY D,** Univ Of Miami, Coral Gables, FL; FR; BFA; Juggling Clb 90; Alpha Lambda Delta; Theatre Arts League Schlrshp; Musical Theatre; Film/Television.

**BOBKO, LISA A,** Longwood Coll, Farmville, VA; JR; BA; Advsry Comm Econ Dpt Chr; Intrnshp Fr Smll Bus Ctr; Alpha Sigma Alpha Vp; Grk Srvc Awd 90; Econ; Law.

**BOBO, BARBARA A,** Univ Of Sc At Union, Union, SC; FR; BS; SGA Frsh VP 90-; Tchr Yr Com; Jr Rtrn; Chemistry; Pharmacy.

**BOBO, MELISSA G,** Lexington Comm Coll, Lexington, KY; SO; BS; Delta Delta Delta 89-; Nrsng; RN.

**BOBO, MICHAEL L,** Univ Of Tn At Memphis, Memphis, TN; GD; DDS; Alumni Cncl 89-90; ASDA 90-; IADR; Phi Eta Sigma 87-90; Beta Beta Beta 89-90; Hons Seminar 87-90; Mu Epsilon Delta 87-89; Kappa Alpha Order Sec 88-90; Cir K Sec 87-90; Dens Lst 87-; Bio Lab TA 89-90; Dentistry.

**BOBOLSKY, LINDA M,** Mount Aloysius Jr Coll, Cresson, PA; SO; Med Assist Club Pres 90-; Ward 2 Election Portage Judge 90-; Food Comm Chrprsn; AS; Med Assist.

**BOCCADUTRE, LISA M,** Trenton St Coll, Trenton, NJ; FR; BA; ASA 90-; Art Ed; Tchr.

**BOCCANERA, CONSTANCE A,** Niagara Univ, Niagara Univ, NY; JR; BS; Pol Sci Frm Pres 88-; Yrbk Stff Actvts Edit 89-; Phi Alpha Delta 90-; Cmps Mnstry 89-; Lw Frm Intrnshp 90; Intrnshp Cngrssmn J La Falce; Chrldr 88-; Pol Sci; Corp Law.**

**BOCCHINO JR, ROBERT L,** Harvard Univ, Cambridge, MA; FR; BA; Dudley Hse Orchstr 90-; Mixed Chr 90-; Fresh Urban Prog 90; Math.

**BOCCUTI, LINDA B,** Emory Univ, Atlanta, GA; GD; MN; Robert W Woodruff Fellow 90-; NAPNAP; DIP Mastin Schl Nursing 68; Cert FNP 81; FNP Pediatric Allergy/Plmnry Grady Mem Hosp 71-; Nursing/Clinical Hlth; Cns/Fnp Pediatrics.

**BOCCUTI, LISA M,** Kent St Univ Stark Cmps, North Canton, OH; SO; BS; Kent St Edn Assoc; Oh Edn Assoc; Sec 88-; Elem Edn.

**BOCHDAM, KRISTA J,** Columbia Greene Comm Coll, Hudson, NY; SO; AS; Phi Theta Kappa 90-; Alpha Chi Omega; Bus Admnstrn; Acctg.

**BOCHMAN, MICHAEL A,** Newbury Coll, Brookline, MA; SO; BS; Fnncl Sec Tres UAW Lcl 1113 90-; Cert 90; Bus/Cmptr Sci; Mngmnt.

**BOCK, ANTHONY J,** Savannah St Coll, Savannah, GA; SO; BS; Amer Soc Cvl Eng 90-; Optmst Clb Tybee Isl V P 90-; Cvl Eng Tech; P E Cvl Eng.

**BOCK, CHRISTINE K,** Longwood Coll, Farmville, VA; SO; BBA; Ambsdrf Delta Sigma Pi; Sigma Kappa Tres 90-; Bsns Admnstrtn Spnsh; Accntng.

**BOCK, WENDY J,** Westminster Coll, New Wilmingtn, PA; SR; BA; Panhellenic Cncl Treas 90-; Mortar Brd 90-; Omicron Delta Kappa 90-; Tau Pi Phi 89-; Phi Mu Panhellenic Cncl Rep 90-; Alpha Phi Omega 89-; Acctg; CPA.

**BOCKLET, R CARY,** Medical Univ Of Sc, Charleston, SC; GD; DMD; SGA Rep 90-; Amercn Stdnt Dntl Assoc Exec Cncl 88-; Stdnt Clincns Of Amercn Dntl Assoc 90-; Ceramic Engr Hon Soc 81-83; Psi Omega 89-; Kappa Sigma 81-; Summer Rsrch Intrnshp 89; Stdnt Clincn Award 90; BS Clemson U 83; Dentstry.

**BOCOCK, DEBORAH S,** Patrick Henry Comm Coll, Martinsville, VA; SO.

**BOCZAR, ANDREA M,** Saint Joseph Coll, West Hartford, CT; FR; BS; Blgy Clb 90-; Pals Clb 90-; Biology; Vet Mdcn.

**BODDEN, LYNN M,** Temple Univ, Philadelphia, PA; SO; Hsng Snt Sec 89-; Yrbk 90-; OAS Strng Cmt 89-; Psychlgy Hon Scty 90-; Alpha Lmbd Dlt 89-; Intlctrl Hert Scty 89-; Phi Sgm Pi 90-; Chrldng 89-90; Otstndng Achvmnt Schlrshp 89-; Pre Phys Thrpy/Psychlgy; Phys Thrpy.**

**BODDEN, STEPHEN S,** Univ Of Miami, Coral Gables, FL; JR; BA; Frnch Clb 88-; Hons Assn 89-F Golden Key 90-; Engl Hon Soc 90-; Frnch Hon Soc 90-; Myers/Alberga Legl Intrn 88-90; Goldsmith/Harris Fncl Anlyst Intrn 90-; J F Pearson Schlrshp 88-; Engl/Frch/Bus Admin; Law.

**BODE, MARGUERITE W,** William Carey Coll, Hattiesburg, MS; FR; BSN; Nursing.

**BODE, WILLIAM C,** S U N Y Coll Of Tech At Frmgdl, Farmingdale, NY; FR; AS; Crmnl Jstc.

**BODEEN, LAURA L,** Christian Brothers Univ, Memphis, TN; JR; BS; Gldn Key 87-; IRS; Math.**

**BODENSTEIN, KARYN R,** Fl Atlantic Univ, Boca Raton, FL; JR; BA; AA; Mgmt.

**BODIFORD, DONNA C,** Univ Of South Al, Mobile, AL; SO; BA; Spec Ed; Tch.

**BODIFORD, FELECIA B,** Univ Of Sc At Columbia, Columbia, SC; JR; BA; Psychlgy Clb 89-; Pacesetter Peer Cnslr Asst W/Frshmn Orien; Gamma Beta Phi 90-; Outstdng Psychlgy Stdnt 90; Pres Lst 90; Psychlgy; Clin Psychlgy.

**BODIFORD, JOSEPH C,** Fl St Univ, Tallahassee, FL; SR; BA; Deans Lst; Ntl Deans Lst; Phi Mu Alpha Sinfonia P; Music; Prof.

**BODIN, PATRICK F,** Univ Of South Al, Mobile, AL; SR; BA; Baptist Union 84-87; IM Ftbll/Bsktbll/Sftbll; Comptrllr 90-; Accntg.

**BODKIN, JAN FORD,** Univ Of Sc At Coastal Carolina, Conway, SC; JR; BA; Rtrning Stdnts Assn; Psi Chi; Deans Lst; Chncllrs Hon Roll 90-; Grl Scts Ldr 89-90; Ftr Telphn Pionrs Amer VP 73-88; Equip Engr Sthrn Bell 72-88; Psychlgy; Cnslng.

**BODKIN, JENNIFER M,** Radford Univ, Radford, VA; SO; BA; Phi Sgm Sgm Pldg Cls Sec; Cmnctns; Advrtsng.

**BODLE, DIANA M,** Ky Christian Coll, Grayson, KY; SO; BS; Educ; Tchng.

**BODNAR, CAROL L,** Duquesne Univ, Pittsburgh, PA; JR; BS; Am Pharmaceutical Assn; PA Pharmaceutical Assn; Phi Kappa Phi; Rho Chi; Thomas Drug Store Inc Intern 90-; Rho Chi Acad Achvmnt Awd 90; Schlrs Awd 88-; J W/Ruth Rhade Meml Schlrshp 90-; Outstndg Coll Stdnt Am Awd 90; IMS 88-89; Pharmacy.

**BODNAR, MARK S,** Univ Of Nc At Charlotte, Charlotte, NC; JR; BA; A J Fletcher Schlrshp; BS Blgy 85; Music; Teach/Envrnmntl Studies.

**BOEHM, CAROL A,** Barry Univ, Miami, FL; SO; BS; Hon Stdnt Assn Hstrn 89-; Res Hall Assn Pres 90-; Stdnt Ldrshp Comm 90-; Stdnt Dvlpmnt Cntr Comm; St Cathrnes Medl Nominee; Biolgy; Diagnstc Ultrsnd Tech.

**BOEHM, JANICE CASON,** Southeastern Coll Of Hlth Sci, N Miami Beach, FL; BS; Acad Stdnt Pharm 88-89; Gold Key 86-; Fresh Hon Soc 85-86; AA FL State U 88; Pharm.

**BOEHM, KURT W,** Duquesne Univ, Pittsburgh, PA; GD; MBA; Iron And Steel Scty 88-; Assoc Mtllrgcl Eng Armco AMC Btlr PA 89-; BS Met E Iowa St Univ 87; Bus; Eng Mgmt.

**BOEHM, LAURA A,** Barry Univ, Miami, FL; SR; BS; Hnr Stdnt Assoc Pres 87-; Ambassador Clb 87-89; Hnrs Prog Cncl 87-; Lambda Sigma Pres 88-; Delta Epsilon Sigma 89-; Kappa Delta Pi 88-; Campus Mnstry; Resident Advsr; Stdnt Tchng; Hnrs Prog; IM Sftbl Vlybl; Math; Educ.

**BOEHMKE, SUSAN SCHIFFMACHER,** Life Coll, Marietta, GA; GD; DC; Gnstd Clb 90-; Actvtr Clb 90-; Mtn Palpation Clb 90-; Jr Leag Buffalo 83-; Buffalo Philharmnc Wmns Comm80-; Amrcn Chrprctc Assn 90-; Inttntnl Chrprctc Assn 90-; BS Canisius Cllg 69; Chrprctc.

**BOEL, KATHRYN E,** Le Moyne Coll, Syracuse, NY; SO; BA; Jdcl Rvw Brd 89; Hstry Acdmy VP 90; Hall Cncl VP 90; Hstry; Law.

**BOENIG, DOREEN G,** Saint Josephs Coll Sufflk Cmps, Patchogue, NY; JR; BA; Dns Lst Suffolk Cmnty Clg 89-90; Phi Alpha Sigma 89-90; AA 90; Elem Ed/Spec Ed; Tchr.**

**BOERSMA, KAREN L,** S U N Y Coll At Fredonia, Fredonia, NY; JR; BS; Tchr Educ Clb; Hosp Tutor 90; Yth Otrch Bg Sr 88-89; Proj Intrn Chldrn Fndtn 89; BA Duke Univ 90; Elem Educ; Tchr.

**BOESE, LINDA S,** Kent St Univ Kent Cmps, Kent, OH; GD; Stdnt ALA 89-90; Lbry Schl Stdnt Assoc 89-90; Beta Phi Mu; Alpha Xi Delta Mbrshp Chr 59-61; PED 82-; Teacher 89; BS Ed Wittenberg Univ 61; MLS 90; Chldrns Lbrn.

**BOESE, SHARON R,** Hillsborough Comm Coll, Tampa, FL; SO; BA; Eclgy Clb Sec 90; AA; Cltrl Antplgst.

**BOESKY, THEODORE E,** Manhattanville Coll, Purchase, NY; FR; BA; Theatre 90; Tennis MVP; Tennis 90.

**BOFILL, JOSE C,** Fl International Univ, Miami, FL; GD; JD; Law Assn Act Chrmn 90-; Radisson Mart Plza Hotel Intrnshp Bar Capt 86-89; AA Miami Dade Comm Coll 84-88; Law.

**BOGAN, JARET L,** Morgan St Univ, Baltimore, MD; SR; BA; Art.

**BOGAN, WILLETTE,** Wilberforce Univ, Wilberforce, OH; SR; BA; Pre-Law Clb Scrty 89; Sigma Omega 90; Pol Sci; Law.

**BOGAR-WRAGA, BARBARA,** Castleton St Coll, Castleton, VT; JR; BS; Non Trad Stdnts Assn; AS 82; Psych; Guidance Cnslr.

**BOGARD, STARLA R,** Univ Of Tn At Martin, Martin, TN; GD; Psychlgy Clb 86-90; Cert/Rl Est; Psychlgy.

**BOGARD, THOMAS E,** Oh St Univ At Marion, Marion, OH; JR; BA; Envrnmntl Grp Pres 90-; Griffen Hnr Soc 90-; OH Air Ntl Grd Sarg 85-; Educ; Sci/Math Tchr.

**BOGAS, EKATERINI,** Saint Andrews Presbytrn Coll, Laurinburg, NC; JR; BS; CHAOS 90-; Alpha Chi; Natl Hnr Scty; Intern NASA; Gnrl Hnrs Pgm 88-90; Bsktbl 88; Chem; Rsrch.

**BOGDANOWICZ, LAURA A,** Hudson Valley Comm Coll, Troy, NY; SR; AAS; Exec Offce Asst; Comp Info Systms.

**BOGDON, MICHELE A,** Univ Of Miami, Coral Gables, FL; SR; MS; Engr Advsry Bd; Natl Soc Arch Engrs 89-; Amer Soc Cvl Engrs Treas 90-; Phi Alpha Epsilon; Chi Epsilon; BS Arch Engr; BS Cvl Engr; Arch Engr-Bldg Syst.

**BOGEN, JOCELYN D,** Clark Atlanta Univ, Atlanta, GA; JR; BA; Soc Of Amer 89-; Alpha Kappa Mu; Lyndon B Johnson Presdntl Congrsnl Award 90; Intrnshp Congrsmn Benjamin Cardin 90; Mass Media/Publc Rltns; Ed.

**BOGER, CINDY D,** Converse Coll, Spartanburg, SC; SR; BA; NAA V P 88; Cmptr Sci/Math Clb V P 88-; Tutor 89-; Deans Lst 88-; Lee Broome Mac Bay Luttrell Intrn 90-; Peat Marwick Intrn; Vybl 87-90; Acctg/Cmptr Sci; Acctg.

**BOGER, SUSAN R,** Kent St Univ Kent Cmps, Kent, OH; SO; Phi Epsilon Kappa 90-; X-Cntry Rning 89-90; Phys Ed; Tchr.

**BOGER, SUSAN R,** Kent St Univ Kent Cmps, Kent, OH; SO; PERD; Crs Cnty Rnng 89-; Phi Epsln Kappa 90-; Physcl Ed; PE Tchr.

**BOGERT, BETHANY A,** Elmira Coll, Elmira, NY; FR; BA; Valdctrn Schlrshp 90-; IM Sftbl; Engl; Educ/Sec Tchr.

**BOGERT, LEE ANN,** Elmira Coll, Elmira, NY; FR; BA; Elem Educ; Spec Educ Tchr.

**BOGERT, SUSANNE J,** Georgian Court Coll, Lakewood, NJ; FR; Acctg/Bus; Actnt.

**BOGGAN, JANET L,** Memphis St Univ, Memphis, TN; SR; BBA; Acctng.

**BOGGESS, KEVIN L,** Union Univ, Jackson, TN; JR; BA; Psychology; Cnslng.

**BOGGESS, RUTH ANNE,** Liberty Univ, Lynchburg, VA; SR; BA; Jr Vars Chrldr 89-90; Prayer Ldr 90-; Asst Secr Athl Dir 90-; Psych; Cnslg.

**BOGGIONI, NICHOLAS A,** Univ Of Toledo, Toledo, OH; GD; JD; Teaching Assist 72-74; Rsrch Assist 75-76; Flwshp 77-78; BA MA U Of NV 72-74; MBA Claremont Grad Schl 83; Law.

**BOGGS, ANGELA A,** Wv Northern Comm Coll, Wheeling, WV; SO; MBA; Engl; Educ.

**BOGGS, ANITA L,** Univ Of Akron, Akron, OH; SR; BS; Lake Elem Vol; PTO Brd Mbr; Brwn Asst Ldr; Sndy Schl Tchr; Bvrg Store Ownr; Tchr Asst/Rdng Tutor; Elem/Spec Ed; MA Spec Ed.

**BOGGS, ERIC M,** Fl Atlantic Univ, Boca Raton, FL; SR; BBA; Alpha Omega Club Pres 89-90; Clg Repblns 88; Hnr Grad 88; Natl Assoc Reltrs; Intl Assoc Corp Real Estate Exec 90-; Profl Real Estate Appraiser 83-; AA Palm Beach Comm Clg 88; Busn Admin; Law.

**BOGGS, LEE J,** Indiana Univ Of Pa, Indiana, PA; SO; BS; Marchng Bnd 89-90; Symph Bnd 90-; Kappa Delta Pi; Phi Mu Alpha Suifonia 90-; Elem Tchr.

**BOGGS, SANDRA K,** Union Coll, Barbourville, KY; FR; BA; Sngrs 90-; Brss Ensmbl 90-; Jz/Pep Bnds 90-; KY All-Collgt Chorus 90-; Dir Music Un Mthdst Chrch; Chrch Music/Rlgn; Music Mnstry.

**BOGGS, THERESA A,** Lexington Comm Coll, Lexington, KY; SO; BA; Med; Radiography.

**BOGGS, WESLEY K,** Miami Chrisitian Coll, Miami, FL; SR; BA; Spiritual Life Chrmn 89; Biblcl Studies/Elem Ed; Tchr.

**BOGLE, DEBORAH A,** Jefferson Comm Coll, Louisville, KY; SO; BBA; Stdnt Sprt Serv Prog Tutor 89-; Talent Rstr Otsdng Mnrity Cmuty Clg Grad; AA; Mktg; Mktg Firm.

**BOGRAD, CARLA B,** Hillsborough Comm Coll, Tampa, FL; SO; AA; SG Sgt At Arms 90-; Eco Clb 90- Scholastic Success Club 90-; Phi Theta Kappa; SSC; Elem Educ.

**BOGUSZ, SCOTT A,** Allegheny Coll, Meadville, PA; JR; BA; Liaisons Leaders Edctnl Spprt; Alden Sclr 88-90; Frank Wilbur Main Schlrshp; Intrnshp A G Edwards Invstmnt Bnkng; Bsbl 88-89; Ecnmcs; Bsns Invstmnt Bnkng.

**BOHACH, CHRISTOPHER J,** Oh Coll Of Podiatric Med, Cleveland, OH; JR; DPM; OPMSA Clin Affrs Dir 90-; Cls V P 89-; Pi Delta V P; Natl Mrt Schlrshp 89; BS Heidlbrg Clg 88; Pod Med.

**BOHANNA JR, JOHN H,** Atlantic Comm Coll, Mays Landing, NJ; SO; AS; ACC; ACC; Englsh Lit; Tchr BA.

**BOHANNAN, THOMAS P,** Memphis St Univ, Memphis, TN; JR; BS; Natl Assoc Emerg Mgrs; Emerg Mgmt Assoc TN; Fire Admin/Protctn Tech; Emerg Mgmnt

**BOHANNON, ALISON H,** Univ Of Southern Ms, Hattiesburg, MS; JR; BA; Phi Mu Sorority; Alumni Assn Sec; Newman Club; Speech Cmnctn Assn; Sigma Nu Aux; Chorale; Jazz Singers; Phi Mu; Dns Lst; Panhellenic Tlnt Award; Speech Cmnctn; Pblc Rltns.

**BOHANNON JR, JOHN R,** Old Dominion Univ, Norfolk, VA; SR; SME 90-; SAE 89-; Dsgn Chllng 90; SAE Ntrl Gas Vhcl Chllng Norman OK; AAS Gen Eng Cntrl VA Cmnty Clg Cum Laude 88; Cert Mchn Tl Cntrl VA Cmnty Clg Cum Laude 87; Cert CAD Cntrl VA Cmnty Clg 88; Eng.

**BOHANON, LISA M,** Tn St Univ, Nashville, TN; SR; BS; Hnrs Pgm; Pr Cnslr 87-88; SWE 90-; Alpha Kappa Mu 89-; Eta Kappa Nu; Alpha Lambda Delta 87-; Alpha Kappa Alpha Philctr 89-90; Otstdng Hnrs Awd; GM Intrnshp 87-88; Tex Instrmnts Co Op 89-; Elec Eng.

**BOHLING, MATTHEW,** Univ Of Sc At Columbia, Columbia, SC; SO; BA; Crusade Christ VP 90-; Hons Prog 89-; Phi Eta Sigma 90-; Marine Bio; Frshwtr Fshrs Biolgst.

**BOHLMANN, RACHELLE L,** Kent St Univ Kent Cmps, Kent, OH; JR; Golden Key; Alpha Epsilon Pi; Pres Lst 90; Deans Lst 90-; Psych.

**BOHMANN, DAVID S,** Bridgeport Engr Inst, Fairfield, CT; FR; ASEE; Cert C T Sch Electrncs 89; ACET Intl Soc Cert Electrncs Tech 89; Electrical; Engr.

**BOHN, JENNIFER S,** Georgian Court Coll, Lakewood, NJ; SO; Bus Clb 90-; Acctg; CPA.

**BOHN, MATTHEW PHILIP,** Univ Of Sc At Columbia, Columbia, SC, SO, BA, Rsdnc Hll Govt Sen 90 ; Rsdnc Hll Assoc 90-; Hll Dsk Asst 90-; Hstry.

**BOHNING, LORI A,** Nova Univ, Ft Lauderdale, FL; GD; MBA; BA Sttetson Univ 87; Bus Admn; Corp Mgt.

**BOHR, LARA E,** Univ Of Louisville, Louisville, KY; SR; BS; SWE VP 90-; ACM Tres 88-90; GE Applncs Co-Op Comm/Spec Proj/Soc Chair 90; KY Soc Of Prof Engrs Axlry Schlrshp; GE Applnc Co-Op Intern 90-; Engr Math/Cmptr Engr.

**BOHRER, SUZANNE M,** Hudson Valley Comm Coll, Troy, NY; SR; AAS; Nrsg.

**BOHUSCH, THERESE A,** Philadelphia Coll Pharm & Sci, Philadelphia, PA; SR; BSMPT; Physcl Thrpy Clb 87; Intrfrat Cncl 88; Alpha Lambda Delta Sec 88-89; Lambda Kappa Sigma Pres 90; Ruth Davies Flaherty Serv Awd; Physcl Thrpy; Physcl Thrpst.

**BOIANO, DANIEL M,** Univ Of Ct, Storrs, CT; SR; SGA 87-88; Frstry/Wldlf Clb 90-; Otdrs Clb 90-; A S Farwell Schlrshp Awd 87-88; A Wadsworth/H Clarke Meserve Memrl Trst Fnd Awd 88; Bsktbll Plyr 86-88; Envrnmntl Tech 88-89; Envronmntl Mgmt; Rsrcs Mgmt.

**BOISCLAIR, MICHAEL N,** Bunker Hill Comm Coll, Boston, MA; FR; BA; Chess Clb 90-; Musician Drums; Anml Sci; Vet.

**BOISROND, PIERRE D,** Nova Univ, Ft Lauderdale, FL; SO; BS; Intl Stdnts Assn Pres 89-; Blk Stdnts Assn 89-; Schlr Awd 90-; Cert Mrt Clb Ofcr 89-90; Hon Awd Schlrshp; Rtrd Prfsnl Schlrshp 89-; Inst Elctrncs Elect Engr Soc 90-; Cmptr Engr.

**BOISSE, MARC A,** Andover Coll, Portland, ME; JR; Biddeford Racers VP 90-; Hmg Pigeon Racing Club Delegate 89-90; Hill Haven Corp; Acttng; Admint.

**BOISSONNEAULT, FAY ANNE,** Elms Coll, Chicopee, MA; JR; Stdnt Ambssdr 88; Deans Lst 88-; Brwnie Ldr 90-; Elms Clg Schlrshp; Elem Educ; Tchng.

**BOISSONNEAULT, KATHLEEN ROSE,** Elms Coll, Chicopee, MA; JR; BA; Phi Alpha Theta; DA Cert Spfld Tech Comm Clg 68; Amer Stds/Elem Educ; Tchr/Lbrn.

**BOISVERT, SCOT M,** Alfred Univ, Alfred, NY; SO; BS; Res Hall Cncl Treas 89-; Keramos; Alpha Lambda Delta 90-; Hnrs Pgm 89-; Res Asst 90-; Ceramic Engnrng.**

**BOITO, ANDREA R,** George Washington Univ, Washington, DC; FR; BS; Pres Schlrshp 90-; Ward Trckng Schlrshp 90-; Statstcs/Comp Sci; Statstcn.

**BOJANOWSKI, JENIFER J,** Bethany Coll, Bethany, WV; JR; BS; Circle K Clb Pres 90-; Psych Clb Stdnt Bd Rep 90-; Soc Distingshc Clgns; Alpha Xi Delta Ritual/Song Ldr 90; Sch Yng Chlrdn Intern Tchr 89-; Psych; Clncl Psych.

**BOJARSKI, CLARE J,** Allegheny Coll, Meadville, PA; SR; Class Officer Sec/Treas 90-; ASG Senator 89-; Dimensions Treas 89-; Bacchus Pres 89-; MAA; Allegheny Comm Exchng 90-; BS; Math; Physics.**

**BOKEKO, DEBBIE L,** Immaculata Coll, Immaculata, PA; JR; BS; Clss Pres 90-; Hons Comm Coll Phila 87-90; Kappa Omicron Nu 90-; Dietetics.

**BOKINSKY, LISA L,** Mount Aloysius Jr Coll, Cresson, PA; FR; Acctg.

**BOKSNER, ELENA,** Univ Of Toledo, Toledo, OH; GD; JD; Wmns Law Stdnt Assn; Deans Lst 90; BA Miami U 90; Law.

**BOLAND, JEANIE P,** Waycross Coll, Waycross, GA; SO; BA; Newspr Busn Mgr 89-90; Phi Theta Kappa Pr Sec 90-; Phi Beta Lamba 88-; Humants Awd 90; Okefenokee Tech Sec Adv Comm 87-90; AA Engl Waycrs Clg; Comm Arts/Publ Rel.

**BOLAND, KATHLEEN M,** Seton Hall Univ, South Orange, NJ; SR; BS; E A Seton Educ Soc 87-88; Kappa Delta Pi 89-; Delta Phi Epsilon Formal Chr 88; I M Ftbl 90; Ele Spec Educ; Spec Educ Tchr.

**BOLANDER, DORINDA D,** Marist Coll, Poughkeepsie, NY; SR; BS; Alpha Chi 90-; CPA Acctg Award 91; Acctg; Law.

**BOLANOS, HELEN,** Univ Of Miami, Coral Gables, FL; JR; BA; Psi Chi; Deans Lst 88-; AA 90; Psychlgy.

**BOLD, SHARON LYNN,** Salisbury St Univ, Salisbury, MD; GD; Radio DJ 88-90; Nws Magzn Rprtr 89-90; Yrbk Asst Edtr 87-89; Wind Ensmbl 86-88; Stdnt Cable TV Prodcr 90; TV Prodctn.

**BOLDEN, ANGELL C,** Howard Univ, Washington, DC; JR; BA; NAACP US Marine Corps Rsrvs; Wmn Arch/Plng Curves; Amers Inst Archs Schlshp 88-; Arch; Law.

**BOLDEN, ERICA S,** Jackson St Univ, Jackson, MS; FR; PHARM; WEB Duboise Hnrs Clg; Chmstry Scty; Yng Scntst Prgrm Schlr; Pres List; Deans List; Chmstry; Phrmclgy.

**BOLDEN, FREDRICA O,** Fl A & M Univ, Tallahassee, FL; FR; PHARM; Rose Buds Hstrn 90-; Gospel Choir; 1st Yr Phrmcy Cls Sec 90-; Phi Eta Sigma; Chmstry; Phrmcy.

**BOLDEN, JENNIFER F,** Fort Valley St Coll, Fort Valley, GA; SR; BBA; Coop Dvlpmntl Engry Prog 88; Alpha Kappa Mu 89; Delta Sigma Theta; Hrtfrd Gvns Schlrshp/Intrnshp 90; Cargill Schlrshp; Ga Scty Of CPA'S 90; Awd Of Excllnce; Bsnss Admin; Accntnt.

**BOLDEN, KIMBERLY D,** Radford Univ, Radford, VA; JR; BSW; Soc Wrk Clb 90-; Baptist Stdnt Union VP 89-; Phi Alpha VP 90-; Phi Kappa Phi; Intrn Womens Resrce Ctr 89-90; Socl Wrk.

**BOLDEN, MAXINE S,** Tougaloo Coll, Tougaloo, MS; SR; BA; Alpha Kappa Mu Pres 90-; Alpha Lambda Delta Bus Mgr 88-89; Delta Sigma Theta; Eng/Pre-Law; Law.

**BOLDEN, MICHAEL J,** Tougaloo Coll, Tougaloo, MS; SR; BA; Stdnt Govt Assoc Repr 89-; Support Svcs V P 89-90; Alpha Lambda Delta Pres 88-89; Alpha Kappa Mu Hstrn 90-; Kappa Alpha Psi Polemarch 89-90; Peer Helpers 89-90; Oper Shoestring Tutorials 88-89; State Farm Ins Co Intern 90; Econ/Acctg; Bsn/Ins.

**BOLDEN, SARA A,** Univ Of Pittsburgh At Bradford, Bradford, PA; SO; AD; Stdnt Nrs Org; Non-Trdtnl Stdnts Org; Nrsng; BSN.

**BOLDING, MELANIE L,** Snead St Jr Coll, Boaz, AL; SO; BS; Phi Theta Kappa 90-91; Microbiology; Med Rsrch.

**BOLDT, WILLIAM A,** Georgetown Coll, Georgetown, KY; JR; BA; Asst Coach Crs Cntry Team 90-; Pastor Ewing Baptst Church Ewing KY; Cert Ferris State Clg Big Rapids MI 68; Relgn; Fmly Cnslng/Pstrng.

**BOLE, ABIGAIL A,** Allegheny Coll, Meadville, PA; SR; BS; Wmn Ensmbl 87-89; Crawford Co READ Ttr 90-; Stu Envrnmntl Awrnss 90-; Phi Beta Kappa; Alpha Chi Omega Chrmn 88-; Alden Schlr 87-; Biol/Envrnmntl Sci.

**BOLE, LAURA C,** Univ Of Ga, Athens, GA; SR; AATCC 88-; Fshn Assc Fshn Mrchndsng Clb 87-88; OH Univ Chrs 87-88; Phi Upsilon Omicron 90-; Intern GA Fmly Cnsmr Sci; Intern The Limited; BSFCS; Trvl Inds.

**BOLEN, CRYSTAL A,** Univ Of South Al, Mobile, AL; SR; BA; Drama Clb 84; UMW 86-87; IMS 84; Asst Yth Dir Jackson 1st UMC 86-88; Aerobics Instr Patrick Henry State Jr Coll 83-84; Mgr Cosmetologist Crystals Style Shop 79-; AS Patrick Henry State Jr Coll 84; Elem Edn; Teach.

**BOLEN, DONELLA S,** Univ Of Akron, Akron, OH; SR; BS; Mrchng Bnd Sectn Ldr 87-; Cncrt Bnd Sctn Ldr 87-; Vrsty Bnd; Cncrt Bnd; Smmr Bnd 89-; Gldn Key 89-; Hnrs Prgrm 87-; Kappa Kappa Psi Tres 89-; Bnd Stf Unfrms Mngr 90-; Unvrsty Key Awrd; Deans Lst; Bsns Mngmnt; Arts Mngmnt.

**BOLEN, DOROTHY L,** Wilmington Coll, New Castle, DE; JR; BA; AAS Delaware Tech/Comm Clg 79; Bhvrl Sci; Psy.

**BOLEN, JANA L,** Meridian Comm Coll, Meridian, MS; SO; BA; Phi Theta Kappa Crrspdng Sec; Aerobics Wght Trng; AS; Elmntry Ed.

**BOLEN, JOY B,** Marshall University, Huntington, WV; JR; BBA; Alpha Kappa Psi; Mrktng-Trans Option; Intl Sales.

**BOLES, ALICIA S,** Birmingham Southern Coll, Birmingham, AL; FR; BA; Conservancy 90-; Quest II; Phi Eta Sigma; Kappa Delta Rec Chrmn 90-; Acctng.

**BOLES, REBECCA DIANE,** Roane St Comm Coll, Harriman, TN; SO; ASOC; Stars Clb; Gamma Beta Phi; Singrs 90-; Physcl Thrpy Asst.

**BOLES, SHELAH,** Univ Of Bridgeport, Bridgeport, CT; SR; BFA; Charles A Dana 89-; Phi Kappa Phi; Cnma; Grad Schl Wrtng.

**BOLES, SONJA D,** Al A & M Univ, Normal, AL; SR; ASSC; Coop Ed Stdnt 89; NASA Marshall Space Flght Cntr/Group Achievmnt Awrd 90; Mathematics; Engr.

**BOLES, VERA M,** Miami Jacobs Jr Coll Of Bus, Dayton, OH; JR; Tai Kwon Do; Bkry Clrk 83-; Bus Admin.

**BOLEWARE, BETH M,** Univ Of Southern Ms, Hattiesburg, MS; SR; BS; Hon Grad 76; Prsbytrn Yth Chr Ldr 89-90; BA Prl Rvr Jr Coll 76; Elem Educ; Tch.

**BOLEWARE, LILLIE A,** Meridian Comm Coll, Meridian, MS; SO; Org Advcmnt Asc Degree Nrsng 90-.

**BOLEY, DEBRA L,** Northwest Al Comm Coll, Phil Campbell, AL; SO; AAS; Phi Theta Kappa 90-; Cmptr Info Sys; Bus.

**BOLGEN, HEATHER L,** Glassboro St Coll, Glassboro, NJ; SR; BA; Crim Just; Law.

**BOLICK, SOPHIE C E,** Univ Of Central Fl, Orlando, FL; SO; BA; Crew Tm; History; Law.

**BOLICK, STEPHANIE R,** Liberty Univ, Lynchburg, VA; JR; BSN; Ythqst Clb 88-90; Lght Clb 89-90; Alpha Lambda Delta 88-; RA 90-; Nrsng.

**BOLICK, SUSAN M,** Nova Univ, Ft Lauderdale, FL; GD; MS; MGMA; Utlztn Mgt/Prvdr Rltns Crdntr Blue Cross/Blue Shld Cntrl FL Rgn; Bchlrs BPS Elizabethtown Clg 84; RN Harrisburg Hosp Schl Nrsng 74; Hlth Serv Admnstrtn.

**BOLIN, JOHN P,** Univ Of North Fl, Jacksonville, FL; JR; Phi Delta Theta Chpln 90-; Hstry/Pol Sci; Law/Frgn Serv.

**BOLING, BRIAN E,** Univ Of Ky, Lexington, KY; FR; BS; Hmwk Htln 90-; Chns Karate Sec 90-; Sngltry Schlp Awd; Natl Mrt Schlp; Elec Eng.

**BOLING, TIMOTHY A,** Northeast State Tech Comm Coll, Blountville, TN; JR; AAS; Engr.**

**BOLINGER, PATTY A,** Wv Univ At Parkersburg, Parkersburg, WV; FR; Frat Ordr Plc Assoc Gurd 90-; Snd Hl Hm Mkrs Pres Elct; Jrnlsm; Nws Rptr.

**BOLIVAR, FEDERICO J,** George Mason Univ, Fairfax, VA; SO; BA; Vllybl 90-; Parks Rec Leisure Stdies; Hotl Mgmt.

**BOLIVAR, SILVIA C,** Fl International Univ, Miami, FL; SR; BS; AA Miami Dade Comm Coll South 83; Educ; Elem Educ.

**BOLJA, DANIEL C,** Barry Univ, Miami, FL; JR; BS; Barry Cuccaneer Sports Ed 89-90; Engl; Tchg.

**BOLLER, JOHN A,** City Univ Of Ny Baruch Coll, New York, NY; GD; MBA; Drg Enfrcmnt Admin 90; Polc Cadt Corp 88-90; AAS Qunsbrg Comm Coll 88; Cert H R Blck Tx Schd 89; Cert Qunsbrgh Comm Coll MBA 87; Bus/Mktng Mngmnt/Acctng; FBI.

**BOLLES, JENNIFER L,** Chattahoochee Vly St Comm Coll, Phenix City, AL; FR; BSED; Science; Scndry Edctn.

**BOLLES, THOMAS P,** Va Commonwealth Univ, Richmond, VA; SR; BA; History; Museum Wrk.

**BOLLHORST, SUSAN K,** Christopher Newport Coll, Newport News, VA; SR; BS; Amer Mrktng Assn 90-; Dean Lst 89-; Sml Bus Inst 90-; Rsrch Asst Bus Prof 90-; Bus; MBA.

**BOLLING, CECIL W,** Univ Of Cincinnati-Clrmnt Coll, Batavia, OH; SO; BA; Deans Lst; Bus; Actnt.

**BOLLING, DOUGLAS L,** S U N Y Coll At Fredonia, Fredonia, NY; SO; BA; Hnrs Prgm 89-; Pi Mu Epsilon 90-; Acdmc Schlrshp 89-; IM Sccr; IM Bsktbll; IM Vllybll 89-; Math.

**BOLLING, ROD A,** Ms St Univ, Miss State, MS; JR; BA; Scty Advncmnt Mngmnt Dir Info Syst 90-; Data Proc Mngmnt Assoc 89-; Pi Sigma Epsilon Asstnt VP Finance 90-; Bus Info Systems; Syst Analysis.**

**BOLLINGER, SUSAN L,** Middle Ga Coll, Cochran, GA; SO; BA; Crmnl Juste Clb Sec 90-; Pltcl Sci; Law.

**BOLLINO III, ANTHONY,** Anne Arundel Comm Coll, Arnold, MD; SO; Athlt Assc Coach 90; Elem Ed; Tchr.

**BOLLMAN, ROBERT E,** Marshall University, Huntington, WV; JR; BBA; Stdnt Govt Assn Sntr 90-; Intrn 90-; Pblc Acctg.

**BOLLMAN, ROBERT M,** Duquesne Univ, Pittsburgh, PA; SO; BM; Prcssn Instrctr Ventures Drm Blgle Corps 90-; 1st Pl Tympahi Prcssive Arts Soc Coll Div 89; 1st Pl Tympahi Drum Crps Intrntnl Indvdl Ensemble Competion 89-87; Music Tchnlgy; Snd Eng.

**BOLOIX, JOSE R,** Miami Dade Comm Coll, Miami, FL; SO; Cert Key Power T Inst 88; Cert Miami T Clg 87; Math Physcs; Elect Eng All Degree.

**BOLT, EDITH J,** Miami Dade Comm Coll, Miami, FL; SO; Phi Theta Kappa; Bus Admin; Intl Finance.

**BOLT, ELLEN L,** Radford Univ, Radford, VA; JR; BS; PE Majors Clb 90-; Vol Asst Vlybl Coach 8th Grade/J V Radford High 90-; IM Sftbl/Vlybl; Phys Ed; Tch P E.

**BOLTIN, C RENEE,** Coll Of Charleston, Charleston, SC; FR; BA; Engl; Law.

**BOLTON JR, JOHN G,** Elmira Coll, Elmira, NY; SR; MS; Pres Law Scty Corning Comm Coll Pres 88-; Paralegal Pursuing Tchng Degree History; AAS Corning Comm Clg 89; Religious History; History Teacher.

**BOLTON, KEVIN W,** Hudson Valley Comm Coll, Troy, NY; FR; US Pstl Serv Mntc MPE; Cert TTC Norman OK; Elec/Elec/Math; Tech/Engr.

**BOLTON, LINDA W,** Western Ky Univ, Bowling Green, KY; SR; Phi Kappa Phi; Sigma Delta Pi Pres; Gldn Key 90-; Intl Trvl Awrd; Lgn Cnty Yng Rpblcnexctv Cmmtt Rep Prty 88-89; Spnsh.

**BOLTON, MARY E,** Appalachian Bible Coll, Bradley, WV; SO; BA; Dcrtns Comm 89-90; Evltn Comm 90-; Schlrshp 90; Bible/Fam Cnslng.

**BOLTON, TRACY L,** Memphis St Univ, Memphis, TN; FR; BSN; Nrsng.

**BOLTZ, LYSBETH C,** Spalding Univ, Louisville, KY; FR; BSN; Phi Theta Kappa 86-87; Pres Awd 85; Labor/Delivery; BS Carson-Newman Colg 89; AD Anderson Colg 87; Nrsng; Nurse.

**BOLTZ, MARY F,** Wagner Coll, Staten Island, NY; FR; Alpha Omicron Pi; Excell German Awd; Deans Lst.

**BOLYARD, LORI A,** Univ Of Akron, Akron, OH; JR; BSN; Nrsng Clb; Gldn Key; Nrsng; Nrs Anesthtst.

**BOMAR, MARY A,** Mary Baldwin Coll, Staunton, VA; SO; BA; Cltrl Actv Cmte 89-90; Concert Choir 89-; Alpha Lambda Delta Pres 90-; Omicron Delta Epsilon 90-; Tch Asst Prncpls/Econ 90; Econ; Econ Rsrch/Bkg.

**BOMBACK, BREANNA M,** Notre Dame Coll, Cleveland, OH; JR; BS; Croation Fratenal Union 84-; Phi Theta Kappa VP Mbrshp 88-; Iota Sigma Pi 91-; Lorain County Co Clg Outstndg Student 90; AS Lorain County Commty Clg 90; Chem; Chem Engrg.

**BOMBARD, THOMAS J,** Univ Of Sc At Aiken, Aiken, SC; FR; BS; Unvrsty Bnd; Sthrn Bell Schlrshp; Comp Sci.

**BOMBARDIER, KEVIN C,** Merrimack Coll, North Andover, MA; FR; BS; Assoc Cmptng Mach 90-; Boston Cmptr Soc; Merrimack Coll Lacrss Tm 90-; Cmptr Sci.

**BOMICH, DANA L,** Comm Coll Algny Co Algny Cmps, Pittsburgh, PA; FR; Arths; Cmunctn/Media.

**BOMMER JR, JOHN S,** Tn St Univ, Nashville, TN; JR; Air Force ROTC Clr Guard Cmdr 88-; AECOMP 90-; Tuskegee Airmen 89-90; Hnr Soc 88-90; Cmptr Sci; Air Force Ofcr.

**BOMMER, WENDI S,** West Liberty St Coll, West Liberty, WV; GD; BA; BA; Engl; Tchr.

**BON, ELIZABETH O,** Vanderbilt Univ, Nashville, TN; FR; BA; Alpha Phi Omega; Deans Lst; Engl Sec Ed; Hgh Schl Engl Tchr.

**BONACHEA, LOURDES M,** Fl International Univ, Miami, FL; SR; BA; Ftr Edctrs Amr VP 87-89; Phi Kappa Phi 90-; Kappa Delta Pi 90-; Stdnt Actvts Awrd; PTA Swtwtr Elm Pres 89-90; PTA Glbrt Prtr Elm Hstrn 90-; AA 89; Elem Ed; Tchng.

**BONADUCE, KARA A,** Widener Univ, Chester, PA; JR; BS; Foreign Lang Club 90-; Lacrosse Manager 88-90; Bus Mgmnt; Human Resources.

**BONAFEDE, BRIAN M,** Daemen Coll, Amherst, NY; SR; BS; Bus Clb Treas 90-; Hmn Serv Clb 90-; Acctg.

**BONAN, DIANA M,** Villanova Univ, Villanova, PA; JR; BA; Prjct Sunshine 89-; Spcl Olympics Med Tm 89-90; Psi Chi; Psychlgy Intrnshp; Outstndng Clg Stdnts Am 89; Deans List 88-; Psychlgy.

**BONANNI, JUDITH D,** Ramapo Coll Of Nj, Mahwah, NJ; GD; BA; Psychology Clb 89-90; Grad Hnrs Cnty Clg Mrs 88; Grad Magna Cum Laude; AA Cnty Clg Morris 88; Psychology; Clncl Scl Wrkr Thrpst.

**BONANNO, LISA M,** S U N Y Coll Of Tech At Frmgdl, Farmingdale, NY; FR; AS; Computer Club; Education; Teacher/Engrng.

**BONANNO JR, VINCENT N R,** Univ Of Rochester, Rochester, NY; SO; Res Advsr 90-; Sigma Chi 89-; Bausch Lomb Schlr; Pol Sci; Law.

**BONARD, NOELLE M,** Auburn Univ At Auburn, Auburn, AL; JR; BS; ACF Ldrshp Comm 88-; Alpha Lambda Delta 88; Phi Eta Sigma 88; Kappa Delta Pi; Deans List 88; Park & Rec Admnstrn Schl Of Ed; Camp Admnstr.**

**BONATESTA, PATRICIA,** Indiana Univ Of Pa, Indiana, PA; SR; BED; Hugger Special Olympics 87-88; Elem Educ.

**BONAVENTURA III, LOUIS,** Atlantic Comm Coll, Mays Landing, NJ; SO; AAS; S Co Amatr Radio Assn Brd Of Dir 89-90; Amatr Radio Emrgncy Serv Vol 89-; Radio Amatr Cvl Emrgncy Serv Vol 90-; Shore Poines Amatr Radio Clb 89-90; Trck Drvr; Amatr Radio Opratr 89-; Off Of Emrgncy Mngmnt Vol 90-; N J Army Mrs Vol; FAA; Comp Syst Tech; Comp Eng.

**BONAVITA, JENNIFER E,** Springfield Tech Comm Coll, Springfield, MA; GD; AS; Grphc Arts Club 89; Dns Lst; Grphc Arts/Cmrcl Art.

**BONCZEK, JOSEPH V,** Le Moyne Coll, Syracuse, NY; JR; BA; Bio Clb 88-; Bus Clb 90-; Dpol Sci Acad 88-; Dlt Mu Dlt 91-; Tri Beta 90-; Big Bro/Big Sis Pgm 90; Proj Comm PIC 90-; Hon Rsrch Proj Bus Admn 91-92; Rgby 88-90; Swmng/Dvng 89-; Bio/Bus Admn; Bus.

**BOND, CHRISTINE,** George Mason Univ, Fairfax, VA; JR; BS; Gldn Ky; Alpha Chi; AAS Northern Virginia Comm Coll 86; Bus; Intrntl Mrktng.

**BOND, DANIEL T,** Tidewater Comm Coll, Portsmouth, VA; SR; MS; Phi Theta Kappa 90-; Outstndng Mnrty Stdnt 90; Grdtd Summa Cum Laude; Dns Lst 89-; Hnr Roll 89-; Acctg; Acct/Clg Prof.

**BOND, DAVID F,** Univ Of Med & Dentistry Of Nj, Newark, NJ; SR; BS; Am Assn Physn Asst 87-; NJ State Soc Physn Assts 88-; Ntl Bd Resprtry Care 85-; Assoc Sci Laboure Coll 83-85; Physcns Asst.

**BOND, FRANK K,** Limestone Coll, Gaffney, SC; GD; AS Trident Tech Clg 86; AS Trident Tech Clb 78; Bsn Adm.

**BOND, L LEE,** Univ Of South Al, Mobile, AL; JR; BS; Fin Mgmt Assc; Assc Intrnl Adtrs; Dbeta Gamma Sgm; Acctg; CPA.

**BOND, LAURA A,** Univ Of Ga, Athens, GA; JR; BSED; Golden Key 90-; Kappa Delta Epsilon 1 VP 90-; Alumni Schlrshp 88-; Early Childhood Educ; Teaching.

**BOND, PAMELA H,** Univ Of Southern Ms, Hattiesburg, MS; JR; BSBA; Acctg; CPA.

**BOND, ROBERT ANDREW,** Univ Of Ky, Lexington, KY; SR; Amer Soc Mech Engr; KY Soc Prof Engrs; USN Nclr Pwr Pgm 81-87; Engr Wtch Supv Qlfd; Fssl Plant; NEC 3355 USN Nclr Pwr Pgm 83; NEC 3365 87; Mech Engr; Power Prod.

**BOND, SHARON R,** Tn St Univ, Nashville, TN; SR; BS; Mu Rho Alpha 89-; William Mdcl Ctr; Lentz Hlth Clinic; Cumberland Hall; Chemistry/Med Rec Adm.

**BOND, TERRI A,** Radford Univ, Radford, VA; SR; BA; Int Vars Chrstn Flwshp 89; Bsn Admn; Tch.

**BOND, TRACEY D,** Radford Univ, Radford, VA; SO; BS; Crmnl Jstc Clb 90-; Hs Cncl 89-90; Hl Cncl 89; Crmnl Jstc; Law.

**BOND, TRISHUN L,** Hampton Univ, Hampton, VA; JR; BS; Natl Assn Blck Actnts; Hampton Bus Clb; Univ Big Bro/Sis Pgm; Alpha Kappa Mu; AICPA Schlrshp 90-; Gnrl Mtrs Schlrshp 90-; Gnrl Mtrs Intrn 89-; Acctg; CPA.

**BONDELL, HOWARD D,** City Univ Of Ny City Coll, New York, NY; FR; BS; Tau Epsilon Phi Pldge Wrdn Edctr 90-; Elec Eng; Eng.

**BONDESON, BART G,** Fl International Univ, Miami, FL; JR; BED; English/Educ; Teacher.

**BONDI, TERESA A,** Univ Of Tn At Chattanooga, Chattanooga, TN; SO; BS; Civl Eng; Eng.

**BONDOC, OANA,** Merrimack Coll, North Andover, MA; SO; BA; Inter Clb V P 89-90; Soc Advncmnt Mgmt V P 89-90; Merrimack Mktg Assn; Mgmt.**

**BONDS, BRENDA M,** Al A & M Univ, Normal, AL; SO; BS; Action Impact Inc; Exec Assist 13 Yrs Total Experience Sectl Capacities 75-; Busn Admin; Hmn Res/Busn Owner.

**BONDS, FRANKIE L,** Christian Brothers Univ, Memphis, TN; FR; BS; Genl Business.

**BONDS, WALTON C,** Union Univ, Jackson, TN; SO; BFA; Phi Delta Theta 89-; Art.

**BONDY, ANGIE L,** Oh DominicN Coll, Columbus, OH; FR; Black And Gold Clb 90-; Tr Gde For The Admssns Office At OH Dmncn; Elem Educ; Kndrgrtn Tchr.

**BONDY, HEATHER L,** Coll Of Charleston, Charleston, SC; SR; BA; Psychlgy Clb Exec Offcr 90-; Psi Chi 89-; Omicron Delta Kappa Gamma 90-; Asstshp Medcl Univ SC Chrnc Pain Mgmt 90-; Psychlgy; MA/IND/ORG Psychlgy.

**BONE, BRANDY L,** Univ Of Tn At Martin, Martin, TN; FR; Acctng; Law.

**BONE, CHANDRA E,** Stillman Coll, Tuscaloosa, AL; FR; Gamma Iota Sigma; Alpha Phi Alpha; Hstry; Law.

**BONENBERGER, KEVIN B,** Salisbury St Univ, Salisbury, MD; SR; BA; Mrktng.

**BONENFANT, DAVID L,** Fl St Univ, Tallahassee, FL; FR; BA; Phi Eta Sigma 90; Im Soccer 90; Bsnss; Mrktng/Fnce.

**BONESTEEL, BETH A,** Mount Saint Mary Coll, Newburgh, NY; SO; BA; Flk Grp; Tutrng 90-; Sp Ktchn 90-; Soc Sci/Elem Ed; Tchr.

**BONET VALLES, RUTH A,** Inter Amer Univ Pr Aquadilla, Aguadilla, PR; FR; BBA; Acctg.

**BONET, MANUEL A,** Univ Politecnica De Pr, Hato Rey, PR; FR; Civil Air Patrol Flght Cmmndr 88-; Orntatn 88-; Ldrshp Emrgncy Srvcs Dstr; Billy Mitchell Awd; Strctrl Dsgn; Engnrng.

**BONET, NILDA R,** Inter Amer Univ Pr Hato Rey, Hato Rey, PR; SO; BA; Assn Of Acctng Stdnts; Bus Admn; Mgmt Econs.

**BONEY, STEPHEN M,** Univ Of South Al, Mobile, AL; SR; BS; Alpha Kappa Psi Mstr Ritual; Yng Vol Actn 84-90; Dns Lst USA 89-90; Acctg; Corp Law.

**BONFANTI, NICOLE M,** Dowling Coll, Oakdale Li, NY; JR; BA; Acctng Assoc 88-; Intrnshp Boces II 90; Intrnshp Maillard Miller/Lilly CPAS; Acctng; CPA.

**BONFOEY, RENEE M,** Pellissippi St Tech Comm Coll, Knoxville, TN; SO; BSN; Deans List 90; Hnr Roll 85-90; AS; Science Physical; Nursing RN.

**BONGIORNO, CHRISTINE L,** Univ Of De, Newark, DE; FR; BS; 4h Clb 90-; Anml Sci; Vet.

**BONGO, DOMINIC A,** Fairfield Univ, Fairfield, CT; FR; BA; Commuter Clb 90-; Bus.

**BONHAM, LONNIE C,** Norfolk St Univ, Norfolk, VA; JR; BS; Alpha Kappa Mu 90-; Zeta Chptr; Nrflk Schl Brd Dstrct; Srfc Wlfr Snr Chf Ymn Us Nvy; Intrdsplnry Stds Mgmt.

**BONHOMME, BRIAN,** City Univ Of Ny City Coll, New York, NY; SO; BA; City Clg Flw 90-; Hist; Rsrch/Ed.

**BONI, ALISON,** Albertus Magnus Coll, New Haven, CT; SO; BA; Vlbl 90-; Psych/Math; Cnslng.

**BONI, TINA M,** Duquesne Univ, Pittsburgh, PA; GD; MA; Psi Chi 88-; Outstndg Coll Stdnts Am 87-; Hon Pgm 89-90; BA IN Univ 90; Psychlgy.

**BONIFAY, MARC D,** Fl St Univ, Tallahassee, FL; SR; BS; Civil Engr.

**BONILLA RIVERA, DAISY R,** Caribbean Univ, Bayamon, PR; SR; BA; Educ Serv English Tutor 83-86; Kappa Delta Phi; Teachers Assoc; Lions Club; AS Comp Sc Bayamon Tech Univ Clg 84; Cert Airline Fund Bayamon Tech/Comm Inst 87; English; Teaching.

**BONILLA, A LUIS,** Wilmington Coll, New Castle, DE; SO; BS; Wlmngtn Trst Co Glf Team Capt 90-; F Comm Co Advsry Brd; Bndmstr Usrs Assoc Brd; Bnkng/Finance; Financl Plning.

**BONILLA, DORIS W,** Medical Coll Of Ga, Augusta, GA; SR; BSN; Hlpng Hnds Chf Admin 87-; Nwspr Artcl Wrk Haiti; Nrsng; Wrld Hlth Org/US Asstnc Intl Dvlpmnt.

**BONILLA, MAGALI Y,** Fl International Univ, Miami, FL; SR; AA Miami Dade Cmnty Clg 89; Crmnl Jstc; Fed Govt Agent.

**BONILLA, WILLIAM J,** Cumberland County Coll, Vineland, NJ; FR; AAS; Hrtcltr Clb; S State Gen Cntrsctrs; P/B Cntrctng Inc Pres 76-82; Cmmrcl Const Estmtr/Dsgn/Bldr 76-89; Hrtcltur; Lndscp Arch.

**BONILLA, ZOBEIDA E,** Univ Of Pr Cayey Univ Coll, Cayey, PR; SR; BA; Cuadro De Hnr De La Rectora 87-; Athltc Cmptns La Lai 88; Scl Sci; Anthropology.

**BONINCONTRI, KIMBERLY L,** Univ Of Ga, Athens, GA; JR; BSED; Erly Chldhd Ed; Elem Schl Tchr.

**BONITATIBUS, DANA L,** Duquesne Univ, Pittsburgh, PA; JR; BS; Ornttn Stff 90-; Phi Chi Theta 89-; Phi Sigma Epsilon 90-; SHARP 90; Dns Lst 90; Mrktng Intnatl Bus; Grad Schl Mrktng Dept Adv.

**BONITO, HOLLI P,** Newbury Coll, Brookline, MA; SO; BA; Stdnt Hall Cncl 89; PAL 90; Deans List 90-; Merit Presntn Award; Emmus 17/18 Church Grp 88; Pie 19 Church Grp 89; Best Video Commrcl Award 90; Outstndng Achvmnt Award; Assoc Deg; Media Tech; TV Prod/Wrt Commrcls/TV Sitcms.

**BONKOWSKI, HOLLY A,** William Paterson Coll, Wayne, NJ; JR; BA; Pi Lambda Theta; Schlrshp Acad Excellence; Alumni Assn Schlrshp; Erly Chldhd Ed/Engl Lit; Tchng.

**BONNAR, LORRAINE,** Wilmington Coll, New Castle, DE; JR; BAS; AA 90; Bsns Pblc Admnstrtn; Prfsr.

**BONNER, APRIL B,** Middle Tn St Univ, Murfreesboro, TN; SO; BS; Advrtsng Clb 90-; Gamma Beta Phi 90; Deans Lst 90; Mass Cmmnctns; Advrtsng.**

**BONNER, CHANTEL J,** Clark Atlanta Univ, Atlanta, GA; SR; MBA; Undergrad Mrktng Clb Chrprsn Pgms 89-90; Deans Lst 89-90; BA 90; Mrktng; Bus.

**BONNER, CONRAD HAMILTON,** Middle Tn St Univ, Murfreesboro, TN; SR; BUS; Assn US Army 83-; Ntl Rfl Assn 75-; Petro/Wtr Lgstcn 90-; US Army.

**BONNER, GRETCHEN R,** Kent St Univ Kent Cmps, Kent, OH; SO; Hnrs Clg 89-; Alpha Lambda Delta 90-; Alpha Phi 89-; IM Vllybl 89-; Psychology.

**BONNER, JEAN A,** Memphis St Univ, Memphis, TN; JR; BA; Wmns Pnhllnc Cncl Pres 90-; Stdt Gvt Assoc Sen 90-; Greek Pblc Rltns Brd Chrmn 89-; Stdt Ambsdr Brd 90-; Order Omega 90-; Mortor Board; Omicron Delta Kappa Pres 90-; Pi Sigma Epsilon VP PR 89-; Gamma Iota Sigma 90-; Alpha Delta Pi Exec VP 88-; Business; Law.

**BONNER, JENNIFER A,** S U N Y Coll Of A & T Morrisvl, Morrisville, NY; SO; AA; Yrbk 89-90; Hnr Stdnt 90-; Intern Offc Agng; Arbcs; AA; Indvdl Stds.

**BONNER, KIA M,** Tuskegee Univ, Tuskegee Inst, AL; SO; BA; FL Clb 89-; Hnr Rl 89-; Psychlgy; Psychlgst.**

**BONNERWITH, BARRY L,** Columbia Greene Comm Coll, Hudson, NY; FR; AS; Math; Engrng.

**BONNETTE, ANGELA,** City Univ Of Ny Baruch Coll, New York, NY; GD; Mdrn Dnc Inst 85-89; Sclgy Clb VP 85-86; Blck Bnkrs Cltn Mbr 89-90; Sndy Sch Tchr 83; Yth Org Brd Dir 89-90; Deans Lst 90; Cty Lwr Stu Serv Hnr Ctn 90; Chrch Choirs Tres 87-89; Chrch Ushr Brd Sec 88-89.

**BONNEY, TAMMY H,** Univ Of South Al, Mobile, AL; SO; BS; Phi Eta Sigma; ASNE 87-; MGCRC 90-; Grdt Newport Nws Shpbldng Dry Dck Dsgn Aprntcshp Pgm 83-85; Ingalls Shpbldng; Elctrcl Dsgnr; Tech Wrtr; Bdgt Anlyst 85-90; Oprtns/Systms Mgmt; Indstrl Mgmt.

**BONNEY-SANTUCCI, REBECCA J,** Old Dominion Univ, Norfolk, VA; SR; BED; Dist Edctn Cl/Am ODU Pres 90; Stdnt Tchr Va Edcn Asso 90-; Golden Key 90-; Iota Lambda Sigma/Old Dominion Un; ASS Tidewater Comm Colg 88; Mrkt Edctn; Mrktg Edctn Tchr.**

**BONO, WENDY R,** S U N Y Coll Of A & T Morrisvl, Morrisville, NY; SO; BA; Elem Ed; Tchr.

**BONO, YVONNE M,** Mount Aloysius Jr Coll, Cresson, PA; FR; Early Chldhd Educ; Open Pre Schl.

**BONOMO, FRANCIS B,** Bridgeport Engr Inst, Fairfield, CT; GD; BSME; Dsgnr 81-87; Dsgn Eng 87; ASAE Nrwlk State Tech Clg 77-79; Mech Eng; Eng/Mngmnt.

**BONOSTRO, LUDOVIC PASCALE,** City Univ Of Ny La Guard Coll, Long Island Cty, NY; JR; AAS; Haitian Clb 88; Deans List; Long Island Jewish Hosp Nrsng Stdnt 89; Jamaica Hosp 90; Elmhurst Hosp 90; Nursing.

**BONSALL, TRACI,** Salem-Teikyo Univ, Salem, WV; SR; Stu Athltc Trnrs Assn 89-; Bsktbl 86-; Sftbl 88-89; Gamma Beta Phi 86-; Lamba Zeta Theta 86-89; Schlr Athlt Yr 89-; Otstndng Sr 90-; BS; Phys Educ/Athltc Trnng.

**BONVINO, ANGELO J,** City Univ Of Ny Baruch Coll, New York, NY; SO; MBA; Italian Clb 89-; Dns Lst 90-; Acctng/Law; Law/CPA.

**BONWILL, MARYELLEN,** Univ Of Bridgeport, Bridgeport, CT; SR; BA; Newspr Stf Wrtr/Copy Edtr 90-; Co Author Univ Pblc Rltns Pln 90; Plns Crdntr; Phi Kappa Phi Ntl; Asst UB Dir Pblc Info 90-; Chrldg Squad Frshmn Yr 88-89; Ad; Pblc Rltns.

**BOODRAM, BASMATTEE,** Dartmouth Coll, Hanover, NH; FR; Yng Democrats 90-; Intl Stdnts Assc 90-; Milan Asian Stdnts Org 90-; Wmn In Sci 90-; Pre Med Hnr Scty 90-; Stdnt Rep; Stdnt Utd Agnst Hate; Big Green Env Scty; Albert Einstein Coll/Medicine Yeshiva Univ 90; Spcl Pgm Sci/Eng City Univ NY 87-; History/Biology/Pre Med; Medicine.

**BOODRAM, DIPNARINE FRANKIE,** City Univ Of Ny Queensbrough, New York, NY; SO; AAS; Phtncs Clb 89-; Laser Inst Amer; Optcl Scty Amer; Tau Alpha Pi 91; Laser Fiber Otpcs Technlgy; Optcl Eng.

**BOOG, RHONDA M,** Salisbury St Univ, Salisbury, MD; SR; BS; Fin Mgmnt Assoc VP 89; Natl Assoc Accntns; Holloway/Marvel PA CPA Firm; Acctg Intnrshp 90-; Acctg; CPA.

**BOOGADES, LINNEA D,** Anne Arundel Comm Coll, Arnold, MD; FR; Anne Arundel Comm Clg Dnc Co 90; Grphc Arts; Adv/Mktg.

**BOOHER, CHARLOTTE A,** Defiance Coll, Defiance, OH; SO; BS; Pres Host 90-; Tutor 90-; Dns Lst 89-; Chem Awd 89-90; Med Tech.

**BOOK, MELISSA L,** Birmingham Southern Coll, Birmingham, AL; FR; BS; Stdnt Alumni Assoc VP Mbrshp 90-; Conservancy 90-; Hanger Cleanup Coord; Alpha Phi Omega 90-; Triangle Clb; Biology; Genetical Engrng Research.

**BOOKBINDER, KARI M,** Yeshiva Univ, New York, NY; GD; BA; Sigma Delta Tau; Deans Lst; BA Stern Clg; MA Azrieu Grad Inst Of Jwsh Ed/Admin; Judaic Studies Ed; MA.

**BOOKER, ALETHA L,** Johnson C Smith Univ, Charlotte, NC; SO; Alpha Swthrt 89-90; Mrchng Gldn Bulls Band; Bio; Lab Bio/Resp.

**BOOKER, CHERYL M,** Livingston Univ, Livingston, AL; SO; BA; Loan Secty Eastover Bank 88-89; Elem Ed.

**BOOKER, EMORY H,** Fl A & M Univ, Tallahassee, FL; JR; BS; Hatchett Pre-Law Cnslr 90-; WI Clb; SBI Hmn Rsrcs-Trng Tchr; Cnslr; TV Taper; Deans Lst; Hon Rl; Fin Intrnshp; Cert Schlrshp/Achvmnt; Bus Admin; Law.

**BOOKER, GARY A,** Howard Comm Coll, Columbia, MD; SO; AA; Cert Achvmnt Dstngsh Acad Perf; Laboratory Sci; Chem.

**BOOKER, HUDSON C,** S U N Y At Buffalo, Buffalo, NY; JR; Golden Key; Non Cmmssnd Offcrs Assoc/Museum Assoc; USA; Philosophy; Law.

**BOOKER, JANET M,** Alcorn St Univ, Lorman, MS; JR.

**BOOKER, KAREN V,** Morgan St Univ, Baltimore, MD; GD; BS; Fncl Exec Inst Awd 90-; Frndshp Bapt Chrch Trustee 90-F Fed Rsrv Bk 73-; Acctg; CPA.

**BOOKER, KARIN M,** Hampton Univ, Hampton, VA; JR; BA; Stdnt Ldrshp Prgm 90-; VA Pr Almn Assoc Prlmntrn 88-; C2asp Ttrl Prgm 90-; Alpha Kappa Mu 90-; Pi Sigma Alpha 90-; Tdwtr Ar Mscns Orchstr 85-; Dn Schlrs Prgm 90; Pltcl Sci.

**BOOKER, KRISTIN M,** Queens Coll, Charlotte, NC; SO; BA; Stdnt Govt Fac Senator 90-; Stdnt Admsns Core Cncl Sec 90-; Queens Orntn Comm Ldr; Kappa Delta Pldg Cls VP Soc Chair 89-; Art/Bus Admin; Advrtsng/Mktg.

**BOOKER, MARTHA C,** Univ Of Tn At Knoxville, Knoxville, TN; SR; BS; MOPS 89-; Beta Gamma Sigma; Beta Alpha Psi; Roddy Schlr 90-; Dupont Schlr; Seymour Cmnty Pk Prjct; Acctg.**

**BOOKER, RENA E,** Meridian Comm Coll, Meridian, MS; SO; BS; Elem Ed; Tchr.

**BOOKER JR, RUSSELL W,** Ms St Univ, Miss State, MS; SR; BS; Soc Amer Forstrs Chrmn 90-; Forstry Clb 87-88; Xi Sigma Pi 90-; Miss Wldlife Fed Schlrshp 89; L Homan Forstry Schlrshp 89-90; Amer Legion Post 81 87-; U S Navy 81-87; Forest Mgmnt.

**BOOKER, STACY M,** Saint Pauls Coll, Lawrenceville, VA; GD; BA; Sclgy Clb Treas 89-; NAACP 90-; Delta Sigma Theta; Vol Svcs 90-; Peer Cnslr 90-; Brian Ctr Vol 90-; D C Gen Hosp Vol 90-; Distr Columbia Gen Hosp Intern 90; Sports Info Stf 90-; Sftbl Capt 87-; Vlybl Co-Capt 89-; Sclgy; Police Ofcr.

**BOOKER, THOMAS E,** Univ Of Tn At Knoxville, Knoxville, TN; JR; Knxvl Trck Clb 88-F Exec Undergrad Prog 89-F Alpha Sigma Lambda; Olden Key 89-; Gamma Beta Phi 89-; US Pstl Serv Qlty Step Awd 90/Merit Awd 89/Postal Clrk 87-; Acctg.

**BOOKHART, CATHERINE L,** Winthrop Coll, Rock Hill, SC; SR; B ED; Wnthrp Eaglts 87-; Stdnt Natl Edctn Assoc 88-; Bg Brthr/Bg Sstr Prgrm 88-90; Elem Edctn; Tchr.

**BOOKMAN, DEBRA M,** Johnson C Smith Univ, Charlotte, NC; GD; BS; FBLA Secty 87-; NABA 89-; SGA 86-90; Alpha Phi Alpha Aux 87-; NAACP 87-; IBM Co-Op 89-; Talent Search 90-; Chrldr Cptn 86-88; BS 90; Acctng; MS.

**BOOKOUT, SHANNON L,** Univ Of Al At Birmingham, Birmingham, AL; JR; BA; Amer Mktg Assn; Golden Key; Bus; Mktg Rsrch.

**BOOKS, HEATHER J,** Germanna Comm Coll, Locust Grove, VA; FR; AA; Phi Theta Kappa; Psych; Clncl Psych.

**BOOKS, LAURIE C,** Mount Aloysius Jr Coll, Cresson, PA; FR; AAS; Intrprtr Clb Asst Treas 90-; Phi Theta Kappa; Sftbl 90-; Intrprtr Trn For Deaf.

**BOOKSER, RYAN T,** Comm Coll Algny Co Algny Cmps, Pittsburgh, PA; SO; BS; Think Tank 90; Forensics 90; Phi Theta Kappa Treas 89-; Educ/Hist.

**BOOMA, ROBIN D,** Ny Univ, New York, NY; FR; BA; Bus; Fnc.

**BOOMER, JEFFERY A,** Anne Arundel Comm Coll, Arnold, MD; FR; Gnrl; Bus.

**BOOMER, JEREMY A,** Univ Of Miami, Coral Gables, FL; FR.

**BOOMHOWER, SPENCER G,** Savannah Coll Of Art & Design, Savannah, GA; JR; BA; Painting; Fine Arts.

**BOONE, BRYAN T,** Univ Of Nc At Asheville, Asheville, NC; JR; Univ Sngrs; Rhpsdy And Blue Shw Chr; UNCA Chrs; Bapt Stdnt Unn; Mgmt Clb.

**BOONE, CHRISTOPHER C,** Univ Of Sc At Columbia, Columbia, SC; SR; BA; Stdnt Govt Sec 87-88; Rsdnc Hll Assoc Sen 90-; Intern Lyn Frnc Stbl Vrdl Corp 89; Frnch; Law.

**BOONE, DAPHNE R,** Va St Univ, Petersburg, VA; SR; BSW; Social Work Club 87-89; Intrnshp Big Bros & Big Sis 90; Cum Laude; Social Work; Case Manager Human Serv Agncy.

**BOONE, JENNIFER B,** Memphis St Univ, Memphis, TN; SR; BA; Crisis Cntr Htln; Asst Psychlgcl Rsrch 87-89; Clncl Psychlgy.

**BOONE, JUDY CARROLL,** Memphis St Univ, Memphis, TN; SO; BB; Burlington No RR Ramp Mgr 76-; Intrmdl Hub Dvn; Marketing; RR Promo.

**BOONE, JWANITA M,** Nc Agri & Tech St Univ, Greensboro, NC; FR; BS; Elem Ed; Tchng.

**BOONE, LAURA S,** Univ Of Ky, Lexington, KY; JR; BS; SADD 88; Math Clb 90; Lances Jr Hon; Delta Gamma Treas 88; Intrn IBM; Math/Sci.

**BOONE, LINDA M,** Livingston Univ, Livingston, AL; SR; BS; Millsaps Sngrs 77-79; Millsaps Plyrs 77-79; Alpha Psi Omega 78; Stdnt Serv Tutor 89; Millsaps Plyrs Bckstge Awd 78; Deans Lst Pres Lst 89-90; United Meth Women Sec 83; Den Ldr Cub Scts 90; Lab Assist Quality Cntrl 87-89; Bio; Lab Tech/Tchr.

**BOONE, LORI L,** Converse Coll, Spartanburg, SC; FR; BA; Wellness Assoc Frshmn Repr 90-; Leaders Pgm 90; Alpha Lambda Delta; Trustee Hnr Schlr 90-; Art.

**BOONE, RHONDA K,** Christopher Newport Coll, Newport News, VA; JR; BSGA; Pre-Law Soc; Phi Theta Kappa 90-; PTA 88-90; AS Tidewater Comm Coll; Crmnl Jstce; Law.

**BOONE, SHELBY H,** James Sprunt Comm Coll, Kenansville, NC; FR; Schl Vol Wallace Elem Schl; Vol Fire Dept 90-; Nursing; RN.

**BOONE, SUSAN G,** Barry Univ, Miami, FL; JR; BA; Ambssdrs Clb PR Dir 90-; Pblc Rltns Stdnt Soc Amer VP 90-; Dnc Line Co-Capt 88-89; Amer Mktg Assn 90-; Chrldng Sqd 89-90; Hunger Clean-Up Clb 89-; Ambssdr Food Drv Chrprsn 90; Cmnctn/Bus; Brdcst Jrnlsm.

**BOONE, TANYA L,** Hampton Univ, Hampton, VA; SO; BS; Bus Clb 90; Bus Mktg.

**BOONE, TARA L,** Ky St Univ, Frankfort, KY; SO; Cncrt Bnd 89-; Shwchoir 89-; Alumni Assoc Ambass 89-90; Deans Lst 90-; Chrldr 90-; Acctg; CPA.

**BOONE, TRACY A,** Al A & M Univ, Normal, AL; SR; BA; Lgstcs Clb Sec 90-; Clstr Clb 90-; Deans Lst 87-; Alpha Kappa Alpha Ivy Lf Rep 90-; Gnrl Mtrs Intern 90; Lgstcs Prcrmnt.

**BOONE, W WAYNE,** Birmingham Southern Coll, Birmingham, AL; FR; BA; Sr Sys Anlyst 78-; Bus; Cmptr Sci.

**BOOTH, CYNTHIA F,** Schenectady County Comm Coll, Schenectady, NY; FR; BS; LPN Brainerd Area Voc Tech Inst 83; Nrsng; RN.

**BOOTH, DENNIS L,** Penn Coll Of Straight Chiro, Horsham, PA; GD; DC; Gonstead Clb 89-90; Frat Ordr Of Elks 86; Wshngtn Chiropractic Assoc 88; Wrld Chrprctc Allnce 89; Sigma Chi Psi Rgnt 89-90; Sigma Chi Psi Sntnl 88-89; BSA Sct Mstr 85-86; Lttl League Sftbl Coach; AAS 72; BS 90; Chiropractic; Pri Practice.

**BOOTH, JESSICA L,** Savannah Coll Of Art & Design, Savannah, GA; SO; BFA; Intl Ord Rainbow Girls Star Officer 89; Art; Illustration Prof.

**BOOTH, JOHN E,** Anne Arundel Comm Coll, Arnold, MD; FR; BSN; Dns Lst 90-; Otstndng Stdnt Awd 90-; VP Untd Masnry Inc 83-89; RN.

**BOOTH, KELLY E,** Univ Of Montevallo, Montevallo, AL; SO; BA; Bus; Acctng.

**BOOTH, LESLIE C,** Indiana Univ Of Pa, Indiana, PA; JR; BS; Educ Of Hrng Imprd.

**BOOTH, MARSHA A,** Cornell Univ Statutory College, Ithaca, NY; SR; Orien 90; Busn Opport Club 89-90; Concet Commission 90; Deans List 90-; CIVITAS; USAC Publicity Officer 89; Varsity Track 89-90; BS; Applied Econ/Busn Mgt.

**BOOTH, TAMMY M,** Univ Of Montevallo, Montevallo, AL; JR; BS; Phlnthrpy Actvts Fr Jvnle Dbts 88; Coll Nght Prps Mke Up Bus Com 89-; Alpha Gamma Delta 88-; Erly Chldhd Elem Educ; Tchr.

**BOOTH, TRACEY D,** Nc Agri & Tech St Univ, Greensboro, NC; SR; BA; Pal-Peer Advsr 89-; Spch Lang Pathology Clb 90-; NAACP 87-88; Hon Stdnt 87-; Zeta Phi Beta 2nd VP 89-; Spch Lang Pathology.**

**BOOTHBY, MICHELLE M,** Saint Josephs Coll, Windham, ME; SR; BED; Nwspr 87-88; Delta Epsilon Sigma; All Am Schlr Coll Awd; Mc Cahill Harvey Schlrshp 88-89; IM 87-88; Elem Educ; Tchng.

**BOOTHBY, RAFAEL A,** Fl St Univ, Tallahassee, FL; SR; BS; Cncl Excptnl Children 89-; Florence Girvin Literary Awrd 90; Minority Comm Clg Transfer Schlrshp 90; Acdmc Ldrshp Awrd; Specl Educ Mental Handicaps; Teaching.

**BOOTHBY, RICHARD S,** Oh Univ, Athens, OH; JR; BA; Glee Clb 89-; Opera Theatre 89-; Phi Mu Alpha Sinfonia; Chr Dir Bapt Chrch; Music Educ; Tch.

**BOOTHE, BARBARA K,** Memphis St Univ, Memphis, TN; SR; Beta Gamma Sigma Pres 88-; Delta Sigma Pi 88-; Omicron Delta Kappa; BBA.

**BOOTHE, BETHANY A,** Liberty Univ, Lynchburg, VA; SR; BS; Lbrty Assn Chrstn Tchrs 89-; Chi Alpha 90-; Kappa Delta Pi 90-; Math Ed; Tchr.

**BOOTS, JANYCE E,** Tomlinson Coll, Cleveland, TN; JR; BS; Yrbk Edtr 90-; Std Snt 90-; Sprtl Life Comm 89-; Phi Theta Kappa 90; AS 90; Mnstry/Educ.

**BOOTS, REBECCA J,** Tn Temple Univ, Chattanooga, TN; FR; BA; Hist; Arch.

**BOOTWALLA, ANYA N,** Univ Of Cincinnati, Cincinnati, OH; JR; BA; Prctcms Univ Cinti Stdnts Dvlpmntl Eng Pgm Tchg Pstn 90-; Sec Ed/Cmnctns Cmprhnsv; Tchr.

**BOOZER, SHAWNDA YOLETE,** Spartanburg Methodist Coll, Spartanburg, SC; FR; BA; SGA Frshmn Sntr 90-; Nwspr Stf Wrtr 90; Yrbk Phtgrphr 90-; Spcl Edctn; Edctnl Instrctr.

**BOOZER, ZACHARY M H,** Univ Of Sc At Columbia, Columbia, SC; JR; BM; Stdnt Advsry Cncl; Pi Kappa Lambda; Music; Prfrmnc Compstn.

**BOPP, VIRGINIA L,** Saint Francis Coll, Loretto, PA; SR; BS; The Mc Carthy Memorl Schlrshp 87-; Greater Beneficial Union Pittsburg Schlrshp 87-; Deans List; AAPA 87-; Physician Assistant.

**BORBAS, JANIS G,** William Paterson Coll, Wayne, NJ; SR; BA; Trnty Luth Chrch; AT And T In NJ Asst Stff Mgr 84-; AAS Txtle Dsgn Fashion Institute Of Tech Magna Cum Laude 79; Mrktng Bus; Mrkt Rsrch Or Advrtsng.

**BORCHARDT, CRAIG L,** Saint Francis Coll, Loretto, PA; SR; BA; Engl Clb Pres 90; Newspapr Staff Membr 87; Spnsh Clb Pres 88-89; Sigma Tau Delta; Hnr Soc; Eagle Scout; Engl-Wrtng.

**BORCHER, LINDA S,** Northern Ky Univ, Highland Hts, KY; SR; BS; IM Wmns Bsktbl Mgr 87-88; Math; Law Enfrcmnt.

**BORDE, HERBY,** Newbury Coll, Brookline, MA; FR; AAS; Marco Polo Trvl Clb Pres 90-; Stu Govt; Dean Lst 90-; Vrsty Bskblt Asst Mngr; Trvl Trsm Mngmnt; Trvl Hsptlty Indstry.

**BORDEN, MICHAEL H,** Hudson Valley Comm Coll, Troy, NY; SO; AS; Pres List 90; Vrsty Bsbl MVP 88-90; Phy Ed; Tch.

**BORDEN, MILA R,** Memphis St Univ, Memphis, TN; JR; BFA; Wmn Act Cltn 90-; Grphc Dsgn; Cmmrcl Art.

**BORDER, ROCHELLE K,** Bowling Green St Univ, Bowling Green, OH; JR; BS; Sprt Mgmt Clb 89-90; Sprt Mgmt Alliance 90-; Alpha Lambda Delta 89-; Goldn Key 90-; Phi Eta Sigma 89-; Phi Kappa Phi; Exrcs/Sprt Sci/Physcl Ftnss; Exrcs Phys.

**BORDERS, AUDRIA L,** Fl A & M Univ, Tallahassee, FL; SO; BS; Hnrs Stndt Cncl 89-; Am Inst Of Chem Engrs 90-; Natl Soc Of Blck Engrs 89-; Phi Eta Sigma; NAACP; Chem Engr.

**BORDO, DIANNE J,** Marywood Coll, Scranton, PA; SR; BS; CEC 88-; Kappa Delta Pi; Spcl Olympcs 89; Md Vlly PTA 85-; Nrthestrn Educ Intrmdte Unt 19; Admin Sec; Assoc 2 LAS Penn State 87; Cmmnctn Dsrdrs; Tchr.

**BORDO, KAREN J,** Marywood Coll, Scranton, PA; JR; BA; Natl Humane Soc 90-; Agency Anml Welfare; People Ethical Trtmnt Anmls; Delta Epsilon Sigma; Lambda Iota 87-88; Intrnshp Asst State Wrkmns Ins Fund; Law.

**BORDSEN, CINDY L,** Central Fl Comm Coll, Ocala, FL; SO; Reg Nurs.

**BORECKI, RICHARD P,** Bridgeport Engr Inst, Fairfield, CT; SO; BS; Perkin Elmer Corp; CSE 83; Elec Engr/Inf Sys Eng.

**BOREMAN, STEPHEN C,** Columbus Coll Of Art & Design, Columbus, OH; JR.

**BORG, CHRISTOPHER K,** Unity Coll, Unity, ME; JR; BS; Wildlife Soc Pres 89-; Wildlife Eclgst/Rsrch Asst Inst Of Ecosystem Studies N Y 90; Aquatic Ecologist/Rsrch Intern IES Millbrook Ny; Wildlife Bio; Endangered Species Rsrch.

**BORGATTI, EVELYN A,** Niagara Univ, Niagara Univ, NY; SR; BA; Psychlgy Clb Niagara Univ; Delta Epsilon Sigma; Psi Chi; Com Prsn Democratic Party NFNY; ASA Bus Adm Niagara Cnty Comm Coll Sanborn NY 87; Psychlgy/Art Sci; Grad Sch/ Tchr Cnslr.

**BORGE, MILIND L,** Columbia Union Coll, Takoma Park, MD; JR; BA; Pre Med Soc Pstr 88-90; Pre Med Soc Tres 90-; Phi Eta Sigma Tres 88-; Alpha Chi 90-; Cmps Mnstrs Ctlyst Cnng 90-; Wltr Reed Army Mdcl Cntr Hstlgy Chm Apprntc 88; Magna Cum Laude 89-; Biology; Medicine.

**BORGES ORTIZ, MARICARM,** Univ Of Pr Cayey Univ Coll, Cayey, PR; GD; BBA; CADE 90-; Hnrs Lst 87-; Bus Admin/ Acctng.

**BORGES VALERO, GLORIA E,** Univ Of Pr Cayey Univ Coll, Cayey, PR; JR; BA; Rectors Hon Lst 90-; Municipal Cncl 88-; Edn Culture Cmsn Pres 88-; Yth Rec Sports Cmsn Sec 88-; Hon Register; Natl Hispanic Schlrshp 88-; Pedagogy Soc Sci; Laws.

**BORGES, GEORGE,** Bayamon Central Univ, Bayamon, PR; FR; MBA; Bsktbl; Accntng.

**BORGES, MARIA C,** Miami Dade Comm Coll, Miami, FL; SO; Mzart Cnsrvtry 90-; Music; Tchr.

**BORING, ALISON A,** Westminster Coll, New Wilmingtn, PA; SO; BM; Music Educ Natl Conf Pres 90-; Cncrt Choir; Intrn Tchng Prog; Mu Phi Epsilon Chorstr; Trustees Schlr; Armco Schlrshp; Mina Grundish Awd; Music Educ; Tchr.

**BORING, JENNIFER M,** Ms St Univ, Miss State, MS; FR; BA; Amer Scty Of Intrr Dsgnrs 90-; Home Econs Assn 90-; Alpha Lambda Delta 90-; Phi Mu Almni Rltns 90-; Intrr Dsgn Home Econs; Intrr Dsgnr.

**BORIRAKCHANYAVAT, SIDHIPORN,** Boston Univ, Boston, MA; GD; Alpha Omega Alpha; Math; Opthmlgy.

**BORISUTE, NURITH M,** Yeshiva Univ, New York, NY; SR; BA; Fine Arts Soc Pre-Law Soc 88; Psych Clb; Clg Rpblcns; BESAMIM 89; Psychlgy; Intrntl Law.

**BORKMAN, WILLIAM C,** Norfolk St Univ, Norfolk, VA; SR; BS; Assoc Genl Cntrctrs Treas 87-; Stdnt Advsry Com Treas 89-; Alpha Kappa Mu 89-; Spartan Alpha Tau 87-89; Tidewater Vlybl Assoc 90-; AS Architectural Drafting 90; Construction Mgmnt.

**BORKOWITZ JR, ROBERT R,** Savannah Coll Of Art & Design, Savannah, GA; FR; MFA; HOW Co Chrmn 90-; BSU 90-; Francis Larkin Mccommon Schlrshp 90; Art; Illustration.

**BORLAND, DAVID J,** Clarkson Univ, Potsdam, NY; SR; BS; Stdnt Sen Sentr 88-89; Clrksn Ambssdrs 90-; Alpha Kappa Psi Pr 89-90; Pres Schlr; Dns Lst; IM; Mgmt/Mktg; Busn Entrpnr.

**BORMAN, MATTHEW DAVID,** Univ Of Sc At Columbia, Columbia, SC; FR; BA; Var Diving Tm; NCAA All Amer/Mtr/ Twr; Metro Conf Chmp 3 Mtr; Deans Lst; Accntng/Fnce; Law Schl.

**BORN, BIEN,** Suffolk Comm Coll Selden Cmps, Selden, NY; SR; BED; Eng.

**BORNE, THOMASINE YVETTE,** Norfolk St Univ, Norfolk, VA; JR; BS; Am Hm Econ Assoc V P 90-; Ombudsman NAS Oceana & VA Yth Ldr Ebenezer Bapt Ch; PTA; Hm Econ Edn; Teach Family Studies.

**BORNSTEIN, TODD J,** Emory Univ, Atlanta, GA; JR; Cncrns Cmte 89-; Food Cmte 89-; Beta Alpha Psi Sec; Deans Lst 88-; Acctng; Law.

**BOROS, LANCEY M,** Queens Coll, Charlotte, NC; SR; BA; NC Stdnt Lgstr Sec St 87-; Harvard Natl Mdl UN Hd Dlgte 88-90; Stdnt Admsn Cr Tr Dir 88-; Ord Omega Grk Hnr Soc 90-; Mrtr Brd Sr Hnr Soc Sec 90-; Phi Alpha Theta 90-; Kappa Delta Soc Phlnthrpy Chr 87-; OASIS 89-; Pol Sci; Law/Pol.

**BOROS, RHONDA L,** Univ Of Nc At Greensboro, Greensboro, NC; SR; BS/BA; Intramrls 89-; Phsy Educ/Math.

**BOROUGHS, LISA R,** Univ Of Tn At Martin, Martin, TN; FR; BS; Yrbk Staff 90-; Assoc Cmptng Mach 90-; Pi Sigma Epsilon ; Phi Alpha Delta; Pltcl Scnc/Pre Law.

**BORRAS, MELISSA R,** Queens Coll, Charlotte, NC; SO; BA; Admssns Core; Phi Mu 89-; Dana/Queens Schlrs; Vllybl 89-; Communications.

**BORRELLI, CHARLES P,** De Tech & Comm Coll At Dover, Dover, DE; FR; DPN; Nrsng Clb; Spec Olympics Vol 87-90; Flag Ftbl Capt 90-; Developmentally Disabled Cnslr 87-; Y; Nrsng; Med Schl.

**BORRERO, ANA I,** Catholic Univ Of Pr, Ponce, PR; GD; MBA; Assoc Educ 87-89; Hnr Rl 89-; BS Univ Catolica De Puerto Rico; BA Educ Univ Catolica De Puerto Rico; Educ.

**BORROWS, JANICE R,** Miami Dade Comm Coll, Miami, FL; SO; BA; Coll Hnrs Pgm 89-; AA; Biology; Medicine.

**BORRUSO, MARGARET C,** N Y Institute Of Technology, Central Islip, NY; JR; BPS; Hsptlty Clb 90-; Stdnt Govt Clbs/ Activ Bd 89-90; Phi Theta Kappa Secy 89-90; Phi Theta Kappa Sec 89-90; Outstanding Frshmn Of Yr 89; Curriculum Achvmnt Awd 90; Stdnt Marshal Cmmncmnt 90; Roundtable For Wmn In Fdserv; Hotel/Rest Admin; Hosp Spprt Serv.

**BORST, CANDI L,** Christopher Newport Coll, Newport News, VA; FR; BS; Bio; Environmntlst.

**BORSUK, JOEY M,** Univ Of Nc At Charlotte, Charlotte, NC; FR; BS; Crim Jstc; Law.

**BORUM, CHRISTINA E,** Southern Coll Of Tech, Marietta, GA; SO; BA; SECME 87-; Natl Hnr Soc; IBM Co-Op 89-; Indl Engr.

**BORUM, GLORIA E**, Univ Of Tn At Knoxville, Knoxville, TN; JR; BA; Beta Gamma Sigma; Supvr 87-; AS Roane State Comm Coll 80; Engl; Tech Writing/Mktg.

**BOS, MARTHA M**, Suffolk Comm Coll Eastern Cmps, Riverhead, NY; JR; BA; Pi Alpha Sigma; Intr Dsgn; Psychlgy.

**BOS, SADIE G**, Univ Of North Fl, Jacksonville, FL; SR; BA; Ltn Amer Lit Clb 90-; Frnch Clb 90-; Gldn Ky 90-; AA Miami Dade Jr Coll Miami 77; Cert French Universite De Rennes Rennes France 75; Spnsh; Tchng And Trnsltn Wrk.

**BOSARGE, FLORA C**, Ms St Univ, Miss State, MS; JR; BA; Almn Dlgts 90-; Res Asst; Asst Dir Stdnt Hlth; Phi Eta Sigma 89-90; Alpha Lambda Delta 89-90; Engl; PHD.

**BOSARGE, LORI A**, Univ Of South Al, Mobile, AL; SR; BS; Soc Cmptng Info Prcsng; Vol Inc Tax Asst 90; Beta Gamma Sigma; Barber Daries Schlrshp 90; Al Soc Of Schlrshp 90; Univ S Al Pres Schlrshp 90; Acctg; Cmptr.

**BOSCH, MINDY S**, Bloomfield Coll, Bloomfield, NJ; JR; Alpha Kappa Psi Sec; Sigma Phi Delta Pres 89-90; Serv & Achvmnt Awds.

**BOSCIA, JOSEPH WILLIAM**, Univ Of Dayton, Dayton, OH; FR; BS; Army ROTC 90-; Taekwon Do; Applchia Clb 90-; Sprr Cdt Awrd Aarotc 90-; Natl Sjrnrs Awrd AROTC 90-; Elec Eng; Army And Elec Eng.

**BOSCO, JENNIFER L**, Univ Of Ct, Storrs, CT; FR; Vol Wrk At Local Day Care Ctrs/Elem Schls 89-; Elem Educ; Schl Admin.

**BOSCO, ROBERT M**, Comm Coll Algny Co Algny Cmps, Pittsburgh, PA; FR; BA; CCAC Demo VP 90-; Sch Nwspr Photo Ed 90-; Ntl Eagle Scout Assoc 88-; BSA Asst Sctmstr 88-; Engr.

**BOSCO, TERESA A**, Teikyo Post Univ, Waterbury, CT; SR; BS; Class Sec 89-; Ambsdr Intrn 89-; AMA 89-; Alpha Chi Mbr 90-; Admsns Intrn 90-; Judicial Bd 90-; AS Bay Path Coll 89; Mktg.

**BOSE, JENNIFER A**, Univ Of Akron, Akron, OH; SR; BS; Outstanding Cllg Stdnts America 89-; Gldn Key; Deans Lst 87-; Alpha Lambda Delta 87-; Kappa Delta Phi 89-; Stow Tchrs Assn Schlrshp 87; Elem Edctn; Tchng.

**BOSE, SANTANU**, Mount Olive Coll, Mount Olive, NC; SO; BS; Intl Clb Pres 89-90; Sci Clb; US Min Achvmnt Awd; Coll Mrshl 89-; Hon Schlr 89-; Pres Lst 89-90; Bio/Chem; Biochemist.

**BOSLET, LEAH J**, Saint Francis Coll, Loretto, PA; SR; BS; Red Key Clb 87-90; Ornttn Asst 88-90; Cosida Dist II Acad All Amer 88; Std Rep Exec Brd PA Soc Physcn Asst; Vlybl 87-90; Physcn Asst.

**BOSMA, MARK A**, Air Force Inst Of Tech, Wrt-Ptrsn Afb, OH; GD; MS; Inst Radio/Elec Engrs 79-; Wrls Inst 72-; Ryl Austrln AF Elec Engr 77-; BE Wstrn Austrln Inst Tech 77; Lgstcs Mgmt.

**BOSS, DANIEL ALAN**, Middle Tn St Univ, Murfreesboro, TN; SO; Envrnmntl Engrng.

**BOSSARD, HEIDI A**, S U N Y Coll Of Tech At Alfred, Alfred, NY; SR; AAS; Chmstry Clb Sec 90-; ACS 89-; Sigma Tau Epsilon 89-; Sr Chem Tech Awd; Chem Tech; Bio Chemistry BS.

**BOSSARD, T DAN-XIA**, Smith Coll, Northampton, MA; SO; BA; ASA Cltrl Chr 89-; Chr 90-; Gld Key Gdng 90-; Dns Lst 89-90; Frst Grp Schlr 89-90; Hrsbck Rdng 89-; Econ.

**BOSSCHER, JUDITH A**, Univ Of West Fl, Pensacola, FL; JR; BA; AA N FL Jr Coll 90; Educ; Tchng Early Chldhd.

**BOSSERT, HEATHER L**, Allegheny Coll, Meadville, PA; SO; BA; Stdnt Srvce Ldrshp Com Chr 89-; Ldrs And Lsns In Educ Spprt 89-; Stdnt Ornttn Advsr; Lambda Sigma 90-; Alpha Delta Pi 89-; Intrn Untd Wy 89-; Lcrsse 89-; Econs.

**BOSSERT, JILL A**, Ny Univ, New York, NY; BA; Assoc Publisher Freelance Wrtr Editor; Creative Wrtng, Novelist.

**BOSSINGER, KELLY ANN**, Erie Comm Coll South Cmps, Orchard Park, NY; SR; Phi Theta Kappa; Intrnshp Buffalo Oxygen Svc.

**BOST-BEY, TIMOTHY A**, Coppin St Coll, Baltimore, MD; SR; BS; Moorish Sci Tmpl Of Amer Inc Sec 87-; AA Essex Comm Coll 89; Cert Southern Career Inst; Mgmt Sci; Bus Admin/Law.

**BOSTER JR, KENNETH B**, Belmont Coll, Nashville, TN; JR; BBA; Flwshp Chrstn Athlts 90-; Bsbl 90-; Fin; Invstmnt Brkr.

**BOSTIC, JANET L**, Limestone Coll, Gaffney, SC; SR; BA; Elem Ed; Teaching.

**BOSTICK, RANDALL W**, Hampton Univ, Hampton, VA; FR; BS; Navy ROTC; IM Bsktbl; Sailing Clb; Computer Sci; Naval Ofcr.

**BOSTICK, YVETTE C**, Miles Coll, Birmingham, AL; JR; MBA; Alpha Phi Alpha; Business; Mngmnt.

**BOSTON, ANTIONETTE**, Shaw Univ, Raleigh, NC; JR; BA; Pblc Admnstrtn Pres 90; Schlstc All-Amer Cllgte Prog; Gold Mdl Hnr Pin; Brng Out Bst Awd; Gspl Choir Yngs Mssnry Ame Chrch 90; AS Wke Tchncl Cmmnty Clg 90; Crmnl Jstce/Pblc Admin; Law Jvnle Rghts.

**BOSTON, BRENDA A**, Radford Univ, Radford, VA; SO; BA; Bapt Un Outrch Dir 89-; Madrgl Sngrs; Radfrd Sngrs; Wmns Chrl Univ Chorus; Frnch Clb; Frnch Rndtbl Hnrs Pgm 89-; Alpha Lambda Delta Sec 90-; Ret Hm Juv Det Ctr 89-; Schlrs Awd 89-; Jo Anne J Trw Awd; Psych.

**BOSTON, CHERYL O**, Univ Of Cincinnati, Cincinnati, OH; JR; BM; Frnch Clb Sec 90; MTNA 89-; Alpha Lambda Delta 89-; Piano Prfrmnce; Prfssr.

**BOSTON, DAVID L**, Chattanooga St Tech Comm Coll, Chattanooga, TN; SO; BA; Art Assoc 88-; Phi Theta Kappa 89-; Hon Pgm 89-; Fine Art/Art Edn; Tch/Studio Art.

**BOSTON, INEZ I**, Saint Josephs Coll New York, Brooklyn, NY; SR; BS; Deans Lst NYCTC; Grad Hon NYCTC 81; Stf Nrse Awd 88; NY State Nurses Assn 81-; Am Nurses Assn 83-; RN 83-; Cardiac Rehab/Care; AAS NYC Tech Coll 81; Cmnty Hlth; Dir Outrch Hlth Edn Prog.

**BOSTON, MONICA**, Anne Arundel Comm Coll, Arnold, MD; FR; AA; Bus Pblc Admn; Bus Fld.

**BOSTON, ORAL W**, Cornell Univ Statutory College, Ithaca, NY; SR; BS; PRSSA 89; Bateman Tm At Crnll 90; Crnll Trk Tm 87-90; Cmmnctn; Intrctve Multimedia Cmptrs.

**BOSTWICK, GEOFFREY RICHARD**, Central Al Comm Coll, Alexander City, AL; FR; BA; Cmmssnr IM Sftbl; Dns Lst; Pres Lst; Hstry; Tchng Bus.

**BOSTWICK, MICHELE K**, Central Fl Comm Coll, Ocala, FL; SO; AS; Deans List; Commty Schlrs; Cert Scarlet Oaks Career Devpmtn Campus 79; Sci; Nursing.

**BOSWELL, ANTONIO D**, Al St Univ, Montgomery, AL; FR; BA; Cmmnctns; Radio Tlvsn Brdcstng.

**BOSWELL, EDMUND O**, Univ Of Sc At Columbia, Columbia, SC; JR; BS; Gamma 88-89; Grk Ldrshp Trng Order Of Omega; Chi Psi Rush Chrmn 89-90; Serv Projects; IM; Busn Admin; Law.

**BOSWELL, JENNY L**, East Tn St Univ, Johnson City, TN; SR; BBA; Amrcn Mrktng Assoc 90-; Phi Kappa Phi; Mrktng Hnr Stdnt 90-; Hlstn Dstrbtng Schlrshp 90-; Vrsty Chrldr Etsu Ftbl & Bsktbl Cptn 89-; Mrktng; Bsns.

**BOSWELL, JULIE A**, Univ Of Tn At Martin, Martin, TN; SO; BA; Hall Assc 89-90; Kappa Alpha Southern Belle 90; Phi Eta Sigma 90; Alpha Omicron Pi Trea 90; Bsn Admnstrtn Awrd 90; Unvrsty Schlr 89; Acct.

**BOSWELL, LEONARD C**, Middle Tn St Univ, Murfreesboro, TN; SO; BS; Nashville Entrtnmnt Assc; AFTRA; Mscn; Radio TV; Ownshp Mass Media Co.

**BOSWELL, STEPHANIE D**, Middle Tn St Univ, Murfreesboro, TN; SR; BS; HPERS Clb 87-; Stdnt Orien Asst 88-; Hmcmng Comm 89-; Rho Lambda 89-; Kappa Delta Pi; Stdnt Tchng Assn; Kappa Delta Mbrshp Chrmn 87-; Fndrsng Prev Chld Abuse 87-; Spec Olympics 88-90; IM 89-; Elem Educ; Tchr.

**BOSWELL, TERRI S**, Fl A & M Univ, Tallahassee, FL; FR; BS; Hon Stdnt; Ldr L Boykin Awd; Cert Schlrshp; Bio; Med.

**BOSWORTH, AMELIA CAROL**, Davis & Elkins Coll, Elkins, WV; JR; BA; Fshn Clb 90-; Phi Beta Lambda 90-; Amer Hrt Assn 88-; Fshn Mrchndsng Mrktng Mgmt; Clthng Stre Ownr.

**BOSWORTH, JULIE K**, Fl International Univ, Miami, FL; JR; BED; Var Chrldng Sqd Co Capt 89-; Vlg Cncl Husng Orgztn 89-; Housing Res Asst 89; FEA 90-; Chi Alpha Theta Soc Chrmn 89-90; Apprctn Awd; Res Asst 89-; Ele Educ; Tch.

**BOSWORTH, RICHARD D**, Barry Univ, Miami, FL; JR; BA; Assoc Arts Weber State Univ 90; Sprt Mgmt.

**BOTELHO, LINDA L**, Providence Coll, Providence, RI; FR; Wind Ensemble 90-; Political Science; Law.

**BOTELHO, LISA M**, Newbury Coll, Brookline, MA; GD; ASSOC; Acctg Assoc 89; Mgmt Assoc; Acctg.

**BOTH, ELFIE K**, Hilbert Coll, Hamburg, NY; FR; AAS; Prsnl Crdntr 88-90; Law; Lgl Asstnt.

**BOTHELLO, DEENA B**, Coll Of William & Mary, Williamsburg, VA; FR; BA; Wlm/Mary Chrs 90-; Hl Cncl Rep 90-; Admssns Asst 90-; Govt; Law.

**BOTKIN, HOLLY A**, Bridgewater Coll, Bridgewater, VA; SO; BS; Brthrn Stdnt Fllwshp 89-; Vrsty Vlybl 89-; Psychlgy; Schl Psychlgst.

**BOTKINS, JENNIFER L**, Ky St Univ, Frankfort, KY; SR; BA; Contact Inc; Head Bkkpr 87-; Psychology.

**BOTTA, NICOLE M**, Mount Saint Mary Coll, Newburgh, NY; JR; BA; Ldrshp Dvlpmnt 90; Spec Olympcs; Hmn Serv/Psychlgy; Cnsl Abusd Chldrn.

**BOTTEGAL, JENNIFER J**, Birmingham Southern Coll, Birmingham, AL; JR; BA; Pre Law Soc; Coll Dmcrst 89-; Cnsrvncy; Hmcmng Cmmtt 90-; Mdl Sen; Phi Eta Sigma; Alpha Lambda Delta 88-; Pi Alpha Sigma 90-; Alpha Kappa Psi 89-90; Kappa Delta VP; Tutor; Otrch Day; Comedy Clb Bnft; Tchr Asst; IM Sftbl 90-; Sthrn Vol Serv; Pol Sci; Law.

**BOTTESCH, JAMES J**, East Stroudsburg Univ, E Stroudsburg, PA; FR; BS; Marine Sci Clb 90-; Tutrl Prog ESU 90-; Grnpce 89-; CRC Prs Fr Chem Achvmnt Awd; Marine Sci; Env Protctn Agcy.

**BOTTIGLIERI, ANN E**, Saint Joseph Coll, West Hartford, CT; JR; BS; Acctg Scty Pres 89-; Bus Scty 89-; Cmmtrs Assoc 88; PALS 89-; CT Yng Wmn Yr Schlrshp Prgm 86-; Cmmnty Acctg Aid Srvds; CT Scty CPA Schlrshp Awrd; Acctg; CPA.**

**BOTTOM, DONALD L**, Ky St Univ, Frankfort, KY; SO; AA; Pre Law Clb 89-; AA 91; Crmnl Juste; Law BA JD.

**BOTTOM, JEANINE S**, Ky St Univ, Frankfort, KY; JR; BA; Early Ele Soc/Behvrl Sci.

**BOTTONI, THOMAS N**, Hahnemann Univ, Philadelphia, PA; GD; MD; Amer Rd Crs Cpr Inst 87-; Lawrnc Twnshp Frst Aid Sqd 86-; CIVITAS; Big Bro Tutr 87-88; Cornl Univ Dns Lst 85-88; Dns Lst 89-90; BS Cornl Univ 88; Med/Trauma Med; Trauma Surg.

**BOTTS, JOSEPH A**, Univ Of Ky, Lexington, KY; SR; BS; ASCE 89-; Sigma Alpha Epsilon Wrdn 89; Civil Engr.

**BOTTS, SHEILA R**, Univ Of Ky, Lexington, KY; GD; PHARM; Ky Acad Stdnt Pharms 89-; Stdnt Actvts Cncl 90-; Res Lf Stf/Res Adv Hl Dir 90-; Phi Lambda Sigma Pres 90-; Rho Chi Soc Pres; Lambda Kappa Sigma; Kappa Alpha Theta Stdnrds Com 86-89; A T Burk Awd; Sftbl 90-; BS Centre Coll 85-89; Clncl Phrmcy.

**BOTWINICK, PAULA J**, S U N Y Coll Of Tech At Frmgdl, Farmingdale, NY; SO; BS; Hort Clb VP 89; Phi Theta Kappa 89; Spec Hnrs Hrtcltr 90; Plng Flds Arb Intshp 90; Clrk Grdn Educ Intshp; Peter Deland Awd Exclnc 89; B F Gdrch Awd Schlstc Mrt 89; L Pynsn Mem Schlp 89; Achvmnt Awd 90; Jpn Soc; Glen Core Btfctn Comm; AAS 90; Ornmntl Hrtcltr; Lndscp Dsgn.

**BOUCEK, BONNIE L**, Univ Of Sc At Aiken, Aiken, SC; FR; English Eduction; Teacher Secondary.

**BOUCHARD, AMY C**, Ky Wesleyan Coll, Owensboro, KY; SR; KY Educ Assoc 88-; KWC IM Prog 89; KWC Pres Schlrshp 85-; Dr M Clay Phys Educ Awd 89; KWC Deans List 89; KWC Sftbl Tm Gt Lks Vly Conf Chmps 86; O'boro Fmly YMCA Prog Stff/Yr 90; BA 90; Phys Educf Teach.

**BOUCHARD, STACY L**, Newbury Coll, Brookline, MA; SR; Phi Theta Kappa; Intrnshp Natl Lsre Grp Bstn; Dns Lst 89-; AAS; Trvl Trsm Mgmt; Trvl Agnt.

**BOUCHER, ANN B**, Newbury Coll, Brookline, MA; GD; AS; Sr Sec 89-; Mngmnt/Mktg.

**BOUCHER, JACQUELINE L E**, Southern Vt Coll, Bennington, VT; SO; BA; Acctg; CPA.

**BOUCHER, KAREN J**, Central Me Medical Center, Lewiston, ME; SR; ADN; Nrsg.

**BOUCHER, KENNETH M**, Norwalk St Tech Coll, Norwalk, CT; SR; Tau Alpha Pi 90-; Phi Theta Kappa 90-; ASME Schlrshp 90-; Glf 90-; Mech Eng.

**BOUCHER, KIMBERLY A**, Longwood Coll, Farmville, VA; FR; BA; Stdnt Ed Assn 90-; Intrntl Stdies Hsng Exec Cncl 90-; Mdrn Lang Clb 90-; Alpha Lambda Delta 90-; Pi Delta Pi 90-; Alpha Delta Pi; Ouststndng Frsh Yr 90-; Paul Douglas Tchng Schlrshp 90-; Longwood Schlr 90-; Frnch; Tchng/Frgn Svc.

**BOUCHER, MARIE E**, Elms Coll, Chicopee, MA; JR; BA; SGA; Jdcl Brd 90; Untd Sts Achvmnt Acdmy All Amrcn Schlr Coll Awrd; Math Scit.

**BOUCHER II, RAYMOND G**, Univ Of Nh Plymouth St Coll, Plymouth, NH; FR; BS; Cmptr Sci.

**BOUCHER, WENDY C**, Dyersburg St Comm Coll, Dyersburg, TN; SO; BA; Phi Theta Kappa 89-; Bsktbl Chrldr 90-; Eng; Sec Ed Tchr.

**BOUCK, JENNIFER E**, Nc St Univ At Raleigh, Raleigh, NC; FR; BS; Alpha Lambda Delta 90; Ordr St Ptrck 90; Deans Lst; Swm 90; Mchncl Eng; Ergnmcs.

**BOUDREAU JR, JOSEPH E**, Springfield Tech Comm Coll, Springfield, MA; GD; Hon Scty Annl Xmas Party 89-90; Alfa Nu Omega 90-; Intrnshp Queens Med Ctr Hawaii 89; Space Shuttle Mission Elect Tech Back Up Operator 81; Audubon Scty 90-; Cousteau Scty 90-; Electro Mech Tech Mass Career Inst 88; Biomed; Clncl Eng.

**BOUDREAU, LAURA L**, Western New England Coll, Springfield, MA; JR; Marketing; Advrtsng/Mrktng Research.

**BOUDREAUX, MICHELE RENEE**, Univ Of Sc At Beaufort, Beaufort, SC; SO; BA; Drama Club 90-; Gamma Beta Phi 90-; Gamma Beta Phi Pres 91-92; Soc Chr 90-; Marine Corps Schlrshp Assoc 90-; Marine Corps Schlrshp; Bowling 90-; Psych; Clinical Thrpy/Join Navy.

**BOUDWIN, KIMBERLY M**, The Kings Coll, Briarclf Mnr, NY; FR; BED; Chrstn Svc Outrch 90-; Vlybl 90-; Math; Tchr Frgn Mssn Fld.

**BOUGH, ERIC D**, Liberty Bible Coll, Pensacola, FL; FR; BA; Ftbl; World Chngrs Pres; Theology; Msnry Pastor.

**BOUGHMAN, BOB G**, Kent St Univ Kent Cmps, Kent, OH; SR; BA; Envrnmntl Awrns Club 90-; Golden Key; Oh Air Natl Guard 179 Tag Mansfield Oh; Clinical Psych.

**BOUGRAND, NANCY K**, Bristol Univ, Bristol, TN; GD; MBA; Pers Execs Assoc Pres; Amer Bsn Wmns Assoc; Dns Lst; Jacksonvle State Univ Dns Lst; Delta Zeta; Cmnty Dev Cncl; Dir Pers Camelot Care Ctrs Inc; MBA Bristol Univ; BS Jacksonvle State Univ 83; Exec Mgmt.

**BOUJAOUDE, GHASSAN GEORGES**, Brescia Coll, Owensboro, KY; JR; BA; Admin Arabian Polyfab Co Al-Khobar Saudi Arabia 78-86; AS 89-90; Grphc Dsgn; Comm Arts.

**BOUKIS, JOHN P**, Georgetown Univ, Washington, DC; JR; BBA; Musi Comedy Prdcr 89-90; Fnce.

**BOULDIN, SHANDER NESHELLE**, Univ Of Southern Ms, Hattiesburg, MS; SR; BS; Afro AM Scty Orgnztn 89-90; IM 87; Crmnl Justice; Law.

**BOULET, KATIE M**, Unity Coll, Unity, ME; FR; MS; Sci; Vet Med.

**BOULWARE, ELIZABETH A**, Spartanburg Methodist Coll, Spartanburg, SC; SO; Drama Clb; Nwspr Stf; Msc Glee Clb.

**BOUMAN, CYNTHIA M**, Univ Of Akron, Akron, OH; SR; BS; ACES 89; Kappa Delta Pi 89; Sigma Delta Pi 90; Golden Key 88; Pi Lambda Theta 90; Elem Ed; Tchr.

**BOUNDS, CHRISTOPHER T**, Asbury Theological Sem, Wilmore, KY; GD; MDIV; Habitat Humnty 88-; Yng Repblcns Sec 88-90; Theta Phi 88-; Bsktbl Tm 89-; BA Asbry Clg 88; MDIV Asbry Theolgcl Sem; Theolgcl; Pstr/Profsr.

**BOUNDS JR, DAVID L**, Christopher Newport Coll, Newport News, VA; JR; English; Tch/Wrt.

**BOUNDS, KEVIN STANFORD,** Birmingham Southern Coll, Birmingham, AL; JR; BA BM; Msc Hstry Prfrmnce; Orchstra Cndctr.

**BOUNDS, MOLLY B,** Univ Of South Al, Mobile, AL; SR; Pres Lst Intrnshp 90; Dns Lst; BS 90; Educ Elem Cert; Elem Educ.

**BOUNOS, MICHAEL S,** Pittsburgh Tech Inst, Pittsburgh, PA; SR; AS; Cert Vale Tech Inst 87; Cmptr Grphcs/Mach Dsgn; Eng.

**BOURASSA, KIMBERLY A,** Endicott Coll, Beverly, MA; SO; BA; Phi Theta Kappa; Work Study 89-; Intrnshp Greater Medica Cable 89; Intrnshp State Mutual Co 90; Deans List 89-; AS; Communications; Broadcast.

**BOURBEAU, TRACIE L,** Univ Of Ky, Lexington, KY; SO; BA; WCEA Tchr Schlrshp; Early Elem Ed; Tch.

**BOURCY, CHRISTINE J,** Radford Univ, Radford, VA; SR; Flr Rep Fr Hse Cncl 88-89; Hse Cncl Treas 88-89; BS; Psychlgy; Sbstnce Abse Cnslr.

**BOURG, BRIDGET L,** Ky Wesleyan Coll, Owensboro, KY; SO; Stu Gvt Assc Sen 89-90; Pnhllnc Cnsl VP 90-; Nwsppr Grk Nws Ed 88; Alpha Chi; Alpha Phi Sigma Pres 90-; Sthrn Cmrnl Jst Assc 89-; Simga Kappa Rep 90-; Prctcm Cty Crt Morgan City 89; BA; Crmnl Jst; Law.

**BOURGELAS, RICHARD T,** Western New England Coll, Springfield, MA; SR; BSME; Amer Soc Mech Eng 89-; Sigma Beta Tau Sec 90-; Peer Tutrng 88-90; Mech Eng.

**BOURGEOIS, AMANDA J,** Univ Of North Fl, Jacksonville, FL; FR; Sci; Optometry.

**BOURGEOIS, BARBARA L,** Ga St Univ, Atlanta, GA; SR; BSED; Golden Key 89-; Mortar Brd 90-; Mu Rho Sigma Hstrn 88-; Pres Plaque; Deans Schlrshp Key; Magna Cum Laude; Early Chldhd Ed; Tch.

**BOURGEOIS, MONIQUE M,** Auburn Univ At Auburn, Auburn, AL; SO; BS; Stdnt Diettc Assn 90-; Phi Eta Sigma 89-; Gamma Sigma Delta 90; Kappa Kappa Gamma Rgstr 89-; IM Bsktbl 90-; Ntrtn/Foods; Rgstrd Diettn.

**BOURGEOIS, STEPHAN J,** S U N Y Coll Of Tech At Frmgdl, Farmingdale, NY; FR; BA; Grphc Cmmnctns; Advrtsng.

**BOURGHOL, PAUL E,** City Univ Of Ny Baruch Coll, New York, NY; JR; MBA; Bdybldg Clb Sec 89-; Thtr Prod 88; Fin/ Invstmnts; Fin/Invstng.

**BOURGOIGNIE, PIERRE-TRISTAN,** Samford Univ, Birmingham, AL; GD; Intl Law Scty Pres 89-; Deans Lst; Phi Elpha Delta Marshall 90-; Honorable Wm M Hoereler US District Crt Intern 90; BA Univ Miami 87; JD Cumberland Schl Law; European Commnty Law.

**BOURKE, ANDREW B,** Univ Of Md Baltimore Prof Schl, Baltimore, MD; GD; MSW; Phi Kappa Phi 90; BA Brandeis Univ 89; Social Work.

**BOURN, RACHEL J,** Carnegie Mellon Univ, Pittsburgh, PA; FR; BS; GCMSO Evnt Crdntr 90; Tartan Nwspr Prod Asstnt 90-; Lambd Sgm; Deanst List; Vrsty Sccr Tm; Grphc Cmnctns Mgmt; Bus/Mgmt.

**BOURNE, JANIS K,** George Mason Univ, Fairfax, VA; SR; BS; Gldn Ky 89-; Alpha Chi 90-; Kappa Delta Pi 89-; Csmtlgst 85-87; Psycl Educ/Hlth; Tchng.

**BOURQUE, DORENE M,** Univ Of Nh Plymouth St Coll, Plymouth, NH; JR; BS; Dean Lst 90-; Pres Lst 90-; Frstyl Ski Tm 84-89; Ski Coach 89-; Mrktng/Ggrphy; Sprts Mrktng.

**BOURS, JENNIFER R,** Indiana Univ Of Pa, Indiana, PA; FR; BS; Music; Edctr.

**BOURY JR, ELLIS M,** Wv Univ, Morgantown, WV; JR; BS; ASCE; Rtry Intl 84-86; Ownr/Optr Elbys Big Boy Rest 83-; Bs 80; Cvl Engr; Bus.

**BOUTIETTE, LISA A,** Elms Coll, Chicopee, MA; JR; BA; Future Tchrs Assn 88-89; Bg Sr/Ltl Sr Clb 88-89; Early Chldhd Educ; Tchng.

**BOUTIN, ROGER R,** Elms Coll, Chicopee, MA; SO; BSN; Nationally Regstrd Emergency Medl Tchn; Nursing; Emergency Nrsng.

**BOUTON, MICHELE L,** Middle Tn St Univ, Murfreesboro, TN; JR; BA; Frgn Lng Clb Sec 90-; Intl Affrs Scty 90-; Phi Alpha Theta 90-; Erth Cmmnctns Orgnztngrnpc; PETA; Wrld Wldlf Fnd; Chrstc Instt; Acctn Crdntr 84-88; Hsty.

**BOUTROS, GEOFFREY H,** Fl Atlantic Univ, Boca Raton, FL; FR; BS; IM; Intl Bus; Bus.

**BOUTWELL, LORELEI T,** Univ Of Southern Ms, Hattiesburg, MS; SR; BA; Stdnt Sports Med Assoc; NATA; Awd D C Leach Schlrshp; AA Jones Cnty Jr Clbe 86; Coaching Sports Admnstrn; Atletic Trnr.

**BOUZGUENDA, KARIMA,** Radford Univ, Radford, VA; JR; BBA; Intl Clb 89-; Stdnt Govt Assn 90-; Frndshp Prog 90-; Frnch Acdmy VA 90; SRS 89-; Oprtns Mgmt; Bus.

**BOVA, JONATHAN L,** Univ Of New Haven, West Haven, CT; JR; BA; JV/VAR Bsbl 89-; Bus Adm.

**BOVE, CHRISTOPHER M,** S U N Y Coll Of Tech At Alfred, Alfred, NY; FR; Alfred St Rsc Tm 90-; Natl Voc Tech Hnr Soc 90-; Sigma Tau Epsilon 90-; IM Sprt 90-; Cnstrctn Mntnc Elect; Elctrcn.

**BOVE, DENISE E,** Hudson County Comm Coll, Jersey City, NJ; SO; BS; Evng Vol Mdwlnds Hosp; Prsntly Admin Asstnt Sr VP; AAS; Educ; Tchg.

**BOVE, GLENN D,** Newbury Coll, Brookline, MA; SO; Radio Clb Prmtns 90-; Phi Theta Kappa 90-; Outstndng Acdmc Achvmnt Awd 90-; V Sccr Co-Capt 90; Media Tchnlgy.

**BOVE, MICHELLE T,** Univ Of Pittsburgh, Pittsburgh, PA; SR; BS; Amer Inst Chem Engrs VP 89-; Engrs Wk Prd-CHE Chrprsn 90; IM Vlybl 89-; Omega Chi Epsilon VP 89-; Natl Gldn Key Druids 89-; Tau Beta Pi 90-; Chi Omega Asst Rush Chrmn 87-; Clb Itln Wmn Schlrshp 87; Lubrizol Schlrshp 89; Chem Eng.

**BOVIER, JAN B,** S U N Y Coll Of Envr Sci & For, Syracuse, NY; SR; Frst Eng Clb Sec 88-; Prsdnt Lst 88-; BS; Envrnmntl Eng.**

**BOVINO, GREGORY K,** Western Carolina Univ, Cullowhee, NC; JR; BS; ROTC Rngr Clb 88-90; Rngr Chall 88-; Ntrl Rsrc Mgmt; Fed Game Warden U S Army Rngr.

**BOWDEN, ALAN G,** Univ Of Nc At Charlotte, Charlotte, NC; FR; BS; Mech Engr; Engr.

**BOWDEN, DOREEN M,** Kent St Univ Kent Cmps, Kent, OH; SR; JD; Pol Sci Forum Treas 89; Alpha Lambda Delta 87; Cum Laude; Assoc Of Arts 89; Bus Mngmnt; Law.

**BOWDEN, ERIC R,** Glassboro St Coll, Glassboro, NJ; SR; BA; Sclgy; Cnslg.

**BOWDEN, GAYNELLE,** Nc Agri & Tech St Univ, Greensboro, NC; JR; BS; Blgy Clb Sec 88-; ACS Sec 89-; SG Sntr 89-; Hon Pgm 90-; Sigma Theta Alpha 90-; Peer Advsr Ldr 90-; MBRS 89-; William Penh Schlrshp 90-; Tutor 90-; Artis P Graves Schlrshp 90-; Blgy; Medcl Rsrch MD/PHD.

**BOWDEN, JENNIFER L,** Va Commonwealth Univ, Richmond, VA; SO; BS; Urban Stdies Stdnt Assoc; Intrnshp Spotsylvania Co Zoning Dept; Urban Stdies/Plnng; Emerg Serv Plnng.

**BOWDEN, JOHN A,** Thomas Nelson Comm Coll, Hampton, VA; SO; BS; Sailing Club 90-; Brickmason 88-; Fin; Real Estate Law.

**BOWDEN, MARY T,** Roane St Comm Coll, Harriman, TN; SO; Gama Beta Phi 89-; Bsktbl Schlrshp 89-90; Bio; Phys Therapy.

**BOWDEN, MAUREEN O,** Univ Of North Fl, Jacksonville, FL; SR; BSH; Nonathltc US Swmmng 85-; Gldn Ky Clb 89-; Phi Kappa Phi; Hlth Prmtn Educ Intrnshp Nvl Hosp Air Sta Jcksnvlle FL; Hly Fam Cath Chrch 84-; PTA 78-; AA Florida Comm Coll Of Jacksonville 87; Hlth Sci Hlth Prmtn.

**BOWDON, THOMAS D,** King Coll, Bristol, TN; FR; BA; Stdnt Ambssdr Pgm 90-; Rsdnt Asst 90-; Tnns/Glf 90-; Deans Lst 90-; Bus; Law.

**BOWE, CHRISTOPHER M,** S U N Y Coll Of Tech At Frmgdl, Farmingdale, NY; SO; MBA; Vrsty Lcrs 90-; Crim Jstc; Psychlgy.

**BOWELL, MARLA J,** Midlands Tech Coll, Columbia, SC; SR; ASSC; Stdnt Assc Dntl Hygn Assc Sec 89-90; Phi Theta Kappa 90-; Pres Hon Roll; Deans List; Dntl Hygn.

**BOWEN, BRENDA RAE,** S U N Y Coll Of Tech At Alfred, Alfred, NY; SO; AA; Criminal Jstc; Law.

**BOWEN, DANA J,** Memphis St Univ, Memphis, TN; FR; BA; Crmnl Jstce Prelaw; Prctce Law.

**BOWEN, DANIEL M,** William Paterson Coll, Wayne, NJ; SO; BA; Hist; Secondary Edn.

**BOWEN, JASON H,** Univ Of Sc At Columbia, Columbia, SC; SO; BA; Club Ftbl 88-89; Phi Eta Sigma; Sigma Phi Epsilon Brother 89-; Chancellors List Fall; Political Sci; Law.

**BOWEN, JUDY,** Elmira Coll, Elmira, NY; SR; BA; Penn/York Opportnts Flr Super/Job Plcmnt Speclst 89; Shltrd Wrkshp/Athns PA; Alfred Univ/NY State Coll Of Art/Dsgn 87-88; Fine Art; Grad Schl/MFA Art Thrpy.

**BOWEN, KRISTINA G,** Coll Of Charleston, Charleston, SC; JR; BS; Stdnt Marshall 90-; Sigma Alpha Phi; Phi Kappa Phi; Omicron Delta Kappa 90-; Peer Mentors 89-90; Bsn Adm; Bsn Mgr.

**BOWEN, LA RETTA ANN,** Strayer Coll, Washington, DC; SO; MBA; Natl Frm Blck Pblc Admin 90-; Amer Soc Ntrs 90-; Cmptr Info Systms.

**BOWEN, PATRICIA A,** Castleton St Coll, Castleton, VT; SO; BA; Psych; Thrphy.

**BOWEN, PAUL A,** Morehouse Coll, Atlanta, GA; JR; BA; New York/New Jersey Clb; Econ; Law.

**BOWEN, SONITA,** Ashland Comm Coll, Ashland, KY; SO; BSC; Acctg Tchnlgy; Actnt.

**BOWEN, TERRA L,** Fl A & M Univ, Tallahassee, FL; JR; NAACP; Kappa Diamond 3; Gspl Choir; Big Sister; Psych Club; Psi Chi Pres 90-; Golden Key; Princeton Univ Summer Rsrch Intrnshp; Superior Perf Schlrshp; Dns Lst; Psych; Clinical Psych.

**BOWEN, TIFFANY L,** Atlantic Comm Coll, Mays Landing, NJ; SO; BA; Intl Clb 89-; Horse Show Asc 87-; Achvmnt Acad 83; Engl/Educ; Ed.

**BOWENS, MICAH L,** Morehouse Coll, Atlanta, GA; JR; BA; Bsn Assoc 88-; Real Estate Clb 89-; Invstmnts Clb Fndr; Hnr Rl; Dns Lst; Gentleman Qualities V P 87; JR Achvmnt Vol; H L Fncl Svcs Intern; San Diego Hsg Auth Intern 90; Cmptr Access Intern 89; Finance; Invstmnt Bnkg.

**BOWENS, SYLVIA M,** Columbia Union Coll, Takoma Park, MD; GD; BS; Critical Care Nurse Frederick Mem Hosp; AA Fred Cmnty Clg 83; LPN Fred Cnty Schl Of PN; Hlth Care/Educ.

**BOWER, LISA D,** Wv Univ At Parkersburg, Parkersburg, WV; JR; ACT Test Asst; Bus Admin; Mgmt.

**BOWER, THOMAS L,** Oh St Univ At Marion, Marion, OH; SO; BA; Math; Elem Educ.

**BOWERMAN, MICHELE R,** Glassboro St Coll, Glassboro, NJ; SO; BA; Pet Therapy; Elem Ed; Tchg.

**BOWERMEISTER, JAY EDGAR,** Memphis St Univ, Memphis, TN; FR; BS; Alpha Lambda Delta; PTA 89-; Cert Springfield/ Clark County 79; Appl A/C Engrng/Busn Mgmnt; Mechnl Code Mgr.

**BOWERS, DEANNA K,** Radford Univ, Radford, VA; FR; MBA; Zeta Tau Alpha Pldg Cls Serv Chr; Elem Ed; Tchr.

**BOWERS, ERIN L,** West Liberty St Coll, West Liberty, WV; SR; BED; U S Army Res Spec 86-; Our Ldy Peace Cath Chrch 87; Elem Educ; Tchg.

**BOWERS, FRANKIE A,** Howard Univ, Washington, DC; SO; BSN; Dorm Cncl Bible Stdy 89-; Campus Chrstn Crsde; Ladies Tubman Quadrangle 89-90; Deans Lst 89-; Awd Acad Schlrshp Trustee 90; Nurs; RN.

**BOWERS, JAMES R,** Ashland Comm Coll, Ashland, KY; SO; MBA; Sr Hlth Physcs Technen 83-90; Bus Admn; Corp.

**BOWERS, JAMIE P,** Univ Of Akron, Akron, OH; FR; Hnrs Clb 90-; Chem Eng.

**BOWERS, JULIE S,** King Coll, Bristol, TN; SO; BS; Ambsdr 90-; Frnch Asstnt 89-; Math Asstnt; Math; Tchg.

**BOWERS, KELLIE M,** Liberty Univ, Lynchburg, VA; SR; Va St Rdng Assn 89-90; Lbrty Assn Chrstn Tchrs 89-; Drm Actvts Drctr 89-90; Kappa Delta Pi 90-; Elem Edctn; Tchr.

**BOWERS, KIMBERLY D,** Univ Of Sc At Lancaster, Lancaster, SC; FR; BS; Baptist Stdnt Union 90; Fin.

**BOWERS, LAURA E,** Fl International Univ, Miami, FL; SR; BED; AA Tallahusee Cmnty Clge 84; Elem Ed; Tchr.

**BOWERS, MICHAEL K,** Ms St Univ, Miss State, MS; JR; BA; Bapt Stdnt Un Dir 90-; Res Hall Govt Soc Chrmn 88-90; Univ Hnrs Prog Nwspr Staff; Res Hall Order 90-; BSU State Nom Comm; IM Spts 88-; Psych; Full Time Chrstn Vocation.

**BOWERS, MONIKA F,** Middle Tn St Univ, Murfreesboro, TN; SO.

**BOWERS, R CHRIS,** International Bible Coll, Florence, AL; JR; BA; Dns Lst; Pres Lst; Acad Schlrshp Awd; Bible; Minister/Bible Sch Tchr.**

**BOWERS, RUTH L,** Adirondack Comm Coll, Glens Falls, NY; SO; BA; Tutr; AA; Elem Ed/Math; Tchr.**

**BOWERS, SANDRA G,** Univ Of Sc At Columbia, Columbia, SC; FR; ASSOC; Nrsng; RN.

**BOWERS, SERENE B,** Anne Arundel Comm Coll, Arnold, MD; FR; BA; Dance Thrpy.

**BOWERS, SHAWNA DENISE,** Univ Of Sc At Aiken, Aiken, SC; FR; AASA 90-; Vocal Ens 90-; BA; Math/Comp Sci; Pgmng/ Analysis.

**BOWERS, TRACY J,** Univ Of West Fl, Pensacola, FL; JR; BS; Deans Lst 90-; AA 90; Elem Educ.

**BOWERS, VICKI E,** Univ Of Miami, Coral Gables, FL; JR; BA; FCA 88-; ICF 90-; Bptst Church; Spcl Olympics 89-90; Vrsty Schlrshp Bsktbl 88-; Psychlgy; Med Schl.

**BOWERY, CINDY MILLSAP,** Northeast State Tech Comm Coll, Blountville, TN; FR; AAS; Amer Dsgn Drftng Assn 90-; Phi Beta Kappa; Notary Plbc St TN 85-; Drftng Dsgn Tech; Mech Eng.

**BOWES, BRIAN N,** Univ Of Rochester, Rochester, NY; JR; BS; Univ Mdcl Ermgncy Rspnc Tm Exec Offcer 88-; Prsh Cncl; Sprts Med Dvsn Athltc Trnr 89; Brghtn Vol Amblnc Mdc 90; Bbl Stdy Grp 90; Delta Upsilon Rush Exec; Deans Lst; EMT Westchester Acdmy 90; Nrsci; MD.

**BOWES, DEBRA A C,** Gaston Coll, Dallas, NC; FR; AD; Theatre Guild Treas; Nursing; Obstetrics.

**BOWES, JOHN E,** Miami Dade Comm Coll, Miami, FL; SO; BS; Miami Bk Fr Intl Vol 90; FL Fd Rcvry Prjct Hmls 90; Hspnc Hrtg Fest Vol 87; Phi Theta Kappa; Hnrs Grad; Hnrs Pgm; Outstndng Acad Achvmnt Cert; FL Bd Rltrs 86-87; Lcnsd FL Real Est Slsmn 86; AA; Eng/Bus Adm; Engineering.

**BOWES, KIMBERLY S,** Allegheny Coll, Meadville, PA; SR; BA; Jr Cls Pres 89-90; Nescstr Schl Radio 88-89; Rsdnt Advsr 90-; Kappa Alpha Theta 89-; Alden Schlr 89-90; Kappa Alpha Theta Schlr 89-; Ims Aerbcs Instrctr 90-; Engl; Law.

**BOWICK, JEAN M,** Univ Of Montevallo, Montevallo, AL; JR; BA; Civitan Clb; Hnrs Prog 88; Alpha Lambda Delta 89f Sigma Tau Delta 90; Carmichael Libr Book Review Awd 89; Engl Intrcltrl Studies; Wrtng.

**BOWIE, AUDREY D,** Daytona Beach Comm Coll, Daytona Beach, FL; GD; AS; Law.

**BOWIE, EVANGELINE D,** Al A & M Univ, Normal, AL; SO; Intl Stdnt Clb; Env Sci; Eng.

**BOWLER, MICHAEL W,** Western New England Coll, Springfield, MA; FR; BA; Deans Lst 90-.

**BOWLER, VENISHA E,** Va St Univ, Petersburg, VA; SR; BS; Stdnt Educ Assoc Pres 90-; Hlth/Phys Educ Majs Clb Sec 90-; Delta Psi Kappa Sec 90; Natl Assoc Advncmnt Of Colored People; Kappa Delta Pi; Hlth/Phys Educ.

**BOWLES, BARBARA,** D Youville Coll, Buffalo, NY; BSN; RNAO 85-; AOM 85; RN England/Canada; SRN Nottingham England 72; Cert Mohawk Clg Hamilton Ontario Canada 85; Nrsng.

**BOWLES, DEBBIE B,** Clark Atlanta Univ, Atlanta, GA; SR; BA; GA Asc Edctrs Chrp 88-; Govt Assc Sec 85-88; Alpha Kappa Mu; Kappa Delta Epsln Chrp 89-; AA Atlanta Jnr Clg 88; Educ; Tchng.

**BOWLES, KIMBERLY L,** Univ Of North Fl, Jacksonville, FL; JR; BA; Amrcn Mgmnt Assn; Undrwrtng Spclst Ins Co; AA FL Comm Clg Jcksnvl 87; Mgmt; Ins.

**BOWLES, LORETTA A,** Longwood Coll, Farmville, VA; JR; BS; Kappa Delta Pi; Elem Ed; Tchg.

**BOWLIN, LORA D,** Roane St Comm Coll, Harriman, TN; SO; BA; Educ.

**BOWLING, BEVERLY D,** Sue Bennett Coll, London, KY; FR; Math/Sci Clb Pres; SGA 90-; Jdcl Cncl; Sci; Phrmcy.

**BOWLING, JOEL A,** Embry Riddle Aeronautical Univ, Daytona Beach, FL; JR; BS; Aeronautical Studies Cmptr Sci; Aviation.

**BOWLING, LEE M,** Union Coll, Barbourville, KY; SO; Sci; Dentristry.

**BOWLING, ROBERT T,** Daytona Beach Comm Coll, Daytona Beach, FL; FR; BA; Comm; Law.

**BOWMAN, BARBARA J,** Wv Northern Comm Coll, Wheeling, WV; SO; BA; PBS Of WV; Natl Arbor Fdtn; Adult Day Cr Ctr; SS Tchr; Chrch Cammp; AD 84; Hmn Serv; Soc Wrk.

**BOWMAN, BRENDA M,** Univ Of Sc At Columbia, Columbia, SC; FR; Bus Admin; Mgmt.

**BOWMAN, CARRIE K,** Univ Of Cincinnati, Cincinnati, OH; SR; BS; Franklin Cty Ct Probation Dept Vol 89-90; Hamilton Police Dept Rsrch Asst Intern; IM Sftbl 87; Crim Just; Law.

**BOWMAN, CHERYL A,** Middle Tn St Univ, Murfreesboro, TN; SR; BSN; Stdnt Nrs Assoc 89-; Nrsng Hon Soc 90-; Resp Thrpst; Asst Appld Sci El Paso Comm Clg 83; Nrsng.

**BOWMAN, CHRISTOPHER KELVIN,** Ky St Univ, Frankfort, KY; SR; SNEA 87-; KAPERD 87-; AAPERD 87-; Tchr Fair Awd KY St Univ; Rcgntn Awd Serv Blazer Lbry 86; Rcgntn Awd Serv 87; BA KY St Univ 88; BS KY St Univ 90; Phy Ed; Tch/Grad Schl.**

**BOWMAN, CHRISTY M,** Univ Of Va, Charlottesville, VA; JR; BSN; Sigma Sigma Sigma 89-; Nrs Asst 89-; Nrsng.

**BOWMAN, DARIN K,** Bridgewater Coll, Bridgewater, VA; SO; BA; Rlgs Actvts Comm 90-; Brthrn Flwshp Strng Com 89-; Lambda Soc; Phlsphy/Rlgn; Mnstry/Tch.

**BOWMAN, JOHN G,** East Tn St Univ, Johnson City, TN; FR; BBA; Acctng; Law.

**BOWMAN, JONATHAN M,** Univ Of Nc At Charlotte, Charlotte, NC; FR; BA; Kappa Sigma; Dns Lst 90-; IM Ftbl/Bsktbl/Soccr 90-; Busn Admin; Mktg.

**BOWMAN, KEITH H,** Broward Comm Coll, Ft Lauderdale, FL; SO; BA; Phi Theta Kappa 90-; Prof Math Tutor 89-; Pres Lst 89-90; Engr.**

**BOWMAN, KELLEY A,** Northern Ky Univ, Highland Hts, KY; SR; BA; Psychlgy Clb 90-; Psi Chi Treas 90-; Delta Zeta Crrspndng Sec Treas 88-; Psychlgy; Obtn Ph D Schl Psychlgy.

**BOWMAN, KIM D,** Ky St Univ, Frankfort, KY; SR; BA; Deans List 88-90; Txtls Clthng/Mrchndse; Buyer.

**BOWMAN, KIMBERLY R,** Middle Tn St Univ, Murfreesboro, TN; FR; BS; Stdnt Nwspr Staff Wrtr; MTSU Yrbk Cmps Life Sctn Edtr; Jrnlsm; Nwspr/Mag Jrnlst.

**BOWMAN, LEIGH A,** Indiana Univ Of Pa, Indiana, PA; JR; BED; March Band 88-90; Delta Omicron Chpln 88-; Elem Edn; Tchr.

**BOWMAN, MARGARET M,** Washington Coll, Chestertown, MD; FR; Vrsty Lacrosse MIP; Vrsty Fld Hcky; Tr Gde/Sub Tchr/Vol Lcl Elem Sch; Fld Hcky; Educ; Elem Tchr.

**BOWMAN, SCOTT A,** Saint Vincents Coll & Seminary, Latrobe, PA; FR; BA; Mth Engnrng; Engnrng.

**BOWMAN, SHANNON L,** Western Carolina Univ, Cullowhee, NC; SO; Pltcl Sci; Law.

**BOWMAN, SUSIE E,** Univ Of Ga, Athens, GA; SR; BED; Kappa Delta Pi 90-; Gldn Ky 90-; Rotaract 88-89; Kappa Delta Pi 90-; Dns Lst 90-; Tutor 90; Educ Awd 89; Miss Hilltopper 89; AA Middle Georgia Coll 89; Early Chldhd Educ; Tchr.

**BOWMAN, TIMOTHY M,** Oh Univ, Athens, OH; SR; BSEE; Barbell Clb; Gldn Key; Tau Beta Pi; Eta Kappa Nu; IEEE; Dow Chem Co Co Op; Elec Eng.

**BOWMAN, TRUDY F,** Kent St Univ Kent Cmps, Kent, OH; SR; BA; Womens Network 89-90; Beta Gamma Sigma; Golden Key; Hnrs Coll 86-90; Dist Schlr Awd; Pres List; Bus Adm-Fin; Auditing.

**BOWMAN-HANZEL, THERESA D,** Methodist Coll, Fayetteville, NC; JR; BED; Circuit Players 88-90; Masque Keys 88-90; Monarch Players Pres 88-90; Thea Schlrshp 88-90; Thea Edctn; Tch.

**BOWRING, NANCY A,** Univ Of Nc At Charlotte, Charlotte, NC; SR; BA; Dns Lst 88-90; Chnclrs Lst; Engl; Hstry/Law.

**BOWSER, ELANA S,** Indiana Univ Of Pa, Indiana, PA; JR; BA; Sgn Lang Clb 89-; Educ Fr Hearg Imprd; Tchr.

**BOWSER, KELLY J,** Indiana Univ Of Pa, Indiana, PA; FR; Elem Ed Cncntrtn Math; Tchr.

**BOWSER, KEN T,** Fl St Univ, Tallahassee, FL; FR; BS; Chem; Engrng.

**BOWSER, SHEILA L,** Westminster Coll, New Wilmingtn, PA; SO; BA; Cmps Nwspr 89-; Lit Mag 89-; Band Sec 89-; Sigma Kappa 90-; Alpha Phi Omega 90-; Girl Sct Ldr 90-; Eng/Thtr; Tchng.

**BOX, ANITA C,** Itawamba Comm Coll, Fulton, MS; FR; AD; Nursng.

**BOYARSKY, BARRY I,** Yeshiva Univ, New York, NY; FR; BS; Engr.

**BOYCE, ANGELA K,** Marshall University, Huntington, WV; FR; BBA; Hll Advsry Cncl; Dns Lst; Acad Schlrshp; Accntng.

**BOYCE, CARI D,** Univ Of North Fl, Jacksonville, FL; JR; BA; Golden Key; Fine Art/Studio.

**BOYCE, DWAYNE F,** Piedmont Tech Coll, Greenwood, SC; JR; BS; Blck Assoc Treas 89-90; NSBE 89-; Acad Advntg 90-; Ebony 90-; Ronald Mc Nair Post Bcclrt Achvmnt Prog Univ Of TN; Upjohn Pharm Intrn; Milliken Txtls Coop 89-; AS; Elec Engr; Human Factors.

**BOYCE, JENNIFER L,** Duquesne Univ, Pittsburgh, PA; FR; DJ Radio; Engl; Law.

**BOYCE, KATINA S,** Jackson St Univ, Jackson, MS; FR; Mass Cmnctns; Pblc Rltns.

**BOYCE, KELLY K,** Goucher Coll, Towson, MD; SO; BA; Stdnt Govt Assoc Rep 89-; French Club 89-; Hse Pres 90-; Chmbr Orchestra; Chmbr Music Grps; Soc Comm Rep; Soc Hon Bd Rep; Recpnt Of German Prz Of Embsy Of The Fedrl Repblc Of Germny; Ballrm Dancing; Frnch/Interntl Rltns/German; Frgn Svc.

**BOYCE, KEVIN H,** City Univ Of Ny Baruch Coll, New York, NY; SR; Trip Orgnzr Prtnr 88; BBA 90; Mktg Mgmt; Entrtnmnt Mktg.

**BOYCE, PAUL K,** S U N Y At Buffalo, Buffalo, NY; JR; BS; ASCE; NSPE; Phi Eta Sigma; Goldn Key; Tau Beta Pi; Cvl Eng.

**BOYCE, STEPHANIE L,** Va Commonwealth Univ, Richmond, VA; SO; BS; Hnrs Prog 89-; Vol Chippenham Hosp Phrmcy 89-; Involved In Chrch Yth Grp 89-; Math/Sci; Physician.

**BOYCE, THOMAS E,** Univ Of Fl, Gainesville, FL; JR; BA; Golden Key 89-; Music/Pych; Grad Schl.

**BOYCE, THOMAS FRED YOUNG,** Univ Of South Al, Mobile, AL; SR; BA; Yng Dmcrts Pres 90-; The Eagles 89-; Kappa Delta Pi; Pres Lst 90-; Deans Lst 90-; US Army E-4 76-80; US Navy E-5 80-84; AA Flknr Univ 88; Ed; Tch/Poltcs/Fmly.

**BOYCE, VALERIE L,** Univ Of Ky, Lexington, KY; SO; BA; Stdnts Rprdctve Choices Publcty Chrmn 90; Deans List 90; Socl Wrk; Socl Admnstrtn.

**BOYD, AMY E,** Temple Univ, Philadelphia, PA; SR; BS; Stdnt Cn Cl Rep Of Phrmcy Class Of 92 90-; Am & Pa Phrmctcl Assoc 89-; Yrbk Comm Chief Edtr; Rho Chi; Alpha Lambda Delta 88; Lambda Kappa Sigma 90-; Deans List 87-; Phrmcy.

**BOYD, BEVERLY R,** Univ Of Al At Birmingham, Birmingham, AL.

**BOYD, CHERYL L,** Memphis St Univ, Memphis, TN; JR; BA; Sound Fuzion Memphis Symphny Pops 89-; Mphs St Univ Sgrs 88-; Academic Schlrshp 89; Perf Schlrshp 90-; Commercial Msc Vcl Perf; Vcl Stdio Wk Comp.

**BOYD, DANA M,** Georgetown Coll, Georgetown, KY; SR; BS; Phi Beta Lambda; Sigma Kappa 89-; Vlybl/Sftbl 87-; Capt 90-; Acctng.

**BOYD, DAVID R,** Tn St Univ, Nashville, TN; JR; BS; Cmptr Sci Clb VP 90-; Assn Excl Cmptr Sci Math Physics; Gldn Ky; Bell Cmmnctns Rsrch Intern 90-; Cmptr Sci; Sftwr Eng.

**BOYD, ELLA R,** Patrick Henry Comm Coll, Martinsville, VA; GD; Data Process Mgmt Assn 90-; Phi Theta Kappa 90-; Stdnt Sprt Svcs Tutor 90-; Hnrs Lst; Dns Lst 89-; Cert; AAS; Cmptr Tech; Data Prcssng.

**BOYD, ERICA L,** Cheyney Univ Of Pa, Cheyney, PA; SO; Pre Law Scty; Vrsty Chrldng; Crmnl Jstc; Law.

**BOYD JR, GARY T,** Northeast State Tech Comm Coll, Blountville, TN; FR; ASSOC; Ntl Rd Bldrs Assc 89-; Cert Asphlt Cncrt Dsgnr; Army 85-89; Diesel Tech; Mech Eng.

**BOYD, GLENDA G,** Nova Univ, Ft Lauderdale, FL; GD; MBA; Mgmnt Clb Bd Dir; Pan Am World Serv Employees Rec Assn Bd Of Dir; Spvsr Procedures/Forms Mgnt; BA 90; AA Brevard Comm Clg 77; Human Resources.

**BOYD, JAMES S,** Univ Of Ky, Lexington, KY; SR; BS; ASME 87-90; Fresh Orntn Ldr 89; Mrtr Bd 88-89; Alpha Lambda Delta 87-88; Phi Eta Sigma 87-88; Sigma Pi Treas 87-90; Eastmn Kdk Schlr 87-89; Sigma Pi Frat Chptr Schlrshp 89; Grk Chptr Serv Awd 89; Mech Eng; Pro Engr.

**BOYD, JANET M,** City Univ Of Ny Queensbrough, New York, NY; JR; AAS; Accntng; Bus.

**BOYD, JANICE R,** Vance Granville Comm Coll, Henderson, NC; FR; AAS; Beta Phi Upsilon; Med Ofc Tech.

**BOYD, JENNIFER M,** Univ Of Fl, Gainesville, FL; SO; BFA; FL Plyrs 89-; Mrchng Bnd 89-90; Wntr Cbr Grd 90; Alpha Lambda Delta 89-; Sigma Tau Sigma; Prsdnts Hnr Rll; FL Under Grad Schlrshp 89-; Thtr Prdctn Cstm Dsgn; Spcl Effcts Mkp.

**BOYD, JOHN T,** Piedmont Tech Coll, Greenwood, SC; FR; DPL; Bldg Cnstrctn.

**BOYD, JOYCE R,** Patrick Henry Comm Coll, Martinsville, VA; SO; Nrsng; RN.

**BOYD, KAREN,** Suffolk Comm Coll Eastern Cmps, Riverhead, NY; SO; AAS; Pi Alpha Sigma; Modern Dnce; Wght Trng; Intr Dsgn.

**BOYD, KAREN R,** Tn Tech Univ, Cookeville, TN; JR; BSN; Local TSNA 90-; BS Trevecca Nazarene Coll 90; Nursing; Ms.

**BOYD, KEVEN C,** Univ Of Sc At Columbia, Columbia, SC; JR; BS; Brwr Gld Schlrshp; Lcnt Awrd; Glgy.

**BOYD, KIMBERLY E,** Univ Of Nc At Asheville, Asheville, NC; SO; BA; Res Hll Asst 89-90; Alpha Xi Delta Hstrn 89-; Grls Clb Sccr Tm; Art; Advrtsmnt.

**BOYD, MARCUS W,** Commonwealth Coll, Norfolk, VA; JR; AAMA; Intshp Med Asst; Dntl Asst HHORC 86-87; Sci; Med Asstng/Lab Tech.

**BOYD, MARY KAY,** Le Moyne Coll, Syracuse, NY; JR; BA; Crss Cntry Capt; Educ Clb Pres 90-; Psych Clb Pblcty Chr 90-; Alpha Sigma Nu 90-; Psi Chi 90-; Intgrl Hnrs Prog Com 90-; Cnfrmtn Grp Ldr 90; Lctr 90-; Rtrt Prog Tm Ldr 90-; Lbrty Prtnrshp Prog Tchng Intrn 89-; Crss Cnty Capt; Pscyh Spcl Educ.

**BOYD, MELANIE A,** Savannah Coll Of Art & Design, Savannah, GA; FR; BFA; Art; Illstrtn.

**BOYD, MERICLE E,** Benedict Coll, Columbia, SC; SR; BA; Art Clb 90-; Alpha Kappa Mu; Deans Lst 88-; Art; Advertising.

**BOYD, MICHELLE R,** Hampton Univ, Hampton, VA; JR; BA; African Studies Clstr 89-; Alpha Kappa Mu 90-; Dana Fndtn Apprncshp Schlrshp 90-; Pol Sci; Univ Tchng.

**BOYD, NANCY E,** Fl Atlantic Univ, Boca Raton, FL; SR; BA; Vol Bayview Elem Schl; Phi Kappa Phi 90-; Bsn/CIS; Law.

**BOYD, REBECCA M,** Univ Of Southern Ms, Hattiesburg, MS; SR; BS; Stdnt Alumni Assn 90-; Hon Stdnt Assn 90-; Gamma Beta Phi 90-; Phi Kappa Phi; Phi Delta Rho; Hon Clb 90-; Otsdng Clg Stdnts Amer 90; Pres Lst 88-; Deans Lst 90; Sec Educ/English; Tch.**

**BOYD, REGINA J,** Johnson C Smith Univ, Charlotte, NC; SO; BED; Pn Afrcn Cncl Fr Blck Awrnss 89-; JC Smith Univ Hnrs Coll 90-; Vlybl Bsktbl 89-; Erly Chldhd Educ; Schl Tchr Educ.**

**BOYD, RICHARD C,** Abraham Baldwin Agri Coll, Tifton, GA; SO; BA; Puppet Mnstry Clb Asst Dir 90-; Music Mnstry Sound Dir 89-; Pres Lst; Erly Chldhd Educ; Tchr.

**BOYD III, RICHARD W,** Embry Riddle Aeronautical Univ, Daytona Beach, FL; SR; BS; AS 90; Avtn Tech.

**BOYD, ROBERT,** Coppin St Coll, Baltimore, MD; JR; BS; Crmnl Jstce; Tchr.

**BOYD II, ROBERT A,** Morehouse Coll, Atlanta, GA; JR; Yrbk Stf Photogrphr 88-; Schl Nwspr Photogrphr 88-; Deans Lst 90-; Intrnshp Sheraton Hotel Mgmnt Trainee 89; Pol Sci; Law.

**BOYD, RONALD S,** Radford Univ, Radford, VA; JR; SAM VP Pgms; Hon Pgm; BBA; Mgkt.

**BOYD, SARAH A,** Fl Jr Coll At Jacksonville, Jacksonville, FL; FR; BA; Hnrs Pro; Music; Tchr.

**BOYD, SONJA B,** Stillman Coll, Tuscaloosa, AL; SO; BA; Trng Choir 89-; Cordell Wynn Hnr Soc 90-; Gamma Iota Sigma; Alpha Kappa Alpha 89-; Engl Cmnctns; Brdcstg.

**BOYD, STEPHANIE R,** Alcorn St Univ, Lorman, MS; JR; BS; Inst Mngmt; Htl/Rstrnt Mngmt.

**BOYD, TABATHA M,** Univ Of Southern Ms, Hattiesburg, MS; SR; BA; Fash Clb 88-90; Stdnt Hm Ec Assn 89-90; Clthng Merch; Bus.

**BOYD, TIMOTHY D,** Coll Of Charleston, Charleston, SC; SO; BA; Bus-Acctg/Spnsh; CPA.

**BOYD, TONYA L,** Vance Granville Comm Coll, Henderson, NC; SR; AAS; Comp Clb 90-; Stdnt Govt Assoc 89-90a; Phi Theta Kappa 90-; Acdmc Achvmnt Schlrshp 89-90; Pauline Neisler Brewer Acdmc Achvmnt Schlrshp 90-; Bsn Comp Prog.

**BOYD, TRACIE M,** Cumberland Coll, Williamsburg, KY; SR; BS; Cmps Bptst Yng Wom 87-88; Sigma Tau Delta Pblcst 90; Love In Action 87-88; Acad Schlrshp 87-; Deans List 89-; Pltcl Sci/English; JD Law.

**BOYD, WILLIAM D,** Middle Tn St Univ, Murfreesboro, TN; JR; BS; HYPERS 89-; Campus Rec Stf 89-; Gamma Beta Phi Socty 89-90; Hnrs Prog 90-; Phi Epsilon Kappa 90-; AS Columbia State Comm Coll 89; Phys Educ; Tchr/Coach.

**BOYDEN, TERRI D,** Springfield Tech Comm Coll, Springfield, MA; SO; AS; Alpha Nu Omega; Cmptr Data Prcssng; BA Prgrmmr.

**BOYDSTON, ALEX K,** Univ Of Al At Huntsville, Huntsville, AL; SR; BSEE; Eta Kappa Nu 90-; Tau Beta Pi; Hon Schlr 90; Pres List NE State Jr Clg 85-86; Deans List Auburn Univ 84; AA Sci NE State Jr Clg 86; Elec Eng.

**BOYENS, LAUREN A,** Schenectady County Comm Coll, Schenectady, NY; SO; AAS; Amer Red Cross 86-90; March Dimes; World Hunger Walk 89-; Proctors Hstrc Lndmrk Theatre 90; Trvl/Tourism/Bsn; Mgmt.

**BOYER, APRIL L,** Allegheny Coll, Meadville, PA; SO; BA; Stdnt Svc Ldrshp Cmt; Kappa Alpha Theta Phlntrpy Chrmn; Alden Schlr; Hist/Pol Sci Cmnctns Arts; Law.

**BOYER, JENNIFER L,** Va Commonwealth Univ, Richmond, VA; SO; BSW; Scl Wrk; Sbstnc Abuse Cnclr.

**BOYER, MICHELE R,** Neumann Coll, Aston, PA; SO; Stdnt Nrs Assoc; Neuman Clg Hon Prog 89-; Wmns Sftbl 90; BSN; Nrsng; RN.

**BOYER, SHANE D,** East Stroudsburg Univ, E Stroudsburg, PA; JR; BA; Cmptr Sci.

**BOYER, SUZANNE L,** Comm Coll Algny Co Algny Cmps, Pittsburgh, PA; MS; Dns Lst 89-; BS Indiana Univ PA 89; Phys Ther.

**BOYER, WENDY M,** Winthrop Coll, Rock Hill, SC; SR; BA; History Club; History; Doctorate History/Writer.

**BOYERINAS, BERNARD T,** Indiana Univ Of Pa, Indiana, PA; JR; BS; Hstry Club 89-90; Pi Gamma Mu 90-; Soc Sci Educ; Tchr.

**BOYERS, JASON O,** Nyack Coll, Nyack, NY; SO; BM; Music Edctrs Natl Cnfrnc VP 89-; Stdnt Govt Acdmc Affrs Offcr 90-; Coll Brass Choir 89-; Coll Chrl Lbrn 89-; Music Educ.

**BOYETTE, SHELIA DANYEL,** Santa Fe Comm Coll, Gainesville, FL; FR; Medicine; Cardiopulmonary Tech.

**BOYKIN, CASSANDRA D,** Old Dominion Univ, Norfolk, VA; SR; BS; Ebony Impact Choir VP 87; Mrktng Ed; Trng/Dvlpmnt.

**BOYKIN, DEBORAH A,** Tn St Univ, Nashville, TN; SR; BS; Stdnt Un Brd Govrs Sec 88-90; Ac Comp Math Clb Sec 89-90; Peer Cnslr 88; Alpha Mu Gamma 90-; Beta Kappa Chi 90-; Gldn Ky; UTK Ronald Mc Nair Achvmnt Flw 90; Co Otstndng Soph 89; John A Merritt Schlrshp Awd 87-; Math; Actrl Sci.

**BOYKIN, DIANE M,** Ms St Univ, Miss State, MS; JR; BA; Ins; Ins Agnt Or Undrwrtr.

**BOYKIN, EARLENE,** Al A & M Univ, Normal, AL; JR; YMTF 90; Stdnt Clstr Org 90; Thespian Scty 90; Deans Lst 90; Awds Hnrs 90; Mjr Pol Sci Mnr Cmptr Sci; Pltcs.**

**BOYKIN, MERRILL A,** Queens Coll, Charlotte, NC; JR; BA; Canterbury Clb Chpln Asst 88-; Religious Life Cmte 88-; Org Agnst Soc Inj/Suf 89-; Pr Schlr 88-; Elem Tchr.

**BOYKINS, KEITH M,** Cheyney Univ Of Pa, Cheyney, PA; SO; AT/T Bell Lab; Elec Tech; Engr.

**BOYLAN, SANDRA M,** Tri County Tech Coll, Pendleton, SC; FR; AS; Alpha Zeta Beta; Med Lab.

**BOYLE, JAMES PATRICK,** Univ Of Tn At Chattanooga, Chattanooga, TN; JR; BS; IEEE Sec 90-; NSPE 90-; Gldn Key 88-; NCEA; Comp Sci/Info Syst; Syst Anlyst.

**BOYLE, JOAN M,** Wilmington Coll, New Castle, DE; BS; Sch Nwspaper 90; Yrbk 90; Delta Epsilon Rho 90-; Phi Theta Kappa 89-90; Deans List; J P Morgan Schlrshp; AA DE Tech Cmnty Clg 87-89; Bus Mgt; Bus/Humn Rsrc Mgt.

**BOYLE, JOANNE M,** Coll Misericordia, Dallas, PA; JR; Marketing Clb; 4-H Clb Prsdnt 88; All Amrcn Schlr; Bsns Mrt Schlrshp; Conlon Schlrshp; Bsns; Mrktng Mgmnt.

**BOYLE, KELLY A,** Wagner Coll, Staten Island, NY; GD; Tri Beta Historian 88-90; Wagner Clg Grant 86-90; Medl Genetics Internship 89-90; BS 90; Biology; Research.

**BOYLE, NICOLE K,** Clark Atlanta Univ, Atlanta, GA; SR; MA; Res Asst; Tutorial Mntrng Prog; Psych Club; Dorm V P 89-90; Natl Hnrs Soc 88-; Psi Chi 90-; NAACP 87-; All Am Schlr; Psych Intrnshp; BA; Clinical Psych.

**BOYLE-PENNINGTON, DEIRDRE K,** Univ Of Fl, Gainesville, FL; SR; Phi Kappa Phi Gldn Key; Amer Phys Thrpy Assc; BS; Phys Thrpy.

**BOYLES, MICHAEL S,** Nc Central Univ, Durham, NC; GD; JD; BA Chpl Hl 87; Law.

**BOYLES, PATRICIA,** Edinboro Univ Of Pa, Edinboro, PA; SO; BFA; Univ Nwspr-Cntrbtng Wrtr 89-; Fine Art; MFA Tch Coll Lvl.

**BOYLES, TINA M,** Wv Univ At Parkersburg, Parkersburg, WV; SO; ASN; Phi Theta Kappa; Pres Schlr; Nrsng.

**BOYNTON, IDA MAY,** Tomlinson Coll, Cleveland, TN; SO; Sngl Prntg Spprt Grp 88-90; Abused Wom Shltr 88-90; Prctcl Mnstrs/Stdnt Mnstrs 90-; Prctcl Job Prep Prog Soc Wrkr Asst 87-88; Phone A Thon Rsr Bsktbl 90; Adlsnt Drug Abuse Grls Grp Hm Asst Cnslr 90-; Wrkstdy Hd/Sci Sec 90-; Ministry; Chaplan/Pstrl/Hman Serv.

**BOYTIM, MICHELLE L,** Univ Of Miami, Coral Gables, FL; JR; Mcrobio/Immnlgy Clb Sec 88-; Golden Key Pblcty 89-F Hons Assn 88-90; Phi Kappa Phi; Phi Beta Kappa; Beta Beta Beta; Rsrch Intrnshp; Mcrobio/Imnlgy; Rsrch.

**BOYTIM-SMAIL, CHRISTINE L,** Indiana Univ Of Pa, Indiana, PA; JR; Assn Chldhd Educ Intl 90-; Educ; Tchr.

**BOZELKO, CHANDRA A,** Princeton Univ, Princeton, NJ; FR; AB; Writer Student Course Guide; Field Hockey.

**BOZEMAN, DECUNDA DUKE,** Alcorn St Univ, Lorman, MS; JR; BS; Hinds JR Clg Agri Club V P 83-84; Mississippi Pst-Scndry Agri Club State Pres 84-85; Clgte Ftr Frmrs Of Amer 90-; Mississippi Lvstck Jdg Team/Jnr Clg Lvl 82-83; Agri Dept Achvmnt Award 90-; Intrnshp USDA Soil Cnsrvtn Svc; Agri Educ; Tchng.

**BOZEMAN, DENNIS P,** Fl St Univ, Tallahassee, FL; GD; MS; Phi Kappa Phi; Garnet Key 89-; Stdnt Govt Cncl Schlrshp 89; FSU Fndtn Schlrshp 90; Alfred I Dupont Fndtn Schlrshp 90; AA Gulf Coast Cmnty Clg 88; BS FL State Univ 90; Mngmnt.

**BOZEMAN, JENNIFER L,** Valdosta St Coll, Valdosta, GA; SO; BBA; Bus; Acctng.

**BOZZA, CHRISTIE,** William Paterson Coll, Wayne, NJ; SR; BA; Litrcy Mag VP 90-; Aid Bomels 90-; Fellwshp; Hum Hnr Pgm 89-; Sen Lautnbrg Intrn; Dns Lst 88-; Engl/Wrtg; Ma.

**BOZZA, JANNET D,** S U N Y Coll Of Tech At Frmgdl, Farmingdale, NY; SO; BA; Spec Educ Aide Huntington Schl Dist 83-; Chldhd Educ; Tchr.

**BRAATEN, LORI J,** Columbia Greene Comm Coll, Hudson, NY; FR; Nrsg; Rn.

**BRABHAM, JONATHAN M,** Univ Of Sc At Salkehatchie, Allendale, SC; Fish/Game Clb 90; Engl; Bsnss.

**BRABHAM II, ROBERT W,** Univ Of Sc At Columbia, Columbia, SC; SO; MMA; Gamma Beta Phi 90-; Media Arts; Film Mkng.

**BRABSON JR, ALAN R,** Hiwassee Coll, Madisonville, TN; FR; BA; Anthrplgy; Antrplgst.

**BRABSON, PAMELA P D,** Pellissippi St Tech Comm Coll, Knoxville, TN; SO; Phi Theta Kappa; Indstrl Engr.

**BRACAMONTE, GRACE F,** Miami Dade Comm Coll South, Miami, FL; SO; BA; Tlnt Rstr Otstndng Mnrty Comm Clg Grads; AA; Crmnl Jstce; Law/Law Enf.

**BRACAMONTE, MIRIAM A,** Springfield Tech Comm Coll, Springfield, MA; JR; BA; Hnr Rl; Coll Karate Clb; Ct Stngrphy/Ct Rptng.

**BRACE, CYNTHIA A,** Elmira Coll, Elmira, NY; SR; BSN; Nrsng Clb VP 90-F Hon Schlr 90-; Nrs Excell Awd; Connelly Nrsng Excell Awd 90; P Kelley Nrsng Awd 89; AAS Nrsng Corning Comm Coll 89; Nrsng; Tch.

**BRACERO, MARIEL,** Inter Amer Univ Pr Hato Rey, Hato Rey, PR; FR; Catequist/Local Chrch Santisima Trinidad 90-; SR GS Cncl 198 Caribbean 90-; Polt Scns; Law.

**BRACEY JR, MITCHELL L,** Richard Bland Coll, Petersburg, VA; SO; BA; Sclgy Anthrplgy; Ed.

**BRACHMANN, CLAIRE R,** Asnuntuck Comm Coll, Enfield, CT; GD; AS; Rd Crss Vol 89-; Ftr Wrtr 86-; Phi Theta Kappa; Sprvsr Assgnd Rsk Dpt 86-91; Psychlgy.

**BRACKBILL, MARLENE L,** Christopher Newport Coll, Newport News, VA; SR; BA; BS Harrsbrg Area Comm Clg 69; Elem Middle Schl; Mstrs Degr.

**BRACKEEN, JOLENE M,** Central Fl Comm Coll, Ocala, FL; SO; AA; Phi Theta Kappa; Biology; Geology.

**BRACKEN, AMY J,** Va Commonwealth Univ, Richmond, VA; JR; BS; SEAC 90-; Rnfrst Actn Com 89-; Gldn Key 90-; Outstndng Stdnt Awd 90-; Sclgy/Anthrplgy.

**BRACKEN, RODDY GENE,** Cumberland Coll, Williamsburg, KY; JR; BS; Bptst Stu Unn Crtv Mnstrs Chr Vllybl 88-; SG Jstc 88-; Sigma Tau Delta 90-; Acdmc Hnr Soc; Engl Schlrshp; Ftbl Hd Mngr 88-90; Engl/Spch/Drama; Mnstry.

**BRACKMAN, SONDRA L,** Roanoke Coll, Salem, VA; SO; BA; Fencing Clb Sec 89-; Fandom Cnfdrtn 90-; KGB Spoof Soc Clb Sec 90-; Clg Hnrs Prgrm 89-; Beta Beta Beta 89-; Tchrs Asst Hstry; Hstry Biology; Archlgst.**

**BRADBERRY, TOBY P,** Truett Mc Connell Coll, Cleveland, GA; SO; Engl; Edn.

**BRADBURY, KAREN D,** Univ Of Sc At Aiken, Aiken, SC; SO; Stdnt Nrs Assoc Pres 90-; Stdnt Nrs Assoc SC 2nd V P; Gamma Beta Phi; Fuld Flwshp; RN MICU Med Clg GA; ADN; BSN; Nrs Anesth.

**BRADDOCK JR, DANNY H,** Ms St Univ, Miss State, MS; JR; BS; Coop Ed Prgm 90-; Gamma Beta Phi 89-; Mech Eng.

**BRADEL, DALLAS A,** Gordon Conwell Theol Sem, S Hamilton, MA; GD; MDIV; Lehigh Univ Choir 82-85; The Bach Choir Of Pittsburgh 89-90; Seminary Choir 90-; Alpha Gamma Delta 82-85; Allegheny Cnty Bar Assoc 88-; Amer Bar Assoc 88-90; Bar Of Commonwlth Of PA 88-; BA Lehigh Univ 85; JD Duquesne Univ Schl Of Law 88; Theology; Christian Educ.

**BRADEN, LADINA A,** Middle Tn St Univ, Murfreesboro, TN; SR; BBA; AA Three Rivers Cmnty Clge 81; Acctng.

**BRADEN JR, WILLIAM F,** Life Coll, Marietta, GA; SR; DC; William Fischer Meml Awd 87-89; AS Ocean Cty Clg 90; Chrprctc.

**BRADFORD, AMY L,** Central Al Comm Coll, Alexander City, AL; FR; BS; SGA Sec 90-; Phi Theta Kappa Treas; Aerospc Eng; Eng.

**BRADFORD, GRETA J,** Tougaloo Coll, Tougaloo, MS; FR; Bsktbl 90-; Poli Sci; Law Schl.

**BRADFORD, KYLE D,** Univ Of Tn At Martin, Martin, TN; JR; BS; Econ Clb; Sigma Alpha Epsilon Treas 89-; Good Lark Schlr 88-; Econ/Finance; Banking.

**BRADFORD, LIBBY G,** Radford Univ, Radford, VA; SO; BM; MENC 90-; PAS 89-; Sugma Alpha Iota; Music Ed; Secndry Sch Music.

**BRADFORD, LISA G,** Abraham Baldwin Agri Coll, Tifton, GA; SO; BA; Actvts Scl Drctr; Psychlgy.

**BRADFORD, LISA J,** Coll Of The Holy Cross, Worcester, MA; FR; BA; Slng Clb 90; Paper Photo Staff 90-; IM Vlybl; Pltcl Scnc; Law.

**BRADFORD, PAMELA L,** Norfolk St Univ, Norfolk, VA; SR; BS; Omega Essnce Clb Inc Thrgh Omega Psi Phi; Army ROTC Rngr Chllnge; Med Spclst In US Army Rsrvs; Psych; Indstrl Psychlgy.

**BRADFORD, PAUL D,** Univ Of Nc At Asheville, Asheville, NC; SR; BA; Chnclrs Collqm 89-; Phi Alpha Theta 90-; Hist; Law.

**BRADFORD, SHERRY L,** Abraham Baldwin Agri Coll, Tifton, GA; FR; Cloggers; Bapt Stdnt Un; Sci; Phys Thrpst.

**BRADFORD, SHIRLEY LOUISE,** Univ Of South Al, Mobile, AL; SR; BS; Acctg Clb V P; Indstrl Acctg; Acctg; CPA.

**BRADFORD, TRACY A,** Central Fl Comm Coll, Ocala, FL; FR; AA; Plu Theta Kappa; Intrn WTRS Radio Statn; Cmmnctns; Law.

**BRADFORD, TRINA L,** Fl A & M Univ, Tallahassee, FL; JR; BA; Astra Clb Sec; Crmnl Jstc; Lwyr.**

**BRADHAM, REATHEA E,** Clayton St Coll, Morrow, GA; SO; BA; Math; Educ.

**BRADLEY, BARBARA C,** Univ Of North Fl, Jacksonville, FL; JR; BED; AA FL Comm Clg 89; Elem Ed; Tch.

**BRADLEY, BEVERLY D,** Owensboro Comm Coll, Owensboro, KY; FR; ADN; Nrsng; RN.

**BRADLEY, BRENT E,** Memphis St Univ, Memphis, TN; SO; BA; Gamma Iota Sigma 90-; Lambda Chi Alpha Sec 90-; St Bd Rgnts Schlrshp 89-; Rsk Mgmt/Maj Corp.

**BRADLEY, BRIAN R,** Univ Of Nc At Charlotte, Charlotte, NC; SO; BA; S/D Coffee Prod Mgr 88-; AAS Purdue Univ 86; Bsn Finance; Bnkg/Finance.

**BRADLEY, CAROLYN L,** Univ Of Sc At Spartanburg, Spartanburg, SC; FR; BS; Sci/Engl/Hstry; Nrs.

**BRADLEY, CHARMAINE T,** Williamsburg Tech Coll, Kingstree, SC; SR; Cosmetology Clb; Sec Cosmetolgist Nail Tech Make Up; Cosmetic Arts.

**BRADLEY, CHRISTINE,** Oh Univ, Athens, OH; GD; DO; Stdnt Advcts Envrnmntl Advcts 90; Alpha Sigma Nu 90; Alpha Epsln Delta 88-90; Vrsty Sftbl 87-89; BS John Carroll Univ 90; Med; Physcn.

**BRADLEY, DANIEL,** Va St Univ, Petersburg, VA; SR; BS; Wilson Magnet HS Acad/Spts Hnr Awd 85-86; Natl Hnr Scty 85-86; Deans List 87-88; Public Admin; Mgt.

**BRADLEY, DONNA L,** Patrick Henry Comm Coll, Martinsville, VA; SO; Patrick Henry Paralegal Assoc Pr/Fndr 90-; Tutor; Deans Lst 90; Hons Lst 90-; Mother Rachel Walker Awrd 90-; Williams/Luck/Williams Atty; Paralegal; Law/U S Govt.

**BRADLEY, EDITH I,** City Univ Of Ny Hunter Coll, New York, NY; JR; BA; Amer Museum Ntl Hstry Vol 86-; Chrstn Choir Dir; Psychlgy; Cnslg.**

**BRADLEY JR, EDWARD E,** Tn St Univ, Nashville, TN; SO; BS; Natl Soc Blck Eng 90-; Natl Soc Archtctrl Eng 90-; Physics Clb Treas 90-; Sigma Tau Delta 90; Hnrs Prog 90-; Tutor 90-; Stu Spprt Srv Tutor 90-; Mssnry Brd; Eng Srvc Awrd 90-; Archtctrl Rsrch Fllwshp 90-; Ronald Mcnair Awrd 90-; Arstcrt Bnd; Archtctrl Eng; Strctrl Eng.

**BRADLEY, EILEEN P,** George Mason Univ, Fairfax, VA; SO; BA; Socty Intl Stds Pres; Socty Intl Stds Sec 90; Intl Actv Comm Chrmn; Gldn Key Actvty Pres; Cath Cmps Mnstry Chrmn 90-; Asstshps 89-; Panama Cnl Comm 89-; IM Ftbl/Aerobics 90-; Intl Stds/Spnsh; Foreign Rel Diplomacy.**

**BRADLEY, GLENN T,** Hudson Valley Comm Coll, Troy, NY; FR; AOS; Phi Theta Kappa 90-; Mchnst Apprntce; Mchng Prcs; Engnrng.

**BRADLEY, HEATHER M,** Peace Coll, Raleigh, NC; FR; BS; Chrstn Assn; Choir 90-; Bacchus/SADD 90-; Fllwshp Chrstn Athltc; Rcrtn Assn 90-; Run Fun Mrthn 90-; Vol Cnstrctn Plygrnd 90-; Pwdr Puff Ftbll 90-; Rehab Cnslng; Subs Abuse Cnslr.

**BRADLEY, KAREN L,** Univ Of South Al, Mobile, AL; JR; BS; Alpha Lambda Delta; Phi Eta Sigma 89-; Beta Gamma Sigma; Mortar Brd; Alpha Chi; Phi Alpha Phi; Phi Mu Tr 90-; Achvmnt Schlrshp 88-; Busn; Acctg.

**BRADLEY, KATHLEEN M,** Univ Of Louisville, Louisville, KY; SR; BS; Stdnt Cncl Cls Rep 90-; Amer Soc Civil Eng 89-; Soc Wmn Eng 89-; Chi Epsilon Sec/Treas 90-; Tau Beta Pi 90-; Golden Key 89-; W B Wendt Civil Eng Awd 90; Tau Beta Pi 89; Civil Eng; Eng.

**BRADLEY, KEITH P,** Salisbury St Univ, Salisbury, MD; SR; BS; Gamma Theta Upsilon; Outstndg Acad Achvmnt Awd; Geogrphy.

**BRADLEY, KEVIN M,** Widener Univ, Chester, PA; SR; BS; IEEE 90-; Licensed Electrician 85-; Elctrcl Engr; Engr.

**BRADLEY, KIMBERLEE A,** Salisbury St Univ, Salisbury, MD; JR; BS; Cyclng Clb 90-; Sprts Medcn Clb 89-; Phys Ed Mjrs Scty 89-; Athltc Trng Intrnshp 87-; Stdnt Athltc Trnr 87-; Phys Ed/Athltc Trng; Athltc Trng.

**BRADLEY, KIMBERLY J,** James Madison University, Harrisonburg, VA; JR; BS; Stdnt Govt Repr 80-81; Otng Clb 80-; VVA Psychlgy Clb 90; Psi Chi Psychlgcl Hnr Soc Treas UVA JMU 90; Vctm Wns Asst Pgm Intrn Cmnwlth Attys Ofc Alexandria VA; JMU Wm Lacrosse JV 89; Psychlgy; Soc Serv/Law/Crim Jstc.

**BRADLEY, KIMBERLY S,** Ms St Univ, Miss State, MS; SO; BS; Amer Chem Soc 89-; Bnd Squad Ldr 89-; Pres Schlrs 89-; Sigma Alpha Iota Sgt At Arms 89-; Stu Of The Yr 89-90; Undrgrad Rsrch Asstnt 89-90; Chem; Rsrch/Dvlpmnt.

**BRADLEY, LISA L,** Fl St Univ, Tallahassee, FL; JR; BA; Ntl Stu Spch/Hrg Assoc; Kappa Kappa Gamma; Cmnctns Dsordrs; Spch/Lang Pathology.

**BRADLEY, LORRAINE M,** Saint Josephs Coll Sufflk Cmps, Patchogue, NY; SR; Natl Bus Hnr Soc 90-; NY Daily News Intrnsp 90; BS; Acctg; CPA.**

**BRADLEY, MARIA E,** Coll Of New Rochelle, New Rochelle, NY; SR; BSN; Sigma Theta Tau Inc 90-; Tns 90-; AAS Westchester Comm Clge 76; Nrsg; RN.

**BRADLEY, MARY V,** Marymount Univ, Arlington, VA; FR; ASID; Acad Schlrshp; Vrsty Vlybl; Bsktbll Mgr; Exercise Physlgy/Blgy; Own Health Clb.

**BRADLEY, MELANIE J,** Duquesne Univ, Pittsburgh, PA; FR; BS; Music Educ; Teach.

**BRADLEY, MELINDA C,** Univ Of Ky, Lexington, KY; SR; BS; Mrchng Bnd 87-89; Cncrt Bnd 87-88; Psychlgy; Cnslng Chld Dvlpmnt.

**BRADLEY, MELISSA C,** Morris Brown Coll, Atlanta, GA; SR; Clge Cncrt Chr; Synsnt Soc; Delta Omicron; BA; Vcl Prfrmcn; Tchg Vc/Chrl Cndctng.

**BRADLEY, MELROSE MC A,** Univ Of Sc At Columbia, Columbia, SC; JR; BA; Judcl Brd 89-; Almni Assn/Legslatv Aid 89-90; Delta Delta Delta Socl Dev Chrmn 90-; Engl/Hist; Law.

**BRADLEY, MICHAEL A,** Univ Of Tn At Chattanooga, Chattanooga, TN; SO; BSE; Phi Delta Theta 90-; Eng; Elec.

**BRADLEY, NANCY L,** Atlantic Comm Coll, Mays Landing, NJ; SO; MPT; Physcl Thrpy.

**BRADLEY, RACHEL J,** Erie Comm Coll, Buffalo, NY; FR; BA; De Graff Mem Hosp Nurs Asst; Nurs; ER Nurs.

**BRADLEY, REBECCA J,** Muskingum Coll, New Concord, OH; SR; BA; Adlt Lrnrs Clb 88-90; Phi Theta Beta Ed Hnrry; Trp Ldr Grl Scts 84; Sec Sls; El Ed.

**BRADLEY, REBECCA W,** Mayland Comm Coll, Spruce Pine, NC; FR; AAS; Pres Lst 90; Dns Lst 90; CNA Mcdwl Tech Comm Clg 82; Med Offc Tech; Hosp Admin.

**BRADLEY, ROBERT L,** Al A & M Univ, Normal, AL; SR; BS; FFA Sec 85-86; Undergrad Normalite Assoc Chpln 88-89; Cir K Pres 88-89; Alpha Zeta 90; Phi Beta Sigma State 2nd Vice 89-; Hopkins Hall Man Of Yr 85; ROTC Schlrshp Awrd 87; Assoc Dean Of Stdnts Awrd 86; Agri Bus Educ.

**BRADLEY, STACIA D,** Ashland Comm Coll, Ashland, KY; FR; MBA; Nwspr Stff Ed Chief 90-; Jrnlsm Stndt Yr 90-; 1st Pl Sprts Wrtng 90-; 2nd Pl Ed Wrtng 90-; KY Stdnt Ldrshp; Engl; Jrnlsm.

**BRADLEY, TENA M,** Meridian Comm Coll, Meridian, MS; SO; AA; Dstrbtv Ed Clbs Amer Sales Chrprsn; Ldrshp Efctvns Dvlpmnt Pgm; Ldrshp Efctvns Dvlpmnt Cert; Fnce/Bkg; Acct Exec/Credit Intrvwr.

**BRADLEY, TODD R,** Ms Gulf Coast Comm Coll, Perkinston, MS; FR; Prk Prmr 90-; Math; Eng.

**BRADLEY, TROY,** Truett Mc Connell Coll, Cleveland, GA; SO; AA; Toastmstrs Intl Spchcrftr; Fl Gospel Bsnmn Flwshp; Lamar/Bradley Aviation Svcs Co-Owner 86-; Cert Aerosp Grnd Equip Tech USAF 82; Cert Law Libr Clrk 90; Bsn Mgmt/Psych; Entreprnr.

**BRADLEY, VALERIE A,** Belmont Coll, Nashville, TN; SO; BBA; Blck Stdnt Awareness Grp Sec 90-; Gamma Beta Phi 89-; Deans Lst 90; Schlrshp Bsktbl 4 Yr; Mktg/Mgmnt; CEO Major Company.

**BRADSHAW, ANGELIQUE MICHELLE,** Central St Univ, Wilberforce, OH; FR; BA; Acctng; Cpa.

**BRADSHAW, BILLY R,** Owensboro Comm Coll, Owensboro, KY; SO; BA; Bsnss Admin; Law Enfrcemnt FBI.

**BRADSHAW, CARLA DIANE,** Meridian Comm Coll, Meridian, MS; SO; AA; Phi Beta Lambda Rptr/Hist 89-90; Cmptr Tech.

**BRADSHAW, FELICIA M,** Fayetteville St Univ, Fayetteville, NC; SR; Kappa Delta Pi Treas 90-; Acad Awd Exclnc; Chrch Chldrns Choir Dir 83-; Sndy Schl Tchr/Preschl Dir 82-; Elem Ed; Tchr.

**BRADSHAW, HEATHER M,** Fl St Univ, Tallahassee, FL; SO; BS; Soc Wmn Eng VP; Phi Eta Sigma; IM Sccr Flg Ftbl; Cvl Eng.

**BRADSHAW, HOLLY H,** Richard Bland Coll, Petersburg, VA; SO; BS, Biology Clb 90-; Deans Lst 90-; Applchn Trl Conf; Amer Hiking Soc; Wrld Wldlfe Fnd; Natl Assn Srch/Rscue; Amer Reg Radlgic Tech 88-; Amer Soc Radlgic Tech 88-; Richmond Srch Rscue; K-9 Alert Srch/Rscue; AA R I Comm Clg 79; Nurs.

**BRADSHAW, NOLAND J,** City Univ Of Ny Baruch Coll, New York, NY; BBA; Econ/Fin Club 90-; Cari Com Club 89-; Finance; Prof.

**BRADSHAW, PAUL S,** Univ Of Ky, Lexington, KY; SR; BA; Cnslng Psychlgst.

**BRADSHER, MARTIN L,** Vance Granville Comm Coll, Henderson, NC; JR; AAS; Indstl Mgmt; Indstl Plnt Mgmt.

**BRADWELL, THOMAS J,** Schenectady County Comm Coll, Schenectady, NY; FR; BA; Chrstn Flwshp Clb 90; Pres Lst; Hmn Services.

**BRADY, CYNTHIA D,** Fayetteville St Univ, Fayetteville, NC; SR; Phi Beta Lambda Pres 88-90; SAM Sec 88-90; Chancllrs Ldr Forum 89-90; Delta Mu Delta 89-90; Cumberland Urb Renew/Beutfcn; BS 90; Busn Admin; Law.

**BRADY, EMILY C,** Univ Of Nc At Greensboro, Greensboro, NC; SR; BS; Stdnt Intrnshp Jones Elem Schl Grnsboro N C 90-; Vol Asst Hgh Fls Elem Schl High Falls N C 90-; Elem Educ; Tch.

**BRADY, FRANK BARCO,** Fl A & M Univ, Tallahassee, FL; SR; BS; Pnlls Gm Offcls Assoc 88-89; Armcn Crmnl Jstc Assoc 90-; AA 89-; Crmnl Jstc.

**BRADY, JEFFREY J,** Univ Of Southern Ms, Hattiesburg, MS; SR; BS; HEA Pres 89-90; Stdnt Dietetic Assoc 89-; Gamma Beta Pi/Kappa Omicron Nu 90-; Amer Dietetic Assoc Fdn Quindara Oliver Dodge Schlrhsp 90-; Dietetics; Hlth Care.

**BRADY, JOHN K,** Fayetteville St Univ, Fayetteville, NC; SR; BA; Pltcl Sci Clb VP 90-; Spch Dbt Clb Sec 88-89; Hstry.

**BRADY, KELLEY M,** Univ Of Cincinnati, Cincinnati, OH; JR; BSN; Nrsng.

**BRADY, KRISTIN M,** Hudson Valley Comm Coll, Troy, NY; SO; BA; Pres Lst 89-; Coop Exprnc 90-; AAS Bsn Admin; Acctg.

**BRADY, MATTHEW K,** Westminster Coll, New Wilmingtn, PA; SR; BS; SAVE; Cncrt Chr; Rsdnc Life Stf; Beta Beta Beta Tres 88-; Intrnshp Dlphn Rsrch Cntr; Hnry Mntn Xi Undrgrd Rsrch; Biology; Marine Biology.

**BRADY, PATRICIA A,** Merrimack Coll, North Andover, MA; JR; BS; Acctng Fnnce Scty; Natl Assn Of Accts; Acad Schl; MA St Schl; Endwmnt Schl; Mn Of Mrrmck Schl; Acctng; CPA.

**BRADY, ROSALEEN A,** Mount Saint Mary Coll, Newburgh, NY; SR; BED; Entrnmnt Edtr Sch Nwspr Edtr 89-90; Sch Nwspr Wrtr 88-90; Ambsdr Clb Tour Guide; Res Lving Cncl Jr Cls Rep 88-90; Ldrshp Dev Series I Grp Ldr 89-90; Admns Rep 88-90; Res Asst 90-; Deans Lst; Stdnt Tchr Intrn 90; BA; English/Educ; H S English Tchr.

**BRADY, TRELLA J,** Univ Of Tn At Martin, Martin, TN; SR; BSW; Socl Wrk Clb 90-; Socl Wrk.

**BRADY, WILLIAM T,** Fayetteville St Univ, Fayetteville, NC; SR; BS; Crmnl Justice Clb 90-; AA Fayettevl Tech Com Clg 88-90; Crmnl Justice; Law Enfrcmnt.

**BRAFFORD II, JAMES E,** Bridgewater Coll, Bridgewater, VA; SO; BS; Pre-Med Soc 89-; Bapt Stdnt Un Cncl 89-; Lambda Soc 90-; Bio; Neurology.

**BRAGASON, ATLI BJORN,** Univ Of Sc At Columbia, Columbia, SC; SR; BS; Amer Mktg Asc 89-; Eurpn Comm Asc Pres 90-; Gldn Key 90; Intl Std Hnr Soc; Acad Exclnc Awd 90; Acad Exclnc Pres Hnr Lst Awd 90; Mktg/HRTA; Intl Bsn.

**BRAGDON, MICHAEL R,** Embry Riddle Aeronautical Univ, Daytona Beach, FL; JR; BS; Civil Air Ptrl 89-; Aero Sci/Flightf Comm Aviation.

**BRAGG, DEBORAH S,** Northeast State Tech Comm Coll, Blountville, TN; SO; AAS; Tau Kappa Epsilon 87-88; Jr Vol H V C Hosp 88-89; Off Sys Tech; Admin Sec.

**BRAGG, EDWARD R,** Alfred Univ, Alfred, NY; SR; BS; Amer Crmc Scty 88-; IM 88; Clg Bowl 89-; Kappa Psi Upsln Soc Chrmn; Trck/Crs Cntry 88-89; Ceramic Eng; Grad Sch Eng.

**BRAGG, ELLEN M,** Beckley Coll, Beckley, WV; SO; BS; Psychlgy; Cnslng.

**BRAGG, HOYT DANIEL,** East Tn St Univ, Johnson City, TN; FR; MA; Alumni Hon Schlrshp; WSP Rgnts Schlrshp; K W Shrp Schlrshp Acctng Exclnc; Bus/Accntncy; CPA.

**BRAGG, RICHARD M,** Springfield Tech Comm Coll, Springfield, MA; SO; BA; Spfd Continental Cablevsn Audio Engr 89-; Telecmunctns; Music/Film.

**BRAGG, TINA ANN,** Al A & M Univ, Normal, AL; SR; MBA; Amer Mktg Assn 88-; Mu Kappa Tau; Delta Mu Delta; Cum Laude; Calhoun Coll 88.

**BRAHAM, RICHARD W,** Fl St Univ, Tallahassee, FL; JR; BA; Intrntl Rltns Clb 89; Video Cntr; Phi Eta Sigma 88-; Dns Lst 89; WJTB AM Intrn; Cmmnctns; Media Prdctn.

**BRAHLER, DANIEL J,** Univ Of Hartford, West Hartford, CT; JR; BS; IM Vlybl Clb MVP 89-90; All-Conf Tns Awd 90-; Var Tns Plyr NAC Champs Capt 88-; Bus Mgmt; Real Estate.

**BRAHLER, DOUGLAS D,** Kent St Univ Kent Cmps, Kent, OH; SO; BA; Russian Clb 89-; Alpha Lambda Delta 90-; Hall GPA Awrd 89-90; Resrv Ofcrs Assoc Awrd ROTC; Russian Lang; Army/Diplomat.

**BRAHLER, LINDA J,** West Liberty St Coll, West Liberty, WV; JR; Spnsh Clb Pres; Stdnt Tutor 90-; Kappa Delta Pi Treas 90-; Spnsh; Tchr.

**BRAHLER, ROBERT B,** Univ Of Akron, Akron, OH; JR; BA; Acctg Assn; RHPB Musc/Comdy Comm; IM Ftbl/Sftbl/Glf/Vlybl; Acctg.

**BRAILEY, BRIAN E,** Middle Tn St Univ, Murfreesboro, TN; SO; BBA; Acctg; CPA.

**BRAIN, CARMEN T,** Fl International Univ, Miami, FL; SO; BMUS; Music Edctrs Ntl Cncl VP 89; Music Ed; Tchr/Bnd Dir.

**BRAINARD, JASON A,** S U N Y Coll At Fredonia, Fredonia, NY; SO; BA; Ski Clb 89-90; WNYF TV 90-; Anthplgy Clb 90-; Anthrplgy.

**BRAITHWAITE, LISA A,** Palm Beach Comm Coll, Lake Worth, FL; SO; AA; Accntng; CPA.**

**BRAITHWAITE, MARIA L,** Comm Coll Algny Co Algny Cmps, Pittsburgh, PA; SO; Deans Lst; Nrsng Career; AD Nrsng 93; Life Sci; Nrsng.

**BRAKEBILL, THOMAS M,** Southern Coll Of Tech, Marietta, GA; SR; BSIET; Inst Indust Eng; Deans Lst 88-90; Eng.

**BRAKER, GENA N,** Converse Coll, Spartanburg, SC; JR; Cncl Excep Chldrn V P; St Lvl PAN; Deaf Educ; Tchng.

**BRALLEY, CHAD L,** Univ Of Sc At Columbia, Columbia, SC; SR; BSBA; Bus Soc; Deans Lst; Intrn Spgs Ind; Mktg; Advtsng.

**BRAM, JENNIFER F,** Dowling Coll, Oakdale Li, NY; JR; BA; Elem Edn; Tchr.

**BRAMAN, JOSHUA C,** Univ Of Miami, Coral Gables, FL; SO; Hmecmg Exec Comm Assoc Chr 90-; Interfrat Cncl 86-; Rho Alpha; Hnrs Stdnts Assoc 89-; Alpha Lambda Delta 90-; Phi Eta Sigma 90-; Zeta Beta Tau Philanthropy Chr 89-.

**BRAMBLEY, MIKA B W,** Embry Riddle Aeronautical Univ, Daytona Beach, FL; FR; BS; Aeeronautical Sci; Pilot.

**BRAME, MARGARET A,** Vance Granville Comm Coll, Henderson, NC; SR; AAS; Norlina Wmns Clb Pres 66-81; Norlina Jr Wmns Clb Pres 81-; Warrenton Lioness Clb Bd Of Dir 81-; 4h Alumni Socty Dist Wnr 73; NC Fed Wmns Clbs St Dept Chmn 86-88; Outstdng Achvmnt Crime Prev Gov Martin 87-88; Bus Admin/Acctng; CPA.

**BRAMER, LAWRENCE R,** Youngstown St Univ, Youngstown, OH; SR; BE; Amer Scty Of Mech Engs 89-; Ta Beta Pi 90-; Mech Eng; Eng.

**BRAMMER, KIMBERLY D,** Univ Of North Fl, Jacksonville, FL; SR; BA; AA FCCJ 90; Engl; Tchr.

**BRAN, JOSE L,** Saint Thomas Univ, Miami, FL; SR; BBA; WSU Crew Clb 87-88; Sccr Clb 89-; Dns Lst 88; Gthrng Plce; Bsns; Mgmt.

**BRANA, MARTA,** Univ Of Pr At Rio Piedras, Rio Piedras, PR; GD; MPA; Willsey Awd 81; BS; Pblc Admin; Govt.

**BRANCH, ELVERT L,** Fayetteville St Univ, Fayetteville, NC; SO; BS; Math; Eng.

**BRANCH, KEVIN W,** Abraham Baldwin Agri Coll, Tifton, GA; SO; BA; ABAL Frstry/Wldlf Clb 88-; Bsbl 89-90; Frstry; Cnsltnt.

**BRANCH, KIMBERLY DEE,** Auburn Univ At Auburn, Auburn, AL; FR; AICHE; Scty Wmn Eng; Baptist Cmps Mnstrs; Alpha Lambda Delta; Phi Eta Sigma; Prjct Uplift Big Sis 90-; Campus Cvitan Hstrn; Deans Lst 90; -; Chem Engineering; Law.

**BRANCH, LA SHANDA D,** Howard Univ, Washington, DC; SO; BS; Texas Club 90-; Howard Univ Hnr Stdnt 89-; Human Dvlpmnt; Pub Hlth.

**BRANCH, MICHELLE E,** Liberty Univ, Lynchburg, VA; SR; BS; Flag Corp/Color Gd 89-90; Stdnt Govt; Big Sis Pgm 89-90; Alpha Lambda Delta 89-; Kappa Delta Pi 89-; LACT Snt Rep; Deans Lst 88-; Elem Ed; Tchr.

**BRANCH, RODERICK V,** Tidewater Comm Coll, Portsmouth, VA; SO; Bsn; Acctng.

**BRANCH, TAMARA Y,** Va St Univ, Petersburg, VA; FR; BA; Acctg; CPA.

**BRANCH, WILLIE E,** Ms Valley St Univ, Itta Bena, MS; SR; BFD; FFA; Chrstn Athltc Ass Ftbl; Lf Grd; Frst Aid; CPR; Pres Lst; Pres Schlr; Lf Svng Cert; Physcl Ed Spec Ed Intern; Ftbl Asstntshp; BSGS Delta St Univ 87; Ed/Sclgy.

**BRAND, KAREADER,** Mary Holmes Coll, West Point, MS; FR; AA; Acctng; Go To MSU.

**BRAND, ROBERTA L,** Duquesne Univ, Pittsburgh, PA; GD; Psi Chi Prsdnt 89-90; Omicron Delta Kappa; Sigma Tau Delta; Sigma Tau Delta; Alpha Gamma Delta Mmbrshp Chrmn 89-90; Cmps Actvts Brd 87-90; Schl Hnr Brd 89-90; Grad Magna Cum Laude; Trck Tm 87-90; MA; Psychology; Chld Psychlgst.

**BRANDENBURG, CHARLES G,** Univ Of Sc At Coastal Carolina, Conway, SC; SR; Bsns Admn/Mrktg.

**BRANDENBURG, KAREN E,** George Mason Univ, Fairfax, VA; SO; BS; Vllybl Leag; Chi Omega 90-; Chrch Actvts 89-; Bus; Accntng.

**BRANDER, CRAIG A,** Va Commonwealth Univ, Richmond, VA; SR; Aoc Advncmnt Mngmnt 90-; Rho Epsicon 90-; BA 90; Bus; Bus Mngmnt.**

**BRANDES, GREGORY P,** Kent St Univ Kent Cmps, Kent, OH; JR; Kappa Kappa Psi Frshmn Bnd Awd; Mstrs Awd; Metcalf Awd; Delta Omicron Smmr Music Schlrshp; Music Prfrmnce; Prfssnl Mscn Tchr.

**BRANDES, KELLEY M,** Va Commonwealth Univ, Richmond, VA; FR; MBA; Hstry.

**BRANDFON, THEA P,** Carnegie Mellon Univ, Pittsburgh, PA; SR; BA; Educ Abroad Comm 90-; Swpstks Capt 88-; Dns Lst 90; Kappa Alpha Theta Stndrds 87-; Greek Cncl Socl Chr 90-; Mister Rogers Nghbrhd Prod Asst 90-; WGBH TV Prod Asst 90-; Denmark Semester 89; IM Soccer/Flr Hcky/Ftbl 89-; Prof Wrtng; Govt.

**BRANDON, MELINDA J,** Siena Coll, Loudonville, NY; SR; BBA; Stdnt Senate Lbrary Comm 89-90; Acctg Clb 87-; Ski Clb 89-; Delta Epsilon Sigma; Magna Cum Laude; R J Schrienep Intrn 90-; Acctg.

**BRANDON, NANCY J,** Marshall University, Huntington, WV; SO; BBA; Phi Eta Sigma 89-; Gamma Beta Phi 89-90; Phi Mu 89; Academic Schlrshp 90-; Health Care Mgmnt; Hosp Admnstrn.

**BRANDON, RONALD C,** Marshall University, Huntington, WV; SR; MBA; BBA; Econ; Bus.

**BRANDT, ELIZABETH G,** Univ Of New Haven, West Haven, CT; SR; BS; Alpha Lambda Delta 90-; MVP 89; Acad Achvmnt Awd; Dns Awd Bsns Admn; Dns Lst 90-; Vars Bsktbl Capt 89-; Bsns Admn; Spts Mgmt.

**BRANDT, MARIA F,** Providence Coll, Providence, RI; JR; BA; Friars Clb 89-; Wrtng Fellow 90-; Tutor; Pub Rltns Intrn; IM Ftbl Chmpn 90; Engl/Bus; Pub Rltns/Ed.

**BRANDT, MICHAEL M,** Univ Of Sc At Columbia, Columbia, SC; SR; BA; Scuba Clb 88-89; Intl Rel; Govt.

**BRANDT, SHELLY A,** Middle Tn St Univ, Murfreesboro, TN; SO; BS; Hnrs Prog 88; Math; Professor.

**BRANDT, STACEY L,** Univ Of South Fl, Tampa, FL; FR; BA; Univ Concert Bnd; Pep Bnd; Intrntl Law.

**BRANDVOLD, KARIN A,** Univ Of Fl, Gainesville, FL; SR; BFA; Floridance Pres 90; Fine Arts Cncl 90; Alpha Psi Omega; Delta Gamma Im 88; Constans Schlrshp 90; ACDFA 89; Dance; Perf/Prdctn.

**BRANDWENE, LESLIE A,** Broward Comm Coll, Ft Lauderdale, FL; SO; CERT; Career Mngmnt; BA San Fran Univ 79; Peralegal; Law.

**BRANDY, CAROL LEE,** Memphis St Univ, Memphis, TN; SR; Soc Human Res Mgmnt 89-; Bus Mgmnt; Human Resources.

**BRANDY, SHERI L,** Ky Christian Coll, Grayson, KY; BA; Priscillas Clb VP; Chrldng Coach 90-; Deans Lst 90-; Kndrgrtn Sunday Schl Tchr 88-; Dntl Asst; Prof Law Sec; Med Sec; Elem Ed; Tchng.

**BRANHAM, BETH CHRISTINE,** Univ Of Sc At Columbia, Columbia, SC; SR; BA; Gamma Beta Phi 90-; Alpha Lambda Delta 89; Psi Chi 89-; Columbia Area Mental Hlth Vol 90-; Law.

**BRANHAM, CAROLYN S,** Radford Univ, Radford, VA; JR; BS; Prsdnts Lst 88; Bnd Bstrs Inc Sec 88; Cmmnctn Sci Dsrdrs.

**BRANHAM, KIMBERLY D,** Univ Of Sc At Columbia, Columbia, SC; SO; BA; Gamma Beta Phi 90-; Deans Lst; Prsdnts Lst; Hstry; Elem Edctn.

**BRANIECKI, DEBORAH L,** Daemen Coll, Amherst, NY; SR; BA; Daemen Clg Art Clb Sec 90-; Kappa Delta Pi Sec 90-; Phi Gamma Mu 90-; Vars Bsktbl Capt 87-; BA Art Educ; Art; Tchr.

**BRANIELLA, JOSE,** Saint Thomas Univ, Miami, FL; SR; BA; Cmptr Sci Assn Fndr Pres; Delta Epsilon Sigma 90-; Circle K 89-90; Goldn Glds Elem 89-90; Dns Lst 89-; U S Achvmnt Acad; Navy Achvmnt Medl; Good Condct Med 88; Soccr Clb 89-; U S Mar Corps Res Sqd Ldr 89-; U S Mar Crps 85-89; Cmptr Sci; Cartgrphr.**

**BRANK, KAREN L,** Johnson C Smith Univ, Charlotte, NC; Pan-Afr Coun/Black Aware Secy 90-; Library Cl; Project Vote Vol 90; Stdnt Orien Ldr 90; Jr Achvmnt Top Seller Rogers H S Chours Outstndng Svc; Scl Work.

**BRANKER, LAURA M,** Fl A & M Univ, Tallahassee, FL; JR; BA; Publ Rels Stdnt Soc Amer PR Dir 90-; Jrnlsm; Publ Rels Spec.

**BRANNAN, MEISHA L,** Univ Of Southern Ms, Hattiesburg, MS; JR; BS; Reflections MS Gulf Comm Coll 89; Prknstn Cmps; Annl Stff 89; VP Lst MS G C Coll 88-89; Deans Lst 90; Psychlgy; Psychlgst PhD.

**BRANNAN, ROBIN M,** Bryant Stratton Bus Inst Roch, Rochester, NY; SR; AOS; Bus Mgmnt.

**BRANNEN, JOSEPH C,** Valdosta St Coll, Valdosta, GA; JR; BA; Intrfrat Cncl; IMS; Ordr Omega; Pi Gamma Mu; Sigma Alpha Epsilon VP 90; Pldg Yr; Athlt Yr; All Amer Ntl Flg Ftbl Chmpnshps; IMS Ftbl/Bkstbl/Vlybl/Sftbl; Pol Sci; Law.

**BRANNEN, PEGGY E,** Abraham Baldwin Agri Coll, Tifton, GA; SO; BS; Phi Theta Kappa; Rcpntst; AS; Speech/Lang Pthlgy; Tchng MS.

**BRANNIGAN, KIMBERLY A,** Elms Coll, Chicopee, MA; JR; BA; Bsns Clb Tres 89-; Eqstrn Tm 88-; Bsns Mgmnt; Accntng.

**BRANNING, TODD P,** Univ Of Miami, Coral Gables, FL; JR; BBA; Business Advisory Cncl; Peer Counseling; Beta Alpha Psi; Deans Lst 89-; Bowman Ashe Academic Schlrshp 88-; NAA 90-; IMS 88-; Acctng; CPA.

**BRANNOCK, DEBBY A,** Vance Granville Comm Coll, Henderson, NC; Tchr Assoc Degree.

**BRANNON, DEANNA M,** Spartanburg Methodist Coll, Spartanburg, SC; SO; AS; Acctg; CPA.

**BRANNON III, LEE R,** Al A & M Univ, Normal, AL; FR; BA; Comm Yth Chr VP 89-90; Eagle Lodge 90-; Psychlgy.

**BRANNON, SUSAN C,** Ms St Univ, Miss State, MS; SR; BA; Alumni Delg 90-; MS St Mjrtte Co-Capt 87-90; Kappa Alpha Chpln 87-; Kappa Delta; Gen Lib Arts/Indstl Psych; Publ Rel/Rl Est.

**BRANON, JONATHAN P,** Johnson St Coll, Johnson, VT; JR; BS; Chesamore Hnr Soc 90-; Envrnmntl Sci.

**BRANSON, KANDI L,** Ky St Univ, Frankfort, KY; JR; BS; Pre-Prfssns Hlth Clb Sec; Alpha Kappa Mu VP; Blgy Mjr Acdmc Sprstr; Deans Lst; Blgy; Med.**

**BRANSON, KATHY W,** Bristol Univ, Bristol, TN; SR; BS; Acctg.

**BRANSON, RALPH MATTHEW,** Oh St Univ At Newark, Newark, OH; FR; Alpha Lambda Delta; Phi Eta Sigma; Eng.

**BRANSON, RHONDA F,** Univ Of Sc At Columbia, Columbia, SC; FR; BA; Bsn; Acctg.

**BRANT, ANDREA,** Indiana Univ Of Pa, Indiana, PA; SO; BA; Soc Sci/Hist; Tchr.

**BRANT, KRISTIN A,** S U N Y At Buffalo, Buffalo, NY; JR; BS; Mngmnt Assc Career Dvlpmnt; Dlta Sigma Pi Pldg Cmmt 90-; Deans List 89-; Ecnmcs Tchng Asstshp; Mngmnt/Bsn Admin; MBA Mngmnt.

**BRANTLEY, DOUGLAS R,** Coll Of Charleston, Charleston, SC; JR; BS; Flwshp Christ Athletes 90-; Phi Kappa Phi; Alpha Phi Omega Sgt Of Arms 89-; Commencement Marshall 89-; CRC Pres Freshman Chem Achiev Awd 88; Med Univ SC Peds PT Tm Intshp 90; Student Athletic Trnr 88-91; Physicial Ed; Physical Therapy.

**BRANTLEY, EMMY L,** Ms St Univ, Miss State, MS; JR; BS; Stdtn Govt Assoc Treas 89-90; Rep 88-89; Bapt Stdnt Un Hlms Cmmnty Coll 88-90; Phi Kappa Phi 90; Kappa Delta Pi 90; Phi Theta Kappa Hlms Cmmnty Coll 89-90; Elem Ed.

**BRANTLEY, JANE L,** Valdosta St Coll, Valdosta, GA; SO; BS; Wsly Fdn 90-; Batgirl Bsbl 90-; Spch/Lang Pthlgy.

**BRANTLEY, JENNIFER R,** Univ Of Sc At Columbia, Columbia, SC; FR; BED; Alpha Lambda Delta; Gamma Beta Phi; Phi Eta Sigma; Elem Tchr.

**BRANTLEY, NORE L,** Fayetteville St Univ, Fayetteville, NC; JR; BS; Cmpgrnd Untd Mthdst Chrch 69; Dntl Assist Sls Leas Assoc Revco Drg Stre 83-88; AS Bus Admin Fyttvle Tchncl Cmmnty Clg 90; Bsnss Admin; Hosp Admin.

**BRANTLEY, PAGE M,** Liberty Univ, Lynchburg, VA; JR; BS; Mrktng Assoc; Amer Mrktng Assoc; Alpha Lambda Delta; Bsnss; Mrktng/Pblc Rltns.

**BRANTLEY, ROBERT MARK,** Middle Ga Coll, Cochran, GA; SO; BS; Nuclear Med.

**BRANTLEY, SANDRA L,** Radford Univ, Radford, VA; JR; BS; Psychology Clb 90-; Tutor 88-; Rsrch 89-; Alpha Lambda Delta Pres 89-90; Psi Chi Pres 90-; Most Outstdng Stdnt Awd 90-; VA Psychol Assn 90-; Assn Wmn In Psychol 90-; Cnslng Psychology.

**BRANTON, REGINA P,** Univ Of Sc At Columbia, Columbia, SC; JR; BA; Rsdnt Stdnt Dvlpmnt Rsdnt Advsr Rsdnt Ad 89-; Strn Proj Asst Tchr 88-89; Govt/Intrntl Stds.

**BRANTON, TRACY A,** East Tn St Univ, Johnson City, TN; SO; BA; Majorette In The Band; Dental Hygiene.

**BRANTSEN, BONNIE L,** Univ Of Miami, Coral Gables, FL; JR; BSN; Natl Stdnt Nrs Assn Univ Of Miami; Pres Hnr Rl 90; Dns Hnr Rl Univ Miami 90; Nrsng.

**BRANYAN, LORI A,** Ky Christian Coll, Grayson, KY; SR; AA; Sci/Engl Comm; Tch.

**BRAREN, OLAF D,** Embry Riddle Aeronautical Univ, Daytona Beach, FL; SR; BA; Nvl Avtn Clb 86-87; GACE Flyng Clb 84-; Dean Lst 86-; Flr Hky/Sftbl/Ftbl 86-90; Air Way Sci; Pro Pilot.

**BRAREN, WAYNE M,** S U N Y Coll Of Tech At Delhi, Delhi, NY; SO; BS; Delhi Anti Grvty Grp Jgglng Clb Pres Fndr 89-; Priorty Erth Env Grp 89-; Adv Du Bois Hl Res Hl Cncl 90-; RA 90-; Priorty Erth Chrmn Earthdy 90; AA SUNY Delhi 91; Env Sci; Wldlf Biol.

**BRASEL, DAWN D,** Roane St Comm Coll, Harriman, TN; SO; Cert In Comp Acct Kee Bus Coll Newport News VI 85; AAS; Bus Mgmt Tech; Acctng.

**BRASFIELD, KINSLEY TODD,** Fl St Univ, Tallahassee, FL; SR; BA; Sports Brdcstr Staff; Tampa Bay Ski Club 86-; Sales/Prod Intern WTXL ABC; Vol Pr Assist Ronald Mcdonald House 90; Golf/Soccer 88-; Media Commtn; Brdctng/Sales/Law.

**BRASFIELD, NICK J,** Univ Of Tn At Martin, Martin, TN; SO; BA; Bus Adm; Htl Mgmt.

**BRASFIELD, TAMMY N,** East Tn St Univ, Johnson City, TN; SR; BS; Phi Kappa Phi 90-; Kappa Omicron Nu 88-; Dns Lst 88-90; All Amer Schlr 89; Fashion Mrchndsng; Retail Mngmnt.

**BRASHEAR, CHERYL L,** George Mason Univ, Fairfax, VA; SR; BSED; Stdnt Educ Assoc 89-; Kappa Delta Pi 90-; Golden Key 90-; Early Tchng.

**BRASHER, JEFFREY D,** Univ Of Montevallo, Montevallo, AL; JR; BS; Psychlgy; Indstrl Psychlgy.

**BRASHIER, KENNETH M,** Greenville Tech Coll, Greenville, SC; FR; ASSOC; Vol Fireman Laurens Ctr Asst Chief 89-90; Mchnst; BEM-6 90; AEM-6; Mech Tchnlgy; Mech Maintenance.

**BRASINGTON, CHANDIS R,** Univ Of Sc At Columbia, Columbia, SC; SR; MS; Gldn Keyf Phi Eta Sigma; Omega Chi Epsilon Prsdnt; Amrcn Inst Chmcl Engnrs Sec; Alpha Delta Pi 89; Carolina Schlr; IM Ftbl; BS; Chmcl Engnrng.

**BRASSARD, ALISON M,** Western New England Coll, Springfield, MA; SR; BA; Stdnt Ltrcy Corps Vol; AA Holyoke Comm Coll 89; Psych; Scl Srvcs Scl Wrk.

**BRASSELL, STEPHEN A,** Villanova Univ, Villanova, PA; SO; BS; Band; AED; Phi Gamma Delta; Barry M Goldwater Schlrshp; Univ PA Traineeship Stdnt; Dns Lst; IM Capt; Bio/Hnrs; Med.

**BRASSINGTON, PETER A,** Coll Misericordia, Dallas, PA; JR; BS; Exec Brd Stu Govt Tres 89-90; Cmptr Sci/Mth Clb Pres 89-; Intl Clb Tres 89-; Cll Msrcrd Hnrs Assn 88-; Nwsppr Asst Sprts Ed 89-; Cmps Mnstry 89-; Peer Ttr 88-; Intern Lehigh Vlly Hosp Cntr; Sccr Tm 88-; Math/Cmptr Sci; Oprtns Rsrch.

**BRASSINGTON, WILLIAM J,** Coll Misericordia, Dallas, PA; SO; BSC; Intl Clb Pres 90-; Cmps Mnstry Brd 90-; Acct; Ecnmcs.

**BRASWELL, BERNICE,** Al St Univ, Montgomery, AL; FR; BA; Bus; Acctng.

**BRASWELL, HARIETT J,** Cecils Coll, Asheville, NC; GD; AS; Ray Tipton Mem Schlrshp 90; Sunday Schl Tchr; Employee Asst Pgm/Cmte Mbr 91; Ofc Admin.

**BRASWELL, MARK E,** Southern Coll Of Tech, Marietta, GA; SR; BS CE; ASCE Pres 89-; ACI; GSPE; Tau Alpha Pi; GSPE Schlrshp 88-; Ga Acad Recgntn Day 90; Ge Engr Tech Stdng Yr 90-; Glaziers Union 82-; Civil Engr Tech; Structl Engr.

**BRASWELL, MONICA R,** Johnson C Smith Univ, Charlotte, NC; FR; BA; Elem Ed; Ed.

**BRASWELL, RHONDA A,** Auburn Univ At Auburn, Auburn, AL; SR; BSN; Sigma Theta Tau 90-; Am Nurses Assoc Ala St Nurses Assoc 84-; Chmbrs Co ASNA Nurse Of Yr 85; Fac Am Heart Assoc 89-; Hospice Inc; Mem Hosp 84-90; ADN Southern Un St Jr Coll 84; Nrsng.

**BRASWELL, SHARON Y,** City Univ Of Ny Med Evers Coll, Brooklyn, NY; SO; BA; Ed; Tchng.

**BRATCHER, BEVERLY A,** Duquesne Univ, Pittsburgh, PA; SR; Cls Sec 87-88; Alpha Tau Delta Pres 89-90; Vols; Sacred Hrt Med Ctr Intrnshp; BSN; Nrsng.

**BRATETICH, STEPHANIE A,** Comm Coll Algny Co Algny Cmps, Pittsburgh, PA; SO; Cmmnctns.

**BRATHWAITE, ANGELA D,** Univ Of Nc At Charlotte, Charlotte, NC; JR; BA; Intr Sorority Cncl VP 89-90; Emergng Ldr Mentr 88-89; NAACP VP 89-90; Alpha Kappa Alpha Secy; Intrnshp With Toyr R Us Human Rsrcs Asstnt 90-; Engl; Human Rsrcs.

**BRATHWAITE, INGER J,** Norfolk St Univ, Norfolk, VA; SR; Intl Stdnt Orgztn; Early Chldhd Educ Clb 90-; Alpha Kappa Mu; Schlrshp Hon Awds Convoctn 89; Ass Clg Bahamas 88; Tch Cert 88; Early Childhood Educ.

**BRATHWAITE, MAURICE H,** City Univ Of Ny Med Evers Coll, Brooklyn, NY; SO; BSC; META Stg Mngr 89-; CASA PRO; Tchrs Asst 90-; Mktg/Mgmt.

**BRATKIV, MARK,** Univ Of Miami, Coral Gables, FL; SR; BBA; Scr Clb V Pres 88-89; Bus Schl Stdnt Gov Sentr 89-90; Orientn Coord 90-; Omicron Delta Kappa 90-; Mortar Brd 90-; Order Of Omega 90-; Lambda Chi Alpha 89-90; Fin; Real Estate.

**BRATON, TRACEY A,** Kent St Univ Kent Cmps, Kent, OH; JR; BS; Rho Phi Lambda; Deans Lst 90-; Rec/Leisure Stdy; Arln Indstry.

**BRATTA, ROBERT A,** Univ Of Tn At Knoxville, Knoxville, TN; JR; BA; Judo Clb; Bus Admin; Bus.

**BRATTON, MARC E,** Univ Of Southern Ms, Hattiesburg, MS; JR; BS; SG 88-; Homcmng Dir; Alumni Assn 88-; Southern Style 90-; Lambda Sigma 89-90; Gamma Beta Phi 89-; Phi Kappa Tau VP 88-; Sports Med Assn 88-; Ath Trng; Med.

**BRAU SOBRINO, ALBERTO,** Univ Politecnica De Pr, Hato Rey, PR; FR; Math; Elect Eng.

**BRAUCH, MICHELLE L,** Methodist Coll, Fayetteville, NC; SO; BS; Bible Sch Tchr; Sundy Sch Tchr; Tutor In Kids At Risk Prog; Marshall For Gradtns; Elem Ed; Tch Deaf Chldrn.**

**BRAUER, PAULETTE J,** Wilmington Coll, New Castle, DE; SR; BSN; Assn Oprtng Rm Nrs VP 90; AD Del Tech & Comm Coll 89; Oprtng Rm Nrs.

**BRAUN, BETH JUSTINE,** Mount Saint Mary Coll, Newburgh, NY; FR; BA; Gaelic Scty; Educ.

**BRAUN, CLINTON J,** Univ Of Sc At Columbia, Columbia, SC; JR; PHD; Rotoract; Ldrshp Dev 89-; Gamma Beta Phi 90; Piedmont Soc 89; Univ Bsn Soc 90; Pi Kappa Phi 90; Econ/Fin; Clg Prof.

**BRAUN, GRETCHEN A,** Western New England Coll, Springfield, MA; JR; BS; SWE; Inst Indust Eng; Stdnt Tchr; Lambda Delta; Indust Eng Dptmnt Awd; Eng.

**BRAUN, JASON J,** Radford Univ, Radford, VA; SO; BA; Tau Kappa Epsilon; Finance/Hist.

**BRAUN, JONATHAN D,** Embry Riddle Aeronautical Univ, Daytona Beach, FL; JR; BS; Chrstn Flwshp Clb Pres; Strmrdrs Surf Clb 89-; Flight Trng Schlrshp 90-; Dayton Bch First Baptist Coll Grp 89-; IM Vlybl/Sftbl 90-; Aerontcl Sci; Prof Pilot.

**BRAUN, MERLE P J,** Va Commonwealth Univ, Richmond, VA; SR; Art Educ Chptr Pres 90; Phi Kappa Phi 90; Dns Hnr Lst 90; Magna Cum Laude 90; GB Hamm Acad Achvmnt Awrd VCU Schl Of Arts 90-; Ruth Hyland Hibbs Schlrshp 89; VA Art Educ Assn 90; Frnds Of Art 90; BFA 90; AA Indian River Comm Coll 85; Art Educ; Art Tchr K-12.

**BRAUN, PATRICK G,** Schenectady County Comm Coll, Schenectady, NY; FR; AS; C W Elston Schlrshp; Bus Admn; Acctg.

**BRAUNGER, LORI M,** Indiana Univ Of Pa, Indiana, PA; FR; BED; CEC 90-; Spec Ed; Tchr.

**BRAUNS, KELLEY J,** Catawba Valley Comm Coll, Hickory, NC; JR; AAS; Sex Equity; Furn Prod Mgmt; Furniture.

**BRAVAKIS, SEAN E,** Univ Of Hartford, West Hartford, CT; SO; BA; Radio Sta At Uni Of Hartford DJ Staff 89-90; Bsbl 89-; Cmnctn; TV Radio/News Media.

**BRAVERMAN, LINDA K,** Univ Of Cin R Walters Coll, Blue Ash, OH; FR; BS; Deans Lst; AS Sinclair Comm Coll 75; AS Southern Ohio Coll 85; Soc Wrk; Substance Abuse.

**BRAVIS, DIANNE L,** Clemson Univ, Clemson, SC; SR; BS; Swimming Tm Co Capt 87-; Athletic Advsry Brd 89-; Golden Key; Rho Phi Lambda; Outstanding Stdts Amer; Black C Clb; NCAA All Amer/Hnrbl Mntn 88-; Atlantic Cst Cnfrnc Tm Chmpns 88-; Spec Olympcs 88-; Parks Recreation Tourism Mgmt.

**BRAVO, ELENA M,** Fl International Univ, Miami, FL; SR; BSN; NSNA 89-; Phi Lambda 90-; Sigma Theta Tau; Feed Homeless Catholic Church 90-; Camillus Hlth Concern; Nrsg; MS Nrsg/Bsn.

**BRAVO, NICK J,** Life Coll, Marietta, GA; GD; DC; Chi Rho; CA St Schlrshp 81; IM Bsktbl 90; Cvln USAF 89; AS Moorpark Coll 84; BS State Univ Of New York 86; Chrprctc.

**BRAVO, SERGIO G,** Fl International Univ, Miami, FL; SO; BS; Faculty Schlrs; Fla Schlrs Schlrshp 89; Fclty Schlrs Schlrshp 89; Natl Hispanic Fund Schlrshp 90; Engrng Electrcl Mechanical.

**BRAVO-CANDELARIA, JENNIFER,** Miami Dade Comm Coll South, Miami, FL; SO; MBA; Phi Theta Kappa Soc Dir Comm Serv Pres Aide; Stu Assoc Envrnmt 90; Bk Schlrshp Thrgh Hnrs Dept; Slctd Tlnt Rstr Otstndg Mnrty Comm Coll 90-; IM Cmptn; Mdrn Lang; Tchr.

**BRAXTON, ARONEYSA D,** Alcorn St Univ, Lorman, MS; FR; BA; Jr Classical League Pres; Magnolia Fed Arts/Civics Clb V P; Clg Bnds Section Ldr; Alpha Phi Omega V P; Club Hero Pres; Elem Educ; Tchr.

**BRAXTON, SCHNETTA T,** Va St Univ, Petersburg, VA; FR; BA; Pol Sci; Law.

**BRAY, CHADWICK M,** Univ Of Sc At Columbia, Columbia, SC; FR; BA; Nwspr Crm Rprtr 90-; Carolina News Prdctn Stf 90-; Res Hl Govt Exec Cncl 90-; Gamma Beta Phi 90-; Habitat For Humanity; Rick Temple Jrnlsm Schlrshp 90-; Deans Lst 90-; IM Ftbl/Sftbl/Ultmt Frsbee 90-; Jrnlsm; Intrntl Crrspndnt.

**BRAY, CRAIG A,** Northern Ky Univ, Highland Hts, KY; JR; BA; German.

**BRAY, LARRY R,** Memphis St Univ, Memphis, TN; JR; BA; Bsktbl Frd Hrdmn Univ 88-89; Sigma Chi 90-; Acctg; Tax Law.

**BRAY, MELODY L,** Clark Atlanta Univ, Atlanta, GA; SO; BS; Chem Clb 90-; Cntrs Disease Cntrl Atlanta GA; Chem; Clncl Rsrch.

**BRAY, SCOTT P,** Clayton St Coll, Morrow, GA; JR; BA; AA 90; Busn; Real Estate Hospitly.

**BRAY, TRICIA D,** Middle Ga Coll, Cochran, GA; JR; BA; Dns Lst 89-90; Assoc; Bsn Admin.

**BRAZ, JEANNE M,** James Madison University, Harrisonburg, VA; JR; BS; Com Instl Efctns 90-; Assn Edn Yng Chldrn 89-; March Royal Dukes 88-; Kappa Delta Pi; Gold Key 90-; Tau Beta Sigma Natl VP 89-; Emerging Ldrs 90; Early Childhd Edn; Teach.

**BRAZAO, STEVEN A,** Embry Riddle Aeronautical Univ, Daytona Beach, FL; JR; BS; Flght Dmnstrtn Tm Sec 89-; Rsdnt Advsr; Deans Lst 88-; Omicron Delta Kappa 90-; Aerntcl Sci; Airln Plt.

**BRAZELL, VELMA A,** Univ Of Sc At Columbia, Columbia, SC; FR; BA; Bsnss Admin Org Mngmnt; Law.

**BRAZELTON, LYNN B,** Hampton Univ, Hampton, VA; SR; BA; Soc Wrk Clb Pres 90-; NAACP 87-; Big Bro Big Str 87-; Alpha Kappa Alpha 89; Pine Chapel Tutor 89-90; Dept Soc Serv 89-; Peninsula Alcoholsm Serv 90-.**

**BRAZEMAN, CRAIG P,** Southern Coll Of Tech, Marietta, GA; SR; BS; ACS Assn 87-; Scttsh Rite Med Ctr Vol 90; Eng Apprntc Textl Mfg 90-; AS De Kalb Clg 90; Qlty Cntrl; Law.

**BRAZZANO, LISA M,** Dowling Coll, Oakdale Li, NY; SO; BA; Nthnl Gffn Glf Tnns Trn 89; Hldy Trbt Cncrt 90; Thm Comm; Prsdntl Hnr Schlrs 89-; Anthrplgy Archlgy.

**BRAZZELL, GARY L,** Saint Andrews Presbytrn Coll, Laurinburg, NC; SO; BA; Round Table 90-; Wrtrs Forum Dir 89-; Theatre 90; Alpha Chi VP; Hon Soc 90-; Hons Prog 89-; Scotland Lit Cncl Tutor 90-; Press Intrnshp Edtrl Asst; Ins Intrn Serv Mrktng; Cmnctns; Mrktng PR/JRNLSM.

**BREA, ARTURO,** City Univ Of Ny Baruch Coll, New York, NY; SR; Computer Clb 89-; Photog Clb 90-; Golden Key; Comp Info Syst; Info Mgmt.

**BREA, LUIS O,** Fordham Univ, Bronx, NY; SO; MBA; Acctng; Law.

**BREADS, SUSAN E,** S U N Y Coll At Fredonia, Fredonia, NY; JR; BS; Girl Schts Rgstr 85-; Natl Hnr Soc 75; Jay Cees Trea 89; Med Tech/Chmstry.

**BREARLEY, JODIE L,** Univ Of Cincinnati, Cincinnati, OH; SR; BS; Clermnt Clg Educ Clb 87-; Gldn Ky; Phi Delta Kappa 88-; Asst Div Chr Humnties 90-; Formr Admn Asst 83-87; AA UC Clrmnt Clg 87; Engl Educ; Tchr/Bsns.

**BREARTON, PAULA S,** Univ Of Cincinnati-Clrmnt Coll, Batavia, OH; SO; BS; Phi Theta Kappa Sec 90-; Mrs Ftnss Wrld Instrctr; Prkng Attndnt 90-; AA; Nclr Med.

**BRECHEISEN, JEANNIE K,** Fl St Univ, Tallahassee, FL; SO; BA; Mrchng Chfs 89-; Tau Beta Sigma 90-; Music; Music Thrpy.

**BRECKER, TIMOTHY T,** Coppin St Coll, Baltimore, MD; SR; BS; Senate 90-; Amer Assn Hlth &E Rec/Dnc 90-; Hon Assn Treas 88-; Alpha Kappa Mu; MD Assn Tchr Educ Outstndng Stdnt Awd; Vrsty Tnns 88-; MD Assn Hlth PE Rec/Dnc Outstndng Stdnt 90-; Adptd Phy Ed; Tchr.

**BREDAHL, SUZANNA C,** Christopher Newport Coll, Newport News, VA; JR; BS; Alpha Chi 90-; Alpha Kappa Psi VP Hmn Rsrcs; Langley Yth Serv Vol Sccr Coach; Deans Lst; Fin; Fin Anlyst.

**BREDESON, GWYN E,** Al A & M Univ, Normal, AL; JR; BS; Intrntl Tstmstrs Clb 89-; Amer Scty Of Mltry Cmptrllrs 88-; Dgree In Lgstcs.

**BREDINE, DAVID W,** Ms St Univ, Miss State, MS; JR; BA; Clg Rpblcns 88-89; Prfsnl Golf Mgmnt Clb VP 88-; Hl Cncl Rep 88-89; Sigma Nu Sec 89-; Dlgt 1st Ntnl PGM Prgrm Mttng 90; Emrgnt Ldr Wrkshp 89; IM 88-; Prfsnl Golf Mgmnt; Golf Prfsnl.

**BREED, CARLENA A,** Clarkson Univ, Potsdam, NY; FR; Accntng Clb; Prsdntl Schlr; Deans Lst; Delta Zeta; Accntng.

**BREEDING, AMY Y,** Union Coll, Barbourville, KY; SO; BA; Scl Sci Clb 90-; Psych; Occptnl Thrpst/Clncl Psychlgst.

**BREEDING, MARK D,** West Chester Univ, West Chester, PA; JR; BS; Athltc Trnrs Clb 90-; Natl Athltc Trnrs Assoc 89-; Pnnsylvn Athltc Trnrs Scty 89-; Phi Eta Sigma; Phi Kappa Theta Srgnt Arms 89-; US Army Rsrv 86-; Clncl Wchst Univ; Clncl Swrthmr Coll; Hcky 90; Athltc Trnng.

**BREEDING, TERESA L,** Roane St Comm Coll, Harriman, TN; FR; AAS; Hlth Sci/Physl Therapist Asst; Medl PTA.

**BREEDLOVE, BRUCE W,** Limestone Coll, Gaffney, SC; SR; BS; Advsry Cncl 90-; Bsn Mgmt; Mgmt St Govt.

**BREEN, ANNE E,** Hudson Valley Comm Coll, Troy, NY; FR; AS; Pres List; Lbrl Arts; Psychlgy.

**BREEN, KATHLEEN M,** Villanova Univ, Villanova, PA; SO; BA; Stdnt Govt Intrnl/Pblc Rltns 90-; Stdnt Snt Arts/Sci Sntr; Sailg Tm Sec 89-; Deans Lst 89-; Alpha Phi 90-; Prjc Sunshine-Vol Our Mother Sorrows 89-; Spec Olympcs Hggr 89-; WA DC Intrnshp; IM Sccr Bsktbl Sftbl Ftbl Capt 89-; Pltcl Sci; Law.

**BREEN, MARY KIMBERLY,** Hudson Valley Comm Coll, Troy, NY; FR; AA; Maxwell Online BRS Div Latham NY QC Spclst 84-; Manpower Temp Serv Sec; Trained 8 Subordinate Stf Ed To Edit Mainframe Cmptr 84-; Lib Arts Humanities/Soc Sci; Publ Inds.

**BREEN-SNOW, HEATHER L,** Coker Coll, Hartsville, SC; JR; BA; Plyrs Drama Clb Sec 89-; Ambssdrs-Stdnt Rcrtng 89-; Cls VP 90-; Yrbk Asst Edtr 89-; Alpha Psi Omega Sec 90-; Cmmssnrs 89-; Natl Deans 89-; William C Coker Schlrshp 88-; Psychlgy/Drama; Clncl Psychlgy.

**BREEZE, TROY L,** Middle Ga Coll, Cochran, GA; SO; BA; Gamma Beta Phi 88-; Mchncl Engnrng.

**BREGANDE-BUCELLA, DENISE,** Neumann Coll, Aston, PA; JR; BS; Stdnt Nurses Assn 89-; Stdnt Rep Core Com 90-; Delta Pi Epsilon Sigma; Hospice Nrsng.

**BREGE, REBECCA L,** Daemen Coll, Amherst, NY; FR; BS; Physcl Thrpy Clnc; Deans Lst 90-; Tuitn Schlrshp 90-; Physcl Thrpy.

**BREGOU, CHRISTINA E,** Liberty Univ, Lynchburg, VA; SO; BS; SGA Senate 90-; Chi Alpha Club 90-; Liberators For Life 89-90; Prayer Ldr 90-; Deans Lst 89-90; Human Ecology.

**BREIDENBACH, JULIE G,** Miami Jacobs Jr Coll Of Bus, Dayton, OH; SR; Cert Sinclair Comm Coll 87; Cert Montgomery Cty JUS 86; Automated Ofc Tchnlgy; Comp Prgmng.

**BREIER, STACY L,** Wagner Coll, Staten Island, NY; SR; BSE; Sngfst Comm Pblc Rel 90; Educ Hnrs; Kappa Delta Pi 90-; Epsilon Delta Omicron Sec 89-; Elem Educ.

**BREIN, CHARLES L,** Hudson Valley Comm Coll, Troy, NY; JR; BBA; Pr Lst; Natl Acad Of Opticianry 78-; AAS Erie Cmnty Clg 77; Acctng/Bus; CPA.

**BREISH, BONNIE M,** Glassboro St Coll, Glassboro, NJ; JR; BA; Clg Nwspr Prod Asst; Clg Radio Sta Pub Serv Asst; Res Asst Res Hls 89-; Cmunctn; Publctn Prod.

**BREITENBACH, SHERILYN P,** Univ Of Cin R Walters Coll, Blue Ash, OH; SO; BSN; Assoc Cinti Bible Clg 70; Nrsng.

**BREITENSTEIN, JONATHAN E,** Georgetown Coll, Georgetown, KY; SR; BS; Greek Cncl Rep 89-90; Interfrat Cncl Pres 89-90; Alpha Lambda Delta 88; Pi Kappa Alpha Crrspndng Scrtry 88; Mrktng/Fnce Dept Awd; Alpha Lambda Delta Awd; Mrktng/Fnce; Law.

**BREITENSTEIN, KELLEY M,** Univ Of Ky, Lexington, KY; JR; BSN; Res Hall Assn Dorm Rep 88-89; Stdnt Govt Assn 88-89; Sftbl Res Hall 88-90; Alpha Lambda Delta 88-89; Sigma Kappa; Schlrshp Awrd 90; Res Advsr 89-90; Deans Lst; Acdmc Exclince Schlrshp 90-; Fmly Nrs Prctnr.

**BREITENSTEIN, LAURA L,** Duquesne Univ, Pittsburgh, PA; FR; BA; Music; Cmpsr/Cndctr.

**BREITHAUPT, BRUCE J,** Univ Of Southern Ms, Hattiesburg, MS; JR; Elec Eng Tech.

**BREITMAIER, CHRISTINE,** Mount Saint Mary Coll, Newburgh, NY; JR; BS; Acctg; CPA.

**BRELAND MURRY, KELLEY D,** Ms Gulf Coast Comm Coll, Perkinston, MS; GD; AS; VP List 90-; Bus; Admin Sec.

**BRELAND, BETTY L,** Ms Gulf Coast Comm Coll, Perkinston, MS; FR; BA; Elem Educ.

**BRELAND, KATY A,** Auburn Univ At Auburn, Auburn, AL; FR; SGA Sprt Cmmtt; Dorm Pres; Gym Clb; Dnkng Drlng.

**BREMER, ERIC C,** Western New England Coll, Springfield, MA; JR; BA; Clss Treas 90-; Intrnshp HP Hood Inc; Vrsty Golf/ IM Sftbl Ftbl Hcky 88-; Mktg; Sls.

**BRENDESE, DAVID A,** Hudson Valley Comm Coll, Troy, NY; SO; BA; Pres Lst 89-; Tennis Team 88; Acctng.

**BRENDLE, APRIL D,** Western Carolina Univ, Cullowhee, NC; FR; BA; Alpha Xi Delta; Radio/Tv.

**BRENEGAN, SHARLYN,** James Madison University, Harrisonburg, VA; JR; BS; Stdnt Educ Assn 90-; Gldn Ky; Kappa Delta Pi Hist; Alpha Chi Omega Opn Hs Chrprsn; Erly Chldhd Educ; Tchr.

**BRENEGAR, JEANNE J,** Christopher Newport Coll, Newport News, VA; SR; Spnish Clb; Alpha Chi; Alpha Kappa Delta; Dept Hnrs; Dns Awd; BA; Spanish; Tchng.

**BRENEK, LAURA M,** Villanova Univ, Villanova, PA; SO; BA; Art Hstry/Engl.

**BRENNAMAN JR, TIMOTHY R,** Central St Univ, Wilberforce, OH; JR; BA; Scty Mech Eng 90-; Bsbl 90-; Mfg Eng.

**BRENNAN, ALVIN L,** Voorhees Coll, Denmark, SC; SR; BS; SGA Pres 90-; Pol Sci Clb Sec 90-; Debate Tm VP 89- AAPS; Alpha Phi Alpha Sec 89-; AA Univ Of NY 89; Pol Sci; U S Congress.

**BRENNAN, CHRISTINE M,** Univ Of New England, Biddeford, ME; JR; BA; Earths ECO Media Co-Ord 90; LOLA Unity Clg Pres 85-87; Stdnt Activities Dept Unity Clg Dir 86-87; Alpha Chi Ntl Hon Soc; Received Fndtn For Seacoast Hlth Schlrshp 90; Unity Cly Im Co-Ed Sftbl 85-86; Human Serv/Cnslng; MPA/D Gvrnr Of Me.

**BRENNAN, COLLEEN A,** Eckerd Coll, St Petersburg, FL; JR; BA; Campus Nwspr Edtr Chief 88-; Mdl UN 89-; Cncrt Choir 88-; Delta Phi Alpha VP 88-; Omicron Delta Kappa 90-; Stu Asstnt Dvlpmnt Ofc 89-; Pol Sci; Law.

**BRENNAN, CYNTHIA,** Medaille Coll, Buffalo, NY; SO; BED; Tch Org Ed Mjrs; Ele Educ/Lit; Tch.

**BRENNAN, JAMIE N,** Univ Of Nc At Asheville, Asheville, NC; SR; MBA; Psychlgy Clb 89-; Cnclng Rp Crs Cntr 90-; Intern Cnclng Etng Dsrdrs 90-; Psychlgy; Prctcng Psyclgy.

**BRENNAN, ROBERT A,** Kent St Univ Geauga Cmps, Burton Twp, OH; BA; SOS Inc; Prgrmr Analyst 90-; Assoc PA Stae Univ EE 83; Cmptr Sci; Cmptr Analyst.

**BRENNEMAN, KEITH R,** Furman Univ, Greenville, SC; FR; BS; Wesley Fndtn 90-; Habitat For Humanity 90-; Phi Eta Sigma; Phi Kappa Phi; Physics; Engineering.

**BRENNEMAN, STEPHEN R,** Garrett Comm Coll, Mchenry, MD; SO; BA; Cmptr Sci.

**BRENNEN, CHERYL L,** Duquesne Univ, Pittsburgh, PA; JR; BS; Math Clb Pres 90-; Math Assoc Amer 90-; Soc Stu Actuaries 90-; Lambda Sigma Advsr Finance Chr 89-; Phi Eta Sigma 89-90; Intrn W/Mby Corp; Math; Stats.

**BRENNEN, WILLIAM J,** S U N Y Coll Of Tech At Frmgdl, Farmingdale, NY; JR; BA; AAS 89; Art Educ.

**BRENNER, ANNETTE M,** Univ Of Akron, Akron, OH; JR; BS; Tstmstrs 90-; Amer Inst Chem Engrs 87-; Tau Beta Pi Pres 89-; Goldn Key 89-; Hon Prog 87-; Natl Collgt Eng Awrd; All Amer Schlr; Engrs Fndtn OH Schlrshp 87-; IM Vlybl; Chem Eng.

**BRENNER, BRUCE RICHARD,** Memphis St Univ, Memphis, TN; JR; BA; SAM Tres 90; SHRM 90; APICS 90; Gldn Key 90; Jaycees Drctr 84-, Mgmnt.

**BRENNER, TRACY L,** Univ Of Ga, Athens, GA; SR; BSED; Dns Lst 90; Delta Phi Epsilon 87-89; Stdnt Tchng; IM Ftbl/Sftbl 87-89; Early Chlchd Educ; Tch K-4.

**BRENNINKMEYER, SEBASTIAN M,** Georgetown Univ, Washington, DC; FR; BA; German Clb/Italian Clb; Mrktng Soc; Psych/Mrktng.

**BRENNY, MICHELLE R,** Judson Coll, Marion, AL; SR; Judsn Amb 88-90; Tr Cls Offcr 88-90; Judsn Schlrs 90-; Dns Lst 90-; Hillcrst Fndtn Awd Excell Psych 89; Otsdng Psych Maj Awd; Annie Rhds Schlrshp 88; Tenns 90-; BS; Psych; Soc Psych.

**BRENT, LUIS A,** Wilberforce Univ, Wilberforce, OH; FR; BA; Natl Assc Blck Accntnts 90-; Stu Govt Assc Treas; Accntng; CPA.

**BRENT, SUZANNE D,** Saint Johns Univ, Jamaica, NY; SR; BS; Kappa Delta Pi 90-; Gldn Key; Deans Lst 89-; AA Cum Laude 89; Elem Ed; Tchg.

**BRENTON, RICHARD M,** City Univ Of Ny La Guard Coll, Long Island Cty, NY; JR; BA; Cntr Bsns Career Values Clb 89; Phi Theta Kappa 90-; Otstndng Srvc Awd 90; Grphc Artsts Gld 90-; Vlntr St Vncnts Hsptl Sprtv Care Prgrm 90; Grphc Dsgnr Illstrtr 80-; Certf Manhattan Comm Clg 79; Certf New Schl Scl Rsrch 89; Englsh Lit; Tchng Wrtng.

**BRENTS, ANNA M,** Ms St Univ, Miss State, MS; JR; Std Asc Comm 90-; IM Flg Ftbl 88-89; Sigma Alpha Epsln Ltl Sis; Alpha Lambda Delta 89-; Phi Eta Sigma 89-; Gamma Beta Phi 89-; Chi Omega Chrmn 90-; Very Spec Arts MS 90-; Untd Way 88-89; Slvtn Army 89-90; Bldg Hsts; Mktg.

**BRENZEL, BETH A,** Swarthmore Coll, Swarthmore, PA; FR; BA; Chrs; Chmbr Sngrs; CPP Belwin Cmpstn Awrd 90-; Natl Gld Of Comm Schls Of The Arts Yng Cmpsrs Awrd; Msc And Hstry.

**BRERETON, DEBORAH M,** Univ Of Sc At Columbia, Columbia, SC; SR; JD; Greeks Against Mismgmnt Of Alcohol 87-; Denas Lst 87 89 90; Pres Lst 90; Soc Prof Jrnlsts 87-90; Alpha Epsilon Rho 87-90; Kappa Delta Sorority 88-90; Carolina Cares 88-90; S C State Museum; Golden Law Firm; Law.

**BRERETON, PHILIPPA A,** City Univ Of Ny City Coll, New York, NY; SR; BSC; Caribbean Stdnts Assn 89; Golden Key 90-; City Clg Flwshp; Mentor/Tutor Mini Clg Prog Risk High Schl Stdnts 87-88; Spcl Ed; Schl Psychlgy.

**BRESCIA, SUSAN F,** Mount Saint Mary Coll, Newburgh, NY; JR; BA; AAS Orange Cnty Comm Coll 82; Engl; Elem/Spec Educ.

**BRESLER, KURT T,** Central Fl Comm Coll, Ocala, FL; SO; BS; Chrstn Spprt Grp; Fla Cert Nursry Prof; Fla Cert Pst Cntrl Oper; FNGA; Qulty Lawn Serv Ownr; Hortcltr; Ornmntl Hortcltr.

**BRESLIN, CHRISTINE E,** Temple Univ, Philadelphia, PA; FR; BS; Marching Bnd 90; Alpha Lambda Delta; Pres Awrd 90; Mktg; Sport Mgmnt.

**BRESNOWITZ, DORIS,** Bergen Comm Coll, Paramus, NJ; FR; AS; Phi Theta Kappa 89-; CPC Intrntl Englewood Cliffs N J 89-; Bus Admin/Mktng.

**BRESSAN, DEBRA A,** Univ Of De, Newark, DE; FR; BS; Intervrsty Chrstn Flwshp Bible Study Grp 90; Blrm Dncng 90; Gold Key; Tri-Beta; Sci Alliance 90-; Smr Intrnshp Smithkline Beecham Cnsmr Brands Microbio Qlty Lab; IM Inner Tube Water Polo; Biotechnology; Genetic Eng/Recombinant DNA.

**BRESSON, TIMOTHY R,** Kent St Univ Kent Cmps, Kent, OH; GD; Air Force Reserve Ofcr Trng Corps Cdt/Lt Col 86-90; Tse Kubndo Club 89-90; BA 90; Pol Sci; Prfsnl Ofcr USAF.

**BRESTENSKY, DEBRA L,** Comm Coll Algny Co Algny Cmps, Pittsburgh, PA; Bus And Pblc Admin; Exec Sec Or Admin Asst.

**BRETCHES, PAMELA L,** Emory Univ, Atlanta, GA; GD; MN; Sigma Theta Tau; Alpha Chi Omega Schlrshp Ofcr 76-79; Natl Assoc Neontl Nrs; GA Assoc Neontl Nrs; Henrietta Egleston Hsptl Chldrn Inc 83-88; Gracy Mem Hosp 88-; BS Auburn Univ 79; BSN Med Clge GA 83; Neontl/Perintl Nrsg; Neontl Nrs Prctnr.

**BRETON, JOHANNE M,** Saint Joseph Coll, West Hartford, CT; FR; BSW; Campus Dorm Council 90-; Frshm Hnrs Symposium 90-; Social Work.

**BRETON, MELANEE S,** S U N Y Coll Of Tech At Alfred, Alfred, NY; FR; RN; Bowling Treas 87; Class Pr 90; Provider Of Care; LPN 90; Nursing; BS.

**BRETZ-SUNDELL, GAIL E,** Christopher Newport Coll, Newport News, VA; JR; BS; Bio Clb Pres 89-; Stdt Ldrshp Instit 89; Stdt Orntn Ldr 89; Alpha Chi 90-; Biol; Genetic Counselor.

**BREUER, JENNIFER M,** Le Moyne Coll, Syracuse, NY; JR; BA; Res Advsr Underclsmn Res Hl 90-; Intl Hse Vol 89-; Vars Cross Country Capt 88-; Cross Country Mid East Conf Champ 88.

**BREWAH, JOHN,** Strayer Coll, Washington, DC; JR; BS; BS Ecnmcs Univ Sierra Leona West Africa 87; Pblc Acctng.

**BREWER, BEVERLY KAY,** Lees Coll, Jackson, KY; SO; Stdnt Bdy Govt Sec 90-; Stdnt Bdy Govt Rep 89-90; Phi Theta Kappa 90; Dns Lst 89-; AA Appld Bus Mgmt; Bus Ed.

**BREWER, BLAIK T,** Middle Tn St Univ, Murfreesboro, TN; SR; BA; VP Tom Brewer Co 88-; Aerospace Adm.

**BREWER, BRUCE H,** Fl A & M Univ, Tallahassee, FL; JR; BA; Coll Nwsppr Edit In Chf 90; FL Comm Col Prss Assn; Awrd 3rd Pl Ftre Gen Clmn Wrtng; 2nd Pl In Dpth Rprtng And 1st Pl Ftre Phto Fr TCC Nwsppr 90; AA Tallahassee Comm Coll 90; Jrnlsm.

**BREWER, CHRISTI L,** Fl St Univ, Tallahassee, FL; JR; BA; Theatre; Law.

**BREWER, DARRELL R,** Ms Gulf Coast Comm Coll, Perkinston, MS; SO; BA; Crim Just; Law.

**BREWER, DEBORAH BAXTER,** Midlands Tech Coll, Columbia, SC; SR; ADN; Red Bank Elem PTA Secty 88-89; Co Chrprsn Just Say No Co-Chrpsn 89-; Secty 69-77; Nursing/Allied Hlth; Nurse.

**BREWER, DENISE B,** S U N Y Coll Of Tech At Alfred, Alfred, NY; FR; AAS; AGC Assc; Amer Cngrs Srvyng/Mpng Ass Fresh Dir; Equine Clb; Peer Tutoring Pgm; Wmn Engnrng Tech Rcrtng Pgm; ASS Grl Sct Ldr; Pres Church; Srvyng Engnrng.

**BREWER, FRANCES J,** Fayetteville St Univ, Fayetteville, NC; JR; BS; PTA Cumberland Co & Ft Bragg Sch Sys 89-; Parent Aide Vol E Car Exch/Exchangette Child Abcuse Prvntn Ctr Inc 90; Math Psych; Edn/Cnslng.

**BREWER, HEIDI A,** Saint Josephs Coll, Windham, ME; FR; Crs Cntry IM Sprts 90-; Bio; Medcn.

**BREWER, JOHN A,** Southern Coll Of Tech, Marietta, GA; JR; BMET; Pep Bnd; Kappa Kappa Pis 86-87; Mech Eng Tech; Prof Mnfctrng Eng.

**BREWER, LEAH S,** William Carey Coll, Hattiesburg, MS; SR; BS; Kappa Mu Epsilon; Math; Tchr.

**BREWER, LISA,** Medical Coll Of Ga, Augusta, GA; SO; DDS; Amer Stdnt Dentl Assn 89-; Amer Dntl Hygn Soc Sec/Treas 83-89; Sftbl; AS Santa Fe Comm Coll 83; Dntstry.

**BREWER, LORI J,** Univ Of Nc At Greensboro, Greensboro, NC; SR; BA; AA Sandhills Comm Coll 89; Elem Ed K-6; Tch.

**BREWER, LYNN A,** Pasco Hernando Comm Coll, Dade City, FL; FR; AA BS; Phi Theta Kappa 90-; Cert CPR 90; Science; Nursing/Doctor.

**BREWER, MARTHA J,** Birmingham Southern Coll, Birmingham, AL; SO; BA; Cnsrvncy Nwsltr Edtr 89-90; Nwspr Layot Edtr 90-; Pub Bd Bus Mgr; Alpha Lambda Delta; Phi Eta Sigma; Alpha Omicron Pi Phlntrpy Chrmn; Habitat Humnty 89-91; Ala Hunts Fndtn Pub Rel Intrn; Ldrshp Dev Crse; English; Jrnlsm.

**BREWER, MELISSA J,** Middle Tn St Univ, Murfreesboro, TN; JR; BS; AS Motlow St Comm Clg 90; Math; Prvt Ind.

**BREWER, PAULA J,** Fl St Univ, Tallahassee, FL; SO; BS; Todays Ntrtn Club Hstrn 89-90; Undergrad Schlrs Fund Schlrshp 89-; Schlrshp 89; Bio; Med Sch.

**BREWER, REBECCA A,** Union Coll, Barbourville, KY; SR; BA; Iota Sigma Nu 90-; BA; Soc/Psych; Grad Schl.

**BREWER, ROBERT H,** Univ Of Ky, Lexington, KY; SR; BS; AS 87; Zoology; Med.**

**BREWER, SHARON K,** Wright St Univ, Dayton, OH; FR; BA; Clg Stdnts Spcl Wish Clb 90-; Stdnt Hons Assn 90-; Alpha Lambda Delta 90-.

**BREWER, SUZY,** Phillips Jr Coll, Jackson, MS; FR; AS; Dns Lst; Prlgl.

**BREWER, TERRY F,** Memphis St Univ, Memphis, TN; SR; BA; Internatl Assoc Arsn Invstgtrs 87-; TN Advsry Cmte Arsn 87-; Fr Spclsts Invstgtr; Fire Prvntn.

**BREWINGTON, MARETTA L,** Methodist Coll, Fayetteville, NC; SO; BA; Cmptr Sci.

**BREWSTER, BECKY L,** Middle Tn St Univ, Murfreesboro, TN; SR; BS; Stdnt Cncl Excptnl Chldrn Stdnt Gvt Rep 90-; Spcl Olympcs 89-; Tns Tm 86-88; Spcl Edctn; Tchr.

**BREWSTER, DARIUS L,** Al A & M Univ, Normal, AL; FR; Stdnt Govt V P 88-89; VICA 87-89; FHA 87-88; Natl Hnr Soc 87-89; U S Army Res 89-; Chrch Svcs Comm 87-; Highst Phy Fitns Score U S Army Trng 89; Boys State Ala Mbr 88; Ftbl/Bsktbl/Ftbl/Bsbl/Soccr 84-89; Drftng Mech U S Army.

**BREWSTER, FRANCES L,** Univ Of Md At Eastern Shore, Princess Anne, MD; JR; BS; Pre-Pro Soc Treas 88-90; Tri Dist Rep Clb Carroll Cnty 89-; Mt Zion Untd Mthdst Choir 87-; Clncl Intrnshp-Physcl Med Dept St Josephs Hosp Stdnt Physcl Thrpst; Physcl Thrpy.

**BREWSTER, PHYLLIS A,** Univ Of Sc At Columbia, Columbia, SC; SO; BA; Carolina Alive 90; Wmns Choir 89-90; Crmnl Justc Assn 89; Young Life Ldr 90; Peer Conduct Board 90; Fear Of Crime Pollster 90; Rsdnt Advsr 90; Mnrty Stdnt Affairs Award; Crmnl Justc; Fdrl Law Enfor.

**BREWSTER, RUDOLPH A,** City Univ Of Ny City Coll, New York, NY; GD; MS; Alum Asso; Alum Var Asso; Black Alum; Cert/Merit/Outstndng Work/Fld Plcmnt Intern 89; Cert Asso/Exam Bd England 84; Biol; Rsrch/Publ Hlth Admin.

**BREWSTER, TINA D,** Univ Of Louisville, Louisville, KY; SO; BSI; Comp Sci; Comp Prog.

**BREWTON, CHRISTOPHER D,** Southern Coll Of Tech, Marietta, GA; JR; BS; Lt US Coast Guard; Engr Ofcr USCGC Storis; AA U Of State NY 83; Elec Eng; US Coast Guard.

**BREY, TERRANCE L,** Ms St Univ, Miss State, MS; SR; BS; Soc Ptrlm Engnrs VP 90-; Ntnl Soc Prfsnl Engnrs; Pi Epsilon Tau Tres Sec 90-; Engnrng.

**BREZICKI, DEBRA A,** Seton Hall Univ, South Orange, NJ; SO; BS; Peer Advsr 90-; Camp Mnstry 89-; Kappa Delta Pi; Ambass 90-; Bus Mgmt; Corp Mgr.

**BRIAN, JOSEPH M,** Univ Of Louisville, Louisville, KY; SR; IEEE 90-; Tau Beta Pi; Electrcl Engrng; Music Indstry.

**BRICE, ANDREW N,** Univ Of Fl, Gainesville, FL; JR; BS; Natl Athletic Trainers Assoc 86-; Natl Strength Conditioning Assoc 89-; Amer Physical Therapy Assoc 90; Phi Kappa Phi 89-; Honorable Discharge USAF Sergeant 85; Natl Schlrshp Natl Athletic Trnrs Assoc 89; Physical Therapy; Sports Medicine.

**BRICE, CHRISTIAN,** Bunker Hill Comm Coll, Boston, MA; SO; AS; Deans List; AS Srvyng Fclty Sci Port U Prince Haiti 83-86; Cert Libry Sci Schelcher Un Frt De France Martinique; Acctg; CPA.

**BRICE, DOANNIE MICHELLE,** Univ Of Tn At Martin, Martin, TN; FR; BS; Bptst Stdnt Un Pblcty Chrmn; Mu Epsilon Delta; Biology; Medicine.

**BRICE, JULIE E,** Wilmington Coll, New Castle, DE; FR; BS; Fin; Fin Mgmt.

**BRICE, MARIEJUDITH J,** City Univ Of Ny City Coll, New York, NY; GD; Inst Elctrcl Elctrnc Engnrs 88-; Gldn Key 90-; Grd Hnrcum Laude 90; Be 90.

**BRICKER, KATRINA M,** Columbus Coll Of Art & Design, Columbus, OH; SO; Illustration; Disney.

**BRICKEY IV, ARTHUR G,** Memphis St Univ, Memphis, TN; SR; BA; Outdr Recrtnl Sprts Clb 88-; IM 87-90; Finance; Bsnss.

**BRICKLES, HETTI J,** Fl St Univ, Tallahassee, FL; SR; Fla Pub Rel Assn Pres 90-; Stdnts Organ Donation Awrns Sec 90; Hnrs/Schlrs 88-; Gldn Key Chrprsn 89-; Lambda Pi Eta Co Chr 90-; Phi Eta Sigma 89-; Acad Schlr 88-; Schl Bds Assn; Intrnshp Msclr Dystrphy Assn; Intrnshp 90; Cmmnctn; Pub Rel.

**BRICKMAN, CHERYL L,** East Stroudsburg Univ, E Stroudsburg, PA; JR; BS/BA; Mngmnt Econs Clb 90-; Econs.

**BRICKNER, ELIZABETH H,** Villanova Univ, Villanova, PA; JR; BA; Spec Olympcs 88-89; Proj Snshn Tutrng/Vstng Hndcpd Chldrn 88-90; Psychlgy; Chld Psychlgy/Cnslng.

**BRICKUS, JOANNA E,** Cheyney Univ Of Pa, Cheyney, PA; SR; BA; Rec Photo Edtr 88-89; Mrchng Bnd Pres 89-90; Concrt Chr Sec 90-; Outstndg Coll Stdnts Am; Bnd Schlrshp; Music Therapy.

**BRIDDELL, RICHELE L,** Va St Univ, Petersburg, VA; SR; BS; Bg Brthrs Bg Sstrs Org Pres 90-; Htl/Rstrnt Mngmnt Clb; Ntnl Soc Fr Mnr Htlrs; Amrcn Hm Ecnmcs Assn; Htl/Rstrnt Mngmnt; Grad Schl.

**BRIDEAU, NICOLE R,** Hudson Valley Comm Coll, Troy, NY; SR; AS; Bus Admin.

**BRIDENBAUGH, GRANT D,** Univ Of Pittsburgh, Pittsburgh, PA; SO; BS; Chem Engr.

**BRIDGEFORTH, TONY G,** Lane Coll, Jackson, TN; JR; BA; Stdnt Chrstn Orgnztn Chpln 90; Soc Sci; Educ.

**BRIDGEMAN, RANDALL C,** Ky St Univ, Frankfort, KY; SR; Pre Law Clb 88-; Stu Spprt Serv 87-90; Dean Lst 88-90; Juvenile Serv Intern 90; Vrsty Glf Capt 89-; Crmnl Just; Law.

**BRIDGEMAN, SHAUN K,** Alcorn St Univ, Lorman, MS; JR; BA; SIFE; Amer Chess Fed 89-; United Wy Yth In Action Stdnt Vol Prog 89-; I M Bkbl Sftbl; Bus Admn; Exe Corp Amer.

**BRIDGERS, WILLIAM D,** Vt Law School, S Royalton, VT; GD; JD; Ordr Gwnsmn 85-86; Phi Kappa Phi 88; Delta Kappa Epsilon Pres 80-85; Frsb 87-88; BA Univ South 86; MPH Univ Al Birmingham Schl Pblc Hlth 88; Envrnmntl Law; Hlth.

**BRIDGES, ALEX V,** Al A & M Univ, Normal, AL; FR; BS; Cmptr Sci; Cmptr Tech.

**BRIDGES, CYNTHIA A,** Anne Arundel Comm Coll, Arnold, MD; FR; AA; Marine Corps Vtrn 87-89; Electrnc Eng; Elctrnc.

**BRIDGES, DEBORAH R,** Chesterfield Marlboro Coll, Cheraw, SC; SO; Scholar Bowl 88-89; President Lst 90-; Cheraw Yarn Mill Schlrshp 90-; Deans Lst 88-89; Presidential Schlrshp 88-89; Omega Psi Phi Top 20 Awrd 88-89; Bsktbl Schlrshp 88-89; Business; Mngmnt.

**BRIDGES, EDDIE,** Nc St Univ At Raleigh, Raleigh, NC; FR; EE; TEMPS 90-; Engineering.

**BRIDGES, JAMES B,** Univ Of Nc At Asheville, Asheville, NC; JR; BA; UNC Hnrs Pgm; AA Caldwell Comm Clg Tech Inst 90; Cmnctns; Prnt Jrnlsm.

**BRIDGES, JENNIFER C,** Rochester Inst Of Tech, Rochester, NY; FR; BA; Intrvrsty Chrstn Flwshp 90-; Hghst GPA Awd 90-; Imgng Sci.

**BRIDGES, JENNIFER R,** Univ Of Sc At Columbia, Columbia, SC; FR; Deans List 90-.

**BRIDGES, KIMBERLY L,** Ms St Univ, Miss State, MS; JR; BS; Bptst Stdnt Un Fresh Cncl 88-89; Alpha Lambda Delta; Phi Eta Sigma; Kappa Delta Pi; Phi Kappa Phi; Mc Cool Schlrshp 89-; Pres Schlr; Edctnl Psych; Cnslng.

**BRIDGES, LISA,** Albany St Coll, Albany, GA; SR; BS; GANS Prsdnt 90-; Nrsng Advsry; Self Stdy Strng Comm; Nrsng Hnr Soc; Delta Sigma Theta; William Hoskins Mmrl Schlrshp 89; GA Leage Nrsng Essay Awd 90; Hsptl Clncl Nrsng Awd; Nrsng; Nrs Prctnr.

**BRIDGES, LYNIA A,** Spartanburg Methodist Coll, Spartanburg, SC; Phi Theta Kappa; Pres Lst 90; Tucapau Bptst Chrch 86-; Grcry Str Bkkpr.

**BRIDGES, MARK W,** Morehouse Coll, Atlanta, GA; SO; BS; Hlth Careers Soc 89-; Florida Clb 89-; Phi Beta Kappa; Golden Key; Outstndg Achvmnt 90-; Bio; Physician.

**BRIDGES, MICHAEL R,** Univ Of Sc At Columbia, Columbia, SC; SO; BS; Coop With Dupont; Mech Engr.

**BRIDGES, MICHELLE R,** Defiance Coll, Defiance, OH; FR; BA; Theta Xi Lil Sis; Bus; Mktg.

**BRIDGES, MISTI M,** Birmingham Southern Coll, Birmingham, AL; FR; Phi Eta Sigma; Alpha Lambda Delta; Alpha Omicron Pi Pnhlnc Del; Dns Lst; Acctg; Corp Law.

**BRIDGES, NOVELLA N,** Jackson St Univ, Jackson, MS; FR; BS; Chmstry Scty 90-; Yng Scntst Prgm 90-; Alpha Lambda Delta; ROTC Awrd Hgh GPA; Tn Tm; Chmstry.

**BRIDGES, PATRICIA L,** Ga Inst Of Tech At Atlanta, Atlanta, GA; SO; BS; US Pstl Serv 81-; Chem Engr.

**BRIDGES, WILLIE R,** Alcorn St Univ, Lorman, MS; SR; Math Clb; Hnrs Org; Army ROTC Colt/Capt; Schlrshp Acad; Math; Actuary.

**BRIDGWATERS, VASHON WILSON,** Fisk Univ, Nashville, TN; SR; MBA; Cmptr Sci Clb; Dns Lst; Delta Mu Delta 90-; Exxon Chem Amer 88-; BS; Bus Admin/Cmptr Sci; Finance.

**BRIEN, MICHELLE M,** Merrimack Coll, North Andover, MA; SO; BA; Big Sister 89-; IM Vlybl 90-; Accntng.

**BRIGGS, BARBARA G,** Bristol Univ, Bristol, TN; GD; MBA; Inst Indstrl Eng Pres; APICS 90; BSIE 86; AS Eng 80; Indstrl Eng Mgmt.

**BRIGGS, CATHERINE M,** Livingston Univ, Livingston, AL; SR; BA; Sigma Tau Delta Pres 90-; Omicron Delta Kappa; Sucarnochee Rvw Ed; Engl; Pblc Rels.

**BRIGGS, CEBRINA M,** Bethune Cookman Coll, Daytona Beach, FL; JR; BS; Rotoract Clb 90-; Bus Hnr Scty 90-; Phi Beta Lambda 90-; Acad Merit Awd 90-; Outstndng Comm Coll Stdnt 90; AA Daytona Bch Comm Coll 90; Business Adm; Mrktng/Advrtsng Exec.

**BRIGGS, DALE G,** Methodist Coll, Fayetteville, NC; JR; BA; Glf Pro; Glf Mgmt Bus; Glf Prfssnl.

**BRIGGS, DEARN M,** Immaculata Coll, Immaculata, PA; SR; BA; Hnr Rl; Entrprnr Rtl Sls; Bus Admin/Econ; Business.

**BRIGGS, DEBRA T,** Johnson C Smith Univ, Charlotte, NC; SO; MBA; Comp Sci Clb; Math/Sci Clb; Comp Sci/Bus.

**BRIGGS, DEREK H,** Fl St Univ, Tallahassee, FL; JR; BA; I M Ftbl Sftbl 88-90; AA 90-; Cmunctns; Radio T V.

**BRIGGS, HARRIET A,** Southern Vt Coll, Bennington, VT; SO.

**BRIGGS, JAMES T,** Daemen Coll, Amherst, NY; SO; BS; Gldn Key 89-; Dns Lst 87-; Phys Thrpy; Mstrs PT Rsrch.

**BRIGGS, JOHN W,** Villanova Univ, Villanova, PA; JR; BA; Nvl Rsrv Offcrs Trng Corp Dpty Oper Offcr 88-; Villanova Envrnmntl Grp 88-; Gamma Theta Upsilon 90-; IM Sccr/Bsktbl Capt 89-; Geography; Naval Officer.

**BRIGGS, JONATHAN E,** Ms St Univ, Miss State, MS; FR; BS; Alpha Epsilon Delta; Gamma Beta Phi Soc; Alpha Lambda Delta; Blgy; Med.

**BRIGGS, RAWLE R,** City Univ Of Ny Queensbrough, New York, NY; JR; BA; Orntn Ldrs Club 89-90; Phi Theta Kappa 90; Alpha Sigma Lambda 90; Talent Roster Cert Of Achvmnt For Dist Acdmc Perf; Customer Serv Rep N Y Tlphn 90-; AA; Pol Sci/Soc; Law.

**BRIGGS, SCOTT M,** Western New England Coll, Springfield, MA; FR; BA; Economics.

**BRIGGS, YOLANDA C,** New Comm Coll Of Baltimore, Baltimore, MD; SR; Cmptr Info Sys.

**BRIGHAM, JENNIFER C,** Newbury Coll, Brookline, MA; SO; Deans List 89-90; Phi Theta Kappa; Fashion Mrchndsng.

**BRIGHAM, LEA M,** Millsaps Coll, Jackson, MS; FR; BS; Fllwshp Chrstn Athlts 90-; Phi Eta Sigma Pres; Kappa Delta Pldg Clss VP 90-; Cmps Mnstry Tm Co Chr Pblcty; Omicrom Delta Kappa Ldrshp Cnfrnc; IM 90-; Eng.

**BRIGHT, BOBBIE JO,** Univ Of Sc At Spartanburg, Spartanburg, SC; SO; BA; Pdmnt Soc 90-; Elem Ed; Tch.

**BRIGHT, MICHELLE L,** Muskingum Coll, New Concord, OH; SR; BA; Fllwshp Christian Athlts Co/Pres 88; Tour Guide 88; Theta Phi Alpha Social Chrmn 89-90; Historian 88-89; Fundraiser 88-89; Resident Asst 89-90; BA; Elmntry Ed; Tch.

**BRIGHTSEN, LORRAINE S,** The Kings Coll, Briarclf Mnr, NY; SR; BA; Yrbk 89-90; FCEA Treas 89-; Deans Lst; Biol Educ; Tch.

**BRIGHTWELL, LINDA K,** Lincoln Memorial Univ, Harrogate, TN; SO; AD; Stdnt Nrs Assoc 89-; Rosedale Baptst Church; Hm Hlth Agncy; Nrsng.

**BRIGHTWELL-SCHNEIDER, LISA C,** Neumann Coll, Aston, PA; SR; BA; Prof Educ Soc VP 90; Deans List 89-; DE Indpndt Ins Agnts 89-; PSEA NEA 89-; Neuman Clg Chld Dev Cntr 86-; Med Soc DE Ins Serv Inc 86; DE Acad Fmly Phsycns 86-; AAS Southside VA Comm Clg 83; Liberarl Studies; Erly Chldhd/Emem Educ.

**BRIGMAN, GLYNNIS DIANNE,** Univ Of South Al, Mobile, AL; SR; BA; Fncl Mgmt Asc 90-; Sndy Schl Tchr Orchrd Bptst Chrch 86-; Fnce.

**BRIGNONI, RUBEN H,** Univ Of Pr At Mayaguez, Mayaguez, PR; JR; BS; Clg Bnds FIM Swmng Wrstlng 88-; ASME 90-; Svnth Day Advntst Med Cdts Corp Pfc E3; Red Cross Vol Lfgrd Dstr Svc 86-; Natl Clgt Eng Awrd 90-; Mech Eng; Eng.

**BRILLHART, EMBER A,** Le Moyne Coll, Syracuse, NY; JR; BS; Sclgy Clb Prsdnt 88-; SG 90-; Frgn Affrs Clb Sec 90-; Amrcn Sclgcl Assn 90-; Alpha Kappa Delta 90-; Tutor 88-; Dstrct Attrny Intrn Prsnt; Sclgy Crmnlgy Crmnl Jstc; Law.

**BRIM, FRANCES YVONNE,** Patrick Henry Comm Coll, Martinsville, VA; SO; BA; Phi Theta Kappa 90-; Spir 89-; Deans List 90; Youth Dir Plsnt View Bptst Chrch 90-; Employed Piedmont Trust Bank Trust Dept Trust Asst; AAS; Accounting; CPA.

**BRIMAGE, CYNTHIA A,** Craven Comm Coll, New Bern, NC; SO; 7th Day Advntst Chrch Asst Tres; Elem Educ.

**BRIMMER, JASON R,** Univ Of De, Newark, DE; FR; BA; Natl Mrt Schlrshp; Engl; Tchr.

**BRIN, LEON Q,** Western New England Coll, Springfield, MA; JR; BS; Photography Clb 90-; Alpha Lambda Delta 89-; Sigma Beta Tau; Vol Fire Dept; Mech Engr.

**BRIN, NICOLE K,** Univ Of Md At Eastern Shore, Princess Anne, MD; JR; Caribbean Clb Natl Assn Blck Accntnts Cmps Cmps Judcl Bd; Minority Hnrs Intrnshp Pgrm; Bus Admin; Accntng/Law.

**BRINDLEY, CLARENCE S,** Northwest Al Comm Coll, Phil Campbell, AL; SO; BA; AD 90; Indstrl Tchnlgy; Mgmt.

**BRINDLEY, KIMBERLEE B,** Univ Of Cincinnati, Cincinnati, OH; SR; BFA; Alpha Epsilon Rho 90; WGRR Promotion/Data Entry 90; Christ Hos Video Prod 90; Brdcstng.

**BRINER, LORI A,** Spalding Univ, Louisville, KY; JR; BSN; Sgm Theta Tau; Nrsng; Pedtrc Nrsng.

**BRINEY, JOHN P,** Livingston Univ, Livingston, AL; JR; BS; AS Shelton State Cmnty Clg; Envir Sci; Engr.

**BRINGAS CASTILLO, JAVIER E,** Inter Amer Univ Pr Hato Rey, Hato Rey, PR; SR; Frgn Stu Orgn 87-89; Arntcl Stu Orgn 87-88; Magna Cum Laude Inter Amer Univ 87-; Cnslr Stu Prgm 87-; Otstndng Aviation Stu Awrd; Amer Assn Arprt Exec Fndtns 90; Airway Cmptr Sci; Air Trffc Cmptrllr.

**BRINGAS, ROSSANA A,** Univ Of Miami, Coral Gables, FL; JR; BA; Psychlgy/Educ; Ph D Psychlgy.

**BRINK, VINCENT E,** Comm Coll Algny Co Algny Cmps, Pittsburgh, PA; SO; BA; Deans List 90; Weight Lftng Comp 2nd Pl; Adv Sales 4 Yrs; Bio Sci.

**BRINKLEY, AMANDA R,** Univ Of Ga, Athens, GA; SR; BSED; Golden Key 90-; Phi Theta Kappa 88-; Kappa Delta Pi 90-; Yth Mssn 89; Hons Day 90-; AA Gordon Coll 89; Erly Chldhd Ed; Tchr.

**BRINKLEY JR, JAMES E,** Alcorn St Univ, Lorman, MS; SO; BA; Charles Harrison Mason Bible Sch Sec 87-89; Chrch God Christ Flwshp Org VP 90-; Hnr Stu Org Tres 90-; Bus Admin; Real Est Bus.

**BRINKLEY, KENDRA S,** Univ Of Tn At Martin, Martin, TN; FR; BS; Phi Alpha Delta; Chi Omega; Acctng; Law.

**BRINKLEY, TRACY R,** Bowie St Univ, Bowie, MD; SR; BS; Delta Mu Delta Bus Pres 90-; Hnr Soc; Dns Lst 90; Ldrshp Awrd; Bus-Mngmt; Law.

**BRINKLEY, YOLONDA R,** Clark Atlanta Univ, Atlanta, GA; JR; BA; Intl Stdnt Org 90-; Dnce Grp Pub Rltns Dir 88-; Alpha Kappa Mu; All Amer Schlr 90-; Frst Amer Inst Frgn Stdy Schlrshp; Frnch/Intl Bus; Intl Law.

**BRINKMAN, DARLENE B,** Bishop St Comm Coll, Mobile, AL; SO; Sci/Math Clb 87-88; Yrbk Phtgrphr 87-89; Hnr Rl 87-90; Dns Lst 88-90; Pres Lst 89-90; Phi Theta Kappa; Phi Beta Lambda 88-89; Intrnshp Deaf Intrprtr Trnr; Wrk Stdy Prog 87-90; Alumni Affairs 87-90; Cub/Boy Scts Of Amer 90-; Univ/S Alabama; Offc Admin; Paralegal Stds.

**BRINKMAN, NICOLE M,** Univ Of Miami, Coral Gables, FL; SR; BMUS; Music Stdnt Cncl; FCMENC Pres; Amercn Choral Dir Assoc Pres; Phi Kappa Phi; Pi Kappa Lambda; Omicron Delta Kappa; Golden Key; Sigma Alpha Iota Sec; Winner Hons Ethic/Profsns Essay Compet; Assoc Tchr Cypress Elem Sch/Arvida Mdl Sch; Music/Ed/Choral; Tchr Of Music.

**BRINKMAN, PATRICIA M,** Hilbert Coll, Hamburg, NY; SO; BA; Thrsdy Nght Lads Bwlng Leag Pr 89-; Hrshoe Soc Clb 86-; Dart Leag Capt 89-; Hopevl Inc Hm Grls Intrn 90-; AA; Crim Just.

**BRINSON, IVY D,** Bryant Stratton Bus Inst Roch, Rochester, NY; SO; ADS; Business; Mgmt.

**BRINSON, SMIRA D,** Clark Atlanta Univ, Atlanta, GA; SO; BS; Intervrsty Chrstn Flwshp; Saturday Sci Acdmy Cmptr Tch Asst; Summer Pgrm Cmptr Tchr Asst; Cmptr Sci; Cmpt Database Pgrmr/Sys Ann.

**BRINSON, SONIA P,** Fayetteville St Univ, Fayetteville, NC; SO; BA; Computer Science Club 89-; Resident Assistant; Computer Science; System Analyst.

**BRINSTON, BRENDA G,** Tougaloo Coll, Tougaloo, MS; SR; Pre-Alumni Cncl Secr 88-90; Wakadzi V P 88-; Willing Workers Amer 87-; BA; Econ/Acctg; Acctg.

**BRINSTON, GLENDA F,** Tougaloo Coll, Tougaloo, MS; SO; BA; Pre-Alumni Cncl; Willing Worker Amer; Engl/Jrnlsm; Jrnlst.

**BRINTON, JONATHAN B,** Gaston Coll, Dallas, NC; FR; AS; Chrltte Life Svng Crew Vol EMS Sqd; AS Underwater Tech FL Inst Of Tech 86; Med; Parmedic.

**BRIONES, CHRISTINE HAZEL O,** City Univ Of Ny Baruch Coll, New York, NY; SO; BBA; Filipino-Am Club 89-; Acctng Soc 90-; Fin-Econ Club 89-90; Beta Alpha Psi 90-; Folklorico Dance Co 90-; Provost Merit Awd 90-; Bus Admn; Acctng.

**BRISCOE, SHERYL S,** Univ Of Rochester, Rochester, NY; FR; BA; Assn Blck Drama/Arts Fshn Shw Prog Mgr 90-; Radnce Dnce Theatr 90; Lv Jy Drm Cncl Pres Elect 90-; Delanosisson Prz 90-; Slvtn Army; Gas Co Intrnshp 89-; Econ/Anthrplgy; Intl Finance.

**BRISEBOIS, MICHELE E,** Univ Of Nh Plymouth St Coll, Plymouth, NH; SR; BA; Admissions Repr 89; Orient Ldr 88; Peer Assist 88-90; Stdnt Senate 87-88; Tutor 89-90; Drmtry Hse Comm 87-89; Class Officer Treas 87-88; Phi Kappa Phi 89; Psi Chi 88; Natl Dns List Mbr 89-90; Outstdng Snr Class Of 1991; Psych; Emplymnt Prsnnl/Lwyr.**

**BRISKMAN, BRIAN L,** Ny Univ, New York, NY; FR; BA; Beta Clb 89-90; Key Clb 89-90; Acdmc Bwl VP 87-90; Media Prod Clb Treas 89-90; SUVAC Fndr/Chrmn; Mgmt Assn Spch Cntst 2nd Plc; Indvdl Dedctn Excllnce Awrd 89-90; Acdmc Bwl Tm 89-90; Flm/TV; TV Prod.

**BRISLIN, DIANNA L,** Georgetown Univ, Washington, DC; FR; MBA; Nomadic Theatre 90-; New Stdnt Orientn 90-; Interntl Bus.

**BRISLIN, MELINDA A,** Ashland Comm Coll, Ashland, KY; JR; BBA; Phi Beta Lambda 90-; Tutor 89; Morehead City League Bsktbl; Cardinal Key; Holy Fam Alum Schlrshp/ACC Acdmc Schlrshp/Gene Gross Schlrshp 88; MSU Transfer Schlrshp 89; Fast Pitch Sftbl Mgr 89-; Basic Bus/Teach; Coach.**

**BRISON, LAURAINE L,** Comm Coll Algny Co Algny Cmps, Pittsburgh, PA; SO; AD; Phi Theta Kappa Treas 90-; Schlstc Achvmnt Awd 90-; Merit Cert 90-; Ofc Mgmt Comp Oper 84-86; Patnt Trans Bld Trans Msgr 86-88; Lgl Sec Spclst.

**BRISSON, MICHAEL J,** Villanova Univ, Villanova, PA; JR; BA; IM Bsktbl/Sftbl Capt 88-; English.

**BRISTER, JO A,** Univ Of Southern Ms, Hattiesburg, MS; SR; BS; AA Southwest MS Comm Coll Summit MS 89; Barbers Lic Brdwy Hair Coll Mc Comb MS 88; Psychlgy; Grad Schl.

**BRITNELL, PATRICK C,** Embry Riddle Aeronautical Univ, Daytona Beach, FL; SR; BS AS; Naval Aviation Clb; AAAE; Civil Air Ptrl; Volusia Cty Hlfwy Hse Vol 89; Deans Lst 89-; Hnr Roll 89-90; Prvt Pilot/Physlgcl Trng FFA 90; Aeronautical Studies; Prof Pilot.

**BRITNELL, VONDA L,** Samford Univ, Birmingham, AL; GD; JD; Trl Advcy Brd Dir 90-; Law Clrk Shleby Co DA 90-; BA Univ Montevallo 88; Law.

**BRITSCH, KRISTINE MARIE,** Fl International Univ, Miami, FL; JR; BA; Occptnl Thrpy Clb 90; Phi Theta 90; Intrnshp At Miamis Chldrns Hosp; Grad From Brwrd Cmmnty Clg 87-89; AA 89; Med Fld; Occptnl Thrpy.

**BRITT, BOBBIE L,** Ms St Univ, Miss State, MS; SR; BA; Psychlgy Clb; SAM; Advsry Comm; Phi Kappa Phu; Psi Chi; Gamma Beta Phi; Psychlgy; Mngmt/Hmn Rsrcs.

**BRITT, DEBORAH C,** Univ Of Nc At Asheville, Asheville, NC; SO; BS; Cncrt Bnd 89-; Rsdnt Asssoc 90-; Entrtnmnt Brd 90-; Phi Eta Sigma 89-; Alpha Delta Piambssdrs 90-; Ambssdr Yr; Hnrs Prgm 89-; Univ Schlr 89; Mrn Blgy.

**BRITT, ERROL W,** Wilberforce Univ, Wilberforce, OH; FR; BS; Blk Ml Cltn; Trk Tm; Ed Wrtng Clb; Pres Schlrshp; Charles Leander-Hill Awd; Deans Lst; IM Bsktbl; Med.

**BRITT, JAMES KEVIN,** Univ Of Southern Ms, Hattiesburg, MS; SR; BA; AA Cph-Lincoln Comm Coll 90; Coachng/Math; Tch/Coach.

**BRITT, NANCY L,** Univ Of Sc At Columbia, Columbia, SC; SR; BAIS; Kappa Delta Epsilon 90-; Elem Ed; Tchng.

**BRITT, SHERRY KAY,** Montgomery Comm Coll, Troy, NC; ASSOC; Assoc; Bus Sec.

**BRITT, T,** Univ Of Sc At Columbia, Columbia, SC; JR; Music; Commrcl Music.**

**BRITT, TRULINDA E,** Nc Agri & Tech St Univ, Greensboro, NC; SO; BS; Alobeaem Acctng Socty Corr Sec; Flwshp Gspl Choir 89-; Alpha Lambda Delta 90-; Delta Sigma Theta; New Bethel Bapt Chrch Yng Adult Choir; NIV Natl Alumni Schlrshp 90-; Acctng Dept Schlrshp 89-; Acctng.**

**BRITTAIN, ALAN D,** Catawba Valley Comm Coll, Hickory, NC; SO; AAS; Comp Sci; Sys Analyst.

**BRITTAIN, AMY L,** Western Piedmont Comm Coll, Morganton, NC; SO; AS; Phi Theta Kappa 90; Math; BA.

**BRITTAIN, BONNIE LYNN,** Univ Of Ga, Athens, GA; SR; BA; Merchnds Assc 90-; Amer Assc Txtl Chem-Colrsts 90-; Alpha Delta Pi 87-; Atlanta Apprl Intrn; Fshn Mrktng; Rtlng.

**BRITTAIN, ELINDER L,** Coll Of Charleston, Charleston, SC; JR; BA; Alpha Dlt Pi; Sls Rep Sthwstrn Co 90; Bus Admn; Fin.

**BRITTAIN, MARTIN L,** Univ Of Sc At Aiken, Aiken, SC; JR; BIS; Grphc Dsgn/Msc; Advrtsg.

**BRITTEN, JAMUSCA DONEVA,** Central St Univ, Wilberforce, OH; SR; Delta Sigma Theta Prlmntrn/Sgt Arms 89-; Stdnt Govt Assc Chf Jstce 89-90; Ntl Assc Ngro Bus/Prfssnl Wmn Clb; Poli Sci; Law.

**BRITTINGHAM, KATHLEEN F,** Va Commonwealth Univ, Richmond, VA; SR; BSN; Surreywood Civic Assn 89-; AA Catonsville Comm Clg 90; Diploma Nrsng Union Meml Hosp Schl Nrsng 70; Nrsng; Hlthcr Mgt.

**BRITTO, FLAVIO V,** East Stroudsburg Univ, E Stroudsburg, PA; SO; BA; Latin Armcn Assoc Scl Chrprsn; Minsi Hll Cncl 90-; IIE Schlrshp 90-; Cmmnctns; Intl Affrs.

**BRITTO, REGIS B,** Univ Of Md At Eastern Shore, Princess Anne, MD; SR; BS; Internatl Food Serv Executives Assoc; Eta Rho Mu; Lowews Lengant Plaza Hotel 89-90; Dip HRA Internatl Clge Hotel Mgmnt Switzerland 88; Dip HRM Inst Hotel Mgmnt Catering Tchnlgy Applies Nutrition India 83; Hotel & Restrnt Mgmnt; Mktg Finance.

**BRITTON, BETH TREVATHAN,** Univ Of Akron, Akron, OH; GD; MA; Cncrt Choir 87-89; Madrigal Sngrs 89-; Golden Key V P 88-90; Phi Sigma Alpha 88-90; Psi Chi Educ/Serv Chrmn 89-90; Support Inc 89-91; BA 90; Comm Cnslng; Cnslng/Tchng.

**BRITTON, BRADFORD E,** Wv Univ At Parkersburg, Parkersburg, WV; FR; AAS; Pres Lst 90-; Mech Eng; Eng Cnstrctn.

**BRITTON, JAMES S,** Hiwassee Coll, Madisonville, TN; SO; BA; Phi Theta Kappa; Pre-Physcl Thrpy; Physcl Thrpst.

**BRITTON, KEITH E,** Univ Of Sc At Sumter, Sumter, SC; SO; BA; Stdnt Govt 90-; Assoc Arfcn Amrcn Stdnts VP 90-; Orttn Ldr 90-; Deans Lst; AA; Econ; Bus Mgmt Govt.

**BRITTON, PATRICK,** S U N Y Coll At Fredonia, Fredonia, NY; JR; Circle K 90-; Hstry Social Studies Scndry Ed; Prfssr.

**BRITTON, ROBYN A,** Central Al Comm Coll, Alexander City, AL; FR; BA; Bus; Mktg.

**BRIXEY, SUZANNE N,** Villanova Univ, Villanova, PA; JR; BA; Cmps Mnstry Coord 88-; Mscl Thtr 90-; RA 90-; Phi Kappa Phi; Psi Chi; Alpha Epsilon Delta 90-; Cmmtt Philadelphia Hmlss 88-; Pres Schlr 88-; Lib Arts Hnrs; Med.

**BRKLJACIC, SUSAN L,** Wv Univ, Morgantown, WV; FR; BA; Mrchng Bnd 90-; Wnd Symphny 90-; Cncrt Bnd 90-; Msc; Educ.

**BROADEN, SHARI D,** Lane Coll, Jackson, TN; JR; Stdnt Natl Edn Assn; Pep Clb; Stdnt Orntn Ldr; Peer Cnslr; Stdnt/Govt Assn; NAACP; SCOPE; Elem Edn; Tchr.

**BROADFIELD, BONNIE K,** Winthrop Coll, Rock Hill, SC; SR; BFA; Amer Soc Intr Dsgnrs 89-; Zeta Tau Alpha Hstrn 89-; Intrnshp Intr Dsgn; Intr Dsgn; Cmmrcl.

**BROADHEAD, JAMES A,** Univ Of Southern Ms, Hattiesburg, MS; SR; BA; Sigma Chi 88-; Kyle Greer Memrl Sprts Awd; IM Sprts; Bus Admin.

**BROADHEAD, JULIE A,** Hudson Valley Comm Coll, Troy, NY; FR; BS; Bsktbl MVP Awrd; Bsktbl Capt; Bus; Acctnt/CPA.

**BROADHEAD, MARGARET A,** Medical Univ Of Sc, Charleston, SC; GD; DMD; Oral Bio Jrnl Clb 90-; Dr Joseph Cleveland Awd 90-; Am Stdnt Dntl Assn 90-; BS Northwstrn Univ 87; Dntstry.

**BROADWATER, JOSHUA B,** Vanderbilt Univ, Nashville, TN; FR; BE; Phi Epsilon Sigma; Alpha Lambda Delta; Engrg/Acstcl.

**BROADWELL, JEFF A,** Bryant Stratton Bus Inst Roch, Rochester, NY; GD.

**BROCATO, JOHN W,** Ms St Univ, Miss State, MS; SR; BA; Art Sci Adv Cncl 89-; Phi Eta Sigma; Phi Kappa Phi 89-; Soc Schlrs; Sigma Tau Delta 90-; Pres Lst Dns Lst 87-; Peyton Wllms Wrtng Awd; Engl; Muscn.

**BROCHU, DOREEN D,** Central Me Medical Center, Lewiston, ME; SR; ADN; Med-Surg Nrsng.

**BROCHU, MICHELLE J,** Notre Dame Coll, Manchester, NH; SO; Erth Day Comm Pblcty Coor 90; Coll 40th Ann Comm Dsgnd T-Shrt 90; Outstndg Stdnt Awd Nom; Pres Deans Lst 89-; Cmrcl Art/Fine Art.

**BROCK, ALISON H,** Hillsborough Comm Coll, Tampa, FL; FR; BA; Mass Cmmnctns; Pblc Rltns.

**BROCK, BETTE J,** Norfolk St Univ, Norfolk, VA; SR; BS; Food Sci/Nutrition Clb V P 88-; Alpha Kappa Mu; Amer Dietetic Assn 88-; Tidewater Nutrition Cncl; Va Dietetic Assn 89-; Va Pblc Hlth Assn 89-; Tidewater Dietetic Assn 88-; Food Sci/Nutrition; MS.

**BROCK, CARLA E,** Fl International Univ, Miami, FL; SR; Amer Med Rcrds Asc 83-; South FL Med Rcrd Asc 83-; Asst Dir Mdcl Rcrds Univ Miami Hosp/Clnc; BS 88-; AS Miami-Dade Comm Clg 80-82; Med Rcrd Admn.

**BROCK, CYNTHIA R,** Tallahassee Comm Coll, Tallahassee, FL; SO; BS; AA 90; Engr; Cvl Engr.

**BROCK, ESTER E,** Union Coll, Barbourville, KY; SO; Baptist Union 90-; Chrldr 89-90; Elem Educ; Tch.

**BROCK, GLORIA J,** Univ Of Sc At Columbia, Columbia, SC; SR; BA; Educ Mjrs Clb Pr 89-; USCA 90; Dns Lst 88-90; Educ Mjrs Clb Schlrshp Pr 89-; Pacesetter 89; Spec Olympcs Hd Gm Offcl 88-89; BA; Elem Educ; Tchr.

**BROCK, JUDITH L,** Univ Of Ky, Lexington, KY; JR; BS; Horticulture Club; T T Jones Memorial Schlrshp 90-; Acctng; CPA.**

**BROCK, JUNE M,** Tri County Tech Coll, Pendleton, SC; SR; AA; Vet Tchnlgy Dept Stdnt Govt VP 89; Stdnt Chptr Of ANAVTA 90; Alpha Zeta Beta 90; Vtrnry Tchnlgy; Vtrnry Tchncn.

**BROCK, LAURIE M,** Univ Of Southern Ms, Hattiesburg, MS; SR; BS; Ftbl Rcrtrs VP 87-; Peer Rcrtrs 88-89; Crim Jstc Assoc 89-; Omicron Delta Kappa 90-; Phi Delta Rho 89-; Gamma Beta Phi 89-; Golden Key 90-; Lambda Sigma 86-; Alpha Delta Pi Pres 86-; Egl Clb 90-; Untd Way 90-; Cncr Soc 90-; Eng/Crim Jstc; Law Schl/Grdt Schl.

**BROCK, LEAH C,** Edinboro Univ Of Pa, Edinboro, PA; SR; BS; Delta Zeta Treas 87-; Panhellenic Cncl Treas 88-89; Nuclear Med Schlrshp 90; Nucl Med Tech; Nucl Phrmcy.

**BROCK, NORMA D,** Clayton St Coll, Morrow, GA; SR; BSN; Baccalaureate Stdnt Nrs Assn Co Pres 90-; Fndtn Tal Schlrshp 89; Amer Hrt Assn; Soc Ambulatory Care Prof; Assn Opertain Rm Nrs; ADN Jr Coll 86; Nrsng.

**BROCK, SHEILA E,** Mobile Coll, Mobile, AL; SO; BA; Phi Theta Kappa 89-; Loxley Schl PTA Pres 85-87; Baldwin Cnty Strawberry Fstvl Bd Of Gov; Educ; Elem Educ.

**BROCK, SHERRY A,** Sue Bennett Coll, London, KY; SO; BA; Intrnng Laurel Cnty Jvnl Srvcs 90-; History; Law Paralegal Sci.

**BROCK, TEELA L,** Comm Coll Algny Co Algny Cmps, Pittsburgh, PA; FR; Spch/Thtr/Bus.

**BROCK, VICKI L,** Cumberland Coll, Williamsburg, KY; JR; BED; Spcl Chldrns Mnstry Tm Ldr 90-; Hghr Calling Sec 88-; Love In Action Tm Ldr 90-; Elem Spcl Ed; Tchg.

**BROCK, WILLIAM D,** Cumberland Coll, Williamsburg, KY; JR; BA; PEMM 85-; Alpha Chi 90-; Ftbl Track Team Cap 85-90; Physical Ed; Teaching.

**BROCKELBANK, SANDRA L,** Univ Of North Fl, Jacksonville, FL; JR; BS; Phi Kappa Phi; AA 90; Nrsng; Rn.**

**BROCKETT, TRACI L,** Bay Path Coll, Longmeadow, MA; FR; Trvl Admin.

**BROCKI, LISA A,** S U N Y Coll At Fredonia, Fredonia, NY; SR; BS; Biol/Chem; Med Tech.

**BROCKINGTON, WAYNE,** Glassboro St Coll, Glassboro, NJ; SR; MSW; Sociology Clb Pres 90-; NAACP Pres 90-; Alpha Phi Alpha Sec 89-90; BA; Martin Luther King Schlr; Stdnt Ldrshp Awrd 90-; Soc Soc Wrk.

**BROCKINSON, JACQUELINE M,** Comm Coll Algny Co Algny Cmps, Pittsburgh, PA; GD; BA; AS 90; Bus Mgmt.

**BROCKWAY, JANET L,** Wagner Coll, Staten Island, NY; FR; Alpha Omicron Pi Asst Mbrshp; Stdnt Activites Brd; Allied Hlth Clb; Blgy; Pre/Med Pdtrcs.

**BROCKWELL, ERIC W,** Univ Of Tn At Martin, Martin, TN; JR; BS; Methdst Mvmnt VP 89-; SGA VP 89-; Opera Theatre; Geogrphy; Feogrphcl Soc/Frgn Svc.

**BROCKWELL, RUSSELL C,** Univ Of Al At Birmingham, Birmingham, AL; SR; MD; Alpha Epsilon Delta 89; Phi Sigma 89; Deans Lst 90; Pres Lst 90; Biological Rsrch Hon; BS; Med.

**BROCKWELL, STEPHANIE L,** Old Dominion Univ, Norfolk, VA; SR; BS; DECA; Iota Lambda Sigma; Sec Educ; Teaching.

**BROD, RACHEL L,** Duke Univ, Durham, NC; FR; Tennis Clb VP; Soc Chrprsn Dorm Hse Cncl 90-; Mjr Attrctns 90-; Prod Intrnshp 90-.

**BROD, ROBIN W,** Southern Vt Coll, Bennington, VT; JR; BA; Acctg; Tax Audtr.

**BRODERICK, JAMES M,** Univ Of Miami, Coral Gables, FL; JR; BA; Amer Fed Mscns; Marine Corps; Muisc.

**BRODERICK, KELLEY L,** Teikyo Post Univ, Waterbury, CT; SR; AS; Equestrn Tm 89-90; Equine Studies.

**BRODERICK, MICHAEL J,** Eckerd Coll, St Petersburg, FL; JR; BA; IM Street Hcky/Sftbl 88-; Mgmt Information Systems; Computers.

**BRODIE, ALLAN R,** Daytona Beach Comm Coll, Daytona Beach, FL; SO; AA; Pres Schlr 90; Deans List 90; Bus; Bnkng.

**BRODIE, PETER L,** Daemen Coll, Amherst, NY; JR; BS; Stdnt Assn Treas 90-; Res Cncl Rep 90-; Orient Head OL 89-; Delta Mu Delta; Camp Mnstry-Comm Svc Coord 90-; NY State Sen Sessn Asst Pgm Jrnl Clrk 90; Admin Stdy-Alld Hlth; Hosp Admin.**

**BRODSKY, TAMMY C,** Albertus Magnus Coll, New Haven, CT; JR; BA; Ltrcy Vol; AA 90; English; Tchng.

**BRODY, AARON L,** Yeshiva Univ, New York, NY; GD.

**BRODY, DREW,** Cornell Univ, Ithaca, NY; FR; USITT Stdnt Chptr Cornell Ed Chrmn; Cornell Theater; IM Sports; Theater Arts/Dsgn; Brdwy.

**BRODZIAK, JO ANN M,** Hilbert Coll, Hamburg, NY; GD; BA; Western NY Paralegal Assoc 90-; AAS Niagara Cnty Comm Coll 89; Legal Asst Career; Social Sci/Legal Studies; Law/Legal Spt Stf.

**BROEKER, WILFRED B,** Embry Riddle Aeronautical Univ, Daytona Beach, FL; JR; BA; Entrtnmnt Com 89-; Hon Rl; Deans Lst; Vlybl 88-89; Aerntcl Sci/Flght; Cmmrcl Pilot.

**BROEMSEN, MELANIE NICOLE,** Kent St Univ Kent Cmps, Kent, OH; SO; Wrestlng Sec 90-; Hons Clg 89-; Phi Alpha Delta 89-90; Alpha Epsilon Pi Aux 90-; Deans Lst 89-90; Bus Schlrshp 89-; Wrestlng Stat 90-; Acctng; Law.

**BROGDEN, BRENDA D,** Vance Granville Comm Coll, Henderson, NC; SO; AAS; Admin Sec; AAS Vance-Grnvl Comm Coll; Admin Off Technlgy; Exec Sec.

**BROGDEN, DEBRA L,** Saint Francis Coll, Loretto, PA; SR; BA; Acctng Club Sec 90-; ACE 89-; Natl Alum Schlr 88-; Deans List 87-; Lynnanne Wingard Schlrshp 89-; PICPA Awd; Acctng; CPA.

**BROGDEN, LARRY R,** Vance Granville Comm Coll, Henderson, NC; FR; AAS; Phi Theta Kappa; Elec; Eng.

**BROGDON, JEANINE L,** Al St Univ, Montgomery, AL; JR; BS; Natl Stdnt Exchnge Chrprsn 90; Coll Schlrs Of Amer; AL St Univ Acad Schlrshp 88; Hnr Rll Stdnt 88-; Comp Info Systms; Systms Anlyst.

**BROJACK, LORI A,** Pa St Univ Main Cmps, University Pk, PA; JR; BA; Stdnt Union Brd VP 88-; Jstc Assc Pres 89-; Pre Law Scty 90-; Phi Eta Sgm; Phi Kappa Phi Pres 90-; Gldn Key 90-; Mrtr Brd; Rlgs Ed Tchr 87-89; IM 89; ICC Dnc Marthn Cmt 90-; Liberal Arts Crclr Afrs Cmt Stdnt Rep 90; D; Admn Justice; Jvnl Law.**

**BROMBERG, LINDA HODGE,** Oh Dominican Coll, Columbus, OH; SO; BA; Amer Medl Techgts 87-; English; Writer.

**BROMFIELD, ANDREW W,** Fl International Univ, Miami, FL; SO; BSC; Org Jamaican Unity 88-89; Caribben Stdnts Assoc 88-89; Natl Soc Prof Engrs 89-; FL Engr Soc 89-; Const; Const Mgmt.

**BROMFIELD, VICTORIA L,** Va St Univ, Petersburg, VA; GD; Scrvi Pres 89; Cmtee Relief Virgin Islanders; BA VSU; Soc/Crmnl Juste; Law/Crmnl Juste.

**BROMHAL, GRANT S,** Wv Univ, Morgantown, WV; SO; Mrchng Bnd; Hon Prog; Amer Chem Soc; Cvl Eng/Math.

**BROMLEY, LAURA S,** Middle Tn St Univ, Murfreesboro, TN; JR; BS; AS Jackson State Comm Clg 90; Soc Sci; Elem Ed.

**BRONCATO, MIANNE L,** Alfred Univ, Alfred, NY; SO; BS; Amaer Mktng Assn Sec 89-; Stdnt Sen Fin Comm; St Judes Chrch Eucharistie Mnstr; Jr Achvmnt Schlrshp; Acctg; CPA.

**BRONKAJ, ANDREW N,** Duquesne Univ, Pittsburgh, PA; SR; BS; Amer String Tchrs Assn 87-; Phi Mu Alpha Sinfonia Hist 89-; IM Tennis 90-; Music; Prof.

**BRONKAN, JANINE ANN,** Univ Of Miami, Coral Gables, FL; SR; BSN; Phi Kappa Phi 90-; Natl Cllgte Nrsng Awrd; Amer Assn Of Oprtng Rm Nrss 85-; RN Oprtng Rm 78-; AA Miami Dade Comm Coll 78; ASN; Nrsng.

**BRONNER, KERRI A,** Southern Vt Coll, Bennington, VT; JR; BS; Bus Clb Pres 89-F Dns Lst 88-; RA 90-; Bus Mgmt/Rsrt Mgmt; Mng Htl/Rstrnt.**

**BRONSKI, JOHN E,** City Univ Of Ny Baruch Coll, New York, NY; JR; BS; Am Soc Notaries; Gold Key 90-; NY State Notary Publ 90-; US Naval Res Petty Ofcr 1st Cls E-6 82-; Pol Sci/Engl; Law.

**BRONSON, CHERYL Y,** S U N Y Coll Of Tech At Frmgdl, Farmingdale, NY; FR; BA; Dorm Socl Comm; Lbrl Arts; Cmnctns.

**BRONSON, CHRISTOPHER M,** Western New England Coll, Springfield, MA; FR; BA; Cope 90; Alpha Lambda Delta 90; Math.

**BRONSON, SHARON L,** Bennett Coll, Greensboro, NC; FR; BS; Gospel Choir 90-; Vrsty Vlybl 90-; Biology; Medicine.

**BRONSTEIN, ALAN,** Beaver Coll, Glenside, PA; GD; Pi Delta Epsilon 67; Alpha Psi Omega 67; Chltnhm Prnts Chllnge Advsry Brd 90-; PA Mont Co & Phila Sci Tchrs Assn 88-; Amer Chem Scty 90-; BA Dickinson Coll 67; M Ed 89; Sci Educ; Tchng.

**BRONSTEIN, GEORGE PHILIP,** Univ Of Miami, Coral Gables, FL; SR; BS; Ltn Amer Std Asn Tr 89-; Amer Soc Cvl Engr 90-; Tau Beta Pi 90-; Chi Epsln; Rsch Asst 90-; BS; Cvl Engr; Strctrl Engr.

**BROOKE, CAROLYN C,** Gaston Coll, Dallas, NC; JR; BA; Pi Gamma Mu 89-90; Cmptr Prfssnl 75-84; Assoc 77; Ed; Tchng.

**BROOKE, JOHYNE P,** Univ Of Cin R Walters Coll, Blue Ash, OH; FR; BS; Phi Theta Kappa; Bio; Med.

**BROOKE, LISA A,** Chattahoochee Vly St Comm Coll, Phenix City, AL; FR; MBA; Frmhse Crscnts; Frmhse Lit Sis; Lbrl Arts.

**BROOKS, ALICIA F,** Tn Tech Univ, Cookeville, TN; FR; BS; Band/Concert Band 90-; Marching Band 90-; Amer Home Econ Assn 90-; TN Home Econ Assn 90-; TN Tech Home Econ Assn V Chrprsn 90-; Alpha Lambda Delta; Home Econ; Interior Dsgn.

**BROOKS, ANTHONY T,** Longwood Coll, Farmville, VA; SR; BS; Greek Cncl 88-; Inter Frtrnl Cncl 88-; ABS Mnrty Mntr 90-; Alpha Chi Rho VP 89-90; Sml Bus Dev Ctrn Intern 90-; Schlrshp 87-88; IM Awd Exc 90-; Finance; Corp Finance.

**BROOKS, ATHENA,** Hillsborough Comm Coll, Tampa, FL; FR; BA; Educ Music; Chrl Dir.

**BROOKS, BETHANY M,** Wv Univ At Parkersburg, Parkersburg, WV; FR; AAS; Phi Theta Kappa; Natl Collgt Nrsng Awrd; Nrsng.

**BROOKS, CHRISTOPHER J M,** Cornell Univ Statutory College, Ithaca, NY; SR; BS; Rsrch Asst Equine Immnlgy Cornell Vet Clg 90-; Grad Cum Laude; Ftbl 87-88; Microbio; Med.

**BROOKS, CLARENCETINE D,** Univ Of Md At Eastern Shore, Princess Anne, MD; FR; Amnsty Intl 90-; Cir K 90-; Ltry Mag Chrwmn; Stdnt Vol; SGA; Deans Lst; Hon Pgm; Law/Soc Hstry; Lwyr/Jdg.

**BROOKS, COLIN N,** Lenoir Rhyne Coll, Hickory, NC; JR; BS; SG DCP 88-; Amnsty Intl Anti-Dth Pnlty Coord 88-; Coll Dmcrts Sec 88-; Alpha Lambda Delta 89-90; Chi Beta Phi 90-; Mu Sigma Epsilon; Theta Xi Edctr 89-; Ntr Cnsrvcy Intrn 90-; Deans Lst 88-; Pres Lst 90; Envrnmntl Mgmt; Eclgst.

**BROOKS, COREY MARIO,** Va St Univ, Petersburg, VA; SO; BS; Assn Pol Sci 90-; Dirty Dozens 89-90; Kappa Alpha Psi; Sammy Youmpg Jr 89-90; Patric Lumumba 90-; Va St Acdmc Achvmnt 89-90; Pol Sci; Law.

**BROOKS, DANA G,** Ms St Univ, Miss State, MS; GD; DVM; Amer Vet Med Assn 87-; Amer Anml Hosp Assn 89-; Yrbk Stf 88-90; Gamma Beta Phi 87-89; Alpha Psi Sec 88-; Dns Schlr 89-90; Asstshp Yerkes Rgnl Primate Rsrch Ctr Atlanta GA 88; Aux Am Vet Med Assn Awd; Vet Medicine; Intl Med/Tch Vet Med.

**BROOKS, DAVID A,** Howard Univ, Washington, DC; GD; MSW; Hon Stdnt Soc 90-; Natl Soc Wrkrs 90-; Biog 91 Al-Am Schlr Coll Dir; 91 Natl Coll Awds Yrbk; Track Tm/X-Cntry 83-85; Boy Scouts Of Am 90-; Coalition For Homeless 89-; Mntl Hlth Cnslng/Cmnty Activist 89-; Soc Wrk; Mntl Hlth Cnslng.

**BROOKS, DAWN M,** Coll Of Charleston, Charleston, SC; SO; BA; Peer Mntr Assoc Pres; German; Intl Law.

**BROOKS, DEBBIE A,** Al A & M Univ, Normal, AL; JR; BS; Urbn Plnng Assn VP 90-; Amrcn Plnng Assn; America Plnng Assn; Alpha Zeta Chnclr; Urbn Plnng.

**BROOKS, DELMA R,** Univ Of Southern Ms, Hattiesburg, MS; BED; Afro Amer Scty Orgn; Dns Lst; Tch Scndry Engl Ltr Obtn Mstrs Dctrte In Engl; BS 90; Engl.

**BROOKS JR, FREDRICK E,** Memphis St Univ, Memphis, TN; JR; State Bd Of Regents Schlrshp; Bus.

**BROOKS, GENA E,** Midway Coll, Midway, KY; SR; BSN; Stdnt Govt Rsdnce Life Sntr 88-89; Stdnt Alumnae Brd Sec 88-89; Phi Theta Kappa 87-89; RN Univ Kentucky Med Ctr 89; ADN Midway Clg 89; Nrsg; RN.

**BROOKS, GERALD RAYMOND,** Nova Univ, Ft Lauderdale, FL; GD; MBA; FL St Cert Bldg Cntrctr; Dsgntd Prprty Mgr RPA; FL Licnsd Rl Est Broker; FL Licnsd Mrtgage Broker; Real Est Mgmt.

**BROOKS, J LEANNE,** Belmont Coll, Nashville, TN; SR; BSW; Soc Wrk Clb Pres 89-90; Gamma Beta Phi; Blue Key Treas 90-; Kappa Delta; Rape/Sexual Abuse Ctr Vol 89-; Soc Wrk; MSW.

**BROOKS, JACQUELYN W,** Univ Of North Fl, Jacksonville, FL; JR; BED; Ftr Edctrs Amrc Treas 89-90; Cncl Excptnl Chldrn 90-; Gldn Key; Kappa Delta Pi; AA St Johns River Cmmnty Coll 89; Spcl Edctn.

**BROOKS, JENNIFER P,** Va Polytechnic Inst & St Univ, Blacksburg, VA; FR; BS; Debate 90-; Chrch Chr 90-; Mtrls Eng; Eng.

**BROOKS, JO E,** Slippery Rock Univ, Slippery Rock, PA; SR; BSED; Sigma Delta Pi Treas/Sec 88-; Lambda Epsilon Delta 89-; Mu Kappa Gamma 88-89; Elem Prctcm Evans Cty Elem 90; Sec Prctcm Butler H S; Stdnt Tchg Northview; Elem Ed/Sec Ed/Spnsh; Tchng Inr Cty Schls.

**BROOKS, JOSEPH M,** Ms St Univ, Miss State, MS; SO; BA; Psychlgy; Law Schl.

**BROOKS, JOY A,** Springfield Tech Comm Coll, Springfield, MA; FR; AS; Med Assist Club; Dns Lst 90-; Notre Dame Folk Choir 86-; Bowling Leagues Sec 67-88; Nrsg Assist Northampton Nrsg Home 76-88; Med Assist.

**BROOKS, KATHLEEN O,** Westminster Coll, New Wilmingtn, PA; SR; BA; SGA 88-89; Yng Repbl Actv Chmn 88-; Kapa Delta Pi 90-; NCTE; Deans List 90; Elem Tchng Intnshp; Elem Ed; Tch.

**BROOKS, KELLIE S,** Univ Of Va Clinch Valley Coll, Wise, VA; FR; BA; Hnrs Prgm 90-; Blgy; Med.

**BROOKS, KELLY D,** Univ Of Akron, Akron, OH; JR; BED; Cncl For Excptnl Chldrn 90-; Res Asst Of Res Halls 90-; Spec Edn/LD; Edn.

**BROOKS, KIMBERLY J,** Wv Univ, Morgantown, WV; SR; BS; Inst Indus Engrs Sec 88-; Lacross Clb Ststcn 87-88; Li Toon Awa 88-89; Alpha Pi Mu 90-; Greensburg Coll Clb Schlrshp 87-; Rsdnc Life Tutor 89-; Indus Engr.

**BROOKS, LANCE H,** Mercer Univ, Macon, GA; FR; BA; Elec Eng.

**BROOKS, LEONORA S,** Jacksonville St Univ, Jacksonville, AL; JR; BSN; Natl Stdnt Nrs Assn; Jdcl Brd; Nrs Ambsdr JSU 90-; St Nrsng Schlrshp 90-; D Sterne Schlrshp 91-; Nrsng; RN.

**BROOKS, LINDA D,** Brevard Coll, Brevard, NC; SO; Natl Assoc Female Exec; AS; Art Prod.

**BROOKS, LISA M,** Tn Wesleyan Coll, Athens, TN; JR; BS; AS Cleveland St Comm Clg 90; Acctg.

**BROOKS, LYNETTE E,** Tn St Univ, Nashville, TN; FR; BA; Univ Fashion Guild Fr Ambassador 90-; Design Concentration Hom Ec; Fashn Dsgnr.

**BROOKS, MARTHA M,** Va Commonwealth Univ, Richmond, VA; SR; BS; Nrsng; Mgt.

**BROOKS, MARY MICHELLE,** Middle Tn St Univ, Murfreesboro, TN; SR; BS; Educ Club 88-89; STEA 90-; Tau Omicron 90-; Kappa Delta Pi 89-; Hmcmng Crt 88-89; AS Motlow St Comm Clg 89; Elem Educ; Teach.

**BROOKS, MICHELLE R,** Central Fl Comm Coll, Ocala, FL; JR; BA; QWL-EI 90; NRLCA 90; Rural Carrier Assoc 89; Gnrl; Ed.

**BROOKS, MONIKA,** Broward Comm Coll, Ft Lauderdale, FL; FR; AS; Constr Bus; RN; Nrsng.

**BROOKS, NANA N,** Fl A & M Univ, Tallahassee, FL; SR; BS; Stdnt Allnc Fr Cltrl Devlpmnt 90-; Psy Hnr Scty; Psychlgy; Clncl Psychlgst.

**BROOKS, NICKI A,** Univ Of Tn At Knoxville, Knoxville, TN; FR; BA; Pre Law Soc; Vol For Christ; Clement Hall Res Assoc; Alpha Lambda Delta; Bus; Law.

**BROOKS, PAMALA RENEE,** Va St Univ, Petersburg, VA; SR; NAACP 90-.

**BROOKS, PATRICIA M,** Univ Of Rochester, Rochester, NY; SR; BS; Soc Wmn Engrs 90-; Optcl Soc Amer 90-; Tau Beta Pi 90-; Adpt A Grndprnt 87-88; Optics Hnrs Thesis 90-; Optics; Engr.

**BROOKS, PATRICK J,** Coker Coll, Hartsville, SC; SR; BA; Fin Cmte; Judcl Cncl; Fac Search Cmte; Natl Bus Merit Awrd Winner 89-; YMCA Vol 90-; Intern E D Jones & Co; Acad All Amer Soccer 89-; Soccer 87-; Golf 89-; BA Coker Clg 91; Mktg; Bus Admin.

**BROOKS, ROBERT W,** Niagara Univ, Niagara Univ, NY; JR; BBA; Acdmc Schlrshp; Presidential Schlrshp; Acctng; CPA.

**BROOKS, RONA N,** Clark Atlanta Univ, Atlanta, GA; SO; BA; Choir 90; Film Soc 87; Key Clb 88-89; Natl Achvmnt Semi-Finalist 88-89; Bus Admin; Mktg Fshn.

**BROOKS, SCOTT C,** Pellissippi St Tech Comm Coll, Knoxville, TN; FR; BA; Phi Theta Kappa; Sci/Math; Elec Engr.

**BROOKS, SHERRY L,** Savannah Coll Of Art & Design, Savannah, GA; SO; BFA; Grphcs Grp 89-; Bacchus 89-; Deans Lst 89-; Dcmntd Wrk 89-; Art; Grphc Dsgn/Advrtsng.

**BROOKS, STACEY M,** S U N Y Coll At Fredonia, Fredonia, NY; SO; BS; Spch Pthlgy Adlgy Scty 90-; Bg Brthr Bg Sstr 90-; Spcy Pthlgy.

**BROOKS, STEVEN TODD,** Univ Of Tn At Chattanooga, Chattanooga, TN; JR; BS; US Achvmnt Acad; Pi Mu Epsilon; Roper Golf Tm 90; Natl Hon Soc 87-88; Golden Key 90; Tau Beta Pi; Specl Svcs Tutor 90; Co-Op Pgm/Engr Roper Clg 89-; Eleanor R Williams Schlrshp 88; Elec Engr.

**BROOKS, TERRI G,** Endicott Coll, Beverly, MA; FR; BA; Acctng.

**BROOKS, VERONICA S,** Bluefield Coll, Bluefield, VA; SR; BSU Cncl Treas 90-; Bluefield Sngrs; BSU Drama; BSU Msns; Consessions Coord Atheletics; Play Our Town 90; Alpha Psi Sigma 89-; Phi Mu Delta 88-; RA 90-; Hlth Intrnshp; Alpha Psi Sigma; AS 89; BS; Hlth; Occptnl Therapy.

**BROOKS, VICKI J,** Oh Dominican Coll, Columbus, OH; SR; BS; Reg MLT ASCP 74-; Lab Tech Mt Carml Med Ctr 78-; AS Clrk Tech Clg 74; Acctg.

**BROOKS, VICTORIA F,** Indiana Univ Of Pa, Indiana, PA; SR; Adults Seeking Knowledge Penn St Univ; Dns Lst; St Josephs Church Choir; Retail Exper 73-88; Tchrs Aid Hrg Imprd/TMR Clsrms; BS Ed 90; Tchr Hrg Imprd; Tchr Hrg Imprd/Schl Admin.

**BROOKS, VIRGINIA M,** Germanna Comm Coll, Locust Grove, VA; GD; AAS; Alha Beta Gamma 90; Cert 90; Secretarial Studies.

**BROOKS, WILLIAM ELLIS,** Univ Of Ky, Lexington, KY; SO; BS; Chess Clb Prsdnt 89-; Cmptr Sci Math; Prgrmmng.

**BROOKS-JONES, BERNICE,** Barry Univ, Miami, FL; GD; MS; Bapt Ch 72-; Usher Bd Sec 87; Sch Instrtnl Aide; Sub Tchr 78-; BLS 90; Cert State FL Dept Edn 89; Liberal Studies; Tchr Elem Edn.

**BROOM, TERI L,** Ga St Univ, Atlanta, GA; SR; BED; Stdnt Ga Assoc Of Edctrs Prog Co-Coord 89; Ntl Cncl Of Tchrs In Math; Blue Key Scl Co-Chrmn 89; Ordr Of Omega 89; Alpha Xi Delta VP 90; Initial Tchr Prep Awd; Sr Awd; Vllybl 87-88; Mddle Chldhd Ed; Tchr Math/Sci.

**BROOM, VERA I,** Atlantic Comm Coll, Mays Landing, NJ; FR; BA; Casino Mktg Rep; Acctg; CPA.

**BROOME, COURTENAY LYNN,** Univ Of Sc At Columbia, Columbia, SC; SR; BS; Gamma Beta Phi 89-; Golden Key 89-; Beta Alpha Psi 90-; Accounting; Public Accounting/Tax.

**BROOME, DOROTHEA M,** Coll Of Charleston, Charleston, SC; JR; BA; Math Clb Co Pres 90-; Phi Theta Kappa 80; Math; Educ; Eng.

**BROOME, JOYCE L,** Piedmont Tech Coll, Greenwood, SC; SO; AA; Psi Beta; Crmnl Justice Intrn 90-; Crmnl Justice; Law.

**BROOME, LENORA M,** Northern Ky Univ, Highland Hts, KY; FR; BS; Ed; Tchg.

**BROOME, SHANNON T,** Univ Of Sc At Columbia, Columbia, SC; JR; Amer Pharm Assn 90-; Bapt Stdnt Union 88-; Lifeguard Trng Instr 89-; Water Sfty Instr ARC 87-91; Revco Intrnshp 90; Dns Lst 88-; Carolina Bdybldng Team 90; Pharm; Med.

**BROOMS, PAUL R,** Univ Of The Dist Of Columbia, Washington, DC; SR; BA; Caribbean Stdnt Assn; Jrnlsm; Med Indus.

**BROOMS, TREZA L,** Fl A & M Univ, Tallahassee, FL; FR; MBA; NAACP 90-; Pres Schlrs Assn 90-; Phi Eta Sigma; Bus; Intl Bus Admin.

**BROPHY, CHRISTINA A,** Temple Univ, Philadelphia, PA; JR; BA; Arch Dsgn.

**BROSSOK, CAROL A,** Savannah Coll Of Art & Design, Savannah, GA; SO; BA; ISID V P; Upholstery Bsn 85-90; AA Centerary Clg For Wmn 75; Interior Design.

**BROTH, RICHARD E,** Yeshiva Univ, New York, NY; SR; BA; SSSJ Pres 89-; Issac Brever Clg For Jud Stds Stdnt Cncl VP 90-; Peer Adv 89-; Food Svc Cmte 89-; Photo Yrbk; Photo Nwspr; Deans Lst 88-; Vlybl; Bio; Med.

**BROTHERS, KECIA N,** Norfolk St Univ, Norfolk, VA; SR; BS; Hnr Rl 90-; Portsmouth Commwlth Attnys Off Intrnshp 90-; Sociology/Crim Just; Law.

**BROTHERS, THERESA M,** Springfield Tech Comm Coll, Springfield, MA; AD 90.

**BROTHERTON, JACQUELINE N,** Middle Tn St Univ, Murfreesboro, TN; FR; BS; Hons Pgm; Delta Zeta Pan Del 90-; Mktg; Bus.

**BROUGH, CARLENE J,** Liberty Univ, Lynchburg, VA; SR; BED; Kappa Delta Pi 90-; Lbrty Assn Chrstn Tchrs 89-90; Upper/Lower Curr Educ; Educator.

**BROUGHTON, DAVID S,** Fl St Univ, Tallahassee, FL; JR; BA; March Band 90; AA Tallahassee Comm Colg 90; T V Brdcstg; News.

**BROUGHTON, SHELLEY S,** Fl St Univ, Tallahassee, FL; SR; Alumni Fndtn 88-90; Seminole Ambssdrs 88-90; Gold Key 90-; Golden Key 89-; Mortar Brd Elctns Chrprsn 89-90; Phi Kappa Phi 90-; Phi Beta Kappa; Delta Delta Delta Soc Dvlpmnt Chrmn 87-; Fclty Undergrad Schlrshp 90-; Med.

**BROUILLARD, CAROL L,** Mount Saint Mary Coll, Newburgh, NY; FR; BA; Sci; Nrsg.

**BROUILLETTE, KIMBERLY B,** Univ Of Nc At Charlotte, Charlotte, NC; SR; BS; Epsilom Sigma Sec/Treas 87-; Boone Schlrshp 90; Dns Lst 90; Stdnt Tchng 88-90; Earth Sci; Advrtsng.

**BROUILLETTE-BEEBE, KAREN L,** Southern Ct St Univ, New Haven, CT; SR; BSN; Crrclum Brd 89-; Sr Bnqt Comm 90-; Ntnl Stdnt Nrs Assn NSNA Sec 87-; Clncl Asst 90; Nrsng; Mtrnl Chld Nrsng MSN.

**BROUS, PAIGE E,** Savannah Coll Of Art & Design, Savannah, GA; SO; BFA.

**BROUSE, JOSEPH D,** Beckley Coll, Beckley, WV; JR; BED; Raleigh Cnty Young Reps Pres 90-; WV For Families Treas 89-; Cand WV House Of Delgts 90; Educ; Pol Sci.

**BROW, DESSERIE H,** Fl St Univ, Tallahassee, FL; SR; BS; Du Bois Scty; Deans Lst 90; Nrsng; Peds Nrse.

**BROWDER, TONYA A,** Univ Of Sc At Columbia, Columbia, SC; JR; BA; Psychlgy Clb 89-90; Grmn Cl BVP 89-90; Hstry.

**BROWDER, WAYNE G,** Univ Of Sc At Columbia, Columbia, SC; SO; BA.

**BROWE, DAVID M,** Christopher Newport Coll, Newport News, VA; FR; BSBA; Mgnt; Enrepreneur.

**BROWER, DAVID L,** Nyack Coll, Nyack, NY; SR; BA; ARA N E Bible Clg 90; Psych.

**BROWER, MARYANN F,** Converse Coll, Spartanburg, SC; SR; BA; Bank Teller; Dental Asst; Psych/Sociology.

**BROWER SR, NEIL B,** Temple Univ, Philadelphia, PA; SO; BS; Dsc Jcky 90; Deans Lst 89-90; Wtr 90-; Phrmcy.

**BROWN BLANKS, KENDRA M,** Ms St Univ, Miss State, MS; SR; Phi Theta Kappa 88-89; Hnrs Grad 89; Magna Cum Laude 90; AA Meridian Comm Clg 89; BA 90; Bus Admin; Govt/Law.

**BROWN, ADRIAN B,** Alcorn St Univ, Lorman, MS; JR; BS; Hnrs Stdnt Org; Alpha Kappa Mu 90-; Deans Lst 88-; U S Achvmnt Acdmy Allamer Schlr 90-; Outstdng Clg Stdnts 88-; Acctng; Financial Analyst.

**BROWN, ADRIEN WESLEY,** Daemen Coll, Amherst, NY; JR; BA; New York St Army Natl Grd 87-; Pi Gamma Mu; Hstry/Govt; Law.

**BROWN, ALICIA D,** Duquesne Univ, Pittsburgh, PA; JR; BA; Phi Kappa Phi; Delta Sigma Pi Secr 88-90; Univ Schlr 88-; Dns Lst 88-; Three Rivers Shakespeare Fest Publ Rels Intern; Engl; Grad Sch.

**BROWN, ALLAN R,** Fl A & M Univ, Tallahassee, FL; SR; BS; Amer Inst Archtct Stdnts Pres 88-; Golden Key; Naoa Schlrshp 90; Arch; Rgstrd Archt.

**BROWN, ALLISON C,** Univ Of Al At Birmingham, Birmingham, AL; JR; BS; Stdnt Occptnl Thrpy Assn 90-; Alpha Gamma Delta 88-90; Occptnl Thrpy.

**BROWN, ALVINA L,** Univ Of Ky, Lexington, KY; FR; BA; SAB 90-; Bio; Med.

**BROWN, AMANDA A,** Union Univ, Jackson, TN; JR; BSBA; Rtldg Hstry Clb Treas 89-; Chrldr; Alpha Chi 90-; Phi Beta Lambda 90-; Mgmt; Ad Sales.

**BROWN, AMMA K,** Bennett Coll, Greensboro, NC; FR; BA; SGA Secty 90-; WICI; Brdct Commtns; TV News Anchor Wmn.

**BROWN, ANDRE J,** Coppin St Coll, Baltimore, MD; SR; Psychlgy Clb Sen 87-; Choir; BS; Psychlgy; Lwyr.

**BROWN, ANDREA C,** Univ Of Southern Ms, Hattiesburg, MS; FR; BS; Socty Physics Stdnts 90-; Hnrs Assn 90-; Physics.

**BROWN, ANGELA J,** Anne Arundel Comm Coll, Arnold, MD; SO; BA; Sntrl Schlrshp 89-; Ldies Of Elks Schlrshp 89-90; AA; Bus Admin; Acctg.

**BROWN, ANGELA L,** Alcorn St Univ, Lorman, MS; SR; BS; Alpha Kappa Mu 89-; Bus Admin; Mgmt.

**BROWN, ANGELA RANAE,** Univ Of Southern Ms, Hattiesburg, MS; JR; BA; Psych; Chld Psych.

**BROWN, ANGELIQUE S,** Fl A & M Univ, Tallahassee, FL; JR; BS; FFEA Exec Bd 89-; Ele Educ; Ele Educ Tchr.

**BROWN, ANGIE W,** Itawamba Comm Coll, Fulton, MS; FR; Nrsng.

**BROWN, ANNETTE F,** Old Dominion Univ, Norfolk, VA; JR; BS; Alpah Chi 90-; Gldn Ky; Soc Wmn 89-; Cvl Eng.

**BROWN, BARRY J,** Marshall University, Huntington, WV; JR; BED; Marshall Action Peaceful Solutions 88-90; Habitat Humanity Vol; Boys Clb Amer Vol 89; IMS 88-89; Cnslg/Rehab; Ther/Clg Prfsr.

**BROWN, BELINDA F,** Univ Of Southern Ms, Hattiesburg, MS; FR; Trck Tm Sprntr 90-; Biol Sci; Premed.

**BROWN, BELINDA M,** Lexington Comm Coll, Lexington, KY; JR; AS; Cmptr Sci; Pgmng.

**BROWN, BETH W,** Merrimack Coll, North Andover, MA; SO; BBA; Co Op Bostn Stck Exch; Finc; Law.

**BROWN, BETHANY C,** Spelman Coll, Atlanta, GA; FR; BSCHE; Chmsty Clb 90-; Ntnl Scty Blck Engrs 90-; Hrns Prgrm Clb 90-; Alpha Lambda Delta 90-; Most Otstndng Frshmn Engrng Stdnt 90-; Best Paper NASA Rsrch Sympsm; NASA Summer Intrshp Lewis Rsrch Ctr; Chmcl Engrng; Chmcl Engr.

**BROWN, BONNES ONEAL,** Alcorn St Univ, Lorman, MS; SO; Bsktbl 89-; Poltcl Scnc; Lawyer.

**BROWN, BRACKEN T,** Dyersburg St Comm Coll, Dyersburg, TN; FR; MD; Biolgy; MD.

**BROWN, BREANNA M,** Fl A & M Univ, Tallahassee, FL; SO; Phi Eta Sigma 89-; Stdnt Asstshp; Chem Engr.

**BROWN, BRENDA A,** Central Fl Comm Coll, Ocala, FL; FR; Law; Legal Assistant.

**BROWN, BRIAN W,** Middle Tn St Univ, Murfreesboro, TN; SO; BM; Music Perf; Tchr.

**BROWN, BRIDGETTE S,** Alcorn St Univ, Lorman, MS; SO; BS; Hons Stdnt Org 89-; Comptr Sci/Appld Math; Comptr Anlyst.

**BROWN, BRUCE A,** Univ Of Akron, Akron, OH; SO; BED; Comp Sci Club; Hnrs Club 89-; Hnrs Prog 89-; Scndry Edn Math Comp Sci; H S Math Tchr.

**BROWN, BYRON A,** Winthrop Coll, Rock Hill, SC; FR; Alpha Lambda Delta 90-; Biology; Med.

**BROWN, CALVIN W,** Limestone Coll, Gaffney, SC; SR; BS; SGA Sntr 87; Cir K Pres 87-88; Cir K Lt Gov 88; Kiwanis Clb 89; Kappa Alpha Chrmn 87; Yth Drug Prvntn Prog 90-; Chldrns Hosp Apprec Awd; H S Asst Coach 87-; Methodist Yth Grp 87-90; Bus Office; Bus Admin; Bus Mgmnt.

**BROWN, CAMI M,** Palm Beach Comm Coll, Lake Worth, FL; FR; BA; Phi Thera Kappa 90-; Deans/Pres Lst 90-; Art; Advrtsng Dsgn.

**BROWN, CAMILLE Y,** Clark Atlanta Univ, Atlanta, GA; FR; MBA; Pep Clb 90-; Techwd Tutrng Pgm 90; Bus; Law.

**BROWN, CAROL JOAN,** Newbury Coll, Brookline, MA; AAS; Optcl Scty 89-; Newenco Cls VP 87-; ASOA Sec; Phi Beta Kappa; Blck/Latin Clb 87; Dorm Pres 86; Big Sis Awrd 86; AME Chrch 87-; BA Skidmore Clg 87; NE Clg Optmtry 88; Ophthlmc Dspnsg; Optmtry.

**BROWN, CAROLINE R,** Mount Olive Coll, Mount Olive, NC; FR; AA; Spnsh Clb; Hon Prog 90-; Chrldr 90-; Elem Educ; Tchr.

**BROWN, CARY R,** Embry Riddle Aeronautical Univ, Daytona Beach, FL; SO; BS; YMCA 86; Natl Hnr Soc Secndry Schls 88-89; Alpha Eta Rho 88-90; ASS Vincennes Univ; Aviation; Commrcl Pilot.

**BROWN, CASSANDRA,** Alcorn St Univ, Lorman, MS; SO; BS; Cmptr Sci/Math Clb 89-91; Gosepl Choir 89-91; Cmptr Sci/Math; Analyst.

**BROWN, CATHERINE L,** Radford Univ, Radford, VA; SO; BA; Alpha Lambda Delpha 90-; Therptc Rec; Occptnl Therpy.

**BROWN, CHAD J,** Middle Ga Coll, Cochran, GA; SO; PHARM; Pharmacy; Trad Druggist.

**BROWN, CHANDRA L,** Wilberforce Univ, Wilberforce, OH; FR; BS; NABA Sec 90-; NSBL 90-; Schlrshp Cargill Inc; Bus; Actnt.

**BROWN, CHARISSA S,** Fl St Univ, Tallahassee, FL; SO; BED; Symphnc Bnd 89-; Flute Choir 89-90; Baroque Flute 90; Phi Eta Sigma Actvty Offcr 89-; Sigma Alpha Iota Pldg VP 90-; Incntv Schlrshp 89; Music Educ/Prfrmnc; Tchr Cnslr.

**BROWN, CHARLENE A,** Univ Of Sc At Columbia, Columbia, SC; SO; BS; Deans Lst Achvmnt 90; Phrmcy.

**BROWN, CHARLOTTE K,** Volunteer St Comm Coll, Gallatin, TN; SO; BBA; Lambuth Mem United Mthdst Chrch Admin Brd/ Cncl On Mnstrs 89; Accntng Co-Op Pstn Wth Allied Automtve Bendix In Gallatin TN 89; AS; Bsnss Accntng; Accntng In Mfg Envrnmnt.

**BROWN, CHERYL L,** Anne Arundel Comm Coll, Arnold, MD; JR.

**BROWN, CHERYL R,** Belmont Coll, Nashville, TN; FR; BS; Tri Beta 90-; SAACS 90-; Gamma Beta Phi; Vol Hosp; IM Vllybll Bsktbll 90-; Physcl Thrpy.

**BROWN, CHRISTA R,** Univ Of Nc At Charlotte, Charlotte, NC; FR; BSW; Phi Eta Sigma 90; Crisis Preg Ctr; Intern Hickory Grove Bapt Ch 90-; Soc Wrk.

**BROWN, CHRISTINA D,** Murray St Univ, Murray, KY; FR; BED; Hstry; Ele Educ.

**BROWN, CHRISTINA J,** Mount Aloysius Jr Coll, Cresson, PA; FR; ADN; Spec Olymp; Medcl Asst Clb; Phi Theta Kapa; Nrsng; RN.

**BROWN, CHRISTINE R,** Midlands Tech Coll, Columbia, SC; GD; BSN; Phi Theta Kappa 89; ADN; Nrsng; MA PHD In Nrsng.

**BROWN, CHRISTOPHER A,** Univ Of Nc At Charlotte, Charlotte, NC; SO; BA; Deans Lst; Wash Sem/Amer Bnkrptcy Inst Intrnshp Pltcl Sci; Vars Sccr Plyr Schlrshp 89-; Pltcl Sci/ Cmnctns Gov CLEGG; Law/Grad Schl.

**BROWN, CHRISTOPHER D,** Georgetown Univ, Washington, DC; SR; BSBA; Stdnt Nwspr Chmn 87-; Bus Day Steering Com Co-Chprsn 88-; Soph/Jr Cls Com 88-90; Deans Lst 87-; First/ Scnd Hon 88-; Public Acctg.

**BROWN, CHRISTOPHER E,** Clark Atlanta Univ, Atlanta, GA; FR; Mass Cmnctns/Radio TV Film; TV Studio Eng.

**BROWN, CHRISTOPHER E,** Fl International Univ, Miami, FL; SR; BSC; AA Miami Dade Comm Coll 89; Cmptr Sci/Math; Pgmmng.

**BROWN, CHRISTOPHER Q,** Western New England Coll, Springfield, MA; JR; BA; Dns Lst 90-; Bus Mgmt.

**BROWN, CHRISTY L,** Middle Ga Coll, Cochran, GA; FR; BA; Erly Chldhd Educ.

**BROWN, CLAIRE HOOPER,** Marymount Manhattan Coll, New York, NY; JR; BA; Alpha Chi 90; Psi Chi; Rsrch Assist Psychtry; Trvl Agncy Mgr 79-85; Psychlgy; Thrpst/Tchr.

**BROWN, COLONY M,** Radford Univ, Radford, VA; SR; Tour Guide; Cmnctns; Publ Rels.

**BROWN, CONNIE JO BARTLOW,** James Sprunt Comm Coll, Kenansville, NC; SO; BED; Engl/Hstry; Elem Ed.

**BROWN, CONSUELA D S,** Claflin Coll, Orangeburg, SC; Deans Lst; Bus Comp Sci.

**BROWN, CRYSTAL M,** Central St Univ, Wilberforce, OH; SR; BS; Prncpls Schlshp 86-87; Deans Lst; Mktg/Mgmt.

**BROWN, CYNTHIA G,** Univ Of Nc At Greensboro, Greensboro, NC; SO; BA; Inter Vrsty Chrstn Fllwshp Socl Coord; Vision; Dns Lst; N C Tchng Fllws Schlrshp; Elem Educ; Psych Cnslr.

**BROWN, CYNTHIA M,** Union Inst, Cincinnati, OH; SR; BA; Publctn Review Bd 90-; Intrnshp At Cncl For Chldrns Svcs 84-85; Cmnty Video Vol 89; Engl; Legal Studies/Tchng.

**BROWN, CYNTHIA R,** Middle Tn St Univ, Murfreesboro, TN; SR; Psychlgy Clb 88; Intrnshp Dept Yth Dvlpmnt S Cntrl Reg Outstdng Vol; ASSOC Mtlw St Comm Coll 89; Psychlgy/Soc Wrk; Chld Psychlgst.

**BROWN, DANIEL F,** Hudson Valley Comm Coll, Troy, NY; SO; BA; Cross Cntry Indr Otdr Trck; Btny; Law.

**BROWN, DARLENE G,** Radford Univ, Radford, VA; SO; BBA; Bus; Acctng.

**BROWN, DAVID A,** Nc Agri & Tech St Univ, Greensboro, NC; JR; BS; Fncl Mngmnt Assoc Pres 90-; Amer Mrktng Assoc VP Finance 90-; Stdnt Govt Assoc Senator 88-; Alpha Lambda Delta 89-; Beta Gamma Sigma; Hoechst Celanese Corp Treas Intern 90; Cargill Inc Oper Intern; Bus Admin; Bnkng.**

**BROWN, DAVID A,** Hudson Valley Comm Coll, Troy, NY; SR; AAS; Otng Clb HVCC 90; Adirondacl Mtn Clb 85-; Mowhawk Hdsn Wheelman 80-; Rsprtry Care; Prfsn Tchnlgy.

**BROWN, DAVID EMSON,** Kent St Univ Kent Cmps, Kent, OH; BBA; Acctg Assoc 89-; Beta Alpha Psi 90-; Intrn Mcgill Pwr Bl/Co CPAS 90-; Christ Luth Chrch Shrn Pa Hd Ushr; Penn St Alumni Assoc 88-; BA 88; Pblc Acctg.

**BROWN, DAVID M,** International Bible Coll, Florence, AL; JR; AA; Pres Lst 90; Deans Lst 89-; Bible/Cmnctns; Religious Jrnlsm.

**BROWN, DAWN KIMBERLEY,** Fl St Univ, Tallahassee, FL; JR; MBA; DBCC Girls Sftbl 88-90; Mst Outstndg Athl 90; Dns Lst 88-; Kappa Kappa Gamma 90-; AA 90; Cmnctns; Publ Rels.

**BROWN, DEBBIE M,** Va Highlands Comm Coll, Abingdon, VA; Bus Tech Mng.

**BROWN, DEBBIE S,** Univ Of Akron, Akron, OH; JR; BA; First Aid Cert; Chld Abuse Rcgntn Cert; Tutor 90-; Latchkey Kids Inc 89-; Elem Edn/Engl; Teach.

**BROWN, DEBORAH A,** Georgetown Univ, Washington, DC; JR; BSBA; Chrldng 88-89; Delta Sigma Pi Treas 90-; Arthur Andersen Ldrshp Conf; Dns Lst; Frst Hnrs; Second Hnrs; IM Vlybl Capt 90-; Pub Acctng.

**BROWN, DEBORAH S,** Univ Of Va Clinch Valley Coll, Wise, VA; SR; BA; AA SE Cmmnty Clg 90; Ed; Tchr.

**BROWN, DEBRA A,** Hampton Univ, Hampton, VA; JR; BS; Hsp Obstetrics Gyneclgy 89-; Nrsng.

**BROWN, DELORES L,** Memphis St Univ, Memphis, TN; JR; BA; Crmnl Jstc Soc; Gamma Beta Phi; Lamda Epislon Chi; Crml Jstc; Law.

**BROWN, DENICE,** Al A & M Univ, Normal, AL; SO; Chrldr; Rsdnts Awrd; Smmr Hnrs Acmdc Rnfrcmnt Prgm.

**BROWN, DENISE MARIE,** City Univ Of Ny City Coll, New York, NY; SR; Emmnl Svnth Day Advntst Chrch 90-; Sigma Theta Tau.

**BROWN, DESWICK,** Howard Univ, Washington, DC; GD; MDIV; Natl Assn Blck Smnrns VP 89-; Rlgn; Clrgy.

**BROWN, DIANA R,** Univ Of Sc At Columbia, Columbia, SC; SO; BA; Mrktg; Bus Admin.

**BROWN, DIONNE M,** City Univ Of Ny Baruch Coll, New York, NY; SR; BBA; Golden Key 90-; Alpha Iota Delta 89-; AA NY City Techncl Clg 88; Mgt; Hlth Care Admnstrtr.

**BROWN, DONALD,** City Univ Of Ny Med Evers Coll, Brooklyn, NY; SO; BS; ACM 89-; Pstl Wrkr; AS; Cmptr Sci; Data Cmmnctns.

**BROWN, DONALD E,** Methodist Coll, Fayetteville, NC; SR; BS; Pltcl Sci/Histy Clb P 90-; Assn US Army 86-; US Army Infntry Ofcr Capt; Pltcl Sci; US Army Ofcr.

**BROWN, DONALD J,** Daemen Coll, Amherst, NY; SR; BS; Stdnt Assn Vice Chr Prgmg 89-; Stdnt Phy Thrpy Assn 88-; IM 86-; Phi Beta Gamma Pres 89-90; Phy Thrpy Sr Intrnshps; Phy Thrpy Chltn Mem Hosp; Phy Thrpy; Priv Prac Orthopdc.

**BROWN, DONNA A,** Lansdale School Of Bus, North Wales, PA; FR; ASB; Med Asst; Med Fld.

**BROWN, DONNA K,** Univ Of Ky, Lexington, KY; JR; Whsprng Hills Chrch Christ; Boy Scouts America Pck Mstr; Cncl Excptnl Chldrn; Outstndng Clg Stdnts Amer; Educ/Spec Educ; Tch.

**BROWN, DYANN L,** Univ Of New England, Biddeford, ME; JR; BA; Yrbk Stf 89-; Day Care Intrn Stf 90-; Human Serv; Day Care Ctr.

**BROWN, EARL A,** Columbia Union Coll, Takoma Park, MD; SO; Singspiration Treas 90-; Delta Sigma Tau Treas 90-; Gospel Choir Fin Adv 90-; Phi Eta Sigma Pres 90-; Acctng/Comp Sci; Acctng Private Pub Govt.

**BROWN, ERIC A,** Catawba Valley Comm Coll, Hickory, NC; SO; Arch Tech; Engr.

**BROWN, ERIC S,** Enterprise St Jr Coll, Enterprise, AL; FR; BA; Sci/Math; Engr.

**BROWN, ERICK C,** Stillman Coll, Tuscaloosa, AL; SO; Stillman Schlr; Blngrth Schlr; Deans Lst; Engl; Pblc Rltns/Educ.

**BROWN, ESTHER T,** Albany St Coll, Albany, GA; SR; MED; Stu Gvt Assc 90-; Pre Almn Clb 87-; Fclty Stff Wvs Clb Rprtr 87-; Alphbtts 87-; NCTE 90-; BA; Engl; Educ.

**BROWN, EVELYN DENISE,** Ashland Comm Coll, Ashland, KY; JR; BS; Appls Brd 87-90; AAS Offc Bus Admn 89; AA 90; Rdlgy.**

**BROWN, EVERARD N,** City Univ Of Ny Baruch Coll, New York, NY; SR; BA; Crbbn Stdnts Assoc 89-; Beta Gamma Sigma; Deans Lst; Sccr 89-; Cert 83; Mrktng.

**BROWN, FAYE,** Northwest Al Comm Coll, Phil Campbell, AL; FR.

**BROWN JR, GEORGE W,** Ky St Univ, Frankfort, KY; FR; Dns Lst 90; Ftbl 90; Pol Sci; Law.

**BROWN, GERALDINE ELLIOTT,** Oh Univ-Southern Cmps, Ironton, OH; SO; BA; Wellnss Clb; Chrch Of God; Comm Ky Colonl; Sec Treas Lads Mnstrs; Hosp Vol; Social Wrk.

**BROWN, GINGER S,** Univ Of Al At Birmingham, Birmingham, AL; JR; BA; Stdnt Occptnl Therapy Assoc Mbrs Serv Committee 90-; Presidental Hnr Rl Mbr 90-; Private Practice Occptnl Therapy Asstnt 90-; Occptnl Therapy; Physical Dysfunction.

**BROWN, GREGORY T,** Comm Coll Algny Co Algny Cmps, Pittsburgh, PA; SR; AS; Body Bldg Clb; 1st Plc Bnch Prss Comp 90; AS Cmptr Sci 86f; Bus/Acctg; CPA.**

**BROWN, GRETA M,** Abraham Baldwin Agri Coll, Tifton, GA; FR; BA; Business; Bus Mgmt.

**BROWN, HALI F,** Univ Of Cin R Walters Coll, Blue Ash, OH; SR; AS; Prgrmmr/Analyst; Cmptr Prgrmmng.

**BROWN, HAYLEY S,** Southern Coll Of Tech, Marietta, GA; JR; BS; IIE 87-; ASQC 87-; Gas Light Co Intrn 88-91; Ind Engr.

**BROWN, HEATHER L,** Clarkson Univ, Potsdam, NY; SO; BS; Clarkson Soc Accntnts 90-; Soc Wmn Mgrs 90-; Natl Assoc Acctnts 90-; Peer Tutor; Pres Schlr 90-; Acctg/Finance; CPA CMA.

**BROWN, HEIDI A,** Casco Bay Coll, Portland, ME; SR; Phi Beta Lambda Prsdnt 89-; Sr Mntr 90-; Trvl Agncy Intrn 90; Deans Lst 89-; Lewiston Rgnl Vctnl Cntr 89.

**BROWN, HENRY L,** Albany St Coll, Albany, GA; JR; BA; Mgmt Assn VP 90-; Exec Rnd Tble Assn VP 90-; Stdnt Govt Assn Stdnt Ldr Fr Com 87-; Alpha Kappa Mu 90-; Alpha Phi Alpha Pres 90-; Inst Fr Educ Oppstnty Intrnshp 90-; Mnrty Otrch Intrnshp Prog; Delco-Remy Intrnshp; Mgmt; Utlze Mngrl Sklls In Mjr Corp Co.

**BROWN, HOLLY A,** Univ Of Ky, Lexington, KY; FR; BA; Res Hall Govt Flr Rep 90-; Deans Lst; Psychlgy.

**BROWN, HOLLY CHRISTINA,** Smith Coll, Northampton, MA; SO; BA; Jpns Clb 89-90; Sazanami Clb Sec 90-; Gld Key Gd 90-; Dns Lst 89-90; Frst Grp Schlr 90; E Asian Stds.

**BROWN, HOWARD R,** Ms St Univ, Miss State, MS; SR; BA; Stdnt Assoc Sen Comm Chr; Res Asst; Asst Hall Dir; Elder Statesmen; Blue Key; Pres Lst 90-; English; Law.

**BROWN JR, HUGH OREN,** Univ Of Ga, Athens, GA; SO; BLA; Intrnshp GA Correctional Industries Eng Dept 90-; IM Sprts; Lndscp Arch.

**BROWN III, J BROOKS,** Univ Of North Fl, Jacksonville, FL; JR; BA; Golden Key; AA FL Cmnty Clg 90; Cmnctns/Sclgy.

**BROWN, JACK BARTON,** Ky St Univ, Frankfort, KY; JR.

**BROWN, JAMES A,** Univ Of Southern Ms, Hattiesburg, MS; FR; BA; Army Spc 88-90; Engl; Wrtr.

**BROWN JR, JAMES E,** Fayetteville St Univ, Fayetteville, NC; FR; MBA; Math/Hstry; Eng/Cmptr Sci.

**BROWN, JAMES S,** Ky St Univ, Frankfort, KY; SR; BA; NAACP 88-; Deans Lst 89-90; Econ; Mgmnt.**

**BROWN JR, JAMES T C,** Va St Univ, Petersburg, VA; GD; Bsn Admin Clb 89-90; Cum Laude 90; Bsn Admin; Achvmnt Cert 87-90; Dns Lst 89-90.

**BROWN, JANICE M,** Johnson C Smith Univ, Charlotte, NC; SO; BA; Dns Lst 90-; Cmptr Sci; Prgmmr.

**BROWN, JANICE P,** Alcorn St Univ, Lorman, MS; JR; BS; Hnrs Stu Org 88-; Stu Govt Senate 90-; Math/Cmptr Clb 89-; Alpha Kappa Mu 90-; Ntl Hnr Soc 87-; Delta Sigma Theta Sor Inc 90-; Full Acdmc Schlrshp 88-; Pres Schlr 90; Deans Lst Schlr 88-; Math; Engr.

**BROWN, JASMINE M,** City Univ Of Ny Med Evers Coll, Brooklyn, NY; AS; Caribbean Stdnt Union Kingsboro Cmnty Clg Pres 80-81; Secr Sci; BS Bsn.

**BROWN, JASON S,** Fayetteville St Univ, Fayetteville, NC; SO; BS; AM Red Cross Bld Dnr 87-90; Lacrosse 89-90; Mchnl Eng; Pilot.

**BROWN, JAYE MARIE,** Gallaudet Univ, Washington, DC; SR; BA; Phi Sigma Iota 90-; English Wrtng/Psych/Spanish; Pblshng/ Educ.

**BROWN, JEANETTE E,** Brewer St Jr Coll, Fayette, AL; SO; Phi Theta Kappa 90-; AAS; Off Admin; Bus.

**BROWN, JEANNE L,** Lenoir Rhyne Coll, Hickory, NC; SR; SNCAE 90-; Intrntl Order Of The Rainbow For Girls Miss Svc 87-; Spanish Club 87-88; Wesley Flwshp 87-88; Band 87-89; Erly Chldhd Ed; Tchng.

**BROWN, JEANNIE R,** Univ Of Sc At Columbia, Columbia, SC; SR; Bsn Soc 88-89; Phi Beta Kappa; Phi Theta Kappa 88-89; Beta Gamma Sigma; Gamma Beta Phi 90-; Schlr Schlp 90-; Peap Schlp 87; IM Vlybl 87; BS; AA Univ MD 89; Mgmt Sci; Prod Mgr.

**BROWN, JELENA J,** Univ Of Nc At Charlotte, Charlotte, NC; JR; Crmnl Just; Law.

**BROWN, JENA L,** Meridian Comm Coll, Meridian, MS; SO; BA; Awarded John C Stennis Inst Schlrshp At MS State Univ Poltcl Sci; Var Tennis 89-; AA MCC; Political Science; Law & Elective Govt.

**BROWN, JENNIFER,** Ky St Univ, Frankfort, KY; SR; BS; Hm Econ Clb Sec 89-; Ldy Dmnd Scl Clb Pres 88-; Chndlr Hll Clb Pre S89-90; Natl Coll Awrd; Deans Lst 90-; Hm Econ Strngthng Awrd 88-; Cncrt Chr Awrd 86-87; Gldn Grls VP 88-; Fshn Mrchndsng.

**BROWN, JENNIFER J,** Pa St Univ Main Cmps, University Pk, PA; FR; BAE; SWE 80-; Alpha Xi Delta Risk Mngmnt 90-; Arch Eng.

**BROWN, JILL M,** Hilbert Coll, Hamburg, NY; FR; AAS; Natl Hnrs Soc 90-; Acad Schlrshp 90; Hnrs List 90-; Leg Asst.

**BROWN, JOHN P,** Middle Tn St Univ, Murfreesboro, TN; SO; BBA; Gamma Beta 90-; Bus Admin.

**BROWN, JOHN T,** Wv Univ, Morgantown, WV; JR; BS; Amer Chem Soc Stdnt Afflts; Golden Key; Trvl Awd Amer Chem Soc Org Chem Div; Chem; Grad Schl Synth Org Chem.

**BROWN, JON B,** Kent St Univ Kent Cmps, Kent, OH; FR; BA; Bus; Acctg.

**BROWN, JOVANKA M,** Univ Of Southern Ms, Hattiesburg, MS; SO; BS; Hll Cncl VP; Rho Eta Alpha; Pschlgy.**

**BROWN, JOYCE V,** S U N Y Coll Of Tech At Alfred, Alfred, NY; SO; Commuter Clb 90-; Alpha Sigma Mu; Phi Theta Kappa; Psi Beta; Literacy Vol Amer 89-; Lib Arts/Ed; Sec Sch Tchr.

**BROWN, JULIE K,** Anne Arundel Comm Coll, Arnold, MD; SO; BA; MD Rec/Pks Co Chr 85-87; US Naval Acad Emplyees Rec Secy 85-89; Arthur Slade Regnl Cathlc Schpublcty Chr 89-90; Tstmstrs 88-89; Corp Cmnctns/Mktg; Intrntl Mktg.

**BROWN, JULIE M,** Univ Of Akron, Akron, OH; SR; BA; BA Of Sci 91; Phy Ed; Ed.

**BROWN, JULIE MARIE,** Medical Coll Of Ga, Augusta, GA; SO; BSN; BA Columbia Coll 88; Pediatrc Onclgy Nrsng.

**BROWN, JULITA Z,** Talladega Coll, Talladega, AL; SR; Engl Mjrs Assn Sec 87-; Stdnt Govt Assn Ambssdr 90-; Stdnt Govt Assn Sntr 87; Zeta Phi Beta Pres 90-; Big Sis Prog 89-; Coretta Scott King Schlrshp 89; Zeta Phi Beta Finer Wmnhd Schlrshp 90-; IM Vlybl 87-; BA; Engl; Tchr/Lwyr Civil/Crmnl.

**BROWN II, K KENNETH,** Juniata Coll, Huntingdon, PA; JR; BA; Pblc Affrs Clb 90-; SG 90-; Res Assn P 90-; Pi Sigma Alpha P 90-; Brumbaugh-Ellis Schlrshp 88-; J C Henry Schlrshp; Sccr 88; Poly Sci Pblc Law; Law.

**BROWN, KAMMY V,** Va St Univ, Petersburg, VA; SR; Bsktbl 86-90; Vllybl 88; BFA Cmmrcl Art/Dsgn 86; Advrtsng Dsgnr Illstrtr.

**BROWN, KARA L,** Univ Of Cincinnati, Cincinnati, OH; SO; BM; 1st Prze Bauer Instr Comp; Stix Mem Schlrshp Afrcn Amer Stdnts; Flute Perf/Music Educ; Orch Perf.

**BROWN, KAREN A,** Univ Of South Al, Mobile, AL; SR; BS; Phi Theta Kappa 87-89; Human Resource Mgrs Treas 90-; Cir K Sec 89-90; Med Ctr Intern; Most Otstndng Bus Stdnt 89; Acdmc Schlrshp 91-; Karate 89; AS Shelton St Comm Coll 89; Personnel & Ind Relations.

**BROWN, KAREN E,** Union Univ, Jackson, TN; JR; BS; Tchr Educ Assoc; Zeta Tau Alpha; Erly Elem Educ; Tchr Own Dy Care Ctr.

**BROWN, KAREN L,** Edinboro Univ Of Pa, Edinboro, PA; FR; BFA; Hnrs Prog 90-; Art; Cmmrcl Art/Grphc Dsgn.

**BROWN, KATHALYN D,** Hampton Univ, Hampton, VA; SR; BA; Choir Pres 87-; Concrt Chr 88-89; Music Edctrs Ntnl Cnfrnce 89-90; Alpha Kappa Alpha 90; Intrnshp Alpha Kappa Alpha Srty Inc 90; Geo Andrews Mem Fndtn Schlrshp 89; Big Brthr Big Sistr Prgrm 89-90; Il Prealumni Assn; Engl; Fdrl Law Enfrcmnt.**

**BROWN, KELLY M,** Univ Of Rochester, Rochester, NY; SR; BA; Mock Trial Org Pres 88-; Meridian Soc 89-; Stdnt Intervwr 90-; Omicron Delta; Econ/Pol Sci; Law.

**BROWN, KENDRA LYNN,** Anderson Coll, Anderson, SC; FR; AD; Gamma Beta Phi; Phi Theta Kappa; Psych.

**BROWN JR, KENNETH A,** Broward Comm Coll, Ft Lauderdale, FL; GD; Amtr Radio Oprtr; WAS WAC WPX DXCC Oprtng Achvmnt Awds; Cum Laude; Internatl Pltfrm Assoc; MAA; AHSME Sbcommtt CAMC; Math Cmptr Sci Instrtr Adj Fac; AS 67; BS Fl Atlantic Univ 69; MED 76.

**BROWN, KENNETH K,** Fl A & M Univ, Tallahassee, FL; FR; BS; SGA 90-; Phi Eta Sigma 90-; Inrds Awd 90-; Univ Cert Schlrshp 90-; FAMU FSU Clge Engrg Dns Lst 90; Vrsty Bsbl 90-; Mech Engrg; Engrg Dsgn.

**BROWN, KERRI C,** Marshall University, Huntington, WV; JR; BA; Gamma Beta Phi; Dns Lst; Ntl Schlstc Coll All Am; Elem Educ; Schl Adm.

**BROWN, KEVIN D,** Univ Of Sc At Columbia, Columbia, SC; FR; BA; IM Bsktbl/Sftbl; Crmnl Just; Law/Law Enfrcmnt.

**BROWN, KIMBERLY E,** Stillman Coll, Tuscaloosa, AL; SO; BA; Cncrt Chr 90-; Chrstn Stdnt Assoc 90; Natl Hnr Scty 88-; Brwn Grl Sct Ldr 87-89; Nrmndy Schl Dstrct Tsk Frc 89-; Grd Amrcn Yth Fndtns Natl Ldrshp Cnfrnc 87; Music.

**BROWN, KIMBERLY F,** Vance Granville Comm Coll, Henderson, NC; SR; AAS; Radiology Clb Treas 90-; NC Soc Of Radiologic Tech 89-; Deans Lst 89-; Radiologic Tech.

**BROWN, KIMBERLY M,** Univ Of Sc At Coastal Carolina, Conway, SC; SR; BA; Cstl Crln Nwspr Stf; Intshp Std Tchr; Grgtwn Hgh Stprs Capt 82-86; Scndry Ed/Engl; Tch.

**BROWN, KIMBERLY N,** Elizabethtown Comm Coll, Elizabethtown, KY; FR; BA; Phi Beta Lambda Secty; Bapt Student Union; English; Tch H Schl.

**BROWN, KRISTA L,** Univ Of Cin R Walters Coll, Blue Ash, OH; SO; BBA; Bus Clb 90; AIESEC; Hmltn Co Dept Hmn Svcs-Acctnt 85-89; AA; Acctng/Fin.

**BROWN, KRISTA M,** Teikyo Post Univ, Waterbury, CT; SO; BS; Acctg; CPA.

**BROWN, KRISTEN A,** Oh Wesleyan Univ, Delaware, OH; JR; BA; Pres Clb VP 89-; Yrbk Org Edtr 89-; Stdnt Fndtn Trgd 90-; Phi Eta Sigma 88-; Phi Soc 89-90; Omicron Delta Epsilon Pub Chrmn 90-; Pres Schlrshp 89-; Deans Lst 88-; Econ; Bus Mgmt.

**BROWN, KRISTEN E,** Duquesne Univ, Pittsburgh, PA; SO; BA; Intl Affairs Comm Mock U N Rep 90-; Russian Clb 89-; Phi Eta Sigma 89-; Lambda Sigma Hstrn 90-; Alpha Phi Pldg Cls Schlrshp Chr 90-; Union Pgm Bd 90-; IM Ftbl/Sftbl Capt 89-; Pol Sci; Law/Govt.

**BROWN, KRISTI LYNN,** Salisbury St Univ, Salisbury, MD; GD; Intrn Div Voctnl Rhbltn 89; Intrn Geriatric Evltn Svc 90; BASW 90; Soc Wrk.

**BROWN, KRISTIE L,** Central St Univ, Wilberforce, OH; SR; BS; Alpha Kappa Alpha 90-; Deans Lst 88-; Wtr Rsrcs Mngmnt; Pblc Envrnmntl Affrs.

**BROWN, KRISTIN C,** Georgetown Univ, Washington, DC; SR; BSBA; Mktg Socty VP 90-; Prog Bd Vice Chr 90-; SG 87-90; Dns Lst 87-90; PALS 90-; 2nd Hnrs 88-90; 1st Hnrs 88-89; Mktg; Cnsltng.

**BROWN, KRISTY L,** Marywood Coll, Scranton, PA; JR; Cls Govt Commuter Repr 83-89; Bsn Adm/Fncl Plng.

**BROWN, LA DENA P,** Fayetteville St Univ, Fayetteville, NC; JR; Alpha Kappa Mu; Alpha Kappa Alpha; US Army 86-88; Mktg; Byr.

**BROWN, LA SHUNDA S,** Tallahassee Comm Coll, Tallahassee, FL; GD; BA; AA; Bus Admin; Mktg.

**BROWN, LA VERNE L,** Old Dominion Univ, Norfolk, VA; FR; BS; Dn Schlrs Prog 90-; Alumni Hons Schlrshp 90-; Chem Engr; Chem.

**BROWN, LAURA E,** Univ Of Southern Ms, Hattiesburg, MS; SR; BS; Stdnt Eagle Clb 89-; Omicron Delta Kappa 90-; Gamma Beta Phi 90-; Gold Key 89-; Outstndg Coll Stdnts Am; Kappa Mu Epsilon 89; Gamma Beta Phi; Outstndg Serv Gamma Beta Phi; Deans Lst 88-89; Pres Lst 90; NCTM 90-; Math/Scndry Edn; Teach High Sch Math.

**BROWN, LAURA S,** S U N Y Coll Of Tech At Frmgdl, Farmingdale, NY; Cooperative Extension; AAS; Ornmntl Horticulture; Int/Ext Lndscps.

**BROWN, LAURI L,** East Tn St Univ, Johnson City, TN; JR; BA; Clown Alley Sec 88-90; Choir 89-; Wesley Fndtn 90-; Stdnt Ul Hnrs Coll 86-87; Hnrs Coll Advsry Bd Sec 87; MS 89-; Spcl Olympics Vol 89-; Amer Red Cross Clowns; Schlrshp Awd Ripon Coll 84; Deans Lst 84-85/90-; Pres Lst 86; Chrldng 85-86; Bus/Mgmt.

**BROWN, LAURIE M,** Saint Pauls Coll, Lawrenceville, VA; JR; BS; Non-Dnmntnl Bible Study Grp 89-; Proj Lit; Proj Reassurance; Sigma Gamma Rho Basileus 90-; Eastern Star; PHA; Intl Y Mens Assn; Cert Elctrnc Comp Prgrmng Inst 88; Bus Mgt; Mortician.

**BROWN, LAVERNE M,** Fl A & M Univ, Tallahassee, FL; JR; MSW; SASW Pres 90-; Phi Alpha Pres 90-; White/Gold Hnr Soc; Zeta Phi Beta; Social Work.

**BROWN, LAWANDA D,** Fl A & M Univ, Tallahassee, FL; FR; MBA; Sch Bus/Indstry Intrnl Audtg Co Stf Auditor 90-; Phi Eta Sigma; Alpha Phi Omega Jewel Org; Bus; Acctg.

**BROWN, LESLIE C,** Univ Of Ga, Athens, GA; JR; BED; Natl Stdnt Spch Lng Hrng Assoc 90-; Alpha Xi Delta St Mgr/Asst Treas 88-; Rs Mny Amer Lng Assoc; Lenn Reed Ldrshp Awd 89-90; Ed/Cmnctn Sci Dsrdrs; Spch Pthlgy.

**BROWN, LINDA,** Spartanburg Methodist Coll, Spartanburg, SC; JR; BS; Blck Allnc Clb 89-90; Afro-Amer Clb 90-; Tutor Serv 89-90; Phi Theta Kappa 90; Dns Lst 88-90; Exclnc Cmptr Applctns 90; Exclnc Psy 88; Offc Info Sys; Cmptr Oper.

**BROWN, LINDA A,** S U N Y Coll Of Tech At Delhi, Delhi, NY; SR; Beta Blockus 90-; Phi Theta Kappa 90-; Broome Ctr Chpl Gld Tres 70-; Girl Scts Am Assc Chrmn 81-83 Natl Dlgt 83; RN Captl Dist Psychtrc Ctr Albany NY; Nrsng.

**BROWN, LINDA C,** Wv Northern Comm Coll, Wheeling, WV; SO; AAS; Allied Hlth; RN.

**BROWN, LINDA K,** Univ Of Cincinnati-Clrmnt Coll, Batavia, OH; Legal Asst; Paralegal.

**BROWN, LINDA M,** Germanna Comm Coll, Locust Grove, VA; SO; BS; AAS; Comp Sci.

**BROWN, LISA A,** Tuskegee Univ, Tuskegee Inst, AL; JR; BS; SNEA 90-; Chgo Clb 88-89; Schlrs Pgm Columbia U; Elem Ed; Tchr.

**BROWN, LISA G,** Middle Tn St Univ, Murfreesboro, TN; SO; BBA; Gamma Beta Phi; Econ; Mgmt.

**BROWN, LISA M,** Glassboro St Coll, Glassboro, NJ; SR; BA; Pblc Rltns Stu Soc Amer Sec 88-; Prctn Glsbr St Coll Stu Rn PR Frm Asstnt Acct Exec 90-; Wm Cmnctns Inc 89-; Gamma Tau Sigma 90-; Pblc Rltns Stu Soc Amer Ntl Gld Key Awrd Sec 90; Cmnctns; Pblc Rltns.

**BROWN, LOIS B,** Savannah Coll Of Art & Design, Savannah, GA; SR; BFA; Intl Tv Assoc Sec 89-; Tlnt Schlrshp 88-; Rprtg Intrn NBC 89-90; Video Prod.**

**BROWN, LORETTA A,** Bloomfield Coll, Bloomfield, NJ; JR; BA; Bus Admin; Insur.

**BROWN, LORINE REED,** Bethune Cookman Coll, Daytona Beach, FL; SR; BA; Zeta Phi Beta; Meals On Wheels Ex Asst 76-; Ext Ctr Sec 87-; NAACP; UNCF; Prof Sec Intl; Womens Resource Ctr; St Pauls Bapt Ch; AA Manatee Comm Coll 84; Rel Ed/Phlsphy; Use Skills To Help Mankind.

**BROWN, LUANNE,** Oh Univ-Southern Cmps, Ironton, OH; SR; BED; Summer Bible Sch Tchr 89-; Sales Dept 90-; Elem Ed; Tchng.

**BROWN, LYNETTE A,** Univ Of South Al, Mobile, AL; FR; BS; Acctg.

**BROWN, LYNNETTE,** S U N Y Coll Of A & T Morrisvl, Morrisville, NY; FR; Cmpus Tutor; Phi Theta Kappa Treas; Sci; Tchr.

**BROWN, MARGARET K,** Wv Northern Comm Coll, Wheeling, WV; GD; AAS; Deans Lst 90; Scrtrl Intrnshp; Otstndng Scrtrl Sci Stdnt 90; Stdnt Mnth 90; Wrtn Hghts Fr Mthdst Chrch; Cert; Scrtrl Sci.

**BROWN, MARK A,** Wagner Coll, Staten Island, NY; FR; BA; Rsdnce Hll Cncl; On Stge Prfrmncs In Mame; Dark Of The Moon; Bys Nxt Dr; Evta; Iota Delta Alpha; MADD Yth Div; IM Sccr Vlybl; Thtre Spch; Actr Dir Tchr.

**BROWN, MARLA Y,** Tougaloo Coll, Tougaloo, MS; SO; BS; Math/Cmptr Sci Clb 90-; Stu Sprt Serv 89-90; Math; Anlyst.

**BROWN, MARY A,** Peace Coll, Raleigh, NC; FR; MBA; Future Bsn Women 90; Choir; Phi Theta Kappa 90; Marshal; Fashion Mrchndsng; Retail Buyer.

**BROWN, MARY E,** Northern Ky Univ, Highland Hts, KY; JR; Biol Soc; Tnns Tm; Alpha Chi Treas; Hosp Vol 89-; Biol; Med Sch.

**BROWN, MARY SANDLIN,** James Sprunt Comm Coll, Kenansville, NC; JR; AD; Bsnss Admin/Data Entry Opr.

**BROWN, MARYBETH,** Duquesne Univ, Pittsburgh, PA; SO; BA; Orientation Staff 90-; Pre Law Soc 90-; SHARP 89-; Delta Zeta; Duquesne Univ Vol; Econ; Law.

**BROWN, MELANIE L,** Ms St Univ, Miss State, MS; SO; BA; Phi Eta Sigma; Psych.

**BROWN, MELINDA,** Univ Of Sc At Columbia, Columbia, SC; FR; BA; Assoc For African-Amercn Stdnts 90-; Bus Admn; Bus Mgt.

**BROWN, MELISSA A,** Univ Of Nc At Charlotte, Charlotte, NC; SR; BA; Gldn Key; Psych.

**BROWN, MELISSA L,** Edinboro Univ Of Pa, Edinboro, PA; FR; BA; Univ Hnrs Pgm 90-; Spch/Hrg Dis; Spch/Lang Pthlgy.

**BROWN, MELODEE D,** Va St Univ, Petersburg, VA; SO; BA; Richmond Pre Alumni 89-; Busn; Syst Analyst.

**BROWN, MICHAEL D,** Al A & M Univ, Normal, AL; FR; BA; Judicial Bd Chf Just 90-; Inter-Dorm Cncl; Nasiha Roho Adinasi Pres 90-; Pol Sci/Engl; Law.

**BROWN, MICHAEL D,** Morehouse Coll, Atlanta, GA; SR; BAS 90; BA Mrehse Clg 90; Mrktng.

**BROWN, MICHAEL N,** Western New England Coll, Springfield, MA; FR; BS; Phrmcy.

**BROWN, MICHAEL T,** Johnson C Smith Univ, Charlotte, NC; JR; AB; Mrchng Bnd Drm Mjr 89-; Concert Jazz Pep Bnds Dir 88-89; Kappa Alpha Psi Pres 90-; R W Johnson Spiritual Chr 87-89; Natl Educ Assn Mbr; All C I A A Mrchng Bd 87-89; Mr July Men Of Smith Calendar 89-90; Psychology; Chld Psychlgts Schl Sys.

**BROWN, MICHELE M,** D Youville Coll, Buffalo, NY; SR; Ftr Tchrs Amr Treas 90; Deans Lst 88-; Rbrt Smth Awrd Spcl Ed 90; BS; Ed Vslly Imprd.

**BROWN, MICHELLE A,** Stillman Coll, Tuscaloosa, AL; JR; BA; Chancellorette Corrspndng Secy; Alpha Swthrt Club Pres 90; Gamma Iota Sigma; Cordell Wynn Hons Progrm; Phi Beta Lambda; Alpha Kappa Alpha Secy; Bus Admn; Acctng.

**BROWN, MICHELLE D,** Clark Atlanta Univ, Atlanta, GA; FR; BS; Alld Hlth Soc Treas; Allied Hlth; Physcl Thrpst.

**BROWN, MICHELLE L,** Memphis St Univ, Memphis, TN; FR; BA; Bsn; Acctg.

**BROWN, MICHELLE M,** Samford Univ, Birmingham, AL; GD; Cumberland Law Review 90-; Law Week Committee 90-; Phi Kappa Phi 89-90; Pi Gamma Mu VP 89-90; Phi Alpha Theta 88-90; Phi Mu VP 89-90; Natl Moot Crt Tm; BA 90; Intl Rltns; Law.

**BROWN, MITZI I,** Clayton St Coll, Morrow, GA; SO; BA; Amer Rd Crs Rcrtr 89-; AS 90; Biology; Dctr Orthpdcs/Spts Med.

**BROWN, MONICA C,** Memphis St Univ, Memphis, TN; SO; BA; SGA Sntr Clge Arts/Sci; Blck Stdnt Assoc 89-; Ed Sprt Pgm Tr Ldr Stdy Sns 89-; Blck Schlrs Unlmtd 90-; Pltcl Sci; Law Schl.

**BROWN, MONTY L,** Univ Of Nc At Charlotte, Charlotte, NC; SO; BSCE; Res Assn 89-90; Hl Cncl 89-90; Intervar 89-90; Delta Sigma Phi Sec; Dns Lst 90-; Chnclrs Lst 89; IM 89-; Cvl Engnrng; Strctrl/Envnmntl Engr.

**BROWN, MORRIS V,** Anderson Coll, Anderson, SC; SO; BA; Lbrl Arts.

**BROWN, MORRY D,** Norfolk St Univ, Norfolk, VA; SR; BS; Pre Mdcl Soc Prsdnt 87-; Chem Clb Tres 89-; Yrbk Copy Edtr 89-90; Beta Kappa Chi Prsdnt 88-; Alpha Kappa Mu 88-; Chem Physcs Awd 90-; IM Bsktbl 87-; Chemistry; Medicine.

**BROWN, NAIMA CHERIE,** Fl A & M Univ, Tallahassee, FL; FR; BA; Sociology; Prof Of Sociology.

**BROWN, NANCY L,** Roane St Comm Coll, Harriman, TN; Criminoloy; Law Enfor.

**BROWN, NATILEE D,** Benedict Coll, Columbia, SC; JR; BA; Gospel Choir 89-90, Jr Cls Cncl; Crmnl Jstc Clb; Hnrs Prog; Alpha Kappa Alpha Sec 89; Tchrs Aid Carver Elem; Crmnl Jstc; State Atty.

**BROWN, NICHOLAS A,** Allegheny Coll, Meadville, PA; SO; BA; Wnd Sym; Rugby 90-; Chem; Med.

**BROWN, NICOLE M,** Mount Saint Mary Coll, Newburgh, NY; FR; Admissions Clb 90-; Tours Of Campus Guide 90-; Var Bsktbl 90-; Comp Sci.

**BROWN, NIGEL A,** Hillsborough Comm Coll, Tampa, FL; FR; BSEE; Sci Math Physcs; Eng.

**BROWN, NOLETER P,** Nc Agri & Tech St Univ, Greensboro, NC; SO; United Chrstn Fllwshp 90-; A/T Fllwshp Gospel Choir 90-; Alpha Lambda Delta Editor 90-; Educ; Elem Educ.

**BROWN, PAMELA E,** Univ Of Sc At Coastal Carolina, Conway, SC; SR; BA; Trck Tm-Malone Coll 84-85; Bus Admin; Mktg.

**BROWN, PAMELA J,** Univ Of Nc At Asheville, Asheville, NC; SR.

**BROWN, PATRICIA A,** Tougaloo Coll, Tougaloo, MS; JR; Delta Sigma Theta Miss Red/White 88; Stdnt Govt Assoc 2nd Altrnte To Miss Tougaloo; Class Scrtry 89; VP Schlr 88; Upward Bound Prog Tutor 90; Hmnty Fstvl/Afrcn Dncr 90.

**BROWN, PATRICIA F,** Daytona Beach Comm Coll, Daytona Beach, FL; SO; BA; Phi Theta Kappa 90-; Pres List 88-; Daytona Bch Symphny Scty; AA 91; Grnd Rpds Symphny Scty; W MI Wmn Exec Chrtr Pres Chrch Orgnst; Engl/Lit; Wrtr.

**BROWN, PATRICIA Y,** Valdosta St Coll, Valdosta, GA; JR; BS; AA Daytona Comm Coll 90; Nursing; RN.

**BROWN, PAUL D,** Commonwealth Coll, Virginia Beach, VA; GD; Bus Adm; Mgmt.

**BROWN, PAUL E,** Univ Of Ga, Athens, GA; SR; BS; Acad Stdnts Phrmcy 90-; Phi Beta Kappa 84-; GA Phrmctcl Assoc 90-; Amer Phrmctcl Assoc 90-; Former US Navy Subs 84-89; BS 84; Phrmcy; Hosp Phrmcst.

**BROWN JR, PAUL W,** Syracuse Univ, Syracuse, NY; FR; BSA Asst Sctmstr 85-; SUNY Coll Envrnmntl Sci Frstry Ntwrk Admn Cstdl Suprvsr 83-; Infrmtn Sci Technlgy; Infrmtn Commnctn Mngmnt.

**BROWN, PAULA K,** Bellarmine Coll, Louisville, KY; JR; BA; St Rbt Bellarmine Schlrshp 88-; Deans Lst 88-90; Acctg.

**BROWN, PEGGY L,** Clark Atlanta Univ, Atlanta, GA; SO; BA; IVOF Mbr 89-; Engl Club Mbr 90-; Hons Progrm Mbr 90-; Deans List 89-90; Engl; Law.**

**BROWN, PENNY L,** Western Carolina Univ, Cullowhee, NC; SO; BS; Cmptr Sci; Cmptr Pgrmmr.

**BROWN, PRISCILLA F,** Pellissippi St Tech Comm Coll, Knoxville, TN; SO; BS; AA; Educ; Elem Educ.

**BROWN, RAHMAN,** Morehouse Coll, Atlanta, GA; JR; BA; NY NJ Club 88-; Omega Psi Phi Frtrnty Inc; Mens IM Bsktbl Capt 88-; Political Sci; Law.

**BROWN, RALPH W,** Kent St Univ Kent Cmps, Kent, OH; FR; BS; Stdnt Med Assn 90-; IM Sftbl/Ftbl/Vlybl 90-; Medicine; Med Dr.

**BROWN, RANDALL T,** Embry Riddle Aeronautical Univ, Daytona Beach, FL; JR; BS; Panair Flying Clb 90-; AA Miami Dade Cmnty Clg 90; Aero Sci; Pilot.

**BROWN III, RAY W,** Christian Brothers Univ, Memphis, TN; SR; BS; Ltry Mag Asst Edtr 90-; Opera Chrs; Symphny Chrs; Alpha Chi 90-; BA Univ Notre Dame 89; Blgy; Envrnmntl Txclgy.

**BROWN, RAYMOND B,** Univ Of Tn At Knoxville, Knoxville, TN; JR; BS; Vrsty Swim Capt 88-; Cndn Natl Swim Tm 85-; Gamma Beta Phi 90-; Gldn Key 90-; Bernard I Dahlberg Memrl Schlrshp; Acctg.

**BROWN, REBECCA A,** O'more School Of Design, Franklin, TN; FR; BA; Amer Scty Interior Designers 90-; Stdnt Govt Assoc Secy; Interior Dsgn.

**BROWN, REBECCA B,** Saint Pauls Coll, Lawrenceville, VA; FR; BA; Newspr Rprtr 90-; Erly Chldhd Edn/Eng.

**BROWN, REBECCA E,** Memphis St Univ, Memphis, TN; FR; BA; Engl Clb Rprtr 90-; Pr Mntr Prog 90-; Hll Cncl Rsdnce Hll Assn Sec; Phi Eta Sigma; Alpha Lambda Delta; Gamma Beta Phi; Hnr Stdnt Assn 90-; Engl; Edtng.

**BROWN, REBECCA F,** Oh St Univ, Columbus, OH; JR; BA; Westerville Civic Symph; Richmond Symph Orch 88-90; Columbus Symph Orch Sub 88; Dns Lst 87-; Church Christ Svc Wrk; Partial Schlrshp Univ Cinc Talent/Acad 87-90; Partial Schlrshp Aspen Music Fest 88; Partial Schlrshp OH State U Acad/Talent; Music; Music Perf/Ed.

**BROWN, RENEE S,** Coppin St Coll, Baltimore, MD; SO; BNS; Sci; RN.

**BROWN, RICKEY C,** Univ Of Ky, Lexington, KY; JR; BS; Golden Key 90-; Full Gspl Busmns Fllwshp Intl Sec 84-86; Deans List; Deans Schlrshp; Acad Excllnc Schlrshp; Swiss Fed Matura Fed Matura Cmmssn/Switzerland 81; Cmptr Scnc.

**BROWN, RICKEY S,** Emory & Henry Coll, Emory, VA; SR; BA; Cmptr Clb Pres 89-; Math Assn Pres 87-; Cmtr Stdnt Org Pblcty Chmn 89-; Blue/Gold 89-; Concert Choir 87-; Alpha Phi Omega VP Serv 88-; Alpha Psi Omega 90-; Oretorio Choir 87-; Opera Wrkshp Lead Roles 87-; Sub Choir Dir Pleasantview Meth Ch; Cmptr Sci.

**BROWN, RITA J,** Seton Hall Univ, South Orange, NJ; SR; BS; Parish Cncl V P 90-; Kappa Delta Pi 89-; Elem Ed/Spnsh; Tch.

**BROWN, RIVA R,** Univ Of Southern Ms, Hattiesburg, MS; SO; Afro Amer Stu Org Pbl Rel Dir 89-90; Yng Dem Tres 90-; Lambda Sigma; Alpha Lambda Delta; Gamma Beta Phi; Jrnlsm.

**BROWN, ROBERT W,** Western New England Coll, Springfield, MA; SR; BSEE; IEEE 90-; Elec Eng.

**BROWN, ROSALYN A,** Fayetteville St Univ, Fayetteville, NC; JR; BS; Math/Comptr Sci Club 90-; Future Alumni Assoc 89-90; Wilmington/Charlotte Club Secy 89-; Alpha Kappa Alpha Reprtr 90-; Comptr Sci; Sftwr Engr.

**BROWN JR, RUSSELL F,** City Univ Of Ny La Guard Coll, Long Island Cty, NY; JR; BA; Crmnl Law.

**BROWN, RUSSELL T,** Gaston Coll, Dallas, NC; SO; AS; Am Red Crs; Gamma Beta Phi Svc Com Chr 90-; Bio/Chem; MD.

**BROWN, SANDRA K,** Beckley Coll, Beckley, WV; FR; BA; Art; Commrcl Art.

**BROWN, SARAH E,** Memphis St Univ, Memphis, TN; JR; BS; Dean Lst; Geog; Gvt.

**BROWN, SCOTT A,** Ashland Comm Coll, Ashland, KY; FR; Law Enfrcmnt; Police Ofcr.

**BROWN, SEAN T,** Hudson Valley Comm Coll, Troy, NY; FR; BA; GM Auto Repr.

**BROWN, SHAWN P,** Newbury Coll, Brookline, MA; FR; BA; 5 Yrs Experience Three Different Food Serv Estblshmnts; Clnary Arts; Clnary Chef.

**BROWN, SHEILA,** Baldwin Wallace Coll, Berea, OH; FR; BA; Prgm Brd 90-; Gspl Chr 90-; Psychlgy Sclgy; Scl Wrk.

**BROWN, SHEILA A,** Ms St Univ, Miss State, MS; SR; BA; Psych Clb 88-; Pre Vet Clb 88-89; Scavma 88-; Phi Kappa Phi 90-; Cir K 88-89; Pres Lst; Deans Lst; Psych.

**BROWN, SHELLY L,** Univ Of Md At Eastern Shore, Princess Anne, MD; JR; BA; Stu Govt Assoc 88-; Nwspr Edtr/Ad Mgr 90-; Senate 90-; All Amer Schlr 90-; Mnrty Rsrch Inst; Sclgy; Law.**

**BROWN, SHERMEL A,** Bloomfield Coll, Bloomfield, NJ; SO; Stdnt Advsry Brd 90-; Brd Trustees Stdnt Rep 90-; Soph Cls Tr 90-; Alpha Kappa Psi Sec 90-; Acctg.

**BROWN, SHERRY A,** Central Al Comm Coll, Alexander City, AL; FR; ASN; Boy Scouts Cub Scout Ldr 85-87; RN.

**BROWN, SHIRELLE L,** Al St Univ, Montgomery, AL; FR; BS; Vcs Prs Gspl Chr 90-; Phi Eta Sigma 90-; Prsdntl Schlrshp 90-; Chmstry; Pre Med.

**BROWN, SHUNDRA D,** Tougaloo Coll, Tougaloo, MS; SR; BA; Yrbk Stff Ed 89-90; Stdnt Natl Educ Assoc 90-; Educ Clb Tres 90-; Elem Educ; Teacher.

**BROWN, SONDRA D,** Alcorn St Univ, Lorman, MS; FR; Interfaith Gospel Chr 90-; Math/Cmptr Sci Clb; Hon Scty 90-; Math/Cmptr Sci; Cmptr Pgmng.

**BROWN, SONJI,** Tougaloo Coll, Tougaloo, MS; SR; BS; Math Cmptr Sci Clbs; Gspl Chr; Alph Lambda Delta; Stu Govt; Delta Sigma Theta VP; Entergy Oprtns Smmr Asst; Math Cmptr Sci; Entrprnr.

**BROWN, SONYA G,** Howard Univ, Washington, DC; SO; BA; Alpha Kappa Alpha; Psychology.

**BROWN, SONYA M,** Somerset Comm Coll, Somerset, KY; FR; MBA; Fnc; Bnk Ofcr.

**BROWN, STACIE L,** Mobile Coll, Mobile, AL; JR; BS; Psi Chi Pres 89-; ICC Innr Clb Cncl 90-; Campus Actvies Brd 90-; Behvrl Sci Clb 90; Alpha Chi 90-; Psi Chi Serv Awd; Psi Chi Serv Awd 91; Gov Hunts Yth Corp 89; Psych/Soc; Clncl Psych/FBI Agnt.

**BROWN, STEPHANIE CHANDLER,** Wallace St Comm Coll At Selma, Selma, AL; SO; BS; Phi Theta Kappa Sec; Biology; Medicine.

**BROWN, STEPHEN L,** Hampton Univ, Hampton, VA; FR; BS; Chrstn Assoc Treas 90-; Campus Mnstry Secr 90-; Pres Eminent Schlrs Awd 90-; IM Bsktbl 90-; Acctg; Mnstry.

**BROWN, STEPHEN P,** Va Commonwealth Univ, Richmond, VA; SR; BS; Natl Prks And Rcrtn Assn Brd Of Dir 90-; Lambda Chi Alpha 84-; Rrl Rcrtn Dev Intrn; Rcrtn And Pks Mgmt; Mncpl Rcrtn.

**BROWN JR, STEPHEN R,** Univ Of Sc At Columbia, Columbia, SC; SO; BA; Work At Fed Res Bnk Of Columbia; Fin; Bnking/Investmnts.

**BROWN, STEVEN H,** Savannah Coll Of Art & Design, Savannah, GA; GD; MFA; Grad Assn; Arts Assn; BA Univ Of Missouri At Kansas City 82; Art; Phtogrphc Arts.

**BROWN, SUNDAI M,** Saint Pauls Coll, Lawrenceville, VA; GD; Alumni Clb Pres 90; Rcrtng Cmmttee 90; Womens Cncl 87; Alpha Kappa Alpha; Hosp Intrn 88; Trck/Fld 87; BA St Pauls Clg 87.

**BROWN, SUSAN C,** Oh Univ-Southern Cmps, Ironton, OH; SR; BSN; Nrsng Sprvsr/Hlth Educ Comm Action Org; Diploma Good Samaritan Hosp Schl/Nrsng 63; Nursing.

**BROWN, SUSAN L,** Providence Coll, Providence, RI; SR; BA; Cum Laude; Grad Hnrs; Humanities; Intl Bus.

**BROWN, SUSAN R,** Univ Of Cincinnati, Cincinnati, OH; SO; BSN; Natl Stdnt Nurs Assoc 88-; Nrsg.

**BROWN, SUZANNA M,** Marshall University, Huntington, WV; JR; BFA; Grphc Dsgn/Art.

**BROWN, TANYA R,** Voorhees Coll, Denmark, SC; SO; Peer Cnslrs 90-; Eye Phi Eye Ettes Scl Clb 89; Acctg.

**BROWN, TANYA S,** Faulkner Univ, Montgomery, AL; SO; BS; Deans Lst 89-; Ldrshp Schlrshp 89-; Hnr Rl Schlrshp 90-; Elem Educ; Tch.

**BROWN, TERRI L,** Univ Of Ky, Lexington, KY; SO; BED; Dir Asst Dscvry Montessori Sch; Elem Ed; Tchng.

**BROWN, TERRY T,** Tuskegee Univ, Tuskegee Inst, AL; SO; Bio-Chem Clb 90-; Hrn Rll 90-; Smmr Intrn-Kaiser Permenente 90; Med Tech; Hemtlgy.

**BROWN, THERESA A,** Bloomfield Coll, Bloomfield, NJ; FR; BA; Vlybl; Bus Mgt; Acctg.

**BROWN, THERESA M,** Milligan Coll, Milligan Clg, TN; SR; BA; Cncrt Choir/Chmbr Sngrs 88-; Lit Mag Edtr 89-; Schl Nwsppr 89-90; Alpha Psi Omega VP 88-; Arts Cncl 88-; Hmnts Awd 89; Frnch Awd 88; Johnson City Area Arts Cncl Intrnshp 90; Cmmncgns/Hmnts; Arts Admin.

**BROWN, THOMAS E,** Medical Univ Of Sc, Charleston, SC; GD; MD; Sprhlth 2000 88; Alpha Omega Alpha Pres 90-; Intrfth Crss Mnstry Hlth Clnc 89-; Thomas Savage Mem Awrd 90-; Rich Schlrshp 90; IM Ftbl Bsktbl 87-; BS East Carolina Univ 83; MA 85; Orthpdc Srgery.

**BROWN III, THOMAS L,** Univ Of Ct, Storrs, CT; JR; BS; UCONN Frstry/Wldlf Clb 90-91; Rnwbl Natrl Rsrcs.

**BROWN, TIMOTHY A,** Birmingham Southern Coll, Birmingham, AL; JR; BA; Kappa Sigma Sec 82-86; Sls Rep 88-; Acctg; MBA.

**BROWN, TIMOTHY L,** Southern Coll Of Tech, Marietta, GA; JR; BSIET; SGA V P 87-88; Sci Club Pres 87-88; Inst Of Ind Engrs 89-; AA Dekalb Coll 88; Ind Engrng.

**BROWN, TIMOTHY M,** Univ Of Sc At Columbia, Columbia, SC; JR; BS; Gamma Iota Sigma Pres; Faculty Schlrshp; IM Bsktbl Soccer Sftbl; Bus-Fin & Ins; Actuary.

**BROWN, TIMOTHY R,** Saint Pauls Coll, Lawrenceville, VA; JR; BA; AA Richard Bland Coll Of Chll & William & Mary 90; LLA Tutor Brunswick Lit Cncl With Laubach Ltrcy Action; Prof Of Eng.

**BROWN, TIMOTHY S,** Univ Of Sc At Spartanburg, Spartanburg, SC; SR; BA; Drama 90-; Gamma Beta Phi V P 88-; Alpha Epsilon Rho 87-88; Cum Laude; Engl.**

**BROWN, TINA M,** Ky St Univ, Frankfort, KY; FR; Univ Bnd Dncr 90-; Columbus Chptr Alumni Schlrshp 90-; Chld Psych.

**BROWN, TODD E,** Muskingum Coll, New Concord, OH; JR; BA; Sprt Bnd Bsns Prsdnt 88-; Jazzbnd 89-; Wnd Ensmbl Pblc Rltns Rep 88-; Lambda Sigma Soc 89-; Omicron Delta Kappa 90-; Snr Hnry; Rsdnt Asstnt 90-; Pblc Affrs Intrnshp; IM Sprts 90-; Bsns Pblc Affrs; Mgmt Finance.

**BROWN, TONY V N,** Univ Of Md At Eastern Shore, Princess Anne, MD; SR; PHD; Hawks Mssg Stf Wrtr 87-89; Actvty Brd 89-; Sclgy Slb 90-; Hnrs Soc 87-; Alpha Kappa Mu 90-; Tchng Intrn 90-; Billiards Tm Cptn 88-; BA; Sclgy.

**BROWN, TRACEY C,** Coppin St Coll, Baltimore, MD; JR; BA; Psychlgy Clb Sec 90-; Psychlgy.

**BROWN, TRACEY M,** Daemen Coll, Amherst, NY; JR; BS; Bus Clb 89-; Drll Tm Treas 90-; Booga Booga Beta Sec Pres 90-; Intrnshp Applnce Instlltn And Srvcs Corp Admin Asst; Bus Mgmt.

**BROWN, TRACI L,** Comm Coll Algny Co Algny Cmps, Pittsburgh, PA; FR; Phrmcy Tech; Cert Phrm Tech N Hlls Sch Hlth Occptns 88; Biol Sci; Sec Educ Tchr.

**BROWN, TRACI L,** Miami Jacobs Jr Coll Of Bus, Dayton, OH; FR; BS; Accntng.

**BROWN, TRACIE L,** Jackson St Univ, Jackson, MS; SO; BED; Band Chpln 90-; Orchestra Prncpl Oboe 89-; Wind Ensemble Prncple Oboe 89-; Alpha Lambda Delta; Delta Sigma Theta; Engl Ed; Tchg.

**BROWN, TRACY GARNETTE,** Va St Univ, Petersburg, VA; SR; BS; FBLA 87-88; AMA 90; Gspl Brsmbl 83-88; Mrktng Mgmt.

**BROWN, TRAVIS L,** Albany St Coll, Albany, GA; JR; Newspapr Rprtr 89; Sigma Tau Delta Pres 90.

**BROWN, TRENA L,** Alcorn St Univ, Lorman, MS; SO; Stdnt Natl Educ Assoc Pres 90-; Hons Stdnt Org 89-; Natl Hon Soc VP 87-; Alpha Kappa Alpha 90-; Elem Educ.

**BROWN, TROY M,** Christopher Newport Coll, Newport News, VA; JR; BA; MSA 88; Mktg/Mgmt; Intl Mktg/Mgmt.**

**BROWN, VALRIE A,** Howard Univ, Washington, DC; JR; BSC; Crbbn Stdnts Assn Pres 90-; Deans Hon Rl/Deans Lst 89-; Gldn Key; Ominicron Nu; Hmn Rsrc Dvlpmnt MBA; Cnsmr Affrs/Mgmt.

**BROWN, VELEKA M,** Alcorn St Univ, Lorman, MS; SO; BA; Spnsh Clb 90-; Dns Lst Kennedy King Clge 90-; Blgy Hnrs 90-; Eng/Cmnctns; Advrtsng/PR.

**BROWN, WANDA L,** Va St Univ, Petersburg, VA; SR; BA; Acctg Clb Treas 89-; CPA Clb 89-; Deans Lst 90-; Tutorng 89-; Acctg; Law/MA Acctg.

**BROWN, WEYLIN N,** North Greenville Coll, Tigerville, SC; SO; BME; Mrchng Bnd P 90-; Jazz Bnd; Pres Clb 89-F Phi Theta Kappa 90-; Etude Musc P 90-; Mst Outstndg Music Stdnt; Mst Outstndg Etude Stdnt; AFA; Music Ed; Bnd Dir/Orgnist.

**BROWN JR, WILL T,** Univ Of South Al, Mobile, AL; JR; Bapt Stdnt Union 89-; Ballet 90-; Modern Dnc 90-; Deans List; Pres List; Elem Educ; Tchr.

**BROWN, WILLIAM A,** Tn Tech Univ, Cookeville, TN; FR; BS; Mrchng Eagle Band 90-; Symphony Band 90-; Hons Prog 90-; Elec Eng.

**BROWN, WILLIAM E,** Univ Of Nc At Asheville, Asheville, NC; JR; BA; Econs Clb Pr 90-; Orientation Ldr; Peer Tuitor For UNCA In Econs 90-; Resrch Asst Dr Kask UNCA Dr Shrogen IA State Univ; Mortgage Bnkrs Of The Carolinas Schlrshp; Econs.

**BROWN, WILLIAM T,** Univ Of Pittsburgh, Pittsburgh, PA; SR; BASW; Generatn Tegthr/Yiste 88-90; Open Doors Handicpd 82-; Golden Key 88; AS CCAC 85; Social Work.**

**BROWN, WILLIE T,** Volunteer St Comm Coll, Gallatin, TN; SO; BS; Gamma Beta Phi; Rdlgy; Rdlgc Tchnlgst.

**BROWN, YVETTE A M,** Barry Univ, Miami, FL; JR; BSC; Jamaican Assc Sec 90-; Crcl K Tres 90-; Big Bro/Big Sis; Dipl Coll Arts Sci/Tech 89; Comp Sci; MIS Drctr/Sr Syst Analyst.

**BROWN, YVETTE R,** Comm Coll Algny Co Algny Cmps, Pittsburgh, PA; FR; Var Bsktbl Sftbl 90-; Acctg; CPA.

**BROWN-MURPHY, JENNIFER L,** Valdosta St Coll, Valdosta, GA; JR; BA; Baptst Stdnt Un 85-86; Youth Dir Apostolic Faith Ctr 89-90; Sundy Sch Tchr 90; Kitzinger W Germany Tchrs Asst Dept Of Defns Dependnt Schls 88-90; AA 90; Erly Chldhd Ed; Tchr/Cnslr.

**BROWNE, BRIAN J,** Univ Of Akron, Akron, OH; JR; BS; Civil Eng.

**BROWNE, JENNIFER ROBIN,** Univ Of Rochester, Rochester, NY; JR; Delta Zeta Rcmmndtn Eff 90-; Alpha Phi Omega; Swimming Vrsty 89-; History; Hstrcl Preservation.

**BROWNE, RICHARD I,** City Univ Of Ny Baruch Coll, New York, NY; JR; BA; Golden Key 90-; Bsn Mgmt; Oprtnl Mgr.

**BROWNELL, PEGGY A,** Lake City Comm Coll, Lake City, FL; SO; AA; Phi Beta Lambda Tres 86-88; Alpha Gamma Delta 86-; Rstr Otstndg Comm Coll Mnrty 90-; AS 88; Sci; Psychlgy.

**BROWNING, BARBARA C,** Valdosta St Coll, Valdosta, GA; JR; BED; W J Powell Co Cust Svc Mgr 84-90; AS Early Chldhd Ed Thomas Clg; Early Chldhd Ed; Tchr.

**BROWNING, BOBBIE P,** Miles Coll, Birmingham, AL; JR; BA; Asst Mgr Sm Retail Store 88-; Social Sci; Social Work.

**BROWNING, CONNIE L,** Lake City Comm Coll, Lake City, FL; FR; AA; Pre-Engr; Cmptr Engr.

**BROWNING, GLEN J,** Ms St Univ, Miss State, MS; SR; BFA; Phi Kappa Phi 90-; Prsdnts Schlr 88-; Intrnshp Unvrsty Tlvsn Cntr 90; Art; Tlvsn Grphcs.

**BROWNING, HEATHER D,** Univ Of Va Clinch Valley Coll, Wise, VA; FR; BS; Pol Sci; Govt Tchr.

**BROWNING, JO ANN P,** Univ Of Ky, Lexington, KY; FR; BACH; Amer Scty Cvl Eng 90-; Scty Wmn Engs 90-; UK Cncrt Bnd And Orchstra 90-; Alpha Lambda Delta; Lambda Sigma; Alpha Gamma Delta 90-; Cvl Eng.

**BROWNING, JUDY L,** Northeast State Tech Comm Coll, Blountville, TN; SO; AAS; Bus Mgmt-Acctg; Acctg.

**BROWNING, MEREDITH L,** Medical Coll Of Ga, Augusta, GA; SR; BS; Phi Mu 87; Nrsng.

**BROWNING, ROY E,** Georgetown Coll, Georgetown, KY; JR; BS; SGA SFCC Elcntns Chr 87; Phi Theta Kappa 90-; AA S Fla Comm Clg 90; Physics/Eng; Res Dsgn.

**BROWNING, STEVEN C,** Univ Of Sc At Columbia, Columbia, SC; SR; MACC; Golden Key 89-; Fin Mgrs Assn 89-; Econs Soc 90-; BS Fin Univ Of SC; BS Econs Univ Of SC; Acctng; CPA.

**BROWNING, TODD A,** Marshall University, Huntington, WV; JR; BBA; Gamma Beta Phi 90-; Lab Asst; Mktg; Sls/Mktg.

**BROWNLEE, TERESA JO,** Meridian Comm Coll, Meridian, MS; SO; VICA St Offcr Hstrn 90-; Nal Lg Nrs 90-; LPN Clss Offcr Pres; Dean Lst 90-; Nrsng.

**BROWNLEE, WARREN R,** Clark Atlanta Univ, Atlanta, GA; SO; BS; Natl Soc Of Blck Engrs Frshmn Advsr 90-; Physcs Club Parlmntrn 90-; NAACP; GM Intrn Pres Tech Club 90; Math Award; Physcsl/Engrng; Mech Engr.

**BROWNLOW, WANDA F,** Al A & M Univ, Normal, AL; SO; BS; Accounting; CPA.

**BROWNRIDGE, TARA A,** Georgian Court Coll, Lakewood, NJ; SR; Sigma Tau Delta 89-90; Sigma Tau Delta 90; CCD Tchr 90; BA; Engl Elem Ed.

**BROYLES, KEVIN E,** Univ Of Tn At Knoxville, Knoxville, TN; SR; BS; Phi Eta Sigma 89-; Beta Gamma Sigma 89-; Gldn Key 89-; Phi Kappa Phi 90-; Delta Sigma Pi Prof Bus 89-; Jr Achvmnt Bus Bscs Instr 90; Paul L Royston Schlrshp 90; Arthur Andersen Co Schlrshp 90-; Acctg; Law.

**BROZAK, GEORGE A,** Oh Univ, Athens, OH; GD; MBA; Mrchng Bnd 86-90; Kappa Kappa Psi VP 86-; Lambda Chi Alpha High Gamma 90-; Grad Asst Mrchng Bnd; BM 90; Music Educ.

**BROZYNA, RANDY M,** Univ Of Tn At Martin, Martin, TN; SO; BS; Assn Cmptng Mchnry Sec/Treas; Phi Eta Sigma; Cmptr Sci.

**BRUBAKER, AMY S,** Univ Of Cincinnati, Cincinnati, OH; SR; BS; Goldn Key; Deans Lst 88-; Kappa Delta Pi 90-; Elem Ed; Tchng.

**BRUBAKER, DERON E,** Bloomsburg Univ Of Pa, Bloomsburg, PA; SO; BS; Deans Lst 90; Envrnmntl Sci; Envrnmntlst.**

**BRUBAKER, JOY B,** Niagara Univ, Niagara Univ, NY; JR; BS; SGA Sec 90-; Ornttn Exctv Brd 90-; Prnts Wknd Cmmtt 90-; Delta Epsilon Sigma; Cmmrc Hmn Rsrc Mgmt.

**BRUCE, CINDY S,** Itawamba Comm Coll, Fulton, MS; SO; BA; Lioness Clb Pres 83-; Lit Cncl Tutor 86-; Spec Ed; Spec Ed Tchr/Adlscnt Psychlgst.

**BRUCE, DAVID C,** Christopher Newport Coll, Newport News, VA; FR; BSA; Acctng; CPA.

**BRUCE, HEATHER A,** Univ Of Ga, Athens, GA; FR; BED; Angel Flght 90-; Coll Rpblcns 90-; Dean Lst 90-; Frnch; Bus.

**BRUCE, JANET M,** Univ Of Montevallo, Montevallo, AL; JR; BA; Bapt Campus Mnstry; Montevallo Wnd Ensmbl; Vol Spch/Hrng Clnc; Zeta Tau Alpha; Angel Flght; Civitari; Univ Ldrshp Schlrshp; Scl Wrk; Med.

**BRUCE, KENNETH H,** Middle Tn St Univ, Murfreesboro, TN; JR; BS; Rcrdng Indstry; Audio Engnrng/Elctrncs.

**BRUCE, KIMBERLY M,** Univ Of Ky, Lexington, KY; JR; BS; NSSLHA VP 90-; KY Charms 89-; Wildcat Lodge Aux Pres 88-90; Phi Alpha Theta 90-; Commtn Disorders; Speech Lang Pathlgy.

**BRUCE, MICHELLE L,** Carson Newman Coll, Jefferson City, TN; FR; Bapt Stdnt Union 90-; Epsilon Alpha Gamma 90-; Carson-Newman 2nd Annl Ldrshp Confrnc.

**BRUCE, RICHARD M,** S U N Y Coll Of Tech At Delhi, Delhi, NY; SR; BS; SADD 90-; NY State Assc Anml Techcn Pres 90-; Extrnshp Pgm 90; Vetrnarn/Sci.

**BRUCE II, YALE B,** Allen Univ, Columbia, SC; SR; BS; Phi Beta Kappa Pres 90-; NAACP VP 87-; Band 89-; Phi Beta Lambda Pres 89-; Phi Beta Sigma; Pres Awd; Phi Beta Lambda Awd; AA Val Comm Coll 87; Mktg; Cpa.

**BRUDENELL, MARK A,** Fl A & M Univ, Tallahassee, FL; JR; PHARM; Asstshp Fl St Particle Accelerator 88; Mbr/Ldr Couples Grp Bible Stdy 90-; US Navy Nuclr Rctr Oper 79-85; Cntrl Rm Oper Pub Utlty Nclr Pwr Plnt 85-88; Intsv Care Unt 89-; Clncl Phrmcy.

**BRUDER, BETH A,** Notre Dame Coll, Cleveland, OH; SO; BA; Res Assoc Brd Rep 89-90; Res Assoc Brd VP 90-; Cls Pres 90-; Lambda Sigma Slctn Comm 90-; Campus Ambsdrs 90-; Ldrshp Awrd 89-; Sr Aquinas/Sr Coltild Awrd Serv 90; IM Vlybl 90-; Grphc Cmnctns; Pblc Rltns.

**BRUDER III, JOSEPH B,** Antonelli Inst Of Art & Photo, Cincinnati, OH; SR; Alpha Beta Kappa Awd Best Artst; Assoc; Cmmrcl Artst.

**BRUECKHEIMER, LEAH C,** Yeshiva Univ, New York, NY; SR; BA; Schl Nwspr Grphc Ed 90-; Max Stern Schlrshp 87-; Judaic Stds; Ed.

**BRUECKMANN, KAREN M,** Radford Univ, Radford, VA; SR; MA; Radio Brd Oprtr 87-; Res Lfe Stf Apprctn Comm 89-; Ambssdrs Vp 90-; Ntl Res Hl Hnry 90-; Deans Lst 90-; BA; Stdnt Dev/Admin.

**BRUECKNER, JENNIFER K,** Univ Of Ky, Lexington, KY; JR; Tau Beta Sigma 88-; Gldn Key 90-; Alpha Lambda Delta 89-; Lambda Sigma Scty 90-; Phi Eta Sigma 90-; Lf Sci Assoc 90-; Pre Dntl Scty 90-; US Deans Lst 88-90; UK Cmmnwlth Schlrshp 88-; US Spr Acdmc Achvmnt Awrd 89; Blgy.

**BRUEGGEMEIER, ANDREA L,** Oh Wesleyan Univ, Delaware, OH; FR; BA; Pres Clb Com Co-Chair 90-; Stdnt Paper 90-; Stdnt TV Station 90-; Phi Eta Sigma 90-; Deans Lst 90-; Jrnlsm/Economics.

**BRUESER, DAWN M,** Va Commonwealth Univ, Richmond, VA; JR; BS; Jack Green/Joe Lewis Schlrshp 88-; Film; Video Prod.

**BRUGGER, MARTHA J,** Oh St Univ At Newark, Newark, OH; JR; BED.

**BRUGGER, MICHELE A,** Oh St Univ, Columbus, OH; JR; BA; Stdnt Envrnmntl Actn Cltn 90-; Jpblc Rltns Stdnt Scty Amrc; Phi Kappa Phi 90-; Mtn Hnrry; Alpha Phi Omega Pldg Trnr Fnc Chrmn 88-; Hnrs Prgm Hnrs Ths 89-; Pblc Rltns Envrnmntl Org.

**BRUGGNER, MARCO K,** William Carey Coll, Hattiesburg, MS; FR; Tennis; Math Tchr; Coach.

**BRUGNETTI, GARY J,** Embry Riddle Aeronautical Univ, Daytona Beach, FL; JR; BS; Stdnt Govt Assn Rep 90-; Substance Awrns Com Rep 90-; Naval Aviation Clb 90-, Stdnt Ldrshp Pgm; IM Hockey/Bsktbl/Vlybl/Sftbl 88-; Aeronautical Stu/Mgmnt; Naval Aviation.

**BRUHNKE, KURT M,** Columbia Union Coll, Takoma Park, MD; FR; BS; Assoc Cmptng Mchnry Pblc Rltns; Phi Eta Sigma 90-; Acdmc Schlrshp 90-; Comp Sci.

**BRUINSMA, DAEYON L,** Anne Arundel Comm Coll, Arnold, MD; FR; AA; Bsnss/Pbl Admin; Accntng CPA.

**BRULEY, ALICE M,** Tougaloo Coll, Tougaloo, MS; SO; BS; Math/Cmptr Sci Clb Sec 90-; Spnsh Clb VP 90-F Gospel Chr Asst Sec 90-; Dept Chrprsn US Acad Acadmc Achiev Schlrshp 90-; Math/Cmptr Sci; Prgrmr.

**BRUMAGIN, JODY R,** Allegheny Coll, Meadville, PA; SR; BS; Wind Symphny 87-; Chrstn Otrch Ldrshp Tm 87-; Alden Schlr 89-; Phi Sigma Iota 90-; Habitat Hmnty Sec Asst 89-90; Phy Thrpy Aide Meadville Med Cntr 88-90; Dept Envrnmntl Rsrcs Intrn 90-; IM Vlybl 88; Biology/Spanish; Phys Thrpy.

**BRUMBALOW, DENNIS C,** Univ Of Nc At Greensboro, Greensboro, NC; SR; BM; Msc Edctrs Natl Conf; NC Msc Edctrs Conf; Phi Mu Alph Sinfonia Sec 89-; Msc; Prfrmnc/Ed.

**BRUMBAUGH, JUDITH A,** Nova Univ, Ft Lauderdale, FL; MBA; Asst Provost; BA Adrian Clg 62; MHE Univ GA 69; Bsn; Tchg.

**BRUMBELOE, ERIN E,** Fl St Univ, Tallahassee, FL; JR; MBA; Acctng Scty Hstrn 90; Phi Eta Sigma; Beta Kappa Alpha; Gld Ky; Kappa Kappa Gamma Phlnthrpy Chrmn; Hghst GPA 90; Offcr Of The Wk; Hmn Rsrce Mgmt.

**BRUMBELOW, PAULA L,** Anne Arundel Comm Coll, Arnold, MD; SO; BA; Amnesty Intl; Sierra Clb; Maryland Gen Assbly Intrn; AA; Geography.

**BRUMBLES, MARILYN H,** Chesterfield Marlboro Coll, Cheraw, SC; FR; Data Proc; Certif Columbia Cmrcl Clg 69; Cmptr Pgm.

**BRUMELL, PEARLENE,** Western New England Coll, Springfield, MA; JR; BSW; Untd Mutly Eql Treas 88-; Div Comm 90-; Soc Sci Clb 90-; Hmcmg Comm 89-90; Vol Wk Spfld Urbn Lge 89-90; Ars Mass Tnts Rts Org Intshp; Scl Wk; Fmly Cnslg.

**BRUMFIELD, CHRISTY A,** Ms St Univ, Miss State, MS; SO; BA; Orntn Ldr; Stdnt Recrtr 90-; Stdnt Assn Cabinet Dir Univ Ser; Lambda Sigma Ed 90-; Alpha Lambda Delta Sec 90-; Phi Eta Sigma; Chi Omega VP; Order Omega; Cardinal Key; Phi Kappa Phi Soph Schlrshp; Acctg; CPA/LAWYER.

**BRUMFIELD, MELISSA G,** Univ Of Ga, Athens, GA; SR; Yound Choreographers Series 89-; Concert Dance Co 89-; Golden Key 90-; Southwestern Co Mgr 90-; Intl Busn; MBA/LAW.

**BRUMFIELD, RODERICK D,** Alcorn St Univ, Lorman, MS; JR; BS; Indstrl Tchnlgy Clb 88; Alpha Kappa Mu; Pres Schlr 90; Bsebl 88-90; Elctrncs/Cmptr Tchnlgy; Indstrl Mngmnt.

**BRUMLEY, CAROLYN R,** Maysville Comm Coll, Maysville, KY; FR; ASN; MCCANS VP 90-; Nrsng.

**BRUMLEY, CATHERINE L,** De Tech & Comm Coll At Dover, Dover, DE; FR; AAS; DA Bryan Inst Mdcl/Dntl Asst 75; Business/Psychology; Human Rsrc Mgt.

**BRUMLEY, HEATHER L,** Northern Ky Univ, Highland Hts, KY; FR; BA; Bio/Chem; Scndry Educ.

**BRUMLEY, KAYRN L,** Northwest Al Comm Coll, Phil Campbell, AL; SO; BS; Yrbk Stf; Phi Theta Kappa; Vlybl Mgr 90-; Frnch Grmn; Intrntl Bus.

**BRUMLEY, LAURA E,** Milligan Coll, Milligan Clg, TN; SO; BA; Scl Affrs Clb 89-90; Nwsppr Asst Ed 90-; Sigma Tau Delta 90-; Engl.

**BRUMLEY, PAUL E,** Univ Of Tn At Chattanooga, Chattanooga, TN; SO; BSE; AS Mt Wachusett Comm Clg Gardner MA 88; Elec Engr Instrmntn.

**BRUMLOW, AMY B,** Ky St Univ, Frankfort, KY; SR; Rsdnt Asst 88-; Tau Beta Sigma Sec 87-; Mrchng/Pep/Cncrt Bands Sec 87-; Lloyd E Alexander Awd 88; All Clgt Band 90; Bio/Chem; Pediatrics.

**BRUMME, BECKY L,** Capital Univ, Columbus, OH; SO; BA; Natl Assn Accntnts 90-; Amer Soc Womn Accntnts; Pub Accntns Soc Ohio; Dns Lst 89-; Acctg.**

**BRUMMERT, RENAE D,** Indiana Univ Of Pa, Indiana, PA; FR; BA; Activities Brd; Drama; Elem Ed; Tchr.

**BRUMMETT, KANDRA J,** Longwood Coll, Farmville, VA; SR; Stu Union Cncrt 88-90; Lngwd Series Prfmng Arts Rcptn Chr 88-90; Sigma Sigma Sigma Robbie Page Mem Chr 88-; Lst Spcl Intrst Hl 89-; Bs; Elem Educ; Tchg.

**BRUMMETT, SUSAN W,** Univ Of Ky, Lexington, KY; SO; BA; Psychlgst.

**BRUNDIGE, AMANDA L,** Univ Of Tn At Martin, Martin, TN; SR; BS; Alaph Tau Omega Little Sister 89-; Ftbl Hostess 87-88; Mcord Hall Assoc 87-88; Pi Sigma Epsilon VP Personnel 90; Chi Omega Actvts Comm Chrprsn 89-90; Deans Lst 89-; Chi Omega Schrlshp; Owl Dangle Awrd; Mrktng; Merchandising.

**BRUNE, MARIBETH,** Univ Of Sc At Columbia, Columbia, SC; SO; PHARM; Stdnt Govt Snte; Res Hall Assoc Hall VP 89-90; Res Hall Advsr 90; Hnrs Clb 89; Delta Zeta 1st VP 89; Var Schlrshps; Im 90; Pharmacy; Phamacutical Doctorite.

**BRUNELL, ANTHONY G,** Univ Of Pittsburgh, Pittsburgh, PA; FR; BS; Elect Engr; Sound Engr.

**BRUNELLE, ANDREA M,** Palm Beach Comm Coll, Lake Worth, FL; JR; BA; Phi Theta Kappa 88-; Pres Schlp 88-90; FL Atlntc Univ Comm Schlp 90-; AA 90; Clncl Psy.**

**BRUNER, KAREN L,** Indiana Univ Of Pa, Indiana, PA; SR; PSEA NEA; Magna Cum Laude; Rural Nwspr Dlvr; BED 90; English; Teacher/Reading Spclst.

**BRUNERMER, DANIEL T,** Pa St Univ Main Cmps, University Pk, PA; FR; BS; Sigma Tau Gamma Mgmt VP; Hbtt Fr Hmnty; Univ Schlr 90-; Elec Comp Eng; Eng.

**BRUNET, M CHRISTINE,** Hillsborough Comm Coll, Tampa, FL; JR; BS; Prsdntl Schlrshp HCC 88-; Fl Acdmc Schlrshp 88-; AA Hllsbrugh Comm Cllg 90; Business; Banking.

**BRUNETTE JR, GLENN M,** Saint Josephs Univ, Philadelphia, PA; SO; ACM Sec 89-; Tutr 89-; Acad Cmptg Ntwrk Cnsltnt 89-; Delmarva Pwr/Lght Intrnshp Sys Analyst 90-; Zenith Data Sys Clgte Rep 90-; St Josephs Univ Pres Schlrshp 89-; Cmptr Sci; Sys/Ntwrk Admin.**

**BRUNETTI, ANTHONY,** City Univ Of Ny Baruch Coll, New York, NY; SR; BBA; Golden Key 90; Endowment Fnd Provosts Schlrshp 89; Deans Lst 88; Accntng; CPA.

**BRUNETTO, MELEAH L,** Radford Univ, Radford, VA; SO; Cthlc Std Asc; Elem Ed; Tchr.

**BRUNGARD, KATHERINE J,** Univ Of Cincinnati, Cincinnati, OH; FR; BS; Nrsng; Oprtng Rm Nrse.

**BRUNI, ANTHONY D,** Comm Coll Algny Co Algny Cmps, Pittsburgh, PA; FR; BA; Bhvrl Sci; Scl Wrk/Psychlgy.

**BRUNI, BONNY G,** Univ Of Nc At Charlotte, Charlotte, NC; JR; BA; Pre Law Scty 89-; Gldn Key; Pi Sigma Alpha; Phi Theta Kappa; Plctcl Science; Law.

**BRUNI, JENNIFER L,** Syracuse Univ, Syracuse, NY; FR; Pblc Rltns Dept Stdnt 90-; Rd Stn; Deans Lst 90; Awrd Acdmc Schlrshp; Cmmnctns Pblc Rltns.

**BRUNICARDI, MARIO O,** Oh St Univ, Columbus, OH; SR; BS; Rfle Clb 88; Phi Kappa Phi; Alpha Lambda Delta; Phi Eta Sigma; Gldn Ky; Hnrs Rcgntn 90-; IM Bsktbl Sftbl 87-; Math; Med.

**BRUNK, DARVIN J,** Lansdale School Of Bus, North Wales, PA; FR; ASB; Library Clb 77-78; Mennonite Vol Serv 78-81; Oper Mgr 89-; Bus Admin/Data Proc.

**BRUNK, LAURA L,** Bridgewater Coll, Bridgewater, VA; JR; BS; Brethrn Stdnt Flwshp 88-; Pin Plyrs Drama Org 88-; Stdnt Educ Assn 90-; Lambda Soc 89-; Int Yth Cab Coord 89-; Pres Schlrshp 88-; Math/Cmptr Sci; H S Tchng.

**BRUNKA, KIMBERLY D,** S U N Y Coll Of Tech At Frmgdl, Farmingdale, NY; FR; AAS; IM Vlybl; Veterinary Sci Tchnlgy.

**BRUNNER, JENNIFER M,** Indiana Univ Of Pa, Indiana, PA; FR; Acctg; CPA.

**BRUNNER, MATTHEW G P,** Oh Univ, Athens, OH; SO; Mrchng Band 89; Jazz Band 89; Glee Clb 90-; Pep Bnd 89-; U Band 89-; Phi Mu Alpha Sinfonia Treas 90-; Ballzando Trmpt Awd 89-90; Trck Tm 89-.

**BRUNNER, ROBIN F,** City Univ Of Ny Baruch Coll, New York, NY; GD; MBA; Rsdent Asstnt Dorm Cobleskill Un 84-85; Drm Cncl Sec 83-84; Orange Key 83-85; Dollars/Snse Mag Wrtr 89-90; Deans List 83-85; Bld Dr 83-90; Ski Clb; DBA; Cmps Cnctn Mag Intrnshp Admn Asst 89-90; Westfield Home Nws Intrnshp Admn Asst 90-; Jrnlsm/Bus Comnctns; Acct Exec.

**BRUNO, ANGELA M,** Univ Of Cincinnati, Cincinnati, OH; SO; ASSOC; Soc Comm Chrmn 90; Stdnt Govt Dept Repr 89-90; Stdnt Life/Svcs Comm 89-90; Soc Wmn Engr 89-90; Newslttr 88-89; Soc Comm 89-; Kappa Delta 90; Co-Op Stdnt For Henkel-Emery Corp Lab Tech 90-; IM; Chem Tech; Pharm.

**BRUNO, ANGELA N,** Emory Univ, Atlanta, GA; JR; BBA; Rush Cnslr Rho Chi 90-; IM Sprts 89-; Kappa Alpha Theta Prchs Fnd Athltc Chrmn 89-; Vrsty Bsktbl 88-89; Accntng; Law/Txtn.

**BRUNO, LISA C,** Adelphi Univ, Garden City, NY; SR; BA; NSSLHA VP 90-; Phi Theta Kappa 87-89; Dns Lst 88-; Trustee Achvmnt Awd 89-; AA Nassau Comm Clg 89; Comm Disrdrs; Spch/Lang Path.

**BRUNO, MICHELLE J,** Kent St Univ Geauga Cmps, Burton Twp, OH; FR; ASSO; Busn.

**BRUNO, PAUL J,** Memphis St Univ, Memphis, TN; JR; BBA; Bus Fnc; Corp Law.

**BRUNO, WILLIAM A,** Fl International Univ, Miami, FL; JR; BS; AOS Culinary Inst Amer 90; Hosptlty Mgmt.

**BRUNOZZI, MARIADORA A,** Neumann Coll, Aston, PA; SR; BSN; Stdnt Nrs Assn 89-90; Sigma Theta Tau; St Francis Of Assisi Awd; Nrsng.**

**BRUNSCHWIG, ELAINE B,** Oh St Univ, Columbus, OH; SR; BS; Self Defense/Kwon Do 87-90; Univ Hnrs Soc 87-; Helix Biol Sci Hnry 88-; Biol.

**BRUNSON, SHANNON L,** Coll Of Charleston, Charleston, SC; FR; BA; Elem Edctn; Tchng.

**BRUNT, MARIA L,** Cheyney Univ Of Pa, Cheyney, PA; FR; BA; Deans Lst; Bus Admin/Acctng; Computer Sci.

**BRUNT, RICHARD T,** Hudson Valley Comm Coll, Troy, NY; GD.

**BRUNT, STEVEN T,** Univ Of Akron, Akron, OH; SR; BS; Natl Eagle Scout Assoc 80-; Nittany Divers 86-87; Stark Co Bicycle Clb 90-; Golden Key 90-; Galen J Roush Mem Schlrshp 90-; Jason/Corrine Summer Schlrshp 90-; United Grinding/Machine Co 87-90; Acctg.

**BRUNTON, CHRISTOPHER S,** George Mason Univ, Fairfax, VA; GD; MBA; Swim Club V P 85-; Amer Alliance Hlth/Phys Educ 90; Kappa Delta Pi; Boy Scouts Amer 82; Stdnt Educ Assn 90; PALS 88-89; Amer Swimming Coaches Assn 85-; Natl Educ Assn 90-; Fairfax Cnty Pblc Schls/Phys Edctr 88-; Phys Educ; Elem Educ.

**BRUNTON, MELINDA A,** Fayetteville St Univ, Fayetteville, NC; GD; Pep Clb 86; Phi Beta Lambda 89-90; IM 89-90; BS 90; Busn; Busn Exec.

**BRUSCA, JAMES P,** City Univ Of Ny City Coll, New York, NY; SR; BA; Stu Nwsppr Edtr 88-; Stu Radio Sta Nws Brdcstr 88; Chess Clb 87; Alpha Lambda Delta; Sigma Delta Chi; WWOR TV Nws Sprts Intern; MSG Cbl Ntwk Sprtdsk Intern 90; Creativity Mag Intern 89-90; Irving Rosenthal Almn Awrd; Almn Schlrshp; Cmmnctns; Jrnlsm.

**BRUSCEMI, VICKI L,** Indiana Univ Of Pa, Indiana, PA; JR; BS; Elem Ed; Tchr.

**BRUSCH, WYNETTE S,** Tuskegee Univ, Tuskegee Inst, AL; SR; BSN; NSNA Sec 87-88; Chi Eta Phi Pres 89-; Anita K Bass Schlrshp 89-90; M S Busn Admin.

**BRUSH, ANNE,** Univ Of Akron, Akron, OH; SR; BFA; Killbuck Vly Hstrcl Soc/Museum Vol 86-; Art/Drwng/Pntng; Clg Art Tchr.

**BRUSH, TIMOTHY SCOTT,** Univ Of Cincinnati, Cincinnati, OH; SR; MFA; ACT Orchd Awrd 89; Strader Schlrshp; Otstndng Almni; Asstshp Univ Of Nw Orlns; BFA; Elec Media Arts; MFA Thtre Prfrmnce.

**BRUSOVANKIN, LEV,** Bunker Hill Comm Coll, Boston, MA; FR; AS; AS Mech Engr Inst Cvl Engr Leningrd USSR 73-76; Radlgy.

**BRUSTAD, CAROLINE E,** Allegheny Coll, Meadville, PA; SR; BA; Phi Sigma Iota 90-; Kappa Alpha Theta 87-; Swm Tm 87-89; French.

**BRUTSMAN, JOSEPH ALDEN,** S U N Y Coll Of Tech At Alfred, Alfred, NY; FR; BA; IM Sccr; Eng Sci; Cvl Eng.

**BRUYN, PASCAL,** Univ Of South Al, Mobile, AL; SO; BA; Sigma Phi Epsilon 90; Educ; Tchng.

**BRUZDA, MARY A,** Seton Hill Coll, Greensburg, PA; SO; BA; Engl; Elem Educ.**

**BRUZEL, LOREN B,** Hillsborough Comm Coll, Tampa, FL; FR; BA; Phys Thrpst.

**BRUZZICHESI, GINA M,** Villanova Univ, Villanova, PA; SO; Hse Cncl Rep 89-90; Deans Lst; Hnrs Pgm/Mjr; Alpha Chi Omega Phlnthrpy Chrmn 90-; Cmnty Svc Rep; Hunt For Hunger Chrmn; Sclgy/Hnrs; Law.

**BRYAN, ALWIN T,** City Univ Of Ny City Coll, New York, NY; SR; BED; NSBE 87-88; Elec Eng; Cmptr Sci.

**BRYAN, ANGELA M,** Comm Coll Algny Co Algny Cmps, Pittsburgh, PA; FR; Ldrshp Clb; Bus Mgmt; Prsnl Admin.

**BRYAN, BONNIE S,** Meridian Comm Coll, Meridian, MS; FR; AA; Phi Beta Lambda 90; Phi Beta Lambda; Busn/Offc Tech/Law; Legal Fld/Acctg.

**BRYAN, CRAIG R,** Univ Of Akron, Akron, OH; JR; BS; Alpha Lambda Delta; Phi Eta Sigma; Golden Key; Im Bsktbl; Fnce; Fncl Anlyst Or Stock Brkr.

**BRYAN, GINA L,** Memphis St Univ, Memphis, TN; SO; BA; Gamma Beta Phi; Bsn; Mktg.

**BRYAN, GRETCHEN A,** Univ Of Akron, Akron, OH; SO; BA; Asst 4h Ldr/Geauga Cnty; Grt Geauga Cnty Frbnd 90-; Blue/Gold Brass Mrchng Bnd Sec Ldr 89-; ASCE; Phi Eta Sigma 89-; Gold Key 90-; Hnrs Club 89-; Kappa Kappa Psi 89-; Otsdng Kybrd Stdnt 90-; Cavanaugh Bldg Schlshp; Civil Engr/Piano.

**BRYAN III, JAMES E,** Univ Of Louisville, Louisville, KY; JR; MENG; IEEE 90-; Woodford R Porter Sr Schlrshp 88-; Elect Eng; Eng.

**BRYAN III, JAMES W,** Union Univ, Jackson, TN; JR; Pblc Rlts Soc 88-; Intr Frtrnty Cncl VP 89-; Hnrry Hstry Clb 88-; Alpha Tau Omega Pres 88-; Mngmnt Mrktng Intern 90-; Glf Tm 88-; Mss Media Cmmnctns; Bus Mgmt.

**BRYAN JR, JIMMY C,** Univ Of Miami, Coral Gables, FL; JR; BBA; Propeller Clb 90-; Dean Lst 90-; Accntng; Cnsltng/Tax Law.

**BRYANT WORKMAN, LEOTA K,** Oh Univ-Southern Cmps, Ironton, OH; JR; BED; Deans List 88-; Engl; Secondary Ed.

**BRYANT, ALAN C,** Savannah Coll Of Art & Design, Savannah, GA; SO; BFA; Illustration.

**BRYANT, ALICIA,** Tuskegee Univ, Tuskegee Inst, AL; JR; Cmps Dgst; SNEA Pres; Kappa Delta Pi; Delta Sigma Theta; Lng Arts; Law.

**BRYANT, AMY C,** Snead St Jr Coll, Boaz, AL; SO; Stdnt Govt Assn Sec 90-; Ambssdrs Pres 89-; Bptst Stdnt Union 90-; Phi Theta Kappa 90-; Early Chldhd/Elem Ed; Tchr.

**BRYANT, ANGELA D,** Coll Of Charleston, Charleston, SC; SR; BA; French/English; Dtc Comparative Lit.

**BRYANT, APRIL J,** Univ Of Nh Plymouth St Coll, Plymouth, NH; FR; BA; Senate Election Comm; Peer Educator; Tutor.

**BRYANT, AVIA N,** Fl A & M Univ, Tallahassee, FL; SR; MBA; NABA; Pres Schlr 87-; Prdntl Insur Amer 89; Dow Crng Corp 90; Deloitte/Touche; Acctg; CPA.**

**BRYANT, BARRY L,** Univ Of Ky, Lexington, KY; SR; Engr Stdnt Cncl VP 90-; ASCE 88-; KSPE 90-; Chi Epsilon Mrshl 90-/88-; Tau Beta Pi 90-; BSCE; Civil Engr.

**BRYANT, BRENDA K,** James Madison University, Harrisonburg, VA; SO; BSN; Nrsng Awd 90-; Hospice Vol 88-; PTA 88-; Nrsng.

**BRYANT, C DENISE,** Savannah Coll Of Art & Design, Savannah, GA; JR; BFA; Illustr.

**BRYANT, CRYSTAL DENISE,** Univ Of Sc At Columbia, Columbia, SC; SR; BA; Dorm Gov Sec Tutr 89-90; Poly Scif Pblc Amdin.

**BRYANT, CYNTHIA M,** Clark Atlanta Univ, Atlanta, GA; FR; BS MS; Oper Pride; Frgn Cltr Clb; SADD; Jr Ushr Bd; Cncrt Bnd; Mrchng Bnd; Orch; Natl Hnr Socty Treas; Hnrs Prog; Maggie B Greene Yth Cncl Rcrdng Sec; Every Hm Crsd; Vac Bible Schl Tchr; Offc Nvl Rsrch Schlrshp; Vrsty Bsktbl/Tns/Sftbl; Chmstry; Med.

**BRYANT, DANA C,** Valdosta St Coll, Valdosta, GA; JR; BED; PAGE; Early Chldhd Ed.

**BRYANT, DANIEL L,** Western Carolina Univ, Cullowhee, NC; SO; BS; Geology; Envrnmntl Engrng.

**BRYANT, DEMETRIA S,** Voorhees Coll, Denmark, SC; SO; BA; Choir 89-; Rcrtmnt Clb Sec 90-; Ntl Hnr Soc 88-89; Frnch Ntl Hnr Soc 88-89; Key Clb 87-89; Dnmrk Insprtnl Choir 89-90; State Choir 88; Cnty Choir 89; Math; Educ.

**BRYANT, DONALD E,** Memphis St Univ, Memphis, TN; FR; BBA; Finance/Geology; Stockbroker/Paleontologist.

**BRYANT, DONNA JILL,** Truett Mc Connell Coll, Cleveland, GA; FR; PHD; Deans Lst Pres Clb 90; Psychlgy; Drug/Alcohol Rcvry.

**BRYANT, DOROTHY L,** Memphis St Univ, Memphis, TN; SO; Gamma Beta Phi Soc; Spvr 78-89; English; Wrtr.

**BRYANT, ETHEL M,** Miles Coll, Birmingham, AL; JR; BS; Socl Sci.

**BRYANT, FEDERICA L,** Va St Univ, Petersburg, VA; SR; BS; ROTC Cadet Btln Cmndr 90-; SAM Rcrdng Sec 89-90; SAM 90-; Whos Who 90; Mltry Ordr World Wars Awd; G C Marshall Awd; Gen Dynmcs Exclnc Awd 90; Cert Achvmnt; Admn Sys Mgmt; 2 Lt U S Army.

**BRYANT, GREGORY D,** Fayetteville St Univ, Fayetteville, NC; SR; BA; PE Clb; Nun Phi Nun VP; IM Sprts Drctr; Psych/Phy Ed/Rec; Naval Intlgnt Srvc/Tchr.

**BRYANT, GWENDOLYN D,** Clark Atlanta Univ, Atlanta, GA; JR; BA; Natl Ed Assoc 88-; Kappa Delta Epsilon 90-; Vlybl Cptn 88-; Bskbl 90; Early Childhood Ed; Tchng.

**BRYANT, JACQUELYN P,** Fl St Univ, Tallahassee, FL; FR; BA; Amer Choral Dir Assn 90-; Phi Eta Sigma 90-; Music.

**BRYANT, JEAN J,** Tri County Tech Coll, Pendleton, SC; Ext Hmkrs Clb Pres; Tchr Aid.

**BRYANT, JENNIFER J,** Faulkner St Jr Coll, Bay Minette, AL; SO; Bus; Acctng.

**BRYANT, JERRON M,** Al St Univ, Montgomery, AL; FR; Math; Acctg.

**BRYANT JR, JOHN L,** Univ Of Nc At Charlotte, Charlotte, NC; SO; Univ Prog Brd Lctrs Dir 89-; Rsdnt Stdnts Assn Natl Comm Coor 90-; Stdnt Almni Ambssdrs Scl Chr 89-; C C Cmrn Mrt Schlr 89-; Rsdnt Advsr 90-; Univ Prog Brd Otstndng Dir 90-; Hmn Srvcs; Stdnt Affrs.

**BRYANT, JUDY F,** Univ Of Sc At Columbia, Columbia, SC; FR.

**BRYANT, JULIANA SEABROOK,** Va Commonwealth Univ, Richmond, VA; JR; BS; Hmn Rltns Cmte 90-; Nws Rprtr WVCW; Stf Wrtr Commonwealth Times 89-90; Soc Prfsnl Jrnlsts 89-; Intrnshp WTVR TV 6 Prdcr; Ms Cmnctns; Rprtr.

**BRYANT, JUSTIN,** George Mason Univ, Fairfax, VA; SO; BBA; Finance.

**BRYANT, KATHLEEN DIANNE,** Norfolk St Univ, Norfolk, VA; JR; BA; Amer Home Ec Assn 89-; VA Home Ec Assn Sec; Nrflk State Amer Home Ec Sec 90-; Alpha Kappa Mu; Acad Achvmnt Awd; Highest Rnkng Stdnt; Amer Red Cross 90; AA Pensacola Jr Clg 89; Home Ec Educ; Tch.

**BRYANT, KATRINA L,** James Madison University, Harrisonburg, VA; JR; BS; Stdnt Sen Rep 89-90; Stdnt ASID 90-; Phi Theta Kappa 89-90; Gldn Key 90-; Phi Omicron Tau 90-; All Amrcn Schlr; Intr Dsgn; Prfssnl Intr Dsgnr.**

**BRYANT, LATASHA J,** Columbus Coll Of Art & Design, Columbus, OH; SR; BFA; Retail Advrtsng.

**BRYANT, LATRELL D,** Memphis St Univ, Memphis, TN; SO; BA; Blk Stdnt Assoc Membrshp Chrprsn 90; Blk Schlrs Unlmted Coord Schlrshp Brkfst 90; SGA Snte Clrk 90; Blk Schlrs Unlmted; Phi Eta Sigma; Alpha Lambda Delta; Foreign Lang Spnsh; Tchng.

**BRYANT III, LEWIS A,** Radford Univ, Radford, VA; SO; BA; Acctg Soc 90-; Econ Clb Treas 90-; Hon Prog 90-; Acctg.

**BRYANT, MELISSA S,** Univ Of Sc At Columbia, Columbia, SC; SO; BA; Kappa Kappa Gamma Frat Ed 90-; Ed; Tchg.

**BRYANT, MICHAEL D,** Morehouse Coll, Atlanta, GA; JR; BA; Pre Law Scty 88-; AT Univ Cntr TX Clb 88-; Hnrs Prgm 88-; Gldn Key; US Achvmnt Acdmy Schlr 90-; Frederick Douglass Ttrl Inst Co Dir 88-90-; Hnr Rll 88-; Deans Lst 88-; Pltcl Sci; Law.**

**BRYANT, NONA E,** Memphis St Univ, Memphis, TN; SR; BA; NAECY Natl Conf 89; Fcltr Rnbws For All Chldrn 90-; Psy Chi Rho 87-88; Wing Capt 88-89; Alpha Lamda Delta 87; Stdnt Mntr Pgm 88; Rsrch Assist 90-; Acad Schlrshp 87-89; Art Schlrshp 88-89; Child Psych.**

**BRYANT, PATRICK C,** Marshall University, Huntington, WV; SR; BBA; Alpha Kappa Psi 88-; Wst Vrgn Scty CPAS 88-; Acctg.

**BRYANT, PATRICK W,** Memphis St Univ, Memphis, TN; GD; Stu Govt Assoc Sntr 87-88; Intrfrat Cncl Pres 87-90; Ordr Omega VP 87-90; Omicron Delta Kappa 88-90; Alpha Tau Omega 86-90; Pres 89-; Stu Ambsdr Brd 87-90; Orntn Guide 88; J Wayne Jhnsn Ldrshp Awrd 89; BA 90; Ldrshp Cnsltnt.

**BRYANT, PHILLIP R,** Ky St Univ, Frankfort, KY; FR; MBA; Chem; Eng.

**BRYANT, RANDOLPH P,** Christopher Newport Coll, Newport News, VA; SR; Pres-Wolftrap Oprtns Inc; BSBA; Fin; Bus.

**BRYANT, SABRINA M,** Monroe Comm Coll, Rochester, NY; SO; BSN; Nrs Extern Strong Memorial Hosp; Nrsg.

**BRYANT, SHEKEDIA L,** Al A & M Univ, Normal, AL; FR; MA; Ford Schlrs Pgm 90-; Dns Lst 90-; Elem Ed; Tchr.

**BRYANT, SIMEON M,** Univ Of Sc At Columbia, Columbia, SC; JR; BS; Phi Theta Kappa 88-; LDS Chrh Financial Clerk/Mens Pres 85-89; Sunday Schl Pres 89-; Busn Admin; Acctng.

**BRYANT, SUSETTE M,** Albany St Coll, Albany, GA; SO; Grayhound Acad Schlrshp Awd 90; Mc Knight Acad Achvmnt Awd; Bsktbl/Vlybl 89-; Acctg; CPA.

**BRYANT, TAMARA E,** Univ Of Rochester, Rochester, NY; JR; BA; Cinema Grp Pers Dir 89-; Undergrad Cognitive Sci Cncl 89-; Tech Asst Linguistics Rsrch; IM Water Polo 89-; Cognitive Sci.

**BRYANT, TERESA A,** Southern Union St Jr Coll, Wadley, AL; FR; Chem; Fshn Mrchndsng.

**BRYANT JR, THOMAS F,** Univ Of Sc At Columbia, Columbia, SC; SO; BA; Asst Foreign Stdnts W/Engl; Intl Studies.

**BRYANT, TRACY L,** Clarkson Univ, Potsdam, NY; JR; BS; Soc Accntnts V P; Circle K 89-91; NAA; Natl Hnr Soc; Alpha Delta Kappa Treas; Pres Schlr 90; Trustee Schlrshp 89-; Robert Smith Awd 89-90; Acctg/Fiance.

**BRYANT, TYRON S,** Lenoir Rhyne Coll, Hickory, NC; SR; Baptist Student Union Pres 87-; Resident Advisor 89-; Lenoir Rhynean Clg Nwspr Staff Wrtr 90-; Christian Serv Awrd; Natl Cllgt Edctrs Awrd; Stdnt Tchr S Caldwell High; BA; History Social Studies Educ; Church Work.

**BRYANT, WENDI A,** Savannah Coll Of Art & Design, Savannah, GA; GD; MFA; Jr Cls Pres 89; Sr Cls Pres 90; Ord Omega 90; Alpha Delta Pi VP 86-90; Tns Tm 86-87; BA Queens Coll 90; Photgrphy; Photogrphr.

**BRYANT, WENDY R,** Alcorn St Univ, Lorman, MS; SR; BS; Bio Clb 88-; Chem Clb 88-; Alpha Kappa Mu 89-; Phi Theta Kappa VP 87-88; Presdntl Schlr; AS Lawson State Comm Clg 88; Chem; Physcn.

**BRYANT, WILLIAM ROBBY,** Ms St Univ, Miss State, MS; SO; BA; Lndscp Archtctr.

**BRYANT-JUDE, YETUNDE A,** Central St Univ, Wilberforce, OH; FR; Vol Spec Olympics 90-; Architechture.

**BRYARS, VICKI M,** Univ Of South Al, Mobile, AL; SO; BS; Ed; Elmntry Ed.

**BRYCE, MARIAN C,** Immaculata Coll, Immaculata, PA; SO; BA; Campus Mnstry 90; Bio Clb 90; Chem Clb 90; Bio Chem; Med MD.

**BRYD, TEANA G,** William Carey Coll, Hattiesburg, MS; SR; BS; Bptst Stdnt Un 87-; All-Am Schlr; AA Lib Arts Jones Co Jr Coll 89; Elem Educ; Tchr.

**BRYK, ERICA L,** Kings Coll, Wilkes-Barre, PA; FR; BA; Communications.

**BRYMER, LEA,** City Univ Of Ny Queensbrough, New York, NY; SO; AAS; Bus; Hmn Rsrcs/Chld Dvlpmnt.

**BRYON, MELISSA L,** George Mason Univ, Fairfax, VA; SR; BS; Early Ed; Teaching.

**BRYSON, ANNETTE,** Atlantic Union Coll, S Lancaster, MA; SR; BA; Mass Media Clb V P 87-88; Hstry Clb Pub Rel 90-; Hstry Dept Newsltr Ed 90-; Phi Alpha Theta 90-; Amnesty Intl; Radio Rep Voice Am Afflte Sta Geneva Switz 89; BA Loma Linda Univ 88; Hstry.

**BRYSON, MOLLY M R,** Stillman Coll, Tuscaloosa, AL; SR; BS; Alpha Kappa Mu Hnr Soc 90-; Gamma Iota Sigma 87; Beta Kappa Chi 90-; Cordell Wynn Hnrs Pgrm 88-; Delta Sigma Theta Treas 90-; All Amer Schlr; Natl Collgt Cmptr Sci Awd; Stlmn Schlr 87-; Dns Schlr Dns Lst 87-; Vlybl Tm Co Capt; Cmptr Sci/Math; MS Sys Eng.**

**BRYSON, SHENERA T,** Fl A & M Univ, Tallahassee, FL; FR; MBA; Phi Eta Sgm 90-; Leander L Boykin Awrd 90-; Hsng Cert Schlrshp 90-; Bus Admn; Bus Mgmt.

**BRYTUS, ROBIN N,** Duquesne Univ, Pittsburgh, PA; JR; BED; Phi Eta Sigma 88-89; Kappa Delta Epsilon 89-; Sharp Vol 88-89; Phone A Thon 88-; Jr Achvmnt 90; Math/Spnsh; Sec Educ.

**BRZEZINSKI, EDWARD L,** Barry Univ, Miami, FL; SO; BA; IMS 89-; Cmps Mnstry 89-; Actvts 89-; Bsbl 89; Crmnl Jstce; Fed Invstgtn.

**BUBB, TRACEY J,** Mary Washington Coll, Fredericksburg, VA; FR; BA; Hl Cncl Pres 90-; Admssns Clb; Vars Swm Tm 90-; Music; Tchr.

**BUBB-DEANE, PATRICIA,** Ny Univ, New York, NY; JR; Acctg Intl; Law.

**BUBLITZ, THERESA M,** Radford Univ, Radford, VA; SR; BS; Stdnt Ed Assn 89-; Dnce Dept Clb 87-88; Kappa Delta Pi Treas 90-; Early/Mdl Ed; Tch.

**BUCANAN, FRANCES JUNE,** Mayland Comm Coll, Spruce Pine, NC; FR; MBA; First Un Natl Bank Cust Svc Rep 73-90; Med Ofc Tech.

**BUCARO, GINA M,** Bergen Comm Coll, Paramus, NJ; SO; AAS; Natl Stdnt Nrs Assn 90-; Dns Lst 90-; Phi Theta Kappa 90-; Nrsng.

**BUCCA-JANACEK, ANNETTE,** Univ Of Med & Dentistry Of Nj, Newark, NJ; GD; Biolgcl Soc 85-87; SGA Schlrshp 84; John Keosian Mem Award 87; Acadmc Exclnc Award 90; BA Rugerts Univ 87; BS 90; Sci/Toxiclgy; Medcl Rsrch.

**BUCCARELLI, REBECCA J,** City Univ Of Ny City Coll, New York, NY; JR; BA; Tns Tm 90-; Ecnmc Scty Clb Treas; Phi Theta Kappa Treas 87-89; AA Borough Manhattan Cmnty Clge 89; Econ/Bsn Mgmt; Fnce.

**BUCCELLATO, JOSEPH,** City Univ Of Ny Baruch Coll, New York, NY; GD; BA; Acctg Soc; Acctnt.

**BUCCELLATO, SALVATORE,** Thomas Nelson Comm Coll, Hampton, VA; SO; BA; AS Mech Engr Tech; Sci; Engr.

**BUCCI, CHRISTINA M,** Univ Of Rochester, Rochester, NY; SO; BA; Nwmn Cmmnty 89-; Chmbr Sngrs Sec 89-; Tiernan Dorm 90-; Meridian Soc 90-; Guthrie Schlr 89-; Gannett Schlar 89-; IM Sccr Co Capt 89-; Biol/Rel; Med.

**BUCCI, JEAN,** Georgian Court Coll, Lakewood, NJ; JR; BED; Humanities; Tchr/Librarian.

**BUCCI, MICHAEL P,** Hartwick Coll, Oneonta, NY; FR; BA; Lbbyng Cncl 90-; Stdnt Snte VP Snte Affrs 90-; Rsdntl Life Stff Rsdnt Advsr 90-; Dns Lst 90-; Fr Pol Sci Stdnt Of Yr 90-; Pol Sci Pre Law; Law.

**BUCCOLA, REGINA M,** Bellarmine Coll, Louisville, KY; SR; BA; Stdnt Nwsppr Edtr 87-; Amnsty Intrntnl Prsdnt 89-; Crdnl Sctn 87-; Soc Prfsnl Jrnlsts 89-; Kappa Gamma Pi; Intrn Dpt Comm Srvcs 89-; Intrn Lsvll Cntrl Area Inc 90; Intrn Brown Frmn Corp; IM Vllybl; Englsh Cmmnctns; Pursue Mastr Englsh.

**BUCH SERAPION, JOHANNIE,** Inter Amer Univ Pr Hato Rey, Hato Rey, PR; FR; Engl; Acctng.

**BUCHAN, CHAUNCEY S,** Univ Of Sc At Coastal Carolina, Conway, SC; JR; BA; Simga Tau Delta; Nelson Schlrshp 90-; Neil Graham Schlrshp; Wellness Clb; Brd Dir Theatr Rpblc; Wrk USC Costal Carolina Admssns Ofc; Engl; Jurnlsm.

**BUCHAN, IRENE F,** Le Moyne Coll, Syracuse, NY; JR; Psych/Spec Educ; Tch.

**BUCHANAN, AARON L,** Univ Of Va Clinch Valley Coll, Wise, VA; SR; Asst Professor Rsrch/Dev 90-; Bsn Mgmt; Mgmt.

**BUCHANAN, ANDREA J,** The Boston Conservatory, Boston, MA; JR; BM; Peer Support Grp 89-; Piand Perf; Musician.

**BUCHANAN, ANNA F,** Emory & Henry Coll, Emory, VA; Dir Womens Hsng Emory & Henry Coll 88-; BA 86; Spanish; Teach.

**BUCHANAN, HOLLY M,** Va Highlands Comm Coll, Abingdon, VA; SO; BA; Deans List; Elem Ed; Teach.

**BUCHANAN, HOPE R,** Clark Atlanta Univ, Atlanta, GA; SO; BS; Hnrs Prgrm 90-; Mntr 90-; Hnrs Prgrm 89-; UNCF Premed Inst 90; Ldrshp Awrd 90-; All AM Schlr Cllgt Awrd 90-; Prsdntl Schlrs Incnt Awrd 89-; Chrldng 89-90; Blgy; Med.

**BUCHANAN, JAMES W,** Middle Tn St Univ, Murfreesboro, TN; JR; BS; Phi Theta Kappa 87-88; Pres Lst 87-88; Dns Lst 88-; Minister Church Og Prophecy 80-; Psych; Psych Asst.

**BUCHANAN, JEANNE K,** Thomas Nelson Comm Coll, Hampton, VA; SO; Firefghtrs Aux VP 78-81; AAS Thomas Nelson; Bus; Sec/Admin Asst.

**BUCHANAN, JULIE L,** Wilmington Coll, New Castle, DE; SO; BSN; RN 76-; RN Milford Mem Hosp Schl Nrsg 74; Nrsg; Inservice Nrsg Instr.

**BUCHANAN, KAREN L,** Univ Of Nc At Asheville, Asheville, NC; SR; BA; Bio; Med.**

**BUCHANAN, MARK A,** Kent St Univ Kent Cmps, Kent, OH; SO; BA; Trmcrate; Alpha Lambda Delta 90-; Bus Admn; Bus.

**BUCHANAN, MATTHEW A,** Mayland Comm Coll, Spruce Pine, NC; FR; BS; Mgmt; Bus.

**BUCHANAN, RITA R,** New Comm Coll Of Baltimore, Baltimore, MD; GD; BA; Comm Share Inc Sec 90-; Phi Theta Kappa 90-; Intrnshp AARP 89-90; Woodmr Nghbr Assn 89-90; Mktg Coord 86-; AA; Socl Wrk; Clin Soc Wrk.

**BUCHANAN JR, ROBERT C,** Memphis St Univ, Memphis, TN; SR; BA; Acctng Tutor Prog Fairleigh Dickenson U 79-80; Acctng Tutor Prog Univ RI 80-81; Deans Lst Fairleigh Dickenson Univ 79-80; Deans Lst Univ RI 80-81; Golf Tm 81-83; Neighborhood Watch 89-; Eagle Flght Sales Trng Seminar 89; Dealer Cert 85; Mrktng; Business Mktg Mgmnt.

**BUCHANAN, ROBIN L,** Univ Of Nc At Greensboro, Greensboro, NC; JR; BS; Phi Theta Kappa; AA 90; Math; Ele Educ.

**BUCHANAN, SANDRA L,** Univ Of Miami, Coral Gables, FL; SR; BS; Bowling Clb Pres 88-; Campus Sprts/Rec Intrst Clbs Fed Chrmn 89-; Microbiology Clb; Gldn Key Chr Best Of Amer Rcrdng Sec 90-; Phi Kappa Phi; Mrtr Bd; Omicrom Delta Kappa; Hnrbl Mntn USA Today All Amer Acad Tm; Rstnt Asst; Microbiology/Immunology; Med.

**BUCHANAN, STACY MICHELLE,** Union Coll, Barbourville, KY; JR; Dns Lst; Spec Olmpycs; Chrldng Schlrshp; Chrldr; Elem Educ; Tchr.

**BUCHANAN, TAMMY L,** Union Coll, Barbourville, KY; JR; Bus Admin; MBA.

**BUCHANAN, THERESA A,** Radford Univ, Radford, VA; SR; BS; SNA; Sigma Theta Tau; Chi Omega; Weight Lftng Clb; Aerobics; BS VA Tech 87; Nrsng.

**BUCHANAN, THERESA D,** Univ Of Sc At Columbia, Columbia, SC; JR; BA; Elem Educ.

**BUCHANAN, TONI MARIE,** East Tn St Univ, Johnson City, TN; SO; Alpha Lambda Delta; Gamma Beta Phi; Assn Rcrd Mgrs/Adminstrtrs; Bus; Acctng.

**BUCHANAN-HILL, CHARLYN A,** Univ Of Cin R Walters Coll, Blue Ash, OH; GD; BA; Intrnshp Mead Imaging Media Tchnlgst 90; Intrnshp Mead Data Ctr Media Tchnlgst; Whtwtr Rftng/Scb Dvng 87-90; Media Tchncn/Mcrofch Prcsr 85-87/89-; Lbry Sci; Lbrn.

**BUCHANNA, REGINALD L,** Al A & M Univ, Normal, AL; SO; Univ Gspl Chr; ROTC; USAR; Engl/Pol Sci; Law.

**BUCHEISTER, KRISTI L,** Commonwealth Coll, Virginia Beach, VA; SR; Law Soc Sec 90-; Dns Lst; Chrch Wmns Clb 90-; Chng From Mgmt To Lgl; Cert Wrd Proc San Jose Reg Voc Ctr 78; Paralgl; Law.

**BUCHENBERG, SARA L,** Defiance Coll, Defiance, OH; GD; BA; AA; Art/Intrr Dsgn.

**BUCHER, JENNIFER R,** Fl St Univ, Tallahassee, FL; FR; BA; Cmmnctns; Brdcstng.

**BUCHER, JOHN P,** Miami Jacobs Jr Coll Of Bus, Dayton, OH; SO; AD; Acctg 67-88; BBA Univ Of Cincinnati 71; Cmptr Prog.

**BUCHER, KAREN ANN,** Teikyo Post Univ, Waterbury, CT; JR; BA; Drm Cncl 88-; Itln Clb 89; Amer Mrktg Assc 89-90; Yrbk 88-89; Deans Lst 89-90; Intrnshp Silver Man Gallery Woodcliff Lake NJ 90-; IM Sprts/Ski Clb 89; Mrktg; Mrktg Mngmt.

**BUCHER, ROBERT W,** Beaver Coll, Glenside, PA; GD; MA; Untd Auto Wrkrs Shp Stwrd 90-; Southampton Sprts Clb; Die Mkr/Shop Stwrd; BA Manchester Coll 73; Ed; Secndry Math Tchr.

**BUCHHEIT, SHERRY L,** Univ Of Sc At Columbia, Columbia, SC; SO; BM; Symphny Orchstr 89-; Chmbr Orchstr 89-; Alpha Lambda Delta 90-; Gamma Beta Phi 90-; Pi Kappa Lambda; Delta Omicron 90-; Msc; Msc Thry.

**BUCHHOP, TODD C,** Embry Riddle Aeronautical Univ, Daytona Beach, FL; SR; BS; Soc Of Commrcl Aviatn Techncns 90-; Maint Flwshp Prog; Deans List 87-; Hon Roll 87-; Cert Airframe/Pwrplnt Mechnc FFA License 90; Aerontcl Studies; Aviatn Techncn.**

**BUCHMAN, BRIAN T,** Coll Misericordia, Dallas, PA; FR; OK; Hon Scty 90-; Bio.

**BUCHMELTER, JENNIFER M,** Duquesne Univ, Pittsburgh, PA; SO; Phi Eta Sigma 90-; Bus/Acctg; Law.

**BUCK, AMY,** Elmira Coll, Elmira, NY; JR; Outing Clb 88-89; Legislative Bd 88-89; Cls Treas 88-89; PAL 88-89; Elem Ed; Tchg.

**BUCK, KATHERINE J,** Chesterfield Marlboro Coll, Cheraw, SC; SO; BA; Early Chldhd Ed; Tchr.

**BUCK, LAURA M,** Mount Aloysius Jr Coll, Cresson, PA; SO; AS; Bus Clb 90-; Mngmnt/Acctng; BS.

**BUCK, LORI M,** Duquesne Univ, Pittsburgh, PA; FR; BS; Msc Edctrs Natl Conf Clgt Chr; Mu Phi Epsln; Msc Ed.

**BUCK, MECHELLE R,** Radford Univ, Radford, VA; FR; BS; Theatre; Alpha Lambda Delta; Comm Sci/Disorders; Spch Pathlgst.

**BUCK, ROBERT A,** New England Coll Of Optometry, Boston, MA; SR; OD; Beta Sigma Kappa; Optmtrc Svc Hmnty 89-; BS Oglethorpe Univ 83; ODNEWENCO; Optmtry.

**BUCK, TIMOTHY E,** Univ Of West Fl, Pensacola, FL; SR; BA; BCM Sec/Treas 90-; AA Gulf Coast Coll 89; Early Chldhd/Elem Ed; Tchr.

**BUCKALEW, SHANNON D,** Wilmington Coll, New Castle, DE; FR; BED; Hmcmng Crt 88-90; SG VP 88; Chrldr Capt 87-90; Elem Ed Hstry; Tch.

**BUCKELEW, MARY J,** Univ Of Ga, Athens, GA; FR; BA; BSU Cncl 90-; Rdct Band; Msc; Thrpst.

**BUCKHAM, ROBIN ROHAN,** Howard Univ, Washington, DC; JR; BA; Intrntnl 90-; Hnrs Diploma 89; IM Sccr 90-; Certf Clg Arts Sci Tchnlgy 89; Archtctr.

**BUCKHANNON, ALISA A,** Pa St Univ Delaware Cty Cmps, Media, PA; SO; BED; English; Teaching.

**BUCKHOLTS, CHARLES D,** Middle Tn St Univ, Murfreesboro, TN; FR; BS; Tau Kappa Epsilon 90-; IM Tnns/Bsktbl/Sftbl 90-; Aerospace; Pro Pilot.

**BUCKINGHAM, JILLIAN B,** Ms St Univ, Miss State, MS; FR; BPA; Gamma Beta Phi; Alpha Lambda Delta; Phi Eta Sigma; Dns Schlr 90; IM Flb Ftbl 90-; IM Vlybl 90-; Acctg; CPA.

**BUCKLAND, REBECCA M,** Beckley Coll, Beckley, WV; SO; BA; AA 90; Soc Sci; Educ.

**BUCKLE, EILEEN P,** Georgian Court Coll, Lakewood, NJ; JR; BA; Coll Nwspr 90-; Trnsfr Club 89-; Dns Schlr 90; English; Writer.

**BUCKLES, SCOTT L,** Sue Bennett Coll, London, KY; FR; BA; Fncng Bnkng.

**BUCKLEY, ANNEMARIE,** Merrimack Coll, North Andover, MA; SR; BA; AM Mktng Assc 90; Merrimck Mrktng Assc 90; Deans List 89; Bsn/Admntrtn; Mrktng.**

**BUCKLEY, CHERIE S,** S U N Y Coll Of Tech At Alfred, Alfred, NY; FR; AAS; AAS Alfred State Clg Alfred NY 81; BS In Nursing.

**BUCKLEY, COLLEEN,** Univ Of Va, Charlottesville, VA; SO; BS; Soc Wmn Engrs Hstrn 89-; Engr Cncl 89; Yrbk Bus Stff 89-90, Golden Key 90-, Phi Eta Sigma 90-, Theta Tau, Fluor Daniel/Massey Schlrshp; Elect Engr.**

**BUCKLEY, DEBORAH S,** Middle Tn St Univ, Murfreesboro, TN; SR; BS; Psychlgst.

**BUCKLEY, DIANE L,** Georgian Court Coll, Lakewood, NJ; JR; BA; Math Assoc Of Am 90-; Pi Mu Epsilon 90-; BSA 86-; AA Brookdale Comm Coll 88; Math; Teach.

**BUCKLEY, GINGER ME GALE,** Univ Of Tn At Martin, Martin, TN; FR; BS; Rsdnc Hall Assoc; Phi Alpha Delta; Zeta Tau Alpha Publc Rltns Chrmn; CWS Under The Shlrshp Chrmn At UTM; Pol Sci; Attnd Law Sch.

**BUCKLEY, GREGORY W,** Wv Univ At Parkersburg, Parkersburg, WV; FR; BS; Buckly Assn Pres 91; Cust Svc Rep Xerox 3 M 85-; Elec Eng.

**BUCKLEY, LISA L,** Fl Memorial Coll, Miami, FL; SR; BA; Delta Sigma Theta VP 90-; PRIDE Tutor 89-; SGA 87-; Hnr Rl 87-; Citibank Intern; Hnr Schlrshp 87-; Urbans Bankers Schlrshp 90-; Business Mngmnt.

**BUCKLEY, LONAS S,** Univ Of Southern Ms, Hattiesburg, MS; SR; BS; Etta Sigma Gamma; Certif Diploma Medl Lab Tchnlgy Awrd Clinical Perfmnc; AS 88; Health; Human Sciences.

**BUCKLEY, MARSHA A,** Meridian Comm Coll, Meridian, MS; FR; Medl Labrty Techn.

**BUCKLEY, SARA J,** Columbia Union Coll, Takoma Park, MD; SR; BS; Stdnt Assn Exec Sec 89-; Phi Eta Sigma; Alpha Chi Repr 90-; Soup Kitchen; Arthur Hauck Award 90; Jrnlsm; News.

**BUCKLEY, STANLEY P,** Ms Coll, Clinton, MS; GD; JS; Coll Law Revw Stf 89-; Phi Delta Phi 89-; Intrnshp Cntrl Ms Lgl Svc 90; Am Jursprdnce Trl Prctc 90; BS 88; Law; Lawyer.

**BUCKMAN, BARBARA N,** Savannah St Coll, Savannah, GA; JR; BSW; Vol Wrk Hmls Shltr 90-; Hospice 90-; Rape Crisis Cntr Inc 90-; Leisure Svcs Bureau 90-; Pi Gamma Mu 90; Alpha Kappa Mu; NASW 90-; NOW; German Cath Coll Socl Wrk 82; Socl Wrk; Mstr Clin Socl Wrk.

**BUCKMAN, CHRISTINE,** Saint John Fisher Coll, Rochester, NY; FR; BA; Drama Clb 90-; WFCX Radio Stn Camps 90-; Peer Advsr Incmg Fr; Alpha Mu Gamma; Teddi Proj Dance Marthn Rsng Fnds Camp Good Days Spec Times Camp; Cnslrs Asst Visa Pgm St John Fshr Athl Asst Thos Jeff Mdle Schl 90; Comm/Jrnlsm; Tele News Anchr.

**BUCKMAN, RENEE J,** Central Fl Comm Coll, Ocala, FL; FR; AS; Stdnt Govt Assoc Stdnt Rep; Prlgl Scty Pres; Phi Theta Kappa; Lgl Asst Stdnt Mbr; Nrs Aid Cert Vo Tech MD 83; Lgl Asst; Law Schl.

**BUCKMAN, ROBERT J,** Middle Tn St Univ, Murfreesboro, TN; JR; BS; Vars Bsbl 87-; Wllns/Ftns; Corp Fitness.

**BUCKNER, BENJAMIN H,** Univ Of Nc At Charlotte, Charlotte, NC; SO; BA; Golden Key; Lit Corp Proj; Psychology Resrch Asst; Var Golf 8990-; Psychology; Clncl Psychologst.

**BUCKNER, BRITT C,** Southern Coll Of Tech, Marietta, GA; JR; BSIET; Inst Indstrl Eng; BSIM Georgia Tech 85; Indstrl Eng; Techncl Sls.

**BUCKNER, JEANNIE T,** Univ Of Southern Ms, Hattiesburg, MS; SR; BS; Am Chmsty Soc Treas 89-; Gamma Beta Phi 88-; Chmsty; Rsrch.

**BUCKNER, JENNIFER L,** Univ Of Fl, Gainesville, FL; SR; BA; Art Hist Assoc VP 90-; Art League Awds Chair; Photo Show Dir 90-; Clsscl Hnr Soc 90-; Kappa Delta 87-; Art Gllry Intrn 90-; Deans List 90-; Pres Hnr Rl 90; Art Hist; Museum Wrk/Art Dir.

**BUCKNER, LAURA A,** Radford Univ, Radford, VA; JR; BS; Stdnt Lf-Spec Evnts Com 89-90; Sigma Tau Delta 90-; Alpha Sigma Alpha Fndrsng Com Head 89-; Engl; Tchr.

**BUCKSON, SUSAN H,** Univ Of Md At Eastern Shore, Princess Anne, MD; JR; BA; Dram Soc; Ftr Educ Of Amer/Eastern Shore Chapt Sec; Wom Bsktbl Tm UMES Capt 89-; Kappa Delta Pi Pres; Otsdng English Mjr; Hnr Stdnt 89-; Capt 89-; English; Teaching.

**BUCKWALTER, DARLENE J,** Cumberland County Coll, Vineland, NJ; FR; Elem Educ/Erly Chldhd.

**BUCKWALTER, MARGARET K,** Univ Of Cincinnati, Cincinnati, OH; FR; Alpha Lambda Delta; Perform Dance Ensembles MCCM Patricia Corbett Pavilion; Ballet; Prfssnl Dncr Bllt Co.

**BUDA, MELISSA A,** Dowling Coll, Oakdale Li, NY; SO; BA; Acctg Soc Pres 90-; Stanley H Kaplan-Chaykin CPA Rvw Repr; Kickline 90-; Acctg; CPA.

**BUDD, CHRISTINE M,** Glassboro St Coll, Glassboro, NJ; JR; BS; Psychlgy Clb Secy 89-; Stdnts Life Secy 89-; Psi Chi Secy; Gamma Tau Sigma; Blgy; Med.

**BUDELL, SANDRA J,** Clayton St Coll, Morrow, GA; GD; DPMA Pres 90-; Natl Assoc 90-; AAS.

**BUDESA, CHRIS I,** Dowling Coll, Oakdale Li, NY; JR; BA; Psi Chi; Psychlgy; Law Enfrcmnt.

**BUDHRAM, ARJUNE A,** City Univ Of Ny Baruch Coll, New York, NY; SR; BA; Algebra Nmbr Thry Grp; Oper Resrch Asst; Math.

**BUDINSKY, THOMAS J,** Univ Of Akron, Akron, OH; JR; BFA; Goldn Key 90-; Deans Lst 87-; Intrnshp Cncptl Imgry 90; Grphc Dsgn/Ilstrtn; Dsgn/Ilstrtn.

**BUDNIEWSKI, RICHARD S,** Schenectady County Comm Coll, Schenectady, NY; FR; AABA; U S Army Communications/ Electronics Spclst 81-87; Pol Sci/Econ; Clg Prof/Admin.

**BUECHEL, ELLEN R,** Le Moyne Coll, Syracuse, NY; JR; BA; Cmps Radio DJ 88-89; Le Moyne Schlrshps 88-; Tchng Elem Schl 88-90; IM Sprts; Engl Cmmnctns; Flm.

**BUEHLER, JAMES F,** Oh St Univ At Newark, Newark, OH; SR.

**BUEL, PENNY M,** S U N Y Coll Of Tech At Delhi, Delhi, NY; SR; BSN; Beta Blckrs 90-; Hosp Nrs 88-; CPN 84; AAS; Nrsng.

**BUEL, REBECCA L,** Saint John Fisher Coll, Rochester, NY; SR; Hstry Clb Ldrshp Dev Tm Prsdnt 89-; Rsdnc Cncl 88-; Winter Olympics Comm 89-; Phi Alpha Theta 89-; Teddi Project Dncr 88-; Cmps Mnstry; Hnr Grd; Deans Exclnc Awd 90-; Hstry Chrmn Asst 88-; IM Bsktbl Vllybl; BA; Hstry; Tchr.

**BUELL, CHARLENE A,** Univ Of Cincinnati-Clrmnt Coll, Batavia, OH; SO; BA; Phi Theta Kappa Nwslttr Asst Ed; Deans Lst; Clermont Chirprctc Intrn; Anatmy/Chem; Chrprctc.

**BUELL, MARY P,** Univ Of Southern Ms, Hattiesburg, MS; JR; BA; Stdnt Almn Assoc 90-; Exrcs Physlhgy C Lb 89-; BACCUS 89-; Phi Theta Kappa 88-89; Gamma Beta Phi; Phi Kappa Ta Lttl Sstr Crr Dvlpmnt Chrprns 89-; Intern; Exrcs Physlgy; Physcl Thrpy.

**BUENAFE, MARK A,** Univ Of Miami, Coral Gables, FL; SR; BS; Pres 100 90-; Sprts Fst Exec Com 90-; LINK Stdnt Vol Srvcs Chrprsn 89-; Gen Hnrs; Psych; Law Bus.

**BUENO, MARIA G,** Midway Coll, Midway, KY; SR; BA; Intl Club Pres 88-89; Phi Beta Lambda Pres 88-89; Phi Theta Kappa 87-; Midway Coll Amb; Aaa 89; Bus.

**BUENVENIDA, TRICIA F,** Boston Univ, Boston, MA; SO; BS; Nwspr Wrtr 89-; Radio Sta 89-; Gldn Key 90-; Alpha Delta Pi VP 90-; Dns Hst; A E Schwartz/Assc Wrtng/Edtng Intshp 89-90; Jrnlsm/Intl Rltns.**

**BUETER, DANIEL J,** Central Fl Comm Coll, Ocala, FL; FR; AA; Boy Sct Trp 196 Asst Sctmstr 89-; Bus; Rstrnt Mgmt.

**BUFALINI, HELEN A,** Geneva Coll, Beaver Falls, PA; FR; Chrstn Cath Clb 90-; Vars Vllybl Sftbl Bsktbl Lttr 90-; Elem Educ; Tchr.

**BUFANO JR, JOSEPH,** Bloomfield Coll, Bloomfield, NJ; JR; Chrprctc.

**BUFF, AMY M,** Western Piedmont Comm Coll, Morganton, NC; SO; AAS; Phi Beta Lambda 89; Gnrl Accnt.

**BUFF, DAWN M,** Fl St Univ, Tallahassee, FL; JR; BA; Hl Govt CO State Univ 89; Phi Kappa Phi 89; Phi Eta Sigma 88-89; Golden Key 90-; Alpha Lambda Delta 88-89; AA 90; Philosophy; Law.

**BUFF, GERALD DAVIS,** Catawba Valley Comm Coll, Hickory, NC; FR; BS; Wstrn Pdmnt Cmmnty Coll Flyng Clb Pres 84-85; Deans Lst 84-86; Sls Rep; BS Avtn Mntnc Sacramento Cty Coll 79-; AS Bus Admn 86; Elctrncs.

**BUFFIN, KELLY A,** Lexington Comm Coll, Lexington, KY; FR; BA; Chrch Yth Grp VP 90-; Econ; Law/Govt Serv.

**BUFFONE, JOHN J,** S U N Y Coll At Fredonia, Fredonia, NY; SR; BS; AS Jamestwn Comm Clg 89; Bus Admin; Mgmt.

**BUFORD, JENNIFER K,** Newbury Coll, Brookline, MA; FR; BA; Nanny; Culinary Arts.

**BUGAJSKI, DAWN L,** Slippery Rock Univ, Slippery Rock, PA; SO; BACHL; HPERD Clb 89-; Phi Eta Sigma 89-; Kappa Psi Delta; Trck And Fld 89-; Phys Educ; Tch Phys Educ.

**BUGARIN, DARWINA S,** Univ Of Sc At Columbia, Columbia, SC; SO; BS; Air Force Rsrv Offcrs Trng Crps Flt Cmmdr 89-; Arnold Air Soc 90-; Deans Lst 89-; Pres Hnr Rl 89-; Sup Perf Awd; Pol Sci; Air Force Officer.

**BUGASH, SUSAN E,** Lebanon Valley Coll, Annville, PA; FR; BS; Slk Squad Mrchng Bnd 90-; Cncrt Choir 90-; Biol Clb 90-; SAFE 90-; Hons Prog 90-; Pres Ldrshp Awd Schlrshp; Biochem; Res.

**BUGGS, SHELIA D,** New Comm Coll Of Baltimore, Baltimore, MD; GD; Hmn Srvc Asst; Scl Wrk.

**BUHLER, CHARLES C,** Univ Of Cincinnati-Clrmnt Coll, Batavia, OH; JR; AS; Bus; Fin.

**BUHLER, MAUREEN A,** S U N Y Coll Of Tech At Frmgdl, Farmingdale, NY; FR; Bus Admn; Cpa.

**BUHRER, STEPHANIE B,** Univ Of Southern Ms, Hattiesburg, MS; SO; BA; DP Comp Oprtr; Bus Ed; Tchng.

**BUHRMANN, JOHN K,** Eckerd Coll, St Petersburg, FL; SO; BA; Frnch Clb Pres 88-89; Nrthwstrn Conn Baming Socty Sec 85-89; Pinewoods Tns Clb 85-89; Jordan Park Hsng Proj St Petersburg 90-; Yale Univ Sci Symposium 88; Weslayan Univ Sci Lecture Series 88; Vrsty Tennis Tm 1st Dbls Tm 85-89; German Lang; Coll Prfssr.

**BUI, HANH D,** Boston Univ, Boston, MA; FR; BS; Sci; Engnrng.

**BUI, HUU QUANG,** City Univ Of Ny City Coll, New York, NY; SR; ME; IEEE; Elec; Eng.

**BUI, HY SI,** Univ Of Southern Ms, Hattiesburg, MS; FR; Tchr; Plymr Sci Physcs; Sci.

**BUI, PHIPHUNG THI,** Bunker Hill Comm Coll, Boston, MA; FR.

**BUI, THANH T,** Felician Coll, Lodi, NJ; JR; BA; Sci Club 88-; Church Choir 88-; Chrch Cmnty Treas 90; Lab Tech 88-; AAS Essex Cmnty Clg 88; Cmptr Sci/Math; Pgmr.

**BUI, TRAM T,** Columbus Coll Of Art & Design, Columbus, OH; FR; Art Clb 87-90; Clmbns Serv Clb Pres 87-90; Spnsh Clb 87-90; Fine Arts; Gllry Ownr.

**BUI, VUONG T,** Harrisburg Area Comm Coll, Harrisburg, PA; FR; BS; Bio.

**BUI, XAY V,** City Univ Of Ny City Coll, New York, NY; JR; Vietnamese Stdnt Assoc VP 89-90; IEEE 90-; Elec Engr.

**BUICK, ALAN J,** Univ Of Miami, Coral Gables, FL; SR; BA; Photo Clb Pres 89-; Beta Gamma Sigma; Sigma Alpha Epsilon 88-; Fin; Law.

**BUIE, MARSHA A,** Valdosta St Coll, Valdosta, GA; SO; BSN; Phi Mu; Sigma Alpha Epsilon Swthrt; Sigma Alpha Epsilon Ltl Sis; Nrsng; Midwfry.

**BUIST, LINDA Y,** City Univ Of Ny Med Evers Coll, Brooklyn, NY; SO; BS; Legal Asst Paralegal Inst 89; CUNV/BOE Mentor; Psychlgy; Chld Psychlgst/Scl Wrkr.

**BUITRAGO RAMIREZ, JAVIER O,** Univ Politecnica De Pr, Hato Rey, PR; FR; Aspr Inc 85-86; Sci Math.

**BUJDOS, BRIAN L,** Syracuse Univ, Syracuse, NY; FR; BA; Newspr Cntrbtng Wrtr 90-; Stdnt TV Sta; Lambda Chi Alpha 90-; WESA AM FM Radion Sta Intrn; Orange Mascot Chrldng; Nwspr/Brdcst Jrnlsm; Wrtr/Rprtr/Anncr.

**BUJOLD, JEANETTE SUSANNE,** Saint Thomas Univ, Miami, FL; SR; BED; Lgl Sec Roca/Assoc; AA Miami Dade Comm Clg N 81; Cert Miami Lakes Tch Ed 84; Elem Ed/Hist; Tchg/Sec Law.

**BUJORIAN, ANNE M,** Univ Of Akron, Akron, OH; SR; BSBA; Pi Sigma Epsilon Pres 90-; Phi Eta Sigma Hstrn 89-90; Pres Ambsdrs 89-; Yrbk 87-89; Mrtr Bd 90-91; Omicron Delta Kappa 90-91; Mu Kappa Tau 89-91; IM Sprts 87-90; Coll Bus Dns Cncl 90-; Outstdng Sr; Top Natl Mktg Stdng 90; Mktg; Visiting Nrs Service.

**BUKKOSY, SARA B,** S U N Y Coll At Fredonia, Fredonia, NY; SO; BA; All Coll Bnd 90; Clncl Psychlgst.

**BUKOVAC, CHRISTINE M,** Marshall University, Huntington, WV; SO; BA; Accntng; CPA.

**BUKOWSKI JR, JOHN A,** Univ Of Sc At Columbia, Columbia, SC; JR; Math Computer Sci Clb Pres 90-; Intl Clb 89-; Computer Lab Asstnt Sr Asst 89-; Omicron Delta Kappa 90-; Phi Mu Epsilon 90-; Presidents Lst 90-; Deans Lst 88-90; Aux Corp Internshp 90-; BSA Asst Sctmstr 88-89; US Army Imagery Analyst 85-89; Computer Sci; Research Dvlpmnt.

**BULAN, ERWIN J,** Cornell Univ Statutory College, Ithaca, NY; JR; BS; Advsr 90-; Ho Nun De Kah; Golden Key; Rsrch Clg Vet Med Anesthetics; I M Tennis Soccer Ftbl Lacrosse 8; Biology Genetics; Med.

**BULKA, SHMUEL R,** Yeshiva Univ, New York, NY; GD; JD; Clb Canada 87-90; Pltcl Sci Soc 87-90; Stdnt Nwspr Sports Edtr 88-90; Deans Lst 88-90; IM Hcky 88-89; IM Bkstbl 89-90; Law; Lwyr.

**BULKLEY, MICHAEL D,** Alfred Univ, Alfred, NY; JR; BSME; ASME; Mech Eng; Energy Conversion.

**BULLARD, BARNABY D,** Univ Of Rochester, Rochester, NY; SO; BA; NROTC 89-; Sigma Nu 90-; Econ; Fin.

**BULLARD, JOSEPH L,** Central Al Comm Coll, Alexander City, AL; SO; AA; Masjid Mahammad IMAM 89-; GED Prog Tutor 90-; Dipl J F Ingram St Tech Coll; Engl; Cmptr Sci.

**BULLARD, N CAROLINE,** Univ Of Montevallo, Montevallo, AL; SR; BA; Engl/Pol Sci; Grad Sch.

**BULLEN, AUDREY V,** S U N Y Coll Of Tech At Frmgdl, Farmingdale, NY; JR; BA; Frgn Lng Clb; AA; Engl.

**BULLEN, JOEL M,** S U N Y Coll Of Tech At Frmgdl, Farmingdale, NY; SR; Radio Engr; Engr.

**BULLER, COLIN A,** Glassboro St Coll, Glassboro, NJ; SR; BA; Econ Clb V P 89-; Peer Rfrl Orntatn Stf 90-; Gamma Tau Sigma 90-; Totor 90; Economics; MBA Finance.

**BULLERS, KRYSTAL B,** Nyack Coll, Nyack, NY; FR; Clg Pblcty Grp 90; Brooklyn Gspl Team 90; Hstry/Phlsphy; Hghr Educ.

**BULLINGTON, GRADY D,** Western Ky Univ, Bowling Green, KY; FR; Chrstn Stdnt Flwshp; Pi Mu Epsilon; Alpha Phi Omega 90; Math.

**BULLIS, LAUREN E,** Castleton St Coll, Castleton, VT; JR; Phi Eta Sigma 89-; Crss Cntry 89-90; Bus; Accntg/Finance.

**BULLOCK HOOPER, LESLIE NAOMI,** Univ Of South Al, Mobile, AL; SR; BS; Soc For Hmn Rsrc Mgrs VP 90-; Data Proc Mgrs Assn VA 90-; Prsnnl Intrn At USA Med Cntr; AA Pat Hnry Jr Coll 80; Mgmt; Srvc Indstry Mgr.

**BULLOCK, ANGELA WINNIFRED,** Fl Atlantic Univ, Boca Raton, FL; JR; Crbbn Stdnt Un Treas 89-; MEAA Schlrsp; AA Miami Dade Cmmnty Coll 90; Fnc; Own Real Est Co.

**BULLOCK, BEVERLY A,** Norfolk St Univ, Norfolk, VA; SR; BS; SVEA 90-; Erl Chldhd Educ; Tchg.

**BULLOCK, CLIFTON G,** Appalachian Bible Coll, Bradley, WV; GD; THB; Married Lfe Cmmttee 89; Mssns Conf Evltn Cmmttee Co-Chrmn 89-90; Mssns Intrn 89-90; Cert Brlngtn Ble Inst 86; Bible; Foreign Mssnry.

**BULLOCK, ELLEN LOUISE,** Asbury Theological Sem, Wilmore, KY; GD; Theta Phi; H S Tchr; Pastr; BA 68; MS Eastrn Ill Univ 84; MA; Chrstn Educ; Pastrte.

**BULLOCK, GAYLYN D,** Holyoke Comm Coll, Holyoke, MA; SO; AA; Untd Prfssnl Hrsmns Assoc Assoc Mbr; Wkr Sqsh Bdmntn Clb Treas 85-87; NZ Tstmstrs Assoc Treas 84-86; Ftr Frmsr Amrc Exchng Stdnt; Lab Tchcn; Accnts Clrk; Accntnts Asst; Shppng Agnt; Hrstrnr; Rdng Instrctr; Bus.

**BULLOCK, HEIDI L,** Furman Univ, Greenville, SC; FR; BA; Amnsty Intrntl 90-; Wrstlng/Vlybl Tm Statscn 90-; Crew Tm; IM 90; Engl; Tchr.

**BULLOCK, KATHLEEN F,** Univ Of Rochester, Rochester, NY; SO; BA; Tiernan Cmnty Svc Spcl Intrst Dorm Secy 89-; Comm On Perfrmng Arts 90; Humor/Satire Magzn 90-; Stdnts Actv In Vol Entrprs; Compeer Vol Prog; Psychlgy; Spcl Ed.

**BULLOCK, LOUISA M,** Norfolk St Univ, Norfolk, VA; FR; BA; Spartan Alpha Tau; Bio; Med.

**BULLOCK, MICHAEL J,** Al A & M Univ, Normal, AL; FR; BS; Deans Lst 90; Presdnts Lst; Mchncl Eng.

**BULLOCK, SCOTT K,** Wilmington Coll, Wilmington, OH; JR; Stdnt Fndtn Scl Chr; Srtma 90-; Start Big Bro Big Sis Prog Clntn Cnty; Sem In Crnvca Mexico 90; Vrsty Ftbl Offnsve Lne Coach 89; Vrsty Ftbl 90; Pscyh And Sclgy; Clncl Psychlgy Ph D.

**BULLOCK, TANYA M,** Western New England Coll, Springfield, MA; FR; BA; Bsn; Banking.

**BULLOCK, TOMMIE C,** Univ Of Southern Ms, Hattiesburg, MS; JR; BSBA; Phi Theta Kappa Alum 90-; Gamma Beta Phi; Acctg.

**BULOTA, LARA A,** Georgetown Univ, Washington, DC; JR; BS; Stdnt Fed Credit Un Tlr 90-; Alpha Lambda Delta 87-88; Pi Beta Phi Asst Rush Chrm; Rugby Clb 87-88; Acctg; Envrnmntl Law.

**BULWIN, DEBRA L,** Duquesne Univ, Pittsburgh, PA; SO; Concert Choir 89-; Show Choir 90-; Deans Lst; Music; Music Mgmnt.

**BUMGARDNER, EMILY K,** Marshall University, Huntington, WV; FR; BED; Phi Eta Sigma; Gamma Beta Phi; Speech Lang Pathology.

**BUMGARNER, JOHN N,** Methodist Coll, Fayetteville, NC; SO; BA; US Army; Pltcl Sci; Fed Gvmt.

**BUMGARNER, PHILLIP W,** Univ Of Tn At Chattanooga, Chattanooga, TN; SO; BSE; Bapt Stdnt Union 88-; Deans Lst 88; Yth Minister E Ridge Bapt Chrch 89-90; IM Wrstlng 90; Engrng Mechncl Cvl.

**BUMGARNER, SUSAN M,** Catawba Valley Comm Coll, Hickory, NC; SO; BA; Psych; Clncl.

**BUMP, MICHELLE D,** Oh Univ, Athens, OH; SR; Natl Hons Soc; Outstndng Sr Dance; Dance.

**BUMPERS, LUCY E,** Livingston Univ, Livingston, AL; SR; Alpha Upsilon Alpha; Pres Lst 89-; Dns Lst 89-.

**BUMPUS, JAMIE E,** Univ Of Tn At Martin, Martin, TN; JR; BS; Scty Prfssnl Jrnlst; Cmps Rdio 90; Cmps Nwsppr Stff 88-; All Amer Schlr; Trvl Stdy Washington D C; Obn Cnty Mgrnt Schl Tchrs Assnt; Hnr Rll 89-; Wrk Stdy 89-; Gooch/Scripps-Howard Comm Dept Schrlshp 88-; Cmnctns; Jrnlsm.**

**BUNCH, NICOLE M,** Fl A & M Univ, Tallahassee, FL; FR; BS; Palm Beach Clb Asst Tr 90-; Hon Roll 90-; Medicine.

**BUNCK, ELIZABETH A,** Fl International Univ, Miami, FL; JR; BS; Natl Ntrtnl Foods Assc 77-; Sthrn Hlth Org 77-; Hotel/Rest Alum Assc 77-; Amer Hm Econ Assc 90-; Fl Hm Econ Assc 90-; Phi Theta Kappa 74-75; Phi Kappa Phi; Schlrshp Fl Hm Econ Assc; Cnslng Ntrtn/Mgmt Hlth Food Stores 77-; BS 77; Hm Econ Ed.

**BUNDICK, JONATHAN E,** Univ Of Md At Eastern Shore, Princess Anne, MD; JR; BS; Hnrs Lst; US Army 90; Rnk E-4 86-; Bus Admin; CPA.

**BUNDICK, RONEEA L,** Johnson C Smith Univ, Charlotte, NC; SO; BA; Choir Minister Music 89-; Asstnt To Hnrs Clg Rector 90-; English Clb 90-; Alpha Lambda Delta 89-; Honors Clg; Presidents List 89; Deans Lst 89-; UNCF Mellon Schlrshp Awrd Wnnr 90-; English; Law.

**BUNDY, DAN L,** Atlanta Christian Coll, East Point, GA; SO; BA; Dns Lst 90; Vars Bsktbl 90-; Ed; Tchg.

**BUNDY, DAVID W,** Univ Of Sc At Columbia, Columbia, SC; JR; BS; AWARE Treas 90-; Natl Fed Of The Blnd 87-; Cmps Mnstrs 90-; Gamma Beta Phi 88-; Phi Theta Kappa 90; Yth Coor Meth Chrch 90-; AA Anderson Coll 90; Psych; Cnslng And Tchng.

**BUNDY, ERICA S,** Glassboro St Coll, Glassboro, NJ; JR; BA; NAACP 86-87; Gateway Cbl Intrnshp 90-; Cmnctns; Media Prod.

**BUNDY, NICOE J,** City Univ Of Ny Baruch Coll, New York, NY; JR; BA; Wmn Color 90; Acctg; Mgmt.

**BUNGARD, TRINA T,** Saint Pauls Coll, Lawrenceville, VA; JR; BA; Cub Scts Den Mthr/Asstnt Cub Mstr 86-88; Cntrbry Clb St Pauls Clg 89-; Alph Kappa Mu; Deans List 88-; Deans Asst Sec 88-; Lawrence Fmly Schlrshp 90-; Grad Elem Educ.

**BUNGARD, WILMA L,** West Liberty St Coll, West Liberty, WV; GD; Sigma Sigma Sigma 84-; Std Tchng; BA Bio 86; BA Educ 90; Bio; Tchng.

**BUNGE, JO ANN A,** S U N Y Coll Of Tech At Frmgdl, Farmingdale, NY; SO; Hnr Scty Indctn 90; Cert Mrt; Deans Lst 90.

**BUNGE, KELLY J,** Indiana Univ Of Pa, Indiana, PA; JR; BS; Sign Lang Clb 88-; Sign In Cstm Coord 89-; Parent Infrmtn Prjct 90-; RA 89-90; Peer Clnslr 90-; Edctn Hrng Imprd; Rhbltatn Cnslr Deaf.

**BUNKER, JAY A,** Univ Of Cin R Walters Coll, Blue Ash, OH; BA; 12 Stp Rcvry Ctv Coord; Assoc; Educ; Educ/Psychlgy.

**BUNKER, LINDA A,** Atlantic Comm Coll, Mays Landing, NJ; SO; Hosp Mgmt; Mgmt.

**BUNKLEY, TODD C,** Hillsborough Comm Coll, Tampa, FL; SO; MBA; Film Prod/Dramatic Arts; Prof Mdl/Prod Actor.

**BUNN, CASSANDRA L,** Fl St Univ, Tallahassee, FL; SR; Lady Sclphntrs 90-; Fllwshp Chrstn Athlts Tres 87-; Seminole Uprsng WVFS Radio Ftr Rptr 90-; Beta Kappa Alpha 89-; Goldn Key 90-; Deans Lst 88-; Sigma Kappa Stndrds Comm 88-; WCPX TV Asst 90; Cmmnctn; Brdcst Jrnlsm.

**BUNN, DONNA RAYE,** Ga St Univ, Atlanta, GA; SR; Stdnt Govt 86-90; PAGE 89-; Wesley Fndtn 86-88; Blue Key; Gldn Key; Phi Kappa Phi; Omicron Delta Kappa; Order Of Omega; Kappa Delta Pi; Phi Mu VP 87-90; P Douglas Tchr Schlrshp; BSED GA St Univ; Early Chldhd Ed; Elem Tchr.

**BUNN, JOEL W,** Saint Francis Coll, Loretto, PA; SR; BA; Amer Acad Physcn Asst; ENA; Fmly Prctc; CVMH Schl Nrs 87; Grtr Jhnstwn Vo-Tech 85; Physcn Asst; Fmly Prctc.

**BUNNING, JULIE A,** Univ Of Ky, Lexington, KY; JR; BA; Sigma Kappa Prnts Clb Chr; Clncl Psy.

**BUNSONGSIKUL, PED,** Univ Of Miami, Coral Gables, FL; SO; BS; First Aid Sqd; Chess Clb; Table Tennis Clb; Biomed Engr; MD.

**BUNTA, HOWARD C,** Univ Of Ct, Storrs, CT; JR; BS; BA Boston Coll 89; Archtctrl Lndscpng.

**BUNTING, DARRIN R,** Oh Univ, Athens, OH; GD; DO; Hillsdale Clg Mns Cncl Treas 87-89; Inter Vars Chrstn Fllwshp 86-90; Chrstn Med/Dntl Soc 90-91; Sigma Zeta Pres 87-90; Beta Beta Beta 87-90; Fmly Prctc Club 90; RA 87-88; Brooks Award 89; Intrnshp Univ Texas Med Brnch 88; Ostepathy; Osteopathic Phys.

**BUNTING, MARIA L,** Jackson St Univ, Jackson, MS; SO; BA; SGA 90-; Chrldr 90-; Drm Clb 89-; Alpha Lambda Delta 89-; Jst Sy No 87-; Pres Lst 90-; Dns Lst 89-; Psychlgy; Law.**

**BUNTY, CHRISTOPHER M,** Ms St Univ, Miss State, MS; SR; BA; Mu Alpa Theta 86; Carpenter 90-; AA E Central Community Clg 88; Biology/Ed.

**BUONO, CHRISTOPHER L,** Hudson Valley Comm Coll, Troy, NY; SO; BA; Bus Mgr Schl Nwsppr Bus Mgr 91-; Rstrnt Mgr 85-90; Bus.

**BUOYE, CATHLEEN M,** William Paterson Coll, Wayne, NJ; SR; BA; Spec Educ; Teach Handicapped.

**BUQUOI, FRANCINE M,** Univ Of Southern Ms, Hattiesburg, MS; SR; BS; NEA 90-; Jr Coll Trans Schlrshp; Deans & Pres Lists 87-; Otstndng Serv Spec Ed 90-; AA Jones Co Jr Coll 89; BS Spec Ed; Spec Ed; Teach Spec Children.

**BURBANK, HARRY M,** Bloomfield Coll, Bloomfield, NJ; BA; Marine Bio.

**BURBICK, JODI L,** Univ Of Ky, Lexington, KY; FR; Ed; Tch.

**BURCH, ANGELA S,** Muskingum Coll, New Concord, OH; SR; BA; Psych Clb 88-; Jazz Ensmbl VP 87-91; Sax Qrtet 87-91; Psi Chi Pres 88-; Omicron Delta Kappa VP 90-; Lambda Sigma 88-89; Simga Alpha Iota VP 90-; Sigma Xi; Cora T Orr Awd; Wm Trumpeter Awd; Undrgrad Rsrch Asst Kent State U 90; Psych.

**BURCH, CASSANDRA M,** Comm Coll Algny Co Algny Cmps, Pittsburgh, PA; FR; AS; Ldrshp Trng I/Ii Cert; Deans Lst; Math; Engr.

**BURCH, THERESA M,** Univ Of Cincinnati-Clrmnt Coll, Batavia, OH; FR; BA; Foreign Lang; German Tchr.

**BURCH, THOMAS H,** Univ Of Ky, Lexington, KY; FR; BFA; Hnrs Prog; U K Theatr; Theatre/Dsng/Tchnlgy; Dsgnr/Dir.

**BURCHETT, ANGELA S,** Univ Of Nc At Greensboro, Greensboro, NC; GD; Student Tchng; BS 90; Ed K-6; Tchng.

**BURCHETT, CYNTHIA C,** Fayetteville St Univ, Fayetteville, NC; GD; BA; Delta Mu Delta Hnr Soc; Bus Admin; Bnkg.

**BURCHETT, GREGORY S,** Univ Of Ky, Lexington, KY; FR; BA; Theatrical Exper Actor/Publcty Mgr 90-; Brdcst Jrnlst.

**BURCHETT, JAMES A,** Georgetown Coll, Georgetown, KY; SR; BA; Phi Kappa Tau Frat 90-91; Emil S Liston Awd Winner For Sch Dist 90; Bsktbl 87-; Bus & Mrktng/Fin; Bus Fin.

**BURCHETT JR, JOEL B,** Radford Univ, Radford, VA; SR; BS; AS New River Cmnty Clg 89; Phys Educ; Tchng/Bsn.

**BURCHETT, SHERRY J,** Wheeling Jesuit Coll, Wheeling, WV; FR; BS; Bio; Vet Med.

**BURCHETTE, LESLIE,** Central St Univ, Wilberforce, OH; SR; BS; Fashion Assc Pres 85-86; Intrgnztnl Cncl 85-86; Wstnghs Mtrls Co Schlrshp 90-; Cmptr Info Systms; Systms Anlyst/Prgmng.

**BURCHFIELD, ALLAN C,** Daytona Beach Comm Coll, Daytona Beach, FL; SO; BS; Army 84-89; Bus; Aviatn Bus/Mgt.

**BURCHFIELD, DAVID C,** Memphis St Univ, Memphis, TN; SR; BA; DPMA; MENSA; Delta Sigma Pi V P; Aviation Ins Undrwrtng V P 69-89; Mgmt Info Systms.

**BURCHWELL, SUSAN R,** Univ Of Ky, Lexington, KY; JR; BA; Mrchng Bnd Hd Drm Mjr; Symphnc Wnds 89-; Elem Ed; Tchng.

**BURDEN, ELIZABETH N,** Owensboro Comm Coll, Owensboro, KY; SO; DVM; Stdnt Assn; Math Clb; POLAR Anthrplgy; Sci Clb; Chem Dscpln Awd; AA; Vet Med.

**BURDEN, GLENDA S,** Univ Of Cincinnati, Cincinnati, OH; JR; BSN; Stdnt Nrs Assn 89-; Nrsng; RN.

**BURDEN, JOE W,** Fl A & M Univ, Tallahassee, FL; FR; BA; Ftbl; Crmnl Justc/Bsn Admin; Lawyer/Own Bsn.

**BURDEN, JOSEPH F,** Western Ky Univ, Bowling Green, KY; JR; BA; Phi Eta Sigma 90; Regents Schlrshp 89-; Dns Lst 89-; Cmptr Sci; Prgrmg/Rsrch.**

**BURDEN, MELISSA A,** Savannah Coll Of Art & Design, Savannah, GA; SO; BACCHUS Pres 89; Pres Cncl 89; Rsdnt Assist 89; Prt Dsgn Ambssdr 89; All Tourn Tm Vllybl 90; Brd Of Trustees Schlrshp Vldctrn 89; Vllybl NAIA 90; Im Vllybl Bsktbl 89; Grphaic Dsgn/Illstrtn; Cmmrcl Arts.

**BURDETT, CINDY K,** Wv Univ, Morgantown, WV; JR; BS; ASP 90-; Kappa Psi Treas; Mxwll Pres Schlrshp 88-; Phrmcy.

**BURDETTE, DEBORAH A,** Saint Catharine Coll, St Catharine, KY; SO; BED; Phi Theta Kappa 90-; W Marion PTO VP 90-; SS Tchr; Bible Schl Tchr; Ophthalmic Tech; Elem Ed English; Teach.

**BURDETTE, DEBRA C,** Abraham Baldwin Agri Coll, Tifton, GA; SO; BED; Dns Lst 90-; Sec Educ/Soc Sci; H Schl Tchr.

**BURDETTE, KIMBERLY D,** Univ Of Montevallo, Montevallo, AL; SO; BA; Church Choir; MCS News Video Techncn 89-; MCS News Dir/Prodcr; AL Publc TV Intrnshp Montgomery Teleprmptr Camera; Deans List; Valedictorian Schlrshp 89-; Pres List 90; Blant Schlrshp 89-; Brdcst Media; News Anchrng/Prodc Dir.

**BURDETTE, LARRY S,** Tri County Tech Coll, Pendleton, SC; SR; SGA Treas 90.

**BURDETTE, RENEE M,** Univ Of New Haven, West Haven, CT; FR; BA; Lbrl Arts; Wrtng Actng.

**BURDETTE, STEVEN G,** Marshall University, Huntington, WV; FR; BA; Sprts Med; Physcl Thrpy/Rehab.

**BURDETTE, SUSAN C,** Univ Of Al At Birmingham, Birmingham, AL; SR; BS; Alpha Sigma Tau Treas 88-; Pres Hnrs; Dns Lst Hnrs; Bus Mktg.

**BURDICK, CHRISTOPHER G,** S U N Y Coll At Postdam, Potsdam, NY; JR; BM; Crane Stdnt Assc Rep; Wnd Ensmbl 90-; Jzz Bnd II; Kappa Delta Pi; Pi Kappa Lambda; Pres Lst 89-; All Amer Schlr; Musc Educ; Tchg.

**BURDICK, HOLLY E,** Univ Of Sc At Columbia, Columbia, SC; FR; Wmns Sccr Clb 90-; Gamecock TV; Communications; Brdcstng.

**BURDICK, KEITH P,** Univ Of New Haven, West Haven, CT; SR; BA; Psychlgy Club VP 87-; Lambda Delta 90-; Psi Chi 88-; Outstndng Psychlgy Award 90-; Sterling Hse Cmnty Svc Award 90; Psi Chi Rsrch Award; EPA; Psychlgy; Clincl.

**BURDICK, PETER B,** Hudson Valley Comm Coll, Troy, NY; SR; AS; Ski Clb 90-; Phi Theta Kappa 90-; Theta Kappa Beta 87-; Pres Lst 90-; Ski Clb 90-; Bus; Fnnce.

**BURDICK, SUSAN E,** Univ Of Sc At Columbia, Columbia, SC; JR; BS; Am Inst Chem Engs; Assn Hon Stdnts; Tau Beta Pi; Omega Chi Epsilon; Chem Eng.

**BURDINE, TONYA J,** Sue Bennett Coll, London, KY; JR; BA; Cncssns/Prd/Promo Comm/Laurel Cnty Fstvl; Phi Theta Kappa; History; Teach.

**BURDITT, ROBERT E,** Christian Brothers Univ, Memphis, TN; SO; BS; Pi Kappa Phi Soc Chrmn 90-; Comp Sci; Prgrmr.

**BURFORD, CYNTHIA A,** Univ Of Tn At Knoxville, Knoxville, TN; SO; BA; Intclgte Fornes Dbte Tm 89-90; Gamma Beta Phi 89-; Gamma Beta Phi Serv Charctr Schsp; Fin; Invstmnt Brkr.

**BURFORD, TARA L,** Indiana Univ Of Pa, Indiana, PA; SR; BED; Elem Ed; Tchr.

**BURGA, CHRISTINA R,** Broward Comm Coll, Ft Lauderdale, FL; FR; AA; Stdnt Govt Assoc Sec 90-; Drama Clb Pres 90-; Comptv Edge Pres Ldrs; Pres Lst 90; Biol; Med.

**BURGA, TIMOTHY W,** Oh Wesleyan Univ, Delaware, OH; SO; BA; Dept Of Agng Intrnshp Wash DC; Marion Co Dmcrtc Prty; Knghts Of Columbs; AS Marion Tech Coll 86; Poli/Govt.

**BURGARD, JESSE F,** Saint Petersburg Jr Coll, St Petersburg, FL; FR; AS; IM Ftbl/Bsbkl 90-; Interdisiplinary Hnrs Studies 90-; Phsy Therapy; Sports Med.

**BURGDORF, PAUL E,** Western Ky Univ, Bowling Green, KY; SR; BS; Hrtcltr Clb 89-; Cmps Crusade Christ 89-; Glden Key 89-; Phi Kappa Phi 89-; Alpha Zeta; IM Bsktbl 90-; AS Vincennes Univ 89; Hrtcltr; Mssn Fld.

**BURGE, VICTORIA B,** Livingston Univ, Livingston, AL; SR; BA; Alpha Upsilon Alpha; AS Patrick Henry Jr Clg 89; Educ.

**BURGE, WILLIAM T,** Appalachian St Univ, Boone, NC; FR; BSCJ; Gamma Beta Phi 90-; Crmnl Jstce; Law Enf.

**BURGENER, MARGARET R,** Longwood Coll, Farmville, VA; JR; BS; Stdnt Ed Assn VP 88-; Phi Kappa Phi; Kappa Delta Pi 89-; Elem Ed; Tchng.

**BURGER, ANDREA J,** Ms St Univ, Miss State, MS; JR; Clg Republ 90-; Rice Hall Repres; Delta Gamma 90-; Compas Club 90; Phi Kappa Tau; IM Flag Ftbl/Sftbl 90-; Sci; Dentistry.

**BURGER JR, DAVID C,** Univ Of Cincinnati-Clrmnt Coll, Batavia, OH; FR; BA; Accntnt 88; Bsnss; Accntnt CPA.

**BURGER, FRANK J,** Ny Univ, New York, NY; JR; BA; Dir Cmptr Serv Sftwr Firm; Creative Writing; Fiction/Drama.

**BURGER, GARY O,** Clemson Univ, Clemson, SC; SO; BS; Prgm Clhn Coll 89-90; Scty Amrcn Frstrs 90-; Clmsn Schlr; Fclty Stff Schlrshp 89-; Frstry Award 89-; Frst Mgmt.

**BURGER, JACQUELINE G,** Middle Tn St Univ, Murfreesboro, TN; JR; BS; Elem Educ; Tchng.

**BURGER, JEFF A,** Univ Of Southern Ms, Hattiesburg, MS; FR; BS; Mrchng Bnd 90; Cncrt Bnd; Polymer Sci Clb 90-; Phi Mu Alpha 90-; Rcmnded Outstndng Fresh Male; Polymer Sci Schlrshp; Polymer Sci; Rsrch/Dvlpmnt.

**BURGER, JONI M,** Oh Univ, Athens, OH; JR; BA; BARC 89-90; Eclgy Clb 89-90; Amnsty Intl 89; Dns Lst 89-; Art; Graphc Desgn.

**BURGER, KRISTINE E,** East Stroudsburg Univ, E Stroudsburg, PA; FR; BA; Fine Arts.

**BURGER, ROBERT W,** Me Maritime Academy, Castine, ME; FR; Pi Kappa Alpha; Marine Trans; Shp Offcr.

**BURGER, TRESSA L,** Middle Tn St Univ, Murfreesboro, TN; SR; Stndt Hm Ec Assoc; Am Hm Ec Assoc; Home Ecnmcs; Fash Merch.

**BURGER, WENDY R,** Spartanburg Methodist Coll, Spartanburg, SC; JR; BS; AA Spartanburg Methodist Coll 90; Physcl Thrpy; MSPT.

**BURGESS, ALANE B,** Western New England Coll, Springfield, MA; FR; BA; Bhvrl Scl/Sci Clb 90-; Alpha Lambda Delta Pres 90-; Sccr 90-; Psychlgy.

**BURGESS, ANISSA,** Spartanburg Methodist Coll, Spartanburg, SC; SO; BS; Blck Alliance Hist Clb 89-; SG 90-; Psi Beta 89-; Deans Lst 89-; AA Spartanburg Meth Coll; Chem/Bio; Med Tech.

**BURGESS, ANNE E,** Radford Univ, Radford, VA; SO; BA; Phi Beta Lambda 90-; Acctg.

**BURGESS, BARNARD,** Al A & M Univ, Normal, AL; FR.

**BURGESS, CHRISTOPHER N,** S U N Y Coll Of Tech At Alfred, Alfred, NY; FR; AOS; Sigma Tau Epsilon 90-; Kamyr Drftng Achvmnt Schlrshp 90-; Drftng.

**BURGESS III, DONALD V,** Ky Christian Coll, Grayson, KY; JR; BS; Stdnt Repr 90-; Msc Ensmbl 89-; Madrigal Singer 90-; Psych; Marriage/Fmly Ther.

**BURGESS SR, JEFFREY A,** Univ Of North Fl, Jacksonville, FL; SR; BA; Phi Kappa Phi 89-; Gldn Ky 87-; Beta Gamma Sigma 90-; Natl Assn Of Home Blders; Lic Gen Cntrctr; Acctng; Law.

**BURGESS, KEVIN P,** Fayetteville St Univ, Fayetteville, NC; SO; Art Club 86-88; Alpha Kappa Mu; Chancellors List 88-; Deans List 86-88; Magna Cum Laude; BA Visual Arts; BA History; Visual Arts & History; Graphic Artist.

**BURGESS, LAURIE A,** Saint Francis Coll, Loretto, PA; SO; BS RN; Stdnt Nrsng Orgnztn Sec 89-; Rd Ky; Jacob Fend Fndtn Schlrshp; IM Vlybl Bsktbl 90; Nrsng; Mtrnty OB Nrsng.

**BURGESS, LINDA S,** Univ Of Fl, Gainesville, FL; JR; BSN; NCNA 90-; Phi Theta Kappa 86-87; NSNA 90-; Stdnt Nurses Assn 90-; Deans List 90-; Presidents List; AA Santa Fe Cmnty Clge 87; Nursing.

**BURGESS, RUSSELL L,** Tri County Tech Coll, Pendleton, SC; FR; AIT; Ind Elect Tchnlgy; Elect Tchncn.

**BURGESS, SCOTT E,** Univ Of Sc At Columbia, Columbia, SC; SR; BA; Grmn Clb 89-; Delta Phi Alpha 90-; Elgl/Grmn; Law School.

**BURGESS, STACY L,** Univ Of Southern Ms, Hattiesburg, MS; SR; BS; Pentecostal Flwshp Pres; Ambsdr Yth Club Treas; Spanish Club; Beta Club; Phi Theta Kappa V P; Sunday Schl Tchr; Red Cross; Rotary Club Scholar; Assoc MS Gulf Coast Cmnty Clge 90; Secondary Ed History; Teach.

**BURGESS, TERENCE M,** Bryant Stratton Bus Inst Roch, Rochester, NY; GD; AOS; Elect Tech.

**BURGESS, WENDY C,** Univ Of Ga, Athens, GA; SR; BSED; Fresh Cncl 87; Stu Rcrtmnt Tm 87-89; Cmps Hmcmng Cmmtt; Z-Clb Tppng Chrmn 87-; Kappa Alpha Theta Rush Chrmn 87-; Engl; Educ Admn.

**BURGIO, DAVID R,** S U N Y At Buffalo, Buffalo, NY; SR; CPA; Young Investors Pr 89-; Acctng Assoc Nws Cmte 90-; Deans Lst; Natl Assoc Of Accts 90-; Deans Lst; Grad Cum Laude; BS; Acctng/Fin.

**BURGO, JOAO J M,** Commonwealth Coll, Virginia Beach, VA; SO; AAS; Alpha Beta Gamma 90-; Pres Lst; Electrncs; Eng.

**BURGOS MONTANE, MARGARITA,** Univ Of Pr Medical Sciences, San Juan, PR; GD; MS; BS 89; Pblc Hlth; Evltn Rsrch.

**BURGOS SANCHEZ, HUGO J,** Univ Of Pr Humacao Univ Coll, Humacao, PR; SR; BA; SMA 87-; Acct Assn 87-; Chess Finals Champ 88-90; IM Sftbl 89-90; Acctng; CPA.

**BURGOS, AMILDA,** City Univ Of Ny City Coll, New York, NY; SR; BA; Alpha Sigma Lambda; NYC Dept Gen Serv Otstndg Emplye 85 Awrd Rcvd Ctys Appl 85-86; Sclgy; Prof.

**BURGOS, JOLIE,** Western New England Coll, Springfield, MA; JR; Prdctn Cntrl Crdntr Cst Anlyst Kollmorgan Corp 85-89; Bus; Fnc.

**BURGOS, JUAN M,** Bunker Hill Comm Coll, Boston, MA; FR; BA; US Army Airborne Inf 86-89; Lib Arts; Law.

**BURGOS, LISIE J,** Inter Amer Univ Pr Hato Rey, Hato Rey, PR; JR; BA; Inst De Banca 87; Hon Stdnt; Comp Prog; Acctg; Law.

**BURGOS, MAYRA J,** Univ Of Pr Medical Sciences, San Juan, PR; GD; MS; NSSHLA Grp Rep 89-; Soc Natl Hstry 89-; Fundacion Puertoigueria Cnsrvcn 89-; Adlgy; PhD.

**BURGOS, SANDRA,** Univ Politecnica De Pr, Hato Rey, PR; SO; Amer Bus Wmns Assoc.

**BURGOS, SANDRA P,** Barry Univ, Miami, FL; FR; BA; Hon Stdnts Assn 90-; Pre-Law; Law.

**BURGOS-COTTO, JAVIER R,** Univ Of Pr Cayey Univ Coll, Cayey, PR; JR; BS; Puertorican Org Extcs Brds; Crps Med Cdts 88-90; Hnr Rl 89-; Ftr Hlth Prfsnls 88-89; Blgy; Med/Surg.

**BURGOS-VAZQUEZ, DRA LUISA ENERY,** Univ Of Pr Medical Sciences, San Juan, PR; GD; MHSA; Pry Lf; Tchr; Qlty Asrnc Assoc 88-; Deans Lst 89-90; Mdcl Tchnlgst; Pdtrtn Mstr Hosp Hlth Srvcs Admn; MT MD Univ PR Schl Med San Juan; MHSA; Admn; Mdcl Admn.

**BURGOYNE, KRIS A C,** Owensboro Jr Coll Of Bus, Owensboro, KY; JR; AS; Comptrzd Ofc Profsnl; Data Mgr Or Spclst.

**BURGREEN, CARL T,** Univ Of Sc At Columbia, Columbia, SC; JR; BA; Hstry Govt And Intrntl Stds; MA Ph D Hstry.**

**BURGUN, CHANELE M,** Le Moyne Coll, Syracuse, NY; JR; BS; Bg Bro/Bg Sr Prog 90-; Spgfld Garden Tutorng Prog 90-; Biol; Med.

**BURI, MARK D,** S U N Y At Buffalo, Buffalo, NY; SO; BS; Accntng Assn; Hnrs Prgrm 89-; Accntng Finance; Law.

**BURK, KEVIN C,** Itawamba Comm Coll, Fulton, MS; SO; BA; Baptist Un 89-; BSU Ensmbl 90-; Phi Theta Kappa 89-; Chem; Engr.

**BURK, KRISTEN L,** Methodist Coll, Fayetteville, NC; FR; BA; Psych.

**BURK, RHONDA L,** Owensboro Jr Coll Of Bus, Owensboro, KY; SO; AS; Deans Lst 89; Hon Lst 90-; Cmptrs; Cmptr Off Prfsnl.

**BURKARD, KAREN L,** Saint John Fisher Coll, Rochester, NY; SO; BA; Svisa 90-; Thomas Jefferson Fisher Partnership 90; Judi Weis Awd; Joseph S/Irene C Skalny Schlrshp 90-; Cmmnctns; Mgmt/Educ.

**BURKE, AMY M,** Walker Coll, Jasper, AL; FR; AS; Science; Funeral Sci.

**BURKE, CANDY L,** Univ Of Ky, Lexington, KY; JR; BED; Commuter Stdnt Brd 89-90; Activities Cncl 89-90; Psychology; Teaching.

**BURKE, CHERYL J,** Central Fl Comm Coll, Ocala, FL; SO; MA; Parent Booster Club CHS Pres 89 ; 1st Grd Lvl CCD Cathlc Church Tchr 89-90; Pre Sch Tchr; Spch Lang/Pathlgy; Spch Thrpst In Publc Schls.

**BURKE, CHRISTINA A,** Duquesne Univ, Pittsburgh, PA; SO; BA; Zeta Tau Alpha Rcrdng Sec; Cross Cntry 90; Intl Bsn; Bnkng.

**BURKE, CHRISTOPHER J,** Air Force Inst Of Tech, Wrt-Ptrsn Afb, OH; GD; MS; Sigma Iota Epsilon 89-90; Air Force Assn 89-90; Amer Inst Aeronatics Astrntcs 89-90; USAF Ofcr; MSA Cntrl Mich Univ 88; BS Univ Notre Dame 85; Logistics Mngmnt; Military.

**BURKE, DAVID M,** Villanova Univ, Villanova, PA; SR; BA; Univ Lit Mag 89-; Phlsphy Clb 89-; Univ Radio Sta 87-89; Phi Beta Kappa; Phi Kappa Phi 90-; Phi Sigma Tau 90-; Villanovans Cncrnd Centra Amer Coord 88-90; Stdnt Coalition Agnst Apartheid Racism Sec Treas 89-; Engl; Wrtng/Pblshng.

**BURKE, DIANA,** Marymount Manhattan Coll, New York, NY; SR; BS; Stdnt Dev Comm 87-; Stdnt Govt 89-; Alpha Chi Secr 90-; Law Sch.

**BURKE, ELIZABETH ERINN,** Smith Coll, Northampton, MA; SR; Head Rsdnt Danes House; Crew; Regln/Biblcl Stds; Certfd Midwife.

**BURKE, HEATHER L,** Va Commonwealth Univ, Richmond, VA; FR; BS; Phi Eta Sigma; Bsn; Acctng.

**BURKE, JENNIFER E,** Widener Univ, Chester, PA; SR; BS; Data Proc Mgmnt Assn Pres 90; Phi Sigma Sigma 88-; Spec Olympics Vol 88-; East Side Ministries Hmwrk Clinic Vol 88-; Bsktbl 88; Mgmnt; Mgmnt Info Sys.

**BURKE, JEWELL J,** Va Highlands Comm Coll, Abingdon, VA; BA; Pres Hon Roll 86-87; Phtgrphy Awrd Dstnctn 88; Phtgrphy Peoples Chce 89; Phtgrphy Hon Mntn 89; J Burke Phtgrphy Stdio Ownr; Phtgrphy Cert 88/90; Phtgrphy/Hmn Serv; Expnd Phtgrphy Bus.

**BURKE, LESLIE K,** Univ Of Sc At Columbia, Columbia, SC; SO; BA; Phi Eta Sgm 89; Psi Chi 90-; Psychlgy.

**BURKE, LUKE I,** Coll Of Health Sci Stony Brook, Stony Brook, NY; GD; MD; AMA; KC; Ancient Ord Of Hibernians; Curriculum Comm; Phi Delta Theta; BA Colgate Univ 89; Med.

**BURKE, MARY M,** Broward Comm Coll, Ft Lauderdale, FL; SO; Stdnt Nwspr So Campus Bureau Chf 90-; Phi Theta Kappa; Nwsltr Ed; Grad Hon Inst; Photofinishing; Jrnlsm.

**BURKE, MARY-JO,** Coll Of Notre Dame Of Md, Baltimore, MD; FR; BA; Choir 90-; Campus Mnstry Sec 90-; Comm Serv 90-; Mntrshp Clvrt Co Crthse 90; Psychlgy; Law.

**BURKE, MAUREEN A,** D Youville Coll, Buffalo, NY; SO; Parish Cncl 88-89; CYO Delegate 87-88; Eucharistic Minister 88-; Physical Therapy.

**BURKE, MELISSA A,** Providence Coll, Providence, RI; JR; BA; Hist Clb 88-; Ed Clb 88-; Dski Clb 88-90; Phi Alph Theta Hstrn 90-; Hist; Tchr.

**BURKE, MICHELLE D,** Nova Univ, Ft Lauderdale, FL; GD; MBA; Intrnshp WPBT Chnnl 2 Pblc Rltns Dept 88; AA Miami Dade Comm Clg 87; BA The Union Institute 89; Acctg; Mgmnt.

**BURKE, PEGGY D,** Cumberland Coll, Williamsburg, KY; SO; BS; FRIENDS VP 90-; Stu Trained Ready 90-; Bptst Chrch S S Tchr; Psych; Schl Psychlgst.

**BURKE, RICHARD A,** City Univ Of Ny Queensbrough, New York, NY; FR; BA; Acctg.

**BURKE, SEAN D,** Concordia Coll, Bronxville, NY; FR; BA; Cmps Chrstn Mnstry 90-; Festival Chorus 90; Tour Choir 90; F K Endwmnt Schlrshp; Elks Fnd Mst Vlble Stdnt Schlrshp; Hon Rporg; Pre Sem/Behvrl Sci; Mnstry/Psychology.

**BURKE, SHAWN PATRICK,** Merrimack Coll, North Andover, MA; JR; BS; Accntng/Finance Scty 90-; NAA 90-; Alpha Kappa Psi Serg/Arms 90-; AS Northern Essex Comm Coll 89; Accounting; Federal Law Enforcement.

**BURKE, SONIA A,** Asnuntuck Comm Coll, Enfield, CT; SR.

**BURKE, STEPHEN P,** City Univ Of Ny Queensbrough, New York, NY; FR; BA; Accounting.

**BURKE, SUSAN A,** Bunker Hill Comm Coll, Boston, MA; FR; AS; Pgm Cncl 90-; Psych.

**BURKE, SUSAN K,** Dowling Coll, Oakdale Li, NY; JR; BA; Tutor Engl/Hmnts Wstrn Civ Acad Sprt Cntr 90-; Sigma Tau Delta; Alpha Chi; Engl; Jr High Sch Engl Tchr.

**BURKE, TERESA,** Miami Dade Comm Coll South, Miami, FL; JR; Csmtlgst 82-86; US Air Force 86-90; Mgmnt US Air Force 89; Cmptrs; Cmptr Cnsltnt.

**BURKE, TRACY W,** S U N Y Coll Of A & T Morrisvl, Morrisville, NY; FR; Biology; Vet.

**BURKE, WILLEL D,** Howard Univ, Washington, DC; JR; BARCH; Architecture/Plng 87-; Amer Inst Architects 90-; Wmn In Arch/Plnng 88-90; Architecture.

**BURKE, WILLIAM J B,** Northeast State Tech Comm Coll, Blountville, TN; SO; BBA; SGA Court Judge 90; NATS 89-90; Phi Theta Kappa 90; Dns Lst 88-90; AAS Northeast State Tech Comm Coll 90; Acctng; CPA.

**BURKERT, KIMBERLY A,** Duquesne Univ, Pittsburgh, PA; JR; BA; Psychology; Rsrch.

**BURKET, MICHAEL C,** Indiana Univ Of Pa, Indiana, PA; JR; BED; USAR Spclst 88-; Cmp Cnslr Meth Yth Grp 87-; Asstnt HS Ftbl Coach 90-; Vrsty Ftbl St Francis Clg 89; Educ/Scndry Sci; HS Sci Tchr.

**BURKETT, ALLISON COLLEEN,** Barry Univ, Miami, FL; SO; BSEE; Natl Soc Blk Engrs 90-; Chpl Usher Rankin Chpl Howard Univ 90-; IEEE 90-; Crbbn Stdnts Assoc 90-; Elec Engr.**

**BURKETT, JANICE G,** Univ Of Ga, Athens, GA; SO; BED; Crcl K Dstrct Treas 90-; Alpha Gamma Delta 89-90; Mddl Schl Ed.

**BURKETT, KAREN M,** Christopher Newport Coll, Newport News, VA; SO; BM; Cncrt Music Clb T; Hons Pgm 89-; Music; Cncrt Pianist.

**BURKETT, MATTHEW W,** Univ Of Akron, Akron, OH; SO; BED; ICF 89-; Aces 90-; Phi Eta Sigma 89-; Army Achvmnt Medal 88; Elem Tchr.

**BURKETT, STEPHEN ERNEST,** Univ Of Sc At Columbia, Columbia, SC; JR; BS; Japnese Clb 90-; Gamma Beta Phi 90-; Ltr Cmmndtn US Sbmrne Frce Pcfc Flt 90; Ltr Cmmndtn USS J Monroe 90; PECE 90; Asst Local Elem Schl Comp Lab; US Navy Submarine Force; Acctg; Intl Bus/Mgmt.

**BURKETT, TIMOTHY A,** Longwood Coll, Farmville, VA; FR; BS; IM Activities; Bsn; CPA.

**BURKHALTER, JOSEPHINE A,** Phillips Jr Coll Spartanburg, Spartanburg, SC; GD; Campus Crusade For Christ; Pres List; Deans List.

**BURKHARD, REBECCA F,** Univ Of Ky, Lexington, KY; FR; BA; Pnhllnc Cncl 90; Alpha Lambd Delta 90; Phi Eta Sigma 90; Lambda Sigma 90; Jrnlsm.

**BURKHARD, SHARON,** Christopher Newport Coll, Newport News, VA; SR; BS; Lions Club Schlrshp 86; State Schlrshp 87; Sftbl Cptn 87-90; All Confrnce Plyr 89; Physcl Ed; Tchng.

**BURKHART, BRADLEY D,** Univ Of Ky, Lexington, KY; FR; PHARM; Phi Eta Sigma; Singletary Schlrshp; Hnrs Stdnt; Pharmacy; Pharmacist.

**BURKHART, CYNTHIA M,** Manhattan Coll, Bronx, NY; FR; BA; Psychlgy; Tchr.

**BURKHART, JO ANN L,** Univ Of Cin R Walters Coll, Blue Ash, OH; GD; BA; Alpha Beta Gamma; Fraud Invstgtrs 89-; Bnk Prtctn Sec/Scrty 89-; Acctg/Law; JD Corp Atty.

**BURKHART, JOANNA L,** Fordham Univ, Bronx, NY; FR; BS; Bsn Admn/Acctng.

**BURKHART, LINDA J,** Salem-Teikyo Univ, Salem, WV; JR; BA; Amer Humanic Assoc Comm Chrprn 90-; Stdnt Govt Repr 90-; Comm Acad Stds Hns Stdnt Repr 90-; Inner Grk Cncl Treas 89-90; Gamma Beta Phi 89-; Delta Mu Pres 90-; Salem Teiyko 1niv Acad Schlrshp 88-92; Bsktbl IMS; Yth/Hmn Serv; Spec Educ/Non Teach.

**BURKHART, LORI A,** Mount Aloysius Jr Coll, Cresson, PA; SO; AS; Chldrns Advcry Assn 90-; Early Chldhd Educ; Tchr.

**BURKHART, LORI S,** Tri County Tech Coll, Pendleton, SC; FR.

**BURKHEAD, PHILLIP L,** Univ Of Cincinnati, Cincinnati, OH; JR; BA; Gldn Key; CCM Hnrs Schlrshp 88-; Dino Santangelo Awrd Cum 1000 89; Prsr Schlr Awrd 1500 90-; Cinn Mgzn Awrd; Anl Best/Wrst Cinn Issue; Best Jass Pianist 89; Jass Stuty Mjr; Flm Score Wrtr/Tchr/Prfmr.

**BURKIN, WENDY J,** Columbus Coll Of Art & Design, Columbus, OH; SO; Stdnt Bible Stdy 90-; Advertising.

**BURKS, CHRISTOPHER W,** Va St Univ, Petersburg, VA; FR; BS; Scl Work Cl Secy 90-; NABSW; USN Rsve; USN; Scl Work; Intnl Scl Wrkr.

**BURKS, DANA D,** Voorhees Coll, Denmark, SC; SR; Deans Lst 89-; Soclgy.

**BURKS, DUANE L,** Emory & Henry Coll, Emory, VA; JR; BS; Young Demos 90-; Wasp Radio 90-; Orientation Ldr 89-90; Pi Gamma Mu; Blue Key 90-; Alpha Phi Omega 90-; Intrnshp At Merrill Lynch Invest Fitm; 90; IM 88-; Bus Mgmnt.

**BURKS, EVA M,** Clark Atlanta Univ, Atlanta, GA; SO; BA; Fnnc Clb Treas 90-; NAACP 89-; Hnrs Prog 90-; Delta Sigma Theta; Chrldr 90-; Bus Fnnc; Invstmnt Bnkng.

**BURKS, LESLIE A,** Va Commonwealth Univ, Richmond, VA; SO; BFA; Phi Eta Sigma; Fshn Merch; Txtl Ind.

**BURKS, PAMELA S,** Asbury Theological Sem, Wilmore, KY; GD; MA; Kappa Delta; Yth Christ Lifeline; IMS; Dr Adult Edn; 1st UMC 89; Forest Hills Meth 90; Montezuma UMC; BA Engl Valdosta State Coll 89; Chrstn Edn; Mnstr.

**BURKS, SARA A,** Chattahoochee Vly St Comm Coll, Phenix City, AL; SO; BED; Elem Educ; Tch.

**BURKS, TABITHA R,** Wittenberg Univ, Springfield, OH; FR; BA; Cncrnd Blck Stdnts Org; Bus Mgmt; Dept Store Mgr.

**BURKS, TERRY L,** Fayetteville St Univ, Fayetteville, NC; FR; Comp Sci; Prgrmmr.

**BURKS II, TONY L,** Morehouse Coll, Atlanta, GA; JR; BA; Std Govt Asc; New Std Ornttn Wk Co-Chrmn; Pre Almni Asc 90-; GTE Schlr 89-; Phlsphy; Law.

**BURKS, TYRONE G,** Al A & M Univ, Normal, AL; SR; Symph/Mrchng Bnd; Hnr Rl 87-88; Cmptr Sci; Sys Analyst.

**BURKS, URSULA VICTORIA,** Newbury Coll, Brookline, MA; Perf Arts Dancers Pres 87; VPAHS Mbr Of St Louis Rep 87; Muny Opera Kids Chorus St Louis; 2nd Runner Up For Dance St Louis 87; Stdnt Of Dance Theatre Of Harlem 87-88; Stdnt Of Alvin Ailen Dance Ctr 89; Bus/Acct; Bus Mgt.

**BURKWHAT, ANITA R,** Univ Of Sc At Lancaster, Lancaster, SC; FR; BA; Ele Educ.

**BURLEIGH, RUTH N,** City Univ Of Ny La Guard Coll, Long Island Cty, NY; Intern Am Red Crs Hmls Shltr 89; Intern Assn Hlp Retrd Chldrn Asst Dev Spec 89-90; Grl Sct Asst Ldr 88; Wrkng Mntly Rtrd 89-; AA Lagrd Comm Coll 90; Hmn Svr; Psychlgy.

**BURLESON, JEFFERY W,** Univ Of Al At Birmingham, Birmingham, AL; Emer Med Tech; Fir Fghtr/Paramed.

**BURLESON, MARSHA L,** Mayland Comm Coll, Spruce Pine, NC; FR; AD; Gen Ed; Elem Ed.

**BURLETTE, BRIGETTE M,** Univ Of Southern Ms, Hattiesburg, MS; JR; BFA; Stdnt Alumni Assn 88-89; Assoc Stdnt Body Spirit Cmtee 88-89; Gamma Beta Phi 89-; Delta Gamma Asst Pldg Ed 88-; Intrn Disney MGM Stdes 89; I M 88; Theatre.

**BURLEY, CATRICE A,** Harford Comm Coll, Bel Air, MD; FR; BA; Math; Comp Sci.

**BURLEY, PAGET L,** Rust Coll, Holly Springs, MS; FR; Stdnt Cncl Pres 89-90; Tech Stdnt Assn Pres 89-90; Chrch Yth Grp 85-; Hon Rll 89-; Pres Lst 90-; Spec Hon Rll 90-.

**BURLEY, PAGET L,** Rust Coll, Holly Springs, MS; FR; Tchnlgy Stdnt Assoc Pres 88-90; Votch Stdnt Cncl Pres 89-90; On Wy Clb 89-90; Hnr Rl Stdnt 89-90; Pres Stdnt 90-.

**BURLEY, SUSAN R,** Va Commonwealth Univ, Richmond, VA; SR; BSBA; Bio/Engl; Bio Rsrch.

**BURLINGAME, SUSAN M,** Univ Of North Al, Florence, AL; FR; BA; Civitan; Zeta Tau Alpha 90-; Bnd; Crmnl Jstc; Law/Crmnlgy.

**BURLINGHAUS, TRACEY L,** Kent St Univ Geauga Cmps, Burton Twp, OH; JR; BA; Kappa Omicron Nu Treas; Golden Key; Fam/Indiv Studies; Day Care.

**BURLINGHAUS, TRACEY L,** Kent St Univ Kent Cmps, Kent, OH; JR; BA; Kappa Omicron Nu Treas; Golden Key; Fam/Indiv Studies; Day Care.

**BURMASTER, JOY E,** D Youville Coll, Buffalo, NY; SR; BS; SOTA VP 89-; Deans List 88-; Occuptl Therapy.

**BURNELL, JAMES D,** Wv Univ, Morgantown, WV; FR; BS; Bnd 90; Hnrs Prgm 90; Hlvt Sphmr Hnrry; Deans Lst 90; Prsdntl Awrd 90; Fndtn Schlr; Elec Com Eng.

**BURNER JR, JERRY L,** Fairmont St Coll, Fairmont, WV; SO; BS; Sigma Epsilon Mrshll 90-; WP Blck Schrlshp 89-; Bus; Mgmt.**

**BURNER, KAREN L,** Lexington Comm Coll, Lexington, KY; SO; AAS; Dntl Lab Tech Assc; Dean Lst; Johnsons Wax Son Dau Schlrshp; Dntl Lab Tech.

**BURNER, NANCY M,** Univ Of Nc At Charlotte, Charlotte, NC; SO; BA; BSU 90-; Spnsh; Chld Psychlgst.

**BURNESS, MARGERIE L,** East Tn St Univ, Johnson City, TN; FR; MD; BS Wash St Univ 78; Med; Physcn.

**BURNETT, DERRICK A,** Birmingham Southern Coll, Birmingham, AL; JR; BA; Pres Stdnt Svc Org 90-; Stdnt Jdcry 90-F Resdnc Hsng Assoc 90-F Mortar Bd; Phi Eta Sigma 90; Alpha Lambda Delta 90; Alpha Phi Omega 88; Triangle Club 89-90; Admnstrtv Intrn 90; Bus Admn/Mgt; Law.

**BURNETT, DIANE,** Sue Bennett Coll, London, KY; FR; MBA; Engl; Ed.

**BURNETT, JAMES B,** Univ Of Sc At Spartanburg, Spartanburg, SC; SO; Business; Intrntnl Mrktng.

**BURNETT, JEFFREY R,** Univ Of Ky, Lexington, KY; JR; BS; Amer Soc Cvl Engrs 89-; Chi Epsilon 88-; Outstndng Fr/Yr 87-88; Rfl Team 88-90; Cvl Eng.

**BURNETT, JOHN EDWARD,** Gaston Coll, Dallas, NC; SO; Elctrcl Htng Ac.

**BURNETT, JOHNNIE B,** Wallace St Comm Coll At Selma, Selma, AL; SO; ASSD; Bsbl Tm 89-; Phi Theta Kappa 89-; Sci; Med.

**BURNETT, KIMBERLY A,** Univ Of Montevallo, Montevallo, AL; SR; BA; AAS SUNY Cobleskl 80; Educ; Teach.

**BURNETT, MELISSA DAWN,** Piedmont Tech Coll, Greenwood, SC; FR; AAS; Bsn; Acctng/Mgmt.

**BURNETT, MIGUEL G,** City Univ Of Ny Baruch Coll, New York, NY; SR; BBA; Clb Caricom Pub Rel 90-; Nwspr Cpy Edtr 90-; Goldn Key; Forgn Stdnt Schlrshp; Prvst Schlrshp; IM Soccr Capt; Cmptr Inf Syst; Mgmt Inf Syst.

**BURNETT, PAMELA J,** Meridian Comm Coll, Meridian, MS; SO; BA; Flwshp Of Christn Athlts; Electn Poll For Amercn Govt; Bsktbl/Sftbl; Engl/Hist; Educ.**

**BURNETT, RITA G,** Fayetteville St Univ, Fayetteville, NC; FR; BA; Tchrs Aid Montessori 90-; Educ; Teach.

**BURNETT, STEPHANIA D,** Middle Ga Coll, Cochran, GA; SO; BA; Acdmc Affrs VP 89; Bsn; Finance.**

**BURNETTE, ANGELA F,** Averett Coll, Danville, VA; SO; BS; All Amer Schlr 90-; Tennis 90-; Math.

**BURNETTE, APRIL G,** Central Fl Comm Coll, Ocala, FL; FR; BA; Elem Ed; Tchr.

**BURNETTE, DANEISE C,** Christian Brothers Univ, Memphis, TN; SR; BA; Fed Exp Comm Vol 87-; Fed Exp Corp Pgrm Mgr Sys Tech Prod Dv; Bus Mngmnt.

**BURNETTE, ELAINE G,** Univ Of West Fl, Pensacola, FL; SR; Intrn Tchr 90-; AS Pensacola Jr Coll 85; BA; Elem Educ; Tchr.

**BURNETTE, JASON E,** Western Piedmont Comm Coll, Morganton, NC; FR; AS; Math; Teaching.

**BURNETTE, KATHY D,** Radford Univ, Radford, VA; JR; BBA; Phi Beta Lambda WCC 88-90; AAS Wytheville Commty Clg 90; Busn Admin; Mgts.

**BURNETTE, LAURA A,** Marshall University, Huntington, WV; SR; BA; Elem Educ.

**BURNETTE, TRACY L,** Univ Of Sc At Columbia, Columbia, SC; JR; Coastal Carolina Hnrs Prgrm; Rho Chi Chptr.

**BURNEY, CHERI D,** Dyersburg St Comm Coll, Dyersburg, TN; FR; Crmnl Just; Law.

**BURNHAM, DAVID E,** Birmingham Southern Coll, Birmingham, AL; SR; BA; Alpha Epsilon Delta 90-; Southern Vol Svcs 90-; Philosophy; MD.

**BURNHAM, JOHN G,** Abraham Baldwin Agri Coll, Tifton, GA; SO; BA; Ag; Tchng.

**BURNHAM, JULIE A,** Fl International Univ, Miami, FL; JR; BS; Scuba Clb 90-; Aquacltr Lab Tchncn Dynasty Marine Assn Inc 89-90; Marine Bio.

**BURNHAM, KRISTY R,** Univ Of Southern Ms, Hattiesburg, MS; JR; BSBA; Acctng; CPA.

**BURNHAM, SYLVIA LEIGH,** Univ Of Ga, Athens, GA; SR; BSED; Gldn Key 90-; Kappa Delta Epsilon 90-; Erly Chldhd Ed; Tchng.

**BURNHAM, TONDIA L,** Alcorn St Univ, Lorman, MS; SO; BS; Mrchng Bnd 89-; Wnd Ensmbl 89-; Indstrl Tech Clb Miss Tech 89-; Dean Lst 89-; Waterways Exper Sta 90; Indstrl Tech/CAD; Grphc Artst.

**BURNHOUSE, TONI L,** Westminster Coll, New Wilmingtn, PA; SO; BA; Stdnt Adm Tm 90-; Alpha Gamma Delta 90-; VISA Svc Tm 89-; Trustees Acad Schlrshp 89; IM Soccer; Psych/Rlgn.

**BURNS, ANDREW NELSON,** Univ Of Tn At Knoxville, Knoxville, TN; JR; BS; Stdnt Govt Bdgtng Cmmtt Stdnt Rghts Rspnsblts Comm 90-; Intr Frtnrty Cncl Brd Dir 90; Ordr Omega Treas 90; Phi Eta Sigma 89-; Otstndng Coll Stdnts Amrc 88-; Gldn Key 90; Beta Alpha Psi; Kappa Alpha Prvnc Undrgrdt Chrmn Treas 88-; Exctv Undrgrdt Prgm 88-; Acctg.

**BURNS, ANDROMEDA S,** Clarkson Univ, Potsdam, NY; JR; BS; Clarkson Soc Accntnts 90-; Acctg; CPA Law.

**BURNS, CHANDRICKA R,** Howard Univ, Washington, DC; SR; BSW; Assn Future Socl Wrkrs 89-; Dorm Cncl 87-88; Pi Sigma Delta 91; Dns Hnr Rl 89-; Socl Sci Awd; Socl Wrk; Clin Socl Wrkr.

**BURNS, CHRISTINE A,** Saint Johns Univ, Jamaica, NY; SR; BS; Goldn Key 89-; Kappa Delta Pi; Deans Lst 88-; Elem Ed; Tchr.

**BURNS, CYNTHIA GUNTER,** Univ Of Sc At Spartanburg, Spartanburg, SC; JR; BA; Psychlgy Clb; Gamma Beta Phi; Hosp RN; ASN Grnvl Tech Coll 79; Psychlgy.

**BURNS, D KYLE,** S U N Y Coll Of Tech At Frmgdl, Farmingdale, NY; FR; Rstrnt Mgmt Assoc 90; Intern Plndm Cntry Clb; Rstrnt Mgmt Assoc.

**BURNS, DERICK J,** Rochester Inst Of Tech, Rochester, NY; FR; BA; Graphic Dsgn/Illustrtn.

**BURNS, DONNA M,** Pa St Univ York Cmps, York, PA; FR; BSED; Biol; Educ.

**BURNS, FAITH K,** Tn Temple Univ, Chattanooga, TN; JR; BS; Stdnt Mssn Fllwshp 89-; Vlybl 90-; Bus Clb 90-; Zeta Tau Row 90-; Cert Word Of Life Bible Inst 88; Word Of Life Schl Of Mssns/Evnglsm 89; Admin Mgmnt/Bible; Bus.

**BURNS, HEATHER A,** Springfield Tech Comm Coll, Springfield, MA; SR; AD; SNAP Baystat Med Ctr 90-; Nurs.

**BURNS, HEATHER M,** Villanova Univ, Villanova, PA; FR; Alpha Chi Omega Jr Panhelnc Rep.

**BURNS, HEIDI M,** Kent St Univ Geauga Cmps, Burton Twp, OH; SO; BS ED; AAS EC Ed Univ Of Cincinnati 80; Elem Ed Cncntrtns Math Engl; Tchng.

**BURNS, JAMES K,** Tallahassee Comm Coll, Tallahassee, FL; JR; BA; Opion Editor Campus Nwspr; AA 90; Comm; Media Comm Jrnlsm.

**BURNS, JONATHAN D,** Marshall University, Huntington, WV; FR; MBA; FMA; Natl Collegiate Bus Mrt Awd; Alpha Kappa Psi VP; IM; Alpha Kappa Psi Delg VP; Natl Cnvntn Dnvr Colorado; Natl Mrt Schlr; Bus Admin; Spts Admin.

**BURNS, JULIE M,** Albertus Magnus Coll, New Haven, CT; SO; BA; Spanish Club SG Secy 89-; Community Corner 89-90; Newspaper Wrtr 90-; IM Yoga Wght Trng Arobics Vrsty Sftbl 89-; Intl Business; Political Sci.

**BURNS, LEATHA L,** Wv Univ At Parkersburg, Parkersburg, WV; SO; AS; Mgmt-Bus; Mgmt.

**BURNS, MARCY C,** Valdosta St Coll, Valdosta, GA; SO; BBA; Coop; Alpha Delta Pi 89-90; Mgt; Law.

**BURNS, MARGARET A,** Univ Of Miami, Coral Gables, FL; JR; BBA; Golden Key 90; Bsnss Admin; Mrktng.

**BURNS, MARILYN JEAN,** Va Commonwealth Univ, Richmond, VA; JR; BSN; Undergrad Admsn Policy/Prgrsn Com 90-; Undergrad Curriculum/Evaluation Com 90-; SNA 90-; Vet Admin Valor Pgm Extrnshp; BS Human Serv VA Tech 85; Nrsng; Critical Care Nrsng.

**BURNS, MATTHEW J,** Hudson Valley Comm Coll, Troy, NY; FR; AAS; Ski Clb 90-; Lib Arts; Cmmnctns.

**BURNS, MENDY R,** Spartanburg Methodist Coll, Spartanburg, SC; FR; BA; Crmnl Jstce; Law.

**BURNS, MOLLY J,** Ms St Univ, Miss State, MS; FR; Bulldog Hostess; Hall Cncl 90-; Niv Hnrs Prog 90-; Hnrs Prog Newsletter Staff 90; Delta Delta Delta Actv Chrmn 90-; Compass Club Treas 90-; Genrl Liberal Arts.

**BURNS, RAYMOND W,** Thomas Nelson Comm Coll, Hampton, VA; FR; AS; Eng.

**BURNS, ROXIE ANNA,** Wilberforce Univ, Wilberforce, OH; FR; BA; Rcvd Cargill Schlrshp; Bus; Cmptr Info Systs.

**BURNS, SAMANTHA A,** Johnson St Coll, Johnson, VT; SR; BA; Peace/Justc Club Pres 89-; Dance Club Pres 89-; Vol Clarina Howard Nichols Ctr; Wmns Shltr 2001 Envir Club 90; VPIRG Pres 90-; Stdnt Coord; Abenaki Rsrch Prjct 90; LEAD Stdnt Ldrshp Pgm 90; Dance Ensemble 89; Psych; Envir/Soc Justice Educ.

**BURNS, SCOTT D,** Univ Of Nc At Charlotte, Charlotte, NC; JR; BA; Brunos Inc Gadsden Al 4 Yrs; Srvc Fds Inc Atlanta Ga 82-89; Engl; Wrtng/Advrtsng.

**BURNS, STEPHEN W,** Middle Tn St Univ, Murfreesboro, TN; FR; BA; Hnrs Prgm 90-; Bus.

**BURNS, TAMMY L,** Queens Coll, Charlotte, NC; SO; BA; Communications Club 90-; Admissions Orientation Ldr 90; The Current Staff 89-; Kappa Delta Sorority V Pres Public Reltns 89-90; Belk Ldrshp Schlrshp 89-; Communictions; Broadcasting.

**BURNS, TRACI C,** Radford Univ, Radford, VA; SR; BS; Ntl Educ Assoc 89-; Spice Co Fndr 90-; Career Assoc Clb Chrprsn 90-; Erly Educ.

**BURNS, WENDY R,** Al A & M Univ, Normal, AL; SR; BS; Ben Marcato Clb Pres 89-90; AL Acad Sci 89-; Alpha Kappa Mu 89-; Pres Schlrs 89-; Alpha Kappa Alpha 90-; MARC Minority Access Rsrch Careers 89-; Recip Saul Wilson Schlrshp; Zoology; Vet Med.

**BURPEE, JENNIFER S,** Newbury Coll, Brookline, MA; SR; AS; Peer Actvty Ldr 90; Magna Cum Laude 90-; Alpha Beta Gamma 90-; Outstndng Acctg Awd 90; Acctg; CPA.

**BURR, GEOFFREY W,** S U N Y At Buffalo, Buffalo, NY; SR; PHD; Cvl Sym 89-; Wnd Ens 86-89; Shsmstrs Ski Clb 86-; Eta Kappa Nu Pres 88-; Tau Beta Pi Treas 88-; Phi Eta Sigma 87-; Gldn Key 89-; IEEE 87-; NSPE 88-; Ordr Engr; Alton Zerby Outstdng Std; N R Carson Outstdng Jnr 90; IM Sccr; BS; BA; Elec Engr; Acad.

**BURR, SHERRI L,** Fl St Univ, Tallahassee, FL; SR; BA; Yrbk Asst Edtr 87-89; Amer Soc Intr Dsgnr 90-; Alpha Clb 89-90; Gldn Ky 89-90; Phi Theta Kappa Treas 88-89; Miss Fla Coll Ct 88-89; Stdnt Recrtr 89; AA Fla Coll 89; Fshn Mrchndsng/Fshn Dsgn; Brdl Cnsltnt/Dgnr.

**BURR, SUSAN L,** Univ Of Tn At Martin, Martin, TN; SR; BS; Hrtcltr Clb Treas 88; Bptst Union 87-; Chi Alpha 88-; Amer Home Ec Assn 90-; Phi Eta Sigma 87-; Phi Kappa Phi; Home Ec; Hmn Serv/Cnslng.

**BURR, TRACEY M,** Salem-Teikyo Univ, Salem, WV; FR; MBA; Nurs; Pediatric Nurs.

**BURR, VIVIAN S,** Belmont Coll, Nashville, TN; GD; BM; Church Ldr 87-89; Cum Laude 89; Deans Lst 90; Kappa Kappa Gamma 86-89; Highland Pk Presby Chrch Cnslr 89; BFA 89; Music.

**BURRAGE, THERESA ANN,** Wilberforce Univ, Wilberforce, OH; FR; BA; Gspl Choir Treas 90-; Cmnctns Clb Sec 90-; Engl; Cmnctns.

**BURRELL, CATHERINE R,** Univ Of Nc At Asheville, Asheville, NC; SR; BS; Phi Eta Sigma 88-; Alpha Xi Delta Quill 90; Prce Mcnbb PR Intrnshp; Trsm Dev Athrty Schlrshp 90; Mrktng Mgmt; Phrmctcl Sls Rep.

**BURRELL, KERRY I,** Schenectady County Comm Coll, Schenectady, NY; SO; AS; Dns Lst 90; Eng; Ed.

**BURRELL, KIMBERLYANN,** Newbury Coll, Brookline, MA; SO; AAA; Freelncd Brdl/Evng Wear; Asst Mgr Cashmeres Of Scotland Ritz-Carlton Htl Boston MA; Fshn Dsgn.

**BURRELL, LYNNE M,** Schenectady County Comm Coll, Schenectady, NY; SO; Prsdnts Lst 90; Silver Key 87; Employee Full Tm Trustees Bnk; Accntng.

**BURRELL, ROBBIE N,** Al A & M Univ, Normal, AL; JR; BS; Busn Admin; Busn Mgt.

**BURRELL, ROSIE M,** Al A & M Univ, Normal, AL; JR; BA; Financl Mgmt Assn Treas; Pres Schlr; Finance; Mgmt.

**BURRELL, SONYA J,** Fl A & M Univ, Tallahassee, FL; SO; Hrn Roll; Dns Lst; Poltcl Sci; Corp Law Atty.

**BURRIESCI, BRIGIDA,** City Univ Of Ny Queensbrough, New York, NY; FR; BA; Bus Admnstrn; Acctg.

**BURRIS, DEANNA L,** Allegheny Coll, Meadville, PA; SO; Alleg Stdnt Govt 89-; Chrprsn Wmns Stds Mjr Comm; Rep Acad Affrs Comm 89-; Lambda Sigma V P 90-; Pr Alchl Educ 90-; Stdnt Svc Ldrshp Comm 90-; Aldn Schlr 89-; Pol Sci/Wmns Stds; Law.

**BURRIS, KATINA R,** Johnson C Smith Univ, Charlotte, NC; FR; Sci Clb; NAACP 90-; Panafrcn Cncl 90-; MBRS; Deans Lst 90-; Tutor; Chmstry; Phrmcy.

**BURRIS, LAURA S,** Mercyhurst Coll, Erie, PA; FR; BM; Opera Theatre 90-; Phi Eta Sigma 90-; Music; Voice Perf.

**BURRIS, ROSHUNDA R,** Wilberforce Univ, Wilberforce, OH; SO; Big Str Assn 89; NAACP 90; Sigma Omega 90; Alpha Kappa Alpha; Cargil Schlrshp; Deans Lst 89-90; Bus; Cmptr.

**BURRIS, SHERI L,** Univ Of Nc At Charlotte, Charlotte, NC; FR; BS; Phi Eta Sigma 90-; Chem; Phrmcst.

**BURRIS, STUART C,** Western Ky Univ, Bowling Green, KY; SO; BS; Chem Hnr Soc 90-; Chmstry.

**BURROUGHS, BRENDA P,** Univ Of The Virgin Islands, St Thomas, VI; SR; BA; Cmtrs Clb Pres 90-; Cmptd; Ntbl Clb 88-; Pres Clb Chrprsn Fndrsng; Phi Beta Lambda Prof Dvlpmnt Comm Asst Chrprsn 89-90; Cmtrs Asst Ofc Stu Afrs; Itrnshp Bkstr 90; Tns Tm 90; Bus Admin.

**BURROUGHS JR, JAMES E,** Abraham Baldwin Agri Coll, Tifton, GA; SO; BBA; Stdnt Gvrnmnt Assn Prsdnt 89-; Blck Prrty Clb Prjcts Comm Chrmn 89-; ABAC Ambsdrs VP 90-; Stdnts Stdnts Prsdnt 90-; SGA Frshmn Sntr Yr 90; Dstngshd Ambsdr Awd; ABAC Pcstr Awd; AS; Accntng; Corp Law.

**BURROUGHS, JULIE M,** Snead St Jr Coll, Boaz, AL; SO; BA; Cntrbry Clb; Phi Thetta Kappa; Gntrsvll Swm Tm Assoc; PTA; Elem Ed.

**BURROUGHS, PAULA D,** Christopher Newport Coll, Newport News, VA; GD; MACC; Alpha Chi; Managerial Acctng Awd; Magna Cum Laude; UMC; AAS Rappahannock Comm Clg 87; USAF Cmptr Sys Analyst 76-84; Acctng; Professor.

**BURROUGHS, RONALD W,** Morehouse Coll, Atlanta, GA; FR; Dorm Pres 90-; Hnrs Prog Clb 90-; Hnr Rl 90; Deans Lst 90-; Boeing Aircraft Intrn; Swm Tm 90-; Poli Sci; Law.

**BURROUGHS, SANDRA L,** Asbury Theological Sem, Wilmore, KY; GD; MA; Coll Cls Ofcr; Lit Mag 67-71; SG 67-71; IM 67-71; Wrld Outrch 86-88; Kngdm Conf 87-89; Ichthus Mnstry 86-; Hosp Aux 76-77; Soph Princ Hmcmng 68; Sr Princ Wtr Wkend 71; Tchr Yr 77; Bsktbl All-Str 71; Lay Mnstry Mthdst Chrch 71-86; Pstrl Cnslng; Pstrl Mnstry/Tchng Coll.

**BURROWS, BERNADETTE TANYA,** American Baptist Coll, Nashville, TN; FR; Baptist Student Union; BA; Busn Mgt.

**BURROWS, ELLA M,** Univ Of Sc At Columbia, Columbia, SC; JR; BS; Stdnt Gvrnmnt Assn Sntr; AS Unvrsty SC Union 90; Engnrng Elctrncs.

**BURROWS, LISA A,** Muskingum Coll, New Concord, OH; JR; BS; Sr Hnry; Omicron Delta Kappa 90-; Sigma Alpha Iota Pres 90-; Beta Beta Beta Treas 90-; Sigma Xi; Clement E Dasch Schlr Awd 90-; Crss Cnty Vars 88-89; Bio; Eclgcl Rsrch.

**BURROWS, LISA L,** Casco Bay Coll, Portland, ME; SR; Sr Mntr 90-; Assc Dgree; Sec Sci Cert Trvl And Trsm; Sec.

**BURROWS, NADETTE ATO,** Al A & M Univ, Normal, AL; SR; BS; NASW 90-; Philippine Amer Assn 90-; Intl Wmns Clb 83-84; Socl Wrk.

**BURROWS, TREVOR D,** City Univ Of Ny Grad School, New York, NY; SR; BA; Hudson Lvl Mmrl Schlrshp 90; Phi Beta Sigma Frat Inc 90; Jrnlsm; Pblc Admnstrtn.

**BURRUSS, IRIS A,** Old Dominion Univ, Norfolk, VA; SR; BA; Coll Dmcrts; Alpha Kappa Alpha VP 90; JC Penney Mgmt/Mchdsng Intrn 90; Mst Outstndng Stdnt; Miss Blck VA 89-90; Mktg Ed; Fshn Mchdsng.

**BURRY, MARK S,** Oh Northern Univ, Ada, OH; GD; JD; Book Awd-Lgl Resrch/Wrtg 90; BA Purdue Univ 89; Law; Attny.

**BURRY, SUZANNE M,** Univ Of Sc At Columbia, Columbia, SC; SR; BA; Dns Lst 87-; Bnd Dnc Tm 88-89; Engl; Tchr/Prof.

**BURSACK, KEITH A,** Glassboro St Coll, Glassboro, NJ; SR; Cls Exec Bd Treas 89; Stdnt Fin Contrl Bd 89-90; Cls Exec Bd Secy 90-; Gamma Tau Sigma 90-; Kappa Sigma Pldg Eductr 89-; Willingboro Police Dept Intrn 90; BA; Law/Jstc.

**BURSE, MONTRE C,** Waycross Coll, Waycross, GA; SO; Std Govt Asc 90; Blck Std Allnc Sec 88-; MAP Tutor 88-; Kappa Omcrn Tau 90; Adpt-A-Schl Pgm Tutor; Tlnt Rstr; Bsn; Cmptr Info Mgmt.

**BURSON, ANGELA E,** Savannah Coll Of Art & Design, Savannah, GA; SR; BA; Stdnt Art Shw 88; Pntng.

**BURSON, PAUL J,** Birmingham Southern Coll, Birmingham, AL; SR; BA; Alpha Sigma Lambda 90-; Alpha Kappa Delta 90-; Omicron Delta Kappa 90-; AAS Jefferson St Jr Clg 89; History Sociology; Graduate School.**

**BURST, MELINDA D,** Univ Of Sc At Columbia, Columbia, SC; FR; BS; Phi Eta Sigma; Coastal Hnr Soc 90-; Deans Lst; Pres Lst; Vllybl 90-; Biol/Applied Math; Cardiac/Neuro Surgeon.

**BURSTYNOWICZ, ROBERT J,** Univ Of Pittsburgh, Pittsburgh, PA; FR; BS; Cvl Eng; Eng.

**BURT, LISA M,** Univ Of Pittsburgh At Bradford, Bradford, PA; SO; BS; Biology Clb 90-; Biology/Chem; Biochem Rsrch.

**BURT, LORI,** East Central Comm Coll, Decatur, MS; SO; BA; New Dirts 90-; Phi Theta Kappa 90-; Pres List; Sunday Schl Tchr; Cosmetologists; Ed; Tchng.

**BURT, SUSAN C,** Univ Of Southern Ms, Hattiesburg, MS; SO; BA; Gamma Beta Phi 90-; Deans Lst 89-; Alpha Delta Pi Schlrshp 89-; Engl; Wrtr.

**BURT, VALARIE A,** Villanova Univ, Villanova, PA; SR; BA; Geog Soc 88-; Gamma Theta Usilon Pres 88-; Phi Kappa Phi; Kappa Alpha Theta 89-; Tchng Asst 89; DVGA; Otstndng Stu Awrd; Alexander Von Humbolt Mdlln; Geog; City Rgnl Plnnng.

**BURT-FRONHOFER, CINDY A,** Castleton St Coll, Castleton, VT; SR; BA; AA Adirondack Comm Clge 89; Cmrcl Art; Grphc Art.

**BURTON, BARBARA Y,** Western New England Coll, Springfield, MA; SR; JD; Acctg Clb 90-; Prelaw Soc 89-; Deans Lst 89-; Grad Cum Laude; BSBA; Law Schl; Attrney.

**BURTON, BETH A,** Wv Northern Comm Coll, Wheeling, WV; FR; Phi Theta Kappa; Acad Schlrshp 90-; Acctg; CPA.

**BURTON, CONNIE S,** Union Coll, Barbourville, KY; SR; BS; Acad Policy Com 90-; Gamma Beta Phi State Pres 88-; Iota Sigma Nu 89-; Deans Lst 87-; Pres Lauratet 88-; Acctg/Bus Admin.**

**BURTON, DEBORAH E,** Marshall University, Huntington, WV; SO; BA; Symph Bnd 89-90; Wind Symph 90; Alpha Chi Omega Pldg Cls Pres; Res Advsr 90-; Busn/Acctg.

**BURTON, JANICE D,** Univ Of Montevallo, Montevallo, AL; SR; BS; Phi Kappa Phi; Omicron Delta Kappa 90-; Lambda Sigma Pi 90-; Kappa Delta Pi Secy 89-; Katherine Vickery Awrd; Linly Heflin Schrlshp; Elem Educ; Teaching.

**BURTON, JOAN PEGG,** Univ Of Nc At Charlotte, Charlotte, NC; JR; BA; Gldn Key 90-; Alpha Delta Pi Chpln 90-; Psychlgy.

**BURTON, JOHN T,** S U N Y Coll Of Tech At Alfred, Alfred, NY; Drftng; Drftsmn.

**BURTON, JULIA A,** Univ Of Nc At Charlotte, Charlotte, NC; SO; BA; Crmnl Justc; DEA/FBI.

**BURTON, KIMBERLY P,** Univ Of West Fl, Pensacola, FL; JR; BA; Phi Theta Kappa Penscaola Jr Clg 90; Dns Lst Dept Educ Univ W Fla; Read Acad Hnrs Penscla Jr Clg 89; EASE 89-; Prof Modl N Y Cty Mdlng Agncy 83-85; AA; Spec Educ/Lrng Dis; Educ/Tchg.

**BURTON, LISA M,** Fl A & M Univ, Tallahassee, FL; JR; BA; Cmptr Infrmtn Sys Clb 90-; White Gold; AA FL Comm Coll 89; Cmptr Infrmntn Sys.

**BURTON, LISA R,** Bowie St Univ, Bowie, MD; FR; BS; Mrchng Concrt Band 90-; Busn Admin; Acctg.

**BURTON, LORI M,** Howard Univ, Washington, DC; SO; BA; Stdnt Assn 90-; Microbiology; Medicine.**

**BURTON, LORRAINE,** James Sprunt Comm Coll, Kenansville, NC; FR; AA; Stdnt Of The Mo Of June; Deans List 90-; Kornegays Knights Karate Team 90-; ETTP Coastal Carolina Cmnty Clg 89; Pre Elem Ed; Tchr.

**BURTON, MONICA E,** William Paterson Coll, Wayne, NJ; SR; BA; APA 89-; NAEYC 88-; Psi Chi 90-; Pi Lambda Theta Ntnl Hon/Prfssnl Asso Edctn 91; Mother/2 Boys; Hosp Swtchbd Oper 87-; Early Chldhd/Psychlgy; Tch; Appl Dev Psych.

**BURTON, NATHAN A,** Tn Tech Univ, Cookeville, TN; SO; BS; SGA Treas 90-; Blck Stdnt Org Treas 89-; Stdnt Admsns Rep 90-; Stdnt Orien Ldr 90-; Tenn Intrcoll State Lgsltr Chf Of Stf Elect; Amer Prod/Invntry Cntrl Socty Pres 89-; Alpha Phi Alpha Treas 90-; Prod/Oper Mgmt/Info Systs; Bus/Entrprnr.**

**BURTON III, ROBERT L,** Al A & M Univ, Normal, AL; JR; BA; US Postal Wkrs Un; Psychlgy; Juvenile Law Enfrcmnt.

**BURTON, SCOTT J,** Manhattan Coll, Bronx, NY; SR; BS; IM Bsktbl/Sftbl Lacrosse 88-; Tau Beta Pi 90-; Epsilon Sigma Pi 90-; Chi Epsilon Treas 90-; ASCE; Tutor 89-90; Cvl Engr; MS Envrmntl Engr.

**BURTON, SUSAN C,** Univ Of Al At Birmingham, Birmingham, AL; JR; ELE; Kappa Delta Pi 90-; Elem Edn; Tchr.

**BURTON, SUZANNA K,** Va Commonwealth Univ, Richmond, VA; SR; Am Crrtnl Assn 90-; Ntl Assn Extrdtn Ofcls 87-90; Outstndg Svc Awd Frfx Co Polc Dept 90; BS 90; Adm Jstce; Adlt Crrctns.

**BURTON, VICTORIA J,** Oh Dominican Coll, Columbus, OH; JR; BA; Hmstd Wms Glf Lg 90-; Outstndg Stdnt 89; 6 4.0 Cert 89; AS Bliss Clge 89; Bsn/Fshn.

**BURTON III, WILLIAM H,** Oh St Univ, Columbus, OH; FR; BSEE; Natl Soc Prof Engrs; Engr Co-Op Prog; Hons Prog 90-; Stadium Schlrshp Dorm 90-; Boy Scoutng Asst Sctmstr 90-; TSA Alumni Mbr 90-; Elec Engr; Comp.

**BURTON, WILMA B,** Fayetteville St Univ, Fayetteville, NC; GD; BA; Alpha Kappa Mu 89-; Delta Mu Delta; Natl Stdnt Bus Lg 90-; Deans Lst 89; Chncllrs Lst 90-; Jms Llv Schlrshp 89-90; NETWORTH Schlrshp 90; Gdyr Schlrshp; AAS; Bus Admn Mgmt.

**BURTON-THEUS, WANDA R,** Union Univ, Jackson, TN; JR; BS; SGA V P 89-; Phi Theta Kappa Hstrn 89-90; AS Jackson St Comm Coll 90; Acctng Bus.

**BURTRAM, SHANNON M,** Univ Of Al At Birmingham, Birmingham, AL; JR; BS; UAB Sch Eng Peer Advsr 88-90; Amer Scty Mech Eng Sec 88-90; Alph Omcrn Pi 90-; UAB Hon Schlrshp 88-; Mech Eng; Eng.

**BURWELL, VINCENT O NEAL,** Central Al Comm Coll, Alexander City, AL; GD; Math/Hstry; Elec Eng.

**BUSBY, DAVID W,** Ms St Univ, Miss State, MS; SR; Fin Mgt Assoc 89-90; Deans List Schlr 89-90; IM Sports 87; BBA 90; Bnkng/Finance.

**BUSBY, JOAN P,** West Liberty St Coll, West Liberty, WV; SO; BS; Assoc RN WUNCC 81; Bus/Mktg.

**BUSBY, KELVIN L,** Denmark Tech Coll, Denmark, SC; SO; ASSOC; Elec Eng.

**BUSBY, PAUL L,** Univ Of Tn At Martin, Martin, TN; SR; BA; Intl Stu Assn Lcl Cnsltnt 87; Psi Chi; Sigma Phi Epsilon Lambuth Coll Soc Chrmn 87; Psych Sclgy; Clncl Psych.

**BUSCEMI, VINCENT J N,** Niagara Univ, Niagara Univ, NY; FR; BS; Pltcl Sci Frm 90-; Phi Alpha Delta 90-; Stdnt Advsry Cncl 90-; Stdnt Offc Asstnt 90-; Pltcl Sci; Law.

**BUSCH, DONALD A,** Bapt Bible Coll & Seminary, Clarks Summit, PA; GD; MDIV; Prfsnl Engr; Chem Engr 84-90; BS Rensselaer Polytech Inst 84; Chrstn Mnstry; Urban Missions.

**BUSCH, MARY ANN,** Wagner Coll, Staten Island, NY; JR; BA; Music Soc 88-; Nwspr 89; Guitar/Flt Ensmbl 88-; Omicron Delta Kappa; Deans Lst; Spnsh Folk Mass Gtrst; Msc; Educ.

**BUSH, BERNARD D,** Glassboro St Coll, Glassboro, NJ; SR; BA; Pub Rel Stdnt Soc Of Amer 89-; Radio Sta Educ Dir 85-86; Camden Co Clg Stdnt Gov Judcl Brd Mbr 86-87; USMC Res Corp Wire Chf 83-87; Comm/Publ Rel; Law.

**BUSH, CAROLYN J,** Bryant Stratton Bus Inst Roch, Rochester, NY; AAS; Tbl Tnns Clb Pres 87-90; Park Table Tnns Lge Sec/Stats 87-90; Swtchbrd/Tlphn Coord 78-; Expdtng Crlk Rchstr Button 64-68; Bsn Mgmt/Acctng; Comm Mgmt.

**BUSH, CHANTEL E,** Elms Coll, Chicopee, MA; JR; BA; Z Club 89-; Prac Robert Ash CPA/CHICOPEE MA 91; Acctng/Busn Mgt; CPA.

**BUSH, DENESE N,** West Liberty St Coll, West Liberty, WV; SR; MBA; Delta Mu Delta 90; Alpha Kappa Psi 90-; US Achvmnt Acad All Amer Schlr; Asstshp At WVU Fr MBA; MS 90; Bus.

**BUSH, JEFFREY L,** Western Carolina Univ, Cullowhee, NC; JR; BA; Res Asst Wm B Harrill; Res Hall; Acctg/Phlsphy.**

**BUSH, JEFFREY W A,** Centenary Coll, Hackettstown, NJ; SO; BA; Psychlgy Clb; Chem Stdnt Instr; Psychlgy Tutor; Pres Lst 90-; Am Psychlgcl Assn; Coll Mntrshp Recpt 90-; Pres Schlrshp Recpt; Heath Awd Otstndg Achvmnt Chem 90; Psychlgy/Engl/Math; Prfrshp.

**BUSH, JENNIFER L,** Providence Coll, Providence, RI; SO; BA; P C Corp; Pastoral Cncl Scl Action Comm 89-; Vars Tennis 89-; Engl; Law.

**BUSH III, JOHN I,** Univ Of Sc At Columbia, Columbia, SC; JR; BS; Gamma Beta Phi 90; Sprts Admn; Clg Athletics.

**BUSH, JOYA M,** American Baptist Coll, Nashville, TN; FR; BA; Class Tr 90-; Inst Healng Racism; Bapt Stdnt Un; Highst Gpa 90-; Natl Hook Up Blck Womn Inc; Assn Comm Org Refrm Now 90-; Biblcl Stds/Theo/Soc; Mnstr/Tchr/Wrtr.

**BUSH, JUDITH G,** Va Commonwealth Univ, Richmond, VA; GD; BS; Phi Beta Kappa 68; NCTM VEA GRCTM 89-; BA Randolph Macon Wmns Clg 68; MS Un VA 70; Math; Tchr Educ.

**BUSH, JULIE M,** Univ Of Akron, Akron, OH; SO; BS; Muscl Entrtnmnt Music Comedy 89-; Mjr Evnts Res Hl Prog Bd 90-; Publ RHC Comms Spec Featrs 90-; Delta Sigma Pi; Educ Fndtns Sml Grp Ldr 90-; IM Sftbl; Sec Educ; Educ/Spnsh/Pol Sci.

**BUSH, KENDRA D,** Concordia Coll, Selma, AL; SO; BA; Red Cross Sec 89-; Ethnic Cnslng; Nwspr Ed Chief 89-; NAACP; High Hon Grad; Engl Edn; Profsr.

**BUSH, KEVIN D,** Alcorn St Univ, Lorman, MS; SO; BA; Mrchng Brvs Bnd; Wnd Ensmbl Sctn Ldr; Cmmnctns; Cmmrcl Art.

**BUSH, MELISSA M,** Hamilton Coll, Clinton, NY; FR; BA; Science Library; Math; Engineering/Medicine.

**BUSH, NYJA N,** Georgetown Univ, Washington, DC; JR; BS; Mktng Soc; Mktng Comm; Vars Sccr; Deans Lst; Second Hnrs; Mktng/Intl Mgmnt.

**BUSH, REGINA,** Clark Atlanta Univ, Atlanta, GA; JR; Kappa Delta Epsilon Co Chair Mbrshp 90-; Deans Lst 89-; Early Chldhd Educ; Teacher.

**BUSH, ROBERT D,** Univ Of Ky, Lexington, KY; SO; BS; Phi Eta Sigma 90-; Sigma Alpha Epsilon Rush Chrmn 89-; Deans Lst 90-; 27 Bsktbl/Ftbl/Rcqtbl 89-; Bio; Optmtry.

**BUSH JR, ROY Z,** Vance Granville Comm Coll, Henderson, NC; SO; AAS; SG Parlmtrn 89-90; Phi Theta Kappa 90-; Stdnt/Mo 90; Deans List 89-; Elctrnc Dept Advsy Cmte; Cert Wake Tech Comm Colg 82; Elctrnc Engrng; Techcn.

**BUSH, SHANNON D,** Fl St Univ, Tallahassee, FL; SR; BS; Gldn Key; Phi Beta Phi; Intrnshp Video Prdctn Hse; AA 89; Media Prdctn Cmmnctn; Flmkng.

**BUSH, SHERITA D,** Univ Of Al At Birmingham, Birmingham, AL; SO.

**BUSHEY III, GEORGE J,** Hudson Valley Comm Coll, Troy, NY; FR; Ski Clb 89-; Outing Clb Pres 89-; Stdnt Senate 90-; Phi Theta Kappa 90-; Peer Tutor 89-; Chem; Engr.

**BUSHEY, JENNIFER LYNN,** Nova Univ, Ft Lauderdale, FL; GD; MIBA; Hons Prog 84-88; Omicron Delta Epsilon 85-88; Circle K; WCCP 89-; Lcnsd All Lines Adjstr 89-; Claims Adjstr Liberty Mutual Ins 89-; BA Eckerd Clg 88; Intl Bus; Intl Law.

**BUSHEY, LISA M,** Mount Saint Mary Coll, Newburgh, NY; SO; BSN; Bacchus Pres 90-; Nrsng Stndt Un Secy 90-; SGA Cls VP; Ambasdr Club 90-; Spcl Olympcs Training Club 89-; New Britain Mem Hosp Vol; Nrsng.

**BUSHNELL, HOLLY J,** Livingston Univ, Livingston, AL; JR; BA; Athltc Clb; Tnns Tm 2nd Sd 90-; AA AS Jefferson Davis State Jr Coll 90; Acctng; CPA.

**BUSHTA, JOHN F,** Oh Coll Of Podiatric Med, Cleveland, OH; JR; DPM; Ohio Pdtrc Med Stdts Assoc Treas 89-; Sports Med Clb 88-; Amer Coll Foot Srgns 90-; Deans List 89-; AS Keystone Jr Coll 86; BS Marywood Coll 88; Podiatry.

**BUSKEL, CARI L,** Memphis St Univ, Memphis, TN; FR; BSEE; Bnd 90-; Peer Mntr Pgm 90-; Gamma Beta Phi; Kappa Kappa Psi 90-; Smmr Intrnshp GE Med Sys; Elec Eng.

**BUSKIRK, JAMES A,** Thomas Nelson Comm Coll, Hampton, VA; FR; BS; Slng Clb; YMCA Swmng Instr 79-; Red Crs 79-; Aquatics Dir; Aquatics Cluster Coord 85-; Engr.

**BUSKO, JOHN F,** Univ Of Akron, Akron, OH; SO; BS; Vol Frfghtr 85-; Welder 75-90; ASME Cert 79-; Welding Dpt Frmn Mach Mfg 86-90; Mech Engr; Design.

**BUSS, MICHAEL E,** Univ Of Sc At Columbia, Columbia, SC; JR; BA; Hstry; Archlgy.

**BUSS, SUSAN M,** Academy Of The New Church, Bryn Athyn, PA; JR.

**BUSSARD, RYAN W,** Oh St Univ, Columbus, OH; SO; BS; Am Ins/Arch Stdnt 89-; Oh St Hon 89-; IM Sftbl/Ftbl 90-; Archtctre.

**BUSSEY, CHRISTOPHER B,** East Tn St Univ, Johnson City, TN; FR; BS; Athletic Trnrs Clb 90; Alpha Lambda Delta 90; Phy Ed/Athletic Trng; Athletic Trnr.

**BUSSJAGER, REBECCA J,** Univ Of Rochester, Rochester, NY; GD; MS; D Lion Organ 87-; Deans List 88-; Stdt Union Stdt Mngr 88-; IM Soccer/Vlybl 86-; Leuremie Scty; Photonics; BS Univ Roch 90; Optics; Engineering.

**BUSTELO, ILEANA E,** Miami Dade Comm Coll North, Miami, FL; SO; BA; Vllybl Tm 89-90; Clncl Psychology; Mntl Hlth.

**BUSTER, ASHLEY T,** Univ Of Sc At Columbia, Columbia, SC; SO; Phys Ther.

**BUSTER JR, TONY M,** Univ Of Southern Ms, Hattiesburg, MS; SR; BS; AA Jones Cty Jr Coll 89; Blgcl Sci; Pollution Cntrl.

**BUSTILLO HERNANDEZ, MARTA M,** Univ Of South Fl, Tampa, FL; GD; MSPH; Pub Hlth Stdnts Assn; Latin Amer Stud Assn; Wmns Intrntl Pub Hlth Ntwk; MALAS Univ Flor 89; BA Univ Puerto Rico 85; Pub Hlth; Rsrch/Tchng/Hlth Pgrms Eval.

**BUSTIN, LISA L,** Univ Of Southern Ms, Hattiesburg, MS; FR; Stdnt Alumni Assn; Alpha Lambda Delta; Lambda Sigma; Schlrshp Tennis.

**BUSTIN, TINA R,** Univ Of Southern Ms, Hattiesburg, MS; FR; BS; Stdnt Alumni Assn 90-; Alpha Lambda Delta/Phi Eta Sigma 90-; Tnns Tm 90-; Optmtry.

**BUSTOS, GREGORIO F,** Saint Andrews Presbytrn Coll, Laurinburg, NC; JR; BA; Wrld Cltr Soc V P 90; Busn Clb 89-; Chess Clb Tr 90-; Alpha Chi; Hnr Soc; Amer Intercltrl Stdnt Exch 88; Dns Lst 90-; Natl Coll Busn Mert Awd 90; Soccr Vrsty 89-; Econ; Intl Busn.

**BUSWELL, RANDAL C,** Me Maritime Academy, Castine, ME; JR; BS; Rugby 89-90; Marine Engr.

**BUTAS, SUSAN M,** Univ Of Akron, Akron, OH; JR; BSN; Phi Eta Sigma 89; Nrsng.

**BUTCHARD, WILLIAM A,** Central Fl Comm Coll, Ocala, FL; SO; BA; Philosophy; Tchng Philosoph.

**BUTCHER, CINDY J,** Wv Univ At Parkersburg, Parkersburg, WV; SO; BED; Elem Ed; Tchg.

**BUTCHER, DIONNE R,** City Univ Of Ny Bronx Comm Col, Bronx, NY; SR; AAS; Phi Theta Kappa Treas 89-; AAS Bronx Comm Clg; Acctg; CPA.

**BUTCHER, JANET L,** Liberty Univ, Lynchburg, VA; SR; BS; Stdnt Nrs Assoc 89-; 1st Bptst Chrch Prmry Dept 88; AA Hyles Anderson Coll 86; Nrsng.

**BUTCHER, JEAN M,** S U N Y Coll Of Tech At Frmgdl, Farmingdale, NY; JR; Early Chldhd Club 89-; SUNY Farmingdale, Anchor Camp For Handcpd Adlts/Chldrn Lfgrd 89-; Restrnt Mgt 87-89; Spcl Ed; Tchng.

**BUTCHER, JOHNNY C,** Univ Of Va Clinch Valley Coll, Wise, VA; SR; Amer Psy Soc 90-; Phi Theta Kappa 88-; Disabled Coal Miner; Psy; Rehab Cnslr.

**BUTCHER, LU ANNE,** Middle Tn St Univ, Murfreesboro, TN; FR; NHS; US Govt Dept Commerce; Pre Law; Law.

**BUTENAS, MARK W,** Merrimack Coll, North Andover, MA; JR; BA; Intr Bsktbl; Bsns; Accnt.

**BUTERA, JOANN R,** City Univ Of Ny Baruch Coll, New York, NY; JR; BA; Acctg Soc 90-; Beta Gamma Sigma; Gldn Key 90-; Deans Lst 89-; Provost Schlrshp 90-; Acctncy; CPA.

**BUTKA, ROBERTA L,** Barry Univ, Miami, FL; JR; BS; Accounting Assoc 88-; Assoc Cmptng Mach 89-; FACE; Honors Assoc 88-; US Dept Energy/Science/Engineering Argonne Ntl Lab; Computer Science/Math; Educ/Research.

**BUTKUS, MARY ANN B,** Teikyo Post Univ, Waterbury, CT; SR; BS; CPA Intern 88-; AS Mattaluck Commty Clg 72; AS Mattatuck Cummty Clg 86; Acctng; CPA.

**BUTLER, ADALGISA,** Western Piedmont Comm Coll, Morganton, NC; FR; BED; Phi Theta Kappa; Spanish.

**BUTLER, ALISON S,** Univ Of Southern Ms, Hattiesburg, MS; SR; BS; Chld Lf Vol; Hm Econ Clb; Pi Beta Phi Censr 90-; Dns Lst; Dns Lst Awd Amng Grks; Fmly Rel Emph Chldlf; Chldlf Spec.

**BUTLER, ANGEL L,** Piedmont Tech Coll, Greenwood, SC; SR; AAS; Stdnt Govt 90-; Publ Serv Clb 89-; Phi Theta Kappa Sec 90-; Psi Beta Sec 89-90; M Underwd Serv Awd Schlrshp 90; Two Intrnshps Dept Yth Svcs 90-; Marshal Tech Clg Grad 90; Crim Just; Cnslr.

**BUTLER, AUDREY J,** Ms St Univ, Miss State, MS; JR; BS; Microbio; Rsrch/Hlth.

**BUTLER, BLAIR A,** Edinboro Univ Of Pa, Edinboro, PA; SO; BA; Physics/Engrng; Phi Eta Sigma 89-90; Physics; Eng.

**BUTLER, CAROLE D,** Bethel Coll, Mckenzie, TN; SO; BS; Stu Govt Rep 90-; TN Educ Assn Treas 90-; Chrstn Iss Orgnztn Treas 90-; Diakonoi; Tnns Tm 89-; Elem Educ; Tchng.

**BUTLER, CAROLYN J,** Middle Tn St Univ, Murfreesboro, TN; SO; BA; SID 90-; Gamma Beta Phi 89-; Chattanooga Area Home Ec Schlrshp; Elther/Caver Smith Schlrshp; Int Design.

**BUTLER, CHRISTOPHER S,** Wv Univ, Morgantown, WV; SO; BS; Bapt Campus Ministeries 90-; City Recreational Assoc; Civil Engrg.

**BUTLER, DEANNA L,** Middle Tn St Univ, Murfreesboro, TN; JR; STEA 88-; Gamma Beta Phi 90-; AAS; Elem Ed; Tchr.

**BUTLER, DEIDRA D,** Washington State Comm Coll, Marietta, OH; FR; AAB; Phi Theta Kappa 90-; AAB 85; Cert 85; Mcrcmptr Appl Tech.

**BUTLER, DEIDREA F,** Jackson St Univ, Jackson, MS; SO; BA; Acctg Soc 90-; WEB Du Bois Hons Clg 89-; Alpha Lambda Delta Miss ALD 90-; Yng Wtnss Chrst Chrch Affltd; Smmr Intrn Bkkpr; Acctg; Publ Acctg/Corp Law.**

**BUTLER JR, DONALD J,** Univ Of Sc At Columbia, Columbia, SC; JR; BA; Southern Bell 87-; Hist; Study In Eng/Grad Sch.

**BUTLER, EARL D,** City Univ Of Ny Baruch Coll, New York, NY; SR; BBA; Frgn Trd Scty Tres 88-; Fin/Ec Scty 90-; Untd Mlysn Stdnt Assc 88-89; Dlt Nu Alph Trnsp Frat 88-; USA Achvmnt 86 Gd Cndct Mdl 86 Ar Asslt Bdg 85; USA 101st Ar Aslt Div 84-86; Intrntl Mktg/Fin; Intrntl Bus.**

**BUTLER, HANNAH C,** James Madison University, Harrisonburg, VA; SR; BA; Univ Chorus 88-; Engl/Psychlgy.

**BUTLER, JACQUELINE VERNEDA,** Atlantic Comm Coll, Mays Landing, NJ; SO; Pre-Law; Law.

**BUTLER, JANE C,** Winthrop Coll, Rock Hill, SC; JR; BA; Boy Scouts Ldr 87-; Kappa Mu Epsilon; Kappa Delta Pi; Sears 69-90; Math; Scndry Educ.

**BUTLER, JOANN P,** Ms Valley St Univ, Itta Bena, MS; GD; BS; Chm Wmn Clb; Univ Hnr Scty; Prsdnt Schlr 90; Cmmnty Srvc Vol; Yth Grp Spnsr; Sec Elem Schl 82-85; Lbrrn Asst Mddl Schl 86-; Elem Ed; Tchr.

**BUTLER, KRISTIN KAY,** Belmont Coll, Nashville, TN; SR; BM; Mscl Theatre 88-90; Sgm Alph Iota Pres 88-; Pres Forum 89-90; Intrnshp Amrcn Fedrtn TV Radio Artists 90-91; Cmrcl Msc; Vocal Prfrmnc.

**BUTLER JR, LANDO,** Itawamba Comm Coll, Fulton, MS; JR; BA; Dns Lst 90; IM Sftbl; Psych; Cnslg.

**BUTLER, LAURA R,** Winthrop Coll, Rock Hill, SC; FR; BME; RUF 90-; MENC 90-; Delta Omicron; Hnrs Alumni Schlrshp 90-; Music; Teacher.

**BUTLER, LAURA S,** Stillman Coll, Tuscaloosa, AL; SR; BA; Chrldr Cpt 87-; Sprts Rprtr Ed 89-; Brdcstg 90-; Delta Sigma Theta 90-; All Amer Schlr Awd; Trck/Fld; Cmnctns; Radio Sls.

**BUTLER, LESLIE A,** Univ Of Rochester, Rochester, NY; SR; BA; Phi Beta Kappa; Stdnt Mngmnt; Hist.

**BUTLER, MARY JO,** Bryant Stratton Bus Inst Roch, Rochester, NY; GD; AOS; Stdnt Cncl; Trvl Clb Pr; Dns Lst 89-; Untd Way 90-; Exec Sec/Word Proc.

**BUTLER, MELINDA E,** Salisbury St Univ, Salisbury, MD; SR; BS; Alpha Omega 90; Beta Beta Beta 90-; Phi Eta Sigma 87-; MD Dist Schlr 87-; Pres Awrd 87-; Richard A Henson Schlr 89-; Bio; Med.

**BUTLER, MICHAEL A,** St Tech Inst At Memphis, Memphis, TN; FR.

**BUTLER, NADINE M,** Univ Of Sc At Columbia, Columbia, SC; SO; BS; SGA 90; Mgmt/Org Clb 90; Blgy Clb 90; Phi Eta Sigma 90; Intergreek Cncl 90; Sigma Xi Chi Fndng Pres 90; Chnclrs Intern 90; Hnrs Coll 90-; Pres Hnr Lst 89-90; Blgy/Marine Blgy.

**BUTLER, REBECCA A,** Hillsborough Comm Coll, Tampa, FL; SO; AA; Chrldng Capt 89-; Stdnt Govt; Athltc Awrd Outstndng Ldrshp Chrldng 90-; Intr Dsgn.

**BUTLER, ROBERT M,** Univ Of Miami, Coral Gables, FL; SR; BSC; Gldn Ky 90-; Pi Mu Epsilon 88-; Provosts Hnr 89-; Cmptr Sci/Math; Cmptr Sci.

**BUTLER, ROBIN D,** Univ Of Southern Ms, Hattiesburg, MS; GD; BS; Neonatal ICU/WELLBORN Nsy Nurse 84-; Nursing; MSN.

**BUTLER, ROBIN L,** Oh St Univ At Newark, Newark, OH; JR; BS; Wmns Sprt Grp 89-; Hon Cmt 90-; Hon Tres 89-; Gldn Key 90-; Hon Schlrshp; Dvlpmnt Educ Tutrng Pgm; Rsrch Asstntshp 89-; Psychlgy; Lgl Psychlgy.**

**BUTLER, SHARON M,** Longwood Coll, Farmville, VA; SO; BA; Frnscs Tm Mgr 89-; Hnr Brd 90-; Alpha Lambda Delta 90-; Alpha Phi Omega 90-; Peer Advsr 90-; Emrgng Ldr Awd 89-90; Ed; Tchg.

**BUTLER, SHAWN M,** S U N Y Coll Of Tech At Alfred, Alfred, NY; SR; BA; Cncrt Chr 90; AS; Erly Chldhd Educ; Erly Chldhd Tchr.

**BUTLER, SHERINA M,** Va St Univ, Petersburg, VA; JR; MBA; Bus Info Sys; Cmptr Analyst.

**BUTLER, SHOBHNA D,** Memphis St Univ, Memphis, TN; SR; PHARM; Sigma Kappa Si 86-87; Phrmcy.

**BUTLER, STACY A,** Glassboro St Coll, Glassboro, NJ; JR; BA; Geog Clb 90-; Hnr Soc 89-; Intern Del Vlly Reg Plnng Cmmssn; Geog/Hnrs; City Rgnl Plnng.

**BUTLER, STEVEN R,** Tn Temple Univ, Chattanooga, TN; SR; R A Torry Soc; Deans List; Chrstn Svc 87-91; Soc Sports; Charc Help; Scndry Ed; Math; Math Tchr H S.

**BUTLER, SUSAN L,** Ga St Univ, Atlanta, GA; SR; BS; Mddl Chld Educ; Tch/Psychlgst.

**BUTLER, THOMAS J,** Piedmont Tech Coll, Greenwood, SC; FR; AA; Acdmc Advntg 90-; Phi Theta Kappa 90-; Phi Theta Lambda; Ambss PTC; Ed Resrc Schlrshp; Nrcts Anyms Rep 89-; Comp Tech; Prgmr.

**BUTLER, THOMAS M,** Western New England Coll, Springfield, MA; SO; Acct; CPA.

**BUTLER, TRACI D,** Union Univ School Of Nursing, Memphis, TN; FR; BSN; Stu Chrstn Assc; Nrsng.

**BUTLER, YOLANDA J,** Jackson St Univ, Jackson, MS; FR; BS; Bapt Stdnt Un 90-; Campus Crusade For Christ 90-; Alpha Lambda Delta Edtr 90-; NAACP 90-; Acdmc Schlrshp; Deans Lst; WEBD Du Bois Hnrs Clg; Mass Communications; Cmmnctns Law.

**BUTLER, ZACK J,** Alfred Univ, Alfred, NY; FR; BS; Vrsty Ski Tm; Elec Engr.

**BUTLER-LUCKING, MICHELE M,** Memphis St Univ, Memphis, TN; SR; BA; ASCE 90-; Civil Engrg.

**BUTNER, JULIE E,** High Point Coll, High Point, NC; SO; BA; Ed; Tchr.**

**BUTOROVICH, PETER A,** S U N Y Coll At Fredonia, Fredonia, NY; JR; AS Jamestown Cmmnty Clg 90; Cmptr Sci; Syst Anlysis/Sftwre Dsgn.

**BUTT, FAUZIA K,** Ma Inst Of Tech, Cambridge, MA; SO; SB; Pre-Med Scty 90; Paksmit 89; Drm Big Sis 90; Bio; Med.**

**BUTTACAVOLI, PAUL V,** Villanova Univ, Villanova, PA; SO; BA; Cmps Mnstry 90-; Hall Cncl Env Ofcr 90-; RA; Phi Kappa Phi; Fncl Aid Ofc Wrk/Stdy 89-; Psycholgy.

**BUTTARO, MARISSA L,** Philadelphia Coll Pharm & Sci, Philadelphia, PA; SR; Stdnt Nwspr APA 87-; Newman Clb 87-; Drama Clb; Alpha Lambda Delta 87-; Rho Chi 90-; Lambda Kappa Sigma Rcrdng S 87-; Wrtng Cntr Peer Tutr; Ntl Pharm Cncl Intrnshp; Chem Asst; Aerbcs Grp; Pharm; Dr Pharm.

**BUTTER VENDRELL, DORIS E,** Inter Amer Univ Pr San German, San German, PR; SR; BA; Orttn Pres 87-89; Stdnt Cncl UIA De Aguedilas Pres 89-90; Rsrch Cntr Aide 90-; Prsbytrn Yth Cmmtt Pres 84-87.

**BUTTERFIELD, O RENEE,** Bunker Hill Comm Coll, Boston, MA; FR; ASSC; BSSC Cert Hgh Sch; Med Radgrphy; Technlgst King Edward Hosp.

**BUTTERI, TRACY A,** Comm Coll Algny Co Algny Cmps, Pittsburgh, PA; GD; Court Rprtrs Org VP 90-; Deans Lst 89-; Cert Achvmnt; Assoc; Court Rprtng.

**BUTTERKLEE, NEIL H,** Ny Law School, New York, NY; GD; JD; Delta Mu Delta 87; Phi Alpha Delta 88-; Law Rev Edtr 90-; Con Edisons Mngmnt Awrd 90; Amer Jurisprdnc Awrd; Natl Rank; Brd Of Dir/United States Fencing Assoc 79-87; Sr Forecast Analyst Con Edison 89-; Forestal Analagy Con Ed 83-89; Law.

**BUTTERMAN, MARIETTE D,** Atlantic Comm Coll, Mays Landing, NJ; SO; BA; Literative French; College Professor.

**BUTTERWORTH, ANNETTE,** O'more School Of Design, Franklin, TN; FR; BA; OFMA Treas; SGA Exec Comm Liaison; SEC Crtfd; NASD 88-90; NSDA Com Chr 88-90; Scrts Ind 81-90; Fshn Mrchndsng/Dsgn.

**BUTTERWORTH, JENNIFER L,** Univ Of Nc At Asheville, Asheville, NC; FR; BS; Intrntl Stdnt Assn 90-; U Hons Pgm 90-; Bio; Gntc Rsrch.

**BUTTERWORTH, KAREN L,** Bay Path Coll, Longmeadow, MA; FR; BA; Glee Clb 90; Intrnatl Frnds Clb; Intrnatl Ordr Or Rnbw For Grls 85-; Prlgl Stds; Law.

**BUTTERWORTH, MELANIE L,** Slippery Rock Univ, Slippery Rock, PA; GD; MA; Un Pgm Brd 87-89; Hl Cncl 86-90; Spnsh Clb Sec 87-89; Phi Eta Sigma 86-88; Phi Eta Sigma 86-88; Sigma Sigma Kappa 89-90; Sigma Delta Pi Sec 88-90; Untd Cerbrl Plsy Swm Pgm 88-89; Spec Oly 87-88; Yth Dev Ctr Vol 87-88; BSW 90; Stdnt Persnl.

**BUTTERY, BELINDA L,** Union Coll, Barbourville, KY; FR; BA; Psychlgy; Psychtry.

**BUTTON, KEITH A,** Elmira Coll, Elmira, NY; SO; BA; Newspaper Mng Ed; Phi Eta Sigma Treas 90-; Phi Beta Kappa Prize; Engl Lit; Envir Law.

**BUTTREY, CHRISTY J,** Univ Of Tn At Martin, Martin, TN; JR; BA; Scty Prof Jrnlsts VP 89-; Spnsh Clb Sec; Phlsphy Forum; Hnrs Smnr 89-; UIM Nwspr Cpy Edtr 89-; Pacer Awd 89-90; Phlsphy/Spanish; Univ Prof Phlsphy.

**BUTTS, DAVID L,** Al St Univ, Montgomery, AL; SO; BA; Math; Engineering.

**BUTTS, SONJA Y,** Shaw Univ, Raleigh, NC; SR; Choir/Band V P 90-; Alpha Kappa Mu; Alpha Kappa Alpha; Achvmnt Awd/ Gold Medals 88-; Am Schlr Awd 88-.**

**BUTWELL, ALICIA E,** Teikyo Post Univ, Waterbury, CT; SR; BA; Res Dir Stdnt Ldr 90-; AS Mattotuck Comm Coll 89; Lbrl Arts; Prof Engl.

**BUTZER, MOLLY M,** Hilbert Coll, Hamburg, NY; SO; BAS; AAS; Busn Admin; Acctnt.

**BUWEMBO, CHRISTOPHER K,** Barry Univ, Miami, FL; FR; BS; Blck Stdnt Org 90-; Sci Clb 90-; Math; Engr.

**BUXTON, CAREY G,** Univ Of Ky, Lexington, KY; JR; BA; Soccer 90; SWE; Phi Eta Sigma; Co-Op NASA 89; Elctrcl Eng.

**BUXTON, CHRISTINE E,** Kent St Univ Kent Cmps, Kent, OH; SR; BS; Pre Med; Medicine.

**BUXTON, SARAH J,** Oh Wesleyan Univ, Delaware, OH; SR; BA; Chrl Arts Scty 88-89; Phi Eta Sigma 88-; The Phi Scty VP 89-; Phi Beta Kappa; Ntnwd Ins Intern 90; KPMG Peat Marwick Intern; Acctng; Adtng.

**BUXTON, SCOTT J,** West Liberty St Coll, West Liberty, WV; JR; BA; Kappa Delta Rho VP 90-; Yth Bsbll League Coach 88-; Scndry Ed; Tchr.

**BUYCK, ROSE R,** Converse Coll, Spartanburg, SC; JR; BA; Y/ Other Y 90; SGA 88; SAC Co Chr/Dance Comm 89; Alpha Lambda Delta 89; Keyboard; Mortar Brd Nom; Cnvrse Schlrs Nom; Chrldr 89-90; Fin/Econ; MA.

**BUZZANCA, MELISSA L,** Georgetown Univ, Washington, DC; SR; BSBA; Hnd-Hnd Fest People W/Mntl Hndcps Pres 89-F Best Buddies 89-; J Georgetwn Radio 89-; Mktg; Bus Non-Prft.

**BUZZARD, JEFFREY D,** Wv Univ At Parkersburg, Parkersburg, WV; SR; BBA; Phi Beta Lambda; AA 89; Bus Mgt.

**BUZZELLI, MAUREEN N,** Comm Coll Algny Co Algny Cmps, Pittsburgh, PA; FR; BS; Med Rcrds Clb 90-; Med Rcrd Tech; Admin.

**BYARD, RACHEL R,** Cornell Univ Statutory College, Ithaca, NY; SO; BS; Il Cing Co Pres 90-; Intl Afrs Grp 90-; Choral; Frnds Frgn Stu 90; Intrn Tmpkns Cnty Envrnmntl Mgt Cncl; IM Ice Hcky/Bsktbl 89-90; Ntrl Rsrcs; Sci.

**BYARD, TINA M,** Methodist Coll, Fayetteville, NC; FR; BA; Engl; Tchng.

**BYARS, SHERRY L,** Ms St Univ, Miss State, MS; SR; MPA; Phi Theta Kappa 87-88; Gamma Beta Phi 88-; BPA; Acctng.

**BYARS, STEPHANIE L,** Winthrop Coll, Rock Hill, SC; JR; BFA; Wrkd Prttm Rsdnc Hl Ofc 90-; Chi Omega Art Chrmn 90-; Deans List 90-; Grphc Dsgn.

**BYBLE, JEREMY S,** Central Fl Comm Coll, Ocala, FL; FR; AS; Deans Lst; Radiation Proctn; Nuclear Engr.

**BYELY, LORISSA,** Franklin And Marshall Coll, Lancaster, PA; FR; BA; Psychlgy.

**BYER, FABIAN A,** S U N Y At Buffalo, Buffalo, NY; SO; DDS; DSA Represt Under Grad Class Pres 87-88; BS 88; Dentsy; Gen Pratice.

**BYERLY II, JEFFREY C,** Coppin St Coll, Baltimore, MD; BED; Ambssdr Clb 90-; Adptd Phys Ed Mjrs Clb 90-; Deans Lst; Cmmnty Srvc Lcl Elem Schls; Adptd Phys Ed Stdnt Asstntshp Emply 89-; NCAA Div I Wrstlng 89-; Adptd Physcl Ed; Tchng Physclly Chllngd Kds.

**BYERS, LORA J,** Wv Univ At Parkersburg, Parkersburg, WV; FR; AAS; Acctg.

**BYERS, LOUISE V,** Univ Of Va, Charlottesville, VA; FR; BAMED; New Gnrtn Cmps Mnstrs 90-; Blck Voices 90-; Frst Yr Liason Hnr Com 90-; Math/Education.

**BYERS, MARY HANNAH,** Univ Of Nc At Asheville, Asheville, NC; SO; BA; Outing Clb Org; IM Soccer Tm; Psychlgy; Clin Prac.

**BYERS, MELISSA D,** Indiana Univ Of Pa, Indiana, PA; FR; BA; Cmnctn Media.

**BYERS, MICHELLE L,** Va St Univ, Petersburg, VA; JR; BA; Agri Sci Org Sec 90-; Agri Educ; Instr.

**BYFORD, SHERI A,** Middle Tn St Univ, Murfreesboro, TN; SR; B ED; Kappa Delta Pi; Elemntary Edctn; Tchr/Admnstrtn.

**BYNUM, AMY N,** Univ Of Southern Ms, Hattiesburg, MS; SR; BS; Alumni Assn 90-; Spch Cmmnctn Assn 90-; Deans Lst; Rtl Clthng Mngr 86-; Spch Cmmnctn; Grad Schl.

**BYNUM, JACQUELINE M,** Va St Univ, Petersburg, VA; SO; BS; Textiles & Clothing; Fashion Design/Mrchdsng.

**BYNUM, KESHA DOREEN,** Bennett Coll, Greensboro, NC; SO; BSN; Slf Dfns 90-; Dns Lst 90-; Hnr Rl 90-; Tutor Rdng 90-; Nrsng; Pediatric Nrsng.

**BYNUM, MONJYA F,** Georgetown Univ, Washington, DC; JR; BS; Cls Comm 89-90; In Roads Inc Intrn Bd 88-; Blck Stdnt Alliance 88-; In Roads Awd 90-; Finance; Invstmnt Bnkng/Fncl Analysis.

**BYNUM, SUSAN R,** Middle Tn St Univ, Murfreesboro, TN; JR; BBA; Gamma Beta Phi 90-; Acctng.

**BYNUM II, WILLIAM D,** Univ Of Nc At Charlotte, Charlotte, NC; SO; BS; Stdnts For Helms Pres 90-; NC Stdnt Leg Pres 90-; Clge Republicans Pres 90-; Tri-Beta Exec Ofcr Of Nwspr Staff 90-; Civitans 90-; Deans List 90-; Stdnt Govt Assoc 90-; Tour Guide 90-; Dir Stdnt Affrs 90-; Class Council 90-; Biology; Medicine.

**BYRD, ANN M,** Converse Coll, Spartanburg, SC; JR; BA; Day Stdnt Assn VP 89-; Habitat For Hmnty 90-; Bus Admin; Mktg.

**BYRD, BRENT A,** Univ Of South Al, Mobile, AL; SR; BS; Amer Mktg Assn 88-90; Sigma Tau Theta 88-90; Pi Kappa Alpha 86-90; Dns Lst; Pres Lst; Mktg; Advrtsg.**

**BYRD, CYNTHIA A,** Waycross Coll, Waycross, GA; FR; BS; Music Clb 90-; Sigma Clb 90-; Phi Theta Kappa VP 90-; Stdnt Gvrnmnt Assn Sec 90-; Ntnl Jr Fllwshp Prgrm 90-; Chmstry Biology; Envrnmntl Safety.

**BYRD, ERIC M,** Central St Univ, Wilberforce, OH; SR; BA; Pol Sci Assmbly Tr 89-90; Pol Sci; Law.

**BYRD, JENNIFER LEIGH,** Radford Univ, Radford, VA; SO; BS; Oprtn Smile Std Asc Sec 89-90f Alpha Omcrn Pi 89-; Jrnlsm/Pblc Rltns.

**BYRD, JOHN F,** Univ Of Sc At Columbia, Columbia, SC; FR; BS; Engnrng.

**BYRD JR, JOHNNIE M,** Fayetteville St Univ, Fayetteville, NC; JR; BA; Crmnl Jstc Clb; AS Fayetteville Tech Comm Coll; Crmnl Jstc; FBI CIA DEA US Mrshl.

**BYRD, JOYCE K,** Central St Univ, Wilberforce, OH; SO; BED; Cmmtr Schlrshp; Instrctr Smltd Drvrs Ed 79-; Spcl Edctn; Tchr.

**BYRD, LAURIE E,** Ms St Univ, Miss State, MS; SR; BPA; Beta Gamma Sigma 89-; Schlrshp; Eubank Betts Achvmt Schlrshp; Pres Schlr; Acctg.

**BYRD, LISA S,** Va St Univ, Petersburg, VA; SR; BS; Acctg Clb 88-90; CPA Clb 88-90; Balt Pre Alumni Clb 88-90; Gspl Ensmble 88-90; Sch Bus Acdmc Awrd 89-90; Acdmc Awrd 89-90; Deans Lst 86-90; Acctg.

**BYRD, LISHA E,** D Youville Coll, Buffalo, NY; FR; Wrkng Yth Dtntn Wrkr; Nrsng; Nrs Prctcnt.

**BYRD, MELANIE P,** Clark Atlanta Univ, Atlanta, GA; FR; BA; NAACP 90-; Acdmc Excllnce Awrd 90-; Acdmc Achvmnt Awrd 90-; Acctg/Finance; CPA.**

**BYRD, MICHAEL J,** Univ Of Sc At Columbia, Columbia, SC; SO; BSBA; AS.

**BYRD, PAULA,** Oh Univ-Southern Cmps, Ironton, OH; SR; BSED; Math; Tchg.

**BYRD, RUSSELL A,** Wv Univ At Parkersburg, Parkersburg, WV; BA; Bnk Tlr; Bus; Acctg.

**BYRD, SHARON D,** Johnson C Smith Univ, Charlotte, NC; JR; BA; Mrchng Band; Exec Bd 90-; Pi Delta Tau; Summer Schlrs Prog Columbia Univ; Elem Edn; Teach.

**BYRD, SHARON R,** Fl A & M Univ, Tallahassee, FL; SR; BS; Orchesis Cntmpry Dnc Thtr 87-88; Chgo Clb 87-89; Orators Clb Coord Mgr 87-90; Deans Lst 88-90; Hon Roll 87-89; Coord Mgr Yr Ortrs Clb; Bus Admin; Mktg.

**BYRD, TIFFINI T,** Fl A & M Univ, Tallahassee, FL; FR; BS; Phi Eta Sigma; Deans Lst; Hon Roll; Phrmcy; Toxicologist.

**BYRDSONG, RUPERT A,** Morehouse Coll, Atlanta, GA; SR; JD; Pre-Law Soc 87-; March Band Sect Ldr Tubas 87-; Hon Pgm Clb VP 87-; Phi Beta Kappa; Gold Key; Sigma Tau Delta 89-; Kappa Kappa Psi 90-; March Band Awd; Ldrshp Awd; IM Track/Bsktbl Capt 87-; BA; Pol Sci; Law.

**BYRGE, DEBBY RENAE,** Roane St Comm Coll, Harriman, TN; SR; Gamma Beta Phi; ASSCTS; Radlgc Tech.

**BYRNE, FRANK J,** Kent St Univ Kent Cmps, Kent, OH; SR; Phi Alpha Delta 87-89; Phi Alpha Theta 87-89; Golden Key 90-; Deans List 87-89; Pres List 90-; Hist; Law.

**BYRNE, JAMES A,** Duquesne Univ, Pittsburgh, PA; JR; BS; Cmmtr Cncl; Pi Sigma Epsilon; Mrktng; Law/Bsnss.

**BYRNE, JANE A,** William Paterson Coll, Wayne, NJ; GD; MED; Spec Ed Clb 88-; BA 84; Spec Ed/Lrng Disblts; Ed/Cnsltg.

**BYRNE, JENNIFER E,** Univ Of Sc At Columbia, Columbia, SC; SO; BS; Applchn Poplr Prog Serv 89-90; IM Vllybl Capt 89-; Engl Educ; Educ.

**BYRNE, JULIE M,** Indiana Univ Of Pa, Indiana, PA; SR; BA; Cncl Exceptnl Chldrn Pres 89-; IM 88-; Spec Edf Tchng Excptnl Chldrn.

**BYRNE, KAREN L,** S U N Y Coll Of Tech At Frmgdl, Farmingdale, NY; GD; AAS; LPN Lewis A Wilson Tech 86; EMT Suffolk Commnty 90; Nursing RN.

**BYRNE, KEVIN F,** Le Moyne Coll, Syracuse, NY; SR; BA; Prgmmng Brd 89-; Radio DJ 88-; Theatre Clb 87-; Lit Mag Edtr 87-; Ornttn 88-; Cmps Mnstry Flk Grp 88-89; SADD 87-89; Vol Crps; Syrcs Pst Snd Rptr Intrn; G Mc Carthy Awd Drmtcs Hnr; Swim Tm Capt 90-; Engl/Comm; Brdcst Jrnlst/Rptr/Actor.

**BYRNE, SEAN M,** Western New England Coll, Springfield, MA; FR; Intrclgte Bkbl; Acctg.

**BYRNES, GARRETT M,** Manhattan Coll, Bronx, NY; SO; BE; Amer Inst Chem Eng; Dns Lst; Pres Schlrshp; N Y State Regents Schlrshp; IM Bsktbl Vlybl; Chem Eng; Eng.

**BYRNS, JOANNE C,** Univ Of Sc At Sumter, Sumter, SC; GD; Deans Lst 90; Ofcrs Wvs Clb/Spkr Chrstn Wvs Clb/Sndy Schl Tchr/Bible Stdy Ldr 67-; Tm Ldr/Mgr 84-90; Mary Kay Csmtcs/Tchr/Mgr OWC Thrft Shp/Intrior Dcrtng Cnsltnt 90-; BA IS 90; Engl/Lbrl Arts; Tchng/Intror Dsgn.

**BYRNS, JOANNE C,** Univ Of Sc At Columbia, Columbia, SC; SR; Deans List 90; Officers Wives Club 67-; Interior Dcrtng; BS.

**BYRNS, SUZANNE W,** Northern Ky Univ, Highland Hts, KY; SR; BA; Elem Tchr.

**BYRON JR, LESTER A,** Nova Univ, Ft Lauderdale, FL; GD; MBA; Sigma Alpha Epsilon Intrmrl Chr 80-84; Ft Ldrdl Bd Rltrs 87; FL Gnrl Cntrctr 87-; Gateway Invstmnts Corp Real Est Dvlpr 84-; BA-FIN Sthrn Mthdst Univ 84.

**BYRON, REBECCA L,** Bellarmine Coll, Louisville, KY; SR; BA; Courier Jrnl Hmn Rsrcs Inters 90; St Robert Bellarmine Schlrshp 87-; Psychlgy; Hmn Rsrcs Admin.

**BYRUM II, CHARLES L,** Catawba Valley Comm Coll, Hickory, NC; FR; AAS; Assoc USA 88-; Army Air Frce Mutl Aid Assoc 88-; Hospce 90-; Inst Mgmt Accts 89-; NC Army Natl Grd Assoc 87-; BSBA Applcn St Univ 89; Bsns Comp Prog.

**BYRUM, STEVEN D,** Anderson Coll, Anderson, SC; SO; BA; Hstry; Mnstry Ed Cnslng.

**BYXBE, DONNA K,** Univ Of Southern Ms, Hattiesburg, MS; JR; BA; Gldn Ky 90-; Psi Chi 90-; Gamma Beta Phi 90-; Hons Clg Schlrshp 89-; Cub Scts Of Amer Ldr 89; Assoc Ofc Persnnl 86-89; Bnkng Clg Fin Aid Sec 83-89; Psych; Thrpst.

# C

**CABALLERO, GEORGE,** Bloomfield Coll, Bloomfield, NJ; FR; ALAS; Sociology; Lawyer.

**CABALLERO, LESLIE D,** Univ Of South Al, Mobile, AL; SR; BA; Elem Ed; Tch.

**CABALLERO, MANUEL E,** Catholic Univ Of Pr, Ponce, PR; SO; BS; Fgn Org 89-90; Grntlgy Org Pub Rel; Dns Hon Lst 90-; Scr Tm Cpt 89; AS; Grntlgy; MS.

**CABALLERO, MYLENE,** Fl International Univ, Miami, FL; SR; BA; Intl Rltns Clb 87-90; French Clb Tutor; Dr D Fernandez Rsrch Asst 89-90; Intl Rltns/French; Intl Stdes.

**CABALLERO, NAIDA,** Holyoke Comm Coll, Holyoke, MA.

**CABAN, DENNIS A,** Univ Of Pr At Mayaguez, Mayaguez, PR; JR; BA; AEIC Luis M Torres 89-; IEEE Talent Show 89; Gen Engr Hnr Soc Dr Jose F Lluch 89-; Natl Hispanic Schlrshp Fdtn Ernest Z Robles 90-; Cmptr/Elctrcl Engr.**

**CABE, JILL C,** Kent St Univ Kent Cmps, Kent, OH; SR; BA; Prog Stdnt Ntwrk 89-; Hnrs Clg 89-; Eng/Hist; Museum Studies.

**CABE, MEREDITH J,** Univ Of Tn At Knoxville, Knoxville, TN; FR; BS; Carrick Hall Res Assoc 90-; Sigma Kappa Pldge Class Pres; La Crosse Ltl Sis; Actg & Bus Law; Bus.

**CABELL, NICOLE C,** Tougaloo Coll, Tougaloo, MS; JR; BA; Nws Edtr/Nwsltr 90-; Awrds Prsv/Impromptu Spch; Engl; Law.

**CABEZA GONZALEZ, CARLOS M,** Univ Politecnica De Pr, Hato Rey, PR; JR; BA; Blr Tch A Schl; Math.

**CABEZAS, IVELICE C,** Miami Dade Comm Coll South, Miami, FL; SO; BA; Ed; Tch.

**CABLE, ALANA M,** Oh St Univ At Newark, Newark, OH; JR; BA; Bsn; Acctg.

**CABLE, KATHY R,** George Mason Univ, Fairfax, VA; FR; BA; Symphonic Band 90-; Wind Ensmble; Nwspr Crspndt 90; Engl; Editor.

**CABLE, MELISSA L,** Union Univ, Jackson, TN; FR; BS; Sigma Alpha Iota; Deans Lst 90; Accntng Finance Msc; Bsns Admnstrtn.

**CABRAL, ANNA R,** S U N Y Coll Of Tech At Delhi, Delhi, NY; SO; BA; AA Suny CO Of Tech At Delhi; Political Science; Law.

**CABRAL, DIANNE,** Newbury Coll, Brookline, MA; JR; Fshn Dsgn.

**CABRE, ADRIANA C,** Duquesne Univ, Pittsburgh, PA; SR; BB; Intl Busn Assoc Pres 89-; Spnsh Clb 87-; Itln Clb 89-; Delta Sigma Pi VP 89-; Busn Dean Advsry Brd 89-; Stdy Abrd Italy; Swmng Tm 87-89; Intl Busn.

**CABRE, MAYRA I,** Univ Of Pr At Rio Piedras, Rio Piedras, PR; SR; Stdnt Cncl 90; AIAS 90; Dns Lst Of Archtctre 88-; Toms Mrvl Archtct Awrd; Dns Schl O Archctre 88-; Hnr Ttn Univ Of PR 88-.**

**CABREARA, JOSEPH,** Fl International Univ, Miami, FL; FR; BEA; Vsl Arts; Phtgrphy.

**CABRERA RAMOS, ANTONIO,** Univ Politecnica De Pr, Hato Rey, PR; FR; Engnrng.

**CABRERA, BRENDA M,** Univ Of Pr At Rio Piedras, Rio Piedras, PR; SO; BBA; Fnce; Fncl Anlyst.

**CABRERA, KATHERINE W,** Fl International Univ, Miami, FL; SR; MS; Pre Med Soc Sec 86-88; Dietetic Assoc 90-; Phi Kappa Phi 90-; ADA 90-; Deans Lst 88-; Dietetic/Ntrtn Dept 90-; Otstndg Acdmc Awrd; BS 88; Dietetics/Ntrtn.

**CACCAMISE, CHRISTINE A,** Univ Of Rochester, Rochester, NY; JR; BA; Soc Physics Stdnts 88-; Physics; Eng.

**CACCIATORE, DESIREE M,** Fl St Univ, Tallahassee, FL; Glden Key 90; Phi Beta Kappa 90; Kash N Karry Schlrshp 87; Leroy Dehman Fndtn Scr 90; BA; History.

**CACDAC, DARBY E,** Saint Thomas Univ, Miami, FL; JR; BA; Cir K Intl Clb Edtr 89; ACM; IEEE; Cmptr Sci Assn; Tnns; AA Miami Dade Comm Coll; Cmptr Sci Math; Eng.

**CACHO, MARVIN O,** Central Fl Comm Coll, Ocala, FL; FR; African Stdnt Union Pres 90-; Spanish Amer Club VP 90-91; Phi Theta Kappa 90-; Cass Casp 90-; Cmnty Schlr 90-; Tutor Soc Tutoring 90-; Most Valuable Plyr Soccer 90; Schlrshp Stdnt For Georgetown Univ 90-; Assoc Deg; Math; Engrng.

**CACO, ROSEMARY M,** Kent St Univ Kent Cmps, Kent, OH; SR; Nursing Home Rec Activity; BA; Psychology; Medical Sales Rep.

**CADDELL, ANGELA R,** Memphis St Univ, Memphis, TN; FR; BA; Chi Alpha Chrstn Fllwshp; Brk Cmps Crusade Chrst; Phi Eta Sigma; Sociology; Crisis Cnslr.

**CADDELL, CAMELA A,** Univ Of Nc At Greensboro, Greensboro, NC; SR; BS; Gamma Sigma Sigma Hall Mgr 88-; Marshall 88-90; Dance Company 89-90; Alpha Lambda Delta 88; NC Tchng Fllws Pgm 87; Orient 88/89; Dance Educ; Tchng/Perf.

**CADDELL, HOLLY L,** Hilbert Coll, Hamburg, NY; FR; ASS; Rsdnts Hll Comm; Alpha Chi Omicron 90-; Lbrl Arts.

**CADE, STEPHANIE C,** Methodist Coll, Fayetteville, NC; SO; BS; Elem Ed; Tchng.

**CADEAU, KATSIA MARIE,** Saint Thomas Univ, Miami, FL; SO; BBA; Intrntl Clb Rep 90; Mnrty Clb 90-; Acctng Clb 90; Actvts Schl Chr 1st Sprno 89-; Hlp Lil Chldrn In Chrch Sndy Schl Tchr 89; Lvly Stne Chrch Of Miami Yth Tm Hd Sec; Bus Mgmt.

**CADEGAN, JULIA A,** West Liberty St Coll, West Liberty, WV; SO; BA; Amensty Intl Pres 90-; Pi Sigma Alpha; Fraisure/Singleton Stdnt Legis Prog; Engl Lib Arts/Pol Sci; Prof Engl/Pol Sci.

**CADENA, GEORGETTE M,** City Univ Of Ny La Guard Coll, Long Island Cty, NY; SR; AAS; Deans List 88-89; Active In CYO; Data Procsng; Comptrs.

**CADET, JUDITH,** Bunker Hill Comm Coll, Boston, MA; FR; MD; Prog Cncl Mbr 90-; Chrldr 90; Nuclear Med; Med Doc.

**CADMAN, PATRICIA A,** Slippery Rock Univ, Slippery Rock, PA; JR; BSED; Mensa 87-; Hon Clb; Acad Hon 89-; Alpha Beta Alpha 89-; Sigma Tau Delta 90-; Stephenson Schlrshp 89-; Pres Schlr 89; Engl Dept Hon; Scndry Edn Engl/Lib Sci; Edn.**

**CADY, JEFFREY ALAN,** Univ Of New Haven, West Haven, CT; SR; BA; Vars Track 87-90; Intrnshp Groton Police Dept 89; Law Enfrcmnt Admin; Bus Admin.

**CAETTA, GINA M,** Kent St Univ Kent Cmps, Kent, OH; SR; BA; Phi Alpha Delta 90-; Wshngtn Prog In Natl Issues 90; Gldn Ky; Intrnshp 90; US Attrnys Offce Nrctcs Intrn; Pltcl Sci Prelaw.

**CAFARARO, RENEE A,** Le Moyne Coll, Syracuse, NY; SO; BS; Sftbl 89-; PE Spec Educ Tchr.

**CAFARELLA, KATHRYN E,** Newbury Coll, Brookline, MA; FR; ASSOC; Trvl Trsm.

**CAFARIELLA, SUSAN A,** Schenectady County Comm Coll, Schenectady, NY; JR; AAS; Bus Mngmnt; Admnstrtr Advrtsng/Sls.

**CAFARO, DONALD V,** Commonwealth Coll, Virginia Beach, VA; GD; Computer Club; Alpha Beta Gama; NCOA: VFW Post 1500; U S Navy 63-90.

**CAFARO, SUSAN,** Comm Coll Algny Co Algny Cmps, Pittsburgh, PA; BA; Nrsng.

**CAFFREY, KERRY B,** Seton Hall Univ, South Orange, NJ; SO; Kappa Delta Pi; Elem Ed; Dwn Dycr.

**CAFFYN, PETER C,** Westminster Choir Coll, Princeton, NJ; SO; BM; Symphnc Choir 89-; Chrch Music 86-; Curch Music; Dirctr.

**CAGAN, HOLLY B,** Nova Univ, Ft Lauderdale, FL; GD; MBA; Deans List 89-; United Way 89-; Barnett Bank 89-; BSBA Un FL 84-88; Fin; Plng.

**CAGE, FELICIA E,** Alcorn St Univ, Lorman, MS; FR; Biology/Pre Med; Doctor.

**CAGLE, KEVIN S,** Middle Tn St Univ, Murfreesboro, TN; FR; BA; Gamma Beta Phi 90-; Bus Ad; Law.

**CAGLE, LISA W,** Southern Coll Of Tech, Marietta, GA; SR; BA; Amer Inst Archtctrl Stdnts 89-90; AA Floyd Coll 88; Archtctrl Engr, Archtct.

**CAGLE, RICHARD S,** Univ Of Tn At Martin, Martin, TN; FR; BA; High Hnr GPA 90; Cmnctns; Brdcstg.

**CAGNO, JOSEPH R,** Rutgers St Un At New Brunswick, New Brunswick, NJ; JR; BS; Clg Cncl; Cncrt Comm 88-; Pre Med/Dent Clb 90-; Alpha Zeta 90-; Bio; Med.**

**CAHANA, ROBERT J,** Univ Of Miami, Coral Gables, FL; SO; BS; Video Flm; Mtn Pctr Bus.

**CAHILL, CARYN T,** Mount Saint Mary Coll, Newburgh, NY; FR; BS; Pre Law; Law.

**CAHILL, CHRISTOPHER M,** Univ Of Sc At Columbia, Columbia, SC; JR; BA; Stdnt Govt Sntr 85-86; Phi Alpha Theta 90-; Assoc Horry-Georgetown Tech Clg 86; Hist.

**CAHILL, DANNY T,** Univ Of New Haven, West Haven, CT; SR; BS; Resd Life Stff Res Asst 89-; Crmnl Jstc Clb 88; Intern W Haven Police Dept; IM Sftbl Vllybl 90-; Crmnl Jstc; USAF/FED Law Enfrcmnt.

**CAHILL, DAWNNA JEAN,** Newbury Coll, Brookline, MA; SO; Cls Rep 90-; Sec 89-; Cert Budett Schl Bsn 89; Acctng/Mgmt; Fncl Mgr.

**CAHILL, MARION K,** Manhattanville Coll, Purchase, NY; JR; BA; Stu Prgrmmng Brd 88-89; Ecnmcs-Mngmnt Clb 89-; Radio Sta 89-; Intern Nelson Pblctns; Sclgy; Jrnlsm/Brdcstng.

**CAI, SYMINTON,** City Univ Of Ny City Coll, New York, NY; GD; Tau Phi Sigma 86-87; Trnst Auth Brk Mech 88-; AAS NY Cty Tech Coll 87; Mgmt.

**CAIAZZA, GERALD T,** Hudson Valley Comm Coll, Troy, NY; JR; BA; Assoc Hudson Vly Cmnty Clg 90; Bsn/Mktg.

**CAICEDO, JEANNIE H,** Fl International Univ, Miami, FL; SR; Inst Indstrl Engr Sec 89-90; Wrthg Schlrshp Acdmc 87-; BS; Indstry/Sys Engr.

**CAILLET, KRISTINE M,** Kent St Univ Kent Cmps, Kent, OH; JR; BA; Rho Phi Lambda; Pi Delta 89-; Recr/Leisure; Ther Recr.

**CAILLOUET, JEFFREY W,** Univ Of Southern Ms, Hattiesburg, MS; SR; BA; Goldn Key 90-; AA Pearl Rvr Comm Coll 89; Psychlgy; Soc Wrk.

**CAIN, CANDANCE B,** Davis & Elkins Coll, Elkins, WV; JR; BS; Stdnt Educ Assn 89-; PT Clrk-A/P Store Elkins Swv 89-; Elem Ed; Tchr.

**CAIN, CAROLYN A,** Univ Of Cincinnati, Cincinnati, OH; SR; MED; Kappa Delta Pi 89-; Beta Alpha Psi Rcrdng Sec 85-87; Hnr Schlrshp 89; Hntr Schlrshp; Hld Askrn Schlrshp; Wmns Clb Hm Lf Chrprns 89-; BED; Erly Chldhd Ed; Tchng.

**CAIN, JEFFERY W,** Piedmont Tech Coll, Greenwood, SC; SO; BA; Elect Eng; Tech Serv.

**CAIN, JEFFREY C,** Univ Of Sc At Columbia, Columbia, SC; JR; Elect Eng.

**CAIN, JENNIFER L,** Univ Of Sc At Columbia, Columbia, SC; FR; Lbrry Asst 90-.

**CAIN, KIMBERLY A,** Washington State Comm Coll, Marietta, OH; SR; AS; Med Lbrtry Tchnlgy Clb 89-; Phi Theta Kappa 90-; Marietta Memorial Hosp Intrn 90-; AM Scty Med Tchlgst 90-; Med Lbrtry Tchnlgy.

**CAIN, LASHAUNDA N,** Al A & M Univ, Normal, AL; SO; SGA Sec 90-; Cls Ofcr 89-90; Hghst Avrg Tlcmnctns 90-; Delta Sigma Theta Achvmnt Awrd 90-.

**CAIN, LYNDOL K,** Piedmont Tech Coll, Greenwood, SC; SO; IM Sports; Phi Theta Kappa 90-; Hon Grad-Eng Grphcs; BSBA Univ SC 76; ADET Piedmont Tech Coll; Dsgn Engr/Drftsmn.

**CAIN, RONALD D,** Ms St Univ, Miss State, MS; GD; Engl Clb 87-88; AT&T Collegiate Inv Chlng 89-90; ACT Schlrshp 86; Deans Schlr 87-90; BBA 90; Bus Admin/Mgmnt.

**CAIN, TRACY D,** Faulkner Univ, Montgomery, AL; SR; BS; Bus.

**CAIN, VICKI L,** S U N Y Coll Of Tech At Alfred, Alfred, NY; FR; AAS; Allegany Cnty Stdnt Rep; Pblc Assist Comm; Amer Legion Aux 90-; Fund Rsng Comm 90-; Chrstn Educ Tm Tchr 90-; Little League T Ball; CNA 86-87; Recptnst/Sec/Elect Assist; Nrsng.

**CAINE, MICHELLE L,** Western New England Coll, Springfield, MA; JR; MBA; Mgr Bsktbl Team 88-; Yrbk Secy 90-; Peer Tutor 89-; Tennis Team 90-; Fin; Law.

**CAINES, DEBORAH A,** Coll Misericordia, Dallas, PA; SR; BS; Educ Clb 89-90; Action Line Lf Hot Line Cnslr 89-; Elem Ed; Tchng.

**CAINES, DEBORAH L,** Savannah St Coll, Savannah, GA; JR; BS; Staff Accntnt CPA Firm; AS Leeward Comm Clg Univ 85; Acctg; CPA.

**CAIRNS, STACY M,** Indiana Univ Of Pa, Indiana, PA; FR; BS; Mrchng Bnd Grd 90-; Crsd Chrst 90-; Scl Stds Ed.

**CAIRO, ADIHELIN,** Fl International Univ, Miami, FL; SR; BA; AA Miami Dade Comm Coll 89; Elem Educ.

**CAISON, DENISE L,** Saint Andrews Presbytrn Coll, Laurinburg, NC; JR; BA; Hll Pres 89-; Hstry Clb Treas 89-; SG 90-; Alpha Chi 90-; Hnr Scty 90-; Pi Gamma Mu 90-; Delta Kappa Gamma Schlrshp 90-; Hstry Educ; Tch.

**CAJIGAO, MARK A,** Wagner Coll, Staten Island, NY; FR; BA; Hon Prog; Theatre/Spch; Tch Educ.

**CALABRESE, FELICIA,** Seton Hall Univ, South Orange, NJ; JR; BA; Elem Educ/Dvlpmnt Dsrdrs; Erly Intrvtn Spclst.

**CALABRESE, JENNIFER M,** Univ Of Cincinnati, Cincinnati, OH; FR; BM; Symphny Bnd 90-; Rprtr Orchstr 90-; Coll Cnsrvtry Msc Hnrs Schlrshp 90; Music.

**CALABRESE, KELSA L,** Newbury Coll, Brookline, MA; SO; Dns Lst 89-; Cert Educ Inst Amer Hotel Motel Assn 89-; Hotel/Rest Mngmnt; Hotel Gst Srvc Mngmnt.

**CALABRIA, JON,** Univ Of Ga, Athens, GA; SR; BA; Rowing Clb Fndg Mbr Univ Rel 90-; GA Stdnts Of Lndscp Archtctr 89-; Biking/Sftbl/Vlybl/Rowing 89-.

**CALABRIS, THOMAS C,** Univ Of Akron, Akron, OH; SR; BS; Co Op Educ W/Va Power 89-90; Elec Engr.

**CALABRO, LYNN M,** Providence Coll, Providence, RI; SR; Pstrl Cncl Treas 87-; Acctg Assn 88-; IM Sports 87-89; Tau Pi Phi; Ernst/Young Tax Intrnshp 89-; Ri Hosp Trust Awd; Blue Crss/Blue Shld Schlrshp Awd 90; Summa Cum Laude 87-; BS; Tax Actnt.

**CALABRO, SEBASTIANO M,** City Univ Of Ny Baruch Coll, New York, NY; SR; BBA; Seek Awd Fr Acad Dstnctn 88; Acctng; CPA/MSTRS Finance.

**CALAFUT, MARIA T,** Marywood Coll, Scranton, PA; SR; BS; Tchrs Of Tomorrow 87-; Crspndnce Comm 87-89; NAEYC 89-; Kappa Delta Pi V P 88-; Delta Epsilon Sigma 88-; Kappa Delta Pi Ldrshp Conf 90; Educ Fclty Liason 90; Elem Educ; Tch.

**CALAME, KATHRYN L,** Univ Of Akron, Akron, OH; JR; BED; Elem Ed/Geo.

**CALAME, LORRAINE O,** City Univ Of Ny City Coll, New York, NY; FR; BSC; Crbbn Std Asc 90-; NY Pblc Intrsts/Rsch Grp 90-; Mtrlgy.

**CALAMETTI, KIMBERLY J,** Univ Of Southern Ms, Hattiesburg, MS; SO; BA; Eagle Connection Sec 90-; Stdnt Alumni Assn Grp Chr 90-; Jr Panhellenic Treas 89-90; Lambda Sigma 90-; Alpha Lambda Delta 89-90; Phi Eta Sigma 89-90; Gamma Alpha Epsilon; Delta Delta Delta Rcrdng Secy; Pol Sci; Law.

**CALARA, KAREN B,** Boston Univ, Boston, MA; FR; BA; Asian Stdnt Un 90-; Filipino Stdnts Clb 90-; The League 90-; Phys Therapy.

**CALCAGNO, ANNA M,** West Liberty St Coll, West Liberty, WV; JR; BS; Chi Beta Phi 90-; Hnrs Prgrm 90-; RA 90; Lrning Cntr Tutr 90; Phrmcy Intrnshp 90; Phrmcy.**

**CALCANO, IVAN,** Inter Amer Univ Pr Hato Rey, Hato Rey, PR; SR; BS; Chld Evang Flwshp Helper 89-; Cmptr Sci; Pgmr.

**CALCHI, CATHERINE L,** Fl Atlantic Univ, Boca Raton, FL; SR; BBA; Phi Kappa Phi; FAU Community Schrlshp; PBCC Presidential Schlrshp; Leisureville Square Schlrshp; AA Palm Beach Comm Clg 89; Mngmnt; Human Resources.

**CALDER, CASSIE J,** Memphis St Univ, Memphis, TN; FR; BS; Bptst Stdnt Union 90-; Peer-Mntr Pgm; Alpha Lambda Delta Treas; Phi Eta Sigma; Math; Pre-Med.

**CALDERON COLON, RAMON,** Inter Amer Univ Pr Hato Rey, Hato Rey, PR; FR; BA; Bsbl Tm; Bus Adm.

**CALDERON SANTOS, ESTEBAN,** Inter Amer Univ Pr San German, San German, PR; GD; BS; Comp Sci.**

**CALDERON, ANA D,** Inter Amer Univ Pr Hato Rey, Hato Rey, PR; JR; AS; Inter-Amer Chrstn Assoc; Valdctrn/Magna Cum Laude 90; AS MIS Columbia Clg 90; Cmptr/Math; Tchr Cmptrs.

**CALDERON, BRENDA L,** Inter Amer Univ Pr Hato Rey, Hato Rey, PR; JR; Crmnl Jstc; Law.

**CALDERON, WELLINGTON A,** Daytona Beach Comm Coll, Daytona Beach, FL; FR; AS; Prsdnts Lst 90; Phtgrphy; Freelance Phtgrphy.

**CALDERON-LEON, GUILLERMO,** Univ Del Turabo, Gurabo, PR; SR; BBA; Nmrcl Cntrl Soc/Aim Tech 88-; Kodak Pro-35 Photo Clb 83-; Tool/Die Makr; CNC Prgrmr; Mfg Sprvsr; Diplma Tool/Die Trning Schl 81; Comp Info Syst; Eng/CIM.

**CALDERONE, NICOLLE I,** Seton Hall Univ, South Orange, NJ; FR; BA; Elem Educ; Tchng.

**CALDWELL, CAROLINE L,** Converse Coll, Spartanburg, SC; FR; BS; Stdnt Gov Assn 90-; Alpha Lambda Delta; Stdnt Vol Svcs 90-; Trus Hnr Schlrshp 90; Acctg.

**CALDWELL, CHANEY E,** Alice Lloyd Coll, Pippa Passes, KY; SR; BA; Elem Educ.

**CALDWELL, CHRISTINE L,** Thomas Nelson Comm Coll, Hampton, VA; GD; AAS; Offc Sys Tech.

**CALDWELL, DAVID P,** Tri County Tech Coll, Pendleton, SC; AIT T; Phi Theta Kappa; Alpha Zeta Beta; MTT; Eng.

**CALDWELL, DEBORAH A,** Univ Of Pittsburgh At Bradford, Bradford, PA; SR; BA; Anthrplgy Clb Pres 90-; Yng Demos Clb Treas 90; Chautauqua Inst Intern; Hmn Rels.

**CALDWELL, DEIDRA K,** Univ Of Al At Birmingham, Birmingham, AL; SR; BS; Stdnt Occptnl Thrpy Assc Chrprsn Actng Tres 90; Phi Theta Epsilon; Pres Lst 90-; Deans Lst 90; Cert Coosa Valley Tech Schl 80; Science; Occupational Therapy.

**CALDWELL, DENNIS L,** Univ Of Akron, Akron, OH; JR; BS; IEEE; Tau Beta Pi; Engr; Elec Engr.

**CALDWELL, ELIZABETH L,** Seton Hall Univ, South Orange, NJ; FR; BED; Frshmn Cls Coun 90-; Dns Lst 90-; Educ.

**CALDWELL, GARY A,** Fl A & M Univ, Tallahassee, FL; SR; Blk Stdnt Un Pres 88; Acad Achvmnt Awd; AA Lake City Cmuty Clg 88; BS Fla A & M Un; Indus Arts Educ; Tch.

**CALDWELL, GREG L,** Meridian Comm Coll, Meridian, MS; SO; Assistantshp 90.

**CALDWELL, JASON T,** Univ Of Tn At Martin, Martin, TN; BA; Army ROTC; Assc US Army ROTC Medal Awd; Supr Cadet Decrtn Awd; Green To Gold Schlrshp; US Army MP Rnk E5 Sgt; Crim Jstc; US Army MP.

**CALDWELL, JEANNE LEIGH,** Fl International Univ, Miami, FL; SR; BA; Phi Lambda Beta Tm Ldr 90-; Dade Cnty Pk/Rcrtn Dept 80-; Pblc Admin; Law.

**CALDWELL, JENNIFER L,** Northern Ky Univ, Highland Hts, KY; JR; Elem Ed.

**CALDWELL, KENNETH L,** Meridian Comm Coll, Meridian, MS; SO; BA; Bsnss Admin; Bsnss Mngmnt.

**CALDWELL, MARGARET ELIZABETH,** Univ Of Nc At Greensboro, Greensboro, NC; JR; BS; Bpt Student Union 88-89; Natl Scty Children Amer Revltn State Chrmn Mt Schls 81-; Natl Scty Children NC 88; NC Sci Tchrs Assoc 90-; First Bapt Church Greensboro Assist Tchr Gyrold Class; Early Childhood Ed; Tchng Kndgrdn Elem.

**CALDWELL, MONTI ELIZABETH,** Univ Of Southern Ms, Hattiesburg, MS; JR; BS; Poralegal Scty 90-; Criminal Justice Assoc 90-; Pre Law Scty 90-; Gamma Beta Phi; Phi Theta Kappa Secty 89-90; Paralegal; Law.

**CALDWELL, NICHOLE R,** Central St Univ, Wilberforce, OH; SR; BA; Psych Clb; Drm Cncl Pres 88-; Natl Assc Ngr Bus Prof Wmn Clb Inc; Sftbl; Psych; Grad Schl/Psychlgst.

**CALDWELL, RAY A,** Va Commonwealth Univ, Richmond, VA; SR; BS; Phi Kappa Phi; Phi Theta Kappa 87-; AAS Patrick Henry Cmnty Clg 88; Chem; Toxicology.

**CALDWELL, SHARON L,** Marshall University, Huntington, WV; SR; MBA; Karate Clb Pres 89-90; Grad Asstntshps 90; Monel Pk Cvc Assc Inc Pres 88-; BBA 89; Bsns.**

**CALDWELL, SONYA T,** Comm Coll Algny Co Algny Cmps, Pittsburgh, PA; FR; AS; Cmptrs.

**CALDWELL, TAMMYE S,** Tn St Univ, Nashville, TN; JR; BS; Socty Wmn Engrs 90-F; Elec Engr.

**CALDWELL, THOMAS P,** Univ Of Tn At Martin, Martin, TN; JR; BS; Bio; Dentstry.

**CALDWELL, WILLIAM C,** Univ Of Miami, Coral Gables, FL; SO; BARCH; AIAS Stdnt 90-; Phi Kapp Aphi; Archtct Trng St AZ 89-; Prctcng Jr Archtct 86-90; BS ASU 86; Architecture.

**CALEMMO, JENNIFER C,** Marywood Coll, Scranton, PA; SO; BA; Tchrs Tmrrw 90-; Adopt Grndprnt 90-; Elem Early Chldhd Educ.

**CALEODIS, GEORGE P,** Oh St Univ, Columbus, OH; SR; BS; Strollers Stdnt Theatrics 87-88; Sigma Epsilon Phi Treas 87-; Phi Beta Kappa 90-; Alpha Lambda Delta 87-; Gldn Ky 89-; Stdnt Instrctnl Aide Dept Math 90-; Biochemistry/Math; Med/Acturial Sci.

**CALERO, ANN-MARGARET,** Fl International Univ, Miami, FL; SO; BA; Pre-Med Soc 90-; Phi Lambda Pi 90-; AS 89-; Bio; Med.

**CALERO, GISELA,** Fl International Univ, Miami, FL; SR; BA; Psychlgy; Clncl Psychlgy.

**CALERO, MIRNA,** City Univ Of Ny La Guard Coll, Long Island Cty, NY; GD; BA; Acctg Clb 88-90; Cmptr Clb 89-90; Dns Lst; Grad Hnrs 90; AAS 90; Cmptr Sci; MBA.

**CALEY JR, A PAUL,** Manhattan Coll, Bronx, NY; FR; BED; Jz Bnd; IM Bsktbl; Eng.

**CALHOUN, AMY M,** Bridgewater Coll, Bridgewater, VA; SO; BA; Brthrn Stu Flwshp 89-; Rsdnt Cnslng; Tutrg 90-; Lambda Soc 90-; Sclgy; Cnslg.

**CALHOUN, DAVID T,** Central St Univ, Wilberforce, OH; JR; Estr Sls Handcp Cmp 88; Ftbl 89-90; Recreatn.

**CALHOUN, DEANDRE W,** Morehouse Coll, Atlanta, GA; FR; BS; Mathletes 90-; Hnrs Prog Clb 90-; Mentor Prog 90-; Hnr Roll 90-; Mathematics.

**CALHOUN, DONYETTA P,** James Madison University, Harrisonburg, VA; JR; BS; Cntmpry Gospel Singers 89-; Univ Orch 88-; Campus Crusade For Christ 89-90; Psi Chi Mbrshp Chr 90-; Omega Essence Ct Chpln 90-; Afro-Am Image Awd; Sch Psych.

**CALHOUN, FELITA Y,** Clark Atlanta Univ, Atlanta, GA; SO; BED; Vol Prjct Sccss; Hms Cmmnty Ctr: Insprtnl Voices Fth Chpln 90-; Math Awd 90-; IBM Offc Aide 90; Atlanta Pblc Schls Aide 86-89; Bsn Ed; Tch.

**CALHOUN, KAREN N,** Emory Univ, Atlanta, GA; SR; BSN; Stdnt Nrs Assn 89-; Hnr Cncl 90-; Sigma Theta Tau 90-; Assc Bacc Awd; Vol Homls Clnc Amer 89-; Cancr Soc ACS 89-; Inv Mgmt 84-89; BBA Univ TN Knxvl 84; Nrsng.

**CALHOUN, LARRY B,** Clemson Univ, Clemson, SC; SO; BS; Forestry Forest Mngmnt; Corp Forester.

**CALHOUN, MARY C,** Austin Peay St Univ, Clarksville, TN; FR; BA; Gamma Beta Phi 90-; Psychlgy Clb 90-; Clncl Psychlgy.

**CALHOUN, MELINDA D,** Bridgewater Coll, Bridgewater, VA; SO; BS; Mt Olivet Sr CBYF Treas 86-; Deans List; Business; CPA.

**CALHOUN, RUSSELL B,** Auburn Univ At Auburn, Auburn, AL; GD; MED; Phi Kappa Phi 90-; Pi Lambda Theta 89-; Prfsnl Assn GA Edctrs 90-; BED 90; Math Ed; Tchr.

**CALHOUN, SUSAN C,** Univ Of Ky, Lexington, KY; SR; Dns Lst 89-; Gldn Key 90-; Psychlgy Thrpy.

**CALI, MARIA F,** Saint Josephs Coll Sufflk Cmps, Patchogue, NY; JR; BA; Chld Study Clb Pub Rltns Ofcr 90-; Sigma Iota Chi 90-; Deans Lst 89-; Orntatn Guide Walk Amer Ch Crprsn 89-; CBS Schlrshp; Kickline 89-; Child Study.**

**CALIX, NANCY C,** Ky St Univ, Frankfort, KY; JR; Intrntl Stdnts Assc Pres 89-; Deans Lst; Elem Educ.

**CALIZ, BRENDA E,** Bayamon Tech Univ Coll, Bayamon, PR; SR; BA; Hon Soc 87-; Assoc Acctg 90; Bsns Admn; Acctg.

**CALKINS, FLOYD TIMOTHY,** S U N Y Coll Of Tech At Alfred, Alfred, NY; SO; AS; Comp Sci.

**CALKINS, JOHN D,** Saint Francis Coll, Loretto, PA; JR; BS; Stdnt Govt Sntr 89-; Athltc Advsry Brd; Crclm Cmte 89-90; Hnrs Pgm 88-; Alpha Kappa Psi Pres; Wood Coop Pgm 90-; Knights Columbus 90-; Boy Scts Amer Eagle 82-; Intrnshp; Mns Bsktbl Mgr 88-; Mgmt/Econ; Mgmt.

**CALKINS, MIA A,** Ny Univ, New York, NY; FR; Jrnlsm; Wrtr.

**CALL, CAROLYN S,** Va Highlands Comm Coll, Abingdon, VA; BA; Alpha Gamma Rho 90-; Phi Theta Kappa 90-; Psychtrc Aide Adlscnt Ward Mntl Hosp; Nrsng Asst Cert Aleghany Comm College Cumberland Md 85; Hmn Srvcs; Socl Wrk/Cnslng.

**CALL, DEBORAH A,** The Boston Conservatory, Boston, MA; SO; BM; Cmmtr Clb Co Chrprsn 90-; Music/Piano Perf.

**CALL, M BETHANY,** Tn Temple Univ, Chattanooga, TN; SO; BS; Psi Delta Rho Pres 90-; Elem Ed; Tchr.

**CALL, WENDY J,** Newbury Coll, Brookline, MA; FR; Interior Dsgn; Interior Dsgnr.

**CALLA, LAURA,** Daemen Coll, Amherst, NY; JR; BS; EMT Cert; Erie Comm Clg 88; Special Ed; Teacher.

**CALLAHAN, COLLEEN MARIE,** Villanova Univ, Villanova, PA; SO; BA; Villanova Stdnt Musical Theatre 90-; Spcl Olympics Vol 89-90; Campus Ministry 89-; French Clb 89-90; Hnrs Prog 89-; English; Teaching.

**CALLAHAN, DAVID L,** Allegheny Coll, Meadville, PA; SR; BA; Phi Sigma Iota; Phi Kappa Psi 87-; Lambda Sigma Publcty Chrmn 88-89; Alden Schlr 87-; Allegheny Cyclng Clb Pres 90-; French; Govt Srvc.

**CALLAHAN, DAVID M,** Germanna Comm Coll, Locust Grove, VA; SO; MBA; Stdnt Gvrnmnt Assn Prsdnt; Cllg Nespr Entrtnmnt Edtr 90-; Finance; Corp Finance.

**CALLAHAN, HARRIET D,** Univ Of Al At Birmingham, Birmingham, AL; SR; BED; Phi Theta Kappa V P Finance 89-90; AA Jefferson St JR Clg 90; Ed; Mdl Schl Sci Tchr.

**CALLAHAN, JOHN R,** East Central Comm Coll, Decatur, MS; FR; BS; Engr Clb 90-; ECCC Plyrs 90-; Mu Alpha Theta 90-; Phi Theta Kappa 90-; Fres Engr Awd 90-; Math; Actuary.

**CALLAHAN, KIMBERLY A,** Univ Of Rochester, Rochester, NY; SO; Engl Cncl Treas; Cir K; Engl; Law.

**CALLAHAN, KIMBERLY ANN,** Georgetown Univ, Washington, DC; JR; BSBA; Orientatn Stf 90; SFCU 89-90; Spirit Comm 89-90; Beta Gamma Sigma; Alpha Lambda Delta 89; Bread For Wrld Vlntr 89-90; Dnc Co 90-; Intl Mgmt/Finance; Law.

**CALLAHAN, MARK E,** Radford Univ, Radford, VA; SR; BA; Univ Ski Clb Pres 89-; Delta Mu Delta; Phi Sigma Kappa Pres 90-; Bus; MBA.

**CALLAHAN, PETER F,** S U N Y Coll Of Tech At Frmgdl, Farmingdale, NY; SO; BA; Soc Mfg Eng Frst V Chrmn 90-; Sftb IM; AAS; Mftrng Eng.

**CALLAHAN, SHAWN M,** Univ Of Scranton, Scranton, PA; SO; BA; Rsdnt Hs Govt Pres 90-; Rsdnt Asstntshp; Prsdntl II Schlsrhp 89-; Acctg.

**CALLAM, MAIRI,** Fl International Univ, Miami, FL; GD; Adjunct Prfsr Ed Dept 90; FL Cncl Soc Stds; Natl Geogrphy Soc; British Govt 86-89; Dade Cty Pblc Schls 90-; MA Hons Univ Edinburgh 85; MS 90; Ed; Tchng.

**CALLAN, HOPE Y,** York Coll Of Pa, York, PA; JR; BSED; Theatre Pblcty 88-; Yrbk 88-; Nu Lambda Tau 89-; Sigma Delta Tau 89-; Dns Acad Schlrshp 88-89; Elem Ed/Math; Tchng.**

**CALLAN, JOSEPH B,** Hudson Valley Comm Coll, Troy, NY; SO; Phi Theta Kappa 90-; Rensselaer Phi Theta Kappa Schlrshp 90-; G Howard Carragan Awrd For Ex In Exp Physics 90-; AS; Elec Eng.

**CALLANAN, SUSAN M,** Newbury Coll, Brookline, MA; SO; AS; Asst Offc Mgr Elec Mfg 84-; Acctng.

**CALLE, SHELLIE A,** Oh St Univ, Columbus, OH; SR; BS; Club Karate 89-; Hnr Soc 87; Golden Key 90; Tutor 90; Excel Schlrshp Award 90; Acad Cmndtn Ohio Hse Repr; Ranco Cntrls Div Schlrshp 87-; Psych; Prsnl/Govt/Cnslng.

**CALLEGARI, JO ANN,** Albertus Magnus Coll, New Haven, CT; GD; BA; Alpha Signa 90-; Harry S Truman Schlrshp 90; Rgstr Vtrs West Haven 81-; BA; Sociolgy.

**CALLEJAS, LUCIO A,** Univ Of West Fl, Pensacola, FL; SR; BS; SASA 90-; Cltrl Actvs Prmtg Latin Amer Cltr; Coop De Vivenda Zapote Norte Honduras Comm Serv 83-89; AHECASP 87-89; Schlrshps 85-87; AA 87; Manuf Engr Tech.

**CALLENDER, JENNIFER A,** Clark Atlanta Univ, Atlanta, GA; FR; BA; NAACP Mbr 90-; Spirits Boosters; Deans List 90-; Bus Admn; Banking Or Fin.

**CALLENDER, KIM V,** Guilford Tech Comm Coll, Jamestown, NC; GD; AAS; Amer Soc Quality Cntrl 90; Boy Scouts Amer Ldr 89; Logistrial Sply Sgt USAR 89; Mgmt.

**CALLEY, DANIEL P,** Boston Coll, Chestnut Hill, MA; SO; BA; Pltcl Sci/Hstry; Law.**

**CALLICOAT, DEBRA W,** Tri County Tech Coll, Pendleton, SC; FR; BS; Cmptr Sci; Prog.

**CALLICUTT, LAUREN L,** Univ Of Southern Ms, Hattiesburg, MS; JR; BS; Stdnt Alumni Assn 90-; Rfrmd Univ Flwshp 88-89; Stdnt Govt Comm 88-89; Phi Mu 88-; Gamma Beta Phi; Gamma Alpha Epsilon Treas; Phi Eta Sigma 88-89; Upsilon Pi Epsilon; Pres Lst,Dns Lst 88-; Cmptr Sci; Prgrmng/Bus.

**CALLIHAN, VALERIE LYNN,** Mount Aloysius Jr Coll, Cresson, PA; FR; ASSOC; Amateur Thtr Grp; Erly Chldhd Advcy Assn; Erly Chldhd Educ.

**CALLIS, DUANE I,** Saint Pauls Coll, Lawrenceville, VA; JR; Math Sci Clb VP 89-; NAACP 89-90; Alpha Kappa Mu; CRC Press Chmstry Awrd 90; Ognc Chmstry Awrd; Biol Awrd 90-; Biol; Dntstry.

**CALLIS, MELINDA M,** Union Univ, Jackson, TN; FR; BA; Bapt Stdnt Un 90-; Singrs 90-; Chi Omega 90-; Art Musc Schlrshps; Art Awds Drwngs; Art; Int Desgn.

**CALLISON, LEA M,** Toccoa Falls Coll, Toccoa Falls, GA; SR; BS; Dorm Cncl Pres 88; RA 89-; Choir 88; Church Choir 90-; Mntl Hlth Ctr Vol; Dns Lst 88-; Cnslg; Marriage/Family Ther.

**CALLOWAY, DANIEL K,** Bridgewater Coll, Bridgewater, VA; JR; BA; Lambda 90-; Mnstr Chrch Brthrn; Dncr Chmpnshp Adjdctr 77-; Fist D Bb La 85; Phlsphy Rlgn.

**CALLOWAY, THERESA B,** William Carey Coll, Hattiesburg, MS; SR; Red Crss; Air Frc Mntl Hlth Nrs 89-; RN Cmpltng BSN; ADN Westark Comm Coll 83; BS Coll Ozarks 81; Nrsng; Nrs Ansthst.

**CALLWOOD, CHERISSE M,** Clark Atlanta Univ, Atlanta, GA; JR; BA; Kappa Delta Epsilon; Early Chldhd Educ; Tchng.

**CALNAN, DEBRA J,** Saint Josephs Coll, Windham, ME; SR; BS; Delta Epsilon Sigma; Beta Imicron Chapter; Vol Rescue Sqd EMT 85-; Fire Dept Aux; Elem Educ; Tchr.

**CALOGERO, DIANE,** Ramapo Coll Of Nj, Mahwah, NJ; SR; MSW; NASW 89-; Natl Org Wmn 89-; World Vsn 87-; Scl Wrk Clb 90; Phi Sigma Omcrn 87; Cum Laude; Cnslng Sev Vol 89-90; BSW; Scl Wrk.

**CALOHAN, ANDREW A,** Ferrum Coll, Ferrum, VA; JR; BS; Soph Cls Ofcr Tres 89-90; Bus Clb 89-; Stu Mntr 89-; Acdmc All Cnfrnc Bsbl 89-90; Bsbl 88-; Bus; Ins.**

**CALTVEDT, SIRI C,** Smith Coll, Northampton, MA; SO; BA; Chrs 89-90; 1st Grp Schlr 90; Comp Sci; Comp Sci/Cndctng.

**CALVELLO, JOHN,** Manhattan Coll, Bronx, NY; FR; BE; Elec Engr.

**CALVERT, AMANDA G,** Livingston Univ, Livingston, AL; SR; BED; Sga Sec 90-; Envoy Schl Hostess 90-; Alpha Chi 90-; Cardnl Key 90-; Omicron Delta Kappa; Phi Mu Panhell Dele 90-; 3rd Runr Up Miss L U; Summr Orntn Intrn 91; IM Sprts; Lang Arts Comp; Educ.

**CALVERT, JULIE D,** West Liberty St Coll, West Liberty, WV; SO; MBA; Chi Omega Actvty Chrmn 89-; Phrmcy.

**CALVERT, KIM S,** Univ Of Al At Birmingham, Birmingham, AL; SO; BS; Wrldwde Chrch Of God 68-; Prgrmmr Anlyst 89-; AS Ambassador Coll 84; Comp Sci.

**CALVERT, LORI A,** West Liberty St Coll, West Liberty, WV; JR; BS; Chi Omega; Bus Admn; Acctg.

**CALVERT, NORIE AFFOLTER,** Morgan St Univ, Baltimore, MD; SR; Amer Soc Hwy Engrs; Hwy Adm Designer 83-; Cvl Engr.

**CALVERT, SHEILA W,** Piedmont Tech Coll, Greenwood, SC; FR; Phi Theta Kappa 90-; Ware Schls Pntcstl Hlns Chrch Drctr Chldrns Chrch 87-; Sec & Tres Wmns Mnstrs Sndy Schl Tchr Lf Lnrs Tchr; Elmntry Edctn; Tchng.

**CALVIN, AARON B,** Johnson C Smith Univ, Charlotte, NC; FR; BA; Educ Orgnzr.

**CALVIN, CHERYL MARIE,** Kent St Univ Kent Cmps, Kent, OH; SR; BM; Gldn Ky; Superior Schlrshp Cert; Music Schlrshp 86-87; Music; Educ.

**CALVIN, SHELIA N,** Alcorn St Univ, Lorman, MS; JR; Math Ed; Tch Secndry Lvl.

**CALVO, CANISHA C,** Tn Temple Univ, Chattanooga, TN; FR; BS; Sigma Delta Rho 90-; Cmptr Info Systs; Cmptr Prgrmr.

**CALVO, MARIA E,** Fl International Univ, Miami, FL; SO; BS; Amer Inst Archtctr Stdnts 90-; Chi Alpha 90-; Dns Lst 90; Phi Lambda Beta; Jr Orange Bwl Fstvl Comm 90-; Intershp Diane Deen Intr Dsgn Inc 90-; Cert Inst Artistic Formation Brivil 90; Art/Intr Dsgn; Intr Dsgn.

**CALZADA PAGAN, RAMON LUIS,** Univ Of Pr Medical Sciences, San Juan, PR; GD; MPH; Puerto Rico Speleological Soc 84-; P R Chem Assn 76-; Amer Chem Soc 78-; Amer Assn Advncmnt Sc 90-; Envirnmntl Hlth.**

**CAMACHO CONTY, MEI LING Z,** Inter Amer Univ Pr Hato Rey, Hato Rey, PR; SR; BA; Un Chrstn Asso 86-88; Am Mdlng Asso Petite Mdl 86; Fundacion Ortega Gasset Ex-Stdnt Asso 90-; Inter Am Un Hon Bd 88-; Hon Prog Stdnts Hon Bd 88-; Hon Prog Stdnt Asso 90-; Alpha Kappa Omicron 85; Spcl Ed Sever Handicap; Psychglgy.

**CAMACHO CRUZ, JO-HANNA,** Univ Of Pr At Mayaguez, Mayaguez, PR; SO; BSME; Assoc Evnglstcl Stdnts 88-; Mech Engr.

**CAMACHO, DARYNELL,** Inter Amer Univ Pr San German, San German, PR; FR; BA; Schl Coop Admin 87; Mu Alpha Phi; Blgy; Lab Tchnlgy.

**CAMACHO, GRISEL,** Inter Amer Univ Pr San Juan, Hato Rey, PR; JR; BA; SPELL 89-; Univ Hon Prog Sec 90 V P Elect; English/Pre Sch Ed; Tch Univ Level.

**CAMACHO, JOANNE,** Central Pa Bus School, Summerdale, PA; FR; ASSOC; Stdnt Lgl Assc; Strng Comm; Lgl; Law.

**CAMACHO, JORGE L LUGO,** Univ Of Pr At Mayaguez, Mayaguez, PR; GD; PHD; Mmbr Assn Stdnts Agrnmy Soils 89-; Hnr Stdnt Agrcltr Fac 87-89; Deans Lst 88-; Hnr Stdnt Agrcltr Apprctn Wk 88; BS; Agrnmy Sos; Sls Chmstry.

**CAMACHO, MARGOT,** Univ Of Pr At Rio Piedras, Rio Piedras, PR; GD; BA; Bible Stdy Grps 87-89; Engl Grad Stdnt Org 88-89; Engl/Spnsh; Tchng/Sprvsr.

**CAMACHO, MARIA HELAN,** Bryant Stratton Bus Inst Roch, Rochester, NY; ASSOC; Acctg.

**CAMACHO-CRUZ, LI-MARIE,** Univ Of Pr At Mayaguez, Mayaguez, PR; SR; BSCE; ASCE 88-; SWE 89-; Tau Beta Pi 89-; Civil Engr.

**CAMANTIGUE, JANETTE F,** Clayton St Coll, Morrow, GA; SO; AAS; Data Procssng; Compt Prgrmmng.

**CAMARA, ARMANDO A,** Bunker Hill Comm Coll, Boston, MA; SO; ASSOC; Bus Admin; Exec.

**CAMARGO, ANNA M,** Fl International Univ, Miami, FL; SR; BS; Police Dept Intrn 90; AA Miami Dade Comm Coll 86; Crmnl Jstce; Law Enfrcemnt.

**CAMASTO, ANGELA M,** Cornell Univ Statutory College, Ithaca, NY; SO; BS; Sage Chpl Chr 89-; ALERT 90-; CIVITAS 90; Vol Srvcs St Francis Hosp; IM Sccr 90; Blgy; Med.

**CAMBRIA, SUSAN,** S U N Y At Binghamton, Binghamton, NY; JR; BS; Accntng/Mngmnt Org 89; Human Rsrce Mngmnt Assoc 90; BS; Mngmnt; Human Rsrces Mgr.

**CAMBRIDGE, SHEVONN NATHANIEL,** Manhattan Coll, Bronx, NY; SR; BSME; Amrcn Scty Mchncl Eng VP; 88-; Pi Tau Sigma; Tau Beta Pi; Epsilon Sigma Pi; Eng CnclIM Bsktbll 89-90; Mchncl Eng.

**CAMDEN, MICHAEL P,** Bethany Coll, Bethany, WV; SO; BS; Pltcl Sci Advsry Cncl 89-; Mdl Untd Ntns VP 89-; Stdnts Agnst Drnk Drvng Treas 90-; Gamma Rho Omicron 89-; Kappa Alpha Corres Sec 90-; BISONS 89-; WA Smstr Prgm; Pltcl Sci; Ed.

**CAMDEN, MICHELE L,** Daytona Beach Comm Coll, Daytona Beach, FL; FR; BA; Psy.

**CAMEJO, FRANKLYN M,** City Univ Of Ny Baruch Coll, New York, NY; JR; BA; Latin Amer Yth Hispanic Soc 89-; Soc Stdnt Actuaries 90-; Actuarial Soc Clb; Actuarial Sci/Math.

**CAMERA, DAVID P,** Kent St Univ Kent Cmps, Kent, OH; JR; BA; Yth Ldr 90-; Alpha Kappa Delta 90-; Pi Gamma Mu 90-; Gldn Ky; IM Bsktbl Vlybl; Sociology; Law/Seminary Yth Pstr.

**CAMERON, BETH K,** Indiana Univ Of Pa, Indiana, PA; SR; BA; Assn Rehab Adv Sec 90-; Stdnt Advsry Cncl ; Cncl For Excep Chldrn; Alpha Gamma Delta Fncl Sec 89-90; Intrnshp Harmarville Rehab Cntr; Rehab; Rehab Cnslr.

**CAMERON, CHERYL D,** Johnson C Smith Univ, Charlotte, NC; SR; MBA; Johnson C Smith Choir 87; Duke Hall Hall Cncl Asst 88-90; Rsdnt Advsr Sr RA 89-90; Cnfrnc Asstnc Asst 87-89; BA 90; Comp Sci; Comp Analyst.

**CAMERON, DAVID,** Comm Coll Algny Co Algny Cmps, Pittsburgh, PA; JR; BA; Allegheny Art Assn VP 90-; Nwspr Msc Clmnst; Mgzn Arts Art Edtr; COOP Art Show; Allegheny Art Assn; AS; Grphc Dsgn; Drct Dsgn Frm.

**CAMERON, GEORGIA JAYNE,** Univ Of Southern Ms, Hattiesburg, MS; SR; BS; Jones Co Jr Clg Crmnl Justice Assoc 90; Gamma Beta Phi; LPN Pearl River Commty Clg 73; Social Rhlbltn; Crmnl Justice Systm.

**CAMERON, HEATHER L,** Northeastern Christian Jr Coll, Villanova, PA; SO; BA; Iota Kappa Sigma Sec 89-90; Sccr 89-90; AA 90; Scl Wrk.

**CAMERON, JANICE,** Bloomfield Coll, Bloomfield, NJ; JR; Alpha Kappa Psi.

**CAMERON, JULIE C,** Univ Of Southern Ms, Hattiesburg, MS; SO; BS; Chemistry; Tchr.

**CAMERON, KAREN J,** Brown Univ, Providence, RI; JR; Gym Instr 88; Alpha Chi Omega Sor Corrs Scrtry 88; Brwn Cmmnty Outrch Prog 88; Brwn U Athletic Schlrshp 88; Ivy League Gym Champs Tm 89-90; All-Ivy Leage Gym Tm 89; Mst Vlble Plyr Awd 89-90; Mst Imp Gym Awd 89-90; Brwn U Womens Vrsty Gym Tm 88; Psychlgy; Bsnss.**

**CAMERON, KIMBERLY S,** Johnson St Coll, Johnson, VT; FR; Prfssnl Wrtng; Jrnlsm.

**CAMERON, LAURA A,** Univ Of Nc At Greensboro, Greensboro, NC; SO; BS; Jr Marshall; Elem Ed.

**CAMERON, MARILYN J,** Marywood Coll, Scranton, PA; JR; BA; Delta Epsilon Sigma 89-; Bus/Acctg; Actnt.

**CAMERON, NANCY E,** Univ Of Southern Ms, Hattiesburg, MS; SR; BA; Spch Pthlgy.

**CAMERON, ROBERT J,** Indiana Univ Of Pa, Indiana, PA; SO; BS; TV Exctv Prdcr ETV 89-; The Pnn Cntrbtng Wrtr 89; Acrn Thtr Prjct Actr 89; Prvst Schlr; Deans Lst 89-; Cmmnctns Md.

**CAMERON, RUSSELL D,** Meridian Comm Coll, Meridian, MS; FR; Bshl.

**CAMERON, TRACI L,** Jackson St Univ, Jackson, MS; SO; BS; Acctng Soc 90-; Mrchng Band 90-; Alpha Lambda Delta Sec 90-; Eqtbl Real Est Int 90-; Acctng; CPA.

**CAMFIELD, DEBORAH A,** Fl International Univ, Miami, FL; FR; BS; Design.

**CAMINITI, SUSAN J,** Ramapo Coll Of Nj, Mahwah, NJ; SR; BA; Delta Mu Delta; Bus Admin; Marketing.

**CAMINO TORRES, JOSE R,** Inter Amer Univ Pr San German, San German, PR; SR; BBABA; Valle Hermosa Rec Assn 87-89; Natl Assn Accntnts 90-; Phi Sigma Alfa; Acctng/Finance; CPA.

**CAMIOLA, LISA M,** William Carey Coll, Hattiesburg, MS; GD; BSN; SGA 87-; Chrstn Flwshp 87-; Amer Red Cross Vol; Elnian Clb Philanthrpc Org 78-; Dns Lst Univ New Orleans 84; Pres Lst 87; Intermed Med Certif S Bapt Hosp 89; Nrsg; Med Sch.**

**CAMIRE, KIM M,** Univ Of New England, Biddeford, ME; SR; AD; Nrsng Clb 89-; All-Am Schlr Awd; CST Maint Med Ctr Sch Surgical Tech 88; Nrsng; Emerg/Trauma Nrsng.

**CAMISA, TERESA K,** Eckerd Coll, St Petersburg, FL; JR; BA; Earth Soc; Psychlgy Clb 88-; Dmcrts Clb 88-; Psychology; Family Therapy.

**CAMM, MELODY L,** Christopher Newport Coll, Newport News, VA; BED; Alpha Kappa Alpha Rsh Crhmn 85-86; Math Sstr GAMES Prgm; Rtl Mgr 86-; BA VA Tech; Ed; Elem Tchr.

**CAMMACK, FLOYD S,** Univ Of Ky, Lexington, KY; JR; BA; Engl; Law.

**CAMMACK, WILLIAM D,** Mt Saint Marys Coll & Seminary, Emmitsburg, MD; SR; BA; George Henry Miles Hon Soc 87-88; Pi Delta Phi; Pi Sigma Alpha; Alpha Mu Gamma; Rev John J Oneil Meml Prize; Track/Field 87-; Pol Sci; Foreign Serv.

**CAMMEL, MICHAEL J,** Kent St Univ Stark Cmps, North Canton, OH; FR; BA; Bus Admin; Owner Comm Cntr.

**CAMMILLERI, ROXANNE M,** Felician Coll, Lodi, NJ; SR; Questing Ed In Chf 88-90; Soph Rep 88; Drama Clb 89-; Amer Art Thrpy Assc 88-89; Clifton Art Assc Scnd Vp 90-; Lcl Nws Artcl Art Intrnshp 90; Drozd Skawinski Awd Schlrshp 87-; Deans Lnchn Hnr Cert 89-90; Art/Vsl Cmnctn Dsgn; MFA Art.

**CAMMILLERI, SANDRA LOUISE,** Felician Coll, Lodi, NJ; SR; BA; Crr Cnslng Nwslttr Crtr Wrtr; Coll Lit Mgzn Pblcty Dir 88-90; Stdnt Govt Rep 89; Spch Cmmnctn Assoc; Pssc Cnty Hstrcl Scty; Pr Spprtr Nw Stdnts 88-; TV Mv Crtc; Shw Hst Intern 90-; Pres Schlrshp 87-; Pblc Rltns Asst; Engl.

**CAMP, ALINE V,** Morgan St Univ, Baltimore, MD; JR; BS; Psychology Club 89-; Beta Kappa Chi; Pi Gamma Mu; Deans Lst 90-; Psychology.

**CAMP, ALLISON J,** Univ Of Sc At Lancaster, Lancaster, SC; FR; BA; Elem Ed; Tchr.

**CAMP, ALLYSON N,** Univ Of Nc At Greensboro, Greensboro, NC; SO; BA; Brdcstng Jrnlsm; Radio/TV.

**CAMP, APRIL LEIGH,** Univ Of Montevallo, Montevallo, AL; JR; BA; Sigma Tau Delta 90-; Jensen Awd; Eng/Intercltrl Stds.**

**CAMP, DAVID R,** Chattanooga St Tech Comm Coll, Chattanooga, TN; SO; BS; Math/Sci Clb Pres 87-88; Beta Clb 87-88; Cmptr Clb 87-; Phi Theta Kappa 90-; Hist Assn 87-; USMC Sci Awd 88; Kodak Intl Nwspr Snapshot Awd 87; Elec Eng/Cmptr Sci.

**CAMP, GINGER C,** Salisbury St Univ, Salisbury, MD; GD; Stdnt Senate Secy 87-89; SNEA 86-; Deans Lst 87-90; BS 90; Elem Educ; Teacher.

**CAMP, LAURA B,** Univ Of Sc At Columbia, Columbia, SC; JR; BA; Kappa Delta Pi; Gamma Psi Delta V P 88-; Erly Chldhd Educ; Spec Educ.

**CAMP, LORI J,** Clayton St Coll, Morrow, GA; GD; Delta Epslon Chi Sec 89-; Deans Lst 90; Delta Epsilon Chi Comp Mgmt Dcsn Mkng/Merch Cat 1st State Comp; Amer Grtngs Merch 84-; AAS; Mktg/Bus Mgmt; Sls Rep.

**CAMPANA, CHRISTOPHER A,** Widener Univ, Chester, PA; SR; BS; Data Proc Mgmt Assoc Treas 89-; Phi Eta Sigma V P; Alpha Chi 90-; Kappa Sigma Treas 88-; Data Proc Mgmt Assoc Reg II Outstndg Stdnt Awd; Mgmt Info Syst; CEO.

**CAMPANALE, DEANA M,** Newbury Coll, Brookline, MA; SO; BA; Bus; Mgmt.

**CAMPANARO, CHRISTOPHER M,** Univ Of Fl, Gainesville, FL; SR; BS; Hbtt Hmnty; IM Ftbl 90; Pre Lgl Hon Soc Wrtr Nwsltr 90-; Gldn Key 89-; Real Estate 90-; Deans Lst 88-; AIREA Apprsl Schlrshp 90; Intrcllgt Trck/Fld Syracuse 87-88; Real Estate/Bus Admin; Law.

**CAMPANELLA, PAULINE,** Oh St Univ At Marion, Marion, OH; SR; OH Edctnl Assoc 87-; Edctn Scty OSUM Sec 90; OH St Almn Assoc; 90 Prairie Edctnl Crdntr; BS Ed; Elem Ed; Tchng.

**CAMPANELLA, TIMOTHY J,** Villanova Univ, Villanova, PA; JR; BA; Republicans Clb 88-; Pre Law Scty 90-; Comm Yth Svc 88-; IM Bsktbl/Sccr/Sftbl Cptn 88-; History; Law.

**CAMPBELL, A HEATHER,** Birmingham Southern Coll, Birmingham, AL; JR; BA; FCA 90-; Cvtn Clb Tres 90-; Amnsty Intrntnl 88-89; Beta Beta Beta 90-; Chi Omega Tres 88-89; Vol Srvc 88-89; S Highland Hsptl Vol 88-; Biology Psychlgy; Orthdntst.

**CAMPBELL, ALEXANDRA P,** Johnson St Coll, Johnson, VT; SR; BA; Chesamore 88-; AS DHVIC Berlin N H 83; Bus; CPA.

**CAMPBELL, AMIE E,** Univ Of Cincinnati, Cincinnati, OH; FR; BM; Sigma Alpha Iota; Trombone Perf.

**CAMPBELL, AMY B,** Indiana Univ Of Pa, Indiana, PA; JR; BED; Stdnt PSEA 90-; Assoc Chldhd Ed Internatl 90-; Dns Lst 90-; Elem Ed; Tchr.

**CAMPBELL, AMY L,** Roane St Comm Coll, Harriman, TN; SO; MBA; Acctg.

**CAMPBELL, AMY MEREDITH,** Birmingham Southern Coll, Birmingham, AL; SO; BS; Fr Ldrshp Dvlpmnt 89-90; Links-Up Cnslr 89-90; Adult Lit Tutor Coord 90-; Alpha Epsilon Delta; Beta Beta Beta; Chi Omega Pldg Cls Pres 90; Amnesty Intl 89; Bsc Conservancy 90-; Bapt Campus Mnstrs 89-90; Intern Walrn; Bio/Psychlgy; Med.

**CAMPBELL, ANDREA D,** Jackson St Univ, Jackson, MS; SO; BS; Ntnl Stdnt Speech Hrng Lng Assn; Speech Comm Orgnztn; NAACP; Speech Cmnctn Dsrdr; Spch Pthlgst.

**CAMPBELL, ANDREW P,** Villanova Univ, Villanova, PA; JR; BA; Academic Hnrs Prog 88-; English/Liberal Arts; Law.**

**CAMPBELL, ANGELA B,** Pellissippi St Tech Comm Coll, Knoxville, TN; SO; AD; Coll Scec Intrntl Clb; Info Sys Tech; Sec/Wrd Prcssng Wrk.

**CAMPBELL, ANGELA L,** Clayton St Coll, Morrow, GA; SO; AS; Bapt Un 89-90; Envrmntl Awareness Clb 90-; Bus Mgmnt; Mgmnt BBA.

**CAMPBELL, ANITA N,** Coll Of Charleston, Charleston, SC; JR; BA; Phi Kappa Phi; Biology Tutor 90-; Biology; Educator.

**CAMPBELL, ANNETTE B,** Univ Of Fl, Gainesville, FL; SR; BSCE; ASCE 89; Tau Beta Pi 90; Golden Key 90; Eng.

**CAMPBELL, BECKY RUTH,** Univ Of Al At Birmingham, Birmingham, AL; SR; TCHR; Criminal Justice Scty 86-87; Deans List; IM Spts/Sftbl/Soccer/Bskbl; Amer Hrt Assoc 90-; United Way 88-89; Chbr Commer 88-89; AB Univ GA 87; Social Studies; Masters Schl Counselor.

**CAMPBELL, BELINDA ANN,** Univ Of Nc At Charlotte, Charlotte, NC; JR; BS; Intervrsty Chrstn Fllwshp 89-90; IM Ftbll, IM Vllybll 89-; Scndry Ed.

**CAMPBELL, BRUCE A,** Univ Of Va Clinch Valley Coll, Wise, VA; JR; BA; Wesley Fndtn 90-; Dean Lst Dist Stu 90-; Hstry; Tchng.

**CAMPBELL, CARMEN D,** Central Va Comm Coll, Lynchburg, VA; FR; MBA; Acctg; CPA.

**CAMPBELL, CARRIE A,** Le Moyne Coll, Syracuse, NY; FR; Clg Tour Guide; Soc; Soc Wrkr.

**CAMPBELL, CHRISTIE L,** Tusculum Coll, Greeneville, TN; SO; BA; Rsdnt Advsr; Vrsty Sftbl 89; Scl Studies; Law.

**CAMPBELL, CHRISTOPHER P,** Tusculum Coll, Greeneville, TN; JR; BA; Stdnt Gov Rep 88-89; Tusculum Drama Dept 88-; Alpha Chi 90-; Engl Scndry Ed; Tchng.

**CAMPBELL, CRAIG K,** Tn St Univ, Nashville, TN; JR; BA; Crmnl Jstc Orgnztn Asst Sec 90-; Spnsh Clb Prsdnt 89-; Gldn Key; Lambda Tau Epsilon; Alpha Mu Gamma 89-; TN Bureau Invstgatn; Crmnl Jstc.

**CAMPBELL, CYNTHIA MICHELLE,** Univ Of Sc At Columbia, Columbia, SC; SR; BA; Kappa Delta Epislon VP; AS Greenville Tech Clge 88; Elem Ed/Psychlgy; Cnslng Chldrn Absd.

**CAMPBELL, DARLENE G,** Central St Univ, Wilberforce, OH; SO; BA; Free Lance Mdl/Sls Rep 80-90; Cstmr Ser Rep 88-89; Pltcl Sci; Law.

**CAMPBELL, DAVID A,** Wv Univ, Morgantown, WV; SR; BS; ASME Pres; Vdo Yazaki Corp Intrnshp; Mech Engr.

**CAMPBELL, DAVID L,** Christopher Newport Coll, Newport News, VA; SO; BS; Hnrs Pgm 89; Engr.

**CAMPBELL, DAWN DE ANN,** Dyersburg St Comm Coll, Dyersburg, TN; SO; BA; Data Proc Mgmnt Assoc; Phi Theta Kappa; Bus/Comp Sci.

**CAMPBELL, DE ANNA K,** Roane St Comm Coll, Harriman, TN; Gen.

**CAMPBELL, DENISE N,** Roane St Comm Coll, Harriman, TN; FR; Medl; Physical Therapy Assist.

**CAMPBELL, DWIGHT L,** Johnson C Smith Univ, Charlotte, NC; SR; BA; US Cst Grd MORE Pgm; Hstry; Law.

**CAMPBELL, ELENA S,** Univ Of North Fl, Jacksonville, FL; JR; BA; Mrchng; Cncrt Bnds; Orchstr Frst Chr 88-90; Stff Wrtr Coll Newsppr 89-90; Alpha Mu Gamma 89-90; Cmmnctns; Pblc Rltns.

**CAMPBELL, ELIZABETH JANE,** Univ Of Sc At Columbia, Columbia, SC; JR; BA; Psi Chi; Kappa Kappa Gamma 88-; MR Center Vol; Craw Clb 88-89; Psychlgy; Ph D.

**CAMPBELL, ERIN M,** Fl St Univ, Tallahassee, FL; FR; BA; Campus Allnce/Litcy V P 91/Secy 90-; Phi Eta Sigma Pres; Busn; Acctng.

**CAMPBELL, FELINA D,** Univ Of Al At Birmingham, Birmingham, AL; SR; BSN; Phi Kappa Phi; Gldn Key 90; Psychlgy; Psychtrc Mntl Hlth Nrsng.

**CAMPBELL, GARY ALLEN,** Union Coll, Barbourville, KY; SO; BBA; Wldrnss Clb 90-; Gamma Beta Phi 90-; Pres Lvrt; US Army 86-89; Acctg; US Army.

**CAMPBELL, GERALD D,** Al St Univ, Montgomery, AL; JR; BA; CIS.

**CAMPBELL, GINGER E,** Univ Of Ky, Lexington, KY; SR; BA; Somerset Comm Coll Stdnt Svp 88-89; Govt Assn; AA Somerset Comm Coll 89; Early Elem Educ; Tchr.

**CAMPBELL, GWENDOLYN D,** Univ Of Sc At Columbia, Columbia, SC; SR; MA; Gamma Beta Phi 86-90; Golden Key 88-90; Kappa Delta Epsilon 88-90; BA S USC 90; Elem Ed; Tchr.

**CAMPBELL, HOPE E,** Univ Of Md Baltimore Prof Schl, Baltimore, MD; JR; BSP; Class 1992 Pres 89-; Stdnt Natl Pharmaceutical Assoc 89-; Acdmy Stdnts Pharmacy; Rho Chi 90-; Research Awrd Grant Neuro Phrmclby 90-; Science Teacher 85-89; BSC Univ West Indies 84; Pharmacy; Clinical Pharmacy.

**CAMPBELL, HULIAN H,** Alcorn St Univ, Lorman, MS; JR; BS; Hnr Stdnt Org 88-; Acctng Clb Sntr 90-; SIFE 90-91; Acctng.

**CAMPBELL, JAMES D,** Liberty Univ, Lynchburg, VA; BS; Phi Alpha Theta; Chancellors Schlrshp 88-89; Hstry; European Mltry Hstry Prof.

**CAMPBELL JR, JAMES R,** Rutgers St Univ At Camden, Camden, NJ; SR; BS; Mktg Clb 89-; Lacrosse Clb 87-88; Ski Club 87-88; Athenaeum; Sigma Nu 88; Deans Lst 87-; Mgmnt/Mktg; Law.

**CAMPBELL, JANET M,** Ny Univ, New York, NY; FR; BA; Cont Ed Schlr; Deans List; Lit/Phlsphy.

**CAMPBELL, JEFFERY G,** Union Coll, Barbourville, KY; SO; BS; SS Music Dir Bapt Chrch 88-; Math; Educ.

**CAMPBELL, JERALD M,** Univ Of Tn At Martin, Martin, TN; JR; BS; Crmnl Jstc; Crprt Law.

**CAMPBELL, JILL L,** Indiana Univ Of Pa, Indiana, PA; SO; BS; Spch Pthlgy Adlgy; Spch Pthlgy.

**CAMPBELL, JOAN A,** Lees Coll, Jackson, KY; FR; BA; Engl; Ed.

**CAMPBELL, JOHN D,** Marshall University, Huntington, WV; JR; Mktng.

**CAMPBELL, JOHN F,** Savannah Coll Of Art & Design, Savannah, GA; GD; MFA; Amer Inst Of Grphc Arts 89-; Grphx Grp Pres 90-; BA In Art Studio St Univ Of New York At Geneseo 89; Grphc Dsgn; Grphc Dsgnr.

**CAMPBELL, KAREN L,** Free Will Baptist Bible Coll, Nashville, TN; JR; BS; Pryr Capt Grp Ldr 90-; Elizabeth Barrett Browning VP 90-; Elem Educ; Tchg.

**CAMPBELL, KATHERINE D,** Allegheny Coll, Meadville, PA; SO; BA; Wmns Ensmbl 89-; Prvsts Com-TACC 90-; Allghny Cstm Shp Tech Dir Asst 90-; Alpha Chi Omega Cmnctns Chrmn 89-; Meadvl Soup Ktchn Vol 89; Phnllnc Pldg Tm 90; Alden Schlr 90; IM Sftbl Tm; Psychlgy-Clncl/Scl Wrk.

**CAMPBELL, KATHLYN J,** Bridgewater Coll, Bridgewater, VA; SO; BA; Day Stdnt Org 89-; Co Ownr C & C Guns 79-; Soc/Hstry Pltcl Sci; Tch Clg Prfsr.

**CAMPBELL, KATRINA C,** Hampton Univ, Hampton, VA; SO; BA; Stdnt Govt 90-; Nwspr 90-; Mass Media Arts; Print Jrnlsm.

**CAMPBELL, KELLY E,** Saint Joseph Coll, West Hartford, CT; JR; Best Buds Chptr Dir 90-; Spec Ed Clb Treas 88-; Chld Stdy Clb 89-90; Amnsty Intrnl 88-; Deans Lst; Res Asst 90-; Ct Robinson Hmntrn Svc Awd Nom; Spec Ed; Tchng.**

**CAMPBELL, KEVIN L,** Youngstown St Univ, Youngstown, OH; JR; BA; IEEE; Elec Engr.

**CAMPBELL, KIMBERLY L,** Univ Of Sc At Columbia, Columbia, SC; FR; BA; Gamma Beta Phi 90-; Psych; Elem Ed.

**CAMPBELL, KRISTI C,** Memphis St Univ, Memphis, TN; SO; BA; Peer Mentr Grp 89-; Alpha Lamda Delta 89-90; Phi Eta Sigma 89-90; Art Hstry.

**CAMPBELL, LEIGH ROBINSON,** Univ Of Al At Birmingham, Birmingham, AL; SO; BS; Alpha Lambda Delta 89-; Ullman Schlrshp Wnr; Vc Chrmn/Pst Chrmn/Tres/Sec/Lbrn Lvl Sprtl Asmbly Bhis Mt Brook; Pst Mbr Dist Tchg Comm; Fed Crtrm Dpty Clndr Rspnsblty; Cert Ntl Assoc Lgl Sec; Psych; Mediation.

**CAMPBELL, LENWASKI O,** Alcorn St Univ, Lorman, MS; SO; BA; Math; Tchr.

**CAMPBELL, LESLIE A,** Lexington Comm Coll, Lexington, KY; SO; ASSOC; Computer Infor Syst; Progr.

**CAMPBELL, LINDA M,** Atlantic Comm Coll, Mays Landing, NJ; FR; Alld Hlth; RN.

**CAMPBELL, LISA A,** Greenville Tech Coll, Greenville, SC; SO; AB; WP Cert; Bus; Sec/Cler.

**CAMPBELL, LISA M,** Lesley Coll, Cambridge, MA; JR; BED; Early Chldhd Educ/Daycare; Tchng.

**CAMPBELL, LISA WILLIAMS,** Bristol Univ, Bristol, TN; SR; BS; TN Pbl Hlth Assoc 89-90; Infort Syst Specialist 90-; Infor Syst Analysis 83-90; AS NE Regional Clg 82; Computer Sci; Computer Sci Mgt.

**CAMPBELL, LYNN E,** Springfield Tech Comm Coll, Springfield, MA; SR; AS; Phys Therapist Clb Sec 89-; Alpha Nu Omega 90-; Deans Lst 89-; Assoc Schuyllal Bus Inst 84; Phys Therapy.

**CAMPBELL, MARCIA J,** City Univ Of Ny Queensbrough, New York, NY; FR; C Step.

**CAMPBELL, MARGARET A,** Univ Of Sc At Coastal Carolina, Conway, SC; SO; BS; Pres Hnr Roll Chancellors Hnr Roll 90; Deans List 90; All Amer Schlr 90; Non Commissioned Officers Assoc 86-89; USAF 83-89; USAF Resvers 89-90; History; Military Historian.**

**CAMPBELL, MARGARET A,** Univ Of Sc At Coastal Carolina, Conway, SC; SO; BS; U S Air Force 83-89; U S Air Force Rsrvs 89-90; Hstry; Law/Govt.

**CAMPBELL, MARY HUNTER,** Christopher Newport Coll, Newport News, VA; SR; BA; Sclgy/Soc Work Clb Pres 89-; Orientation Ldr; Stdnt Govt Assn Pres Cncl 90-; Alpha Kappa Delta; Advsry Brd; Soc Work/Grntlgy.

**CAMPBELL, MATTHEW C,** Memphis St Univ, Memphis, TN; FR; BA; Jrnlsm; T V/Radio Rprtr/Naval Officer.

**CAMPBELL, MICHAEL F,** Kent St Univ Kent Cmps, Kent, OH; JR; BBA; Flr Hcky Clb 90-; Kung Fu Clb; Otstndg Coll Stu Amer 89-; Alpha Lambda Delta 89; Indstrl Mgmnt.

**CAMPBELL, MINDY L,** Radford Univ, Radford, VA; SO; BA; Poltcl Sci; Civil Svc.

**CAMPBELL, NATALIE R,** Univ Of North Fl, Jacksonville, FL; FR; IMANI 90-; AASU 90-; Pres Schlrshp; Chld Psych.

**CAMPBELL, PATRICIA A,** Sue Bennett Coll, London, KY; SO; BA; Phi Theta Kappa 89; Bkkpr Deputy Clrk Admin Offce Of Crts 81; Accntng; CPA.

**CAMPBELL, ROBERT B,** Niagara Univ, Niagara Univ, NY; SR; BS; Amer Inst Bio Sci Pres 88-; Amer Chem Soc 88-; St Vincent De Paul Soc Pres 90-; Sigma Xi; Multicltrl Issues Comm 89-; African Amer Stdnt Advsry Bd Comm 90-; Jstc Peace Cncl 89-; Dstngshd Stdnt Awd Excell Bio 90-; Bio/Chem; Med.

**CAMPBELL, ROBERT P,** Atlantic Comm Coll, Mays Landing, NJ; SO; AS; Phi Theta Kappa; Govt Prchsng Assn NJ; Deans Lst; Prncpl Prchsng Asst; Bus Mngmnt; BA Profssnl Prchsng.

**CAMPBELL, ROBERT S,** Clarkson Univ, Potsdam, NY; FR; BS; Natl Ski Patrol 90-; Ski Clb; IM Ftbl; Vars Bsebl; Bsn-Mgmt Info Syst; Syst Analyst.

**CAMPBELL, RODRICK W,** Springfield Tech Comm Coll, Springfield, MA; FR; MBA; Computer Science; Engineering.

**CAMPBELL, ROY L,** Ms St Univ, Miss State, MS; JR; BS; IEEE; MS Bptst Lay Mnstry Yth Coord 86-; Vclst 86-; Eta Kappa Nu; Alpha Lamda Delta 89-; Univ Hon Pgm 89-; Outstndng Hon Jr; Pres Lst 89-; Phase I Univ Hon Cert 90; Elect Eng.

**CAMPBELL, RUTHANNA J,** Beckley Coll, Beckley, WV; SO; Assoc Degree In Business; Psychology; Mstrs Psychology.

**CAMPBELL, SCOTT T,** Siena Coll, Loudonville, NY; SR; BS; Fin Club 87-; Pre Law Club 87; Traffic/Safety Appeals Board 88-90; Gnrl Elctrc Corp 90-; IM Sports 87-89; Fin; Bnkng.

**CAMPBELL, SHARON F,** Daytona Beach Comm Coll, Daytona Beach, FL; FR; BA; Ntl Grdn AD LITEM 7th Dist Fl Aptd Grdn; By Scts Am Tusarora Dist WEBLOS Ldr 90-; De Land Ltl Lg Bsbl Tm Mom; Hlth/Rehab Svcs Recp Vol 90-; Crmnl Jstc; Law.

**CAMPBELL, SHERRY L,** Union Coll, Barbourville, KY; JR; UC Hmcmng Ct Mbr 89-90; Chrldng; Dance Tm Co-Capt 88-90; Elem Ed K-4; Tchr.

**CAMPBELL, STACEY RANELL,** Univ Of Sc At Columbia, Columbia, SC; SO; BMU; Symp Orch 89; Alpha Lambda Delta Cnsl 90; Phi Eta Sigma 90; Music Ed; Tchr.

**CAMPBELL, STEPHANIE D,** Alcorn St Univ, Lorman, MS; FR; BE; BA; Bsnss Ed.

**CAMPBELL, TAMMY A,** Fl International Univ, Miami, FL; JR; BS; Cmps Mnstry 88-90; Occptnl Thrpy Scty 90-; Pi Theta Epislon; Deans Lst 90-; Pi Theta Epsilon 90-; AA Univ Sth FL 90-; Occptnl Thrpst.

**CAMPBELL, TAMMY L,** Univ Of Ky, Lexington, KY; JR; BA; Ukans 90-; KY Romance Writers 90-; Psychology.

**CAMPBELL, TIMOTHY D,** Southern Coll Of Tech, Marietta, GA; SR; BS; Electrcl Engrng Tchnlgy.

**CAMPBELL, TODD A,** Gaston Coll, Dallas, NC; SO; MBA; Stdnt Govt 90; AA; AS; Accntng/Bsnss Admin; Bsnss.

**CAMPBELL, TRACEY L,** Auburn Univ At Auburn, Auburn, AL; SR; MS; Natl Cncl Tchrs Math 90; Otstndng Undgrdt 89-90; Exercise Physlgy; Hlth Rltd Occptn.

**CAMPBELL, VICTORIA L,** Davis & Elkins Coll, Elkins, WV; JR; BS; Rep To The Bd Of Trustees 90-; Jennings-Randolph Ldrshp Prog 90-; Panathon Cntctng Slumni; Alpha Chi; Beta Alpha Beta 90-; Hons Assoc Prog Treas 88-; Phi Beta Lambda 88-; Alpha Chi Omega Treas 88-; F J Daniels Award 89-; Acctng/Fin; CPA.

**CAMPBELL III, WILLIAM E,** Livingston Univ, Livingston, AL; FR; BA; Delta Chi Tr 90-; Var Bsbl Mgr 90-; Intl Affrs; Intl Bnkg.

**CAMPER, KEVIN E,** Liberty Univ, Lynchburg, VA; SO; BED; Players Clb; Bsbl; Sprt Admnstrtn; Prf Bsbl Mgmt.

**CAMPERO, JENNIFER L,** Gallaudet Univ, Washington, DC; SO; Class 93 Asst Chmn Fndrsng 89-90; Dallas Assn Deaf Inc Chmn 90; Stdnt Body Govt Asst Chmn Fndrsng; Govt/Cmncntn Arts.

**CAMPION, DENISE M,** Central Pa Bus School, Summerdale, PA; FR; AS; Stdnt Govt; PBL; Chld Care Mgmt; Tchr Of A Day Care.

**CAMPION, KEVIN J,** Providence Coll, Providence, RI; FR; BA; Radio Sptscstr Prod 90-; Bg Bro/Sr 90-; Dns Lst 90-; IM Rugby Bsktbl Sccr 90-; Pol Sci/Bsns; Law.

**CAMPIONE, GINA MARIE,** Atlantic Comm Coll, Mays Landing, NJ; FR; Phrmcy/Tchng.

**CAMPNEY, CHRISTIE S,** Western New England Coll, Springfield, MA; SR; BSW; Residence Hall Assc 88; Behovioral Social Science Clb 89-; Intrnshp Hmpdn Cnty Spr Crt Pbtn 90-; Alumni Assc Awrd Excllnc.

**CAMPO, CHRISTINA K,** James Madison University, Harrisonburg, VA; FR; BS; Coach Vol Spec Olympcs 90-; Cmps 90-; CCM 90-; Cmps Crsd Chrst 90-; Art; Art Thrpy/Msc.

**CAMPO, JAIRO,** Saint Thomas Univ, Miami, FL; Dir Lib Columbiano Sec; Colombian Deputy; Universidad Libre Colombia Ecnmst; Riffle Assn Of Fla; Sacred League; Spnsh Lit/Educ; Bed Columbia.

**CAMPOLA, MARK W,** Schenectady County Comm Coll, Schenectady, NY; GD; AD; Hotel Mngmnt; Own Hotel.

**CAMPOS FELICIANO, JOHANNA R,** Catholic Univ Of Pr, Ponce, PR; JR; BSC; Youth Assoc Assmbly Chrstn Chrchs VP 88-; Science; Nurse.

**CAMPOS, GUADALUPE,** City Univ Of Ny Baruch Coll, New York, NY; JR; BA; AAS Borough Manhattan Cmuty Clg 86; Off Admn/Tech; Managerial Position.

**CAMPOS, JOSE A,** Miami Dade Comm Coll South, Miami, FL; SO; BA; US Army Srgnt; Sprvsr UPS; Hstry; Archtctr.

**CAMPOS, JOSHUA J,** Daytona Beach Comm Coll, Daytona Beach, FL; FR; AA; Busn/Advrtsng; Mgmt.

**CAMPOS, PAMELA S,** Columbia Union Coll, Takoma Park, MD; GD; BS; Fin Plnng Anlyst 85-; Bus Admin; Mgmt Comp Sci.

**CAMPOS, RODNEY E,** Embry Riddle Aeronautical Univ, Daytona Beach, FL; GD; BS; Arcrft Eng; Eng.

**CAMPOS, ROSA A,** Inter Amer Univ Pr San Juan, Hato Rey, PR; GD; BA Un Puerto Rico 86; Juris Doctor; Law.

**CAMPOS-DOLIVEIRA, PEDRO F,** Univ Of Miami, Coral Gables, FL; SR; BBA; Squash Clb Pr 90-; Soccer Clb 90-; Phi Theta Kappa Fndrsng Dir 89-; Clg Hons Pgm; Beta Gamma Sigma; Provosts Hon Rl 90-; Deans Lst 88-; Vlyble IM Champ; AA Miami-Dade Cmnty Clg 90; BBA; Fin; Bnking.

**CAMPS, JORDI,** Fl International Univ, Miami, FL; JR; BA; Math Tutor Lrng Ctr 90-; Acctg/Finance; CPA Law.

**CAMRON, TIM J,** Fl A & M Univ, Tallahassee, FL; FR; BA; Vrsty Ftbl; Lndscp Dsgn.

**CAMULAIRE, FRANTZ,** City Univ Of Ny City Coll, New York, NY; SO; PHD; Engr Ret Pgm; RCMS; NACME; Con-Ed Schlrshp; Engr Aid Intrn; Mech Engr.

**CANADA, BRODERICK N,** Al A & M Univ, Normal, AL; SO; BA; Soc Sci Clb; Pep Clb; SGA Frshmn Class Treas 89-90; Sigma Tau Epsilon; Alpha Phi Alpha Corr Sec 90-; Deans List 89-; IM Ftbl 89-; Am Red Cross Bld Dnr 89-; Elem Schl Tchr; Elem Ed; 8th Grade Engl Tchr.

**CANADA, JESSE A,** Union Univ, Jackson, TN; SR; BS; Vlntr Ynglf Ldr 87-; Sigma Alpha Epsilon 87-; Psychology.

**CANADA, JOAN E,** Univ Of Charleston, Charleston, WV; SO; BA; Alpha Lambda Delta; Dns Lst 89-; AWANA Chrch Orgnztn Ldr 87-; AA; Psych; Law.

**CANADA, LAURA J,** Univ Of Southern Ms, Hattiesburg, MS; SR; BS; ACS Sec 89; Hon Cncl Exe Cmtee 89; Hon Stdnt Assn 87; Alpha Lambda Delta 88-90; Omnicron Delta Kappa 90-; Phi Delta Rho 90; Delta Zeta Schlrshp Chrmn 88-; Angel Flight 87-89; Monsanto Chem Co Intrn 90-; Chem; Med Rsrch.

**CANADA, WEYLIN I,** Hampton Univ, Hampton, VA; SO; BS; Exec Cncl 90-; Bus Clb Stndt Govt 90-; Fla Pre Alumni Treas 90-; Boys Clb 90-; Intrn Dean Witter 90-; Fin; Secrtes Brkr.

**CANADY, MARIA L,** Fl Atlantic Univ, Boca Raton, FL; SR; Bus Mgmt; Tchng.

**CANAFF, ROGER A,** Univ Of Nc At Charlotte, Charlotte, NC; JR; BA; Stdnt Leg Lt Gov 90-; Stdnt Leg Gov; Stdnt Govt Assoc Chr Of Leg; Pol Sci; Law.

**CANAGANAYAGAM, DHARINI,** Elms Coll, Chicopee, MA; SO; BSC; Chem Clb Co Pres 90-; Ornttn Advsr 89-; Std Amb 89-90; Intl Clb 89-; Fresh Chem Achv Awd 89; Intl Std Grnt 89-; Bio/Chem; Med/Surgery.

**CANAGANAYAGAM, SHIVANTHI,** Elms Coll, Chicopee, MA; BA; Intl Clb; Ambsdr Orntatn Advsr Liturgical; Dance Grp; Choir; Intl Stdnt Schlrshp; Cert Colombo Intl Sch 89; Bus Mgmt/ Acctg; Acctg.

**CANALE, TAMELA L,** Coll Of Charleston, Charleston, SC; JR; BA; Lang Asstnt In Spanish Dept 90-; AA Trident Tchnl Clge 90; Spanish; Teaching.

**CANALE, TONY D,** Manhattan Coll, Bronx, NY; FR; BS; Cvl Eng; Eng.

**CANALES, MICHAEL J,** Western New England Coll, Springfield, MA; JR; BA; Tennis 90-; Coach :YMCA Bsktbl 88-90; Johnson Elem Schl Prog 88-89; History; Professor.

**CANCIO, JOSE A,** Univ Of Pr At Mayaguez, Mayaguez, PR; JR; BS; Amer Chem Soc Stdnt Affliatt 89-; Hnr Brd 89-; Phi Sigma Alfa 88-; NCSSA 90-; Dns Lst 89-; Chem; Med.

**CANDEE, BERTON W,** S U N Y Coll Of Tech At Alfred, Alfred, NY; FR; AAS; NY Patriot Soc Indvdl Lbrts Assn 81-86; Cmcl/Rsdntl Elctrcn 78-; Electro/Mech Eng; Mnfctrng/Ind.

**CANDEE, JAY A,** Bridgeport Engr Inst, Fairfield, CT; JR; BSEE; ASEE Waterbury St Tech Coll 85; Elec Eng.

**CANDELARIA MARRERO, GERMAN R,** Univ Of Pr At Rio Piedras, Rio Piedras, PR; SO; BBA; Math.

**CANDOCIA, FRANK M,** Fl International Univ, Miami, FL; GD; MS; BS 90; Sci; Elec Eng.

**CANDREVA, SCOTT R,** Saint Josephs Coll Suffolk Cmps, Patchogue, NY; JR; BS; Bus Clb Treas 88-; Sigma Iota Chi 89-; Delta Mu Delta Treas 90-; Acdmc Schlrshp Awrd 88-; Mncpl Pblc Wrks Mngmnt Intern 90-; Bwlng Tm 89-; Accntng; CPA.**

**CANDY, MARY JO,** Springfield Tech Comm Coll, Springfield, MA; BS; Physl Therapy Assist Club 89-; Alpha Nu Omega 90-; Grad Cam Lau De; Amer Phys Therapy Assoc 90; Friends Holyoke Range 89-; Aetna Life/Casualty Claims Dept 83-88; Exer Sci; Specialize Muscle.

**CANEDO III, RICARDO B,** Oh Wesleyan Univ, Delaware, OH; FR; BA; Hrzns Intrnatl 90-; Acctng Comp Sci; Bus.

**CANEJO, SHIRLEY M,** Newbury Coll, Brookline, MA; FR; Intr Dsgn.

**CANFIELD, CAROLYN T,** Lenoir Rhyne Coll, Hickory, NC; SR; BA; Sign Troupe 87-90; Newman Clb 88-90; Chapel Cncl 88-90; Mu Sigma Epsilon 90-; Broyhill Ldrshp Mntr Prog 88-89; Kappa Delta 88-; Circle K 87-88; Sp Ed HI/ELEM Ed; Tchr.

**CANFIELD, KATHRYN M,** Univ Of Nh Plymouth St Coll, Plymouth, NH; SO; BS; Crisis Prgnancy Cntr Vol; Lctr At Chrch; Pres Lst 90-; Elem Ed; Tchng.

**CANGANI, CAMILLO,** Univ Politecnica De Pr, Hato Rey, PR; JR; BA; Engr.

**CANGIALOSI, ANDRIANA M,** Radford Univ, Radford, VA; SR; BSW; Natl Assoc Of Soc Wrkrs 90-; Rho Lambda 90-; Phi Alpha Pres 90-; Alpha Sigma Tau Fndrsng/Exec Cncl 89-; Elbert H/Evelyn S Waldron Schlrshp 90-; Srch Comm Dean Clg Of Ed/ Human Dev 90-; Tour Guide 90-; Greek Wk Co Chrprsn 90-; Soc Wrk; Pvt Cnslr LCSW.

**CANGIANO, JEANETTE,** Miami Dade Comm Coll, Miami, FL; SO; AA; Phi Theta Kappa 89-; William Mc Knight Emphasis Excellence Schlrshp 90; Linda Ray Infant Ctr Vol 89-90; Exec Assist Greater Miami Host Comm; Phy Therapy; BS.

**CANINO, MICHAEL J,** Glassboro St Coll, Glassboro, NJ; JR; BA; PROS; Stdnt Govt Assoc Treas; Stdnt Fncl Control Bd; Gamma Tau Sigma; Newspaper Stf Wrtr; Literary Mag; Albert J Taylor Schlrshp; Bando Karate; Engl/Philosophy; Ed.

**CANIPE, CARISA V,** Catawba Valley Comm Coll, Hickory, NC; FR; SADD 87-88; Bio/Elem Ed.

**CANIPE, JENNIFER A,** Univ Of Sc At Columbia, Columbia, SC; SR; BS; Amer Soc Mech Engrs 88-; Inst Electrcl/Electrnc Engrs 86 88; Duke Power Co Co Op Clb Soc Chrprsn 88, Otstdng Clg Stdnt Amer 90; Deans Lst 89; I M Stbl 89; Mech Engr.**

**CANN, RENEE N,** Howard Univ, Washington, DC; GD; MSW; Natl Collgt Social Sci Awrd 90; Natl Assoc Social Workers 90-; BA York Univ 89; Social Worker; Child Welfare.**

**CANNATA III, EDWARD N,** Radford Univ, Radford, VA; SO; BA; Schl Nwspaper Phtgrphr 90; Jz Bnd Ld Tnr 90; Comp Sci.

**CANNATA, LISA,** S U N Y Coll Of Tech At Frmgdl, Farmingdale, NY; SO; AS; Stdnt Un Brd 89-90; Fr Orientatn Org Comm 89-90; Whlhs 89-90; Lbrl Arts; Elem Ed.

**CANNATGELLI, LORETTA M,** Wilmington Coll, New Castle, DE; SO; BA; NAEYC; Behavior Sci; Thrpst.

**CANNAVAN, JACQUELINE E,** Saint Thomas Univ, Miami, FL; SR; BA; Pltcl Actn Clb Pres 89-; SG 89-; Delta Epsilon Sigma Pres 90-; Delta Phi Epsilon Hstrn/Pblc Rltns 90-; Cir K 89-; IM Sprts 89-; Poly Sci; MBA.

**CANNELLA, LAUREEN A,** City Univ Of Ny Queensbrough, New York, NY; SO; BS; PA Of Bronx HS Of Sci 90-; PA Of PS 91 88-; Phi Theta Kappa 89-90; QCC Chptr Of Cny Womens Coalition; Woman Of Exclnc Award; George Alterman Award; AS; Physcl Thrpy.

**CANNELLA, TIMOTHY P,** Christopher Newport Coll, Newport News, VA; JR; BSBA; Amer Mktng Assoc; Omicron Delta Epsilon; Amer Cancer Scty Bqudson Spts Boosters; Deans List; Econ/Fin; Fin Plng.

**CANNICK, HARVIETTA ELAINE,** Savannah St Coll, Savannah, GA; FR; BA; Rape Crsis Cnslr; Sfe Shltr; Sec Savannah St Clg 89-; Soc Wrk; Soc Wrkr/Elem Educ.

**CANNIZZARO, CHARLES A,** East Tn St Univ, Johnson City, TN; GD; Orntn Comm 88-; Acdmc Prmtns Comm Class 87-; Alzheimers Disease Support Grp; Class Pres; Alpha Omega Alpha; Am Med Assn 87-; Am Phys Thrpy Assn 87-; Am Med Stdnt Assn 87-; Rsdncy Johns Hopkins Rehab Med Prog Sinai Hosp Baltimore; Rehab Med.

**CANNON, CHARLES E,** Valdosta St Coll, Valdosta, GA; SO; BS; NSPE Pres 90-; ACM 90-; Pres Freehmon Schlr 90; Dip Valdosta Tech Inst 87; Elec Engr.

**CANNON, CRAIG L,** Southern Coll Of Tech, Marietta, GA; SR.

**CANNON, DIANA S,** Coll Of Charleston, Charleston, SC; SO; BS; Geology Cl 89-; Biol Cl; Marine Biol; Marine Bioligst; Envmntl Studies.

**CANNON, GARY W,** Brewer St Jr Coll, Fayette, AL; SO; BA; Phi Theta Kappa; Engr.

**CANNON, GEORGIA A,** Coll Of Charleston, Charleston, SC; JR; BED; Coll Hnrs Prog; Omicron Delta Kappa; Alpha Phi Omega; IM Vlybl Sftbl Ftbl; Elem Educ; Tchr.

**CANNON, JAMES T,** Mobile Coll, Mobile, AL; SR; BA; Mnstrl Assc 87-89; Bptst Stdnt Union 87-89; Alpha Chi Vp 89-; Theta Alpha Kappa Vp 89-; Sigma Tau Delta Vp 89-; Rcgntn Potntl Fr Futr Accmplshmnt; Pres Lst; Deans Lst; Relgn/Engl; Ph D Theology/Phlsphy.

**CANNON, JUDY P,** Troy St Univ At Dothan, Dothan, AL; SR; BS; Phi Theta Kapa Pblc Rltns Ofcr 80-82; Gamma Beta Phi; Fe Soph Of Yr 82; Early Cty Mntl Health; AS Bainbridge Jr Coll 82; Psychology; Cnslng.

**CANNON, KEISHA L,** Clark Atlanta Univ, Atlanta, GA; FR; BA; Deans Lst; Pol Sci; Intl Relations.

**CANNON, LEANNE R,** Indiana Univ Of Pa, Indiana, PA; SR; BS; Dns Lst 89; MENSA; Tchg Lrng Dis Eaton Mdl Sch; Spec Ed.

**CANNON, MARTHA J,** Univ Of Sc At Columbia, Columbia, SC; GD; BSN; WMU; Nrsng Hon Soc; Gamma Beta Phi; Cum Laude BSN Grad; AAMA Pres 89; Urolgy Nrs; Nrsng.

**CANNON, MELANIE R,** Winthrop Coll, Rock Hill, SC; SO; BA; Stdnt Ntnl Edctn Assn 90-; Cncl Excptnl Chldrn 90-; Spcl Edctn; Tchng.

**CANNON, STEPHANIE A,** Seton Hall Univ, South Orange, NJ; SO; BS; Kappa Delta Pi; Stdnt Intrnshps 90; Chldrns Inst Stdnt Tchr; E Orng YMCA; Spec Ed; Tchr Hndcpd.

**CANNON, TRACY L,** Atlantic Comm Coll, Mays Landing, NJ; GD; BA; Phys Thrpy Assoc 88-90; Career Day Vol 89-90; PTAP Vol 90; Mem Hosp Intrn 89-90; AAS Atlantic Comm Clg 90; Biology; MS Phys Thrpy.

**CANNON, YVONNE M,** Central St Univ, Wilberforce, OH; JR; BS; Psi Chi Natl Hon Soc VP 90-; Alpha Kappa Mu 89-; Alpha Kappa Alpha; Minrty Accs Resrch Carrs 90-; Am Bus Wmn Assn 88-; Chrlding Squad Co-Capt 89-; Psych; Psychologist.

**CANO-ALICEA, NOEMI,** City Univ Of Ny Bronx Comm Col, Bronx, NY; SO; BS; Phi Theta Kappa IOC Rep 90; Phi Theta Kappa; Deans Lst 89-90; DA Intrnshp 90; Tlnt Rstr Coll Brds Coll Schlrshp Serv 90; Brnx Comm Coll Fndtn Schlrshp 90; Prnt Advct Lf Off Mngmnt Assn Inst Fndmntls Lf Ins Crs 80; AAS; Crmnl Jstce/Poltcl Sci; Law.

**CANOCELIS, CARLOS C,** Miami Dade Comm Coll, Miami, FL; SO; Dean Lst 89-90; Full Tuition Schlrshp NWSA 89-; Otstndng Acdmc Achvmnt 90-; Schlrshp Inter Amer Music Soc 90; Music; Music Cmpstn.

**CANODY, THOMAS E,** George Mason Univ, Fairfax, VA; SR; BS; Stdnt Educ Assn 89-; Wrestling 86-90; Erly Chldhd Educ; Tchng.

**CANON, ANDREA L,** Univ Of Southern Ms, Hattiesburg, MS; JR; BA; Right To Life Org 88-; Boosting Alcohol Consciousness 88-; Cncrng Hlth Univ Stdnts Stdnt Alumni Assoc 88-; Pi Beta Phi 88-; Each One Teach Hattisburg Edn Literacy Proj 90-; Cncl Psychlgst.

**CANONGE, HECTOR A,** City Univ Of Ny Baruch Coll, New York, NY; SR; BBA; Frgn Trade Soc T 89; Frgn Trade Soc P 90-; Golden Key 90-; Fresh Orient Svcs Ldr 89; 42nd Annul Stdnt Conf US Affrs W Pnt Dlgt 90; I H Kellar Awd P; H Wollman Prz; Intrntl Mktg; Intrntl Corp Law.

**CANSECO HERNANDEZ, ROBERTO,** Univ Politecnica De Pr, Hato Rey, PR; SO; BS; Mech Engrng.

**CANTAVE, PIERRE J,** S U N Y Coll Of Tech At Frmgdl, Farmingdale, NY; JR; Soc Mfg Eng 89-; Ba Tech; Mfg Eng.

**CANTELMI, ROSE A,** City Univ Of Ny Baruch Coll, New York, NY; JR; BA; History; Intl Bsn.

**CANTER, HARRY J,** Anne Arundel Comm Coll, Arnold, MD; SO; BA; Athletic Hnr Rl; Vars Golf; Financial Mgmtn.

**CANTER, JAMES R,** Lenoir Rhyne Coll, Hickory, NC; FR; BA; Hstry.

**CANTEY, KIMBERLY E,** Coker Coll, Hartsville, SC; FR; FCA 90-; CHOICE 90-; Vrsty Vllybll Sftbll; IM Bsktbll Vllybll 90-; Physcl Ed.

**CANTON, ALBERT G,** Youngstown St Univ, Youngstown, OH; SO; BA; IIE; Eng; Ind Engr.

**CANTOS, CHRISTINE M,** Fl St Univ, Tallahassee, FL; JR; BS; Radio Sta News Anchor 90-; Wmn In Cmunctns 90-; Fla Acad Schlrshp 88-; Hon Schlrshp 88-; Acad Trans Schlrshp; AA Edicon Comunty Clg 90-; Communications; Pub Rltns Radio.

**CANTRELL, ANDRIA N,** Univ Of Nc At Asheville, Asheville, NC; SR; BA; Sclgy Clb 89-; Sclgcl Hnr Scty; Sclgy Awrd; Qlty Frwrd; Sclgy.

**CANTRELL, CARA-KRISTEN D,** Oh Wesleyan Univ, Delaware, OH; SR; Vrsty Fld Hcky Cptn 87-; Vrsty Lacrosse 87-; Stdnt PE Brd; Kappa Kelta Phi 90-; Otstndng Clg Stdnts Amrca 87-; Delta Delta Delta Spnr Chrmn 87-; Ba; Physcl Edctn; Edctn.

**CANTRELL, DELANO BROWN,** Midlands Tech Coll, Columbia, SC; SO; ADN; Phi Theta Kappa; Parmdcs Instrctr ACLS/BTLS Instrctr; Paramedic; Flght Parmdc Prvdnc Lf Rch; Parmdc Cert Chipola Jr Clg 76; Nrsng; MSN.

**CANTRELL, DONNA J,** Central Al Comm Coll, Alexander City, AL; SO; BA; Comp Sci; Prgrmng.

**CANTRELL, LORI ALESIA B,** Univ Of Sc At Spartanburg, Spartanburg, SC; SR; BA; Piedmont Soc 89-; Kappa Delta Pi 89-; Dean Lst 88-; Pres Hnr Rll 88-; Elem Educ; Tch.

**CANTRELL, LORI C,** Univ Of Tn At Martin, Martin, TN; SR; BS; Stdnt TN Edn 88-; Phi Kappa Phi; Deans Lst 89-; Edn; Teach.

**CANTRELL, LYNN D,** Livingston Univ, Livingston, AL; SO; BA; Pnhlnc Cncl Sec 90-; Histrcl Soc 90-; Alpha Sigma Tau Treas 89-; IM Sprts Sftbl 89-; Erly Chldhd Ed/Hist; Tchng.

**CANTRELL, MARY E,** Univ Of Ga, Athens, GA; JR; Cmmnvrsty Tchrs Asst 90-; Alpha Gamma Delta 89-; IM Indr Sccr 90-; Erly Chldhd Educ; Tch.

**CANTRELL, MARY J,** Fl St Univ, Tallahassee, FL; JR; BA; Stdnt Cltn Agnst Aprthd/Rcsm 89-90; Stdnt Mvmnt Soc Jstc Tres 90-; Intrn Judge Harris P Hines 90; Superior Ct; Marietta GA; Anthrplgy, Tchng Wrtng Rsrch.

**CANTRELL, PATRICIA A,** Ashland Comm Coll, Ashland, KY; SO; Dmcrt Clb; Nrsng.

**CANTRELL, RACHEL A,** Middle Tn St Univ, Murfreesboro, TN; SR; BS; Perf Arts Co Pres 89-90; Blue Moves Dance Co Co-Fndr 89; Hnrs Stdnt Assoc Steering Comm 89-; Natl Hnrs Semester Morrocco; Jrnlsm/Engl; Mag Wrtr/Edtr.

**CANTRELL, REGINA D,** Volunteer St Comm Coll, Gallatin, TN; SO; BA; FCA Carson-Newman Clg 89-; BSU Carson-Newman Clg; Nursing.

**CANTRELL, SCOTT D,** Ms St Univ, Miss State, MS; SR; Phi Alpha Theta; Intra Ftbl Bsktbl Sftbl Bsbl 87-89; BS; Soc Studies; Tchr Coach.

**CANTWELL, CYNTHIA D,** Univ Of Tn At Knoxville, Knoxville, TN; JR; BA; Amer Mrktng Assoc 90-; Phi Eta Sigma 88; Alpha Xi Delta Treas 90-; Marketing; Research/Development.

**CANTWELL, PAULA T,** Univ Of Ri, Kingston, RI; JR; BS; Sigma Theta Tau; Dns Lst 90-; Cranston Gen Hosp LPN 89-; LPN Cmnty Clg RI 76; BS Bio Westfield State Clg 87; Nrsg.

**CANTY, CAROL A,** Benedict Coll, Columbia, SC; SR; BSS; Deans Lst 87-90; Prsdnts Lst; Vllybll 86-90; Thrptc Rcrtn.

**CANTY, KEVIN M,** S U N Y Coll Of Tech At Frmgdl, Farmingdale, NY; SO; BA; Grocry Store Mgr 86-; Bus; Acctg.

**CANUPP, JOHN R,** Faulkner St Jr Coll, Bay Minette, AL; SO; BA; Mscns Clb Pres; Intrmntl Music Awrd 90; Drctrs Awrd Frshmn Music Awrd 90; Jazzbnd Awrd; Music; Studio Musician.

**CAO, LAN T,** Richard Bland Coll, Petersburg, VA; SO; AS; Rotaract Club Pres 89-; Hon Ct Rep 90-; SGA Rep 90-; Bon Homme Richard Wrtr 89-90; Mnemosyne Prose Edtr 90-; Ricard Blands Plyr Stg Mrg/Actress 90-; Pores List 90; Talnt Roster Of Outstndng Mnrty Comm Clg; Im Vlybl/Tennis 90-; Intrntl Rltns; Diplmtc Wrk.

**CAPALDO, ROSEMARY,** Dowling Coll, Oakdale Li, NY; SO; Dance Choreograph Sabatino Verlezza 90; Engl; Clncl Psych.

**CAPANNA, LYNN R,** Wv Univ, Morgantown, WV; JR; BSW; Socl Work Org 90-; Socl Work; Grad Schl.

**CAPDEVILA, EVELYN,** Miami Dade Comm Coll, Miami, FL; FR; AS; Physcl Thrpy Asst.

**CAPE, CYNTHIA M,** Anderson Coll, Anderson, SC; SO; BS; Trojettes Treas 89-90; Gamma Beta Phi V Pres 89-90; J Lacy Mcclane Awrd; Ldrshp Schlrshp; Mktng.

**CAPECCI, PIERO,** Muskingum Coll, New Concord, OH; JR; BS; Tri Beta V Pres 89-; Sigma Xi; Stag Club Sec/Treas 89-; Biology; Medicine.

**CAPEL, PATRICIA P,** Fayetteville St Univ, Fayetteville, NC; JR; BA; Art Clb 90; Deans Lst 90; Mnrty Bsnss; Spksmn For Beauty/Fitness Wk; VP Of Chrch Choir; Hair Dsgnr; Visual Arts/Mrktng; Cmmrcl Artst Intrior Dsgn.

**CAPELLA-PRATTS, JOSE M,** Inter Amer Univ Pr San German, San German, PR; JR; BA; Psychology Stdnts Assn 90-; Acad Excellence Psychology Awd 90-; Psychology; Presby Minister.

**CAPERS, CHRISTOPHER F,** Univ Of Pittsburgh, Pittsburgh, PA; FR; BA; Blk Action Soc 90-91; Natl Soc Blk Engrs V P 90-92; Shc Engr Impact Prog Inrds V P; G E Intrn 90-91; Chnclr Schlrshp 91-; Engr.

**CAPERS, DWAIN A,** Al A & M Univ, Normal, AL; FR; Acctng; CPA.

**CAPERS, TOSHA A,** Morris Brown Coll, Atlanta, GA; SO.

**CAPERS, TRAVIS D,** Univ Of Sc At Columbia, Columbia, SC; FR; Bus Mgmt Sci.

**CAPERTON, THAD A,** Ms St Univ, Miss State, MS; FR; BA; TV News Hl Cncl Sec 90-; Phi Eta Sigma; Gamma Beta Phi; Lambda Sigma; Kappa Alpha; Sam Dudley Comm Schlrshp 90-; Prsdnts Schlr 90-; Cmmnctn; TV Prdcr.

**CAPILLE, SUSAN E,** Atlantic Comm Coll, Mays Landing, NJ; SO; AAS; Nrs Clb 90-; Ntl Stu Nrs Assoc Inc 90-; ASSE Exchng Pro Hst Prnt 88-; Nrsg.

**CAPIOLA, NANCY E,** Univ Of South Al, Mobile, AL; SR; BS; Deans Lst 90-; Soc Hmn Rsrc Mngrs; Assn Soc Prsnl Admn; BS; Hmn Rsrc Mgmnt; HRM Cnsltng Prsnl Mgt.

**CAPITTI, LISA M,** Montclair St Coll, Upr Montclair, NJ; SO; BA; Psychlgy.**

**CAPIZZANO, MICHAEL S,** Springfield Tech Comm Coll, Springfield, MA; SR; BS; Alpha Nu Omega 90-; AS; Elec Rbtcs Tech; Eng.

**CAPLAN, PAMELA J,** Univ Of Fl, Gainesville, FL; SR; BS; Chrldrs 86; Phi Kappa Phi; Delta Delta Delta Hstrn Pblc Rltns Corr 85; Natl Coll Awrd; Chrldrs 86; Amrcn Assoc Physcn Assts 89-; Flrd Assoc Physcn Assts 89-; BS 88; BSPA; Physcn Asst Med.

**CAPLE, MARGARET A,** Coll Of Charleston, Charleston, SC; SO; BA; Stdnt Alum Assn; Alpha Delta Pi 89-; IM Sports 89-; Psych; Child Psychlgst.

**CAPOBIANCO, WILLIAM F,** Methodist Coll, Fayetteville, NC; FR; BS; Cmps Escort Svc; Fayetteville Roadrunners Soccer Coach; Soccer 90; Phys Educ; Tchng.

**CAPOCCI, JOHN A,** Iona College, New Rochelle, NY; SO; BA; Pltcl Sic; Law.**

**CAPOGROSSI, TRICIA A,** Univ Of Ga, Athens, GA; SR; BSW; Natl Assoc Of Soc Workers 90-; Ga Rtrdtn Ctr Vol 90-; Winter Spec Olympcs Vol; Gamma Sigma Sigma 90-; Soc Work Intern Ctrl St Hosp C & A Unit; Soc Work Intern Fine Finish MR Ctr 90-; Soc Work.

**CAPONE, CARLA,** Glassboro St Coll, Glassboro, NJ; JR; BS; Glassboro State EMS 89-; Bio; Grad Sch.

**CAPORALI, JANEL,** Marywood Coll, Scranton, PA; JR; BS; Math Clb 89-; Kappa Mu Epsilon 90-; Bsktbl Tm 88-90; Math/Sec Educ; Tchr.

**CAPOTE, CAROLINA M,** Ms St Univ, Miss State, MS; SR; BA; Spnsh Grman.

**CAPOTE, MARIA LOURDES,** Ny Univ, New York, NY; SR; BA; Alph Sgm Lmbd; Deans List; CWA 1101 Shop Stwrd; The Vigilia; Swthng Equip Techcn; Art Hist; Law Sch.

**CAPOTOSTO, MONICA E,** Univ Of Akron, Akron, OH; JR; BA; Kappa Kappa Gamma; Art Edn; Teach.

**CAPOZZI, DAVID A,** Rutgers St Univ At Camden, Camden, NJ; SR; BS; Mktg Assn 90-; Fndng Cngrsmn Bus Schl Stdnt Cngrss Rtgrs 90-; Anthaneum; Phi Kappa Sigma Pres 90; Melitta Intl Schlrshp Acdmc Exclnce 90; IM Sftbl/Ftbl 87-; Phi Kappa Sigma Educ Schlrshp 90; Rtgrs Bus Schl Awrd Outstndng Mgmt Stdnt; Bus Mgmt; Law Schl.

**CAPOZZI, MICHAEL J,** George Mason Univ, Fairfax, VA; SR; BS; Acctg Clb 88-; Cyclng Clb 88-90; Golden Key 90-; Cmnty Tax Aid 90; IM Ftbl/Bsktbl 89-90; Acctg; Mgmrl Adtr.

**CAPOZZOLO, PATRICK E,** Daytona Beach Comm Coll, Daytona Beach, FL; FR; AS; Phtgrphy; Dcmntry Phtgrphr.

**CAPPADONIA, THOMAS E,** Utica Coll Of Syracuse Univ, Utica, NY; SR; BS; Data Procsng Mgt Assoc 80-81; Alpha Sigma Lambda 90-; Deans List 89-90; Cont Eductn Award For Outstndng Clg Perfrmnc; Progrmr/Anlyst 83-; Comptr Asst 80-81; AAS Morrisville Ag/Tech Clg 82; Bus Admn; Info Sys Mgt.**

**CAPPEL, ANITA L,** Univ Of Cincinnati, Cincinnati, OH; SO; BA; Nrsng.

**CAPPELLO, LORI A,** Bloomfield Coll, Bloomfield, NJ; FR; Cmmctns.

**CAPPIELLO, SCOTT C,** Va Polytechnic Inst & St Univ, Blacksburg, VA; FR; BS; Stdnt Govt Pblc Rltns Sec 90-; Stdnt Almn Assoc; Nwsppr Prdctn Ed 90-; Bradley Elec Eng Schlrshp; Almn Prsdntl Schlrshp 90-; Hahn Eng Schlrshp 90-; Comp Eng.

**CAPPIELLO, ZINA B,** Lehigh Univ, Bethlehem, PA; FR; BA; Chrldng 90-; Alpha Gamma Delta; Bio; Doctor.

**CAPPLEMAN, WADE B,** Blue Mountain Coll, Blue Mountain, MS; SR; BA; Psy Club 90-; Ministerial Alliance 90-; Tippah Co Child Serv Student Wrkr 90; No MISS Medl Ctr Student Chpln; Dumas Bapt Chrh 90-; US Air Force Secty/Trng Syst 81-89; AS Comm Clg Air Force 87-88; Bible/Psy; Pastor/Counselor.

**CAPPOLA, KIMBERLY A,** Fl International Univ, Miami, FL; SR; BA; Brd Gvrnrs 90-; Intl Dance Exerc Assn 90-; Phi Kappa Phi 90-; Phi Lambda Beta 90-; Sclgy; Mstrs Ntrtn Dietetics.

**CAPPS, JUDY W,** Bristol Univ, Bristol, TN; JR; BA; Indpndnt Tele Pioneer Assc VP; Ladies Aux Brstl Shrine Clb Sec; Utd Way Bluff Cty VP; Cost Svc Analyst; AS; Bus Adm/Acctng.

**CAPPS, KELLIE C,** Univ Of Nc At Greensboro, Greensboro, NC; JR; BA; AEYC 88-89; Elem Schl Intern; Child Devl; Elem Tchr.

**CAPPS, MARK A,** Western Ky Univ, Bowling Green, KY; JR; PH D; Phi Kappa Phi 90; Pres Schlr 88-90; Deans Lst 90-; Pharm; Rtl Pharm.

**CAPRILES-QUIROS, JOSE A,** Univ Of Pr Medical Sciences, San Juan, PR; FR; MPH; Beta Beta Beta 78-81; San Juan City Hosp Pediatrics Ec Alumni Socty Pres 89-; Puerto Rico Hrt Assn Pediatric Resuscitation 89-; Straight Intrnshp Pdtrcs 81-82; Rsdnt Pdtrcs 82-84; Flwshp Neonatal Perinatal Med 84-86; Puerto Rico Med Assn; Med/Biology; Pub Hlth/Acad Medicine.

**CAPSIS, CHARLES,** Univ Of Cincinnati, Cincinnati, OH; FR; BFA; Alpha Epsilon Rho; Brdcstng; Radio/TV.

**CAPUTI, CHRISTOPHER D,** D Youville Coll, Buffalo, NY; SR; MS; Std Physcl Thrpy Asc 89-; Ornttn Vol 90; Accrdtn Comm 90-; Skating Asc Blnd/Hndcppd 89-90; Physcl Thrpy.

**CAPUTO, LEONARD S,** City Univ Of Ny Brooklyn Coll, Brooklyn, NY; FR; BS; Italian Clb Sec; Alpha Phi Delta; Phys Engr.

**CAPUTO, MICHELE J,** Fordham Univ, Bronx, NY; SO; BS; Cmmtng Assn Gnrl Assmbly; Dante Italian Amrcn Soc; Deans Lst 89-; All Amrcn Schlr; Accntng; Corp Lawyer CPA.

**CAPUTO, MICHELLE C,** Duquesne Univ, Pittsburgh, PA; SO; BA; Theater Co Hstrn 89-; Sign Waves 89-90; Phi Eta Sigma 89-; Mgmnt Info Sys; Sys Dsgnr.

**CARA, THOMAS J,** Univ Of Miami, Coral Gables, FL; SR; BBA; Golden Key Corrspndg Sec; Beta Gamma Sigma; Phi Kappa Phi; Johnson Johnson Sls Intrn; Fin; Cert Fin Anlyst.

**CARABALLO GONZALEZ, FELIX M,** Univ Of Pr Cayey Univ Coll, Cayey, PR; FR; BA; Bus Adm Clb; Acctng; Law.

**CARABALLO, CARMEN M,** Univ Of Pr At Mayaguez, Mayaguez, PR; SO; Assn Stdnts Psych 89-; Stdnts Orient 90-; Mu Alpha Phi 89-; Matricula De Honor 89-; Natacion 89-90; Psych; Clncl Psych.

**CARABELLO, CHRISTIAN D,** Villanova Univ, Villanova, PA; JR; BA; Stdnt Govt 90-; Sclgy Clb; Spcl Olympcs; Phi Beta Phi; Dns Lst 90; Phi Beta Phi; Bxng 90; IM Bsktbl Sftbl 88-; Sclgy; Prfssr.

**CARABETTA, HEATHER A,** Western New England Coll, Springfield, MA; JR; BA; Rsdnt Advsr 89; Deans List 89; Encntr Jvnl Dlnqncy 90; Indpndnt Stdy Jvnl Crts 90; Intrnshp Crrctns Pre/Release; Crmnl Justice; Crrctns.

**CARABETTA, KIMBERLY K,** Radford Univ, Radford, VA; JR; BS; Campus Dining Hl Spvsr 88-; Phi Beta Lambda; Zeta Tau Alpha; Vlybl Stat 90-; Adm Syst.

**CARABETTA, SHANNON M,** Elmira Coll, Elmira, NY; SO; BS; Scl Pol Union 89-90; Amnsty Intrntl 89-90; Cmmnty Serv Wth Hm For The Aged 90; Anthrplgy.

**CARABINA, MATTHEW S,** Univ Of New Haven, West Haven, CT; SR; BS; Intrnshp Fdrl Bur Invstgtn 88-; Crmnl Justc; Law Enfrcmnt.

**CARACCI, LAURA A,** Hudson Valley Comm Coll, Troy, NY; FR; BS; Phrmcy Tech; Cert Orthst Surgcl Grmnts Custm Stckngs; Cert Camp Inst Appl Tech 86; Cert Jobst Inst 86; Sci; Phrmcst.

**CARACO, DEBORAH S,** Cornell Univ Statutory College, Ithaca, NY; SO; BS; Symphonic Bnd 89; Marching Bnd 90; Alpha Phi Omega; Deans List 89-; Engrg.

**CARACO, MICHAEL P,** Hudson Valley Comm Coll, Troy, NY; JR; BA; Sigma Alpha Epsilon Upr Cncl 88-90; AAS 90; Math Tchr.

**CARACOSTIS, KIKI H,** Univ Of Tn At Knoxville, Knoxville, TN; SR; BS; Phi Kappa Phi 90-; Beta Gamma Sigma 90-; Golden Key 89-; Beta Alpha Psi VP Prjcts 90-; Delta Sigma Pi Fctly Rltns Comm Chr 90-; Accounting; Tax Accounting.

**CARAMBO, CRISTOBAL R,** Fl International Univ, Miami, FL; FR; BED; Ntl Hnr Soc 67; Chem/Ed; Tchr.

**CARATINI, MIGDALIA,** Inter Amer Univ Pr San Juan, Hato Rey, PR; GD; JD; Law.

**CARAVETTE, PETER M,** Pasco Hernando Comm Coll, Dade City, FL; SG Rep 89-; Ltl Lgue Coach 89-; Alpha Epsilon Delta; Tau Kappa Epsilon; Cum Laude Hon; Deans Lst 82-86; D Haskell Awrd; Pres Lst 90-; IM Rqtbl Chmpn; Extrardnry Mnstr; BS Loyola Univ; Hlth; Prctitnr.

**CARAWAY, CHAD D,** Univ Of Southern Ms, Hattiesburg, MS; JR; BS; Stdnt Nurses Assn So MS; Bapt Stdnt Un Exec Cncl 88-; Bapt Nrsng Flwshp 90-; Sp 4/E 4 US Army 84-88; AA Jones Cnty Jr Coll 90; Nrsng; Msnry Nurse.

**CARAWAY, JOHN W,** Lincoln Univ, Lincoln Univ, PA; SR; BA; Chem Club VP 87-; French Clug 89-F Spanish Club 87-88f Alpha Chi Treas 89-F; Sigma Xi; Beta Kappa Chi 90-; Oak Ridge Assoc Univ Nuclear Enegy Trng Schlrshp 89-; Amer Chem Scty Awd; IM Assist Coach 89-90; Chemistry; Research.

**CARAWAY, JULIE FAYE,** Meridian Comm Coll, Meridian, MS; SO; BA; DECA Rprtr 89-90; Delta Epsilon Cia Rprtr 89-90; Deans List 90-; Finance/Bnkng.

**CARBALLEIRA, DANIEL V,** Union Inst, Cincinnati, OH; SR; BA; Cntr Grp Cnslng 88-; S E Mnstrs Fclttr 83-; Frlnc Dsply Dsgnr 80-; Psych; Fmly Cnslng.

**CARBERRY, LINDA K,** Newbury Coll, Brookline, MA; SO; Clss Rep 90-; Nghbrhd Rlf Fnd Pres 90; Quincy Interfaith Shhltrng Cltn Bus Mgr 90-; Acctg; Mngrl Acctnt.

**CARBERT, TIMOTHY L,** Embry Riddle Aeronautical Univ, Daytona Beach, FL; JR; AAS; Scty Of Cmmrcl Avtn Techs; Arspce Scty 90; Arcrft Mtnce.

**CARBON, MARIANNE,** Comm Coll Algny Co Algny Cmps, Pittsburgh, PA; FR; BA; Dontn Art Fndrsr Wmns Shltr; AS Art Inst Pgh 89; Art Educ; Tchr.

**CARBONE, CHRISTINE M,** Marist Coll, Poughkeepsie, NY; JR; BS; Alpha Chi 90-; Sigma Zeta 90-; Hdsn Vly Schlrshp 88-; Cmptr Sci.

**CARBONE, DAVID G,** Univ Of Miami, Coral Gables, FL; JR; BA; Drm/Bgl Crps Bloomington IN 90-; Mrchg Bnd; MENC 91; Drm/Bgl Crps Orlando FL 90; Phi Theta Kappa 90; Mrchg Bnd Instrctr Braddock Sr Hgh Schl 90-; AA Hnrs Edison Cmnty Clg 90; Musc Educ; Prcssn Instr/Jdg Hgh Schl Drm/Bgl.

**CARBONE, JOHN A,** Temple Univ, Philadelphia, PA; JR; BSME; ASME Sec 90-; AA Montgomery Cnty Comm Coll 89; Mech Engr.**

**CARBONE, LINDA M,** Holyoke Comm Coll, Holyoke, MA; SO; AA; Tutor 90-; Art Awd; Dns Lst; Grphcs Photogrphy/Composition 80-; Visual Art; Cmrcl Photogrphy.

**CARBONE, STEPHEN,** Georgetown Univ, Washington, DC; SO; BSBA; Std Acad Advsr; New Std Ornttn Pgm 90-; Dns Lst 89-; Intl Busn Mchns Acctng Asst 90; Acctng.

**CARBONELL, EDWARD G,** City Univ Of Ny City Coll, New York, NY; JR; BS; Mnrty Access To Rsrch Careers/Natl Hnr Soc; Ward Medal For Hist/Hnrs Rsrch Chem; Biochemistry; Med.

**CARBONNEAU, CAROL M,** Central Me Medical Center, Lewiston, ME; FR; AD; Girl Scouts Ldr Trp Ldr 84-87; Schl Nrsng Parltm 90-; Wrkd Special Needs Childrenn; Nursing; Ed In Nrsng.

**CARBONNEAU, DANIEL P,** Western New England Coll, Springfield, MA; JR; BA; Peer Rvw Bd Chrprsn 90-; Stdnt Snte Sntr Lge 91; Stdnt Rep Stdnt Afrs Cmtee 90; Alpha Kappa Delta; Stdnt Ambsdr; Legal Intrn 90-; Sociology; Law.

**CARCICH, JACQUELINE S,** Georgian Court Coll, Lakewood, NJ; SO; BS; VP Of Class 89; Stdnt Affrs 89; Sprts Wrtr; Dstrct 31 Conf Tm Soccer 89-90; Frshmn Of Dist Bsktbl 89-90; Jersey Nine Stdnt Athlete 89; Bsktbl Var 89-90; Soccer Var 90; Accntng; CPA.

**CARD, ANDREA D,** Fl International Univ, Miami, FL; SR; BS; Med Lab Sci/Chmstry; Med.

**CARD, AYANNA N,** Fl A & M Univ, Tallahassee, FL; FR; Architectural/Construction Eng Tech; Drftr.

**CARD, HEIDI A,** Endicott Coll, Beverly, MA; SO; AS; Peer Tutor Chmstry 90-; Vrsty Clb Soccer 89-; Phi Theta Kappa; Phi Theta Kappa; Soccer 89-; Med Allied Hlth; Dntl Hygnst.

**CARD, JODY A,** Marshall University, Huntington, WV; SR; Tchr Art Opprtnty Pgm Marshall Univ 90; Gamma Beta Phi 87-88; Nom Stdnt Tchr Yr 90-; Deans Lst 89-; Grad Summa Cum Laude; BA; Art Educ K-12; Art Tchng.

**CARDAMONE, GINA L,** Duquesne Univ, Pittsburgh, PA; JR; BS; Natl Assoc Rtl Drggsts 89-; Acdmy Stdnts Phrmcy 90-; Amrcn Phrmctcl Assoc 90-; Natl Hnr Scty 88-; Phrmcy.

**CARDEN, CARLA M,** Univ Of Ga, Athens, GA; SR; BSED; Bapt Stdnt Union 87-; Alph Lmbd Dlt 87-; Gldn Key 88-; Otstndng Clg Stdnt Amer 88-; Soc Sci Educ.

**CARDEN, CHAD N,** Ga Coll, Milledgeville, GA; FR; BBA; Deans List 90-; Bus; Mgmnt.

**CARDEN, CHERYL A,** Univ Of West Fl, Pensacola, FL; JR; BA; AAS Okaloosa Walton Comm Clg 89; Elm Educ; Tch.

**CARDEN, CHERYL L,** Walker Coll, Jasper, AL; SO; BS; Wmns Dorm Cncl Pres 90-; Stdnt Govt Assn Soph Rep 90-; Stars/Bars Stf Copy Ed 90-; AS; Bio; Med Sch.

**CARDENAL, MARIA C,** Lenoir Rhyne Coll, Hickory, NC; SR; BA; Pgrm Bd 89-; Newman Clb 89-; Intrntl Clb 89-; Alpha Lambda Delta 89-; Mu Sigma Epsilon 90-; Omicron Delta Epsilon 90-; Dns Lst 89-90; Bus Admin; Bus Mngmnt.

**CARDENAS, GARY E,** Univ Of Miami, Coral Gables, FL; SR; BBA; Lambdea Chi Alpha Schlrshp Chrmn 88-; Pres 100 88-; Data Procsng Mgt Assoc VP; Beta Gamma Sigma; Phi Kappa Phi 90-; Golden Key 89-; Paideta Greek Acadmc; Outstndng Sr In Comptr Info Sys; Fencing 87-88; Comptr Info Sys; Mgt.

**CARDENAS, WALDO,** Fl International Univ, Miami, FL; SR; BS; FEA; Chldrns Home Soc Mclamore Chldrns Ctr Norma Rae Infant Ctr 89-; Faith Comm Ch Miami Yng Adults Singles Mnstry Dir 89-; Intl Bnkg Ofcr Adjustor 81-; AA Miami Dade Comm Coll 85; Elem Edn; Teach.

**CARDER, AMBER J,** Wv Univ, Morgantown, WV; SR; BSJ; Am Advrtsng Fed VP 87-90; Kappa Tau Alpha; Gldn Key 89-; Intern Waynesburg Obserer Rprtr 90; Intern Parkersburg News/Sentinel 90; Cert Direct Mktg Coll Inst 90; Jrnlsm; Advrtsng.

**CARDIN, ANN M,** Newbury Coll, Brookline, MA; FR; Retail Mngr 87-90; Mrchndsr 90-; Mrktng.

**CARDIN, H E,** Church Of God Sch Of Theology, Cleveland, TN; MDIV; Senior Pastor Trion Church Of God Prophecy; Theology; Mnstry.

**CARDINALE, MICHAEL A,** Providence Coll, Providence, RI; SO; BA; Accntng.

**CARDONA, ANDRES,** City Univ Of Ny Baruch Coll, New York, NY; SO; MBA; Offce Assist 90; Baruch Clg Dept Of Mdrn Lang/Cmprtve Lit; Invlved Wth Intrntl Fllwshp Spnsred By Intrntl Pen Frnds; Bsnss Admin; Fnce/Mngmnt.

**CARDONA, CARALI G,** Catholic Univ Of Pr, Ponce, PR; JR; BA; Amer Scty Prsnl Adm 89; Hnrs Pgm Stdnt Advsry Comm 89-; Bus Hnr Scty; Hnr Scty; Deans Lst 89-; Comm Ldrshp; Hnrs Schlrshp 89-; Finance; Mba.

**CARDONA JR, CARLOS J,** Univ Of Pr At Rio Piedras, Rio Piedras, PR; JR; BA; Univ P R; Soc Sci; Law.

**CARDONA, IRIS R,** Univ Of Pr Medical Sciences, San Juan, PR; GD; MD; AMA 87; Deans Lst; Pblc Hlth; Pblc Hlth Sp Peds.

**CARDONA-REICH, CARMEN E,** Nova Univ, Ft Lauderdale, FL; GD; M HSA; Hspnc Amer Clb VP 90; Sthestrn Scty Of Hosp Phrmcst 89; FL Phrmctcl Assn 89; Swnnee Vly Phrmcst Assn 90; Prcptr Univ Of PR Coll Of Phrmcy 87; Clncl Instrctr; Amer Scty Of Hosp Phrmcst 86; BS PH Univ Of Puerto Rico Coll Of Pharmacy 72.

**CARDONITA, DONNA L,** Albertus Magnus Coll, New Haven, CT; JR; BA; Deans List 86-88/89; Phi Theta Kappa; Xi Theta 87-; Intrnshp Dean/Admin Servs 88; Brd Of Educ/Data Proc Mgmnt Info Systs/Fscl Serv 89; AS So Cntrl Comm Clg 88; Comm/Corp/Promo Pblc Rltns; Adv.

**CARDOSO, ARMANDO P,** Saint Thomas Univ, Miami, FL; MBA; MDCC Stdnt Govt VP 83; Jewish Fdn TV Intrnshp 87; WCIX Chnnl 6 Intrnshp 87-; NADTP 90-; Limelite Studios Dskto Pblshr 88; Cad Dsgnr/Cal Engr; Adv Dsgnr Mendive/Gonzalez CPA 86-90; Pblshng Spclst/Miami Chldrns Hosp/Intl Ped; Mgmnt Info Syst; Art Dir.

**CARDOZA, MICHELLE M,** Saint Josephs Coll New York, Brooklyn, NY; SR; BS; Rgstrd Nrs 86-; AAS 86; Hlth Admn.

**CARDUCCI, ANGELA J,** Duquesne Univ, Pittsburgh, PA; SO; BA; Cmps Nwsppr Nws Edtr 89-; Dean Lst 90-; Prnt Jrnlsm; Jrnlsm/Pblc Rel.

**CARDUCCI, KIMBERLY A,** S U N Y Coll At Fredonia, Fredonia, NY; SO; BA; Acctng; CPA.

**CARDWELL, DEBORAH L,** Kent St Univ Kent Cmps, Kent, OH; JR; BA; Psychlgy; Cnslng.

**CARDWELL, HEATHER A,** Allegheny Coll, Meadville, PA; SR; BS; AMDA Jr Brd Mbr 88-90; Alden Schlr 87-88; Dist Alden Schlr 89-90; Frank Wilbur Main Flw 90-; Track 88; Econ; Busn.

**CARDWELL, JOAN B,** Birmingham Southern Coll, Birmingham, AL; JR; BA; Adlt Stds Mntr 90-; Adlt Stds Advsry Cncl 90-; Ornttn Pr Advsr 90-; Dns Lst 90; Amer Phys Thrpy Assn 80-; Phys Thrpy Assn 80-; Lcnsd Phys Thrpst Asst 78-; AAS Southern Union State Jr Coll 78; Cert Phys Thrpy Univ Of AL Birmingham 78; Bus Admin; Mgmt Hmn Rsrcs.

**CARDWELL, STAN G,** Asbury Theological Sem, Wilmore, KY; GD; MDIV; HAND Fd Bnk Dir; Habitat Humanity VP; Beeson Schlr 89-; Mech Eng 85-89; BS W Vir Univ 84; Ordained Mnstry Untd Meth Chrch.

**CARE, D DESIREE,** Goucher Coll, Towson, MD; SO; BA; Open Cir Theatre; Pres Schlrshp 89-; Deans Schlr 89-; Engl/Drama; Actng.

**CARECCIA, SHARON L,** Old Dominion Univ, Norfolk, VA; JR; BS; Soc Mfg Engrs 2nd V Chr 90-; Natl Soc Prfsnl Engrs 90-; Tau Alpha Pi Pres 88-; Golden Key 90-; Delta Sigma Lambda Hstrn 88-; AA Montgomery Clg 82; Draftsman US Navy 2nd Cls Petty Ofcr 83-87; Mfg/Mech Engr.

**CAREY, ANNASTASIA M,** City Univ Of Ny Baruch Coll, New York, NY; JR; BA; Mrktng Soc 87-88; Dns Lst 87; AA Coll Bahamas 88; Statistics; Rsrch.

**CAREY, AUDRA L,** Marshall University, Huntington, WV; JR; BA; Majorette 89-; Gamma Beta Phi 90-; Alpha Kappa Psi 90-; Alpha Xi Delta; Deans Lst; Bus Educ.

**CAREY, DAVID E,** Oh Univ-Southern Cmps, Ironton, OH; FR; BED; Awrd Rec Jan Michael Long Oh St Sen; Awrd Rec Mark Malon Oh Hse Rep; Deal Lst; Sale Rep; Hstr; Elem Educ Tchr.

**CAREY, DELICIA E,** Al A & M Univ, Normal, AL; FR; BA; Natl Soc Blck Eng 90-; Fresh Hnr Rll; Pres Awrd Fresh; Conf Offcl; Math; Corp.

**CAREY, DONNA J,** Wilmington Coll, New Castle, DE; SR; BA; Bnkng Offcr Crdt Analyst II 83; AA Wesley Clg Dover DE 79; Bus Mgt/Bnkng/Fncng; Bnkng Fld.

**CAREY, DOUGLAS E,** Marshall University, Huntington, WV; SO; BBA; Acctg.

**CAREY, JAMESE C,** Fl A & M Univ, Tallahassee, FL; FR; MBA; Stdnt Govt Assn Comm Co Chr 90-; Econ Clb; Phi Eta Sigma Chpln; Busn; Econ.

**CAREY, JODY E,** Univ Of Ga, Athens, GA; SR; BSED; Kappa Delta Epsilon 90-; Phi Kappa Phi; Gldn Key 90-; Early Chldhd Educ; Tchng.

**CAREY, LYNNE M,** Clark Atlanta Univ, Atlanta, GA; JR; BA; Mktg Clb 90-; Spnsh Achvmnt Awds 89-90; Natl Coll Busn Mrt Awd 90-; All Amer Schlr Awd 90-; Busn; Acctg.

**CAREY, RENEE M,** Indiana Univ Of Pa, Indiana, PA; SR; BS; Pstl Clb 90; Dance Co 87; Prnts Anonymous; Prctcm; Media; Resrc Intrnshp; PR; Cmmnctns Media; Entrntnmnt Law.

**CAREY, SALLY L,** Union Coll, Barbourville, KY; FR; BA; BSU 90-; CAB 90-; FCA 90-; Deans Lst; Acad/Swim Schlrshps; Lady Bullfrog Swim-Dive Team 90-; Bus; Acctg.

**CARGILE, PATRICIA E,** Univ Of Montevallo, Montevallo, AL; SR; BED; Alpha Gamma Delta 87-88; Stdnt Tchng; Erly Chldhd Elem Ed; Tch.

**CARGILL, LANCE A,** Johnson C Smith Univ, Charlotte, NC; FR; BA; Iota Phi Theta; Bnkg/Finance; Fncl Advsr.

**CARGILL, MICHELE A,** Cornell Univ Statutory College, Ithaca, NY; SR; BS; Ho Nun De Kah; Gldn Key 90-; Phi Kappa Phi 90-; Alpha Phi Schlrshp Chr 88-; Genetics; PH D Rsrchr/Professor.

**CARIDDI, MARIANNE K,** Rivier Coll, Nashua, NH; BFA; Rcpnt On My Own Tme Art Awrd Digitl Equip Corp 88; Mmbr Grnt Scrbs 89-; Vol Sth Mrrmck Chrstn Kndrgrtn 90-; Emply Digitla Equip Cor Admn Sec 80-90; Assoc Bus Sci Castle Coll 76; Art; Art Rltd Art.

**CARIK, JOSEPH M,** Duquesne Univ, Pittsburgh, PA; SR; BS; Beta Gamma Sigma; Amrcn Prdctn Invntry Cntrl Scty 83-; Bus Admn; Sr Systms Engnr.

**CARINI, KAREN M,** Univ Of Sc At Columbia, Columbia, SC; JR; BA; Assn For Early Chldhd Educ 88-90; New Rvr Vly Agency For Mentally Ret Vol 89-90; Campus Coalition For Literacy; Gamma Beta Phi Soc; Elem Educ.

**CARL, ANN L,** Univ Of Cincinnati-Clrmnt Coll, Batavia, OH; SR; Student Ambassador 90-; AAA; Admin Support Co Op; Secretarial.

**CARL, KEVIN M,** S U N Y Coll Of Tech At Frmgdl, Farmingdale, NY; SO; ASSOC; Engr Sci Club Treas; Sftbl Team; Fld Supv MRI Mfg Firm Domestic/Intrnal Instltns; Elec Engr.

**CARL, SCOTT E,** West Liberty St Coll, West Liberty, WV; JR; BS; US Coast Grd 3rd Class Port Scrtymn; Intrnshp OH Cty Sheriffs Dept; Crmnl Just; Law Enfrcmnt Offcr.

**CARLA, CARLA R,** Univ Of Southern Ms, Hattiesburg, MS; JR; Univ Sthrn Ms Chrldr; Assoc Stdnt Bdy; Deans Lst; Phi Mu Dir; Bsktbl/Ftbl Chrldr.

**CARLBERG, CHARLENE MARIE,** Pasco Hernando Comm Coll, Dade City, FL; SO; BA; PTK; Hghst Hons; AA 90; Educ.**

**CARLBERG, STEVEN S,** Rochester Inst Of Tech, Rochester, NY; FR; BA; Rprtr Mgzine Humor Wrtr 90-; IM Bsktbll Capt 90-; IM Vllybll Capt 90-; Comp Sci; Artfcl Intllgnce.

**CARLE, NANCY A,** Univ Of Sc At Coastal Carolina, Conway, SC; FR; Phi Eta Sigma; Pol Sci; St Dept.

**CARLESS, THOMAS G,** Univ Of Miami, Coral Gables, FL; JR; BA; Orng Bwl Comm Asct Mbr 87-; Vars Tnns 86-88; Acctng/Bsn Law.

**CARLETON, JULIE M,** Univ Of Sc At Aiken, Aiken, SC; SO; BS; Alpha Kappa Psi; Alpha Gamma Delta 89-90; Wyatt Dev Co-Op Ed; Bus Admin; Prof.

**CARLETON, LINDA L,** Merrimack Coll, North Andover, MA; SO; BA; Blgy Clb 89-90; Yrbk Staff 89-90; Biology/Genetics.

**CARLILE, MANNA M,** Daytona Beach Comm Coll, Daytona Beach, FL; SO; AS; Prsdnts Lst 88-90; Deans Lst 89; Acctg.**

**CARLIN, MICHAEL JAMES,** Southern Coll Of Tech, Marietta, GA; FR; BS; US Navy; Partnr Audio Bsns 90-; Engr Elec.

**CARLIN, MICHELE L,** Pa St Univ Main Cmps, University Pk, PA; JR; BS; Stdnt Govt Exectv Hsng Cncl 88-; Rsdnt Asst Orttn Ldr 89-; Ln Shr 90-; Hmn Dvlmnt; Vol Nrsng Hms 88-; BACCHUS Pres 89-90; Hmn Dvlmnt Fmly Stds: Adlt Dvlmnt Agng.**

**CARLINE, KIMBERLY A,** James Madison University, Harrisonburg, VA; SR; BS; Inter-Hall Coun Exec Sec 87-89; Cl Org Exec Sec 89-90; Stdnt Edctn Asso 88-90; Asso/Edctn/Yng Chldrn 88-90; Deans List 89-90; Pres List 90-; IM Fld Hockey/Bsktbl 87-90; Early Chldhd Edctn; Tch.

**CARLINO, CRAIG J,** S U N Y At Buffalo, Buffalo, NY; GD; MBA; Univ Buffalo Acctg Assoc Pro Dir 90-; Univ Buffalo Rugby Ftbl Clb 88-89; Ski Clb 88-89; Phi Eta Sigma 88-; Beta Alpha Psi Sec 90-; Deans Lst; Acctg.

**CARLISLE, CHRISTOPHER A,** Georgetown Univ, Washington, DC; FR; BA; Bus; Intl Fin.

**CARLISLE, CHRISTY A,** Birmingham Southern Coll, Birmingham, AL; FR; BS; SGA Comm 90-; Triangle Clb; Chorale; Cncrt Choir/Hilltop Singers .0-; Phi Eta Sigma; Alpha Lambda Delta; Alpha Omicron Pi 90-; Erly Chldhd Educ; Teacher.

**CARLISLE, LAURA L,** Univ Of Southern Ms, Hattiesburg, MS; SO; BA; Chi Omega Derby Chrmn; Sgm Alpha Epsln Ltl Sis VP; Clthng Mrchndsng; Regnl Mgr Rtl Indstry.

**CARLISLE, SAMANTHA A,** Univ Of Al, Tuscaloosa, AL; SO; Gamma Beta Phi; Delta Zeta; Bsns; Hlth Care Mgmt.**

**CARLISLE, WILLIAM TODD,** Samford Univ, Birmingham, AL; GD; JD; Cmbrlnd Law Review Edtr Chf 90-; BS 88; Law; Corp Law.

**CARLISLE III, WOODSON S,** Va Commonwealth Univ, Richmond, VA; JR; BA; Dns Lst 90; Acctng; Bsn Exec.

**CARLL, CAROLINE J,** Webber Coll, Babson Park, FL; JR; BS; Fash Clb 90-; Phi Theta Kappa; AS Palm Beach Jr Clg 84; Bus Admn; Fshn Rtlng.

**CARLO HERNANDEZ, ILEANA,** Inter Amer Univ Pr Fajardo, Fajardo, PR; SR; BBA; Assoc Bsn Admin 90-; Hnrs Lst 90-; Acctng; CPA.

**CARLO, GRISELLE E,** Inter Amer Univ Pr San German, San German, PR; SR; BMT; Microblby Students Assoc 88-90; Biology; Medl Techgt.

**CARLO JR, RADAMES,** S U N Y Coll Of A & T Morrisvl, Morrisville, NY; SO; AA; Latin Amer Orgztn 90-; SG 90-; Friars Clb 89-; RA 90-.

**CARLOW JR, MICHAEL F,** Hudson Valley Comm Coll, Troy, NY; JR; BA; Phi Theta Kappa 90-; Cmptr Sci Inf Sci.

**CARLSON JR, ALLEN L,** S U N Y Coll At Fredonia, Fredonia, NY; SR; BA; Soc/Anthrplgy Clb 90-; Alpha Kappa Delta 90-; Outstdng Achvmnt Awd Hum Svc 89-; Rosa Parks Schlrshp; Hse Prnt Grp Hm 88-; AA Jmstwn Comm Coll; Soc; Msw Soc Wrk.

**CARLSON, BEVERLY A,** George Mason Univ, Fairfax, VA; SR; BS; Stdt Educ Assoc; Golden Key: Kappa Delta Pi; Schrlshp Fairfax City; Brnch Amer Assoc Univ Women; Early Education; Teaching.

**CARLSON, CHERON D,** Oh St Univ, Columbus, OH; SR; BA; Columbus City Power Coed Vlybl 88-; Alpha Lambda Delta 87-88; Phi Eta Sigma 87-88; Kappa Alpha Theta 87-89; Grove City Jaycees 87-89; Japanese Inst Schlr 88-; Ohio Distngshd Schlr 89-; Intl Trade Consultant Asst; Japanese Intl Studies; Intl Trade Commnctns.

**CARLSON, GEORGE A,** Univ Of Akron, Akron, OH; JR; BSME; Hnrs Clb 88; Amer Soc Of Mchncl Eng 90; Tau Beta Pi; Eng Co-Op At BF Goodrich; Mchncl Eng; Eng.

**CARLSON, JEANNE M,** Univ Of Cincinnati, Cincinnati, OH; JR; BED; Kappa Delta Pi 90-; Phi Theta Kappa 90; Elem Educ; Tchr.

**CARLSON, JEREMY E A,** S U N Y Coll Of Tech At Alfred, Alfred, NY; FR; MBA; IM Hockey; Eng Sci; Eng.

**CARLSON, KELLY K,** Atlantic Comm Coll, Mays Landing, NJ; SO; BA; Hstry/Govt Clb Sec; Judicial Review Bd.

**CARLSON, KIERSTIN K L,** Cornell Univ Statutory College, Ithaca, NY; SO; Wldlf Soc; Habitat Hmnty; Ntrl Rsrcs; Vet Med.

**CARLSON, KIRSTEN L,** Nyack Coll, Nyack, NY; SR; Cls Ofcr 89-; Yrbk; Orntn Innr Cty Otrch; Stdnt Svc Cmt; Intrnshp Nyack Mdl Schl; BA; Psychlgy.

**CARLSON, KRIS G,** S U N Y Coll At Fredonia, Fredonia, NY; JR; BS; Amer Ptrlm Inst Awd Outstanding Grad 84; AS U Of Pittsburg 84; AS Jamestown Comm Clg 90; Bus Admin/Mgmnt; Politics.

**CARLSON, MARION L,** Georgian Court Coll, Lakewood, NJ; JR; BA; Re Entry Women Clionaes Trnsfr 90-; Socl Wrk; De La Salle Clb; NJ Cncl Lrng Disb; Phi Alpha Theta 90-; Vol Rec Prog Assn Retarded Citizens ARC; Dns Lst Brookdale Comm Coll 88-90; Tutor Engl Non Native Spkr Cls 90; Spec Educ; Elem/Hstry Educ.

**CARLSON, MELANIE F,** Wilmington Coll, New Castle, DE; SR; BS; AS BIS Goldey Beacom Clg 84; Acctng.

**CARLTON, BARBARA D,** Mount Olive Coll, Mount Olive, NC; JR; BS; Art Clb 88-89; Dsgn Communications Hist 90-; Pres List 88-; Art Schlrshp 88-; Pblsh Essay Lit Magzn 89; Visual Communicaitons.

**CARLTON, ROBERT L,** Western Piedmont Comm Coll, Morganton, NC; SO; AS; Yng Mens Clb 76-77; Phi Theta Kappa 90; Mchncl Drftng; Cmptrs; Bsnss Cmptr Prog.

**CARLUCCI, JOSEPH R,** Villanova Univ, Villanova, PA; JR; BA; IM Bsktbll/Sftbll 87-; Boxing Clb 89; Project Sunshine 89; Psi Chi; Psychology.

**CARLYLE, EDWARD A,** Southern Coll Of Tech, Marietta, GA; JR; BS; IEEE; NSPE; Tau Alpha Pi; Elec Eng; Robtcs.

**CARLYLE, MICHAEL J,** Southern Coll Of Tech, Marietta, GA; SR; BS; Srvyng/Mpng Soc Georgia Pres 89-; Stdnt Govt 89-; Intermural Indoor Soccer 89-90; Civil Engr Tech.

**CARMACK, JONATHAN E,** Free Will Baptist Bible Coll, Nashville, TN; FR; BA; Master Mens Sec 90-; Ch Training Asst Dir 90-; William Jennings Bryan Soc; Bsktbl/Vlybl; Scndry Edn; Marines.

**CARMACK, KELLY M,** Univ Of Tn At Martin, Martin, TN; FR; BS; Block Bridle Clb 90-; FFA Treas 90-; Soc Hnrs Seminar Stdnts 90-; Chi Omega 90-; State FFA Ofcr Treas 90-; Animal Sci; Food Indstry.

**CARMAN, ANN L,** S U N Y Coll Of Tech At Delhi, Delhi, NY; SR; BA; Ski Clb 89-90; Phi Theta Kappa 90-91; Sftbl 89-91; AAS 91; Acctg; CPA.

**CARMAN, CHRISTINE L,** West Liberty St Coll, West Liberty, WV; JR; BA; SWE 88-89; Hnrs Pgm 88-89; Alpha Kappa Psi V P Mbrshp 90-; Delta Gamma 88-; SBI; Acctg; CPA.

**CARMEN, ALICEA L,** Inter Amer Univ Pr Hato Rey, Hato Rey, PR; FR; Scl Wrkr Assn; Scl Wrk.

**CARMICAL, VERONICA R,** Cumberland Coll, Williamsburg, KY; FR; BA; Math Sci Clb 90-; Edwin Gould Fndtn Schlrshp 90-; Math/Engl; Law.

**CARMICHAEL, GAIL A,** Valdosta St Coll, Valdosta, GA; JR; BA; Erly Chldhd Educ; Tchr.

**CARMICHAEL, RITA L,** Concordia Coll, Selma, AL; SO; Acad Awds; AA; Bus Educ; Mgmnt Firm.

**CARMICHAEL, SARAH H,** Univ Of Ga, Athens, GA; JR; BSED; Comm Univ Vol Orgnztn 90-; Big Brother Big Sister; Inter Scty Cncl Repr 89-90; Kappa Delta Epsilon; Tau Phi Delta 88-90; Early Childhood Educ; Teacher.

**CARMICHAEL, VERONICA L,** Oh St Univ At Newark, Newark, OH; JR; BA; Stdnt Sent Sentr 90; Bsktbl Capt 89-; Engl; Law.

**CARMODY, PATRICK J,** Anne Arundel Comm Coll, Arnold, MD; SO; AA; Optmst Clb Coach 90-; Bsktbl Leg; Vlntr Firfghtr; Prmdc Anne Arndl Cnty 88-; EMT D Certf AACC 90-; CRT AACC 89-; Emrgncy Med; Paramedic.

**CARMONA BENITEZ, GESENIA,** Univ Of Pr Humacao Univ Coll, Humacao, PR; SO; FBLA 87-89; All Amer Schlr Awrd.

**CARNAHAN, DOUGLAS G,** Defiance Coll, Defiance, OH; SR; BA; Fresh Snte; Judcl Cmtee; Lambda Beta 87-; Acad Advsr In Voctnl/Tech Clg Rspr Thrpy; I M Sftbl; Amer Assn Rsprtry Care; Ohio Soc Rsprtry Care; Popular Rotbcrft Assn; Cardio Pulmnry Dir; AS Ind Voc Tech Clg 83; Bus Admn; Hosp Admn.

**CARNAHAN, JENNIFER K,** Univ Of Cincinnati, Cincinnati, OH; FR; BM; Stdnt Alumni Cncl 80-; Alpha Lambda Delta 90-; Ohio State Fed Tchrs Regnl/Natl 90-; Hon Mntn Natl Endwmnt Arts 80; Artist Cmptn Sing; Three Arts Schlrshp; Song Recital; Vocal Performance; Operatic/Recital Perf.

**CARNAHAN, LISA J,** Fl St Univ, Tallahassee, FL; JR; BS; Lamda Pi Eta 90-; Trnsfr Stdnt Schlrshp; Pres Schlrshp; AA St Petersburg Jr Clg 90; Cmnctns; Mngmnt.

**CARNAHAN, PAMELA C,** Broward Comm Coll, Ft Lauderdale, FL; JR; BA; AA 90; Secndry Ed; Engl Tchrr.

**CARNAHAN, SHARON M,** West Liberty St Coll, West Liberty, WV; JR; BA; Ttr 89-; Kappa Phi 90-; Phi Alpha Theta; Sigma Tau Delta 90-; Wmns Sftbl Co Capt 88-; Engl.

**CARNES, ANNE F,** Univ Of Sc At Columbia, Columbia, SC; SO; BA; Thomas Gibons Mangum Schlrshp 89; AA; Sociology; Soc Wrk.

**CARNES, GINGER M,** Univ Of Sc At Columbia, Columbia, SC; JR; BS; Assoc 89; Finance; Bus Exec.

**CARNES, KERRY J,** Wv Univ At Parkersburg, Parkersburg, WV; SO; AS; SNA 90-; Thomas Betty Harris Schlrshp 87; Hosp Crtcl Care Inern; OH Nrs Assn; Marietta Sfty Serv Cmmndtn 86; Amer Nrs Assn; LPN Muskingum Area Jnt Voc Schl 84; Nrsng; BSN/ACLS/CCRN.

**CARNES, LISASUE H,** Univ Of Sc At Lancaster, Lancaster, SC; FR; AS; Hsewf/Mthr Two Bys; Math; Acctg.

**CARNEY, DAWN M,** Eckerd Coll, St Petersburg, FL; JR; BA; Cheerleading 88-; Rsdnt Advsr Dorm Residence 89-; Work Schrl Prog Bk Str Cshr 88-; Pinellas Cnty Vol Ass Youth Motivator 89; Elementary Education; Instruction.

**CARNEY, DEBORAH L,** Coker Coll, Hartsville, SC; SR; BA; SC Ar Natl Grd 78-; Psych.

**CARNEY, DONALD J,** Comm Coll Algny Co Algny Cmps, Pittsburgh, PA; Assoc In Sci; Acctng; CPA/MBA Acctng.

**CARNEY, ELIZABETH A,** Univ Of Southern Ms, Hattiesburg, MS; JR; BA; Elem Educ; Tchng.

**CARNEY, ELIZABETH A,** Smith Coll, Northampton, MA; SO; BA; Mass PIRG Treas Proj Coord 89-; RCA Wrkshp Fcltr 90-; SOS Dorm Repr 89-90; Amer Studies; Educ.

**CARNEY, JON K,** Columbus Coll Of Art & Design, Columbus, OH; FR; BA; Army Natl Guard Spec E4 90-; Pres Lst; Army 86-90; Indstrl Dsgn; Indstrl Dsgnr/Illustr.

**CARNEY, LORA R,** Saint Catharine Coll, St Catharine, KY; FR; AAS; Phi Theta Kappa Sec; Bus; Tchr.

**CARNEY, WILLIAM C,** Univ Of Sc At Columbia, Columbia, SC; BAIS; APICS; Bus Admn; Mfg.

**CARNIVAL, BARBARA ANN,** East Stroudsburg Univ, E Stroudsburg, PA; FR; BS; Aerobics Clb; Psych Assc 90-; Hnrs Pgm 90-; Psych; Child Psych.

**CARO, DANIEL C,** S U N Y At Buffalo, Buffalo, NY; GD; MBA; Gldn Key 89-; Grad Asstntshp Systm Analyst Prgrmr 90-; IM Hcky Sftbl; BS; Mrktng MIS Bsns; Corp Law.

**CARON, CHRISTANY A,** Elms Coll, Chicopee, MA; FR; BA; Intrdprtmntl Stds; Ed.

**CARON, KENNETH M,** Tufts Univ, Medford, MA; SO; Cath Newsltr Co Edtr 90-; Bostn Rd Clb Cyclng Tm 90-; Sigma Nu Schlrshp Chrmn; Boy Scts Amer Asst Sctmstr 89-; Eagle Sct; Tufts Cyclng Tm 90-; Mech Eng; Mfg/Desgn.**

**CARON, KRISTINE R,** Merrimack Coll, North Andover, MA; FR; Mktg Asc 90-; Intl Bsn Clb; Alpha Kappa Psi 90-; Intl Bsn; Foreign Serv/Trade.

**CAROZZA, CHRISTINE A,** Duquesne Univ, Pittsburgh, PA; FR; BS; St Frncs Hlth Sys; Assoc Comm Clg Beaver Co 87; Sci; Phrm.

**CARPENTER, ALEXANDRA C,** Palm Beach Atlantic Coll, W Palm Beach, FL; FR; BA; Phi Beta Lambda Secy 90-; Wrkshp Cmnty Vol Prog; Supper Hons Schlr; Pres List; GPA Award; Bus Admn/Acctng.

**CARPENTER, BELINDA S,** Wv Univ, Morgantown, WV; SO; BS; Chrstn Stdnt Fllwshp 90-; Dns Lst 90; Dns Lst KCC 89-90; IM Vlybl Ky Chrstn 89-90; Socl Wrk.

**CARPENTER, CAROL L,** Univ Of Akron, Akron, OH; JR; BA; Psychlgy Clb; Cmpns Chrst; Tr Akron Cntrl Hwr Wrtng Lab 90-; Hmn Dvlpmnt Lrng Sml Grp Fcltr 89-90; Alpha Lambda Delta 89; Golden Key 90; Kappa Delta Pi; Gen Acdmc Schlrshp Akron U Zeta Chptr Delta; Eng/Sclgy/Psychlgy; Cnslng.

**CARPENTER, CHARLES C,** Christian Brothers Univ, Memphis, TN; SO; BA; Cmps Nwspr Clmnst 89-; Assn Cmptng Mchnsts; Zeta Umgaba Grand Poo-Bah; Knights Clmbs Cncl 6156 Dpty Grnd Knght; Deans Lst; IM Athltcs 89-; AAS Richlnd Coll; Comp Sco/Sclgy; Intl Comp Pgmg.

**CARPENTER, CONNIE J,** Wv Univ At Parkersburg, Parkersburg, WV; SO; BA; St Josphs Hosp; Hmn Res Mgmt; Mgmt.

**CARPENTER, HEATHER D,** Oh Univ-Southern Cmps, Ironton, OH; SO.

**CARPENTER, HOLLY M,** Newbury Coll, Brookline, MA; SR; AS; SGA Sntr 88-89; Stdnt Union Actvts Board 88-89; Phi Theta Kappa; Dns Lst 88/90; Girl Scouts 77; Admin Assist; Office Mgr 89; Cmptr Sci; Sys Anlyst.

**CARPENTER JR, JOHN A,** Hillsborough Comm Coll, Tampa, FL; FR; BS; Eng.

**CARPENTER, JULIA E,** Univ Of Sc At Columbia, Columbia, SC; JR; BA; Kappa Kappa Gamma 2nd VP; English; Busn.

**CARPENTER, KRISTIN D,** Marshall University, Huntington, WV; JR; MBA; Acctg Clb 89-; Cmps Crsd Christ 88-; Gamma Beta Phi 89-; Deans Lst 89-; Acctg; CPA.**

**CARPENTER, KRISTINE A,** Immaculata Coll, Immaculata, PA; FR; BA; Campus Ministry 90-; Commty Orchestra 90-F Cue/Curtain 90-; Chemistry; Sci Related Field.

**CARPENTER, LA FRANCE L,** Johnson C Smith Univ, Charlotte, NC; SO; BA; Yrbk Stff 90-; Pan Afrcn Cncl 90-; Miss Soph 90-; Alpha Lamda Delta 89-; Bus/Mrktng; Educ.

**CARPENTER, LINDA S,** Middle Tn St Univ, Murfreesboro, TN; SR; Stdnt TN Educ Assoc 88-; Kappa Delta Pi .0-; Gamma Beta Phi 87-89; Summa Cum Laude Columbia St Comm Clg 89; Magna Cum Laude Mddl TN St Univ; AS Columbia St Comm Clg 89; Elem Teacher.

**CARPENTER, LORI D,** Wv Northern Comm Coll, Wheeling, WV; SO; Lthse Bapt Ch; KAAS; Med Lab Tech; Hstotechngst.

**CARPENTER, MARK W,** Ky St Univ, Frankfort, KY; FR; Elec Engr.

**CARPENTER, MARY K,** Univ Of Southern Ms, Hattiesburg, MS; FR; BS; Stdnt Alumni Assoc 90-; Alpha Lambda Delta 90-F Phi Eta Sigma 90-; Gamma Beta Phi 90-; Delta Delta Delta 90-; Im Ftbl/Vlybl 90-; Physcl Thrpy.

**CARPENTER, MELISSA K,** Ky St Univ, Frankfort, KY; SO; BA; Phys Thrpy Aide 90-; Cert Acdmic Achvmnt; Sci; Phy Thrpy.

**CARPENTER, MICHAEL J,** Methodist Coll, Fayetteville, NC; SR; BS; A G Rgmntl Asc VP 90-; US Army 82 Airborne 75-; AA 89; Pol Sci/Bsn Admn; Pblc Admn.

**CARPENTER, NEVEDIA R,** Blue Mountain Coll, Blue Mountain, MS; JR; BS ED; Phi Beta Lambda Pres 90-; MS Assn Eductrs 90-; Euzelian 90-; Coner Bus Awd 90-; Guyton Bus Schlrshp 89-; Bus Educ Ldrshp Awd 90-; Bus Educ; Tch Bus.

**CARPENTER, ROBIN J,** Union Inst, Cincinnati, OH; SR; BA; Bus; Fin Plnng.

**CARPENTER, RONICA L,** Univ Of Fl, Gainesville, FL; SR; BSN; Sigma Theta Tau; Fla Nurs Assn; Stf Nurs Bone Marrow Unit; Dip Mobile Infirmry Sch Nurs 68; Nurs; Crtcl Care Nurs.

**CARPENTER, SANDRA RENEE,** Elon Coll, Elon, NC; FR; BA; Coll Bowl; Hstry; Tchg.

**CARPENTER, SARAH G,** Becker Coll At Leicester, Leicester, MA; SR; Travel Hsptlty Clb 90; Phi Theta Kappa Pres 89; Intrnshp; Travel/Tour; Travel Cnsltnt.

**CARPENTER, SCOTT A,** Old Dominion Univ, Norfolk, VA; JR; BS; Tau Beta Pi Ctlgr; Pi Tau Sigma; Theta Tau Corr Sec 89-; US Nvy Actv Dty; AS Tidewater Comm Coll; Mech Eng.

**CARPENTER, SCOTT E,** Univ Of Pittsburgh At Bradford, Bradford, PA; JR; BA; Sigma Mu Trea 89-90; IMS; Mngmnt; Mrktng.

**CARPENTER, SHERRY L,** Bowling Green St Univ, Bowling Green, OH; FR; Univ Hnrs Prgrm 90-; Alph Lambda Delta; Deans List; Mthmtcs/Cmptr Science.

**CARPENTER, SUZAN S,** Valdosta St Coll, Valdosta, GA; SR; MSED; NSSLHA 87-; ASHA 87-; DAV MS Scty 82-; PVA 82-; USAF Ar Trffc Cntrllr 82; BSED; Spch Lngge Pthlgy.

**CARPENTER, TERI L,** Schenectady County Comm Coll, Schenectady, NY; FR; ASSOC; Travel/Tourism; Travel Agency.

**CARPENTIERI, CHRISTIE M,** Teikyo Post Univ, Waterbury, CT; FR; BS; Dorm Cncl Pub Rels 90-; Interior Design Clb 90-; Deans Lst; Religious Tchr Asst 88-; PR Schlrshp 90-; Campus Act 90-; Int Design.

**CARPER, BARBARA BELTZ,** Va Commonwealth Univ, Richmond, VA; SR; BSN; Phi Kappa Phi; Golden Key Soc; RN; AAS Piedmont VA Cmnty Clg VA 86; Cert Pottsville Hosp PA 44; Nrsng; Admnstrtr.

**CARPIN, TRACEY A,** Daemen Coll, Amherst, NY; SR; BS; Specl Olympcs Vol 90-; Arthrts Foundatn Vol 89-90; BS; Phys Thrpy; Phys Thrpst.

**CARPINELLI, KENNETH-SCOTT,** Glassboro St Coll, Glassboro, NJ; SR; BA; SGA Chr 86-; Cncl Off-Cmps Lvng Pres 88-; Bur Serv Org VP 89-; Std Actv Brd 86-89; S J Hghr Educ Cnsrtm Alchl/Drug Abse SGA 90-; Psy Dpt 90-; Psy.

**CARR, ALAN K,** Savannah Coll Of Art & Design, Savannah, GA; SO; BEA; Whelan Schlrshp 89-; Illust.

**CARR, CHERELL M,** Spelman Coll, Atlanta, GA; FR; NSBE 90-; Spelman Chem Clb 90-; Alpha Lambda Delta; Parsons Schlrshp; Eng Hnr Roll/Awd; Hnrs Pgm Hnr Roll/Deans Lst 90-; Chemistry; Chem Eng.

**CARR, CHRISSI J,** Middle Tn St Univ, Murfreesboro, TN; SO; BS; NAACP 90-; Ntnl Assn Blck Accntnts; Alpha Kappa Psi 90-; Allen Chapel AME Church Yth Dept Pres 88-; Accntng; CPA.

**CARR, CYNTHIA L,** Univ Of Southern Ms, Hattiesburg, MS; JR; BA; Phi Theta Kappa 89; Assoc Copiah Lncln Cmmnty Clg 90; Elem Ed; Tchr.

**CARR, DAVID W,** Middle Tn St Univ, Murfreesboro, TN; JR; BS; Hlth Phys Ed Rcrtn And Sfty Clb 89-; Phi Epsilon Kappa Treas; Auto Prts 85-; Phys Educ; Alld Hlth.

**CARR, DONALD T,** Fl Atlantic Univ, Boca Raton, FL; JR; BA; Dive Clb 89-; AA Palm Bch Comm Coll 89; Intl Bus; Bus Mgmt.**

**CARR, ERIC J,** Univ Of Md Baltimore Prof Schl, Baltimore, MD; JR; BS MT; Pre-Med Scty 88-90; Cls Ofcr 90-; Deans Lst 89-90; IM 88-90; Med Tchnlgy; Medicine.

**CARR, ESTER L,** Coppin St Coll, Baltimore, MD; SR; BS; Chr 90-; SIFE 90-; Pi Gamma Mu; Ronald Mcnair Schlr; AA Kittrell Coll 72; Soc Sci; PHD Adult Ed Grntlgy.

**CARR, GLENN D,** Western New England Coll, Springfield, MA; JR; BS; Schl Nwspr Stf Wrtr 90-; Ecnmcs; Bnkng/Brkrg.

**CARR, JAMES L,** Univ Of Nc At Charlotte, Charlotte, NC; SO; BS; USAF E-4 85-89; Accntng.

**CARR, JENNIFER,** Stockton St Coll, Pomona, NJ; FR; BS; Glgy Clb; Rehab Hosp 90-; Glgy; Med/Dntstry.

**CARR, JENNIFER ANN,** Univ Of Sc At Columbia, Columbia, SC; SO.

**CARR, JILL F,** Univ Of Nc At Asheville, Asheville, NC; SR; BA; Ornttn Ldr 90-; Psi Chi; EUREKA Grant; Rsch Grant 90; Clncl Psy.

**CARR, JOEL S,** Univ Of Ga, Athens, GA; SR; BA; Res Asst 89-90; Phi Theta Kappa; Dns Lst; Hstry.

**CARR, JONATHAN J,** Cayuga County Comm Coll, Auburn, NY; FR; MBA; Judo 90; Rcqtbl 90-; Eng Clb 90-; Mech Eng; Eng.

**CARR, KRISTI A,** Liberty Univ, Lynchburg, VA; SR; MBA; Psi Chi; Pres Cbnt Stu Govt; Dorm Pryr Ldr; Kidsquest; Alpha Lambda Delta 87-; BA; Psych; Psychlgst/Chld Adlcnt.

**CARR, MARY BETH,** Oh St Univ, Columbus, OH; SR; BS; Helix Blgcl Sci Hnry 88-; Gldn Key 90-; Alpha Lambda Delta 88; Phi Eta Sigma 88; Intrnshp US Frst Serv Blgcl Aide 88-89; Rsrch Asst; Mlcr Gntcs; Biochem.

**CARR, MICHAEL,** Central St Univ, Wilberforce, OH; SO; BA; Computer Aided Drafting Engr.

**CARR, MICHAEL L,** Hillsborough Comm Coll, Tampa, FL; SO; AA; Stdnt Govt; Phi Theta Kappa 89-; AS 90; Comp Info Systms; Prgrmmng.

**CARR, MYSHANTE C,** Benedict Coll, Columbia, SC; SO; Vybl; Bus Admn; Mgmt.

**CARR, PAMELA,** Tougaloo Coll, Tougaloo, MS; JR; BA; Stdnt Recruiter; Pol Sci Clb Sec 90-; Alpha Kappa Alpha; Comm Invlvmnt 89-; Grad Edn Mnrty Pgm New York Univ 90; Pol Sci; Law.

**CARR, PAULA,** Tougaloo Coll, Tougaloo, MS; JR; BA; Pre-Hlth Clb; Alpha Kappa Alpha; Comm Invlvmnt 89-; Wash State Univ Rsrch; Univ MS Med Ctr Rsrch; Chem; Surgeon.

**CARR, RHONDA J,** Hillsborough Comm Coll, Tampa, FL; AS; Nrsng; Crtcl Cr.

**CARR, SANDRA,** Tougaloo Coll, Tougaloo, MS; FR; SPEN 90-; Alpha Lambda Delta; Natl Beta Club 89-; Presidential Schlr 90-; UNCF Citicorp Fellow 90-; Biology; Medicine Cardiopediatrician.

**CARR, SHANNON T,** Colby Sawyer Coll, New London, NH; SR; BA; Alpha Chi Assoc 88-89; Alpha Chi Pr 89-; Tchng Asst 90-; Baccalaureate Awrd In Psych; Psych; Forensic Sci.

**CARR, THOMAS L,** Univ Of Nc At Charlotte, Charlotte, NC; JR; BA; Gldn Key; Phtgrphc Prnts Exhbtd; Phtgrphc Eqpmnt Sls 83-; Anthrplgy; Curation Educ.

**CARR, TUNYA A,** Memphis St Univ, Memphis, TN; JR; BA; Adult Student Assoc; Natl Brd Rlts 85-; Grad Rltr Inst; SCYA Shelby County Yth Authorty; Mgt; Busn Admin.

**CARR, VALERIE L,** Alcorn St Univ, Lorman, MS; SO; Bus Admin; Bus Firm.

**CARRANCHO, MICHAEL J,** Merrimack Coll, North Andover, MA; SR; Merrimack Entrepeneurial Ntwrk V P 90-; MENSA 90-; AS N Shore Comm Clg 89; Civil Eng.

**CARRANO, CHRISTINA M,** Univ Of Miami, Coral Gables, FL; JR; BA; Pre Lgl Scty 90-; Hon Assc 90-; Soclgy; Law.

**CARRASQUILLO, EDGARDO,** Univ Del Turabo, Gurabo, PR; BA; Psych Cl Pres 90-; Psychlgy; MA Ph D.

**CARRASQUILLO, ROSA E,** Univ Of Pr At Rio Piedras, Rio Piedras, PR; JR; Gldn Key; Soc De Estdnts De Histr 90-; Hstry; Hstry Tchr.

**CARRASQUILLO-SALIB, JAVIER A,** Univ Of Pr At Mayaguez, Mayaguez, PR; SR; BS; Pre Med Clb Pres 88-89; Math Stdnts Assoc Publ Rels 90; SEMI 90; Clg Dns Lst 87-90; Clg Rstr Otstndng Mnrty Stdnts Grad 88; Getsemani 90; Subgrad Sci Inv Asst 88-89; Chem Olympiad 1st Pl 89; Microbiol.

**CARRATALA, MABEL,** Miami Dade Comm Coll South, Miami, FL; SO; AA; The Catalyst Stf Wrtr 90-; Ed; Tchr.

**CARRENA, LUIS OSWALD,** Bridgeport Engr Inst, Fairfield, CT; JR; BS; AS NSTC; Engr.

**CARRENO, MARISOL,** Miami Dade Comm Coll South, Miami, FL; SO; BA; Wrk Cmprhnsv Cncr Rsrch Grp Inc Sec Dty Clrcl 90-; Ntl Hspnc Rcpnt Tlnt Rstr Dist Acdmc Prfmc Two Yr Coll; AA; Mrktg; Bus.

**CARRERAS, MARIA DELCARMEN COLON,** Inter Amer Univ Pr Hato Rey, Hato Rey, PR; GD; BA; SGA Pres 88-89; Embamer Funl Dir 87-; Tae Kwon Doo Scuba Dvng 86; Beta Beta Beta 88-; Msclr Systrphy Assoc Vol; Suma Cum Laude Pol Sci; Cum Laude Genl Average; Pol Sci; MA/CRIM Just.

**CARRERAS, MARIANA,** Miami Dade Comm Coll South, Miami, FL; SO; BA; 1991 Region IV Brain Bowl Tourn 90-; Clg Lit Mag Publ Artist 90-; MDCC Intercampus Brain Bowl Tourn 90-; Phi Theta Kappa; Clg Hnr Schlrshp Pgm; 24/25 Annual Stdnt Show Art Exhib 90-; Fine Arts; Professor Fine Arts.

**CARREROU, AILEEN,** Miami Dade Comm Coll South, Miami, FL; JR; BA; GSA Cncl Trp Ldr 89-; Sigma Phi Epsilon 87-89; Tlnt Rstr Otstndg Mnrty Comm Coll Grads; Spcl Educ; Tch.

**CARRIBON, MAHALIA M,** City Univ Of Ny City Coll, New York, NY; JR; Urban Legal Studies Assoc 87-; Golden Key 90; Trintociti Achvrs 88-90; Deans Lst 89; Congrsmn C B Rangel Intrn/Ofc Asst 88-89; Headley/Zeitlin Esquires Intrn 90; Urban Legal Studies; Law/Intl Judge.

**CARRICK, JENNIFER C,** D Youville Coll, Buffalo, NY; FR; BA; Student Assoc Sen 90-; Writers And Artists Assoc 90-; Catalyst Ed In Chief; Lambda Sigma Soc; Spcl Ed; Tch.

**CARRICO, AMY L,** Marshall University, Huntington, WV; FR; BBA; Deans Lst 90; Bsnss; Hosp Adminstrtr.

**CARRICO, CHRISTOPHER D,** Univ Of Ky, Lexington, KY; JR; BS; Dntstry Soc Prsdnt 89-; Gldn Key 90-; Deans Schlrshp; Mcrblgy; Dntstry.**

**CARRICO, DONNA R,** Beckley Coll, Beckley, WV; FR; Soc Wrk.

**CARRICO, LISA J,** Marshall University, Huntington, WV; SO; BA; SOAR 89-; Baptist Campus Ministries 89-; Flute Ens 90-; Gamma Beta Phi; Elem Math Educ.

**CARRIER, MAURICE R,** Me Maritime Academy, Castine, ME; JR; Cadet Shpng Hnr 90; Ftbl 88-89; Engnrng; Mrchnt Marine.

**CARRIERE, ANDREA M,** Coll Of New Rochelle, New Rochelle, NY; SO; BS; Business/Econ; Law.**

**CARRIERE, MICHAEL S,** Univ Of Southern Ms, Hattiesburg, MS; SO; MBA; Hon Soc 86-87; Phi Kappa 85-87; Acadmc Decathln Team 87; Rugby Team 90-; Bus Admin; Intl Bus.

**CARRIG, WILLIAM M,** S U N Y Coll Of Tech At Alfred, Alfred, NY; GD; AAS; Phi Theta Kappa; Floriculture Prod; Greenhouse Mgr.

**CARRIGG, ELIZABETH R,** Univ Of Sc At Columbia, Columbia, SC; FR; Hnrs Rcpnt 90-; Deans Lst 90-; Mrktg.

**CARRIKER, LYNN GAYLE A,** Winthrop Coll, Rock Hill, SC; SR; BSHED; New Start Std Assc VP; WINHECON VP 90-; Std Govt Rep; Kappa Delta Pi; Palmetto St Tchrs Assc; S Buton Memrl Ed Fund Schlrshp; B Feezor Schlrshp Fndtn; Amrcn Busnss Wmns Assc Chr 88-; Food Serv Dir 90; Hme Ec Ed.

**CARRILES, ALFREDO J,** Miami Dade Comm Coll South, Miami, FL; JR; BA; Cntrl Univ Venezuela Bsbl 87; Aviation; Engineering.

**CARRILLO, FLAVIO,** Univ Of Miami, Coral Gables, FL; JR; Chss Treas 89; Gldn Key 90; Frnds Music Schlrshp 90-; Richard Mcewen Shlrshp; Erpn Stds Salzburg Austria 90; Erpn Stds Eichstatt Germany; Natl Gld Piano Tchrs 88; Music Thry Cmpstn; MFA DMA.

**CARRILLO, HECTOR O,** Univ Of New Haven, West Haven, CT; SR; Occptnl Sfty Hlth.

**CARRILLO, JORGE H,** Univ Politecnica De Pr, Hato Rey, PR; FR; BA; Mech Eng; Eng.

**CARRILLO, LUIS C,** Nova Univ, Ft Lauderdale, FL; GD; MBA; Sys Engr Mcdonnell Douglas Missile Sys Corp; BSEE FL Inst Of Tech 87; Elec Eng/Micro; CEO.

**CARRILLO, NIVIA SARA,** Inter Amer Univ Pr Hato Rey, Hato Rey, PR; FR; Blgy; Mcrblgy.

**CARRINGTON, BRUCE H,** Radford Univ, Radford, VA; JR; BS; Sclgy/Anthrplgy; Rsrch.

**CARRINGTON, PAMELA R,** Radford Univ, Radford, VA; SO; BA; Bio Clb 90-; Gspl Choir 89-; Alpha Lambda Delta 89-; Bio; Physcn.

**CARRINGTON, PAUL C,** Averett Coll, Danville, VA; SR; Sci Assoc VP 89-; AAS Danville Comm Coll 89; Bio.

**CARRINGTON, SHERRY L,** Norfolk St Univ, Norfolk, VA; SO; BS; Spartan Alpha Tau 90-; English; Writer.

**CARRINGTON, TERRON M,** Fl St Univ, Tallahassee, FL; SO.

**CARRINGTON, TRACEY L,** Freed-Hardeman Univ, Henderson, TN; FR; BBA; Phi Lambda Omega; Acctg; CPA.

**CARRINGTON, VANNESSA E,** Clark Atlanta Univ, Atlanta, GA; FR; BA; Psychlgy; Clncl.

**CARRIZOSA, ANA M,** Univ Of Miami, Coral Gables, FL; SO; BS; Microbiology Clb Hstrn 90; Latin Amer Stdnts Assn V P 90; Dance Clb 90; Phi Eta Sigma 89; Microbiology/Immunology; Med Rsrch.

**CARROLL, AVIVICE,** Clark Atlanta Univ, Atlanta, GA; SO; Stdnt GA Assn Educators Asst Sect 90-; Kappa Delta Epsilon 90-; Natl Hnr Soc 90-; Early Chldhd Educ; Prof Tchr/Educ.

**CARROLL, CANDACE L,** Clayton St Coll, Morrow, GA; JR; BA; Chem Rbbr Co Frshmn Achievemnt Awd For Chem 90; Math Awd 90; AA 90; Schlstc Achievemnt Awd 90; Math; Sftwre Eng.

**CARROLL, CARLA R,** Heidelberg Coll, Tiffin, OH; FR; BA; Hll Cncl Flr Rep 90-; Psych; Cnslng.

**CARROLL, CAROL S,** Univ Of North Fl, Jacksonville, FL; JR; BA; Phi Theta Kappa 88-; Deans List 87-; Schlrshp 87-89; AA FL Comm Clg 89; Delem Ed; Tchng.

**CARROLL, CLIFFORD A,** Radford Univ, Radford, VA; JR; BBA; PBL; Acctg; CPA/MBA/PHD.

**CARROLL, FLORENCE GREEN,** Univ Of The Dist Of Columbia, Washington, DC; Delta Mu Delta; Alpha Kappa Alpha 68; Toastmasters Fed Reserve Bd Pres 90; Fed Reserve Bd Acctg Analyst Div Reserve Bnk Op/Pymnt Sys 83-.

**CARROLL III, GEORGE T,** Univ Of Akron, Akron, OH; JR; BS; Socty Auto Engrs 90-; Co Op Educ Prog W/Figgte Intl; Mech Engr; MBA.

**CARROLL, HARLAN P,** Kennesaw St Coll, Marietta, GA; FR; BS; Phi Eta Sigma 90-; Biol; Miltry.

**CARROLL, JANICE P,** Livingston Univ, Livingston, AL; SO; BS; Acctg; CPA.

**CARROLL, JOY LEE,** Chattanooga St Tech Comm Coll, Chattanooga, TN; SO; Clgte Sec Intl 89; Phi Theta Kappa 90; Deans Lst 88.

**CARROLL, JULIE M,** S U N Y Coll At Fredonia, Fredonia, NY; SR; BED; Elem Ed; Tchng.**

**CARROLL, KEVIN D,** Univ Of Akron, Akron, OH; SR; BS; Gldn Ky; Alpha Sigma Lambda; Beta Gamma Sigam; KPMG Peat Marwick Fndtn Schlrshp; Galen Roush Mem Schlshp; Accntng; CPA.

**CARROLL, KIMBERLY P,** Univ Of Sc At Columbia, Columbia, SC; SO; MBA; Alpha Epsilon Delta; Gamma Beta Phi; Alpha Chi Omega 90-; Bio; Med Schl.

**CARROLL, LEIGH E,** Bowling Green St Univ At Huron, Huron, OH; SO; BA; PTO Vol; Drmtry Govt Treas 89; Dns Lst; Catawba Is Vol Fire Dept Sec 90-; Elem Ed.

**CARROLL, LISA M,** Oh Dominican Coll, Columbus, OH; FR; AA; Eagle Forum 87-; Ascension Lthrn Chrch Pre Schl/Sndy Schl Tchr 90-; Franklin Cnty Fmly Day Care Prvdrs Assn Action For Chldrn 89-; Erly Chldhd Educ; Tchr.

**CARROLL, MICHAEL J,** Mt Saint Marys Coll & Seminary, Emmitsburg, MD; SR; BS; Hong Cmtee Exe Bd 87-89; Peer Grp Cnslr 89-90; Publcty Cmtee 90-; Delta Mu Delta 89-; Alpha Mu Gamma 90-; G H Miles 87-; Pres Schlrshp 87-; Deans Lst 87; I M Ftbl Bkbl Sftbl 87-; Bus/Fin Spanish; Intl Bus.

**CARROLL, MICHAEL W,** Coppin St Coll, Baltimore, MD; SR; BA; Bsn Mngmnt.

**CARROLL, PAMELA A,** Gallaudet Univ, Washington, DC; GD; MA; Stdnt Cncl Excptnl Chldrn VP 87-88; Cncl Armcn Instrctrs Df Pres 90-; Kappa Delta Pi Sec 90-; Gldn Key; Kappa Delta Pi Sec 90; Sigma Kapa Schlrshp Chrmn; COMSERV; Mrnrs Sec 85-86; Wllm Zplln Awrd; Emblm Clb Schlrshp; BS 89; Df Ed.

**CARROLL, PATRICIA LYNN,** Fl International Univ, Miami, FL; SR; MBA; AA Miami Dad Comm Clg 89; Bus; Acctg.

**CARROLL, ROBERT J,** Nova Univ, Ft Lauderdale, FL; GD; MBA; BS 89; Bus; Mgmt.

**CARROLL, SARAH S,** Greenville Tech Coll, Greenville, SC; FR; AS; Dns Lst 90-; Finance 84-89; Engr.

**CARROLL, SCOTTY D,** Fl St Univ, Tallahassee, FL; SR; BS; ROTC; Engr Hon Soc; IM; Elec Engr.

**CARROLL, YAZMIN C,** Univ Of Al At Huntsville, Huntsville, AL; SO; Wrld Exper Coor; Elect Eng; Dsgn.

**CARROTHERS, DIANN L,** Wv Northern Comm Coll, Wheeling, WV; FR; AAS; CNA Mc Kinley Voc Schl 72; Hlth; Rsprtry Care Thrpy.

**CARRUTH, NATALIE O,** Ms Univ For Women, Columbus, MS; JR; BS; Miss Assn Eductrs 90-; Asst Tchr Sullgnt Elem Schl 90; Elem Educ; Tchng.

**CARSCH, RUTH G,** Univ Of Cincinnati, Cincinnati, OH; SR; BFA; Sigma Delta Tau Assist Hse Mgr 87-; Thtr Dsgn/Prdctn; Thtr.

**CARSON, CAROLINE P,** Univ Of Sc At Columbia, Columbia, SC; SO; BM; Cncrt Choir; Wmns Chrs; Philhrmnic Chrs; Opera Wrkshp; Tutr; Chrch Chr; Ushr; SE Bach Chrl Ensmbl; Invttnl Tour Germany; Charleston Symphny Sngrs Guld; Scottish Scty; Music Ed; Ed.

**CARSON, CHRISTINA M,** Fayetteville St Univ, Fayetteville, NC; SO; Drama Clb/Young Repubs/FBLA/STDNT Govt Pr; Deans Lst; Blood Dr; Christmas Dr-Falcon Childrens Home; Track; IM Sports; Pol Sci; Law.

**CARSON JR, DORSEY R,** Ms St Univ, Miss State, MS; SO; BA; S A Traffic Appeals Ct Chrmn 89-; Activ Bd 90-; Yng Democrats Of MI 90; Alpha Lambda Delta 90-; Phi Eta Sigma 90-; Sigma Phi Epsilon IFC Rep 90; Schlrshp Comm 89-; S A Elections Cmmsn Co Chrmn 90-; Nwspr Photog/Wtr 89-; Pol Sci; Law.

**CARSON, GEORGE S,** Univ Of Ky, Lexington, KY; JR; BS; SGA Chrmn Acdmc Rghts 89-90; Amer Inst Chem Engrs SE Rgn Prlmntrn 88-; Omicron Delta Kappa 89-; Gldn Key 90-; Lances Jr Mens Honry 89-; Tau Beta Pi 90-; Phi Sigma Kappa Pres 88-; Vol Amer 89; Big Bro/Big Sis Lexingtn 88-; Gods Pntry 90; Chem Eng; MS/CHEM Eng/MBA.

**CARSON, GLORIA J,** Saint Joseph Coll, West Hartford, CT; SR; BA; Almn Vol; Deans Lst 88-; Hnrs Sympsm 89; Pltcl Sci.**

**CARSON III, JAMES,** Memphis St Univ, Memphis, TN; SR; BPS; Univ Clg Schlp 90; Cnslng.

**CARSON, JAMES M,** Cumberland County Coll, Vineland, NJ; FR; Stdnt Sennate 90-; Horticulture.

**CARSON, JUANYALE M,** Chattanooga St Tech Comm Coll, Chattanooga, TN; FR; BS; Phi Theta Kappa 89-; Tlnt Rstrs Cert Acad Achvmnt; Sign Lang Cert; AS; Bsn Admin; Mgmt.

**CARSON, MARSHA L,** Lincoln Univ, Lincoln Univ, PA; SR; BA; Usher Bd 90-; Pittsburgh Clb 90-; Russian Clb V P 90-; Dobro Slovo; Phi Sigma Iota; Alpha Mu Gamma; Campus All Star Challenge; Sales Clerk 87-89; FBI File Clerk 89-90; Russian; Trnsltn/Intrpret Ed.

**CARSON, MARTY RAE,** Queens Coll, Charlotte, NC; SR; BA; Soph Cls Pres 89-90; Dorm Sntr 88-89; Soph Hnry Cncl; Beta Beta Beta; Belk Schlr 88-; Dana Schlr 89-90; Bus Admin/Cmptr Emphasis; Retail Sls.

**CARSON, MARY LAHR,** Coker Coll, Hartsville, SC; JR; BA; Envrnmntl Clb 90-; Cultrl Arts Comm 90-; Art Clb 88-; Fr/Soph Clss Offcr; Yrbk Asst Ed 89-90; Ambsdr 89-; Crew Team 89-; Stdnt Ltrcy Corps 90-; May Ct 88-90; C W Coker Acdmc Schlrshp; Phtgrphy.

**CARSON, MARY P,** William Paterson Coll, Wayne, NJ; JR; BS; Rsdnc Lf Rsdnt Asst 90-; Chmcl Soc VP 90-; BACCHUS 89-90; Delta Psi Omega 89; RA Acdmc Achvmnt Awd 90; Crs Cntry 88; Chmstry; Chmstr/Glgy.

**CARSON, RANDAL J,** Daemen Coll, Amherst, NY; SO; BS; Stdnt Actvties Assn VP; Sigma Chi Phlnthrpy Chr 89-90; Phys Therpy; Rehab.

**CARSON, SHAWN W,** Wv Univ At Parkersburg, Parkersburg, WV; JR; AAS; Crmnl Juste; Law Enfrcmnt.

**CARSON, STEPHANIE DAWN,** Univ Of Tn At Martin, Martin, TN; SR; BS; Math Clb 89-; STEA 89-; Phi Kappa Phi; Alpha Delta Pi; Tchrs Asst In Math Lab 90-; Hnrs Smnr 89-; Pnhllnc Rep VP 90-; AS Dyersburg State Comm Coll 89; Math Educ; Tchng.

**CARTAGENA VILLANUEVA, ENID M,** Univ Of Pr Cayey Univ Coll, Cayey, PR; FR; Hon Assn 90-; Soc Sci; Psychology.

**CARTE, MATTHEW L,** Ms St Univ, Miss State, MS; FR; BS; Bptst Stu Unn VP Cmmtt; IM Sccr; Cmptr Eng; Eng.

**CARTE, PATRICK J M,** Univ Of Charleston, Charleston, WV; SR; BA; Psych Clb Pres 88-; Tutor; Covenant House Intern; Cmnty Hlts Ctrs Intern; Pi Gamma Mu Secr/Treas 90-; Psi Chi; Pi Gamma Mu Schlrshp; Psych Awd; Acad Achvmnt Cert; Amer Pol Sci Assoc 90-; Hosp Med Affairs Corp Study Coord; Psych; Hlth Care.

**CARTEE, KATHI BIHL,** Oh Univ-Southern Cmps, Ironton, OH; SR; BA; Golden Key; Gamma Pi Delta; Deans Lst Morehead St U; Deans Lst Shawnee St U; Deans Lst OH U; Advsry Cncl Impct Drg/Alchl Abuse Pgm; Sthrn OH Task Frc Dmestc Vlnc; AA W/ Hnrs Shawnee St U 86; Psych; Hmn Svcs.

**CARTEE JR, M LEWIS,** Univ Of Ga, Athens, GA; SR; BED; Coach Sccr 87-88; Hstry Educ; Tch.

**CARTER, ADISA T,** Morehouse Coll, Atlanta, GA; FR; BS; Hnr Sprgm 90-; Hnr Rll 90-; John Hope Prjct 90; Comp Sci; Comp Prgrmmr.

**CARTER, AMY D,** Univ Of Ga, Athens, GA; SR; BSED; Dance Co Pres 88; Yng Choreogrphrs Series Scrtry 89-90; Golden Key 89; Ldrshp 90; Kappa Delta Epsilon 90; Blue Key; Deans Lst 89; Dance Ed; Dance/MFA/TCHR.

**CARTER, AMY N,** Middle Tn St Univ, Murfreesboro, TN; FR; BA; Crmnl Justce Soc Nwsltr Rprtr 90-; Gamma Beta Phi 90-; Crmnl Jstce; Law.

**CARTER, ANGELIA A,** Clark Atlanta Univ, Atlanta, GA; SR; BA; Stdnt GA Assc Edctrs VP 90-; Pblcty Chr Prsn 89-90; Tsk Frc 88; All Amer Schlr; BA; Educ; Tchng.

**CARTER, ANNA K,** Ms Univ For Women, Columbus, MS; SR; MS; Ntl Stu Spch Hrng Lang Tres Assoc Tres/Vp 89-; Mdlg Squad Asst 87-89; Pres Lst; Deans Lst; Otstndg Stu Spch Pthlgy 89; Hrvy Crmwl Acdmc Schlrshp 90-; Hzrd Acdmc Schlrshp 90-; BS, Audiology; Grad Sch.**

**CARTER, APRIL M,** Valdosta St Coll, Valdosta, GA; JR; Heart Assoc Pres; Blood Dr.

**CARTER, AVIS D,** Blue Mountain Coll, Blue Mountain, MS; JR; MAESP 90-; TWIGS Pres 82-83; Elem Ed; Elem Tchr.

**CARTER, BETTY LOU,** Volunteer St Comm Coll, Gallatin, TN; SO; BA; Gamma Beta Phi 90-; Bus; Acctg.

**CARTER, BRENDA L,** Univ Of Southern Ms, Hattiesburg, MS; JR; BSN; Amer Hrt Assoc CPR Instrctr 87-; Dntl Tchncn U S Navy; U S Navy Nrs 82-; AS Central Tx Clge 89; Nrsg; U S Navy Nrs.

**CARTER, BRIAN T,** Univ Of Nc At Asheville, Asheville, NC; SO; BA; Pol Sci Hon Soc Sec 89-90; Drama; Film.**

**CARTER, BRUCE,** Al A & M Univ, Normal, AL; SO; Bapt Stndt Un; Stdnt Drg Tsk Frc; Hnr Stdnt; Busn Mgmt; Mgr.

**CARTER, CANDY L,** Anne Arundel Comm Coll, Arnold, MD; FR; JD; Paralegal Law; Law.

**CARTER, CAROLINE J,** Saint Thomas Univ, Miami, FL; SR; Airline & Travel Agency Associated Schools Inc Personnel 87.

**CARTER, CARY B,** Univ Of Tn At Martin, Martin, TN; JR; BS; Teach Mens Bible Cls; Veterinary Medicine; DVM.

**CARTER, CATHERINE S,** Univ Of Southern Ms, Hattiesburg, MS; SR; Gamma Beta Phi 90-; Kappa Omicron Nu 90-; Goldn Key 90-; AAS Jones Cnty Jr Coll 88; Fmly Lf Studies Chld Lf; Chld Lf Pro.

**CARTER, CHAWNETTE C,** Middle Tn St Univ, Murfreesboro, TN; JR; MTSU Vars Chrldr 88-; Erly Chldhd Educ; Elem Sch Tchr.

**CARTER, CHERI C,** Memphis St Univ, Memphis, TN; SR; BA; Mngmnt Infmnt Systms; Systms Anlyst.

**CARTER, CHRIS S,** Middle Tn St Univ, Murfreesboro, TN; SR; Jr Coll Bsbl Vrsty 86-88; Spec Olympc Hlpr 86-88; Gamma Beta Phi 87-; AD Martin Mthdst Coll 88; BS MTSV; Aerospce/Prfsnl Pilot.

**CARTER, CHRISTOPHER M,** Univ Of Akron, Akron, OH; FR; BS; Rcrtnl Events Comm 90-; Phi Eta Sigma; Hnrs Pgm 90-; IM Bsktbl; Chem Engr.

**CARTER, CHRISTY L,** Univ Of Tn At Martin, Martin, TN; SR; BSE; STEA; Gamma Beta Phi; Explr Asst Ldr; Church Yth; Comm Clg Schlrshp; Gooch Schlrshp; Hist; Tch.

**CARTER, CINDY A,** Univ Of Southern Ms, Hattiesburg, MS; SR; BS; Soc Prof Jrnlsts; Ord Of Omega; Delta Gamma Hs Mgr 90-; Jrnlsm Intern; Radio TV Film; Brdcst Jrnlsm.

**CARTER, DARLENE,** Norfolk St Univ, Norfolk, VA; SR; Hlth Educ Clb Amer; Grad Hon 90; Oper Brkng Through 90; Ch Bldg Fnd Prmtns Dir 90-; Cmt; Nrflk Comm Svc Brd Crdntr 90; Say No To Drgs Pgm; Hlth Ed; Comm Hlgh Edctr.

**CARTER, DE WAYNE O,** Al A & M Univ, Normal, AL; FR; BS; Lambda Sigma Pi 90-; Math Clb 90-; Am Math Assn; Class Treas 90-; SGA 90-; Church Yth Grp 89-; Pres Awd 90; Pres Cup 90-; Comp Sci/Math; Sftwr Eng.

**CARTER, DEBORAH K,** Va Highlands Comm Coll, Abingdon, VA; SO; BA; Phi Theta Kappa Pres 90-; All Amer Sclr; Pres Hnr Roll 89; Dns Lst 90-; Amer Red Cross; Bsn Admin; Internatl Bsn.

**CARTER, DENINE T,** Hampton Univ, Hampton, VA; FR; BS; Stdnt Mntrshp Prog 90; Sapphire Pom Pom Sqd; Ele Educ.

**CARTER, DENISE R,** Wilberforce Univ, Wilberforce, OH; JR; BA; United Charities 90; Soc Work.

**CARTER, DENNIS M,** Univ Of South Al, Mobile, AL; JR; BA; Dns Lst 88-90; St Vincent De Paul 89-; US Pstl Serv Mgr 86-; Acctng.

**CARTER, DETRIA D,** Talladega Coll, Talladega, AL; JR; Engl Club 88; Newspr 89; SGA 88; Alpha Chi; Alpha Kappa Alpha V P 89; Engl/Jrnlsm; Law.

**CARTER, DONNA J,** Miami Dade Comm Coll North, Miami, FL; SO; AA; Lbrl Arts; Cmnctns.

**CARTER, EBONY M,** Alcorn St Univ, Lorman, MS; SO; BA; Acctng; CPA.

**CARTER, FELICIA R,** Alcorn St Univ, Lorman, MS; JR; BA; Sec Sci.

**CARTER, GAIL A,** Salisbury St Univ, Salisbury, MD; SR; BA; Radio 87; Sci Clb 87-; Pi Sigma Alpha 90-; Dns Lst 90-; Leg Intrn MD Gen Assmbly; Attny Gen Cnsmr Affrs Intr 90; Pltcl Sci; Pblc Admin.

**CARTER, JAMES S,** New England Coll Of Optometry, Boston, MA; GD; OD; Phi Beta Kappa 83; Phi Alpha Theta 83; BA Un/R I 83; Optmtry; Rsrch.

**CARTER, JANET L,** Methodist Coll, Fayetteville, NC; SR; MBA; SGA VP 89-90; SIFE Pres 89-90; Magna Cum Laude; Outstndng Stdnt Awd; ABWA 87-89; Utd Way 87; BS 90; Bus Amn.

**CARTER, JASON W,** Univ Of Al At Birmingham, Birmingham, AL; SR.

**CARTER, JAVETTE S,** Hampton Univ, Hampton, VA; JR; BA; Nw Jrsy Pre Almn Clb 89-; Bus Clb 89-; NAACP 89-90; Acctg.**

**CARTER, JEFFREY A,** Chesterfield Marlboro Coll, Cheraw, SC; FR; BA; Plyrs Art Socty; Dns Lst 90-; Pres Lst 90-; Musc/Vocl Prfrmnc; Tchr.

**CARTER, JEFFREY ALAN,** Wv Univ, Morgantown, WV; SO; BSIE; Inst Indstrl Eng Treas 90-; Pi Mu Epsilon 90-; Tech Asst Ctr Entrprnl Stud 89-; Indus Eng, Cnsltng Eng.

**CARTER, JEFFREY L,** Abraham Baldwin Agri Coll, Tifton, GA; SO; BED; Science; Wildlife Mgmnt/Teaching.

**CARTER, JENNIFER D,** Valdosta St Coll, Valdosta, GA; SO; BA; Symphny Orchstra 90-; Cncrt Band 1st Chair 89-; Mrchng Band Sctn Ldr 89-; Sigma Alpha Iota; GA Msc Edctrs Assn; Bptst Stdnt Union; GMEA Piano Cmptn 90; Deans List; Msc Prfrmnc.

**CARTER, JENNIFER L,** Al St Univ, Montgomery, AL; FR; Beulah Mssnry Bptst Chrch; Yng Adlt Choir; Jr Ushr Brd; Pres Of Ushrbrd 87-90; Hnr Roll; Mass Cmmnctns; Brdcst Jrnlst.

**CARTER, JENNIFER M,** Western New England Coll, Springfield, MA; FR; BS; Grls Tnns Tm 90-; Acctg/Engl; Mstrs Cmnctn.

**CARTER, JENNIFER M,** Merrimack Coll, North Andover, MA; FR; BA; Drmtc Scty 90; Bg Brthrs Bg Sstrs 90; Bus Mgmt Mgmt Info Systsm.

**CARTER, JENNIFER S,** Univ Of Sc At Columbia, Columbia, SC; SR; MA; Phi Beta Kappa 90-; Golden Key 89-; Gamma Beta Phi 89-; Mc Duffie Sr Engl Awd 90; Columbia Brd Rltrs Million Dlr Clb; BA 90; Engl; Coll Lvl Tchng.

**CARTER, JESSE H,** Wv Inst Of Tech, Montgomery, WV; SO; BA; Intrnshp VA Power 90; Intrnshp Union Carbide; Chem Eng.

**CARTER, JOHN C,** William Carey Coll, Hattiesburg, MS; JR; BLA; Blgy/Rlgn/Lib Stds; Mnstry Bl Tchr.

**CARTER, JOHN N,** Anne Arundel Comm Coll, Arnold, MD; FR; BA; Comptr Sci; Comptr Indstry.

**CARTER JR, JOHN T,** Univ Of Sc At Columbia, Columbia, SC; JR; BM; Music; Tchr.

**CARTER, JOSEPH W,** Univ Of Nc At Asheville, Asheville, NC; FR; BS; Phi Eta Sigma 90; Chncllrs Lst 90; Mchncl Eng; Eng.

**CARTER, JULIA A,** Univ Of Nc At Asheville, Asheville, NC; JR; BA; Univ Hnrs Stdnt Lst 90; UNCA Dns Lst; Chnclrs Lst 90; UNCA 90; Psychlgy; Cnslng/Clin Psychlgst.**

**CARTER, KATHERINE R,** Middle Tn St Univ, Murfreesboro, TN; SR; BED; Spcl Ed; Tchr.

**CARTER, KATHY A,** Univ Of Nc At Charlotte, Charlotte, NC; FR; BA; Deans Lst; Chmstry; Phrmcst.

**CARTER, KATHY L,** Middle Tn St Univ, Murfreesboro, TN; SR; BS; Elem Ed; Tchr.

**CARTER, KEITA A,** Strayer Coll, Washington, DC; SO; BS; Acctg Clb; Acctg; CPA.

**CARTER, KELLI-AN J,** Va Commonwealth Univ, Richmond, VA; JR; BS; Res Hl Std Asc Pres 86-87; Phi Theta Kappa 88-; Summa Cum Laude 90; Dns Lst 90-; AS 90; Mktg; Pblc Rltns/Mktg.

**CARTER, KELLY E,** Fl A & M Univ, Tallahassee, FL; FR; BS; FAMU Pres Schlrs Assn; Fresh Class Govt Comm Chrmn 90-; Math Soc Advsry Board; Amer Soc Stdnt Actuaries; Phi Eta Sigma 90-; Actuarial Intern Allstate Insur Co; Acturial Sci; Property/Cslty Insur.

**CARTER, KELLY J,** West Liberty St Coll, West Liberty, WV; SR; MBA; Tutrng Serv 80-90; BA; Sec Soc Sci Ed; Tchr.

**CARTER, KELLY S,** Fl A & M Univ, Tallahassee, FL; SO; BA; Natl Blck Accntns Assn; Phi Eta Sigma; Nwmn Clb; Accntng; CPA.**

**CARTER, KIMBERLY D,** Utica Jr Coll, Utica, MS; SO; Nwspr Staff Reptr 89-90; Phi Theta Kappa 90-; English; Tchr Author.

**CARTER, KOBIE RANDALL,** Hampton Univ, Hampton, VA; FR; BA; Fla Pre Alum Assn Parlmntrn 90-; Busn Clb 90-; Fr Hnrs Pgm 90-; Dns Lst 90-; Eminent Schlrs Awd 90-; Finc; Fincl Anlyst.

**CARTER, LEIGH A,** Anne Arundel Comm Coll, Arnold, MD; SO; BA; Vol Tudor; Phi Theta Kappa; Dns Lst 89-; AA; Elem Educ; Math Tchr.**

**CARTER, LINDA K,** Watterson Coll, Louisville, KY; SR; BED; Acctng; Cpa.

**CARTER, LINDA W,** Univ Of Pittsburgh, Pittsburgh, PA; GD; MSN; Sigma Theta Tau 85-; Delta Epsilon Sigma 84-; Amer Nrs Assoc 86-; PA Nrs Assoc 86-; Intl Soc Nrs Cncr Cr 89-; Amer Cncr Soc Brd Dir 89-; Nrs Hope 87; Chem Educ Com 89-; Vol Yr 87; Spkrs Bureau Awd 87; Publ Educ Lf Svr Awd 87-88; BSN Carlow Clg 86; Med Srgcl Nrs; Onclgy.

**CARTER JR, LONNIE J,** Tri County Tech Coll, Pendleton, SC; SR; Alpah Zeta Beta 90-; Phi Theta Capa 89-90; Apprenticeship For Robert Bosch Corp 89-; AS.

**CARTER, LONNIE S,** Al St Univ, Montgomery, AL; JR; BS; Soc For Advncmnt Of Mgt 90-; Hon Roll 88-; Mktg; Real Est.

**CARTER, MARIAN V,** Hampton Univ, Hampton, VA; FR; BED; Stdnt Chrstn Assoc 90-; Gspl Chr 90-; Pres Eminent Schlrshp 90-; Math Ed.

**CARTER, MARY D,** Western Piedmont Comm Coll, Morganton, NC; SO; BS; AA; Bus; Admin.

**CARTER, MELANIE WILMET,** Alcorn St Univ, Lorman, MS; JR; BS; Hon Stdnt Orgnztn; Math/Cmptr Sci Clb Sec 90-; Alpha Kappa Mu; Deans List; Allen Chrstn Endeavor Leag; Pres Schlr; Math; Bus.

**CARTER, MELISSA L,** Univ Of Pittsburgh At Bradford, Bradford, PA; SO; BA; Biology Clb 90-; Beta Beta Beta Biological Soc 90-; Theta Sigma Delta Act Dir 89-; Biology; Med.

**CARTER, MICHAEL C,** James Sprunt Comm Coll, Kenansville, NC; FR; BS; Ag; Tchng.

**CARTER, MICHAEL M,** Fl St Univ, Tallahassee, FL; FR; MBA; IM Ftbl Sftbl 90-; Bus/Fin.

**CARTER, MICHAEL R,** City Univ Of Ny John Jay Coll, New York, NY; JR; BS; Ftnss Ctr; Law.**

**CARTER, MICHAEL SHANNON,** Univ Of Tn At Knoxville, Knoxville, TN; FR; MT; Mrchng Bnd; Pep Bnd; Prcssn Ensmbl; Stl Drms; Wnd Ensmbl; Cncrt; Music Ed; Tch Music.

**CARTER, MICHELLE A,** Elms Coll, Chicopee, MA; SO; BA; Chmstry; Envrmntl Chmst.

**CARTER, MONICA D,** Univ Of Md At Eastern Shore, Princess Anne, MD; JR; BA; Telecomm Clb 90-; Delta Sigma Theta VP; Dns Lst Hnree 89-90; Cert Acdmc Achvmnt 90; Dns Lst Hnree 90-; Engl; TV Prodctn.

**CARTER, NANCY R,** Union Univ, Jackson, TN; SR; BA; Stdnt Tenn Educ Assoc 89-; Annual Stf Copy Edtr 88-90; Dorm Cncl SGA Sntr 89-90; Kappa Delta Prsnl Enrchmnt Prog Chrmn 89-; Deans Lst 90; Elem Educ; Teach.

**CARTER, NANCY S,** Va St Univ, Petersburg, VA; GD; BA; Nrth Elem PTA Treas 86-88; Clncl Hghts Spec Educ Advsry Comm 88-90; Kappa Delta Psi 89-; Metro Life Schlp; Pres Awd 88-90; Scl Stds; Tchr.

**CARTER, PAULINE J,** Methodist Coll, Fayetteville, NC; SR; BS; Beta Beta Beta Treas 88-; Methodist Clg Chem Scty 90-; Internship Wake Forest Univ 90; BS; Biology Chemistry; Research Perfusionist.

**CARTER, RENEE J,** Hocking Tech Coll, Nelsonville, OH; SR; BSS; Deans List; AAB; Mgmnt Info Syst; Analyst.**

**CARTER JR, RICHARD P,** Univ Of Sc At Columbia, Columbia, SC; FR; BS; SGA 90-; Gamma Beta Phi 90-; Stdnt Yr 90-; Cmmncmnt Mrshll 90-; Stdnt Asst; Pres Lst; Intra-Cmps Bsktbl Co-Capt 90-; Pre-Med/Blgy; Med.

**CARTER, SANDRA L,** Dyersburg St Comm Coll, Dyersburg, TN; FR; BA; Mdrn Wdmn Am Pres 87-88; Jr Yth Clb Pres; Phi Theta Kappa; Lauderdale Co Hd Start Vol 88-89; Sub Tchr 89-90; Hist; Elem Edn.

**CARTER, SCOTT D,** Univ Of Nc At Charlotte, Charlotte, NC; SO; BS; US Fencing Assoc; Purdue Fncng Clb; Biochem; Grad Sch.

**CARTER, SHARON R,** Methodist Coll, Fayetteville, NC; JR; BA; Blck Stdnt Mvemnt 88-; Acctg.**

**CARTER, SHERRI K,** Radford Univ, Radford, VA; FR; BA; Business; Mrktng Dir.

**CARTER, SHERWYN M,** Ny Univ, New York, NY; JR; BA; Stdnt Cncl Sch Cont Ed Alt Sen 90-; AAS NYU 90; Bsn-Intl Studies; Law.

**CARTER, STEPHANIE L,** Univ Of Tn At Martin, Martin, TN; SO; BS; Amer Chem Soc 90-; Bapt Yth Flwshp 85-; Alpha Omicron Pi 90-; I M Bkbl 90-; Pre Med; Med.

**CARTER, T PAMETTE,** Beckley Coll, Beckley, WV; FR; BA; State Teen Talent Awd 89; Ch Of God Asst Tchr 90; Sls Assoc 90-; Day Care; Ele Educ.

**CARTER, TABITHA A,** Salisbury St Univ, Salisbury, MD; SR; MBS; Stdnt Natl Ed Assn 89-; Stdnt Tchng 90; Elem Ed; Tchr.

**CARTER, TACITA A,** Bethune Cookman Coll, Daytona Beach, FL; FR; BA; Tennis Tm; Yrbk Stff Colayout Edtr; Gspl Chr; Blgy; Neonatlgy.

**CARTER, TERRI H,** Memphis St Univ, Memphis, TN; SR; BSET; Students Unlimited Ters 89-90; SGA Senate Engrg Chr 89-90; Scty Mnfty Engrs 90-; Elec Engrg; Engrg.

**CARTER, TERRI J,** Oh Univ-Southern Cmps, Ironton, OH; SO; AAB; Grtr Emmanuel Intl Rec Sec; Fllwshp Chrchs/Mnstrs Yth Dept Treas; Offc Admin Tchnlgy.

**CARTER, THOMAS R,** Ky Wesleyan Coll, Owensboro, KY; JR; Sigma Phi Epsilon VP 89-; Gus E Paris Schlrshp 90; Cmmn Wlth Attrnys Offc Intrnshp; Rummase Kamuf Yewell Pace/Condon Lw Intrnshp 89-90; Glf/Crss Cntry Tms 88-; Poli Sci; Law.

**CARTER, TRACY L,** Univ Of Rochester, Rochester, NY; JR; BA; Engl; Tchng.

**CARTER, TRAVIS L,** Fayetteville St Univ, Fayetteville, NC; JR; BS; Marching Band; Symphonic Band; Jazz Band; Precussian Ensemble; Kappa Kappa Psi V Pres ,9-; Yth Conservation Camp Intern Outdoor Ed Dir 90-; Music Education; Superintendant Of Schls.

**CARTER, VALERIE E,** Jackson St Univ, Jackson, MS; SO; BA; Hnrs Coll 89-; Bus Admn; Acctg.

**CARTER, VANESSA L,** Alcorn St Univ, Lorman, MS; FR; Stdnt Natl Educ Assn 90-; Fd Srvce Com Hmcmng Com; Crntn Com; Hnrs Stdnts Orgnztn; Vlybl Tm; Elem Educ; Tchr.

**CARTER, WANDA D,** Fl A & M Univ, Tallahassee, FL; JR; BS; Valencia Comm Clge Gspl Chr 87-89; Yng Wm Mv 87-89; Fl Ftr Ed Amer 90-; AA Valencia Comm Clge 89; Elem Ed; Tchg.

**CARTER, WENDY RENE,** Alcorn St Univ, Lorman, MS; FR; BS; Alpha Phi Omega Swthrt Sec; Cmptr Sci; Oprtr.

**CARTER, WILEY SEAN,** Marshall University, Huntington, WV; SO; BA; Alpha Chi Rho Educator 89-90; Acctg; CPA.

**CARTER-FARMER, REGINA M,** Elmira Coll, Elmira, NY; SR; MS; Amercn Cancer Soc; Amercn Heart Assoc; Natl Assoc Of Pediatric Nrs Assocts/Practnrs; Nrsng Emr Dept 74-; Nrsng.

**CARTHRON, JAMES A,** Clark Atlanta Univ, Atlanta, GA; SR; BS; Ntl Tchncl Soc Scrtry 89-90; Exp Bio Clb; Hosp Intrn; Mdcl Schl Intrn; Deans Lst; Chmstry; MD.

**CARTIER, ANDREA D,** Univ Of Southern Ms, Hattiesburg, MS; JR; BS; Hall Govt Sec 88-89; I M Ftbl; A F ROTC Admn Ofcr 88-; Gamma Beta Phi; Lambda Eta Pi 90-; Arnold Air Soc Deputy Cmdr 88-; Amer Lgn Schlstc Exclnc Awd 88; Radio T V Film; Telecmunctrs Rsrch.

**CARTIER, KELLI A,** Springfield Tech Comm Coll, Springfield, MA; SR; AS; Phys Thrpy Asst Clb 88-; Alpha Nu Omega 90-; Phys Thrpy Asst.

**CARTLEDGE, LAURA ANN,** Univ Of Sc At Aiken, Aiken, SC; FR; BS; Schol Hon Awd; Pres List; Acctng; CPA.

**CARTMELL, JEFFREY S,** Univ Of Rochester, Rochester, NY; SO; Hillel Co Chrmn 89-; Stdnt Sen 90-; Amer Soc Of Mech Engrs; Chi Phi Sec 90-; Mech Engr.

**CARTRETTE, COBY G,** Winthrop Coll, Rock Hill, SC; FR; BA; Winhecon 90-; Hmn Rsrce Mgmt Soc; Alpha Lambda Delta Pres 90; Louis Rhame West Schlr 90-; Pres Lst 90; Bsn Admin/Acctg; Law.

**CARTWRIGHT, AMY B,** Oh St Univ At Newark, Newark, OH; FR; BA; Hon Soc Hons Pgm 90-; Math Tutr 90-; Act Prctr 90-; Alpha Lambda Delta; Phi Eta Sigma; Utica Sertoma/Serteen Schlrshp 90-; Nwark Tchrs Assn Schlrshp 90-; OSU Hons Schlrshp PEO Schlrshp; Allied Med Prof; Med Dietetics.

**CARTWRIGHT IV, CLARENCE M,** Mount Olive Coll, Mount Olive, NC; FR; BA; Flwshp Of Chrstn Athlts 90-; Vrsty Bsbl 90-; Hstry; Educ.

**CARTWRIGHT, KATHY-ANN M,** Western New England Coll, Springfield, MA; JR; BA; Fincl Mgmt Assc 90-; Acctg Assc 90-; Caribbean Cltrl Exchng; Tae Kwon Do Clb; Inter Cltrl Orgnztn; Nassau Cruises Ltd Acctg 86-; BSL Laurention Univ 85; AA Clg Bahamas 82; Bus Acctg; CPA.

**CARTWRIGHT, KIMBERLY A,** George Mason Univ, Fairfax, VA; SR; BS; Hlth Educ.

**CARTWRIGHT, KRISTY S,** Middle Tn St Univ, Murfreesboro, TN; FR; BA; Elem Edn; Tchr.

**CARTWRIGHT, LAURIE A,** Duquesne Univ, Pittsburgh, PA; SO; BS; Field Hcky/Lock Haven Univ 83-87; Ambulance Vol; BS 87; Nurs.

**CARTWRIGHT, LISA BETH,** Univ Of Tn At Martin, Martin, TN; JR; Stdnt Tchr Educ Assn 90-; Chi Omega Pres 88-; Elem Educ; Tchr.

**CARTWRIGHT, RYAN C,** Niagara Univ, Niagara Univ, NY; SO; BA; Mktg Clb 89-90; Tax Serv Elderly 90-; Tutrd Niagara Univ 89-90; Sftbl 90-; Acctg; CPA.

**CARTY, LINDA E,** Fl A & M Univ, Tallahassee, FL; JR; Amer Phrmctcl Assoc 90-; Stdnt Natl Phrmctcl Assoc 90-; Phi Theta Kappa Natl V P 89-; Flwshp Bio-Med Rsrch Pgm Univ MI 90-; Space Life Sci Trng Pgm NASA 89-90; Cmnty Clg Schlrshp 90-; PC Miami-Dade Cmnty Clg 85; AA Miami-Dade Cmnty Clg 90; Phrmcy.

**CARTY, PATRICK K,** Glassboro St Coll, Glassboro, NJ; SR; BA; Glassboro Mrchng/Concert Bnds 87-89; Lit Pblctn 88-90; NJ Pirg 87-90; Stdnt Govt Treas 90-; Library Comm 89-90; Gamma Tau Sigma 90-; Alpha Chi Rho V P 88-; Alpha Phi Omega 90-; Deans Lst 88-; AFL-CIO Mcguire Schlrshp 88-; Hist/Scndry Educ; Tchr.

**CARTY, SHARON K,** Glassboro St Coll, Glassboro, NJ; SR; Phi Alpha Theta 90; Glcstr Co Hstrcl Scty 88; Ntl Cncl For Scl Studies Of NJ 89; BA; Cert Scl Studies Tchr NJ; Mstry; Tchr Secndry Ed.

**CARUCCI, LAURA R,** Cornell Univ Statutory College, Ithaca, NY; JR; BS; IM Bsktbl; Sccr Leag Catholic Cmmnty; Ho Nun De Kah; Dean Lst 89-; Mcrbiol; Med.

**CARUSO, AMY E,** Glassboro St Coll, Glassboro, NJ; FR; MBA; Cmnctns; Media/Bus.

**CARUSO, CHRISTINE,** Seton Hall Univ, South Orange, NJ; SR; Kappa Delta Phi; BA; Psychlgy/Elem Ed.

**CARUSO, DENISE MARIE,** Providence Coll, Providence, RI; JR; BA; Dvlmnt Wstrn Cvlztn Stdnt Rep 88-89; Intrnshp US Cngrsmn Ronald Machtley 90-; IM Flg Ftbl Bsktbl 89-; Pltcl Sci; Law.

**CARUSO, JANIS M,** Memphis St Univ, Memphis, TN; MD; Boy Scts Of Amer Den Ldr 88-; Med Soc Wrkr 87-89; ABED Univ Mich 73; MSW Univ Of Mich 75; MSED No Ill Univ 80; Pre Med.

**CARUSO, MARK D,** Teikyo Post Univ, Waterbury, CT; JR; BS; AS Mattatuck Comm Clge 90; Mgmt; Prsnl/Hmn Rsrce Mgmt.

**CARUSO, SILVIA L,** Duquesne Univ, Pittsburgh, PA; JR; BSED; Deans Lst 88-; Education Schlrshp 90-; Competitive Schlrshp; Scndry Math Ed; Tchng.

**CARUTHERS, CHRISTINE L,** Univ Of Southern Ms, Hattiesburg, MS; SR; BA; Stdnt Act Voice Envrnmnt 90-; Cmps Choice Pres 89-; Univ Hnrs Coll 89-; Phi Delta Phi; Philosophy; Tchng.

**CARUTHERS, TIMOTHY N,** Univ Of Fl, Gainesville, FL; SO; BA; Excptnl Ple Vol 90-; Bsn; Ins.**

**CARVALHO, SUSAN R,** Comm Coll Algny Co Algny Cmps, Pittsburgh, PA; SO; MOTA; Soc Art Crfts 89-; Doll Artisan Gld 88-; Uppr St Clair Leag Arts 86-; AM Schl Mdrd Boostr Soc Pblcty Chrmn 83-; AA Los Angeles Comm Clg 70; BA Unvrsty CA Berkeley 72; Occptnl Thrpy.

**CARVER, DENNIS L,** Coppin St Coll, Baltimore, MD; FR; Prncpl Achvrs 90; Cmnwlth Plus 90; Hon Pgm 90-; Hse Dlgts Schlrshp 90; Pres Acad Ftns Awrd 90; Pol Sci; Law.

**CARVER, EDWARD T,** Univ Of Akron, Akron, OH; JR; BS; Ntl Hon Soc; Mu Kappa Tau; R/H Mitten Schlrshp; Bus Adm; Intl Mktg/Bus.

**CARVER JR, JACKY E,** Roane St Comm Coll, Harriman, TN; SO; AS; Blgy; Med.

**CARVER, JAMES T,** Livingston Univ, Livingston, AL; FR; BA; Bapt Campus Ministries Host 90-; IM Ftbl 90-; Busn; Acctng.

**CARVER, MICHELLE L,** Tn St Univ, Nashville, TN; SR; BS; Crmnl Jstce Org Sec 87-; Stdnt Un Brd Govrs 90-; Univ Mrchng Cncrt Bnds Sec Ldr 87-; Gldn Ky Nw Mbr; Lambda Tau Epsilon VP 89-91; Alpha Kappa Alpha Sorority Inc 90-; Natl Assoc Adv Clrd People 87-89; Int TN St Legsltr Hs Rep; Res Adptd In Name; Crmnl Jstce/Psych; Corp Atty.

**CARWAY, CHARLES,** Ny Univ, New York, NY; JR; BS; Ancnt Ord Hibrns; Prog Anlyst; Inf Sys/Econ; MIS.

**CARWILE III, CORNELIUS T,** Christopher Newport Coll, Newport News, VA; JR; BS; Pi Lmbd Phi Soc Comm; Bio Marine.

**CARWILE JR, FREDERICK E,** Norfolk St Univ, Norfolk, VA; FR; BS; Spartan Alpha Tau; Bus; Fncl Plnr.

**CARWISE, ANDRETA K,** Fl A & M Univ, Tallahassee, FL; SO; Gospel Choir 89-90; Pres Schlr Assn 89-90; Phi Eta Sigma 90; Allstate Ins Co Intrn 89-; Math; Actuarial Sci.

**CARY, CHRISTOPHER D,** Ky Wesleyan Coll, Owensboro, KY; SO; BA; Golf Capt 89-; Flwshp Chrstn Athls 89-; Bsn; Law.

**CARY, DONNA M,** Schenectady County Comm Coll, Schenectady, NY; SR; AAS; Actvt Brd VP 88-89; Kntcky Drby Cncsn Stnd Mngr 90; Prsdnts Lst 89-90; Dns Lst 90; Chrldng 88-89; Htl/Rstrnt Mngmnt.

**CARY, JASON S,** Hudson Valley Comm Coll, Troy, NY; FR; BS; Crmnl Jstc; U S Army Ofcr.

**CARY, PATRICIA D,** Alcorn St Univ, Lorman, MS; SR; BS; Dghtrs Amrcn Rvltn 86-87; Intrntnl Stdnt Clb 88-90; Ordr Estrn Str 90-; Phi Beta Lambda Sec 89-90; All Amrcn Schlr Cllgt Awd 90-; Bsnsn Admnstrtn; Hmn Rsrc Mngr.

**CARY, TIM J,** Okaloosa Walton Comm Coll, Niceville, FL; FR; AA; Phi Theta Kappa 90-; Pres Lst And Dns Lst 90-; IM Ftbl And Bsktbl 90-; Bus; Rstrnt Mgmt.

**CARY, TIMOTHY A,** Radford Univ, Radford, VA; SR; BS; Phi Theta Kappa 88-89; Amry ROTC 89-; Hstry; Educ.

**CARY, YVONNE M,** Vance Granville Comm Coll, Henderson, NC; SO; Alternate Stdnt Gov 90-; Acad Schlrshp 89-; Tech Dipl; Chldhd Ed; Tch.

**CASABURRI, TARA M,** City Univ Of Ny Baruch Coll, New York, NY; SR; BA; Tchrs Tmrrw 88-; Deans Lst 88-; Engl; Prfssr Engl Lit.

**CASACCHIA, ROBERT J,** Youngstown St Univ, Youngstown, OH; SR; BS; Mngr; BS Penn St Univ 76; Cvl Eng; Envrnmntl Eng.

**CASACCI, KATHLEEN M,** S U N Y At Buffalo, Buffalo, NY; GD; DDS; Am Dntl Assn 89-; Am Stdnt Dntl Assn 89-; Am Assn Wmn Dntsts 89-; Delta Sigma Delta Hist; William Tucker Schlrshp 90-; RT LRT Mt St Marys Hosp 79; BA; Dntstry.**

**CASANOA, NANETTE G,** Coll Of Charleston, Charleston, SC; GD; MSTRS; PTA; Guardian Ad Litem Prog 89-; Lbrry Sci.

**CASANOVA, JOSE LUIS,** S U N Y Coll Of Tech At Alfred, Alfred, NY; FR; Sci Cl 90-; Intnl Cl 90-; Aerosp; Engrng.

**CASANOVA, VIRGINIA L,** De Tech & Comm Coll At Dover, Dover, DE; SO; AAS; Phi Theta Kappa 90-; Deans Lst 89-; Acdmc Incntv Schlrshps 89-; Comp Pgmg; Comp Cnsltng Bus.

**CASAS, CRISTINA,** Fl International Univ, Miami, FL; SR; BS; Hall Cncl Sec 90-; Scl Cltrl Prgrmmng Comm Sub Chrprsn 89-; SG Chrprsn 90-; Srvcs Comm 89-90; Prgrmmng Comm Chrprst; Sfty Comm 90-; Elem Edctn; Prfsnl Edctr.

**CASAS, OMARA J,** Miami Dade Comm Coll, Miami, FL; SO; BA; Deans Lst; Miami Rght Lf; Miami Chrstns Cr; Dade Vtrs Rgstrtn Dr; Crs Prgncy Cntr; Lgl Sec US Atty Offc 87-; BA Florida Bible Coll 75; Engl.

**CASCADDAN JR, RICHARD O,** Central Fl Comm Coll, Ocala, FL; SO; BA; Phi Theta Kappa; Pltcl Sci; Law.

**CASCINI, KATHLEEN A,** Middle Tn St Univ, Murfreesboro, TN; SO; BA; Foreign Lang; Bus.

**CASCO, OSWALDO,** Ky St Univ, Frankfort, KY; SO; BA; Grp Intl Stdnts; Acad Educ Dev Ambsdr Honduras Stdy US 89-; Pub Admin.

**CASDIN, CHRISTOPHER WENDELL,** Univ Of Va, Charlottesville, VA; SO; BA; Phi Eta Sigma 90-; Clsscs; Flm Edtg/Scrn Wrtng.**

**CASDORPH, CARLA F,** Marshall University, Huntington, WV; JR; MBA; Gamma Beta Phi; Spch Pthlgy; Thrpy.

**CASE, ANTONE V,** Niagara Univ, Niagara Univ, NY; JR; BA; Deans Lst 88-; Alpha Kappa Psi V P 90-; I M Bkbl Sftbl Capt 88-; Acctg; Mgmt.**

**CASE, FRAN M,** Alcorn St Univ, Lorman, MS; SR; BSN; Hi Hnrs; Cum Laude; AA 89; BS; Nrsg.

**CASE, LORI N,** Roane St Comm Coll, Harriman, TN; SO; BS; Raider Corp 89-; Assoc Degree; Bus Admin; Prsnnl/Lbr Relatns.

**CASE, MICHELE L,** Syracuse Univ, Syracuse, NY; FR; BSN; SGA Sec 90-; Nrsng; RN.

**CASE, PAUL C,** S U N Y Coll Of Tech At Alfred, Alfred, NY; SR; Amer Cngrs Srvyng/Mpng; ACSM 88-89; AAS 90-; Srvyng/Cnstr Engr; Prfsnl Land Srvyng.

**CASE, STACY L,** Univ Of Southern Ms, Hattiesburg, MS; JR; BS; Campus Newspapr Staff Wrtr 90; Stdnt Alumni Assoc/Sthrn News Jrnl; Frmr Fndrsng Chrmn/VP Scty Of Prof Jrnlsts 90; Gamma Alpha Epsilon Pres; Gamma Beta Phi; Kappa Delta Mag Chrmn/VP Of Pldge Class; Im Co-Rec Ftbl; AA 90; Brdcst Jrnlsm/Pol Sci; Brdcst Orprnt Jrnlst.

**CASEBOLT, SUSAN B,** Fl International Univ, Miami, FL; SR; BA; FIU Acctg Assoc 90; Natl Acctng Assoc 90-; BA Univ Of Central Florida 85; Acctg.

**CASELL, ALANA C,** Univ Of Va Clinch Valley Coll, Wise, VA; FR; BS; Educ.

**CASEMAN, ABBY L,** Oh Univ, Athens, OH; FR; BM; Natl Assoc Music Thrpy 90-; Sigma Alpha Iota Cl Sec 90-; Music Thrpy; RMT.

**CASEY, ANNA M,** Miami Jacobs Jr Coll Of Bus, Dayton, OH; SO; AS; Total Group Services Of Ohio 90-; Word Processing/Sec; Ins.

**CASEY, BETH C,** Cornell Univ Statutory College, Ithaca, NY; JR; BS; Stdnt Asmbly Envrnmntl Com 89-; Stdnt Advsr 89-90; Res Advsr 90-; IM Soccer Capt 90-; Bio Sci; Envrnmntl Sci/Cnsrvtn.

**CASEY, DONNA M,** Hood Coll, Frederick, MD; FR; BA; Hood Thtr 90-; Mgmt; Administrator.

**CASEY, FRANCIS X,** Univ Of Ct, Storrs, CT; SO; BS; Rnwld Ntrl Rsrcs; Water Rsrc Mgt.

**CASEY, JOHN B,** Villanova Univ, Villanova, PA; SR; JD; Trck And Fld Crss Cnty 87-; BA; Psych; Law.

**CASEY, KENNETH S,** Univ Of Miami, Coral Gables, FL; SR; PHD; Soccer Clb Pres 87-; Pgm Cncl 88-90; Golden Key 90-; Res Asst 88-; Marine Sci Summer Flwshp 88-89; Outstndg Clb Sport Pres 90; Phys Oceangrphy; Tchg/Rsrch.

**CASEY, MARK T,** Niagara Univ, Niagara Univ, NY; SO; BA; Niagara Univ Plyrs 89-; Chapel Choir Sngrs 89-; Outreach Ply 90-; Niagara Univ Hons Prog 90-; Theatre/Music; Music Perf.

**CASEY, MARY C,** Providence Coll, Providence, RI; JR; BA; Spec/Elem Educ; Tch Deaf/Hrng Imprd.

**CASEY, MAUREEN C,** Air Force Inst Of Tech, Wrt-Ptrsn Afb, OH; GD; MS; Alpha Psi Omega 68-71; Sigma Iota Epsilon 90; AF Assoc; Aircraft Pilots/Ownrs Assoc; BA Cntrl Mi U 71; MS 86; Info Rsrce Mngmnt; Career Offcr USAF.

**CASEY, PAMELA D,** Livingston Univ, Livingston, AL; SR; BS; Bus Admn/Cmptr Sci; Cmptr Pgmr.

**CASEY, PAMELA M,** Colby Sawyer Coll, New London, NH; FR; BS; Sftbl 90-; Vrsty Bsktbl 90-; Sprts Sci; Athltc Trnng.

**CASEY, PATRICIA L,** Memphis St Univ, Memphis, TN; SR; BS; Gldn Key 89-; Memphis State Unv Wvs Schlrshp 88-89; Family Srvcs 90-; Edctn; Tchr.

**CASEY, PETER F,** Merrimack Coll, North Andover, MA; SR; BSBA; Prsdntl Schhlr; Deans List 87-; Alpha Kappa Psi Sgt At Arms 90-; Morris Goodman Schlrshp Awd 90; Acctg; CPA.

**CASEY, SANDY S,** Midlands Tech Coll, Columbia, SC; SR; ASN; Ntnl Asso/Neonatal Nrs; Nrsg/Hlth Sci; Neonatal Intsv Care Nrsg.

**CASEY, SHANNON A,** Owensboro Comm Coll, Owensboro, KY; FR; BA; Sci; Cmptr Sci.

**CASEY, SHERYL L,** Univ Of Cincinnati, Cincinnati, OH; SR; BA; Cir K Clb Chptr Mgmnt 89-; Golden Key; AA Fla St Uiv 86-88; Spec Educ; Tchng.

**CASEY, WANDA GAIL,** Univ Of Montevallo, Montevallo, AL; SR; BS; Alpha Lmbd Dlt 88-; Kappa Dlt Pi 89-; Lmbd Sgm Pi 90-; Phi Kappa Phi; Alph Lmbd Dlt Schlrsp; Pres List 89-; Meth Chrch Fun Tyme 80-86; Grl Sct Ldr 74-79; Educ/Elem/Math/Sci.

**CASH, AMY L,** Longwood Coll, Farmville, VA; SR; BS; Cls Rep 90-; SEA 89-; IM/CMPS Rcrtn 86-; Educ; Tch.

**CASH, HERBERT J,** Vance Granville Comm Coll, Henderson, NC; SO; AA; Crmnl Juste Clb 89-90; Marshall 90-; Pres Merit Awd 90-; Crmnl Juste; Police/Crctnl Offcr.

**CASH, JAMES D,** Univ Of Ga, Athens, GA; SR; BS; Bpt Student Union 89-; Food Giant 83-84; Natl Bnk GA 84-87; Trust Co Bnk 87-88; Belk 88-; Early Childhood Ed; Tch Children K-4.

**CASH, LYNN M,** Radford Univ, Radford, VA; SO; BBA; Rdfrd Unv Ambsdrs Chrprsn 89-; Stdnt Lifes Cncrt Comm Mmbr 89-; Accntng; Bsns.

**CASHER, DAVID S,** Widener Univ, Chester, PA; SR; BS; Stdnt Govt Rep 87-; Ord Of Omega 90; Alpha Tau Omega Pres 87-; Acad Hnrs 90; Deans Lst 90; AS Brndywn Clg 86-88; Bus Mgmnt; Mktng.

**CASHWELL, KAREN A,** Fayetteville St Univ, Fayetteville, NC; SO; BA; Cnclrs Lst 89-90; Deans Lst 90-; Bus Admin; Loan Offcr.

**CASILLAS, DAVID,** Evangelical Semimary Of P R, Hato Rey, PR; GD.

**CASILLI, KRISTEN,** Providence Coll, Providence, RI; SR; BS; Ice Hockey IMS 87-; Mktg.

**CASIMIRE, TERESA A,** City Univ Of Ny Baruch Coll, New York, NY; JR; BA; Club Caricom; Bus Communication; Public Rltns.

**CASINO JR, WILLIAM ARNOLD,** Hillsborough Comm Coll, Tampa, FL; FR; AA; US Navy Nuclear Power Plnt Op 82-88; Eng.

**CASKEY, JULIE A,** Queens Coll, Charlotte, NC; SO; BA; ACLU Brd Dir 90-; Jaycees 90; PIE Ttr 90; Duke Power Co 87-; Engl.

**CASLER, DAVID S,** Fl Atlantic Univ, Boca Raton, FL; SR; Amer Mrktng Scty VP; Delta Sigma Chi; AA Univ Of Florida 89; BBA; Mrktng; Mgmt Cnsltng.

**CASO, ALEXANDER A,** Univ Of Miami, Coral Gables, FL; SO; BS; Cvl Engr.

**CASON, LINDA C,** Tri County Tech Coll, Pendleton, SC; FR; BA; Creatv Wrtng Grp; Alpha Zeta Beta; Abney Fndtn Schlrshp; R Bosch Corp Elec Assmbly; Engl; Wrtng.

**CASPAR, DANA J,** Univ Of Ky, Lexington, KY; FR; BPHAR; Pre Pharm Clb 90-; Chnclr Schlrshp; Deans List; Pharm Clg Arts Sci; Pharm Hosp.

**CASSAGNOL, HANS P,** Saint Johns Univ, Jamaica, NY; FR; BA; Billards; Bsebl/Bsktbl 90-; Librarian; All Amer Schlr 90; ASAA Awd 90; Bio; Med.

**CASSAZZA, LINDA G,** Univ Of Fl, Gainesville, FL; SR; BS; Stdnt Hlth Otrch Tm 90-; Fl Acdmy Of Physicians Assts 90-; Stdnt Assoc Physician Assts 90-; Alpha Delta Pi Hs Mgr 86-89; AA 89; Physician Asst.

**CASSELL, DIANA L,** Davis & Elkins Coll, Elkins, WV; JR; BA; Alpha Chi; All Amrcn Shclr 90-; Art Ed.**

**CASSELL, LISA B,** Univ Of Southern Ms, Hattiesburg, MS; SO; MS; Spch Lang Scis; Spch Pthlgy.

**CASSELL, SHERI L,** Univ Of Sc At Columbia, Columbia, SC; SR; BA; Bapt Stdnt Un P R Chr 87-90; Phi Beta Kappa; Gamma Beta Phi 88-89; Phi Eta Sigma 87-; Kappa Kappa Gamma Pldg Asst 89-; K E Grbr Schlrshp 87-; Pres Lst 88; Dns Lst Coll Jrnslsm 87-90; Jrnlsm/Advrtsng; Vet Schl.

**CASSIDAY II, JOHN R,** Univ Of Akron, Akron, OH; SR; BS; Dns Lst 85-90; Intrnshp 89; Acctg.

**CASSIDY, GREGORY A,** Univ Of Sc At Columbia, Columbia, SC; FR; BED; Bapt Stdnt Union 90-; Chem Eng; Eng.

**CASSIDY, SEAN W,** Villanova Univ, Villanova, PA; JR; BA; Chinese Clb Pres 88-; Yng Life Asst Ldr 87-; Phi Kappa Phi; Omicron Delta Epsilon; Litrgcl Mnstr 90-; Balloon Day Fnd Raisr Coord 88-; Mid-Atlntc Watr Polo-Acdmc All Conf 90-; Watr Polo 88-; Econ; Intrnatn Bus.

**CASSIDY, SINDY J,** Univ Of Montevallo, Montevallo, AL; JR; BS; Kappa Delta Pi 90-; Chi Omega 88-; Ece Elem Educ; Elem Tchr.

**CASSIDY, THOMAS E,** Georgetown Univ, Washington, DC; SO; BS; Fnnce Intrntl Bus; Law.

**CASSON, KERSTIN A,** Savannah Coll Of Art & Design, Savannah, GA; JR; Painting Clb; Painting; Tchg.

**CASSORLA, SHIRA LEA,** Allegheny Coll, Meadville, PA; SR; MAA Stdnt Chptr Chrtr Mem Co Chr 89-; Nwsppr Lyt Ed Cpy Ed 88-90; Stdnt Orttn Advsr; Alpha Phi Omega Sec Hstrn 87-; Alden Schlr 87-89; BS; Mth.**

**CASTAGNA, RICH J,** City Univ Of Ny Queensbrough, New York, NY; FR; Civl Air Patrl; Alpha Beta Gamma; Cmptr Prgmmg/Acctg.

**CASTANEDA, JANENE B,** City Univ Of Ny Queens Coll, Flushing, NY; SO; BS; Biology Hnr Soc; Biology; Medicine.**

**CASTANEDA, MAGDALENA,** Fl International Univ, Miami, FL; FR; AA; Deans Lst 90-; Church Choir 78-; Catechism Instructor 86-; Communicaions; Public Relations.

**CASTANER, WANDA I,** Univ Of Pr At Rio Piedras, Rio Piedras, PR; SR; BA; Assn Phys Educ Sec 90-; Gldn Ky 90-; Phy Educ; Phslgy Exercise.

**CASTANO, CLAUDIA N,** Fl International Univ, Miami, FL; JR; BS; Future Edctrs Amer 89-; Hnrs Cncl Repr; Ambsdr; Kappa Delta Pi V P; Talent Roster Certif Achvmnt 88; Outstndg Achvmnt Svc 90; Learn-To-Read Vol 89-; AA Miami-Dade Cmnty Clg 90; Ed; Rdg Spclst.

**CASTEEL, DEBRA ANN E,** Widener Univ, Chester, PA; JR; BA; Acctg Soc 90-; Hnrs Pro; Acctg; CPA.

**CASTEEL, SARA E,** Milligan Coll, Milligan Clg, TN; SR; BS; Exec Cncl Secr 89-; Delta Kappa 88-89; Johnson City Med Ctr Hosp Wellness Ctr Intern; Bsn Adm/Hlth-Phys Ed; Fitness Mgmt.

**CASTELLANI, CHRISTOPHER C,** S U N Y Coll Of Tech At Delhi, Delhi, NY; FR; Cross Country 90; Building Trades.

**CASTELLANO, JENNIFER P,** Coll Misericordia, Dallas, PA; JR; BS; SOTA 88-; Cls Secy 90-; Phi Theta Epsilon 89-; Cmapus Minstry Progrm Coor 89; Orentn Cnslr 90; Occuptnl Thrpy.

**CASTELLANO, JOHN R,** Fl Atlantic Univ, Boca Raton, FL; SO; BS; Bsn Adm; Law.

**CASTELLANOS, ELSA A,** Fl International Univ, Miami, FL; JR; BA; Phi Eta Sigma 88-; Educ; Tchr.

**CASTELLANOS, JUAN C,** Inter Amer Univ Pr Hato Rey, Hato Rey, PR; SO; BS; Aviation; Engrng.

**CASTELLANOS, MONICA M,** Univ Of Miami, Coral Gables, FL; SO; BA; Hurricane Prdctns 90; Ad Clb 90; Newspapr Staff Wtr/Movie Critic 90; Amer Advrtsng Fdrtn 90; Music Schl Vol 89; Vol For Prometeo Theater Grp 89; Hnrs Day Awd For Prometeo Theater Grp, Deans Lst 90; Cmmnctns Flm Prod/Engl; Flm Actng/Prdctn.

**CASTELLAW, DARYL C,** Southern Coll Of Tech, Marietta, GA; SR; BS; Bapt Stdnt Union 90-; Inst Elec/Electrnc Eng 90-; Pres Cert Acad Excell 90; Deans Lst 90-; Elec Eng Tech; Eng/Bus.

**CASTELLAW, TERESA L,** Univ Of Sc At Columbia, Columbia, SC; SO; BA; Srfsde Un Mthdst Sr Hgh Adlt Ldr; Elem Ed.

**CASTELLI, ROSARIA MARIA,** Barry Univ, Miami, FL; JR; BA; Nwspr Rprtr 90-; Pblc Rltns Stdnt Soc Amer; Cmmnctn Dpt Prdctns Rprtr; Barry Unvrsty Undrgrd Hnr Soc 90-; Phi Theta Kappa 89-; Soc Prfsnl Jrnlsts; Ntnl Fdrtn Press Wmn; Ntnl Clgt Cmmnctn Art Awrds Wnnr 90-; Brdcst Cmmnctn; Brdcst Jrnlst.**

**CASTELLI, SALVATORE A,** Embry Riddle Aeronautical Univ, Daytona Beach, FL; JR; BS; Avation; Airline Pilot.

**CASTELLINO, ANTHONY J,** Colby Sawyer Coll, New London, NH; JR; BS; Trdtns Scl Chrmn 90-; Trthln Clb 90-; Sprng Flng Mrktr 90-; SHAC 90-; Phi Gamma Delta 88-; Phlnthrpy Comm 90; Vol Work Univ AX Med Ctr; Food Serv 90; Clncl Path Lab Intshp; IM; Bio; Med.

**CASTELLINO, HEATHER A,** Temple Univ, Philadelphia, PA; JR; BA; Pre-Law Soc 89-; Golden Key 90-; Ted Feschuk Mem Awd; Temple Ambler Run For Leukemia 90; Pol Sci; Law.

**CASTELLON, GUSTAVO A,** Fl International Univ, Miami, FL; JR; BA; Mngmt Info Sys/Fin; MA Bus.

**CASTELLUCCI, CHRISTINA R,** Seton Hall Univ, South Orange, NJ; SR; BS; Seton Hall Chorus 87-; Theater Grp 87-; Madrigal Ensemble 87-; Kappa Delta Pi 88-; Ruth Foley Schlrshp 90; IM Vlybl 87-; Elem Educ; Teacher.

**CASTER, KARLA Y,** Hampton Univ, Hampton, VA; SO; BS; Stdnt Recruitment Prog 90-; Hmn Ecol Clb; Dietetics/Hmn Nutrition.**

**CASTIGLIA, KIM E,** S U N Y Coll At Fredonia, Fredonia, NY; SR; BA; Trinity Luth Chrch; SUNY Fredonia Soph Educ Awd; Aide Comm Nrsry Schl Montessori Nrsy Scl; Taught Sunday Schl; AOS Comm Art Bryant Stratton Buffalo N Y 80; Erly Chldhd Educ; Tchr.

**CASTILLERO, TANIA STELLA,** Catawba Valley Comm Coll, Hickory, NC; SO; BA; Stu Gvt Assn Sen 90-; Psych Clb; Cmmnty Srvc; Chld Psychlgy/Cmmnctns; PR/CLD Psychlgy.

**CASTILLO HAUTAU, ELISA M,** Univ Of Pr At Mayaguez, Mayaguez, PR; SO; Psych Stdnts Clb 89-; Peer Cnslr Drg-Alchl Abuse Ctr 90-; Smmr Asst Purdue Univ; Scl Sci-Psych; Cnslng.

**CASTILLO VAZQUEZ, MARIA S,** Univ Politecnica De Pr, Hato Rey, PR; FR; BSIE; Indus Engr.

**CASTILLO, DONALD A,** City Univ Of Ny City Coll, New York, NY; SR; BS; Cmptr Sci; Engr.

**CASTILLO, ILSA Y,** Inter Amer Univ Pr San German, San German, PR; FR.

**CASTILLO, ISANDER M,** Hillsborough Comm Coll, Tampa, FL; FR; Medicine Health Allied; Radiogist Tchnlgst.

**CASTILLO, JOANNE L,** Catholic Univ Of Pr, Ponce, PR; SR; BA; Campus Mnstry Chorus Kings Clg PA 86; Club Futuros Maestros Catholic Univ PR 88; Dean List Ed Dept 88-; Spcl Ed.

**CASTILLO, LAZARO DANIEL,** Me Maritime Academy, Castine, ME; SO; BA; Nvl ROTC 90-; Deans Lst 89-; Pres Lst 89-; Capt Lst 90; USN 84-89; Marine Sys Engr.

**CASTILLO, LINDA D,** Miami Dade Comm Coll, Miami, FL; SO; AA; Bus Admn.

**CASTILLO, MARIA-GABRIELA,** Fl International Univ, Miami, FL; JR; BA; CASA 90-; Phi Theta Kappa 89-; Comm Serv Awrd Miami Dade Comm Clg 89; Grad With Highest Hnrs 89; AA Miami Dade Comm Clg 89; Elem Educ; Teaching.

**CASTILLO, MARICEL,** Saint Thomas Univ, Miami, FL; SO; Chrldr Capt 90; Delta Phi Epsilon 90; Social Studies Ed; Law Schl.

**CASTILLO, OLMAN O,** Univ Of West Fl, Pensacola, FL; BA; Spansh Amer Stdnt Assoc Pres 90-; Otstdng Stdnt Ind Tech 90-; Fla Dept Int Educ Schlrshp 90-; L H Perkins Schlrshp; AA Waukesha Cty Tech Clg 87; Mech Eng Tech.

**CASTILLO, ROSELLA L,** Daytona Beach Comm Coll, Daytona Beach, FL; SO; AA; Phi Theta Kappa Actvts Chrpsn 89-; Rotaract Intrclgt Clb 90-; Phi Theta Kappa; Pres Lst; Math; Actuary.

**CASTILLO, THOMAS A,** Fl International Univ, Miami, FL; SO; BA; Soc Stds; Educ.

**CASTLE, CATHERINE L,** Va Highlands Comm Coll, Abingdon, VA; SO; AS; Lung Assn Comm 90-; Cncr Soc 88-; Boostr Clb Sec 88-89; Natl Csmtlgy Assn 79-; VA Csmtlgy Assn Pres 85-; CES Cert VPI 83-88; D Carnagee Cert 82; Image Assoc Cert 84; VA Acdmy Hrstylng Cert 79; Salon Ownr 79-; Lbrl Arts; Bus Mgmt.

**CASTLE, GERALD S,** Bristol Univ, Bristol, TN; SO; BS; Admsns Crdntr; Business.

**CASTLE, JULIE K,** Peace Coll, Raleigh, NC; FR; AA; SGA Prlmntrn; Ntl Assc Acctnts Chmn 90; Phi Theta Kappa 90-; Sigma Delta Mu 90-; Res Asst; Dns List Dstnctn; Marshal; IMS; Intnl Bus.

**CASTLE, PATRICIA D,** Bristol Univ, Bristol, TN; SO; BS; Sec; Bus.

**CASTLE, VICKI W,** Oh Univ-Southern Cmps, Ironton, OH; SR; BESA; Flatwoods Womens Clb Pr 80-89; Amer Leg Aux; Camp Fire Ldr Pr 90; Hist.**

**CASTLER, JEFFREY D,** Siena Coll, Loudonville, NY; SR; BBA; Radio DJ 88-89; Acctng Club 90-; Nwspaper Arts/ Entrtnmnt Edtr 90-; Acctng.

**CASTLES, K PAGE,** Clemson Univ, Clemson, SC; SR; BS; SC Pks/Rcrtn Scty 90-; Cntrl SPMA Sales Comm 87-88; Snow Ski Clb 88-89; Advrtsng Intern 90; Hotel Intern 89; Kappa Sigma Frat Swthrt 90; Deans Lst 90; IM Bsktbl/Sftbl/Rcqtbl 87-91; Cert Ed Inst Amer Hotel/Motel Assc 90; Pks/Rcrtn Trsm Mgmt; Sales Advrtsng Rsrt Mgmt.

**CASTNER, JANET B,** Fl St Univ, Tallahassee, FL; SR; IM Soccr 88; Kappa Alpha Ltl Sistr 88; Elem Schl Intrn; BS; Elem Ed; Tchr.

**CASTO, SHELLY A,** Wv Univ At Parkersburg, Parkersburg, WV; SO; AAS; Crmnl Jstc Org 90-; Phi Theta Kappa 90-; Ohio Adult Parole Authority Intrn Wash Cnty Prob; MOCA 76-; VFW Aux; Crmnl Jstc; BA Parole/Prob Offcr.

**CASTO, TODD R,** Oh Univ, Athens, OH; JR; BS; Soc Mfg Engrs 1st Vchrmn 89-; Acdmc Achvmnt 89-; Univ Rcyclng 90-; Stdnt Cncl 90-; Eng Co-Op 88-; Soc Mfg Eng Schlrshp 90-; Indstrl Tech; Mfg Eng.**

**CASTON, BRENDA M,** Union Univ, Jackson, TN; SR; BS; Acctng Club VP 88-; FCA 87-; Union Univ Stdnt Fndtn Hosts 88-89; Alpha Chi 90-; Chi Omega Treas 87-; Im Athlt Award 89; Acctng; CPA.

**CASTON, DANIEL W,** Longwood Coll, Farmville, VA; SR; BS; Biology Clb Pub Chr 89-; Beta Beta Bet A Pres 90-; Alpha Chi Rho Hist Chptr Mgr 87-; Biology; Otdr Rec Fld Biology.

**CASTON, STANLEY,** Alcorn St Univ, Lorman, MS; JR; BA; Mrchg/Concert Bnd 87-; Interfaith Gospel Choir 88-; Stdnt Sen 88-; Kappa Kappa Psi Pres 87-; Engl/Cmnctns Soc Treas 89-90; NAACP 89-; Cls Asst 90-; Engl/Mass Cmnctns; Phtgrphy/Ed.

**CASTOR, NORMA R,** Endicott Coll, Beverly, MA; FR; BA; Drama Clb Lead Role 90; Peer Tutor Si Leader; Intrnshp/Town Crier Asst Wrtr/Edtr; Cmmnctns; Jrnlst.

**CASTRANOVA, LINDA J,** Wv Northern Comm Coll, Wheeling, WV; FR; BA; Phi Theta Kappa; Spcl Educ.

**CASTRILLI, LORI,** Seton Hall Univ, South Orange, NJ; SR; Spcl Olympics 89-; Comm Serv Cncl 87; Kappa Delta Pi; BS; Elem Edn/Dvlpmntl Disabilites; Tchr.

**CASTRO GONZALEZ, NEXA MAGALLY,** Univ Politecnica De Pr, Hato Rey, PR; FR; MBA; Taller De Teatro Ladi Tres Asst Mngr 89-; Academia De Refinamiento Y Modelaje Refine Mdl 87-89; Engnrng.

**CASTRO VEGA, SARA,** Univ Del Turabo, Gurabo, PR; SR; BA; Cert Hi Hnr Acdmc 85-; Dept Educ Por Exclette Lbr Educ 90; Dept Educ Marstea Aux 86-90; Scl Wrk 86; BA; Spnch; Tchr.

**CASTRO, CARLA L,** Cleveland Inst Of Art, Cleveland, OH; SR; BFA; SG Sec; Art Therapy Intrn; Clevlnd Museum Art TA; Painting; Art Thrpy.

**CASTRO, DAISY C,** Saint Thomas Univ, Miami, FL; SR; BA; Delta Epsilon Sigma 90-; Intrnshp WBFS TV 33 Miami; Cmmnctns Arts; TV Prom/Advrtsng.

**CASTRO, DIANE,** Wagner Coll, Staten Island, NY; JR; BA; Alpha Omicron Pi Awd; Bsn Admin; Mktg Exec.

**CASTRO, ELIA M,** Miami Dade Comm Coll South, Miami, FL; GD; BA; Boy Scts Ldr 90-; Cuban Bsbl Leag Asst Coach 90-; AA; Educ; Sci Tchr.

**CASTRO, EMA M,** Miami Dade Comm Coll, Miami, FL; FR; MBA; Sci; Bus Admin/Nrsng.

**CASTRO, JHACCO,** Glassboro St Coll, Glassboro, NJ; GD; MBA; Stdnt Govt Assoc Sen Chm 88-89; Pol Sci Club Pres 88-89; Middle States Steering Comm Stdnts Rep 89; Pi Sigma Alpha 90; BA 90; Pol Sci.

**CASTRO, LESLIE,** Univ Of Pr At Rio Piedras, Rio Piedras, PR; JR; AM Chem Soc 89-; Gldn Key 90-; Chmstry.**

**CASTRO, LESLIE J,** Fl International Univ, Miami, FL; SR; BA; Intern Federal Bureau Of Prisons/Lgl Tech 90; IM Sports 88-90; Pgm 88-90; Crmnl Justc; Law.

**CASTRO, ODALYS,** Fl International Univ, Miami, FL; SR; BA; AA Miami Dade Comm Coll; Soc Wrk Publ Affairs.

**CASTRO, VIVIAN,** Fl International Univ, Miami, FL; SR; BA; EES; AA Miami Dade Comm Clg 88; Clin Psych.

**CASTRO-SANCHEZ, MARIA R,** Univ Of Pr Humacao Univ Coll, Humacao, PR; JR; BBA; Acctg; CPA.

**CASTROMAN, SUZANNE V,** Fordham Univ, Bronx, NY; SO; BA; Hspnc Scty Ltn Amer Yth 89-; La Undd VP; Jrnl Of Phlsphy And Scl Sci Edit 90-; Stdnt Ntwrkng Admssns Prog Coor; Emer Med Srvce Clb; Pce Clb; Pre Law Scty; Ssqcntnnl Ambssdr 90-; Econs Math Pol Sci; Law.

**CASTRONOVA, BRIAN J,** Embry Riddle Aeronautical Univ, Daytona Beach, FL; SR; BAS; Raquetball; Cert 90; Aviation Tech/AMT Avionics; Airline Maint.

**CASTRONOVA, NINA M,** Univ Of Rochester, Rochester, NY; SR; BA; Spnsh Clb 88-89; Eucharistic Mnstr 88-90; Sndy Sch Tchr Newman Comm; Fmly Ctr Chld Therapy/Rsrch Intern; Chrldng 88-; Clncl Psychlgy.

**CASTRONUOVO, KENNETH J,** City Univ Of Ny Baruch Coll, New York, NY; SR; BA; Golden Key; Bsn Comm; Law.

**CASTURO, ROBERT M,** Duquesne Univ, Pittsburgh, PA; SR; BS; Bus Mgnt; Mgr.

**CASURSO, ANNMARIE E,** Wagner Coll, Staten Island, NY; JR; BS; Radio Sta 88-; Acctg Soc 88-; Commtr Clb Tr 88-; Delta Mu Delta; Althea Tr 90-; Omicron Delta Kappa Tr 90-; Peer Tutrng 90-; Intrnshpnorthfld Svgs Bk; Dr Chs Kramer Schlrshp 88-; Acctg.

**CASWELL, DAVID E,** Catawba Valley Comm Coll, Hickory, NC; FR; AAS; Cmptr Engr Tech; Engr-Dsgn.

**CASWELL, SANDRA M,** Univ Of Nh Plymouth St Coll, Plymouth, NH; SR; BS; Pi Gamma Mu; Presidents Lst; Deans Lst; Social Sci Educ; Teacher.

**CATALA, ADIRENNE M,** Dowling Coll, Oakdale Li, NY; SR; MBA; Untd Tchrs Of Trade; Natl Hnr Soc 88-90; Stdnt Tchg 89-90; BA Dowling Coll 90; H S J V Gym Coach Hd Coach 86-89; Smithtown Gental Schl Dist; Suffolk Cnty Comm Coll; Masters MA Fla Intrntl Univ; Specific Lrng Disb; Tchr Coll Prof Educ.

**CATALDI, DIANA M,** Univ Of Cincinnati, Cincinnati, OH; JR; BM; Cnsrvtry Music Trbnl Secy 89-; Alpha Lambda Delta 89; Golden Key; Sigma Alpha Iota; Frnklin Bens Acad/Tlnt Schlrshp 89; Vocal Perf; Opera Sngr/Prfssr.

**CATALDO, SUSAN J,** Univ Of Ri, Kingston, RI; JR; Golden Key 90-; Nursing.

**CATALINA, SHELLI R,** Ct Coll, New London, CT; FR; BA; IM Rep/Env Coord/Tour Guide 90-; IM Vlybl/Dance Clb/House Cncl 90-; Dorm Host/Coll Exec Bd 90-; Mentor 90-; Cool Exec Bd Planning Dir 90-; Psych/Child Dev.

**CATANZANO, TARA M,** Hofstra Univ, Hempstead, NY; JR; BA; Bio; Med.**

**CATANZARO, FRANK C,** Duquesne Univ, Pittsburgh, PA; JR; Acctg; Law.

**CATCHES, JULIA G,** Univ Of Fl, Gainesville, FL; SR; BFA; CMENC 90-; Phi Kappa Phi 90-; Edith Pitts Schlrshp; Msc Tchrs Natl Assn; FL St Msc Tchr Assn; Gainesville Msc Tchrs Assn; Orgnst Chrch; Prv Piano Instr; AS Pensalola Jr Coll 75; Music Educ.

**CATE, AIMEE PAIGE,** Univ Of South Al, Mobile, AL; SO; Dnce Team 90-; Campus Crsde Mnstry; Dnce/Theatr Gld 89-90; Phi Mu 89-90; Wmn Vtrs League 89-; Peer Cnslr Bptst Chrch 90-; Scndry Educ/Lang Arts; Tch.

**CATE, DIANNA M,** Middle Tn St Univ, Murfreesboro, TN; JR; BS; Phi Theta Kappa 89; Gamma Beta Phi; Tau Omicron; Hwss Coll Hrs Shw 89; Anml Sci.

**CATE, STEPHANIE A,** Univ Of Tn At Knoxville, Knoxville, TN; FR; BA; Quest Yng Life Ldr 90-; Bapt Stdnt Un Exec Cncl Rec 90-; Coll Ensemble 90-; Bus; CPA.

**CATE, SUSAN L,** Le Moyne Coll, Syracuse, NY; JR; BA; Wlsn Art Gllry Comm Stu Liason 90-; Art Clb Vp/Pres 89-; Phlsphy Clb Pres 90-; Psych Clb 89-; Bio Clb; Opn Hs Comm; Nwspr; Cncl Clbs 89-; Beta Beta Beta; Psi Chi 90-; Phi Sigma Tau Pres 90-; Phi Theta Kappa Sec 86-87; Nwmn Clb Pres 86-87; Bio; Biomed Ethcs.

**CATE, WILLIAM B,** Univ Of Tn At Martin, Martin, TN; SR; BS; Stdnt Afflts Amer Chem Scty Pres 87-; Mu Epsilon Delta Vp 88-; Beta Beta Beta 89-; Tchg Asst Bio 90-; IM 90-; Bio/Chem; Med.

**CATELLI, RONALD T,** Saint Thomas Univ, Miami, FL; JR; BA; Tau Epsln Phi Brother Elect 88-; DIM Ftbl Bkstbl Sftbl Hcky 88-; Pol Actn Clb 88-; Tau Epsln Phi Brother Elect 88-; Pol Sci; Law.

**CATER, LISA A,** Alcorn St Univ, Lorman, MS; JR; AA Copaih Lincoln Jnr Clg 81; Bsn Admn.

**CATER, SHANNON F,** Anderson Coll, Anderson, SC; SO; AA; Cmps Mins Jrny Tm 89-; Stdntalumni Cncl 90; Hnrs Pgm 90; Gamma Beta Phi Pres 89-; Acctng; BA/CPA.

**CATER, STEPHEN P,** Univ Of Sc At Columbia, Columbia, SC; JR; BM; Afa Andersn Clg 90; Music.

**CATES, MICHAEL F,** Union Univ, Jackson, TN; SR; BM; Std Asst Bnd Dir 84-85; WHBE Radio/WCTA Radio 89-; WIRJ Radio; AS Jcksn St Comm Clg 85; Msc Educ; Tchr.

**CATES, PAULA T,** Voorhees Coll, Denmark, SC; SO; BS; Cls Sec 89-90; Pre Med/Pre Dent Clb 89-; Omega Psi Pyi Swthrt 90-; Chrldr 89-90; Biolgy; Admn Nrs/RN.

**CATHCART, ANN S,** Piedmont Tech Coll, Greenwood, SC; SO; ASSOC; Psi Beta 90-; Hmn Srvcs.

**CATHERWOOD, CHERI L,** Univ Of Pittsburgh At Bradford, Bradford, PA; JR; BA; SGA 90-; Athltc Comm 90-; WDRQ DJ Sec 88-90; Ornttn Asst; Actv Cncl; Psi Chi 90; Intshp Sgrbsh Rspt Hm 90-; Sccr Mgr Vars Ltr 90-; Psy; Scl Psy/PHD.

**CATHEY, ROBIN E,** Memphis St Univ, Memphis, TN; JR; BA; Acctng; MBA.

**CATINCHI, KATHERINE H,** Cornell Univ Statutory College, Ithaca, NY; Pre Vet Soc 89-; Livestck Show 89-90; Minority Undrgrad Vetrnry Assoc 89-; PR Stdnt Assoc Of Cornell 89-90; Living Lrng Ctr Outrch/Progrmng Comm; Amercn Soc Of Anml Sci Schlstc Achvmnt Award 90-; Saul T Wilson Schlrshp USDA; Animal Sci; Vetrnry Medcn.

**CATLEDGE, ANDREA B,** Kent St Univ Kent Cmps, Kent, OH; FR; BA; Campus Crusade; Oscar Ritchie Book Schlrshp; Hulda Smith Acad Awd; Flg Ftbl/Aerobics; Math/Cmptr; Bus/Acctng.

**CATLETT, JILL A,** Univ Of Tn At Knoxville, Knoxville, TN; FR; Vol Cmmnty 90-; Alpha Lambda Delta 90-; Bsn; Acctng.

**CATLETT, JUDY L,** Cumberland County Coll, Vineland, NJ; SO; BS; Fncng Clb Sec 89-; Multi Cltrl Clb; Mu Theta Alpha; Phi Theta Kappa Sec 90-; AS; Blgy; Med.

**CATLETT, RAMONA I,** Pellissippi St Tech Comm Coll, Knoxville, TN; SO; BA; Std Govt Asc VP 90-; Phi Theta Kappa 90-; Bptst Std Un 89-90; Outstdng Std Govt Asc Ldr VP 90-; Bsn; Mgmt.

**CATLIN, SCOTT J,** Univ Of Rochester, Rochester, NY; JR; BS; AF ROTC Grp Cmmndr 88-; Rugby 88-; Optical Scty Of Amer 90-; Tau Beta Pi 90-; Arnold Air Scty Area Logistics Offcr 89-; Wells Awrd; Genl Dynamics Ldrshp Awrd; Scty Of War 1812 Awrd; Optical Engrng; Law.

**CATLIN, TAMMY R,** Univ Of Rochester, Rochester, NY; SO; BA; Pol Sci; Econs.

**CATO, PATRICK W,** Spartanburg Methodist Coll, Spartanburg, SC; FR; BA; Deans Lst 90; Bsnss Mngmnt; Mnge Real Estate Agncy.

**CATOE, CRYSTAL M,** Univ Of Sc At Columbia, Columbia, SC; FR; Mech Engr.

**CATON, MELODY B,** Roanoke Bible Coll, Elizabeth Cy, NC; SR; BS; Cls Sec 87; V Pres 89; Treas; Salutatorian; Chrstn Educ; Tch.

**CATONE, SUSAN J,** City Univ Of Ny La Guard Coll, Long Island Cty, NY; FR; BSN; Phi Theta Kappa; Psi Beta; Nrsng Stdnt; Sci; Nrsng.

**CATRICALA, ELIZABETH,** Saint Joseph Coll, West Hartford, CT; FR; BA; Econ/Fin; Law.

**CATRON III, FRED M,** Emory & Henry Coll, Emory, VA; SR; Commuter Stdnt Org Pres 90-; Tour Guide Assoc 90-; Blue/Gold Soc 90-; Dominion Bnk Intrn 90; Almn Ofc Emory Henry Clg Ofc Asst; AA S Virginia Highlands Comm Clg 89; Bsn/Mgmt.

**CATTONI, DEANNA L,** Slippery Rock Univ, Slippery Rock, PA; JR; BS; Knsother Clb 88-90; Phi Sigma Pi 90-; Phi Epsilon Kappa Sec 90-; Deans Lst 89-90; Knsther; Phys Ther.

**CAU, AMY P,** Birmingham Southern Coll, Birmingham, AL; FR; Pep Bnd 90-; Southrn Choral 90-; Prtnrshp 90-; IM Sccr Bsktbl; Intl Tutoring; Alpha Phi Omega 90-.

**CAUDILL, DEBORAH J,** Univ Of Ky, Lexington, KY; JR; BA; Prshng Rfls Exec Offcr 89-; Psi Chi; Army Natl Grd Scnd Lt 88-; Psych; Cnslng Psych.

**CAUDILL, DELENA D,** Alice Lloyd Coll, Pippa Passes, KY; SR; BA; Phi Beta Lambda Sec 89-; Clg Radio Clb Stlatstcn 87-; Alpha Chi Reg Rep 89-; Caney Schlstc Soc 88-; Phi Beta Lambda Sec 89-; Salutatorian; Otsdng Sr Bus Admn; Bbus Admn/Mktg Mgt; Banking.

**CAUDILL, JACQUELINE L,** Oh Univ-Southern Cmps, Ironton, OH; SR; BSS; Gamma Pi Delta; Open Door Bapt Chrch; Rec Inst Adlt Ed Pro/Aftr Sch Care Instr; AA 89; Thrpctc Red Mgt; Sclgy.

**CAUDILL, LA CRETIA C,** Union Coll, Barbourville, KY; SO; BA; Bptst Std Un 90-; Union Clg Choir 90-; Mlchr Frnck Choir 90-; Hndbls Choir 90-; Trnslvn Univ Choir 89-90; Trnslvn Univ Mdrgls 89-90; Dns Lst 90-; Natl Mrt Schlp 89-; KY Rvr Coal Co Schlp 89-; Vcl Music; Audio Rec Tech/Performer.

**CAUDILL, MICHELLE LYNN,** Western Ky Univ, Bowling Green, KY; SO; BS; Ntl Stdnt Nrs Assc 90-; KY Assc Nrsg Stdnts Sec 90-; Ogden Rsrch Schlrs 89-; Phi Eta Sigma 89-; Untd Wy Bg Sistr 89-; WKU Pres Lst 90-; Deans Lst 89-90; Nrsg; Nrs Anthtst.

**CAUDLE, DARICE L,** Georgetown Univ, Washington, DC; JR; BSBA; Gospel Choir 88-90; Ntl Assoc Of Blk Accntnts 89; Blk Stdnts Alliance 88-90; Inroads Intrn Wth Arthur Andersen/Corp 90; Acntng; Pblc Accntng.

**CAUDLE, GLORIA DEANNE,** Gaston Coll, Dallas, NC; SO; BA; Gamma Beta Phi; Bus Adm; Mgmt/Bus.

**CAUDLE, JENNIFER M,** Univ Of Al At Birmingham, Birmingham, AL; SR; Undrgrd Stdnt Gvrnmnt Assn Lgsltr 89-; Film Srs Comm Tres; Ntnl Orgnztn Wmn Sec 88-89; Omicron Delta Kappa 90-; Sigma Tau Delta 90-; Gldn Key; Phi Beta Phi; UAB Hnrs Prgrm 87-; Clarence B Hanson Brmnghm Nws Schlrshp; Englsh; Clg Prfsr Englsh.

**CAUFIELD, FRANKLIN E,** Methodist Coll, Fayetteville, NC; GD; BS; Boys Scouts Scmstr 79-86; Knights Dir 79-84; Stdnt Ed Assoc 89-90; Deans List 90-; Grad Cum Laude; Assoc US Army 83; Stdnt Ed Assoc 89-90; Army NCO Of Year 88; Army Fmly Of Year Panama 84; Pursue Career Elem Ed; Ed; Elem Teacher.

**CAUFIELD, MARK J,** Ms St Univ, Miss State, MS; JR; BA; Prof Golf Mgmnt Clb Almn Cntct 89-; Intern Racine Cntry Clb; IM Sprts 89-; Intern Blackhawk Cntr Clb; Mrktng/Prof Golf Mngmnt; Golf Pro.

**CAUGHMAN, PATRICK B,** Univ Of Sc At Columbia, Columbia, SC; SO; BA; Cmptr Sci; Prgmmr.

**CAULDER, LINDA M,** Vance Granville Comm Coll, Henderson, NC; AA; Wrtrs Cir 90-; Phi Theta Kappa 90-; Academic Achvmnt Schlrshp 90-; Ptry Cntst 89-90; Math.

**CAULLETT, ALAN B,** Fl Atlantic Univ, Boca Raton, FL; JR; BS; Hall/Fame Datyona Comm Colg 78; Phi Kappa Phi 90-; AS Daytona Bch Comm Colg 78; AS AA Palm Bch Comm Colg 90; Cmptr Info Sys; Syst Anal.

**CAUPP, CHERYL A,** Univ Of Sc At Columbia, Columbia, SC; SO; BS; Pgm Union Treas 90-; Gamma Beta Phi; Frnds Baruch Inst Schrlshp 91-; Sci; Marine Bio.

**CAUSEY, LYNN N,** Limestone Coll, Gaffney, SC; SO; BS; All Amer Schlr Collgt Awrd 90-; Sec/Acctg Dept; Bus Admin; Mgmt.

**CAUSEY, PEGGY C,** Hillsborough Comm Coll, Tampa, FL; SO; BA; Alpha Gamma Theta; Plant City Chmbr Commerce Yth Recreational Committee; Jr Womens Clb; PTA; Chrmn Strawberry Festival Gift Shop; Schlrshp Downtown Tampa Bus Profssnl Wmns Clb; English Educ; Teacher.

**CAUSEY JR, ROBERT W,** Univ Of Sc At Spartanburg, Spartanburg, SC; JR; BS; Choir Dir; Gamma Beta Phi; Deans Lst 90-; Bus; Mgmt/Admin.

**CAUSSE, SUZETTE V,** Univ Of Southern Ms, Hattiesburg, MS; SR; BS; Actvts Cncl 87-; Hl Cncl V P 87-89; PRSSA 88-90; Spch Cmnctn Assoc 89-90; Publ Rels Intern; Spch Cmnctn; Hlth Care Publ Rels.

**CAVA, NICOLE M,** Indiana Univ Of Pa, Indiana, PA; FR; BA; Phi Sigma Pi; Ofc Admin; Mngmnt.

**CAVAGGIONI, LUIGINA,** Marymount Manhattan Coll, New York, NY; SR; MA; Alpha Chi; Valedictorian; Gold Crss/Gld Mdl Pol Sci Dept; Gerard Schlr; Curian Schlr; Silver M Awrd; Dean Lst 87-; Hnrs Colloquia 89-90; A H Nells Schlrshp; VP Lark Labs 78-87; Sales Mngr 70-78; Asst Mngr Imprt Exprt Milan Italy 66-70; BA; Pol Sci/Intl Stu; Dplmtc Serv.

**CAVAGNARO, AUGUSTINE J,** Univ Of Nc At Asheville, Asheville, NC; SO; BS; BS Bsn Mgmt 88; Math/Sci; Mech Engr.

**CAVAGNARO, JEFFREY D,** Univ Of Cincinnati-Clrmnt Coll, Batavia, OH; JR; BED; Ed Clb; Phi Theta Kappa 83; Tutored Prsnrs Lbn Crrtnl Inst 90; Tutored Tngrs Amelia Crisis Rnwy Centr 90; Chamber Commerce Otstndng Bsn Stdnt Awrd 83-84; AS; Hstry/Math Mjr; Tchng Hgh Sch.**

**CAVAGNARO, JEFFREY D,** Univ Of Cincinnati, Cincinnati, OH; JR; BED; Educ Club; Phi Theta Kappa 90-; Tutor Lebanon Corr Inst 90; Tutor Amelia Crisis Rnawy Shltr 90; Chmbr Cmmrc Awd/Outsdng Bus Stdnt 83-84; Assoc Bus Mgt/Assoc Sec Ed; Math/Hist; Teaching.

**CAVALIER, RONALD A,** Western New England Coll, Springfield, MA; FR; PHARM; Stdnt Sen 90-; Alpha Lambda Delta 90-; IM Sftbl Flg Ftbl; Phrmcy; Clin Phrmcy,Indstry Rscrch.

**CAVALIERE, JOHN N,** Schenectady County Comm Coll, Schenectady, NY; FR; AAS; Elec Tch Clb 90-; Govt Assoc Sen 90-; Elec; Eng.

**CAVALIERE, ROBERT J,** Widener Univ, Chester, PA; JR; BS; Acctg Soc 90-; Econ Soc 90-; Ldrshp Soc; Hon Prog; Acdmc Achvmnt PA Inst CPA 90; Trnsfr Schlrshp Widener Univ 90-; PA Inst Of CPA; AA DE Co Comm Coll 90; Acctg; CPA.

**CAVALLARO, FRANK A,** Rutgers St Univ At Camden, Camden, NJ; SR; BA; Acctng Soc; Tau Kappa Epsilon Treas 88-; Deans List 89-; Acctng Intrnshp; Im Ftbl/Bsktbl/Sftbl; Young Repblcns Assoc; Bus; Acctng.

**CAVALLO, ANNE T,** Elms Coll, Chicopee, MA; GD; Alpha Lambda Delta 87-90; Marguerite Pelletier Frgn Lang Awd 90.

**CAVALLO, MICHELLE L,** Albertus Magnus Coll, New Haven, CT; SR; BA; Stdnt Gov Clss Pres 87-; Peer Cnslr 90-; Rec Comm 89-; Sci Tchr 90-; Soup Ktchn 89-; Grmmr Schl Tutr 90-; Intrnshp Ear/Nose/Throat/Fcl Plstc Surgy Ofc 90; Bio/Sclgy; Med.

**CAVANAUGH, CHRISTOPHER B,** Allegheny Coll, Meadville, PA; FR; Drmtry Stdnt Brd 90-; Delta Tau Delta 90-; Stdnt Athlt Hnr Rll 90-; Vrsty Golf 90-.

**CAVANAUGH, DANIEL M,** Springfield Tech Comm Coll, Springfield, MA; SO; AS; Alpha Nu Omega; Deans Lst; Pscyhlgy; Lawyer.

**CAVANAUGH, DARLENE D,** Central Pa Bus School, Summerdale, PA; SR; Allied Hlth Clb 89-; Med Asst.

**CAVANAUGH, PETER J,** Norwalk St Tech Coll, Norwalk, CT; SO; AS; Phi Theta Kappa; Indstrl Mgmnt; Elctro Mchncl.

**CAVANNA, CHRISTINE M,** Univ Of Scranton, Scranton, PA; JR; BS; Lcrs Stats; Wmns Bsn Hnr Soc; Bsn Hnr Soc; Acctng; CPA.

**CAVE, LAKECHEA T,** Clark Atlanta Univ, Atlanta, GA; FR; Dorm Step Tm 90-; Inspirational Voices Faith 90-; Sparklers Band Capt 89-; Top Ten 89-90; Spirit Boosters 90-; Acctg; CPA.

**CAVE, TRACY L,** Coll Misericordia, Dallas, PA; SR; BA; Stdnt Occptnl Thrpy Assc 87-; Orientn Cnslr 88-89; Tutr 88-89; Sftbl Athl Schlrshp 87-90; Lvl II Fldwrk Geisinger WY Vly; Lvl II Fldwrk Binghamton Psychtrc Ctr; Sftbl Cpt 87-90; Occptnl Thrpy; Alld Hlth.

**CAVENAUGH, DONNA SHOUP,** James Sprunt Comm Coll, Kenansville, NC; SO; James Sprunt Acad Schlrshp 90-; Deans Lst 90-; AA; Engl; Tchr.

**CAVENDER, ELIZABETH M,** Middle Tn St Univ, Murfreesboro, TN; SO; Stu Tchr Educ Assn VP 90-; Hmn Sci Assn 89-; TN Hmn Sci Assn 89-; Amer Hmn Sci; Kappa Delta Pi 90-; Gamma Beta Phi; Alpha Delta Pi Edctn Brd 90-; Schlrshp; Albert Carver Smith Schlrshp; Erly Chldhd Educ; Tchr Kndrgrtn.

**CAVENDISH, RICHARD C,** Fl St Univ, Tallahassee, FL; JR; BA; Psi Chi Treas; AA Tallahassee Cmmnty Clg 90; Psychlgy; Psychlgcl Rsrch.

**CAVERO, IGNACIO,** Savannah Coll Of Art & Design, Savannah, GA; SO; BFA; Grphc Dsgn; Advrtsng.

**CAVESE, JULIE A,** Allegheny Coll, Meadville, PA; SO; BA; Orchss Dnce Co; Art Gllry Asst 89-; Coll Rdio Sttn; Psi Chi 90-; Kappa Kappa Gamma 90-; Aldn Schlr 90; Psychlgy; Indstrl Clncl Psychlgy.

**CAVICCHIA, ROCHELLE L,** Kent St Univ Kent Cmps, Kent, OH; SR; BA; Panhllnc Coun V P 88-; Hall Coun; Golden Key; Rho Lambda; Pi Alpha Delta; Delta Gamma 87-; County Publ Def Intnshp 90; Un Schlrshp 87-; Svc Awd 90; IM Aerob; Pol Sci; Law.

**CAVICCHIO, THERESA,** Neumann Coll, Aston, PA; JR; BA; Psi Chi; Acdmc Achvmnt Awd Sociiology 90; Deans List Delaware Cnty Comm Clge 81-90; Deans List 90-; Mayors Commission On Literacy Cmnty Y 89-90; Vlntr Literacy Tutor; Admnstrtve Employee Relatins Specialist 82-87; AAA DE Cnty Cmnty Clge 90-; Liberal Studies/Psychology; Social Services.

**CAVINESS, DEBBIE,** Memphis St Univ, Memphis, TN; JR; BPS; Sub Abuse Cnslr Memphis Rec Cntrs; Ind Stds; Cnslng.

**CAVINESS, ELAINE T,** Memphis St Univ, Memphis, TN; SR; BPS; Mphs Pub Libr Stf Org Pres 82-88; Gamma Beta Phi Prog Chrpsn Exec Bd 87-; Phi Theta Kappa Sec 79-81; DPMA 89; SAM 89; Grtr Untd Wy Mphs 89-; Jr Achvmnt Vol Tchr 90; Chrch Lvng God Mssnry 90-; Tn Pre-Prof Law Stdnt; AS 81; MIS Paralgl Stds; Law.

**CAVLOVIC, THERESE A,** Fl St Univ, Tallahassee, FL; SR; Fin Soc 90-; BS; Fin.

**CAVNAR, MICHAEL S,** Livingston Univ, Livingston, AL; SR; BED; Ftbl; Coll Ftbl Stdnt Coach 86-; Engl/Hist; Tchng Law.

**CAVROS, G MICHAEL,** Western New England Coll, Springfield, MA; JR; BS; Phtgrphy Club; IEEE; Tutor 90-; AS Springfield Tech Comm Coll 89; Elctrcl Eng.

**CAVUTO, LISA M,** Elmira Coll, Elmira, NY; SO; BS; Stdnt Actves Bd; Psi Chi; Pupil Asst Lrng 90; Pres Schlrshp 89; Psychology; Psychlgcl Cnslg/Rsrch.

**CAWLEY, BRIDGET,** S U N Y At Binghamton, Binghamton, NY; SO; BA; Nwsppr Wrtr; Lit Rhtrc Pltcl Sci; Jrnlsm Law.**

**CAWLEY, CATHERINE M,** Schenectady County Comm Coll, Schenectady, NY; FR; AAS; Phi Theta Kappa; Ltrcy Vol Amer 86-89; Trvl/Trsm.

**CAWLEY, NANCY LYNN,** Commonwealth Coll, Virginia Beach, VA; SR; BA; Assoc 90; Med Tchnlgst.

**CAWRSE, ELLEN E,** Univ Of Akron, Akron, OH; SR; BS; Cmnctv Dsrdrs.

**CAWTHORNE, WILLIAM R,** Wv Univ, Morgantown, WV; SO; BS; Hall Cncl Treas 89-90; Inst Of Elect & Elctr Engrs 90-; Chimes; Alpha Phi Omega; Phi Kappa Phi 90; Elect & Comp Engrng.

**CAY PEREZ, ZORAIDA,** Univ Del Turabo, Gurabo, PR; SR; 4h Clb.

**CAYLOR, SUSAN M,** Pellissippi St Tech Comm Coll, Knoxville, TN; SO; BED; Vision Volunteer 90; Elem Educ.

**CAYNOR, RICKY A,** Marshall University, Huntington, WV; SO; Mgmt.

**CAYS, STEPHEN E,** West Chester Univ, West Chester, PA; JR; BS; W Chester Univ Hnrs Prog 89-; Musid Educ; Tchr.**

**CAYTON, JOHN J,** Bristol Univ, Bristol, TN; GD; MBA; Prof Artst; BBA.

**CAYTON, SHIRLEY J,** Bristol Univ, Bristol, TN; GD; MBA; Life Rsrc Brd 89-; VP Nrsg Med Cntr 89-; BSN 78; MN 80; Mgmt.

**CEBERT, MARIE CARMEL,** Al A & M Univ, Normal, AL; GD; Beta Beta Beta Chrprsn 88; Dorm Cncl Rep 87-89; Red Crs Vol 87-90; Grad Rsrch Asst; Sci Plympiad Rep 88-; Coop Extnsn Progrm Sci Tutor; Grad Tchng Asst 88-89; Mgc Cty Tnns Clb 90-; AL Acdmy Of Sci 88-89; NAACP 90-; BS Sthrn CT St U 81-85; Chem; Medcn.

**CEBULA, MARC C,** Hilbert Coll, Hamburg, NY; FR; Law.

**CEBULAR, DEANNA V,** Georgetown Univ, Washington, DC; JR; BSBA; Dorm Cncl Drm Prsdnt 88-89; Jr Cls Comm 90-; Sr Cls Comm; Sprt Comm 88-; Schl Bsns Admn 90-; Stdnt Advsr 90; Accntng Soc 90-; Amrcn Asst Mgmnt Intrnshp 89; Price Wtrhse Intrnshp 90; Cllgt Cngrsnl Schlr 88-; Deans Lst 88-; Accntng; Gvrnmnt Pblc Accntng CPA Law Schl.

**CECCHETTI, LUCIA,** Ramapo Coll Of Nj, Mahwah, NJ; SR; BA; Intl Stds; Intl Rltns.

**CECERE, CHRISTA A,** Manhattan Coll, Bronx, NY; JR; BSCE; Std Govt Lgstr 90-; Amer Soc Cvl Engrs 89-; Mnhtn Engr Nwsltr Edtr; Chi Epsln; Clmbs Day Comm Ynkrs Rep 89-; Engr Asst 90-; Engr Asst; Miss Columbus 89-90; Cvl Engr.

**CECH, SHARLA K,** Daytona Beach Comm Coll, Daytona Beach, FL; FR; AS; Chorus 82-83; FBLA 85-86; Spnsh Ovrseas 83; Sng In Cndlelght Choir Dsny Wrld 87; AA Vlencia Cmmnty Clg Orlando Fl 83; LAS 87; Med Trnscrptn Med Scrtry; Med Rcrds Tchncn.

**CECIL, AMY CHRISTINE,** Youngstown St Univ, Youngstown, OH; FR; Cntrns; Dns Lst 90-; Eng.

**CECIL, CYNTHIA D,** Chattahoochee Vly St Comm Coll, Phenix City, AL; FR; BA; Sec 90; Lib Arts; Advrtsng.

**CECIL, DEANNA L,** Univ Of Ky, Lexington, KY; JR; BA; Deans List; Excellence Schlrshp Cert; Letter Recognition Eastern State Hosp Vol Wrk; Psychology; Graduate School.

**CECIL, JOSEPH M,** Lexington Comm Coll, Lexington, KY; SO; AAS; Bus; Mgr.

**CECIL, MARY A,** Univ Of Ky, Lexington, KY; JR; BSN; Flag Corps 88-90; Deans Lst 89-90; All A Deans Lst 90; Natl Cllgt Nrsng Awrd 89; Bapt Hosp E Extern Prog; Veterans Admin Stdnt Prog 89-; Flag Corps Color Grd 88-90; Nursing; RN.

**CECIL, PATRICIA A,** Fort Valley St Coll, Fort Valley, GA; JR; BSN; Student Tutoring Corps; Phi Kappa Phi 86-; BA Mercer Univ 86; Nursing.

**CECIL, VERONICA ERVENA,** Tn St Univ, Nashville, TN; JR; BS; Natl Soc Arch Engrs Pres 90-; Physics Clb 89-; Astrology Clb 89-; NAACP 89-; Gresham Smith/Partners Arch Tech II 90; Assoc Nash State Tech Inst 83; Arch Engr/Constr/Structures; MBA.

**CECILIO JR, LAURO P,** Univ Of Med & Dentistry Of Nj, Newark, NJ; SR; CRTT; BS Med Tech Univ St Tomas Manila Philippines 76; MD Far East Univ 80.

**CECKOWSKI, WENDY L,** Holyoke Comm Coll, Holyoke, MA; FR; BS; Cmptr Info Sys; Pgmng.

**CEDENO-SILVA, JEANNETTE,** Catholic Univ Of Pr, Ponce, PR; SO; AIESEC 90; Hnrs Pgm 89-; Sec Sci; Law.

**CEESAY, FANTA JALAMANG,** Rust Coll, Holly Springs, MS; SO; Intl Assoc 89-; Gamma Sigma Sigma; Pres Lst 89-.

**CEESAY, SOFFIE B,** Univ Of The Dist Of Columbia, Washington, DC; SR; BBA; Cambia Stdnts Assn Perm Sec 86-; Jalibaa Nwsltr Cambians US Assn Fndr 87-; Phi Sigma Pi; Com Sldrty People Of El Salvador Fund Drv Sprvsr 87-89; Book Drv Cambodian Stdnts Orgnzr 88-91; Cmptr Info Systs Sci; Intl Bus Admin.

**CEFKIN, MARTHA M,** Broward Comm Coll, Ft Lauderdale, FL; SO; BA; Phi Theta Kappa; Elem Ed; Tch.

**CEGAN, SARAH C,** Memphis St Univ, Memphis, TN; JR; BA; English Clb Prog Chr 90-; Aas Everett Cmuty Clg 85; English; Law.

**CEJKOVSKY, STEPHEN E,** Mount Saint Mary Coll, Newburgh, NY; SO; BA; Dfrnt Stgs Drama Clb 89-; Clarion Asst Edtr In Chf 90-; Bacchus 90-; Ralph Schlr; Hnrs Allnc 90-; Ambsdr Clb 90-; Comm; Radio Brdcstng.

**CEKALSKE, BARBARA A,** Hilbert Coll, Hamburg, NY; GD; Socty Stdnt Accntnts 89-; VITA; Phi Theta Kappa 89-.

**CELESTE, CLAUDINE M,** Niagara Univ, Niagara Univ, NY; SO; MA; Psychlgy; Cnslr.

**CELESTE, JEFFREY C,** Mount Olive Coll, Mount Olive, NC; FR; Singers 90-; Visual Comm; Advrtsng.

**CELIO, JORGE D,** Ny Univ, New York, NY; BAMBA; AIESEC Uruguay V P 84-88; Block Assoc Fndrsng; Gen Elec Intrn 88; Joffplann Laroche Info Spclst 88; Progrmr Anlyst 87; Bachelor Engr 82; Intl Stdes; Law.

**CELLA, BETH A,** Univ Of Miami, Coral Gables, FL; SR; SGA Undrsec 87-89; SAMS Prog Dir 88-89; IM Stdnt Adv Brd 90-; Alpha Kappa Psi 90-; Lambda Chi Alpha Ltl Sr Treas 88-; Carni Gras Chrprsn 90-; London Eng Royalhrsgrd Hotel Sls/Mkt Intrnshp 90; Stdnt Conslt Sys Grp Intrn 90; Mgmt; Hosptlty/Mgmt.

**CELLA, MARY C,** Longwood Coll, Farmville, VA; JR; BS; Psychlgy.

**CELLINI, DENA M,** Mount Saint Mary Coll, Newburgh, NY; JR; BS; Stdnt Bus Assoc 88-; Jr Cl Rep 90-; Res Living Cncl Sr Rep; Deans List 89-; Hnrs Alliance 90-; Bus Mgmt Admn.

**CEN, XI BING,** City Univ Of Ny Baruch Coll, New York, NY; JR; BBA; Chns Cltrl Clb; Chns Chrstn Flwshp; Gldn Key; Acctncy; CPA.

**CENATUS JR, HERVE,** Union County Coll, Cranford, NJ; SO; Talent Roster; Engr.

**CENSABELLA, LISA M,** Iona College, New Rochelle, NY; SO; BA; Stdnt Gov Sophmr Rep 90-; Frshmn Orient Grp Sprvsr 90-; Sftbll 89-; Crmnl Justice; Lawyer.**

**CENTENO, BAYARDO B,** Southern Coll Of Tech, Marietta, GA; SR; BEET; Jvtd Ctlc De Atlnta 88-; Tau Alpha Pi 88-; Lcl Olmpc Gms Math 1st Pl 81; Ntl Olmpc Gms Math 3rd Pl; Dns Lst 88-; IEEE 89-; AMA 91; Elec Eng Tech.

**CENTER, BRIAN C,** Ms St Univ, Miss State, MS; SO; BS; Bio Engr Soc 90-; Pres Schlr 90-; Bio Engr.

**CENTER, SUSAN G,** Middle Tn St Univ, Murfreesboro, TN; JR; BSN; SNA; Nursing Dept; LPN Shelbyville Voc-Tech Schl 81; Nursing.

**CENTER, TRACY D,** Clemson Univ, Clemson, SC; SO; BS; Sccr Clb 89-90; Alpha Lambda Delta 90-; Rho Phi Lambda; Prks/Rec/Trsm Mgmt.

**CENTODUCATI, SANDRA M,** Cornell Univ Statutory College, Ithaca, NY; SO; BA; Progrmng Bd 89-; Kappa Delta; Fld Hockey 89-90; Im Sftbl/Vlybl 89-; Anml Sci; Medcl Fld.

**CEPARSKI, JEFFREY J,** S U N Y Coll Of Tech At Alfred, Alfred, NY; FR; AS; AAS Cayoga Cnty Cmnty Clg 87; Cmptng Grphcs Engr Tech.

**CEPEDA PIZARRO, CARMEN S,** Univ Metropolitano, Rio Piedras, PR; JR; BA; Tlnt Clb 87-; Hnr Assoc 87-; Spnsh/Math; Elem Ed/Lng Arts.

**CEPEK, THOMAS C,** Comm Coll Algny Co Algny Cmps, Pittsburgh, PA; SO; BED; Phi Theta Kappa; Acctg.

**CEPHAS, ANGELA D,** Bennett Coll, Greensboro, NC; FR; BA; Bsn; Bsn Admin.

**CEPHAS, JEROME L,** Livingston Univ, Livingston, AL; FR; BA; Acctg.

**CEPPAGLIA, PAUL A,** S U N Y Coll At Fredonia, Fredonia, NY; JR; BS; Audro Engr Soc; Chorus; Band; Cmptr Lab Proctor; Newman Ctr Muscn; Pi Kappa Lamba; Deans Lst 88-; Sound Recrdng Tech; Record Engr/Prodctn.**

**CERCONE, BETH ANN,** West Liberty St Coll, West Liberty, WV; SR; BA; Scec 90-; Elem Ed/Spcl Ed & Erly Chldhd Ed; Tchr.

**CERCONE, LISA A,** Slippery Rock Univ, Slippery Rock, PA; SO; BA; Sigma Sigma Sigma; Deans Lst; Spnsh; Trnsltr/Intrprtr.

**CERDA, ELIZABETH,** Univ Of Miami, Coral Gables, FL; FR; Cir K 90-; Fed Cuban Stdnts 90-; Biology Clb 90; Alpha Lambda Delta 90; Serv Awd 90-; Biology; Med.

**CERITTO, HOLLY L,** Elms Coll, Chicopee, MA; SO; BA; Stdnt Ambssdrs 89-; Rsdnt Cnsl 90-; Soph Shw Msc Dir 90-; Prlgl Stds; Law.

**CERJA, STACY L,** Indiana Univ Of Pa, Indiana, PA; FR; Kappa Delta Pi; Elem Educ; Tchg Fld.

**CERRA, JOAN E,** Coll Misericordia, Dallas, PA; JR; BS; FNA Co Advsr 90-; PSEA; Red Cross; ASN Robert Packer Hosp Schl Nrsng 77; Nrsg; Schl Nrs.

**CERRATO, KIMBERLY D,** Univ Of North Fl, Jacksonville, FL; JR; BS; Data Prcssg Mngmt Assc; Phi Theta Kappa 90; Pres Lst 89-90; Deans Lst 90; Co Op Martin Marietta; Ntl Org Fr Wmn 89-; Jax Fed Svgs Bnk 85-90; CSX Cmmrcl Srvcs Co Op; AA FL Cmnty Clg 90; Cmptr Sci/Info Sys; Cmptr Cnsltnt/Tchr/Trnr.

**CERRELLI, ROWAN K,** Anne Arundel Comm Coll, Arnold, MD; SO; BS; Jaycees 88-; Nursing.

**CERRITELLI, E GREGORY,** Univ Of New Haven, West Haven, CT; SR; BS; Crmin Jstc Clb 87-90; Crim Jstc; Law Schl.

**CERRUTO, DAWN M,** Glassboro St Coll, Glassboro, NJ; SO; BA; Glssbr Vc Chc VP; Ltry Mag 89-; Cnm Wrkshp 90-; Cmmnctns.

**CERRUTO-NOYA, PATRICIA C,** Elms Coll, Chicopee, MA; JR; Intl Clb; Spanish Clb; Bus Clb; I M Bkbl; Intl Stdes/Spanish; Trnsltr/Liaison Bolivia.

**CERVINI, CARLO,** Manhattan Coll, Bronx, NY; FR; BE; Engr.

**CERVINO, KRISTEN A,** Univ Of Rochester, Rochester, NY; JR; BA; Glee Clb 88-; Prtnrs Reading 89-; IM Flr Hcky Vllybll 88-; Engl; Law.

**CESARE JR, JOSEPH G,** Georgetown Univ, Washington, DC; SR; BS; Ftbl Tm 87-90; Ftbl Asst Coach 89; Jr/Sr Cls Com 89-; Deans Lst 89-; US Trade Rep Intern 90-; Vrsty Ftbl Outstndng Back Awd; Finance/Intl Mgmt; Invstmnt Bnkng.

**CESAREO, MATTHEW T,** S U N Y Coll Of Tech At Delhi, Delhi, NY; FR; AOS; Rsdnt Asst 90-; Auto Mchncs.

**CESARIO, TRACEY K,** Coll Of William & Mary, Williamsburg, VA; FR; BA; TSA 90-; Delta Gamma Soc Chrmn Asst 90-; Camp Shkspear Asst Dir; Williamstown Theatre Fstvl Apprntce; Theatre Plays Actng/Dir 90-; Publcty Aid 90-; Theatre Bkbl Tm Chrldr 90-; Theatre/Art Italian; Theatre Act/Dir.

**CESARZ, NANCY L,** Mount Aloysius Jr Coll, Cresson, PA; FR; AS; Cardiovsclr Tech; Hlth Field.

**CESEFSKE-HILL, SANDRA L,** Brewer St Jr Coll, Fayette, AL; FR; ASBS; Engl/Educ; Tchng.

**CESSNA, DENNIS E,** Me Maritime Academy, Castine, ME; JR; BS; Propeller Clb 90-; Deans Lst 90-; Commandants Lst 90-; Cadet Trng Cruise 90-; Commercial Fisherman 81-88; Engineering; Merchant Marien Ofcr.

**CESTERO, FRANCISCO J M,** Univ Of Pr At Mayaguez, Mayaguez, PR; JR; Comp; Eng.

**CHABOT, CHARLES V,** Allegheny Coll, Meadville, PA; SR; BA; Stdnt Art Soc Sec 89-90; Camps Nwspr Phtgrphr 88-; Aldn Schlr 87-; Studio Art/Phtgrphy; Svc Mgmt.

**CHACH, MARGARET M,** Teikyo Post Univ, Waterbury, CT; SR; BA; Acdmc Achvmnt Awrd 90; AS 90; Mrktng.

**CHACON BAIZ, SONIA,** Inter Amer Univ Pr San German, San German, PR; SR; BA; Mayaguez Voc Schl 84; Spel Educ.

**CHACON, HUMBERTO,** Miami Dade Comm Coll North, Miami, FL; SO; BS; Natl Hspnc Hon Soc 89-; AA 90; Crmnl Jstce Admin/Engl; Law.

**CHACON, JEAN-PIERRE,** Univ Of Miami, Coral Gables, FL; JR; BS; Crmnl Jstc/Brdcstng; Law.

**CHACONAS, DOROTHY,** Univ Of Sc At Columbia, Columbia, SC; SR; BS; Ltrcy Prog Clrndn Cnty SC 88; AA USC Sumter 89; Bus Mgmt.

**CHACONAS, JUDY ANN,** Columbia Union Coll, Takoma Park, MD; JR; Hlth Rprtr For The American Hosp Assoc Washington DC; Hold A Master Barber Licns In MD; Hlth Care Admn.

**CHADAJO, JOSHUA E,** Bates Coll, Lewiston, ME; FR; BA; Hll Govt Pub Dir 90-; Rdio Music Dir 90-; Jewish Cltrl Cmmnty 90; Alld Actn 90-; Dana Schlr; 2M Bsktbll Sftbll 90-; Math; Bus Admn.

**CHADWICK, CHRISTINA L,** Ms Gulf Coast Jr Coll Jeffersn, Gulfport, MS; FR; BA; Phi Theta Kappa; Bus; Acctg.

**CHAFFEE, NATHAN A,** S U N Y Coll Of Tech At Alfred, Alfred, NY; SO; BA; Stdnt Rev Brd 90-; IM Vlybl 89-90; Deans Lst 89-; AS; Engr.

**CHAFFIN, GREGORY S,** Brewer St Jr Coll, Fayette, AL; SO; BA; AA; Bus Mgmt.

**CHAFIN, JENNIFER L,** Middle Ga Coll, Cochran, GA; SO.

**CHAGNON, TERRI L,** Lesley Coll, Cambridge, MA; SO; BS; Lit Mag Ed Fctn Sctn 89-; Crrnt Issues Forum 90-; Harvard U Mdl UN Dlgt 90-; Schlr 89-; Currclm Comm 90-F; Elem Ed; Tchr.

**CHAHIN, ROBERTO P,** Fl International Univ, Miami, FL; SO; BBA; Amnsty Intl 89-90; Fin/Intl Bsns.

**CHAHOUD, BELKIS J,** Miami Dade Comm Coll North, Miami, FL; SR; BA; Bus Admin.

**CHAI, MELISSA M,** Va Commonwealth Univ, Richmond, VA; JR; MED; NEA 89-; VEA 89-; Gldn Key 90; OCSA 87; Dns Lst 86-90; Hnrs Prgm; N N Schlrshp 86-90; VA Undergrad Schlrshp 86-90; BA; Engl Ed; Edctnl Admns.

**CHAIN, ANDREA L,** Carson Newman Coll, Jefferson City, TN; FR; Alpha Lambda Delta Treas; Phi Eta Sigma Treas; Carson Newman Hon Org; Math/Sec Edn; Tchr.

**CHAIRVOLOTTI, EDWARD F,** Nova Univ, Ft Lauderdale, FL; GD; MBA; AA Brevard Cmnty Clg 83; BSBA Univ Cntrl Florida 86; Bsn; Corp Fin.

**CHAKRAVARTY, ARUP,** Tampa Coll, Tampa, FL; JR; BSC; Dir Lst; Deans Lst 89-; AS; Cmptr Info Sci; Sys Analyst.

**CHALFANT, MELISSA J,** Duquesne Univ, Pittsburgh, PA; SO; BA; Dns Lst 90-; Media Prdctn Cmmnctns; Rcrdng Snd Eng.

**CHALK, ALISHA R,** Phillips Jr Coll Spartanburg, Spartanburg, SC; JR; AS; Comp Clb; Pres Lst; Deans Lstf; Data Proc; Jr Pgrmr.

**CHALKER, JAMES L,** S U N Y Coll Of Tech At Alfred, Alfred, NY; JR; BT; Sys Engrng Dept Dresser-Rand Steam Turvine Motor/Genrtr Div 87-; AAS 87; Elec Engrng.

**CHALMERS, KEVIN M,** Longwood Coll, Farmville, VA; JR; BS; Stdnt Govt 90-; IM Brd Pr 90-; Acad Advsry Comm 90-; FRESH Hall IM 90-; Marshall Orientn Ldr; Chem; Res/Analytcl Testng.

**CHAM, WEI TIONG,** S U N Y At Buffalo, Buffalo, NY; JR; BS; SE Asia Stdnt Assn; Bdmntn Clb; Clara Hendershot Schlrshp 90-; Acctg/Finance; CPA Cnsltnt.

**CHAMBERLAIN, CARRIE T,** Dowling Coll, Oakdale Li, NY; SR; Natl Assoc Educ Of Yng Chldrn Assoc 90-; NY St Educ Emtnlly Dstrbd; Dowling Clg Deans List; Alpha Chi; Big Bro/Big Str Org; Acad Schlrshp; AS Suffolk Comm Clg 89; Spec Educ; Teacher.

**CHAMBERLAIN, CHERYL D,** Middle Tn St Univ, Murfreesboro, TN; SR; BBA; Society Advancement Mngmt 87; AMA 87-89; Church Singles Pres 87-89; Music Chorister/Sunday School 87-89; Teacher 87; Kappa Alpha Theta 87; Killgore Schlrshp 87; Mngmnt; Business Admin/Human Resorces.

**CHAMBERLAIN, DEBORAH J,** Schenectady County Comm Coll, Schenectady, NY; FR; AAS; Paralgl.

**CHAMBERLAIN, JANEL M,** Glassboro St Coll, Glassboro, NJ; SO; BA; Psych.

**CHAMBERLAIN, MARISSA A,** Elmira Coll, Elmira, NY; SO; BA; Phi Eta Sigma.

**CHAMBERLAIN, STEVEN D,** Oh Univ, Athens, OH; SO; BA; IEEE 90-; Elect Eng; Eng.

**CHAMBERLIN, CHRISTIAN L,** Siena Coll, Loudonville, NY; FR; Vars Sccr; Engl; Law/Tchng.

**CHAMBERS, ANN MARIE,** Ky St Univ, Frankfort, KY; SR; BS; Clss Govt Treas 90-; Alpha Kappa Mu 90-; Sigma Gamma Rho Fin Sec; Txtls/Clthng/Mrchndsg; Cstm Dsgn/Advrtsg.

**CHAMBERS, ANNA J,** Univ Of Ga, Athens, GA; JR; BED; Gamma 88-; Phi Mu Schlrshp Chrmn; IM Sftbl; IM Flg Ftbl; Erly Chldhd Educ; Elem Tchr.

**CHAMBERS, BROOKE S,** Waycross Coll, Waycross, GA; SO; BA; Judicry Cncl 90-; Dns Lst 90; ABA; Bus Admin; Acctg.

**CHAMBERS, CASSANDRA E,** Spartanburg Methodist Coll, Spartanburg, SC; SO.

**CHAMBERS, DENNIS C,** Marshall University, Huntington, WV; SR; Acctg Clb 90-; NDL; AA Ashland Comm Coll; Acctg.

**CHAMBERS, JILL G,** Univ Of Nc At Greensboro, Greensboro, NC; SR; Willomore Bap Church Choir Spcl Music Soloist Sun Schl Tchr 84-; Bible Schl Sub Tchr; Outstanding Clge Stdnts Of Amer; Deans List 88-90; Scholar 87-88; Honors Convocation 88; Grad Hnrs Recogntn Letter; Potncl Rotary Schlrshp Awd; Erly Chldhd Ed; Teach.**

**CHAMBERS, JIMMY E,** Snead St Jr Coll, Boaz, AL; FR; BS; Phi Theta Kappa 90-; Pres Lst 90-; Calculus Awd 90-; Cmptr Engrg.

**CHAMBERS, JUDE M,** Western Ky Univ, Bowling Green, KY; SO; BGS; Farmer 85-; Indstrl Arts/Horticulture; Woodwrkng/Lndscp.

**CHAMBERS, KARLENE T,** Fl Memorial Coll, Miami, FL; JR; BS; FMC Stdnt Gvmt; Jamaica Clb; Alpha Kappa Mu; Alpha Kappa Alpah Srty Inc Dlt Et Chpt; FL Mem Clg Hon Schlrshp 88-; Bus Admn; Mgmt MBA.

**CHAMBERS, KATHARINE ELIZABETH,** Univ Of Sc At Columbia, Columbia, SC; FR; BA; Alpha Lambda Delta; Gamma Beta Phi; Journalism; Public Realtions/Advertising.

**CHAMBERS, KELLY D,** John C Calhoun St Comm Coll, Decatur, AL; FR; BA; Sftbl; Pham.

**CHAMBERS, LEATRICE C,** Alcorn St Univ, Lorman, MS; SR; BS; Blgy Clb Ms Blgy; Khem Clb; NAACP Snt Rep 89-; Blgy-Pre-Med; Physcl Thrpst.

**CHAMBERS, MELANIE R,** Univ Of Tn At Knoxville, Knoxville, TN; FR; BA; Acctg; CPA.

**CHAMBERS, TERESA KIM,** Greenville Tech Coll, Greenville, SC; SR; AHS; Stdnt Amer Dntl Hygn Assoc 89-; Dntl Hygn.

**CHAMBLIN, CARLTON D,** Birmingham Southern Coll, Birmingham, AL; SO; BA; Stdnt Govt 90-; Stdnt Alumni Assn 89-; Southern Vol Serv 90-; Alpha Lambda Delta; Phi Eta Sigma Pres; Art Hist; Architecture.

**CHAMBLISS, ALONZO,** Va St Univ, Petersburg, VA; SR; BA; Indus Educ/Tech Acad Schlrshp; Indus Educ/Tech; Mech Engr.

**CHAMBOLA, CHRISTINE M,** Comm Coll Algny Co Algny Cmps, Pittsburgh, PA; FR; BA; Cert Dntl Asst; Cert Dntl X-Ray; Oral Surg Ofc Mgr; Nrsng; RN.

**CHAMDANI, ISMAWAN E,** Southern Coll Of Tech, Marietta, GA; SR; BS; GSPE Bd 90-; Indonesisan Stdnt Assn Pres 89-90; Tau Alpha Pi 90-; Vrsty Tns 87-89; Mech Eng; Mfg Eng.

**CHAMP JR, RICHARD C,** Embry Riddle Aeronautical Univ, Daytona Beach, FL; SO; BS; Vetrns Assoc 89-; Wireman HES; US Army 86-88; Bus Mgt; Aviation Law.**

**CHAMPIGNY, MICHAEL D,** Springfield Tech Comm Coll, Springfield, MA; SO; BS; Alpha Nu Omega 90-; Comp Sci; Sftwr Engr.

**CHAMPION, BRETT R,** Walker Coll, Jasper, AL; SO; ASSC; Stdnt Govt Assn Pres 90-; Explrrs Clb Soph Fvrte; Phi Theta Kappa; Clncl Pscychlgst.

**CHAMPION, FRED L,** East Carolina Univ, Greenville, NC; SR; BFA; Visual Arts Comm 89-90; Flms Comm 89-; Spec Cncrts Comm Chrprsn 89-; Univ Un Hon Soc 90-; Alpha Kappa Epsilon Iota; Outstndng Stdnt Un Membr 89-90; AA Acctg Clvlnd Comm Coll 86; AA Bus Admin 86; Txtl Dsgn; Grad Schl.

**CHAMPION, JEFFREY A,** Univ Of Nc At Greensboro, Greensboro, NC; SR; BMUS; Univ Orch Prncpl Oboe 89-; Univ Wnd Ensmbl Prin Oboe 90; Chorale Grad Woodwnd Quintet; Pi Kappa Lambda; NC Tchng Fellow; Sibm Watson Schlr; Dns Lst; Univ Mrshl; Stdnt Excel Awd; Stone Awd For Excel Perf; Music Educ Oboe Perf; Perform/Tch.

**CHAMPION, MELISSA A,** Middle Tn St Univ, Murfreesboro, TN; SR; BS; Delta Zeta; Engl; Law.

**CHAMPION, REBECCA A,** Gardner Webb Coll, Boiling Spg, NC; FR; BA; Cmmtr Clb; Hnr Rl; Acctng; CPA.

**CHAMPION, SANDRA H,** Univ Of Al At Birmingham, Birmingham, AL; SR; BS; Phi Theta Kappa Secy 86-88; OES 86-; Deans List; AAS Gadsden St Comm Colg 88; Radlgc Sci.

**CHAMPION, WANDA R,** Comm Coll Algny Co Algny Cmps, Pittsburgh, PA; JR; BA; African Amer Schlstc Achvmnt Awd 90; Dns Lst 88-; Engl; Tchr.

**CHAN LAM, TERRY H,** City Univ Of Ny City Coll, New York, NY; SO; BS; Comp Sci; Eng.

**CHAN SETO, LIN SAI,** City Univ Of Ny Baruch Coll, New York, NY; JR; MBA; Gnrl Offc Mngr Phoenix Bldrs Inc 88-F; Acctg; Bus.

**CHAN TACK, KIRK M,** Univ Of Miami, Coral Gables, FL; FR; BSC; Trndd Tbg Stdnts Assoc Treas 90-; Chmstry Clb; Nwsppr Clmnst 90-; Alpha Lmabda Delta; Hnrs Stdnts Assoc; Prvsts Hnr Rll; Sngr Schlrshp; Comp Sci Chmstry.

**CHAN, AMY M,** Cornell Univ Statutory College, Ithaca, NY; JR; BS; MBSA Chf Fncl Offcr 90-; Chinese Stdnts Assn 88-; New York Chinese Bapt Chrch 82-; Alpha Phi Omega 89-; John Mc Mullen Schrshp; S2m Sprts Capt 88-; Appl Econ/Bus Mgmt; Acctng/Bus.

**CHAN, ANGELA W,** Duquesne Univ, Pittsburgh, PA; JR; BA; Intl Stndts Org 88-90; Phi Eta Sigma; Beta Alpha Phi; Beta Gamma Sigma; Fnc; Intl Bus.

**CHAN, BELINDA P,** City Univ Of Ny Baruch Coll, New York, NY; SR; Chinese Chrstn Flwshp VP 89-90; Finance Econ Soc 90-; Gold Key 88-; Beta Gamma Sigma 88-; Ch Un Brethren Exec Sec 90-; Baruch Endwmnt Schlrshp Awd 88-90; BBA.

**CHAN, BETTY,** City Univ Of Ny Baruch Coll, New York, NY; SR; BBA; Mbr Acctg Soc 90-; Phi Beta Kappa 87; AAS La Guardia Comm Clg 88; Acctg.

**CHAN, CHUI,** S U N Y At Buffalo, Buffalo, NY; GD; DDS; Denistry.

**CHAN, CHUN F,** City Univ Of Ny Baruch Coll, New York, NY; SO; BBA; Acctg; Actnt.

**CHAN, DENNIS A,** S U N Y At Binghamton, Binghamton, NY; SO; Asian Stdnt Union Art Prod; Mgmt.

**CHAN, DOREEN W,** City Univ Of Ny Baruch Coll, New York, NY; SR; BA; Beta Gamma Sigma; Gldn Key; Deans Lst; Beta Alpha Psi; Acctg.

**CHAN, DOROTHY D,** Northeastern Univ, Boston, MA; BS; Intrnshp Coopers Lybrand Tax Preparer; Acctg Economics; CPA.**

**CHAN, HUNG M,** City Univ Of Ny Baruch Coll, New York, NY; JR; Badminton Sec; Acctng; Golden Key.

**CHAN, JENNIFER,** Cornell Univ Statutory College, Ithaca, NY; SO; BS; High Rise Hall Cncl Co-Chair 90-; Rsdnc Life Com; Chinese Stdnt Assn Pblctns Asst Ed 90-; Cornell Symphony Orchestra 89-; Chinese Bible Study/Choir 90-; Red Carpet Soc 90-; Clg Ag/Life Sci Ambssdrs 90-; Nutrition; Med.

**CHAN, JENNY,** S U N Y At Buffalo, Buffalo, NY; SO; BA; Stdnt Assn Asst Treas; Asn Amer Stdnt Union 90-; Chnse Stdnt Assn 89-; Delta Phi Omega Sec 90-; Comm Actn Corps 90-; IM Vlybl 89-; Bus Mgmt.

**CHAN, KAM W,** Coll Of Charleston, Charleston, SC; JR; BS; Bapt Stdnt Unio COC BSU Rep Cty Wide; Phi Kappa Phi; Alpha Chi Sigma; Chem.

**CHAN, KOK KUAN A,** City Univ Of Ny Baruch Coll, New York, NY; JR; BA; Badminton Clb Pres/Treas 89-90; Un Malaysian Stdnt Assn Treas; Beta Alpha Psi; Acctg; Auditing.

**CHAN, KWOK FAN,** City Univ Of Ny City Coll, New York, NY; SR; MS; Cmptr Sci.

**CHAN, LAI CHU,** City Univ Of Ny Baruch Coll, New York, NY; SR; BA; Actrl Sci, Actry Bnkng.

**CHAN, MAI,** City Univ Of Ny Baruch Coll, New York, NY; JR; BBA; Acctng Scty; Gldn Ky; Intrnshp Bnkrs Trst Corp NY Admin 90; Acctncy; CPA.

**CHAN, MEI KUEN,** City Univ Of Ny La Guard Coll, Long Island Cty, NY; SO; Hong Kong Clb Tres 90-; Acctg Clb 89-; Otstndng Contrbtn Awrd; Svc Awrd; AS; Acctg/Data Prcsng.

**CHAN, MEI N,** City Univ Of Ny Baruch Coll, New York, NY; SO; BA; Hong Kong Stdnt Assn Pres; Badminton Clb; Acctntng; CPA.

**CHAN, SHUE WING ALBERT,** Bridgewater Coll, Bridgewater, VA; FR; BS; Econ/Bsn.

**CHAN, STEVEN HO,** Cooper Union, New York, NY; SO; BE; Mthmtcl Assn Amrca 89-; Rsrch Rcyclng Plrd Btrs Tchr Asstnt 90; Rsrch Chmcl Rctns Chmcl Tchrs Asstnt; Smltn Prcs Cmptr Sftwr; Ping Pong Cmptn IM; Chmcl Engnrng.

**CHAN, SUSAN C,** City Univ Of Ny Baruch Coll, New York, NY; JR; BA; Stdy Abrd/Paris; Deans List 90-; Pres Schlr 89-; Bus; Mgmnt.

**CHAN, TERRENZ-CHING,** City Univ Of Ny Baruch Coll, New York, NY; JR; BA; Acctg Assn 89-; Acctg; CPA.

**CHAN, THERESA Y,** Smith Coll, Northampton, MA; SR; BA; Amer Chem Scty Treas 90-; Sr Cls 90-; Lawrence Hse Cncl Treas 89-90; Phi Beta Kappa 90-; Sigma Xi; Serv Orgnztns Of Smith Rep 88-89; Hnrs Thesis Resrch Proj 90-; Intrnshps Molecular Genetics 89-; Intnshp Genetic 88; Biology; Medicine Acdmc Mdcn.

**CHAN, WAI K,** City Univ Of Ny La Guard Coll, Long Island Cty, NY; SO; AAS; Phi Theta Kappa; Technen Digitrk Elec Inc; Comp Info Syst; Elec Eng.

**CHAN, WAI M,** Univ Of Rochester, Rochester, NY; SO; BS; Chinese Stdnts Assn Cinema Grp 89-; Japan Interest Grp 90-; Cmptr Sci; Cmptr Prgrmr.

**CHAN, WARREN,** City Univ Of Ny Baruch Coll, New York, NY; JR; CSA 90-; Acctng; Audtr.

**CHAN, XU-DONG,** City Univ Of Ny La Guard Coll, Long Island Cty, NY; SO; Bilngl Chinese Paraprfsnl 88-; Eng; Tchr.

**CHAN, YUK YIN,** City Univ Of Ny Baruch Coll, New York, NY; JR; BA; Gldn Key 90-; Acctng.

**CHAN, YUNG,** Wv Univ, Morgantown, WV; FR; BSEE; Chinese Stdnt Assoc; Hnr Prog; Elect Engrng.

**CHANASAR, KRONGKAEO,** Univ Of Sc At Lancaster, Lancaster, SC; FR; BS; Hnrs Soc Treas Elect; Pres Hnr Roll 90-; Marshall; Bio; Med.

**CHANCE, CALLY R,** Univ Of Nc At Greensboro, Greensboro, NC; JR; BFA; Dancer; Alpha Lambda Delta; Phi Beta Kappa Book Awd; Cmptvte Schlr 89-; Deans Lst 89-; Dance; Thrpst.

**CHANCE, ELIZABETH HENSLEIGH,** Univ Of Southern Ms, Hattiesburg, MS; SR; Phi Kappa Phi 89-; Kappa Mu Epsilon 90-; Math Assoc Of Amer 90-; Pres List 88-; Outstndng Young Woman Of Amer 84; Math; Secndry Ed.

**CHANCE, KIMBERLY G,** Univ Of Ga, Athens, GA; JR; PHARM; Acad Stu Pharmcy 90-; Outstndg Coll Stu Am 89; Kappa Psi Little Sistr; Alpha Delta Pi Intrm Chrmn 88-89; Intrnshp Vets Admin Hosp; Fast Pitch Sftbl Augusta Coll 90; Pharmacy.

**CHANDEL, LEENA K,** Memphis St Univ, Memphis, TN; SR; BA; Psych.

**CHANDLER, AMY D,** Middle Tn St Univ, Murfreesboro, TN; SR; Bapt Stdnt Un 87-; Dance Club 87-; Deans List; YWCA Domestic Violence Ctr; Asst Dance Instr Middle Tn Acdmy Of Dance 90-; Dance Instr 90-; BS 91; Psych; Masters Degree/Teach Coll Level.

**CHANDLER, ANDREW W,** Winthrop Coll, Rock Hill, SC; SO; BS; Action For Food V P 89-; Winthrop Coalition For Homeless 89-; SGA 90-; Alpha Lambda Delta 90-; Omicron Delta Kappa; Pi Kappa Phi Secy 90; IM Greek Games 90-; Pol Sci; Pblc Admin.

**CHANDLER, BEVERLY A,** Snead St Jr Coll, Boaz, AL; FR; Diploma New World Clg Bus 84; Ed; Elem Tchr.

**CHANDLER, CAMILLE A,** Middle Tn St Univ, Murfreesboro, TN; SR; Hall Pres 86-87; SGA Advtsng 86-87; Stdnt Intr Dsgnrs Advtsng Chrmn 89; Alpha Omicron Pi Pld Sec 88-90; I M 86-; Ele Educ; Wrtr/Illustr.

**CHANDLER, CARLA R,** Univ Of Hartford, West Hartford, CT; FR; BMUS; MENC 90-; Outng Clb 90-; Sigma Alpha Iota; Vio Perform; Perform Chmbr/Orchstrl.

**CHANDLER, JON C,** Auburn Univ At Auburn, Auburn, AL; SO; DP Mgt Assc 90-; Computer Engineering.

**CHANDLER, KRISTIE F,** Univ Of Al At Huntsville, Huntsville, AL; JR; BA; Scty Wmn Eng 90-; Marshall Bptst Yth Assc Vp 86-87; Sec Mt Carmel Bptst Chrch 87-90; Intergraph Mech Dsgn Co-Op 89-; Snead St Jr Clg Vrsty Bsktbl Schlrshp 87-88; Mech Eng; Appld Spce Mech.

**CHANDLER, LAURA B,** Ms St Univ, Miss State, MS; JR; BA; Gamma Beta Phi; Alpha Lambda Delta; Phi Kappa Phi; Sigma Tau Delta; Pres Schlr; Engl; Tchg.

**CHANDLER, LILA H,** Central Fl Comm Coll, Ocala, FL; SO; ADN; Nrsng; Cr AIDS Ptnts.

**CHANDLER, MARLA R,** Averett Coll, Danville, VA; SO; BA; Beta Beta Beta 90-; Averett Ldrshp Schlrshp; IM Vlybl 89-90; Bio; Phys Ther.

**CHANDLER, MICHAEL D,** Union Univ, Jackson, TN; JR; BED; Phi Mu Alpha Sinfonia Frat Ed Ofc 90-; Msc Ed; Clg Msc Prof/Church Mscn.

**CHANDLER, MICHAEL L,** Tri County Tech Coll, Pendleton, SC; SO; BA; Phi Theta Kappa; Ind Mgmt.

**CHANDLER, RACHEKE A,** Al A & M Univ, Normal, AL; SO; STIX Percussion Sect.

**CHANDLER, ROBERT S,** Univ Of Sc At Columbia, Columbia, SC; JR; BA; Intrdscplnry Studies; Law.

**CHANDLER, SALLIE K,** Lane Coll, Jackson, TN; JR; BA; Sclgy.

**CHANDLER, VERONICA L,** Univ Of Sc At Sumter, Sumter, SC; SO; BED; Early Chldhd Educ; Tchng.

**CHANDRASEGARAM, DHAYALINI,** Claflin Coll, Orangeburg, SC; FR; BSC; Yrbk 90-; Hons Progrm 90-; Alpha Sweethrt; Deans List 90; Bio/Chem; Medcn.

**CHANDRASENA, BANI,** Western New England Coll, Springfield, MA; SO; BA; Intrntl Stdnts Assc Sec 90-; Acctg.

**CHANEY, ASHLEY D,** Univ Of Sc At Columbia, Columbia, SC; FR; Natl Fresh Hnr Soc; Phi Eta Sigma; Dean Lst Wingate Bptst Coll; Engl; MBA.

**CHANEY, CHRISTOPHER M,** Eastern Ky Univ, Richmond, KY; FR.

**CHANEY, KRIST W,** Union Univ, Jackson, TN; SO; BM; Sigma Alpha Iota; Msc; Clg Prfssr.

**CHANEY, LEIGH A,** Itawamba Comm Coll, Fulton, MS; SO; BED; Choir 89-; Elem Ed; Tchr.

**CHANEY, RITA J,** Muskingum Coll, New Concord, OH; FR; BED; Elem Ed.

**CHANG, CHI CHING,** S U N Y At Buffalo, Buffalo, NY; SO; BA; Bsns Mgmt; Mgr.

**CHANG, CHIA-LING,** Manhattan School Of Music, New York, NY; SO; BACHL; Bachelor Degree Sophomore; Harp Perforn; Musician.

**CHANG, DANNY T,** Fl St Univ, Tallahassee, FL; JR; BA; Fla Pub Intrst Rsch Grp V-Chr 90-; Stdnt Govt Vdeo Ctr Prod Asst 89-90; Lib Stds Hon Prog; IM Scr 89; Pyscs/Comp Sci; Engr.

**CHANG, EMILY B,** Colgate Univ, Hamilton, NY; FR; BA; Tae Kwon Do Club Instr 90-; Work Study Huntington Gym Black Belt 2nd Degree; Sanford Field House Bldg Spvsr 90-; Phi Eta Sigma 90-; Alpha Chi Omega 90-; Rsrch Intern Grant; Chem; Med.

**CHANG, HORACE S L,** City Univ Of Ny City Coll, New York, NY; SR; BE; IEEE 90-; Tau Beta Pi 90-; Golden Key 90-; Deans Lst 87-; Elect Eng; Eng.

**CHANG, JAEHYUN,** Ms St Univ, Miss State, MS; SR; MBA; ME Hanyang Univ 86; Bus.

**CHANG, JOHN T,** S U N Y At Buffalo, Buffalo, NY; SR; MBA; Alpha Pi Mu; Deans Hnr Lst 89-; Tbl Tns Trnmnt Frst Pl 87; Bllrd Trnmnt 1st Pl 88; Blrd Trnmnt Frst Pl 90-; Mgmnt Engnrng.

**CHANG, JUDY C,** Univ Of Al At Huntsville, Huntsville, AL; SR; BS; IEEE 82-; ACM 82-90; Intergraph Corp Cmptr Grphcs Sys Sftwr Dvlpmnt; BS Fu Jen Univ Taiwan 78; MA Univ New Brunswk Canada 80; MS Univ Tenn 83; Elec Eng.

**CHANG, LEA-WEI,** Univ Of Rochester, Rochester, NY; SO; Go Clb 90-; Comp Int Flr Dir Art Comm 89-; Fncng Tm 89-; Psych; Law.

**CHANG, MARIA A,** Fl International Univ, Miami, FL; FR; BAMBA; Bus; Admin.

**CHANG, RICHARD Y,** Harvard Univ, Cambridge, MA; FR; BA; Admissions Cncl 90-; Polo Club 90-; Equestrian Tm 90-; Anthropolgy; Law/Bus.

**CHANG, RITA M,** Cornell Univ Statutory College, Ithaca, NY; JR; BS; Chinese Assn Sec 88-; Gldn Ky 89-; Alpha Phi Omega; Mcrcmptr Applctns TA; Bus Mgmt/Mrktng; Accntng.

**CHANG, TANYA K,** Ga St Univ, Atlanta, GA; FR; BBA; Accntng.

**CHANG, WEI,** City Univ Of Ny Baruch Coll, New York, NY; JR; Acctg.

**CHANG, WEI-JEN,** Savannah Coll Of Art & Design, Savannah, GA; GD; MFA; Graphix Grp 90-; Intl Assn 90-; Lab Asst/Tutor 90-; Envrnmntl Graphic Dsgnr Leicester City Cncl UK 87-88; HND Higher Natl Dip UK 88; Graphic Dsgn; Advrtsng.

**CHANKO, MELISSA E,** Le Moyne Coll, Syracuse, NY; JR; BA; I M Soccer Vybl 89-; I H Intl Hse; Deans Lst 89; Big Str/Big Bro 88; Extrnshp Law Off 90-; Yth Agnst Cancer Co Chrmn 87; Hstry; Law.

**CHANNELL, ANGELA LYNN,** Ms St Univ, Miss State, MS; JR; BSED; Bptst Stu Unn 90-; Kappa Delta Pi 90-; Gamma Beta Phi 90-; Hinds Cnnctns 89-90; Pres Schlr; IM Sprts 90; Art Educ; Educ.

**CHANNELL, GLENN M,** Univ Of Toledo, Toledo, OH; SO; BS; Amrcn Inst Chmcl Engnrs 89-; Phi Eta Sigma 89-; Tau Beta Pi Sec; Theta Tau; Scout UT Tres 89-; Ntnl Mrt Schlr; AICHE Otstndng Soph; US Achvmnt Acdmy Eng Awd; All Amrcn Schlr; Chmcl Engnrng.**

**CHANNELL, JENNIFER L,** Atlantic Comm Coll, Mays Landing, NJ; FR; Phi Theta Kappa; Hnrs Prog; Atlantic Cnty Vol 90-; Lit Eracy Vol; Vllybl; Psychology; Soc Wrk.

**CHANSKY, NEYSA D,** City Univ Of Ny Queensbrough, New York, NY; SO; BS; Alpha Beta Gamma 86; AAS Queensborough Cmnty Clg; Cmptr Info Syst; Pgmr/Syst Analyst.

**CHANTO, ALEXANDRA,** Univ Of South Al, Mobile, AL; SR; BA; Latin Amer Stdt Assoc Pres 89-; Cncl Exceptional Children 89-; Education; Special Education.

**CHAO, CHUN-HSIN,** Manhattanville Coll, Purchase, NY; FR; BA; Intrntl Club 90-; Econ/Mgt Club 90-; Econ; Sr Auditor.

**CHAO, KAN Y,** City Univ Of Ny City Coll, New York, NY; JR; BS; Biochem; Med.

**CHAO, PEI-LI,** Univ Of Md Baltimore Prof Schl, Baltimore, MD; SR; BS; Smithsonian Assoc; Phi Kappa Phi; Med Lab Tech; AA Tuan-Per Jr Coll Taiwan 80; Med Technology; Lab Scientist.

**CHAPDELAINE, JOHN C,** Barry Univ, Miami, FL; SR; BS; ATC Aeroclub NCOA 88-90; Deans Lst 90; U S Air Force 84-88; Flight Simulator Eng 88-; AS U Of SC 88; Tech; Bus Admin.

**CHAPIN, AMY L,** Bryant Stratton Bus Inst Roch, Rochester, NY; GD; AOS; Acctng; Tax Acctnt.

**CHAPIN, STACEY L,** Kent St Univ Kent Cmps, Kent, OH; SR; BBA; Mrchng Band 87; Golden Key 90-; Acctng; CPA.

**CHAPLICK, DANIEL R,** Clarkson Univ, Potsdam, NY; JR; BS; Interfrat Sports Dir 90; Sigma Delta Hse Mgr 89; Cmnty Svc Potsdam 89-90; Clarkson Phone-A-Thon; Alumni Phone-A-Thon; Clarkson Trustees Schlrshp 87-88; Intrnshp Carrier; Ind Mktg; Sales/Adv.

**CHAPLIK, IGOR,** Univ Of Miami, Coral Gables, FL; FR; BS; Orntn Asst; Alpha Lambda Delta; Kappa Sigma; Provosts Hnr Roll; Hghts Pldge; Deans Lst; Bio; Med.

**CHAPLIK, TRICIA J,** Kent St Univ Kent Cmps, Kent, OH; SR; BBA; AIESEC Exec VP 88-; Gldn Key 90-; Deans Lst 87-; Mktg.

**CHAPLIN, CHAD L,** Wv Northern Comm Coll, Wheeling, WV; Forensics Tm 88; Stdnt Cncl 89-90; Deans Lst 87-; Phi Beta Lambda 90-; Bsktbl Cancer Benefit 87-; AA 90; SBA 90; Law MS JD.

**CHAPLIN, JOHN M,** Anne Arundel Comm Coll, Arnold, MD; SO; BS; AAS Maryland Drftng Inst 79f; Eng.

**CHAPLIN, LA TONYA E,** Claflin Coll, Orangeburg, SC; SR; BA; NAACP 88; Delta Sigma Theta; Alpha Sweet Heart 87-; Hnr Roll 89-90; Stdnt Support Svcs Acad Ach Award 90-; BA; Sclgy; Soc Wrk/Cnslng.

**CHAPLIN II, ROBERT A,** Nyack Coll, Nyack, NY; SR; BS; Brooklyn Gspl Tm 87-88; Elem Ed; Tchng.

**CHAPMAN, ALANNA B,** Kent St Univ Kent Cmps, Kent, OH; FR; BS; Newman Clb 90-; Outstndng Svc Awd; Bio.

**CHAPMAN, ANGELA B,** Emory & Henry Coll, Emory, VA; SR; Intern Blue Ridge Job Corps Marion VA Cnslr 90; Pysch/Art.

**CHAPMAN, BRIAN J,** Newbury Coll, Brookline, MA; SO; AB; Cls Rep 90; Mgr Expressway Inc Logan Intl Airprt Trcking Ind 85-; Bsns; U S Sen.

**CHAPMAN, CARISSA L,** Ky Wesleyan Coll, Owensboro, KY; FR; BA.

**CHAPMAN, CRYSTAL M,** Univ Of Nc At Asheville, Asheville, NC; SR; BA; AA Brevard Clg 89; Psy; Tchr.

**CHAPMAN, DONNA K,** Itawamba Comm Coll, Fulton, MS; JR; BED; Mdlng Sqd 84-86; Drama Clb 84-85; Hmcmng Ct 86; Delta Epsilon Chi Sec 84-86; Ply Prdctn 84; Stage Crew 85; AAS Itawambo CC 86; Math; Elem Ed.

**CHAPMAN, DONNA M,** Va Commonwealth Univ, Richmond, VA; SR; BA; Pol Sci Scty Sec 90-; Coopertv Educ Pgm 90-; Hse Dlgts Intrn 90-; Pol Sci; Pblc Admnstrn.

**CHAPMAN, EMILY A,** Colby Coll, Waterville, ME; FR; BA; Wkly Nwsppr Stff Wrtr 90-; Wnd Ensmbl 90-; Wdwnd Qntt 90-; Engl; Athr Ed.

**CHAPMAN, FREDA L,** City Univ Of Ny Baruch Coll, New York, NY; JR; BBA; COAP 87; COAP Cnslr; Acctng; CPA.**

**CHAPMAN, GINA M,** Old Dominion Univ, Norfolk, VA; GD; BA; Golden Key 90-; Iota Lambda Sigma 90-; Intrnshp S C Johnson Wax; Mrkt Ed/Mgt; Hmn Rsrc.

**CHAPMAN, GRETCHEN R,** Univ Of Southern Ms, Hattiesburg, MS; SO; BA; Stdnt Alumni Assoc Sec; Clg Repubs Pub Rels; Speech Cmctn Assn; Pi Tau Chi; Chi Omega 89-; Gamma Beta Phi; Lambda Sigma; Speech Cmctns.

**CHAPMAN, J DALE,** Coker Coll, Hartsville, SC; JR; BA; Ed; Tchr.

**CHAPMAN, JENNIFER J,** Marshall University, Huntington, WV; FR; MBA; Bus; Acctg.

**CHAPMAN, JEREMY W,** Embry Riddle Aeronautical Univ, Daytona Beach, FL; JR; BS; MAA 90-; AMA 84-; Tau Alpha VP 89-; Omicron Delta Kappa; Army ROTC Cadt Cap 88-; Selectd To Spk At Natl MAA Convntn; ROTC Colorgrd Asst Commndr; IM Sftbl; Aircrft Engrng; Aircrft Rsrch/Devlpmnt.

**CHAPMAN, KAREN LYNN,** Roane St Comm Coll, Harriman, TN; FR; AS; Occptnl Thrpy; Occptnl Thrpst.

**CHAPMAN, KAREN S,** Marshall University, Huntington, WV; SR; BBA; Alpha Kappa Psi V P Admin 90-; Prichard Schl Bd Acad Schlrshp 90-; Mktng; Bus Educ.

**CHAPMAN, KERI L,** Indiana Univ Of Pa, Indiana, PA; SR; BS; Actvts Bd Grphcs-Chrprsn 87-89; Artst Series 90-; TV/RADIO Stations 90-; Intrnshp Media Grp -Prod Hs Columbua OH Prod Asst 90; Grad Magna Cum Laude; Cmnctns; Film/Video Prod.

**CHAPMAN, KEVIN H,** Univ Of Southern Ms, Hattiesburg, MS; SR; BS; Stdt Eagle Club 90-; Hotel/Restaurant Mangement.

**CHAPMAN, KEVIN L,** Univ Of Sc At Columbia, Columbia, SC; FR.

**CHAPMAN, KEVIN R,** Ohio Valley Coll, Parkersburg, WV; SO; AA; Acpla Qtrt 89-; Chrs/Chrl 89-; Tmthy Clb; Alpha Tau Sigma 89-; Bible/Relgn; BA Mnstry/Mssns.

**CHAPMAN, LILA L,** Univ Of Akron, Akron, OH; SR; BA; Sec Ed Eng/Hist; Tchr.

**CHAPMAN, MEGAN S,** Univ Of Ct, Storrs, CT; SR; BS; Intrclgt Hrs Shw Assc Sec 87-; Block/Brdl Clb Tres 89-90; Eqstrn Tm Cptn 89-; Alpha Zeta Chnclr 89-; Sigma Alpha Pres 90-; Intrclgt Horse Shw Assc Schlrshp; Donald Mccollugh Mem Ldrshp Awd; NE Stdnt Afflt Outstndng Animal Sci Sr; Agriculture; Animal Sci.

**CHAPMAN, MELINDA D,** Columbia Union Coll, Takoma Park, MD; SR; BS; Bus Clb 87-; Phi Eta Sigma 87-; Alpha Chi; Theta Alpha Beta 90-; Amer Red Cross 90-; Amer Heart Assoc 90-; MD Distinguished Honor 88-; Acctg/Minor Computer Sci; CPA Accountant.**

**CHAPMAN, MICHAEL P,** Mount Olive Coll, Mount Olive, NC; SO; BS; USAF Nco; Photo Snsrs Mntnc Spcl; AAS 90; Bus Mgmt; Cmsnd Offcr.

**CHAPMAN, MIRA JANEL,** Lenoir Rhyne Coll, Hickory, NC; SR; BS; Flwshp Chrstn Ath 87-89; Bapt Stdnt Un 90-; Sftbl 87-; Biology; UNC Wilmington Maine Biology.

**CHAPMAN, NORMAN L,** Univ Of Sc At Sumter, Sumter, SC; FR; BA; IM Bsktbl; Bus; Stck Brkr.

**CHAPMAN, SARAH K,** Coker Coll, Hartsville, SC; SO; BA; Choice Clb 89-; Coffee Hse Comm Chr 89-; Coker Sngrs 89-90; Milestone Staff Phtgrphr 89-; Comsnrs Co-Head 90-; Ambsdrs 90-; Charles W Coker Schlrshp 89-; Coker Comm Chr Yr Awd 90-; Phtgrphy/Bus Adm; Prof Phtgrphr.

**CHAPMAN, SHERRY L,** Univ Of Sc At Spartanburg, Spartanburg, SC; FR; Mdl Untd Ntns; Mth Clb; Sci Clb; Intrntl Orgn; Fndrs Scty; Fndrs Schlrshp; Math; Educ.

**CHAPMAN, TANYA A,** Morgan St Univ, Baltimore, MD; SR; BSW; Soc Work Admn.

**CHAPMAN, TONY R,** Lexington Comm Coll, Lexington, KY; SO.

**CHAPMAN, TREVAR O,** Univ Of Sc At Sumter, Sumter, SC; FR; BA; Auto CAD Operator Interlake Matl Hndlng 89-; ASSOC Sumter Area Tech Clg 89; Comp Sci; Engr.

**CHAPMAN, WILLIAM S,** Tri County Tech Coll, Pendleton, SC; SO; AS; KAPPA; Ntnl Grd Assn; Machine Tool Tchnlgy.

**CHAPPELL, CYNTHIA L,** Allegheny Coll, Meadville, PA; SR; BA; Phi Sigma Lota 91; Kappa Kappa Gamma Pdge Educ 88-; WPGH Fox 53 Intrnshp 90-; Var Tennis Tm 89-90; Cmunctn Arts.

**CHAPPELL, GINGER MULVEHILL,** Univ Of Al At Birmingham, Birmingham, AL; SR; Teaching Pinson Elem; Teaching Washington Elem; BS; Elem Ed.

**CHAPPELL, GREGG S,** Castleton St Coll, Castleton, VT; SR; BED; Stdnt Assn Pres 90-; Stdnt Educ Assn 90-; Tadashii Krate Do Yonkyu 87-; Kappa Delta Pi Pres 90-; Kappa Delta Phi Chpln/Hstrn 90-; Allen Broilette Schlrshp 90; Awd Recog 90; IM Ftbl 87-; Elem Educ; Tchr.

**CHAPPELL, JOSEPH CHARLES,** Southern Coll Of Tech, Marietta, GA; SR; BA; Tau Alpha Pi 89-; IIE 89-; Amer Soc Quality Control 90-; Tau Alpha Pi 89-; BA Southern Clg Tech 90; Indstrl Engr Tech; Engr.

**CHAPPELL, LISA M,** Univ Of Sc At Columbia, Columbia, SC; SO; BA; Bapt Stdnt Un Cncl 90-; Writing Awd 90; Eng; Teach.

**CHAPPELL, LISA M,** Tn Tech Univ, Cookeville, TN; SR; BS; Newman Org Pres 87-; Alpha Mu Gamma 88-; Kappa Omicron Nu 90-; Intern Fixtur-World Designs 90; Deans Lst 87-90; Home Econ/Int Dsgn; Designer.

**CHAPPELL, MOLLY DE TREVILLE,** Converse Coll, Spartanburg, SC; SR; Stdnt Govt Assoc 87-; Stdnt Admission Bd 89-; Stdnt Actvts Comm Movie Hd 88-89; Safe Homes/Childrens Shelter Vol Coord 89-; Ltl Sis Pgm 89-; Continuum Care Spec Friend Vol 90-; VIP Character Dev Pgm 90-; Dept Yth Svcs Intern; Sclgy/Psych; Scl Wrkr.

**CHAPPELL, SUE A,** Ky Wesleyan Coll, Owensboro, KY; JR; BA; SGA Sntr 89-; James Graham Brown Scty 88-; Alph Chi 90-; Sclgy/Hmn Rsrcs Admn Clb 89-; James Graham Brown Schlrshp 88-; Untd Meth Mnstrs Schlrshp 88; Hmn Rsrcs Admn; Soclgy Tchng.

**CHAPPINE, KATHLEEN S,** Widener Univ, Chester, PA; SR; BS; Acctng Socty VP 87-89; Wmns Sftbl Tm Co Capt 87-; Acctng.

**CHARALAMBOUS, PANAYIOTA A,** Univ Of Sc At Coastal Carolina, Conway, SC; JR; BA; Intl Clb Secy 90-; Bus Clb 90-; AS Tidewater Comm Clg 89; Mktng.

**CHARANIA, SHIRIN F,** Emory Univ, Atlanta, GA; JR; BBA; Intl Assoc Chrprsn 88-; Pre Law Soc 89-; Intl Bsns Assoc 90-; Alpha Phi Omega 89-90; Vol Emory 89-90; Cir K 88-90; Peer Cnslr 89-; Fin; Intl Corp Law.

**CHARD, WILLIAM I,** Widener Univ, Chester, PA; SR; BS; Acctg Soc 88-; Penn Inst Of Cert Pblc Acctnts 88-; Moose Ldg 90-; Prvt Pilot; Phi Kappa Phi; Lambda Chi Alpha 88-; Acdmc Hnrs 87-; Acctg; CPA.

**CHAREST, JILL M,** Western New England Coll, Springfield, MA; SO; BA; Fnc; Bus.

**CHARITONENKO, STEPHANIE,** Univ Of Tn At Knoxville, Knoxville, TN; JR; BA; AIESEC Pres 89-90f Fncng Clb VP 89-90; Invstmnt Clb Fndr 89-; BSACD 89-90; Undrgrd Exec Prog 89-90; Golden Key 89-; Gamma Beta Phi 90-; Alpha Kappa Psi 89-90; Spec Olympcs Vol Med Tm 87-; Nshvl/Knxvl Cty Mssns Vol Coord 87-; Cir K Coord 89-90; Fin/Jpns; Csnltnt/Dept Of St/Ambssrd Int Advr.

**CHARITY, PAMELA L,** Hahnemann Univ, Philadelphia, PA; JR; MD; AMSA Adlscnt Sbstnce Abse Prjct Instrctr 90; Fischer Acad Schlrshp; Amer Coll Of Physns; Amer Acad Physn Assts; Physn Asst; BS Alderson Broaddus Coll 79; Med; Prmry Cre Med.

**CHARKOW, GAIL L,** Dowling Coll, Oakdale Li, NY; GD; MA; Cum Laude; BED Spcl Edn/Elem 90; Edn; Teach.

**CHARLES, ALFRED,** Miami Dade Comm Coll, Miami, FL; SO; Math/Sci; Eng.

**CHARLES, ALICIA A,** Middlesex County Coll, Edison, NJ; SR; AAS; Soc Stdnt Radiogrphrs 90-; Certif Acad/Outstndg Achvmnt State NJ Dept High Ed; Alice Jackson Stuart Awd Acad Excell; Radiogrphy Ed; Nucl Med.

**CHARLES, CAROLYN G,** Savannah St Coll, Savannah, GA; SR; BS; Stdnt Govt Assn 87-88; Sieee Pres 90-; Electronics; Engr.

**CHARLES, CHERYL L,** Bellarmine Coll, Louisville, KY; JR; BA; Math Assn Am 90-; Delta Epsilon Sigma 90-; IMS 89-; Math/Comp Sci.

**CHARLES, CORTLANDT J,** City Univ Of Ny Bronx Comm Col, Bronx, NY; JR; BA; Phi Theta Kappa 90; Dean Lst 88-90; Bus Cmptrs; Cmptr Infrmtn Systms.

**CHARLES, DARRELL D,** Al A & M Univ, Normal, AL; FR; BA; Vrsty Bsktbl; SGA Nmntng Cmmtt 90-; Dean Lst 90-; Hnr Rll 90-; Engl; Law.

**CHARLES, EDNA R,** Snead St Jr Coll, Boaz, AL; SO; BS; Phi Theta Kappa 89-; Admin Asst; Bsn.

**CHARLES, JEAN E,** S U N Y Coll Of Tech At Frmgdl, Farmingdale, NY; GD; BS; Bus Clb 89-; Haitian Stdnt Org Co-Advsr 89-; Deans Lst 89; Pres Lst 90; Phi Theta Kappa 90; AS 90; Bus/Acctg.**

**CHARLES, KAY J L,** City Univ Of Ny Baruch Coll, New York, NY; SR; BA; Deans Lst; Ntnl Deans Lst; Elglsh Lit; Edctn.

**CHARLES, ROSA C,** City Univ Of Ny Baruch Coll, New York, NY; SR; BBA; Gldn Ky 90-; Beta Gamma Sigma; Admn Asst 86-; AAS NYC Tech Clg 84; Fin; Fin Anlyst.

**CHARLES, VLADIMIR,** Miami Dade Comm Coll North, Miami, FL; JR; MBA; Blck Stndt Un; Haitian IBO Clb 88-; Delta Iota Delta 90-; AA; Architecture/Design.

**CHARLES, WENDY J,** Univ Of Sc At Columbia, Columbia, SC; FR; BA; Snw Sk Clb 90-; Chld Psychlgst.

**CHARLESTON, CYNTHIA M,** Tougaloo Coll, Tougaloo, MS; FR; Bio; Pre Med.

**CHARLESWORTH, HEATHER L,** Pa St Univ Altoona Cmps, Altoona, PA; FR; BS; Hnrs Pgm 90-; Tutor 90-; Engineering; Comp Eng.

**CHARLEVILLE, STEPHEN C,** Univ Of Cin R Walters Coll, Blue Ash, OH; FR; AA; Lbrl Arts.

**CHARLOCK, BETTE A,** Fl International Univ, Miami, FL; JR; BA; AA Miami Dade Comm Clg 89; Lang Arts; Elem Educ.

**CHARLOP, ZIPPORA F,** Yeshiva Univ, New York, NY; JR; BA; Math.

**CHARLOT, VERA S,** Univ Of Southern Ms, Hattiesburg, MS; SR; BA; Air Frc ROTC 89-; Afro Amer Stdnt Org 90-; Phi Kappa Phi; Gamma Beta Phi 90-; Arnold Air Soc 90-; Air Frc ROTC Schlrshp; U S Air Frc 84-89; Eng; Prfsr/Athr.

**CHARLSON, STEPHANIE M,** Univ Of Akron, Akron, OH; SO; BED; ACES 90-; Stdnt Lf VP 90-; Alpha Lambda Delta 90-; Phi Eta Sigma 90-; Math; Tchng.

**CHARPENTIER, CHRIS J,** Kent St Univ Kent Cmps, Kent, OH; JR; IM 88-; Gldn Ky; Delta Sigma Pi; Bus Mktng/Mgmnt.

**CHARRON, AMY ELIZABETH,** Southeastern Ma Univ, N Dartmouth, MA; SO; BSBA; Rsdnc Halls Cngrs 88-89; Rsdnt Asstnt Yr 90-; Nrsng Psychlgy.

**CHARRON, CYNTHIA L,** Clark Univ, Worcester, MA; FR; BA; Psychlgy; Cnsllng.

**CHARTRAND, ANITA D,** Newbury Coll, Brookline, MA; SR; AD; Raytheon Co; Bus Mngmnt; Bus.

**CHARTRAND, SUZANNE M,** Univ Of Cincinnati, Cincinnati, OH; FR; BA; Alpha Lambda Delta 90-; Brdcstng; TV/LAW.

**CHASE, CHRISTOPHER W,** East Tn St Univ, Johnson City, TN; GD; MD; Admissions Comm 89-; Alpha Omega Alpha Pres; Mc Graw Hill Awd 89; BA Univ TN 86; Med; Gen Surg.**

**CHASE, DOUGLAS W,** Univ Of Nh Plymouth St Coll, Plymouth, NH; FR; BS; Bus; Gen Mgmt.

**CHASE, ELISHA A,** Hampton Univ, Hampton, VA; SO; BA; Church Yth Choir 87-; Univ Gspl Choir 89; Pltcl Sci Clb/Wmns Senate 90-; Nmntd GTE Acdmc All Am Wmns Vlybl Tm 90; Most Outstndng Fresh Vlybl 89; Coachs Awd Vlybl 90; Vrsty Vlybl 89-; Pltcl Sci; Entrtnmnt Law/Schl Tchr Govt/Hist.

**CHASE, JABAL L,** Tougaloo Coll, Tougaloo, MS; FR; MBA; Econ/Acctng; Law.

**CHASE, KAFI N,** Fl A & M Univ, Tallahassee, FL; FR; BS; Physics; Scintst.

**CHASE, LISA B,** Lincoln Univ, Lincoln Univ, PA; SR; BS; Sclgy Clb 90-; Dance Trp 87-89; Dean Lst; All Amer Schlr; Crmnl Jstc/Sclgy; Law.

**CHASE, MARY JO,** Siena Coll, Loudonville, NY; SR; BBA; Intrnshp Ge R/D; Rmn Cath Chrch Mnstr 89-; Acctg; Stf Acctnt.

**CHASE, REBECCA A,** Bay Path Coll, Longmeadow, MA; SO; Theatre Workshop; AS; Paralegal; Law/Criminal Justice.

**CHASE, SUSAN E,** Univ Of New Haven, West Haven, CT; JR; BS; W Haven Vtrns Assoc Awd Acdmc Exclnc 88-; Mktg Stdnt Yr Nmn 90; Bsn Admin; Orgnztnl Psychlgy.

**CHASE, TODD P,** Barry Univ, Miami, FL; SR; BPS; Offcr Mnth 86; Offcr Qrtr 90; Deans Lst Pres Lst 90; Plc Bnvlnt Assoc 84-87; Frtrnl Ordr Plc 90; Plc Offcr 84-; Prfssnl Stds.

**CHASE II, WILLET D,** Ga Military Coll, Milledgeville, GA; FR; AA; ROTC Advncd Course 90-; Phi Theta Kappa 90-; Outstndg Engl Stdnt; Outstndng Pol Sci Stdnt; Pol Sci; Law/U S Army Ofcr.

**CHASKO, MARY A,** Duquesne Univ, Pittsburgh, PA; JR; BA; 5 Yrs Invntry Cntrl Clrk For 2 Mdrt Btr Wmns Fshn Strs; Assoc Spec Bus 85; Engl; Prof.

**CHASMER, SUSAN D,** Bergen Comm Coll, Paramus, NJ; SO; AAS; Mstr Grdnrs Of Brgn Cnty 89-; By Scts Dn Ldr 90-; Zlgcl Scty Of NJ 84-; Dns Lst 84-; Phi Theta Kappa 90-; Prprtrs Evr Grn Hrtcltrl Srvcs 89-; Cert Rutgers Cooperative Extension Paramus NJ 89; Ornmntl Hrtcltre; Lndscpe Archtct.

**CHASON, ERIC D,** Brevard Coll, Brevard, NC; SO; AA; Clg Mrshls Chief Mrshl 90-; Stdnt Tutor 89-; Frshmn Schlr Awrd 90; Sphmr Schlr Awrd 91; Pres Awrd Achvmnt; IM 89-90; Ecnmcs; Law.

**CHASON, KELLY D,** Brevard Coll, Brevard, NC; FR; BS; Envrnmntl Awrnss Grp 90-; Stdnt Tutor 90-; Simms Schlrshp 90-; Math Science Schlrshp; Blgy.

**CHASSAGNE, SABRINA,** Fl International Univ, Miami, FL; JR; Alpha Phi Sigma 91-92; I M Sftbl; Crmnl Juste; Law Sch.

**CHASTAIN, CYNTHIA B,** Gaston Coll, Dallas, NC; SO; AS; Med Ofc Tech.

**CHASTAIN, LYNN M,** Univ Of Southern Ms, Hattiesburg, MS; SO; BA; Lbry Sci; Tchr.

**CHASTAIN, RON M,** Marshall University, Huntington, WV; SR; BA; Pi Kappa Phi Wrdn 89-90; Intrnshp Shrwn Wms 90-; Bsns; Acctng.

**CHASTAIN, SAMUEL W,** Southern Coll Of Tech, Marietta, GA; SR; BS; Inst Of Indstrl Engs; Sigma Pi VP 87-; Intr Frat Cncl Schlrshp Awrd 90-; Indstrl Eng Tech; Intrnatl Bus And Distrbtn.

**CHASTAIN, SUSAN A,** Tri County Tech Coll, Pendleton, SC; SO; CDA; Chld Dev Asst; Day Cr/Pre Sch.

**CHASTAIN, T B,** Univ Of North Fl, Jacksonville, FL; JR; BA; Gldn Ky; Pi Kappa Phi; Free And Accptd Masons; Shrine; Asst Dir Cstmr Rspnse CSX Trnsprttn; AA Florida Comm Coll At Jacksonville 89; Bus.

**CHASTAIN, VICTORIA E,** Univ Of Cincinnati, Cincinnati, OH; FR; BM; CCM S Symphony Band; Chamber Music; Alpha Lambda Delta; Music-Flute; Symphony Performer Clge Flute.

**CHASTANG, EDWIN J,** Alcorn St Univ, Lorman, MS; FR; BA; NAACP; Hnr Stdnt Org; SGA Election Commission; Hnr Soc; Bus Mgmnt; Corporate Law.

**CHATAKONDU, RAMADEVI,** City Univ Of Ny Queensbrough, New York, NY; SR; Comp Sci.

**CHATANI, DEEPA H,** Univ Of Miami, Coral Gables, FL; SO; BBA; ISA; Sindhi Assn S FL; CIS; Syst Anlys.

**CHATFIELD, RUTH H,** Birmingham Southern Coll, Birmingham, AL; GD; BA; Phi Alpha Theta; Alpha Sigma Lambda; Hstry.

**CHATHAM, KAREN L V,** Va Commonwealth Univ, Richmond, VA; SR; BS; Sigma Theta Tau; Phi Kappa Phi; Sigma Zeta; Natl Gldn Key Hnr Scty; Alpha Kappa Psi; BSBA 84; Nrsng; Emrgncy Nrsng.

**CHATLAND, LAURA S,** D Youville Coll, Buffalo, NY, FR, MS; SPTA 90-; Catalyst 90-; AAU Power Level Vlybl Capt 90-; Interclgt Wmns Vlybl 90-; Phy Thrpy; Outptnt Rehab/Sports Rehab.

**CHATMAN, ANDRE B,** Clark Atlanta Univ, Atlanta, GA; SR; Pan-Hellenic Cncl Rep 88-90; Pep Clb Sctn Ldr 87; Career Hlth Fair 89; Kappa Alpha Psi Kpr Of Rcrds 88; Amrcn Cncr Scty Vol; Camilla Nrsng Hm Intrnshp 90; BS; Allied Hlth Cmmnty Hlth Ed; Pblc Hlth Admin.

**CHATMAN, CASSANDRA N,** Alcorn St Univ, Lorman, MS; SO; BS; Hnr Rll 90-; Engl Tchng; Tchng.

**CHATMAN, TONY M,** Coppin St Coll, Baltimore, MD; SR; BA; Jaycees Legis Dir 89-90; (AACP 87-; Psyc Clb Sec 90-; N Shore Anml League 88-; Chl Psychlgy.

**CHATMON, RODDRICK L,** Fort Valley St Coll, Fort Valley, GA; SR; MS; Psych Advsry Com Chrmn 90-; Psych Clb Pres 90-; Alpha Kappa Mu 90-; Nom Natl Collgte Stdtn Govt Awrd 90-; Nom All Amer Schlrs Intrnshp Chrtr Lake Hosp; Bgn Grad Stds GA Coll; BA; Psych; Psychlgst.**

**CHATTERTON, ELLIS K,** Ms St Univ, Miss State, MS; JR; BS; FAA Instr/Cmmrcl Plt Cert/Instrmnts Rtng; Cotton Belt Aviation STF MGS; Phi Eta Sigma 90-; Alpha Lambda Delta 90-; Sigma Gamma Tau; Acad Schlrshp 88-92; Teledyne Brown Engr/ Merit Stdnt Emp Awd 88-; Aerospace Engr; Airline Pilot.

**CHAU, ANH L,** Temple Univ, Philadelphia, PA; SR; BS; Rho Chi; Dr M L King Jr Awd; Deans Lst; Stdnt PPA ASHP PSHP; Pharm.

**CHAU, HILDA,** Newbury Coll, Brookline, MA; SR; Outstndng Acas Achiev Plq; Deans Lst; Herman Geist Smpl Rm 83-; AA Newbury Coll Brookline MA 89-; Fash Dsgn.

**CHAU, KIM N,** Onondaga Comm Coll, Syracuse, NY; BA; Wmn Info Syracuse; Arch.

**CHAU, THAO THI LE,** Memphis St Univ, Memphis, TN; FR.

**CHAUDHRY, BARBARA L,** Ny Univ, New York, NY; FR; AAS; Cmptrs.

**CHAUDHRY, SAEED MOHAMMAD,** S U N Y Coll Of Tech At Frmgdl, Farmingdale, NY; SR; Asn Clb 90-; Acctg Scty 90-; Hnrs Cert Bus Dpt 90; AS; BA; Bus Mgmt.

**CHAUDRY, SHAHIDA N,** New Comm Coll Of Baltimore, Baltimore, MD; JR; Rsprtry Thrpy; RT.

**CHAUHAN, JENNIFER D,** Villanova Univ, Villanova, PA; SR; Orntn Cnslr 90; Phi Beta Kappa 91; Phi Kappa Phi 90; Eng Hnr Soc 91; French Hnr Soc 90; Alpha Chi Omega Sec 88-90; Acdmc Pres Schlrshp Full Tuition 87-; Joseph J Gildea OSA Awd Mod Langs 91; BA 91; Eng/French; Law.

**CHAUHAN, NILESH D,** Ga Inst Of Tech At Atlanta, Atlanta, GA; FR; BEE; Lamda Sigma; Phi Eta Sigma; Ford/Pele Sccr Schlrshp 90; Hennessy Schlr/Athlt Schlrshp 90; Elec Engr.

**CHAUVIGNE, BRIGITTE J,** Univ Of Nc At Greensboro, Greensboro, NC; JR; BA; Nrsng.

**CHAUVIN, MARY CATHERINE,** Univ Of Nc At Greensboro, Greensboro, NC; SR; BS; Phi Theta Kappa 89; Marshalls; Spec Olympics Swmng Instctr 89; Covington Schlrshp 88; All Amer Schlrs; Marshalls; Jay Cees 89-90; Mgr Night Clb; AS Guildford Tech Comm Clg 89; Math/Phy Sci; Educ/Peace Corps.

**CHAVEL, SIMEON B,** Yeshiva Univ, New York, NY; SR; BA; Aliyah Clb Pres; Stdnt Pblctns Gvrng Bd 89-; Radio Sta Gst Hst 90; Stdnts Sprtl Revival Sct Jwry Educ Pgmr; Gmilut Hasidm Clb 90; Bellein Schlr Acdmc Excllnc; 1st Prz Essay Gnrl Sbjct; Engl; Rbbnt.

**CHAVEZ, TERESITA,** Univ Of Miami, Coral Gables, FL; FR; Alpha Lambda Delta 90-; Delta Gamma 90-; Jrnslm Pol Sci; Rprtr.

**CHAVEZ, VIRGINIA L,** Princeton Univ, Princeton, NJ; FR; BA; Frshmn Sngrs 90-; Mngr/Lghtwght Ftbll 90-; Cmmty House 90-; Intrnshp Sntr Dennis Deconcini DAZ; Ftbll; Law.

**CHAVIS, PAMELA AMANDA,** Western Carolina Univ, Cullowhee, NC; SR; March Dimes-Walk Amer; Zeta Phi Beta Pres 89-; BSW; Scl Wrk.

**CHAWLA, POONAM,** George Mason Univ, Fairfax, VA; JR; BA; Assn Indian Stdnts 89-; Alpha Chi ; Gldn Key; Alpha Lamda Delta 90-; Deans Lst 90-; Schlrshp; Acctg; Corp/Pblc Acctg.

**CHAYT, STEVE B,** City Univ Of Ny City Coll, New York, NY; SO; Asbestos Abatement Co Intrnshp; ASBESTOS Supv Lic NY St/Cty/Fed; Cvl Eng/Archtctr.

**CHEAH, HOW YAN,** Univ Of Ky, Lexington, KY; FR; BSEE; Malysn Stdnt Org; Elec Eng.

**CHEAK, TERESA M,** Univ Of Ga, Athens, GA; SR; BED; Earth Day Edn Comm 90; Alpha Lambda Delta 87-; Kappa Delta Pi; Elem Edn; Teach.

**CHEAN, PONG CHUON,** Univ Of South Al, Mobile, AL; SR; BSC; Asian Student Assoc Treas/VP 90; Diploma Intl Clg Malaysia 89; Accounting.

**CHEATHAM, DAVID L,** Lincoln Univ, Lincoln Univ, PA; JR; BS; Russian Clb 88-89; Acct Clb 90-91; Hnrs Pro 88-89; Ecnmcs; Fncl Anlyst.

**CHEATHAM JR, ROBBIE S,** Univ Of Ga, Athens, GA; JR; BS; Dns Lst 90-; AA Reinhardt Coll 90; Socl Sci Educ; High Schl Tchr.

**CHEATHAM, SHANNON R,** Univ Of Al At Birmingham, Birmingham, AL; SO; MBA; Psych; Phy Thrpst.

**CHECCHI, JOSEPH C,** De Tech & Comm Coll At Dover, Dover, DE, GD, BS; Tau Alpha Pi 90-; Otstndng Grad Awrd; AAS Cmptr Eng; AAS Electrnc Eng; Cmptr Eng.

**CHEEK, JARROD W,** Clark Atlanta Univ, Atlanta, GA; SO; BA; BSU 88-90; Clg Choir 88-90; All-Amer Schlr Cllgte Awd 90-; Ftbl 88; Accntng; CPA.

**CHEEK, JASON S,** Univ Of Sc At Columbia, Columbia, SC; FR; BA; Res Hl Govt; Bsn Finance; Law.

**CHEEK, KIMBERLY A,** Univ Of Nc At Greensboro, Greensboro, NC; SO; BS; Serv Wth Dsbld Stdnts 90; Chld Dvlpmnt/Pre-Schl Ed.

**CHEEKS, ARIZONA G,** Concordia Coll, Selma, AL; GD; AA; SGA; AL Schl Offc Spprt Prsnnl; A M E Chrch YPD Dir 87-; Cert Trenholm St Tech Coll 67; Lbrl Arts; Bus Admin.

**CHEESMAN, CHRISTINE M,** S U N Y Coll At Fredonia, Fredonia, NY; SO; BA; Vol Wrk Comm 87-; Rlgs Educ Tchr 90-; Phi Alpha Theta; Stdy Abrd Ireland; Spcl Educ.

**CHEEVER, MARVELLE C,** Barry Univ, Miami, FL; GD; BA; Cert Achvmnt 90; Mssnry Scty St Luke Cousin Mem AME Chpln; AA 90; Bell South Pblshng/Advrstsng Svc Order Clrk; Business Adm; Mgmt.

**CHEEVES, REGINA C,** Comm Coll Algny Co Algny Cmps, Pittsburgh, PA; SO; BA; Deans List; Rosetta Ct Comm Enrchmnt Prgrm Pres; Cert Us Army Prevntve Med Spec 86; Nrsng; Nntl Care Nntlgy.

**CHEFITZ, DANIEL E,** Yeshiva Univ, New York, NY; GD; JD; Pol Sci Soc 87-90; Model U N Tm 88-90; Vrsty Bsktbl 87-90; BA 90; Pol Sci; Law.

**CHEGNE, PECK K,** Strayer Coll, Washington, DC; SR; BS, Dc Gama; DCIS 89; DM London Chmbr Of Cmmrce/Indstry 85; Cmptr Info Syst.

**CHELGREN, KAREN E,** Indiana Univ Of Pa, Indiana, PA; SR; BED; Oremus Pres 87-90; Elem Educ; Tchr.

**CHELL, CAROLINE M,** D Youville Coll, Buffalo, NY; GD; BSMS; Vrsty Figure Sktng 82-83; Stdnt Phy Thrpy Assn 88-90; Sr Hon Soc 89-90; Acdmc Achvmnt Awd Phy Thrpy 89; Rsrch Achvmnt Awd; Rgstrd Rsprtry Thrpst 87-; Rsprtry Thrpst 87-88; BS Univ Wstrn Ontario London Ontario 85; Cert 87; Phy Thrpy.

**CHELST, DOV N,** Yeshiva Univ, New York, NY; JR; BA; Nwspr Assoc Copy Edtr 90-; Jrnl Wrtr 89-; Math/Physics.

**CHEMAN, ERICKA JEAN FAITH,** S U N Y Coll At Fredonia, Fredonia, NY; SR; Kappa Delta Pi 90-; Pi Kappa Lambda; MENC 88-89; Kappa Delta Pi 90-; Pi Kappa Lambda; BM; Music Educ; Tchr.**

**CHEMIDLIN, CHRISTINE A,** Newbury Coll, Brookline, MA; SO; AS; Htl Mgmt.

**CHEMMANNOOR, SINDHU,** City Univ Of Ny Baruch Coll, New York, NY; SO; BBA; Clb India Treas 89-; Acctg.

**CHEN, AMANDA Z,** Cornell Univ Statutory College, Ithaca, NY; JR; BS; Clb Amrcn Scty Blgcl Sci 89-90; Extrcrrclm Cmmtt Agrcltr Coll 89-; Chns Stdn Assoc; Emrgncy Mdcl Srvc 90f; Bio Chmstry; Med.

**CHEN, AN,** City Univ Of Ny La Guard Coll, Long Island Cty, NY; SO; AS; Asst Pattrn Mkr 87-88; Cmptr Sci; Applctn Prgrmr.

**CHEN, ARJENE WANG-C-C,** Ms St Univ, Miss State, MS; JR; BA; Chns Stdnt Assn Pres 90-; Pres Schlr 89-; BA Chns Cltr Univ; Fine Art; Grphc Dsgnr.

**CHEN, CARL C,** Fl International Univ, Miami, FL; SR; BSEE; Sigma Alpha Mu 88-; Physics; Elctrcl Engr.

**CHEN, CHENG-HSIUNG,** Oh Univ, Athens, OH; JR; BS; Cmmctn/Cmptr Auto 78-87; Electcl; Engrng.

**CHEN, CHIUN HUNG,** City Univ Of Ny City Coll, New York, NY; SO; BA; ASME; Mchncl Engr; Engr Mgmt.

**CHEN, CHONG,** Univ Of Miami, Coral Gables, FL; SR; BBA; Intl Bus Assoc 90-; Tennis Clb Pres 90-; Golden Key; Beta Gamma Sigma 90; Smith Barney Intrnshp 90-; Acad Exclnc Awds 90-; Bowman ASHE Schlrshp 90-; Intl Fin/Mktg; Grad Sch.

**CHEN, CONNIE H,** Cooper Union, New York, NY; FR; BS; Soc Of Women Engrs 90-; IEEE 90-; Shinese Stdnt Assoc 90-; Elec Tengr.

**CHEN, EVELYN I,** Univ Of Miami, Coral Gables, FL; FR; Chinese Stdnt Assn 90-; Sugarcane 90-; Frnds Singapore 90-; Alpha Lambda Delta 90-.

**CHEN, FEI,** Univ Of Sc At Beaufort, Beaufort, SC; MBA; Chinese Trdtnl Mrtl Arts Assc Tres 82-84; AK Public TV Vol 89; Bsktbl/Field/Track Jinan Univ 80-84; BA Jinan Univ Guang Zhou China 84; Business Adm; Intl Trade.

**CHEN, FRANZ C,** Univ Of Miami, Coral Gables, FL; FR; BS; Chinese Assn; Elec Eng.

**CHEN, HUAN X,** Bunker Hill Comm Coll, Boston, MA; FR; BS; Cert ESL Prog Boston 90; Math/Pltcl Stdes Awd; Acctg; Acctg; CPA.

**CHEN, JULIE,** Univ Of Ga, Athens, GA; JR; BS; Asian Stdnt Union Treas 89-90; Asian Amer Stdnt Assn 90-; Dean Lst 89-; Hon Entrnc 88-89; Gntcs; Rsrsh/Gntc Eng.**

**CHEN, LI-TEH,** City Univ Of Ny City Coll, New York, NY; SR; BT; Han Wave Chns Stdnt Assn 88-; ASHRAE 87-; ASME 88-; Gldn Key 89-; Phi Theta Kappa 89-; Tau Phi Sigma 89-; Sigma Epsilon Tau 89-; Jeffrey Ballet Co 88; W A White Inst 88; Schlrshps NYCTC 86-90; Deans Lst 86-90; AAS NYC Tech Coll 88; Electro-Mech Tchnlgy; Eng.

**CHEN, LIANE H,** City Univ Of Ny Baruch Coll, New York, NY; JR; BA; Acctng.

**CHEN, MEIVILE,** Cooper Union, New York, NY; JR; Chns Stdnt Assoc; Elec Eng.

**CHEN, MICHELLE M,** Univ Of Sc At Columbia, Columbia, SC; JR; BSME; Sumphny Orchestra 88-; Alpha Lambda Delta 88-; Phi Eta Sigma 88-; Music Schlrshp; NSF Fnd For Rsrch Im Mech Engr 90; Blackmon Schlrshp Mecn Engr 89-; Engr.

**CHEN, MIKE S,** Harvard Univ, Cambridge, MA; JR; BA; House Comm Sec; House Grill Gen Mngr; House Opera Ad Mgr; Habitats/Homeless; Boston Marathon 90; New York City Marathon 90; Lghtwght Crew 88-89; Biology; Medicine.**

**CHEN, RICHARD,** Coll Of Health Sci Stony Brook, Stony Brook, NY; GD; MD; BS Stanford Univ 89; Med; Physcn.

**CHEN, SHIH-LIN L,** City Univ Of Ny Baruch Coll, New York, NY; SO; BBA; Acctnt Soc; Acctng.

**CHEN, SOON YIK,** Univ Of South Al, Mobile, AL; SO; BS; Asean Stdnts Assn 90-; Fin; Mgr.

**CHEN, SZU-WEI,** Jersey City St Coll, Jersey City, NJ; SR; MBA; Intl Stdnts Assn; Chns Stdnts Clb; Deans Lst; AA Wrld Coll Jrnlsm Taiwan 88; BS 89-; MBA/MIS.

**CHEN, VICKY H,** Cooper Union, New York, NY; FR; BS; Soc Of Women Engrs 90-; Chinese Stdnt Assoc 90-; IEEE 90-; Elec Engr.

**CHEN, WENDY FANG,** The Julliard School, New York, NY; JR; BA; CD Rcrdng Piano Soloist Grieg Schumann; Piano Concertos London Philharmonic Orch; Alice Tully Hall Lncln Ctr Debut Recital; Mozart Piano Concerto Carnegie Hall; Pres Schlrs Arts 88, Awd 1st Lvl Natl Fndtn Advncmnt Arts 88; Piano/ Cmpstn; Pianist/Cmpsr.**

**CHEN, WENXIONG,** Greenville Tech Coll, Greenville, SC; SO; AS; Natl Deans Lst 90; BA Shanghai Nrml Univ 68; Telecmnctn; Eng/Bilngl.

**CHEN, XIAOBO,** Savannah Coll Of Art & Design, Savannah, GA; GD; BA Chinese People Univ 85; MFA; Phtgrphy; Phtgrphr.

**CHEN, YANG Z,** City Univ Of Ny City Coll, New York, NY; SO; BA; Cmptr Sci; Prgmmr.

**CHEN, YANQIN,** City Univ Of Ny Baruch Coll, New York, NY; SO; BA; Finance Invstmnt; Law.

**CHEN, YIMIN,** Cooper Union, New York, NY; JR; BE; Amer Soc Cvl Engrs; Chi Epsilon Treas; Hnrs Lst 90-; Tutn Schlrshp; Cvl Engrg.

**CHEN, YONG DONG,** City Univ Of Ny Baruch Coll, New York, NY; SR; BA; NY State Soc CPA; Publ Acctg.

**CHEN, YONG Q,** Bunker Hill Comm Coll, Boston, MA; FR; AA; Frst 2nd Prize Rcpnt 91; Bnkr Hill Comm Clg; Stdnt Exhbt Cmptn; BS Foshan Tchrs Clg China 84; Lbrl Arts Cmmnctn Fine Arts; Grphc Dsgnr.

**CHEN-CHENG, HENRY,** Cornell Univ Statutory College, Ithaca, NY; FR; BA; Chess Clb 90; Adelphic Awd 90; Bio; Med.

**CHENAULT, DEBRA D,** Memphis St Univ, Memphis, TN; FR; BSN; Phi Eta Sigma; Alpha Lambda Delta; Gamma Beta Phi; Nrsng; Surgical Nurse.

**CHENEY, BRIAN C,** Manhattan School Of Music, New York, NY; FR; BM; Schl Of Music Res Pres 90-; Natl Schlr 90-; Deans Lst 90-; Singer; Opera.

**CHENEY JR, WILLIAM H,** Emory Univ, Atlanta, GA; SR; MBA; Hmbldr Mrtge Loan Ofc 85-; Bsns Admn; Mgmt Consl.

**CHENG, JENNY Y,** Lasell Coll, Newton, MA; SO; AS; Intl Stdnt Clb Treas 90-; RMTC Adv Brd Chrprsn 90-; Bus Hon 89-; Bus Admin; Mgr.

**CHENG, KING-KWAN,** Lesley Coll, Cambridge, MA; SO; BA; Asian Stdnt Clb Sec 89-90; AHANA 89-; Lesley Schlr 89-91; Erly Chldhd Educ; Erly Chldhd Tchr.

**CHENG, KWUN-TSEE,** City Univ Of Ny Baruch Coll, New York, NY; GD; BBA; Hong Kong Stdnt Assn; Finance.

**CHENG, NOLAN,** Rutgers St Un At New Brunswick, New Brunswick, NJ; SO; BA; Frshmn Clcl 89-90; Png Png Org 89-90; Swmmng 89; Phi Eta Sigma 89-; Rstrnt Mgr 87-; Cert Acdmc Achvmnt 89-990; Deans Awrd Excllnc 89-90; BA; Bus Admn; Bus Law.**

**CHENG, SU YING,** City Univ Of Ny Baruch Coll, New York, NY; SR; BBA; Goldn Key; Deans Lst 89-90; Acctg.

**CHENG, TINA J,** Cornell Univ Statutory College, Ithaca, NY; JR; BS; Horsemans Assoc Foalwatch Chrmn Pres 89-; Alpha Phi Omega Natl Co-Ed Serv Frat 90-91; Teaching Asstnt Animal Sci 265 Horses 91; Summer Intrnshp At Univ CA Animal Sci 91; Equestrian Team 88-89; Drill Team 91; Animal Science; Vet.

**CHENG, TZI YUN L,** Christian Brothers Univ, Memphis, TN; SO; BS; Intrcltrl Clb Prsdnt; Delta Sigma Pi 90-; Accntng; Bsns.

**CHENG, YIN WAI,** Capital Univ, Columbus, OH; SO; BA; ISA Tres 90-; Ecclesia Bible Stdy Pres 90-; Nrsng/Medcn; Dr.

**CHENG, YUEN,** Univ Of Tn At Martin, Martin, TN; FR; Tbl Tns 90-; Chem Engr.

**CHENNIKARA, JASMINE M,** Manhattan Coll, Bronx, NY; FR; BS; Mnrty Stdnt Un 90-; Eng.

**CHENOWETH, BARBARA L,** Prince Georges Comm Coll, Largo, MD; FR; AA; Ntl Antivivsctn Soc/Amer Antivivsctn Soc; Hnrbl Mntn Poetry Wlrd Poetry; Gldn Poet Awrd 90; Educ; Elem Tchr.

**CHENOWETH, SHIRLEY J,** Davis & Elkins Coll, Elkins, WV; SR; AS; Stu Nrs Assoc Sec/Tres 90-; Hnrs Assoc; Nrsg.

**CHERER, DEAN TALBOT,** Norfolk St Univ, Norfolk, VA; JR; BS; Physics; Sec Educ.

**CHERIAN, ANN,** Colby Sawyer Coll, New London, NH; SR; BS; Asian Stu Orgn 89-90; Key Assn 90-; Chrch Sr Chr 87-90; Adelaide Nichols Schlr 88-; Intern Clincl Obsrvr Sports Med Div Chldrn Hosp; Stu Athltc Trnr 90; Sprts Sci/Athltc Trnng; Sci Fld.

**CHERIZIEN, CLORAINE,** City Univ Of Ny Med Evers Coll, Brooklyn, NY; SO; BA; Assoc Yth Stdnts Pres 78-82; Frenc' Teach Anse-A Veau 76-80; BA Schl Of Law Gonaives Haiti 78-82; Educ.

**CHERRY, ANNETTE M,** Defiance Coll, Defiance, OH; SR; BS; Enfrcmnt Sprvsr Lucas Cnty Child Support Enfrcmnt Agncy 88-; Crmnl Just.

**CHERRY, HENRY J,** Tn St Univ, Nashville, TN; SR; BS; Gldn Key 90-; ADN Motlow St Comm Coll 80; Natural Sci; Nurse Anethesia.

**CHERRY, JACQUES J,** Tuskegee Univ, Tuskegee Inst, AL; SO; BA; Al St Assc Hlth Phys Ed Rcrtn/Dnc VP 89-; Human Dvlp Rsrch Inst Mnrty Indvdls Univ NC; Track Tm 89-90; Phys Ed; Sprts Med/Sprt Sci.

**CHERRY, KAREN A,** Emory Univ, Atlanta, GA; SR; BBA; Black Stdt Alliance Arts Comm Chr 87-; Rsdnc Life 88-; Ldr 88-; Beta Gamma Sigma; Honor Society 88-; Poynter Institute Media Studies/Journalism 87-; Marketing/Management; Research.

**CHERRY, MICHAEL W,** Memphis St Univ, Memphis, TN; JR; BA; Gamma Beta Phi; Phi Sigma Kappa Treas; Memphis Motor Sports Inc Acctg Intrnshp; Acctg; CPA.

**CHERRY, SARAH N,** O'more School Of Design, Franklin, TN; JR; BA; Stdnt Govt Arts Cmte; Graphic Arts; Freelance Illust.

**CHERRY, TARA Y,** Memphis St Univ, Memphis, TN; SO; BA; Biology; Doctor.

**CHERRY, WENDI D,** Va St Univ, Petersburg, VA; SO; BA; Textiles Apparel Merch Mngmnt Pr 90-; Big Bros/Big Sis Org 90-; Gospel Choir 89-; Reginald Lewis Schlrshp; Marching Bnd 89-90; Merch Mgmnt; Retail Buyer.

**CHERRY, WILLIAM L,** Savannah St Coll, Savannah, GA; GD; Pi Gamma Mu 90-; Crmnl Jstc; Navy/Law.

**CHERU, FENTAW MOKONNEN,** Ny Institute Of Tech Ny City, New York, NY; SR; BT; Nu Ypsilon Tau; Elec Eng Tech.

**CHERVENAK, THOMAS M,** Charles County Comm Coll, La Plata, MD; FR; AA; Bsn Admn.

**CHERY, JO ANNE,** City Univ Of Ny Queensbrough, New York, NY; SR; BBA; Data Proc Clb; Cmptr Pgm/Ofc Adm-Tech; Ofc Adm-Tech.

**CHERY, MIRLANDE,** Bloomfield Coll, Bloomfield, NJ; SR; BS; SDA Church Sinai Sabbot School Sec 87-89; E Benezer SDA Church V Pres 89-90; Acctg; CPA.

**CHESAK, DAVID P,** Univ Of Rochester, Rochester, NY; SR; BA; Phi Beta Kappa; Psi Chi; Psych/Bio; Med.

**CHESEN, KATHLEEN M,** Savannah Coll Of Art & Design, Savannah, GA; JR; BA; Drama 89-90; Poem Pblshd Natl Lbrry Of Poetry; Grphc Dsgn Artst.

**CHESNET, DAWN M,** Western New England Coll, Springfield, MA; JR; BA; Social Work.

**CHESNEY, JULIE A,** Milligan Coll, Milligan Clg, TN; JR; BS; Acdmc Affrs Comm 90-; Sprtl Life Comm 90; Hnr Code Comm Sec 90-; Cir K 89-; Delta Kappa 90-; Rcpnt Prsdntl Schlrshp 88-; SAT Schlrshp 88-; Chrch Schlrshp 90-; Deans Lst 88-; Ntnl Assn Accntnts Otstndng Schlstc Achvmnt; Accntng Bsns Admnstrtn; CPA.

**CHESNUTT, ELIZABETH M,** Saint Andrews Presbytrn Coll, Laurinburg, NC; FR; Psychlgy.

**CHESS, KARRIE-ANN D,** Central St Univ, Wilberforce, OH; SR; BSED; Elem Educ; Tch.

**CHESS, KIMBERLY A,** Va St Univ, Petersburg, VA; SR; BA; Gspl Choir Tres 86-90; Scl Wrk Clb 88-90; NY Pre Alumni Clb 86-87; Sclgy; Scl Wrk.

**CHESSER, STEPHANIE L,** Hillsborough Comm Coll, Tampa, FL; FR; BS; Biolgy; Dntstry.

**CHESSES, PAULINE,** George Mason Univ, Fairfax, VA; FR; BA; Business; Bus Admin.

**CHESTER, KAREN L,** Manatee Comm Coll, Bradenton, FL; FR; BA; English Ed; Law.

**CHESTER, RICHARD T,** Nova Univ, Ft Lauderdale, FL; GD; MBA; AICPA FICPA HFMA SACP; Cntrlr; BBA Fl Intl Univ 82; CPA St Of Fla 84; Hlth Care Damn.

**CHESTINE, STEPHANIE L,** Gaston Coll, Dallas, NC; SO; AAS; Bsn Tech; Acctg.

**CHETNIK, MATHEW R,** S U N Y Coll At New Paltz, New Paltz, NY; FR; RHSA Sec 90-; NACURH Dlgt; Hl Govt Rep 90-; IM Vlybl; Engl/Crtv Wrtng Theatre; Pblshng.

**CHETRAM, BRIAN S,** Ma Inst Of Tech, Cambridge, MA; FR; BS; Chess Clb; I M Ice Hcky Bkbl Sftbl Vybl; Info Tech; Engr.

**CHETSAS, ALEX,** Hellenic Coll/Holy Cross, Brookline, MA; FR; BA; Boston Diocese Retreats Stf/Cnslr 90-; Boston Diocese Summer Camp Pgm Staff 90; Dns Lst 90; Greek Orthodox Church Tchr 88-90; Cust Serv Rep 88-90; Religious Studies; Elem Ed.

**CHEUNG, CLARE YUN-KAM,** Newbury Coll, Brookline, MA; FR; BA; Bus Mngt.

**CHEUNG, HEALKAN,** Cooper Union, New York, NY; FR; BSE; Elec Engr.

**CHEUNG, HONGWAH DOMINIC,** William Paterson Coll, Wayne, NJ; JR; BS; Comp Soc Pres; Upsilon Pi Epsilon Sec 90-; Comp Sci; Sys Analysis.

**CHEUNG, JUN G,** S U N Y At Buffalo, Buffalo, NY; SR; IEEE 89-; Gldn Key 90-; Eta Kappa Nu 90-.

**CHEUNG, LUCIA SHUK YING,** Univ Of Sc At Columbia, Columbia, SC; FR; BA; Cock Asian Assn; Alpha Lambda Delta; Gamma Beta Phi; Dns Lst; Pres Lst; Chem Eng; Eng.

**CHEUNG, MAN Y,** Fl International Univ, Miami, FL; FR; Math; Engrng.

**CHEUNG, MARCUS K,** Coll Of Charleston, Charleston, SC; JR; BA; Math/Bus Admin; Actuary.

**CHEUNG, MUI,** Fl A & M Univ, Tallahassee, FL; FR; BS; Chem Club; Asstng FCSCM Pre Clg Progrm; Chem Tutor; Chem; Rsrch.

**CHEVEREZ, DANIEL H,** Univ Of Pr At Mayaguez, Mayaguez, PR; JR; Plnfctn Com 90-; Clcls Cmpttn; Hnr Prog 90-; Ttr Spcl Srvcs Fed Prog 90-; Math; BSEF.

**CHEVERIE, BRIAN D,** S U N Y Coll At Fredonia, Fredonia, NY; SR; BA; WCVF FM Prod Mngr 89-90; WNYF Tel Prod 90; Ethos PR Mngr; NYARNG 199 Army Band 89-; ASA Niagara Cnty Comm Clg; Comm; Grad Schl.

**CHEW, BEE SIAN,** City Univ Of Ny Baruch Coll, New York, NY; SR; Un Malaysian Stdnts Org Sec 88-90; Dance Clb 89-90; Clb Acctnts Skng Hgts; Com Mem Asia Wk 89; Beta Gamma Sigma 89-; Gold Key; Deans Lst 86-90; Beta Alpha Psi 90-; Cmnty Tax Aid; Vol Visually Impaired Stdnts; Helpline 87; Acctg.

**CHEW, CATINA L,** Memphis St Univ, Memphis, TN; FR; BA; Black Stdnt Assoc; Acctng; CPA.

**CHEW, KET-KWEN KENNETH,** Oh Univ, Athens, OH; JR; BS; Golden Key; Elec Eng.

**CHEW, SOO PETER J,** Oh Wesleyan Univ, Delaware, OH; JR; BA; Campus Prog Brd Pres 90-; Univ Film Series Pres 89-; Univ Judicial Syst Std Adv 90-; Mortar Brd Omicron Delta Kappa; Omicron Delta Epsilon Pres 90; Phi Soc Pres ; Order Of Omega Treas 90-; Pi Mu Epsilon Treas 90-; Chi Phi Sec Risk Ins Mgr 89-; Economic Mgmnt & Acctg; Invstmnt Banking.

**CHI, SUSAN K,** Univ Of The Dist Of Columbia, Washington, DC; SR; MBA; DPMA 88-90; African Stdnts Unity 87-90; Cameroon Stdnt Assc Sec 87-; Ngemba Cult Grp Fncl Sec 89-; J P Henry Awd 89-90; BA UDC 90; Humna Dvlpmnt Rsrcs.

**CHI, YU TIEN,** Central Fl Comm Coll, Ocala, FL; SO; BA; Slvr Sprngs Wldlf Prsrvtn; Acctg Cmptr; AA 90-; Bus Admin.

**CHIA, CUONG Q,** City Univ Of Ny Baruch Coll, New York, NY; SO; BBA; Chinese Assn; Mgmt.

**CHIACCHIARO, MARIA,** Georgian Court Coll, Lakewood, NJ; GD; BS; Phi Theta Kappa 84-86; Dns Schlr 89-; Stf Acctnt 90-; AS Mddlsx Cnty Clg 86; Acctng.

**CHIAPPUTI, SHARA L,** Univ Of Med & Dentistry Of Nj, Newark, NJ; SR; AA; Cert Inst Totowa 86; Dntl Hygn; Chrprctc.

**CHIARAVALLOTI, VICTORIA NINA,** Dowling Coll, Oakdale Li, NY; SR; BBA; Big Sister; Stdnt Bus Assc 89-; Deans List 88-; Bus Mgmt; Law.

**CHIARELLA, APRIL E,** Youngstown St Univ, Youngstown, OH; SO; BSE; Centurians; SAMPE 90-; Matrls Eng.

**CHICHESTER, KEITH R,** Newbury Coll, Brookline, MA; FR; AAS; Stdnt Govt Assn 90-F Radio Clb 90-; Drama Clb 90-; Media Tech; TV.

**CHICK, JANE M,** Jersey City St Coll, Jersey City, NJ; JR; BED; Cncl Excptnl Chldrn 90-; Kappa Delta Pi 90-; Spec Ed; Tchr.

**CHICK, MARTHA M,** Endicott Coll, Beverly, MA; SO; BA; House Cncl Treas 89-90; Psychology Clb; Shpmtes 89-; Phi Theta Kappa 90-; RA 90-; V A Hosp Hmls Vet Rehab Intrn; Ski Clb 90-; Psychology; Cnslng Phsy/Law.

**CHICKY, RONALD JOHN,** Worcester St Coll, Worcester, MA; JR; BA; Psi Chi; Harriet Bishop Schlrshp; Dns Lst 89-; Psychlgy/ Engl/Phlsopy; Cnslng/Tchng/Wrtng.**

**CHICOTEL, ANTHONY M,** Muskingum Coll, New Concord, OH; SO; BA; Lambda Sigma 90-; Tau Kappa Epsion Treas 89-; Wshngtn Smstr Bar Assoc Intern; Hnr Bnqt 90-; Rgby Clb; Pol Sci Engl.

**CHICOVSKY, PAMELA S,** George Mason Univ, Fairfax, VA; JR; MIS Decision Sci.**

**CHIDI, PAUL CHUKUMALINI,** Norfolk St Univ, Norfolk, VA; SR; BS; VICA Clb; Natl Tech Tchrs Assn Nigeria; Tchr; Ind/Voc Educ; Tchng.

**CHIGIRA, KUMI,** Newbury Coll, Brookline, MA; SR; ASSOC; Mgmt.

**CHIKOWORE, MARTHA J,** Marymount Manhattan Coll, New York, NY; JR; BA; Tennis; Phys Trng; Priv Sec Zimbabwe Msn 88-; Intl Bus/Mktg; MA Intl Stds.

**CHILCOTE, DON M,** Univ Of Rochester, Rochester, NY; SR; Hcky Clb 88-89; Glee Clb 90-; Biology; Bus.

**CHILCOTE JR, STEPHEN P,** Garrett Comm Coll, Mchenry, MD; SO; BA; Drm Clb 87-88; Pi Kappa Phi 87-88; Estrn Erpn Hstry.

**CHILDERS, BETH A,** Marshall University, Huntington, WV; JR; BA; Natl Stdnt Speech Lang Hearing Assoc 90-; The Gamma Beta 89-90; Speech Path/Audio.

**CHILDERS, CHRISTOPHER T,** Marshall University, Huntington, WV; SO; BA; Bsbl Otfld 89-90; Acctg.

**CHILDERS, GLENDA S,** Northwest Al Comm Coll, Phil Campbell, AL; GD; AAS; Phi Theta Kappa 89-; Offc Mgmt/ Sprvsn; Offc Admin.

**CHILDERS, GWEN M,** Western Piedmont Comm Coll, Morganton, NC; FR; AAS; Med Asstng Clb 90-; Am Assn Med Asstnts 90-; Stdnts Christ 90-; Phi Theta Kappa Alpha Gamma Mu; Med Assisting; Cert Med Asstnt.

**CHILDERS, JAMI M,** Ashland Comm Coll, Ashland, KY; FR; MBA; Bsn; Acctg.

**CHILDERS, JERI L,** Oh Univ-Southern Cmps, Ironton, OH; SR; BA; Natl Hnr Soc 88-; Stdnt Ldrshp Awd 89-90; Psychology; DHHS Clms Rep.

**CHILDERS, JOHN T,** Central Fl Comm Coll, Ocala, FL; SO; BA; Phi Theta Kappa; Science; Phys Thrpy.

**CHILDERS, KIT D,** Lees Coll, Jackson, KY; SO; Cncl 90-; Phi Theta Kappa VP 90-; AA; Jrnlsm.

**CHILDERS, LANNA J,** Ms St Univ, Miss State, MS; SO; BA; Gamma Beta Phi; Math; Educ.

**CHILDERS, MELISSA N,** Western Piedmont Comm Coll, Morganton, NC; SO; AAS; Deans Lst; Bus Admin.

**CHILDERS, REGINA NANETTE,** Northwest Al Comm Coll, Phil Campbell, AL; SO; ADN; Phi Theta Kappa 89-; Lpn Nrsng Excell Awd 89; Cert N W Al St Tech Clg 89; Sci; R N.

**CHILDERS, TERESA L,** Oh Univ-Southern Cmps, Ironton, OH; SR; Dean Lst; S S Tchr 87-; Chrch Pianist 87-; BSED; Tchng Cert; Elem Schl Tchr.

**CHILDERS JR, TERRY O,** Univ Of Ga, Athens, GA; JR; Bsbl Tm 88-; Ed Psych.

**CHILDERS, TODD D,** Memphis St Univ, Memphis, TN; SR; BBA; E MISS Jr Clg Ltr/Ftbl 84; Lcnsd Brkr/Dlr Vp; Natl Assc Brkr/Dlrs 86-90; Mrktg/Mrktg/Dist/Promtn/Sls.

**CHILDRESS, DAMALI A,** Fl A & M Univ, Tallahassee, FL; FR; MBA; OH Clb 90-; Phi Eta Sigma 90-; Kodak Schlrshp; Bus.

**CHILDRESS, DONNA JILL,** Univ Of Tn At Martin, Martin, TN; SO; BA; Peer Enblng Prgrm Pep Ldr 90-; Undrgrd Alumnicncl 90-; Ldrs Rsdnc 89-; Phi Eta Sigma VP 90-; Soc Hnr Stdnts 89-; Hnrs Smnr 89-; Pi Sigma Epsln 90-; Alpha Omicron Pi Mmbrshp Edctn 89-; Unv Srvc Awd; All Amrcn Schlr; Accntng; CPA.

**CHILDRESS, ELLEN E,** Fayetteville St Univ, Fayetteville, NC; SR; BS; Chnclrs Lst; Englsh; Tchr.

**CHILDRESS, EUGENE DAVID,** Ms St Univ, Miss State, MS; SR; BS; Inst Indstrl Engrs 87-; Soc Mfg Engrs 90-; Alpha Pi Mu 88-; Phi Kappa Phi 90-; Gamma Beta Phi 88-; Pres Lst 87-; Gr Amer Fdrl Svngs/Ln Acdmc Schlrshp 85; Univ Acdmc Schlrshp 85; Indstrl Eng; Applctn Engr.

**CHILDRESS, MICHELLE E,** Univ Of Cincinnati-Clrmnt Coll, Batavia, OH; FR; ASSOC; Comp Pgm.

**CHILDRESS, RHONDA W,** Univ Of Tn At Martin, Martin, TN; SR; BS; Chrch Of Chrst Stdnt Ctr; Deans Lst 86-90; Mu Epsilon Delta; Im Ftbl Sftbl; Hlth Care Mngmnt; Hosp Admin.

**CHILDRESS, TIFFANY L,** Meridian Comm Coll, Meridian, MS; FR; Phi Theta Kappa; Engl; Law.

**CHILDS, ALKEISHA L,** Bowie St Univ, Bowie, MD; FR; BS; NAACP 90-; Gd Srs Treas 90-; Gspl Choir 90-; Hon Rl 90; Dns Lst 90; Kappa Swthrt Pres; Bsktbl Tm 90-; Math/Educ; Tchr.

**CHILDS, CHRISTINE J,** Le Moyne Coll, Syracuse, NY; JR; BS; Lacrosse Clb 88-89; Organic Chem Rsrch 90-; Bio; Optometry.

**CHILDS, JOHN DAVID,** Nova Univ, Ft Lauderdale, FL; SR; MBA; Swtchng Srvcs Super 87; Eng 87-89; Admn 89-; BS 90; Prfssnl Mgmt.

**CHILDS, PATRICK LEE,** Nova Univ, Ft Lauderdale, FL; GD; MBA; Phi Kappa Tau Prlmntrn 68-70; Natl Hnr Soc 65-66; Mission Bay Aquatic Trg Ctr 89-; Hoosier Schlr 66; IM Sftbl/Bwlng 67-70; First Treas E Sprng Lk Hmwnrs 84-85; Stf Mgr Exec Frcst Sthrn Bell 70; BA Univ Evansville 70; Intl Bus; Dvlp/Mkt Cmptr App Prog.

**CHILDS, SANDRA L,** Elizabethtown Coll, Elizabethtown, PA; SO; BS; Cir K 89-90; Newman Cl V P 89; Campus Gold Pres 89-; SOTA 89; Alpha Lambda Delta Treas 90; Pi Theta Epsilon; Dstngshd Fresh Awd 90; Deans Lst 90; Ocuptnl Thrpy; Ocuptnl Thrpst Pediatreics.**

**CHILES, MARY BELLE,** Coll Of Charleston, Charleston, SC; JR; BA; Stdnt Alumni Assn 89-; Sigma Iota Rho 90-; Hon Pgm 88-; Harrison Randolph Schlr 88-; German; Intl Bus.

**CHILLARI, NINA L,** Wv Univ, Morgantown, WV; JR; BSW; Kappa Delta 88-; Soc Work; Psych.

**CHILTON, ANNE L,** Longwood Coll, Farmville, VA; SR; MBA; Forensics Team 89; Hnrs Prgrm 87-89; Virginia Special Olympics BS 90; Reading Spclst; Tchng.

**CHILTON, DEAN A,** Schenectady County Comm Coll, Schenectady, NY; FR; BS; Bus; Phrmcy.

**CHILTON, STACY,** Univ Of Nc At Greensboro, Greensboro, NC; SO; BS; Dtcs; Clncl Dttn.

**CHIN KIT-WELLS, MEELIN D,** S U N Y At Buffalo, Buffalo, NY; GD; DDS; Zoolgy Assc 89; Carbn Std Assc 87; Phi Beta Kappa 85-89; Beta Kappa Chi; Gldn Key; Zoolgy Dept Awd 89; Lab Asst86-89; Tchg Asst 88; Zoolgy Dept Awd 89; Schl Dentl Nrs Dist La Brea Trin 84-85; Schl Dentl Nsr Cert Govt Trin Mnstry Hlth 83; Dentl Med; Dentsry.

**CHIN, ADRIENNE,** Miami Dade Comm Coll, Miami, FL; JR; ASBA; Wrd Lgl Prcsr 86-; Certf Intl Crrspndnc Schl; Nrsng; Med.

**CHIN, CYNTHIA A,** Medical Univ Of Sc, Charleston, SC; JR; BSN; SNA; SGA; Forest Lakes Civic Clb Treas 86-; Loss Cntrl Mgr Carolina Shpng 77-89; BS Winthrop Coll 76; Nrsng.

**CHIN, CYNTHIA S,** Cornell Univ Statutory College, Ithaca, NY; SO; BA; Sigma Delta Tau; Bio; Med Schl.

**CHIN, DEANNE E,** Univ Of Sc At Columbia, Columbia, SC; FR; BA; Hatfield Mem Schlrshp 90-; Music/French; Profsnl Symphny/Orchstra.

**CHIN, DIANA S,** Providence Coll, Providence, RI; SR; BS; Yng Rpblcns 87-88; Brd Prgmmrs 88-89; Mktg; Rtl/Adv/Sls.

**CHIN, EDWARD H,** Univ Of Miami, Coral Gables, FL; SR; MD; Hnrs Stdnt Assn 88-89; Stdnt Gvrnmnt Undr Sec 88-89; Lit Magazine Edtr Brd 88-90; Gldn Key; BA; Pltcl Sci; Med.

**CHIN, HOI,** Pellissippi St Tech Comm Coll, Knoxville, TN; FR; Engr/Tchr.

**CHIN, JENNIFER F,** Manhattanville Coll, Purchase, NY; FR; BA; Nwspr; Pol Sci; Govt.

**CHIN, JENNY,** Wagner Coll, Staten Island, NY; SO; BS; Stdnts 4 Planet Earth Intrvrsty; Chrstn Flwshp; Engl Clb; Alethea; Omicron Delta Kappa; Sigma Tau Delta; Kappa Delta Pi; Zeta Delta Alpha; Elem Ed; Tchng.

**CHIN, KIN KEONG,** Univ Of Tn At Martin, Martin, TN; JR; BS; Mgmt Adm Data Systems.

**CHIN, LILLIAN,** City Univ Of Ny Baruch Coll, New York, NY; JR; BBA; Mgmt.

**CHIN, MAVA Y,** Fl Atlantic Univ, Boca Raton, FL; SR; BA; Fin Mngmnt Assn; Delta Sigma Pi Treas; Lf Ins Million Dollar Rnd Tbl 88-89; Ins Indstry; Dip/Bnkng Chartered Inst Bnkrs London 87; Bus; Fin.

**CHIN, NICOLE A,** Fl International Univ, Miami, FL; FR; Pre Med Soc 90-; Biology; Med.

**CHIN-LUE, ROLAND LINCOLN,** Univ Of Miami, Coral Gables, FL; FR; Biology; Medicine.

**CHIN-YOU, NEIL B,** Fl International Univ, Miami, FL; SO; MBA; Math; Eng.

**CHINEA, CARLO,** Univ Of Pr At Mayaguez, Mayaguez, PR; SR; BA; Formula Racing Tm Pblc Rltn S Coord; NACME Schlrshp 88-; Math; Mech Engr.

**CHING, CHAM Y,** Univ Of South Al, Mobile, AL; SO; BSC; Amer Mktg Assoc 90-; Internatl Stds Clb; Amer Pltcl Sci Assoc; Dns Lst 90-; Bsn Frtrnty; Internatl Bsn; Intl Trd/Govt.

**CHINNIS, SHANNON C,** Livingstone Coll, Salisbury, NC; SO; BS; Stdnt Govt Assn Secy 90-; Stdnt Ldr Org Pres 90-; Prayer Meeting Choir Secy 89-; Alpha Kappa Alpha 90-; Hnrs Premed Acad Baylor Clg; Minority Ldrshp Schlr; US Achvmnt Acad 90-; Cros Cntry Capt 89-; Trck/Fld Cap 89-; Biol; Obstetician.

**CHIOCCARIELLO, CARMINE J,** Daemen Coll, Amherst, NY; FR; BS; Ski Clb; Dns Schlrshp; Pres Schlrshp; Dept Schlrshp; Dns Lst; Phys Therapy.

**CHIONG, LISA J,** Oh Dominican Coll, Columbus, OH; SR; BA; Library Sci; Law.

**CHIONG, TERESITA M,** Univ Of Fl, Gainesville, FL; JR; BS; Outstndg Acad Achvmnt Awd 87; AA Miami Dade Cmnty Clg 88; Aerosp Engr.

**CHIPIWALT, ANNA A,** Va Commonwealth Univ, Richmond, VA; SR; BS; Phrmcst Tech 85-; Engr Dsgn Drftsmn 70-85; Dnc Instr 75-; Acctg; CPA.

**CHIPLEY, DI ANNA W,** Meridian Comm Coll, Meridian, MS; FR; AD; Nrsng; RN.

**CHIPMAN, KAREN L,** Dyersburg St Comm Coll, Dyersburg, TN; SO; AB; Data Prcsng Clb 89-; Phi Theta Kappa 90-; Bus; Cmptr Pgmr.

**CHIPMAN, YVONNE M,** Univ Of Pittsburgh, Pittsburgh, PA; GD; Sigma Theta Tau; Amer Red Crs Dir 85-; Natl Lgue Nurs; Nurs Edctr 67; MSN 91.

**CHIRIAC, ROXANA,** City Univ Of Ny Baruch Coll, New York, NY; SO; BBA; Intl Mktg; Bus.

**CHISENHALL, MARK A,** Univ Of Nc At Charlotte, Charlotte, NC; JR; BA; Sociology.

**CHISENHALL, MELANIE S,** Northern Ky Univ, Highland Hts, KY; SO; BA; Pltcl Sci; Law.

**CHISHOLM, ERIK D,** Fayetteville St Univ, Fayetteville, NC; FR; BS; Litrcy Prog 90-; Deans List 90-; Hnry Achvmnt Awd; Chemistry.

**CHISHOLM, LATASHA R,** Lincoln Univ, Lincoln Univ, PA; FR; BS; Laser Clb; Engrs Clb 90-; Hahnemann Univ Grad Sch Smr Rsrch Pgm Talent Mnrty Stdnt; Chem; Pharmaceuticals.

**CHISHOLM, MARIA A,** Univ Of Ga, Athens, GA; SR; PHARM; PMA 90-; ASP 90-; Phi Lamdba Sigma Pres 90-; Dns Advsr Bd 89-; Dns Lst 89-; Wall Mart Schlrshp; Allen/Hansbury Schlrshp; Rgnt Schlr; BS Georgia Clg 89; Pharm.

**CHISHOLM, TAMARA R,** Longwood Coll, Farmville, VA; SR; BSBA; Amer Mktng Assoc 90-F Delta Sigma Pi 89-; Mktng Mgt 90-; Advisory Grp; ASBA Piedmont Vl Commty Clg 89f; Busn Admin; Busn Mgt.

**CHISHTY, SHAHERYAR A,** Oh Wesleyan Univ, Delaware, OH; FR; BA; Entertainment Comm 90-; Deans List 90-; Phi Eta Sigma 90-; Omicron Delta Epsilon 90-; Var Cross Cntry Indoor Trac Outdoor Track; Economics French: Business.

**CHISLER, CATHARINE JEWEL,** Alderson Broaddus Coll, Philippi, WV; JR; BA; Bapt Campus Mnstrs Steering Cncl 89-90 88-; Chrstn Grp Support Grp Ldr 89-; Stdnt Ed Assoc 89-; Stdnt Ed Assoc Treas 90-; Cncl Except Chldrn 89-; Cnsl Except Chldrn Treas 90-; Assoc Wmn Stdnts 89-90; Clgte 4-H 88-; Elem Ed/Spec Ed SLD; Ed/Tchr.**

**CHISLEY, KARMILLA V,** Univ Of Md At Eastern Shore, Princess Anne, MD; JR; BA; Crmnl Law; Law.

**CHISM, EDDIE L,** Oh St Univ At Newark, Newark, OH; FR; BS; Hnr Stdnt 90-; Hstry.

**CHISM, JANET M,** Northeast Ms Cc, Booneville, MS; FR; BS; Deans List 90; Phi Theta Kappa 90-; Sftbl 90-; Elem Ed; Tch.

**CHISM, LARRY L,** Cheyney Univ Of Pa, Cheyney, PA; SR; BSED; Plntrm Asst 90-; Otstndng Acdmc Achvmnt Awrd 90; Assoc Indstrl Chmstry 75; Sci.

**CHISM II, WILLIAM W,** Fl International Univ, Miami, FL; SO; BS; Flyg Wrkng Arcrft; Cmpng; Hntng; Fshng; Tnns; Golf; Faculty Sholars Schlrshp 89-; Arfrm Pwr Plnt Lcns TX Aero Tech 89; Physcs; Rsrch.

**CHISOLM, ADRIENNE J,** Johnson C Smith Univ, Charlotte, NC; SO; BA; Intl Mrchng Band 90-; Pep/Cncrt Band 89-90; Hall Cncl Sntr; Nwspr Rprtr 90; Deans List 89-; Cmnctns Arts; Jrnlst/Radio Brdcstr.

**CHISTOLINI, JENNIFER L,** Merrimack Coll, North Andover, MA; FR; Law Soc Treas; Math/Chem; Envrnmntl Rsrch/Govt.

**CHITA, JULIE,** Univ Of Med & Dentistry Of Nj, Newark, NJ; JR; CERT; Spch Cmmnctn Clb 83-85; Order Omega 85; Chi Omega Pres 83-85; Otstndng Stdnt Ldrshp; BA 85; Physcl Thrpy.

**CHITWOOD, TERESA I,** Volunteer St Comm Coll, Gallatin, TN; SO; BS; Engl/Sec Educ; Tchr.

**CHIU, CHI-HUNG,** Cooper Union, New York, NY; FR; BE; Hong Kong Stdnt Assoc NY Univ 90-; Elect Engr; Engr.

**CHIU, HANG,** The Boston Conservatory, Boston, MA; FR; BM; Msc; Prfmr.

**CHIU, SUSAN A,** Ma Inst Of Tech, Cambridge, MA; FR; BS; Chinese Stdnt Clb 90-; Math Assn America 89-; Amrcn Mthmtcl Assn 8-; New York Acdmy Sci 89-90; Arsta Ntnl Hnr Soc 87-90; Archon Key Clb 89-90; Vrsty Trck 89-90; EE Appld Math; Engnrng.

**CHIZMAR, KATRINA T,** Carnegie Mellon Univ, Pittsburgh, PA; SR; BS; Assn Ind Mgmnt/Econ Pres 89-; Stdnt Advsry Cncl 90-; Bus Advsry Cncl Rep; Beta Gamma Sigma Co Pres 89-; Mrtrbd 89-; Andrew Carnegie Soc Schlr; Financial Acctng Tchg Assist; Univ Schlrshp; IM Vllybl/Bsktbl; Ind Mgmnt; Financial Cnsltnt.

**CHLOPECKI II, ALEXANDER J,** D Youville Coll, Buffalo, NY; SO; BSMS; Stdnt Assoc Treas 89-; Stdnt Physical Therapy Assoc 89-; Lambda Sigma 90-; Physical Therapy.

**CHMIELEWSKI, CAROLYN M,** Manhattanville Coll, Purchase, NY; SO; BA; Plyrs Guild VP 89-; Hnr Schlrshp 89-; Deans Lst 90-; Dnc/Theatre; Actress.

**CHO, HYUN JIN,** Anne Arundel Comm Coll, Arnold, MD; FR; Cmptr Sci.

**CHO, MIN K,** Georgetown Univ, Washington, DC; JR; BA; Fncl Mgmt Assn; Korean Stdnt Assn 89-; Frst Hnrs Dns Lst 89-; Comm Action Coalition Stf 90-; Chase Manhattan Bnk Intrnshp Fncl Analyst; Finance; Corp Finance.

**CHOATE, KIMBERLY F,** Christopher Newport Coll, Newport News, VA; SR; BA; Psychlgy Lab Asst; Psychlgy; BS Nrsng.

**CHOI, ANNIE H,** City Univ Of Ny Baruch Coll, New York, NY; GD; Cmptr Qntttv Mthds Clb 90-; Chns Stdnt Assoc Treas 86-87; SGA 86; BBA 90; Comp Info Systms.

**CHOI, DAVID,** Ny Univ, New York, NY; SO; AAS; NYU Hsng Assist Cmptr Coord 90-; Bus Mgmnt.

**CHOI, HI SUN,** Cooper Union, New York, NY; SR; BE; Korean Stdnt Assn Cooper Union 88-; Tau Beta Pi; Chi Epsilon Sec 90-; Hunter Coll Deans Lst 86; Deans Lst 88-90; Amer Soc Cvl Eng 88-; Soc Wmn Engrs 88-; Tuitn Schlrshp 88-; Gnrl Elctrc Fndtn Schlrshp; Cvl Eng; Eng.**

**CHOI, HUNN,** Asbury Theological Sem, Wilmore, KY; SR; MDN; Vrsty Sccr Kalamazoo Coll 78-79; Amer Inst Astrontcs/Aerontcs 82-88; Amer Scty Mech Engnr 82-88; BSE/MSE Univ MI 82; Thlgy/Rlgn; Smnry Tchng/Parish Mnstry.

**CHOI, HYUNG S,** City Univ Of Ny Baruch Coll, New York, NY; SR; BBA; Gldn Ky 90; Acctg; CPA.

**CHOI, JI MI S,** Marymount Manhattan Coll, New York, NY; SO; BA; Stdnt Govt Exec Brd VP 90-; Stdnt Nwspr Edtr Chf 89-; Intl Stdnts Clb Pres 89-90; Engl/Comms Arts; Telejrnlsm/Frelnce Wrtr.

**CHOI, MEI NGAN STELLA,** Bunker Hill Comm Coll, Boston, MA; FR; Wrd Prcsng; Offc Edctn Tchng.

**CHOI, MYUNG C,** Temple Univ, Philadelphia, PA; JR; BS; Korean Assoc Chf Ed 90; Golden Key; Elctrcl Engr.

**CHOI, SHEUNG F,** Long Island Univ C W Post Cntr, Greenvale, NY; SR; Chmstry Clb Sec 87-; Blgy Clb 87-; Phi Eta Sigma 87; Kapp Mu Epsilon 89-; Delta Sigma Pi Chncllr 89-; Sigma Delta Omega 90; Hmcmng Kng 90; CREC Chmstry Awrd, Dean Shclrshp 90.

**CHOICE, BRANDON K,** Clark Atlanta Univ, Atlanta, GA; JR; BA; NAACP 90-; Hmcmng Comm; Mktg Clb Pres; Yrbk Stff Org Chr 90-; Acdmc Schlrshp 89-; Un Ngro Coll Fnd Schlrshp; Top Tn Fr Males Awrd 88; Hon Roll 89-; Intrnshp; NE Fndrsr Chrprsn Phi Beta Lambda; Bus Admin; Mktg.

**CHOJECKI, DOBROCHNA M,** William Paterson Coll, Wayne, NJ; SR; BA; Polish Wmns Alliance Miss Plonia 90 80-; NJ Speech/Lang/Hrng Assn 89-; Speech Path Clb 89-90; Delta Phi Epsilon Rec Sec 88-; Adopt A Grmr Schl/Almn Fndtn 90-; Cystic Fbrs Fndtn 88-; Anorexia Nervosa/ 88-; Speech Lang Path; Ph D Comm Dsrdrs.**

**CHOLAK, RAMONA A,** Wv Northern Comm Coll, Wheeling, WV; FR; Sierra Clb Washington Cty Hmn Scty 80-; Claysville Prnt Tchrs Orgnztn 88-; Phi Theta Kappa; UVNCC Stdnt Mnth; WVNCC Acad Schlrshp; Elem Educ; Elem Tchr.

**CHOMYCZ, WILLIAM M,** Hudson Valley Comm Coll, Troy, NY; FR; AOS; Intrnshp Adams Chev; Gen Mtrs Auto Mech; Automtv Tech.

**CHON, WENDY C,** City Univ Of Ny Queensbrough, New York, NY; SO; BA; Le Cercle Francais Pres 89; Humanities Clb Sec 90; Stdnt Orient Ldrs Org 90; Phi Theta Kappa VP 90; NY Pblc Intrst Rsrch Grp 89; Nahtaly Levy Mem Schlrshp 89-90; AA; Awd Of Acad Excllnce In Frnch 89-90; Deans Lst; Ecnmcs; Tchr Of Scl Sci.

**CHONG, CAROL C,** Nova Univ, Ft Lauderdale, FL; GD; MBA; SE Soc Hosp Phrmcst; Amer Pharm Assoc; Asstnt Drct Phrmcy; BS 84.

**CHONG, FEE CHING,** Univ Of Md At Eastern Shore, Princess Anne, MD; SR; Eta Sigma Delta 90; BSC Hotel Rstrnt Mgmt; FLB Dip Crans Montana Swztrlnd 88; Hotel/Rstrnt Mgmt.

**CHONG, GABRIEL,** Univ Of Sc At Columbia, Columbia, SC; SO; Internatl Stdt Union 89-; Alpha Lamda Delta 90-; Habitat Humanity; Ltrcy Am; Cmnctn; Scl Wrk/Cnslg.

**CHONG, HYE-SIL,** Western Ky Univ, Bowling Green, KY; SO; BA; Chrstn Stdnt Fllwshp 90; Phi Eta Sigma 90-; Acctng.

**CHONG, HYUNSOO,** Radford Univ, Radford, VA; SR; BBA; Asian Assoc Pres 89-; Intl Clb 88-; Delta Mu Delta 90-; Korean Army 85-88; Mktg.

**CHONG, JIT CHEE,** Univ Of Al At Huntsville, Huntsville, AL; JR; BA; Eta Kappa Nu; Tau Beta Pi; Elec Eng.

**CHONG, KET MING,** City Univ Of Ny La Guard Coll, Long Island Cty, NY; GD; BBA; Phi Theta Kappa; Outstndng Acad Achiv Awd 90; Cert Admin Mgmt/Inst Admin Mgmt U K 83; AS Bus Admin Laguardia Comm Coll 90; Fnc/Invstmnts.

**CHONG, YEW-KEONG,** Ms St Univ, Miss State, MS; SO; BSC; MSA 90-; Gamma Beta Phi 90-; Thomas Nelson Intrnshp Prog; Elec Eng.

**CHONG, YOOJUNG K,** Rockland Comm Coll, Suffern, NY; SO; BA; Orchestra 81-89; Dns Lst 89-; Sftbl 85; AAS; English/Ecnmcs; Law Intrnatnl Bsn.

**CHONGSIRIWATANA, SONGSDHIT,** Piedmont Coll, Demorest, GA; FR; BS; Elec Eng.

**CHOO, POO DEE,** Univ Of Southern Ms, Hattiesburg, MS; SR; Cert 81; Elec Engr.

**CHOON, MARK YEW-KONG,** City Univ Of Ny Baruch Coll, New York, NY; JR; Collegiate Sci/Tech Entries Prog 87-; Cmptr Clb; Bowling 90-.

**CHOON, MICHELLE L,** Elms Coll, Chicopee, MA; SO; BA; Stndt Actvts Cmmt 89-; Cmmnctn Science Dsrdrs Clb Rep 89-; Rsdnt Cncl 89-90; Ldrshp Pin 90; Cmmnctn Science Dsrdrs; Speech Pthlgy Adlgy.

**CHOONG, VI-EN,** Allegheny Coll, Meadville, PA; SO; BS; Stdnt Govt Cncl 89-90; Math Assn Of Amer 89-; Asian Studies Hs 90-; Lambda Sigma 90-; Allegheny Vols 90-; Doane Schlr; Howard Hughes Med Inst Grant Resrch Asst; Pen Midwest Sci Cluster Math Intrhshp; Dominoes Pizza Tm Tennis Capt 90-; Physics; Engrng.

**CHOPRA, PAUL,** Birmingham Southern Coll, Birmingham, AL; JR; BS; Alpha Phi Omega Sgt At Arms 88-; Intl Stdnts 90-; Lab Asst 89-; Alpha Epsilon Delta; Beta Beta Beta; Alpha Phi Omega Srvc Awd 90-; Dns Lst 90-; NASA Spc Cmp Cnslr 88; Hosp Vol 90-; Wldlf Rescue 90-; Red Crs 90; Habitat For Hmnty 90; TA Usher Gld; Biology; Med Dr.

**CHOROCO, CAROLINA S,** Columbus Coll Of Art & Design, Columbus, OH; FR; BA; Art; Phtgrphy.

**CHOROSZY, CHERYL J,** Saint Josephs Coll, Windham, ME; GD; BS; Sprkds 88-89; Yrbk 90-; Bus Admn; Mngmnt.

**CHOT, MICHAEL LUL,** Interdenominational Theo Ctr, Atlanta, GA; JR; MASTE; Pastor Tchr; Dipl St Paul Untd Thlgcl Coll Limuru Kenya 78-80; Sociology Relgn; Pastr/Tchr.

**CHOU, WILLIAM B,** City Univ Of Ny Baruch Coll, New York, NY; SR; BBA; Asian Assn Pres 84-87; ACM 89-; IEEE Cmptr Soc; Cmptr Prgmr Anlyst 88-; Cmptr Syst.

**CHOU, YU,** City Univ Of Ny Baruch Coll, New York, NY; SO; BA; Int Mktg.

**CHOU, YU-SHU J,** Univ Of Miami, Coral Gables, FL; JR; BS; Fncng Clb VP 90-; Glf Clb 89-; Frst Aid Sqd 90-; Phi Sigma Tau Treas 90-; Alpha Epsilon Delta 90-; Rsrch; Biol; Med.

**CHOU, YUAN M,** George Mason Univ, Fairfax, VA; FR; BA; Fr Cntr 90-; Blck Stdnt Assn 90-; Dns Lst 90-; IM Ftbl 90; Intrnatl Bus.

**CHOUDHURY, WASIM K,** City Univ Of Ny Baruch Coll, New York, NY; SR; BBA; Newspapr Wrtr 90; Accntng; CPA.

**CHOUINARD, TERRENCE P,** Memphis Academy Of The Arts, Memphis, TN; FR; BFA; LA Care Art League 90-; Illstrtn; Art Educ.

**CHOUINARD, TERRENCE P,** Memphis Academy Of The Arts, Memphis, TN; FR; BFA; La Care Art Lgue 90-; Arts Rcgntn/Tlnt Srch 91 Awrd; Portfolio Schlrshp; Vlybl; Illstrtn/Grphc Dsgn; Art Ed.

**CHOW, LAI-SAU,** City Univ Of Ny Queensbrough, New York, NY; SO; BA; Orntl Scty Clb 87; Alumni Assc; Alpha Beta Gamma 87-; Cert Achvmnt; AS Queensborough Cmmty Clg; Ecnmcs; Banking.

**CHOW, MAGGIE,** City Univ Of Ny City Coll, New York, NY; SR; BE; Chinese Chrstn Fwlshp V P Treas 88-90; Math Soc; Engr Soc; IEEE Mbr 88-; Cnslr Chinese Immigrants Vol 86-87; Tch Summer Prog 88; Chinese Clgte Merit Schsp; City Clg N Y Schlrshp; Chinese Chrstn Herald Crusdrs; Engr.

**CHOW, MEI-LING,** Broward Comm Coll, Ft Lauderdale, FL; SO; BED; Elem Educ; Sci Tchr.

**CHOW, MING-HO,** Univ Of Sc At Columbia, Columbia, SC; SR; BS; Hong Kong Stdnt Assn Pres 90-; Intl Stdnt Assn 90-; IEEE 89-90; Tau Beta Pi 89-; Gamma Beta Phi 89-90; Elect/Comp Eng; Eng.

**CHOW, TAT K,** City Univ Of Ny Baruch Coll, New York, NY; JR; BBA; Chinese Chrstn Flwshp 89-90; Econ/Fnc Soc; Golden Key; Intrntl Fnc.

**CHOW, WAI WINNY,** Va Commonwealth Univ, Richmond, VA; JR; BA; Mrktng.

**CHOW-SCHUPNIK, KAREN,** Atlantic Union Coll, S Lancaster, MA; SO; BS; Clg Choir 90-; Pres Schlrshp 89-90; Merit Schlrshp 89-; Med Tech; Med.

**CHOWDHARY, AJAY K,** Barry Univ, Miami, FL; SO; Chess Clb 87-88; Bsnss.

**CHOWDHURY, SHAHNAZ P,** Bennett Coll, Greensboro, NC; SO; BS; Comp Sci Math Clb 90-; Intl Stndts Clb 89-90; Plyr Hll 90-; Bnnt Schlrs Prgm; Zeta Phi Beta; Prsdntl Schlr 89-; Elec Eng.

**CHOWENHILL, DAVID T,** Hudson Valley Comm Coll, Troy, NY; SO; BA; Cmps Radio 90-; Crdc Tchncn 88-89; New Schl Cntmpry Radio 86; Psychlgy; Psychlgst.

**CHOY, CORINNA S,** City Univ Of Ny La Guard Coll, Long Island Cty, NY; SO; AAS La Guardra; Acctng; Acctnt.

**CHOY, KIT SHAN,** S U N Y At Buffalo, Buffalo, NY; JR; BA; Stdnt Assmbly 90-; Eta Kappa Nu 90-; Phi Eta Sigma 90-; Tau Beta Pi 90-; IEEE 90-; Elec Engr/Cmptr Sci; Engr/Cmptr/Bus.

**CHRABASCZ, ERIC,** Western New England Coll, Springfield, MA; FR; ME; Eng.

**CHRABASZCZ JR, JOHN J,** Western New England Coll, Springfield, MA; SR; Fncl Mgmt Assc 87-; IM Sprts 87-; Kghts Clmbs Cncl 90-; Acad Ach Awd; BA; Fnce; Cmptr Cslt.

**CHRAIBI, MALIKA,** Comm Coll Algny Co Algny Cmps, Pittsburgh, PA; SO; AS; ARC 90; Wstrn Psychtrc Inst Clncs John Merck Pgm; Univ Pgh Chld Dvlpmnt Ctr 90; Chld Dvlpmnt/Chld Care; Bhvrl Thrpst.

**CHREBET, JENNIFER L,** Glassboro St Coll, Glassboro, NJ; SO; BA; Schl Nwsppr 89-; Stdnt Actvts Brd 89-; Cmmnctns Jrnlsm.

**CHRISANTHUS, KEITH A,** Hellenic Coll/Holy Cross, Brookline, MA; GD; MDIV; Sigma Epsilon Phi Pres 83-; Stdt Gvt VP 88-; Deans List 88-; Rho Pi Phi 87-; Orthodox Actnln Stdt Co Dir 89-; Cmps Mnstry 88-; Amer Bible Scty Awd 90; Gargas Mem Schlrshp 89; IM 83-; Amer Pharm Assc 86-; Ohio State Alumni Assc 88-; Theology; Pastoral Counseling/Priesthood.

**CHRISCO, P DAVID,** Tn Temple Univ, Chattanooga, TN; GD; Phi Psi Sigma Scty Ntl; Alpha Epsilon Theta Scty TTU; Psychology; Counseling/Teaching.

**CHRISMAN, CHAD E,** Radford Univ, Radford, VA; FR; BS; Bus.

**CHRISMAN, SANDRA L,** Radford Univ, Radford, VA; SO; Hon Pgm; Music; Bus.

**CHRIST, DIANE L,** Davis Coll, Toledo, OH; SO; AA; Stdnt Advsry Bd Chrprsn/Prmtn 89-; Pres/Deans Lst 89-; Interior Desgnr 90-; The Collaborative Inc Intern90; The Wallpaper Studio Inc Intern; Interior Dsgn; Res/Cmrcl Design.

**CHRIST, TRACY M,** Mount Aloysius Jr Coll, Cresson, PA; FR; DIPL; Srgcl Technlgst Clb 90-; Srgcl Tchnlgy; Srgcl Tchnlgst.

**CHRISTAKOS, MARIA,** City Univ Of Ny Hunter Coll, New York, NY; FR; BA; Grk Clb; Ed.

**CHRISTEN, JOHN PAUL,** Univ Of Pa, Philadelphia, PA; JR; BS; US Senate Fnce Cmte Intn 90; Fnce/Mgmnt/Pol Sci; Fncl Svcs Indus.

**CHRISTENSEN, CELESTE A,** Lexington Comm Coll, Lexington, KY; BA; Phys Asst.

**CHRISTENSEN, JARRET R,** James Madison University, Harrisonburg, VA; FR; BBA; Amnesty Intl 90-; EARTH 90-; Inter-Vars Chrstn Flwshp; Dns Lst 90; Pres Lst; Bsn Mgmt; Exec.

**CHRISTENSEN, WESLY W,** East Stroudsburg Univ, E Stroudsburg, PA; FR; BA; Hnrs Prog 90-; Math & Chem Tutor 90-; Acdmc Schlrshp 90-; Cert Of Merit Dept Of Chem 90-; Military Duth Army 3 Yrs Germany 87-90; Chem/Med Tech/Math.

**CHRISTENSON, AMY BETH,** D Youville Coll, Buffalo, NY; FR; Sg 90-; Tutor 90-; Lamda Sigma Chr Comm; RA; Elem Educ/Math; Tch.

**CHRISTIAN, ANGELA C,** Oh Univ-Southern Cmps, Ironton, OH; SR; BED; Kappa Delta Pi 90-; Deans List 88-94: Clifford E/Jean Peters Alen Schlrshp 88-90; Trumbo Schlrshp 88-90; Elem Educf Tach.

**CHRISTIAN, ANGELIA B,** Al A & M Univ, Normal, AL; SO; BS; Assn Rsrch Enlghtmnt 88-; Logistics Analyst/Cmptr Pgrmr; Untsvl Area Voctnl Tech Cntr 82; Physics/Math; Eng Physics.

**CHRISTIAN, ANTHONY D,** Comm Coll Algny Co Algny Cmps, Pittsburgh, PA; SO; BA; Engr Clb 89-; Outstndg Acad Stdnt Awd 90-; IM Bsktbl; Engr/Arch; Arch Engr.

**CHRISTIAN, CARL H,** Johnson C Smith Univ, Charlotte, NC; SO; BS; NAACP; Soup Ktchn; Mddl Sch Tutor; Hon Pgm; Deans Lst; Comp Sci.

**CHRISTIAN, CONNIE C,** Western Piedmont Comm Coll, Morganton, NC; AA; SS Teacher; Csmtlgy Prog Coordntr; Burke Acad Of Csmtc Art 84-; Bus Admin.

**CHRISTIAN, DARIC M,** Savannah Coll Of Art & Design, Savannah, GA; SO; BFA; Photo Grp Show Coord; Photo Tech At Phtgrphy Bldg; Shows At Cty Mrkt; 2 Shows At Shphrdstwn Mens Clb 90; Photogrphy; Wrkng Artst Art Prof.

**CHRISTIAN, DAVID E,** Duquesne Univ, Pittsburgh, PA; JR; BA; Acctg; CPA.

**CHRISTIAN, DIXON L,** Univ Of Md At Eastern Shore, Princess Anne, MD; Phi Beta Sigma Sec 88-89; Caribbean Clb Intl Pres 89-90; Pre Prof Socty Pre Med 90-; Phi Beta Sigma.

**CHRISTIAN, ETHYL JANE S,** East Tn St Univ, Johnson City, TN; SR; Gamma Beta Phi; Holston Conf Sec Assn 88-; Ch Pianist; Ch Sec 88-; Bus Admin; Ofc Mgr.

**CHRISTIAN, FREYA L,** Hampton Univ, Hampton, VA; SO; BS; NAACP 90; Bsnss Clb 89; African Studies Cluster 90; Tutor 90; SG 90; Accntng; Corp Law.

**CHRISTIAN, HAVEN MATTHEW,** Marshall University, Huntington, WV; JR; BBA; Fnncl Mgmt Assn; Gamma Beta Phi 89-; Alpha Kappa Psi Mstr Of Rtls 90-; Fnnce; Invstmnt Bnkng.

**CHRISTIAN, KEVIN L,** Middle Tn St Univ, Murfreesboro, TN; SO; Engl; Writer.

**CHRISTIAN, KEWANDA P,** Tuskegee Univ, Tuskegee Inst, AL; JR; BSN; Untd For Christ; Natl Nurs Hon Soc; Nrsng Award; LPN; Nrsng.

**CHRISTIAN, MARTHA J,** Birmingham Southern Coll, Birmingham, AL; JR; BS; SGA 89-90; Sthrn Chrstn Flwshp Exec Brd 89-; Nwspaper Edtr 90-; Phi Eta Sigma 89; Omicron Delta Kappa 90-; Alpha Epsilon Delta 90-; Alpha Lambda Delta 89; Pres Stdnt Serv Org 90-; Chem; Med.

**CHRISTIAN, QUINCEY J,** Fl Memorial Coll, Miami, FL; FR; BA; Bus Admn; Bus.

**CHRISTIAN, RANDY G,** Middle Tn St Univ, Murfreesboro, TN; SR; BBA; US Air Frc Accmdtn Mdl; US Air Frc Achvmnt Mdl; Inspctr Gnrl Supr Prfrmr; Two Rvrs Bptst Chrch; US Air Frc Explsv Ordnc Dspsl Spclst 83-90; Acctg; CPA.

**CHRISTIAN, TERRI L,** Lancaster Bible Coll, Lancaster, PA; SO; BS; Yrbk Editor In Chf 90-; Intl Stdnt Fllwshp Pres 90-; Conestogans 89-; Missions; Foreign Mssnry.

**CHRISTIAN, THOMAS J,** Christian Brothers Univ, Memphis, TN; FR; B CHE; Deans Lst; Amer Inst Chem Engrs; Chem Engr; Med Sch.

**CHRISTIAN, WAKULLA B,** Hudson Valley Comm Coll, Troy, NY; SR; AAS; Stdnt Gvrnmnt Sntr 90-; Crtfd Pblc Hsng Mngr 87; Bsns Admn/Mrktng.

**CHRISTIAN, WENDY A,** Fl St Univ, Tallahassee, FL; JR; BA; NSSLHA 90-; BCM 87-90-; Phi Theta Kappa 88; AA Okaloosa-Walton Cmnty Clg 89; Speech Path.

**CHRISTIANSEN, CYNTHIA L,** Hudson Valley Comm Coll, Troy, NY; SR; BS; Erly Chldhd Clb 89-; Prdsdnts Lst 89-; Elem Edctn; Tchr.

**CHRISTIANSEN, ERIC M,** Tallahassee Comm Coll, Tallahassee, FL; SO; Schl Nwspaper Opinion Editr 90-; Engl/Math; Jrnlsm/Educ.

**CHRISTIE, JERRYANN E,** Christopher Newport Coll, Newport News, VA; SR; Minority Stdnt Assoc; U S Navy; BSGA; Govt Admin.

**CHRISTIE, LORI A,** Cumberland Coll, Williamsburg, KY; SO; BA; Envir Awareness Comm 90-; Dorm Hse Cncl Flr Repr 89-90; Dns Lst 89-; All-Amer Schlr 90-; Engl.

**CHRISTIE, LYNN A,** Drew Univ, Madison, NJ; JR; BA; Chrle Mdrgl Sngrs 89-; Fntsy Gme Clb Sec 90-; Nwsppr Phto 89-; PAR Pr Cnslr 90-; Drew Schlr 89-; Dns Lst 89-; IM Bwlng Dir 89-; Engl; Wrtr.**

**CHRISTIE, MICHAEL D,** Univ Of Nc At Charlotte, Charlotte, NC; JR; BA; SG 89-; Hon Prog Pres 88-; RA 89-; Envrnmntl Endavrs 90-; Comm Ser 90-; Dsbld Stdnt Mntr 89-; MT Spkr House Intrn 90-; Pltcl Sci; City Cunty Plnr.

**CHRISTIE, MONICA E,** City Univ Of Ny Bronx Comm Col, Bronx, NY; SR; AD; 4-H Clb 77-83; Drugs Hosp/Hlth Cr Emplys Union 87-; Nrsng.

**CHRISTIE, RYAN V,** S U N Y Coll Of Tech At Frmgdl, Farmingdale, NY; SO; BA; Caribbean Stdnt Org Treas; Rsdnt Assist 90; Trk/Fld; Bsnss; Mrktng.

**CHRISTINE, CHARLES W,** Temple Univ, Philadelphia, PA; SO; IAEEE 90-; Elec Eng; Comp Applctns.

**CHRISTIS, STELLA,** City Univ Of Ny Baruch Coll, New York, NY; JR; Acctg.

**CHRISTMAS, DEBRA H,** Univ Of Sc At Columbia, Columbia, SC; SR; BA; Sc Sea 88-89; AS USC Sumter 89; Early Chldhd Educ; Tchng.

**CHRISTNER, BRUCE G,** Univ Of Sc At Columbia, Columbia, SC; FR; BA; Art Studio; Professor.

**CHRISTNER, CRYSTAL L,** Ringling School Of Art, Sarasota, FL; SR; BFA; Selby Schlrshp 90-; Freelance Artist 77-; AA Manatee Cmnty Clg 89; Illustr; Freelance Artist/Wrtr.

**CHRISTNER, CRYSTAL W,** Ringling School Of Art, Sarasota, FL; SR; BFA; 4-H Clb Asst Ldr 89; Deans Lst Manatee Comm Coll 87; Selby Schlrshp 90-; Pres Lst Rnglg Schl Art/Dsgn 90-; Free-Lnc Artst; AA Manatee Comm Coll 89; BFA Rnglng Schl Art/Dsgn; Illstrn; Wrt/Ill Chldrns Bks/Free Lnc.

**CHRISTODOULOPOULOS, CHRISTINA,** Smith Coll, Northampton, MA; SO; BA; Some Dsgn Intrnshp 90; Asstnt Set Dsgnr 90-; Theatre; Scene Dsgn.

**CHRISTODOULOU, SAVVAS E,** City Univ Of Ny City Coll, New York, NY; JR; BE; Greek Club; Eta Kappa Nu; Tau Beta Pi; Golden Key; IEEE; Elec Eng.

**CHRISTOPH, JESSICA L,** George Mason Univ, Fairfax, VA; JR; BSW; Scl Wrk Stdnt Assc 90-; Golden Key 90-; Scl Wrkr/Chld Wlfr.

**CHRISTOPHE, REVERE J,** William Carey Coll, Hattiesburg, MS; SR; BA; Pres List 90; Intrnstnl Narcotic Ofcr Assc 87-; Natl Narcotic Ofcr Assc 87-; D; Law Enfrcmnt Ofcr Fdrl Drg Tsk Frc 77-; Bus Admn; Law Enfrcmnt.

**CHRISTOPHER, BIRNEY C,** Bloomfield Coll, Bloomfield, NJ; SO; BA; Cmptr Info Sys; Prgmg.

**CHRISTOPHER, DORNIS C,** Fl Memorial Coll, Miami, FL; SO; BA; Acctg; Lawyer.

**CHRISTOPHER, GINGER A,** Univ Of Tn At Martin, Martin, TN; SR; BA; Advrtsng Mgr Stdnt Nwspr 90-; Phi Chi Theta Soc Chmn 89; Alpha Delta Pi Lil Sis Soc Chmn 89-90; PR Intrnshp Univ TN Memphis Hlth Sci Ctr; Mktg/Pub Rel; Advrtsng/Pub Rel.

**CHRISTOPHER, JILL S,** Univ Of Ky, Lexington, KY; SO; BSN; Stdnt Ath Club; Frshmn Clcn V P Worship 89-90; Phi Eta Sigma; Deans List; Nurse Anesthetist.

**CHRISTOPHER, LISA,** Franklin And Marshall Coll, Lancaster, PA; JR; Campus Tour Gde 89-; Stdnts Agnst MS Asst Sec 88-; Res Asst; Blck Pyrmd Sr Hon Soc; Charles A Pana Schlr; Alpha Phi Schlrshp Chrmn; CRC Chem Achvmnt Awd 89; Hckmn Hughes Schlr Intrn 90-; Vol Rec Awd; Chem; Dr.

**CHRISTOPHER, LISA A,** Univ Of Akron, Akron, OH; JR; BS; Gldn Key; Acctng; CPA.

**CHRISTOPHER, MARC CONRAD,** Marshall University, Huntington, WV; SO; BA; Prog Dir Unitarian Univ; Former USM Purple Hrt Vet 68; Engl/Soc Stdies; Sec Educ.

**CHRISTOPHER, MARK J,** Memphis St Univ, Memphis, TN; SO; BBA; Deans Lst 90; Fin; Invstmnts/Bnkg.

**CHRISTOPHER, MARY ELIZABETH,** Tn St Univ, Nashville, TN; GD; MA; Literary Gld Prsdnt 89-; Delta Mu Delta 89-90; Asstntshp; BS Englsh 90; Englsh; Tchr.

**CHRISTOPHER, PATRICIA C,** Cecils Coll, Asheville, NC; SO; Literacy Assoc; Acctng; Computer Sci.

**CHRISTOPHER-STRAYHORN, ROBERT,** Howard Univ, Washington, DC; JR; BARCH; Amer Inst Arch Stdnts 90-; Amer Heart Assoc Chrmn/Fndrsng 89; BACA Mntr 90-; Hakan Corley Assoc Intrn; Plng Dept UNC Med Sch Intrn 90; Water Polo Chrmn Coach 89-; Arch.

**CHRISTOU, ANTHOULA STEPHANOU,** Jersey City St Coll, Jersey City, NJ; JR; BA; Intl Org 90-; Prfsnl Nrs Clb 90-; SEA 90-; BED Nrsng Schl Cyprus 89; Nrsng; Tchr.

**CHRISTOU, PETER A,** Villanova Univ, Villanova, PA; FR; BA; Mrchng Band 90-; Pep Band 90-; Jazz Ens 90-; Dns Lst 90-; Pol Sci; Law.

**CHRISTY, JANE Y,** Cumberland County Coll, Vineland, NJ; SO; BA; Nwsppr Edtr 89-; Stdnt Senate 90-; Phi Theta Kappa Tres 90-; Latin Amrcn Clb 89-90; Wmns Clb Pres 66-; Chmbr Fo Cmmrc 89-90; Cmbrlnd Cnty Mntl Hlth Brd Sec 87-; Am Hrt Fnd Sec 87-; Mc Schrnk Co Sec 56-66; Drchstr Shpbldng Corp Sec 66-68; Cmmnctns/Lbrl Arts; Pblc Rltns.

**CHRISTY, NOEL L,** William Jennings Bryan Coll, Dayton, TN; FR; BS; Hilltop Players; Prctcl Chrstn Invlvmnt; Elem Ed; Tchr.

**CHRISTY, SCOTT M,** Univ Of Scranton, Scranton, PA; SO; BA; Sec House Govt Sec 90-; Humn Res Assn 90-; Univ Tour Guide 90-; Res Asst; Mgmt Acctg; Acctnt.

**CHRISTY, STEWART E,** S U N Y Coll At Fredonia, Fredonia, NY; SR; BA; Deans Lst 88-; Psychlgy; Cnslng.**

**CHROMCZAK, TERESA M,** Le Moyne Coll, Syracuse, NY; SR; Orient Cmmttee; Proj In Cmmnty Vol Tutor; Pre-Law Cmmttee; Clg Newspapr; Brd Dir For Clg Radio Vrsty Chrldr Engl Clb Pblcty Dir 89-90; Chrldr 88; Pblc Rltns Intrn Wth Depart Of Scl Serv; Engl; PHD In Engl.

**CHROMY, JENNIFER E,** Savannah Coll Of Art & Design, Savannah, GA; SO; BFA; Drama Clb 90-; Intr Dsgn; Comm Dsgn.

**CHRONISTER, JAMES B,** Univ Of Pittsburgh, Pittsburgh, PA; FR; BS; Cncl 90-; Ski Clb; Phi Eta Sigma 90-; Tennis; Engr; Mtrl Sci.

**CHRSITOPHER, DWAYNE L,** Morehouse Coll, Atlanta, GA; FR; BS; Pac West Clb; Deans List; Pol Sci; Law.

**CHRYSOSTOMOU, ANDREAS COSTA,** City Univ Of Ny Baruch Coll, New York, NY; JR; BBA; Hllnc Soc Sprvsr 88-; Acctg Soc 89-; Beta Gamma Sigma; Gldn Key; Alpha Beta Psi; St Dmtrs Orthdx Chrch Yth Clb 88-; Grk Cyprt Stdnt Assn Pres 88-90; Endwmnt Fund Prvsts Schlrshp 88-; Deans Lst 88-; LCC Acctg London Chmbr Cmmrc 86; Actncy; CPA.**

**CHRZAN, LAWRENCE J,** Comm Coll Algny Co Algny Cmps, Pittsburgh, PA; SO; BS; AS; AS 90; Indstrl Eng.

**CHRZANOWSKI JR, FRANCIS A,** Ursinus Coll, Collegeville, PA; SR; BS; USGA Exec Jdcry Brd 89-; Brdwd Chem Soc 87-; Brwnbck Andrs Premed Soc Tres 87-; Cub/Key 89-; Beta Beta Beta 88-; Phi Lambda; Sigma Xi; Mu Epsilon Rho 87-; Merck Awrd; Deans Lst 87-; Intrnshp Mcneil Cnsmr Prods Co 89-; Swmg Capt 87-; Chem; Med.

**CHU, ANDREW K,** Cooper Union, New York, NY; JR; BS; Tau Beta Pi; Eta Kappa Mu; Var Bwlng Capt 89-90; Elec Eng.

**CHU, CHENG L,** George Mason Univ, Fairfax, VA; SO; Chinese Stdnt Assn Treas 90-; Pre Bus; Accnt.

**CHU, CHIA LIN,** Ma Inst Of Tech, Cambridge, MA; FR; B; Bio; Med.

**CHU, CRISTINA L,** Dartmouth Coll, Hanover, NH; FR; BA; Tae Kwon Do Clb 90-; Cttn Awd 90.

**CHU, EDDIE,** City Univ Of Ny City Coll, New York, NY; JR; BA; Archtctr.

**CHU, JEANNY C,** City Univ Of Ny Baruch Coll, New York, NY; JR; Gldn Key; Alpha Beta Psi; Acctg Cpa.

**CHU, MEI F,** Univ Of North Fl, Jacksonville, FL; SO; BA; Acctng.

**CHU, WAN TAO ARVID,** Univ Of Akron, Akron, OH; JR; BS; Hng Kng Stdnt Assoc VP 89-; Amrcn Scty Mchncl Eng 89-; Scty Autmtv Eng 89-; Gldn Key; Mchncl Eng.

**CHUA, CHEE THIAN,** Univ Of Al At Huntsville, Huntsville, AL; SR; BS; Foon Yen Alumni Assoc; Tau Beta Pi; Eta Kappa Nu; Elec; Elec Engrg.

**CHUBB, KRISTINA L,** Memphis St Univ, Memphis, TN; SO; Univ Singers 90-; MENC 90-; Music Ed; Teacher.

**CHUE, SUSAN E,** Fl International Univ, Miami, FL; JR; BS; AA So Fla Comm Clg 90; Physical Education; Teaching.

**CHUI, WAI YEE,** Ithaca Coll, Ithaca, NY; FR; BS; IM Bsktbll 90-; Athltc Trnng; Trnr.

**CHUMLEY, SUSAN CAROL COY,** Ky St Univ, Frankfort, KY; SO; ASN; Mercer Cnty Elem Schl PTO Pres 86-89; Mercer Co High Schl Academic Bstr Clb; Sec 74-79; Hlth; Nrsng.

**CHUN, ANDERSON,** City Univ Of Ny La Guard Coll, Long Island Cty, NY; SO; BSEE; Math; Engr.

**CHUN, CARLOS J,** Nyack Coll, Nyack, NY; JR; BS; NU Rocks; Deans Lst; Yth Mnstry.

**CHUN, ELLEN E,** Smith Coll, Northampton, MA; SO; KASS Soc Chrm 89-90; Vllybl Capt 90-; Phlsphcl Soc; Frst Grp Schlr 90-; Intern Kim Chang Lee Intl Law Frm Korea; Crew 89-90; Vrsty Vllybl 90-; Phlsphy/Anthrplgy; Law.

**CHUNG, CLAUDINE C,** Fl International Univ, Miami, FL; FR; BA.

**CHUNG, JEAN,** Univ Of Sc At Columbia, Columbia, SC; FR; BA; Carolina Pgm Un Video Cnnctns/Cltrl Arts Comm 90; Adv/Jrnlsm; Adv Exec.

**CHUNG, KATY W,** Univ Of Sc At Columbia, Columbia, SC; FR; BS; Asian Amer Assn 90-; Marine Sci; Marine Blgst.

**CHUNG, KIRK M,** Nova Univ, Ft Lauderdale, FL; GD; MBA; BSCE/BSCS Univ Of Miami 87.

**CHUNG, KITIKORN,** Univ Of Sc At Lancaster, Lancaster, SC; FR; BSE; Hnrs Soc V P Elect; Deans List; Comp; Engrng.

**CHUNG, MANH HUNG,** Fl St Univ, Tallahassee, FL; SR; BS; Radio Club; IEEE; Hnr Soc; SWE; Rgnt Schlrshp Fund 88-90; AA Tallahassee Cmnty Clg 90; Elctrcl Engr; Engr.

**CHUNG, WILLIAM Y,** Columbus Coll Of Art & Design, Columbus, OH; FR.

**CHURA, CONNIE M,** Mount Aloysius Jr Coll, Cresson, PA; FR; AS; Phi Theta Kappa; By Scts Amer Parent Vol 89-; Hotel Rest Mngmnt; Cert Comm Nrsng Srvc 79; Hotel Rest Mngmnt; Fd Srvc Mngmnt.

**CHURCH, DAVID A,** East Tn St Univ, Johnson City, TN; SO; BA; Chamber Choir 89-; Mens Ensemble 89-; Cmptr Sci; Acctg.

**CHURCH, DESTA A,** Memphis St Univ, Memphis, TN; GD; BSET; Soc Mfg Engrs Sec 88-; Soc Wmn Engrs; Univ Sngrs/Vocal Jz Ensmbl 88-90; Goldn Key 88-; Phi Eta Sigma 87-88; Miss Mphs St Univ 89-90; Outstndng Sr Awrd 90-; Mfg Eng; Eng.

**CHURCH, KEVIN BRENT,** Oh St Univ At Newark, Newark, OH; SO; Cmptr Info Sci; Cmptr Grphcs/Sftwr Dsgn.

**CHURCH, ROBERT G,** Dowling Coll, Oakdale Li, NY; JR; BS; Fnd Mbr LISAICU; Mgr Clg Radio; Orntn Ldr; Limba Schlp; Pres Hnry Schlp; Cmptr Sci; Cmptr Prgm.

**CHURCHILL, BRIAN S,** Bunker Hill Comm Coll, Boston, MA; FR; BA; Sclgy; Law Enfrcmnt.

**CHURCHILL, VESTA J,** Memphis St Univ, Memphis, TN; SR.

**CHURCHWELL, BARBARA G,** Chattahoochee Vly St Comm Coll, Phenix City, AL; SO; BA; SGA 90-; Gamma Beta Phi; SS Tchr Phil Bptst Chrch 90-; Preschl Chr Dir 90-; Elem Ed; Tchg.

**CHURCHWELL, JEFFERY L,** Chattahoochee Vly St Comm Coll, Phenix City, AL; FR; BA; Stdnt Govt Assoc 90-; PA Bapt Chrch Choir Mbr 88-; Swift Txtl Ind Supv 90-; Maint Cert Colmbs Tech Voc Sch 87-88; Bsns Supv/Mgmt; Uppr Supv Mgmt.

**CIACCI, DAVID C,** Case Western Reserve Univ, Cleveland, OH; FR; BS; Wrstlng 90-; Matrl Sci/Eng.

**CIAFONE, JOHN JOSEPH,** Ny Univ, New York, NY; SR; BA; Pre-Law Soc 90-; Mock Trial Clb 90-; Debate Tm 90-; Speech Tm 90-; Chamber Deputies 90-; Phi Beta Kappa 90-; Pi Sigma Alpha 90-; Alpha Kappa Delta 90-; Omicron Delta Epsilon 90-; Dns Circle 90-; NYM Schlr 90-; Pres Circle 90-; Pol Sci/Econ; Lawyer-Judge.**

**CIAGLO, TERRI A,** Western New England Coll, Springfield, MA; FR; Rsdnc Lf Pres; Vrsty Bsktbl/Sftbl; Law.

**CIAMACCO, ANTONELLA TERESA,** Immaculata Coll, Immaculata, PA; JR; BA; Modern Foreign Lang Assoc Treas 88-; Ed Clb 89-90; Italian Cultural Soc 88-; Sigma Delta Pi 89-; Immacalata Clg Hnr Soc 89-; Dns Lst 88-; Spnsh; Intl Bsn.

**CIAMPA, LISA A,** Memphis St Univ, Memphis, TN; SO; BS; Treas Agnt Fdrl Exprss Corp; Dipl Taylor Inst 85; Educ/Elem; Tch.

**CIANCETTA, JOSEPH B,** Wv Northern Comm Coll, Wheeling, WV; FR; BA; Phi Theta Kappa; Lector 88-91; Acctg; Acctnt.

**CIANCI, NORIE A,** Univ Of Nh Plymouth St Coll, Plymouth, NH; JR; BS; NAA; Rugby 90-; Deans Lst 89; Pres Lst 90; Myrtle Grover Schlrshp; Acctng; CPA.

**CIANCI, STEPHEN R,** Widener Univ, Chester, PA; SR; MBA; Tutor Ec/Calculus 89-90; Phi Eta Sgm 87-; Omcrn Dlt Epsln 89-; Alpha Chi; Phi Kappa Phi; Natl Ftbl Fndtn/Clg Hall Fame Schlr Athlt Awrd 90; Ftbl 87-; BS Mgt; Mdl Atlntc Conf Hon Roll 89 90; Acad All Amer Nominee 89 90; Fin; Prfsnl Money Mgt.

**CIANCIO, JOCELYN D,** Endicott Coll, Beverly, MA; SR; ASSOC; Bsnss Clb 89; Stdnt Orient Ldr 90; Shpmtes Clb 90; Phi Thetta Kappa 90; Intrnshps Marths Vineyrd Co-Op Bnk 90; Nom For Pres Awd; Bsnss Admin; Bnkng.

**CIANCIOLA, BARBARA A,** Immaculata Coll, Immaculata, PA; JR; BA; Immaculate Hon Soc 90-; Psychlgy; Elem Ed.

**CIANI, MICHAEL A,** Methodist Coll, Fayetteville, NC; SO; BA; Rsdnt Advsr; Ambssdr; Bsebl; Phy Ed; Admin.

**CIARAMELLA, TERRI A,** Duquesne Univ, Pittsburgh, PA; SR; Acdmy Stu Phrmcy 89-; Rho Chi Hstrn Chrmn 50th Annvrsy Com.

**CIARCO, SHAUNA,** Seton Hall Univ, South Orange, NJ; JR; BS; Natl Cncl Tchrs Engl; Kappa Delta Pi 89-90; Stdnt Tchg Intern 89-; Ed/Engl; Elem Tchr.**

**CIARICO, ROBIN E,** Duquesne Univ, Pittsburgh, PA; SR; Alumni Rltns Tm 89; Lambda Sigma Pres Advsr 89-; Beta Alpha Phi 90-; IM Vlybl Capt 87-90; Sftbl; BS/BA; Mktg; Wstnghse Purch Dept.

**CIBIK, ERIK C,** Duquesne Univ, Pittsburgh, PA; FR; BS; APHA 90-; NARD 90-; Phrmcy Schlr 90-; Deans Lst 90-; Phrmcy.

**CICCO, TONINA,** Saint Johns Univ, Jamaica, NY; FR; BA; Business; Mrktng/Real Estate.

**CICH, LISA A,** Univ Of Akron, Akron, OH; JR; BSCHE; Amer Inst Chem Engrs VP 87-; Alpha Gamma Delta Chrmn 88-; Air Prdcts/Chem Intshp; Chem Engr; Env Engr.

**CICHANOWSKY, MARKO,** Temple Univ, Philadelphia, PA; SR; BS; PA Scty Hosp Pharm Treas 89-; Phi Delta Chi 89-; Rho Chi 90; US Navy Rsrvst Persian Gulf/War Duty Dec 90; IM Vlybl 89-; Pharm.

**CICILEO, CURT J,** Univ Of Louisville, Louisville, KY; SR; MENG; ASCE 89-; Wght Clb; Tau Beta Pi 89-; Internshps; 2M Rcqtbll Sftbll; AAS Bes:; Cvl Eng.

**CIESLINSKI, BRIAN E,** S U N Y At Buffalo, Buffalo, NY; GD; Archtct Grdt Stdnt Assc Pres 90-; Admssns Cmmt Schl Archtct 89-; Tchng Asst Schl Arch 90-; AM Inst Archt Stdnts 87-; Tchng Asst Schl Archt 90-; AAS Arch SUNY Alfred 87; BPS Marc SUNY Buffalo 89-; Arch; Archtct.

**CIESONES, RONALD A,** Western New England Coll, Springfield, MA; SO; BA; Fin Clb 90; Mktg Clb 90; Alpha Lambda Delta 90-; Bus; Acctg.

**CIESZYNSKI, JEFFREY E,** Schenectady County Comm Coll, Schenectady, NY; FR; AAS; SG 90-; Elec Tech Clb 90-; Scty Mnfg Engs Schlrshp 90-; A Dabul Achvmnt Awrd 90-; US Nvy Elecs Tech 89; Wlts Elec 90; Elec Eng Tech; Elec Eng.

**CIGLER, JODI M,** Univ Of North Fl, Jacksonville, FL; FR; BA; Bus; Acctg.

**CIHAN, NERKIZ,** City Univ Of Ny John Jay Coll, New York, NY; JR; BA; Am Tutor Assn Treas 87-; Intrnshp Queens Supreme Ct; Legal Studies; Law.**

**CILANO, KRISTEN A,** S U N Y Coll At Fredonia, Fredonia, NY; SR; MA; Stdnts Stdnts Sec 89-90; Fredonia Hamburg Teach Intrnshp 90-; BS Ed; Lib Sci Edn; Teach.

**CILLAN, MARCIA L,** Georgetown Univ, Washington, DC; JR; BA; Georgetown Pgm Bd Mrktng Chr 90-; Mrktng Scty 89-; ALEEEC Accnt Exec 89-; Delta Sigma Pi VP Alumni Bnfts 89-; Gamma Phi Beta Pldg Pres 88-89; Tutor 89-90; Intl Yth Hall Fame Intl Prjct Crdntr 90-; MD Prfrmng Troupe; Intl Mgmt/Mrktng; Intl Business Law.**

**CILLES, BERNADETTE DEIS-DE,** Edison Comm Coll, Fort Myers, FL; SO; BA; Pi Nu Epsilon Corr Secr 73-75; St Andrews Church CCD Tchr 89-; Univ Hosp Wmns Aux/Vol 85-86; Tchr/Bilingual Tutor 87-; AAS SUNY ATC 75; AA 90; Early Chldhd/Elem Ed; Tchg.

**CILYOK, CARLA J,** Western Ky Univ, Bowling Green, KY; JR; BSBA; Fnce; Corp Fnce.

**CIMAGLIA, BRIDGET E,** S U N Y At Binghamton, Binghamton, NY; FR; BS; Tutrng 90-; Econ; Mktg Rsrch.

**CIMINO, GLORIA J,** Cumberland County Coll, Vineland, NJ; SO; BA; Math; Tchng.

**CIMINO, JOSEPH B,** Le Moyne Coll, Syracuse, NY; SO; BS; Acctg Soc 90-; Bus Clb 90-; Jos A Ciminio Food Brkrs Inc Intrnshp; Vrsty Lacrosse; Acctg Econ; CPA.

**CIMINO, SCOTT,** S U N Y Coll Of Tech At Frmgdl, Farmingdale, NY; JR; BE; AS 90; Mech Eng.

**CINQUANTO JR, LOUIS A,** Embry Riddle Aeronautical Univ, Daytona Beach, FL; SO; BS; Aero Sci; Prof Aviation.

**CINQUEMANI, KAREN,** Wagner Coll, Staten Island, NY; JR; BS; Nwpr Wrtr 89-; Actvts Brd 90-; Telephone Fndrsr 90; Omcrn Dlt Kappa VP 90-; Alethea Sec 90-; Beta Beta Beta VP 90-; Alpha Sgm Omega Ltl Sis Tres 88-; St Vincents Med Ctr; Lab Asst; Cmps Comm Chest Chrty Orgnztn 89-90; Acad Schlrshp; Bio; Medcn.

**CINQUINA, ANTHONY R,** City Univ Of Ny Baruch Coll, New York, NY; JR; BBA; Cmptr Info Sys; Analyst.

**CINTRON HERRERA, MARIA M,** Inter Amer Univ Pr Hato Rey, Hato Rey, PR; GD; Gum Laude; BBA.

**CIOCCA, HOLLY A,** Temple Univ, Philadelphia, PA; SO; BED; AS Spec Tech Art Inst Phila 88; Sec Ed/Hstry; Tchr/Clg Prof.

**CIOCI, AMANDA S,** Bay Path Coll, Longmeadow, MA; SO; BA; Deans Lst 90; Sftbl 90; ASS; Bus Admin.

**CIOFFI, LORRAINE A,** Hudson Valley Comm Coll, Troy, NY; FR; Sci; Dentl Hygiene.

**CIPOLLA, KRISTA-ANNE,** Niagara Univ, Niagara Univ, NY; SO; BA; Hstry; Tchr.

**CIPRIANI, FAITH A,** Schenectady County Comm Coll, Schenectady, NY; FR; BA; Clnry Arts; Chef.

**CIRILLO, MARIA V,** Duquesne Univ, Pittsburgh, PA; SO; Pitt Band 90; Pre-Health Soc; Phi Eta Sigma 90-; Biology; Medicine.

**CIRNE, EUNICE A,** Bloomfield Coll, Bloomfield, NJ; SO; Stdnt Ambssdrs 89-; Stdnt Alumni Assn Pres 89-; Stdnt Ldrshp Prog 89-; Nwspr Co-Edtr 90-; Mntrshp Prog 90-; Pltcl Sci; Law.

**CIRONI, JENNIFER LYNN,** Univ Of Cincinnati, Cincinnati, OH; SO; BN; Emerging Ldrs 89-90; Navigators Bible Study Ldr 90-; Gampus Crusade Christ 89-; Deans List; CURE 90-; Benjaman Pilhashy Schlrshp; Nursing; Medicine.

**CISSE, FATOUMATA,** Benedict Coll, Columbia, SC; SR; BS; Intl Stndts Assoc 88; Natl Stdnt Bus Lg Treas 90; Alpha Chi; Phi Beta Lambda 90; 1S Agncy Intl Dvlpmnt Schlrshp 89-; Bus Admn.

**CISZ, MARK MICHAEL,** Cornell Univ Statutory College, Ithaca, NY; SR; BS; RA 90-; Cornell Demcrts Treas 89-; Nwspaper Treas 90-; Marion A/A Leon Fellow Shp Fund 90; Bruce A Failing Sr Bus Pln Award 90; Dorman Fmly Bus Cnsltng Award 90; Appld Econ/Bus Mgt/Fin; Bus/Fin.

**CISZEK, MICHAEL J,** Univ Of Rochester, Rochester, NY; SO; BS; Phi Kappa Tau Rsh Chrmn 90-; Elec Eng.

**CITARELLA, LILLIAN I,** Fl International Univ, Miami, FL; SR; BA; Ftr Edctrs Amrca; Kappa Delta Pi; Kappa Delta Pi 89-90; Offc Sec VP Sec 90-; Hnrs Cncl Prsdnt VP Assn Cncl; KDP Bk Drv Chrmn 90-; Adopt Trp Comm Exec Brd 90-; Clg Edctn Movie Prty Fndrsr Chrmn 90-; Otstndng Prtcptn Awd Achvmnt 89-; Erly Chldhd Admnstrtn Edctn.

**CITY, VELISCIA E,** Univ Of Southern Ms, Hattiesburg, MS; SR; BA; Rsdnc Hall Assn 88-89; Hall Cncl Sec 88-89; Yng Dmcrts 88-89; Coop Educ Intrnshp 90-; IM Sftbl 87-89; Psychlgy; Scl Wrk.

**CIUFFO-BYRNE, MARIANNE,** Newbury Coll, Brookline, MA; SO; AS; MA Prlgl Assoc 90-; Grl Scts Dsy Ldr 90-; Phi Theta Kappa 79-80; Deans Lst; MA Real Est Lcnse 84-; Glr Scts Amrc Dsy Ldr; Tchr Aid; Tlmrktr; Cstmr Srvc; ; Prlgl Stds; Cmmnctns Law.

**CIULLA, JULIE,** Merrimack Coll, North Andover, MA; SR; BS; Deans Lst 89-; Uprclssmn Acdmc Schlrshp 89-; Bus Admin; Hmn Rsrces Admin.

**CIUNCI, ADRIENNE L,** Widener Univ, Chester, PA; JR; Soc Advncmnt Mgmnt VP Spkrs 90-; Acctg Soc 89-; Phi Sigma Pi Hist 90-; Deans Lst; Merit Schlrshp; Acctg.

**CIVIELLO, THERESA M,** Merrimack Coll, North Andover, MA; SO; Amer Mrktng Assoc; Sigma Phi Omega; Ims Sprts Bsktbl.

**CLABAUGH, LYNNE M,** Central Pa Bus School, Summerdale, PA; FR; ASB; Brkaway Wkend Ldr Advtsng; Vybl 90-; Bus Mgmt; Small Bus Mgr.

**CLABOUGH, JOHNATHAN D,** Univ Of Al At Huntsville, Huntsville, AL; JR; BSE; Mech Engr; Engr.

**CLABOUGH, JONATHAN D,** Univ Of Al At Huntsville, Huntsville, AL; JR; BS; Mech Engr; Engr.

**CLABOUGH, SUZANNE E,** Univ Of Tn At Knoxville, Knoxville, TN; SR; BA; MCA Records Intern; Brdcstg; Music Bsn/Record Industry.

**CLAGER, JENNIFER L,** Univ Of Dayton, Dayton, OH; FR; BA; Scty Wmn Eng 90-; Xmas Cmps Vol 90; Hnrs Pgm 90-; Cercona Intern; IM Scr/Bsktbl 90-; Dayton Wmns Sccr Tm 90-; Engnrng; Chem Eng.

**CLAGGION, LINDA Y,** Norfolk St Univ, Norfolk, VA; GD; First Yr Tchr Of Yr.

**CLAIBON, ROSEMARI L,** Al St Univ, Montgomery, AL; SR; JD; Alpha Kappa Alpha; Nws Rptr Anncr 89-; BA; Law.

**CLAIR, BARBARA,** Fl International Univ, Miami, FL; JR; BS; Jr Wmns Clb; Nwcmrs Alumn; Paralgl Assoc Reg Sls Mgr; AA Broward Comm Clg 90; Elem Educ/Erly Chldhd Spec; Tchr.

**CLAIR, GINETTE M,** Univ Of Fl, Gainesville, FL; JR; BA; Hnrs Inst Bcc 88-90; Hghst Hnrs BCC 90; AA Broward Cmnty Clg 90; Acctg; CPA.

**CLAMP, BECKY J,** Univ Of Sc At Columbia, Columbia, SC; SO; BA; Phi Eta Sigma 90-; Pres List 90-; Acctg; CPA.

**CLANCY, JOHN J,** Univ Of Rochester, Rochester, NY; SR; BS; ASME 89-; Dir Greek Affairs 90; Alumni Task Force; Deans Lst 90; Pledge Cls; Delta Kappa Epsilon Pres 88-; Mech Eng Rsrch Asst; IM Bsktbl/Ftbl/Sftbl 87-; Mech Eng.

**CLANCY, PHYLLIS A,** Wilmington Coll, New Castle, DE; SR; BSN; Deans List; Head Nurse; Nursing; Nursing Administration.

**CLANCY, THERESA A,** Duquesne Univ, Pittsburgh, PA; JR; BA; Bus Mrktg; Sales Ads.

**CLANZY, GREGORY L,** Morgan St Univ, Baltimore, MD; SR; BS; Alpha Epsilon Rho Spc Asst To Adv 90-; WEAA FM Radio Intrnshp 90-; Mgr; Telecomm; Radio News/Talkshow.

**CLAPP, MAUREEN F,** Univ Of Cincinnati, Cincinnati, OH; JR; BS; Kappa Delta Pi; NAEYC; U S Army Reserves Sgt 79-; Sel F Employed; Early Chldhd; Tchr.

**CLAPPER, MICHELLE L,** Fairleigh Dickinson Univ, Teaneck, NJ; FR; Res Life Cncl; Rookie Year 90-; Hnrs Lst/Dns Lst 90; Vars Vlybl/Sftbl; Marine Bio/Envrmntlst.

**CLAPPROOD, KELLI L,** Univ Of Miami, Coral Gables, FL; FR; Sigma Delta Tau 90-; Psychology; Dvlpmntl Psychologist.

**CLARE, MARILOU S,** Oh Univ-Southern Cmps, Ironton, OH; JR; BA; Gamma Pi Delta 89-; AA; Sociology; Soc Svcs.

**CLARK, ALICE MICHELE,** East Carolina Univ, Greenville, NC; SR; BME; MENC 87-; Gamma Beta Phi 87-88; Pi Kappa Lambda 90-; ECU Marshall 89-90; Music Ed; Tch.

**CLARK, ALISON L,** Casco Bay Coll, Portland, ME; SR; BS; Natl Scty Pblc Acctnt; Acctg; Tax Prprtn.

**CLARK, AMANDA STRONG,** Middle Tn St Univ, Murfreesboro, TN; SO; BA; Spec Sls Rep; Ownr Socks Plus 90-; Mktg; Sls.

**CLARK, ANGELA D,** Oh St Univ, Columbus, OH; FR; BS; Stdnt Alumni Cncl 90-; Almuni Schlr Grtr Cincinnati 90-; Univ Hon Soc 90-; Delta Delta 90-; Biochem; Rsrch.

**CLARK, ANNE ELISE,** Western Ky Univ, Bowling Green, KY; SR; Bptst Stdnt Un Pres 88-; Beta Beta Beta 90-; Res Hall Assn Asst 89-; Phi Kappa Phi; Univ Hon Prog 88-; Outstndng Sr Spnsh Stdnt 90-; WKU Equstrn Team; H S Truman Schlrshp Nominee 90-; Biochem; Vet Med.

**CLARK, APRIALE H,** Catawba Valley Comm Coll, Hickory, NC; FR; BA; Stdnt Govt Sen 90-; Gamma Beta Phi; Educ Erly Chldhd; Tchr.

**CLARK, BARBARA MARIE,** Owensboro Jr Coll Of Bus, Owensboro, KY; SR; AS; Med Office/Cmptr Office.

**CLARK, BARBARA S,** Bristol Univ, Bristol, TN; SR; BS; Stdnt Actvty Comm Pres 88-90; Draughons Junior Clg; Stdnt Of The Quarter Award 89; Bsn Admin.

**CLARK, BENDIK L,** Univ Of Nc At Asheville, Asheville, NC; SR; BS/BA; Hnrs Prgrm; Hrst Llms Pr 90-; IM Sftbl/Ftbl; Envrnmntl Sci; Blgy; Tchr.

**CLARK, BENJAMIN ELROY,** Northwest Al Comm Coll, Phil Campbell, AL; GD; Dsl Mechs.

**CLARK, CATHERINE A,** Eastern Ky Univ, Richmond, KY; FR; AS; Bapt Stdnt Union 90-; Nrsg; Nrsg-Med.

**CLARK, CHARITY R,** Elmira Coll, Elmira, NY; FR; BA; Sftbl 90; Hist; Hotel Mngmnt.

**CLARK, CHERYL L,** William Carey Coll, Hattiesburg, MS; SR; BS; Hnrs 90-; Elem Edctn; Tchr.

**CLARK, CHRISTOPHER L,** King Coll, Bristol, TN; GD; BA; AA Tri Cities St Tech Inst 83; Busn/Econ/Acctg.

**CLARK, CIMBERLIE D,** Winthrop Coll, Rock Hill, SC; JR; BS; Accntng Clb; NAA; Chi-Omega 88; Accntng; CPA.

**CLARK, COLLEN,** Univ Of Fl, Gainesville, FL; SR; BHS; Shands Hosp Neo Natal Int Cr Prnt Sprt Grp 85-; Stdnt Occup Ther Assoc 89-; PN Class Sec 76-78; Santa Fe Schlr 89; Golden Key; Princeton House Intrnshp; Uprch Pavilion Intrnshp; Early Intervntn Ctr; AA Santa Fe Cmnty Clg 89; Occup Ther.

**CLARK, CYNTHIA H,** Univ Of Al At Birmingham, Birmingham, AL; SR; BS; Ohio Sta Univ Ski Clb; Cystic Fbrsis Cmp Friends Inc 87-90; Elpha Chi Omega Exe Panhellenic Delgte 88-89; Bapt Mem Hosp; Pro Rehab; Occptnl Thrpy.

**CLARK, DANIEL G,** Univ Of Tn At Martin, Martin, TN; SO; BE; IEEE; Phi Eta Sigma 90-; :Us Achvmnt Acdmy All Amrcn Schlrs 90-; Coop Jcksn Utlty Dvphi Kappa Phi Cert; Natl Coll Eng Awrd 90; Elec Eng.

**CLARK, DAVID M,** Marshall University, Huntington, WV; SR; BA; Acctng Clb 90-; WVSCPA 90-; Acctng.

**CLARK, DAVID R,** Bellarmine Coll, Louisville, KY; JR; BA; Soc Hmn Rsc Mgmt 89-; Ldrshp Educ/Dvlpmnt 89-; Pres Ldrshp Soc 88-; Bsn Admn; Law.

**CLARK, DAVID S,** Va Commonwealth Univ, Richmond, VA; JR; BA; School Of The Arts Student Show At The Anderson Gallery; Painting & Printmaking Sculpture; Owner Oper.

**CLARK, DEBBIAN JECCIO,** City Univ Of Ny Med Evers Coll, Brooklyn, NY; Coll Thtrcl Assoc 89-; Math Natrl Sci Clb 90-; Dean Lst 90-; Blgy; Gynclgst.

**CLARK, DEBORAH E,** Le Moyne Coll, Syracuse, NY; JR; BS; Delta Mu Delta; NY State Notary Public 88-; AAS Canton Agri Tech Coll 85; Acctg.

**CLARK, DELNITTA M,** Wilberforce Univ, Wilberforce, OH; SR; BA; Acctg.

**CLARK, DOUGLAS B,** Radford Univ, Radford, VA; SO; BA; Outdoors; Hnrs Prog 89-; Art; Tchng Bus.

**CLARK, DOUGLAS H,** Cumberland County Coll, Vineland, NJ; SO; AAS; Phi Theta Kappa 90-; Ornamental Horticulture; Lndscp Horticulture.

**CLARK, DRENA E,** Univ Of Sc At Columbia, Columbia, SC; SR; Psi Chi 88-90; AS Univ South Carolina Lncstr 89; BS 90; Psychlgy.

**CLARK, EDITH SAMANTHA,** Winthrop Coll, Rock Hill, SC; JR; BS; Natl Ed Assn Sec 90-; Kappa Delta Pi; Alpha Lambda Delta 89-; Elem Ed; Tchng.

**CLARK, EDWARD S,** Western Piedmont Comm Coll, Morganton, NC; SO; AA; Acdmc Pwr Lftrs Assn VP 90-; Bus Mgmt; BS/PHYSCL Ftnss.

**CLARK, ELIZABETH A,** Radford Univ, Radford, VA; SO; RV Hons Prog 89-; Sftbl 89-90; Info Sys; Comp Mgt.

**CLARK, ETHEL J,** Meridian Comm Coll, Meridian, MS; FR; DECA Treas 90-; MS Htl Mtl Cnvntn 90; Hlpng Eldrly Cmnty; Hgh Hnr Awds; Asst Cnclmns Lnchn 90; Cnslr Advsry Cmte; Olympc Fst; Rstrnt Htl Mgmt.

**CLARK, EVA M,** East Tn St Univ, Johnson City, TN; FR; Math/Spnsh Tutor 90-; Math/Spnsh Tutor 90-; Soccer 90; Biomed Engr.

**CLARK, GAIL I,** Va Commonwealth Univ, Richmond, VA; JR; BSN; Emer Nrses Assoc; Beta Sigma Phi; ADN Casper Clg Casper Wy 81; Nrsng.

**CLARK II, GARY D,** Ashland Comm Coll, Ashland, KY; SO; BA; Phi Beta Lambda 89-90; AA; Bus; Acctg.

**CLARK, HOLLY A,** Le Moyne Coll, Syracuse, NY; SO; Stdnt Sen Dorm Repr 90-; Acctg Soc 90-; Hnrs Pgm 90-; Edward M O'donnell Medal 89-90; Le Moyne Acad Schlrshp 89-; Dns Lst 89-; IM Vlybl/Bsktbl/Soccer 89-; Acctg; CPA Bsn Law.

**CLARK, IRVIN R,** Fl A & M Univ, Tallahassee, FL; SR; BS; Poltcl Sci Club 87-89; Ftbl Co-Capt 87-; Poltcl Sci; Law Schl.

**CLARK, JACQUELINE D,** City Univ Of Ny Med Evers Coll, Brooklyn, NY; SO; Caribbean Amer Stdnts Assoc Treas 89-; Medgar Evers Theatrical Assoc Treas 90-; Medgar Evers Acctg Clb NABA; Dr Mattie Cook Mem Schlrshp Awd; Dns Lst 89-; Certif Acad Achvmnt 90; Acctg/Finance; CPA.

**CLARK, JACQUELINE D,** Oh Univ-Southern Cmps, Ironton, OH; JR; BAS; Dns Lst 89-; Psych/Soclgy; Clin Psychgst.

**CLARK, JACQUELYN L,** Tuskegee Univ, Tuskegee Inst, AL; SO; BS; AIEHE 89-; NSBE 90; NOBCCHE; Brstl Myrs Sqbb Coop Eng 90-; NALME Schlrshp Rcpnt 90-; Dns Lst Hnr Rll 89-; IM 90; Chem Eng; Rsrch And Dev.

**CLARK JR, JAMES E,** Me Maritime Academy, Castine, ME; FR; BA; Stdnt Govt VP; Vrsty Ftbl 90-; Pwr Eng Technlgy; Eng.

**CLARK, JAMES P,** Univ Of Louisville, Louisville, KY; JR; BS; Sthrn Indiana Tbl Tnns Assc 89-; Vly Chpl Plyr Chrch Pnst 88-; Systm Oprtr Saber BBS Sysop; Cooperative Intrnshp Inf Systms Dvlpmnt 91; Intrntl Dcmnt Adtr Untd Prcl Svc 88-90; Inf Sci/ Data Prcsng; Systms Anlyst.**

**CLARK, JANE S,** Western Ky Univ, Bowling Green, KY; SO; BA; Delta Sigma Pi 90-; Acctg; CPA.

**CLARK, JANETT O,** Mary Holmes Coll, West Point, MS; FR; ASSC; Dns Lst; Hnr Lst; Elem Educ Tchr.

**CLARK, JASON G,** Haverford Coll, Haverford, PA; FR; BS; Vrsty Bsktbl; Math.

**CLARK, JASON G,** Univ Of North Fl, Jacksonville, FL; JR; BA; Grnpce 90-; Wrld Wldlfe Fndtn 90-; UNF Dns Lst 90; FCCJ Dns Lst; AA FL Comm Coll At Jacksonville 90; Lit; Film Drctn.

**CLARK, JEAN E,** Univ Of Southern Ms, Hattiesburg, MS; SR; BA; AA Jones Co Jr Coll 89; Socl/Rehab Serv.

**CLARK, JENNIFER L,** Daytona Beach Comm Coll, Daytona Beach, FL; FR; BS; Vol Vk Cedar Hse Juv Boys; Psych; Clncl Psych.

**CLARK, JENNIFER R,** Univ Of Al At Birmingham, Birmingham, AL; JR; BA; Stdnt Occptnl Therapy Assc; Occptnl Therapy Svc Com; Mntn TOP Staff Mbr; AL Mntl Hlth Spcl Interest Sctn; IM Sftbll/Vlybll; Occptnl Therapy; Rgstrd Occptnl Therapist.

**CLARK, JODI P,** Univ Of Miami, Coral Gables, FL; JR; BS; Bio Clb; Alpha Epsilon Delta; Golden Key 90; Ntl Hnr Scty 90; Pres Hnr Roll; Deans Lst; Bio Chem; Med.

**CLARK, JOELLEN L,** Widener Univ, Chester, PA; FR; Vrsty Bsktbl 90-; Chmstry; Engrg.

**CLARK, JONATHAN RAYMOND,** Georgetown Coll, Georgetown, KY; SO; BS; Pres Hs Assn VP; Flwshp Chrstn Athlts 89-; Bnd 89-; Alpha Lambda Delta Pres 90-; Beta Beta Beta Scl Chrmn; Amer Chem Soc 90-; W I Lewis Memrl Schlrshp; Blgy; Med.

**CLARK, JOSEPH W,** Morehouse Coll, Atlanta, GA; FR; BA; NAACP Pres 90-; Hon Prog Rcrdg Secret 90-; M L K Jr Intl Chpl Asst 90; Philosophy; Law.

**CLARK II, JUDE J,** Fl A & M Univ, Tallahassee, FL; SR; BA; BA; Physical Therapy.

**CLARK, KAREN L,** Franklin And Marshall Coll, Lancaster, PA; SO; BA; Hbtt Hmnty Pres 89-; Hlng Arts Clb 89-; Ttrng 90-; Sght Snd 89-; Blgy; Mdcl.

**CLARK, KAREN N,** Emory & Henry Coll, Emory, VA; FR; BS; Fr Hons Schlrshp 90-; Julian Brown Schlrshp 90-; Creed Fulton Schlrshp; Chem; Res.

**CLARK, KARIN J,** Univ Of Cin R Walters Coll, Blue Ash, OH; SO; AA; Bus.

**CLARK, KATHLEEN M,** Cumberland County Coll, Vineland, NJ; AAS; Advsry Comm 90-; Phi Theta Kappa 90-; Anatomy/ Phys Tutor 89-90; Outstdng Stdnt 90-; Hlth Sci/Radiography; Spec Proc Tech.

**CLARK, KATHLEEN VIRGINIA,** Central Fl Comm Coll, Ocala, FL; FR; AA; Tchr.

**CLARK, KATHRYN A,** Ms St Univ, Miss State, MS; SR; BA; Pres Schlr 90-; Ed; Tchr.

**CLARK, KATHRYN ANN,** Tn Temple Univ, Chattanooga, TN; SR; AA; Hghlnd Pk Bptst Church; Sign Choir; Summa Cum Laude; AA TN Temple Univ; AS George Washington Univ; Sign Lang Interpretation; Intrprt Ed.

**CLARK, KELLY L,** Elmira Coll, Elmira, NY; SR; BS; Radio Station Scrtry 87-90; Speech/Hrng Tchr Cert Speclztn; Tchr.

**CLARK, KENNETH J,** Univ Of Hartford, West Hartford, CT; FR; BS; Ski; IM Sports; IEEE; Pres Acad Schlrshp; Deans Lst; Crss Cntry/Trck; Cmptr Eng.

**CLARK, KENNETH R,** Sc St Coll, Orangeburg, SC; SO; Gnltmn Soc Clb 90-; FCA 90-; Pres Schlr Awrd Slv Mdl; Bus Hnr Rll 89-; Dean Lst 89-; ASCS Ag Prog Asst Intern; Vrsty Ftbl 89-; Agrbsnss; Bus Govt Mngmnt.

**CLARK, KENYON H,** Univ Of Nc At Asheville, Asheville, NC; SO; BS; Phi Eta Sigma; Elctcl; Music.

**CLARK, KERRY L,** Western Ky Univ, Bowling Green, KY; SR; BS; Kntcky Pub Hlth Assn Mbrshp Chr 90-; Flwshp Christian Ath 90-; Phi Eta Sigma 87-88; Gldn Ky 89-; Phi Kappa Phi; Ogden Schlrshp Ogden Schl 89-; Pres Schrlshp 88; Dns Scholav 89-90; Dns Lst 87-90; Comm Hlth; Epidemiology.

**CLARK, KIM ANN,** Boston Univ, Boston, MA; SR; BS; Occptnl Thrpy/Wrk-Rltd Prog/Assmnts Athr K Jacobs/Title Hm Bsd Emplymnt; Occptnl Thrpy.

**CLARK, KIMBERLY M,** Auburn Univ At Auburn, Auburn, AL; SR; AL/NATL Educ Assn 89-; Natl Cncl Tchrs Of Math 89-; AL Cncl Soc Studies 90-; Phi Theta Kappa 88-; Pi Lambda Theta 89-; Phi Kappa Phi 90-; SUSJC Vllybl 88; Sunday Schl Tchr; Youth Cncl; BS 90; Scndry Educ/Math/Hist; Tchr.

**CLARK, KRISTEN E,** Columbia Union Coll, Takoma Park, MD; JR; BS; Vlybl Clb Co-P 88-89; Cum Laude; Tch-A-Kid 89-90; Vlybl Clb Co-P 88-89; Hlth Ftnss Mgmt; Admin Hosp.

**CLARK, KRISTIN M,** Bowling Green St Univ, Bowling Green, OH; SO; Sat Morn Rcrtn Prog Stu Dir 90-; Alpha Lambda Delta; Phi Eta Sigma; Kappa Delta Act Chrmn 90-; Hghst GPA Pldg Kappa Delta Sor 90; IMS; Sprt Mngmnt; Mrktng/Sprts.

**CLARK, LEANNE,** Glassboro St Coll, Glassboro, NJ; GD; BA; Engl Hnr Soc 88-90; Engl.

**CLARK, LISA,** Indiana Univ Of Pa, Indiana, PA; SR; BED; Elem; Tchr.

**CLARK, LISA G,** Radford Univ, Radford, VA; FR; BA; Cmnctns; Pblc Rltns.

**CLARK, LISA M,** Univ Of Cincinnati, Cincinnati, OH; SR; Eta Sigma Gamma; Dns Lst 90-; Hlth; Hlth Ed.

**CLARK, LYNETTE C,** Tn St Univ, Nashville, TN; SR; Univ Clg Cmptr Clb Sec 87-89; Plyrs Gld Hstrn 88-; Cmps Pblctn Edtr 87-90; Hnrs Pgm 88-; Soc Prof Jrnlst 88-90; Alpha Kappa Alpha VP 89-; TN Leg Intshp Pgm; BS; Spch/Comm/Theatre; Pblc Rltns.

**CLARK, MADONIA A,** Fl St Univ, Tallahassee, FL; SO; BS; AA Gulf Coast Cmnty Clge 90; Elem Ed; : Teach Elem Ed.

**CLARK, MARIA G,** Rivier Coll, Nashua, NH; FR; BA; Bridal Consltnt Julies Timeless Tradtns Nashua NH 88-; Elem Tchr.

**CLARK, MARY ANN,** Univ Of Miami, Coral Gables, FL; FR; BA; IM Sports 90-; English Criminal Justice; Law.

**CLARK, MARY M,** Cumberland Coll, Williamsburg, KY; JR; BA; Stdnt Admsns Stf 89-; Lamp Yrbk Stf 90-; Coll Theatre 90-; Sigma Tau Delta Sec/Hstrn 90-; Engl; Pblshng/Edtr/Lit Agnt.

**CLARK, MATTHEW H,** Duquesne Univ, Pittsburgh, PA; JR; BA; Mortar Brd Sect; Phi Alpha Thota; Alpha Phi Omega Pres; Alpha Phi Omega Pres; Duquesne Univ Vlntr 90-; Deans List 88-; Duquesne Univ Miu Var Swing Captn 89-; History/Criminal Justic.

**CLARK, MELESA A,** Oh Univ, Athens, OH; JR; BFA; STYLE Pres; UAL Secty; Pi Beta Phi Art Rep 88-; Design Promtional Flyers L Bnd 89-; Assist Gallery 90-; Studio Art; Busn.

**CLARK, MELINDA A,** King Coll, Bristol, TN; SR; Acctg.

**CLARK, MELISSA L,** Westminster Coll, New Wilmingtn, PA; SO; BA; Soc Comm Panhel 90-; Stdt Gvt; Phi Mu Asst Rush Chr 90-; Business Administration.

**CLARK, MICHAEL J,** Bowling Green St Univ At Huron, Huron, OH; FR; BA; Soc Of Mfg Eng; Alpha Lambda Delta; Ntl Hnr Soc; In Top 10% Of Class 90; Elctrcl Eng; Eng.

**CLARK, NANCY J,** Central St Univ, Wilberforce, OH; JR; Fin/Invstmnt Soc VP; Clg Bus Ambssdrs Clb Pres; Vllybll; Hnrs Clb; Deans List; Penney Drv For Hmlss Sec; Walk A Thon/Homeless Sec; Intrnshp Gen Elec Arcrft Engns Auditing Dept; Acad Athlt Vlybl; Acad Athlt/Yr; Finance; Law/Corp Lawyer.

**CLARK, OTELIA S,** Norfolk St Univ, Norfolk, VA; GD; Tidewater Child Care Assoc; VA Early Chldhd Assoc; Natl Hdstart Assoc; Cum Laude 90; STOP Assoc 72-; S E Tidewater Opport Proj Inc 72-; CDA Certif Univ MD 79; BS ECE 90; Early Chldhd Ed; MA.

**CLARK, PATRICIA A,** Ms St Univ, Miss State, MS; JR; BS; Mss Hm Econ Assoc Vc Chr90-; Hm Eco Clb Treas 88-; Army ROTC Sctchgrd Pres 88-90; Hll Cncl 89-90; Stdnt Assoc Intr Dsgnrs 88-; Delta Gamma Asst Art Chrmn88-; Lambda Chi Alpha Lttl Sstr; Stdnt Spprt Srvcs 88-; Otstndng Achvmnt Awrd MHEA Vc Chr; Hm Econ Intr Dsgn; Intr Dsgn.

**CLARK SR, PAUL BROWN,** Coppin St Coll, Baltimore, MD; JR; BS; Essex Cmnty Clge Deans Highest Hnr 89; Assoc Art With Honors 89; Mgmnt Sci.

**CLARK, PAULA-LYNN,** Barry Univ, Miami, FL; SO; BS; Barry Buccaneer Bsnss Mgr 90; Advnced Scuba 90; Barry Dncelne 89-90; Aquanaut In Undrwtr Rsrch Expdtn 90; Bio; Envrnmntl Marine Sci/Vet Med.

**CLARK, PEGGY J,** Life Coll, Marietta, GA; GD; Chiropractic Tech RT ACRRT.

**CLARK, PEGGY M,** Norfolk St Univ, Norfolk, VA; SR; BA; Soc Clb 86-90; NAACP 87-90; Alpha Kappa Delta 88-90; Cmnwlth Intrnshp Attny Ofc; Hon Rl 87-88; Cum Laude; Sociology; Grad Schl.

**CLARK, R RUSTY,** Northwest Al Comm Coll, Phil Campbell, AL; SO; Bsbl 89-; Math & Sci; Secndary Ed.**

**CLARK, RICHARD P,** Columbus Coll Of Art & Design, Columbus, OH; JR; BFA; Pres Lst 90-; Deans Lst 88-89; Fine Art/Illus; Chldrns Book Writing.

**CLARK, RICHARD T,** City Univ Of Ny City Coll, New York, NY; FR; BA; Anthroplgy; Anthrplgy/Academic.

**CLARK, ROBERT A,** Providence Coll, Providence, RI; JR; BA; Deans Lst 88-; Hist; Law.

**CLARK, ROBERT N,** Suffolk Comm Coll Eastern Cmps, Riverhead, NY; SO; BS; Crpntr/Cnstrctn Wrkr 86-89; Biochem; Rsrch Sci.

**CLARK, ROSE M,** Middle Tn St Univ, Murfreesboro, TN; SR; BS; SHEA 87-; THEA 87-; AHEA 87-; Intrnshp Mdl Tn Med Ctr Cnslr 90-; Vlybl/Sftbl 89-; AD David Lipscomb Univ 84-86; Soc Wrk/Fmly/Cnsmr Stds.

**CLARK, RUTH E,** Al A & M Univ, Normal, AL; GD; Mrktng Clb 87-90; Pres Schlr Scty 89-90; Phi Beta Lambda Pres 89-90; Delta Sigma Theta 89-; BS 90; Mrktng.

**CLARK, SANDRA S,** Savannah St Coll, Savannah, GA; SO; BS; Bd Of Trustees Of Young Life; Kindrgrtn Tchr; Elem Ed.

**CLARK, SCOTT M,** Rutgers St Un At New Brunswick, New Brunswick, NJ; FR; BS; Phi Eta Sigma 90-; Elec Eng.

**CLARK, SHANNON K,** Fl Coll, Temple Terrace, FL; SO; BS; ARETE 89-; CRST Sec 89-; YWTO 89-; Pi Gamma Chapt Phi Theta Kappa Pres 89-; Acdmc Awd Bio 89-90; Acdmc Awd Chem 90-; Deans List Every Sem 89-; Med Lab Sci; Scientist.

**CLARK, SHANNON R,** Univ Of Sc At Aiken, Aiken, SC; FR; Bus Admin; Mktg.

**CLARK, SHARIN J,** Univ Of Nc At Greensboro, Greensboro, NC; SR; Jazz Dance Troupe 87-88; Resid Hall Council VP 89-90; Staff Edtr Nwsltr 89-90; Alpha Phi Alpha Swthrt Court; Neo-Black Scty 87-88; Bluford Elem Schl 90; IM Vlybl Tm 87; BS 90; Education; Tchr.

**CLARK, SHELAGH R,** Midway Coll, Midway, KY; SO; AA; Hrse Patrl 89-; Phi Theta Kappa 89-; Grl Scts Ldr 89-; Explrers; Mdway Coll Equstrn Team 89-; Equine Mgmt; Frstry.

**CLARK, SHERYL L,** Va St Univ, Petersburg, VA; SR; NAACP; Publ Adm Clb Secr 87-; ROTC; VA Cncl Hmn Rights Intern 90; VA State Water Contr Bd Intern 90-; Vlybl; BS VA State Univ; Publ Adm; Law/Crim Just.

**CLARK, SHIRLEY L,** Va Highlands Comm Coll, Abingdon, VA; RN; Nrsng.

**CLARK, STEVEN B,** East Tn St Univ, Johnson City, TN; SR; BS; Assn US Army; Phi Kappa Phi 89-; Gamma Beta Phi 88-; Gen Geo C Marshal Ldrshp Awd; Engr Tech Fclty Awd; Engr Tech; Aviation Offcr.

**CLARK, SUSAN M,** Univ Of Southern Ms, Hattiesburg, MS; SR; MBA; Gldn Key; Phi Kappa Phi; Beta Gamma Sigma; Beta Alpha Psi Treas 90; Chevron Flwshp; John Palmer Grad Fllwshp; MBA Assc; BS 90; Pblc Acctng.

**CLARK, TANYA N,** Clark Atlanta Univ, Atlanta, GA; SO; BA; Engl Clb 90-; Outrch Comm Chr 89-; Hons Pgm; Outrch Comm Chr 89-; NAACP 89-90; UNCF Andrew W Mellon Pgms Flwshp 90-; Engl, Tch Coll/Wrt Chldrns Books.

**CLARK, TED J,** Catawba Valley Comm Coll, Hickory, NC; FR; AAS; Journeyman Book Bndr Mchn Oprtr R R Donnelley/Sons 90; Rec Grnds Mgt; Entrprnr.

**CLARK, TERESSA L,** Oh Univ-Southern Cmps, Ironton, OH; SR; BSED; Dns Lst 89-; Elem Educ; Schl Psychlgst.

**CLARK, THOMAS M,** Embry Riddle Aeronautical Univ, Daytona Beach, FL; SR; BS; Dns Lst; Arntcl Stds; Cmrcl Plt.

**CLARK, TRACEY L,** Fl Inst Of Tech, Melbourne, FL; JR; BAEE; SWE Sec 89-; IEEE 88-; Instrmntl Eng Intern Com 89-; Elec Eng Intern Octaphone; St Awrds Archtrctr 87-89; Elec Eng.**

**CLARK, TRACI M,** Anne Arundel Comm Coll, Arnold, MD; FR; Vol Time At Severna Pk Sr High 90; Art; Dsgn.

**CLARK, TYRONA E,** Fl A & M Univ, Tallahassee, FL; SR; BA; English Lit Gld; Pub Adrs Ancr 89; Bkbl Tm 88-; Big Bro/Big Str; Vybl Capt 89-; English; Lit Prfsr.

**CLARK, VALERIE ANN,** Saint Joseph Coll, West Hartford, CT; SO; BA; Fishers Island Yth Cmtee 90-; French/Russian; Ele Sch Tchr.

**CLARK, VALERIE MARIE,** Hillsborough Comm Coll, Tampa, FL; SO; BA; HELP 90-; State Rep Jim Davis; Phi Theta Kappa 90-; Pblc Rltns/Pltcl Sci; Crprt Law.

**CLARK, VELISA D,** Howard Univ, Washington, DC; GD; Alpha Kappa Alpha 70-; Englsh Grad Asstntshp 76-78; Aids Tsk Frc; MA 74; BA William Carrey Clg 72; MARS 90; Rlgs Stds; Englsh Lit.

**CLARK, VICKIE L,** Univ Of South Al, Mobile, AL; JR; BE; AICHE 90-; SWE 89-; Tau Beta Pi; Phi Eta Sigma 89-; Alpha Lambda Delta 89-; Chem Eng.**

**CLARK, VICTORIA M,** Christopher Newport Coll, Newport News, VA; JR; BA; Momitary Awrd Otstndg Dntl Asstnt Wrkg US Army 87; Dntl Asstnt 78-88; Cert Dntl Asstnt 78; AA 90; Psych; Clncl.

**CLARK, WENDY M,** Abraham Baldwin Agri Coll, Tifton, GA; SO; Science; Physcl Thrpy.

**CLARK JR, WILLIAM B,** Cumberland Coll, Williamsburg, KY; FR; BA; Mrchng Band 90; Cncrt Band; Jazz Band 90-; Bptst Union 90-; High Hons 90-; IM Sports 90; Rlgn; Evnglsm.

**CLARKE, AMY J,** Le Moyne Coll, Syracuse, NY; JR; BS; Dns Lst 89-; Bio; Physician.

**CLARKE, ANNA M,** Univ Of The Virgin Islands, St Thomas, VI; SR; Sigma Stars Club 87; Caribbean Assoc 85-90; NASW 89; Zeta Phi Beta Grmmts 89-90; SW Hosp Soc Wrk Intrn 89-90; BSW Clark Atlanta Univ 90.

**CLARKE, BEVERLY A,** Livingston Univ, Livingston, AL; SR; BS; Stars AL Dance Line 88-90; Ltl Sis Red Rose 87-; Psy Clb 90-; IM Sftbl; BS; Sclgy; Scl Wrk.

**CLARKE, CHARLES O,** Piedmont Tech Coll, Greenwood, SC; SO; AS; Phi Theta Kappa 90-; Outstndg Grad Eng Grphcs; Ftbl/Sftbl 89-; Eng Grphcs Tech; Cvl Arch Eng.

**CLARKE, CHERYL A,** Univ Of Toledo, Toledo, OH; GD; JD; Black Law Assn VP 89-; Lgl Ethics Assn Chr 89-; Wmn Law Assn 90-; Dns Lst 90-; Toledo Law Review Edtr 90-; Stdnt Bar Assn 89-; Dean Srch Comm 90-; MADD 84-; NAACP 78-; Crdntr Alt Sntncng Las Vegas Mncpl Ct 84-89; BS Rchstr Inst Tech 76; Law.

**CLARKE, IAN C,** Fl A & M Univ, Tallahassee, FL; FR; BS; NSBE 90-; Noncmsnd Ofcrs Assoc 88-; Phi Eta Sigma VP; Army Natl Grd 90-; Dns Lst 90-; Army Cmndtn Mdl 90; Army Achvmnt Mdl 88; Ftbl; Elctrcl Engrg; Engr.

**CLARKE JR, JAMES R,** Alfred Univ, Alfred, NY; SO; BS; Tae Kwon Do Clb 90-; Amer Crmc Soc 90-; Alpha Lambda Delta Sec/Treas 90-; Keramos 90-; Tnns 89-; Crmc Engr; Dvlpmnt Engr.

**CLARKE, JAMIE M,** Hillsborough Comm Coll, Tampa, FL; SO; APSO 90-; Eclgy Clb 90-; Tau Kappa Epsilon Aux 86-87; APSO Otstndng Serv 90-; Optcnry.**

**CLARKE, JODIE L,** Muskingum Coll, New Concord, OH; JR; BA; Stdnt Snt Sec 90-; Cntrbrd Sgn Shp 89-; Coll Chr Chmbr Sngrs 88-; Lambda Sigma Pres; Snr Hnrry; Omicron Delta 90-; Phi Theta Beta; 4 H Clb Advsr 90-; Hndcppd Awrnss Prgm Fcltr; Elem Ed.

**CLARKE, JULIE A,** Muskingum Coll, New Concord, OH; JR; BA; Cncrt Chr 88-; Chmbr Sngrs 89-; Lambda Sigma 89-90; Omicron Delta Kappa 90-; Sr Honorary 90-; Edctn Honorary 90-; Chi Alpha Nu 89-; Intrnshp Psychlgy Adlscnts; Elmntry Edctn; Tchng.

**CLARKE, JULIE D,** Univ Of Al At Birmingham, Birmingham, AL; SO; BA; Cmmnctn Arts; Pblc Rltns.

**CLARKE, KATHY-ANNE R,** Tuskegee Univ, Tuskegee Inst, AL; FR; DVM; BS Univ Of The West Indies 88; Vetrny Medcn.

**CLARKE, MARY BETH,** Bridgeport Engr Inst, Fairfield, CT; SO; BSEE; Spec Olympics 85-; Conn Light/Power 85-; USAF 80-84; CL-P 85-; Elctrcl Engr.

**CLARKE, MAUREEN A,** Temple Univ, Philadelphia, PA; SR; BS; Physical Ed; Cardiac Rehab.

**CLARKE, SEAN,** S U N Y Coll Of Tech At Frmgdl, Farmingdale, NY; FR; BS; Latrin Amer Org 90-; Jewish Org Sec 90-; Radio DJ; USMC Rsrvs Lnc Corp 88-; Cert USMC 89f; Engr.

**CLARKE, SHARON N,** Univ Of South Fl, Tampa, FL; GD; MPH; Publ Hlth Stdnt Assoc 89-; Dns Lst 90-; Malik Melody-Malik Sigma Psi Pres 86-; Outstndg Yng Wmn Am 88; Mtrnl/Child Hlth Traineeshp 90; Delores A Auzenne Flwshp 90-; Amer Publ Hlth Assoc 90-; Natl Assoc Scl Wrkrs 90-; Publ Hlth Advsr 88 89; Publ Hlth/Scl Wrk.

**CLARKE, TAMMY L,** Western New England Coll, Springfield, MA; JR; BA; Bowling 88-89; Psych/Scl Wrk; Psych Hosp.**

**CLARKE, TAMMY R,** Central Fl Comm Coll, Ocala, FL; SO; BA; Envir Club V P; Hstry/Engl; Tch.

**CLARKE, THERESA B,** Memphis St Univ, Memphis, TN; SR; BA; Memphis African Violet Soc Sec 90-; Memphis Zoological Soc/Trauma Soc; Emerg Room RN 86-; Dip Meth Hosp Sch Nrsng 85; BLS Instr ACLS Instr 90 BILS; Finance; Hosp Admin/Risk Mgmnt.

**CLARKSON, ELIZABETH S,** Univ Of Sc At Columbia, Columbia, SC; FR; BS; FCA 90-; Dance Tm; Campus Crusade 90-; Alpha Lambda Delta 90-; Bsns Admnstrtn.

**CLARY, GRETCHEN L,** Univ Of Nc At Charlotte, Charlotte, NC; SO; BS; Phys Thrpy 90; Ntwrk Anmls; Chnclrs Lst 90; Bio; Phys Thrpy/Doctor.

**CLARY, KIMBERLY FAY,** Univ Of Sc At Columbia, Columbia, SC; FR; BA; Gamma Beta Phi 90; Founders Schlrs 90-; Elem Educ; Elem Tchr.

**CLASS, WENDY G,** Liberty Univ, Lynchburg, VA; SR; BA; Lbrty Assn Chrstn Tchrs 87-; Pryr Ldr 88-89; Sprtl Lf Dir 89-; Alpha Lambda Delta 87-; Kappa Delta Pi Corr Sec 88-; Deans Lst 87-; Chrldng 87-; Elem Ed; Tch.

**CLASSEN, STEPHANIE J,** Univ Of Sc At Columbia, Columbia, SC; SR; Intrntl Readg Assc; Pres Hnr Rl; Gamma Beta Phi; Deans Lst; Stdnt Tchr; AS Univ SC At Salkehatchie 89; BA Univ SC At Aiken; Elem Educ; Tchr.

**CLATTERBUCK, AIMEE L,** Radford Univ, Radford, VA; JR; Cncl Excptnl Chldrn 90-; Stdnt Life Concert Comm Sec 88-; Panhellenic Assist Rush Chrmn; Rho Lambda; Rho Chi; Phi Sigma Sigma V P 89-; Wrtng Across The Curriculum 90-; Early/Spec Educ; Tchr.

**CLAUDIO, ANA MARIE,** Catholic Univ Of Pr, Ponce, PR; GD; BA.

**CLAUDIO, REINALDO,** Univ Of Pr Medical Sciences, San Juan, PR; JR; DMD; Amer Stdnt Dntl Assoc 88; Omicron Kappa Upsilon 90; Ntl Cllgte Med Prof Awds; BA 88; Dntstry; Oral/Mxllfcl Srgn.

**CLAUSELL, FELICIA,** Alcorn St Univ, Lorman, MS; FR.

**CLAWSON, JULIE R,** Indiana Univ Of Pa, Indiana, PA; FR; BS; Chem.

**CLAWSON, TINA L,** Univ Of Sc At Columbia, Columbia, SC; SR; BS; Phi Beta Kappa 90; Beta Gamma Sigma 90; Bsn Admin; Fin.

**CLAXTON, KRISTI L,** Middle Tn St Univ, Murfreesboro, TN; SR; BS; Dstrbutn Clrk Austin Prdcl Srvc; Elem Ed; Tch.

**CLAXTON, LISA A,** Univ Of Sc At Columbia, Columbia, SC; JR; MBS; Smmr Stdnt Intrnshp Wstnghs 90-; Bus-Acctg.**

**CLAXTON, MICHELLE,** Cumberland Coll, Williamsburg, KY; SR; BA; Data Prcssng/Sec Prctce.

**CLAY, BONNIE J,** Ashland Comm Coll, Ashland, KY; FR; BA; Bus; Acctg.

**CLAY, BRIAN G,** Morehouse Coll, Atlanta, GA; FR; BA; Bsn Adm; Law.

**CLAY, CATHERINE E,** Univ Of Richmond, Richmond, VA; FR; Frat/Sorority Flwshp 90-; Cmps Crusade Christ; IM Bsktbl; Elem Ed Engl; Tchr.

**CLAY, CHRISTINA E,** Ms St Univ, Miss State, MS; SO; BS; Microbiology; Phrmctcl Sales.

**CLAY, GINA B,** Oh Univ-Southern Cmps, Ironton, OH; SO; Dental Asst; Educ.

**CLAY, JOHN N,** Ny Univ, New York, NY; FR; BS; AA Bellarmine Coll 78; Cmptr Sci.

**CLAY, JONNHY RENEE,** Marshall University, Huntington, WV; SR; BED; Ofc Tech Advsry; Jdg CECWV; Pi Omega Pi; Exec Sec; Prlegl 76-88; Bus Educ; Tchng/Ofc Mgmt.

**CLAY, LAURA E,** Marshall University, Huntington, WV; SO; BED; Campus Entert Unlimited Chr Pos 90-; Classical Assoc Treas 90-; Resid Hall Advisory Council 89-; Deans List 90-; Mu Tutoring Serv 91; Math/Elem Ed; Ed.

**CLAY, LORI F,** Kent St Univ Stark Cmps, North Canton, OH; FR; BA; Ambsdr 90-; Spec Educ; Tch Dvlpmntly Hndcpd.

**CLAY, RICHARD A,** Wv Univ, Morgantown, WV; SR; BS; AICHE 88-89; Tau Kappa Epsilon 87-88; Aiche Kanawha Vly Chpt 86-87; Deans List 88-90; IM Athletics 86-; Chemcial Engrg; Process Engr Rhone Poulenc.

**CLAY, SHAUNDRA D,** Clark Atlanta Univ, Atlanta, GA; JR; BA; Fin Clb Chr Pub Rel 88-89; Acctg Clg 88-; Alpha Kappa Alpha Sec 89-; Allst Ins Intern; Acctg.

**CLAYBON, KIMBERLY J,** Fayetteville St Univ, Fayetteville, NC; SR; BS; Math/Cmptr Sci Clb Pres 90; Nrthwstrn Comm Ensmbl 84-86; Kappa Alpha Psi Sec 84-85; Alpha Kappa Alpha Chrprsn Comm 85-; Chnclrs Lst 89-90; Dns Lst 89-; Ind Achvmnt Awd 88; St Stephen Bapt Chrch SS Tchr; Coop Educ Army Corps Of Eng 89-; Math/Comp Sci; Engr.

**CLAYCOMB, LEAH M,** Duquesne Univ, Pittsburgh, PA; BA; SHARP 89-; Ski Clb 89-; Phi Eta Sigma 89-; Lambda Sigma 89-; Kappa Delta Epsilon 89-; CEC 89-; Spcl Elem Ed.

**CLAYPOOL, LISA L,** Univ Of Cincinnati-Clrmnt Coll, Batavia, OH; FR; Phi Alpha Iota Mmbr; Hstry Art Englsh; Grphc Artst.

**CLAYPOOL, STEPHEN TRAVIS,** Univ Of Ky, Lexington, KY; FR; BS; Stdnt Athl Cncl; Bptst Stdnt Un; Bptst Stdnt Un Chr; Phi Eta Sigma; IM Sftbl Bsktbl; Chem Engr; Engrng.

**CLAYTON, CAMILLA,** Fayetteville St Univ, Fayetteville, NC; JR; BA; Bus Admin/Mngmnt.

**CLAYTON, CANDACE ANNE,** Univ Of Sc At Columbia, Columbia, SC; FR; SGA; Alpha Lambda Delta; Dns Lst 90; Cncrt Bnd; Retlng.

**CLAYTON, CATRENIA N,** Morehead St Univ, Morehead, KY; FR; BA; Little Sister Omega Psi Phi 90-; Psychlgy; Computers.

**CLAYTON, ERIC D,** Bethune Cookman Coll, Daytona Beach, FL; FR; BA; Exec Bd Chrmn Stdnt Rel 90-; Out State Clb 90-; Blck Awrns 90-; Da Tribe Sec 90-; Math Tutor 90-; Men Dstnctn Sec 90-; Radio Brdcst Serv DJ 90-; Merit Schlrshp 90-; UNCF Schlrshp 90-; Alpha Phi Alpha Schlrshp 90-; Math/Sci; Cmptr Pgrmmr.

**CLAYTON, HERBERT L,** Al St Univ, Montgomery, AL; SR; BS; AFROTC Corps Comndr; Arnold Air Soc; Pres Awd Mltry Excell; Cmndrs Awd; AFROTC V Cmndnts Awd 90; Pilot AFROTC; Cmptr Sci; Pilot US Air Force.

**CLAYTON, LAKITSIA V,** Fl A & M Univ, Tallahassee, FL; FR; FAMU Connection 90-; Phi Eta Sigma 90-; Jrnlsm; Brdcstdng.

**CLAYTON, LISA R,** Stillman Coll, Tuscaloosa, AL; SO; BS; Pre Prof Sci Clb; Gamma Iota Sigma 90-; Cordell Wynn Hnrs Prog; Natl Coll Sci Awrd; Biol; Phrmcy.

**CLAYTON, PAMELA V,** Tougaloo Coll, Tougaloo, MS; SO; BA; Math/Comp Sci Clb 90-; Stdnt Ldr 90-; Pre-Eng/Phys Sci Clb; Alpha Lambda Delta 90-; Alpha Kappa Alpha; Natl Lab Smmr Rsrch Prtcpnt; Math.

**CLAYTON, PATRICIA L,** Roane St Comm Coll, Harriman, TN; SO; AAS; Bus Mngmnt; Cmptr Prgrmmr.

**CLAYTON, WILLIAM R,** Memphis St Univ, Memphis, TN; GD; BSEE; Gamma Beta Phi 88-90; Tau Beta Pi 90-; EIT State TN 90; Elec Engr; Sys Engr.

**CLEAR, KIMBERLY A,** Boston Coll, Chestnut Hill, MA; SO; BSN; Mendel Clb 89-90; Nursing Senate Tr 89-; Paraprofessional Ldrshp Grp 91-; NSNA; Deans Lst 89-; Nursing.

**CLEARMAN, CURTIS A,** Meridian Comm Coll, Meridian, MS; SO; BA; Rite Choice Distrbrs Pres 87-; Busn; Engrg.

**CLEARY, DANIEL A,** Univ Of Cin R Walters Coll, Blue Ash, OH; FR; PC; Comp Sci Clb VP 90-; Phi Theta Kappa 90-; Deans Lst 90-; Mgr Itln Rstrnt; BBA 88; Comp.

**CLEARY, GERALYN M,** Univ Of Cincinnati-Clrmnt Coll, Batavia, OH; SO; AA; Phi Theta Kappa 90-; Womonways; Socl Wrk; BSW.

**CLEARY, JANET J,** Hudson Valley Comm Coll, Troy, NY; SO; Have Chldrn/Wrk Acctg Fld; FCC Lcns; Bus Amin; Acctg.

**CLEARY, NORA MARIE,** Elmira Coll, Elmira, NY; SR; Educ Clb 88-; Kappa Delta Pi; Lrng Pgm Pupil Asstnc 90-; Deans Lst 90-; BS; Educ; Tchr.

**CLEARY, TIMOTHY J,** Manhattan Coll, Bronx, NY; FR; IM Sftbl; IM Bsktbl 90-; Engineering.

**CLEAVER, LAURA A,** Dyke Coll, Cleveland, OH; SO; ASSOC; Paralegal Sci; Novelist.**

**CLEAVES, DARLA D,** Memphis St Univ, Memphis, TN; SR; BS; Bellevue Bptst Chrch; RN Bptst Memrl Hsp 78-85; RN Dplma Baptist Mem Hsp Nrsg Schl 78; Elem Educ; Tch.

**CLECKLER, APRIL D,** Wallace St Comm Coll At Selma, Selma, AL; FR; BED; Rbkhs Mscn 90-; Pres Lst; Math; Tchng.

**CLECKLER, JUDY D,** Wallace St Comm Coll At Selma, Selma, AL; SO; MBA; Plant Supvsr; AS 90; Psychlgy; Soc Wrkr Counslr.

**CLEERDIN, JESSICA T,** Rutgers St Un At New Brunswick, New Brunswick, NJ; FR; Engl; Tchng.

**CLEERE, ALICE L,** Univ Of Montevallo, Montevallo, AL; FR; Bio Clb; Alpha Delta Pi Rcrdng Sec; Med Tchnlgy.

**CLEGG, DEITRA L,** West Liberty St Coll, West Liberty, WV; SO; BS; Tchrn Trnng Grnt; Edgfwd Prmry Mddl Schl PTA Cmmtt Chrmn 89-; AAS 89; Math; Tchng.

**CLEGG, MELINDA J,** Univ Of Nc At Greensboro, Greensboro, NC; SR; BSN; Assn Nrsng Stdnts Sec 89-; Nrs Chrstn Flwshp; Gldn Chain Socl Chrprsn 90-; Sigma Theta Tau; Marshal; Outstdng Coll Stdngs Of Amer; Nrs Asst Duke Univ Med Cntr; Nrsng; Surgical.

**CLEGHORN, BETHANY G,** Fl International Univ, Miami, FL; SR; BA; Intrntl Fd Srvce Execs Assn 90-; Acad Achvmnt Schlrshp; AA Miami Dade Comm Coll 89; Hsptlty Mgmt; Fd Srvce Mgr.

**CLEGHORN, LENA L,** Northwest Al Comm Coll, Phil Campbell, AL; SO; BA; Sci Clb 90-; Phi Theta Kappa 90-; Ed.

**CLEGHORN, MELANIE E,** Univ Of Ga, Athens, GA; SO; BSED; Delta Gamma 90-; Erly Chldhd Ed; Tchr.

**CLELAND, KENT D,** Oh Univ, Athens, OH; SR; BMUS; Orch 87-; Jazz Ensemble 87-; Trombone Choir 87-; Tuba Ens 87-; Pi Kappa Lambda 90-; Alpha Lambda Delta 88-; Outstndng Soph 89; Fresh 88; Music Theory; Educ.

**CLEM, JAMES S,** Samford Univ, Birmingham, AL; SR; Cmbrlnd Trial Acad Board Chief Judge 90-; ATLA Natl Trial Team Advcte 90-; Bst Advcte Haley Trial Comp 90-; Amer Jrnl Trial Advcry 90-; USAF Jag Capt; JD.

**CLEM, PETER T,** Daytona Beach Comm Coll, Daytona Beach, FL; FR; AA; Math; Cvl Engr.

**CLEMANN, JULIA T,** Univ Of Sc At Columbia, Columbia, SC; FR; BA; Interntl Club 90-; Alpha Mu Gamma; Phi Eta Sigma; Sigma Xi Chi 90-; Internatl Bus.

**CLEMENICH, KELLY M,** John Carroll Univ, Cleveland, OH; FR; BA; Yrbk Clb Photog Ed 90-; Frnch Clb 90-; Finance Clb 90-; Dance Marathon Comm Actvts Comm; Achvmnt Awd Excell French; Finance/Frnch; Bnkg/Invstmnts.

**CLEMENS, MELODY H,** Defiance Coll, Defiance, OH; SO; BA; Elem Educ; Certif Kindergarten Educ.

**CLEMENS, MICHAEL P,** Saint Vincents Coll & Seminary, Latrobe, PA; JR; BA; Stdnt Intrn MPL Corp Buckhannon 89-; Acad Schlrshp St Vincent 88-; Cmptng Inf Sci; Sftwr Eng.

**CLEMENT, DARNELL O,** Howard Univ, Washington, DC; SR; BA; AIA 88-; APSA 89-90; Ftbl 87-88.

**CLEMENT, EMILY G,** The Johns Hopkins Univ, Baltimore, MD; JR; BSN; BS Univ MD 83; Nrsg.

**CLEMENT, JENNIFER A,** S U N Y Coll Of Tech At Frmgdl, Farmingdale, NY; SO; AA; Excel Awrd 90-; Librl Arts/Sci; Physcl Thrpy Ba Ma.

**CLEMENT, MATONSA Y,** Clark Atlanta Univ, Atlanta, GA; SO; BA; Vol United Way; Beta Si; Deans Lst; Mass Media Arts; Radio TV Film.

**CLEMENT, NICOLE M,** Hobart And William Smith Coll, Geneva, NY; FR; BA; Big Sis; Pres Schlr; Emerson Schlr; Pol Sci/Spnsh; Law.

**CLEMENT, PAUL D,** Pellissippi St Tech Comm Coll, Knoxville, TN; SO; AAS; Soc Mfg Eng Sec/Treas 90-; Tau Alpah Pi Sec/Treas 90-F Lambda Chi Alpha VP 86-87; Mech Eng Tech Outstndng Stdnt Awd 90-; Mech Eng Tech; Eng.

**CLEMENT, THOMAS G,** Middle Tn St Univ, Murfreesboro, TN; FR; BM; Band Blue Section Ldr 90-; Phi Mu Alpha Sinfonia; Music Ed; Tchr.

**CLEMENTE, ANNE-MARIE,** The Boston Conservatory, Boston, MA; JR; BFA; Dance; Perform/Own Studio.

**CLEMENTS, ANGEL Y,** Va St Univ, Petersburg, VA; FR; BS; Pltcl Sci; Law.

**CLEMENTS, BRIAN JACK,** Chattahoochee Vly St Comm Coll, Phenix City, AL; SO; AAS; Gamma Beta Phi; Pres Lst 90-; Sprngr Opera Hs; Cmptr Sci; Actng/Busn.

**CLEMENTS, DIANA L,** Univ Of West Fl, Pensacola, FL; SR; BA; Alpha Sigma Lambda 90; SCEC Stat Nwlsttr Ed; UWF Mntr 88-90; AA 89; Spcl Ed; Tchng.

**CLEMENTS, DORDINA M,** Chattahoochee Vly St Comm Coll, Phenix City, AL; FR; AA; Deans List 90-; Child Care Dvlpmnt; Tchng & Child Care.

**CLEMENTS, JENNIFER L,** S U N Y At Buffalo, Buffalo, NY; SR; MBA; Ntl Acctg Assn Dir Mem Attndnc 89-; Acctg Assn 89-; Prcsn Mrchng Brfcs Drl Tm 90-; IN Vlybl/Sftbl 87-; Mgrl Acctg.

**CLEMENTS, MICHAEL O,** Livingston Univ, Livingston, AL; JR; BS; Alpha Chi; Pres List; Deans List; Math/Comptr Progrmng.

**CLEMENTS, RUTH B,** Christopher Newport Coll, Newport News, VA; SR; BA; Ed Dept Hnrs; Magna Cum Laude; Dns Lst; AAS Thomas Nelson Cmnty Clg 85; Elem Ed; Tchg.

**CLEMENTS, SANDI L,** Winthrop Coll, Rock Hill, SC; SR; BS; Kappa Delta Pi Ed Hnry Org Treas 90-; Cmps Bapt Yng Wmn Pres 88-; Bapt Stdnt Un 88-; Kappa Delta Pi Treas 90-; SNEA 90-; NEA 90-; Hngr Org Crp Walk 87-90; Pres Lst 90-; Deans Lst 89-90; IM Sftbll 89; Erly Chldhd Ed; Tchng Admn.

**CLEMENTS, TRACY L,** Kent St Univ Kent Cmps, Kent, OH; JR; BA; Hl Cncl 88-90; All Cmps Prgrmng Brd 88-89; Nw Stdnt Ornttn Instrctr; Gldn Key Natl; Omicron Delta Kappa; Twnhl II Crisis Intrvntn Htln Paraprfsnl; Psychlgy; Mrg & Fmly Thrpy.

**CLEMENTS, WENDELL KENT,** Saint Petersburg Jr Coll, St Petersburg, FL; SO; BA; Bsn Adm; Hosp Adm.**

**CLEMMER, PHILLIP A L,** Beckley Coll, Beckley, WV; SO; BS; Hnrs Prog 90-; GED St Of W Va 88; Bus Admn.

**CLEMONS, BARBARA L,** Western Ky Univ, Bowling Green, KY; SR; BA; SNEA 87-; NCTE 88-; KCTE 90-; Phi Kappa Phi 89-; Golden Key 89-; Phi Eta Sigma 88-; Spcl Olym Vol; Pres Schol 87-; Engl/Allied Lang Arts; H C Tchr.

**CLEMONS, CAROLE N,** Ky St Univ, Frankfort, KY; JR; Phi Beta Lambda Histrn; Army Rsrv Ofcr Trng Corp Cadet Corp; Tnns/Bsktbl/Trck/Crss Cntry; Math/Sci; Cvl Eng.

**CLEMONS, CHARLES L,** Lincoln Univ, Lincoln Univ, PA; JR; BS; Rssn Clb Chrmn 88; Omega Psi Phi Chpln 90-; Tutor 88-; Samuel Robinson Schlrshp 90; Med Cntr Intrn 90; Thrptc Rcrtn Intrn; Thrptc Rcrtn; Clncl Thrptc Rcrtn Spclst.

**CLEMONS, CORETTA Q,** Winthrop Coll, Rock Hill, SC; JR; BS; Assoc Of The Ebonites 89-; Ebonites Gospel Choir 89-; Progrm For Acadmc/Career Enhncmnt 90-; Phi Eta Sigma 88-; C W Posts Long Islnd Univ Co Op Progrm 88-89; Food/Nutrition; Dietitn.

**CLEMONS, KAREN S,** East Tn St Univ, Johnson City, TN; JR; BS; Euclid Ave Bptst Chrch Yth Tchr; AA Univ Of FL 87; Interior Design; Comp Drftng Dsgn.

**CLEMONS, SANDRA G,** Western Ky Univ, Bowling Green, KY; SO; BS; Phi Eta Sigma 89-; SNEA 89-; Newman Cl 89-; Pres Schol 89-; Early Chldhd Ed; Tchr.

**CLEMONS, SHANNON D,** Nc St Univ At Raleigh, Raleigh, NC; FR; Peer Mentor; Stately Ladies.

**CLEMONS, SUSAN C,** Univ Of Ky, Lexington, KY; SO; BED; Cllgns/Acad Excel; Early Elem Ed.

**CLEMONS, TENE TRA N,** Jackson St Univ, Jackson, MS; FR; Alpha Lmbd Dlt Hstrn; Biolgy; Phys Thrpst.

**CLENDENEN, SHERYL M,** Fl A & M Univ, Tallahassee, FL; FR; Pblc Spkng Clb; Fndtns Spch Clb; Acctg; CPA.

**CLERE, KIMBERLY L,** Ashland Comm Coll, Ashland, KY; SO; ADN; Nrsng.

**CLERVIL, ROSENIE,** Newbury Coll, Brookline, MA; GD; AS; Business.**

**CLEVELAND, DARRELL LANIER,** Morehouse Coll, Atlanta, GA; FR; MBA; Gspl Choir 90-; Mntrg Pro 90; Otstndg Blck Schlr; Fl Alumni Cnsrtm Hist Blck Inst 89; Bus Admin; Acctg.

**CLEVELAND, DENICE D,** Gordon Coll, Barnesville, GA; JR; BS; Grad Magna Cum Laude 90; Stngrphr; AS Gordon Coll 90; Bus Admin; Bus Offce.

**CLEVELAND, JANE M,** Salisbury St Univ, Salisbury, MD; SR; BS; IM Sports 87-; Chldrns Theatr Prod Lead Role 88; Alpha Omega 87-; Beta Beta Beta 89-; Phi Kappa Phi 90-; Phi Eta Sigma 87-88; R Henson Schlrshp 88-; Coaches Acad Awrd 90-; Var Sftbl Cap 89-; Biology.

**CLEVELAND, MARY C,** Ms St Univ, Miss State, MS; JR; BA; Psychlgy Clb 90-; Psychlgy; Orgnztnl Psychlgy.

**CLEVELAND, SHANNON M,** Univ Of Sc At Columbia, Columbia, SC; FR; BA; Engl; Jrnlsm.

**CLEVENGER, DEBRA L,** Methodist Coll, Fayetteville, NC; FR; BA; Acctg.

**CLEVENGER, ERIC P,** Univ Of Pittsburgh, Pittsburgh, PA; JR; BS; Mech Eng; Eng.

**CLEVENGER, NANCY L,** Comm Coll Algny Co Algny Cmps, Pittsburgh, PA; SO; Bsnss; Mngmnt.

**CLEVENGER, NICOLE Y,** Tusculum Coll, Greeneville, TN; JR; BA; DAR Grant; Social Studies; Scndry Ed.**

**CLEVENGER-BILLHEIMER, KAREN R,** Marshall University, Huntington, WV; SR; BA; Cnslng/Rhbltn.

**CLEVERSLEY, DIANE,** S U N Y At Buffalo, Buffalo, NY; GD; BA; Gldn Key 90-; Rsrch Asstshp Dr Paul A Toro Ph D 90-; Clncl Psychtrc Intrvwr Rsrch; Psychlgy/Soc Sci Intrdscplnry; Psychlgy.

**CLEVINGER, ANTHONY M,** Broward Comm Coll, Ft Lauderdale, FL; SO; BA; Phi Beta Lambda 90-; Hon Soc 90-; Deans Lst E TN St 90; Pres Lst 90; Bus Admin; Bus Mngmnt.

**CLEVINGER, KATHERINE J,** Emory & Henry Coll, Emory, VA; FR; BS; Emory/Henry Hnrs Schlp; Psy; Med.

**CLEVINGER, MELANIE A,** Radford Univ, Radford, VA; SO; BA; Campus Judcl Brd/Judcl Appls Brd; Hon Prog; Poltcl Sci; Crmnl Law.

**CLIFFORD, ANNE K,** Villanova Univ, Villanova, PA; FR; BSN; Flag Sqd 90-; Saferides 90-; Nrsng.

**CLIFFORD, CYNTHIA A,** Univ Of Ky, Lexington, KY; JR; BED; Miami Symphony Orch 88-89; Alpha Rhi Pan Rep 88-89; Ele Educ Sci; Ele Sci Tchr.

**CLIFFORD, JACKIE L,** Endicott Coll, Beverly, MA; SO; AS; Model In Pbl Reltns Dir 90-; Phi Theta Kappa 90-; TV Prod Intern 90; News Reptr Intern 90; Commtns; TV Film.

**CLIFT, E DANIEL,** Coker Coll, Hartsville, SC; FR; BA; SGA Crrclm Com-Rep 90-; Deans Lst; Top 10; Vrsty Sccr 90-; Acctg Fin; Corp Law.

**CLIFT, FREIDA,** Lexington Comm Coll, Lexington, KY; FR; BA; Nrsng.

**CLIFT, KIMBERLY B,** Middle Tn St Univ, Murfreesboro, TN; FR; Wsly Sngrs 90-; Esprt Sngrs 90-; Chmbr Choir 90-; Std Cncl 90-; Soc Prof Jrnlst 90-; Delta Zeta Chr 90-; Phlnthrpy Spch/ Hrng Imprd; Host TV Show; TV Rptr; Cntrls Nwspr Rptr/ Phtgrphr 90; Mass Comm; TV Rptr/Anchr.

**CLIFT, LINDA A,** Marywood Coll, Scranton, PA; SO; BS; Biol Clb 90-; Accntng 89-90; AS N E Inst Educ 85; Biol/Phrmcy.

**CLIFTON, CAROL R,** Middle Tn St Univ, Murfreesboro, TN; JR; BS; Math Org Pres 88-; Assoc Cmptrg Mchnry Rfrshmnt Chrprsn 90-; Assoc Stu Bdy Hs Rep 90-; Pi Mu Epsilon Sec/Tres 89-; Gamma Beta Phi 89-90; Tau Omicron 90-; Gamma Iota Sigma 90-; Stats/Sctrl Org 90-; Math Assoc Amer; Math; Actrl Sci.

**CLIFTON, CHARLENE E,** Middle Ga Coll, Cochran, GA; FR; Bapt Stdnt Union 90-; Educ Clb 90-; SGA Sec Elect; Bsbl Concession Stnd Wrkr; Math; Educ.

**CLIFTON, CHERYL A,** Savannah St Coll, Savannah, GA; JR; BA; C/S Ntnl Bk Cred Anal; Baugher/Fox CPA'S Atlanta Ga; Acctng; CPA.

**CLIFTON, CHERYL R,** Univ Of Nc At Greensboro, Greensboro, NC; SR; Commuter Assoc 87-; SNCAE 88-90; Alpha Lambda Delta 87-88; Kappa Omicron Nu 90-; Marshals 89-; Exclnce Awd; Dns Lst 87-; Summa Cum Laude; IM Sports 88-90; BS; Child Dvlpmt; Ed.

**CLIFTON, CHRISTINA M,** Savannah St Coll, Savannah, GA; JR; BA; Mrn Blgy Clb 90-; Beta Beta Beta 90-; Ntrl Sci/Eclgy; Wldlf Mgmt.

**CLIFTON, KELLY L,** Univ Of Nc At Greensboro, Greensboro, NC; SR; BS; UNCG AEYC Assc Ed Yng Chldrn Sec 89-; Kappa Omicron Nu Ntnl Home Ec Hnr Scty 89-; Chld Develp; Ed.

**CLIFTON, KIMBERLY D,** Patrick Henry Comm Coll, Martinsville, VA; FR; BS; Stdnt Govt Assoc 90-; Deans List; B/B Trucking Co Ofc Mgr; Ofc Sys/Bus; Ofc Mngng.

**CLIFTON, MARK A,** Patrick Henry Comm Coll, Martinsville, VA; SO; BS; Stdnt Govt Pblc Rltns Comm 90-; Fin Comm 90-; Phi Theta Kappa; Big Bro/Big Sis; Dns Lst 90; Sprmrkt Mgr 84-90; Acctg; CPA.

**CLIFTON, NANCY M,** Daytona Beach Comm Coll, Daytona Beach, FL; SO; AA; Phi Theta Kappa; Meth Chrstn Sch Bd 90-; ACE Pres 89-; Supvr Word Process Univ Rsrch Corp 89-; Edn; Math Tchr Middle Sch.

**CLIFTON, ROBERT E,** Univ Of Montevallo, Montevallo, AL; SR; BS ED; Phi Kappa Phi; AS Alexander City Jr Clg 89; Phys Educ; Recrtn.

**CLIFTON, SHARON D,** Salisbury St Univ, Salisbury, MD; JR; BA; IM Flr Hcky Vlybl Sftbl Aerobcs 88-; Frshmn Hnr Soc 89-; Elem Educ; Tchr.

**CLIFTON, TASHA L,** Stillman Coll, Tuscaloosa, AL; FR; Sci Clb; Ford Schlr; Gamma Iota Sigma; Bio; Pre-Med.

**CLINARD, PAMELA A,** Univ Of Nc At Greensboro, Greensboro, NC; JR; BS; Elem Educ; Tchng.

**CLINCHY, KELLY-ANNE,** Smith Coll, Northampton, MA; SO; BA; Pre Hlth Soc 90-; Mossping 89-90; First Grp Schlr 90-; Deans Lst 89-; SOS Vol Nurs Hm 90-; Chldrn Hosp Vol 90-; Var Sftbl 89-; Biology; Med Doc.

**CLINE JR, CHARLES A,** Valdosta St Coll, Valdosta, GA; SR; BS; ACM 90-; Alpha Chi V P 90-; Pi Mu Epsilon; AAS Cmnty Clg Air Force 89; Cmptr Sci.

**CLINE, CHRISTOPHER M,** Univ Of Nc At Charlotte, Charlotte, NC; FR; BS; Math; Tchng.

**CLINE JR, DANNY O,** Wv Univ, Morgantown, WV; SO; Hon Prog 89; Math Clb; AICHE 90-; Ordr Grail; Pres Schlrshp 89; PPG Indus Schlrshp Chem Engr 90; Phi Kappa Phi Fresh Recgntn; Chem Engr; Rsrch.

**CLINE, JANET M,** Chattahoochee Vly St Comm Coll, Phenix City, AL; SO; BA; Gamma Beta Phi; Erly Chldhd Educ; Tchg.

**CLINE, KAREN R,** Cecil Comm Coll, North East, MD; SO; AA; Phi Theta Kappa 90-; Bsn; Admn.**

**CLINE JR, KEITH A,** Univ Of Akron, Akron, OH; JR; BS; Grk Ldrshp Cncl 89-90; Interfrat Cncl Rep 89-90; Golden Key 90; Beta Gamma Sigma 90; Phi Eta Sigma/Alpha Lambda Delta 88-89; Delta Tau Delta Dir Of Acad Affrs 89-90; Smmr Intrnshp Wth J M Smucker Co; Kershner Schlr Ntl Awd From Delta Tau Delta 88; Accntng; CPA.

**CLINE, MELISSA A,** Longwood Coll, Farmville, VA; JR; BS; Std Govt 89-90; Intl Ordr Rnbw Grls Advsr 83-90; AAS Cntrl VA Comm Clg 90; Elem Ed; Tch.

**CLINE, MICHAEL S,** S U N Y Coll Of Tech At Alfred, Alfred, NY; FR; BSPHD; Phrmcy; Rsrch/Bus.

**CLINE, MOLLY ANN,** Patrick Henry Comm Coll, Martinsville, VA; SR; AAS; SPIRE Natl Hnr Soc 90-; DPMA; Cmptr Prgmng.

**CLINE, NATHAN S,** Univ Of Sc At Columbia, Columbia, SC; FR; BA; Staff Reprtr/Photo Richland Northeast Nwspr; U Of SC Pr Lst 90-; U S Army Team Chf 86-89; U S Army Reserve 89-; Journalism; Photo Jrnlst.

**CLINE, WILLIAM A,** Oh Univ, Athens, OH; GD; DO; Fmly Prctsc Clb; Stdnt Ostpthc Mdcl Assoc; BS 86; Ostpthy.

**CLINGER, CARL A,** Wv Univ, Morgantown, WV; FR; BS; Scuba Clb; Fencing Clb; Engr; Chem Engr.

**CLINKSCALES, JANEL,** Johnson C Smith Univ, Charlotte, NC; SO; Hnrs Clg; Sftbl/Bsktbl; Cmmnctns; Pblc Rltns.

**CLINNER, CHRISTOPHER A,** Univ Of Montevallo, Montevallo, AL; FR; BS; Phi Alpha Mu 90-; Msc Phrmcy; Med.

**CLINTON, CHANTELL,** Lincoln Univ, Lincoln Univ, PA; JR; BA; Bus Clb 88-; Bsktbll Tm 88-90; Bus Admn.

**CLINTON, KENAN D,** Ms St Univ, Miss State, MS; FR; Gamma Beta Phi; Alpha Lambda Delta; Sigma Phi Epsilon; Law.

**CLIPPINGER, ANTHONY L,** Univ Of De, Newark, DE; FR; BA; IM Vllybll Sftbll; Hstry.

**CLIPPINGER, CAROLYN J,** Oh Univ, Athens, OH; SO; Music Ed Natl Conf Treas 89-.

**CLIPPINGER, TRICIA L,** Radford Univ, Radford, VA; JR; BS; SEA 90-; Hnrs Pro 89-; Kappa Delta Pi Pres; Fld Hcky Tm 88-; Erly Educ; Tchr.

**CLISHAM, KATHRYN C,** Merrimack Coll, North Andover, MA; SO; Psych Clb; Educ Clb 89-; IM Sprts; Sftbl; Bsktbl 89-; Psych/Educ Cert; Tchr/Elem Ed.

**CLITES, HEATHER A,** Saint Francis Coll, Loretto, PA; SO; BSN; Phi Delta Kapp Soc Chrprsn 90; Red Key; Nrs Org 89; IM Bsktbl/Sftbl 89; Nrsg; Anesthesia.

**CLIVE, NICHOLAS A,** Georgetown Univ, Washington, DC; JR; BS; Mentor Prog Pres 89-; Mktng; Entrepreneurial.

**CLOCK, GERARD P,** City Univ Of Ny Grad School, New York, NY; GD; PHD; Smnr Ldr 89; Intrnshp Chld Dev Ctr Jwsh Brd Chldrns Srvcs 89; Golden Key 88-; Deans Lst 87-90; BA 90; Hstry; Tchg.

**CLOMAN, JAMES F,** Ms St Univ, Miss State, MS; SR; BBA; Fma 90-; Finance; Investment Bnkng.

**CLONINGER, JEROME M,** Catawba Valley Comm Coll, Hickory, NC; FR; BS; Sigma Nu NSCU 87; Mt Pisgah Luth Chrch 89-; Conover Chair Co 88-; Hstry; Tchr.

**CLONINGER, THOMAS S,** Univ Of Tn At Chattanooga, Chattanooga, TN; FR; BS; Engrg Mechl; Engr.

**CLONTZ, TERESA L,** Western Piedmont Comm Coll, Morganton, NC; SO; AS; Phi Beta Lambda 89; Bus Adm.

**CLOONAN, KELLY M,** Le Moyne Coll, Syracuse, NY; SO; BA; NAA; Acctg Soc; OCC Dns Lst 89-90; Dns Lst; Averson/Klinetop CPA 90-; Acctg; CA.

**CLORE, JUNE A,** Univ Of Ky, Lexington, KY; JR; Dnc Ensmbl Sec 88-90; SADD; Cmps Crsd Chrst Bbl Stu Ldr 90-; Alpha Hnrry 88-; Dean Lst 88-; Alpha Delta Pi Chpln 88-; Chrch Chrgrphr Yth 90-; Vllybll 90; Swmmng Synchrnz Swmmng; Soc Wrk; Law.

**CLOSE, JAMES M,** Kent St Univ Kent Cmps, Kent, OH; FR; Clg Bowl 90-; Campus Crusdae For Christ 90-; Alpha Lambda Delta 90-; Bus; Acct.

**CLOSE, KRISTIE L,** Oh St Univ, Columbus, OH; FR; BS; SWE; Alpha Chi Omega; Deans Lst; Indstrl/Syst Eng.

**CLOSE, MICHAEL LAWRENCE,** Cornell Univ Statutory College, Ithaca, NY; JR; BS; EARS Cnslng Srvc 89-; Cntrl Aftr Schl Prgm Chldrn; Hon Nun De Kah 90-; Gldn Key 90-; Cornell Blgcl Fld Station Internship Awrd Smmr Intern 90; Otdr Edctr Intership; Blgcl Sci; Vet Med.

**CLOTHIER, DI ANNA L,** S U N Y Coll Of Envr Sci & For, Syracuse, NY; SO; BS; NSPE 88-; Green Peace 87-; Animal Rights; Wmns Org; Youth Ctr Vol 89-90; Grad With Hnrs 90; CLC Schlrshp 88-; Letter Of Apprctn Grt Lks Nvl Brig 90; AS Clg Lake County 90; Forestry; Engr.

**CLOUD, KAREN L,** Georgian Court Coll, Lakewood, NJ; SR; BA; Spcl Ed.

**CLOUD, LA DON D,** Central St Univ, Wilberforce, OH; SO; BA; Accntng Clb Treas 90-; Dean List 90; Accntng; CPA.

**CLOUD, NATALIE H,** Valdosta St Coll, Valdosta, GA; JR; BED; Emplyd 1st Fdrl Svngs Bnk 84-; Assoc Bainbridge Coll 84; Sci; Mddl Chldhd Ed; Tchr.

**CLOUD, TRACY L,** Memphis St Univ, Memphis, TN; SR; BS; Outstndng Sophmn 88-89; Child/Family Studies; Law/Phd Child/ Fmly Stds.

**CLOUDEN, YNELLA N,** Va St Univ, Petersburg, VA; SO; AHEA Sec 89-; VHEA Hstrn; 4h Extnsn Svc Vol 90-; Clthng Cnstrctn Tchng Intern.

**CLOUGH, ARCHIE R,** Waycross Coll, Waycross, GA; SO; BA; Bus Clb 90-; Acctg; Acctnt.

**CLOUGH, DAVID H,** Liberty Univ, Lynchburg, VA; SR; BS; Elem Ed; Tchng.

**CLOUGH, DEANNA MARIE,** Elms Coll, Chicopee, MA; JR; BSW; Hmn Svce Asso 87-89; Stdnt Scl Work Org Co-Treas 90-; YMCA Intnshp 87-88; Monson Dvlpmntl Cen Intnshp 88-89; Monson Dvlpmntl Cen MRWI 81-90; AS Colg STCC 89; Scl Work.

**CLOUSE, DACY C,** Roane St Comm Coll, Harriman, TN; FR; BS; Wmns Stdnt Orgnztn 90; Gamma Beta Phi; Mthmtcs; Scndry Edctn.

**CLOUSE, JAMES J,** Alfred Univ, Alfred, NY; JR; BS; Jazz Ens 88-; Cncrt Bnd 88-; Orchstr 88-; Amer Clg Hlthcr Exec Treas 90-; Natl Asc Acctnts Treas 89-90; Alpha Lambda Delta; Delta Mu Delta; Sigma Alpha Mu Treas 90-; Admn Cntrl Med Ctr/ Hosp; Hlth Care Plng/Mgmt/Bus Admn; Hlth Care Admn.

**CLOUSER, KIMBERLY S,** S U N Y Coll At Fredonia, Fredonia, NY; SR; BS; Nwspr; WNYF T V; Dance Marathon MDA; Emcee/Dncr 87-; Usher Corps; Apld Cmunctn Assn; Dance Cncrts; Entrnmnt Bd; Hon Prog 86-90; Upper Cls Buddy; Welns Clb; Sashion Show; Artpark Intrnshp; Pub Rltns Mktg; Cmunctn/ Media; Pub/Med Rltns.

**CLOW, KIMBERLY A,** Colby Sawyer Coll, New London, NH; SR; BS; Intrnshp River City Arts; Bujs Admn; Mrktng/Pub Rltns.**

**CLOWERS, HOLLY E,** Ms St Univ, Miss State, MS; FR; BS; Hnrs Prog 90-; Phi Eta Sigma; Gamma Beta Phi; Alpha Lambda Delta; Beta Beta Beta; Mcrblgy; Rsrch MS.

**CLOWSER, CAROL L,** Radford Univ, Radford, VA; SR; BS; Math; Tchng.

**CLUM, CRISS PATRICK,** Oh Univ, Athens, OH; SR; BSEE; Stdnt Govt Ohio U Lncstr 87; Delta Upsilon Ohio State U 85-86; Wrte Cmptr Prog; Elctrcl Eng.

**CLUM, INHO,** Oh Univ, Athens, OH; JR; BSEE; Tau Beta Pi 90-; Deans Schlrshp 90-; AAS 90; Elec Engrg; Engr.

**CLUNAN, PATRICK H,** Memphis St Univ, Memphis, TN; FR; BA; Tutor Core; TN Brd Rgnts Schlrshp Dean Lst 90-; IM Ftbl Bsktbl Sftbl; Bsns Admnstrtn; Accntng.

**CLUNIE, SHARON,** Andover Coll, Portland, ME; SR; AS; Med Asstng.

**CLUTS, KEVIN L,** Wright St Univ Lake Cmps, Celina, OH; JR; BA; Stdnt Snt Tres 90-; Natl Assc Soc Wrkrs 90-; Intrnshp OH Dept Hmn Svcs; Chldrns Svcs; Fairborn Sr Ctzns Ctr; Soc Wrk; Prvt Soc Wrk Prctc.

**CLYATT, ANGELA D,** St Tech Inst At Memphis, Memphis, TN; FR; BS; TN Brd Rgnts Schlshp 90 ; Pres Lst 90-; Fnc; Law.

**CLYNE, DEBORAH G,** Fl Atlantic Univ, Boca Raton, FL; JR; BA; Frrs St Univ SGA 88-90; Htl Sla Mrktng Assoc; Intl Imprf Lght Cmm; Natl Hnr Scty; Deans Lst 89-; Deans lst 90; Intern Fd Srvc Mgmt; Imprvd Swmmr 90; AAS 90; Intl Bus.

**CMIELEWSKI, DAWN M,** Hudson County Comm Coll, Jersey City, NJ; SO; BA; Erly Chldhd Educ; Sch Tchr.**

**COAKLEY, SHEILA H,** Univ Of Nc At Greensboro, Greensboro, NC; SR; BSN; LPN Sandhills Cumm Clg 81; Nurs.

**COATES, CARA D,** Middle Tn St Univ, Murfreesboro, TN; FR; BA; Chrs 90-; Chmbr Choir 90-; Shw Choir 90-; Jz Ensmbl Voclst 90-; Dance Clb 90-; Rim-Wrtrs 90-; FCA 90-; Music Indstry; Sngr/Sngwrtr/Audio Eng.

**COATES, DEBORAH K,** Longwood Coll, Farmville, VA; JR; BA; Hnr Prog 89-90; AS Danville Comm Coll 90; Biology; Vet Med.

**COATES, ELIZABETH D,** Lesley Coll, Cambridge, MA; JR; BS; LINC Pblcty 88-; Womanthought Mag Stf 90-; Natl Stdnt Campaign Against Hunger 88; Rosies Place/Oakdale Hse/Hunslet Hse Leads England 89; Caspar Emerg Serv Cntr 89; Hmn Svcs/ Sclgy/Psych/Lit; Wrkg Subst Abuse.

**COATES, FREDA M,** Fayetteville St Univ, Fayetteville, NC; FR; Mrchng/Pep/Symph Bnds 90-; Able Lady Of Mnth 90-; Deans Lst 90-; Spec Tlnt Awd 90-.

**COATES, LINDA M,** Tougaloo Coll, Tougaloo, MS; SO; BS; Stdnt Spprt Srvcs 89-; COGIC Clb Treas 90-; Alpha Lambda Delta 90-; Econ/Acctg; CPA.

**COATES, MONIQUE R,** Endicott Coll, Beverly, MA; SO; AS; Peer Tutor 90-; Dns Lst 89-; Finance E Ins Prem Fnc 88-89; Hosp Trust 81-84; RI Auto Ins Plan Serv Offc 84-88; Cert Hall Inst 89; Lib Arts; Intl Rel.

**COATES-SMITH, RENEE,** Niagara Univ, Niagara Univ, NY; SR; BA; Stf Rprtr 89; Dns Lst; Tutoring Srvc Niagara Comm Cntr/Grls Clb; Engl Educ.

**COATS, DAVID KEITH,** Univ Of Sc At Columbia, Columbia, SC; SR; BA; Mrchng Bnd 87-88; Symphnc Bnd 87; Prcssn Ensmbl 87; Alpha Phi Omega 87-; Engl/Bus; Vet Med.

**COATS, MICHELLE L,** Longwood Coll, Farmville, VA; SR; Bpt Student Union Chr 87-88; Camerata Singers 86-90; Intervarsity Christian Flwshp Bible Study Ldr 88-90; Sigma Alpha Iota Chpn 88-89; BA 90; Music; Music Ministry.

**COATS, TIMOTHY W,** Old Dominion Univ, Norfolk, VA; GD; MS; Martial Arts Clb 86-90; Black Belt Soc 89-; Pi Tau Sigma 88-; Tau Beta Pi Pres 89-; Grad Teach Asstntshp 90; BS; Mech Eng.

**COBB, ALLISON A,** Simmons Coll, Boston, MA; FR; BA; Yrbk Stff 90-; French/Cmmnctns.

**COBB, BARRY S,** Univ Of Nc At Chapel Hill, Chapel Hill, NC; GD; JD; Moot Ct Tm; Pi Sigma Alpha; Phi Beta Kappa; Phi Delta Phi; Dns Lst 90-; Amer Jurisprudence Awd 90; BS 89; Law.

**COBB, CAROLYN J,** Bishop St Comm Coll, Mobile, AL; FR; Alpha Epsilon Nu 90; Woodcock Pta Comm Chr 74-87; Mae Ganes Pta 81-83; Williamson HS Pta Sec 86-87; Cert Erly Chldhd 90; Elem Educ.

**COBB, CAROLYN Y,** Univ Of Nc At Greensboro, Greensboro, NC; GD; SNCAE 88-90; BS 90.

**COBB, CHRISTINE,** City Univ Of Ny Queensbrough, New York, NY; FR; Cmptrs; Cmptr Prog.

**COBB, DANIELLE N,** Jackson St Univ, Jackson, MS; SO; BA; Amer Mrktng Assn 89-90; St Joseph Hosp Fnnc Intern; INROADS WI; Bus/Fnnc; Fnncl Anlyst/Bdgt Mngr.

**COBB, DE JUANA M,** Al A & M Univ, Normal, AL; FR; BS; Natl Soc Of Blck Engrs; Inst Of Electrcl/Electrnc Engrs Dsgn Team; Elec Engr Tech.

**COBB, GARY A,** Hillsborough Comm Coll, Tampa, FL; SO; BA; Phi Theta Kappa; Auto Bdy Rpr 77-89; Acctg/Fin; CPA/ADVSR.

**COBB, JACQUELINE A,** Fl International Univ, Miami, FL; SR; Future Educators Of Am 90-; Phi Kappa Phi; Deans List 87-; Grad With Hnrs; AA Miami Dade Comm Coll 89; Elem Edn; Law.

**COBB, KELLY A,** Univ Of Sc At Columbia, Columbia, SC; FR; BS; Bptst Un 90-; Acdmc Achvmnt Awd 90; Blgy; Med/Ob.

**COBB, MARILYN,** Ms Gulf Coast Comm Coll, Perkinston, MS; SO; Wesley Club 89-; Phi Theta Kappa Treas 90-; Stdnt Svc Award 89-90; Hall Of Fame MS Gulf Coast Cmnty Clg 90-; Bus; Acctng.

**COBB, PAMELA A,** Glassboro St Coll, Glassboro, NJ; JR; BA; Acme Mkts Cust Svc Rep/Cashier; AA Camden Cty Clg 89-90; Hstry; Tchg.

**COBB, STACIE M,** Middle Tn St Univ, Murfreesboro, TN; SR; BS; Natl Assoc Female Exec; Amer Mgmt Assoc; Gamma Beta Phi; Phi Gamma Phi 87-; Annual Psyclgy Awd; CSCC Hmng Queen; CSCC Otsdng Acad Achvmnt Athlete; CSCC Psychology Awd; Var Bkbl; CSCC Capt 87-89; AS Columbia Clg 89; Ssychology.

**COBB, SUSAN L,** Middle Ga Coll, Cochran, GA; JR; BS; Stdnt Govt Assoc Sen 88-90; Actvts Comm 89-90; Bat Girl 88-90; AS 90; Fin; Ins.

**COBB, SUSANNAH G,** Peace Coll, Raleigh, NC; FR; BA; Granddaughter/Daughter Clb 90-; Sigma Delta Mu 90-; Ragland Schlrshp Cambridge Univ; Tennis Schlrshp 90-; Acad Schlrshp 90-; Vars Tennis; Econ; Law.

**COBBLE, JULIE A,** Univ Of Ky, Lexington, KY; SO; Coll Acdmc Excllnc; Ovrnght Hstss 89-; Pre Law Clb; Hi Eta Sigma 89-; Delta Gamma 90; Deans Lst 89-; Prsdntl Schlrshp 89-; Pltcl Sci.

**COBBLER, VIRGINIA R,** Piedmont Tech Coll, Greenwood, SC; FR; AS; Omega Chi Phi Theta Kappa; Baptst Womans Mission Un 89-; Deans List 90-; Bus; Acctng/Mgt.

**COBBOLD, ISHMAEL F,** City Univ Of Ny Bronx Comm Col, Bronx, NY; SO; AS; SERC; Phi Theta Kappa VP; Tutorg Serv 90-; OCD; Cngrssnl Cert Mrt 89; Tlnt Rstr Cert Achmvmnt; Deans Lst; WP Bronx Edctnl Opprtnty Cntr 89; Bus Admin Acctg; CPA.

**COBBS, CYNTHIA A,** Allen Univ, Columbia, SC; SO; Cls Treas 89-90; Soph Cls Exec Comm Secy 90-; Eductr; : Tcher.

**COBBS, JEFFREY TAFT,** Univ Of Sc At Columbia, Columbia, SC; JR; BME; Music Ed Natl Conf Clb 90-; March Bnd; Concert Bnd 90-; Symphonic Bnd; Gamma Beta Phi; Delta Omicron 90-; Mnrty Stdnt Awd Acad 90-; Music Edn/Psychlgy; Teach/Clncl Psychlgst.

**COBIN, MARLA R,** Franklin And Marshall Coll, Lancaster, PA; FR; BA; Reach VP; Cltn Choice; Lncstr Assn Rtrd Ctzns; Dana Schlr; Hrns Lst; Deans Lst 90-; Psychology; Clncl Chld Psychlgy.

**COBLE, DARIN W,** Vance Granville Comm Coll, Henderson, NC; FR; BA; Bus.

**COBLER, TONIA D,** Northern Ky Univ, Highland Hts, KY; SO; BA; GUNK Geography Clb; Sec Ed Mddl Grds Soc Studies; Tchr.

**COBURN, CHRISTOPHER R,** Old Dominion Univ, Norfolk, VA; BS; SAE 88-; Tchncl Eng Gleasman Corp 90; AAS SUNY Alfred 90; Eng Tchnlgy; Auto Arntcl Eng.

**COCCIOLO, BARBARA M,** Univ Of North Fl, Jacksonville, FL; SR; BA; Phi Kappa Phi; Jcksnvll Lgl Assts Inc; Lel Asst Selbert Selber 88-; Mrktng.

**COCCOLUTO, RALPH E,** Coll Of Charleston, Charleston, SC; FR; BFA; Artist 87-; Hspntr Mason Prntr 87-; Fine Art; MA/ FINE Arts.

**COCHRAN, CAROLINE M,** Memphis Academy Of The Arts, Memphis, TN; SO.

**COCHRAN, DAVID J,** Univ Of Miami, Coral Gables, FL; SR; BA; Amrcn Inst Archtctr Stdnts 89-; Sigma Phi Epsilon 87-; Natl Coll Archtctr Dsgn Awrd; Intrmrl Hcky 87; Arch.

**COCHRAN, JASON T,** Lexington Comm Coll, Lexington, KY; FR; BS; Deans Lst 90; Tchr.

**COCHRAN, JULIE A,** Univ Of New England, Biddeford, ME; SO; Stdnt Senate 89-; U Of ME Barachute Clb Sec 88-89; Am Red Crs Instr/Vol 90-91; Phys Therapy.

**COCHRAN, KRISTIE E,** Southern Coll Of Tech, Marietta, GA; SO; BS; Inst Indstrl Engrs 90-; Sigma Alpha Omega Soc Chrmn 90-; Indstrl Eng; Tech Sales/Dstrbtn.

**COCHRAN, KRISTIN L,** Converse Coll, Spartanburg, SC; FR; BA; Stdnt Admsns Bd 90-; Dns Lst 90-; Stdnt Cnsltnt Campus Wrtg Cntr 90-; Engl/Pshcylgy/Sec Educ; Engl Professor.

**COCHRAN, RACHEL D,** Birmingham Southern Coll, Birmingham, AL; SR; Yng Dem 87-; Psi Chi 88-; Sigma Tau Delta 89-; Engl Rsrch Intrn 89-90; Cum Laude; Engl/Psychlgy; Orgnztnl Psychlgy.

**COCHRAN, STEVEN A,** Indiana Univ Of Pa, Indiana, PA; SR; BED; Phi Sigma Pi Pres 88-; I M Bkbl Bwlng 88; Stdnt Acctg Assn 88-89; Provost Schlr; Para Prfsnl Lrng Ctr Tutor 90; Mc Farland Schlrshp 89; Math; Tch.

**COCHRAN, TAMMI O,** Al A & M Univ, Normal, AL; JR; BS; Free Entp Clb; Math Clb; Mktg Clb; Delta Sigma Theta Treas 90-; Co-Op AL A/M; Co-Op US Frstry Serv; Cmptr Prgmmr; Mktg/Cmptr Sci.

**COCHRAN JR, WILLIAM L,** Salisbury St Univ, Salisbury, MD; GD; MBA; AA Frederick Comm Coll 88; BS 90; BS 90; Bus Admin; Entrprnr.

**COCKE, LAURA A,** Central Va Comm Coll, Lynchburg, VA; FR; AAS; Bus Admn; Cmptr Prgrmmng.

**COCKERHAM, RHONDA M,** Univ Of Cincinnati-Clrmnt Coll, Batavia, OH; SO; BA; Infant Lrng Proj; Chief Child Care Wrkr STEP; Wkng BSW Currently Wkng Childcare Wrkr Children Home; Social Work; Masters Social Wk.

**COCKERHAM, SCOTT J,** Old Dominion Univ, Norfolk, VA; FR; Old Dominion Hons Prog 90-; NROTC; Nmntn US Naval Acdmy; IM Sports.

**COCKLIN, MICHAEL R,** U S Coast Guard Academy, New London, CT; JR; Scuba Clb Pres 89-; Indoor Soccr Clb 88-; SNAME 90-; Spec Olympcs Vybl Trnmnt Coor; Tutor Mntor Prog 88-; Var Soccer 88-; Marine Engr/Naval Arch; Engr.

**COCKRELL, ALLISON A,** Univ Of Sc At Aiken, Aiken, SC; SO; BA; Cmps Crsd Christ 90-; Gamma Beta Phi 90-; Sthrn Bell Schlrshp; Sci/Occptnl Thrpy.

**COCKRELL, ANGELIA J,** Middle Tn St Univ, Murfreesboro, TN; SR; Creative Sociology Awd 90; Youth Diversion Prog; BS Middle TN State Univ; Psychology; Ph D Clinical Psychology.**

**COCKRELL, GRACE,** Faulkner Univ, Montgomery, AL; JR; BA; Biology; Dermatologist.

**COCKRUM, DARA K,** Itawamba Comm Coll, Fulton, MS; SO; Nursing.

**COCKS, ALICIA I,** Messiah Coll, Grantham, PA; BA; Wmns Ensble 90; Wrld Chrstn Flwshp 90-; Wmns Tennis; Math; Scndry Educ.

**COCKS, ANITA L,** Fl St Univ, Tallahassee, FL; JR; BM; Phi Theta Kappa 88-90; Sigma Alpha Iota Tres; Brevard Clg Prsdnt Awd 90; AFA Brvrd Clg 90; Msc; Bssn Prfrmnc.

**CODER, DEBORAH A,** Niagara Univ, Niagara Univ, NY; SR; BBA; Acctg Assoc 90-; Dns Lst 88-; Delta Epsilon Sigma 89-; PTA Newfane Treas; Friends 22 Mothers Clb Chrmn 90-; Auditing Intern First Bapt Church; AAS Niagara Co Cmnty Clg 88; AA 77; Acctg; CPA.

**CODER, SUSAN L,** Middle Tn St Univ, Murfreesboro, TN; SR; Assoc Stdnt Body Sprme Chr Juste 82-84; Ct Juste; Gamma Iota Sigma Treas 84-85; Tn Tchr Cert 90-; BBA 85; Fin; Tch.

**CODY, CHRISTANA M,** Birmingham Southern Coll, Birmingham, AL; SO; BFA; Art Leag 89-; Trngl Clb 90-; Habitat Hmnty; Art/Pntng/Grphc Dsgn; Advrtsng.

**CODY, CYNTHIA S,** Defiance Coll, Defiance, OH; SR; BS; Alpha Chi 90-; Phi Alpha Theta; Elem Educ; Tchng.

**COE, JASON CHRISTOPHER,** Columbia Union Coll, Takoma Park, MD; FR; MBA; Phi Eta Sigma 90-; Bus/Psychlgy; Admn.

**COE, LAURIE A,** Liberty Univ, Lynchburg, VA; JR; BS; Flwshp Chrstn Ahlts Comm 90-; Intvars Chrstn Flwshp 89; Clgt Bible Stds 88-89; Good Smrtn Ctr Tchr; Crs Cntry/Trck 90-; Physcl Ed; Educ/Coaching.

**COELLO, MARCELA E,** Univ Of Sc At Columbia, Columbia, SC; JR; PRSSA 90-; Andina Publicidad BBDO In Guayaquil Ecuador 90; Advtsng; Adv Agnt.**

**COEN, MARIE W,** Radford Univ, Radford, VA; SR; BS; AAS Wytheville Comm Clg 89; BS Radford Univ; Educ; Elem Tchr.

**COEY, WILLIAM G,** Univ Of Akron, Akron, OH; SR; BS; Fincl Mgmt Assn; Busn Admin/Finc; Corp Atty.

**COFAN, NANETTE MARIE,** Bayamon Tech Univ Coll, Bayamon, PR; JR; AFAP 90-; AS 90; Computer Science; Programming.

**COFER, SCOTTY L,** Livingston Univ, Livingston, AL; SO; Wesley Foundation 90-; IM Spts; Phys Ed; Coach Tch.

**COFFEE, LAURA G,** Georgetown Univ, Washington, DC; SO; BSBA; Ye Dmsdy Bk Yrbk Stff 90; Prtstnt Prog Brd 90-; GAAP WV St Chr 90-; Acctng; Accnt.

**COFFELT, BELINDA S,** Snead St Jr Coll, Boaz, AL; SO; BS; Phi Theta Kappa; Pres Lst; Pres Awrd; Phrmcy; Hosp Phrmcst.

**COFFER, WILLIAM D,** Clark Atlanta Univ, Atlanta, GA; SO; Inspirational Voices Faith Gospel Choir Bus Mngr; Math Excellence Awd Precalculus Tutor; Bus Admin; Marketing.

**COFFEY, DALLAS R,** Sue Bennett Coll, London, KY; SO; BS; Deans List 90-; Busn; Acctng.

**COFFEY, DAVID SCOTT,** Western Ky Univ, Bowling Green, KY; JR; BS; Phi Kappa Phi; Phi Eta Sgm 89-; Eli Lilly Co; Chem; Ph D Srch Chem.

**COFFEY, KEVIN M,** Radford Univ, Radford, VA; SO; BS; Hs Cncl Dm Hl Rep; Rugby Clb; Cmnctns; Sprts Cstr.

**COFFEY, SHEILA M,** Sue Bennett Coll, London, KY; SO; BED; Pep Clb 89-90; PTA 87-; Dorthea Pentecostal Chrch 87-; AA; Socl Sci; Elem Educ.

**COFFEY, TINA LOUISE,** Univ Of Nc At Charlotte, Charlotte, NC; SR; BA; Res RSA 89-; Hll Cncl VP 8-; Deans Lst 87-89; Chncllrs Lst 90-; IM Ftbll; Scl Wrk.

**COFFIN, DEBORAH A,** Daytona Beach Comm Coll, Daytona Beach, FL; FR; BA; Busn.

**COFFIN, DENISE R,** Schenectady County Comm Coll, Schenectady, NY; FR; BA; Phi Beta Lambda 90-; Bus.

**COFFIN, SHERI L,** Syracuse Univ, Syracuse, NY; SR; BARCH; Architecture Stdnt Org 87-; Architecture Nwsltr 89-; Study Abroad Florence Italy 90; Architecture.

**COFFINGER, JOHN J,** S U N Y Coll Of Tech At Delhi, Delhi, NY; FR; AAS; Assoc Gen Cntrctrs Amer VP 90-; Voc Indstrl Clbs Amer Comp Jdg 90-; Phi Theta Kappa 90-; Assoc Gen Cntrs Amer VP 90-; Bldg Constr; Coll Prof.

**COFFMAN, CAROLYN CANDACE,** Univ Of Rochester, Rochester, NY; JR; BA; Phi Theta Kappa; Anthropology Medl Applied.

**COFFMAN, ERIC D,** Univ Of Akron, Akron, OH; SR; BS; Fin Mgmt Assc 90-; Hon Clb 86-; Cmps Fcs 86-90; Fin Mgmt Assc Hon Scty; Hon Pgm 86-; Gldn Key 88-; Intrnshp Paine Webber 90-; Fin; Undrwrtng.

**COFFMAN, HOLLY A,** Longwood Coll, Farmville, VA; SR; Peer Hlpr 89-; Curry Hl Cncl Sec 88-90; SEA; Psi Chi 90-; Dns Lst 88-90; Crp Wlk Spnsr/Coord 89-90; VA Dpndnt Schlrshp 87-; BS; Elem Educ/Psychlgy; Tch.

**COFFMAN, J STEVEN,** Marshall University, Huntington, WV; JR; BA; Acctg Clb 90-; Res Hl Assoc 88-; Phi Eta Sigma 89-; Acctg; CPA.

**COFFMAN, MARSHA L,** Davis & Elkins Coll, Elkins, WV; SR; Phoenix Alliance Hstrn Drug Alcohol Awareness Group Hstrn 90-; Campus Crt Rep 90-; Flag Corp Cap 87-89; Hnrs Assoc; Psychology Club 90-; Sun Schl Tchr 5-6 Grade 90-; Dens List 89-; Psychology; Counseling Psychology.

**COFFMAN, RAYMOND D,** S U N Y Coll Of Tech At Frmgdl, Farmingdale, NY; FR; Bus; Mgmt.

**COFFMAN, STEPHANIE L,** Bridgewater Coll, Bridgewater, VA; SO; BS; Lambda 90-; Deans List 89-; Soclgy.

**COGAN, SONYA R,** Endicott Coll, Beverly, MA; SO; AS; Deans Lst 90; Fclty Schlrshp 89-; Connoisseur Mag Intrnshp Photo Dept 90; C Sanders Studio Intrnshp Asst; Phtgrphy; Advtsng/Fshn.

**COGAR, CARWYN J,** Concord Coll, Athens, WV; SR; BS; Readng Cncl 88-89; Alpha Chi 89-; AS Beckley Clg 71; Ed/Multi Sbjts; Cnslng.

**COGEN, SHANNON HOPE,** Birmingham Southern Coll, Birmingham, AL; SO; Stdnt Alumni Assoc 89-; Conservancy 89-; Partnership Steering Comm 89-; Alpha Lambda Delta; Phi Eta Sigma; Phi Eta Sigma; Chi Omega; Res Hl Assoc Corr Secr 90; Dana Intern Natl Conf Christians/Jews; Hmn Res Mgmt; MA.

**COGGINS, ALLAHNA A,** Univ Of Miami, Coral Gables, FL; SO; BS; Psych; Med.

**COGGINS, LESLIE M,** Univ Of Sc At Columbia, Columbia, SC; FR; BS; Assoc Hnrs Stdnts; Alpha Lambda Delta 90-; Phi Eta Sigma 90-; Hnrs Coll 90-; Mathematics; Professor.

**COGGINS, MARK D,** Univ Of Sc At Columbia, Columbia, SC; JR; BS; Gamma Beta Phi 89-; Gldn Ky 90-; Pres Hon Rl 90-; Dns Lst 89-; Pres Schlrshp 90-; USCS Fndrs Schlrshp 90-; Wlmt Pharm Schlrshp 90-; Pharm.

**COGGINS, MARNIE E,** Univ Of Southern Ms, Hattiesburg, MS; JR; BS; Kappa Mu Epsilon 89-; Gamma Beta Phi 89-; Dmnd Drlngs 88-90; Math.

**COGHILL, GLENNIS WILSON,** Tri County Tech Coll, Pendleton, SC; JR; Ntnl Assc Women Const; Wldng; Indstrl/ Engrng Tchngy; Wldng Instrc.

**COGHILL, PENNY D,** Averett Coll, Danville, VA; JR; BS; Stdnt Fndtn 90; Deans Lst 90; Accntng; Intrnl Adtr Or CPA.

**COGMAN, DENISE N,** Western New England Coll, Springfield, MA; SO; BSW; Minority Orgnztn Asst Treas 89-; Alpha Lambda Delta 90-; Social Work; Teaching.

**COGSWELL, DONALD J,** Salisbury St Univ, Salisbury, MD; SR; MA; Republican Club 89-; American Legion 71-; Phi Kappa Phi; Phi Alpha Theta; Pi Gamma Mu 90-; English; Writing/ Publishing.

**COHEN, ABBA Y,** Yeshiva Univ, New York, NY; GD; MA; Dean Lst; Magna Cum Laude; BA 90; Psych.

**COHEN, ABRAHAM G,** Yeshiva Univ, New York, NY; JR; BA; IM Bsktbl Cptn 90-; Aliyah Clb Fndr 90-; SSSJ 89-; Hnrs Soc; JSS; NHS; PHLNTHRPY Soc 89-90; Fd Hmls Co Chrmn 89-90; AIPAC VP 90-; Statistcs Cmptr Oprtr Asstnt TA 90-; Shcick Spr Hoops Chrmn 89-; Ecnmcs; Bsns.

**COHEN, AHAMED I,** Columbus Coll Of Art & Design, Columbus, OH; JR; BA; Schlrshp; Soccer 90-; Graphic Artist 85-89; Cert City & Guilds Or London Inst 89; Adv Design; Art Dir.

**COHEN, ALICE M,** City Univ Of Ny Queensbrough, New York, NY; SR; AAS; Phi Theta Kappa 89; Alpha Beta Gamma 88; PTA Pres 83-85; P A Jewish Ctr Religious Schl Pres 82-84; Assist Bkkpr 80; Cert 89; Med Assist/Tech Sec; Med Rcrds Admin.

**COHEN, BARAK A,** Cornell Univ Statutory College, Ithaca, NY; JR; BS; YMCA Sccr Coach 89-; Ski Clb 89; Deans Lst 87-; Hughes Schlr; IM; Bio; Rsrch.

**COHEN, BRADLEY W,** Averett Coll, Danville, VA; SR; BA; Hmcmng Ct/King 88-; Eqstrn Clb 87-89; Rugby Clb 87-89; Deans Lst 90-; Pi Kapp Phi 88-; Police Deptofcr 87-; Lf Svng Crew 88-; Chrldr; Law Enfrcmnt; Police.

**COHEN, DANA L,** Western New England Coll, Springfield, MA; SR; SCOPE Scrty Prod Crw 86-88; MUSO Prod Asstnt Mgr 87-88; Psi Chi 90-; Deans Lst 88-90; Grad BA Cum Laude; BA; Psychlgy.

**COHEN, ELIZABETH J,** Cornell Univ Statutory College, Ithaca, NY; JR; NY Wmns Stdy Assoc; Psi Chi; Gldn Key VP; Hu Nu De Kah; Bst Amer Pro; Drug Free Pro One To One Big Sis/Big Bro Pro; YES; Elmira Psychtrc Cntr Intrn; Comm Serv Recog Pro; Educ; Clncl Psychlgy.

**COHEN, ERIC ARIEL,** Broward Comm Coll, Ft Lauderdale, FL; JR; BA; AA 90; Biology; Med.

**COHEN, GREG A,** Broward Comm Coll, Ft Lauderdale, FL; FR; BA; Phi Theta Kappa 90-; Coll Repbl; Hons Inst 90-; Pres Lst 90; Jrnlsm; Sprtswrtr.

**COHEN, ILENE M,** Clark Univ, Worcester, MA; JR; MBA; Plyrs Scty 88; Concrt Chr 88; Stdy Abrd Spain; Bus/Mngmnt; Bus.**

**COHEN, JACQUELINE I,** Univ Of Rochester, Rochester, NY; JR; BA; Alumni Assn VP 89-; Pnhlnc Cncl Rep; Pres Cncl 89-90; Reunion Cncl Capt; Order Omega 90-; Sigma Delta Tau Pres 88-; Pol Sci Intrnshp; Pol Sci/Psychlgy; Law.

**COHEN, JARA M,** Va Commonwealth Univ, Richmond, VA; SR; BS; Innovative Images Asst Dir 90-; Pub Rels Stdnt Soc Of Amer 90-; Golden Key; Kappa Tau Alpha; Intrnshp Mntl Hlth Assoc; Cmctns; Pub Rels.

**COHEN, JOHN A,** Saint Andrews Presbytrn Coll, Laurinburg, NC; JR; BA; Psychlgy Clb Offcer 90-; Nwsppr 90-; Deans Hnr Rll 89-; Chld Stds:.

**COHEN, LAURIE M,** Fl International Univ, Miami, FL; SR; BA; Phi Theta Kappa 90; Psi Chi Rdrdng Sec; AA Miami Dade Comm Coll 89; Psych; Orgnztnl Psych.

**COHEN, LORI A,** Univ Of Sc At Columbia, Columbia, SC; JR; BA; Gamma Beta Phi 88-90; Phi Theta Kappa 89-90; Retailing.

**COHEN, MARC L,** S U N Y Coll Of Tech At Frmgdl, Farmingdale, NY; SO; BA; Alpha Beta Gamma 89; Bus Admin; Bnkng.

**COHEN, MARTIN D,** Univ Of Al At Birmingham, Birmingham, AL; JR; BA; Deans Lst 90; Pres Hon; Fitness Spclst Hlth Ed; Corp Fitness.

**COHEN, MEREDITH L,** Univ Of Miami, Coral Gables, FL; SR; BA; Beta Gamma Sigma; Phi Kappa Phi; Golden Key 89-; Zeta Beta Tau/Lit Sis 88-90; R E Lic Gold Coast R E Schl 88; Fince; R E Invstg.

**COHEN, MITCHELL A,** Temple Univ, Philadelphia, PA; GD; JD; Gldn Key 89-; Dscplnry Com; Deptmntl Hon Crmnl Justc Dept; Deans Lst Law Sch; Phi Alpha Delta Spkrs Com 90-; ABA Law Stdnt Div; Intrn Phil Dist Atty Offc; Deans Lst Undrgrad 80-81 89-90; Cert Apprctn Dean Amblr Cmps 89-90; Law.

**COHEN, R J,** Emory Univ, Atlanta, GA; JR; BBS; Nwspr Jrnlst 90; Spkr Prog Chrmn 89; Beta Gamma Sigma; Ordr Omega; Kappa Kappa Gamma Treas 89; Ambsdr 88-89; Deans Schlr 88-; Hotel Intern 90-; Bus Mgmt; Mgmt Cnsltng.

**COHEN, SETH A,** Yeshiva Univ, New York, NY; JR; BA; James Striar Schl/Hebraic Stds VP 90-; Assoc Ed Mddl Estrn Affrs Pol Paper 89-; Deans List 88-; Pre Law Soc 89-; Excllnc Jrnlsm Awd 90; Var Bsktbl Tm 88-; Soc/Speech; Law.

**COHEN, SHERRIE L,** Univ Of Sc At Columbia, Columbia, SC; FR; BA; Hillil VP 90-; Emerging Ldr Prog; Sfty Com; Delta Gamma Asst Secr; Delta Gamma Hnr Roll; Acctg.

**COHEN, STEPHEN D,** Nova Univ, Ft Lauderdale, FL; GD; MBA; Coral Spgs Chmbr Cmmrce 88-90; Grtr Hllywd Chmbr Cmmrce 87-88; Kiwanis Clb 88-90; Bnk Brnch Mgr; AA Broward Comm Coll 84; BA FL Atlntc Univ 86; Finance/Bnkng.

**COHEN, STEVEN R,** Fl International Univ, Miami, FL; JR; BBA; Miami Christian Clg Cls Vp 00-02; Miami Christian Clg Lbry Awd 87; AA Miami Christian Clg 89; Bus; Law.

**COHEN, THOMAS F,** Ny Univ, New York, NY; JR; BA; Lit Sdts; Professor.

**COHENOUR, ROSEMARIE,** Wv Univ At Parkersburg, Parkersburg, WV; SO; Acdmc Schlrshp; Pre Schl Mothers Assn Pres 87-; BS WV Inst Tchnlgy 79; Drftng Eng.

**COHN, BRADLEY M,** Univ Of Cincinnati, Cincinnati, OH; SR; BS; Cncl Exceptnl Chldrn; Alpha Lambda Delta; Kappa Delta Pi; Gldn Key; Summer Session Schlrshp; Josephine /Justin Rollman Schlrshp; AS Elec Eng Tech 89; Spcl Ed/Tchr.

**COHN, DAVID M,** Univ Of Sc At Columbia, Columbia, SC; SR; JD; Hll Scty Pres 87-; Stdn Tgovt Elctns Cmmssn Dpty Cmmssnr 89-; Assoc Hnrs Stndts Rep; Gamma Beta Phi 88-; Gldn Key 89-; Phi Beta Kappa 90; Prsdnts Lst 87; Dean Lst 87; Stdnt Asst Dvsn Rsrch 88-; IM Tnns Tbl Tnns 87-; B Ar Sc; Law.

**COHN, KLARA J,** Univ Of Sc At Columbia, Columbia, SC; FR; BS; Hillel Pres 90-; Assn Hnrs Stdnts 90-; Gamma Beta Phi; Math.

**COHOON, PETER S,** Hillsborough Comm Coll, Tampa, FL; SO; AS; Phi Kappa Phi; Phi Theta Kappa; Beta Alpha Psi; Constuction Fin Mgt Assoc; ABA Manatee Jr Clg 80; BA Univ S Flr 82; Archtl Engrg; Const Mgt.

**COHOON, SAMUEL S,** Pa St Univ Delaware Cty Cmps, Media, PA; SO; BA; Philosophy.

**COHOON, SHERYL B,** Chattanooga St Tech Comm Coll, Chattanooga, TN; GD; Singn Hnds 89-; Psi Beta Sec 89-; Hamltn Co Bapt Assn WMU 88-; Moccasn Bnd Grl Sct Cncl Ldr 88-; AS 89; Interprtr Trng; Educ.

**COHRON, J GEORGE,** Tn St Univ, Nashville, TN; GD; Outstdg Clg Stdt Am 89; Stdt Tchr Ed Assoc 90-; Bd Govnrs Apostoloc Coalition 85-; Founded Pastoring Madison United Pentecostal Church; Assoc Art Dgr Gulf Cst Comm 81; BA Sci; Biology; Tchg.

**COIANTE, PAUL R,** Eckerd Coll, St Petersburg, FL; SR; BA; SAM 89-; Athlt Awrd; Athltc/Acdmc Schlrshps; Var Bsbl 87-; Bus Mgmt.

**COINER, HEATHER K,** Indiana Univ Of Pa, Indiana, PA; JR; BED; Concrt Danc Co 90-; Pi Delta Phi 90-; Engl/Frnch; Sec/Coll Educ.

**COIT, JEFFREY A,** Me Maritime Academy, Castine, ME; JR; BS; Rgmntl Bnd Bndmstr 88-; Fr Brgd Fr Mrshl 88-; Bgdc Amblnc Corp Mdshpmn Liason 88-; Amatuer Radio Clb VP 88-; TV St ME Dmg Cntrl Sqd Fr Mrshl 89; Prpllr Clb US 89-; Twnsnd Mass Cvl Dfns Tm 88-; ME Cert EMT 88-; Cstn Fr Dept 88-; Meth Chrch Chr 88-; Marine Engr Tech.

**COIT, VALERIE S,** Savannah Coll Of Art & Design, Savannah, GA; SO; BFA; Illstrtn; Chldrns Book Illstrn Edtrl Illstrn.

**COKER, ANNIELOU VIRGINIA L,** Fl A & M Univ, Tallahassee, FL; JR; BED; Tchr Aid 68-73; Offc Mgr 75-; AA Lake City Cmmnty Coll 68; Elem Ed; Tch.

**COKER, CHARITY L,** Univ Of Al At Birmingham, Birmingham, AL; SO; BA; Spnsh/Intrntl Stdys; Peace Corp Gov UN.

**COKER, MICHAEL C,** Williamsburg Tech Coll, Kingstree, SC; AA; Stu Govt Assn Pres 90-; Phi Theta Kappa; Psych.

**COKER, MYTSI L,** Converse Coll, Spartanburg, SC; FR; Yng Rpblcns/Stdnt Govt Assn 90-; Wmn Invld For A Sfr Envir 90-; Ys-4s Yrbk/Skit Comm Mbr/Chr 90-; Converse Ldrs Pgm 90-; Phonathon 90; Bio Lab Assist 90-; Bio/Chem; Med.

**COKER, PAIGE E,** Univ Of South Al, Mobile, AL; FR; BA; Pblc Rltns Stdnt Scty; Amnsty Intl; Kappa Delta 90-; Cmmnctn Arts; Brdcst Jrnlsm.

**COKER III, WILLIAM LINWOOD,** Saint Andrews Presbytrn Coll, Laurinburg, NC; SR; BS; Lab Asst Pgm 88-; CHAOS 90-; NSF Smmr Pgm-UT Knxvll 90; Chmstry; Rsrch.

**COLACO, ALLAN J,** Univ Of Miami, Coral Gables, FL; SO; BBA; Hnrs Stdnts Assn 89-; Indian Stdnts Assn 89-; Amnesty Intl 90-; Prog Cncl 90-; Alpha Lambda Delta 90 ; Phi Eta Sigma 90-; Sngr Schlrshp 89-; Rsdnt Asst; Pres Lst 89-90; Dns Lst 89-91; Scuba Trng/Cert; Acctng; CPA.

**COLAIACOVO, DAREN J,** Radford Univ, Radford, VA; SR; Fnncl Mngmnt Assn VP 90-; IM Flr Ftbl Capt Wtr Polo 89-; Sigma Phi Epsilon 87-; NCAA Div I Lcrss Tm Capt 87-; BBA; Fnnc; Fnncl Anlyst.

**COLANDREA, SABRINA,** Felician Coll, Lodi, NJ; JR; Bus Mgmnt; Law.

**COLANGIONE, RAPHAEL E,** Alfred Univ, Alfred, NY; FR; AS; Play Acting 90; AU Tlthn-Annl Fndrsr 90-; Alpha Lambda Delta; Bus/Admin; Acctg.

**COLANTONIO, ANTHONY J,** Georgetown Univ, Washington, DC; FR; BS; Intl Rltns Com 90-; Coll Rpblcns 90-; IM Sftbl 90-; La Crosse 90-; Biology; Medical Doctor.

**COLANTUONO, LISA A,** Ny Institute Of Tech Ny City, New York, NY; FR; Amer Inst Of Archtctre Stdnts 90-; Bchlrs Of Arctctre; Archtctre.

**COLARUSSO, DEAN V,** Newbury Coll, Brookline, MA; SR; BA; Encrgmnt Awd Fshn Mrchndsng 90; Fshn Mrchndsng.

**COLARUSSO, OLINA,** Merrimack Coll, North Andover, MA; JR; BS; Ornttn Com Coor 88-; Cmmtr Cncl Sec 89; Tr Gde 89-; Acad Achvmnt Schlrshp 87-; Amnsty Intrntl USA 86-; Sllvn Blle And Co CPA 89; Able Rgrs And Sllvn CPA; The Bstn Co 90-; Acctng; CPA.**

**COLASTIN, BEATRICE,** Saint Thomas Univ, Miami, FL; JR; BA; Mnrty Stdnt Union VP 90-; Stdnts Global Prsrvtn; Hon Soc; Acctg/Mgt; Mstrs Degree.

**COLBERG, MONICA T,** Ga Inst Of Tech At Atlanta, Atlanta, GA; FR; BS; Slng Clb; Alumni Assoc; Soc Hispanic Prof Engrs; Alpha Chi Omega Asst Actvts 90-; Techwood Tutoirial 90-; Otsdng Fres Awd; Xerox Awd; Vlybl IMS; Chem Engr.

**COLBERT, BRIAN R,** Univ Of Akron, Akron, OH; SO; BS; Res Hall Gvmt Flr Rep 89-; Co-Op Ed Pgm Figgie Intl Co; IM Ftbl/Vlybl/Sftbl/Golf89-; Civil Engrng.

**COLBERT, CATHERINE R,** Voorhees Coll, Denmark, SC; SR; BA; Pltcl Sci Clb Prsdnt 89-90; Economic Entrprs Assn SIFE 90-; Dbtng Tm Prsdnt 88-; Delta Sigma Theta; Tutrl Srvcs Asst 88-; Deans Lst 88-; Mrt Awd; Vly Bl Tm Cptn 90-; Pltcl Sci; Law.

**COLBERT, CHRISTIE J,** Itawamba Comm Coll, Fulton, MS; FR; BA; Dns Lst 90-; Elem Educ.

**COLBERT, LINDA M,** Western Ky Univ, Bowling Green, KY; SR; Deans Lst 88-89; Assoc Art 89; Engl.

**COLBERT, TIMOTHY E,** Ms St Univ, Miss State, MS; FR; Pre Med; Phys Thrpy.

**COLBURN, KRISTAL B,** Univ Of Southern Ms, Hattiesburg, MS; FR; BA; Eagle Club Phi Mu Rep 90-; Alumni Assn V P 90-; Stdnts Against Drunk Driving V P 90-; Alpha Lambda Delta 90-; Phi Eta Sigma 90-; Gamma Beta Phi 90-; Lambda Sigma 90-; Phi Mu 90-; Deans Lst 90; Gamma Alpha Epsilon Awds 90; Psychology; Ind/Org Psychologist.

**COLBURN, LORETTA J,** Brewer St Jr Coll, Fayette, AL; SO; BS; Phi Beta Lamda; Phrmcy.

**COLBY, JULIE E,** Ms Gulf Coast Comm Coll, Perkinston, MS; FR; Phi Theta Kappa.

**COLDEN, COLLEEN M,** Neumann Coll, Aston, PA; SO; BA; Comm Club 89-; Nwspr Writer 90-; Mag Phtgrphr; Hnrs Prog 89-; VIVA 89-; Deans List 90-; Varsity Awd Intercoll Spts Capt 90-; Acdmc/Athltc Exclnc Awd; Bsktbl Sftbl NAIA Intercoll IM Capt 89-; Comm Arts; Dir Of Motion Pictures.

**COLDIRON, WILLIAM B,** Marshall University, Huntington, WV; SR; BBA; Rpblcn Natl Com 89-; Coll Rpblcns 89-; Gldn Key 89-; Omicron Delta Epsilon Sec/Tres 90; AS OH Univ 89; Business; Acctng/Physics/Engineering/Comp Sci.

**COLE, ALICE M,** Univ Of Montevallo, Montevallo, AL; FR; Alpha Lambda Delta; Gen Crclm.

**COLE, ANDREA MARIE,** Miami Jacobs Jr Coll Of Bus, Dayton, OH; Assoc; Fash Merch; Bus.

**COLE, CASAUNDRA J,** Columbus Coll Of Art & Design, Columbus, OH; SR; BFA; Stdnt Cncl Sec 90-; Blck Stdnt Allince Sec 90-; Illstrtn; Art Thrpy.

**COLE, CATHEY T,** Union Univ School Of Nursing, Memphis, TN; FR; BSN; TN Mthrs Assoc 84; Drummonds Hm Ext Clb Pres 83-84/86-87; Untd Meth Wm Tres 76-; Meth Chrch Trste 86-; TN Yng Mthr Yr 84; Nrsg.

**COLE, CEDRIC D,** Al A & M Univ, Normal, AL; FR; BS; Dns Lst 90-; IM Bsktbl 90; Mktg.

**COLE, CHRISTINA M,** Emory Univ, Atlanta, GA; SR; Res Advsr; Soph Advsr; Rho Lambda 90; Alpha Delta Pi Pres 90-; BBA; Otstndng Svc Grk 90-; IM Sftbl Scr 88-; Mktng.

**COLE, CHRISTY K,** Memphis St Univ, Memphis, TN; SR; BA; Gldn Ky 89-; Engl.

**COLE, DALE E,** East Tn St Univ, Johnson City, TN; FR; BA; Stdnt Govt Assoc Sntr; Blk Affrs Assoc; Rsdnt Hsng Assoc Pres; Pres Prde; Mu Nu Lambda; Alpha Phi Alpha Dir Of Ed Serv; Im Sprts; Bsnss; Law.

**COLE, DANIEL JOHN MC CARTHY,** Hudson Valley Comm Coll, Troy, NY; SR; AAS; Peer Ed Pgm 90-; PATHS 90-; Phi Theta Kappa; Alpha Xi Sigma; Pres Lst 90-; Tmwrk Hlthy Cmps Pnl 90; Adctns Wmn/Rcvry Expo; Mastoranglo/Arnold Acad Schlrshp 90-; Intern Leonard Hosp Biochem Rehab 90-; Sbstnc Abuse Awrns Spkng 89-; Scl Wrk Psychlgy/Addiction; Msw/Cac.

**COLE, DEBORAH L,** Univ Of Sc At Columbia, Columbia, SC; JR; BS; Phrmcy.

**COLE, DEBRA J,** Fl International Univ, Miami, FL; JR; BS; Cec 90-; Aa Miami Dade Comm Coll 90; Spec Ed/Spcfc Lrng Dsblts; Tchr Speclst.

**COLE, DIANE L,** Univ Of Med & Dentistry Of Nj, Newark, NJ; SR; MPT; BS Roaoke Clg 86; Phy Thrpy.

**COLE, DONALD F,** S U N Y At Buffalo, Buffalo, NY; JR; BS; Univ Buffalo Acctg Assoc 90; Phi Eta Sigma 89-; Univ Hon Prog 88-; Under Grad Tchr Asst 90-; G Cafer Mem Awd 90-; Acctg; CPA.

**COLE, ELIZABETH A,** Birmingham Southern Coll, Birmingham, AL; JR; BA; Fresh Ldrshp Clss 88-89; Hmcmn Cmmtt 89; Trngl Clb 89-90; Phi Eta Sigma Sec/Tres 89-; Alpha Lambda Delta Sec 89-90; Sigma Tau Delta 90-; Alpha Chi Omega Chpln 90-; Omicron Delta Kappa 90-; Mrtr Brd Pres; Pres Stu Srvc Orgn 90-; DANA Intern; Engl; Chrstn Educ.

**COLE, ELIZABETH M,** Memphis St Univ, Memphis, TN; JR; BSN; Sci; Nrsng.

**COLE, ERIC D,** Memphis St Univ, Memphis, TN; JR; Elec Eng; Eng.

**COLE, GREGORY,** Univ Of Southern Ms, Hattiesburg, MS; SR; BS; Phi Theta Kappa 87; Golden Key 90-; Beta Gamma Sigma; Metro Conf Commsnrs List 88-90; W B Harlan Awd Otstndng Jr Cl Bus Stdnt 89; Varsity Bsbl 89-90; AA Meridian Comm Coll 88; Bus Admn; Bus Exec.

**COLE, HERBERT E,** Univ Of South Al, Mobile, AL; JR; BS; Marine Corps 84-87; Elem Ed; Tchr.

**COLE, JENNIFER K,** Savannah Coll Of Art & Design, Savannah, GA; JR; BA; Sewanee Outing Clb 87-89; Univ South Wmns Lacrosse Tm 87-89; Univ South Snow Ski Tm Wmns Cptn; Grphc Dsgn.

**COLE, JONATHAN H,** Northwest Al Comm Coll, Phil Campbell, AL; SO; Schlrs Bowl 89-; Dns Lst 90; Pres Lst 90-; Zoology/Marine Bio; Rsrch.**

**COLE, KIMBERLEY E,** Hampton Univ, Hampton, VA; JR; BA; Pol Sci/Pre-Law Clb 88-; Big Bro/Sis 90-; Mrch Bnd 90-; Alpha Kappa Mu 90-F; Cntrl VA Lgl Aid Soc Vol 90-; Woodrow Wilson Flwshp; Pol Sci.**

**COLE, LA TONYA,** Guilford Tech Comm Coll, Jamestown, NC; Talent Roster 90-.

**COLE, LESLEA RENAE,** Marshall University, Huntington, WV; SR; Delta Omicron; Wind Symph 88-90; Symph Band; Mrchg Band; Pep Band; Brass Ensmbl; Tuba Quartet; Sweet Adelines Barbershop Chorus; Gamma Beta Phi; MENC; Bd Regents Music Schlrshp 87-; Barbershop Quartet 90-; Music Ed.

**COLE, LYNN M,** Comm Coll Algny Co Algny Cmps, Pittsburgh, PA; SR; AS; Phi Theta Kappa; BS Carlon Clg 84; Rsptry Thrpy; MS.

**COLE, MARGE,** Bryant Stratton Bus Inst Roch, Rochester, NY; GD; AOS; Legal Sec.

**COLE, MICHAEL G,** Columbia Union Coll, Takoma Park, MD; JR; Pre Law; Psi Chi; Sigma Tau Delta Treas; Natl Deans Lst 88-; U S Acad Achvmnt 88-; Acad All Amer 89-; Engl/Psychlgy; Law.

**COLE, OLIVER GEORGE,** City Univ Of Ny Bronx Comm Col, Bronx, NY; SO.

**COLE, PATRICIA A,** Lane Coll, Jackson, TN; SR; BA; Elem Ed.

**COLE, PATRICIA A,** Univ Of Tn At Martin, Martin, TN; JR; BA; Elem Educ.

**COLE, PENNY M K,** Beckley Coll, Beckley, WV; SO; BSW; Summers Continous Care Ctr; Jmpng Branch Tabernacle; Girl Sct Ldr; Summers Cty Schl Prctcl Nrsng LPN 79; Soc Sci.

**COLE, PETRA M,** Central Fl Comm Coll, Ocala, FL; FR; AA; Phi Theta Kappa 90-; Sci; Med.

**COLE, RUSSELL T,** Middle Tn St Univ, Murfreesboro, TN; SR; Summr Intrn Tenn Publ Svc Comm; IM Bsktbl/Sftbl; BBA 90; Econ; Govt.

**COLE, SANDRA D,** Univ Of Tn At Martin, Martin, TN; FR; Ldrs In Resdnce 90-; Blck Stdnt Assn 90-; BSA Choir 90-; Alpha Phi Alpha 90-; Bus; CPA/ACCTNT.

**COLE, SHERRY M,** Patrick Henry Comm Coll, Martinsville, VA; FR; Dean Lst 90-; Hstry/Math; Tch.

**COLE, SUSAN L,** Old Dominion Univ, Norfolk, VA; SR; BSME; Tau Beta Pi VP; Pi Tau Sigma; Amer Soc Mech Eng; Soc Lgstcs Eng; Schlrshp Soc Lgstcs Eng 90-; Chrch; Coop Stu Virginia Power; BS VR Poly Inst 76; Dsgn Eng.

**COLE III, THOMAS W,** Clark Atlanta Univ, Atlanta, GA; JR; BA; Psych Clb 90-; Hnrs Clb 90-; Alpha Phi Alpha 90-; Intrnshp Cty Oakland Ca; Fr Guide 90; Soccr 90-; Psych; Counslr/Tchr.

**COLE, VICKY K,** Maysville Comm Coll, Maysville, KY; SO; AD; Staff Nrs LPN; Nrsg; RN.

**COLE, VIKKI SHANNON,** Madisonville Comm Coll, Madisonville, KY; SO; AS; Deans Lst 89-; Bnkg/Bus; Acctg.

**COLE, YOLANDA D,** Al St Univ, Montgomery, AL; JR; BED; Bio/Engl; Educ.

**COLEBROOK, ASHLAR S,** Univ Of Miami, Coral Gables, FL; SO; BBA; Univ Miami Brdg Clb 90-91; Fin; Law.

**COLEGROVE, THERESA L,** Mansfield Univ, Mansfield, PA; FR; BA; Sdl Clb 90; Ski Clb 90; Trck/Fld 90-; Elem Ed/Erly Chldhd; Dycr/Tchr.

**COLEMAN, ANGELA,** Al A & M Univ, Normal, AL; FR; BS; Fr Hnr Rll 90-; Dns Lst 90-; Comp Sci; Prgrmmr.

**COLEMAN, BRAD ANDREW,** Univ Of Sc At Columbia, Columbia, SC; FR; BS; Edn; Tchr/Coach Pys Edn.

**COLEMAN, BRENDA S,** Oh Univ-Southern Cmps, Ironton, OH; SO; BFA; Grphc Dsgnr 87-; AS; Grphc Dsgn.

**COLEMAN, CARLETON F,** Al St Univ, Montgomery, AL; SO; BS; AF ROTC Drl Tm Clr Grd Asst Drl Tm Cmdr 90-; ASU Hornt Yrbk Stf Prf Rdr 89; Perry Co Chptr Amer Rd Crs Mbr 88-90; Untwn Cvc Leag 88-; Soph Enrchmnt Prog Intrn; Biol; Med.

**COLEMAN, CAROL J,** Hillsborough Comm Coll, Tampa, FL; JR; AS; Rad Club 90-; Acad Exclnc HCC Hnrs Cnvctn 90-; Radiology.

**COLEMAN, CHRISTIE L,** Savannah St Coll, Savannah, GA; FR; BA; Psych Clb 90-; Chld Psych.

**COLEMAN, CONNIE L,** Middle Tn St Univ, Murfreesboro, TN; FR; BA; Erly Chldhd; Edn.

**COLEMAN, CRYSTAL S,** Middle Tn St Univ, Murfreesboro, TN; JR; BS; Rho Lambda; Tau Omicron; Psi Chi; Chi Omega VP; Miss Middle Tenn St Univ; Psychology; Clin Psychology.

**COLEMAN, DANA M,** Coppin St Coll, Baltimore, MD; SR; Video Prod Clb V P; Yrbk Comm Ed; Clg Newspaper Stf Phtgrphr; BS; Engl/Media Arts; Photojrnlsm/Newspaper.

**COLEMAN, DAVID W,** Ms St Univ, Miss State, MS; SO; BA; Eng Stdnt Cncl; Univ Chrstn Stdnt Cntr Chrch Of Chrst; Gamma Beta Phi; IM Vlybl; Eng; Mech Eng.

**COLEMAN, DWAYNE C,** Univ Of Southern Ms, Hattiesburg, MS; SO; BA; Hnrs Stdnts Assn 89-; Phi Eta Sigma 89-; Phi Kappa Phi; Awd Of Excel 89; Hnrs Coll Schlrshp 89; Engl; Univ Prof.

**COLEMAN, GARY M,** Georgetown Coll, Georgetown, KY; SR; BS; Beta Beta Beta Biological 88; Alpha Lambda Delta 88; Eta Delta Phi 90; Phi Kappa Tau Frtrnty 88; Bio; Med Schl.

**COLEMAN, GLADYS D,** Univ Of Southern Ms, Hattiesburg, MS; FR; Afro-Amer Stdnt Org 90-; Teen Connctn 89-90; Spnsh Clb 89-90; Dstnctn Grad 89-90; All St/All Str Team MVP 89-90; Comp Sci; Data Prcssr.

**COLEMAN, JAMAL I,** Clark Atlanta Univ, Atlanta, GA; FR; BA; Sprt Bstrs; Schl Msct 90-; Stdnt Govt; Mr Frshmn 90-; Univ Cntr Frshmn Cncl 90-; Pblc Rltns.

**COLEMAN, JANICE E,** Atlantic Comm Coll, Mays Landing, NJ; FR; BA; Asst Child Care Cen 90; Elem Ed; Tch.

**COLEMAN, JEAN,** City Univ Of Ny Baruch Coll, New York, NY; SR; BBA; Fr Ornttn Ldr 89-90; Psychlgy Clb 89; Gldn Key 89-; Deans Lst 87-; Brch Endwmnt Fnd Mrt Awrd 88-90; Bwlng 86-87; Hmn Rsrcs Mgmt.**

**COLEMAN, JENNIFER R,** Univ Of Sc At Columbia, Columbia, SC; FR; BE; Bapt Union Flwshp Comm 90-; IM Sftbl Coach 90-; Chem Engr.

**COLEMAN, JOEL A,** Tri County Tech Coll, Pendleton, SC; SR; AS; Tech Sprt Coord 89-; AS 84; Data Proc; Cmptr Prgrmg.

**COLEMAN, KAREN N,** Tri County Tech Coll, Pendleton, SC; SR; AS; Offc Asst 89-; Cert 90; Data Proc; Cmptr Prgmg.

**COLEMAN, KAREN V,** Radford Univ, Radford, VA; GD; BS; Children Church Dir 89-; Ft Chiswell H S Band Booster Pr 87-89; BS; Early Educ.

**COLEMAN, KIM Y,** Central St Univ, Wilberforce, OH; JR; BS; All Amercn Schlr 90-; Natl Clgt Bus Merit Award 90-; Mktg; Rsrch.

**COLEMAN, LAURA D,** Radford Univ, Radford, VA; FR; BA; Appalachian Evts Cmtee 90-; Tutor 90-; Alpha Lambda Delta 90-; Psychology; Sch Psychlgy.

**COLEMAN, MARIAN V,** Alcorn St Univ, Lorman, MS; SO; BSN; Nrsng Clb 90-; Nrsng; Srgcl.

**COLEMAN, MARILYN A,** Univ Of Sc At Columbia, Columbia, SC; SR; Afro; NAACP; MAP 87-; Cngrsnl Schlr; Bsktbl Dorm Activities; Mgmnt.

**COLEMAN, MARK E,** Faulkner Univ, Montgomery, AL; JR; BA; Bskbl; Assoc Sci Aquinas Jr Clg 88-90; Busn Admin.

**COLEMAN, MAXIE L,** Piedmont Tech Coll, Greenwood, SC; FR; ASSOC; Phi Theta Kappa; Flg Ftbl Sftbl; NAACP; Bldg Constrctn Tchnlgy; Contractor.

**COLEMAN, NICKY AARON,** Northeast State Tech Comm Coll, Blountville, TN; JR; MBA; U S Marine 77-86; Accountant Security Services 85-88 88-90; Auto Repair Business-Owner.

**COLEMAN, OWEN A,** Neumann Coll, Aston, PA; SR; BA; Schl Papr Artst 90-; Engl/Art; Artst.

**COLEMAN, PAMELA K,** Kent St Univ Kent Cmps, Kent, OH; SO; BA; Engl; Law.

**COLEMAN, PATRICK G,** Atlantic Comm Coll, Mays Landing, NJ; JR; BS; Future Bus Ldrs Of Amerc Phi Beta Lambda VP 88-90; NJ FBLA Regnl Competitv Evnt Jdg 90; Phi Kappa Sigma Rush Chrmn Rho; Caesers Hotel/Casino Emplyee Of Mo Publc Area Suprvsr 84; Phi Beta Lambda 90; Acctng; CPA.

**COLEMAN, PATRICK L,** Morris Brown Coll, Atlanta, GA; SR; BA; Georgra All Coll Bnd 87-89; Cncrnd About Chldrn Tutorial Prog Sec 88-90; Outstdng Yng Mn Of Amer 88-89; Dns Lst 89-90; Ftbl Outside Ln Bckr 89-90; Mass Comm; TV/FLM Prdcr/Dir.

**COLEMAN II, RICHARD EDWARD,** Va St Univ, Petersburg, VA; FR; BA; Mass Comm Clb 90-; Lang/Lit Clb Treas 90-; Hon Clg 90-; Jr Deacon Star Bethlehem Bapt Ch 89-; Mst Otsdng Mass Comm Stdnt; English; Law.

**COLEMAN JR, ROBERT L,** Christian Brothers Univ, Memphis, TN; JR; BS; Intrnshp City Memphis Gvrmnt Data Systems; Cmptr Sci; Systms Analyst.

**COLEMAN, ROBIN E,** Piedmont Tech Coll, Greenwood, SC; JR; ASSOC; Phi Theta Kappa 90-; Greenwd Milk Sfty Tm; Comp; Comp Pgmr.

**COLEMAN, SCOTT K,** Ky St Univ, Frankfort, KY; JR; Scl Studies Educ Awd; Rsrch Asst Bhvrl/Scl Sci; Pres Schlrshp 90-; Yth Bsktbl Coach 86-89; Scl Studies Educ; H S Tchr.

**COLEMAN, SHEILAH L,** Univ Of Rochester, Rochester, NY; SO.

**COLEMAN, SHERRI T,** Univ Of Southern Ms, Hattiesburg, MS; JR; BS; Gold Tndrs Pes 89-; Alpha Swthrt Clb 90-; Afro Amer Stdnt Orgn 90-; Gamma Beta Phi 90-; Afro Amer Achvmnt Awd 89-; Elem Educ; Tch.

**COLEMAN, SHERRY L,** Va St Univ, Petersburg, VA; SR; BS; CPA Clb Pres 90-; Acctg Clb Treas 89-90; Advsry Com 90-; Acctg.

**COLEMAN, STEPHEN A,** Kent St Univ Kent Cmps, Kent, OH; SR; BA; Gnrl Stds Degree 83; US Marines 83-87; Mrtrs Prmtns; Brtndr; Cnstrctn Job; Fnce/Real Est; Corp Fnce.

**COLEMAN, STEPHEN E,** Univ Of Tn At Martin, Martin, TN; SR; BS; Crim Just Soc VP 88-90; Crim Just; Law.

**COLEMAN, TARA N,** Morgan St Univ, Baltimore, MD; SR; BS; Psychlgy Clb 90-; Psi Chi 90-; Beta Kappa Chi 90-; Promethean Kappa Tau 88-; Phi Eta Sigma 90-; MARC Schlr Mnrty Acs Rsrch Crs 90-; NIDA Intrn 90; Psychlgy; Clncl/Exprmntl Psychlgy.

**COLEMAN, THOMAS H,** Chattanooga St Tech Comm Coll, Chattanooga, TN; SO; AAS; Hlth Physics Soc Pres 90-; Phi Beta Kappa; Intrnshp Oak Rdg Natl Lab 90; Watts Bar Chrch Of God; Hlth Physics; Radtn Prtctn.

**COLEMAN, TOI L,** Fl A & M Univ, Tallahassee, FL; FR; MBA; Club Ohio 90-; Bsn; Acctg.

**COLEMAN, TONI R,** Middle Tn St Univ, Murfreesboro, TN; FR; Math; Tchr.

**COLEMAN, TONYA R,** Valdosta St Coll, Valdosta, GA; SO; MBA; Wmns Bsktbl Prog 89-; Speech/Lang Pthlgy; Schl Systm.

**COLEMAN, TRACY L,** Middle Ga Coll, Cochran, GA; SO; AS; Phi Beta Lamda; Young Democrats Club; Deans List; Merit List; Optimist Club; Pre Law; Law.

**COLEMAN, VICKIE M,** Univ Of South Al, Mobile, AL; SR; BA; Hnr Stdnt 90; AA Faulkner State Clg 90; Erly Chldhd Educ.

**COLEMAN, WENDY R,** Al St Univ, Montgomery, AL; SO; BA; Theatre Arts; Gospel Chior; Bapt Union Chr 90-F Acad Hon Soc; Pres Hon Soc; Muisc/Thtre.

**COLEMAN, ZRENDA M,** Memphis St Univ, Memphis, TN; SR; BA; Blck Schlrs Unlmtd; Phi Eta Sigma; Crmnlgy/Crmnl Jstce; Law Sch.

**COLERANGLE, JOHN B,** Tuskegee Univ, Tuskegee Inst, AL; SR; DVM; AVMA 87-; AAHA 87-; Merks Awrd; Hon Roll/W Africa 79-81; BS Univ Sci/Tech 82; Vet Med; Txclgst/Lab Anml Med.

**COLES, CRISTA L,** Allegheny Coll, Meadville, PA; SO; BS; Newman Clb Assn Cmptng; Mach Math Assn Amer; Allegeheny Vlntrs; Alden Schlr; Intrcoll Sccr; Math; Actrl Sci.

**COLES, KIMBERLY A,** Va Commonwealth Univ, Richmond, VA; JR; BA; J Novick Schlrshp 90-; Golden Needle Awd; M R Novick Schlrshp; Art; Fashion Dsgn.

**COLES, TINA P,** Savannah St Coll, Savannah, GA; SR; BA; Peer Cnslr SGA Asst 88-; Tigers Roar Peer Cnslr 90; Amer Red Crs Vol 84-88; Amer Red Crs Yth Bd V P 87-88; Lector Cmunn Mnstr Church 86-; A Crummell Humanities Sem Pre Grad Stdes Boston Univ; Enlgish Lit; Tch Sec MA.

**COLEY, DARNELL D,** Tuskegee Univ, Tuskegee Inst, AL; SO; BS; Drctr Acdmc Affrs Stdnt Govt 90-; Pltcl Scnc Clb Sec 90-; Miss Pre-Law Scty 90-; Hnr Stdnt 90-; Pltcl Scnc; Law.

**COLEY, GREGORY A,** Univ Of Nc At Charlotte, Charlotte, NC; SO; BA; Bptst Stdnt Un; Cmps Chrstn Fllwshp 90-; Deans Lst 90; Deans Lst; Ultmt Frsb Sftbll; Hstry; Cmps Mnstr.

**COLEY, JILL MONIQUE,** Radford Univ, Radford, VA; SR; Ofcr Mgr; BS 90; IDS/CHLD Dev; Yth Advct.

**COLEY, KATHLEEN,** Concordia Coll, Selma, AL; SO; BA; Bsn.

**COLFLESH, SUSAN A,** Neumann Coll, Aston, PA; JR; Llanerch Fire Co Amb Corp Emt Lt 87-; Acdmc Exclnc Awd 88-90; Sftbl 89-90; Nrsng; Crtcl Care Emerg Rm Nrs.

**COLGROVE, EVELYN D,** Ohio Valley Coll, Parkersburg, WV; SO; BA; Pep Clb Pres 71-72; Phi Kappa Gamma 70-72; AA 72; Bus.

**COLIER, RACHEL,** Ramapo Coll Of Nj, Mahwah, NJ; SR; BA; Stdnt Govt VP 90; Radio Sta Wrpr DJ 87-89; Tutor 89; Pi Sigma Alpha Chrprsn 90-; Phi Alpha Theta Pres 90-; Oxford Hons Schlrshp 87-; Acad Achvmnt Schlrshp 87-; Pol Sci.

**COLINEAR, NICHOLAS P,** Duquesne Univ, Pittsburgh, PA; SO; BS; Ftbl Tm 89-; Bus Admin Finance/MIS/MKTG.

**COLL BORGO, MANUEL E,** Univ Of Pr At Mayaguez, Mayaguez, PR; SO; MSCE; Hnr Lst; Natl Cllgt Mnrty Ldrshp Awrd; Cvl Engrng.

**COLL, ANABELLE A,** Univ Of Pr At Mayaguez, Mayaguez, PR; SR; BSIE; Job Fair 91; Alpha Phi Mu 90; Tau Beta Pi 90; IIE 89; Eta Gamma Delta 88; Indus Engr; Engr.

**COLL, PATRICIA J,** Comm Coll Algny Co Algny Cmps, Pittsburgh, PA; FR; AS; PTA Pres 85-86; Nrsng; Spclzd Nrs.

**COLLADO DELGADO, MIGDALIA,** Inter Amer Univ Pr San German, San German, PR; JR; BA; CSI 90-; Sec Sci; Exec Sec.

**COLLADO, LILLIAN E,** Inter Amer Univ Pr San German, San German, PR; SO; Hnr Pgm 89-; Cuadro De Hnr Del Rector 89-; Camara Juvenil 89-; Prg Hnr Int; Recinto; Placa 90; Cert; Mktg; Own Bsn/Entertainmnet.

**COLLAZO GONZALEZ, MELISSA,** Univ Politecnica De Pr, Hato Rey, PR; SO; Design; Mech Engr.**

**COLLAZO, ANA M,** Fl International Univ, Miami, FL; JR; BA; Edctn.

**COLLAZO, JACKELINE,** Bayamon Central Univ, Bayamon, PR; SO; BA; Assoc Tech Ed; Scts Lisiados Bys; Ptt Mdl; Srvc Bys 89; Srvc Old Prnt 90; Cert Awrd Hnrs; Rnng 89; Mdl 88; Rcpntst; Edctnl Tech; Prfssnl.

**COLLAZO, JAIME M,** S U N Y Coll Of Tech At Frmgdl, Farmingdale, NY; SO; BA; Deans Lst 90; Lbrl Arts.

**COLLAZO, JUAN A,** Inter Amer Univ Pr Hato Rey, Hato Rey, PR; SR; BA; AECT 79-; ICIA CTS 79-; Dir Audiovisual Div; Bus Adm; Law.

**COLLAZO, PEDRO J,** Inter Amer Univ Pr Hato Rey, Hato Rey, PR; FR; Engl; Basic Admin.

**COLLAZO-PEREZ, CARLOS E,** Univ Of Pr At Rio Piedras, Rio Piedras, PR; SO; BARCH; AIAS 90-; Archtctr.

**COLLAZZI, CHARLES L,** Bergen Comm Coll, Paramus, NJ; Phi Theta Kappa 85-; Comms Tech 71-; AAS; Bsns; Human Res Mgmt.

**COLLEN, VICKY M,** University Of Findlay, Findlay, OH; FR; BA; Pre-Vet Clb 90-; Chrch Rel Tm; Tau Omega Pi; Sci; Vet Med.

**COLLERAN, MAURA G,** Saint Francis Coll, Loretto, PA; SR; Sftbl Cptn 87-; Mgmt; Mktg.

**COLLETT, DANNY J,** Lexington Comm Coll, Lexington, KY; SO; Church; Homeless Vol; Chem Dep Vol; Aud Sports Vol; Res/Cmrcl/Hist Restoration Contrctr; Phys Therapy; Paint/Sculp.

**COLLETT, SUSAN K,** Univ Of Akron, Akron, OH; JR; BFA; Gold Key; Folk Schlp Awd Art; AS Columbus St Comm Clg 74; Art.

**COLLETT, SUZETTE E,** Salisbury St Univ, Salisbury, MD; SR; BA; Graphic Design; Illustrator/Teacher.

**COLLETTE, CYNTHIA M-H,** Bay Path Coll, Longmeadow, MA; GD; BS; Deans Lst 89-; Maroon Key 90-; Intrnshp Desert Shield/Storm Vol; Bus Admin.

**COLLETTI, DARLA R,** Va Commonwealth Univ, Richmond, VA; JR; BS; Natl Hnrs Scty; Magna Cum Laude; USAF; AS Northeran Vl Commty Clg 90; Busn Admin.

**COLLETTI, KAREN A,** City Univ Of Ny Queensbrough, New York, NY; FR; Phi Theta Kappa; Sec Queens Distrct Attrny Offc 88-; Biology; Pharmacy.

**COLLEY, BRADLEY T,** Wright St Univ Lake Cmps, Celina, OH; SO; AAS; Schlrshp Scty Mfg Eng; Electrnc Eng Tec; Electrnc Techcn.

**COLLEY, DAVID M,** Marshall University, Huntington, WV; BA; Gen Sci Ed; Tchng.

**COLLEY, MEGAN S,** Va Commonwealth Univ, Richmond, VA; JR; BA; Pnhllnc Treas; Phi Eta Sigma; Golden Key; Phi Sigma Sigma Asst Pldg Mstrss/Pres 90-; Ntl Kdny Fndtn 90-; Cnfdrcy Musm Intrnshp; Hstry/Educ; Tchg/Law.

**COLLEY, MELISSA D,** Univ Of Al At Birmingham, Birmingham, AL; FR; BA; Elem Ed.

**COLLEY, NICOLE R,** Catawba Valley Comm Coll, Hickory, NC; FR; BA; Hstry; Tchng.

**COLLIER, ADRIENNE,** Daemen Coll, Amherst, NY; SO; BA; Chrch Chrst Sndy Schl Tchr; Choir; Goldome Bnk Intrnshp Comm Lndng Intrn 88; Hlth Care Plan Intrnshp Med Rec Intrn 90; Dns Lst; Econ; Inv Bnkg.

**COLLIER, BENITA P,** Jackson St Univ, Jackson, MS; FR; BA; Pol Sci; Law.

**COLLIER, BETTY L,** Memphis St Univ, Memphis, TN; SR; BBA; Golden Key 90-; Phi Kappa Phi; Beta Gamma Sigma; Magna Cum Laude; RN; RN Meth Hosp Sch Nrsg 86; Mgmt Info Syst; Comp Pgm/Analysis.

**COLLIER, BETTY R,** Univ Of North Fl, Jacksonville, FL; JR; BA; Gldn Key; Deans Lst; Prsdnts Lst; Chamber Cmmrc Ambssdr; Sls Mgmt; Prsdnts Clb 87; AA FL Cmmnty Coll 90; Bus; Sls Mgmt.

**COLLIER, BREKITA T,** Clark Atlanta Univ, Atlanta, GA; FR; Bio; Pedtrcn.

**COLLIER, CHARISSE N,** City Univ Of Ny Baruch Coll, New York, NY; GD; Cmptr Quantitative Mthds Soc 90; CQMS 90; Cert Acad Achvmnt Plcmnt On Dns Lst 90; Cert Outstndng/ Dedicated Svc CQMS Club 90; BBA 90; Sys Analysis/Dsgn; MS Cmptr Sci/Engr.

**COLLIER, DAVID L,** Snead St Jr Coll, Boaz, AL; SO; BS; Chf Petty Officer U S Navy Rsrv; Elect Tech; Mgmnt.

**COLLIER, DOROTHY M,** Roane St Comm Coll, Harriman, TN; SO; AS; Gamma Beta Phi; Nursing.

**COLLIER, ELLEN C,** Tn St Univ, Nashville, TN; SR; BS; Crim Just Org 89-90; Juvenile Court Intern 90-; Data Entry Tech; Gourmet Culinary Prfsnl; Certif Amer Inst Tech 86-87; Crmnlgy; Law.

**COLLIER, JEFFREY T,** Central Fl Comm Coll, Ocala, FL; SO; BS; SGA 90-; Brain Bwl Capt 89-; IM Ftbl/Vlybl 90-; Phi Theta Kappa 90-; ICF Ldr 90-; AA; Sci; Cmptr Engr.

**COLLIER, JOAN S,** Memphis St Univ, Memphis, TN; Law Ofc Mgr Horne Peppel Gomes PC 89-; BA Univ TN Knoxville 88; Paralegal Studies; Law Sch.

**COLLIER, KEVIN E,** Fl St Univ, Tallahassee, FL; SR; BME; Mrchng Chfs Sctn Ldr 89-; Wnd Orchstra; Chmbr Wnds; Kappa Kappa Psi Dst Coord 88; Music; Educ.

**COLLIER, KIMBERLY L,** Miami Jacobs Jr Coll Of Bus, Dayton, OH; FR; AS; Collegiate Secretaries Intl; Info Processing; Ofc Mngmnt.

**COLLIER, KIMBERLY P,** Ms St Univ, Miss State, MS; SO; BA; Rsdnc Hall Cncl Flr Repr 90-; Gamma Beta Phi 90-; Med Rcrds Admin.

**COLLIER, LAURA E,** Univ Of Southern Ms, Hattiesburg, MS; FR; BS; Mrchng Bnd 90-; Gamma Beta Phi 90-; Arch Engr Tech.

**COLLIER, MATTHEW P,** Bowling Green St Univ, Bowling Green, OH; SR; BS; Stdnt Cnstrctn Mgt Assn 88-; Deans List 88-; Coop City Akron 88-; IM Athltcs; Cnstrctn Mgt Tchnlgy; Cnstrctn Eng Prfsn.

**COLLIER, MICHELLE L,** Roane St Comm Coll, Harriman, TN; BA; STARS 89; Sarah Kegley Schlp 89; AA; Art; Adv.

**COLLIER, PEARLIE K,** Fayetteville St Univ, Fayetteville, NC; SR; MPM; Stdnt In Free Entrprs Co Edtr 90-; Acctng Assoc Secy 90-; Zeta Phi Secy 89-; Schlrshp To Univ Of MD College Park MD For Grad Studies; Fayettevl State Univ Acadmc Schlrshp 90-; BS; Publc Mgt; Publc Sectr.

**COLLIER, RHETT W,** Hillsborough Comm Coll, Tampa, FL; SO; AA BS; Comp Sci; Comp Graphics Tech.

**COLLIER, SHELIA M,** Tn St Univ, Nashville, TN; SR; BS; Golden Key; Sigma Tau Delta; Amer Red Cross Dr Coord 89-90; Dipl NW AL Techl Inst; Psych/English; Student Serv Higher Ed.

**COLLIER, TIFFANY L,** Duquesne Univ, Pittsburgh, PA; FR; BS; SHARP Prgm 90-; Phi Eta Sigma; Lambda Sigma Scty; Founders Awrd 90; Phrmcy.

**COLLIER, TIJUANA D,** Al A & M Univ, Normal, AL; SO; BS; Army ROTC Schlrshp Cadet Sgt 90-; Bapt Union 89-; Acad Hnr Rl 89-; Acad Schlrshp 90-; Army Schlrshp 90-; Chrldr 90-; Cmptr Sci; Syst Analyst.

**COLLIER-BREWER, TEBLE ANN,** Univ Of Tn At Martin, Martin, TN; SR; Vanguard Thtr 87-90; Hnrs Sem Soc 87-89; Phi Eta Sigma 87-90; Phi Kappa Phi 88-90; Ord Omega 89-90; Alpha Epsilon Rho 88-90; Brdcstng Gld 87-90; Zeta Tau Alpha 87-90; Intern WSMV 89; Intern WBBJ 90; Cmmnctns Dept 88-89; IM Swmmng 88; BS 90; Cmmnctns.

**COLLIFLOWER, AMY B,** Culinary Inst Of America, Hyde Park, NY; FR; AOS; Bakers Clb 90-; Stdnt Focus Grp; High Deans List 90-; Red Cross Bldmbl; Extrnshp Ocdntl Rstrnt Washington DC; Clnry Ars; Chef.

**COLLINGSWORTH JR, LARRY N,** Embry Riddle Aeronautical Univ, Daytona Beach, FL; SO; BS; Aviation Elctrncs.**

**COLLINS, AMY E,** The Kings Coll, Briarclf Mnr, NY; SR; BS; Ftr Chrstn Edctrs Asc VP 88-90; RA 89-90; Brndywn Nrsng Home Otrch 89-; Std Tchng 90; Elem Ed; Tchr.

**COLLINS, ANTOINETTE,** Abraham Baldwin Agri Coll, Tifton, GA; FR; SGA Sntr 90; Econ; Fin.

**COLLINS, BONITA K,** S U N Y Coll Of Tech At Alfred, Alfred, NY; SR; BA; Ergo Lit Mag Edtr 89-; High Schlstc Hnrs For Crrclm; Outstndng Stdnt For Crrclm; Engl; Wrtng.

**COLLINS, CATHERINE M,** Springfield Tech Comm Coll, Springfield, MA; SR; BA; Asst Coach Sftbl Tm; Sci; Envrnmntl Intrprtn.

**COLLINS, CHRISTOPHER P,** S U N Y Coll Of Tech At Frmgdl, Farmingdale, NY; FR; AS; Nursing.

**COLLINS JR, CLIFFORD W,** Cuyahoga Comm Coll, Cleveland, OH; FR; BA; Coop Educ 91; Cert Cuyahoga Vly Joint Voc Sch 90; Arch.

**COLLINS, COURTNEY A,** Villanova Univ, Villanova, PA; SO; BA; SADD 89-90; Delta Delta Delta Public Reltns Ofcr 90-; Special Olympics 89-; Hunger Awareness Week Event Chrprsn 90-; Deans Lst 89-90; English/Business; MBA Law.

**COLLINS, DARCY C,** Newbury Coll, Brookline, MA; SO; AS; Cls Rep 90-; Dns Lst 90-; Stdnt Pys Thrpst Asst 90-; Phys Thrpy.

**COLLINS, DENISE M,** Saint Andrews Presbytrn Coll, Laurinburg, NC; SO; BA; Drama Club; Hnrs Pgm 89-; Psych.**

**COLLINS, DONNA P,** Memphis St Univ, Memphis, TN; JR; BA; Adult Stdnt Assoc 90-; Phi Kappa Phi; Adult Schlrshp 90; AEDP MS Delta Cmnty Clg 78; Psych.

**COLLINS, DOROTHY J,** Liberty Univ, Lynchburg, VA; JR; BS; Alpha Lamda Delta 89-; Math.

**COLLINS, DOROTHY S,** Comm Coll Algny Co Algny Cmps, Pittsburgh, PA; FR; RN; Crtfd Nrsng Asst; Nrsng.

**COLLINS, GLORIA G,** Univ Of Southern Ms, Hattiesburg, MS; JR; Gamma Beta Phi 89; Hattiesburg Police Dept 85-; Law Enforcement; Pol Sci; Law.

**COLLINS, GREGORY S,** Wv Univ, Morgantown, WV; JR; BS; Elec Engrg; Engrg.

**COLLINS, GWYNETTA M,** Al St Univ, Montgomery, AL; FR; BA; Phi Eta Sigma; Blgy Chmstry; Med.

**COLLINS, JANINE ANGELISA,** Al St Univ, Montgomery, AL; JR; BS; Yng Demo 89-90; Pol Sci Clb Tres 90; Pi Gamma Mu; Zeta Phi Beta; Pol Sci; Dfns Attrny.

**COLLINS, JENNIFER K,** Fl St Univ, Tallahassee, FL; SO; MBA; Phi Eta Sigma Sec 90-; Comm Disorders; Speech Path.

**COLLINS, JENNIFER L,** William Paterson Coll, Wayne, NJ; JR; BA; Humanities Club; Hons Progrm 88-; Mayrs Fld Advsry Comm Secy 90-; Frnds Of Long Pond Iron Wrks Histrcl Comm 88-; Garden State Schlrshps 89-; Equestrn Team 89-; Engl/ Wrtng/Envrnmntl Sci.

**COLLINS, JENNY B,** Western New England Coll, Springfield, MA; JR; BA; Magna Cum Laude 90; AA Bay Path Clg 90; English Communications; Higher Educ.

**COLLINS, JERRY D,** Univ Of South Al, Mobile, AL; GD; Pres Lst; Deans Lst; Intrnshp USA Med Ctr; Prsnl/Indust Rltns; Prsnl Admnstr.

**COLLINS, JO L,** Marshall University, Huntington, WV; SO; ATBED; Intrhl Govt Cncl Treas 89; Hl Advsry Cncl Sec 90; Athltc Trnrs Assc; Sprts Med/Hlth Educ; Phys Thrpy.

**COLLINS, JOANN F,** Howard Univ, Washington, DC; SO; BA; Amer Soc Intr Dsgn 90-; Amer Inst Arch 89-90; Slowe Hl Drm Cncl Parlmntrn 90-; Intr Dsgn.

**COLLINS, JOHN M,** Memphis St Univ, Memphis, TN; SO; BA; Stdnt Cncl Pres 89-; Nwsppr Rprtr 90; Spnsh Clb Offcr 90-; Phi Eta Sigma; AATSP Natl Spnsh Exm 89; Wrstlng Tm 90; Intnatl Rltns; US Embssy.

**COLLINS II, JOSEPH O,** Tuskegee Univ, Tuskegee Inst, AL; SR; BS; NSBE 88-90; Stdnt Govt Cls Rep 88; Eta Kappa Nu 88; Alpha Kappa Mu 88; Epsion 88; US Army ROTC Battalion Cmndr 89; Kappa Alpha Psi Exchequer 90; Army ROTC Schlrshp; IM Ftbl Capt 86-88.

**COLLINS, JOYCE A,** Univ Of Tn At Martin, Martin, TN; SR; BS; Wldlf Scty Exec Brd 89-90; 1SAA All Amrcn Schlr 89-90; Mu Epsilon Delta Treas 89-89; Otstndng Stdnt Ntrl Rsrcs Mgmt 89-90; Wldlf Blgy.

**COLLINS, JULIE A,** Middle Ga Coll, Cochran, GA; SO; BSA; Animal Sci; Rsrch.

**COLLINS, KAREN M,** Univ Of Sc At Columbia, Columbia, SC; JR; BAIS; Elem Ed; Tchr/Guidance.

**COLLINS, KATHLEEN M,** Providence Coll, Providence, RI; FR; BA; Stdnt Congrs Rep 90-; Im Bsktbl 90-.

**COLLINS, KATHRYN D,** Union Coll, Barbourville, KY; SR; Sci Clb 89-; Stnbrry Eclgy Awrd; Mmrl Awrd; Sr Blgy Awrd; Blgy Chmstry Dnstry.

**COLLINS, KERI A,** Middle Tn St Univ, Murfreesboro, TN; FR; NRSNG; Alpha Omicronpi 90-; Jr Vrsty Chrldr 90-.

**COLLINS, KERI S,** Fl Coll, Temple Terrace, FL; FR; BA; Acete Crest; Phi Theta Kappa; Elem Educ; Tchg.

**COLLINS, LARRY D,** Middle Tn St Univ, Murfreesboro, TN; SR; BS; Hlth/Physcl Ed/Rec/Sfty Clb Sec 90-; Spec Evnts Comm 86-88 90-; Bptst Std Un 86-88 90-; W E Elliott Schlp 86; Intshp Dvsn Frstry; Bethany Kline Schlp; Prks/Rec.

**COLLINS, LESLIE V,** Fisk Univ, Nashville, TN; SR; BS; Psychlgy Clb 88-; Wesley Fndtn 87-; Univ Deans Lst 89-; Psychlgy/Phlsphy; Cnslng.**

**COLLINS, LISA K,** Univ Of Sc At Spartanburg, Spartanburg, SC; SO; Gamma Beta Phi 90-; Piedmont Soc Sec 89-; Phrmcy.

**COLLINS, MARK,** Embry Riddle Aeronautical Univ, Daytona Beach, FL; SO; BS; AMT Avncs; Avtn Maint Tchnlgy.

**COLLINS, MARTHA J,** Western Ky Univ, Bowling Green, KY; SR; BA; Phi Kappa Phi; KY Lbry Assoc 79-; Asst Lbrn Mary Wood Weldon Mem Lbry 76-; AGS 89; Lbry Media Educ; Public.

**COLLINS, MARY DAN,** Univ Of Ky, Lexington, KY; FR; Pre Phrmcy Clb 90-; Alpha Lambda Delta 90-; Phrmcy.

**COLLINS, MARY E,** Univ Of Scranton, Scranton, PA; SR; BS; Bus Club; Soc Acctng Stdnts: Ski Club; Track Club; Pre-Law Soc; Becker Rep; Delta Mu Delta 90-; Omega Besta Sigma Sec/Treas 88-; United Mind Workers; Hill Nbrhd Assn; Hand In Hand Prog; Magna Cum Laude; Natl Bus Merit Awd; IM; Acctng; CPA.

**COLLINS, MARY F,** Central Fl Comm Coll, Ocala, FL; SO; BA; Phi Theta Kappa 90-; Eng.

**COLLINS, MICHAEL E,** Samford Univ, Birmingham, AL; GD; JD; Cmbrlnd Law Rvw Mbr; Envir Law Soc 90; Sports/Entrnmnt Law Soc 90; BA Univ Tennessee 89; Law.

**COLLINS, MICHAEL H,** Faulkner St Jr Coll, Bay Minette, AL; JR; BS; Pres Lst; Envir Sci; Envir Prtctn Agncy.

**COLLINS, OLETHA,** Clark Atlanta Univ, Atlanta, GA; SO; BA; Allen Chaple Chrch AME Chr Mbr; Chrldng 89-90; Nrsng; Med Schl.

**COLLINS, REBECCA A,** Beckley Coll, Beckley, WV; FR; Comp Prcssng; Comp Prog.

**COLLINS, RICARDO M,** Case Western Reserve Univ, Cleveland, OH; FR; BS; Natl Soc Bick Engrs; Mnrty Schlrs Prog; Mnrty Assn Advncmnt Tech; Mrchng Bnd; Biomed Eng Lab Tech 90; Chem Eng.

**COLLINS, RICHARD S,** Hahnemann Univ, Philadelphia, PA; JR; MD; BA Rutgers Univ; Medcn; Surgery.**

**COLLINS, ROGER F,** West Liberty St Coll, West Liberty, WV; JR; BS; Crmnl Jstc; Law.

**COLLINS JR, RONALD B,** Coppin St Coll, Baltimore, MD; SR; BS; ROCA 86-90; Army Mltry Intllgnc Offcr; Cmptr Sci; Cmptr Prgmmng.

**COLLINS, RONALD L,** Kent St Univ Kent Cmps, Kent, OH; JR; BA; Soclgy Clb Pres; Creativity Clb Mbr; Fncng Clb Mbr 89-F; Archlgy.

**COLLINS, SANDRA A,** Salisbury St Univ, Salisbury, MD; GD; MSW; Scl Wrk Clb 88-; Collgm 86-; Phi Alpha Theta 87-; NASW 90-; Bertha Reynolds Soc; Phi Mu 88-; Coach Spcl Olympics 89-90; Intrn Easter Seals Soc 89-90; Intrn Shrnrs Hosp Crpld Chldrn 90-; BSW 90; Scl Wrk; Chld Wlfr.

**COLLINS, SANDRA J,** Radford Univ, Radford, VA; SR; BBA; Amercn Mktg Assoc Secy 90-; Phi Kappa Phi 90-; Mktg; Mktg Rsrch.

**COLLINS, SHAN M,** Villanova Univ, Villanova, PA; SR; BA; Econ Scty 90-; Phi Kappa Phi; Deans Lst 87-; Adam Smith Awd; IM Sftbl/Bsktbl/Vlybl/Flg Ftbl; Economics.**

**COLLINS, SHARON K,** Salisbury St Univ, Salisbury, MD; SO; BS; Purdue Schlrs Assn Sec/Tr 89-; Natl Assn Of Accts 90-; Phi Eta Sigma 90-; MD Dist Schlr/Deans Lst 89-; Purdue Schlr 89-; Hons Pgm Awd 90-; Bus.

**COLLINS, STEPHANIE R,** Univ Of Sc At Columbia, Columbia, SC; FR; BA; Gamma Beta Phi; Chemistry/Sci; Pharmacy.

**COLLINS, STEPHEN H,** Piedmont Tech Coll, Greenwood, SC; GD; Sc Army Natl Grd; Acdmc Achvmnt Awrd; Ems Brd 89-; Paramdc 89-; Prmdc Instrctr.

**COLLINS, SUSAN L,** Owensboro Comm Coll, Owensboro, KY; SO; BS; Yth Dir Webb Mem Untd Meth Chrch 90-; Farm Home Advsry Cmt; AA Madisonville Comm Clg 90; Elem Ed/Engl; Tchr.

**COLLINS, SUSAN L,** Anne Arundel Comm Coll, Arnold, MD; SO; BS; Cmptr Sci; Cmptr Prgrmmr.

**COLLINS, TIFFANY R,** Fl A & M Univ, Tallahassee, FL; FR; BA; Hstry; Law.

**COLLINS, TIM W,** Ky St Univ, Frankfort, KY; JR; BS; Kiyojute Ryu Kempo Karate 2nd Dgr Blck Blt 88-; Hnrbl Ordr KY Clnls 88-; Mchncl Engnrng.

**COLLINS, TONIA M,** Al St Univ, Montgomery, AL; SO; BSW; Whitney Young Soc Wsork Club Sec 90-; Kappa Delta Pi 89-; Zeta Phi Beta; Hnr Roll Stdnt 90-; Soc Work; Cnslng.

**COLLINS, VICKY C,** Tn St Univ, Nashville, TN; FR; BA; Assoc Yng Chldrn; Ed Cmte; Hd Strt Pgm; Spec Rcgntn Prfsnlsm; CDA Natl Assoc Yng Chldrn 88; Erly Chldhd Ed; Tch.

**COLLINS, WENDY K,** Ms St Univ, Miss State, MS; JR; Cncl Excptl Chldrn 90-; Inter Res Hall Cncl Dir PR; Ntl Res Hall Honry; Gamma Betta Phi 90-; Ed; Spec Ed.

**COLLINS, WILLIAM E,** Middle Tn St Univ, Murfreesboro, TN; JR; BS; Brdcst Cmmnctns; Newscaster.

**COLLINS, YOLANDA N,** Oh St Univ, Columbus, OH; FR; BS; Under-Repr Psych Stdnts 90-; Frshmn Fdtn Pgm 90-; Mentor Pmg 90-; Mnrty Schlrs Pgm 90-; Hnrs Peer Supp Pgm 90-; Ldrshp OH State 90-; Hl Cncl Secr; Ldrshp OH State I Co-Chr; Psych; Chld Psych.

**COLLINSON, SANDRA T,** Bowie St Univ, Bowie, MD; SR; BS; Ed Clb 90-; Phi Theta Kappa 71; Kappa Delta Pi 90-; AA Anne Arundel Cmnty Clge 71; Erly Chldhd/Spcl Ed.

**COLLINSWORTH, AMY M,** Univ Of Sc At Columbia, Columbia, SC; FR; BA; Deans Lst 90-; Hnrs Clg 90-; Vlybl Schlrshp 90-; Biomedcl Eng.

**COLLISTER, DIANE,** Chattanooga St Tech Comm Coll, Chattanooga, TN; SO; AS; Resp Care Stdnt Assoc Pres 90-; Chat State Stdnt Rep TN Soc For Resp Care Brd 90-; Chattanooga State Stdnt Govt Cab Mbr 90-; Phi Theta Kappa 90-; Amer Assoc Of Resp Care 90-; TN Natl Guard Sgt 88-; Hutcheson Med Ctr Resp 89-; Respiratory Care.

**COLLUM, KEVIN L,** Northwest Al Comm Coll, Phil Campbell, AL; SO; BA; Phi Theta Kappa; Pres List; Deans List; Sec Ed/ Bio/Chem; Clg Prfsr.**

**COLLUM, RICKY D,** Valdosta St Coll, Valdosta, GA; SR; BS; Cmps Actvts Brd Flms Chrmn; Undr Grad Jrnl Ed; Rsdnt Asst Snr Ast; Alha Lamda; Coll Ambssdrs; GA Sclgcl Assoc; Coop Edctn Stdnt US Mrshls Srvcs; Asst Krt InstrctrIM Sftbll; IM Ftbll Capt; Crmnl Jstc Anthrplgy; Law.

**COLLURA, PATRICIA M,** West Chester Univ, West Chester, PA; SR; BA; Amerisure Inc; Psych; Trng/Dev.**

**COLLYER, MARCELLA L,** Thomas Nelson Comm Coll, Hampton, VA; FR; AS; US Navy 2nd Clss Instrmntmn; Sci; BS/ BIO/ENVRNMNTL Sci.

**COLMAN, ALFREDO C,** Belmont Coll, Nashville, TN; SO; Intrntl Stdnt Assc Pblc Rltns 90-; Kaleidoscope Cmps 90-; Music; Chrch Msc.

**COLOMBO, MARLENE J,** Wv Univ At Parkersburg, Parkersburg, WV; FR; BA; AS Mountain St Coll 90; Bus; Acctng.

**COLON BAEZ, CARMEN M,** Inter Amer Univ Pr Barranquita, Barranquitas, PR; SR; BA; Hon Lst 90-91; Sec Sci.

**COLON CORTES, MAGDA J,** Inter Amer Univ Pr Hato Rey, Hato Rey, PR; JR; Social Clb De Futuros Trbjdores Sociales 90-; Hnr Roll Cuadro De Hnr De La Univ 90-; Humannidades; Social Work.

**COLON MARTINEZ, BRENDA,** Bayamon Central Univ, Bayamon, PR; JR; BA; United With Christ Church Grp 88-; Comp Sci.

**COLON ORTIZ, NIDIA L,** Univ Of Pr Cayey Univ Coll, Cayey, PR; JR; Samael Aun Weior Hand Bells Chrs 90-; Cert Colegio Univ De Cayes 88-; Accounting.

**COLON PEREZ, BETSY I,** Inter Amer Univ Pr Hato Rey, Hato Rey, PR; JR; BED; Sec Acctg Dept 87-; Spnsh/Lit/Edtg; Exec Sec.

**COLON SANTIAGO, WILFREDO,** Inter Amer Univ Pr San German, San German, PR; SR; Water Polo Tm ADAM 84-88; P R Natl Water Polo Tm 86-88; Phi Eta Mu 88; Hnrs Stdnts 89-; BBA Major Finc Acctg; Acctg/Finc; MBA.

**COLON, DAGMAR E,** City Univ Of Ny Queensbrough, New York, NY; SO; Shtkn Karate 89; Lbrl Arts; Psychlgy.

**COLON, GEORGIANA S,** Inter Amer Univ Pr San Juan, Hato Rey, PR; GD; JD; Law Rvw 89-; Phi Alpha Delta 89-; Summa Cun Laude Hghst Hnr; BS Boston Coll 88; Accntng/Cmptr Sci; Law.

**COLON, GISELLE M,** Inter Amer Univ Pr San Juan, Hato Rey, PR; SR; Amer Bar Assoc 89-90; Law Reivew 89-90; BS Boston Clg 85; Law.

**COLON, GLADYS,** Univ Of Pr Cayey Univ Coll, Cayey, PR; FR; BA; Hnr Clb Rctr Of Univ Coll Of Cayey 90-; Sci; Drmtlgst.

**COLON, HILDA M,** Inter Amer Univ Pr San Juan, Hato Rey, PR; FR; Prfsnl Assn Grad Stdnt Crmnl Juste 85; Magna Cum Laude 71; Summa Cum Laude 86; Fwlshp Amer Assn Advncmnt Sci; Pres Rotavian Ladies; Altrusan Wmn; Labor Rltns Ofcr; State Ins Fund; MA 86; BA 71; Soc Sci; Law.

**COLON, JOSE F,** Univ Of Pr At Rio Piedras, Rio Piedras, PR; SO; Miembro Del Programa De Estudios; De Honor; Bio; Med.

**COLON, JOSE M,** Inter Amer Univ Pr Hato Rey, Hato Rey, PR; SO; BA; Univ Hsng Cmte 89; Comp Sci; Syst Anal.

**COLON, JOSE MARTINEZ,** Inter Amer Univ Pr Hato Rey, Hato Rey, PR; SO; BA; Tec Mdlc; Doc.

**COLON, JUAN M,** Univ Of Pr At Rio Piedras, Rio Piedras, PR; SO; BS; SG 90-; Hnr Roll Ntrl Sci 89-; Biology; MDPHD.

**COLON, KENNY W,** Univ Of Pr At Rio Piedras, Rio Piedras, PR; SO; Nwspr 89; Hon Stdes Prog 90-; Sociology; Law.

**COLON, LILLIAN M,** Univ Of Pr Cayey Univ Coll, Cayey, PR; FR; BA; Crcl Chem; PH Rec Assc Bnd 88-; Nu Upsilon Psi; Science; Medicine/Pediatrician.

**COLON, MARCILYN,** Univ Of Pr Medical Sciences, San Juan, PR; SO; BES; Stdnt Cncl Clge Hlth Ald Prfsns Sec 90-; Aspcts Hlth Ed 93 Cls; Prsbytrn Chrch Chrs VP 89-; Amer Hrt Assoc 90-; Hnr Rl Lst 90; Pblc Hlth; Hlth Ed.

**COLON, MARIA J,** Inter Amer Univ Pr San German, San German, PR; SO; BA; Sectrl Sci.

**COLON, MARIE CARMELITE,** Bunker Hill Comm Coll, Boston, MA; Nrsng.

**COLON, MAYRA,** Univ Of Pr Cayey Univ Coll, Cayey, PR; SO.

**COLON, PEDRO L,** Inter Amer Univ Pr San German, San German, PR; GD; BED; Club CEMI; Hist; Law.

**COLON, RODRIGO A,** Georgian Court Coll, Lakewood, NJ; JR; BS; Deans Schlr 88-90; March Of Dimes Walk-Amer; Childrens Aid Soc Vol Proj Live 85; Jr Achvmnt-Vol Project Bus 90-; J P Morgan Syst Ofcr 83-; Bus Admin; MBA.

**COLON, ROSALYN,** Univ Of Pr Cayey Univ Coll, Cayey, PR; JR; BBA; Cuadro De Hon De La Rectora; Ntl Hispnc Schlr Awd 88-89; Bus Adm/Acctg; Auditng.

**COLON-LARRAURI, IRIS J,** Univ Of Pr At Rio Piedras, Rio Piedras, PR; SR; Assn Of Jrnlsm Stdnts 89-; Assn Advrtsng/Pub Rltns Stdnts 89-; Goldn Key 89; BA 90; Pub Cmnctn.

**COLON-NEVAREZ, IVELISSE,** Univ Of Pr At Rio Piedras, Rio Piedras, PR; SR; Hijas De Maria Daughters Of Mary Santiago Apostol Parish 80-; Assoc De Caricaturistas De Puerto Rico 89-90; Prog Estudios De Hnr De La UPR 86-; Prog Estudiantes Orientadores U Of PR Mbr 87-88; Gen Fine Arts; Cartooning & Animation.

**COLONDO JR, ROBERT C,** Mount Aloysius Jr Coll, Cresson, PA; SO; BS; Crmnlgy; Law.

**COLOSIMO, ROBERT J,** Southeastern Coll Of Hlth Sci, N Miami Beach, FL; GD; PHARM; Stdnt Govt 88-90; Acad Of Stdnts Of Phrmcy 87; Amer Soc Of Hsptl Phrmcy 90; Schl Deans Lst 87; Rho Pi Phi 87-90; Deans Lst 87; Svrl Small Schlrshps; Phrmcy Sci.

**COLPITTS, KELLY J,** Newbury Coll, Brookline, MA; FR; BA; Acctng.

**COLSON, LEE S,** Univ Of Al At Huntsville, Huntsville, AL; JR; BSEE; Instrumentation Specialist 85; Engr.

**COLSTON, DEREK J,** Alcorn St Univ, Lorman, MS; SO; BA; Pre Med Clb 90-; FAM Mason 90-; Pre Phrmcy/Biol; Phrmcst.

**COLSTON, LORA E,** Al St Univ, Montgomery, AL; SO; BA; Bus Educ; Sec Tchr.

**COLTON, KRISTEN K,** Georgetown Univ, Washington, DC; JR; BSN; Sigma Theta Tau; Dns Lst 90-; Bsktbl Mgr 88-; Nrsng.

**COLUCCI, JAMIE M,** Univ Of Rochester, Rochester, NY; SR; BA; Vrsty Pep Bnd Cndctr 89-; Undrgrd Cgntv Sci Cncl Sec 90-; Undrgrd Mgmnts Stds Cncl Bsns Mngr 90-; Deans Lst; Cgntv Sci; Indstrl Lbr Rltns.

**COLUCCI, MARY L,** Boston Univ, Boston, MA; SR; MD; MA Medcl Soc 87-; Amer Medcl Stdnt Assn 90-; Amer Medcl Assn; Alpha Omega Alpha 90; BA 87; Med; Dgnstc Rdlgy.

**COLUCCI, MONICA M,** Fl International Univ, Miami, FL; FR; BED; Edn.

**COLUCY, JAMIE S,** Kent St Univ Kent Cmps, Kent, OH; JR; BA; Dns Lst; IMS; Hmn Rsrce Mgmt; Sprts Bhvr.

**COLVIN, ANN T,** James Madison University, Harrisonburg, VA; FR; BS; Amnsty Intl 90-; EARTH 90-.

**COLVIN, BRIAN M,** Neumann Coll, Aston, PA; JR; BS; AS Delaware Cnty Comm Coll 90; Mgt Info Sys/Bus Admin; Sys Analyst/Cons.

**COLVIN III, GERALD D,** Birmingham Southern Coll, Birmingham, AL; JR; BA; Prgrmg Brd Bnd Chrmn 89-; Pblctns Brd 89; Sthrn Vol Serv 88-; Sigma Tau Delta; Alpha Lambda Delta 89; Phi Eta Sigma 89; Sigma Alpha Epsilon VP 88-; Mccoy Tutrng Pro 90-; Intrnshp US Cngrsmn Tom Bevill; Admin Intrnshp Ofc Dvlpmnt; Engl; Law.

**COLVIN, MAUREEN,** Pellissippi St Tech Comm Coll, Knoxville, TN; SO; BA; Phi Theta Kappa; Alpha Theta; Free Lance Phtgrphr 86-; Soc Work; Indvdl Cnslng.

**COLVIN, REBECCA J,** Jacksonville St Univ, Jacksonville, AL; SR; BS; Asso Nrsg Stdnts 90-; Ntnl Sdtnt Nrs Asso 90-; Am Asso Crtcl Care Nrs 90-; Sigma Theta Tau; Omicron Delta Kappa 90-; Nrsg; MSN; Clncl Nrs Speclst.

**COLWELL, COURTNEY R,** Univ Of Miami, Coral Gables, FL; SO; BA; Motion Pictures; Scrptwrtng.

**COLWELL, JASON D,** Hudson Valley Comm Coll, Troy, NY; SR; Pres Lst 89-.

**COLWELL, JOAN M,** The Johns Hopkins Univ, Baltimore, MD; JR; BSN; SGA 90-; Cls Pres 90-; Nrsng Hnr Grnt 89-90; Merit Schlr 90-; Kelley Schlr 90-; Ped Nrsng.

**COLWELL, JUDY E,** Mount Aloysius Jr Coll, Cresson, PA; SO; AS; Occptnl Thrpy Clb 89-; Phi Theta Kappa 90-; AA IN Univ PA 79; Occptnl Thrpy; Occptnl Thrpy Asst.

**COLWELL, MATTHEW,** Columbia Greene Comm Coll, Hudson, NY; SO; Bsebl/Bsktbl 89; AAS; Crmnl Jstce; US Scrt Serv.

**COLWELL, RACHEL L,** Georgian Court Coll, Lakewood, NJ; FR; BA; Pi Delta Phi; Engl; Tchng.

**COMA, CAROL M,** West Liberty St Coll, West Liberty, WV; SR; BA; Bd Drctrs Gvnr 89-90; Prgrmng Bd 90-; Comm Accrdtn 90-; Amblnc Clb 89-90; Gamma Sigma Tau Ltl Strs Co-Pres 88-89; Scl Sci.

**COMBEST, PAMELA G,** Christopher Newport Coll, Newport News, VA; SO; BS; USAF 80-90; AAS Comm Coll Air Force 89; Bus Mgmt; Law Comm Svc.

**COMBIE, EGBERT FRANCIS,** Al A & M Univ, Normal, AL; SR; BA; OMS Clb Pres 90-; Dept Offce Sys Mgmt Awrd; Schl Bus/Econ Awrd; Cert 90; Cert Univ W Indies 86; Bus Ed; Tchr.

**COMBIE, ELENA-DOMINIQUE,** Howard Univ, Washington, DC; JR; BA; Arch/Pln Sdnt Govt Pres 89-90 2nd Yr Rep 88-89; Tau Sigma Delta 88-; Gldn Ky; Dc Artwrks Assist Coord 88-90; Chabette Wrkshp 90; Barrier Free Access Conf 90; Tchng Assist 88-90; P Roberts Harris Intrnshp; Arch.

**COMBS, BRYAN K,** Univ Of Sc At Columbia, Columbia, SC; SR; BS; USC Naval ROTC Unit Sply Ofcr 89-; Beta Gamma Sigma; Phi Theta Kappa 88-89; Dutch Fork Chrstn Church 89-; Chief Machinist Mate US Navy 81-; AAS Clg Lk County Grayslake IL 89; Bsn Adm; US Navy Sply Corps.

**COMBS, CARRIE W,** Piedmont Bible Coll, Winston-Salem, NC; SR; BA; Choir 89-90; Missions Flwshp 89-90; Kappa Epsilon Beta 89-90; Summa Cum Laude 90; Deans Lst 89-90; Accts Mgr 90-; BS NC St Univ 87; Bible.

**COMBS, CHRISTIE L,** Ms St Univ, Miss State, MS; JR; Mrchg Bnd 88-90; Symph/Concert Bnds 88-90; Res Asst 90-; Beta Beta Beta; Microbio; MS Nrsg.

**COMBS, GAYLE D,** Sue Bennett Coll, London, KY; SO; BS; Sigma Nu; USAA All Amer Schlr; Phi Beta Kappa; Appalachian Cmnts Chldrn Brd 90; Psych; Psychlgst.

**COMBS, GREGORY L,** Univ Of Va Clinch Valley Coll, Wise, VA; JR; BS; Psychlgy Clb 90-; Farmer Vet US Army; AS SW VA Comm Coll 86; Psychlgy/Sociology; Cnslng.

**COMBS, JAMES H,** Georgetown Univ, Washington, DC; FR; BA.

**COMBS, JENNIFER LEE,** Univ Of Ky, Lexington, KY; JR; BED; Alpha Gamma Delta Music 90-; Math; Teacher.

**COMBS, KAREN C,** Ky Wesleyan Coll, Owensboro, KY; SR; BA; Phi Theta Kappa 88; Phi Beta Lambda 87-; Pres Schlrshp 89-; AAS Madisonville Comm Coll 89; Bus.

**COMBS, MELISSA R,** S U N Y Coll Of Tech At Frmgdl, Farmingdale, NY; FR; AAS; Firearms Clb Sec; Adv Art/Dsgn; Prod Art/Art Dir.

**COMBS, MICHAEL D,** Wv Univ, Morgantown, WV; SR; MBA; IEEE 87-; Dns Lst 89-; Ordr Of The Grl 88; Alpha Pi Mu Rcrdng Sec 89; Tau Beta Pi; Gldn Ky Sec 89; Grad Asstnshp; BSIE 90; Indstrl Eng Bus Admin; Eng.

**COMBS, STEVEN D,** Univ Of Ky, Lexington, KY; FR; EE; Stdnt Activies Brd 90-; Phi Eta Sigma; Alpha Lambda Delta; Dns Lst 90; IM Bsktbl Ftbl 90-; Engr; Elec Engr.

**COMEAU, CHERYL,** City Univ Of Ny Baruch Coll, New York, NY; SO; BA; Radio 89-90; Bus Jrnlsm; Jrnlst.

**COMEAUX, SUSAN F,** Middle Tn St Univ, Murfreesboro, TN; FR; BA; Paralgl 86-89; Pltcl Sci; Law.

**COMELLA, KAREN M,** Memphis St Univ, Memphis, TN; JR; BA; Peer/Mntr Pgm 89-; Gamma Beta Phi 89-; Phys Therapy.

**COMER, ALEJANDRO J,** Morehouse Coll, Atlanta, GA; SO; BA; NAACP; Cmptr Dsci Clb 90-; Hon Roll Awrd; Untd Negro Clg Fnd Otstndng Stdnt 90-; Denver Police Athltc Leag Ftbl Orgnztn 88-90; Cmptr Sci.

**COMER, CHANNA L,** City Univ Of Ny Baruch Coll, New York, NY; SO; BBA; Admn Asst 89-; Bus Mgmt; Humn Rsrc Mgmt.

**COMER, HONEY B,** Univ Of Sc At Columbia, Columbia, SC; FR; BA; Wmn Stdnts Assn 90; Alpha Lambda Delta; Phi Eta Sigma; Early Chldhd Ed; Tchr.

**COMER, JAMES M,** Walker Coll, Jasper, AL; SO; MBA; Educ; Law.

**COMER, JOAN V,** Columbia Union Coll, Takoma Park, MD; SR; BSHC; Assoc Crtcl Cr Nrs AACW 80-; ACLS; RN; Crtcl Cr Nrs 76-; Asst Coord Surgcl ICU; ADN Marymount Clg Assoc Deg Nrs 74; Hlth Cr; Hlth Cr Admn.

**COMER, KATHY L,** Beckley Coll, Beckley, WV; SO; MA; Elem Educ/Lrng Dsblts; Tch.

**COMER, KEVIN S,** Old Dominion Univ, Norfolk, VA; SR; BSET; SME 89-; ASHRAE 90-; Faclty Awd Acad Exlcnc Engr Tech; Grad Flwshp NASA 91-; AAS Blue Ridge Comm Clg 89; Mech Engr; Engr.

**COMERFORD, LESLIE S,** Coll Of Charleston, Charleston, SC; SR; BS; Fllwhsp Chrstn Athlts 87-89; CEC 88-; AAMD Treas 89-90; Fcltyhnrs Lst; Ed Spcl Ed.

**COMERFORD, NICOLE J,** Indiana Univ Of Pa, Indiana, PA; JR; Sgn Lang Clb Sec/Hstrn 88-; Kappa Delta Pi 90-; Provost Schlr 89-; Ed Hrng Imprd; Tchng.

**COMESANAS, ELIZABETH,** Univ Of Miami, Coral Gables, FL; JR; BA; English; Educ.

**COMET, DOUGLAS L,** Univ Of Miami, Coral Gables, FL; JR; BBA; Hons Assoc; Sigma Chi Intrm Chrm 89; Law; Chemistry.

**COMIS, THOMAS R,** Hudson Valley Comm Coll, Troy, NY; SR; BA; Schenectady Co Comm Clg Jazz Ensmbl 84; AFM 80-84; VAMC 86-88; Engl/Lib Arts; Sls Rep/Musician.

**COMMA, NEVILLE X,** City Univ Of Ny City Coll, New York, NY; SO; BA; Male Mntrshp Pgm Sec 90-; Alpha Phi Alpha Dir Ed Act 90-; D A Sex Crime Univ 90-; Urban Leag Stds/Afrkn Stds; Law.

**COMMAROTA, LAURA M,** Western Carolina Univ, Cullowhee, NC; JR; BS; WWCU 88-90; Radio Lab Asst For WCU; Asst Dir/ Sound Designer For One Act Play; Alpha Lambda Delta 89-; Speech/Theater Arts Hon Cncl 90-; Alpha Epsilon Rho Pr 88-; Pisgah G S 89-90; Deans Lst 88-; Stdnt Mrshl At Grad 90; IMTENNIS/SOCCER/SFTBL 88; Radio/TV.

**COMO, JAMES A,** Niagara Univ, Niagara Univ, NY; SR; BS; Rape Prvntn Instr 87-; Nwspr 90; Univ Soc Blck Blts 87-89; Alpha Phi Sigma 90-; Jujutsu Sr Instr Blk Blt 88-; East Cst Krt 7th Annl Niagara Fls Opn Krte Trnm Jdg 90; BMT Clg Of AF 89; Crmnlgy/Justice; Law Enfrcmnt.

**COMPE, LISA E,** Hudson Valley Comm Coll, Troy, NY; FR; BA; Bsn; CPA.

**COMPELL, CHRISTOPHER J,** East Stroudsburg Univ, E Stroudsburg, PA; SR; MS; Hl Cncl Pres 89; Assoc Comp Mach Treas 89-; Univ Yrbk 87-88; Sigma Xi Sci Awd; Res Asstshp; IMS Ftbl Bsktbl Sftbl Capt 87-; BS 91; Comp Sci; Res/Devl.**

**COMPOSTO, CAROLYN,** Elmira Coll, Elmira, NY; JR; BA; Bus Clb 89-; Dns Lst 87-; Hnrs Schlr Awd; Hands Of Chrst Awd 89; AA Corning Comm Coll 89; Acctng; CPA.

**COMPTON, BEVERLY L,** Central Fl Comm Coll, Ocala, FL; SO; AS; Sci; RN.

**COMPTON, BRENDA M,** Patrick Henry Comm Coll, Martinsville, VA; SO; AAS; Ofc Systms Tech; Exec Sec.

**COMPTON, CINDY G,** Univ Of Sc At Spartanburg, Spartanburg, SC; SO; BA.

**COMPTON, CYNTHIA J,** Coll Of Charleston, Charleston, SC; SO; BS; Bsn Admn.

**COMPTON, ELLENA C,** Memphis St Univ, Memphis, TN; JR; BA; PRSSA; Campus Dem St Sen Rep Elect; Kappa Kappa Gamma 87-88; Intl Paper Corp Cmmnctns Intern 90; Northwest Airline Intern 90; Fed Exp Global Cmmnctns Intern; PRSA Schlrshp; Otstndng Chptr Pres PRSSA; Pub Rltns/Eng; Corp Cmmnctns.

**COMPTON, GREGG S,** Central Al Comm Coll, Alexander City, AL; BA; Pblc Spkr Fr Free As An Egle Prog; Elecs Tech At JF Ingram Tech Coll; Math; Acctng.

**COMPTON, JAMES T,** Western Carolina Univ, Cullowhee, NC; JR; BS; NRM Clb 90-; US Forest Service; AAS Haywood Tech College 84; Natural Resource Mgt Forestry.

**COMPTON, JANICE A,** Wilmington Coll, New Castle, DE; JR; BSN; Fclty Stdnt Rep 90-; Act Chr Cvc Assn 85-90; RN 77-; Dip Lancaster Gen Hosp Schl Nrsng 77; Nrsng.

**COMPTON, JEROLD,** Univ Of Va Clinch Valley Coll, Wise, VA; SR; BS; SGA 90-; Phi Theta Kappa 88-89; Psych/Sclgy; Indstrl/Orgztnl Psych.

**COMPTON II, JOE W,** Univ Of Ky, Lexington, KY; SR; BA; Singletary Schlr; Gaines Flwshp; Trvlng Schlrs Schlrshp; Jrnymns Jrnl Schlrshp; Engl German Philosophy.

**COMPTON, KRISTAN M,** Columbus Coll Of Art & Design, Columbus, OH; FR; Illus/Advrtsng Dsgn.

**COMPTON, LORA B,** Northeast State Tech Comm Coll, Blountville, TN; SR; BA; INDT; Welding.

**COMPTON, LORIE A,** Radford Univ, Radford, VA; FR; BS; Nrsng; RN.

**COMPTON, LORILEE E,** Univ Of Ga, Athens, GA; BSED; Intrnshp Athens Tutrl Cntr 90; AS 88; Educ Psych; Thcg.

**COMPTON, MARILYN G,** Univ Of Sc At Columbia, Columbia, SC; SR; BS; Deans List 87-; New Salem Baptist Church Sunday Scl Sec 90-; Employed Full Time Southern Ceatings Inc 73-; Busn; Acctng.

**COMPTON, THERESHA D,** Morris Brown Coll, Atlanta, GA; SO; Key Club VP 88-; FBLA Sec 87-; Sociology Clb 89-; Ntl Honors Scty 85-.

**COMSTOCK, JORDAN B,** Fl St Univ, Tallahassee, FL; SR; Frgn Exch Stdnt Nrwy 88; Art Hstry; Crtr.

**CONA, DAVID J,** West Chester Univ, West Chester, PA; SR; BS; Gtr Ensmbl Pres 87-; Msc Ed Natl Cnfrnc VP 89-; Chr VP 87-90; Hnrs Asoc 87-; Deans Lst; Music Ed.

**CONANT JR, STEPHEN H,** Saint Andrews Presbytrn Coll, Laurinburg, NC; JR; BA; Phlsphy Clb Pr 90-; Dns Lst 88-; Phlsphy/Relgn; Schlr.

**CONARD, KAREN A,** Comm Coll Algny Co Algny Cmps, Pittsburgh, PA; SO; BA; Scndry Educ Bus; Tchng.

**CONARD, SHIRL W,** Univ Of Pittsburgh, Pittsburgh, PA; JR; BS; Ctr Exec Ed Admin Asst 88-; Army Cmmssry Sls 90; Wrhse Wrkr 90f Day Care Wrkr 89; Omega Chi Epsilon VP 90-; Wayne Rawley Fun Pittsburgh Fndtn 90-; Eagle Sct Awd; Eng Hons Schlrshp; Chem Eng.

**CONATSER, GREYDON G,** Tn Temple Univ, Chattanooga, TN; JR; BS; AAS Gainesville Coll; Cmptr Info Sys; Mission Wrk.

**CONATY, MARGARET M,** City Univ Of Ny Bronx Comm Col, Bronx, NY; GD; AAS; Phi Theta Kappa; AAS; Nrsng.

**CONAWAY, CHARISSA E,** Va St Univ, Petersburg, VA; SR; Mktg Clb VP 89-90; Alpha Kappa Alpha 90-; Acad Achvmnt Awds 89-; Mktg/Mgmnt/Food Mktg; Sls Mgmnt.

**CONAWAY, CHERYL L,** Univ Of Miami, Coral Gables, FL; SO; BA; Bus Schl Cncl Advsry Brd; Hnrs Stdnt Assn 90-; Henry King Stafford Schlrshp 90-; Acctng; CPA.

**CONAWAY, JUANITA L,** Univ Of Charleston, Charleston, WV; FR; AA; Telephone Interviewer 90-; Paralegal Law; Prlgl Spclzg Cvl Aspects Law.

**CONAWAY, TIMOTHY J,** Univ Of Nc At Charlotte, Charlotte, NC; SR; BA; AA Mitchell Comm Clg 89; History; Ed/Tchng.

**CONCANNON, CRAIG M,** Ms St Univ, Miss State, MS; SR; BA; Symphonic Band 87-; Hall Counceil 87-89; Forum Mag Awd 90; Prism Mag Art Dir 90-; Art; Graphic Dsgn.

**CONCEICAO, MARIA C,** Suffolk Comm Coll Eastern Cmps, Riverhead, NY; SO; Pi Alpha Sigma; Econs.

**CONCEPCION FIGUEROA, WANDA I,** Inter Amer Univ Pr Hato Rey, Hato Rey, PR; SO; Pre Lgl Assoc Treas; Hnr Scty 90-; BA Interamerican Univ 89; Jstc Crmnl; Lawyer.

**CONCEPCION JIMENEZ, SAUL,** Caribbean Univ, Bayamon, PR; SR; BA; ITC Jr Coll Engl Grp VP 87; Christ Mmry Bnd Slst 87; Ftre Secs Assn 87; Engl Clb 88; Yth Assn Christ Co Hrs; Yth Assn Chrsit Co Hrs Sec; ASS ITC Jr Coll Ponce De Leon Ave RP PR 85; Cert Wang Computers Inc 86; Crmnlgy Scl Scis And Educ; Law.

**CONCEPCION MARQUEZ, SHEILA E,** Inter Amer Univ Pr Hato Rey, Hato Rey, PR; SO.

**CONCEPCION, MELANIE,** Dutchess Comm Coll, Poughkeepsie, NY; SO; Achvmnt Awd Outstndng Mnrty Coll Grad; AS; Bus Admn; Cpa.

**CONCINO, JENNIFER C,** Mt Saint Marys Coll & Seminary, Emmitsburg, MD; SO; BA; IM Bsktbl 89-; Amnsty Intrntl 90-; Pi Sigma Alpha 90-; Dns Lst 89-; Pol Sci; Corp Lwyr.

**CONDE, NICOLE D,** Va Commonwealth Univ, Richmond, VA; FR; BS; Medicine; Nursing.

**CONDE, NORA ELENA,** Fl International Univ, Miami, FL; JR; BA; Scl/Cltrl Plng Comm Stu Govt 89-90; Intl Wk Co Chr 89; Thrsdys Bay 89-90; Ntl Crmnl Jstc Hnr Soc 90-; Amnsty Intl 89; Envrnmtl Awrns Grn Pc 89; Wmn Vctms Dstrs Cmpgn 90-; Deans Lst 90-; Crmnl Jstc; Law.

**CONDE, ZULEMA L,** Fl International Univ, Miami, FL; JR; BA; Future Edctrs Am 90-; French Hon Soc Treas 88-; Deans List 90-; AA Miami Dade Comm Clg 90; Elem Ed; Tchr/Prncpl.

**CONDEE JR, ROBERT L,** Marshall University, Huntington, WV; JR; BBA; Roxalana Hilltoip Townhouse Assoc Pres; Supervisor Peabody Coal Co 87-90; Management.

**CONDIA, ANTHONY M,** Univ Of Cincinnati, Cincinnati, OH; SR; BS; Army Rsrv Offcr Trn Corp Btln Cmndr; Rngr Team 90; Army Airbrn Schl 90; US Army ROTC Advnce Cmp 90; Pi Kappa Delta 90-; Deans Lst 89-; Crmnl Jstce; Army Offcr.

**CONDIO, TRUDY,** Bunker Hill Comm Coll, Boston, MA; FR; BA; Dean Lst; Wmn Shltr Htln Wrkr; Narcotic Annyms Sec; Law.

**CONDIS, MYRNA,** Miami Dade Comm Coll South, Miami, FL; SO; BA; Talent Roster Cert Achvmnt; Cmrcl Arts/Grphc Dsgn; Advrtsng.

**CONDO, MORGAN J,** Oh Dominican Coll, Columbus, OH; SO; Habitat For Humanity 89-; Greenpeace 89-; Envrnmntl Hlth Profsnl; Cross-Dscplnry-Bus; Envrmntl Law.

**CONDON, CHERI A,** The Boston Conservatory, Boston, MA; SO; BA; Music Theatre; Broadway.

**CONDON, KEITH B,** Dowling Coll, Oakdale Li, NY; SR; BBA; Acctg Soc 90; Acad Svc Ctr Peer Tutor 88; Acctg; CPA.**

**CONDON, SARAH E,** Radford Univ, Radford, VA; SO; BA; Radford Univ Hnrs Prog; Elem Educ; Tchr.

**CONDOS, CAROL R,** Ny Univ, New York, NY; JR; BA; Engl; Wrtng.

**CONDOS, MICHAEL J,** Hellenic Coll/Holy Cross, Brookline, MA; JR; BA; Smnrn 90-; Dns Lst 90-; Fltly Co Scrty Offcr Prt Tme 90-; LUTCF National Assn Of Life Underwriters 87; Rlgs Stds; Prsthd Clrgy.

**CONDRON, JENNIFER J,** Kent St Univ Kent Cmps, Kent, OH; SO; BA; Orientation Instrctr; Hnrs Clg 89-; Asst Disabled Std; Presdntl Schlrshp 89-; Rsdntl Staff Advsr; Engl; Tch.

**CONE, AMANDA L,** Fl St Univ, Tallahassee, FL; JR; BS; Phi Theta Kappa 89-90; Golden Key 91; Deans List; Crmnl Jstc; FBI.**

**CONE, BRIAN S,** Univ Of Southern Ms, Hattiesburg, MS; JR; Bio/Premed; Med.

**CONE, LESLIE A,** Univ Of Ga, Athens, GA; SO; BA; Educ; Tch.

**CONE, MARTHA JENNIFER,** Univ Of Nc At Greensboro, Greensboro, NC; JR; BED; Music; Tch.

**CONE, SHANNAN N,** Univ Of Sc At Salkehatchie, Allendale, SC; SO; BS; Chem.

**CONERLY, CATHERINE M,** Georgian Court Coll, Lakewood, NJ; JR; BA; Crt Pg Edtr 90-; Soc Comm Pres 89-; Sgima Tau Delta; Engl/Elem Ed; Tchr/Bus-Pub Rltns.

**CONERLY, ELIZABETH A,** Ms St Univ, Miss State, MS; SR; BS; IEEE; Mu Alpha Theta Sec 87-89; Drill Tm Hinds Cmunty Clg 86-87; Elect Engr.

**CONERLY, RHONDA C,** Morris Brown Coll, Atlanta, GA; JR; BS; Psych V P 88-; Hnrs Clb 90-; Yrbk Stf 89-90; Gldn Ky; All Amer Awd; Alpha Swthrt Org Sec 88-; Minority Summer Rsrch Prog 90; Morris Brown Clg Acad Schlrshp 88-; Alcohol/Drug/ Mntl Hlth Admn 90-; Dvlpmntl Psychologist.

**CONERY, DANIEL G,** Univ Of Rochester, Rochester, NY; SR; BA; Tchng Asst 90; Lab Asst; Vars Ftbl 87-90; Mech Eng.

**CONEY, MOLLIE L,** Fayetteville St Univ, Fayetteville, NC; JR; BS; Cllgt Sec Intl 90-; Kappa Delta Pi Pblc Rltns Rep 90-; Alpha Kappa Mu; Sec Intrnshp Admin Asst; Deans Lst 89-; Deans Lst/ Hon Grad 83-85; Bwlng 90; Chrch God Christ Mssnry 80-; Prspctv Lgl Sec; AS B/SS Midlands Tech Coll 85; Bus/Offc Admin; Lgl Sec.

**CONEY, ZATANYA D L,** Tougaloo Coll, Tougaloo, MS; FR; BA; 1st Pl Drama Comp; Pres Schlr 90; Economics; Bus.

**CONFER, KENNETH A,** Oh St Univ, Columbus, OH; FR; BSBA; Alpha Lambda Delta 90-; Phi Eta Sigma 90-; Hnr Soc 90-; Flg Ftbl Co-Capt 90-; Bsn; Law.

**CONGDON, MELISSA L,** S U N Y Coll At Fredonia, Fredonia, NY; SR; Crinos Dnc/Gymnstcs Arts 84-; Psi Chi; Htln Vol 90-; Tri Cnty Chem Dpndncy Intrn; Cum Laude; AA Jamestwn Comm Coll 89; BA; Psychlgy; Rcrtnl Thrpy.

**CONGEL, SUZIE M,** Old Dominion Univ, Norfolk, VA; JR; BA; Pi Beta Phi VP 90; Cmptr Engnrng.

**CONKELTON, AMY R,** Duquesne Univ, Pittsburgh, PA; JR; BS; Yrbk Edtr 88-; Pblctns Brd Rep 88-; Ideas Std Dir 88-90; Acad Tutor 88-; Educ/Engl.

**CONKEY, DARLA J,** Ky Christian Coll, Grayson, KY; SR; BS; Elem Ed; Tchng.

**CONKLE, JEFFREY W,** Union Coll, Barbourville, KY; SO; BED; Vrsty Tns; Bsns.**

**CONKLE, KERI LYNN,** Clayton St Coll, Morrow, GA; SR; Elem Tchr.

**CONKLIN, BOBRA M,** S U N Y Coll Of Tech At Frmgdl, Farmingdale, NY; FR; BA; Acctng Soc; Bsn; Mgmt/Acctng.

**CONKLIN, KATHYRN M,** Newbury Coll, Brookline, MA; FR; ASSOC; Cert Kinyon Campbell Bus Sch 87; Acctng.

**CONKLIN, KHRISTINE M,** Berkeley Coll Of Westchester, White Plains, NY; SO; BA; Phi Beta Lambda Hstrn 89-; Phi Theta Kappa; Intrnshp IBM Corp 90-; AAS.

**CONKLIN, LAURA J,** Eckerd Coll, St Petersburg, FL; SO; BS; Drom VP; Slvtn Army; Ford Apprntc Schlr; Ntl Presbytrn Schlrshp; Hons Schlrshp; Sailng Tm 89-90; Psych.

**CONKLIN, MARK W,** Western New England Coll, Springfield, MA; SR; BA; Indl Psy.

**CONKLIN, MARK Y,** Salisbury St Univ, Salisbury, MD; SR; BS; Sailing Clb 89-; Chesopeake Bay Yacht Racing Assn 85-; Delta Mu Delta 90-; Bus Mngmnt/Info Sys.

**CONKLIN, STEPHEN P,** Univ Of Al At Huntsville, Huntsville, AL; SR; BSEE; IEEE 90-; 10 Yrs Exp Engrng; Elec Engrng.

**CONLEE, TERRI KAY,** Univ Of Tn At Martin, Martin, TN; SO; BA; Block/Bridle 90-; Agronomy Clb 90-; Clg FFA 90-; Alpha Omicron Pi Hist Rptr 90-; Intl Studies; State FFA Rprtr 90-; Ambassador To Amer Royal 90-; Ag; Law.

**CONLEY, ANTOINETTE,** Bloomfield Coll, Bloomfield, NJ; JR; BA; Paralgl Diploma Betty Owen Bus Schl; Crmnl Justice; Lwyr.

**CONLEY, CHARLOTTE J,** Snead St Jr Coll, Boaz, AL; FR; AAS; Bapt Cmps Mnstrs; Phi Theta Kappa; Dats Prcsng; Cmptr Fld.

**CONLEY, DEBBIE K,** Memphis St Univ, Memphis, TN; SO; BA; SGA; Std Actv Cncl; Delta Gamma; Bsn.

**CONLEY, JAMES ALAN,** Univ Of Al At Birmingham, Birmingham, AL; SR; AAS; SG Comm Affrs Comm Chr 90-; Prog Rep 90-; Hlth Rel Prfsns Advsry; AS Jefferson State Comm Coll 85; Rsprtry Thrpy; Trauma Cntr.

**CONLEY, KATHRYN J,** Ashland Comm Coll, Ashland, KY; SO; BA; Phi Beta Lambda 90-; Drug Info Unit Pro Pr Educ 90-; Schlrshp 89-; Hlth Admin; Law.

**CONLEY, KERI A,** Duquesne Univ, Pittsburgh, PA; FR; Campus Mnstry; Print Jrnlsm.

**CONLEY, MARY F,** Coll Of Charleston, Charleston, SC; FR; BS; Stu Govt Sen 90-; Biol Clb 90-; Fllwshp Chrstn Athlts; Phi Mu; Mrn Biol; Rsrch.

**CONLEY, MICHAEL ALLEN,** Univ Of Ky, Lexington, KY; SR; BSCE; Amrcn Soc Cvl Engnrs Tres 90-; Tau Beta Pi; Evl Engnrng.

**CONLEY, MICHELLE A,** Al A & M Univ, Normal, AL; SR; Erly Chldhd Clb; NNACP; Bptst Stdnt Un; Yrbk Stf; Pep Clb Pres 87-; Mrchng Bnd; Kappa Delta Pi; Rgstrd Rdr 87-; Dns Lst/ Hnr Rl 87-; Erly Chldhd Ed.

**CONLEY, RIKKI L,** Savannah Coll Of Art & Design, Savannah, GA; FR; BFA; Art; Cmrcl Art/Advrtsg.

**CONLEY, SARAH T,** Western New England Coll, Springfield, MA; FR; Radio Station DJ; Sch Lit Mag Writer; Psychlgy.

**CONLEY, WENDA H,** Alice Lloyd Coll, Pippa Passes, KY; SR; Kappa Delta Epsilon 89-; Deans Lst 89-90; Deans Dstngshd Lst; AA Prestonburg Comm Coll 88; Education.

**CONLIN, KELLY A,** Villanova Univ, Villanova, PA; FR; Amnesty Intl 90-; Committee Yr Of Diversity 90-; Japanese Clb 90-; Englsh/Philosophy/Japanese; Law Schl.

**CONLON, LISA A,** Central Fl Comm Coll, Ocala, FL; AA; Ntl Assn Rltrs 86-; Rltr Assoc 86-; Gen Stds; RN.

**CONN, JOYETTA,** Spelman Coll, Atlanta, GA; FR; BA; Treas Fresh Dorm 90-; Tour Guide; Extrnl Affairs Brd Treas 90-; Yng Ambtns Muslim Grp Sec 90-; Hon Roll 90-; Comm Serv Awd 90-; Gamma Phi Delta Pres; Emmaus House; E R Carter Elem Schl; Orientation Ldr; Sis/Sis Connection; Ecnmcs/Child Dvlpmnt; Bus/ Ed.

**CONN, KYLE L,** Vance Granville Comm Coll, Henderson, NC; SO; BA; Hist Clb Pres 89-90; Sci Clb 89-90; Schlrshp; Trnsf Schlr 90-; Deans Lst 89-; Bskbl 89-90; AA 90; Psycl Educ/Sprts Med; Teachr/Trnr.

**CONN, LAURA W,** Univ Of Ky, Lexington, KY; JR.

**CONNAH, JENNIFER W,** Univ Of Ga, Athens, GA; JR; BERD; Kappa Delta Pi; Erly Chldhd Educ; Teacher.

**CONNELL, CAROLYN C,** Univ Of Sc At Columbia, Columbia, SC; SR; BA; Delta Zeta Co Chrmn Fndrsng 88-89; Pol Sci; Law.

**CONNELL JR, EDWARD P,** Univ Of Ms Main Cmps, University, MS; FR; Im Ftbl Bsktbl Tennis Wtr Polo; Phi Eta Sigma; Alpha Lambda Delta; Almbda Sigma; Gamma Beta Phi; Phi Delta Theta Corrspnd Sec; Habitat For Hmnty; Chncllrs Hnr Roll; Im Tennis Ftbl 90.

**CONNELL, MELISSA ANN,** Univ Of Sc At Columbia, Columbia, SC; FR; BA; Bus; Offc Mgm.

**CONNELL, NANCY R,** Univ Of Va Clinch Valley Coll, Wise, VA; SR; BS; Darden Soc 88-; Dean Lst 87-; Stemp Acdmc Schlrshp 87-; Bus Pbl Admn; Mngr.

**CONNELL, NICOLE E,** Newbury Coll, Brookline, MA; FR; Exprssns Clb; Fshn Dsgn; Clthng Dsgnr.

**CONNELL, SUSAN E,** Catawba Valley Comm Coll, Hickory, NC; FR; AS; Dns Lst 90-; Acctg.

**CONNELL, WILLIAM R,** Lexington Comm Coll, Lexington, KY; SO; BA; Acad Tm Capt 89-; Confed Air Force Col 89-; Hist; Profl Military.

**CONNELLY, ALEXANDRA E,** Univ Of Sc At Columbia, Columbia, SC; FR; BA; Bus; Law.

**CONNELLY, AMY B,** Mt Saint Marys Coll & Seminary, Emmitsburg, MD; JR; BA; Campus Mnstry 88; George Henry Miles Hnr Scty Campus Scty Pres 88; Phi Alpha Theta Treas 90; Vlybl IM 90; History; Law.

**CONNELLY, GARY P,** Duquesne Univ, Pittsburgh, PA; SO; BA; Univ Fndrs Schlrshp; Tennis Tm; Crmnl Justice; Law.

**CONNELLY, JAY PAUL,** Univ Of Ga, Athens, GA; JR; Recr Mgr Clb 90-; GA Recr/Pks Assoc 90-; IM Bsktbl/Sftbl/Tennis/Golf/Billiards 90-; Kappa Delta Pi; Grady Mem Hosp Therapeutic Recr 90; ACUI Table Tennis 90.

**CONNELLY, LAUREEN A,** Providence Coll, Providence, RI; SR; BA; Stdnt Nwspr Edtr Chf 90-; Featrs Edtr 89-90; Clg Lit Mag Edtr 89-; Magna Cum Laude; Intrn Pub Rltns Asst Ocean Sta Phys Hlth Pln; Pub Rltns Intrn Advtsng Agcy; English; Pub Rltns.

**CONNELLY, MATTHEW M,** Elmira Coll, Elmira, NY; FR; BS; Lacrosse 90-; Crmnl Jstc; Law Enfrcmnt.

**CONNELLY, MAUREEN T,** S U N Y Coll At Fredonia, Fredonia, NY; SO; BFA; Vol Wrk Newmann Ctr Chrch; Dclg Chr; Art; Dart Thrpy.

**CONNELLY, PETER A,** The Boston Conservatory, Boston, MA; SO; BFA; Cnsrvtry Prestns; Thtr Dept Asstshp; Prod Dept Asstshp; Mscl Thtr.

**CONNELLY, SUSAN K,** Univ Of Sc At Columbia, Columbia, SC; FR; BA; Phi Eta Sigma; Dns Lst 90-; Bsn; Acctg.

**CONNER, ALBERT A,** Bowie St Univ, Bowie, MD; SR; BS; Acctg Clb 88-; Acctg; CPA.

**CONNER, ANGELA MARGUERITE,** Northeastern Christian Jr Coll, Villanova, PA; SO; ARTS; Alpha Chi Omega Scty; CLOCS Brd Mbr; Pres Schlrshp; Resid Assit; Vlybl/Sftbl Cptn; Math; Tchr.

**CONNER, BETHANN,** Livingston Univ, Livingston, AL; SO; BA; Stdnt Rvw Ed; Internatl Scty Pts 90-; Al St Ptry Scty 90-; Strhd Athen; Tw Pms Pblshd 90-; Indctd Natl Athrs Rgstry 90-; RA Rgstrd Athr Natl Cmte Gov 90-; Eng; Prfsnl Fctnl Wrtr.

**CONNER, CHENA,** Ms St Univ, Miss State, MS; JR; BA; Phi Kappa Phi; RA; Psychology; Clinical Psy.

**CONNER JR, DANA H,** Univ Of Sc At Columbia, Columbia, SC; FR; BA BS; Rsdnt Hl Govt Rep 90-; Dns Lst 90; Biology; Exper Psychlgy.

**CONNER, JEAN C,** Va Commonwealth Univ, Richmond, VA; SR; BS; Amer Soc Trng/Dvlpmnt 90; Golden Key 90; Ed; Hmn Rsrc Dvlpmnt.

**CONNER, JEFFREY A,** City Univ Of Ny Baruch Coll, New York, NY; SR; BBA; Radio Statn Prgrm Dir 88-; Schlr Advsry Bd 88-90f Beta Gamma Sigma; Golden Key; Schlrshp Bernard M Baruch Grant; Schlrshp NY State Regents Bd; Fin; Corp Fincng.

**CONNER, KEITH F,** Ms St Univ, Miss State, MS; SO; BS; Bptst Stu Unn 89-; Phi Eta Sigma 90-; Alpha Lambda Delta 90-; Eta Kappa Nu 90-; IEEE 89-; Acdmc Schlrshp 89-; Inst Nclr Pwr Oprtns Schlrshp; IM Sprts 89-; Elect Eng.

**CONNER, KEVIN T,** Al St Univ, Montgomery, AL; FR; Redshirt Frshmn Ftbl; Pol Sci/Pre-Law; Lawyer.

**CONNER, MEREDITH L,** Gaston Coll, Dallas, NC; SO; BA; Spkr Annl Md Wntr Smnr Of AEYC; Otstndng Stdnt 90-; Arts And Scis 90-; Pres Lst 90-; Elem Educ; Tchr.**

**CONNER, MICHAEL D,** Pellissippi St Tech Comm Coll, Knoxville, TN; SO; BA; Math; Acctg.

**CONNER, TAMI L,** Univ Of Sc At Columbia, Columbia, SC; JR; BA; Coker Clg Un Bd 89-90; Coker Clg Stdnt Govt Assn 88-90; Yrbk Stf Edtr 89-90; Univ Theatre Plyrs 90-; Alpha Psi Omega 88-; Gamma Beta Phi 90-; Sigma Tau Delta 90-; Coler Clg Cmsnrs Orgztn 89-90; Univ S C Aiken Pcstr Orgztn 90-; Lit/Theatrical Arts; Clg Prfsr.

**CONNER, TANJIALA L,** Alcorn St Univ, Lorman, MS; SO; Yrbk Staff 89-; Deans Lst 89-; Alpha Kappa Alpha 90-; Acctng.**

**CONNER, TINA D,** Univ Of Tn At Martin, Martin, TN; SR; Fshn Mchdsng Assn Pub Rltns/Treas 89-; Amer Home Ec Assn Sec 90-; Sowells Clthng Intrn.

**CONNER, WENDY J,** Longwood Coll, Farmville, VA; SO; BA; Longwd Schlr 89-; Math; Tchg.

**CONNERS, TRACY J,** Saint Joseph Coll, West Hartford, CT; SR; Deans Lst; BS; Spcl Edctn; Tchr.**

**CONNOLLY, ALLAN K,** Univ Of Cincinnati-Clrmnt Coll, Batavia, OH; FR; BBA; Schlrshp AB/RALPH Dolly Cohen Foundation; Acctg; CPA.

**CONNOLLY, BRENDON,** Univ Of Miami, Coral Gables, FL; SO; AS; Hnrs Stdnts Assoc 89-; Bio Chem; Medical.

**CONNOLLY, DAWN M,** Newbury Coll, Brookline, MA; FR; BS; Prlgl Stds; Crmnlgy And Law.

**CONNOLLY, KARL J,** Salisbury St Univ, Salisbury, MD; SR; Olympia/Yorks Pk Ave Atrium NY Art Show; UMES Grp Show; Natl Art Awds Illstrtn; Rgnl Awds Pntng.

**CONNOLLY, KIM M,** S U N Y Coll At Fredonia, Fredonia, NY; SR; BS; Acctg Soc 90-; John T Kennedy Meml Awd 91; Acctg; CPA.

**CONNOLLY, KRISTEN L,** Niagara Univ, Niagara Univ, NY; SR; BS; Vctm Wtnss Assnce Prog Intrn 89; Acad Excllnce Awrd 89; Assoc Hilbert Coll NY 89; Crmnl Jstce; Law Rltd Fld.

**CONNOLLY, LORAINE A,** Villanova Univ, Villanova, PA; SO; BA; Pep Bnd 89-90; Latin Tutor For Childs Pgm 90-; Classical Studies; Med.

**CONNOLLY, MICHELE C,** S U N Y Coll Of Tech At Frmgdl, Farmingdale, NY; JR; BA; Busn Admin; Mktng/Mgt.

**CONNOLLY, TRICIA A,** Barry Univ, Miami, FL; SO; BS; IM Vlybl 89; Pres Lst 90; Dns Lst 90-; Sftbl 89-; Sprts Med; Athl Trng/Phy Thrpy.

**CONNOR, ADRIAN L,** Va St Univ, Petersburg, VA; SO; Bsebl; Hotel/Restaurant Mgmt Clb; Feed Food Hmeless Salvation Army; Walt Disney World Intern.

**CONNOR, CINDY E,** Edinboro Univ Of Pa, Edinboro, PA; SO; BS; Ski Clb Ofcr; Krt Clb; Hnrs Pgm; Art Ed; Tchr.

**CONNOR, COLETTE B,** Suffolk Comm Coll Eastern Cmps, Riverhead, NY; SO; BA; Hsptlty Clb; Wine Clb; Comp Clb; Phi Theta Kappa; Phi Alpha Sigma; Long Island Rstrnt Assn Schlrshp; AAS; Bus.

**CONNOR, DIONNE A,** Univ Of Md At Eastern Shore, Princess Anne, MD; JR; BS; Carbbn Intl Clb; Hon Pgm; Crmnl Juste; Law.

**CONNOR, JEFFREY V,** Univ Of Sc At Columbia, Columbia, SC; SO; BAIS; Pres Lst Dist; Dean Hnr Lst; AA; Psychlgy; Bus.

**CONNOR, KIMBERLY E,** Providence Coll, Providence, RI; JR; BA; Big Bro & Big Sis 90-; Characteriohcs Of Excptional Child Club 88-; Special Olympics 89-90; IM Flag Ftbl Soccer 89-90; Elem/Spcl Ed; Teaching Canselling.

**CONNOR, KIMBERLY J,** Providence Coll, Providence, RI; SR; BA; Englsh; MA Edctn.

**CONNOR, PATRICK O,** Coppin St Coll, Baltimore, MD; JR; BS; Science Clb 90; Hnrs Scty; Deans List 90; Chrch Tutor; Blgy; Medicine.

**CONNOR, SCOTT D,** Owensboro Comm Coll, Owensboro, KY; SO; BA; SGA Sphmr Rep 90-; Scty Physcs Stdnts 90-; Math Assoc 90-; Math Awrd 90-; AS; Elec Eng; Eng.

**CONNOR, TRISTAN K,** Univ Of Sc At Columbia, Columbia, SC; FR; BA; Bsktbl Tm 90-; IM Sftbl 90-; Marine Bio.

**CONNOR, WILLIAM ERIC,** Univ Of Nc At Asheville, Asheville, NC; JR; BA; RHA 90-; Art Frnt Clb 90-; Orientn Ldr 90-; Ldrshp Rtrt 89-90; Deans Lst 89-; Delta Kappa Theta Hstrn 88-; IM 89-; Art; Studio Phtgrphr.

**CONNORS, CAROLYN J,** Newbury Coll, Brookline, MA; SO; AS; New England Aquarium/Audoron Scty/Covsteau/Scty/Wrld Wldlf Federation; Acctns Payble Oper Sprvr 72-89; Paralegal; Law.

**CONNORS, KEITH R,** Edinboro Univ Of Pa, Edinboro, PA; JR; BABS; Physics/Eng 90-; Phi Eta Sigma 89-; Alpha Chi; Gen Telephone Schlrshp 88; Edinboro Oxford Schlrshp 89; Physics; Elect Eng.

**CONNORS, KELLY ANN,** Siena Coll, Loudonville, NY; SR; BS; Delta Sigma Pi Hist 89-90; Alpha Kappa Alpha; Fin Intrn W/Lee & Leforestier Pc 89-; Pres Lst 90-; Crew Tm 87-88; Fin; Law.

**CONNORS, KEVIN P,** Oh Wesleyan Univ, Delaware, OH; SO; BA; Big Pal Ltl Pal Pgm 90; Tutor; Rcyclng Cntr Vol 89-; Deans List 89-; Greek Acad Hon Scty 89-; Phi Kappa Psi Tres 90- Bus Mgr 91 Comm Svc Chrmn 90-91; Operation Entrprse Mgmt Smnr; IM Sccr Bsktbl Vlybl 89-; Ec Mgmt/Envrmntl Stds; Peace Corp.

**CONOVER, BETTY L,** Edinboro Univ Of Pa, Edinboro, PA; SR; BS; Psychology; Psyd.

**CONOVER, LINDA D,** Glassboro St Coll, Glassboro, NJ; SR; BA; Vrsty Fld Hcky 87; Psychlgy; Sbstnc Abs Cnslr.

**CONOVER, ROBIN S,** Smith Coll, Northampton, MA; SR; BA; Stdnt Gov Assn Sen 90-; Clss Rep 90-; Jdcl Brd Dewey Hse 90-; Hons Pgm 90-; Stdnts Aid Soc; News Dept News Wrtr 88-89; Deans Lst; Brds Chmbrs Comrc/Wrtrs Grp New England Wmns Press Assn; Engl/Music.

**CONRAD, ALISON K,** Univ Of Sc At Columbia, Columbia, SC; JR; BS; Gamma Beta Phi; Bus Admin/Mis; Comp Pgmr/Syst Anlyst.

**CONRAD, JAMES A,** Oh Univ, Athens, OH; JR; BS; Alpha Lambda Delta; Tau Beta Pi; Golden Key; Camp Crsd Christ; IM Sprts; Mech Eng.

**CONRAD, JENNIFER L,** Georgian Court Coll, Lakewood, NJ; SO; BA; MAA 90-; Pi Mu Epsilon; Math; Tchng.

**CONRAD, JENNIFER S,** Drew Univ, Madison, NJ; FR; BA; Beta Beta Beta 90-; Ctr Soc Otrch 90-; Deans Lst 90-; Schlr 90-; Psychobiology; Med.

**CONRAD, MELANIE A,** Springfield Coll, Springfield, MA; FR; Thtr 90-; Mrn Key Clb; Orttn.

**CONRAD, ROBIN L,** Wv Univ At Parkersburg, Parkersburg, WV; FR; Office Skills.

**CONRAD, SAMANTHA N B,** Schenectady County Comm Coll, Schenectady, NY; FR; AS; Drama Clb 90-; Cert Schenectady Cnty Cmnty Clg 90-; Psychlgy/Drama; Acting.

**CONRATH, CARL F W,** Univ Of Rochester, Rochester, NY; SO; BS; IEEE; GE Summer Intrnsp 90; Army ROTC Schlrshp; Elec Engrng.

**CONROD, TOSHIRO N,** Alcorn St Univ, Lorman, MS; SO; CYO; Dns Lst 89-.

**CONROW, LARRY L,** Columbus Coll Of Art & Design, Columbus, OH; FR; Art.

**CONROY, CHRISTINA S,** Widener Univ, Chester, PA; SR; BS; Actvs Comm 87-90; Pblcty Chrmn 90-; Phi Sigma Sigma Pnhlnc Dlgt 89-90; Vol Serv 88-; Bus Mgmt; Hmn Rsrc Dept.

**CONSAGA, ANTHONY J,** Pace Univ At Pleasantville, Pleasantville, NY; SR; BBA; Deans Lst 88-89; Bsnss Mngmnt; Bsnss.**

**CONSEDINE, TRACEY A,** S U N Y Coll Of Tech At Alfred, Alfred, NY; SO; BA; Stdnt Sen Pres; Stdnt Rghts; Stdnt Sen VP 90; Stdnt Lf; Stdnt Sen Exec Char 90; Krt Clb; Coll Cncl 90; Trffc Appls Brd Rep; Cndct Cd Brd Ltms Rep; Nclr Wst Cmm Pres; Sp Ktchn Vol 89; SICA 90f Krt Clb 90; Elem Ed.

**CONSERVA, CARI A,** Bentley Coll, Waltham, MA; FR; MBA; SADD; Bentley Pres Awrd; AC; Acct.

**CONSOLO, LUCILLE R,** Albertus Magnus Coll, New Haven, CT; SO; BA; Poltcl Sci.

**CONSTABLE, FRANCINE M,** Coll Misericordia, Dallas, PA; FR; Radiology/Mgt; Medl Nucheal.

**CONSTABLE, GEORGE A,** City Univ Of Ny Baruch Coll, New York, NY; SO; Pre-Med; Med/Pdtrcn.

**CONSTANCE, JENNIFER K,** Le Moyne Coll, Syracuse, NY; SO; Std Prgmmng Brd Rec Chm; Ski Clb 89-; Vars Clb 89-; Vars Sccr 89-; Pol Sci; Law.

**CONSTANCE, WENDY A,** Fayetteville St Univ, Fayetteville, NC; JR; PHD; Psych Clb; Psych.

**CONSTANTIN, CRISTINA,** City Univ Of Ny Baruch Coll, New York, NY; SO; BA; Psy; Med.

**CONSTANTINE, NICHOLAS P,** Life Coll, Marietta, GA; JR; BS; Constead Clb 90-; Dns Lst; Lic Optcn; AS Manatee Jnr Clg 77; AS Hlsbrgh Comm Clg 83; Chrprctc.

**CONSTANTINIDES, LAURA VELEZ,** Jersey City St Coll, Jersey City, NJ; SR; BSN; Sigma Theta Tau VP; Cert Apprctn NYC EMS 84; Nrsng Rsrch Awd; Deans Lst Bronx Comm Coll 80-81; Continuity Care 90-; RN 81-; AAS Bronx Comm Coll 81; Nrsng; Hlth Admin.

**CONSUL, KEVIN C,** Saint John Fisher Coll, Rochester, NY; SR; BS; Academic Tutor; Mngmnt; MBA.

**CONTADINO, ROSE M,** Manhattanville Coll, Purchase, NY; SO; BFA; Deans Lst 89-; Art; Advrtsng/Cmrcl Artst.**

**CONTAKES, CHRISTOPHER R,** Univ Of Pittsburgh, Pittsburgh, PA; JR; BS; Delta Tau Delta 88-; Inf Sci; Telcomm.

**CONTE, SUSAN J,** Fl St Univ, Tallahassee, FL; JR; BS; PACE Treas 90-; Nghbrhd Hlth Ctr Bd Of Dirs 90-; Admnstrtr Fmly Practc Resdncy Prog Tallahassee FL 82-90; AA Becker Jr Clg Worcester MA 71; Soc Sci; Public Admn.

**CONTE, TINA MARIE,** Albertus Magnus Coll, New Haven, CT; JR; BA; Sociology; Crmnl Jstc.

**CONTI, ERIC M,** Duquesne Univ, Pittsburgh, PA; FR; BS; Phi Eta Sigma; Pharmacy.

**CONTI, LAURIE E,** Merrimack Coll, North Andover, MA; SR; BA; Pltcl Sci Law.

**CONTINO, MARSHALL P,** Univ Of Nc At Asheville, Asheville, NC; JR; Rsdnt Life Staff Rsdnt Asst; Phi Eta Sigma 89; Buttheads Scty 90; Intrnshp Stdyng Aluminum Alid Depostion; Cross Cntry Trck 89; Macon Cnty Cltrl Arts Cncl 87; Nantahala Plyrs 87; Envrnmntl Science; Research.

**CONTRATTI, LINDA K,** S U N Y Coll Of Tech At Alfred, Alfred, NY; FR; Dorm Cncl 90-; Extra Crclr Vlybl/Sftbl 90-; NAA Awd Excellence Bus 90; Acctg Cert Krissler Bus Inst 89; Bus; Ct Rprtr.

**CONTRERAS, BEATRICE CHAVEZ,** Duquesne Univ, Pittsburgh, PA; SR; BSBA; AMA 90-; Spansh Clb 90-; Japanese Amer Soc 90-; Melln Bnk N A 78-90; Intl Offcr 87-90; Mktg; Finc; Busn.

**CONVERSE, NATHAN J,** Univ Of Akron, Akron, OH; JR; BED; Golden Key 90-; Elem Educ; Teaching.

**CONVEY, ANGELA C,** Memphis St Univ, Memphis, TN; SR; BSN; RN Chldrns Hosp; Nrsng.

**CONWAY, DANIELLE M,** Howard Univ, Washington, DC; GD; JD; Cntrcts Rsrch Asstnt 90-; Crt Tm Cmptns Edtr; Ntnl Nr Soc Scabbard Blade Exec Offcr 88-; Dstngshd Mltry Grad ROTC 89; Phi Delta Phi Hstrn 90-; Sigma Phi Rho 88-; Corp Intrntnl Lar.

**CONWAY, FELICIA Y,** Converse Coll, Spartanburg, SC; FR; BA; Cir K 90-; Stdnt Vol Srvcs 90-; Stdnt Adv Comm 90-; Dance Tm 90-; Soclgy/Intl Busn.

**CONWAY, JUDITH P,** Clayton St Coll, Morrow, GA; JR; BSN; GA Assn Nrsng Stdnts 88-90; Intrntl Awrnss Clb 89-90; Vlg Atlanta Wmns Mnstries Vlntr 88-; Atlanta Union Mssn Wmns Div Vlntr 90-; Atlanta Care Ctr Crsis Prgncies Sprtr 88-; Nrse Extrn Grady Mem Hosp Atlanta 89; Nrsng; Mdwfry-Matrnl Chld Hlth.

**CONWAY, KENDRICK L,** Univ Of Tn At Martin, Martin, TN; FR; BA; Ftbl; Arts/Sci; Comp Scintst.

**CONWAY, LYNN M,** Hudson Valley Comm Coll, Troy, NY; SR; AAS; Paul Luther Awd Acad Exclnc Crmnl Jstc; Crmnl Jstc; Prbtn Offcr.

**CONWAY, PATRICIA G,** Rivier Coll, Nashua, NH; SO; BA; Aerobics Instrctr 90-; Lift Wghts 89-; Res Hall Cncl Fl Rep 89-90; Paralgl Stds; Law.

**CONWAY, PHYLLIS A,** S U N Y Coll Of Tech At Alfred, Alfred, NY; SO; AA; Phi Theta Kappa; Receptionist; Allied Health; Nrsng.

**CONWAY, TERRI L,** Christopher Newport Coll, Newport News, VA; SO; BA; Captn Yrbk Busn Mgr 89-90; Student Govt Assoc VP Acad Affairs 90-; Student Ldrshp Inst; Order Of Omega; Gamma Phi Beta 90-; Student Orient Ldr; Political Sci; Tchr.

**CONWELL, TESS-ELLA J,** Univ Of Md At Eastern Shore, Princess Anne, MD; SO; BS; Bio Clb; Ch Sunday Sch; MARC Mnrty Acess Rsrch Careers Pgm; IM Vlybl; Bio; Pediatrician/Rsrch.

**CONZONE, SAMUEL D,** Alfred Univ, Alfred, NY; FR; Tae Kwon Do Clb 90-; Hockey Clb Capt 90-; Lambda Chi Alpha Epsilon; Co-Op PASNY; Ceramic Engr; Patent Lawyer.

**COOK LEGGE, TAMMY R,** Belmont Coll, Nashville, TN; SR; BSN; Stdnt Nrs Assn; Gamma Beta Phi 82-84; Deans Lst; RN; AON Belmont 85; Nrsng; Nrsng Educ.

**COOK, ANGELA M,** Mayland Comm Coll, Spruce Pine, NC; AS; Busn Cmptr Prgmg.

**COOK, BUFFY J,** Middle Tn St Univ, Murfreesboro, TN; FR; BA; Gamma Beta Phi; Tri Beta 90-; Otsdng Gen Chem Stdnt Of Yr Awd; Mary C Dunn Schlrshp; Chem/Biology; Medicine/Cardiologist.

**COOK, CASANDRA L,** Univ Of Nc At Charlotte, Charlotte, NC; FR; BA; Spnsh; Trnsltn.

**COOK, CHARLES D,** Randolph Macon Coll, Ashland, VA; FR; BA; Judcl Brd; Admssns; Kappa Alpha; Vrsty Lacrss; Bus Econ.

**COOK, CHRISTOPHER F,** Fl Baptist Theological Coll, Graceville, FL; SR; BTH; Deans Lst 85-87/90-; Stephen Ministries 88-90; Habitat For Humanity 88-89; New Tribes Missions Trng 85-88; DIP New Tribes Bible Inst 87; AA Palm Bch Jr Clg 82; Missionary.

**COOK, CINDY K,** William Carey Coll, Hattiesburg, MS; GD; BS LSU 90; Bio; Educ.

**COOK, CRAIG C,** Itawamba Comm Coll, Fulton, MS; SO; BS; Ftbl 89-90; Engineering.

**COOK, CYNTHIA L,** Elmira Coll, Elmira, NY; JR; BA; Outling Club 88-89; Tompkins Dorm Cncl Treas 89-90; Bus Clb 90-; St Jos Hosp Fdn Intern 90-; IM Vlybl/Sftbl 88-; Ecnmcs/Bus Mgmt; Hospt Admin.

**COOK, DEBRA S,** Germanna Comm Coll, Locust Grove, VA; SO; AA; W Clyde Locker Memrl Schlrshp 90-; Gen Stdies.

**COOK, DOUGLAS M,** Hillsborough Comm Coll, Tampa, FL; FR; AS; Ceramic Tilesetter 81-88; Legal Asstng; Law.

**COOK, GREGORY R,** Univ Of North Fl, Jacksonville, FL; SR; BA; Asst Supvr CSX Cmrcl Serv 84-; Cmnctns/Pol Sci; Law.

**COOK, JAMES D,** Memphis St Univ, Memphis, TN; SR; BS; Chancellors List 87-90; Elect Engrng.

**COOK, JASON L,** Ithaca Coll, Ithaca, NY; SO; BA; Coll Rep VP 89-; Tbl Tns Clb 90-; Pre Law Socty Sec 89-; Oracle Socty Comm Mbr 89-; Dns Lst 89-; TA Acctng/Lbr Rel; Dns Lst; Bus Mgmt; Law.**

**COOK, JEFFREY M,** Embry Riddle Aeronautical Univ, Daytona Beach, FL; SO; BS; Wrstlng Clb 89-; Scuba Clb 90-; Ldrshp Prgm; Lambda Chi Alpha Exec Comm 89-; YMCA Vol 89-; Hgh Schl Coach 89-; Aerntcl Sci; Arln Trnsprt Pilot.

**COOK, JENNIFER L,** Wilmington Coll, Wilmington, OH; JR; Yrdk Sctn Edtr 90-; Stdnt Fndtn 90-; Hall Rep 88-89; Green Key; Delta Omega Theta Sec Elect; Sertoma 90-; Stdy Cuernavaca Mexico 90; Stdnt Athl Trnr 88-89; Intrnshp Fmly Rcvry Srvcs Alcohol/Drug Abuse Inc; Psychlgy/Sociology; Clin Chld Psychlgy.

**COOK, JULIE C,** Univ Of Sc At Columbia, Columbia, SC; FR; Bapt Stdnt Un 90-; Res Hl Soc Comm 90-; Jrnlsm; Pub Rel.

**COOK, KATHY L,** Lexington Comm Coll, Lexington, KY; FR; ADN; Julia Ewan PTA Brd Membr 88-; Cert Nrsng Asst Cardnl Hill Hosp 90-; Nrsng; RN.

**COOK, KENNY A,** Spartanburg Methodist Coll, Spartanburg, SC; FR; ASS; Bsbl; Bus.

**COOK, KIMBERLY E,** Providence Coll, Providence, RI; FR; BA; Pep/Jazz/Cncrt Bnd; Vlybl 90-; Elem Education.

**COOK, KIMBERLY M,** Lesley Coll, Cambridge, MA; JR; BA; LINC Lrnng Nghbrhd Comm 89-90; Lincoln Hancock Schl Quincy MA; Erly Chldhd Edctn Day Care.

**COOK, KRISTIE E,** Cumberland Coll, Williamsburg, KY; FR; Love In Action 90-; FCA 90-; MENC 90-; Frgn Msns.

**COOK, LEIGH F,** Univ Of Ga, Athens, GA; SR; Symph Band 1st Chr 87-90; Mrchng Band 88-89; Stdnt Affair Nwspr Edtr In Chf 88-90; Music Schlrshp; BS Ed; Eng Edn; Hi Sch Tchr.

**COOK, LINDA H,** Averett Coll, Danville, VA; JR; BS; Comm Life Assoc; Phi Theta Kappa; Pres Lst; Deans Lst; AAS 90; Acctg.

**COOK, LUCRETIA L,** Univ Of Md At Eastern Shore, Princess Anne, MD; JR; BS; Phi Theta Kappa 90; Dns Lst 89; Pres Lst 90; Phys Thrpy; Phys Thrpy; Phys Thrpy Prctce.

**COOK, MARY LOU W,** Univ Of Sc At Columbia, Columbia, SC; SR; BA; Trinity Meth Church Choir 90; Co-Drctr Chldrns Church Trinity UMC; Pres Lst 90; Deans Lst 84-85/90; English/Art Hstry; Tech Wrtng/Tchng.

**COOK, MELANIE D,** Gordon Coll, Barnesville, GA; JR; BBA; Pi Sigma Epsilon Pldg Sprng; Phi Beta Lambda 89/90; Phi Theta Kappa 90; March Of Dimes Spnsrd By Walk-A-Thon Delta Air Lines 90; Cum Laude Grdte; BA 90; Mktg; Mktg Repr.

**COOK, MELISSA J,** Castleton St Coll, Castleton, VT; SR; BS; Specl Weekends Comm Chrprsn 88-; Stdnt Educ Assoc Secy 88-90; Outing Clb Sec 87-89; Kappa Delta Phi 89-; Phi Eta Sigma VP 88-; Shorey Harvey Schlrshp 90; Abel E Leavenworth Ldrshp Awrd 90; Clg Serv Awrd 89; Vrsty Sccry 87; Elem Special Educ.

**COOK, MICHAEL E,** Hampton Univ, Hampton, VA; FR; BS; ROTC 90-; Army Med/Dental Rgmnt 86-; Nrsg; Nrs Anesthetist.

**COOK, MICHAEL S,** Univ Of Ga, Athens, GA; SO; BED; Geog; Tchr.

**COOK, MICHELLE E,** West Liberty St Coll, West Liberty, WV; FR; BA; Natl Hnr Soc 90-; Shaw Schlrshp 90-; Bsn; Acctg.

**COOK, NANCY D,** Kent St Univ Kent Cmps, Kent, OH; SO; BSMD; Stdnt Suppring Stdnts 90-; Alpha Lmbd Dlt 89-90; Super Circuit 90-; Cert Nrs Aid 85-86; Med Trnscrptnst/Sec 87-89; Bio; Medcn.

**COOK, PATRICIA S,** Comm Coll Algny Co Algny Cmps, Pittsburgh, PA; SO; AS; Ntrtn/Food Mgmt Clb 89-; Dns Lst 88-; Phi Theta Kappa 90-; St Malachy PTG 86-; Pttsbrg Diet Asc 89-; Diet Tech/Bsn Mgmt; Dttcs.

**COOK, PAUL L,** Fl A & M Univ, Tallahassee, FL; JR; BA; Fut Fl Educ Amer Tres 90-; Afro Amer Stu Union 90-; Phi Beta Sigma Pres 88; AA 90; Elem Ed.

**COOK, REGINA L,** Univ Of Tn At Martin, Martin, TN; JR; BS; Alpha Gamma Rho 90-; Schl/Bus Deans Advsry Comm; Phi Chi Theta Pres 90-; Admin Serv; Clrcl/Mgmnt.

**COOK JR, RUSSELL E,** Western New England Coll, Springfield, MA; SR; BS; IEEE V-Chrmn 90; Sigma Beta Tau Pres 90-; Lambda Delta 90-; Elec Eng.

**COOK, SHANNON L,** Univ Of Sc At Columbia, Columbia, SC; SO; Orntn Co-Ldr 90-; Nrsg.

**COOK, SHARON L,** Univ Of Nc At Greensboro, Greensboro, NC; SR; BSN; Amer Assn Post Ansths Nrs; N C Assn Post Ansths Nrs Tres 88-90; Nrsng; Crcl Care Nrs.

**COOK, STEPHEN R,** Niagara Univ, Niagara Univ, NY; JR; Clss Govt Treas 88-; Orntn Exec Brd 89-; Acad Snte 90-; Sigma Alpha Sigma 90-; Delta Epsilon Sigma 90-; Amer Inst Of Blgcl Scis 90-; Amer Chem Scty 90-; Ngra Univ Comm Actn Prog 90-; Echrstc Mnstr 90-; Rsdnt Asst 89-; Otstndng Fr Awrd 89; Blgy; Med.

**COOK, SUZANNE BALDWIN,** Coll Of Charleston, Charleston, SC; FR; Actvts Bd 90-; Emtnly Hndcppd Cnslr; Art Psychlgy; Art Thrpy.

**COOK, SUZANNE M,** Abraham Baldwin Agri Coll, Tifton, GA; FR; BS; The Stallion Sch Nwspaper Stf Wrtr 90-; Phi Beta Kappa; Meteorlgy; Physcl Meteorlgst.

**COOK, TAWIANA LYNN,** Univ Of The Dist Of Columbia, Washington, DC; JR; BA; Cert Intl Corrp Schl 85; Cett Columbia Schl Brdctng 88; Journalism/English; Christmn Ed.

**COOK, TIMOTHY L,** Oh Univ, Athens, OH; SR; BS; ROC Rch Out Cmps 88-; Eta Kappa Nu 89-; Theta Tau 89-; Coop Gen Electric Arcrft Engns 90-; Sftbl/Vlybl 89-; Elctrcl Engrg.

**COOK, TRACEY M,** Northwest Al Comm Coll, Phil Campbell, AL; SO; BS; Phi Theta Kappa 89-; Elem Ed; Tchr.

**COOK, VALARIE R,** Morris Coll, Sumter, SC; SR; BS; Stdnt Natl Ed Assoc Secy 90-; Alpha Kappa Mu Secy 90-; All Amercn Schlr Winner; Natl Collgt Ed Award; Elem Ed; Tchng.

**COOKE, AMY D,** Union Univ, Jackson, TN; SR; BS; Psychlgy/Soc Clb 90-; Pi Gamma Mu 90-; Psych; Psychtrst.

**COOKE, AUDRA M,** Roger Williams Coll Bristol, Bristol, RI; FR; BS; Sftbl; Psychlgy; Chld Psychlgst.

**COOKE, CHANDRA D,** Columbia Union Coll, Takoma Park, MD; SO; BA; Mms Wrd 89-; Scl Cmmtt 89-; !sprtl Cmmtt 89-; Drm Clb 90-; SG Prsdntl Sec; Psi Chi; Theta Alpha Beta 89-; Lvs Fhs 89-90; Engl.

**COOKE, COLLEEN T,** Catawba Valley Comm Coll, Hickory, NC; FR; AA; Accntng.

**COOKE, CRISTA N,** Mount Olive Coll, Mount Olive, NC; JR; BS; Ltr Outstndng Rcrd Univ Tn 90; Acctg; Acctnt/CPA.

**COOKE, KATHERINE L,** Ms St Univ, Miss State, MS; JR; BED; Gamma Beta Phi; Kappa Delta Pi; Elem Educ; Tchng.

**COOKE JR, KEVIN R,** Ky St Univ, Frankfort, KY; SO; BS; SGA 90-; Cmpt Sci Clb 89-; Natl Soc Blck Eng 89-; Stdnt Ambassador Sec 90-; Alpha Phi Alpha Sec 90-; U S Dept Of Interior Intrnshp; U Of Wis Summer Rsrch Prog; Math/Cmptr Sci; Cmptr Aided Dsgn.

**COOKE, MARVIN A,** Clark Atlanta Univ, Atlanta, GA; FR; BA; Michigan Clb 90-; Political Sci; Law.

**COOKE, MELANIE R,** Al St Univ, Montgomery, AL; JR; BS; Cmmtr Std Asc 90-; Gnrl Elem Ed; Tch.

**COOKE, MICHELE R,** Roane St Comm Coll, Harriman, TN; SO; BS; Math; Scndry Ed.

**COOKE, SUZETTE M,** Barry Univ, Miami, FL; FR; BA; Jamaican Assn; BSO; Vol Wrk At Camillus Hse With Campus Ministry; Mktg/Adv; Art.

**COOKE, THOMAS M,** Kent St Univ Kent Cmps, Kent, OH; SR; BA; Army ROTC; Goldn Key; Prshng Rfls 87-; Poltcl Sci; US Army.

**COOKE, TINA MARIE,** East Stroudsburg Univ, E Stroudsburg, PA; GD; MA; Daytop Vllg Inc Intrnshp Psychlgcl Tstg Asst 89-90; BS; Cnslng; PhD Psychlgy.

**COOKUS, TAMMY A,** Anne Arundel Comm Coll, Arnold, MD; SO; BS; Deans Lst 89-90; Elem Tchr.

**COOLEY, CHERIE M,** Nc Agri & Tech St Univ, Greensboro, NC; JR; BA; Bennett Schlr 89; Speech Cmmnctns; Lwyr.

**COOLEY, CHRISTOPHER L,** Ms St Univ, Miss State, MS; SO; MBA; Accountin.

**COOLEY, ELIZABETH M,** Univ Of Sc At Aiken, Aiken, SC; SO; BS; Bst Buds 90-; Chem Clb; Gamma Beta Phi; GPA Awrd; Chem; Med.

**COOLEY, KATHLEEN,** Western New England Coll, Springfield, MA; JR; BA; Western New England Acctg Assoc 90-; Alpha Nu Omega 89-90; David W Quadrozzi Tax Conslt Intrnshp; PTC PTO ARTS Council 89-; AS Bus Admin Acct Springfield Tech Cmnty Clge 90; Acctg; CPA.

**COOMES HAIRE, CHRISTINA A,** Ky Wesleyan Coll, Owensboro, KY; JR; BA; Max Bareiss Physcs Awd 89; E Munday Schlrshp Awd; Math Physcs; Scndry Educ Tchr.

**COON, KATHERINE F,** Lesley Coll, Cambridge, MA; JR; BED; Acdmc Hnrs 89-; Erly Chldhd Educ; Tchg.

**COON, LISA D,** Christopher Newport Coll, Newport News, VA; SR; BA; Early Chldhd Ed; Tchng.

**COON, LON B,** Le Moyne Coll, Syracuse, NY; JR; BS; Work For UPS 90-; Bus Admnstrn; Mktg Mgmnt.

**COONER, JENNIFER L,** Fl St Univ, Tallahassee, FL; SR; BS; Mgmt Inf Sys Assoc 89-; Chi Omega House Acc Mgr 87-; Deans List 88-90; Mgmt Inf Sys; Comp Cnsltn.

**COONEY, CONSTANCE M,** Johnson St Coll, Johnson, VT; SR; BA; Chesamore Hon Soc 88-; VT Cursille Rector 79-; Art Tchr.

**COONEY, DENISE L,** Univ Of Cincinnati, Cincinnati, OH; JR; BSN; Nrshg; Emerg Nrs.

**COONEY, JENNIFER E,** Castleton St Coll, Castleton, VT; JR; BA; Art Stu League 89-; STEP Lrng Cntr Tutor 90-; Cstltn In Lndn 90; Phi Eta Simga; Pres Schlrshp; Art; Grphc Dsgn.

**COONEY, KELLI COLLEEN,** Le Moyne Coll, Syracuse, NY; FR; BA; Karate Clb; Var Chrldg; Dvg; Bus Mrktg; Intl Ads.

**COONEY, LAURIAN W,** Nova Univ, Ft Lauderdale, FL; GD; Nrthrn Plns Rsrce Cncl; Kappa Delta; Ordr Of Eastrn Str; MT Hlth Cr Assn; MT Herefrd Assn; Amer Herefrd Assn; Nrsng Hm Admin; BSN MT St Univ 68; MBA 90; Nrsng/Bus; Admin/Hlth Cr.

**COONEY, ROBERT E,** Univ Of Rochester, Rochester, NY; SR; BA; Tae Kwon Doe 87-; Bill; Envmntl Studies.

**COONROD, STEPHEN L,** Lexington Comm Coll, Lexington, KY; SO; BA; Dns Lst; Caterng Consltnt Local Rest 89-; Engl/Educ; Tchg.

**COONS, KY LYNNE,** Hudson Valley Comm Coll, Troy, NY; FR; Early Chldhd; Tchr.

**COOPER, ALISON N,** James Madison University, Harrisonburg, VA; SO; BS; AEYC 90-; Alpha Phi 90-; Chi Phi Aux; Psych/Erly Chldhd Ed; Elem Schl Tchr/Chld Psy.

**COOPER, ALLEN L,** Nova Univ, Ft Lauderdale, FL; GD; MBA; Pricing Anal; BS Ks St Un 81.

**COOPER, ANGIE L,** Livingston Univ, Livingston, AL; FR; AD; Nrsg; RN.

**COOPER, ANTHONY E,** Central Fl Comm Coll, Ocala, FL; SO; AS; Amer Nclr Soc 90-; Hlth Physcs; Hlth Physcs Tchncn.

**COOPER, APRIL L,** Ky Christian Coll, Grayson, KY; SO; BS; Concert Choir 90-; Destiny 91-; Music Perf.

**COOPER, BAZETTE P,** Radford Univ, Radford, VA; JR; BS; Theatre Costumer Assit 89-90; Crisis Hotline Trainer 85-89; Dsgn/Cnstrct Bus 75-; Opera Soc Costumer 89; Theatre/Perf Arts; Plywrght/Costumer/Actress.

**COOPER, BRIAN J,** S U N Y Coll Of Tech At Alfred, Alfred, NY; JR; AAS; Natl Jr Coll Acad Wrstlng Tm 90-; Dns Lst Alfrd St Coll 90-; Alfrd St Wrstlng Tm 90-; Mech Dsng Eng; Eng.

**COOPER, CHARLOTTE,** Tougaloo Coll, Tougaloo, MS; FR; BA; Math Clb 90-; Pre Hlth Clb 90-; Vol Miss Bptst Med Cntr 90-; Math; Physcl Thrpst.

**COOPER, CHRISTINE C,** Ny Univ, New York, NY; FR; BA; Prjct Mgr; AA 84; Intl Stdy; Bus.

**COOPER, CLARE E,** Memphis St Univ, Memphis, TN; SR; PTA; Psychlgy; Adlgy/Spch Pthlgy.

**COOPER JR, CURTIS V,** Savannah St Coll, Savannah, GA; SR; BA; Bnd VP 87; Pol Sci; Law.

**COOPER, DANA M,** Tn St Univ, Nashville, TN; JR; BS; Natl Assn Advncmnt Clrd People Press/Pblcty Chair; Nwspr Illstrtr; Alpha Gamma Tau Treas 89-; Alpha Kappa Mu; Yrbk Edtr In Chief; Studio Art/Grphc Dsgn.

**COOPER, DANIEL E,** Salisbury St Univ, Salisbury, MD; SR; Intl Assn Bus Cmnctrs 89-; Amer Mktg Assn 90-; Rsdnc Hall Assn 88-89; Phi Eta Sigma 87-88; Cmps Lf Awd 89-90; IM Ftbl Bsktbl Sftbl Flr Hcky 87-90; BA 90; Cmnctns; Phrmctcl Sls.

**COOPER, DAVID M,** Ms St Univ, Miss State, MS; GD; Otdr Soc Pres 89-90; CAB 89-90; Coll Rpblcns 89-90; Pres Hon Rl 90; BA 90; Gnrl Bus; Sls.

**COOPER, DAVID W,** West Liberty St Coll, West Liberty, WV; JR; BS; Delta Mu Delta; Kappa Delta Rho Almni Chrmn; Accntng; Accntnt.

**COOPER, DAWN M,** Roane St Comm Coll, Harriman, TN; FR; Psych; Nrsng.

**COOPER, DONNA C,** Tn Temple Univ, Chattanooga, TN; SO; BA; Elem Educ; Tchng.

**COOPER, ELTON B,** Chattahoochee Vly St Comm Coll, Phenix City, AL; FR; BA; Columbus Foundry Q A Foreman 87-; Bus; Q A Mgr.

**COOPER, JAMILLE T,** Manhattanville Coll, Purchase, NY; SR; BA; Blck Un 88-; SOAR 88-90; Beta Beta Beta Tres 90-; Manhattanville Hnr Schl; Blgy Rep 88-89; Untd Negro Clg Fnd 90; Premdcl Smmr Inst; Biology; Med.

**COOPER, JAVON S,** Nc Agri & Tech St Univ, Greensboro, NC; SR; BS; ACS 87-89; Tutor 88-89; Biomed Res Spprt Pgm 88-90; Omega Psi Phi 90-; Monsanta Chem Intrn 89-; Pre Doctrl Pgm UNC Chapel Hill 90; Chem; Dentstry.

**COOPER, JOHN T,** Bridgeport Engr Inst, Fairfield, CT; SO; BS; ASEM Norwalk St Tech Coll 86; Elec Eng; Eng.

**COOPER, JULIE D,** Radford Univ, Radford, VA; SR; Nrsng Class Pres 89-; Ntnl Stdnt Nurses Assn 89-; IM Bsktbl Sftbl 87-89; BSN; Nrsng; RN.

**COOPER, JULIE M,** Garrett Comm Coll, Mchenry, MD; SO; AA; Elem Ed.

**COOPER, KAREN D,** Faulkner St Jr Coll, Bay Minette, AL; SO; BAS; Gamma Phi Beta Rush Comm 90-; Bryce Mental Hosp Vltr 90-; BED Baldwin County Brd Ed 90; Public Relations; Law.

**COOPER, KELLIE A,** Daytona Beach Comm Coll, Daytona Beach, FL; FR; AA; Mntl Hlth Assoc Vol 89; Engl; Pblshng.

**COOPER JR, KENNETH L,** Potomac St Coll, Keyser, WV; FR; BA; Circle K Pres; Christian Youth Fellowshp VP; SG Rep; Bio; Medcn.

**COOPER, KIMBERLY H,** Ms Gulf Coast Comm Coll, Perkinston, MS; SO; BS; VP Lst 89-; PTO 89-; AA MS Gulf Cst Comm Coll; Sci; Nrsng.**

**COOPER, KIMBERLY K,** Savannah Coll Of Art & Design, Savannah, GA; GD; AIGA Grphc Dsgn Clb 89-; Layout Artst; BFA Svnnh Clg Art Dsgn; Fine Arts/Grphc Dsgn; Dsgnr Advrtsng Agncy.

**COOPER, LORI R,** Livingston Univ, Livingston, AL; FR; BS; Bsns.

**COOPER, MARY LYNN,** Glassboro St Coll, Glassboro, NJ; JR; BA; Psych Clb 90-; Dns Lst; Psych.

**COOPER, MELANIE A P,** Tri County Tech Coll, Pendleton, SC; FR; AA; Engl; Tchr.

**COOPER, MELISA A,** Middle Tn St Univ, Murfreesboro, TN; SR; BA.

**COOPER, MELISSA ANN,** Roane St Comm Coll, Harriman, TN; SO; Math; Med/Eng.

**COOPER, MICHAEL A,** Univ Of Cincinnati, Cincinnati, OH; SR; BS; Cadugea Pre Med Soc 90-; Sunday Schl Sec 77-; Chmstry Clb 90-; Grmn Stdnt Yr 90-; Gldn Ky Natl Hnr Soc 90-; Univ Cinc Hnrs Schlrshp 90-; A T & T Elec Eng Intrnshp 87-89; Biochmstry/Pre Med; Med.**

**COOPER, NATHAN,** Clark Atlanta Univ, Atlanta, GA; JR; BS; Math Cmptr Sci Clb 86-; Natl Soc Blck Eng 86-; Pi Mu Epsilon 90-; Prof Lawyer Taylor Awrd; Joseph Dennis Schlr 90-; D & L Packard Schlr 89-; All Amer Schlr Coll Awrd; Math Elect Eng; Elect Eng.

**COOPER, NEALETTE R,** Coppin St Coll, Baltimore, MD; SO; BS; Mgt Sci; Accnt.

**COOPER, OMER A,** Watterson Coll, Louisville, KY; GD; DIP; 2nd Pl Adv Contst; 1st Pl Art Fun Contst; Commrcl Art.

**COOPER, REBECCA S,** Boston Coll, Chestnut Hill, MA; SR; BS; Natl Stdnt Nrs Assc 88-; Gldkey 89-; Sigma Theta Tau; Alpha Sigma Nu; Grtr Boston Undergrad Conf Biothethics; Helen Fuld Fellow 90; Nrsng; Cardiac/Med.

**COOPER, SAMUEL P,** Univ Of Tn At Knoxville, Knoxville, TN; JR; BS; Clg Republ Vice Chrmn 89-; TN Clg Republ Fed E Region Dir 89-; Exec Udrgt Prog 90-; Beta Gamma Sigma 90-; Phi Eta Sigma 89-; Beta Alpha Treas 91; Alpha Kappa Psi Acad Achiev Awd 89-90; KPMG Peat Marwick Shlrshp; Acctng; CPA.

**COOPER, SEAN O,** Fl A & M Univ, Tallahassee, FL; JR; BS; Kemetic Math Soc 90-; Natl Soc Of Black Engrs 89-; Pepsi-Cola Intrnshps 88-90; Life-Getr Better Schlrshp 88-90; Acad Awrd FAMU Tennis Tm 89-90; Tennis Capt 89-; Math; Actuarial Sci.

**COOPER, SHARI L,** Old Dominion Univ, Norfolk, VA; SR; BA; ASCE 90-; Chi Epsilon 89-; Tau Beta Pi 89-; USAA Coll All Amer Schlr Awd 89; USAA Coll Awd All Amer Schlr At Lrg 90; USAA Natl Coll Engr Awd 89; Cvl Engr.**

**COOPER, SHARON L,** Memphis St Univ, Memphis, TN; SO; BS; Math; Teach.

**COOPER, SONIA C,** Beckley Coll, Beckley, WV; SO; BA; Hnrs Prgm; Mdcl Offc Admn.

**COOPER, SONYA D,** Paine Coll, Augusta, GA; GD; BS; Sociology Club 90- Omega Pearl Dean Of Pledges 86-; Int Youth Devopmnt Augusta 88-; Paine College Bookstore Stdnt Asstnt; Sociology; Social Worker Or Psychology.

**COOPER, STACY D,** Middle Tn St Univ, Murfreesboro, TN; SO; BS; Natl Hnr Soc 88-89; Nursing.

**COOPER, SYNAE L,** Lincoln Univ, Lincoln Univ, PA; FR; Gospel Ensemble; Militants Christ; Gospel Steppers Secr; Engl Ed; Law.

**COOPER, TAMARA L,** East Central Comm Coll, Decatur, MS; FR; AA; Stdnt Ed Assoc Pres 90-; Warrior Corp Pres 90-; Pres Cncl 90-; Phi Theta Kappa Secr; Recruiter; Math Awd 90-; Sec Ed Awd 90-; IMS 90-; Math; Tchr.

**COOPER, TONI L,** Richard Bland Coll, Petersburg, VA; FR; AA; Pltcl Sci; Law.

**COOPER, TRACEY A,** Anne Arundel Comm Coll, Arnold, MD; FR; AA; US Coast Guard Chief Radioman E-7 80-; Cmptr Ntwrk Mngmnt; Coast Grd Cmmnctns.

**COOPER, WYNEL S,** Salisbury St Univ, Salisbury, MD; JR; BA; Herbert D Brent Schlrshp 90-; Msc; Piano Pedagogy/Prfrmnc.

**COOPERMAN, AMY C,** Eckerd Coll, St Petersburg, FL; SO; BA; Choir 89-; Madrigal Ensmbl 89090; Pop Ensmbl 90-; Rotary Clb 90; Human Dev Serv; Wellness.

**COOPERMAN, JOELLE,** Univ Of Miami, Coral Gables, FL; SR; BS; Sugarcns Bat Grl 87-; Pres 100 Ambsdr 89-; Stdnt Govt Sen 87-89; Phi Kappa Phi 89-; Gldn Key 89-; Psi Chi 88-; Phi Sigma Sigma Rsh Chrmn 88-; Natl Kdny Fndtn 88-; Fundy P R Chr 88-89; Jrnl Clin Chld Psych Auth 89-90; Adv/Psych; Ent Law.

**COOTAUCO, M EMILY,** Franklin And Marshall Coll, Lancaster, PA; SO; SG Rep 89-90; Chi Omega Hstrn 90-; Elderlink 90-; SAMS 90-; Ecnmcs; Med Schl.

**COOTS, ALAN F,** S U N Y Coll Of Tech At Alfred, Alfred, NY; GD; Automotive.

**COOTS, CHARLES J,** Union Coll, Barbourville, KY; JR; BS; Tnns 89-90; Edctn; Mthmtcs; Tchr.

**COPA, ISABEL C,** Univ Of Miami, Coral Gables, FL; JR; BBA; Fdrtn Cbn Stdnts 89-; Alpha Kappa Psi Pldg VP; Deans Lst 90; Mgmt Mrktng; Intl Bus.

**COPE, CATHY A,** Western Ky Univ, Bowling Green, KY; JR; BS; Phi Kappa Phi 90-; Cmptr Sci; Cmptr Pgmr.

**COPE, GARY G,** Volunteer St Comm Coll, Gallatin, TN; SO; Gama Beta Phi 90-; Natl Hm Bldrs Assoc 86-; Nasvll Mddlt Tnn Hm Bldrs 86-; AS; Bus.

**COPE, MARVIN L,** Cumberland County Coll, Vineland, NJ; FR; AS; Laurel Lake Rescue Squad 91; Law Enforcement US Marine 82-90; Crmnl Justc; Law Enfrcmnt.

**COPELAND, BESSIE S,** Piedmont Tech Coll, Greenwood, SC; SO; AS; Phi Beta Lambda Pres 89-; Phi Theta Kappa 90-; Derrick Schlrshp 90-; County Bk Schlrshp 90-; Outstndg Curriculum Stdnt 90-; Admin Specialist; Bsn; Clg Instr.

**COPELAND, BRIAN C,** Southern Coll Of Tech, Marietta, GA; JR; BS; ACM 88-; Tau Alpha Pi 90-; Vet U S Army; Cmptr Sci; Sftwr Engrg.

**COPELAND, CAROL A,** Fl St Univ, Tallahassee, FL; SR; BS; Psi Chi 90-; Gldn Key 90-; Phi Theta Kappa 88-89; NBWA Schlrshps 90; Trnsfr Schlrshp 90-; FIBER 89-90; Fla Cmmcnts Assn 90-; AA Tallahasee Comm Coll 89; Psychlgy; Cmmnctns.

**COPELAND, CASSANDRA C,** Daytona Beach Comm Coll, Daytona Beach, FL; FR; BS; Ecnmcs; Prfssr.

**COPELAND, COURTNEY C,** Duquesne Univ, Pittsburgh, PA; JR; BA; Stdnt Govt Assn Sen 90-; Pub Rltns Stdnt Soc Of Am V P 89-; Orntn Prog Chp 90-; Zeta Tau Alpha Hstrn 89-; UWCA 90-; Intrn Peoples Nat Gas Co; Corp Comm/Eng Writing; Pub Rltns/Sales.

**COPELAND, DAWN A,** Faulkner Univ, Montgomery, AL; SR; BA; Cncrt Chr Sctn Ldr 87-; Pied Pipers 90-; Encore Dinner Thtr 90-; Phi Lambda 90-; Zeta Tau Alpha Msc Chrmn 88; Auburn Univ Thtr Asstshp 88; Outstndng Coll Stdnts 87; AL Shkspr Fest 90; Theatre; Actress.

**COPELAND, ERICA C,** Fl A & M Univ, Tallahassee, FL; FR; BS; NAACP; Phi Eta Sigma; Chmcl; Eng.

**COPELAND, JENNIE M,** James Madison University, Harrisonburg, VA; GD; MED; Alpha Gamma Delta Pnhlnc Rep 89-90; Psychlgy Grad Asstntshp; AACD 90-; VCA 90-; BA Psychlgy 90; Cnslng; Elem Sch Cnslr.

**COPELAND, JENNIFER D,** Truett Mc Connell Coll, Cleveland, GA; FR; BS; Math; Actuary.

**COPELAND, JOYCE R,** Vance Granville Comm Coll, Henderson, NC; JR; AAS; Busn Cptr Prog.

**COPELAND, JULIE C,** Univ Of Tn At Chattanooga, Chattanooga, TN; SR; BS; Vrsty Bsktbl 87-; ASME ASCE SWE 88; Tau Beta Pi 90-; Pi Mu Epsilon 88-; Gldn Key 87-; TN Vlly Authrty Intrn; Eng/Mech; Eng.

**COPELAND, LESHONDA E,** Univ Of Miami, Coral Gables, FL; SO; BA; Insprtnl Concert Choir VP 89-; Untd Black Stdnts Secy 90-; Bus; CPA.

**COPELAND, PAMELA R,** Tn St Univ, Nashville, TN; JR; BS; AE-COMP 89-; Comp Sci Clb 90-; Clrk-Typst US Army Corps Engrs Nashvl Dist; Comp Sci; Comp Anlyst.

**COPELAND, VYTA N,** Wilberforce Univ, Wilberforce, OH; FR; BA; Radio Clb 90; Univ Choir 90f Gspl Choir 90; Deans Lst; Cmmnctn.

**COPENHAVER, MICHELLE K,** Univ Of Fl, Gainesville, FL; FR; Bsn; Mrktng.

**COPES, CHARLENE P,** Va Commonwealth Univ, Richmond, VA; SR; BSN; Gldn Key; Phi Kappa Phi Sigma Theta Tau; Dplm Sci Nrsng St Lukes Hospschl Nrsng 80; Nrsng.

**COPES, ERIC B,** Cheyney Univ Of Pa, Cheyney, PA; JR; Hotel/Restaurent Mgmt Clb Pres 90-; Intrnshp Penn State; Ftbl 90-; Hotel/Rstrnt Instnl Mgmt; Advncmnt Mgmt.

**COPES, JASON B,** Thomas Nelson Comm Coll, Hampton, VA; SO; AA; Prof Phtgrphr.

**COPLAN, DAVID A,** Univ Of Pittsburgh, Pittsburgh, PA; SR; Bach Scl Wrk Clb 89-; Stdnt Exec Cncl Actng Pres/Treas 89-; Stdnt Rep Crrclm Comm 89-90; Sigma Phi Epsilon Sec 90; Stdnt Ldrshp Awd Alumni Assn 90-; IM Bsktbl 90-; BASW; Scl Wrk; MSW/MPA.**

**COPLER, CAROLINE E,** Radford Univ, Radford, VA; SO; SEA 89-; House Cncl 89-90; Deans Lst 90-; Elem Educ.

**COPLEY, MELISSA M,** Ashland Comm Coll, Ashland, KY; SO; AD; Nrsng.

**COPP, JODI L,** Central Pa Bus School, Summerdale, PA; FR; ASB; Stdt Legal Assoc 90-; Cllgte Scrtrs Itnl; Legal Assistant; Law.

**COPPEDGE, CHERITA DAWNE A,** Jackson St Univ, Jackson, MS; FR; B; Cmps Crsd Chrst Srvnt Tm Ldr 90-; Jr Rcrtr JSU 90-; Math; Bus/Educ.

**COPPETO, ELLEN K,** Saint Joseph Coll, West Hartford, CT; SO; BA; Chld Stdy/Psychlgy; Tchr.

**COPPOCK, PATTI L,** Tn Wesleyan Coll, Athens, TN; JR; BS; Coll Bblcl Stds Awrd; AS Cleveland St Comm Coll; Hmn Srvcs; Scl Wrk.

**COPPOLA, CHRISTINE C,** Wagner Coll, Staten Island, NY; SO; BA; Acctng Socty Sec 90-; Dns Lst 89-; Bus; Acctng.

**COPPOLA, DIANNA L,** Schenectady County Comm Coll, Schenectady, NY; SO; ASSOC; Pres List 85-; Phi Theta Kappa; BPWC Yng Career Wmns Cntst Rcgntn 88; Med Ins Verifer/Clctn; Acctg.

**COPPOLA, MARTIN R,** Glassboro St Coll, Glassboro, NJ; SR; BA; Pr Lst 87-89; Deans Lst 89-; Prof Rdng/Wrtng Tutor 89-; Sub Tchr 89-; Mobile DJ; CERT Philadelphia Spinal Tutorium 81; AA Camden Cnty Clg 89; Lib Arts/Cmctn; Author/Tchr/Theologian.

**COPUS, JEFFREY D,** Anne Arundel Comm Coll, Arnold, MD; FR; AA; IM Wrstlng; Arch.

**CORBETT, CHANDA C,** Lincoln Univ, Lincoln Univ, PA; JR; BA; Stdnt Ldr 90-; Chnse Clb Sec 90-; Gspl Ensmbl 89-; Alpha Chi; Psi Chi Vp; Delta Sigma Theta Pres 90-; Alliance Rsrch Opprtnty Prog Univ MI 90; Psychlgy.

**CORBETT, CHET E,** Teikyo Post Univ, Waterbury, CT; SR; BS; AS Mattatuck Comm Coll 89; Engl; Grad Schl.

**CORBETT, DERRICK B,** Nc Agri & Tech St Univ, Greensboro, NC; SO; BA; Natl Clgt Comm Arts Awd; NCA/T Acad Awd; Pres Schlp 89; Sprts Edtr WNAA-FM 89-; Radio Prsnlty 90-; Asst Sprts Info Dir 89-; Brdcst News; Sprtscstr.

**CORBETT, JENNIFER L,** Kent St Univ Trumbull Cmps, Warren, OH; SO; BS; Ambsdr 90-; Hugh Obrien Yth Ldrshp Smnr Cnslr 87-; Pres List; Elem Educ; Tchr.

**CORBETT, JERRY D,** James Sprunt Comm Coll, Kenansville, NC; SO; Kenansville E Bapt Asso; Mt Olive Policemans Bettmnt Asso Chpln 88-; Kenansville E Minis Asso; Police Offcr Mt Olive Police Dept 88-; BLET Wayne Com Colg 88; Crmnl Jstce; Probtn Parole; SBI Agent.

**CORBETT, JONATHAN R,** Tomlinson Coll, Cleveland, TN; SO; BA; Chess Club Pres 90-; In Touch Grp Ldr 90-; Acdmc Curriculum Comm Stdnt Rep 90-; Phi Theta Kappa Pres 90-; AS; Eng; Mnstry Eng Tchr.

**CORBETT JR, JYON L,** Univ Of Al At Birmingham, Birmingham, AL; GD; BS; Clms Adjstr Rsk Apprsr 86-90; BS Mrktg 86; Mchncl Eng.

**CORBETT, KERI A,** Fl International Univ, Miami, FL; FR; Cmctns; Broadcst Jrnlsm.

**CORBETT, LE ANNE M,** Mount Olive Coll, Mount Olive, NC; JR; BA; Mbr AF 87; AS; Cmmnty Clg AF 91; Phrmclgy Science; Phrmcst.

**CORBETT, RONALD A,** Univ Of Louisville, Louisville, KY; GD; BES; IEEE 88; Golden Key 89; Tau Beta Pi 90-; Eta Kappa Nu 90-; Elect Engr.

**CORBIN, CAROLYN M,** Univ Of Cincinnati, Cincinnati, OH; SR; BS; Kappa Delta Pi 90-; Univ Hnr Schlrshp 89-; Schl Sci/Math Assoc 90-; Elem Ed; Tchg.

**CORBIN, JULIE N,** Truett Mc Connell Coll, Cleveland, GA; SO; MBA; Bptst Stu Unn 89-; Rotaract; Chrldr Co Capt 89-; Sftbl Schlrshp 89-; AA; Phys Ed Hlth Ed; Educ Cchng.

**CORBIN, LYNN S,** Blue Mountain Coll, Blue Mountain, MS; JR; BS; Phi Beta Lambda Sec/Treas; 1st Pl PBL St Admn Asst Typist 90-91; Concord Bapt Ch Organist 84-; Bus Edn; Teach.

**CORBIN, PAMELA S,** Milligan Coll, Milligan Clg, TN; JR; BA; Serv Seekrs 89-; Dns Lst; Educ; Spec Educ.

**CORBIN, PERRY S,** Ky Wesleyan Coll, Owensboro, KY; SO; BS; Sigma Zeta Treas; Pre Profsnl Soc 90; Physcs Dept Award; PB/S Chem Co Award; Chem.

**CORBITT, CHRISTIE L,** Chattahoochee Vly St Comm Coll, Phenix City, AL; SO; BS; Gamma Beta Phi; Vrsty Sftbl Tm Capt 89-; Engr/Mttllrgy; Engr.

**CORCINO RIVERA, JOSE H,** Univ Politecnica De Pr, Hato Rey, PR; FR.

**CORCORAN, BRIAN J,** Le Moyne Coll, Syracuse, NY; JR; BS; Resident Advsr 90-; Res Hall Council V Pres 88-; Judicial Review Brd 89-; Internatl House 90; IM Soccer 88-; Bus Admnstrn; Personnel Mgmnt.

**CORCORAN, CANDACE M,** James Madison University, Harrisonburg, VA; FR; BBA; Acctg.

**CORCORAN, KELLY A,** Castleton St Coll, Castleton, VT; FR; BA; Stdnt Ed Assn 90-; Math Clb 90-; SADD 90-; Tutoring 90-; Deans List 90-; IM Vlybl 90-; Math Ed; Tchng.

**CORCORAN, KEVIN A,** Univ Of Miami, Coral Gables, FL; FR; BM; Music Educ/Instrmntl; Bnd Drctr.

**CORDANO, JENNIFER B,** Bloomfield Coll, Bloomfield, NJ; SO; BSN; Soph Cls VP 90-; Bloomfld Clg Nrsng Stdnt Assc VP 90-; Ldrshp Stdnt Alumni Assn VP 89-; Stdnt Ambsdrs 90-; Hnrs Prgrm 89-; Sigma Phi Delta 90-; Nrsng; Nurse.

**CORDASCO, CARLA M,** Univ Of Med & Dentistry Of Nj, Newark, NJ; DMS; SDMS 90-; Valedictorian Berdan Inst 85; Med Asst 86-; Ultrasound.

**CORDEIRO, LUCY M,** Albertus Magnus Coll, New Haven, CT; FR; Accounting; Real Estate Lawyer.

**CORDER, CALANDRA Y,** Stillman Coll, Tuscaloosa, AL; SR; BA; Cmnctn Assoc Pres; NAACP Pltcl Chr; Sr Cls Sec; Bg Bro/Bg Sis; Dns Lst; Mst Outstndng Comm Stdnt; Cmnctns/Eng; Elem Schl/Spch.

**CORDER, JENNIFER L,** Middle Tn St Univ, Murfreesboro, TN; SR; BS; Alpha Delta Pi Asst Guard 88-89; Elem Educ; Elem Schl Cnslr.

**CORDERO CASTRO, MARTHA I,** Inter Amer Univ Pr Aquadilla, Aguadilla, PR; FR; BA; Crmnl Jstce; Law.

**CORDERO DELGADO, MADELINE,** Univ Of Pr Humacao Univ Coll, Humacao, PR; SR; BBA; AUEC; AUEG; Brd Stdnts Admin Rep 88-89; AUETA 88-89; Basic Educ Dept Math Tutor 90-; Cert Schlrshp Hon Stdnts 88-90; Bus Admin; Acctg-CPA.**

**CORDERO LUCIANO, VIVIAN C,** Inter Amer Univ Pr San German, San German, PR; SO.

**CORDERO, EDGAR,** Univ Of Pr At Mayaguez, Mayaguez, PR; SO; NACME 89-90; IM Bsktbl 89-; Mech Engr.

**CORDERO, LORNA E,** Miami Dade Comm Coll South, Miami, FL; SO; BA; Vol Arvida Mddl Schl Vol Clrk 90-; Vol Sr Crm Prvntn Vctms Asst Prgm Tlphn Frnd; Tlnt Rstr Cert Achvmnt; Otstndng Acdmc Achvmnt Awrd 90; Psychlgy; Clncl Psychlgst.

**CORDERO, ROSE MARY,** Fl International Univ, Miami, FL; JR; BA; Elem Ed; Tch.

**CORDERO-ACABA, ROBERTO,** Univ Of Pr At Mayaguez, Mayaguez, PR; SO; BS; Engrng Hnr Rl; Natl Cllgt Mntry Ldrshp Awrd; Track Field 90; Electrcl Engrng.

**CORDES, JENNIFER L,** Elmira Coll, Elmira, NY; FR; BA; Coll Mascot 90-; Pol Sci; Law.

**CORDIER, BRUCE R,** S U N Y At Buffalo, Buffalo, NY; SR; BS; Inst Elec/Electrncs Eng 89-; Elec/Cmptr Eng.

**CORDIER, PHILIP A,** Duquesne Univ, Pittsburgh, PA; JR; BA; Phi Alpha Theta 90-; Kappa Simga Phi 89-; Hstry; Law.

**CORDNER, VICTORIA ANNE,** Old Dominion Univ, Norfolk, VA; JR; BS; Order Of Omega Treas; Alpha Phi Pres 88-; Mst Outstndg Mbr Alpha Phi 90; Schl Yr Rcgnzd By Old Dom U Stdnt Svcs; Mktg/Educ; Advrtsg.

**CORDOBA, ANGELINA RENEE,** Fl A & M Univ, Tallahassee, FL; JR; BSW; Phi Alpha Social 90-; Social Sci Award; Cheerleader 89-; Social Work; Cnslr Chldrn/Fmls.

**CORDONIO, DENISE M,** S U N Y Coll At Fredonia, Fredonia, NY; JR; BS; Spctrm Entrtnmnt Brd 88-90; Shrtn Hrbrfrnt Ftnss Cntr Intern; Bus Amdn; Mrktng Advrtsng.

**CORDOVA, LIZA M,** Smith Coll, Northampton, MA; SR; MS; Hse Cncl 88-90; Phi Beta Kappa; Sigma Xi; Res Asst Inst Neurobiol PR 89; Asst Sci Lib 88-; BA; Biol.

**CORDOVA, ROBERTO E,** Inter Amer Univ Pr San Juan, Hato Rey, PR; GD; Exec Clb 82-85; IAU Deans Lst 90; Acdmc Schlrshps; IMS; Mortgage Bnkrs Assn; Corp/Commrcl Bnkr 86-; MBA St Louis Univ 85; BS St Louis Univ 83; Finance; Attrny/Invstmnt Bnkng.

**CORDOVA, SUSANA R,** Fl International Univ, Miami, FL; SR; BS; Future Educ Of Amer Sec 89-; Kappa Delta Pi 90-; Deans Lst 90-; AA Miami Dade Cmnty Clg 89; Elem Educ; Schl Admin.

**CORDOVA, WALDO G,** Univ Politecnica De Pr, Hato Rey, PR; SO; BSEE; BS Univ De PR 90; Elctrnc; Biomed Engrg.

**CORDOVA, YNES,** Univ Of Pr Medical Sciences, San Juan, PR; SR; BA; Rdlgc Tchnlgst Axl Mtr Hosp; Rdlgc Tech 87; Hlth Sci.

**CORDRAY, TRACY L,** Coll Of Charleston, Charleston, SC; SO; BS; Lutheran Stdnt Movement 89-90; Alpha Chi Sigma Rptr; Alpha Epsilon Delta 90-; Fwlshp Chemical Rsch; Teachers Asstnt Chem Lab 90-; Biochemistry; Medicine.

**COREA, SHARMINI D,** Bloomfield Coll, Bloomfield, NJ; Int Clb Slppry Rck Univ Spec Evnts Offcr; Delta Phi Chi 90; Intl Bus.

**CORELLA, CHRISTINE,** Univ Of Miami, Coral Gables, FL; SR; BM; Band 85-; TUBA 88-; CMENC 86-; Tau Beta Sigma 87-; Ntl Dns Lst 89-90; Music Educ.**

**COREY, DAVID E,** Norfolk St Univ, Norfolk, VA; SR; BS; Phi Mu Alpha Snfn Asst Dean Pldgs 84-; Msc Edctrs Natl Conf 87-88; Tabernacle Asmbly God Suffolk Hd Trustee 88-; Msc Educ; Bnd Dir/Prof Msc.

**COREY, HEATHER A,** Elmira Coll, Elmira, NY; SR; BA; Sprts Ed Schl Nwspr 87-90; Career Asst 88-; Psi Chi 89-; Law Intrnshp 90-; Phi Beta Kappa 90; Vars Mns Bsktbl Statstcn 87-; BA; Psych; Law.

**COREY, MARSHA L,** Ms St Univ, Miss State, MS; SO; BA; Cmpss Clb VP; Delta Delta Delta; IM Sprts; Educ; Elem Educ.

**CORI, LINDA A,** Livingston Univ, Livingston, AL; SR; BS; Nwsppr Ad Sls/Typsttr 89-; Omicron Delta Kappa 90-; Alpha Sigma Tau Treas 89-; Early Chldhd Educ; Tchr.

**CORIANO, BRENDA I,** Univ Of Pr At Rio Piedras, Rio Piedras, PR; JR; BBA; Natl Stu Exch 90-; Accntng Stu Assn 89-90; Hana Schlrshp 90-; IM Vllybl 90-; Accntng; CPA.

**CORIELL, PAUL R,** Oh St Univ, Columbus, OH; SO; BS; Stdnt Rsrc Cnsrvtn 89-90; Alpha Lambda Delta 90; Pheta Sigma; Upsilon Pi Upsilon; Stadium Schlrshp 89-; Dns Lst 89-; Lndscpe Arch.

**CORKEN, ERIN MICHELLE,** Univ Of Cincinnati, Cincinnati, OH; JR; BFA; Alpha Epsilon Rho 90-; Radio Ancr WWEZ 90-; Brdcstng/Film.

**CORLESS, TRACEY A,** Fl St Univ, Tallahassee, FL; JR; BA; Seminole Ambassadors 90-91; Psychology Hnr Scty 90-; Psi Chi Hnr Scty 90-; Psychology; Business.

**CORLEW, ARTHUR E,** Castleton St Coll, Castleton, VT; JR; BS; Radio Clb 87; Physical Educ Clb V P 91-; Asst Coach Bkbl 90-; I M Bkbl Vybl 87-; Ped Edu; Tch/Coach.

**CORLEY, CHAD J,** Belmont Coll, Nashville, TN; FR; BBA; Deans Lst 90-; IM Bsktbl; Music Bus; Rcrdng Engr.

**CORLEY, CHAD J,** Belmont Coll, Nashville, TN; FR; BCOMM; Acadmc Schlrshp 90-; Im Bsktbl; Recrdng Inds Mgt; Recrdng Engr.

**CORLEY, DEIRDRE L,** Univ Of Sc At Columbia, Columbia, SC; FR; BA; Gamma Beta Phi; Bus/Fin.

**CORLEY, HARRY R,** Univ Of Sc At Columbia, Columbia, SC; SR; Geophysics; Envrnmntl Sctr.

**CORLEY, JENNIFER L,** Dyersburg St Comm Coll, Dyersburg, TN; SO; AAS; DPMA Pres 90-; SGA; Phi Theta Kappa; DPMA Cmptr Pgmmng Schlrshp 89-90; Cmptr Sci; Cmptr Pgmmng.

**CORLEY, LAUREN K,** Univ Of Sc At Columbia, Columbia, SC; JR; BA; Gamma Beta Phi 90-F Alpha Delta Pi 88-; Richland Rershaw Solicitors Offc 90-; Engl; Law Schl.

**CORLEY, MICHAEL S,** Univ Of Tn At Chattanooga, Chattanooga, TN; SO; BME; Math Hon Soc; Mgt Inter GEICO Corp 89-90; BSBA Am Univ 89; Mech Eng.

**CORLEY, SHANNON S,** Fl St Univ, Tallahassee, FL; JR; BA; AA 90; Cmnctns Dsrdrs; Spch/Lng Pthlgst.

**CORLEY, STEPHANIE J,** Univ Of Sc At Columbia, Columbia, SC; FR; BA; Frshmn Cncl Carolina Cares; Ronald Mc Donald House Vol; Alpha Delta Pi Histrn 90-; Jrnlsm; Brdcstng.

**CORLEY, TODD L,** Le Moyne Coll, Syracuse, NY; SR; BS; INROADS/UPSTATE NY Inc Brd Dir 87-; Bus Clb VP PR 90-; Cmmtt Race Rltns 90-; Martin Luther King Jr Urban Leg Schlrshp 87-; INROADS Intern 87-; IM Bsktbl 87-; Fnnc/Bus Admn; Fnncl Anlyst.

**CORMIER, KIMIC S,** Clark Atlanta Univ, Atlanta, GA; FR; BS; St Marys Acad Mrchg/Concert Bnd 88-; Cncl Sr Coord 89-; Varsity Vlybl 87-; Hnr Scty; Tambourine/Fan Clb 88-; Hstrc Second Bptst Youth Chr 87-; Youth Dept 87-; Sidney J Bartholemy Acad Achvmnt Awd 90; All Amer Schlrs; Business; Marketing.

**CORN, LISA J,** Univ Of South Al, Mobile, AL; SR; BS; SGA 88-89; Beta Alpha Psi Pres 90-; Phi Chi Theta VP Mbrshp 89-; Acdmc Achvmnt Schlrshp; Pres/Deans List; IM Sftbl; Acctg; Spcl Agent CIO/IRS.**

**CORN, MARA J,** Queens Coll, Charlotte, NC; SO; BA; Amnesty Intl Treas/Sec 90-; Natl Assn Acctnts Sec; Natl Org Wmn; Belk Schlr 89-; Alternate Dana Schlr; Natl Clgte Bsn Merit Awards; Oasis; Intrnshp NCNB; Intrnshp Stndrd Sand/Silica Co; Intrnshp Touch Of Gold Corp; Soccer Ldrshp 89-; Acctg/Cmptr Infor Sys; CPA.

**CORNACCHIA, CHRISTINA,** Franklin And Marshall Coll, Lancaster, PA; FR; BA; Bens Undrgrnd Stdnt Clb Hostess; Hse Cncl Rep 90; Chi Omega; Bsnss; Bsnss.

**CORNATZER, JODI L,** Univ Of Nc At Charlotte, Charlotte, NC; SR; BA; Pep Clb 87-89; Cls Cncl 90-; Bapt Flwshp Prog Dir; Psych; Spec Educ; Adult Mntl Rtrdtn Serv.

**CORNELIUS, BETTYE J,** Snead St Jr Coll, Boaz, AL; SO; AS; Chrch Scl And Spcl Prjct Coor; Phi Theta Kappa; Dns Lst 89-; Lit Mag Poet; ESPO VP 90-; AASOP 85-; Cert Snead State Jr Coll 77; Cert H & R Block Income Tax; Cert Lynelles Cake Decorating 86; Data Prcssng Tech; Comp Sci BS.

**CORNELIUS, HOLLY D,** Jefferson Comm Coll, Louisville, KY; Crss Cntry Capt; Bsktbll; Trck; Red Cross; Sftbll; Vllybll.

**CORNELIUS, JAMES D,** Saint Catharine Coll, St Catharine, KY; SO; BA; AA; Psych/Hstry; Busn/Educ.

**CORNELIUS, JENNIFER R,** Memphis St Univ, Memphis, TN; JR; BA; Paralegal; Law.

**CORNELIUS, TROY W,** Middle Tn St Univ, Murfreesboro, TN; JR; BBA; Stu Govt Assoc; Vol St Comm Coll Sntr 89-90; SGA; Lbry Comm; Vol St CC 89-90; Otstndg Serv Awrd; Vol St CC; Summa Cum Laude Grad; IM Sftbl Coach 88-90; Coed Leagues Prks/Rec Dept Plyr Coach 89-90; AS 90; Mgmnt; Corp.

**CORNELIUS, YOLANDA T,** Allen Univ, Columbia, SC; FR; BA; Bus Admin.

**CORNELL, ELEANOR E,** Kent St Univ Kent Cmps, Kent, OH; SR; BS; Stark Co Schl Fdsrvc Assnpres 88-90; Gldn Ky; Fd Srvc Sprvsr 82-; Chef Mgn 74-82; AS Culinary Inst Amer 74; Hsptlty Mgmt/Bus; Pblc Admn.

**CORNELL, GREGORY M,** Ky St Univ, Frankfort, KY; FR; Pre-Hlth Clb 90-; Ftbl/Track; Dns Lst; Acad All-Amer 90-; Bio/Pre-Med; Geriatrics.

**CORNELL, JON DAVID,** Duquesne Univ, Pittsburgh, PA; FR; Ftbl 90; Phrmcy.

**CORNER, ADERO A,** Tougaloo Coll, Tougaloo, MS; SO; BS; Class Parl 90-; Student Govt Assoc VP; Alpha Phi Alpha; Boy Scouts Ldr 90-; Mr Dehonair; Krogers Mgrs Trn Intshp 90; IM; Physics; Engrg.

**CORNETET, CATHY-MARI,** Emory Univ, Atlanta, GA; JR; BSN; Dns Lst 89-; Prfsnl Sngr; Ownr A Dogs Dreen; AA Hartford Cnsrvtry Msc 75; Nrsg.

**CORNETET, CATHY-MARI,** Saint Joseph Coll, West Hartford, CT; JR; BSN; Profsnl Singer; Ownd Dog Grmng Bus; AD Hartford Consrvtry Of Music 75; Nrsng.

**CORNETT, BRADLEY W,** Univ Of Tn At Knoxville, Knoxville, TN; JR; BS; Course Eval Cmte Dir 89-; Delta Delta Beta Educ Ofcr 90-; Stdnt Govt Sntr 90-; Gamma Beta Phi Scl Cmte Chrmn 89-; Phi Kappa Phi 90-; Omicron Delta Kappa; Bus Mngmnt; Law.

**CORNETT, HEATHER HART,** Ashland Comm Coll, Ashland, KY; SO; Water Safety Instctr; CPR Instctr; First Aid Instctr; Cmptr/Lbry Aid Hager Elem; Elem Ed.

**CORNETT, JERI B,** Valdosta St Coll, Valdosta, GA; SR; BSN; Prnt Tchr Org; SNA Sec 88; MADD; Sigma Theta Tau; March Dimes Blck Coord 83-; Nrsng.

**CORNETT, JOHN G,** Univ Of Ky, Lexington, KY; JR; BA; Clg Democrats 88-; Pi Sigma Alpha; Lt Govt Campaign Intern 90-; Oswald Research/Creativity; Scl Sci Awd; Pol Sci; Law.

**CORNETT, MARY A,** Middle Tn St Univ, Murfreesboro, TN; FR; BS; Gamma Beta Phi; Pre Prfssnl.

**CORNETT, MISTY M,** East Central Comm Coll, Decatur, MS; FR; Bnd 90-; Cntrlt 90-; Flg Ftbl 90-; Bsn Admin; Acctng.

**CORNETT, ROBIN M S,** Univ Of Fl, Gainesville, FL; SR; BS; SHRM Soc Cmtee Chrmn 90-; French Clb; Beta Gamma Sigma; Golden Key 90; Alpha Lambda Delta 88; Sigma Tau Sigma 89-; Alpha Kappa Psi Mobd Cmtee Chrm 90; Fla Undgrad Schlr 88-; Sch Bd Humn Rsrc Intern; I M Sprts 88-; AA 90; Mgmt; Intl Bus.

**CORNETT, VINCE W,** Ms St Univ, Miss State, MS; SO; BS; Cthlc Stdnt Assoc 89-; IEEE 90; Gamma Beta Phi 90-; Phi Eta Sigma 90-; Eng.

**CORNISH, KARLEEN GAYLE,** S U N Y Coll Of Tech At Alfred, Alfred, NY; FR; AD; Belmont Grange 88-; Deans List 90-; Phi Theta Kappa; Human Svc.

**CORNISH, MICHAEL A,** S U N Y Coll Of Tech At Delhi, Delhi, NY; FR; BA; Yrbk 90-91; Swmng Clb 90-91; USAF Plmbr Vetrn SRA 86-90; Actv USAF Rsrvs Hvy Equip Oper SRA 90-91; Cert Suny Delhi Plmbg/Htng Pipftng 90-91; Stdnt Suny Oswego Vol Tech Teaching Trad Sbjct Dgr 91-; Cert Suny Delhi Lfgrd Trng; Voc Tech Trad Sub; Vo Ed Tchr Plmbng/Htng.

**CORNISH JR, ROBERT V,** Samford Univ, Birmingham, AL; GD; Amer Jrnl Trl Advcy Chrmn For Artide; Appellate Advcy Prog Trl Jrnl; Deans Lst; NC Bar Assn; AB Davidson Clg 89; Law; Atty.

**CORNISH, SABRINA Y,** Fl A & M Univ, Tallahassee, FL; JR; BSW; Mbr Bapt Cmps Mnstry FAMU; Mbr NAACP; Natl Hon Scty Soc Wrkrs; Phi Theta Kappa Scty; AA Degree Palm Beach Comm Clg 90; Soc Wrk; Prs Career Clncl Soc Wrk.

**CORNISH-TOMAINO, CYNTHIA,** Castleton St Coll, Castleton, VT; SR; BED; Assn Sprvsn/Crrclm Dvlpmnt 89-90; Kappa Delta Pi 90; Frmr Shoreham Elem Schl Brd Dir/Co-Chr; Spec Ed Aide; Bed Castelton St Coll; Elem Ed/Spec Ed; Tch.

**CORNN, DEBORAH RAE,** Sue Bennett Coll, London, KY; SO; BA; Spnsh/Lang Clb Sec 90-; Flwshp Cntmpry Collegians 90-; Sigma Nu 90-; Destination Grad Tutor 90-91; Engl; Lib Sci.

**CORNWELL, MICHELLE,** Saint Josephs Coll, Windham, ME; SR; BA; Soc Clb Treas 87-; Ski Clb 87-89; Spurwink Schl Intrnshp 90; Soc; Law.

**COROA, TAMMY L,** Mount Saint Mary Coll, Newburgh, NY; JR; BD; Ambsdr Ldr 89-; Orntn Ldr 90; Deans List 90-; Hon Allnc Co Chrmn 90; Bus; Law.

**CORONA, MARIBETH A,** Georgian Court Coll, Lakewood, NJ; JR; BA; Clg Glee Clb V P 88-; Hstry Clb 89-; Clg Nwspr Editor 89-; Phi Alpha Theta; Comm Sears Trng Exellence Awd; Hist; Jrnlsm.

**CORP, NANCY S,** Central Pa Bus School, Summerdale, PA; FR; ASSO; SLA 90-; NALA 90-; Lgl Studies; Law.

**CORPENING, KEITHON R,** Al A & M Univ, Normal, AL; JR; BS; Nw Clstr Orgnztn; Kappa Alph A Psi Vce Ple Mrch; Mltry Acad Achvmnt Awrd; Dstngshd Mltry Stdnt; Hnr Rll; Comp Sci; Sftwre Eng.

**CORPREW, TALYA T,** Va St Univ, Petersburg, VA; JR; BA; Dean Lst 90-; Jack Jill America VP Chesapeake VA Bch Chptr Links Heir Link Cheaseapke Wmns Clb; Pblc Admnstrtn Bsns Admnstrtn; Bsns Admnstrtn.

**CORPSTEIN, KREG K,** Ms St Univ, Miss State, MS; SR; MBA; Cath Stdnt Assoc 87; Phi Eta Sigma 87-88; Delta Chi Schlrshp Chrmn 90; BBA; Bsnss Admin; Mrktng.

**CORRA, JERI L,** Bapt Bible Coll & Seminary, Clarks Summit, PA; SR; Mrrd Stdnt Assn 87-; Shphrdss 87-; Alpha Gamma Epsilon 90-; AA Sec 89; BS Bible; Bible Yth Wrk; Psychlgy Cnslng.

**CORRALES, CATHERINE,** Bloomfield Coll, Bloomfield, NJ; SO; BA; Coll Nwspr Ed 90-; Presbytrn Wmn USA Enblr; Deans Lst High Hons 90-; Hist; Ed.

**CORREA DE JESUS, WYRIE I,** Inter Amer Univ Pr San Juan, Hato Rey, PR; GD; Cuadro De Hon Summa Cum Laude 89; Beca De Hon Summa Cum Laude 88-90; Natl Hispanic Schlrshp Fund 89; Asistente De Catedra 89-90; JD 90 Summa Cum Laude; Jurdis Doctor.

**CORREA, GERALDINE C,** Fl St Univ, Tallahassee, FL; SO; BS; Hns Schlrs 89-; Alpha Epsilon Delta 90-; Prnts Anonyms; Hnrs Fnshr 90; IM Vlybl Dorm Leag 89; Bio/Pre Med; Physcn.**

**CORREA, JULIETTE D,** Saint Marys Coll Of Md, St Marys Cy, MD; SR; JD; Dns Lst 88; BA; Corp Law.**

**CORREA, LARISA A,** City Univ Of Ny La Guard Coll, Long Island Cty, NY; GD; BA; Acctng Clb 89-90; Bake Sale 89-; Stdnt Protest 89-; Phi Theta Kappa 89-; Coop Intrnshp Jordan Mcgrath Case & Taylor Inc 90; Talent Roster Otstndng Min Stdnts 90-; AAS Acctg 91; Acct; CPA.

**CORREIA SANTIAGO, DEREK W,** Univ Politecnica De Pr, Hato Rey, PR; FR; BA; Eng.

**CORREIA, ISABEL S,** Bunker Hill Comm Coll, Boston, MA; SO; CS; Tlnt Rstr 90-; Cert Achvmnt; Mat/Cmptr; Engr.

**CORREIA, LINDA M,** Newbury Coll, Brookline, MA; FR; AS; Accntg Clrk Cambridge Svngs Bank 90-; Dns Lst 90-; Mrt Schlrshp 90-; Acdmc Schlrsph E Cambridge Yth Grp 90-; Media Mngmnt; Mngr TV Sttn.

**CORRELL, BRIAN D,** Univ Of Nc At Charlotte, Charlotte, NC; JR; BS; Psychlgy Clb VP 90-; Crmnl Jstce Assoc VP; Psi Chi 90-; Rsrch Asst 90-; Res Advsr; Crmnl Jstce/Psychlgy; Cncl Psychlgst.

**CORRES, VILMA,** Univ Of Pr Cayey Univ Coll, Cayey, PR; SR; Beta Beta Beta 90-; Natl Sci; Medl Techlgy.

**CORRIEA, KEVIN A,** City Univ Of Ny Baruch Coll, New York, NY; SO; BBA; Clb Caricom Pub Rltns Ofcr 90; Stndt Govt Lwr Coun 90-; Soc Human Rsrc Mngmnt; Human Rsrc Mngmnt.

**CORRIGAN, ANNE D,** Norfolk St Univ, Norfolk, VA; JR; BA; Early Chldhd Ed; Tch.

**CORRIGAN, KATHLEEN M,** Oh Univ, Athens, OH; SO; BA; IM Sccr Sftbl 89-; Cmps Radio 90-; Peer Advsr; Grphc Dsgn; Advrtsng.

**CORRIGAN, MICHAEL L,** Indiana Univ Of Pa, Indiana, PA; SO; Stdnt Govt Rep 89-90; T V Edtng Supv 90-; U O Varner Schlrshp 89-90; I M 89-90; Cmunctns; T V Prod.

**CORRIHER, JASON D,** East Carolina Univ, Greenville, NC; SO; BS; Deans Lst; Res Advsr 90-; Biolgy; Med/Pedatrcs.**

**CORRIVEAU, DEBORAH R,** Fl International Univ, Miami, FL; GD; Outstndng Acad Achiev Awd 86; Tchr Sheridan Hills Elem; BS 87; MS 90; Elem Ed.

**CORRIVEAU, JEFF D,** Springfield Tech Comm Coll, Springfield, MA; JR; BA; College Theater Productions; Natl Hnr Soc 90; Assoc In Liberal Arts 90; Theater; Acting.

**CORROU, DANIEL R,** Le Moyne Coll, Syracuse, NY; FR; BS; Envrnmntl Cltn 90-; Prjcts Comm 90-; Intrntnl Hse 90-; Cool Confrnc.

**CORRY, ELIZABETH A,** Nova Univ, Ft Lauderdale, FL; GD; MBA; Inst Indust Eng; Alpha Pi Mu; Hlth Info Sys Soc; Soc Hlth Sys; Emplyd Shands Hosp Pstn Mgmnt Engr; BSIE Univ S FL Tampa FL 88.

**CORSARO, GENA L,** S U N Y Coll At Fredonia, Fredonia, NY; SO; BS; Cert Merit Awds/Schlstc Achvmnt; Girl Scts; SS; Med Sec/Area Hosp 81-88; Elem Educ.

**CORSETTI, LISA J,** Glassboro St Coll, Glassboro, NJ; JR; BA; Ad Clb 88-91; PRSSA 89-90; Cmnctns; Law.

**CORSI, ALDO B,** Univ Of New Haven, West Haven, CT; JR; BS; Coop Educ Intrn; Cntr Lrng Rsrcs Stdnt Tutor 90; Eng.

**CORSI, ANN K,** Cornell Univ Statutory College, Ithaca, NY; SR; PHD; Mrchng Bnd Sctn Ldr 87-90; EARS 88-; Gldn Ky 89-; No Nun Dekah 89-; Phi Kappa Phi; Gamma Sigma Delta 90-; Delta Delta Delta 89-; Biol Hnrs Prgrm 90-; Howard Hughes Schlr 89-; Clare Booth Luce Fllwshp Univ CA; BS; Molecular/Cell Biol; Acdmc Rsrch.

**CORSI, JILL D,** Niagara Univ, Niagara Univ, NY; SO; BA; Psych.

**CORSI, MARC A,** Oh Univ, Athens, OH; SO; BSEE; Eng.

**CORSO, JERRINE JANET,** Hillsborough Comm Coll, Tampa, FL; GD; ASN; Stdnt Nrsng Organ 90-; Natl Assn Aeromedical Comm Spec 89-; Phi Theta Kappa 90-; LPN Tampa Gen Hosp 78-; Cert LPN Brewster Voc Schl 75; EMT Red Cross 75; Nrsng; Bus.

**CORSON, LAURA B,** Cornell Univ Statutory College, Ithaca, NY; SO; BS; Cornell Natl Shclrs 89-; Alpha Epsilon Delta 90-; Hon Nun Da Ka Als 90-; Alpha Epsilon Delta 90-; Delta Delta Delta Sor 90-; Tompkin Cmnty Hosp Aux Vlntr 90-; Red Carpet Soc 89-; Cornell Natl Schlrs Serv Comm 89-; Bristol Byers Intern 90; Biology; Research Or Medicine.

**CORSON, PAUL J,** Franklin And Marshall Coll, Lancaster, PA; JR; BA; Envir Actn Alnc Exec Cmte 89-; Rsn Clb 89-; Tsk Frc Sxl Awrns 90-; Grmn/Rsn Dept Trvl Awd 89-90; Dana Schlr 90-; Rsn Stds/Econ.

**CORTE, JAMES R,** Eckerd Coll, St Petersburg, FL; JR; BS; Hbitat Hmnty 88-; Cncln Undergrad Rsrch Acdmc Indstrl Undrgrad Rsrch Flwshp 90-; ACS Travel Awrd 90-; Ford Schlr 90-; IM; Chmsty; Acdmcs.

**CORTES PINEIRO, IVETTE,** Fl St Univ, Tallahassee, FL; SR; BA; Stdnt Advsry Cncl; Cmtee Mbr 90-; Alumni Pow Wow Cmtee Chrm 90-; Golden Key 90-; French Hon Soc 90-; Dobra Slova 90-; French/Russian; Univ Prfsr.

**CORTES, AIDA I C,** Inter Amer Univ Pr Hato Rey, Hato Rey, PR; SO; Latinoamerican; Aestheticians Asosc; Geographers Assoc; Deans List; Law Fraternity VP; San Juan Grdns Resid Assoc Sec; Criminal Justice/Political Scie; Law.

**CORTES, AMPARITO,** Univ Of Pr At Rio Piedras, Rio Piedras, PR; SR; USAGA Karate Assn; Brown Belt; Hnr Grp UPR Ntrl Sci Fclty 89; Hnr Grp UPR 89; Biology.**

**CORTES JR, JOSE H,** Columbia Union Coll, Takoma Park, MD; FR; Fr Cls Chpln 90-; Senate Sen; Stdnt Mnstrl Assn VP; Phi Eta Sigma 90-; Camps Mnstries Assc Dir; Theolgy; Clergy.

**CORTES, LENORA MALDONADO,** Caribbean Univ, Bayamon, PR; BED; Marriage Clb 89-90; AD Inst Tech Jr Coll 79; Edn; MA.

**CORTES, LOYDA E,** Bayamon Tech Univ Coll, Bayamon, PR; SR; BA; Hnrs Lst Bayamon Tech U Clg 88; Flour Fndtn Schlrshp 89; Assoc Degree 90; Bsnss Admin; Accntng.

**CORTES, ROBERTO,** Inter Amer Univ Pr Hato Rey, Hato Rey, PR; JR; BS; Bio; Med.

**CORTES-CRUZ, ANGEL L,** Univ Of Pr At Rio Piedras, Rio Piedras, PR; SO; Consejo Stdnt De Hmndades 90-; Spnsh Lit/Lngustc.

**CORTES-PEREZ, JUDITH BINDA,** Catholic Univ Of Pr, Ponce, PR; BA; Hnr Dean List; Cath Church Sec; PTA; BA ED; Elem Educ Gen.

**CORTES-SALAS, REINALDO,** Univ Del Turabo, Gurabo, PR; BA; Police Dept Assoc; Jr Clg Hnr; Sgt Police Dept; BA; Crmnlgy; Law.

**CORTESE, SARAH B,** Univ Of Sc At Spartanburg, Spartanburg, SC; FR; BS; Psych; Cnslng Svc.

**CORTEZ, MAGALY,** City Univ Of Ny Baruch Coll, New York, NY; GD; Frgn Trade Scty 89-90; Phi Theta Kappa 88; Alph Phi Dlt 90-; Wlk Amer; AAS Borough Manhattan Comm Clg 88; Mgmt; Bus Intrntl.

**CORTICO, ROSARIA M,** Wagner Coll, Staten Island, NY; SR; BS; Theatre 86-90; Art Adm; Theatre Mgt.

**CORUM, JONATHAN M,** Fl Coll, Temple Terrace, FL; SO; BA; Omega Chi Pres 89-; Phi Theta Kappa 90-; Alpha Clb 90-; Top Engl Stdnt 90-; Deans Lst 90-; AA; Ltrtr; Tchng.

**CORVINO, MARIE,** Newbury Coll, Brookline, MA; FR; ASSOC; Class Repr 90; Dns Lst 90.

**CORWIN, JENNIFER,** Oh St Univ At Marion, Marion, OH; JR; BS; DE Lioness Clb Treas 83-; Ed Soc 90-; Pi Lambda Theta 90-; Summa Awd; AA 90; Ed.

**CORY, CAROL,** Widener Univ, Chester, PA; JR; BSEE; Soc Womn Engrs IEEE; Tau Beta Pi; Alpha Chi; Coop Gen Elec Aerospace; Electrcal Engrng.

**CORYEA, JILL A,** Elmira Coll, Elmira, NY; FR; BS; Phi Eta Sigma; Purchsng Schlrshp; Mktng Intrnshp; Busn/Mktg; Mktg.

**COSBY, CHRISTOPHER D,** Old Dominion Univ, Norfolk, VA; JR; BSEE; IEEE 90-; Hon Prg 89-; Univ Bnd/Orchstr 89-; Gldn Ky; Alpha Chi 90-; Chrch Wrk Prg 89-; Soph Yr Awd 90; Undgrad Rsrch Asst; Eng Dns Lst 89/91; Elec Eng; Engrng.

**COSBY, CHRISTY L,** Lincoln Univ, Lincoln Univ, PA; SR; BS; Sclgy Clb Cmps Big Bro/Sis Pgm; Phlsphy Clb VP; Spnsh Clb; CIC SROP 90; Sclgy; Tchng.

**COSBY JR, DAVID L,** Fl A & M Univ, Tallahassee, FL; JR; BA; Chptr NAACP; Schl Bus/Indust SBI Svcs; Mntr/Mntee Pgm Coord VP; Mngr/Dir Cls-Ups Dir 90-; Ntl Beta Clb; Alpha Phi Alpha 89-; Alpha Phi Alpha 89-; IM Bsktbl; Bus Admin; Law/Corp Mgmt.

**COSBY, DONNA Y,** Saint Pauls Coll, Lawrenceville, VA; SR; BS; Natl Sci Math Clb Pres 90-; Enrllmnt Mgmt Scty 89-; Bg Brthr Bg Sstr Org 90-; Zeta Phi Beta Pres 90-; Schlrshp 89-90; Asst Univ ND 90; Vllybll 90-; Blgy Chmstry; Clncl Sci.

**COSBY, GAILIEN J,** Lincoln Univ, Lincoln Univ, PA; JR; BS; Gospel Ensmble Sec 90-; Natl Assn Advncmnt Colored People; Chinese Clb; Iota Eta Tau; Alpha Chi; Pi Sigma Alpha; Wyatt B Johnson Prize; Laurence Foster Jr Prize; Dr J Finton Speller Schlrshp; Publ Affairs; Law.

**COSBY, PAMELA D,** Al St Univ, Montgomery, AL; SO; BA; Math Ed; Tch.

**COSCETTE, ELISENA,** S U N Y Coll Of Tech At Frmgdl, Farmingdale, NY; SO; Pioneer Stndrd Elctrncs Sls; Comp Info Syst; Syst Anlys.

**COSCULLUELA, ANA R,** Miami Dade Comm Coll, Miami, FL; SO; BA; Paralegal Real Est/Financing/Corp Law; Bus/Finance; Law.

**COSE, DEBRA R,** Univ Of Al At Birmingham, Birmingham, AL; SR; AA; SPTO 90-; APTA 90-; Afflte Assmbly; Srvce Prjct 90-; BS 88; Phys Thrpy.

**COSENTINO, LISA MARIE,** Elmira Coll, Elmira, NY; JR; BS; Vrsty Soccer Capt 88-; Sftbl 88-; Orientation Ldr 89-90; Intrnshp Willard Psychtrc Ctr 90; Psychlgy; Law Schl.

**COSENZA, CHRISTINE C,** Albertus Magnus Coll, New Haven, CT; SR; BA; Lit Mag Cpy Ed 90; AMC Newspapr Scrd Hrt U Newspapr Cpy Ed Rprtr 89; Engl Clb 90; Pax Christi Campus Mnstry 89-90; Intrn Tlk Shw Prod 90; Intrn PSA Dir Anncr 89-90; Fncng 90; Mjr Engl/Mnr Cmmnctns; Radio Brdcstng.

**COSGRIFF, HEATHER A,** Kent St Univ Kent Cmps, Kent, OH; SO; Bus; Mrktng.

**COSGROVE, DEAN W,** Pasco Hernando Comm Coll, Dade City, FL; GD; ADN; Pres Nrs Paramedic; Pres Owner Total Ftns Spts Med 85-; Prof Triatlow U S A 89-; AAAS S T Pet J C 82-83; BSPHD Columbia Pacific Univ 84-86; Nrsng; Rhbltn/Ped RN.

**COSGROVE, DONI M,** Lancaster Bible Coll, Lancaster, PA; SO; BA; Dorm Asst 90-; Dir Hmecmg Ct 90-; Soccer Stats 89-; Bible/Chrstn Ed-Missions; Msnry Svc Europe.

**COSGROVE, KATHLEEN M,** Lesley Coll, Cambridge, MA; SR; BS; Stdnt Govt Treas 90-; Cthlc Cmmnty 88-; Acdmc Hnrs Lst 87-; Emrld Key 87-; Tchng Asst 89-; Ed.

**COSKER JR, THOMAS,** Worcester Poly Inst, Worcester, MA; SO; BA; Outing Club VP 89-; Charles O'thompson Scty 89-90; Varsity Soccer 89-; Mechl Engrg; Engrg.**

**COSLETT, JOHN M,** Marywood Coll, Scranton, PA; SO; BS; Tutrg 90-; Bus Bscs Prog Jr Achvmnt 90; Acctg; CPA.

**COSMANO, CATERINA C,** Elmira Coll, Elmira, NY; JR; BS; Stdnt Actvts Brd Gen Mbr 89-; Dorm Cncl Flr Repr; Kappa Delta Pi; Elmira Clg Key Award 88; Elem Educ; Tchr.

**COSME SANTOS, RUTH,** Univ Of Pr At Rio Piedras, Rio Piedras, PR; SR; MLS; Hnr Stdnt Grad Schl Librarianshp; Lbry Asst 83-; BA 74; Lbry Sci; Librarianshp.

**COSME, MADELINE MARQUEZ,** Bayamon Central Univ, Bayamon, PR; FR; BA; Acctg.

**COSMO, FREDRIK C,** Va Commonwealth Univ, Richmond, VA; SO; BS; Tennis Tm; Cmptr.

**COSNER, CHARLOTTE A,** Va Commonwealth Univ, Richmond, VA; SR; BA; Bptst Std Un 90-; Lbry Intshp Museum Cnfdrcy; Latin Amer Hstry; Intl Rltns.

**COSPELICH JR, LAWRENCE W,** Ms Gulf Coast Comm Coll, Perkinston, MS; FR; MBA; Delta Club 90-; Elec Engr.

**COSS, CATHERINE M,** Univ Of Toledo, Toledo, OH; GD; JD; BA Muskingum Coll 89; Law.

**COSSACK, TRACEY E,** Marywood Coll, Scranton, PA; JR; BS; Cmps Mnstry Chrprsn 88-; SGA Treas; Vol In Actn Vp; Kappa Delta Pi 90-; Educ; Tchg.

**COSTA, BETSEY A,** Univ Of Sc At Coastal Carolina, Conway, SC; FR; ASN; Acclrtd Crdc Lf Spprt-Instrctr 89-; LPN 83-; Nrsng; RN.

**COSTA, CARMEN R,** Felician Coll, Lodi, NJ; JR; BS; Bus Sec 90; Bus.

**COSTA, CHRISTODOULOS N,** City Univ Of Ny Baruch Coll, New York, NY; GD; MBA; Hellenic Clb 87-90; Acctng Socty 87-90; Dns Lst 87-90; Schlrshp; Finance; Acctng.

**COSTA, FRANK A,** Schenectady County Comm Coll, Schenectady, NY; FR; AS; AAS Hudson Vly Cmnty Clg 90; Music; Music/Prfrmnc/Bus.

**COSTA, IDA J,** City Univ Of Ny Baruch Coll, New York, NY; JR; BA; Dns Lst 90-; Acctg; CPA.

**COSTA, MICHELLE,** Coll Of New Rochelle, New Rochelle, NY; SO; BA; Sisters Sec 90; Jdcl Bd 90; Natl Hnr Scty 89; Spec Ed; Tchr.

**COSTA, NICOLE D,** Univ Of Southern Ms, Hattiesburg, MS; FR; Symphony 90-; Deans Lst 90-; Pi Beta Phi 90-; IM 90-; Jrnlsm.

**COSTAS, CINDY M,** Catholic Univ Of Pr, Ponce, PR; JR; BA; Natl Bus Hnr Socty; Natl Coll Bus Merit Awd; Eta Gamma Delta.

**COSTELLO, DANIEL J,** Valdosta St Coll, Valdosta, GA; FR; BA; Mrtrs Srvc Mdl 89; Ar Frc Cmmdtn Mdl 80-; Ar Frc Achvmnt Mdl 85; Ar Frc Otstndng Awrdarmd Frcs Expdntry Mdl 83; Non Cmmsssnd Offcrs Prfssnl Mltry Edctn Grad Rbbn 85; USAF Snr Mstr Sgt; Bus; Mgmt.

**COSTELLO, DAWN M,** Barry Univ, Miami, FL; GD; BS; Envrnmntl Clb Sunrise FL; Racal-Milgo 88-; Tech Spclst Pgmr; AAS Prospect Hall Coll 86; Comp Sci.

**COSTELLO, ELAINE D,** Siena Coll, Loudonville, NY; SR; BS; Lacrosse Clb Cptn 87; Intrnshp General Elec Schenectady NY 90; Fld Hcky Cptn 87; Mrktng/Mngmnt; Intrntnl Bsn.

**COSTELLO, HEATHER M,** Univ Of Sc At Columbia, Columbia, SC; SO; BSN; Tech Thtr; Editor Ltry Mag Editor 88-89; Poetry Pblshd 84/85/87/89; Gamma Beta Phi; Key Club Intl Sec 83-85; Red Cross Vol 83-89; Newspr Mst Outstndg Editor 84-85; Sgntr Mag Bst Ntn 83/84/85 83-85; Nrsg; Hm Hlth Care.

**COSTELLO, JILL C**, Univ Of Ky, Lexington, KY; SR; BS; Student Alumni Assoc 89-90; Club Mgrs Assoc Amer VP 89-90; Htl Rest Inst Mgt Club Social Chr 87-90; Kappa Omicron Nu; Golden Key 90-; ACUBH I/NACUFS Fd Serv Insterhp Prog Penn Univ 89; Dietetics.

**COSTELLO, KATHLEEN**, Springfield Tech Comm Coll, Springfield, MA; Spec Olympcs; Bdybldng Natl Lvl.

**COSTELLO, ROBERT**, Fl Atlantic Univ, Boca Raton, FL; SR; BBA; U S Coast Guard 84-89; AA Cmuty Clg R I 82; Bus Mgmt; Mgmt.

**COSTERO, RAUL**, Fl International Univ, Miami, FL; SR; BS; AAPHERD 90-; Deans Lst 88-; Amer Sr H S Intern; AA Miami-Dade Comm Coll 88; Sthrdg Sr Hgh-Vrsty Bsktbl Asst Coach; Scndry Phy Ed; Phy Ed Tchr/Mns Bsktbl Coach.

**COSTIN, DEXTER R**, Fl A & M Univ, Tallahassee, FL; SO; BS; Gospel Choir 90-; White/Gold; Mech Eng; Auto Dsgn.

**COSTINE, MATTHEW**, Wagner Coll, Staten Island, NY; SR; Guitar Lute Ens 86-90; Tau Kappa Sigma Sec 87-90; Intrnshp Island Rec Inc Asst 89-90; Arts Admin; Music Busn.

**COSTNER, GEORGE RYAN**, Ky St Univ, Frankfort, KY; JR; BA; Stdnt Crt Jstc 90-; Spnsh Clb 89-; Pre-Law Clb 89-; Deans Lst 89-; Al-Ka-Pals; Alpha Kappa Alpha Schlrshp 88; Ksy Alumni Schlrshp 90; Vrsty Ftbl 88-; Crmnl Juste.

**COSTNER, KEVIN L**, Univ Of Nc At Charlotte, Charlotte, NC; SR; BA; Golden Key 90-; Wisc Mem Schlrshp 87; Dens Lst 87-; Chnclrs Lst 88-90; English; Wrtr.

**COSTNER, LINDA BOLDING**, Lenoir Rhyne Coll, Hickory, NC; SR.

**COSTNER, SANDRA B**, Gaston Coll, Dallas, NC; FR; ADN; LPN; Nrsng.

**COSTNER, SUSAN M**, Coll Of Charleston, Charleston, SC; SO; BA; Math Clb Sec 90-; Math; Tchr.

**COTE, DAVID D**, Western New England Coll, Springfield, MA; SR; Fncl Mgmt Assoc 89-; Tennis Capt 89-; Tennis 87-; BA; Finance; Bsn.

**COTE, JACQUELINE M**, Marywood Coll, Scranton, PA; FR; BA; Ornttn Cmmtt 90-; Clss Sec; Hnrs Prog; Art Educ; Tchr.

**COTE, JENNIFER**, Western New England Coll, Springfield, MA; SR; BA; Lit Corps; Deans Lst 90; Tutor 87; Psychlgy.

**COTE, KAREN C**, Fl Atlantic Univ, Boca Raton, FL; SR; Amer Mrktng Assoc 89; Pres Lst Brwrd Cmmnty Clg 88-89; Sndy Schl Tchr 89-90; Assist To Chrmn Of Mrktng Dept Dr P Korgaonkar Prsnl Assist 90; BA; Bsnss Mngmnt; Small Bsnss Ownrshp.

**COTE, RYAN C**, Cornell Univ Statutory College, Ithaca, NY; SR; Ad Agcy Accnt Exec 89-; PRSSA 88-89; Orientation Cnslr 89; Concert Commission 88-89; Beta Theta Pi PR 88-; Beta Philanthrpc Guild 88-; Yng Rubican Advrtsg Intern 90; Dns Lst 90-; IM Soccer/Sftbl/Ftbl/Vlybl; BS Cornell Univ; Appl Econ/Bsn Mgmt; Advrtsg/Law.

**COTELLESSE, JOANNA M**, Temple Univ, Philadelphia, PA; SR; BS; Rho Chi; Phrmcy.

**COTHERN, WILLIAM W**, Middle Tn St Univ, Murfreesboro, TN; SO; BS; Block/Bridle Clb 90-; Pre-Vet Soc 90-; Kelly Jarrell Mem Schlrshp 90-; Thrush Fndtn Schlrshp; Animal Sci; Vet.

**COTHRAN, JEREMY T**, Univ Of Sc At Columbia, Columbia, SC; SR; BS; IEEE 89-; Gldn Ky 88-; Eta Kappa Nu; Elec Comp Eng; Eng.

**COTHRAN, KIMBERLY K**, Univ Of Nc At Asheville, Asheville, NC; SR; BS; USAA All Amer Scholar 90-; BS; Bus Admnstrn; Mktg.

**COTHREN, LISA R**, William Carey Coll, Hattiesburg, MS; SR; BS; Bptst Stdnt Union 87-; Phi Theta Kappa 87-89; Omicron Delta Kappa 89-; AA SW MS Comm Coll 89; Elem Ed; Tchng.

**COTHRON, JOHN A**, Middle Tn St Univ, Murfreesboro, TN; SO; BA; Hnrs Stdnt Assn 90-; Hstry; Educ.

**COTILLA, MARIA D**, Miami Dade Comm Coll, Miami, FL; JR; BA; St Vin Pl Chrts Contrbtr 90-; St John B Chrch Mbr/Cntrbtr 90-91; AHEAD Schlrshp 90; Deans Lst MDCC 89-; Tutor/Trsnltr Frnch/Spnsh 70-88; Librn INRA Cuba 64-66; Frnch Trnslr Allnc Fran Hvna Cuba 83; BCLRT Inst Sec Educ Hvna Cuba 54; Frnch/Engl; Psychlgy.

**COTLET, LACRAMIOARA G**, Liberty Univ, Lynchburg, VA; FR; BS; Math; Edctn.

**COTNER, CHRYSTAL R**, Univ Of Akron, Akron, OH; SR; ACES 89-; Intrntl Clb Treas 88-; Alpha Lambda Delta/Pi Eta Sigma 89-; Golden Key 90-; Kappa Delta Pi; Univ Schlrshp.

**COTNEY JR, NOAL L**, Univ Of Al At Birmingham, Birmingham, AL; JR; Acctg.

**COTRONEO, PETER A**, Wagner Coll, Staten Island, NY; GD; Omicron Delta Kappa 90-; Kappa Mu Epsilon Pres 90; Comp Prggmng Intrnshp US Navy 90; BS 90; Math; Artfcl Intllgnce Prgrmmng.

**COTTEN, JAMES K**, Memphis St Univ, Memphis, TN; SR; BA; Phlsphy; Tchng Rsrch.

**COTTER, CASEY A**, Wellesley Coll, Wellesley, MA; FR; BA; Intl Rels Clb Model UN Del 90-; Clg Govt Sen 90-; Stdnt Org Fndg Comm 90-; Clg Demos 90-; NH Yng Demos Natl Comm Wmn 89-; Alpha Beta Phi Fndg Sis 90-; IM Crew Tms 90-; Soccer Mgr 90-; Econ/Intl Rels; Govt Svc.

**COTTER, ELIZABETH J**, Glassboro St Coll, Glassboro, NJ; FR; BA; Venue Mag 90; Cmnctns Radio/TV; TV/BRDCSTNG.

**COTTER JR, JOHN J**, Vt Law School, S Royalton, VT; FR; JD; The Defender St Michaels Clg Nws Edtr 82-83; BA St Michaels Clg 83; Law.

**COTTER, PHILIP J**, Drexel Univ, Philadelphia, PA; FR; BS; ROTC; Eng.

**COTTER III, ROSS RAINER**, Samford Univ, Birmingham, AL; GD; Amer Jrnl Trial Advocacy 90-; Cordell Hull Legal Rsrch/Wrtng Fllwshp; BA Cum Laude Auburn Univ 88; J D Cumberland Schl Of Law; Law.

**COTTER-GUDE, MARY JOSEPHINE**, Fl A & M Univ, Tallahassee, FL; SR; BS; APHA 89-; SAPHA 89-; Rho Chi 90-; Magna Cum Laude; Mc Neil Cnsmr Prdcts Awd; Deans Lst 89-; AA Pasco Hernando Comm Clg 86; Phrmcy.

**COTTINGHAM, CARLA ANNE**, Univ Of Sc At Columbia, Columbia, SC; SR; BA; Clg Hnrs Prog 87-; Alpha Lambda Delta 87-88; Phi Beta Kappa 89-90; Gamma Beta Phi 89-; Magna Cum Laude; Bruce Welge Ctznshp Awd 87-88; Francis Bradley Outstndg Soph Engl Awd 88-89; George A Wauchop Sr Engl Awd 90-; Engl; Tchr/Prfssr.

**COTTINI, EMMA PATRICIA**, Columbia Greene Comm Coll, Hudson, NY; GD; MS; Ski Clb VP 83-84; Co-Ed Vlybl IM 83-84; Mmbr Intrntl Rotorget Clb 82-83; 88 Olympc Trls Tae Kwan Do Olympc Trnng Cntr; Certfd Wtr Sfty Instrctr Lfgrd Instr; Blck Blt Instrctr Klees Tae Kwon Do Schls; BS SUNY Crtlnd 86; MS Clg St Rose 90; Elem Edc Physcl; Tchr Scndry Math.

**COTTLE, LISA L**, Mount Aloysius Jr Coll, Cresson, PA; SO; BS; Circle K 88-89; Food Serv Comm 88-90; Stdnt Serv; Chrldng 88-89; AS 90; Biolog Sci; Med Tech.

**COTTO FIGUEROA, NILDA I**, Inter Amer Univ Pr Hato Rey, Hato Rey, PR; JR; BA; Sec Sci; Bus Admin.

**COTTO NIEVES, MARIA H**, Univ Of Pr At Mayaguez, Mayaguez, PR; SO; BA; Elect Eng; Eng.

**COTTO SANTIAGO, MICHAEL A**, Univ Of Pr At Mayaguez, Mayaguez, PR; JR; Hon Stdnt Engr; Chem Engr.

**COTTO, ANNETTE**, City Univ Of Ny Baruch Coll, New York, NY; SR; BS; Catechism Tchr; Paraprfssnl Educ Asst; AAS Kingsborough CC 84; BS Ed; Educ; Bus Tchr.

**COTTO, MANUEL A**, Ny Univ, New York, NY; BS; NYC Dept Transp Safety Ed 90; Vlntr Awd 88-; Queens Hosp Center; Queens Borough Pres Claire Shulman; St Elizabeth Church Pastoral Cncl Comm 89-; NY Treas Ofc Gen Motors Corp 69-; Computer Graphics Spclst Audio Visual Supvr; Human Serv Humanities; Advisor Counselor.

**COTTOM, SHERRY G**, Comm Coll Algny Co Algny Cmps, Pittsburgh, PA; ALA; Cert Median Sch 79; D; Sex Edctr.

**COTTON, ELESHIA**, Alcorn St Univ, Lorman, MS; SO; BS; Bus Admin; Corp Exec.

**COTTON, KELLY C**, Fl Atlantic Univ, Boca Raton, FL; JR; BA; AA Broward Comm Coll 89; Mktg; Law.

**COTTON, MELANIE F**, Univ Of Al At Birmingham, Birmingham, AL; SO; BS; Occptnl Therpy.

**COTTON, NORMAN L**, Livingston Univ, Livingston, AL; JR; BS; Cmptr Sci.

**COTTON, SHERICE L**, Jackson St Univ, Jackson, MS; FR; BA; Sweetheart; Enslish Business; Bus Admnstrn.

**COTTON III, THOMAS E**, East Stroudsburg Univ, E Stroudsburg, PA; SR; BS; Assoc Cmptng Mchnry AMC Pres 87-; Univ Pgmng Cnsl 87-; Chs Clb 90-; Cmptr Sci; Sftwr Engrg.

**COTTRELL, AMY L**, Union Coll, Barbourville, KY; JR; BS; Delta Delta Delta 89-90; Bus Adm/Bus Educ/Mrktng; Tchng/Bus Admn.**

**COTTRELL, PAMELA G**, Marshall University, Huntington, WV; SR; BBA; Gamma Beta Phi VP 90- Soc Chrmn 88-; Acctg Clb 89-; Alpha Xi Delta 87-88; Tutrng Serv 89-; Deans Lst 87-; Aerobc Instrctr 90-; BBA; Acctg; Audtng.

**COTTRILL, MARI C**, Memphis St Univ, Memphis, TN; SR; BBA; MSU Adult Stdnt Assoc; Phi Theta Kappa 90-; Phi Kappa Phi; Hon/Svc Mortar Brd; Achvmnt Recgtn Awrd 90-; Sales Clerk/Bank Teller/Tutor; AA Shelby State Cmnty Clg Memphis 90; Intl Bus; Languages.

**COTTRILL, MELISSA S**, Wv Univ At Parkersburg, Parkersburg, WV; JR; BA; Elem Ed; Tchr.

**COTY, BERNADETTE R**, Brescia Coll, Owensboro, KY; JR; NSSHA 90-; BS; Spch Pthlgy/Adlgy.

**COUCH, BRIAN E**, Univ Of Louisville, Louisville, KY; JR; BS; AICHE 90; Tau Beta Pi 90-; Speed Sch Deans Lit; Chem Eng.

**COUCH, DEBORAH K**, Middle Tn St Univ, Murfreesboro, TN; SR; BA; Phi Kappa Alpha 76-77; Girl Scout Brownie Ldr 86-90; Bus; Educ.

**COUCH, JENNIFER L**, Milligan Coll, Milligan Clg, TN; SR; BS; Nwspr Stff-Rprtng/Edtng 89-91; Phtgrphy 89-90; Sigma Tau Delta; Big Bro/Big Sis Pgm 90-; Intrnshp Prdctn 90; Nws Intrnshp; Cmnctns; Nws Reprtng.

**COUCH, SARAH L**, Union Coll, Barbourville, KY; SR; BS; Deans Lst 88-; To 12 Wmn On Campus 90-; Alpha Psi Omega 89-; Tennis/Sftbl 88-.

**COUCH, VALERIE A**, Indiana Univ Of Pa, Indiana, PA; SO; BED; Elem Ed; Tchng.

**COUCH-GOODMAN, KENDRA B**, Tomlinson Coll, Cleveland, TN; SO; Frshmn Cls Tres 84-85; Drama Clb 84-85; Prsdnts Lst 90-; IM Bsktbl Sftbl 84-85; TSSAA Bsktbl Offcl 89-; Certf Inst Fncl Edctn 88-89; Real Est.

**COUCHON, MARY E**, City Univ Of Ny Baruch Coll, New York, NY; SR; PHD; Psi Chi 90-; Golden Key 90-; Psychlgy Dept Schlr; Mr/Ms Baruch Fitness Posedwn; Psychlgy; Hlth Psychlgy.

**COUF, MARILYN J**, Fl International Univ, Miami, FL; SR; BA; Bed Temple Univ 65f; Hosp/Hotel Mgmnt; Professor.

**COUGHENOUR, GAIL SOPHIA**, West Chester Univ, West Chester, PA; SR; Hndcp Vol 90-; Outstdng Snr Awd Fnlst; Intshp Mntgmry Ftns Ctr; Physcl Ed Schlp 90; M Hrshy Schl Schlp 87-90; IM Rgby 87-88; Exer Sci/Phys Ed; Crdc Rehab.

**COUGHLIN, DAWN M**, Bryant Stratton Bus Inst Roch, Rochester, NY; FR; Sec Clb; Bapt Yth Grp 87-; Deans Lst; Word Process; Secretarial.

**COUGHLIN, DONNA J**, Hillsborough Comm Coll, Tampa, FL; SO; BA; Music Club Secy 89-90; Alpha Beta Beta Secy 90-; Phi Kappa Theta Secy 90-; Vol Tutor Reading VLP 89-90; Svc Award Music Club Secy 89-90; Svc Award Phi Theta Kappa Secy 90-; Music; Perfrmnc/Tchng.

**COUGHLIN, ELLEN F**, Univ Of Tn At Knoxville, Knoxville, TN; JR; MBA; Gamma Beta Phi 90-; Gldn Key 90-; Beta Gamma Sigma; Sigma Delta Pi; Delta Delta Delta Mrshl 88-; TN Schlrsh Pgm 88-; Mktg; Law.

**COUGHLIN, JOSEPH M**, Wv Univ, Morgantown, WV; JR; BS; Scty Ptrlm Eng Vp; Pi Epsilon Tau; Deans Lst 88-90; Outstndg Fr 88; Ptrlm Eng.

**COUGHLIN, TARA A**, Villanova Univ, Villanova, PA; FR; BA; Cmps Mnstry 90-; Hsptlty Mnstr; Crew 90-; Pltcl Sci.

**COULOMBE, ANNETTE T**, Univ Of New England, Biddeford, ME; SR; BA; SOTA 89-; Lfstyls Allnce Pres 89-; Alpha Chi 90-; Natl Cncl Thrptc Rcrtn Cert 85-; Amer Occptnl Thrpy Assn 90-; Cert Thrptc Rcrtn Asst 85-; AS Thrptc Rcrtn Univ Of Southern Maine 85; Occptnl Thrpy; Advncd Stdy In Occptnl Thrpy.

**COULSON, CHRISTINE A**, Patrick Henry Comm Coll, Martinsville, VA; SO; BA; Phi Theta Kappa; Elem Schl Tutor:; Cmnctns/Mktg; Advrtsng.

**COULSON, LESLIE A**, Univ Of Toledo, Toledo, OH; GD; Law Rvw 88-90; Intl Law Soc 88-89; Lgl Rsrch/Wrtng Awd 88; Lgl Ethcs Awd 90; Deans Lst 90; Law Clrk US Mgstrt-Jdgmarc L Goldman US Dstrct Ct 90-; JD Univ Toledo Coll Law 90; BS W MI Univ 87; Law.

**COULTER, BRENDA K**, West Liberty St Coll, West Liberty, WV; SO; WVA Assoc Of AAA'S Cmptr Usrs Grp 90; Clg Hnrs Prog; Ft Clrk Cmmnty Assoc Treas 84-88; Tmple Bapt Chrch Music/Choir Dir 84-89; Sftwre Instlltn Tchncn For Ohio Vlly Clrksbrg Whlng WV; Cmptr Info Syst; Bsnss.

**COULTER, DAVID P**, Coll Of Charleston, Charleston, SC; SR; BA; TV Phtgrphy Intrnshp; Pltcl Sci; Tlvsn Videographer.

**COULTER, JULIA B**, Medical Coll Of Ga, Augusta, GA; SR; BS; Sigma Theta Tau; Nrsng.

**COULTER, LA DONNA JILL**, Saint Catharine Coll, St Catharine, KY; FR; Stdnt Sen V P Pres Elect 90-; Agri Club Pres 90-; Livestock Jdgng Tm 90; Phi Theta Kappa 90-; Comm Coll Tutoring Prog 90-; Agri Bus.

**COULTER, LAURA A**, Elmira Coll, Elmira, NY; SO; BA; Pal Prog 90-; Phi Eta Sigma; Elem Educ/English; Teacher.

**COULTER, LISA D**, Fayetteville St Univ, Fayetteville, NC; JR; BA; Army Blades VA Tech 73-74; Corps Of Cadets Squad Ldr 73-75; Cert Cmndtn US Ambassador Peru 87-89; Ofcrs Wives Clubs/Assoc 76-; Genl Mgr EGP US Embassy Lima Peru 87-89; Pol Sci; Fed Serv.

**COULTER, RHONDA K**, Fl St Univ, Tallahassee, FL; JR; BS; Wesley Fndtn Untd Mthdst Cmps Mnstry 89-; Hnrs Schlrs Assoc 89-, Sigma Sigma Sigma 89-90; STARS; Schlrshp 89-; Schlrs Schlrshp 89-; Dns Lst 89-; IM Sftbl; AA Lib Stds Hnrs Pgm 90; Elem Ed; Tchr.

**COUNCE, GAYLE E**, Middle Tn St Univ, Murfreesboro, TN; SR; BBA; Tau Omicron 88-; Gamma Beta Phi 88-; Rho Lambda 89-; Sigma Iota Epsilon 89-; Belta Zeta Treas 87-; Otstndng Sr 90-; Deans List/Hnr Roll 87-; Bus Admn; Mgmt Fin.

**COUNCIL, MATTIE L**, Univ Of Sc At Columbia, Columbia, SC; FR; BS; Stdnt Govt Assoc VP 90-; Gamma Beta Phi 90-; Comp Sci; Eng.

**COUNCIL, RENEE V**, Fayetteville St Univ, Fayetteville, NC; SR; BA; Speech Choir; Yrbk Staff; Drama Guild; Intrnshp FSU In Radio 90; Intrnshp FSU TV 88; Filming Bsktbl Games At FSU 90; BA 90; Speech/Theatre; Speech Pathology.

**COUNTRYMAN, DAWN R**, Univ Of Cincinnati, Cincinnati, OH; SR; BED; Kappa Delta Pi 89-; Golden Key 90-; AA S State Comm Colg 90; Elem Ed; Tch.

**COUNTS, CYNTHIA D**, Va Commonwealth Univ, Richmond, VA; SR; BFA; Ruth Hibbs Hyland Schlrshp 89-90; Ntnl Arts Edctn Asso 90-; Art Edctn; Tch.

**COUNTS, HOPE W**, Memphis St Univ, Memphis, TN; JR; BA; Council Movies Comm Sec 89; United Methodist Stdnt Ctr Sec 89; Publcty Dir 89; Criminal Justice; Law School.

**COUPE, MELISSA E**, Merrimack Coll, North Andover, MA; FR; BS; Biology; Med.

**COUQUIAUD, LAURENT**, Hudson Valley Comm Coll, Troy, NY; FR; AA; Nwspr; Phi Theta Kappa; Tutor; : Var Tennis; Independent Stdes; Visual Prfrmg Arts.

**COURNOYER, PATRICIA M**, Endicott Coll, Beverly, MA; FR; ASSOC; Bsn Club 90-; Hall Cncl Treas 90-; Hnrs Pgm 90-; Edwards Ins Agncy Intern 90-; Bsn Admin; Mgmt.

**COURSEY-GRAY, KELLY M,** Allegheny Coll, Meadville, PA; JR; Stdnt Art Soc 89-; Alden Schlr 89-90; Lambda Sigma 89-90; Stdnt Orientation Advsr 90-; Doane Prize Art Hstry 90; Art History; Prfssr/Gllry/Museum.

**COURT, ALAN C,** Nova Univ, Ft Lauderdale, FL; BBA 72; MBA 90.

**COURTNEY, ANGELA H,** Univ Of Sc At Columbia, Columbia, SC; SR; Ed Mjr Club Pres 90-; Gamma Beta Phi 90-; Grad Hnrs 91; BA 91; Early Childhood Ed; Tchng.

**COURTNEY, CAROL D,** Va Commonwealth Univ, Richmond, VA; SR; BGS; Gldn Key 90-; Intl Bd Of Stndrds/Prctcs For CFP'S 87-; Inst Cert Fncl Plnrs 87-; Public Brdcstng Fld 66-83; Fncl Srvcs Area; AA Keystone Jr Coll La Plume PA 66; CFP Coll Fncl Plng Denver CO 87; Hmn Rel; Trng/Dev.

**COURTNEY JR, DAVID LONG,** Univ Of Sc At Columbia, Columbia, SC; SR; BA; Acctg; CPA.

**COURTNEY, ESTHER MARIE,** Trident Tech Coll, Charleston, SC; FR; AA; Natl Advrtsng Fed 90-; Commercial Graphics; Graphic Artist.

**COURTNEY, TRISHA K,** Univ Of Cincinnati-Clrmnt Coll, Batavia, OH; SO; BA; Chrch; Cmptr Sci; Sys Analyst.

**COURTNEY, VERONICA A,** Ny Univ, New York, NY; FR; AA; Lbrl Arts; Astrphyscs/Law.

**COURTS, CHRISTOPHER E,** Marshall University, Huntington, WV; JR; BA; Fin Mgmt Assn 91-; Inter Frat Cncl V P 89-91; Greek Race Rltns Cmtee 91; Omega; Pi Kappa Alpha Pres 91-92; K C 89-91; Chld Prtctn Tm 89-91; Wmns Lgue Of Huntington; Fin; Law.

**COURTS, MELINDA D,** Alcorn St Univ, Lorman, MS; SO; ASN; MASN 90-; Excep Schlrly Achvmnt 90-; Pres Schlr 90; Curr Comm 90-; Magna Cum Laude; Highst Hnrs; LHA AHA 88-90; Intl Assn Hosp Hltcr Cntrl Serv 88-; LPN Alex Vo Tech 80; CRCST Purdue Univ 88; Nrsng; Bsn/Msn.

**COURTS, PAUL HUBERT,** Johnson C Smith Univ, Charlotte, NC; JR; Mecklinburg Grp Home 90-; Autistic Mntl Patients Publ Dfndrs Ofc Internshp; Psychlgy Crmnl Jstce; Law.

**COURTWRIGHT, TINA D,** Univ Of Akron, Akron, OH; SR; BA; Chrch Chr 90-; Univ Chr 89; Gldn Ky; Psychlgy Elem Educ; Tchng Psychlgst.

**COUSER, MAURICE T,** Morehouse Coll, Atlanta, GA; JR; Bus Assoc 88-; Chptr NAACP 89-; Deans List 88-; Morehouse Acadmc Schlrshp 88-.

**COUSIN, MAXINE B,** Chattanooga St Tech Comm Coll, Chattanooga, TN; SO; Data Proc Mgmt Assn Stdnt Chptr; Blck Stdnt Assn; Mrt Awd Tenn Leg Blck Caucus; Natl Congr Blck Womn; AAS Mckenzie Clg Tenn Weslyn 79; Inf Syst Micro Cmptrs.

**COUSIN, STEVEN A,** Interdenominational Theo Ctr, Atlanta, GA; GD; MDIV; BA Un AL 84; Bible/New Testament; Mnstry.

**COUSINS JR, D L,** Univ Of Sc At Columbia, Columbia, SC; SO; BS; Westinghouse Savannah River Co Employee 88-90; AS Midlands Tech Clg 88; Mech Eng; Eng Mgmt.

**COUSINS, MARIA I,** Tn Temple Univ, Chattanooga, TN; FR; BA; Bnd; Soccer Tm; Vlybl Tm; Theta Mo Rho; Psych.

**COUTURE, LAURIE-ANNE J,** Johnson St Coll, Johnson, VT; JR; BA; Psych; Med.

**COUTURE, SHARON D,** Western New England Coll, Springfield, MA; JR; BS; Biology; Engr.

**COUTURE, SR GUYLEANE I,** Rivier Coll, Nashua, NH; SR; BA; Campus Mnstry Pax Chrsti 88-; Music Mnstry 88-; Pryr Grp Tm Ldrshp 88-89; Concern Vol Tm Ldrshp 90; Wlkathon/Cropwlk For Hngr 88-; Thnksgvng Bskts 88-90; Tchrs Aid; Yth Mnstry Vol 87-89; Psychlgy.

**COUTURIER, ALICIA K,** Coll Of Charleston, Charleston, SC; SR.

**COUTURIER, KRISTIN A,** Univ Of Sc At Columbia, Columbia, SC; SO; BA; Gamma Beta Phi; Delta Delta Delta Mrshl 89-; Ed; Tchr.

**COVARRUBIAS, PAULA T,** Cleveland Inst Of Art, Cleveland, OH; SO; BFA; AICA Schlrshp 90-; Pntng; Exhbtng Pntr.

**COVE, SUSAN F,** Fl Atlantic Univ, Boca Raton, FL; SR; BA; Accntng Stu Assc 90-; Kiawanis Schlrshp; Amer Bus Wmns Assc Schlrshp; AA Palm Beach Jr Coll 89; Pblc Accntng.

**COVELL, SANDRA D,** Columbia Union Coll, Takoma Park, MD; FR; BA; Phi Eta Sigma 90-; Theta Alpha Beta 90-; Exhibition Gym Tm 90-; Engl/Hlth Mgmt; Ed.

**COVENY, KRISTIN K,** Va Commonwealth Univ, Richmond, VA; FR; BA; Pre Phrmcy Clb 90-; Phi Eta Sigma Sec; Carver Proj; Deans Lst 90-; Top 1 Pct Cls Awd 90-; Pre Phrmcy.

**COVERSTON, LUCINDA J,** Central Fl Comm Coll, Ocala, FL; SO; Spanish Clb 90-; AA; Pre Bus; Bus Acctntng.

**COVERT, KERI A,** S U N Y Coll Of Tech At Alfred, Alfred, NY; FR; AAS; Clg Ag Ldrs Clb 89-90; Intrnshp With FMHA 90; Ag Bus.

**COVERT, TONYA M,** S U N Y Coll Of Tech At Alfred, Alfred, NY; SO; AAS; 4000 Presdlt Schlrshp Geneseo Univ; Acctng; CPA.

**COVIELLO, JILL A,** Teikyo Post Univ, Waterbury, CT; FR; BA; Engl; Educ.

**COVINGTON, BERNADETTE,** Savannah Coll Of Art & Design, Savannah, GA; GD; BFA; Grphc Dsgn Clb 88-90; Study Abrd Pgm 90; Amsterdam News Intern Column Dsgnr 87; Biltmore Textiles Intern Pattern Dsgnr 86; AS Endicott Clg 85-87; Grphc Dsgn; Advrtsg.

**COVINGTON, CAROL L,** Middle Tn St Univ, Murfreesboro, TN; SR; BS; STEA 90-; Kappa Delta Pi; Acctng; Elem Ed.

**COVINGTON, CHRISTINE M,** Elmira Coll, Elmira, NY; SO; BS; Stdnt Assn Pres; Amnsty Intrntl Pres 90-; Scl Pltcl Union 90-; LISP 89-; Hons Schlr 89-; Stdnt Mrshll; Spch/Hrng; Pathlgst/Ther.

**COVINGTON, STEPHANIE S,** Hampton Univ, Hampton, VA; SO; BS; Bus Clb 90-; Bus Enrchmnt Educ Prog; Dns Lst 89-90; Finance; Corp Law/Invstmnt Bnkng.

**COVINGTON, TONY M,** Middle Tn St Univ, Murfreesboro, TN; SO; BA; Aerospace; Pilot.

**COVINGTON, VAUGHN K,** Cheyney Univ Of Pa, Cheyney, PA; SO; BA; Bus Clb; Bsktbl; Bus.

**COVINGTON, VIVIAN A,** Jackson St Univ, Jackson, MS; JR; BA; AMA V P; Alpha Lambda Delta; Phi Beta Lambda; Acad Schlrshp; At/T Intern; Mktg; Bsn.

**COWAN, ANESHA M,** Ms St Univ, Miss State, MS; SR; MBA; Elite Rcrtng Org; MAHO; SEAHO; Mnrty Acdmc Exc Awd 86-90; Ldrshp Fellow; Res Hll Drctr Asst 90; Jackson Chmbr Comm Ldrshp Awd; BBA 90; Alpha Lambda Delta; Phi Eta Sigma; Gamma Beta Phi; Omicron Delta Kappa; Alpha Kappa Alpha Pres 89-90; Mrktng/Business; Mgmt.

**COWAN, CYNTHIA DIANE,** Wv Univ At Parkersburg, Parkersburg, WV; GD; BS; Intl Dance/Exercise Assn Fndtn Cert Instr 88-; Tutor/Chem-Bio Sci 90-; Phi Theta Kappa; Delta Delta Delta; Sigma Phi Epsilon 85-87; Nu Tau Omega-Grntlgy Advsr 88-89; Mon-Valley Eldercare 87-88; Nrsg; Med Schl.

**COWAN, DAVID E,** Dyersburg St Comm Coll, Dyersburg, TN; SO; AAS; Chrst Ambsdrs Asmbly God 83-86; Chrch Chr 83-89; Cert Ripley St Area Voc Tech 86; Cert Ripley St Area Voc Tech 88; Bsn Admin Bnkg; Mgmt Bnkg.

**COWAN, DERRICK A,** City Univ Of Ny Baruch Coll, New York, NY; SR; BBA; Asst Cntrlr Mjr Invstmnt Frm; Accntng; CPA Pltcl Sci.

**COWAN JR, FREDRICK H,** Radford Univ, Radford, VA; SR; BS; Biology Clb 89-; Univ Emer Med Serv Treas 89-; Pi Gamma Mu 90-; Alpha Chi Rho Schlrshp Chrmn 89-; Deans Schlr Nom 90-; Dns Lst 89-; Biology; Medicine.

**COWAN, M BENJAMIN,** Univ Of Miami, Coral Gables, FL; JR; BA; Interfrat Cncl VP; Pres 100 89-; AGLO Dlgt; Paideia Co-Fndr 90-; Gldn Key 90-; Zeta Beta Tau 90-; S Walzer Awd 89-; Provosts Hon Rl 89-90; IM Sftbl 90-; H K Stanford Schlrshp 88-92; Marine Affrs/Bus; Law.

**COWAN, SHERRI L,** East Carolina Univ, Greenville, NC; SR; BFA; Crftsmen East 90-91; VAF 90-91; Art Enthsts Schlrshp; Artwrk Shown ECU; Art Metal Design.

**COWAN, SHERRY L,** Salisbury St Univ, Salisbury, MD; SR; BS; Rsprtry Thrpy Stdnt Assn Pres 89-90; Omicron Delta Kappa; Phi Kappa Phi; Rsprtry Thrpy.

**COWAN, THERESA M,** Mount Aloysius Jr Coll, Cresson, PA; SO; BA; Stdnt Govt Assn Pres 90-; Bus Clb VP 90-; Yrbk Staff 90-; Jdcl Brd 90-; Cmnctns; Pblc Rltns.

**COWARD, DANIEL R,** Piedmont Bible Coll, Winston-Salem, NC; SO; BA; Ensmbl; IM Sprts Sccr/Tnns; Deans Lst; Music Voice; Chrch Music Chrl Dir-Sngwrtr.

**COWARD, JOSEPH D,** Univ Of Sc At Coastal Carolina, Conway, SC; SR; BA; The Mgt Organization Club Pres 90-F Busn Club 89-; SGA Rep 90-; Phi Alpha Delta 89-; Cstd Caroling Clg Intershp 90-; Hnrs Ind Field Study 90; Red Cross 90-; Mgnt/Finance; Self Employment.

**COWARD, JULIET F,** Univ Of Sc At Columbia, Columbia, SC; SO; BA; Acctg/Finance; CPA.

**COWARD, MICHAEL A,** Southern Coll Of Tech, Marietta, GA; SR; BSEET; Elec Eng Tech.

**COWARD JR, PAUL A,** Piedmont Bible Coll, Winston-Salem, NC; JR; BA; Stdnt Cncl VP 88-; Prchrs Fllwshp; Bulldogs VP 90-; Sccr 87-88; Bible Bblcl Studies; Pstrt.

**COWARD SR, SURRANO,** New Comm Coll Of Baltimore, Baltimore, MD; GD; BA; Philosphy; HS Teacher.

**COWART, KATHRYN E,** Univ Of Sc At Columbia, Columbia, SC; SO; BS; Kappa Delta Edtr 89-; Dean Lst 89-; Biol/Pre Med; Mdcl Schl Pdtrcs.

**COWART, TIMOTHY J,** Va Commonwealth Univ, Richmond, VA; SO; MFA; Gymn Club 90; Activ Prog Brd; Freshman Class Elected Class Rep 90-; USMC Resv Lance Corpeal; Theatre; Acting/Dance.

**COWDEN, SHARON F,** Pellissippi St Tech Comm Coll, Knoxville, TN; FR; BA; Intl Clb VP 90-; Geo; Intl Bsn.

**COWDREY, AINSLIE L,** Va Commonwealth Univ, Richmond, VA; JR; BS; Intrnshp; Mass Cmnctns; Advrtsng.

**COWGILL, DARREN S,** Wilmington Coll, New Castle, DE; SR; BS; Phi Theta Kaap 85-86; Lambda Alpha Omega VP 85-86; Cmmnty Cvc Assn; AS Delw Tech Comm Coll 86; Bus Mngmnt; Bus Mngr.

**COWHERD, ANN B,** Middle Tn St Univ, Murfreesboro, TN; FR; MBA; Bus/Mktg.

**COWLES, JENNIFER L,** Univ Of Ga, Athens, GA; JR; BSED; Early Chldhd Educ; Tch.

**COWLING, JACK D,** Univ Of North Fl, Jacksonville, FL; SO; BS; Fnnc Invstmnt Soc; Fnnc; Prtfl Mngr.

**COWSERT, TRENT W,** Univ Of Tn At Martin, Martin, TN; JR; BS; Phi Eta Sigma 90-; Kappa Alpha Order 89-; Hnrs Smnr Schlrshp 89-; Acctng; Cpa.

**COX, ALICIA A,** Univ Of Ky, Lexington, KY; SR; BS; Ky Acdmy Stu Phrmcy Mbr 89-; Ky Phrmcsts Assoc 89-; APHA Amer Phar Assoc 89-; Alpha Chi 88-; Lambda Kappa Sigma 89-; SCODAE 89-90; Boot Strp Awrd; Deans Lst 90-; Phrmcy; Comm.

**COX, AMY L,** Univ Of Pittsburgh At Bradford, Bradford, PA; SR; Comp Ad Lrng Cntr 90f Math Ttr 88-89; Alpha Lambda Delta 87-90; Magna Cum Laude; Emp Eastman Kodal Co; BS 90; Comp Sci.**

**COX, ANGELA D,** Fl A & M Univ, Tallahassee, FL; FR; BA; Hnr Rl 90; Dns Lst; Natl Achvmnt Schlr 90; Bio/Chem; Med Rsch/Biochem.

**COX, ANGELA L,** Miami Dade Comm Coll, Miami, FL; BS; Otstndng Acad Achvmnt Awrd; PSI 88-; Law; Legal Asstnt.

**COX, ANGELA L,** Univ Of Tn At Martin, Martin, TN; SR; BA; Stdnt Govt Assn Elctn Commsnr 88-89; Almni Cncl 90-; Dnce Ensmble 88-90; Phi Kappa Phi; Sigma Delta Pi; Ordr/Omega Sec/Treas 90-; Phi Eta Sigma 88-; Pi Sigma Epsilon VP Pub Rltns 90-; Alpha Omicron Pi Schlrshp Chrmn 88-; Chrldr 89-; Spnsh; Intl Bus.

**COX, ANTHONY D,** Hampton Univ, Hampton, VA; FR; MBA; Mens Cncl 90-; Deans List 90-; Bsn Mngmnt/Engrng; Mngmnt/Engrng/Airplane Plt.

**COX, BRENT A,** Univ Of Tn At Martin, Martin, TN; JR; Phi Alpha Theta VP; Ernest P Wilma Newby Schlrshp; 31st TN Inf Reg Co E CSA Org 82-; Living Hist Assoc Chmn 82-; Conf Leather Works Owner 85-; Hist; Ph D.

**COX, CAMMIE R,** Fl Inst Of Tech, Melbourne, FL; FR; BS; Marine Mml Stdng Ntwrk 90-; Marine Bio; Vet Med.

**COX, CHRISTENE C,** Cumberland County Coll, Vineland, NJ; SO; AAS; Dns Lst; Nrsng; RN.

**COX, CINDY C,** Barry Univ, Miami, FL; JR; BSN; BS Florida Intl Univ 82; BS 82; Nrsng.

**COX, CLIFFORD D,** S U N Y Coll Of Tech At Frmgdl, Farmingdale, NY; FR; GPA Cert 90; Elect Eng Tech; Eng.

**COX, DARLENE E,** De Tech & Comm Coll At Dover, Dover, DE; FR; Cmptr-Data Prcssng.

**COX, DEBBIE KAY,** Middle Tn St Univ, Murfreesboro, TN; SR; BA; Kappa Delta Pi 89-; Gamma Beta Pi 89-; Elem Ed.

**COX, DEBRA SUE,** Savannah Coll Of Art & Design, Savannah, GA; SR; BFA; ASID 90; Hnr Roll 88; Art Hstry; Intr Dsgnr.

**COX, DOUGLAS G,** Bowling Green St Univ, Bowling Green, OH; JR; BS; Frederick C Stone Mem Schlrshp; IM Bsktbl/Ftbl/Sftbl; Mech Engr.

**COX III, EARL F,** Elmira Coll, Elmira, NY; JR; BA; Orntn Ldr 88-89; Stdnt Ambsdr 88-90; Psi Chi 90-; Hon Schlr 88-; Deans List 89-; PAL 88-; Phi Beta Kappa; Dsccr La Crosse Hckry 88-; Psychlgy; Phys Thrpst.

**COX, ELIZABETH SHERMAN,** Ms Coll, Clinton, MS; GD; JD; MBA Fnc/Mgmt U Notre Dame 86; BA Bio Sci U MS 83; Law; Corp-Bus Law.

**COX, ERIC J,** Kent St Univ Kent Cmps, Kent, OH; SR; BA; Stu Govt Pres 89-90; Stu Data Prcssng Mngmnt Assn 88-; DPMA; Tnns 87-88; Bsktbl 87-89; Cmptr Oprtr Prgrmmr Tech Wingfoot Films 90-; AS Kent St 89; Cmptr Sci; Anlyst.

**COX, ERIN L,** Endicott Coll, Beverly, MA; JR; BS; Cls Pres 90-; Admsns Hnr 88-; Psychlgy Clb 90-; Dns Lst 88-; Franker Schlrshp; Endicott Grnt; Phi Theta Kappa 90-; Orntn Ldr 89-; Fndrsng Pres 90-; Prmtng Endicott 88-; Admsns Asst 90-; Intrnshp Erly Intrvntn Pgm Asst 89-; Psychlgy; Med/Psychtry.

**COX, GERI A,** Valdosta St Coll, Valdosta, GA; JR; BED; Assoc In Sci Abraham Badlwin Ag Clg 90; Speech Lang Path.

**COX, GREGORY D,** Oh Northern Univ, Ada, OH; GD; JD; Phi Delta Phi 88-; Brabson Schlrshp 88-; Brd Regents Flwshp 88-90; Intrnshp Lim City Pros Ofc 90; BA Urbana Univ 88; Law.

**COX, JOHN D,** Univ Of Nc At Charlotte, Charlotte, NC; SR; BA; Math Assn 89-; Math; Tch.

**COX, JOHN M,** Marshall University, Huntington, WV; JR; Natl Guard Clp E-4; Fin; Ins.

**COX, JUDITH L,** Hudson Valley Comm Coll, Troy, NY; SO; BA; Awd Grad With Hnrs Pres Lst; Spnsh; Intrprtr.

**COX, KATHY A,** Univ Of Cincinnati, Cincinnati, OH; SR; Stdnt Alumni Cncl 87-90; Stdnt Nrs Assoc Chrprsn 88-; Clncl/Navajo Rsrvtn; BSN; Nursing; Psychiatric.

**COX, KEVIN D,** Middle Tn St Univ, Murfreesboro, TN; SR; Band Of Blue 87-90; Woodwind Quintet 87-90; Double Reed Ens 87-90; Phi Mu Alpha Chapln 89-90; Tenn Vly Winds 88-; Band Apprec Awd 89-90; Otstdng Sect Ldr Awd 89-90; Pep Bnd 87-90; BM.

**COX, KEVIN H,** Univ Of Tn At Martin, Martin, TN; FR; BS; Blck/Brdl Clb 90-; Soc Hon Smnr Stdnts 90-; Anml Sci; Vet Med.

**COX, LARRY DARYL,** Livingston Univ, Livingston, AL; SR; AS; Sftbl 87-; Drftng; Indust Eng.

**COX, LINDA H,** Univ Of West Fl, Pensacola, FL; SR; BA; Chrch Sec 70-; Piano Tchr; Elem Ed; Tch.

**COX, MARGARET C MCD,** Fl International Univ, Miami, FL; SR; BS; Otrch Comm Frst Untd Meth Chrch Miami Chrprsn; Cert Ed Univ Londong England 70; Assn Curriculum Sprvsn Dvlopmnt Nat Assn Educ Yng Chldrn; Hmrm Tchr Untd Ntns Intrnl Sch N Y 74-85; Tchr Gd Hp Schl St Croix 86-89; Spec Educ; Tchng.

**COX, MARSI M,** Auburn Univ At Auburn, Auburn, AL; GD; Scr Swthrts Pres 88-90; Phi Kappa Phi 90-; Pi Lambda Theta 89-90; BSED 90; Erly Chldhd Educ.

**COX, MARTHA J,** Univ Of Pittsburgh At Bradford, Bradford, PA; FR; BA; Alpha Lambda Delta; Sci/Chem/Math; Phrmcst.

**COX, MARVIN J,** Northern Ky Univ, Highland Hts, KY; JR; Hist; Tch Coll.

**COX, MELISSA A,** Al St Univ, Montgomery, AL; FR; Educ.

**COX, MONICA M,** Livingston Univ, Livingston, AL; SO; BED; Edn; Teach.

**COX, REGINALD ARNELL,** Fl A & M Univ, Tallahassee, FL; SO; BA; NOMA 90-; AS Drftng/Dsgn Palm Beach Comm Clg 90-; AA; Architecture.

**COX, RICKY J,** Ms Coll, Clinton, MS; GD; JD; Law Stdnt Bar Assn Sntr; Lambda Chi Alpha VP 88; Alumni Fdrtn Schlrshp; BGS LA St Unvrsty 90; Law.

**COX, ROBERT J,** Inter Amer Univ Pr Hato Rey, Hato Rey, PR; SR; BA; Mktg.

**COX, ROBYN F,** Bridgewater Coll, Bridgewater, VA; SO; BS; Lutheran Church Handbell Choir 90-; Bus Admin/Acctng; CPA.

**COX, RONALD B,** Univ Of Sc At Aiken, Aiken, SC; SO; BS; Gamma Beta Phi 90-; C L Jolly Mem Chnsllrs Schlrshp 90-; Pitney Rowes Schlrshp 90-; Bus Mgmt; Law.

**COX, SANDRA E,** Memphis St Univ, Memphis, TN; SO; BM; Marching Ban 90; Wind Ensmbl; Venezuela Music Ensmbl 90-; Golden Key 87-; Beta Phi Sigma Theta Tau; Toured Caracus Veneruda March 91; Deans List 89-90; Whos Who In Amer Nursing 90; Memphis Sexual Asslt Resc Cntr 89-; BSN 84; MSN 87; Music Performance; Ph D Music Therapy.

**COX, SHANE T,** Truett Mc Connell Coll, Cleveland, GA; FR; BA; Baptist Stdnt Union Pres; Rotaract; Phi Theta Kappa; BSU Summer Missnry; Ministry.

**COX, SHIRLEY ANNE,** Northeast State Tech Comm Coll, Blountville, TN; SO; AAS; Lib Schlrshp 89-; Ofc Sys Tech; Med Transcrptnst.

**COX, STACEY M,** Anderson Coll, Anderson, SC; SO; BA; Phi Theta Kappa 90-; Bus/Acctng.

**COX, STEVEN T,** Va Commonwealth Univ, Richmond, VA; SR; BS; Drug Clrk 90; Phrmcy Tech 89; Stock Clk 87-88; Projectionist 89-87; IM Table Tennis Champ 89; IM Bsktbl 88; Vars Bsbl; Chem; Chem Sales.

**COX JR, THOMAS,** J Sargeant Reynolds Comm Coll, Richmond, VA; GD; BS; Intrn Bthlhm Ctr ADC Asst Supv 90-; Comm/Pblc Afrs.

**COX, THOMAS H,** Birmingham Southern Coll, Birmingham, AL; FR; BA; Hilltop Nws Stff 90-; Rsdnc Hl Assn 90-; Alpha Phi Omega 90-; Mthdst Bi-Cntnnl Schlrshp 90-; Hstry Engl; Coll Prfssr-Hstry/Jrnlsm.

**COX, TIMOTHY W,** Univ Of Al At Huntsville, Huntsville, AL; FR; BSEE; U S Marine Corps 86-90; Elctrncs Radar Repairman; Marine Reserves 90-; Elect Engrng.

**COX, TINA A,** Brescia Coll, Owensboro, KY; GD; BS; Brescia Sci Assn 86-; ONCE Cnslr For Brescia 90; Outstndng Sec Educ Stdnt Tchr; Bio; Tchr.

**COX, TINA R,** Alice Lloyd Coll, Pippa Passes, KY; SO; BA; Schlstc Achvmnt Awd; Acctg; CPA.

**COX, TOSHA Y,** Central St Univ, Wilberforce, OH; FR; BA; Bus Admn; Fin.

**COX, VALERIE A,** Tallahassee Comm Coll, Tallahassee, FL; FR; AA; Psychlgy; Cnslng.

**COX, VIRGINIA L,** Fl A & M Univ, Tallahassee, FL; JR; BS; Chi; Chi Omega Alumnae Jr Leg Tallanassee Admiss 88-; Intn Tallahassee Nurs 90-; BS Brenah Clg 75; Landscape Design.

**COX-FILMER, KATHRYN MARY,** Providence Coll, Providence, RI; SR; BS; Hlth Srvc Admnstrtn Clb 88-; Asst Athltc Drctr G Alaimo Spvsr 89-; Prvdnc Clg; Hlth Srvcs Admnstrtn; Hsptl Admnstrtn Finance.

**COXE, DALE S,** Lenoir Rhyne Coll, Hickory, NC; FR; MBA; Vars Vlybl Starter 90-; Vars Sftbl Starter 90-; Circle K Svcs Club 90-; Acctg; CPA.

**COXE, ROBERT B,** Univ Of Nc At Asheville, Asheville, NC; JR; BA; Outing Clb Pres 89-90; Bapt Stdnt Un 89-90; Bio Clb Pres; Herbarium Asst 89; Bio; Rsrchr.**

**COXON, JENEE C P,** Savannah St Coll, Savannah, GA; SR; BS; Beta Beta Beta Treas 89-; Beta Kappa Chi Chpln 90-; Alpha Kappa Mu 90-; Sigma Gamma Rho; Am Cyanamid Intern; Fisk Univ Premed Inst 90; Bio; Elctrn Mcrscpy.

**COXWELL, NORA C,** Univ Of West Fl, Pensacola, FL; SR; Alpha Sigma Lambda 90-; BA; AA Jefferson Davis Jr Coll 75; Elem Ed; Tchng.

**COY, DONNA C,** Embry Riddle Aeronautical Univ, Daytona Beach, FL; FR; BS; AAAE; Caribbean Assc; Brthrs Wind; Arntcl Sci.

**COY, DOUGLAS L,** Univ Of Pittsburgh At Bradford, Bradford, PA; JR; BA; Nwspr Edtr 89-; Literarymag 89-; R C Laing Creative Arts Awd 91; Wrtng; Jurnlsm.

**COY, MARIE S,** Indiana Univ Of Pa, Indiana, PA; SO; BED; ACEI; Ed.

**COY, MICHAEL A,** Alfred Univ, Alfred, NY; SR; BS; Am Ceramic Soc 87-; Natl Inst Ceramic Engrs 88-; Tau Beta Sigma 89-; Alpha Lambda Delta 87-; Regent Schlrshp; Martin Welch Schlrshp; Coining Glass Wrks Schlrshp; Ftbl 87; Ceramic Eng; Grad Sch.

**COYER, JOYCE A,** Univ Of Charleston, Charleston, WV; SR; BS; Math Educ.

**COYLE, CHRISTINE L,** Rutgers St Univ At Camden, Camden, NJ; SR; BS; Schl Bus Stdnt Cngrss Sec 89-90; Acctg Soc 87-; Athenaeum; Gamma Tau Chi 89-; Acctg Intrnsp Jos Hatch CPA; Acctg; CPA.

**COYLE, EVANGELINE,** Saint Catharine Coll, St Catharine, KY; FR; AAS; Phi Theta Kappa; Lang/Child Care; Day Care Ctr.

**COYLE, KELLY A,** Saint Catharine Coll, St Catharine, KY; FR; BS; Phi Theta Kappa 90-; Econ; Intl Commerce.

**COYLE, WILLIAM J,** Northern Ky Univ, Highland Hts, KY; JR; BABS; Biolgcl Soc 90-; Am Soc Clncl Pthlgsts 85-; AAS Cincinnati Tech Clg 85; Chem/Bio; Med/Chem Rsrch.

**COYNE, HOPE E,** Georgian Court Coll, Lakewood, NJ; SR; BS; Hndcpped Bsktbl Assist; MR Adlts Vol; Bsnss Admin; Law Tax Corp.

**COYNE, KARI L,** S U N Y Coll Of Tech At Alfred, Alfred, NY; SR; BA; AA; Elem Ed.

**COYNE, MICHELE A,** Villanova Univ, Villanova, PA; JR; BA; Stdnt Union 89-90; Homeless Comm 90-; Pre Law Soc 90-; Phi Kappa Phi; Pi Beta Phi Chptr Hstrn 89-; Engl/Poltcl Sci; Law.

**COYNE, PATRICK H,** Comm Coll Algny Co Algny Cmps, Pittsburgh, PA; SO; BA; Avtn Clb; Pttsbrgh Lcrss Clb; Avtn Mgmt; Plt.

**COYNE, SUSAN E,** Univ Of Ga, Athens, GA; JR; BSED; PES Clb; Alpha Lambda Delta 88; Gamma Beta Phi 88; GAHPERD; Kappa Alpha Theta Stndrds Chrmn 88-; Pnhllnc Rush Cnslr; IM Ftbl/Sftbl 88-; Exrcs/Sprts Sci; Corp Wellnss Dir.

**COYNE-CROWLEY, SANDRA J,** Western New England Coll, Springfield, MA; GD; BS; Ronald Mcdonald Hse Bd Of Dir 86-; RMCD Bd Of Dir; Assoc STCC Armory Sq Spfd 75; Mgmt; Advocacy.

**COZART, STEVEN M,** East Carolina Univ, Greenville, NC; FR; BFA; Sigma Phi Eta 90-; Undergrad Show Hnrbl Mntn; Graphic Design; Advrtsng/Printing.

**COZZOLI, MARK S,** Univ Of Akron, Akron, OH; SR; BS; Sigma Iota Epsilon; Deans List 88-; Hmn Rsrc Mgr.

**CRAAN, ALAIN A,** Saint Thomas Univ, Miami, FL; SR; Cir K 89-F Intrntl Stdnt Org Brd 90-; Tutr Stff Asst 88-; Acad Sprt Ctr; Bus Mgmt; Intrntl Fnc.

**CRABLE, LORRAINE E,** Fl St Univ, Tallahassee, FL; JR; BS; Dstrbtv Ed Clb Am 79-80; Garnet Key Hstrn 90-; Chrch Yth Cnslr 90-; Church Sun Schl Tch 87-89; AA Dgr Awrded Hnrs 90; Natl Assoc Fml Exc 86-87; Campfire Girls 86; AA Fl Domnty Clg Jcksvlle 90; Elem Ed; Reading Spec.

**CRABTREE, BARBARA A,** Univ Of Miami, Coral Gables, FL; FR; BFA; Mnrty Theatre Ens 90; Hons Prog 90; Theatre Perf; Perf.

**CRABTREE, DIANA L,** Oh St Univ At Marion, Marion, OH; SR; BA; Educ Soc 90-; OH State Mentrshp Prog 90-; Cmnty Band 87-; Juvnile Detntn Ctr Tchrs Aide; Sci Fair Judge; Deans List 89-; Truman Schlrshp 90; Educ; Tchng.

**CRABTREE JR, JAMES C,** Vance Granville Comm Coll, Henderson, NC; SR; AE; Comp Clb Chrmn Pub Cmte 89-; Mc Donalds Corp 3 Yrs Crwprsn/7 Yrs Mngmnt; Comp Pgm.

**CRABTREE, JERRY W,** Union Coll, Barbourville, KY; FR; Flwshp Chrstn Athletes 90-; Bapt Stdnt Un 90-; Deans Lst; Vrsty Bsebl 90-.

**CRABTREE, JOHN C,** Univ Of Tn At Martin, Martin, TN; SO; BS; Assoc For Cmptng Mchnry Stdnt Cptr Pres; Cmptr Sci; Sftwre Eng.

**CRABTREE, KEITH L,** Appalachian St Univ, Boone, NC; FR; BA; Bus; Worker.

**CRABTREE, KIMBERLY M,** Ms St Univ, Miss State, MS; SR; Engl; Tech Wrtng/Edtng.

**CRABTREE, PATRICK M,** Middle Tn St Univ, Murfreesboro, TN; SR; BBA; Reserve Ofcrs Trng Corps Cadet Mjr 90-; Blue Brigade Drill Tm Cmmndr 90-; Crossed Sabres Exec Ofcr 90-; Gamma Beta Phi; Sigma Clb; Kappa Delta Pi; Beta Gamma Sigma; Gamma Iota Sigma; Deans Lst; Pres Schlstc Exclnc Awrd; ROTC; Finance Insurance; Army Ofcr/Finance Corps.

**CRABTREE, RAYMOND,** Marshall University, Huntington, WV; SR; BBA; Phi Delta Theta Treas 90-; Acctng Clb 88-; Natl Mgmtn Assoc 90-; Gamma Beta Phi 88-89; W Va Soc CPAS 90-; Hntng JCS Lcl Dir 87-89; Dns Lst 87-; Acctng; CPA.

**CRABTREE, SCOTT H,** Coll Of Charleston, Charleston, SC; JR; BA; Phlsphy Clb 89-; Allnc Planet Earth; Phlsphy; Law.

**CRABTREE, SHAWN D,** Western Ky Univ, Bowling Green, KY; JR; BA; Scl Wrk; Ther.

**CRABTREE, SUSAN D,** Univ Of Ky, Lexington, KY; JR; BA; Engl; Law.

**CRACRAFT, CHRISTOPHER,** Youngstown St Univ, Youngstown, OH; JR; BE; IEEE 88-; Amrcn Nclr Soc Sec 90-; Jau Beta Pi 90-; Gldn Key 90-; YSU Cntrns 90-; Elctrcl Engnrng.

**CRADY, LINDA S,** Ky St Univ, Frankfort, KY; SR; BA; Engl; Ed.

**CRAFT, ANTONIO F,** Ms Gulf Coast Comm Coll, Perkinston, MS; FR; BED; VP List 90-; Computer Sci; Engineering.

**CRAFT, CHRISTI A,** Defiance Coll, Defiance, OH; JR; BA; Alpha Chi V P; Acad Schlrshps 89-; Untd Meth Womn V P 88-; Chrst Corp Yth Ldr 90-; Engl/Readng; Sec Educ.

**CRAFT, CURTIS P,** S U N Y Coll Of Tech At Alfred, Alfred, NY; FR; Alfrd St Coll Phtrgrphy Clb; Lbrl Stdy.

**CRAFT, DAWN M,** Columbia Greene Comm Coll, Hudson, NY; SO; BS; Crmnl Jstce Clb Pres 90; Columbia Co Corr Ofcr 91; Crmnl Jstce; Pol Ofcr/Comms Ofcr.

**CRAFT, ELAINE L,** Univ Of Ky, Lexington, KY; SR; BSN; Gldn Key 89-; Soc Nrsg; Sigma Theta Tau; Hgh Dstnctn; RN UK Med Ctr Lexington KY; RN Kings Daughters Schl Nrsg Ashland KY 71; Nrsg.

**CRAFT, KATHLEEN D,** Univ Of Southern Ms, Hattiesburg, MS; SR; BS; Actvts Cncl 87-; Paralgl Scty 89-; Intrntl Rels Clb 89-90; Gamma Beta Phi 90-; Grl Scts; Exchng Stdnt Univ Swansea 88-89; Deans Lst 88-; Lcrss 88-89; BS; Poli Sci; Law.**

**CRAFT, KIMBERLY K,** Univ Of Al, Tuscaloosa, AL; SR; Jrnlsts Assn 89-90; Coll Rpblcns 89; Kappa Tau Alpha 90-; Phi Theta Kappa 88-; Sigma Delta Chi Sec 90-; Nwspr Intern 90; Tourism Nwsltr Stf Writer; Tabloid Ed; Ted/Peg Serrill Schlrshp 90-; Buford Boone Meml Schlrshp 90-; Wal-Mart Schlrshp; Jrnlsm; Rprtr.**

**CRAFT, LYDIA R,** Milligan Coll, Milligan Clg, TN; SR; BS; Prlgl Commnctns.

**CRAFT, MAURICE L,** Alcorn St Univ, Lorman, MS; JR; BA; Cmptr Sci Clb; Math Clb; Alpha Kappa Mu; Cmptr Sci/Applied Math; Pgmmng.

**CRAFT JR, PAUL E,** Ms St Univ, Miss State, MS; SR; BS; Stdnt Assn Dir Univ Serv 89-90; Univ Hon Prog 87-88; Univ Lbrary Comm 90-; Lambda Sigma Edtr 88-89; Phi Eta Sigma 89; Phi Gamma Delta Rec Sec 87-; Circle K Sec/Treas 90-; Un Way Vol Tutr 89-90; Univ Hon Prog 89; Aerospce Eng.

**CRAFT, VICKIE A,** Clark Atlanta Univ, Atlanta, GA; JR; BA; Stdnt Msc Educ Natl Conf Sec 89-90; Phlhrmnc Soc; Mrchng Cncrt Bnds Sec Ldr 88-90; Kappa Delta Epsilon VP 90-; Alpha Kappa Mu; Delta Sigma Theta; Dns Lst 88-; Msc Educ; Vocal Perf Tchng.

**CRAGHEAD, TONYA M,** Radford Univ, Radford, VA; SO; BS; Sigma Tau Delta 90-; Erly Edn; Te Ach K-5/Later Masters In Sch Adm.

**CRAGWALL, JOHN C,** Univ Of Cin R Walters Coll, Blue Ash, OH; SO; ABA; BA Cincinnati Bptst Coll 74; Indstrl Mgmt.

**CRAIG, AIMEE A,** Fl St Univ, Tallahassee, FL; SO; BA; Russian Club; Phi Eta Sigma 90-; Dns Lst 89; Russian Mktng; Law.

**CRAIG, ANGELA D,** Patrick Henry Comm Coll, Martinsville, VA; SO; BA; Phi Theta Kappa 90-; Psychlgy; Cnslng Psychlgy.

**CRAIG, CAREY H,** James Madison University, Harrisonburg, VA; SR; BS; RCIA Membership; AAS Lord Fairfax Comm Clg; Early Childhood Educ; Teacher.

**CRAIG, CATHY L,** Marshall University, Huntington, WV; FR; BS; Elem Ed; Tchr.

**CRAIG, CATHY L,** Owensboro Comm Coll, Owensboro, KY; SO; BA; Scl Wrk; Crmnl Scl Wrkr.

**CRAIG, CURT B,** Morehouse Coll, Atlanta, GA; SO; BA; Spc Endvrs Clb Prlmntrn 90-; Hnrs Pgm 89-90; Ronald E Mc Nair Schlr 89-; NASA Intrn 90-; IM Bsktbl 90-; Math; Engr.

**CRAIG, DIANE,** Concordia Coll, Selma, AL; SO; Phi Theta Kappa VP 90-; Cmptr Sci; Cmptr Pgmr.

**CRAIG, FRANCIS JON,** Indiana Univ Of Pa, Indiana, PA; SR; WIUP TV 90-; Vdgrphr 90-; Prdcr Evngns 90-; Alpha Epsilon Rho 89-; Intrnshp Cble Vsn Of Grtr Jhnstwn Prgrmmng Prdctn Dept; Cmmnctns Media Thtre; TV Prdctn.

**CRAIG, JOSEPH M,** Wallace St Comm Coll At Selma, Selma, AL; SO; BS; IM Ftbl Univ AL Ski Clb 88-89; AS; Info Comp Sci; Proc/Mgmt.

**CRAIG, MICHAEL P,** Memphis St Univ, Memphis, TN; JR; BA; Covington Fire Dept Lt Trng Ofc 81; TN State Fr Sch Instrctr 85-; Intrntl Scty Fr Svc Instctr 86-; Covington Fr Dept Trng Ofcr Lt 81-; AS Dyersburg State Comm Clg 74; Fr Admn; Fire Svc.

**CRAIG, MICHAEL R,** Comm Coll Algny Co Algny Cmps, Pittsburgh, PA; SO; IM Bsktbl 90; Acctg.

**CRAIG, PENRYN LEE,** Univ Of Ky, Lexington, KY; SR; MCR; BA; Drg Alchl Cnslng.

**CRAIG, ROBERT A,** S U N Y Coll At Fredonia, Fredonia, NY; JR; BA; WCVF Fredonia 90-; Itrn Corng Inc 87-; AS Crng Comm Coll NY 90; Fin/Mktg; Bus Mgmt/Prof.

**CRAIG, SHELBY L,** Broward Comm Coll, Ft Lauderdale, FL; SO; AA; Phi Theta Kappa Sec 90-; Deans Lst 89; Pres Lst 90; Elem Ed; Tch.

**CRAIG, SUSAN M,** Georgian Court Coll, Lakewood, NJ; JR; Coll Advsry Brd Mem; Deans Schlr Mem; PTA Exec Brd; Site Dir YMCA Lacey Twnshp 88-; BA; Spec Ed; Tchr.

**CRAIG, TAMARA R,** Univ Of Ky, Lexington, KY; SR; BA; KY Cncl Soc Stdies 90-; Deans Lst; Elem Ed; Tch.

**CRAIG, TERRENCE J,** Howard Univ, Washington, DC; SR; BA; Goldn Key 89-; Phi Alpha Theta 90-; Schl Of Cmnctn Trstee Schlrshp 89-; Intrnshp WUSA Sprts Dept 90-; Brdcst Prod; Video/Flm Edtr/Cameramn.

**CRAIG, TONYA L,** Coll Of Charleston, Charleston, SC; SO; BED; Elem Educ; Tchr.

**CRAIG III, WILLIAM B,** Marshall University, Huntington, WV; JR; BA; CCC 90-; PROWL 90-; Var Babl Tm 89-; Southern Conf Athletc Acad Awd 90; All Amer Acad Candte 91; Bsbl Southern Conf Ptchr Wk 91; Mktg; Sls.

**CRAIN, DEREK G,** Morehouse Coll, Atlanta, GA; FR; MEE; UMOJA Brd Chrmn 90-; US Nvl Rsrvs; Natl Scty Blck Eng Brd Mmbr 90-; NSBE Otstndng Mmbr Yr Awrd 90-; Gen Elec Intern; Elec Eng Math; Eng.

**CRALL, KIMBERLY A,** Salisbury St Univ, Salisbury, MD; SR; Amer Mktg Assn Exec VP Membrshp 90-; Phi Beta Lambda 89; Fndrsng Vol United Way 89; Mktg Rsrch Intrnshp 90; AA A Arundel Comm Coll 89; BS; Bus Admin/Mktg.

**CRAM, MARGARET M,** Immaculata Coll, Immaculata, PA; SR; BA; Math Clb Treas 90; Sigma Zeta 90-; Vlybl 90-; Math/Cmptr Sci; Systms Anlys.

**CRAME, MARIA-ELENA NACINOPA,** De Tech & Comm Coll At Dover, Dover, DE; GD; BA; CSI Treas/Secr 89-; Dns Lst 89-; Outstndg 1st Yr Clgte Secrs Intl Secr 89-90; Church Jesus Christ Ltr Day Saints Libr; Cmptr Oper Del Tech Terry Campus 90-; AAS; Hmn Res Appar Dsgn; Fshn Dsgnr.

**CRAMER, CHRISTY M,** Hudson Valley Comm Coll, Troy, NY; SR; BA; Erly Chldhd Clb Mtng Advsr; Acad Hon 89-; Awrd Acad Achvmnt/Ldrshp 89-; Elem Ed/Psychlgy/Soclgy/Tchr/Cnslr.

**CRAMER, COLLEEN M,** Salisbury St Univ, Salisbury, MD; GD; Psi Chi 90; Deans Lst 89-90; Schlr Athlete 89-90; State Lacross Champs 89; Lacrosse 89-90; ; Ba 90; Psychology; Doctorate.

**CRAMER, GRAYCE E,** Indiana Univ Of Pa, Indiana, PA; SR; BSED; Kappa Delta Pi 90-; Provsts Schlr 89-; Dns Lst 89-; Skng Tchg Pos Elem Educ; Elem Educ; Tchg/Wrtg.

**CRAMER, KEVIN E,** Widener Univ, Chester, PA; FR; BA; Phi Delta Theta; Ftbl 90; Chem Engrg.

**CRAMER, RANDY W,** Nova Univ, Ft Lauderdale, FL; GD; MBA; Amer Scty Law Enfrcmnt Trnrs; Detective Cmndr Hernando Cty Shrf Ofc 90-; BA Wstrn IL Un 81; Bus Mgmt; Law Enfrcmnt Admn.

**CRAMER, SUSANNE,** Fl International Univ, Miami, FL; SR; BA; Phi Eta Sigma 86-; Psi Chi 90-; Phi Kappa Phi; Clncl Psychlgy.

**CRAMER, TEDDY T,** Hillsborough Comm Coll, Tampa, FL; SO; Phi Theta Kappa 89-; Engl; Mass Cmmnctns.

**CRAMER, TRACY J,** Tn Temple Univ, Chattanooga, TN; FR; BA; Zeta Tau Rho 90-; Soc Wrk.

**CRAMER, TRACY L,** Univ Of Cincinnati-Clrmnt Coll, Batavia, OH; SO; BA; Ed Clb VP 89-; Chrch Schl Coord 90-; Jr Hgh Yth Grp Advsr 90-; Elem Ed; Tchng.

**CRAMP, BRETT R,** Univ Of Cincinnati, Cincinnati, OH; JR; BFA; Music Theatre.

**CRAMPTON, RITA M,** Le Moyne Coll, Syracuse, NY; SR; JD; Salamander Co Edtr; Sr Show; Chrldr; BA; Sr Ctzns Dinner; Intl House Fst Hngr; English Clb 90-; Soclgy Clb; Pre Law Soc; Choral Soc; Folk Grp; Ski Clb; Pi Gamma Mu 89-; Alpha Kappa Delta 90-; Citzns Schlrshp Awd 90-; Deans Lst; English/Sociology; Law.

**CRANDALL, HEIDI C,** Hudson Valley Comm Coll, Troy, NY; FR; AS; Nrsng/Bio.

**CRANE, ALLISON L,** Univ Of Miami, Coral Gables, FL; SO; BA; Sigma Delta Tau Fnd Rsr Scl Chr 90; Peer Cnslr; Sigma Delta Tau; Hist/Jrnlsm; Law.

**CRANE, ANNA T,** Boston Coll, Chestnut Hill, MA; SR; Natl Stdnt Nrs Assn 89-; Gldn Key 90-; Sigma Theta Tau; Nursng.

**CRANE, BILLY RAY,** Asbury Theological Sem, Wilmore, KY; GD; M DIV; Frgn Lang Clb 84-86; Gtheta Phi 88-; Summa Cum Laude 86; AA KY Mtn Bible Coll 84; BA Asbury Coll 86; Thlgy; Prsh Mnstry/Rlgs Educ.

**CRANEY, KRISANN,** S U N Y Coll At Oswego, Oswego, NY; FR; BS; Hl Cncl Flr Repr 90-; Recycling Comm Pres 90-; Actvts Comm V P 90-; Red Cross Bld Dr 90-; TV Show 90-; Vocal Perf Winterfest 90; Dns Lst 90-; Res Asst; Aerobics Clb 90-; Elem Ed/Math; Tchr.

**CRANFORD, AMY R,** Catawba Valley Comm Coll, Hickory, NC; SO; BA; Comm Art & Adv Design; Graphic Design.

**CRANFORD, JENNIFER A,** Capital Univ, Columbus, OH; SO; BSN; Dnc Tm 90-; Stdnt Ambssdr 89-; Stdnt Affrs Rep 90-; Pi Phi Epsilon Srrty Rep 90-; Chrldr 89-90; Nrsng.

**CRANMER, KYLE P,** East Stroudsburg Univ, E Stroudsburg, PA; SO; BS; ACM Pres 90-; Chess Clb Treas 90-; Hon Prg 89-; Comp Sci/Math; Rsrch Artfcl Intllg.**

**CRAPPS, SUE T,** Univ Of Sc At Columbia, Columbia, SC; SR; BA; Pres Hon Rl 89-; Outstndng Stdnt Midlnds Tech Coll 88; Outstndng Sr USC; Wrkr Bnk; Day Cr Wrkr; Psychlgy; Bus Mgmt.

**CRATER, MINDY S,** Pa St Univ Main Cmps, University Pk, PA; FR; BS; Edn; Elem Tchr.

**CRAUN, MELISSA A,** Univ Of Akron, Akron, OH; FR; BA; Chrch Grp 90-; Dns Lst; Math; Tchr.

**CRAUN, NANEVA W,** Daytona Beach Comm Coll, Daytona Beach, FL; SO; ADN; Vietnam Vetrans Of N Fl Chrmn Pow 90-; Sci; Medicine.

**CRAUSWELL, AMY B,** Univ Of Al At Birmingham, Birmingham, AL; JR; ASSOC; Stdnt Phy Thrpy Org 90-; Phy Thrpst Asst.

**CRAVATT, ANN M,** Univ Of West Fl, Pensacola, FL; JR; BED; Stdnt Cncl For Excptnl Chldrn 90-; U S Jaycees Pensacola Fl Sec 85-; Fed Govt In Ca Buyers Sec; St Of Fl HRS/CMS Dist Perinatl Sec; City Of Pensacola Lib Audio Visual Clrk; Police Dept Idntfctn Clerk D E Operator; Spec Ed LD & EH; Teach.

**CRAVE, SHARON QUINN,** Univ Of West Fl, Pensacola, FL; JR; BA; Phi Theta Kappa 89; USN Vet; AA Pensacola Jr Coll 90; Elem Ed; Teach.

**CRAVEN, GILBERT O,** Univ Of Southern Ms, Hattiesburg, MS; FR; BME; USM Symphnc Wind Ensmbl; USM Jazz Lab Band; Mrchng Band; Phi Mu Alpha Sinfonia; Music Educ.

**CRAVEN, JENNIFER N,** Savannah Coll Of Art & Design, Savannah, GA; SO; Astrnmy Clb 90-; Paintg Clb 90-; Painting; Painter.

**CRAVEN, JEROME D,** Middle Tn St Univ, Murfreesboro, TN; JR; BA; Aerospace Maint; Avtn Tech.

**CRAVEN, MICHAEL J,** Univ Of Ky, Lexington, KY; SR; BA; Psychlgy; Indstrl Org.

**CRAVEN, VALERIE L,** Univ Of Ga, Athens, GA; JR; BSED; Bptst Stdnt Union 88-89; Phi Theta Kappa VP 88; AS Gainesvil Clg 90; Erly Chldhd Ed; Tchng K/4.

**CRAVER, TRINA M,** Columbia Greene Comm Coll, Hudson, NY; FR; Bus.

**CRAVER, ZACHERY J,** Columbia Greene Comm Coll, Hudson, NY; FR; AOS; Vars Bsktbl Capt 90-; Sci/Hstry; Engr.

**CRAVEY, DANA A,** Valdosta St Coll, Valdosta, GA; SO; Antioch Church Asst RA 89-; Treas Lcl Church RA Grp 88-; Sprts Med/Educ; Athltc Trng/Clncl.

**CRAWFORD, AUNDREA L,** Univ Of Southern Ms, Hattiesburg, MS; SO; Hlth Sci; Nrsng.

**CRAWFORD, BRENT D,** Southern St Comm Coll, Sardinia, OH; FR; BA; Png Png Sftbl Bsktbl; Sci; Comp Eng.

**CRAWFORD JR, CARL W,** East Tn St Univ, Johnson City, TN; FR; BS; Deans Lst 90; Outstndng Comp Sci Frshmn 90-; Comp Sci.

**CRAWFORD, CAROL ANN,** Marymount Manhattan Coll, New York, NY; SR; MA; Natl Clgt Hons Cncl 90-; Asst Dir MMC Gallery 88-; Guest Artist MMC Dance Dept; Prfsnl Ballet Dncr With Dance Theatre Harlem 78-88; Cert Dance Theatre Harlem 86; Art Ed; Entrprnr.

**CRAWFORD, CAROLYN A,** Western New England Coll, Springfield, MA; SR; BSBA; Acctg Assn 89-90; Deans Lst 89-90; Acctg; Tax Law.

**CRAWFORD, CAROLYN BURLESO,** Memphis St Univ, Memphis, TN; SR; BED; Chldrns Cncl 89-; Surg Nurs; AS Univ Ark 77; Ele Educ; Tch.

**CRAWFORD, CHRISTINE L,** Indiana Univ Of Pa, Indiana, PA; SO; BED; Res Hall Assn Wing R Ep 89-90; Cmpus Compact 89-; Kappa Delta Pi 89-; Cir K Intl Pres 90-; Wmn Stdnt Ldrshp Awd 90-; Schlrshp 90; Provost Schlr 90; Biology Educ; Tch Sec Sch.

**CRAWFORD, CRAIG A,** George Mason Univ, Fairfax, VA; SO; BA; Bus; Ins.

**CRAWFORD, DIANNE D,** Univ Of Sc At Columbia, Columbia, SC; SO; BA; AAS Tri Cnty Tec 73.

**CRAWFORD, DONNA L,** Johnson C Smith Univ, Charlotte, NC; SO; BA; Soc Opport Sci Clb Treas 89-; Friends Ensmbl Gospel Chorus Chpln 89-90; Frshmn Hnrs 89-90; Bio; Ph D Cell Bio.

**CRAWFORD, DOUG R,** Embry Riddle Aeronautical Univ, Daytona Beach, FL; SR; BS; Aviatn Tech; Aircrft Maint.

**CRAWFORD, EDNA D,** Univ Of Tn At Martin, Martin, TN; SR; BS; Beta Alpha Psi 81-82; Zeta Tau Alpha 74-76; Bus Admin Mgmnt.

**CRAWFORD, EDWARD E,** Univ Of Sc At Columbia, Columbia, SC; FR; BA; Sci; Aerospace Eng.

**CRAWFORD, FARLEY C,** Central Fl Comm Coll, Ocala, FL; FR; AA; Electronics; Electronics Eng.

**CRAWFORD, FLO A,** Wv Univ At Parkersburg, Parkersburg, WV; FR; BA; Chrch; Girl Scts; Beautician 66; Engl; Mnstry.

**CRAWFORD, GLENN A,** Ky Christian Coll, Grayson, KY; FR; BS; Led Mddl Grds Engl Schl Stds.

**CRAWFORD, GLYNNIS M,** Fayetteville St Univ, Fayetteville, NC; JR; BS; Non Trad Stdnts Orgnztn 90; Bus Admn; Mktg Mgr/Rep.

**CRAWFORD, JACK J,** S U N Y Coll Of Tech At Alfred, Alfred, NY; FR; Babe Ruth Bsbl Coach 90-; Bus; Acctg.

**CRAWFORD, JENIFER L,** S U N Y Coll Of Tech At Alfred, Alfred, NY; FR; AS; Agrcltr; Flr Mrchndsng.

**CRAWFORD, JOHN ROBERT,** Western Ky Univ, Bowling Green, KY; SR; BA; Phi Kappa Phi; Mass Cmmnctns/Psyc; Tchng.

**CRAWFORD, JOSEPH D,** Embry Riddle Aeronautical Univ, Daytona Beach, FL; SO; BA; Sailing Clb 90-; Alpha Eta Rho VP; Aeronautical Sci; Flight/Pilot.

**CRAWFORD, JOSEPH R,** Kent St Univ Kent Cmps, Kent, OH; JR; BA; Golden Key; Hnrbl Mntn All Mid Amer Cnfrnce; Acad All Mid Amr Cnfrnce; Vrsty Bsbl 88-; Finance/Bus Mngmnt; Finance.

**CRAWFORD, JUANITA G,** Va St Univ, Petersburg, VA; SO; Political Science; Law.

**CRAWFORD, KELLEY L,** Saint Joseph Coll, West Hartford, CT; SR; BS; Dance Clb Grp Prsdnt 87-; Amnsty Intrntnl Tres 89-; Chld Stdy Clb 89-; Deans Lst 88-91; Elem Edctn.**

**CRAWFORD, KRISTIN R,** Radford Univ, Radford, VA; FR; MBA; Comm Disorders; Spch Lang Pthlgst.

**CRAWFORD, LEAH G,** Lexington Comm Coll, Lexington, KY; FR; AAT; AIAS 90-; KSA CSI Trdshws; NAWIC Schlrshp Awd 90-; Architecture Tech; Cvl Eng/Bldg Const.

**CRAWFORD, MARCELLA T,** Ashland Comm Coll, Ashland, KY; FR; ABA; Cnty Oldtimers Brkfst Clb Sec/Treas 88-; Natl Mgmnt Assn 80-; March Of Dimes 86-87; Jnr Achvmnt Advsr 75; KY W Va Gas Co 78-90; Bus Admin.

**CRAWFORD, MEGAN A,** Univ Of South Fl, Tampa, FL; FR; BA; IM Vlybl/Sftbl Capt 90-; Themis; Univ Hon Prog; Russian.

**CRAWFORD, MEREDITH J,** Coll Of Charleston, Charleston, SC; FR; BA; French/German; Intl Bus.

**CRAWFORD, NANCY L,** Indiana Univ Of Pa, Indiana, PA; JR; Elem Educ.

**CRAWFORD, PRISCILLA A,** Atlantic Comm Coll, Mays Landing, NJ; SO; AA; Chld Dev/Educ; Preschl Dir/Tchr.

**CRAWFORD, ROSALYNN Y,** Jackson St Univ, Jackson, MS; FR; BA; Bptst Stdnt Un; Yng Scntsts Pgm; Alpha Lambda Delta; Blgy/Predntstry; Orthdntst.

**CRAWFORD, SHAWN W,** Memphis St Univ, Memphis, TN; FR; BS; Engr Tech; Engr.

**CRAWFORD, STEPHEN J,** Univ Of Sc At Columbia, Columbia, SC; FR; BS; By Scts Amer Egle Sct 82-; Crim Just; Law Enfrcmnt.

**CRAWFORD, THEODORE B,** Univ Of Nc At Charlotte, Charlotte, NC; SR; MA; Nc Real Est Lic 88-; UPS 87-; BA 90; Geogrphy; Real Est Devlpmnt.

**CRAWFORD, TIFFANEY A,** Alcorn St Univ, Lorman, MS; JR; BA; Engl Educ; Tchr.

**CRAWLEY, ADRIENE R,** Norfolk St Univ, Norfolk, VA; SR; BA; AERHO 88-89; Resdnt Asst 89; Mass Cmnctns; Publc Rltns.

**CRAWLEY, DWIGHT E,** Hampton Univ, Hampton, VA; FR; BA; Chr 90-; Blgy; Med.

**CRAYCRAFT, KELLY J,** Westminster Coll, New Wilmingtn, PA; JR; BA; Cncrt Pp Bnds Lbrrn 89-; Estblshd Srvce Tms 88-; Rsdnt Lfe Stff 89-; Kappa Delta Pi; Alpha Phi Omega Rcrdng Sec 89-; Estblshd Srvce Tms Ttrng; Tchng Asst 4th Grde; Elem Educ; Tchng.

**CRAYTON, AUDLEY L,** Al A & M Univ, Normal, AL; SR; Intrntl Stdnt Assn Clb Act Asst 88-; Hon Roll; Deans Lst; Chrch Comm Svcs; Prntg Prdctn/Mgt.

**CRAZE, CAROLINE C,** Univ Of Nc At Charlotte, Charlotte, NC; SR; BA; Yng Rpblcns; ETC Magazine Features Edtr; Englsh; Cpywrtng Edtng.

**CREA, ANDREA A,** Rivier Coll, Nashua, NH; FR; BED; Adm Cmte 90-; Deans Lst 90-; Proj Hug 90-; Educ.

**CREAGER, ROBERT MICHAEL,** Western Ky Univ, Bowling Green, KY; SO; BS; Bus Econ.

**CREAMER, DAVID W,** S U N Y At Buffalo, Buffalo, NY; JR; BS; Schussmeisters Ski Clb 89-; Delta Sigma Pi VP Prof Actvts 90-; IM Ftbl 88-90; Business; Finance.

**CREAMER, JOHN W,** Tallahassee Comm Coll, Tallahassee, FL; JR; Pres Awrd 90; Dns Lst 90; AA 90; Crmnlgy; Law.

**CREARY, HILARY A,** Broward Comm Coll, Ft Lauderdale, FL; FR; AA; Food Mrchndsr 85-; AS Alphacomm Coll Jamaica 81; Law.

**CREARY, PAULINE H A,** Morgan St Univ, Baltimore, MD; SR; BS; Econ Clb Pres 89-; Stdnt Rep Fac Stdnt Com Sch Bus Mgmnt 90-; Pi Gamma Mu; Omicron Delta Epsilon Pres; Four Yr Schlrshp Natwest Trust Corp Bahamas Ltd; Emplymnt Natwest Trust Corp Bahamas Ltd 80-87; Smr/Chrstms Emplymnt 87-90; Econ; Invstmnt Banking/Trust.

**CRECENTE, BRIAN D,** Anne Arundel Comm Coll, Arnold, MD; SO; BA; Stu Nwsppr Bus Mgr 89-; Stu Lit Mag Co Edtr 90-; Stu Assn Rep 89-; Otstndng Stu Ldrshp Awrd; AA; Jrnlsm/Nws/Edtrl/Photo.

**CREDE, SUSAN M,** Saint Francis Coll, Loretto, PA; JR; BA; Plus 1 88-; Scl Wrk Clb Sec 88-; Adpt/Grndprnt 88-; Alpha Delta Mu; Scl Wrk.

**CREECH, JIMMY L,** Wilmington Coll, New Castle, DE; SO; BA; American Heart Assn Instr; Bsn Mgmt.

**CREED, JAMES L,** Atlantic Comm Coll, Mays Landing, NJ; SO; AAS; Phi Theta Kappa 90-; Stdnt Red Phys Thrpy; Phys Thrpy Asst.

**CREEK, JENNIFER L,** Univ Of Southern Ms, Hattiesburg, MS; JR; BS; AS 90; Spch/Lang Pathology.

**CREEK, KELLY S,** Middle Tn St Univ, Murfreesboro, TN; SO; BS; Math; Tchng.

**CREEKMORE, DEBORAH A,** Al A & M Univ, Normal, AL; SR; BA; Vol Fire Dept; NYSP; PTA; YMCA/SFTBL Coach; Hist/Pol Sci; Tchr.

**CREEKS, STACEY L,** West Liberty St Coll, West Liberty, WV; SO; Bnd 89-; 4h 89-90; Scndry Educ; Tch.

**CREEL, ANDREA B,** Wallace St Comm Coll At Hncvll, Hanceville, AL; FR; BA; Psych; Adol Psych.

**CREEL, DONALD J,** Univ Of Al At Birmingham, Birmingham, AL; SR; BS; Amer Assoc Rsprtry Thrpst 86-; Pblshd Ribaviria 90; Perinatal/Pediatric Update Resptry Thrpst 90; Miss Scty Rsptry Thrpst Anl Sem 90; Quarterly In Hs Prstns Rsprtry Updates RN/PHYSCNS; Crtcl Cr Trnsprt Tm; Allied Hlth Admin; Dept Dir/Admin Hosp.

**CREER, DEBRA,** Ms Gulf Coast Comm Coll, Perkinston, MS; SO; BS; Min Ldrshp Soc 90-; Nursing; Sci.

**CREGAR, DAYNA L,** William Paterson Coll, Wayne, NJ; SR; BA; Math Clb Treas 86-89; Stdnt Act Pgmng Brd 89-; Math Educ.

**CREHAN, DENNIS L,** Roanoke Bible Coll, Elizabeth Cy, NC; JR; BS; BS Soclgy Towson State Univ Balt MD 76; Biblical Studies; Prchr.

**CREIGHTON, DENISE L,** George Mason Univ, Fairfax, VA; SO; BS; Bus; Dcsn Sci.

**CRELL, TESS,** Commonwealth Coll, Virginia Beach, VA; GD; BED; Ofc Admn Club Pres 90-; Clgt Secrtrs Intrntl BA Beach Campus Pres 90-; Alpha Beta Gamma 90-; Profsnl Secrtrs Intrntl 90-; Paralegal.

**CREMENS, PAMELA C,** Lesley Coll, Cambridge, MA; JR; BED; Girl Sct Brownie Ldr 90-; Lesely Coll Acdmc Excllnc Awd 90; YMCA Pres Awd 90; Spec Ed; Tch.

**CREMO, JULIA M,** Indiana Univ Of Pa, Indiana, PA; SR; BS; Assn Rhblttn Advcts Pres 90-; Rehab; Rehab Cnslr.

**CRENSHAW, ANJANETTE D,** Tuskegee Univ, Tuskegee Inst, AL; JR; BS; Natl Soc Black Engrs 89-90; Alpha Kappa Mu 90-; Alpha Phi Alpha Sweetheart Court 90-; Eastman Kodak Scholar 88-; Track Cross Cntry 88-89 90-; Elec Engrng/Physics.

**CRENSHAW, BILLY J,** Chattahoochee Vly St Comm Coll, Phenix City, AL; SO; AD; Natl Fire Protctn Assn 90; Field Instrctr Ga State Fire Acdmy 83; Prmtd Suppression; Lt 90; Fire Sci; Fire Admin.

**CRENSHAW, CYNTHIA K,** Queens Coll, Charlotte, NC; SO; BA; Chmbr Sngrs; Chorale; Order Of Omega; Pres Cncl; Delta Omicron; Kappa Delta Sng Ldr 89-90; Chld Abuse Fndrsng; NCMTA Convention Soloist 90-; Charlotte Wmns Clb Schlrshp Awd; B-Ball Natl Anthm; Music Educ; Tch H S Chorus.

**CRENSHAW, KELI A,** Ms Gulf Coast Comm Coll, Perkinston, MS; FR; Cncrt/Mrchng Band Sctn Ldr 90-; Delta Clb 90-; Phi Theta Kappa 90-; Electrical Eng.

**CRENSHAW, LINETTE A,** Va St Univ, Petersburg, VA; FR; BS; TAP; Pre-Law Soc; ROTC; Color Guard E4; Alumni Schlrshp; Dns Lst 90-; Corp Allied/Signal Matching Gift Schlrshp; Pol Sci; FBI.

**CRENSHAW, REDERICA A,** Saint Pauls Coll, Lawrenceville, VA; FR; Bus Admin.

**CRESAP, ELIZABETH ANNE,** Oh St Univ At Marion, Marion, OH; JR; BA; AA 90; Art Ed/Psychlgy; Ed/Thrpy.

**CRESCENZI, LISA J,** Hillsborough Comm Coll, Tampa, FL; JR; BA; Math Edn; Scndry Edn.

**CRESCI, CHRISTINA M,** Kent St Univ Kent Cmps, Kent, OH; SR; BA; Alpha Kappa Delta 90-; Pi Gamma Mu 90-; Gldn Key 90-; Lrnsg Dvlpmnt Ctr Mth Ttr 89-; Sclgy; Law.

**CRESPO LA SALLE, DANIEL,** Univ Politecnica De Pr, Hato Rey, PR; FR; Indtl Engrg.

**CRESPO, MYRIAM,** Univ Of Pr At Rio Piedras, Rio Piedras, PR; JR; BA; Golden Key Soc 89-; Intrntl Aikido Fed 90-; US Aikido Fed 90-; Hon Pgm 89-; Mcrobio Lab Asst 88-; Bio; Med Career.

**CRESWELL, A MICHELLE H,** Univ Of Tn At Martin, Martin, TN; SR; BA; STEA 88-; Phi Eta Sigma; Phi Kappa Phi 90-; Gooch Schlrshp 88-89; Charles Vaughn Schlrshp 90-; Edn; Teach.**

**CRESWELL, LAURA A,** Mary Baldwin Coll, Staunton, VA; JR; BA; Fine Arts Assoc Pr 88-; RA; Theatre; E Nottingham Arts Hon Soc 90-; Omicron Delta Kappa VP; Museum Reg NY Cooper Hewitt 90; Clctns Asst 89; Museum Educ Woodrow Wilson Birthplace; Arts Mngmnt; Museum Curator.

**CRESWELL, PAUL A,** Piedmont Tech Coll, Greenwood, SC; SO; AS; Deans Lst 90; Elctrnc Eng.

**CREW, LAURA E,** Ms St Univ, Miss State, MS; JR; BA; Band 89-90; Alpha Lambda Delta 89-; Gamma Beta Phi 89-; Psych; Wrk With Hndcppd Chldrn.

**CREWS MURDY, VICTORIA L,** Univ Of Southern Ms, Hattiesburg, MS; SR; BSW; Cert Act Trvl Schl 88; Cert Barbizon Schl Of Mdlng 86; Scl Wrk.

**CREWS, BRANDI R,** Waycross Coll, Waycross, GA; SO; AA; Stdnt Nwsppr 89-; Aux Entrprs Comm 90; Phi Theta Kappa; Trnsfr Schlrshp To Brewton Parker Coll; Psychlgy; Chld Cnslg.

**CREWS, CAROL L,** Kent St Univ Kent Cmps, Kent, OH; SR; BA; Prog Stdnt Ntwrk 87-89; Stdnts For Peace Pres 88; Golden Key; Crtve Stdnt Awd 87; Sherri Jo Luft Mem Awd 88-89; Ctr For Intrntl Ed Exchnge Wrkcmp Grp Ldr 87; Anthrplgy; Ntrl Sci Illstrtn.

**CREWS, CINDY Q,** Vance Granville Comm Coll, Henderson, NC; GD; AAS; Phi Theta Kappa 90-; Pres Merit Awd; Self Emplyd Farmer 77-; Bus Admin; Accntnt Frm Bks/Tchr.

**CREWS, CINDY R,** Radford Univ, Radford, VA; SO; BED; Hs Cncl; Educ; Spec Ed Tchr.

**CREWS, GWYNDOLYN ANNE,** Marshall University, Huntington, WV; SR; BA; Blck Un Stdts; Delta Sigma Theta Pres 88-90; MURAL Vol 89-; LEAD; Stdnt Asst Corp Of Engrs 89-90; Dns Lst 87-90; Educ.

**CREWS, JANET GAYLE,** Vance Granville Comm Coll, Henderson, NC; FR; BA; Phi Theta Kappa; Clg Trnsfr Schlr; Ed; Tchng.

**CREWS, JENNIFER Q,** Al St Univ, Montgomery, AL; JR; BA; Soc Advncmnt Mgt VP 90-; Natl Outstndng Clg Stdnts Am 89-; Phi Eta Sigma 88-; Delta Mu Delta Sec; Alpha Kappa Mu; Phi Mu Alpha Chpln 89-90; VITA; Acctg; CPA.

**CREWS, KIMBERLY J,** Univ Of Tn At Martin, Martin, TN; JR; BS; STEA 90-91; Tri Beta; Sec Ed.

**CREWS, LEONARD J,** Inter Amer Univ Pr Hato Rey, Hato Rey, PR; FR; BA; Hstry; Acctg.

**CREWS, REBECCA L,** Middle Tn St Univ, Murfreesboro, TN; SR; BS; Outstndg Stdnt Qlty Cntrl; Eng Tech; Eng.

**CREWS, TYNIA M,** Univ Of Southern Ms, Hattiesburg, MS; JR; BS; Amer Mktg Assn 90-; Dixie Darlings Dance Tm 88-; Stdnt Alumni Assn 88-; Lambda Sigma 89-90; Kappa Delta Sec 90-,Schlrshp 89-90; Drg Alcohol Awrns Wks 89-; PGA Annual Golf Clsc; USM Ldrshp Schlrshp 88-89; Dns Lst 88-; IM Vlybl Sftbl Bdmtn; Mktg.

**CRIBB, EMILY M,** Fl International Univ, Miami, FL; SR; BBA; Acctg Assoc 90-; Beta Gamma Sigma; Natl Dns Lst 89-90; Acctg; CPA.

**CRICHTON, DAVID R,** Tn Temple Univ, Chattanooga, TN; SR; Children Ministries 87-; Res Asst 89-; Phi Phi Phi 90-; Ministerial.

**CRICHTON, PATRICIA M A,** Coll Of Charleston, Charleston, SC; JR; BA; French; Transltn.

**CRIDDLE, JOEY W,** Itawamba Comm Coll, Fulton, MS; FR; Neumo Tai 90-; Respiratory Therapy; Medicine.

**CRIDDLE, JULIE A,** Ms St Univ, Miss State, MS; SO; BA; DPMA; Fin Svcs Comm; Alpha Lambda Delta; Retail Mgmt; Bsn Infor Sys; Cmptr Analysis.

**CRIDER, MICHAEL D,** Old Dominion Univ, Norfolk, VA; GD; Tau Alpha Pi 89-90; Gldn Key 89-90; EIT Exam 90; AAS Blue Ridge Comm Clg 88; AA/S Blue Ridge Comm Clg 87; BS Elect Eng Tech; Mstrs Elect Eng.

**CRIGLER, HEIDI D,** Radford Univ, Radford, VA; SO; Phi Sigma Pi; Spts Med; Phys Thrpy.**

**CRILLY, ANNEMARIE,** Kings Coll, Wilkes-Barre, PA; FR; BS; Hon Prog 90-; Ele Educ; Tch.

**CRIM, DAVID E,** Univ Of Al At Huntsville, Huntsville, AL; SO; BS; Stdnt Aide NASA; Elec Eng.

**CRIPE, PATRICIA S,** Antonelli Inst Of Art & Photo, Cincinnati, OH; GD; Alpha Beta Kappa Soc; Assoc Degree Intr Dsgn Antonelli Inst Of Art Phtgrphy.

**CRISAFULLI, TIMOTHY P,** Le Moyne Coll, Syracuse, NY; FR; BA; Hstry.

**CRISCI, ALESANDRA,** Albertus Magnus Coll, New Haven, CT; SO; BA; Art Clb Tr 88; Bookkeeper/ Bartending PT 88-; Psych/Tchr.

**CRISCUOLO, DAVID S,** Neumann Coll, Aston, PA; FR; BA; Slghtn Schl Tutoring 90-; Schl Nwspr 90-; Hnrs 90-; Engl; Tch Hgh Schl.

**CRISCUOLO, NANCY ANN,** Neumann Coll, Aston, PA; SR; BA; Prffnl Educ Scty Treas 87-; Psychlgy Clb 87-; Deans Honor List; Elem/Early Childhood Educ; Teaching.

**CRISCUOLO, RITA J,** Erie Comm Coll, Buffalo, NY; SR; Chld Care Clb 90; NAYECE; AAS Chld Care.

**CRISP, JAMES W,** Owensboro Comm Coll, Owensboro, KY; SO; BA; Anthropology Clb Pres 88-89; Sci Clb 88-; Scty Physics Stdnts 90-; Discipline Awrd Anthropology 90; Discipline Awrd Art; Assoc In Arts 89-90; Assoc In Sci 90-; Architecture.

**CRISP, KIMBERLY R,** Middle Tn St Univ, Murfreesboro, TN; SO; Human Sci; Foods/Nutrition.

**CRISP, MITZI M,** Alice Lloyd Coll, Pippa Passes, KY; SR; BA; Sr Cls Ofcr Sec/Treas 90-; Kappa Delta Epsilon 89-; Deans Lst 88-90; Dstngshd Deans Lst 90-; Math/Eng; Teach.

**CRISP, RHONDA A,** Winthrop Coll, Rock Hill, SC; FR; BS; Alpha Lambda Delta Treas 90-; Math; Tchng.

**CRISPELL, VALERIE J,** Nassau Comm Coll, Garden City, NY; FR; BS; Hon Clb 90-; Theater Clb 90-; Math/Sci; Med Rcrds Admin.

**CRISPIN, WENDY A,** S U N Y Coll At Fredonia, Fredonia, NY; SO; BA; Sclgy/Anthrplgy Clb 90-; Birth Cntrl Infrmtns Cntr 90-; Ldrshp Dvlpmnt Prog 89-; Dean Lst 89-; Share Care Fmly 89-90; BCIC 90-; Cmmnty Srvc Affltd Chrch 89-; IM 89-; Sclgy/Crmnl Jstc; Law.

**CRISS, DONALD R,** Wv Univ At Parkersburg, Parkersburg, WV; FR; MS; Geology; Earth Scie.

**CRISSINGER, MICHELE L,** Kent St Univ Kent Cmps, Kent, OH; JR; BA; Intrntnl Film Soc VP 88-90; Alpha Lambda Delta; Englsh; Rsrch Pblshng Edtng.

**CRISSMAN, FAE M,** Univ Of Sc At Columbia, Columbia, SC; FR; BS; Cmps Cltn Ltrcy 90-; Air Frc ROTC 90-; Emrgng Ldr 90; Alpha Lambda Delta; Gamma Beta Phi; Phi Eta Sigma; Assn Hon Stdnts 90-; Air Frc ROTC Smstr; Math; Law.

**CRISSMAN, MICHELLE D,** Univ Of Pittsburgh, Pittsburgh, PA; SO; SAE 87-; USACM; Alcoa Tech Cntr 85-; Stff Tech Anlyst; Cvl Eng Applctns; Assoc Triangle Institute Of Technology 83; Math And Sci; Eng Cvl.

**CRISTE, THOMAS P,** Saint Francis Coll, Loretto, PA; JR; BS; Acctg Club Sec 89-; Delta Sigma Phi 89-; ACFC Academic Elite Team 89-90; Ftbl 88-; Acctg; Cpa.

**CRITCHER JR, JOSEPH D,** Va Highlands Comm Coll, Abingdon, VA; SO; AAS; Law Enfrcmnt Clb 89-; Choir 90-; Phi Theta Kappa 90-; Pol Sci; Law Enfrcmnt Ofcr.

**CRITE, DEBORAH A,** Nc Agri & Tech St Univ, Greensboro, NC; GD; Delta Sigma Theta Pres 86-87; BA Elon Clg 87.

**CRIVELLO, FRANCES M,** City Univ Of Ny Baruch Coll, New York, NY; JR; BBA; Italian Soc 88-; Finc Econ Soc 90-; Mktg Mgmt; Mgmt.

**CROAK, MICHELE L,** Western Carolina Univ, Cullowhee, NC; JR; BSW; Flwshp Of Chrstn Athlts 90-; Soc Wrk Clb 90-; Stdnt Orientatn Ldr; Alpha Xi Delta Sor Rtl Chrmn 88-; Pi Kappa Alpha Rtl Chrmn 88-; Yth-At-Rsk Vlntr Prog 90-; Psychtrc Hosp Intrnshp 90; Chrldr/Ftbl Bsktbl 88-91-; Soc Wrk; Ma Soc Wrk.

**CROALGARRAWAY, EILEEN C,** City Univ Of Ny Baruch Coll, New York, NY; JR; BA; Dipl Agric Univ Guyana 75; Acctg.

**CROCCO, LORI A,** Embry Riddle Aeronautical Univ, Daytona Beach, FL; FR; BS; Aviation Bus Admin; Profl Pilot.

**CROCE, JENNIFER C,** Univ Of Cincinnati, Cincinnati, OH; JR; BED; Campus Crusade For Chrst Ldrshp Tm 86-90; Gldn Key; Hnr Stdnt Assn 86-; Kappa Delta Pi 90-; Dns Lst 86-90; Univ Hnrs Prog 86-88; Schlrshp Rcpnt 85-; Math/Speech; Tchr.

**CROCE, MATTHEW A,** Rutgers St Un At New Brunswick, New Brunswick, NJ; SO; BS; Biology; Medicine.**

**CROCENELLI, THERESA M,** Allegheny Coll, Meadville, PA; SO; BS; Chorus Womens Ens 89-; Allies Spec Visits Chm 90-; Lambda Sigma Ritual Chm 90-; Alpha Gamma Delta Standards Chm 90-; Barry Goldwater Schlrshp; Summer Undergrad Rsrch Univ Of Pittsburgh; IM Vlybl 89; Chem; Med MD.

**CROCKER, AGNES J,** William Carey Coll, Hattiesburg, MS; JR; BSN; Nrsg.

**CROCKER, ANGELIQUE M,** Pa St Univ Erie-Behrend Coll, Erie, PA; FR; BA; Alpha Sigma Alpha Asst Edtr Elect; Acctng; CPA.

**CROCKER, CHARLES E,** Emmanuel Coll Schl Chrstn Min, Franklin Sprg, GA; SR; MA; Sngrs 87-90; Co Cptn IM Tm 89-90; Gerald Atkinson Mem Schlrshp 89; Exclnc Wrtn Eng Awd 89; Pstrng Woodburn Bptst Chrc; AA 87-89; BA 89-; Thlgy/Biblical Lng; Pstr.

**CROCKER, DEBORAH C,** Univ Of South Al, Mobile, AL; SR; BA; SCEC; Phi Kappa Phi; Alpha Chi ; Kappa Delta Pi; Spcl Edn; Teach.

**CROCKER, EUGENIA A,** Limestone Coll, Gaffney, SC; SR; BA; Bsktbl Capt 87-90; Untd Blck Std 89-90; Chrkee Cnty DSS Intshp; BA; Scl Work; Chldrns Prtctv Serv.

**CROCKER, JONATHAN L,** Fl International Univ, Miami, FL; SO; BA; Bus; Acctg.

**CROCKER, KERI H,** Univ Of Montevallo, Montevallo, AL; SR; BA; German Clb; SGA Sntr 89; Intl/Intercultural Clb; Alpha Gamma Delta Act Chmn 87-88; German Wrk Pgm Intrnshp; European Travel Intrnshp; Coll Night Purple Wmns Athletic Ldr 90-; Intl/Intercultural Studies; Masters Edn.

**CROCKER, LISA A,** Clemson Univ, Clemson, SC; JR; BS; SCRPA 90-; Hort Club; Deans List; Intern U S Fish Hatchery; Intrnshp U S Army Corps Of Engrs; Intern S C Wildlife & Marine Res 90-; Parks Rcrtn Trsm Mgmt; Resource Mgmt.

**CROCKER, PATRICIA A,** Christian Brothers Univ, Memphis, TN; SO; Acct.

**CROCKER, ROBERT MITCHELL,** Univ Of South Al, Mobile, AL; JR; BA; Ala Bowhntrs Assoc 90-; Natl Rifle Assoc 87-; Const Paper Ind 87-87; Res Chldcare Orphaned Neg Abused Childrn 87-; Bus Mngmt; Cnsltng.

**CROCKER, STACEY L,** Univ Of Louisville, Louisville, KY; SO; MENG; Scty Of Wmn Engs 90-; Amer Inst Of Chem Engs 90-; Phi Eta Sigma 89-; Intrn Ashlnd Oil Inc; Chem Eng; Cntrl Systms Eng.

**CROCKETT, JENNIFER L,** Univ Of Tn At Martin, Martin, TN; SO; BFA; Flr Sen Hsng Assn 89-90; Natl Thespian 87-; Alpha Omega; Alpha Phi Omega 90-; Asst Dorm Brwng Hall Yng Art Awd 89-; Fine/Perf Arts; Dir Actng Career.

**CROCKETT, KRISTEN A,** Cornell Univ, Ithaca, NY; FR; BS; Habitat For Hmnty; Wmns Crew Rwng Tm 90; Bus Mgmt; Mktg Exec.

**CROCKETT, RAYMOND L,** Marshall University, Huntington, WV; FR; Sprgfst Fshn Comm Co Chr; Educ Fair Asst Coord; Deans Lst 90-; Erickson Alumni Ctr; Hlth Care Mgmnt/Law; Hosp Admin/Lawyer.

**CROCKETT, REBECCA A,** Coll Of Charleston, Charleston, SC; FR; BA; Business; Investment Broker/Banker.

**CROFT, DENETRESS Y,** Jackson St Univ, Jackson, MS; SO; BA; Alpha Lambda Delta 89-; Acdmc Schlrshp 89-; Bus.

**CROFT, IVAN A,** Davis & Elkins Coll, Elkins, WV; FR; BA; Theatre Set Dsgn/Creation 90-; Intrcol Var Sccr Trvlg Squad 90-; Psych; Hmn Rsrc Mgmt.

**CROFT, TAMMY R,** Central Fl Comm Coll, Ocala, FL; SO; AA; Phi Theta Kappa 91-; Envrnmentl Hygn; Envrmntl Sfty.

**CROLLEY, BEVERLY C,** Univ Of Sc At Columbia, Columbia, SC; JR; BA; Student Ed Club 89-; Kappa Delta Pi; Acad Schlrshp 89-; Licensed Prac Nurse 83-; AA Univ SC 90; Licensed Prat Nurse Lancaster Schl Practical Nrsng 83; Early Childhood Ed; Tchr.

**CROMER, ANGELA L,** Bridgewater Coll, Bridgewater, VA; JR; BS; Stdnt Snte 90-; Alpha Chi 90-; Daystdnt Orgztn Pres 89-; Stdnt Cnslrs 88-; Alpha Chi 90-; Lambda Soc 89-; Clg Alumni Assn Sr Schlrshp; Educ/Biology; Tch.

**CROMER, SABRINA R,** Hampton Univ, Hampton, VA; FR; BS; Chem Clb 90-; Afrcn Stds Clstr 90-; Nnew Generatns 90-; Offc Navl Res; Chem; Psychtry.

**CROMPTON, DAVID C,** Worcester St Coll, Worcester, MA; FR; BS; Rado Asst Prmtn Dir 90-; Psychlgy; Tchr.

**CROMPTON, KATHRYN E,** Tn Temple Univ, Chattanooga, TN; FR; AA; Campus Quest 90; Sign Lang Intrprtr; Spec Educ.

**CROMPTON, LINDY,** Lexington Comm Coll, Lexington, KY; GD; RN; BA FL Presbyterian/Eckerd Clg 74; Nrsg.

**CROMWELL, ELIZABETH J,** Central Fl Comm Coll, Ocala, FL; SO; ADN; Stdnt Nrs Assn; Phi Theta Kappa; Comm Schlrs; Pres Lst 90; Deans Lst; Wmns Prgnancy Cntr Stff Cnslr Vol 89; Nrsng.

**CRON, DIANE V,** Univ Of Nc At Greensboro, Greensboro, NC; SO; BA; Music/Psych; Psychlgst.

**CRON, ROBERT L,** Bowling Green St Univ, Bowling Green, OH; JR; BA; Stdnt Cnstrctn Mgmnt Assn 90-; Rudolf Libbe Cnstrctn Mgmt Tchnlgy Schlrshp; Frmr Vlntr Fireman; Cnstr Industry Cvl Eng 86-90; AAS Edison St Comm Clg 90; Tchnlgy; Cnstrctn Tchnlgy.

**CRONEMILLER, KRISTEN L,** Indiana Univ Of Pa, Indiana, PA; SR; BS; Bkbl Schlrshp 87-; Proj Stride Tutor 89-90; Bkbl Capt 89; Ele Educ; Tch.

**CRONIN, ANN M,** Marymount Manhattan Coll, New York, NY; SR; BBA; Stdnt Gvrnmnt Advsr 89-; Wld Lng Islnd Nassau Comm Clg VP 88-90; Deans Lst; Accnt Exctv Advrtsng Prmtn NBC NY; Bsns Mgmt; Nrsng.

**CRONIN, MICHELLE R,** Le Moyne Coll, Syracuse, NY; SO; BA; Liberty Prtnrshp Pgm 90-; Engl/Cmnctns/Edn; Write Mag/Nwspr/Teach.

**CRONIN-GERVAIS, BRIAN J,** Daytona Beach Comm Coll, Daytona Beach, FL; JR; Amsty Intl Green Peace; Phoenx Soc; Env Anti Terrosts; Dns Lst; Pres Lst 89-; Soc; Tchng/Res/Corp.

**CRONK, CALVIN P,** Newbury Coll, Brookline, MA; SR; Boston Area Bicycle Coalition; Boston Area Serv Commt Serv Rep 90-; Boston Area Serv Commt Asst Secty; Deans List 90; Vtm Era Veteram; Computer Sci; Software Engrg.**

**CRONK, ROBERT J,** Univ Of Rochester, Rochester, NY; JR; BA; Otng Clb Treas 90-; Cinma Grp Chrmn; PEW Mdwst Sci Cmp; Putnam Math Compt; Math; Bsns.

**CROOK, ANDREW J,** Brown Univ, Providence, RI; FR; BS; Cmps Wrk Frc Sprvsr 90-; Pgm Lbrl Medcl Educ 90-; Theta Dlt Chi 90-; Bsktbl 90-; Bio; Medcn Pedtrcs.

**CROOK, RHONDA G,** Liberty Univ, Lynchburg, VA; SR; BS; Mrchng Bd 87-89; Liberty Assn Chrstn Tchrs 88-; Kappa Delta Pi 89-; Alpha Lambda Delta 88-; Elem Educ; Tchng.

**CROOKER, MELISSA A,** Columbia Greene Comm Coll, Hudson, NY; SO; BS; Nrsng Clb 89-; Dean Lst 89-; Pres Lst 90; AS; Nrsng.

**CROOKS, ANN-MARIE M,** Hillsborough Comm Coll, Tampa, FL; FR; AA; Hillsborgh Comm Clg; Theatr/Aernctcs; Actng/Corp Pilt.

**CROOKS, DAWN R,** Union Univ, Jackson, TN; SR; BA; Panhllnc Cncl Tr 88-90; Hmcmg Comm Co Chrmn 88-90; Stdnt Fndtn Tr Chrmn 88-90; Hnrs Stdnt Assn Sen 87-90; Sigma Tau Delta Sec/Treas 88-90; Zeta Tau Alpha Pr 87-90; All Amer Schlrs 89-90; Chmbr Comm Intrnshp 89-90; IM 87-90; Engl; Tchr.

**CROOKS, MATTHEW B,** Comm Coll Algny Co Algny Cmps, Pittsburgh, PA; FR; Psi Beta 90-; Dns Lst 89-; Psych; Cnslng/Soc Wrk.

**CROOKSTON, CAROLYN D,** Kent St Univ Kent Cmps, Kent, OH; SR; BBA; Beta Alpha Psi; Beta Gamma Sigma; All-Am Awd; Deans Lst; Pres Lst; AAS 89; Acctg; CPA.

**CROOM, CHRISTOPHER A,** Univ Of Sc At Columbia, Columbia, SC; JR; BS; Gamma Beta Pi 89; Pi Tau Sigma Pres; Pres Schlrshp 88-; Fluor Daniel Schlrshp 90-; Ohio Aerospace Inst/NASA Intrnshp; Mech Eng; Rsrch.

**CROOM, KATHRYN L,** Mount Olive Coll, Mount Olive, NC; FR; BS; Schlr Schlrshp; Bus Mgmt; Mgmt Pstn.

**CROOMS, DERRICK G,** Al A & M Univ, Normal, AL; SO; BA; Symph/Mrchng Band 89-; Alpha Phi Alpha; King Star Masonic Lodge 90-; Hnr Roll 89-; Deans Lst 89-; Business; Acctnt.

**CROSBIE, SCOTT A,** Univ Of Ky, Lexington, KY; JR; BA; SGA Stdnt Bdy Pres; Army ROTC Advnced Air Asslt 89; Lances Jr Mens Hnry 90; Omicron Delta Kappa; Farm Hse Scl Chrmn 89; Gods Pntry 88; Shrnrs Hospt Vol; Lxngtn Urbn Co Ambssdr 90; SABS Prnts Of Yr Essay Cntst Wnnr 90; Acad Awd 89; Pol Sci; Law.

**CROSBY, AMBER R,** Thiel Coll, Greenville, PA; FR; BA; Thiel Sgntr Asc Chrp; Spch/Hrng Sci; Spch Pthlgy.

**CROSBY, AVA M,** Univ Of Southern Ms, Hattiesburg, MS; JR; BS; Jdcl Brd; Prlgl Soc Sec 90-; AASO Achvmnt Awd; Prlgl Stds.

**CROSBY, BARBARA A,** Univ Of Sc At Columbia, Columbia, SC; JR; BA; Edctn Mjrs Clb Corres Sec 90-; Erly Chldhd Ed; Tchng.

**CROSBY III, CHARLES H,** Middle Ga Coll, Cochran, GA; SO; BBA; Gamma Beta Phi 89-; Acctg; CPA.

**CROSBY, COLIN A,** Fl A & M Univ, Tallahassee, FL; FR; BA; Carribbean Club 90-; Phi Eta Sigma 90-; Bio; Medcn.

**CROSBY, ELIZABETH R,** Univ Of Southern Ms, Hattiesburg, MS; JR; Kappa Delta Pi; Elem Ed; Tchr.

**CROSBY, FAYE E,** Wagner Coll, Staten Island, NY; FR; BA; Psych.

**CROSBY IV, FREDERIC GIFFORD,** Wagner Coll, Staten Island, NY; FR; BA; Vrsty Trck 90; Engl.

**CROSBY, JUNE C,** Clarkson Univ, Potsdam, NY; SR; BS; Theatre Pr 89-; Vol Svcs Tutoring Coord 88-; APICS Pr 89-; Intrnshp At Pratt/Whitney Aircraft 90; Ind Mngmnt; Grad Schl.

**CROSBY, JUNE E,** Univ Of Southern Ms, Hattiesburg, MS; JR; BA; Phi Eta Sigma; Med Rsrch.

**CROSBY, KATHLEEN M,** Duquesne Univ, Pittsburgh, PA; SO; BS; Res Hll Assn Cmmtt Chrprsn 90-; Acdmy Stu Phrmcy 90-; Kappa Psi Srg Arms 89-; Cmps Mnstry 89-; Open Hse 89-90; Big Sis Fresh 90-; Dean Lst 89-; Pres Schlrshp 90-; Phrmcy Awrd 90-; IM Vllybl Sftbl Capt 89-; Phrmcy.

**CROSBY, MOSETTA E,** Tougaloo Coll, Tougaloo, MS; SR; BA; Alpha Kappa Alpha; Girl Scout Trp Ldr; Econ; Law.

**CROSBY, RICKY E,** Alcorn St Univ, Lorman, MS; JR; MBA; Ftbl 90-; Crmnl Jstce; Law.

**CROSBY, WENDY R,** Longwood Coll, Farmville, VA; FR; BS; Bapt Stdnt Un; ROTC; Bio Clb; Hon Pgm; Bio; Vet Med.

**CROSKEY, JENNIFER M,** Univ Of Akron, Akron, OH; FR; BSME; Mech Engr; Biomed Engr.

**CROSLIN, KIMBERLY Z,** Savannah St Coll, Savannah, GA; FR; BA; Comp Eng/Sci.

**CROSS, ADRIENNE C,** Radford Univ, Radford, VA; JR; BBA; Opratns Mgmt; Big Bus.

**CROSS, BRIAN J,** Westminster Coll, New Wilmingtn, PA; JR; BS; Interfrat Cncl Schlrshp Chr 90-; Sigma Mu; Varsity Ftbl; Bio; Med.

**CROSS, CAMISSA J,** Marshall University, Huntington, WV; SR; BA; IM 88-; Univ Chorus 88; Hall Advsry Cncl 88; MU Band 88-; Kappa Delta Pi; Alpha Xi Delta Pblcty 88-; MUS Conf Stf; Marshall Majorette Co Capt 88-; Elem Educ.**

**CROSS, DEBBIE M,** Newbury Coll, Brookline, MA; FR; MBA; Bus Mg/Psychology; Personal Rep.

**CROSS, DEBORAH K,** Univ Of Al At Birmingham, Birmingham, AL; JR; BS; Amer Physcl Thrpy Assn; Amer Occptnl Thrpy Assn; Alpha Eta 78; Amer Phys Thrpy Assn; Rehab/Commicare Stff Physcl Thrpst Asst; AAS Physcl Thrpy 78; Occupatnl Thrpy.

**CROSS, DELORIS MC CLAM,** Columbia Union Coll, Takoma Park, MD; SR; BA; CABW Treas 84-86; Rainbow Coalition 86-; NAACP 80-; FMC Recruiting Team 86-; Ford Motor Credit Co Branch Oper Mgr 79-; AA Prince Georges Cmnty Clg 87; Bus; Fin Mgr/Invstmnt Bnkr.

**CROSS, DONALD A,** Roane St Comm Coll, Harriman, TN; FR; BS; Cmptr Club 90-; Brd Rgts Schlshp; Freshman Math Awd; Cptr Sci; Cptr Prgr.

**CROSS, ERNEST L,** Davis & Elkins Coll, Elkins, WV; FR; BA; Psych.

**CROSS, JANET V,** S U N Y Coll At Fredonia, Fredonia, NY; JR; BS; Phi Theta Kappa 89-; AAS Jefferson Comm Coll 90; Genetic Eng; Med Rsrch.

**CROSS, JANICE H,** Hillsborough Comm Coll, Tampa, FL; AS; ADN; Nursing.

**CROSS, JENNIFER L,** Univ Of Akron, Akron, OH; GD; BS; Golden Key Vp 89-; Beta Gamma Sigma 90-; R C/Katherine Musson Schlrshp; Indstrl Mngmt; Mtrls Mngmt.

**CROSS, JOHN K,** Univ Of Tn At Martin, Martin, TN; SO; BS; Crmnl Jstc Soc; Pi Kappa Alpha Alumni Soc; Crmnl Jstc; Law.

**CROSS, KAREN M,** Christian Brothers Univ, Memphis, TN; JR; BA; Gamma Theta Phi 91; Eng; Personnel Mgmt.

**CROSS, LAURA A,** Dowling Coll, Oakdale Li, NY; SR; BA; Kappa Delta Pi; AAS Suffolk Co Comm Coll 89; Elem Educ; Tchng.

**CROSS, LOREN E,** Univ Of Cincinnati, Cincinnati, OH; FR; BS; Elem Educ; Tchr.

**CROSS, LORIE,** Gallaudet Univ, Washington, DC; FR; BA; Pres Schlr 90; Ed; Tchr.

**CROSS, RENEE A,** Genesee Comm Coll, Batavia, NY; FR; MBA; Sftbl; Math; Eleme Ed.

**CROSS, TAMMY A,** Middle Tn St Univ, Murfreesboro, TN; JR; BA; Chrldng Capt 87-89; Elem Ed; Tchng.

**CROSSEN, SUZANNE M,** Univ Of Sc At Columbia, Columbia, SC; FR; BS; Mid-Carolina Ophthlmic Med Assoc 89; Assoc Of Tchncl Prsnnl In Ophthlmlgy 89; SC Lions Eye Bnk 90; SC Eye Inst 87; COT Joint Cmmssn Allied Hlth Pers 85; Bio; Physcn/Tchr.

**CROSSGROVE, ANDREW T,** The Kings Coll, Briarclf Mnr, NY; SO; BA; Vlybl; Jazz Ens/Cncrt Ens; Mscl Pit Orch; Chrstn Serv Otrch; Rlgn/Bblcl Stds; Yth Pstr.

**CROSSIN, KATHLEEN,** Widener Univ, Chester, PA; JR; BA; Mgmt-Acctg.

**CROSSLEY, LEE A,** Le Moyne Coll, Syracuse, NY; JR; BA; Stdnt Progmmng Brd Jr Sr Pres 90-; Booth Ruskin Drama Clb Hs Mgr 90-; Major Arcana Hse Mgr 90-; Pre Law Scty 88-; Englsh Clb 88-; Orntn Committee 90-; Alpha Sigma Nu 90-; Deans Lst 88-; Winter Spring Olympics Offcl 88-; Englsh Literature/Pltcl Sci; Corp Attny.

**CROSSLEY, SHEILAH M,** Columbia Union Coll, Takoma Park, MD; GD; BS; Takoma Pk Artsts Gld Prog Coord; Creatv Shrng Wrtng Grp; Org Mgmt; MA Tchng.

**CROSSWRIGHT, DELORIS A,** Central St Univ, Wilberforce, OH; SR; BS; AA Cuyahoga Cmnty Clg 86; Scl Wrk; Clncl Scl Wrk.

**CROTEAU, DEBORAH L,** Univ Of Rochester, Rochester, NY; SR; BS; Biochem Soc 90-; Biochem; MS.

**CROUCH, ALLISON M,** Univ Of Sc At Columbia, Columbia, SC; JR; BA; Art Hstry; Arts Mgmt.

**CROUCH, CONNIE E,** Northeast State Tech Comm Coll, Blountville, TN; GD; AAS; Finance.

**CROUCH, DEBORAH RUPPE,** Univ Of Sc At Columbia, Columbia, SC; SR; Gamma Beta Phi 89-; NSNA 89-; Red Crs Vol; Mary Black Schl Nrsng Outstdng Std 90-; Hnr Grad; Roebuck BSA Sec/Treas 88-90; ADN Mary Black Schl Nrsng.

**CROUCH, JENNIFER P,** Muskingum Coll, New Concord, OH; SO; BA; Clg Nwspr 89-; Phi Alpha Theta 90-; Sigma Tau Delta; First/Second Yr Schlr 90-; Engl/Hist; Writer.

**CROUCH, KATHLEEN FULLER,** Nova Univ, Ft Lauderdale, FL; GD; MS; US Drsg Fed; Hosp Eating Dsordrs Intrn; Fl Frlnc Wrtrs; Human Sci; Cnslg Mntl Hlth.

**CROUCH, LORA KRISHNA,** Univ Of Sc At Lancaster, Lancaster, SC; FR; MBA; Sci; Phrmcy.

**CROUCH, RONDA L,** Oh Univ, Athens, OH; SO; BA; Stdt Art Thrpy Orgnztn Treas 89-; Art Thrpy Psychlgy.

**CROUCH, SHANE M,** Central Fl Comm Coll, Ocala, FL; SO; BA; Phi Theta Kappa 90-; AA; Bus Admn.

**CROUSE, BETHANY J,** Goucher Coll, Towson, MD; SR; BA; Stdnt Govt Assoc Treas 88-; Commtng Stdnts Org Secy 87-; Phi Beta Kappa 90-; Deans Schlr 88-; Bls Of 1905 Flwshp 80-; Truman Schlrshp Nomn 88-89; Econ/Engl; Econ Profsr.

**CROUSE, BILL R,** Central St Univ, Wilberforce, OH; SO; BS; Army ROTC 89-; US Ariborne Schl 90; US Army 62nd Army Bnd Ft Bliss TX 86-89; Chem; US Army/Chem Eng.

**CROUSE, KIMBERLY L,** Univ Of Sc At Columbia, Columbia, SC; JR; Drama Clb 86-88; Intrntl Clb 90; Phi Theta Kappa 88-89; Hnr Scty 90; Acad Merit Schlrshp 87-88; Elem Ed; Spcl Ed.

**CROUSE, PAUL E,** Beckley Coll, Beckley, WV; SO; AS; Legal NCO U S Army Sgt 79-86; Drl Sgt U S Army Rsrv Stf Sgt 86-; Law.

**CROUSE, REBECCA A,** Goucher Coll, Towson, MD; SO; BA; Sga Exec Bd Finc Chr 90-; Modl Sen Co Chr 90-; Cmtng Stdnts Org V P 89-90; Dns Schlr 89-90; CAUSE V P; Wrtng Ctr Tutr 90-; Gov Sumnr Intrnshp Pgm Intrn; Gndr Publc Pol Sem Asst; Dns Ldrshp Sem 90; Pol/Publ Pol; Law.

**CROUSE, SUSAN L,** Univ Of Nc At Greensboro, Greensboro, NC; JR; BM; Mrshls; Hnr Frtrnty; Musc Hnr Frtrnty; Mu Phi Epsilon; NC Tchg Fllw; Deans Lst; Musc Educ; Tch.

**CROUSER, CHAD R,** Slippery Rock Univ, Slippery Rock, PA; FR; BS; Assn Hlth/Physcl Ed/Dnce 90-; Hall Cncl Flr Rep 90-; Phi Eta Sigma 90-; Phi Sigma Pi 90-; Sprts Mgmt/Phys Ed; Tchr.

**CROUSHORE JR, WILLIAM S,** Duquesne Univ, Pittsburgh, PA; SR; BA; Acad Stdnts Pharmacy 89-; Natl Assoc Retail Drgst 90-; Phi Delta Chi 88-; Kiwanis Clb Schlrshp 89-90; Pharmcy; Vet Med.

**CROUT, N EUGENE,** Univ Of Miami, Coral Gables, FL; SR; BM; Fndng Mbr SCI 90-; Provost Hnr Roll; Dsns Lst; Music Cmpstn.

**CROUTHAMEL, KAREN K,** Medaille Coll, Buffalo, NY; SR; BS; Tch Assn Sec 90-; Niagara Frntr Rdng Cncl 90-; Alpha Chi 90-; Amer Bus Wmns Assn VP 81-82; Intrclb Cncl Wstrn NY Jr Dlgt 83-; AAS Hilbert Coll 82; Educ/Tchng.

**CROW, DARREN R,** Western Piedmont Comm Coll, Morganton, NC; SO; AS; Pep Clb 87-89; NC Schlr 89; Tnns 87-89; Phrmcy.**

**CROWDER, AMY L,** Univ Of Sc At Columbia, Columbia, SC; JR; BAIS; Kappa Delta Epsilon 90-; Early Chldhd Ed; Tchr/Admin.

**CROWDER, JASON B,** Jackson St Univ, Jackson, MS; FR; BA; Political Sci Clb 90; Journalism.

**CROWDER, LORI C,** Univ Of Montevallo, Montevallo, AL; SR; Al Cncl Scl Study 90-; Stu Ntl Educ Assoc 90-; Phi Kappa Phi; Lambda Sigma Pi 90-; Pres Lst 88-; Deans Lst 87-; Stu Tchg Tchr; Soph/Jr/Sr Hnrs Awrd Coll Educ 88-; BS 90-; Erly Chldhd; Tchg.

**CROWE, CYNTHIA J,** Manhattanville Coll, Purchase, NY; JR; Shaw Choir 88; Hndcp Awrnss Cmmttee Assist Coord 90; Pre-Law Scty 89-90; Wshngtn Smstr Prog Crmnl Jstce 90; Stdnt Advsr; Intrnshp Hlth/Hmn Serv Dept 90; Inspctr Gnrls Offce; Fld Offce; Pol Sci; Law.**

**CROWE, ELIZABETH M,** Western Piedmont Comm Coll, Morganton, NC; SO; PHARM; SGA Chncllr 90; Membrshp Cmmttee Chrprsn 90; Lrng Rsrce Cmmttee Sec 90; Deans Lst 89; Chrch Sec 85-90; Phrmcy Tchncn At Grace Hosp In Morganton NC 90; Sci Bio/Chem; Pharmacy.

**CROWE, FRANCES E,** Immaculata Coll, Immaculata, PA; SR; Cue/Curtain 87-89; Debate Tm 88-89f Educ/Psych Clubs 88-; Tau Kappa Delta 90-; Psych Intrnshp Partial Hosp 90-; Stdnt Teach 90-; BA; Psych/Elem Educ.

**CROWE, JASON A,** Al A & M Univ, Normal, AL; SO; BS; Natl Egle Sct Assn; Scty Of Amer Frstrs; Scty Fr Crtve Anchrnsm Lcl Dpty Knght Mrshl; ROTC Army Rngr Co XO 90-; Frstry; Mltry Cvl Srvce.

**CROWE, JESSE J,** Wallace St Comm Coll At Selma, Selma, AL; SO; BS; Phi Theta Kappa 89-; James B Allen Awd; AS; Cmptr Info Sys; Pgrmng.

**CROWE, JOHANNA L,** Birmingham Southern Coll, Birmingham, AL; FR; Stdnt Alumni Assoc 90-; Frshmn Ldrshp Dev Cls 90-; Dns Lst 90-; Bio/Chem; Biomed Engr.

**CROWE, KAREN,** S U N Y Coll Of Tech At Frmgdl, Farmingdale, NY; JR; BA; AAIS CIS 90; Cmptr Sci; High Tech.

**CROWE, LORI A,** Univ Of Sc At Columbia, Columbia, SC; SO; BA; Ideas/Issues Cmmttee CPU; Engl Psych Mnr; Cmmnctns.

**CROWE, RANI D,** Oh Univ, Athens, OH; FR; BFA; Conver Partners; Theatre; Acting.

**CROWE, ROXANA E,** Western Ky Univ, Bowling Green, KY; JR; Assctd Std Govt Affrs Chrmn 89-; Sprt Mastrs 90-; Chi Alpha Sec 89-; Phi Kappa Phi; Pi Delta Phi Pres 89-; Phi Eta Sigma 90-; Sigma Delta Pi; Pres Schlr 89-; French/Elem Ed.

**CROWE, SONYA E,** Middle Ga Coll, Cochran, GA; FR; BS; Elem Educ.

**CROWE, STACY D,** Jones County Jr Coll, Ellisville, MS; FR; BA; Math; Tchr.

**CROWE, THERESA L,** Anne Arundel Comm Coll, Arnold, MD; SO; BA; Deans Lst 89-; English; Clg English Prfsr.

**CROWELL, BETTY A,** Univ Of Tn At Martin, Martin, TN; SR; Peer Enblg Prog Pep Ldr 90-; All Sng Co Coor 90-; Alpha Phi Omega Pres 90-; Stdnt Afrs Srvc Awd 90-; Bst Pldg 89; Bst Actv Alpha Phi Omega 90-; Educ; Tchg.

**CROWELL, BILLIE J,** S U N Y Coll At Fredonia, Fredonia, NY; SO; BA; Bus; Mrktng.

**CROWELL, CLARA KAY,** Univ Of Tn At Knoxville, Knoxville, TN; SR; BA; Art Clb Sec 88-; Law/Gvt Clb Sec 88-; Gamma Beta Phi 88-; Phi Theta Kappa 88-; Public Administration.

**CROWELL, JEFFREY A,** Univ Of Cincinnati, Cincinnati, OH; FR; BA; Brdcstng; Studio Rcrdng Engnr Prdcr.

**CROWELL, KRISTEN S,** Univ Of Fl, Gainesville, FL; JR; BS; US Vlybl Assc 85-; Mrtr Brd 90-; Phy Thrpy Intrnshp Gainesville Vets Admin Med Ctr; Hmcmg Vlybl Trnmnt 89-; AA; Phy Thrpy; MS.

**CROWL, CHRISTIANNA N,** Univ Of Miami, Coral Gables, FL; JR; BM; Alpha Lambda Delta 89-; Phi Eta Sigma 89-; Music & Acdmc Schlrshp 89-; Schlrshp To Attend Summewr Music Prog-Salzburg Austria 89-; Sportsfest 90-; Music-Kybd Perf; Performer In Voice & Piano.

**CROWLEY, ALYSON C,** Georgetown Univ, Washington, DC; FR; BS; Bsn Adm/Amer Govt; Acctg.

**CROWLEY, CINDY M,** Ms St Univ, Miss State, MS; FR; BA; Nwsppr Phtgrphr; Zeta Tau Alpha 90-; State Strider 90-; Sci; Phys Thrpy.

**CROWLEY, CORRINE B,** William Carey Coll, Hattiesburg, MS; JR; BSB; SG Treas 89-90; Drainage Dist Cmsnr 82-88; Ctzns Advsry Comm Sec 81-85; LDS Pblc Cmnctns Dir 82-86; Dept Of Hmn Svcs Elgblty Case Wrkr 90; Bsn Admin; Lobbist/Cmnctns.

**CROWLEY, DEBRA L,** Saint Josephs Coll, Windham, ME; SR; BS; Ski Clb 87-89; Superkids 89; Dns Lst 90; Hnrs Lst 88-89; Rsdnt Asst 89-90; Calendar Comm 90-; Dev Comm 89-90; R A Selection Comm 89-90; Stdnt Tchng 90; Most Imprvd Vrsty Vlybl 88; IM Vlybl/Sftbl 87-; Elem Educ; Tchr.

**CROWLEY, DONALD A,** Christopher Newport Coll, Newport News, VA; JR; BSIS; Mntnc Elctrcn Aprntc 85-; AAS 81; Info Sci; Cmptrs/Bus Mgt.

**CROWLEY, MAUREEN M,** Syracuse Univ, Syracuse, NY; SR; BARCH; Amer Inst Archtctr Stdnt Chptr Tres 88-89; Sch Archtctr Pr Advsng Pgm 88- Crdntr; Archtctr.

**CROWLEY, MEGHAN D,** Long Island Univ Southampton, Southampton, NY; SO; BA; Road Rally 89-90; Merit Flwshp 89-; Hon Pgm 89-; Hghst GPA 89-; Hon Schlrshp Merit Fllws Schlrshp 89-; Chld Psychlgst.**

**CROY, ANGELA L,** King Coll, Bristol, TN; FR; BS; World Chrstn Flwshp 90-; Nrsng Hm Mnstry 90-; Engl/Bible/Religion.

**CROY, CHARLIE J,** Concord Coll, Athens, WV; FR; BA; Activities Bd VP; Alpha Psi Omega; Theatre Wrkshp; Communication Arts; Pblc Rltns.

**CROYLE, ACACIA J,** Peace Coll, Raleigh, NC; SO; BA; Clg Schlrs 89-90; SGA RA 90-; AA; Engl; Educ.

**CROYLE, RODNEY D,** Piedmont Tech Coll, Greenwood, SC; FR; AS; Mchn Tl; Tl/Die.

**CROZIER, ROBERT A,** Univ Of Rochester, Rochester, NY; SR; BA; Grk Wk Awrds; Grk Wk Games; Deans Lst 87-; Alpha Delta Phi Jdcl Chr 88-; Robert Wood Johnson Med Sch Biochem Flwshp 90; IM Bsktbl Capt 87-; Bio; Med.

**CRUCE, ROBERT K,** Univ Of Montevallo, Montevallo, AL; FR; BS; Pre Med; Phys Thrpy.

**CRUCIANI, CAROLYN G,** S U N Y Coll Of Tech At Frmgdl, Farmingdale, NY; SO; AAS; Store Mgr; Cert SCCC 85; Hortcltr; Sprvsry Pstn.

**CRUDELE, FRANK P,** Broward Comm Coll, Ft Lauderdale, FL; AS; VICA 75-76; OPBRA 86-89; DAPBA 86-89; IAFF 78-; Firefighter; Fire Sfty Instrctr; Paramedic Drvr Eng; Fire Sci.

**CRUESS, MARY CATHERINE,** Webber Coll, Babson Park, FL; SR; BS; Alpha Kappa Psi Secy 77-80; Asst Contrlr Citrus World Inc 86-; Bus Mgt.

**CRUISCE, KAREN M,** Hudson Valley Comm Coll, Troy, NY; SO; ASSOC; Pres Lst 90-; Audit Clrk Matthew Bender Co 85-90; Cmptr Info Sys; Sys Analyst.

**CRULL, TIMOTHY E,** Marshall University, Huntington, WV; JR; BA; Mrchng Bnd 88-; Hl Adv Cncl 89; Cnstrctn Mgmt.

**CRUM, CANDACE D,** Ms St Univ, Miss State, MS; JR; BS; Gamma Beta Phi 90-; Kappa Delta Phi 90-; Phi Mu 90-; Pres Schlr 90-; AA NE MS Comm Coll 90; Elem Ed; Teacher.

**CRUM, KATHY G,** Oh Univ-Southern Cmps, Ironton, OH; JR; BA; Dns Lst 90-; Ironton Med Ctr Med Rec Intern; Ofc Tech Certif; Ofc Tech; Ofc Adm BA.

**CRUM, LETHE C,** Al A & M Univ, Normal, AL; SO; BA; Acad Hnr Rl 90-; ABC Tlvsn 90-; Radio Jzz; Trck/Crss Cntry 89-90; Tlcmnctns; Brdcstr.

**CRUM, MARY E,** Alice Lloyd Coll, Pippa Passes, KY; JR; BA; Pre Med Hlth Svcs Club 83-85; Deans Distngshd List 83-85; 90; Chem Award 84; Lab Asstnt 84-85; Sub Tchr 87-; Engl/Sci; Tchng.

**CRUM, ROBERT J,** Radford Univ, Radford, VA; SR; MDIV; Bapt Union Pr 90-; Pi Gamma Mu 89-; BS; Hstry/Soc Sci; Seminary.

**CRUM, SUE A,** Norfolk St Univ, Norfolk, VA; SR; BSHSM; Hlth Serv Mgmt; Alpha Kappa Mu; VA Bch Hlth Dept Intrn; AS BA 89; RN Wash Cty Hosp Sch Nsg 70; Hlth Serv Mgmt; Admn.

**CRUMBLEY, RAFAAEL P,** Al A & M Univ, Normal, AL; SO; BS; Natl Hon Soc; Alpha Phi Alpa Sec; Acctg; CPA.

**CRUMLEY, JOE F,** Abraham Baldwin Agri Coll, Tifton, GA; FR; Cert Paramedic 73-; Cmptr Sci; Cmptr Analyst/Cons.

**CRUMMETTE, LE ANNE E,** Radford Univ, Radford, VA; SR; BS; Intervarsity Chrstn Flwshp Pres 89-90; Phi Kappa Phi; English; Technical Writing.

**CRUMP, JULIE A,** Lesley Coll, Cambridge, MA; SO; BA; Stdnt Govt Assn Dir Pub; LINC 89-90; Lesly Lrng Ctr Peer Tutr 90-; Nat Sci/Educ.

**CRUMPLER, JACKIE S,** Fl International Univ, Miami, FL; SR; Sub Tchr Dade Cnty Pblc Schls 89-; AA Miami Dade Comm Coll 88; BS 90; Educ; Tchr.

**CRUMPTON, KIMBERLY D,** Wallace St Comm Coll At Selma, Selma, AL; JR; BA; Deans Lst; Pres Lst; Elem Edn.

**CRUMPTON, TIFFANY L,** Stillman Coll, Tuscaloosa, AL; SO; BS; Yrbk Stff Sec 90-; Sigma Gamma Iota 89-; Eckerd Schlr 89; Chemistry; Pharmacy.

**CRUMPTON, WENDY L,** Univ Of Al At Birmingham, Birmingham, AL; JR; Alpha Gamma Delta Rtl Chrmn 90-; Psych/Blgy; Phys Therapy.**

**CRUSER, WAYNE W,** S U N Y Coll Of Tech At Alfred, Alfred, NY; SR; BA; Engl Tutor/Cnslng Tech/Sclgy; Clthng Strs/Rstrnts Mngrs 78-88; Pltcl Sci; Prsnl Mdtn/Arbtrtn.

**CRUT, FELIPE CASTRO,** Inter Amer Univ Pr San Juan, Hato Rey, PR; GD; DJ; Natl Assn Invstgtr 87-; Intl Narcodic Offrs Assn 87-; Intlgnt/Org Crime Invstgtn 87-; Law Schl; Summa Cum Laude 90; Vet Admin Awd 79; BA I A U 90; Cert Comisionadao Seyuro De P R 88; Doctor Juris/Bus Admin; Law.

**CRUTCH, YVETTE M,** Va St Univ, Petersburg, VA; JR; BA; Bsn Admin Club 90-; Corp Orient Pgm 89-90; Fin; Invstmnt Bnkng.

**CRUTCHER, FELECIA D,** Memphis St Univ, Memphis, TN; SR; BED; Gamma Beta Phi 90-; Black Schlrs Unltd 90-; Trckng Prog 88-; Sigma Gamma Rho Recrdng Sec; Elem Educ; Teacher.

**CRUTCHFIELD, BRIAN K,** Longwood Coll, Farmville, VA; JR; BFA; Newsmagazine Pres 89-; Excursion Clb 88-89; Intrntl Stdies House Plnng Cmmt 89-; Alpha Lambda Delta 88-; Phi Kappa Phi; Kappa Pi Pledge Ed 89-; Interior Archtrl Dsgn.

**CRUTCHFIELD, STEPHEN E,** Emory & Henry Coll, Emory, VA; FR; BA; Cmptr Sci; Sys Anlyst.

**CRUTCHLEY, BARBARA J,** Univ Of South Fl, Tampa, FL; JR; BA; Emrgncy Med RN; AS/NRSNG Canton Coll Canton NY 73; Fine Arts-Studio; Art Fld.

**CRUTCHLEY, JULIE A,** Salisbury St Univ, Salisbury, MD; GD; Pgm Board 88; Lambda Iota Tau; Phi Mu Sorority Hstrn 89-90; BA 90; AA Frederick Cmnty Clg 88; Engl; Tech Editing.

**CRUTE, AARON L,** Va St Univ, Petersburg, VA; FR; BA; Info Sys; Prgmmr Anlyst/Engr.

**CRUTE, GLORIA F,** Va St Univ, Petersburg, VA; SR; BA; Yrbk Stt 89; Gspl Choir 89; Dorm Pres Whiting Hall Pres 90; New Generations Cmps Mnstrs 87-88; Incentive Awd/Admin Systs Mgmt Dept 87; BA VA State Univ 91; Bus Admin Systs Mgmt; Admin Exec.

**CRUZ BELLO, ZULMA,** Univ Of Pr Medical Sciences, San Juan, PR; SR; BS; Sci Clb 87; Rlgus Actves; Stdnt Cncl 87; Pres Clsrm Yng Amer 87; Summa Cum Laude 90; AS 90; Biology; Med Tech.

**CRUZ CANCEL, DALIALYS,** Inter Amer Univ Pr Hato Rey, Hato Rey, PR.

**CRUZ CASTRO, VANESSA I,** Caribbean Univ, Bayamon, PR; SR; BA.

**CRUZ CRISOSTOMO, MAGDA DE J,** Inter Amer Univ Pr Hato Rey, Hato Rey, PR; FR; Assoc Stdnts Promo English Lang 90-; Aviation.

**CRUZ CRUZ, ARTURO A,** Bayamon Tech Univ Coll, Bayamon, PR; GD; Acctg Stdnts Assn 87-90; Knights Of Columbus 85-; Magna Cum Laude; BA 90; Acctng; CPA.

**CRUZ CRUZ, ROLANDO I,** Univ Of Pr At Mayaguez, Mayaguez, PR; SR; BS; Tau Beta Pi 89-; Phi Kappa Phi 90-; RUM Deans Lst 87-; Cmptr Eng.

**CRUZ DIAZ, OSVALDO,** Inter Amer Univ Pr San German, San German, PR; FR; High Hnrs; Engineering/Electronics.

**CRUZ FELICIANO, MARIEL,** Inter Amer Univ Pr San German, San German, PR; SR; Hon Prog 90; Radiology Tech.

**CRUZ HERNANDEZ, ELVIN O,** Univ Of Pr At Rio Piedras, Rio Piedras, PR; SO; BBA; Assn Acctg 90-; Deans Lst 90-; Acctg.

**CRUZ LOPEZ, ANGEL,** Inter Amer Univ Pr Hato Rey, Hato Rey, PR; JR; BA; Spnsh; Mrktg.

**CRUZ NARVAEZ, CARMEN E,** Univ Of Pr Cayey Univ Coll, Cayey, PR; SO; Smmr Cmps Org 88-89; Deans Lst 90-; Pstrl Jvnls Grp Pres 89-90; Ctznshp Mdl 89-90; Scl Sci.

**CRUZ NAVARRO, SANDRA E,** Univ Of Pr Humacao Univ Coll, Humacao, PR; SO; Coll Hon Soc 90-; CUH; AJC.

**CRUZ PEDRAZA, CARMEN L,** Univ Of Pr Cayey Univ Coll, Cayey, PR; FR; Yng Grp Ctlc Chrch 87-89; Hgrs Crea 87-90; Toquigrafio En Ingles Y Espanol; Bachillerato.

**CRUZ RIVERA, ROSA D,** Univ Of Pr At Mayaguez, Mayaguez, PR; JR; BA; Amer Chem Scty 89-90; Natl Scty Prfsnl Eng 90-; Hon List Chem Eng Dept 89-; Chem; Eng.

**CRUZ RODRIGUEZ, JUAN ALFREDO,** Univ Of Pr At Mayaguez, Mayaguez, PR; SR; BA; Soc Microbio 88-89; Natural Sci Awd 90; Hnr Rl 88-90; IM Bsktbl 89-90; Life Technologies Lab Tech Intern 90; Indstrl Microbio; Ph D Microbio.

**CRUZ ROMAN, ROSA E,** Inter Amer Univ Pr Hato Rey, Hato Rey, PR; BA; Sec Sci.

**CRUZ ZENO, EDGARDO M,** Univ Of Pr At Mayaguez, Mayaguez, PR; JR; BSEE; IEEE 89-; Deans List 88-; Hon Roll 88-; Elec Eng.

**CRUZ, ANA L,** Inter Amer Univ Pr San German, San German, PR; SR; BA; Nrsng Assoc 89-; Acdmc Awrd 89-90; Hnr Cert 89-90; Nrsng Acdmc Excllnc Awrd 90-; Sci; Nrsng.

**CRUZ JR, ANTHONY,** Univ Of South Fl, Tampa, FL; JR; BA; Pre-Law Soc 90; Arts/Sci Hnr Soc 90-; Golden Key 90-; Dns Lst 90-; AA 89; Hstry/Spch Comm; Law.**

**CRUZ, AWILDA,** Inter Amer Univ Pr Hato Rey, Hato Rey, PR; FR; BBA; Acctg; CPA.

**CRUZ, CECILY,** City Univ Of Ny Queensbrough, New York, NY; FR; AAS; Holy Rosary Chrch Prsh Cncl 89-; Choir 87-; St Marys Hosp Chldrn Vol 90-; Nrsng.

**CRUZ, CYNTHIA,** Coll Of New Rochelle, New Rochelle, NY; SR; BSN; NSNA 88-; CODE 89-; Sigma Theta Tau; Med Asst 85-88; Nrsng.

**CRUZ, CYNTHIA,** Univ Of Pr Medical Sciences, San Juan, PR; GD; BA; Magna Cum Laude 86-87; Ldrshp/Hmnsm Awd; Phys Thrpy Clin Instrctrs Cncl Pr Chptr 87-; Puerto Rico Lung Assn 87-; Phys Thrpy Instrctr 87-; Pub Hlth/Maternal Chld Hlth; Univ Professor.

**CRUZ, DOMINGO G,** Yale Univ, New Haven, CT; FR; BA; Intrn For S C Johnson Wax; Hist; Law.

**CRUZ, ELENA M,** Barry Univ, Miami, FL; FR; Hnrs Stu Assc 90-; Chmstry; Eng/Med.

**CRUZ, ERICSON SANTOS,** Va Commonwealth Univ, Richmond, VA; FR; BFA; Fncng 90-; Cmmnctn Arts; Art Drctn.

**CRUZ, GERARDO J,** Univ Of Ct, Storrs, CT; FR; BS; Polo Clb 90-; Polo Prctcm Asst Instrctr 90-; CT Vrsty Polo Tm 90; Anml Sci.

**CRUZ, HECTOR L,** Fayetteville St Univ, Fayetteville, NC; JR; BS; Med Tech Cert Amer Med Tech Assn; Med Tech 81-; AS Ntl Hlth Inst 81; Bio; Med.

**CRUZ, KISHA E,** Western New England Coll, Springfield, MA; FR; BA; UN Mutually Equal 90-; Acctng Assc; Alpha Lambda Delta; Alpha Kappa Psi; Adlt Literary Corp Tutor; Acctng.

**CRUZ, LUZ IDALIA,** Univ Of Pr Cayey Univ Coll, Cayey, PR; FR; Cuadro De Honor Del La Rectora; Colegio Univ De Cayey Pres Clsrm 90; Pres De La Assn Civica Y Rec De La Comunidad Buena Vista En Cayey P R; Escritora Para La Revista La Linterna Colabroadora; History; Law.

**CRUZ, MICHELLE L,** Endicott Coll, Beverly, MA; FR; BA; Vbllbl Vrsty Team; Cmptr Applctns Bsn.

**CRUZ, NELCIA,** Univ Of Miami, Coral Gables, FL; JR; BA; Stdnt Govt Sntr Exe Sec 89-90; FBG AKA Sorty Rep; Alpha Kappa Alpha Sor Rep; Public Dfndrs Off Intrn Paralegal Asst 89-; AA Daytona Bch Cmuty Clg 89; Crmnl Juste; Law.

**CRUZ, RICHARD,** Miami Dade Comm Coll North, Miami, FL; SO; AA; Bsnss Mngmnt; Law.

**CRUZ, RICHARD A,** Bunker Hill Comm Coll, Boston, MA; FR; BS; Elect/Cmptr Eng.

**CRUZ, ROCIO,** Caribbean Center For Adv Stds, San Juan, PR; GD; MS; SHRUM Pblc Rltns 90-; BS U Of Puerto Rico 89; Ind Psychology.**

**CRUZ, VANESSA,** Univ Of Pr At Rio Piedras, Rio Piedras, PR; SO; BA; Litr Cntst 90; Chem Prctr 90-; Hon Rgstr 90-; Bio; Medcn.

**CRUZ, VIRGINIA,** Southeastern Ma Univ, N Dartmouth, MA; SO; BA; Nrsng.

**CRUZ-HERNANDEZ, GIGI R M,** Univ Of Pr At Rio Piedras, Rio Piedras, PR; GD; MLS; Schl Lbry/Info; Sci Stdnt Cncl; TA Dr Susan Freiband Invstgtn Pblshd 90; TA Dr Consuelo Figueras Micro Cmptr Lab 90-; BA 88; Lbrnshp; Med Lbrnshp.

**CRUZADO, PABLO,** Univ Of Pr Cayey Univ Coll, Cayey, PR; JR; BS; Rctrs Hon Soc 88-; Phi Delta Gamma 88-; Tnns 88-; Ntrl Sci/Blgy; Med.

**CRUZEN, MARGARET E,** Columbia Greene Comm Coll, Hudson, NY; SO; BA; Photogrphy Clb 89-; Aircraft Owners/Pilots Assoc; Catskill Daily Mail Newspaper; Bryant Farms Nursery; Stdnt Pilot Certif; Humanities-Engl; Aerontcs.

**CRYSER, JULIE R,** Wv Univ, Morgantown, WV; JR; BA; Sigma Phi Omega; Kappa Tau Alpha; Phi Kappa Phi; AA Jrnlsm Potomac State Coll 90; Jrnlsm; Stf Wrtr/Edtrshp.

**CRYSTAL, VALERIE,** City Univ Of Ny Grad School, New York, NY; SR; Geology Soc VP 90; Geology Dept Stdnt Rep; Sigma Gamma Epsilon 90-; Michael Duchin Schlrshp 90; Helen Biren Schlrshp 90; Grad W/Hon; WPCF 90; BS; Bio/Geology; Envrnmntl Plng.

**CSAKY, MELINDA C,** Univ Of Akron, Akron, OH; JR; BS; ASME 88-; Tau Beta Pi; Alpha Lambda Delta 89-; Phi Eta Sigma 89-; Mchncl Engnrng; Engnrng.

**CSONKA, MARY E,** Fl Coll, Temple Terrace, FL; SO; Arete 89-; YWTO 89-90; Phi Theta Kappa 90-; AA.

**CSONKA, STEVEN D,** Comm Coll Algny Co Algny Cmps, Pittsburgh, PA; JR; AS; Corr Adm; Law.

**CUADRO GONZALEZ, ADNERIS,** Univ Politecnica De Pr, Hato Rey, PR; FR; History; Engr.

**CUADRO GONZALEZ, ANDERIS,** Univ Politecnica De Pr, Hato Rey, PR; FR; Hstry; Eng.

**CUASURD, TANGINIKA S,** Inter Amer Univ Pr San German, San German, PR; SO; BA; Rdrs Clb; Sas Isidro Labrador Chrch 87-; Yngs Cath Action Sabanna Grande P R 87-; Mktg; Comm.

**CUBBIN, KATHLEEN P,** Philadelphia Coll Pharm & Sci, Philadelphia, PA; GD; BS; Newspaper Edtrl Stf 90-; Apha IPSA ASP 87-; SG 90-; Alpha Lambda Delta 89-; Rho Chi; Alpha Phi Omega 89-; SHAPE Brd 90-; Chemistry TA 88-89; Deans Lst 87-; Intl Pharmaceutical Intern Holland 90; Cross Cntry Vrsty 87-89; Pharmayc/Anglo Amer Stds; Law/Pharmacy.

**CUCCARO, KIMBERLY D,** Ms St Univ, Miss State, MS; SO; NAA 90-; Gamma Beta Phi 90-; Alpha Lambda Delta 90; Pres Lst 89-; Acctng; CPA Law.

**CUCKSEE, LISA C,** Univ Of Al At Huntsville, Huntsville, AL; SR; BS; Am Soc Civil Engrs Treas 89-; Civil Eng; Envrnmntl Eng.

**CUDA, REBECCA A,** Allegheny Coll, Meadville, PA; SO; BA; Bio/Chem; Mrne Biolgst.

**CUDD, HAZEL A,** Univ Of Sc At Columbia, Columbia, SC; FR; BAIS; Encore Clb V P; Cmptr Clb.

**CUDDY, HOLLY M,** Univ Of Pittsburgh, Pittsburgh, PA; JR; BA; Chldrns Hosp Nrsrgry Wng 88-89; Intrn Stdnt Carnegie Mellon Chld Care Ctr Tchrs Aide 90-; Chld Dvlpmnt; Ph D/Rsrch Bldn/Hndcpd Chldrn.

**CUDGEL, MONICA L,** Fort Valley St Coll, Fort Valley, GA; FR; BA; Pep Clb 90-; Bus; Mktg.

**CUDNIK, DEBORAH K,** Bethany Coll, Bethany, WV; JR; BA; Fr Actvts Cncl 89; Stdnt Brd Of Govs Rep 90; Gamma Sigma Kappa; Lambda Iota Tau; Phi Mu Pres 89-; IM Sftbl 89-; Engl; Pblshng.

**CUE, KAREN S,** Univ Of Sc At Columbia, Columbia, SC; SO; BA; Ed Major Clb 90-; Pentecostl Assmbls Wrld Carolina 90-; State Cncl/Mnstrl Wives Asst Secy; Elmntry Ed; Tchng/Middle Schl.

**CUERIA, STEPHANIE R,** Memphis St Univ, Memphis, TN; FR; BA; Jrnlsm.

**CUERVO, CRISTINA ISABEL,** Fl International Univ, Miami, FL; FR; Church Serv Crp 87-.

**CUETO, CARLOS A,** Davis Coll, Toledo, OH; SO; ASSO; Aviatn; BS Airline Pilot.

**CUETO, JOSE L,** Univ Of Sc At Spartanburg, Spartanburg, SC; JR; BA; Rotaract Clb; Hnr Rl 89-; Tennis MVP 89-; Busn Admin; Intl Busn.

**CUEVAS ARVELO, EDGAR,** Univ Of Pr At Mayaguez, Mayaguez, PR; JR; BA; Hon Sch 88-90; AS Univ Of P R In Arecibo 89; Magna Cum Laud; Comp; Engr.

**CUEVAS, CECILIA,** Inter Amer Univ Pr Hato Rey, Hato Rey, PR; FR; Psychlgy Assoc 90-; Psychlgy; Psychlgst.

**CUEVAS, DARRYL L,** Univ Of Southern Ms, Hattiesburg, MS; SR; BS; Gldn Key 90-; Gamma Beta Phi 90-; AA Ms Gulf Coast Comm Clg Jeffrsn Davis Cmps 86; Bsn Admin; Mngmnt Info Systms.

**CUEVAS, MARGARET H,** Univ Of Southern Ms, Hattiesburg, MS; JR; BS; Pol Sci; Jrnlsm.

**CUEVAS, MARY A,** Fl International Univ, Miami, FL; SR; BED; FEA 90; Kappa Delta Pi 90-; AA Ml Dade Cmmty Clg 86; Elmntry Ed; Ed MS.

**CUFFEE, LORI J,** Commonwealth Coll, Virginia Beach, VA; SR; Fash Clb 90-; Blk Hist Month Chair; Alpha Beta Gamma 90-; Fash Meerch; Buyer/Consultant.

**CUICHTA, DAVID L,** West Liberty St Coll, West Liberty, WV; JR; BS; Delta Mu Delta; Phi Theta Kappa 89-90; AAS WV Nrthrn Comm Coll 90; Bus Admin; Retl Mgmt.

**CULBERT, BRIAN K,** East Tn St Univ, Johnson City, TN; SR; BS; Tech Ed Colgt Assoc Pres 88-90; Epsilon Pi Tau 90-; Tech Ed; Tchng.

**CULBERT, GREGORY S,** Morehouse Coll, Atlanta, GA; SO; BS; Pre Alumni Soc 90-; Pre Law Soc 89-; NAACP 90-; AUC LA Clb 89-; Alpha Kappa Delta; Hon Roll Status 90-; Soclgy; Law.

**CULBERTSON, DIANE C,** Northern Ky Univ, Highland Hts, KY; GD; CERTI; SNEA; CWENS 71-74; Kappa Delta Pi; Med Techlg Intshp Jewish Hptl Cinti OH 75-74; Synchronized Swimming Club 70-74; PTA; ASCP 74-; Regist Mdl Techologist 74-; BS Eastern KY Univ 70-74; Elem Ed; Tchng.

**CULBERTSON, JOHN DAVID,** Univ Of Sc At Columbia, Columbia, SC; FR; BS; Frshmn Coun USC Stdnt Govt Pres 90-; Air Force ROTC 1st Yr Cdnt 90-; Hnrs Coll 90-; Kappa Sigma 90-; ROTC Awd; Biology; Med.

**CULBERTSON, PAMELA M,** Univ Of Sc At Columbia, Columbia, SC; SR; BS; Math Clb 89-; Pi Mu Epsilon; Alpha Mu Omega; Intrnshp/Math Tchr; IM Aerbcs 90; Cert Mohawk Vly Comm Coll 84; BS 87; Math; Educ.

**CULBERTSON, RANDALL K,** Tn Tech Univ, Cookeville, TN; JR; BS; Plant Soil Sci Clb 90-; Delta Tau Alpha 90-; Agri; Horticulture.

**CULBREATH, CHANDRA D,** Wilberforce Univ, Wilberforce, OH; SO; BA; Cls Actvts Comm 90-; Sigma Omega 90-; Sociology.

**CULLEN, EDWARD V,** Lancaster Bible Coll, Lancaster, PA; FR; BA; Smr Cmp Cnslr; Chrstn Cnslr/Msnry.

**CULLEN, HEATHER E,** Marshall University, Huntington, WV; FR; BA; Bus; Mgmt.

**CULLEN, MAUREEN E,** Villanova Univ, Villanova, PA; FR; BA; Spec Olympics Vol; Proj Sunshine; Delta Delta Delta; Pom Squad; Psychlgy; Medicine.

**CULLEN, THERESA,** Saint Vincents Coll & Seminary, Latrobe, PA; FR; BA; Pscyh Clb Sec Cls 90-; In Touch Clb Ornttn Comm 90-; Psychology.

**CULLEN, TIMOTHY O,** Embry Riddle Aeronautical Univ, Daytona Beach, FL; SR; BS; Avtn Maint Tech.

**CULLER, ELLEN F,** Univ Of Sc At Columbia, Columbia, SC; JR; BS; Piedmont Soc 90-; Kappa Delta Pi; Elem Edn; Tchr.

**CULLER, SUSAN L,** Cornell Univ Statutory College, Ithaca, NY; SO; BA; Campus Crusade Christ; Rd Key; Indr/Outdr Trck; Microbio.

**CULLIFER-CREWS, CYNTHIA,** Troy St Univ At Dothan, Dothan, AL; SR; BA; AL Ed Assoc 90-; Erly Chldhd Intern; Dstngshd Stdnt; BA; Erly Chldhd Ed.

**CULLIMORE, KEVIN R,** Eckerd Coll, St Petersburg, FL; SR; BA; Hstry Phlsphy Sci; Prfsr.

**CULLINS, SHANNON MARIE,** Fl St Univ, Tallahassee, FL; JR; BA BS; Club Ad 89; English Hon Prog 90-; Med Cmunctns/English Lit; Advtsng.

**CULLOP, DELTER E,** Va Highlands Comm Coll, Abingdon, VA; BA; Deans Lst 89-90; Lttl Leg Bsbl Coach Ftbl Chilhourie HS Tchdwn Clb 87-; Crrctns 77-; Edctn Englsh Hstry; Tchr.

**CULLOP, DONNA B,** Emory & Henry Coll, Emory, VA; JR; BA; Stdnt Va Educ Assn 90-; Sigma Mu Schlrshp Soc; Phi Theta Kappa 81-; Smyth Cty 4h Adult Ldr 83-; 4-H Tech 86-90; AAS Wytheville Cumm Clg 83; Interdisciplinary English; Ele Educ.

**CULMER, NARTARLIE,** Central Fl Comm Coll, Ocala, FL; FR; AS; Natl Stdnt Nrs Assn Inc; Phi Theta Kappa; Nrsng.

**CULP, PHYLLIS L,** Central Al Comm Coll, Alexander City, AL; SO; BA; SGA 90-; Phi Theta Kappa 90-; Dns Lst; Tennis/Swmng/Weight Lftng; Bus Coop Prog; TA 90-91; Elem Educ/Engl; Tchr.

**CULP, STEVE M,** Berklee Coll Of Music, Boston, MA; FR; BA; Jzz Ensmbl 90-; Cmmnty Bnd 90-; Intrn Hgh Schl Accmpnst 90-; Hnrs Awrd 90-; Music.

**CULPEPPER, ART S,** Univ Of Southern Ms, Hattiesburg, MS; SR; BS; Engl; Univ Instrctn.

**CULPEPPER, JUDY L,** Univ Of Fl, Gainesville, FL; GD; Little Sister Pi Kappa Phi 70-72; Phi Chi Theta Pres 71-72; Alpha Chi Omega Corre Sec 68-72; Wmn Of The Year 82; Amer Bsn Wmns Assn 82; New Tribunes Ten Mst Inflntl Wmn 83; Rpblcn Prtys Nom Cnty Cmsn 82/86/90; Bsn Mgmt.

**CULPEPPER, KELLY E,** Mobile Coll, Mobile, AL; FR; BA; Ed; Tchng.

**CULPEPPER, LINDA PARRAMORE,** Western Carolina Univ, Cullowhee, NC; JR; BA; German Soc 90-; Phi Alpha Theta V Pres 90-; Pi Gamma Mu; ASCP/HT 81-; Hstry; Amer Hstry.

**CULPEPPER, SANDRA L,** Univ Of Southern Ms, Hattiesburg, MS; SO; BS; Nrsg.

**CULPEPPER, STEPHEN H,** Univ Of Al At Huntsville, Huntsville, AL; FR; BS; Alpha Lambda Delta; 4 Yr Hon Schlrshp; Elec Eng.

**CULTER, JAN M,** Northern Ky Univ, Highland Hts, KY; SR; BA; Jrnlsm; Pblc Rltns.

**CULTER, ROGER C,** Univ Of Louisville, Louisville, KY; SO; MENG; Musician; Eng/Math/Cmptr Sci.

**CULTON IV, EUGENE,** Univ Of Ky, Lexington, KY; FR; BA; Phi Eta Sigma; Cvl Eng.

**CULVER, ALISHA H,** Union Univ School Of Nursing, Memphis, TN; JR; BSN; Natl Stdnt Nrs Assn; Nrsng.

**CULVER, ALLEN E,** Univ Of Louisville, Louisville, KY; SO; BS; Fern Creek Vol Fire Dpt 83-; Info Sci/Data Prcsng; Cmptr Prgmmng.

**CULVER, JORDAN N,** Univ Of Miami, Coral Gables, FL; SR; Intrvrsty Chrstn Flwshp Bible Ldr 87-89; Campus Mnstry Intrn 89-; Goldn Key 89-; Music Stdnt Cncl Keybnd Rep 88-89; Omicron Delta Kappa; Phi Kappa Phi; Pi Kappa Lambda; Gen Hon.

**CULVER III, LOUIS D,** Edison Comm Coll, Fort Myers, FL; SO; BA; MENSA 78; Amercn Chem Soc 79; Phi Theta Kappa 84; Dr H W Kane Medal Of Hon 84; Colonial Saber Biochem Award 83; Matsushita Ach Award 82; Deans Award Basic Scis 83; Biochem; Medcn.

**CULVER, MILTON L,** Univ Of Montevallo, Montevallo, AL; FR; BA; Hon Pgm 90-; Alpha Lambda Delta 90-; Daens Lst 90-; Pres Awd Excllnc Wrtng 90-; Engl; Jrnlsm.

**CULVERHOUSE, TRICIA A,** Fl St Univ, Tallahassee, FL; JR; BSN; SNA; Dlt Gamma Soc Chrmn 90; Grn Peace; Ballinger Mem Schlrshp; Nrsng; Medcn.

**CUMBEE, LAURA L,** Valdosta St Coll, Valdosta, GA; SR; BED; Pilot Clb Fitzgerald 89-; Ocilla Bapt Ch 81-; Early Chldhd Edn; Teach.

**CUMBERLAND, ANNE,** Watterson Coll, Louisville, KY; FR; Lbrty Chptr OES 245; Prlgl.

**CUMBLIDGE, CHRISTY M,** Univ Of Cin R Walters Coll, Blue Ash, OH; FR; MBA; Psych.

**CUMBO-JONES, CAROLYN A,** Norfolk St Univ, Norfolk, VA; SR; MA; Stdnt Govt Assoc Repr 90-; Evening Clg Stdnt Senate 89-90; Epsilon Tau Sigma V P 87-88; Alpha Kappa Mu V P 87-; AS Tidewater Cmnty Clg 86; BS; Urban Affrs; Pol/Hmn Res Adm.

**CUMMINGS, ANGELA D,** Marshall University, Huntington, WV; SO; 4-H Clb Sec 90-; Gamma Beta Phi 89-; Phi Eta Sigma 90-; Hlth/Sci; Hlth Educ.

**CUMMINGS, ANGELA L,** Radford Univ, Radford, VA; JR; BA; Clgte Chrstn Life 90-; Yth Grp Ldr 90-; Bible Quiz Tm 90-; Educ; Tch.

**CUMMINGS, ANTHONY L,** Marshall University, Huntington, WV; SR; BA; Bsn Mktg.

**CUMMINGS, CHERIE M,** Duquesne Univ, Pittsburgh, PA; SO; BA; Frnch Clb VP 90-; Cmps Mnstry Chrch Chr 89-; Intrntl Bus Assn 90-; IM Spts 89-; Duquesne Univ Vol 89-91; Integrated Hnrs Pgrm 89-; Fndrs Awd/Incentive Grnt 89-; ROTC 3 Yr Schlrshp 90-; Intrntl Bus Acctng; Accntng Big 6 Firm.**

**CUMMINGS, COREY A,** Siena Coll, Loudonville, NY; SR; Judicial Brd Stdnt Advocate 89-90; Harvard Natl Model United Nations Delg 89-; Pre Law Club 88-; Delta Epsilon Sigma 90-; Alpha Kappa Alpha 90-; General Elec Co-Op Intrnshp 90-; BBA; Accounting; CPA.

**CUMMINGS, DEBORAH L,** Univ Of Sc At Columbia, Columbia, SC; JR; BA; Gamma Beta Phi; Part Time Secty; Early Childhood Ed; Tchng K-4.

**CUMMINGS, ENDYA M,** Fl A & M Univ, Tallahassee, FL; JR; MBA; Blk Stdnt Un; Acctg Soc; Min Bus Stdnt Assc; Blk Stdnt Ldrshp Conf; AA Fl Comm Coll Jacksonvl 90; Acctg; CPA.

**CUMMINGS, JENNIFER E,** Kent St Univ Kent Cmps, Kent, OH; SO; BS MD; Univ Pres Lst 90-; Intrgrtd Lfe Scis; Med.

**CUMMINGS, KATHLEEN M,** Wilmington Coll, New Castle, DE; SR; BA; Newspr The Voyager Ftr Edtr; Yrbk; Delta Epsilon Rho 90; Dns Lst 88-; Intrnshp 88; Cmnctn Arts; News.

**CUMMINGS, KEITH A,** S U N Y Coll At Fredonia, Fredonia, NY; SR; BS; Spectrum Entrtnmnt Brd Bus Chrprsn 90-; Delta Mu Delta 90-; Grad Hons; Bus Admin/Finance; Fincl Mgt.

**CUMMINGS, RAIFORD G,** William Carey Coll, Hattiesburg, MS; JR; BS; Flwshp Chrstn Athlts 88-; Bapt Stdnt Union 88-; Sci Clb 88-; Omcrn Dlt Kappa 90; Glf Cst Athletic Conf Hon Roll 90; Gami Chi Big Bro 88-; Vrsty Bsbl 88-; Chem; Medcn.

**CUMMINGS, RICHARD C,** William Carey Coll, Hattiesburg, MS; JR; BS; Flwshp Chrstn Athlts 88; Bapt Stdnt Union 88-; Sci Clb 88-; Alpha Ch 90; Omicron Dlt Kappa 90; Gulf Cst Athltc Conf Hon Roll 88; Gammi Chi Big Bro 88-; Vrsty Bsbl 88-; Chem; Medcn.

**CUMMINGS, RICHARD L,** Alfred Univ, Alfred, NY; JR; Beta Gamma Sigma 90-; Delta Mu Delta 90-; AS Bus Admin Alfred St Coll 74; AAS Real Est Alfred St Coll 90; Bus Admin; Mngmnt.

**CUMMINGS, SCOTT R,** S U N Y Coll Of A & T Morrisvl, Morrisville, NY; Stdnt Govt Rep 89-; Jzz Ensmbl 89-; Cncrt Bnd 89-; Rsdnt Asst 90; Hstry; Secndry Edctn.

**CUMMINGS, STEPHEN R,** Memphis St Univ, Memphis, TN; SR; BS; Park/Rcrtn Soc Treas 89-90; Rcrtn/Pk Admin; Pk Rngr-Natl Pk Serv.

**CUMMINGS, TAMARA L,** Appalachian Bible Coll, Bradley, WV; SO; Drmtc Arts Chrstn Wtns Troupe Sec 90-; Drama Tm 89-90; Advncd Bibl Cert 90; Spec Ed; Chrstn Ed.

**CUMMINGS, TAMMY L,** S U N Y Coll At Fredonia, Fredonia, NY; JR; BA; Bdgt Apprprtns Cmmtt Exec; Drm Cncl Sec; SGA; Bus Clb; Intern Darine Lk Mrktng; IMS; Bus Admn/Mrktng; Advrtsng/Spnsrshp.

**CUMMINGS, WENDI A,** Indiana Univ Of Pa, Indiana, PA; SR; BS; Women In Cmctns Inc Sec 90-; Amer Soc For Trng/Dev 90-; Soc Of Prof Jrnlsts 87-88; Provost Schlr 89-; Pub Affrs Intrnshp; Cmctns Media; Pub Rels.

**CUMMINGS, YOLANDA A,** Memphis St Univ, Memphis, TN; SO; BBA; Black Stdt Assoc 89-; Resident Assist; Peer Mentor; Gamma Beta Phi; Black Scholars Unlimited; Acounting; Law.

**CUMMINGS-JACKSON, ROSEANNE T,** City Univ Of Ny Baruch Coll, New York, NY; SO; BBA; WBI 88-89; WCI; CEMOTAP 90-91; Natl Piano Aud 86; Amer Clg Of Mus 87; Natl Guild Of Piano Tchrs 88; Intl Piano Rcrdng Awrd 88; NFSM 87; Sonatina Medal Piano Guild USA 87; Exec Intrnshp 88; Acctng; CPA.

**CUMMINS, DEBRA Y,** Wv Univ At Parkersburg, Parkersburg, WV; SR; BA; Phi Theta Kappa; Elem Edn.

**CUMMINS, JENNIFER J,** Indiana Univ Of Pa, Indiana, PA; JR; BA; Pnhllnc Cncl VP 90; Alpha Xi Delta VP 89-; Pltcl Scnc; Law.

**CUMMINS, JONATHAN M,** Univ Of Sc At Columbia, Columbia, SC; SR; BS; Sport Adm Clb Pres 88-90; Pres Hnr Rl 89-90; Dns Hnr Rl 88-90; Soccer 90; Pres Intern Sr Intern 88-90; Sport Adm; Law/Intl Bsn.

**CUMMINS, MARY J,** Northern Ky Univ, Highland Hts, KY; SR; BSW; Scl Wrk Clb 89-; Dns Lst.

**CUNAGIN, CHERYL A,** Cumberland Coll, Williamsburg, KY; SR; MBA; Stdnt Alumni Assoc VP 89-90; Foreign Lang/Cltres Clb Sec/Treas 88; Phi Beta Lambda 88; J T Vallandingham Awd; Acad Schlrshp 87; Hgh Hnr Roll 88; BA; Mngmnt; Accntng.

**CUNDIFF, KENYETTA A,** Norfolk St Univ, Norfolk, VA; SR; BA; Psychology Clb 88-; Alpha Kappa Mu 90-; Psi Chi 89-; Peer Grp Cnslr 90-; Alumni Acdmc Schlrshp 90-; Cluster Acdmc Excllnc Schlrshp 88-90; BA; Psychology; Psychiatrist.

**CUNDIFF, MICHAEL L,** Marshall University, Huntington, WV; JR; Rsdnc Hl Assn RA 90-; Empl As Co-Op With US Dept Treas Bureau Of Pub Debt Stdnt Trainee Stf Asst; Finance; Govt.

**CUNEFARE, RICK L,** Limestone Coll, Gaffney, SC; SR; BS; Hnr Grad Magna Cum Laude 90; Deans Lst 89-; Bus Admin/Mgmnt; Financial Analyst/MBA.

**CUNIC, GEORGE D,** Comm Coll Algny Co Algny Cmps, Pittsburgh, PA; FR; Engr.

**CUNNIFFE, REGINA B,** Molloy Coll, Rockville Ctr, NY; JR; BS; Nrsg Acdmnc Brd Repr 90-; Nrsg Clb 89-; Glc Soc 90-; Sigma Theta Tau; Delta Epsilon Sigma; Omicron Alpha Zeta; CCD Instrctr 86-89; Intrnshp St Francis Hosp; Natl League Of Nrsg Comm; Practiced Nrsg In Pineville Clinic; Nrsg; Clncl Nrs Spclst.

**CUNNINGHAM, ALLISON E,** Glassboro St Coll, Glassboro, NJ; SR; BA; Psych; Tchg.

**CUNNINGHAM, AMY BETH,** Univ Of Tn At Martin, Martin, TN; SR; Soc Prof Jrnlsts; Adv Chrmn Miss UTM; Coor Pnhllnc Fshn Shw; Chi Omega Pnhllnc 86-; Stu Affrs Serv Awrd; IM; BA; Cmmnctns Pblc Rltns.

**CUNNINGHAM, AMY D,** Cedarville Coll, Cedarville, OH; FR; BS; Symphnc Bnd 90-; Eng Soc 90-; Pep Bnd 90-; Dean Lst 90-; IM Sftbl; Mech Eng; Eng.

**CUNNINGHAM, AMY M,** Hilbert Coll, Hamburg, NY; SO; AAS; Profl Asstnts Clb Sec/Treas 90-; Alpha Beta Gamma 91; Ofc Tech; Admin Asst.

**CUNNINGHAM, ANGELA L,** Memphis St Univ, Memphis, TN; FR; BA; BSA Models 90-; Choir 90-; Black Stdnts Assn; Black Schlrs Unlimited; MIS.

**CUNNINGHAM, BARBARA A,** Neumann Coll, Aston, PA; SO; BSN; SNA 90-; Delaware Cnty Comm Coll 89-90; Pres Hon Roll; Nrsn RN BSN; MSN Mstr Nrsng.

**CUNNINGHAM, CAROL L,** Saint Francis Coll, Loretto, PA; SR; BS; Educ Clb 87-89; Delta Epsilon Sigma; Clg Hnr Soc; PA Scnc Teach Enhncmnt Prog Clarion Univ 90; Elem Educ; Teach.

**CUNNINGHAM, CHRISTOPHER J,** Univ Of Pittsburgh, Pittsburgh, PA; SO; BS; Cstng Clb 90-; Engr Std Cbnt Rep 90-; ASM 90-; Glbrt Slr Schlp; Dns Lst; Mtrls/Sci Engr.

**CUNNINGHAM, CLIFTON L,** Fayetteville St Univ, Fayetteville, NC; FR; Biology; Military.

**CUNNINGHAM, DEBBIE F,** Univ Of Al At Birmingham, Birmingham, AL; SR; CERT; SOTA Parlmntrn 90-; SHRPS 90-; Dns Lst 90; Pres Hnrs; Chrldr 87-; Occup Thrpy Asst.

**CUNNINGHAM, DONNA M,** Fl International Univ, Miami, FL; JR; Natl Cncl Scl Studies; AA Miami-Dade Cmnty Clg 90; Scl Sci Sec Ed; Tchg.

**CUNNINGHAM, GAYLE A,** Univ Of New England, Biddeford, ME; SR; BS; UNESOTA 89; Non-Trad Stdnt Clb 89; AOTA 79; MEOTA 87; COTA US Army 79; BA Psychlgy St Martinis Clg 87; US Army COTA 79-88; Occptnl Thrpy.

**CUNNINGHAM, GINA,** Barry Univ, Miami, FL; SR; BA; BPW Grnpce 87-; Art; Artst Art Tchr.

**CUNNINGHAM, JACQUELINE,** Talladega Coll, Talladega, AL; SR; BA; German Club VP 89; Pre Alumni Council 87-88; Math Club; Alpha Kappa Alpha Pre 89-; Deans List; Pres II Schlrshp; Albert Schwecter German Awd; UNCE Awd; Math/Computer Sci; Engrg.

**CUNNINGHAM, JEFFREY M,** Univ Of Nc At Asheville, Asheville, NC; SO; MBA; Atmospheric Science; Mtrlgst.

**CUNNINGHAM, JILL A,** Saint Elizabeth Hosp Sch Nurs, Utica, NY; FR; ASN; Grl Scts Asst Ldr 89-; Cncr Vol; Hrt Assc Vol; Nrsng.

**CUNNINGHAM, JOSEPH J,** Pa St Univ Main Cmps, University Pk, PA; SR; BS; IM Ftbl/Sftbl/Crs Cntry 89; Hon Soc VP 88-89; Gold Key 89-; Tau Beta Pi 89-; Eta Kappa Nu 89-; Kappa Theta Epsilon; Pres Awd 87-88; Campus Advsry Ldrshp Awd 88; Deans Lst 87-89; Vrsty Vlybl 87; Elec Eng.**

**CUNNINGHAM II, MICHAEL E,** Marshall University, Huntington, WV; JR; BA; Acctg; Bus Law.

**CUNNINGHAM, PAULER R,** Miami Dade Comm Coll North, Miami, FL; SO; BA; AA Bus Admin; Bus Admin; Pub Bus Amdin.

**CUNNINGHAM, ROBERT M,** Univ Of South Al, Mobile, AL; JR; BS; Alpha Chi; Bus-Fin Depstry Inst Mgt; Bnkg Scrtes/Law Sch.

**CUNNINGHAM, SCHWANNA T,** Morris Brown Coll, Atlanta, GA; JR; MBAJD; Accntng Clb; Hnrs Clb; Gldn Key; Ladies Of Roylty Vp 90-; Im Bsktbl; Oakrdg Mnrty Stdnt Admnstrtv Smr Intrnshp; Accntng; Law.

**CUNNINGHAM, SHARON A,** Kent St Univ Geauga Cmps, Burton Twp, OH; SO; BS; Crs Cntry 90; Blgy; Mdcl.

**CUNNINGHAM, SHAUNTAY D,** Fl International Univ, Miami, FL; SR; BS; Bptst Cmps Mnstry 89-; Intern Metro Dade Co 90-; Bsktbl Tm 89-; AS Broward Comm Coll 89; Prks Rec Mgmt; Hlth Srvcs Admn.

**CUNNINGHAM, SHERRY L,** Wv Univ At Parkersburg, Parkersburg, WV; FR; BA; Asst Mgr/Sec/Gen Mgr; Acctng.

**CUNNINGHAM, SHIRLEY,** Al St Univ, Montgomery, AL; FR; NAACP; 21st Cntry Yth Ldrshp; Phi Eta Sigma; Air Frc ROTC; Crmnl Jstce; Lawyer USAF.

**CUNNINGHAM, STEVEN G,** Jackson St Univ, Jackson, MS; FR; BS; Biology; Med.

**CUNNINGHAM, VENESSA C,** Univ Of Al At Birmingham, Birmingham, AL; SO; AS; Stdnt Occptnl Thrpy Assc; AL Occptnl Thrpy Assc; Cert Carver State Tech Clg 85; Hlth Rltd; Occptnl Thrpy Asstnt.

**CUNNINGHAM II, WILLIAM C,** Univ Of Sc At Columbia, Columbia, SC; SR; BA; Pi Kappa Phi Hstrn 82-85; USAF Trng Ribbon; USAF Lngvty Serv Awd Rbbn; USAF Good Cndct Mdl; USAF Achvmnt Mdl Oak Leaf Clstr; USAF Outstndng Unit Awd Oak Leaf Clstr 86-90; BA Prsbytrn Coll 85; Media Arts; Media Prod.

**CUOMO, KARIN K,** Christopher Newport Coll, Newport News, VA; GD; BSBA; Alpha Chi 89-; Stdnt Cnslr SBAI 90-; Mktg/Mgmt Dept Hon 90; Mktg/Mgmt; Fin Sec Fld.

**CUPELES MATOS, ISRAEL,** Inter Amer Univ Pr San German, San German, PR; FR; BA; DECA 88-90; Math Clb 87; MDA; Mdl Dstrbtv Clb Amer; Blgy; Doctor.

**CUPIL, CRAIG C,** Central St Univ, Wilberforce, OH; GD; BS; Natl Assoc Ind Tech; Deans List; Alpha Kappa Mu; Stdnt Ambssdr; Ind Eng Tech; Co-Op Corp Of Engrs Engr Trainee; IM Bsktbll; Ind Engr Tech.

**CUPIT, DANA R,** Ms St Univ, Miss State, MS; SO; BA; Cmps Crsd Christ 89-; Phi Kappa Phi; Walt Disney World Clg Prog; Bus/Mrktng; Buyer.

**CUPP, CALVIN R,** Pellissippi St Tech Comm Coll, Knoxville, TN; FR; BA; Drama Clb; Phi Theta Kappa; Math; Scndry Ed.

**CUPP, TERRY L,** Anne Arundel Comm Coll, Arnold, MD; SO; BA; Phi Theta Kappa; BA UMBC 87; Hstry; Law.

**CUPPLES, BRETT G,** Ms St Univ, Miss State, MS; SO; BA; Cum Laude AAS; AAS St Tchncl Inst AT Mmphs 90; Archtctr; Architect.

**CURCIO, KRISTINE,** Saint Francis Coll, Brooklyn, NY; JR; Stdnt Govt Sntr 89-90; Chrstn Scty 90; Duns Scotus 90; Big Apple Gms Rcrtnl Assist 88; Cmmssnr Acad Hnr Roll For NE Conf 88; Athletic Bsktbl Schlrshp Capt 88; BS; Mngmnt; Law.**

**CURCIO, TYSON J,** S U N Y Coll Of Tech At Alfred, Alfred, NY; FR; MBA; Dorm Cncl 90-; IM Sftbl 90-; Arch Engr.

**CURCIO, VERONICA L,** S U N Y Coll At Fredonia, Fredonia, NY; SR; MSW; Soc Wrk Intrn 90; Grad Magna Cum Laude; E Coll Sci Cnfrnce; BA; Sociolgy; Grad Schl.

**CURD, KAREN A,** Lexington Comm Coll, Lexington, KY; SO; Data Prcsng Mgmt Assn Mmbrshp Chrprsn 90-; Cmptr Sci.

**CURETON, KATHERINE A,** Johnson C Smith Univ, Charlotte, NC; SO; Kappa Alpha Psi 89.

**CURFMAN, BRIAN K,** Marshall University, Huntington, WV; SR; BBA; Lambda Chi Alpha Frat 86-90; ACM 89-90; Cmptr Sci; Sys Anlyst.

**CURL, CYNTHIA S,** Oh Univ, Athens, OH; GD; DO; ACS 86-89; Sprts Med Clb 89-; Sigma Sigma Phi V P 90-; Cum Laude; Var Vlybl Sftbl 85-86; BS Baldwn Wallc Clg 89; Medicine.

**CURLEE, KENNEY L,** Central Al Comm Coll, Alexander City, AL; FR; AAS; Deans Lst 90-; Comp Sci.

**CURLEE, TRACEY C,** Tallahassee Comm Coll, Tallahassee, FL; SO; AA; Branell Coll 89; Ace Awd Tallahassee Comm Hosp 90; Nurse Tech Branell Coll 89; Med Ph D; Doctor.

**CURLER, MARGIE L,** The Boston Conservatory, Boston, MA; JR; BM; Bstn Cnsrvtry Chrstn Flwshp Prtcpnt 90-; Bstn Cnsrvtry Comm Serv Clb VP 90-; Sigma Alpha Iota Prtcpnt 90-; Tlnt Rstr Cert Achvmnt 87-88; Annabelle Jones Rose Mem Schlrshp 85-86; AA 87-88; Music; Opera.

**CURLEY, CATHERINE R,** Univ Of Rochester, Rochester, NY; SR; BA; Outsd Spkrs Comm 88-; Pol Sci Cncl 87-; Stdy Ahrd Peer Adv 90-; Sigma Delta Tau Pub Chmr 88-; London Prog 90; Pol Sci; Own Bus.

**CURLEY, DENNIS P,** Fl St Univ, Tallahassee, FL; SR; BA; IEEE 89-; FAMU 90-; Golden Key 90-; Phi Beta Kappa 90-; USAF Reserves SSGT 86-; Sucrdrup Tchlgy Engreg Intern Assoc Egr 88-; AA; Engr; Elec Engrg Contractor.

**CURLEY, JACQUELINE JEROME,** Saint John Fisher Coll, Rochester, NY; JR; BS; Spch Scty Pres 87 VP 88; Intrnatl Frndshp Clb Pres 88; Phi Theta Kappa Pres 89; Bus Dept Of Econs Awrd 88; GICO Schlrshp Awrd 89; Pres Schlrshp 89-; IMB Mrktng Awrd; PTA VP 90; GS Ldr 90; Elem Schl Ttr 88; Prsbytrn Chrch Chr; Bus Mrktng.

**CURLEY, JAMERYL A,** Central Fl Comm Coll, Ocala, FL; SO; BA; Brain Bowl Acad Tm 90-; AA 90; English Educ; Prfsr.

**CURNOW, DANIEL A,** Brevard Coll, Brevard, NC; SO; BA; Ambssdr 90-; Video Yrbk Exec Prod 90-; Rsdnt Asst Hnr Dorms 90-; Phi Thetta Kapa; Bsn Mngmnt.

**CURRAIS, MARIA V,** Univ Of Miami, Coral Gables, FL; SO; BA; Pol; Law.

**CURRAN, MAUREEN E,** Albertus Magnus Coll, New Haven, CT; SO; BA; Nwspr Edtr; Lit Mag Edtr 89-; Engl Clb 90-; Amnsty Intl 90-; Tutor/Vol 90-; Engl.

**CURRAN, TRACY E,** Bunker Hill Comm Coll, Boston, MA; FR.

**CURRAY, TERESA G,** Middle Tn St Univ, Murfreesboro, TN; SR; BS; Statistics Actrl Orgnztn Pres 90-91; Math Orgnztn 89-; Pi Mu Epsilon 89-; Gamma Iota Sigma VP Admnstrtn 89-; Gamma Iota Sigma Ins Schlrshps 89-; Math Actrl Sci.

**CURREN, CATHERINE G,** Univ Of Montevallo, Montevallo, AL; JR; Biology Clb; Chmstry Clb; Montevillo Envrnmntlsts; Alpha Lambda Delta; Omicron Delta Kappa; Kappa Mu Epsilon; Alpha Gamma Delta VP; League Anml Welfare; Phmrcy.

**CURREN, JOLYNN Z,** Elmira Coll, Elmira, NY; JR; BA; Phi Betta Kappa; Csmtlgst 86-; Csmtlgst Hair Care Careers 86; Assoc Corning Comm Coll 89; Socl Sci; Elem Educ.

**CURRENCE, LISA M,** Howard Univ, Washington, DC; JR; BS; Nat Stdnt Spch/Lng/Hrng Assoc VP; Stdnt Govt Assoc Repr 90-; Howard Sk Clb; Gldn Key; Frederick Douglass Hnr Soc Pres; Myrs Advsry Cmte Rsrcs Bdgt Yth Rep 87-; Trst Schlrshp Awd 90-; Cmsn Pblc Hlth Imnztn Dvsn Intrn 90-; Rqtbl Clb; Spch/Lng Pthlgy.

**CURRENT, EMILY M,** Fl St Univ, Tallahassee, FL; FR; BA; Glee Clb 90-; Jazz Pop Ensmbl 90-; Blues Lab 90-; Amer Chrl Dir 90-; Fla Msc Educators 90-; Msc; Msc Educ/Hgh Schl Chr.

**CURREY, LYNN M,** Univ Of West Fl, Pensacola, FL; JR; BA; Pensacola Jr Coll Sftbl Tm Capt 2nd Yr 88-90; Univ W FL Sftbl Tm 90-; Phi Theta Kappa 88-90; FCCAA Acdmc Awd 88-89; FCCAA Acdmc Awd 89-90; NCCAA All-Amer Acdmc Awd 89-90; Sftbl Tms; AA Pensacola Jr Coll 90; Math; Educ.

**CURREY, MARY NOELLE,** Univ Of Tn At Chattanooga, Chattanooga, TN; SR; BEE; IEEE Pres 88-; Natl Soc Prof Engrs VP 90-; Soc Wmn Engrs Pres 90-; Tau Beta Pi 90-; Mrtr Brd 89-90; Gldn Key 89-; Sigma Kappa 90-; Kappa Chi Epsln 88-90; Paul Crts Jr Mrm Awd; Tau Beta Pi Flwshp; Sigma Kappa Acad Exclnc Awd; Elec Engr; Acstcl Engr.

**CURRIE, CHRISTIE J,** Univ Of Tn At Martin, Martin, TN; SO; BS; Grkfst Comm Co Chrmn 90-; Phi Eta Sigma; Alpha Omicron Pi Schlrshp Chrmn; Serv Awrd 90; Psych; Law.

**CURRIE, LINDA H,** Averett Coll, Danville, VA; SR; BS; Hmn Rsrc Dvlpmnt.**

**CURRIE, SHARON A,** Univ Of Md Baltimore Prof Schl, Baltimore, MD; SR; BA; Stdnt Govt Treas 89-; Admssns Comm 88-89; Curriculum Comm 90-; Hon Smnr 89-90; Rho Chi 90-; Phi Kappa Phi 90-; Lambda Kappa Sigma 90-; Elder Educ 89-; Prnc Frdrck Vol Fire Dept Ladies Aux 88-; Natl Assn Rtl Drgst Rsrch Grnt 90; Phrmcy; Cmnty Phrmcy.

**CURRIER, GERALD C,** S U N Y Coll Of Tech At Alfred, Alfred, NY; FR; AS; Sigma Tau Epsilon; Drafting Tchngl Illstrtn; Drftng Engnrng.

**CURRIER JR, JOHN K,** Appalachian Bible Coll, Bradley, WV; SO; BA; Sprtl Lfe Cmmttee 89-90; Soph Class Offcr VP 90; Grace Gspl Chrch Daniels WV 89-90; Cmptr Prog/Analyst 84-89; AS NH Tech Inst 85; Diploma Rl Schl Of Phtgrphy 80; Bible/Thlgy; Pstrl Mnstry.

**CURRIN, DAVID L,** Nc St Univ At Raleigh, Raleigh, NC; SO; BS; Horticulture Clb 90-; Hort Sci Schlrshp 89; Dns Lst; IM Bsktbl 90-; Lndscp Hort.**

**CURRIN, DAVID N,** Vance Granville Comm Coll, Henderson, NC; SO; BSN; Stdnt Govt Rep 89-90; Class Sec Treas 90-; Rowan Waltrs Schlrshp 90-; State Psychtrc Hosp; ADN Vgcc; Nrsng.

**CURRY, ALISHA D,** Fl A & M Univ, Tallahassee, FL; FR; BA; Alpha Swthrt 90-; Images Mdlng Trp 90-; Psych; PHD.

**CURRY, ANDRETTE V,** Univ Of Tn At Martin, Martin, TN; SO; Elem Educ; Tchr.

**CURRY, CAROLYN,** Central St Univ, Wilberforce, OH; GD; Stdnt Govt Pres 89-90; Untd States Achvmnt Acad 90; Natl Mrt Schlr 90-; Asstnt Adtr State OH 90-; BS Cntrl State Un 90; AAS Sinclr Comm Clg 87; Acctg; CPA.**

**CURRY, DAVID W,** Indiana Univ Of Pa, Indiana, PA; SR; BSED; Phi Sigma Pi 88-90; Pi Kappa Phi Chap 90-; Dns Lst 87-; Provosts Schlr 87-90; Vars Swmng/Dvng Capt 87-; Gen Sci; Tchg.

**CURRY, DONALD R,** Va St Univ, Petersburg, VA; JR; BA; Class Ofcr Treas 91-; Acctg Clb 89-; Pan Hellenic Cncl; Acctg; Auditor.

**CURRY, ERIN C,** Duquesne Univ, Pittsburgh, PA; JR; BS; Music Thrpy Clb Secy 88-; SG Rep 88-89; Mortar Bd; Pi Kappa Lambda; Mu Phi Epsilon Pres 89-; Univ Vol 90-; Deans Lst 88-; Music Therapy.

**CURRY, JENNIFER J,** Miami Univ At Middletown, Middletown, OH; FR; BA; Jrnlsm; Envrnmntl Rptng.

**CURRY, JOY C,** Memphis St Univ, Memphis, TN; FR; BA; Rehbltn Educ; Speech Pathology.

**CURRY, KAREN B,** Mount Olive Coll, Mount Olive, NC; JR; BS; Presidents List; Marshall For The 90- Chief 90-91 Jr Class 90-; Cashier 85-; AAS Clark Cnty Cmnty Clge 88; Bus Mgmnt; Retail Mgmnt.

**CURRY, LISA M,** Fairfield Univ, Fairfield, CT; FR; Chrldng 90-; English; Law.

**CURRY, MARSHA J,** Kent St Univ Kent Cmps, Kent, OH; GD; Library Science.

**CURRY, MELISSA A,** West Liberty St Coll, West Liberty, WV; FR; BS; Spanish Club VP; Orientn Stf; Hons Progrm; James B Brennan III Schlrshp; Tutor/Cnslr; Chrldr 90-; Medcl/Surgcl Nrs.

**CURRY, ROBERTA A,** Indiana Univ Of Pa, Indiana, PA; SR; BS; Kappa Delta Pi 89-; Deans Lst; PSEA 90-; NEA 90-; Summa Cum Laude; Jdg Elctns 89-; PTA 82-; Seamstress; Brdl Cnsltnt; Elem Edctn; Tchr.

**CURRY, STEPHANIA D,** Nc Agri & Tech St Univ, Greensboro, NC; SR; BS; S-NEA 88-89; NC Cncl Tchrs Math; Collgt All-Amer Schlr 90; Stdnt Tchng; Elem Ed; Tch.

**CURRY, TINA M,** Marshall University, Huntington, WV; SR; BBA; Acctng Clb; AS Southern WV Comm Clg; Acctng.

**CURTI, SERGIO L,** Duquesne Univ, Pittsburgh, PA; FR; BS; Spnsh Clb VP 90-; Intrnatl Stdnts Orgnztn 90-; Sr Awrds Com; Phi Eta Sigma; Bus Admin; Hsptlty Mgmt.

**CURTICE, JENNIFER T,** Univ Of Ga, Athens, GA; SO; BS; Communiv 90-; Chld Life Assoc Treas; Chldrns Hlth Assocf Dns Lst 90-; Alpha Gamma Delta 89-; Red Cross Bone Marrow Donor 90; IM Sftbl; Chld Family Dvlpmt; Chld Life Spec.

**CURTIN, CHRISTIAN J,** George Mason Univ, Fairfax, VA; SO; BA; Fr Cntr 90-; US Snte Intrn 90; Cntr Acad Sccss Awrd 90; Bus Acctng.

**CURTIN, DAVID T,** S U N Y Coll At Fredonia, Fredonia, NY; SR; MM; Piano Clb 88-; All Coll Bnd Sax 88-90; Pi Kappa Lambda 89-; Phi Beta Kappa; Magna Cum Laude; Tchng Asst Piano Univ Louisvl; BM; BA; Music/Engl; Music/Tchr.

**CURTIN, JEFFEREY M,** Liberty Univ, Lynchburg, VA; SO; BS; Otstndng Frshmn Achvmnt Awrd Comp Sci 89-90; Comp Sci Math.

**CURTIN, RANDY K,** Oh Univ, Athens, OH; GD; DO; Stdnt Osteopthc Med Assn; Amer Med Stdnt Assn; Sigma Sigma Phi; Natl Osteo Hnry Pres 90-; Amer Osteo Assn; Ohio Osteo Assn; Amer Soc Clin Pathgsts; BS Edinboro Univ Penns 78; Osteo Med.

**CURTIS, AMY L,** Bethel Coll, Mckenzie, TN; SO; BA; Creative Wrtng Interest League 90-; Bethel Beacon Reporter 90-; English; Novelist.

**CURTIS, BRUCE L,** Middle Tn St Univ, Murfreesboro, TN; SR; BS; Hipers Clb 90-; Phys Educ; Tch/Coach.

**CURTIS, CHRISTINA A,** Colby Sawyer Coll, New London, NH; SR; BA; IM Sprts Dorm Repr 89-90; Wrkd For Boston Celtics PR Offc 90; USIA 91; Vlybl Capt 89-90; Alpine Ski Tm 87; Lacrosse 87-; Sprt Mgmnt; Mrktng/Adv.

**CURTIS, GARY HUGH,** Univ Of South Al, Mobile, AL; SR; BS; SGA 88-90; Sci/Math Clb VP 88-89; Amer Red Crs Vol 89-90; Phi Theta Kappa VP 88-90; Phi Theta Kappa VP 89; Std Serv/Bio Tutor 89-90; HCOP; Rtry Rehb Hosp Vol 89; MHCOP 89; Natl Gvr Asc 90; Amer OT Asc 89-90; AS 90; Thrptc Rec; Prgm Dir.

**CURTIS, JANET C,** Samford Univ, Birmingham, AL; FR; BS; Assc Of Nsg Stdnts 90-; Natl Stdnt Nsg Assc 90-; Nsg Externship; Nursing; Rn.

**CURTIS, JILL,** Endicott Coll, Beverly, MA; SO; Stdnt Orientation Ldr Grp Ldr 90; Shipmates 90-; Intrnshp I Bridgeport Jewish Comm Ctr 90; Intrnshp II Bright Horizons Day Care Ctr 4 Yr Old Asst Tchr; Early Chldhd Edn/Day Care; Tchr.

**CURTIS, KRISHA D,** Alcorn St Univ, Lorman, MS; FR; Mrchng Bnd 90-; Snds Dyamite; Alpha Phi Omega Swthrt 90-; Cmmnctns; Brdcstr.

**CURTIS, MAUREEN J,** Teikyo Post Univ, Waterbury, CT; SR; BS; Rose Trauig Schlrs VP 90-; Orntatn 90; Hspc Vlntr; Crisis Cntr Vol; Ldrshp Awd; Sxl Asslt Crisis Cntr Intrn; Chrstn Ed Brd Sec 87-; Cong Chrch Fllwshp Comm Chprsn Comm; Sciology; MSW MDIV.

**CURTIS, MEREDITH A,** Middle Tn St Univ, Murfreesboro, TN; SR; BA; Future Accntnts Assn Sec/Treas; Beta Alpha Psi 90-; Acctng; CPA.

**CURTIS, RICHARD A,** Memphis St Univ, Memphis, TN; SR; BA; Compndng Supv Schrng Plough 83-; Matls Plnng Cntrl Schrng Plough Inc; Bsns Mgmt.

**CURTIS, ROBIN L,** Univ Of Tn At Martin, Martin, TN; FR; Chem; Pharm.

**CURTIS, THERESA M,** Univ Of Southern Ms, Hattiesburg, MS; SR; PHD; Hnrs Clg; Untd Way; Sxlt Asslt Crisis Cntr 89-90; Jr CYO Advsr 88-90; Gnrl Hnrs 90; Clncl Psychlgy.

**CURTIS, TRACEY LYNN,** Univ Of Fl, Gainesville, FL; JR; BA; Wom Ldrshp Conf Comm; Cmbr Sngrs/Orchestra/Mus Theatre/ Chmbr Music Accmpnst 88-92; Mortar Brd Treas; Alpha Kappa Psi Prof Chrmn 90-; Innsbrck Ambssdr Awd Schlrshp; H A Buddy Bishop Jr Bus Schlrshp; Funk Awd Most Otsdng Fres Piano Stdnt 88-89; Finance/Music; Bus.

**CURTIS-ATTOH, BRENDA,** Coll Of New Rochelle, New Rochelle, NY; SR; The 185/225 Prkhl Ave Tenants Assoc Sec; Faith Chrstn Cntr Chrch Tchr 89-; Law; Scl Wrk.

**CURTISS, CYNTHIA L,** Univ Of Charleston, Charleston, WV; SR; Capito Assoc Nursing Stdnt 87-; Amer Red Cross Vol 87-; Natl Nursing Hnr Soc.

**CURTISS, KATHERINE P,** Kent St Univ Geauga Cmps, Burton Twp, OH; FR; BS; Cross Country 89-90; Police Dispatcher/ Officer; Engr; Cvl/Envir Engr.

**CURTSINGER, ANNA R,** Georgetown Coll, Georgetown, KY; SR; Alpha Lambda Delta; Otstndng Coll Stdnts Of Amrca; Usaa Schlstc Al Amrcn Soc; Stdnt Mmb Ky Soc Of Cpas; Im Bsktbl; Acctng/Cmptr Sci; Cpa.

**CURTSINGER, CARL E,** Spalding Univ, Louisville, KY; SR; BS; Spalding Ambsdrs VP 89-90; Spalding Spctrm Edtr 87-90; Delta Epsilon Sigma 89-91; Kappa Gamma Pi 90-; Alpha Psi Omega 89-; Acadmc Hnrs Lst 88-; Humana Inc Corp Ofc; Vllybl; Cmmnctns; Edtr Prdcr Drctr.**

**CUSA, MARC R,** S U N Y At Binghamton, Binghamton, NY; JR; BS; Cmps Rcrd Str Co-Op Mgr 89-; Orch/Bnd/Prcsn Ensbl Perc Prcpl Plyr 88-; Radio Sta Apprtnc; Dns Lst 90; Tchng Asst Fin Mgmt; IM 88-; Mgmt; Media/Mktg.

**CUSACK, PATRICK P,** American Univ, Washington, DC; FR; BA; Radio Sta; Delta Tau Delta; Rssn/Soviet Stds/Intrnl Bus.

**CUSANO, CHRISTOPHER A,** Univ Of Rochester, Rochester, NY; SR; BA; Religion.

**CUSHING, CATHERINE A,** Fl St Univ, Tallahassee, FL; SR; BS; Cncl Except Chldrn 89-; Alpha Gamma Delta 87-; Spec Ed LD ED VE; Tch Except Stdnts.

**CUSHMAN, DAVID H,** Western Carolina Univ, Cullowhee, NC; JR; BS; Asstnt Actvts Dir Fish/Wldlf Scty Paul Smiths Clg 88-89; Deans List 90-; Avid Otdrsmn Hntng Fshng Trpng Slng; Mattituck Gun Clb; NRA; N Amer Hntng Clb; NY State Rfl/Pstl Assc; AAS Paul Smiths Clg 87-89; Cert Sthwstrn Comm Clg; Natrl Rsrc Mgmt; Prk Rngr/Fed Game Wrdn.

**CUSHMAN, KAREN,** City Univ Of Ny Baruch Coll, New York, NY; JR; BBA; Std Govt Sec 89-90; Jwsh Clb 88-; Brch Schlr 88-; Dns Lst 89-; Truman Schlp 89; Mktg; Bsn.

**CUSICK, CYNTHIA T,** Colby Sawyer Coll, New London, NH; SO; BA; Deans Lst; Sales Clrk; Arts Mgmt/Art Hstry; Museum/ Tch.

**CUSICK, DANIEL P,** Comm Coll Algny Co Algny Cmps, Pittsburgh, PA; SO; BA; Engr; Cvl Engr.

**CUSSAT, CHRISTOPHER L,** Duquesne Univ, Pittsburgh, PA; FR; BA; Campus Mnstry 90-; Univ Vol 90-; Cllgt YMCA 90-; Pre Law Scty 90-; Sclgy Criminal Justice; Law.

**CUSTER, ANNE,** Westminster Coll, New Wilmingtn, PA; SR; BA; Univ Of Pittsburgh Non Crdt Film Crse 79; Chatham Clg Pittsturgh PA Cmnctns 81-82; Penn State Univ Beaver PA Cmnctn Mjr 87; Deans List 88-90; John Orr Schlrshp; Pi Sigma Phi 89-90; Gen Acadmc Schrlshp 89-90; Wm R Jamison Schrlshp 89-90; Relgs Cmnctn.

**CUSTER, BRYAN G,** Wv Univ, Morgantown, WV; SR; Amer Inst Arntcs/Astrntcs 89-; Phi Kappa Phi 89-; Sigma Gamma Tau 89-; Tau Beta Pi 90-; Sigma Phi Omega 88-; Gldn Key 89-; BS; Arspc; Engrg.

**CUSTODIO, CRISTINA M,** Harvard Univ, Cambridge, MA; FR; BA; Natl Mdl UN Admin Stf Dir Dlgte Srvc 90-; Undrgrdt Admsns Cncl Stf/Hsts 90-; PR Stdnt Assoc 90-; Internatl Rltns Cncl 90-; Phillip Brooks Hse/Msn Hl Cnslr 90-; Asst U PR; IM Vlybl 90-; Hstry/Lit; Law/Govt.

**CUTCHEMBER, HILDA A,** Morgan St Univ, Baltimore, MD; FR; BS; Soph Cls Sntr Prlmnt; Educ Afrs Co Chrmn; Govt Oprtns Co Chrm; NASA Summer Prog; Cvl Engr; Engr.

**CUTCHIN, ALLAN H,** Fl A & M Univ, Tallahassee, FL; JR; BS; Whte/Gold; Ntl Cllgte Schlrs Assoc; 7 1/2 Yrs Actve Dty In US Army; AA U Of Md 89; Pol Sci/Pbl Admin; Army Offcr/ Law.

**CUTCHINS, CHRISTINE M,** Christopher Newport Coll, Newport News, VA; FR; Psychlgy Elem Ed; Tchr.

**CUTE, SAMANTHA L,** Indiana Univ Of Pa, Indiana, PA; SR; PSEA 88-; NEA 89-; ASCD 89-; NCTM; Alpha Gamma Delta Song Chr 89-; Deans Lst 90-; Outstndng Grek Schlr; Spec Olymps 90; Elem Ed.

**CUTHBERT, WENDY L,** Castleton St Coll, Castleton, VT; SR; BA; Kappa Delta Pi 90-; Elem Ed; Tch.

**CUTHPERT JR, CLARENCE,** Savannah St Coll, Savannah, GA; SR; MPA; Crmnl Jstce; Fed Law Enfrcmnt.

**CUTLAR, KENYA M,** Howard Univ, Washington, DC; JR; BS; Ldies Of Quad Soc Clb 88-; Campus Crsde Chrst Bible Stdy Ldr 88-; Lip Sync Comm 89-; Entrtnmnt Comm 89-90; Campus Pals Co-Chr Nght Trs 90-; Natl Comptitv Schlrshp 88-; Deans Lst 89-; Natl Deans Lst 90; Phys Therpy Aide; Phys Therpy.**

**CUTLER, JEFFREY G,** Univ Of Akron, Akron, OH; JR; BS; Civil Engrng; Masters Of Sci CE.

**CUTLER, JENNIFER A,** Mary Baldwin Coll, Staunton, VA; JR; Stdnt Sen Sentr 90-; Cosmos Intrntl Clb 90-; Mnrty Wmn Unty 90-; Hons Lst 89-90; Deans Lst 90-; PEG Merit/Ldrshp Awd 90-; Psych; Wmns Advcy.

**CUTLER, JOYCE M,** Life Coll, Marietta, GA; SO; DC; ICA 90-; ACA 90-; Gnstd Stdy Clb; Plptn Inst 90-; Clss Sec 90; Cllgte Fld Hcky Natl Chmps 84; La Crsse Intrcllgte 86; Tchr 88; BS Old Dominion U 86; Chrprctc.

**CUTLER, MELISSA J,** Alfred Univ, Alfred, NY; SR; BS; Soc Of Women Engrs Pres 87-; Amer Ceramic Soc 89-; ASM Intl 90-; Phi Kappa Phi; Tau Beta Pi 90-; Alpha Lambda Delta 87-; Keramos 88-; Corning Inc Summer Intrn 89-90; Manville Schlr 89-90; ASM Intl Schlr 90; Engr.

**CUTLIP, KENNETH W,** Tusculum Coll, Greeneville, TN; SR; BA; Big Buddy Prog; Bsktbl Captn 87-; Computer Science & Math; Air Force Pilot.

**CUTSHAW, JUDITH M,** Univ Of Southern Ms, Hattiesburg, MS; SO; BS; Gamma Beta Phi 90-; Lit Gld 87-; Elem Educ; Tch.

**CUTSHAW, KIMBERLY D,** Tusculum Coll, Greeneville, TN; SO; BS; Cls V P 90-; Bio; Tchr.

**CUTTER, ALAN S,** Yeshiva Univ, New York, NY; JR; BA; IM Bsktbl; Ntl Conf Syng Yth Advsr; Psych; Scl Wrk.

**CUTTER, KIMBERLY S,** Colby Sawyer Coll, New London, NH; JR; BA; Stdnt Govt VP/SEC/TREAS 88-90; Key Assoc Actvts Chrprsn 89-; Outing Club 89-; Deans List 90-; Windy Hill Lb Schl 89-; Cmptr Lb Mntr 90-; Kearsage Elem Schl Prctn; Mens Bsktbl Mngr 90-; Wom La Crosse Mngr 89-90; Chld Stdy/ Psych Minor; Teacher.

**CUTTER, MARGARET S,** Cleveland Inst Of Art, Cleveland, OH; JR; BFA; MS Wmns Com Sec; Knickerbocker Artists; Salmagundi Clb; NY May Show 89; Cleveland Museum Art; Ohio Watercolor Soc; Signature; Watercolor Instr; Our Lady Wayside; Interior Dsgnr/Art Cons/Instr; Painting.

**CUTTER, TODD D,** S U N Y Coll At Fredonia, Fredonia, NY; SO; BS; All Coll Bnd; Jz Bnd; R T Callahan Awrd; Fredonia Schlr Awrd; Undrgrad Asstshp Comp Lab; Coll Tutrng Serv; Comp Sci; Prgrmng.

**CUTTS, DAVID R,** Univ Of Ky, Lexington, KY; JR; BS; Gldn Key 90-; Otstndng Stdnt Eng Phys Morehead St Univ 88-89; Gen Chem Achvmnt Awd Morehead St Univ 89-90; Engrng.

**CUTTS, MATTHEW D,** Univ Of Ky, Lexington, KY; FR; BS; Krte Clb 90-; Alpha Lambda Delta 90-; Sigma Gamma Sigma 90-; Cmptr Scnc.

**CUTTS, SONIA L,** Univ Of Al At Huntsville, Huntsville, AL; JR; BS; Natl Soc Blck Engrs Sec 90-; Blck Stdnts Assn 89-; Eta Kappa Nu Treas 90-; Alpha Lambda Delta Sec 87-88; Order Omega 90-; Alpha Kappa Alpha Pres 90-; Lancer 90-; 3m Mnrty Stdnt Schlrshp 90; GPA Awd 90; Elec Eng.

**CUVELIER, CHARLES J,** Memphis St Univ, Memphis, TN; SR; BS; Stdnt Actvts Cncl Pres 89-90; Advntr Qst Physcl Chllng Crs Fcltr 90-; Mrtr Brd Pres; Omicron Delta Kappa PR Offc 90; Phi Eta Sigma; Beta Beta Beta Blgy Scty; Rc Prks Assoc; Natl Rcr Prks Assoc Std Brnch Sec 88; Prk Rcrtn Scty Treas 88-89; Blgy.

**CVETNICK, ERIC L,** Garrett Comm Coll, Mchenry, MD; SO; RN; Nrsng; RN.

**CWALINA, AMY M,** George Mason Univ, Fairfax, VA; SR; BSED; Stdnt Educ Assn 90-; Alpha Omicron Pi PR Chr 87-; Erly Educ; Tchr.

**CYFERS, JEROME T,** Marshall University, Huntington, WV; SO; BA; 4h VP 88-89; Ntnl Hnr Scty 88; Cmmty Serv 87; Chrch Worker 87; Bsn Mngmnt; Mngmnt.

**CYHAN, TAMARA M,** Catholic Univ Of America, Washington, DC; FR; BA; Radio D J; IM Water Polo; Psychology; Cnslr.

**CYNAMON, BARBARA P,** Comm Coll Algny Co Algny Cmps, Pittsburgh, PA; Word Proc.

**CYPHER, NEAL A,** Liberty Univ, Lynchburg, VA; FR; BA; Youthquest Club 90-; Lght Ministries Club 90-; Acts 5-42 Prog 90-; Im Bsktbl/Ftbl/Sftbl/Indr Soccer Mgr 90-; Youth Ministries; Youth Pastr/Evanglst.

**CYPHERT, KATHLEEN M,** Kent St Univ Kent Cmps, Kent, OH; SR; BBA; AAB 87; Finance.

**CYPHERT, PATRICK A,** Wv Univ, Morgantown, WV; SR; BSEE; IEEE 89-; Natl Hon Soc 85-87; Elec Engr; MSEE.

**CYR, CHRISTINE G,** Portland School Of Art, Portland, ME; FR; BFA; Hrns Lst 88-; Grp Shw ME Wtrclr Cngrss Sq Gllry Portland ME 90; BA Univ Maine-Portland 76; Paintg; Prfssnl Artist.**

**CYR, CHRISTY M,** Central Fl Comm Coll, Ocala, FL; SO; BA; Bsn; Bnkg.

**CYR, JENNIFER,** Seton Hall Univ, South Orange, NJ; SO; BSE; Eliz Ann Seton Educ Assn 90-; Kappa Delta Pi 90-; Psi Chi 90-; Alpha Gamma Delta 89-; Stdnt Tchr Lincln Elem Schl/Jeff Schl 90-91; Jr Var Chrldng Capt 90-; Elem Educ/Psych; Guid Cnslr.**

**CYR, JULIE A,** Saint Josephs Coll, Windham, ME; FR; BA; SGA 90-; Hall Cncl Pres 90-; Intrhl Cncl 90-; Dns Lst 90-; Superkids 90-; IM 90-; Sociology; Fmly Cnslr.

**CYR, KATHY J,** Colby Sawyer Coll, New London, NH; FR; Vstd The Eldrly 90; Sftbl.

**CYR, PETER J,** Providence Coll, Providence, RI; SO; BA; Rugby; IMS; Soc Sci; Law.

**CYR, ROBIN L,** Saint Josephs Coll, Windham, ME; JR; BSBA; Pre Law Soc Pres; Flk Grp 88-89; Stf Acctnt Intern; Acctg; CPA Law.

**CYRUS-CHARLES, RUDOLPH G,** City Univ Of Ny Med Evers Coll, Brooklyn, NY; GD; BS; Ex-Tchrs Assoc Treas 90-; Mutual Assoc Pres 87; Eucharistic Mnstr Our Lady Of Refuge; Magna Cum Laude; Ntl Cthlc Ed Assoc; Elm Schl Tchr; Cert Grenada Tchrs Clg UWI 79-81; Dip Ed; Acctg.

**CZAPALA, CAROLYN E,** Univ Of Sc At Columbia, Columbia, SC; FR; BS; Nrsng.

**CZAPIENSKI, ELAINE C,** Western New England Coll, Springfield, MA; SR; BS BA; Parenta Assn Cathedral High Schl Spgfld MA 90-; Systs Trnr Mass Mutual Life Ins Co Spgfld MA 01119; Cmptr Info Systs; Systs Analyst Trnr.

**CZAPOR, MICHELLE C,** Bay Path Coll, Longmeadow, MA; SO; BS; Phi Beta Lambda Treas 89-; Golden Z Club 90-; Res Asst 90-; Maroon Key 90-; Acctg; CPA.

**CZARNECKI, ANDREA,** Villanova Univ, Villanova, PA; JR; BA; Spanish Clb Treas 88-89; Hs Cncl Envrnmntl Offcr 89-90; Stdnt Un 88-89; Phi Beta Kappa 90-; Phi Kappa Phi 90-; Villanova Hnrs Prog 88-; Kappa Kappa Gamma Phlnthrpy/V P 88-; Spec Olympics 88-; Hmlss Comm 88-; Gen Arts/Pre Med; Med Schl.

**CZEKAJ, JENNIFER C,** Univ Of Rochester, Rochester, NY; SO; BA; Undrgrad Phlsphy Cncl 89-; Intrvarsty Christn Flwshp 90-; Hill Ct Dorm Cncl Rep; Delta Zeta Chpln/Fndrsng 89-; Alpha Phi Omega Mu Lambda Petitng Grp 90-; U Of R D Lions 90-; Deans List 89-; Bausch/Lomb Schlr 89-; Varsty Wmns Swim Tm 90-; Phlsphy Of Sci/Logic; Ed.

**CZEKALLA, GERD H,** Univ Of Akron, Akron, OH; JR; BA; Tnns Vars Tm 88-; AS Art Vincennes Univ 88-90; Bsn Mgmt; Intl Bsn.

**CZERNETZKY, DONNA J,** Bunker Hill Comm Coll, Boston, MA; JR; AAS; Bsn/Lgl-Wrd Proc; Lgl Secr.

**CZERWINSKI-BROWN, LYNN M,** D Youville Coll, Buffalo, NY; SR; BSN; Stdnt Nurses Assn 89-; Sigma Theta Tau 89-; AS Erie Comm Coll; Nrsng; Med Surgical Flr.

**CZUCHREY, KIMBERLY H,** Garrett Comm Coll, Mchenry, MD; SO; BS; Govt Altnt Soph Rep 89-; Nwspr Edtr 88-; Literary Mag Edtr 87-; Phi Theta Kappa Pblc Rltns Off 90-; Chorus Usher 86-; Zion Chrstn Acad Tch Asst 86-; All Amer Cllgt Schlr; Meritorious Schlr Awdd Frostburg State Univ; BA 90; AA 90; English; Teaching.

**CZURI, FRANK N,** Duquesne Univ, Pittsburgh, PA; JR; BED; Phi Theta Kappa 89; Singer Entrtnr 65-; Scndry Math; Tchr.

# D

**D AGATI, DEBORAH A,** Merrimack Coll, North Andover, MA; JR; BA; Alternative Voice Engl Clb 89-90; Nwspr Ad Dir Ed Chf 90-; Music Ministry 85-; Aide Hndcpd 85-89; Breadloaf Wrtng Pgrm; Engl; Tchng.

**D AIELLO JR, NICHOLAS M,** Univ Of Sc At Columbia, Columbia, SC; JR; BS; US Army Bnd 74th Army Bnd 86; Exrcse Sci Scitfc Fndtns; MS Phys Thrpy.

**D ALESSANDRO, LUCI-ANN M,** Le Moyne Coll, Syracuse, NY; SR; BS; Accntng Soc 89-; Prjcts In The Cmmnty 87-88; Accntng; CPA.

**D ALESSIO, PATRICIA A,** Georgian Court Coll, Lakewood, NJ; JR; BA; Sigma Tau Delta; Engl; Tch.

**D ALICANDRO, JOHN P,** Temple Univ, Philadelphia, PA; SR; Deans Lst 87-; IEEE 87; BSEE.**

**D ALOIA, ANTONELLA,** Providence Coll, Providence, RI; SO; BA; Art Clb 89-90; Stdnt Fclty Org 90-; Arts Hnrs Lbry 89-; Hmnts; Art/Art Hstry.

**D AMATO, CHRISTOPHER M,** Univ Of New Haven, West Haven, CT; SR; Forensic Clb Secr 90-; Forensic Sci.

**D AMATO, DEBORAH E,** Univ Of Md Baltimore Prof Schl, Baltimore, MD; JR; BS; SGA VP 90-; ASP Tres; Rho Chi Hstrn; Giant Food Inc Schlrshp 89; Becton Dickenson Giant Food Schlrshp; MD St Delegate Schlrshp 90; Deans Lst 90; Pharmacy; Pharmacist.

**D AMATO, VALERIE A,** Comm Coll Algny Co Algny Cmps, Pittsburgh, PA; SO; BA; DGS Invstmnt Treas 88-89; Tax Para/Prfssnl DGS/CO89-; Acctnt.

**D AMBROSIO, LISA M,** Glassboro St Coll, Glassboro, NJ; GD; BA; Psychlgy Clb 88-90; Deans Lst 89-; Psychlgy; Hosp Admin.

**D AMICO, ALISA A,** Mount Saint Mary Coll, Newburgh, NY; SO; BA; Cls Sec 90-; BACCHUS 89-; Yrbook Co Edtr 90-; Hnrs Alliance 90-; Ambssdr Clb 90-; Hstry/Pol Sci/Sec Educ; Tchr.

**D AMICO, CORINNE M,** Dowling Coll, Oakdale Li, NY; SO; BA; Pres Schlr; Sosd Hosp Vol; Bio/Physcl Thrpy.

**D AMICO, FRANK A,** Bloomfield Coll, Bloomfield, NJ; JR; BA; APICS; Mtrl Mgr; Bsn.

**D AMICO, JUDITH E,** Winthrop Coll, Rock Hill, SC; JR; BA; Pi Sigma Alpha Sec; Mary Hough Swearingen Schlrshp 90-; Eliz China Watkins Schlrshp; Kate V Wofford Schlrshp; Pol Sci.

**D AMICO, MICHAEL J,** Merrimack Coll, North Andover, MA; SO; BA; Bio Club 89-; Psychlgy Club 89-; Bio; Chld Psychlgst.

**D AMICO, NICOLE,** Seton Hall Univ, South Orange, NJ; FR; BS; Elem Ed/Psychlgy; Tchr.

**D ANDREAMATTEO, LISA M,** Niagara Univ, Niagara Univ, NY; JR; BS; Soc Wrk.

**D ANGELO, JANE A,** William Paterson Coll, Wayne, NJ; SR; BA; Once Again Stdtns In Schl Pr 89-; Kappa Delta Pi 87-; Phi Alpha Theta Sec 89-90; Pi Lambda Theta 88-; Alumni Assoc Outstndng Stdnt Awrd 89; Environmntl Protection Cmte Sec 86-; Hist Tchr.

**D ANGELO, RENEE M,** Bryant Stratton Bus Inst Roch, Rochester, NY; FR; ACS; Acctg.

**D ANGELO, VALERIE,** S U N Y Coll Of Tech At Frmgdl, Farmingdale, NY; FR; Dns Lst 90; Physcl Thrpy.

**D ANTONIO, CARLA F,** Kent St Univ Kent Cmps, Kent, OH; SR; BS; KCFR 89-90; Cert Apprctn Intrshps Btrd Wmns Shltr; Chld Advct Stow HS; Adlt Lstrn 90; Indvdl Fmly Study Fmly Life; Educ Psych.

**D ANTONIO, ROBERT J,** Siena Coll, Loudonville, NY; SR; BS; Radio Stn Prog Dir 87; Alpha Kappa Alpha; Intrnshp NYS Ed Dept 90; Im; Mrktng/Mngmnt.

**D APOLITO, PAUL NICHOLAS,** Castleton St Coll, Castleton, VT; SR; Campus Radio Station Stn Mgr 90-; Coll Repblcn Pub Rltns Off 90-91; Coll Nwspr Col Wrtr 89-; Assn Collgt 90-; Dns Lst 89-; BA; Tlvsn Doc Cls Prod Dcmntry Vrmnts 200th Prsntl 90-; Comm/Phylsphy Minor; Law Schl.

**D APRILE, ROSE C,** Central Fl Comm Coll, Ocala, FL; SO; Psych; Soc Wrk.

**D AQUINO, RITA L,** Manhattan Coll, Bronx, NY; SR; MSCHE; SWE 87-; AICHE 87-; Engr Cncl Mod 90-; Tau Beta Pi Tr 89-; Omega Chi Epsilon Sec 90/Vp 89-; Deans Hon Lst; Grad Fellow:; Prutton Medal For Chem Engr; Bro Leo Call Medal; Draddy Medal For Engr; BSCHE; Chem Engr.

**D ARATA, RICHARD E,** Embry Riddle Aeronautical Univ, Daytona Beach, FL; FR; AA; Haggai Inst For Advnced Ldrshp Trng Assoc Trstee 84; St Matthews Epscpl Chrch; Ocean Terr Cndmn Assoc Pres/Chrmn Of Brd 84-88; Sve Chldrn Spnsr 82; Wrld Vsn 84; Plce Bnvlnt Assoc 84; Plce Athletic League 85; Fthr Flngns Boys Twn 85; Aviation Maint Tchnlgy.

**D ARBANVILLE, STEPHANIE A,** Wagner Coll, Staten Island, NY; SR; MA; Stu Nwspr Edtr In Chf 87-89; Stu Lit Mag Edtr In Chf 87-90; Wgnr Coll Engl Clb Pres 89-; Omicron Delta Kappa Soc 89-; Sigma Tau Delta 89-; BA; Engl; Educ.

**D ARCY, CATHERINE S,** Broward Comm Coll, Ft Lauderdale, FL; FR; BA; Phi Theta Kappa 90-; Ofc Mgr; Elem Educ; Tchr.

**D ARCY, GLEN R,** Schenectady County Comm Coll, Schenectady, NY; SO; BS; Pres List 90-; Deans Lst; AS; Math/Cmptr Sci; Tch.

**D ARPINO, KATHY F,** S U N Y Coll Of Tech At Alfred, Alfred, NY; SR; AAS; Bus Admin.

**D AVIS, CYNTHIA M,** Boston Univ, Boston, MA; SR; BS; Habitat For Humanity 89-; Intrclgt Water Polo Tm 88-89; Phys Ther.

**D ESTIENNE, MICHAEL K,** Hudson Valley Comm Coll, Troy, NY; FR; BS; Cmptr Prgmg.

**D OLIVIERA, AMY E,** Eckerd Coll, St Petersburg, FL; SR; BA; Eckerd Coll Hon Pgm 87-; Jvnl Dbts Fndtn 90; Beta Prvntn Pgm-Tutor 89; Cntr Agnst Sps Abs-Cnslr 88; Prschl Spnsh Educ Intrn 90; IM Vlybl Sftbl 87-; Hmn Dvlpmnt Serv; Pdtrc Nrsng.

**D SIDOCKY, DANIEL R,** Kent St Univ Kent Cmps, Kent, OH; SR; BA; Amer Mrktng Asc 90; Fncl Mgt Assc; Gldn Key 90; Finance; Fncl Anlyst.

**D SOUZA, GERALDINE F,** Oh Wesleyan Univ, Delaware, OH; SO; BA; Envrnmnt/Wldlf Clb 90-; Hrzns Intl 90-; Zlgy Stdnt Brd 89-; Phi Soc; Intrnd Chesapeake Wldlf Snctry 90-; Zlgy; Vet Med.

**D SOUZA, SAMIRA,** Coll Of New Rochelle, New Rochelle, NY; SR; BS; Bus Brd 90-; Intl Stdnts Clb Treas 89-90; Glee Clb 90-; Hon Lst 88-; Hon Prog Pub Comm Co-Chr 90- Nwsltr 88-90; Campus Mnstry 89-90; Revlon Intrn; Cerard Hamon Inc Intrn; Landphny; Bus/Frnch; Mktg.

**D SURNEY, JENNIFER L,** Va Commonwealth Univ, Richmond, VA; FR; BS; Phi Eta Sigma 90-; Red Cross 90-; Gen Sci; Occptnl Thrpy.

**DA COSTA, CHRISTOPHER G,** Wilberforce Univ, Wilberforce, OH; FR; BOS; Bsktbl Tm 90-; Mss Media Cmnctns; Sprtscstg.

**DA ROCHA, GINA MARIE,** S U N Y Coll Of Tech At Frmgdl, Farmingdale, NY; SO; AS; Early Chldhd Clb Asst Treas 90-; Deans Lst 89-; Early Chldhd; Spec Ed Tchr.

**DA SILVA, PAULA C,** Southeastern Ma Univ, N Dartmouth, MA; SO; BA; Nursing.

**DA SILVA, RACHAEL A,** Savannah Coll Of Art & Design, Savannah, GA; SO; BA; Soccer Clb 90-; Hlpng Our Wrld Comm 90-; Stdnt Serv/Actvties Prog VP 90-; Deans Lst; Chart House Rstrnt; Illstrtn; Mktg/Advtsng.

**DABNEY, MATT K,** Univ Of Tn At Martin, Martin, TN; SR; BS; Natl Assn Of Bus Ecnmsts 90-; Natl Assn Of Acctnts; Econmcs Clb; Deans Lst; Pi Sigma Epsilon VP Finance 90-; Sigma Alpha Epsilon Her 88-; All Nighter; Economcs/Finance; Finance.

**DABROWSKI, PETER A,** Columbia Union Coll, Takoma Park, MD; SR; Busn Club 90-; Bksbl Starter 88-; BS 91; Busn Finance; Navy.

**DABSON, THERESA A,** Wilmington Coll, New Castle, DE; GD; Ladies Glf Assn 85-; Reebok Profsnl Instrctrs Alliance 84-; Dean Lst 87-; Arthrts Fndtn V Chrprsn 89; Grl Scts Of Amer Ldr 86-87; Mcdnlds Chmpnshp Mrshl 88-; De Clms Assn; Pro Chose Of De 90-; Mdse Mngr 75-78; Finance Dept 78-81; Bus; Bus Mngmnt Ins.

**DACE, TRACY D,** Alcorn St Univ, Lorman, MS; FR; BS; Fr Class Sen 90-; NAACP Bapt Stdnt Un 90-; Econ Clb Soc Sci Soc 90-; Econ; Tchr.

**DACIUK, JULIA W,** West Chester Univ, West Chester, PA; SO; BSAT; Athltc Trng.

**DACUK, JENNIFER M,** Seton Hall Univ, South Orange, NJ; SO; BSN; Nrsng Stdnts Assn Soph 90-; Alpha Phi Sor Chpln 90-; Nrsng; Neontl ICU Nrs.

**DADLANI, MANJU H,** Univ Of New Haven, West Haven, CT; JR; BS; Cmptr Clb 88-89; Natl Hnr Soc 87-; Chem Awd 89; Elect Eng.

**DAESCHLER, SANDRA MAC INTOSH,** East Stroudsburg Univ, E Stroudsburg, PA; SR; BA; Psychology Assoc Sec 89-90; Psi Chi Pres 89-; Sigma Xi Science Honors Award 90; BS Psych 90; VA Sociology 90; BS; Psychology Sociology; Clinical Psychology.

**DAETWYLER, ASHLEY A,** Va Commonwealth Univ, Richmond, VA; JR; BS; Alpha Lambda Delta 89-; Golden Key; Hnrs Prog 90-; Biol; Med.**

**DAFFIN, PAMELA A,** Talladega Coll, Talladega, AL; SR; BA; Sr Cls Senator SGA 90-; Bus/Econ Clb 88-; Alpha Chi 90-; Natl Hrn Soc 88-; Delta Sigma Theta V P 88-; Bus Admin; Bus.

**DAG, MUSTAFA,** Tallahassee Comm Coll, Tallahassee, FL; FR; BS; Intrnatl Orgnztn; Phi Theta Kappa; Dns Lst 90; Pres Lst; Elec Eng; Eng.

**DAGENAIS, GRADY J,** Syracuse Univ, Syracuse, NY; FR; BA; Archtctr.

**DAGESSE, GINA L,** Univ Of Nh Plymouth St Coll, Plymouth, NH; SR; BA; Bsktbl 87-88; Elem Ed; Tchng/Admin.

**DAGG, JAMES M,** Air Force Inst Of Tech, Wrt-Ptrsn Afb, OH; GD; MS; Sigma Iota Epsilon; Assc Cmptg Mchnry; Inst Mngmnt Sci; Oper Rsrch Analyst Fr DOD 89-; BA Summa Cum Laude Wright St Univ 81; Lgstcs Mngmt; Artfcl Intllgnce.

**DAGGETT, KIMBERLY G,** Albertus Magnus Coll, New Haven, CT; SO; BA; Italian Clb; Amnsty Internatl; Bsn Clb; Acctng Clb; Pr Cnslng: Drm Actvts; Tutor Acdmc Dvlpmnt Ctr; Dns Lst; Clark Schlrshp; Hearst Fndtn Schlrshp; Bsn/Rmnc Lng; Internatl Bsn/Itln/Spnsh.

**DAGGETT, TERESA L,** Univ Of Nh Plymouth St Coll, Plymouth, NH; FR; BA; Stdnt Gov VP 90-; Vol Work 90-; Res Asst Wmns Rugby Tm 90-; Delta Zeta 90-; Plymouth Schlr 90-; Pres Lst 90; Elem Educ; Tchr.

**DAGLEY, JOANNE B,** Thomas Nelson Comm Coll, Hampton, VA; SR; AAS; Hon Soc 82-84; Magna Cum Laude 82-84; Suma Cum Laude; Licnsd Vetrnry Techncn; Medcl Lab Tech Sentora Norflk Genrl; AAS Blue Ridge Cmnty Clg 84; Medcl Lab Technlgy.

**DAGOSTINO, JILL A,** Saint John Fisher Coll, Rochester, NY; SR; BS; Acctng 89-; Phi Theta Kappa 87-89; Fncl Exec Inst Top Stdnt 90-; NYS Socty CPAS Top Acctng Stdnt 90-; Intrnshp Bonadio Insreo & Co 90-; Acctng; CPA.

**DAHER, OSAMA W,** Liberty Univ, Lynchburg, VA; JR; BS; Acctng Asc Clb 90-; Acctng; CPA PHD Fnce.

**DAHL, JULIE A,** S U N Y Coll At Fredonia, Fredonia, NY; SR; MA; French Pres 87-; Alpha Mu Gamma Treas 88-; Pi Delta Phi 89-; Kappa Delta Pi 90-; Tchr Assist 89; Ultimate Frisbee Clb 90-; BA; French; French Prfssr.

**DAHL, KERI L,** Univ Of Southern Ms, Hattiesburg, MS; SO; BA; Elem Ed; Tchng.

**DAHL, STACY M,** Wilmington Coll, Wilmington, OH; FR; BA; Qst Envrnmntl Cncrns Grp 90-; Pr Fclttr 90-; Frnds Cmps Mtng 90-; Ht Mls Prgm; Wrk Cheyenne Rvr Indian Rsrvtn; Asst Engl Prfssr Bill Guthrie Engl Prctcm 425; Orttn Ldr; Pc Stds Psychlgy; Psychlgst.

**DAHLBERG, VERONICA I,** Christopher Newport Coll, Newport News, VA; SO; BA; Nwspr Stfwtr; History; Tchng/Freelance Wtng.

**DAHLHAUS, MICHELLE A,** Saint Francis Coll, Loretto, PA; SO; BS; Scl Wrk Clb Pres 90-; Adpt Grndprnt Pgm Coord 89-; Dns Lst 90-; Scl Wrk; Fmly Cnslng.

**DAHLING, SANDRA A,** Anne Arundel Comm Coll, Arnold, MD; SO; BA; Phi Theta Kappa; Crssng Grd Assn Prsdnt 84-90; Prgrm Asst Cnty Altrntv Sentence Prg 90-; AA; Sociology; Cnslng.

**DAHLKE, MARK A,** Limestone Coll, Gaffney, SC; SR; BA; US Navy Lt/6260 74-; AS Mohegan Cmnty Clg; Bus Admn Mgt.

**DAI, ZHENG,** Bay Path Coll, Longmeadow, MA; SO; BA; Bsn Admn; Bsn.

**DAIDONE, BERNADETTE,** Bloomfield Coll, Bloomfield, NJ; FR; BA; Bus Mgmt; Cmptr Spclst.

**DAIL, JEFFREY L,** Univ Of Sc At Columbia, Columbia, SC; SO; BS; Deans List 90; Dsgn Assoc Wouthern Bell 79-; Elec/Comp Eng.

**DAIL, MELISSA M,** Palm Beach Atlantic Coll, W Palm Beach, FL; FR; Bapt Campus Mnstrs; Wrkshp; Psych.

**DAIL, MICHELE,** Daemen Coll, Amherst, NY; JR; BSW; Bus Clb 90-; Pi Gamma Mu 90-; Hmn Srvcs Clb Dmn Coll 90-; Scl Wrk; Cse Mgmt.

**DAIL, SHERRIE M,** Fayetteville St Univ, Fayetteville, NC; FR; BS; Criminal Justice.

**DAILEY, CRETIA J,** Univ Of Al At Huntsville, Huntsville, AL; SO; BS; Math Clb 88-89; SWE 88-90; Hon Schlr 88-90; Elec Engr; Engr.

**DAILEY, MARY JANE,** Univ Of Akron, Akron, OH; SR; BA; Chrch Sftbl Lg; Vol Tutor; Golden Key 89-; Acad Schlrshp 87-; Deans Schlrshp Awd; Deans List 87-; Var Indoor Trck 87; Var Trck 87; Sec Educ/Comm Comprhnsv; Lang Arts Educ/Tchr.

**DAILEY, RUTH A,** Livingston Univ, Livingston, AL; JR; Busn.

**DAILEY, AMY B,** East Stroudsburg Univ, E Stroudsburg, PA; SR; Stdnt Snte Srn Sntr 89-; SOAR Peer Educator 90-; UPC Film Comm 89-; Psych Assn V P 89-; Omicron Delta Kappa; Ntl Ldrshp Hnry Soc; Alpha Phi Omega Pres 89-; Crisis Suicide Hotline 89-90; CEO Stdnt Tutor 88-; Psych/Sclgy/Crmnl Justc Admin; C A Cnslr.

**DAILY, LAUREEN V,** Tempie Univ, Philadelphia, PA; SR; Dns Lst 90; BA; Engl; Jrnlsm.

**DAIMLER JR, STEPHEN J,** George Mason Univ, Fairfax, VA; JR.

**DAINS, DIANA LYNNE,** Miami Jacobs Jr Coll Of Bus, Dayton, OH; SR; Mary Martha Cir; Waynesville Untd Meth Chrch; Bookkpr.

**DAISE, MICHAEL A,** Reformed Episcopal Seminary, Philadelphia, PA; GD; MDIV; Eliza/Louisa Dean Prize 89-90; Joseph D Wilson Meml 90; Free C Kuehner Meml 90; Presbyterian Ch Pastoral Intrn 89-; Theology; Minis.

**DAISLEY, DAWN,** Duquesne Univ, Pittsburgh, PA; SR; BS; SGA 88-89; Omicron Delta Kappa Pres 89-90; Beta Gamma Sigma 90-91; Phi Eta Sigma; Lambda Sigma 88-89; Pres Amb To Univ Pres 89-; Mgmt Inf Sys.

**DAISLEY, RACQUEL E A,** Howard Univ, Washington, DC; SR; BS; Nwsltr Edtr; ASP 90-; Golden Key 90; Rho Chi Hstrn; Kappa Psi; Stdnt Intern NCL/FDA Dist Proj Pilot Proj Coord 90; Phrmcy; Clinical & Cnsltnt Phrmcy.

**DAISLEY, SEAN E A,** Univ Of Pr At Mayaguez, Mayaguez, PR; SO; Elect Utlty.

**DALBEC, DIANE E,** Univ Of Sc At Columbia, Columbia, SC; FR; Alpha Lambda Delta; Phi Eta Sigma; Delta Zeta Pldg Sec; Engl.

**DALE, DEBRA J,** Mercer Univ Schl Of Pharm, Atlanta, GA; FR; PHARM; Amer Scty Of Phrmcsts 90-; Amer Scty Of Hosp Phrmcsts 90-; Phi Delta Chi Intra Frat Rep 90-; BS Tennessee Tech Univ 90; Phrmcy; Hosp Or Comm Phrmcy.

**DALE, JANICE S,** Western Piedmont Comm Coll, Morganton, NC; SO; AAS; Paralegal Assn Pres 89; Creative Wrtng Clb 90; Phi Theta Kappa 90-; Ambsdrs Prog 90-; R R Becker Atty At Law Emplee; Paralegal Tech; Paralegal.

**DALE, JASON P,** Western Piedmont Comm Coll, Morganton, NC; SO; AAS; Phi Theta Kappa 90-; Vlntr Fire/Rscue 90-; Bus Admin; Bus Instr.

**DALE, JEWELL D,** Va Highlands Comm Coll, Abingdon, VA; SO; AAS; Lebanon Cmmnty Fllwshp; Chr Singls Assn; Sec 87-; CIS; Data Prcsng Tchncn.

**DALE, LINDA B,** Oh Wesleyan Univ, Delaware, OH; FR; BA; Choral Art Soc 90; Fllwshp Of Chrstn Athletes 90; Phi Eta Sigma; Math; Sec Math Ed.

**DALE JR, LOWELL B,** Va Highlands Comm Coll, Abingdon, VA; SO; Alpha Gamma Rho 89-; Grad High Hnr; Eng.

**DALE, THERESA A,** Salisbury St Univ, Salisbury, MD; SR; Dance Co Sec 89-; NAA 90-; VITA; Cum Laude; BS; Acctg; CPA.**

**DALESANDRO, COLLEEN M,** East Stroudsburg Univ, E Stroudsburg, PA; JR; Psychlgy Club 89-90; Lab Medcn Club Treas 90-.

**DALEY, DONALD C,** Hudson Valley Comm Coll, Troy, NY; SO; AAS; Deans Lst 90; Alchlsm Cnslr 90; Fndtn Schrlshp Prsdnt Lst 90; Yth Cntr Mntr Asst; Jst Sy No Co Fcltatr 9(; Hmn Srvcs.

**DALEY, KATHLEEN H,** Lesley Coll, Cambridge, MA; SR; BA; Horizons Fnd-Intrnshp; Erly Chldhd Ed.

**DALEY, KATHLEEN P,** Oh St Univ At Marion, Marion, OH; SR; BA; Gold Key 88-; Psychlgy; Med.

**DALEY, KIMBERLY M,** Daytona Beach Comm Coll, Daytona Beach, FL; FR; AA; Telecomm; Brdcst Jrnlsm.

**DALEY, LAURA A,** Univ Of Fl, Gainesville, FL; JR; Cddlr Prgm Shnds Hosp 89; Alpha Lamba Delta 88-; Gldn Key; Prsdnts Hnr Rl 89-; Stdnt Occptnl Thrypy 90-; Amrcn Occptnl Thrpy Assoc; Delta Chi 89-; Prsdnts Hnr Rl 89rcmmndtn Prctcm; Occptnl Thrpy.

**DALEY, LINDA M,** Southern Vt Coll, Bennington, VT; SR; BS; Tstmstrs Intl 90-; Ntry Pblc 89-; !crdt Cllctns Sprvsr; AAS 90; Bus Mgmt.

**DALEY, TRALENE M,** Columbia Greene Comm Coll, Hudson, NY; FR; BA; Acctng.

**DALGADO, NYMPHA G,** Va Commonwealth Univ, Richmond, VA; GD; MA; Yrbk Comm 87; Tchrs Comm 88-89; Midwifery Aga Khan Univ 88; BSN Nrsg Virginia Commonwealth Univ 90-; Nrsg.

**DALKE, CHRISTINA M,** Fl St Univ, Tallahassee, FL; JR; BA; Cmps Crsd For Chrst Prayer Comm 90-; Girl Scouts 89-; Santa Cruz Summer Msns Proj 90; Bolivia Summer Missions Proj; Smith Coll Vrsty Crew 89-90; Math; Tchr.

**DALLACQUA, KRISTEN,** Dowling Coll, Oakdale Li, NY; SO; Intl Clb 90-.

**DALLASTA, KARENANN,** Manhattan Coll, Bronx, NY; JR; BSEE; IEEE 85-; Res Asst E Hill Dorm 90-; Instrmnt Soc Amer 85-89; Inside Sls Rep 84-89; Elec Eng.

**DALLE, JEANETTE L,** S U N Y At Buffalo, Buffalo, NY; SR; MENG; Inst Indstrl Engr 89-; Amer Soc Qulty Cntrl 90-; Intrn Port Auth NY/NJ 90; Deans Lst 90; BSIE; EIT; Indstrl Engr.

**DALLEY, CARLENE,** Middle Ga Coll, Cochran, GA; JR; MED; Dns Lst 90; AAS Erly Chldhd Ed; Spch/Lng Pthlgy; Spch Pthlgst.

**DALLMAN, CHRISTINE A,** Toccoa Falls Coll, Toccoa Falls, GA; SR; BS; Camps Nwspr Edtr 90-; Dns Lst 90-; Ivan Drthy St John Msns Schlrshp 86-87; Wmns Bsktbl 85-86; Jrnlsm/Pub Rel; Ling/Transltn.

**DALMAU, TERESITA,** Caribbean Center For Adv Stds, San Juan, PR; SR; PHD; Psychology; Rsrch.

**DALOIA, DANIEL M,** Bridgeport Engr Inst, Fairfield, CT; JR; BS; Masons 89-; Soc Mnfctrng Eng 89-90; Textron/Lycoming; Cert St Of CT 76; Apprntcshp Sheet Metal Wrk; Mech Eng.

**DALPIAZ, HEATHER JOY,** Coll Misericordia, Dallas, PA; SR; Hstry/Pre Law Clb 90-; Tutor 90-; Alternative Lrnrs Pgm Note Tkr 90-; Kappa Gamma Pi 90-; Delta Epsilon Sigma 90-; Knight Of Columbus Awd; IM Tennis; Intern Atty Leslie Wizelman 90-; Natl Clgt Bus Merit Awd; BA; History; Law/Tchr.**

**DALRYMPLE, SCOTT LORING,** Georgetown Univ, Washington, DC; JR; BSBA; Acctg Soc; Deans List 88-; James Edward Miller Chapman Mem Schlrshp 90-; BSBA; Acctg; Bus/Law.

**DALSANIA, SARAJU C,** Fl St Univ, Tallahassee, FL; SR; MD; Scuba Club 89; Alpha Epsilon Delta 89; Lbrl Stds W/Hnrs Snr Chem Award; BS; Bio Chem; Med.

**DALTON, ANNE K,** Anne Arundel Comm Coll, Arnold, MD; SO; AA; Engl/Hstry; Wrtg/Hmestdg.

**DALTON, ANNMARIE E,** Georgian Court Coll, Lakewood, NJ; SR; BA; Psychlgy Clb Sec/Treas 87-89; Yrbk Sr Ed 89-; Cncrt Bnd 87-; Psi Chi 89-; Sigma Phi Sigma 89-; Kappa Gamma Pi; Psychlgy Dept Awd; Dns Mdl; Psychly; Schl Psychlgst.

**DALTON, BETTY ANN,** Univ Of West Fl, Pensacola, FL; SR; BS; Pensacola Dntl Hygn Soc; Amer Dntl Hygn Assn; AS Pensacola Jr Coll 87; Voc Educ; Tch Dntl Hygn.

**DALTON, CAREY B,** Pellissippi St Tech Comm Coll, Knoxville, TN; SO; AS; Bapt Stdnt Union 89-; Vision Vol 89; Walland Untd Meth Chrch; Ltr Rcmndtn For Karla; Pre Eng; Mech Eng.

**DALTON, CONNIE S,** Marshall University, Huntington, WV; SR; BA.

**DALTON, CRYSTAL L,** Nc Agri & Tech St Univ, Greensboro, NC; SR; BS; Pi Omega Pi 89-; Alpha Lambda Delta 88-; Future Adms & Execs Of Am 89-; Chandellors Seminar For Careers 90; Zeta Phi Beta Schlrshp 87-; Am Bus Womens Assn Schlrshp 89-; Am Inst CPA Schlrshp 89-; Bus Edn/Econ.**

**DALTON, CYNEVA L,** Peace Coll, Raleigh, NC; SO; BA; Future Bus Women 89-; Phi Theta Kappa 90-; AA/AS; Bus; Info Syst.

**DALTON, DIANE M,** James Madison University, Harrisonburg, VA; SR; MED; Spec Educ Stdnt Advsry Comm 90-; Hrrsnbrg Bptst Clg Chrl 89-; Folk Dance Ensem 88-89; Golden Key 90-; Kappa Delta Pi 90-; Chcl Excptnl Chldrn Hist 89-; Grad Magna Cum Laude; Pres List 89-; Deans List 89; Paul Douglas Tchrs Schlrshp Loan; Spec Educ; Teacher.

**DALTON, GAYLA M,** Eastern Ky Univ, Richmond, KY; SR; BS; Rgstrd Med Asst; AA Eastrn KY Univ 74; Cert Clark Cty Comm Clg 85; Med Tchnlgy.

**DALTON, JENNIFER ANN,** Longwood Coll, Farmville, VA; SR; Fedtn Student Soc Wrks Pres 89-90; Alpha Delta Mu; Cum Laude.

**DALTON, KATHRYN R,** Radford Univ, Radford, VA; JR; BS; Stdnt VA Ed Assn; Law Enfrcmnt Cert New Rvr Comm Coll 84; Frnsc Sci Cert New Rvr Comm Coll 84; Spec Ed; Tchr.

**DALTON, LAURA D,** Univ Of Ga, Athens, GA; SR; BED; Educ Psych; Educ.

**DALTON, NANCY E,** Univ Of Sc At Columbia, Columbia, SC; FR; Carolina Mrchng Band 90-; Carolina Cncrt Band 90-; Tau Beta Sigma; Soccer 90-; Advrtsng/Pblc Rltns/Jrnlsm.

**DALTON JR, RICHARD M,** Bethany Coll, Bethany, WV; JR; BA; Stdnt Bd Gov Repr; Delta Tau Delta V P 90-; Hstry; Law.

**DALTON JR, ROBERT P,** George Mason Univ, Fairfax, VA; SR; Symphnc Bnd 87-90; Jzz Bnd 88-90.**

**DALTON, STEVEN M,** S U N Y Coll Of Tech At Delhi, Delhi, NY; SO; BA; Outdoors Club 90-; Music Club 89-90; Phi Theta Kappa 90-; Academic Hnrs 89-; AAS; Environmental Studies; Forestry.

**DALTON, VERNA E,** Ashland Comm Coll, Ashland, KY; SO; Instr Assist; ILC; Sndy Schl Tchr; Assoc 90; JTPA 90; Ofc Admin; Nrsg.

**DALTON, WILLIAM A,** Univ Of Rochester, Rochester, NY; JR; Sgm Chi Pres.

**DALTON, WILLIAM C,** Bethany Coll, Bethany, WV; FR; BA; Amer Chem Scty; Tri-Beta; Bio; Dr.

**DALY, DEANNA R,** Fl St Univ, Tallahassee, FL; SR; MS; NSSLHA V P; Swthrt Pi Kappa Phi 88-89; Alpha Clg Co Dir 90-; Deans Lst 90; Cert Spch; SLPA; DPR; Spch/Lang Path.

**DALY, DONNA ANNE,** Georgian Court Coll, Lakewood, NJ; FR; Mdcl Asstnt; Wrtr; Sec 87-; Englsh Elem Edctn; Elem Tchr.

**DALY, JANE ELIZABETH,** Coll Of New Rochelle, New Rochelle, NY; JR; BA; Class President 90-; Big Bro/Big Sisters 89-90; Hnr List 89-90; Deans List 88-89; Bsktbl 88-; Sftbl 90; History.

**DALY, LISA S,** S U N Y Hlth Sci Cent Brooklyn, Brooklyn, NY; JR; BSN; Stdnt Hlth Advsry Comm; AARP Schlrshp Awd; K Of Pythias Schlrshp; Notary Public (YS; Admin Asst Bnkng/Finance 81-88; BA SUNY Binghamton Harpur Coll 81; Nrsng.

**DALY, TARA M,** Boston Coll, Chestnut Hill, MA; FR; BA; La Crosse; Bsnss.

**DAMAN, WILLEM A,** Univ Of Miami, Coral Gables, FL; JR; BA; Pre-Lgl Soc 89-; Hnr Std Asc 89-90; Alpha Lambda Delta; Peer Cnslr 90-; Intshp Sen Grhms; Hstry; Law.

**DAMAS, SAGINE,** City Univ Of Ny Kingsborough, Brooklyn, NY; SO; BA; KCCS Rd Stn Nws Wrtr 90; KCC Hnrs Optn Prgm Sec 90; AA Kingsborough Cmmnty Coll; Psychlgy; Law.

**DAMASK, DIANE L,** Atlantic Comm Coll, Mays Landing, NJ; JR; BA; Ch Choir 80-; Ch Clrk 80-; Pilgrim Acad Bkbl Coach 87-; Acad Div Servs Coord 83-; AA 90; Literature.

**DAMASK, MICHELLE C,** Atlantic Comm Coll, Mays Landing, NJ; JR; BA; Frshmn Club Pres 89-90; Sci Club 89-90; Earth Day Exec Bd 90; Theater 89-90; Phi Theta Kappa VP 89-90; Church Choir 86-; Trvlng Puppet Team Dir 87-; Peer Mentor Peer Cnslr 89-; Deans List 88-90; AA 90; Psychlgy; Cnslr For Abused Chldrn.

**DAMBREVILLE, DOMINIQUE,** City Univ Of Ny La Guard Coll, Long Island Cty, NY; SR; AAS; Phi Theta Kappa; Acctg; CPA.

**DAME, MARILYN C,** Hudson Valley Comm Coll, Troy, NY; SO; Spec Educ; Tchr.

**DAME, SANDRA J,** George Mason Univ, Fairfax, VA; SR; BS; Elec Comm 88; Rsdnt Stdnt Assn 88-89; Educ Assn Sec 89-; Gldn Key; Alpha Phi 88-; Elem Educ; Tchr.

**DAMIANI, AILEEN,** Fl International Univ, Miami, FL; FR; Cmptr Sci/Art; Grphc Dsgn.

**DAMIANI, GINA E,** Manor Jr Coll, Jenkintown, PA; GD; AS; Sch Newspaper 90-; Stdnt Cncl 90-; Alpha Beta Gamma 89-; Court Rep Demos 89-; Highest GPA Awd 89-; Top Court Rep Stdnt Awd 89-; Svc Awd 90-; Court Rep Intern 90-; Court Rep.

**DAMICO, GREGORY M,** Bethany Coll, Bethany, WV; FR; Frshmn Activities Cncl 90-.

**DAMON, PATRICK J,** Garrett Comm Coll, Mchenry, MD; SO; BA; Yth Grp Treas 85-; Asst Trust Dept 89-; Asst Mngr Pzz Prlr 87-; Dean Lst 90-; Biol/Educ; Educ.

**DAMOUDT, SYLMA R,** Univ Of Pr At Mayaguez, Mayaguez, PR; JR; MBA; SWE 89-; Hnr Stdnt Cert Alphia Pi Mu 90; Free Rgstrtn Hnr Stdnt 89-90; Indus Engr.**

**DAMRON, DEBORAH M,** Colby Sawyer Coll, New London, NH; SR; BS; Rsdntl Asst Hd Res Asst 89-; Key Assoc 88-; Pr Tr 89-; Alpha Chi Assoc 89-; SAC 89-; Dana Farber Cncr Inst Intrnshp Asst Clncl Scntst; Sawyer Flwshp 90-; Dartmouth Mary Hitchcock Hosp Vol 90-; Sftbl 90-; Blgy; Med.

**DAMRON, JOELLE C,** Univ Of Akron, Akron, OH; JR; BAMA; NSSLHA 90-; ASHA 90; Golden Key 90; Medal For Hghst GPA On Tennis Tm; Tennis 88-90; Speech Pthlgy/Adlgy.

**DANAHY, DARREN D,** Schenectady County Comm Coll, Schenectady, NY; FR; AAS; Music; Music Bsnss.

**DANDENEAU, NICOLE A,** Southern Vt Coll, Bennington, VT; FR; BA; Sunrise Family Rsrc Ctr Asst; 4 Internship; Day Care Mgmt.

**DANEK, GABRIELLE M,** Cornell Univ Statutory College, Ithaca, NY; SO; BA; Sage Chapel Choir 89; Fresh Orntatn Cnslr 90; Red Carpet Hstng 90-; Ho Non De Kah; IBM E Fishkill Pre Prfsnl Coop Summer Job; I M Soccer; Physics; Sci Industry.

**DANEY, WINONA Y,** Univ Of Sc At Columbia, Columbia, SC; JR; Omega Psi Phi 88-89; Tp Twnty Achvmnt Awd Morris Clge; Ed Erly Chldhd; Tchg.

**DANFORTH, DARYL R,** Western New England Coll, Springfield, MA; SR; BSBA; Vlybl; Twin Peaks Gazette; Deans Lst 88-; Mngmnt.

**DANFORTH, WILLIAM BARRY,** Abraham Baldwin Agri Coll, Tifton, GA; SO; Animal Sci.

**DANG, DIEMNGOC T,** Univ Of Miami, Coral Gables, FL; FR; BS; Mcrbiolgy Clb 90-; Vietnms Clb 90-; Micrbio/Imnlgy; Medcn.

**DANG, LY C,** Cooper Union, New York, NY; FR; BE; Elec Eng; Eng/Busn.

**DANG, MAI-TRANG D,** Univ Of Rochester, Rochester, NY; JR; BS; Vtnm Std Asc Pres 88-; Asian Amer Asc Exec 88-90; S Afrcn Awrns Comm 89-; Take-Five Pgm; Mech Engr.

**DANG, PHUONG T,** Univ Of Rochester, Rochester, NY; JR; BS; Vietnamese Stdnt Assn Prsdnt 88-; Chrls Drew Prmdcl Soc 88-; Math Clb; Ldrshp Crtfct; Actrl Schlrshp; Appld Math; Biostatistician.

**DANG, TOAN THI,** Univ Of Akron, Akron, OH; SR; BS; Vietnamese Chrstn Yth Grp Treas 89-; Vietnamese Evang Church Pianist 88-; Alpha Lambda Delta 88-; Ph Eta Sigma 88-; Golden Key 88-; Elem Ed.

**DANG, VINH NGOC,** Univ Of Akron, Akron, OH; SR; BS; Elem Ed.

**DANGERFIELD, NINA L,** Jackson St Univ, Jackson, MS; FR; BA; Pol Sci Clb 90-; Pre-Law Clb 90-; Alpha Lambda Delta; Pol Sci; Intl Lawyer.

**DANGERFIELD, SHELLY K,** Oh St Univ At Newark, Newark, OH; FR; Dntl Hygn; Denstistry.

**DANGLER, ELLEN S,** Mount Holyoke Coll, South Hadley, MA; FR; BA; Law Scty 90-; Math Clb 90-; Math; Teaching.

**DANGLOVITCH, BRENDA S,** Indiana Univ Of Pa, Indiana, PA; FR; Elem Educ; Tchr.

**DANGO, TRACY A,** Newbury Coll, Brookline, MA; JR; BA; Kiwanis Clb Cambridge 90-; COM Electric Energy Svc Repr 84-; Bsn Mgmt.

**DANIEL, CHRISTOPHER A,** Northern Ky Univ, Highland Hts, KY; SR; BS; Mktg; Sls/Rsrch.

**DANIEL, CHRISTY R,** Middle Ga Coll, Cochran, GA; SO; AS; Political Sci; Brdctng.

**DANIEL, COLETTE O,** Va Union Univ, Richmond, VA; SR; BS; Stdnt Vir Educ Assn 88-; Comm Schlrs 90-; Tau Beta Sigma Pr 90-; Erly/Elem Educ; Tch.

**DANIEL, DESSIE R,** Jackson St Univ, Jackson, MS; SR; Community Mrchng Bnd 88-89; Phi Theta Kappa; Asso Degree Of Arts Degree Southwest MS Comm Clg 89; Soc Wrk.

**DANIEL, ELENA,** Central St Univ, Wilberforce, OH; FR; BSC; Flwshp Chrstn Std; Intl Std Asc; Mfg Engr.

**DANIEL, GREGORY C,** Fl A & M Univ, Tallahassee, FL; FR; BA; Comp Info Syst Clb; Comp Info Syst; Comp Sci.

**DANIEL, JANIE J,** Union Univ, Jackson, TN; FR; BA; Nrsg; Mntl Hlth Nrsg.

**DANIEL, RAMONA L,** Walker Coll, Jasper, AL; SO; BA; Vly PTA Pres; Ad Vlrm Tax Cmte Co Chrmn; Ins Sec; Sales Sec; Sprvsg Sec; Ed; Lrng Dsblts.

**DANIEL, ROBERT P,** Memphis St Univ, Memphis, TN; JR; BS; Coll Bowl 90-; Phi Kappa Phi 90-; Chi Beta Phi VP 90-; Sigma Pi Sigma 89-90; Univ TN Sci Allnc Fllw 90; FL State Univ Smmr Jr Fllw; Physcs.

**DANIEL, TAMARA J,** Rivier Coll, Nashua, NH; FR; BA; Paralgl Soc 90-F Modrn Lang Soc 90-; Paralg Studies; Law.

**DANIEL, TRACY D,** Alcorn St Univ, Lorman, MS; SO; Hnrs Crrclm Prog 90-; Deans List 89-; Educ Bus; Teacher.**

**DANIEL, WILLIAM R,** Oh St Univ, Columbus, OH; FR; BA; Flag Ftbl Capt 90-; Bus/Mktg; Med/Optometry.

**DANIELE, CARMELA C,** Springfield Tech Comm Coll, Springfield, MA; Itln Tchr Istituto Magistrale Regina Margherita Salerno Italy 78; Engl; Law.

**DANIELL, EMMA P,** Mobile Coll, Mobile, AL; SR; BS; SLATE Pres 89-; KDE Pres 89-; Alpha Chi 89-; Ed; Tchr.

**DANIELLO, STEVEN,** Mount Saint Mary Coll, Newburgh, NY; SO; BA; Yng Demcrts; AAS Five Towns Clg 90; Acctg; CPA.

**DANIELLY, JULIE M,** Mercer Univ Schl Of Pharm, Atlanta, GA; SR; PHARM; ASHP Rep; Chrstn Std Un Sec 90-; APLA/ASP; Beta Beta Beta; Kappa Epsln Chpln; Parke Davis Clncl Intshp; BS GA Tech 83; Pharm.

**DANIELS, ANDREW B,** Dyersburg St Comm Coll, Dyersburg, TN; FR; BS; Math Clb Treas 90; Spnsh Clb 89; Phi Theta Kappa 90-; Vr Bapt Chrch SS Sprtndnt 83; Hstry Educ; Hstry Tchr Coach.

**DANIELS, ANGELA D,** Fayetteville St Univ, Fayetteville, NC; GD; MA; NCEA; Magna Cum Laude; N C State Schlrshp; Supr Acad Achvment Awd; PTA; BS 90; Ele Educ; Tch.

**DANIELS, ANNA E,** Univ Of Ky, Lexington, KY; FR; Phi Eta Sigma; Phrmcy.

**DANIELS, APRIL C,** Saint Johns River Comm Coll, Palatka, FL; SO; Phi Theta Kappa.

**DANIELS, BARBARA S,** City Univ Of Ny Grad School, New York, NY; GD; MS ED; Alpha Beta Gamma; Natl Bus Educ Assn Awd Of Merit; Empire State Flwshp; Natl Bus Educ Assn; Schl Sec; AAS Queensborough Comm Coll 76; BS 90; Bus Educ; Tchg.

**DANIELS, CAMMIE C,** Christopher Newport Coll, Newport News, VA; SR; Alpha Chi 90-.

**DANIELS, CHRISTOPHER C,** Univ Of Akron, Akron, OH; FR; BS; Mech Eng.

**DANIELS, DARCY J,** Notre Dame Coll, Cleveland, OH; JR; BS; AIBS Bio Club; Campus Ambsdr; Bio; Medcl Technlgst.

**DANIELS, DAVID L,** Univ Of Sc At Columbia, Columbia, SC; FR; BS; Natl Soc Blck Engrs 90-; Assoc African Amer Stdnts 90-; Phi Eta Sigma; Dns Lst 90-; Top Ten 90-; Top Minority Stdnt 90-; Elctrcl/Cmptr Engr; Engr.

**DANIELS, DENISE J,** Notre Dame Coll, Cleveland, OH; JR; BS; Notre Dame Nutrition Assn Pres; Bio Club; Cmps Ldrshp Brd; Cmps Ambsdr; Dietetics; Clncl Dietitian.

**DANIELS, DENNIS J,** Jackson St Univ, Jackson, MS; SO; BA; Psy.

**DANIELS, DOREEN NANCY,** Meridian Comm Coll, Meridian, MS; SO; VICA 89-90; Bptst Stdnt Union Setup Chrmn 88; Obiadah Homemakers 75-90; Center Hill Commt Clb 75-90; Sta Home Hlth Serv LPN 86; LPN 83; Cmptr Tchnlgy Operator/Prgrmmr.

**DANIELS, ELAH A J,** Oh Wesleyan Univ, Delaware, OH; SR; Edtr In Chf Owl 89-90; Edtr In Chf Wordworks 89-90; Edtr 88-89; Phi Beta Kappa; Sigma Tau Delta 89-; Hnrs 90-; Magna Cum Laude 90-; BA 90; Eng; Claims Rep.

**DANIELS, JAMI S,** George Mason Univ, Fairfax, VA; JR; BS; Deans Lst 89-; Bus Acctg; Acctg/Fin.

**DANIELS JR, JERALD E,** Univ Of Sc At Columbia, Columbia, SC; JR; BS; Bdy Bldg Clb Pres 89-90; Antqs; Dns Lst 90; Pwrlftng Cntsts 89; Blgy/Exrcs Sci; Med Fld.

**DANIELS JR, JOSEPH W,** Howard Univ, Washington, DC; GD; MDIV; Benjamin E Mays Schlr 88-; Summa Cum Laude; Tyms Awrd Exclnc; BA Amer Un 82; MA 84; Divinity; Ministry.

**DANIELS, KAREN L,** Western Ky Univ, Bowling Green, KY; JR; BS; Assn Undrgrd Geneticists V P; Panhellenic Assn Sec; Chem Hnr Soc; Phi Kappa Phi 89-; Phi Eta Sigma 88-; Beta Besta Beta 90-; Alpha Epsilon Delta 90-; Alphi Xi Delta V P; Recombinant Genetics; Med Rsrch.

**DANIELS, KARLA Y,** Canisius Coll, Buffalo, NY; FR; Buffalos Mnrty Intern Prog; Psychlgy.

**DANIELS, KENNETH M,** Valdosta St Coll, Valdosta, GA; JR; BBA; Phi Kappa Phi; Beta Gamma Sigma; Accntng; CPA.

**DANIELS, KIMBERELY D,** Radford Univ, Radford, VA; FR; BA; Intl Thespian Soc 89-90; Win Ens & Jazz Band 90-; Concert Band & Pep Band 90-; Natl Beta Club 88-90; Sigma Alpha Iota/Espressivo 90-; Perf On Spring Hnrs Recital; Music Edn.

**DANIELS, LEONARD N,** Cheyney Univ Of Pa, Cheyney, PA; JR; BS; Kappa Delta Pi; R J Reynolds; Nabisco Mnrty Schlrs Awd; NAACP; Elem Edctn; Edctnl Admnstrtn.

**DANIELS, LORI J,** Marshall University, Huntington, WV; FR; BBA; Phi Eta Sigma; Gamma Beta Phi; Bsns/Acctg; Accnt.

**DANIELS, MARK A,** Averett Coll, Danville, VA; SR; BS; Phi Theta Kappa 88; AA Prince Georgs Cmmnty Cllg 89; Avtn; Cmmrcl Arline Pilot.

**DANIELS, MARY ANN,** Roane St Comm Coll, Harriman, TN; BA; Bus; Acctnt.

**DANIELS, MARY GAIL,** Univ Of Sc At Columbia, Columbia, SC; JR; BSN; NSNA 90; SNA 90; Golden Key 84-86; Phi Eta Sigma 83-86; Gamma Beta Phi 83-85; Acad Achvmnt Award 86; Award Acad Excel 86; Guardian Ad Litem 90-; LDS Hme Mgmt Tchr 90-; BS 86; Nrsg; Anesthetist.

**DANIELS, MARY K,** Meridian Comm Coll, Meridian, MS; GD; AA; Phi Theta Kappa; Schlrshp Belhavn Clg; Nrsng; BS RN.

**DANIELS, MICHAEL L,** Al A & M Univ, Normal, AL; SR; BS; STIX Inc Pres 89-; Mrchng Maroon/White Bnd 88; Kappa Kappa Psi 90-; Alpha Phi Alpha Par 90-; Soc Pres Schlrsh 88-; Deans Lst 88-; Hon Rl 88-; Comp Sci; Comp Eng.

**DANIELS, OASSIE J,** Livingston Univ, Livingston, AL; SR; BS; UCTE 90-; AA Patrick Henry State Clg 89; Spcl Ed LD; Tchr.

**DANIELS, PAMELA R,** Middle Ga Coll, Cochran, GA; SO; BUSS; Student Gvt Assoc Treas/Sean 90; Rataract; Bpt Student Union 89-; Phi Beta Lambda; Superlative; Tns Tm Cpt 90-; Busn; Acctng.

**DANIELS, PATRICIA A,** Wilmington Coll, New Castle, DE; JR; BSN; Dstngqshd Hnrs Schl Nrsng 81-84; Dlwr Nrs Assoc 90; Cert 84; Nrsng.

**DANIELS, PATRICIA S,** Broward Comm Coll, Ft Lauderdale, FL; SO; BA; Phi Thetta Kappa; Empire Mortgage Grp Inc 87-; United Mortgage Srvcs 84-87; Bus Admin; Acctng CPA.

**DANIELS, PAULA K,** Memphis St Univ, Memphis, TN; FR; BA; Bible Stdy Grp 90-; Engl Clb 90-; Dscssn Grp 90-; Blck Schlrs Unlmtd 90-; Trident Hon Soc 90-; IM Sftbl/Bsktbl 90-; Ed; Navl Offcr/Ed.

**DANIELS, SCOTT R,** Univ Of Nc At Charlotte, Charlotte, NC; JR; BA; Pre Law Soc 90-; SG Cmmtr Rep 90-; Omicron Delta Kappa 90-; Kappa Alpha Order Pres; UNCC Div I Sccr Vars Lttr 88-89; Pol Sci; Law.

**DANIELS, SHANNON L,** Valdosta St Coll, Valdosta, GA; SR; BED; Dean Lst; AA Abraham Baldwin Coll 90; Erly Chldhd Educ.

**DANIELS, SHELLY A,** Endicott Coll, Beverly, MA; SR; AS; Phi Theta Kappa 90-; Frshmn Intrn Grphc Dsgnr Clifford Nicol Prntng 90; Sr Intrn Dsgnr Oriental Rug Rvw Mgzn 90; Ofc Repr Laconia Weirs Chmbr Cmrc; Mdl Osheas Dept Str; Admin Asst; Cmrcl Art; Dsgnr.

**DANIELS, SUZANNE,** Univ Of Ga, Athens, GA; JR; BSPHR; ACS 89-90; Alpha Epsilon Delta 90-; Deans Lst 89-90; AA Valdosta St Clg 90; Pharm.

**DANIELS, TODD M,** Western New England Coll, Springfield, MA; SR; Deans Lst 89-; Grad Cum Laude; Delta Mu Delta; AS Greenfield Com Clg 89; BSBA; Cmptr Info Syst; Cmptr Prgrmmr Analyst.

**DANIELS, TODD M,** Miami Univ, Oxford, OH; FR; MBA; Mm Mrktng Entrprss 90-; Rsdnc Hll Cncl Chrmn 90-; IM Sprts 90-; Phi Kappa Psi 90-; Intl Bus.

**DANIELS, VICKI L,** Spalding Univ, Louisville, KY; SR; BS; Elem Educ; Tchng.

**DANIELS, WILLIAM F,** Saint Andrews Presbytrn Coll, Laurinburg, NC; SR; BA; Hon Soc 89-; Belk Southern Pines NC; Engl; Ministry.

**DANIELS, WILLIE E,** Fl International Univ, Miami, FL; SR; BA; Chrch Yth Royal Ambssdrs Cnslr 86-89; Estrn Arlnes Mtrl Dstrbtn Cntrl 63-89; Assoc Miami Dade Cmmnty Clg 63; Elem Ed; Tchr Cnslr.

**DANIELSON, JUDITH I,** Univ Of West Fl, Pensacola, FL; SR; BS; Mrchng Bnc Fstvl Chrs 83-84; Sigma Alpha Iota 84-86; Emerald Cst Cmm Bnd 88-90; Elem Educ/Erly Chldhd; Tchng.

**DANISHANKO, JOANN E,** Coll Misericordia, Dallas, PA; FR; BA; Alld Mdcl Careers; Vldctrn Kngstn Cls 89-90; Rdgrphy.

**DANISHEFSKY, SUSANNAH J,** Yeshiva Univ, New York, NY; GD; Cmptr Sci Clb Hd Oper 88-89; Torch Actvts Comm Org Lecture Series 87-88; Dns Lst; Summa Cum Laude; Outstndg Stdnt Cmptr Sci; Bsktbl 84-85; MS Columbia Univ 90; Cmptr Sci-Telecmnctns.

**DANISKA, KIMBERLY L,** Kent St Univ Kent Cmps, Kent, OH; JR; BA; Orntn Instr 90-; Lambda Pi Eta Sec; Alpha Lambda Delta 89-; Gldn Ky; Orntn Hon Soc; Pi Delta Sec 89-90; Sigma Sigma Sigma Sec Educ Dir 90-; Rhetrc/Comm.**

**DANKS, JULIE L,** Kent St Univ Kent Cmps, Kent, OH; FR; BA; Alpha Lambda Delta; Erly Chldhd Edn; Elem Sch Teacher.

**DANKU, JOHN M C,** Central St Univ, Wilberforce, OH; FR; BS; Flwshp Of Chrstn Stdnts Comm Coord; Intl Stdnts Assoc 90-; Hnrs Club; Carbondale Proj; Rsrch Asst; Water Resources Mgmt; : Engrng/Med.

**DANKULIC, ALLISON N,** Kent St Univ Kent Cmps, Kent, OH; SO; BED; SHIP 89-; NAD Natl Assoc Of Deaf; Deaf Edn.

**DANN, JENNIFER L,** Rensselaer Polytechnic Inst, Troy, NY; SR; BS; Stdnt Orntn Steerg Com 89-; Pnhllnc Rush Cnslr Coord; Cls Cncl Sec 88-89; Phi Sigma Sigma Pres; Envrnmntl Eng; Educ.

**DANN, LAURIE E,** Univ Of Fl, Gainesville, FL; SR; BFA; Art Hist 88-89; Golden Key 88-; Sigma Tau Sigma Hnry Tutor Soc 88-; Art Hist; Admin.

**DANN, ROBIN J,** Newbury Coll, Brookline, MA; BA; Cls Rep; Acctn Rep; Mgmnt.

**DANNENBURG, ANDREA,** Wilmington Coll, Wilmington, OH; FR; BA; Cincinnati Bicycle Clb 90-91; Intrnshp Longbranch; German Dept Of State 84-87; Agri Sci.

**DANNER, ANTWOINNE M,** Al A & M Univ, Normal, AL; FR; BA; Art Clb; Acdmc Hnr Rll 90-; Deans Lst 90-; Art; Crtnst.

**DANNER, LOLITA Y,** Gaston Coll, Dallas, NC; SO; BS; Blck Awrns Cltn Treas 90-; NAACP; Hist; Corp/Div/Law.

**DANON, EYAL N,** Fl International Univ, Miami, FL; JR; BS; Amer Htl/Mtl Assoc 88-90; Phi Theta Kappa 89-90; Grad W/Hnrs 88-90; FL Intl Univ Merit Schlrshp; Martial Arts Clb 90-; AS Daytona Bch Cmnty Clg 90; Hosptlty Mgmt; Ph D Bsn Mgmt.

**DANQUAH, JUBILANT BOAKYE,** Interdenominational Theo Ctr, Atlanta, GA; JR; MDIV; Afrcn Smnrns Assoc Cnstn Cmte Chrprsn; Internatl Assoc Sec; Hsp Brd Ghana 86-88; Assoc Pstr, Mntly Rtrd Schl Brd Ghana 89-90; New Edubiase Sec Schl Brd 81-85; Ghana Natl Assoc Tchrs; Ghana Meth Pstrs Flwshp Sec 88-90; Asanteman Assoc; Thlgy/Old Tstmnt Blcl Stdy; Thlgn/Prfsr.

**DANTA, MARISABEL,** Miami Dade Comm Coll South, Miami, FL; SO; Hndcpd Serv Tutor; Hnrs Pgm Comm; Sci Soc; Intl Clb Treas; Phi Theta Kappa Comm 90-; Snt Trnsfr Schlp; Hspnc Fnd Schlp; Mc Knight Schlp; Annl Hnrs Day; Tlnt Rstr 90-; Outstdng Acad Achvmnt Cert; Dns Lst; AA; Cmptr Sci; Sys Anlst.

**DANTINO, FRANCIS D,** Le Moyne Coll, Syracuse, NY; JR; BS; Mktg Clb 90-; Radio 90-; Proj Cmnty 89-; Finance/Mgmnt Info Sys.

**DANTZLER, BRADLEY T,** Nova Univ, Ft Lauderdale, FL; GD; MBA; 1st Chrch Nazerene; MBA; Comm Real Est Fin; Comm R E Dvlpmnt.

**DANZER, GARY J,** Ashland Comm Coll, Ashland, KY; SO; BS; Ashland Comm Coll Tuition Schlrshp; Phrmcy.

**DANZY, DAREN D,** Savannah St Coll, Savannah, GA; JR; Mnrty Engr Cncl Pres 88-; Res Cncl Actvty Coord 90-; Tiger Yrbk Stf Edtr Chf 88-90; Amer Chem Soc 88-; Amer Inst Chem Engrs Pres 88-; Stdnt Enhncmnt Clb Pres 90-; Intercat Inc Intrn; Mst Imprvd Engr Tech Stdnt 90; Otsdng Yng Men Amer 89-90; Chem Engr; Engr.

**DARA, KATHLEEN M,** Georgian Court Coll, Lakewood, NJ; SR; Sigma Tau Delta 90-; Eng; Grdt Schl.

**DARABANT, CHRISTIAN T,** Academy Of The New Church, Bryn Athyn, PA; FR; Pre-Med/Art, Med/Grnl Dsgn.

**DARAGO, CARMEN R,** Kent St Univ Kent Cmps, Kent, OH; SO; BA; Hons Clg 89-; Bus; Accnt.

**DARAK, CARLA M,** Kent St Univ Kent Cmps, Kent, OH; SO; BA; Med Assn 90-; Dns Lst 89-90; Pres Lst 90; Bio; Med.

**DARBY, LANORA JANE,** Univ Of Sc At Columbia, Columbia, SC; JR; BS; Numbers Bytes Clb; Cmptr Sci; Pgrmr.

**DARBY, LISA D,** Univ Of Nc At Greensboro, Greensboro, NC; JR; BSN; Deans Lst Natl Cllgt Nrsng Awd 90-; Unit Sec Hosp Emrgncy; Bowman Gray Schl Med; BA UNC-CHPL Hill 85; Nrsng.

**DARBY, TINA A,** Broward Comm Coll, Ft Lauderdale, FL; SO; AA; Intl Clb Sec; Hnrs Inst 90-; Phi Theta Kappa VP 90-; Plntn Gen Hosp Vol; Comp Edge; Medicine; Surgery/Pediatrics.

**DARCY, KENT R,** Providence Coll, Providence, RI; SO; BA; Wght Lftng Clb 90-; Pol Sci; Law.

**DARDEN, DENISE E,** Fayetteville St Univ, Fayetteville, NC; FR; BA; Illusions Mdlng Clb; Lady Broncho Vlybl Tm; Hstry Educ; Jr Hgh Schl Tchr.

**DARDEN, LORNETTE D,** Univ Of Southern Ms, Hattiesburg, MS; JR; BA; Pryr Time Flwshp 90-; Stdnt Almni Assn 90-; ROTC Rngr Chlng Team; Army ROTC Schlrshp 90-; Dept Army Supr Cadet Awrd 90-; US Army Natl Guard 89-; US Army Actv Duty 85-89; AA J Davison Jr Coll 90; Bus; US Army Comssnd Offcr.

**DARDER GONZALEZ, IVELISSE D,** Inter Amer Univ Pr Hato Rey, Hato Rey, PR; FR; Mdlng Acdmy Lady Mdlng Schl; Psychlgst.

**DARGAN, LOUISE F F,** Coll Of Charleston, Charleston, SC; JR; BA; Flwshp Of Chrstn Athlts; Salt/Lght; Omicron Delta Kappa; Chi Omega Sec 89-90; Engl.

**DARGAN, VERONICA DENISE,** Allen Univ, Columbia, SC; SR; Bus Mgr Stdnt Govt 90-91; Dean List 89-; Pres List 90; Alpha Kappa Alph Inc Sec; Brian Cntr Cola SC; Norting Ctr 90; Cosmtlgst Lscn Marion Cty Voc Ctr 85; Soc Wrk.

**DARGIS, ROBBIN L,** Springfield Tech Comm Coll, Springfield, MA; SO; AA; Crmnl Jstc; Law Enfrcmnt.

**DARLING, CHRISTINE C,** Philadelphia Coll Pharm & Sci, Philadelphia, PA; GD; MPT; Phys Thrpy V P 88-89; Agape 86-88; Adopt A Grndprnt Prog 86-88; Tutoring Prog 87-88; IM Vllybl 87-90; BS; Phy Thrpy.

**DARLING, CHRISTINE L,** Allegheny Coll, Meadville, PA; SO; BA; Peer Educ 90-; Nwspr Spts Wrtr 89-; Lambda Sigma 90-; Crs Cntgry Indr Otdr Trck 89-; Pol Sci; Law.

**DARLING, MELANIE A,** Ithaca Coll, Ithaca, NY; FR; MA; Gerontology Club 90-; Geriatric Phys Therapist.

**DARLING, MICHELLE L,** Notre Dame Coll, Cleveland, OH; FR; BA; Stdnt GOA Sntr 90-; Frshmn Cls VP 90-; Bacchus Fndr 90-; Deans Lst; Bsns.

**DARLING, PATRICK W,** Univ Of Pittsburgh At Bradford, Bradford, PA; FR; BA; Pharm.

**DARLINGTON, SHAWN C,** Ny Univ, New York, NY; FR; BS; Stck Chllnges; Deans Asst; Merrill Lynch Wall St Intrn; Finance; Entrprnr.

**DARMANIN, GINA M,** Fl International Univ, Miami, FL; SR; BS; Phi Lambda Hnr Soc; HFTA Tr 90-; Grnd Hotl Intrn Supvsr 90; AA Browrd Comm Clg 89; Hosp Mgmt; Rest Mgmt.

**DARNALL, ELIZABETH LEIGH,** Volunteer St Comm Coll, Gallatin, TN; SO; AS; Tau Alpha Pi V P 89-; Civil Engr; Paramedic Med.

**DARNALL, TERRA L,** Ky St Univ, Frankfort, KY; SO; BA; Erly Elem Ed.

**DARNELL, BARBARA L,** Northern Ky Univ, Highland Hts, KY; SO; BS; Blgcl Soc; Cincinnati Zoo CREW; Chrldrs; Cmps Mnstry 89-90; SG Dance Comm 89-90; Pre Vet Biology; Vet Animan Reprdctv Rsrch.

**DARNELL, K LEE,** Catawba Valley Comm Coll, Hickory, NC; SO; AAS; EMS Soc Hstrn 90-; EMS Advsry Comm 90-; EMS Exctv Comm 90-; Arlngtn Vol Fr Dpt Frfghtr EMT 85-; W Ydkn Vlntr Fr Dpt Lt 90-; Emrgncy Mdcl Sci.

**DARNELL, KIMBERLY D,** Blue Mountain Coll, Blue Mountain, MS; SO; BA; Stdnt Govt Assn Sec 90-; Engl Clb 89-; Koinonia 89-; Modenian Socty VP 89-; Kings Troupe Drama Tm 90-; Bapt Stdnt Union Frshmn Cncl 89-90; Marquis Of Rose For Modenian Socty 90-; Cls Favorite 90-; Bess Hutchins Spnsh Awd; Engl/Psychlgy; Tchr.

**DARNELL, KRISTEN L,** Lesley Coll, Cambridge, MA; SO; Clss Brd 90-; Deans Advsry Cncl 90-; Orient Comm 90-; Rade Schl TA Intrn 90; Mddl Schl TA Intrn 90; Acad Hons 89-; Sccr Clb Co-Capt 89-; Mdl Schl Ed-Lit; Engl Tchr.

**DARNOLD, BARBARA A,** Wv Univ At Parkersburg, Parkersburg, WV; FR; BA; Mgmt; Bsn.

**DAROOWALLA, FARZANA S,** Kent St Univ Kent Cmps, Kent, OH; FR; BS; India Assoc 87-; Zorastrian Assoc 87-; Alha Lambda Delta; Hnrs Coll; Deans Lst 90-; Pdtrc Nrs.

**DARR, KELLY L,** Oh St Univ At Newark, Newark, OH; FR; BS; Choir; OSU Newark Judicial Bd; Alpha Lambda Delta; Phi Sigma; Phi Eta Sigma; Psychlgy; Law.

**DARRAH, TERI L,** Elmira Coll, Elmira, NY; SR; BS; Vol Rape Crisis Ctr 89-; Elem Educ; Tchng.

**DARROW, JESSICA A,** Univ Of Cincinnati, Cincinnati, OH; JR; BSN; Nrsg; Ansthtst.

**DART, KEITH B,** Fl Coll, Temple Terrace, FL; FR; BA; Phi Beta Lambda; Kappa Omicron Athletic Dir; Rent-A-Student; Hnr Rl; Deans Lst; IM Sports; Mrktng; Advertising.

**DARVILLE, LA LANIA N,** Fl Memorial Coll, Miami, FL; JR; BA; Bahamian Cnctn Tres 90-; Nwspr Stf Wrtr; SGA Artst 88-89; Cert Apprctn Intl Stu Org; Bus Admin.

**DARVISH, ABDOLREZA,** Anne Arundel Comm Coll, Arnold, MD; SO; AA; Intl Stdnt Assn 88-; Phi Theta Kappa; Tau Alpha Phi 89-; AA; Elect Engr.

**DAS, MONIKA,** Memphis St Univ, Memphis, TN; JR; BA; Pres Indian Stu Assoc Pres; Rotrct Clb India Sec 87; Univ Psych Dept Grad Assoc Sec 87; BAMA Hnr Soc India Sec 86-87; Passed Bchlrs Hnrs/Dstnctn; Tbl Tens; BA 85-87; Psych; Cnslr.

**DAS, SUSAN F,** Bellarmine Coll, Louisville, KY; GD; BA; Concord Nwspr 87-90; Cum Laude; Cmnctns.

**DASH III, LOUIS,** Central St Univ, Wilberforce, OH; JR; BA; Music Stdnts Cmtd Cncrnd Pres 89-; NAACP VP 89-90; Deans Lst 90-; Phi Mu Alpha Sinfonian Pres; Presser Awd 90-; Wegmanis Schlrshp Awd; Vlybl/Track; Vocal Performance.

**DASHAWETZ, STANISLAUS,** Boston Coll, Chestnut Hill, MA; SO; OK Amer Yth Assn 90-; Std Nrs Asn 90-; Chrst King Chrch Comm VP 90-; Mjr Infntry USA 69-89; BED Northeastern 69; MED Troy St 87; Nrsng; Anaesthesia.

**DASHEFSKY, MICHAEL G,** Univ Of Rochester, Rochester, NY; JR; BA; RAD Entp 89-; Omcrn Delta Epsln; Pblc Dfndrs Ofc Intshp; John Mairs Prz Econ Awd; Ecnmcs; Law.

**DASHER, BONITA D,** Univ Of North Fl, Jacksonville, FL; SR; BA; Golden Key 89-; Phi Kappa Phi; AA St Johns River Jr Clg 75; Acctg; CPA.

**DASWANI, ANJU A,** Rutgers St Un At New Brunswick, New Brunswick, NJ; FR; BA; Douglass Asian Wmns Assn 90-; Assn Indians At Rutgers 90-; Commuter Stdnt Assn 90-; Douglass Merit Schlr 90-; Daily Targum 90-; Caellian Nwspr Staff Wrtr 90-; Indian Nwsltr; Merit Schlr; Douglass Hons Prog; Douglass Voorhees Schlrshp; Bus/Psychlgy; Cnsmr Psychlgst.

**DATA, DEREK C,** Univ Of Akron, Akron, OH; SR; BA; Acctg Assn 89-; Beta Alpha Psi 90-; Intrnshp Cohen/Co; E S Hurst Acctg Schlrshp; Senatr Acadmc Rcgntn 89-; Acctg; MBA/CPA.

**DATELLE, DAVID C,** Le Moyne Coll, Syracuse, NY; JR; BA; Jdcl Rvw Brd 90-; Pol Sci Acdmy 88-; Acdmc Affrs Cmmtt 90-; Alpha Sigma Nu 90-; Pi Gamma Mu; HEPP/STEP Prog Tutor/Cnlsr 90; Intern Wash D C Law Frm; Cert Washington Cntr; Pol Sci; Law/Jrnlsm.

**DATRES, JULIE L,** Duquesne Univ, Pittsburgh, PA; JR; BA; Drama Clb Hstrn 89-; Grmn Clb Sec 89-90; Rssn Clb 90-; Stu For Peach 89-; Grnpc 88-; Intern St Sen Michael Dawida 90; Grmn Cnslt Awrd Prfcncy; Pol Sci/Grmn/Rssn; Intl Affrs.

**DAUBENSPECK, DAWN M,** Brevard Coll, Brevard, NC; FR; Coll Bnd/Cllgt Sngrs 90-; Music Educ; Tchng.

**DAUBER, JAMI L,** Univ Of Fl, Gainesville, FL; GD; MM; Band 86-90; Orchstra 86-90; Chmbr Sngrs 88-90; Golden Key 88-; Sigma Alpha Iota 88-; Tau Beta Sigma VP 87-; Symphnc Band Dirs Award 89; Im 86-87; J J Finley Gen Music Stdnt Tchr 88; Howard Bishop Mdl Sch Intrnshp 90; Jazz Studies; Tch.

**DAUER, ANN M,** Univ Of South Al, Mobile, AL; SR; BS; Lab Tchncn Wstwtr Trtmnt Plnt; Hlth Edctn; Mstr Degree Tchng.

**DAUER, LLOYD J,** Valdosta St Coll, Valdosta, GA; JR; BS; Crnrstn United Meth Chrch; LAMP; Clowndes Cnty Vol; Moody AFB Swm Tm; USAF; AS Avionics Tech Comm Coll Air Frc 89; Trad/Indus Educ; Msnry.

**DAUGETTE, ELISA DORSEY,** Converse Coll, Spartanburg, SC; SR; BA; Stdnt Govt Assn 88-; Stdnt Dev Com 90; Stdnt Advsry Cncl 89-; Stdnt Actvts Com 90; Cncl Fr Excptnl Chldrn 90-; Cnvrse Dnce Ensmble Pres 89-; Ornttn Elctns Chrmn 90-; Excllnce In Ldrshp Schlrshp 87-; Educ Of Hrng Imprd; Tchng.

**DAUGHDRILL, PAULA S,** Univ Of Ga, Athens, GA; SR; BSW; Soc Wrk Clb; Goldn Key 90-; Chld Wlfr Trneeshp Grnt 90-; Rcgntn UGA Hon Day 90; Soc Wrk; Chld Wlfr.

**DAUGHERTY, CHARLES M,** Ms St Univ, Miss State, MS; SR; BA; Fshn Bd 87; Un Activities Cncl 87; ASLA; ASID 87; Lndscp Arch; Ecolgy Dsgn Dvlpmnt.

**DAUGHERTY, CHRISTOPHER J,** Univ Of Tn At Knoxville, Knoxville, TN; FR; BA; Stdnt Alumni Assn; Exec Undrgrad Bus Pgm; Phi Eta Sigma; Alpha Lambda Delta; Alpha Tau Omega Fin Chrmn 90-; Stdnt Athltc Trnr TN Lady Vols 90-; Bus.

**DAUGHERTY, DAVID LEE,** Wittenberg Univ, Springfield, OH; FR; BA; Cycling Club; AIBS; IM Sports; Phi Eta Sigma; Resid Advisor; Tour Guide; Chemistry; Research.

**DAUGHERTY, MICHAEL T,** Wilmington Coll, Wilmington, OH; SR; BA; Citation Exclnc Engl Lit; Lgl Aid Soc Greene Co Ohio Intshp; Law Schl Univ Dayton; Engl; Law.

**DAUGHERTY, MONICA K,** Univ Of Akron, Akron, OH; SR; Resdnc Hall Progrm Bd Mjr Evnts 88-89; RA Liason 90-; Hall Govt 88-89; Concert Choir 87-89; Golden Key; Kappa Delta Pi; Natl Resdnc Hall Honry; BS; Elem Ed; Tchr.

**DAUGHERTY, RENEE M,** Tn Tech Univ, Cookeville, TN; SO; BS; TTHEA 90-; THEA 90-; AHEA 90-; Alpha Lambda Delta 90-; Kappa Omicron Nu; Phi Mu 89-; Home Econ Awd 90; Home Econ Educ; Tchr.

**DAUGHERTY, SARAH R,** Northern Ky Univ, Highland Hts, KY; SR; BME; CMENC 90-; Chorale 87; All Clgte Choir; Mus Educ; Choral Cndctng.

**DAUGHERTY, SCOTT E,** Univ Of Louisville, Louisville, KY; JR; M ENG; SG Secy 90-; Phi Eta Sigma 90-; Golden Key; ASME 90-; Alpha Phi Omega 90-; Coop Engrng Intnshp; Mechncl Engrng; Engrng.

**DAUGHERTY, SHARON K,** Oh St Univ At Newark, Newark, OH; SR; BS; Phi Sigma 87-89; AA; Elem Educ; Tchng.

**DAUGHERTY, TERESA M,** Ms St Univ, Miss State, MS; JR; BA; Miss Reading Assn 90-; Uniiv Assn Eductrs Pres 90-; Miss Assn Chldrn Under 6 90-; Intl Reading Assn 90-; Natl Educ Assn 90-; Southern Assn Chldrn Under 6 90-; Miss Reading Assn Schlrshp 90-; Ele Educ; Tch.

**DAUGHTRY, CHERISE L,** Norfolk St Univ, Norfolk, VA; SO; BS; Gospel Exprsn Chr 90-; DNIMAS 89-; Spartan Alpha Tau 90-; Schlrshp Dororetz Natl Inst 89-; Cmptr Sci; Sys Analyzing.

**DAUGHTRY, SEAN K,** Morehouse Coll, Atlanta, GA; SO; BS; Chem Clb Prlmntrn 90-; Endvr Space Clb Chr 90-; Cmps All Star Chlng 90-; Hnrs Pgm Chr 89-; Mc Nair Schlr 90-; Mntr John Hope Prjcts; NASA Smmr Intrn 90-; Chem.

**DAULTON, RENEE DAWN,** Univ Of Ky, Lexington, KY; SO; BA; Pi Mu Epsilon; Pi Beta Phi; Math; Tchr.

**DAUM, LORETTA,** Dowling Coll, Oakdale Li, NY; SR; MA; Kappa Delta Pi 90-; Cum Laude Acdmc Schlrshp 90; Brownie/Cub Scout Ldr 81; Spcl Educ Tchr; AAS 84; Certf Deaf Studies 84; Spch Lang Pthlgy.

**DAUPHINAIS, KEVIN D,** Temple Univ, Philadelphia, PA; JR; BA; IM Indoor Soccer Capt 90; IM Soccer 89; IM Vlybl Capt 88; Golden Key 89-; Arch.

**DAURA, DAMON P,** Univ Of Med & Dentistry Of Nj, Newark, NJ; GD; MPT; Rutgers/UMDNJ Phys Therapy Mstrs Pgm Govt Cls Rep/Treas 90-; Am Phys Therapy Assn Dlgte 90-; Clb Rugby 86-89; Phi Delta Theta 87-; Newton Meml Hosp Intrnshp 90; Chambersburg Hosp Intrnshp 89; BA Gettysburg Coll 90; Phys Therapy.

**DAURA, DAWN A,** Bloomfield Coll, Bloomfield, NJ; JR; BA; Res Lf Comm 90-; Deans Lst W/Hon 88-; Alpha Omega Epsilon Pres 88-; Sftbl/Vlybl 88-; Psychlgy; Chld Psychlgst.

**DAUSA, YUDIT,** Univ Of Miami, Coral Gables, FL; SR; BA; Acdmc Achvmnt Awrd; Bowman Ashe Schlrshp 89-; Provosts Lst Dns Lst 87-; BA; AA Miami Dade Comm Coll 89; Bus Mngmnt Organ; Law.

**DAUZUK, DARLENE B,** Coker Coll, Hartsville, SC; BS; Bus.

**DAVALIUS, LINDA F HIRSCHLER,** Marywood Coll, Scranton, PA; SO; BA; TV Marywood Traffic Dir; Irish Step Dancers Mothers Clb Pres 89; PTO Little People Day Care Schl 84; PTA Neil Armstrong Schl 86; Mchnst/Wstn Cntrls Archbld PA 78-87; Cert Johnson Schl Tech 78-79; Radio/TV; TV Production.

**DAVAR, VIKRAM,** Cooper Union, New York, NY; FR; BEE; Vlntr Corps 90-; Greens 90-; Medtn Clb 90-; Inst Elec/Elctrncs Eng 90-; Multpl Sclrsis Wlkthn; Eng.

**DAVE, ALPA R,** Fl Southern Coll, Lakeland, FL; SO; BA; Beta Beta Beta; Bio; Med.**

**DAVELLO, TRACI E,** Univ Of Akron, Akron, OH; FR; Engl; Elem Educ.

**DAVENPORT JR, CHARLES W,** Atlantic Comm Coll, Mays Landing, NJ; SO; Crmnl Justice; Police Ofcr.

**DAVENPORT, CYNTHIA L,** Longwood Coll, Farmville, VA; SR; Stdnt Educ Assoc; Sigma Kappa 89-; BS; Elem Educ; Tchr.

**DAVENPORT, DEBRA L,** Univ Of Tn At Martin, Martin, TN; SR; MA; Older Stdnt Assoc Secy 89-90; Phi Kappa Phi; Psi Chi Secy 89-90; Phi Eta Sigma; Summa Cum Laude; Outstndng Stdnt Awrd; Circuit Crt Genl Sessions Crt Deputy Clrk; Clncl Psychlgy.

**DAVENPORT, HEIDI J,** Oh Univ, Athens, OH; JR; BME; Tau Beta Pi; Golden Key; Mech Eng.

**DAVENPORT, JO F,** Bristol Univ, Bristol, TN; FR; AD; Paralegal.

**DAVENPORT, JOSEPH D,** Southern Coll Of Tech, Marietta, GA; SR; BSMET; Amer Soc Mech Eng 89-; GA Soc Prof Eng 89-; Tau Alpha Pi; Qlty Cntrl Champ Yr 90; BSMET; Mech Eng; Eng Dsgn.**

**DAVENPORT, LEA ANN,** Univ Of Ky, Lexington, KY; SO; BA; SG 89-; Undrgrad Cncl 90-; Grk Actvty Steerg Com; Alpha Almbda Delta; Phi Eta Sigma VP 89-; Kappa Alpha Theta Rec Sec; Deans Lst 89-; Blgy; Med.

**DAVENPORT, MEREDITH A,** Central Fl Comm Coll, Ocala, FL; FR; Stndtintern At First 90-; Baptist Church/Ocala; Cmptr Sci/Religion; Youth Ministry.

**DAVENPORT, SHARON T,** Univ Of Ky, Lexington, KY; SR; Phys Ed Advsry Comm Repr 86-88; Vars Soccer/Ice Hockey/Lacrosse Capt 84-88; H S Soccer Hd Coach/J V Asst/Vars 88-; Lexington Yth Ice Hockey Coach 89-; Thoroughbred Bloodstock Research 89-; BA Wesleyan Univ 88; Math; Ed/Tch.

**DAVENPORT, VALERIE S,** Ms St Univ, Miss State, MS; FR; BME; Garner Hl Cncl IM Chrmn 90-; IM Cncl 90-; Blnd Otdr Lsr Dvlpmnt 88-; Lamda Sigma; Gamme Beta Phi; Soc Wmn Eng 90-; Hnrs Prog 90-; Pres Schlr 90-; Rsrch Asst 90-; Mech Eng.

**DAVENPORT-DIAZ, KAREN A,** Tidewater Comm Coll, Portsmouth, VA; SO; MBA; Outstanding Minority Comm Clg Grad; Hist/Educ; Tch.

**DAVES, ROBBIE B,** Western Piedmont Comm Coll, Morganton, NC; FR; BA; Clg Nwspr Stf; Phi Theta Kappa; Wesleyan Childrens Clb Asst 88-; Blue Ridge Juv Diab Fndtn 88-; Sprts Crspndnt Morganton News Herald; Journalism.

**DAVES III, ROEL D,** Savannah Coll Of Art & Design, Savannah, GA; SO; BFA; Paintg/Illstrtn; Artst.

**DAVID, BRENDA,** Univ Of North Fl, Jacksonville, FL; JR; BS; Gldn Key 90-; Cncr Soc Chrprsn 90-; Otstndng Achvmnt Awd Cntr Exprntl Lrng; Deans Lst 90-; Pilot Clb Acdmc Awd; Aerobics Fitness Assn America ; Ntnl Strngth Cndtng Assn; YMCA Fitness Tstng Coord; AA FL State Unv 89; Hlth Science; Physical Therapy.

**DAVID, ELISA M,** Univ Of Rochester, Rochester, NY; SR; BA; Intrntl Lvng Ctr Scl Dir 88-; Intntl Assn Fiest Chr 88-89; Newman Comm Prsh Cncl 88-; Ldrshp Awd 89-90; Pltcl Sci/Intrntl Rltns.

**DAVID, GEOFFREY C,** Univ Of Cin R Walters Coll, Blue Ash, OH; SO; BA; Computer Sci; Prgr.

**DAVID, JANET K,** Davis & Elkins Coll, Elkins, WV; SR; BA; Stdnt Ed Assn; Hons Assn Sigma Tau Delta Pres 90-; All-Amer Schlr; Engl Acad Achiev Awd; Engl; Tchr.

**DAVID, KATHRYN E,** Bellarmine Coll, Louisville, KY; SR; Stdnt Assmbly Rep Stdnt Govt Class Rep 88-89; Mock Trial Tm 89-90; Res Hal Govt 87-89; Delta Epsilon Sigma 89; Pres Schlrs Prog Cmmnctns Coord 87; Crdnl Sctns Hnr Prog 87; Intrnd As Cmmnctns Coord For Campus Recycled Prog 89-90; Cmmnctns; Pbl Rltns.

**DAVID, LAURA J,** Univ Of Fl, Gainesville, FL; SR; BA; Amer Mktng Assn 89-90; Beta Gamma Sigma 90-; Golden Key 89-; Alpha Lambda Delta 88-; Phi Eta Sigma 88-; Sigma Tau Sigma 89; Arthur Ahsw Mem Schlrshp 90-; Mgmnt; Bnkng.**

**DAVID, MYRIANTHE S,** City Univ Of Ny Baruch Coll, New York, NY; JR; BBA; Grk Clb 88-; Dns Lst 89-90; Golden Key 90-; Beta Gamma Sigma; Acctg; Mba.

**DAVID, RANDAL LEE,** Roane St Comm Coll, Harriman, TN; FR; AS; Sls Prsn; AS Roane St Comm Coll 87; BS Tenn Tech Univ 89; Radlgc Tech/Envrnment Fld.

**DAVID-COLON, CARMEN M,** Univ Of Pr At Rio Piedras, Rio Piedras, PR; SR; Natl Assc Soc Sci; Natl Assc Math; Natl Hnr Scty.

**DAVIDOFF, LAURA ANN,** Cornell Univ, Ithaca, NY; FR; BS; Govt; Law.

**DAVIDOFF, SOLOMON H,** Univ Of Cincinnati, Cincinnati, OH; GD; BFA; The News Recrd Stf Wrtr/Colmnst 87-; Clifton Magazn Fictn Edtr 90-; Film Soc Honry Mbr 89-; Natl Brdcst Soc 87-; Pres 89-90; Soc Of Profsnl Jrnlsts 89-; Gold Recrd Award; Rosemary Hanlon Schlrshp; Wrtng Cert; Brdcstng.

**DAVIDS, RACHEL J,** Alfred Univ, Alfred, NY; JR; BS; Natl Career Wmns Assoc 90-; Adopt-A-Youth 90-; Dance Theatre 89-90; Alpha Lambda Delta 89-; Delta Mu Delta; Pacioli; Fncl Mgmt Assoc Treas; Natl Assoc Acctnts 90-; Acctg; CPA.

**DAVIDSON, AUGUSTINE V,** Germanna Comm Coll, Locust Grove, VA; FR; AA; Literacy Vol; Past Prnt Policy Pres/Head Strt Warreton 84-85; Lib Arts; Humanitarian Field.

**DAVIDSON, BENJAMIN C,** Middle Ga Coll, Cochran, GA; SO; BE; Bptst Stdnt Un 89-; Outstndng Soph Eng Math Stdnt; IM Ftbl/Bsktbl/Sftbl; Indstrl Eng.

**DAVIDSON, CECILIA M,** Univ Of South Al, Mobile, AL; SO; BS; Natl Assoc Homebuilders 85-90; Natl Assoc Realtors 83-90; Real Estate Dvlpmnt Hmbldg Relocation Resdntl Proprty Mngmnt 83-90; Intl Mrktng Statistics; Mrktng Mngmnt.

**DAVIDSON, CHRISTOPHER,** Barry Univ, Miami, FL; SR; BS; Acctng Assoc 89-; Phi Theta Kappa 87-; Acctnt Intrnshp At Keller Indstrs 90; Acctng Exclnc Award FL Inst Of CPAS 90-; AS Broward Cmnty Clg 89; Acctng; CPA.

**DAVIDSON, CHRISTY L,** Northern Ky Univ, Highland Hts, KY; SR; BM; CMENC 87-88; Alpha Chi 89-; Dean Lst 89-; Hnrs Dean Lst 86-; Schlrshp 87; Otstndng Wmn Grad Awrd; Music; Tchr.

**DAVIDSON, DEBRA K,** Fayetteville St Univ, Fayetteville, NC; JR; BS; Elem Ed; Tchr.

**DAVIDSON, HEATHER R,** Southern St Comm Coll, Sardinia, OH; FR; BA; CAP; Trustee Acad Schlrshp 90-; Comp Eng; Graphic Dsgn.

**DAVIDSON, JEANETTE M,** Wv Univ, Morgantown, WV; FR; BED; Mrchng Bnd 90-; Germn Clb 90-; Psych; Chld Psych.

**DAVIDSON, JENNIFER L,** Univ Of Pittsburgh, Pittsburgh, PA; SO; BS; Soc Of Wmn Eng 89-; Phi Eta Sigma 89-; Deans Lst; Eng Physics.

**DAVIDSON, JENNIFER L,** Middle Tn St Univ, Murfreesboro, TN; FR; BS; Mass Cmmnctns; Advtsng.

**DAVIDSON, KAREN E,** Middle Tn St Univ, Murfreesboro, TN; SR; Wrk Schlrshp 88-; Hnr Rl/Deans Lst 88-; Gamma Beta Phi 90-; Beta Alpha Psi 89-; BBA MTSU; Acctng.

**DAVIDSON, LEIGH A,** Tn Tech Univ, Cookeville, TN; SO; BS; Hm Econ Assc Pres; Chrstn Stdnt Ctr; IM Athltcs; Kappa Omicron Nu; Orntn Asst; Phi Kappa Phi Outstndg Awd; Mullbro Awd; Chld/Fmly/Hm Econ; Chld Lfe Spec.

**DAVIDSON, MICHAEL W,** Middle Tn St Univ, Murfreesboro, TN; FR; BS; Jr Chamber Of Com Awd; Vol In Phys Ther At Donelson Hosp; Phys Ther.

**DAVIDSON, PIPER L,** Kent St Univ Kent Cmps, Kent, OH; SR; BA; Psych Club 87-; Psi Chi; Psych.

**DAVIDSON, SHEILA D,** Univ Of Southern Ms, Hattiesburg, MS; SR; MS Nrse Assn; Northcrest Bapt Ch; Cert Emerg Nrse; Nrse Emerg Dept; BS; ADN Meridian Comm Coll 87; Nrsng.

**DAVIDSON, SHERYL D,** Univ Of Montevallo, Montevallo, AL; SR; BS; Hon Pgm 87-89; Hsng/Rsdnt Lf Pgm RA 88-90; Cthlc Cmps Mnstrs 87-90; Lambda Sigma Pi 90-; Omicron Delta Kappa 89-; Phi Kappa Phi; Cir K 87-89; Mvallo Assn Hmn Serv 89-; Alpha Gamma Delta Stndrds Chmn 88-; Ldrshp Schlrshp 87-; Scl Wrk; Yth Mnstry.

**DAVIDSON, SUSANNAH,** Smith Coll, Northampton, MA; FR; BA; Nwspr Entrtnmnt Ed 90-; Epheblans 90; 1st Grp Schlr; Engl; Editing/Publshng.

**DAVIDSON, TAVETIA C,** Tougaloo Coll, Tougaloo, MS; FR; Gospel Choir; Recgntn Otsdng Achvmnt Gospel Choir 90-; Math/Cmptr Sci.

**DAVIDSON II, TIMOTHY A,** Univ Of Sc At Columbia, Columbia, SC; FR; BA; Dorm Rep 90-; IM 90-; Intl Affrs; Govt Wrk.

**DAVIDSON, TRACY ANN,** Teikyo Post Univ, Waterbury, CT; SO; BA; Intrcoll Eqstrn Tm 89-; Dns Lst 89-; Eqne Sci; Bus Mgmt.

**DAVIDSON, VERA D,** Univ Of Cincinnati, Cincinnati, OH; SR; BED; Intrnatl Rdng Assn; Natl Sci Tchrs Assn; Tchrs Applyng Whle Lang; Gldn Ky; Phi Theta Kappa; Univ Dns Lst; Grls SE Cncnnti Sccr Assn Inc Cch 90-; By Scts Sec 90-; GS Trp Ldr 90-; Cb Scts Treas Dn Ldr 90; Educ; Elem Tchr.

**DAVIE, JULIANNE J,** Merrimack Coll, North Andover, MA; FR; BA; Pi Theta Epsilon; Psychlgy; Chld Psychlgst.

**DAVIES, ANGELA L,** Univ Of Nc At Greensboro, Greensboro, NC; JR; BS; Food/Nutrition Clb 90; Food/Nutrition/Fd Serv Mgmnt; Catering.

**DAVIES, JEFFREY J,** Columbus Coll Of Art & Design, Columbus, OH; FR; BA; U S Cylcng Fed 84-; Merit Schlrshp 90; Fine Art-Illustrtr; Sulpture/Illustrtr.

**DAVIES, JENNIFER A,** Clarkson Univ, Potsdam, NY; SO; BA; Scty Of Wmn Mgrs 90; Delta Zeta PR; Mgmt Info Systms; Comp Bus Anlyst.

**DAVIES, JENNIFER C,** Georgetown Univ, Washington, DC; JR; BSN; Ntl Stdnt Nrs Assn 90-; Stdnt Nrs Assn Pres 89-; Tau Beta 86-; Slng Var 88-90; Nrsng.

**DAVIES, MICHAEL J,** Radford Univ, Radford, VA; SO; BS; Alpha Lambda Delta 89-; Pi Gamma Mu; Crim Justice; Law.

**DAVIES, RACHEL E,** Goucher Coll, Towson, MD; JR; BA; Hse Cncl Hs Pres 90-; Career Devlpmnt Bd 90-; Intrnshp WDAY Radio Fargo ND 90; Cmnctns; Film.

**DAVILA AYALA, MARIA V,** Inter Amer Univ Pr Hato Rey, Hato Rey, PR; JR; MBA; Bell Cllctrs Clb; Eng Wife Clb; Brd Dir Urb Vista Bella S; Matcor Inc S To P; Law.

**DAVILA, MARIA I,** Univ Politecnica De Pr, Hato Rey, PR; SR; BSIE; Inst Ind Engrs 90-; Ind Eng.

**DAVILA, MATILDE,** Caribbean Univ, Bayamon, PR; JR; BA; PTA Treas 90; Tchr; Elem Ed; Tchr.

**DAVIS SNYDER, KRISTY K,** Defiance Coll, Defiance, OH; JR; BA; Hon List; Cstmr Svc Spclst; Assc NW Tech Clg 88; Acctg/Bus Mgmt.

**DAVIS, AHMED J,** Morehouse Coll, Atlanta, GA; FR; BA; Dorm Cncl Sec 90-; NASA Spce Endvrs Clb 90-; Deans Lst; Hon Roll; IM Vlybl Co-Capt 90-; Chem; Chem Engr.

**DAVIS, AMANDA L K,** Univ Of Southern Ms, Hattiesburg, MS; SR; Sigma Psi Alpha Scl Chrmn 87-89; BS 90; Accntng; CPA.

**DAVIS, AMY L,** Emmanuel Coll, Franklin Spg, GA; FR; BA; Cllgt 4-H Clb Pres 90-; Schl Paper 90-; 4-H Ctznshp Awd 90; IM Ftbl 90; History/Pltcl Sci; Law.

**DAVIS, AMY S,** Albany St Coll, Albany, GA; JR; BS; Alpha Hi Sigma Sec/Tres 90-; Alpha Kappa Mu 90-; Cmps All Star Challenge Tm 89-; Pres Schlr 88-; Criminial Justice; Government.

**DAVIS, AMY S,** Abraham Baldwin Agri Coll, Tifton, GA; FR; BA; Std Govt Asn Sntr 90-; Spch Pthlgy.

**DAVIS, ANA C,** Univ Of Miami, Coral Gables, FL; FR; BA; Pre Legal Soc 90-; Hon Stdnts Assn 90-; Provsts Hon Rl 90-; Alpha Kappa Psi 90-; Acctg/Pltcl Sci; Law.

**DAVIS, ANDREA C,** Univ Of Sc At Columbia, Columbia, SC; SR; BAIS; Elem Ed; Tchng/Admn.

**DAVIS, ANGELA M,** Cecils Coll, Asheville, NC; GD; Dns Lst 90-; Grdtd Hnrs; Trvl; Trvl Indstry.

**DAVIS, ANGELA W,** Univ Of North Fl, Jacksonville, FL; JR; BBA; Gldn Key; Mngmt.

**DAVIS, ANGELIQUE R,** Al A & M Univ, Normal, AL; SR; BS; Stdnt Govt Assoc Treas 90-; Fncl Mgmt Assoc Treas 90-; Intrdrm Cncl 90-; Delta Mu Delta 89-; Delta Sigma Theta Pres 90-; Yng Cthlc Adlts 87-; Ryder Systems Inc Intrn 88-; Jackie Robinson Fndtn Schlr 87-; Bsn Fnce; Fncl Anlyst.

**DAVIS, ANISSA A,** Fl A & M Univ, Tallahassee, FL; FR; Phi Eta Sigma 90-; Sci; Nrs.

**DAVIS, ANITA K,** Union Coll, Barbourville, KY; FR; BA; Iota Sigma Nu Frsmn Awrd 90-; Bsn; Tchng.

**DAVIS, ANNABELLE T,** Howard Univ, Washington, DC; JR; BARCH; Amer Inst Arch Stdnts 88-; Arch/Plnng Stdnt Assn 88-; Tau Sigma Delta 89-; Keyettes V P 86-88; Intrnshp Glave Newman Anderson Architects 89; Architecture.

**DAVIS, ANTOINE L,** Wilberforce Univ, Wilberforce, OH; SR; BA; Il Pre-Almni Pres 86-; SGA Elec Comm 90; Blk Ml Cltn Treas; Phi Eta Psi Sgt 90-; Trck Tm 89-90; Clncl Psychlgy.

**DAVIS III, ARCHIE,** Univ Of Pittsburgh, Pittsburgh, PA; SR; BSW; Crmnl Justc Clb Treas 89-90; Assoc Crrctns Admin Allegheny Comm Coll 89; Scl Wrk Admin; Hosp Admin.

**DAVIS, BARBARA A,** Univ Of Al At Birmingham, Birmingham, AL; JR; BA; Erly Chldhd/Elem; Tchr.

**DAVIS, BARBARA K,** Georgetown Univ, Washington, DC; SO; BSN; Alpha Phi Omega Pub Chrmn 90; Repubs; Natl Stdnt Nurses Assoc; Sigma Theta Tau; Nursing; Admin.

**DAVIS, BENITA J,** Voorhees Coll, Denmark, SC; SO; BS; Debate Team 90-; Concert Choir 90-; Drama Club 90-; Choir Psi Phi; Deans List 89-90; Svc And Support To SGA 90-; Comptr Sci; Sys Progrmr.

**DAVIS, BENJAMIN L,** Columbus Coll Of Art & Design, Columbus, OH; FR; BFA; 1st Church Of Nazarene Choir & Clge Career Group; Schlrshps 90; Art & Design; Illustration.

**DAVIS, BEVERLY S,** Roane St Comm Coll, Harriman, TN; SO; BA Bus Management Sup 90.

**DAVIS, BOBBI R,** Fl A & M Univ, Tallahassee, FL; SO; Tm Tchrs Educ For Mnrty Stdnts Chrprsn 90; Rmp Prog; Summr Prog Fr Mnrty Stdtns; AA Debree; Elem Educ Psych; Law Tch.

**DAVIS, BRAD I,** Milligan Coll, Milligan Clg, TN; JR; BS; IM Sftbl/Vlybl 88-; Sci/Bus; Eng/Bus.

**DAVIS, BRADLEY M,** Univ Of Tn At Martin, Martin, TN; JR; BS; Mrchng Symphnc Bnds 88-; Kappa Alpha Ordr 90-; Scndry Ed.

**DAVIS, BRETT C,** Central Al Comm Coll, Alexander City, AL; SO; BA; Science; Physcl Therapy.

**DAVIS, BRIAN E,** Ashland Comm Coll, Ashland, KY; FR; AAS; Nrsng.

**DAVIS, BRIAN K,** Memphis St Univ, Memphis, TN; SR; BA; English.

**DAVIS, BRIAN K,** Va Commonwealth Univ, Richmond, VA; JR; BS; Urban Studies Stdnt Assn Pres 90-; Univ Bnd 88-89; Intrnshp Cnty Plnng Comm; Deans Lst; Schlor Awd Acad Excellence 90-; Urban Studies/Plng; Plnnr.

**DAVIS, CANDICE J,** Paine Coll, Augusta, GA; FR.

**DAVIS, CANDICE N,** Clark Atlanta Univ, Atlanta, GA; SO; BA; Engl Clb 89-; Engl Hnrs Scty; Banner Carrier 89-90; Majorette 90-; Engl Ed; Law Tchg.**

**DAVIS, CARL E,** Nc Agri & Tech St Univ, Greensboro, NC; SR; BS; Natl Scty Of Blck Engs 90; NAACP 90; Exclsvly MD Clb Pres 87-; Natl Cllgte Eng Awrd; Intrnshp With Corning Inc 90; Elec Eng.

**DAVIS, CARLA R,** Univ Of Tn At Martin, Martin, TN; JR; BS; SGA Chf Jstc 89-90; Phi Chi Theta 90-; Spc Olympcs 90-; Phi Chi Theta 90-; Rcyclng Prjct 89-; Internatl Bsn; Trd.

**DAVIS, CAROLYN J,** Hillsborough Comm Coll, Tampa, FL; FR; AA; Phi Theta Kappa; Mass Communications; Radio.

**DAVIS, CARRIE F,** Valdosta St Coll, Valdosta, GA; SO; BA; Rd Dmnds Ar Clb Pres Lttl Sstrs 90-; Erly Chldhd Ed; Tchng.

**DAVIS, CARRIE R,** Memphis St Univ, Memphis, TN; SO; BA; Ten Step 90-; Psy; Thrpy.

**DAVIS, CASSANDRA L,** Al St Univ, Montgomery, AL; FR; Hnr Rll 90-; Bus; Accntng.

**DAVIS, CATHERINE A,** Jackson St Univ, Jackson, MS; JR; Blgy Scty Sec 89; Bapt Stdnt Unn; NAACP; Alpha Lambda Delta 88-; Beta Beta Beta VP 90-; Beta Kappa Chi Sec 90; Alpha Kappa Mu; Delta Sigma Theta; Mnrty Accss To Rsrch Crrs Schlr 89-; Intrnshp Natl Cntr Fr Txclgcl Rsrch; Blgy; Tchng And Rsrch.

**DAVIS, CATHERINE L,** Fairmont St Coll, Fairmont, WV; FR; BS; Cmptr Sci; Cmptr Pgmr.

**DAVIS, CATHY D,** Anderson Coll, Anderson, SC; SO; AA; Math; Bus.

**DAVIS, CATHY S,** Univ Of North Fl, Jacksonville, FL; SR; BS; Sigma Theta Tau 90-; St Vincents Hosp 80-; Staff RN RRT 88-; Pulomary Rehab Dept 88-; AS Resp Therapy 80; AS Nursing 85; Nursing.

**DAVIS, CHARLES E,** Daytona Beach Comm Coll, Daytona Beach, FL; SO; BA; Naval Aviatn Clb 90-; Lambda Chi Alpha 89-91; Pres Lst 90-; IM Fncng 90; IM Vlybl 90-; Poli Sci; US Army Ofcr.

**DAVIS, CHARLES LOUIS,** Univ Of Southern Ms, Hattiesburg, MS; SR; Phi Kappa Tau Hse Mgr 90-; Lambda Chi 90; Hensel Phelps Constr Co.

**DAVIS, CHARLYN G,** Marshall University, Huntington, WV; SR; BS; Pros Vp 90; Intrnshp Hca Rvr Prk Hsptl; Stdnt Mmbr/Wtra & Atra; Thrptc Rcrtn; Dir Actvty Thrpy Ofc.

**DAVIS, CHERIE L,** Univ Of Sc At Columbia, Columbia, SC; SO; BA; LPN 89-; Psychlgy; Cnslng.

**DAVIS, CHERYL D,** Clark Atlanta Univ, Atlanta, GA; SO; BS; Deans Lst 89-90; Engl/Jrnlsm/Hstry; Radio/TV/FLM.

**DAVIS, CHRISTIAN D,** Univ Of Miami, Coral Gables, FL; JR; BA; Hnr Cncl 90-F SG Chr Acad Affrs Comm 90-; RA 89-; Omicron Delta Kappa ; Gldn Key; Sigma Tau Delta; Iron Arrow Schlrshp 90; Priv Stds Prog; Jackson Mem Hosp Rsrch; Crew Tm JV Crew 88-89; Engl Lit; Physician.

**DAVIS, CHRISTINA K,** Univ Of Charleston, Charleston, WV; JR; BA; Phi Eta Sigma 88-89; Elem Ed; Tchr.

**DAVIS, CHRISTINE LOUISE,** Salisbury St Univ, Salisbury, MD; SR; BS; Resdntl Asst 88-89; Resdnc Hall Cncl Rep 87; Advsr 88-89; Deans List 88-; Presdntl Schlr 87-; Senatrl Schlr 87-; MD Distngshd Schlr; NASAGSFC/WFF Intrnshp 90-; Im Aerobics 88; Chem.

**DAVIS, CHRISTOPHER L,** Southern Coll Of Tech, Marietta, GA; JR; BS; Amrcn Soc Cvl Engnrs 90-; Amrcn Soc Crtfd Engnrng Tchntns 87-88; AS Cvl Engr Tech Chttnga St Tech Cmmnty Clg 88; Cvl Engnrng Tchnlgy.

**DAVIS, CHRISTOPHER W,** Kent St Univ Kent Cmps, Kent, OH; SR; BA; Fin/Real Est; Plng.

**DAVIS, CLAUDIA L,** Univ Of Sc At Columbia, Columbia, SC; JR; BS; Gamma Orgnztn; Psi Chi 89-; Kappa Delta 90-; Psych Indpndnt Stdy; Psychlgy; Rehab Cnslr.

**DAVIS, CLAUDIA LYNNE,** Univ Of Miami, Coral Gables, FL; JR; BBA; Tsk Force Subst Abuse 89-; Peer Cnslng; Intl Hs Res 89-; Golden Key Pr 90-; Alpha Kappa Psi 90-; Dns Lst 89-90; Prvsts Lst 90; Pres Lst; Intl Finc/Mktg; Retail.

**DAVIS, COLLEEN F,** Lesley Coll, Cambridge, MA; SO; BED; Flr Hcky 89-; Sccr Tm 89-; Ltrry Mag 89-; Acad Hnrs Lst 89-; LINC 90-; Rsdnts Lfe Advsry Brd 90; Chld Cre Srvce 90; Mddle Schl Sci Math; Educ Tch.**

**DAVIS, CORA J,** Saint Josephs Coll New York, Brooklyn, NY; GD; BSC; Amrcn Assoc Nrs; Ny St Nrs Assoc; Amrcn Assoc Crtcl Cr Nrs; Deans Hnr Rl; Md Cntr Crdc Intnsv Cr; Icu Prcdr Cmt; Hlth Admnstrtn; Mba/Ms Cmnty Hlth.

**DAVIS, COREY B,** Georgetown Univ, Washington, DC; FR; BA; Grgtwn Invstmnt Allnc 90-; Natl Assoc Blck Acctnts; INROADS Hstn Treas 90-; Internshp Frst Cty Bnk 90-; Trck; Crss Cntry 90-; Intl Fnc; Invstmnt Bnkng.

**DAVIS, CORINA E,** Kutztown University Of Penna, Kutztown, PA; FR; BFA; Communication Design.

**DAVIS, CYNDEE M,** Greenville Tech Coll, Greenville, SC; FR; AA; Bsnss/Accntng; CPA.

**DAVIS, CYNTHIA M,** Univ Of Southern Ms, Hattiesburg, MS; SR; BA; MAE 90-; Jr Clg Hnr Achvmnt Awd; AA Jones Cnty Jr Clg 89; Elem Educ; Teach/Mstrs Deg.

**DAVIS, CYNTHIA Y,** Fl A & M Univ, Tallahassee, FL; JR; BSW; BACCHUS; NAACP; Phi Alpha; Natl Scl Sci Awd; Scl Wrk.

**DAVIS, DANA M,** Radford Univ, Radford, VA; JR; BA; Cir K Intrntl 89-; Stdnt Govt Comm; Hnrs Prog; Alpha Lambda Delta 89-; Sigma Delta Pi Vp 90-; Phi Kappa Phi; Deans Lst; Spnsh; Govt.

**DAVIS, DANIA J,** Univ Of Southern Ms, Hattiesburg, MS; SR; BS; Stdnt Alumni Assn 87-89; Golden Girls 88-89; Diamond Darlings 87-89; Delta Gamma 87-; Rho Chi 88-90; Nwspr Prod 89-; Deans Lst 89-; IM Flgftbl/Vllybl 87-89; Jrnlsm/Advrstng; Mktng.

**DAVIS, DANIEL D,** Ms Gulf Coast Comm Coll, Perkinston, MS; FR; ABM; Band Gld Sctn Ldr 90-; IM Ftbl Sftbl; Msc; Air Force Bnd.

**DAVIS, DANIEL S,** Univ Of Al, Tuscaloosa, AL; JR; BED; La Mesa Espaa; IM Ftbl Captn 90; Res Assistant 90-; Ed H S; Teaching/Coaching.**

**DAVIS, DARLENE S,** Spalding Univ, Louisville, KY; SR; MA; Bus/Profsnl Women Of St Matthew VP; Delta Sigma Epsilon 90-; St Joseph Chldrn Hm Chrprsn 82-; Soc Sci AS Univ Of Louisville 86; Radiolgy Cert Bellarmine Univ 75; Cmnctn/Psychlgy.

**DAVIS, DAVID R,** Morehouse Coll, Atlanta, GA; SO; BA; Hnrs Pgm 89-; Mass Media Arts Soc Pres 90-; Mass Comm; Brdcst Jrnlsm/Tlvsn Prod.

**DAVIS, DAWN M,** Univ Of Nh Plymouth St Coll, Plymouth, NH; JR; BA; Rugby Clb Sec/Capt 89-; Pltcl Sci; Law.

**DAVIS, DAWN M,** Tn Temple Univ, Chattanooga, TN; SR; BS; Wesly Soc; Alpha Epsilon Theta; Pi Epsilon Rho Tr; Pryr Grp Ldr; Sundy Schl Tchr; Natl Dns Lst 88-; Bio; Fornsc Scntst.

**DAVIS, DEBORAH A,** Va Commonwealth Univ, Richmond, VA; SR; BS; Stdnt Educ Assn 90-; Phi Kappa Phi; BBA Coll Of Wm/ Mary 77; Educ; Elem Tchr.

**DAVIS, DEBORAH S,** Miami Jacobs Jr Coll Of Bus, Dayton, OH; GD; AD; Bus Admin.

**DAVIS, DENISE A,** Fl International Univ, Miami, FL; JR; BA; FIU Acctg Assoc 89-; Phi Eta Sigma 89-; Acctg; CPA.

**DAVIS, DETRICE R,** Alcorn St Univ, Lorman, MS; SR; BS; Soc Socl Work Clb 87-; Soclgy/Socl Work.

**DAVIS, DIANA M,** Coll Of Charleston, Charleston, SC; SO; BA; Alumni Assn; Zeta Tau Alpha Treas 89-; Bus/Frnch; Intl Bus.

**DAVIS, DIANA N,** Univ Of Sc At Columbia, Columbia, SC; SR; BS; Clb Mgrs Assn Amer 90-; Gamma Beta Phi Pgm Comm 88-; Eta Sigma Delta 89-; Goldn Key Hstrn 90-; Appld Prof Sci Tchr Yr Comm HRTA Rep Comm Mbr; Pres Lst 88-90; Htl/Rest/ Toursm.

**DAVIS, DIANE E,** George Mason Univ, Fairfax, VA; JR; BS; Decision Scie Club 90-; Symphy Orchestra 89-; Racqubit Club 90-; Golden Key; Alphi Chi; Decision Scie; Operations Res.

**DAVIS, DIONNA R,** Morris Brown Coll, Atlanta, GA; SO; BA; Mrktng Clb 89-90; Mck Trl Tm 90-; Phi Beta Lambda Sec; Natl Cncl Ngr Wmn 90-; NAACP 90-; Bus.

**DAVIS, DON K,** Marshall University, Huntington, WV; SR; BA; Scl Stds; Tchr.

**DAVIS, DONALD P,** Univ Of Al At Birmingham, Birmingham, AL; SO; BA; Lcnsd/Ordained Minister; Prison Inmate Cnslng/ Yth Minister 88-; Cert Rhema Bible Trng Ctr 88-90; Political Sci; Government.

**DAVIS, DONNA L,** Snead St Jr Coll, Boaz, AL; SO; Pres Lst; Bsnss Admin; Accntng.

**DAVIS, DOUGLAS W,** Western New England Coll, Springfield, MA; JR; BSBA; Labrador Rtrvr Clb Pioneer Vly Tres 87-; Acctg Clrk 88-; ASBA Sprngfld Tech Comm Clg 90; Acctg; CPA.

**DAVIS, E JANETTE,** Radford Univ, Radford, VA; SR; BS; Kappa Delta Pi Sec 89-; Alpha Lambda Delta 87-88; Erly/Mid Edn; Teach.

**DAVIS, EDDIE,** Brewton Parker Coll, Mount Vernon, GA; SO; BA; Inner-Greek Council 90-; Council Of Intramural Activities CIA 90-; Phi Chi 89-; Sigma Phi Sigma Pres 89-; Prsdntl Ldrshp Schlrshp 89-; All Star Flag Ftbl Team; All Star Sftbl Team IM 89-; Recreation; Director.**

**DAVIS, EMILIE K,** Georgetown Coll, Georgetown, KY; JR; BA; Phi Mu VP 89-; Pha Little Sis; Baptist Stdnt Union Pres 89-; Stdnt Govt 89-90; Alpha Lambda Delta Treas 89-; Eta Delta Phi; Sigma Gamma Sigma Secy 88-89; Intern Georgetown News Times 89-90; English; Journalism.

**DAVIS, FAITH E,** Broward Comm Coll, Ft Lauderdale, FL; FR; AA; Phi Theta Kappa 90-; Phi Beta Lambda 90-; Pres Lst 90-; Math; Law.

**DAVIS, FRA LENA A,** Alcorn St Univ, Lorman, MS; JR; BS; SIFE 90; Alpha Kappa Alpha; Bus Admin; Advrtsng Exctve.

**DAVIS JR, FRED M,** Pellissippi St Tech Comm Coll, Knoxville, TN; SO; AFP; Otdrs Clb; Vol Fr Christ; Phi Theta Kappa Cmps Rep; Intrnshp Prsnttn Techs; Grphc Dsgn; Dsgn Illstrtn.

**DAVIS, GABRIELLE M,** Univ Of Southern Ms, Hattiesburg, MS; FR; BS; SADD Secy 90-; Stdnt Eagle Clb 90-; Stdnt Alumni Assoc 90-; Gama Beta Phi 90-; Alpha Lamda Delta 90-; Phi Eta Sigma 90-; Bsktbl 90; Educ; Elem Spec Educ.

**DAVIS, GAIL L,** Nc Central Univ, Durham, NC; JD; VP First Yr Class 88-89; Wmns Caucus Vice Chrprsn 88-; Black Law Stdnts Assn 89-90; Law Jrnl Edtr In Chf 89-; Moot Ct Intra Schl Cmptn Coord 89-; Phi Delta Phi; BS Howard Univ 87; Law/ Zoology.

**DAVIS, GAY W,** Valdosta St Coll, Valdosta, GA; SR; BS; Alpha Chi; PAGE; NEA GAE 90-; Sub Tchr 74-76; Secr 84-89; Early Chldhd; Tch.

**DAVIS, GEORGE D,** Middle Tn St Univ, Murfreesboro, TN; FR; BA; Eng; Dsgn Engr.

**DAVIS, GINA E,** Owensboro Comm Coll, Owensboro, KY; Eng; Edn.

**DAVIS, GINGER R,** Memphis St Univ, Memphis, TN; JR; BA; Communication; Air Traffic Control FAA.

**DAVIS, GLENROY L,** Cheyney Univ Of Pa, Cheyney, PA; SR; MA; Tst Mstrs Spch Clb 90; Asst Nws Dir WCSR Rdio 88; Chyny Rcrd Sprts Edit 90; IM Nwslttr Edit 90; Sprts Anncr 90; WVOX Rdio Brdcstr NY; Actng Cge Thtre Mt Vrnn NY; BA Cheyney Univ 90; Brdcstng And Thtre; Sprts Jrnlsm.

**DAVIS, GUERRY M,** Tn Tech Univ, Cookeville, TN; SR; BS; Stdnt Nurses Assn Pres 90-; Natl Stdnt Nurses Assn Cnvtn Deleg 90-; Phi Kappa Phi 89-; Sigma Theta Tau 90-; Mortar Bd 90-; Margaret Perry Ldrshp Awd; TN Assoc Stdnt Nurses Ldrshp Awd TTU Chapt; Nrsng.

**DAVIS, HALEY T,** Univ Of Rochester, Rochester, NY; SR; BS; Scty Wmn Eng VP 88-; Amrcn Scty Mchncl Eng 90-; Tau Beta Pi 90-; Delta Gamma 89-; Deans Lst; Mchncl Eng.

**DAVIS, HAWANYA S,** Fl A & M Univ, Tallahassee, FL; FR; BED; Omega Esnc VP 90-; STARS Tutor 90-; Spcl Educ.

**DAVIS, HEATHER H,** Valdosta St Coll, Valdosta, GA; JR; BS; Alpha Beta Gamma 88-90; Hnr Stdnt 88-90; Deans List; BA Abraham Baldwin Ag Clge 90; Math; Teacher.

**DAVIS, HOLLIE S,** Middle Tn St Univ, Murfreesboro, TN; FR; BS; Art Ed; Tchg/Ind Studio.

**DAVIS, IDA K,** Univ Of Miami, Coral Gables, FL; SR; MBA; Alumni Mentor Prog 90-; Cncl Prsdnts Chr Scl Comm 90-; Honors Prog 88-; Beta Gamma Sigma 89-; Beta Alpha Psi Chr Scl Comm 90-; Golden Key 88-; Alpha Kappa Psi Pres 88-; Vol Income Tax Asst; Ntl Hispanic Schrl Awd; Accounting.

**DAVIS JR, IVAN R,** Tn St Univ, Nashville, TN; SR; BS; NAACP 89-; Blck Stdnt Alliance Pres 87-88; Alchl/Drg Educ Comm 87-88; Outstndng Ldrshp Awrd; Hstry/Sociolgy; Bus Law.

**DAVIS, JACQUELINE S,** Lexington Comm Coll, Lexington, KY; AAS; Rdlgy Tech.

**DAVIS, JAMES F,** Capital Bible Seminary, Lanham, MD; GD; THM; Evngls Theol Soc; Envirnmntl Eng US EPA; BSME Univ WI 85; New Test Lit; Mssnry.

**DAVIS, JAMES M,** S U N Y At Buffalo, Buffalo, NY; JR; BS; Intl Norton Ownrs Assoc; Tau Beta Pi; Eta Kappa Nu; Elec Eng.

**DAVIS, JAMES W,** Middle Tn St Univ, Murfreesboro, TN; JR; US Navy Rsrv 90-; Arnold Air Socty 88-89; Kappa Alpha Order 89-; Aerospace Stds; Prof Pilot.

**DAVIS, JANA D,** Longwood Coll, Farmville, VA; SO; AME; Msc Edctrs Ntl Cnfrnc Vp 89-; Sigma Alpha Iota Tres 90-; Hull Schlrshp 90-; Msc Edctn; Tchng.

**DAVIS, JEFFREY ALLEN,** Western Carolina Univ, Cullowhee, NC; JR; BS; Anthrplgy Clb 89-; Natl Ggrphc Scty 90-; Flklre Scty 90-; Pi Gamma Mu; NC Div Of Archvs And Hstry Intrn; Anthrplgy Ggrphy; Natl Pk Srvce.

**DAVIS, JEFFREY D,** Alcorn St Univ, Lorman, MS; FR; BA; Innerfaith Gospel Choir; Bio; Pre-Med.

**DAVIS, JEFFREY S,** Kent St Univ Kent Cmps, Kent, OH; JR; BS; Golden Key; Sigma Tau Delta 90-; Kappa Delta Pi; Undergrad Studies Comm Dept Of Engl 90-; ATTEP; Engl/Soc Studies; Tch.

**DAVIS, JENNIFER A,** Georgian Court Coll, Lakewood, NJ; SR; BA; Freehld Art Scty VP; Art/Ed; Hgh Schl Tchr.

**DAVIS, JENNIFER L,** Vance Granville Comm Coll, Henderson, NC; FR; AS; Sftbl 89-; Vllybl; Math/Cmptr Sci; Prgrmr.

**DAVIS, JENNIFER LA VERNE,** Saint Augustines Coll, Raleigh, NC; FR.

**DAVIS, JEREMY T,** Univ Of Tn At Martin, Martin, TN; JR; BED; Biol; Tch.

**DAVIS, JILL M,** Converse Coll, Spartanburg, SC; FR; BA; Stdnt Chrstn Assoc 90-; Cnvrs Wllnss Assoc Frshmn Rep 90-; Stdnt Govt Assoc 90-; Alpha Lambda Delta 90-; Ed; Elem Tchr.

**DAVIS, JOAN D,** Greenville Tech Coll, Greenville, SC; SO; AA; Beta Sgm Phi; Electro/Com Inc Ofc Mgr 85-; Exec Secy Dipl Forrest Clg 65; Genrl Educ; Interior Dsgn BA.

**DAVIS, JOHN B,** Newbury Coll, Brookline, MA; SO; BA; Shpng/Rcvng/Ware House Wrk; Acctg.**

**DAVIS, JOHN M,** Fl St Univ, Tallahassee, FL; JR; BS; Interclgte Stds Inst; Phi Theta Kappa 90; Lambda Alpha Epsilon; Dns Lst Schl Crmnlgy 90; AA Gulf Coast Comm Clge 90; Crmnlgy; Fed Law Enfrcmnt.

**DAVIS, JOHN S,** Ms St Univ, Miss State, MS; SO; BA; Enlg; Pblshng/Wrtng.

**DAVIS, JOY M,** Univ Of New Haven, West Haven, CT; SR; BA; Day Stdnt Govt; Black Stdnt Union 88-; Gosp Dir/Anncr; Orient Ldr 89-; Res Asst 90-; Alpha Lambda Delta 89-; Deans Lst 89-; Natl Deans Lst 85-; Gospel Ancr 90-; Keybrd Gosepl Choir 90-; Deans Ldrshp Award 90-; M L King Jr Schlrshp Awrd 90; Music.

**DAVIS, JULIANNE LEIGH,** Fl International Univ, Miami, FL; JR; BA; Cert Otstndng Schrl 89-90; Natl Crmn Jstc 90-; Hnr Scty; Deans Lst 89-; Otstndng Schlr 90; Crmn Jstc.

**DAVIS, JULIE A,** Univ Of Nc At Charlotte, Charlotte, NC; SR; BCA; Bptst Stdnt Un; Stdnt Un; Deans Lst; Awrded Artst Pstn; Flg Ftbl Vlybl Bsktbl Sftbl Sccr Ofcl Sftbl Bsktbl; Vsl Art Tchr Crtfctn; Grphc Dstn Tchr.

**DAVIS, JULIE C,** Roanoke Bible Coll, Elizabeth Cy, NC; SO; Yrbk; Mstrs Sng Grp; Edtr Yrbk; Encrgmnt Comm Co Chrprsn 89; Cls Hstrn 89-; Rcrutmnt Grp 90; I M Bkbl Sftbl 89; Bible; Cmptr Prgrmr.

**DAVIS, KARA L,** Univ Of Nc At Charlotte, Charlotte, NC; FR; BA; Archtctre; Prfssr.

**DAVIS, KAREN S,** Coker Coll, Hartsville, SC; SO; ABA; Secy; AAB Morehead St Univ 82; Psychology; Admin/Prsnl Mgt/ Cnslng.

**DAVIS, KARLA O,** Santa Fe Comm Coll, Gainesville, FL; SO; BA; Mklng Fnd Brd Of Dir Rec Sec 89-; Phi Theta 90-; Coll Hon Prog 90-; Futr Kpr Of Drm Awrd 89; Outstndng Comm Coll Mnrty Stdnt; Hon Cncl Rsrch Papr Cntst; AA Santa Fe Comm Coll; Hosp Vol Prog 86; Telecmnctns/Nwsrprtng; Brdcstng/Media.

**DAVIS, KATHERINE M,** Univ Of Rochester, Rochester, NY; JR; BA; Undergrad Engl Cncl V P 88-90; Strng Mem Hosp 89-90; St Jos Shltr 88-89; J Hook Danc Co 88-; Eng Dept Hnrs Pgm; Natl Endwmnt Hum; Engl; Acad.

**DAVIS, KATHLEEN A,** Columbia Greene Comm Coll, Hudson, NY; FR; AS; Vol Twn Durham Amblnc Sqd; Oak Hill Vol Fir Co Lds Axlry; Amrcn Rd Crss Dstr Asst; Nrsng; Nrsng Physcns Asst.

**DAVIS, KATHRYN L,** Univ Of Nh Plymouth St Coll, Plymouth, NH; SR; BA; Admsn Rep 89-; Orient Ldr 89-90; Kappa Delta Pi Pres 89-; Iota Delta Chi Acad Chair 89-; Bsktbl Chrldr 90; Elem Edn; Teach.

**DAVIS, KAY F,** Va Commonwealth Univ, Richmond, VA; SO; BA; Engl/Relgs Studies; Technel Wrtng.

**DAVIS, KEITH BRADLY,** Cincinnati Bible Coll & Sem, Cincinnati, OH; SO; BA; AA Cincinnati Bible Clg; Philosphy; Law.**

**DAVIS, KELLY M,** Central Al Comm Coll, Alexander City, AL; SO; BA; Edwina Mitchell Hghst Achiev Awd; AA; Bus.

**DAVIS, KEN L,** Middle Tn St Univ, Murfreesboro, TN; JR; BFA; Ownr Essx Mntnc Svc 88-; Grphc Dsgn.

**DAVIS, KENNETH S,** Wv Univ At Parkersburg, Parkersburg, WV; SO; BA; Deans Lst 90; Ims Bsktbl 89; Accntng; CPA.

**DAVIS, KENNETH W,** Broward Comm Coll, Ft Lauderdale, FL; SO; BA; AA 90; Bio; Chrprctc.

**DAVIS, KEVIN D,** Ky St Univ, Frankfort, KY; FR; BS; Bio Awd; USDA Bio Tech Intern; Bio; Med.

**DAVIS, KIM M,** Al A & M Univ, Normal, AL; JR; Office Sys Mgt Clb 89-; Alpha Kappa Alpha VP; Office Sys Mgt.

**DAVIS, KIP A,** Fl Atlantic Univ, Boca Raton, FL; FR; Var Bsbl; Acctg; CPA.

**DAVIS, KIRK R,** Oh Univ, Athens, OH; GD; ACS 88-89; Commtr Act Brd 88-89; Honr Rl 88-89; Sigma Sigma Phi; Ftbl Capt 88-89; BS Baldwn Wallace Clg 89; Med/Osteopthy; Doctr.

**DAVIS, KRISTIN L,** Valdosta St Coll, Valdosta, GA; FR; AB; Jrnlsm; Brdcst Nws.

**DAVIS, KRYSTAL N,** Va St Univ, Petersburg, VA; JR; Tdwtr Pre Alumni Clb 88-90; Data Prcsg Mgmt Assoc 90-; Delta Sigma Theta Prlmntrn 90-; Bus Info Systms; Cmptrs.

**DAVIS, KWI C,** Kent St Univ Kent Cmps, Kent, OH; JR; BS; Acctg Clrk 87-90; Engr.

**DAVIS, LA TONYA V,** Bennett Coll, Greensboro, NC; FR; BA; Pol Sci; Crim Law.

**DAVIS, LEINDA N,** Al A & M Univ, Normal, AL; JR; BS; Stu Drg Tsk Frc 90-; Soc Wrk Clb Treas 90-; NAACP 90-; Alpha Kappa Alpha; Vol Meals Whls 90-; Miss Soc Wrkr; Soc Wrk.

**DAVIS, LESLI D,** Greenville Tech Coll, Greenville, SC; SO; Dns Lst; Elem Ed; Tchg.

**DAVIS, LESLIE D,** Comm Coll Algny Co Algny Cmps, Pittsburgh, PA; SO; BA; Soc Wrk.**

**DAVIS, LISA A,** Univ Of Fl, Gainesville, FL; JR; BA; Rsdnt Asst; AA UF; Thtre; Cstmng.

**DAVIS, LISA C,** Mount Olive Coll, Mount Olive, NC; SR; BS; Ed Ofc Prsnl NC Lenoir Cnty LCAEOP NCAEOP 86-; Bkkpr Sys Oper Lenoir Cnty Schls 86-; Assoc Acctg Lenori Comm Coll 86; Acctg.

**DAVIS, LISA G,** Emory Univ, Atlanta, GA; SO; BS; Dooleys Dools 90-; Intrclb Cncl 90-; Cltrl Actvty Comm 89-90; Oxford Flwshp 89-; Cthlc Clb 89-; Stu Admsns Assoc 89-; Alpha Epsilon Upsilon 90-; Mu Epsilon Delta Pres 90-; Coll Rpblcns 89-90; Rotaract 90-; Res Advsr 90-; Bio; Med.**

**DAVIS, LORI A,** Peace Coll, Raleigh, NC; SO; BA; Coll Nwspr 89-; AA; Sclgy; Crmnl Juste.

**DAVIS, MARCIA ANGELA,** Ny Univ, New York, NY; SO; BA; Citibnk NY Admnstrtv Asst; AA NY Univ 90; Orgnztnl Cmnctn; Pblc Admin.

**DAVIS, MARCY A,** Fl A & M Univ, Tallahassee, FL; FR; BS; Pres Schlrs Assoc 90-; Cmptr Inform Systems Clb 90-; Phi Eta Sigma; Intl Paper Co/Intern 90-; Computer Inform Systems; Systems Analysis.

**DAVIS, MARIA Y,** Tn Tech Univ, Cookeville, TN; SR; Amer Home Econ Assoc 89-90; Tenn Technological HEC Assoc 89-90; German Clb 89-90; College Republicans 89-90; Alpha Mu Gamma 87-90; Phi Mu 89-90; Phi Mu Lady Of Yr 89-90; Internship With Hesses East Town 90.

**DAVIS, MARLON O,** Jackson St Univ, Jackson, MS; FR; BS; Dance Ens 90-; Alpha Lambda Delta 90-; NASA-STDP-EOS Schlrshps Intrnshp; Inroads Internshp; Pr Lst; Deans Lst; Comp Sci.

**DAVIS, MARTHA R A,** Central St Univ, Wilberforce, OH; SO; BS; Comptr Sci/Math Clb Pres 90-; Prshng Rfls 89-; Zeta Phi Beta Sec 90-; SHP Sec 89-; Dns Lst 89-; Cllg Hnrs 89-; Army ROTC 4 Yr Schlrshp 89-; Math/Accntg; Engnrng.

**DAVIS, MARY C,** Longwood Coll, Farmville, VA; SO; BFABA; Ambassadors Soc Chr 90-; Inter Religious Cncl Treas 90-; Baptist Union Pblcty 90; Alpha Lambda Delta 90-; Longwood Schlrs 89-; Kappa Pi; Phi Kappa Phi; Deans Lst; Art; Educator/Dsgnr.

**DAVIS, MELANIE H,** Univ Of South Al, Mobile, AL; SO; BA; Ed; Tchr.

**DAVIS, MELINDA H,** Fl International Univ, Miami, FL; SR; BS; Stdnt Govt Assn Sntr 90; Stdnt Dietetic Assn Pres 90-; Phi Theta Kappa Treas 88-89; Amer Dietetic Assn 88-; Dietry Tchncn Yr Miami Dietc Assn 90; AS Dietry Tchncn Palm Bch Comm Coll 89; Dietcs/Ntrtn; Clcnl Dietcs.

**DAVIS, MELINDA R,** Univ Of Sc At Columbia, Columbia, SC; SO; BAIS; Deans List 89-; Elem Ed; Tchng.

**DAVIS, MELISSA A,** Cedarville Coll, Cedarville, OH; FR; BS; Swrdbrs Extnsn Tm-Chrstn Svc 90-; Elem Ed Clb 90-; Mech Eng.

**DAVIS, MICHAEL W,** Christopher Newport Coll, Newport News, VA; FR; BS; Nuclear Refueling Techn; Math/Biology; Neurosurgery.

**DAVIS, MICHELE L,** Middle Tn St Univ, Murfreesboro, TN; SR; BS; Phi Mu Delta 87-; Meharry Med Clgs Biomed Sci Pgm 89; Lab Vol Alvin C York Vets Hosp; Bio; Med Tech/Med.

**DAVIS, MICHELLE L,** Ky St Univ, Frankfort, KY; SR; BA; SG 86-87; Cnslng/Plcmnt Trophy 90; Mktg.

**DAVIS, MICHELLE R,** Fisk Univ, Nashville, TN; SO; BS; Ohio Fisk 89-; Physics; Stdnt Senate Serv 89-; YWCA 89-; Deans Lst 89-; Summer Studies Prog; Physics.**

**DAVIS, MICHELLE R,** Univ Of Nc At Wilmington, Wilmington, NC; FR; BS; Med Tchnlgy; Med.

**DAVIS, MONICA L,** Univ Of Tn At Martin, Martin, TN; SR; BA; Med 89-; Atrium Hl Sntr 86-88; Tri Beta 89-; Psi Chi 88-; Chi Omega 86-89; Bio; Med.

**DAVIS, MONICA S,** Bowie St Univ, Bowie, MD; FR; BA; Dns Lst; Math.

**DAVIS, MONTIE G,** Memphis St Univ, Memphis, TN; SR; BSEE; Sales Spprt Rep 89-; BS Rhodes Cllg 85; Elctrcl Engnrng.

**DAVIS, MYRA E,** Westminster Coll, New Wilmingtn, PA; JR; BA; Stdnts Acton Value Envrnmnt VP 89-; Lit Mag; Art League; Psi Chi 90-; Omicron Delta Kappa 90-; Pi Sigma Pi; Alpha Phi Omega VP Mbrshp 89-; Hons Stdnt; Art; Clncl Psychlgy.

**DAVIS, NIKEL D,** Va St Univ, Petersburg, VA; SR; Big Bro/Big Sis Org 88-; Acctg Clb 89-; CPA Clb 90-; Alpha Mu Gamma 89-; Westinghouse Intern 90; BS; Acctg; CPA.

**DAVIS, NILES C,** Univ Of Cincinnati-Clrmnt Coll, Batavia, OH; FR; BA; Phi Theta Kappa Rgnl Nwsltr Edtr 90-; Maintenance Tech Holiday Inn Cinti North 86-; Comp Sci; Med.

**DAVIS, PAULETTE E,** Univ Of The Dist Of Columbia, Washington, DC; JR; BBA; Acctng Club Secy 90-; Training Spclst 80-90; AA Montgomery Clg 80; Bus/Admn; Publc Acctnt.

**DAVIS, PENNY K,** Western Ky Univ, Bowling Green, KY; JR; BS; Phi Kappa Phi; Ogden Coll Of Sci Schlrshp Rcpnt 88-; Pres Schlrs List 88-; Biochem; Med Rsrch.

**DAVIS, PRENTISS R,** Alcorn St Univ, Lorman, MS; FR; BS; IM Chmpns 90-; Blgy; Dctr.

**DAVIS, PRESTON H,** Embry Riddle Aeronautical Univ, Daytona Beach, FL; SO; BS; Lambda Chi Alpha 89-; Flight Stdnt Advsry Bd; San Antonio Intl Airport Intern 90; Tennis 89-; Flight; Prfsnl Pilot.

**DAVIS, PRESTON L,** Spartanburg Methodist Coll, Spartanburg, SC; FR; BA; Crmnl Jstc Clb 90-; Clg Chrstn Mvmt 90-; IM Sftbl/Bsktbl 90; Habitat Hmnts; Crmnl Jstc; Law.

**DAVIS, RACHEL E,** Alcorn St Univ, Lorman, MS; Cmnl Jstc; Law.

**DAVIS, RANDAL LEE,** Roane St Comm Coll, Harriman, TN; FR; Clinton Whlsi Co Slsprsn 89-; AS 87; BS TN Tech Univ 89; Rdlgc Tchnlgy; Envrnmntl Flds.

**DAVIS, RASHID F,** Morehouse Coll, Atlanta, GA; JR; Engl Clb; 165th TAG GA Air Ntl Guard; Engl; Law.

**DAVIS, RAY L,** Harding Grad School Of Relig, Memphis, TN; GD; MA; Tstmstrs Pres; Mnstr Chrch Of Chrst; BA W TX St Univ 82; Rlgn; Mnstry/Tchng.

**DAVIS, REBECCA E,** Western New England Coll, Springfield, MA; SR; BA; Prelaw Clb 89-; Max Y Litman Engl Prz; Engl; Law.

**DAVIS, REBECCA L,** Wilmington Coll, New Castle, DE; FR; BED; Deans Lst 90-; Sec State Farm Ins; Elem/Spec Ed; Tch.

**DAVIS, REBECCA S,** Catawba Valley Comm Coll, Hickory, NC; SO; AAS; Stu Govt Sen 90-; Dean Lst 90-; Eng Tech/Mngmnt; Eng.

**DAVIS, RICHARD A,** Cornell Univ Statutory College, Ithaca, NY; SO; BS; Ice Hockey; Mktg; Medicine.

**DAVIS, RICHLYN PATRICE,** Univ Of South Al, Mobile, AL; SO; BA; Sigma Tau Delta 90-; Delta Sigma Theta 90-; Scndry Educ; Tchr.

**DAVIS, ROBERT A,** Fl Atlantic Univ, Boca Raton, FL; SR; BBA; AA Palm Bch Cmnty Clg 87; Bsn; Mgmt.

**DAVIS, ROBERT L,** Central St Univ, Wilberforce, OH; SO; BA; Church Percussionist 87-; Drama Clb 89-90; Phi Beta Sigma Pr 89-90; CIS.

**DAVIS, ROBERT M,** Columbus Coll Of Art & Design, Columbus, OH; SO; BA; CCAD Rptr 90-; Adv Dsgn.

**DAVIS JR, ROGER K,** Coll Of Charleston, Charleston, SC; SO; BA; Music.

**DAVIS, ROXANNE R,** Davis & Elkins Coll, Elkins, WV; SR; BS; Cmmnctn Clb VP 89-; Intnatl Stdnt Orgnztn 89-; Hnrs Assn Pres 87-; J Rndlph Ldrshp Assn 89-; Phi Beta Lambda Treas 89; Stdnt Almn Assn 88-; Acad Achvmnt Awrds 88-; L Nwtn Thms Schlr 89-; Cmmnctn; Media.

**DAVIS, SAMMY L,** S U N Y Coll Of Tech At Alfred, Alfred, NY; FR; BA; Human Serv; Parole Ofcr.

**DAVIS, SANDRA J,** Le Moyne Coll, Syracuse, NY; JR; BA; Math Clb 88-; MAA 90-; Natl Clgt Fgr Sktng Chmp 90-; Pi Mu Epsln 90-; Fltn Fge Sktng Clb Instctr; Rsch Exp Undgrad OSU; Math; Grad Schl.

**DAVIS, SANDRA J,** Saint Josephs Coll New York, Brooklyn, NY; SR; BS; Chf Exctv Offcrs Clb Prsdnt 89-; Grdtn Comm; Deans Lst; Vldctrn; NYPC; Estrn Star 80-; Sr Sys Analyst 89-; Tchncl Spprt Spec 86-; Hmn Rsrc Mgmnt; Cmptr Rsrch Mthdlgy.

**DAVIS, SANDRA L,** Univ Of Cincinnati, Cincinnati, OH; JR; BA; Assoc Raymond Walters Clg 90; Math; Elem Ed.

**DAVIS, SAUNDRA D,** Mount Saint Mary Coll, Newburgh, NY; SR; BA; Alpha Chi 90-; Hon Allnc; Spec Ed Asst 87-88; ASS Orng Co Comm Coll 85; Psych; Tchng/Psychlgst.

**DAVIS, SCOTT R,** Ky Mountain Bible Coll, Vancleve, KY; FR; BS; Biolgy; Dntstry.

**DAVIS, SHAJUANDA L,** Univ Of Southern Ms, Hattiesburg, MS; SO; BA; Crmnl Jstce Assn; Rsdnce Hll Assn 90-; Afro Amer Stdnt Orgnztn 89-; Gamma Beta Phi; Crmnl Jstce; Law.

**DAVIS, SHARMANE P,** Allegheny Coll, Meadville, PA; SR; BA; Advnmnt Bck Cltre Chrprsn 87-; Aleghny S Zfrica Sch Func Coord 89-; Allegheny Bckks Intl Sprt 89-90; Lambda Sigma 88-89; Soup Kitchen Vol 89-; Clg Alden Schlr; Res Dir 90-; English; Law.

**DAVIS, SHARON H,** Univ Of Nc At Greensboro, Greensboro, NC; JR; BS; Univ Mrshl; All Amer Schlr; Elem Ed/Hstry; Tch.

**DAVIS, SHARON L,** Albany St Coll, Albany, GA; SR; BA; Brd Of Mgrs Stdnt Ldr 88-90; Clge Gospel Choir 88-90; Miss Sophmore 88-89; Miss Charm 89-90; Sigma Tau Delta; English; Law School.

**DAVIS, SHAWN L,** Central St Univ, Wilberforce, OH; SO; BA; Pol Sci Assmbly 90; Phlsphy Engl Pol Sci; Entrtnmnt Cvl Rghts Law.

**DAVIS, SHEILA M,** James Sprunt Comm Coll, Kenansville, NC; FR; AS; Business; Cmptr Progrmmr.

**DAVIS, SHEILA M,** Northern Ky Univ, Highland Hts, KY; FR; BSN; Epsilon Alpha Gamma 90-; Nrsg; OB Nrs.

**DAVIS, SHERRY B,** Davis & Elkins Coll, Elkins, WV; SO; BA; Jennings Randolph Ldrs Prog; Freeman J Daniels Award For Hghst Rnkng Frshmn 90; Acadmc Achvmnt Award For Hghst Rnkng Stdnt In Hlth Mjr 90; Bsktbl Tm Cptn 89-; Tatiana Jardetsky Award For Frgn Lang 90; Crs Cntry Tm 90; Hlth Ed/Spansh.

**DAVIS, SHIRLEY D,** Wv Univ At Parkersburg, Parkersburg, WV; FR; AA; Sec Prkns Oil-Gas Inc 89-; Rltr Fair Prc Rlty 90-; Bus; Pblc Rltns Mdtr.

**DAVIS, SHUVON E,** Univ Of Ky, Lexington, KY; JR; BA; Blck Stu Unn 89-; Univ KY Blck Voices Sec 89-; Natl Pan Hllnc Cncl Chrprsn; Delta Sigma Theta VP; Spnsh; Tchng.

**DAVIS, STACY L,** Muskingum Coll, New Concord, OH; JR; BS; Am Chem Socty Treas 88-; Vol Prgrm House Coord 89-; Wind Ensmbl 88-; Omicron Delta Kappa 89-; Sigma Chi; Med Awrd; IM; Chem; Dntstry.

**DAVIS, STEPHANIE L,** Va St Univ, Petersburg, VA; SR; BA; Assoc Intl Stdy Pblc Rltns 90-; Spnsh Clb Pres/Sec 86-88; Ntl Hnr Soc Frgn Lang Stu 90-; Cir K Pres/Sec 86-88; AS 88; Cmpltn Frgn Pro 89; Intl Stdy; Intl Mrktg Cnsltnt.

**DAVIS, STEPHANIE M,** Tuskegee Univ, Tuskegee Inst, AL; SO; BS; Pre-Vet Clb 90-; Georgia Clb 90-; Vlybl/Bsktbl Ltrmn Sweater 90-; Animal Sci/Pre-Vet; Vet.

**DAVIS, STEVEN C,** Barry Univ, Miami, FL; FR; Hlthgrp 90-; Boy Scouts Am Eagle Scout 89; Rec Div Mgmnt/Eng.

**DAVIS, STEVEN J,** Fl International Univ, Miami, FL; JR; BA; FMA Aths Dir 89-90; FMA Mbr 89-; Phi Theta Kappa 87-88; FMA Hon Soc 89-; Recg Otstndng Acad Achvmnt Intl Bsns 91; AA Miami Dade Comm Clg 89; Fin/Intl Bsns; Law/Intl Bsns.

**DAVIS, SUSAN J G,** Nova Univ, Ft Lauderdale, FL; GD; MS; FL Org Nrs Exec/CNMA Rgn I Sec 90-; Amer Assn Crtcl Cr Nrs CCRN 75-; Amer Hrt Assn 80-; Cert Nrsng Admin; Cert Crtcl Cr Nrsng; AACN-CCRN Rgnl Plnng Bd; FONE/CNMA Rgn I-Sec 90-; BBA FL Atlntc Univ 90; BSN Graceland Coll; Hlth Serv Admin; Hlth Cr Admin.

**DAVIS, SYLVIA L,** Bristol Univ, Bristol, TN; JR; BS; Martin Marietta Energy Systems 74-; Tn Eastman Co 70-; Bus Admin; Mgmt/Prsnl/Pblc Rltns.

**DAVIS, SYLVIA M,** Fort Valley St Coll, Fort Valley, GA; FR; BS; Pre Vet; Veternrn.

**DAVIS, TAMMY M,** Piedmont Tech Coll, Greenwood, SC; SO; BS; Belk 90-; Crtv Actvts Chldrn; Hnrs 90-; Deans Lst 90-; Edctn; Tchr.

**DAVIS, THERESA M,** Va Commonwealth Univ, Richmond, VA; SR; BS; Hon Pgm 87-89; Phi Kappa Phi; Sigma Theta Tau; Valor Stdnt Vet Admin Med Ctr; ICU Nurse.

**DAVIS, TIMOTHY S,** Old Dominion Univ, Norfolk, VA; JR; BS; Pi Tau Sigma Pres 90-; Co Op NASA LARC 89-; Mech Engr/Mech.

**DAVIS, TORIANO L,** Howard Univ, Washington, DC; FR; BSA 90; Archtct/Planning.

**DAVIS, TRACEY A,** Norfolk St Univ, Norfolk, VA; JR; BS; Bus Mgt.

**DAVIS, TRACY L,** Alcorn St Univ, Lorman, MS; SO; BS; NAACP 90-; Eastern Star Secy 90; Psych Cl 90-; Alpha Kappa Mu 90; Deans List 89-; Psychlgy; Indus Orgztl Psychlgy.

**DAVIS, TRACY N,** Univ Of Ga, Athens, GA; JR; BLA; Gsla 90-; Bnd 88-; Wrldwd Dscplshp Assc; Sigma Lambda; Sigma Alpha Iota Scl Chrprsn 89-; Bg Sistrs 88-89; IM Sftbl 90; Lndscp Archtctr/Hrtcltr.

**DAVIS, TRACY V,** Medical Coll Of Ga, Augusta, GA; JR; BS; BSA Awrds 88; BS Bio GA Clg 89; Nursing; Anethisist.

**DAVIS, VALARIE C,** Al A & M Univ, Normal, AL; FR; BA; Lit Clb; Bptst Stu Unn; Dean Lst 90; Pres Awrd Rcpnt 90; Elem Educ.

**DAVIS, VANNESSA L,** Teikyo Post Univ, Waterbury, CT; SR; BA; Std Govt Asc Sntr 88-90; Psy Clb 87-; Agro-Amer Asc 87-90; Dns Lst; Psy/Sclgy; Cnslng.

**DAVIS, VIVIAN R,** Longwood Coll, Farmville, VA; SR; BA; SEA; Minority Mentors; Commuter Assoc; Kappa Delta Pif Alpha Lambda Delta; Louise Brightwell Watson Meml Schrlshp 89-; Elem Educ; Teach.

**DAVIS, WAKISHA L,** Fl Atlantic Univ, Boca Raton, FL; FR; PASA 90-; Business; Acctg.

**DAVIS, WAYNE,** Johnson C Smith Univ, Charlotte, NC; JR; Foreign Club; Acctng; Bus.

**DAVIS, WENDY RENEE,** Fl St Univ, Tallahassee, FL; SR; BA; Garnet Key 90-; Dns Lst 89-90; AA Gulf Coast Cmnty Clg 89; Elem Ed; Tch.

**DAVIS, WENDY S,** D Youville Coll, Buffalo, NY; SO; BS; Phys Therpy Assn 89-; Adpt-A-Grndprnt 89-; Crnvl Comm 89-; Lambda Sigma 90-; Phys Therpy.

**DAVIS JR, WILLIAM A,** Univ Of Sc At Columbia, Columbia, SC; SO; BS; Fr Cncl SGA 89-90; Gamma Beta Phi; Phi Beta Lambda; Intrnshp Bst Wstrn Hotl 90; Deans Lst 90-; IM Flg Ftbl/Sftbl Capt 89-; Hotel/Rstrnt Trsm Admin.

**DAVIS JR, WILLIAM H,** Vanderbilt Univ, Nashville, TN; FR; Alpha Lambda Delta; Phi Eta Sigma; Kappa Sigma; Gamma Beta Phi 90; Robert C Byrd Schlrshp 90; Engl; Law.

**DAVIS, WILLIAM P,** Oh Univ, Athens, OH; SO; BFA; Wrote Music Mag; Chimes; Art/Phtgrphy; Tchr Or Envrnmntl Law.

**DAVIS, WILLIE,** Defiance Coll, Defiance, OH; SR; BA; Amer Mktng Assoc VP Advtng 89-90; Computer Club Treas; Tau Phi Phi Chrmn Activ 90-; Financial Exec Awd 90-; Natl Clgt Miniority Ldrshp Awds; Mktng/Finance; Finance.

**DAVIS, YOLANDA F,** Ky St Univ, Frankfort, KY; SR; BS; Natl Soc Blck Engrs Pres 90-; NAACP 87-; Eng Clb 87-90; Alpha Kappa Mu 89-; Delta Sigma Theta 89; Big Bro/Big Sis 89-; Most Outstndng Math Major 90-; Hghst GPA Grk 89-; Hghst GPA Co-Op Pgm 90-; Vlybl 87-88; Elect Eng; Eng.**

**DAVIS, YOLANDA S,** Lexington Comm Coll, Lexington, KY; SO; BS; KY Police Pistol League Sec Treas 81-; Frtrnl Ordr Police 79-; Amrcn Plygrph Assn 81-89; Intrntnl Assn Wmn Police 79-89; Police Offcr Dctv Polygraph Exmnr Fngrprnt Idntfctn; Pharmacy.

**DAVIS, YVONNE N,** Univ Of Sc At Aiken, Aiken, SC; SR; BS; SC Emplymnt Scrty Cmsn; AA Un Maryland 86; AS Un SC Sumter 90; Fin; Govt Fin.

**DAVISON, JACALYN S,** Edinboro Univ Of Pa, Edinboro, PA; JR; BS; Beta Beta Beta 90-; Alpha Chi 90-; Hnrs Pgm; CPUB Award; Bio; Rsrch/Micro Bio.

**DAVISON, KIMBERLY R,** Univ Of Southern Ms, Hattiesburg, MS; SR; BS; Stdnt Almn Assoc; AMA; Delta Sigma Pi VP Prfssnl Actvts 90-; AA Assoc Arts 87-89; Mrktng.

**DAVISON, TERRILL L,** Fisk Univ, Nashville, TN; SR; BS; Pol Sci Clb 88-; Nebraska Clb 88-; Pi Sigma Alpha; Alpha Kappa Alpha; UNCF Schlrshp; Dns Lst; Pol Sci; Law.

**DAVISON III, VERNON A,** Northwest Al Comm Coll, Phil Campbell, AL; Dns Lst 90; Pres Lst; Aircrft Maint.

**DAVOODY, FERRIDHUN R,** Memphis St Univ, Memphis, TN; SO; BBA; Acctg.

**DAVY, LARRAINE B,** Glassboro St Coll, Glassboro, NJ; SR; BA; Phi Alpha Theta; AA Burlingtn Co Clg 90; Hstry; Bsns/Govt.

**DAVY III, THOMAS E,** Columbia Union Coll, Takoma Park, MD; SR; BS; Clss Pres 90-; Sigma Phi Epsilon Clss Pres 81-84; US Nvy Hosp Crps 78-; Hlth Cr Admn.

**DAWE, SCOTT A,** Fl Atlantic Univ, Boca Raton, FL; SR; BBA; AA Palm Bch Cmnty Clg 89; Bus Mngmt; Rtl Mngmnt.

**DAWES, LINNEA M,** Norfolk St Univ, Norfolk, VA; SR; BS; Psych Clb 89-; Psi Chi; Alpha Kappa Mu 89-; VA Clgiate Hons Cncl 89-; Smmr Prog Undrgrd Mnrty Vrgns Partcpnt; Psych; Clncl Psych.

**DAWKINS, NATALIE O,** Felician Coll, Lodi, NJ; AAS; NJNS 2nd VP 90-; Cls VP 89090; Sci Clb VP 89090; Peer Spprtr 89-; Tr Guide Frshmn Stdnts 88-89; Hmlrs Shltr St Anestasia 88; Nrs Extrnshp Hcknsck Mdcl Cntr 90-; Acdmc Schlrshp 89-; Deans Lst 89-; Nrsng; Med.**

**DAWKINS, RUSSELL D,** Morehouse Coll, Atlanta, GA; SO; BA; Bsns Mgmnt; Pre Law.

**DAWKINS, SHELL-LEE B,** Univ Of Montevallo, Montevallo, AL; SR; Kappa Delta Pi.

**DAWKINS, SUSAN E,** Christian Brothers Univ, Memphis, TN; SO; BS; Auditorm Lghtng Coor 90-; Tech Theatre Lghtng Set 89-; Telecmnctns; Info Sys Mgt.

**DAWLEY, KENNETH S,** Mount Saint Mary Coll, Newburgh, NY; SR; BA; Student Ambassador 88-89; Student Nwspr 87-89; Hnrs Alliance 90-; Prestl Schlrshp 88-; Bsbl 87-89; Communications; Law.

**DAWS, WILLIAM D,** Cumberland County Coll, Vineland, NJ; SO; Phi Theta Kappa 89; AA; Bus Admn.

**DAWSEY, KRISTIN A,** Anne Arundel Comm Coll, Arnold, MD; FR; BA; FTA; Spec Olympcs; Elem Educ; Tchr.

**DAWSON, AMY HERRON,** Univ Of West Fl, Pensacola, FL; SR; BA; Grad Magna Cum Laude; AA Pensacola Jr Coll 76; Erly Chldhd Elem Educ; Tchng.

**DAWSON II, CARLOS L,** Hinds Comm Coll, Raymond, MS; FR; BA; Math; Eng.

**DAWSON, CATHERINE,** Tuskegee Univ, Tuskegee Inst, AL; GD; BS; Stdnt Occptnl Thrpy Clb 90; Amer Occptnl Thrpy Assn 90; AL Occptnl Thrpy Assn 90; Alpha Kappa Mu 90; Dns Lst 90; Emnt Schlr 90; Stdnt Prsntr ALOTA Cnfrnce 89; Occptnl Thrpy; Occptnl Thrpst.

**DAWSON, CHRISTINE G,** George Mason Univ, Fairfax, VA; FR; Best Buddies 90-; Engl/Bus; Jrnlst.

**DAWSON, CHRISTOPHER B S,** Middle Tn St Univ, Murfreesboro, TN; SO; BS; Math; Air Crft Dsgn.

**DAWSON, DOUGLAS D,** Kent St Univ Kent Cmps, Kent, OH; SR; BBA; Sigma Alpha Zeta Co Fndr 87-; Untd Wy Fndrsr 88-90; Pres Dean Lst; Gldn Ky; Phi Kappa Tau Pres 88-90; Acdmc Schlrshp Educ Excl; Grad Magna Cum Lade; Clarion Univ Vrsty Fltbl 86-88; BBA; Mst Otstnding Mmbr Delta Clas Pres 88; Fnnce; MBA Hlth Care Indrs.

**DAWSON, EILEEN GAYLE,** Fl International Univ, Miami, FL; JR; BA; Engl; Educ.

**DAWSON, EVELYN L,** Va Commonwealth Univ, Richmond, VA; JR; BA; AA P G Comm Coll 75; Hstry; Rsrch.

**DAWSON, JOHN W,** Kent St Univ Kent Cmps, Kent, OH; JR; Asst Track Coach Strtsbro Hgh Schl; ATTEP; Kappa Delta Pi; Ftbl Ohio St Univ 87-88; Scndry Educ/Geog/Hist/Pol Sci; Tchr.

**DAWSON, JOYCE L,** Widener Univ, Chester, PA; SR; BA; Acctg Soc Pres 88-89; Yrbk Stf 89-; Stdnt Govt Treas 88-89; Phi Eta Sigma; Alpha Chi; Deans Lst; Phi Sigma Sigma 88-89; Mnstry Tutr 89-; Res Asst 88-; Coopers/Lybrand Intrnshp 90; Tutr 88-; Ambsdr; Financl Mngmnt Soc Schlrshp Awrd; Acctg.**

**DAWSON, JOYCE R,** Averett Coll, Danville, VA; SR; BS; Sci Clb Sec 89-90; Beta Beta Beta; Phi Eta Sigma; Alpha Chi; Vol Mem Hosp 88; Bio/Chem; Med Tech.

**DAWSON, JULIE A,** Glassboro St Coll, Glassboro, NJ; SO; BA; Cntrbtr Coll Ppr 89; Cntrbtr Coll Mag 89-90; Hnrs Prgm 89-; Pm Plbshd 90; Sico Foundation Schlrshp; NJ Distngshd Schlr; Engl; Free Lnc Wrtng.**

**DAWSON, KAYE P,** Truett Mc Connell Coll, Cleveland, GA; SO; BSN; Sundy Sch Tchr 80-; Church Pianist 80-; Nrsng; RN.

**DAWSON, MARIE Y,** City Univ Of Ny La Guard Coll, Long Island Cty, NY; ASSOC; Acctng.

**DAWSON, MARK L,** Waynesburg Coll, Waynesburg, PA; FR; Tau Kappa Epsilon; Engl; Adv/Law.

**DAWSON, MICHAEL R D,** Univ Of Miami, Coral Gables, FL; FR; BA; Org Jamaican Unty Pblc Rltns Ofcr 90-; Sccr Clb 90-; Prvst Hnr Rl 90-; Deans Lst 90-; Bwmn Ashe Schlrshp 90-; Mlyns Grdns Yth Clb Scl Dir 87-90; Mst Otstndg Employe Brgns R Us 89-90; IM Sccr/Bsktbl 90-; Bus Admin; Finance.

**DAWSON, PAMELA L,** Jackson St Univ, Jackson, MS; FR; BS; Alpha Lambda Delta SGA Rep; Alpha Lamba Delta; Indust Tech; Cmptr Tech.

**DAWSON, SHARYN A,** Daytona Beach Comm Coll, Daytona Beach, FL; FR; BA; Jaycees VP 89-; Bkkpng Srvc Bsns 87-89; Crtf Wldng PRUTI; Bsns Accntng.

**DAWSON, SHEREEN R,** Howard Univ, Washington, DC; GD; MSW; ROTC Cadet 87; Army Rsrve Unit Mltry Offcr 86-89; BS Ball State U 89; Scl Wrk; Sbstnce Abse.

**DAWSON, THERESA F,** George Mason Univ, Fairfax, VA; JR; BS; Govt/Pblc Admin.

**DAWSON, WENDY N,** Middle Tn St Univ, Murfreesboro, TN; SR; BS; Pi Gamma Mu 90-; Amer Psych Assoc Stdnt Affiliate 90-; Psych; Ph D-Clncl Psych.

**DAY, ANGELA D,** Dyersburg St Comm Coll, Dyersburg, TN; SO; BS; Newspaper Ed 90-; Stdnt Govt Assoc 90-; Bapt Stdnt Union Res 89-; Phi Theta Kappa 90-; Stdnt Support Svcs Tutor 90-; AS Dyersburg State Cmnty Clg; Chem/Bsn; Engr.

**DAY, BARBARA J,** Norfolk St Univ, Norfolk, VA; SR; Stdnt VA Educ Assc 90-; BS Widener Univ 78; Erly Chldhd; Tchg.

**DAY, CATHLEEN M,** Georgian Court Coll, Lakewood, NJ; JR; BA; Psychlgy Clb 89-; Psi Chi 90-; Schl Psychlgst.

**DAY, CHRISTOPHER M,** Univ Of Miami, Coral Gables, FL; FR; BS; Collegium Musicum; Band Of The Hour 90; Choral 90; Alpha Lambda Delta 90; Phi Mu Alpha Sinfonia; Amer Soc Civil Engr; Civil/Ocean Engr; Coastal/Ocean Engr Abrd.

**DAY, DIANE G,** Georgetown Coll, Georgetown, KY; SR; BS; Band; Oratorio Chrs; Hmcmng Show Bnd 88-89; Kappa Delta Sng Ldr 90-; Elem Ed; Teaching.

**DAY, DOVER,** Piedmont Tech Coll, Greenwood, SC; SR; Heating/Vent/Air Cond; Engr.

**DAY, GAIL DENISE,** Fl International Univ, Miami, FL; SR; BS; AA Miami Dade Comm Coll 88; Soc Wrk; Clncl Soc Wrkr.

**DAY, GLENDA D,** Alcorn St Univ, Lorman, MS; SR; BSN; MS Assoc Student Nurses 90-; Higher Ed Appre Awd; Nursing.

**DAY, GLORIA A,** Elms Coll, Chicopee, MA; SR; BA; Phi Theta Kappa Mbr 89; Intrnshp Pioneer Vly Railroad Acctng Clrk; Bus Coop At Oconnell Companies Acctng Asst 88-89; AS Holyoke Comm Coll 89; Acctng/Bus; CPA.

**DAY, HEATHER E,** Temple Univ, Philadelphia, PA; SO; BA; Ntl Syndctd Tlvsn Shw Hst 89-; Dnc Prty; Deans Lst 90-; Natl Spksprsn Ant Drg; Arbcs Instrctr 90-; Cmmnctns; Rdl Tvsn Flm.

**DAY, JACK W,** Radford Univ, Radford, VA; SR; BA; Clg Republ 89-; Pi Gamma Mu 89-; Alpha Phi Omega Sgt At Arms 90-; Polt Sci; Law.

**DAY, JANE A,** Owensboro Comm Coll, Owensboro, KY; FR; AAS; Hmn Serv; Soc Wrk/Hmn Serv.

**DAY, JE NELL L,** Lexington Comm Coll, Lexington, KY; SO; BA; Deans List; Asst Mgr Hanover Towers Condominums 90-; Mgt/Mktg; Hotel Mgt/Mktg.

**DAY, JEFFREY O,** Unity Coll, Unity, ME; FR; BS; Conservation Law Clb 90-; Wldlfe Clb 90-; IM Vlybl 90-; Pk Mgmt; Ranger/Law Enfrcmnt.

**DAY, KESHA N,** Alcorn St Univ, Lorman, MS; FR; BA; Acctg; CPA.

**DAY, KIMBERLY A,** Teikyo Post Univ, Waterbury, CT; JR; BS; Paralgl Clb Co-Fndr/Pres 90-; Natl Paralgl Assn 90-; Deans Lst; Delta Sigma Pi 89-; Recgntn Awrds; Lgl Asst; Law.

**DAY, LINDA S,** Anson Comm Coll, Ansonville, NC; JR; ASSC; AS Degree Legal Sec Sci CPCC 82; Acctng Bus Comp Prgrmmng.

**DAY, LISA B,** Univ Of Tn At Knoxville, Knoxville, TN; SO; BS; Bapt Stdnt Union 90-; Alpha Lambda Delta 89-; Bsn; Acctg.

**DAY, REBECCA H,** Univ Of Al At Birmingham, Birmingham, AL; SR; Med Rec Clb Tr 89-; Pres Lst 90-; Amer Med Rec Assn; Tenn Med Rec Assn; BS; BS; Med Rec/Psych; Med Rec Admin.

**DAY, RUSSELL S,** Univ Of Sc At Columbia, Columbia, SC; SR; MBA; Assistanship; BS Univ Sc; Marketing; MBA.

**DAY, SHARON J,** Ms St Univ, Miss State, MS; JR; BBA; Bsbl Bt Grl 89-; Bnd 88-90; Gamma Beta Phi 88-; Beta Alpha Psi; Acctg; CPA.

**DAYA, BHANUBEN M,** Emory & Henry Coll, Emory, VA; JR; BED; Indian Cltrl Comm 89-; SVEA; Enlgish; Teacher.

**DAYE, KELLEY N,** Lincoln Univ, Lincoln Univ, PA; SR; BA; Thurgood Marshall Law Soc; French Clb 88-; Ctr Pub Plcy/Dplmcy; Alpha Swthrt; Big Bro/Big Str; Pltcl Sci Clb; V P Extrnl Afrs; Co Author Book Rvw; Rsrch Asst; Intl Rltns/French.

**DAYS III, KENNETH D,** Morehouse Coll, Atlanta, GA; SR; BA; Pre Law Soc 87-; Bus Assn 89-; Pol Sci Soc 90-; Dean Lst 89-; Hnr Rll 89-; Big Bro 90-; Middledays Flm Prod Fndr 90-; Bank Intern 88-89; Pol Sci; Law/Real Est Dvlpmnt.

**DAYTON, JANIS ANN,** Bowling Green St Univ At Huron, Huron, OH; JR; Fri Nght Hix 90-; Nu Fau Treas 85-89; Alumni Schlrshp 90-F Deans Lst 88-; Elem Ed/Math; Tch.

**DAYTON, THOMAS M,** Duquesne Univ, Pittsburgh, PA; JR; BS; Bsn; Acctg.

**DAYTZ, RHONDA B,** Fl International Univ, Miami, FL; JR; BA; AA Broward Cmnty Clg 89; Graphic Art.

**DAZA, NELSON,** City Univ Of Ny Baruch Coll, New York, NY; JR; BBA; Hispanic Scty 89-; Proudst Schlrshp; Acctg; Law.

**DAZEN, DEVON D,** Wv Univ, Morgantown, WV; SO; BS; Mech Eng.

**DE AGUIAR, EDWARD,** Fl International Univ, Miami, FL; SO; BS; Asst Sls Mgr 88-; Chem/Physcs; Rsrchr/Prfssr.

**DE ANGEL, EDWIN,** Univ Of Pr At Mayaguez, Mayaguez, PR; SR; BS; Tau Beta Pi; Phi Kappa Phi; IEEE; Deans Lst; Elec Engnrng; Ms.

**DE ANGELIS, FRANK J,** Elizabethtown Coll, Elizabethtown, PA; SO; BA; Pol Sci Clb Sec/Treas 89-; Pre Law Sec Treas 89-; Stdnt Senate 89-; IM Sftbl Capt 89-; Hist; Law.**

**DE ANGELIS, JOANNE M,** Strayer Coll, Washington, DC; SO; BSCS; Strayer Colg Schlrshp 90-; Cmptr Info Sys; Prog/Anal.

**DE ANGELIS, MICHELLE L,** Univ Of Cincinnati, Cincinnati, OH; FR; BA BS; Cntmpry Arts Cntr; Betty Jane Hull Schlrshp; French; Educ.

**DE ARMAS, JUAN C,** Fl International Univ, Miami, FL; SR; BS; Inst Elec/Elctrncs Eng Inc 90-; Sci; Elec Eng.

**DE ARMENT, DANIEL W,** Juniata Coll, Huntingdon, PA; SO; BA; Brrstrs Clb 90-; Acdmc Dvlpmnt Com 90-; Pltcl Sci; Law.

**DE ARMOND, ANGELA R,** Savannah Coll Of Art & Design, Savannah, GA; JR; BFA; Tutor 89-; Savannah Art Show 88; Festival Sidewalk Arts; SCAD Records 88-; Painting/Art Educ.

**DE BAENE, DEBRA K,** Univ Of Miami, Coral Gables, FL; JR; BS; SME 90-; IIE 90-; SWE 90-; RN Int Care Unit Mercer Co Hosp 84-85; ADN Black Hawk Clg 84; CAD Certif Black Hawk Clg 89; Indstrl-Mfg Engr.

**DE BARTOLO, TINA M,** Univ Of North Fl, Jacksonville, FL; SO; BA; Amer Mgmt Assoc 91; Zeta Tau Alpha 89-90; Bus; Acctg.

**DE BEER, IZANNE,** Univ Of Sc At Columbia, Columbia, SC; SR; BS; USC Fencing 89-90; Fllwshp Chrstn Athletes 89-; Golden Key 90-; Chi Delta Chi 90-; USC Schlrshp 90-; Mc Meekan Schlrshp 90-; U S Army Natl Guard 90-; Biol; Genetic Rsrch.

**DE BIASE, DAVID C,** Bridgeport Engr Inst, Fairfield, CT; SO; BSEE; Elctrnc Tchncn Hbbll Inc 89; ASEE Grtr New Hvn State Tech 87; Elctrcl; Eng.

**DE BIASE, ELIZABETH R,** S U N Y Coll At Fredonia, Fredonia, NY; SR; Tonmeister Assn Bylws 88-; Audio Eng Soc Trea 88-; Piano Clb 88-89; Nwmn Cntr 89-; Squires Prod Inc Intern 90; Hnrs Rctl Appld Piano; BS; Snd Rcrdng Tech; Audio Eng.

**DE BIASI, LISA M,** Univ Of Nh Plymouth St Coll, Plymouth, NH; SR; Ftbl Chrldr 88; Mary Lyon Hse Comm 87; Admssns Rep Tour Gde 89; Hlth Mjrs Clb VP 90; Plymouth State Schlr 87-90; Hlth; Crprte Hlth.

**DE BIASI, LORI MICHELLE,** Providence Coll, Providence, RI; SR; BA; Asst Copy Edtr Schl Nwspr; Big Bro/Sis 88-; Pstrl Cncl Mbr Spcl Evnts/Soc Action/Fndrsng Com 90-; Spcl Olympcs Vol 88-; IM; Hmnts; Pblc Rltns.

**DE BLAKER, DONNA M,** Springfield Tech Comm Coll, Springfield, MA; GD; Alpha Nu Omega 90-; Data Proc Deptmntl Awd; Quaboug Rgnl Schl Com 87-88; Warren Elem Schl Com 86-87; Assoc; Comp Info Syst.

**DE BLASIO, ROBBIN M,** Seton Hall Univ, South Orange, NJ; SR; BSE; Vltr Serv Div 88-; Drama Wkrshp 90-; Research Assist; Kappa Delta Pi 90-; Assoc Retarded Citz 88-; Speical Olympics 90; Camp Fatima 90; Elem Ed/Special Ed; Tchr Hndcprd.

**DE BLOK, MELISSA M,** Holyoke Comm Coll, Holyoke, MA; FR; Dean Lst 90-; Vet/Anml Sci; Vet Tech.

**DE BOBEN, JENNIFER L,** Univ Of Nc At Greensboro, Greensboro, NC; SR; BS; Zeta Tau Alkpha 89-90; AA Santa Fe Comm Coll 88; Elem Ed.

**DE BOER, BARBARA G,** Queens Coll, Charlotte, NC; SO; BA; Alpha Delta Pi Schlrshp Svc Chrmn 90-; Rlgs Lf Comm; Order Omega; OASIS 89; Intrnshp Florida Hosp 90-; Natl Collegiate Bus Mrt Awd; Soccer Tm 89-90; Acctntng; CPA.

**DE BOER, MICHAEL J,** Liberty Univ, Lynchburg, VA; SR; BABS; Alpha Lambda Delta 88-; Hnrs Prog 90-; Res Asst 90-; Rlgn; Clrgy.

**DE BOER, MICHELLE A,** Liberty Univ, Lynchburg, VA; FR; BS; IM Vlybl 90-; IM Bstkbl 90; Alpha Lambda Delta; Math; Tchr.

**DE BOER, SCOTT W,** Liberty Univ, Lynchburg, VA; SR; BS; SGA Sntr 88-; VP Cabinet 90-; Rsrch/Rcyclng Comm Chrmn 89-; Deans Lst; Grad Summa Cum Laude; IM Glf; Govt/Frgn Affrs; Intl Poltcs.**

**DE BOK, SANDRA J,** Anne Arundel Comm Coll, Arnold, MD; SO; BA; Vol Riverdale Fire Dept 89-; Bus Mrktng; Law.

**DE BOLT, ROSS R,** Emory & Henry Coll, Emory, VA; FR; BS; IMS Ftbl Bsktbl Sftbl; Economics; Business.

**DE BOOM, JAN L,** Webber Coll, Babson Park, FL; SR; MBA; Dn Lst 86-; Doke Hackney Manley CPA Frm 89-; BS; Bsns Admn; CPA.

**DE BRACCIO, DENISE J,** Univ Of Ky, Lexington, KY; JR; BA; Peace Studies Grp 89; Hons Progrm 88-89; Betty Walsh Morris Schlrshp; Farquhar Poetry Award; Litery Magzn Award 89; Deans List 87-90; Engl/Psychlgy; Writing.

**DE BUSK, JOHN H,** Pellissippi St Tech Comm Coll, Knoxville, TN; GD; BA; TN Vly Prsnnl Assn 90; Rtrct 90; Bus; Mgmt.

**DE CAIRES, DIONNE L,** City Univ Of Ny Baruch Coll, New York, NY; SO; BBA; Mgmnt; Law.

**DE CANDIDO, ANN MARIE,** Md Coll Of Art & Design, Silver Spring, MD; FR; ASSOC; Anml Actvst; Visual Comm; Educ.

**DE CARDENAS, EDUARDO G,** Univ Of Miami, Coral Gables, FL; SR; BA; Geo Club 89-; Phi Beta Kappa 90-; Golden Key 90-; Alpha Kappa Psi 89-; IM Bsktbl; Econs/French; Law.

**DE CARLO, HELEN M,** Comm Coll Algny Co Algny Cmps, Pittsburgh, PA; SR; AA; Phi Theta Kappa 90-; Attndnc Asst Pgh Brd Ed Cty Pgh 89-; Ed.

**DE CARLO, TODD M,** Allegheny Coll, Meadville, PA; SO; Cmptr Science.

**DE CARO II, JOHN C,** Univ Of Sc At Columbia, Columbia, SC; JR; BS; Ntl Exchng 90-; Delta Sigma Ph Phlnthrpy Chr 89-90; Deans Lst 90; Fnc; Invstmnt Anlysis.

**DE CARPIO, DINA M,** Indiana Univ Of Pa, Indiana, PA; SR; BED; Engl Clb Pres 88-89; PA Intcllgt Engl Clb 87-90; Natl Cncl Tchrs Engl 90; Engl; Tchr.

**DE CESARIS, MIKE,** S U N Y Maritime Coll, Bronx, NY; JR; BE; Weight Lftng Clb 88-; Auto Clb 90-; Admirls Lst 88-90; Honour Co 88-89; Elec Eng.

**DE CHARIO, GINA M,** Hillsborough Comm Coll, Tampa, FL; SO; AS; Stndt Govtmnt 82-83; French Club Pres 83-85; Inter Club Council 84-85; Phi Theta Kappa 90-; Hnrs Convocation; Hotel/Restuarant Mgmnt; Hotel Mgmnt.

**DE CLERCK, RUSSELL A,** Manhattan Coll, Bronx, NY; SR; MS; ASME 89-; SAE 89-; Pi Tau Sigma 89-; Phi Kappa Psi 85-; BS 91; Engr.

**DE COSTA, KIMBERLY E,** Fl Atlantic Univ, Boca Raton, FL; SR; MBA; Pres Hnr Lst; Deans Lst 89-; :Bba 90; Finance.**

**DE COSTA, MELISSA J,** Trenton St Coll, Trenton, NJ; FR; BA; SADD 90-; Radio Nws Prgm 90-; Amrcn Mrktng Assoc 90-; Coll Hnr Scty 90-; Crlck K 90-; Acctg; CPA.

**DE COSTE, JENNIFER M,** Univ Of Hartford, West Hartford, CT; FR; BME; Chr Slst 90-; Univ Plyrs Ld Rl 90-; Vc Hnr Srctl Rnkd 1st Clss 90-; Deans Lst 90-; Music Vc Emphs; Music Edctn.

**DE COTES, CAROL J,** Hillsborough Comm Coll, Tampa, FL; SO; AA; Art/Art Hstry Tchr.

**DE COUD, NEDRA S,** Tuskegee Univ, Tuskegee Inst, AL; SR; DVM; Amer Vet Medl Assoc 87-; Amer Animal Hosp Assoc 87-; Phi Zeta Rho 89-; Hills Schlrshp 88; Merck Awrd; BS Univ Calif LA 85; Vet Medicine; Small Animal Practioner.

**DE CRACKER, DANIEL J,** S U N Y Coll Of Tech At Alfred, Alfred, NY; FR; BA; Dean List 90-; Mech Engr.

**DE CUNZO, CHRISTINE MARIE,** S U N Y Coll Of Tech At Frmgdl, Farmingdale, NY; SO; MBA; Erly Chldhd Club Secy; Deans List; CYO Vlybl Coach; Girl Scouts; BA; Elem Ed; Tchng.

**DE CUNZO, DONNA M,** Fl International Univ, Miami, FL; JR; BS; SG 90-; Dietetic Assoc 90-; Phi Beta Kappa 88; ADA 90-; FDA 90-; MDA 90-; FPHA 90-; Sports/Cardio Nutritionists 90-; CV Program 90-; Deans List 89-; Dietetics/Nutrition; Sports Nutritionist.

**DE DOMING, LYNORE A,** Newbury Coll, Brookline, MA; SO; Acctg Mgr Const Industry; Bus Mgmt; Arch Engr.

**DE DOMINICIS, MARGARET A,** Erie Comm Coll, Buffalo, NY; GD; Chld Care Clb 90-; AAS; Chld Care; Soc Serv/Chld Psychlgy.

**DE FAZIO, KIMBERLEY A,** Wv Univ, Morgantown, WV; JR; BSN; Nrsng.

**DE FAZIO, PAMELA J,** Niagara Univ, Niagara Univ, NY; FR; BED; Engl Educ; Dctr Engl Tch Coll.

**DE FIGUEIREDO, SUSAN L,** Univ Of Fl, Gainesville, FL; SR; BA; Art History Assn 89-; Goza Art History Award 90-; Art History; MA.

**DE FINIS, YVONNE L,** Temple Univ, Philadelphia, PA; SR; BSN; Sigma Theta Tau; Nrsng; Perinatal Nrsng.

**DE FREESE, MICHELE L,** The Kings Coll, Briarclf Mnr, NY; SR; BS; Stu Msn Flwshp Conf Coord 88-90; Future Chrstn Educ Assoc Pub Chairprsn 88-; Elem Educ; Tchng.

**DE FREEST, JANET I,** Johnson St Coll, Johnson, VT; JR; BA; Rgby 90-; Chsmr; Vol Srvcs; Elem Ed; Spcl Ed.

**DE FREEZ, KRISTEN E,** Univ Of Al At Huntsville, Huntsville, AL; SO; BS; UAH Hon Pgm 89-; Soc Women Engrs 89-90; Kappa Delta Sor VP 89-; Panhellenic Schlrshp Awd 90-; Kappa Delta Schlrshp Awd 90; UAH Full Tuition Schlrshp 89-; IM Vlybl; Aerospace Eng.

**DE FREITAS, MARSHA S,** Washington State Comm Coll, Marietta, OH; SR; AD; MLT Clb 89-; Med Lab Tech; Med Lab.

**DE FRIESE, ROBERT A,** Chattanooga St Tech Comm Coll, Chattanooga, TN; SO; BA; Phi Theta Kappa 90-; Deans Lst; Stdnt Merit Awrd 91; Acad Work Schlrshp 88-; Restaurant Mgr; AA; Hist; Educ.

**DE FUSCO, MARK,** Fl International Univ, Miami, FL; SR; MPA; Police Offcr 81-; AA Miami Dade Comm Coll 88; BA; Pol Sci/Pbl Admn; Pblc Plcy/Admn.

**DE GARADY, STEVEN CHRIS,** Coll Of Charleston, Charleston, SC; FR; BS; Cmptr Engr; Engr.

**DE GASPERIS, VINCENT J,** Fl Atlantic Univ, Boca Raton, FL; SO; BS; Jewish Cmmnty Cntr 89-; Sftl Leag 89-; Cllg Bsns Deans Lst 89-; Prsdntl Schlrshp; Accntng; Pblc Accntnt.

**DE GOLYER, DAVID L,** Elmira Coll, Elmira, NY; SR; Corning Comm Coll; Engl Lit; Law.

**DE GOLYER, ROSEMARY K,** Catholic Univ Of Pr, Ponce, PR; SR; BA; TESOL 90-; Engl Tchr; Engl; Mastrs.

**DE GRAFFENREID, ASHLEY,** Stillman Coll, Tuscaloosa, AL; SO; BS; Cordell Wynn Hnrs Pgm; Gamma Iota Sigma 89-; Sclgy/Blgy; Ocptnl Thrpy.

**DE GRAFFENRIED, DAWN S,** Birmingham Southern Coll, Birmingham, AL; FR; BS; Phi Eta Sigma; Alpha Lambda Delta; Alpha Chi Omega Sistrhd Sprt Chr 90-; Acctg; Law/Corp.

**DE GRAFFINREED, CHERYL G,** Bloomfield Coll, Bloomfield, NJ; SO; Bus Admin; Imprt/Exprt Bus.

**DE GRANDIS, VALERIE A,** East Stroudsburg Univ, E Stroudsburg, PA; FR; BS; Polyglot Clb 90-; Intl Clb; Foreign Lang; Interpreter U N/Intl Bsn.

**DE GRAW, LYNNE K,** Mount Saint Mary Coll, Newburgh, NY; JR; BSN; Amrcn Cncr Soc; Amrcn Hrt Assn; NYSNA; NLN; ICU CCU Rpblc Hlth Nrsng Slvn Cnty; ASSOC Degree Appld Orange Cnty Cmmnty Clg Sci Nrsng 79; Nrsng; Pblc Hlth Nrs.

**DE GRAY, RENAE A,** Endicott Coll, Beverly, MA; SR; AS; Fshn Dsgn Cl Co-Pres 90-; Orntn 90; Thea Brandies Univ Intern; Fshn Dsgn; Retail; Pattern Drftg.

**DE GREGORIO, DAWN M,** Indiana Univ Of Pa, Indiana, PA; JR; BA; Assn Chldhd Educ Intl Sec 89-; Provost Schlr 89-; Kappa Delta Pi 89-90; Project Stride Tutor 89; Educ; Elem.

**DE GROOT, ANDREAS R,** Hudson Valley Comm Coll, Troy, NY; JR; BS; Intl Stdnts Clb VP 90-; Outing Clb; Chem; Chem Engr.

**DE GROOT, TIMOTHY G,** Fl St Univ, Tallahassee, FL; JR; BA; Acctng Soc; Phi Theta Kappa Secy 88-F Beta Alpha Psi; Tanglewood Elem Mntrs 89-90; Dept Of Learning Asstnc Tutors 89-90; AA Edison Cmnty Clg 90; Acctg; CPA/PHD.

**DE GRUY, KARMA,** Univ Of Montevallo, Montevallo, AL; FR; BA; Crmchl Lbrry Bk Rvw Awrd Fr Div; Engl; Frlnce Wrtng.

**DE GUIA, FRANKLIN G,** Anne Arundel Comm Coll, Arnold, MD; SO; BS; Spcl Olympcs MD; Anne Arundel Cnty Srvy Ld By AACC 89; O'conor Piper Flynn Real Estate Lcnsng Schl; Crmnl Jstce; Law.

**DE GUZMAN, ARMIL,** Le Moyne Coll, Syracuse, NY; SR; BS; Indstrl Rel Jr Class Assoc Rep 87-, Amer Red Cross First Aid Instr 90-; Outstanding Clge Stdnts Of Amer 89-90; IM Bsktbl 89-; Indstrl Relations.

**DE GUZMAN, CHERRY M,** Anne Arundel Comm Coll, Arnold, MD; FR; BA; Cmptr Sci.

**DE HAAS, DEBRA L,** Longwood Coll, Farmville, VA; SR; BA; Lambda Iota Tau 90-; Poem Pblsh Lit Mag 90; William L Frank Schlry Bk Awrd; Engl; Pblc Rlts/Pblshng.

**DE HART, KIMBERLY S,** Western Carolina Univ, Cullowhee, NC; SR; BA; Stdnt Comm Against Acquantance Rape 89-; English Clb 87-; Chi Alpha Delta 89-; Alpha Lambda Delta; Sigma Tau Delta 87-; Deans Lst 87-; Western Gold 88-; NC Prospective Tchr Schlrshp Loan 88-; Crum Schlrshp 90-; Ramsey Schlrshp 90-; English; Tchng Secndry Educ.

**DE HART, ROBERT A,** Middle Tn St Univ, Murfreesboro, TN; JR; BA; Musc; Prfrmnc/Tchg.

**DE HOLLANDER, ROBIN M,** Univ Of Sc At Columbia, Columbia, SC; SO; BA; Mrchng Bnd 89-; Cncrt Bnd 89-90; Symphnc Bnd Cvc Bnd 89-; Delta Omicrom; Tau Beta Sigma; Music Educ; Tchr.

**DE HOMBRE, CRISTINA M,** Nova Univ, Ft Lauderdale, FL; GD; MBA; Beta Alpha Psi 80-82; ALCPA Schlrshp; Ldrshp 89; FICPA; AICPA 83; CPA 83; MBA 91; BBA 82; Acctg; CPA.

**DE JARNETTE, KATHRYN J,** Mary Baldwin Coll, Staunton, VA; FR; BA; SG 90-; Art Clb 90-; RA; Psych TA; Art Hist/Psych; Grad Schl/Art Hist/Museum.

**DE JARNETTE, LISA J,** Longwood Coll, Farmville, VA; GD; Stdnt Educ Assc 89-90; Lmbd Iota Tau 88-90; Sgm Kappa Srty VP Mbrshp 87-90; Grk Cncl 88-90; BA 90; VA Tchng Cert; Engl; Educ.

**DE JESUS CASAS, GILBERTO J,** Univ Politecnica De Pr, Hato Rey, PR; FR.

**DE JESUS CLAUDIO, MIRIAM M,** Bayamon Central Univ, Bayamon, PR; SR; Pstrl Yth Mnstry Pres 87-89; Sr Maria Rafaela Brdng Sch Orphnd Abse Yng Girls Cnslr 89-; Doc Degree Psychlgy.

**DE JESUS PADRO, ANNETTE A,** Inter Amer Univ Pr Hato Rey, Hato Rey, PR; JR; BA; Acctg.

**DE JESUS SEDA, JESSICA,** Inter Amer Univ Pr San German, San German, PR; FR; Dstrbtv Ed Amer 88-90; Clb 4 H 80-83; Grls Sct 77-79; Cert Hgh Ave Acdmc Indx Pgm San German Interamericana; Cert Eng Fstvl 90; Alphbtcl Ordr Rcrd Eldrly Hm; Mdl Dstrbtv Ed Amer; Cert Cls Up Fndtn; Pre Schl Ed; BED.

**DE JESUS, BRENDA MARANGEL,** Univ Of Pr At Rio Piedras, Rio Piedras, PR; JR; BA; Prog De Estudios De Hon Sec 90-; Biology; Med.

**DE JESUS, DAVID J,** S U N Y Coll Of Tech At Frmgdl, Farmingdale, NY; SO; BA; Acctg Soc 89-; NSPA; Bear Strns Intrn 90; Acad Hnrs Schlrshp; Acctg/Finc; Inv Bnkr.

**DE JESUS, DIANA I,** S U N Y Coll Of Tech At Frmgdl, Farmingdale, NY; FR; LASO Sec 90-; Islndr Yrbk Cpy Asst 90-; Bus Admn.

**DE JESUS, ELSA MILAGROS,** Univ Of Pr Cayey Univ Coll, Cayey, PR; FR; BA; Cdro De Hnr De La Rectra Mrgrta Bntz Univ De PR Cayey; Engl; Trnsltr.

**DE JESUS, GAMALIER,** Univ Of Pr At Rio Piedras, Rio Piedras, PR; SR; BA; Gldn Key 90; Hon Pgm Pres 90-; Marc Flw Mnrty Accs Rsrch Careers Asstnt Invstgtn 89-; U MN UROP Trainee 90; Psychlgy; Clncl Psychlgst.

**DE JESUS, LOURDES M,** Inter Amer Univ Pr Hato Rey, Hato Rey, PR; FR; Acctng; Hnr Grp; Math; Acctng.

**DE JESUS, MARITZA H,** Inter Amer Univ Pr Guayama, Guayama, PR.

**DE JESUS, TRACY,** City Univ Of Ny City Coll, New York, NY; SO; MBA; PRES 89-; City Coll Hon Pgm 89-; RCMS 90-; Mech Eng.

**DE JESUS, VERONICA,** Univ Of Sc At Sumter, Sumter, SC; SO; BA; ISO Sec 90-; CAB 90-; Pace Comm; Union For Peace Dom Rpblc Pres 87-89; Comm Prog Dom Rpblc VP 86-88; Ldrshp Org Dom Rpblc 85-89; CASS Schlrshp; Vlybl/Sccr/Sftbl; Bus Mgmnt.

**DE JESUS-ALICEA, DERMIS EDITH,** Univ Of Pr Medical Sciences, San Juan, PR; SR; MA; Juv Ecum Univ 87-89; Cons Stdnts Fclty Ed 88-89; CPRS 89-90; Soc Hnr Stdnts 88-89; NSSHLA PR 89-; Verano Misionero 88-90; Pastoral De Sordos Catolicos; Premio Civismo Eugenio Maria De Hostos; Stdnts Sobrslte CPRS-RCM; Dns Lst 88-90; Spch/Lang Pthlgy; Spch/Lang Pthlgy Ph D.

**DE JESUS-ALPERT, MICHELE A,** Widener Univ, Chester, PA; JR; BS; Elec Engr; Engr.

**DE JESUS-PEREZ, JENNIE,** Catholic Univ Of Pr, Ponce, PR; JR; BA; Ftr Bsn Ldrs 87-88; Bsc Tm Cmptrs Usrs Tchr 88; Brd Hnr 87-; Gd Exclnc 89; Emply Mtvtn Awd Spkr; Cmnwlth Dt Prcs Asst EDP 75-76; Mgmt Info Systms Dir 76-; BED Puerto Rico Univ 75; Bsn Admin; Mgmt.

**DE JESUS-RUIZ, VANESSA A,** Univ Of Pr Medical Sciences, San Juan, PR; GD; MS; NSSHLA 90-; Audiology Cls Dir V P 90; P R Tchrs Assn 85-90; Spec Educ Tchr 85-90; BED Univ P R 85; Audiology; Ph D.

**DE JONGE, LANEY F,** Birmingham Southern Coll, Birmingham, AL; SR; BS; Hbtt Hmnty 89-; Sthrn Vol Serv 89-; Alpha Lambda Delta 87-; Phi Eta Sigma 88-; Mrtr Brd 89-; Alpha Kappa Psi 89-; Kappa Delta Pblc Rltns 88-; Deloitte/Touche Ldrshp Conf; Acctng/Engl.

**DE JOSEPH, CHRISTOPHER B,** S U N Y Coll At Fredonia, Fredonia, NY; SO; BA; Vrsty Sccr 89-90; Pol Sci; Law Enfr/ FBI.

**DE KEMPER, DEBORAH K,** Central Fl Comm Coll, Ocala, FL; JR; BA; Phi Theta Kappa Hstrn; Alpha Ru Rho; Psych Intrn Coop Pgm; Instr Mntl Hlth; AA Cntrl FL Comm Coll 90; Pblc Admin.

**DE KOK, CAROLYN J,** Savannah Coll Of Art & Design, Savannah, GA; FR; BFA; Fine Arts-Phtgrphy.

**DE LA CERRA, MANUEL F,** Ma Inst Of Tech, Cambridge, MA; FR; BS; Inter Frat Rltns Chrmn 90-; Concrete Canoe Team 90-; Zeta Psi Soc Chrmn 90-; Local Recycling Ctr Vol 90-; Bsbl/Bsktbl/Ftbl 90-; Civil/Env Eng; Env Law.

**DE LA COVA, ROSE M,** Univ Of Miami, Coral Gables, FL; SR; MED; Goldn Key 90-; Engl; Tchng.

**DE LA CRUZ SANTIAGO, YSHA M,** Inter Amer Univ Pr Hato Rey, Hato Rey, PR; FR; MBA; Hnr Scty Offc 90-; Acctg.

**DE LA CRUZ, ENRIQUE M,** Rutgers St Univ At Newark, Newark, NJ; SR; Bio Clb 88-89; Biomed Res Pgm 87-; Beta Beta Beta 90-; Clg Hnrs Pgm 89-; Acad Accom Awd 87-88; BA Rutgrs Newark; Cell Bio/Biochem; Phd Academia.**

**DE LA CUEVA DE-SORGE, PATRICIA,** Cleveland Inst Of Art, Cleveland, OH; FR; BFA; Cmnty Dsgn Comm Medina Steering Bd Mbr 88-; Garfield Elem PTO Envir Comm Chrprsn 90; Mtrl Hndlng Engr 80-81; Visual Fine Arts; Indus Dsgn.

**DE LA HORRA, LILLIAN S,** Fl International Univ, Miami, FL; GD; MS; NAEA; BA Univ Miami 73; AA Miami-Dade Comm Coll 72; Art Educ; Tchr.

**DE LA OSA CRUZ, STEVEN M,** Elmira Coll, Elmira, NY; SR; BA; 1917 Prize In Eng; AS Corning Comm Coll 89; Eng Lit; Scndry Edn.

**DE LA OSA, DAVID M,** Miami Dade Comm Coll, Miami, FL; FR; Paella Schlrshp 89-; English; Philosophy/Literature.

**DE LA PUERTE, GLADYS B,** Newbury Coll, Brookline, MA; ASSOC; Barry Controls 88-; Acctng; Mgt.

**DE LA TORRE DAVILA, SAREIDA,** Inter Amer Univ Pr Hato Rey, Hato Rey, PR; SO; ADESIRU Capitulo Vet; Hnr Roll 90-; Cert Fontocha Acad 88; Cert Puerto Rico Educ Dept 89; Bio; Med/Pedtrcn.

**DE LA TORRES MORALES, WILMARIE,** Inter Amer Univ Pr San German, San German, PR; FR; BA; Math/Physics; Engrn.

**DE LA VEGA, ERICH,** City Univ Of Ny City Coll, New York, NY; SR; BA; Hist Clb 88-89; Math Clb 90-; Bishp Hill Prz Exclnc Cnstnl Law; Swmng Tm Co Capt 87-; Pre Law; Law.

**DE LACY, LYNLY A,** Liberty Univ, Lynchburg, VA; SR; BS; Band Secr 89-; MENC; Instrmntlst Yr 90-; Instrmntl Msc; Conductg.

**DE LAMA-LI, ANUBIS,** Univ Of Miami, Coral Gables, FL; JR; BS; Hon Stdnt Assn 89-90; Pi Mu Epsilon VP 90-; Phi Kappa Phi 89-; Miami Music Clb Schlrshp 88; Pres Hon Rll 89-90; Physcs/Math; Appld Math.

**DE LANCEY, STORI L,** Oh St Univ At Newark, Newark, OH; JR; BED; Phi Sigma 90-; AA; Elem Ed.

**DE LAUDER, SAUNDRA F,** Howard Univ, Washington, DC; GD; PHD; Stdnt Senate Scl Cncrns Actvties Comm 80-81; Prjct Upward Bnd Chem Instrctr 83-84; Math Instrctr Prjct Upward Bnd IL 88; Prncpl Schlrs Prgrm 88; Beta Kappa Chu 85; Tchng Asst NCAT Univ Of IL And Howard Univ Chem Depts 83-; EPA Fllwshp 86; Chmstry; Rsrch Chmstry.

**DE LAURIER, ROBIN MICHELLE,** Fl International Univ, Miami, FL; FR; BA; Law Asc; Delta Phi Epsln Chr; Pol Sci; Lawyer.

**DE LAY, FAYE L,** Western Carolina Univ, Cullowhee, NC; JR; Std Mrshll Vol Shriners Crppld Chlrdrn Hsptl; Sigma Tau Delta; Engl; Pblshng.

**DE LEEUW, ELISA L,** Liberty Univ, Lynchburg, VA; SO; BS; Deans Lst 89-; Engl; Pblshng.

**DE LELLA, DIANE M,** Nova Univ, Ft Lauderdale, FL; Fin Mgrs Soc Pres 89; VP; BA FL Intrntl Univ 81; MBA 90.

**DE LEMOINE, CLAUDINE,** Saint Thomas Univ, Miami, FL; FR; Biolgy; Med.

**DE LEO, DAWN A,** Lesley Coll, Cambridge, MA; SR; Thtr Mrj Role; Intern MASS Hlfwy Huses Inc Cnslr 90-; Intern Belmont Brookline Schl; BA; Cnslng Psych.

**DE LEON, FREDDIE,** Univ Of Pr Medical Sciences, San Juan, PR; GD; MS; Amer Cnfrnc Govt Indus Hygnsts 90-; Puerto Rico Fed Sfty Hlth Cncl 90-; Cum Laude 88; Magna Cum Laude; BS Interamerican Univ PR 88; MS Univ PR; Sci/Envrnmntl Hlth.**

**DE LEON, TANIA,** Boricua Coll, New York, NY; SR; MPH; HIV Coun Phleb NY St Dept Hlth 90; Med Lab Tech Mandl Schl 79; Pblc Hlth; Intl Hlth.

**DE LEON-RIVERA, JESSENIA,** Bayamon Central Univ, Bayamon, PR; JR; Bus Adm Assc 89-90; 4-H Clb 89-90; Toa Alta Cthlc Church 88-89; Chrch Chr 90-; Scrtrl Sci.

**DE LILLE, SHARILYN G,** Abraham Baldwin Agri Coll, Tifton, GA; SO; BA; Phi Beta Lambda Sec/Treas 88-89; Awd Merit ABAC Spch Forum 89; Dstngshd Achvmnt Awd 90; Deans List; Bus; Intl Mgt.

**DE LILLO, MARK A,** Georgetown Univ, Washington, DC; SR; BS; Stdnt Serv Com 87-89; Vol H S Coach 87-; Deans Lst 87-; Vrsty Ftbl 89-; Vrsty Chrldr Co-Capt 87-89; Fin.

**DE LOACH, AMANDA R,** Central Al Comm Coll, Alexander City, AL; SO; AS; Vllybl 89-90; Cmptr; Cmptr Sci.

**DE LOACH, DANIEL F,** Univ Of Miami, Coral Gables, FL; SR; BS; Golden Key 90-; Beta Gamma Sigma; IM Ftbl/Bsktbl/ Rcqtbl; Economics; Surf The World.

**DE LONG, BEVERLY A,** Hillsborough Comm Coll, Tampa, FL; FR; AA; Art; Cmmrcl Artst.

**DE LONG, MICHELE L,** Marshall University, Huntington, WV; JR; BA; Spnsh Soc 88-89; Phi Eta Sigma 88-89; Sigma Delta Pi Sec 89-; Rotary Intl Ambsdr Schlr; Spnsh; Scndry Educ.

**DE LORENZO, MAUREEN H,** Immaculata Coll, Immaculata, PA; SR; BA; Hon Soc 90-; Cert Bus; Cert French; Cert Art; English; Public Rltns.

**DE LORM, GEOFFREY S,** Savannah Coll Of Art & Design, Savannah, GA; FR; BARCH; Whelan Schlrshp 90-; Archtctre.

**DE LOS REYES, MONINA SAN LUIS,** Bloomfield Coll, Bloomfield, NJ; SR; BS; Alpha Chi 90; Alpha Kappa Psi 90; Acctng; CPA.

**DE LOUIS, JOSEPH,** Univ Of Pittsburgh, Pittsburgh, PA; SR; BA; Gldnkey 89-; Tffc Accdnt Prvntn Fndtn Asst 85-; Frtm Schl Eng Trm Hnr Stdnt; Mchncl Eng.**

**DE LUCA, ANGELA M,** S U N Y Coll At Postdam, Potsdam, NY; JR; BM; MENC 89-; NASA Sec 89-; Phi Eta Sigma Stdnt Advsr 89-90; Kappa Delta Pi 89-; Sigma Alpha Iota V P 89-; Music Educ.

**DE LUCA, BERNARD J,** Oh St Univ, Columbus, OH; SR; BFA; Univ Dance Co 88-89; Dept Dance Schlrshp 88-; Summa Cum Laude; Arts/Sci Awd Excell Schlrshp; MD Dance Theatre 85-86; Pittsburgh Dance Alloy 86-88; Dance; Athl Trng Dancers.

**DE LUCA, PETER D,** Temple Univ, Philadelphia, PA; SO; BS; De Luca Fuel Oil Inc VP 87-; Hlth Phys Educ; Tchr.

**DE LUCA, RENEE S,** George Mason Univ, Fairfax, VA; GD; MA; Psych Clb 88290; Cntr Serv Lrng 88; Pnhlnc Rush Cnslr 89; Psi Chi 89-90; Gldn Key 87-90; Otstndg Coll Stu Amer 87-90; Alpha Chi Omega 87-90; Magna Cum Laude 90; Pres Lst 88-90; Deans Lst 87-88; BA 90; Indstrl Org Psych.

**DE LUCCA, EDNA FRANCES MARIA,** Univ Of Southern Ms, Hattiesburg, MS; SR; BSN; Gamma Beta Phi; Stdnt Nrs Assn Southern Miss Corr Sec 90-; BS Univ N O 88; Lambda Chi Alpha U Nw Orlns White Rose 83-86; Hgh Schl Sci Tchr 88-90; Nrsng Psychlgy Mnr; Nrsg.

**DE LUCCA, MARCIO R,** Univ Of Southern Ms, Hattiesburg, MS; FR; Cond Ilha Do Sul VP 88-89; TEC Natl Radio Inst 90; Radio/Tlvsn/Film; Tv Prod.

**DE LUCIA, ANGELA,** Kent St Univ Kent Cmps, Kent, OH; JR; BFA; Frnds Armcn Art Btlr Inst Armcn Art; KSC Prgrmmng 88-; Gldn Ken; Alpha Lambda Delta; Phi Alpha Theta 89-; Schlrshp 88-; Hstry.

**DE LUQUE, SANDRA BEATRICE,** Fl International Univ, Miami, FL; JR; BA; Fla Intl Univ Colombian Clb 90-; Latin Amer Ins Assn 87-88; Summer Intrnshp Carlond Ins Agncy Conn 89; Coll Bds Outstdng Grad Mnrty Stdnts 89; AA Miami Dade Comm Coll 89; Intl Bus/Mktg; Overseas Mktg.**

**DE MAIO, TONI A,** Dowling Coll, Oakdale Li, NY; SR; BBA; BA Suffolk Cnty Comm Coll; Bus Admin/Mktg.

**DE MARCO, JO ANN,** Ms St Univ, Miss State, MS; GD; DVM; Ntl Pres Schlrshp Awd; BS Mntclr St Coll 89; Vet Med; Vetrnrn.

**DE MARIA, CHRISTINE M,** Seton Hall Univ, South Orange, NJ; SR; BSED; Phi Alpha Theta VP 89-; Kappa Delta Pi Hstrn 89-; R Foley Schlrshp 89-; Acdmc Schlrshp 87-; Ornmntl Irn Wrkrs Schlrshp 88-; Scndry Educ/Hstry; Tchr.

**DE MARIA, ROSEANN,** S U N Y Coll Of Tech At Frmgdl, Farmingdale, NY; SO; Erly Chldhd Clb 89-; Dante Fndtn Schlrshp 89-; Ctchst Tchr 89-; Asst Aide Martin Ave Schl; Asst Aide Little Vlg Schl 90; Ed; Tchr.

**DE MARSE, DANIELLE J,** S U N Y Coll Of Tech At Alfred, Alfred, NY; FR; AAS; Yrbk Stf 90-; Scty Mnfctrng Engnrs 90-; Ntl Cmptr Graphics Organ 90-; Tour Guide Alfred State Cllg; Stdt Ambsdr Alfred State Cllg 90-; Cmptr Graphics Eng Tech; Aerospace Eng.

**DE MARTINI, TERESA A,** Barry Univ, Miami, FL; FR; BA; Scrbrd Kpr Scr/Bsktbl 90-; Asst Sprts Info Drctr 90-; Bus.

**DE MARTINO, LENORE,** Fl International Univ, Miami, FL; JR; BA; Future Ed Am; Phi Sigma Sigma 88-; Deans Lst 89-; Elem Edn; Teach.

**DE MARZO, BRIAN,** Wagner Coll, Staten Island, NY; JR; BA; Theta Chi 89-; Busn Admin; Mgmnt.

**DE MASI, ANN M,** Davis & Elkins Coll, Elkins, WV; JR; BS; Spanish Clb 89; Mrktng Mngmnt.

**DE MATTEO, LORI A,** Ny Univ, New York, NY; JR; Deans Lst 90-; Educ Schlr 90-; NAFE 89-; AAS 79-81; Org Cmnctns; Bus.

**DE MERSSEMAN, WILLIAM P,** Asbury Theological Sem, Wilmore, KY; GD; Organizer/Coach Bsbl Tm Gen Mngr 88-; Icthus Christian Music Fstvl Asst Prog Coord 88-; Senior Chapel Serv 90; IM Bsktbl/Ftbl/Tennis/Bsbll; Pstr Gilchrist Pk Untd Meth Chrch; MDIV 90; Theology; Ministry.

**DE MICHAEL, CHRISTOPHER P,** Kent St Univ Kent Cmps, Kent, OH; SR; MBA; IMS 87-; Delta Upsilon Fndg Fthr/Tres 88-; BA; Finance; Mgt.

**DE MINICO, LINDA R,** Univ Of Nh Plymouth St Coll, Plymouth, NH; CERT; BBA Univ MA 72; Mktg/Art Ed; Tch.

**DE MITCHELL, SULEICA M,** Fl International Univ, Miami, FL; SR; BA; Chldrns Hm Soc; Otstndg Stu Yr 89; Hnrs Schlrshp 89; Comm Coll Trnsfr Schlrshp 90-; AA Hghst Hnrs 90; Clncl Psychlgy.

**DE MOND, MARILYN J,** Univ Of Toledo, Toledo, OH; SR; BS; Schlstc Rcgntn 90-; Pres Hnr Lst; Deans Hnr Lst 89-; Amer Scty Trng/Devlpmnt 90-; Sr Luter Leag Advsr; Admnstrtv/Sls Exprnc 72-; AS 88; Hmn Rsrcs; MBA/ORGNZTNL Dvlpmnt.

**DE MOND, MARLISA H,** Univ Of Miami, Coral Gables, FL; JR; BA; Psychlgy; Chld Psychlgst.

**DE MOSS, JENNIFER L,** Ky Wesleyan Coll, Owensboro, KY; SO; BS; Pre Prof Soc 89-; Sigma Zeta 90-; Sigma Kappa VP Mbrshp 89-; Bio; Med.

**DE MOTT HASENAUER, SANDRA L,** Rochester-Hall-Crozer Dvty Sch, Rochester, NY; GD; MDIV; Bapt Alliance Co Cnvnr 89; Yth Tsk Frc 90-; Stdnt Cabinet; BA SUNY Geneseo 87; Mnstry.

**DE NAULT, SHARON A,** Marywood Coll, Scranton, PA; JR; BA; Kappa Gamma Psi 68-70; PTA Sec 85-86; Cncr Soc/Rch Rcvry 81-; Artist Art 88-; Prt Ownr Fabrctng/Steel Jusquanna Stdio; Ownr S T Lersige 83-87; Co Ownr Overland Hrs Trlr 85-87; Art/Fine Arts Appld; Mstrs Ther.

**DE NEEN, ANDREA E,** Univ Of Rochester, Rochester, NY; SO; BA; Dnc Trp Brd Mbr/Chrgrphr 89-; Rlgn Psychlgy; Mdcn.

**DE NEZZA, MARCY A,** The Boston Conservatory, Boston, MA; FR; BFA; Musical Theatre Core Pub Relations 90-; Black Artists Assoc Choregrapher 90-; Assistanceship In Theatre Div AV-SOUND Operator 90-; Auditions Big Sister 90-; Music Theatre; Performing Arts.

**DE NICOLA, RICHARD V,** S U N Y Coll Of Tech At Delhi, Delhi, NY; SR; IM Ftbl Capt 90-; Pr Tutor; AAS; Cvl Engr; Inspctr.

**DE NOIA, CAROLYN K,** Radford Univ, Radford, VA; JR; BS; Pblc Rltns Clb; Sr Cls Hstrn; Sigma Sigma Sigma Chrmn; Speech/Communications; Advertising.

**DE NOVI, OLGA L,** Fl International Univ, Miami, FL; SR; BS; Amer Dietc Assoc; BS Biol Univ Simon Bolivar 81; Fd Sci Univ Simon Bolivar 85; Dietcs/Nutrn; Publ Hlth.

**DE NOYERS, MICHELLE L,** Clarkson Univ, Potsdam, NY; SR; BS; Ski Clb; Photo Clb; Ntl Yth Ldrshp Cnfrnc; Rgnts Schlrshp; Brmbl; Mktg; Fnce.

**DE OLDEN, BARBARA ANN,** D Youville Coll, Buffalo, NY; SO; BS; Two-Bit Players Drama Clb Pres 87-90; Stdnt Govt Repr 87-88; Res Cncl Pres; Stdnt Phys Ther Assoc 90-; CCC Tour Guide 87-89; Sci Clb 89-90; Ambassador 90-; Corning Hosp Vol P J Dept 87-88; Phys Ther Intern St Joes Hosp 89-; AS Corning Clg; Phys Ther.

**DE OLIVEIRA, LOREN D,** Univ Of Sc At Columbia, Columbia, SC; FR; Cmps Actv Brd 90-; Intl Std Org 90-; Spnsh; Tch.

**DE PACE, CHRISTINE F,** S U N Y Coll Of Tech At Frmgdl, Farmingdale, NY; FR; Acctg Soc Pub Rltns 90-; Bus Clb Pres; NAA 90-; Actvty Brd; Alpha Beta Gamma; Dsrt Strm Support Fndrsr; Spec Olympcs Vol; Acctg/Bus Admin.

**DE PALMA, JOSEPH F,** Widener Univ, Chester, PA; JR; BS; Ecnmcs Clb Pres 90; Ldrshp Prog 90; APICS VP; Bsnss Mngmnt/ Ecnmcs.

**DE PALMA, MELISSA A,** Providence Coll, Providence, RI; FR; IM Sccr Ftbl; Trps Vstng Eldrs Nrsng Hm; Sccr Ftbl; Math.

**DE PALMA, MICHELLE LAURETTE,** Dowling Coll, Oakdale Li, NY; SR; BA; Suffolk Cnty Cmnty Clge 87-89; Visual Arts; Art Tchr.

**DE PALMA, PATRICIA,** Tri County Tech Coll, Pendleton, SC; SO; RN; Hlth Sci; RN.

**DE PAOLI, GINA MARIE,** The Boston Conservatory, Boston, MA; SO; BED; Stdnt Govt Tres 90-; Msc Edctr Natl Conf Pres; Deans List 89-; Sgm Alph Iota Sec; BCM Wnd Ensmbl; Msc Educ; Tchng/Prfrmnc Clrnt.

**DE PASCALE, DANIELLE M,** Seton Hall Univ, South Orange, NJ; JR; BSN; Natl Stdnt Nrs Assoc 89-; Nrsng.

**DE PASS, EARL J,** City Univ Of Ny Baruch Coll, New York, NY; JR; African Stdnts Assn Sec 89-; Offc Stdnt Dvlpmnt 90-; Dpt Blck Hspnc Stds Pblshr Mlti Cltrl Jrnl; Awd Otstndng Accmplshmnts Clb Actvts 90; Cmmnctns; Multi Media Infrmtn Systms.

**DE PENA JR, REYNALDO A,** City Univ Of Ny Baruch Coll, New York, NY; SR; BBA; CQMS 88-; Chess Clb; Gldn Key 88-; Beta Gamma Sigma 90-; Endwmnt Fnd Prvst Schlp; Cmptr Info Sys; Cmptr/Ntwrk Engr.

**DE PIORE, WILMA J,** Univ Of Sc At Columbia, Columbia, SC; JR; BS; Trck/Crss Cntry; Pres Lst; Habitat For Humanity; Athlete Of Yr; Crss Cntry/Trck; Exercise Sci; Phy Thrpy.

**DE POLO, AMY M,** Endicott Coll, Beverly, MA; FR; BA; Busn Clb 90-; Engl Hnrs 90-; Windwrd Gft Shp Intrnshp Asst Mgr 90-; Busn Admin; Mgr.

**DE POY, MICHELLE L,** Morehead St Univ, Morehead, KY; FR; BS; Mrchng Bnd; Pep Bnd; Math Clb; Gamma Beta Phi; Fr Hnree Phi Kappa Phi; Acad Hnrs Awrd Fr Mntng 4.0 GPA; Math; Hgh Schl Tchr.

**DE PRIEST, CYNTHIA G,** Oh Univ-Southern Cmps, Ironton, OH; SO; AAB; Cert 90; Ofc Admin Tech; Ofc Mgr.

**DE PRIMO, JIMMY P,** Tn Temple Univ, Chattanooga, TN; JR; BS; Cncrt Choir 90-; Alpha Omega Delta 90-; Bsktbl IM 90-; Bus Admin; Bnkg.

**DE RIENZO MANNION, MARIE C,** Mount Saint Mary Coll, Newburgh, NY; JR; BA; Sch Bus Drvr 80-; AA Prange Cty Cmnty Clg 90; Pol Sci/Hstry; Elem Ed-Spec Ed Tchr.

**DE ROCHE, KRISTY L,** Unity Coll, Unity, ME; SO; BS; Hlth Cncl Sec 90-; Edtr Clg Nwspr 90-; Wildlfe Clb 89-; Deans Lst 89-; Emerg Resns Grp; Crs Cntry Rng 89-90; AS; Wildlfe Biology.

**DE RODRIGUEZ, JANET RIEFKOHL,** Inter Amer Univ Pr San Juan, Hato Rey, PR; FR; BA; Rl Est Brkr Palmas Del Mar 90-; Ownr Palmas Video 87-; Assn Stdnts Grnca Clg 88-89; Univ Humacao 88-89; Magna Cum Laude Bchlr Degree/Bsn; BA Clg Univ Humacao 89; Law; Rl Est/Corp/Crmnl Lwyr.

**DE ROSIER, CHARLES D,** Savannah Coll Of Art & Design, Savannah, GA; FR; MBA; Phtgphy; Cultrl Phtgphy.

**DE RUE, ANGEL L,** Glassboro St Coll, Glassboro, NJ; FR; BA; SCEB Sec 90-; Cmmnctns Jrnlsm.

**DE SANCTIS, DINO R,** Duquesne Univ, Pittsburgh, PA; SR; BS; Alpha Tau Omega 87-; IM Sprts; Alpha Tau Omega 87-; Field Stdy Bus Admn 90; Acctg; CPA.

**DE SANTIS, CHRISTOPHER,** Broward Comm Coll, Ft Lauderdale, FL; SO; AA; Phi Theta Kappa 90-; Pres Lst 90; Crmnl Justice; Law Enfrcmntt.

**DE SANTIS, MARISA S,** Dickinson Coll, Carlisle, PA; SO; BA; Yrbk Spec Evnts Edtr 89-; Coll Bwl 89-; Russn Clb 89-; Spnsh Clb 89-; Itln Clb 89-; Russn Lang Stdy Moscow; IM Vlybl Capt 89-; Spnsh/Rssn.**

**DE SANTO, VANETTA R,** S U N Y Coll Of Tech At Frmgdl, Farmingdale, NY; SO; PH D; Lbrl Arts Hon Scty 90-; ASSC Sunny Fdale; Lbrl Arts; Law Psychlgy.

**DE SCHON, MARGARET L,** Univ Of North Fl, Jacksonville, FL; JR; BSH; Hlth Sci; Cmnty Hlth.

**DE SENA, MICHELLE,** Dowling Coll, Oakdale Li, NY; SR; BBA; Dns Lst; Mrktng; Mrktng Mgr.

**DE SEYN, MELANIE M,** Elmira Coll, Elmira, NY; SR; Actvts Brd Tchnl Dir 87-; New Stdnt Orttn Prnts Wknd Chrpersn 90-; Kappa Delta Pi; BS Ed; Elem Ed; Tchng.

**DE SILVA, GINIGE L,** S U N Y At Buffalo, Buffalo, NY; SR; MS; Sri Lanka Stdnt Assoc Treas 88-90; Tau Beta Pi; Eta Kappa Nu; Golden Key; Grad Engr Dept Hnrs; Mary Capen Mem Awd 89; Dns Hnrs Lst; BS; Elctrcl Engr; Engr.

**DE SILVA, JAMES T,** Ny Law School, New York, NY; Moot Crt Cpmt 89-; Std Serv Tutor; Jrnl Hmn Rghts Edtr 90; Intshp Snr Std 90-; Law Clrk; Dpty Atty Gnrl 87-90; Corp Cnsl 90-; BA Niagara Unv 85; Law.

**DE SIMONE, DEBRA A,** Saint Johns Univ, Jamaica, NY; SR; BS; Phi Theta Kappa 87-89; AAS Nassau Comm Clg 89; Spec Ed; Tchng.

**DE SIMONE, JEAN D,** Glassboro St Coll, Glassboro, NJ; JR; BS; Amer Chem Soc Tr 89-; C W Newcombe Schlrshp Awd 90-; Intrn Mbl Res Dev; Anml Hlth Tech Vet Hosp; AAS Camdn Cnty Clg 81; Chem/Bio; R/D.

**DE SIMONE, ROSE,** Atlantic Comm Coll, Mays Landing, NJ; SO; AAS; CSA 89-90; Deans Lst 89-; Vlybl; Culinary Cert 89-; Culinary Arts; Chef.

**DE SISTO, JOHN A,** Georgetown Univ, Washington, DC; JR; BA; Ftbll 88-; Fncs; Bnkg.

**DE SOUZA, KEVIN A,** Fl A & M Univ, Tallahassee, FL; FR; BS; Deans Lst 90; IM Sftbl Tm; Cvl Engrng.

**DE SOUZA, RACHEL LINDA,** Univ Of Sc At Columbia, Columbia, SC; JR; BS; Amer Mktg Assn Camp Prgrmng; Kappa Alpha Theta; Ct Appntd Spec Advct; Bus; Mktg.

**DE SPAIN, EMBRA D,** Univ Of Tn At Martin, Martin, TN; SO; BS; Natl Blck/Brdl Clb 89-; Cir K Intl 89-90; Church Christ Stdnt Cntr 89-; Agri; Anml Rprdctn/Gntcs.

**DE SPAIN, MICHELLE L,** Wagner Coll, Staten Island, NY; SR; BA; Plyrs 89-; Trnty Univ Plyrs 87-89; Choir 88-89; Omicron Delta Kappa 89-; Alpha Lambda Delta 88-; Alethea 89-; Deans Lst 88-; Summa Cum Laude Grad; Theatre.

**DE STEFANO, MICHELLE L,** Univ Of Pittsburgh At Bradford, Bradford, PA; SO; BS; SGA 90-; Bio Clb Pres 89-; STARS 89-90; Alpha Lambda Delta Pres 90-; Beta Beta Beta Secr; Zeta Alpha Chi 90-91; Jo Anne Trow Awd; IM Sftbl/Bsktbl 90-; Bio; Optemetry.

**DE STEFANO, TRACY A,** William Paterson Coll, Wayne, NJ; JR; BA; SGA Humanities Rep 90-; Mobilization Comm; Constitution Judicial Bd 90-; Cert Belleville 90; Engl; Professor.

**DE STEPHANO, MARK W,** Le Moyne Coll, Syracuse, NY; FR; BA; Modern Lang Alliance 90-; WLMU Campus Radio Station 90-; French; Ed/Intl.

**DE TARDO, JILL L,** Univ Of North Fl, Jacksonville, FL; JR; BA; Tstmstrs 88-90; AFAA 89-; Phi Theta Kappa 88-90; Comm Coll Reg Schlrshp 89; Summa Gum Laude St Johns River Comm Coll 89; AA 89; Engl Lit; Law.

**DE TESO, DAVID R,** Univ Of Nh Plymouth St Coll, Plymouth, NH; SR; BA; Tutor 87-88; Comm Vol 90-; Pi Gamma Mu; Outstdng Snr Pol Sci; Pol Sci; Env Law.

**DE TREUX, BARBARA R,** Manor Jr Coll, Jenkintown, PA; SO; Alpha Beta Gamma 90-; Bus Admin; Hmn Rsrc Mgmt.

**DE VAI, TEKLA,** City Univ Of Ny Queensbrough, New York, NY; BA; Cmmnq Asst Ed 89-90; Hmnts Clb Pres 90-; Stdnt Orttn Ldrs 90-; Alpha Sigma Lambda; Phi Theta Kappa; Thomas R Jennings Mem Awrd; Arnold Smithline Simon Trefman Awrd 90; Friends Of Library Awrd; John Wmanigaulte Mem Awrd; Engl Lit; Tchng.

**DE VAN JR, STANLEY M,** Morehouse Coll, Atlanta, GA; JR; BS; SGA Acdmc Affrs Com 90-; Spelman Coll Extrnl Affrs Bd 90; Xerox SCEL Intrn 90-; Techbnd Pre-Eng Pgm 89; Rensselaer Plytech Inst Baltimore Awd Math; Outstndng Fresh-AVC Dual Degree 88-89; Math/Eng.

**DE VANEY, THOMAS A,** Livingston Univ, Livingston, AL; JR; BS; Mthmtcl Assc AM; Phi Eta Sigma; Alpha Chi; Bsbll; Mthmtcs; Engr.

**DE VARONA, EMELINA I,** Univ Of Pr At Rio Piedras, Rio Piedras, PR; SR; BBA; All Amer Schlr Collgt Awd 89-; Natl Collgt Bus Mrt Awd 89-; Admin Asst 80-; Acctg; CPA.

**DE VAULT, KATHLEEN E,** Oh St Univ, Columbus, OH; SR; Theatre Lghtng Dsgnr/Stage Mgr 88-; Dorm Paper Edtr 87; Dorm Cncl 86-87; Outstndng Schlrshp Awd; Theatre Schlrshp 89-90; Fresh Schlr 86; Theatre/Engl; Grad Schl.

**DE VAULT, LAURA I,** James Madison University, Harrisonburg, VA; JR; BA; Psychlgy Clb 87-; Psychlgy; Cnslng Psychlgy.

**DE VAULT, MARSHA L,** Wv Univ, Morgantown, WV; FR; BA; Elec Cmptr Eng.

**DE VECCHIS, SHARON LYNN,** Atlantic Comm Coll, Mays Landing, NJ; FR; AAS; Nrsng; RN.

**DE VELLIS, DAVID M,** Amherst Coll, Amherst, MA; FR; BA; IM Soccer Indoor/Outdoor; IM Bsktbl/Vlybl/Sftbl; Sci/Lib Arts; Med.

**DE VENDRA, STACY L,** Marshall University, Huntington, WV; JR; BA; Gamma Beta Phi; Sigma Delta Pi Pres; Phi Eta Sigma; Intl Affrs/Spnsh; Intl Rltns.**

**DE VERA, NEYRISSA M,** Comm Coll Algny Co Algny Cmps, Pittsburgh, PA; FR; BA; Mrktng; Bus.

**DE VILLIERS, ANA V,** Univ Of Miami, Coral Gables, FL; FR; BA; Jrnlsm And Pol Sci; Bus Law Or Intrntl Law.

**DE VINEY JR, MICHAEL R,** Ms Gulf Coast Comm Coll, Perkinston, MS; FR; Kds Blck 90-; Thtr 90; Acdmc Hnrs Prgm 90; VP Lst 90; Chmstry; Pdtrc Crdlgst.

**DE VITO, GARY R,** City Univ Of Ny City Coll, New York, NY; GD; BE; ASCE Sec Am Rr Engr Assn 89-90; Coll Concrete Canoe Clb; Shapiro/Wrght Ctznshp Awd; Cvl Engr Dept Stdnt Adv Comm 89-90; Gldn Key 89-90; Tau Beta Pi VP 89-90; Chi Epsilon VP 89-90; Tutoring; Am Soc Mltry Engrs Schlrshp; Engr-Trng Cert; Cvl Engr; Constr Mgmt.

**DE VIZIO, JENNIFER,** Bergen Comm Coll, Paramus, NJ; SO; AS; Phi Theta Kappa; BA Wm Paterson Coll 85; Nrsng.

**DE VOLLD, STANYA L,** Ky Christian Coll, Grayson, KY; SO; BS; Stdnt Govt Spiritual Ldr 90-; Trvlg Ensmbl 90-; Sign Lang Clb 89-90; SG 89-; Concert Choir Awd; Horton Piano Schlrshp 90; Elem Ed; Tch.

**DE VORE, LEIGH A,** Winthrop Coll, Rock Hill, SC; JR; BED; MENC 90; Delta Omicron 90; Music; Tch.

**DE VORE, MYRA C,** Ms St Univ, Miss State, MS; SR; BS; Scotch Guard Army ROTC Ltl Sis 90-; Pi Omega Pi Pres 90-; Pi Omega Pi V P 89-90; Phi Beta Lambda State MS Rep/Rep 89-; Farm House Ltl Sis 89-; Francis N Matthews Mem Schlrshp 90-; Pres/Dns Schlr 89-; ABS Draughons Jr Clg 83; Bsn Ed; Tchg.

**DE VORE, RICHARD S,** Northeastern Christian Jr Coll, Villanova, PA; SO; BED; Vly Rd Chrch Chrst Cls Instrctr 90-; Bethanna Hm Chldrn Hs Prnt 88-; AA Nrthstrn Chrstrn Jr Clg; Elem Edctr; Chrstn Edctr.

**DE VOS, DAVID G,** Bryant Stratton Bus Inst Roch, Rochester, NY; SO; BA; Deans List 89-90; Elctrncs; Eng.

**DE WALT, PATRICIA,** Univ Of Sc At Columbia, Columbia, SC; JR; BA; Elem Edn; Teach.

**DE WANE, CATHERINE TARA,** Livingston Univ, Livingston, AL; SR; BS; AAHPERD 90-; Pres Lst; Aerobics Instr; Earthday 90; Candy Striper 87; Phys Ther Asstntshp 89-; Diving Tm Capt/All State 87-; Hlth/Phys Ed; Pers Trng/Nutr Cnslg.

**DE WEERDT, ELLEN G,** Southern Vt Coll, Bennington, VT; SR; BS; Acctg; CPA.

**DE WEES, TRACY L,** Wv Univ At Parkersburg, Parkersburg, WV; FR; AAS; Offc Admin; Exec Sec.

**DE WIRE, LAURIE S,** Asbury Theological Sem, Wilmore, KY; GD; MBA; Stdnt Govt Assn-Asbury Sem Pres 91-; Yth Chrst Wrk W/Incrcrtd Yth Stf Prsn 90-; Sigma Alpha Iota Sng Ldr 86-; Recrtn Prof Chrstn Sng Grp Entrnr 86-89; BA Susqhna Univ 86; Chrstn Educ.

**DE WITT SALVIE, CHRISTINE M,** Smith Coll, Northampton, MA; SR; BA; Phi Beta Kappa 88-; Schlr 89-90; Dns Lst 87-; Valdictrn 89; AA Berkshr Comm Clg 89; Elem Educ.

**DE WITT, LACY D,** Univ Of Ga, Athens, GA; SR; BS; Bptst Stdnt Union Exec Cncl 87-; IM; Golden Key 87-; Alpha Lambda Delta 88-; Gamma Beta Phi 88-; Kappa Delta Epsilon 90-; Tutr; Law Co Stdnt Ldr 90; Math Educ.

**DE WITT, MINDY S,** Miami Jacobs Jr Coll Of Bus, Dayton, OH; FR; Natl Hon Soc 89-; Applied Bus; Trvl/Tourism.

**DE WOLFE, KATE S,** Colby Sawyer Coll, New London, NH; SR; BS; Stdnt Govt Jr V P Sr Sec Treas 89-; Chlhd Clb 89-; Res Hl Stf 88-90; Tchng Asst 90-; Stdnt Tchng Intrn; Var Bkbl Cap 88-; Early Chldhd Educ; Tch.

**DE ZARRAGA, MARIA T,** Univ Of Miami, Coral Gables, FL; SR; BS; PRSSA; Wmn Cmnctns; Stf Wrtr UM Sch Cmnctn Nwsltr; Phi Kappa Phi; Phi Theta Kappa; Hmls Prjct St Augustine Cthlc Chrch; Provosts Hnr Rl/Deans Lst; Pblc Rltns Intrnshp Mercy Hosp Miami Fl; Cert Acdmc Achvmnt; AA 89; Pblc Rltns; Corp.

**DEACONEASA, GINETTA,** City Univ Of Ny Baruch Coll, New York, NY; SO; BBA; Qlty Serv Circle Of Ll Svng Bnk Repr; Romanian Yth Commnty; Bus Acctng; Fincl Acctng.

**DEAL, ANGELA,** Pa St Univ Delaware Cty Cmps, Media, PA; FR; BA; Lions Eye News Edtr 90-; Lbrl Arts; Art Educ.

**DEAL, MARIE E,** Univ Of Sc At Columbia, Columbia, SC; GD; ADN; Hons Prog 90-; Chldbrth Ed Of Beaufort Regis/Treas 89-; Prentl Instrctr 89-; Lab Phlebotnst 88-; AS USC Beaufort; Nrsng; Earn MSN In Midwfry.

**DEAL JR, RICHARD BURDON,** Radford Univ, Radford, VA; SR; BS; Comp Sci Clb 89-; Radford Notpub Pres 89-; First Annual Prgrmng Cntst 2nd Place 90-; Comp Sci; Dvlpmnt Prgrmr.

**DEAMON, TINA MARIE,** Middle Tn St Univ, Murfreesboro, TN; SR; BA; Fine Arts Com Math Org 90-; Stdnt Tchrs Ed Assn 90-; Stdnt Home Ec Assn 89-; Preschl Tchr; Early Chldhd Ed; Tch K-8.

**DEAN, AMANDA C,** Meridian Comm Coll, Meridian, MS; SO; Rdlgc Tech Stdnt Assn; Coll Ambass; Coll Act Brd; Comm Coll Ambass; LEAD; 4-H Pres 89-90; Rdlgc Tech.

**DEAN, ANDY A,** Univ Of Al, Tuscaloosa, AL; FR; BS; Cmptr Based Hon Pgm 90-; Hon Pgm 90-; Mallet Assembly Hon Pgm 90-; Fr Forum Hon 90-; Lambda Sigma 90-; Friend Campus Pgm 90-; Sys Analysis/Legal Philosophy; Law.

**DEAN, ANGELA D,** Meridian Comm Coll, Meridian, MS; FR; BA; Activities Bd; Ambassadors; Phi Theta Kappa; Phi Theta Kappa; Bus; CPA.

**DEAN, CAROL L,** Va St Univ, Petersburg, VA; JR; BS; VA State Univ Gspl Ensmble 88-89; Ladies Billiards Chmpn 88; Schl Bsn Award 88-89; Dns Lst 88-90; IM Bsktbl 88; Bsn; Cmptrs.

**DEAN, CAROL M,** Embry Riddle Aeronautical Univ, Daytona Beach, FL; SR; BS; FPWA 88-; Stdnt Ct Jstc 89-90; Orientation Ldr 89-90; Aero Sci Assist 90-; Aero Sci; Airline Pilot.

**DEAN, DENISE L,** Clarkson Univ, Potsdam, NY; SR; BS; Scty Accts 87-90; Student Orient Serv 88-90; Ski Club 87-89; Omega Delta Phi Cmmt Ldr 88-; Trustees Schlrshp 87-; Acctng; CPA.

**DEAN, EDDIE L,** Union Coll, Barbourville, KY; JR; BS; Cmtr Cncl VP 90-; Sci Clb 88-; Gamma Beta Phi 90-; Trmco Chmstry Awrd 89-90; Physcs Awrd 89-90; Vrsty Tnns 90-; Chmstry/Physcs; Rsrch.

**DEAN, JEFFREY L,** Univ Of Southern Ms, Hattiesburg, MS; SR; MS; Prog Cncl 87; Baptist Union 87-; Crmnl Just Assn 88-; Deans Lst 88-; IM 87-; BS; Crmnl Just; Fed Prob Officer.

**DEAN, JENNIFER L,** Savannah Coll Of Art & Design, Savannah, GA; SO; BFA; Graphic Dsgn; Graphic Dsgn; Graphic/Comm Arts.

**DEAN, KAREN DAWN,** Memphis St Univ, Memphis, TN; SR; BFA; AA Bauder Coll Atlanta 89; Fine Art; Tchr.

**DEAN, KEVIN R,** Samford Univ, Birmingham, AL; GD; JD; Dlgte Natl Mdl UN Stdnt Dir 88; Chrstn Lgl Scty 90; Mltry Jstce Scty; Pi Gamma Mu VP 89; Amer Jrnl Of Trl Advccy 89-; Intrnshp Hon Edward S Smith Jdge 90; US Ct Of Appls For The Fed Crct; Egle Sct By Scts 86; BA Valdosta St Coll 87; AA; Law; Attnry.

**DEAN, LAURIE WYNISE,** Ky St Univ, Frankfort, KY; SO; BA; Chrldr; Txtls/Clthng/Merch; Dept Str Byr.

**DEAN II, MATTHEW E,** Averett Coll, Danville, VA; JR; BS; SG Treas 88-; Bptst Stdnt Un 88-; Pi Kappa Phi Wrdn/Chpln 88-; Stdnt Fndtn Pres 90-; Mssn Stmnt Comm 89-90; Judicl Brd Co-Chr 90-; Y Kelly Schlr 90-; Cougar Spirit Awrd 89-90; Psychlgy; Clncl/Cnslng Psychlgy.

**DEAN, MICHELLE T,** Fl St Univ, Tallahassee, FL; GD; MSW; NASW 90-; Scuba Clb 89-; 1st Cls Training 89; Phi Alpha; Phi Alpha; Alpha Tau Omega Swthrt 89; Asstncshp Dean Stdnts Wmns Cncrns 90; Intrnshp Dondon Gardens Latch Key Cnslr 89; Scl Wrk Clncl Trck; PHD Psychology Cnslng.

**DEAN, PAMELA C,** Holyoke Comm Coll, Holyoke, MA; FR; AA; Econ Awrd; Grn Key; Prsdnt EXCEL Cnstrctn Corp; Acctg; CPA.

**DEAN, RHONDA K,** Univ Of Southern Ms, Hattiesburg, MS; SR; BS; State Farm Ins Empl; Psychology.

**DEAN, ROGER KEITH,** Univ Of Nc At Charlotte, Charlotte, NC; SR; BA; Psychlgy Clb 89-; Psi Chi 89-; W Disney Wrld Coll Prog 90; IM Swmng 89; Psychlgy; Soc Psychlgy.

**DEAN, SHALAGH C,** Merrimack Coll, North Andover, MA; FR; BS; Yrbk 90-; Benzene Ring 90-; Entrepeneurial Ntwrk 90-; Deans List 90-; Chem.

**DEAN, STEVEN K,** Western Carolina Univ, Cullowhee, NC; FR; Bio; Optometry.

**DEAN, TIMOTHY A,** Univ Of Al At Huntsville, Huntsville, AL; JR; BS; Coop Edn Stdnt 89-; Selected As NCEA Natl Coll Engrng Awd; All Am Schlr At Lrg Div By USSA; Pi Kappa Alpha 87-88; Coop Stdnt Emplyr SRS Tech; IM Ftbl 87 Bsktbl 88-89; Elect Engrng.

**DEAN, TOMMY S,** Livingston Univ, Livingston, AL; JR; BS; Albm Hstrcl Scty; Pre Law Scty; Phi Eta Sigma Pres; Pi Kappa Phi; Trsts Ldrshp Schlr; Bus Admn; Law.**

**DEAN, TONICA R,** Cincinnati Metropolitan Coll, Cincinnati, OH; Deans List/Pres List; Phi Beta Lambda; Outsdtng Day Student Nominee; Certif Natl Career Inst 89; Certif Fed Tax Serv 89.

**DEAN, TRACI L,** Indiana Univ Of Pa, Indiana, PA; SO; BS; Speech Path/Audio; Speech Ther.

**DEANE, KATHERINE M,** Univ Of Pittsburgh, Pittsburgh, PA; SO; BSN; NSNA Snap; Phi Eta Sigma; Hnry Mcnl Schlrshp 90; Nrsng.

**DEANHOFER, LISA H,** Coll Of Charleston, Charleston, SC; JR; BS; Acctng Asc; Omcrm Delta Kappa 90-; Hnrs Pgm 88-; Rebecca B Herring Acctg Schlp; Acctng; CPA.

**DEAR, JULIE A,** Ms St Univ, Miss State, MS; JR; BS; Clg Reps 90-; Chi Omega 88-; Pres Lst 90; IM 88-90; Bio; Phy Thrpy.

**DEARCHES, CLAUDE K,** Ms Gulf Coast Comm Coll, Perkinston, MS; SO; BA; Delta Club; Phi Beta Kappa; Hnrs Prog; Elec Engrg.

**DEARING, KELLE B,** Valdosta St Coll, Valdosta, GA; SO; BS; All Amer Schlr; Natl Clgte Nrsg Awd; CNA N Fla Jr Clge 89; Nrsg; RN.

**DEARLOVE, TERRENCE A,** City Univ Of Ny Med Evers Coll, Brooklyn, NY; FR.

**DEARMAN, JEREMY K,** Univ Of Southern Ms, Hattiesburg, MS; JR; BA.

**DEARMAN, ROBBIN M,** Univ Of Southern Ms, Hattiesburg, MS; SR; BA; Anthrplgcl Soc 90-; Dns Lst 90-; Pres Lst 89; Htl Nght Adtr 84-; Anthrplgy.

**DEARSTYNE, CAROL J,** Hudson Valley Comm Coll, Troy, NY; FR; AA; AAS Acctg 81; Lbrl Arts/Hstry; Educ.

**DEARTH, JODI L,** Kent St Univ Kent Cmps, Kent, OH; JR; BA; All Cmps Prgmg Bd Flm Chrpsn 90-; Nw Stdnt Orient Instr 90-; NACA Reg Delg 90; Kent St Volgo Grad; USSR Exchg; Hon Coll Schlrshp 88-; Intl Rltns; Frgn Svc.

**DEARTH, NANCY A,** Hillsborough Comm Coll, Tampa, FL; FR; AA; Receptionist; Humanities.

**DEATON, ANGELA MOORE,** Ms St Univ, Miss State, MS; GD; MBA; Coll Rpblcns; Sctch Grd; Union Pgm Cncl; Trnsprtn Clb; Univ Hall Fame; Omicron Delta Kappa; Crdnl Key; Mu Kappa Tau; Phi Eta Sigma; Alpha Lambda Delta; Gamma Beta Pi; Pi Sigma Epsilon; Delta Gamma 86-90; Coll Bus Grad Asstshp; BBA 90; Bus Admin; Mktg.

**DEATON, ANN MICHELLE,** Univ Of Nc At Asheville, Asheville, NC; FR; BA; Thtr 90-; Hnrs Prog 90-; Phi Eta Sigma 90-; Awrd Otstndng Drama Stu 90-; Wrtng Cntst 90-; Drama; Dir Stg/Flm.

**DEATON, BETTY A,** Union Univ, Jackson, TN; SR; BS; Psychlg Socilgy Club; Phi Theta Kappa Recrdng Secty 88-89; Alcoholism Counselor; Social Wrk Psy; MSW.

**DEATON, FRANK J,** Hudson Valley Comm Coll, Troy, NY; SO; AS; Acctg Ofc Key Svcs Corp 89-; Bus Acctg; CPA.

**DEATON, MARK,** Lees Coll, Jackson, KY; SO; BA; ADAPT; Computer Prgrmng.**

**DEAUX, REBECCA LYNN,** Christopher Newport Coll, Newport News, VA; JR; BA; Offcrs Wvs Clb 90-; Grmn Tchr W Germany 89-90; NM Lcnsd Rltr 84-087; Fine Arts; Tchr.

**DEAVERS, MARK G,** Bridgewater Coll, Bridgewater, VA; SO; BS; Debate Clb P 89-; Phi Beta Lambda 90-; Econ Clb 90-; Bus Admin Acctg/Econ; CPA.

**DEAVOURS, DEBORAH R,** Univ Of Al At Birmingham, Birmingham, AL; JR; BS; SGA Pres 74-75; Nurs Cert 75; BSN 89; Nurs Anesthesia; CRNA.

**DEBARBA, ELIZABETH A,** Teikyo Post Univ, Waterbury, CT; JR; BS; Rose Travrig Treas 91; BPW; Quality Assurance Mgr; Mgmnt; Consultant.

**DEBERTOLIS, PATRICIA A,** Mount Saint Mary Coll, Newburgh, NY; SO; BA; BACCHUS Treas 89-; CARE Chrpsn; Clarion Stffwrtr 90-; Hnrs Alliance 90-; Ambssdr Clb 90-; Cmmtt Pstn O Sexual Hrssmnt; Engl/Ed Cert; Thcr.

**DEBISH, TRACY DENISE,** Fl International Univ, Miami, FL; SR; FEA 90-; J Doran Crs Fnd 89-; Var Chldrns Hosp 86; Dns Lst 90; Educ.

**DEBNAM, BRETT A,** Univ Of The Dist Of Columbia, Washington, DC; JR; BA; Acctng Cpa.

**DEBNAM, KELLY G,** James Madison University, Harrisonburg, VA; SR; MSW; Swthrt Chi Phi 89-; BS James Madison Univ; Soc Wrk.

**DEBORDE, MARK A,** Ashland Comm Coll, Ashland, KY; SO; ASOD; Fncl Aid Ofc Wrk/Stdy; Vet Admin; Sci; Optmtry Prvt Prac.

**DEBREE, JEFFREY W,** Univ Of North Fl, Jacksonville, FL; SR; BS; Data Prcsng Mgr Of Edctnl Comm Cr Un; AA Fl Jr Coll 84; Comp Sci; Prgmr.

**DEBROT, JACQUES L,** City Univ Of Ny City Coll, New York, NY; SR; Phi Beta Kappa; Summa Cum Laude; Harvard English Fellow Prize; BA 90; MA; English; Writer Professor.

**DEBSKI, JEFFREY M,** Duquesne Univ, Pittsburgh, PA; SO; BS; Acctng Assn; Phi Eta Sigma 89-; Dns Lst 89-; Westinghouse Co; Acctng Bus; MBA.

**DEBSKI, RICHARD E,** Univ Of Pittsburgh, Pittsburgh, PA; SR; BS; Var March Band 88-; Am Soc Mech Engr 88-; Gold Key 88-; Au Beta Pi 89-; Pi Tau Sigma 89-; Phi Eta Sigma Memb Cmte 87-; Bethany Church 87-; Tchr Asst Engr Dsgn Rsrch Cen/CMU; USAA All Am Schol; Deans List; Mech Engrng; Biomechanics.

**DEBUS, JEFFREY RICHARD,** Hudson Valley Comm Coll, Troy, NY; FR; Hudsonian Wrtr 90-; Pres Lst 90-; By Scts Cb Mstr 89-; Tlcmnctns Tech Bus Ownr 75-90; Math/Physcs; Elec/Tlcmnctn/Eng.

**DECASTRO CARLO, FLOR DE MARIA,** Inter Amer Univ Pr San German, San German, PR; JR; BA; Art Stdnts Assn 90-; Amigos Museo Arte De Ponce; Fine Arts; Artist/Educ.

**DECASTRO, HECTOR J,** Inter Amer Univ Pr Hato Rey, Hato Rey, PR; GD; MBA; Amer Mrktng Assc; BA; Bus Adm/Mrktng; Finance/Mrktng.

**DECHANT, LAURA M,** Neumann Coll, Aston, PA; FR; BS; Hnr Prog 90; Nrsng.

**DECHENE, TRACI ALLEN,** Univ Of Nh Plymouth St Coll, Plymouth, NH; JR; BA; Blknp Plnng Brd 89; Erly Chldhd Clb; Kappa Delta Pi Hstrn 90-; Fld Hcky; Harriet Faunce Trst Schlrshp 88-; Frgn Lngge Dept Fllwshp 90-; Pres Lst; Schlr Atlte 89; Erly Chldhd Educ Physclgy; Prfssnl Chld Care.

**DECHENT, MARY C,** Lenoir Rhyne Coll, Hickory, NC; SR; BA; Fools Christ Sec 90; Sign Trp 89; Chplns Cncl 87-89; Early Chldhd Educ; Tchr.

**DECHRISTOPHER, CAROLYN,** Atlantic Comm Coll, Mays Landing, NJ; JR; BA; Provdnc Hs 90-; Deans List The Art Inst Of Phila; AA 90; Psychlgy/Soc Wrk; Jvnl Dlngncy.

**DECKER, ANN AUSTIN,** Memphis St Univ, Memphis, TN; SO; BA; Memphis Ad Fed/The Amer Cancer Soc; Acct Exec; Marketing.

**DECKER, BRENDA L,** Le Moyne Coll, Syracuse, NY; SR; BS; Bsns Clb 90-; Mrktng Clb 90-; AS Cayuga Comm Clg 88; Bsns Admn.

**DECKER, CARLA J,** Owensboro Jr Coll Of Bus, Owensboro, KY; FR; AA; Hon List; Med Off Asst.

**DECKER, DAWN M,** S U N Y Coll Of Tech At Alfred, Alfred, NY; FR; AAS Olean Business Inst 79; Exec Sec; Cvl Srvce.

**DECKER, EARL N,** Tn Temple Univ, Chattanooga, TN; GD; BS; Alpha Epsilon Theta; GA Mental Hlth HST 89-; Psych.

**DECKER, HERBERT M,** Nova Univ, Ft Lauderdale, FL; GD; MBA; Jr Achvmnt 85-88; Instrmnt Soc America; BS Rtgers 74; Mgmnt.

**DECKER, RANDY C,** Cornell Univ Statutory College, Ithaca, NY; SR; BS; Tau Epsilon Phi Almni Chrmn 89-; Educ.

**DECKER, SHAWNA L,** Marshall University, Huntington, WV; SO; BS; I M 90-; Gamma Bea Phi 90; Phi Eta Sigma 90-; Math/French Educ; Tch.

**DECKER, SYDNEY R,** Eckerd Coll, St Petersburg, FL; SR; BA; Campus Tour Guide 87-; Stdnt Amb 88-; Co-Curr Coord 87-90; Omicron Delta Kappa 88-; Deans Lst 87-; Voters Reg Deputy Reg 87-; Omicron Delta Kappa VP 88-; Spcl Talent Awrd 87-; Church/Campus Schlr 87-; Como Perf Co Dancer 88-90; Intl Bus; Ma Intl Mngmnt.

**DECKLER, TAMMY L,** Oh St Univ At Marion, Marion, OH; SO; BED; Lit Mag Co-Ed 89-; SGA Ldrshp 90-; Envnmtl Cl 90-; Phi Eta Sigma 89-; Alpha Lambda Delta 89-; Griffin Soc 89-; Marion YMCA 89-; Tour Gde 89-; Sci Fair Judge/Help 90-; Albert Schweitzer Colloquium 89-90; Bilngl Elem Ed; Bilngl Tchr.

**DECKOP, KEVIN J,** Hilbert Coll, Hamburg, NY; FR; MBA; Soccer 90; Southline Fire Co Vol; Acctng; CPA.

**DECLERCQ, KAREN A,** Univ Of Toledo, Toledo, OH; GD; JD; Phi Kappa Phi 89-; Hons Schlrshp 89-90; Amer Jurisprdnc Awd 90-; De Arce Koch Schlrshp 90-; Prestg Schlrshp Awd; RN Chrg Nrs In Acute Cornry Cr Unit 75-; BS 90; Law.

**DECOWSKI, NOELLE M,** Coll Misericordia, Dallas, PA; FR; BS; CMSOTA 90-; IM; Occup Ther.

**DECROO, NICOLE L,** Indiana Univ Of Pa, Indiana, PA; JR; BS; Red Cross Lifeguard Intr 86-; Delta Gamm VP Pledge Ed; Math; Tchr Secondary Level.

**DEDDA, GABRIELLA,** Villanova Univ, Villanova, PA; SO; BA; Italian Clb; Delta Delta Delta Spnsr Chrmn; Spec Olympcs Asst Ofcr; Economics.

**DEDE, EDGAR K,** Wv Univ, Morgantown, WV; SO; BS; Arspc Eng; Eng.

**DEDERICK, HEATHER L,** Clarkson Univ, Potsdam, NY; SO; BS; Mrktng/Tech Cmmnctns; Pbl Rel.

**DEDGE, BETTY S,** Anne Arundel Comm Coll, Arnold, MD; SO; BS; Phi Theta Kappa 90-; Acad Achiev Awd 90-; Pres Merit Schlrshp Towson State Univ MD; AA; Acctg; Fnc.

**DEDIOS, SEVERIANO,** City Univ Of Ny City Coll, New York, NY; SR; BA; NYPIRG Sml Clms Crt Actn Cntr CCNY 87; Italian Amrcn Stdnt Assn 86-90; Kappa Delta Rho Temple Unvrsty 88; Gnrl Mtrs Schlrshp 90; Ntnl Mdl Untd Ntns Hnrbl Mntn 89; CCNY 87-89; Pltcl Sci; Law Tchng.

**DEDMAN, JAMES D,** Southern Coll Of Tech, Marietta, GA; SR; BA; City Sftbl/Bsktbl 88-; Bapt Stdnt Union 88-; Phi Eta Sigma 87-; Co-Op 88-90; IM Bsktbl 89-90; Elctrcl Engr; Engr.

**DEE, LEOPOLD,** Univ Of Miami, Coral Gables, FL; FR; BBA; Bus Admin; Entrepreneur.

**DEE, RENIDA,** Alcorn St Univ, Lorman, MS; SO; BS; Pro-Nrsng Clb 89-; Hon Stdnt Org 90-; US Achvmnt Acdmy 90-; Deans Lst 90-; Pres Lst; Nrsng; Pediatrcs Nrs.

**DEE, SALLY A,** Commonwealth Coll, Virginia Beach, VA; SR; Fun Runs/Volunteer For Homeless Shelters.

**DEEB, CHRISTINE M,** Western New England Coll, Springfield, MA; SR; Plymth Hall Pres 89; Hall Assoc Pres; Gate Way Pres 90; Lambd Dlt 89; Stdnt Lf Awrd 89; Internship Hamilton Standard; Acctg.

**DEEDS, CHRISTA L,** Appalachian Bible Coll, Bradley, WV; SO; BA; Chorale 89-; Elem Ed; Tchng Elem Schl.

**DEEL, PATRICK S,** Columbus St Comm Coll, Columbus, OH; SR; AAS; Mktng; Advtng.**

**DEEM, LAURA R,** Livingston Univ, Livingston, AL; JR; BS; Sprts Mdcn Clb Treas 90-; Psychlgy Clb Treas 90-; Flwshp Chrstn Athlts 89-; Robert Gilbert Wrtng Awd 88; Swede O Unvrsl Schlrshp; Vlybl/Ftbl 90-; Cert Bsc Emrgncy Mdcl Tchncn 90-; Athltc Trng; Cert Athltc Trnr Hgh Schl/Clnc.

**DEEM JR, RICHARD M,** Washington State Comm Coll, Marietta, OH; FR; ASSOC; Amer Hrt Assn Wash Cnty Ems Assn; Warren Twp Vol Fire Dept; 17 Yrs Kardey Sys Inc 74-90; 17 Yrs Firemn; 16 Yrs Emt 74-; Fire Inst 85-; Nrsng.

**DEEN, SUE-ELLEN,** Daytona Beach Comm Coll, Daytona Beach, FL; SO; BA; Phi Theta Kappa; Fdng Pgm Hmls Vol 90; Mssns Otrch Wld Chlng Hmls NYC 89; Dns Lst 89; Pres Lst 90-; Cnlsr Yths Chrst 90; Mgrnt Wrkrs Mnstry Vol 89; Psy; Cnlsr.

**DEERE, PAULA R,** Middle Tn St Univ, Murfreesboro, TN; SO; BSN; LPN; Nrsng Sci.

**DEERING, DE SHAWN N,** Saint Johns River Comm Coll, Palatka, FL; SO; BA; Black Union Treas 90-; Schl Nwspr 90-; AA; Poli Sci; Law.

**DEERING, GAIA A,** Southern Vt Coll, Bennington, VT; SR; BSW; Afrmtv Actn/Sexl Hrsmnt Rep 89-; LGBA 88-; Hnrs Comm Stu 90-; Scl Wrk; Grad Sch.

**DEES, CANDY L,** Univ Of South Al, Mobile, AL; JR; BS; Phi Mu 89-; Elem Educ.

**DEES, DEBBIE A,** Ms St Univ, Miss State, MS; SR; BS; Educ Psych; Cnslg.

**DEES, SUSAN DONNETTE,** Ms Gulf Coast Comm Coll, Perkinston, MS; FR; Hons Pgm; Dance Tm Capt; Banking/Fin; Corp Law.

**DEES, TERESA E,** Faulkner St Jr Coll, Bay Minette, AL; SO; BA; Phi Theta Kappa; Deans List; Pres List; Nrsng.

**DEES, VIRGINIA A,** Ms St Univ, Miss State, MS; JR; BA; Stdnt Assoc Govtl Affairs Comm 89-90; Canterbury Episcopal Fllwshp Grp Ldr 89-; Activities Brd Div Hd 90-; Stdnt Assoc Asstnt Atty Genl 90; Pre Law Scty 90-; Stndng Comm Pblctns Brd Comm Vice Elctns; Presidents Schlr 90; Wash Ctr Intrnshp; Political Sci; Law.

**DEESE, CRYSTAL S,** Winthrop Coll, Rock Hill, SC; JR; BA; Karen Zaman/Assoc Legal Asst 88-; AS Central Piedmont Comm Coll 90; Pol Sci; Atty.

**DEESE, DAMON M,** Valdosta St Coll, Valdosta, GA; SO; BA; Acctng; Law.

**DEESE, JAN M,** Abraham Baldwin Agri Coll, Tifton, GA; SO; AASAA; BSU 89-; Criminal Justice; Georgia Wildlife Fed 90-; Wakulla Co Horsemans Assn 89-; Crmnl Justice/Art.

**DEESE, JEANNA L,** Catawba Valley Comm Coll, Hickory, NC; GD; SSN; Cmrcl Art; Ads.

**DEESE, JULIE M,** Univ Of Montevallo, Montevallo, AL; SR; BS; Cmps Otrch 89-; Pnhllnc Assn Pres; Lambda Sigma Pi; Chi Omega Pnhllnc 90-; Elem Educ; Tchr.

**DEESE, KENDAL M,** Fl St Univ, Tallahassee, FL; FR; PR Com GCLC 90; PR Com Hmcmng 90; Deans Lst; Pi Beta Phi 90-.

**DEESE, MARY O,** Chesterfield Marlboro Coll, Cheraw, SC; SO; AAS; Comp Prog; Educ.

**DEESE, RALPH L,** Fayetteville St Univ, Fayetteville, NC; SR; BS; Orien Ldr 89-; Peer Cnslr 90-; Human Rael Cncl; Beta Kappa Chi 90-; Kappa Delta Pi 90-; Alpha Kappa Mu 90-; Stdnt Advsry Dsplnry Comm 90; Dns Lst 88-; Outstdng Acad Achvmnt; Psychlgy Intrnshp; Psychlgy; Ph D Clin Psychlgy.

**DEETS, SHERI A,** Va Commonwealth Univ, Richmond, VA; GD; BS; Paid Intern VA Assc Of Broadcasters 90; Mass Comm/Brdcst Jrnlsm; Radio Ancr/Newsprsn.

**DEFENDINI-RODIGUEZ, LOURDES M,** Inter Amer Univ Pr San Juan, Hato Rey, PR; GD; JD; ANED 89-; CED 90-; Jlaw Rv 90-; Dean Lst 89-; Magna Cum Laude; Awrd Bst Stdnt 87; BA Univ PR 87; Hmnts; Law.

**DEFFREN, JULIE A,** Univ Of Cin R Walters Coll, Blue Ash, OH; FR; BA; Deans Lst; Bus Admin; Acctg.

**DEFRIES, DAVID J,** Univ Of Richmond, Richmond, VA; FR; BA; Phi Delta Theta 90-; Natl Mrt; Hstry; Law.

**DEGANUS, ADADE A,** Univ Of Md At Eastern Shore, Princess Anne, MD; FR; BS; Afrcn Asc; Tnns; Agri/Bsn; Bnkng.

**DEGEN, JAMES B,** Univ Of Akron, Akron, OH; SR; BS; AICHE Reg Conf Purdue Univ; Intnshp W/I Ind; Chem Engg; Law.

**DEGENHARDT, DONNA R,** Univ Of Pittsburgh, Pittsburgh, PA; JR; BS; Otdrs Clb 90-; Carnegie Lbry 90-; Intrn Alghny Cnty Dept Spcl Serv/Mntnc Oprtns; ASCP 83-; IIE Tres 90-; Med Lab Tech 85-; AAS 83; Cert 81; Indstrl Engr.

**DEGENHART, GAIL M,** Univ Of Sc At Columbia, Columbia, SC; JR; BA; Assn Hnr Stdnts 88-; Mbr SC Coll USC Hnrs Coll 88-; SC Coll Acdmc Schlrshp 88-; Wmns Vrsty Golf Tm 88-90; Accntng; CPA.

**DEGIULE, BERNHARDT D,** Hudson Valley Comm Coll, Troy, NY; SO; ABET; Tau Alpha Pi; AAS; Electronics.

**DEGLI, JENNIE L,** Coll Of Charleston, Charleston, SC; SO; Alph Adelta Pi; Hghly Dstngshd Hnrs Lst; Dstngshd Hnrs Lst 90; Almn Assoc Schlrshp; Elem Ed.

**DEGLOW, CHERYL,** Northern Ky Univ, Highland Hts, KY; JR; BSW; Fine Arts; Cincinnati Botanical & Zoological Society; Parent Teachers Org; Social Work; Licensed Social Worker.

**DEHAAN, KATHRYN E,** City Univ Of Ny Med Evers Coll, Brooklyn, NY; JR; BS; Legal Sec 86-; Mngmnt.

**DEHANEY, DONALD R,** Coppin St Coll, Baltimore, MD; JR; BA; Mngmnt Science; Bsn.

**DEHLITSCH, NICOLE L,** Morgan St Univ, Baltimore, MD; JR; BA; Elec Engrg.

**DEHN, BETSY J,** Casco Bay Coll, Portland, ME; FR; AS; Acctng.

**DEHNER, CYNTHIA A,** Cumberland Coll, Williamsburg, KY; SR; Flwshp Chrstn Athlts 90-; BED; Elem Ed; Tchr.

**DEIBEL, LEANN C,** Univ Of Akron, Akron, OH; JR; Golden Key 90-; Kappa Delta Pi; Ed.

**DEIBLER, CATHERINE J,** D Youville Coll, Buffalo, NY; GD; Campus Mnstry 87-88; Stdnt Assoc 88-89; Stdnt Physical Thrpy Assoc 87-88; Lambda Sigma 88-89; Natl Honor Scty 86-; Outstndng Stdnts Amrca; Physical Thrpy.

**DEICHMANN JR, CHARLES F,** Embry Riddle Aeronautical Univ, Daytona Beach, FL; SR; AAS; Frmn 85-; AOS Alfred State Coll 85; Avtn Mtnce; Mgmt.

**DEILY, KRISTINE,** Alfred Univ, Alfred, NY; FR; Frshmn Rsdnt Hall Gvrnmnt Prsdnt 90-; Dance Co 90-; Chrldng 90-; Alpha Kappa Omicron; Ldrshp Wrkshop; IM Sccr 90-; Biology; Med.

**DEINHART, LYNN M,** Hilbert Coll, Hamburg, NY; FR; AA; PWP 90-; PTA Eden Ele 90-; Human Serv; Soc Welfare.

**DEINHART, STACI L,** S U N Y Coll At Fredonia, Fredonia, NY; JR; BED; Dorm Cncl Soc Chrmn 90-; Tchrs Edn Clb 90-; Co-Ed Sports IM Partcptnt 88-; Elem Edn; Tchr.

**DEIS, THOMAS A,** Univ Of Pittsburgh, Pittsburgh, PA; SR; BS; AM Ceramic Scty 90; ASM Intrntnal 88; TMS 88; Otstndng Senior; Grad Sch Eng Rsrch Fellowship; BS; Material Science; Grad Sch Eng.

**DEISE, JENNIFER A,** Radford Univ, Radford, VA; SO; Circle K; Alpha Lambda Delta; Info Sys Mgt.

**DEITZ, LAURA D,** Meridian Comm Coll, Meridian, MS; SO; BS; Ldrshp Effctvnss/Dvlpmn Prog 90-; Phi Theta Kappa Exec Brd/Hist 90-; Med Lab Tech.

**DEKLE, JENNIFER S,** Univ Of Miami, Coral Gables, FL; SO; BS; Pgm Cncl; Concert Choir Pblcty 90-; Wmns Choir 89-90; Delta Gamma Pldge Class Pres 89-90; Dns Lst 90; Hnrs Stdnt 89-90; J W Pearson Acad Schlrshp 89-; Cmnctn/Psych; Mgmt.

**DEL BENE, ALLISON MARIE,** Anne Arundel Comm Coll, Arnold, MD; JR; AD; SPCA; Nrsg.

**DEL C ZAYAS, MILDRED,** Univ Politecnica De Pr, Hato Rey, PR; JR; BA; Calasanz HS Sec 87; Leos Club; Lions Club; Sci; Indus Engr.

**DEL CARMEN, ALEJANDRO,** Fl International Univ, Miami, FL; SR; BS; Alpha Phi Sigma 90-; Acad Crim Just Sci; Intrnshp Hialeah Pol Dept 90; AA Miami Dade Comm Clg 89; Crim Just; Law.

**DEL FAVERO, ANDREA R,** Univ Of Sc At Columbia, Columbia, SC; SO; BS; Baker Res Hll Govt Pres 90-; Mrchng Bnd 89-; Peer Cndct Brd; Delta Sigma Pi VP; NJ Lic Intern Mortuary Sci 90-; Pldg Sem 90; Dean Lst 90; Bus Admn; Fnrl Dir.**

**DEL FAVERO, JILL A,** City Univ Of Ny Queensbrough, New York, NY; SR; Tau Alpha Pi VP 90-; Phi Theta Kappa 89-; Col John C Lackas Awd 91; AAS Queensbrgh Comm Coll; Comp Eng Tchnlgy; Elect Eng.

**DEL GRECO, STEPHEN A,** Univ Of Nc At Asheville, Asheville, NC; JR; BS; Amer Metrlgcl Soc Stdnt Chptr 90-; Stdnt Govt Sen 88-89; Prof Assn Diving Inst 85-; Mastr Scuba Dvng Inst; Pres Emplymnt Natl Oceangrphc Atsmphrc Assn 90-; AA St Pete Jr Clg Clrwtr Fl 90; Atmsphrc Sci; Phd Tch Univ.

**DEL GROSSO, RICHARD,** City Univ Of Ny City Coll, New York, NY; SR; BA; Phi Theta Kappa 82; Alpha Sigma Lambda; Engl; Ed.

**DEL PADRE, HEATHER G,** Teikyo Post Univ, Waterbury, CT; SO; MBA; Mst Pts Ernd Intrcoll Hrs Shwng 89-90; Intrcoll Hrs Shwng 89-; Pre-Vet; Vtrnrn.

**DEL PIZZO, DENNIS DANIEL,** Dowling Coll, Oakdale Li, NY; SO; Acctng.

**DEL POPOLO, ERIKA D,** Kutztown University Of Penna, Kutztown, PA; FR; BED; Reading; Tchr.

**DEL PRINCE, KATHLEEN M,** Columbus Coll Of Art & Design, Columbus, OH; SR; United Way Man To Man Woman To Woman 89-90; Sccr Clb 87 89; BFA; Book Illustration.

**DEL RIO MORA, ALEXANDER,** Univ Politecnica De Pr, Hato Rey, PR; GD; Math; Elect Eng.

**DEL RIO JR, LUIS RAUL,** Radford Univ, Radford, VA; SR; BA; Pol Sci Scty 90-; Hse Cncl Flr Rep 87; Intrgovt Cncl Stdnt Rep 90-; IM Sccr 90-; Pol Sci; Govt Law.

**DEL ROSARIO, JAYNE,** Anne Arundel Comm Coll, Arnold, MD; SO; BA; Serv Clb VP 90-; Ft Tchrs Clb Presi Hnrrm Awd; Engl; Educ.

**DEL SONNO, SCOTT T,** Daytona Beach Comm Coll, Daytona Beach, FL; FR; BA; Math; Archtctr.

**DEL VALLE MOJICA, KIOMARIE,** Univ Politecnica De Pr, Hato Rey, PR; SO.

**DEL VALLE, DANIEL A,** Suffolk Comm Coll Selden Cmps, Selden, NY; SO; BS; Adlnte Fo Sfflk Cnty Brd 90; La Union Hspna Brd Sec 90-; NYS Dvsn Hmn Rghts Brd 90; Frnch Clb VP 83; Assn Of Bilngl Chem Dpndnce Cnslrs Chr 89-; Otstndng Mnrty Stdnt; Cltn Fr Prvntn Of Alchlsm And Othr Chem Dpndncs 90-; CAC; Hlth Scis; Nrsng Scl Wrk Mntl Hlth.

**DEL VALLE, NORIE,** Fl International Univ, Miami, FL; FR; BA; Engl; Pblshng.

**DEL VALLE-EMMANUELLI, ANTONIO L,** Univ Of Pr At Rio Piedras, Rio Piedras, PR; JR; BS; Pre Med Stdnts Assn 90-; Beta Beta Beta 90-; Phi Sigma Alpha Beta Chptr 89-; Schl Natl Sci Dns Lst 90-; Bio; Dentistry.

**DEL VECCHIO, FRANCINE E,** Savannah Coll Of Art & Design, Savannah, GA; SO; BFA; Fiber Arts Clb 90-; Effing Schlrshp 90; Fiber/Txtl Dsgn Photo.

**DEL VISCIO, JOHN A,** Providence Coll, Providence, RI; FR; BS; Ski Clb; IM Bsktbl; Chem.

**DEL-SETTE III, HERMES W,** Schenectady County Comm Coll, Schenectady, NY; FR; BA; Telecommunications.

**DEL-VALLE-LOPEZ, PEDRO A,** Univ Of Pr At Rio Piedras, Rio Piedras, PR; GD; MLS; Lbry Info Science Cncl Pres 89-; Mcrcmptrs Lab TA 90-; BS 88; Lbry/Info Science; Info Science.

**DELA CRUZ, LIEZL A,** Columbia Coll, Columbia, SC; JR; BA; Yrbk 90-; Cultural Diversities Com 90-; Alpha Lambda Delta 89-; Omicron Delta Kappa; Chi Beta Phi Sec 90-; Wrld Poetry Gold/ Silver Poet 89-; Deans Lst 89-; Vlybl 89-90; Bio Pre-Med; Medicine.**

**DELACOTTE, STEPHANE L,** City Univ Of Ny Baruch Coll, New York, NY; JR; BBA; Finance; Invstmnt Banking.

**DELAFUENTE, TANIA M,** Radford Univ, Radford, VA; JR; BS; Early Edctn; Tchng.

**DELAHOUSSAYE, JAMES DARRIN,** Morehouse Coll, Atlanta, GA; SR; BA; Natl Soc Blck Eng 87-; Big Bro Big Sis 88-; Frederick Douglas Ttrl Prog 88-; Delco Moraine NDH GMC Intern 89-; Physc; Mech Eng.

**DELAINE, DEBRA D,** Tuskegee Univ, Tuskegee Inst, AL; SR; MS; Alpha Phi Alpha 86-; Florida Clb; Res Prgrmmng Asst 89-; BS; Psych.

**DELAINE, JULENE R,** Livingston Univ, Livingston, AL; SR; Matrons Pres 89-; Kinter Cush Distr Wmn Conv Fld Wrkr.

**DELANCY, PATRICIA M,** Coll Of Charleston, Charleston, SC; FR; Amnesty Intl Campus Grp 90-; Hons Pgm 90-; Anc Hist; Educ.

**DELANEY, ANN L,** Dowling Coll, Oakdale Li, NY; GD; MSED; Kappa Delta Pi; Acdmc Hnr Schrlshp 89-90; Grl Scts Ldr 90-; Yth Dev Corp Rdng Tutor 89-90; Bkkpr/Accntnt; AAS Suffolk Cnty Comm Clg 89; Bs 90; Ed; Tchr/Accnt.

**DELANEY, ANNETTE,** Villanova Univ, Villanova, PA; SO; BA; Delta Gamma 89-; Vrsty Bsktbl 89-; Commnctns; Sprts Brdcstg.

**DELANEY, LISA A,** Univ Of The Dist Of Columbia, Washington, DC; JR; BA; Hnrs Prog 88; Cert Acad Excel 90-; Dns Lst Awd 90-; Wash Cnsltng Grp Inc 90-; Acctng; CPA.

**DELANEY, LOLO M,** Schenectady County Comm Coll, Schenectady, NY; SR; LPN; Phi Pheta Kappa; EMT 2 SCCC; Aos 1 SCCC; Nursing.

**DELANEY, SHERYL M,** Erie Comm Coll, Buffalo, NY; GD; AS; Phi Theta Kappa Treas 90-; Sci; Chrprctc.

**DELANO, GINA M,** S U N Y Coll Of Tech At Alfred, Alfred, NY; SR; AAS; Karate 89-90; Stu Tutor; Crt Rprtg.

**DELANY, MARGARET A,** Univ Of Cincinnati-Clrmnt Coll, Batavia, OH; SO; BA; Auxier Schlrshp 90-; Chrtr Oak Flr Cvrng Bkkpr 84-; Acctg; CPA.

**DELARGY, KAREN J,** Molloy Coll, Rockville Ctr, NY; JR; BS; Scnc Club Treas 90-/88-; Fourrager Awds 4 Consctv Smstrs Deans List 88-90; Mens Bsktbl Mgr/State 90-; Intrdscplnry Stds/Scnc.

**DELEKTA, ANNE P,** Kent St Univ Kent Cmps, Kent, OH; SR; BA; Fencing 89-; Prog Bd 87-89; Stdnts For Peace 87-88; Alpha Lambda Delta; Sigma Tau Delta; Pi Gamma Mu; Anthroplgy Awd; Golden Key 90; Anthropology; Prof/MA Phd.

**DELEO, JOHN C,** S U N Y Coll Of Tech At Alfred, Alfred, NY; FR; Photo Clb 90; Sigma Tau Epsilon; Electrns; Elec Tech.

**DELESLINE, CHARLENE K,** Wilberforce Univ, Wilberforce, OH; SO; BA; ROTC 89; Sigma Omega 89; Sigma 90; Bsktbl 90; Psychlgy.

**DELGADILLO, ELIZABETH V,** Miami Dade Comm Coll South, Miami, FL; SO; BA; Phi Theta Kappa Offcr Comm Serv; Awd Co-Op Educ Cmpltn 90; Tlnt Rstr Cert Achvmnt; Outstndng Achvmnt; Bus; Info/Mgmt Sci.

**DELGADILLO, MARINA,** Fl St Univ, Tallahassee, FL; SR; BA; Ad Clb 89-; Untd Ltn Soc 89-; Gldn Key 90-; Phi Theta Kappa 87-88; Tinsley Adv; Grad Magna Cum Laude; Dns Lst; AA Miami Dade Comm Clg 88; Adv/Comm; Grad Schl.

**DELGADO CABALLERO, JOSE M,** Univ Politecnica De Pr, Hato Rey, PR; SO; BS; Sci; Mech Engr.**

**DELGADO MORALES, FRANCISCO J,** Univ Of Pr At Rio Piedras, Rio Piedras, PR; SR; BA; Hon Stdnt 90-; Architecture Dsgn.

**DELGADO RIVERA, VILMARIE,** Univ Of Pr At Rio Piedras, Rio Piedras, PR; SR; Acctg; CPA.

**DELGADO ROMERO, DENISE,** Inter Amer Univ Pr San German, San German, PR; SR; BS; Tri Beta 90-; Intrnshp Smmr Mnrty Accss To Rsrch Trng 90; Asst Rsrchr 90; Intrnshp Rsrch Inst Of Intramer Univ Of PR 89; Blgy; Elem Schl Tchr.

**DELGADO, AITSSA N,** Fl International Univ, Miami, FL; SR; BS; FEA 90-; AA Miami Dade Comm Coll 89; Educ; Elem Tchr.

**DELGADO, ALAIN,** Univ Of Miami, Coral Gables, FL; SR; BS; Hsptl Vlntr 89-; Biology; Mdcl Dctr.

**DELGADO, CHRISTINE M,** Fl International Univ, Miami, FL; JR; FEA 90-; Dns Lst 88-; Elem Ed; Edtr.

**DELGADO, ELIZABETH,** City Univ Of Ny Baruch Coll, New York, NY; SR; BBA; Deans Lst NY City Tech 87; Deans Lst; AAS NY City Tech Coll 87; Comp Info Syst.

**DELGADO, MICHAEL ANTHONY,** City Univ Of Ny City Coll, New York, NY; SR; BSEE; Elec Eng Stdtn Assn Stdnt Rep 87-88; Caribbean Stdnt Assn 88-F Golden Key 90-; Tau Beta Pi; Eta Kappa Nu; Pgm Rtntn Eng Stdnt Tutr 89-; Seek Rsrch Fndtn Tutr 89-; City Coll Pro Prep Tm Ldr 90-; EE Cert Coll Art/Sc/ Tech 85-88; Elec Eng.

**DELGADO, REINALDO,** Miami Dade Comm Coll, Miami, FL; JR; BS; Ftr Edctrs Amer 89-90; Cmps Nwspr 90-; Engl Ed; Tchng/Cnmtgrphy.

**DELGADO, ROBERTO J,** Hillsborough Comm Coll, Tampa, FL; FR; AA; AA; Biology; Phrmcy.

**DELGROSS, KURT D,** Kent St Univ Kent Cmps, Kent, OH; SR; BA; Weight Club Mgr 89-; Deans List 90; Otstndng Ldrshp Awd Stdnt Actvts 89-90; Otstndng IM Employee Awd 89-90; Bodybuilding Champ; Psych; Corp Fitness Or Spts Psych.

**DELGROSSO, ANNETTE,** D Youville Coll, Buffalo, NY; SO; BSW; Scl Wrk Assoc V P; Fmly Chldrns Serv; Scl Wrk.

**DELISLE, ANGELIQUE E,** Holyoke Comm Coll, Holyoke, MA; SO; BA; Green Key; Deans Lst 90; Nurs Asst 88-89; Ele Educ.

**DELISLE, LYNN E,** Central Fl Comm Coll, Ocala, FL; SO; AA; Retail Sls Mgr U S Shoe Corp; Ele Educ; Tch.

**DELL ANGELO, TABITHA,** Atlantic Comm Coll, Mays Landing, NJ; FR; AA; Educ; Tchng.

**DELLA GIUSTINA, MAUREEN E,** Western New England Coll, Springfield, MA; FR; BS; Alpha Lambda Delta; Acctng; Intl Bus.

**DELLAMORA, ELIZABETH R,** Oh Wesleyan Univ, Delaware, OH; JR; BA; Cncl Stdnt Affrs 88-90; Fd Comm Sec 89-90; Camps Pgm Brd Sec 88-89; Dns Lst 90; Schlr Hnr Stdnt 88-; Kappa Delt A Pi; Delta Gamma Rec Sec; IM; Var Swmng Capt 88-; Elem Educ; Elem Schl Tchr.

**DELLAROSE, LAURIE A,** Duquesne Univ, Pittsburgh, PA; JR; BS; Cls VP 88-; Tour Guide; Phi Lambda Sigma 90-; Phi Kappa Phi 90-; Lambda Kappa Sigma Chrmn 89-; Lctr St James R C Chrch 85-; Thrft Drug Intrn 90-; Swmg 90-; Phrmcy.

**DELLARTE, SUZANNE E,** Marywood Coll, Scranton, PA; JR; BFA; Art Clb 89-90; Delta Epsilon Sigma 90-; Dns Lst 88-; Illust.

**DELLECAVE, RHODA A,** Marywood Coll, Scranton, PA; JR; BS; Kappa Mu Epsilon 90-; AS 88; Math; Tchr.

**DELLERBA, AMY M,** Newbury Coll, Brookline, MA; FR; AS; Fash Merch.

**DELLICARRI, JEANNE,** Villanova Univ, Villanova, PA; SO; BA; Alpha Chi Omega Pnhlnc Dlgte; Hstry/Popltcl Sci; Law.

**DELLIGATTI, SCOTT R,** Univ Of Pittsburgh, Pittsburgh, PA; SR; MBA; Pi Tau Sigma Pres 89-; Golden Key 89-; Intrn Westinghouse 90; Assoc Westmoreland Comm Clg 84; Engr; Dsgn.

**DELLINGER, CARI C,** Longwood Coll, Farmville, VA; SO; BFA; Vrsty Bsktbl; Art/Grphc Dsgn; Art.

**DELLINGER, MICHELLE D,** Univ Of Nc At Charlotte, Charlotte, NC; FR; BA; Acctng.

**DELLINGER, SALLIE J,** Univ Of Tn At Knoxville, Knoxville, TN; JR; Christian Stdnt Ctr 88-; Chorale 89; Phi Eta Sigma 88-89; Gamma Beta Phi 89-; Golden Key 90-; Phi Kappa Phi; Beta Alpha Psi 90-; Gamma Sigma Sigma 89-90; IMS Vlybl Ftbl Co Capt 88-; Acctng; CPA.

**DELLINGER, TIMOTHY C,** Gaston Coll, Dallas, NC; SO; BS; Art; Cmrcl Art/Grphc Dsgn.

**DELLIQUARDRI, MARIA L,** Univ Of Pittsburgh, Pittsburgh, PA; JR; BSA; Pre-Law Soc 90-; Prism 89-; Gldn Key 90-; Exxon Exclnc Awd; Info Sci; High Tech/Cmptr Law.

**DELLOSO, MICHELLE M,** Univ Of Sc At Columbia, Columbia, SC; SR; BS; Sprts Admn Clb 88-; NCAA All Amer Sftbl 88-; Olympc Fstvl Gold Mdlst 88-90; Div I Sftbl Plyr Capt 88-; Practicum Raybestos Bzakettes 89-90; Sprts Admn; Athletic Mgmt/Mktg.

**DELMANTO, JANINE R,** Georgian Court Coll, Lakewood, NJ; GD; PH D; Mndl Soc Treas 88-89; Pre Med Clb 89-; Deans Lst 89-; Flwshp Grad Schl UMDNT; Flwshp Undrgrad Smmr Rsrch Univ Med/Dntstry NJ 90; BS; Pthlgy; Rsrch Scntst.

**DELMONTE, JENNIFER M,** Lasell Coll, Newton, MA; FR; AS; Soccer 90; Fashion Bd; Honor Lst 90; Fashion Merch; Fashion Dsgnr.

**DELNUOVO, LISA A,** Fl Atlantic Univ, Boca Raton, FL; JR; BA; Pi Kappa Phi 88; Hon Rl 89-90; Deans Lst 89-90; Pres Lst 90; Bus Mgmt; Envrnmntl Law.

**DELONG, STEPHANIE A,** Radford Univ, Radford, VA; JR; BS; Early/Middle Ed; Tch Elem/Middle Schl.

**DELOZIER, DEBRA J,** George Mason Univ, Fairfax, VA; SR; BSED; Stdnt VA Educ Assn 89-; Kappa Delta Pi 90-; Golden Key 90-.

**DELP, CHRISTINA L,** Radford Univ, Radford, VA; FR; MBA; Bus; Acctg.

**DELP, JANE E,** Univ Of Md Baltimore Prof Schl, Baltimore, MD; SR; BS; Stdnt Amer Dntl Hygiene Assn; Dntl Hygiene.

**DELPH, RODERICK E,** Morehouse Coll, Atlanta, GA; JR; BA; Re Law Soc 88-; English Clb 88-; Morehouse Bus Assn 88-; Hon Rl 88-; Deans Hon 88-; F Douglass Tutrl Prog 88-89; Big Bros/ Strs Atlanta 88-89; Res Asst 90-; English; Corp Law.

**DELPRETE, CATHERINE M,** Villanova Univ, Villanova, PA; FR; BA; Spec Olympics 90-; Alpha Chi Omega 90-.

**DELUCA, CLAUDINE C,** City Univ Of Ny Baruch Coll, New York, NY; GD; BBA; Ldr 89; Am Mrktng Assoc 89-90; Deans List 89-; Carter Wallace Intrnshp; Bay Ridge Amb Org 86-87; Mrktng Mgmt.

**DELUCA, MELISSA M,** Oh St Univ, Columbus, OH; SR; BA; Hall Govt Pblcst 88-89; RA 89-90; Gldn Ky 89-; Phi Kappa Phi 90-; Conf Hsng Asst 88-; Acdmnc Exclnc Schlrshp Awd 90; IM Flg Ftbl 87-88; Psychology; Phd/Indstrl Organ Psychlgy.

**DELUKE, BETH L,** Schenectady County Comm Coll, Schenectady, NY; FR; AS; Duanesburg Fire Co Auxilary Prsdnt 86-; Astrocooks 4-H Clb Sewing Ldr 90-; Tchrs Aide 88-; Librl Arts Tchr Ed; Tchr Scndry Lvl Spcl Ed.

**DELVA, GAETANE Y,** Univ Of Rochester, Rochester, NY; FR; BA; Radiance Dnc Troupe 90-; African/Caribbean Cltrl Clb 90-; Dns Lst 90; Nrsng/Hlth Admin; RN Hlth Admnstrtr.

**DELVIN, CLYDE H,** Middle Tn St Univ, Murfreesboro, TN; JR; 4-H Clb 88-89; Alpha Gamma Rho; Agrcltr; Eng.

**DEMACOPOULOS, ELENI E,** Ringling School Of Art, Sarasota, FL; RA 90-; Big Sis; Ringling Vol 89-90.

**DEMARAY, PHILLIP I,** Liberty Univ, Lynchburg, VA; FR; BA; Bus Admn.

**DEMAREE, JUANITA C,** Lexington Comm Coll, Lexington, KY; FR; BS; HSO 90-; Mrry Snshne Poetry Clb; Cvl Eng/Math.

**DEMAREE, MARGOT M,** Ky St Univ, Frankfort, KY; SR; Soc Wrk Clb Treas 89; Mbr NASW; Deans Lst; WTLA Gospel Choir 87-; Co Op Awd Cnslng Plcmnt Off 90-; BA; Soc Wrk; MSW/ SOC Wrk.

**DEMARIA, LAURA L,** Wagner Coll, Staten Island, NY; SR; Chrldng Coach 87; Tutor 87; Omicron Delta Kappa 88; Alethea 88; Sigma Theta Tau 90; Deans Lst 87; Intrnshp 90; BSN; Nrsng; Peds.

**DEMASTUS, KIMBERLY A,** Salisbury St Univ, Salisbury, MD; SR; BA; Psychlgy Clb 90-; Psi Chi; Deans Lst 90; Psychlgy.

**DEMBOSKY JR, JOHN A,** Indiana Univ Of Pa, Indiana, PA; SO; BS; Geoscience Clb 89-; Sigma Gamma Epsilon; Provosts Schlr; Deans Lst 89-; Foundation Distinguished Achiver 89-; Educ Earth Space Sci.

**DEMBOSKY, MARY F,** Chesterfield Marlboro Coll, Cheraw, SC; AA; Alpha Omicron Pi 82-84; Kangaroos Pouch 87-; BGS U MD Clg Pk 88; Comp; Hsptl.

**DEMCHOCK, KIMBERLY M,** Saint John Fisher Coll, Rochester, NY; SO; BS; Acctng Club 89-; Pre Reg Helper 89-; Prctpnt In Heveron Laschenski Walpool P C Prog; Trustee Schlrshp 89-; Deans Liszt 89-; Acctng.

**DEMEL, KURT C,** Oh Wesleyan Univ, Delaware, OH; FR; BA; Pres Clb Comte Chr 90; Amnesty Intrnl 90; Campus Prgrmng Board 90; Deans List/Fclty Schlr; Jvnl Dlqncy Cntr Vlntr 90; Hsptl 89; Vlntr 89; IM; Chmstry/Foology/German; Medicine.

**DEMENT, DANA L,** Middle Tn St Univ, Murfreesboro, TN; SR; BS; Phi Mu Delta 89-; Math Clb 90-; Pan Cncl 90-; Rho Lambda; Gamma Beta Phi 89-; Tau Omicron 90-; Chi Omega Sec; Outstndng Sr; Outstndng Soph In Chi Omega 89-90; Chem; Med.

**DEMERS, GERARD,** Atlantic Comm Coll, Mays Landing, NJ; SO; BA; Chmstry; Phrmcy Med.

**DEMERS, MAUREEN A,** Johnson St Coll, Johnson, VT; SR; BA; Chesamore Hon Soc VP 90-; Elem/Spcl Edn; Tchr.

**DEMETRIOU, ALEXANDRA,** S U N Y Coll Of Tech At Frmgdl, Farmingdale, NY; SR; MA; Academic Achvmnt Awd; Liberal Arts Dept; Lib Arts; Occptnl Thrpy.

**DEMICCO, ANGELA M,** Teikyo Post Univ, Waterbury, CT; JR; BA; Acctg; CPA.

**DEMIRAL, ZEHRA G,** Edinboro Univ Of Pa, Edinboro, PA; JR; BS; Phi Eta Sigma 89-90; Beta Beta Beta 90-; Hnrs Pgrm 89-; Hnrs Schlrshp 89; Stdy Abrd Hnrs Schlrshp 90; Trck Fld 89-; Biology; Med/Ped.

**DEMM, CAROLYN C,** Univ Of Nc At Charlotte, Charlotte, NC; SR; Intrsor Cncl Dlgt 88; Grk Wk Chair Chrmn 89; Actvts Bldg Bd Chrmn 89; Chi Omega Scl Chr Schlrshp Chr 89-90; Safe Drive Vol 89; 1NCC Escrt Serv 90; Jay Cee Vol 88-89; Chi Omega Sis Yr 88-89; IMS 86-90; Cert Katharine Gibbs Schl; Engl.**

**DEMMIN, GARY T,** S U N Y Coll At Fredonia, Fredonia, NY; JR; BS; Fredonia Jazz Wrkshp; Fredonia Jazz Jazz Ensemble 88-89; Deans Lst; Rcratn Dept Cmuty Jazz 87-; Grayline Sghtseng/Tursm Niagara Falls; Cmptr Sci; Progrmng/Sftwre Dsgn.

**DEMOPULOS, DEMETRI T,** Hellenic Coll/Holy Cross, Brookline, MA; GD; MDIV; Phi Kappa Phi 76-; Gamma Sigma Delta 77-; Amer Assn Advncmnt Sci 80-; Genetics Soc Amer 84-; Rsrch Scientist/Genetics 85-89; PHD Univ Wis 85; MS Iowa State Univ 77; Theology; Clergy/Tchng.

**DEMPSEY, CAROLINE C,** Elms Coll, Chicopee, MA; SR; MBA; Student Ambrdr Big Sister Little Sister Prog; Yrbk Comm Resident Council; Soph Show; Resid Advisor Rose William Dorm 89-90; Hd Resid Advisor Rose William Dorm 90-; Ldrshp Awd 89-90; Soccer 88; Elms Clg Assist Dean Students; Ed; Elem Ed Tchr.

**DEMPSEY, DANIEL D,** Marshall University, Huntington, WV; JR; BBA; Fin; Fin Advsng.

**DEMPSEY, JEROME D,** Tn St Univ, Nashville, TN; JR; BS; Amer Soc Cvl Engrs 87-; Cum Laude 86; Big Bro Fdn Fnd Rsr 86-; Amer Hrt Asc 88-; Barge/Wggnr/Smnr/Cnn Env Dsgnr 86-; AS Chttnga St Tech Comm Clg 86; Cvl Engr.

**DEMPSEY, MICHAEL T,** S U N Y At Albany, Albany, NY; SO; BBA; Ftbl Bsbl 90-; Acctg; Fin.

**DEMPSTER, ROBERT M,** Methodist Coll, Fayetteville, NC; JR; Stu Jdcl Crt 87-88; Intrfrat Cncl 87-; Sigma Omega Chi Pres 88-; Pi Kappa Phi VP 87-; Marshall Grad 87; Var Bsktbl 88-89.

**DEN BLEYKER, MARC A,** Widener Univ, Chester, PA; SO; BA; Ambssdr; Vrsty Soccer 89-90; Engr.

**DENARDO, HEIDI L,** Indiana Univ Of Pa, Indiana, PA; GD; BED; Sigma Kappa; Proj Strd Internshp 89-; BS Educ 91; Elem Schl Cnslng; Cnslr.

**DENBOW, CINDY L,** Andover Coll, Portland, ME; SR; ASSOC; Hgst Hnr Awd; Vita; Accntng.

**DENDINGER, JENIFER W,** Univ Of Ms Medical Center, Jackson, MS; JR; BSN; NSNA 90-; MS Assc Stdnt Nrs 90-; Deans Lst Hinds Jr Coll 90; Deans Lst; NW Rankin PTO Cndy Sale Chrmn 88; BA LA St Univ 80; Nursing.

**DENDOR JR, EDWIN H,** Univ Of North Fl, Jacksonville, FL; GD; BT; Undrwtr Tech Assn Sec Treas 85; Knghts Of Clmbs 3rd Dgree 88-; Alpha Epsilon FIT 85; Dns Lst 85; Undrseas Med Assn Assoc 85-; NE FL Bldrs Assn 89-; FL EMT 88-; AS FL Institute Of Technology 85; AA FL Comm Coll Of Jacksonville 83; Tech; Cnstrctn.

**DENDY, DIANNE,** Piedmont Tech Coll, Greenwood, SC; SO; Phi Beta Lambda 90-; Phi Theta Kappa 90-; Clg Ambssdr 90-; Cert; Cmptr Tech; Cmptr Oper.

**DENECKE, DANIEL G,** S U N Y Coll At Fredonia, Fredonia, NY; SR; Pi Kappa Lambda; BM; Music.

**DENEEN, MICHELE,** Lesley Coll, Cambridge, MA; JR; BED; Erly Chldhd Assn AC Pres 89-90; SG/AC 89-90; Phi Theta Kappa AC 88-90; Val AC 90; ASSOC Aquinas Clg 90; Educ; Erly Chldhd Educ.

**DENEKE, JENNIFER K,** Cumberland Coll, Williamsburg, KY; SO; BA; Bsktbl 89-; Cis.**

**DENEUMOUSTIER, COLETTE A,** Bunker Hill Comm Coll, Boston, MA; SO; BA; Acctng.

**DENG, CHUN HUA,** City Univ Of Ny La Guard Coll, Long Island Cty, NY; JR.

**DENHAM, MICHELLE S,** Saint Andrews Presbytrn Coll, Laurinburg, NC; SR; BA; Day Cr Asst Dir Presch Tchr 86-89; Elem Educ; Tchr.

**DENHAM, RICHARD S,** S U N Y Coll Of Tech At Alfred, Alfred, NY; SO; BS; Drm Cncl 89-; AS Alfred State Coll; Bus Admn; Mgmt.

**DENIS, DARLA A,** Holyoke Comm Coll, Holyoke, MA; SO; BS; Phi Theta Kappa 90-; Deans Lst 90-; Ralph Hosford Prize Excell Bio; West Spngfld Anml Hosp Vet Tech; Vet Anml Sci; Vet Biotech.

**DENIS, MARCEL PIERRE,** City Univ Of Ny City Coll, New York, NY; SR; BA; Govt & Law Soc Pres 90-; Stdnt Govt Ombudsman 89-90; Sen 87-88; Urban Legal Studies & Black Studies; Law.

**DENIS, REGINE,** Saint Thomas Univ, Miami, FL; JR; BA; Drama Clb V P 88-; Fin.

**DENISON, DODIE M,** Mary Washington Coll, Fredericksburg, VA; FR; BS; Amssns Clb 90-; Art Clb 90-; RA; Psych/Tchng Cert; Pre-Schl Tchr.

**DENKER, TODD R,** City Univ Of Ny Baruch Coll, New York, NY; SO; BS; Tenns 89-90; Schlrs Pgm 88-; Im Bsktbl; M I S.

**DENMAN, JEANNIE M,** Methodist Coll, Fayetteville, NC; SO; Mnrch Plymkrs; Coll Bowl; Spcl Educ Clb Stdnt Cncl Fr Excptnl Chldrn 90-; Phi Eta Sigma; Spcl Educ Elem Educ; Tchng.

**DENMAN, SUE H,** Fl Baptist Theological Coll, Graceville, FL; SR; Cls Sec 90-; BRE; Religious Educ; Cnslr.

**DENMARK, DEBRA M,** Fl St Univ, Tallahassee, FL; JR; BA; Phi Theta Kappa 88-90; Pres Lst At N FL Jr Clg 88-90; Dns Lst 90-; Univ Trnsfr Schlrshp 90-; Clercl/Bnkng 77-90; AA N FL Jr Clg 90; Elem Educ; 3rd Gr Tchr.

**DENNARD, NAKEISHA N,** Stillman Coll, Tuscaloosa, AL; SO; BS; Biology.

**DENNERY, PATRICIA A,** Wilmington Coll, New Castle, DE; JR; BS; AAS Salem Community Clg 84; Busn Mgt; Mgt.

**DENNEY, CYNTHIA A,** Roane St Comm Coll, Harriman, TN; FR; AS; LPN Jesse Holman Jones Hosp 78; Nursing.

**DENNEY, JILL K,** Radford Univ, Radford, VA; SO; BS; Intervrsty Chrstn Fllshp 89-; Alpha Lambda Delta; Hnrs Pgm; Dr Chas Martn Schlrshp; Mary Ann Jennings Hovis Schlrshp 90-; Chem; Med.

**DENNIE, PAULA A,** Coppin St Coll, Baltimore, MD; SR; BSN; Amer Assoc Critical Care Nrs 87-; RN 82-; Certif Critical Care Nrsg 90-; AS Northshore Cmnty Clg 82; Nrsg.

**DENNIN, PETER J,** Georgetown Univ, Washington, DC; JR; BSBA; Stdnts Georgetown Inc Dir Bk Co-Op 90-; Emerg Resp Med Svc Crew Chf 90-; Mark Mc Getrick Mem Awd; Publ Acctg.

**DENNING, GINGER A,** Hudson Valley Comm Coll, Troy, NY; SO; AAS; Hmn Serv/Soc Wrk.

**DENNING, JENNIFER L,** Univ Of Nc At Charlotte, Charlotte, NC; SR; BA; Swim Tm; Delta Zeta IM Rep 88-89; Deans Lst 89-90; Psych.

**DENNIS, ANTHONY J,** Va St Univ, Petersburg, VA; FR; BA; Mrktg Wth Advrtsg Cncntrtn.

**DENNIS, BONNIE M,** Oh St Univ, Columbus, OH; SR; BFA; Golden Key; Arts/Sci Awd 90; Schlrshp Undergrad Stdnt Art Cnptn 88; Jurors Awd Best Show 88; Art; Artst.

**DENNIS, BRIAN W,** Univ Of Ky, Lexington, KY; FR.

**DENNIS, CARMA J,** Union Univ, Jackson, TN; SO; BA; Stdnt Tchr Ed Assn 90-; Stdnt Act Cncl Advsry Brd; Rutldg Hnry Hist Clb 90-; Phi Alpha Theta 90-; Kappa Delta Ed 89-; Scl Stds; Tchng.

**DENNIS, CHARLES E,** Univ Of Ga, Athens, GA; SO; BLA; Phi Theta Kappa 89-90; Nurseryman Landscape Grdn Desgr Illustr; Env Design; Landscape Arch.

**DENNIS, DANIEL P,** S U N Y Coll Of Tech At Canton, Canton, NY; SR; Rsdnt Asst 90-; Phi Theta Kappa Snt Rep 90-; Outstndng Sr Man; Ski Tm Cpt 89-90; Civil Engrg Tech; Civil Engr.

**DENNIS, GREGORY,** Piedmont Bible Coll, Winston-Salem, NC; JR; THB; Thlgy; Pstr.

**DENNIS, JAMES P,** Spartanburg Methodist Coll, Spartanburg, SC; SO; BA; SGA Sen 90-; Phi Theta Kappa 89-; Psi Beta 90-; Phi Beta Lambda VP; AA; Rl Est.

**DENNIS, JASON E,** Oh St Univ At Newark, Newark, OH; FR; Engl; Elem Ed.

**DENNIS, JUDY E,** Williamsburg Tech Coll, Kingstree, SC.

**DENNIS, KATHRYN E,** Ms St Univ, Miss State, MS; FR; BS; Campus Crusade For Christ 90-; Gamma Beta Phi; Alpha Lambda Delta; Phi Eta Sigma; Deans Lst 90; Pres Lst; Mech Eng.

**DENNIS, KATIE M,** East Central Comm Coll, Decatur, MS; AAS; Gospel Chr 89-90; IM Flg Ftbl 88-89; IM Bsktbl 88-89; AAS; Chld Care Sprvsn Tech; Chld Care BA.

**DENNIS, KIMBERLY,** Norfolk St Univ, Norfolk, VA; JR; BA; Gospel Choir; Pltcl Sci Assn; Yng Dems Assn; Pltcl Sci; Pblc Admin.

**DENNIS, MELANIE L,** Liberty Univ, Lynchburg, VA; SR; BS; Virginia Psychlgcl Assc 90; AM Psychlgcl Assc 90; Psi Chi Sec 90; Intrnshp/Presbyterian Home Children; Psychlgy/Human Serv/Cnslng.

**DENNIS, MICHAEL G,** Yeshiva Univ, New York, NY; SR; BA; Chem Clb 90; Sigma Delta Rho 88-; Rsdnt Cncl Chrmn 88-; Fd Srvs Com 89; Scrty Concl 89; Dns Lst; Blgy; Med.

**DENNIS, MICHAEL V,** Univ Of Nc At Charlotte, Charlotte, NC; FR; BS; Inroads Charlotte Inc 88-; Phi Eta Sigma 90-; Elec Eng Intrnshp Pelton Crane 90-; Chancllrs Lst 90; Elec Eng.

**DENNIS, SCOTT A,** Oh St Univ At Marion, Marion, OH; SR; BS; Acctg.

**DENNIS, SCOTT E,** Memphis St Univ, Memphis, TN; SR; BSET; Comm Tech 89-; Dean Sel Comm Herff Clg Eng 90-; Dns Lst 89-; Order Eng 89-; BSET 90; Syst Eng.

**DENNIS, TAMI L,** Univ Of Rochester, Rochester, NY; JR; BAMS; Intrvrsty Chrstn Flwshp Exec Brd 90-; Clg Democrats Tres 90-; Omcrn Dlt Epsln; Msc Intrst Flr Cbnt Mbr 89-; BA Economus/MS Pblc Plcy; Pblc Plcy.

**DENNIS, YVONNE L,** Indiana Univ Of Pa, Indiana, PA; JR; IM Spd Ftbl Vlybl 89-; Elem Ed; Tchng.

**DENNISON, JOHN DAVID,** Univ Of Fl, Gainesville, FL; SR; All Amer Hnrs SEC Chmpns 200 Medley Relay 90-; SEC Academic Hnr Rl; Swm Tm 88-; BS.

**DENNISON, MELONIE S,** Western Ky Univ, Bowling Green, KY; JR; ADN; KY Assc Nsg Stdnts 90-; Reg Nrsg.

**DENNISON, PATRICIA J,** Univ Of Akron, Akron, OH; JR; BA; Alpha Lambda Delta 89-; Phi Eta Sigma 89-; Beta Gamma Sigma; Delta Sigma Pi 90-; Dns Lst 88-; Pres Schlrshp 88-; Golden Key; Mgmt.

**DENNISON, SARAH J,** Marshall University, Huntington, WV; JR; BBA; Alpha Kappa Psi Sec 90-; Acdmc Tuition Wvrs 88-; Natl Assn Prchng Mngmnt Schlrshp 90; Dean Lst 88-; Mrktng; Advrtsng.**

**DENNY, EILEEN M,** Albertus Magnus Coll, New Haven, CT; JR; BA; Cmmtr Rep Jr Class 90; Vol Amer Red Cross 88; Wrk As Emer Med Tchncn; Bio; Rsrch Med.

**DENNY, MICHAEL P,** City Univ Of Ny City Coll, New York, NY; JR; BA; Msc Dept Exec Comm 90-; Nwspr Edtr 89-; Msc Clb 90-; Ford Fdn Flwshp 89-; Natl Endwmnt Hmnts Yngr Schlrs Awd 90; Prof Guitarist 78-; Msc; Clg Tch.

**DENSLER, SHEILA L,** Antonelli Inst Of Art & Photo, Cincinnati, OH; GD; AS; AD 89-; Interior Design; Arch.

**DENSMORE, TARA D,** Shorter Coll, Rome, GA; SO; BA; Epsilon Sigma 89-; Brdcstng/Radio Tv; Cmnctns.**

**DENSMORE, TERRI ANITA,** Univ Of Sc At Aiken, Aiken, SC; SR; AD; Treas 90-; Nrsng Clss 90-; Gamma Beta Phi; Pres Hnr Rll 89-; Oprtng Rm Nrsng.

**DENSON, CANDACE L,** Miami Dade Comm Coll North, Miami, FL; SO; AA; Elem Educ; Tchr.

**DENSON, CAROLYN,** Columbia Union Coll, Takoma Park, MD; SR; Bwlng Clb; MNCPPCC Admnstrtv Asst 88-; Church Clerk; Vol Coach Bsbl; BS Columbia Union 90; Bus Admin; Self Emplyd/Bus Admin.

**DENSON III, LEE A,** Va Commonwealth Univ, Richmond, VA; GD; MD; MIT Vol For Yth Dir 84-88; AMA/AAFP 89-; Sigma Xi 87-; Lambda Chi Alpha Hse Mgr; A D Williams Summer Rsrch Flwshp 90; SNAME Natl Schlrshp 85-86; Rsrch Asst 85-88; MIT Dept Of Ocean Engrs 85-88; Vrsty Lacrosse 82-84; Medicine.

**DENT, DE ANDREA MICHELLE,** Alcorn St Univ, Lorman, MS; FR; BA; Mrchng Band/Cncrt Band 90-; Wood-Wind Ensemble Soloist 90-; Career Edctnl Grp Pres 90-; Patient Escort Baptist Med Princeton Hosp; Elem Ed/Msc Ed; Tchr/Msc Dir.

**DENT III, HOWARD,** City Univ Of Ny Baruch Coll, New York, NY; SR; BBA; NAACP Treas 85-; Yth Chr Treas 86-; Yth Actn Cmmtt Yth Lsn Stt Lcl Lvl; Gldn Key 90; Deans Lst 87-; Inbds Intern 88-; Brch Schlr Awrd 87-; Rgnts Schlrshp 87; Fnc Invstmnts.

**DENT, JEFFREY L,** Claflin Coll, Orangeburg, SC; JR; BS; NAACP 90-; Habtat Hmnty; Hon Prog 88-; US Brkly Prtnrshp Prog 87-; Math; Educ.

**DENT, LA SANDRA L,** Central St Univ, Wilberforce, OH; SR; BS; Soc Wrk Org 88-; Clmbs Pre Alumni Assc 88-; Black Awrnss Comm 87-; Alpha Kappa Alpha Srty 90-; Deans List 87-; Honors Roll 87-; Social Welfare; Graduate School.

**DENT, VICTORIA RENEE,** Univ Of Sc At Columbia, Columbia, SC; JR; BS; Retlng Nwsltr Contributing Edtr 90-; Chi Omega 89-; Deans Clg Rtlng Indpent Styd Crd; Fashion Merchng; Law Schl Grad.

**DENTES, MATTHEW J,** Cornell Univ Statutory College, Ithaca, NY; SO; MBA; Crss Cntry Trck 90; Ho Nun De Kah; Bus/Mrktng; Mngmnt.

**DENTON, AMY V,** Clemson Univ, Clemson, SC; SO; BS; SNA Cmnty Hlth Dir 90-; CCC; FCA; Alpha Lambda Delta; SNA; Weight Clb; Nrsg; Med/Physician.

**DENTON, ANGEL C,** Northeast State Tech Comm Coll, Blountville, TN; SO; Cmptr; Eng.

**DENTON, BRIAN L,** Tn Tech Univ, Cookeville, TN; SR; BA; Tech Cllgt FFA Treas 90-; Delta Tau Alpha 90-; Agri Educ; Tchr.

**DENTON, DAVID THOMAS,** Univ Of Sc At Columbia, Columbia, SC; SR; BA; Otstndng Ynm Mn Amrc 89; Msn; Shrnr; Amrcn Lgn; Armr Assoc; Natl Grd Assoc; Natl Prpn Gs Assoc ; SC Prpn Gs Assoc; Dntns Gs Cmpny; Prtnr Lckhrt Car Wsh; AS 82; Intrdscplnry Stds.

**DENTON, MICHELE L,** Saint Joseph Coll, West Hartford, CT; SO; BS; Cmmtr Asc 90-; Spec Ed; Tch/Cnsl.

**DEOPERSAUD, SAVITRI A,** City Univ Of Ny City Coll, New York, NY; SO; BA; Engl; Law.

**DEPP, DONA B,** Georgetown Coll, Georgetown, KY; SR; BS; Stdnt Govt Assn; Georgetown Coll Chrl; Georgetown Coll Bd; Eta Delta Phi; Phi Beta Lambda Bus Frat Soc Chrmn 90-; Kappa Delta Sor Pres 89-90, Sec 88-89; Mktng/Fin; Bnk Exmnr.

**DEPTO, DARON M,** Mount Aloysius Jr Coll, Cresson, PA; FR; Crdvsclr Inntrnshps/Teach Hosp; Natl Spanish Hnr Soc; Cardiovasculat Tech.

**DEPTO, KATHLEEN A,** S U N Y Coll At Fredonia, Fredonia, NY; JR; BA; AA Jmstwn Cmmnty Coll 90; Art; Tch Coll Lvl.

**DERAGON, DONNA M,** Fl Southern Coll, Lakeland, FL; FR; BA; Big Buddy Prog; I M Sftbl Soccer Dorm Rep; Stdnt Un Bd; Phi Eta Sigma; Fresh Hon Awd GPA; English; Law.

**DERBORT, MICHELLE J,** Memphis St Univ, Memphis, TN; SR; BPS; Pre Law Society 90-; Gamma Beta Phi 90-; City Attorney Paralegal Intern; Legal Asst Cert 90; Paralegal Services; Law.

**DERBY, ANDREA L,** Christopher Newport Coll, Newport News, VA; FR; BA; Styron Schlr Schlrshp; Deans Lst 90-; Hon Pgm 90-; Psychlgy; Dvlpmntl Therapist/Marriage/Fmly.

**DERENBURGER, JOHN A,** Wv Univ, Morgantown, WV; SR; BSPHA; Acdmy Stdnts Phrmcy Treas 89-; Rho Chi 90; Gldn Key 81; Kappa Delta Pi VP 80; Pi Mu Epsilon 81; Key Clb Spnsr 82-; BS Ed 82; Chem Inst 82-89; Magna Cum Laude 82; Bys Tns/Grls Vlybl Coach; Dns Awd WVU Schl Pharm; Rho Chi Awd WVU Schl Pharm; Pharmacy.

**DERICKSON, CHRISTINE LYNN,** Defiance Coll, Defiance, OH; SO; BS; Intervars Chrstn Flwshp Clb; Stdnt Newspaper; Cross Country; Alpha Xi Delta; Commuters-In-Action Secr/Treas; Stdnt Scl Wrk Assoc; Chamber Singers Ensmbl; Spring Play; LPN Assoc OH; Natl Assoc Scl Wrkrs; LPN; Scl Wrk; BA MA Scl Wrk.

**DERICO, AGGIE,** Fl A & M Univ, Tallahassee, FL; SR; BS; FAMU 87-; FAMU Gspl Chr 87; Yng Wmns Aux; Hstry/Afr Amer Stds; Tchr/Prncpl.

**DERIFIELD, LOIS H,** Ashland Comm Coll, Ashland, KY; SO; Scndry Educ.

**DERILUS, OSIAS,** Tomlinson Coll, Cleveland, TN; FR; Sun Sch Tchr 88-90; Sec Yth 87-89; VP 89-90; Phtgrph Yr Bk 90-; Photog Centre D Etudes Phogrpahy Haiti 84; Eng Ft Lauderdale Clg 89; Ministry.

**DERING II, FRED W,** Fl International Univ, Miami, FL; SR; BS; Delta Delta Phi; Phi Kappa Phi; Beta Theta Pi; IM Sftbl; FIU Broward Cmps; Hsptlty Mgmt; Hotel/Rstrnt Mgmt.

**DERISE, JESSICA J,** Central Fl Comm Coll, Ocala, FL; SO; BA; Campus Diplomats Sec 90-; Phi Theta Kappa Sec 90-; Intrnshp; News Asst WMOP Radio; Engl; Engl Prof.

**DERMOND, ANDREA L,** Widener Univ, Chester, PA; SR; BS; Acctng Soc 88-; PA Inst CPAS 89-; Natl Assoc Acntnts 90-; Omicron Delta Epsilon 90-; VITA; Acctng.

**DEROCHER, SHEREE LAUREEN,** Univ Of Sc At Columbia, Columbia, SC; SO; BS; Laurel Bay Mddl Schl Tutor; US Marine Corps/Lgl Spclst Sgt/E-5 87-; Bus; Bus Law.

**DEROSSETT, ROBERT WAYNE,** Bellarmine Coll, Louisville, KY; SR; BA; Acctng Asso Treas 87-; Pres Soc 87-; Delta Sigma Pi; Delta Sigma Pi Pres 88-; Acctng Fac Merit Awd; Acctng; CPA.

**DERR, JILL R,** Indiana Univ Of Pa, Indiana, PA; SR.

**DERR, PAULA M,** Auburn Univ At Auburn, Auburn, AL; SR; Hsptlty Stdnt Assn 89-; Clb Mngrs Assn Of Amer 90-; Eta Sigma Delta VP 90-; Lit Sis Delta Sigma Phi 88-, BS; Hsptlty Mgmt.

**DERREBERRY, BRIAN W,** Univ Of Akron, Akron, OH; JR; BS; Mechanical Engrng.

**DERRICK, JERRY M,** Memphis St Univ, Memphis, TN; SR; BS; Tri Beta 86-; Oil Spill Clean Up Kodiak Katmai AK 89; Bio; Rsch.

**DERRICK, MELISSA LEE,** Mount Saint Mary Coll, Newburgh, NY; SO; BA; Nwspr 90-; Flk Grp 89-; Choir 89-; Hnrs Allnc Sec 90-; Ralph Schlr; Cmmnctn Arts; Media/Pblc Rltns.

**DERRICKS, IDA D,** Ms St Univ, Miss State, MS; JR; BA; M Clb Tr; Bsktbl Tm Capt 90-; Acad All-Amer; Alpha Kappa Alpha Sec 90-; Black Awrns Awd 89-; Acad All Sec 90-; Bus Tech; Tchr.

**DERRICKSON, BRYAN H,** Morehouse Coll, Atlanta, GA; SO; BS; Occptnl Hlth Careers Scty 90-; Phi Beta Kappa; Spanish Natl Hnr Scty; Gldn Key; Natl Eye Inst Lab Asst 90-; Natl Inst Of Health Lab Asst 90-; Morehanse Schl Of Medicine Lab Asst 90-; Biology/Spanish; Professor.

**DERROW, MELODY A,** Bridgewater Coll, Bridgewater, VA; SR; BS; Lambda Soc 88-; Alpha Chi 89-; Omicron Delta Akappa 90-; Bsktbl Vlybl Tnns 87-; Bus Admin; Hmn Rsrc Mgmt.

**DERSIN, JENNIFER L,** Coll Of Charleston, Charleston, SC; SO; BS; Cntr Stg 90-; Psi Chi; Psychlgy; Scl Psychlgst.

**DERSTINE, CHRISTOPHER W,** Ursinus Coll, Collegeville, PA; SR; BS; Intervars Chrstn Flwshp Pres 87-; Org Commuting Stdnts Treas 87-; Beardwood Chem Soc 87-; Kappa Mu Epsilon 90-; Cub/Key Soc 90-; Tennis 87-89; ACS Div Polymer Chem 89; Amer Inst Chem Stdnt Awd; William L Lettinger Achvmnt Awd; Chem; Chem Rsrch.

**DERWID, KURT E,** Bloomfield Coll, Bloomfield, NJ; FR; BA; Pre Chrprct Clb 90; Achvd Hgh Hnrs 90-; Dean Lst 90; Chrprctr.

**DES PLAINES III, EDWARD R,** Springfield Tech Comm Coll, Springfield, MA; SO; BS; STCC Ski Clb 90-; Alpha Nu Omega 90-; US Army Vet 4 Yrs Actve 2 Yrs Inactve; Comp Rpr Spclst 89; Physcs; Thrtcl Or Appld Physcs.

**DES ROCHER, CHRISTOPHER J,** Clarkson Univ, Potsdam, NY; JR; BA; Fin Mngmnt Assn 90-; Archery Clb 89-; Natl Rifle Assn; Knights Of Columbus 88-; Fin Econ; Bnkng Fin Plng.

**DESAI, HIRENKUMAR B,** Univ Of Ky, Lexington, KY; SO; BA; Finance; Law.

**DESAI, MANISH M,** Middle Ga Coll, Cochran, GA; SR; BSIE; Inst Indstrl Eng; Alpha Pi Mu; AS 89; Indstrl Eng; Eng.

**DESAI, MEETESH S,** Univ Of Miami, Coral Gables, FL; SR; BA; India Stdnts Assoc Adtr 89-90; Golden Key 89-; Sigma Tau Delta; IM Scr 88-89; Eng; Med.

**DESALLIERS, CHANTAL J,** Rivier Coll, Nashua, NH; FR; BA; Acctg; CPA.

**DESANTIS, KIMBERLY A,** Univ Of Akron, Akron, OH; SR; BA; Gall Govt 87-89; Kappa Delta Pi; Pi Delta Phi; Golden Key; Deans List; Elem Edn; Teach.

**DESCHAMBAULT, NICHOLE M,** Univ Of New England, Biddeford, ME; FR; BS; Phys Thrpy Clb 90-; Deans Lst 90-; Phys Thrpy; Reg Phys Thrpst.

**DESCHENES, ADAM W,** Becker Coll At Leicester, Leicester, MA; SO; AS; Dns Lst 89-90; IM Bsktbl/Flr Hcky/Vrsgy Glf; Phys Educ; Athl Dir.

**DESDUNES, MARLENE D,** Johnson C Smith Univ, Charlotte, NC; JR; Acadmc Comm SGA Chrprsn 90-; Soclgy/Soc Wrk Club Secy 90-; Shaki Mdlng Troupe Ass Hosp Chr 90-; Alpha Swthrts VP 90-; Collabrtv Lrng Tea Tutot/Team Ldr 90-; Stdnt Orientn Ldr 90-; Soclgy; Soc Wrk/Jvnls.

**DESHARNAIS, BRIAN M,** Merrimack Coll, North Andover, MA; SO; BA; Ironworks Gym 90-; Deans List 89-; Science; Civil Engrng.

**DESHAZO, MICHAEL A,** Univ Of Al At Birmingham, Birmingham, AL; JR; BA; Blazer Bnd 87-; Wind Ensmbl 87-; Gldn Key; Pres Hnrs Lst 89-; Dns Lst 90; Music Hstry.

**DESHLER, KRISTIN M,** S U N Y Coll Of Tech At Frmgdl, Farmingdale, NY; GD; AAS; Offc Mgmt Clb 89-; Lgl Offc Mgmt Clb Treas 90-; Deans Lst 89-; Lgl Intrnshp Manhattan Law Firm; Lgl Fld; Law.

**DESIR COLIMON, DIERY Y,** Inter Amer Univ Pr San German, San German, PR; SO; BA; Hon Soc 90-; Bud Phi Eta Cnslr 89-; Soccr; Comp Sci; Prog.

**DESLAURIERS, CHRISTINA M,** Saint Joseph Coll, West Hartford, CT; SO; BA; Cls VP 89-90; Madonna Drm Sec 89-90; PALS 89-; Engl/Pol Sci; Law.

**DESLAURIERS, DOMINICK E,** Western New England Coll, Springfield, MA; SR; BS; Biology Clb VP 88-; Vrsty Sccr Cptn; Biology; Physical Therapy.

**DESMARAIS, LYNNE A,** Univ Of North Fl, Jacksonville, FL; SO; BBA; Betah Sigma Phi; Accntng; CPA.

**DESMARAIS, STEVEN A,** Newbury Coll, Brookline, MA; FR; AS; Cnstrctn Foreman 86-89; Cert Control Data Inst 86; Bsn; Acctng.

**DESMOND, ANGELA J,** Univ Of New England, Biddeford, ME; SO; BED; Elem Ed; Tch.

**DESMOND IV, THOMAS A,** Fl St Univ, Tallahassee, FL; SR; Gldn Ky 87-; FAMU FSO Eng Hnr Scty Pres 88-; IEEE 87-; AIAA 90-; BSEE 90; Elec Eng.

**DESO, KENNETH P,** Western New England Coll, Springfield, MA; SR; BA; Accntng Assoc 90-; Bwlng Clb 87-88; Deans Lst 89-; Accntng.**

**DESPAIN, AMY,** Savannah Coll Of Art & Design, Savannah, GA; SO; BFA; Deans Lst 89-; Ambsdr; Ilstrtn; Frlnc.

**DESPEAUX, LANDON D,** Memphis Academy Of The Arts, Memphis, TN; SR; BFA; Dean Lst 88-; Sigma Alpha Epsilon 85; Inter Wdlf Phtgrphy Asst 90; BA Memphis Coll Art; Cert Woodland Schl Phtgrphy 87; Cmmrcl Photo.

**DESPORT, WILLIAM D,** Kent St Univ Kent Cmps, Kent, OH; JR; BBA; Computer Sci; Systems Analyst.

**DESPOTH, DEBRA L,** Univ Of Akron, Akron, OH; SO; BA; Deans List; Acctng; CPA.**

**DESPOTOPOULOS, PETER GEORGE,** The Boston Conservatory, Boston, MA; SO; BA; Cnsrvtry Astntshp 90-; Cnsrvtry Schlrshp 90-; Danny Sloan Dnc Co Prncpl Dncr 87-88; New Ehrlich Thtr Actr 89-90; Boston Blt 85-86; Alvin Ailey Dnc Thtr 86-87; Cert New Ehrlich Thtr 89-90; Mscl Thtr; Actng.

**DESPRES, DAWN B,** Springfield Tech Comm Coll, Springfield, MA; SO; BA; Rcgntn Lst Tunxis Comm Coll 90; Bay State Medcl Hosp-Vol 89; Hlth/Medcl Fld; Nrsng.

**DESRAMEAUX, RODNEY,** Fl International Univ, Miami, FL; JR; BSW; Scl Wrk.

**DESROCHERS, CHRISTINE A,** Niagara Univ, Niagara Univ, NY; SO; BA; Ski Club 89-; Lcnsd Csmtlgst 89-91; Bsn Commerce.

**DESROCHERS, LISA A,** Boston Univ, Boston, MA; SR; BA; Sargent Coll Stdnt Coun Sr Cls Phys Thrpy Rep 90-; Gldn Ky 89-; Vrsty Sftbl 87-90; Stdnt Ath Recgntn Acdmc Achvmnt 87-90; Sargent Coll Dns Lst; IM Bsktbl Vlybl Sftbl 87-; Phys Thrpy.

**DESROSIERS, CAROL F,** Hudson Valley Comm Coll, Troy, NY; SO; AAS; N E Subcntrctrs Assn 89-; Prt Ownr Of Desrosiers Const Co; Math; Engr.

**DESSELLE, SHAWNA D,** Georgetown Univ, Washington, DC; SO; BBA; Georgetown Pgmng Brd 90-91; Dorm Pgmng Brd 90-91; Bus Sch Strng Cmt 90-91; GUICE Vol Tchrs Aid Hyde Elem 90-91; Vol Teller GU Stdnt Credit Union 90-91; Deans List 89-91; Tnns IM Tm 89-90; Intrntl Bus; Law.

**DEST, SUSAN C,** Univ Of Ct, Storrs, CT; SR; BA; Plnt Sci; Hrtcltr.

**DESTIN, CINDY A,** Central Fl Comm Coll, Ocala, FL; SO; BA; Prnt Advsry Cmmtt Chrprsn 90-; Sth Smtr Sftbll Assoc Cch; Art Ed Cnsllng; AA 90; Fn Arts Ed.

**DESZCZ, ERIC J,** S U N Y Coll Of Tech At Alfred, Alfred, NY; FR; Schlrshp From Electrical Prods Unlimited In Olean NY; Electrician.

**DESZELL, DANIEL J,** Broward Comm Coll, Ft Lauderdale, FL; SO; AS; Sprvsr 87-89; AS Owens Tech Coll 85; Cert Atlantic Voc Schl 88; Electronics; Bio Med Engr.

**DETESCO, JENNIFER L,** John Carroll Univ, Cleveland, OH; SO; BA; Psi Chi; Psy; Indtl Psygt.**

**DETMER, SARA E,** Northern Ky Univ, Highland Hts, KY; FR; Hlth Physcl Educ; Edctn.

**DETRICK, HEATHER E,** Teikyo Post Univ, Waterbury, CT; JR; BS; Papanazzo Hl Cncl V P; Japanese Peer Guide; Certif Ldrshp; Equine Mgmt.

**DETTWEILER, SUSAN L,** Longwood Coll, Farmville, VA; SR; Stdnt Educ Assn 88-90; IM Sprts Capt 88-89; Stdnt Tchng 90-91; BS 90; Elem/Scndry Educ; Tchr.

**DETWEILER, PHILIP N,** Tallahassee Comm Coll, Tallahassee, FL; SO; Chrch Yth Grp Pres 89; AA; Acctg; CPA.

**DETWILER, MARK G,** Embry Riddle Aeronautical Univ, Daytona Beach, FL; SR; BA; Nvl Aviation Clb 87-88; IM Sftbl 90-; Aerospc; Arln Pilot.

**DEURINGER, URSULA I,** Anne Arundel Comm Coll, Arnold, MD; SO; BA; Supplemental Instrctn Ldr Acctng I Stdnts; Cust Srvc Rep 86-88; Cust Srvc Asst Mngr Magazine Washington D C; Cert Fleet Bus Schl 85; Bus; Human Resources.

**DEURLEIN, EMILY M,** Indiana Univ Of Pa, Indiana, PA; SO; BA; Educ; Rehab.

**DEUTSCH, CHERYL A,** Fl International Univ, Miami, FL; SO; Alpha Kappa Psi Sec; Delta Phi Epsilon Fndrsr 90-; Bus; Corp Law.

**DEUTSCH, MELISSA N,** Univ Of Rochester, Rochester, NY; JR; BA; Grss Rts; Sigma Delta Tau 90-; EAT; Comp Peer Cmmnty Pr 89; Cnslr; Trm Abrd 90; Deans Lst 88-; Tchr Asstng Psychlgy; Sigma Delta Tau 88-; Cmmnty Pr Cnslr 90; Fld Hcky 90; IMS 90; Psychlgy.

**DEVADASON, ANNE MAIDA LAWRENCE,** Columbia Union Coll, Takoma Park, MD; SR; BS; Chrstn Nrs Assoc India; Clg Hnr Rl; Dns Lst; Alpha Chi; Amer Publ Hlth Assoc; Gen Nrsg Cncl U K SRN; Tchr Nrs Gen Nrsg Cncl U K STD; Canadian Exec Svc Overseas; Vol Dominica British W Indies 71; RN State Bd Nrs MD VA Distr Columbia; Hlth Adm; Nrsg/Hlth Adm.

**DEVANE, VICTORIA LYNN,** Valdosta St Coll, Valdosta, GA; JR; BFA; GA Theatre Conf 88-; Southeastrn Theatre Conf 88-; Lowndes Assn Retarded Citizens; Theatre.

**DEVANEY, DEANNA LYNNE,** Lesley Coll, Cambridge, MA; SO.

**DEVANEY, PHILIP C,** Toccoa Falls Coll, Toccoa Falls, GA; SR; BS; Winning Choral Compostition Moody Bible Inst 85; Antioch Bapt Chrch 90-; Minister Music 86-88; Cert Moody Bible Inst 85; Music Composition; Music Instrctn.

**DEVAUL, MARGIE D,** Tougaloo Coll, Tougaloo, MS; SR; BA; Chrldr 87-88; Pre Alumni Assoc 89-; Intrnshp Abused Neglected Sr Citizens; Alpha Sweetheart 88; Sclgy/Psycholgy; Sociologist.

**DEVEAUX, SHANISE N,** Bunker Hill Comm Coll, Boston, MA; SO; AA; Dean Lst; Hmn Serv Intern; Hmn Srvcs; Psychlgy.

**DEVENDORF, JOAL R,** Wesley Coll, Florence, MS; FR; BA; Chr/Ensmble VP; SG 90-; Lit; Law Enfrcmnt.

**DEVENEY, STACY A,** Middlesex County Coll, Edison, NJ; JR; AS; Phi Theta Kappa; Dntl Hygn.

**DEVENS, NATALIE F,** Atlantic Comm Coll, Mays Landing, NJ; SO; AS; Gnrl Studies; Bus Admin.

**DEVER, DAVID A,** Pa St Univ Delaware Cty Cmps, Media, PA; FR; BS; Outstndg Acad Achvmnt Fr Yr Awd; Mech Eng.

**DEVER, L DANIEL,** Bluefield Coll, Bluefield, VA; JR; Alpha Phi Sigma 89-; Phi Mu Delta Pres 90-; Pres Schlrshp 88-; Wyatt A Winkler Schlrshp 89-; Vlybl; Bsn; Bsn Mgr.

**DEVERELL, CONNIE K,** Univ Of Ga, Athens, GA; SR; BS; Bapt Stu Union IM Dir 87-; IM Bsktbl/Flg Ftbl/Sftbl/3 On 3 Vlybl/Wlybl 87-; Tm Capt 87-; Phi Lambda Sigma 90-; Rho Chi; Lambda Kappa Sigma; Roche Cmnctns Awrd; Revco Intrn 89-; Hmltn Med Cntr Intrn 90-; Accptnc To Post Bs Phrm : Sch; Phrmcy; Hosp Clncl Phrmcst.

**DEVERS, KIMBERLY A,** Univ Of Ky, Lexington, KY; GD; KASP 90-; Gldn Ky 87-; Phi Eta Sigma 86-; Smith Kline Fllwshp; BA Chem U Of Louisville 89; Pharmacy.

**DEVIES, DEBBY LYNN,** Hillsborough Comm Coll, Tampa, FL; AS; Wrkd With Rd Crss At Mcdll AFB Vol; Like To Obtain 4 Yr Degree; Nrsng; Get BS In Nrsng.

**DEVILLE, TERRENCE S,** Univ Of Ky, Lexington, KY; JR; BARCH; Kappa Alpha Ordr; Archtctre.

**DEVILLIER, JOHN M,** Fl St Univ, Tallahassee, FL; JR; BA; Futr Educrs Amer; Bg Brthrs/Bg Sistrs 90-; IM Ftbl/Vlybl/Sftbl Capt 88-; AA Okaloosa-Walton Comm Coll 90; Educ/Hstry; Tchng/Admin.

**DEVINE, AILEEN M,** Immaculata Coll, Immaculata, PA; SR; Stdnt Govt Sec 87-; Earth Day Cmte Chrmn 90-; Class Cmtes 87-; Mac Mentor/Big Sister Pgm Chrmn 89-; Yrbk Edtr 90-; Immaculata Hon Soc 89-; Intl Hist Hon Soc; Alpha Theta; Natl Hon Soc; Kappa Gamma Pi 88-; Campus Mnstry 87-; Econ Bus Admin; Law.

**DEVINE, MARY A,** Oh Wesleyan Univ, Delaware, OH; SR; BA; Politics Gov Stdnt Board 90; Wesleyan Stdnt Fndtn 88; Gift Fund Committee; Pi Sigma Alpha 90; Phi Sigma Iota 90; Phi Beta Kappa; Big Little Sister Prgm 88-90; Career Serv Cnt Intern 90; Varsity Soccer 87; Politics Govt/French; Foreign Service.

**DEVINNEY, BRIAN F,** Duquesne Univ, Pittsburgh, PA; JR; BA; Deans List 88-90; IM Ftbl 88-89; History; Law.

**DEVINO, ROBERT S,** Utica Coll Of Syracuse Univ, Utica, NY; SR; BA; Phi Alpha Theta; Morelli Mem Schlrshp; Twn Westernville NY Histrcl Soc; Rome NY Histrcl Soc; Histrn 416th Bombardmnt Wng Griffiss AFB NY; AAS Comm Coll Air Force 90; AAS Comm Coll Air Force 89; Hist; MLS Syracuse U.

**DEVINS, JULIE M,** S U N Y Coll At Fredonia, Fredonia, NY; SR; JD; Stdnt Assoc Rep; Operations Procedures Comm Stdnt Assoc; Legal Serv; Intrnshp Harris Evans Fox Chesworth 89; BA; AAS 89; Sclgy/Crmnl Justice; Law.

**DEVIR, ILAN,** City Univ Of Ny City Coll, New York, NY; SR; BE; Am Soc Mech Engrs Treas 90-; Stdnt Advsry Grp Mech Eng Dept Executive Com 90-; Mech Eng Awd Copy Of Marks Mech Engrs Hndbk Offers ASME 90-; City Coll Soccer Tm Plyr 88-89; Mech; Eng.

**DEVIR, STEPHEN J,** Alfred Univ, Alfred, NY; JR; BA; Delta Sigma Phi Food Serv Mgr 90-; Vrsty Track/Field.

**DEVLIN, ELLEN E,** Seton Hall Univ, South Orange, NJ; SO; SNA 90-; Stdnt Hlth Aide; Deans Lst 89-; Burdette Tomlin Meml Hosp Schlrshp 90-; Nrsng.

**DEVLIN, KELLY A,** Salisbury St Univ, Salisbury, MD; SR; BSN; Std Nrs Assc 90-; Nrsg; RN.

**DEVOOGD, AMY,** Va Commonwealth Univ, Richmond, VA; SR; BFA; Pntng/Prntmkng.

**DEVORE, DEIDRA G,** Oh Northern Univ, Ada, OH; SO; BS; Alpha Omicron Pi Tr; Asst Tr 90-; Acctg.**

**DEW, ANGELA FRANKLIN,** Ms St Univ, Miss State, MS; JR; BA; Campus Actvts Bd Lecturn 89-90; Psych Clb 89-; Soc Schlrs; Phi Eta Sigma 89-; Dev Fdtn Schlrshp 90-; Phi Kappa Phi 90-; Psi Chi 90-; Gamma Beta Phi 90-; Pres Schlr 89-; Research Asst; Schlrs Recognition Day 90-; Psych; Indstrl Psych.

**DEWAN, BINDU,** George Mason Univ, Fairfax, VA; SO; BA; Acctg; CPA.

**DEWAR, DENISE A,** Albertus Magnus Coll, New Haven, CT; SO; BA; Pax Christi 89; Engl Clb; UMC Wrshp Cmmssn Yth Rep 88; UMC Cmmn Stwrd 88; AA 91; Engl; Ed/Jrnlsm.

**DEWAR, HEATHER L,** Eckerd Coll, St Petersburg, FL; SR; BA; Org Of Stdnts V P 89-; Stdnt Alum Cncl 89-; AIDS Prvntn Grp 89-; Omicron Delta Kappa 90-; Meals On Wheels Vol 89-; ASPEC/STDNT Liason Tsk Frc Cochr; Comotion Dance Theatre Chrtr Mbr 88-; Cmps Mnstry Schlrshp 87-; Spec Tlnt Schlrsshp; Human Dvlpmnt Serv; Elderly Serv.

**DEWEESE, CARRIE J,** Oh St Univ At Newark, Newark, OH; FR; BA; Phi Eta Sigma; Alpha Lambda Delta; Hnrs Soc; Vet Asstnt; Pre Vet Med.

**DEWESE, ARLIEDA P,** Univ Of Sc At Columbia, Columbia, SC; SR; BA; Blck Awrnss Grp 90-; AA USC At Lancaster 90; Nrsng; Clncl Nrs Spclst.

**DEWEY, BRIAN T,** Southern Vt Coll, Bennington, VT; SO; ASHRACE Cmte Chrmn 89-; Bodokai Karate 81-; AAS SUNY Delhi 87; Mngmnt; Engr.

**DEWEY, JANIS G,** Johnson St Coll, Johnson, VT; SR; BA; Chesamore Hnr Soc; Am Leg; Bus Mgmt/Acctng; Auditor.

**DEWEY, MATTHEW H,** Univ Of Sc At Columbia, Columbia, SC; SO; BA; Sandhill Mag Fiction Awd; COSU Frshmn Achvmnt Schlrshp; Enligh; Novelist/Professor.

**DEWEY, SHELLY C,** S U N Y Coll At Fredonia, Fredonia, NY; SO; BS; Math; Tchr.

**DEWEY, WILLIAM C,** Memphis St Univ, Memphis, TN; GD; SPECI; Alpha Epsilon Delta Treas; BA Princeton Univ 87; Med.

**DEY, CHARLTON W,** Radford Univ, Radford, VA; SO; BA; Mktg.

**DEYAMPERT, NICOLE M,** Fl A & M Univ, Tallahassee, FL; FR; BS; Natl Soc Black Eng; Pres Schlrs Assoc; NASA Schlrs Assoc; Phi Eta Sigma Soc; Intrnshp NASA Goddard Sp Flght Cntr; Chem Eng.

**DEYETTE, RACHEL I,** Wesleyan Univ, Middletown, CT; FR; BA; Cncrt Chr 90-; Crdnl Ky 90-; Wlkng Escrt 90-; Chadbourne Prz 90-; Govt/Ecnmcs; Law/Pblc Affrs.

**DEYOT, LISA M,** S U N Y Coll At Fredonia, Fredonia, NY; SR; MA; Psych Clb Pres 89-; Spnsh Hnr Soc 90-; Natl Foreign Lang Hnr Soc 90-; Internship; Merit Awd; Tchrs Asst 90; Trck/ Field State Champ 88-89; BA; Psych.

**DEYTON, BOBBIE J,** Truett Mc Connell Coll, Cleveland, GA; SO; BED; GAE 89-; Chld Dvlpmnt Assoc; CDA Crdntl Natl Counc Erly Chldhd Prof Recogntn; CDA Advsr Tchrs Stf; Erly Chldhd Educ.

**DEYTON JR, CLARENCE S,** Mayland Comm Coll, Spruce Pine, NC; SO; AA; Phi Theta Kappa; Bio; Teach.

**DEZARN, CATHERINE M,** Northern Ky Univ, Highland Hts, KY; SR; BS; Psych Clb 88-; Psi Chi Sec 88-; Alpha Chi 89; Bk Grnt 89-90; All Acad Tm 89; Drll Tm 88; Psych; Nrsng.

**DEZARN, KRISTIE M,** Cumberland Coll, Williamsburg, KY; JR; BS; Math Clb Sec 90-; Sigma Tau Delta VP 90-; Deans Lst 88-; Engl/Math; Tchr.

**DEZURA, KIMBERLY A,** Univ Of Pittsburgh, Pittsburgh, PA; SO; Scty Wmn Engrs 89-; Amer Inst Cheml Engrs 90-; Res Stdnt Assoc 90-; Hand In Hand Festival 90-; Engrng Deans Lst 90-; Chem Engrng.

**DHALLA, DIMPLE,** Fl International Univ, Miami, FL; SO; BS; Pre Med Scty Sec 90-; Chmstry Clb; Sclgy Anthrplgy Clb; Alpha Epsilon Delta; Blgy; Med.

**DHALWALA, RITU S,** George Mason Univ, Fairfax, VA; JR; BS; Violin 83; Vol At Leewood Nrsng Hm 89; Bsnss Admin Accntng; Accntng Fnce.

**DHANA, FIDEL D,** Fl International Univ, Miami, FL; JR; SGA 88-89; Orgn W Indian Stu; Phi Theta Kappa 88-89; Accntng; CPA.

**DHARMASAPUTRA, ROBERT,** Univ Of Miami, Coral Gables, FL; SO; BS; Indonesia VP 90-; Hnr Assn 90-; Alpha Lambda Delta 89-; Pi Eta Kappa 89-; Cmptr Engnrng; Capoulting.

**DHARMAWAN, LIZA,** Radford Univ, Radford, VA; SR; BBA; Fncl Mgmt Assoc 90-; Intl Clb 87-89; Asian Assoc 88-89; Delta Mu Delta 90-; Finance; Bsn.

**DHOOGE, SUSAN M,** Savannah Coll Of Art & Design, Savannah, GA; SR; BFA; Photo Club 87-88; OVP Fire Dept; Explorer Post Pres/Capt 87-88; Choir 87-88; Dns Lst 88-90; REACH Tchr 87-89; CPA 87-89; Schlstc Art Awds 88; Francis Larkin Mc Common Schlrshp 88-; Crew Team 88-90; Phtgrphy.

**DI BELLA, ANN M,** Villanova Univ, Villanova, PA; SR; DMD; Phi Sigma; Dns Lst 89-; Dance Ensmbl 89-; BS Bio; Bio.

**DI BELLO, CHARLENE M,** Edinboro Univ Of Pa, Edinboro, PA; JR; BA; Psych Clb; Am Psychlgcl Assoc; Am Psychlgcl Soc; CEC; Psi Chi; Psych; Dvlpmntl Psychlgst.

**DI BENEDETTO, MARIA I,** Villanova Univ, Villanova, PA; JR; Gamma Phi; Kappa Kappa Gamma; Specl Olympcs/Rush Cnslr For Grk Systm; Dns Lst; Flg Ftbl/Grk Week Sprtng Evnts; Engl; Law.

**DI BIASE, KELLY K,** Indiana Univ Of Pa, Indiana, PA; SR; BED; PSEA 90-; Elem Edn; Publ Sch Edn.

**DI BONA, WENDY L,** Bay Path Coll, Longmeadow, MA; SO; Glee Clb Ky Nts VP 89-; Stdnt Govt 90-; Res Asst; Vlybl Coord; AS; Human Svcs; Indstrl Psychlgy.

**DI BUONO, CHRISTOPHER M,** Atlantic Comm Coll, Mays Landing, NJ; SO; AA/BA; Ski Clb 89-; Stdnt Govt Rep 90-; Pltcl Sci; Govt Law.

**DI CARLO, DIANE F,** Westchester Comm Coll, Valhalla, NY; SR; BA; Fclty Stdnt Assc Pres 90-; Bdgt Com Chrprsn 90-; Stndt Pgrmng Com Chrprsn 89-90; Alpha Beta Gamma 89-; Stdnt Sen Exec Bd 89-; Hnrs Cnvctn Hnrs Grad; AS; Accounting; Cpa.**

**DI CESARE, JILL M,** Old Dominion Univ, Norfolk, VA; JR; BS; Mrktg Ed Trng Spec; Mrktg/Advrtsg/Trng.

**DI CICCO, JULIA A,** Oh Univ, Athens, OH; GD; DO; UAAO 88-; AMSA 88-; Sprts Med Clb 88-; Sigma Sigma Phi 90-; Pi Beta Phi 85-; Rsrch Flwshp 89; BS OH Univ 88; Zlgy; Med.

**DI CICCO, M JACQUELINE,** Ms Univ For Women, Columbus, MS; SO; BS; Advsry Cncl 90-; Phi Beta Lambda 90-; Torch; Bus Clss Schlr; GPA Awd; Amer Inst Bnking/Golden Trngl P 84-91; Fncl Wmn Intrntl 87-89; Career Bgnngs; Bnk Bus Dvlpmnt VP; Cert MS Schl Bnkng 86; Bus Damin; Trng.

**DI CICCO, ROSE M,** Kent St Univ Kent Cmps, Kent, OH; SR; BA; Amer Soc Interior Dsgnrs 90-; Golden Key; Kappa Omicron Nu 90-; Sheri Jo Luft Mem Award 90; Dns Lst 89-; Interior Design.**

**DI CIOCCIO, DANA L,** Albertus Magnus Coll, New Haven, CT; JR; BA; Arts Clb 90-; Hrt/Cncr Assn; Mtn Bike; Psych/Art.

**DI DOMENICO, PATRICK V,** Le Moyne Coll, Syracuse, NY; SO; BS; Pltcl Sci Acdmy 90-; Pre Law Soc 90-; Mrtl Arts/Self Dfns Smnrs Instrctr; Pltcl Sci; Law.

**DI DONATO, CARRIE,** William Paterson Coll, Wayne, NJ; FR; BS; Math Tchr.

**DI FIORE, MARIANNINA,** Teikyo Post Univ, Waterbury, CT; JR; BS; Pop Clb NJ Sec 87-; Notary Pblc 89-; Scrty Svngs/Loan Teller 88-; Re/Max Prop Unltd Rcptnst; BS; Mgmt/Bsn Admn.

**DI FONZO, DENISE A,** West Liberty St Coll, West Liberty, WV; SO; BA; Fshn Mktg Clb; Alpha Xi Delta; Fshn Mktg; Retail Buyer.

**DI FRANCESCO, CHRISTINA F,** Saint John Fisher Coll, Rochester, NY; SR; BA; Cir K Pres 89-90; Cmps Mnstry Cncl 90-; Amm B Martin Schlrshp Awd 89-90; NW Dist Dstngshd Pres Awd 89-90; Wrk Stdy Stdnt Yr Awd 89-90; Engl/Sclgy; Law/Scl Wrk.

**DI FRANCESCO, GINA,** Seton Hall Univ, South Orange, NJ; SR; BA; Kappa Delta Pi 90-; AA Union Cnty Clg 89; Psy; Elmntry Schl Tchr.**

**DI GIACOMO, DIANA P,** Bunker Hill Comm Coll, Boston, MA; SO; Bus Mgmt; Mrktng.

**DI GIACOMO, JENA M,** Univ Of Akron, Akron, OH; SR; BS; Spanton Res Hall Govt Sec 87-88; Natl Assoc For Female Exec; Pi Sigma Epsilon Co Dir Of Orntn 89-; Am Mutual Life Assoc Schlrshp 89-90; Sls & Mrktng Execs Of Akron Stdnt Of Month 90; Bus; Mrktng.

**DI GIORGIO, ANDREA L,** Niagara Univ, Niagara Univ, NY; SO; BA; Psychlgy Club 90-; Croquet Club; Hons Prog 89-; Psychlgy.

**DI GREGORIO, DEANNA L,** Strayer Coll, Washington, DC; SR; BS; Alpha Chi 90-; Hon Rl 90-; Dns Lst 90-; Pres Lst 90-; Bus Adm; Mgmt.

**DI JOSEPH, PAUL J,** Temple Univ, Philadelphia, PA; JR; BS; Amer Soc Of Mech Eng 89; Im Bsktbl Sftbl 88-90; Mech Eng; Eng.

**DI LAPO, MARTINA D,** Daemen Coll, Amherst, NY; JR; Kappa Delta Pi; Spec/Elem Ed.

**DI LEO, ANDREA,** Univ Of Nh Plymouth St Coll, Plymouth, NH; FR; BA; Pace 90-; Plymouth Schlr; Bus Mgmt; Law.

**DI LEO, BRENDA A,** Fordham Univ, Bronx, NY; SR; BS; Cltrl Affrs Com Pres 89-; Acctng Scty 89-; Beta Gamma Sigma 90-; Alpha Sigma Nu; Beta Alpha Psi Crrspndng Sec 90-; VITA 90; Dns Lst 87; Dltte And Tche Intrn 90; Summa Cum Laude; BS; Acctng; CPA.

**DI LEONARDO, LINDA M,** Univ Of Pittsburgh, Pittsburgh, PA; SR; BS; Info Sci; Comp Spclst.

**DI LORETO JR, ROMEO ANTHONY,** Savannah Coll Of Art & Design, Savannah, GA; GD; MFA; Art Gllry 87-; Intl Stdnts Clb VP 90-; Acdmc Cncl Rep 88-89; Stdnt Excptnl Prms 89; Deans Lst 90-; Art Exhbtns 85-89; Dffld Bys Hcky Clb Asst Cch 84; Phtgrphy 90-; Prps Fllwshp 90-; Sl Grp Exhbtns 84-; Intern Dn Snydr Tchng 90; Bdmntn Tm 83-84; Phtgrphy.

**DI MAIO, MARIA A,** Clark Univ, Worcester, MA; SO; BA; Jazz Wrkshp Treas 90-; Italian Scty 90-; Cmprtv Lit.**

**DI MARCO, THOMAS A,** Salisbury St Univ, Salisbury, MD; SO; BS; Perdue Schlrs Assoc 89-; Phi Eta Sigma 89-; Bus Admin; Mgmt Info Systms.

**DI MARIA, SARA G,** City Univ Of Ny Baruch Coll, New York, NY; SR; BS; Ed.

**DI MARO, JENNIFER L,** Patrick Henry Comm Coll, Martinsville, VA; FR; Bsn.

**DI MARTINO, MARIA T,** Teikyo Post Univ, Waterbury, CT; SR; RCVD; BS 90; Mktg.

**DI MASCIO, CINDY L,** S U N Y Coll Of A & T Morrisvl, Morrisville, NY; FR; Yrbk Edtr In Chf 90-; Hall Cncl 90-; Swim Tm Stats 90-; Nitrition/Sports Stds.

**DI MASCIO, MICHAEL G,** Newbury Coll, Brookline, MA; SO; BA; Rstrnt Sprvsr At Ndhm Shrtn Htl; Fd Srvce Mgmt; Rstrnt Mgmt.

**DI MATTEO, CHERYL K,** Merrimack Coll, North Andover, MA; JR; BA; Hist Mjr Mnr Spnsh Elem Ed; Elem Tchr.

**DI MATTIA, MARGARET,** Notre Dame Coll, Cleveland, OH; SO; Notre Dame Ed Cncl Sec/Trea 90-; Elem Ed/SLD; Tchng.

**DI MEO, DOROTHY DENISE,** Va Commonwealth Univ, Richmond, VA; SR; BS; Sigma Theta Tau; Phi Kappa Phi; Gldn Key 90-; Nrsng.

**DI MEO, MARIA,** Hudson Valley Comm Coll, Troy, NY; FR; AS; Pres Lst 90-; Gen Stds.

**DI MOLFETTA, CHRISTINE F,** Wagner Coll, Staten Island, NY; JR; BSE; Kappa Delta Pi; Alpha Tau Mu 88-; Phi Mu Alpha Sinfonia 90-; Spec Educ; Tchg.

**DI MURO, DAVID E,** Univ Of North Fl, Jacksonville, FL; SR; BA; Finance; Auditg.

**DI MUZIO, DAWN E,** Liberty Univ, Lynchburg, VA; FR; BS; Acctg/Fin; Acctg/Bus.

**DI NARDO, CHRISTOPHER C,** Savannah Coll Of Art & Design, Savannah, GA; SO; BA; Illustration.

**DI NUCCI, ADRIENNE M,** Western New England Coll, Springfield, MA; FR; BA; Bus; Mktg.

**DI PAOLA, DOUGLAS,** Fl Atlantic Univ, Boca Raton, FL; SR; BBA; Bsns Admnstrtn; Mgmnt.

**DI PAOLO, LORI ANNE,** Fairfield Univ, Fairfield, CT; FR; Bio; Med.

**DI PAOLO, MICHELLE A,** Johnson St Coll, Johnson, VT; SR; Grad Comm; Pres List; Prac I Kids Sch Pre Sch 89-90; BAEEDECE; Practcm II Johnson Elem Sch Grade 1 90-; Elem Ed/Erly Chldhd; Tchr.

**DI PASQUALE, ANDREA J,** Oh Univ, Athens, OH; SR; BFA; ACD 88-89; Golden Key 88-; Grphc Dsgn Dpt 90-; Intrn; IM Vlybl/Bsktbl; Fine Art; Grphc Dsgn/Illstrtn.

**DI PASQUALE, RON C,** West Liberty St Coll, West Liberty, WV; SO; BED; AA Art Inst Pittsbgh 83; Biol; Tchr.

**DI PERSIO, CHRISTOPHER R,** Adelphi Univ, Garden City, NY; SO; BS; Tutor 90-; AA Nassau Comm Clge 89-; Physc; Prfsr.

**DI PIETRO, FRANK J,** Fl International Univ, Miami, FL; JR; BACC; Acctg Mgr/Cmptrlr; Acctg; CMA CPA.

**DI PIETRO, MICHELE G,** Georgetown Univ, Washington, DC; JR; BS; Stdnt Fedrl Credit Un Opertv Mgr 90-; Delta Sigma Pi Pres/Treas 90-; Coopers/Lybrand Intrhsnp 90-; Acctng; Publc Acctng.

**DI PRESSO, JEANNE M,** S U N Y Coll Of Tech At Frmgdl, Farmingdale, NY; SO; AS; Am Dntl Hyg Assoc 88-; Dntl Hyg Scty 88-; Std Am Dntl Hyg Assoc 88-; Dns Lst 89-; Dntl Asst; AS; Dntl Hygiene.

**DI PRIZIO, FRANK,** Bunker Hill Comm Coll, Boston, MA; FR; ASSOC; Mgmt.

**DI RENZO, DINA M,** Glassboro St Coll, Glassboro, NJ; SR; BA; Ad Dyn Acct Exec 90-; Ad Clb Stf Wrtr 89-; NJPIRG 87-; Red Crs Intrn 90-; Retl Adv Intrn 90-; Comm Adv; Copywrtng/Acct Mgmt.

**DI RIENZO, CINDY A,** Lasell Coll, Newton, MA; SO; Stdnt Govt Dorm Rep 89-90; Intl Clb V P 89-90; Travel Clb 89-90; Bus Hon 89-; Greater Boston Cnvntn Vstrs Bur; Var Sftbl 89-90; AS; Bus; Hotel Admn.

**DI RIENZO, DEBRA A,** Saint John Fisher Coll, Rochester, NY; SR; MA; Delta Epsilon Sigma 87-; Pi Gamma Mu 87-; Alpha Mu Gamma 87-; Pres Schlrshp 87-; Deans Lst 87-; Rgnts Schlrshp 87-; BA; Anthrplgy.

**DI SANTO, DANIELLE M,** City Univ Of Ny Queensbrough, New York, NY; SR; CSI 90-; Dist Attrnys Offc Sec/Wrd Prcsr 86-88; AAS; Admin Sec.

**DI SCIPIO, MARIANNE,** Daytona Beach Comm Coll, Daytona Beach, FL; FR; BA; Phi Theta Kappa; Sugar Mill Elem; Epiphany Ch; Waitress Ryans Steakhouse; Sci; Medical.

**DI SIMONI, SUSAN W,** Marywood Coll, Scranton, PA; SO; BA; Our Lady Snows R C Church Lctr 88-; Bgng Experience Fcltr 85-88; Waverly Wmns Clb; Natl Assn Med Staff Sec 85-; Bus Mgr Spch Thrpsts; Soc Sci/Pub Admin; Hlth Care.

**DI STEFANO, CARMEN,** Bergen Comm Coll, Paramus, NJ; SR; AA; Phi Theta Kappa; NJ Dept Of Lbr.

**DI STEFANO, PAMELA G,** Univ Of Pa, Philadelphia, PA; JR; BSE; Food Serv Ind/Own Catering Firm/Rstrnt; Mgmt.

**DI STEFANO, SAVERIO P,** Fl Atlantic Univ, Boca Raton, FL; JR; BBA; Cmptr Info Sys; Sys Anlyst.

**DI SUNNO, CARMEN M,** Cornell Univ Statutory College, Ithaca, NY; JR; BS; Eqstrn Tm 89-; Tae Kwon Doe Tm 89; Gldn Ky 90-; Ho Nun De Kah 90-; Alpha Epsilon Phi; Admin Tchng Asst; Fnnce; Cnslng.

**DI VINCENZO, JOSEPH P,** S U N Y At Buffalo, Buffalo, NY; JR; BA; Acctg Assn; Natl Assn Pblc Actnts; Gldn Key; Beta Alpha Psi; WNY Chptr Msclr Dystrphy Assn; SERTOMA Clb; Buffalo Chldrns Hosp Tlthn Com; NY State Rgnts Schlrshp Awd Wnnr; Acctg; Pblc Acctg.

**DI VITO, DOREEN M,** Niagara Univ, Niagara Univ, NY; SR; Natl Assn Acctnts 89-; Acctg Soc 89-; Alpha Kappa Psi Pub Rltns Chrmn 90-; IRS Vol Intrnshp; BBA; Acctg; CPA.

**DI VITO, THOMAS S,** Memphis St Univ, Memphis, TN; SO; BSN; ROTC Treas 90-; Nursing Sch Stdnt Assoc 89-; Natl Defense Medal 90-; Navy Nurse Corps Officer Candidate 89-; U S Navy Active Duty 85-; BA Beaver Coll 84; Navy Nurse Corps Officer.

**DIABO, JENNIFER D,** Fl International Univ, Miami, FL; FR; BA; Std Serv Comm 90-; Bsn Mktg/Adv; Intl Bsn.

**DIACONT, MATTHEW W,** Bloomsburg Univ Of Pa, Bloomsburg, PA; FR; Acctg/Econs; Corp Law.

**DIACONT, WILLIAM D,** Richard Bland Coll, Petersburg, VA; FR; BA; Cmptr Sci; Sys Anlyst.

**DIACONU, ALEN S,** Lenoir Rhyne Coll, Hickory, NC; JR; MBA; Indpndnt Intl; US Embssy Offc Clrk 87-88; Hm Rd; Glbtrttr; Bus Admn.

**DIACONU, MIRELA,** Lenoir Rhyne Coll, Hickory, NC; SO; MBA; Alpha Lambda Delta; BA 87; Acctg.

**DIAGO, MARIANA,** Georgetown Univ, Washington, DC; JR; BS; Con Amrcn Stdnts Assn Scl Chrprsn 90-; Phi Eta Sigma 89-; Finance.

**DIAL, JIMMI D,** Livingston Univ, Livingston, AL; JR; BS; Elem Educ; Teacher.

**DIAL, KELLI K,** Salisbury St Univ, Salisbury, MD; SR; BA; Dance Company Pres 87-; Frshmn Orientation Instrctr 89-; Phi Eta Sigms Pres 87-; Stdnt Asst Blackwell Lbry 88-; Phi Kappa Phi 90-; Omicron Delta Kappa 90-; Amer Mktng Assn 89-; Achvmnt Ky Awd 88-89; Cmps Lf Awd 89-90; Mst Ltsndng Sr Awd 90-; Comm Arts/Minor Mktng; Mktng.**

**DIAL JR, WILLIAM B,** Waycross Coll, Waycross, GA; SO; BA; Busn Club 90-; Acctng.

**DIALECTAKI, PHIVI,** Atlantic Union Coll, S Lancaster, MA; SR; BA; Sorbone IV Univ Of Paris 88; French.

**DIAMANTE, ROBERT,** Portland School Of Art, Portland, ME; SO; BFA; Stdnt Rep Body Frsh/Soph Rep 89-; Maine Vol Litrcy Prog Bd Mbr/Tutor In Training; Alterntv Mdms Artsts Who Raise Mny For People With Aids Publc Rltns/Prs Org 90-; Photogrphy; Photo Jrnlsm/Grad Sch.

**DIAMOND, CECIL DAVID,** Union Coll, Barbourville, KY; SO; BA; Fellowship Christian Athletes 90-; Social Sci Clb; Gamma Beta Phi 90-; Natl Guard Spec E4 88-; Deans Lst 90-; Ftbl 90-; English Sociology; Teach Coach.

**DIAMOND, DANA B,** Nova Univ, Ft Lauderdale, FL; GD; MBA; Natl Org Wmn 79-86; Yng Dmcrts TX 79-86; Univ TX Alumni Assn 83-; Schlstc Achvmnt 88-; Boca Raton Chmbr Commerce/Cnvntns/Trsm Com 88-; Mtng Plnrs Intl 90-; Spctrm Cnfrnc Plnrs Inc Pres 88-; BBS Univ TX 83; Bus Admin Finance.**

**DIAMOND, GREGORY D,** Univ Of Sc At Columbia, Columbia, SC; FR; BSBA; Thrtr Prod 90-; Pre Law Thtr; Law.

**DIAMOND, JOSHUA P,** Longwood Coll, Farmville, VA; JR; BS; Rsrv Offcrs Trng Crps 90-; Chrch Tns Clss Tchr; Thtr Actr 89; Gst Hnrry Ldrshp 90-; Phi Mu Epsilon; Scty Physcs Stdnts 90-; Physcs Math; Hlcptr Plt Elctrncs.

**DIAMOND, ROBERT H,** S U N Y At Buffalo, Buffalo, NY; FR; BS; Chem Engr.

**DIAMOND, SETH C,** Univ Of Rochester, Rochester, NY; SO; BA; Mrdn Soc Stdnt Vlntrs Admssns 89-; Chi Phi Sec 89-; Vrsty Swim Tm 89-; Ecnmcs; Accntng Finance.

**DIAMOND, TRACY R,** Wilmington Coll, New Castle, DE; FR; BA; Deans Lst 90; Sci-Ele Educ.

**DIAO, WEI,** Smith Coll, Northampton, MA; GD; PHD; SG Beijing Univ 86-87; Class Govt 88; Intl Org/Asian 87-90; Phi Beta Kappa 88-; Samuel Econs Prize 90; First Grp Schlr 88-90; Magna Cum Laude; Econs.

**DIAS, MARIO N,** Univ Of Pittsburgh, Pittsburgh, PA; SO; BS; Dbt Union 89-90; Chncllrs Nmnee Schlrshp; Milliken Eng Schlrshp; Elect Eng; Eng.

**DIAZ ALVAREZ, LIDSY,** Univ Of Pr At Rio Piedras, Rio Piedras, PR; JR; BA; Finance Assoc 90-; Dns Lst 89-90; Finance; Law.

**DIAZ DIAZ, RUY V,** Inter Amer Univ Pr San Juan, Hato Rey, PR; GD; JD; Sga Rep 88-90; Am Bar Assoc 87-; Deans Lst 88-; Prac Attrny; BS 87; Crmnlgy.**

**DIAZ MARGUEZ, MERCEDES,** Inter Amer Univ Pr Hato Rey, Hato Rey, PR; JR; Assc Crstn Unvrstr 89-90; Ascacn De Hon Mdl De Hon 88-89; Grdcn Esvl Spr Jsf Pstrn; Ftrs Ldrs Del Cmrc De Amer Dipl 87-88; CC Cert Contbld Esc Sup Josefa Pstrn 89; Ninguna; Bchlrt Admnstrcn De Emprs Con Una Conntrcn En Sistms Cmptrzds De Inf Gen; Matmtc; Trmnr Mi Careera Y Graduarmepara.

**DIAZ ORTIZ, PEDRO,** Univ Of Pr Medical Sciences, San Juan, PR; SR; BHS; Rdlgc Tech Assn 83-; Rltr; Admn; Law.

**DIAZ RIVERA, LINDA J,** Inter Amer Univ Pr San Juan, Hato Rey, PR; GD; JD; Deans Lst 78-85; Asociacion De Sico Logos De P R 91; Carribean Assoc Trro Prog 86; J Harris Flwshp Best Stdnt 87; Deans Lst 78-85; Master Clncl Psychology; MA Univ P R 85; Law; Doctor Clncl Psychlgy/Master Law.

**DIAZ RIVERA, WANDA S,** Univ Of Pr Medical Sciences, San Juan, PR; GD; MS; Ftr Hlth Prfsnl Assc 88-90; Actvs Free Hlth Svc Chldrn 90-; BS Un PR 90; Actvts Free Hrng Tests Old People 90-; Natrl Sci; Audiology M S.

**DIAZ SEPULVEDA, ANAED,** Inter Amer Univ Pr San German, San German, PR; SR; Cuada De Honorde La 88-; Univ Interamer; De Puerto Rico Recinto De San German.

**DIAZ VALDES, OSCAR L,** Inter Amer Univ Pr Guayama, Guayama, PR; SO; BA; Boy Scts Amer Patrl Ldr 83-87; Grnt ICI Phrmctcl Inc 89; HGA Grad Instr Tech 90; Frst Gov Stdnt Conf Rep; AD Inst Tera Guayama P R 90; Elec; Elec Eng/Math Bs.

**DIAZ, BARBARA M,** Fl International Univ, Miami, FL; SO; BA; Phi Lambda; Vntltd Asstd Chldrns Cmp Oprtns Crew; Deans Lst 90; Spcl Olympcs Asst 90; Bsns Admnstrtn; Accntng.

**DIAZ, CHRISTINA M,** Univ Of Miami, Coral Gables, FL; SR; BBA; Hon Stdnts Assn 87-; Pre Legal Soc 88-; Golden Key 90-; Alpha Kappa Psi VP 89-; Henry King Stanford Schlrshp 87-; Acctg; Law.

**DIAZ, DAISY,** Miami Dade Comm Coll North, Miami, FL; GD; BS; Phi Theta Kappa 90-; Talent Rstr Cert Achvmt; Outstdg Acdmc Achvmt MDCC N; Grad Highest Hnrs; Gymnstcs; AA MDCC N 90; Psychology.

**DIAZ, DAMARIS,** Fl International Univ, Miami, FL; JR; BA; Amrcn Cancr Soc 88-; AA 90; Accntng; CPA.

**DIAZ, DAVID T,** Univ Politecnica De Pr, Hato Rey, PR; SO; BSCE; Chrch Yth Org Pres 88-; Crs Cntry Capt 85-; Engr; Cvl Engr.

**DIAZ, DONABEL V,** Commonwealth Coll, Virginia Beach, VA; SO; AAS; Cmptr Sci Clb 90-; Cmptr Sci.

**DIAZ, EDGARDO J,** Univ Of Pr At Mayaguez, Mayaguez, PR; JR; BSME; ASME 90; SAE 90-; ASHRAF 90-; Tau Beta Pi; Eng Dept Hon Brd 88-; Eng.**

**DIAZ, EDWARD J,** George Mason Univ, Fairfax, VA; FR; MBA; Bus/Law.

**DIAZ, ELIK A,** Univ Politecnica De Pr, Hato Rey, PR; SO; BA; Scuba Dvng/Snrklng; Bdybldg; Comp Eng; Comp Grphcs Anmtn/Hrdwr Dsgn.

**DIAZ, ELKIN A,** Miami Dade Comm Coll South, Miami, FL; SO; St Catherine 89-90; Univ Miami Tbl Tns Clb 89-90; Assoc Engrs Fla 89-; Engrg Mchncl.

**DIAZ, IVAN J,** Nova Univ, Ft Lauderdale, FL; GD; DBA; Sdtnt Cncl Prs Clg 68-69; Toastmasters 89; BBA U Of Puerto Rico 69; Mgmnt; Bus.

**DIAZ, JUAN CARLOS,** Saint Thomas Univ, Miami, FL; SR; BA; Stdnt Advsry Coun 90-; Yth Ldrshp Dvlpmnt Proj Metro Dade Cnty 89-; Prop Admin 81-; AS Fla Intrnl Coll 90; Pub Admin; Doctorate Mngmnt.

**DIAZ, JUDY G,** Fl St Univ, Tallahassee, FL; JR; Peer Facilitator Prog 89-90; Baccus 89-90; Buena Vida Rtrmnt Comm Intrnshp 90; Excptnl Acad Perf Awd Multicltrl Stdnt Spprt Cntr 90-; Intrprsnl Commnctn; Prsnl Mgmt.

**DIAZ, MARIE E,** City Univ Of Ny La Guard Coll, Long Island Cty, NY; SO; BA; Acctg; Law/Bus Admnstrtn.

**DIAZ, MARIO J,** Miami Dade Comm Coll, Miami, FL; Cmptrs; Engr.

**DIAZ, MARITZA,** Inter Amer Univ Pr Hato Rey, Hato Rey, PR; FR; Math Awrd.

**DIAZ, MARK,** Univ Of Miami, Coral Gables, FL; JR; Beta Gamma Sigma; Beta Alpha Psi; Recrtnl Dept 85-; Deans Lst 88-; Pres Lst 90; Ftbl.

**DIAZ, PATRICIA,** Miami Dade Comm Coll, Miami, FL; FR; BA; Bus.

**DIAZ, RAFAEL A,** Inter Amer Univ Pr Hato Rey, Hato Rey, PR; SO; BS; US Navy Vet; Aviation Elect Sys.

**DIAZ JR, RAMON,** Springfield Tech Comm Coll, Springfield, MA; JR; BS; Radio; Hnr; AS 90; Comp Sci.

**DIAZ, RAYMOND A,** City Univ Of Ny City Coll, New York, NY; SR; BSMD; Matasanos Spanish Club Pres 87-89; Third Wrld Org Secy 88; Golden Key 88-; Bio Med; Medcn.

**DIAZ, SUSIE FERNANDEZ,** Univ Of Pr At Rio Piedras, Rio Piedras, PR; JR; Jesus Grp 89-; Gldn Key; Univ Stu Rdr Blnd 89-; Tutor Math; Tch Smr Cmp Chrch 90; Hnrs Cert Sci/Math 90; Sci.

**DIAZ, WENDY D,** Fl International Univ, Miami, FL; JR; BA; Grace Church 88-; AA Miami-Dade Comm Clg 90; Bus Admnstrtn; Acctg.

**DIAZ-ORTIZ, ANGEL L,** Univ Del Turabo, Gurabo, PR; SR; BBA; Stu Chr 86; Hnr Brd; Judo 86-87; Cmptr Inf Systms; CPA PHD.

**DIAZ-VICIEDO, MARIA C,** Univ Of Miami, Coral Gables, FL; SR; BA; Schl Msc Almn Assc Schlrshp; AA Miami Dade Comm Coll 89; Vcl Prfrmnc; Prof Sngr.

**DIBBINI, MICHAEL A,** Ny Univ, New York, NY; SR; DDS; Omicron Kappa Epsilon; Xi Psi Phi 90-; Deans List 89-90; BA SUNY 87; Dentstry; Surgry.

**DIBBLE III, SHERMAN L,** Tn Temple Univ, Chattanooga, TN; SO; BS; Mens Vllybl Clb 90-; Bus Clb 90-; Sigma Chi Delta 90-; Acctng; Bus/Finance.

**DICE, KATHLEEN,** Comm Coll Algny Co Algny Cmps, Pittsburgh, PA; FR; AD; Med Asst.

**DICE, SHARON V,** Fayetteville St Univ, Fayetteville, NC; SO; BS; Wrtrs Clb 90-; Prealumni Cncl 90-; Gold Medal Academia 89-; N C State Schlrshp 90-; Elem Ed/History.

**DICHIARA, LONA L,** Ms St Univ, Miss State, MS; SR; BA; Delta Delta Delta VP 78-82; W Point Jr Aux Tres 84-90; Amer Cance Soc 83-; Hm Grdn Clb 87-; BA 82; Elem Educ; Tchr.

**DICK, ANDREW E,** Hillsborough Comm Coll, Tampa, FL; JR; AA; Prjct Lit; MIS Bus; Bnkng/Actuarial BA.

**DICK, CHRISTIAN S,** Peace Coll, Raleigh, NC; FR; MBA; Drama Cl; Phi Theta Kappa; Sigma Delta Mu; Engl; Publshg.

**DICK III, HENRY N,** Univ Of Southern Ms, Hattiesburg, MS; SR; BSBA; Univ Appeals Comm 90-; Bckr Rvw Cmps Rep; Beta Alpha Psi 90-; Phi Chi Theta 90-; NAA; Pi Kappa Alpha Treas 89-; Coop Educ Stdnt 89-; Acctg; Pblc Acctng/Law.

**DICK, STEVEN C,** Univ Of North Fl, Jacksonville, FL; SR; BA; Poli Sci Soc; Phi Theta Kappa; Gldn Ky; Phi Kappa Phi, Pblc Dfndrs Ofc Intrnshp; AA St Jhns Rvr Comm Clg 90; Crmnl Jstc; Law.

**DICKENS JR, FRANK T,** City Univ Of Ny City Coll, New York, NY; JR; PRES 87-; NSBE 88-; Pi Tau Sigma; Hewlett Packard Co 88-90; Mech Eng.

**DICKENS, KIMBERLY A,** Marshall University, Huntington, WV; GD; MA; SGA Sntr 89-; Campus Crsde 88-; Delta Kappa Pi 90-; Phi Delta Kappa 88-; Red Crss 86-; Un Way Fndrsng Comm Chrprsn 89-90; Comp Clss Tchr 90-; Orientatn Coord 90-; Ed; Tchng.

**DICKENS, MELANIE D,** Univ Of Ga, Athens, GA; SO; BED; Math; Math Educ.

**DICKENS, PEGGY C,** Ky Wesleyan Coll, Owensboro, KY; GD; Ky Wesleyan Sngrs 85-89; Brass Ens/Jazz Bnd 85-89; Deans Lst 87-89; Outstndng Clg Stdnts Of Amer 87; MENC Pres Of Stdnt Chptr 85-90; BME 90; Tchng Music In Publ Schls.

**DICKERSON, ARCOLA L,** Memphis St Univ, Memphis, TN; MBA; MEA TEA; Tchr City Schls 78-; Ed.

**DICKERSON, BARBARA L,** Daemen Coll, Amherst, NY; SO; BS; Booga Booga Beta Soc Clb Tres; Yng Rpblcns 88-; Stu Athltc Trnr 89-90; Emerg Sqd 87-88; IM Brmbl Capt 87-90; Phys Thrpy; Phys Thrpst.

**DICKERSON, CHRISTINE L,** Univ Of New Haven, West Haven, CT; FR; BA; Arch; Int Dsgn.

**DICKERSON, DARREN D,** Union Univ, Jackson, TN; JR; BS; AS Jackson State Cmmnty Coll 90; Comp Sci; Comp Prgrmmr.

**DICKERSON, DEANNA K,** Univ Of Nc At Greensboro, Greensboro, NC; JR; BS; Church Yth Cncl/Cnslr 89-; REC Cross CPR/FIRST Aid Inst; Frshmn Schlrs Awd 89; Rsrch Asst 90-; Headstart Tstng 90-; Child Dvlpmnt/Fmly Rltns; Mdcl Child Lf Spec.

**DICKERSON, DEBRA L,** Wilmington Coll, New Castle, DE; SR; BS; Delta Epsilon Rho 90-; Admin Asst 88-; AS DE Tech And Comm Coll 87; Acctng; Comp Prgrmmng.

**DICKERSON, DOUGLAS K,** Guilford Tech Comm Coll, Jamestown, NC; SR; BA; Crim Justc Clb 87-90; Natl Talent Roster 90-; United Parcel Svc Supv 88-; Crim Just; Mgmt.

**DICKERSON, JUANITA S,** Vance Granville Comm Coll, Henderson, NC; SR; AAS; Pres Merit Awrd 90; Therapeutic Rec.

**DICKERSON, LEE ANN,** Memphis St Univ, Memphis, TN; SO; BA; Alpha Lambda Delta Edtr 89-; Cmps Crsd Chrst 89-90; Essay Cntst 90; Acad Exclnc Schlp 89; Crmnl Jstc; Cnslng.

**DICKERSON, LINDA F,** Memphis St Univ, Memphis, TN; SO; BSN; Blck Schlr; Deans Lst; LPN; Cmptr Oprtr; Sci; Nurs.

**DICKERSON, LINDA L,** Va Commonwealth Univ, Richmond, VA; JR; BA; Orgnst; Fairmont Chrstn Chrch Chldrns Chr; Msc Ed; Tchr.

**DICKERSON, MELISSA L,** Davis Coll, Toledo, OH; FR; ASSC; Advsry Brd Sec 90-; Admin Sec.

**DICKERSON, MYNA C,** Ms St Univ, Miss State, MS; JR; BA; Bldkfriars Drama Soc Prsdnt 90-; Unvrsty Chr 88-89; Alpha Psi Omega 90-; Cmmnctn; Prfsnl Theatre Actrs.

**DICKERSON, YOLANDA M,** Morris Brown Coll, Atlanta, GA; SO; USAA Natl Awd Wnr 89-90; Hon Lst Soc MBC 89-; Sigma Dove Org 89-; Chrldr 90-; Cmrcl Music/Rcrdng; Snd Engr Rcrd Co.

**DICKERSON-MAYO, TAMMY R,** Bethel Coll, Mckenzie, TN; JR; BA; Diakonoi V P 90-; Advncmnt Wmn Assn 90-; Clg Mnstrl Schlrshp 90-; Cumbrland Presbytrn Wmns Schlrshp; Rlgn; Prfsr Rlgn.

**DICKERT, NICCI S,** Saint Vincents Coll & Seminary, Latrobe, PA; JR; BS; NAA 89; Bsn Forum Trea 89; Charley Bros Acct Intrn 90; Acct.

**DICKERT, TANYA J,** Georgian Court Coll, Lakewood, NJ; JR; BA; Varisty Soccer GCC 88-89; Student Gvt Assoc Commuter Council Rep 88-; Deans List 88-89; Deans List 90-; Varisty Soccer 88-89; Hmnts/Elem Ed; Tchr.

**DICKEY, DANIEL W,** Kent St Univ Kent Cmps, Kent, OH; SR; BA; Mens Clb Vlybl Tm Mgr/Coach 90-; Pltcl Sci; Law.

**DICKEY, DEBORAH M,** Oh Wesleyan Univ, Delaware, OH; FR; BA; Wmen In Sci; Chemistry; Med Rsrch.

**DICKEY, ISAAC L,** Alcorn St Univ, Lorman, MS; JR; BS; Mrchng Bnd 88-; Intrfth Gspl Choir 89-; Biolgy; Dntstry.

**DICKINSON, CYNTHIA P,** Univ Of Montevallo, Montevallo, AL; JR; BS; Educ/Gen Sci; Tch.

**DICKINSON, DENISE C,** Patrick Henry Comm Coll, Martinsville, VA; SO; BA; Phi Theta Kappa; AS 90; AS 90; Psychlgy; Educ.

**DICKINSON, GA ROY L,** S U N Y Coll Of Tech At Alfred, Alfred, NY; SR; BS; Sci; Inds Eng.

**DICKINSON, GAROY L,** S U N Y Coll Of Tech At Alfred, Alfred, NY; SR; BS; Hghr Edn Awds; AS; Indstrl Eng.

**DICKINSON, GINGER ANN,** Southern Vt Coll, Bennington, VT; FR; BA; Studnt Assn Tres; Clg Stdnt Secrty Sprvsr 90-; Accntng.

**DICKINSON, JAMES J,** Hillsborough Comm Coll, Tampa, FL; SR; AS; Nuclear Med Club Treas 89-; Sigma Pi Sigma 83; BS Ball State Univ ,3; Nuclear Med Tchnlgy.

**DICKINSON JR, JOHN J,** Temple Univ, Philadelphia, PA; SO; Penn Dept Transport Intern; Dns Lst 90-; Elctrcl Engr.

**DICKINSON, KIMBERLY A,** Thomas Nelson Comm Coll, Hampton, VA; BA; Admin Asst; Pltcl Sci; Prlgl/Law.

**DICKMAN, GREGORY J,** Northern Ky Univ, Highland Hts, KY; SR; BA; IM Bsktbl; Acctg; CPA.

**DICKS, LISA L,** Univ Of North Fl, Jacksonville, FL; SR; BA; Golden Key; Kappa Delta Pi; AA Lake City Cmnty Clg 89; Elem Tchr.**

**DICKSON, ADRIENNE M,** Mount Holyoke Coll, South Hadley, MA; FR; Camp Cnsrvtn Cltn.

**DICKSON, BARBARA LYNETTE,** Tri County Tech Coll, Pendleton, SC; SO; BS; Alpha Zeta Beta 90-; Abney Schlrshp 90-; SAEOPP Schlrshp; Early Chldhd/Elem Educ; Tch.

**DICKSON, BELINDA J,** Memphis St Univ, Memphis, TN; SR; BA; Psychology; Counseling/Alcohol/Drugs.

**DICKSON, CHARLES W,** Catawba Valley Comm Coll, Hickory, NC; SO; AS; Deans Lst; Hrtcltr; Natl Rsrcs Mgmt.

**DICKSON, EDNA K,** Union Univ, Jackson, TN; SO; BS; Alpha Tau Omega Sweetheart 90-; Psychlgy Clb 89-; Psychlgy; Cnslr.

**DICKSON, HEATH C,** Univ Of Sc At Columbia, Columbia, SC; FR; BA; ARETE; Real Est Slsmn I Lic 90-; Bus Admin; Real Est.

**DICKSON, KATHERINE A,** Indiana Univ Of Pa, Indiana, PA; SR; Cmps Crsde Fr Christ Scl Chrprsn 86-; SADD 88-90; BACCHUS 88-90; Deans Lst 86-; Elem Educ; Tchg/Cnslg.

**DICKSON, MEREDITH L,** Anderson Coll, Anderson, SC; SO; BA; Phi Theta Kappa 89-; Gamma Beta Phi 89-; Tutor Awd; AA; Psy.

**DICKSON, PIERRE D,** Columbia Union Coll, Takoma Park, MD; SR; BS; Asst Dir ONE 86; Cnslr 82-86; Cls Repr 89-; Fld Trng Ofcrs Sch Instr 88-90; Prince Georges Cty Police Detective 85-; Org Mgmt; Hstry.

**DICUS, JIMMY P,** Tampa Coll, Tampa, FL; JR; BA; ROTC 89-90; Phi Beta Lambda; Sigma Nu 89-90; ROTC Hgh Physcl Trng Awd 90; Mgmt/Mktg; Ofcr U S Army.

**DICUS, LAURA ANN,** Middle Tn St Univ, Murfreesboro, TN; JR; BS; Gamma Beta Phi 90-; Alpha Kappa Psi Busn; Chi Omega Wmns 89-; Psych; Humn Res Mgmt.

**DIDAS, LEANNE M,** S U N Y Coll Of Tech At Alfred, Alfred, NY; FR; BA; Human Services; Counseling.

**DIDELOT, JULIE A,** Bowling Green St Univ At Huron, Huron, OH; FR; BS; Alpha Lambda Delta; Social Wk; Juvenile Corrtns.

**DIDICH, MICHELLE A,** Univ Of Akron, Akron, OH; SR; BA; RHPB Pblcty Comm 87; Golden Key 89-; Acad Schlrshp 89; Top Female Stdnt Ath 88; Co-Op Cntrl Intell Agncy Grphc Dsgnr 90-F Crss Cntry/Trk 87-89; Grphc Dsgn; Art Dir.

**DIDIER, DAVID,** Miami Dade Comm Coll, Miami, FL; JR; Boukan Clb VP 90; Cert Achvmnt; North Shore Hosp Phlbtmst Intern; Cert Phlbtmy.

**DIDIER JR, HENRY N,** Fl St Univ, Tallahassee, FL; JR; BA; Alumni Fndtn 90-; Seminole Ambsdrs 90-; Phi Kappa Phi 90-; Gold Key VP 90-; Beta Gamma Sigma VP 90-; Sigma Iota Epsilon 90-; Alpha Taul Omega PR Of 90-; Omega Alpha Rho 90-; Orntn Stf 90-; Orntn Trnr; Shotokan Karate Karate Clb Pres 88-; Bus; Law.

**DIDION, TAMARA D,** Bowling Green St Univ At Huron, Huron, OH; JR; BED; Elem Ed/Early Chldhd; Teacher.

**DIEGNAN, RICHARD P,** Providence Coll, Providence, RI; SR; Finance Clb 90; IMS 87-; Tau Pi Phi; A T T Intern 89-90; Cum Laude; BS; Finance; Network Svcs.

**DIEGO, JACQULINE,** Fl International Univ, Miami, FL; SR; BS; Commrcl Ins 86-; AA Miami Dade Co Clg 84; Elem Ed.

**DIEGUEZ, GLORIA,** Fl International Univ, Miami, FL; JR; BS; Future Edctrs Amer 90-; Kappa Delta Pi; AA Miami Dade Comm Coll 88-90; Elem Educ; Educ Cnslng.

**DIEHL, BRIGID M,** George Mason Univ, Fairfax, VA; SR; BA; Schlrshp N VA Asso Of Yng Chldrn; Early Chldhd Educ; Tchr.

**DIEHL, DAVID L,** Univ Of Tn At Martin, Martin, TN; SR; BS; Phi Kappa Tau 82-83; IM Ftbl/Sftbl 90-; Envrnmntl Geolgy.

**DIEHL, JENNIFER,** Anne Arundel Comm Coll, Arnold, MD; FR; BA; Amer Sgn Lngge Clb VP 90-; Sci.

**DIEHL, JENNIFER A,** Univ Of Pittsburgh, Pittsburgh, PA; FR; BSN; Ski Clb 89; NSNA 90; NSA 90; Deans Lst 89; Alpha Tau Delta 90; Chi Omega Asst VP 90; Hghst QPA Awd 90; Nrsng.

**DIEHL, JENNIFER S,** Fl St Univ, Tallahassee, FL; SO; BA; Intrntnl Affrs Soc 89-; Women Glee Clb 90-; Phi Eta Sigma 89-; Gold Key 90-; Omicron Delta Kappa 90-; Tlphn Cnslng Rfrl Srvc 90-; Best Wmn Soph Stdnt Yr 90-; Intrntnl Affrs Spnsh; Law.

**DIEHL, JULIA M,** Radford Univ, Radford, VA; SR; Delta Mu Delta 89-; Phi Kappa Phi; Deans Lst; Accntng Soc 89-; BBA; Accntng; Mgmnt.

**DIEHL, KELLY L,** Saint Francis Coll, Loretto, PA; SR; MA; Bsktbl Statstcn 89-; Tutor 88-; Delta Epsilon Sigma 90-; Sigma Tau Delta 89-; SFC Hnr Soc 90-; Dns Lst 87-; Pres Schlrshp 87-; BA; Engl; Grad Schl.

**DIEHL, LISA M,** Shippensburg Univ, Shippensburg, PA; SO; BED; Assc Chldhd Ed Intl VP/SEC; Keystone Rsrc Edctn Pgm; Peer Cntct; Wmns Ctr Vol; Big Bro/Big Sis 90-; Scotland Schl Vet Chldrn Tutor 89-; Aerobics 89-; Acad Achvmnt/Univ Schlr Recognition 90-; Elem Ed/Erly Chldhd; Elem Tchr.**

**DIEHL, SHERIE L,** Saint Francis Coll, Loretto, PA; SR; BS; Ed Clb 87-; Red Key Clb Thtr 88; Rght Lf Org VP 89-; Gamma Sigma Sigma VP/SEC 89-90; Dorothy Day Ctr Pls Spc Frnds Wd Cp Sp Ktchn 87-; Elem Ed; Tchg.

**DIEHM, CHRISTIAN A,** Salisbury St Univ, Salisbury, MD; JR; MBA; Engl Psychlgy; Tchr.

**DIELMAN, CHRISTINE M,** Memphis St Univ, Memphis, TN; SR; BA; Stdnt Activities Cnsl 87; Phi Kappa Phi 88; Golden Key 88; Gamma Beta Phi 87; Phi Eta Sigma 87; Psychology; Cnslr.**

**DIELSI JR, ANTHONY CARMEN,** Univ Of New Haven, West Haven, CT; JR; ASCE 88-; Alpha Lambda Delta; Alpha Lambda Delta; AS; Cvl Engnrng; Engnrng.

**DIENER, KURT,** Fl International Univ, Miami, FL; FR; Intl Student Clb 90-; FPIRG 90-; Crew 90-; Bus; Mngmnt.

**DIEROLF, SUSAN J,** Duquesne Univ, Pittsburgh, PA; GD; Orientation Stf 87-89; Beta Alpha Phi 87-90; Phi Chi Theta V P 87-90; SHARP 86-90; Accntnt Info Sys; BS Bus Admin 90; Acctng; Mgmnt.

**DIETRICH, BAERBEL H,** Univ Of Sc At Columbia, Columbia, SC; JR; BMED; Columbia Philharmonic Orch 87-; Palmetto String Trio 88-; Dns Lst 86-; USC String Proj Tchr 86-; Music; String Tchr.

**DIETRICH, BARBARA J,** Univ Of Akron, Akron, OH; SR; BFA; Glnd Ky 89; Presdntl Schlr 87-; Natl Paper Box Pkg Regl Dsgn Wnr 90; Intrnshps Buffalo Area Advtsng Agncy 89-90; IM; Graphic Dsgn; Mktng Dsgn Pkgng.

**DIETRICH, DENISE A,** Kent St Univ Stark Cmps, North Canton, OH; FR; BED; SEA; Comm Choir 90-; Cncr Bnft Cncrt 90-; Bchwd Stds; Hnrs Rctl 90; Pres Lst; Erly Chldhd Educ; Tchng.

**DIETRICH, JON D,** Salisbury St Univ, Salisbury, MD; GD; Concert Choir 87-90; Intrntl Thespian Soc Drama Club 88-; Theatre Prodctns 88-90; Deans List 89-90; Choral Concert Tour Of Germany 90; Guerrieri Univ Ctr Music Mjr Award; BA 90; Entertnr.

**DIETSCH, JULIE,** Oh St Univ At Marion, Marion, OH; JR; BED; NEA 90-; Dns Lst; AAS Owens Tech Clg 85; Elem Ed/Sci Ed; Tchr.

**DIETZ, CHRISTINE J,** Tn Temple Univ, Chattanooga, TN; SR; BA; BSU Cleveland St Comm Coll Wrshp Chm 85-86; Alpha Epsilon Theta Tn Temple Univ 88-; Tn Bapt Childrens Home Inc Psych Intern; Psych/Mnstrl Cnslng; Marriage & Family Cnslng.

**DIETZ, HOLLY L,** Auburn Univ At Montgomery, Montgomery, AL; FR; BED; Phi Eta Sigma 90-; Early Chldhd Ed; Tchr.

**DIETZ, JOHN D,** Western Piedmont Comm Coll, Morganton, NC; SO; AAS; Phi Theta Kappa; Trck Drvr; Bus; Trfc/Trans.

**DIETZ, MARGUERITE R,** Allegheny Coll, Meadville, PA; JR; BA; Lambda Sigma 89-90; Kappa Alpha Theta Schlrshp Dpty 89; Alden Schlr Allegheny 89-91; Vars Vlybl Co Capt 88; Poltcl Sci; Govt.

**DIETZ, SHARON F,** Kent St Univ Kent Cmps, Kent, OH; SR; BBA; Golden Key Pres 89-; Beta Gamma Sigma 89-; Deans List 87-; Pres List; Eastern Star 63-; Bus Mgr 74-; AA 89; Mrktng.**

**DIETZ, SHIRLEY G,** Birmingham Southern Coll, Birmingham, AL; SR; BA; Music Stdnts Comm 90-; Elizabeth May Meyer Awd 88; AL Music Tchrs Assn 90; Alys R Stevens Piano Competition 90-; Music; Educ.

**DIEZ-DE-ONATE, BEATRIZ M,** Fl International Univ, Miami, FL; SR; BA; AA/AS Miami Dade Comm Clg 89; Specl zd Trng Erly Chldhd Ed Miami Dade Comm Clg 89; Elem Ed; Tchng.

**DIEZ-DE-ONATE JR, JORGE,** Barry Univ, Miami, FL; SR; BS; Magna Cum Laude; Cafe Ideal Inc Operations Mgr 81-; AA Miami Dade Comm Coll 88; Mgmt Inf Sys; Intl Bus.

**DIFFEE, DERRICK E,** Longwood Coll, Farmville, VA; SR; Rgby Clb 87-; Delta Pres/Socl Chrmn 90-; BS; Crmnl Law.

**DIFFENDERFER, LAURA A,** Mount Aloysius Jr Coll, Cresson, PA; SO; AA; Intrprtr Clb 89-; Bacchus 90-; Sftbl; Intrprtr Trng.

**DIGBY, RANDALL L,** Univ Of Sc At Columbia, Columbia, SC; JR; BA; Entrpnrl; Own Bus.

**DIGGES III, RANDOLPH E,** Univ Of Toledo, Toledo, OH; GD; JD; Alumni Recgntn Awd 89-; Alumni Fund Schlrshp 90-; Amrcn Juriprudence Awds 89-; BA OH St Unvrsty 88; Law.

**DIGGINS JR, JOSEPH P,** Westminster Coll, New Wilmingtn, PA; JR; BA; Stu Govt Assn Tres; Stu Govt Assn Chap 90-; Tau Pi Phi 90-; Omincron Delta Kappa 90-; Chpl Stff Mssn Intrp Awrnss 90-; Accntng.

**DIGGS, KELLY D,** Nc Agri & Tech St Univ, Greensboro, NC; JR; BS; ASHRAE 89; Tau Beta Pi 90; Alumni Schlr 87; ASHRAE Schlrshp; Cross Cntry Trck/Fld 87-89; Archtctrl Eng; Eng Tchncl Sales.

**DIGGS, MARGARET E,** Bunker Hill Comm Coll, Boston, MA; FR; AD; Med Rdgrphy; Med Rgstrd Rdlgy Tchncn.

**DIGGS, MARILYN L,** Wilmington Coll, New Castle, DE; FR; BA; Soc Of Black Americans 90-; Black Hist Comm Sec 90-; U S Air Force SSGT/E5 83-; Criminal Justice; Law.

**DIGGS, ROBERT O,** Va St Univ, Petersburg, VA; SR; BS; Ecnmcs Clb 90; Pltcl Involvment Com Fndr/VP 88; VA Statesman Nwspr Staff 88; Iota Phi Theta Pres 84-85; Ecnmcs; Ecnmst/Fed Rsrv.

**DIGH, ANDREW D,** Univ Of Nc At Asheville, Asheville, NC; JR; BA; Mbr Math Assn Amer Stdnt Chptr Camps 88-; Phi Eta Sigma 88-; Chncllrs Lst 88-; Math.

**DIGLIO, MICHELE G,** Fl International Univ, Miami, FL; GD; NOW 90-; FRIRG; Sigma Phi Alpha 90-; Sigma Phi Delta 89-; Crmnl Jstc Hnr Soc; Legal Ad Soc 89; Spouse Abs Inc 90; Crmnl Jstc Artcl; AA Valencia Comm Coll 89; BS 90; Crmnl Jstc; Lwyr.

**DIHARCE, CECILIA,** Fl International Univ, Miami, FL; FR; Elem Educ.

**DIKE, IFEANYI S,** Cheyney Univ Of Pa, Cheyney, PA; GD; BS; Tstmstrs 87-; Bus Clb 89-; Intrntl Assn Sec Gen 88-89; Acad Recog; Klass Mem Clb VP 87-; BS 89-; Bus Admin Acctg; Corp Law.

**DIKEAKOS, MARIA V,** Cooper Union, New York, NY; SO; BSCE; Grk Clb 89-; Grk Orthdx Yng Aadlt Leag 90-; Hllnc Cmmnty Yth Cncl 90-; Soc Wmn Eng 89-; Cvl Eng.

**DILDAY, KEVIN W,** Mount Olive Coll, Mount Olive, NC; SO; BS; Schlrs Prog 89-; Bys Clb 90-; Bsktbl Asst 89-; Bus Mgmt; Law.

**DILEO, HEIDI A,** Fl Atlantic Univ, Boca Raton, FL; GD; SADD Ldr 86-; Natl Assoc Accntnts 90; Natl Accntng Hnr Scty Candidate 90; Alpha Tau Omega 87; Envrnmntl Protection Agcy 86-88; Child Care Lcl Business 86-90; Track Tennis Swim 86-; BBA 90; Acctng.**

**DILKS, MICHAEL S,** Wilmington Coll, New Castle, DE; SO; BS; Avtn Mgmt; Flight.

**DILL, ANDREW BRENDAN,** Coll Of Charleston, Charleston, SC; FR; BS; Fllwshp Of Chrstn Athletes 90; Hnrs Prog Stdnt Assoc 90; Deans Lst; Pres Lst; Bio Pre-Med; Mdcl.

**DILL, PATRICIA L,** Ms St Univ, Miss State, MS; FR; BA; Psych Club; Alpha Lambda Delta; Gamma Beta Phi; LPN; Psych; Cnslng.

**DILLARD, ALLISON L,** Univ Of Ky, Lexington, KY; JR; BA; Frnch Clb 90-; Cncrt Com 88-90; Pi Delta Phi Sec; Pi Beta Phi 88-; Alzheimers Assn 90-; Engl/Frnch; Prfssr.

**DILLARD, CHRISTOPHER R,** Roanoke Coll, Salem, VA; SO; BBA; Bsbl Clb Fnd Rsng Chrmn 90-; Intr Frat Cncl 90-; Kappa Alpha Ordr Pres 90-; Acctng; CPA.**

**DILLARD, CINDY W,** Univ Of Montevallo, Montevallo, AL; JR; BS; Chmstry Clb 89-; Phi Kappa Phi; Kappa Mu Epsilon; Chmstry Awrd 89-; Hghst Hnrs 89-; Chmstry.

**DILLARD, DARLENE M HARMON,** De Tech & Comm Coll At Dover, Dover, DE; FR; AAS; Phi Theta Kappa; Vol Kent General Hsop; Sales; Arch Eng/Interior Dsgn.

**DILLARD, DAVID L,** Patrick Henry Comm Coll, Martinsville, VA; SO; MA; Blck Stdnt Assn 90; ASSC; Elec Tech; Eng.

**DILLARD, JERRY W,** Univ Of Al At Birmingham, Birmingham, AL; SR; BSEE; Eta Kappa Nu; Tau Beta Pi 90; Elctrcl Eng.

**DILLARD, JOHN W,** Memphis St Univ, Memphis, TN; SR; BA; Cmptr Repair Tech 84-; ASET State Tech Inst Memphis; Eng Tech NICET; Elect Tech; Eng Tech.

**DILLARD, KRISTINE M,** Columbus Coll Of Art & Design, Columbus, OH; JR; BFA; Illustration.

**DILLE, JODY M,** Defiance Coll, Defiance, OH; FR; BED; Tchrs Asst Hnry Cnty Pblc Schls 85-; Psy/Sclgy; Educ/Spec Ed.

**DILLE, WANDA J,** Wv Univ At Parkersburg, Parkersburg, WV; GD; MBA; Toastmasters Intl Div Lt Gov 87-88; WVA Interstate Fair Com Chrpsn 73-; Accountant At G E Plastics; BS Glenville State Coll 90; Acctng.

**DILLEY, BETH A,** Garrett Comm Coll, Mchenry, MD; FR; BS; Dns Lst; Hnr Rl; Elem Ed.

**DILLEY, KRISTEN L,** Rutgers St Un At New Brunswick, New Brunswick, NJ; FR; NSPIRG 90-; Cncrt Orgn 90-; Wmn Stu; Coll Prfssr.

**DILLIGARD, LATONYA L,** Johnson C Smith Univ, Charlotte, NC; JR; BA; Engl Clb 89-; Johnson C Smith Univ Nwspr Stf 90-; Alpha Chi 90-; Alpha Kappa Mu; Sigma Tau Delta; Alpah Kappa Alpha Corres Sec 89-; Pres Lst; All Amer Schlr; Engl; Law.

**DILLING, KLAUS F,** Univ Of Sc At Columbia, Columbia, SC; JR; BA; IM Sccr; Ecnmcs; Intl Bus.

**DILLINGER, BETTY L,** Oh St Univ At Marion, Marion, OH; SR; BED; Univ Educ Scty 90-; Tchrs Aide Tiffin City Schls 76-89; Elem Educ/Sci; Tch.

**DILLMAN, MELISSA G,** Watterson Coll, Louisville, KY; SR; ACT; Cmptr Pgm; Pgmr/Syst Analyst.

**DILLON, BOBBIE L,** Saint John Fisher Coll, Rochester, NY; SR; BA; Nwspr Wrtr 89-; Otstndnt Adlt Stdnt; Mktg Hghr Educ Pltnm Awrd; Admsn Mktg Achvmnt Awrd; Wmn Cmnctns; Wrtr/Edtr Clg Cmnctns 90-; AAS Comm Clg Finger Lakes 89; Cmnctns/Jrnlsm; Pblc Rltns.

**DILLON, CAROLYN K,** Owensboro Comm Coll, Owensboro, KY; FR; HS; Humn Serv; Soc Wrk.

**DILLON, CLAIRE M,** Rutgers St Un At New Brunswick, New Brunswick, NJ; FR; BA; Acctg; CPA.

**DILLON, CRAIG J,** Alcorn St Univ, Lorman, MS; FR; BS; ROTC Prcsn Drlltm Sgt; Slvr ROTC Mdl Sgt; Sns Amrcn Rvltn Awrd Sgt; Acctg; CPA.

**DILLON, DAWN M,** Belmont Coll, Nashville, TN; SR; BS; Dns Lst; Elem Educ; Elem Schl Tchr.

**DILLON III, HAROLD D,** East Tn St Univ, Johnson City, TN; GD; MD; Phi Kappa Phi 77-; Fgtr Pilot US Air Frc 8-89; Med; Pilot/Physcn.

**DILLON, JANET E,** Oh Univ, Athens, OH; FR; Soccr Clb 90-; Phys Therpy; Asst.

**DILLON, MARK A,** Wv Univ, Morgantown, WV; JR; BS; IEEE; Tau Beta Pi; Electrical Eng; Eng.

**DILLON, MATTHEW E,** Oh Univ-Southern Cmps, Ironton, OH; SR; MBA; Bus Mgt.

**DILLON, MICHAEL J,** Univ Of Cincinnati, Cincinnati, OH; SR; BA; OH Natl Guard Sgt; Golden Key; Probation/Parole Vol; IM Bsktbl/Sftbl; AAS 90; Crmnl Jstc; Law.

**DILLON, MICHELLE K,** Mount Aloysius Jr Coll, Cresson, PA; SO; AD; Phi Theta Kappa 90-; Mcd Lab Tech; Med.

**DILLON, PAMALA J,** Eckerd Coll, St Petersburg, FL; JR; BA; Sch Nwspr Copy Edtr 88-90; Model Un Ntns Del To Harvard Natl Mun 89-90; Intl Stdnt Assoc 89-90; Jazz Ens Tenor Sax 89-90; Kennedy Twnshp Girls Sftbl Asst Ch; London Prog 90; Intl Stdnt Exch Prog Univ Amsterdam; IM Sports 88-90; Pol Sci/Intl Studies; Foreign Serv.

**DILLON, SARAH ELIZABETH,** Liberty Univ, Lynchburg, VA; JR; BS; Psychlgy Clb 90-; Va Psychlgcl Assoc; Alpha Lambda Delta 88-; Psi Chi Psychlgy VP Actvts; Psychlgy Hmn Serv/Cnslng; Agncy/Soc Wrk.

**DILLON, TANA S,** Univ Of Akron, Akron, OH; SR; BED; English; Teaching.**

**DILLON, WES P,** Milligan Coll, Milligan Clg, TN; FR; BS; Student Govt Pres 90-; Christian Ministers Assoc; Deans List 90-; Bible; Preaching Ministry.

**DILLS, DAVID R,** Atlantic Comm Coll, Mays Landing, NJ; FR; Zet Beta Tau Sec 90-; IM Bsktbl 90-; Commctns.

**DILS, MICHELE M,** S U N Y Coll At Fredonia, Fredonia, NY; JR; BA; BACCHUS Treas 89-; Amnsty Intl 90; Pblc Rlts Intern; Dean Lst; Cmmnctns; Pblc Rlts.

**DIMALANTA, CAROLYN B,** Temple Univ, Philadelphia, PA; FR; BA; OAS 90-; Sterring Comm 90-; Alpha Lambda Delta 90-; Delta Zeta Histrn 90-; OAS Schlrshp 90-; Chem; Medcn.

**DIMALANTA, ERIC C,** Univ Of Akron, Akron, OH; JR; BA; Amer Inst Chem Eng 90-; Goldn Key 90-; Phi Gamma Delta Awrds Chrmn 90-; Amer Red Crss 90; Asst Eng 89-; Chem Eng; Law.

**DIMELER, JENNIFER L,** Drexel Univ, Philadelphia, PA; FR; BS; Middletwn Area Stu Hlprs 87-90; Am Inst Of Physcs; Stu Reprtr; Phi Eta Sigma; Pi Sigma Pi; Deans List 90; Hall Fdtn Schlrshp 90; Rotry Schlrshp 90; Physics/Stmospheric Sci; Physicist.

**DIMENNA, JENNIFER L,** Univ Of Sc At Aiken, Aiken, SC; FR; BS; Math; Tchng.

**DIMITRI, GINA S,** S U N Y Coll Of Tech At Frmgdl, Farmingdale, NY; FR; BA; Asstnt Coach Soccer; Mdcl Ofc Mgmnt.

**DIMITRIOU, DEACON SAMUEL,** Hellenic Coll/Holy Cross, Brookline, MA; SR; M DIV; Stdnt Gvmt VP 90-; Stdnt Gvmt Sec 88-89; Hndbk Comm 90-; Deans Lst 87-90; YAL Treas 87-88; Hosp Mnstry Chpln 90-; Altar Grp Ldr 90-; Chntr 87-; IM 87-; Lay Asst St Nicholas 89-90; Ordnd Mnstr; BA Hellenic Coll 89; Thlgy; Priest.

**DIMKPA, PRINCE UZOMA,** Howard Univ, Washington, DC; GD; PHD; Cosmopolitan Clb Pres 87; Mbr At Large Communications Cncl 90; Guest Spkr Cultural Affrs 90-; Graduate Asstnt 90-; Graduate Stdnt Of Yr Cmmnctns; BA Salesian Univ Italy 83; MA Morehead St Univ Ky 86; Communication.

**DIMOCK, NANCY L,** Manhattan School Of Music, New York, NY; JR; BM; Oboe Perf; Msc.

**DINARDI, DAWN M,** Le Moyne Coll, Syracuse, NY; SO; BA; Acctg Soc Jdcl Review Sys 90-; Human Serv Assoc 90-; Intercoll Vlybl 89-90; Orntn Com; Eucharistic Mnstr 90-; Big Sis Pgm 90-; Hghr Edn Opprtnty Pgm Tutor 90-; Capt Winter/Spring Olympics 90-; Acctg.

**DINES, PAMELA M,** Itawamba Comm Coll, Fulton, MS; SO; DPMA; Comp Tech; Cmptr Data Entry.

**DING, HOU-WU,** Univ Of South Al, Mobile, AL; JR; Chinese Assoc Intl Stu Oa 90-; Assc Of SE Asian Nation Intl Stdnt Ofc 90-; Engr Assoc Pr 88-89; Deans Hon Lst 90-; Nanya Schlrshp 87-89; Pr Lst 87-89; Tennis Clb/Chess Clb 87-89; AS Nanya Jr Clg Taiwan 88; Bus Admin; Fin.

**DINGESS, KRISTY L,** Marshall University, Huntington, WV; SO; BA; Phi Mu; Dns Lst; Grk Hnr Rll; Acad Nick Jo Rahall Schlrshp; Spch Pthlgy And Adlgy; Pthlgst Adlgst.

**DINGLASAN, MAIRA P,** Hillsborough Comm Coll, Tampa, FL; FR; BA.

**DINGLER, AMY K,** Birmingham Southern Coll, Birmingham, AL; JR; BA; Southern Chorale 88; Cncrt Choir 90-; Intl Stdnts Tutor 88; Deans List 89-90; Omicron Delta Kappa 90-; Chi Omega Comm Serv Chmn/Sngldr/Soc Chrmn 88-; Adult Lit Crdntr 89-90; Vol Corp Govrnrs Awd 90-; Deans Advsry Com 90-; Hist; MA.

**DINGLEY, PAMELA A,** Ri Coll, Providence, RI; FR; BA; Fine Art.

**DINGMAN, DAVID L,** Univ Of Louisville, Louisville, KY; SO; MA; Engr.

**DINGUS, CHERYL C,** Univ Of Va Clinch Valley Coll, Wise, VA; JR; BA; Phi Theta Kappa Mt Empire CC 90; AS Mt Empire CC 90; Engl; Tchng.

**DINGUS, SHANNON S,** East Tn St Univ, Johnson City, TN; JR; BS; Elec; Engr.

**DINH, HONG-DIEM N,** Univ Of Nc At Charlotte, Charlotte, NC; SO; BA; Deans Lst; Chncllrs Lst 90; Cameron Morrison Schlrshp 89-; Math; Scndry Educ.**

**DINH, HUONG,** Springfield Tech Comm Coll, Springfield, MA; SR; Elec Tech; Engr.

**DINH, MIEN,** Hudson Valley Comm Coll, Troy, NY; FR; Elctrcl Engr Tech; Engr.

**DINH, THUY AI X,** Smith Coll, Northampton, MA; SO; Vietnamese Clb 89-; Prhlth Clb 89-; Newman Clb 89-; Serv Organz Smith 89-; Blakeslees Schlrshp Genetics; Intrshp Stdyng Anthcynin; Blgcl Pgmnt; Blgy; Med.

**DINH, TUAN TRONG,** Catawba Valley Comm Coll, Hickory, NC; FR; BS; Vietnms Refugee Boy Sct 89-90; Vietnms Scr Clb 90-; Vietnms Tbl Tns Clb 90-; Elec Engr.

**DINIZULU, YAO O,** Fl A & M Univ, Tallahassee, FL; FR; BA; Stdnt Rntl Rts Hsng Cmmtt Stff Mbr 90-; Yng Hll Drmtry Pres 90-; Mdl Epcrn Mdlng Cmpny 90-; FAMU Hsng Cert Schlrshp 90; Intern Cty Cnclmn Stan Michels; Pblc Admn; Law.

**DINKINS, CANDICE W,** Univ Of Nc At Greensboro, Greensboro, NC; SR; BS; AEYC 89-90; Deans Lst 90-; Gibson/Clutts Schlrshps 90-; Rural Hall Elem Intrn; Tutr Northwest Mddl Schl 90-; Elem Educ; Tchr.

**DINKINS, CLEOTHA A,** Tougaloo Coll, Tougaloo, MS; SO; BA; Spt Serv 90-; Math/Cmptr Sci Clb 90-; Alpha Lambda Delta; Columbia Brdcstng Sys Schlrshp 90-; UNCF Carnegie Mellon Flw; Math/Cmptr Sci; Pgrmmr.

**DINKINS, MICHELLE K,** Central Fl Comm Coll, Ocala, FL; SO; BA; Schlrshp Showchoir; PEO; Cert Apprctn; Wmns Clb; Intrn Wyomina Elem Schl; IM Vlybl/Sftbl; Elem Educ; Tchr.

**DINKINS, VICTORIA G,** Fort Valley St Coll, Fort Valley, GA; SR; BS; Agri Demie Forum Pres 90-; Agric Econ 88-; Coop Dvlpmnt Enrgy 88-; Alpha Kappa Mu Sec/Treas 90-; Alpha Kappa Alpha Pres 90-; Oglethorp Power Coop Intrnshp 89-90; Agri Econ; Bus.

**DINNEN, KEVIN JOSEPH,** Barry Univ, Miami, FL; FR; BA; Ptchr Barry Univ Bsbl Tm 90-; Sprts Admin.

**DINOPOULOS, KAREN L,** Rivier Coll, Nashua, NH; JR; BA; Drct Comm Arts Cncl Exec Brd 88-; Wst Sbrbn Crtve Arts Schls Cncl 88; Spec Elem Educ; Tchng.

**DINSMOOR, DEBORAH Y,** Emory Univ, Atlanta, GA; SR; BSN; Sigma Theta Tau; Emory Student Nurses Assoc; GE Student Nurses Assoc; Deans List 90-91; Nursing Assoc Schlrshp 91; Sigma Theta Tau Schlrshp 91; Jr League Greater Alton IL; Former HS/COMMTY Clg Tchr; BS Ed Univ TX 72; Nursing; Maternal Child Nursing.

**DINSMORE, HELENE M,** Casco Bay Coll, Portland, ME; SR; Sr Mntr 90-; Miss Atlntc Cst.

**DINSMORE, WENDY A,** Hudson Valley Comm Coll, Troy, NY; GD; AEMTP; Pres List 90; AEMT Vol Ambulance 89-; Stained Glass Artist 81-; BA Castleton St Coll Vt 84; Art Glass; Physicians Asst.

**DINWIDDIE, MICHELLE L,** Univ Of Cincinnati-Clrmnt Coll, Batavia, OH; FR; BA; Admin Assoc Quantum Chem 89-; Bus Admin; Chem Indust.

**DION, ANNE-MARIE J,** Central Me Medical Center, Lewiston, ME; FR; ASN; Mdcl Ctr Rdlgy 87; Drug Stre Hm Hlth 84; Sci Nrsng.

**DIOP, SEYDINA ISSA HENRY,** Central St Univ, Wilberforce, OH; SO; BA; Intl Org; Math/Cmptr Sci; Hnr Assn; NAACP; NSBE; Moslem Assn; Intl Schlrshp; ROTC Romper Ribbon; Hnr Stdnt; Deans Lst; Karate; Cmptr Sci/Eng; Aero Eng.

**DIPIETRO, JOY MARIE,** Atlantic Comm Coll, Mays Landing, NJ; SO; Educ; Tchr.

**DIPKO, BARBARA J,** Saint Francis Coll, Loretto, PA; JR; BA; Redkey Spec Evts Coord 88-; Adpt A Grndprnt 88-; Psychlgy Clb 88-; Vlybl 90-; Trck 89-; Psychlgy; Dnc Mvmnt Thrpy.

**DIRR, SUSAN R,** Mount Saint Mary Coll, Newburgh, NY; SR; MBA; BA; Elem/Spec Educ; Tchr.

**DISAMAN, DEBRA S,** Embry Riddle Aeronautical Univ, Daytona Beach, FL; SR; BS; Aerntcl Sci; Comm Avtn.

**DISANTIS, DIAN,** Cleveland Inst Of Art, Cleveland, OH; JR; BA; ARLIS/NA Chptr Chr 89-90; Prnt Clb Of Cleveland Trustee 88-; Cleveland Socty Cntmpry Art Trst 88-; Phi Beta Mu 79-; NOVA; Art Librarian; BS Ball State Univ 58-61; MLS Kent State Univ Lib Schl 77-79; Painting Mjr; Tchng.

**DISARIO, DANNY D,** Temple Univ, Philadelphia, PA; SR; BSCE; Amer Soc Civil Engrs 89-; Natl Hnr Soc; IM Sftbl Bsktbl Golf; Civil Engrng.**

**DISHER, HAROLD L,** Univ Of Sc At Columbia, Columbia, SC; GD; BS; Bus Mgmt.

**DISHER, KAREN B,** Ny Univ, New York, NY; FR; BFA; Jazz Ensmbl 90-; Orch 90-; Tisch Schl Arts Fresh Mntr; Flm/TV; Anmtn.

**DISPENZA, THERESE M,** Nova Univ, Ft Lauderdale, FL; GD; MBA; Fnd Rsng Cnsltnt 90-; Grt Amer Opprtnts; BSBA Shippensburg U 81; Intrntl Bus; Mktg.

**DISQUE, LISA,** Xavier Univ, Cincinnati, OH; FR; BA; Yng Dem 90-; Intl Affairs; Intl Law.

**DISTEFANO, LISA M,** Va Commonwealth Univ, Richmond, VA; SR; Advtsg Cl; Advtsg; Advtsg/Copywrtr.

**DISTLER, SETH W,** Oh Wesleyan Univ, Delaware, OH; FR; BA; Bnai Brith Hillel Org 90; Sprtswtr/Brdcstr For Campus Chnnl TV Stn 90; Sprts Wrtr For Schl Newspapr; Phi Eta Sigma; Deans Lst 90; Chi Phi; Assist To Sprts Info Offce 90; Jr Inter-Frat Cncl Pldge Class Rep; Jrnlsm; Sprts Brdcstng.

**DITCHKUS JR, JOHN,** Marywood Coll, Scranton, PA; JR; BA; High Point Rod/Gun Clb 88-; Endless Mtn Skydvrs Clb 88-; Delta Epsilon Sigma 90; Nurs; CRNA.

**DITTMAN, AMY J,** Univ Of Southern Ms, Hattiesburg, MS; SR; BS; Angel Flight Cmndr 88-; SADD PR 90-; Dept Res Life Stf RA/HALL Dir 88-; Gamma Beta Phi 90-; Phi Delta Rho, Pi Tau Chi 90-; Rho Eta Alpha 89-; IMS Ftbl/Sftbl 87-; MS Assn Hsng Ofcrs; SE Assn Hsng Ofcrs; Cnslng Psychlgy; Stdnt Dvlpmnt.

**DITTMAR, LYNNE E,** Univ Of Fl, Gainesville, FL; FR; MBA; Alpha Lambda Delta; Phi Eta Sigma; Acctg; CPA.

**DITTO, GREGORY P,** Southern Coll Of Tech, Marietta, GA; SR; BS; IEEE 89-; Deans List 88-; Comp Eng Tchnlgy.

**DITTO, RAMONA R,** Brescia Coll, Owensboro, KY; JR; KY Ed Assn 90-; Bsktbl Cpt 88-; IM Sprts 88-.

**DITTY, GERALD L,** Temple Univ, Philadelphia, PA; JR; BS; PA Phrmctcl Assn; Kappa Psi; Phrmcy.

**DIVEN, ELIZABETH ANNE,** Indiana Univ Of Pa, Indiana, PA; FR; BA; Educ/History Track; Tch.

**DIVINCENZO, ANGELA J,** City Univ Of Ny La Guard Coll, Long Island Cty, NY; SO; AS; Phi Theta Kappa 90-; Mnhtn Psych Cntr Awrd Vol Serv 89-90; Rehab Asstnt Nrsg Home 86-; Occptnl Thrpy.

**DIVINCENZO, JOSEPH A,** Embry Riddle Aeronautical Univ, Daytona Beach, FL; FR; AS; Big Flts Vol Fire Dept Lt 90; Big Flts Fire Co Inc 85-; Aerontcl Sci; Arln Pilot.

**DIVINE, KATHLEEN W,** Savannah Coll Of Art & Design, Savannah, GA; SO; BFA; Phtjrnlsm.

**DIX, ANGELA R,** Univ Of Sc At Columbia, Columbia, SC; JR; BA; Pcstrs Clb; Educ Mjr Clb; ASSOC 90; Erly Chldhd Educ; Tchr.

**DIX JR, JOSEPH,** Al St Univ, Montgomery, AL; FR; Hnr Stu; IM Bsktbl 90-; Cmnctns; Brdcstg.

**DIX, MARTIN T,** Averett Coll, Danville, VA; FR; BS; Phi Eta Sigma; Deans Lst 90; Pr Lst; Sci; Criminology.

**DIXON SMITH, ROBIN R,** Cumberland Coll, Williamsburg, KY; SR; Phi Beta Lambda Pres 88-; Stu Free Entrprs 88-; Stu Govt Sen 87-88; J T Vallindingham Hnr Soc 90-; Bptst Stu Unn 87-; Fllwshp Chrstn Athlts 87-; Acdmc Schlrshp 87-; Otstndng Accntng Stu Awrd; Tnns Capt 87-89; BS; Accntng; CPA.

**DIXON, ALANNA C,** Morgan St Univ, Baltimore, MD; FR; Phi Eta Sigma 90-; Alpha Lambda Delta 90-; Hugh O'brian Yth Fndtn Alumni Assn Nwslltr Edtr/Sec 87-91; Cmptr Sci; Cmptr Aided Rsrch.

**DIXON, ALICIA M,** Univ Of Miami, Coral Gables, FL; FR; BA; IM Vlybl 90-; Gen Hnrs Prog 90-; Kappa Kappa Gamma 90-; Sportsfest 90; Law.

**DIXON, ANDREA N,** Brevard Comm Coll, Cocoa, FL; SO; AA; Cmps Cncl Sec 90-; Afrcn Amer Std Un Pres 90-; Pres Ldrshp Conf 90-; Ldrshp Awd 90-; Serv Awd 90-; Acctng; CPA.

**DIXON, ANGELA,** Livingston Univ, Livingston, AL; SR; Pres Lst; Deans Lst; BS; Spec Ed LD; Tchng.

**DIXON, ANGELA L,** Al A & M Univ, Normal, AL; SO; BA; Kappa Alph Psi 89-90; Frd Fndtn Schlr Pgm 89-90; Hon Roll 89; Deans List 89:; Ford Foundation Schlr Pgm 89-; Eng; Corprt Atty.

**DIXON, ANGELIA S,** Alcorn St Univ, Lorman, MS; JR; BA; Hons Org 90-; Alpha Kappa Mu 90-; Natl Hon Soc 90-; Deans Lst; All-Amer Schlr; Bus Admin/Mgmnt.

**DIXON, ANJANETTE L,** Morgan St Univ, Baltimore, MD; JR; BA; Univ Chr 89-90; Cmps All Str Chlng Tm 89-; Cmps Nwspr 90; Grant Brett Promethean Kappa Tau 88-; Phi Eta Sigma 88-; Alpha Lambda Delta 88-; Lgstv Intrn MD Gen Asmbly; Hstry; Law.

**DIXON, ANTOINE L,** Al A & M Univ, Normal, AL; JR; BS; Mktg Clb 90-; Stdnts In Free Ent VP 90-; Human Res VP; Co-Op U S Forest Svc 90-; Acad Schlrshp; Mktg; Rsrch/Cnsltnt.

**DIXON, BOBBIE R,** Univ Of North Fl, Jacksonville, FL; SO; BFA; AA; Fine Arts; Cmrcl Art.

**DIXON, BOBBY A,** Northwest Al Comm Coll, Phil Campbell, AL; SO; BA; Crmnl Jstc; Law.

**DIXON, BOBBY J,** Fayetteville St Univ, Fayetteville, NC; SR; BS; Mrktng Educ Cllgte Div 89; Coll Dmcrts 89; Dns Lst 90; Wrkd St And Natl Pltcl Cmpgns; Cmbrlnd Cnty Schls Prme Tme Aftr Schl Prog Area Sprvsr 90-; Scl Sci Educ Hstry; Edctr.

**DIXON, BRIAN J,** Wv Univ, Morgantown, WV; FR; BA; Ind Eng; Engr.

**DIXON, CHANDRA E,** Alice Lloyd Coll, Pippa Passes, KY; FR; BA; Tutor; Dns Dist Lst 90-; Sftbl; Educ/Math/Engl; Prfssr.

**DIXON, CHERYL A,** Radford Univ, Radford, VA; SR; BS; Tri M VP 88-; IM Vlybl 89; IM Bwlng; Kappa Mu Epsln VP 89-; Phi Kappa Phi 90-; Foundation Schlrshp; Otstndng Stdnt 90-; Statistics; Biostatistician.

**DIXON, DEIRDRE D,** Bridgewater Coll, Bridgewater, VA; SR; BS; Acctg Tchng Asst 90-; Bus Admn; Acctg CPA.

**DIXON, DOMINIC J,** Fayetteville St Univ, Fayetteville, NC; SR; BS; NC Schlrshp 88f Deans List 89-; Wrestling 88; Biology; Marnie Biologist/Envrt.

**DIXON, DONNA R,** Mobile Coll, Mobile, AL; SR; BSU 86-87; SLATE 86-87; Deans List 88-; NCEA USAA.

**DIXON, GLORY M,** Atlanta Christian Coll, East Point, GA; FR; BS; Stdnt Govt; Bty Pgnt Rnnrup 81; Rcqtbll Tnns Vllybll; Bbl Bus Music.

**DIXON, JOHN G,** Oh Univ, Athens, OH; JR; BFA; Wtr Pl Tm 89; Ultmt Frsb Tm 90-; Yrbk Phtgrphr; Advrtsng Phtgrhy Internshp; Phtgrphy; Advrtsng Phtgrphy.

**DIXON, JULIE A,** James Sprunt Comm Coll, Kenansville, NC; FR; BS; Nrsg.

**DIXON, KATHY D,** Howard Univ, Washington, DC; SR; Amrcn Inst Archtctr Stdnts Pres 88-89; Mrylnd Clb Sec 87-89; Tau Sigma Delta Pres 89-Gldn Key; Barch; Archtctr.

**DIXON, LESLEY D,** Clayton St Coll, Morrow, GA; JR; BS; AA Clayton State Clg 90; Psych; Cnslr.

**DIXON, LILLIE B,** Sinclair Comm Coll, Dayton, OH; SO; AFA; Chrch Artst/Yng People; Bible Stdy Tchr; Cmrcl Artst; Prof.

**DIXON, LYNNE J,** Atlantic Comm Coll, Mays Landing, NJ; SO; Elem Ed; Tch.

**DIXON, MALETHA L,** Jackson St Univ, Jackson, MS; FR; BA; Alpha Lamda Delta; C F Moore Schlr 90-; Acctg; CPA.

**DIXON, MARY A,** Garrett Comm Coll, Mchenry, MD; FR; AA; Cert Wilma Boyd Career Schl 87; Lib Arts; Advrtsng.

**DIXON, MARYANN M,** Davis & Elkins Coll, Elkins, WV; JR; BS; Stdnt Assmbly 90; Hnrs Assoc Scrtry 90; Jennings Randolph Ldrshp 90; Beta Alpha Beta 90; Phi Beta Lambda VP 89; Alpha Phi Omega VP 88; Ntl Cllgte Bsnss Merit Awd 90; Mngmnt/Mrktng.

**DIXON, MICHAEL R,** Liberty Univ, Lynchburg, VA; SO; BA; Sheperds Clb 90; Licensed Southern Baptist Minister; AA; Religion.

**DIXON, NANCY J,** Converse Coll, Spartanburg, SC; SO; BMED; Class Rept To Hnr Brd 89-; Stdnt Chrstn Assoc 89-; Stndt Govt Assoc 89-; Alpha Lamda Delta 90-; Crescent Soph Serv Org Pres 90-; Stdnt Vlntr Serv Pres; Converse Clge Schl Music Concerto Contest Winner Soloist Pianbo Spartanburg Symphny; Music Education; Ministry.

**DIXON, NICOLE F,** Fisk Univ, Nashville, TN; SR; BS; Delta Sigma Theta; Trvlrs Ins Intern 90; Bsktbl/Trck/Fld/Crs Cntry Capt; Pol Sci; Law.

**DIXON, RHONDA R,** Alcorn St Univ, Lorman, MS; SO; MBA; Alpha Kappa Alpha Assist Secy; Acctng; CPA.

**DIXON JR, ROBERT E,** Carnegie Mellon Univ, Pittsburgh, PA; SO; Sign Lang Clb 90-; English; Advtsng.

**DIXON, ROBIN R,** Middle Tn St Univ, Murfreesboro, TN; SO; BS; HCHS Bnd Pres 90; Hnrs Dplm; Beta Clb; Hnrs Schlrshp; Pltcl Science; Law.

**DIXON, SCOTT A,** S U N Y Coll Of Tech At Canton, Canton, NY; SR; Phi Theta Kappa 90-; Acctg; COA.

**DIXON, SCOTT E,** Univ Of Southern Ms, Hattiesburg, MS; SR; MBA; Inter Frat Cncl 89; Pi Kappa Alpha Pblc Rltns 88-; Grad Assist Mktng Dept; Vars Chrldr Capt 89-92; BSBA; Bus/Finance.

**DIXON, SHERRY L,** East Tn St Univ, Johnson City, TN; SO; BA; Bsn; Acctng.

**DIXON, STACY S A,** Ms St Univ, Miss State, MS; SR; BA; Anthrplgy Clb Pres 87-; SCPAE VP 89-90; Alpha Lambda Delta; Phi Kappa Phi 90-; Soc Schlrs; Lambda Alpha 90-; Pres Schlr 88-90; Otstndg Anthrplgy Stu 89-90; Cobb Inst Archlgy Undrgrad Rsrch Asstntshp 87-; Anthrplgy.

**DIXON, STEPHANIE R,** Ashland Comm Coll, Ashland, KY; SO; BS; Deans Lst 90-; Waitress; Psychlgy; Psychatry.

**DIXON, TAMMY G,** Cumberland Univ, Lebanon, TN; SR; BA; Alpha Lambda Delta Sec 88-; Alpha Chi VP 90-; Intern State Sen Robert Rochelle 89; Scl Sci.**

**DIXON, TAMMY G,** West Liberty St Coll, West Liberty, WV; SR; Amer Chrl Dirs Assn 88-; MENC 89; Kappa Delta Pi 88-; BA 90; Msc Educ; Msc Educ Prfrmnce.**

**DIXON, THOMAS R,** Kent St Univ Kent Cmps, Kent, OH; SO; BS; Stdnt Med Assoc 89-; House Council 89-90; Univ Ski Clb 89-90; Alpha Lambda Delta 89-; Sherri Jo Luft Mem Awrd; Bio/Pre Med.

**DIXON, TONYA M,** Comm Coll Algny Co Algny Cmps, Pittsburgh, PA; FR; BA; Accntnt; Govt Accntnt.

**DIXON, TRACEY L,** Middle Tn St Univ, Murfreesboro, TN; SR; TN Donar Svcs; Amer Cncr Soc; BS Belmont Clg 89; Tchng.

**DIXON, VANESSA S,** Lee Coll, Cleveland, TN; JR; Alpha Chi 88-; Alpha Epsilon Delta 90-; Delta Zeta Tau Pres 89-; Alha Gamma Chi; Hnrs Schlrhsp 88-; CRC Chmstyr Awrd 90; Bsktbll Chrldr 89-990; Blgy; Physcl Thrpy.**

**DIXON, WILMA L,** Abraham Baldwin Agri Coll, Tifton, GA; SO; AD; GA Stdnt Nurse Assn 90-; Am Heart Assn; Cystic Fibrosis Assn; LPN Valdosta Tech 85; Nrsng RN.

**DIXON JR, WINSTON M,** Bloomfield Coll, Bloomfield, NJ; JR; BA; Lcrss 89-90; Psychlgy; Law Schl Bus.

**DIXON, ZELMA M,** Va St Univ, Petersburg, VA; JR; BA; Art Clb Sec 89; Cmmrcl Art/Dsgn.

**DIZE, TRACI B,** Salisbury St Univ, Salisbury, MD; SR; BS; Phi Kappa Phi; Kappa Delta Pi; Phi Eta Sigma; Elem Educ; Tchng.

**DIZON, ERWIN M,** Ny Univ, New York, NY; JR; BUS; Acct Rep; Act Sci; Actuarial Soc Amer.

**DO, JAMES H,** Columbia Union Coll, Takoma Park, MD; SR; Cert Natl Inst Paralegal 90; Accntng; Law.

**DO, LONG D,** Harrisburg Area Comm Coll, Harrisburg, PA; SO; BA; Vietnamese Org Pres 89; Outstndng Mnrty Cmmnty Clg Achivmnt Awd 90; Multi-Cltrl Advsry Cmmttee Mrtrs Serv Awd 90; Eng.

**DO, YUSUK,** Old Dominion Univ, Norfolk, VA; SO; Biochem; Med.

**DOAN, DOAT,** Patrick Henry Comm Coll, Martinsville, VA; SO; ASS; Stdnt Support Svcx At PHCC 90-; Deans List 90-; Indstrl Electrncs Technlgy; Engr.

**DOANE, KRISTI L,** Va Highlands Comm Coll, Abingdon, VA; FR; AAS; Alpha Gamma Rho Sec; Cntrl Fdlty Schlr; Offc Tchngly.

**DOATY, SIDNEY J,** Birmingham Southern Coll, Birmingham, AL; JR; BA; Mktg/Bsn Admin; Mktg Exec.

**DOBAN, DENISE M,** Comm Coll Algny Co Algny Cmps, Pittsburgh, PA; SR; MPT; Fllwshp Chrstn Athlts Offcr 84-86; Sftbl Co Cpt 84-86; BS Clarion Univ 86; Phys Thrpy.

**DOBB, ERIN S,** Converse Coll, Spartanburg, SC; SR; BA; FCA; SCA; SCSEA; Sndy Schl Tchr; Sccr Coach; Vars Sccr Plyr; FCA; Elem Ed; Bus.

**DOBBELAERE, MONIQUE ANNETTE,** Savannah Coll Of Art & Design, Savannah, GA; FR; MA; Art; Tch/Hstrc Prsrvtn.

**DOBBINS, CHRISTINE M,** Christopher Newport Coll, Newport News, VA; JR; BA; Compus Tr Committee Student Orient; Ldr Selec Commt; Campus Activ Brd/Student Orient Ldr 90-; Omega Treas; Gamma Phi Beta Officer 90-; Ed; Tchng.

**DOBBINS, LOUISE M,** Comm Coll Algny Co Algny Cmps, Pittsburgh, PA; FR; AD; Nrsng.

**DOBBINS, TABBETHA A,** Lincoln Univ, Lincoln Univ, PA; SO; BS; Beta Kappa Chi; Asst Rsrch Prjct 90-; Physcs.

**DOBBS, LEAH S,** Auburn Univ At Auburn, Auburn, AL; SR; MED; Phi Alpha Theta 89-; Alpha Gamma Delta 87-; Clg Night/Bus Cabinet 90-; Christine Griffith Callahan Schlrshp 87; BS; Educ.

**DOBBS, MELISSA A,** Wallace St Comm Coll At Selma, Selma, AL; FR; AS; Deans Lst 90; Accntng/Bsnss; CPA.

**DOBBY, TEALA A,** Ms St Univ, Miss State, MS; JR; BS; Phi Eta Sigma/Gamma Beta Phi 88-; Alpha Epsilon Delta 90-; Delta Delta Delta 88-; Pre Med/Microbio; Med.

**DOBEREINER, MICHAEL B,** S U N Y At Buffalo, Buffalo, NY; GD; MA; BA Oswego State Univ 90; AAS Onondaga Comm Coll 83; Architecture.

**DOBIN, JOSHUA W,** Yeshiva Univ, New York, NY; SO; BA; NYSIPAC 89-; Pre-Law Soc 89-; March Of Living-Holocaust Meml 88; Var Bsktbl 89-; Hist; Law.

**DOBNIKAR, LAURA J,** Broward Comm Coll, Ft Lauderdale, FL; SO; Pres Lst; Gen Sales 88-; AA 91; Busn Admin; Acctg.

**DOBOS, LORI A,** Youngstown St Univ, Youngstown, OH; FR; BA; Psych.

**DOBRONSKI, CECELIA R,** Ms Univ For Women, Columbus, MS; SO; BA; Bench/Gavel Clb 90-; Lntrn Hon; Prlgl; Law Schl/Lwyr.

**DOBSON, DUANE F,** Ms Gulf Coast Comm Coll, Perkinston, MS; JR; BA; Delta Clb 90-; Phi Theta Kappa 90-; Dean Lst 88-; VP Lst 88-; Bsbll 88-; AA; Math; Eng.

**DOBSON, MONTE R,** Draughons Jr Coll Nashville, Nashville, TN; FR; AS; Data Proc Mgmt Assn Pres; Pres Lst; Comp Sci; Info Syst.

**DOCKERY, BARBARA J,** Northwest Al Comm Coll, Phil Campbell, AL; SO; MBA; Phi Theta Kappa 89-; Pres Lst 88-; Dns Lst 90; Finance; Fncl Plng.

**DOCKERY, DANA M,** Western Piedmont Comm Coll, Morganton, NC; FR; Computer Engrng.

**DOCKERY, LEONARD S,** Norfolk St Univ, Norfolk, VA; SO; Dnimas Stdnt Assn Parlmntrn 90-; IEEE Pub Chrmn 90-; NROTC Schlrshp 89-; Alpha Kappa Mu; IM Bsktbl/Ftbl 90-; Elec Eng; U S Navl Intell Offcr.

**DOCKERY, REBECCA A,** Georgetown Coll, Georgetown, KY; JR; BA; Stdnt Exec Cncl Media & Pblcty Chr; Stdnt Ct Of Review Justice 89-; Faculty Comm Sec; Phi Alpha Theta; Alpha Lambda Delta Sec 89-; Phi Beta Lambda St Pres 88-; Kappa Delta Sec 89-; Trustees Schlrshp 88-; Writing Lab Tutor 89-; Georgetonian 89-; Hist & Pol Sci; Law.

**DOCKERY, STEPHANIE A,** Chattanooga St Tech Comm Coll, Chattanooga, TN; FR; Comp Prgrmmr.

**DODD, ANGELA MARIA,** Strayer Coll, Washington, DC; SR; MBA; BSBA; Bus Admn; Bus Mgmt.**

**DODD, CHRISTINE L,** Fayetteville St Univ, Fayetteville, NC; SO; BS; AS Quinsigamond Cmmnty Clg 89; Math/Ed; Ed.

**DODD, DAVID D,** Univ Of Southern Ms, Hattiesburg, MS; JR; BS; Plymer Sci Clb 88-; Soc Plstcs Engrs 90-; Phi Kappa Tau; Sftbl Bsktbl Vlybl 88-; Polymer Sci; Medcl.

**DODD, DEBORAH L,** Middle Tn St Univ, Murfreesboro, TN; FR; BS; Deans List 90-; Business; Office Management.

**DODD, JAMES E,** Brevard Coll, Brevard, NC; SO; BA; Semester Abroad Austria; Cross Cntry Indoor Track Outdoor Track 89-; AA; Bus Admn; Auto Industry.

**DODD, KIMBERLY D,** Ms Univ For Women, Columbus, MS; JR; BS; Delta Cnnctn P/R Rcrttmnt Miss Delta Comm Clg 89-90; Delta Dncrs/Imprssns Mdlng 88-90; Bnch/Gavl Prlgl/Miss Univ/Wom 90; Nu Epsilon Delta; Paralegal Law.

**DODD, MARGARET J,** Univ Of Nc At Greensboro, Greensboro, NC; JR; BS; NCAEYC 90; NC Prspctve Tchr Schlr 88-; Chld Dev Fam Rltns; Elem Educ.

**DODD, REBECCA N,** Ms St Univ, Miss State, MS; JR; BS; Std Asc Intrs Dsgnrs Treas; Home Ec Clb Sec; Adv Cncl Rep 90-; Dns Lst 88-; Pres Lst 90-; Cls Rep PRJC 86-87; String/Pearls Dancer 86-87; Home Ec/Intrn Dsgn.

**DODD, RICHARD W,** Nova Univ, Ft Lauderdale, FL; GD; MBA; Brandon Masonic Ldg 114 F & A M 81-; ISSA 89; CSI 90-; Mgr Info Secrty GTE Data Serv 80-; BS 89; AS 81; Cert; Bus; Cmptr Bus Wrk.

**DODD, TARA L,** Seton Hall Univ, South Orange, NJ; JR; BS; Kappa Delta Pi 90-; Dns Lst 89-; Elem Ed/Psy; Tchr/Cnslr.**

**DODD, VALERIE D,** Central St Univ, Wilberforce, OH; FR; BA; ROTC Army Marauder Battalion; Dns Lst 90-; Pol Sci; Corp Law.

**DODD, WILLIAM J,** Ms Gulf Coast Comm Coll, Perkinston, MS; SO; Bsktbl/Golf 83-89; Hosp Admin.

**DODDATO, JENNIFER A,** Univ Of Nc At Charlotte, Charlotte, NC; JR; BA; Stdnt Escrt Serv 89-; Phi Eta Sigma 89; Intrdscplnry Hon Soc 88-; Gldn Key 90-; Alpha Delta Pi Intrsor Cncl Dlgt 89-; Psychlgy/Crmnl Justc; Law Enfrcmnt.

**DODDS, MATTHEW J,** Carnegie Mellon Univ, Pittsburgh, PA; SR; BS; Mortar Bd Treas 90-; AIESEC; CMU Invstmnt Grp; Dns Lst 89 90; Stdnt Envir Action Comm; Finance.

**DODDS-ABRAHAM, SARAH E,** Univ Of Cincinnati-Clrmnt Coll, Batavia, OH; SO; BA; Deans Lst 88-; Lbrl Arts/Psych; Mnstr.

**DODGE JR, DOUGLAS W,** Me Maritime Academy, Castine, ME; SO; BS; Nautical Science.

**DODGE, JAMES PAUL,** S U N Y Coll At Fredonia, Fredonia, NY; JR; BA; Beta Beta Beta; Im Bsktbl/Brmbl; Tecombinant Gene Technlgy; Rsrch.

**DODGE, LYNN M,** Manatee Comm Coll, Bradenton, FL; FR; AA; Engl; Elem Educ.

**DODGE, MAGGIE M,** James Sprunt Comm Coll, Kenansville, NC; FR; Cmmrcl Art/Advrtsng; Graphic Dsgnr.

**DODGE, MARGARET T,** Hillsborough Comm Coll, Tampa, FL; SO; BA; Phi Theta Kappa Sec; 16 Yrs In Sls/Mrktng; Pub Rltns.

**DODRILL, FREDERIC S,** Old Dominion Univ, Norfolk, VA; JR; BS; Phi Theta Kappa 88-90; Phi Theta Tau; AAS Blue Ridge Comm Clg 90; Eng; Mech Eng Tchnlgy.

**DODSON, ALAN R,** Univ Of Nc At Charlotte, Charlotte, NC; SR; BA; Asctn Bsn Std 85-87; Psi Chi; Sigma Chi 85-87; Dns Lst 84-85 90-; AA Co Adtr 87-89; Sd Lns Mktg Asc Acctnt 89; RDH Tire/Trtrd Co Acctnt 89-; BSBA Univ NC Chpl Hl 87; Psy; MBA.

**DODSON, ANDREW W,** Atlantic Comm Coll, Mays Landing, NJ; SO; ASSC; Fll Tm Aprntc Crpntr 87-; Gen Stds.

**DODSON, BOBBY D,** Hillsborough Comm Coll, Tampa, FL; SO; MSCS; Math Merit Awd 90-; Cmptr Oper Mgr 90-; AS Tampa Tech Inst 83; AA 90-; Cmptr Sci; Rsrch/Dvlpmnt.

**DODSON, CYNTHIA D,** Young Harris Coll, Young Harris, GA; FR; BS; Phi Theta Kappa 90-; Phi Delta Pres Elect 90-; Dorcus Sec Elect 90-; Wrk Stdy Prog Coll Infrmry Sec 90-; Sci; Phys Therpy.

**DODSON, DORIS R,** Young Harris Coll, Young Harris, GA; SO; Phi Theta Kappa VP 89-90; Vol In Serv Own Nghbrhd Chrprson 89-90; Var Tns 88-90; Otstndg Soph 90; Spat Serv Awrd; Acdmc Tns Awrd Mst Vlbl 90; Tennis 88-90; Finance; Scl Wrk.**

**DODSON, GWINDA B,** Central Al Comm Coll, Alexander City, AL; FR; BS; Phi Theta Kappa 90-; Ele Educ; Tch.

**DODSON, KIMBERLY J,** Hagerstown Jr Coll, Hagerstown, MD; FR; AA; Cmptr Sci; Prgrmmr.

**DODSON, LINDA M,** Wright St Univ Lake Cmps, Celina, OH; SR; ELMED; Gldn Ky 90-; U S Achvmnt Acdmy 90-; Kappa Delta Pi 90-; CCD Educator 88-; Amer Rd Crs Bld Mbl 81-; MLT ASCP Bd Rgstry Amer Soc Clin Pathlgsts 81; MLT Lim Meml Hosp 81, Sci, Tchng.

**DODSON, RALPH EDWARD,** Vance Granville Comm Coll, Henderson, NC; SO; AAS; Std Gvt VP 90-; Cmptr Clb; Currclm Comm Std Rep; Phi Theta Kappa Pres 90-; Optmst Clb Pres 85-86; MD S DE Dist Optmst Int Lt Gvrnr 86-87; Bus Comp Prog; Progmr/Fed Govt.

**DODSON, ROBIN L,** Germanna Comm Coll, Locust Grove, VA; GD; ASSC; Alpha Beta Gamma; Bus Mgmt; Mgmt Govt Fld.

**DODSON, SUSAN A,** Pellissippi St Tech Comm Coll, Knoxville, TN; SO; Elem Educ.

**DODSON, TAMRA K,** Univ Of Ky, Lexington, KY; SR; Stdnt Athltcs Cncl 90-; Bapt Stdnt Union 89-90; Amer Soc Civil Eng 88-90; Tau Beta Pi 89-; Chi Epsilon 89-; Gldn Ky 89-; Civil Eng.

**DODSON, YLONNE A,** Univ Of The Dist Of Columbia, Washington, DC; SR; BA; Acctng Club Pres 90-; Bus Comm Club 90-; Annual Tax Clinic 90-; Harvest Dr Chp 90; Schlstc Awd 89-; Acctng; CPA/LAW.

**DOE, TRACY A,** Univ Of Sc At Columbia, Columbia, SC; JR; Deans List 89; Nursing; RN.

**DOEGE, LINDA H,** Univ Of West Fl, Pensacola, FL; SR; BS; Co-Dp NCTS N823 NAS Pnscla FL; AS Pnscla Jnr Clg 88; Elec Engr Tech.

**DOEGE, SHARON ANN,** Univ Of Md At Eastern Shore, Princess Anne, MD; JR; BA; Engl; Publc Rltns.

**DOERING, CYNTHIA L,** Univ Of Akron, Akron, OH; SO; BA; Dance; Prfrmnc.

**DOERR, APRIL E,** Comm Coll Algny Co Algny Cmps, Pittsburgh, PA; SO; BA; Lib Arts.

**DOERR, TRACI R,** Indiana Univ Of Pa, Indiana, PA; SR; PA St Educ Assn; Cncl Excptnl Chldrn; Delta Zeta Pnhllnia Rep; Proj Stride; Elem Ed; Tchng.

**DOERSCHNER, CHRISTINE,** Western Carolina Univ, Cullowhee, NC; SR; BS; Stdnt Advsry Bd Math Dept 89-; Stdnt Advsry Bd To Dean 90-; Amer Socty Stdnt Actuaries; Alpha Lambda Delta 89-; Phi Kappa Phi 90; Natl Coll Math Awd; Frshmn Math Awd 89; Sr Math Awd; W Carolina Bnd Dncr 88-90; Math; Actuarial Sci.

**DOERTER, LAURA R,** Univ Of Tn At Knoxville, Knoxville, TN; SO; BS; Exec Undrgrdts 90-; Pny Clb 85-; Alpha Lambda Delta 90-; Phi Eta Sigma 90-; Gamma Beta Phi 90-; Beta Lambda Delta; Alpha Gamma Delta Crspndng Sec 90-; Bsn; Mgmt.**

**DOGGETT, DONNA M,** Nova Univ, Ft Lauderdale, FL; GD; MBA; Dns Lst 83 85; Addctns Cnslr Since 85; BA Converse Clg 85; Pol; Emp Asstnce Prog.

**DOGGETT, KIMBERLY E,** Ms St Univ, Miss State, MS; SR; BA; Beta Alpha Psi 89; Phi Kappa Phi 89-90; Summa Cum Laude; Wm Trnr Schlrshp 90; Accntng.

**DOGGETT, KRISTINA L,** Salisbury St Univ, Salisbury, MD; SR; BA; Rsdnc Hl Assn 87-; Rsdnt Asst 88-; 2M Sprts 87-; Lambda Iota Tau; Ltl Sis Minerva Sigma Alpha Epsilon VP; Engl; Tchr.

**DOGGETT, TELICE,** Wilberforce Univ, Wilberforce, OH; JR; Natl Assn Blk Accts Chrprsn Mbrshp 90-; Natl Stdnt Bus League; Acctg.

**DOHENY, HEATHER E,** Coll Misericordia, Dallas, PA; SR; BA; St Alumni Assn Prsdnt 88-; Cls Offcr Prsdnt 87-88; Deans Lst 90-; Wmn Moose Moose Ldg 1320 Lnsdale 90-; Jay Dugan Schlrshp Rcpnt 88-; PA Attrny Gnrls Ofc Madraid Fraud Dvsn Intrnshp 89; Lbrl Stds Pre Lar; Law Schl Gonzaya Unvrsty.

**DOHENY, MATTHEW A,** Allegheny Coll, Meadville, PA; JR; BA; Stdnt Gov Pres 90-; Edtr Camps Nwspr 90-; Tr Guide Dir 89-; Allies Ldrs Dir 89-; SOA 90-; Inter Jdg Grdn Mlr 90-; Var Ftbl 88-; Pol Sci; Law.

**DOHERTY, ELIZABETH A,** Providence Coll, Providence, RI; SO; BS; Big Sis; Tchng Asst; IM Bsktbl; Fnnc; Stck/Bnkng.

**DOHERTY, JAMES F,** Merrimack Coll, North Andover, MA; FR; BA; Bus.

**DOHERTY, SHAWN P,** Savannah Coll Of Art & Design, Savannah, GA; JR; BA; Photogrphy; Commerecial/Fine Art Phtgrphr.

**DOHME, LILLIAN M,** Univ Of Cin R Walters Coll, Blue Ash, OH; FR; AA; Upsilon Psi; Elem Educ Math; Tchng.

**DOIRON, SHERRY D,** Thomas Nelson Comm Coll, Hampton, VA; JR; AAS; Data Proc Mgmt Assoc; Med Facility; Cmptr Info Syst/Pgmg; Cmptr Pgm.

**DOLAN, BRENDON J,** Villanova Univ, Villanova, PA; SO; BA; Habitat For Humanity 89-; Proj Sunshine 89-90; Litrgcl Mnstry Prog 90-; IM Sftbl 89-; Educ/Hstry; High Schl Tchr.

**DOLAN, DANIEL T,** Memphis St Univ, Memphis, TN; SR; BA; Phi Theta Kappa 88-; Phi Alpha Theta 89-; Phi Kappa Phi; NROTC Trdnt Hon Soc 90-; Nvl Inst 88-; Navy ROTC 90-; IM Bsbl; AWANA Chrstn Yth Clbs Amer Ldr 89-; USN; Enlstd Cmmssng Pgm 83-; AA Chaminade Univ Honolulu 89; Hstry; Navy.**

**DOLAN, DARLENE K,** Spalding Univ, Louisville, KY; JR; BS; NEA; Pi Lambda Theta; Elem Edn; Teach.

**DOLAN, JENNIFER L,** East Carolina Univ, Greenville, NC; GD; MBA; Epsilon Phi Tau 88-; Vrsty Record Holder 86-; Fresh Record Holder 86-; Swimming Team 86-; Industrial Tech; Statistical Process Control.

**DOLAN, JILL E,** Middlesex County Coll, Edison, NJ; FR; AS; Rdlgy.

**DOLAN, KATHLEEN S,** Elmira Coll, Elmira, NY; SR; Deans List 90-; Hnrs Scholar, Kappa Delta Pi, BS Cornell Univ 87; Speach & Hearing; Speech Pathologist.

**DOLAN, LISA K,** Univ Of Scranton, Scranton, PA; SO; BS; Admsns Tour Guide 90-; Peer Tutor 90-; Crew Club 90-; Womens Bus Hon Soc 90-; Natl Collgt Bus Merit Award 90-; Deans List 89-; Acctng; Public Acctng.

**DOLAN, LYNN A,** William Paterson Coll, Wayne, NJ; SR; Kappa Delta Pi; Alpha Kappa Delta 89-; Deans Lst 89-90; Swm Tm Co Capt 69-71; NJEA NAEYC 91-; Grl Sct Ldr/Cb Sct Den Mthr/Rlgs Ed Tchr/Swm Tm Coach 81-89; Swm Tm Coord/Swm Instr 81-89; Sub Tchng; BA 90; Ed.

**DOLAN, MARIA,** George Mason Univ, Fairfax, VA; SR; BS; Soc Wrk Stdnt Assoc Secy 89-; Resdnt Advsr RA 90-; Co-Ed Touch Ftbl Co Cptn 87; Soc Wrk; Fmly Thrpy/Soc Wrk.

**DOLBOW, DIANNA L,** Central Fl Comm Coll, Ocala, FL; SO; BA; Phi Theta Kappa 90-; AA CFCC 90; Elem Ed; Tchr.

**DOLCE, JENNIFER L,** Fl St Univ, Tallahassee, FL; SR; BA; Fin Soc Prfd Stck 90-; Cthlc Yth Grp/Svc Clb 90-; Phi Beta Lambda 88-89; FSU Nttkng Hrng Imprd Stdnts 90-; PBCC Stdnt Yr Eng Lit/Art Hstry/Econ 88-90; Phi Beta Lambda St Ldrshp Conf 1st Pl Bus Prncpls 90; AA Plm Bch Comm Coll 90; Fin; Law Schl.

**DOLEJS, CHRISTOPHER M,** Bethel Coll, Mckenzie, TN; JR; BA; Bethel Stdnt TN Educ Assc 90-; Soc Svc; Hist Tchr.

**DOLEY, STACY J,** Fl A & M Univ, Tallahassee, FL; SO; BS; Jrnlsm Clb 90-; Jrnlsm.

**DOLFI, MICHAEL J,** Old Dominion Univ, Norfolk, VA; SR; MET; Stdnt Govt Sntr 89; SME 89-90; SAE 90-; Elec Jrnymn 79-; Mech Eng.

**DOLIN, DAVID M,** Marshall University, Huntington, WV; SR; BBA; Alpha Kappa Psi 90; Deans List 90-; Mrktng; Sls/Mgmt.

**DOLIN, SHARON K,** Oh Univ-Southern Cmps, Ironton, OH; FR; BA; Girl Scts Drvr 86-; Poli Cand Awrns 85-; Med Ofc Asst 86-; Psych; Clncl Psych.

**DOLINAK, CYNTHIA A,** Marywood Coll, Scranton, PA; JR; BA; 1st Pl Hghr Educ Wk Essay Cntst 90; Hnrbl Mntn Crtv Wrtng Natl Undrgrad Wrtng Cmptn Delta Epsilon Sigma 90; Engl; Scndry Educ.

**DOLINGER, SHAYNA G,** Richard Bland Coll, Petersburg, VA; SO; BA; Span Clb 88; Pltcl Sci Clb 88-; Yrbk Stf Edtr 88; Equestrian Prptl Trophy 84-90; Equestrian; AS 90; Govt; Law.

**DOLL, FREDA E,** Wv Univ At Parkersburg, Parkersburg, WV; AAS; Chrch Chrst; Wrkng AAS Dgr Offc Admn.

**DOLL, JENNIFER E,** Univ Of Sc At Columbia, Columbia, SC; FR; BS; Gamma Beta Phi; Piedmont Fndrs Schlr 90-; Nrsng; BSN Nrsng.

**DOLL, JOACHIM K,** Univ Of The Dist Of Columbia, Washington, DC; SO; BS; Stdnt Plng Orgnztn Undrgrad Pres; Urban/Rgnl Plng; Plcy Mkng/Cnsltng.

**DOLL, KRISTIN L,** Bowling Green St Univ, Bowling Green, OH; JR; BS; Sprt Mgmt Alliance Pub Chr 88-; Amer Mktg Assn 90-; N Amer Soc Sprt Mgmt; Goldn Key 90; Alpha Lambda Delta 89; Sat Rec Prog 89-90; Sprt Mgmt; Sprt Mktg/Prmtn.

**DOLLY, LINDRELL A,** Hampton Univ, Hampton, VA; FR; BA; Womens Senate 90-; Hons Clg 90-; Pr Eminent Schlr 90-; Pr Schlrshp 90-; Bus; Cpa.

**DOMAN, LATIF S,** Morehouse Coll, Atlanta, GA; JR; BA; &A/S Jrsy Clb 88-90; Pre-Law Soc 88-; Pltcl Sci Soc 89-; Intrnshp W/Sntr Bill Bradley NJ 90; Pltcl Sci; Law.

**DOMANSKI, ROBYNNE MARIE,** Indiana Univ Of Pa, Indiana, PA; FR; BA; Judicial Bd 90-; Hmcmng Ct 90-; Dns Lst 90-; Adopt Grndprnt 90-; St Thomas Moore Pryr Grp 88-; Commnctns; Pub Rltns/Mktng.

**DOMARADZKI, LAURA,** S U N Y Coll Of Tech At Frmgdl, Farmingdale, NY; FR; Hons List 90; Bus Admin/Mgt.

**DOMBARD, ANDREW J,** Haverford Coll, Haverford, PA; FR; BA; Physics/Astronomy; Planetary Resrch.

**DOMBROSKY, MADOLINE C,** Owensboro Jr Coll Of Bus, Owensboro, KY; SO; AD; Cert Cmptrs 89; Cmptrzd Offc Prof.

**DOMBROWSKI, CLAUDIA A,** Christopher Newport Coll, Newport News, VA; FR; BS; Pharm.

**DOMBROWSKI, DANIEL S,** Va Commonwealth Univ, Richmond, VA; FR; BS; Bio/Chem; Bio Profsr.

**DOMEN, MICHELLE L,** Kent St Univ Kent Cmps, Kent, OH; SR; BA; Undergard Stds Comm 90-; Phi Alpha Delta 90-; Alpha Pi Sigma Alpha T 90-; Golden Key 90-; US Attrnys Ofc Intrn; Pres Lst 90; Deans Lst 88-90; Pltcl Sci; Law.

**DOMENCIC, MARK,** Comm Coll Algny Co Algny Cmps, Pittsburgh, PA; FR; BA; Comtra Cltrl Cntr Thtr; Dinner Pianist; Music.

**DOMENCIC, PAUL L,** Comm Coll Algny Co Algny Cmps, Pittsburgh, PA; FR; BA; Civic Light Opera 90-; Jr Mendelssohn Choir 90-; Comtra Comm Theatre Actor/Sngr; Librl Arts.

**DOMENCIC, PETER L,** Comm Coll Algny Co Algny Cmps, Pittsburgh, PA; SO; BED; Poetry Pblshd; Phi Theta Kappa 90-; Hghst Hnrs; AA; Engl; Tchng.

**DOMERESE, SUSANNA M,** Ms Univ For Women, Columbus, MS; JR; BA; Educ; Elem Educ.

**DOMINGO, BRENDA E,** Boston Univ, Boston, MA; FR; BS; AHANA 90-; Cncrt Orch 90-; NOBCCHE Annl Conf 90-; Longy Schl Music Asstshp Mgr 88-; Polaroid Corp Asst Engr 90; Natl Dir Msc Wrtrs; Mech/Arspc Engr.

**DOMINGO, GLORIA M,** Fl International Univ, Miami, FL; JR; BS; Phi Lambda 90-; Phi Kappa Phi 91; FL Undergraduate Scholar 88-; Participant In Student Hnrs Mentor Prog 90; Biology; Biotechnology.

**DOMINGUES, AIRES C,** George Mason Univ, Fairfax, VA; JR; BS; Golden Key 90; Schl Dns Lst 89; Dscn Sci; Cnsltng.**

**DOMINGUEZ ROSADO, JOSE A,** Univ Politecnica De Pr, Hato Rey, PR; SO; BSEE; Sci; Elec Eng.

**DOMINGUEZ, CHRISTOPHER W,** Univ Of Nc At Asheville, Asheville, NC; SR; Deans List 90-; BA; Psychlgy; Dctr Clncl Psychlgy.

**DOMINGUEZ, EDUARDO L,** Miami Dade Comm Coll, Miami, FL; SO; BA; Metro Nwsppr Edit In Chf 89-; Hnrs Prog Stdnt Advsry Com 90-; Paella Strng Com 90-; Phi Theta Kappa Pblctns Chrmn 89-; Fctly Snte Schlrshp; Bowman Ashe Schlrshp; Otstdng Hnrs Stdnt Dept Of Lngge Arts 90; AA; Jrnlsm; Pblshng.**

**DOMINGUEZ, JAVIER,** Univ Of Pr Cayey Univ Coll, Cayey, PR; JR; BS; Future Ldrs Of Hlth Prof 90-; Hnr Soc; Hnr Tuition 90-; Nat Sci Prog; Med/Obstetrician.

**DOMINGUEZ, MARIA E,** Miami Dade Comm Coll South, Miami, FL; SO; BA; AA; Psy; Psygt.

**DOMINGUEZ, OLAF,** Miami Dade Comm Coll, Miami, FL; SO; AA; Sci; Medcn.

**DOMINICK, DAVID ALAN,** Daytona Beach Comm Coll, Daytona Beach, FL; FR; BA; Photo Fine Art; Advrtsng.

**DOMINICK, DEBRA S,** Piedmont Tech Coll, Greenwood, SC; SR; Outstdng Grad Radiologic Tech; Radiologic Tech; Medical.

**DOMINKOVICS, KARIN A,** Barry Univ, Miami, FL; SO; BA; Acctng; Law.

**DOMINO, MARK F,** S U N Y At Buffalo, Buffalo, NY; SR; MENG; Natl Soc Prfsnl Engrs 90-; Inst Elctrcl/Elctrnc Engrs 89-; Engr Stdnt Assoc 89-; Eta Kappa Nu Sec/Initiation Chr 89-; Tau Beta Pi Initiation Chr 89-; Golden Key 89-; Elctrcl Engr Intern 90; BS; Elctrcl Power Engr.

**DOMITROVITS, JOHN P,** S U N Y Coll Of Tech At Delhi, Delhi, NY; FR; AOS; Ski Club 90-; Outdoors Club 90-; Elec Motors/Controls; Elec Contractor.

**DOMM, CHRISTINE A,** Syracuse Univ, Syracuse, NY; FR; BA; Natl Cllgte Nrsng Awrd; Dns Lst 90; Nrsng; Rgstrd Nrse Spclzng In Crdlgy.

**DOMMISSE, BETTINA D,** Christopher Newport Coll, Newport News, VA; JR; Portsmouth Acad Med Aux Rec Sec 87-89; Wstrn Brnch High Sch PTA 87-89; Dip Groote Schuur Hosp/Carinus 70; Nrsng Coll Capetown South Africa; Elem Edn; Teach.

**DOMOGALA, DEBRA A,** Saint Joseph Coll, West Hartford, CT; FR; BED; Fr Hon Symposium; Chld Study; Teach.

**DOMON, PATRICK A,** Niagara Univ, Niagara Univ, NY; SO; BS; Army ROTC Drill Tm Sec 89-; Rngrs Clb 89-; Crmnl Jstce; Law Enfrcmnt.

**DOMPREH, JEFFREY K,** Central St Univ, Wilberforce, OH; JR; AASU Pr 89-90; NCBC Wrkshp Dir 89-90; SGA Act Chrmn 89-; Alpha Kapa Mu Tr; Kappa Alpha Psi Sec; Deans Lst 89-; Tennis/Vlybl Capt 89; Sci; Physics Tchr.

**DOMST, WENDY A,** Hilbert Coll, Hamburg, NY; FR; Sftbl; Bus Admin.

**DONADIO, KEVIN C,** Villanova Univ, Villanova, PA; JR; BA; Scuba Clb Pres 88-90; Pre-Law Socty VP 90-; Hist Clb; Natl Hist Hnr Socty; Phi Kappa Phi; Powr-Lftng Clb; BA; Hist; Law.

**DONAGHEY, MICHAEL F,** S U N Y Coll Of Tech At Frmgdl, Farmingdale, NY; SO; BS; Flyng Clb 90-; AAS; Aviatn.

**DONAHOE, KRISTINE M,** Indiana Univ Of Pa, Indiana, PA; SR; BS; Alice Paul Hs Dmstc Vlnc Cntr Vol 87-90; Outstndng Stdnt Tchr Awd 90; Educ; Tchr-Admin.

**DONAHUE, KATHERINE M,** Nova Univ, Ft Lauderdale, FL; GD; MBA; Acad Of Mngmnt; Assoc For Prctnr In Infctn Cntrl 81; Phi Theta Kappa 78; Acad Of Mngmnt; Assoc For Prctnrs In Infctn Cntrl 81; Sls Rep; BA 81; Bsnss Admin; Bsnss.

**DONAHUE, NANCY J,** Indiana Univ Of Pa, Indiana, PA; JR; BA; Assn Chldhd Edn Intl VP 90-; Early Chldhd Edn; Teach.

**DONAHUE, PATTI L,** East Stroudsburg Univ, E Stroudsburg, PA; SO; BS; Wrk Study 89-; Hon Stdnt Assoc 89-; Deans List 89-90; Comptr Sci; Comptr Progrmng.

**DONAHUE, TIA E,** Merrimack Coll, North Andover, MA; SR; BA; Colg Demo Pres 88-; UN Mdl Head Delg 88-89; Pol Sci Soc 87-; Yrbk 90; Phi Alpha Theta 90-; Truman Schlrshp 88; Legstve Intn 90; Pres Schol; Pol Sci; Publ Admin; Prof.

**DONALD JR, DAN A,** Abraham Baldwin Agri Coll, Tifton, GA; SR; Horticulture Clb 89-90; Dist Achvmnt Lst 90; Deans Hon Lst 90-; Pres Lst 90; Red Cross Cert Inst 84; Golden Eagle Cntry Clb Intrn 90; Scuba Cert 87; IM Basktbl/Ftbl 89-90; Golf Crse Super; Asso Of Amer; Pest Lic; Golf Crse Super.

**DONALD, STEPHEN D,** Ga Inst Of Tech At Atlanta, Atlanta, GA; FR; BA; Navy ROTC Schlrshp/Pgm; Sailing Tm; Soccer Tm; Physics Math; Elec Eng.

**DONALDSON, AMY W,** Bridgewater Coll, Bridgewater, VA; SR; BS; Concert/Stage Bnd 88-; Pre Med Soc 87-; Alpha Chi Pres 89-; Lambda Soc 88-; Stdnt Cnslr 87-89; Tutor 87-90; Vol High Schl Tchr 90-; Pres Merit Schlrshp 87-; Lab Assist 87-; Biol; Grad Schl/Rsrch.

**DONALDSON, ANTHONY K,** Fl A & M Univ, Tallahassee, FL; JR; BA; Art Clb Dsgn Comm 90-; Art.

**DONALDSON, CANDI M,** Daemen Coll, Amherst, NY; SO; BFA; Drama Clb 90-; Art Clb 90-; Admissions Asst 89-; Psi Xi Omicron Asst Secr 90-; Cmnty Svc 89-; Liberty Partnership Mentoring Pgm; Grphc Dsgn/Art Ed.

**DONALDSON, EDWARD B,** Oh St Univ, Columbus, OH; SR; BS; Soc Exp Geophscsts; Natl Well Wtr Assoc; Geo Soc Of Amer; Phi Kappa Phi 90; Deans List 88-90; Sigma Gamma Epsilon 89; Sigma Awd 88; AB Dolly/Rlph Schlrshp 90-; United Parcel Serv; Tech Asst Dr Jeff Daniels OH St Univ; USN Nuclear Pwr Prog; Geology; Grad Schl/Duke.

**DONALDSON, JAMES T,** Saint Andrews Presbytrn Coll, Laurinburg, NC; SR; MS; Fishing Scty Pres 89-; Dorm Council 88-89; RA 89-90; Class Hnrs; Alpha Chi 90-; Deans List 88-; Forest Serv Vltr 88; Clg Wrkstdy Awd 87-90; Brunnenburg Exchg 90; Forest Serv Trl Speclt 89-; BA; Philosophy/Nature; Einvtl Sphere.**

**DONALDSON, JEFFREY T,** Memphis St Univ, Memphis, TN; SR; BA; Gamma Beta Phi 87-; Phi Alpha Theta 90-; Gldn Key 90-; Marcus W Orr Schlrshp; Hstry; Rsrch.

**DONALDSON, LISA E,** Duquesne Univ, Pittsburgh, PA; SR; BA; Stdnt Accntng Assn Prscnt 88-; Jdcl Rvw Brd Gvrnmnt; IM Vllybl Cptn 90-; Beta Gamma Sigma 90-; Beta Alpha Phi 89-; Imicron Delta Kappa; Phi Kappa Phi; Phi Eta Sigma 88-; Otstndng Clg Stdnts America 88-; Phi Chi Theta Sec 88-; Accntng; Kpmg Peat Mariwich.

**DONALDSON, LORI K,** Union Univ, Jackson, TN; JR; BSBA; Acctg Clb 90-; Gamma Beta Phi 90; Phi Beta Lambda 90; Alpha Delta Pi Soph Mem Lrg 88-90; Wrk Schlrshp 88-90; IM Ftbl 88-89; Mgmt/Mktg; Own Bus.

**DONALDSON, TAMRA RENEE,** Univ Of Tn At Martin, Martin, TN; SR; BS; STEA; Edctn.

**DONALDSON, TRACY A,** Pa St Univ Altoona Cmps, Altoona, PA; FR; BS; Alpha Lambda Delta; Nrsng; Nrs Ansthtst.

**DONARUMA, PATRICIA,** City Univ Of Ny Queensborough, New York, NY; SO; 25 Pls Clb 89-; NYPIRG 89-; Perf Arts Srs 89-; Phi Theta Kappa 90-; Tutor 90-; Std Ornttn Ldr Vol 89-90; Inctv Awd Day Std; Ray Ricketts Mem Awd; Wmns Clb Awd; PS 159 PTA 84-; Rosary Soc 84-; Hrlstylst; PT Engl Tutor 90-; Hlth Educ.

**DONATELLI, FRANCES,** Endicott Coll, Beverly, MA; JR; AA; Ltry Magazine 88; Psych Clb 91; Phi Theta Kappa 87-88; Phi Theta Kappa 87-88; Psychlgy/Sclgy Awrd Class 88f Magna Cum Laude 88; Phi Theta Kappa Schlrshp 88; Psychlgy; Psychlgst.

**DONATI, MATTHEW D,** Wv Univ, Morgantown, WV; FR; BS; Engineering; Industrial Engineering.

**DONATO, CHERIE L,** James Madison University, Harrisonburg, VA; SR; BS; CCM Cath Org 87; CEC 87; Psyc Club; Ski Club; Madison Outing Club; Golden Key 89; Vol Daycare/Camelot Nrsg Home 90; Cncl Excep Chldrn; Psych; Chld Psychlgst.

**DONATO, CHRISTINE A,** Siena Coll, Loudonville, NY; SR; BA; Rep Rsdnt Hall Cncl 88-89; Mgr Hcky 90-; Phi Alpha Theta; Legsltv Asstnt Sen M J Tully NY State Senate; Pol Sci; Govt.

**DONATO, KATHRYN L,** Schenectady County Comm Coll, Schenectady, NY; FR; AAS; Bus Prgrmng/Sys.

**DONATO, LISA RAE,** Fl Atlantic Univ, Boca Raton, FL; SO; BA; FAU Sb Dv Clb; Bus.

**DONAVANT, TAMMIE W,** Patrick Henry Comm Coll, Martinsville, VA; SO; BA; Hstry; Elem Tchr.

**DONCASTER, DAVID J,** Embry Riddle Aeronautical Univ, Daytona Beach, FL; SR; BS; Ldrshp Dvlpmnt Pgm 90; Entrnmnt Comm 90-; Nvl Avtn Clb 87-88; Wlybl IMS 88; Flght; Airline Pilot.

**DONCHEY, AMY SARAH,** Atlantic Comm Coll, Mays Landing, NJ; JR; BA; Glassboro SGA; Key Club; AS Atlantic Comm Coll; Spcl Ed; Tchng.

**DONDELINGER, MICHAEL K,** Chattahoochee Vly St Comm Coll, Phenix City, AL; FR; AS; Sci; Engr.

**DONEGAN, LISA A,** Le Moyne Coll, Syracuse, NY; JR; BA; Engl Clb 90-; Firehse Theater 88-; Choral Soc 88-90; Deans Lst 89-; IM Wlybl 88-90; Engl; Lib Sci Rsrch.

**DONEGAN, LORI A,** Middle Tn St Univ, Murfreesboro, TN; SO; BA; Finance; Banking.

**DONELLA, DONNA A,** Georgetown Univ, Washington, DC; SO; Intl Rel Clb 89-; Alumni Phone-A-Thon 89-; Intl Bsn/Minor Govt; Corp Law.

**DONELSON, HEATHER L,** Immaculata Coll, Immaculata, PA; SO; BA; Educ Club 89-90; Daycare Ctr Vol 89-90; Psych/Elem Educ; Tchr.

**DONELSON, PEGGY J,** Univ Of Tn At Martin, Martin, TN; SO; BA; Scl Wrk; MSW.

**DONES SANCHEZ, BETZAIDA,** Inter Amer Univ Pr San German, San German, PR; JR; BA; Assn Est Orntdores 90-; Bio; Med Tech.

**DONG, CONNIE C,** S U N Y Coll Of Optometry, New York, NY; SR; OD; Beta Sgm Kappa 89-; BA Un PA 88; Psychlgy; Optmtry.

**DONG, HOA V,** Bunker Hill Comm Coll, Boston, MA; FR; Liberal Arts.

**DONG, KIMBERLY A,** Ms St Univ, Miss State, MS; FR; BA; Natl Mrt Schlr 90-; Hnrs Pgm 90-; Engl; Law.

**DONKO-HANSON, P KWAME A,** Univ Of Rochester, Rochester, NY; JR; BA; African/Caribbean Cultural Clb Fndr/Pres 89-; Thurgood Marshall Pre Law Soc; All Campus Judicial Cncl Justice; J V Bsktbl 88-89; Philosophy; Corp Law.**

**DONLON, DEBORAH A,** S U N Y Coll At Fredonia, Fredonia, NY; JR; BA; Army Res Ofcrs Trng Corps 1st Lt 89-; Delta Phi Epsilon 88-89; IM Bsktbl Sccr Vllybl; Bsns Fin.

**DONNELL, LISA A,** Hillsborough Comm Coll, Tampa, FL; SO; BA; Phi Theta Kappa 90; Pol Sci Sclgy; Law.

**DONNELLY, DANIELLE M,** City Univ Of Ny Baruch Coll, New York, NY; JR; BA; Mktg; Cnsltnt.

**DONNELLY, JEFFREY J M,** Bunker Hill Comm Coll, Boston, MA; JR; BM; Dart Tm Rep; Snd Rcdng Tech.

**DONNELLY, KATHLEEN A,** Le Moyne Coll, Syracuse, NY; SR; BS; Hmn Srvcs Assoc Pres 87-; Blgy Clb 87-; Nwsppr Stff 89-; Beta Beta Beta 88-; Deans Lst; Hmn Srvcs Assoc Pres 87-; Cmps Mnstry; Blgy Rsrch Asst 89; Rsdnt Hosp Admn 90; Blgy.

**DONNELLY, LEE A,** Univ Of Nc At Asheville, Asheville, NC; SR; BA; Stdnt Nwsppr 89-; Stf Wrtr/Phtgrphr 8-; Actvts Paper Staff Photog 90; Dns Lst 90; Socty Prof Jrnlsts 89-; Intrnshp Price/Mc Nabb Advrtsng/Pub Rel 90; Bele Chere Fstvl Voc 90; WCQS FM Pub Radio; Hsptlty Indstry; AAS 86; Mass Comm; Advrtsng/Pub Rel.

**DONNELLY, TINA C,** Radford Univ, Radford, VA; SO; SGA VP; Delta Zeta Tres; Bus Mrktng; Mrktng.

**DONNER, GREGORY J,** Daemen Coll, Amherst, NY; JR; BA; Art Clb 90-; Art; Tchr.

**DONNER, VICKY L,** City Univ Of Ny City Coll, New York, NY; SO; BA; City Clg Flwshp; Pol Sci; Prfsr/Rsrch/Ph D.

**DONOHEW, CONNIE R,** Wv Univ At Parkersburg, Parkersburg, WV; ECG Tech Jackson Gen Hosp.

**DONOHUE, BRIAN PATRICK,** Capital Bible Seminary, Lanham, MD; SO; Stdnt Govt Sntr/Soc Chmn 86-87; Pres Rugby Clb Pres 85-86; Sr Advsr 86-87; Intermediate Hon 86; Sigma Chi 85-87; Asst Yth Pastor 88-90; Rugby; Corp Cntrlr 88-89; Firm Mgr 89-90; Dir Op 90-; Biblical Studies; Mnstry.

**DONOHUE, CHRISTIAN D,** Villanova Univ, Villanova, PA; SO; BA; Stdnt Pgm Cncl 89-90; Stdnt Theatre Actor 89-90; Phi Kappa Phi; Omicron Delta Kappa; Stdnts Against Drvg Drunk V P 90-; Psych; Med.

**DONOHUE JR, DANIEL T,** Saint Leo Coll, Saint Leo, FL; SO; BS; Hl Judcl Brd Chrmn 90-; Tau Kappa Epsilon 90-; Law.**

**DONOHUE, ELOISE W,** Hilbert Coll, Hamburg, NY; SO; AA; Phi Beta Lambda Pres 90-; Comeback Clb 90-; Alpha Beta Gamma; Ladies Auxil VFW Post 1419 Hamburg 90-; Girl Scouts USA Ldr 85-; Bus/Lib Arts; Bus Mgmnt/Personnel Admin.

**DONOHUE, JULIE A,** Univ Of De, Newark, DE; FR; BS; Fshn Mrchndsng Clb 90-; Fshn Mrchndsng; Bus.

**DONOHUE, KRISTEN A,** Univ Of Akron, Akron, OH; JR; BSBA; FMA 90; Hnr Key; Deans Lst 89; Im Aerobics 89; Fnce; Law Schl.

**DONOHUE, MARY C,** Fl International Univ, Miami, FL; SR; BS; Stdnt Intern VAMC Miami 90-; Gold Coast ATRA; Amer Therapeutic Recreation Assoc Natl; Recr Mngmnt; Therapeutic Recreation.

**DONOHUE, MATTHEW P,** Manhattan Coll, Bronx, NY; JR; BE; Bagpipe Bnd Drum Sgt; Stdnts For Life VP; Voyagers; Natl Engr Hon Soc; Mech Engr Soc; Deans Lst; Amer Soc Of Mech Engrs; Soc Of Auto Engrs; Soup Kitchen; Big Bros; IMS; Mech Engr; Law.

**DONOVAN, CHRISTINE M,** Newbury Coll, Brookline, MA; FR; ASSOC; Innkprs Clb VP 90-; Cert 90; Cert 90; Htl Rst Mgmt.

**DONOVAN, DANIEL W,** Bowling Green St Univ, Bowling Green, OH; SR; BS; Im Adv Brd VP 90-; Clb Soccr VP 89-90; Clg Educ Allied Prof Undergrad Cir Comm; Goldn Key; Otstdng Clg Stdnts Amer; Spec Olympcs Comm Trnmnt; Int Univ Cin Athl Dept; Natl Im Rec Sprts Assn; Sprts Mgmt.

**DONOVAN, JEAN D,** Ny Univ, New York, NY; JR; BS; Info Sys/Mgmnt; Admin/Mgmnt.**

**DONOVAN, JENNIFER E,** S U N Y Coll At Fredonia, Fredonia, NY; JR; BSED; Intrntnl Cir K Edtr Pblc Rltns 89-; Spch Pthlgy Adlgy Soc Sec 89-; Kappa Delta Pi; Spch Pthlgy Adlgy.

**DONOVAN, JENNIFER L,** Abraham Baldwin Agri Coll, Tifton, GA; SO; BED; Drama Tm 89-; Stdnt Nwsppr Stf Wrtr 90-; Stdnt Bd Arts Sec; Deans Lst 90-; Clggng Tm 89-; Engl; Educ.

**DONOVAN, KAREN D,** Univ Of Tn At Martin, Martin, TN; FR; BS; Physcl Thrpy Clb Treas 90-; Mrchng Bnd 90; Mu Epsilon Delta 90-; Physcl Thrpy.

**DONOVAN, KIRSTEN C,** Univ Of Hartford, West Hartford, CT; JR; BA; V P Stdnt Ath Bd V P; Players Asst Comm; Acdmc All Am Awd & Deans List 89-; Varsity Sftbl Tm; Org Communication.

**DONOVAN, MARY LYNNE,** Northern Ky Univ, Highland Hts, KY; SR; BA; Smmr Fllwshp; Dns Cncl; IM; Asst Natl IM Assn In Cncnnti; Phys Educ; Grad Schl.

**DONOVAN, STACEY L,** Lesley Coll, Cambridge, MA; FR; Catholic Cmmnty 90-; Gulf Crisis Timeline 90-; Gulf Crisis Hotline; Deans List 90-; Softball; Early Childhood Educ; Teacher.

**DONOVAN, TERESA A,** City Univ Of Ny Hunter Coll, New York, NY; GD; MS; NSSIWA Pr 87-; Rusk Inst Vol 90-; BA Penn St Univ 89; AAS Nassau Comm Clg 87; Comm Sci; Spch Path.

**DONOVICK, ROBYN LYNN,** Georgetown Univ, Washington, DC; JR; BSBA; Newspapr Sprts Wtr 88-89; Share Our Strngth 88; Amnsty Intrntnl 88; Phi Theta Kappa 89; Share Our Strngth 88; Advntge Intrntnl Intrn; Deans Lst 88; Mngmnt Cert Dist Of Clmba 90; Rstrnt/Bar Mgr 88; Cert Mntgmry Clg 88; Mrktng; Law.

**DONOWAY, LISA R,** Univ Of Md At Eastern Shore, Princess Anne, MD; JR; BA; Art Educ; Tchr.

**DONTINO JR, PHILIP T,** Ny Chiropractic Coll, Glen Head, NY; GD; DC; Amer Chrprctc Assn 88-; Intrnatl Chrprctc Assn 88-; NY St Chrprct Assn 90-; Phi Chi Omega 88-; Theta Delta Chi 87; Bdn St Mssn 87; Dirs Asst 90-; Srvce Awrd; Dstngshd Clncns Awrd; Clnc Rsdnt; IM Sftbl 90; BS Univ Of Rochester 87; Mlclr Gntcs; Chrprctc.

**DOOD, LAURA L,** Bapt Bible Coll & Seminary, Clarks Summit, PA; SO; Puppet Team 89-.

**DOODY, SEAN E,** Me Maritime Academy, Castine, ME; SO; MBA; Propeller Clb US Port ME Maritime Acad 89-90; Cadet Shipping Pgm; Sailed Oil Tnkr Cstl Corp Cadet; Marine Eng; Eng.

**DOOLEY, JENNIFER A,** King Coll, Bristol, TN; JR; BS; Psychlgy Dept Rsrch Asst 90-; Psychlgy; Spch/Hearing Disorders.

**DOOLEY, MICHAEL L,** Faulkner Univ, Montgomery, AL; SR; BS; Vrsty Bsktbll Capt 90; Fdrl Jnr Fllwshp Rpgm 87-; Crr 91; Bus Mgmt.

**DOOLEY, RITA L,** Univ Of Montevallo, Montevallo, AL; JR; BS; Stdnt AL Educ Assoc; Centrala Rdng Cncl 90-; Elem Educ; 2nd Gr Tchr.

**DOOLEY, TRACY T,** Univ Of Va, Charlottesville, VA; SO; BA; VA Rdng Tm Sec 89-; Vol Madsn Hse ER 90-; Vol Rdrs Vsly Imprd 90-; Phi Eta Sigma VP Initatn 90-; Spnsh/Lngstcs; Intrprtr/Trnsltr.**

**DOOLIN, KATHLEEN G,** Univ Of Ky, Lexington, KY; SR; BA; Phi Beta Kappa; Golden Key; Psychology.

**DOOLING, JENNIFER A,** Columbia Union Coll, Takoma Park, MD; FR; BS; Cabin John Vol Fire Dept EMT-A 89-; Nrsg.

**DOOLING, JENNIFER L,** Saint Joseph Coll, West Hartford, CT; FR; BA; Psych Clb; St Francis CCD Pgm 90-; Engl; Media/Tchr.

**DOOLITTLE, KATHI G,** Saint Joseph Coll, West Hartford, CT; JR; BS; Chr 88-90; Chmbr Chr 88-90; Amnsty Intl 88-; Music Clb 89-; 4 H VP 86-; FFA Almn; Engl; Corp Wrtng.**

**DOOMES, EDWARD E,** Morehouse Coll, Atlanta, GA; SO; BS; Natl Soc Blck Engrs; Eastman Kdk Schlr 90-; Chem.

**DOPERAK, MARCIE J,** Indiana Univ Of Pa, Indiana, PA; FR; BA; Assoc Chldhd Edn Intl 90-; Elem Edn; Ed Admin.

**DOPICO, PABLO G,** Univ Of Southern Ms, Hattiesburg, MS; SR; BS; Amer Chem Assoc Stdnt Afflte 87; Hnrs Stdnt Assoc 87; Polymer Sci Clb; Omicron Delta Kappa 89; Phi Kappa Phi 88; Phi Eta Sigma 87; Lambda Sigma Treas 88-89; Mst Outstndng Frshmn Mle 87-88; Phi Kappa Phi Bowl 90; Hall Of Fame 90; Trck/Fld 87-; Polymer Sci; U Prof.

**DORAN, CINDY M,** Mount Aloysius Jr Coll, Cresson, PA; SO; BA; Spcl Olympcs Chrmn 90; Cmps Mnstry Assn VP 89-; Bacchus VP 88; Mdrgls Chrmn 88-; Deans Lst 90; Yr Bk Stf Phtgrphr 88-; Stdnt Prgrmmng Brd 89-; Stdnt Ldr Hrrcn Hugo Fnd Rsr 90; AS Bnrl Stds Mnt Aloysius Jr Clg 90; Englsh Lit Scndry; MA Degree.

**DORAN, COLLEEN L,** Oh Northern Univ, Ada, OH; FR; BA; Alpha Lambda Delta; Psi Sigma; Kappa Phi Almni Offcr; Chld Psychlgy.

**DORAN, DAVID S,** Northeast State Tech Comm Coll, Blountville, TN; BA.

**DORAN, MARY E,** Coll Of Charleston, Charleston, SC; SR; BS; Amer Assn Mntl Rtrdtn VP 89-; Cncl Excptnl Chldrn 89-; Hghly Dstngshd Hon Lst 89-; Dstngshd Fclty Hon Lst 89-; Spec Ed; Emtnlly Hndcppd Dvlpmnt Thrpst.

**DORAS, SHARON B,** City Univ Of Ny Med Evers Coll, Brooklyn, NY; FR; Wst Indian/Caribbean Clb; Computer Science; Programmer.

**DORCAS, DEAN W,** United States Naval Academy, Annapolis, MD; SR; Scuba Clb 89-; Aikido Clb 90-; Omcrn Delta Epsln 89-; Hvywght Vars Crew 87-90; Ecnmcs; Nvl Avtn.

**DORE, TINA M,** Belmont Coll, Nashville, TN; FR; BBA; Offc Hrngs/Appls Clrk 86-; Financl Anlyst.

**DOREY, DEBORAH S,** Liberty Univ, Lynchburg, VA; FR; MBA; Alpha Lambda Delta; Accntng; Bsnss.

**DORFMAN, LYNDA,** Saint Josephs Coll New York, Brooklyn, NY; GD; Hlth Care Admin.

**DORGAN, DANA L,** Univ Of Pa, Philadelphia, PA; SO; Amnsty Intl Treas; Mag; Wing Rep Dorm Dorm Rep 90; Alpha Chi Omega 90-; Prjct Sunshine Vol Tutor 90; French/Spnsh/Engl; Intl Law.

**DORIAN, MICHAEL L,** Memphis St Univ, Memphis, TN; FR; BA; Real Estate.

**DORIN, GENYA,** Memphis St Univ, Memphis, TN; FR; Sigma Alpha Epsilon Ltl Sr 90-; Med; Nrsng/Phys Thrpy.

**DORIO, BOBBI ANN,** Ny Chiropractic Coll, Glen Head, NY; SR; DC; Yrbk Cmtee 90-; Dynamic Esntls 90; Bus Card Cmtee 90; Alpha Zeta Scribe 85; X Ray Prfcncy Dipl; BS Rutgers Univ 88; Chirop.

**DORIO, DENISE M,** Fordham Univ, Bronx, NY; SR; BS; Mrktng Soc 90-; Alpha Mu Alpha; Mrktng; Tchng.

**DORIS, ANDREW H,** Fl A & M Univ, Tallahassee, FL; BS; Racal Milgo Bsktbl League 90-; AS Miami Dade Comm Coll 89; Elec Engr.

**DORKOFIKIS, SOPHIA,** Fordham Univ, Bronx, NY; JR; BA; Fin Soc 90-; Cultrl Arts Clb; Rose Hill Soc; Fin Mgmt Assoc; Fin Hon Soc; Intrnshp Cowen; Fin; Fin Anylst.

**DORMAN, BONNIE G,** Memphis St Univ, Memphis, TN; SR; BA; Golden Key; Hmn Rsrc Mgmt.

**DORMAN, DAWN E,** Wilmington Coll, New Castle, DE; SR; MBA; Phi Theta Kappa 83-85; US Army Mltry Intlgnce Sgt 78-82; Dns Lst 83-85; Dns Lst 89-90; CPA Exam Nov 89; AAS Delaware Tech/Cmnty Clg 85; CPA State Delaware Bd Acctncy; Acctg; CPA.

**DORMAN, DREW M,** Franklin And Marshall Coll, Lancaster, PA; FR; Coll Dems; IM Tnns And Bsktbl; Phi Kappa Tau; NCEA; Hstry.

**DORMAN, STUART M,** Univ Of Sc At Columbia, Columbia, SC; JR; BA; Amer Mktg Assn VP Fndrsng 90-; Intl Stdnt Exch 90-; Prog Prtcpnt Home Univ; Mktg; Cnsltncy.

**DORN JR, ALLEN A,** Me Maritime Academy, Castine, ME; SR; Prpllr Clb 87-90; Rgmnt Mid-Shpmn/Bravo Co Exec Offcr B Co 90-; Alpha Phi Omega Exec Cncl 87-; Bsktbl 88-; Emrgncy Medcl Tech/Bgduc Amblnc Corps 88-; Castine Vol Fire Dept 87-; BS; Marine Eng Tchnlgy; Marine Engr.

**DORN, EDWARD R,** Univ Of Nc At Charlotte, Charlotte, NC; JR; BA; Meth Presby Campus Ministry Pres 89-90; United Religious Ministries Co Chair; Religious Studies; Campus Minister.

**DORN, JASON L,** Old Dominion Univ, Norfolk, VA; SO; BS; Tau Beta Pi; Chi Epsilon; Golden Key; Civil Eng; Envrnmntl Eng.

**DORN, STEPHANIE T,** Bridgewater Coll, Bridgewater, VA; FR; BA; Pol Sci; Law.

**DORNA PESQUERA, REBECCA,** Univ Of Pr At Rio Piedras, Rio Piedras, PR; SR; Assn Advrtsng/Pub Rltns Stdnts 89-; Fdrtn Flm/Tlvsn Stdnts 90-; Goldn Key 89-; BA; Pub Cmnctn.

**DOROGI, SARA R,** S U N Y Coll At Fredonia, Fredonia, NY; SO; BA; Spectrum Entertainment Brd 89; Theatre.

**DOROSHUK, TERRY R,** Tomlinson Coll, Cleveland, TN; SO; BA; Stdnt Govt Pres 90; Bsktbl 89-90; Spiritual Lfe Cmmttee 89; Phi Theta Kappa 89; Pres Lst 90; Ministry.

**DOROUGH, JANET E,** Univ Of Montevallo, Montevallo, AL; JR; BED; Educ; Tch.

**DOROZENSKI, BETH-ANNE M,** Ringling School Of Art, Sarasota, FL; SO; BFA; Schlrshp Frances Hook; Schlrshp Naples Art Assn; Pres Awrd; Fine Art; Tchr.

**DORR, KIMBERLY L,** Univ Of New England, Biddeford, ME; SR; BS; BS; Occptnl Thrpy.

**DORRIS, ANGELA L,** Oh St Univ At Newark, Newark, OH; SO; BSBA; I M Vybl Capt 89; Hon Soc 90-; Acctg/Bus; CPA.

**DORRIS, APRIL D,** Western Ky Univ, Bowling Green, KY; SR; BS; Phi Beta Lambda Sec 89; Soc Hmn Rsrce Mgmt V P 90; Beta Gamma Sigma Pres 90-; Omicron Delta Kappa 90-; Phi Kappa Phi 90-; Phi Eta Sigma 88-; Delta Sigma Pi Schlrshp Key; Outstndng Mgmt Stdnt; Schlr Clg Bsn; Mgmt; Hmn Rsrcs.

**DORRIS, DONALD F,** Memphis St Univ, Memphis, TN; JR; BSEE; W TN Histrcl Soc; Assoc Of The US Army; Natl Guard Assoc; Certfd Instrctr San Diego Cmnty Clg Dist; AS Univ Of NY Regene 88; Elec Engr.

**DORRIS, TRENA G,** Middle Tn St Univ, Murfreesboro, TN; SO; BA; Gamma Beta Phi 90-; Kappa Delta Phi; Elem Educ; Tchr.

**DORSA, JOANNE C,** Atlantic Comm Coll, Mays Landing, NJ; FR; Strawbridge/Title Clthr Custsvc 90-; Edctn; Sign Lang Tchr.

**DORSETT, DWIGHT AUGUSTUS,** Tuskegee Univ, Tuskegee Inst, AL; FR; BS; Pre-Vet Med Assn; Bahamian Stdnts Assn Sec; Intrntl Stdnts Assn; Anml Sci; Med/Vet Med.

**DORSEY, ANTHONY C,** Morehouse Coll, Atlanta, GA; SO; BA; Stdnt Natl Med Assoc Fnd-Rsg Comm 90-; Hlth Careers Soc Prlmntrn Elect; Inspirtnl Voices Faith Choir 90-; PSI Mntly Disbld Population Asst Cnslr 90; Bio/Pre-Med; Med-Ob.

**DORSEY, BRIAN,** Lincoln Univ, Lincoln Univ, PA; SR; MS; Eng Clb 90-; PRIME 79-; Beta Kappa Chi 83-84; BS; Advncd Sci/Eng Rnfrcmnt Flwship 90-; Summer Intrnshp Honeywell Inc Sprcndctr Rsrch; Physics; Prs Career Elect Eng.

**DORSEY, CAROLYN R,** Alcorn St Univ, Lorman, MS; SR; BA; Soc Work Clb Prlmntrn 90-; Claiborne Cnty Mass Choir; Ord Estrn Str Str Pnt 87-90; Radio Dsptchr Shrff Dept 90-; Soc Work; Law Enfrcmnt.

**DORSEY, DARRELL K,** Truett Mc Connell Coll, Cleveland, GA; SO; BED; Emplyd Bsc EMT/PRMDC 82; Cert Bsc EMT N Ga Tech Clarkesville Ga 82; Cert Prmdc Lanier Area Tech Gainesville Ga 84; Hstry; Tch.

**DORSEY, ERIK S,** Md Coll Of Art & Design, Silver Spring, MD; SR; Ski Clb; Lft Wts Ski Pnt; AD; Cmmnctns; Phto Jrnlst Art Dir Advrtsng.

**DORSEY, JACQUETTA E,** Coppin St Coll, Baltimore, MD; FR; BS; Stdnt Hnrs Assn 90-; Comm Serv 90-; Dns Lst; Mgmt Sci; Cpa.

**DORSEY, KEVIN R,** West Liberty St Coll, West Liberty, WV; SR; BS; Math; Cmptr Prgrmng.

**DORSEY, LAURA B,** Norfolk St Univ, Norfolk, VA; SR; BS; Mgmt Clb 87; Delta Sigma Theta 89-; Ntl Coll Bus Merit Awds 89; Pgrmr Assoc Sovran Fncl Corp 89-90; Mgmt Cmptr Info Sys; Cmptr Oper/Mgmt.

**DORSEY, MARETTA S,** Paine Coll, Augusta, GA; SO; BS; Vlybl/Sftbl Capg 90; Biol; Engrng.

**DORSEY, NATHANAEL H,** Tn Temple Univ, Chattanooga, TN; SR; BA; Chpl Pstr 89-; Pstrl Stds.

**DORSEY III, PERCELL,** Newbury Coll, Brookline, MA; BA; Deacon New Covenant Chrstn Ctr Boston; Treas Metco Pgrm Dover Strgn Brnch; Assoc Propty Off Draper Lab.

**DORSEY, RAY A,** Coppin St Coll, Baltimore, MD; JR; BS; Mgmnt Sci; Grad Sch.

**DORSEY, RENALDO U,** Univ Of Al At Birmingham, Birmingham, AL; JR; BS; UAB SHRP SSA Cmmnty Affairs Cmmt Co/Chrmn 89; Rdgrphy Class Rep Senator 89; AL Scty Radiologic Tech 89; UAB NAACP 88; Pres List UAB 90; Hnr Roll/Faulkner Univ 89; AAS Faulkner Univ Bham; Radiological Science; Medical.

**DORSEY, SARA J,** Tn Temple Univ, Chattanooga, TN; SR; BS; Sunday Sch Tchr/Yth Ldr 89-; Elem Edn; Tchr.

**DORTA MARTINEZ, JOSE,** Inter Amer Univ Pr Hato Rey, Hato Rey, PR; BA; Clb Ntc Arcb 80-; Cngrjs Ytch Clb 80-; Achvmnt Mdl 90; Bchlrshp.

**DORTCH, SCHONA S,** Savannah St Coll, Savannah, GA; SR; BS; Beta Beta Beta 90-; ID Natl Eng Lab Asst 90; Bio; Dntstry.

**DORTCH, YASMIN A,** Tn St Univ, Nashville, TN; JR; BS; Scl Wrk Clb 89-; Alpha Delta Mu; Alpha Kappa Alpha 90-; Big Sis; Pr Cnslr 90-; Scl Wrk; Med Scl Wrkr.

**DORTON, JOHN K,** Ma Inst Of Tech, Cambridge, MA; FR; BS; Archtctr Mech Eng; Eng.

**DORWART, STEPHANIE J,** Duquesne Univ, Pittsburgh, PA; JR; BS; Kappa Delta Epsilon 90-; Math Educ; Tchr.

**DORWAY, OSCAR P,** City Univ Of Ny City Coll, New York, NY; SO; BCE; PRES; CSU; Civil Eng.**

**DOS SANTOS, AGUINALDO J,** City Univ Of Ny La Guard Coll, Long Island Cty, NY; SO; BA; Psych Clb; Deans Lst 89-; Phy Theta Kappa VP 90-; Intrn Asst Mgr; Biogrph Cinema Asst Mgr 90-; Thtr/Flm; Actng/Dir/Plyrtng.

**DOSCH, LAURA K,** Muskingum Coll, New Concord, OH; JR; BA; Cntrbd 89-90; Blck/Gold Club 88-89; Tour Guide 89; Kappa Mu Epsilon; Math; Advrtsng.

**DOSKY, DOUGLAS A,** Oh Dominican Coll, Columbus, OH; SR; BS; Soccer Tm Capt 90; IM Soccer Clb Crdntr; Ftrnl Order Police 89-; Grad Cum Laude 87; AS Columbus State Comm Clg 87; Math; Tchr/Prfsr Math.

**DOSS, FRANCES B,** Univ Of Montevallo, Montevallo, AL; SR; Yrbk 89; Phi Theta Kappa 87-; Kappa Delta Pi 89-; Chi Omega 89-; Pres Ldrshp Schlrshp 89-; BS; Elem Ed; MS.

**DOSS, JENNIFER D,** Univ Of Sc At Columbia, Columbia, SC; SO; BS; Phi Eta Sigma 90-; Dns Lst 89-; Chancllrs Lst 90; Acctg/Busn Admin.

**DOSS, MARILYN J,** Elon Coll, Elon, NC; SO; Math; Tch.**

**DOSS, SHARON D,** Univ Of Southern Ms, Hattiesburg, MS; JR; BS; Afro Amer Stdnt Organ Awds 89-; Zeta Phi Beta; Elem Educ; Tchng.

**DOSS, STEVEN R,** Ky Wesleyan Coll, Owensboro, KY; GD; BA; Ky Wesleyan Psychlgy Clb Pres 90-; Psy Chi; Clin Prctcm Vly Inst Psychtry 90-; Nwsppr Mgmt Pblshr 76-88; Psychlgy; Doctorate/Psychlgy.

**DOSS, SUSAN R,** Univ Of Sc At Columbia, Columbia, SC; SR; BS; Deans Lst 90-; Cmptr Sci.

**DOSTER, DEANNA L,** Univ Of Tn At Martin, Martin, TN; JR; BS; Chi Alpha; Hm Ecnmcs; Fshn Mrchndsr.

**DOSTER, DENISE E,** Bethany Coll, Bethany, WV; SR; BA; Lacrosse Clb Treas 89-; SIFE Treas 88-; Soc Bus Stdnts Govt Rep 89; Gamma Sigma Kappa 89-; Kalon 90-; Omicron Delta Epsilon 90-; Pi Gamma Mu; Kappa Mu Epsilonm; Soc Clgte Jrnlst; Ph Mu Treas 89-; Otsdng Jr Wmn 89-90; Econ; Intl Econ/Rltns.

**DOSTER, MALCOLM K,** Morehouse Coll, Atlanta, GA; JR; BA; Coll Bus Assn 88-90; DC Metro Clb 88-90; Jr Achiev 90-; Perry Homes Bys/Grls Clb; Dept Nvy Mltry Sealft Cmmnd; IM Bsktbl/Ftbl 88-; Acctg; CPA.

**DOSTIE, YVETTE D,** Georgian Court Coll, Lakewood, NJ; SR; BS; Delta Mu Delta 90-; Hnrbl Mntn Bsn Admin; Dns Lst 87-; Mgna Cum Laude; Bsn Admin; Hmn Rsrc Mgmt.

**DOTSON, CHERYL B,** Ashland Comm Coll, Ashland, KY; SO; AAS; Stdnt Govt Rep 90; Boy Scts Of Amer Dn Ldr/Cubsct Cmsnr 89-; Comp Info Sys; Prgrmr.

**DOTSON, ELIZABETH J,** Glenville St Coll, Glenville, WV; SO; BA; Ladies White Rose 89-90; 4-H Pres Rainbow 80-; Edn Engl; Teach.**

**DOTSON, HAROLD S,** Univ Of Md At Eastern Shore, Princess Anne, MD; SO; Spanish Hnr Soc 87; Senatorial Schlrshp Cert 90; Acad Achvmnt Cert 90; IM Ftbl/Bsktbl; Acctng; Law.

**DOTSON, KEVIN E,** Univ Of Tn At Knoxville, Knoxville, TN; JR; BS; Bapt Stdnt Un Dir Of IMS; Furman Sngrs 89-90; Univ TN Concert Choir 90; Beta Gamma Sigma; Sigma Mu Alpha Statstcl Soc Pres; Clg Educ Serv Corps Furman Univ 89-90; Statstcs; Statstcl Consltng.

**DOTSON, KIMBERLY ANN,** Marshall University, Huntington, WV; SR; BBA; Natl Mgmnt Assn 89-; Alpha Kappa Psi Chrmn 88-; Serv Com Chair 90-; Deans Lst 86-; Mgmnt/Mktg; MBA.

**DOTSON, LAURA W,** Gaston Coll, Dallas, NC; JR; AS; Accntng; CPA.

**DOTSON, MARY H,** Ms Valley St Univ, Itta Bena, MS; SR; BS; Assoc Cmptng Mchnry Treas 90-; Cmptr Sci Math Clb Sec 90-; Stdnt Afrs Brd Stdnts Undergrdte Pgm 90-; Beta Kappa Chi 90-; Dns Lst 88-90; Ltr Aprctn NASA Rsrch Prjct 90; AA Miss Delta Jr Clge 87; Cmptr Sci/Info Syst; Cmptr Pgmr.

**DOTSON, SARAH THERESA,** Univ Of Sc At Columbia, Columbia, SC; SR; Angel Flght Org Scrtry 89; Delta Gamma Alumnae Chrprsn 88-90; BS; Intrnshp Visual Mrchndsng San Diego Ca; Retlng; Ed Prfssnl.

**DOTSON, STACEY L,** Univ Of Tn At Martin, Martin, TN; SO; BS; PEP 90-; Pcr Annual Staff 90-; Stdnt Ambssdr 90-; Chi Omega Jr/Sr Pnhllnc Del/Tres Pan Cncl 89-; Ldrs Res Schlrshp; Ernest/Fannie M Hdgcck Schlrshp; Chrldr Schlrshp; Biology; Grad Deg.

**DOTSON, THOMAS L,** Western Ky Univ, Bowling Green, KY; FR; BS; Sigma Alpha Epsilon; Pr Schlr 90-; Physics.

**DOTSON, TONY W,** Univ Of Ky, Lexington, KY; SR; BS; Alpha Epsilon Delta 90-; Sigma Kappa Sigma 90; Bio Club 88-90; Yrbk Stf 88-90; Varsity Bsktbl 88-90; SMADT; Deans List 88-; Clg Schlrs Of America; Mens Bsktbl Frshmn Of The Jr 90; Mens Varsity Bsktbl Oakland Cty Clg 88-90; Bio/Chem; Medcn.

**DOTTIN, DANNY B,** Mount Saint Mary Coll, Newburgh, NY; FR; BA; Chrstn Flwshp Clb 90-; BSU 90-; Bio; Med/Pdtrcn.

**DOTY, MARY B,** Union Univ, Jackson, TN; SR; BS; Campus Bapt Yng Wmn Pres 89-; Bapt Stu Union Cnsl 87-; Psych/Sclgy Clb 89-; Pi Gamma Mu Sec 90-; Phi Theta Kappa 88-89; AA 89; Scl Wrk.

**DOTY, SALLY B,** Ms Coll, Clinton, MS; GD; JD; Envrnmntl Law Assn Treas 90-; Miss Yng Lawyrs; Hon Crt Juste; Phi Delta Phi; Appellate Advcry Awd 90-; Circuit Ct Intrn; BA Miss Univ Wmn 88; Law.

**DOTY JR, WILLIAM M,** Univ Of Al At Huntsville, Huntsville, AL; JR; BS; Alpha Lambda Delta VP 88-89; Eta Kappa Nu Brdg Crspndt 90-; Tau Beta Pi; Hnr Schlrshp 87-; Hnr Schlr 88-; Elec Engr.

**DOUCETTE, JUDY L,** Univ Of West Fl, Pensacola, FL; JR; BA; Phi Theta Kappa 90-; AA Pensacola Jr Coll 90; Spec Educ SLD; Educ.

**DOUCETTE, SAMUEL F,** Albertus Magnus Coll, New Haven, CT; SR; Cmmtr Cncl Class Rep 89-90; Nwspapr Wrtr 90-; Stdnt Serv Comm 90-; Tau Pi Phi 90-; BA; Econ; Rmn Cthlc Prsthd.**

**DOUGHERTY, AMIE E,** Univ Of Ky, Lexington, KY; SO; BA; Stdnt Athletics Chcl 89-; Univ Ky Vybl Tm 89-; Lances Jr Hon; Kappa Delta Sor Prlrmntrn 90; Vybl Tm; Biology/Pre Med; Med Pedtrcn.

**DOUGHERTY, BRIAN D,** Methodist Coll, Fayetteville, NC; SR; BS; Theatre Grp; Bsns Admn; Indstry.

**DOUGHERTY, CHRISTY L,** Univ Of Ky, Lexington, KY; JR; BA; Math Clb; Epsilon Delta; Delta Gamma Corr Sec; Math; Teacher.

**DOUGHERTY, DARLA R,** Savannah Coll Of Art & Design, Savannah, GA; SO; BA; Graphc Desgn; Advrtsng.

**DOUGHERTY IV, GEORGE F,** Piedmont Bible Coll, Winston-Salem, NC; SR; BA; Beta Sigma Phi VP 88-89; Chorale Pres 90-91; All Amer Schlr 90-91; Dns Lst 89-90; Delta Epsilon Chi 90-; Scr 87; Music; Grad Schl Trmpt Perf.

**DOUGHERTY, JAMES B,** Hampton Univ, Hampton, VA; FR; BARL; Archtctre Achievemnt Awd; Amer Lgn Mdl; Army ROTC Schlstc Achievemnt Rbbn; Architecture.

**DOUGHERTY, JENNIFER REBECCA,** Univ Of Sc At Columbia, Columbia, SC; FR; BA; Univ Rd Stn DJ; Emrgng Ldrs; Brdcst Jrnlsm; Law.

**DOUGHERTY, KATHLEEN E,** Neumann Coll, Aston, PA; SO; BSN; Natl Stdnt Nrs Assoc 89-; Stdnt Nrs Assoc Repr 89-; Dns Lst 89-; Sftbl 90-; Aston-Beechwood Vol Fire Co 86-; Collingdale Vol Fire Co 1 90-; EMT DE Co Cmnty Clg 88; Nrsg.

**DOUGHERTY, LEA M,** Marywood Coll, Scranton, PA; SR; BSW; SG Cmtr Rep 90-; Vlntrs Actn VP 89-F Caritas Pres 89-90; Kappa Gamma Pi; Delta Epsilon Sigma; Pi Gamma Mu; Alpha Delta Mu; Hosp Intern; Bsktbl Stats; Scl Wrk; MSW.

**DOUGHERTY, MARINA L,** Lansdale School Of Bus, North Wales, PA; BA; Cert Accntng Mngmnt 88-90; Accntng Mngmnt; CPA.

**DOUGHERTY, MELISSA R,** Univ Of Akron, Akron, OH; FR; BA; Hon Clb 90-; Hon Pgm 90-; Phi Eta Sigma 90-; Schlrshp 90-; IM Vlybl 90-; Acctg; CPA.

**DOUGHERTY, REGINA M,** Marywood Coll, Scranton, PA; SO; BA; Publ Rels Stdnt Soc Amer; Newspaper Copy Ed; Amer Advrtsg Fed; Psych Clb; Act 101 Ldrshp Cncl 90; BPO Ladies Aux Pres 86-87; Wmns Clb V P 88-89; Publ Rels/Advrtsg; PR Adv Free-Lance Wrtg.

**DOUGHERTY, SCOTT A,** Indiana Univ Of Pa, Indiana, PA; SO; BS; Crcl K Vp 89-90; Sgn Lng Clb VP 90-; Mrchng Bnd 89-; Phi Mu Alpha Sinfonia Sec 90-; Ed Hrng Imprd.

**DOUGHERTY, WENDY S,** S U N Y Coll At Fredonia, Fredonia, NY; SR; BA; Amer Pol Sci Assn 90-; Piano Clb 88-89; Chautauqua Cnty Hm 88-90; Pi Sigma Alpha; Tchg Asst; Pol Sci; Law.

**DOUGHLIN, CHARLES H,** City Univ Of Ny Baruch Coll, New York, NY; JR; BBA; Club Caricomf Intrvrsty Chrstn Flwshp; Bd Of Dir/Stdnt Govt; Chrch Yth Dept Treas 88-89; VP 88-89; Comm Grp 88-89; Occup Hlth Sfty Rep 88-89; Cstms Clrk/Lgl Clrk; Finance; Fncl Analyst.

**DOUGHTY, ROSA G,** Thomas Nelson Comm Coll, Hampton, VA; FR; Art.

**DOUGHTY, THADDEUS J,** Saint Leo Coll, Saint Leo, FL; SR; ROTC Cadet Capt 89-; Delta Epsilon Sigma 89-; Chester Taylor Schlr 89-; Full Schlrshp To Law Schl; Dns Lst 88-; IM Bsktbl Chmps 90; BA Crmnlgy; Crmnlgy; Attend Law Schl.**

**DOUGHTY, VICTORIA L,** Radford Univ, Radford, VA; JR; BS; Soc Coll Jrnlsts Pr 87-89; Blcksbrg Fellwshp Chrch; Wavy 10 Sprts Asst 87-88; Prod Asst 85-87; Video Fshn Prod Asst 90-; Comm; Entertnmnt News.

**DOUGHTY, WAYNE E,** Me Maritime Academy, Castine, ME; FR; BA; Sec Baete; Fldhs Wrkstdy 90-; IM 90-; Pwr Engrg; Engrg.

**DOUGLAS, ANGELA A,** Indiana Univ Of Pa, Indiana, PA; JR; BED; Penn St Educ Assn 90-; Symph Bnd 88-89; Res Hl Assn 88-90; Dns Lst 89-; IM Vlybl; Elem Educ; Tchg.

**DOUGLAS, APRILE L,** Fl A & M Univ, Tallahassee, FL; FR; Phi Eta Sigma 90-; Fresh Pharm Cls Queen 90-; Pharm.

**DOUGLAS, BRANDY M,** Univ Of South Al, Mobile, AL; FR; BA; Circle K 90-; Alpha Lambda Delta; Phi Eta Sigma; Elementary Education; Teacher.

**DOUGLAS, CAROLE A,** Northeastern Univ, Boston, MA; JR; BS; Phi Kappa Phi 90; Pres Awrd 90-; Ernest & Young Intern; MA Hghr Ed Asst Corp Audit Intern 88-; Accntng; Law.**

**DOUGLAS, CHRISTALAN D,** Southern Junior Coll, Birmingham, AL; FR; Nwsppr; Dns Lst.

**DOUGLAS, DESMOND M,** Fordham Univ, Bronx, NY; JR; BS; All Amrcn Schlr 90; Beta Alpha Psi 90; Beta Gamma Sigma 90; VITA 90; Fordham Acdmc Schlrshp 88-; Martin J Keane Mem Prz Acctg 90-; Pblc Acctg; Corp Law.**

**DOUGLAS, EARL RAY,** City Univ Of Ny La Guard Coll, Long Island Cty, NY; GD; Radio Sta Music Dir 88-; Phi Theta Kappa 90-; Intrn WNEW-FM 89-; Lib Arts/Cmmnctns/Engl.

**DOUGLAS, ELIZABETH M,** Univ Of Nc At Greensboro, Greensboro, NC; SO; BM BA; Coll Msc Ed Natl Conf Sec 90-; Presbyterian Hse Pres 89-; Env Awrns Fndtn 89-; Undergrad Msc Hstry Exc Awd; Suncg Mrshl; Tchng Prctcm East Davidson HS 90; IM Bsktbl 90; Intl Trmpt Gld 87-; Msc Ed/Msc Hstryf Coll Prof Music.

**DOUGLAS, HORATIO M,** Va St Univ, Petersburg, VA; JR; BS; Bsn Admn Clb 88-89; Tdwtr Pre-Almni 88; Dorm Jdcl Rep 90-; IM Sprts 88-; Bsn Admn; Entprnr.

**DOUGLAS, JAMES H,** Valdosta St Coll, Valdosta, GA; JR; BS; Process Cntrl Asst; Elec Eng; Process Cntrl Eng.

**DOUGLAS, JULIET S,** Memphis St Univ, Memphis, TN; FR; BA; Spnsh Clb 90-; Hl Cncl Rep 90-; Res Hl Asc Rep 90-; Phi Eta Sigma; Sexual Assault/Date Rape Std Task Frc MSU; Spnsh; Lib Sci.

**DOUGLAS, KATHERINE E,** Va Commonwealth Univ, Richmond, VA; JR; BA; Pol Sci Scty 90-; Pre Law Clb 90-; Gldn Key 90-; Deans List 90-; Rchmond Ballet 84-; Pol Sci/Phlsphy; Law/Dplmcy.

**DOUGLAS, KENT B,** Columbus Coll Of Art & Design, Columbus, OH; SO; BFA; Fine Arts; Freelance Illus.

**DOUGLAS, KIMBERLY A,** Castleton St Coll, Castleton, VT; JR; BA; Rdio Dsc Jcky 90-; Crmnl Jstc Clb 89-; Tour Gd 88-; Admsns Hst Crdntr 90-; Nrth Scrbrgh Grng Vol 88-; Coll Clb Prtlnd Schlrshp 88-89; Maine Schlrshp 90-; Nrth Scrbrgh Grng Schlrshp 88-89; Im Vlybl 90-; Crmnl Jstc/Spnsh/Psychlgy.

**DOUGLAS, LAURA A,** Tri County Tech Coll, Pendleton, SC; SR; AAS; Phi Theta Kappa 90-; Industrial Electronics.

**DOUGLAS, LESLIE A,** Elmira Coll, Elmira, NY; JR; BA; Ins/Trvl Ind; AS Corning Comm Clg 90; CPA.

**DOUGLAS, MAILE A,** George Mason Univ, Fairfax, VA; SO; BA; Deans Admission Prog 89-; Business Hnr Soc 89-; Deans List 89-; Business; Law & Business.

**DOUGLAS, MARCIA H,** City Univ Of Ny Baruch Coll, New York, NY; GD; BBA; Sigma Alpha Delta Rec Sec 90-; Beta Gamma Sigma; Sr Prgrmmr/Anlyst 86-; AAS NY Cty Tech Clg CUNY 86; Cmptr Info Syst; Prgrmmr/Anlyst.

**DOUGLAS, MARQUIL D,** Univ Of Sc At Columbia, Columbia, SC; FR; BA; UMOJA; Alpha Lamda Delta; Dns Lst; Cmptr Sci.

**DOUGLAS, MELISSA RENEE,** Lexington Comm Coll, Lexington, KY; SO; BA; Amer Red Crs; Hm Proj Oper Desert Shld; Cassidy Ele Tch; Ele Educ; Tch.

**DOUGLAS, REBECCA L,** Vanderbilt Univ, Nashville, TN; SO; BA; Hnr Cncl; Arts Sci Cncl; Vanderbuddies 89-; Alpha Omicron Pi 89-; Communication; Law/Jrnlsm.**

**DOUGLAS, REBECCA L,** Ashland Comm Coll, Ashland, KY; FR; BA; Acctng; CPA.

**DOUGLAS, SANDRA L,** Marshall University, Huntington, WV; SR; BS; Amer Mktg Assn; Soc Adv Mgmt; Alpha Kappa Psi 90-; Jr Achvmnt; Dns Lst; Concordia Clg 89; Mktg; Mgmt Retail Estblsmnt.

**DOUGLAS, TENESHA M,** East Tn St Univ, Johnson City, TN; FR; BA; Alph Lmbd Dlt; Acad Achvmnt Awrd; Clncl Psychlgst.

**DOUGLAS JR, THOMAS L,** Samford Univ, Birmingham, AL; GD; JD; Cumberland Intl Law Soc Pres; Amer Jrsprdnc Bk Awrd; Corp Extern AL Title Co; Amer Bar Assn; BS Univ AL 84; MBA Univ AL 89; Law.

**DOUGLAS, TRACY S,** Thomas Nelson Comm Coll, Hampton, VA; SO; Elec Engr.**

**DOUGLAS, VICTORIA J,** Washington Coll, Chestertown, MD; FR; BA; Hist Soc 90-; Lab Asst Acad Cmptng Ctr 90-; City Wilmington Port Wilm Intl Trade; Awd Dstnctn Fresh Common Seminar 90-; Pre-Law.

**DOUGLAS, VIRGINIE,** Greenville Tech Coll, Greenville, SC; SO; BSEET; Elctrncs; Eng.

**DOUGLASS, CARMEN J,** Memphis St Univ, Memphis, TN; SR; BA; Gamma Beta Phi; Mortar Bd 90; Risk Mgmt.

**DOUGLASS, DIANNA M S,** Memphis St Univ, Memphis, TN; SR; BA; Pblc Rltns Stdnt Soc Amer PR Dir 90; Macedonia Untd Meth Chrch Nwsltr Ed 90; Alumni Schlrshp Awd Jrnlsm 89; Macedonia Untd Meth Chrch 87-90; Past Yth Dir; Sndy Schl Sprntndnt; Sndy Schl Tchr; Pennaco Hosiery; Jrnlsm; Pblc Rltns.

**DOUGLASS JR, HARRY W,** Indiana Univ Of Pa, Indiana, PA; JR; BA; Univ Radio DJ 90- Stdnt Engr 90- Undrwrtng Dir; Alpha Epsilon Rho 90-; Apaches Clb Hockey 88-90; Cmnctns Media.

**DOUGLASS, JOHN A,** Livingston Univ, Livingston, AL; SR; BS; Ftbl Tm 87-; History; Law.

**DOUKHNAI, ALEXEI V,** Atlantic Comm Coll, Mays Landing, NJ; SO; AAS; Comp Systms Tchnlgy.

**DOUROUX, VICKI DAWN,** Univ Of Sc At Columbia, Columbia, SC; JR; BA; Soc Of Profsnl Jrnlsts; Clg Of Young Repblcns; Alpha Epsilon Rho; Zeta Tau Alpha; Intrnshp As WIS-TV Columbia SC; Jrnlsm; Law.

**DOUTT, DORI ELLEN,** Slippery Rock Univ, Slippery Rock, PA; JR; BA; AA Butler Cty Comm Coll 90; Exercise Physlgy; Phys Therapist.

**DOUVILLE, FRANCIS,** Atlantic Union Coll, S Lancaster, MA; SO; French Club Pres 89-; Physcl Thrpy; Thrpst/Biolgcl Rsrch.

**DOVE, BRADLEY R,** Central Fl Comm Coll, Ocala, FL; FR; AS; Ind Elect; Cert 90; Elctrncs; Ind Elect Tchncn/Engr.

**DOVE, DAVID C,** Univ Of Miami, Coral Gables, FL; SO; BA; Psychology/Sociology; Social Psychologist.

**DOVE, LISA R,** Univ Of Cincinnati, Cincinnati, OH; JR; BSN; Minrty Stdnt Nrs In Action Treas 90-; Untd Black Assoc 88-89; Nrsng/Hlth.

**DOVER, GARCELLE A O,** Bloomfield Coll, Bloomfield, NJ; SO; BS; Orng Yth Ensmbl Chpln 90-; Cmmnty Serv Sec 88-; Pre Prof Biol; Med.

**DOVER, JUNIUS A,** Univ Of Tn At Knoxville, Knoxville, TN; SR; BS; Exec Clb; Beta Gamma Sigma; Acctng; CPA.

**DOVER, KAREN H,** Univ Of Tn At Chattanooga, Chattanooga, TN; JR; BS; Tenn Scenc Rvrs Assn; Boy Scts Amer; Bg Bro Bg Sis; Bstn Brnch Assn; Appl Chem Text Crpt Ind; BS Tenn Tech Univ 84; Chem Eng; Oper/Tech Serv Mgmt.

**DOW, CHRISTINE F,** Teikyo Post Univ, Waterbury, CT; FR; AS; Stu Govt Assoc Lbrl Arts Sntr 90-; Phi Theta Kappa; Ldrshp Awrds; Gen Stdy.

**DOW, JEFFREY A,** Bridgeport Engr Inst, Fairfield, CT; JR; BE; AE Wtrbry St Tchncl Clg 90; Math; Engnrng.

**DOW, KATHLEEN M,** Elms Coll, Chicopee, MA; FR; AS; Cls 1994 Sec; Ambdsr; Fld Hcky/Lcrse 90-; Comm Sci Dsrdrs.

**DOW, ROBERT L,** Alcorn St Univ, Lorman, MS; FR; BA; Acctg; CPA.

**DOWARD JR, OSCAR W,** Al A & M Univ, Normal, AL; SO; BA; Army ROTC 89-; Alpha Phi Alpha; Hstry Pltcl Sci; Edctn.

**DOWD, CHRISTOPHER J,** Western New England Coll, Springfield, MA; SR; BS; Pol Sci Club 90-; Cmnty Fstvl 88-89; Deans List 90-; Campus Ctr Bldg Suprvsr 89-90; Athltc Asst 90-; Varsty Bsbl 87-; Cert Teacher Ed Prog; Govt; Tchng/Govt.

**DOWD, JENNIFER A,** Providence Coll, Providence, RI; JR; Resdnc Bd Mengher Hall Pres 89; Apt Complx Cncl Apt B Chrmn 90; Big Bro/Sistrs 89-; Habitat For Humanity Pastrl Cncl; Intrnshp St Joseph Hosp Providence RI; Im Fld Hockey/Flg Ftbl 89-; Hlth Policy Mgt; Hosp Admn.

**DOWD, JOHN J,** Boston Coll, Chestnut Hill, MA; FR; Yng Rpblcns; Pltcl Sci Clb; Ftbl Mgr; IM Bkstbl; Pltcl Science; Law.

**DOWD, PETER J,** City Univ Of Ny Queensbrough, New York, NY; SO; BA; Dns Lst 90; Psy.

**DOWDLE, MICHELLE R,** Western Carolina Univ, Cullowhee, NC; SR; Univ Plyrs 90-; Alpha Epsilon Rho Sec 88-90; Tutor Spec Serv Trnstn Proj 90; Univ Deans List 87-; Outsdng RTV Stdnt Yr 90; Otsdng Achvmnt Awd 89; Radio T V/Cmunctns; Pub Rltns.

**DOWDY, AMY L,** Univ Of Tn At Martin, Martin, TN; SO; BSOT; Pre Occ Thrpy Clb; Amnsty Intl; Mu Epsilon Delta; Biol Occup Thrpy.

**DOWDY, JILL D,** Univ Of Sc At Columbia, Columbia, SC; FR; BA; Natl Scty Black Engrs; Assoc Of Hnrs Stdnt; Assoc Of Afro Amer Stdnts; Carolina Prog Union; Alpha Lamba Delta; Minority Asstnt Peer; Energy Ldr; Presidents Lst; English; Education.

**DOWDY, PAULA A,** Tri County Tech Coll, Pendleton, SC; FR; BEDBA; Alpha Betta Zetta; IE; Engrng.

**DOWELL, DUANE N,** Coppin St Coll, Baltimore, MD; JR; BA; Crmnl Jstc Soc Cpn St Clg Asst Delg 87-; Peer Ambsdr Clb Grp Spkr 90-; NAACP Prsdnt 90-; Omega Psi Phi Prsdnt; Prjct 2000 Mntr Prgrm Orgnzr; US Marine Corp 84; Rsrv; Crmnl Jstc Pltcl Sci; Drctr Jvnl Srvcs.

**DOWELL, MEDINA L,** Univ Of Tn At Martin, Martin, TN; SO; BS; Phi Eta Sigma; Bus Admin; CPA.

**DOWELL, REBECCA S,** Univ Of Cincinnati, Cincinnati, OH; SR; BM; Ohio Cllgte Music Edctrs Assoc Sec 89; Lambda Sigma 88-89; Golden Key Ntl Hon; Mortar Brd; Sigma Alpha Iota 87-89; Kappa Kappa Gamma Schlrshp Chr 89; Pi Kappa Lambda Outstndng Soph Awd 89; Music Ed; Tchr HS Music.

**DOWEY, DENA M,** Mount Aloysius Jr Coll, Cresson, PA; FR; AS; Legal Assist; Law.

**DOWLESS, ANGELA M,** Christopher Newport Coll, Newport News, VA; JR; BSBA; Phi Eta Sigma 86-87; Alpah Kappa Psi Hist; Alpha Delta Pi 86; Mktng.

**DOWLESS, KATHERINE L,** Fl International Univ, Miami, FL; FR; BS; Hist; Crmnl Jstce.

**DOWLESS, KIMBERLY DAWN,** Univ Of Miami, Coral Gables, FL; JR; BA; Psi Chi V P; Psych/Spec Ed; Ed.**

**DOWLING, HEATH ADAM,** S U N Y Coll Of Tech At Alfred, Alfred, NY; SO; BA; Radio DJ 90-; Awrd For Bst Prog; Elec Eng.

**DOWLING JR, ROBERT J,** Tufts Univ, Medford, MA; FR; Chem; Med.

**DOWLING, TRACY E,** Villanova Univ, Villanova, PA; SR; BA; Ofc Rsdnc Lf Hd Rsdnt 89-; Prjct Sunshine Vlntr Orgnztn 88; Pi Sigma Alpha 89-; Delta Gamma Pnhlnc Dlgt; Hnrs Sqnc Lbrl Stds 88-; Deans List 88-; Pltcl Sci Hstry Phlsphy Mgmt; Pblc Rltns.

**DOWLUT, MOONEEB M,** Catawba Valley Comm Coll, Hickory, NC; FR; AAS; Furn; Prod.

**DOWNARD, CHRISSONDRA D,** Central Oh Tech Coll, Newark, OH; JR; ASSOC; Somerset Amer Legion Post #58 88-; Phi Theta Kappa 90-; Sectrl Sci.**

**DOWNARD, PAULINE DENISE,** Atlantic Comm Coll, Mays Landing, NJ; SO; AAS; Nrs Clb Pr 90-; Nrs Clb 89-90; Natl Stdnt Nrs Assn 90-; Dns Lst 89-; Phi Theta Kappa 90; LPN Camdn Cnty Voc Tech Sicklrvl Nj 74; Nrsng; Phd.

**DOWNARD, STEVE R,** Embry Riddle Aeronautical Univ, Daytona Beach, FL; JR; BS; Water Ski Club Sec 89-; Orientation Team 89-; Var Golf Team 88; Stdnt Ldrshp Dvlpmnt Prog; Deans List 90; Aeronautical Studies/Mgmnt; Prfsnl Pilot.

**DOWNER, JULIE L,** Gaston Coll, Dallas, NC; FR; AS; Bio; Nrsng RN.

**DOWNES, JAMES LAWRENCE,** Saint Josephs Coll, Windham, ME; SO; BA; Lit Mag Edtr 90-; SGA Voting Mbr 90-; IM Ftbl/Vlybl; Engl; Wrtr.

**DOWNEY, BRIAN C,** Boston Univ, Boston, MA; FR; BS; Nwman Hse 90-; Trustee Schlrshp 90-; IM Sccr/Vlybl/Innrtb/Wtr Polo 90-; Biomed Eng; Med.

**DOWNEY JR, JAMES A,** Liberty Univ, Lynchburg, VA; SO; BS; Ftbl 89-; Govt/Bsn Mgmt; Law.

**DOWNEY, MARK M,** Ky St Univ, Frankfort, KY; SR; BA; SNEA Sec/Treas 90-; KY Ed Asc Stdnt Pgm Ofc Exec Comm; KY Ed Asscstdnt Bd; Natl Cncl Soc Studies 90-; Lit Vol Amer 90-; Accntnt; Fncl Dir Real Est Bd; ASB Ctr Degree Studies 88; BS CA Coast Univ 89; Scndry Ed/Soc Studies; Tchng.

**DOWNEY, NINA P,** Manhattanville Coll, Purchase, NY; SR; BA; Manhattanville Dance Ensemble VP/PRFRMR 87-; Class Com 90-; Manhattanville Theatre Dept Stage Mgr/Prfrmr 87-89; Deans List 90-; O Clair Poetry Prize 90-; Capezio Dance Awd 90-; Rcgnzd Clg Pres Outstndng Cntrbtry; Engl Lit.

**DOWNEY, TOSHA D,** Clark Atlanta Univ, Atlanta, GA; FR; NAACP Sgt Arms 90-; Prtnrs Excell 90-; Hnrs Pgm 90-; Natl Hnr Soc 89-90; Inter Var Chrstn Flwshp 90-; Yng Life 88-90; All Amer Schlr 90-; Educ; Tchng.

**DOWNING, CARLOTTA M,** Meridian Comm Coll, Meridian, MS; FR; AAD; Hortcltre Cl 90-; Deans List 90-; Voices/Joy Mass Choir; Supv Flower Bulb Co 80-90; St Mark Y Methodist Ch Pastor Parris Cmte Chpsn 89-; Hortcltre Technlgy; Busn/Hortcltre Field.

**DOWNING, EUGENE R,** Portland School Of Art, Portland, ME; JR; Ultmt Frsbee Red Tide Tm 89-; Soc Nrth Amer Gldsmths.

**DOWNING, JAMES E,** Springfield Tech Comm Coll, Springfield, MA; JR; BA; Natl Skeet Shtng Assn 84-; Trnsfr Cmpct Pgm 90; Bus Mgmt.

**DOWNING, JAMES N,** Western New England Coll, Springfield, MA; SR; NSEE; Alpha Nu Omega 84-86; Sgm Beta Tau 89-; Laser Electro/Optcs Fclty Awrd 86; Otstndng Achvmnt Awrd 86; Dept Awrd WNEC 89; Optcl Dvlpmnt Tech 86-89; SPIE Intrntl Scty Optcl Eng 86-; AS Lsr Electro Optcs Tech STCC 86; Electro Optics Eng.

**DOWNS, CAMBERLEIGH ANGEL,** Middle Tn St Univ, Murfreesboro, TN; SR; BS; Peer Cnslr 87-89; Drama Club 87-89; Ltry Clb 87-89; Hon Engl Soc 87-89; Hon Hstry Soc 87-89; Hon Wrld Cvlztn Soc 87-89; Phi Ro Pi 87-89; Phi Theta Kappa Sec/Treas 87-89; Gamma Beta Phi 87-89; Acdmc Schlrshp 87-; Psychlgy; Psychlgst-Dctrt/Open Prvt Prctc.

**DOWNS, CHARLES E,** Milligan Coll, Milligan Clg, TN; JR; BA; Scl Affrs Comm Chr 88-; Sec Pardee Hl 90-; Pres; Eagle Scout 88-; Vars Sccr 88-; Comm; M Div/JD.

**DOWNS, HEATHER E,** Memphis St Univ, Memphis, TN; JR; BSED; Bptst Stu Unn Cmmnctns Chrmn 90-; Educ Spprt Prog Ttr 89-; Kappa Delta Pi; Acdmc Excl Schlrshp; Marine Corps Schlrshp; Fndtn Schlrshp; Elem Educ/US Stds; Tchng.

**DOWNS, JENNIFER D,** Cumberland Coll, Williamsburg, KY; FR; BA; FCA 90-; Tchng Asst 90; Crcltn Wrkr; Elem Ed; Tchr.

**DOWNS, JESSICA E,** Univ Of Nh Plymouth St Coll, Plymouth, NH; FR; BA; Forgn Lang Soc 90; Tutor Spanish; English.

**DOWNS, KAREN MARIE,** Comm Coll Algny Co Algny Cmps, Pittsburgh, PA; GD; MA; Insur Claims Exam; BS Slippery Rock St Colg 80; Studio Art/Art History; Tch.

**DOWNS, SCOTT R,** Bloomfield Coll, Bloomfield, NJ; SR; BA; Lcrs Clb 88-; Dns Lst 90-; Alpha Kappa Psi Mstr Rtls 90-; Zeta Phi Epsilon Sec 87-; Intrnshp TV Stn; Scr Capt 89-90; Bsn Admin.

**DOWNS, TIFFANY A,** Univ Of Southern Ms, Hattiesburg, MS; JR; BA; Bapt Stdnt Union Exctve Cncl 90; Stdnt Alumni Assoc; Lambda Delta 88; Hnrs Clg 90; Bapt Stdnt Union; Deans Lst 88-90; Pres Lst; Im Ftbl; Scl Rhbltn Serv; MA Prof Thrpst.

**DOXTATER, LILLIAN L,** Erie Comm Coll, Buffalo, NY; FR; AAS; Ofc Tech; Legal Sec.

**DOYLE, CHRISTINE R,** Longwood Coll, Farmville, VA; FR; BS; Bapt Stdnt Union 90-; Dorm Govt 90-; Psych; Elem Ed.

**DOYLE, DEBBIE SKAGGS,** Western Ky Univ, Bowling Green, KY; SO; AAS; Phi Eta Sigma 90; Deans List/Pres Schlr 89-; Chas Roy Martin Schlrshp 90-; Den Ldr 89-; Right To Life Assoc 88-; Offc Mngr; Bus; Offc Mngmnt.

**DOYLE, ELAINE E,** Northern Ky Univ, Highland Hts, KY; SO; BA; BAWAC Agncy Prctcm Exprnc 90; Mntl Hlth/Hmn Ser; Prfrmng Arts.

**DOYLE, ELIZABETH L,** Alcorn St Univ, Lorman, MS; SO; ASN; NSNA 88-; Nrsg; OB RN.

**DOYLE, GORDON E,** Northern Ky Univ, Highland Hts, KY; FR; BA; Alpha Delta Gamma Rcrdng Sec 90-; Bsbl 90-; Bsns; Cpa.

**DOYLE, JANET T,** Western New England Coll, Springfield, MA; SR; Aerobics/Wlkng/Rnng/Crmacs; MA Mutula Life Ins Co Title Plcy Chng Asst 82-; AS BA Springfield Tech Comm Coll 82; Bus Admin; Insur Indust/Bkng Admin.**

**DOYLE, JENNIFER K,** Bellarmine Coll, Louisville, KY; JR; BA; Theatre Pres 89-90; Psych Clb 89-; Assoc Equality 90-; Psi Chi; Delta Sigma Pi; Campus Msntry Music Mnstr/Chmn 89-; Parish Yng Adult Grp 90-; Pres Schlrs 88-; Foreign Lang Schlrshp; St Robert Bellarmine Schlrshp 88-; Psychlgy; Cnslr/Therapist.

**DOYLE, KATHLEEN M,** Bunker Hill Comm Coll, Boston, MA; SO; BED; Cert Early Chlhd 89-90; Educ; Tchr.

**DOYLE, KIMBERLY ANN,** S U N Y Coll At Fredonia, Fredonia, NY; JR; BA; Acctg Soc 89-; VITA 90-; SBI; Acctg.**

**DOYLE, MARILYN M,** Atlantic Comm Coll, Mays Landing, NJ; FR; EOF Hnr Roll 90; Emplyed By Arlnes 83-86; Assist Msles Mmps Rblla Prog; Assist To ACC Schl Nrse Hlth Offce 90; Pa Intrlne Clb PIC Clb Arlne Clb 84-86; Assoc In Applied Sci/Bsn; RN.

**DOYLE, MICHAEL G,** Lexington Comm Coll, Lexington, KY; FR; BA; Deans List; Cmmctns; Radio/Advtsg.

**DOYLE, RODNEY T,** City Univ Of Ny Baruch Coll, New York, NY; SR; BA; Sigma Alpha Delta; Pentcstl Crusaders Of The WI Cptn 87-; Christ Ambsdrs Dept Of The Calvary Pentcstl Chrch Grp Ldr 89-; Purchsng Dept; BA Assov Of Bus Exec London England 89; Acctng; Law.

**DOYLE, SHAWN C,** Schenectady County Comm Coll, Schenectady, NY; JR; BA; Clnry Arts; Chf.

**DOYLE, SHAWN J,** Morehouse Coll, Atlanta, GA; FR; BS; Natl Scty Black Engnrs; Elec Engnrng.

**DOYLE, STEPHANIE A,** Catholic Univ Of America, Washington, DC; SO; BA; Vlybl Clb 89-; Hon Soc; Sch Frnds TA 89-; Elem Edn; Teach.

**DOYLE, THOMAS J,** Saint Josephs Univ, Philadelphia, PA; GD; Natl Hnrs Scty 79-80; Phi Theta Kappa 79-80; Fraternal Order Police 70-; Police Chiefs Assoc Southeastern PA 85-; DE Vly Chiefs Police 88-; Grad Schl Crim Justice Awd; Phila Commty Clg Outstndng Alumni 89; Criminal Justice; Law Enforement.

**DOYLE-ZABELSKI, KATHLEEN M,** Georgian Court Coll, Lakewood, NJ; SR; BA; Deans Lst 88-90; Cmtee Wmn Dist 8 Dover Twnsp; Paralegal; Humanities; Tch.

**DOYNOW, AARON A,** Ny Univ, New York, NY; JR; BA; Dns Lst 90; AA 90; Jrnlsm; Law.

**DOYON, ROBERT L,** Ringling School Of Art, Sarasota, FL; SO; BFA; Pres Lst 89-; AICA Intrnshp; Set Cnstrctn Epcot Cntr/MGM Stdios 81-89; Fine Arts/Sclptr; Set Dsgnr.

**DOZER, LORI L,** Otterbein Coll, Westerville, OH; FR; BA; Epsilon Kappa Tau 90-; Trck Tm 90-; Sprts Med.

**DOZIER, CORBIE E,** Univ Of Sc At Columbia, Columbia, SC; FR; Rsdnc Hl Assoc Sntr 90-; Stdnt Govt Rtntn Comm; Mdl Untd Ntns Undr Sec Gen; Natl Rsdnc Hl Hnrry; Advertising; Grphc Advrtsr.

**DOZIER, DEROLYN D,** Al A & M Univ, Normal, AL; SR; BS; Natl Soc Blck Engrs; Assn Cmptng Mchnry; Co-Op Crne Army Amntn Actvty; Comp Sci; Prgrmr/Anlyst.

**DOZIER, MEIRA HAVA,** Univ Of Sc At Columbia, Columbia, SC; SO; BS; Psychology Clb Pres 90-; Coastal Earth Envrnmntlst Scty; Eastern Surfing Assoc; Psi Chi; Phi Eta Sigma; Alpha Mu Gamma; Psychology; Research.

**DOZIER, VERA M,** Commonwealth Coll, Virginia Beach, VA; SO; Prsdnts Lst; Exctv Ofc Admnstrtn.

**DRAFT, KIMBERLY D,** Nc Agri & Tech St Univ, Greensboro, NC; SR; BS; PTA; Deans Lst 89-90; Tchr Asst Yr 89; Elem Edctn; Tchng.

**DRAFT, SANDRA E,** Piedmont Tech Coll, Greenwood, SC; SR; DIPL; Resp Thrpy.

**DRAFTS, SCOTT P,** Univ Of Sc At Columbia, Columbia, SC; JR; BA; Bus Mgmnt Info Sys.

**DRAGO, MICHAEL CHRISTOPHER,** S U N Y At Binghamton, Binghamton, NY; FR; BA; Hinman Prdctn Co 90; Woodswrld Newspapr 90; Pol Sci.

**DRAGOMIRE, HEATHER J,** Ohio Valley Coll, Parkersburg, WV; FR; BA; Sigma Social Clb 90-; Exclnc Rsrch Awd 90-; Good Sprtsmnshp Awd 90-; Res Asst Schlrshp; Ele Educ.

**DRAGONE, MONICA L,** Comm Coll Algny Co Algny Cmps, Pittsburgh, PA; JR; BA; Deans Lst 90-; Spec Ed.

**DRAHEIM, TIMOTHY A,** Livingston Univ, Livingston, AL; SO; BA; IFC; SADD; Tau Kappa Epsilon V P 89-; Tau Kappa Epsilon Bro/Qrtr; Deans List 90-; IM; Cleaner L U Hon Awd 89-; Biol, Biolgst.

**DRAIN, JUDY A,** Anne Arundel Comm Coll, Arnold, MD; FR; BSW; Chld Care Bd 87-; Cnsl Yth Mnstrs Dir; Off Mgr 81-87; Soc Wrk; Cnslng.

**DRAINE, CHANEL D,** Va St Univ, Petersburg, VA; JR; BA; Accntng Clb Ms Accntng; NABA; Deans Lst; Alpha Kappa Alpha; Chldrn Hm Vol; Bapt Chrch; Cntrl Intllgnce Agncy; Accntng; CPA.

**DRAKE, AUDREY DIANE,** Univ Of Southern Ms, Hattiesburg, MS; SR; BS; Hotel Restaurant Tourism Mngmnt Clb 90-; Domestics Sftbl Tm; Hotel Restaurant Tourism; Trvl Admin.

**DRAKE, DAVID A,** Wv Univ At Parkersburg, Parkersburg, WV; SO; BS; Elect Sci; Elect Eng.

**DRAKE, JASON CHAD,** Roanoke Chowan Comm Coll, Ahoskie, NC; FR; !; ACES Sec 90-; Flwshp Chrstn Ath 90-; Math; Hghst Acad Av 90-; !; Sci; Coach.

**DRAKE, KATHLEEN C,** Univ Of Al At Birmingham, Birmingham, AL; SR; BS; Pi Beta Phi; Alumni Clb; 1ST Nazarene Daycare/Kndrgrtn Tchr/Bkkppr 90-; BA Auburn Univ 88; Socl Wrk.

**DRAKE, MID J,** Univ Of Al At Birmingham, Birmingham, AL; SO; NAACP; Birmingham Bd Rltrs; US Army 85-89; Elem Ed.

**DRAKE, PATRICE L,** Al A & M Univ, Normal, AL; SO; BA; Marching Bnd 89-; Business; Administrtor.

**DRAKE, PENNY L,** Western Ky Univ, Bowling Green, KY; SR; BA; Psi Chi 90-; Phi Kappa Phi 90-; Gldn Key 90-; Sclgy.

**DRAKE, RHONDA A,** Univ Of Montevallo, Montevallo, AL; SO; BS; Rsdnce Hll Assn Sec 90-; Erly Chldhd Elem Educ; Tchng.

**DRAKE, RUTH K,** Univ Of Southern Ms, Hattiesburg, MS; SR; BSW; Soc Wrk Clb 90-; Soc Wrk.

**DRAKE, SONJA M,** S U N Y Coll Of Tech At Alfred, Alfred, NY; SO; BA; Commtr Cncl 89-; Sigma Tau Epsilon 90-; Phi Theta Kappa 90-; Alfred Hons Clb 89-; Lit Vol Of Amer 90-; Pres Schlrshp 89-; Soc Sci; Law.

**DRAKE, SPENCER B,** Middle Tn St Univ, Murfreesboro, TN; GD; MS; Bio Clb 86-88; Sigma Alpha Epsilon 87-90; Deans Lst 90; Hon Rl 90-; Cumberland Bulldogs Bsbl Tm 83-84; Wellness/Fitness; Prof.

**DRAKE, TRACI D,** Fayetteville St Univ, Fayetteville, NC; SO; BS; Hstry; Tchng Or Rsrch.

**DRAKEFORD, CHRISTINN T,** Dutchess Comm Coll, Poughkeepsie, NY; SO; BA; Gl Sftwre Dev Mgr; Exec Sec Admin Asst Krissler Bus Institute 77; Comp Info Systms; Bus Comp Sftwre.

**DRAKEFORD, KESHA T,** Va St Univ, Petersburg, VA; SO; BA; Jdcl Brd Affrs 90-; RA 90-; Alpha Mu Gamma VP; Pol Sci; Law.

**DRAPELA, ANNA M,** Notre Dame Coll, Cleveland, OH; JR; BA; Clss Pres 90-; RSA 90-; Sigma Alpha Mu Lttl Sis 90-; Elem Educ; Tchr.

**DRAPER, DEANNA A,** Belmont Coll, Nashville, TN; FR; BBA; Belmnt Undergrad Adm 90-; Hnrs Pgm Belmnt Clg; Acctg.

**DRAPER-PELAEZ, CAREN L,** Atlantic Comm Coll, Mays Landing, NJ; FR; BA; Tutrd Macro Econ 90; Schlrshp Atlantic Elec 90; Chem; Pharm.

**DRAUGHN, KELLY L,** Univ Of Nc At Chapel Hill, Chapel Hill, NC; FR; BA; Pre Pharm Clb 90-; Medcn; Pharm.

**DRAUGHN-BUTTRAM, GAIL DENISE,** Roane St Comm Coll, Harriman, TN; FR; BS; Pre-Med; Rdlgy.

**DRAWDY, KATHY J,** Univ Of Sc At Columbia, Columbia, SC; JR; BA; AA 90; Ed; Tchr.

**DRAY, JENNIFER S,** Fl International Univ, Miami, FL; JR; BA; Hillel 86-89; Hebrew U Of Jerusalem In Israel 86-87; AA Brwrd Cmmnty Clg 90; Hosp Mngmnt; Hotel/Rstrnt Mngmnt.

**DRAYTON, ANGENIQUE R,** Fl A & M Univ, Tallahassee, FL; FR; MBA; Hnr Rl 90-; Bus Admin; Mrktg.

**DRAYTON, LYNDA G,** Univ Of Sc At Columbia, Columbia, SC; SR; BS; Amer Mktg Assn VP Cmnctns 90-; Gamecocks Advctng Mtr Mgmt Alchl VP 89-90; Ldrshp Mntr Pgm 90; Phi Beta Kappa; Gldn Key 89-; Gamma Beta Phi 89-; Kappa Delta Sec 90; Mktg; Mktg/Sls/Mgmt.

**DRAYTON, TOYE S,** Livingstone Coll, Salisbury, NC; SO; BA; Bsktbl,Vlybl,Trck,Fld Capt 90-; Bus; Acctg.

**DRAYTON-WILLIAMS, LORRAINE,** City Univ Of Ny City Coll, New York, NY; SR; BA; Para Prof Asst Pblc Schl Sys; AA Bronx Comm Coll 73; Elem Ed; Tchr.

**DRAZIN, HEATHER I,** Univ Of Rochester, Rochester, NY; SO; BA; Hillel Co-V P 89-90; IM Inrtb Wtr Polo; IM Flr Hcky; Adpt Grndprnt; Big Bro/Big Sis; Psych/Rlgn; Clncl Psych.

**DREAPER, LAURA C,** Univ Of South Al, Mobile, AL; SO; BS; Alpha Chi; Scndry Educ/Soc Sci; Tchng.

**DREHER, DAWNITA C,** Lincoln Univ, Lincoln Univ, PA; SR; BA; NAACP 89-; Bus Clb 88-; Big Bro/Str Prog 90-; Deans List 88-; Alpha Chi; Delta Sigma Theta 89-; Pblc Plcy/Dplmcy Acad Pgm 89; Sr Schlstc Awd Ecnmcs 90-; Renwick Awd 90-; Ecnmcs/Finance; Analyst.

**DREHER, ELIZABETH C,** Fl St Univ, Tallahassee, FL; JR; BA; Rsdnt Asst Cmps Hsng 90-; Cmmnctns Hstry ; Interprsnl Cmmnctns.

**DREHER, JOSEPH B,** Elmira Coll, Elmira, NY; JR; BA; ELACI Coord Stdnt Life 89-; Fellowship Intl Relations Tchng Fellow; IM Soccer Sftbl 90; Political Sci Intl Relations.

**DREIFUSS, MICHAEL L,** City Univ Of Ny Baruch Coll, New York, NY; SR; BBA; Inf Syst Consltnt; AS Queensborgh Comm Clg 78; Finc; Incl Mgmt/Corp.

**DREITZER, MICHAEL F,** Cornell Univ Statutory College, Ithaca, NY; SR; JD; Radio Sprtscstr Mrng Sports 88-; Trdtn Flwshp Chair 87-; Ambssdr 87-; Am Assn Ag Lwyrs; Alpha Epsilon Pi Rush Chair 88-90; IM Soccer/Sftbl 87-; Lgsltv Intrn Ofc US Sntr Tom Harkin 90; Ecnmc Rsrch Serv USDA Ag Ecnmst; Ag Lwyr.

**DREIZE, LIVIA REBBEKA,** Catholic Univ Of Pr, Ponce, PR; GD; JD; Law Review Ed Biblgrphy 90-; Htl Sls/Mktg Assoc 87-88; Amer Bar Assoc Stdnt Div 89-; Phi Alpha Delta 90-; Annual Acad Competition; High Cls Grade Evidence/Crmnl Law 90-; BS FL Intl Univ 88; Law.

**DREMBUS, DEBORAH C,** James Madison University, Harrisonburg, VA; JR; BS; CEC 88-; Ctr Fr Srvc Lrng 90-YARC 88-; Golden Key 90-; Kappa Delta Pi 90-; Spcl Educ; Tch.

**DRENGA, CRAIG,** Springfield Tech Comm Coll, Springfield, MA; SR; BA; New England Trl Riders Assc Chrmn 89-; Intrntnl FAHQ Riding Team VP 87-; AS 90; Elctrncs; Bsn Ownrshp.

**DRENNAN, MARCIA E,** Erie Comm Coll, Buffalo, NY; FR; BED; Chld Care Clb; First Rspndr Heart Assn; Right To Life; Bravnic Ldr; HOPE Org; Leukemia Socty; Early Chldhd Educ; Wrtng/Chldrn.

**DRENTEN, ELAINE M,** Bowling Green St Univ At Huron, Huron, OH; FR; BA; Stdnt Actvts Cnsl Rep 90-; Beta Sigma Phi 86-; Elem Ed.

**DRESBACH, DANA R,** Indiana Univ Of Pa, Indiana, PA; JR; BS; TV Station Mktg Dir 90-; Alpha Epsilon Rho 89-; Intrnshp Brdcstng Fld; Cmnctns Media; Pblc Rltns/Prmtns Brdcstng.

**DRESCH, RUSSELL A,** Old Dominion Univ, Norfolk, VA; SR; BSEE; IEEE 90-; Eta Kappa Nu Pres 89-; Elect Eng; Dsgn Eng.

**DRESCHER, MELISSA A,** Columbia Greene Comm Coll, Hudson, NY; SO; BBA; Phi Theta Kappa VP 89-; AAS; Mktg/Advrtsng.

**DRESS, CHRISTOPHER M,** Christian Brothers Univ, Memphis, TN; FR; MD; Chorale 90-; CORE 90-; Beta Beta Beta Bio Hon Soc 90-; Tau Kappa Epsilon Histrn 90-; Bio; Pediatrician.

**DRESS, LISA L,** East Stroudsburg Univ, E Stroudsburg, PA; SR; BS; Psychlgy Assc 90-; Mntl Hlth Wrkr Intern; Psychlgy; Wllnss Mngmnt.

**DREW, DANNY CARL,** Tn St Univ, Nashville, TN; GD; PHD; Ecnmcs Clb Pres 90; Std Free Entrprs Grp Chr 90; Nwspr 87-89; NAACP ; Advsr Hmcd Rdctn Prgm; Nw Dem Movemnt; Naval Resrv Drl Tm; Yeoman; Edtrl Awd; Post Bcclrt Fllwshp Wayne St Unv; BEE Cert Cllg Lake Cnty Chicago 88; Gert Gnnr 88; Econmcs; Tchr/Resrch/Advs.

**DREW, ELAINE M,** Kent St Univ Kent Cmps, Kent, OH; FR; BS; Bio Clb 90-; Alpha Lambda Delta 90-; Bio/Pre Med.

**DREW, KAREN E,** Univ Of Ga, Athens, GA; JR; PHD; ASP Pgm/Publcty Comm 90-; Lambda Kappa Sigma Scl Chr 90-; IM Bsktbl/Sftbl 90-; Pharm.

**DREW, TRENTON L,** Thomas Nelson Comm Coll, Hampton, VA; SO; AS; Honda Excllnc Schlrshp Awd 90-; T Nelson Comm Coll Awd; BA Bus-Fin.

**DREWERY, KIMBERLY D,** Ms St Univ, Miss State, MS; SO; Dairy Sci Cl 90-; Dairy Prod Judging Tm 90-; Dairy Sci; Publ Hlth Inspctn.

**DREWES, ANGELA D,** Fl St Univ, Tallahassee, FL; SR; BS; Prnts Anyms Vol; Hnrs Thesis 90-; Psi Chi 90-; Phi Theta Kappa 87-; AA St Johns River Comm Clg 89; Psychlgy; Ph D Psychlgy.

**DREWES, KAREN E,** Christian Brothers Univ, Memphis, TN; SR; Ntl Assoc Of Accntnts 89; Alpha Chi 90; Delta Sigma Pi VP 88; BA; INTRNSHP Wth Arthur Andersen/Co 89; Delta Sigma Pi S Rgn Cllgn Of Yr; Accntng; CPA.

**DREWRY, KATHY E,** Univ Of Tn At Martin, Martin, TN; FR; BS; Alpha Omicron Pi Pldg Clss Prsdnt 90; Jr Vrsty Chrldr 90-; Intl Bus.

**DREXLER, CHERYL A,** Wilmington Coll, Wilmington, OH; SO; BA; Stdnt Fndtn; Quest Envrnmntl Awrenss Clb; Sigma Delta Pi; Alpha Phi Kappa; Spnsh.

**DREYHAUPT, SCOTT Y,** Univ Of Sc At Columbia, Columbia, SC; FR; BA; Fencing Club 90-; Lambda Chi Alpha Educ Chrman 90-; Biology; Medicine.

**DREZEK, CRAIG D,** Teikyo Post Univ, Waterbury, CT; SO; BA; Stdnt Gov Assn Treas 90-; Soph Cls Pres 90-; Budget Comm Chrmn 90-; Alpha Chi; Stdnt Orientation Ldr Coun 89-; PSC 90-; Vrsty Bsktbl 2 Yr Starter 89-; Acctg; CPA.

**DRIGGERS, WESLEY J,** Valdosta St Coll, Valdosta, GA; SR; PH D; Brain Bowl Team Sci Div Capt 87-89; Corinth Bapt Chrch 85-; Phi Theta Kappa Treas 88-89; Alpha Epsilon Delta 90-; Phi Kappa Phi; Alpha Chi; Full Schlrshp 87-; Hstry Awds; Math Awds; Socl Sci Awd; Vlybl Bm 89; Biology; Mdcl Csrch.

**DRILLING, GARY,** Univ Of Fl, Gainesville, FL; SR; BS; Delta Omicron 87-; Golden Key; Deans Schlr; Outstndng 2 Yr Grad; Amer Phys Ther Assn 89-; AA Palm Bch Comm Coll 88; Phys Ther.

**DRIPPS, MELISSA E,** Clayton St Coll, Morrow, GA; JR; BBA; AA 91; Admin Bsn Emphasis Mrktng; Mngmnt.

**DRISCOLL, ANNMARIE P,** Merrimack Coll, North Andover, MA; JR; BA; Stdnt Gov SG 88-89; Dncng 90-; Bus; MBA.

**DRISCOLL JR, KENNETH B,** Western New England Coll, Springfield, MA; JR; BA; Wght Lftng Clb Treas 90-; WNEC Acctg Assn; Alpha Nu Omega 89-90; Tnns/Shck Spr Hoops; AS STCC 90; Acctg.

**DRISCOLL, KEVIN M,** S U N Y At Buffalo, Buffalo, NY; JR; BA; Acctng Assoc 90-F Schmtrs Ski Club 88-; Golden Key; Beta Alpha Psi Comm Secy; IM Bskbl Vlybl; Acctng; Public Acctng.

**DRISCOLL, LESLIE,** Univ Of Fl, Gainesville, FL; SR; BME; Fighting Gater Mrchng Bnd 88-; Cllgt Music Edctrs Ntl Cnfrnc 88-; Tau Beta Sigma VP 88-; Univ Fl Summer Bnd Cmp Stf 90; J J Finnley/P K Yonge HS Stdt Intrnshp 90; AA 91; Music Educator.

**DRISCOLL, LINDA J,** Univ Of Nc At Charlotte, Charlotte, NC; SR; BA; Phi Kappa Phi; Golden Key; Deans List; Chancellors List 90; Psychlgy/Soclgy.

**DRISCOLL, MARY E,** Assumption Coll, Worcester, MA; SR; Assmptn Clg Chorale 87-; Chapel Choir VP 88-; Ecumenical Wrshp Cmmt 89-; Delta Epsilon Sigma 90-; UN Way AM Intrn 88-90; Lthrn Adlt Day Hlth Intrn 90-; Salutatrn Class 91 Assmptn Clg Grad Summa Cum Laude 91.**

**DRISCOLL, PATRICIA,** Long Island Coll Hosp Of Nrsng, Brooklyn, NY; FR; AAS; Nrsng Rn.

**DRISCOLL, SANDRA S,** Salisbury St Univ, Salisbury, MD; SR; BA; Scl Wrk.

**DRISKILL, TONYA ANNETTE,** Franklin Coll, Paducah, KY; FR; CERT; Nrsng/Med Tech.

**DRISLANE, DAVID C,** Newbury Coll, Brookline, MA; FR; ASSO; Trvl/Tourism; Airline Indus.

**DRIVER, BRIDGETTE N,** Memphis St Univ, Memphis, TN; FR; BA; BSA 90-; SGA Leg Asst 90-; Phi Eta Sigma; Alpha Lambda Delta; BSU; Alpah Kappa Alpha; Gamma Beta Phi 91; Memphs St Univ Ldrshp Schlrshp 90-91; Pol Sci; Corp Law.

**DRIVER, JASON B,** Vanderbilt Univ, Nashville, TN; FR; BE; Biomed Engr Soc 90-; Biomed Engr Soc Fres Repr 90-; Phi Eta Sigma; Alpha Lambda Delta; Gamma Beta Phi; Biomed Engr; Medicine.

**DRIVER, JOSEPH H,** Samford Univ, Birmingham, AL; GD; JD; Law Rvw; Phi Alpha Delta 90-; Pres Schlrshp 90-; Deans Lst 90; Am Jur Awd 90; BS Auburn Univ 89; Law; Attrny.

**DRIVER, LORI A,** Univ Of Fl, Gainesville, FL; SR; BS; SOTA VP 90-; Phi Kappa Phi 89-; Morton Plnt Hosp Schlrshp 86-; AA 89; Ocptnl Thrpy.

**DRIVER, MARTHA E,** Catawba Valley Comm Coll, Hickory, NC; SO; Arch Drftsprsn.

**DRIVER, ROBERT E,** Duquesne Univ, Pittsburgh, PA; JR; Stdnt Govt Assn 90-; New Entrprnrs Of Amer Fndr Chrmn; Phi Chi Theta VP 90-; Phi Chi Theta Pres; Fnnce; Prsnl Fnncl Plnng.

**DRIVER, TANYA L,** Belmont Coll, Nashville, TN; FR.

**DROEGE, KARLA J,** Lenoir Rhyne Coll, Hickory, NC; SR; Theta Xi Ltl Str 88-; Plymkrs Pres 87-; Mu Sigma Epsilon 90-; Alpha Psi Omega Pres 88-; Fresh Drama Awd 88; Pearl Setzer Deal Plymkr Awd 90; Deans Lst 87-; BA; Thtr Arts; Prof Thtr.

**DROESE, MICHAEL D,** Univ Of Miami, Coral Gables, FL; SO; SOJ; Alpha Tau Omega Chptr Mgr 86-88; Deans List 88-; Crmnlgy; Law.

**DRON, CAROLYN SUE,** Savannah Coll Of Art & Design, Savannah, GA; GD; MFA; ISID 90-; BSPA Unv AZ 59; Intr Dsgn; Ktchn Dsgnr.

**DROSCHAK, KRIS A,** Univ Of Pittsburgh, Pittsburgh, PA; FR; BSN; NSNA 90-; Nrsng.

**DROSKY, TODD C,** Fl St Univ, Tallahassee, FL; SO; BS; Delg Repbl Conv 90; Pol Sci; Law.

**DROST, KIRK F,** Univ Of Fl, Gainesville, FL; SR; BSCE; Amer Scty Of Cvl Eng 89; Scty Of Auto Engnrs 88-90; Tau Beta Pi 90; Pi Eta Sigma 88; Fl Eng Scty JETS Chrmn 88; Ntl Scty Of Prof Engnrs 90; Fl Engnrng Scty Pres Awd; Fl Acad Schlrshp; Henry Bauch Schlrshp; Eng Deans Lst; Cvl Eng.

**DROST, NANCY J,** Mount Aloysius Jr Coll, Cresson, PA; FR; Phi Theta Kapp; Zeta Delta.

**DROTT, STACEY L,** Univ Of Southern Ms, Hattiesburg, MS; FR; BS; Hon Stdnt Assn 90; Alpha Lambda Delta 90-; Phi Eta Sigma 90-; Alpha Epsilon Delta 90; Delta Gamma Asst Pldg Eductr 91; Gamma Beta Phi; Hon Clg 90-; Psychology/Pre Med; Med.

**DROUT, MICHAEL D C,** Carnegie Mellon Univ, Pittsburgh, PA; GD; Newspr; Ice Hockey Club; Phi Kappa Theta Stwrd/Hse Mgr 86-90; Andrew Carnegie Merit Schlrshp 86; Stanford Univ Fllwshp; MA Stanford Univ.

**DROZDICK, JOHN,** Franklin And Marshall Coll, Lancaster, PA; JR; BA; Amer Chem Soc Pres 88-; Sym Wnd Ens 88-; Jazz Ens 88-; Mu Upsln Sigma Chrmn 89-; ACS Anlytcl Chem Awd; Isaac E Roberts Prize; Dns Lst; Hnrs Lst 88-; Chem/Pre-Med; Med.

**DRPIC, INGRID G,** Fl Atlantic Univ, Boca Raton, FL; JR; BA; Ltl Sistr Sigma Chi Frat 89; Intrnshp WFLX TV 29 W Palm Bch FL; AA Palm Beach Cmnty Clg 90; Cmnctns; TV Brdcstg.

**DRUELL, STACI L,** Winthrop Coll, Rock Hill, SC; FR; BA; Chrl 90-; Jazz Voices 90-; RUF BSU 90-; Msc Vcl Prfrmnc; Tchng.

**DRUM, DEBORAH L,** Univ Of Miami, Coral Gables, FL; GD; BA; Intrnshp Dept Envrnmntl Resrc Mgmt; Beta Beta Beta; Mrn Affrs/Anthrplgy; Envrnmntl Rsrc Mgmt.

**DRUMGOOLE, SEAN L,** Morehouse Coll, Atlanta, GA; SO; BA; Morehouse Bus Assn Exec VP 89-; IL Assn VP/ INSTITUTIONS 89-90; Perspective Stdnt Seminar VP Acad 90-; Deans Lst 90-; Pres Schlr 90-; BA Intern Northern Trust Bank 90-; Bnkg/Finance; Corp Lawyer.

**DRUMHELLER, SHARON L,** Fl St Univ, Tallahassee, FL; SR; Stdnt Hlth Advcy/Resp Tm Pres 88-90; Gld Ky Ldrshp Hon Comm Serv Chrmn 89-; Semnle Ambsdrs 89-; Phi Eta Sigma 88-; Gldn Ky 89-; Mortr Brd Elec Ofcr 90-; Beta Kappa Alpha; Chi Omega Nwsltr Edtr 88-; Hmcmng Comm 89; Pnhllnc Nwsltr Edtr 90; Comm/Publ Rels; Publ Rels/Mrktng Hlth Cr Ind.

**DRUMMOND, ANDREA DEE,** Samford Univ, Birmingham, AL; SR; Natl Trial Tm 90-; Amer Jrnl Trial Adv 89-; Author The Villareal Decision; Amer Juris Prud Book Awrd 89; Amer Juris Prud Book Awrd Decedenta 90; Cumberland Trial Adv Brd 89-90; Pi Beta Phi; Judge C Najjar Cir Ct 89; Law.

**DRUMMOND, APRIL M,** Va St Univ, Petersburg, VA; SR; BS; Big Bro/Sis Org 89-; Bus Admin Clb T 90-F Jdcl Affrs Comm 89-; Alpha Kappa Alpha 90-; Acad Achvmnt Awd; Bus Admin-Fnc; Fncl Anlyst.

**DRUMMOND, DONNA L,** Va Commonwealth Univ, Richmond, VA; SO; BS; Dns Lst Schlr 90-; IM Sftbl; Admin Jstc; Fed Govt.

**DRUMMOND, MELISSA J,** Univ Of Southern Ms, Hattiesburg, MS; SO; BS; Acad Schlrshp 90-; Scnc Educ; HS Scnc Teacher.

**DRUMMOND, STACIE D,** Radford Univ, Radford, VA; SO; BS; Bus Mgmt/Psychlgy.

**DRURY, JENNIFER G,** Ms St Univ, Miss State, MS; SR; MA; Sigma Tau Delta 89-; NEA 88-; Tutor 89; BS; Sec Endl Educ; Tchr.

**DRURY, JOHN W,** Middle Tn St Univ, Murfreesboro, TN; FR; BS; Chemsty Club; Gamma Beta Phi 90-; Chemistry; Med.

**DRURY JR, MICHAEL E,** Rutgers St Un At New Brunswick, New Brunswick, NJ; FR; IM Sftbl 90; Bwlng 90; Bus/Mktg; Advtsng.

**DRURY, NANCY L,** Univ Of Southern Ms, Hattiesburg, MS; JR; BSN; Kappa Delta 88-; Nrsg; RN.

**DRUST, JOHN M,** Seton Hall Univ, South Orange, NJ; SR; BS; Beta Gamma Sigma 90-; Lctr St Cecelias 87-; Echrstc Mnstr St Cecelias 89-; Deans Lst 87-; Acad Schlrshp 87-; Klein/Fein Schlrshp; Acctg; Prv/Pblc Acctnt.

**DRYDEN, CATHERINE E,** Anderson Coll, Anderson, SC; FR; BA; Phi Theta Kappa; Phtjrnlsm; Phtgrphy.

**DRYER, AARON A,** Oh St Univ At Newark, Newark, OH; SO; BA; Multi-Cltrl Stdnt Org; Alpha Lambda Delta; Phi Eta Sigma; Fresh Fndtn; Fin; Law.

**DRYER, AMY L,** Smith Coll, Northampton, MA; JR; BA; Sc Chr 89-90; Hmlss Vol 89-90; Doshisa Univ Envrnmntl Clb; Dean Lst 88-; Frst Grp Schlr 88-90; Assc Kyoto Prog 90-; Crew 88-89; E Asian Stu Japns; Prfssr.

**DRYMON, LISA A,** Georgian Court Coll, Lakewood, NJ; SO; Nwspr Wrtr; Wmns Clb; Ed; Tch.

**DRZYMALA, JEFFREY A,** Widener Univ, Chester, PA; JR; BA; Phi Eta Sigma 89-; Alpha Sigma Phi 90-; Intrnshp Ernst Young; Acctg; CPA.

**DU BOIS, DEANA J,** Central Fl Comm Coll, Ocala, FL; Passo Cnty Abate 90-; Patriot Missile 87-; Office Sys; Bus Admin.

**DU BOIS, FRANCES M,** Cumberland County Coll, Vineland, NJ; SO; AAS; Intern Cmbrlnd Rhbltn 899-90; Commnty Srvc Scl Wrk; Scl Wrk.

**DU BOIS, MONIQUE J,** Johnson C Smith Univ, Charlotte, NC; SO; BA; R W Johnson Spiritual Choir 89-; NAACP 89-90; Psych Clb 90-; Psych; Chld Psych.

**DU BOIS, ROBERT E,** Central Fl Comm Coll, Ocala, FL; SO; AA; Boy Scouts Amer Eagle Scout; Math/Sci Hon Clb 89-; Spkr Serv; U S Navy Good Cnduct Awd; Engr; BSEE BA Hstry Sec Hstry Tchr.

**DU BOSE, ANJA H,** Univ Of Southern Ms, Hattiesburg, MS; JR; BS; Gold Key 90-; UPE; DOW Chem Outstndg Jr Awd Nominee; Cmptr Sci/Stats; Cmptr Sci.

**DU BOSE, JULIE Y,** Winthrop Coll, Rock Hill, SC; SR; BS; Spec Edn; Teach.

**DU BOSE, MARY ANNE,** Univ Of Sc At Columbia, Columbia, SC; JR; Spcl Event Cmte Chmn 88; Fllwshp/Chrstn Busn Maj V P 88; Kappa Delta Epsilon 90; Early Chldhd Ed; Tch.**

**DU BRY, JOHN G,** Catawba Valley Comm Coll, Hickory, NC; FR; AS; AA Hawkeye Inst Tech 73; Elctrncs; Machinist Supv.

**DU CHANOIS, GREGORY M,** Univ Of North Fl, Jacksonville, FL; JR; BT; Gldn Key; Dns Lst FCCJ; Grad W/High Hnrs AA Degree FCCJ; Dns Lst; AA Fla Comm Coll Jcksnvl 88; Elec Engr Tech.

**DU CHARME, KENNETH R,** Bunker Hill Comm Coll, Boston, MA; FR; BS; Natl Grd 89-; US Army Mltry Intelligence Berlin 86-89; Physics; Eng.

**DU FRESNE, MARY KAY,** Univ Of North Fl, Jacksonville, FL; SR; BA; Kappa Delta Pi; Gldn Ky; Educ; Elem Educ.

**DU MOND, JON MICHAEL,** Fl St Univ, Tallahassee, FL; JR; BS; Stdnt Dorm Govt Pres 88-89; Yng Demo 88-90; Gldn Ky 89-; Phi Eta Sigma 89-; Zeta Beta Tau Pres 89-; John M Olin Intrnshp; Econs; Bnkng/Fin.

**DU PLAIN, JENNIFER R,** Kent St Univ Stark Cmps, North Canton, OH; FR; BA; Bus/Cmptrs.

**DU PLESSIS DE RICHELIEU, SARAH,** Radford Univ, Radford, VA; JR; BA; Intl Forgn Lang Hnr Stdnt; Cert Univ Angers France 90; French; Tchng.

**DU PREE, DE LON A,** Johnson C Smith Univ, Charlotte, NC; FR; Johnson C Smith Intl Mrchg Bnd 90-; Concert Bnd 90-; Hnrs Clg 90-; Mens Homeless Shelter Vol; Appl Math; Math.

**DU PREE JR, LOUIS S,** Savannah Coll Of Art & Design, Savannah, GA; JR; BFA; Thtr Co 90-; Berkeley Artst Bld 88-90; Woodmen Wrld 85-; Video; TV.

**DU PRIEST, SONJA L,** Central Al Comm Coll, Alexander City, AL; SO; BA; Phi Theta Kappa; Bsn; Bsn Mgmt.

**DU QUETTE, MICHAEL J,** Cumberland County Coll, Vineland, NJ; SO; BA; Mktng; Sales/Mktng New Products.

**DU VALL, ERIC B,** Western Piedmont Comm Coll, Morganton, NC; FR; AS; Computer Prog; Analyst/Programmer.

**DU VALL, MARILIN S,** Chatfield Coll, Saint Martin, OH; SO; BA; Emrgncy Med Dsptch; Ntry Pblc Rcrds 86-; Art Engl; Cmmrcl Art Advrtsng.**

**DU, DIEM CHAU D,** Anne Arundel Comm Coll, Arnold, MD; JR; Intrntnl Stdnt Assn Mmbr 89-90; Tau Alpha Pi Mmbr 89; Amrcn Soc Cvl Engnrng Mmbr; Deans Lst 90; Hnr Lst 88; Cvl Engnrng.

**DUARTE, ESTELA M,** Univ Of Miami, Coral Gables, FL; SR; MA; Orntn Asstnt Incmng Trsnfr Stdnt OA 90; Kappa Sgm Swthrt 87-; BA; MSTR Tutor Pgm Tutor Psychlgy 88; Rsrch Asstnt Grad Stdnt Psychlgy 90-; Psychlgy; Schl Psychlgst.

**DUBAY, DARLENE A,** Univ Of Pittsburgh, Pittsburgh, PA; GD; MSN; Sigma Theta Tau 85; AACN PNA 80-91; CCRN 86-91; BSN 85; ADN Mt Aloysius Jr Clg 79; Nrsng Ed; Tchng.

**DUBBS, MICHAEL E,** Univ Of Sc At Columbia, Columbia, SC; JR; BA; Sailing/Windsurfing Club 89; Golden Key; Sigma Phi Epsilon Alumni Relation Dir 89-90; Adopt-A-Hwy Prog 88-; MS Walk For Life; Deans List 88-; :Im Vlybl Raquetbl 88-; Finance Mrkting; Attend Grad Sch MIB.

**DUBE, KIMBERLY A,** Andover Coll, Portland, ME; GD; Typing Award; Shorthand Award; Internship Legal Secretary John M Whalen PA; Assoc Degree; Secretarial; Legal Secretary.

**DUBE, PAULE,** Fl International Univ, Miami, FL; JR; BA; DEC Cegep De La Pocatiere 83; AA Broward Cmmnty Coll 90; Bus; Acctg.

**DUBEAU, ERNEST W,** Chesterfield Marlboro Coll, Cheraw, SC; SO; BA; Gen Stds Bus; Bus.

**DUBERSTEIN, SHANI B,** Univ Of Miami, Coral Gables, FL; SR; BS; Pblc Rltns Stdnt Scty Am Pres 89-; Pres 100 88-; Stdnt Actvty Fee Allctn Cmt 89-90; Phi Kappa Phi 88-; Gldn Key 89-; Frshmn Orntn Stff 88-90; Sgm Alph Epsln 88-; Fresh Orntan Stdf 88-90; Hurrican Honois Ftbl Rcrtng 88-; Pres Hon Roll 87-; Pblci Rltns/Mkrge; Banking.

**DUBEY, ANASUYA L,** Franklin And Marshall Coll, Lancaster, PA; JR; BA; Intl Club 88-; Spanish Club 88-90; Sigma Delta Pi 89-; Habitat Humanity 88-90; Tutor SATS 90-; Dana Intshp; English/Spanish; Communications.

**DUBIN, ALLISON M,** Univ Of Fl, Gainesville, FL; SR; BHSMT; Coll Rpblcns 89; Amer Scty Of Med Tech 89-; Med Tech.

**DUBINSKY, STEVEN R,** Clarkson Univ, Potsdam, NY; SO; BSC; NCAA Dvsn I Hcky Vrsty 89; Mrktng Mngmnt.

**DUBOIS, PAMELA,** Tn Temple Univ, Chattanooga, TN; FR; Bus Mnstry 90-; Alpha Kappa Rho 90-; Sctrl; Bus.

**DUBOSE, CARRICK M,** Morehouse Coll, Atlanta, GA; SR; BA; Bsn Assoc 87-; Pre-Law Soc 88-; Pltcl Sci Soc 88-; Hnr Roll 89-; Kappa Alpha Psi Pres 88-; Feel Safe Scrty Intern 90; Pltcl Sci; Law.

**DUBOSE, LISA A,** Univ Of West Fl, Pensacola, FL; JR; BA; AA Pensacola Jr Coll 90; Erly Chldhd/Elem Edn; Teach.

**DUBUISSON, TRACY L,** Univ Of Southern Ms, Hattiesburg, MS; SO; BS; Eagle Clb 90-; Gamma Beta Phi 90-; Freeport Mcmoran Schlrshp; Busn; Acctnt.

**DUBUQUE, KRISTIE A,** Castleton St Coll, Castleton, VT; JR; BA; Stdnt Govt Treas 89-90; Radio State Prnslty 88-; SEA V P 90-; Phi Eta Sigma 88-; Kappa Delta Pi 90-; Elem Spec Ed/ Reading; Tchr.

**DUBY, ELIZABETH A,** Western New England Coll, Springfield, MA; JR; Meadows East Hlth/Fitness Ctr Asst Mgr 85-; Certif Intl Dance/Exercise Assoc 90; Aerobics Instr Aerobics/Fitness Assoc Amer; Mktg; Sales.

**DUCA, MICHELLE E,** Ms St Univ, Miss State, MS; JR; BBA; Beta Gamma Sigma; Gamma Beta Phi 88-90; Mu Kappa Tau; Pi Sigma Epsilon 90-; Delta Delta Delta Soc Dvlpmnt Chrmn 88-; Pres Lst 88-; Deans Lst 88-; Natl Merit Schlrshp 88-; Ctzns Schlrshp 90-; Acdmc Schlrshp 88-; Mktg Rsrch; Mktg Rsrch Anlyst.

**DUCATE, RUTH L,** Univ Of Sc At Columbia, Columbia, SC; JR; BA; Yrbk Stf Bus Mgr 90-; Grphcs.

**DUCHEINE, SANDRA,** Fl International Univ, Miami, FL; SO; BS; Fnce; Corp Lawyer.

**DUCKARDT, CLAUDIO D,** Fl International Univ, Miami, FL; SR; BA; Spec Ed; Ed Mntly Rtrd.

**DUCKERSCHEIN, INGO T,** Richard Bland Coll, Petersburg, VA; FR; BS; Spnsh Club; Mgmt/Fin; Intl Fin.

**DUCKWORTH, AMY POLLARD,** Univ Of Montevallo, Montevallo, AL; SR; BS; Phi Theta Kappa Pres 88-89; Lambda Sigma Pi; Kappa Delta Pi Pres 90-; Phi Theta Phi; Stdnt Spprt Serv Tutor 90; Pres Ldrshp Schlrsp 89-; Most Outstndg Undrgrad Mjr Awd ECE; Early Chldhd/Elem Ed; Tchng.

**DUCKWORTH, ANDREW G,** Univ Of Akron, Akron, OH; JR; BS; Acctg Assoc Dir Soph 90-; Beta Alpha Psi Conf Dir; Beta Gamma Sigma; Alpha Lambda Delta 89; Phi Eta Sigma 89; VITA; USMC 84-88; Acctg.

**DUCKWORTH, DIANE,** Ms St Univ, Miss State, MS; JR; BA; Stdnt Assn Serv Com 89-90; Activities Brd Lctrn Com 90; Bptst Stdnt Union; Order Omega Pres; Mortar Brd Elctns Chrmn; Phi Kappa Phi 90-; Sigma Tau Delta; Chi Omega VP 90; Ltl Theatre 88-90; Blood Dnr 90; Beautfl Hwy Prjct 90-; Engl; Tchng.

**DUCKWORTH, ERIKA N,** Fl A & M Univ, Tallahassee, FL; JR; BA; Stdnt Nwspr Fetrs Edtr 88-; Delta Sigma Theta 90-; Summer Intrn Nwspr 90-; Summer Intrn Greensboro Nws/Rcrd; Exclnt Achvmnt Schlr 88-; Jrnlsm; Nwspr Jrnslm.

**DUCKWORTH, MORIE M,** Meridian Comm Coll, Meridian, MS; SO; BA; MCC Diamond Dolls; MCC I M Bowling Tm; MCC Pen Pals; Phi Theta Kappa; Acctng; CPA.

**DUCKWORTH, STEFANIE A,** Muskingum Coll, New Concord, OH; JR; BA; Fellowshp Christian Athletics 88; Dorm Council Rep 90; Phi Sigma Iota 89; Acct Honorary 90; Delta Gamma Theta 89; Lambda Sigma 89-90; Omicron Detta Kappa 90; Ohio Lottery Intn 89-90; Track Cross Countrysch Rec Hldr 88; Acct French; International Acct CPA.

**DUCLOS, THEODORE J,** Central Fl Comm Coll, Ocala, FL; SO; AA; Math And Sci Hnrs Clb 90-; Phi Theta Kappa; Blwng And Glf; Eng; Mech Eng.

**DUCOT-UTSETT, MINERVA,** Catholic Univ Of Pr, Ponce, PR; JR; BA; Credit Union Brd Sec 87-90; Mgmt; Bus Mngr.

**DUDA, KIM C,** Middlesex County Coll, Edison, NJ; FR; AAS; SADHA 90; Dntl Assist 85; Applied Sci Dntl Hygne.

**DUDA, NICOLE M,** Fl Atlantic Univ, Boca Raton, FL; JR; BA; Ntnl Law Camp 90; Pol Action Commttee Plm Bch Jr Clg 88; Phi Kappa Phi 90; Beta Gamma Sigma 89; Cities In Schls 88; Phi Theta Kappa 88; Pres Lst 90; Deans Lst 90; Acad Hnrs Lst 88-89; Grad PBJC Hghst Hnrs; AA 89; Intrntl Bsnss; Law.

**DUDA, ROGER H,** U S Military Academy, West Point, NY; FR; BS; Cadet Band 90-; Life Sci.

**DUDAC, YVETTE C,** Saint Joseph Coll, West Hartford, CT; FR; BA; Dns Lst 90-; Iadarola Math Mem Awd; Math/Cmptr Sci.

**DUDDEY, GAIL E,** Northern Ky Univ, Highland Hts, KY; FR; BSW; Sndy Schl Tchr St Pius X Parish 90-; St Johns Soc Svc Cinn OH 90-; Scl Wrk.

**DUDDY, STEPHANIE L,** Bellarmine Coll, Louisville, KY; SR; BA; Psych Clb 89-90; Bsktbl Cmp Cnslr 87-90; Psi Chi 90-; Deans Lst 87-; Kappa Gamma Pi; Ldy Knght Almn Assc Awd; Fred J Karem Schlstc Achvmnt Awd; Ten Broeck Hsp Intrnshp 90; Bsktbl Co Cpt 87-; Psychlgy.

**DUDE, RICHARD A,** Livingston Univ, Livingston, AL; SO; ADN; Dns Lst 90; Pres Lst; Union Jrnymn Crpntr; Nrsng.

**DUDEK, PAUL T,** Glassboro St Coll, Glassboro, NJ; JR; BA; Stdnt Activities Bd 90-; Glassboro State Emergency Squad SGT 90-; Stdnt Govt Assn 90-; Gamma Tau Sigma 90-; Stdnt Trustee 89-; Eagle Scout/Asst Scoutmaster; Peer Referrel/Orientation Staff 90-; Psychology; Clinical/Cnslng Psych.

**DUDLEY, BEVERLY K,** Middle Ga Coll, Cochran, GA; SO; BS; Assn Life Undrwrtrs; Career Agnt GA Frm Bureau Mtl Ins Co Macon GA; Psych; Cnslng.

**DUDLEY, ELIZABETH D,** Radford Univ, Radford, VA; JR; BA; Mrktg.

**DUDLEY, TARA A,** Marywood Coll, Scranton, PA; FR; BS; Pres Schlrshp; Cmmnctn Dsordrs; Speech Pthlgst.

**DUDLEY, TASHA L,** Al St Univ, Montgomery, AL; JR; BA; PRCA 90-; Yrbk Stff; John Marshall Metro Gen Schlrshp Awrd 88-89; Acdm Schlrshp 88-; Cmmnctns; Pblc Rltns Cnsltnt.

**DUDLI, JOHANNA L,** Temple Univ, Philadelphia, PA; JR; BA; Athltc Trnrs Clb 90-; Rsdnt Asstshp 90-; Phys Educ Athltc Trnng; Sprts Med.

**DUDRICK, DAVID FRANCIS,** Franklin And Marshall Coll, Lancaster, PA; FR; BA; Radio Sta Cmps 90-; IM Bsktbl/Vlybl 90-; John Mrshl Schlr 90-; Dnsysn Soc 90-; Engl; Law.

**DUDZIC, TRACI-LEE,** Univ Of Rochester, Rochester, NY; SO; BA; Cmptr Vlntr Orgnztn 90-; Strng Mmrl Hsp Vlntr 90-; Psychlgy; Psychlgst.

**DUDZINSKI, KIMBERLY A,** Duquesne Univ, Pittsburgh, PA; JR; BS; Acad Stdnt Phrmcy 89-; Amer Phrmctcl Assoc 89-; Natl Assoc Retail Drgsts; Dns Lst; Holy Family Yth Grp Pres 87-88; CCD Tchr 88-; Church Lector 87-; Giant Eagle; Phrmcy.

**DUEITT, DAVID R,** Ms St Univ, Miss State, MS; SR; BA; Psychlgy Clb; Coll Rpblcns; Pre Law Scty; Sftbll; Psychlgy.

**DUELL, MARK E,** Oh St Univ, Columbus, OH; SR; BS; Cir K Lt Govnr 87-; Clg Bowl Tm; Gldn Key 89-; OH Hon Pgm 87-; Math/Physcl Sci 90; IM Sftbl Sftbl Umpire Sprts Trivia Bwlng Bsktbl Tm Capt 87-; Physc Economics; Law.

**DUERR, ANDREA ROWEN,** Le Moyne Coll, Syracuse, NY; SR; Env Coalitn Sec 87-; Outing Clb Pres 88-; Art Clb VP 87-90; Amnsty Intl Philo Clb VP 87-90; Psi Chi; Intl Hse Publ Dir 88-90; Psych/Biol; Env Sci.

**DUES, CHERYL A,** Fayetteville St Univ, Fayetteville, NC; JR; BS; US Army/Combat Medic Srgt 86-89; NC State Schlrshp Acad 90; Amer Fdrtn Govt Emply; US Military Vtrn; AS Univ State Of NY 88; Chem; Med Rsrch.

**DUFFACK JR, WILLIAM C,** Samford Univ, Birmingham, AL; GD; JD; Amer Jrnl Of Trial Advcy 89-; Sigma Alpha Epsilon; Pub Dfndrs Offc Intrn 90; Cumberland Rcqtbl Chmpn 89-90; BA FLA State Univ 88; JD Samford Univ; Engl; Law.

**DUFFAU, AMY L,** Fairleigh Dickinson Univ, Rutherford, NJ; FR; BA; English; Writing.

**DUFFUS, KEVIN M,** D Youville Coll, Buffalo, NY; SR; MS; Intshp Lutheran Mdl Brooklyn NY; Kessler Inst W Orange NJ; Physical Therapy.

**DUFFUS, MEGAN S,** Miami Univ, Oxford, OH; FR; BA; Bnd Rep 90-; Phi Eta Sgm 90-; Alph Lmbd Dlt 90-; Dlt Omcrn Prfsnl Wmns Msc Hon Scty; Tau Beta Sgm Hstrn Pldg Cls; Msc Educ.

**DUFFY, CHRISTINA F,** Georgian Court Coll, Lakewood, NJ; SR; BA; Trnsfr Clb 89-; De La Salle Clb 90-; Sigma Phi Sigma 90-; Evcharistic Mnstr 90; AA Middlesex Cnty Clg 83; Soc/Elem Educ; Teach.

**DUFFY, DIANA,** Seton Hall Univ, South Orange, NJ; SR; Elizabeth Ann-Seton Clb Educ Mjrs 89-; Spec Olymp 88-; Math Clb 87-88; Kappa Delta Pi 88-; Delta Phi Epsilon Hstrn Fndng Sis 88-; IM Ftbl Champs 89-; BS; Dvlpmntl Dsrdrs.

**DUFFY, ELISE Y,** Univ Of West Fl, Pensacola, FL; SR; BA; Kappa Delta Pi 89-; Deans Lst 89-; Cert Dental Asst 83-; Florist/ Designer/Dental Asst; AS Cert Dental Asstng Pensacola Jr Clg 83-88; Tchr.

**DUFFY, MICHAEL D,** Univ Of Sc At Sumter, Sumter, SC; SR; BA; Aprn Phlsphcl Soc VP 88-89; Schl Nwspr Phtgrphr 88-90; Stdnt Ed Assn Pres 89-90; Elem Ed; Tchng.

**DUFFY, PATRICIA L,** Oh St Univ At Newark, Newark, OH; FR; BED; Pataskala Pks/Rec Coach Soccer; Kirkesville PTO V P Room Mother; Forgn Lang/Engl; Elem Tchr.

**DUFFY, PETER R,** Villanova Univ, Villanova, PA; FR; BS; Data Procng Mgt Assoc 90-; Financial Mgt Assoc 90-; Acad Advmnt Tutor; Spl Olympics Games Commt; Deans List 90-; IM Bskbl Tm Cptn; Busn Admin; Corp Finance.

**DUFFY, VINCENT E,** Manhattan Coll, Bronx, NY; SR; BSEE; IM Indoor Soccer Capt 88-89; Bill Byron Mem Run Wnr 89 88-89; Sch Radio DJ 88-89; Eta Kappa Nu Pres 90-; St Patrick Yth Grp Retreat Ldr Grp Ldr 90; IBM Waison Labs Wrk Study Engr 88-; Turkey Trot 2nd Pl 89; Elctrcl Engr; Patent Law.

**DUFOUR, LYNN M,** Juniata Coll, Huntingdon, PA; FR; BED; Elem Ed; Tchng.

**DUFRESNE, CAROL J,** Univ Of Miami, Coral Gables, FL; GD; BARCH; Cnmtc Arts Cmmssn 90-; Arch Lctr Comm 90; Urbn Dsgn Cmptn 90; Arch Hstry Asst 89-90; Urbn Plnnr; MA Univ MD 83; Arch.

**DUFRESNE, CHRISTINE M,** Merrimack Coll, North Andover, MA; JR; BA; Sigma Phi Omega Treas 89-; Intercultural Clb 90-; Intl Bus Clb Pres 90-; Deans Lst; Sigma Phi Omega Treas 89-; I M Capt 88-; Bus Admn; Intl Bus.

**DUFTLER, MELISSA J,** Univ Of Rochester, Rochester, NY; JR; BA; Panhlnc Cncl Treas 89-; Vol St Agnes Hosp 83-; Deans List 90-; Ordr Of Omega; Sigma Delta Tau Exec Panhlnc Rep 88-; Meridian Soc Vol; Hlth/Soc/Psychlgy; Hlth Rltd.

**DUGAL, BRENT R,** Embry Riddle Aeronautical Univ, Daytona Beach, FL; JR; BS; Aerontcl Studies; Pilot.

**DUGAN, ELIZABETH T,** Univ Of Rochester, Rochester, NY; SO; BS; Navy ROTC 89-; Var Vlybl 89-90; Crew 90; Optcl Engr; Navy.

**DUGAN, JOYCE P,** The Johns Hopkins Univ, Baltimore, MD; JR; BSN; Jr Cls Stdnt Govt Sec 90-; V A Schlrshp 90-; Tchg Asst; Med Sec Admin Asst 77-90; AA Duffs Busn Inst 77; Nrsng; Mstrs Degr.

**DUGAN, MARK W,** Univ Of Rochester, Rochester, NY; SR; BA; Sigma Chi Steward 90-; Psychlgy; Bus Mgt.

**DUGAN, THERESA A,** Wv Univ At Parkersburg, Parkersburg, WV; JR; AS; Criminal Justice Organization 87; Deans Honor List 89-90; Phi Theta Kappa; WV Legislative Prog Honor Stdnts 89-90; Criminal Justice; Corrections/Probtn/Parole.

**DUGAN, TIMOTHY,** City Univ Of Ny Baruch Coll, New York, NY; JR; Amer Mktg Assn V P Prmtns 90-; Pres Schlrshp 88-; Mktg.

**DUGAS, MOREAU,** Fl A & M Univ, Tallahassee, FL; SR; BS; Acad Schlrshp; All Amer Schlr Clgt Awrd; Assc Miami Dade Comm Clg 90; Electrnc; Eng.

**DUGGAN, CATHERINE A,** Univ Of Sc At Columbia, Columbia, SC; SR; BA; Kappa Delta Pi 90-; AA 89; Early Childhood Ed; Teaching.

**DUGGAN, JOY FAITH,** Univ Of Sc At Coastal Carolina, Conway, SC; SO; BA; Yth Dir Shepherd Of Sea 90-; Elem Edn; Tchr.

**DUGGAN, KATHLEEN GORMAN,** Ny Law School, New York, NY; SR; JD; Legal Assoc Of Women 88-; Tchng Flw 90-; Rsrch Asst 90; Jrnl Of Human Rights 89-90; High GPA; Phi Alpha Delta 89-; ABA/LSD 89-; Bell Sys 68-73; Stdnt Intern Hon Burton R Lifland Chf Judge Bnkrptcy Ct SDNY; BA Fordham Univ 68; Law.

**DUGGAN, KELLEY D,** Dowling Coll, Oakdale Li, NY; SR; BA; Spcl Ed/Elmntry Ed; Tchr.

**DUGGER, JANELLE O,** Pellissippi St Tech Comm Coll, Knoxville, TN; SO; BA; Soc Stdys; Tchr.**

**DUGGER, PATRICIA LUCY,** Tallahassee Comm Coll, Tallahassee, FL; JR; BA; Engl; Wrtng/Tchng.

**DUGGER, PATSY M,** Dyersburg St Comm Coll, Dyersburg, TN; SO; AS; Ownr/Oper Dugger Sectrl Svc 86-; Acctg.

**DUGGINS, ROBIN R,** Univ Of Tn At Knoxville, Knoxville, TN; GD; DVM; Eqstrn Clb 89-; SCAVMA Tres 90-; Equine Clb Treas 90-; Gamma Sigma Delta 90-; Prcptrshp Equine Serv; BA 88; Vet Med.

**DUGLAS, ALANA K,** Clark Atlanta Univ, Atlanta, GA; JR; BA; Orntn Guide Corp 90-; Dncrs 90; Alpha Kappa Alpha Membrshp Co-Chair 89-; Mass Media Arts; Film Prod.

**DUHART JR, BENJAMIN T,** Fl A & M Univ, Tallahassee, FL; FR; BA; Chem Clb 90-; Phi Eta Sgm 90-; Bionr Smr Pgm 90; IM Vlybl Capt 90-; Chem; Med Chem Phrmclgy.

**DUHON, JAMES B,** Univ Of Southern Ms, Hattiesburg, MS; SO; BA; Karate Clb Tres 89-; Hnrs Stdnts Assn 89; Intrntnl Affrs Frnch; Analyst Offcr.

**DUITZ, VERED,** Pellissippi St Tech Comm Coll, Knoxville, TN; SO; BFA; Art.

**DUKE, ANTON L,** Univ Of Tn At Martin, Martin, TN; SR; BS; FCA; SGA; BSU Servant Singers Bapt Church; Phi Kappa Phi; Phi Eta Sigma; Alpha Gamma Delta Big Bro; Art-Sci Awd; Gulf S Confce All Acad Hon Prog; Adopt/Schol Prog; Athl Bd; Drug Ed Comm; Var Ftbl 87-; Biol/Pre Med; Med Schl.

**DUKE, CYNTHIA A,** Central Al Comm Coll, Alexander City, AL; FR; BA; Sci; RN.

**DUKE, DEBORAH C,** Livingston Univ, Livingston, AL; SR; Crdnl Key 90-; Alpha Chi 90-; Alpha Upsilon Alpha 90-; Stdnt Tchng Elem Schl; Elem Ed; Tchng.

**DUKE, HELEN R,** Roanoke Coll, Salem, VA; FR; Neriah Bapt Ch Yth Grp; Alpha Lambda Delta; Peer Tutor; Vlybl; Music; Elem Edn.

**DUKE, JOEY D,** Samford Univ, Birmingham, AL; GD; JD; Amer Jrnl Of Trial Advocacy Research Wrtng Editor 90-; Deans Lst; Cordell Hull Research Wrtng Fellow 89-; BA Univ Ala 87; Law.

**DUKE, JOHN S,** Duquesne Univ, Pittsburgh, PA; SR; BA; Phi Eta Sigma 88; Rho Chi 90-; Phi Delta Chi 89-; Dns Lst 87-; Conemaugh Vly Mem Hosp Phrmcy Intrnshp 90-; Phrmctcs; Hosp Phrmcy.

**DUKE, RAYNANZA L,** Watterson Coll, Louisville, KY; BA; Law.

**DUKE, SUSAN J,** Univ Of Sc At Columbia, Columbia, SC; JR; BA; Stdnt Govt Assoc Sen 87-88; Young Repblcns 88-89; Anthroplgy Stdnts Assoc 88-; Interdisplnry Studies/Elem Ed; Ed Admnstrtr.

**DUKELOW, NANCY J,** D Youville Coll, Buffalo, NY; FR; MS; Cmps Mnstry; SOTA; Lambda Sigma; Dns Lst; Occptnl Thrpy.

**DUKES, AMY L,** Winthrop Coll, Rock Hill, SC; SR; MBA; Acctng Clb Pres 87-; Natl Assn Acctng 89-; Baptist Stdnt Un 87-; Phi Kappa Phi V P 90-; Omicron Delta Kappa V P 89-; Alpha Lambda Delta V P 88-89; Alpha Kappa Psi V P 87-; Cir K 87-89; Winthrop Schlr 89-; Wall Strt Jrnl Awd; Bus; Acctng.

**DUKES, CYNTHIA L,** Univ Of Fl, Gainesville, FL; JR; BS; Amer Inst Chem Engr 90-; Tau Beta Pi; CRC Press Chem Achvmnt Awd 89; S & A Restrnts 87; AA Hon Hillsborough Comm Clg 89; Chem Engr/Waste Mgmt.

**DUKES, DEBORAH J,** Marshall University, Huntington, WV; SR; BBA; Natl Mgmt Assn 89-90; PROWL 89-; Prmtm Campus Crsde For Chrst 89-; X-Cntry/Trck 87-90; Mgmt; Corp Mgr.

**DUKES, DERRONICA L,** Jackson St Univ, Jackson, MS; FR; BA; Clss Sec 90-; Bptst Stdnt Un Choir 90-; Dunbr Drmtc Gld 90-; Alpha Lambda Delta 90-; Acctg; Corp Law.

**DUKES, DONNA D,** Miles Coll, Birmingham, AL; SR; BA; Bptst Stdnt Un Pres 87-; Pltcl Sci Clb Pres 89-90; Chpl Anncr Mdtn Ldr Ldr 88-; Soc Prsdntl Schlr Div Pres 88-89; Intrn Rep Lewis Spratt AL Lgsltr; Vldctrn Summa Cum Laude; Pltcl Sci; Edctn Rfrm Law.

**DUKES, ERIK W,** William Carey Coll, Hattiesburg, MS; JR; BS; FCA Pres 890; SGA Rep Allied Sciences 90-; Omicron Delta Cappa 90-; Alph Chi 90-; GCAC 90-; Frshm Sci Awd 88-89; Bsktbl 88-; Biology/Chemistry; Doctor.

**DUKES, LA SHONDA Y,** Tougaloo Coll, Tougaloo, MS; SO; BA; Psych Clb 90-; Haram Bee Staff 90-; Stdnt Support Svcs Tutor; Alpha Lambda Delta 90-; Alpha Kappa Alpha Sor Inc; Pr Schlr 89-; Psych.

**DUKES, SHEA A,** Coll Of Charleston, Charleston, SC; JR; BED; CEC 90-; AAMR; Panhellenic Clcl Pres 89-; Omicron Delta Kappa 90-; Zeta Tau Alpha Exe Ofcr 88; Spec Educ; Tch.

**DUKES, SHEDRICK L,** Fl A & M Univ, Tallahassee, FL; JR; BA; RHA Pres 88-; ROTC 88-; Top Rl ROTC Cls 90-; Trck Im Ftbl Sftbl 88-89; Engr; Elect Engr.

**DUKOVICH, LISA A,** Duquesne Univ, Pittsburgh, PA; SR; BS; Scty Hmn Rsrc Mngmt 90-; Univ Annl Dnce Mrthn Asst Chrmn/ Co Chrmn 89-90; Delta Zeta Pres/Rcrdg Sec 90-; Univ Vol 90-; Hmn Rsrc Intrn QED Communications; Hmn Rsrc Mngmt.

**DUL, JAMES P,** S U N Y Coll Of Tech At Alfred, Alfred, NY; FR; BS; Const AL Blades/Sons Inc Hrnl NY; AA 69-71; Chem; Envrnmtl Engr.

**DULAI, SARBJOT S,** Va Commonwealth Univ, Richmond, VA; GD; MD; BS Duke Univ 89; Medicine.

**DULANEY, SUSAN M,** Univ Of Cincinnati-Clrmnt Coll, Batavia, OH; FR; BA; Phi Theta Kappa; Alpha Iota Theta; Stdnt Ambsdr; PTA/PTO 87-; Nrsng/Cmptrs; Nrsng.

**DULEY, JANESE Y,** Volunteer St Comm Coll, Gallatin, TN; SO; BSEE; Tlphne Pnrs Of Amer Athltcs Chrprsn 90; Natl Math Awrd; Assc Institute Of Electronic Tech 85; Elec Eng; Eng.

**DULIK, KAREN,** Univ Of Sc At Columbia, Columbia, SC; SR; Soc Undrsea Wrld Prsdnt 90-; IM Sftbl 88-; Stdnt Gvrmnnt Assn Clb Rep 88-; Omicron Delta Kappa 89-; Phi Beta Kappa 90-; Hnrs Prgrm 87-; Rsrch Asstntshp 90; IM Sftbl 88-; BS; Marine Sci.

**DULIK, KAREN,** Univ Of Sc At Coastal Carolina, Conway, SC; SR; Scty Undrsea Wrld Pres 90-; Stdnt Govt Assc Clb Rep 88-; Hnrs Prog Cncl Sec 89-; Omicron Delta Kappa 89; Phi Beta Kappa 90-; Hnrs Prog 87-; Smmr Rsrch Asstshp 90; IM Sftbl 88-; BS; Marine Sci; Grad Schl.

**DULIN, DANNA L,** Miami Jacobs Jr Coll Of Bus, Dayton, OH; SO; Miami Jacobs; Hghr Accntng; CPA.

**DULISSE, DEBORAH A,** Mount Saint Mary Coll, Newburgh, NY; JR; BA; Phi Theta Kappa 89-90; Natl Assn Acctnts Awd Excell Busn 90; Orng Cty Comm Col; Cert Mrt Outsdng Schl Achvmnt Acctng 90; OCCC Acad Achvmnt Awd Excell Schlrshp 90; AAS Orng Cnty Comm Clg 90; Acctg.

**DULL, AMY L,** Miami Jacobs Jr Coll Of Bus, Dayton, OH; FR; AS; Sci; Med.

**DULL, ROBIN K,** James Madison University, Harrisonburg, VA; SR; BS; Natl Assoc Ed Yng Chldrn 88-90; Campus Crusade Christ 87-90; Gldn Key; Pres Lst; Dns Lst; Paul Douglas Tchr Schlrshp; Phi Delta Kappa Future Edctr Schlrshp; Early Chldhd Ed; Tchr.

**DULMAINE, JENNIFER L,** Elms Coll, Chicopee, MA; SO; BA; Orttn Advsr; Grl Scts Prgm Dir; Grl Sctng 89-; All Amrcn Schlr Coll Awrd; Elem Ed.

**DULONG, ANDREA M,** Albertus Magnus Coll, New Haven, CT; JR; BA; Engl Clb Pres; Brkwtr Lit Mag Edtr-In-Chf; Engl; Tchng.

**DUMAS, DAVID M,** Ms St Univ, Miss State, MS; SR; BA; Pres Lst; BS La Tech Univ 89; Jrnlsm; Wrtr/Edtr/Consltnt.

**DUMAS, DORA A,** Talladega Coll, Talladega, AL; SO; BA; Alpha Phi Alpha Swthrt; All Amercn Schlrs Award; Natl Collgt Minrty Ldrshp Award; Fin/Bnkng.

**DUMAS, DORTHEA KAY,** Asbury Theological Sem, Wilmore, KY; GD; MDIV; Commodities Progrm Dir; Career Consltnt 62-72; Legsltv Asstnt 72-87; Christn Bookstore Ownr 86-89; BLS St Edwards Univ 85; Gen Divnty; Pastor.

**DUMAS, ERNEST R,** Univ Of Nh Plymouth St Coll, Plymouth, NH; FR; BA; Hist; Archaeology.

**DUMAS, EVETTE M,** Ms St Univ, Miss State, MS; JR; Elem Ed; Tchr.

**DUMAS, KIMBERLY M,** Fl A & M Univ, Tallahassee, FL; FR; BA; Striker Dance Org Mbr 90-; Crmnl Jstc/Comptr Info Sys; Law.

**DUMAS, LORI A,** Hampton Univ, Hampton, VA; JR; Stdnt Chrstn Assn Co Chrprsn/Pres 90-; Upsilon Pi Epsilon; Alpha Kappa Mu; Beta Kappa Chi; Bell Cmnctns Eng Schlrshp; Bell Cmnctns Intrnshp.

**DUMAS, ODESSA E,** Stillman Coll, Tuscaloosa, AL; JR; Elem Educ; Tchr/Princpl.

**DUMAS, RANDALL E,** Univ Of Southern Ms, Hattiesburg, MS; FR; BS; Vllybl Tm 90-; Hnrs Clg 90-; Bio Chem/Pre Med; Med.

**DUMAS, STACIE M,** Niagara Univ, Niagara Univ, NY; SO; BS; Drm Cncl 90-; Crmnl Jstc; Law.

**DUMBROSKI, LAUREN K,** Univ Of Nc At Greensboro, Greensboro, NC; JR; BS; Natl Org Scl Wrkrs Pres 90-; Gldn Chain; Phi Mu Dir 89-; States Attrny Offc Mntgmry Co Intrn 90; Kenya E Africa Intrn; Scl Wrk; Law.

**DUMIN, JO ANN,** Rensselaer Polytechnic Inst, Troy, NY; SR; BS; Wmns Athletic Assn 87-; Stdnt Orntatn Co Chprsn 88-; Govr Athletes Agnst Drnk Drvng; Phalanx Rensselaers Sr Hon Soc 90-; Fresh Advsng Prog Biology Mbr 88; Deans Srch Cmtee 89; Lab Assnt 90-; W Stanton Mr RPI Awd; Bus Conf 90; Var Bkbl; Biology; Ph D Biochemistry.

**DUMMER, CHRISTINE L,** Univ Of Rochester, Rochester, NY; SR; BAMS; Deans Lst 87-; Meliora Rcpnt; AS Monroe Cmmnty Clg 89; Ecnmcs Pblc Plcy Anlysis; Law.

**DUMPHY, WILLIAM C,** Wv Univ, Morgantown, WV; JR; BS; Pi Tau Sigma; Mech Engr; Engr.

**DUNAC, DONALD,** Inter Amer Univ Pr San German, San German, PR; FR; BS; AA 90; Blgy; Med.

**DUNAGAN, STAN P,** Univ Of Tn At Martin, Martin, TN; SR; BS; Intr-Frat Cncl Pres 90-; Phi Kappa Phi 90-; Phi Eta Sigma 89-90; Kappa Alpha Order Pres 89-90; Sigma Xi Rsrch Grnt 90-; Cert Merit Arts/Sci 90-; Geolgy; Geolgst.

**DUNAWAY, ANDREA L,** Univ Of West Fl, Pensacola, FL; SR; BA; Elem Educ.

**DUNAWAY, ERIC K,** Morehouse Coll, Atlanta, GA; SO; BA; Morehouse Glee Club 89-90; Political Sci Club 89-; Dorm Council 89-90; Hnr Rl 89-; State Dept Divis Human Resor 90; Political Sci; Law.

**DUNAWAY, TAMMERA S,** Univ Of Ky, Lexington, KY; SO; BA; Vocl Music Awd 89; PTA; Clin Psych.

**DUNAWAY, TENA M,** Univ Of Southern Ms, Hattiesburg, MS; JR; BS; Phi Theta Kappa; Alpha Of Miss; AA Copiah Lincoln Comm Clg 90; Psychology.

**DUNBAR II, DENNIS J,** Siena Coll, Loudonville, NY; SR; BS; Delta Epsilon Sigma; Intrnshp Lawrence Hlthcare Admin Svcs; Mktg/Mgmt; Fnc/Insur.

**DUNBAR, SHARLENE A,** Va St Univ, Petersburg, VA; SO; BS; Acctg.

**DUNCAN, ANGELA K,** Emory & Henry Coll, Emory, VA; SR; BA; SVEA; Sigma Mu; Phi Theta Kappa 88-89; Phi Delta Kappa; Chrstn Stdnt Mvmnt 87-89; JH Brunner Awrd 89; Spnsh-Ed; Tchng/Scndry Schls.

**DUNCAN, ANGELA KIMBERLY,** Univ Of Sc At Columbia, Columbia, SC; SR; MPER; Baptist Stdnt Union 87; Kappa Kappa Gamma 88-89; Alumni Schlrshp 87-; Emplymnt Rltns; BA; Psychology/Bus; Hmn Rsrc Dvlpmnt.

**DUNCAN, BOBBIE B,** Va Highlands Comm Coll, Abingdon, VA; SO; AAS; Phi Theta Kappa/Alpha Gamma Rho Tres 89-; Acctg/Cmptr Cert Inf Systms; Advncd Cmptr Inf Systms; Electrncs; Cmptr Techcn.

**DUNCAN, BRIAN L,** Middle Tn St Univ, Murfreesboro, TN; SR; MBA; Ohio Vly Cnfrnc Cmsnrs Hnr Rl 88-; Tns Buck Bolin Sprtsmnshp Awd 90; OVC Indr Tns 5 Sngls Rnrp 90; OVC Indr Tns 3 Dbls Rnrp 90; Tns Tm 88-; BBA; Fnce; Fncl Cnsltnt.

**DUNCAN JR, CHARLES W,** Northeast State Tech Comm Coll, Blountville, TN; SO; AS; Math/Comptr Prog; Sftwer Anlyst/Tchr.

**DUNCAN, CHRISTOPHER L,** Union Univ, Jackson, TN; GD; BS; Flwshp Chrstn Athl 88-; Bapt Stdnt Union 86-; Asst Bsebl Coach 90-; Sigma Delta V P 89-; Ltl League Coach 88-; Natl Phys Ed Hlth/Recr Awd; Vars Bsebl 86-90; Stdnt Tchrs Ed Assoc 89-; AS Jackson State Cmnty Clg 88; BS; Hlth/Phys Ed; Coach/ Teach.

**DUNCAN, CHRISTY L,** Ms St Univ, Miss State, MS; SO; BS; Bapt Stdnt Un 89-90; Phi Eta Sigma; Alpha Lambda Delta; Gamma Beta Phi; Alpha Gamma Delta 90-; Robert C Byrd Schlrshp 89; MSU Acdmc Schlrshp 89-; Mohasco Corp Schlrshp 90-; Engl Ed; Tchng.

**DUNCAN, DENISE R,** Montgomery Comm Coll, Troy, NC; SO; AAS; Ssg; Pres List; Acctg/Bus Admin.

**DUNCAN, ELIZABETH A,** Longwood Coll, Farmville, VA; JR; Psychlgy Clb 90-; Sclgy/Anthrplgy Clb 90-; Ordr Omega VP 90-; Psi Chi 89-; Alpha Kappa Delta 90-; Delta Zeta VP 89-; Psychlgy/Sclgy; Crmnl Juste.

**DUNCAN, HAZEL A,** Univ Of Tn At Martin, Martin, TN; SO; BS; Collegiate 4h 90-; Phi Eta Sigma 90-; Woodmen Wrld Lodge 938 90-; Erly Chldhd Educ.

**DUNCAN, HUBERT A,** Roane St Comm Coll, Harriman, TN; SO; Judiciary 90-; USGA Assoc 90-; Gamma Beta Phi 89-; Great Performing Athletes Awd; Deans Lst; Varsity Bsktbl; IM Sftbl 89-; Hist; Law.

**DUNCAN III, JAMES L,** Univ Of Southern Ms, Hattiesburg, MS; SR; Rotaract; Gamma Beta Phi Dir Cmty Serv; Alpha Epsilon Delta; Kappa Sigma Dir Pblctns; Deans List; BS 90; Biological Science; Medicine.

**DUNCAN II, JAMES R,** Greenville Tech Coll, Greenville, SC; SO; AB; Natl Chefs Assn 90-; Golf Trnmnt; Tennis Tour; Culinary Arts; Chef.

**DUNCAN, JANICE C,** Middle Tn St Univ, Murfreesboro, TN; JR; BS; Band Of Blue Guard Cptn 89; Hnr Roll 88-90; Deans List 88-90; Psychlgy; Cnslng.

**DUNCAN, JENNIFER L,** Wv Univ, Morgantown, WV; SR; BSCE; ASCE 89-; Cvl Engr; Envr Engr.

**DUNCAN III, JOHN D,** Randolph Macon Coll, Ashland, VA; FR; Hons Prog; Lambda Chi Alpha; Res Asst; Vars Ftbl; Bsbl; Bsns/Econs.

**DUNCAN, JONATHON L,** Middle Tn St Univ, Murfreesboro, TN; SO; Gamma Beta Phi 90-; Tau Kappa Epsilon; BBA; Mrktng.

**DUNCAN, KAREN S,** Middle Ga Coll, Cochran, GA; SO; BED; Gamma Beta Phi 90-; Quiz Bowl 90-; Math Ed.

**DUNCAN, KEVIN DEAN,** Savannah Coll Of Art & Design, Savannah, GA; JR; BFA; Grphc Dsgn; Creatv Dir.

**DUNCAN, MEARLENE J,** Fl A & M Univ, Tallahassee, FL; JR; BA; FFEA; Circle 1 Willowhead MB Ch VP 89-; Natl Coll Ed Awd 90-; Theta Omega Soc 76; All Am Schlr 89-; White/Gold Hon Soc FAMU; Ford Fndtn Schlr; PTO; NAACP; Bible Study Stdnt; Msnry Soc 75-; AS Edn Thomas Coll 77; Elem Edn; MA Doc Degree.**

**DUNCAN, PENNY M,** Middle Tn St Univ, Murfreesboro, TN; SR; BBA; Gamma Beta Phi 89-; Phi Kappa Phi 89-; Phi Theta Kappa 87-; Gamma Iota Sigma 89-; Allstate Ins Co Schlrshp 90-; AA Hiwassee Clg 88; Fin; Insur Claims/Undrwrtng.

**DUNCAN, RHESA S,** Univ Of Sc At Columbia, Columbia, SC; SO; BA; USAF 84-88; Honbl Disch; SCANG Honbl Disch 89; Nrsng; Med.

**DUNCAN, SAMANTHA J,** Univ Of Ma At Amherst, Amherst, MA; SO; MA; Cmnctn Disorders Clb Frsh/Soph Rep 89-; March Band 89-; Spitfire Indoor Winter Guard 89-; Gold Key; Cmnctn Disorders; Audiology.**

**DUNCAN, SONJA S,** Jackson St Univ, Jackson, MS; SO; BS; Bio Clb; Alpha Lambda Delta; Beta Beta Beta Prlmntrn 90; Bio; Med Schl.

**DUNCAN, STEVEN R,** S U N Y Coll Of Tech At Alfred, Alfred, NY; FR; MBA; Bus Admin; Acctng.

**DUNCAN, TRICIA M,** Northern Ky Univ, Highland Hts, KY; FR; BED; Ed; Elem Tchr.

**DUNCAN, WILLIAM W,** Ms St Univ, Miss State, MS; SR; BA; Yrbk 88-89; Spnsh Clb 88-89; Sigma Tau Delta 90-; Phi Alpha Theta; Engl; Prfssr.

**DUNDEE, ISABELLE M,** Salisbury St Univ, Salisbury, MD; SR; MBA; SNEA; Kappa Delta Pi; Elem Educ; Tchng.

**DUNFORD, ANNETTE G,** Methodist Coll, Fayetteville, NC; SR; Vol Wrk Fayttvl Tech Comm Coll NC 90-; Vol Wrk Red Crs Ft Bragg NC 90-; Rgstrd Dntl Hygnst 89-90; AS Appl Sci Fayttvl Tech Comm Coll 89; Blgy/Pre Dntl; Dntl Schl.

**DUNFORD, MELISSA K,** Va Highlands Comm Coll, Abingdon, VA; SO; AAS; Phi Theta Kapa 89-; Bus Mgmt; Rtl Store Mgmt.

**DUNGAN, CHRISTOPHER M,** Free Will Baptist Bible Coll, Nashville, TN; JR; Alpha Chi Omega 87-; Chrstn Srvc Org 87-; Bsktbl 87-89; BA; Physcl Ed/Blgy; Dr Chiro.

**DUNHAM, CYNTHIA J,** Atlantic Comm Coll, Mays Landing, NJ; SO; BS; Prof Flrl Dsgnr; Cert Nurse Asst; Phys Thrpy.

**DUNHAM, GARY T,** Ms Univ For Women, Columbus, MS; SR; BSN; Tenn Tom Chptr Emerg Nrs Assn Treas 89; BS Gnrl Mtrs Inst 70; AD Univ Mississippi For Wmn 89; Nrsg.

**DUNIGAN, JOY A,** Savannah Coll Of Art & Design, Savannah, GA; JR; BFA; Amer Inst Grphc Arts; Grphc Dsgn Prdctn Rm Asst; Asstnt Intrnshp Thompson 90; Sprtng Gds Slkscrn Artst; Grphc Dsgn.

**DUNITHAN, TIFFANY S,** Garrett Comm Coll, Mchenry, MD; SO; AA; Hoyes Un Meth Yth Grp Treas 87-90; SGA Fr Rep 89-90; Sadd Clb; Dns Lst 89-; Phi Theta Kappa 89-; Soc/Behvrl Sci; Gdnce Cnslr.

**DUNKLE, AMY M,** Marshall University, Huntington, WV; JR; BA; Erly Chldhd Ed; Edctr.

**DUNKLE, LEIGH A,** Marietta Coll, Marietta, OH; FR; BA; Alpha Lambada Delta; Chi Omega 90; Merrit Schlrshp; English; Publshng.

**DUNKLE, RAYMOND H,** Univ Of Akron, Akron, OH; SR; BS; Stdnt Tstmstrs Tres 89-; Accntng Assn 89-; Beta Gamma Sigma; Gldn Key; Alpha Lambda Delta; Phi Eta Sigma; Beta Alpha Psi Tax Cnfrnc Coord 90-; Vlntr Income Tax Asstnc Prgrm; Sr Rcgntn Awd; Accntng; Pblc Accntng.

**DUNLANY, JOSEPH B,** Youngstown St Univ, Youngstown, OH; FR; BME; Materials Engr.

**DUNLANY, MICHELLE E,** Brescia Coll, Owensboro, KY; SO; BS; NEA-SP Sec 90-; Little Theatre Troupe 90-; Stdnt Ambass 89-; Alpha Chi 90-; Chrldr 89-; Elem Educ; Tchng.

**DUNLAP, APRIL M,** Bethany Coll, Bethany, WV; SO; BS; Amer Chmcl Soc Sec 89-; Gamma Sigma Epsilon; Chmstry Awrd; Chmstry; Rsrch Orgnc.

**DUNLAP, CARL W,** Central Fl Comm Coll, Ocala, FL; SO; BA; Marion County Sheriffs Explores Pres 84-; Emergency Squad 89-; Criminology; Law Enforcement.

**DUNLAP, CHARLES L,** Columbia Greene Comm Coll, Hudson, NY; FR; AS; Karate Assn Yllw Blt 90-; Vllybl 90-; Biol/Chmstry; Rsrchr.

**DUNLAP, CHARLES SCOT,** Pellissippi St Tech Comm Coll, Knoxville, TN; FR; IE ACCOD 88; Cmptr Sci; Mech Engr.

**DUNLAP, TABITHA J,** Rockingham Comm Coll, Wentworth, NC; FR; Art; Cmmrcl Artst.

**DUNLAP, TINA L,** Roane St Comm Coll, Harriman, TN; SO; ASS; Amer Dntl Hygnsts Assn; ADAA 85-; Cert Dntl Asst; CDA St Tech Knox Tn 85; Hlth/Dntl Sci; Dntl Hygnst.

**DUNLEAVY, KATHLEEN T,** City Univ Of Ny La Guard Coll, Long Island Cty, NY; SO; BA; Phi Theta Kappa 90-; Para Prof Ed 88-; Engl; Ed.

**DUNMAN, AMY M,** Radford Univ, Radford, VA; JR; Hnrs Pgm 90-; Alpha Lambda Delta 88; Sigma Kappa Chrprsn 90-; Adopt-A-Hwy; Prjct Alzheimers Disease; Canned Food Drive; Ted Dalton Schlrshp; Acad Schlrshp 88; IM Sports; Sports Med; Phys Thrpy.

**DUNN, ALBERTA E,** Roane St Comm Coll, Harriman, TN; SO; AAS; Gamma Beta Phi; Physical Therapy; Physical Thrpst Asst.

**DUNN, ASHLEIGH A,** Mobile Coll, Mobile, AL; SR; BA; Stdnt Govt; Mbl Clge Trng Chr Pres 88-; Drm Tm; Stdnt Repr Org; Frgn Lng Clb; Bptst Stdnt Un; Sigma Tau Delta Pres 90-; Alpha Chi Vtng Dlgte 89-; Ms Mobile Clge 1st Rnr Up; Schlstc Tlnt Awds 89; Mdrn Frgn Lng Awd; Eng/Frgn Lng; Tch Frnch/Eng.

**DUNN, BETHANY S,** Salisbury St Univ, Salisbury, MD; GD; BS; Phys Edn Majors Soc Treas 87-90; Soccer Clb VP Capt 86-89; Res Hall Cncl 86-88; IM Rec Act 86-90; Schlstc All-Am 88; Citizens Cert Merit 88; Cum Laude 90; Campus Life Awd 89; NCPEHA 88; MAHPERD 87-; Phys Therapist Asst 90-; BS 90; Phys Therapy.

**DUNN, CAROL E,** Ms St Univ, Miss State, MS; SR; BFA; Phi Kappa Phi 90-; Deans Lst 90; Pres Lst; Kappa Pi 90-; Dux D Lux Intrnshp; AA 88; Art; Prtrt Artist.

**DUNN, CATHERINE D,** Central Al Comm Coll, Alexander City, AL; FR; Phi Theta Kappa; Bus Admn; Corp Law.

**DUNN, COLIN J,** Niagara Univ, Niagara Univ, NY; FR; BA; IM Bsktbl; Economics; Law.

**DUNN, COLLEEN MARIE,** Central Fl Comm Coll, Ocala, FL; FR; MBA; Phi Theta Kappa; Hospice Citrus Cty; Good Spirit Fndtn; Admn Coord 88-; Assn Female Executives 90-; Bus.

**DUNN, D CASSANDRA,** Wilberforce Univ, Wilberforce, OH; Natl Student Busn League Secty 88-; Cuy Ctyn Brd Elec Deputy Reg; Class Treas; Deans List 89-; Yth Counslr Assist Collinwood Comm Serv 88; Vtlr Rep Rean Comm 89-; Psy Emphasis; Clinical Psy.

**DUNN, DANIEL G,** Alfred Univ, Alfred, NY; FR; BS; Mech Eng.

**DUNN, JAMES A,** Asbury Theological Sem, Wilmore, KY; SR; MDIV; Wesleyan Smnry Fndtn Chpln 89-; Intrntnl Soc Theta Phi 89-; Pstrl Intrn Browns Chpl Wslyn Ch 89-; Stdnt Chpln VA Hsptl 90; IMS 88-; BA Rlgn Brtlsvl Wslyn Cllg OK 88; Mnstrl Stds; Pstrl Mnstry.

**DUNN, JAMES C,** Hudson Valley Comm Coll, Troy, NY; FR; AAS; Cvl Eng Technlgy; Cnstrctn/Drftg.

**DUNN, JAMI B,** William Carey Coll, Hattiesburg, MS; JR; BS; SGA Rep 89-; Elm Ed; Tchng.

**DUNN, JENNIFER M,** Central Fl Comm Coll, Ocala, FL; FR; BA; Dns Lst; Asstshp In Cntrl FL Comm Coll Lbrry; 20 Hr Tchng Cert CFCC 90; Erly Educ.

**DUNN, KATHLEEN R,** Providence Coll, Providence, RI; JR; BA; The Cowl Sch Nwspr Stf Wrtr 90-; Res Bd Dorm Treas 88-89; Pltcl Sci; Law.

**DUNN, KEVIN S MC S,** George Mason Univ, Fairfax, VA; JR; Dept Army Cvln Serv 79-90; Urbn Plnng; Indpndt Conslt Bsns.

**DUNN, KRISTYN C,** Johnson C Smith Univ, Charlotte, NC; FR; Shaki Mdlg Trp 90-; Stu Chrstn Assoc 90-; Advncd Frshmn Stdy 90-; Inrds Org; Inrds Intrnshp GE Capital; Ecnmcs.

**DUNN, MICHAEL C,** Longwood Coll, Farmville, VA; JR; BA; ROTC 88-90; Tau Kappa Epsilon; VFW Medal/Citation Ldrshp 90; Anthrplgy.

**DUNN, MICHAEL JOHN,** Oh Univ, Athens, OH; JR; BSEE; Karate Clb Instrctr 88-; Dale Carnegie Course Grad Asst 87-88; Cmptng/Lrng Srvcs Lab Asst 88-90; Alpha Lambda Delta 89-90; Tau Beta Pi 90-; Awd Dns Schrshp 89-90; Elec Engr.**

**DUNN, MICHELLE E,** Hudson Valley Comm Coll, Troy, NY; FR; AAS; Hudson Vly Comm Clb H O Amstutz Awd Acad Achvmnt 90-; Intrn Cmptr Info Serv; Pres Lst 90-; 1st Nationwide Bnk Fin Serv Spvr 87-90; Cmptr Info Sys; Cmptr Prgrmr.

**DUNN, SEAN MICHAEL,** Bridgewater Coll, Bridgewater, VA; FR; BA; Undermined.

**DUNN, SHANNON L,** De Tech & Comm Coll At Dover, Dover, DE; SO; IM Sftbl 89-90; Crmnl Jstc; Law Enf.

**DUNN JR, THOMAS G,** Truett Mc Connell Coll, Cleveland, GA; FR; Phi Theta Kappa; Ecnmcs; Law.

**DUNN, THOMAS M,** Allegheny Coll, Meadville, PA; SO; BA; Outing Clb Pres 90-; Curriculum Com Acting Stdnt Chair 89-; Ldrs/Liasons Edctnl Spt 90-; Psi Chi; Vail Mntn Rescue Grp 88-; Alden Schlr 89-90; IM Soccer Capt 89-90; Psychlgy; Edn.

**DUNN, TIMOTHY D,** Univ Of Tn At Martin, Martin, TN; JR; BS; Prk Recrtn Adv Clb Pres 89-; All Amer Schlr Awrd 90-; Leslie Duke Awrd; Dean Lst 90-; Prk Rcrtn Admn.

**DUNN, TIMOTHY K,** Daemen Coll, Amherst, NY; FR; BA; Physcl Thrpy.

**DUNN, WENDI L,** Meridian Comm Coll, Meridian, MS; SO; AA; Schlrs Bowl Tm 90; Activities Brd 89; Ambssdrs 89; Phi Theta Kappa 89; Chrch Yth Grp 89; Yth For Undrstndng Intrntl Exchnge 90; Engl; Med.

**DUNNAVILLE, BUFFY S,** Ky St Univ, Frankfort, KY; JR; BA; NAACP; Fllwshp Chrstn Athlts 88-89; Attndt; Sigma Gamma Rho Pres 90; Sftbll Tm 90-; Physcl Ed Tchr.

**DUNNE, MARTHA F,** Univ Of Cincinnati, Cincinnati, OH; JR; BFA; Clg Cnsrvtry Musc Trbnl Sntr 89-; Stdnt Snte Clg Sntr 90-; CCM Dnc Ensmbl 88-90; Hnrs Stdnt 88-; Kappa Delta Pnhlnc Dlgt 90-; Univ Hnrs Schlrshp 88-; Dnc; Bllt Prfrmnc.

**DUNNING, DAVID J,** Univ Of Southern Ms, Hattiesburg, MS; SR; BMED; Bnd Cncl 90-; Phi Mu Alpha Sinfonia VP 90-; Drm Mjr USM Mrchng Bnd 90-; Instr Music; Instr Music Educ.

**DUNNING, DEBORAH A,** Univ Of Fl, Gainesville, FL; JR; BS; Recreat Soccer Lge 87-90; Golden Key; Alpha Lamda Delta 90-; 87-; Pres List 87-90; Deans List 87-; IM Soccer/Sftbl 87-; Physical Therapy.

**DUNNING, JAMES M,** Univ Of Nc At Charlotte, Charlotte, NC; SR; BA; Amer Inst Arch Stdnts V P 90-; Stdnt Cncl 87-; Phi Kappa Phi 89-; Omicron Delta Kappa 90-; Crw Ldr Charlotte Habitat Hmnty 87-; Charlotte AIA Trvlng Fllwshp 90; Ireland Chnclrs Lst 89; Top 10th 90-; Arch.

**DUNNING, WANDA J,** Thomas Coll, Waterville, ME; JR; Accntng Scty 88; Yrbk 89-90; Alpha Chi 90; Pres Lst 88; Accntng/Cmptr Info Syst; CPA.**

**DUNPHY, JULIANE,** Middle Tn St Univ, Murfreesboro, TN; JR; BBA; Tau Omcrn Pres; Gamma Beta Phi; Alph Mu Alph; Deans List Hon Roll; Mktg; Rtl Mgm/Advrtsng.

**DUNPHY, SHEILA K,** Union Univ, Jackson, TN; SR; BS; STEA 89-; Alpha Chi 90-; Phi Theta Kappa 88-89; Magun Cum Laude JSCC 89; Magna Cum Laude UU; AS Jackson St Comm Coll 89; Elem Educ; Tch.

**DUNSHEE, STEVEN W,** Clarkson Univ, Potsdam, NY; SR; BS; GM Technel Advsr 88-90; Assoc Mtllrgst 86-88; Mltng Dept Rlf Sprvsr 84-85; Phi Kappa Phi; Plnt Scrty Offcr 76-86; Phi Theta Kappa 85-89; Cmnctn Awrd 89; Ldrshp Awrd 89; Pres Schlr 90-; AAS Canton ATC 76; Mgmt; Indstrl Mgmt.

**DUNSMORE, SUZANNE ELISE,** S U N Y At Buffalo, Buffalo, NY; SR; BPS; Archt Desgnr/Drftr; Asst Constr Mgr; AAS 81-83; Archtecture.

**DUNSON, BRADLEY S,** Hillsborough Comm Coll, Tampa, FL; FR; BA; Church Chrmn 90-; Phi Theta Kappa; Air Force Achvmnt Mdl 89-; US Air Force 85-89; Math; Engnrng.

**DUNSON, DEBRA L,** Tn St Univ, Nashville, TN; GD; MS; Grad Asstntshp 90-; AS Nashville St Tech Inst 88; BS 90; Chemistry; Instructor.

**DUNSON, LISA M,** Converse Coll, Spartanburg, SC; SO; BA; Baptist Stdnt Union VP 89-; Pre-Law Soc Sec 90-; Stdnt Adm Brd 89-; Alpha Lambda Delta; Crescent 90-; Pols/Rel; Soc Ministry.

**DUNSTON JR, PHILIP M,** Interdenominational Theo Ctr, Atlanta, GA; GD; MDIV; Stdnt Govt Pres 90; Morehouse Sch Of Relgn Flwshp 89-; Theta Phi 90-; Deans List 89-; Alpha Phi Alpha 80; UNCF Schlrshp 90; Benjamin E Hays Schlrshp Nom 90-; Bsktbl Coach 90-; BBA NC Central Univ 83; Biblicl Studies; PhD Homiletics/Worshp.

**DUNWOODY JR, BOBBY J,** Ms Gulf Coast Comm Coll, Perkinston, MS; SO; BED; Mrchng Bnd Drum Capt 89; Symp Bnd Sctn Ldr 90; Bapt Stdnt Union; Hstry; Tchr.

**DUONG, KHANH,** City Univ Of Ny La Guard Coll, Long Island Cty, NY; SO; Math Competition 89-90; Outstanding Math 90; Computer Science.

**DUPALY, DENISE M,** Duquesne Univ, Pittsburgh, PA; SR; BS; Amer Phrmctcl Assn 89-; Natl Assn Retail Drgsts 89; Phi Eta Sigma 88-; Rho Chi; Amer Diabetes Assn 89-; Juv Diabetes Fndtn 89-; Phrmcy Intrnshp Retail Phrmcy 89-; Acad Chlng Rsrch Stdnt Ohio State U; Phrmcy; Phrmctcl Rsrch.

**DUPEE, JUDITH M,** Oh St Univ, Columbus, OH; SR; BS BA; Gold Key Hon Soc 88-; Pi Mu Epsilon; Scarlet/Gray Schlrshp 90-; Dept Of Math Undergrad Recog Pgm; Univ Womens Clb Schlrshp 89-90; Miyo Kawai Mem Awrd 88-89; Arts/Sci Awrd 90; OH State House Of Rep Cmdtn; Math/Japanese.

**DUPKOSKI, PATRICIA A,** East Tn St Univ, Johnson City, TN; JR; BBA; Alpha Lambda Delta 89-; Gamma Beta Phi 90-; Bus; Mgmt.

**DUPLAK, YAROSLAVA A,** Le Moyne Coll, Syracuse, NY; SR; MS; Ukrainian PLAST Orgn Reg Dir 87-; Psych Clb 87-88; Intgrl Hnrs Prog 87-; Dean Lst Hnrs 87-; Beta Beta Beta 88-; Elmcrest Chldrns Cntr Intern; Acdmc Schlrshp 87-; Ukrainian Frtrnl Assn Schlrshp 87-; IM Vllybl 87-88; BS; Biol/Psych; Envrmntl Eng.

**DUPLESSIS, DAVID HUNTER,** Western Ky Univ, Bowling Green, KY; SR; BS; Scabbard/Blade 88-; Beta Beta Beta 88-; Phi Kappa Phi 89-; Pres Schlr 87-; Rsrv Ofcrs Assn Awd 90; Bio/Chem.

**DUPLISSEY, BONNIE L,** Christopher Newport Coll, Newport News, VA; GD; BED; Stdnt VA Ed Assn 89-; Suffolk Cty Rdng Cncl 89-; Beta Sigma Phi Xi Beta Iota Pres 82-; Obici Hosp Prntl Sblng Edctr Tchr 81-; AA Tidewater Comm Coll 86; Elem Ed; Kndrgrtn Tchr.

**DUPONT, DAWN,** Springfield Tech Comm Coll, Springfield, MA; FR; Hon 90; Cosmetology.

**DUPPE, KATHERINE M,** Duquesne Univ, Pittsburgh, PA; FR; BA; Acad Of Stdnts Of Phrmcy 90-; Natl Assn Of Rtl Drggsts 90-; Phi Eta Sigma; Lambda Sigma; Univ Vols 90-; SHARP 90-; Dns Lst 90-; Dirs Circle 90-; Founders Awrd Schlrshp 90-; Phrmcy.

**DUPRAS, THOMAS A,** Hudson Valley Comm Coll, Troy, NY; FR; AOS; Automotive; Auto Tchncn.

**DUPREE, CURTIS M,** Anne Arundel Comm Coll, Arnold, MD; SO; BS; U S Ar Frc; AA Comm Clg Ar Frc 89; Eng.

**DUPREE II, LARRY G,** Vance Granville Comm Coll, Henderson, NC; SO; BS; Phi Theta Kappa; Comp Sci; Syst Anlyst.

**DUPREY, JOSE A,** Univ Of Pr Cayey Univ Coll, Cayey, PR; JR; ROTC 88-; Coll Bus Sctrn 89; Bsktbll Tm 90-; Jdean Hnr 89-; Bsktbll Tm Mgr; Bus Admn; Bus Mgmt.

**DUPUIS, JACQUELYN G,** Fl St Univ, Tallahassee, FL; SR; BME; ACDA 90-; CMENC 90-; Phi Theta Kappa MCC 85-86; AA Manatee Comm Coll 86; Cert Sklls/Cert Mscl Prfrmnc MCC 86; Muisc Ed-Chrl; Tch.

**DUPUIS, JUDITH A,** Colby Sawyer Coll, New London, NH; JR; Stdnt Acdmc Cnslr 88-89; Nrdc Ski Tm 87-88; Erly Chldhd Ed; Tchg K-3.

**DUQUETTE, EUGENE J,** Univ Of Nh Plymouth St Coll, Plymouth, NH; FR; Cnstrctn Sprntndnt; Assoc Degree Laconia Tech Clg 71; Civil Eng.

**DURAHA, KAREN D,** Columbia Union Coll, Takoma Park, MD; JR; Premedical Scty Pres 90-; Schl Yrbk 89-90; Phi Eta Sigma 88-90; Alpha Chi 90-; Frshmn Chem Stdnt Of Yr 88-89; Biology Dept Awrd 89-90; Carnegie Inst Stdnt Research Asstnt 90-; Vlybl Tennis Vrsty Tms 90-; Biology; Molecular Biologist.

**DURAI, MARIE A,** Univ Of Sc At Coastal Carolina, Conway, SC; JR; Soc Studies; Tch.

**DURALL, SHARON E,** Univ Of Ky, Lexington, KY; SR; BS; Math Clb 89-; Natl Cncl Tchrs Math 90-; Phi Beta Kappa 90-; Pi Mu Epsln 90-; Sallie E Pence Math Awrd 88-90; Otis Sngltry Acad Schlrshp 87-; Andrew Jackson Grdnr Schlrshp 87-; Math; Tchng.

**DURAN, PAOLA,** Miami Dade Comm Coll North, Miami, FL; SO; Tennis MVP 89-; Sprts Soc Otstndng Athlete 90-; Gerrie Walklet Sprtsmnshp Awd; Vrsty Tns; Cmptr Sci.

**DURAND, GILBERT CLAUDE,** Inter Amer Univ Pr San German, San German, PR; FR; BS; Math; Eng.

**DURAND, JONATHAN M,** Western New England Coll, Springfield, MA; SR; BS; Deans Lst 90-; Grd Cum Laude; ASEET 89; Tchnol Mgmt.

**DURAND III, LOUIS,** Atlantic Comm Coll, Mays Landing, NJ; SO; BA; Cert S Jersey Prfssnl Schl Bus 88; Bus; Intl Bus/Mrktng.

**DURANT, RUTH P,** Univ Of Miami, Coral Gables, FL; FR; BA; Barbados Comm Col Chr 87-89; Barbados Schlrshp 90; Bowman Ashe Schlrshp 90; Arch.

**DURANTE, PAT L,** Merrimack Coll, North Andover, MA; JR; BS; ACM Chrprsn 87-; All Amer Schlr; Cmptr Sci Awd; Cmptr Sci; Software Engrng.

**DURBIN, CHRISTOPHER M,** Univ Of Cin R Walters Coll, Blue Ash, OH; JR; BS; Physics Clb Pres; Elec Engr.

**DURBIN, KAREN L,** Northern Ky Univ, Highland Hts, KY; JR; BA; Geo Clb GUNK Sec 89-; Psy Clb 88-; Phi Alpha Theta 90-; Psi Chi 90-; Psy.

**DURBIN, KELLI E,** Univ Of West Fl, Pensacola, FL; FR; BA; Cert Acad Exc 90; MIRA Awd Tlnt Schlrshp 90; Music; Mscn/Tchr/Performance.

**DURBIN JR, ROBERT C,** Villanova Univ, Villanova, PA; JR; BS; Intrprsnl Exprnce Wrkshp Pres 89-; Upsilon Pi Epsilon; Phi Kappa Phi; Phi Sigma Tau; Prjct Snshne 88-; Comp Sci.

**DURBIN, STEPHEN R,** Bellarmine Coll, Louisville, KY; SO; BA; Acctg Assn 89-; Deans Lst 90; Intrnshp-Fields Howard & Assoc 90-; Acctg/Comp Sci; Acctg.**

**DURBIN, STEVEN C,** Clemson Univ, Clemson, SC; SO; BS; Adventurers Guild 90-; IM Ftbl/Sftbl 90-; Bsn Mgmt; FBI Spec Agent.**

**DURDEN, DEBRA A,** Univ Of Fl, Gainesville, FL; SR; BD; Ntl Art Ed Assn; Golden Key; Art Ed; Elem Schl Art Tchr.

**DURDEN, RONALD W,** Univ Of South Al, Mobile, AL; SR; BFD; SHAPE Clb 89-; ASAHPERD 89-; Cty Hlth Clb Intrn; Exrcs Physlgy/Phys Ed.

**DURELL, TODD E,** Anne Arundel Comm Coll, Arnold, MD; SO; AA; Architecture.

**DUREN, CARLA C,** Hampton Univ, Hampton, VA; FR; BA; Gospel Chr 90-; Pompon Sqd Chrgrphr 90-; Honor Rl; Psych; Psycho Thrpy.

**DUREN, MELANIE A,** Univ Of Montevallo, Montevallo, AL; SO; BED; Drama Chorus; Early Chldhd/Elem Ed; Tchr/Cnslr.

**DUREZA, ROWENA I,** Goucher Coll, Towson, MD; SR; Maria Morales Spnsh Dance Cmpny 85-; Club Asia Sec 90; Cmtng Stdnts Org Treas 89-90; Phi Beta Kappa; Dns Schlr 88-90; BA; French; Educ.

**DURHAM, DISA N,** Univ Of Sc At Columbia, Columbia, SC; SR; BS; Bus Admn; Mrktng.

**DURHAM, GERI S,** Greenville Tech Coll, Greenville, SC; SO; SAPHA; Dntl Hygiene.

**DURHAM, KYLE A,** Hahnemann Univ, Philadelphia, PA; GD; MD; AMWA 90-91; AMSA Tsk Frc; Armed Frcs Hlth Prof Schlrshp Prog 89-; Wm Goldman Schlrshp 90; BS/BA Univ Pittsburgh 89; Cert Univ Pittsburgh 89; Medicine; Med Career US Navy.

**DURHAM, LAURA S,** Averett Coll, Danville, VA; GD; BS; Danville Jaycees Pres; Va Jaycees Progmn 89-90; Medl Assit Yr 86; Outstndng Jaycee Jr 88-89; AAMA Secty 87; Brd Dir Cancer Scty 84-87; Medl Assist Phys Office; CMA AAMA Certif Brd 83; Busn Mgt; Medl Field Mgt Sales.

**DURHAM, LETRICE A,** Clark Atlanta Univ, Atlanta, GA; SR; BA; Fin Clb 89-; Ntl Coll Bus Mrt Awd 89-; Beta Gamma Sigma 89-90; Psi Beta Lambda 88-89; Atlnta Chpt Fin Exec Inst Schlrshp 89-90; Bus Adm/Fin; Fin Insts Examnr FDIC.

**DURILLA, JUDITH A,** Wilkes Univ, Wilkes-Barre, PA; FR; BA; Circle K Intl 90-; Stdnt Hlth Advsry Cncl 90-; Schlr 90-; Biochemistry; Ophthalmology.

**DURIVAGE, SCOTT A,** Hudson Valley Comm Coll, Troy, NY; SO; BA; Explorer Post 477 87-; Cross Country Track Outdoor Track 89-; Busn; Computer Busn Field.

**DURKAY, MARK C,** Saint Francis Coll, Loretto, PA; SO; BA; Adopt A Grndprnt 89-90; Spec Frnds Hndcpd Pople 89-90; Plus 1 Yng Chldrn 89-; Hnrs Pgrm 89-; Dns Lst 89-; Elem Educ; Tchng.

**DURKEE, ELIZABETH M,** Lesley Coll, Cambridge, MA; SR; Dorm Cncl 84-85; Sra 85-86; Cmmtr Clb 89-; Haven From Hngr 85-; New Sound Cncrts 90-; Revere Comm Couns Ctr 89-90; Mass Eye/Ear Infirmiry 88-89; Mass Adptn Rsrc Exch 88-89; Grotonwood Bapt Yth Grp Ldr 83-87; NE Fmly Inst 89-; Hmn Srvcs; Socl Wrk.

**DURKIN, CHRISTOPHER T,** Lexington Comm Coll, Lexington, KY; JR; BS; Biology; Marine Bio.

**DURKOS, ELAINE S,** Hudson Valley Comm Coll, Troy, NY; GD; BPS; Soc Diag Med Sonogrphrs 90-; Sonogrphrs Cont Ed 90-; Amer Soc Rad Tech 83-; Rad Tech 70-; Certif Glens Fls Hosp Sch Rad Tech 69; Adirondack Cmnty Clg 66; Ultrasound; RDMS.

**DURLAND, FRANCES JEAN,** Univ Of Sc At Columbia, Columbia, SC; SR; BA; Bahai Comm No Myrtle Bch SC Chmn 90-; Sociology; MA Publ Hlth.

**DURLOCK, DEBRA L,** Va Highlands Comm Coll, Abingdon, VA; SO; BA; Pres Hnr Rl 87-; Zenith Fuel Syst Cost Acctnt 84-; Certif Supv 88; Advncd Acctg 90; Acctg.

**DURNWALD, CELESTE P,** Kent St Univ Kent Cmps, Kent, OH; FR; BS; Intragated Life Sci; Med.

**DURR, ADRIANNE J,** Clark Atlanta Univ, Atlanta, GA; SO; BA; Urbn Lge 89-; Natl Asc Bsn Prof Wmns Clb; Bsn Admn; Mktg.

**DURR, LAURA A,** S U N Y Coll At Fredonia, Fredonia, NY; SR; BS; Fstvl Chorus 90-; Drm Cncl 87-; Omicron Delta Epsilon 90-; Bsns Admn; Mgmt.

**DURR, MARY CHRISTINE,** Comm Coll Algny Co Algny Cmps, Pittsburgh, PA; SO; ASSOC; Photogrphy Clb 89-; PTA 88-; Svc Indstrs; Paralgl; Law.

**DURR, PASHA O,** Bowling Green St Univ, Bowling Green, OH; FR; BA; Cltn Fr Trnscltrl Enhncmnt Treas 90-; Bus Admin; Corp Lwyr.

**DURRAH, GRETTA L,** Phillips Jr Coll Spartanburg, Spartanburg, SC; GD; AAS; Mgmt.

**DURRANCE, GORDON EUGENE,** Chattahoochee Vly St Comm Coll, Phenix City, AL; MBA; Educ/Hist.

**DURRILL, ELIZABETH A,** Univ Of Nc At Greensboro, Greensboro, NC; SR; BED; Golden Chn Marshal; Intrnshp 5th Grd Clsrm; Lndsport Cnslr Camp Pinecliffe ME Asst Lndsprts Dir; Bsktbl Co-Capt; Elem Ed; Tchng.

**DURROUGH, BRIDGETT R,** Al St Univ, Montgomery, AL; JR; Cmtr Stdnt Assoc 89-; Easter Seal Soc Vol; Acctg; CPA.

**DURST, KIMBERLEY E,** Kent St Univ Kent Cmps, Kent, OH; FR; BS; Alpha Lambda Delta; Hon Coll; Occptnl Therapy.

**DURST, RACHAEL L,** Widener Univ, Chester, PA; FR; BA; Natl Asc Acctnts; PICPA; Phi Eta Sigma 90-; Pres Acad Schlp 90-; Int Clgt Vlybl/Trck Tms 90-; Acctng/Spnsh.

**DURST, ROBIN M,** Indiana Univ Of Pa, Indiana, PA; SR; BS; Cncrt Dnc Cmpny; PSEA; Elem Ed.

**DURST, RUSSELL A,** Bowling Green St Univ, Bowling Green, OH; FR; Bus; Mktg/Acctg.

**DURU, IFY BEATRICE,** Bloomfield Coll, Bloomfield, NJ; SR; Deans Lst 85-87; TX All St Nrsng Schlrshp Awd 85-87; Acad Cmptv Schlrshp Awd 85-87.

**DUSSAULT, KATHLEEN A,** Univ Of New England, Biddeford, ME; SR; BS; UNESOTA Pres 90-; Poetry Clb Sec 90-; MEOTA Stdnt Liaison 90-; Amer Occup Thrpy Assn ASCOTA Rep 89-90; Rural Maine Hlth Proj 90-; Occup Thrpy; Pediatric Occup Thrpst.

**DUSSAULT, MICHELLE L,** Endicott Coll, Beverly, MA; FR; BA; Fld Hockey Team 87-90; Bsn Clb 90; NH Attrny Gnrls Off Intrnshp; Hnrs Stdnt; Bsn.

**DUTCH, BARBARA J,** Atlantic Comm Coll, Mays Landing, NJ; SO; BFA; Chldrns Thtr/Chrl 89-; Dns Lst 90-; Gen Studs/Art; Fashn Dsgn/Art.

**DUTCHER, RENEE M,** Va Commonwealth Univ, Richmond, VA; JR; MS; Phi Eta Sigma 89; Phy Thrpy.

**DUTEIL, ARLENE M,** Inter Amer Univ Pr Hato Rey, Hato Rey, PR; SO; MBA; Psy Asc; BA 90; Univ Del Sagardo Corazon Santurce 88; Psy; Doctor Psy.

**DUTEY, JENNIFER L,** Marshall University, Huntington, WV; FR; BA; Phi Eta Sigma 90-; Bus Mgmt; Corp Atty.

**DUTKOVIC, TANYA L,** Pa St Univ Main Cmps, University Pk, PA; FR; BA; Std Advsr Clg Bsn; Alpha Gamma Delta Chr; Bsn; Insurance.

**DUTKOVICH III, FRANK M,** Duquesne Univ, Pittsburgh, PA; SO; BS; Tamburitzans 89-; Acctng.

**DUTTA, KAUSHIK R,** Franklin And Marshall Coll, Lancaster, PA; SO; BA; Cricket Clb VP 90-; Intl Hse Co-Chrmn; Coll Nwspr Jrnlst; Dana Schlrshp; Math Teach Asst; Prtcpnt Modelng Cntst; Math/Bus Admin; Math Rsrch.

**DUTTON, HEATHER ANN,** Savannah Coll Of Art & Design, Savannah, GA; SO; BFA; Fshn Dsgn.

**DUTTON, LISA C,** Hillsborough Comm Coll, Tampa, FL; FR; BSN; Nrsng.

**DUTTON, SANDRA LEIGH,** Dyersburg St Comm Coll, Dyersburg, TN; FR; AS; Phi Theta Kappa 90-; Nrsg.

**DUTTON, VICKY W,** Va Commonwealth Univ, Richmond, VA; SR; BS; Scty Hmn Rsrc Mgmt Dir Prgrmmng 90-; AS JS Reynolds Cmm Coll 84; Bus Admn Mgmt; Hmn Rsrcs.

**DUTY, CHERYL E,** Va Polytechnic Inst & St Univ, Blacksburg, VA; FR; BS; SWE Sec 90-; Coll Bwl 90; YMCA Stdnt Envir Prog Educ Chr 90-; VI Tech Rclcng 90-; Bradley Schlr Elec Eng; Pres Lst 90-; Dns Lst 90-; Elec Eng; NASA Coop.

**DUVA, LINDA D,** Vt Law School, S Royalton, VT; GD; JD; Law Review Hd Notes Ed 89-; Am Jurisprudence Awd Contracts 88; Am Jurisprudence Awd Cmrcl Law 90; BA Dartmouth Coll 87; Law.

**DUVAL, BRIAN M,** Savannah Coll Of Art & Design, Savannah, GA; FR; BA; Photogrphy; Natr/Frlnce Photo.

**DUVAL, RAYMOND L,** Bloomfield Coll, Bloomfield, NJ; JR; BA; Bus.

**DUVAL-LA FLAMME, KAREN C,** Springfield Tech Comm Coll, Springfield, MA; SO; BS; Clg Theatre 90; Advncd TV Prdctn 90-; Trnsfr Stdnt Westfield State Clg; Ran Elctrnc Fld Prdctn Camera Two Moto Crs Shts For Power Sprts Videao CA; BS Mass Cmnctns; Mass Cmnctns; Mjr Prdctn Mnr Jrnlsm.

**DUVALL, ANNE M,** Ms St Univ, Miss State, MS; SO; BA; Am Inst Architecture Stdnts 89-; Gamma Beta Phi; Arch Fndtn Ms Awd Hls Petproducts Dsgn Cmptn; Architecture.

**DUVALL, PAUL S,** Oh St Univ At Marion, Marion, OH; SO; BS; Phi Eta Sigma 90-; Alpha Lambda Delta 90-; Data Proc; Cmptr Prgrmr Anlyst.

**DUVENDECK, DEBRA J,** Oh Univ-Southern Cmps, Ironton, OH; SO; BSN; Aerbcs 90-; Euchre Trnmnts 90-; Deans Lst 90-.

**DVORAK, ANDREA M,** Georgetown Univ, Washington, DC; SO; BA; Bus Admin.

**DVORAK, BONNIE J,** Comm Coll Algny Co Algny Cmps, Pittsburgh, PA; BA; Nrsng Asst; Cert PA Nrs Asst 90; Nrsng.

**DVORAK, JAMES K,** City Univ Of Ny Baruch Coll, New York, NY; JR; BBA; Mgmnt; Indstrl Eng.

**DVORIN, ADAM L,** Glassboro St Coll, Glassboro, NJ; SR; BA; Pblc Rltns Std Soc Amer Exec 89-; Radio Hst 87-; Std Nwspr Wrtr 87-; Gamma Tau Sigma 90-; Kappa Sigma; Sprts Info Std Asst 87-; Comm/Pblc Rltns.

**DVORSHAK, ANDREW J,** Radford Univ, Radford, VA; JR; BBA; Coll Of Bus & Econ Undergrad Advsr 90-; Brdcstr Radio 90-; Stdnt Life Cncrt Comm 90; Mrktng; Envrmntl Rspnsblty Cnsltng.

**DWAN, ROBIN K,** Winthrop Coll, Rock Hill, SC; JR; BFA; Sigma Sigma Sigma; Natl Stdnt Exch; Grphc Dsgn; Advrtsg.

**DWOREK, MICHELLE L,** Dekalb Coll, Decatur, GA; SO; BA; Acdmc Achvmnt Awrd 90; Bus; Accntng.**

**DWORJANYN, LARISSA X,** Univ Of Sc At Columbia, Columbia, SC; JR; BS; French Clb 88; Mrchng Bnd 90; Gamma Beta Phi 89-; Golden Key 90-; Delta Sigma Pi VP; Natl Stdnt Exchng 90; Bus.

**DWYER, BARBARA,** Atlantic Union Coll, S Lancaster, MA; SO; SOWK; Yrbk Edtrs Asst 89-90; Tchr Of Tomorrow Sec 89-90; Socl Wrk; Socl Wrkr.

**DWYER, JENNIFER A,** James Madison University, Harrisonburg, VA; SR; BS; Golden Key 90-; Kappa Delta Pi 90-; Early Chldhd Ed; Tchr.

**DWYER, JENNIFER L,** Christopher Newport Coll, Newport News, VA; SO; BA; Honcncl 89-; Yrbk Asst Edtr 89-; Orentatn 90-; Ldrshp Inst 90-; English.

**DWYER, JILL M,** Seton Hall Univ, South Orange, NJ; FR; BA; Hon Pgm; Bus; Acctg.

**DWYER, KATHLEEN A,** S U N Y Coll Of A & T Morrisvl, Morrisville, NY; FR; AS; Silver Bullets Jr Drum Corp 89-90; Nursing.

**DWYER, KIMBERLY S,** William Paterson Coll, Wayne, NJ; JR; BA; Math.

**DWYER, MARLENE F,** S U N Y Coll Of Tech At Frmgdl, Farmingdale, NY; SO; AAS; Erly Chldhd Clb 89-; Erly Chldhd; Day Care Cartaker.

**DWYER, SANDRA E,** Univ Of Miami, Coral Gables, FL; SR; BS; Master Tutor Pgm 88-90; Rsrch Asst Mobility Proj Univ Miami Dr Eric Vernberg 90-; Cnslng Psychlgy.

**DWYER, SEAN M,** Wagner Coll, Staten Island, NY; SO; BA; Sigma Tau Delta; Engl; Law.

**DWYER, TERI L,** Univ Of Cincinnati, Cincinnati, OH; SO; BS; Kappa Delta Phi; Elem Ed.

**DYAR, CHANDA L,** Univ Of Sc At Columbia, Columbia, SC; SR; BSN; Stu Nrs Assoc Edtr/Hstrn 88-; Yrbk Stf Asst Bus Mgr 89-90; Mary Blck Mem Hosp Auxlry Schlrshp 87-; 500 Hr Awrd 87; Nrsg Extrn Sprtnbrg Reg Med Cntr 90; Chnclrs Lst 90-; Nrsg; Trauma.**

**DYBAS, MICHAEL J,** S U N Y Coll At Fredonia, Fredonia, NY; SR; BS; Pi Mu Epsilon; Phi Theta Kappa 79-80; Deans Lst 78-83 90-; Trangle Frat 77-; Stdnt Tchng Asst 90-; NJCAA Bwlng 78-80; Cstmr Engr/Comp Syst 84-90; BS Rochstr Inst Tech 83; AAS Fltn-Mntgmry Comm Coll 80-; Comp Sci; Prog/Sftwr Engrng.

**DYCHE, LISA MARIE,** Broward Comm Coll, Ft Lauderdale, FL; FR; BA; Narcotics Anonymous Grp Svc Rep; Pres Lst 90; Psych/Scl Wrk; Psychotherapy.

**DYCK, THOMAS L,** Central Fl Comm Coll, Ocala, FL; SO; BA; Phi Theta Kappa; Bus Admin; Acctng.

**DYDYNSKI, DONNA M,** Glassboro St Coll, Glassboro, NJ; JR; BA; Psych Clb 90; Vol Orgnztn Brlngtn Cnty 90-; Strwbrdge & Clthr Employee 86-; ASS Burlington County Coll 85; Psych; Psychlgst.

**DYE, CHRIS M,** Oh Univ, Athens, OH; FR; BS; James Hall Cncl; Secr; IM Brmbl; Chemistry; Chemical Engr.

**DYE, GEORGE W,** Univ Of Nc At Charlotte, Charlotte, NC; JR; BS; IM Stdt Fld Sup 88-; Phi Kappa Sigma Acad 88-; Geography.

**DYE JR, JOSEPH F,** Univ Of Ky, Lexington, KY; SR; BARCH; AIAS 88-90; Stdnt Cncl Mem; Scnd Yr Dsgn Awrd 89-90; Thrd Yr Dsgn Awrd 90; Deans Lst; Archtctr.

**DYE, OZA R,** Univ Of Montevallo, Montevallo, AL; JR; BS; SGA Pblcty Chrmn 89-; SAEA Hstrn; Alpha Lambda Delta 89-; Prsdnts Lst; Ed; Elem Schl Cnslr.

**DYEL, VICKI E,** Hillsborough Comm Coll, Tampa, FL; JR; BA; Ofc Admn 79-90; Lib Arts; Law.

**DYER, AMY LEIGH,** Univ Of Ga, Athens, GA; JR; Ammnvrsty Athens Tutrl Svc 89-; Golden Key 89-; Kappa Delta Epsilon 89-; Erly Chldhd Ed; Tch.

**DYER, DEBORAH L,** Gallaudet Univ, Washington, DC; GD; MA; Pres Schlr 90; Bilng/Bcltrl Intrn IN Schl Deaf; BA Univ NH Durham 89; Linguistics; Deaf Ed/Rsrch.

**DYER, GABRIELLE,** Savannah Coll Of Art & Design, Savannah, GA; FR; Smr Intrshp Mrktg Dept Melvin Simon/Assoc 90.

**DYER, JASON P,** Brewer St Jr Coll, Fayette, AL; SO; MBA; Stdnt Cons Assn 89-90; Band & Chorus 89-; Otstndng Band Stdnt 90-; AS; Chem; Biochem.

**DYER, KRISTI A,** Colby Sawyer Coll, New London, NH; JR; BS; Stdnt Govt/Class Offcr Sec/Treas 88-89; Clg Mag Asst Sprts Ed 88-89; Var Clb Yrbk Phtgrphr; Deans Lst; Ntl Athltc Trnrs Assoc 89-; Key Assoc Pblcty Chr; Clg Alcohol Plcy Cmmttee 90; Res Staff RA RC 89-90; Tchng Assist 90-; Sprts Med; Athletic Trnr/Phy Thrpy.

**DYER, MARJORIE V,** Fl International Univ, Miami, FL; SR; BHSA; Flrd Nrs Assoc Dstrct Fv 87-; Cmmnty Hlth Sth Dd Nrs Chrprsn 89-90; Prctnr Grp; Phi Kappa Phi 90-; Deans Lst 90-; Otstndng Schlr Cert 90-; Flrd Nrs Assoc 86-; Amrcn Nrs Assoc Brd Cert 87-; ARNP 82; RN Cnm 75 79; Hlth Srvc Admn; Chf Exctv Offcr Lwyr.

**DYER, NATALIE C,** Univ Of Tn At Martin, Martin, TN; FR; BS; Mrchn Bnd Drm Mjr 90-; Symphnc Bnd; Alpha Omicrn Pi Almn Rltns; Indstrl Psychlgy.

**DYER, PAMELA K,** Wilberforce Univ, Wilberforce, OH; FR; BA; Chr 90-; Drm Clb; B E Assoc Shft Mgr 90; Mktg; Advrtsng.

**DYER, RACHELLE L,** Middle Tn St Univ, Murfreesboro, TN; SR; BA; Assoc For Cmptng Mchnry 90; BS Tenn Tchnlgcl U 90; Hstry; Tchng.

**DYER, RHONDA J,** Univ Of Montevallo, Montevallo, AL; JR; BA; Kappa Dlt Pi Hstrn; Alpha Gamma Dlt 88-; Deans List 90-; Pres List 90; Erly Chldhd Elem Educ; Tchng.

**DYER, SHERRIE K,** Union Univ, Jackson, TN; GD; BS; Psychology Clb 89-; Pi Gamma Mu 90-; Psychlgy; Cnslng.

**DYER III, WILLIAM B,** Samford Univ, Birmingham, AL; GD; JD; Snr Cls Pres; Jnr Cls Rep 90-; Fresh Cls Rep 89-90; Kappa Alpha; IEEE 82-; Snr Engr 86-89; Law.

**DYES, SHUN L,** Al St Univ, Montgomery, AL; SR; BA; Pan Hellenic Panel Voting Rep 90-F Kappa Alpha Psi Natl Voting Delagate 90-; YMCA Yth Supervisor 88-89; Christian Love MB Church Yth Counselor 87-88; Chicago Boys Club Spl Ed Dir 90-; Hnr Roll 90-; Busn Finance; Corp Law.

**DYESS, CYNTHIA R,** Univ Of South Al, Mobile, AL; SR; BED; Kappa Delta Pi; Cert Med Asst Capps Clg 85; LPN Hobson Tech Clg 82; Early Childhd Educ.

**DYGERT, DANIEL D,** Hudson Valley Comm Coll, Troy, NY; SO; ASC; ECM Club 90; Deans List; Sci/Appld; Elec Maint.

**DYKE, JANIS M,** Univ Of North Fl, Jacksonville, FL; SR; BSH; Phi Kappa Phi; Alpha Omicron Pi; Agng Adlt Stds: Nrsng Hm Admn.

**DYKE, TERESA S,** Marshall University, Huntington, WV; GD; MAT; Grad Stdnt Cncl 90-; Phi Delta Kappa 90-; Grad Asstshp 90-; BS 90; Educ; Tchng.

**DYKEMA, KRISTEN C,** Univ Of Cincinnati, Cincinnati, OH; SR; BA; Civic Orch/Chgo Violinist 85-; Aspen Music Fstvl Violinist 85-; N KY Comm Orch Cncrtmstr 90-; Columbus OH Symp Orch Violinist; Lex KY Phlhrmnc Orch Violinst 89-90; Ernest Heerman Mem Schlrshp 89; Music; Violinist/Major Symp Orch.

**DYKEMA, TAMARA D,** Tallahassee Comm Coll, Tallahassee, FL; FR; BA; Sci; Tchg.

**DYKEMAN, KATHY A,** Univ Of Cincinnati, Cincinnati, OH; FR; BA; Frnch Clb 90-; Grk Week Com 90-; Hmcmng Com 90-; Stdnt Govt Dir Aux Serv 90-; Alpha Lambda Delta; Chi Omega; Tour Gd Univ 90-; Outstndng Com Mbr Stdnt Govt; Hghst GPA Pldg Cls Sor; Intl Rltns/Pltcl Sci; Frgn Serv/Untd Ntns.

**DYKEMAN, MELISSA M,** George Mason Univ, Fairfax, VA; SR; BED; Golden Key 90-; Elem Educ; Teacher.

**DYKES, BETSY MICHELLE,** Middle Ga Coll, Cochran, GA; FR; BA; Crmnl Jstc Clb 90-; Law/Cnslng.

**DYKES, EVELYNN R,** Univ Of Al At Birmingham, Birmingham, AL; FR; BS; Hon Pgm 90-; Early Med Sch Acptnce Pgm 90-; Phi Sigma Delta; Bd Trustees Prfmr; Bio; Physician.

**DYKES, JAMES E,** Schenectady County Comm Coll, Schenectady, NY; FR; AS; Pythagorean Soc P C Users Grp Pres 90-; ELT Cl; Drama Cl; Stdnt Gov Senator; Pres List; Stdnt Rschr; Lab Asst; Curriculum Cmte; Screening Cmte Tchr Excel Awd; Asso/Non Destruct Test; USN Sub Fce Mtce/Opt Tech Asst Sys Mgr Goddard Sp Cen NASA; Math/Sci; Elec Engrng.

**DYKES, LORI A,** East Tn St Univ, Johnson City, TN; FR; MBA; Alpha Lambda Delta 90-; Bus; Bus Admin.

**DYKES, SHANNON P,** Univ Of Md At Eastern Shore, Princess Anne, MD; SO; Airway Sci; Cmrcl Pilot.

**DYKES, WESLEY A,** Univ Of Southern Ms, Hattiesburg, MS; SO; BA; Marching Bnd; Jazz Bnd 90-; Symphonic Bnd 90-; Phi Mu Alpha Sinfonia 90-; Deans Lst 90-; Music Educ; Band Dir.

**DYL, MICHELLE E,** Rutgers St Un At New Brunswick, New Brunswick, NJ; FR; BA; Scarlet Key; Housing Floor Repr 90-; Stdnt Govt 90-; Gamma Phi Beta; Acctg; CPA.

**DYLL, DARCY A,** S U N Y Coll At Fredonia, Fredonia, NY; JR; BS; Inter Grk Coun Pub Rltns 90-; Delta Mu Delta 90-; Natl Soc Pershing Rifles 89-; Delta Phi Epsilon Rsh Chrmn 88-; ROTC; Brmbl; Acctntng; Army Ofcr 2nd Lt.

**DYMKOWSKI, LEA BUFFY,** Temple Univ, Philadelphia, PA; SR; Drm Snt 87-88; Jdcl Brd Sec 89-90; Alpha Lambda Delta 86-87; Gldn Key 87-88; Psychlgy Hnrs Prgm 88-90; BA 90; Psychlgy.

**DYMON, ANNMARIE A,** Western New England Coll, Springfield, MA; JR; BS; DPMA 90-; Dns Lst 89-; Cmptr Info Syst; Cmptr Pgm.

**DYNAK, DOROTHY S,** Western New England Coll, Springfield, MA; FR; Acctng.

**DYSART, CHARLES SCOTT,** Piedmont Tech Coll, Greenwood, SC; GD; Phi Theta Kappa 90-; Dns Lst 90-; Bsktbl/Sftbl; Chrch Bsktbl/Sftbl; Grnwd Mlls Weaver; Indl Mgmt; Engr.

**DYSART, DENNIS A,** Bridgewater Coll, Bridgewater, VA; SO; BS; SG 90-; Stdnt Affrs 90-; Cum De 90-; Lambda Soc 90-; Hons Schlrshp; Track/Fld; Bus Admin/Econs; Bus Law.

**DYSART, JEAN N,** Roane St Comm Coll, Harriman, TN; SO; BS; Deans Lst 90-; Hlth Physcs Techncn 88-; AAS Ashvl Buncombe Tech Comm Coll 88; AAS Roane St Comm Coll; Eng; Hlth Physcst.

**DYSON, CARLA D,** Western Piedmont Comm Coll, Morganton, NC; FR; Intr Dsgn Clb; Clb Nwsltr Ed; Intr Dsgn.

**DYSON, HOLLY A,** Commonwealth Coll, Virginia Beach, VA; SR; AAS; St James AME Chrch Schlrshp; Red Crss Vlntr; Fash Clb; Deans Lst; Fash Merch; Bus Admin.

**DYSON, LISA R,** Longwood Coll, Farmville, VA; JR; BS; Stdnt Cncl Excptnl Chldrn VP St Brd 89-; Res Asst 90-; Psi Chi 90-; Geist VP; Peer Hlprs Chrprsn Mrktng 88-; Jr Mrshl; Dns Lst 90-; Psych/Spec Educ; Chld Psych.

**DYSON, MIRANDA,** Univ Of Sc At Columbia, Columbia, SC; FR; BA; Chem Engr.

**DZIECH, SARA J,** Univ Of Cin R Walters Coll, Blue Ash, OH; FR; AAB; Acctg.

**DZIEZYNSKI, KRISTINE,** Teikyo Post Univ, Waterbury, CT; SR; BA; Drama Clb 87-90; Alpha Chi; Presidential Schlrshps 89-; Deans Lst 87-; AS Univ Conn 89; Business Mngmnt.

**DZIJA, JENNIFER A,** Elms Coll, Chicopee, MA; SR; BA; Math; Actarial Studies.

**DZIKOWSKI, CHRISTINA,** Allegheny Coll, Meadville, PA; SR; BA; Choir 88; Panhellenic Cncl Pblc Rltns Chr 89-90; Lambda Sigma 88-89; Order Of Omega 89; Alpha Delta Pi 88; Alden Schlr 87; Stdnt Assist Ofc Pblc Affairs 87; Mortimer E Graham Schlr 90-; Engl; Tchng.

**DZIOK, JENNIFER A,** Germanna Comm Coll, Locust Grove, VA; FR; AAS; Amer Crmnl Jstce Assoc 90-; IM Vllybl 90-; Pol Sci; Law.

**DZION, MICHELE D,** Univ Of Akron, Akron, OH; JR; BS; Mu Kappa Tau; Pi Sgm Epsln VP Cmnctns 90-; Robert/Helen Mitten Schlrshp; Acad Schlrshp 90; Mktg.

**DZIUBICH, CHRISTINA M,** Brescia Coll, Owensboro, KY; FR; Student Govt Assoc 90-; Circle K Treas 90-; Freshman Pres 90-; Elem Ed; Tchng.

**DZUBAN, DANIEL N,** Kent St Univ Kent Cmps, Kent, OH; JR; BA; Sem Stdy In Wash DC; Res Hl Adv; Pi Sigma Alpha; Gldn Ky; Hons Clg 88-; Delta Tau Delta Pldg Cls Pres; Parlgl Lgl Cnsl For Eldrly Wash DC; Paralgl Intrn DE Co Prosctr 89; Deputy Clrk DE Muncpl Crt 88; Vars Ftbl 89; Pol Sci; Law.

**DZUPINKA, GEORGE JOHN,** S U N Y Coll Of Tech At Alfred, Alfred, NY; FR; BA; Electrncs; Elect Engr.

# E

**EADDY, ELIZABETH ANN L,** Univ Of Sc At Columbia, Columbia, SC; SR; BS; Deans Lst; Pres Lst 90; Stdnt Of Yr Mgmt; Chrch Choir Dir/SS Tchr 86-; Lgl Sec 70-; AA Wlmsbrg Tech Coll 86; Mgmt; Law.

**EADDY, JOY L,** Univ Of Sc At Columbia, Columbia, SC; JR; BS; Stdnt Orient Ldr 90; Cncrt Bnd 89; Phi Eta Phi 88; Golden Key 89; Alpha Lambda Delta 88; Beta Alpha Psi Corr Sctry 90; Accntng; Tax.

**EADDY, KASSANDRA,** Morris Coll, Sumter, SC; SO; BA; Peer Counselor 90-; Fine Arts; Advertising Agent.

**EADES, DESIREE L,** Coppin St Coll, Baltimore, MD; FR; BA; English; Law/Professor.

**EADS, BARRY K,** Brewer St Jr Coll, Fayette, AL; FR; BS; Phi Theta Kappa; Brewer Biology Awd; Amer Heart Assn80; BCLS Instr; W Ala Engr Med Serv; EMT Instr; Natl Reg Paramedic; LPN; Ambulance Serv Dir; LPN 75; Cert Paramedic 79; Nurs/Sciz; Nurs Admn.

**EADY, APASRA D,** Johnson C Smith Univ, Charlotte, NC; JR; BS; Pres Grenfld Hall 90-; Alpha Lappa Mu; Acctng.

**EADY, SCHENTERIAL M,** Ga Inst Of Tech At Atlanta, Atlanta, GA; FR; BS; Global Site Analysis Intern; IM Bsktbl/Vlybl; Econ/Bsn Mgmt; Own Bsn.

**EAGAN, TIMOTHY J,** Gaston Coll, Dallas, NC; FR; AS; Machnst 2nd Shft Leadmn Ingersoll Rand Pump Serv Charlotte 89-; Phys Sci; Engr.

**EAGEN, KERRY K,** Elmira Coll, Elmira, NY; SR; BS; Leag Intern Spch Pthlgst Sec 89-; Dean Lst 89-; Spch Hrng; Pthlgy.

**EAGLE, ELEANOR,** Saint Andrews Presbytrn Coll, Laurinburg, NC; FR; BA; CSO; Comm Thtr Dncr; CAR VP; Elem Ed; Tch.

**EAGLE III, EVERETT W,** Radford Univ, Radford, VA; JR; BS; Cmpgn Vol; UPE; Plnt Nwsppr; Tmstr Mbr; Mrktg; Grad Schl/US Mltry Offcr.

**EAGLES, MARILYN B,** Seton Hall Univ, South Orange, NJ; JR; BS; Brownie Ldr; Sunday Sch Tchr; Clsrm Mother; Township Wmns Clb; Sch Libr Vol; Gas Co Home Economist; Institutional Fd Sls; BA Montclair State Clg 68; Nrsg.

**EAKER, ANTHONY D,** Ms Gulf Coast Comm Coll, Perkinston, MS; SO; BME; Guitar Orch USM 89-; Hnrs Pgm 89-; Phi Theta Kappa 90-; De Molay Chpln 85-; Outstndg Perf Clscl Guitar Awd 89-90; Completion Hnrs Pgm MGCCC Awd 89-; Dns Endowmnt Perf Awd Clscl Guitar Univ S MS; Guitar Msc Ed/Perf; Tchg Clg/Perf.

**EAKES, BRIAN M,** Christopher Newport Coll, Newport News, VA; SR; BS; SGA 90-; Budget/Finance Com 90-; Coll Hon Soc Class Rep 90-; Alpha Chi 90-; Acctg; Law.

**EAKES, JAMES D,** Old Dominion Univ, Norfolk, VA; JR; BS; Phi Theta Kappa 87-89; Cvl Eng.

**EAKES, JANET L,** Memphis St Univ, Memphis, TN; JR; BA; Phi Kappa Phi; Delta Zeta Chrmn 90-; Bsn; Acctng.

**EAKES, JO A,** Meridian Comm Coll, Meridian, MS; SR; LPN; Hlth; Nsg.

**EAKES, KEVIN W,** Appalachian St Univ, Boone, NC; FR; BM; Assoc Educs; Tchng Fllws; Gamma Beta Phi; Tchng Fllws Exec Cncl Rep; Dns Lst; Music Educs Awd/Schlrshp; Spkr Natl Clgt Hons Cncl; Spkr NC Cllgt Hons Conf; Music Educ.

**EAKIN, EDNA J,** Al A & M Univ, Normal, AL; FR.

**EAKIN, RAYMOND J,** Youngstown St Univ, Youngstown, OH; JR; BE; Inst Elec Electrnc Eng Pr; Elec Eng.

**EAKINS, ANGELA D,** Wv Univ At Parkersburg, Parkersburg, WV; JR; BA; Dns Lst Mrshl Univ 88-89; Dns Lst WVU-P 90; Bus; Mgmt.

**EAKINS, CHAJUANDA,** Lincoln Univ, Lincoln Univ, PA; JR; Acctg Clb 89-; Frnch Clb 90-; Hd Mngr/Stattcn Mens Bsktbl 88-; Acctg; CPA.

**EALY, BARBARA R,** Fayetteville St Univ, Fayetteville, NC; SO; BS; Chrldng 89-90; Mrchng Bnd 90-; ABLE 90-; Hon Prog 89-; Acctg.

**EAMES, ARLYN C,** Univ Of New Haven, West Haven, CT; JR; BS; Alpha Lambda Delta 90-; Eta Sigma Delta; Trvl/Tourism Admnstrtn; Mtng/Trvl Plnr.

**EAMES, RYAN E,** Univ Of Nh Plymouth St Coll, Plymouth, NH; SO; BED; Dns Lst 90; Pres Lst; Elem Ed; Tch.

**EANS, SORENNA M,** Univ Of Md Baltimore Prof Schl, Baltimore, MD; GD; MD; Amer Soc Mcrblgy 87-88; Amer Med Stu Assn 88-89; Jvnl Dbts Fndtn Med Stu Wrkshp 90; Gldn Ky; Phi Sigma 87-88; Sigma Alpha Omicro; Phi Kappa Phi; Alpha Omega Alpha VP; Chncllrs Schlrshp 83-87; MA Dist Schlrs Schlrshp 83-87; IM Vllybl Sftb 88; BS 88; Med.

**EARBY, KIMBERLY S,** Alcorn St Univ, Lorman, MS; SO; BS; Deans Lst 89-; Bio/Med Tech; Med Tech.

**EARDLEY, LAURA J,** East Stroudsburg Univ, E Stroudsburg, PA; SR; Spch Cmnctn Assn 88-; Phi Sigma Sigma 89-; BA; Spch Cmnctns; Publ Rel.

**EARGLE, CAROL D,** Piedmont Tech Coll, Greenwood, SC; SR; AA; Psi Beta 90-; Human Serv; Tchr.

**EARGLE, DEE A,** Winthrop Coll, Rock Hill, SC; SO; Big Bro/Big Sis 89-90; Glee Clb 90-; Epsilon Sigma Alpha 90-; Specl Educ; Elem Guidance.

**EARHART, CYNTHIA S,** Gallaudet Univ, Washington, DC; SR; BS; German Club 87; Orient Club 90; Food Comm Gally Zoo 87; Dcrtn Comm Snwbll 88; Delta Phi Epsilon; Mgmt/Entrepreneurial.

**EARL, DAVID R,** Bowling Green St Univ, Bowling Green, OH; FR; BA; Aerotechnlgy; Airln Trnsprt Pilot.

**EARL, ELIZABETH J,** Saint Joseph Coll, West Hartford, CT; SR; BS; Chr 89-90; Sigma Theta Tau; Nrsng.

**EARL, LA SHONE D,** Central St Univ, Wilberforce, OH; FR; BA; Engl; Corp Law.

**EARL, MIA D,** Alcorn St Univ, Lorman, MS; SR; BS; ROTC 86-; Hon Soc Pershng Rfls Sec 88-; Miss Nrsng 88-89; Collgt Awrd 90-; Biolgy; Hlth Ed/Nrsng.

**EARLE, ANGELA K,** Limestone Coll, Gaffney, SC; JR; BA; Accts Payagle/Traffic Advsr Hamricks Inc; Lavonia Bapt Church Minister Msc; Bsn; Acctg.

**EARLE, ERIN K,** Fl International Univ, Miami, FL; SO; BA; Spec Ed; Tchr.

**EARLE, REGINA M,** Newbury Coll, Brookline, MA; FR; Sr Offc Asst 88-; Cert Univ London 80; Cert Univ Cambridge 83; Admin Asst.

**EARLE, RICHARD H,** Fayetteville St Univ, Fayetteville, NC; SO; BS; 4.0 Club; Armed Forces Cmntcns Electrncs Assoc; Assoc Of US Army; Retires Army Ofcr; AA San Jose City Clg 60; BA San Jose State Univ 62; Math; Tchng.

**EARLES, KIMBERLY D,** Averett Coll, Danville, VA; FR; BS; Cmptr Sci; Cmptr Pgmr.

**EARLEY, APRIL J,** Bryant Stratton Bus Inst Roch, Rochester, NY; AS; Word Prcsng Sec; Admin Asst.

**EARLEY, CLARISSA K,** Central St Univ, Wilberforce, OH; JR; BA; Phi Kappa Mu 88-; Univ Tour Choir Sctn Ldr 88-; Cncrt Chorale Cbnt 89-; Univ Hnrs Prog 88; Phi Mu Alpha VP 89-; Poetry Awd/Creative Wrtng 89-; Prncpls Schlrshp Awd 88; Otstdng Chrl Mbr 90-; Radio TV Commnctn; Intl Affrs.

**EARLS, KEYETRA F,** Alcorn St Univ, Lorman, MS; FR; BA; Vllybl; Cmptr Sci.

**EARLY, DANIEL E,** Univ Of Nc At Asheville, Asheville, NC; FR; BS; Undergrad Rsrch Jrnl 90-; Undergrad Rsrch Flw 90-; Chem; Rsrch Chemist.

**EARLY, THERESA L,** Ky St Univ, Frankfort, KY; SR; BA; Stdnt Govt Sntr 86-88; Cheerleader Co-Capt; Intrnshp W/Frnkln Cnty Rgnl Jail; Track/Cross Cntry Capt 86-90; Sclgy; Law.

**EARNEST, AMY E,** George Mason Univ, Fairfax, VA; SO; BS; Dcsn Sci Clb 90-; Alpha Lambda Delta 90-; Coop FDIC; Mgmt Info Syst; Pgmg Comp.

**EARNEST, JENNIFER S,** Union Univ, Jackson, TN; FR; Ed; Elem Ed.

**EARNEST, PAMELA K,** Chattahoochee Vly St Comm Coll, Phenix City, AL; SO; BS; Sci; Phrmcy.

**EARNEST, TARA E,** Edinboro Univ Of Pa, Edinboro, PA; SO; ASPCE; Psych Cl 90; Photo Cl; Phi Eta Sigma Treas 90-; Hon Prog; Dr R E Ackerman Psych Schlrshp 89-90; Schlrshp/Summer Abroad/Oxford Un 90; Engrng; Envnmtl Engrng.

**EARNHARDT III, WILLIAM F,** East Tn St Univ, Johnson City, TN; SR; MBA; Assc Gen Cntrctrs Amer Tres 88-; Natl Assc Hm Bldrs 90-; Prof Assc Dvng Inst; Epsilon Pi Tau; Deans Lst; Co-Op TN Eastman Co 89-90; BS; Construction Eng Tech; Mgmt.

**EARNST, KEVIN L,** Univ Of Al, Tuscaloosa, AL; FR; BS; Phi Eta Sigma; Alpha Lambda Delta; Deans Lst 90-; Pres Schlr 90-; Harriet/Walter Smith Engr Schlrshp; IM Sccr/Glf 90; Aerspc/Elect Eng; Eng.

**EASLER, CINDY L,** Univ Of Sc At Spartanburg, Spartanburg, SC; SR; BA; Univ Bus Soc 88-; Treas 89-90; Frshmn Advsry Cncl 88-; V Pres 89-; Grad Univ Ldrshp Dvlpmnt 88-90; Intrnshp Spartanburg Childrens Shelter 89; Bus Admnstrn; Marketing.

**EASLER, SHARI S,** Greenville Tech Coll, Greenville, SC; FR; Clerk Typust Receptionist; Certif; Engrg Graphics; Computer/Design.

**EASLEY, JEROME A,** Ms Univ For Women, Columbus, MS; SR; BS; Paralegal Assn Treas 90-; Historical Scty 90-; SMAE 89-; Paralegal; Law.

**EASLEY, PAIGE LOUISE,** Savannah Coll Of Art & Design, Savannah, GA; JR; BFA; Illstrtn Soc 88-89; Jwlrs Clb Sec 90-; Coll Deans Lst 88-; Grl Scts USA 76-; Frncs/Lskn/Mccmmn Schlrshp 88-; Ilstrtn.

**EASLEY, ROY L,** Ms St Univ, Miss State, MS; SR; BS; Frstry Clb 890-90; Wildlf Soc 89-90; Soc Amer Frstrs; Phi Kappa Phi; Xi Sigma Pi; Acad Achvmnt 87-88 90-; Frstry/Wldlf.

**EASLEY-WITCHER, TERRI L,** Patrick Henry Comm Coll, Martinsville, VA; SO; MS; Non-Tradtl Students Orgtn VP 90-; Student Advisory Council; Phi Theta Kappa 90-; Sergeant USAF/AIR Force Reserve 83-89; Learning Disblts; Middle/H Schl Instr.

**EASON, ADAM G,** Middle Ga Coll, Cochran, GA; SO; BS; SGA Sntr 90-; Harris Res Hall VP 90-; Clg Rppglcns Clb Svp 90-; Gamma Beta Phi Hnry Mbr 90-; SADD Treas 90-; Stdnts Actvs Comm Advsr 90-; Harris Res Hl Rm Asst 90-; Bapt Stdnt Un Mbr 89-; Soph Sprltv Awd 90-; SADD Awd 90-; Biochemistry; Medicine.

**EASON, KATHY D,** Chattanooga St Tech Comm Coll, Chattanooga, TN; FR; Med Rcrd Tchnlgy.

**EASON, NICOLE,** Anne Arundel Comm Coll, Arnold, MD; SO; Dance Co 90-; Psychlgy; Chld Psychlgst.

**EASON III, THOMAS G,** Southern Coll Of Tech, Marietta, GA; SR; BSMET; ASME Chrmn 88-; Bldg Hmn Pwrs Vhcl 88-; Coop Glfstrm Arspc Corp 87-90; Eng; Grad Sch.

**EASTEP, TERESA D,** Bridgewater Coll, Bridgewater, VA; SO; BS; SG 89-; Pre Med Soc 90-; Vlybl 89-90; Bio; Med.

**EASTER, ANGELA C,** Greensboro Coll, Greensboro, NC; FR; BS; Cmmtr Clb 90-; Stdnt Asst In Acad Comp Cntr And Comp Wrtng Cntr 90-; Tutor 90-; Bus Admin; Bus Admin Mgmt Acct Comp Porgrmmr.

**EASTER, BRENDA J,** Wv Univ At Parkersburg, Parkersburg, WV; FR; AAS; Bus Admin.

**EASTER, KELLY A,** Springfield Tech Comm Coll, Springfield, MA; SR; AS; Ski Clb Treas 88; Radiation Therapy Tchnlgy.

**EASTER, STEPHANIE L,** Wv Univ At Parkersburg, Parkersburg, WV; Bsn; Acctng.

**EASTERLIN, AMY D,** Univ Of Sc At Columbia, Columbia, SC; FR; BA; Stdnt Govt Assn Sec 90-; Annl Stff Stdnt Life Edtr 90-; Gamma Beta Phi 90-; Erly Chldhd Ed.

**EASTERLING, JEFFREY J,** Univ Of Sc At Columbia, Columbia, SC; FR; Bsbl Tm 90-; Bsns Admn.

**EASTERLING, SARAH T,** Univ Of Ky, Lexington, KY; JR; BA; Wildlife Soc; Golden Key; Wildlife Rsrch; Naturalist; 4-H Pgm Asst; BS Eastern KY Univ 85; Elem Edn; Tchr.

**EASTERLY, DAVID A,** Univ Of Akron, Akron, OH; JR; BA; Acctg Assn 88-; Intrnshp Acctg Publ Acctg Firm; Publ Acctg.

**EASTERLY, DONALD W,** Univ Of Akron, Akron, OH; JR; BS; Intrnshp Public Acctg Firm; Acctg; Public.

**EASTERLY, MARSHA L,** Daemen Coll, Amherst, NY; SO; BS; Spcl Olympcs 89-; VA Hosp 90-; IM Vlybl/Bsktbl 90-; Physcl Thrpy.

**EASTERWOOD, ALLYSON G,** Univ Of Southern Ms, Hattiesburg, MS; SR; BSBA; Beta Gamma Sigma 90-; Beta Alpha Psi 89-; Delta Delta Delta Almna; Pres Lst Schlr; F Kenamnd Acctg Thry Awrd; Asst Dir Mssn Frnds Frst Bptst Chrch 90-; Bptst Yng Wmn 87-; Acctg; Pub Acctg.

**EASTHAM, EVELYN L,** Ashland Comm Coll, Ashland, KY; SO; BA; Acctng; Law.

**EASTMAN, ALAN W,** Univ Of Sc At Coastal Carolina, Conway, SC; FR; BS; Hon Prog; Phi Eta Sigma; Marine Sci; Marine Biolgy.

**EASTMAN, EDWARD R,** Coll Of Charleston, Charleston, SC; JR; BS; Omicron Delta Kappa 90-; Corp U S Marine Corps Elite Recnsnce Unit 84-88; Biology; Ph D College Prof.

**EASTMAN, SHANNON L,** Ms St Univ, Miss State, MS; SO; BS; Clg Repblcns 90-; Kappa Delta Asstnt Rush Chrmn; Adult Literacy 90-; Biology; Medicine.

**EASTMAN, STEPHANIE P,** Immaculata Coll, Immaculata, PA; JR; BS; Cub Scout Asst Den Ldr/Tr Yth Clb 90-; VP Epsc Church Women 89-; Bus Owner/Licensed Realtor/Resrch Asst 80-89; AA Cmnty Clg Of Delaware Co 70; Psych.

**EASTON, ERIN A,** Va Commonwealth Univ, Richmond, VA; JR; BS; Psi Chi 90-; Golden Key Secy; Phi Mu Schlrshp Chmn 90-; Psychlgy; Adol Coun.

**EASTON, JAMES P,** S U N Y Coll At Fredonia, Fredonia, NY; SO; BA; Bsn; Mktg.

**EATMON, JAMES L,** Radford Univ, Radford, VA; SR; BS; Geography; Info Systems.

**EATON, AMANDA K,** Carnegie Mellon Univ, Pittsburgh, PA; FR; AB Tech 90-; Chmcl Engnrng.

**EATON, ANGELA C,** Vance Granville Comm Coll, Henderson, NC; FR; AAS; Phi Theta Kappa; Deans Lst 90; Schlstc Schlrshp; Bus Cmptr Pgmng.

**EATON, HEATHER R,** Univ Of Tn At Martin, Martin, TN; SO; Stdnt Aflt Amer Chem Scty 89-90; Phi Eta Sigma 90-; Alpha Omicron Pihsmngr 89-; Meth Sundy Schl Tchr 89-; Adopt A Hwy Pgm 89-; Deans Lst 89-; IM; Pharmacy.**

**EATON, MARY A,** Itawamba Comm Coll, Fulton, MS; SO; BPA; Phi Beta Lambda Pres 89-; Indn Dlgtn 89-; Stdnts Fr Entrprs VP 90-; Deans Lst 90-; Acctg.

**EATON, STEVEN A,** Central Fl Comm Coll, Ocala, FL; FR; BS; Phi Theta Kappa; Eng; Eng Mgmt.

**EATON, THERESA M,** Commonwealth Coll, Virginia Beach, VA; SO; Amer Assn Of Med Assts 90-; MSP Navy Wives Grp Pr 90-; Med Admin; Nursing.

**EAVES, KATHERINE A,** Union Univ, Jackson, TN; SR; Acctg Clb; Rutledge Hist Soc; Pre-Legal Soc; Stdnt Senate; Panhellenic Cncl; Hon Pgm; Alpha Chi; Chi Omega Rush Ofcr; Schlrs Excell Recpt; IM Bsktbl; BS; Acctg; CPA.

**EAVES, PAMELA C,** Univ Of Sc At Columbia, Columbia, SC; JR; BS; Pharmacy.

**EAVES, TINA R,** Univ Of Ky, Lexington, KY; JR; BED; Campus Crusade 89-; SAVE; ADD 90-; Delta Zeta Points Chrmn 88-; Spcl Edn/Early Elem Edn; Tchr.

**EBAUGH, MELISSA S,** Va Commonwealth Univ, Richmond, VA; SR; BS; Psychlgy; Psychtrc Nrsng.

**EBBELER, CHARLES E,** Tri County Tech Coll, Pendleton, SC; SO; ACJ; Crmnl Jstc; Law Enfrcmnt.

**EBBERT, BETH A,** Radford Univ, Radford, VA; SO; BS; Dns Lst 90-; Educ; Tchr.

**EBE, DAWN,** Oh St Univ, Columbus, OH; SR; BA; Circle K Intrnl Dist K/Family Chair 87; Alpha Lambda Delta/Phi 87-88; Romophos 88-89; Bucket/Dipper 89-90; Arts/Science Excllnc Acdmncs Awrd 90; Western Psychtr Inst Clinic Intrnshp 90; Psychlgy; Phd.

**EBELHAR, STACIE R,** Owensboro Comm Coll, Owensboro, KY; SO; BS; Bus; Acctng.

**EBELING, CINDY M,** Gallaudet Univ, Washington, DC; FR; BA; Nwspr Rep 90-; Stdnt Body Gov Hstrn; Stdnt Body Govt Sec; Hon Stdnt Org 90-; Stdnt Rep Natl Clgiate Hons Cncl 90.

**EBERHARD, MELANIE,** Westminster Choir Coll, Princeton, NJ; JR; BM; Symphnc Choir 89-; Organ Perf; Psy.

**EBERHARDT, NATALIE J,** Oh Univ, Athens, OH; FR; BFA; Alpha Lambda Delta; Art; Grphc Dsgn.

**EBERSBERGER, KASEY,** Comm Coll Algny Co Algny Cmps, Pittsburgh, PA; SO; Aviators Clb 90-; Phi Theta Kappa 89; Pilot.

**EBERSOLE, KERRY A,** Marywood Coll, Scranton, PA; SR; BA; Ski Clb 88-89; Karate Clb 88-89; Sigma Pi Mu 88-90; Pi Gamma Mu 89; Prelaw-Eng; Law.

**EBERT, DONNA A,** Rutgers St Univ At Camden, Camden, NJ; SR; BS; Mgmt; Mktg Advrtsng.

**EBLE, LYNN M,** Univ Of Montevallo, Montevallo, AL; FR; BS; Cvtn Clb; Alpha Lambda Delta; Soc Stds; Tch.

**EBLIN, CHRISTINE R,** Oh St Univ At Marion, Marion, OH; FR; MBA; Psychlgy; Law.

**EBLIN II, DANNY L,** Oh St Univ At Marion, Marion, OH; FR; Psychlgy Clb 90-; Phi Eta Sigma 90-; Alpha Lambda Delta 90-; Engnrng; Elctrcl Engnrng.

**EBY, ELIZABETH A,** Philadelphia Coll Pharm & Sci, Philadelphia, PA; GD; MPT; Phy Thrpy Clb 86-; Upsilon Sigma Phi Pres 87-; Chrldng 86-88; BS; Phy Thrpy.

**EBY, HUMBERTO S,** Fl International Univ, Miami, FL; JR; BBA; Fnnc/Intl Bus; Mny Mngmnt.

**EBY, KERRY R,** Middle Tn St Univ, Murfreesboro, TN; SR; MBA; Coll Repblcns Clb; AOPA 87-89; Dorm Prest; IM 86-87; Phi Kapp Phi 90-; Phi Kappa Phi 90-; Phi Beta Lambda 87-; Gamma Beta Phi Sec 87-; Vrsty Chrldr 89-; Southeastern Arprt Mngrs Assc Schlstc Schlrshp 90-; All Amer Schlr 88-90; Plt Lic; Strategio Mngmnt; Aviation Mngmnt.**

**EBY, KRISTIN L,** Univ Of The Arts, Philadelphia, PA; FR; BFA; Vlybl League 90; Dance; Brdwy Dnc Company.

**EBY, VALERIE DENISE,** Univ Of Al, Tuscaloosa, AL; FR; BS; Fr Frm 90-; Cmmrce And Bus Admin Stdnt Exec Cncl 90-; Rho Epsilon 90-; Delta Zeta Pldge Clss Treas 90-; Almni Assc Schlrshp 90-; Comp Mgmt; Bus.

**ECCLI, DORENE,** Georgetown Univ, Washington, DC; SR; BSBA; Acctg Soc 89-; Chi Omega 87-90; Acctg; Publ Acctg.

**ECHAVARRIA ROJAS, ALEJANDRO F,** Jersey City St Coll, Jersey City, NJ; SR; BA; Stdnt Act Offce Brookdl Comm Clg 88; Adv Clb Schlrshp; Dist Schlr Brkdl Comm Clg 89; ASBEE Schlrshp Awd; Indr Trck Fld 89; AAS Brookdl Comm Clg 89; AA 89; Media Arts; Mstrs Film Prod.

**ECHELBERGER, MARY ANN,** Va Commonwealth Univ, Richmond, VA; GD; MD; Vol Wrk Local Free Clinic 88-; Phi Eta Sigma; Phi Kappa Phi; Sys Analyst Undergrad 78-87; BS 88; Med; Psychlgy.

**ECHEVARRIA, KEITH A,** Springfield Tech Comm Coll, Springfield, MA; SO; BA; Alpha Nu Omega 90; Vars Bsebl 90; Cmnctns; Telecmnctns.

**ECHEVARRIA-CORTES, WIHELMA,** Univ Of Pr At Rio Piedras, Rio Piedras, PR; JR; Pre-Med Assn 88-; Beta Beta Beta 88-; Deans Lst 89-; Gldn Key 90-; Sci; Med.

**ECHEVARRIA-ROSADO, ROSALINE,** Univ Of Pr At Mayaguez, Mayaguez, PR; SO; BA; Amer Mktg Assn 90-; Dns Lst Schl Busn 89-90; Admin VPR Mayagz Camps 90-; Mktg; Advrtsng/Law.

**ECHOLS, ANDREA D,** Ms St Univ, Miss State, MS; JR; BA; Crrctns Assoc 89; Pre-Law Scty 89; Sclgy/Crmnl Jstce; Crmnl Attrny.

**ECHOLS, CAROLE M,** Clark Atlanta Univ, Atlanta, GA; JR; BA; Pol Sci Clb; Pre-Law Soc; OACC; NAACP; Big Sis Pgm; Pol Sci/Intl Rel; Coop Law.

**ECK, TRACY J,** Indiana Univ Of Pa, Indiana, PA; SR; BED; Stdnt Govt 87-88; Deans Lst; Alpha Sigma Tau VP/PLDGE Cls 90-; Metacognitive Strategies Proj IN Sch Dist 90; Study Skls Pgm Ftbl Tm; Stdnt Teach Fox Chapel HS Pittsburg; Scndry Soc Sci Edn/Hist; Teach.**

**ECKARD, DANA L,** Univ Of Tn At Chattanooga, Chattanooga, TN; SO; BS; SWE; Chem Engr.

**ECKARD, LORI D,** Lenoir Rhyne Coll, Hickory, NC; JR; BA; Sigma Kappa Alumni; Art; Graphics/Animation.

**ECKE, APRIL LYNN,** Ms St Univ, Miss State, MS; FR; M Clb 90-; Phi Eta Sigma 90-; Lambda Sigma 90-; Prsdnts Lst 90; Athltc Hnr Rl 90; Crs Cntry Trck Vrsty 90-; Hstry Gvrnmnt; Scndry Ed.

**ECKEL, EMILY J,** Comm Coll Algny Co Algny Cmps, Pittsburgh, PA; BS; Pgh Pblc Schls Cbntry Advsry Comm; Dsgnr/Woodwrkr; BFA Carnegie Mellon Unv 71; Occptnl Thrpy.

**ECKENROAD, TODD A,** Saint Francis Coll, Loretto, PA; FR; BS; Hnr Prgrm 90-; Ftbll 90; Accntng; CPA.

**ECKENRODE, DENISE M,** Mount Aloysius Jr Coll, Cresson, PA; JR; BA; Bus Admin; Acctng.

**ECKENRODE, JENNIFER A,** Saint Francis Coll, Loretto, PA; SO; BS; Hnrs Prog 89-; Acctng Club 89-; Schlr Awd 89-; Acctng CPA.

**ECKENRODE, KIMBERLY L,** East Tn St Univ, Johnson City, TN; SR; BS; Gamma Beta Phi; AAS; Eng Dsgn Grphcs; Eng Tchnlgy.

**ECKENRODE, MARY ELAINE,** Saint Francis Coll, Loretto, PA; SO; BS; Lic Prac Nurse; Crim Just/Soc.

**ECKERT, JEANE F,** Anne Arundel Comm Coll, Arnold, MD; SO; BA; Cntr Spc Iss Soc Forum 90; Phi Theta Kappa; Psychlgy.

**ECKERT, MARK A,** Villanova Univ, Villanova, PA; JR; BA; Spec Olympcs 90-; Prjct Snshn; Intrnshp Kewalo Basin Marine Mammal Lab; Vlybl 90-; Psychlgy; Grad Schl/Neuro Sci Clncl Nrpsychlg.

**ECKERT, PATRICIA A,** Coll Misericordia, Dallas, PA; SR; BS; CEC; AS Lunerne Cnty Comm Clg 89; Spec Educ; Tch.

**ECKERT, VIRGINIA E,** Kent St Univ Geauga Cmps, Burton Twp, OH; FR; BA; Lgl Sec-Benesch Friedlander Coplan/Aronoff; Bus/Cmnctns.

**ECKES, AUDRA L,** Univ Of Md At College Park, College Park, MD; FR; BS; Stdnt Govt Mnthly Nwsppr Phtgrphy Ed 90-; Mrchng Bnd 90-; Cncrt Bnd 90-; Jrnlsm.

**ECKHARDT, SEAN L,** Bowling Green St Univ, Bowling Green, OH; SO; BS; Visual Comm Tech Organ; Visual Comm Tech; Print Indstry.

**ECKHARDT, VALERIE Y,** Liberty Univ, Lynchburg, VA; SR; BS; Psych Club 90-; Clg Repubs 89-; Psi Chi 90-; VPA 90-; Mental Hlth Ctr 89-90; Liberty Godparent Home For Preg Women 90-; Psych.

**ECKLER, JEFFREY M,** Bowling Green St Univ At Huron, Huron, OH; JR; BA; VIA Yth Clb 89-; Deans Lst 89-; Elem Edn/Spanish; Teach.

**ECKMAN, DEBORAH M,** Bryant Stratton Bus Inst Roch, Rochester, NY; SO; AOS; Bus Mgmt Clb Sec 90-; Rochester Brnch Ltrcy; Amer; BA SUNY 71; MLS Uni HI 72; Bus Mgmt.

**ECKMAN, PETER M,** Va St Univ, Petersburg, VA; SO; MS; US Cycling Fed 89-; Richmond Velosport Signet Bank Cycling Tm 89-; Deans Lst 90; Architecture.

**ECKMEIER, ANNETTE L,** Fayetteville St Univ, Fayetteville, NC; JR; BA; Art Clb Pres 90-; PTA 90-; NCAE-NEA 90-; Chclrs Lst Acdmc Achvmnt Awrd 90-; AA/AS SE Comm Coll 88; Art Ed; Prfssr.

**ECKSTEIN, AMY L,** Univ Of Med & Dentistry Of Nj, Newark, NJ; JR; BS; Amer Acad Phy Asst; N Y Dept Hlth Aids Survlnc Unit 87-89; BA St Univ N Y 85; Physcn Asst.

**ECKSTEIN, CINDY D,** Daemen Coll, Amherst, NY; SO; BS; Aphus 88-; Hillel 88-; Pep Bnd 88-89; Phi Eta Sgm 89-; Spec Olympcs 90-; Comm Actn Cops 88-; Baird Point Amblnc Corps 88-89; IM Vlybl Bsktbl Co Capt 88-; Comm Action Corps Vetrns Hosp; ECMC Buffalo Gen; Sisters Hosp; Phys Thrpy.

**ECKSTROM, CHRISTOPHER A,** Embry Riddle Aeronautical Univ, Daytona Beach, FL; SR; BS; Prelas Assn Aviation Stdnts 90-; Sr Cls Cncl 90-; Aircraft Owners Pilots Assn 90-; Lambda Chi Alpha Hstrn; Daytona Bch Chmbr Commerce; Vllybl Hcky Ftbl Golf; Aeronautical Stds; Avatn Law.

**ECLAVEA, DIANA A,** Niagara Univ, Niagara Univ, NY; SO; BS; Hnrs Pgm; Blgy; Med.

**ECONOMIDES, CONSTANTINE Z,** Villanova Univ, Villanova, PA; SR; JD; Spcl Olympics Vol 90; Pi Sigma Alpha 90-; Deans Lst; Cum Laude; BA; Political Sci; Law.

**EDDEY, KARA L,** Westminster Coll, New Wilmingtn, PA; SR; BA; Ltrgcl Dance; Cncrt Chr; Pep Bnd; Phi Alpha Theta; Alpha Phi Omega VP Flwshp; Hstry Rsrch Asst; Hstry; Tchr/Trnsltr.

**EDDINGS, JOLIETTE M,** Fl A & M Univ, Tallahassee, FL; FR; Pres Schlrs Assn 90-; Phi Eta Sigma 90-; Intrnshp Eng Cnsltng Frm; Cvl Engrng.

**EDDINGS, MARILYN A,** Univ Of Al At Birmingham, Birmingham, AL; SO; BA; Cncl Excptl Chldrn; Dvsn Lrng Dsblts Cncl Excptl Chlrn; Cncl Chldrn Bhvr Dsrds; AL Cncl Excptl Chldrn; AL Cncl Chldrn Bhvr Dsrdrs; AM Arts Assc 90-; Tght Strss Mngmnt Clss Pelham 89-; Pblc Lbry Fcltr Yng Athrs Conf; Asst Cnltn 78-90; Special Ed/Emtnl Cnflt; Tch Svrly Emtnl Cldrn.

**EDDINGTON, AMY J,** Univ Of Tn At Martin, Martin, TN; SR; Tae Kwon Do Clb Sec 88-89; Tae Kwon Do Trnmnt 89.

**EDDINS, CARY L,** Univ Of Tn At Knoxville, Knoxville, TN; JR; BA; Weightlifting Club Treas 89-; Amer Mktg Assoc 90-; Executive Undergraduates 89-; Gamma Beta Phi; Phi Eta Sigma 90-; Alpha Lambda Delta 90-; Delta Sigma Pi Hd Prof Cm; Delta Gamma Ast Treas 90-; Fred M Roddy Schlrshp 89; Mod Woodman Schlrshp 89; Business; Marketing.

**EDDINS, WILLIAM D,** Univ Of Sc At Columbia, Columbia, SC; JR; BS; Columbia Clg Wind Ensmbl 90-; Gamma Beta Phi; BA Marshall Univ 85; Marine Sci; Marine Biologist.

**EDDLEMAN, DENISE W,** Wallace St Comm Coll At Selma, Selma, AL; JR; BS; Kappa Delta Pi; Bptst Preschl Tchr 87-; Spch/Lang Pthlgy; Tch.

**EDDLEMAN, MITZI S,** Univ Of Nc At Charlotte, Charlotte, NC; JR; BS; Phi Theta Kappa Central Piedmont Comm Coll 89-; Advsry Brd Crrctnl Srvc Prog 90-; Intern Kannapolis Police Dept 89-90; AAS Central Piedmont Comm Coll 90; Crmnl Jstc; Fed St Govt Agncy.

**EDDY, CAROLYN M,** Univ Of Al At Birmingham, Birmingham, AL; FR; BA; Psychology Club; Chld Psychlgst.

**EDDY, EILEEN C,** Univ Of New Haven, West Haven, CT; SR; Hnr Soc; Eta Sigma Delta Intl Hosp Mang Soc; Cum Laude; Sales Mgr Ramada Hotel; AS Keene State Clg 87; BS; Hotel/Rest Mgmnt; Sls.

**EDDY, KAREN,** Castleton St Coll, Castleton, VT; JR; BA; Poltcl Discussion Grp Secy 88-90; Demcrtc Actn Comm Pres; Alpha Chi; Acadmc Exclnc Award Hist Dept; Rescue Sqd Vol 85-; Hist; Publc Polcy.

**EDDY, MELISSA J,** Memphis St Univ, Memphis, TN; SO; BA; Pnhllnc Cncl Extnsns Chr; Gamma Beta Phi; Delta Gamma 90-; Bus; Lwyr.

**EDDY, MICHAEL C,** Ramapo Coll Of Nj, Mahwah, NJ; SR; BS; Delta Mu Delta; Co-Op Ed Stdnt UPS Hmn Rsrcs Dept Adm Asst 89-; IM90-; Adm/Bus Info Syst; Syst Analyst.

**EDEMBA, EDMUND I,** Al A & M Univ, Normal, AL; JR; BSC; Intl Stu Assc Sprts Edtr 88-89; Dr C Marlbury Acdmc Hnrs 89; Bst Fresh Acdmc Hnrs 88; Mst Otstndng Sccr Plyr 89-90; Sccr 88-; Accntng.

**EDEN, SAMANTHA D,** City Univ Of Ny Queensbrough, New York, NY; SO; BA; Nrsng.

**EDENS, ANITA G,** Middle Tn St Univ, Murfreesboro, TN; SR; BA; Horsemans Assoc 87-88; Animal Scnc; Hrs Brdng Farm.

**EDENS, JASON W,** Univ Of Ga, Athens, GA; SO; BED; Stdnts Envrnmntl Awrnss 90-; Athns Pc Cltn 90-; Rsdnt Asst; Alpha Lambda Delta; Hnrs Prgm; Deans Lst; Cltrl Ggrphy.

**EDENS, MYLISSA S D,** Ms St Univ, Miss State, MS; FR; BS; Chi Alpha 90; IM Vlybl 90-; Anml Sci; Vet.

**EDER, MARY E,** Northern Ky Univ, Highland Hts, KY; FR; BAS; Eng/Theater; Writing.

**EDEY, COLIN N,** Morehouse Coll, Atlanta, GA; SO; BS; New York/New Jersey Clb 89-90; Bus Assn 90-; J P Morgan Morgan Guaranty Trust 88-; Bnkng/Finance.

**EDGAR, CHRYSTINE M,** Atlantic Comm Coll, Mays Landing, NJ; SO; AAS; Nrsng Clb; Flwshp Shr Mem Hosp; Nrsng.

**EDGAR, COLON G,** Inter Amer Univ Pr Hato Rey, Hato Rey, PR; GD; BA; SG V P 87-88; ASW 89-90; Red Cross 90-; Arts; Soc Wrk.

**EDGAR, KIMBERLY M,** Va Commonwealth Univ, Richmond, VA; JR; BA; Biology Clb; Phi Eta Sigma 89-; Gldn Key; Med Clg VA 90-; Biology; Med Tech.**

**EDGAR, SHELIA R,** Clemson Univ, Clemson, SC; SR; BS; Stdnt Nurses Assc 90-; Sigma Theta Tau 90-; Nrsng.

**EDGAR, WILLIAM WALKER,** Ms St Univ, Miss State, MS; SR; BBA; Stdnt Rcrtr 90-; Sigma Chi Pldg Trnr 89-90; Chrty Prjcts; United Way; Amer Diabetes Assn; Palmer Hm Chldrn 89-90; Deans Lst 88-89; Pres Lst 89; IM Flg Ftbl 88-90; Mgmt/Ecnmcs; MBA/LAW.

**EDGE, ANGELA B,** Owensboro Comm Coll, Owensboro, KY; FR; Nursing.

**EDGE, ANGELA D,** Itawamba Comm Coll, Fulton, MS; FR; Mirror Stf; Phi Theta Kappa; Educ; MED.

**EDGE, DEBRA J,** Univ Of Sc At Columbia, Columbia, SC; SR; BA USC Coastal Carolina Col; Educ/Psychlgy; Chld Psychlgy.

**EDGE, FRANCIS S,** Spartanburg Methodist Coll, Spartanburg, SC; SO; BA; Hstry Clb 89-; PTK Clb 90-; AA; Hstry; Hstry Prfssr.

**EDGE, MELODY E,** Ky Wesleyan Coll, Owensboro, KY; JR; Stdnt Govt Chrprsn; Psychlgy Clb 89-; Stdnt Orien Ldr; Dns Lst 88-; Alpha Chi 90-; Coll Schlrs Am; Sigma Phi Epsilon 89-; Frnd/Frnd Prog; Psychlgy Tutr 90-; RWC Sngrs/Rngrs/Insprtns 88-; Oak/Ivy Nom; Pres Schlrshp 88; Wdfd B Tntmn Schlrshp; Psychlgy/Msc; Clncl Psychlgst/Grntlgst.

**EDGE, RUTH A,** Athens St Coll, Athens, AL; SR; BED; The ATHENIAN ASC Campus Nwspr Edtr Chief 89-; Paper Calhoun Clg Nwspr 87-89; Phi Theta Kappa; Kappa Delta Pi; Pi Tau Chi; ASC Wlkng Tm March Of Dimes Wlk Amer Chrpsn 90-; Early Childhood/Elem Ed; Tch Public Schl.

**EDGELL, ALISON R,** Daytona Beach Comm Coll, Daytona Beach, FL; FR; BA; Cmnctns; Dir/Wrtr/Prdcr Films.

**EDGELL, DALE R,** Univ Of Miami, Coral Gables, FL; SR; MSPT; Wrstlng Clb VP 87-89; Sccr Clb 88-90; Pre-Physcl Thrpy Clb 87-90; Sigma Chi Rep 87-; Pres 100 88; IM Sprts 87-; BHS; Physcl Thrpy.

**EDGELL-HAMMOND, MARLENE W,** Wv Univ At Parkersburg, Parkersburg, WV; SR; BA; Denex Corp Mgr Lab Serv; AS 88; Human Rsrc Mgmt.

**EDGERTON, DIANE V,** Radford Univ, Radford, VA; SR; BSN; Sigma Theta Tau; Nrsng.

**EDGERTON, ELIZABETH A,** Univ Of Sc At Columbia, Columbia, SC; SO; BA; Busn Admin; Acctng.

**EDGERTON, MICHAEL T,** Univ Of Ky, Lexington, KY; FR; BA; Phlsphy Clb Stu Rep Crclm Plan Comm 90; Acdmc Exclnc Schlrshp; Deans Lst; Phlsphy; Pblsh Poetry.

**EDGETT, LISA M,** Wells Coll, Aurora, NY; FR; BA; Class Tr 90-; French Clb Tr; Chamber Orch 90-; Free Library 90-; Orientation Cmte; Intrnshp Southern Cayuga Central Schl; Romance Lang; Tchr/Law.

**EDGHILL, MICHAEL E,** Fl International Univ, Miami, FL; FR; BS; Mech Eng.

**EDGSON, SUSAN,** Fl International Univ, Miami, FL; JR; BA; Gymnstcs Coach 88-; Phi Theta Kappa Drctr 88-89; Fncl Mgmt Assc; Inst Crdt Mgmt England 90-; Schlrshp 89; Hnrs Pgm 89; Outstndng Stdnt Intl Bus 90; AA Miami Dade Comm Coll 89; Finance/Intl Bus; Law.**

**EDINGTON, LISA L,** Columbus Coll Of Art & Design, Columbus, OH; FR; BFA; Fine Arts; Intr/Dstrl Dsgn.

**EDISON, CHRISTINE A,** Lincoln Univ, Lincoln Univ, PA; JR; BA; Acctg Clb 90-; Track 88-90; Acctg/Bsn Adm; Acctg.

**EDKINS, JODI A,** Elmira Coll, Elmira, NY; SR; BS; League Of Intern Speech Pathologists Pres 90-; Legislative Board Sec 88-89; Judicial Board 88-; Natl Student Speech Lang Hearing Assoc 90-; Pupil Assistance In Lrng 87-89; English 2nd Language Tutor 89-; Speech Language Pathologist.

**EDLER, GREGORY T,** Univ Of Sc At Columbia, Columbia, SC; JR; BA; Radio Sta Exec Bd; DJ Columbia Hall Stdnt Govt; Flr Rep; Media Arts.

**EDMINSTER, WILLIAM C,** Cumberland County Coll, Vineland, NJ; FR; BA; Horticulture Clb Treas; Horticulture; U S Dept Forestry.

**EDMISTEN, LORI A,** Tn Temple Univ, Chattanooga, TN; SR; BS; Hs Tres 88-89; Hs Pres 89; Stu Tchg; Chrldr 89-90; Educ; Tchr.

**EDMOND, SONYA L,** Jackson St Univ, Jackson, MS; SO; BED; Elem Ed; Tchr.

**EDMONDS, GARY L,** Al A & M Univ, Normal, AL; JR; BS; U S Army ROTC 89-; Phi Theta Kappa 89; Tau Alpha Psi; Acdmc Hnrs Awd 90-; Inst Elctrcl Elctrncs Engrs 90-; Non Cmsnd Ofcrs Assoc 86-; U S Army 81-89; Elctrcl Engrg Tchnlgy; Engr/U S Army.

**EDMONDS, KIM L,** Fl A & M Univ, Tallahassee, FL; FR; PHARM; Phi Eta Sigma; Kappa Epsilons Rosebuds 90-; Phrmcy.

**EDMONDS, MELANIE R,** East Tn St Univ, Johnson City, TN; SR; Otstndng Bus Ed Stdnt 90-; Stdnt Tchr Ed Assc 90-; TN Bus Ed Assc 90-; Natl Bus Ed Assc 90-; BS; Bus Ed; Tchr.

**EDMONDS, NANCY LEACH,** Univ Of Cin R Walters Coll, Blue Ash, OH; FR; BED; Vlntr Vctms Svc Ctr; Scl Wrk; Grief Cnslr.

**EDMONDS, WENDY B,** Catholic Univ Of America, Washington, DC; JR; BA; Phi Theta Kappa 85; Lgl Sec 79-83; Educ; Tchr.

**EDMONDSON, CHRISTOPHER D,** Univ Of Cincinnati-Clrmnt Coll, Batavia, OH; FR; Hosptlty Mgmt.

**EDMONDSON, EDWARD O,** Morehouse Coll, Atlanta, GA; FR; BA; Bsn Admin; Acctng.

**EDMONDSON, SHEILA M,** Middle Tn St Univ, Murfreesboro, TN; JR; BA; Kappa Delta Pi 90-; Tau Omicron 90-; Elem Edn; Tchr.

**EDMONSON, OWEN V,** Ms St Univ, Miss State, MS; SO; Stdnt Assoc Sntr 90-; Roadrunner Stdnt Rcrtr 89-; Cmpss Clb Chrmn Intrnl Affrs 89-; Gamma Alpha Epsilon Pres 90-; Ordr Omega V P; Alpha Lambda Delta Treas 90-; Gamma Beta Phi Crdnl Key 90-; Phi Eta Sigma 90-; Ntl Assoc Actnts 89-; Delta Gamma; Acctg; CPA.

**EDMONSON, RANDALL A,** Ms St Univ, Miss State, MS; GD.

**EDMUNDS, AMY KA,** Comm Coll Algny Co Algny Cmps, Pittsburgh, PA; SO; BA.

**EDMUNDS, LORI J,** Georgian Court Coll, Lakewood, NJ; GD; MA; Psychology Club 89-90; Re-Entry Womens Club 88-90; Psi Chi 89-90; Grad Cum Laude With AA 88; Grad Magnum Cum Laude With BA 90; Dean Schlr Awd 89-90; AA Ocean Cnty Clge 88; BA 90; Psychology; Child Psychologist.

**EDMUNDSON, MATTHEW L,** Univ Of Al At Huntsville, Huntsville, AL; SO; BS; Alpha Lambda Delta 90-; Hnr Schlr 89-; Almni Schlp 89-90; Hnrs Schlp 89-; Elec Engr.

**EDMUNDSON, TIFFANY L,** Coll Of Charleston, Charleston, SC; SR; BA; Vsl Arts Clb Pres 88-90; Stdnt Nwspr Clmnst 89-; Omicron Delta Kappa 90-; Alpha Phi Omega Rgnl Cnfrnc Plnr 88-90; Fn Arts Schlr Art Hstry 88-; Exchng Clb Schlr 87-88; Fine Arts; Cmnty Serv.

**EDNEY, ALVIN D,** Alcorn St Univ, Lorman, MS; SO; Natl Hnr Soc; Alpha Phi Alpha 90-.

**EDNEY, ELIZABETH A,** Brevard Coll, Brevard, NC; FR; BS; Phi Theta Kappa; Vrsty Tnns 90-; Sci.

**EDONMI, REX U,** Roane St Comm Coll, Harriman, TN; SO; BA; Bapt Student Union 89-; Deans List; Acad Achiev Awd; Talent Roster Mintry Cmm Clg Gr; Chartered 74-; Inst Bankers London; Acctng; CPA.**

**EDOUARD, KATY,** Miami Dade Comm Coll North, Miami, FL; SO; BA; AA; Psychlgy/Soc Sci; Cnslng/Thrpy.

**EDSALL, MARK A,** Me Maritime Academy, Castine, ME; SO; Rifle Club Shrpshtr 90-; Mstrs List 90-; Marine Engr.

**EDUARDO, BAS R,** Univ Of Pr At Mayaguez, Mayaguez, PR; Jgng/Wghtlftng; Hon Dipl; Elect Eng.

**EDWALL, MARI ANN V,** Univ Of Cincinnati-Clrmnt Coll, Batavia, OH; FR; Childrens Support Grp Coord; Yng Peoples Beginning Explt Coord; Septd Divorced/Renornied Grp Brd Mbr; Orgd Bible Study Church 89-90; Social Concerns Commt Chrprn 87-88; Nursing; PN.

**EDWARD, COMPTON A,** Vance Granville Comm Coll, Henderson, NC; SO; VGCC Vctnl Clb Exec Com Mbr 90-; Virgilina Msnc Ldg Wrshpfl Mstr 87; BA Bus Mgmt/Ecnmcs NC St Univ Raleigh NC 79; Elect/Ind Maint; Sprvsr.

**EDWARD-JENKINS, GWENETH V,** Ny Univ, New York, NY; SO; BS; Sttstcl Asst UNICEF 85-; AAS 90; Cert Compucenter London 80; Infrmtn Systms.

**EDWARDS VIDAL, DERICK A,** Univ Politecnica De Pr, Hato Rey, PR; FR.

**EDWARDS, ALEXIS L,** Clark Atlanta Univ, Atlanta, GA; FR; BA; Spirit Bstr Clb 90-; Jrnlsm; Authr/Nwspaper Jrnlst.

**EDWARDS, AMANDA G,** Va Commonwealth Univ, Richmond, VA; JR; BS; Treehs/Clnl Assn Pres 88-90; Hlth Admin Clb 90-; Univ Hsng Task Frc 89-90; Area Nwsltr 90-; Riverside Convlscnt Cntr-Smithfield Admin Intrn; Jane Jones Thornton Awd Rsdnt Asst; VA Hlth Cr Assn Schlrshp 90-; Hlth Care Mgmt Long-Term Care; Hlth Admin.**

**EDWARDS, AMY L,** Itawamba Comm Coll, Fulton, MS; SO; BA; Spec Edn; Teach.

**EDWARDS, ANGELA H,** Mary Baldwin Coll, Staunton, VA; JR; BA; Fine Arts Clb Co Chrwmn 89-; Stu Senate 90-; Hnr Schlr Soc 88-; Cosmos 89-; Mnrty Wmn Unity 89-; Bailey Schlrshp 88-; Margarett Kable Russell Awrd; Art Hstry; Film.

**EDWARDS, ANGELA M,** Christopher Newport Coll, Newport News, VA; JR; BS; Rvrsde Hosp Vol; Tennis/Chrldng 88; Bio; Physical Thrpy.

**EDWARDS, ANGELA M,** Northern Ky Univ, Highland Hts, KY; SO; BA; Stdnt Athltc Clb 89-90; Delta Gamma Soroity 89-90; Spanish/Jrnlsm.

**EDWARDS, ANTHONY GUYNN,** Bristol Univ, Bristol, TN; GD; MBA; Clg Bsbl Capt 82-86; Bsbl Golf; Forceman Golf Clb Pres 90-; AS 86; BA 87.

**EDWARDS, APRIL L,** Fayetteville St Univ, Fayetteville, NC; JR; Bus Admin/Finace; Corp Law.

**EDWARDS, BARBARA C,** Pellissippi St Tech Comm Coll, Knoxville, TN; SO; AAS; DPMA VP 90-; Phi Theta Kappa 90-; Alpha Beta Gamma; DPMA Gateway Chptr Schlrshp Awrd 90; Admn Asst; Bkkpr; Dntl Asst; Sec; RDA Cert Knox Co Schls Dental Asst Prog 85; Cmptr Sci; PC Trnng Spprt Data Base Spec.

**EDWARDS, BARTLEY N,** Univ Of Fl, Gainesville, FL; FR; BS; Delta Chi; Sprngbrd Dvng Tm; Psychlgy; Med.

**EDWARDS, BRUCE E,** Mayland Comm Coll, Spruce Pine, NC; FR; ASSC; Tnns Tm Ashvlle Bncmb Tech Coll 87; Ck Le Grdn Restrnt 85; Fd Svce Mgmt Cleveland Comm Coll 90; Bsc Ckng Mayland Comm Coll; Clnry Arts Rstrnt Fd Srvce Mgmt; Chf Entrprnr.

**EDWARDS, CARLEEN M,** Nc Agri & Tech St Univ, Greensboro, NC; JR; BS; Inst Electricl Elctrncs Engnrs; Tau Beta Pi; Eta Kappa Nu; Alpha Lambda Delta; Delta Sigma Theta; Naval Undrwtr Systm Cntr Schlrshp Intrn; Electrcl Engnrng; Engnrng.

**EDWARDS, CAROLYN C,** Vance Granville Comm Coll, Henderson, NC; GD; ABA; Scts Clbmstr; Otstndng Vol Awd 4-H; Dietary Mgrs Assoc; Cert Dietry Mgr Univ FL Gainesvl FL 86-87; Bsns; Bsns Admn.

**EDWARDS, CAROLYN R,** Univ Of Bridgeport, Bridgeport, CT; SO; BA; Blck Stdnt Alliance 89-; Co-Chrmn Mltcltrl Advsry Comm Co-Chrmn; Natl Assn Negro Bsn/Prof V P 89-90; Wmns Club Yng Adult Div; GE Tchng Schlrshp Pgm 89-; Engl; Tchng.

**EDWARDS, CATHERINE M,** Univ Of Sc At Columbia, Columbia, SC; JR; BA; Mdl UN; Phi Beta Kappa; Mtr Brd Pres; Omicron Delta Kappa; Delta Delta Delta; Intern US Sen Frtzbllngs; Intl Stds.

**EDWARDS, CHAD J,** Bridgewater Coll, Bridgewater, VA; FR; BA; Var Bsktbl Var Golf 90-; Hstry/Pol Sci; Coaching.

**EDWARDS, CHRISTOPHER S,** Univ Of Sc At Columbia, Columbia, SC; JR; BS; Midlands Astronomy Clb 90-; Society Physics Stdnts; Sigm Api Sigma; Physica Math; Astronomy.

**EDWARDS, DANNY H,** Old Dominion Univ, Norfolk, VA; JR; BS; Prvt Plt 89-; Soc Mfg Engrs 90-; Gldn Key; Dns Lst 90-; Summa Cum Laude 90; Diploma Drftng/Dsgn Dnvl Comm Clg 90; Mech Engr Tech; Pilot.

**EDWARDS, DARLENE,** Wilmington Coll, New Castle, DE; SR; BS; Pres Lst Brandywine Clge 75-76; Schlrshp 76; Dns Lst Brandywine Clge 84-88; Evngn Dvsn Schlrshps Goldey Beacom Clge 84-87; ICI Phrmctcls Newark De; AS Brandywine Clge 77; AS Goldey Beacom Clge 88; Bsn Mgmt; Bsn.

**EDWARDS, DARNELL S,** Tuskegee Univ, Tuskegee Inst, AL; SR; BS; Bnd 88-; All Str Chlng Tm; Hnrs Pgm 87-; Omega Psi Phi 90-; By Scts Amer Jr Asst Sctmstr 80-89; Natl Brthrhd Hnr Cmprs Cmpng Prmtns Chrmn 83-89; Egl Sct 86-87; Arspc Engrg/Physcs; Engrg.

**EDWARDS, DAVID M,** Cornell Univ Statutory College, Ithaca, NY; SR; Phi Delta Theta 88-; Lacrosse 87-; BS; Bus Mngmnt/Mrktng.

**EDWARDS, DEBORAH Y,** Va St Univ, Petersburg, VA; JR; BA; Admin Jstc Clb; Sclgy; Law Enfrcmnt.

**EDWARDS, DENISE K,** Radford Univ, Radford, VA; SR; BS; Vsl/Prfmng Arts; Thtr Acting.

**EDWARDS, DIXIE C,** Itawamba Comm Coll, Fulton, MS; SO; EXED; Spcl Edn.

**EDWARDS JR, DONALD W,** Va St Univ, Petersburg, VA; GD; MS; Alpha Kappa Mu 90-; Phi Beta Lambda 90-; DPMA V P 88-89; ROTC Btln Cmdr 86-90; Ranger Dtchmnt Cmdr 87-90; Bapt Un V P 88-90; H S Truman Schlrs Clb 87-90; ROTC Schlrshp; M A Braadford Schlrshp; ALCOA Schlrshp; Pres Lst; Deans Lst; BS; Mgmt Info Sys.

**EDWARDS, DONNA R,** Ms St Univ, Miss State, MS; JR; Phi Mu Sprts Chrprsn 89; Oktibbeha Cnty Hosp; MS State Ticket Ofc 88-; IM Bsktbl/Vlybl 88-90.

**EDWARDS, DWYLA M,** Al St Univ, Montgomery, AL; SO; BS; Cmptr Info Sys; Data Prcsg.

**EDWARDS, GEORGIA A,** Gallaudet Univ, Washington, DC; SO; Sec Black Deaf Stu Un 89-90; Theatre Awds 88-90; Drama; Educ.

**EDWARDS, GEORGIANA L,** Atlantic Comm Coll, Mays Landing, NJ; SO; Elem Educ.

**EDWARDS, GLENDA KAY,** Northwest Al Comm Coll, Phil Campbell, AL; SO; BA; Phi Theta Kappa 90; Pres Lst; Phys Ther.**

**EDWARDS, HEATHER L,** Univ Of Sc At Columbia, Columbia, SC; SO; BA; RHA 89-90; RH Gvmt 89-90; RA 90-; Intlctl Pgm Sem 90; RH Dsk Super; Intrdscplnry Studies; Tch Elem Schl.

**EDWARDS, HOLLY M,** Univ Of Akron, Akron, OH; SR; BA; Cncl Ed Stdnts 89-; Rdng Clb; Yng Reps 89-; Deans Lst 90-; IM Sprts Bsktbl/Touch Ftbl 87-; Elem Ed; Tchng.

**EDWARDS, JAMES R,** Christian Brothers Univ, Memphis, TN; JR; BS; Ecnmcs Finance; Fdrl Law Enfrcmnt.

**EDWARDS, JAMIE,** Va St Univ, Petersburg, VA; SO; BA; SGA Comm; Alpha Kappa Alpha; Big Brothers/Sis; (AACP Sec 90-; Acad Achvmnt Awd 89-90; Pub Admin; Law.

**EDWARDS, JASON A,** Ms St Univ, Miss State, MS; JR; BS; Gamma Beta Phi 87-88; Univ Hons Prog 87-88; Cooperative Ed Prog 88-; Mech Eng.

**EDWARDS, JILL M,** Marywood Coll, Scranton, PA; JR; BA; AAF V P 90-; PRSSA 90; NE Pa Ad Club 90-; Newspr Entrnmnt Edtr 90-; Gann-Dawson Advrtsg/Pblc Rltns Intern; AS Penn State Univ 89; Cmnctn Arts; Advrtsg/Pblc Rltns.

**EDWARDS, JOEL EUGENE,** Md Inst Coll Of Art, Baltimore, MD; SR; BFA; 2 Man Exib; Stdnt Cen Gallery 90; Undergrad Exhib 85-; AIRA Exhib NYC N Y; Deans List; Cum Laude; AUCA N Y Studio Studio Prog; Illus Colg Catalog/Courses 90-; Fine Arts/Paingint; Artist.

**EDWARDS, JOHN K,** Univ Of South Fl, Tampa, FL; GD; MPH; Sigma Xi 88-; Tchng Asstshp 85-87; Sigma Xi Grnt 88; Rsrch Assocshp 87-89; Ultmt Frsbee Team 85-89; Qlty Assrnce Offcr/Co Wtr Syst 90-; MS 88; Evnrnmntl Hlth/Zoolgy; Hlth Regltn.

**EDWARDS, JOHN T,** Fl St Univ, Tallahassee, FL; JR; BA; Tchng Awds Comm 90-; Stdnt Adv Comm 90-; Golden Key 90-; Hnrs Schlrs Pgm 88-; Humanities.

**EDWARDS, JUDY C,** Univ Of Sc At Coastal Carolina, Conway, SC; SR; BS; Educ Clb; Elem Chldhd Educ; Tchr.

**EDWARDS, KAREN,** Univ Of Tn At Martin, Martin, TN; FR; BSW; Scl Wrk Clb 90-; Scl Wrk.

**EDWARDS, KARLA A,** Oh Dominican Coll, Columbus, OH; SR; BA; Beta Sigma Phi Pres 74-; PTA Treas 89-90; Atmn Wds Hmwnrs Co Pres; Lbrry Sci.

**EDWARDS, KARMECITHIA L,** Al St Univ, Montgomery, AL; FR; BA; Cmnctns; Brdcst Jrnlst.

**EDWARDS, KELLI L,** Radford Univ, Radford, VA; FR; Day Care Schlrshp.

**EDWARDS, KIMBERLY E,** Borough Of Manhattan Comm Coll, New York, NY; SO; BBA; Phi Theta Kappa 88-90; AAS 90; Off Admn/Tech; Mgmt.**

**EDWARDS, KIMBERLY J,** Oh St Univ At Newark, Newark, OH; JR; BS; Mortor Board 90; Elmntry Ed; Tchng.

**EDWARDS, KIMBERLY M,** Richard Bland Coll, Petersburg, VA; SO; BA; Chrldr 89-; Psychology; Edctn.

**EDWARDS, LA JUAN C,** Miami Dade Comm Coll North, Miami, FL; SO; BA; Untd Blck Stdnts; Brdcst Jrnlsm; News Anchr/Lwyr.

**EDWARDS, LAUREN E,** Bethany Coll, Bethany, WV; FR; Amnesty Intl 90-; English; Law.

**EDWARDS, LAURIE,** Columbia Union Coll, Takoma Park, MD; JR; BA; Alpha Sigma Beta VP Mktg 87-; Phs II Com 89-90; Shrt-Tm Msn Wrkr Hndrs 89; Stdnt Mssnry Ebeye MI Pthfndr Ldr Phs Ii Dir Sbbth Schl Ldr 89-90; Bus Adm/Mktg; Intl Law.

**EDWARDS, LEE A,** Ms Univ For Women, Columbus, MS; JR; BS; Bus Acctng; CPA Law.

**EDWARDS, LESLIE J,** Univ Of Tn At Knoxville, Knoxville, TN; FR; Kappa Delta 90-; Sigma Alpha Epsilon 90-; Hghst Hnrs Dns Lst 90; Fred M Roddy Schlrshp 90-; Bsn; CPA.

**EDWARDS, LINDA ANN,** Middle Tn St Univ, Murfreesboro, TN; JR; MBA; Crisis Ctrs 85-; LAA Armstrng Clg Brkly CA 74; Cmptr Sci.

**EDWARDS, LYNN E,** Univ Of Ga, Athens, GA; SR; MED; Chld/Fmly Dvlpmnt 89-; Page 90-; Phi Mu Assist Treas 89-90; BED; Early Chdhd Educ; Educ.

**EDWARDS, M ABIGAIL,** Coll Of Charleston, Charleston, SC; FR; BA; Stdnt Govt Sec Stdnt Bdy/Senator 90-; Fllwshp Chrstn Athlts 90-; Glee Club 90-; Hnrs Clg 90-; High Dist List 90-; Fdn Brchr/Prstgs Alumni Blcklck Pprs; Dance Tm 90-; Poltcl Sci; Law Dplmt.

**EDWARDS, MAMON C,** Al A & M Univ, Normal, AL; SO; BS; Hme Econs Assns; Bapt Stdnt Unn 90-; Eliza Patton Schlrshp 90-; Kappa Omicron Nu; Hosp Fd Systm Mgmt; Lgstns.

**EDWARDS, MELISSA A,** Northern Ky Univ, Highland Hts, KY; SR; BA; Blgcl Soc 90; Biology; Medicine.**

**EDWARDS, MICHAL A,** Alcorn St Univ, Lorman, MS; JR; BA; SGA Pres; Karate Clb; Cmnctns.

**EDWARDS, MITCHELL W,** Stillman Coll, Tuscaloosa, AL; SR; BS; Sociological Assoc 90-; Alpha Kappa Mu; Cordell Wynn Hnrs Pgm; Masonic Lodge; Alpha Phi Alpha Chaplain/Dir Ed Actvts 90-; Stillman Schlr; Bapt Church; Interdiscplnry Stds/Sclgy/Psych; Scl Psych.

**EDWARDS, NICHELLE A,** Tn St Univ, Nashville, TN; JR; BS; Pep Clb 88-89; Stdnt Elctn Cmmssn Sec 90-; Spch Cmm; Tlvsn Pblc Rltns.

**EDWARDS, NICOLLE L,** Johnson C Smith Univ, Charlotte, NC; SO; BA; Accntng; CPA.

**EDWARDS, PATRICK C,** Bloomfield Coll, Bloomfield, NJ; FR; BA; Chrch Jesus Chrst; Bus Admin; Bus Mgr/Owner.

**EDWARDS, PAULETTE,** Al St Univ, Montgomery, AL; GD; SOS Ldr 88-; Gldn Ambssdr 89-; SGA Sen 88-90; Pi Gamma Mu 89-; Delta Sigma Theta Trea 90-; Intern AL Attrny Gen Offc Cvl Rghts Div 90; BS; Crmnl Jstc; Law.

**EDWARDS, PEGGY A,** Univ Of Md At Eastern Shore, Princess Anne, MD; SO; BS; Wmns Bsktbl 89-90; Acctg; CPA.

**EDWARDS, PRISCILLA O,** Christopher Newport Coll, Newport News, VA; SR; BSN; Alpha Chi 90; Amer Rd Crs 79-; AACN Comm Act Comm Local Amer Assoc Crit Cr Nrs 86-; Bapt Yng Wmn Central Hill Chrch Svp 90-; CCRN 88-; RN Diplma Louise Obia Schl Nrsng 82; Nrsng; MSN.

**EDWARDS, RAMONA D,** Rutgers St Univ At Camden, Camden, NJ; JR; BA; Acctng Soc; Summer Mgmnt Intrnshp Prog 90; ; Ba Rutgers St Univ 87; Acctng; CPA.

**EDWARDS, RONALD D,** Ms Gulf Coast Comm Coll, Perkinston, MS; FR; Ftbll Capt 90-; Blgy; Gntc Eng.

**EDWARDS, S ELAINE,** Comm Coll Algny Co Algny Cmps, Pittsburgh, PA; FR; MBA; Dntl Asst 78-90; Bsns Mgmt Trvl Trsm; Bsns Bsns Mgt.

**EDWARDS, SHARI N,** Barry Univ, Miami, FL; FR; BS; Clrk Typst 90-; Mgmnt; Occptnl Thrpy.

**EDWARDS, STACY M,** Fl A & M Univ, Tallahassee, FL; FR; BA; Grphc Dsgn/Jrnlsm; Grphc Arts.

**EDWARDS, SUSAN C,** Belmont Coll, Nashville, TN; FR; BA; Chrstn Music Soc 90-; Bptst Stdnt Union 90-; Tom T Halls Anmlnd Bnft 90; Kenny Rogers CP Tlthn; Sammy Davis Jr Vrty Clb Tlthn; Deans Lst 90-; Sqr Dncng; Music Bus; Entrtnr/Tlnt Agncy Owner.

**EDWARDS, TAMMY L,** Comm Coll Algny Co Algny Cmps, Pittsburgh, PA; FR; BA; Lib Arts; Ph D Psychlgy.

**EDWARDS, TERESA L,** Vance Granville Comm Coll, Henderson, NC; SO; AAS; Comm Coll Ambsdr; Acadmc Achvmnt Schlrshp; Gen Ofc Tech; Comptr Oper.

**EDWARDS, THOMAS C,** S U N Y Coll Of Tech At Alfred, Alfred, NY; FR; AS; Elec Clb Sec 90-; Cncrt Bnd 90-; Sigma Tau Epsilon 90-; Elec Cnstrctn; Elec Bus.

**EDWARDS, TINA L,** Wv Univ, Morgantown, WV; JR; BS; Amer Soc Cvl Eng; Cvl Engrng.

**EDWARDS, TISHA N,** Hampton Univ, Hampton, VA; SO; BS; Wmns Snte 90-; High Hnr Roll 89-91; Acctg; CPA.

**EDWARDS, TRACY L,** Albertus Magnus Coll, New Haven, CT; SR; BA; Engl Clb 90-; Phlsphy Clb 88-89; Yale Univ Spec Stdnt Status 88-; WELI 960 AM Radio Intrn 89; Com Tech Closed Circuit Telev Sta Intrn; WTNH TV Chnl 8 Action News Intrn 90; Cmmnctns; Advrtsng/Televsn.

**EDWARDS, YASMIN J,** City Univ Of Ny City Coll, New York, NY; SR; BA; Assn Cmptng Mchnry 89-90; Cadeucus 88-; Blgy; Med.

**EDWARDS-EL, WILLIAM R,** Coppin St Coll, Baltimore, MD; JR; BS; Moorish Sci Temple Of Amer Inc Brnch Tmpl Chrmn 87-; Elem Educ; Teacher.

**EFAW, TRACIE M,** Wv Univ, Morgantown, WV; SR; BSN; Ntl Stdnt Nrses Assoc 90; Sigma Theta Tau; Nrsng.

**EFF, RENEE M,** Cornell Univ Statutory College, Ithaca, NY; JR; BS; Hillel 89-; Summer Intrnshps RPR Phrmctcls 89-; Microbio; Phrmctcl Rsrch.

**EGAN, ELIZABETH A,** Western New England Coll, Springfield, MA; FR; BS; Bus Mgmt; Bus.

**EGAN, KATHLEEN,** Kent St Univ Kent Cmps, Kent, OH; FR; BA; Int Dsgn.

**EGAN, MARY T,** Niagara Univ, Niagara Univ, NY; SO; Soccer 89-90; Bus Cmrce; Mktg.

**EGAN, MICHELLE R,** The Kings Coll, Briarclf Mnr, NY; SO; BA; Fr Cls Offcr N E Bibl Clg Sec 89-; Schl Nwspr N E Bibl Clg Asst Edtr 89-90; Elem Educ; Tchg.

**EGBERT, ROBERTA L,** Univ Of Cincinnati, Cincinnati, OH; SO; BED; Nwspaper Wrtr 90-; Eta Sigma Gamma 90-; Amer Red Crss Instrctr; La Leche League Prfssnl Liaison 81-; Intl Lactn Cnsltnts Assn 85-; Lactatn Cnsltnt; Hlth Prmtn/Educ; Dir Hlth Educ Prog.

**EGER, KIM DAVID,** Christopher Newport Coll, Newport News, VA; JR; BA; Stdnt Govt Assn Human Rel Chmn 90-; Stdnt Assn VA Rep 90-; Frnch Clb Pub Rcrtr 90-; Alpha Chi; Sigma Tau Delta VP; Amnesty Intl 90-; Engl Dept Asst 90-; Frnch; Intl Bus/Jrnlsm.

**EGGART, LAUREL MARAIST,** Univ Of Sc At Columbia, Columbia, SC; SO; MBA; Acctg; CPA.

**EGGERS, ANN MARIE L,** Central Fl Comm Coll, Ocala, FL; SO; AA; Kndrgn Techr Aide Marion Co Schl Brd 88-; Word Procng Dipl Cleary Clg 87; Elem Ed; Tchng.

**EGGLESTON, CHAUNCY R,** Tuskegee Univ, Tuskegee Inst, AL; SO; BS; Pres Schlrshp 89; Mech Eng.

**EGGLESTON, MICHELE L,** Neumann Coll, Aston, PA; SO; BSN; SNA 90-; Glenolden Yth Clb Coach 87-90; AD Delaware Cnty Comm Clg 89; Nrsng; Med Srg Nrsng.**

**EGGLESTON, SHERONICA F,** Al A & M Univ, Normal, AL; JR; BS; Deans Lst Hnr Stdnt 88-; Biology; RN.

**EGIPCIACO, DONALINE I,** Inter Amer Univ Pr San German, San German, PR; FR; CSI; Comp Sci; Sec Comp.

**EGLESTON, SIDNEY D,** Ashland Comm Coll, Ashland, KY; SO; MBA; Outstndng Bus Mgt Stdnt 90-; AAS; Bus; Admn.

**EGNACZYK, KIMBERLY A,** Univ Of Pittsburgh, Pittsburgh, PA; SO; BSN; Nrsng.

**EGNER, JOHN E,** S U N Y Coll Of A & T Morrisvl, Morrisville, NY; SO; AS; Strght Forwrd Educ Grp; Ind Stds; Drg Alchl Cnslr.

**EGUT, JOHN V,** Univ Of Akron, Akron, OH; SR; BS; Fin/Bus Admin; Cmmrcl/Res Real Est Fin.

**EHLERS, JENNIFER S,** Villanova Univ, Villanova, PA; SO; BA; Amnesty Intrntnl Tres 90-; Literary Mag Asst Edtr 90-; Envrnmntl Grp 90-; Englsh; Pblshng Jrnlsm.

**EHLERS, JULIE A,** Villanova Univ, Villanova, PA; SO; BA; Schl Nwspr Stff Rprtr 89; Amnsty Intrntnl 90-; Lit Mag Asst Ed 90-; Hons Pgm 89-; Engl; Wrtng.

**EHLMAN, JENNIFER R,** Cumberland County Coll, Vineland, NJ; SO; Bus; Acctng.

**EHMANN, CHRISTINE M,** Univ Of Rochester, Rochester, NY; SO; BED; Stdnt Govt Rep 89; Intrn Mnre Cnty Leg 90; Hlth Sci; Educ.

**EHRBAR, HOLLY Y,** Colby Sawyer Coll, New London, NH; BED; Sls Sec/Mrktng Repr/Mngr/Hostess/Waitress; AS Quinnipiac Clg Hamden CT 74; Chld Stdy Prog; Treacher.

**EHRHARDT, KIRK V,** Univ Of Sc At Columbia, Columbia, SC; SO; BA; Deans Lst 89; Jrnlsm; Wrtng/Pblshng.

**EHRHART, TABITHA A,** Oh St Univ At Marion, Marion, OH; FR; BS; Psych Clb 90-; Alpha Lambda Delta 90-; Phi Eta Sigma 90-; Sci; Dntl Hygiene.

**EHRLICH, KISSA,** Bunker Hill Comm Coll, Boston, MA; FR; BA; Deans Lst; Engl; Law.

**EHRLICH, SIMONE,** Fl International Univ, Miami, FL; JR; BA; Fl Intl Univ Acctng Assoc; Phi Lambda Beta; Acctng; CPA.

**EHRLICH, STEPHEN E,** Hofstra Univ, Hempstead, NY; JR; BBA; SGA Prgrmmng Apprtn Comms 90-; Cmmtr Stdnts VP 89-; Booster Clb Acctng Soc 88-; Beta Alpha Psi; Beta Gamma Sigma; Activties Ldgrshp Awrd; Sclr Of The Yr; Acctng; Law.**

**EIBEN, LAURA L,** Radford Univ, Radford, VA; JR; BS; SEA 89-; CEC 90-; Kappa Delta Pi 89-; Early/Spec Educ; Teach.

**EICHEN, DEAN K,** Daemen Coll, Amherst, NY; JR; BS; Physcl Thrpy Clb; Jrnl Clb; US Cycling Fdrtn 87-90; Deans Lst 90-; Physcl Thrpy.

**EICHENBAUM, DWAYNE S,** Univ Of Miami, Coral Gables, FL; SO; BBA; Sigma Chi Ktchn Mgr 89-; Chrldg 89; Acctg; Tax Law.

**EICHENLAUB, BOBBIE D,** Northern Ky Univ, Highland Hts, KY; JR; BA; Scndry Educ/Engl; Tchng.

**EICHHORST, STEPHANIE A D,** Southern Ct St Univ, New Haven, CT; JR; BA; Grmn Clb 89-; Sci Clb 90-; Alpha Chi 90-; Gen Physics Ii; Erly Chldhd Educ; Tch.**

**EICHIN, ALYSE M,** Univ Of Ga, Athens, GA; SR; BED; Stdnt Govt Soph Sntr 89; Stdnts Cncrnd Alcohol/Drug Awrns 89; Kappa Delta Epsln 90-; Alpha Delta Pi Actvty Chrmn 87-; Chrldng Coach Ftbl 87; Stdnt Tch Australia; I M Flag Ftbl 87; Mdle Sch Math/Sci; Tch.

**EICHMAN, GAIL T,** Kent St Univ Kent Cmps, Kent, OH; SR; BA; Indiv/Fmly Studies; Child Care Cnsltnt.

**EICHNER, ROBIN C,** Manor Jr Coll, Jenkintown, PA; GD; Alpha Beta Gamma; Outstndng Fresh Awd 90-; Miss Cngnlty Awd; Assoc; Sec Sci; Bus Admin.

**EICHORN, KEVEN B,** Univ Of Southern Ms, Hattiesburg, MS; JR; Alumni Assn 90-; Athletic Trnrs Clb; Natl Athletic Trnrs Assn 90-; Phi Kappa Tau 90-; Athletic Trnr; Athl Trng/Biol; Tch.

**EICHTEN, MOLLY T,** Long Island Univ C W Post Cntr, Greenvale, NY; SR; BS; Kappa Mu Epsilon 89-; Psi Psi Psi Pres 89-; Deans Lst 87-; H B Huntley Mem Awrd 90; C F Adler Awrd; Bsktbl 87-89; Math; Actuary.

**EICHWURTZLE, VIRGINIA H,** Northwest Al Comm Coll, Phil Campbell, AL; SO; AAS; Phi Theta Kappa; Ofc Admin.

**EICKHOLT, MELISSA K,** Hillsborough Comm Coll, Tampa, FL; FR; Bus; Mgt.

**EICOFF, CHARMAINE D,** Central Fl Comm Coll, Ocala, FL; GD; AS; IDSAC 90-; Phi Theta Kappa; Ocala/Slvr Spgs Rtry Clb Acdmc Schlrshp 90-; Pres Lst; Intrnshp Lcl Archtcts Offc; Deans Lst; Cert 89; Intrr Dsgn Tchnlgy; Intrr Dsgn.

**EIDELMAN, JEFFREY B,** S U N Y Coll Of Tech At Delhi, Delhi, NY; SR; Plumbing Heating Pipefitting Air Conditioning Refrigeration 90-; Plumbear.

**EIDENS, MICHELLE F,** Liberty Univ, Lynchburg, VA; FR; BA; Ythqust Clb 90-; Educ; Ele Sch Tchr.

**EIDSON, SUSAN S,** Chattanooga St Tech Comm Coll, Chattanooga, TN; SO; AAS; Phi Theta Kappa 89-; Dns Lst 89-; Caroline Holt Natl Nrsng Schlrshp 90; Hlth Sci Schlrshps 89-; Mbr Woodland Park Bapt 82-; Church Choir Chattanooga TN; Nrs Intrn; Nrsng; RN Labor/Delivery.

**EIDSVIG, ELISABETH,** Fl Atlantic Univ, Boca Raton, FL; JR; BA; Phi Kappa Phi; AA Palm Bch Comm Clg 90; Finance.

**EIGNER, BEVERLIN,** Benedict Coll, Columbia, SC; SR; BSW; Soc Wrkrs Club 88-; NASW 88-; Alpha Chi Hnr 89-; Yth Svcs Intern 90; US Army 82-87; US Army Reserve 87-; AS Midlands Tech Clg 88; Soc Work; MSW.

**EIGNER, TONY S,** Stillman Coll, Tuscaloosa, AL; SR; BA; Exec Council SGA 88-89; Pride Phi Prestige 90-; Sphstctn Unlmtd Mdlng Trpe 87-90; Gamma Iota Sigma 88; Phi Theta Alpha; Alpha Phi Alpha; IM Bsktbl 88-89; Hstry; Law.

**EIKELHOF, ESTHER,** S U N Y Coll Of Tech At Frmgdl, Farmingdale, NY; GD; AAS 90; Aerospace Tchnlgy; Financial Mgr.

**EILAND, IDA M,** Rust Coll, Holly Springs, MS; SO; BA; NAACP 90; Crimson Schlr/Hnrs Trk Prog 89; Schlrshp; Pres Lst 89; Deans Lst 90; Bsnss Admin; Mngmnt.**

**EILAND, JONATHAN E,** Al A & M Univ, Normal, AL; FR; Big Bro Am 88-; Ambassadors Clb VP 89-90; Drama Clb 89-90; Spnsh/Sci Clb 89-90; Hi-Y Clb 89-90; Arts Cncl 89-90; Nation Fire Fighter 89-; Tchrs Aide Edn Awd 89-90; Tennis/Golf 86-; Fstry.

**EILAND, SHERI B,** Univ Of Montevallo, Montevallo, AL; FR; BS; Eng.

**EILRICH, DALE B,** Oh Wesleyan Univ, Delaware, OH; SR; BA; Cncl Stdnt Affrs Geo Rep 90-; Big Pal Ltl Pal; Yrbk Act; Phi Eta Sigma 89; Phi Soc 88; Omicron Delta Kappa; Omicron Delta Epsilon V P 84-; Var Bsktbl 87-; BA; Econ Mgmt; Consltng/Bnkg.

**EIMER, TIMOTHY C,** Beaver Coll, Glenside, PA; GD; Undergrad Phila Clg Bible Pres 82-83; Stdnt Govt Pres Snr/Soph Cls 84-85; Phi Dlt Kappa 90-; Natl Sci Tchrs Assc 89-90; BS Phila Clg Bible 85; MA Beaver Clg 90; Rcpnt Grad Intrn Schlrshp 88-90; Daniel Richner Stdnt Athlt Awrd; Sci Educ; Sci Edctr.**

**EINBINDER, KERRY M,** Fl International Univ, Miami, FL; SR; BED; Student Tchng; Interns Intershp I II III; Elem Ed; Tchr.

**EISBERG, CHRISTOPHER J,** Cincinnati Bible Coll & Sem, Cincinnati, OH; JR; BMUS; Come Alive Sngrs Summer Trvlng Tm 89-; Music/Voice; Music Tchr.**

**EISENAHRDT, JEAN M,** Castleton St Coll, Castleton, VT; JR; Ath Trnrs Clb 88-; VT Natl Grd 88-; Nordic Ski Tm Biathlon 88-; Actv Military Dty In Saudi Arabia 172 Psc; Jr Natl Biathlon Tm 87-89; Cism Biathlon Tm 90; Sprts Med; Ath Trng/P T.

**EISENHARDT, ELIZABETH A,** Villanova Univ, Villanova, PA; SO; BA; Nwspaper Photogrphr 89-; Spcl Olympcs Vol 89-; Hist.

**EISENMESSER, BRETT H,** City Univ Of Ny City Coll, New York, NY; JR; BS MD; Hon Soc 89-; Bio Med; Doctor.

**EISNER, LISA M,** Newbury Coll, Brookline, MA; FR; ASSOC; Clinical Internship; Assoc Massasoit Comm Clg; Phy Thrpy Assist; Pediatrics.

**EISNER, TERI,** City Univ Of Ny Queensbrough, New York, NY; SO; AA; Deans Lst 90-; Phi Theta Kappa; Social Sci/Psych; Clncl Psychologist.

**EISON, TRACIE D,** Voorhees Coll, Denmark, SC; SR; BS; Soc Sci Clb 89-; Soclgy; Soc Wrkr.

**EISWERTH, STEVE G,** Nova Univ, Ft Lauderdale, FL; GD; MBA; Clg Repubs PR Chrmn 84; Alpha Tau Omega 82-85; Territory Sales Repr 87-; BA Univ TN 86; Strategic Plng; Mktg/Cust Serv.

**EJEKAM, MICHAEL C,** Fl International Univ, Miami, FL; FR; BSC; Intl Stdnts Clb 90-; Black Stdnts Union 90-; Hons Pgm Soc 90-; Hons Cmte 90-; Rotaract Clb; IM Soccer 90-; Econs; Law/Bus.

**EJEM, THERESA O,** Al A & M Univ, Normal, AL; GD; BS; Food Sci Clb 87-90; Pres Schlrstc Clb 88-90; Chrch Choir 87-88; Food Sci.

**EJERCITO, JOAN C,** Mount Saint Mary Coll, Newburgh, NY; SR; BS; Pblc Rel Assn 88-89; Stu Bus Assn 88-89; Gaelic Soc 90-; Schl Ppr 90-; Cmpgn Mngr 90; BA; Engl; Mdcl Rcrd Admn.

**EJIOGU, KINGSLEY C,** Hellenic Coll/Holy Cross, Brookline, MA; SR; BA; Assc Nigerian Stu 87-88f Yrbk Clb Edtr In Chf; Flash Magz; Assc Hnr Stu; Intern Jstc Rsrc Inst; WASC Emmanuel Coll Nigeria 79; Hmn Dev/Rel Stu; Law.

**EKE, CHINWE C,** Howard Univ, Washington, DC; SO; BARCH; Afrcn Stdnt Assoc Sec 90-; Tae Kwon Do; Archtctr.

**EKECHI, CHIDI U,** Kent St Univ Kent Cmps, Kent, OH; SO; MBA; Vol Coach/Referee Kent Yth Pks/Recr 87-; Hulda Smith-Graham Awd Schlrshp 90; Soccer 89-; Mgmt/Econ; Bsn/Econ.

**EKHOLM, CARL W,** Savannah St Coll, Savannah, GA; JR; BS; USAF Rtrd Msgt; Elctrncs Tech; Engr.

**EKHOLM, STACIA M,** Univ Of New England, Biddeford, ME; JR; ASN; Nur Assoc Me Med Ctr; Nurs; R N.

**EKINS, JAMES P,** Western Carolina Univ, Cullowhee, NC; JR; BS; Outdoor Activities Com 88-; Mtn Bike Racing Tm 90-; Nat Res Mgt Clb 89-; Natl Park Serv Intern 90; Varsity Open Canoe Tm Asst Coach 88-; Geo Sci; Natl Park Serv Ranger.

**EKKENS, MELINDA J,** Columbia Union Coll, Takoma Park, MD; FR; BS; Phi Eta Sigma; Mdcl Tchnlgy; Mdcl Tchnlgst.

**EKOKU, KOKOME B,** City Univ Of Ny Kingsborough, Brooklyn, NY; SO; BA; Hons Optim Clb 90; AAS; Bus; Acctng.

**EKPO, ENE LAZARUS,** Southern Coll Of Tech, Marietta, GA; JR; BTECII; Elec Eng.

**EKPO, MWENI U,** Tougaloo Coll, Tougaloo, MS; FR; BA; Clg Concrt Chr 90-; Stdnt Govt Assn; Alpha Lambda Delta 90-; Music Awd 90-; Engl/Music; Law.

**EKUBAN, CYNTHIA E,** Seton Hall Univ, South Orange, NJ; FR; Blck Stdnt Union 90-; Rsdntl Actvts 90-; M L King Jr Stdnt Assn 90-; Elem Ed/Psychlgy; Elem Ed.

**EKWUGHA, COMFORT C,** Al A & M Univ, Normal, AL; SR; BS; Schl Bus Org; FMA; Acdmc Hon; Lrng Rsrcs Cntr Asstshps 87-88; Schl Agri Dept Food Sci 89-90; Mbr St Charles Aglcn Chrch Hntsvll 89-; Grad Lvl Degree Comp Sci; Fin; Comp Sci.

**EL MASRI, ANIS B,** Lexington Comm Coll, Lexington, KY; FR; BA; Deans Lst; Architecture Tech.

**EL-AMIN, ALICIA J,** Univ Of Al At Birmingham, Birmingham, AL; SR; BED; Chem/Spnsh; Medicine.

**EL-GHOUCH, MOHAMAD MUHIEDDINE,** Old Dominion Univ, Norfolk, VA; SR; MS; ISA 87-88; Alpha Chi Epsilon 88; BSEET 90; Cmptr Engr; Engr.

**ELAM, MATTHEW,** Univ Of Cincinnati, Cincinnati, OH; JR; BS; Crmnl Just; Law Enfrcmnt.

**ELAM, PAULA D,** Alcorn St Univ, Lorman, MS; FR; BS; Spec Educ; Tch.

**ELAM, SALLY A,** Lexington Comm Coll, Lexington, KY; FR; BA.

**ELBAUM, JEFFREY C,** Ny Univ, New York, NY; GD; Cystc Fbrsis Chrty Org 89-; Clg Dntstry 90-; Univ Pittsburgh 84-85; Alpha Omega 87-; Pi Lambda Phi Sec 84-87; Sccr/Bsktbl; Bronx Lebanon Hsp; Albert Einstein Hsp; Oral/Mxllfcl Srgry Res Montefiore Bronx NY; DDS; Dntstry; Oral/Mxllfcl Srgry.

**ELBAZ, VERONIQUE M,** James Madison University, Harrisonburg, VA; SR; French Clb 87-88; Clarinet Choir 87-88; Psych Clb 89-; Golden Key 90-; Psi Chi 89-; Ctr Svc Learning 88-90; BS; Psych; Cnslg Psych.

**ELBERT, BRUCE B,** Univ Of Ky, Lexington, KY; JR; BS; Ballroom Dnce Scty VP 89; Stdnt Athletic Cncl 89; Keeneland Hse Cncl 89; Bio Pre-Med; MD.

**ELBERT, DENNIS M,** Bellarmine Coll, Louisville, KY; SR; Stdnt Gvrnmnt; Stff Wrtr Schl Newspapr; Stdnt Sr Rep 88; Ambssdrs Cmmttee; Math Assoc Of Amer; Drm Govt Flr Rep; Orient Advsr 90; Delta Epsilon Sigma 90; Delta Sigma Pi VP 90; Deans Lst 88-90; Intrnshp Actrl 89; Im Bsktbl Vllybl Flshbl; Math Actrl Sci.

**ELDER, CAROLYN H,** Bloomfield Coll, Bloomfield, NJ; GD; BA; Alpha Sigma Lambda 90; Alpha Chi 90; Psi Chi 89; Mental Hlth Intrnshp 90; ARRT Am Soc Of R T 89-; NJSRT Radiogrphc/Radiothrpy 74-; Staff Rdtn Thrpst 75-; RT-R UMDNJ 75; Soc Dvlpmnt; Clinical Psych/Divinity.

**ELDER SR, JAMES R,** Pellissippi St Tech Comm Coll, Knoxville, TN; FR; AAS; Stdnt Govt Assn Treas V P 90-; Tenn Intercigte Sta Leg Sntr 90-; Phi Theta Kappa 90-; Tau Alpha Phi; U S Army Warrant Ofcr Assn Chapt Sec 88-89; U S Army Qtrmstr Warrnt Ofcr 63-89; Engr; Cmptr Drftng.

**ELDER, JANET M,** S U N Y Coll At Fredonia, Fredonia, NY; SR; BA; Phi Theta Kappa 89; Alpha Kappa Delta; Intrnshp Wrkplc Lit Of Dunkirk NY; Mayville Div Ethan Allen 73-88; BA; ASS Jamestown Cmnty Clge 89; Sclgy; Soc Wrk.

**ELDER, JOSEPH MERRITT,** Univ Of Ga, Athens, GA; Camp Ynts Schlrshp Piedmnt Clg 88-90; Trnsfr Stdnt Schlrshp Univ Ga 90-; K L Waters Schlrshp Phrmcy Schl 90-; Phrm D Pgm.

**ELDER, KAREN MC ANLIS,** Univ Of Toledo, Toledo, OH; GD; JD; Fedlst Soc 90-; Grad Asst Public Cmunctn 87-88; BA 84; MA 88; Law.

**ELDER III, ROBERT J,** Tallahassee Comm Coll, Tallahassee, FL; SR; BA; Pi Kappa Alpha; AA Tallahassee Cmnty Clg 90; Acctng; Tax Attrny.

**ELDER, ROBIN L,** Univ Of Sc At Columbia, Columbia, SC; FR; BA; Frshmn Achvmnt Wrtng Awd; Chnclrs Lst; Prsdnt Lst; Vrsty Sftbl 90-; Psychology; Psychologist.

**ELDER, TRUDY J,** Kent St Univ Kent Cmps, Kent, OH; SR; BBA; RHO Epsilon Sec 90; Intnl Assc Corp Real Est Excvtvs; KSV Fnc Assc; Golden Key; Pres List/Deans List; Harwood Memorial Schrshp; Finance/Real Est; Corp Real Est.

**ELDRED, GREG B,** Univ Of Miami, Coral Gables, FL; SO; BA; Army ROTC 89-90; Stf Rptr 90-; Scrty Asst Cmps Scrty; Gnrl Hnrs 89-90; Hnrs Std Asc 90-; Natl Ftbl Fdn Hall/Fame Awd; Schlp Notre Dame 89-; F Steele Mntl Attd Awd 89; Acad All-St Tm; Natl Hnr Soc 85-89; Jrnlsm Awds 89; Jrnlsm/Engl; Law.

**ELDRED JR, JAMES L,** Old Dominion Univ, Norfolk, VA; FR; BS; Tau Alpha Phi 90-; US Navy 90; Elec Eng Tech.

**ELDRED, JEREMY G,** Elmira Coll, Elmira, NY; SO; BA; Phi Beta Kappa Prize; Hstry.

**ELDREDGE, ALISON L,** Univ Of Nh Plymouth St Coll, Plymouth, NH; SO; BA; Wmns Track; Psi Chi 90-; Salem Hse Neglctd/Abused Chldrn; Natl Hnrs Soc 90-; Plymouth Schlrs Awd 89-90; Dns Lst 89-90; Pres Lst 89-; Psych; Clncl Psych.

**ELDREDGE, KARMA J,** Coker Coll, Hartsville, SC; JR; Clcnl Psych; Ph D.

**ELDRETH, DORIS P,** Catawba Valley Comm Coll, Hickory, NC; FR; Natl Orgztn Wmn 89-; Off Mgr Multi City Foods Inc; Bus Admn; Legal Asstng.

**ELDRIDGE, ALICIA C,** Marshall University, Huntington, WV; FR; BA; SGA Ste 90-; Phi Eta Sigma; Chem/Phy; Secdry Ed.

**ELDRIDGE, DONNA R,** Univ Of South Al, Mobile, AL; SR; MBA; Propeller Club Of U S Port Of Mobile 90-; Delta Nu Alpha 90-; Deans List 90-; Pres List; Delta Nu Alpha; Schlrshp Gulf Coast Traffic Club 90; Propeller Club Of U S Port Mobile 90-; Social Serv/Hmn Resc Worker 88-89; BS; Bus Mgmnt; Transportation Mgmnt.

**ELDRIDGE, HARRIETT C,** Univ Of Cincinnati, Cincinnati, OH; SR; BS; Gold Key 90-; Voorhees Hon Schlrshp 90-; Art Dir Amer Fed Of Adv Cnsltnts 82-85; Pr Mc Gregor Thompson Mc Gregor 86-89; Crim Just; Juv Rehab.

**ELDRIDGE, JANICE M,** Tn Temple Univ, Chattanooga, TN; FR; BS; Stdt Govt VP; 85-86; Stdt Cncl 84-85; Stdt Cncl Repr Class Repr 87-89; Yrbk Stf Jr Editor 84-87; Jr/Sr Com Pres 87-88; Sr Lunch Com Tutor 88-89; Stdt Aides Hgh Schl Tchr Asst Tchr Engl/Sci 86-89; Bsktbl Cpt 85-89; Sftbl 85-89; Hstry Law; Corp Lawyer.

**ELDRIDGE, JENNIFER L,** Northern Ky Univ, Highland Hts, KY; JR; BED; SNEA; Engl Tutor Vol 87-; Wlk-Amer 89-; Spec Ed Asst 90-; Scnd Grd Asst 90-; Jr Clss Mrshl; Elem Ed.

**ELDRIDGE, KAREN A,** Trinity Coll, Burlington, VT; FR; BA; Applied Phtgrphy; Phto Jrnlst.

**ELDRIDGE, MARK W,** Univ Of Ky, Lexington, KY; SO; Amer Inst Chem Engrs 90-; Chem Engr.

**ELEFTHERIOU, STEPHANIE M,** Smith Coll, Northampton, MA; JR; BA; French Clb German Clb 88-89; Intrntl Stdnts Org 88-90; Porcupine Rag Humor Mag 88-90; 1 Grp Schlr 89-90; Ruth Forbes Eliot Poetry Prize 89-90; Engl Lit; Pblshng.

**ELENCHIK, PAMELA M,** Coll Misericordia, Dallas, PA; JR; BS; Educ Clb Pres/Sec 89-; Peer Tutrng 89-; Elem Educ; Tchng.

**ELENGO, CHRISTINA M,** Albertus Magnus Coll, New Haven, CT; SR; MA; Pax Chrsti 90-; BA; Psychlgy.

**ELEY, PARIS L,** Univ Of Nc At Charlotte, Charlotte, NC; SO; BS; Bapt Stdnt Union; Blck Stdnt Union; Sch Newspaper Prod Asst; Bio; Med.

**ELEY, ROBYN M,** Oh Northern Univ, Ada, OH; FR; BA; OH Nrthrn Chms Bll Chr 90-; Mck Trl 90-; Drm Hll Wng Rep 90-; Pol Sci Hstry; Law.

**ELEY, STACY L,** Alcorn St Univ, Lorman, MS; JR; BS; Acctg Clb; SGA Miss Jr 90-; Hon Stdnts Org 88-; Alpha Kappa Mu 90-; Phi Beta Lambda Treas 89-; Estrn Star 90-; Pres Schlr 89; Deans Lst Chlr 88-; Acad Schlrshp 88-; Hmntrn Schlrshp 88-89; Acctg; Emplyee IRS.

**ELFARRA, ABDELGHANI K,** Univ Of Louisville, Louisville, KY; JR; MENG; NCSA; IEEE 89-; GE Applncs Applnc Park Louisvl KY 90-; Elctrcl; Eng.

**ELFMAN, AMY M,** Lasell Coll, Newton, MA; SO; BA; Lbrl Arts.

**ELFORD, JENNIFER A,** The Boston Conservatory, Boston, MA; SO; BFA; Jose Limon Dance Co Dancer; Dance.

**ELGAALI, MAGDELDIN A,** Ms St Univ, Miss State, MS; SR; Amer Assoc Agri Engrs 89-; Internatl Stdnts Assoc 87-; Trng Pgms Hgh Schl Stdnts 84-86; AS Cayahoga Comm Clge 86; BS; Ag Engrg.

**ELGIN, BRUCE LANE,** Patrick Henry Comm Coll, Martinsville, VA; SO; BA; NTSO Treas 89-90; Phi Theta Kappa 89-; Spire 90-; Collinsville Jaycees 90-; Circular Knit Mech 81-; AAS; Acctg; CPA.

**ELGIN, HOLLI M,** Indiana Univ Of Pa, Indiana, PA; SO; BS; Provost Schlr; Engl Educ; Tchg.

**ELGIN, WILLIAM L,** Tri County Tech Coll, Pendleton, SC; FR; ASSC; Lng Brnch Bapt Chrch Asst SS Tchr 89-; Wst Pnt Pprll Sprvsr Trnee; Txtle.

**ELIAS, ANTHONY A,** U S Military Academy, West Point, NY; FR; BS; 2nd Rgmnt Co A 90-; Cmpltd Cdt Bsc Trng 90-; Cdt Fld Trng; Dns Lst 90-; Armr Mchnzd Infntry Air Dfnse And Fld Artllry Trng Ft Knox; Dstngshd Cdt 90-; Bxng Gymnstcs Swmmng 90-; Chem Bsc Sci Stds Life Scis; Med.

**ELIAS, LISETTE G,** Western New England Coll, Springfield, MA; SO.

**ELIAS, RASCHAA E,** Clark Atlanta Univ, Atlanta, GA; FR; BED; Mrchng Bnd 90-; Cncrt Bnd 90-; Hnrs Prgrm; Early Chldhd Edctn; Tchng.

**ELIE, SHERRY ANN B,** Fl St Univ, Tallahassee, FL; SR; BS; Caribbean Assn; Gldn Key; Phi Kappa Phi; Du Bois Hnr Soc; SCEC; Deans Lst 87-90; FL Mltcltrl Spprt Cntr Awrds; AA; Lrnng Dsblts Emtnl Dstrbncs; MS Spcl Edctn.

**ELKHATIB, GHADA M,** Davis Coll, Toledo, OH; FR; IBD; Int Design.

**ELKINS, CHARLOTTE W,** Itawamba Comm Coll, Fulton, MS; FR; Sierra Clb Fulton Reg Chrmn Mbrshp Comm; Dental Asst; Radlgc Tech.

**ELKINS, JUDITH P,** Univ Of Cincinnati, Cincinnati, OH; SO; BS; Deans Lst 89-; Nutrition; Dietetics.

**ELKINS, KIMBERLY A,** Ky St Univ, Frankfort, KY; SO; Ohio Clb 89-90; Chrldr 90; Physcl Thrpy; Sprts Med.

**ELKINS, RONI JO,** Fl International Univ, Miami, FL; GD; BA; AA 86; Elem Ed.

**ELLEN, DANIEL M,** Ny Univ, New York, NY; SO; BS; Peers Ears Stdnt Cnslng Srvc Cnslr 89-90; Speech Debate Soc 89-90; IM Vlybl Cptn 89-90; AA; Bsns; Finance Mgmt.

**ELLER, DORIS J,** West Liberty St Coll, West Liberty, WV; SR; Kappa Delta Phi; BA; Elem Educ/Erly Chldhd.

**ELLER, HANSELENA R,** Central Wesleyan Coll, Central, SC; FR; MBA; Law And Educ; Lawyr Tchr.

**ELLER, JAMES J,** Hillsborough Comm Coll, Tampa, FL; SO; BSCH; Phi Theta Kappa; Math; Engrg.

**ELLER, JOHN H,** Brevard Coll, Brevard, NC; FR; BA; Glf Schlrshp Brvrd Coll; Brvrd Coll Golf Tm; Prof Glf Mgt; Dir.

**ELLER, NICOLE B,** Daemen Coll, Amherst, NY; JR; BS; APTA 90-; Intrnshp Buffalo Pt Sportscare/Assoc Ther; Phys Ther.

**ELLER, SHERRY A,** Wv Northern Comm Coll, Wheeling, WV; FR; ASSOC; Project Best Schlrshp 90-; Bus Admn; Bnkng Mgmt.

**ELLETT, ANGEL N,** Va Commonwealth Univ, Richmond, VA; SO; BS; Phi Eta Sigma 90-; Sigma Sigma Sigma 90-; Biol; Enviro Studies.

**ELLI, R THOMAS,** Indiana Univ Of Pa, Indiana, PA; JR; BED; UMWA 87-; Nrthrn Cambria Rec; Elem Educ; Tchg.

**ELLIAS, RANDI L,** Franklin And Marshall Coll, Lancaster, PA; SO; BA; Choral Scty 89-90; Envrnmntl Actn Allnce 90; Mrshll Schlr; ACS Awd For Orgnc Chem; Chem; Law/Envrnmntl Chem.

**ELLINGBOE, PATRICIA J,** Atlantic Comm Coll, Mays Landing, NJ; SO; Bsn Admin; Bnkng.

**ELLINGER WOODSON, DELTHA T,** Mary Baldwin Coll, Staunton, VA; GD; BA; Abraxas House Cnslr 87-88; Regn Ten Comm Svcs Cnslr 90; Aug Cnty Schl Brd Tchr 87-; AAS Blue Ridge Comm Clg 87-89; Soc/Tchr Cert Pgm; Educ.

**ELLINGSWORTH, TERESA R,** Clarkson Univ, Potsdam, NY; SR; BS; Natl Assoc Acctnts Stdnt Aflt Grp Sec 88-; Clarkson Soc Acctnts 89-; Bsn Clb 88-89; Phi Theta Kappa Treas 88-; Phi Kappa Phi 90-; AS Jefferson Cmnty Clge 89; Acctng; CPA.

**ELLINGTON, CHAD K,** Fl International Univ, Miami, FL; FR; BS; Rd Dsc Jcky 90-; Mass Comm.

**ELLINGTON, YVONNE L,** Claflin Coll, Orangeburg, SC; SR; BA; Stdnt Chrstn Assoc Treas 90-; Stdnt Gov Assoc 2nd Attndt Miss Claflin 90-; ROTC Clb 87-90; Natl Soc Scbbrd/Blde Jrnlst 88-89; Alpha Kappa Alpha Corsp Sec 90-; Dns Lst; Hon Rl; Natl Dns Lst; Soclgy; Soc Wrk/Law.

**ELLINGWOOD, JENNIFER A,** Allegheny Coll, Meadville, PA; JR; BA; Clg Chrs 88-89; Amnsty Intrntl; Psi Chi; Kappa Alpha Theta 89-; Tchrs Asstnt/Tutr Fr Psych Dpt; Alden Schlr 89-90; Psychlgy.

**ELLIOT, DENISE L,** Savannah Coll Of Art & Design, Savannah, GA; SR; Crew.

**ELLIOT, VANESSA E,** Tougaloo Coll, Tougaloo, MS; SO; BA; SG Miss Frshmn 89-90; Alpha Lambda Delta Sec 90-; Upward Bnd; Tutor 90-; Hlth Care/Intern; Clinical Chld Psychlgst.

**ELLIOTT FRIEND, NINA J,** Davis & Elkins Coll, Elkins, WV; GD; ASN; SNA 90-; Acadmc Awd 90-; LPN Mon Co Vo Tech 81; Nrsng.

**ELLIOTT, ADAM T,** Georgetown Coll, Georgetown, KY; JR; BS; Pi Kappa Alpha Schlrshp Chrmn 89-; Outstndg Pre-Engrg Stu; Pre-Engrng; Mech Engrng.

**ELLIOTT, ALASTAIR C,** Univ Of Miami, Coral Gables, FL; FR; BS; Amer Soc Cvl Engrs 90-; Cncl Intl Stu Org 90-; Org Jamaican Unity 90-; Alpha Lambda Delta; Hnr Stu Assoc 90-; Ntl Coll Engr Awrd; Cvl Engr.

**ELLIOTT, ANGELITTA P,** Howard Univ, Washington, DC; JR; BSW; Bsktbl 88-; SW Seneca Clg N York On 88-90; Soc Wrk; Prfsnl Soc Wrker.

**ELLIOTT, AUDREYLYNN,** Radford Univ, Radford, VA; FR; BA; Prsbytrn Org; Ncrt Bnd 90-; Alpha Lambda Delta; Musc Bus.

**ELLIOTT, AVIS A,** Va St Univ, Petersburg, VA; JR; BA; Intrntnl Stds Clb; Hstry Clb 89-; Pltcl Sci Clb; Alpha Mu Gamma 90-; Red Cross 89-; Spnsh Tutor 89-; Martin Lthr Prtr Hstry Awd 89; Dpt St Frgn Srvc Inst Intrn; Frt Lee Fmly Spprt Grp; Intrntnl Stu Pltcl Sci; Frgn Srvc.

**ELLIOTT, BEVERLY E,** Winthrop Coll, Rock Hill, SC; SO; BED; Cncl Exptnl Chldrn 90-, Alpha Lambda Delta 89-; Spec Ed.

**ELLIOTT, BRIAN J,** Univ Of New Haven, West Haven, CT; FR; BA; Crmnl Jstce; Law.

**ELLIOTT, CARLA R,** Brewer St Jr Coll, Fayette, AL; SO; BED; Deans Lst; Math Chmstry; Scndry Ed.

**ELLIOTT, CY F,** Univ Of The Dist Of Columbia, Washington, DC; SR; BBA; UDC Acctg Clb 88-; UDC Bus/Finance Clb 89-; Gd Nghbrs Clb Treas 87-; Acctg; CPA.

**ELLIOTT, CYNTHIA L,** Univ Of Tn At Martin, Martin, TN; JR; BS; Yrbk Edtr 88-; Comm Clb 88-90; Tapherd Aapherd 90-; Phi Epsilon Mu 89-; Phi Epsilon Delta 88-89; Habitat Humnty 90-; Inner City Dev 90-; M Hart Schlrshp 88-; Phys Educ; Corp Ftns.

**ELLIOTT, DAWN G,** Abraham Baldwin Agri Coll, Tifton, GA; SO; BA; AS; Erly Chldhd Educ.

**ELLIOTT, EDDIE G,** Coker Coll, Hartsville, SC; SR; BS; Army Natl Gurd Mstr Sarg; Georgetwn Steel Corp Elec Engr; AS Cntr For Degree Studs 89; Bus Mgmt; Elec Engr.

**ELLIOTT, ELISON J,** City Univ Of Ny City Coll, New York, NY; GD; JD; Gov Law Scty Pres 87-88; Pltcl Dir 88-90; Day Stdnt Gov Pltcl Dir 88-89; Sub Rosa Chrmn Dir 89; Gldn Key 89-90; 4h Yth Dvlpmnt Prgrm 90; Rosenberg Humphrey Fllw Pblc Plcy Rsrch 89-90; Intrn Cngssnl Bdgt Off NRCD Dvsn 89; Intnl Law/Dvlpng Nations; Pblc Offc.

**ELLIOTT, GLYNIS J,** Clark Atlanta Univ, Atlanta, GA; SR; BA; Early Chldhd Educ Clb 90-; BA; Early Chldhd Educ; Tchr K-4.

**ELLIOTT, GORDON E,** Wilmington Coll, New Castle, DE; JR; MBA; De FOP Lodge 86-; Lt Dewey Bch Police Dept 84-; AS De Tech Clg 89; Crmnl Justc; Chf Police.

**ELLIOTT, GWEN M,** Radford Univ, Radford, VA; SR; BBA; Amer Mktg Assn 90-; Hs Cncl Treas 88-89; Phnllnc-Schlrshp 90-; Zeta Tau Alpha; Mst Outstndng Sr Mktg; Mst Outstndng Sr ZTA; Mktg.

**ELLIOTT, JEREMY S,** Univ Of Sc At Columbia, Columbia, SC; SR; BS; Fncl Mngmnt Assoc Sec 90; FMA Ntl Hnr Soc; Phi Betta Kappa; Beta Gamma Sigma; Beta Alpha Psi; Campus Coalition For Litrcy; Thomas J Robertson Bnkng Schlrshp 90; Fnce Accntng; Big 6 Accntng.

**ELLIOTT, JODI L,** Wv Northern Comm Coll, Wheeling, WV; FR; BA; Math/Sci Lab Asst; Acctg.

**ELLIOTT, JOHNATHAN V,** Pfeiffer Coll, Misenheimer, NC; SR; Hstry Clb Pres 87-; Symphnc Cncrt Choirs 89-; By Scts Amer Asst Sctmstr 88-89; Phi Alpha Theta Treas 90-; US Achvmnt Acad 90-; Otstndng Clg Stdnts Of Amer 87-; AB; Hstry; Law.**

**ELLIOTT, JULIA D,** Univ Of North Fl, Jacksonville, FL; JR; BA; Kappa Delta Pi; Elem Educ.

**ELLIOTT, KAREN E,** Middle Tn St Univ, Murfreesboro, TN; SO; BS; CSTEA 89-; SOA 90; Gamma Beta Phi 90-; Elem Educ; Elem Tchr.

**ELLIOTT, KELLY G,** Birmingham Southern Coll, Birmingham, AL; SO; Triangl Clb 90-; Kappa Mu Epsilon 90-; Phi Eta Sigma VP 90-; Alpha Lambda Delta 90-; Alpha Chi Omega Rec Sec 89-; Alpha Phi Omega 90-; Stdnt Vol Serv 90; Dana Intrnshp 90-; Math.

**ELLIOTT, KELLY J,** Western Ky Univ, Bowling Green, KY; SO; BS; Assoc Stdnt Govt VP 89-90; Phi Eta Sigma 89-; Beta Beta Beta 89-; Alpha Epsilon Delta; Alpha Omicron Pi 90-; Outstndng Stdnt Afrs Comm Prsn 90; Bio/Chem; Medcn.

**ELLIOTT, MARA S,** Tallahassee Comm Coll, Tallahassee, FL; SO; BA; Deans Lst; Engrng.

**ELLIOTT, MATTHEW T,** Bethany Coll, Bethany, WV; FR; BA; Socl Sci; Politics.

**ELLIOTT, MICHAEL W,** Univ Of Al, Tuscaloosa, AL; FR; BS; Phi Eta Sigma; Alpha Lambda Delta; Eng.

**ELLIOTT, MICHELLE D,** Daytona Beach Comm Coll, Daytona Beach, FL; FR; BA; Deans Lst; Pres Lst; Bnk Tlr; Food Srvc; Acctg; CPA.

**ELLIOTT, MIRIAM E,** Birmingham Southern Coll, Birmingham, AL; SO; BA; Hnrs Prog; Triangle Club; Pres Stdnt Serv Org; Admn Intern Office Of Adult Studies; IM Bsktbl Vlybl; Bus Admn; Mrktng/Entrepreneur.

**ELLIOTT, NATHAN,** Livingston Univ, Livingston, AL; JR; BS; Sci/Math Scty 89-; Math Assc Amer VP 89-; Wsly Fndtn Pres 89-; Alph Chi; Wesley Fndtn Intrn 89-; Chrstn Ldrshp Awrd; MAA GPA Awrd; Math/Bio; Tchng/Methdst Mnstry.

**ELLIOTT, NIGEL H,** Tuskegee Univ, Tuskegee Inst, AL; FR; DVM; SCAVMA; Ornt/Wlcm Comm Chrmn 90-; B Sc U W Indies Mona Jamiaca WI 88; Vet Med.

**ELLIOTT, PAULETTE D,** Watterson Coll, Louisville, KY; ASSOC; Church Usher Sec; USA Dntl Asst 86-90; Acctg.

**ELLIOTT, RAYMOND E,** Anne Arundel Comm Coll, Arnold, MD; FR; BS; Sociology; Education.

**ELLIOTT, SCOTT M,** The Boston Conservatory, Boston, MA; SR; BFA; Afro Am Artist Assoc 89-; SGA 89-; House Of Reps 90-; Dance Dept Rep 89-; Class Pres 90-; Class Marshal 90-; Boston Cons Asstshp In Dance 89-; Dance Perf; Joining Dayton Ballet Co Ohio.

**ELLIOTT, STEPHANIE L,** Truett Mc Connell Coll, Cleveland, GA; SO; BS; Animal Science; Horse Breeding/Training.

**ELLIOTT, TOMMY,** Rust Coll, Holly Springs, MS; FR; Dns Lst/Hnr Rl 90-; IM All Star Bsktbl; IM Capt 90-; Math; Scndry Ed/Tchng.

**ELLIOTT, WANDA L,** Middle Tn St Univ, Murfreesboro, TN; SO; BS; Gamma Beta Phi 90-; Psych; Cnslng.

**ELLIOTT, WILLIAM F,** Univ Of Montevallo, Montevallo, AL; SR; Bsbl George Wallace Jr Clg 85-88; BS 90; Physcl Ed; Tchg Physcl Ed.

**ELLIOTT, WILLIAM G,** Furman Univ, Greenville, SC; FR; BSBED; Flshwp Chrstn Athlts 90-; Bapt Stdnt Union Sec 90-; Phdi Eta Sgm 90-; Clgt Eductnl Svc Corps 90-; Physcs Fclty Awrd; Physcs; Teach.

**ELLIOTTE, MARK B,** Radford Univ, Radford, VA; FR; BA; Hist.

**ELLIS, ANGELA DENISE,** Fl A & M Univ, Tallahassee, FL; SO; BA; Amer Poetry Assn 87-; Pub Rltns Soc Amer Promo/Serv Chrprsn 90-; Phi Eta Sigma 89-; Natl Assn Blck Jrnlsts 90-; Jrnlsm Endwmnt Schlrshp; Pub Rltns; Corp.**

**ELLIS, BARBARA A,** Volunteer St Comm Coll, Gallatin, TN; BA; Gamma Beta Phi; Hnr Rl; Dns Lst 89-91.

**ELLIS, BRIAN K,** Mount Olive Coll, Mount Olive, NC; JR; BS; Psychlgy Clb Hstrn 90-; Psi Chi; NC State Govt Intern; AA Johnston Comm Clg 89; Psychlgy.

**ELLIS, BRYAN P,** Birmingham Southern Coll, Birmingham, AL; FR; BA; Computer Sci; Consulting.

**ELLIS, CASEY A,** Univ Of Sc At Columbia, Columbia, SC; FR; BS; Sltudent Assist/Student Wlkr; Student Council Schlrshp Marshall; Nursing.

**ELLIS, CATHY LEANNE,** Pellissippi St Tech Comm Coll, Knoxville, TN; SO; AA; Vsn Vol 89; Jrnlsm/Ms Cmnctns; Pblctns/Mgzn Ed.

**ELLIS, CHANTE M,** Hampton Univ, Hampton, VA; FR; Terpschrn Danc Co Trs Arnd The St Rep Univ 90-; Intrnshp Exxon Co 90-; Cmptr Sci; Cmptr Analyst.

**ELLIS, CLIFFORD E,** Roane St Comm Coll, Harriman, TN; FR; BA; Alld Hlth; Phy Thrpy.

**ELLIS, CRISTINA M,** Valdosta St Coll, Valdosta, GA; SO; BED; Early Chldhd Ed; Tchng.

**ELLIS, CYNTHIA J,** Owensboro Comm Coll, Owensboro, KY; FR; BS; Amnsty Intl; Commonwealth Schlrshp; Accntng; CPA/LAW.

**ELLIS, DAVID S,** Univ Of Ga, Athens, GA; FR; AB; Wesley Fndtn 90-; Clge Rpblcns 90-; Alpha Lambda Delta 90-; Hnrs Pgm/Cert Acdmc Achvmnt; Hstry; Tchg.

**ELLIS, DEBORAH L,** Milligan Coll, Milligan Clg, TN; JR; BS; Cncrt Chr Drll Tm; Nwsppr; Yrbk; Cmmnctns; Msc Thrpy.

**ELLIS, DOROTHY SHOOK,** Univ Of Montevallo, Montevallo, AL; SR; Phi Theta Kappa; Kappa Delta Pi 87-; Omicron Delta Kappa; Lambda Sigma Pi 87-; Phi Alpha Theta 89-; AA Jefferson State 89; BA; Scl Scis.

**ELLIS, GARY M,** Middle Tn St Univ, Murfreesboro, TN; JR; BS; Deans List; Cntr Abused Chldrn Vol; Psychlgy; Industral Psychlgst.

**ELLIS, GEORGE,** Bloomfield Coll, Bloomfield, NJ; SR; BA; Psych Clb V P 89-90; Psi Clb; Washington Acad Tchr Aide Emtnly Chldrn Intern 89-; Psych; Clncl Psych.

**ELLIS, GEORGE W,** Roane St Comm Coll, Harriman, TN; SO; BS; Crmnlgy; Law.

**ELLIS, GWENDOLYN E,** Univ Of Cincinnati, Cincinnati, OH; GD; ED; Faculty Senate Repr 89-; Grad Ed Assoc Secr 89-; Tenure/Appropriation Comm 89-90; Phi Theta Kappa 89-; Kappa Delta Pi 89-; Phi Beta Lambda 80-89; Outstndg Yng Wmn 81; Blck Wmns Caucus 85-87; Srch/Screen Comm 84-86; Sch Psych/Spec Ed; Univ Prfsr/Rsrchr.

**ELLIS, JAMES L,** Cincinnati Bible Coll & Sem, Cincinnati, OH; GD; MAMRE; Yth Mnstr 80-87; Prchng Mnstr 90-; Bth Ozark Bible Clg 82; Cnslng Rlgs Edctn.

**ELLIS, JAMIE C,** Middle Tn St Univ, Murfreesboro, TN; FR; BS; Chemistry; Medicine.

**ELLIS, JANET B,** Winthrop Coll, Rock Hill, SC; SR; BSW; Phi Kappa Phi 90; Dept Mngr Rtl Store 85-88; AS Gen Bus York Tech Coll 81; Scl Wrk.

**ELLIS, JANIE Y,** Stillman Coll, Tuscaloosa, AL; GD; Sclgy Clb Pres 89-; Rtrct Clb 88-; Natl Leag Advncmnt Educ 88-; Deans Lst; Cordell Wynns Hon Pgm; Sclgy/Elem Ed; Educ.

**ELLIS, JAYNIDA M,** Tougaloo Coll, Tougaloo, MS; FR; Hon Rl 90-; Chem; Pre Med/Pharm.

**ELLIS, JENNIFER R,** Tn St Univ, Nashville, TN; JR; BA; Univ Nwspr Mng Edtr 88-; Stdnt Elec Comm 90-; Univ Peer Cnslr 89-; Gldn Ky; Alpha Kappa Mu Frgn Lang Hon Soc Sec 89; Soc Prof Jrnlsts Pres 89-90; Natl Assoc Blck Jrnlsts 90-; Alpha Kappa Alpha Sorty Inc Ivy Leaf Rep 90-; Mass Comms; Mrktng Res.

**ELLIS, JOHN T,** Ms St Univ, Miss State, MS; SR; BS; ACM; Gamma Beta Phi; Phi Eta Sigma 87-; Alpha Lambda Beta 88-; Theta Tau 90-; IBM Coop 88-; Anderson Cnsltng Schlrshp; Univ Hnrs Prog 87-; Acdmc Schlrshp 87-; Comp Engrng.

**ELLIS, JUELDA,** Roane St Comm Coll, Harriman, TN; SO; AS; Bsn Ed; Secr.

**ELLIS, JULIE M,** Wallace St Comm Coll At Hncvll, Hanceville, AL; FR; Larry G Cooke CPA 90-; Bus; Acctg.

**ELLIS, KATHY D,** Univ Of Nc At Charlotte, Charlotte, NC; SR; BA; Emergng Ldrs 86-87; Dns Lst 89-; Alpha Delta Pi 87-; Pol Sci; Grad Schl.

**ELLIS, KRISTI M,** Southern Coll Of Tech, Marietta, GA; FR; BS; Nrsng; Nrsng Ansthst.

**ELLIS, LA DEIDRA A,** Fl A & M Univ, Tallahassee, FL; SR; BS; Tau Beta Sigma V P; Non Geek Cncl V P 89-90; Golden Key; White & Gold; Delta Sigma Theta; Deans Lst; Intrn Eaton Corp; Bus Admn/Pltcl Scif Corp Law.

**ELLIS, LAUEEDA L,** Roane St Comm Coll, Harriman, TN; SO; Gamma Beta Phi; Gamma Beta Phi 88-; Magna Cum Laude; Associates; Mgmnt & Finance.

**ELLIS, MARK L,** Univ Of Ga, Athens, GA; JR; BSED; DECA 89-; IM Ftbl 90-; Mktng Ed; Mdl Supply Sales.

**ELLIS, MELANIE A,** Marshall University, Huntington, WV; JR; BA; All Amer Schlr; Acctg; CPA.

**ELLIS, PAULA J,** Saint Catharine Coll, St Catharine, KY; FR; Stdnt Senate Jdcl Bd; Htlh; Dntl Hygeine.

**ELLIS JR, R PARK,** Belmont Coll, Nashville, TN; JR; Music/Engl; Mscn/Engl Prof.

**ELLIS, RANDY L,** Oh Wesleyan Univ, Delaware, OH; JR; BA; Stdnt Govt Jdcl Afrs 90; Dintr Fratrnty Cncl 89-90; Phi Eta Sgm Phi Scty; Omicron Dlt Kappa; Mortar Brd; Ordr Omega; Phi Eta Sgm; Sgm Chi Schlrshp Chr 88-; Stdnt Schlr 90; Vrsty Crs Cntry Indr/Otdr Trck 88-90; Intrntl Bus/Spnsh; Bus.

**ELLIS, SALLY B,** East Tn St Univ, Johnson City, TN; SR; BS; Kappa Omicron Nu Rep 90-; Phi Kappa Phi; Kappa Delta Pi; Amer Hm Ec Assoc Chr 90-; Amer Hm Ec Assoc State 1st V Chr; Harryett Blackwell Schlrshp 89-90; Clemmer Schlrshp 89-90; Best All Around 89-; Voc Hm Ec Ed; Tch.

**ELLIS, STEPHANIE A,** Tougaloo Coll, Tougaloo, MS; JR; Gspl Chr Asst Dir; Afrcn Amer Stds Assn 90; Impct Gspl Grp VP 90; Econs; Law Bus.

**ELLIS, SUSAN R,** Villanova Univ, Villanova, PA; JR; BA; Orntn; Career Plnng Cnslr 90-; Spec Olympcs 89-90; Phi Kappa Phi; Omicron Delta Kappa; Ord Of Omega; Delta Gamma Treas 90; Econs; Mgmt Consltg.

**ELLIS, TANIA,** Fl St Univ, Tallahassee, FL; JR; BS; Sigma Alpha Epsilon AMX 89-90; Mktg; Sales/Phrmctcls.

**ELLIS, TODD D,** Univ Of Sc At Columbia, Columbia, SC; JR; MBA; NAACP Treas 88-; Assoc Afro-Amer Stdnts; Res Advsr; RA; Natl Hnr Soc 89-; SGA 90; SC Telco Fed Credit Union Bd 89-; Minority Asst Peer 90-; Dns Lst 89-; Weightlftg Tm; Med Dr.**

**ELLIS, TONY L,** Savannah St Coll, Savannah, GA; JR; Beta Kappa Chi 90-; Alpha Kappa Mu 90-; Computer Clb; Newtonian Scty 90-; Retired Offcrs Assoc Schrlshp Rcpnt; US Navys Enlisted Cmmssng Prog 90-; US Navy STG 2 85-; Math; Naval Nuclear Propulsion Program.

**ELLISH, YAACOV,** Yeshiva Univ, New York, NY; SR; BA; Psi Chi VP 90-; Psych Clb 90-; Amer Psychlgcl Assn 90-; Dns Lst 88-; Res Advsr Drm Cnslr 90-; Ivan P Tillem Pgm Proj SAGES 89-; Karate Orng Blt 88-89; Psych; Educ.

**ELLISON, ANGELA A,** Middle Tn St Univ, Murfreesboro, TN; SO; BBA; Fresh Hon Stdnt Yr 89-90; Bus; Corp Exec.

**ELLISON, BRIAN S,** Snead St Jr Coll, Boaz, AL; SR; BS; Stdt Escort Serv 87-; Pi Kappa Phi Chrmn Cmnty Serv 87-; Athletic Trainer 90; Exercise Sciences; Physical Therapy.

**ELLISON IV, DAVID G,** Coll Of Charleston, Charleston, SC; SO; BS; FCA 90-; St Philips Episcopal Church; Bus Law; Air Force Law.

**ELLISON, DAVID M,** Univ Of Cin R Walters Coll, Blue Ash, OH; SO; Sci Pre Med; Med.

**ELLISON, JARED K,** Tuskegee Univ, Tuskegee Inst, AL; JR; BS; Pltcl Sci/Debate Clb 89-90; GA Clb/Savannah GA Clb 89-; GM Schlrshp 90-; Hnr Roll 89-90; Track/Field 89-90; Pltcl Sci; Atty/Fed Judge.

**ELLISON, MARY E,** Le Moyne Coll, Syracuse, NY; JR; BS; Yrbk Stf 90-; Intl Hs 88-; Psi Chi 90-; Empr St Chlngr Tchg Schlrshp 89-90; Paul Douglas Tchrs Schlrshp 89-90; Clncl Psych.

**ELLISON, SHARON C,** Lexington Comm Coll, Lexington, KY; SO; ADN; Nrsng; RN.

**ELLISON, TERRY KAY CULP,** Wallace St Comm Coll At Selma, Selma, AL; GD; AS; Pres/Deans Lsts; Bus Admin.

**ELLISOR, JONATHAN L,** Harvard Univ, Cambridge, MA; FR; Chrstn Impact 90-; Crimson Key Soc 91; Frshmn Ftbl 90-; Hist; Intl Bus Law.

**ELLISTON, DANIEL A,** Central Fl Comm Coll, Ocala, FL; JR; PHARM; Acad Stdnt Pharm; Yrbk Asst Edtr; Stdnt Govt Assc VP 88-90; Phi Theta Kappa 87-; Rho Pdi Phi Rope Link Edtr 90-; Our Lady Springs Yth Grp 87; Chrldr 89-90; AA 90; Intrnshp Marion Comm Hosp Pharm 88-89; Intrnshp Walgreens Pharm; Pharm.

**ELLISTON, JEAN A,** Univ Of Tn At Martin, Martin, TN; JR; Stdnt Govt Assn; Educ/English; Tch/Wrt.

**ELLIXSON, DAPHNE C,** Piedmont Comm Coll, Roxboro, NC; FR; AAS; Flrnc Ave Bapt Chrch Treas 84-90; Sub Tchr 80-89; Comp; Data Cmmnctns.

**ELLSWORTH PIMENTEL, MYRIAM,** Inter Amer Univ Pr Hato Rey, Hato Rey, PR; JR; BA; Assn Pol Sci; Pol Sci; Pol Analyst.

**ELLSWORTH, BRUCE,** Rutgers St Univ At Camden, Camden, NJ; JR; BS; Rutgers Acctg Soc 90-; Rutgrs Mktg Clb 90-; Athenem Hnr Soc; Natl Assn Acctnts 90-; Dns Lst 90-; Acctg.

**ELLSWORTH, SHERELL L,** Hillsborough Comm Coll, Tampa, FL; FR.

**ELLUM, PETER V,** Mount Saint Mary Coll, Newburgh, NY; SO; BA; Oper Desert Shld Storm; IM; US Marine 90-; Bus Mgmnt; Law.

**ELMERA, MARIE M,** Bloomfield Coll, Bloomfield, NJ; SO; BA; Nrsng; Med Schl.

**ELMORE, CHISTI R,** Lexington Comm Coll, Lexington, KY; SR; Alpha Sigma Tau; Sigma Tau Lil Sis 87-89; Pldg Queen; Miss Knockout 87-89; Miss Body Beautiful; Schlrshp High Grade Chrldg 90-; Chrldr 87-; Sports 87-; Psych/Dntl Hyg; Dntl Hyg.

**ELMORE, DAMON E,** Savannah St Coll, Savannah, GA; SO; BA; All-Star Challenge Team 90; Drama Society 89; Political Science Club 89; Omega Psi Phi 90; Summer Intrnshp 91; Sarah Mills Hodge Schlrshp 90; Political Science; Law.

**ELMORE, KATHARINE N,** Univ Of Nc At Greensboro, Greensboro, NC; FR; BM; U Show Chr 90-; Intrvrsty Chrstn Flwshp 90-; Alpha Lambda Delta 90-; Music Ed; Tch Chr.

**ELMORE, MICHAEL W,** Gaston Coll, Dallas, NC; FR; BS; Phys Therapy; Sportsmed Spclst.

**ELMORE, PAMELA S,** Wallace St Comm Coll At Selma, Selma, AL; SO; BS ED; AS BA 83; Math; Algbra Tchr.

**ELMORE, PHILLIP C,** Alfred Univ, Alfred, NY; FR; BA; WALF Radio Statn Dj; Alpha Lamda Delta; Bus; Acctg.

**ELMORE, SHEA,** Savannah Coll Of Art & Design, Savannah, GA; FR; BA.

**ELOVECKY, SUZANNE M,** Teikyo Post Univ, Waterbury, CT; FR; BA; Paralegal Clb Pres; Acad Awd $1000 90-; Paralegal Stds; Law.

**ELPERS, LORI A,** Brescia Coll, Owensboro, KY; JR; BS; Natl Student Speech Language Hearing Assoc; Vlybl Tm; Alpha Chi Sec; Deans Lst 89-; Vlybl; Speech Hearing; Speech Pathoogist.

**ELPHICK, THERESE I,** Niagara Univ, Niagara Univ, NY; SO; BA; Flms Cmt 90-; Psychlgy Clb 90-; Hon Pgm 90-; Chld Psychlgst.

**ELROD, DAVID J,** Oglethorpe Univ, Atlanta, GA; SO; BBA; Acctng Clb; Natl Soc Pblc Acctnts; Phi Eta Sigma; Exec Rnd Table; Acctng Intrn MSI Inc 89-; Acctng.**

**ELROD, DON B,** Ky Wesleyan Coll, Owensboro, KY; SO; BS; Pre-Prof Soc; Sigma Zeta; Sigma Phi Epsilon; Pres Schlrshp; Dns Lst; Karen D Fisher Physics-Chem Schlrshp; Abernathy Chem Awd; Charles J Majors Mem Schlrshp; Chem/Pre-Engr; Chem Engr.

**ELSAMOULY, ABDELFATTAH,** City Univ Of Ny Queensbrough, New York, NY; SR; AAS; Deans Lst 90; Rest Mngr; Music Elctrnc Tech; Engr.

**ELSIS, DINA MARIE,** S U N Y Coll Of Tech At Frmgdl, Farmingdale, NY; FR; MBA; Spec Educ; Spec Ed Tchr.

**ELSNER, CONNIE,** Univ Of Miami, Coral Gables, FL; SR; MBA; Advrtng Assn 88-89; Phi Kappa Phi 90-; Gldn Ky 90-; Phi Theta Kappa 88-; AA Miami Dade Comm Coll 87; BA; Mrktng; Advrtsng-Mrktng.**

**ELSTON, JAMES W,** Columbus Coll Of Art & Design, Columbus, OH; SO; BFA; Pblctn Grphcs Edtr 90-; Bible Stdy 90-; Primetime Advrtsng 90; Illusration.

**ELSTON, JOSEPH E,** Wright St Univ Lake Cmps, Celina, OH; SO; AAS; Scty Manuf Engrs Secty 90-; Tchl Study Emphasizing Statistics.**

**ELSTON, TANYA K,** Coll Of Charleston, Charleston, SC; SR; Blgy Clb 89-; Phi Kappa Phi; Blgy; Eclgy.

**ELSWICK JR, RAYMOND E,** Ashland Comm Coll, Ashland, KY; SO; BA; Acctng; Law.

**ELTER, CANDICE M,** Duquesne Univ, Pittsburgh, PA; SO; BSBA; Phi Eta Sigma 89-; Deans Lst 89-; IM 89-90; Bus.

**ELVESTROM, JENNIFER C,** Fl St Univ, Tallahassee, FL; JR; BS; Pre Law Soc 90-; Gldn Key 90; Pi Gamma Mu 90-; Deans Lst 89; Intrntnl Affrs Hstry; Law.

**ELVY, EUKLYN A,** City Univ Of Ny La Guard Coll, Long Island Cty, NY; GD; BS; Ntl Soc Of Blk Eng 90; Blk Awarenes Coord Cmmttee 90; Phi Theta Kappa 88; AAS 90; Cmptr Eng Tech; Eng.

**ELWOOD, LAUREEN E,** Bridgeport Engr Inst, Fairfield, CT; JR; BA; Dsgn Tchncn; AS 90; Elec Eng.

**ELY, DOUGLAS J,** Newbury Coll, Brookline, MA; FR; AS; Radio Clb 90; Radio Stn DJ Sprts Dir 90; Bsktbl 90; Cmmnctns; Radio DJ Sprts Anncr.

**ELY, MARK A,** Univ Of Nc At Asheville, Asheville, NC; SO; BA; Bus.

**ELY, STEPHANIE K,** Radford Univ, Radford, VA; JR; BS; Fshn Scty 88-; Kappa Omicron Nu; Phi Sigma Sigma Sprt Chmn/Frml Chr 89-; Awd Fr Hghst GPA Phi Sigma Sigma 90-; Fshn Mrchndsng; Fshn Stylst.

**EMANUEL, AKO Y,** Jackson St Univ, Jackson, MS; FR; Sigma Pi Sigma; Physcs; Rsrch.

**EMANUEL, MARTIN D,** George Mason Univ, Fairfax, VA; SR; BS; Dcsn Science 90; MIS Clb; Alpha Chi 90-; Gldn Key 90-; Brd Drctrs Cmmnty Assn 90-; Mgmnt Infmtn Systm.

**EMANUEL, MEGHAN K,** Marshall University, Huntington, WV; SR; BED; Cntrbry Fllwshp VP 88-; Untd Mthdst Stdnts 90; Gamm Beta Phi Fnd Rsng Comm Chrr 88-; Kappa Delta Pi 89-; Elem Ed.**

**EMBERLEY, SARAH A,** Lesley Coll, Cambridge, MA; JR; BED; Erly Chldhd Educ/Mdte Spec Needs; Tch.

**EMBLETON, BARBARA DIANE,** Roane St Comm Coll, Harriman, TN; SO; Sec Sci Cert 85; Hlth Physics Cert.

**EMBRESCIA, AMANDA,** Georgetown Univ, Washington, DC; SO; BA; Choice 90-; SBA Mntr Prg 90-; Intrnshp/Amer Inns Of Ct Fdn; Intl Bus/Law.

**EMBRY, ANNIE L,** Southern Junior Coll, Birmingham, AL; SO; BS; PTO Rm Mthr 87-; Prblm Analyses Tm 90-; US Air Natl Guard Cls Ldr 90; Most Outstndg Stdnt 90-; Hghst Qlty Point Avg 90-; Girl Scout Trp Ldr 89-; Cmptr Op 87-89; Safety Tech/Cmptr Op 89-; AAS So Jr Coll 83; Elec Engr Tech.

**EMBRY, BRYCE T,** Fl Coll, Temple Terrace, FL; SO; BA; Stdnt Anthology Editor 90-; Math Tutor 90-; Writing Tutor 90-; Phi Theta Kappa VP 90-; Alpha Clb 90-; Outstndng Math Stdnt 90-; Outstndng Bible Stdnt 90-; Awrd Outstndng Stdnt Greek I 89-90; Physical Sci Math; Teaching.

**EMBRY, LOVELLA R,** Wilberforce Univ, Wilberforce, OH; FR; BA; Ntl Stdnt Bus Leag 90-; Deans Lst 90-; Cargill Schlrshp; Kappa Swthrt; Acctg; CPA.

**EMBRY, SEAN R,** Old Dominion Univ, Norfolk, VA, SR, BS BA; Golden Key 90-; Man Inf Sys; Prgrmr/Analyst.

**EMEOTT, MATTHEW KEVIN,** Savannah Coll Of Art & Design, Savannah, GA; FR; BA; Soccer 90-; Architecture; Furniture Designer.

**EMERICK, ROBERT C,** Hillsborough Comm Coll, Tampa, FL; SR; AS; Nuclear Med Clb 89-; Phi Theta Kappa 90-; Nuclear Med; Public Health.

**EMERLING, REBECCA A,** Cornell Univ, Ithaca, NY; FR; BS; Red Crpt Soc 90-; Dairy Sci Clb 90-; Trdtns Schlrshp 90-; Ecnmcs.

**EMERSON, GARETH R,** Univ Of Tn At Martin, Martin, TN; FR; BS; Bus Mgmt.

**EMERSON, PATRICIA A E,** Univ Of Nc At Charlotte, Charlotte, NC; JR; BS; Intrnshp Adlt Prob/Parole NC 90-; Crmnl Justice; Law Enfrcmnt.

**EMERSON, PAUL R,** Kent St Univ Kent Cmps, Kent, OH; SR; BBA; Fin Assoc 89-90; Golden Key 90-; IM Flag Ftbll 88; Finance.

**EMERSON, RANDALL J,** Northeast State Tech Comm Coll, Blountville, TN; FR; Soccer; Diesel Mech.

**EMERT, HERBERT G,** East Stroudsburg Univ, E Stroudsburg, PA; JR; BA; Assn Cmptng Mchnry 88-; Intrvrsty 88-; WESS Radio Anncr Smmr Pgm Dir 88; Pgmr 90-; Drftsmn 88-89; Assmblr 86-88; Assoc Mech Engr 85; Assmblr 82-; Chf Engr/Anncr 81; Tutor 88-; Comp Sci; Comp Smltn/Tch/Coll Lvl.

**EMERY, GREG V,** Hartwick Coll, Oneonta, NY; FR; BA; Jazzwick 90-; Jazz Combo 90-; Pep Band 90-; Phi Mu Alpha Sinfonia; Dana Assc; MIROR VP Pblc Rltns; IM Vlybl/Sccr 90-; Art.

**EMERY, MARGARET M,** Univ Of Sc At Columbia, Columbia, SC; SR; BA; Alpha Chi Omega Sor 88-; Tutor 90; Deans Lst 89-; Ele Educ; Tch.

**EMERY, R JAMES,** Castleton St Coll, Castleton, VT; SO; Pol Discsn Grp 89-; Histry Clb 89-; Stdnt Assoc Sen; Sem In-London; Hnrs Prog History 90-; Hstry Hnrs Prgm; Jrnalism.

**EMIG, CRYSTAL J,** Central Pa Bus School, Summerdale, PA; FR; AS; Cntrl 4-H Dairy Clb Sec 86-89; Acctg.

**EMIG, JOHN R,** Kent St Univ Kent Cmps, Kent, OH; SR; PHD; Pi Mu Epsilon 89-; Harshbarger Schrlrshp; Math.

**EMINGER, BARBARA J,** Defiance Coll, Defiance, OH; SR; BS; All AM Schlr; Elmntry Ed; Tch.

**EMLER, HEATHER J,** George Mason Univ, Fairfax, VA; SR; BSED; Operation Smile Corres Rcrdr; Stndt Educ Assn 90-; Gldn Ky; Dean Lst 89; Kappa Delta Pi; Dorothy Mcdermont Educ Schlrshp 90; IM Sftbl; Early Educ; Tchr.

**EMMANUEL, WILLIE P,** Ms St Univ, Miss State, MS; JR; BSC; Agronomy; Agri-Seed Tech.

**EMMERT, JULIE A,** Oh Univ, Athens, OH; FR; BA; Art Clb Pres 87-; Stdnt Cncl 87-; 4-H Clb Pres 87-; Deans List; Jr Fair Brd Pres 87-; Ctznshp Washington Focus 88; 4-H Clb Congress 87; Artist Yr; Golf Tm 88-; Child Dvlpmnt/Bus; Day Care Mgt.

**EMMERT, KATY S,** Univ Of Nc At Greensboro, Greensboro, NC; JR; BSN; Univ Cthlc Cntr Pres; Natl Cllgt Nrsng Awd; Nrsng.

**EMMERT, TONYA,** Univ Of Cincinnati, Cincinnati, OH; JR; BA; Alpha Phi Omega; Elem Educ/Engl; Tchg.

**EMMERTZ, KATHLEEN A,** Univ Of De, Newark, DE; FR; BED; Elem Educ; Tch.

**EMMETT, JILL E,** Lincoln Memorial Univ, Harrogate, TN; SR; ASN; Vrsty Chrldr Capt 87-90; SGA Treas 88-; Stdnt Nurses Assoc; Alpha Chi 89-; Homecoming Queen 89-90; Nursing.

**EMMI, NANCY,** Neumann Coll, Aston, PA; SO; BA; Cmmnctns Clb Sec 90-; Schl Nwsppr Wrtr 90-; Thtr Ensmble Prod Mgr 90-; Cmmnctn Arts; Advrtsng.

**EMMONS, MARYANNE E,** Liberty Univ, Lynchburg, VA; FR; Mrchng Bnd; Cncrt Bnd; Hnrs Prog 90-; Paul Douglas Educ Schlrshp 90-; English; Sec Educ.

**EMOND, SUSAN A,** Univ Of New England, Biddeford, ME; JR; BS; Campus Night Life Clb 88-89; Stdnt Occptnl Therapy Clb 90-; Res Asst 89-; Deans Lst 88-; Occptnl Therapy.

**EMPOLITI, STEVEN M,** Georgetown Univ, Washington, DC; SR; BSBA; Yng Rpblcn Clb 87-; Betta Gamma Sgm; Natl Fin Mgmt Hon Scty; Psi Chi; Almn Assc Wrkr Asstnt Dir/Admn 88-; Fin/Intrntl Mgmt; Fin Anlyst.

**EMRICH, ALLISON G,** Univ Of Tn At Martin, Martin, TN; SR; BS; Hnrs Seminar Pgm 87-; Order Omega; Phi Kappa Phi 90-; Phi Eta Sigma 87-; Mu Epsilon Delta 88-90; Beta Beta Beta Hstrn 89-; Zeta Tau Alpha 1st V P 87-; Bio.

**EMRICH, GEORGE F,** Jefferson Comm Coll, Watertown, NY; FR; Vrsty Golf; Deans Lst; Physical Ed; Tchr/Coach.

**EMRICK, VIRGINIA L,** Glassboro St Coll, Glassboro, NJ; GD; MA; Cnm Wrkshp 89-90; Rd/TV Assoc 89-90; Sgnt Ed 86-87; Kappa Delta 86-; Grdt Asst Grphc Cmnctn 90-; Tchnlgy Ctr Glassboro St; PR Intrnshp Mt Sinai Hosp; BA 90; Cmnctns; Entrtnmnt Pblc Rltns.

**ENCARNACION, JOANNA P,** Boricua Coll, New York, NY; JR; Outstndng Merit/Accompmnt; Christian Hrld Ministry 87-; Parents Support Grp.

**ENCINAR, ELONIDO,** Miami Dade Comm Coll, Miami, FL; FR; Phi Theta Kappa; Elec Eng.

**ENDEMANN, KYLE E,** S U N Y Coll Of Tech At Alfred, Alfred, NY; FR; BA; Mrktng Clb 90-; Deans Lst; Bus Admn; Hosp Ed Admn.

**ENDERLE, DEWEY M,** Univ Of Cincinnati, Cincinnati, OH; FR; BED; Arch Eng Tech; Arch.

**ENDERS, DARBY E,** Univ Of Al At Birmingham, Birmingham, AL; SR; BSAH; FL Lcnsd Dntl Hygnst; AS Pensacola Jr Clg 84; Hlth Admnstrtn; Hsptl Hlth Admnstrtn.

**ENDERS, KAREN K,** S U N Y Coll Of Tech At Alfred, Alfred, NY; FR; Stdnt Employee Yr; Deans List.

**ENDERS, LAURA E,** Univ Of New Haven, West Haven, CT; JR; BS; Am Soc Mech Engs 90-; Order Engs; Deans List; Swmng 87-88; Mech Eng.

**ENDICOTT, MAREVA L,** Marshall University, Huntington, WV; FR; BA; Phi Eta Sigma; Acctng.

**ENDICOTT, SHERRY L,** Marshall University, Huntington, WV; FR; BA; Gamma Beta Phi Soc; Lbry/Offc Asst; Acctg; CPA.

**ENDLISH, JASON LEE,** Bowling Green St Univ, Bowling Green, OH; SR; BA; Never Again Pres 90-; Goldn Key 90-; Epsilon Pi Tau; Pi Kappa Phi Exec Sec 90-; PUSH 90-; Cooper Indstrl Prod Intrnshp 90; Mfg Eng.

**ENDOH, TOSHIHIKO,** Univ Of Tn At Martin, Martin, TN; JR; BS; Wldlf Bio; US Fish/Wldlf.

**ENDREDI, AMANDA A,** Coll Of Charleston, Charleston, SC; JR; BA; Vsl Arts Clb Pres 90-; Omcn Ddlt Kappa; Bus Admn; Fin.

**ENDRES, CARRIE L,** Hudson Valley Comm Coll, Troy, NY; FR; Pres Lst 90; Acctg; CPA-ACTNT.

**ENDRES, DALE A,** Univ Of Cin R Walters Coll, Blue Ash, OH; FR; Lic Mnstr Church Of God Cleveland Tenn; Mach Oper; Mfg Engr; Engr/Mnstry/Chrstn Educ.

**ENDRES, DIANA M,** Hudson Valley Comm Coll, Troy, NY; FR; AS; Nursing; RN.

**ENDRES, SARAH G,** Columbia Union Coll, Takoma Park, MD; FR; BS; Phi Eta Sigma; Math/Elect Eng.

**ENDRIZZI, MATTHEW G,** Fl St Univ, Tallahassee, FL; FR; Fr Ml Stdnt Yr 91; IM Ftbl Sftbl 90-.

**ENG, FLORENCE,** City Univ Of Ny Baruch Coll, New York, NY; JR; BA; Chinese Stdnt Assoc 88-; Acctg Soc 90; Chinese Cultr Clb 88-; Dns Lst 88-; Gldn Ky 89-; Amer Mktg Assoc; CUNY Women Excel Awrd; Mktg; Advtsng.

**ENG, GLORIA L,** Bergen Comm Coll, Paramus, NJ; GD; BA; Deans Lst 86; Soc Sec Admin 67-; AS; Sociology; Pub Admin.

**ENG, JACK,** City Univ Of Ny Baruch Coll, New York, NY; SR; BBA; Cmptr Infor Sys; Cmptr Sys Analyst.

**ENG, MICHELE,** City Univ Of Ny Baruch Coll, New York, NY; SO; BA; Bsn; Acctng.

**ENG, SUSAN Y,** City Univ Of Ny Baruch Coll, New York, NY; SR; BBA; Frshmn Smnr Ldr; Retail Trade Scty; AM Mrktng Assc; Gldn Key; Beta Gamma Sigma; Mrktng; Mrkt Rsrchr.**

**ENGEL, DOUGLAS LEONARD,** S U N Y At Buffalo, Buffalo, NY; GD; MARC; Golden Key 89-; Schlr Ath Hons 87-89; JV MVP Ftbl 87; Vars Ftbl 88-89; PBS 90; Arch.

**ENGEL, JOHN J,** Univ Of Sc At Columbia, Columbia, SC; SO; BA; Coll Rep 89-; Sigma Chi Sec 90-; Intrnshp Sen John Warner S C Rep Party 90; Sigma Chi Flag Ftbl IMS; Pol Sci; Law.

**ENGEL, KIMBERLY LYNNE,** Univ Of Cincinnati, Cincinnati, OH; SR; BS; Gldn Ky 90-; Kappa Delta Pi 90-; Oh Army Ntl Grd 87-; BS; Spcl Educ; Tchng.

**ENGEL, KRISTIN E,** Indiana Univ Of Pa, Indiana, PA; FR; BA; Band; Engl Educ; Tchr.

**ENGEL, MARC L,** Cornell Univ Statutory College, Ithaca, NY; SR; BS; PRSSA Treas 87-; Oxford Union Scty; Curriculum/Study Abrd/Execl Tchg Comm; Phi Kappa Phi; Gamma Sigma Delta; Golden Key 90-; Ho-Nun-De-Kah Hnr Scty 89-; Ambr 87-; Tutor 88-; Applied Econ/Busn Mgt; Law/Comedy.

**ENGEL, VICKI L,** Univ Of South Fl, Tampa, FL; JR; BS; Dnc Tm 90-; Kappa Delta Pi; Thms 89-; Gldn Key; Mrtl Brd; Kappa Delta Frml Chrprsn 89-; Bst Str Awd; Dns Lst 89-; Math Ed; Tchg.**

**ENGELBRACHT, CHARLES W,** Univ Of Rochester, Rochester, NY; SO; BS; Scty Phys Students 89-; Shotaokan Karate Club 88-F Campus Literary Mg 88-90; German Lang Awd 88; Phys/Astrom; Astronomer.

**ENGELHARDT, ANDREA M,** Univ Of Miami, Coral Gables, FL; SR; Price Waterhouse Auditg Intern 90; BBA; Auditor.

**ENGELKE, BRYANT O,** Academy Of The New Church, Bryn Athyn, PA; JR; BA; Mind Altering Sub Comm 89-; Mech Designer 80-89; Edn/Psych; Teach/Clinical Psych.

**ENGELKEN, LARA H M,** Univ Of The Dist Of Columbia, Washington, DC; FR; BA; High Hon 90-; Deans Lst; Intrnshp Round House Theatre Bckstg Asst 88; Sch Prod Asst Stage Mgr 90; Theatre Arts; Theatre Dir.

**ENGLAND, CHRISTOPHER M,** Kent St Univ Kent Cmps, Kent, OH; GD; BBA; Arnld Air Scty Frst Ltnt 86-88; Mortar Brd 89-90; Beta Gamma Sigma 89-90; Gldn Key 89-90; Delta Sigma Pi Schlrshp Key; Superior Schlrshp; Sherrie Jo Luft Memorial Awrd Otstndng Schlstc Achmnt; US Ntnl Cllgt Awrd Business; Bsn Mngmnt; Human Resources Mngmnt.

**ENGLAND, JENNIFER A,** Fl St Univ, Tallahassee, FL; JR; BS; Golden Key 90-; Alpha Soc 88-; Alpha Delta Pi 88-; Vol Ronald Mcdonald House 88-; Leon Co Start Ctr; Atty Gen Office Criminal; Deans List 89-90; AA 90; Crmnlgy; Law.

**ENGLAND, MELISSA A,** Northern Ky Univ, Highland Hts, KY; FR; BA; Hons Club 90; French Frgn Lang Award; Engl/Secndry Ed.

**ENGLAND, WILLIAM L,** Univ Of Pittsburgh, Pittsburgh, PA; SR; MSW; Stdnt Exec Cncl 90-; Intern St Francis Medical Ctr 90-; BASW; Social Work.

**ENGLANDER, SOPHIA T,** Univ Of Miami, Coral Gables, FL; JR; BA; Dmcrtc Party St FL St Com Wmn 66-78; FL St Fair Athrty Cmsnr 89-; Miami Bch Hsng Athrty Cmsnr 63-67; Miami Bch Bd Rltr 75-; Political Science.

**ENGLE, AMY L,** Univ Of Nc At Charlotte, Charlotte, NC; SO; BA; Emrgng Ldrs 89-90; Choir 89-91; English; Teaching.

**ENGLE, BETTY A,** Roane St Comm Coll, Harriman, TN; GD; Cert 90-; Med Trnsprtn; Med Fld.

**ENGLE, BRIAN D,** S U N Y Coll At Oswego, Oswego, NY; FR; BS; Stdnts Agnst Drvng Drunk Asst Pres 90; Res Hall Cncl 90; Cert Life Guard 87 90; Educ; Tch.

**ENGLE, CHARLES R,** Univ Of Cincinnati, Cincinnati, OH; JR; BS; Taekwondo Clb Treas 87-89; Res Hl Asc VP 87-88; Mrtr Brd Sec; Tau Beta Pi Pres; Eta Kappa Nu; Sigma Phi Epsln Cntrl; Elec Engr.**

**ENGLE, DANNY R,** Sue Bennett Coll, London, KY; FR; MA; Pep Clb 90; IM Sprts 90-; Sgm Nu VP; Phi Theta Kappa; Acad All Amer; Marshel Of Sue Bennett Clg; Psychlgy; Prvt Prctc.

**ENGLE, DOUGLAS H,** Oh Univ, Athens, OH; GD; Athena Yrbk Phtgrphr 86-87; Intrnshp Chlstn Gztte WV Phtgrphr 90; Athens Mssngr Phtgrphr 87-90; Eddie Adams Wrkshp 90; Rprtr; BFA 90; Phtjrnlsm.

**ENGLE, JOEL M,** Univ Of Southern Ms, Hattiesburg, MS; JR; BS; Golden Key 90-; Gamma Beta Phi 89-90; Assoc Jones Cnty Jr Clg 89; Ind Tech; Eng.

**ENGLE, KANDICE D,** Mary Baldwin Coll, Staunton, VA; SR; BA; Sen Stdnt Rep 90-; Hnr Schlr 87-; Stdnt Rep Adv Brd Vistrs 88-89; Sigma Tau Delta 89-; Phi Alpha Theta; Baily Schlr 87-; Engl; Law.

**ENGLE, MARY M,** Chatfield Coll, Saint Martin, OH; SO; Factry Wrkr.

**ENGLE, SHERRI L,** Sue Bennett Coll, London, KY; SO; Phit Beta Lambda Treas/Pres 89-; Flwshp Clg Clgts 90-; Stdnt Govt Assc Jdcl Cncl 90-; Sigma Nu 89-; Bus; Hlth Cr Admin.

**ENGLEMAN, CONNIE J,** Miami Jacobs Jr Coll Of Bus, Dayton, OH; GD; AS; Bus Admin; Retail/Whlsl Groc Mgmnt.

**ENGLER, AMY M,** S U N Y Coll Of Tech At Alfred, Alfred, NY; FR; ASS; Bnd Treas 90-; Bus Admin.

**ENGLESON, ERIC J,** City Univ Of Ny Baruch Coll, New York, NY; JR; BBA; Acctg.

**ENGLISH, ALFRED R,** Howard Univ, Washington, DC; GD; JD; Stdnt Bar Assoc Class Rep 89-90; Future Interest Inner City Tutorial Prog Chrprsn 89; Envrmntl Help Soc Chrmn Fund Raising 90-; Law Journal 90-; Alpha Phi Omega V P 82-83; Amer Jurispurdence Awd 90; Merit Schlrshp 89-; Clrkshp Paul Hastng Janofoky Walker; Marketing; Law.

**ENGLISH, ALLISON C,** Duke Univ, Durham, NC; SO; BA; Drama 89-; NC Wrtrs Ntwrk; Hstry.**

**ENGLISH, ANAYANSI A,** Eckerd Coll, St Petersburg, FL; SO; BA; Coll Nwsppr Rprtr 89-; Spnsh Hnr Scty; Wrtng Cntr Cnsltnt 89-; Cmmnctns Spnsh; Jrnlst.

**ENGLISH, CAROL A,** Marywood Coll, Scranton, PA; SO; BA; Amer Dietetic Assoc 90-; Stdnt Dietetic Assoc 90-; Kappa Omicron Nu 89-; Marywood Stdnt Dietetic Clb Treas; Kappa Omicron Nu Schlrshp 89-; Dietetics.

**ENGLISH, CHANTEL M,** Va Union Univ, Richmond, VA; SO; BED; Comm Schlrs 90-; Cls Treas 90-; Michael A Bradford Schlrshp; Early Chldhd Educ; Tchr.

**ENGLISH, CHRISTOPHER L,** Hudson Valley Comm Coll, Troy, NY; Sci; Med Fld.

**ENGLISH, DENA R,** Univ Of Sc At Columbia, Columbia, SC; SR; BA; Gamma Beta Phi 89-; Pi Mu Epsilon 90-; Gldn Key 89-; Assoc 89; BA; Math.

**ENGLISH, JENNIFER L,** Duquesne Univ, Pittsburgh, PA; FR; BA; Phi Eta Sigma 90-; Deans Lst 90-; Computer Progmmng; Prog Analyst.

**ENGLISH, KIMBERLY S,** Comm Coll Algny Co Algny Cmps, Pittsburgh, PA; JR; AS; Nrsng Sci; RN.

**ENGLISH, LESLIE MONIQUE,** Va St Univ, Petersburg, VA; JR; BA; Mrktng Mgmt Bus Admn.

**ENGLISH, MERIDTH R,** Univ Of Sc At Lancaster, Lancaster, SC; FR; BS; Bsn/Mktg; Sales.

**ENGLISH, ROBIN L,** Winthrop Coll, Rock Hill, SC; FR; BS; Envrnmnts Biology.

**ENGLISH, TRESSA L,** Comm Coll Algny Co Algny Cmps, Pittsburgh, PA; FR; BA; Lbrl Arts; Crmnlgy.

**ENGLISH IV, WILLIAM D,** Southern Coll Of Tech, Marietta, GA; SR; BS; Comp Eng.

**ENGLUND, LYNN A,** Hilbert Coll, Hamburg, NY; SO; BA; Paralegal Assn Pres 89-; Soc Stdnt Accnts Treas 89-; VITA 90-; Natl Merit Schlr US Achvmnt Acdmy 90; AAS 90; Acctg; Law.**

**ENGQUIST, JONATHAN T,** Ny Chiropractic Coll, Glen Head, NY; GD; DC; Phi Chi Omega; Bread/Life Programs Fund Raising; Cum Laude; BA Assumption Cllg 86; DC Ny Chiro Clg; Chiropractic.

**ENGRAM, MICHELLE LAPRIESE,** Fl International Univ, Miami, FL; JR; BS; Cvl Affrs Assn Sec 89-; Frndshp Clb Treas 87-; FBLA; Hnrbl Dschrg; AA Miami Dade Comm Coll 88; Bus Educ/Pub Adm; Tchng Fld.

**ENGSTROM, IAN C,** Memphis St Univ, Memphis, TN; FR; BSCE; Memphis Opera Chorus 89; Alpha Lambda Delta; Civil Eng; Eng.

**ENGSTROM, KEVIN E,** Villanova Univ, Villanova, PA; JR; By Scts Adlt Ldr 89; Yng Athlts Of Amer 88-; Wtr Polo Cch VHS US Wtr Polo 90-; Tau Kappa Omega VP; Hbtt Fr Hmnty 90; Crbrl Plsy Fr Dlwre Cnty 90; Vrsty Wtr Polo; Dte Rpe Pr Cnslr Fr Vllnva Grk Org Dir; Intrn Cnty Of Ornge EMA 90-; Ggrphy And Pol Sci; Law.

**ENLOW, DAWN E,** Univ Of Sc At Columbia, Columbia, SC; SO; BAIS; Phi Beta Kappa 89-90; Elem Ed; Tch.

**ENLOW, MELINDA S,** Northern Ky Univ, Highland Hts, KY; SR; BA; Rdlgy.

**ENLOW, PAULA J,** Univ Of Ky, Lexington, KY; JR; BED; Epsilon Delta 88-; Hist; H S Tchr.

**ENNIS, JUDI A,** Wilmington Coll, New Castle, DE; GD; MA; PGH-SRGRY; Admin Sprvsr Hosp; Tchng Tech Coll; Cstl Hosp; BSN W/Hon; AD 75; Nrsng; Tch Nrsng.

**ENNIS, TRACEY E,** Bloomfield Coll, Bloomfield, NJ; GD; BA; Pep Squad Treas; EOF Prog; Advsy Bd; Fam Svcs Intern 90; State Fam Svc Speclst 90-.

**ENOCH, BOBBY G,** Va St Univ, Petersburg, VA; JR; BA; Accntng Clb; Ntl Assoc Of Blk Accntnts; Im Sprts 88; Accntng; CPA.

**ENOKI, TOMOKO,** Univ Of Sc At Columbia, Columbia, SC; SO; BA; Nomura Securities Co 88-90; AA Tokoyo Wmns Chrstn Univ 88; Intl Studies.

**ENOS, ROBERT T,** Coll Misericordia, Dallas, PA; SR; BA; Nwspr Wrtr 89-90; Madrigal Dinner Prfrmr 88-; Natl Stdnt Hon Assn 89-; Fac Prvt Sec Misericordia 88-; Storer Cable Cmnctns Wrtr; Engl; Pro Wrtr.

**ENOUS, CHRIS CORNELIUS,** Schenectady County Comm Coll, Schenectady, NY; JR; BMA; Deans Lst 90; Pres Lst 90-; Benigh Enous Fund Bd Mbr 89-; Mdcl Asst 84; BMA Stratford Schl 84; Dietitian.

**ENRICO, REBECCA J,** Liberty Univ, Lynchburg, VA; SO; BS; Kappa Delta Pi Corres Sec; Elem Edn; Elem Tchr.

**ENRIGHT, DONNA-JEAN MARIE,** Fl International Univ, Miami, FL; SR; BA; Sccr 87-; AS 89; Phys Ed.

**ENS, KRISTINE M,** Georgian Court Coll, Lakewood, NJ; SR; BA; Clinoaes Clb 89-; Phi Alpha Theta VP 89-; Dns Lst 88-; AS Ocean Cnty Coll 89; Hstry; Bus.

**ENSLEY, GREGORY A,** Al St Univ, Montgomery, AL; SO; Treas Of My Hnr Drm 90; Intrn At White Cnsldted Indstries 90.

**ENSMINGER, RYNELL L,** Liberty Univ, Lynchburg, VA; SR; Lbrty Nrsng Stdnts Assn 89-; Flwshp Chrstn Ath 89-90; Yth Quest 89-90; Nrsng Intrnshp Cntrl Afrcn Repblc; BS; Nrsng.

**ENSMINGER, VALERIE E,** Western Ky Univ, Bowling Green, KY; SR; BSN; SGA Rep 77; Gamma Beta Phi 76; Sigma Theta Tau 88; KY Assn Nrsng Stdnts 78-; Amrcn Assn Nphrlgy Nrs Tchncns 81-82; Alpha Delta Pi 75-78; Bptst Yng Wmn Thrd Bptst Chrch Pres 84-86; RN Co 80-; AS 79; BS 79; Nrsng.

**ENTERKIN, ROBIN K,** Univ Of Al At Birmingham, Birmingham, AL; SR; MA; Phi Theta Kappa 89-; Gldn Key 90-; Alpha Kappa Delta; AA Jefferson St Comm Clg 89; Sclgy.

**ENZOR, SAMANTHA B,** Coker Coll, Hartsville, SC; SO; BA; Ambssdr 89-; Chrldr 90; Fr/Soph Cls Sec; Crw Rce Tm; Psychlgy/Cnslng.

**ENZWEILER, KEVIN A,** Northern Ky Univ, Highland Hts, KY; SR; BS; Amer Chem Soc Pres 88-; Bio Soc 86-88; Sci-Fi Clb Treas 86-87; Alpha Chi 89-; Outstdng Grad Chem; Cncl Undgrad Rsch Acad Ind Rsch Flwshp 90; Dns Schlp 90-; Flag Ftbl 90; Chem/Bio; Grad Scl Chem/Indstry.

**EOBBI, LORI A,** Glassboro St Coll, Glassboro, NJ; JR; Gymnstcs 89-; Gamma Tau Sigma; Phi Sigma Sigma 90-; Psychlgy.

**EPEL, NIKKI,** Univ Of Central Fl, Orlando, FL; FR; BA; Surf Clb Clb Coord 90-; Lambda Chi Alpha 90-; Frshmn Hnrs Cnvctn 90-; Deans Lst; IM Wmns Sccr/Hcky 90-; Communications.

**EPHFROM, LATRICHA,** Jackson St Univ, Jackson, MS; FR; BS; Alpha Lambda Delta; GSA 78-; Deans Lst; Math; Tchg.

**EPIFANIO, IRIS M,** Univ Of Miami, Coral Gables, FL; JR; BA; Panamenian Intrntl Stdnt Assoc 89; Intrntl Fnce/Mrktng; Fnce.

**EPLER, DANIEL ELIJAH,** Ohio Valley Coll, Parkersburg, WV; SO; BA; SG Pres; Theta Soc Treas; Ed Of Newspapr Ed 89; Highlander Awd; Accntng; Tchr.

**EPLEY, REBECCA LEWIS,** Middle Tn St Univ, Murfreesboro, TN; SR; BA; SHEA 90-; Clearview Baptist Church; Nutrition; Reg Dietician.

**EPPERS, MELISSA R,** Univ Of Montevallo, Montevallo, AL; SR; BA; Psi Chi Pres 90-; Alpha Delta Pi VP 88-89; Fclty Awrd Rsrch Excllnc; Chrlder 87-89; Crs Cntr Vol 90-; YMCA Yth Cnslr 90-; Arbc Instrctr 90-; Psychlgy Spnsh; Grad Schl.

**EPPINGER, CATHERINE E,** Villanova Univ, Villanova, PA; JR; BA; Villanova Crew 88-; Delta Gamma 89-; Proj Sunshine 88-; Elem Educ/Psych; Elem Schl Guidance/Soc Wrk.

**EPPLEY, JAMES H,** Embry Riddle Aeronautical Univ, Daytona Beach, FL; JR; BS; SADD Pres 90-; CARAL 90-; Aeronautical Sci; Commercial Pilot.

**EPPLEY, KATHLEEN M,** Indiana Univ Of Pa, Indiana, PA; SR; BSED; PSEA 88-; Elem Educ; Tchr.

**EPPLEY, MARY FRANCES,** Mount Aloysius Jr Coll, Cresson, PA; FR; ADBSN; Lcnsd Prctcl Nrse; Nrsng.

**EPPLEY, SUSAN H,** Cecils Coll, Asheville, NC; GD; AAS; Comp Sci/Bus Admin Acctg.

**EPPS, ALLAN E,** Univ Of Sc At Columbia, Columbia, SC; JR; BS; Wrld Wldlf Fnd; Elec Engr.**

**EPPS, BONNIE I,** Emory Univ, Atlanta, GA; GD; MSN; Emer Nurs Assn 88; Emer Nurs; Dip Piedmont Hosp Sch 73; Nurs Admn.

**EPPS, CYNTHIA A,** Savannah Coll Of Art & Design, Savannah, GA; GD; BFA; Grphc Dsgn Clb 88-90; Dns Lst 87-90; Vlybl; Grphc Dsgn.

**EPPS, DENILLE E,** Ky St Univ, Frankfort, KY; FR; BED; Mrchng Bnd 90; Cncrt Bnd; Trck Tm 90-; Sec Educ Math; Tchng.

**EPPS, DENISE HOPE,** Univ Of Southern Ms, Hattiesburg, MS; SR; MS; Stdnt Speech Hrng Assoc Pres 89-; Signing Eagles 90-; Etoile Du Bard Schlrshp; Speech Pathology.

**EPPS, ESTELLE F,** Norfolk St Univ, Norfolk, VA; SR; BVS; AMA S 89-; Mass Cmnctns Assn Chpln 88-; Hampton Rds Clk Media Pro 89-; Alpha Kappa Mu 90-; Alpha Eplison Rho 90-; Mass Cmnctns; Pblc Rltns.

**EPPS, JUSTIN N,** Morehouse Coll, Atlanta, GA; FR; BS; Glee Clb; Hnr Roll; Mrktng; Law.

**EPPS, WANDA JOYCE MOUZON,** Williamsburg Tech Coll, Kingstree, SC; FR; ASSOC; Stdnt Govt Assn 90-; Dean List 90-; Acctnt.

**EPSTEIN, ANNE R,** Emory Univ, Atlanta, GA; SR; BBA; Wind Ensmbl 87-; Jazz Ensmbl Sect Ldr 87-; Saxophone Quartet 87-; Dns Lst 87-; Beta Gamma Sigma; Mu Phi Epsilon Pres 89-; Bus/Msc; Jwlry Indstry.

**EPSTEIN, ERIC R,** Univ Of Rochester, Rochester, NY; JR; BA; Sigma Chi; IM Soccer/Sftbl/Polo Capt 88-; Econ.

**EPSTEIN, MARGARET M,** Saint Johns Univ, Jamaica, NY; SR; BS; Hmn Svcs Clb S 88-; Exprnc Coll Pgm; Golden Key 89-; Dorothy Day Awd; Gold Medal; Comm Vlntr; AA Bor Manhattan Comm Coll 75; Hmn Svcs; Scl Wrk.

**EPSTEIN, PAMELA D,** Univ Of Rochester, Rochester, NY; SR; BA; D Lions Org 88-89; Intrnshp Altrntvs Battered Women 90; Phi Sigma Sigma Tribune 88-; Intrnshp London Eng Wstmnstr N Conservative Assoc 90; Grad Cum Laude; Crew Coxwain 87-88; Psy; Therapy Psy.

**EPSTEIN, WENDY JILL,** Cornell Univ Statutory College, Ithaca, NY; SO; BA; COMPASS Intl Mag Bsn/Publ Rels 89-; European Cmnty Simulatns 90-; Dns Lst 89-; 4 Yr NY State Regents Schlrshp; Delta Gamma 90-; Thomas Gullota Nassua Cty Exec Intern 89; Defense Dept Soviet/E Europe Affrs Extern; Cmnctns/Intl Rels; Govt.

**EPTING, KAREN A,** Schenectady County Comm Coll, Schenectady, NY; SO; AAS; Data Entry Ld Clrk; UCS Coord; Asst Info Serv Sprvsr; Comp Pgmg/Syst; Data Proc Comp Pgmg.

**ERAMO, KRISTINA R,** Univ Of Cincinnati, Cincinnati, OH; FR; BA; Std Cncl 87-90; Ski Clb 87-90; Hgh Schl Bld Drvs 88-90; Alpha Lambda Delta 90-; SELF Pres 87-90; Fld Hcky 87-90; Nrs.

**ERBECK, GREGORY D,** Univ Of Cincinnati, Cincinnati, OH; SR; BM; Internatl Assoc Jazz Educators Pres 87-; Music Ed Assoc Class Rep 88-; Music; Music Education.

**ERBELDING, LISA M,** Kent St Univ Kent Cmps, Kent, OH; SR; Acctg Assc Scl Comm 89-90; Golden Key; Outstndg Clg Stdnts Amer; Beta Gamma Sigma; Alpha Beta Gamma; Deans Lst 86-90; Pres Lst; Hnrs Dy Cnvctn; BBA; Acctg; CPA.

**ERBY, LEAH D,** Univ Of Tn At Martin, Martin, TN; FR; Hnrs Seminarl Prog 90-; Soc Hnrs Seminar Stdnts 90-; Math/Cmptr Scnc.

**ERCOLINO, JOANNE M,** S U N Y Coll Of Tech At Frmgdl, Farmingdale, NY; FR; AS; SADHA 90-; Dntl Hygn; Dntst.

**ERDY, ANGELA S,** Oh Univ, Athens, OH; SR; BFA; Paintg/Art Hstry; Paintg Cnsrvtn.

**ERFANI, SADI,** Cornell Univ Statutory College, Ithaca, NY; JR; BS; Persian Stdnts Assn 89-; Microbiology Stdnt Advsr 90-; Soccer Starter 88-; Microbiology; Med.

**ERGAS, REBECA,** Fl International Univ, Miami, FL; SO; Psychlgy.

**ERICKSON, COURTNEY A,** Cornell Univ Statutory College, Ithaca, NY; JR; BS; Mag Wrtr 90-; RESULTS 89-; Pgm Comm Living Lrng Ctr Secr 89-90; Alpha Phi Omega 90-; Habitat Humanity 90-; Asst Sports Info 89-; Wrtr Newspaper 90-; JV Bsktbl Mgr 90-; Cmnctns; Law.

**ERICKSON, DAVID WILLIAM,** Savannah Coll Of Art & Design, Savannah, GA; SO; BARCH; Amer Inst Archtctr Std; Golf; Archtctr.

**ERICKSON, ELDINE H,** Commonwealth Coll, Virginia Beach, VA; SR; AAS; 1 Yr Temp Med Offcs/Hosp 83-84; 7 Yrs Cnstrctrn; 3 Yrs Offc Utility Insp; Med Offc Mgmt; Med Trnscrptn.

**ERICKSON, MIA K,** Radford Univ, Radford, VA; JR; VAHPERD 90; AAHPERD 90; Virginia Rcrtn/Park Soc; Red Cross Water Sfty Instr 87; YMCA; Spec Olympics 88; Nw Rvr Vlly Agncy For Mntly Rtrd; US Wtr Ftns Instr 90; Thrptc Rcrtn; Rsrch Aquatic Rhbltn.

**ERICKSON, PATRICIA ANN,** Cornell Univ Statutory College, Ithaca, NY; JR; BS; Stu Rep 88-89; N Cntry Comm Coll NY; Cntrbtr Sch Nwspr 88-89; Deans Lst NCCC 87-89; Deans Lst; Tutor/Pr Cnslr Stu Serv 87-89; Deans Spcl Awrd 88-89; Deans Lst 88-; Amer Assos Zoo Kprs 84-; Prevet Soc 90; Bio; Vet Med.

**ERICKSON, THOMAS H,** Kent St Univ Geauga Cmps, Burton Twp, OH; CERT; Sigma Delta Chi 68-69; Hartsgrove Vol Fire Dept Asst Chief 85-90; U S Army 1st Lt 70-71; Sales Engr; BSJ Ohio Univ 65-69; Comp Tech.

**ERIKSSON, ANN E,** City Univ Of Ny Queensbrough, New York, NY; Envrnmntl Clb 90; Deans Lst Qnsbrgh Cmmnty Clg 90.

**ERION, JACQUELINE M,** Bowling Green St Univ, Bowling Green, OH; JR; BA; Vsl Cmmnctn Tchnlgy Orgnztn 90-; Epsilon Pi Tau; Rcvd Alumni Bk Schlrshp; Ferris St Unvrsty 88; Vsl Cmmnctns Prnt; Mgmt Pblshr.

**ERIQUE, MARISOL ARCEO,** Miami Dade Comm Coll, Miami, FL; FR; St John Bosco Catechist Assn Mtng/Nws Rep 89-; St John Bosco Sch CCD Rel Tchr 87-; Chldrns Mass Instr 85-; Math; Edn.

**ERIXTON, VICKY G,** Valdosta St Coll, Valdosta, GA; SR; BBA; AA 89; Acctg.

**ERJAVEC, JOSEPH F,** Kent St Univ Kent Cmps, Kent, OH; JR; BS; Amer Inst Of Archtctre Stdnts 90; Ntl Merit Schlrshp 86-87; Diocesan Comp Schlrshp 86 87; Archtctre BS Chem BA; Archtctre Enrgy Dsgn.

**ERLY, STEPHEN C,** James Madison University, Harrisonburg, VA; GD; Prog Bd 88-90; Alpha Phi Omega 89-90; Earth Envrmntl Advcte 89090; BS 90; Mktg Mgt Prince Georges Clg 84; Psychology/Mktg Mgt; Bus Mgt.

**ERMALINSKI, JEFFERY M,** George Mason Univ, Fairfax, VA; SR; GMU Dive Club 88-89; Sigma Chi 88-; Coop At MCI 89-90; BS Decision Sci; MIS; Sys Engr.

**ERMER, DAVID R,** Memphis St Univ, Memphis, TN; SR; BS; Mc Allister Phys Schlrshp; Barber Awd Excl In Physics; Physics.

**ERMER, JAMIE L,** Northern Ky Univ, Highland Hts, KY; FR; BS; Nrsg.

**ERMILIO, JENNIFER A,** Univ Of Va, Charlottesville, VA; SO; BA; Cntrbry 89-; Stdt Allnce VA Envrmt Rcyclg Tm Ldr 89-; Alpha Xi Delta Acdmc Achvmt Chrprsn 90-; Madison Hse 90; Extrnshp Am Red Cross; Psychlgy.**

**ERNEST, CAROLE A,** Univ Of Nh Plymouth St Coll, Plymouth, NH; JR; BS; Mensa; AS Mc Intosh Clg 84; Elem Ed; Tchr.

**ERNEST, DOUGLAS M,** West Liberty St Coll, West Liberty, WV; JR; BS; Phi Theta Kappa 88-; Delta Mu Delta; Bus Adm; CPA.

**ERNST, KEITH R,** S U N Y Coll Of Tech At Alfred, Alfred, NY; SR; Senate; Exec Chrmn 89-90; Senate Fin Chrmn 88-90; Actvts Cncl Wllsvl Pres Finance 87-88; AAS Atmtv Srvc; AAS Trck Dsl Eqpmnt; Engnrng.

**ERNST, KIRSTEN M,** Smith Coll, Northampton, MA; SO; BA; Hmr Mag 89-90; Lit Mag 89; MASSPIRG; Tutor Nail Crew 89; Cmprtve Lit; Pblshng.

**EROSS, ERIC J,** Allegheny Coll, Meadville, PA; SR; BS; IM Sprts; Tri Beta 87-; Theta Chi Chptr Cnslr 90-; Alpha Phi Omega 87-89; Alden Schlr 89-90; Neurobiol; Med Schl.

**ERRANTE, COLLEEN,** Trenton St Coll, Trenton, NJ; FR; BA; Hnrs Prgrm 90-; Math; Tchr.

**ERRICHIELLO, LAURETTA A,** Newbury Coll, Brookline, MA; SO; AS; Hlth Science.

**ERRICKSON, AMANDA L,** Bridgewater Coll, Bridgewater, VA; FR; BS; Mu Epsilon Mu Hstrn Treas; IM Aerobics; Hm Ec; Intr Dsgnr.

**ERRICO, MICHAEL W,** Merrimack Coll, North Andover, MA; SR; BA; Psych Clb 88-; Psi Chi 90-; Tutor; Ice Hcky; Phlsphy.

**ERSKINE, KIMBERLY A,** Northeastern Christian Jr Coll, Villanova, PA; JR; BA; Psychology; Counseling.

**ERSKINE, LAURIE M,** Andover Coll, Portland, ME; SR; ME Natl Bank Vrs Pstns In AP And Ln Dept 89-; Acctng; Acct Sec Co Ownr Fam Const Bus.

**ERSOFF, NORRIE L,** Univ Of Miami, Coral Gables, FL; SR; BA; Latin Am Stdnts Assoc 89-; French Club 89-90; Org Jewish Stdnts 88-90; Golden Key 90-; Hnr Stdnts Assoc 88-; Alpha Epsilon Phi Pldg Cl V P 89-90; Amensty Intl 90-; Eart Alert 89-; Proj Noah Envrmntl Grp 89-90; Latin Am Studies; Un Nations/Foreign Serv.

**ERTAC, YUSUF,** S U N Y At Buffalo, Buffalo, NY; SO; BS; Trksh Stdnt Assn 89-; Bus Admin; Acctng.

**ERTEN, GUZIN,** Colby Sawyer Coll, New London, NH; SO; BA; Lit Mag Editor 89-90; Drama 90-; Theatre 90-; Stdnt Govt V P; Res Educ Staff Res Asst 90-; Key Assn; Video News Mag Prod 90-; Windy Hill School Promo Video Co Prod 90-; Comm; Brdcst News.

**ERTL, ERIKA A,** Niagara Univ, Niagara Univ, NY; JR; BSN; Yrbk Stff Clss Edtr 88-90; Bnd Fltst 88-89; Delta Epsilon Sigma; Sigma Theta Tau; Natl Stdnt Nrs Assn Pres 88-; Circle K Sec 90-; NUCAP 88-90; Chldrns Hosp Intrn; Campus Mnstry Flk Grp 88-; Natl Collgt Nrsng Awrd 90-; Sigma Theta Tau Nrs Awrd; Nrsng; Neontl Nrs.

**ERTL, SCOTT N,** Va Commonwealth Univ, Richmond, VA; SR; BS; Rcyclg Initiave Fndr 89; Jglg Tm Dir 88-; Plng Bdgt Com Rep; Dns Lst 88-; Hnrs Prog 88-; Rsrch Intrshp 89-90; Indpndt Stdy Elem Schl Syst 88-; Psychlgy Ed; Theraplay.

**ERTWINE SR, DOUGLAS M,** New Comm Coll Of Baltimore, Baltimore, MD; SO; AA; Human Serv Asst; Psychlgst.

**ERVIN, MARCUS STACKHOUSE,** Coll Of Charleston, Charleston, SC; JR; BS; Actvts Brd 90-; Alpha Epsilon Delta Treas 90-; Kappa Alpha 89; Schl For The Blnd 88-; Bttrd And Absd Chldrn Vol 89; Chldrn Hosp MUSC 89-; Vrsty Swmmng 90; Pre Med Blgy Chem Psych; Pedtrcn.

**ERVIN, SHARON R,** Union Univ, Jackson, TN; SR; BS; Stdnt Tchrs Educ Assn 90-; Bptst Yng Wmn VP 86-; Bptst Stdnt Union 86-; Elem Ed; Tchr.**

**ERVIN, SONYA R,** Liberty Univ, Lynchburg, VA; JR; BS; Pryr Ldr; Psi Chi; Psych; Cnslr.

**ERVIN, THOMAS C,** Radford Univ, Radford, VA; SO; BS; Nwspr Cir Mgr 89-; Sociology; Educ.

**ERVIN, TONYA L,** Hudson Valley Comm Coll, Troy, NY; SR; BA; Bsn/Acctng; Acctnt.

**ERWIN, DONNA S,** Piedmont Tech Coll, Greenwood, SC; AS; Phi Theta Kappa 90-; New Hope Presbyterian Sunday Sch Tchr 87-; Outstndg Cmnty Vol 87-90; Secr Forrest Clg 67; Med-Hlth Care.

**ERWIN, GINA C,** Univ Of Al At Birmingham, Birmingham, AL; SR; BA; Sec Edctn Math Tchr.

**ERWIN, LAURA A,** Oh Univ, Athens, OH; FR; BFA; Ecology Clb 90; Planned Prnthd; Fine Arts; Ceramics.

**ERWIN, PAIGE N,** Ms St Univ, Miss State, MS; SR; Concrt Chr 87-; Reveille Stf 88; Refrmd Univ Flwshp 89-; Phi Kappa Phi 89-; Kappa Pi 86-; ALAS 86-87; Acdmc Schlrshp 86-90; Coll Photo Finlst 89-; Art Awds 88-; Grphc Dsgn; Dsgnr/Portrtst.

**ERWIN, ROCHELLE Y,** Fayetteville St Univ, Fayetteville, NC; SO; BS; Cert Rutledge Coll 89; Cmptr Sci; Anlyst.

**ERWIN, SCOTT L,** Ms St Univ, Miss State, MS; SO; BS; Choir 90-; RUF 90-; Comp Sci; Progrmr.

**ERWIN, SHIRLEY R,** Coppin St Coll, Baltimore, MD; SR; MED; Cls Pres 90-; Cls Sen 90-; Hons Assocs VP 89-; MD Assoc Of Tchr Edctrs Bd 90-; Ronald E Mc Nair Achvmnt Prog Schlr 90-; Deptmntl Acadmc Hons Citation 90; Natl Blck Chld Dev Inst 90-; Towanda-Keyworth Nghbrhd Org Pres 90; Human Grwth/Dev; Measrmnt/Evalutn.

**ESCALET MOJICA, ROBERTO,** Univ Politecnica De Pr, Hato Rey, PR; FR; History/Psychology; Engineering.

**ESCHENBACH, ANGELA M,** Northern Ky Univ, Highland Hts, KY; FR; Eng.

**ESCOBAR, EMMA I,** Antillian Adventist University, Mayaguez, PR; SO; BS; GPA Awd 90-; Yth Church Ldr Dir 90-; Child Choir Dir; Bio/Nursing; Dr.

**ESCOBAR, RICARDO,** Univ Of Miami, Coral Gables, FL; SR; BS; Natl Scty Architectural Engrs Treas 90-; Columbian Stdnts Assoc 88-90; Natl Scty Prof Engrs 89-; IM Sccr 88-; Cvl Engrng; Architectural Engrng.

**ESCOFFERY, COURTNEY G,** City Univ Of Ny Med Evers Coll, Brooklyn, NY; FR; BS; Accts/Cmptrs; Invest Bnkng.

**ESCRIBANO GONZALEZ, GILBERTO,** Univ Politecnica De Pr, Hato Rey, PR; FR; Fshng Clb 90-; Sci; Eng.

**ESCRIBANO MARRERO, NESTOR R,** Inter Amer Univ Pr Hato Rey, Hato Rey, PR; BA; Cmptv Chess 79-80; Assoc 82; Lbry Awrd 81-82; Pol Sci; Law.

**ESCRIBANO SANCHEZ, DIANA,** Bayamon Tech Univ Coll, Bayamon, PR; JR; BA; Hon Stdnt List 89-; Rlgs Chr Pntcstl Chrch; Rlgs Yth Clb 85-; Magna Cum 90; BAD Bayamon Tech Unv Clg 90; Bus Admn/Acctg; Mstr Degree/CPA Cert.

**ESCUDERO, ENRIQUE A,** Fl International Univ, Miami, FL; JR; BACC; Clg Brd Talent Rstr Dstngshd Acad Prfrmnc 90; Cert Cmpltn Coop Ed 88; Clg Brd Otstndng Mnrty Stdnt 89-90; Asst Cntrlr Frzn Fd Dstrbtrshp Miami FL 87-90; AA Miami Dade Comm Clg 90; Acctg; CPA.

**ESCUTARY, TERESITA S,** William Paterson Coll, Wayne, NJ; SR; BA; Spec Ed Clb 89-90; NJEA; Spec Ed; Dvlpmntl Dsblties/ESL Cert.

**ESDAILE, RON STEUART MICHAEL,** Al A & M Univ, Normal, AL; JR; BS; Caribbean Stdnts Assoc Public Rltn Ofcr 90-; Intl Stdnt Assoc Editor In Chief 90-; Urban Plng Assoc Parliamentarian 89-; Most Outstndng Intl Stdnt Schl Agri Hm Econ; Urban Regional Plng.

**ESDINSKY, MARY B,** Mount Aloysius Jr Coll, Cresson, PA; SO; Assn Surgical Tech 90-; Deans Lst 90; Surgical Tech.

**ESHELMAN, MELISSA G,** Lansdale School Of Bus, North Wales, PA; WP; Deans Lst; Bsns Scrtrl W Prcsng.

**ESHENAUR, RICHARD D,** Kent St Univ Kent Cmps, Kent, OH; FR; Chem.

**ESKEDAL, LEE A,** Schenectady County Comm Coll, Schenectady, NY; SO; DC; Chrprctc Asst 90-; Lib Arts/Math/Sci; Chrprctr.

**ESKEW, TASHIA,** Clark Atlanta Univ, Atlanta, GA; SR; BA; Beta Gamma Sigma; Phi Beta Lambda 89-; AA Roxbury Comm Coll 89; Bus Admin; Entrepeneurship.

**ESKIN, ALYSSA M,** Fl International Univ, Miami, FL; SR; BS; Cncl Excptnl Chldrn 90-; Future Edctrs Am 90-; Pi Kappa Phi 90-; Phi Lambda 90-; AA Miami Dade Comm Clg 90; Spcfc Lrng Dsblts/Spcl Ed; Edctr.

**ESKIOGLOU, STAVROS,** Bunker Hill Comm Coll, Boston, MA; SO; AS; SAGA Intl Intern; Bsn Adm; Import/Export Bsn.

**ESMAY, BRIAN M,** Tampa Coll, Tampa, FL; SR; BBA; Summa Cum Laude; Bnvlnt/Prtctv Order Elks 88-; Business Adm.

**ESPADA, DAISY L,** City Univ Of Ny Baruch Coll, New York, NY; JR; BED; Brooklyn Professional Wmns Orgnztn; Ofc Automation Clb 90; Golden Key 90; Deans Lst; NY Wmns Bus Assoc Schlrshp 90; Proofreading Awrd Lotus 123 Database Iii; Natl Puerto Rican Forum Teaching Awrd; Pblshng 87-; AAS 87; Ofc Automation; Professor.

**ESPADA, PEDRO J,** Inter Amer Univ Pr Fajardo, Fajardo, PR; FR; BA; Bsns Admnstrtn; Stdnt Assn; Unvrsl Jesus Chrst 89-; Certf Acdmc Achvmnt; Certf Cooprtn; Accntng; Accntnt.

**ESPADA-MIRANDA, AMARILYS,** Caribbean Center For Adv Stds, San Juan, PR; GD; MS; Scty Hmn Res Mgt Caribbean Ctr Chptr Student 89-; Div Amer Psych Assoc Scty Indtl Org Psy Inc 90-; Assoc Psciol Puerto Rice 90-; Comite Timo/N De Estudianted F 89-90; Assoc De Estudiantesde Psicoloria 90; Indstl Org Psy Phd.

**ESPEJO, BARBARA M,** City Univ Of Ny La Guard Coll, Long Island Cty, NY; SR; Acctng.

**ESPINA, FRANCISCO J,** Inter Amer Univ Pr Hato Rey, Hato Rey, PR; SR; BA; Acctg Stdnts Assoc 89-; Acctg; CPA.

**ESPINAL, GLENNYS A,** City Univ Of Ny City Coll, New York, NY; SO; BS; Biology; Medicine.

**ESPINET, ERIKA W,** Univ Of Al At Birmingham, Birmingham, AL; SR; BA; Ballet; English Lang Arts; Secndry Educ.

**ESPINOSA, CORINA J,** George Mason Univ, Fairfax, VA; FR; BA; PAW; Crew; Frnch; Trnsltr Dsgnr.

**ESPINOSA, CRISTINA M,** Univ Of Miami, Coral Gables, FL; JR; BA; Hmcmng Exec Comm 90-; Pres 100 89-; Phi Beta Kappa; Phi Kappa Phi; Mortar Brd; Intrn US Sen Bob Graham 90-; Pom/Dnce Tm 89-; Soc/Engl; Law/Govt.

**ESPINOSA, GABRIELA,** Endicott Coll, Beverly, MA; SO; Bus Admn; Mgmt.

**ESPINOSA, JOSE A ROSADO,** Caribbean Univ, Bayamon, PR; BSCE; Engr Stdnts Assoc 90; PR Natrl Hist Soc; N Amer Vegtrn Soc; BA Magna Cum Laude 78; Hnrbl Mntn Univ Lit Cntst 78; Lit Poetry/Ftns/Ntrl Ntrtn Snclng/Orgnc/Frmng; BA 78; Engr; Civil.

**ESPOSITO, DAVID F,** Dowling Coll, Oakdale Li, NY; SR; BA; Dns Lst; Dns Lst Hnrs; Acdmc Hnr Schlrshp; Mbr Pi Alpha Sigma; Intrnshp Allstate Chem Bnk; AA Suffolk Comm Coll 88; Fin; Bnkng.

**ESPOSITO, MICHAEL A,** Univ Of Nc At Charlotte, Charlotte, NC; SR; BA; AIAS 90-; Crss Cntry 86-; Architecture.

**ESPOSITO, TRACEY L,** Albertus Magnus Coll, New Haven, CT; SR; BA; Intrnshp Gannett Outdr CT 90; Intrnshp KC101 Radio Sta Noble Brdcstng 90; Cmmnctns; Advrtsng/Promo.

**ESPRIT, ULREC J,** Tn St Univ, Nashville, TN; SR; BA; Intl Club 88; Golden Key 90; Betta Kappa Chi; Emory Univ Summer MCAT Prog; Biology; Med.

**ESPY, MICHAEL W,** Memphis St Univ, Memphis, TN; BA; Memphis St Pockt Billrds Champ 89-; AS Kalamazoo Vly Comm Coll 89; Math; Educ.

**ESSER, TRACY A,** George Mason Univ, Fairfax, VA; SR; MBA; SEA 88-90; NEA 88-; Trap/Skeet Tm 88-90 Coachs Awrd 90; BSED George Mason Un 90; Ed; Tchr.

**ESSEX, CALVIN S,** Al A & M Univ, Normal, AL; SR; BS; Stdnt Natl Ed Assn 90-; Agrnmy Clb Treas 88-90; Cir K; Alpha Kappa Mu Pres 89-90; Kappa Delta Pi Pres 89-90; Pres Schlrs Soc 88-; Alpha Zeta VP 88-89; Clgt FFA Advsr 90-; Cir K VP 87-88; Stdnt Cncl 89-; Agribus Ed.

**ESSICK, APRIL D,** Univ Of Nc At Greensboro, Greensboro, NC; JR; BS; Assoc Of Arts Surry Cmmnty Clg; Mddle Grades Ed Math/Sci.

**ESSIG, RICK J,** Grove City Coll, Grove City, PA; FR; BS; Nu Delta Epsilon 90-; Vrsty Bsbll 90-; Fnc.

**ESTABROOK, LEZLIE HOPE,** Lesley Coll, Cambridge, MA; SO; BED; Womanthought Mag Art Staff 90-; Church Choir/Bell Choir 89-; LINC 90-; Acad Hons Lst 90; Fld Hockey 90; Elem Tchr Math/Sci.

**ESTABROOKS, APRIL D,** Rivier Coll, Nashua, NH; JR; BA; Fllac Collaborative 88-90; Rspt Care Prvdr 89-; Art Educ; Elem Tchr.

**ESTEE, CHERYL W,** Coll Of Charleston, Charleston, SC; JR; BS; Stndt Port Clb 90-; SC State Ports Auth Intrnshp; S Atlantic/Caribbean Ports Assn; SC State Ports Auth Schlrhsp; Bus Admin; Intermodal Trans/Logistics.

**ESTELA, JULIO I,** Inter Amer Univ Pr Hato Rey, Hato Rey, PR; JR; Acctng Assn; Unmgu Mrthn Assn; Sttd Cvl Dfnse Agncy Emer Mgmt 90-; Hnr Lst 88-; Hnr Awrd Cert 90; Acctng; Lwyr.

**ESTEP, DUANE E,** West Liberty St Coll, West Liberty, WV; GD; Hnrs Cncl 87-89; Dns Lst; Australia Amer Exchng 88; Ftbl 87-89; Orntrng 88; SWC Tch Ftbl Lg; AAU Grls Bsktbl Coach 90-; Phys Ed Tchr 90-; CHS Tns Coach; JMHS Grls Bsktbl 90-; BA 90; Phy Ed; Tchr/Coach.

**ESTEP, JENNIFER A,** Tn St Univ, Nashville, TN; FR; BS; Crmnl Jstce; Law Enfrcmnt.

**ESTEP, LEAH M,** Mount Aloysius Jr Coll, Cresson, PA; FR; ASN; Class Rep 90; PTK Treas 90; Nrse Intrn Mrcy Hosp; Nrsng.

**ESTEP, LESLIE D,** Roane St Comm Coll, Harriman, TN; SO; Rdlgc Tech Clncl Awrd; AS; Sci; Mgmt.

**ESTEP III, PRESTON W,** Cornell Univ Statutory College, Ithaca, NY; JR; MS; Hughes Schlr; Musicn/Music Tchr 83-89; Cell/Moleculr Biol; Res.

**ESTEP, TERESA K,** Oh Univ-Southern Cmps, Ironton, OH; GD; BA; Deans Lst 89; Gamma Pi Delta 88; BA; Elem Ed; Tchr.

**ESTERLE, REBECCA S,** Univ Of Akron, Akron, OH; FR; BS; Amer Chmcl Scty Stdnt Affiltes; Phi Eta Sigma; Alpha Lambda Delta; Chmstry; Chmcl Eng.

**ESTES, CHERYL D,** Hampton Univ, Hampton, VA; FR; BA; Dean List; Pres Emnt Schlrs Awd; English/Elem Educ; Admin Educ.

**ESTES, D CHRISTOPHER,** Faulkner Univ, Montgomery, AL; SR; BS; Yng Rpblcns Dbt Tm 88-; Orch 88-90; Chrus Acpla 88-89; Epsilon Phi Upsilon VP 89-90; Kappa Sigma Phi 90-; Mntgmry Fmly Vlnc Pgm Chldrn Ther 90-; IM Ftbl/Bsktbl/Bsbl/Vlybl; Psych/Bible; Clncl Psych.

**ESTES, DEBRA S,** Brewer St Jr Coll, Fayette, AL; SO; BS; PTA 85-; Typst Antch Bapt Chrch 88-; Grl Scts Amrc Ldr 88-89; Ntry Pblc 79-; Albm Kdny Fndtn Inc Sec 87-; Sec Prsdnt Bnk 79-90; Cert 78; Scl Sci.

**ESTES, JEFFERY J,** Ms St Univ, Miss State, MS; JR; BA; Nwspr 87-89; Phi Beta Lambda Pres 88-89; Pres Cncl Repblcns 88-; Dns Schlr 90-; Pres Schlr; TN Tom Toursm Cncl Proj; Pol Sci/Publ Admn; Publ Rels/Persnl Mgmt.

**ESTES, PAMELA F,** Snead St Jr Coll, Boaz, AL; SO; Phi Theta Kappa; Bus; Accntng.

**ESTES, SABRINA P,** Ms St Univ, Miss State, MS; SO; Gamma Beta Phi; Phi Mu 90-; Comm Of 82; IM Flg Ftbl Sftbl 89-; Englsh; Law.

**ESTES, STEVEN D,** Univ Of South Al, Mobile, AL; SO; BA; Assoc Jstc Stdnt Govt 90-; Coll Rplbcns 89-90; Sigma Chi 90-; Prsdnts Lst 90; Bus Admn.

**ESTES, TAMMARA M,** Longwood Coll, Farmville, VA; SR; BS; Std VA Educ Asc Pres 90-; Std Educ Asc Pres 89-90; Alpha Lambda Delta 89-; Phi Kappa Phi; Kappa Delta Pi 88-; Sigma Kappa Chr 89-; GEIST Pres; Ambsdr 89-; RA 90-; Ornttn Ldr Chrmn 90-; Elem Ed.

**ESTEVES, JAVIER F,** Univ Politecnica De Pr, Hato Rey, PR; SO; BED; Utd St Army Sgt Frst Cls; Army ROTC 88-90; IM Bkstbl 90-; Mech Engnrng.

**ESTEVES, NANCY,** Univ Of Pr At Mayaguez, Mayaguez, PR; JR; BA; Indstrl Engr Hnr Brd 88-; Rolodx Schlrshp 89-90; Indstrl Engrng.

**ESTHER, CHRISTY J,** James Madison University, Harrisonburg, VA; JR; BS; Intrvrsty Chrstn Flwshp Pres 88-; Psi Chi 90-; Intrnshp Harrisnburg Offc Prob Parole; IM Tennis; Psychlgy; Chrstn Mnstry.

**ESTIME, NADAL P,** Miami Dade Comm Coll North, Miami, FL; SO; BA; Educ Tlnt Srch Clb Treas 90-; Bkbl Tm Mgr 88-90; Bus Admn; Bus.

**ESTRADA, MICHELLE D,** Marywood Coll, Scranton, PA; FR; BA; Vlybl Clb 89-90; Nrsng Clb 90-; Multicltrl Clb 90-; Natl Hon Soc 89-90; Nrsng/Ntrl Sci.

**ESTRADA, STEPHANIE J,** Univ Of Ga, Athens, GA; GD; PHARM; Zoolgy Clb Vp 88-90; Blck/Brdl 88-89; Pre Vet Clb 87-89; Phi Beta Kappa 90-; Mrtr Brd 89-90; Golden Key 89-; Beta Beta Beta 88-; Alpha Lambda Delta 88-; Phi Kappa Phi 90-; Symphnc Bnd 87-88; UGS Frst Hnr; UGA Elmn Schlr; Ntl Mrt Schlr; Phrmcy.

**ESTREET, ALLEGRA D,** Ny Univ, New York, NY; FR; BFA; Mntr; Trstee Schlr; Dance; Prfrmr.

**ESTRELLA, JANE M,** Merrimack Coll, North Andover, MA; FR; Hse Mgr On Stagers Sec 90-; Psychology/English; Chld Adlsnt Psychlst.

**ETHEART, PASCALE V,** Fl International Univ, Miami, FL; SO; BA; Blck Stdnt Un Hstrn 90-; Phi Eta Sigma 90-; AOP Schlrshp 89-; Eng; Jrnlsm.

**ETHEREDGE, VERONICA E,** Mobile Coll, Mobile, AL; SR; BS; Alpha Chi; Kappa Delta Epsilon; Gen Sci Awd; Sec Educ Awd; S S Tchr; Clerk Stngrphr II Hwy Dept; Ultra Sound Tech Asst; Composite Sci; Tch.

**ETHERIDGE, JUAN C,** Nc Agri & Tech St Univ, Greensboro, NC; SR; BS; IEEE 88-; NSBE 88-; TBTT; Dept Defense Co-Op Nvl Underwtr Syst Ctr NUSC 89-; Elctrcl Engr.

**ETHERIDGE, MELODY B,** Univ Of Ga, Athens, GA; JR; BED; Phi Theta Kappa 87-90; Kappa Delta Phi 90-; Lavonia Jr Srvc League; Hmnts Awd 90; Excel Wrtn Engl Lang; Dstngshd Awd Merit BSA 87; Cub Mstr 86-89; Treas Lavonia Carneville Ltl League 86-88; Long Dist Oper/Bookkeeper/Prsnl/Payroll; Middle Schl Educ; Tchng.

**ETHERIDGE-AUGUSTE, JENNIFER,** City Univ Of Ny Baruch Coll, New York, NY; SR; BBA; Gldn Key 90-; Cum Laude; Brkrg Indstry 83-; AA NYC Tech Coll 83; Finance; Cpa.

**ETIENNE, CECILEY M,** Anderson Coll, Anderson, SC; FR; AA; Anderson Coll Hnrs Prog; Bus Admin; Banking.

**ETKIN, WILLIAM B,** Glassboro St Coll, Glassboro, NJ; FR; BA.

**ETKINS, RAYMOND E,** City Univ Of Ny Baruch Coll, New York, NY; SR; BBA; AAS Borough Of Manhattan Comm Coll 89; Fnnce And Invstmnts; Bnkng.

**ETO, TAISKE,** S U N Y At Buffalo, Buffalo, NY; BS; AM Mrktng Assc VP 90-; Mrchng Drill Team/Vrsty Show Cmmt Dir Advrtsng 90-; Beta Gamma Sigma 90-; Gldn Key 90-; Ishida Seminar Meiji Univ Japan EVP 87-88; Mrktng Intrn Entrnmnt Equip Corp; Deans List; Kendo Clb Meiji Univ Japan Cptn 87-88; Bsn Mktng; Intntnl Bsn.

**ETRE, SUZANNE A,** Providence Coll, Providence, RI; SO; BA; Pstrl Cnsl Chrprsn Soc Actn Cmtee 90-; Habitat Humanity 89; Spec Olympcs 89; Soc Wrk.

**ETTER, DAVID E,** Salisbury St Univ, Salisbury, MD; GD; Hon Soc; I M Sftbl Vybl Bkbl Ftbl 86-90; AA 87; BA 90; Hstry; Bus.

**ETTER, MARK E,** Univ Of Ky, Lexington, KY; FR; BS; Phi Eta Sigma; Bsbl Tm; Physcs; Dr.

**ETTERS, BENJAMIN PAUL,** Memphis St Univ, Memphis, TN; SR; BBA; Phi Gamma Delta 85-86; Hmn Rsrcs Mgmt; Lbr Rltns.

**ETTRICH, KEVIN D,** S U N Y Maritime Coll, Bronx, NY; FR; BS; Hon Sectn 90-; Admrls List 90-; Color/Hon Guard 90-; Rugby 90-; Matrine Transprtn; Bus.

**ETUFUGH, ALOZIE N,** Manhattan Coll, Bronx, NY; SO; BSEE; Ntl Soc Blck Engr VP; IEEE; Elctrncs Clb; Elec Engr.

**EU, MAY-LIN E,** Gallaudet Univ, Washington, DC; SO; BA; Asian Pacific Assn Cong Rep 90-; Crrspndg Sec 90-; VP; BA 89-; Elem Educ; Tchr.

**EUBANK, THOMAS KYLE,** Univ Of Southern Ms, Hattiesburg, MS; SR; USM Sprts Med Assn 88-90; Gldn Key; Gamma Beta Phi; Delta Tau Delta Srgnt Of Arms 88-90; BS; ATC Natl Athl Trnrs Assn; Athl Trng.

**EUBANKS, KIMBREL S,** Clayton St Coll, Morrow, GA; SR; ABJ; Yrbk Stff Assoc 89-; Gldn Key 90; Rp Crss Cntr Nrthst Treas; Univ Deans Lst 89-; Clytn St Coll Deans Lst 90; Intern Mrkt Cntr PR Dept; Pblc Rltns.

**EUBANKS, LEAH T,** Memphis St Univ, Memphis, TN; SR; BA; Dance Co 88-; English; Dance Wrtng.

**EUBANKS, MARK J,** Liberty Univ, Lynchburg, VA; SO; BS; Cir K VP; Bio; Med Dr.

**EUBANKS JR, REAVIS THAYER,** Univ Of Nc At Asheville, Asheville, NC; JR; BA; Hstry.

**EUBANKS, STEPHEN S,** Castleton St Coll, Castleton, VT; JR; BS; Freestyle Ski Club Treas 88-; Im Bsktbl 88-; Cycling Club 90-; Radio Sta DJ 88-; Kappa Delta Phi Philntrpc Coordntr 88-; Tennis Team Co Cptn 88-; Bus Admn/Fin/Econ; Invstmnt Brkr.

**EUDY, ANGELA L,** Univ Of Nc At Charlotte, Charlotte, NC; JR; BA; Gldn Ky 90-; Biol; Tch Sec Schl.

**EUDY, JOHN DEWAYNE,** Mayland Comm Coll, Spruce Pine, NC; FR; AAS; Acctng.

**EUDY, REBEKAH L COOKE,** Mayland Comm Coll, Spruce Pine, NC; GD; LIC; Deans Lst/Pres Lst 89; Csmtolgy; Beautcn/Tchr.

**EUGENE, ANISSA J,** Tougaloo Coll, Tougaloo, MS; JR; BA; Psychlgy Clb 90-; Pan-Afrcn Ed Ntwrk 88-90; Psychlgy; Cnslr.

**EUI HYANG, KIM,** Barry Univ, Miami, FL; SR; BED; Gtr Clb 86-87; Brd Edctn Lcl Pblc Offcl 82-85; Tchr Cert 89; Erly Chldhd.

**EULAU, LISA M,** City Univ Of Ny Queens Coll, Flushing, NY; FR; BA; NYPIRG 90-; Amnsty Intl 90-; Deans Lst 90-.

**EURY, ANGELA R,** Univ Of Nc At Charlotte, Charlotte, NC; SR; BA; Psychlgy Clb 89-; Crt Apntd Spec Advct 90-; Amer Psychlgcl Assoc; Psi Chi 90-; Frnd Fmly 89-; Hlp Ln Untd Wy 88-89; Crs Asstnc Mnstry 88; Rsrch Asst 90; Intrnshp Chldrns Law Ctr 90; Internshp Fmly Outrch; Psychlgy.

**EUSEBIO, KARLA E,** Univ Of Pr At Rio Piedras, Rio Piedras, PR; SR; BS; Math Cmptr Sci Assn 89-90; Gldn Ky 90-; Hnrs Pgrm 88-; Dns Lst 90-; GTE Spacenet Schlrshp 87-; Math; Cmptr Sci.

**EVAKISE, LYDIA NAMONDO,** Howard Univ, Washington, DC; GD; MSW; African Stdnt Assn V P; Treas; Fin Sec 90-; Assn Ftr Soc Wrkrs 87-90; Hosp Dialysis Soc Wrkr 89-90; Prbytrn Chrch Outrch Coord 90-; BSW 90; Cmnty Org/Mgmt; Soc Work.

**EVANCAVICH, LISA M,** Marywood Coll, Scranton, PA; FR; Art/Interior Dsgn.

**EVANCHO, MICHAEL E,** Saint Vincents Coll & Seminary, Latrobe, PA; SR; BA; Alpha Sigma Lambda 89; Intrnshp 90; Swanson Analysis Syst Inc 89; Deans Lst 87; Elctrncs Tchncn 73-75; Retl Sls 76-86; Ast Penn Tchncl Inst 73; Cmptng Info Sci; Prog/Analyst.

**EVANKO, ELAINE M,** West Liberty St Coll, West Liberty, WV; SR; BA; BS Bio WV Univ 89; Scndry Ed/Bio; Tchr/Pharm Sales.

**EVANS, ALECIA M,** Ky St Univ, Frankfort, KY; JR; BA; Gspl Ensmbl 89-; Dns Lst 88-90; Delta Sigma Theta Hstrn 89-; Smr Intrnshp USDA Frmrs Hm Adm Clrk 89-; Mgmt/Mktg.

**EVANS, AMY D,** Univ Of Ms Main Cmps, University, MS; SR; Gldn Ky 90-; Gamma Beta Phi 89-; Alpha Epsilon Delta Sec 89-; Beta Beta Beta 88-; Alpha Omicron Pi Rec Sec 88-; Emerg Rm Vol 90; BA; Biol; Med Sch.**

**EVANS, AMY E,** Univ Of Sc At Columbia, Columbia, SC; FR; BA; Alpha Delta Pi Schlrshp Com 90-; Crlna Crs 90-; Rd Crss Vol; Dns Lst USC; Jrnlsm; PR.

**EVANS, AMY G,** Waycross Coll, Waycross, GA; FR; BS; Phi Theta Kappa; Computer Sci; Systems Analyst.

**EVANS, ANGIE R,** Alcorn St Univ, Lorman, MS; FR; BED; Elem Educ.

**EVANS, ANNE N,** Radford Univ, Radford, VA; FR; BA; Envrnmntl Actvsts 90-; Ed.

**EVANS, BARBARA A,** City Univ Of Ny Baruch Coll, New York, NY; JR; BA; Amrcn Mrktng Assoc 90-; Gldn Key; Prvst Schlrshp Blcr Fmly Schlsrhp 90-; Assoc Lgl Admn 88-89; Lgl Admn 87-; Mrktng Mgmt.

**EVANS, BRENT D,** Fl Memorial Coll, Miami, FL; SR; MBA; Alpha Kappa Mu; Greyhnd Schlrshp 88; Irma Bridgette Roganoff Schlrshp 89; Forrest Flmmng Trst Schlrshp 88; BA; Mgmt; Bnkg.

**EVANS, CASSANDRA L,** Univ Of Miami, Coral Gables, FL; JR; BA; Inspratn Cncrt Choir Pres 89-91; Biology Clb 89-90; United Blk Stdnts 88-91; Hurricane Honeys V P 90-91; House Tutor 88-89; Crmnl Juste; Law Sch.

**EVANS, CATRISSE L,** Al St Univ, Montgomery, AL; FR; BA; Bus Mgt/Acctng.

**EVANS JR, CHARLES N,** Marshall University, Huntington, WV; JR; BED; Im Trck Team Chmp; Adlt Fitns; Cardiac Rehab.

**EVANS, CHERYL LYNN,** Anne Arundel Comm Coll, Arnold, MD; FR; Biology; Vet.

**EVANS, CRISTINA,** Broward Comm Coll, Ft Lauderdale, FL; SO; BABEA; Pres List 90-; Thea; Acting/Techn; Thea/Film.

**EVANS, CYNTHIA R,** James Madison University, Harrisonburg, VA; SR; MED; Psych Clb 88; Outing Clb 87-88; Psi Chi 89; Premed Schlrshp 87; BS; Cnslng.

**EVANS, DANA J,** Roane St Comm Coll, Harriman, TN; FR; AAS; Nrsng; RN.

**EVANS, DAVID B,** Garrett Comm Coll, Mchenry, MD; SO; BA; Phi Theta Kappa; High Hon; Lib Aid/Asst 90-; Best Math Rsrch Paper/Best Math Proj Awds; AA; Native Am Studies/Hist; Teach.

**EVANS, DAVID W,** Marywood Coll, Scranton, PA; JR; BS; Kappa Delta Pi 90-; Math Scndry Ed; Tchng.

**EVANS, DEBORAH K,** George Mason Univ, Fairfax, VA; JR; BS; Scl Wrk Stdnt Assoc Pres; Social Work.

**EVANS, DENISE A,** Daytona Beach Comm Coll, Daytona Beach, FL; FR; Engl; Educ.

**EVANS, ELLEN J,** Emory Univ, Atlanta, GA; GD; MSN; Sigma Theta Tau 86-; Phi Beta Kappa 84-; ANA 86-; BA Rockford Clg 84; Nrsg.

**EVANS, FELICIA L,** Comm Coll Algny Co Algny Cmps, Pittsburgh, PA; GD; BA; Geriatric Nurse; Home Hlth Care Aide; Clerk III CNA Ins Co 87-; AS; HHC/GN Cert 86; Bus Mgt; Corp Law.

**EVANS, FLOYD RAY,** Morehouse Coll, Atlanta, GA; JR; BA; Recrtmnt V P 88-90; Drama Cl 88-; Law Soc 88-; SGA 89-90; Hon Roll/Deans List; Cosby Show Intrn:; Pol Sci; Entrnmnt/ Sports/Law; Agent Prodctn.

**EVANS, HARRIETT A,** Oh Dominican Coll, Columbus, OH; SO; BA; Amer Nrsng Assn Cert Cmmnty Hlth Nrsng; Dir Nrsng Licking Co Hlth Dept; RN Holzer Hosp Schl Nrsng 65; Hlth Admn.

**EVANS, JACQUELINE D,** Northern Ky Univ, Highland Hts, KY; AD; Nrsg; Srgcl Nrs.

**EVANS, JANET LYNNE,** Mount Vernon Coll, Washington, DC; FR; BA; Stdnt Govt Assoc Sec/Acct Cls 94; US Glbl Stdies Clb Sec/Acct; Orntn/Acad Adv; Smmr Intrnshp NJ Hsng Mort Fin Agcy Res Asst 91; Intl Stdies.

**EVANS, JEAN M,** Univ Of Bridgeport, Bridgeport, CT; GD; MS; Ltry Mag-Housatonic Comm Coll Edtr 89; Dana Schlr 90; Phi Theta Kappa 89; Housatonic Comm Coll Hon Soc VP 88-89; Grad Intrnshp-Darien H S Sub Tchr; Drs Louise-Anthony Soares Schlrshp; Cmmncmnt Awd; Ltrtr 90-; Summa Cum Laude 90; Educ-Scndry Lvl Engl; Engl Tchr-Scndry Lvl.**

**EVANS, JEFFREY L,** Oh St Univ At Newark, Newark, OH; SO; BSED; Hnr Soc 89-90; Dns Lst 89-90; Symphony Orch 85-; Data Processor 90; Mstr Lrn Sys; Educ; Tch.

**EVANS, JENNIFER L,** Kent St Univ Kent Cmps, Kent, OH; JR; BA; SGA Sec 88-89; Psychlgy Clb VP 90-; Gold Key; Psi Chi VP 90-; Bible Stdy 90-; Cmps Crsds Chrst 90-; IM Vlybl/Sftbl 89-; Psychlgy; Cnslng.

**EVANS, JERMAINE L,** Brevard Coll, Brevard, NC; FR; AA; Blk People In Unity Pres; French Clb; Proj Inside Out 90-; Music; Educ.

**EVANS, JUDY J,** Kent St Univ Kent Cmps, Kent, OH; SO; BS; Tdy Tmrrw Prgm 89-90; Prsdnts Lt; Math.

**EVANS, KAREN B,** Univ Of Tn At Martin, Martin, TN; JR; BS; MED 90-; Schlrshps Acdmc/Ldrshp 89-; Blgy; Med.

**EVANS, KATHY J,** Alcorn St Univ, Lorman, MS; SR; BS; MS Assn Stdnt Nrses VP 89-; Nation Stdnt Nrs Assn; Stdnt Rep Fclty Advsry Comm 90-; Spirit Nrsng Awd; Outstdng Stdnt 87-; Nrsng; Peds.

**EVANS, KATHY S,** Washington State Comm Coll, Marietta, OH; FR; AAS; Soc Serv; Soc Wrkr.

**EVANS, KELLY E,** Indiana Univ Of Pa, Indiana, PA; JR; BED; Big Bros/Big Sistrs; Elem Ed; Tchng.

**EVANS, KENNETH L,** Univ Of Tn At Knoxville, Knoxville, TN; SR; Bapt Stdnt Union 87-; Phi Kappa Phi 90; Dlt Nu Alph 89; E Ward King Schlrshp 89-90; New England Cncl Lgstcs Mgmt Schlr; William Way Jr Schlrshp 90; Logstcs/Trnsprtn; Indstry.

**EVANS, KEVIN G,** Wilmington Coll, Wilmington, OH; SR; MPA; Stdnts Envrnmnt; Green Key 90-; Cngrsnl Intrn 90-; AB; Pltcl Sci; Pub Admn.

**EVANS, KIRK N,** Johnson C Smith Univ, Charlotte, NC; FR; BA; Soc Sci; PHD.

**EVANS, KRISTI E,** Bridgewater Coll, Bridgewater, VA; SR; BS; Mu Epsilon Mu Pres; Res Cnslr; Co Curricular Awd Ldrshp; BS; Hm Econ; Educ.

**EVANS, KRISTI L,** Ms Gulf Coast Comm Coll, Perkinston, MS; FR; Stdnt Cncl VP 90-; Bptst Union Pres; MS Sound Show Grp 90-; Clg Hnrs Prgrm 90-; Schlrs Bowl Team 90-; Dance Team 90-; Phrmcy; Phrmcy.

**EVANS, KRISTIN D,** Univ Of Southern Ms, Hattiesburg, MS; SO; BA; Stdnt Alumni Assoc VP 90; Gamma Beta Phi; Lambda Sigma 90-; Alpha Lambda Delta; Phi Chi Theta VP; Banking/ Finance.

**EVANS, LINDA S,** Wv Univ At Parkersburg, Parkersburg, WV; FR; Bsns; Acct.

**EVANS, LISA ANNE DIES,** Volunteer St Comm Coll, Gallatin, TN; SO; BS; Gamma Beta Phi 90-; Math Lab Tutor 90-; Sml Animal Dietitian; Sr Citizen Vol Pgm; Ofc Mgr Lebanon Animal Hosp; AS Magna Cum Laude; Math; Sec Ed MA.

**EVANS, LISA W,** Univ Of Al At Birmingham, Birmingham, AL; SR; BS; Amer Mktg Assn; Pr Hons Lst 90; Deans Lst; Hosp Hltchare Mktg 88-; Hosp Bus Dev Dir; Bus/Mktg; Psych Hlthcare.

**EVANS, LURLEEN C,** City Univ Of Ny Baruch Coll, New York, NY; SR; BBA; Pi Slpha Alpha; Pan Hellanic Cncl Of Grtr New York VP 90-; Delta Sigma Theta Pres 89-90; Publc Admn; Grad Schl Of Univ Of KS For MDA.

**EVANS, LUTRESHA R,** Alcorn St Univ, Lorman, MS; FR; Nrsng.

**EVANS, LYNDA M,** Hillsborough Comm Coll, Tampa, FL; SO; Phi Theta Kappa 90-; Rdlgc Thchnlgy.

**EVANS, LYNETTE S,** S U N Y Coll At Fredonia, Fredonia, NY; SR; BED; Tchr Edn Clb; Vol Tutor Pgm; BCIC; Kappa Delta Pi VP 90-; Edn.

**EVANS, LYNNE W,** Portland School Of Art, Portland, ME; SR; BA Southern Vermont Coll 77; Grphc Dsgn; Free Lance Dsgnr.

**EVANS, M MICHELE,** Univ Of South Al, Mobile, AL; GD; MED; Kappa Delta Pi 90-; Gras Asstshp 90-; Army Achvmnt Mdl 89; Pres Lst 88-; Army Cmmndtn Mdl 86; Deans Lst 88; US Army Rsrvs 86-; Bsktbl/Sftbl Offcls Assn 89-; BA Univ AL 82; BS Univ S AL 90; Phys Ed/Exrcse Physlgy; Tchng/Coachng.

**EVANS, MARGARET C,** Va Commonwealth Univ, Richmond, VA; SR; BSN; Schl Nrs/Psychtrc Staff Nrs; AAS John Tyler Comm Clg 78; Nrsng; Fmly Nrs Prctnr.

**EVANS, MARY C,** Owensboro Comm Coll, Owensboro, KY; FR; BA.

**EVANS, MATTHEW S,** Embry Riddle Aeronautical Univ, Daytona Beach, FL; SO; BS; Army ROTC; Sons/Am Revltn; Silver ROTC Medal; IM Sftbl/Bsktbl/Ftbl; Aerontcl Sci; Prfssnl Pilot.

**EVANS, MELINDA S,** Univ Of Ga, Athens, GA; SR; BSED; Gldn Key 90-; Natl Stdnt Spch Lang Hear Assoc 89-; Newton Cnty Mntl Hlth Ctr Prac 90; Ednl Psychlgy; Audiology.

**EVANS, MELISSA A,** Castleton St Coll, Castleton, VT; SR; BS; Kappa Delta Pi; Elem Edctn; Tch.

**EVANS, MEREDITH RACHELLE,** Clark Atlanta Univ, Atlanta, GA; FR; BS; Hist Soc; Phlhrmnc Soc; NAACP; Hon Pgm; Pres Schlr Awd; Hon Roll; All-Amer Schlr; BA; Jrnlsm/ Histh; Wrtr/Prof.

**EVANS, MICHAEL R,** Univ Of Fl, Gainesville, FL; JR; BS; Stdnt Hon Ct Assoc Juste 89-; Pre Legal Hon Soc 88-90; Fin Mgmt Assn 90-; Golden Key 90-; Pub Dfndrs Off Invstgtr Intrn 90; Fin/Spch; Law.

**EVANS, MILETTE L,** Fl A & M Univ, Tallahassee, FL; SR; BS; Clss Sec 87-88; Amer Med Rcrd Assn 89-; Stdnt Med Rcrd Assn P 90-; FL Med Rcrd Assn; Pres Schlr Exclsr Awd 89-; Med Rcrd Admin.

**EVANS, MONICA M,** Clark Atlanta Univ, Atlanta, GA; JR; BA; Mktg Clb VP Elect; Miss Jr 90-; NAACP 89-; Beta Gamma Sigma; Mngmnt Trne 89; Northern Telecom Intrn 90-; Bus Admin; Mktg/Sls.

**EVANS, PAMELA J,** Kent St Univ Kent Cmps, Kent, OH; JR; BSN; Stdnts Prof Nrsng 89-; Orntn Instr; Natl Leag Nrsng 89-90; Alpha Lambda Delta 89-; Sprtd Instr; Nrsng; Nrsng Admn/Peds.

**EVANS, PETER C,** Bridgewater Coll, Bridgewater, VA; SO; BA; Rd Asst Prgm Drc; Nwsppr Art Drctr; Art.

**EVANS, REBECCA A,** Kent St Univ Kent Cmps, Kent, OH; JR; BA; Vlybl Co Rec 89-; Campus Crusade 90-; Stu Govt Tres 88-89; Gldn Key; Delta Sigma Pi Jr VP Scl Actvs; Bus; Mgmt.

**EVANS, REBECCA A,** Garrett Comm Coll, Mchenry, MD; FR; BA; Vybl 90-; Acctg.

**EVANS, RHONDA L,** Kent St Univ Kent Cmps, Kent, OH; JR; BA; Pre Law Clb 90-; Itln Clb 90-; Orientn Instrctr Bst Syllbs Dev; Golden Key Outstndg Jr Schlrshp; Poli Sci Clb Pres; Cmnty Hsp; Sherri Jo Lutt Meml Awd; Ft Steuben Mall Schlrshp 88; Poli Sci; Law.

**EVANS, RISE C,** Univ Of Cin R Walters Coll, Blue Ash, OH; SO; BSW; Suicide Crisis Line; Soc Work; Psy D Clinical Psychogolist.

**EVANS, ROBERT,** Va St Univ, Petersburg, VA; SR; BA; NAACP V P 88-89; Mktg/Mgmt; Mgmt Analsty.

**EVANS, ROBYN E,** Valdosta St Coll, Valdosta, GA; FR; BS; Blzn Brgd Mrchng Bnd 90; Nrsng.

**EVANS, RONDAI,** Yale Univ, New Haven, CT; JR; BA; Inroads Hnr Awd; Yale Heinz Schlr; Intrn Mobay Chem Co; Arch; Med Doctr.**

**EVANS, SANDRA E,** Neumann Coll, Aston, PA; JR; BA; Prof Ed Scty Pres 90-; AA DE Cty Comm Coll 90; Erly Chldhd Ed/ Elem Ed; Tchr.

**EVANS, SARAH E,** Radford Univ, Radford, VA; SO; Hstry/Art Hstry; Museum.

**EVANS, SCOTT J,** Univ Of New England, Biddeford, ME; JR; ADN; Nrsng Stdnt Clb Pres 90-; Stdnt Nrs Assn By-Law Com 90-; Nrsng.

**EVANS, SHARI ELIZABETH,** D Youville Coll, Buffalo, NY; SR; BS; Cum Laude; Dns Lst 89-; AAS Bryant Strattn 88; Mgmt; Finc.

**EVANS, SHARON E,** Oh Univ, Athens, OH; JR; BFA; RHA Sntr 87; Stu Art Thrpy Orgn; Art Thrpy.

**EVANS, SHAWN D,** Fl A & M Univ, Tallahassee, FL; FR; BA; Acctng.

**EVANS, TERESA RENEE,** Marshall University, Huntington, WV; SR; BS; Cmps Entrnmnt Unlmtd Chrprsn 84-86/89; Hmcmng Dance Comm Chrprsn 86/87/90; Stdnt Ctr Gvrng Brd Chrprsn 90-; ACM; Stdnt Assistanship/Dean Of Stdnt Affairs Rsrch 90-; Girl Scout Ldr 88-89; Cmptr Sci.

**EVANS, W KENNETH,** Allegheny Coll, Meadville, PA; JR; BA; Jzz Bnd/Wnd Symphny 88-; Vol Spprt Admssn Almn 89-; Radio Sta 88-; Lambda Sigma; Ecnmcs/Pol Sci; Ecnmc Law.

**EVANS, WENDY L,** Univ Of Sc At Spartanburg, Spartanburg, SC; SR; BA; Psych Clb VP 89-; Problem Hotline/Lifeline Vice Chrmn 90; Peer Educ 90; Psych; Family Ther.

**EVANS, WILLIAM B,** Oh St Univ At Newark, Newark, OH; FR; BS; Phi Sigma; US Navy Hnrble Sdschrg; Ag.

**EVANS-WIDENHOUSE, JOY,** Western Carolina Univ, Cullowhee, NC; JR; BSW; Pi Gamma Mu; Phi Alpha; Smky Mntn Comm Thtre Asst Dir 90-; Unty Reg Yth Trtmtn Ctr Vlntr 90-F Cmptr Cnsltn Co Ownr 82-89; AS Sthrn Coll 78; Scl Wrk; Admin/Cnslng.

**EVATT, KEVIN C,** Tri County Tech Coll, Pendleton, SC; SR; DPLMA; State Pipe Wldng Comp; Cert 90; Wldng; Cnstrctn.

**EVE, SHELLEY RENEE,** Univ Of Ga, Athens, GA; SR; BSED; Kappa Delta Epsilon Fndrsng Chr 90-; Gldn Key; Pro Assn GA Edctrs; Athens Tutrl Cntr 90; Early Chldhd Educ; Tchng.

**EVELETH, LYNDA S,** Univ Of Akron, Akron, OH; SR; MS; Intrnshp Univ Akron Atltc Trng Sports Med Sprvsr 86-90; BSED; Sports Med.

**EVEN, JULIE A,** Ms Coll, Clinton, MS; GD; JD; Phi Delta Phi VP 90-; IM Sftbl Vlybl Tns; BA 88; Law.

**EVENSEN, MARY A,** Glassboro St Coll, Glassboro, NJ; SR; BA; Intrn NATPE Convntn; Storer Cbl Local Channel Intrn; Cmnctns/Radio/TV Film; BA Early Chldhd Ed.

**EVERETT, ALICE E,** Univ Of Miami, Coral Gables, FL; FR; MBA; Innr Cty Fndtn; Hrrcne Hns; Untd Blck Stdnts; Fr Ornttn Prog Orttn Asst; Gldn Achvr; Cap Schlr; Sprts Fst; Comp Info Systms Econs; Corp Law.

**EVERETT, AMY L,** Meridian Comm Coll, Meridian, MS; SO; AA; Batgrl; Ambssdrs; Elem Educ; Tch.

**EVERETT, BRUCE W,** Univ Of Ga, Athens, GA; JR; BSCFD; George Montgomery Schlrshp; Washington Presbyterian Chrch 72-; Ltl League Umpire 90; Chld/Fmly Dvlpmnt; Cnslr.

**EVERETT, CINDY CAROL,** Murray St Univ, Murray, KY; FR; BS; Stdnt Alumni Assoc 90-; Bapt Stdnt Union Frshmn Ldrshp Tm 90-; Lead; Hnrs Pgm 90-; Math Dept Uprclsmn Schlrshp; Math; Clg Prfsr.

**EVERETT, GLORIA J,** Meridian Comm Coll, Meridian, MS; SO; Phi Beta Lambda.

**EVERETT, GREGORY L,** Univ Of Nc At Charlotte, Charlotte, NC; SR; BCA; Blck Stdnt Un 87-88; Ntl Arts Educ Assoc; Comm Minrty Concrns 89-90; IM Bsktbl Ftbl Sftbl 87-; Dns Lst 89-90; Bny/Smth Fn Art Awd 90; Visl Arts; Grphc Artst/Tchr/Prof.

**EVERETT, KATRINA L,** Univ Of Md Balt Cnty Campus, Catonsville, MD; SO; BS; Intrvrsty Chrstn Flwshp; Alpha Sigma Alpha Schlrshp Chr; Blgcl Sci.**

**EVERETT, MATTHEW W,** Univ Of Ky, Lexington, KY; SR; BS; Otstndng Physc Stu 89-; IM Bsktbll 86-89; BS Georgetown Coll 90; Cvl Eng.

**EVERETT, RAYMOND,** Va St Univ, Petersburg, VA; SR; BS; Mrktg Clb Pres 88-; Phi Beta Lambda 90-; Stu Advsry Cncl Sch Bus 90-; Hnrs Deans Lst 88-90; Alpha Phi Alpha; Cert Acdmc Achvmnt 90-; Acdmc Awrds Pin 90; Mrktg; Cnsltnt.

**EVERETT, RITA A,** George Mason Univ, Fairfax, VA; GD; BS; Stdnt Educ Assn 87-; Phi Mu 87-; BS; Early Ele Educ; Tch.

**EVERETT, SAMANTHA F,** Volunteer St Comm Coll, Gallatin, TN; SO; BA; Acctng Clb 89-90; Acctng; Cpa.

**EVERETTS, ANNGINA D,** Middle Tn St Univ, Murfreesboro, TN; FR; BA; Tutor Math Hist; Intern Congressman Jim Cooper 90; Staff Asst Con Jim Cooper 90; Historic Preservaton.

**EVERHEART, HENRY H,** Al St Univ, Montgomery, AL; FR; BA; Sci; Eng.

**EVERITT, LORI R,** Univ Of Akron, Akron, OH; SO; BS; AICHE 90-; Hnrs Clb 89-; Alpha Lambda Delta 89-; Phi Eta Sigma 89-; Pi Mu Epsilon; Explrer Pst 2177 Vp 86-; Rsrch Asst Chem Eng Dpt 90-; Chem Eng.

**EVERS, DANIEL C,** Wright St Univ Lake Cmps, Celina, OH; FR; Mechanical Engineering; Engineering.

**EVERS, KIM E,** Ms Coll, Clinton, MS; GD; Ms Defense Lawyers Assoc 90; Amer Bar Assoc 90; County Bar Assn Sec/Treas 90-; Law Review 88-90; Phi Delta Phi; Amer Jurisprudence Awd Ethics 89; Ms Def Lawyers Reginald Gray Schlrshp; Legal Assoc 90-; JD 90-; BS USM 87; Law.

**EVETTE, AMY L,** Winthrop Coll, Rock Hill, SC; SO; BS; Dinkins Un 89-90; Envrnmntl Awrnss 90; Psychlgy Clb 89-90; Alpha Lambda Delta 90-; Psi Chi; Sigma Sigma Sigma 90-; Circle K; Stdy Abrd Prog/Univ Lndn; Psychlgy; Clncl Psychlgst.

**EVIRS, RICHARD K,** Middle Tn St Univ, Murfreesboro, TN; JR; BS; Intra Frtrnty Cncil Judcl Bd Justice; Pi Kappa Alpha Rush Chrmn; Tv Prdctn; Motion Pcture Indstry.

**EVITTS, JOYCE J,** Owensboro Comm Coll, Owensboro, KY; SO; Hmn Servs; Cnslng/Soc Work.

**EVORA, IDELSY B,** Fl International Univ, Miami, FL; SR; Fin Mgmt Assoc 89-; Rotaract Sec 90-; Jr Achvmnt 90; Intrnshp Wrld Trd Ctr Asst Mbrshp Coord 90-; BBA; Fin/Intl Bsns.

**EWALD, JOHN E,** Southern Coll Of Tech, Marietta, GA; JR; BS; Exchng Std Englnd 90; Pres Lst; Dns Lst; Tau Kappa Epsln Chrmn 89; Coop Atlanta Gas Lght Co 88-90; IM Sftbl 89; Indl Engr Tech; Cnsltnt.

**EWAN, JILL S,** Atlantic Comm Coll, Mays Landing, NJ; SO; Travel/Tourism; Airline Ticket Agent.

**EWERS, KAREN L,** Commonwealth Coll, Norfolk, VA; SO; AAS; Commonwealth Recorder Editor 90-; Alpha Beta Gamma 90-; Medical.

**EWERS, KASSIE J,** Capital Univ, Columbus, OH; SO; Ambssdr 89-; Nrsng.

**EWING, BRADFORD S,** Memphis St Univ, Memphis, TN; SR; BA; Mktg; Cmrcl Bkg/Invstmts.

**EWING, DENISE L,** Barry Univ, Miami, FL; JR; Pres Lst Barry Univ 89; Dns Lst 89-90; Bahamas Inst Of Bnkrs 84-; Bahamas Inst Bnkrs 84-; Exch Cntrl Asst Cntrl Bnk Of Bahamas 81; Exch Cntrl Asst Cntrl Bnk Of Bahamas 81-; Econ/Finance; Bnkng.**

**EWING, KAREN L,** Alcorn St Univ, Lorman, MS; SO; MASN; NSNA; OAADG; SA Pres; Pres Schol; Helene Fuld Nsg Fllwshp; Class Treas 90-; Jonesville Jr Guild Civic Cl; Nrsg.

**EWING, MARY ELIZABETH,** Marywood Coll, Scranton, PA; SO; BFA; AHSA 85-89; AMHA 76-90; CRC 88; Orient; Tutor 90; VIA 89; Ski Clb 90; Intr Dsgn.

**EWING, VALERIE P,** Bowie St Univ, Bowie, MD; SR; BS; Hnrs Prgrm; Ntnl Urbn Leg; Prnt Tchr Assn Tres 90-; NAACP; AS Solano Cmmnty Clg 86; Mgmnt; Tchng.

**EXHEM, MICHAEL C,** City Univ Of Ny La Guard Coll, Long Island Cty, NY; JR; AAS; Asst Ntwrk Admn; Telecomm; Telecomm Spec.

**EXUM, BRENDAN M,** Hudson Valley Comm Coll, Troy, NY; FR; AOX; Scuba Dvng Jrnlsm Clb 86-; Skiing 76-77; Nwspr Edtr 87-88; Dns Lst 90-; Mdl Car Rcng Lang Clb H S 86-88; Phi Theta Kappa 90-; Soccer Ltrd 86-88; Audiosears Corp Apprntc Tool Mkr 89-90; AOS Hudson Vly Comm Coll; Mach Proc; Eng/Dsgn Auto.

**EXUM, HOPE,** Brandywine Coll Of Widner Univ, Wilmington, DE; SO; AS; Styles/Images Clb 90; Bermans Intern; AS; Fshn Merch; Buyer.

**EYER, GINA G,** Northern Ky Univ, Highland Hts, KY; JR; BA; Anthropology Club Pres 90; Stdnt Sclgy Org Treas; Awarded Michael Zalla Mem Grant; Anthropology/Phlsphy; PHD Anthropology.

**EYETSEMITAN, FRANCISCA,** S U N Y Coll Of Tech At Alfred, Alfred, NY; SR; AS; Chrtrd Inst Bnkrs London England 85; ACIB Chrtrd Inst Bnkrs London 85; Acctg.

**EYINK, RENEE M,** Wright St Univ Lake Cmps, Celina, OH; FR; AAB; Med Admin; Secretary.

**EYLER, DEBRA L,** Ulster County Comm Coll, Stone Ridge, NY; FR; Nrsng.

**EYOB, JERUSALEM,** Selma Univ, Selma, AL; SO; BA; Miss Selma Univ; Blck Blt Art Cult Ctr; Dns Lst; Cheschire Hm Clb 86-89; Lions Clb 88-89; Wildlf Clb 87-89; Hnr Soc Awd; Med Tech; Dr.

**EZEIRUAKU, ELO S,** Glassboro St Coll, Glassboro, NJ; SR; BA; Co Pub Dfndrs Intrn; Deans Lst; AS Camden Co Coll 90; Jstce; Law.

**EZEKWE, BENJAMIN U,** Va St Univ, Petersburg, VA; JR; BS; Accntng Clb Bus Prmtns 90-; CPA Clb 88-; Intl Stu Clb VP; Dean Lst 88-; Big Sis/Bro 90-; Coca-Cola USA Intern 90; Ftbll 88-89; Accntng.

**EZELL, ANTOINE C,** Fl A & M Univ, Tallahassee, FL; SR; BA; NAACP 88-; Bg Bro/Bg Srs 88-90; Math Tutor 90-; Omega Psi Phi Basils 88-89; Quaker Oats Intrnshp 90; Allstate Ins Intrnshp Anlyst; Supr Perf Schlrshp; Vars Ftbl; Masonic Ord; Bsns Admn; Fin.

**EZELL, BELINDA L,** Univ Of South Al, Mobile, AL; SR; BS; Alpha Lambda Delta 89-; Alpha Chi 90-; Phi Eta Sigma 89-; Educ; Elem Educ.

**EZELL, CHRISTY L,** Univ Of Sc At Spartanburg, Spartanburg, SC; JR; BA; Univ Bus Socty 90-; Piedmnt Socty Sec 89-; Gamma Beta Phi 89-; Ldrshp Dvlpmnt Prgrm 90-; Bus Admin/Mktg; Advrtsng Sls Agnt.

**EZELL, KARLA J,** Wv Univ At Parkersburg, Parkersburg, WV; SR; BA; AA Ohio Vlly Coll 89; Educ.

**EZELL, KYLA A,** William Carey Coll, Hattiesburg, MS; SR; BS; Bapt Stdnt Un; Sci Scty; Gamma Chi; Mss Wllm Cry Coll 89; Physcl Ed; Athltc Dir.

**EZELL, LISA R,** Univ Of Southern Ms, Hattiesburg, MS; SR; BS; Baptst Stdnt Union 89-; Stdnt Eagle Club 89-; Paralegal Soc 89-; Gamma Beta Phi 88-; Phi Eta Sigma 88-; Golden Key 89-; Paralegal Studies; Legal Assistant.

**EZELL, TERRESA C,** Ms St Univ, Miss State, MS; SO; BA; Gamma Beta Phi 90-; Phi Eta Sigma; Hnrs Prog 89-; Commtns; Public Relations.

**EZELL, WALTER L,** Al A & M Univ, Normal, AL; SO; BS; Mktg Awd 90-; Mktg/Bsn; Mktg Spec.

**EZEOKOLI, DONNA M,** Bloomfield Coll, Bloomfield, NJ; JR; BS; Acctg; Mgmnt Acctg.

**EZZELL, BRENDA S,** James Sprunt Comm Coll, Kenansville, NC; GOT Spclty; Scrtry.

**EZZYK, PATRICIA G,** Patrick Henry Comm Coll, Martinsville, VA; SO; Ntrdtnl Stdnt Assns; Phi Theta Kappa Spire; RN.

# F

**FABELO, MICHELLE D,** Univ Of Pr At Rio Piedras, Rio Piedras, PR; SO; BA; AIESEC; Acctng; Acctng; Bus Admin.

**FABER, KEVIN M,** D Youville Coll, Buffalo, NY; JR; MS; Tri Beta Pres 89-90; Cmps Mnstry 88-89; Stdnt Phy Thrpy Assn 89-; Dns Lst; Presdntl Hnrs Schlr; Wndsr Smith Awd; Phy Thrpy; Priv Prctc.

**FABER, MARK S,** Methodist Coll, Fayetteville, NC; FR; BS; Phi Eta Sigma; Vars Tennis 90-; Bus.

**FABER, SHERI L,** Oh St Univ, Columbus, OH; SR; BS; Hnrs Pr Spprt Prgm; Gldn Key; OSU Hsptl Vol; Rep Trmn Schlrshp; IM Sccr Tai Kwon Do; Psychlgy Pre Med.

**FABIAN, CHARLES P,** Kent St Univ Trumbull Cmps, Warren, OH; SO; BA; Acctg Stdnt Yr; Mgr Gas/Convenience Stores EMRO Mrktng Co 78-89; Acctg; CPA.

**FABIAN, JAMES JOSEPH,** Univ Of Akron, Akron, OH; JR; BA; Acctg Assoc 90-; Gldn Ky; Acctg; CPA.

**FABIAN, TRICIA A,** Univ Of Charleston, Charleston, WV; JR; Clg Nwspr Rptr; Psi Chi; Alpha Lambda Delta; Vars Sftbl Pitcher; Psychology.

**FABIANO, REBECCA,** Univ Of Hartford, West Hartford, CT; SO; BA; Afrrican Amer Stdnt Assoc 89-; Task Force To Work With The Dean 90-; Advisory Comm 90-; Teaching Esh & Spanish 90-; B Ed; Spanish; Teaching.

**FABIANO, TRICIA A,** Le Moyne Coll, Syracuse, NY; SR; Orientation Com 88-; BA Engl; Tchng.

**FABICH, PAULA M,** Westminster Coll, New Wilmingtn, PA; JR; Frshmn Orentation Jr/Sr Coord 89-; VISA 90-; Habitat For Humanity 90-; Kappa Delta Pi 90-; Omicron Delta Kappa 90-; Mortar Bd; Kappa Delta 89-; Lambda Sigma Tours Chr 89-90; Elem Educ; Tchng.

**FABISCH, JASON P,** Trenton St Coll, Trenton, NJ; FR; BA; Mech Engr.

**FABO, BRIAN G,** Univ Of Cincinnati, Cincinnati, OH; JR; BSAET; Amer Inst Arch Sdnts; Photo Clb Treas 89-90; Amer Inst Cnstrctrs Sec 88-89; Tau Alpha Pi Pres 90-; Scepter Soc; Alpha Lambda Delta; Coll Apld Sci Assoc Grad Yr 90; Dept Cnstrctn Sci Soph Yr 90; Muriel Gilligan Excl 90; Archtctrl Eng; Reg Arch.

**FABRIZIO, ANTHONY M,** City Univ Of Ny Queensbrough, New York, NY; AAS; Tau Alpha Pi Sec; Deans Lst 90-; Ttrng Fllw Stdnts 86-; Lttl Lg Cch Sttcn 88-; Snr Drftsmn 87-; Dsgn Drftng Comp Grphcs; Own Cmpny.

**FABRIZIO, STEVEN E,** Univ Of Sc At Columbia, Columbia, SC; JR; BS; Rsdnc Hall Sntr 88; Omicron Delta Kappa; Phi Eta Sigma 90; USC Cstl Carolina Cllg Hnrs Cncl 88-; Cstl Carolina Deans Lst 88-; Cstl Carolina Chnclrs Hnr Roll 89-; Cstl Carolina Trck Tm MVP; Biology; Medicine.

**FACCONE, MICHAEL A,** Stevens Inst Of Tech, Hoboken, NJ; SR; MS; Stvns Ambssdrs 87; IEEE 88; Ntl Scty Of Profssnl Eng; NJ Scty Of Prof Eng 87; BS; Cmptr Sci; Cmptr Scntst.**

**FACEY, MONIQUE L,** Cornell Univ Statutory College, Ithaca, NY; JR; BS; Stu Hlth Alnc Chrprsn Comm Actvs 88-; Blck Biomed Tech Assoc 90-; Crnl Univ Prgmg Brd 90; Stu Hlth Clnc Vol 88-90; Well Baby Clncl Serv 90; Cert Aprctn Hlth Advct Trng 89; Deans Lst 89-; Bio Sci; Med.

**FACHET, PATRICK M,** Methodist Coll, Fayetteville, NC; FR; BS; Vrsty Bsbl; Bus Admn; Accntnt.

**FACKLER, ERIC G,** Franklin And Marshall Coll, Lancaster, PA; JR; BA; Amer Chmcl Soc 88-; Healing Art Clb 89-; John Marshall Schlr 88-; Spaulding Fllwshp; Sccr 88-90; Chmstry; MD.

**FACTEAU, DIANE E,** Hudson Valley Comm Coll, Troy, NY; FR; AA; Erly Chldhd Clb; Phi Theta Kappa; PTA 90-; Med Sec 72-75; Erly Chldhd; Tchr.

**FADDE, CATHRYN A,** Marymount Manhattan Coll, New York, NY; SR; BA; Pol Sci & Intl Studies.

**FADDEN, THOMAS J,** Mansfield Univ, Mansfield, PA; FR; BA; Wind Ensmbl; Jaz Ensmbl; Sax Quartet; Kappa Kappa Psi Histrn; Music Ed; Tchng.

**FADELEY, ROBERT G,** Kent St Univ Geauga Cmps, Burton Twp, OH; SO; Solon Players 90; Telecmnctns Engr 69-; Bsn; Cmptr Sci.

**FADEM, JESSICA A,** City Univ Of Ny Baruch Coll, New York, NY; SR; BBA; Advrstng Soc Dir Cmpgn 89-90; AMA 89-90; Dean Lst 89-90; Gldn Ky 90-; Feit Schlr 89-90; Nwsppr Advrtsng Sale Assc Schlrshp; Mrktng Cmmctns Pres Asst 90-; Advrtsng Mrktng; Advrtsng Accnt Mngmnt.

**FAECHER, ELIZABETH J,** Univ Of Nc At Chapel Hill, Chapel Hill, NC; GD; JD; Jrnl Of Interntl Law/Cmmrcl Regltn; Persnl Comm; Plcmnt Comm; BA Harvard/Radcliff Clg 88; Magna Cum Laude; Law.

**FAGAN, DEIRDRE M,** Georgian Court Coll, Lakewood, NJ; JR; BA; Psychlgy Clb 89-; Psi Chi Sec 90-; Psychlgy/Mktg; Law.

**FAGAN, VIRGINIA,** S U N Y Coll Of Tech At Frmgdl, Farmingdale, NY; FR; BA; Vet Med; Wldlf Rsch/Cnsrvtn.

**FAGER, M GENEVIEVE,** Ms St Univ, Miss State, MS; GD; MA; Kappa Delta Edtr 87-; Fshn Brd 89-; Stf Wrtr Nwspr 90-; Phi Kappa Phi; Pi Delta Phi 89-; Sigma Tau Delta 89-; Kappa Delta 87-; Miss MS St Unv 89-; Dpt Engl Tchr Asst; Std Asc Hsng Gde Wrtr; BA; Engl; Wrtng.

**FAGERSTROM, JENNIFER W,** Univ Of South Al, Mobile, AL; SO; BA; Presidental Schlr 90-; Early Chldhd Educ; Teacher.

**FAGG, ANGELIA R,** Shepherd Coll, Shepherdstown, WV; FR; BA; Marching Bnd/Wind Ens 90-; Christian Stdnt Union 90-; Hons Dorm Hs Cncl 90-; Music/Orch.

**FAGO, DALE L,** Christopher Newport Coll, Newport News, VA; SO; BSA; Acctg.

**FAGTANAC, LEILA LOVELLE,** Univ Of Sc At Columbia, Columbia, SC; SO; BA; Chmstry/Biol/Physics; Phrmcy.

**FAGUNDES, LICINIA B,** Newbury Coll, Brookline, MA; SO; Fash Dsgn; Pattern Mkr/Dsgnr.

**FAHERTY, KATHLEEN M,** James Madison University, Harrisonburg, VA; SR; BS; Assoc For The Ed Of Yng Chldrn Pres 89; Golden Key 89; Kappa Delta 89; Early Chldhd Ed; Tchr/Schl Admin.

**FAHEY, DEANN L,** Newbury Coll, Brookline, MA; JR; BA; Sec; Bus Mgmt/Acctg; Corp Cntrlr.

**FAHNESTOCK, CRAIG A,** Central Pa Bus School, Summerdale, PA; FR; ASSOC; Phi Beta Lambda; Vllybl; Mss Media; Music/Vdeo Fld.

**FAHRENBACK, CAROLYN C,** Univ Of Akron, Akron, OH; SR; BS; Tstmsters 89-; Tri Cnty Yth Athltcs Coach 90-; Flwshp Chrstn Athlts 87-88; Mu Kappa Tau 89-; Beta Gamma Sigma 90-; Golden Key 89-; Pi Sigma Epsilon Evnt Chrprsn 88-; Vrsty Sftbl Mt Vernon Nazarene Clg 87-88; Mrktng; Phrmctcl Sls.

**FAHRENBACK, MARIANNE K,** Ringling School Of Art, Sarasota, FL; JR; BFA; Pres Lst 89; Deans Lst 87; Graphic Dsgn.

**FAHRINGER, ROBIN R,** Univ Of Sc At Columbia, Columbia, SC; SO; BA; Yrbk Univ GA 89-90; Alpha Phi Omega Pldg Cls VP 90-; Hon Coll 89-; Alumni Schlrshp Univ GA 89-90; IM Sftbl Univ GA 89-90; Psychlgy/Elem Ed; Tchng/Clncl Psychlgy.

**FAIELLO, RAQUEL J,** Kent St Univ Kent Cmps, Kent, OH; JR; BM; Pi Kappa Lamda; Barthel Piano Schlrshp; Msc Perf; Music Perf/Piano.

**FAILE, AARON K,** Winthrop Coll, Rock Hill, SC; JR; BA; Psych 90-; Psi Chi 90-; Pres Lst 90-; Yth Dir 89-; Psych; Clin Psych/Psychlgst.

**FAILE, ALLISON L,** Winthrop Coll, Rock Hill, SC; SO; BFA; Bapt Stdnt Unn 90; Alpha Lambda Delta 89-; Intrn Polcy Mgmt Systms Corp SC; Pres Lst 90-; Intrr Dsgn; Rsdntl Cmmrcl Dsgn.

**FAILE, STACY M,** Winthrop Coll, Rock Hill, SC; FR; BA; Natl Stdnt Edctrs Assoc 90-; Alpha Lambda Delta 90-; Ed.

**FAILE, TIMOTHY M,** Liberty Univ, Lynchburg, VA; FR; BA; Biblical Studies; Lngstcs/Bible Trnsltn.

**FAILOR, ANGELA K,** Central Pa Bus School, Summerdale, PA; SR; Bus Clb Treas; Deans Lst; Rotary Schlrshp 89.

**FAILS, DAVID K,** Al A & M Univ, Normal, AL; SR; BS; Msnc Clb 88-; GM Pwrtrn Div Intrnshp Eng Spprt 90; Elec Elecs Tech; Elec Eng.

**FAIN, CHRISTOPHER J,** Morehouse Coll, Atlanta, GA; SR; BA; Psychlgy Assn 89-; Calif Clb 87-; Dns Lst 90-; Hnr Rl 90-; Morehouse/Spelman Mntr Prog 88-; Psychlgy; Clin Psychlgst.

**FAIN, JULIE A,** Univ Of Ky, Lexington, KY; SO; MBA; SAC 89-; Phi Eta Sigma 89-; Deans List 89-; English; Education/Law/Writing.

**FAINER, CHRISTOPHER A,** Albertus Magnus Coll, New Haven, CT; SO; BA; Frnch Club 89-; Coll Peer Cnslng 90; Math; Math Educ.

**FAIR, DONALD A,** Pa St Univ Berks Cmps, Reading, PA; FR; BA; Lion Ambassadors 90-; Penn Plyrs 90-; Ag Clb 90-; IM; Agric; Syst/Mgmnt/Tech.

**FAIR, FREDERICK J,** Fl A & M Univ, Tallahassee, FL; SR; BA; AROTC Btlln Cmmndr 90; Dstngsh Mltry Grad; George C Marchall Awd; Phi Beta Sigma; All Amrcn Schlr; AROTC Pres Schlrshp Awd; Im Bsktbl Ftbl 89; AA Troy State U 89; Crmnl Jstce; Army Avtn.**

**FAIR, LORI D,** Piedmont Tech Coll, Greenwood, SC; SO; AD; Cmptrs.

**FAIR, SONYA L,** Temple Univ, Philadelphia, PA; SR; BSN; Nrsng Pres 89-; Stdnt Nrs Assn 89-90; Sigma Theta Tau Intl; Natl Ordr Omega 87-; Delta Sigma Theta Pres 86-87; Nrs Extrn Tmpl Univ Hosp 89-; Nrsng; PhD.

**FAIR, STEVEN A,** Spartanburg Methodist Coll, Spartanburg, SC; FR; Bsktbl Tm; Math; Chldhd Educ.

**FAIR, VANNESSA M,** Alcorn St Univ, Lorman, MS; FR; BA; Bus Admn; Publc Ofcl.

**FAIRALL, LONNIE D,** Oh St Univ At Newark, Newark, OH; FR; BA; Alpha Lambda Delta; Phi Eta Sigma; Sci; Vtrnry Med.

**FAIRBROTHER, PHILIP W,** Western Carolina Univ, Cullowhee, NC; SR; BA; BS 77; Engl.

**FAIRCHILD, RON P,** Fl A & M Univ, Tallahassee, FL; JR; MA; Amer Inst Arch Stdnts Treas 88-89; AIAS 89-90; AA Broward Cmnty Clg 89; Arch.

**FAIRCLOUGH, DAWN MARIE,** Hudson Valley Comm Coll, Troy, NY; FR; ASSC; Assc; Erly Chldhd; Tchng.

**FAIRFAX II, DAVIS J,** Valdosta St Coll, Valdosta, GA; FR; BS; Cmptr Sci.

**FAIRFAX, STEPHANIE M,** Memphis St Univ, Memphis, TN; FR; Bnd Twrlr 90-; Physcl Thrpy.

**FAIRLEY, DEEDEE D,** Al St Univ, Montgomery, AL; FR; BED; Hnrs Convctn; Elem Educ/Erly Chldhd Dev; Tch.

**FAIRLEY, KIM M,** Ms Gulf Coast Comm Coll, Perkinston, MS; FR; AS; Dietary.

**FAIRLEY, PATRICK N,** Ms St Univ, Miss State, MS; SR; BS; Beta Beta Beta; Bio Sci; Med.

**FAIRLEY, STEPHEN G,** Liberty Univ, Lynchburg, VA; SO; BS; Lght Clb/Ythqst Clb 89-90; Shphrds Clb Rcrtmnt Dir 90-; Intercollgt/On Camp Debate Tm 89-; Alpha Lambda Delta Cmnctn Dir 90-; Coll Rpblcns 89-90; Urban Outrch 89-90; Pryr Ldr 90-; On-Cmp Debte Tm Ldrshp Awd 89-; Pastrl Stds; Pstr/Cnslr.

**FAIRLEY, TENA M,** Ms Gulf Coast Comm Coll, Perkinston, MS; SO; BA; AS MGCCC Perkinston; Crmnl Jstc; Law.

**FAIRWEATHER, JAMES A,** Hudson Valley Comm Coll, Troy, NY; SO; AS; Phi Theta Kappa 90-; G Hwrd Crrgn Awrd; Engnrng Sci; Physcs.

**FAIRWEATHER, ROBERT J,** Manhattan Coll, Bronx, NY; FR; BS; I M; Engr; Cvl Engr.

**FAISAL, MOHAMMAD Z,** City Univ Of Ny La Guard Coll, Long Island Cty, NY; SO; BS; Calculus Clb 89-90; Elec Eng.

**FAISCA, HEIDI E,** Univ Of Pr Cayey Univ Coll, Cayey, PR; FR.

**FAISON, BRIAN D,** Morehouse Coll, Atlanta, GA; JR; BA; Pol Sci; Law.

**FAISON, GENEVIEVE S,** Fayetteville St Univ, Fayetteville, NC; SO; BS; Yrbk Artst 89-; Delta Sigma Theta Treas; Biol; Med.

**FAISON, JENNIFER,** Nc Agri & Tech St Univ, Greensboro, NC; JR; BED; Phys Edn Club Pres 90-; Peer Advsng Ldrshp Prog 90-; Teach Flws Prog 88-; Alpha Lambda Delta Mbr 88-89; Talented Ungrad Mnrty Rsrch Flwshp Prog U Of Tx; Summer Worker Duplin Co Bd Of Edn 89-; Vlybl Track 88-; Hlth Phys Edn; Coach.

**FAJARDO, ARNEL M,** Fl St Univ, Tallahassee, FL; SO; BS; Chem/Chem Eng.

**FAJARDO, MARIA ARLENE E,** City Univ Of Ny City Coll, New York, NY; SO; BS; Phlpn-Amer Org 90-; Caduceus Soc 90-; Chem; Med/Heart Surgeon.

**FAJARDO, SILVIA B,** Univ Of Miami, Coral Gables, FL; SR; BS; Frnch Clb Hon Stdnts Assn 87-89; Phi Eta Sigma; Alpha Lambda Delta; Golden Key 87-; Phi Kappa Phi; Phi Beta Kappa; Alpha Epsilon Delta Pres/VP Sclpl Rprtr 88-; Deans List; Vice Prvsts Hon Roll; Bio; Med.**

**FAJARDO-GODOY, ANA S,** Univ Of North Fl, Jacksonville, FL; SR; BA; Intl Stdnts Assn 90-; CSX Trnsprtatn Intrn; Micro Cmptr Rpr Tech 86-; Assoc Apld Sci 86-87; Elect Engr; Engr.

**FAKHER, SEPIDEH,** Gallaudet Univ, Washington, DC; SO; BA; Intl Stdnt Advsry Bd; Math Tutor; Pres Schlr 90-; Leon Auerbach Math Awd 90; Biology; Dentist.

**FAKHOURY, RUBA A GHANI,** Univ Of Nc At Asheville, Asheville, NC; SR; BS; Cmptr Sci; Busn.

**FAKHREDDIN, ASSEM M,** Old Dominion Univ, Norfolk, VA; SR; Elec Eng Tech; MA.

**FAKIR, ALI AHSAN,** S U N Y Coll Of Tech At Alfred, Alfred, NY; SR; AAS; Internatl Clb 89-; Phtgrphy Clb/Archtctr Clb 90-; Ergo Clb 90; Clge Pr Tr Math/Physcs 90-; Dns Lst 90-; AAS; Archtctrl Engrg Tchnlgy; Lsncd Cvl Engr.

**FAKLA, ISTVAN,** Nova Univ, Ft Lauderdale, FL; GD; MIBA; Sccr Schlrsp 84-87; BA 88; Intl Bus.

**FALANA, KATHLEEN Y,** Fl A & M Univ, Tallahassee, FL; SR; BS; Photog Intern; Photography.

**FALBER, SHAWNA J,** S U N Y Coll At Fredonia, Fredonia, NY; SR; BCHLR; Phi Theta Kappa 89-; Deans List 87-90; Rodger C Seager Presdntl Schlrshp 90-; All Amer Schlrshp Clgt Awrd; Assc Sci Bus Admn JCC Jamestown Comm Clg 89; Acctg; CPA.

**FALCETO, RUTH M,** Va Commonwealth Univ, Richmond, VA; SR; BS; Mss Rchmnd Bty Pgnt; Gldn Ky 90; Fr Natl Hnr Scty 89; Dns Lst; POS SPA; Law.

**FALCIONI, CINDY L,** Teikyo Post Univ, Waterbury, CT; GD; AS; Phi Theta Kappa; Deans Lst 90-; Excllnc Early Chldhd Educ; Dipl Acdmy Bus Careers 88; Early Chldhd Educ; Presch Tchr.

**FALCO, LAURA A,** Middlesex County Coll, Edison, NJ; SR; AS; Radlgst Tech.

**FALCO, SHERI L,** Univ Of Nc At Charlotte, Charlotte, NC; JR; BA; Stu Govt; Mdl UN; Clss Pres; Res Lf Offc; Hll Cncl; RA; TREE; Phi Eta Sigma 89-; Hrns Prog 89-; RA Hghst GPA 89-90; Mst Otstndng Del 90-; Amer Bnkrptcy Nst Intern; IM Ftbll Vllybl 89-90; Pol Sci; Law.

**FALCON, ANNE M,** Northern Ky Univ, Highland Hts, KY; SO; BED; Frmr Arlns Flght Attndnt 77-79; Edctnl Tchng.

**FALCON, LAURA,** Univ Of Pr At Rio Piedras, Rio Piedras, PR; SO; BS; Nat Sci; Med.

**FALCON, SANDRA ANA,** Miami Dade Comm Coll, Miami, FL; SO; AA; World Vision; Schlrshp Brazil 90-; Tennis 89-90; AA 90-; Pol Sci; Intl Law.

**FALCONE, DENISE J,** Atlantic Comm Coll, Mays Landing, NJ; SO; Psychlgy; Soc Wrk.

**FALCONE, GINA M,** Providence Coll, Providence, RI; SR; BA; Apt Cmplx Cncl Pres 90-; Stdnt Cngr Mem Rep 90-; Res Brd Dorm Pres 88-89; Pi Mu Epsilon 89-; RI State Intrnshp Pgm 90-; IM Bsktbl 87-; Math Mnr Bus; Acctg.

**FALCONE, KIMBERLY J,** Indiana Univ Of Pa, Indiana, PA; GD; CESI 90; PTA Prvt Tutor; Deans List IN Un Of PA; Red Cross; Stdnt Tchng; Vlybl; BS Elem Ed IN Univ Of PA; Elem Ed; Tchr.

**FALCONE, MICHELLE R,** Kent St Univ Kent Cmps, Kent, OH; SR; Amer Soc Intr Dsgnrs Pblcy 88-90; Italian Clb Treas 89-90; Internshp Stouffer Hotels Rsrts 89-90; Wghtlftg Clb 88-90; BA 90; Interior Dsgn; Dsgnr.

**FALEIRO, BRIAN J,** Fl International Univ, Miami, FL; SO; BS; Phi Eta Sigma 90-; Eng; Mech Eng.

**FALER, TRACY A,** Ms St Univ, Miss State, MS; SR; MBA; Fashion Focus 87-89; Delta Force 90-; Gamma Beta Phi 87-; Phi Alpha Theta; Mu Kappa Tau 90-; Delta Delta Delta Msc Chrmn 87-; Pres Wlkng Awrd; Pres Schlr; Deans List 89-; INS BA; Mrktng/Bsn; Advtsng.

**FALES, JODY ALLEN,** Univ Of Fl, Gainesville, FL; JR; BMED; Mrchng Bnd 88-; Jazz Bnd I 88-; Symphnc Bnd 88-; Kappa Kappa Psi 90-; Msc Ed/Cmpstn; Tchng.

**FALESTO, MARIA D,** Daemen Coll, Amherst, NY; SR; BS; Spec Olympics 90; Massage A Thon 89-; Hlth Fr 90; IM Volybl 90; Phy Thrpst Asst 84-; AAS Orange Cnty Comm Coll 84; Phy Thrpst.

**FALGIER, BRENDA J,** Gallaudet Univ, Washington, DC; Rit-Gally Wkend Comm Pblcty Dir 90; Deans Lst 90; Vllybl 89-90.

**FALIERO, KAREN M,** Bunker Hill Comm Coll, Boston, MA; FR.

**FALIVENE, CAROLINE P,** Middlesex County Coll, Edison, NJ; FR; AA; Mgr 80-90; Dental Assistant 90-; BA Monmouth Clg 84; Dental Hygiene; Hlth Serv Dentistry.

**FALK, JULIE S,** S U N Y Coll At Fredonia, Fredonia, NY; JR; BA; Bus; Htl Rstrnt Mngmnt.

**FALKE, JEFF A,** Fl Atlantic Univ, Boca Raton, FL; JR; BA; Finance; Business.

**FALKENSTEIN, CHRISTY L,** Eckerd Coll, St Petersburg, FL; JR; BA; Rep Club 88; Leg Cncl Rep Day Stdnts 88; Day Stdnt Assoc 88-; Soc Adv Of Mgmt; N/A At Eckerd; Vol St Petersburg Acdmy For Blind 88; Vol Suncoast Chldrns Drm Fund; Envrmntl Watch Prog For Endangered Sea Turtles 88-; IM Vlybl 88-89; Mgmt; Corp Atty.

**FALL, DEGUENE,** City Univ Of Ny City Coll, New York, NY; SR; Int Studies Clb 89-; Ins Intrn Paris 88; Univ De Tech France 88; For Lang; Int Studies.

**FALLAD, MERCEDES C,** Miami Dade Comm Coll North, Miami, FL; SO; AA; Cmptr Sci Assoc Treas 90-; Cmptr Sci Engr; Math/Cmptr Pgm.

**FALLAW, DAVID E,** Univ Of Sc At Aiken, Aiken, SC; SR; BA; Gamma Beta Phi 88-89; Pacer Jaycees Sec 90-; Schlstc Achvmnt Awd 88-; Bsns/Fin.

**FALLAW, MARK E,** Univ Of Sc At Columbia, Columbia, SC; SR; BBA; Pacer Jaycees Pres 90-; Gamma Beta Phi 88-90; Busn Adm Mgt.

**FALLEN, KIMBERLEY D,** Longwood Coll, Farmville, VA; SR; BS; Chem Clb 90-; Stdnt Affiliate Am Chem Soc; IM Bwlng 88; Deans List 87; Vol Asst B/B Lab; Achvmnt Awd Golden Corral; Chem.

**FALLEY, MARISA N,** S U N Y Coll Of Tech At Delhi, Delhi, NY; GD; BA; Culinary Tm 90-; Soccer 90-; Htl Resort Mgmt; Hsptlty Indstry.

**FALLIN, DAVID B,** Nova Univ, Ft Lauderdale, FL; GD; MBA; U S Patents 4,891,805 - 4,998,244 Awd 90-; BSEE Purdue Univ 84; Mktng Fin; Eng Mngmnt.

**FALLIS, SANDY,** Livingston Univ, Livingston, AL; GD; BS; IM Sftbl Tm Capt 89-90; All Star Sftbl Tm 89-90; IM Vlybl Bsktbl 87-90; Tau Kappa Epsilon Ltl Sr 89-90; Hmcmng Swthrt Tau Kappa Epsilon 90; Nrsng.

**FALLON, JUSTINE,** Univ Of Ct, Storrs, CT; JR; BS; Hall Cncl 90; Coop Ed Intrn; Ntrl Rsrces; Envrnmntl Cnsltng.

**FALLON, KATHLEEN J,** Teikyo Post Univ, Waterbury, CT; SR; Stdnt Govt Sec 85-86; Rsdnt Asst 90-; BS; Hmn Rsrc.

**FALLON, THERESA,** Univ Of Miami, Coral Gables, FL; JR; BSN; NSA; Tae Kwon Do Assn 2nd Degree Red Belt; PTA Chrmn/Budget Com 89-; Hospice Inc Vol 88-; Hospice Dade Cnty Vol Yr 89-; Hospice Inc Corp Vol Yr; BA Univ MA 82; Nurse Practitioner.

**FALLOWS, KATHIE A,** Saint Andrews Presbytrn Coll, Laurinburg, NC; SO; BS; CHAOS 89-; Ste Ldr; Coll Radio Sta D J 89-90; Hall Cncl; Theatre Prod Runr 89; Gen Hnrs 89-90; Comm Outrch Pgm 89; Otstdng Fr Chem Awd 90; Soph Hnrs; IM Bwlng 1st Pl 89; Chem; Tchng.**

**FALLS, KAY F,** Oh Univ-Southern Cmps, Ironton, OH; SR; BS; Kappa Delta Pi Honr Ed Soc 90-; Gamma Pi Delta 90-; Psych Aide 80-; Elem Ed/Mnr Psych; Tchr/Schl Psychlgst.

**FALLS, LAWRENCE D,** Newbury Coll, Brookline, MA; SR; Chef; Rest Proprtr.

**FALS, ANGELA M,** Univ Of Miami, Coral Gables, FL; SO; Bio Clb V P 90-; Colombian Stdnt Assoc 89-; Bio; Med.

**FALSETTA, DIANA,** Fl St Univ, Tallahassee, FL; FR; BA; Phi Eta Sigma; Kappa Alpha Theta Asst To VP Fnce 90; Im Bwlng Tm 90; Accntng; Accntng CPA.

**FALUS, JUDITH,** Univ Of Hartford, West Hartford, CT; JR; BS; Sigma Delta Tau 89-; Hebrew Home Volntr; AA; Accntng.

**FALZARANO, VICKIE J,** Elms Coll, Chicopee, MA; FR; BA; Mktg.

**FALZONE, CHERYL L,** Univ Of Akron, Akron, OH; SR; BS; Golden Key 89-; Kappa Delta Pi 89-; IM 88-; Ed; Tchr.

**FAMA, DONNA A,** Molloy Coll, Rockville Ctr, NY; JR; BA; Math Clb VP 90-; Educ Clb; Molloy Kickline; Omicron Alpha Zeta; Mu Sigma Mu Pr 90-; Delta Epsilon Sigma; Sons Italy; Math; Educ.

**FAMADAS, NELSON E,** Harvard Univ, Cambridge, MA; FR; BA; Crmsn Nwsppr Bus Edit; PR Stdnt Assn At Hrvrd Rdclffe 90-; Dtls Mag Coll Pnl Pnlst; Econs; Bus.

**FAMBRO, TAWANA DI-ANN,** Hudson Valley Comm Coll, Troy, NY; GD; AAS; Afrcn Amer Stdnt Allnc 89-; EOP Clb 89-; Mnrty Mntrng Prog; Mnrty Schlrshp 89-90; Dns Lst 90; Pres Lst 90; Cert Acad Achvmnt; Educ Oppor Prog; Acctng; CPA.

**FAMBRO, WANDA R,** Central St Univ, Wilberforce, OH; FR; BS; SGA 90; Deans Lst 90; Bsnss Admin Option CIS; Syst Analyst.

**FAN, KAI KEI,** Cooper Union, New York, NY; FR; BED; Tnns/Tbl Tnns; Elec Engr.

**FAN, QING,** Old Dominion Univ, Norfolk, VA; GD; MS; IEEE Mmbr; IEEE Cmptr Soc; Tau Beta Pi; Alpha Chi; ODU IEEE Dgtl Lgc Hrdwr Cntst; Magna Cum Laude; Grad Tchng Asstnshp 90-; BSEE 90; Cmptr Engnrng; Engnrng.

**FAN, RICK V,** City Univ Of Ny Baruch Coll, New York, NY; SR; BBA; Beta Alpha Psi Acctng Tutor 89-; Acctng.

**FANCEY, MARCELLA M,** Fl St Univ, Tallahassee, FL; GD; PHD; Psi Cen 90; Gldn Key 90; BS; Psychlgy; Academic Psychlgy.

**FANCHER, ELIZABETH D,** Univ Of Al At Birmingham, Birmingham, AL; SR; BA; Vybl Tm 88-89; Early Chldhd Educ; Tch.

**FANCHER, KEVIN A,** Univ Of Cincinnati-Clrmnt Coll, Batavia, OH; FR; BA; Ind Arts Tchnlgy; Scndry Educ.

**FANCHER, MARSHA G,** Univ Of Al At Birmingham, Birmingham, AL; JR; Alpha Lambda Delta 90-; Pre-Pharm; Pharmacy.

**FANCHIER, TINIA M,** Univ Of Tn At Martin, Martin, TN; FR; BS; Wildlife Soc 90-; Agronomy Clb Envir Repr 90-; Clgte 4-H 90-; Proj Recycle Treas; Schlrs Org Envir Repr 90-; Envir Mgmt; Rsrch/Imprvmnt.

**FANEITE, MAYLER ALBERTO,** City Univ Of Ny La Guard Coll, Long Island Cty, NY; SO; BS; Cmptr Soc IEEE 89-; Lib Cmptr/Info Sci 90-; Sci; Eng.

**FANELLI, DAMIAN A,** East Stroudsburg Univ, E Stroudsburg, PA; SO; BA; Coll Nwspaper Staff Wrtr 90; Eng Club; Litry Supp Editor/Publ Poet; Deans List 90; Eng/Wrtng; Jrnlsm/Creative Wrtr.

**FANELLI, FLORENCE E,** Georgian Court Coll, Lakewood, NJ; FR; BA; Mndl Soc Clb 90-; Rlgs Edctn Tchr 90-; Cmps Mnstry Rep 90-; Frnch Ntnl Hnr Soc Prsdnt; Georgian Crt Clg Schlrshp 90-; French; Trnsltr Intrprtr.

**FANELLI III, THOMAS J,** Glassboro St Coll, Glassboro, NJ; SR; BA; Theta Chi Treas 89; Intrnshp US Customs Svc; Crmnl Jstc; Fedrl Law Enfrcmnt.

**FANG, NING YAN,** Duquesne Univ, Pittsburgh, PA; SO; BS; Scntfc Assoc For Eng In Wangting Pwr Plnt PRC 84-89; Assist Eng For Auto Cntrl Syst In Wangting Pwr Plnt 84-89; Cert Shanghai Elctrc Pwr Inst PRC 84; Mngmnt Info Syst; Bsnss Tchnques In Asia.

**FANG, YIWEI,** City Univ Of Ny Baruch Coll, New York, NY; JR; BBA; Acctng/Ecnmcs; Fncl Advsr/Anlyst.

**FANKELL, TARA M,** Bowling Green St Univ At Huron, Huron, OH; SO; ASSOC; Hlth Info Tech; ART Parlgl.

**FANN, LORI S,** Middle Tn St Univ, Murfreesboro, TN; SR; BS; ARMS 90-; Gamma Beta Phi 89-; Humane Fndtn 88-; Recording Indstry Mngmnt; Artist Mngmnt.

**FANN, STEPHEN A,** Methodist Coll, Fayetteville, NC; FR; BS; Phi Eta Sigma; Biology; Medicine.

**FANN, TERESA S,** Middle Tn St Univ, Murfreesboro, TN; FR; CERT; Busn; Legl Asst.

**FANNIN, ANGELA J,** Morehead St Univ, Morehead, KY; SO; BA; Gamma Beta Phi; Delta Gamma Fdtn Chm; Deans List 90-; Elem Ed; Tchr.**

**FANNIN, JENNIFER A,** Univ Of Ky, Lexington, KY; SO; BA; Alpha Delta Pi Pledge V P 89-90; Engl Lit; Law.

**FANNING, ANDREW W,** Univ Of Rochester, Rochester, NY; SR; Rgby Clb 89-90; Coll Deans Lst 87-; Optcl Engf.

**FANNON, ANGELA L,** Fl St Univ, Tallahassee, FL; FR; BA; Music Minor 90-; Stdnt Govt; IM Sports; Phi Eta Sigma; Eng/Bus; Law Sch.

**FANO, VICTOR M,** Bloomfield Coll, Bloomfield, NJ; FR; Prchrprctc Clb; Sci Chrprctc.

**FANT, ANDREA M,** Coll Of Charleston, Charleston, SC; SR; BS; Stdnt Cncl Excptnl Chldrn 88-; Amer Assoc Mntl Rtrdtn 89-; Educ Clb 87-89; Hgh Dstngshd Hon Rl 90; Spec Ed; Tchr.

**FANT, JOSEPH S,** Saint Pauls Coll, Lawrenceville, VA; FR; BS; Bus; Mngmnt.

**FANT, MONICA D,** Central St Univ, Wilberforce, OH; SR; Deans List 90-; Flwshp Chrstn Stdnts; Elem Ed; Tchr.

**FANTASIA, MARIA P,** Saint Josephs Coll New York, Brooklyn, NY; SR; Art Clb 88-; Yrbk Div Pg 90; Sigma Iota Chi 89-; BA; Chld Study; Elem Sch Tchr.**

**FANTAUZZI, JOHN A,** Siena Coll, Loudonville, NY; SR; BA; Trck Clb 87-88; Bg Brthrs Bg Sstrs 90; Delta Epsilon Sigma; Smstr Prgm; Intrnshp 89; Econ.

**FANTE, RASHELL L,** West Liberty St Coll, West Liberty, WV; SR; BS; Nwspr 89-; Cmmnctns; Pblc Prctcnr.

**FARABAUGH, LISA A,** Indiana Univ Of Pa, Indiana, PA; FR; BED; Sign Lang Clb 90-; Fndtn Dstngshd Achiever 90-; Ed Hear Impaired/Early Chldhd; Educator.

**FARABAUGH, PATRICK G,** Indiana Univ Of Pa, Indiana, PA; SO; BA; Cmnctns.

**FARABEE, JOY J,** Auburn Univ At Auburn, Auburn, AL; SR; BS; Natl Orgnztn Fr Wmn 90; Amnsty Intrnatl 88; Kappa Omicron Nu; Fshn Inc 87-; Fshn Mrchdsng; Rtl.

**FARABUGH, JULIE A,** Saint Francis Coll, Loretto, PA; FR; BS; Accntng; CPA.

**FARACI, MICHELLE M,** Univ Of Rochester, Rochester, NY; SO; BA; Cormpeer Vltr Org; Hist Awd 90; Pre Med/Psy; Psychiatry.

**FARAGALLI, CRAIG M,** Pa St Univ Delaware Cty Cmps, Media, PA; FR; BA; Ovrbrk Strttrs Cmc Clb; Bus Admin.

**FARBANIEC, RENAY,** Georgian Court Coll, Lakewood, NJ; FR; Coll Sftbl 90-; Bus Clb 90-; Acctg; Acctnt.

**FARBER, GREGORY A,** S U N Y At Buffalo, Buffalo, NY; GD; DDS; Hbrt Mscns Cllctv Pres 86-88; Sccr; Omicron Kappa Upsilon 88; Hbrt Deans Lst 88; ASDA 88-; Sigm Aphi 84-88; Tckr Schlrshp 89-; Cncr Scty Fllwshp 89; Chmstry Awrd 88; Sccr Tm Indr Hckry 88-; BS 88; Dnstry.

**FARBMAN, SETH A,** Yeshiva Univ, New York, NY; FR; BA; Psychlgy; Law.

**FARDINPOUR, KOUROSH,** Hillsborough Comm Coll, Tampa, FL; FR; AA; Sci Math; Eng.

**FARE, BRIDGET M,** S U N Y Coll At Fredonia, Fredonia, NY; JR; BS; Res Asst 90-; Tr Gde 89-; Sprdnc MDA 89-; WNYF TV 89-; WCVR AM FM 89-; Blmbl 89-; Newman Cntr Rlgs Educ Instr 90-; WIVB TV CBS Afflt Buffalo NY Intrn; WWKB Radio Buffalo NY Intrn/Wrtr 89-90; Louis C Adler Schlrshp Pblc Rlts Intrn; Cmmnctn/Pol Scnc; Brdcst Jrnlsm.

**FARESE, MICHELLE L,** Ramapo Coll Of Nj, Mahwah, NJ; JR; BS; Rsdent Stdnt Assoc VP Is 88-89; Stdnt Govt Repr 88-89; Pgm Cncl Repr 89-90; Delta Mu Delta; Dns Lst 88-90; Intrnshp Asst Acctnt 90-; Acctng; CPA.

**FARHAN, ISAM M,** Embry Riddle Aeronautical Univ, Daytona Beach, FL; SR; BS; Islmc Cntr Of Dytna Bch 88-; MAA 89-; SAE 89-; BS; Arntcl Eng; Eng.**

**FARIA, LAURIE A,** Merrimack Coll, North Andover, MA; FR; BA; Yrbk Art Stff 90; Pi Theta Epsilon; Bus Mrktng Advrtsng.

**FARIAS, PEDRO J,** City Univ Of Ny City Coll, New York, NY; JR; BA; Anthroplgy.

**FARIER, PATRICK E,** Al A & M Univ, Normal, AL; JR; Crbbn Stdnts Assoc 89-; FR Prs Award 89-90; Hnr Rl; Deans Lst; Acctg.

**FARINA, ANTHONY G,** Villanova Univ, Villanova, PA; JR; BA; Vlnv Sngrs 90-; Key Clb 88-90; Knghts Clmbs 88-; Hnrs Prgm 88-90; IM Bsktbll 89-; Phlsphy.**

**FARINA, DIANNE R,** Radford Univ, Radford, VA; SR; MBS; Tri M Math Clb; KME Math Hnrry Scty; Mdcl Coll VA Grad Bststs Fllwshp; Acctg Clrk; BS; Biosttstscs.

**FARINA, JEANMARIE,** Saint Francis Coll, Loretto, PA; JR; BA; Orntn Asst 89-; Red Key 88-; Plus 88-; Adpt Grndprnt 88-; SAIL 90-; SFC Sngrs 88-; Cin Shwcase 90-; Stdnt Rep Adv Cncl 89-; Phi Sigma Iota; Psych.

**FARINA, KOETHI Z,** Birmingham Southern Coll, Birmingham, AL; FR; Phi Eta Sigma/Alpha Lamua Delta; Hab Humanity; Econ; Law Schls.

**FARINAS EXPOSITO, ROSSANA L,** Univ Of Miami, Coral Gables, FL; JR; BBA; Baptist Hosp; Specl Olympics Buddy 89-; Orange Bowl 90; Pol Sci; Diplo/Nutrition.**

**FARINAS, ANABEL,** Fl International Univ, Miami, FL; SR; MBA.

**FARIVAR, FARHAD F,** Southern Coll Of Tech, Marietta, GA; SR; BSMET; Mchncl Engnrng; Mstrs Bio Mdcl Engnrng.

**FARKAS, ROBERT J,** George Washington Univ, Washington, DC; FR; BA; Stdnts Sldrty/Dmcrcy Estrn Europe 90-; Spnsh Clb 90-; Euro Clb 90-; Intl Affairs; Foreign Svc.

**FARLER, IVY D,** Volunteer St Comm Coll, Gallatin, TN; FR; AAS; Radlgy; X Ray Tech.

**FARLEY, ANNEMARIE,** Albertus Magnus Coll, New Haven, CT; SO; BA; Poltcl Sci; Law.

**FARLEY, CONSTANCE A,** Methodist Coll, Fayetteville, NC; SR; BS; NTEA 90-; Transfer Schlrshp; Merit Schlrshp; Ret Tchr Assoc Schlrshp; Church Action Haymont Meth Church; AAS Fayetteville Tech Cmnty Clge 89; History Educ; Teaching HS.

**FARLEY III, FRANK D,** Georgetown Coll, Georgetown, KY; SO; BS; Hmcmng Shws The Times Of Our Lives Cast 89; The Music Man Lead 90; Clg Nwspr Spts Edtr 89-90; Choir 89-90; Sel Choir 89-90; Alpha Lambda Delta 89-; Beta Beta Beta 90-; Lambda Chi Alpha VP 90-; IM Sftbl Bsktbl Vllybl 89-; Biol; Med.

**FARLEY, GREGORY S,** Duke Univ, Durham, NC; FR; BS; Project CHANCE 90-; Chapel Usher 90-; NROTC 90-; Biology; Oceanography/Marine Biology.

**FARLEY, JILL K,** Marshall University, Huntington, WV; JR; BS; Blgy; Envrnmntl Scnc.

**FARLEY, KAREN L,** Wv Univ, Morgantown, WV; SR; BSN; Stdnt Nrs Assc 90-; Mrchg Bnd 86-88; Alpha Xi Delta; Outstndg Acad Achvmnt Awd 87; Nrsg.

**FARLEY, LINDA F,** Walker Coll, Jasper, AL; FR; MBA; Winston Co PTO 83-90; Btr Bus Bureau 87; Amer Lng Assn 78-90; Phi Theta Kappa; Fdshr AL/WLKR Co Pub Rltns 87-88; Un Way-Wlkr Co 90; Deans Lst 90-; Wnstn Co Ltl Lgue Sec 85-86; Cert Off Mgmt 90; Cert Comp Wnstn Co Voctnl 84; Psychlgy; Marriage/Fmly Cnslr.

**FARLEY, ROSE T,** Glassboro St Coll, Glassboro, NJ; SR; BA; PRSSA Hstrn 90-; Advrtsng Clb 89-; Yrbk 90-; Miss GSC 88-; Gamma Tau Sigma 90-; Aerobics Instrctr; Comm Lbrl Arts; Advrtsng.

**FARLEY, SHANNON M,** Duquesne Univ, Pittsburgh, PA; FR; MBA; Phi Eta Sigma 90-; Univ Vol 90-; Deans Lst 90; Hlth Sci; Med.

**FARLEY, TONYA L,** Marshall University, Huntington, WV; SO; BBA; Majorette 89-90; Res Adv 90-; Clg Bsns Acrdtn Comm 90-; Soph Hmcmng Attdnt Fnlst 90; Res Hl Assoc 90-; Gamma Beta Phi; Alpha Kappa Psi 90-; Acctg; CPA.

**FARLOW, DEBORAH G,** Defiance Coll, Defiance, OH; JR; BS; Hbtat For Humnty 89-; Intrcllgte Spch Tm 90-; Parkview Mthdst Schl Nrsg Almn Assc 90-; St Johns Lthrn Chrch Choir 90; RN Hsptl Hm Care Nrsg; Lcnsd Hm Day Care; RN Parkview Mthdis Schl Nrsg 82; Cmnctn/Mrktg; Med Mrktg.

**FARLOW, GINA MARIE,** Radford Univ, Radford, VA; JR; BA; AAS New River Com Clg 89-90; Nrsg.

**FARMER, BARBARA A,** Univ Of Tn At Martin, Martin, TN; FR; BED; Scndry Edctn Bsns; Tchng.

**FARMER, BONNIE E,** Limestone Coll, Gaffney, SC; SO; BS; Natl Assn Acct 90-; AS/ACCTG Rutledge Bsn Clg 80; Bsn Mgmt; Acctg.

**FARMER, BRETT G,** Univ Of Southern Ms, Hattiesburg, MS; FR; Stdnt Eagle Clb; Hstry; Mktg.

**FARMER, CYNTHIA A,** Thomas Nelson Comm Coll, Hampton, VA; FR; BED; Educ; Tchr.

**FARMER, DEBERAH SUE,** Spalding Univ, Louisville, KY; SR; BA; NSSLHA Pres 90- Sec 89-90; Pi Lambda Theta Hstrn 90-; Delta Epsilon Sigma 90-; Kappa Gamma Pi; Dream Factory 87-; Worship Comm Secy 82-; Yng Adlt Ministry Bd Mbr 82-85; Deans Lst 89-; Sls Assoc Lazarus; Communicative Disorders; Speech/Lang Path.

**FARMER, EDWARD S,** Univ Of Ky, Lexington, KY; SR; BSCE; Ky Trans Cab Schlrshp 87-; Dns Lst 90; Eng; Cvl Eng.

**FARMER, ERIC E,** Clark Atlanta Univ, Atlanta, GA; GD; BS; Pre Prof Hlth Soc 83-85; Alld Hlth Soc 87-; Prkwd Reg Hosp; BS; Med Rec Admin.

**FARMER, FRANK W,** Univ Of Pittsburgh At Bradford, Bradford, PA; JR; BS; Karate Club 88-90; EMS Club 89-90; Thtr 88-90; IM Bsktbl/Ftbl 90; Bsn Mgmt; Phys Thrpy.

**FARMER, GEORGE A,** Univ Of Sc At Columbia, Columbia, SC; FR; BA; Frnch Clb; Lthrn Brthrhd 90-; Jrnlsm; Advtsng.

**FARMER, JANET H,** Abraham Baldwin Agri Coll, Tifton, GA; SO; AA; Early Chldhd Educ; Cnslng/Gdnc.

**FARMER, LINDA FAYE,** Univ Of Sc At Aiken, Aiken, SC; SO; BFA; Art/Grphc Dsgn; Illustr.

**FARMER, LISA M,** Univ Of Sc At Columbia, Columbia, SC; JR; BA; Art; Illustrator.

**FARMER, MELANIE S,** Univ Of Nc At Greensboro, Greensboro, NC; SR; BS; Inter Var Chrstn Flwshp Exec Comm 87-; Leisure Assoc 88-90; V C Rec Fdn Schlrshp 90-; Intrnshp Regnl Rehab Ctr; IM Bsktbl Vlybl 89-90; Rec Therapy.

**FARMER, PAULA D,** Fl A & M Univ, Tallahassee, FL; FR; BA; ROTC 90-; Schlrshp Awd Dept Of Army 90-; Nrsng; MP Otstrtcs/Gynclgy.

**FARMER, QUINN E,** Memphis St Univ, Memphis, TN; SR; BBA; Whitehaven Jr Sprts Assoc Hd Ftbl Coach 89-; Pres Escrt U S Army 85-88; Mgmt; Mgmt Psitn.

**FARMER, RICHARD G,** Piedmont Tech Coll, Greenwood, SC; SO; ASSOC; Eletrncs; Eng.

**FARMER, SHURRON M,** Fl A & M Univ, Tallahassee, FL; FR; Biol/Pred Med Soc; Pres Schol Asso; Biol/Pre-Med; Dr/Rsrch.

**FARMER, STEFANIE M,** Cheyney Univ Of Pa, Cheyney, PA; JR; BA; Ambassadors Club 90; Rcrtn Club 88-; Stdnt Affairs 88-89; Newspr/Yrbk Staff Assist Editor 89-90; Roh Phi Lambda; Ethnic Mnrty Soc Female Schlrshp 90; Denver Water Dept Smmr Hlp 89-90; Indus/Cmrcl Rcrtn; Indus Rcrtn Mgr.

**FARMER, TANYA M,** Middle Tn St Univ, Murfreesboro, TN; SO; BS; Vlyvw Yth Grp 87-; Chr 89-; Psychlgy; Grad Schl/Tchng Coll.

**FARMER, TARA G,** Univ Of Sc At Columbia, Columbia, SC; SR; BS; Bapt Stu Union 86-; Intrdscplnry Studies; Tch.

**FARMWALD, HEATHER R,** Kent St Univ Geauga Cmps, Burton Twp, OH; JR; BA; Akron Allnc Chrch Tutr; Elem Ed; Tchr.

**FARMWALD, JANICE D,** Kent St Univ Kent Cmps, Kent, OH; SR; BA; Prsnl Asst ASM Intl 89-90; Assoc Bus Mgt Kent State Univ 89-90; Bus/Hmn Rsrc Mgt.

**FARNELL, JOSEPH CROCKETT,** Nova Univ, Ft Lauderdale, FL; GD; MBA; Alpha Tau Omega 81-86; Cmrcl Cnstrctn Prjct Mgr 86-; BBA 86; Real Estate Dvlpmnt.

**FARNHAM, ADAM H,** S U N Y Coll Of Tech At Alfred, Alfred, NY; SR; BS; Acdmc Intgrty Comm; Alfred ISA Sec 90-; Sigma Tau Epsilon 90-; Natl Vo-Tech Soc; Deans Lst 90-; Instrmnt Soc Amer Schlrshp; AS Alfred St; Elec Eng.

**FARNHAM, DEBORAH L,** Unity Coll, Unity, ME; JR; BS; Woodsmen Tm 90-; Envrnmntl Sci.

**FARNHAM, JAMES P,** S U N Y Coll Of Tech At Alfred, Alfred, NY; FR; BS; Elect Eng.

**FARNHAM, NICHOLE ALISON,** Western New England Coll, Springfield, MA; SO; BA; Psychlgy; Prsnl.

**FARNSWORTH, ELAINA,** Univ Of North Fl, Jacksonville, FL; SR; BM; UNF Jazz Ensmbl 87-; UNF Cncrt Bnd Lbrn 87-90; UNF Vcl Jazz Ensmbl Soprano 87-88; Gldn Key 87-; Music Schlrshp Jazz 87-89; UNF Acdmc Schlrshp 90-; Music; Sng Cmpsg Wrtg Tchg.

**FARNSWORTH, JENNIFER J,** Longwood Coll, Farmville, VA; JR; BS; Alpha Kappa Delta; Intrnshp; Scigy; Scl Serv Admin.

**FARNSWORTH, MAYA A,** Univ Of New England, Biddeford, ME; JR; BS; Earth ECO Clb 90-; Lbrry Assn Treas 90-; Envir Sci; Plnt Sci.

**FARO, DENISE,** City Univ Of Ny Baruch Coll, New York, NY; SR; BBA; Beta Alpha Psi V P 90-; Beta Gamma Sigma 90; Dns Lst 85-90; Baruch Endowmnt Fund Merit Awd; Acctg.

**FARR, LAURIE P,** Villanova Univ, Villanova, PA; SO; BA; Psychology; Early Chldhd Educ.

**FARR, ROCHELLE R,** Clark Atlanta Univ, Atlanta, GA; FR; Acctg; CPA.

**FARR, TANZA C,** Ms Coll, Clinton, MS; GD; JD; Amer Inns Of Court 90-; Law Review Note/Comment Ed 89-; Broker 86-88; BA Mississippi State Univ 85; Law; Lawyer.

**FARR, VIDA JEAN,** Univ Of Ga, Athens, GA; SR; BSW; Ntl Assoc Scl Wrkrs; Otstndg Emply Psych Hlth Serv 89; Chrtr Wnds Hosp 89-90; Psych Hlth Serv 87-89; Scl Wrk.

**FARRAJ, ROBERT,** Philadelphia Coll Pharm & Sci, Philadelphia, PA; FR; MS; Amer Pharmctcl Assn; Alpha Lambda Delta; Kappa Psi; Pres Schlrshp; Assoc Mem Amer Museum Ntrl Hist; NYS Rgnts Schlrshp; Pharm/Bus; Dr.

**FARRAND, HEIDI J,** Wv Univ At Parkersburg, Parkersburg, WV; SO.

**FARRAR, LISA A,** James Madison University, Harrisonburg, VA; SO; BSN; Univ Pgm Brd 90-; Hl Cncl Flr Repr 90-; Bptst Stdnt Un 89-; Lettie Pate Whitehead Schlrshp 90-; Nrsg; RN/ONCLGY.

**FARRAR JR, ROLAND B,** Central Piedmont Comm Coll, Charlotte, NC; FR; BSET; Deans Lst 90-; Comp Eng Tech; Engnrng/Svc.

**FARRAR, SEAN E,** U S Military Academy, West Point, NY; FR; Brgde Exec Offcr; Ushrs; Vrsty Bsbl; Ring And Crst Com; IM Ftbl; Math; Career Army.

**FARRAR, TARRICE Y,** Va St Univ, Petersburg, VA; FR; BS; Drm Treas 90-; Bsktbl Mgr 90-; Cmptrs; Sys Anlyst/Eng.

**FARRELL, ANDREA L,** Anne Arundel Comm Coll, Arnold, MD; SO; BS; Schlr/Athlete Fmle 90; Soccer 89; Erly Chldhd Ed; Kndrgrtn Tchr.

**FARRELL, DIANE,** Indiana Univ Of Pa, Indiana, PA; JR; BED; Actvts Bd 88; PSEA; Phi Sigma Pi Hstrn 89-91; Provost Schlr 90-; Deans List 88-; Elem Edn; Teach.**

**FARRELL JR, DON J,** Univ Of Cincinnati, Cincinnati, OH; SR; BFA; Mscl Theatre; TV/RCRDG; Swm Coach/Instr; Lfgrd; Wrstlr; Bsbl; Muscl Theatre; Stg Prfrm.

**FARRELL, DONNA MARIE,** Va Commonwealth Univ, Richmond, VA; SR; BFA; Cmmnctn Arts Assn 88-; Schl Of Arts Stdnt Advsry Comm 90-; Stdnt Art Space Comm 90-; Schwarzschild Visual Mrchndsng Illus Awd; Stdnt Advsr; Fshn Art/Advrtsng; Illustration.

**FARRELL, JOHN J,** Manhattan Coll, Bronx, NY; SR; BSEF; Radio 86-; Eta Kappa Nu 89-; Tau Beta Pi 90-; Elec Engr.

**FARRELL, PATRICIA E,** Catholic Univ Of America, Washington, DC; JR; BA; Fools For Jesus Treas 89-; Campus Mnstry 89-; Early Chldhd Ed; Tchr.

**FARRELLY, CHRISTINE A,** Saint Joseph Coll, West Hartford, CT; JR; BA; Hstrcl Soc; Acad Res Ctr Tutor 90-; Curatrl Intrn; Intrnshp Exhbt Coord Oliver Ellswrth Hmsd; Publ Hstry.

**FARREN, SHANNON D,** Western New England Coll, Springfield, MA; FR; BA; Rsdnt Hall Assn Repr 90; COPE 90; Rsdnt Advsr; Alpha Lamba Delta V P; Psych; PHD.

**FARRENTINE II, JOHN N,** Univ Of South Fl, Tampa, FL; SO; BA; Fne Arts Stdnt Coll Cncl Pres 90-; Stdnt Thtre Prdctns; Undergrad Tchng Awrds Com; Thtre Arts; Actng Film.

**FARRIA, KAMEEL A,** City Univ Of Ny Queensbrough, New York, NY; SO; AAS; C-Step; Bsktbl Trn/Tennis Tm Mgr/Player; Literacy Vol Of Am Tutor; Comp Prgmng; Comp Tech.

**FARRIS, CARLA L,** Univ Of Sc At Columbia, Columbia, SC; JR; BA; Gldn Key 90-; Natl Assn Rltrs; Hrbison Bptst Chrch; Rltr 83-; Mill Dollar Clb 84-85; AA-SOC Sci Coll Sequoias-CA 72; Psychlgy; Cnslng.

**FARRIS, DAWN C,** Univ Of Al At Birmingham, Birmingham, AL; SR; BS; Grd Cum Laude; Psychlgy; Real Estate Law.

**FARRIS, GREGORY W,** Univ Of Tn At Knoxville, Knoxville, TN; JR; BA; Cstmr Serv Sprvsr 80-; Fnce; Invstmnt Mgmt/Rsrch.

**FARRIS, REBECCA J,** Memphis St Univ, Memphis, TN; SR; Phi Theta Kappa 87-88; Cum Laude 88-89; BBA; Mgt; Law.

**FARRIS, REGINA L,** Univ Of Montevallo, Montevallo, AL; SR; BS; Montevallo Assn Hmn Serv Prjct Chrprsn 89-; Lucille Griffen Awd; Scl Wrk; Medcl Scl Wrk.

**FARRIS, SONYA J,** Wallace St Comm Coll At Selma, Selma, AL; SO; AS; Sci.

**FARRISH, LISA J,** Cumberland Coll, Williamsburg, KY; JR; BS; Love In Action Stdnt Coord ,8-; Math Sci Clb 90-; Baptist Union Cncl 88-; Mtn Otrch Dir Of Info 88-; Softball 88-; Math; Teaching.

**FARROKHNEJAD, FARROKH,** Va Commonwealth Univ, Richmond, VA; JR; BS; Bio; Dentistry.

**FARROW, DAVID N,** Cumberland County Coll, Vineland, NJ; SO; BS; Bethel Commandment Church Dir; Drama Clb; Asst Scout Master; Eagle Scout; Bd Elders Bethel Commandment Church Treas; Phi Theta Kappa; AS 90; Mktg; Fshn Dsgn.**

**FARROW, WILLIAM MARSHALL,** Columbia Union Coll, Takoma Park, MD; SR; BS; Acctng Club; MENSA; Phi Mu Alpha; Sinfonia; Diabetes Assn; Bldng Matrl Usage Epxrt; Profsnl Hardware Deg From Natl Retail Hardware Assoc; Natl Physique Comm; Heart Assocs Hlth/Wellns Expo 89; Bus Mgt/Acctng; Law MBA.

**FARRRUGGIO, STEPHANIE,** Coll Of Insurance, New York, NY; FR; Ralph Bell Schlrshp 90-; Spnsrshp Schlrshp 90-; Actrl Sci; Actry.

**FARRY, GREGORY SCOTT,** Univ Of Rochester, Rochester, NY; SR; BA; Delta Kappa Epsilon 88-; NROTC 87-91; IM Sports 87-; Pol Sci; Offcr Career.

**FARWELL, SUSAN A,** Hillsborough Comm Coll, Tampa, FL; FR; AA; Physcn Ofc Mgr/Bkkpr 69-90; Cert Dent Asst Rochester Dental Asst Sch 68; Medcn; Physcn Asst.

**FAS, OLGA M,** Univ Of Pr At Mayaguez, Mayaguez, PR; SR; BA; Phi Alpha Delta; Sor Mu Alpha Phi Pres Scl Com 89-90; Hstry Amer; Law.**

**FASANO JR, JOSEPH F,** Bloomfield Coll, Bloomfield, NJ; FR; BS; Bus Mgmt; Bus Exec.

**FASANO, MARIA A,** Daemen Coll, Amherst, NY; GD; BA; Lambda Lota Tau 86-; Masterson Schlrshp 86; Eng.

**FASANO, TERESA R,** Dowling Coll, Oakdale Li, NY; SR; BA; Tutor 90-; Dns Lst CW Post/Suffolk Cmnty Clg/Dowling Clg 87-; CW Post Acad Frat 87; State Senate Campaign Intern 90; Patrick Halpin Schlrshp 90; Scl Sci; Law.

**FASINO, RICHARD B,** Le Moyne Coll, Syracuse, NY; SO; BA; Radio DJ 89-; Karate Clb 90; Chldrns Tutor 90-; Bus Fin; Bus.

**FASOLDT, THOMAS M,** Capital Bible Seminary, Lanham, MD; GD; MA; Teacher; BS SUNY Oswego; Theology; Missions Education.

**FATA, ROSARIA,** Albertus Magnus Coll, New Haven, CT; JR; BA; Frshmn Cls Treas 88-89; Amnsty Internatl Pres 89-90; Jr Cls Ofcr Pres 90-; Dixwell Q Hs Vol 88-89; Vrsty Vlybl 88-89; Itln/Frnch; Intrprtn/Trnsltn/Tchg.

**FATIGANTE, DAWN M,** Univ Of Pittsburgh, Pittsburgh, PA; FR; BS; Yrbk 90-; Blgy; Physcl Thrpy.

**FATIGANTE, PAMELA A,** Saint Francis Coll, Loretto, PA; SR; BSN; Natl Cathlc Hon Soc 90-; Hon Soc 90-; Nrsng.

**FATSIS, NECTARIOS,** Hellenic Coll/Holy Cross, Brookline, MA; JR; BA; Stdnt Govt Exec Comm Sec 89-; Recyclng Comm 87-89; GOYA Hd Advsr 86-89; Anognosan Schlrshp 88; Im Bsktbl 90; Rel Stds.**

**FATTORE, JOSEPH S,** Temple Univ, Philadelphia, PA; SR; AIAS 89; Deans List; Cum Laude; Kappa Delta Rho 89-90; Achtctr; Reg Archtct.

**FATUROTI, YEMI,** Univ Of South Al, Mobile, AL; JR; BS; Acctng Clb 90-; Tutor 89; Rugby Capt 86-87; St Josephs Clg Ipswich England; Acctng/Fnce; MBA.

**FATZYNYTZ, RICHARD,** Salisbury St Univ, Salisbury, MD; JR; BA; Deans Stdnt Advsry Cncl 90-; Tau Kappa Epsilon Pres 90-; Loyola Fdrl Schlrshp Awd 89-; IM Sftbl Bsktbl Flr Hooked Ftbl; Bus; Mgmt.

**FAUGL, ANN M,** Univ Of Sc At Aiken, Aiken, SC; JR; BS; Engl Educ.

**FAUL JR, CARLOS A,** Univ Of Southern Ms, Hattiesburg, MS; SR; Gldn Key; Tuba Intrntl; Handsboro Untd Meth Chrch; Intrn Sound Stage Rcrdng Studio; Ftbl Mrchng Bnd; Bsktbl Pep Bnd; Orchstr; AA Msc Ms Gulf Coast 89; BA Electrncs Technlgy Ms Gulf Coast Jr Clg 87; Music Indstry.

**FAUL, MEGHEAN R,** Newbury Coll, Brookline, MA; FR; AI Peer Activity Ldr 90-; Culinary Christmas Charity Proj 90-; Externship Geneva On The Lake Pantry Cook; Cert 90-; Culinary Arts; Chef.

**FAULCON, GEORGEANNA,** Saint Pauls Coll, Lawrenceville, VA; FR; BS; Mathematics.

**FAULDS, WENDY K,** Saint John Fisher Coll, Rochester, NY; SR; BA; Spanish Cl Pres 90-; French Cl V P; Yrbk Cmptr Ed 87-; Alpha Mu Gamma 88-; Pi Delta Phi; Intnl Studies Asso; Camp Good Days/Spcl Times Work Vol; Forgn Study Un/Salamanca Spain 89-90; Spanish; Chrstn Minis/Mssnry.

**FAULHABER, WILLIAM D,** Andover Coll, Portland, ME; SO; AA; Hon Soc 90-; Stdnt Of The Mod 90; VITA 89-; Lobster Fisherman 88; Owner Bills Finest ME Seafood 90; LA Acctng; Bus Admin; CPA.

**FAULK, ANNA C,** Belmont Coll, Nashville, TN; SR; Msc Bus Stu Adv Brd 88-; Alpha Chi 89-; William G Hall Schlr 88-; BBA; Bus; Msc Inds.

**FAULK, KELLY D,** Hampton Univ, Hampton, VA; SR; Stdnt VA Edn Assn 89-; Elem Edn Clb 89-; Vrsty Sftbl Tm 89-90; Kappa Delta Pi 90-; BS; Elem Edn.**

**FAULK, TAMERA L,** Faulkner St Jr Coll, Bay Minette, AL; SO; Dance Co; Deans List 90-; Law Psychology; Lawyer.

**FAULK, TAMMIE M,** Memphis St Univ, Memphis, TN; JR; BFA; Campus Crsde For Chrst VP 89-; Gldn Ky; Intr Dsgn.

**FAULKENBERRY, CARREN L,** Middle Tn St Univ, Murfreesboro, TN; SR; DTA 89-; FFA VP 86-; Young Farmers & Homemakers Sec 87-90; Agribusiness; Teaching.

**FAULKENBERRY, DANA L,** Univ Of Sc At Columbia, Columbia, SC; SO; BA; AA; Art; Advrtsng.

**FAULKENBERRY, RHONDA J,** Winthrop Coll, Rock Hill, SC; SO; BED; Early Chldhd Educ; Tchng.

**FAULKNER, DIANA N,** S U N Y At Albany, Albany, NY; JR; BA; Dnc Mdlng Ttrng Stdnts; Tri Delta; Pltcl Sci.

**FAULKNER, KAREN D,** Pellissippi St Tech Comm Coll, Knoxville, TN; SO; BS; Alpha Beta Gamma; Acctg.

**FAULKNER, KATHERINE A,** Univ Of Southern Ms, Hattiesburg, MS; SR; BS; Minds Comm Clg Chr/Ensmbl 87-88; Golden Key; AA Comm Clg 89; Psych.

**FAULKNER, LAURA G,** Converse Coll, Spartanburg, SC; SO; BA; Stdnt Admssns Brd Co Char 89-90; Coll Rep Treas 90-; Nwsppr Kybrd Cmmnty Advsr; Stdnt Vol Srvc; Crscnt; Deans Lst; Engl.

**FAULKNER, REBECCA L,** Univ Of Tn At Martin, Martin, TN; SR; BS; Stdnt Dietetics Assc Fndr; Amrcn Dietetics Assc 89-; GSA; Home Ec; Dietetics.

**FAULKNER, SANDRA F,** Itawamba Comm Coll, Fulton, MS; BSN; Ntnl Fedtn LPN; LPN 88-; Nrs Cert Prac Itawamda Comm Colg 88; Nrsg; MSN.

**FAULLS, KATHLEEN A,** Glassboro St Coll, Glassboro, NJ; JR; BA; Deans List 88-90; Math; High Schl Math Tchr.

**FAUROT, SUSAN D,** Auburn Univ At Auburn, Auburn, AL; JR; BS; AWARE Vc Chrprsn 90-; Theata XI Ltl Sis; Cir K Cmt Hd 90-; Crisis Cntr Brd Rep 90-; Proj Uplift Big Sis 90-; Asstnt Stdy Marriage/Fmly Thrpy 90-; Best New Mbr 90; Fmly/Chld Dvlpmnt; Cnslng.

**FAUSEY, PAMELA A,** Radford Univ, Radford, VA; SO; BA; Bus; Mktg.

**FAUST, KAREN J,** Va Highlands Comm Coll, Abingdon, VA; GD; AAS; Judiciary Com 90; Phi Theta Kappa 90-; Alpha Gamma Rho 90-; Intrnshp Abuse Alt Cnslr 90-; Schlrshp VA Cncl Soc Welfare 90; Hairdresser; Human Serv/Psy Soc; Substances Abuse Therp.

**FAUX, JENNIFER A,** Rochester Inst Of Tech, Rochester, NY; FR; BFA; Polished Brass 90-; IM Flr Hcky 90-; Phtgrphy.

**FAUX, SUSANNE M,** Univ Of Md At Eastern Shore, Princess Anne, MD; JR; BS; Amer Phys Thrpy Assn 90; Phys Thrpy Assist 85-; AA Comm Clg Of Baltimore 85; Phy Thrpy.

**FAVA, DOREEN L,** Cumberland County Coll, Vineland, NJ; FR; BA; Trea Vineland Jr Wmns Clb 82-87; Cert Pod Surgcl Asst 87-; Sci; Nrsng.

**FAVA, JENNIFER A,** Univ Of Ma At Amherst, Amherst, MA; JR; BS; NRPA Natl Rcreatn/Pks Assn; Goldey Key 90-; Stdnt Rep Faculty 90; Rcrtn Rsrcs Mgmt; Rcrtn/Leisure Serv.

**FAVALE, G MICHAEL,** Cornell Univ Statutory College, Ithaca, NY; SR; JD; Rsdnt Advsr 90; Codes/Jdcl Cmmttee 89; Ambssdr For CALS At Crnll; Golden Key 89; Gamma Sigma Delta; Tchng Assistnt For Intro To Mass Media 89; Tchng Assistnt For Oral Cmmnctns 90; Im Ftbl Sftbl Vllybl Sccr Wtr Polo 87; BS; Law.

**FAVALORO, CRISTINA E,** Villanova Univ, Villanova, PA; JR; BA; Pre Law Soc 90-; Pi Beta Phi 89-; Pltcl Sci; Law.

**FAVARO, GINA SUE,** Univ Of Sc At Columbia, Columbia, SC; FR; BS; Hotel/Rstrnt/Tourism Adm; Resort Mgmt.

**FAVERS, ALEXIS M,** Comm Coll Algny Co Algny Cmps, Pittsburgh, PA; BA; Cert ICM Sch Bus 77; Cmptrs; Cmptr Sci.

**FAWCETT, KIMBERLY A,** Rivier Coll, Nashua, NH; SR; Dean Lst 88-; BA; Elem/Spcl Educ; Tchng.

**FAY, LISA A,** Univ Of Cin R Walters Coll, Blue Ash, OH; SO; AS; Ntnl Acdmc Hnr Soc; Deans Lst 88-; Cmmrcl Art Pstr Wrk Apprdn Pstrs 89-; Maga Cum Laude; Cmmrcl Art; Cmmrcl Grphc Artst.

**FAY, MICHELLE E,** Merrimack Coll, North Andover, MA; SO; BA; Orntn Cmmtt 89; Big Brother/Sister Greater Lawrence 90; IM Basktbll; Bsn; CPA.

**FAYARD JR, JIMMY O,** Ms Gulf Coast Comm Coll, Perkinston, MS; FR; BA; V Pres Lst 90-; Engl; Tchg.

**FAYE, PAULA D,** Coll Of Charleston, Charleston, SC; JR; BS; Army ROTC Francis Marion Clg 88-89; Hghly Distngshd Faclty Hons 90-; AA Trident Techncl Clg 90; Elem Ed; Tchng.

**FAYE, REBECCA J,** Marywood Coll, Scranton, PA; FR; BA; Ski Clb; Wind Ensmbl; Campus Choir; Alpha Mu Gamma; French/Span Educ; English Secnd Lang Educ.

**FAYET, TRACI D,** Saint Andrews Presbytrn Coll, Laurinburg, NC; FR; BS; Ntnl Model United Ntns Clb; Bio; Med.

**FAZAL, SHAFEEK,** City Univ Of Ny City Coll, New York, NY; SR; BE; Indn Cltrl Clb; Gldn Ky; Tau Beta Pi; Cuny Schlrshp; Elec Eng; Eng.

**FAZI, NICHOLAS M,** Duquesne Univ, Pittsburgh, PA; SR; BA; Commtr Cncl 87-88; Fin Mgmt Assoc 89-; Pittsbrgh Soc Fincl Anlysts 90-; Beta Alpha Phi 89-; Phi Chi Theta Corres Sec 89-; Fin; Mgmt.

**FAZIO, CHRISTINA E,** Fl Atlantic Univ, Boca Raton, FL; SR; BBA; Phi Kappa Phi; Cmnty Clge Schlrshp 87-; AA Broward Cmnty Clge 89; Internatl Bus.

**FAZIO, DANA,** Villanova Univ, Villanova, PA; FR; BA; Hse Cncl VP Dorm 90-; Muscl Prod 90; Delta Gamma Soc Chrmn; Chrty Fndrsr; Spec Olympcs Vol Bddy 90; Sociolgy/Psychlgy.

**FAZZARI, JENNIFER L,** Cornell Univ Statutory College, Ithaca, NY; SO; BS; Scty Creative Anachronsim 90-; Law Enformnt Explorer Post #58 Lieut 87-; Deans List; Natl Resources; Envtl Conservation.

**FAZZARO, MARY E,** Glassboro St Coll, Glassboro, NJ; SR; BA; Phi Theta Kappa 87-88; Phi Alpha Theta Pres 89-90; M Livingston Awd Sr Hstry 90; St Mary Magdalen Ch; Rsrch Dir Millville Army Airfld; AA Cumberland Cty Clg 88; Otsdng Yng Wmn Amer Awd; Hon Grad; History/Sec Educ; H S History Tchr/Guidance.

**FAZZINO, CRISTINA M,** Mount Saint Mary Coll, Newburgh, NY; SR; BS; Stdnt Bus Assn V P 89-90; Stdnt Bus Assn; Ldrshp Awd Sdtnt Bus Assn; Blck Party Weekend Spnsrd Carnival; AAS Orange Cnty 86; Mgmnt Comm Coll; Bus Mgmnt/Admin; Law Degree.

**FAZZINO, TABITHA G,** Fl St Univ, Tallahassee, FL; SR; BS; Pre Law Soc 89-; Intl Affrs Soc 90-; Pi Gamma Mu Pres; Phi Eta Sigma 87-; Intrnshp Senate Mjrty Offc FLA 90; AA 90; Pol Scnc/Hist; Public Admin/Urb Reg Plnng.

**FAZZOLARI JR, FRANK S,** West Liberty St Coll, West Liberty, WV; SR; Kappa Delta Rho IM Rep 88-; Crrctns Acdmy Intern 90; BS W Liberty St Coll; Crmnl Jstc; Crrctns.

**FEAGIN, JAMES RUSSELL,** Coker Coll, Hartsville, SC; SR; BA; Rcrtr; Bus Mgmt; Prsnnl Mngr.

**FEAGIN, JOY D,** Emmanuel Coll Schl Chrstn Min, Franklin Sprg, GA; SR; BA; SGA; Plyrs Tm Ldr Clss Sec 88-89; SGAE; IMS Pres 88-89; Drm Cncl; FSAC Ststcn; Hnr Grad; Sndy Schl Tchr 87-; Cnvlscnt Cntr Wrkr 88-89; Internshp Falcon Chldrsn Hme; IM Bsktbll 90-; Dir Chldrns Mnstrs; AA 89; Flgn; Chrstn Jrnlsm.

**FEARNBACH, HEATHER,** Western Carolina Univ, Cullowhee, NC; JR; BA; Yrbk Staff; Yr/Stdnt 90-; Ntnl Hon Cnfce; Alpha Lamda Delta; Tutor 90-; Horatio Helder Schlrsp 90-; Mc Clure Schlrsp 90-; Crum Schlrshp; Southn Regnl Coun Schlrshp; Hon Prog; Deans List; Engl; Law.

**FEARS JR, LARRY R,** Bellarmine Coll, Louisville, KY; SR; BA; Omicron Delta Epsilon; Intl Hon Soc Econ; Wall St Jrnl Stdnt Achvmnt Awrd; Econ; Mgmt/Finance.

**FEASEL MC DONALD, LORI,** Atlantic Comm Coll, Mays Landing, NJ; JR; BS; NJ Occptnl Thrpy Assn Pblc Rltns; AAS 90; Occptnl Thrpy.

**FEBEL, KAREN S,** Univ Of Cincinnati, Cincinnati, OH; FR; BS; Cmps Bnd 90-; Alpha Lambda Delta 90-; Hnr Stdnt Assoc 90-; NASA Lewis Rsrch Cntr Intrnshp 90; Nursing.

**FEBLES, CARLOS F,** Fl International Univ, Miami, FL; SR; Fncl Mgt Assoc Pres; Soc Advncmnt Mgt VP Prog 90-; BA; AA 89; Finance; Law.

**FEBONIO, DENISE A,** Rivier Coll, Nashua, NH; JR; BA; PTA 90-; Legal Sec/Bnk Supvrsr; Lib Studies.

**FEBRES, ARRAYO Y,** Univ Of Pr At Rio Piedras, Rio Piedras, PR; JR; Aspr De P R Clb De Cvrns De Salad 87-; Cuadro De Hon Del De Cano Fcltd Cncn Ntrl 90-; Volrt Allhosp De Avea Dr Carolina El Lab Clnc 88; Tchnlg Media.

**FEBRES-CORDERO, ZULEMA,** Univ Of Miami, Coral Gables, FL; SR; BSME; Amer Sty Mech Eng Ald Sgnl Sec 89; Amer Scty Htng Rfrgrtng Ar Cndtng 90-; People Intrntl 87-; Real Corp Ofc Asst 83-90; Mech Eng.

**FECCIA, DEBORAH M,** Newbury Coll, Brookline, MA; ASSOC; Byr Data Gen Crp; Assoc 89; Fshn Mrchndsng.

**FECHNER, SHIRLEY F,** Union Univ School Of Nursing, Memphis, TN; FR; BSN; Csmtlgst Enrri Schl Beauty 80; Nrsng/Sci.

**FEDDER, TAMARA B,** East Carolina Univ, Greenville, NC; JR; BFA; Pres Lst Carenet Comm Coll 88-89; Deans Lst Carolina 90; Stdnt Store Schlrshp Envrn Dsn Proj Undergrad Shw; Cartrt Comm Coll Tnns Tm 89; Envrnmntl Dsgn; MA Arch.

**FEDDERS, KENNETH O,** Central Fl Comm Coll, Ocala, FL; SO; BA; Marion Co Shrf Dept Ptrl Dpty; Crim Law; Law Enfrcmnt.

**FEDELE, PHYLLIS A,** Commonwealth Coll, Virginia Beach, VA; FR; AAS; Ofc Admin Clb Sec 90; Coll Sec Intl 90-; Legal Ofc Admin; Paralegal.

**FEDELE, RAELYNN B,** Marshall University, Huntington, WV; SO; BA; Bus Admin; Mgmt.

**FEDER, DARRIN M,** William Paterson Coll, Wayne, NJ; SR; BA; Stdnt Govt Assn Hmnts Rep 89-; Hstry Clb Pres 88-89; Natl Org Reform Marijuana Laws Pres 89-; Stdnt Mobilization Comm Pres 89-; Phi Alpha Theta 89-; Prog Actn Network Fndr/Crdntr; Juv Educ/Awrns Proj Bd 90-F; Hstry/Pol Sci; Activist.

**FEDER, KEVIN W,** Niagara Univ, Niagara Univ, NY; SO; Rsdntl Asstnt; Heritage Cntr Vlntr; Excptnl Edctn; Tchng.

**FEDER, MARK A,** Yeshiva Univ, New York, NY; SR; BA; Yeshiva Coll Philanthropy Soc 90-; Har Sinai Chapt NCSY 89-; Psi Chi VP 90-; Samuel Belkin Schlrshp Pgm 89-; Psychlgy/Edn.

**FEDERICK, VALENCIA D,** Bennett Coll, Greensboro, NC; SR; BS; Stdnt Almni Assn 89-90; Campus Grl Scout 90-; Stdnt Govt Prlmntrn 90-; Alpha Kappa Alpha Phylctr 90-; T Hlgt Awrd 87-88; USAA All Amer Schlr 90-; Bennett Coll Mer Schlr 90-; Biolgy; Rsrch Scntfc.

**FEDERICO, ALISA M,** Villanova Univ, Villanova, PA; JR; BA; Vllnv Ski Clb 88-; Phi Kappa Phi; Omcrn Delta Kappa; Delta Gamma 88-; Nat Mrt Schlr; Pres Schlr; Crew Tm Vars Cxswn 88-; Hnrs/Pol Sci; Intl Affrs.

**FEDGCHIN, BRIAN D,** Providence Coll, Providence, RI; FR; BS; AIESEC; Yrbk Stff; Hnrs Prog; Dns Lst; IM; Blgy; Med.

**FEDOR, KELLI T,** Niagara Univ, Niagara Univ, NY; JR; BA; Scl Wrk Actn Clb Sec 89; Hnr Std 89-; Scl Wrk.

**FEDORCHAK, NICOLE S,** Villanova Univ, Villanova, PA; FR; BA; Pi Beta Phi; Lbrl Arts.

**FEDORKO, HOLLY M,** Mount Aloysius Jr Coll, Cresson, PA; FR; Peer Tutor; Phi Theta Kappa 90-; Paralegal.

**FEDRICK, THOMAS P,** Old Dominion Univ, Norfolk, VA; SR; BS; AMA VP 90-; Pi Kappa Phi 87-; Trning/Dvlpmnt Cncpts Inc Intrn 90; Sec Educ/Trn Spec; Org Trn/Dvlpmnt.

**FEE, JOHN P,** Univ Of Tn At Knoxville, Knoxville, TN; JR; BS; Fincl Mgmt Assc Soc Chrmn 90-; Beta Gamma Sgm; Fincl Mgmt Assc; IM Tm Capt 89-90; Jack York Fin Schlrshp; Fin.

**FEELEY, CATHLEEN M,** Saint Andrews Presbytrn Coll, Laurinburg, NC; JR; BA; Dns Lst; Chrstn Athl Assn; Outstdng Frshmn Awd Schlrshp; Soccer Schlrshp; Wmns Soccer Capt; Engl/Math/Hlth; Bus/Acctng.

**FEELEY, RYAN G,** Colby Coll, Waterville, ME; FR; Nwsppr Wrtr 90-; Engl; Tch.

**FEENER, SUZANNE M,** Clarkson Univ, Potsdam, NY; SR; Mktg/Mis Soc Pres 89-; Amercn Mktg Assoc 90-; Soc Of Women Mgrs; Omega Delta Phi Alumni Secy 88-; BS; Mktg.

**FEENEY, BROOKE C,** Salisbury St Univ, Salisbury, MD; SR; BA; Psych Clb 90-; Stdnt Asst Admssns Offce 87-; Phi Kappa Phi 90-; Psi Chi 90-; Phi Eta Sigma 88-; Psych Mjr Engl Mnr; Grad Schl Chld Pscyh.

**FEENEY, MICHAEL M,** Embry Riddle Aeronautical Univ, Daytona Beach, FL; JR; BS; IM Sftbl/Ftbl/Bsktbl 89-; Eagle Scout BSA; IM 89-; Aeronautical Stds Mgmt; Prof Arntcs Pilot.

**FEENEY, REBECCA L,** Savannah Coll Of Art & Design, Savannah, GA; FR; BFA; Stdnt Actvts Cncl 90-; Grphc Dsgn; Advrtsng.

**FEENY, NORAH C,** Ursinus Coll, Collegeville, PA; SR; BS; Psi Chi 90-; Deans Lst 89-; Intrnshp Prkmn Vlly Mid Sch 90; Fndng Sufdna Found Acdmc Exclnc 90; Psychology Anthropology Soc; Phd.

**FEGHALI, FADI M,** Univ Of Sc At Columbia, Columbia, SC; JR; BA; Wtr Dwnhl Skg; Hntg; Rftg; Tns; Dns Lst 88-90; Bsn Info Systms; Systms Anlyst.

**FEHLHABER, JENNIFER A,** Belmont Coll, Nashville, TN; SR; BA; Chrstn Music Soc 90-; Dns Lst 90-; Music; Sound Re-Infrcmnt.

**FEHRMAN, JOHN M,** Commonwealth Coll, Virginia Beach, VA; SO; Eng.

**FEHSENFELD, DELBERT A,** Liberty Univ, Lynchburg, VA; JR; BA; Eng; Psychlgy.

**FEIGH JR, JOHN M,** Christopher Newport Coll, Newport News, VA; JR; BSGA; Rotract Clb 89-90; SGA VP 89-90; Pre-Law Soc VP 90-; Cum Laude 90; TCC Dist Std Awd 90; Nwprt News Shpbldng 84-88; ASS Tidewater Comm Clg 90; Govt/Lgl Stds; Law/Govt Admn.

**FEILD JR, JOHN M,** Valdosta St Coll, Valdosta, GA; SR; Pi Gamma Mu Pres 90-; Pre Law Awrd 90-; Intrnshp Law Ofc David Mallis 90-; BA; Pol Sci; Law.

**FEINGLASS, MARY B,** Univ Of North Fl, Jacksonville, FL; JR; BS; Natl Gldn Key 90-; Phi Kappa Phi 90-; Diploma St Marys Hosp Schl Nrsng 81; AA Santa Fe Comm Clg 87; Nutrition; Dietician.

**FEINGOLD, DANIEL L,** Univ Of Rochester, Rochester, NY; JR; BA; Meridian Scty Trs; Deans Lst 88-; Tau Kappa Epsilon; Bio; Med.

**FEINMAN, AMY E,** Indiana Univ Of Pa, Indiana, PA; SO; BA; Cncl Excptnl Chldrn Pres 90-; Hillel Treas 89-90; Sigma Tau Alpha Sec; NCAA 1st Tm Sftbl; Deans Lst; Intrcllgt Sftbl; Spec Ed; Tchr.

**FEINSTEIN, SHERRIE L,** Shepherd Coll, Shepherdstown, WV; FR; BA; Bacchus Treas 90-; Stdnt Govt Sntr 90-; Hse Cncl Wing Rep 90-; Delta Zeta Pnhlnc Rep 90-; Orntn Asst; Cmcntns; Jrnlsm.

**FEIST, FRANCES A,** Univ Of Cin R Walters Coll, Blue Ash, OH; Rgstrd Nurse.

**FEIT-SEIDMAN, SUSAN S,** Yeshiva Univ, New York, NY; SR; BA; Advrtsng Intrnshp Ntl Kidney Fndtn C Schwartzappel Mem Awd Excell Phlsphy 90-; Phlsphy; Frlnc Advrtsng/Phlsphy Ph D.

**FEITL, E J,** Univ Of Pittsburgh, Pittsburgh, PA; JR; BS/BA; AICHE 89-; Ovrll Dptmntl Eng Wk Chrprsn; Tau Beta Pi Rcrdng Sec 89-; Omega Chi Epsilon Co Vp 89-; Merit Schlrshp 87-; Almni Assc Hnrs Schlrshp 87-; Proctor/Gamble Intrnshp 90; IM Ftbl 87-89; IM Vlybl 89-; Chem Eng/Hstry/Phlsphy Sci; Eng.

**FEKETE, ILONA E,** Univ Of Nc At Asheville, Asheville, NC; SO; BA; Vero Bch Jaycees 90-; Wmns Vlyvbl UNCA Tm 90-; USUBA 90-; Deans Lst 90-; Womns Vllybl 90-; Biology; Edctn Hlth Prmtn.

**FELDBERG, MARNIE A,** Univ Of North Fl, Jacksonville, FL; FR; BBA; Stdnt Gvrnmnt Assn Sntr 91; Bacchus Peer Theatre Tres 90-; Unv Hsng Advsry Cncl Brd Mmbr 90-; Phi Beta Lambda Hstrn 90-; Bsns; Corp Financing.

**FELDBUSH, MARK A,** Columbia Union Coll, Takoma Park, MD; SO; BS; SG Sprtl VP; Phi Eta Sigma Hstrn 90-; Cmps Mnstry Dir Drm Grp 90-; Brdcstng/Thlgy; Relg Cmmnctns.

**FELDER, ARTHUR M,** City Univ Of Ny Baruch Coll, New York, NY; JR; BBA; Golden Key 90; Mrktng Advrtsng.

**FELDER, JENNIE R,** Denmark Tech Coll, Denmark, SC; GD; AD; Pres List 90-; Deans List 90-; Human Srvces Club 90-; Miss Human Srvces 90-; Alpha Delta Omego; Human Srvces; Social Wrk.

**FELDER, JO-ANN MARNEE,** Va St Univ, Petersburg, VA; SO; BA; Stdnt Govt Assoc Pres; Assoc Of Pol Scntsts Pres; Tdewtr Pre-Alumni Assoc Sec 90; Pre-Law Scty 89; NAACP 90; XAMPLES 90; Deans Lst 89; SCHEV 90; Pol Sci; Crmnl Law.

**FELDER, JOE V,** Al A & M Univ, Normal, AL; FR; BA; Acctng; Acct.

**FELDER, KIMBERLY J,** Indiana Univ Of Pa, Indiana, PA; SO; BA; Nrsng.**

**FELDER, LAURIE S,** Univ Of Southern Ms, Hattiesburg, MS; SR; BED; NEA 89-; AA 89; Educ; Elem Ed.

**FELDER, PAMELA T,** Benedict Coll, Columbia, SC; SO; BA; Acctg Assn 90-; Phi Beta Lamba; Trustee Schlr 89; Pres Lst 90; Deans Lst 89; Acctg; CPA.

**FELDHOUSE III, HAROLD E,** Cleveland Inst Of Art, Cleveland, OH; FR; BFA; Vsl Cmnctn/Grphc Dsgn; Advrtsng.

**FELDMAN, LAUREN K,** Univ Of Ga, Athens, GA; SO; BS; Hillel; Neo Pgn Scty; Alpha Epsilon Delta 90-; Alpha Lambda Delta; Psych Pre Med; Pysch Rsrch.**

**FELDMAN, MARINA A,** City Univ Of Ny La Guard Coll, Long Island Cty, NY; SO; AS; Serv For Aged 89-; Comm Hlth Prog 90-; Home Hlth Attendant; Med Recptnst; BA Music 87; Cert 89; Med Sci; Nrsng.

**FELDMAN, RACHEL S,** Univ Of Ct, Storrs, CT; SR; BS; Univ Ct Forestry Wldlfe Clb 89-90; Deans Lst 90; Pi Lamda Phi Ltl Str 88-89; Rsrch Asst Kenya Africa 90; I M Vybl 89-90; Animal Sci; Wldlfe Cnsrvtn.

**FELDNER, ANGELA M,** Washington State Comm Coll, Marietta, OH; GD; Nrsg Clb 90-; Nrsg; LPN.

**FELESKY, CAROLINE V,** Duquesne Univ, Pittsburgh, PA; BS BA 90.

**FELGENHAUER, TYLER N,** Cornell Univ, Ithaca, NY; FR; Mech/Cvl Eng.

**FELIBERTY, MELBA,** Ny Univ, New York, NY; FR; BA; League Unified Coop Hispanic Amer; Inter Sorority Council Repres AHANA; Tau Sigma Phi Pres 90-; Psy; Law.

**FELICE, MICHAEL P,** S U N Y Coll Of Tech At Frmgdl, Farmingdale, NY; JR; BT; Smithtown Fire Dept 3rd Asst Chief 79-; Assoc Engr Fire Rsrch Corp 80-; AAS 89; Manuf Eng.

**FELICIANO ALICEA, JOSE,** Inter Amer Univ Pr San German, San German, PR; JR.

**FELICIANO BURGOS, ARLENE,** Inter Amer Univ Pr San German, San German, PR; FR; BA; Erly Admssn Treas 90-; HOSA Hlth Asst 90-; Vlybl Tm Cpt 90-; Med; Phys Thrpy.

**FELICIANO HERNANDEZ, ROCIO DEL,** Univ Of Pr Medical Sciences, San Juan, PR; GD; MBS; Natl Stdnt Spch Lang Hrng 87-; BS 90; Spch Pthlgy.

**FELICIANO VALENTIN, FELIX,** Inter Amer Univ Pr Aquadilla, Aguadilla, PR; SO; JAJ 90-; Chorus; Muncpl Dance Grp; Nicest Emplyr 89-90; Rlgus Serv Soc 90-; Sec Educ.

**FELICIANO, ALEXANDER,** Univ Of Pr At Mayaguez, Mayaguez, PR; JR; BA; Amer Inst Cheml Engrs 90-; Chemical Egrg.

**FELICIANO, AMY,** Central Fl Comm Coll, Ocala, FL; FR; BA; Stdnt Govt Rep; Phi Theta Kapa SGA Rep; Psi Beta SGA Rep; Advocacy For Human Rights Cmte 90-; Psych; Prison/Police Dept.

**FELICIANO, KATHARINA,** Inter Amer Univ Pr Aquadilla, Aguadilla, PR; FR; BMT; Hlth; Med Tech.

**FELICIANO, VICTOR R,** Chattahoochee Vly St Comm Coll, Phenix City, AL; SO; BA; TV Sports Intern 90; AAS; Radio/TV Brdcstg; Sports Brdcstg/Advrtsg.

**FELICIANO, YESENIA,** Inter Amer Univ Pr Hato Rey, Hato Rey, PR; FR; BA; Bsns Admn.

**FELIX, ALLISON P,** Univ Of Sc At Columbia, Columbia, SC; JR; Schlrshp Play Mrchng Bnd; Wnd Ensmbl/Symphny; Engl; Tchng.

**FELIX, NELSON E,** Univ Politecnica De Pr, Hato Rey, PR; GD.

**FELIXBERTO, FERNANDO FAURILLO,** Old Dominion Univ, Norfolk, VA; JR; BS; US Navy 84-; Cmptr Engr; Engr.

**FELKER, KIMBERLY F,** Univ Of Tn At Martin, Martin, TN; JR; BS; Stdnt Mbr Sctn Amer Hm Econ Assoc 1st Vc Chr; Stdnt Agnst Drnk Drvrs; Zeta Tau Alpha Rtl Chrmn 90; Spec Olympcs Aid; Gen Hm Ec; Dy Cr Wrkr/Chld Lf Spclst.

**FELLER, BLAIR,** Nova Univ, Ft Lauderdale, FL; GD; MBA; Instrmnt Soc Amrc; Rgstrd Prfssnl Eng; BSEE 72; AA 70.

**FELLINGER, KAREN A,** Savannah Coll Of Art & Design, Savannah, GA; SR; Illustration Clb 89-90; Deans Lst Dutchess Comm Clg 87-89; Deans Lst 90-; AAS Dutchess Comm Clg 90; Illustration/Art; Med Illustrator.

**FELLOWS, STARLA D,** Union Univ, Jackson, TN; JR; BS; Flwshp Chrstn Athltcs 90-; Bptst Stdnt Un 90-; Stdnt Ldr Frshmn Cnslr 89-; Alpha Tau Omega 90-; Ms Clrk Co 89-90; Natl Hnr Soc 81-; Phi Eta Sigma 88-; Chi Omega Cr Dv Chr Pldg Cls Pres 90-; IM Vlybl 90-; Fnc/Econ; Econ Dvlpmnt.

**FELLS, PATRICIA A,** Miles Coll, Birmingham, AL; SR; BS; Pres Schlr 90-; Alpha Kappa Alpha Prlmntrn; Outstndng Stdnt Scl Wk Intern 88-89; AAS Lawson St Comm Coll 89; Scl Sci; Cnslng/Law.

**FELMET, CAMILLA H,** Catawba Valley Comm Coll, Hickory, NC; GD; AAS; Stdnt Govt Assoc Sen 89-; Rotar Act Clb Pres/V P 90-; Gamma Beta Phi 89-; Lit Mag Asst Ed 90; Bsn Adm; Mgmt.**

**FELMLY, REBECCA L,** Kent St Univ Kent Cmps, Kent, OH; SO; BA; Crmnl Justice/Pre-Law.

**FELOSO, STACI A,** Indiana Univ Of Pa, Indiana, PA; SR; BED; Cncl Excep Chldrn 87-90; Phi Mu Natl Pldg Cls VP 88-90; IMS; Educ Excep Chldrn; Tchr.

**FELSENTHAL, STEVEN M,** Yeshiva Univ, New York, NY; SR; BA; SG Pres 90-; Clg Repubs Pres 89-90; Cls Pres 87-89; Dramatics Soc 90-; Dns Lst 89-; Hebrew Hnrs Soc 89-90; Newspaper 87-90; Alpha Psi Omega 90-; NSCY Advsr 87-; SSSJ 89-; SIPA State Exec Bd 89-90; Publ Def Svc Intern 90; Drama Gypsy Awd 87-88; Pol Sci; Law Rabbinical Sch.

**FELTNER, LINDA A,** Oh St Univ At Marion, Marion, OH; SR; BA; Psych Clb 87; Griffin Soc 89; Psych.

**FELTON, ANGELA E,** Christopher Newport Coll, Newport News, VA; GD; BA; Bptst Std Un Pres 85-; Art Clb 87-; SGA Hist 87-88; Phi Theta Kappa 85-88; Ordr Slvr Fthr 87; Supr Ctznshp Awd 87; Flrl Dsgnr 87-; AA Chowen Clg 87; Fine Arts; Art Ed.

**FELTON, AUDREY IRIS,** Jackson St Univ, Jackson, MS; SR; BA; Phi Beta Lambda 89-; Acctg Soc 89-90; Finance Clb 90-; Alpha Chi; Alpha Kappa Mu; Phi Kappa Phi; Dns Lst 88-; Finance; Fncl Plnr.

**FELTON JR, EUGENE,** Morehouse Coll, Atlanta, GA; JR; NAACP 89-; Pre Alumni Assoc 89-; Pol Sci Soc Rprtr 88-; Gldn Key; Boys Mntrg Pro; IM Vlybl; Pol Sci; Law.**

**FELTON, SONYA A,** Norfolk St Univ, Norfolk, VA; JR; BS; IEEE Prog Chrprsn 90-; Math Clb; Yrbk Stff; Spartan Alpha Tau; Math; Actry.

**FELTS, STACEY L,** Stevens Inst Of Tech, Hoboken, NJ; FR; BE; Glee Clb 90-; Weight Clb 90-; NJ Schlr 90-; Stevens Flw 90-; IM Sftbl/Vlybl 90-; Envrnmntl Eng; Law.

**FELTY, LORA J,** Northern Ky Univ, Highland Hts, KY; SR; BA; Baptst Stdnt Un 87-; Pres Ambsdr 89-; LALINK Pres 90-; Sigma Tau Delta 90-; Engl Secndry; Tchng.

**FELTY, PAUL R,** Ashland Comm Coll, Ashland, KY; SO; Resp Ther.

**FENDELET, QUENTIN A,** Merrimack Coll, North Andover, MA; FR; MBA; IM Tennis/Sftbl 90-; Deans Lst 90-; Vrsty Hockey 90-; Acctg; CPA.

**FENDER, MYRA G,** Univ Of Sc At Columbia, Columbia, SC; SR; BS; Beta Alpha Psi 90-; Pres List 90-; Qual Work-Life Chpsn 85; Acctng; CPA.

**FENDER, ROBERT GREGORY,** Univ Of Nc At Charlotte, Charlotte, NC; JR; BA; AFROTC Pldg Cls Pres 90-; Gldn Key 90-; Sigma Nu; Air Force Assoc 90-; Air Ntl Guard Stf Sgt 89-; USAF Vet; Hstry; Mgmt.

**FENG, LARRY,** Oh Dominican Coll, Columbus, OH; SR; BA; Tau Pi Phi 88-; Fin Exec Inst Educ Awards Pgm 90; Peer Cnsltn 90; Bsn Admin Tutor 90; Mktg Intrnshp/Ntnwde Insur; Mktg Intrnshp/Son Of Heaven Exhbtn 89; Advrtsg Intrnshp/Saatchi/Saatchi Advrtsng 88; Bsn Admin; Mktg/Advrtsng.

**FENHAGEN, MICHELLE L,** Univ Of Fl, Gainesville, FL; SR; BHSC; Clg Hlth Rlts Prof Cncl OT Rep 89-; Std OT Asc 89-; Cmmtr Cncl 87-89; Gldn Key 89-; MD Dist Schlr 88; Grtc Rsch Intrn; FL OT Asc 89-; Amer OT Asc 89-; Occptnl Thrpy.

**FENIO, KENLY G,** Barry Univ, Miami, FL; FR; All Thtre Prdctns; Thtre; Law.

**FENNELL, ALECIA L,** Valdosta St Coll, Valdosta, GA; JR; BBA; Stu Asst Inst Rsrch/Plng; AA 90; Acctg; Cert Intrn Audtr.

**FENNELL, ANGELA M,** Univ Of Southern Ms, Hattiesburg, MS; JR; BA; Stdnt Alum Assn; Dixie Darling 90-; Deans Lst 88-; Delta Gamma Rtls Chrmn 88-; Occptnl Thrpy.

**FENNELL, SERINA R,** Va St Univ, Petersburg, VA; SO; BS; Acctg.

**FENNEMA, CRISTINA M,** Fl International Univ, Miami, FL; JR; Stdnt Dietetic Assc 89-; Deans List 89-; Dietetics/Nutrition.

**FENNER, ALFRED R,** Va St Univ, Petersburg, VA; SO; BS; Big Bro/Sis; Bsn Admn; Inv Banking.

**FENNER, BARBARA E,** Central St Univ, Wilberforce, OH; JR; BA; St Agstn Cath Chrch Jmstwn OH CCD Inst; Thrptc Prog Sprngvw Dev Cntr; Soc Work Clark St Spgfld OH 89; Elem Educ; Teacher.

**FENNER, GAYLE L,** Miami Jacobs Jr Coll Of Bus, Dayton, OH; FR; AB.

**FENNER, MARSHA W,** Elmira Coll, Elmira, NY; JR; BA; Outing Clb 88-; Chmbr Sngrs Accmpst 88-; Lit/Artstc Pblctn Edtr 88-90; Phi Beta Kappa 90-; Pres Schlshp; Hnrs Schlr 88-; IM Vlybl/Bwlng/Sftbl; Clsscl Stds/Phlsphy.

**FENSKY, WESLEY R,** Univ Of New Haven, West Haven, CT; JR; BS; Crmnl Jstc; Law.

**FENSTERMACHER, TRACI J,** Widener Univ, Chester, PA; FR; BS; Soc Wmn Eng 90-; Am Soc Mech Eng 90-; Soc Auto Eng 90-; Wmns Crs Cntry; Wmns Sftbl 90-; Mech Eng; Engrng.

**FENTERS, DANIEL B,** Univ Of Sc At Coastal Carolina, Conway, SC; SR; BS; Psych; Scl Wrk.

**FENTRESS JR, MICHAEL L,** Univ Of Vt & St Agri Coll, Burlington, VT; FR; BA; Phi Delta Theta; Pol Sci; Law.

**FENWICK, STACY D,** Owensboro Comm Coll, Owensboro, KY; FR; BA; Math; Accntnt.

**FEO, DAVID A,** Central Fl Comm Coll, Ocala, FL; FR; BA; Accntng; CPA.

**FERDINANDI, PETER,** Seton Hall Univ, South Orange, NJ; JR; BS; Stn Hll Acctng Clb 90-; IM Sprts 88-; Rgby VP 88-; Bus; Acct.**

**FERDINANDS, SHIREEN L,** Smith Coll, Northampton, MA; FR; BA; Stdnt Gov Sen; Career Dvlpmnt Offc House Rep; Gldn Key Campus Tour Guide; Stdnt Orgnztns Smith Vol Tutor 90-; Hmltn Lrng Cntr Prjct Head; Law Intrnshp Rcrds Clrk; Gov/Frnch; Law.

**FERENC, ALANA M,** Saint Johns Univ, Jamaica, NY; FR; BA; Frnch Clb 90-; Pre Law Scty 90-; Univ Hnrs Prgm 90-; Deans Hnr Lst 90-; Pre Law; Law.

**FERENC, KELLY ANN,** Hudson Valley Comm Coll, Troy, NY; FR; Bus/Ofc Exec.

**FERENCE, MARY J,** Saint Vincents Coll & Seminary, Latrobe, PA; JR; BS; Biology Club 88-90; Chem Club 88-; Physics Club 90-; Ski Club 88-; Yrbk 89-; Sports Frndship Days 88-; Hosp Observation Prog 89-; Literac Prog 89-; Tour Guide 89-; Campus Ministry 88-; Resch Intern Pittsburgh Energy Tchnlgy Ctr 90-; Biology Chemistry; Medicine.

**FERENCZI, DESIREE,** Glassboro St Coll, Glassboro, NJ; SR; BA; SGA Sntr 89-; Snr Cls Dir 90-; Lit Frm 89-; Gamma Tau Sigma 90-; Epsln Theta Sigma 90-; Almni Schlr; Dns Lst; Engl; Pblshng.

**FERGENBAUM, MARK I,** Savannah Coll Of Art & Design, Savannah, GA; JR; BFA; AABA St Petersburg Jr Clg 86; Archtctr/Intr Dsgn.

**FERGUS, CYNTHIA WILLIAMS,** Strayer Coll, Washington, DC; SR; BS; Ntl Assc Fml Exec 85-; Acct Admin Chase Manhattan Bnk NY NY 80-88; Fincl Plnnr Frst Investors Corp Norfolk VA 88-89; Bus Admin; Mngmnt.

**FERGUSON, ALAN E,** Morehouse Coll, Atlanta, GA; SO; BA; Mntrng Pgm 90-; Bsn Asc 90-; Blck Std Asc Chrmn 88-90; Hnr Rl 90-; Inroads Intrn 90; Wall St Jrnl Outstdng Bsn Soph 90; Vars Ftbl 88-89; Fnce; Banking.

**FERGUSON, ANGELA D,** Univ Of Southern Ms, Hattiesburg, MS; JR; BA; Phi Eta Sigma 89; Mu Phi Epsilon Sec 90-; Grmn/Frnch; Intnl Dplmcy.**

**FERGUSON, CAROL,** Cuyahoga Comm Coll, Cleveland, OH; GD; AD; Tlnt Rstr Coll Schlrshp Srvc; Phi Theta Kappa; Bus; Law/Mgmt.

**FERGUSON, CASSANDRA TYIESE,** Memphis St Univ, Memphis, TN; SR; BA; Pre Law Scty; Stdnt Govt Assoc 86-; Blk Stdnt Assoc 86-; Mnrty Affrs VP 86-88; Pi Sigma Alpha 90-; Rmdl Dvlpmntl Trng Vol; Blck Schlrs Unlmtd 88-; Bg Sstr Vol 86-; Vtr Rgstrtn 86-87; Lgsltv Intern; Bnd Schlrshp MTSU; Pltcl Sci Intl Stds; Corp Law.

**FERGUSON, CATHIE S,** Blue Mountain Coll, Blue Mountain, MS; JR; BS; Elem Ed; Tch.

**FERGUSON, CHRIS J,** Univ Of Sc At Columbia, Columbia, SC; JR; BA; Dorm Govt Treas 90; Astrnmy Instctr/Lab Tchr 89-; IM Ftbl/Sftbl; Hstry/Educ; Tchr.

**FERGUSON, CINDY K,** East Central Comm Coll, Decatur, MS; FR; BS; Stdnt Educ Orgnztn; Mu Alpha Theta; Phi Theta Kappa; Paul Douglas Tchrs Schlrshp; Elem Educ; Tchr.

**FERGUSON, CYNTHIA H,** Bellarmine Coll, Louisville, KY; JR; BA; NEA-SP Educ Clb 88-; Elem Ed/Engl; Tchng.

**FERGUSON, DANIEL B,** Salisbury St Univ, Salisbury, MD; SR; BA; Engl.

**FERGUSON, DARLENA S,** Marshall University, Huntington, WV; JR; BA; NSSHLA 89-; Bptst Yth Assn Sec/Treas 90; Ntl Mrt Spcl Schlrshp 88-; Cmmnctns Dsrds; Spch Pthlgst.

**FERGUSON, DAVID A,** Duke Univ, Durham, NC; FR; BA; Natl Soc Black Engr 90-; Mag Prdctn Staff 90-; Black Stdnt Assn 90-; Elctrcl Engr.

**FERGUSON, DAVID RUSSELL,** Univ Of South Al, Mobile, AL; SO; BA; Russian Clb Treas; Scndry Edn; Edn Russian.

**FERGUSON, DEBORAH J,** Faulkner St Jr Coll, Bay Minette, AL; SO; AS; Fmly Spprt Grp Ala Army Natl Grd 80-; Spec Educ Paraprof 87-; Elem Educ; Educ Ms.

**FERGUSON, DESIREE C,** Lincoln Univ, Lincoln Univ, PA; JR; BS; Spch Clb Pres 89-; Educ Clb V P 88-; Dance Troupe 88-; Alpha Chi 90-; Lder Ntwrk 89-90; Lecitures/Rectl Cmtee 89-; Dance Troupe MVP 89090; Dance Troupe 88-; Early Chld Ele Educ; Educ Admn.

**FERGUSON, DOLORES P,** Garrett Comm Coll, Mchenry, MD; SO; BS; Hstry.

**FERGUSON, DONNA J,** Seton Hall Univ, South Orange, NJ; FR; BS; Polish Falcons 75-; St Casimirs Chrch Lctr 86-; Kappa Dlt Pi; Scndry Educ/Engl; Tchng.

**FERGUSON, ELIZABETH J,** Fayetteville St Univ, Fayetteville, NC; SO; BS; Dns Lst; Bnkg; Assoc Minot State Univ 78; Acctg; CPA.

**FERGUSON, JAMES E,** Roane St Comm Coll, Harriman, TN; SO; AA; Bsn Admn; Trnsprtn Spec.

**FERGUSON, JANIS R,** Rivier Coll, Nashua, NH; FR; BS; Acctng.

**FERGUSON, JASON S,** Univ Of Tn At Knoxville, Knoxville, TN; FR; Std Govt Asst Dir; Phi Eta Sigma Dir; Alpha Lambda Delta; Kappa Alpha Ordr Chmn 90-; Acctng; Law.

**FERGUSON, JERMAINE A,** Fl A & M Univ, Tallahassee, FL; FR; BA; Leander L Boykin Schlr; Brdcst Jrnlsm; Flm TV Prdcr.

**FERGUSON, JOANNA L,** Georgetown Coll, Georgetown, KY; FR; BA; SGA 90-; Sigma Kappa Pldg Cls VP 90-; Var Chrldr 90-; Chem.

**FERGUSON, JULIE E,** Davidson Coll, Davidson, NC; SO; BA; Ambsdrs Pres 89-; Wstmnstr Flwshp Serv Crdntr 89-; Cncrt Choir 89-; Spncer Eating House 90-; St Govt Intrnshp; SH Bell Hnr Schlrhsp 89-; Presbytrn Chrch Schlrshp 89-; Psych; Tchg.**

**FERGUSON, JUNE A,** Univ Of Akron, Akron, OH; SO; BA; NSSLHA; Cmmctve Disorders; Spch Path.

**FERGUSON, KAREN K,** Immaculata Coll, Immaculata, PA; SR; BSN; Immclta Cllg Org Of Reg Nrs; Univ Immclt Clg 90-; Dns Lst 89-90; Amer Red Crs Nrs; Natl Fed Bsns Prof Wmn 71-84; Vol St Maximillian Kolbe Cath Chrch Westtown PA; RN Asbury Sch Of Nrsg Salina KS 84; Nrsng; MA Nrsng.

**FERGUSON, KATHY M,** Ms St Univ, Miss State, MS; SR; BA; Phi Theta Kappa 87-; Gamma Beta Phi 89-; Phi Kappa Phi; Engl.

**FERGUSON, KEITH M,** Christopher Newport Coll, Newport News, VA; JR; BSA; Acctg.

**FERGUSON, KELLI K,** Marshall University, Huntington, WV; SR; BA; IM Vllybl Capt 87-90; IM Sftbl 87-; Alpha Chi Omega Mystag 89-; CEC 90-; Spec Educ; Tchr.

**FERGUSON, KYLE R,** Univ Of South Al, Mobile, AL; SR; SHAPE Clb Pres; Pres Lst; Deans Lst; BA S E MO State 90; Phy Ed; Scndry Ed.

**FERGUSON, LINDSEY N,** Vanderbilt Univ, Nashville, TN; FR; BS; Alpha Delta Pi; Molecular Bio; Med.

**FERGUSON, LORI A,** Univ Of Nc At Greensboro, Greensboro, NC; JR; BA; Assoc Educ Yng Chldrn Pub Comm Chrprsn 90; Human Env Sci Marshls 90; AS Western Piedmont Comm Clg 87-89; Child Dev Svcs.

**FERGUSON, MICHAEL D,** Fl St Univ, Tallahassee, FL; SO; BS; Mrchng Chfs Ldr 89-; VP Stdnt Affrs Advsry Bd 89-; Lib Stds Hnrs Prog 89-; Mech Engr.

**FERGUSON, OLA MARIE,** James Madison University, Harrisonburg, VA; GD; MA; Psychlgy Clb 88-90; Advrtsng Clb 89-90; Psi Chi 89-90; Alpha Chi Omega 86-90; Ind/Orgnztnl Psychlgy.

**FERGUSON, PATRICIA A,** Univ Of Tn At Knoxville, Knoxville, TN; JR; BS; Office Mgr/Data Prcsng Mgr Cnstrctn Ind/Typesttr Prdctn Mgr Bus Jrnl; Dsktp Pblshng Eng Asst; Gen Bus; Comp Sftwr Rep.

**FERGUSON, PORSETTA A,** Marshall University, Huntington, WV; FR; Columbia Gas Transmission 90; Inroads 89-; Acctng.

**FERGUSON, RICKY D,** Radford Univ, Radford, VA; JR; BA; Oak Level Ruritan Clb Pres 86-; Basset Rescue Squad Inc Hstrn 88-; W Piedmont Pony League 86-; Natl Assoc Sprts Offcls 86-; Natl Fdrtn Intrschlstc Offcls Assoc 86-; Mthmtcs; Sec Ed.

**FERGUSON, ROSALIND A,** Spartanburg Methodist Coll, Spartanburg, SC; FR; BA; Tutor 90-; Phi Theta Kappa 90-; Pres List 90-; Outstndng Minority Commcoll Grad; Stdnt Trustee; Enlgish/Comp Sci Exc Awds 90-; Business; Cpa/Financial Cnsltnt.

**FERGUSON, SCOTT L,** Univ Of Ky, Lexington, KY; SR; BA; Boy Scts AM Asst Scout Master 75-82; Order Demolay 79-83; Sigma Delta Pi VP; Spanish; Trnsltr Civil Srv Immigration.

**FERGUSON, SHANNON R,** Western New England Coll, Springfield, MA; SR; BA; Peer Advsr/Stdnt Tchng Asst 90-; Mgmnt Assocf Intl Assoc; Deans List 89-; AA Clg Of Bahams 89; Bus Mgmnt.

**FERGUSON, TAMMY M,** Union Coll, Barbourville, KY; JR; BS; Hstry/Engl/Sec Cert, Educ.

**FERGUSON, TRACI E,** Hampton Univ, Hampton, VA; SR; Stdnts Va Educ Assn Tr 89-90; Educ Clb; Kappa Delta Pi; All Amer Schlrs; BS; Elem Educ; Tchng.

**FERGUSON, VICKIE L,** Owensboro Jr Coll Of Bus, Owensboro, KY; FR; Prsdnts Lst 90-.

**FERGUSON, WANDA L,** Art Inst Of Atlanta, Atlanta, GA; AB; Entrntmnt Mgmt Grp 90; Music Bsns; Perf/Bsns Mgmt.

**FERGUSON, WILLIAM M,** Marshall University, Huntington, WV; GD; MS; Grad Stdnt Cncl Mem; AICPA Mem 87-; WVSCPA 89-; Publ Acctg 87-; CPA Am Inst Of CPA 89; BBA Acctg 86; Acctg; Teach/Publ Practice.

**FERIA, DEAN R,** Fl International Univ, Miami, FL; JR; BA; Fin; Bnkg.

**FERL, SUZANNA R,** Triangle Inst Tech Erie, Erie, PA; FR; AS; Mech CADD.

**FERLAND JR, RUSSELL J,** Providence Coll, Providence, RI; JR; BA; Psi Chi 90-; Psychlgy; Law.

**FERM, MARK A,** Alfred Univ, Alfred, NY; FR; BA; Alpha Lambda Delta; Delta Sigma Phi; Vrsty Sccr Tm 90-; Acctng.

**FERMIN, JANET P,** City Univ Of Ny City Coll, New York, NY; SR; BA; 3rd Wrld Org 87; Matasanos Treas 87-88; Bio; Med.

**FERNANDER, CECILE D,** Fl International Univ, Miami, FL; SR; BSC; Bahamian Stdnts Assn 89-90; Intl Stdnt Club 89-90; Fllw Org Amer States 91; Hlth Svcs Admin; Hosp Admin.

**FERNANDER, ELOISE M,** Tuskegee Univ, Tuskegee Inst, AL; SO; BSC; Assc Gnrl Cntrctors Vp 90-; Assc Cnrl Cntrctrs Sec 91-; Cnstrctn Sci Mngmnt; Eng.

**FERNANDER, TIESCHKA C,** Clark Atlanta Univ, Atlanta, GA; FR; BA; Mgmt/Mktg.

**FERNANDES, ANTOINETTE M,** Memphis St Univ, Memphis, TN; SO; BED; Ltl Strs Crimson Cross 90-; Peer Mntr 90-; Bacchus 89-; Delta Gamma Corr Sec 89-; Deans Lst 89-; Early Chldhd Ed; Tch.

**FERNANDES, NICOLE,** Bloomfield Coll, Bloomfield, NJ; FR; BA; Pre-Chrprctc Clb 90-; Mntrng Prog 90-; Deans Lst; Hghst Hon; Pre-Chrprctc.

**FERNANDEZ BETANCOURT, DIANA,** Univ Politecnica De Pr, Hato Rey, PR; GD; BA; Mech Eng.

**FERNANDEZ, AIDA C,** Fl International Univ, Miami, FL; JR; BA; Wld Trkys Frst Aid Clb Sec 88-; Amer Red Crs Frst Aid Inst 89-; Phi Theta Kappa 87-89; Int Dsgn Assc Sec 90-; AA Miami-Dade Comm Coll 89; FL Real Est Lcns Bent Rodgers Schl Real Est 89; Engineering; Int Dsgn.

**FERNANDEZ, ALBERTO,** Inter Amer Univ Pr San Juan, Hato Rey, PR; GD; JD; Amer Bar Assoc LSD Dir 89-; Intr Amer Law Rev 89-; Phi Alpha Delta Treas 88-; BA Clark Univ 88; Law.

**FERNANDEZ, ALEX,** Merrimack Coll, North Andover, MA; JR; BS; IEEE Chrmn; ASES Northern Essex Comm Clg 90; Elect Engr.

**FERNANDEZ, ALFREDO M,** Univ Of Miami, Coral Gables, FL; JR; BS; Bio Clb 88-89; Phi Kappa Phi 90-; Golden Key 89-; Pres Hon Roll; Provost/Hon Roll; Deans List; Bio; Med.

**FERNANDEZ, ANGELICA T,** Yeshiva Univ, New York, NY; JR; BA; N Amer Jwsh Stdnt Ntwrk NY Rgnl Chrmn 88-89; Pres Cncl BBH-JACY Chrmn 89-90; Spch Arts Frm Pres 89-; Psychlgy; Psychtry/Med Sch.

**FERNANDEZ, BIELCA A,** City Univ Of Ny Queensbrough, New York, NY; FR; AS; Deans Lst 90-; Office Tech; Adm Asst.

**FERNANDEZ, BRIDGET A,** Temple Univ, Philadelphia, PA; JR; BS; Vrsty Tennis 90; Physical Ed; Physical Therapy.

**FERNANDEZ, CESAR A,** City Univ Of Ny City Coll, New York, NY; SO; BA MA; Econ Soc 90-; Econ; Law.

**FERNANDEZ, GUSTAVO ADOLFO,** Alfred Univ, Alfred, NY; SO; BA; Ibero Amer Stdnt Ynion Sec 90-; Inst Ind Engrs 90-; Ind Engrs Awd Alfred Univ; Ind Eng.

**FERNANDEZ, IJALU,** Lincoln Univ, Lincoln Univ, PA; JR; Activities Prgrm Brd 90-; Chinese Clb Sec 90-; Alpha Chi; Alpha Mu Gamma; Schlrshp Ntnl Taiwan Normal Univ Mandarin Trng Cntr.

**FERNANDEZ, IVONNE D,** Miami Dade Comm Coll South, Miami, FL; SO; BA; AA 91; Psych.

**FERNANDEZ, JONATHAN L,** Nova Univ, Ft Lauderdale, FL; GD; CPA; BSC U Of WI 84; Accntnt; Admin.

**FERNANDEZ, KRISTINA I,** Univ Of Pr At Rio Piedras, Rio Piedras, PR; JR; Choir; Concert Choir; Cmnctns; Jrnlsm.

**FERNANDEZ, LETTICIA,** Cumberland County Coll, Vineland, NJ; FR; Psychlgy; Indstrl Psychlgst.

**FERNANDEZ, LIZBETH,** Fl International Univ, Miami, FL; SR; BS; Kappa Delta Pi Sec 88-; Future Edctrs Am 87-; Elem Ed.

**FERNANDEZ, LYNN M,** Miami Dade Comm Coll, Miami, FL; SO; BA; Bsnss/Law.

**FERNANDEZ, MARIA C,** Miami Dade Comm Coll South, Miami, FL; SO; AA; Tlnt Rstr Otstndng Mnrty Stdnt; Pharm/ Chem.

**FERNANDEZ, NIELSEN Q,** City Univ Of Ny City Coll, New York, NY; SO; BS; Presb Hsp Allen Pavillion 90-; Biol; Med.

**FERNANDEZ, NORMA,** Fl International Univ, Miami, FL; SO; BA; Fclty Schlr; Comp; Comp Sci.

**FERNANDEZ, ONEIDA,** City Univ Of Ny Baruch Coll, New York, NY; SR; BBA; Rcyclng; Mrch Dms; Phi Theta Kappa 88; Alpha Beta Gamma 88; Golden Key 90; Sigma Iota Epsilon; SHRM PR; AS Queensborough Comm Clge 88; Hmn Rsr Mgmt; Tch.

**FERNANDEZ, OSCAR G,** Oh Wesleyan Univ, Delaware, OH; FR; BA; Middle Hgh Schl Tutor; Ntnl Hnr Society VP 90; Clbs/ Actv Choral Art Scty Mbr 90; Eng Major; Tchng.

**FERNANDEZ, OSVALDO C,** Inter Amer Univ Pr Guayama, Guayama, PR; FR; BA; Bsktbl 90-; Crmnl Jstc; Law.

**FERNANDEZ, RAMON RUIZ,** Bayamon Central Univ, Bayamon, PR; FR; BA; Spnsh Clb Ldr 89-90; Sci Invstgtn Clb 88-89; Coop Ssn 89-90; Ftr Tchr Assn 90-; Vctnl Cnslng Brkdwn Fvr Cnslr 87-88; Bkstbl 88-89; Phy Ed Dsbld Chldrn.

**FERNANDEZ, RAUL E,** Miami Dade Comm Coll South, Miami, FL; JR; MBA; AA MDCC 90; Finance.

**FERNANDEZ, RICHARD,** Broward Comm Coll, Ft Lauderdale, FL; SO; AA; Phi Thetta Kappa; Alpha Eta Rho 89-90; Pres Lst 90; Bsn.

**FERNANDEZ, ROBERTO A,** Life Coll, Marietta, GA; GD; Gonstead Clb 90-; Point Zero Clb; AA Miami Dade Cmnty Clg 89; Chiropractic.

**FERNANDEZ, SUSANA M,** Miami Dade Comm Coll South, Miami, FL; SO; MBA; Phi Theta Kappa Pres; Stu Assoc Envrnmt Sec 90; William Mcknight Schlrshp 90-; Otstndg Bus Stu Hnr Cnvctn 90-; Otstndg Acdmc Achvmnt Awrd 90-; IM Cmptn 90-; Htl Mgmnt.

**FERNANDEZ, SYLVIA C,** Univ Of Miami, Coral Gables, FL; JR; BBA; Hillel 88-89; Hnrs Stdnt Assn; Psi Beta VP 90-; Gldn Key 89-; Beta Gamma Sigma 89-; Phi Eta Sigma 89-; Beta Alpha Psi 89-; Dns Lst 88-; Pres Hnr Rl 89-; Sngr Full Schlrshp 88-; Sprtsfst 90; Acctng/Psychlgy; Rsrch Psychlgy.

**FERNANDEZ, TANYA,** Fl International Univ, Miami, FL; SR; MBA; SGA 87-89; Amer Mktg Assn 90-; Italian Clb Sec 87-88; Phi Kappa Pi 90-; Phi Eta Sigma Sec 88-; Beta Gamma Sigma; Jacobson Advtsng Agcy Intrn; Vybl 90-; BBA; Bus; Mktg.

**FERNANDEZ, TARA L,** Univ Of Fl, Gainesville, FL; JR; BSN; Nrsg Stdnt Assoc Rec Secr 90-; Nrsg Clg Cncl Jr Repr 90-; Golden Key 90-; Campus Organized Against Rape 89-; Chi Omega 89-; AA Univ FL 90; Nrsg.

**FERNANDEZ, TOURE,** Cheyney Univ Of Pa, Cheyney, PA; SR; BA; Alkebu-Lan Nation Inc Pres 89-; Deans List 89-; Judith Stark Writing Contest 88; Cmnty Clge Speech Contest 89; Campus All Star Challenge; Psychology; Psychological Consultant.

**FERNANDEZ, VIVIAN R,** Univ Of Pr At Rio Piedras, Rio Piedras, PR; FR; BA; Stdnt Cncl Rm Rep 86-90; Clss Ofcrs Pres/ VP 86-90; Spts Cncl P R Ofcl 89-90; Jr Natl Hon Soc Hstrn 86-87; Natl Hon Soc 88-90; 2004 Olymp Comm Vol Mbr 90-; Valdctrn 89-90; Vllybl Jr Vars Vars 86-89; Mrktng.

**FERNANDEZ JR, W WARREN,** Univ Of Miami, Coral Gables, FL; SR; BS; Diving Clb; Clmbng/Hkng Clb; Natl 89-; Lambda Chi Alpha 89-; Physcs.

**FERNANDEZ-BOFILL, RAMON,** Univ Of Miami, Coral Gables, FL; FR; Alpha Lambda Delta 90-; Art.

**FERNANDEZ-MIRA, ELISA,** Fl International Univ, Miami, FL; GD; Hnr Mntrs Prgrm 88; Phi Kappa Phi 90-; Certf 90; Certf French Alliance Universite De Nancy Paris 85; French; MS Htl Fd Srvc Mgmnt.

**FERNANDEZ-RIERA, YADIRA,** Univ Of Miami, Coral Gables, FL; SR; BSN; RN; ICU Nurse; Diplma RN Jackson Mem Hosp Schl Of Nursing 83; Nursing; MSN.

**FERNANDO, BERNADETTE D,** Elms Coll, Chicopee, MA; FR; BSC; Elms Clg Intl Clb 90-; Clg Of Chem Clb 90-; Orient Adv For Orient At Elms 90; Chem Achvmnt Awrd At Elms 90-; OL Colombo Intl Schl 90; Bio/Chem; Med.

**FERRAGONIO, MELISSA J,** Duquesne Univ, Pittsburgh, PA; FR; BA; Law.

**FERRAIOLO, JACK D,** Albertus Magnus Coll, New Haven, CT; FR; BA; Stdnt Activities Brd 90; VP Frshmn Class 90; Act 2 Theater; Deans Lst 90; Chrch Clwn Clb 90.

**FERRAN, SARAH C,** Miami Dade Comm Coll South, Miami, FL; SO; AA; Phi Theta Kappa; Coral Way Merchnts/Owners Assoc Sec; Phtgrphr Antique Dlr/Rstrer; Human Biology; Nursing.

**FERRAO, JOAQUIN E,** Fl International Univ, Miami, FL; FR; BA; Clge Rpblcns 90-; Internatl Rltns; Frgn Serv Career.

**FERRAR, CHERYL M,** Oh St Univ, Columbus, OH; SR; BS/ MA; Alpha Lambda Delta 87-; Phi Eta Sigma 87-; Arts/Sci Excel Schlrshp 90; Excel Math Award; Dns Lst 87-; Math; Tchr.

**FERRAR, GEORGE C,** Gordon Conwell Theol Sem, S Hamilton, MA; GD; MDIV; Vineyard Christian Fellowship; Exhibited Photos; Mc Gill Univ Schrlshp; Ntl Press Photographers Assoc; Tchng Evening Clg Courses Graphic Desig; MS Mass Comm Boston Univ 84; BA English Lit Mc Gill Univ 77; Ministry.

**FERRARA, JO ANN M,** Coll Misericordia, Dallas, PA; SO; BA; Stdnt Occup Thrpy Assoc 89-; Stdnt Hnrs Assoc 89-90; Peer Tutor 90-; Hnrs Schlrshp 89-; Occupational Therapy.

**FERRARA, MARC B,** Univ Of De, Newark, DE; FR; MBA; Vrsty Rcqtbl Clb V P 90-; Self-Defns; Mktg/Oprtns; Corp Exec.

**FERRARA, PATRICIA D,** Newbury Coll, Brookline, MA; GD; Cls Rep Eng Crmnl Law Litigatin; Paralegal; Law.

**FERRARI, GINA C,** Endicott Coll, Beverly, MA; FR; BA; Learn Cncl 90-; Hnrs Prog 90-; Internship; Hotel Rest Mngmnt.

**FERRARI, KAREN A,** Univ Of Sc At Columbia, Columbia, SC; FR; BS; Alpha Lambda Delta Cncl; Phi Eta Sigma; Chi Omega Schlrshp Chrmn; Pres Lst 90; Most Schlrly; Emrgng Ldrs Prog; Htl/Rstrnt/Trsm Admin; Htl/Trsm Mgmt.

**FERRARI JR, RICHARD J,** Wv Univ, Morgantown, WV; GD; IEEE 89-; Eta Kappa Nu 90-; Tau Beta Pi 90-; Deans Lst 89-; BSEE 90; Elect Eng.

**FERRARO, ANNE MARIE,** Rensselaer Polytechnic Inst, Troy, NY; GD; MS; Union Exec Brd Pres 88-; Pep Band Mgr 86-; Stdnt Orient Chrprsn 87-; Phalanx Ldrshp Hnry Soc Pres 88-; Upsilon Pi Epsilon 88-; Phi Sigma Sigma Rush Chrprsn 87-90; Wmns Ice Hockey 90-; Cmptr Sci; Cnsltng.

**FERRARO, CHRISTINE A,** Endicott Coll, Beverly, MA; FR; Sol Ldr; Orien Ldr; Intrnshp The Essex Asst Actvts Dir; Gerontology.

**FERRARO, SHARON,** S U N Y Coll Of Tech At Delhi, Delhi, NY; SR; Prmsng Schlrs Schlrshp Awrd 90; Prcptrshp Delhi Anml Hosp; Westbrook Vet Clnc NY; AAS Equine Sci 83; AAS Vet Tech; Vet Tech.

**FERRAVANTI, KIM S,** Dowling Coll, Oakdale Li, NY; SR; BBA; Cigna Ins 87-; Mgmt; Bus.**

**FERREE, KIMBERLY S,** Fl St Univ, Tallahassee, FL; SR; BS Appalachian St Univ 81; Acctng; Cpa.

**FERREIRA, CUSTODIO J S,** Univ Of Rochester, Rochester, NY; SO; Scty Hispanic Prof Engrs Pres 90-; Am Inst Chem Engrs 89-90; Amer Scty Mecl Engrs Prog Chrmn; Bausch/Lamb Schlr 89-; Engrg; Mechl Engrg.

**FERREIRA, DARREN V,** Hillsborough Comm Coll, Tampa, FL; SO; BA; Phi Theta Kappa 90-; AA; Natural Sci; Med.

**FERREIRA, ELIZABETH,** Rivier Coll, Nashua, NH; SR; BA; Modern Lang Clb Pres 87-; Campus Newspaper 89-90; St Joseph Soc 87-; Portuguese Continental Union 87-; Stdnt Tutor 88-; Portuguese Cont Union Schlrshp; Union St Jean Bapt Schlrshp; Frnch/Spnsh; Law/Interpreting.

**FERREIRA, SUZANNE LOURENO,** Gallaudet Univ, Washington, DC; JR; Bisonettes Clb 89-; Deans Lst 87-90; MVP Bkbl Sftbl 87-; Bus Mgmt/Cmptr Sci; Sys Anlyst.

**FERRELL, ELAINA J,** Univ Of Miami, Coral Gables, FL; SR; BA; WVUM Campus Radio News Dir 87-88; Earth Alert Envir Clb 88-; Hnrs Stdnts Assoc 87-; Alpha Lambda Delta Hstrn 88-89; Henry King Stanford Schlrshp 87-; Harrison Book Prize Hnrs Achvmnt; Politics/Ecology; Envir Pol/Actvsm.

**FERRELL, KAREN D,** Univ Of Tn At Martin, Martin, TN; SO; BS; Geogrphy; Trvl/Toursm.

**FERRELL, LISA A,** Middle Tn St Univ, Murfreesboro, TN; SR; BA; Scty Intl Affairs Pres 88-; TN Assoc Political Sci Student Chrmn 88-90; Yng Clg Republ 88-; Pi Gamma Mu 90-; Pi Sigma Alpha 89-; Alpha Mu Gamma 90-; Psi Chi 90-; Alpha Omicron Pi VP 87-; Kappa Alpha Order Southern Bell 88-; Intl Reltns; Law Schl.

**FERRELL, MICHAEL DAVID,** Vance Granville Comm Coll, Henderson, NC; JR; AAS; Vet Admin Med Ctr; Radiologic Tech; Radiography Imaging Rssrch.

**FERRELL, PETRA C,** Davis & Elkins Coll, Elkins, WV; FR; BA; Ortr Scty 90; Hstry; :.

**FERRELL III, WILLIAM B,** Marshall University, Huntington, WV; JR; BS; WV Amer Academy Of Family Physicians 85-; Family Medicine Foundation Vol; Amer Academy Of Family Physicians Asst To Ex Dir; Business; Assoc Mgmnt.

**FERRELL JR, WILLIAM T,** Coppin St Coll, Baltimore, MD; SR; Psych Clb 1ST VP 90-; BS; Business/Counseling Psych.

**FERRER LARACUENTE, MARITZA I,** Inter Amer Univ Pr San German, San German, PR; BA; Beta Beta Beta Asst; Hon Cert 90-; Bio/Microbio; Med Tech.

**FERRER, ERNESTO JUAN,** Univ Of Pr At Rio Piedras, Rio Piedras, PR; FR; Math; Mech Eng.

**FERRER, IRELA,** Miami Dade Comm Coll, Miami, FL; SO; BS; Math; Edn.

**FERRER, JACINTO ROBLES,** Caribbean Univ, Bayamon, PR; JR; Red Cross Pr 87; Sci Clb; Hon Mention 87; Prize In Sci 87; GPA Awrd 90; Bsktbl 88-89; Sci Educ; Med.

**FERRER, JESSICA E,** Inter Amer Univ Pr Hato Rey, Hato Rey, PR; FR.

**FERRER-FRAU, RAYMA M,** Univ Of Pr At Rio Piedras, Rio Piedras, PR; SR; BA; Scty Of Hstry Stdnts 1st Dir 90; Hostess Intrntl Olymp Cmmttee 89; Dstngshd Stdnt 89; Hnr Awd Free Tuition 89; History; PHD Tchng/Rsrch.

**FERRERA, CARLOS,** Barry Univ, Miami, FL; BA; Dir Admin Svcs; Bus Mgmt.

**FERRERAS, SOLYMAR,** Georgetown Univ, Washington, DC; FR; BA; Puerto Rican Assn 90-; Latin Am Assn Sec 90-; CAHA 90-; Govt; Law.

**FERRERI, MARK A,** Seton Hall Univ, South Orange, NJ; SO; BED; Kappa Delta Pi; Hist; Teach/Law.

**FERRETTI, ENRICO F,** Newbury Coll, Brookline, MA; MED; Silver Key 83-84; Summa Cum Laude; Hnrs Certs; AS Food Serv Mngmnt; Food Serv Mngmnt; Tchr.

**FERRIE, SUSAN V,** Fl St Univ, Tallahassee, FL; SR; BS; Hnrs & Schlrs Prog Rec Chr 87-89; Habitat For Humanity 90-; Phi Eta Sigma 88-; Beta Kappa Alpha 88-; Golden Key 88-; Phi Kappa Phi 88-; Sigma Kappa Schlrshp Chr 88-; Dist Coll Of Am; Fin/ Multinatl Bus; Fin Mgmt.

**FERRIGNO, JOSEPHINE N,** Georgetown Univ, Washington, DC; FR; BS; Deans Lst 90; SGC Intrn 90; Frnch; Intl Law.

**FERRILL, ALISA L,** Radford Univ, Radford, VA; SR; Stdnt Ed Assoc; Deans Lst; BS; Early Chldhd Ed; Tchr.

**FERRILL, JULIE D,** Ms St Univ, Miss State, MS; SR; BS; Air Force ROTC Cdt Mjr 89-; Bptst Stdnt Un 89-; Arnold Air Soc 90-; Gamma Beta Phi 90-; Beta Beta Beta; AA Pearl Rvr Jr Clg 89-; Microbiology; Air Force Offcr.

**FERRIN, JACQUELINE L,** S U N Y Coll Of Tech At Delhi, Delhi, NY; SO; BED; Assoc Trvl Exec 90-; Phi Theta Kappa 89-; Htl Mgt.

**FERRIOLA, VINCENT F,** Widener Univ, Chester, PA; SR; BS; Wdnr Univ Acctg Scty 87-90; Alpha Chi 89-; Phi Eta Sigma 87-88; Phi Kappa Phi; Lambda Chi Alpha 89-; Acctg.

**FERRIS, ANNA-MARIE,** John Tyler Comm Coll, Chester, VA; FR; Tchrs Asst Yth Cnslr Retail Sls 90-; Engl Tchr.

**FERRIS, BROOK,** Longwood Coll, Farmville, VA; FR; BSBA; Geology Geography; Envrnmntl Sci.

**FERRIS, CYNTHIA D,** Truett Mc Connell Coll, Cleveland, GA; SO; BED; Engl; Tchr.

**FERRIS, KATHERINE RUTH,** S U N Y Coll Of Tech At Alfred, Alfred, NY; SR; BS; Adpt Yth 89-90; Yrbk 88; Ski Clb 88-89; Sigma Chi Nu Alfrd Univ 90-; Ski Clb 88-89; AAS; Blgy Mdcl Lab Tchnlgy.

**FERRO, ANN MARIE,** Georgian Court Coll, Lakewood, NJ; SR; BS; Bus Clb 87-89; Pi Dlt Dphi VP 90-; Cert Mgmt/Mktg; Bus Admn; Bnkg.

**FERRO, JANET M,** Fl International Univ, Miami, FL; FR; BA.

**FERRO, MANUEL E,** Univ Of Miami, Coral Gables, FL; FR; BA; Crew Tm 90-; Math; Cmptr Sci.

**FERRO, MONICA A,** Md Coll Of Art & Design, Silver Spring, MD; JR; AS; Mnthly Nws Blltn Bd Serv Amer Corp Coord 90-; Visual Comm; Advrtsng.**

**FERRO, PATRICIA A,** S U N Y Coll Of Tech At Frmgdl, Farmingdale, NY; SR; AS; SGA 89-; AAS Bus Admin 81; Nrsg; Obstrcs.

**FERRON, CHADD W,** Columbus Coll Of Art & Design, Columbus, OH; SR; Soc Illstrtrs; Stdnt Exhbtn Awd; Illstrtn.

**FERRON, NATALIE E,** Fl Atlantic Univ, Boca Raton, FL; SR; BA; Acctg Stdnts Assn Brd Dir; Phi Kappa Phi; Lflng Lrng Soc Schlrshp Awd 90-; Acctg; CPA.

**FERRY, COLLEEN K,** Saint Josephs Coll, Windham, ME; SR; BSN; Stdnt Nrses Assn Sr Clss Rep 87-; Sigma Theta Tau; Vars Sccr 88-89; Nrsng; RN.

**FERTAL, KELLY E,** Xavier Univ, Cincinnati, OH; FR; BA; Mrktng Clb 90; Irsh Clb Pre Law Scty 90; Mrktng; Mstrs Bus.

**FERY, PATRICIA A,** Fl International Univ, Miami, FL; SR; BA; Hotel/Food/Trvl Assoc 90; Jazz Dncng/Rcqtbl/Tennis/Smmng 89-90; Hosp Mgmnt; Hotel.

**FERZIGER, ARI A,** Yeshiva Univ, New York, NY; JR; BA; SG Sntr 90-; Nwspr Gvrng Edtrl Bd 89-; Phlsphy Soc VP 89-; Sigma Delta Rho 89-; Phlthrpy Soc 89-; YUSSR Comm Fin Coord 90-; Deans Lst 89-; Vrsty Tnns Tm 89-; Phlsphy.

**FESI, DE VONNE ANGELA,** Univ Of Southern Ms, Hattiesburg, MS; SR; BA; Sears Dept Mgr 76-85; Slf Emplyd 85-87; Engl; Tchr/Prfssr.

**FESQUET, VICTORIA A,** Va Commonwealth Univ, Richmond, VA; SR; MBA; Hnrs Prog Virginia Cmnwlth Univ 86-; BA; Engl; Wrtg.

**FESSENDEN, MARK D,** Middle Tn St Univ, Murfreesboro, TN; SR; AS Gen Bsns Admn Vol St Comm Clg 85; Mass Comm; Publ Rels.

**FESSLER, JEFFREY J,** Ny Law School, New York, NY; GD; JD; Schl Law Rvw Artcls Edtr 90-; Amer Inst Of Cerf Pblc Acctnts 87-; NJ Soc Cerf Pblc Acctnts 87-; BS Univ Of MD 85; CPA 87; Law/Acctg.

**FESTA BROWNE, GINA R,** Atlantic Comm Coll, Mays Landing, NJ; GD; Amer Culinary Federation 89-; Sci Clb 88; Culinary Arts; Chef.

**FESTER, TRACI E,** Antonelli Inst Of Art & Photo, Cincinnati, OH; GD; Stdnt Govt 90-; Alpha Beta Kappa 89-; Pres List 89-; ASSC Deg Fshn Mrchndsg; Mrktg Cert Mrktng Educ Glen Este Career Ctr 89; Fshn Mrchndsg; Fshn Byr/Arlne Stwrdss.

**FETANAT, GHOLAM H,** Bunker Hill Comm Coll, Boston, MA; SO; ASSOC; Sccr 89-90; Acad Achvmnt Med Asst 86-87; Dns Lst Bnkr Hl Comm Clg 89-91; MSRT; Beth Israel Hosp 90-; Intrn X Ray Texh 89-91; Med Asst Un Tech Inst 86-87; Radiol; BS Radiol.

**FETTERER, AINA L,** Mount Olive Coll, Mount Olive, NC; GD; BS; Jr Achievemnt VP 74-75; ABWA 88; Phi Theta Kappa 82-88; Pres Lst 90; Sprvsr Admin Assist Head Of Data Prcssng 84; AAS Wayne Cmmnty Clg 85; AAS 88; Bsnss Mngmnt; CPA.

**FETTERMAN, KATHLEEN M,** D Youville Coll, Buffalo, NY; SR; BA; FTA Pres 90-; Hnr Soc 90-; Bio Clb 89-90; Order Orioles 90-; Bio Sec Ed.

**FETTY, GLENN A,** Wv Univ At Parkersburg, Parkersburg, WV; FR; BS; Phi Beta Kappa 90; Chem; Analytical Chmst/Envir.

**FEULA, PRISCILLA V,** Felician Coll, Lodi, NJ; SO; BA; Dns Lst 90; Cmptr Sci; Sys Analyst.**

**FEW III, WALTER L,** Morehouse Coll, Atlanta, GA; SO; BS; Hnrs Prog Clb 89-; TN Clb 89-90; Hlth Careers Scty 89-90; Early Idntfctn Prog Biomed Rsrch Brown Univ; Biology; Cardiology.

**FIACCO, DANA M,** Schenectady County Comm Coll, Schenectady, NY; FR; Hdsn Mhwk Fgr Sktng Clb 81-; Clnry Arts.

**FIACCO, KRISTIN F,** Eastern Nazarene Coll, Wollaston, MA; SO; BA; Evangelicans For Socl Actn 90-; Jazz Ensmbl 90-; Wind Ensmbl 89-; Nwsppr 89-; Sigma 89-; Intrnshp Tchng Wrtng 90; Math Cmptr Lab Asst 90; Scuba Cert 89; Engl/Phlsphy; Law.**

**FIALA, TYSON E,** Savannah Coll Of Art & Design, Savannah, GA; JR; BA; Illustration/Graphic Dsgn; Commercial Art.

**FIALKOV, JONATHAN M,** Allegheny Coll, Meadville, PA; JR; BS; Beta Beta Beta VP 89-; Alden Schlr Deans Lst 89-90; Intrnshp Pstn Mansour Med Ctr 90; Bio; Med.

**FIANNACA, JOSEPH S,** Univ Of Rochester, Rochester, NY; SR; BA; Rsrch Vol/Rochester City Schls 88-; Vars Ftbl 87-88; Club Hockey Capt 87-90; Dns Lst 88-90; Psi Upsilon Treas 87; Indpndnt Stdy Wrkr Mtvtn 89-90; Soc Comparisons 90-; Psych; Law.

**FIATO, RITA A,** Hudson Valley Comm Coll, Troy, NY; SO; AAS; Crim Just.

**FICARROTTA, JOSEPH P,** Queens Coll, Charlotte, NC; SO; MBA; Stdnt Govt Assn Treas; Campus Jdcl Bd Sec 89-90; Pres Asst 90-; Janusian Ordr Hon Soc 90-; Pi Kappa Phi Treas 90; Admsns Core 90-; Dana Schlr 90; Deans Lst 89-; Orntatn Cmtee Chrmn 90-; I M 89-90; Bus Admn/Acctg; Bus/Acctg CPA.

**FICHETOLA, LINDA,** Atlantic Comm Coll, Mays Landing, NJ; SO; AS; Nrsng Clb 90-; Nrsng.

**FICHTER, BARBARA A,** Univ Of Pittsburgh, Pittsburgh, PA; SR; BS; Pedology Comm Clg Allghny Cnty 87; Chld Dev; Spec Educ.

**FICHTER JR, GERALD A,** Le Moyne Coll, Syracuse, NY; SR; PHD; Hstry Acdmy Hstry Clb Sec Tres 88-; SADD Orgnzr 89-90; Phi Alpha Theta 89-; Pi Gamma Mu 90-; Dean Lst 87-; Big Bro Big Sis Regnl Asst 87-89; HEOP Prog Mntr 88-; Head Tutor 88-90; Stu Tchr 90-; IM Bsketbl Ftbl Vllybl Capt 87-; BA; Hstry Erly 19th Cent Amer; Coll Prfssr.

**FICK, LISA A,** Univ Of Southern Ms, Hattiesburg, MS; SR; BS; Social Rehabilitation Serv; Psychology.

**FICKIES, MARY M,** Savannah Coll Of Art & Design, Savannah, GA; SR; BFA; ASID 89-90; ISP 90-; Chrprsns Awd; Dipl Durham Coll Appld Arts/Tchnlgy 87-89; Intr Dsgn; Rtl Dsgn.

**FICKLING, ELIZABETH WHITLEY,** Univ Of Sc At Columbia, Columbia, SC; JR; BS; Dorm Govt 90-; Phi Eta Sigma V P 90; Pharm; Med.

**FICORILLI, LYNNE M,** Daemen Coll, Amherst, NY; SR; BSN; Western NY Breastfeeding Ntwrk Bd Of Dir 89-; RN; AAS Niagara Cnty Comm Clg 82; Nrsng; Lactation Spclst.

**FIDLER, AMY D,** Marshall University, Huntington, WV; JR; BA; Amer Clge Of Health Care Executives; Health Care Mgmnt; Hosp Admnstrtn.

**FIDLER, REBECCA S,** Glassboro St Coll, Glassboro, NJ; FR; BA; Psychlgy Clb 90-; Hnrs Prgm 90-; Psychlgy.

**FIDO, MARY ANN,** Albertus Magnus Coll, New Haven, CT; JR; BA; Sr Undrwrtr/Corp Asst Sec Natl Rnsrnce Corp Stmfrd Ct; Bsn; Rnsrnce Undrwrtg.

**FIEDEL, JESSICA L,** Fl St Univ, Tallahassee, FL; FR; BS; Bus; Hsptlty Admin.

**FIELD, CARRIE F,** Newbury Coll, Brookline, MA; Intrnatl Stdnts Orgnztn Yng Entrprnr Clb VP; Mrktng.

**FIELD, CHRISTOPHER R,** Lehigh Univ, Bethlehem, PA; FR; Jazz Ens 90-; Grdn St Schlr; Grdn St Artist.

**FIELD JR, LONNIE D,** De Tech & Comm Coll At Dover, Dover, DE; SO; AAS; DPMA 89-; Phi Theta Kappa 90-; Data Proc; Prgrmr.

**FIELD, SHANE M,** Edinboro Univ Of Pa, Edinboro, PA; SO; BSCS; Phi Eta Sigma 90-; Cmptr Sci; Sys Anlys.

**FIELD, SHERRI A,** Univ Of New England, Biddeford, ME; FR; BS; Cert CPR; RA; Schl Jdcl Bd Stdnt Appeal Jdg; Mdcl Biology; Medicine.

**FIELDEN JR, ROBERT L,** Roane St Comm Coll, Harriman, TN; SO; BA; AS Engr; Mech Engr; Engr.

**FIELDER, MONTE C,** Me Maritime Academy, Castine, ME; FR; AS; Fire Brigade Mrshl; Yacht Clb; Lt Raymond Fire Dept 80-; Castine Fire Dept 90; Flght Instr 87; Bus; Marina Mgmt.

**FIELDHOUSE, HEATHER A,** Univ Of Cincinnati, Cincinnati, OH; FR; BSN; Air Force ROTC P A Asst; Incentive Awd; Rsrv Offcros Assn Bronze Awd; I M Vybl 90-; Nurs; Air Force.

**FIELDS, ALAN P,** City Univ Of Ny Baruch Coll, New York, NY; SR; Day Sessn Stdnt Govt Uppr Cncl 89-; Clb Caricom 87-; W Indian Cultrl Clb 87-; Beta Gamma Sigma; Psi Chi; Beta Gamma Sigma Alumni NYC Mdl; Cecelia S Cohen Mem Awd; Provosts Schlrshp 87-89; BBA; Acctg; Mgmt.

**FIELDS, ANNE MARIE,** Muskingum Coll, New Concord, OH; GD; BA; Chas Dwl Ldrshp Awrd 85; Crw Cptn 84-85; Ntnl Cncl Thrptc Rec Certf; Cncl Fr Excptnl Chldrn Va Prks & Rec; Thrptc Rec Spec; Nctrc 85-; Bs Msu E Lnsng Ml 83, Elem Ed/Lrng Dsblts; Tchr.

**FIELDS, BOBBIE J,** Univ Of Nc At Charlotte, Charlotte, NC; JR; BA; Gldn Ky; Alpha Kappa Delta; Bkkpr/Accntnt 81-; Sclgy; Soc Sci.

**FIELDS, CHAD O,** Kent St Univ Kent Cmps, Kent, OH; JR; BA; Cllgt Bus Assn Trea 90-; Fnnc/Real Est.

**FIELDS, DAVID B,** Univ Of Rochester, Rochester, NY; JR; BS; Weightlifting; Optical Soc; Tau Kappa Epsilon Pylortes 87-; IM Bsktbl; Optical Engr; Engr.

**FIELDS, DAVID C,** Southern Coll Of Tech, Marietta, GA; SO; Deans Lst; IM Sccr; EET; Elec Engr.**

**FIELDS, EDWIN K,** Va St Univ, Petersburg, VA; SR; BS; Bus Dept Awds 86-; USAF 81-; Bus Info Sys; Pgrmmr/Anlyst.

**FIELDS, ENOS M,** Sue Bennett Coll, London, KY; SO; BA; Hon Stdnt Jet Mech Sch Navy 85; Navy AD 3 85-89; Jet Engine Mechanic USS Ranger; Telocommunications; TV.

**FIELDS, GENETTE E,** Benedict Coll, Columbia, SC; SR; BS; Crmnl Just Treas 88-; Alpha Chi; Alpha Kappa Mu; Alpha Kappa Alpha; Crmnl Just; Cnslr.

**FIELDS, JACQUELINE,** Southern Junior Coll, Birmingham, AL; FR; Sci; Nrsng.

**FIELDS, JODI L,** Salisbury St Univ, Salisbury, MD; SR; BED; Coach JV Sftbl; Phi Eta Sigma 87-90; Cum Laude Grad Hon 90; Elem Ed; Elem Tchr.

**FIELDS, KIMBERLY M,** Nc Agri & Tech St Univ, Greensboro, NC; JR; BA; Digit Cir Secty 90-; ACM; SAFE Vltr; Proj Uplift Vltr; Intern Gen Elec 90-; Computer Sci.

**FIELDS, KIMBERLY M,** Al A & M Univ, Normal, AL; FR; BS; Stix Sweetheart 90-; Hmn Rsrcs Office Aide 90; Hnr Roll 90; Music Schlrshp 90-; Chrch Orgnst; Elem Ed; Music.

**FIELDS, LAURIE M,** City Univ Of Ny Queensbrough, New York, NY; SR; AAS; Ni-Prg 89-90; Bus/Mngmt.

**FIELDS, LINDA K,** Wv Univ At Parkersburg, Parkersburg, WV; SO; AAS; Data Prcssng.

**FIELDS, LISA J,** Univ Of Sc At Columbia, Columbia, SC; JR; Nu Beta Pi; Tutor Stdnts 14-17; Educ; Teach.

**FIELDS, LISA JO,** Union Univ, Jackson, TN; SO; Church Activities Calvary Baptist 90-; Occupational Therapy.

**FIELDS, MARCUS D,** Morehouse Coll, Atlanta, GA; JR; BA; Hon Rl 89-; Math Excl Awd 89-90; Appt Air Frc Acad 88; Air Frce ROTC Schlrshp 89-; Bsns; Bnkng.

**FIELDS, MARSHALL A,** Northern Ky Univ, Highland Hts, KY; SR; BS; Chrstn Ch Deacon/Com Chmn 81; Cincinnati Belting/Trnsmsn 89-; AS Cincinnati Tech Coll 87; Inds Tech Manuf; Dsgn Eng.

**FIELDS, MERCEDES P,** Va St Univ, Petersburg, VA; SR; Alpha Kappa Mu Sec 89-; Tmpry Agncs Olsten/Manpwr/Kelly; AAS John Tyler Comm Coll 88; Bus; Grad Schl/Tchng.

**FIELDS, RHONDA C,** Greenville Tech Coll, Greenville, SC; SO; ADN; Nursing RN; Oncology.**

**FIELDS, RITCHIE L,** Tn Tech Univ, Cookeville, TN; SO; BA; Business Mgmt.**

**FIELDS, ROBERT W,** Columbia Univ, New York, NY; FR; BA; Horace Mann Theatre 90-; Church Lang Trade Rusian Engl 90-; Engl; Wrtr/Theatricl.

**FIELDS, SHELLY L,** Marshall University, Huntington, WV; FR; BA; Alpha Chi Omega 90-; Wrk/Stdy Admssns Offce 90-; Acctg; CPA.

**FIELDS, STACY A,** Univ Of Charleston, Charleston, WV; SO; BA; Professional Business Club; Alpha Lambda Delta; Acctng; CPA.

**FIELDS, TAMIKA L,** Alcorn St Univ, Lorman, MS; JR; BA; Hrld 89-; Yrbk Stff 90-; Hon Stdnts Org 88-; Kappa Upsilon 90-; Kappa Mu; Pres Schlr 89-90; Engl/Cmnctns; Pblc Rltns.

**FIELDS, TARSHA D,** Johnson C Smith Univ, Charlotte, NC; SO; BS; Alpha Sweet Heart; Stdnt Govt 89-; Univ Choir 90; Bus Admn; Mgmt.

**FIELDS, TISHA Y,** Hampton Univ, Hampton, VA; FR; BS; AICHE; SCA; NSBE; Eminent Awd; Sthrn Co Srvcs Schlrshp/ Intrnshp; Chem Eng; Eng/Physcn.

**FIELDS, TRACY R,** Univ Of West Fl, Pensacola, FL; JR; BED; Black Stdnt Un 88-90; Alpha Kappa Pres 89-; Elem Edn.

**FIELDS, VALERIE K,** Univ Of Nc At Chapel Hill, Chapel Hill, NC; FR; BA; Carolina Assoc Blck Jrnlsts 90; Kappa Alpha Psi 90; Jrnlsm/Mass Cmunctns; Pub Rltns.

**FIELDS, VERONICA R,** Clark Atlanta Univ, Atlanta, GA; JR; BA; IN Clb 88; Yrbk Stff 89; Nwspr Stff 90; Jrnlsm; Prnt Jrnlsm.

**FIELDS, WILLIAM H,** Comm Coll Algny Co Algny Cmps, Pittsburgh, PA; SO; Peer Tutor; Highland Dr Vet Admin Med Ctr 82-; Biolgcl Sci; RN.

**FIELY, TAMMY L,** Mercer Univ Schl Of Pharm, Atlanta, GA; JR; Acad Stdnts Pharm 90-; Pharmcy.

**FIENBERG, JEFFREY B,** Saint Vincents Coll & Seminary, Latrobe, PA; JR; BS; Psycology Clb; Pre Law Clb; History; Law.

**FIETZE, PAMELA A,** Univ Of Rochester, Rochester, NY; SO; BS; Biol Soc 90-; Sftbl; Deans Lst 90-; Biol; Dentistry.

**FIFER, CRYSTAL S,** Va Commonwealth Univ, Richmond, VA; JR; BSN; SNA 90-; Tckh Vol Rsc Sqd Crhmn Brd 88-; Flg Ftbll 90; EMT State VA 00 ; Hlth Sci; Nrsng.

**FIGARO, RICHARD C J,** City Univ Of Ny City Coll, New York, NY; SR; BENG; Trntcty Pres; ASCE 90; SBE; Gldn Key 90; Chi Epsilon 90; Tau Beta Pi; Rsrch Career Mnrty Schlrs; Var Sccr 90; Cvl Engr.

**FIGAS, WILLIAM F,** Robert Morris Coll, Coraopolis, PA; FR; BA; SAM V P; Commuters Assn; Lambda Sigma; Tutor; Merit Schlrshp 90-; Finance; Bnkng.

**FIGEL, JOHN A,** Washington State Comm Coll, Marietta, OH; Tres Apstlc Chrstn Chrch; Mbr LU 5760 USWA; Cert 76; EET; Elctrnc Engr.

**FIGGINS, JUSTIN E,** Univ Of Rochester, Rochester, NY; JR; BA; Res Advsr 90-; RLAC 90-; Order Omega 90-; Phi Kappa Tau Rsh Chrmn 90-; Oper Welcom Home 90-; Merrill Lynch Intern; Cross Country Track 88-; Econ/Pol Sci; Mktg.

**FIGHTMASTER, ADRIENNE G,** Univ Of Ky, Lexington, KY; JR; BBA; Deans Lst 90; Mgmnt/Comm.

**FIGUERAS, ANITA R,** S U N Y Coll Of Tech At Canton, Canton, NY; SO; BS; Omega Alpha Cl 90-; Acad Tutor; Phi Theta Kappa Chpsn Schlrshp Cmte 90-; Form Admin Asst/Cnfce Cen; BA Potsdam Colg SUNY 73; Acctg; CPA.

**FIGUEROA GAMERO, ROSA,** Inter Amer Univ Pr Hato Rey, Hato Rey, PR; SO; BA; Math; Engr.

**FIGUEROA GARCIA, MARILY,** Univ Of Pr At Mayaguez, Mayaguez, PR; SO; BA; IEEE; Untd St Achvmnt Acdmy 90-; NACME; Indstrl Engrg.**

**FIGUEROA IGLESIAS, JOSE F,** Caribbean Center For Adv Stds, San Juan, PR; GD; PH D; SHRM 90-; MBA Univ Turaba 85; MS 90; Ind Org Psychlgy.

**FIGUEROA LOPEZ, SKARLET D,** Inter Amer Univ Pr San German, San German, PR; SO; Almni Assn Fndtn Vocal; Vol 88-90.

**FIGUEROA MALDONADO, ELVIA M,** Inter Amer Univ Pr Hato Rey, Hato Rey, PR; SR; BS; Tri Beta 90-; Magna Cum Laude; Microbiology; Occptnl Hlth.**

**FIGUEROA MORALES, WILFREDO,** Bayamon Central Univ, Bayamon, PR; GD; BA; Educ Media Assn Sec 89-90; Tech Educ; Instrctr Dsgnr.

**FIGUEROA MUNOZ, ANGEL R,** Catholic Univ Of Pr, Ponce, PR; SO; 1st Hon 90-; Smng Awd 87-88; SSS 90-; UCPR 90-; Math; CPA.

**FIGUEROA NARVAEZ, SANDRA IVETTE,** Univ Of Pr Medical Sciences, San Juan, PR; JR; MA; Ophtalmic Tech Assn PR 89-; Sci; Hlth Sci.

**FIGUEROA ROJAS, PATSULIVIA,** Bayamon Central Univ, Bayamon, PR; GD; BSN; Inst Nrsng Pr; SNA 90-; Cert Hnr Prac Nrsng 86; Cert Prac Nrsng 86; Cert Admin Poguenos Negocis 89; Cert Ceramic 89; Nrsng; Law/Nrsng.

**FIGUEROA VAZQUEZ, LUMARIE,** Inter Amer Univ Pr Hato Rey, Hato Rey, PR; FR; Accounting.

**FIGUEROA, ALBERT,** Strayer Coll, Washington, DC; SR; BA; Alpha Chi 90-; Pi Kappa Phi 83-; VA Army Ntl Grd Sgt 86-; Harris Schlrshp 90; Acctg; CPA.

**FIGUEROA, ANNETTE MARIE,** Univ Of Pr At Rio Piedras, Rio Piedras, PR; SO; Hnr Rl Dr Carlos Ramos 90-; Biol; Med.

**FIGUEROA, GERARDO A,** Univ Politecnica De Pr, Hato Rey, PR; JR; Lap 87-88; Club De Ciencias Pres 87-89; Sis De Tutrs De Epsnol Tutr 87; Ninos Escikhas Ldr De Tropa 88; Math; Egnra Mecanica.**

**FIGUEROA, IRIS V,** S U N Y Coll At Fredonia, Fredonia, NY; JR; Hispanic Sic Treas 87-88/90-; Un Alumni Cncl 90-; Wellness Clb Sec; Hist Hon Soc; Pol Sci Hon Soc; Albany Intern Pgm Albany NY; IM Racquetbl; BA SUNY Fredonia; Intl Rel/Law; Lawyer.

**FIGUEROA, JOCELYN LLORENS,** Catholic Univ Of Pr, Ponce, PR; JR; BA; Acctng Asso PR 89-; Hon Prog 88-; NBHS Secy; Acctng; Law.

**FIKE, CHAD E,** Garrett Comm Coll, Mchenry, MD; FR; AA; Evnglcl Free Chrch Yth Grp 90-; Wldlf Mgt.

**FILBRUN, LEANN,** Miami Jacobs Jr Coll Of Bus, Dayton, OH; GD; AS; Stdnt Advsry Committee 89-; Cllgt Secrtrs Intl; Presidents Lst 90-; Directors Lst 89; Business; Exec Secretarial.

**FILEGER, DAVID M,** Fl Atlantic Univ, Boca Raton, FL; GD; BBA; Corp Mgmt.

**FILEGER, F ELIZABETH,** Eckerd Coll, St Petersburg, FL; SR; BA; Yng Rep Clb 87-89; Psychlgy Clb 88-90; Hnr Schlrshp 87-; Trng 90; Intern; Ply Thrpy; Cnslng Prs 90; Intrmrl 87-89; Chld Psychlgy.

**FILES, PAMELA L,** Davis Coll, Toledo, OH; SO; AAS; Owens Ill 74-; Acctg.

**FILIANO, AMY E,** Immaculata Coll, Immaculata, PA; SO; BA; Campus Mntry 89-90; Psych.

**FILION, MARGARET A,** S U N Y Coll At Fredonia, Fredonia, NY; JR; BS; Otdr Act Unlmtd Clb At Monroe Comm Coll Sec 88-89,Pres 89-90; Stdnt Rn T V Sta; AS Monroe Comm Coll 90; Comm/Media Arts; Sound Rcrdng Eng.

**FILIPEK, DORENE CILETTI,** Duquesne Univ, Pittsburgh, PA; GD; BSBA; Amer Mktg Assn; Phi Eta Sigma; Lambda Sigma Prlmntrn 88-; Magna Cum Laude Grad; Intgrtd Hnrs Prog; Mktng.

**FILITSKE, LAURIE B,** Indiana Univ Of Pa, Indiana, PA; FR; BA; Adlt Stu Assn; Dean Lst 90-; Orville Redenbaucher Sec Strt Schlrshp 90; Prnt Coord Prnt Infr Prjct 90-; Hrng Imprd Educ; Tchng.

**FILLER, TRACY A,** Saint Francis Coll, Loretto, PA; FR; BS; Bio Clb 90-; Trvl/Rec Comm 90-; Cinema Shwcs 90-; Hnrs Pro 90-; Deans Lst 90-; IM; Bio; Marine.

**FILLINGAME, DONALD C,** Univ Of Cincinnati-Clrmnt Coll, Batavia, OH; JR; Gldn Key; AS 90; Fnc/Acctng.

**FILLINGIM, LAUREL K,** Univ Of South Al, Mobile, AL; JR; BA; Baptist Christian Ministry 90-; Alpha Chi; Sec Educ Scl Sci; Teach Middle Schl.

**FILLION, MICHELLE F,** Saint John Fisher Coll, Rochester, NY; JR; BA; BASIC; Alpha Mu Gamma 88-; GTE Academic All Amer 89; State All Star Tm 90; Vlybl Tm; Psychology; Teach.

**FILLIS, PHOEBE R,** Fl A & M Univ, Tallahassee, FL; SR; Schlpr Stf Writer; Lit Vol Am Tutor; Intern Wakulla News Rprtr; Intern Tallahassee Democrat Stf Writer; Lace Crafts Mag Asst Ed; LUA Cert Walculla Cnty FL 88; Sub Teach Cert Mnroe Cnty FL 78; Jrnlsm/Eng; Publ Info Wrk Govt.

**FILOMENA, CHRISTOPHER D,** Univ Of Akron, Akron, OH; JR; BSBA; Akron Brick/Blck Meml Schlrshp 90-; Finance; Bus Cnsltnt.

**FILOMIA, JUDITH M,** Fl International Univ, Miami, FL; SR; Big Sis/Big Bro; AA Miami-Dade Cmnty Clg 89; Elem Ed.

**FILOSOF, JANA,** City Univ Of Ny Baruch Coll, New York, NY; JR; BBA; Mktg; Advtsng.

**FILPO, MARTHA E,** Manhattan Coll, Bronx, NY; JR; Mnrty Stdnt Un Pres 90-F Coll Sen 90-; Coll Lgsltr 89-; Pen Swrd VP Elect; AICE 90-; Scty Hspnc Prfsnl Eng 89-; Cmps Mnstry 89-; Rsdnt Asst RA; Mobil Rsrch Devlp Corp Intern 90-; IM Vllybll 89-; Chmcl Eng; Prct Eng.**

**FIMBEL, JULIE C,** Western New England Coll, Springfield, MA; JR; BA; Data Prcsng Mgmt Assoc 90-; Bowling Club 90-; Lambda Delta 89-90; Delta Mu Delta; Inrnshp At Travellers Ins Co; Bowling Tm 90-; Comp Inf Sys; Sys Analysis.

**FINAN, MARGARET L,** Georgetown Univ, Washington, DC; SO; BSBA; Nw Stdnt Orntn Stf Asst 90-; Stdnt Adv Prog Stdnt Adv 90-; Soph Cls Comm 90-; 1st Hons 90-; 2nd Hons 89-90; Acctg/Philosphy; Acctg.

**FINCH, CABELL B,** Bristol Univ, Bristol, TN; GD; Bus.

**FINCH, DENISE B,** Northeastern Christian Jr Coll, Villanova, PA; SO; ASSOC; Choir Secy 87-89; Bowling 90-; Deans List 90-; Pres List 90-; Pres Schlrshp; Tchrs Aide Hennigan Elem Sch 88-90; Elem Ed; Tchr.

**FINCH, ELIZABETH D,** S U N Y Coll At Fredonia, Fredonia, NY; SR; BS; GSA Ldr 74-; Deans List 89-; YWCA; Acctg; Public/Hlthcr Acctg.

**FINCH, JEFFERY S,** Northeastern Christian Jr Coll, Villanova, PA; FR; AA; Vcs Of Prse Chrs Dir 90-; Gsplrs Chrs 90-; Dns Lst; Bible; Mnstr.

**FINCH, SARAH A,** Univ Of Tn At Martin, Martin, TN; SR; STEA 89-; AS Dyersburg St 88; Elem Educ; Tchr.

**FINCH, TANYA KAY,** Ms St Univ, Miss State, MS; JR; BA; Band 85-; Gamma Beta Phi; Phi Theta Kappa 88-90; Dns Lst 88-89; Pres Lst 89-; Communctns.

**FINCH, WILLIAM R,** Old Dominion Univ, Norfolk, VA; SR; MBA; Beta Gamma Sigma 90; Srvc Mgr 83-; AS Tidewater Cmnty Clg 88; BS 90; Mngmnt.

**FINCHER, AMY L,** Univ Of Nc At Charlotte, Charlotte, NC; JR; BS; Geogrphy; Lctnl Anlys.

**FINCHER, PAMELA J,** Butler County Comm Coll, Butler, PA; SO; BSN; Nrsng Clb 89; Phi Theta Kappa 90; AAS; Nrsng.**

**FINCK, MARGIT R,** Lesley Coll, Cambridge, MA; SR; BS; Cls Offcr Prsdnt 89-; STEP Stdnt Exchng Prgrm Brdfrd Englnd 89-90; Lesley Clg Hnrs Stdnt 88-91; Emrld Key Soc 88-; Acdmc Rspnsblty Comm Stdnt Rep 89-; Hmn Srvcs.

**FINCKE, LESLIE M,** Georgetown Univ, Washington, DC; FR; BA; Dns Lst 90-; Scnd Hnrs 90-; Hnrs Stdnt 90-; Vrsty Fld Hcky 90-; Engl; Pblshng Or Educ.

**FINDLAY, ABIGAIL R,** Methodist Coll, Fayetteville, NC; FR; BSC; Clg Tennis Tm 90-; Bus Admin.

**FINDLEY, MICHAEL C,** Capital Bible Seminary, Lanham, MD; GD; M DIV; Assn Old Crows 82-86; NAM Capt USMCR 90; 1st Allnc Chrch Sndy Schl Tchr 89-; US Govt Actv Mltry 82-86; USMCR 87-90; BA Univ CO 82; Thlgcl Studies; Chrstn Mnstry.

**FINE, AARON L,** Oh Univ, Athens, OH; SO; BFA; Art League 89-; UAL Juried Show 90-; Paintng; Studio Artist.

**FINE, JOANNA K,** Fl St Univ, Tallahassee, FL; JR; BS; Wmn Cmnctns Inc 90-; Cncl Hnr Soc 90-; Gldn Key Nwsltr Edtr 89-; Lambda Pi Eta; Sigma Sigma Sigma Ed Dir 89-; IM 89; Bus Cmnctns; Mgt.

**FINE, LESLIE A,** Tn Tech Univ, Cookeville, TN; SR; BS; AHEA 89-90; THEA 89-90; Bowling League Treas; Home Ec Ed; Teach.

**FINE, RONNY L,** Oh St Univ, Columbus, OH; JR; BLA; Lndscp Archtcr.

**FINEBERG, ALISON B,** Univ Of Rochester, Rochester, NY; SO; BA; Merdn Soc 89-; Dorm Cncl 90-; Univ Deans Lst 89-; Kappa Delta Hs Mngr Schlrshp 89-; Lcl Pgmg Rsrch Asst WCNY-TV 24 90; Pltcl Sci/Psychlgy; Jrnlsm.

**FINELLE, ANNETTE E,** Marywood Coll, Scranton, PA; SR; BFA; Delta Epsilon Sigma 89-; Prfrmnc Lrng 91-; Advtsng Graphics; Grphcs Dsgnr.

**FINGER, DEREK A,** Life Coll, Marietta, GA; GD; DC; SA 88-; Chi-Rho Sec 89-; AA Manatee Cmnty Clg 87.

**FINGER, ROBERT N,** Syracuse Univ, Syracuse, NY; SR; BARCH; Fac Tenure/Reappointmnt Com 90-; Nom Architecture Schlrshp; Architecture.

**FINGERER REICHEL, ANDREA M,** Yeshiva Univ, New York, NY; GD; MA; Yrbk Ed; Spch Pathology/Audiology Clb; Natl Hon Soc; JPSY; Awd Spch/Lang; Audiology.

**FINGERHUT, CHRISTINE G,** Villanova Univ, Villanova, PA; SO; BA; Spnsh Clb; Sigma Delta Pi; Pi Beta Phi; Engl.

**FINK, ALLISON R,** Allegheny Coll, Meadville, PA; SO; BS; Orntatn Advsr; Alden Schlr 89-90; Kappa Alpha Theta 89-; Economics; Corp Mgmt.

**FINK, ANNE M,** Thomas Jefferson Univ, Philadelphia, PA; JR; BSN; Misericordia Campus Mnstry Coord 88-90; Peer Cnslr 88-90; Tutor 88-90; Stdnt Hnrs Assoc 88-90; Nrsg.

**FINK, CONSTANCE L,** S U N Y Coll Of Tech At Frmgdl, Farmingdale, NY; SO; AS; Med Lab Tech Clb 89-; Snrs Med Labs Schlrshp; Lng Bch Mem Hosp; Med Lab Tech.

**FINK, DEENA N,** Yeshiva Univ, New York, NY; SR; BA; NY State Israel Pltcl Actn Comm Camp Lsn 89-90; Cpy Ed The Bus Rvw 89-90; Bus Stff Observer 89-90; Stern Coll Drmtc Soc Treas 90; Sy Syms Schl Bus Dnnr Chrprsn 90-; Sy Syms Schl Bus 90-; Joint Bus Soc; Mktg; Pblc Rltns.

**FINK, HOLLY B,** Lancaster Bible Coll, Lancaster, PA; JR; BS; Cmptr Pgmr/Mktg Grphc Dsgn 88-; DJ Contemp Chrstn Radio Sta 87; AS Radio/TV York Clg PA 84; Cmnctns; Multi Media Prod/Desk Top Publshg.

**FINK, JENNIFER K,** Marywood Coll, Scranton, PA; SO; BFA; Art Clb; Kappa Pi Sec; Art/Dsgn/Illstrtn.

**FINK, MARTIN JAN,** Middle Tn St Univ, Murfreesboro, TN; JR; Pre Vet Med Soc Pres 89-; Delta Tau Alpha 90-; Alpha Gamma Rho ABS Repr 89-; Outstndng Anml Sci Stdnt 89; Outstndng Pre Vet Stdnt; Dns Lst 89-; Vet Med; Gen Prctnr.

**FINK, TRACY L,** Glassboro St Coll, Glassboro, NJ; FR; BA; Chrmns Awrd Biolgy Acad Exclnc Bio 90-; Bio; Envrnmntl Stds.

**FINKE, ANNE M,** Villanova Univ, Villanova, PA; FR; BA; IM Soccr 90-; Crew 90-; Spec Olympcs; Math/Ed; Tchng.

**FINKEL, GALINA,** Univ Of Tn At Knoxville, Knoxville, TN; FR; Bsnss Mngmnt/Psychlgy.

**FINKELSTEIN, ALAN D,** City Univ Of Ny Baruch Coll, New York, NY; JR; BA; Trvl Clb 89-; Deans Lst 88-; Goldn Key 90-; Acctg; CPA.

**FINKELSTEIN, ANDREA L,** Ny Univ, New York, NY; SR; BA; Alpha Sigma Lamba; Fndrs Day Hnrs Convocation; Dns Lst 89-; Intrntl Stdnt; Tchng/Hist.

**FINKELSTEIN, ARIANA D,** Rutgers St Un At New Brunswick, New Brunswick, NJ; JR; BS; Mrchng Bnd 88-; Stdnt Advsrs 89; Stdnt Embsdrs; Pre Vet Med Clb 88; Golden Key; Mu Upsilon Alpha 88; Pub J Dairy Sci 74; Animal Sci; Vet.**

**FINKENBERG, DAVID,** Fl International Univ, Miami, FL; SR; BS; Hotel Food/Trvl Asc 90-; IM Sprts 88-; AA Union Cnty Clg 88; Hosp Mgmt.

**FINKLE, JOSHUA,** Gallaudet Univ, Washington, DC; JR; Im Asst Coor 87-88; Kappa Sigma; Psychlgy; Schl Psychlgst.

**FINKLEA JR, KENNETH M,** Memphis St Univ, Memphis, TN; SR; BS; USMC Sgt Hon Dischg; Comp Tech; Elec Eng; Engrng.

**FINLAND, JASON B,** Valdosta St Coll, Valdosta, GA; FR; BA; Alpha Lambda Delta Sec 90-; Deans Lst; Bsns.

**FINLAY, BOBBIE J,** Nova Univ, Ft Lauderdale, FL; GD; MS; FL Assoc Quality Assurance Prof 88-; Qlty Imprvmnt Asst 87-; ASN Broward Comm Clg Ft Lauderdale FL 73; BSN Fla Internation Univ Miami FL 77; Admin/Mgmnt; Hlth Serv Admin.

**FINLEY, CHRISTA L,** Univ Of Akron, Akron, OH; SR; BS; Akron Cncl Ed Stdnts 89-; Golden Key 90-; Kiwanis Schlrshp 90-; Dns Schlr Pgm; IM Sprts 89-; Elem Ed; Tchg.

**FINLEY, DON C,** Univ Of Sc At Columbia, Columbia, SC; SO; BS; Comptr Sci; Comptr Progrmmng.

**FINLEY, KARA S,** Furman Univ, Greenville, SC; FR; BS; WISER Pres 90-; Rsdnt Hsng Assn Exec Offcr 90-; Stdnt Govt Lectd Mmbr; Phi Eta Sigma; Pi Mu Epsilon; The Delphian 90-; Stdnts Fr Wmns Awrnss Co Pres 90-; CESC Vol 90-; Fllwshp Of Chrstn Athlts 90-; Dns Lst 90-; Wmns Sccr Tm 90-; Math Comp Sci; Comp Bus.

**FINLEY, KEVIN W,** Northern Ky Univ, Highland Hts, KY; SO; BS; Yrbk 88-89; Cmptr Sci Clb; Rsrch Flwshp; Cmptr Sci; Prgrmr Cnsltnt.

**FINLEY, LILKA E,** Fl A & M Univ, Tallahassee, FL; SR; BS; Stdnt Govt Assoc Jr Sntr 89-90; Stdnt Natl Pharmaceutical Assoc; Amer Pharmctl Assoc; Alpha Kappa Mu Sec 90-; Beta Kappa Chi; Phi Eta Sigma 87-; Kappa Epsilon 88-; Alpha Kappa Alpha 89-; Pharmacy; Pharmaceutical Practitioner.

**FINLEY, SARAH C,** Union Univ, Jackson, TN; JR; BA; Pblc Rltns Scty; Rutledge Hnry Hstry Clb; Alpha Psi Omega; Zeta Tau Alpha Pldg Serv Chrmn; Nrsng Hm/Mnstry/Visitation; IM Sftbl; Educ Elem; Teach Elem/Speech.

**FINN, DANIEL B,** Univ Of Rochester, Rochester, NY; JR; BA MA; Frisbee Clb 88-; Bridge Clb VP 88-; Math Clb 90-; Bausch/Lomb Schrshp 88-; Cigna Actuarial Schlrshp 90-; Aetna Actuarial Intrnshp; Vlybl 89-90; Math; Actuary.

**FINN JR, DONALD E,** Radford Univ, Radford, VA; SR; BS; Social Sci; High Sch Tchr.

**FINN, JOHN B,** Le Moyne Coll, Syracuse, NY; JR; BS; Std Snt Rep 90; Acctng Soc; IM Bsktbl/Sccr/Ftbl; Delta Mu Delta; KPMG Peat Mrwk Intshp 90-; Pblc Acctng.

**FINN, LAURA M,** Hudson Valley Comm Coll, Troy, NY; GD; BA; DPMA 90-; Pres Lst 90; Dns Lst 90; Hdsn Rhd Rvr Rnrs Clb; Econ.

**FINN, SHAWN M,** Ky Wesleyan Coll, Owensboro, KY; SR; BA; Parnassus Soc Lit Mag Ed 87-; Alpha Chi 89-; Engl; Sign Lang Interpreting.

**FINN, WILLIAM F,** Hudson Valley Comm Coll, Troy, NY; SO; BED; Crmnl Jstc.

**FINNE, ANNA E,** Univ Of Va Clinch Valley Coll, Wise, VA; SR; MA; Judd Lewis Soc VP 88-; Hnr Crt Repr; Nwspr Asst Ed 88-90/89-; Darden Soc; Chi Delta Rho Sec 88-89/88-; Cir K Internatl Sec 87-89; Woodrow Wilson Vstng Flws Cmte 90-; Hnrs Pgm; Magna Cum Laude; IM Vlybl 87-88; Ancnt Hstry; Prfsr.

**FINNEGAN, BRIAN R,** Cornell Univ Statutory College, Ithaca, NY; SO; BS; Econ.

**FINNEGAN, KIMBERLY A,** Immaculata Coll, Immaculata, PA; SO; BA; Sclgy/Educ; Tchng.

**FINNEGAN, MAUREEN P,** Siena Coll, Loudonville, NY; SR; MBA; Stdnt Evnts Bd Prgmng Pres 89-; Hrvd Mdl UN 89-; Stdnt Sen 89-; Stdnt Jud Bd 90-; Alpha Kappa Alpha; Phi Alpha Theta; Alpha Mu Gamma; Poli Sci Hon Prgm 89-; Pres Lst; Dns Lst; IM Grls La Crosse 88-89; BA; Poli Sci/Frgn Lang; Law.

**FINNEGAN, SHARILYNN M,** Univ Of Sc At Columbia, Columbia, SC; SO; BS; Acstcl Soc Amer 89-; Ntl Flute Assoc 87-; Finnish Mnstry Educ Schlrshp 88; Fnlandia Fndtn Schlrshp 88; U Of S Carolina Music Schlrshp 88; Sub Flute/Piccolo Grnvl Symphny 89-; Cmpct Disc Rcrdg Frmon Civic Bnd 90-; BMUS 86; Mech Engr.**

**FINNEGAN, THOMAS W,** Atlantic Comm Coll, Mays Landing, NJ; SO; Tau Kappa Epsilon TKE 90; Crmnl Justice; Law Enf Off.

**FINNELL, PAMELA D,** Tn Temple Univ, Chattanooga, TN; ASSO; Chrstn Svc Hnr Rl; Bsktbl Tm 89-; Gen Educ; Coach/Tchr.

**FINNER, RAMON T,** Morehouse Coll, Atlanta, GA; JR; BA; NAACP 89-90; Hist Majors Club 90-; Phi Alpha Theta; Coll Intern Mayors Office Milwaukee Wi; Hist; Teach.

**FINNERTY, WILLIAM BOONE,** Georgetown Univ, Washington, DC; FR; MBA; Deans Lst; Inr Cty Wrk; Hlpg Hmls Gvg Blnkts/Food Hmls Strtd Myslf; Hcky; Acctg; Law.

**FINNEY, AMBER C,** Memphis St Univ, Memphis, TN; FR; BS; Rfrmd Univ Fllwshp; Alpha Gamma Delta; Lvng Arms Vol Wrk Med; Ed; Elem Tchr.

**FINNEY, KAREN J,** Daytona Beach Comm Coll, Daytona Beach, FL; FR; BA; Ed.

**FINNEY, LISA A,** Temple Univ, Philadelphia, PA; SR; MPT; Goldn Key 89-; Theta Pi Theta 90-; BA; Phys Thrpy.

**FINNICUM, DEBBIE J,** Wv Northern Comm Coll, Wheeling, WV; FR; BED; Swimming Instrctr Coach 76-; CRNA Belmont Jefferson JVS Audit Div 83; English; Teaching.

**FINNIN, LISA M,** Marywood Coll, Scranton, PA; SO; BFA; Art Clb 89-90; Graphic Dsgn Lab Tchcn 90; Fmly Festival Day; Marywood Deans Lst; Montgomery Cnty Comm Clg Deans Lst 89-90; Campus Ministry; Art Educ; Teaching.

**FINNK, JENNIFER L,** Hillsborough Comm Coll, Tampa, FL; FR; BA; Educ/Math; Tchr.

**FINOCHIO, KATHLEEN A,** Le Moyne Coll, Syracuse, NY; JR; BA; SG 89-90; Budget Comm 89-90; Orchestra 88; Intl Hse Jail Mnstry 90-; Ida Benderson Sr Ctr Intern; Salv Army Golden Age Intern; Hnrs Proj; Sclgy; Hlth Adm.

**FINSTER, LINDA J,** Univ Of Nc At Asheville, Asheville, NC; SR; BS; Full Tuition Schlrshp 89-90; Sales/Mktg Clb 89-90; Dir Mktg Coll Inst Chicago Il; Empl Smoky Mtn Forest Prod/Mktg Spclst; Mktg Mgmt; Bus Direct Mktg.

**FINTONIS, FAITH H,** Endicott Coll, Beverly, MA; SO; AS; Endicott Players Drama Clb 89-; Phi Theta Kappa 90-; Intrnshp Edtl Bstn; Gnrl Edctn; Psychology.

**FIOCCHI, CINDY L,** Cumberland County Coll, Vineland, NJ; FR; AD; Phi Theta Kappa 90-; Pres Lst 90; Deans Lst; Bus; Acctg.

**FIORDELISI, SUZANNE L,** Coll Of New Rochelle, New Rochelle, NY; GD; BA; Eng/Lit.

**FIORE, CHRISTINE A,** Rivier Coll, Nashua, NH; SR; BA; Perspective Campus Newspaper Ed-Chf 88-; Blues Express Asst Dir 89-; Images 89 Asst Ed 88-89; Concord Cmnty Msc Sch Support Dir Dev Intern 90-; BA; Cmnctns; Mktg/PR.

**FIORE, DANIEL A,** Carnegie Mellon Univ, Pittsburgh, PA; JR; BS; Univ Law Soc VP 90-; IM Vllybl Capt 88-; Scotch N Soda Thetr Org Actr/Wrtr 88-89; Phi Eta Sigma 88-89; Lambda Sigma Pres 89-90; Phi Alpha Theta 90-; Andrew Carnegie Soc Schlr 90-; Carnegie Mlln Undergrad Res Grnt 90-; Hstry/Pol Sci; Crim Atty/Law.

**FIORENZA, RICHARD J,** Barry Univ, Miami, FL; SO; Pres Schlrshp; Lutheran Brotherhd Schlrshp 89-; Male Scholar/Athlete Awd 90-; Varsity Bsebl 89-; Sports Mgmnt; Athletic Admin.

**FIORESI, MICHELLE M,** Univ Of Montevallo, Montevallo, AL; JR; BS; Cmps Otrch; Alph Dlt Pi Stndrds 89-; Deans List; Vlybl Bsktbl Sftbl Orchs 88-90; Cnslng/Guidnc; Cnsl/Chrstn Wrk.

**FIORINI, KAREN J,** Marywood Coll, Scranton, PA; SO; BA; Cncl Excptnl Chldrn Pres 89-; Tchrs Tmrrw 89-; Vols Actn 89-; Sigma Pi Epsilon Delta; Spec Ed/Elem Ed; Spec Ed Tchr.

**FIQUEROA, BETZAIDA,** Dowling Coll, Oakdale Li, NY; SR; BSPLS; Huntington Hd St Tchr 86-89; Fmly Res Entrprs Cnslr Mgr 87-90; CDA LIDS 89; Soc Wrkr.

**FIRESTONE, PATRICIA L,** Radford Univ, Radford, VA; SR; BS; Plyrs Guild 88-; Kappa Omicron Nu 90-; Phi Kappa Phi; Envrnmntl Dsgn.

**FIRNSTEIN, MARC R,** Univ Of Rochester, Rochester, NY; JR; BA; IFC 88-89; Delta Kappa Epsilon Rush Chmn; Varsity Bsebl 88-90; Econ; Grad Studies.

**FIRST, DAWN M,** Slippery Rock Univ, Slippery Rock, PA; SR; BA; French Clb; Pi Delta Phi Prsdnt 90-; French; Trnsltr Intrprtr.

**FIRTELL, LESLIE A,** Univ Of Rochester, Rochester, NY; JR; BA; Rho Chi; Psi Chi; Sigma Delta Tau Scl Chrwmn 90-; WOKR-13 Nws ABC Afflte; Psychlgy; Nws Prdctn/Law.

**FIRTH, CAROLYN L,** D Youville Coll, Buffalo, NY; GD; BS; Std Occptn Thrpy Asc 87-; Res Cncl 87-88; Food Serv Comm; Lambda Sigma Sec 88-89; Snr Hnr Soc 90-; Pres Hnr Schlp 87-; NYS Rgnts Schlp 87-; Occptnl Thrpy.

**FISANICK, DAVID,** Saint Francis Coll, Loretto, PA; GD; BSW; Intrnshp Adult Prob Office Laurel Crest Manor & Altntv Comm Rsrc Ebersburg Pa 89-; Cambria Co Juvenile Det Ctr 90-; AS Mt Aloysius Jr Coll 89; Soc Work.

**FISANICK, MARY ANNE,** Univ Of Pittsburgh, Pittsburgh, PA; GD; BSN; Sigma Theta Tau 90; Mercy Hosp Intern 90; Onclgy Nrsng Soc 88-; Hosp Evening Dir Nrsng 88-; Diploma Mercy Hosp Schl Nrsng 83; Nrsng.

**FISCHEL, PETER C,** Univ Of Miami, Coral Gables, FL; JR; BS; Scuba Safety Diver 90-; Trnsfr Advsry Buddy Sys Advsr 90-; Crew 90-; Marine Sci/Biol; Envrnmntl Eng.

**FISCHER, ANNE M,** Fl International Univ, Miami, FL; SR; BS; Deans List 88-; Licensed Acupunturist; Ph D Univ CA Santa Cruz 85; BS Univ CA Berkely 76; Physical Therapy.

**FISCHER, AUDREY A,** Univ Of Cincinnati-Clrmnt Coll, Batavia, OH; SO; BA; Clermnt Cnty Scl Clb Prnts Without Prtnrs 90-; Phi Theta Kappa 90-; Vlybl Tnns 90-; Mktg; Mktg Mgmt.

**FISCHER, BRIDGETTE M,** Univ Of Montevallo, Montevallo, AL; JR; BS; Orchs Dnc Cmpny 90-; Mntg Stff Acdmc Ed 90-; Prpl Vctry Chrldr 90; Kappa Omicron Nu; Delta Gamma PR Chrmn 90-; Rtl Mrchndsng.

**FISCHER, DANIEL,** Univ Of South Al, Mobile, AL; SO; BS; European Stdnt Assn; Tennis Clubs Switzerland; Bus Mgmt Mrktng; MBA.

**FISCHER, DERESA,** Le Moyne Coll, Syracuse, NY; SR; BS; Natl Assoc Acctnts 89-; Delta Mu Delta 89-; Horace Landry Schlrshp 90; WS Smith Memorial Awrd; Crss Cntry 89-90; Acctg; CPA.

**FISCHER, ELIZABETH A,** Univ Of Sc At Columbia, Columbia, SC; JR; BA; Res Hall Gvmt Pres 88-90; Mensa Inc 89-; Gamma Beta Phi Sec 88-; Gldn Key 90-; Sigma Delta Chi Pub Chr 88-; Dow Jones Schlrshp; Mensa Ltd Schlrshp; St Rcd Schlrshp; GA Press Edctnl Fdn Schlrshp; Scripps Howard Fdn Schlrshp; Journalism; Copy Editing.

**FISCHER, JENNIFER,** William Paterson Coll, Wayne, NJ; SR; Lit Mag Ed In Chf 88-90; Res Lite Res Asst 90-; Deans List 89-; Alum Assn Schlrshp 90-; Garden St Schlr 88-; Zeta Beta Tau Little Sis Rep 88-; Eng Intrnshp; Nom For Grad Asstshp; Res Asst 90-; Eng Wrtng/Minor Film; Editing Wrtng.

**FISCHER, MICHELLE A,** Mt Saint Marys Coll & Seminary, Emmitsburg, MD; SR; BS; Sci Clb Pres 87; Admssns Stdnt Assist 89; Beta Beta Beta 90; Geo H Miles Sec 88; Ntl Cath 89; Phlsphy; Frgn Lang HS 89; Campus Mnstry 89; Hugh J Phillips Prze 88; Amer Med Prof Awd 90; Daniel Mannion Schlrshp 90; All Amer Schlr; Im Bsktbl MVP 89; Bio; Med.

**FISCHER, SHAWNE D,** Coll Of Notre Dame Of Md, Baltimore, MD; FR; BA; Yrbk Phtgrphr 90-; Kymry Frshmn Rep 90-; Emrgng Ldr Prgrm 90-; Cmptr Sci.

**FISCHER, TERESA A,** Hillsborough Comm Coll, Tampa, FL; SO; MS; Mallickvdt Awd 77; Amer Soc Radlgc Tech 78-; Amer Assn Med Dosmtrsts 85-; Reg Rad Tech 78-; Reg Rad Thrpst 80-; Cert Med Dosimtrst 88-; AAS Carteret Tech Inst 77; Cert Univ Vir Schl Radtn Onclgy 80; Med Physcs.

**FISCHER, TRACEY L,** Allegheny Coll, Meadville, PA; SR; PHD; Christian Outreach 89-; German 89-; Lifeguarding/Swmmng Instrctr 89-; Alden Schlr 87-; Phi Sigma Iota; Tutor 87-; Study Abraod W Germany; :IM Sports 87-; German/Lit; Intl Bus.

**FISCHETTI, ANGELA P,** Schenectady County Comm Coll, Schenectady, NY; GD; PTA Prsdnt 88-90; Phi Theta Kappa 88-; Sec Assn 88-; Cmmnty Hmn Srvcs 88-; Sec; Bsns Admnstrtn.

**FISCHGRUND, MEG R,** City Univ Of Ny City Coll, New York, NY; SR; BS; Washu Acdmy Physcl Ftns Disciple; Physcl Edctn; Spcl Edctn.

**FISCUS, PATRICIA L,** Webber Coll, Babson Park, FL; SO; BS; Fshn Clb 89-; Ret Mgmt/Fshn Merch; MS/APPRL Txtls.

**FISH, BRIAN S,** Kent St Univ Geauga Cmps, Burton Twp, OH; FR; BA.

**FISH, JEFFREY M,** Cornell Univ Statutory College, Ithaca, NY; FR; BS; Symphonic Bnd 90-; Stdnt Lvstck Show; Cornell Cath Comm 91; Biology; Vet.

**FISH, JOHN A,** Johnson St Coll, Johnson, VT; SR; BS; Johnson State Cross Cntry Tm Dist Champ 86-87; Phys Educ Tchr.

**FISH, JONATHAN E B,** Va Commonwealth Univ, Richmond, VA; SO; BSC; AIESEC VP; Acctng; Law.

**FISH, KEVIN D,** Me Maritime Academy, Castine, ME; JR; BS; Striker Stf 89-90; Bravo Co Hnr Co 89-90; Fresh Cruise Awd 89; Soccer 88-90; Ntcl Sci.

**FISH, KIMBERLY J,** Limestone Coll, Gaffney, SC; SR; BED; Vol Wrk Sth Mtn Chrstn Camp Rd Crss Wtr Sfty Instrctr 89-90; NCATA 86-88; Elem Ed.

**FISH, LISA L,** Fl International Univ, Miami, FL; SO; BA; Phi Eta Sigma; Engl; Tchng.

**FISH, SHARI M,** Indiana Univ Of Pa, Indiana, PA; GD; VETS; Alpha Gamma Delta VP Frat Educ; Chrldng; BS Ed; Elem Educ.

**FISH, SHERI ANNE,** Southeastern Ma Univ, N Dartmouth, MA; SO; BSN; Ophtlmc Asst; Cert Sthestrn Tech Inst 84; Nrsng; Ophthlmc.

**FISH-PARCHAM, CHERYL D,** Howard Univ, Washington, DC; GD; Orchstr; So Othrs Mght Eat; MSW; BA.

**FISHBACK, GLENN R,** Fl St Univ, Tallahassee, FL; SR; BS; IEEE 90-; Engr Hnr Soc 90-; Bsktbl/Sccr/Sftbl 88-; Elec Engr.

**FISHBACK, JANET L,** Ky Christian Coll, Grayson, KY; JR; BS; Radio Stdnt Mgr 89-; Drama 89-; Cncrt Choir Dstny 89-90; Dns Lst 88-; Hands Of Praise Co Dir 88-; Priscillas 90-; Bsktbl 88-89; Elem Educ; Tchr.**

**FISHER, AIMEE J,** Nazareth Coll Of Rochester, Rochester, NY; FR; BS; Camps Mnstry; Soc Just Comm; Env Club; Lifgrdng; Bio.

**FISHER, ALISIA H,** Memphis St Univ, Memphis, TN; JR; BBA; Gamma Beta Phi 86-; GMAC F/I Consltnt; Mgmt; Law.**

**FISHER, ASHLI C,** Art Inst Of Atlanta, Atlanta, GA; FR; Waiting For Apprvl Intrnshp; Psych/Peds; Chld Psychlgst.

**FISHER, BARRY G,** Niagara Univ, Niagara Univ, NY; SO; BA; Glf Tm 90-; IMS 89-; Delta Epsilon Sigma; Alpha Kappa Psi 90-; Acctng; CPA.

**FISHER, BRIAN K,** Coker Coll, Hartsville, SC; FR; BA; Env Clb 90-; Drama Clb 90-; Coffeehouse Cmte 90-; Nwspr 90-; Commissioners; Adv Brd 90-; Asst Nwspr Edtr; Top Ten Stdnt Awrd; Deans Lst 90-; IM Vlybl; Cmctns; Humorist/Doodle Virtuoso.

**FISHER, CATHY C,** Middle Tn St Univ, Murfreesboro, TN; SO; BS; Dance 87-; Kappa Delta Pi; Eary Child Tchr.

**FISHER, CHRISTINA A,** Univ Of Montevallo, Montevallo, AL; JR; BA; SAEA; Kappa Delta Pi 90-; Albm Schl Cnslrs Schlrshp 88-; Vd Crly Hlt Schlrshp 88-; Brns Schlrhsp 90-; ECE Elem Ed; Tchr.

**FISHER, CYNTHIA D,** Hilbert Coll, Hamburg, NY; SO; AAS; Prof Sec Clb Sec 89-90; Sec Sci/Exec; Admin Asst.

**FISHER JR, DAVID M,** Univ Of Nc At Chapel Hill, Chapel Hill, NC; FR; BS; Biology; Orthodontist.

**FISHER, DEBORAH K,** Lexington Comm Coll, Lexington, KY; FR; AD; Nrsng; Trauma Cntr.

**FISHER, DONNA-JEAN M,** Cumberland County Coll, Vineland, NJ; JR; AAS; Phi Theta Kappa 88-90; Deans Lst 88-90; Pres Lst 90; BS Stockton State Coll; AAS 90; Comp Sci; Pgmr Edctnl Sftwr.

**FISHER, DOUGLAS W,** Glassboro St Coll, Glassboro, NJ; SO; BA; Radio Sta News/Sprts Announcer 90-; Liberal Arts; Comm/Jrnlsm.

**FISHER, DOUGLASS HAYDEN,** Richard Bland Coll, Petersburg, VA; FR; BA; Stdnt Ldr Cath Yth Rtrt 90-; Cert Safety Instr.

**FISHER, ELIZABETH M,** Univ Of Rochester, Rochester, NY; SR; BA; Sigma Delta Tau 88-; Campus Y 90-; Family Care Pgm 90-; Tutor 90-; Inst European Studies Madrid Spain 90; IMS 88-90; Mgmnt Cert; Spnsh; Bus/Mgmnt/Human Resources.

**FISHER, ERIC J,** Morehouse Coll, Atlanta, GA; FR; BA; Hnr Rl 90-; Shrine Tmple 74 Schlrshp 90-; Geo W Wilson Ldg 101 Schlrshp; Bus; Law.

**FISHER, FRANK T,** Univ Of Pittsburgh, Pittsburgh, PA; FR; BS; Fessenden Trott Eng Schlrshp 90-; Natl Mrt Semi Fnlst 90-; Mech Eng/Math; Engr.

**FISHER, GINA A,** City Univ Of Ny Bronx Comm Col, Bronx, NY; JR; BA; Edctn Soc VP 89; Ltrcy Mag; Phi Theta Kappa 89; Tlnt Rstr Otstndng Mnrty; Cmmnty Clg Grad; Intrnshp Asst Sprts Rsrch Coord Wrld Leg Ftbl USA Ntwrk; Intrnshp Stdnt Tchr CS 44 Brnx 89; Englsh; Cmmnctns.

**FISHER, GREGORY M,** Clarkson Univ, Potsdam, NY; SR; BA; Ski Club VP 85-86; AMA Amer Mktng Assoc 89-; Peer Advisor 89-; General Mgr; AS Suny Cable Skill 84-86; Mgt/Mktng.

**FISHER, JANNIFER K,** Alcorn St Univ, Lorman, MS; JR; Bio Clb 90-; Deans Lst 89-; Hlth Sci/Phys Therapy.

**FISHER, JO ANNE,** Central Pa Bus School, Summerdale, PA; FR; BS; Legl Stdnts Assn 90-; Crim Just; Law Enfrcmnt.

**FISHER, JODY JOHN,** S U N Y At Buffalo, Buffalo, NY; SR; BS; Omega Rho 90-; Intern Comptek Rsrch 90-; Indstrl Eng; Eng.

**FISHER, JOHN J,** East Stroudsburg Univ, E Stroudsburg, PA; SO; BA; Bus; Acctg.

**FISHER, KAREN M,** Duquesne Univ, Pittsburgh, PA; SR; BSBA; Beta Alpha Sec 90; Alpha Gamma Delta Activities Chrmn 90; Intrnshp Lhormer Real Estate Agncy; Bsn Real Est/Mrktng; Real Est Develp.

**FISHER, KATHERINE L,** Oh Univ-Southern Cmps, Ironton, OH; JR; AB; Rnbw Clb Grls 86-; Frnd Lbry 89-; 1st Presbytrn Chrch 74-; Alpha Lambda Delta Rep 90-; Golden Key; Cncl Psych.

**FISHER, LAINIE M,** Fl St Univ, Tallahassee, FL; JR; BA; Mamie Tyner Ed Schlrshp 90-; Deans List; AA Okaloosa Walton Comm Clg 90; Ed; Scl Sci Ed.**

**FISHER, LAURE A,** Wilmington Coll, New Castle, DE; SR; BSN; Amer Assn Crtcl Cr Nrses; RN In Crtcl Cr Unit; ADN DE Tech/Commnty Coll 86; Nrsng.

**FISHER, LEONA L,** Mayland Comm Coll, Spruce Pine, NC; FR; Dns Lst 90-; Bio/Math; Path/Cytlgy.

**FISHER, MARIA A,** Univ Of Akron, Akron, OH; JR; ACES 90-; Alpha Lambda Delta 89-; Elem Educ; Tchr.

**FISHER, MARIA P,** Univ Of Akron, Akron, OH; SR; BSN; Ntnl Assc Stdnt Nurses 90-; Gldn Key 89-; Sigma Theta Tau; Deans List 87-; USAA All AM Schlr Large Division 90-; Ntnl Cllgt Nrsng Awrd; Nrsng.

**FISHER, MARJORIE C,** Salisbury St Univ, Salisbury, MD; SO; BS; Geographic Soc; Phi Eta Sigma; Happening Diocese Of Easton Lay Dir; Yth Ldr 87-; Geography; Tchr.

**FISHER, MARK L,** Middle Tn St Univ, Murfreesboro, TN; SO; BS; Gamma Beta Phi 90-; Alpha Eta Rho; Aerospace; Pilot.

**FISHER, MEGHAN E,** Schenectady County Comm Coll, Schenectady, NY; FR; AAS; Ed; Tchng.

**FISHER, MONISA A,** Univ Of Nc At Asheville, Asheville, NC; FR; BA; Bapt Stdnt Union 90; Cmmnctns; Law.

**FISHER, NATHAN W,** Middle Tn St Univ, Murfreesboro, TN; JR; BS; Delegate Southern Invitation/Deep South; Intl Rltns; Grad Schl.

**FISHER, NICOLE L,** Mary Baldwin Coll, Staunton, VA; JR; BA; Stdnt Snt Co Chrwmn 88-; Amer Chem Scty Pres 88-; Omcrn Dlt Kappa; Alph Lmbd Dlt 89-; Beta Beta Beta; Iota Sgm Pi; Math Tutor 90-; Chem; Medcn.

**FISHER, SANDRA A,** Memphis St Univ, Memphis, TN; SR; BSED; Elem Educ; Teach.

**FISHER, SANDRA D,** Western Carolina Univ, Cullowhee, NC; GD; BS; Soc Wrk Clb Treas 89-; Bapt Un; Hall Cncl 86-87; Child Dev Cmsn Intrn 90; Soc Wrk.

**FISHER, SCOTT PEARCE,** Radford Univ, Radford, VA; JR; BBA; Intl Acad Mktg/Mgmt 89-90; BUS-PAC Undergrad Advsr 90-; Delta Mu Delta 90-; Psi Chi Treas; IM Soccer/Vlybl 89-; Hmn Res Mgmt/Psych; Bsn Cnsltg.

**FISHER, SHARON L,** Memphis St Univ, Memphis, TN; SR; BA; Nwspr Edtr 89-90; Soc Prof Jrnlsts VP 89-; Kappa Tau Alpha 90-; Chi Omega 86-87; Mike Mc Gee Gridiron Schlp 90-; Best Ftr Wrtr Daly Hlmsmn Awd 89-90; Outstdng Nwspr Std Awd 90-; Jrnlsm/News Edtrl; Fiction Novelist.

**FISHER, SHERRY ANN,** Salisbury St Univ, Salisbury, MD; GD; US Army Career Soldr 78-; AA Univ MD 86; BS 90; Mgmt.

**FISHER, STANLEY M,** Mayland Comm Coll, Spruce Pine, NC; SR; Automtv Body Repair.

**FISHER, STEPHEN A,** Medical Coll Of Ga, Augusta, GA; JR; BSN; Undrgrd Prog Comm; GANS; Pi Kappa Alpha; Army ROTC Schlrshp; GA Army Natl Gd; Nrsng; Admin.

**FISHER, SUSAN S,** Univ Of Sc At Columbia, Columbia, SC; SO; BS; Acctg.

**FISHER, TAMMY D,** Memphis St Univ, Memphis, TN; SR; BA; Fashion Board 80-81; Alpha Delta Pi Treas 80-82; Commt Organ 90-; Trnsplnt Fund USA Henderson; Staff Acct 89; Acct Bsn.

**FISHER, TAMMY W,** Thomas Nelson Comm Coll, Hampton, VA; FR; Nwspr Stf Ed 90; Eng Tech Gannett Fleming Inc; Eng.

**FISHER, TOBIN J,** Univ Of Al At Birmingham, Birmingham, AL; JR; BS; Alpha Epsilon Delta Sec; Phi Sigma; Gldn Key; Dns Lst/Pres Hnrs 88-; Ntrl Sci; Med.

**FISHER, TODD A,** Slippery Rock Univ, Slippery Rock, PA; SO; PSAHPERD 89-; PHERD 89-; Phi Eta Sigma 89-; Deans Lst 89-; JV Sccr 89; IM Street Hcky/Indr Sccr 89-; Sport Mgmt/Bus Admin/Spnsh; Mtrsprts Auto Rcg.**

**FISHER, TONYA M,** Howard Univ, Washington, DC; JR; BA; Alain Locke Phlsphcl Soc 88-; Hnrs Pgm 88-; Lib Arts Hnrs Asc 88-; Stdnt Ambsdr 89-; Gldn Key 90; Ntnl Cmptitv Schlrshp 88-; Dns Lst 89-; Phlsphy; Law.**

**FISHER, TRACY J,** S U N Y Coll Of Tech At Alfred, Alfred, NY; SO; BS; Biotech Clb Pres 90-; Socl/Behav Sci Clb 89; Phi Theta Kappa; Sigma Tau Epsilon 89-90; Kinship Yth Srvcs Vol; Proj Shape 90; AAS Alfred State Coll; Genetics; Rsrch.

**FISHER, VICKI G,** Middle Tn St Univ, Murfreesboro, TN; SR; BBA; Tau Omcrn 90-; Gamma Beta Phi 90-; Beta Alph Psi Sec 90-; Beta Gamma Sgm 90-; FAA 90-; Intrnshp Rogers Grp Inc; Acctg; CPA.

**FISHER, VINESSIA T,** Fl A & M Univ, Tallahassee, FL; JR; BS; FL A & M Gospel Choir 89-; Inst Of Ind Engrs; NASA Schlrs Assn Treas 90-; Intrnshp Marshall Space Flight Ctr 90; Stennis Space Flght Ctr; Champion Intl Paper Co 87-89; AA Pen Jr Clg 89; Indust Engr.

**FISHER-VINES, ANNETTE,** Newbury Coll, Brookline, MA; FR; AA; Hickory Schl Schlrshp Awd 84-85; PBS; Foundation Assist Grants Mgmt Assoc 90-; Certif The Hickory Schl Boston MA 85; Mktng/Busn Mgt; MBA.

**FISK, SHEILA K,** Northern Ky Univ, Highland Hts, KY; SO; AS; RE Sls Licnc KY State Bd Of Rltrs 84; Bookkpr Cert Southwestrn Clg Of Bus 88; Humn Svcs; Chem Depndncy.

**FISKE, MARTINE M,** Castleton St Coll, Castleton, VT; JR; BA; Hstry Clb Pres; Stdnt Educ Assn 89-; Outing Clb 89; Tchrs Asst Hstry 90; Deans Lst 88-; USAA Amer Schlrs; Hstry/Sec Educ; Tchng.

**FISTER, PAMELA A,** Univ Of Cin R Walters Coll, Blue Ash, OH; JR; MBA; AA Raymond Walters Clg 90; Psy; Clncl Psy.

**FITCH, DEBRA R,** Northern Ky Univ, Highland Hts, KY; GD; Scl Wrk Clb; Natl Assoc Scl Wrkrs; Deans Lst Hnrs; Awrd Jvnl Srvcs; Scl Wrk.

**FITCH, JULIE A,** Va Commonwealth Univ, Richmond, VA; SR; BS; SNA Pres 90-; SNAU Bdmbr 90-; Sigma Theta Tau; Alpha Sigma Chi; MCU Hosp Med Respiratory ICU Intrn; Capt Nurs Ftbl Sftbl Vybl Tms 89; Nurs; Masters Degree.

**FITTEN, TEKOIA D,** Tuskegee Univ, Tuskegee Inst, AL; JR; Finance Club 90-; Amoco Intrnshp Chicago IL 90-; Thurgood Marshall Schlr 89-; Business; Finance.

**FITTERLING, MICHAEL A,** Univ Of South Fl, Tampa, FL; JR; BA; Datiuus Anderson Univ; Fine Arts; Cptn/Charter Serv.

**FITTING, CYNTHIA C,** Radford Univ, Radford, VA; SO; BA; Bllng Hse Cncl Adv 89-; Inter/Res Hl Cncl Brd 89-; Pgm Clrnghse Chrp 89-; Alpha Lambda Delta Pres 90-; Outstdng Std Awd Fresh 89-90 Soph 90-; Natl Res Hl Hnry 89-; Bsn; Bsn Admn.

**FITTON, NANA S,** Liberty Univ, Lynchburg, VA; SR; BS; LACT 90-; Kappa Delta Pi 90-; Cum Laude; Educ; Tchr.

**FITTRO JR, RONALD G,** Univ Of Pittsburgh, Pittsburgh, PA; GD; MSN; RN Plng Comm 90-; Sigma Theta Tau 90-; PA Nrs Assn; Nrs Admin; BSN 90; Admin; Htlchr.

**FITTS JR, JAMES R,** Holyoke Comm Coll, Holyoke, MA; FR; BA; Co Fndr Friends Of Bill W; Lrng Asst Ctr Tutor; Bus; CPA.

**FITTS, LISA MARIE,** Middle Tn St Univ, Murfreesboro, TN; SR; BS; Engl; Tchr.

**FITZ, DAVID A,** Univ Of Southern Ms, Hattiesburg, MS; SR; BSBA; Gldn Key 90-; Beta Gamma Sigma; Gamma Beta Phi; Deans Lst 88-; Deans Lst 89-; Accntng.

**FITZGERALD, ALEXANDRA S,** Smith Coll, Northampton, MA; JR; BA; Stdnt Gov Assn Clss VP 90-; Nwspr Wrtr 89-; Hse Cncl Clss Rep 88-90; Schlr 89-90; Edtrl Intrn/New Chorus Mag 90; Ed Intrn CT Mag 90; Advrtsng Intrn Barry Blan/Prtnrs 89; Engl/Econ; Law/Jrnlsm.

**FITZGERALD, AMANDA KATHLEEN,** Thomas Nelson Comm Coll, Hampton, VA; SO; AAS; Exec Sec Wrd Prcssng; Dvsn Sec.

**FITZGERALD, HEATHER L,** Univ Of Cincinnati, Cincinnati, OH; FR; BM; Music/Piano Perf; Tchr/Perfmr.

**FITZGERALD, HOKE S,** Univ Of North Fl, Jacksonville, FL; SR; BSN; AORN; 1LT Fla Natl Grd; Flglr Hosp Oper Rm Nrs; ADN Polk Comm Clg 84; AA Polk Comm Clg 89; Nrsng.

**FITZGERALD, JAMES W,** Univ Of Rochester, Rochester, NY; SO; BA; Soc Actvts Brd Trea 90-; Dorm Cncl Pres 90-; All Cmps Jdcl Cncl 90; Cmmmnty Srv Dorm; Intern Congressman La Falce; Pol Sci.

**FITZGERALD, JEFFREY L,** George Mason Univ, Fairfax, VA; FR; MBA; IM Sprts Offcl 90-F Franklin Co Pssttrs 89-; Intrn Cngrssmn L F Payne; JV Chr Sqd; Bus; Fnc/Acctg.

**FITZGERALD, KATHLEEN J,** Fl International Univ, Miami, FL; SR; MS; Deans Lst 89; Deans Lst 90; Deans Lst 90; NCAA Wmns Sccr Cptn 86-89; BS 90; Edctn; Admnstrtn.

**FITZGERALD, KELLEY A,** Univ Of Cincinnati-Clrmnt Coll, Batavia, OH; FR; BA; Township Fields/Tavern Mgr; Nrsg.

**FITZGERALD, KRISTINE R,** Radford Univ, Radford, VA; JR; BS; Psych Clb 88-89; Crmnl Justice Clb Co VP 88-; Phi Gamma Mu; Lambda Alpha Epsilon 88-; Criminal Justice; Law Enf.

**FITZGERALD, MARK S,** Old Dominion Univ, Norfolk, VA; SR; BSEET; Gldn Ky; AAS Blue Ridge Comm Coll 89; Dipl Blue Ridge Comm Coll 87; Elect Eng Tech.

**FITZGERALD, MICHAEL W,** Coppin St Coll, Baltimore, MD; SR; BS; Jaycees 87-; NAACP 88-; Alpha Kappa Mu 90-; Psych Clb 90-; BS; Psych; Subst Abse Cnslr.

**FITZGERALD, SEAN,** Bunker Hill Comm Coll, Boston, MA; SO; AA Bunker Hill Comm Clg; Psych; Clncl Psych.

**FITZGERALD, SEAN C,** Teikyo Post Univ, Waterbury, CT; FR; BA; Varsity Bsktbl; Lib Arts; Law Enfrcmnt.

**FITZGERALD, SHANNON L,** Radford Univ, Radford, VA; FR; BA; Deans Lst 90-; Biolgy; Marine Biolgy.

**FITZGERALD, SHARON K,** James Madison University, Harrisonburg, VA; SO; BASN; Nrsng.

**FITZGERALD, WAYNE H,** Schenectady County Comm Coll, Schenectady, NY; SR; Adctns Cnslng Conifer Pk Scotia NY 2 Yrs; Hmn Srvcs; MSWCAC Thrpst.

**FITZGERREL, WILLIAM W,** Asbury Theological Sem, Wilmore, KY; SO; MDIV; Postdoctoral Fellow Univ NM Sch Med 74-76; Fed Am Soc Exper Bio Presentation 72-74; Methodist Church Pastor 89-; Assoc Prof Bio 76-82; Instr Bio 89-; BA Univ TX Austin 66; Ph D Univ TX Hlth Sci Ctr Dallas 74; Theology; Pstrl Mnstry.

**FITZHARRIS, LAURIE M,** Univ Of Sc At Columbia, Columbia, SC; SO; BS; SC Clg 89; Alpha Epsilon Delta 90; Carolina For Kids In Dngr 90; Var Schlrshps 89; Deans Lst 90; Bio-Pre Med; Med.

**FITZMAURICE JR, THOMAS N,** Dowling Coll, Oakdale Li, NY; SR; BBA; Rllr Hcky Clb Dir/Coach 88-; Bsn Mgmt; MBA.

**FITZPATRICK, AMY K,** Ms St Univ, Miss State, MS; SR; Pre Vet Clb; IM Vlybl; Band Sqd Ldr 89-; Microbiology; Veterinarian.

**FITZPATRICK, ANITA C,** Univ Of Ky, Lexington, KY; SR; PHD; KASP 88-90; Rho Chi 89-; KSHP Hosp Phrmcy Awd 90-; KY Soc Hosp Phrmcsts 90-; BS Univ KY 78; MS Univ KY 81; Chem; Clncl Phrmcy.

**FITZPATRICK, BRIAN W,** Univ Of Nh Plymouth St Coll, Plymouth, NH; SO; BS; Pres Lst 90; Mdle Schl Coach; Soc Sci Educ; Teach.

**FITZPATRICK, ERIN R,** Univ Of Southern Ms, Hattiesburg, MS; JR; BA; Gold Key 90-; Beta Gamma Sigma 89-; Phi Chi Theta 90-; Delta Gamma 87-; Lamar Cnty Bnk Awd Schlrshp 90-; Pres Lst 89-90; Deans Lst; Acctg; CPA.

**FITZPATRICK, JOHN J,** Duquesne Univ, Pittsburgh, PA; SO; BA; Sign Waves 89-; Alpha Phi Omega Sec 90-; Greek/Latin Tutor Clsscs Dept; Classics/Theology.

**FITZPATRICK, KELLEY L,** Lexington Comm Coll, Lexington, KY; SO; ADN; Nrsng; Nrs Ansths.

**FITZPATRICK, LESLIE R,** Univ Of Ga, Athens, GA; SR; BSED; Kappa Delta Pi; Assc Dgr Dekalb Comm Clg 89; Educ; Tchr.

**FITZPATRICK, PAMELA A,** Northern Ky Univ, Highland Hts, KY; JR; BA; Bio Soc 89-; Hlth Sci; Physcl Thrpy.

**FITZPATRICK, ROBERT J,** Radford Univ, Radford, VA; SO; BA; Pltcl Sci/Hist; Law.

**FITZSIMMONS, AMI L,** Univ Of Pittsburgh At Bradford, Bradford, PA; JR; BS; Bsktbl Capt 88-; Alpha Lambda Delta 89-; Univ Schlr; All Conf Tm 88-; Bus Mgmt; Acctnt At Large Firm.

**FITZSIMONS, STUART A S,** Univ Of South Al, Mobile, AL; JR; BED; Sccr Snblt 1st Tm 90; All Sth Rgn 3rd Tm; Vrsty Sccr; Phys Educ.

**FITZWATER, KATHERINE MICHELLE,** Newbury Coll, Brookline, MA; FR; BA; Culinary Arts.

**FIUMARA, DINO S,** Duquesne Univ, Pittsburgh, PA; SO; B ED; Msc Edctn Piano.

**FIUMARA, THERESA E,** Univ Of Nc At Greensboro, Greensboro, NC; SR; BS; Alph Chi Omg Schlrshp 89-; Sintrnshp Sternberger Elem Sch 90; Elem Ed; Tchng.

**FIUTEM, STACEY L,** Western New England Coll, Springfield, MA; SO; BA; Fin; Inv Adv.

**FIVEK, KAREN E,** Univ Of Med & Dentistry Of Nj, Newark, NJ; GD; MS; Am Dietetic Assc; NJ Dietic Assoc ; BS Rutgers Univ 86; Nutrtn.

**FIVES, GREG,** S U N Y Coll Of Tech At Frmgdl, Farmingdale, NY; JR; AA; Pres Lst 89-90; Dns Lst 89-; Fr Schlrshp Awrd 90; Lib Arts/Pre Hlth; Physcl Thrpy.

**FIX, MELANIE D,** Radford Univ, Radford, VA; SO; BS; Bio Clb/Amer Chem Soc 89-; Repubs 90-; Bacchus; Tutor 90-; Bio; Med.**

**FIX, ROBERT W,** Pa St Univ Main Cmps, University Pk, PA; SO; Chess Clb Secy 89-; AICHE 90-; Alpha Kappa Lambda Secy 90-; Chess Team Cap 89-; Chem Eng; Eng.**

**FIXLER, MICHAEL A,** Univ Of Miami, Coral Gables, FL; FR; BBA; Pre-Legal Scty 90; Hnr Stdnts Assoc 90f Sigma Alpha Mu Ims; Bsnss Law/Cmptr Info Syst; Law.

**FIXLER, SEEMA,** Yeshiva Univ, New York, NY; SR; Sigma Delta Rho 87-90; Fine Arts Soc 87-90; Drmtcs Soc 87-90; Cls Sec 89-90; Deans Lst 87-90; Prjct Ezra 89-90; BA/BLGY 90; AA/JDAIC Studies 90; Entrtnmnt Spkr First Annl Bd Dir Dnnr Stern Coll Wmn; Blgy; Optmtry.

**FIXLER, SHARON M,** Barry Univ, Miami, FL; JR; BS; Athletic Trnr; Hunger Clean Up; Sports Med; Phys Therapy.

**FIXLER, SUSAN A,** Atlantic Comm Coll, Mays Landing, NJ; SO; AAS; HSMA; Dns Lst 89-; Mark G Etess Mem Schlrshp 90; Ed Inst Amer Hotel/Motel Assoc Certifs 89-; Hosptlty Mgmt; Hosptlty Mgmt/Mktg.

**FIZER, CECILIA A,** Concord Coll, Athens, WV; SR; MS; Theta Pi 89-90; Cardinal Ky 89-; Kappa Delta Pi 89-; Dns Lst 88-; BS Ed 90; Concord Coll Undgrd Schlshp Recpnt 89-90; Grad Magna Cum Laude; BS 90; W V Stdnt Natl Educ Assn 90-; Wmns Resource Cntr Bd Dir 85-86; Math/Comp Sci; Coll Prof.

**FLACINSKI, BETH A,** Univ Of Pittsburgh At Bradford, Bradford, PA; FR; AD; Stdnt Nrss Orgnztn 90-; Nrsng.

**FLACK, BLAIR T,** Nc Agri & Tech St Univ, Greensboro, NC; SR; BS; Stu Natl Educ Assn 90-; Assn Chldhd Edctrs Intl 90-; Yng Dmcrts; Dean Lst 89-; Natl Yth Sprts Prog 90; Elem Educ; Tch.

**FLACK, JOHN M,** Anne Arundel Comm Coll, Arnold, MD; SO; AA; Bsns Gnrl; Mgmt.

**FLACK, TIMOTHY W,** Memphis St Univ, Memphis, TN; JR; BA; Hist; Law.

**FLAGG, ANDREA L,** Daemen Coll, Amherst, NY; JR; BS; Stdnt Phys Therapy Assn; Alpha Phi Omega; Phys Therapy.

**FLAGG, EDWARD A,** Tallahassee Comm Coll, Tallahassee, FL; JR; BA; Lit Mag Fctn Edtr; AA 90; Eng; Tchr/Author.

**FLAHERTY, CLAIRE E,** Georgetown Univ, Washington, DC; JR; Blue/Gray Clb 89-90; Var Slng Tm 89-90; Finance.

**FLAHERTY, KATHLEEN E,** Univ Of Fl, Gainesville, FL; SR; BS; Wmn Rsrc Cntr Wash Univ 85-87; Stu Agnst Sexism Wash Univ 85-87; Wmn Caucus 85-87; Bus Admn/Mrktng; Mrktg Rsrch/QC/RSK Mgmnt.

**FLAHERTY, LAURA L,** Bunker Hill Comm Coll, Boston, MA; SO; BA; Htl/Restrnt Mgt; Food/Bevrg Dir.

**FLAHERTY, MARY ELLEN,** Saint Josephs Coll, Windham, ME; JR; BS; SGA 90-; Hall Cncl 90-; Res Asst 90-; Elem Ed Assn 90-; Spr Kids Scl Svc Clb Pres 90-; Intrnshp Lcl Schl 90-; Elem Ed; Clssrm Tchr.

**FLAHERTY, SHARON,** William Paterson Coll, Wayne, NJ; JR; BA; Hghst Schlstc Avrg Ward; Gen AA Awrd; BCC 90; AA 90; Spnsh Lgl Trnsltn.

**FLAHERTY, THOMAS J,** City Univ Of Ny Queensbrough, New York, NY; JR; BA; AA Queensborough Cmnty Clg 90; Cmmnctns Arts/Sci; Media Prod.

**FLANAGAN, DENISE A,** Univ Of Nc At Charlotte, Charlotte, NC; JR; BSW; Soc Wrk.

**FLANAGAN, LINDA A,** William Paterson Coll, Wayne, NJ; SR; BA; Stdnt Accntng Soc VP 88-; Cmps Rep Bckr CPA Rvw Crs 90-; Vol Income Tax Asstnc 90; Schlrshp New Jersey Soc Pblc Accntnts 89; Intrnshp R D Hntr Co; Accntng; CPA.

**FLANAGAN, PATRICIA B,** Hilbert Coll, Hamburg, NY; FR; AAS; Bkkpr 86-89; Crmnl Jstc; Yth Cnslng.

**FLANARY, BEVERLY J,** Northeast State Tech Comm Coll, Blountville, TN; FR; AAS; Chem; Chem Tech.

**FLANIGAN, ELIZABETH J,** Univ Of Sc At Columbia, Columbia, SC; JR; BED; Kappa Delta Pi 90-; Chrch Ed Com 87-; Women Of ELCA Pres 88-89; Elem Ed; Tch.

**FLANIGAN, JAMES A,** S U N Y At Buffalo, Buffalo, NY; JR; MBA; Fncl Mgmt; Invstmnt Bnkg.

**FLANIGAN, KRISTIE J,** Salem-Teikyo Univ, Salem, WV; FR; BA; Deans Lst; Edctn Hstry; Tchng.

**FLANIGAN, REBECCAH N,** Memphis St Univ, Memphis, TN; FR; BBA; Stdnt Ct Just; Ambass Brd; Econ; Urbn Plng.

**FLANNERY, CHARLES G,** County Coll Of Morris, Randolph, NJ; FR; BA; SAPB; Amnesty Int.

**FLANNERY, LEE-ANNE S,** East Stroudsburg Univ, E Stroudsburg, PA; FR; Med; Occptnl Thrpy.

**FLANNERY, PATRICIA,** Georgian Court Coll, Lakewood, NJ; JR; BS; Delta Mu Delta Treas 90-; Township Meritous Serv Awd; Gertrude Turner Mahon Schlrshp 88-; Acctg; CPA.

**FLASINSKI, MARY ANN,** Widener Univ, Chester, PA; SR; BS; Eucharistic Minstr St Josephs Church Aston PA; Human Rsrc Mgr Crystal Brands Inc Womens Apparel Grp 76-90; Mgt/Human Rsrcs; Human Rsrc Mgt.

**FLATLEY, SHERRY L,** Univ Of Md At Eastern Shore, Princess Anne, MD; SO; BS; Cllgt Agri Sci Clb 89-; Deans Lst 87-89; USDA Intrn 90-; Agri Schlrshp 90-; Sntrl Schlrshp 90-; IM Sftbl 90; PTA Boy Scts; Agri-Bus; MS Agri Fin/Econ Farm Mgmt Ext/Fin.

**FLAUTT, KRISTIN H,** Ms St Univ, Miss State, MS; FR; MBA; Fshn Brd 90-; Rdrnr; Lamda Sigma 90-; Gamma Beta Phi 90-; Phi Eta Sigma 90-; Pi Mu 90-; IM Ftbl Sftbl; Bsns Cmmnctns; Mrktng Pblc Rltns.

**FLAVIUS, LERA,** Univ Of Sc At Columbia, Columbia, SC; SO; Intl Org 90; Afr Amrcn Assoc; Actvts Brd 90-; Bus Admn.

**FLAX, SANDRA J,** Clark State Comm Coll, Springfield, OH; SO; AAS; Art Clb 89; Phi Theta Kappa 89; Deans Lst 88; Lit Art Pblctn 89; Exhbts Awd 89-90; Sprng Flng Art Tm 89; Cmmrcl Art; Grphc Dsgnr Illstrtr.

**FLE, CLAUDINE J,** Univ Of The Dist Of Columbia, Washington, DC; SR; BA; Mrktng Clb UDC 89-; Polyglor Clb UDS 88-; Phi Sigma Pi; Mrktng; Intl Bus.

**FLEARY, VERA,** City Univ Of Ny Med Evers Coll, Brooklyn, NY; SR; AS Se 90.

**FLECHA, WENDY A,** S U N Y Coll Of Tech At Frmgdl, Farmingdale, NY; SO; BS; Lib Arts/Sci Clb VP 89-; Phi Theta Kappa 89-90; Back Stage Theater Co 89; Phi Theta Kappa 90-; Math Hnr Socty; Lib Arts/Sci VP 90-; Toys For Tots 90; Mrch Of Dimes Walk A Thon 90; Pide In Frmngdale Day 90; Lib Arts/Sci Chrmns Acad Exc; Lib Arts/Sci; Pre Prof Cnctrn.

**FLECK, TARYN B,** Villanova Univ, Villanova, PA; SO; BA; Spec Olympcs; Hugger Crmnes Cmtee; Dorm Hse Cncl Sec Tread; Reading Tutor; Kappa Alpha Theta Sec Pldge Cls; I M Flag Ftbl Capt; Psychology; Clncl Psychlgy.

**FLEECE, NICK A,** Wv Univ, Morgantown, WV; SR; BS; Cir K 90-; N Cntrl WV Coal Mng Inst; Amer Soc Mchncl Engrs 87-; IM Ftbl 90; Mchncl Engrg.

**FLEECE, STEPHEN E,** Emory Univ, Atlanta, GA; SR; BBA; Delta Tau Delta 87-; Interfrat Cncl 88-89; Stdnt Admssns Assn 87-88; Bus Schl Hnr Cncl 90-; Bus Admin; Bus Cnsltng.

**FLEEGAL, ERIC B,** Liberty Univ, Lynchburg, VA; SR; BS; Assc Comptng Machnry; Lbrty Hon Pgm; Natl Eagle Sct Assc; AS Comm Co; Cmptr Sci; Systms Eng.

**FLEENOR, JENNIFER S,** Univ Of Va Clinch Valley Coll, Wise, VA; FR; BA; Phi Upsilon Omega; Biology; Sec Educ.

**FLEENOR IV, JOHN P,** Ms St Univ, Miss State, MS; FR; BA; Bapt Stdnt Un 90-; AIAS 90-; Tenn St Soccr Assn 90-; Miss St Soccr Assc Ref; IM Soccr/Ftbl 90-; Architecture.

**FLEENOR, SCOTT W,** Wv Univ At Parkersburg, Parkersburg, WV; FR; Mstrs Clb 89; Radio Chrstn Music Prog; AS; Bsnss Admin.

**FLEETWOOD III, THOMAS C,** Life Coll, Marietta, GA; GD; DC; Vlybl 89; Sftbl 87-90; Phi Beta Kappa 90; Phi Kappa Phi 90; Golden Key 89-90; Magna Cum Laude; BAAS Univ Delaware 90; Chir.

**FLEGAL, RALPH P,** Wilmington Coll, New Castle, DE; JR; BS; Vfw Post 615 Jr Vice Cmdr; Phi Theta Kappa Treas 88-; Criminal Justice; Law.

**FLEISCHER, BONNIE M,** Georgetown Univ, Washington, DC; SR; BSBA; BIS Assoc Dir 87-; Intl Rels Clb Conf Coord 87-; SGA Comms Comm 88-89; Tour Gds/Ushrs VP 87-; Acad Comp Adv Comm 90-; Currclm Stndrds Bd 90-; Porsche Crs N Amer Fin Intrn 90; Crew Tm Coxswain 87-88; Intl Bsns/Fin; Intl Bsns Law.

**FLEISCHER, FLAVIA SAMELLA,** Gallaudet Univ, Washington, DC; FR; BA; HSO 90-; IM Bsktbl And Sftbl Cch 90-; Engl And Govt; Law.

**FLEISCHER, MICHAEL I,** Life Coll, Marietta, GA; GD; DC; Mtn Palptn Cl Instr; Gonstead Cl 90-; SOT Cl; Lung Asso; BS Stockton St Colg 74; Chiro; Biol.

**FLEISCHHAUER, AMELIA M,** Columbia Greene Comm Coll, Hudson, NY; Deans Lst; Presidents Lst; Intrnshp Catskill Police Dept 85-86; Intrnshp Subs Abuse Certif 90-; AAS CGCC 86; BA SUNY Albany 88; Crim Just Substance Abuse.

**FLEISCHMANN, TOBI E,** Stockton St Coll, Pomona, NJ; JR; BA; Crt Cncl Org Cmps Actvts 90-; Bus Mrktng; Advrtsng Byr.**

**FLEISHER, MICHELE B,** The Kings Coll, Briarclf Mnr, NY; SR; Future Christian Educ Assoc VP 90-; Hmcmng Repr Decrtng Comm 89-90; Nwspr Typist 88-90; CSO Brandywine Nrsng Hm 87-88; RA 89-90; Coreen Cook Schlrshp 90; Fld Hcky 88-89; BS; Elem Educ; Teaching.

**FLEITAS, IVONNE M,** Fl International Univ, Miami, FL; SR; Stdnt Govt Senatr 90-; Law Assn 90-; Natl Org For Wmn 90-; Phi Kappa Phi; Phi Lambda 90-; Sigma Sigma Sigma 90-; All Abrd Prog 88-89; Acdmc Achvmnt Awrd; Outstndng Mnrty Commnty Coll Grad 89; Poltcl Sci Dept Annual Bk Awrd; AA 89; Poltcl Sci; Law.

**FLEMING, ANGELA,** Alcorn St Univ, Lorman, MS; FR; BA; Bus Admin; Mngmnt Est Cmptr Co.

**FLEMING, ANNE E,** Univ Of Tn At Martin, Martin, TN; SO; Yrbk Stff 90-; Bsbl Batgrl 89-90; Pi Sigma Epsilon 90-; Chi Omega 90-; Arts/Sci.

**FLEMING, ARMARIA J,** Va Commonwealth Univ, Richmond, VA; SO; BA; Blck Stdnt Alliance 89-90; Rcgnzd Acad Excell Ofc Mnrty Stdnt Affairs 90-; Soc Wrk; Indstrl Psychlgy.

**FLEMING, DENSEL V,** Alcorn St Univ, Lorman, MS; SO; BA; Mrchng Bnd Drm Mjr 89-; Intrfth Gspl Chr Chpln 89; Men GQ/GRT Qlty Pres 90-; Smmr Rsrch Opprtnty Pgm UIUC; Agri Ecnmcs; Dctrt Ecnmcs.

**FLEMING, DONNA D,** Univ Of Md At Eastern Shore, Princess Anne, MD; SR; BA; Kappa Alpha Psi Aux Sec 88-; Nwspr Wrtr 90-; Cmnctns Clb 89-90; Jrnlsm Lab Intrn; Wmns Clb Sftbl Tm 90; Engl/Cmnctns; Print Media/Jrnlsm.

**FLEMING, GARY A,** Wv Univ, Morgantown, WV; SR; BS; SAE 88-; ASME 88-; MENSA Ltd Of Amer 85-; Gldn Ky 90; Schlrs Prog 87-; Tau Beta Pi 90-; Pi Tau Sigma 90-; Tchng Asstshp; Athltc Schrlship Lttrmn 89-; Vrsty Dvng Tm 87-; Mech Eng; MSME.

**FLEMING, GREGORY D,** Toccoa Falls Coll, Toccoa Falls, GA; SR; BA; AA 90; Biblcl Stdies; Chrch Plntr.

**FLEMING, JILL M,** Tougaloo Coll, Tougaloo, MS; SR; Ed Clb 90-; Natl Ed Assoc 90-; Ed; Tchng.

**FLEMING, JODIE L,** Oh Univ, Athens, OH; JR; BFA; Inrntl Stdnt Union Soc Chr Pgmng Bd 89-; Art Leag 88-; Gldn Key; Rsdnt Vol Athns Mntl Hlth Ctr; Prntmkg/Art Hist; Fine Arts.

**FLEMING, JONATHAN C,** Univ Of Southern Ms, Hattiesburg, MS; SR; BS; Gamma Beta Phi 90-; Ads; Cpywrtg.

**FLEMING, JULIE A,** Fl St Univ, Tallahassee, FL; JR; BS; Stdnt Alum Fndtn VP 89-90; Cncl Hnr Soc Chrmn; Sem Ambssdrs; Mortr Brd VP 90-; Phi Kappa Phi Goldn Key 90-; Beta Kappa Alpha; Gold Key 90-; Kappa Alpha Theta; Wal Mart Corp Intrnshp Hm Offc Bentonvl Ark; AA 90; Mktg/Spnsh; Hisp Mktg.

**FLEMING, KAREN M,** Columbus Coll Of Art & Design, Columbus, OH; FR; BA; CCAD Spcl Schlrshps; Prvs Plc Dsptchr/Crctns Offcr; Cert 87; Ads Dsgn; Grphc Artst.

**FLEMING, KASSANDRA D,** Howard Univ, Washington, DC; JR; Nws Dir Radio; Co-Hst Sptlght WHMM-TV Chnl 32; Natl Asc Blck Jrnlsts; Fred Dgls ; Gldn Key; Dns Lst; Soc Prof Jrnlsts; NABJ; Std Ambsdr; Big Bro/Sis Pgm; WTTG Intrn; WHUR Intrn; Brdcst Jrnlsm/Bus Admn; Grad Schl MBA Mktg.

**FLEMING, KATHLEEN A,** Marywood Coll, Scranton, PA; SO; BA; NCAA Fld Hockey; Spanish Tutor; Orientn Comm; Cmnctns/Radio/TV.

**FLEMING, KIMBERLY A,** Peace Coll, Raleigh, NC; FR; AA BA; Ntnl Assc Acctnts Pres; Acdmc Exclnc Awrd; Admssns Asst; Prsdnts Aide; Bsn/Acctng; CPA.

**FLEMING, KRISTI L,** Meridian Comm Coll, Meridian, MS; SO; MBA; Phi Beta Lambda; AA; Acctg; CPA.

**FLEMING, MARK A,** Franklin And Marshall Coll, Lancaster, PA; SO; BA; Im Ftbl 90; Tour Guide; Phi Kappa Tau 90-; Hons List 89-90; Deans 90-; Adadmc Schlrshp; Varsty Soccer 89-; Bus Admn.

**FLEMING, PERRYN B,** Davis & Elkins Coll, Elkins, WV; SR; BS; Kappa Alpha Theta 65-67; All Amer Schlrs Clgte Awd 90-; Natl Clgte Ed Awd; Davis Elkins Clge Acdmc Achvmt Awd; Natl Ed Assoc 90-; WV Ed Assoc 90-; Elem Ed; Tchg.

**FLEMING JR, ROBERT B,** Univ Of Sc At Columbia, Columbia, SC; JR; BS; Clg Rpblcns 89-90; IEEE 90-; Alpha Lambda Delta 89; Golden Key 90-; Stdnt Eng 89-90; Summer Intern SCPSA; IM Ftbl/Bsktbl 88-; Elec Eng; Eng Power Co.

**FLEMING, SCOTT M,** Duquesne Univ, Pittsburgh, PA; SO; BA; SG 90; Ski Clb 89; Deans Lst; Delta Sigma Pi 89; RA; Mis; Mngmnt.

**FLEMING, SHANNON R,** Fl A & M Univ, Tallahassee, FL; FR; Political Sci; Lawyer.

**FLEMING, STEVE E,** Wilberforce Univ, Wilberforce, OH; JR; BA; TN Pre-Almni Asc 88-; Blck Male Cltn 89-; Std Govt Assc Actv Comm 89-; Dns Clb 88-; Rdng Lab Aide; Std Emplye Year 90-; Std Year 90-; Most Pplr Std 90-; IM Bsktbl Champ 90-; Elem Ed.

**FLEMING, TODD D,** Schenectady County Comm Coll, Schenectady, NY; JR; BA; ECN Hudsn Vly Comm Clg 88-89; Elec Eng.

**FLEMING, VIRGINIA S,** Chesterfield Marlboro Coll, Cheraw, SC; FR; AA.

**FLEMINGS, JON ANN,** Alcorn St Univ, Lorman, MS; FR; Ky Success Clb Pres 89-90; Univ Hon Clb 90-; M Marietta Smnr Intrn 90; Acctg.

**FLEMMING, CHARMAINE A,** Univ Of Sc At Columbia, Columbia, SC; SR; BA; Deans List 90-; Hist; MAT Bio.**

**FLEMMING, DENZIL M,** City Univ Of Ny Med Evers Coll, Brooklyn, NY; SO; BE; Ntrl Sci Clb VP 89-90; ASC 86-88; Engr; Cvl Envrnmtl.

**FLEMMING, MAURIA A,** Immaculata Coll, Immaculata, PA; SR; BMUS; Cue & Crtn Drma Clb Sec 87-90; Chrl 87-; Drctr Anl Vrty Shw 87-; Mdrgls Drctr 87-90; Nwsppr Stff Rprtr Wrtr 87-88; Orchstra 88-; Alpha Psi Omega 89-; Greenpeace 89-; Sadd 89-90; Edctn; Msc/Drma Flds.

**FLEMMING, VALERIE J,** George Mason Univ, Fairfax, VA; JR; BS; Gldn Key; IM 88; Mrktng.

**FLESCH, RITA M,** Oh Dominican Coll, Columbus, OH; FR; BA; Bncho Natl Bnk 75-; Bus; Bnkng.

**FLESHER, ERIK A,** Columbus Coll Of Art & Design, Columbus, OH; SR; BA; Grnpc 88-; PETA 89-; Pres Lst 88-; Deans Lst 86-87; Illstrtn; Frlnc Artst.

**FLESHMAN, SHIRLEY R,** Beckley Coll, Beckley, WV; SO; B ED; Tch 4yr Old Sndy Schl Cls Swl Vly Bptst Chrch 89-; Tchbgng Prschl 87-; Mlti Sbjcts; Tchng K-8.

**FLESHMAN, STEPHANIE GRAY,** Cumberland County Coll, Vineland, NJ; FR; AA; Stdnt Sen; Trojan Chorus; Tutoring; Deans Hnr List; Vlybl; Earn Doctorate In Eng.

**FLESHNER, SHARON K,** Beckley Coll, Beckley, WV; SO; BA; Amer Chrprctc Assn 83-; Flschnr Clncl Chrprctc Asst 83-; Psychlgy.

**FLETCHER, CYNTHIA A,** Livingston Univ, Livingston, AL; SR; Psychlgy Clb Pres 90-; Cardinal Ky Tres 89-; Alpha Chi 89-; Dept Awrd Hghst GPA; Almn Awrd Otstndng Achv; Magna Cum Laude; BS; Sclgy; Psychlgy.

**FLETCHER, JEFFREY D,** Liberty Univ, Lynchburg, VA; JR; BS; Stdnt Govt Assoc Sntr; Cir K Clb; Clge Rpblcns 88-90; Alpha Lambda Delta 89 ; Anne Arundel Co Yth Cncil 88-; Govt; Law.

**FLETCHER, KENT L,** Univ Of Al At Huntsville, Huntsville, AL; JR; BS; Inter Frat Cncl Rep 87; Alpha Lambda Delta 87; Pi Kappa Alpha Treas 87-88; Teledyne Brown Eng 88-; Co Op Stdnt; Elect Eng.

**FLETCHER, KEVIN T,** Princeton Univ, Princeton, NJ; FR; AB; Army ROTC 90-; Tutor Inner City Chldrn 90-; Urban Actn 90; Superior Cdt Awd 90-; Heritage Fndtn Intrn Wash D C; Econ.

**FLETCHER, LEIGH M,** Wv Univ, Morgantown, WV; SR; BS; Frasure-Singleton Awd 89; Am Adv Fdrtn V P Hd Fund-Raising 89-90; Schlrs Prog Ldrshp Awd 87-; Mortar Bd 90-; Golden Key 89-; Phi Kappa Phi Otstndng Frshm N 87-88 90-; Kappa Tau Alpha 90-; Alpha Delta Sigma; Jrnslm; Advtsng.**

**FLETCHER, MARESSA DE ANN,** Emory & Henry Coll, Emory, VA; JR; BA; Phi Theta Kappa 90-; Sec 87-88; Mine Acctnt Asstnt Island Creek Coal Co 88-; AAS SVCC 86-88; AAS 87-88; Acctg/Cmptr Sci; CPA.

**FLETCHER, MARGAREECE,** Memphis St Univ, Memphis, TN; JR; BBA; Mgmt Info Syst.

**FLETCHER, MARGARET A,** Va Commonwealth Univ, Richmond, VA; GD; MED; Rcyclng Cprtv Treas 89-; Stdnt Ed Assn 90-; BA 84; Mddl Ed.

**FLETCHER, MATTHEW H,** Marshall University, Huntington, WV; JR; BA; Gamma Beta Phi 90-; Tau Kappa Epsilon 86-91; Vet USAF; Exec Asst Htngtn Chb Comm; Fin; Law.

**FLETCHER, REBECCA H,** Ms St Univ, Miss State, MS; JR; BS; Educ Psychlgy; HS Cnslng/Psychmtry.

**FLETCHER, TARA A,** Clark Atlanta Univ, Atlanta, GA; SO; BA; Pre-Prof Hlth Soc 90-; Atlanta Univ Cntr Mentor Prog 90-; Hnrs Prog 89-; Howard Hughes Shclr 89-; Biology; Med.

**FLETCHER, TRACY D,** Univ Of Cin R Walters Coll, Blue Ash, OH; FR; Guest Jrnlst Clg Paper; Liberal Arts.

**FLETT, BONNIE L,** Va Commonwealth Univ, Richmond, VA; GD; MD; Stdnt Psych Soc 89-; Amer Med Stdnt Assn 90-; Stdnt Fmly Prctc Assn Org Comm 90-; Stdnt Tchng Aids To Stdnts 89; NIH Summer Cancer Fllwshp 90; BS Wake Forest Univ 88; Med: Doctor.

**FLETT, DIANA J,** Va Commonwealth Univ, Richmond, VA; SR; BS; Pbl Rltns Intern YMCA 90; Mss Cmmnctns; Publ Rltns.

**FLEURY, DAWN M,** Western New England Coll, Springfield, MA; SR; BA; Peer Advsr 90-; Res Hall Assoc Treas 89-; Delta Mu Delta; AA Holyoke Cmuty Clg 89; Acctg.

**FLEWELLYN, THOMAS,** Central St Univ, Wilberforce, OH; SO; BA; Psi Chi 90-; NAACP; Dns Lst; Prnce Hl Masons; Intrnshp Philip Crosby Assoc; Psych.

**FLICK, LORI A,** Immaculata Coll, Immaculata, PA; FR; BA; Cmps Tr Guide; Acdmc Schlrshp Per Yr Immaculate; Ray Kroc Awd Mcdonalds 90; Miss Teen Harford Cnty 90; Tns Tm 90-; Chemistry; Dietetic.

**FLICK, MATTHEW A,** Bridgewater Coll, Bridgewater, VA; FR; BS; Chem; Med.

**FLICK, STEPHANIE L,** Indiana Univ Of Pa, Indiana, PA; JR; BS; Res Hall Assn Pres 90-; Campus Crusade Christ; Cncl Excptnl Chldrn 89-; PSEA 90-; Natl Res Hall Hon; Spcl Olympics 89-; Jump Rope Am Heart Assn; Edn Excptnl Stdtns; Teach.**

**FLICKENSCHILD, STEPHEN C,** S U N Y Coll Of Tech At Alfred, Alfred, NY; FR; AAS; Eng; Architect.

**FLICKER, MICHAEL T,** Temple Univ, Philadelphia, PA; SR; Vars Athl Trainer 87-; Golden Key 89-; Alpha Lambda Delta 87-; Natl Athl Trnrs Assn 89-; Estrn Athl Trnrs Assn 89-; Athl Trnr; Vol Athl Trnr OCHS; Hcky Cmp Athl Trnr; Moyer-Liburd Award 87/89; Outstndng Snr PE; EATA Schlrshp 90; Phsy Educ/Athl Trng.

**FLICKINGER, CRAIG W,** Oh Wesleyan Univ, Delaware, OH; SR; BA; Phi Scty; Peat Marwick Adt Intrn; Vrsty Bsbll 88-90; Acctng; CPA.

**FLICKINGER, GREGORY L,** Oh Univ, Athens, OH; SO; RCIA; St Vincent De Paul; Deans Schlrshp; Pres Acad Brkfst; Var Ftbl; Chem Engr.

**FLICKINGER, THERESA F,** Al A & M Univ, Normal, AL; FR; Ord Of Moose Sr Regent; Natl Assn Female Execs 90-; Exec Secy Dean/Univ Clg 88-; Bus Admin; Mgmnt/Admin.

**FLICKINGER, TRACEY L,** Indiana Univ Of Pa, Indiana, PA; FR; Deans Lst 90-; Psychlgy.

**FLIK, YORK M,** Univ Of Miami, Coral Gables, FL; SR; Karate Clb 87-; Anthropology Clb 89-; Golden Key; Phi Kappa Phi; Annual Anthropology Dept Awrd; BA; Anthropology.

**FLINT, GREGORY D,** Northwest Al Comm Coll, Phil Campbell, AL; SO; BA; Phi Theta Kappa 89-; Bsktbll Mst Vlbl Plyr 90-; James B Allen Awrd 90-; Vsty Bsktbll; Acctg; Bus.**

**FLINT, NICOLE,** East Central Comm Coll, Decatur, MS; FR; BA; Sigma Sigma Mu Tau; Worrior Corps Sec; Cls Fav; Mu Alpha Theta; Phi Theta Kappa Treas; Frank F Leatherwood Schlrshp; Pres Lst; Dns Lst; Vrsty Bsktbl; IM Sprts; Bio Sci; Dntstry.

**FLIPPIN, KENYANN G,** Univ Of Nc At Chapel Hill, Chapel Hill, NC; GD; JD; Univ NC Hldrnss Moot Court Team; Craven Moot Court Cmptn Comm; Amer Bar Assn 90; Rsrch Assist Prof Elizabeth Gibson 90; UNC Schl Law Chncllrs Schlr 89; BM West Virginia Univ 89; Law.

**FLIPPO, DONNA J,** Northwest Al Comm Coll, Phil Campbell, AL; SO; BA; Bus; Acctng.

**FLISSLER, ALLEN C,** City Univ Of Ny Baruch Coll, New York, NY; SR; BBA; Clge Acctng Soc 88-90; Dns Lst 90; Intrnshp First Boston Corp 89-90; Acctng.

**FLLOYD JR, PERCY W,** William Carey Coll, Hattiesburg, MS; SR; BS; Southern Christian Stdnt Cntr VP 88-89; Future Ldrs Apprctn Day Honoree 90; Fin; Ins Claims Adjstr.

**FLODEN, HEATHER E,** Georgian Court Coll, Lakewood, NJ; FR; BA; Biochem; Phrmclgy Rsrch.

**FLOER, ANDREA,** The Boston Conservatory, Boston, MA; FR; BM; Voice Prfrmnc; Opera.

**FLOOD, DANA L,** Brescia Coll, Owensboro, KY; SR; BS; Natl Ed Assoc Stdt Prog 90-; Cncl Excptnl Chldrn 90-; Dns Lst 90-; Spec Ed LBD; Tchg.

**FLOOD, TERRI J,** Spalding Univ, Louisville, KY; SO; BS; Ele Educ; Tch.

**FLOORE, REBECCA L,** Univ Of Ky, Lexington, KY; JR; BA; Natl Ath Trnrs Assn 89-; Ky Ath Trns Soc 89-; S Eastern Ath Trnr Assn 89-; Dns Lst 90; Ath Trnr Vlybl Ftbl Tns 89-; Exercise Sci; Exercise Physiology.

**FLOORE, TODD T,** Univ Of Ky, Lexington, KY; SR; BA; Geogrphy.

**FLORA, RAY A,** Radford Univ, Radford, VA; JR; BS; Phy Educ Majrs Clb 90-; Tutor 89-; IM Bsktbl/Sftbl/Vlybl 89-; Hlth/Phys Educ; Tchg.

**FLORA JR, WILLIAM A,** Old Dominion Univ, Norfolk, VA; SR; BS; IEEE 89-; IEEE Computer Scty 90-; Deans List Fox 89-; Elec Engrg Techlgy; Engrg.

**FLORER, TRACY ELLEN,** Northern Ky Univ, Highland Hts, KY; SR; Fllwshp Chrstn Athlts 87-89; Ornttn Ldr 90-; Hnrs Lt 90; SNEA 90-; Sigma Kappa 87-; Brksvll Chrstn Chrch Pnst Tchr 87-; IM Vllybll 90; Bus Ed.

**FLORES MUNOZ, JUAN CARLOS,** Univ Of Pr At Mayaguez, Mayaguez, PR; JR; BA; Chem; Eng.

**FLORES VALENTIN, RAFAEL,** Inter Amer Univ Pr Arecibo Un, Arecibo, PR; SO; Aspen-In-Action Vocal; Soc Soc Para Dinamoca Hmn; Pres IG DDP Supv; Com Eval IGGDD; Grad Mizpa; Grad Air Lines; Grad Air Machines.

**FLORES, ALEXIS R,** Univ Of Central Fl, Orlando, FL; FR; BSASE; Air Force ROTC 90-; Arnold Air Society; Engnrng; Aerospace Engnrng.

**FLORES, ANNABELLA,** Valdosta St Coll, Valdosta, GA; SR; Ga Sclgcl Assoc 90-; Soc Intl Stu Sec 90-; Alpha Kappa Delta Ofcr 90-; DFCS Intk Wrkr; Otstndg Sr Sclgy/Anthrplgy 90-; Durrenberger Awrd; BA; Sclgy; Intl Study.

**FLORES, BRUNILDA,** Catholic Univ Of Pr, Ponce, PR; SR; Our Ldy Vlvanera Cthlc Schl Coord 89-; Engl Tchr Elem/Scndry Lvl 79-.

**FLORES, CAROLINA,** Manhattan School Of Music, New York, NY; FR; BA; Tchr Clg Pool 90-; Piano/Theory Prof 88-90; Finalist Natl Piano Comp 84; Hnr Prizes 84; Chamber Music Recitals; DMA Madrid; Piano; Perf Pianist.

**FLORES, ELSA R,** Ma Inst Of Tech, Cambridge, MA; FR; BS; Project Interphase 90; Chem Engnrng.

**FLORES, EUGENIA,** Univ Of North Fl, Jacksonville, FL; JR; Natl Hnr Scty 87-88; Phi Kappa Phi 90-; Blgy; Med.

**FLORES, MARGARITA,** Ramapo Coll Of Nj, Mahwah, NJ; SR; BA; Intl Stdnts Org Treas 88-; Org Latin Unity Pres 89-; Ordr Oak Hon Soc 90-; Lambda Tau Omega; Inrds Intrn-Intrnd Nabisco Co; Bus-Comp Info Syst.

**FLORES, SIRVONNER B,** Hampton Univ, Hampton, VA; JR; BSN; Stdnt Nrs Assoc VA 88-90; Sigma Theta Tau; Nrsg Extrnshp Sentara Norfolk Gen Hsp Hspce Unit; Grl Scts Ldr 90-; Yth Mnstry Coordntr 90-; Nrsg; Nrsg Edctr.

**FLORES-RODRIGUEZ, MARILYN,** Bayamon Central Univ, Bayamon, PR; SO; BA; Assn Busn Adm; Army Assoc; Comm Busn Adm; ROTC; Stdnt Act 89-; Mktg Sl Mgmt 89-; Lybl; Bsktbl; Engl/Spnsh; Acctg/Mktg/Cmptr.

**FLORIMONT, BARBARA L,** Georgian Court Coll, Lakewood, NJ; JR; BA; Re Entry Wmn 87-; Engl.

**FLORIMONTE, ELAINE,** Radford Univ, Radford, VA; SO; BA; House Cncl Sec 90-; Rsdnt Assist; Art Educ; Tchng.

**FLORIO, LAINA,** S U N Y Coll Of Tech At Frmgdl, Farmingdale, NY; SO; AAS; Bus Admin; Bus Mgmt.

**FLORY, DOUGLAS M,** Comm Coll Algny Co Algny Cmps, Pittsburgh, PA; SO; AS; USMCR Dsrt Strm Vet CPL 88-; AOPA 90-; FAPA 89-; Mnvlly Lthrncks 88-; Avtn; Pilot.

**FLORY, DOUGLAS R,** Defiance Coll, Defiance, OH; SO; BA; F B Gorrell Meml Schlrshp 90-; J F Coressel Schlrshp 90-; Math; HS Tchr.

**FLORY, HILDA M,** Va Commonwealth Univ, Richmond, VA; JR; BS; Civitan 89-; Hnrs Prog 89-; Pharmacy.

**FLOURNOY, CHARLES D,** Bloomfield Coll, Bloomfield, NJ; SO; MBA; Bsktbl Team 90-.

**FLOWERS, ANDREA R,** Wilmington Coll, Wilmington, OH; SR; BS; Aggies Club Pres 87-; Clgte 4-H Sec 87-90; Leader Schlr Chrmn 87-; Delta Tau Alpha Pres 89-; Green Key 88; Delta Theta Sibma Ltl Sis 88-; Hourglass Nwsedtr 88-; Wilmington News Jrnl Intrn Wrtr 89; Clinton Mem Comm Intrn; Agri-Commf Pub Rltns.

**FLOWERS, DEBRA J,** Christopher Newport Coll, Newport News, VA; JR; BA; 2nd Presby Church 90-; Kindergarten Aide; AS Thomas Nelson 90; Elem Ed; Schl Psychologist.

**FLOWERS, FELICIA M,** Jackson St Univ, Jackson, MS; SR; BS; Assn/Comp Mach 88-; Natl Soc/Blck Engr 88-; Pi Mu Epsilon Sec 90-; Alpha Kappa Mu Pres 90-; Alpha Chi 89-; Phi Kappa Phi; Delta Sigma Theta; Bell Comm Rsrch Intern; Acdmc Schlrshp; Hnrs Coll; Comp Sci; Sftwr Systms Dvlpmnt.

**FLOWERS, JEFFREY TYRONE,** Howard Univ, Washington, DC; SO; BA; DE Club VP 90-; Bskbl 90-; Architecture.

**FLOWERS, JENNIFER L,** Longwood Coll, Farmville, VA; JR; BS; Soc Physcs Stdnts 90-; Amer Inst Physcs 90-; Phi Kappa Phi; Pi Mu Epsilon; Dns Lst 89-90; Sxth Anl Math Cntst 90; Physcs/Math; Cmptr.

**FLOWERS, JO ANN,** Al A & M Univ, Normal, AL; SO; Ofc Syst Mgmt; Govt Secr.

**FLOWERS, JOHN E,** Univ Of Sc At Columbia, Columbia, SC; JR; BS; Elec/Cmptr Eng; Artificial Intellegence.

**FLOWERS, JOY L,** Comm Coll Algny Co Algny Cmps, Pittsburgh, PA; FR; Assoc 81; Wrd Prcsg Spclsts; Tchg.

**FLOWERS, JULIE D,** Univ Of Tn At Martin, Martin, TN; JR; BA; Pre-Phys Ther Clb Pres 89-90; Phi Eta Sigma; Mu Epsilon Delta Treas 90; Arts/Sci Awd; Phi Kappa Phi; Pre-Prof Awd; IMS; Phys Ther.

**FLOWERS, KENNETH J,** Pellissippi St Tech Comm Coll, Knoxville, TN; GD; BAS; SME V Chrmn 89-90; Assoc Appld Sci/Mech Engr Tech 90; Mech Engr Tech.

**FLOWERS, MARIA D,** Fayetteville St Univ, Fayetteville, NC; JR; BS; Alpha Kappa Mu Sec/Treas 90-; Zeta Phi Beta 89-; Brd Elcts Stdnt Gov 90-; Alpha Kappa Mu Sec/Treas 90-; Crmnl Just; Cnslr/Prbtn/Prl Ofcr.

**FLOWERS, MARK E,** Oh St Univ At Newark, Newark, OH; SO; BA; Hon Soc 89-; Bsebl Co-Capt 90-; Math; Civil Eng/Surveying.

**FLOWERS, SHANTEL D,** Tn St Univ, Nashville, TN; SO; NAACP Asst Sec 90-; INROADS 89-; Gen Mtrs Intrnshp Stdnt Engr 90-; Elec Eng.

**FLOWERS, SHARON A,** Univ Of Sc At Columbia, Columbia, SC; SR; Kappa Delta Epsln 89-; Delta Zeta 86-; Bapt Young Women 90-; Pres List 90-; D; Natl Cncl Chld Abse; Mrchng Bnd Dnc Tm 87-88; BAIS; Elem Educ; Tchr.

**FLOWERS, SHERRY KAY,** Emory Univ, Atlanta, GA; GD; MN; PTA; NACOG; RN Pediatrics; Dip Piedmont Hosp Sch Nurs 75; Nurse Mid Wife; Cert Nurs Midwife.

**FLOWERS, TONYA M,** Southern Coll Of Tech, Marietta, GA; GD; MTM; NAACO Pres 88; Southern Tech Diplmt Bd Mbr 87-90; Natl Soc Of Blck Engrs Spcl Evnts Chrprsn 87-; Cobb Cnty NAACP Yth Achvmnt Award 88-89; BS Apparel Engrng 90; OSHA Certfctn 90; Technel Mgt.**

**FLOWERS, TRACEY E,** Memphis St Univ, Memphis, TN; SR; BBA; Hl Cncl 88-; Gamma Beta Phi 89-; Black Schlrshps Unltd 89-; Res Advsr; Mgmnt Info Syst; Analyst/Progmmr.

**FLOWERS JR, WILLIS E,** Limestone Coll, Gaffney, SC; SO; BS; Catawba Lodge 56 AFM Deacon 90-; Scottish Rite 90-; N Amer Shrine 90-; Amer Soc Of Quality Control 85-; Mgr Qlty Assurance Homelite Textron 88-; BA; Bus Mgmnt; Qlty Assurance Mgmnt Exec.

**FLOYD, ANDREA ARLENE,** Southern Coll Of Tech, Marietta, GA; SR; BSIET; Gearing Up Orient Phm Pr 86-90; Tech Sls Clb 80-; Diplomats Pr 88-89; Peer Fac 90; Alpha Soc 86; Alpha Delta Pi Exec VP 86; Sigma Pi Chrprsn Little Sis; Inst Indust Engrs; Ronald Mc Donald House 85-90; Acad Schlrshp IBEW 85; Indust Engr.

**FLOYD, BRIAN,** Al St Univ, Montgomery, AL; JR; BA; Phtgrphy Clb 89-; Pblc Rltns Cncl VP 89-; Blck Entrtnmt TV Intrn 89-90; Sprts Nws Ntwrk Coop 89-90; Pblc Rltns; Produce Music.

**FLOYD, CARRIE L,** Hillsborough Comm Coll, Tampa, FL; FR; AA; Spcl Ed.

**FLOYD, CHARLES K,** Ga Coll, Milledgeville, GA; JR; BA; Beta Beta Beta 90-; Biol; Lab.

**FLOYD, CHRISTY C,** Univ Of Nc At Greensboro, Greensboro, NC; FR; BA; Hall Cncl Rep 90-; Gamma Sigma Sigma; Nursing.

**FLOYD, DELLA M,** Univ Of Sc At Columbia, Columbia, SC; SR; BA; Yng Rpblcn Clb 87-88; Jdcl Brd 87-88; Delta Delta Delta Sec 87; Elem Ed; Tchg.

**FLOYD JR, HAROLD M,** Phillips Jr Coll Spartanburg, Spartanburg, SC; FR; Cert 89; Business Mngmnt; Mrktng Purchasing.

**FLOYD II, JAMES LEE,** Univ Of Sc At Coastal Carolina, Conway, SC; SO; BA; Coastal Bus Clb 90-; Mssn Chrch Jesus Christ Latter-Day Snts 88-90; Bus Admin.

**FLOYD, JERRY SCOTT,** Middle Ga Coll, Cochran, GA; SO; AS; Eng Clb 86-; Natl Soc Prof Eng 86-; Soph Eng Awd 90; Elec Eng.

**FLOYD, JUDY A,** Memphis St Univ, Memphis, TN; SR; BBA; Ntl Hnrs Scty 90; Deans Lst 80; Memphis Tn Assoc; Volvo Tm Tennis/Phillips Capt 90; Accntng; Bsnss.

**FLOYD, KIMBERLY L,** Richard Bland Coll, Petersburg, VA; SO; AS; Bsn.

**FLOYD, LISA A,** Williamsburg Tech Coll, Kingstree, SC; SO; BS; Sci; Mdl Techlg Chemistry.

**FLOYD, LYNDA G,** Tn Temple Univ, Chattanooga, TN; SO; BA; Choir 90-; Engl; Tchr/Mssnry.

**FLOYD, MICHELE B,** Univ Of Sc At Columbia, Columbia, SC; JR; BS; Gama Beta Phi 90-; AS Orangeburg Calhoun Tech Clg 77; Acctg; MA Txtn.

**FLOYD, MICHON A,** Central St Univ, Wilberforce, OH; SO; BS; Acctg Clb; Pres Schlrshp 89-; Acctg; Financl Anlyst.

**FLOYD, PETAL Y,** Albany St Coll, Albany, GA; SR; Gspl Chr 86-87; GA Assn Nrs 88; Rlgs Life Orgnztn 86-88; Schl Nrsng Hnr Soc; Zeta Phi Beta Pres 89-; Panhellenic Cncl Pres 89-; US Army Spirit Nrsg Awd; BS; Nrsng; Law.

**FLOYD, ROTINA D,** Westmoreland County Comm Coll, Youngwood, PA; SO; BED; Mon Vly Lit Cncl; Tchrs Ed.

**FLOYD, SHERRY P,** Univ Of North Fl, Jacksonville, FL; JR; BBA; Armcn Mgmt Assoc; Gldn Key; Frst Un Natl Bnk Tllr 86-; AS Bus Admn Mgmt 86; Mrktng Mgmt; Bus.

**FLOYD, SHERYL D,** Univ Of Montevallo, Montevallo, AL; SO; BS; Alpha Lambda Delta 89-90; Deans Lst Samford Univ 89; Deans Lst 90; Indstrl Psychlgy.

**FLOYD, SONYA L,** Al St Univ, Montgomery, AL; FR; Phi Eta Sigma; Bsktbl Tm 90-; Math; Engr.

**FLOYD, TAMARA G,** Middle Tn St Univ, Murfreesboro, TN; SO; BS; Gamma Beta Phi; Pol Sci; Law.

**FLOYD, TONYA L,** Chattahoochee Vly St Comm Coll, Phenix City, AL; FR; AS; Cmptr Sci; Cmptr Sys Analyst.

**FLOYD, TOSHJA D,** Jackson St Univ, Jackson, MS; JR; BA; Pol Sci-Pre Law Club 88-; Pierian Lit Soc 89-; Acdmc Hnrs Cncl 89-; Phi Kappa Phi; Sigma Tau Delta 90-; Alpha Lamda Delta 89-; Alpha Mu Gamma 90-; SROP Ind Univ 90; Pres Schlr 88-; Eng/Pre Law; Law.

**FLOYD, VALERIE A,** Coppin St Coll, Baltimore, MD; SR; BS; Pan Hellenic Cncl Sec 90-; Hon Prog 86-88; Zeta Phi Beta Treas Sec 89; Mgmt Sci Acctg; Accnt.

**FLOYD, VICKIE C,** Fayetteville St Univ, Fayetteville, NC; SR; BA; Math/Comp Sci; Grad Schl.

**FLUDD, OLIVIA V,** Hampton Univ, Hampton, VA; SR; BS; Natl Assoc Black Accts 90-; Alpha Kappa Mu 90-; Acctg; CPA.

**FLUKE, DENISE F,** Bethany Coll, Bethany, WV; SO; BA; Jz Bnd 89-90; Im Sprts 90-; Alpha Xi Delta Astnt Tres; Elem Ed; Tchng.

**FLUKER, WAKITA S,** Norfolk St Univ, Norfolk, VA; SO; Alpha Tau 90-.

**FLUMERFELT, SUSAN J,** Cornell Univ Statutory College, Ithaca, NY; JR; BS; Golden Key 90-; Kossoff Awd Otsdng Bus Pln Cmpltd Prsnl Entprs Prog; Deans Lst 88-; Bus Mgmt/Mktg; Bus Mgmt.

**FLY, MILDRED LEIGH,** Ms St Univ, Miss State, MS; SO; BA; Ldr Arts Sci Prog; Gamma Beta Phi 90-; Deans Lst 90-; Psychlgy.

**FLYNN, ALICE J,** George Mason Univ, Fairfax, VA; GD; Gldn Key 90-; Dept Of Navy 80-85; Vredenburg & Co 85-86; AA Chas Co Comm Clg 85; BS 90; Bus; Gvrnmnt.

**FLYNN, ANGELA L,** Middle Tn St Univ, Murfreesboro, TN; BS; ANA Prssa; Mntl Hlth Ornttn Instrctr 84-; AS Rn 84; Mss Cmmctns.

**FLYNN, COLLEEN E,** Union Univ, Jackson, TN; FR; BS; BSU 90-; Bio; Vetrnry Medcn.

**FLYNN, DEBORAH A,** Clarkson Univ, Potsdam, NY; SR; BS; Clarkson Radio Bsn Dir; Scty Women Mngrs 87-; MIS; Prgrmmr Anlyst.

**FLYNN, ELLEN M,** Dowling Coll, Oakdale Li, NY; SR; BA; Clg Newspaper; Orientation Leader; Academic Standards Comm Rep; Alpa Chi VP 89; Kappa Delta Pi; Honors Schlrshp; ATC Schlrshp; Social Science; Social Studies Tchr.

**FLYNN, GWENDOLYN L,** Middle Tn St Univ, Murfreesboro, TN; FR; BBA; Chi Omega 90; Acad Schlrshp Univ TN 90; Mgmt; Htl Mgmt.

**FLYNN, HEATHER C,** Fl International Univ, Miami, FL; JR; BFA; Frddck Brtchr Co Prncpl Dncr 87-88; Bllt Rndlph Prncpl Dncr; Nw Wrld Schl Coll Dnc Ensmbl Schl Rep 89-; Deans Lst 89-; Dncng Lf 89; Arbcs Agst Adsschl Rep Dnc Fstvl; Schl Rep Dnc Fstvl; Dance; Law.

**FLYNN, JAMES S,** Clarkson Univ, Potsdam, NY; SR; BS; Pres Lst 90; Deans Lst 89-90; Chenango Brdge Fire Co Inc 87-; Acctg.

**FLYNN II, JOSEPH C,** Coll Misericordia, Dallas, PA; JR; BS; Acctng Clb Pres; SGA Treas 90-; Stdnt Nwspr Sprts Ed 88/Nws Ed 89; Bsn Clb 90-; Pr Tutor 89-90; Hstry Pre Lw 88-90; IM Ftbl/Vlybl/Sftbl 90-; Acctng/Mgmt; Acctnt.

**FLYNN, KATHLEEN A,** Middle Tn St Univ, Murfreesboro, TN; SO; BSN; T Ball Team Mthr; Relg Educ Vol Tchr; Nrsng; Hosp Surgry.

**FLYNN, KEITH B,** Niagara Univ, Niagara Univ, NY; JR; BS; Ski Clb 89-; Swmmng Tm 88-8 9; Bus Mgmt Hmn Rsrcs; Upper Lvl Mgmt Intl Corp.

**FLYNN, KIRSTEN R,** Me Maritime Academy, Castine, ME; FR; BS; Univ VT Crew Clb 89-90, Big Buddies/Amer 89; Vrsty Slng Tm 90-; Marine Biologist Ocean Scnc; Rsrch/Envrn Prtc.

**FLYNN, SEAN M,** Fl St Univ, Tallahassee, FL; JR; BA; Amer Mktg Assn 90-; Phi Kappa Phi 90-; Intl Bus; Corp Exec.

**FLYNN, SHIRLEY G,** Univ Of Ky, Lexington, KY; SR; Amer Soc Mech Engrs Treas 90-; AIAA VP 90-; Pi Tau Sigma; Alpha Omicron Pi; RA 90-; Mech Engr.

**FLYNN, THERESA M,** Middle Tn St Univ, Murfreesboro, TN; JR; BS; Gamma Beta Phi 90-; Wrk Schlrshp Awrd MTSU 88-; Mss Cmmnctns; Rd TV Mgmt.

**FLYNT, TIMOTHY D,** Ms St Univ, Miss State, MS; JR; BS; Frstry Clb 90-; Scty Amer Frstrs 90-; Xi Sigma Pi; Alpha Omega 89; Vrsty Ftbl/Tnns 89; Frst Mngmt.

**FOAN, WENDY L,** Elms Coll, Chicopee, MA; FR; BSN; Ambssdr 90-; Ornttn Advsr; Rainbow Grnd Offcr 84-; Grnd Crss Clr 90-; Dean Lst; Nrsng.

**FOARD, HEATHER J,** Univ Of Nc At Charlotte, Charlotte, NC; FR; BA; Hl Cncl; Nrsg.

**FOCARINO, MARY,** City Univ Of Ny Queensbrough, New York, NY; JR; AAS; Bus Mgmt/Mktg.

**FODERA, ROSALIA,** Lasell Coll, Newton, MA; SO; ASSOC; Bus Admin.

**FOEHL, STACEY A,** City Univ Of Ny Queensbrough, New York, NY; SO; BA; Alpha Beta Gamma 89; Deans Lst 90-; Psych; Bus Admin.

**FOEHR, DAVID J,** Villanova Univ, Villanova, PA; JR; BS; Engr Bg Bros; AICHE; Tau Beta Pi; Dns Lst 88-90, Chem Engr; MBA Tech Mgmt.**

**FOELLER, ANN-JEANNINE,** Univ Of Toledo, Toledo, OH; GD; JD; Bar Asso 90-; Moot Ct Bd 90-; Am Bar Asso 90-; Oh Bar Asso 90-; Toledo Wmns Bar Asso 90-; Beta Gamma Sigma 84-; Beta Alpha Psi 84-86; Phi Alpha Delta Vice Jstce 90-; Lgl Edctn Cmte 91-; Am Jurispndce Awd 90; Acctng; Law.

**FOERTH, MARY ANN,** City Univ Of Ny Queensbrough, New York, NY; GD; BA; Phi Theta Kappa 90-; Alpha Sigma Lambda 90-; Dns Hnr Lst 88-90; Legal Sec; AA; Urban Studies Env; Law Gov.

**FOGAH, GRACE-ANN L,** Atlantic Union Coll, S Lancaster, MA; JR; Blck Chrstn Union Pub Rel 90-; Spnsh; Educ.

**FOGAN, JACK D,** Wilmington Coll, New Castle, DE; SR; BA; BA; Crmnl Jstc; Law.

**FOGAROS, JOHN R,** Western Ky Univ, Bowling Green, KY; SO; BS; Phi Beta Sigma 89-90; Sigma Chi Treas 89-; Wrstlng IM; Acctg.

**FOGARTY, DEANNE M,** Univ Of Pittsburgh At Bradford, Bradford, PA; FR; BS; Telemktg; Alpha Lambda Delta VP; Lambda Xi Sgt Arms; RA; Hstry/Pol Sci; Law.

**FOGARTY, ELEANOR A,** Immaculata Coll, Immaculata, PA; SR; BA; Socty Adv Mgmt Pres 87-; Outsdrs Clb Co Chr 87-; Mdrn For Lang Assn; Hnr Socty VP 88-; Delta Epsilon Sigma; Kappa Gamma Pi; Chldrns Theater 87-; Cmps Mnstry; Habitat For Hmnty; Dns Lst 87-; Acad Schlrshp 87-; Econ/Bus Admin; Info Mgmt.

**FOGEL, ALTER S,** City Univ Of Ny Brooklyn Coll, Brooklyn, NY; SR; BS; Clg Newspapr Ed-In-Chief 88; Stdnt Govt 89; Golden Key Scty; Cntry Fair Awd; Stdnt Govt Serv Awd 90; Lfetme Serv Awd; Golden Pen Awd 90; Intrn Asst To CPA 90; Alpha Sigma Lamda Awd; BA Tlmdcl Smnry Oholei Torah 90; Accntng; Attrny.

**FOGLE, CHRISTOPHER M,** Wilmington Coll, Wilmington, OH; FR; BA; Stu Elec Comm 90-; Flwshp Chrstn Stu 90-; Chorale 90-; Var Wrstlg 90-; Scndry Educ; Tchr.

**FOGLE, CONNIE J,** Middle Tn St Univ, Murfreesboro, TN; JR; BA; NEA 89-; STEA 90-; Spcl Ed Elem Ed; Tch.

**FOGLE, MELISSA D,** Hampton Univ, Hampton, VA; FR; BA; Bus Clb 90-; Bus/Finance; Company Owner.

**FOGLEMAN, MICHAEL J,** Univ Of Sc At Columbia, Columbia, SC; FR; BS; Karate Clb 90-; Fncng Clb 90-; Hnrs Clg 90-; Math Physics; Rsrch.

**FOGLIETTI, JODI L,** Univ Of Sc At Columbia, Columbia, SC; SR; BA; Adv Club Secy 90-; IFAW 89-; Save/Chldrn 89-; PVA 90-; Busn Admin/Mrktg; Cmmctns/Sls.

**FOGLIETTI, JODI L,** Univ Of Sc At Coastal Carolina, Conway, SC; SR; Advrtsg Clb Secr 90-; Dns Lst 87-; IFAW 89-; Save-The-Children 89-; PVA 90-; BA; Bsn Adm/Mktg; Cmnctn/Sls.

**FOGT, JASON E,** Univ Of Cincinnati, Cincinnati, OH; FR.

**FOIL, JAY H,** Univ Of Southern Ms, Hattiesburg, MS; SR; BS; Arnold Air Scty Dpty Cmndr 89-90; Physics; Air Force Ofcr.

**FOKSEANG, BRIGITTE M,** City Univ Of Ny Baruch Coll, New York, NY; JR; BBA; Cmptr Info Sys; Sys Analyst.

**FOLDOE, LARRY E,** Toccoa Falls Coll, Toccoa Falls, GA; SR; BA; Mrrd Stdnt Assoc VP 89-; Delta Epsilon Chi; PTO Exc Com 89-; BA; BS 74; Pstrl Mnstrs.

**FOLEY, BRENDA A,** Villanova Univ, Villanova, PA; FR; Stdnt Pgmg Cncl; Hmls Com; Alpha Epsilon Delta; Alpha Phi; Hmlss Com Emmaus Rtrt Vol; Deans Lst; Crew; Sci; Medcl.

**FOLEY, COLLEEN A,** Nc Central Univ, Durham, NC; BA Boston Coll 83; Engl; Law.

**FOLEY, CRISTINA A,** King Coll, Bristol, TN; SR; BA; Nw Stdnt Ornttn Com 86; Schl Plys 88; Chr And Cllgm 86-; Hnrs In Soph Engl Lit 87; Hnrs In Wstrn Civ 87; Hnrs In Intrmdte Frnch 88; Engl; Free Lnce Wrtng.

**FOLEY, EILEEN,** Eckerd Coll, St Petersburg, FL; GD; BA; Phi Theta Kappa 87-; Outstndng Stdnt In Engl/Creatv Actvties 89; Phi Theta Kappa Awrd 88; SAFE Vol Crisis Cnslr 85-88; Nghbrhd Crm Wtch Capt 87-89; Sec/Cmptr Bckgrnd 65-85; AA St Ptrsbrgh Jr Coll 89; Engl; Lit.

**FOLEY JR, HENRY W,** Widener Univ, Chester, PA; JR; BSEE; IEEE 90-; Tau Beta Pi Pres; Phi Kappa Phi 90-; ASEE Delaware Tech Comm Coll 89; US Navy Rdr Tech Cmmrcl TV Maint Eng 89; Eng; Cmmnctn Elecs.

**FOLEY, IAN D,** Niagara Univ, Niagara Univ, NY; SR; BA; Niagara Univ Ftr Tchrs Clb 82-; Delta Epsilon Sigma 90-; Pi Lambda Theta 90-; Sigma Tau Delta 90-; Eng Ed; Mdl Schl Lng Arts Tchr.

**FOLEY, LA DONNA J,** Christopher Newport Coll, Newport News, VA; SR; BSA; The Natl Assn Acctnts 90-; BS Rdfrd Univ VA 85; Acctg; CPA/MNGMNT Acctg.

**FOLEY, MARION L,** Lesley Coll, Cambridge, MA; JR; Alliance Colorguard Greater Boston Citations Jr Drum & Bugle Corp Instr 88-89; Summer Intern Bull HN Inf Sys Inc 88-; Erly Chldhd Edn.

**FOLEY, MELANIE R,** Univ Of Tn At Martin, Martin, TN; SO; BS; Univ Schlrs Org VP 89-; Phi Eta Sigma; Mu Epsilon Delta Pledge VP 89-; Alpha Omicron Pi Asst Treas 90-; Bio; Med.

**FOLEY, MICHELLE,** Colby Sawyer Coll, New London, NH; JR; BA; Rsdnt Assist 89-90; Dance Clb Sec/Treas; Psych; Bsnss/Psych.

**FOLEY, ROGER W,** Le Moyne Coll, Syracuse, NY; SR; JD; Acad Affrs Comm 90-; Pre-Law Soc 88-; Pol Sci Acad 88-; Pi Gamma Mu 90-; Phi Sigma Tau 90-; BA; Pol Sci; Law.

**FOLEY, SHARON F,** Cumberland Coll, Williamsburg, KY; SR; BA; USAA All-American Scholars; High Hnrs 88-; Deans List 88-; Data Processing Secretraial Sci; Cmptr/Sec.

**FOLEY, THOMAS J,** Bryant Stratton Bus Inst Roch, Rochester, NY; SO; ADS; Acctng; CPA.

**FOLEY, THOMAS P,** Univ Of Al At Birmingham, Birmingham, AL; FR; Hmcmng Com 90-; Springfest Com 90-; ASME Sec 90-; Pres Lst; Deans Lst; Mech Eng.

**FOLEY, TIMOTHY L,** Old Dominion Univ, Norfolk, VA; JR; BSEET; Quail Unlmtd 86-; Elctrncs; Engnrng.

**FOLEY JR, WILLIAM M,** Hudson Valley Comm Coll, Troy, NY; SO; BA; Gen Contrctrs Assn; Alpha Chi Rho; AAS Hudsn Vly Comm Clg; Const Mgmt; Cvl Eng.

**FOLGER, DEBORAH K,** West Liberty St Coll, West Liberty, WV; JR; BA; Chi Beta Phi; Ordr Estrn Star 89-; Unit Meth Ch 83-; Wheeling Clinic 87-89; CST Cert 77; Biology/Chem; Educ.

**FOLINO, JILL A,** Fl St Univ, Tallahassee, FL; SR; BS; Ldy Sclphntrs; Phi Eta Sigma; Gldn Key; Mrtr Brd; Omicron Delta Kappa Mrtr Brd; Beta Kappa Alpha Mmbrshp Exc 90-; Kappa Dleta Chptr Sec 89-90; Intern Vctm Wtnss Unt; Intern Rsswll Hs Dtntn Cntr 88-90; Scl Wrk.

**FOLINO, TAMMY D,** Univ Of Fl, Gainesville, FL; SR; MACC; Ldrshp 87-88; Amer Mktg Assn Rsrch Chrmn 89-; AIESEC Chrmn 90-; Self Comm PR Chr 88-89; Alpha Lambda Delta; Deans Lst 89-; Beta Gamma Sigma; Sigma Tau Sigma Coord 88-; Alpha Omicron Pi Swthrt Rush Chr 88-; Comm Vlntr 90-; Mktg; Acctng.

**FOLK, BRIAN M,** Siena Coll, Loudonville, NY; SR; BS; Amer Chmcl Soc Stdnt Afflte; Siena Clge Chem Club 87-; Radio Statn Prog Dir 87-88; Sigma Pi Sigma 90-; Scientific Rsch Hnr Soc; Chem Awd; Intern Sterling Rsch Group A Div Of Sterling Drug Sr Rsch Tchn 90-; Chemistry; Ph D Oreganic Chem.

**FOLK, DEBRA LYNN S,** Univ Of Sc At Spartanburg, Spartanburg, SC; SR; BS; Red Crs; Nrsng.

**FOLKENFLIK, DAVID P,** Ms Coll, Clinton, MS; GD; JD; Deans Lst 87-88; BA Univ S Fla 88; AA St Ptrsbrg Jr Clg 86; Law.

**FOLKERTH, LAURA R,** Oh St Univ, Columbus, OH; SR; BS; Phi Kappa Phi; Mathematics; Mathematics Eng.

**FOLKERTS, JANE A,** Methodist Coll, Fayetteville, NC; JR; BS; Stu Educ Assoc 90-; Chld Care Tech Stu Yr 88; Chld Care Intrnshp 87-88; Vlybl 86-87; AAS 88; AS 89; Elem Ed; Tchg.

**FOLLAND, NORA T,** Webber Coll, Babson Park, FL; SO; BA; Stdnt Govt Treas 89-90; Fshn Clb 90-; Fshn Rtlng; Rtl Byr.

**FOLMER, EMILY J,** Oh Univ, Athens, OH; FR; BED; Art; Art Tchr.

**FOLSOM, TAMMY L,** Fl A & M Univ, Tallahassee, FL; SR; AA No FL Jr Coll 89; Elem Edn.

**FOLSTER, MICHELLE M,** Mount Saint Mary Coll, Newburgh, NY; JR; BA; Cmmtr Cncl VP 90-; Nwsppr Stff Wrtr 90; Deans Lst 89-; Mrktng Intern; Cmmnctn Arts.

**FOLTZ, ANGELA M,** Lock Haven Univ, Lock Haven, PA; FR.

**FOLZENLOGEN, JANICE R,** Univ Of Cin R Walters Coll, Blue Ash, OH; FR; Golden Key 87; Sigma Theta Tao 87-; RN 87-; BSN 87; Pharm.

**FOMENKO, PATRICIA P,** Southern Vt Coll, Bennington, VT; FR; BA; Trout Unlmtd Hoosuck Sec Trea 88-; BRCC Brd Dir Sec 90-; RT St Joseph Hosp 69; Bus/Accntng; Mngt.

**FONAROV, ILYA,** Fl International Univ, Miami, FL; SO; BSN; SGA Pblcty Chr 89-; Brd Gvrnrs; Scl/Cltrl; Phi Lamda Beta 90-; Tau Epsilon Phi Scrb Bnnr Chr 89-; SGA Bnnr Cntst Awds 90; IM Bsktbl/Ftbl 89-; Nrsng.

**FONDA, ANDREW R,** Radford Univ, Radford, VA; SO; BA; Bsns; Mrktng.

**FONG, AMY HSIAO MING,** Georgetown Univ, Washington, DC; JR; CPA; AIESEC Mrktng Rep 88-89; Chlng Georgetwn Physcl Dsability Tres Awrns Clb 90-; Deans Lsts 90-; Fnlst Cmmnwlth Exchng Prgrm 89; Intrn Sanwa Bnk Ca 90; Accntng Intrnl Mgmnt; CPA.

**FONG, NEIL A,** Fl International Univ, Miami, FL; FR; Pre Med Soc; Fac Schlrshp; Chem/Bio; Med.

**FONG, WAI H,** City Univ Of Ny Baruch Coll, New York, NY; SO; Beta Alpha Psi; Acctg; CPA.

**FONKE, JEROME E,** Life Coll, Marietta, GA; GD; DC; Capt USAF Sprtd Frm Srvce 83; BS East Carolina Univ 76; MS Univ Of Arkansas 81; Chrprctc; Dr Of Chrprctc.

**FONS, BENJAMIN A,** Ga Inst Of Tech At Atlanta, Atlanta, GA; SR; BEE; Gold Key 89-; Elec Eng/Mgmnt.**

**FONSECA, GWENDOLYN F,** Tufts Univ, Medford, MA; SO; BA; Williams Clg Mystic; Seaport Maritime Stds Pgm; Anthrplgy; Law.**

**FONTAINE, LORETTA A,** S U N Y At Buffalo, Buffalo, NY; SR; AIAS; Stdt Editorial Brd Intersight; UB Honors Prog; NY Telephone Schrlshp; BPS; Architecture.

**FONTAINE, MARYANNE L,** William Carey Coll, Hattiesburg, MS; JR; BSN; Nrsng.

**FONTAN, CHRISTIE A,** Univ Of Southern Ms, Hattiesburg, MS; SO; BA; Bus; Acctg.

**FONTANA, DANILO,** Bunker Hill Comm Coll, Boston, MA; SO; Amnsty Intl Clb 89-90; Stdnt Cncl Sen Vce Chrprsn 89-; Brd Trstees Stdnt Trstee 90-; Alpha Kappa Mu 90-; Phi Theta Kappa 90-; Peer Adv 89-90; Acad Excl Awd 89-90; Pres Ldrshp Awd 90-; AA; Econs/Env Sci; Law.

**FONTANA, LAURA L,** Univ Of Tn At Martin, Martin, TN; SR; BA; STEA 90-; Alpha Omicron Pi 87-90; Alpha Tau Omega Ltl Sistr Sr Pnhlnc 87-90; IM S 86-90; Erly Chldhd Ed; Tchng.

**FONTANESE, ELIZABETH A,** D Youville Coll, Buffalo, NY; JR; MPT; Stdnt Phys Thrpy Assoc 89-90; USAF Rsrv SSGT 87-; Work For Caterer; Phys Thrpy.

**FONTANESI, MOLLY L,** Villanova Univ, Villanova, PA; JR; BA; Cmpsu Mnstry 89-; Tri Delta 89-; Chi Alpha 90-; Phi Kappa Phi; Cmmn Arts; Law.

**FONTANEZ, BARBARA J,** Nyack Coll, Nyack, NY; SR; Clg Chrl Pres 86-90; MENC Pres 88-90; Orchstra/RA/MSC Dept Asst; Hnr Soc; Crtfct Mrt Otstndng Svc Clg Cmnty; BMUS 90; Msc Tchr.

**FONTE, JEAN-NATE,** City Univ Of Ny Kingsborough, Brooklyn, NY; GD; BA; Deans Lst 90; Sftbl 86-87; AAS Kingsborough Comm Clg; Communications; Advertising/Music Prod/Eng.

**FONTIANE, LA LORIA,** Tougaloo Coll, Tougaloo, MS; JR; BA; Tougaloo Clg Gspl Choir; Pltcl Sci Clb; Alpha Lambda Delta; Delta Sigma Theta; Gamma Psi; Pltcl Sci Intrnshp; Pltcl Sci; Clg Prfsr.

**FONTZ, DAVID M,** Anne Arundel Comm Coll, Arnold, MD; FR; MA; Psychology.

**FONVIELLE, LINDA M,** Abraham Baldwin Agri Coll, Tifton, GA; JR; PHARM; Phi Theta Kappa; Physics/Chem/Math Tutor; Phi Theta Kappa; Prmcy Tech; Pharmacy.

**FOO, G TREVOR,** Barry Univ, Miami, FL; SR; BA; Comp Sci Assoc Pres 88-90; Data Proc Mgmt Assoc 88-; Snny Ils C C Yth Grp Dir 89-90; Phi Theta Kappa Publ Rels 88-; MDCC CIS Dept Awds 89-90; Hon Mntn ; Fl Clg Stdnt Of Yr 90; AA Miami-Dade Comm Clg 90; Comp Inf Sci; Mgmt.

**FOOSE, GARY J,** Wv Univ, Morgantown, WV; JR; BS; Am Soc Cvl Engr Sgt 90-; Chi Epsilon Sec-Treas 90-; Cvl Engr.

**FOOSHEE JR, JOHN D,** King Coll, Bristol, TN; JR; BA; Cmps Crsd Christ Ldr 89; Jericho Pryr Wlk Pryr Ldr Orgzr/Sprvsr; Stdnt Govt-Cnstn Rvsn Com Jr Rep; Pres Hon Rl 90; A..-Amer Schlr; Pi Kappa Alpha 89-90; Hghlnd Pk Prsbtrn Chrch Smmr Stf Intrn 90-; Bible/Rlgn; Pstr.

**FOOSHEE, SIDNEY G,** Univ Of Ky, Lexington, KY; SR; BA; Mrchng/Pep Band 87-; Shotokan Karate Clb 89-; Psi Chi 88-; Intern Harris Psychological Svc Ctr 89-; Psychology; Phd Industrial/Org Psych.

**FOOTE, ALICIA C,** Georgetown Univ, Washington, DC; JR; BSN; Cmps Mnstry 88-; Sigma Theta Tau 90-; Nursing/Pre Med.

**FOOTE, GARY L,** Valdosta St Coll, Valdosta, GA; SR; BBA; Phi Kappa Phi; Alpha Chi; Beta Gamma Sigma; Alpha Epsilon Alpha Chrmn Nwslttr; USAF 82-; AAS Comm Coll AF 89; Accntng; Pblc Indstrl Govt Accntng.

**FOOTE, MELANIE D,** Mary Washington Coll, Fredericksburg, VA; FR; Bushnell Hl Cncl Sec 90-; Bushnell Hl Jdcl Bd Sec 90-; IM Vlybl 90-; Psychlgy/Spnsh; Chld Psychlgst.

**FORAKER, SHANNON K,** Memphis St Univ, Memphis, TN; SR; BBA; Alpha Lambda Delta 89-; Delta Epsilon Phi 86-; Phi Kappa Phi 91-; Golden Key 89-; Intrnshp Intl Bus Smith Nephew Richards 90-; Intl Bus; European Intl Afrs U S Govt.**

**FORBES, BLAIR L,** Univ Of The Dist Of Columbia, Washington, DC; SO; BA; Assn Srgcl Tchnlgst 90-; Schl Hlth Care Sciences 88; Physcl Thrpy.

**FORBES, JOHN W,** Univ Of The Virgin Islands, St Thomas, VI; SR; BA; Accntng Assoc Pres 90-; Prsdnts Clb; Deans Lst; Tennis 90; Vlybl Clb Tres; Accntng; Cpa.

**FORBES, ROCHELLE N,** Bethune Cookman Coll, Daytona Beach, FL; GD; Bus Rotaract Clb; Cncl Person-At-Lg Stdnt Govt; Womens Snt Chapln; Bus Hons Soc; Hon Roll; Rec Natl Clg Bus Merit Winner 90; Alpha Kappa Alpha Treas/Mbrshp Chrmn; Army SROTC Basic Trng 89; Shell Oil Intrnshp Admin Asst 90; Marching Bnd; BS; Mngmnt; Grad Schl.

**FORBES, SONYA A,** Tougaloo Coll, Tougaloo, MS; FR; BS; Pre Hlth Clb 90-; Alph Lmbd Dlt Chpln; Bio; Medcn.

**FORBES, THOMAS E,** Birmingham Southern Coll, Birmingham, AL; FR; BS; Alpha Lambda Delta; Phi Eta Sigma; Math; Elect Eng.

**FORBES, WENDY A,** Univ Of Miami, Coral Gables, FL; JR; BS; Rsdnt Asst 90-; Mrtr Brd 90-; Delta Gamma Pres 88-; Hnrs Pgm 88-; Mtn Pctrs/Art Hstry; Scrn Wrtng.

**FORBIS, NANCY M,** Queens Coll, Charlotte, NC; JR; Natl Assoc Accts; Mortar Brd Pi Epsilon Alpha; Natl Clgt Busn Merit Awd 89-; Dana Schlrshp 90-; NC Beal Estate Broker/Christ Lutheran Chrh; Charlotte Brd Reltrs/Various Civic Activities; Busn/Acctng; CPA.

**FORBUS, KEVIN L,** Central Al Comm Coll, Alexander City, AL; FR; BS; Deans Lst 90; Eng; Cmptr Eng.

**FORCIER, CHARLES J,** Villanova Univ, Villanova, PA; SR; BA; Blue Key 89-; Boxing Tm 87-89; Chi Alpha 89-91; Pi Kappa Alpha 89-; Intern KYW TV Philadelphia; Comm Arts; Sprts Public Rltns.

**FORD, ANGELA YVETTE,** Memphis St Univ, Memphis, TN; JR; BBA; Blck Student Assoc 90-; Gamma Beta Phi 89-; Golden Key 90-; Blck Schlrs Unlmtd 89-; Beta Gamma Sigma; INROADS Intern 88-; INROADS Schlr Yr 90; Busn; Risk Mgr.

**FORD, BOYD D,** Mount Aloysius Jr Coll, Cresson, PA; FR; BA; Fd Svc Cmte 90-; Dvlpmntl Studies Prog Tutor; Crmnlgy; Law.

**FORD, BRADLEY DON,** Memphis St Univ, Memphis, TN; JR; Amer Mrktg Assoc 90-; Bsktbl/Bsbl/Trck 90-; BA; Bus; R/D.

**FORD, CAROL C,** Radford Univ, Radford, VA; SO; BED; Phi Sigma Sigma; Spec Ed; Tchr.

**FORD, CAROL L,** Claflin Coll, Orangeburg, SC; JR; BA; NAACP 89-90; Hnr Roll 88-89; Dns Lst 89-90; Acad Award 89-; Bsktbl 88-; Sclgy; Law Enfor.**

**FORD, CAROL M,** Glassboro St Coll, Glassboro, NJ; SR; BA; Epsilon Theta Sigma 90; Engl; Pblctns.

**FORD, CAROLINE E,** Atlantic Comm Coll, Mays Landing, NJ; FR; AAS; Phi Theta Kappa; Phys Thrpy Asst; Physcl Thrpst.

**FORD, CATHY L,** Andover Coll, Portland, ME; SR; Natl Assoc Accntnts90-; VITA 90; Hnr Scty 89-; Intern Chmbr Cmmrc 90; Cncl Acctncy 90-; AAS Actg; AAS Bus Admn; Acctg Bus Admn.

**FORD, CRAIG,** Univ Of Southern Ms, Hattiesburg, MS; JR; Soc Prfsnl Jrnlst 90; Radio T V New Dir Assn; Radio Sport News Stdnt; Radio In Depth Stdnt; Radio T V Film; Brdcst Jrnlsm.

**FORD, DARRELL L,** Erie Comm Coll South Cmps, Orchard Park, NY; SR; AAS; Cmptr Repair Tech; Elctrcl Engr.

**FORD, DAVID M,** S U N Y At Buffalo, Buffalo, NY; SR; PHD; AICHE Stdnt Chptr 89-91; Phi Eta Sigma 87-; Tau Beta Pi Comm Chrmn 89-; SUNY AB Presidential Hnrs Schlr; SUNYAB Sr Fllwshp Chemcl Engrng; Summa Cum Laude Grad; Allied Signal Corp Grant; BS; Chemical Engrng; Engrng Research.

**FORD, DEMETRA D,** Univ Of Sc At Columbia, Columbia, SC; FR; Assoc Afrcn Amer Stu 90-; NAACP 90-; Engr.

**FORD, DIONE M,** Central St Univ, Wilberforce, OH; FR; Cntrl State Univ Deans List; Bus Mgmt.

**FORD, DOUGLAS E,** Fl International Univ, Miami, FL; SR; BA; Enlghtnmnt Entrprs Soc 89-; Sigma Tau Delta; Engl; Tchng.

**FORD, DOUGLAS EDMOND,** Pellissippi St Tech Comm Coll, Knoxville, TN; GD; Tau Alpha Pi 89-; Phi Theta Kappa 89-; AAS; Chmcl Engnrng; Tchncn.

**FORD, EDWIN E,** Savannah St Coll, Savannah, GA; SR; Crmnl Jstc Clb 88-; Deans List/Hnr Rl/Pres Deans Lst 87-; Tiger Phi Tiger 86-; Athltc Schlrshps; Drew Schlrshp; William E Grant Awd; MVP Sprng Gm 87; Pres Deans Lst; Ftbl Tm Cpt 86-90; Crmnl Jstc; Fed Law Enfrcmnt.

**FORD, ELEANORA R,** Christopher Newport Coll, Newport News, VA; JR; BS; Stdnt Govt Assoc 88-90; Natl Assoc Accntnts Pres 89-90; Mnrty Stdnts Assoc 88-90; Stdnt Ldrshp Inst 89; Intrnshp CPA Frm; Acctg; CPA.

**FORD, EVA V,** Hudson Valley Comm Coll, Troy, NY; GD; AAS; Gold Key Tour Guide 89f Theatre Clb Dir 89; Deans Lst 89f Pres Lst 89; Cashier; Bkkpr; Accntng; Own Grnhse Bsnss.

**FORD, FELISA C,** Jackson St Univ, Jackson, MS; SR; PHD; Pltcl Sci Pre Law Clb; Alpha Lambda Delta 88-; Phi Kappa Phi; Alpha Kappa Alpha VP 89-; Prsdnts Lst; Deans Lst Schlr Hnr Dvsn; BA; Pltcl Sci Intrntnl Rltns; Tch Unvrsty Lvl.

**FORD SR, GLENN J,** Coppin St Coll, Baltimore, MD; SR; BS; AA Essex Comm Coll 89; Mgmt Sci/Psychlgy; Daycr Sprvsr/Alchl-Drg.

**FORD, GURTH A,** Tuskegee Univ, Tuskegee Inst, AL; JR; BA; Bahamian Stdnts Assn Treas 90-; Intrntl Stdnt Assn 89-; Intrntl Stdnt Scr Tm Cl 89-; Fld Tech Cmptr Centre Ltd 87-89; Assoc Arts Electrncs Coll Bahamas; Elec Eng/Math; Eng/Tchng.

**FORD, HOLLY A,** Univ Of Cincinnati, Cincinnati, OH; JR; BFA; News Record Stf Wrtr; Dns Lst; Guardian Angels Catholic Church 90-; Consrvtry Schlrshp 90-; Brdcstg; Critic-Film/Art/Music.

**FORD, IAN S,** Univ Of Sc At Columbia, Columbia, SC; JR; BA; Resid Hall Senator 90-; St Thomas Moore Folk Chr 90; Flwshp Christian Athl 90; Phi Beta Kapp; Golden Key 90-; Alpha Lambda Delta 88-; Rural Mission Workcamp 90-; Freshman Contact Prog 90-; K; Political Sci; Law.

**FORD, JACKIE R,** Stillman Coll, Tuscaloosa, AL; SO; BA; Bnd Swthrt 89-; Cls Ofcr Tres 90-; Amer Soc Wmn Acctnts Comm Stu Actvs 90-; Gamma Jota Sigma 90-; Cordell Wynn Hnrs; Phi Beta Lambda Bus Tres 90-; Delta Sigma Theta; Alpha Phi Alpha Tres 89-; Aids Peer Educ; USAA All Amer Schlr; Bus Admin; CPA.

**FORD, JACQUELINE D,** Univ Of Montevallo, Montevallo, AL; SR; Stdnt Govt Assn Sntr 87-; Stdnt Ala Educ Assn 90-; Omicron Delta Kappa 90-; Kappa Delta Pi 90-; Alpha Hon Soc 87-; Alpha Delta Pi 87-; Cls Fvrte 87; Head Rush Cnslr 90-; Ldrshp Schlrshp 87-88.

**FORD III, JAMES,** Valdosta St Coll, Valdosta, GA; FR; BM; Blzn Brgd; Vldsta Symphny Orch; Jazz Ensmbl; Music Educ; Tchr.

**FORD, JEANNE J,** Atlantic Comm Coll, Mays Landing, NJ; SO; BA; Bus.

**FORD, JEFFREY B,** Al A & M Univ, Normal, AL; JR; Alpha Kappa Mu 90-; Deans Lst 88-; Pres Schlr 89-; Smr Apprntcshp 88; Brkhvn Natl Lab Smstr/Smr Prog; Biolgy/Chemstry; Med.

**FORD, JOHN E,** Merrimack Coll, North Andover, MA; JR; BA; Biology Club/Natl Rifle Assoc VP Bio Club; Natl Trapping Assoc; Natl Wldlf Rehab Assoc/No Andover Boxing Clb; Men Of Merrimac Schlrshp; CRC Achvmnt Awd; Biology; Medicine.

**FORD, JUANAKEE,** Vance Granville Comm Coll, Henderson, NC; FR; AS; Phi Theta Kappa 90-; Accounting; Acctng Fed/Govt.

**FORD, KENITRA J,** Howard Univ, Washington, DC; SO; BA; Club Detroit 89-; Jazz Stds; Career Music.

**FORD, KIMBAL D,** Univ Of Ky, Lexington, KY; SR; BPHAR; KY Acdmy Stu Phrmcy 89-; Stu Cmmtt Drg Awrnss Educ 89-90; Phrmcy Pltcl Actn Cmmtt; Kappa Psi Scl Chrmn 89-; Sigma Chi 88-; Vrsty Bsbl 86-87; Phrmcy; Clncl Phrmcy.

**FORD, KRYSTAL LISETTE,** Hampton Univ, Hampton, VA; FR; BA; Pol Sci; Law/Crmnl.

**FORD, LA TANYA R,** Ky St Univ, Frankfort, KY; SR; BA; SGA Sec 90-; Alpha Kappa Alpha Sec 90-; Prsdntl Schlrshp; Bsns Mgmnt.

**FORD, LACY ANN,** Bridgewater Coll, Bridgewater, VA; SR; BS; Stdnt Educ Assn 89-; Im; Elem Educ; Tchng.

**FORD, LAURA C,** Roane St Comm Coll, Harriman, TN; SO; BA; STARS Art Clb 89-; Lit Clb VP 89-90; Audio Visl Clb 90; Otstndng Spkr Awd 89-90; Merit Awd Roane St Art Comp 89-; Meret Awd TN St Comm Clg Art Comp; Fine Art; Photgrphr.

**FORD, LOKITHA T,** Central St Univ, Wilberforce, OH; FR; BA; Comp Inf Sys Club; Deans List; IM Sftbl; Bus Admn/Fin; Fin Cnsltnt.

**FORD, LUCY R,** East Tn St Univ, Johnson City, TN; SO; Alpha Lambda Delta.

**FORD, MARIA PIERCE,** Fayetteville St Univ, Fayetteville, NC; SO; BS; Chncllrs Schlr; Bio/Sci Clb; Ft Bragg Offcrs Wvs Schlr Awd; Chncllrs Lst; Dns Lst; Hnr Std Awd; Bio/Ed; Tchr.

**FORD, MELISSA A,** Univ Of Pittsburgh At Bradford, Bradford, PA; SO; BS; Psych Clb Treas 90-; Photo Clb 89-90; Psi Chi Pres; Alpha Lambda Delta 90; Amer Psych Assoc; Psych.

**FORD, MICHAEL C,** Univ Of Southern Ms, Hattiesburg, MS; JR; Soc Prof Jrnlsts 90-; Radio TV Nws Dir Assoc; MAPBA Stdnt Contst 1st Pl Radio Spt Nws; SPJ Mrk Excl Contst 1st Pl 90; Marvin Reuben Schlrshp; Radio/T V/Flm; Brdcst Jrnlsm.

**FORD, MICHAEL L,** Ms St Univ, Miss State, MS; JR; BS; AAS N E MS Comm Coll 85; CET Natl Inst 90; Trade/Tech; Eng.

**FORD, NICOLE Y,** Univ Of Sc At Columbia, Columbia, SC; FR; BA; Cncl 90-; Mnrty Asst Peer Pro; Assoc Afrcn Amer Stu 90-; NAACP 90-; Cthlc Yth Org 89-; Psych; Corp Law.

**FORD JR, RICHARD,** Johnson C Smith Univ, Charlotte, NC; JR; BS; MBRS; IM Bsktbl; Chem; Indust.

**FORD, ROBERT T,** Middlesex Comm Coll, Bedford, MA; SO; BS; Crmnl Justice Assoc Pres 87-88; Concord Dist Ct Concord MA 87-88; Westford Police Dept 87; Reading Police Dept 87-89; Danvers Police Dept 87-89; Pol Sci; Law.

**FORD, RODRICK D,** Johnson C Smith Univ, Charlotte, NC; SR; Engl Hnr Soc 90; Athletic Trnr Ftbl BB Tms Spec Asst 86; BA; Pblc Rltns; Sprts Mngmnt.

**FORD, STEVEN G,** Pellissippi St Tech Comm Coll, Knoxville, TN; SR; ASSOC; Tau Alpha Pi; Phi Theta Kappa 90-; Purch Agnt; Mech Engr Tech.

**FORD, TAMARA H,** Lexington Comm Coll, Lexington, KY; FR; BA; Deans Lst 90; Cert Fugazzi Clg 82; Nrsg.

**FORD, TIMOTHY FRANCIS,** Slippery Rock Univ, Slippery Rock, PA; JR; BA; PA State Assn HPERD 90; SRU HPERD 90; Nom VP HPERD; Pi Epsilon Kappa 90; Phi Sigma Pi 90-; Me Peing Cheng Schlrshp; Deans Lst 89-90; W Chester U Ftbl Vars; Hlth/Phys Ed; Tchr/Coach.

**FORD, TRAVIS M,** Memphis St Univ, Memphis, TN; GD; Edward A Hamilton Frfghtr Schlrshp 89; TN Frmns Assc 89; Intrntl Frfghtr 85-; Metro Fire Dept 85-; BA 90; Assc Nashville State Tech Inst 82.

**FORD, WILLIE M,** Tn St Univ, Nashville, TN; JR; BS; Peer Cnslr Pgm 89-90; Hon Pgm 87-; Cmptr Sci Clb 89-; Mead Mnrty Schlrshp 90-; Rock Island Arsenal Intrnshp 89-90; Cmptr Sci; Analyst.

**FORDE, EVERTON D,** Columbia Union Coll, Takoma Park, MD; SR; BSC; Un Way Cmpgn Sol 86-89; Wldlfe Cnsvtn Intnl; Smithsonian Inst Mem 88-89; Exptnl Acad Prfmnce Montgomery Colg 90; Psych Nrs Barbados N W Med Svcs Coord MD SPA; Dipl Nrsg Barbados Schl/Nrsg 79; Hlth Care Admin; MBA Admin/Hlth Store.

**FORDER, NORMAN H,** Unity Coll, Unity, ME; SO; BA; Soccer Mgr 90; Bsktbl Mgr 89; Dns Lst 89-; Cnsrvtn Law Enfrcmnt; Law Enfrcmnt.

**FORDHAM, AMY M,** Univ Of Southern Ms, Hattiesburg, MS; JR; Fash Mrchndsng.

**FORDHAM, CINDY L,** Univ Of Sc At Columbia, Columbia, SC; FR; BA; Phi Eta Sigma; Psychlgy; Scl Wrk.

**FORDHAM, MICHELLE,** Ms St Univ, Miss State, MS; SO; BS; Block/Brdl Clb 89-; Pre-Vet Clb 89-; Meat Jdgng Tm; Gamma Beta Phi 90; Alpha Lambda Delta 89-90; Phi Eta Sigma 89-90; Anml Sci/Pre-Vet Med; DVM.

**FORE, DEBRA F,** Fayetteville St Univ, Fayetteville, NC; SO; BS; Acctg; CPA.

**FORE, JAMES S,** Gaston Coll, Dallas, NC; BIP; Dallas Gospel Lights 90-F; Mechl Drafting/CAD.

**FORE, JANET M,** Univ Of Southern Ms, Hattiesburg, MS; JR; BS; Blldg Brk MGCCC Perk Campus Rep 90; ADULT 89-90; Grad W/Hons MGCCC 90; Dns Lst; AA MGCCC Perk Campus 90; Soc Wrk.

**FORE, JIMM D,** Radford Univ, Radford, VA; SR; BS; Amer Mktg Assn 90-; Intrshp W/Sthwstrn Regl Nrsg Cncl Cmnwlth VA 90-; IM Ftbl/Bsktbl/Sccr/Sftbl/Vlybl Coach/Plyr 87-; Mktg; MBA Mktg Rsrch.

**FOREHAND, BEVERLY E,** Western Ky Univ, Bowling Green, KY; SO; BAMBA; Herald Staff Features Wrtr 89-90; Museum Stdnt Assist 89-; Zepyrus Poetry Pblctn 89-90; Psi Eta Sigma 90-; Deans/Pres Lsts 89-; Two Ten Schlr 89-; Cherry Hts Schlrshp 89-; Mary Clinard Schlrshp 89; Engl Lit/Hnrs Hist; Hist.

**FOREMAN, AMY L,** Ky Wesleyan Coll, Owensboro, KY; SR; BA; Ky Ed Assoc Stdnt Prog Pres 88; Bapt Stdnt Union Pres 87; Stdnt Govt Sntr 88; Alpha Chi 89; Sigma Kappa 88; Lit Sis To Sigma Alpha Mu 89; Pres Schlrshp; Ntl Cllgte Ed Awds Wnnr; Cum Laude; Elm Ed; Tchr.

**FORET JR, JOHN B,** Livingston Univ, Livingston, AL; SO; Schlrshp Ftbl Ltr 89-; Physcl Thrpst Asst.

**FORGRAVE, KATHERESA M,** Oh St Univ At Newark, Newark, OH; FR; BA; Newark Camp Hon Soc 90-; Alpha Lambda Delta 90-; Phi Eta Sigma 90-; Vlntr Licking Mem Hosp 90-; Occ Ther.

**FORHAN, CARL E,** Christian Brothers Univ, Memphis, TN; JR; BS; Kngts Columbus 90-; IEEE; Tau Beta Pi VP; Cmps Mnstry 88-; IM 88-; Teens Encntr Christ 87-; Intern Procter/Gamble Engnr; Elec Engrng.

**FORIZS, THORA L,** Villanova Univ, Villanova, PA; FR; BA; Res House Cncl Soc Awareness Officer 90-; Hnrs Prog Stdnt; Deans List; Econ & Jap Lang; Hsptlty Hotgels Rstrnt.

**FORLANO, BARTHOLOMEW F,** Cornell Univ Statutory College, Ithaca, NY; SR; PHD; Pre-Vet Soc V P 88-; Ag Ambsdrs 87-; Parish Cncl 89-; Ho-Nun-De-Ka 90-; Acad Athl 89; Ftbl Vars Ltrmn 90 87-90; BS; Animal Sci; Vet Med.

**FORMAN, FAY L,** Univ Of Southern Ms, Hattiesburg, MS; SR; BA; Kappa Delta; Psychology.

**FORMAN, HARRIET E,** Saint Josephs Coll New York, Brooklyn, NY; BS; B'nai B'rith Wm VP 70-; Natl Cncl Jwsh Wm 75-; Admin Alrgy/Imnlgy Dept Long Is Clge Hosp Brooklyn NY; Mgmt; Hmn Rsrcs.

**FORMAN, JOSEPH S,** Hudson Valley Comm Coll, Troy, NY; FR; Im Bsktbl; Finance/Real Estate.

**FORMAN, RHONDA D,** Beaver Coll, Glenside, PA; GD; CERT; Yrbk Stf Advsr 85-90; Accrdtn Steerng Comm 88-90; Grace Bible Chrch 84-; NCTM 84-90; ATMOPAV 84-90; BA Messiah Coll 84; MED 89; Biblcl Stdies.

**FORMAN, SANFORD J,** Univ Of Nc At Asheville, Asheville, NC; SR; BA; Wrtrs Gld Ed 88; Grn Ftrs 86-88; Rnssnc Gld Asst Dir 84-85; Engl Hnr Scty; Zeta Beta Tau Scl Crhmn 83-; Grnpc PETA Hmnst Mvmnt; Deans Lst 88-; Bst Pt 87; Carl Sandburg Ptry Awrd 90; IM Sccr; IM Ftbll 86-88; Cert Drg Trtmnt Cnslr; Ed; Law Schl.

**FORMICHELLA, LORI A,** Long Island Univ C W Post Cntr, Greenvale, NY; SR; BFA; Coll Nwspr Colmnst 87-; Psi Psi Psi Pres 89-; Peer Cnslr 90; Phi Eta Sigma 87-; Phi Eta; Hnrs Pgrm/Mrt Flwshp 87-; Tri Psi Pres 89-; Pub Rltns Yth Mrt Awd; DIET Arts Awd Schlrshp Univ 89-; Pub Rltns; PR Pub/Jrnlsm.

**FORMY-DUVAL, ELIZABETH H,** Peace Coll, Raleigh, NC; SO; AA; SG Cmtee Chrmn 90-; Yrbk Edtr 89; Drma Clb Yng Rpblns Chrstn Assn 90; Phi Theta Kappa 90-; Frgn Stdy Schlrshp 90-; Acad Excnlc Awd 90; I M Bkbl; Fletcher Music Awd 89-90; Jrnlsm; Brdcst Jrnlsm.

**FORNASH, LINDA M,** Bunker Hill Comm Coll, Boston, MA; SO; Hotel/Restrnt Mgt.

**FOROUGHI, SHAHRZAD,** Kent St Univ Kent Cmps, Kent, OH; SR; BS, IISEA 88-; Dwnhll Ski Clb 89-; Hsptlty Food Serv Mngmnt; Own Estblshmnt.

**FORREST, BRENDA L,** Ashland Comm Coll, Ashland, KY; SO; Nrsng.

**FORREST, KIMBERLY L,** Univ Of Southern Ms, Hattiesburg, MS; FR; BS; RHA 90-; Hall Coun 90-; Gamma Beta Phi 90-; Psychology; PHD.

**FORRESTER, PAMELA J,** Roane St Comm Coll, Harriman, TN; FR; AAS; Gamma Beta Phi; Bsn/Acctng; Acctnt.

**FORRIDER, SCOT A,** Columbus Coll Of Art & Design, Columbus, OH; FR; BA; Indstrl Dsgn.

**FORSEE, JAMIE J,** Methodist Coll, Fayetteville, NC; JR; BS; Self Emp Bookkeeper; Acctng; Cpa.

**FORSHEY, TRICIA L,** Indiana Univ Of Pa, Indiana, PA; JR; BS; Phi Sigma Pi 89; Elem Educ; Tchr.

**FORSLING JR, PHILIP T,** Univ Of Cincinnati, Cincinnati, OH; GD; Brdcstng Trbnl Chr 88-; Alpha Epsln Rho 89-; Cmmnty Rec Brd 90-; Radio Prod 88-; BFA; Brdcstng; Tlvsn/Radio Prod/Prgmmng.

**FORSYTH, TERESA L,** Central Fl Comm Coll, Ocala, FL; SO; BS; Phi Theta Kappa 81-82; Legal Scty Judicial Assist 82-; AS 82; Elem Ed; Elem Schl Tchr.

**FORSYTHE, CHRISTINE A,** Radford Univ, Radford, VA; FR; CSA Treas; Math; Tchng.

**FORSYTHE, KIMBERLEY A,** Union Univ, Jackson, TN; JR; BA; Stdnt Actvts Cncl 88-89; Stdnt TN Educ Assn Sntr; Union Univ Sngrs 88-89; Lingual Murdi 90-; Sndy Schl Tchr 90-; Jr Hgh Grls Sftbl Tm Asst Coach; Mjsty-BSU Msc Ensmble Accmpnst 89-90; BSU IM Sftbl 88-89; Elem Ed; Blngl Educ.

**FORSYTHE, NANCY J,** Oh Univ, Athens, OH; SR; Alpha Lambda Delta 87; Alpha Xi Delta Pldg Brd 87-; Intrn Rlty Theater Colmbs OH; BFA; Acting.

**FORSYTHE, SHANE A,** Salisbury St Univ, Salisbury, MD; SO; BS; Outdr Clb 89-; IM Vlybl 89; Cmp Cnslr Amer Diabetes Assn 90; Elec Eng; Bio-Med Engr.

**FORT, HEATHER L,** Univ Of Bridgeport, Bridgeport, CT; SR; BS; Phi Kappa Phi 90-; Outstndng Fresh Awd 88; Fash Merc/Rtl.

**FORT, JEFFREY P,** Broward Comm Coll, Ft Lauderdale, FL; SO; A; Music; Music Prfrmnc.

**FORTE, ANDRE M,** Le Moyne Coll, Syracuse, NY; SR; JD; Stu Sen 87-90; Pol Sci; Alpha Sigma Nu 90-; Wash Cntr Inter Pres 90-; TRW Schlrshp; Bsbl; IM Bsktbl Sftbl Wllybl 87-; Cmmnty Kit Vol 87-90; Huntington Fmly Cntr Vol 87-88; Eisen Rome P L Paralegal 90-; BA; Pol Sci/Frnch; Attrny/Jdg.

**FORTE, MAURICE,** Jackson St Univ, Jackson, MS; JR; BA; Asso Cmpting Mchnry Cl; Pu Mu Epsilon; Alpha Lambda Delta; Beta Kappa Chi; Summer Intern IBM Rscrch Triangle Park N C 90; Sci; Cmptr Sci.

**FORTE, STEVEN G,** Va Commonwealth Univ, Richmond, VA; JR; Sigma Phi; Gldn Ky; AA SUNY Frmngdl 80; Bio; Dntstry.

**FORTENBERRY, JULIA A,** William Carey Coll, Hattiesburg, MS; JR; BS; Hon Prog 89; Chldrns Dir 87-90; Tchr Asst 85-89; Ele Educ; Tch Ele Educ.

**FORTENBERRY, TINA M,** Phillips Jr Coll Spartanburg, Spartanburg, SC; FR; Bsns Accnrnt; Accntng Firm.

**FORTENBERRY, WILLIAM P,** Ms St Univ, Miss State, MS; SO; Clg Rep; Alpha Lambda Delta; Gamma Beta Phi; Phi Eta Sigma; Kappa Alpha; IM Ftbl; Bus; Law.

**FORTH, CHARISSA M,** Fl St Univ, Tallahassee, FL; JR; BA; Falmouth Acdmy Alumni Assoc 88-; Deans Lst 90-; Fla Public TV Intern; AA 90; Communications; Media Prodctns.

**FORTH, SHARON M,** Roberts Wesleyan Coll, Rochester, NY; FR; BED; PIE; Sftbl; Sec Engl Tchr.

**FORTHMAN, SHANNON H,** Univ Of Sc At Columbia, Columbia, SC; JR; BA; Psychology.

**FORTICH, MERCEDES E,** Fl Atlantic Univ, Boca Raton, FL; JR; BBA; Pres Awd 88-; Vldctrn Awd 88-89; Fl Undrgrdt Schlrs Fnd 88-; Bsn Admin; Mgmt/Fnce.

**FORTIN, JOHN P,** Central Fl Comm Coll, Ocala, FL; SO; Math/Sceince Hnrs Clb 90-; Phi Theta Kappa 89-; Deans List; Pres List; ASEET; Elctrncs.

**FORTIN, RONALD E,** Nova Univ, Ft Lauderdale, FL; GD; MBA; Sr Prdct Eng; BS 82; Bus; Mktg.

**FORTIN, TOM,** Nova Univ, Ft Lauderdale, FL; GD; MBA; Demos Sftbl Tm 85-; Sigma Phi Epsilon VP 80-; Prfsnl Engr 89-; Sr Dsgn Engr Pratt Whitney 85-; BSME Univ Florida 84; ME Univ Fl 88; Bsn; Engrg Mgr.

**FORTINO, ELIZABETH A,** Daemen Coll, Amherst, NY; FR; BS; Spec/Elem Ed; Ed.

**FORTNER, DOUGLAS COMMODORE,** Catholic Univ Of America, Washington, DC; SR; MA; Phi Beta Kappa; Phi Sigma Tau 89; Pi Gamma Mu; Phi Eta Sigma 88; War Mem Schlrshp 87; Eliz Brcknrdge Cldwll Mem Fllwshp 88-89; Rev T Brhny Fllwshp 89; BA; Loughran Schlrshp 90; Phlsphy.**

**FORTSON, HEATHER C,** Fl St Univ, Tallahassee, FL; SR; MA; Smnl Uprsng 90; 1800 Scnds 90-; FSU Dept Dnc 88-90; Kappa Kappa Gamma 88-90; Wfsu Tv Internshp; BS; Flm.

**FORTSON, JEFFERY B,** Morehouse Coll, Atlanta, GA; SR; BA; Bus Assoc 87-; Sls/Mktg Inst; G M Schlr; Mobil Oil Schlr; Deptmntl Hon; Cum Laude; Top Slsprsn Sls/Mktg; Quaker Oats Intrn; Hon Rl; Mktg; District Sls Mgr.

**FORTUN, JOSEFINA MARIA,** Fl International Univ, Miami, FL; SR; Acctng Assn VP 90-; Phne Com Chr Prsn 90; Natl Assn Of Accts 89-; Vol Incme Tax Asst 88 ; Bach In Acctng; Acctng; MBA.

**FORTUNA, JONATHAN P,** West Liberty St Coll, West Liberty, WV; JR; BA; Hlltp Plyrs 88-; Chmbr Choir 88-89; Chorus 88-89; Alpha Psi Omega VP 89-; Engl Lbrl Arts; Dsgn/Cstm/Intrr.

**FORTUNA, SCOTT A,** Me Maritime Academy, Castine, ME; SO; BS; Clss VP 89-; Dean Slst 87-; Coprtv Intern Untd Tchnlgs; Pwr Eng; Vrsty Ftbll 89-; Pwr Eng Tchnlgy; Eng.

**FORTUNE, CARLYLE S,** Bayamon Central Univ, Bayamon, PR; SR; BA; Order Friars Prchrs 87-; Phlsphy; Prsthd.

**FORTUNE, LORI A,** Univ Of Tn At Martin, Martin, TN; JR; BS; UT Martin Fresh Chrldr Capt 88-; UT Martin Vrsty Chrldr Capt 89-; NCA Stff Instrctr 90; Deans List 90-; Chi Omega Chpln 88-; Spirit Comm Chrmn 90; FCA 90-; Dscpl Now Chrstn Cnslr 90-; Elem Educ; Elementary School Teacher.

**FORTUNE, MARK A,** Columbia Union Coll, Takoma Park, MD; FR; BS; Alpha Sigma Beta Bus Clb 90-; Phi Eta Sigma 90-; Bus Admin/Comp Sys; Hosp Admin.

**FORTUNE, WILLIAM T,** Univ Of Al At Birmingham, Birmingham, AL; FR; BA; Trck/Fld 90-; Alpha Delta Lambda 90-; Acctg; Corp Law.

**FOSBRINK, RONALD D,** Edinboro Univ Of Pa, Edinboro, PA; FR; BAPO; Pol Sci; Intl Rltns.

**FOSCHIO, DEBORAH A,** S U N Y At Buffalo, Buffalo, NY; SO; BS; Sarah Helen Kish Memrl Schlrshp; Bus Admin; Mgmt.

**FOSHEE, SHEILA A,** Ms Gulf Coast Comm Coll, Perkinston, MS; SO; BS; MGCCC Perkettes, Bulldog Babes Batgirl; Phi Theta Kappa; Delta Clb; Chem/Bio Sci.

**FOSKEY, KEVIN H,** Va St Univ, Petersburg, VA; FR; BA; Deans Lst 90-; Bus Admn; Mgr.

**FOSS, WENDY DENISE,** Univ Of Cincinnati, Cincinnati, OH; JR; BS; Amer Dtc Assoc 89; Eta Sigma Gamma; Ntrtn; Dtcs.

**FOSSESIGURANI, YVONNE A,** Manhattanville Coll, Purchase, NY; FR; BA; Chorus Treas 90-; Stdnt Vol Ntwrk 91-; Mktg Intrn 90-91; Wmns Lacrosse 91-; Psych; Cnslng.

**FOSTER, ALAN D,** Bridgewater Coll, Bridgewater, VA; JR; BA; St Jude Chldrns Rsrch Hosp Vol; Bike A Thon; Lambda Soc 90-; I M Bkbl Sftbl 88-90; Cert Draftng Blue Ridge Comm Clg 87-; Hlth/Physical Educ; Tch.

**FOSTER, AMY M,** Univ Of Cincinnati, Cincinnati, OH; GD; MSED; Rly Cats 87-88; Gldn Key; Delta Delta Delta Asstnt Scl 87; BSED 90; Educ; Tchr.

**FOSTER, ANDRE L,** Draughons Jr Coll Nashville, Nashville, TN; SR; AS; Pres Lst; Dns Lst; Bus Mgmt.

**FOSTER, ANGELIA S,** Univ Of Southern Ms, Hattiesburg, MS; SR; BA; Marching Bnd 89-90; Anthropology Scty Reporter 89-; Copiah Lincoln Band 87-89; Lambda Alpha 90-; Gamma Beta Phi 90-; AA Copiah Lincoln Comm Clg 89; Anthropology; Teaching Govt.

**FOSTER, APRIL L,** Coll Of William & Mary, Williamsburg, VA; FR; AB; Lit Mag Prod Stf 90-; Soclgy.

**FOSTER, BRENDA E,** Rivier Coll, Nashua, NH; JR; BA; AS Cmptr Tech 85; Ele Educ.

**FOSTER, CATHLEEN ELIZABETH,** D Youville Coll, Buffalo, NY; SO; BSMS; Camps Mnstry 89-; Cmmtr Cncl 90-; Latin Amer Stdnt Org 89-90; Dietcs.

**FOSTER, CATHY M,** Miles Coll, Birmingham, AL; SR; BS; Std Spprt Serv 89-; Cmps Hnr Clb; Hnr Rl Cert 89; Pres Schlr Cert 90; Scl Sci.

**FOSTER, CHRISTOPHER A,** Pellissippi St Tech Comm Coll, Knoxville, TN; SO; AAS; Elec Engr Tech.

**FOSTER, CYNTHIA D,** Tn Temple Univ, Chattanooga, TN; FR; BA; Ofc Mgmt; Mgmt.

**FOSTER, CYNTHIA D,** Univ Of Sc At Columbia, Columbia, SC; GD; BS; Amnsty Intrntl 90-; Psychlgy Clb 90-; Piedmont Clb 90-; Gamma Beta Phi Scty 90-; Usc Hon Pgm 90-; Amer Scty CLU CHFC 90-; SC Insurance Agent; ASSOC Degree Sptbg Meth Clg 81; Tech Sec Degree Sptbg Tech Clg 72; Intrdscplnry Stds; Ins Agncy Mgr.

**FOSTER, DARRYL D,** Tuskegee Univ, Tuskegee Inst, AL; SO; BS; NSBL Natl Soc Bsn Ldrs 90-; NAACP 90-; Accts NABA 90-; Yng Mns Dvlpmnt Clb Shady Grove Msnry Bptst Chrc Sec 90-; Intrn IBM; Dns Lst Tuskegge U; James Albert Johnson Mem Awd; Acctg; CPA/LAW.

**FOSTER, DAVID E,** Hudson Valley Comm Coll, Troy, NY; FR; AAS; Amer Assn Resp Care 90-; D Cushman Schlrshp; NYSSRC Schlrshp 90; Resp Care Prctitnr; Resp Therpy.

**FOSTER, DONNA M,** S U N Y Coll Of Tech At Frmgdl, Farmingdale, NY; SR; ASN; Nursing; RN.

**FOSTER, DORIS G,** Benedict Coll, Columbia, SC; SR; BA; SC Ed Assoc Pres 89; T L Duckett Ed Assoc 88; Mnrty Access To Tchr Ed MATE 88; Alpha Kappa Mu 90; Alpha Chi 90; Elem Ed; Tchr.

**FOSTER, EMERSON COLYER,** Oh St Univ, Columbus, OH; GD; MA; Golden Key; Acdmc Ldrshp Serv Awrd 89; Scarlet And Grey Schlrshp; African Amer Schlr Awrd; Commendation From Ohio Hse Of Repr; BA 90; Educ Technology; Training HRD.

**FOSTER, GARY W,** Univ Of North Fl, Jacksonville, FL; SR; BA; Rsrch Asst Eminent Schlr 90-; AA FCCJ; Bus/Accntng Sys; Sys Anlys.

**FOSTER, JANET E,** Tuskegee Univ, Tuskegee Inst, AL; SO; BS; Florida Club; Aerospace Engineering.

**FOSTER, JOHN EDISON,** Jackson St Univ, Jackson, MS; SR; BS; Scty Physcs Stdnt Pres 87-; Phi Kappa Phi; Tutor 87-; Sprt Grp Hon Div 87-; Gldn Key; Pres List 87-; Physcs; Astrnt/Scntst.

**FOSTER, JULIE A,** Ga St Univ, Atlanta, GA; SR; BED; Gold Key 90-; Phi Kappa Phi; BED 91; Early Chldhd.

**FOSTER, KARA L,** Va Commonwealth Univ, Richmond, VA; SR; BS; Rchmnd Mem Hsp Sch Nrsng 84; Nrsng; Fmly Nurse Prctnr.

**FOSTER, KELLY M,** Central Fl Comm Coll, Ocala, FL; SO; Phi Theta Kappa 89-F Math/Scnc Hnrs Clb 89-; Phi Theta Kappa 89-; AA CFCC; Phys Thrpy.

**FOSTER, KIMBERLY S,** Longwood Coll, Farmville, VA; JR; BS; Yrbk Cpy Wrtr 90-; Nwspr Cntct 90-; ICF 88-90; Kappa Pi 90-; Sigma Kappa Hist 90-; Hnr Symposium Spkr 90-; Otsdng Jr Awd 90-; IM Sftbl; Art Educ.

**FOSTER, LARRY S,** Univ Of Nc At Charlotte, Charlotte, NC; JR; BA; Alld Hlth Clb 88-; Prog Brd 90; Blgy Pre Med; Med.

**FOSTER, LAUREN,** Saint Josephs Coll New York, Brooklyn, NY; SR; BA; Police Offc NY City 82; Hsng Athrty; AAS Elizabeth Seton Clg 80; Bsn Admin Humn Resources Mgmt; Law Schl.

**FOSTER, LE ANN,** Union Univ, Jackson, TN; JR; BS; Bptst Stdnt Un 88-90; Stdnt Fndtns 89-; Alpha Chi 89-; Sigma Zeta 89-; Chi Omega Pnhllnc 88-; Biolgy; Phys Therpy.

**FOSTER, LIBBY A,** Univ Of Ga, Athens, GA; SR; Stdnt Coun/Excep Chldrn 90-; Golden Key 90-; Kappa Delta Pi; Spcl Edctn; Mental Retrdtn Tchr.

**FOSTER, LISA G,** Fl International Univ, Miami, FL; SO; BA; Sccr Tm; Fin/Intrntl Bus; Crprte Law.

**FOSTER, LISA L,** Alcorn St Univ, Lorman, MS; SR; BS; Young Writers Clb 88; Nwspr Clb 88; Phi Theta Kappa 88; Alpha Mu Gamma; Hlth Science; Pblc Hlth.

**FOSTER, LORI A,** Middle Tn St Univ, Murfreesboro, TN; SO; BA; Ntl Coll Awd Wnr Math/Comp Sci; Math; Actrl Sci/Statcs.

**FOSTER, MARIA A,** Tuskegee Univ, Tuskegee Inst, AL; GD; Stdnt Chptr Am Vet Med Assn 87-; AAZV 87-; AWV 87-; DVM; BS; Vet Med; Small Anml Prctc.

**FOSTER, MELINDA K,** Marshall University, Huntington, WV; JR; BA; Res Hl Assoc Repr 88-; Intra-Hl Govt Cncl Secr 89; Gamma Beta Phi 89-90; Kappa Delta Pi; Res Advsr 90-; Res Schlr 88-89; Dns Lst 88-; IM Vlybl/Sftbl 88-; IM Swim 88-; Miss Amity Miss WV USA Pageant 90; Soph Hmecmg Attndnt Semifin 89; Elem Ed/Spec Ed; Tchr/Principal.

**FOSTER, MIA J,** Univ Of Md At Eastern Shore, Princess Anne, MD; JR; BS; Eta Rho Mu; Eta Sigma Delta; Htl/Rest Mngr; Bus Mgmnt.

**FOSTER, MICHAEL S,** Livingston Univ, Livingston, AL; SO; BS; Ftbl 89-90; Indstrl Technology; Industrial Technology.

**FOSTER, MICHELLE,** Indiana Univ Of Pa, Indiana, PA; SR; BS; Stdnt Govt Assoc 87-88; Assoc Chldhd Ed Intrnatl 90-; Delta Phi Beta Fndng Mbr Assoc Sec 87-; Prjct Strd 90; IM Vlybl 88-; Elem Ed.

**FOSTER, MICHELLE J,** Trevecca Nazarene Coll, Nashville, TN; FR; BS; Ministry Outreach Tm 90-; Church Choir 90-; Legacy Layout/Writer 90-; Hnrs Porg 90-; Acctng/Busn Adimin; CPA.

**FOSTER, NADYNE L,** Comm Coll Algny Co Algny Cmps, Pittsburgh, PA; SO; AS; Paralegal; Law.

**FOSTER, NORMA K,** Radford Univ, Radford, VA; JR; BA; Phi Sigma Iota Pres 90-; French; Intl Bus.

**FOSTER, PATRICIA A,** Univ Of Tn At Chattanooga, Chattanooga, TN; JR; BSE; Amer Soc Cvl Eng Pres 90-; Ntl Soc Prof Eng 90-; Soc Wmn Eng 90-; Tau Beta Pi Treas; Golden Key 90-; Phi Eta Sigma/Alpha Lambda Delta 89-; Mortar Brd; Hsng Pgm Comm 90; Brock Schlr 88-; Soc Wmn Cnstrctn Schlrshp 88-; Cvl Eng.

**FOSTER, REBECCA J,** Kent St Univ Kent Cmps, Kent, OH; JR; BA; Usvba Vlybl 90-; ASID 88-; IM Bksbl/Sfbl Tm Cptn 88-; Pi Delta Hlth Fitn 89-90; Intshp Stouffers Hotels; Listed Deans List 88-; Listed Pres List 90-; Usvba Club 90-; Interior Design.

**FOSTER, REVONDA A,** Univ Of Tn At Martin, Martin, TN; SR; Sga 88-; Pre Law Clb 88-; Res Hsng Assn V P 88-90; Univ Schlrs Rep 88-; Phi Alpha Delta 89-; Alpha Gamma Delta Prl Chrmn 88-90; Cir K Nrsng Hm Chrmn 89-90; T N St Leg Intrn 90; IM Vlybl 88-; BS; Pol Sci/Econ; Law Schl.

**FOSTER, RICHARD B,** Nova Univ, Ft Lauderdale, FL; MBA; Ski Clb ASB Rep 86-90; DECA Clb 87-88; IM Sprts Tm Capt 85-90; BS Wash St Univ 90; Busn; Proj Eng.

**FOSTER II, RICHARD C,** Memphis St Univ, Memphis, TN; SO; BS; Actvts Cncl Mv Cmmtt 90-; Educ Spprt Prog Ttr 89-; Ornttn Guide 90-; Hnrs Stu Assc 89-; Alpha Lambda Delta 90-; Phi Eta Sigma 90-; Gamma Beta Phi; Chi Beta Phi; Otstndng Chmstry Awrd 90; SAC Cmmtt Mmbr Yr 90-; Joanne J Trow Awrd; Math.

**FOSTER, SONYA P,** Bennett Coll, Greensboro, NC; SR; BA; Acctg/Bus Clb 90-; Cmps Girlscts 86-89; Inter Res Cncl Pres 88-90; All-Amer Schlr Clgt Awd; Acctng.

**FOSTER, STACIE J,** Univ Of Charleston, Charleston, WV; FR; BA; Paralegal; Psych.

**FOSTER, STACY C,** Ms Univ For Women, Columbus, MS; JR; BS; Phi Theta Kappa Sec 89-; Deans Lst; Pres Lst 88-; Acctg; CPA.

**FOSTER, STEPHANIE R,** Univ Of Va Clinch Valley Coll, Wise, VA; FR; BA; Psychlgy; Elem Ed.

**FOSTER, THERESA M,** Salisbury St Univ, Salisbury, MD; SR; BS; Gamma Theta Upsilon 90-; Geogrphy; Physcl/Envrnmntl Sci.

**FOSTER, THERESA MARIE,** Coppin St Coll, Baltimore, MD; SR; BSW; Scl Wrk Assoc Sec 89-; Deans Lst 89-; AA 79; Scl Wrk.

**FOSTER, TIMOTHY G,** Garrett Comm Coll, Mchenry, MD; FR; Tutor 90; Theater Cnstrctn 90; Math/Sci; Tchr.

**FOSTER, TONYA L,** Patrick Henry Comm Coll, Martinsville, VA; SO; AAS; Bus Admn; Acctg.

**FOSTERLING, SALLY A,** Gaston Coll, Dallas, NC; FR; BA; Acctg.

**FOTIA, CRISTA M,** Indiana Univ Of Pa, Indiana, PA; JR; BSED; VTA 89-90; Erly Chldhd Ed; Tch.

**FOTOVICH, ELIZABETH J,** Univ Of Al At Huntsville, Huntsville, AL; JR; BE; Eta Kappa Nu Rec Secr 90-; Tau Beta Pi 90-; Alpha Lambda Delta Pres 88-; Elctrcl Engr; Engr.

**FOUCHEY, TRINA G,** Tri County Tech Coll, Pendleton, SC; FR; AAS; Bus Ldrs Tmrrw 90-; Bwlng Sec/Treas; Cert N Harris Co Coll 89; Acctg.

**FOULES, LISA B,** Alcorn St Univ, Lorman, MS; SR; BS; Psychlgy Clb; SNEA Swpa Asst Sec 90-; Cncrt Chr; Univ Chr; Lgcl Assoc; Hnr Rll; Univ Chr; Psychlgy; Clncl Psychlgst.**

**FOUNTAIN, STEPHANIE JO ANN,** Univ Of South Al, Mobile, AL; SR; BA; Scndry Ed/Math; HS Tchr.

**FOUNTAIN, WARREN GRANT,** Middle Ga Coll, Cochran, GA; SO; MBA; Phi Beta Lambda 90-; Jpns Lang Cert 87-; Lfgrdng 90-; Cert MTC Provo UT 87; Bsn/Intl.

**FOUNTAINE, CRAIG,** Va St Univ, Petersburg, VA; SO; BA; Bapt Stdnt Union Pres 90-; Mass Cmmnctns Clb 90-; Lit/Lang Clb 90-; Alpa Mu Gamma 90-; Engl.

**FOURMAN, MARLENE L,** Sinclair Comm Coll, Dayton, OH; FR.

**FOURNIER, DEBRA A,** Colby Sawyer Coll, New London, NH; JR; BA; Stdnt Alumnae Assc 89-; Orntn Stf 90; Course Evltn Cmt; Alpha Chi 90-; Stdnt Cnslr 90-; Intrnshp Wmns Cnslng Ctr; Tchng Asstnt; Vrsty Tnns 89-; Psychlgy; Cnslng.

**FOURNIER, KEITH F,** Univ Of New England, Biddeford, ME; SO; BA; Schlr Athlete Of Yr Awd 89-; Deans Schlrshp Awd 90-; Vrsty Soccer/Lacrosse 89-; Med Bio; Medicine.

**FOURNIER, LISA M,** Western New England Coll, Springfield, MA; SR; BSBA; Delta Mu Delta; Ofc Public Relations At Western New England Clge 88-; AS In Bus Admnstrn Bay Path Jr Clge 88; Mgmnt In Eng Communication Track; Business.

**FOURQUREAN, SUSAN L,** Univ Of Ga, Athens, GA; CERT; Std Tch; BS Intrl Frnshngs; BS Auburn Univ 85; Mddl Schl Educ.

**FOUSE, ALLEAN O,** Tn St Univ, Nashville, TN; SR; Scl Wrk Clb 89-; Stu Union Brd Govrs Brd 90-; Explsn Comm Chrprsn 90-; Hnrs Pro 88-; Beta Kappa Chi 89-; Gldn Key Pres 90-; Vndrblt Army ROTC Schlrshp 89-90; Otstndg Cdt 89-90; SUBG Bsktbl Cocapt 90-; Bio; OB/GYN.

**FOUSHEE, PAULA M,** Brescia Coll, Owensboro, KY; JR; BS; Stdnt Govt Assn 88-89; Math Clb 90-; Class Treas 89-90; Chrldr 88-89; Appld Math.

**FOUST, CHARLOTTE D,** Univ Of Nc At Charlotte, Charlotte, NC; SR; BCA; Vis Arts; Illstrtn/Pntng Studio.

**FOUST, GREGORY N,** Memphis St Univ, Memphis, TN; JR; BIS; Amer Assoc Resprtry Care 73-; Tenn Soc Resprtry Care VP 73-; Amer Lung Assoc Tenn 87-; Bsbl Jackson St Comm Clg; Tech Dir Respirtry Care 74-78; AS Resp Therapy N W Miss Jr Clg 73; Hlth Admin; Education.

**FOUST, JOHN D,** Oh Univ, Athens, OH; SR; BS; ASME 88-; Marching 110 Sec Ldr 87-90; Singers Sec Ldr 88-89; Tau Beta Pi Treas 90-; Golden Key 88-; Natl Soc Pfrsnl Engrs 88-; Co-Op W/ Cooper Pwr Tools APEX Div 89-90; Deans List 88-90; Mechanical Engrng; Materials Or Process Engrn.

**FOUTS III, JAMES P,** Univ Of Ky, Lexington, KY; FR; BS; Stdnt Athl Comm 90-; IM Ftbl Bsktbl Cap 90-; Biolgy; Phd In Med.

**FOUTS, KARLA L,** Univ Of Ga, Athens, GA; SR; BSED; IM Bsktbl; Early Chldhd Ed; Tchr.

**FOWLE, SCOTT R,** Schenectady County Comm Coll, Schenectady, NY; FR; ASSOC; Culinary Arts; Hotel Mgmnt.

**FOWLER, ALISON A,** Vance Granville Comm Coll, Henderson, NC; GD; Csmtlgy.

**FOWLER, CARLA D,** Clark Atlanta Univ, Atlanta, GA; JR; BA; Dns Lst 89-90; Busn Admin/Finc; Corp Law.

**FOWLER, CONNIE G,** Univ Of Ga, Athens, GA; SR; BSED; Mbr Stu Prof Assoc Ga 90-; Deans Lst 90-; Erly Chldhd Educ; Tchg.

**FOWLER, CRYSTAL LYNN,** Phillips Jr Coll Spartanburg, Spartanburg, SC; FR; Wrd Prcssng; Wrd Prcssr Bkkpr.

**FOWLER, DAVID M,** Wv Univ At Parkersburg, Parkersburg, WV; FR; Bus Admin; Acctg.

**FOWLER, DEBORAH M,** Gordon Coll, Wenham, MA; FR; BA; Hmlss Mnstr; Wom Choir; Hnrs List; English; Missions Work.

**FOWLER, ELIZABETH C,** Bob Jones Univ, Greenville, SC; FR; BA; Chi Sigma Phi; Guid/Conslng/Psych; Adolscnt Cnslr.

**FOWLER, FALVO M,** Columbia Union Coll, Takoma Park, MD; SO; BA; Poetry Soc Of India Mbr 89-90; Natl Religious Brdcstrs; Cmnctn; Brdcstnt/TV Prodctn.

**FOWLER, JAMES L,** Piedmont Tech Coll, Greenwood, SC; GD; AS; Psi Beta; Phi Theta Kappa; Outstdng Grad Crrclm; Lions Clb Brd Dir; SC Law Enf Asn; Amer Jail Asn; Amer Corr Asn; SC Corr Asn; SC Jail Admn Asn; Chrch Cncl; Dpty Grnwd Cty Shrffs Dpt; Jail Admn; Crmnl Jstc; Law Enf.

**FOWLER, JOHN B,** Univ Of Sc At Columbia, Columbia, SC; SR; BS; Phi Beta Kappa; Tau Beta Pi Cataloguer 89-; Chem Eng; Medicine.

**FOWLER, JOYCE L,** Middle Tn St Univ, Murfreesboro, TN; SO; BA; Finance-Rl Est; Rl Est Appraiser.

**FOWLER, JULIA A,** Univ Of Sc At Columbia, Columbia, SC; FR; BA; Dnce Co; Gamma Beta Phi; Chi Omega; Theatre; Actrss/ Drama Tchr.

**FOWLER, KIMBERLY H,** Volunteer St Comm Coll, Gallatin, TN; FR; AAS; Microcomputer Acctg; Acctnt.

**FOWLER, LEISA R,** Univ Of Ky, Lexington, KY; SR; Stdts Against Violation Envrmt 89-; Amnesty Internatl 88-; Phlsphy Clb 90-; Slvtn Army 90-; Rpblcn Party KY Intrnshp; Cngrsmn Larry J Hopkins Intrnshp; BA; Pltcl Sci/Phlsphy; Law.

**FOWLER, MARGARET S,** Kent St Univ Kent Cmps, Kent, OH; JR; BA; Lambda Alpha Epsilon; Golden Key; Mid-Amer Conf Cmsnrs Awrd; Pr Lst 90; Var Track/Field 89-; Psych; Crim Just.

**FOWLER, MARKAL G,** Univ Of Southern Ms, Hattiesburg, MS; GD; BS; Crmnl Jstc; Law.

**FOWLER, MARY S,** Walker Coll, Jasper, AL; SO; MBA; Stdnt Govt Assn; Phi Theta Kappa; Pres Lst; Red Garter Schlrshp; Kiwanis Clb Schlrshp; State AL Acad Schlrshp; Psychlgy; Psychoanalysis.

**FOWLER, NORMAN E,** Middle Tn St Univ, Murfreesboro, TN; SR; BS; Cmptr Scnc; Sftwr Dsgn.

**FOWLER, REBECCA D,** Roane St Comm Coll, Harriman, TN; SO; AAS; Offc Admin/Wrd Prcssng.

**FOWLER JR, ROBERT A,** Bapt Bible Coll & Seminary, Clarks Summit, PA; FR; BSM; Cncrt Chr 90-; Music Ed; Tchr.

**FOWLER, ROBERT S,** Univ Of Southern Ms, Hattiesburg, MS; FR; BME; Mrchng Bnd 90; Wnd Ensmbl; Deans Endwmnt Prfrmnc Awd 90-; Instrmntl Msc Educ; Educ.

**FOWLER, RONALD K,** Fl A & M Univ, Tallahassee, FL; SO; BA; Ntl Soc Blck Engrs; Commodores Clb; Phi Eta Sigma; Deans Lst; Presschlr; NROTC Schlrshp; Life Gets Better Schlrshp; Cmndg Ofcrs Recog Awrd; AFCEA Hnr Awrd; Mdshpmn Mo; Bp Intrn; 2M Bsktbl; Elec Engr.**

**FOWLER, SABRINA-PAIGE T,** Univ Of Sc At Columbia, Columbia, SC; SR; Intrnshp Erly Chldhd Ed; BA Ed Univ SC Cstl CA Clg; Tchng.

**FOWLER, STEPHANIE R,** Birmingham Southern Coll, Birmingham, AL; FR; Alpha Lambda Delta 90-; Phi Eta Sigma 90-; Pi Beta Phi Asst Tres 90-; Biology; Medicine.

**FOWLER, TERESA N,** Saint Peters Coll, Jersey City, NJ; JR; BS; Collins Chem Soc; Mendel Clb; Biol; Med.**

**FOWLER JR, THOMAS E,** Le Moyne Coll, Syracuse, NY; JR; BA; Pre Law Scty 88-; Pol Sci Acad 88-; Rsdnce Hll RA 90-; Intgrl Hnrs Stdnt 89-; Pol Sci Crmnlgy; Law.

**FOWLER, THOMAS L,** Fayetteville St Univ, Fayetteville, NC; SR; BS; Soclgy Clb 88-90; Alpha Kappa Mu 90-; Kappa Delta Pi 89-; Hgst GPA In Geogrphy Awd 90-; Geogrphy; Govt.

**FOWLER, TODD D,** Urbana Univ, Urbana, OH; JR; BA; Jr Trnmt Bowlers Assoc VP; S Eastern OH Bowlers Prprtrs Assoc Pres 89-; 4-H VP 79-90; Hnr Scty; Pres Schlrsph; Finance/ Ecnmcs; Banking.**

**FOWLER, WILLIAM R,** Marshall University, Huntington, WV; SO; BA; Cmptr Sci.

**FOWLKES JR, ALVIN C,** Va Commonwealth Univ, Richmond, VA; SO; BS; African Amer Schlr Prog 89-; Activities Planning Brd 90-; Project BEST 89-; Deans List 90-; Business; Advertising.**

**FOWLKES, NANCY DUNAWAY,** Savannah Coll Of Art & Design, Savannah, GA; GD; MFA; Clg Art Assoc; Natl Art Ed Assoc 84-89; Ark Art Ed Assoc 84-89; Soc Of Chldrns Bk Wrtrs Illstrtrs 90; Stephens Awd For Outstndng HS Tchng 88; Prsntr Of Crrclm Cncpts 87; Brd Of Dir Scrty Svngs Bnk 82-89; PEO Sistrhd 78; BA; Illstrtn; Clg Tchng Chldrns Bk Illstrtn.

**FOWLKES, VICKI L,** Middle Tn St Univ, Murfreesboro, TN; GD; BS; Gamma Beta Phi; Pub Serv Intrnshp 89-; Pre Law Intrnshp 90; Pol Sci; Lawyer.

**FOX, ATHENA L,** Univ Of Nc At Chapel Hill, Chapel Hill, NC; GD; JD; Phi Alpha Delta Clrk 88-; Crmnl Clinc Rsrch Asst 90-; Bar Cert; BA U N C Asheville 88; Law.

**FOX, BETHANY G,** S U N Y Coll At Fredonia, Fredonia, NY; SR.

**FOX, BRUCE S,** S U N Y Coll Of Tech At Delhi, Delhi, NY; SO; MBA; Intrntl Fd Srvce Exec Assn Pres 89-; Htl Sales And Mrktng Assn Dir Of Prmtns 89-; Gamma Delta Iota Pldge Mstr 90-; Hosptlty Stdnt Of The Yr 90-; Htl And Rsrt Mgmt.

**FOX, CANDICE R,** Mount Aloysius Jr Coll, Cresson, PA; SO; AS; Yrbk 90-; Orientation Ldr 90-; Legal Asst Stud; Law.

**FOX, DANIEL W,** Birmingham Southern Coll, Birmingham, AL; SO; BA; Circle K 90-; Jazz Band 90-; Model Senate Staff 89; Alpha Lambda Delta Secr 90-; Phi Eta Sigma 90-; Frshmn Chem Awd 89-90; Chem; Med Sch.

**FOX, DARLA R,** Wallace St Comm Coll At Selma, Selma, AL; FR; BS; VP List 90; Pres List; US Army Sec; Pschy; Cnslr.

**FOX, DEBBIE L,** Univ Of Al At Huntsville, Huntsville, AL; FR; Alpha Lamdba Delta; Chi Omega; Cir Intl 90-; Vltr Adult Ed Ctr; Hnr Schlrs List 90-; Engrg.

**FOX, DEBRA N,** Duquesne Univ, Pittsburgh, PA; SO; BA; Sign Waves 90-; YMCA Pal Prog 90-; Campus Mnstry 89-; YWAM 90-; Mnstrs In Action 89-; Intern Dry Tavern Comm Pharmcy 89-; Pharmacy.

**FOX, JANICE A,** Middle Tn St Univ, Murfreesboro, TN; SR; BS; Health With Biology Minor; Public Health Ed.

**FOX, JEFFREY A,** Univ Of Ky, Lexington, KY; SR; BA; Sigma Pi 86-88; Psych; Phys Ther.

**FOX, KAREN S,** Univ Of Miami, Coral Gables, FL; SR; BM; Msc Thrpy Clb Sec; Natl Assoc Msc Thrpy; S Fl Msc Thrpy Ntwrk; Dns Lst 90; Dns Lst U Hartford 86-87; Med Phtgrphy Dept Roswell Prk Mem Inst 89; Tlnt Schlrshp 88; Tlnt Schlrshp Harlt Schl Msc 86-88; Msc Thrpy; Msc Thrpst.

**FOX, KATHLEEN M,** Merrimack Coll, North Andover, MA; JR; BA; Yrbk Comm 90-; Poltcl Sci Soc 90-; Outreach Experience 89-; Amnesty Internatl Mbr 90; Pol Sci; Law Sch.

**FOX, KEENA A,** Univ Of Southern Ms, Hattiesburg, MS; FR; Afro-Amer Stdnt Org 90-; Comp Sci; Pgmg.

**FOX, KEVEN H,** Middle Tn St Univ, Murfreesboro, TN; GD; Beta Theta Pi 87-88; Sigma Clb Treas 89-; Bus; Fin Ins.

**FOX, KRISTA L,** Univ Of Cincinnati-Clrmnt Coll, Batavia, OH; SO; ASSOC; Kappa Delta Pi 87; Gldn Ky 87; Big Bro Big Sis 89-; GS Ldr 89-; Univ Hnrs Schlrshp 87; Benjamin Philhalsy Schlrshp 87; IM; B Ed 87; Hosp Mgmt; Mgr Of Brd Unt.**

**FOX, KRISTIN P,** S U N Y Coll At Fredonia, Fredonia, NY; SO; BFA; Concert Choir 89-90; Alpha Psi Omega; Gary Eckhart Awrd Techncl Prodctn; Santa Fe Opera Props Apprntc; Theater; Prodctn Stg Mngmnt.

**FOX, MARY ELIZABETH,** Univ Of Sc At Columbia, Columbia, SC; JR; BA; Yrbk Edtr 88-; Prtfl Ltry Mgzn; Univ Nwsppr Asst Nws Ed 90; Gamma Beta Phi 88-90; Alpha Lambda Delta 88-89; Phi Eta Sigma; Omicron Delta Kappa; Delta Zeta 89-90; Rmsr Schlrshp 88-; Schlrshp Deans Schlrshp; Engl; Mgzn Edtr.

**FOX, MICHELLE L,** Univ Of Nc At Asheville, Asheville, NC; FR; BA; Stdnt Govt Fr Senator 90-; Stdnt Govt Soph Senator Acad Affairs Com Chmn; Phi Eta Sigma 90-; Alpha Delta Pi 90-; Chrldng Co-Capt 90-; Lit; Edn/Admin.

**FOX, REBA J,** Roane St Comm Coll, Harriman, TN; FR; BSN; LPN 83; Crtcl Cr Nrsng 88; Nrsng.

**FOX, SANDRA M,** Broward Comm Coll, Ft Lauderdale, FL; JR; BA; Drmtry Stdnt Govt VP 85-86; Alpha Tau Omega Lttl Sstrs 86-88; Prsdntl Asst ; Clnt Aqstn Prgrmmr; Brnch Offc Trdr; Elem Ed.

**FOX, SHARON P,** Univ Of Sc At Columbia, Columbia, SC; SO; BS; Hmcmng Comm 89-90; Womens Stdnt Assn 90-; Delta Delta Delta 89-; IM Spts 89; Erly Chldhd Edn.

**FOX, SUSAN L,** Indiana Univ Of Pa, Indiana, PA; SR; BED; PSEA; ACEI 90-; Kappa Delta Pi 89-; Prvst Schlr 89-90; Brody Schlrshp 90-; Elem Ed; Tchng.

**FOX, TAMMY S,** Tusculum Coll, Greeneville, TN; SR; BS; Bus Admin.

**FOX, TERESA L,** Middle Tn St Univ, Murfreesboro, TN; SR; BS; Pi Gamma Mu; Intrnshp Dprtmnt Yth Dvlpmnt; Crmnl Jstc Adm Sclgy; Cnslr.

**FOXWELL, LEONARD N,** Salisbury St Univ, Salisbury, MD; JR; BA; Pltcl Sci Clb Pres 89-; Sclgcl Scty VP; Yng Dem Mmbrshp Drctr; Phi Eta Sigma 89-; Phi Sigma Alpha; Pltcl Sci.

**FOY, KIMBERLY A,** Georgian Court Coll, Lakewood, NJ; SR; BA; Stdnt Gvmt Pres 90-; De La Salle Ed Clb Pres 90-; Trnsfr Clb Sec/Treas 89-90; Cliones Hstry Clb 89-; Stdnt Afrs Comm Rep 90-; Res Asst Pgrm RA 90-; Deans Schlr 89-90; Hstry/Elem Ed; Tchr.

**FOY, TAMMY L,** Duquesne Univ, Pittsburgh, PA; JR; BA; Commuter Asst Transfr Asst; Univ Vol; Deans List 90-; Points Of Light; Vol Corps Ldr 90-; Vol Recgntn Award; Elem Ed; Tchr.

**FRAAS, TONYA K,** Mercer Univ Schl Of Pharm, Atlanta, GA; GD; PHD; Acdmy Stdnts Phrmcy Com Chrprsn 88-; Am Soc Hosp Phrmcsts 89-; Cncl Stdnts 88-; Rho Chi Pres 90-; Phi Lambda Sigma VP 91-92; Chrstn Stdnt Union Pres 89-90; Mercer Univ Acdmc Prfrmnc/Standard Com 90-; Red Cross Comm CPR Instrctr; Phrmcy; Doctorate Phrmcy.

**FRACASSA, STEPHANIE R,** Manhattan School Of Music, New York, NY; SR; BM; Vocl Perf; Oper Perf.

**FRACHETTI, PATRICIA A,** Le Moyne Coll, Syracuse, NY; SO; BA; Vrsty Swim Tm 90-; Acctng; CPA.

**FRACK, TRICIA L,** Univ Of Pittsburgh, Pittsburgh, PA; SO; BSN; NSNA 90-; SNAP 89-; NSA; Phi Eta Sigma 90-; Deans Lst 89-; Nrsng; Practitioner.

**FRADO, WENDY B,** The Boston Conservatory, Boston, MA; FR; BFA; Mscl Theatre; Prfrmnc.

**FRAELICH, MELODEE L,** Univ Of Akron, Akron, OH; JR, BSN; Nursing; Neo Natal ICU.

**FRAELICH, SANDRA A,** Wilmington Coll, New Castle, DE; JR; BS; DE Nurses Assoc 90-; Intl Wildlife Coalition Green Peace; RN Mdl Ctr DE 89-; MDL Subgical Certif Amer Nurses Assoc 89; Nursing.

**FRAGA, IVONNE,** Univ Of Pr At Rio Piedras, Rio Piedras, PR; SR; BBS; Pre Mdcl Stdnts Assoc 90; Amrcn Chmcl Scty 90; Gldn Key 90; Hnr 88-89; Yth Cmmssn; Mtrcl Hnr; Schlrshp Gldn Key Natl Hnr Scty; Schrlshp Bnc Pplr; Blgy.

**FRAGOSO, RUBEN C,** Princeton Univ, Princeton, NJ; JR; BA; Chicano Caucus 88-; Hispanic Bsn Soc 89-; PRIMOS Pres/Fdr 90-; Mellon Stafford Mnrty Exch Pgm Stanford Univ 90; Moleclr Bio; Ph D.**

**FRALEY, COURTENAY NICOLLS,** Samford Univ, Birmingham, AL; GD; JD; Cmbrlnd Trial Brd/Envrnmntl Law Soc; Phi Alpha Delta 90; Fnlst Haley Trial Comp/Client Cnslng Comp 90-; Deans Lista; Pi Beta Phi/Tau Theta Chi 84-88; Cngrssnl Intrn Hnrbl Bart Gordon; BA 84-88; Grad Lad Schl; Atty.

**FRALEY, DEBORAH L,** Concord Coll, Athens, WV; FR; BS; Activities Board 90-; Acctg.

**FRALEY, ROBERT C,** Univ Of Sc At Columbia, Columbia, SC; FR; Psych; Tchng.

**FRAME, SHANNON A,** East Tn St Univ, Johnson City, TN; FR; BS; Alpha Lambda Delta; Elem Ed; Tchg.

**FRAMIL, RONALD S,** Atlantic Union Coll, S Lancaster, MA; JR; BM; Nw Englnd Yth Ensmbl; Hnrs Cr Prgm 88-; Vllybll Clb 88-; Cll Prfrmnc.

**FRANC, TAMY C,** Duquesne Univ, Pittsburgh, PA; SR; BA; Acctg; CPA.

**FRANCE, ALICE R,** Coll Of Charleston, Charleston, SC; SO; Yrbk Stff 89-90; Hnrs Prgm Stdnt Assoc Nwslettr Stff 89-90; Bbl Stdy 89-; Dlphn Schlrshp; Clss Schlrshp; Engl.

**FRANCE, KEVIN C,** East Carolina Univ, Greenville, NC; FR; BFA; Art; Adv.

**FRANCES, ANTONIO C,** Va St Univ, Petersburg, VA; SR; BFA; Art Club VP 89-; Acadmc Award Pins 89-; Acadmc Achvmnt Award 90; Ftbl 87-89; Commrcl Art/Dsgn; Adv/Illustrtn/Freelnc Wrk.

**FRANCES, CORTES BELLO,** Univ Of Pr Medical Sciences, San Juan, PR; GD; MSN; BSN U PR Arecibo 86; Nrsng.

**FRANCESCHI, SONIA E,** Univ Of Pr Ponce Tech Univ Col, Ponce, PR; SO; BA; Acctng Stdnts Assn VP 89-; Hnr Scty 89-; Acctng; Lawyer.

**FRANCESCHINI, GILBERTO A,** Univ Central Del Caribe, Cayey, PR; GD; MD; Pre Med Clb 82-83; Biology Clb 82-83; Intramrcn U Hnr Soc 84-85; Deans Lst Acadmc Avrg Cthlc U PR 82-83; Cum Laude Intramrcn U Pr 88; BA Intramrcn U PK 88; BS Intramrcn U PR 88; Medicine; Surgery.

**FRANCESCONI, MARIA M,** Colby Sawyer Coll, New London, NH; JR; BSN; Stdnt Nrs Assoc Pres 90-; Res Dir Res Ed Staff 89-; Alpha Kai 90-; Nrsg.

**FRANCIS, BRENDAN C,** Barry Univ, Miami, FL; JR; BS; Bahamian Clb Meda Cnsltnt/ VP 90-; Intrntl Stdnt Org 88-90; Tri Beta 88-; Knights Columbus 90-; Fresh Yr; Lyford Lay Schlr; Bio; Med.

**FRANCIS, CAROL K,** Longwood Coll, Farmville, VA; SR; Stdnt Educ Assn; Bptst Stdnt Un; Intrvrsty Chrstn Flwshp; Kappa Delta Pi; Alpha Lambda Delta Sec/Treas 88-89; Phi Kappa Phi; Alpha Lambda Delta Sr Bk Awrd; BS 90; Elem Ed; Tchng.

**FRANCIS, DAVID J,** Saint Francis Coll, Loretto, PA; FR; BS; Stdnt Activities Assoc 90; Psychlgy Clb; Psychlgy.

**FRANCIS, DENNIS J,** Univ Of Sc At Columbia, Columbia, SC; FR; Pol Afrs Cmt Sec; Debating Tm; Lacrosse Co Capt; Pol Sci; Lawyer.

**FRANCIS, ELIZABETH M,** Fl St Univ, Tallahassee, FL; JR; BS; Seminole Ambadrs Sec 90-; Stdnt Alumni Fndtn Lady; Garnet/Gold Girls; Pi Beta Phi Panhellenic Rep 88-; Pi Beta Phi Cmpus Chrmn 88-; Gamma Grks Advctng Mgmt Alcohol; GCLC Rep 90-; Nurs.

**FRANCIS, GARY F,** Marshall University, Huntington, WV; GD; MBA; River Cities Un Way Bd/Dir; Schl Bd Our Redeemer Luthrn Ch Pres 88-; Prod Mgr BASF Corp Huntington WV 87-; BSCHE WV Un 75; Busn Mgmnt.

**FRANCIS, GILLIAN D,** Rutgers St Un At New Brunswick, New Brunswick, NJ; FR; MBA; Schl Newspaper; Pltcl Sci Clb; Natl Hnr Scty; Finance/Political Sci; Law.

**FRANCIS, JACQUELINE C,** Georgetown Univ, Washington, DC; SR; BSBA; DC Schl Prjct Vol Tutor 90; Yrbk Edtr 89-90; Bsn Mntrs Pgm 89; New Std Ort 89; Big Bro/Sis Pgm 89; Natl Elks Fdn Schlp 87-88; Bernard Mcdonough Schlp 88-; Rhodes Schlp; Fnce; Bnk/Cnsltng.

**FRANCIS, JULIE M,** Alfred Univ, Alfred, NY; SO; BS; Alpha Lambda Delta 89-90; All Amer Schlr 90; Soccer 89-; Bsn Adm; Mktg.

**FRANCIS, MARIE A,** Bethune Cookman Coll, Daytona Beach, FL; JR; BA; Alpha Angels VP 90-; Tutr/Yth Motvatr-Kenan Prgrm 89-; Alpha Mu Gamma; Delta Sigma Theta Sec 90-; Dns Lst; Hnr Rll; Elem Ed.

**FRANCIS, MAXINE B,** Bowie St Univ, Bowie, MD; SR; BS; Kndrgrtn Tch 87-; Dip Ed Micro Tchrs Coll Jamaica WI 84; Erly Chldhd/Spec Ed; Schl Admin.

**FRANCIS, MONIQUE M,** Fisk Univ, Nashville, TN; SR; BA; Meharry Cath Assoc Pres 89-90; Intnatl Stdnt Org Sec 90-; Sci Club V P 88-89; Mortar Bd Gold Key Chapt 90; Deans List 89-; WEB Dubois Hnrs Prog 90-; AA Coll Of Bahamas 89; Cert Coll Of Bahamas 90; Bio; Phrmcy/Edn.

**FRANCIS, SHARON C,** Morgan St Univ, Baltimore, MD; SR; BS; Bio Clb Sec 90-; Beta Kappa Chi Pres 90-; Alpha Kappa Mu; Mntry Access Rsrch Careers Schlrshp Stdnt Advsr 90-; Lucy V Warrington Awd Excell Dvlpmnt Bio; Deans Lst; Bio; Ph D Physiology.

**FRANCIS, SHERONNA M,** Clark Atlanta Univ, Atlanta, GA; SR; BS; Morehouse ROTC Bttln Assn Admn Offc 88-90; Math Dept Ttr 90-; Meto Trans Athrty 88-; Math; Fnnc/Actrl Sci.

**FRANCIS, WENDY P,** Barry Univ, Miami, FL; FR; BS; Black Stdnt Org 90-; Bus Mgt.

**FRANCIS-SMITH, AMY LEIGH,** Univ Of West Fl, Pensacola, FL; SR; BA; Drama; Dns Lst; AA Okaloosa-Walton Comm Clg 90; Educ; Tchng.

**FRANCISCO, ALICE REGINA,** Fordham Univ, Bronx, NY; JR; BS; Jr Comm Intl Debutantes Ball 87-; Philippine Amer Club 88-; Acctng Stcy 89-; Prepfnl KPMG Peat Marwick 90-; Fordham Dance Tm 90-; Public Acctng.

**FRANCISCO, DWAYNE B,** Univ Of Ky, Lexington, KY; SR; BS; Sidney Missionary Bapt Chrch; Amer Socty Cvl Engrs; Order Of Omega; Pi Kappa Phi Fndrsng Chr 89-90; ASE Morehead State Univ 90; Cvl Engr.

**FRANCISCO, JENNIFER M,** Oh St Univ At Newark, Newark, OH; FR; PHR; Natl Hnr Soc 90-; Phrmcy.

**FRANCISCO, PAMELA L,** Ms St Univ, Miss State, MS; SR; MS; Scty Of Wmn Engs Pres; Eng Stdnt Cncl Rep; Natl Scty Of Blck Engs Com Mmbr; Gamma Beta Phi Scl Chrprsn; Alpha Pi Mu Sec Treas; Rsdnt Asst Of Rsdnce Hll; Kodak Schlrshp; Indstrl Eng Dept Cmmndtn; Indstrl Eng Stdnt Of Mnth; BS; Indstrl Eng.

**FRANCISCO, SHARON K,** Longwood Coll, Farmville, VA; SR; BS; Bptst Un 89-; Chi Alpah 90-; ICF 88-; Alpha Phi Omega Hstrn 87-; IM Flg Ftbl 86-87; Ed; Elem Ed.

**FRANCISCUS, WILLIAM T,** Comm Coll Algny Co Algny Cmps, Pittsburgh, PA; FR; BA; Cmptr Sci.

**FRANCKOWIAK, LORI L,** Ms Univ For Women, Columbus, MS; SR; BA; NAA 90-; Acctng Hnry 90-; Phi Beta Lambda 90-; AF Ofcrs Wifes Clb 88-90; Yth For Understanding Host Parent 89; AA Miss Gulf Coast Comm Clg 89; Business Acctng; CPA.

**FRANCO COLON, MAYRA LEE,** Inter Amer Univ Pr Hato Rey, Hato Rey, PR; FR; Medicine.

**FRANCO, ALVARO,** Univ Of Southern Ms, Hattiesburg, MS; SR; Beta Gamma Phi 90-; Lttr Rcgntn Otstndng Acdmc 83-84; US Navy 87-; BS Unvrsty Sthrn MS 90-91; Cmptr Sci; Cmptr Engnrng.

**FRANCO, JONATHAN S,** S U N Y Coll Of Tech At Frmgdl, Farmingdale, NY; GD; BEET; IM Rcqtbl Vlybl Sftbl Wtrplo; Elect Eng Tchnlgs; Eng.**

**FRANCO, MARISOL,** Univ Of Pr At Mayaguez, Mayaguez, PR; FR; BSCHE; Cthlc Apstlc Grp 90-; Lg Mr; Chem Engrg.

**FRANCO, MARK S,** Univ Of Charleston, Charleston, WV; SO; BA; Actvts Bd 90; Math Ed; Tchr.

**FRANCOIS, JACQUES OLCY,** Miami Dade Comm Coll, Miami, FL; GD; Haitian Bookan Clb; Stdnt Retention Ctr; Math Tutor; Grad W/Hnrs; Outstndg Acad Awd; Multiple Yr Awd; AA Miami-Dade Cmnty Clg 90; Math.**

**FRANCOIS, KRISTA M,** James Madison University, Harrisonburg, VA; JR; BS; Catholic Cmpus Mnstry 88-; CEC 90-; Ctr Serv Lrng 88-90; Mortar Bd; Kappa Delta Pi; Spec Educ.

**FRANCOLINI, SCOTT A,** Bryant Coll Of Bus Admin, Smithfield, RI; FR; 1st Rnk Clss; Vars Sccr; Fnc; Bus.

**FRANCOLINO, BARBARA R,** Cabrini Coll, Radnor, PA; SO; BA; Pool Clb 89-90; Bio Clb 89-90; Stdnt Govt Rep 89-; Acctg Assn Sec/Treas 89-; PA Inst CPA 90-; Phonathon 89-; Deans Schlrshp 89-; Cabrini Deans Lst 90-; Deans Schlr 89-; Acctg; CPA.**

**FRANCZAK, ALICIA,** Saint John Fisher Coll, Rochester, NY; SR; Deans Lst 89-90; BA; AA 75; Psychlgy; Psychlgy Rltd Emplymnt.

**FRANCZAK, MARY ELIZABETH,** Miami Dade Comm Coll Med Centr, Miami, FL; SR; BA; Stdnt Senate 90-; Phi Theta Kappa 90-; Rcvd James J Mcknight Schlrshp; AS 91; Phys Thrpy.

**FRANEK, ANN MARIE T,** Temple Univ, Philadelphia, PA; SR; BS; PA Phrmctcl Assn; Rho Chi VP 89-; Phi Delta Chi 88-; W W Smith Sr Excllnc Awd 90; Phrmcy.

**FRANK, CHARLES F,** Embry Riddle Aeronautical Univ, Daytona Beach, FL; JR; BA; Orange Cty Off Roaders 86-; Noving Co Ownr; Lawn Serv 87; Airframe Cert; Powerplant Cert; Avionics/Mgt; Aerospace.

**FRANK, DAWN E,** Lansdale School Of Bus, North Wales, PA; GD; CERT; Prchsng Dept Sec; Wrd Prcssng; Sec.

**FRANK, JEAN H,** City Univ Of Ny La Guard Coll, Long Island Cty, NY; SO; AS; Busn Admin.

**FRANK, REBECCA J,** Oh St Univ, Columbus, OH; SR; Jwsh Stdnt Actvts Bd Mbrshp Chrmn 88-90; Coll Dmcrts 90-; Phi Alpha Delta 87-; Mirros Pblc Rltns/Scl Chrmn 88-89; Alpha Xi Delta Asst Schlrshp Chrmn; Untd Jwsh Appl Co-Chrmn 88-89; Sntr L Fishers Cmpgn Ohio Attrny Gnrl Prdctn Asst 90-; Ecnmcs; Law-JD.

**FRANK, SHERRY L,** Univ Of South Al, Mobile, AL; SR; BS; SHAPE 90-; Kappa Delta Pi 90-; PTSA Mbrshp Chrmn 90-; Sndy Sch Dir 89-; Phys Educ; Tchr.

**FRANKE, BETTY L,** Kent St Univ Kent Cmps, Kent, OH; SO; BSN; SPN; Pathfinder Clb 71-74 Cnslr 86-; Chrch Brd/Fin Cmt 75-; Assc Home Ec Andrews Un 71; Nrsng.

**FRANKE, MELANIE L,** Univ Of Sc At Union, Union, SC; FR; Encr Clb 90-; Hstry Awrd 90-; Psych; Cnclng.

**FRANKE, MICHAEL A,** Hudson Valley Comm Coll, Troy, NY; SR; AAS; Grdtd With Hnrs; Paul Luther Mem Award; Amer Inst Bnkng; Fleet/Norstar Data Svcs Corp 90-; Crmnl Justc; Law.

**FRANKE, MICHAEL E,** Northern Ky Univ, Highland Hts, KY; SO; BA; SG V P; Ord/Omega; Pi Kappa Alpha Pledge Ed 90-; ROTC Schlrshp; Jewish War Vet Awd 90-; Intnl Studies; Frgn Affr.

**FRANKE, SANDRA R,** Univ Of Ga, Athens, GA; SR; BSED; All Campus Homecmng Comm 89-90; Greek Wk 88-89; GA Girl 89-90; Golden Key 89-; Kappa Delta Epsilon 89-; Deans List 88-; Kappa Alpha Theta Song Ldr 87-; Kappa Alpha Theta Serv Comm 88-; Miss GA Spirit Rep 88; Theta Lady Awd; Erly Chldhd Ed; Teaching.

**FRANKEL, KEVIN A,** Manhattan Coll, Bronx, NY; JR; BS; Phto Clb 90-; AICHE VP 89-; Omega Chi Epsilon Treas 90-; Tau Kappa Epsilon 89-; Dns Lst 88-; IM Bsbl Bsktbl 89-; Chem Eng.

**FRANKERT, FRANK R,** Comm Coll Algny Co Algny Cmps, Pittsburgh, PA; FR; BA; Eng.

**FRANKET, DION D,** Univ Of Sc At Columbia, Columbia, SC; SR; PHD; Physcs Soc 88-; Hnr Assoc 87-; Pi Mu Epsilion 90-; Sigma Pi Sigma; Hnrs Pgm 87-; Sigma Pi Sigma; Pi Mu Epsilon 90-; Hnr Schlrshp 87-; Bsktbl/Flr Hcky/Scr/Vlybl 87-; BS; Physcs; Elem Prtcl Physcs.

**FRANKFURT, DAVID M,** Oh Wesleyan Univ, Delaware, OH; SR; BA; MUB PUB Comm VP 87-; Yrbk Sprts Ed 89-90; TV Stn Anchr/Prdcr 87-90; USA Ntwrk Smr Intrshp Assoc Pro 90; TV Chnl 4 Columbus Intrn 90; Swmtm/Crs Cntry/Trck 89-90; Brdcst Jrnlsm; Sprts Prdcr.

**FRANKFURTH, JILL A,** Oh Wesleyan Univ, Delaware, OH; SR; BA; Stdnt Adv WCSA 90-; Sigma Chi Lil Sis 88-90; Acctng; Auditor.

**FRANKLIN, BEVERLY G,** Univ Of South Al, Mobile, AL; SR; BS; Kappa Delta Pi; Law Spouse Clb Pres 85-86; Deans Lst 90; Mortar Bd; Mobile Bar Assoc 89-; Sec; ASN FL Comm Coll Jacksonville 89; Elem Edn; Teach.

**FRANKLIN, CHARLENE J,** Dutchess Comm Coll, Poughkeepsie, NY; SO; BA; Blck Stdnt Union; Most Outstndng Mnrty Stdnt Comm Coll 90-; AS/SCI; Phrmcy.

**FRANKLIN III, CHARLES E,** Univ Of Southern Ms, Hattiesburg, MS; JR; BA; Egl Clb 90-; Alpha Beta Gamma/Phi Theta Kappa 89-90; Mktg; Phrmctcl Sls.

**FRANKLIN, CINA S,** Univ Of Tn At Martin, Martin, TN; FR; Blck Stdnt Assc; Hnr Roll 90-; Schlrshp Fall; Acctng; Acctnt.

**FRANKLIN, DAVID M,** Valdosta St Coll, Valdosta, GA; FR; MBA; Engl; Law.

**FRANKLIN, DONALD E,** Univ Of Sc At Columbia, Columbia, SC; SO; BS; Math Chem Physcs; Eng.

**FRANKLIN, EDWARD P,** Union Univ, Jackson, TN; SR; MED; Phi Theta Kappa 87-90; Sigma Tau Delta Sec 90-; Fclty Awd; Hmnts Awd; NEA/TEA; AS Jackson St Comm Clg; BA; Engl; Tch.

**FRANKLIN, JASON A,** Univ Of Pittsburgh, Pittsburgh, PA; FR; BA; Univ Schlr; I M Bkbl; Indus Engr.

**FRANKLIN, JOHN L,** Fl St Univ, Tallahassee, FL; GD; MD; Phi Beta Kappa 90-; Delta Tau Delta 87-90; Med; Dctr.

**FRANKLIN, KIMBERLY B,** Mayland Comm Coll, Spruce Pine, NC; SO; AAS; Phi Theta Kappa Tres 90-; Bus Admn.

**FRANKLIN, KIMBERLY C,** Gaston Coll, Dallas, NC; FR; Gamma Beta Phi; Woodmen Of Wrld 87-; Math; Scndry Edn.

**FRANKLIN, LESLIE A,** Al St Univ, Montgomery, AL; SO; Cmptr Info Systs; Cmptr Analyst Prgrmr.

**FRANKLIN, MATTHEW P,** Lord Fairfax Comm Coll, Middletown, VA; FR; AAS; Co Advsr Frdrck Co Shrffs Cdts Lt 88-; FFA Treas 85-; Sci Clb 90; RB Harper Awrd; Bus Mgmt; Law Enfrcmnt.

**FRANKLIN, MELISSA D,** Lenoir Rhyne Coll, Hickory, NC; JR; BA; Sigma Kappa VP 89-90; Big Sis 89-; Rock A Thons Alzhmrs Disease 89-; Crop Walk 88; March Of Dimes 89; Exercise Phslgy Intrn; Chrldr Capt 90-; Tchng Cert; Corp Fitness.

**FRANKLIN, NANCY J,** Niagara Univ, Niagara Univ, NY; SR; BBA; Natl Acctg Assoc 90-; Frnkln Trffc Srvc 81-90; Acctg.

**FRANKLIN, RHONDA M,** Wallace St Comm Coll At Selma, Selma, AL; FR; Spnsh Clb 89-90; Nrsng; RN.

**FRANKLIN, SANDRA A,** S U N Y Coll Of Tech At Frmgdl, Farmingdale, NY; SO; NYSAAEYC NAEYC 89-; Mult Sclerosis Soc N Y; Erly Chldhd; Tchng Spec Nds Chldrn.

**FRANKLIN, SANDRA K,** Western Piedmont Comm Coll, Morganton, NC; SO; BA; Phi Beta Lambda Tr 90-; P Hutchns Schlrshp; Ii Pl Acctg St Ldrshp Conf; Dns Lst; Acctng.**

**FRANKLIN, SERENA Y,** Lincoln Univ, Lincoln Univ, PA; SR; Spnsh Clb Sen; Bsns Clb Sec; US Army Res Spec; Natl Assoc Adv Clrd People; Longvty Serv Rbbn Spec; BA; Bsns Admn; Org Mgmt.

**FRANKLIN, SUSAN L,** Wallace St Comm Coll At Selma, Selma, AL; SO; Cheerleader; Ambassador; Phi Theta Kappa Pres 0-; Soc Dist Amer Jr Clge Stdnts 89-; Historic Pilgrimage Hostess 76-; Battle Of Selma Hostess 88-; Selma Dallas Cnty Recycling Com 90-; Outstndg Stdnt 90-; Cheerleader 90-; Math; Civil Engrng.

**FRANKLIN, TESSA L,** Alcorn St Univ, Lorman, MS; SO; BA; Engl/Lit; Tchr.

**FRANKLIN, THOMAS A,** Fl Atlantic Univ, Boca Raton, FL; JR; BBA; SGA Acdmc Excllnc Physcs Physcl Sci 88-89; Cmmty Coll Acdmc Achvmnt 88; Assoc Enrgy Eng 88-; Amrcn Inst Plnt Eng 90-; Mgmt; Comp Info Systms.

**FRANKLIN, THOMAS N,** Va Commonwealth Univ, Richmond, VA; FR; BS; VCV Hnrs Pgm; Phi Eta Sigma; Psi Chi; Rsrch Intrnshp Psychlgy; Top One Prcnt Frshmn Cls; Psychlgy/Pre Med; Med.

**FRANKLIN, TONYA L,** Fl A & M Univ, Tallahassee, FL; Wlkr Ford Comm Ctr Vol 90; Baby Rattler Day Care Ctr 89; Hnr Std 89-90; AA Tallahassee Comm Clg 89; Crmnl Jstc/Scl Wlfr; Law.

**FRANKLIN, WAYNA R,** Clark Atlanta Univ, Atlanta, GA; SO; BED; Blck Stu Allnc Hmncmng 90; Queen 90; Alpha Kappa Alpha; Coor Hst Blck Stu Wknd 90; Psych; Chld Psychlgst.

**FRANKLIN, WILLIAM M,** Univ Of Ky, Lexington, KY; SR; BS; Cvl Eng; Envrnmntl Eng/Law.

**FRANKO, CAROL M,** Duquesne Univ, Pittsburgh, PA; FR; BS; Italian Club; Tauburntiza Ensemble; Phi Eta Sigma Orchestra Ldr; Lambda Sigma; Tamburitzan Schlrshp; Liberal Arts/Sci.

**FRANKO, MARY C,** Clarion Univ Of Pa, Clarion, PA; SO; BSBA; Sigma Sigma Sigma; Finance/Real Estate.**

**FRANKS, ADARRYL L,** Stillman Coll, Tuscaloosa, AL; FR; BA; Gamma Iota Sigma; Comm Brdcst; History Tchr.

**FRANKS, DAWN E,** Fl International Univ, Miami, FL; JR; Activities/Ldr Facty Schlrs Social 87; Faculty Schlr 87-; Accepted Competivite Physical Therapy BS Prog 91; Assoc FIU 89-90; Physical Therapy; Dir Burn Unit/Wound Care Dp.

**FRANKS, KATHY M,** Commonwealth Coll, Virginia Beach, VA; SO; AA; Hnr Roll/Deans List/Prest List; Vlybl/Spring Fling; Messiah Luthn Coed Sftbl Tm; Exec Office/Legal; Secty.

**FRANKS, RITA SUE,** Northwest Al Comm Coll, Phil Campbell, AL; FR; ASSOC; Diploma; Nursing.

**FRANQUEZ, MARIA LOURDES,** Miami Dade Comm Coll, Miami, FL; SO; AA; Travel/Tourism Mgmnt; Travel Agency Mgr.

**FRANS, KERENZA T K,** Webber Coll, Babson Park, FL; SO; BA; Cntrl Fla Htl/Mtl Assn 89-; Intl Stdnt Clb 89-; Sdtnt Hosp Mgmnt 90; Intrsnshp Grosvenor Resort 90; Cert Amer Hotel Assn 89-; Cert 89-; Vars Tennis; Hotel/Rest Mgmnt; Acctng.

**FRANSON, TODD G,** Savannah Coll Of Art & Design, Savannah, GA; SR; BFA; Photo Grp VP 89-; Photography/Graphic Dsgn; Advrtsng.

**FRANTZ, PAMELA A,** Immaculata Coll, Immaculata, PA; SR; BA; Peace/Just Comm; Intrntl Rltns Co; Psych Clb Sec 90-; Psi Chi Sec 90-; Intrnshp Ken Crest Chld Dvlpmnt Ctr; Psych; Cnsling.

**FRANZ, JOSEPH D,** Univ Of Akron, Akron, OH; JR; BA; Dns Cncl; Phi Eta Sigma Treas/Snr Advsr; Alpha Lambda Delta Pres; Beta Gamma Sigma V P; Mu Kappa Tau Mktg Hnry; Cprtve Educ Exper Color Tile; Mktg/Bsn; Mktg Rsrch/Sales.

**FRANZ, JOSEPH N,** S U N Y Coll Of Tech At Alfred, Alfred, NY; SR; AS; Almni Assn Phnthn; Natl Vo Tech Hon Soc Sec/Treas 90-; Sigma Tau Epsilon 89-90; IM Flr Hockey/Ftbl; Drftng/Cad.

**FRANZ, LORRAINE M,** City Univ Of Ny La Guard Coll, Long Island Cty, NY; SO; AA; Intrn Little Dolphin Nrsry Schl; Chld Care/Dev; Chld Psychlgst.

**FRANZ, TRAVIS T,** Oh Univ-Southern Cmps, Ironton, OH; SO; BA; Fine Arts; Graphic Designist.

**FRANZEN, NOELLE L,** Radford Univ, Radford, VA; FR; BA.

**FRANZREB IV, JOHN E,** City Univ Of Ny Baruch Coll, New York, NY; SR; BA; Gold Key; Value Line Inv Survy; Mobl Oil Corp; Valve Line; Finc; Inv Analyst.

**FRASE, MELISSA J,** Kent St Univ Kent Cmps, Kent, OH; JR; BA; Psych Clb VP 89-; Hse Cncl Pres 89-; Nw Stdnt Orntn Stdnt Instr 88-90; Kent Intrhl Cncl 89-; Orntn Hon Soc Schlrshp Chrprsn 89-; Gldn Ky; Psi Chi VP 89-; Alpha Lambda Delta 88-; Twnhl II Crisis Hlpln 90-; Phi Beta Kappa; Dns Lst 89-90; Psych; Chld Psych.

**FRASER, ALLISON K,** Univ Of Ky, Lexington, KY; SO; BA; Soccr Clb Treas 90; Alpha Gamma Delta IM Chrmn; Engl; Hgh Schl Engl Tchr.

**FRASER, ANDREA S,** Norfolk St Univ, Norfolk, VA; SR; BS; Fshn Shw Mdl 89-90; You Gotta Get Yours 89-90; E T Marshall Schlrshp 87; Mss Cmmnctn; Pblshng.

**FRASER, CHARLES H,** Manhattan Coll, Bronx, NY; GD; BS; Elec Clb; Natl Soc Blck Eng Sec 89-90; Eta Kappa Nu; IEEE 87-; Royal Naval Coll 78; Tech Ofcr Guyana Dfns Force; Royal Nvy Schl Wpn Eng 81; Elec Eng; Eng.

**FRASER, CHARLOTTE D,** Pellissippi St Tech Comm Coll, Knoxville, TN; SO; AAS; Pres Cncl 90-; Tau Alpha Pi Pres 90-; Psi Delta Chap; Phi Theta Kappa 89-; Fclty Cncl Schlrshp Awd 90; Cmptr/Drftg/Dsgn; Eng.

**FRASER, DIANE T,** Atlantic Comm Coll, Mays Landing, NJ; SO; BA; AA; Psychlgy/Soc Serv.

**FRASER, KATE E,** Emory Univ, Atlanta, GA; JR; BSN; Nurse Assoc Pres 90-; GA Assoc Nursing Stdnts 2nd V Pres 90-; Omicron Delta Kappa; Alpha Phi Omega Pldgemstr 89-90; Nursing.

**FRASER, KEITH L,** Southern Coll Of Tech, Marietta, GA; SR; BA; Toastmasters Intl 90-; United Chess Fed 80-82; Intrnshp Furniture Maker 86-87; Mech Engrng.

**FRASER, RICHARD A,** Salisbury St Univ, Salisbury, MD; SR; BS; Otstndng Stdnt Finance; Deans Lst 88-; Delta Mu Delta 90-; Stdnt Athlt Hnr Roll 90; Phi Beta Lambda 88-; Intrn Wheat First Scrts 90; Intrn Entrprs Lsng Clg Pk MD 90; Hnr Roll SSU 88-89; Vrsty Bsbl 88-90; Bsns; Fnncl Plnng.

**FRASIER, HOYT J,** Northeast State Tech Comm Coll, Blountville, TN; FR; BA; Hstry.

**FRATANGELO, MICHAEL R,** Siena Coll, Loudonville, NY; SR; BBA; Glf Tm 87-; Ski Clb 89-; Nwspr 89; CPA Intern 90; Outstdng Acad Athlt; Acctg; CPA.

**FRATARCANGELO, EDWARD P,** Alfred Univ, Alfred, NY; SR; BA; Vrsty La Crosse Capt 88; Mrktng; Mrktng Mngmnt.

**FRATER, FITZGERALD A,** City Univ Of Ny Bronx Comm Col, Bronx, NY; SO; AA; Paralegal Soc 90-; Phi Theta Kappa 89-; Law.

**FRATER, JOEL L,** Cheyney Univ Of Pa, Cheyney, PA; SR; BS; Rec Clb 90-; Intl Assn Org Sec 90-; Res Councl 90-; Dns Lst 90-; Rho Phi Lambda; Ambssdr Corps 90-; Food Dr Comm 90; Comm Ctr Intrn; Vlybl/Sftbl/Soccr/Table Tenns; Cert G C Fostr Clg 87; Cert Moneague Tchrs Clg 82; Rec; Rec Thrpy.

**FRATERRIGO, ROBERT,** City Univ Of Ny City Coll, New York, NY; GD; BET; Phi Theta Kappa 89-; Golden Key 89-; Bsbl 87-; AAS Bronx Comm Coll Of CUNY 89; Electromechanical Engrng Tech; E & D Engr.

**FRATES, LAURA L,** Western New England Coll, Springfield, MA; FR; BA; Ovrnght Hstss 90-; Fesh Focus Grp 90-; Alpha Lambda Delta Treas 90-; Deans Lst 90-; Acctg; CPA.

**FRATINI, COLLEEN M,** Univ Of New England, Biddeford, ME; JR; BA; Stu/Almn Phnthn 90; Echrstc Mnstr Cmps Chrch 89- Kndrgrdn Tchr Aide 90; Jvnl Dtctv Aide Biddeford; Hmn Srvcs; Cnslng Drug Rehab.

**FRATOLILL, APRIL J,** Univ Of Sc At Columbia, Columbia, SC; SR; BA; Carolina Clsscs 89-; Cncl Psych.

**FRAWLEY, CAROLYN M,** S U N Y Empire St Coll, Saratoga Spg, NY; GD; BA; AAS 90; Crmnlgy.

**FRAYLER, MICHAEL T,** Saint Josephs Coll, Windham, ME; FR; Soccer 90; Math; Actuary.

**FRAZEE, CAROL A,** Garrett Comm Coll, Mchenry, MD; FR; AA; Clrcl; Elem Ed; Tchr.

**FRAZER, AMY L,** Columbus Coll Of Art & Design, Columbus, OH; SO; BA; Illustration Adv Dsgn; Magazine Freelance.

**FRAZER, CYNTHIA R,** Longwood Coll, Farmville, VA; JR; BS; Longwood Ambrs Treas 89-; Alpha Lambda Delta 88-; Recpt Hull Ridgeway 89-90; Pre Mdl; Psychiatry.

**FRAZER, LORETTA I,** Univ Of Sc At Columbia, Columbia, SC; JR; BA; Greenville Cty Lbry Stf Assc; Lbrn Asst Greenville Cty Lbry 89-; Humanities/Intrdscplnry; Prof Librarian.

**FRAZER, SUSAN O,** Birmingham Southern Coll, Birmingham, AL; JR; BA; Cnsrvcny 90; Alpha Lambda Delta; Phi Eta Sigma; Kapp Delta Phlthrpy 90-/88; Acctg Asst 90-; Intrnshp WBP/B; Robert Henry Kirkland Acctg Merit Schlrshp; Acctg.

**FRAZIER, BARBARA WHEAT,** De Tech & Comm Coll At Dover, Dover, DE; SO; AA; Hmn Serv Org Sec 90-; Big Bro/Sis; Hmn Serv/Bhvrl Sci; Spec Educ/Excptnl Chldrn.

**FRAZIER, BERNICE L,** Central St Univ, Wilberforce, OH; SR; Alpha Kappa Mu VP 90-; Cltn Of 100 Blck Wmn 88-; Mt Clvry Bapt Ch Chr 76-; Cncrnd CSU Plce Wfs Assn Chrprsn 88-; Natl Bus Lgue 89-; Cnsltnt PR; AS Miami Jacobs Jr Coll Dayton OH 75; Cmmnctn; PR.

**FRAZIER, BRUCE S,** Middle Tn St Univ, Murfreesboro, TN; FR; BM; Music/Instrmntl Prfrmnce.

**FRAZIER, CAROL L,** Jacksonville St Univ, Jacksonville, AL; SR; BS; Amer Heart Assn Basic Life Support Instr; Grdtd Cum Laude GSCC 78; AD Gadsden State Cmnty Clg 78; Nrsg/Sci.

**FRAZIER, CHARLENE K,** Albany St Coll, Albany, GA; JR; Math And Comp Sci Clb 89-; Alpha Kappa Mu Sec 90-; Alpha Kappa Alpha Sec 90-; Comp Sci; Systms Anlysts.**

**FRAZIER, ELISA A,** Savannah Coll Of Art & Design, Savannah, GA; JR; BA; Photography; Photo Journalism.

**FRAZIER, JAMIE L,** Univ Of Cin R Walters Coll, Blue Ash, OH; SO; AAB; Med Offc Admin; Hosp Admin.

**FRAZIER, JEFFREY S,** Vance Granville Comm Coll, Henderson, NC; SR; Elect Club 87-; Deans List Hnr Roll 89-90; Intrnshp IBM; Math Skilled Awd; Sftbl Bsktbl; Cert 87; Cert 88; Elect Prog Mech Engr.

**FRAZIER, JULIE A,** Oh Dominican Coll, Columbus, OH; SR; BA; Camp Mnstry 89-; Psi Chi 90-; Kappa Gamma Pi; Delta Epsilon Sigma; Chlds Wrtng Awd 89; Stdnt Tchr Yr; Vars Sftbl 87-89; Ed Cert; Psych/Engl; Dvlpmntl Psych.

**FRAZIER, JULIE C,** Univ Of Sc At Columbia, Columbia, SC; FR; MBA; Carolina Pgm Union 90-; Alpha Lambda Delta; Alpha Phi Omega; Jrnlsm; Brdcst Jrnlst.

**FRAZIER, KATHRYN L,** Western Carolina Univ, Cullowhee, NC; FR; BA; Stream Watch 89-90; Adopt A Hwy 89-90; Art/Philo; Educ.

**FRAZIER, KATRINA E,** Fl A & M Univ, Tallahassee, FL; SR; BS; Vars Chrldr Capt 88-; Future Educ Amer 90-; Stdnt Assn Tchr Educ Ldr 89-90; Save The Children Prog 88-89; Elem Educ.

**FRAZIER, KELLI M,** Univ Of Nc At Wilmington, Wilmington, NC; FR; BA; Psychlgy; Psychiatrist.

**FRAZIER, KIMBERLY J,** Oh Dominican Coll, Columbus, OH; SR; BA; Ntl Assoc Of Deaf 90; Dghtrs Of Amer Rvltn 80; Prctcm Sign Lang 89-90; Cert Dntl Assist; Sign Lang Intrprtr 75-90; AS Columbus State Cmmnty Clg 90; Cross Dscplnry Studies Psych; Wrk Wth Deaf.

**FRAZIER, MARJORIE G,** Emory Univ, Atlanta, GA; GD; MN; Grad Nrss Assn Pres 90; Cncl Of Pres Of Stdnt Govt Assn 90; Omicron Delta Kappa; Sigma Theta Tau Intrntl; Woodruff Fllwshp 89; Amer Nrss Assn 88; GA Nrss Assn 88; ADN Floyd College Rome GA 82; Grntlgy Mntl Hlth.

**FRAZIER, MARVIE S,** Jackson St Univ, Jackson, MS; FR; Hon Coll 90; Bailey-Wiggins Mnrty Schlrshp Spch Lang Pthlgy 90; Spch Pthlgy.

**FRAZIER, MINYON K,** Clark Atlanta Univ, Atlanta, GA; SO; BS; Fin Clb Sec 89-; Dancers 89-; Bus Fin; Mngmnt.**

**FRAZIER, MONICA C,** Al St Univ, Montgomery, AL; JR; BA; Gospel Choir Sec 88-; Stdtn Orientation Serv Ldr V P 89-; Phi Eta Sigma Asst Sec 89-; Beta Kappa Chi; Alpha Kappa Alpha 90-; Stdnt Rsrch Asst U Of AL; Chemistry; Medicine.**

**FRAZIER, ORIE D,** Wilmington Coll, New Castle, DE; SR; BS; Armasn Chldrns Assn Mntr 87-88; Grl Scts Arm Sr Grl Sct Ldr 85-87; Phldlph Ftrs Mntr; Olympc Org Cmmtt Gd Interprtr 87-88; USAF 78-89; US Pstl Srvc; AAS Cmmnty Coll Air Force 84; AA Pikes Peak Cmmnty Coll 83; Bus Mgmt; Cnsltng.

**FRAZIER, OUIDA L,** Alcorn St Univ, Lorman, MS; FR; BS; Hon Stdnt 90-; Dns Lst 90-; Pre-Med/Bio; Med/Pdtrcs.

**FRAZIER, REGINALD W,** Morehouse Coll, Atlanta, GA; FR; BA; Ntnl Soc Black Engnrs 90-; Math Clb 90-; Frederick Douglass Tutrl Prgrm 90-; NSBE Member Of The Yr 90-; Hon Roll; Math; Mech Eng.

**FRAZIER, RICHARD T,** Birmingham Southern Coll, Birmingham, AL; GD; BS; Adlt Studies Stdnt Advsry Cncl Mntr 87-; Adlts Studies Alumni Rep 90-; Omicron Delta Kappa 90-; Deans Lst 86-; Elctrnc Tchncn; Comp Info Syst.**

**FRAZIER III, ROBERT E,** Morehouse Coll, Atlanta, GA; JR; BS; Comp Sci Club 90-; Matheletes Club Math Tutor 89-; NAACP 88-; Comp Sci; Software Dvlpmnt.

**FRAZIER, SCOTT A,** Defiance Coll, Defiance, OH; SO; BA; IM Sftbl/Ftbl Capt; Thetas Xi; Deans Lst; Track/Field Varsity; Math; Actuarial Sci.

**FRAZIER, SHEILA L,** Fayetteville St Univ, Fayetteville, NC; SR; MA; Assn US Army 88-; Warrant Offcr Assn; Eastern Star 87-; US Army Warrnt Offcr 75-; BS; Psychlgy; Cnslng.

**FRAZIER, SHERRIA D,** Univ Of Southern Ms, Hattiesburg, MS; SR; Golden Key 90-; Beta Alpha Psi 90-; Phi Beta Lambda 88-90; Acctg; CPA.**

**FRAZIER, THOMAS M,** Univ Of West Fl, Pensacola, FL; JR; BA; Phi Theta Kappa 89-; Spcl Ed; Tchng.

**FRAZIER, TRAVIS C,** Univ Of Ky, Lexington, KY; SO; BA; Yng Artists; Hstry/Art Studio; Archlgy.

**FRECHETTE, CHRISTOPHER S,** Widener Univ, Chester, PA; SR; BS; Acctg Soc; Penn Inst Cert Pub Assoc; Acctg.

**FRECHETTE, MIKELL B,** Savannah Coll Of Art & Design, Savannah, GA; JR; BA; Arts Cncl; Indpndnt Stdy Txtl Dsgn; Belize CA Prmtv Art Stdy Sabatacle; Dsgn Asstntshp; Int Dsgn/Textl; Artist.

**FREDENBURGH, DANIEL P,** Norwalk St Tech Coll, Norwalk, CT; SR; AS; Tau Alpha Pi Pres 90-; Phi Theta Kappa Pres 90-; Bsbl 90; Elec Engnrng Tech.

**FREDERICK, AMY E,** Univ Of Ky, Lexington, KY; FR; BA; Cosmo Clb 90-; Germn; Intrpretr.

**FREDERICK, CONA D,** Hillsborough Comm Coll, Tampa, FL; JR; BS; Stdnts For Schlstic Success Pres 87-90; SGA 88-90; Phi Theta Kappa V P 88-; Phi Beta Lambda Prlmntrn 88-90; Caribbean Stdnt Assn 90-; Cmptr Prgmng Awd 89; AA Hillsborough Comm Clg 90; Cmptr Info Sci; Cmptr Sftwr Spclst.**

**FREDERICK, KIMBERLY J,** Youngstown St Univ, Youngstown, OH; SO; BE; IEEE; Natl Soc Prfssnl Engrs 90-; YSU Centrns 90-; Awrd Schlstc Hon; Awrd Schlrshp Outstndng Achvmnt; St OH Cert Achvmnt; Elec Eng.

**FREDERICK, LORI C,** Memphis St Univ, Memphis, TN; SR; BPS; Break 87-90; Gamma Beta Phi 89-; Dns Lst; Nghbrhd Chrstn Ctr Tutor 89; Intrn Paralgl Parrish Shaw Law Frm; Mortarbrd Nom; Paralgl Cert; Parlgl Stdies; Parlgl In Law Frm.

**FREDERICK, LU ANNE C,** City Univ Of Ny City Coll, New York, NY; SR; BSN; Sigma Theta Tau; Nursing.

**FREDERICK, RHONDA A,** Univ Of Akron, Akron, OH; SR; BA; Elem Educ; Tchr.

**FREDERICK, ROBERT T,** Univ Of Pittsburgh, Pittsburgh, PA; SO; BA; Phi Eta Sigma 90-; Engr Hnrs Schlrshp; Co-Op Pgm Swanson Analysis Syst Inc Mech Engr; IM Soccer; Mech Engr; Engr.

**FREDERICK, RONALD J,** Ramapo Coll Of Nj, Mahwah, NJ; SR; Psych Clb 90-; Deans Lst; Mst Otstndg Stu; Estrn Psych Assoc Conf; Actors Equity Assoc 88-; Clncl Psych.

**FREDERICK, SUSAN M,** George Mason Univ, Fairfax, VA; SR; BSED; Erly Educ; Tch.

**FREDERICK, TAMMY J,** James Sprunt Comm Coll, Kenansville, NC; FR; ADN; Sci; Nrsng.

**FREDERICK, TIMOTHY S,** Wv Univ, Morgantown, WV; SO; BSCHE; AICHE 90-; Tau Beta Pi 91; Phi Kappa Phi 90; Outstndng Frshmn Schol 90; Pres Schlrshp 89-; Chmcl Engrng.

**FREDERICKS, ELLEN E,** Glassboro St Coll, Glassboro, NJ; JR; BA; Pnhllnc Cncl Del; Rsdnt Stdnt Assoc Hnrs Drm Sec 90-; Pblc Rltns Stdnt Scty Armc 90-; Phi Beta Lambda Pres 89-90; Theta Pi Omicron Almn Rep; Great Gorge Resort Intern; 2nd Plc St Phi Beta Lambda Cmptn 89-90; Berkeley Coll Almn Schlrshp 88; AAS 90; Cmmnctns Plbc Rltns.

**FREDERICKS, ERA IDETTE,** Univ Of The Virgin Islands, St Thomas, VI; SR; BAAA; Explrs Clb Sec 89; Pre-Law Assoc Sec/Treas 90; Photogrphy Clb Treas 90; Pres Clb; FBLA Chrprsn Of Prof Cmmttee 89; The Cmfrtrs Hosp Vstn Grp; Erly Admssn Prog; Bsnss Admin Fclty Awd; BA; AA; Bsnss Admin; Law.

**FREDERIKSEN, ALAN B,** Univ Of Fl, Gainesville, FL; JR; BSEE; UF Clb Sccr; Elec Engr.**

**FREDRECK, JENNIFER L,** Villanova Univ, Villanova, PA; JR; BA; Stdtn Govt 88-89; Cmmnctn Arts Hnr Scty; Cmmtt Hmlss 88-89; Crew 89; Cmmnctns; Law.

**FREDRICK, LISA N,** Schenectady County Comm Coll, Schenectady, NY; Hosptlty Clb VP 90-; HVCC Thtr Co 90; Intern Walt Disney World Co; Pres Lst 90; AAS Hudson Valley Comm Coll 90; Htl Rest Mngmnt.

**FREDRICKS, VIVIAN M,** Methodist Coll, Fayetteville, NC; JR; BS; Alpha Chi 90-; PTA M R Williams Schlr VP 90-; NCATA Chr 90-; Tchr Asst Elem Schl 85-; Elem Ed; Tchr.

**FREDRICKSEN, BERNICE R,** Fl St Univ, Tallahassee, FL; JR; BS; Flambeau Wrtr; Sls/Mgmnt; AA Tallahassee Comm Colg 90; Engl Edctn: Tch.

**FREDRICKSON, JAN N,** S U N Y Coll At Postdam, Potsdam, NY; FR; BA; Hl Cncl Sec; Yrbk Sec 90-; Dnc Ensmbl; Phi Eta Sigma Pres 90-; Deans List 90-; Fclty Dnc Cncrt; French/Spanish; Trnsltr/Intrprtr.

**FREE, SHAWN M,** Wilmington Coll, Wilmington, OH; FR; BS; Bsktbll 90; Bus; Acctnt.

**FREEDMAN, BENJAMIN J,** Yeshiva Univ, New York, NY; SR; BA; Sigma Delta Rho 87; Chmstry Clb VP 88-90; Orient 89-90; Drmtcs Scty 90; Mensa 87; Deans Lst 87; Ntl Cncl For Synagogue Yth Rgnl Advsr 89-90; Tutor 87; Roth Merit Schlrshp For Biomed Rsrch 90; Chpl Of Four Chplns Cmmnty Serv Awd 87-88; Bio; Med.

**FREEHAN, CATHERINE JO,** Georgetown Univ, Washington, DC; SR; Natl Stdnt Nrs Assn 88-; Schl Nrsng Acdmc Cncl Chrprsn 89-; Dance Co Stdnt Chrgrphr 89-; Sigma Theta Tau 89-; Deans Lst 87-; IM Bsktbl 87-88; BSN; Nrsng.

**FREELAND, ANITA S,** Wv Univ At Parkersburg, Parkersburg, WV; SO; AAS; Spncr Prmry Cntr Vol 90-; Spncr S Bptst S S Tchr 89-; Cert Arch Moore Vo Tech 88; Nrsng; RN.

**FREEMAN, ALEACNA T,** Al A & M Univ, Normal, AL; FR; BS; Delta Kappa Pi; BS; Engl; Scl Wrk.

**FREEMAN, ANGELA K,** Lexington Comm Coll, Lexington, KY; FR; AS; Nrsg.

**FREEMAN, ANSON J,** Wilberforce Univ, Wilberforce, OH; JR; BA; Crmnl Jstc Comm Chrmn 89-; Elec Comm Chrmn 89-90; Const Comm Chrmn 89-; Alpha Kappa Mu 90-; Andrew W Mellon Fllwshp; Achvmng/Serv Awd Wilberforre 90-; NAACP; YMCA; Philosphy; Educ.

**FREEMAN, BRIAN S,** Univ Of Miami, Coral Gables, FL; FR.

**FREEMAN, CAREY L,** Univ Of Ga, Athens, GA; JR; BED; Dean Lst 90-; Educ; Tchr.

**FREEMAN, CAROL,** Atlantic Comm Coll, Mays Landing, NJ; FR; CERT; Appld Sci.

**FREEMAN, CHARLENE R,** Meridian Comm Coll, Meridian, MS; SO; AA; HOSA; VICA Sec; AA Jones Jr Clg 89; Med Record Tech; Med Record Asst Dir.

**FREEMAN, CHRISTIAN C,** Savannah Coll Of Art & Design, Savannah, GA; FR; BFA; Fine Art; Teach Fine Art.

**FREEMAN, CLAIRE E,** Castleton St Coll, Castleton, VT; SR; BA; Summer Intrnshp Rgst Ctzn 90; Arts/Entrnmnt Reporter Torrington CT; Corp Cmmnctns; Jrnlsm.

**FREEMAN, DEBRA R,** Wilmington Coll, New Castle, DE; SR; BABS; Delta Epsilon Rho; Rcptnst; AAS Delaware Tech/Comm Clg 89; Crmnl Jstce/Psychlgy; Educ/Law.

**FREEMAN SR, DENNIS RAY,** Norfolk St Univ, Norfolk, VA; JR; BS; Head Cocah Larkspur/Salem Pirates Bsbl Lttl League; Alpha Kappa Mu; Ata Alpha Tau Alpha Tx Jr Coll; Instrctr; AS; Elec Tech/Cmptr Sci; Offcr US Navy.

**FREEMAN JR, GARRY L,** Univ Of Al At Huntsville, Huntsville, AL; JR; BS; IEEE Actvts Chrmn 90-; ASME 90-; SEDS 90-; Hnrs Schlr; Elec Eng.

**FREEMAN, GINA M,** Union Univ School Of Nursing, Memphis, TN; SR; Hlth Occup Stdnts Of Amer Pr 89-; Stdnt Govt Rep 90-; Nursing.

**FREEMAN, GINA R,** Univ Of Nc At Greensboro, Greensboro, NC; SO; BS; NC Prspctvs Tchrs Schlrshp 89-; Wrk Stdy Chld Care Ed Prgrm 89-; Intrnshp; Elem Edctn; Tchr.

**FREEMAN, HOLLY J,** Univ Of Fl, Gainesville, FL; SR; BS; Stdnt Cncl Secr 88-90; Sigma Theta Tau; Phi Kappa Phi; Golden Key; US Publ Hlth Svc Intern 90; BSN Univ Central FL Clg Nrsg 87; Phrmcy.

**FREEMAN, JANET FEY,** Univ Of Md At Eastern Shore, Princess Anne, MD; JR; BS; Intl Fd Svc Exec Assoc; Phi Theta Kappa; Ducks Unltd; Ocean City Dune Assoc; Worchester Gdn Clb; Natl Demo Wmns League; AA Wor-Wic Tech Cmnty Clg 90; Htl/Rstrnt Mgnt; Tch Cmnty Clg.

**FREEMAN, JO ANNE,** Wv Univ At Parkersburg, Parkersburg, WV; SR; BA; Assn Chldrn/Adults W/Lrng Dsblts Past Pres 85-; LPN Early Intervntn; Hlth Care Admin.

**FREEMAN, JOHN R,** S U N Y Coll Of Tech At Alfred, Alfred, NY; FR; ASSOC; Peer Tutoring Prog Tutor 90-; IM Bsktbl; Constr Engr.

**FREEMAN, JOHN W,** Newbury Coll, Brookline, MA; Deans Lst; Cmnty Ctr VP; Digital Equip; Cert Northeastern Univ 89/90; Bus Mgmnt; Comp Sci.

**FREEMAN, KELLY K,** Susquehanna Univ, Selinsgrove, PA; FR; Natl Big Bros/Big Strs Treas 90-; Symphonic Band; Friends Proj; Alpha Lambda Delta; Sigma Alpha Iota Pldge Cls Pres; Deans Lst 90-; Best New Proj; Acctg; Lawyer.

**FREEMAN, KENNETH A,** Univ Of Med & Dentistry Of Nj, Newark, NJ; GD; MPT; Stdt Hlth Advsry Comm VP 83-; Stdt Awd Clncl Excell; Deans List 89-; Amer Physical Therapy Assoc 89-; Amer Medical Writers Assoc 90-; BS Brigham Young Univ 84; Physical Therapy; Brain Injury Rhbltn.

**FREEMAN, KRISTIE A,** Ms Gulf Coast Comm Coll, Perkinston, MS; SO; Phi Theta Kappa Sec 89-; Band 89-; Stdnt Cncl Exec Secy 89-; Hnrs Forum 89-; Homecoming Ct 89-; Spec Hnrs 90; Hall Of Fame 90; BS; Acctng; CPA.

**FREEMAN, LETTIE L,** Fl A & M Univ, Tallahassee, FL; FR; MBA; Phi Eta Sigma; Accntng; Bus/Corp Law.

**FREEMAN, LINDA K,** Methodist Coll, Fayetteville, NC; SO; BA; Stage Band 90; Chapel Pianist 89; FCA; Frshmn Ldrshp Grp 89; Stdnt State Conf Grp Ldr; Engl.

**FREEMAN, LYNN L,** Alcorn St Univ, Lorman, MS; SO; BS; Gspl Choir Org; ROTC Org; Psychlgy.

**FREEMAN, MARANDA J,** Univ Of Nc At Charlotte, Charlotte, NC; SO; BS; Pre Law Soc; Golden Key; Deans Lst 89 90; Crmnl Juste; Law.

**FREEMAN, MARIA R,** Muskingum Coll, New Concord, OH; JR; BA; Adult Lrnrs Club 90-; Psy Chi 90-; Intrnshp Coshoctn Cnty Drug Cncl 89-90; Psych Assist 90-; Red Cross; SOCCA; Den Ldr; Legal Sec; AAS Muskingum Area Tech Clg 90; Psych/Sclgy; Cnslng.

**FREEMAN, MARK M,** Southern Coll Of Tech, Marietta, GA; SR; BSARC; AIAS 89-; Tau Alpha Pi 90-; Archtctrl Intrn 87-; Architecture.

**FREEMAN, MARY BETH,** Univ Of South Fl, Tampa, FL; GD; MSPH; Marine Corps Marathon; Phi Kappa Phi 80-; US Pblc Hlth Traineeship Schlrshp; BS Univ FL 80; Biostatstcs/Epdmlgy.

**FREEMAN, MICHAEL R,** Univ Of Southern Ms, Hattiesburg, MS; FR; BA; Ortr Chrs 90; Prk Mgmt; Outdr Rcrtn.

**FREEMAN, MICHELLE L,** Univ Of Sc At Columbia, Columbia, SC; SO; BA; Dlt Tau Omega 89-90; Acctg/Cmptrs.

**FREEMAN, PATRICIA L,** Christopher Newport Coll, Newport News, VA; JR; BA; SG 87; Hstry Clb 87; Chrldng 87-88; Hstry; Law.

**FREEMAN, SALLIE M,** Limestone Coll, Gaffney, SC; FR; BA; Yth Drctr Chrch 90-; S C Accountancy Bd 87-; Bus; Accntng.

**FREEMAN, SHANNON G,** Clarkson Univ, Potsdam, NY; SR; BS; Ski Clb 87-88; Smstr Abrd Pgm 89-90; Vars Lacrss/Sccr 87-; Mgmt Info Sys; Vet Sci.

**FREEMAN, SIDNEY E,** Mount Saint Mary Coll, Newburgh, NY; SR; BA; Res Lvng Cncl Rep 90-; Bplc Rltns Assn Pres 89-; Blck Stu Unn 87-; Soup Ktchn 89-; Bstkbl 87-; Bsbl Tm 87-; Pblc Rltns.

**FREEMAN, SONYA V,** Norfolk St Univ, Norfolk, VA; SR; BA; Practicum Intrnshp Holiday Hs Portsmouth VA Mntly Retarded Chldrn; Cncl Psychlgy.

**FREEMAN, SPRING R,** Christopher Newport Coll, Newport News, VA; SO; BSIS; Info Sci; Computer Programmer.

**FREEMAN, STEPHANIE L,** Old Dominion Univ, Norfolk, VA; JR; BS; ODO DECA VP; Mrktng Edctn; Mrktng Edctn Tchr Coord.

**FREEMAN, TRICIA J,** Toccoa Falls Coll, Toccoa Falls, GA; SR; BA; Dorm Cncl Pres 88-90; Early Chldhd Educ; Tchng.

**FREEMAN, TYRONDA M,** Wilberforce Univ, Wilberforce, OH; FR; Dns Lst 90-; Chrldr 90-.

**FREEMAN, VELINDA,** Nc Agri & Tech St Univ, Greensboro, NC; FR; BA; Alpha Lambda Delta 90-; NC Tchng Fllwshp Schlrshp; Pblc Schl Exprnc Tchr/Cls Asst 90-; Elem Ed/Psychlgy; Educ/Dctrt Psy.

**FREEMAN-KIRBY, PATRICIA S,** Hudson Valley Comm Coll, Troy, NY; SO; BS; PTA; Read Runners Clb; AS 90; Pol Sci; Intl Bus.

**FREEMON, RACHEL L,** Fl International Univ, Miami, FL; GD; MPH; D Auzenne Flwshp 90-; Genl Schlrshp 90-; Am Dietetic Assn 85-; Am Assn Diabetic Edn 90-; BS Tuskegee Inst 85; Publ Hlth; Hlth Promo.

**FREENEY, LISA R,** Tn Temple Univ, Chattanooga, TN; SR; Stdnt Bdy Ofc Co-Pres 88-89; Rho Alpha Tau Actvts Drctr 87-88; Chrldr 87-88; Moccassin Bend Mntl Hlth Hosp Intern 90; Psych; Sm Bus Ownrshp.

**FREER, STEFANIE A,** Allegheny Coll, Meadville, PA; JR; BA; Alghny Comm Exchng 89-90; Aldn Schlr 89-90; Ecnmcs; Crprt Mngmnt Or Govnmnt.

**FREEWALT, JOLEE A,** Limestone Coll, Gaffney, SC; JR; SGA Pres 89-; Hnrs Prog 88-; Kappa Delta Kappa Pres 89-; Chrldng 90-; Sccr; Elem Educ; Law Schl.

**FREIBERG, SANDY,** Cornell Univ Statutory College, Ithaca, NY; JR; BS; Cls Cncl 89-; Cncrt Cmmssn 89-; Stdnt Run Adv Agncy Acct Strtgst 90-; Golden Key 90-; Cornell Ntl Schlr 88-; Mrktg/Bus Mgt; Bus.

**FREIHAGE, ERIKA L,** James Madison University, Harrisonburg, VA; SO; BA; Stdnt Ambssdrs Treas; Emrgng Ldrs Prog; Ordr Of Omega; Alpha Chi Omega KROP Chrmn; Psych; Chld Psych.

**FREIHAUT, DONNA L,** Mercer Univ Schl Of Pharm, Atlanta, GA; PHARM; Cncl Stdnts 90-; ASP 90-; GSHP 90-; Rho Chi Pres; GSHP PR 90-; ASHP 90-; BS St Louis Univ 81; Phrmcy; Clncl Phrmcy.

**FREILE, JUAN J,** Clarkson Univ, Potsdam, NY; SR; BA; Phi Theta Kappa VP 88-89; Mltcltrl Clb 87-89; Theta Sci Tres 90-; IM 87; AS Jefferson Comm Coll 89; Fnnc; Bnkng.

**FREILER, JOHN F,** William Paterson Coll, Wayne, NJ; SO; BS; Ntrl Sci Clb 90-; Army Natl Grd 88-; Hnrs Pgm; Blgy; Bpsychlgy; Physcl Thrpst/MS.

**FREIMARCK, DEBRA L,** Hampton Univ, Hampton, VA; SO; BSN; Admnstrtv Stenogrphr 73-78; US Army 78-87; Military Police; Military Wrkng Dog Hndlr Trng; NCO; Instrctr At Military Wrkng Dog Schl; Nrsng; RN.

**FREIRE, KERRY J,** Rivier Coll, Nashua, NH; FR; BA; Paralgl; Lawyer.

**FREITAG, MARK A,** Edinboro Univ Of Pa, Edinboro, PA; JR; BAMA; Hnrs Prog 88-; Pi Mu Epsilon VP 89-; Phi Kappa Psi Treas 89-90; PA State Athletic Conf Acdmc Athlete 88-90; Mens Tnns Tm 88-; Math; Clg Professor.

**FREITAS, ELIZABETH F,** City Univ Of Ny Baruch Coll, New York, NY; SR; JD; Deans List Pi Gamma Mu Natl 85-; Betta Gamma Mu; Golden Keys; U S Intl Trade Comm Intern 85-86; BA Politics Cath Univ Of Am 85; BBA Intl Bus Baruch Coll CUNY; Intl Law.

**FRENANDEZ, MANUEL,** Fl International Univ, Miami, FL; JR; BA; Engl.

**FRENCH, ALICE D,** Univ Of Tn At Martin, Martin, TN; SO; BSN; SNA 90-; Phi Eta Sigma 90-; Nrsg; Ansthtst.

**FRENCH, FARABE L,** Univ Of Md At Eastern Shore, Princess Anne, MD; SR; Phys Thrpy.

**FRENCH, FRANK E,** Strayer Coll, Washington, DC; SO; BS; Alpha Chi; Dept Crctns Vol 89-; Wash Hilton Htl Sprvsr 80-; AAAC Strayer Clge; CP/GCE Univ London 67/69; Acctng; CPA.

**FRENCH, JENNIFER A,** Univ Of New England, Biddeford, ME; SO; BA; Physcl Thrpy Clb 90-; Vrsty Sftbll 90-; Physcl Thpry; Med.

**FRENCH, KARA-JANE,** Univ Of North Fl, Jacksonville, FL; FR; BA; Physcs/Eng.

**FRENCH, MARC D,** Western New England Coll, Springfield, MA; JR; BA; Pr Ttrng 89-90; Ftbll 88-89; Comp Info Systms; Scrt Srvc.**

**FRENCH, MARY E,** Hudson Valley Comm Coll, Troy, NY; SR; AS; Pres Lst 90; Cub Sct Ldr 87-89; Bus Admn; Tlcmmnctns.

**FRENCH JR, RICHARD B,** Embry Riddle Aeronautical Univ, Daytona Beach, FL; SO; Waterski Club 90; Naval Aviation Club; Aeronautical Science; Pilot.

**FRENCH, ROBERT E,** Johnson C Smith Univ, Charlotte, NC; SO; BA; Corp Acctg.

**FRENCH, TERENCE,** Trenton St Coll, Trenton, NJ; SO; BA; Coll Radio DJ/NEWS Ed 90-; SGA Treas 90-; Intl Rel Cncl 90-; Socty Hnr Stdnts 89-; Lakeside Stdnt Govt Treas 89-; Comm Advsr; Garden State Distngshd Schlr; Coll Schlr; I Vlybl; Poli Sci; Law.**

**FRENCL, JOSEPH E,** Cumberland Coll, Williamsburg, KY; SO; BS; Math Club VP 90-; T E Mahan Award; Math Tutor 90-; Math/Physics; Grad Sch/Tchng.

**FRENEY, DENISE E,** Averett Coll, Danville, VA; JR; BS; Stu Fndtn VP; Delta Xi Zeta VP 90-; Eqstrn Stu/Bus Admn; Stbl Mngmnt.

**FRENI, MARIO J,** Merrimack Coll, North Andover, MA; FR; BE; IM Sports 90-; Retreat Pgm 90-; Delta Phi Kapps 90-; Engr.

**FRENNIER, JENNIFER M,** S U N Y Coll Of Tech At Delhi, Delhi, NY; SR; AAS; N Y St Assn Vet Tech; Intern Palmer Vet Clinic 90; Chrldng/Track & Field Capt 89-; Vet Tech; Bio-Med Rsrch.

**FRENTZEN, SUSAN J,** Univ Of Nh Plymouth St Coll, Plymouth, NH; SR; BA; Assn Non/Trdtnl Stdnts Pres 90; Wmns Caucus 88-89; Intrnshp League NH Crftsmn Prsntr PR Assist 90; 6th Natl Conf Clg Wmn/Stdnt Ldrs; Wshgnt SC Psc Prsntr 90; Plymouth Friends Arts Vol 90-; Boy Scouts Amer Dn Ldr 90; Mktg/Engl/Art; Sml Bsn Mktg.

**FREPPON, DEBORAH M,** Lexington Comm Coll, Lexington, KY; SR; ASSOC; Amer Soc Interior Dsgnrs 88-89; Intern Corporex Constr 90; Intern Batson/Assoc 90; Intern Drees Cmpny 88; Univ Kentucky Vlybl Club Pres 87-90; BA Univ Kentucky 89; AA Midway Junior Clg 86; Arch Tech.**

**FRERE, RALPH E,** Daytona Beach Comm Coll, Daytona Beach, FL; SO; BA; SE Cntr Photographic Soc 90-; Retail Industry 83-; Fine Arts; Photographer.

**FRERE, TUERE N,** Syracuse Univ, Syracuse, NY; FR; BA; Math; Bus.

**FRERES, JULIE M,** Univ Of Southern Ms, Hattiesburg, MS; FR; BS BA; Amnsty Stdnt Lbrtn Orgnztn 90-; Hnrs Stdnt Assc Stdnt Eagle Clb 90-; Co Chrdrm Envrnmntl Cmmt 90; Phi Eta Sigma 90; Otstndng Frshmn Wmn 90-; IM Myhlldorm IM 90-; Psychlgy/Art; Art Thrpy/Crt Psychlgist.

**FRERET, GRACE S,** Univ Of Southern Ms, Hattiesburg, MS; JR; BS; Kappa Mu Epsilon; Gamma Beta Phi; Math.

**FRERICHS, LISA M,** Univ Of Tn At Martin, Martin, TN; GD; BA; Bio/Chem; Res Lab.

**FRESE, GLENN R,** Univ Of Miami, Coral Gables, FL; SR; BS; Hurricn Cncrt Prod 89-; WVUM Radio Exec Brd 88-90; Ord Omega; Sigma Phi Epsilon Rsh Chrmn 87-; Sony Music Intrnshp 89-; IM Ftbl Sftbl 87-90; Comm/Flm/Pol; Music Law.

**FRESHOUR, RICHARD C,** Wv Northern Comm Coll, Wheeling, WV; SO; BA; Cmctns; Radio Brdcstng/TV.

**FRETT, RENARD W,** Christopher Newport Coll, Newport News, VA; SR; Mnrty Stdnt Assc VP 89-; Acctng; Cpa.**

**FREUND, REBECCA L,** Univ Of Miami, Coral Gables, FL; FR; BS; Hnrs Stdnt Assoc 90-; Orientation Asstnt; Miami Committment 90-; Delta Gamma 90-; Sportsfest IM Tennis 90-; Archtctrl Engrng.

**FREY, CATHERINE L,** Bapt Bible Coll & Seminary, Clarks Summit, PA; SO; BA; Hgst GPA Theology 89; Word Lfe Bible Inst 89; Cnslng; Wmn Cnslng.

**FREY JR, DENNIS A,** Carnegie Mellon Univ, Pittsburgh, PA; SR; BS; Ice Hockey Club Pres 87-; Hist Soc Co Chair 89-; Mortar Bd 90-; Phi Eta Sigma Histrn 87-89; Lambda Sigma 87-89; Phi Alpha Theta; Deans List 88-; Univ Hons; Mktg Intrnshp; Hist; Profsr.

**FREY, JEANIE M,** West Chester Univ, West Chester, PA; JR; BED; Kappa Delta Pi 90-91; Elem Educ; Tchr/Sch Admn.**

**FREY, LAURA L,** Kent St Univ Kent Cmps, Kent, OH; JR; BBA; Finance Assn Sec 90-; Golden Key; Delta Sigma Pi 90-; Ecnmcs; Law/Bus.

**FREY, NANCY E,** Broward Comm Coll, Ft Lauderdale, FL; SO; BA; Exceptional Stdnt Ed; Special Ed Tchr Autisti.

**FREYDINA, BELLA D,** Bunker Hill Comm Coll, Boston, MA; FR; Acctg/Engl.

**FREYRE CABRERA, MILITZA,** Inter Amer Univ Pr Hato Rey, Hato Rey, PR; JR.

**FREYTAG, CAMILLA GAY,** Roane St Comm Coll, Harriman, TN; SO; AA; Plc Sci.

**FRICK, DAVID A,** Atlantic Comm Coll, Mays Landing, NJ; FR; BA; Bus; Indpt Bus.

**FRICK, PHILIP A,** Univ Of Ct, Storrs, CT; JR; BS; Cnn PIRG Elctd Brd 88; Frgn Lng Hs Alsopa 88; Frgn Lng Hs Alsopa Pres 89; Block I 90; Block II 90f; Rnwbl Ntrl Rsrcs.

**FRICKS, EVETTE N,** Alcorn St Univ, Lorman, MS; SR; BS; Sr Clss Queen 90-; NAACP VP 89; Jr Clss Treas 89-90; Phi Beta Lambda Pres 89-90; Alpha Kappa Alpha Hdgs 90-; Deans Lst 89-90; Trk 89; Bus Admin; Grad Schl.**

**FRIDAY, DIANE LYNN,** Univ Of North Fl, Jacksonville, FL; SR; BA; Spnnkr Cntrbtng Wrtr 89-; Gldn Key Cmmnctns Crdntr; Sigma Phi Epsilon Lttl Sstr 82-; Jcksnvll Jycs 89-; Dntl Asst 72-90; Cmmnctns Prnt Jrnlsm; Nwsppr Mag Wrtng.

**FRIDAY, PAULINE B,** City Univ Of Ny City Coll, New York, NY; SR; BA; Hosp Stf Fncl Analyst Univ Hosp; Sclgy; Bus Admin/Law.

**FRIDSHAL, HILARY,** Univ Of New Haven, West Haven, CT; JR; BS; Chmstry Clb Pres 90-; Frnsc Sci/Chmstry; Law.

**FRIEBELY, JOHN D,** Clarkson Univ, Potsdam, NY; SO; BS; Un Brd Trvl Comm 90-; Potsdam Ice Crnvl Gen Chrmn 90-; Nwspaper Advtsng Mgr; Alpha Chi Rho Asst Treas 90-; Finance; Sls/Cnsltng.

**FRIED, ZANDRA M,** William Paterson Coll, Wayne, NJ; FR; BA; Elem Ed; Tchr.

**FRIEDEL, THOMAS J,** Univ Of Akron, Akron, OH; SO; Res Hall Gvmnt Flr Rep 89-; Acctng Assc Direc Fresh/Soph Mtgs 89-; Beta Alpha Psi 90-; Intrnshp Acctng; IM Sports Tm Coach 89-.

**FRIEDLINE, SUZANNE M,** Fl St Univ, Tallahassee, FL; SR; BFA; Phi Kappa Phi 90-; Dbr Slv 90; Delta Delta Delta 87-88; Thtr Actng.

**FRIEDMAN, ERIC S,** Cornell Univ, Ithaca, NY; FR; Writer Cncl Daily Sun; Deans Lst; IM Ftbl 90; Child Dvlpmnt.

**FRIEDMAN, SETH P,** Duquesne Univ, Pittsburgh, PA; SO; BA; Psych Clb; Spring Fling Comm; Psych; Law.

**FRIEDMAN, STACEY A,** Univ Of Miami, Coral Gables, FL; SR; BA; Gldn Key 89-; Psi Chi; Phi Beta Kappa; Phi Kappa Phi 89-; Psychlgy.

**FRIEDRICHSEN, KAREN A,** D Youville Coll, Buffalo, NY; FR; MBA; Cmps Mnstry Sec 90-; Wrtrs Clb 90-; Frnds Nght Pple 90-; Hnrs Prog 90-; Phys Thrpy.

**FRIEDSAM, KRISTEN L,** Middle Tn St Univ, Murfreesboro, TN; SR; Stdnt Gvt Treas 88-89; NEA 90-; TEA 90-; Chrldr Co Cptn 86-88; AS Aquiras Jr Clg 88; Tchng Cert; Spcl Ed/Elem Ed; Tchng.

**FRIEL, BRIGID K,** Le Moyne Coll, Syracuse, NY; JR; BA; Phlsphy/Rlgn; Wrtg/Tchg.

**FRIEL, CHRISTA S,** Union Univ, Jackson, TN; FR; BM; BSU 90-; Revival Tm 90-; Music; Music Mnstry.

**FRIEND, KIMBERLY R,** Oh Univ-Southern Cmps, Ironton, OH; JR; BED; Scl Stdy; Educ.

**FRIEND, TARA D,** Univ Of Pa, Philadelphia, PA; SO; BABS; Nwspapr Finance Dept Stff 90-; Jwsh Soc Actn Comm 89-; Wharton Wmn 89-; B Franklin Schlr 90-; J Wharton Schlr Sec 89-; Kappa Delta Almni Rltns Chr 90-; Deans Lst 89-90; W M Ware Awrd Exclince; Finance/Psychlgy; Bnkng.**

**FRIEND, WENDY L,** Coppin St Coll, Baltimore, MD; JR; BS; Crmnl Jstc Clb; Crmnl Jstc; Law.

**FRIERMAN, JUDITH L,** Fl Southern Coll, Lakeland, FL; JR; BS; Stdnt Un Bd 88; Alpha Omicron Pi 88-; Deans Lst/Pres Lst 89-; Art Asst FL Tile; IMA 89-; Art Comm; Cmrcl Artist.**

**FRIESS II, MICHAEL A,** Kent St Univ Kent Cmps, Kent, OH; JR; BBA; Admin Offcr.

**FRIEZ, SUSAN E,** Teikyo Post Univ, Waterbury, CT; JR; BS; Alpha Chi; Gnrl Studies; Psychlgy.

**FRIGON, DIANE M,** Springfield Tech Comm Coll, Springfield, MA; SR; AS; Bus Clb Pres 90-; Vol Spec Olympics 89-; Bus Clb Achvmnt Awd; Bd Of Rgnts Awd; Natl Assn Ins Wmn 90; Bus Finance; Commnctn.

**FRILEY, DETRA L,** Al St Univ, Montgomery, AL; JR; BA; Cmptr Infrm Sys; Anlyst.

**FRINGER, JEANNE M,** Univ Of Rochester, Rochester, NY; SO; BS; Intl Lvng Cntr Pres 90-; Dean Lst 89-; Biochmstry; Rsrch.

**FRINK, LISA J,** Fl International Univ, Miami, FL; SR; BS; Dietetic Assn Hstrn 90; Nutrition/MD Schlrshp 90-; Amer Med Tchnlgsts 83-90; Reg Med Asst 83-90; AA BCC 89; Dietetics/Nutrition.

**FRISBEE, MARLA K,** Christian Brothers Univ, Memphis, TN; SO; Natl Assoc Acctnts 90-; Ambssdr Brd 90-; Zeta Tau Alpha Treas 90-; Pr Cnslr 90-; Bus Acctg.

**FRISCH, STEPHANIE A,** Duquesne Univ, Pittsburgh, PA; FR; BS; Pres Schlr 90-; Phrmcy Schlr; Phrmcy.

**FRISHMAN, SCOTT P,** Duquesne Univ, Pittsburgh, PA; SO; BA; Alpha Tau Omega Treas; Finance; Corp Law.

**FRISOLI, GREGORY V,** Cornell Univ Statutory College, Ithaca, NY; JR; BS; Trck/Fld 89; Tae Kwon Do 90-; Zeta Psi Treas 89-; Mrrl Lynch Prc Fnnr/Smith Intrn; NY Acad Sci Intrn 88; Agri Ecnmcs; Mgmt.

**FRISONE, DOROTHEA A,** Schenectady County Comm Coll, Schenectady, NY; FR; BA; Bookkeeper; Acctg.

**FRISSELL, MARK R,** Savannah Coll Of Art & Design, Savannah, GA; GD; MFA; SPA 90-; Habitat For Hmnty; Stone Cnsrvtn Intrn Mt Kisco NY; BS 87; Hstrc Prsrvtn; Frntr Cnsrvtr.

**FRISSELL, NICOLE A,** Hillsborough Comm Coll, Tampa, FL; SO; BA; Phi Theta Kappa Pres 90; Rcyclng Pgm Fndr 89-90; Acad Exclnc Math 89-; Forestry; Land Mgmt.**

**FRITCHY, LORRE A,** Eckerd Coll, St Petersburg, FL; SR; BA; The Siren/Triton Tribune 87-; Bskblt Mgr 88; Vlybl Mgr 87; Deans List 88-; Sunshine Clg Conf Athletic Hnr Rl; Little League Sftbl Coach 89f Spel Oly; Secty Super XXIII Sptfst 87-88; 5k Turkey Trot 5k Run Shelter 88-89; Creative Wrtng; Wrtng Cpywtng Title Wtng.

**FRITTS, ANGELA D,** Roane St Comm Coll, Harriman, TN; GD; Clgte Sectry Internatl 89-90; Ways & Means Comm Scrpbk Comm; Gamma Beta 89; AAS 90; English; Exctv Sectry.

**FRITZ, ANN M,** Indiana Univ Of Pa, Indiana, PA; SR; BED; PA St Educ Assn 90-; Kappa Delta Pi 90-; Provosts Schlr 89-90; Deans Lst 88-; Sally B Johnson Schlrshp/Awd 90-; Swim Tm Capt 88-; Elem Ed; Tchng.

**FRITZ, CATHERINE A,** Ms Univ For Women, Columbus, MS; SR; BS; NAA 89-; DPNA Secy 89-; Phi Kappa Phi; Acctng Hntry 90-; USAF NCOIC Cnsldtd Tool Kit/Automatic Flght Cntrl Systms Spclst 82-88; CIS; Cmptrs/Acctng.

**FRITZ, JENNIFER Y,** Northeast State Tech Comm Coll, Blountville, TN; FR; AAS; Yth Grp Central Holston Chrstn Church 90-; Dns Lst; Ofc Syst Tech; Secr/Recptnst.

**FRITZ JR, JOHN A,** Jersey City St Coll, Jersey City, NJ; SR; BS; Pre Med Soc; Biology Clb; Untd Ntns Yth Cncl; Intrntnl Ocngrphc Fndtn; Deans Lst 88-89; Police Actvts League; Greenville Phrmcts Orgnztn; Microbiogy Rsrch Intrn; Biology Major; Mdcl Schl.

**FRITZ, STACY L,** Univ Of Akron, Akron, OH; SO; BA; Prog Brd Chrprsn 90-; Cncl Educ Stu 90-; Phi Eta Sigma 90-; Educ; Tchng.

**FRITZGERALD, ROBERT J,** Univ Of North Fl, Jacksonville, FL; JR; BSCS; Prgrmmn Tm; Assn Cmptr Mach 90-; Gldn Ky; Phi Kappa Phi; Dean Lst 89-; Cert Exmplry Prfrmnc; AA 90; Cmptr Sci; Eng.

**FRIZSELL, DANIEL M,** Univ Of Nc At Asheville, Asheville, NC; FR; BS; Jazz Bnd; Music; Audio Eng.

**FRIZZELL, TERRY L,** Nc Agri & Tech St Univ, Greensboro, NC; JR; AE; Tau Beta Pi; Explrer Sct Advsr 90-; Acad Awd Cert/Deans Lst 88-; Arch Eng.

**FRIZZI, MARY E,** Indiana Univ Of Pa, Indiana, PA; SO; BREHB; Natl Rhbltn Assc 89-; Nwmn Stdnt Assc 89-; Cncl Excptnl Chldrn Tres 89-; Assc Rhbltn Advcts 89-; Deans List 90; Rhabltn; Cnslr.

**FRKANEC, JENNIFER M,** Castleton St Coll, Castleton, VT; FR; BFA; BACCHUS 90-; Drama Clb Hstrn Pblcty 90-; Cncrt Chr 90; PAIRS Cnslr; Mst Otstndng Frshmn 90-; Theatre Arts; Entrtnmnt Indstry.

**FROBERG, DENISE A,** Le Moyne Coll, Syracuse, NY; SR; MA; Radio Drctr 89-; Hl Cncl Rep 89-90; Dolphin Nwspr Stf Wrtr 87-89; Deans Lst 90-; Red Cross Vol 87-88; Intrntnl Hse Vlntr 88-; Cltrl Rsrcs Cncl Syracuse Pr Intrn; Radio Intrn 89; Chrldng 88-; Cmmnctns; Pblc Rltns.

**FROEMKE, DAVID L,** Fl St Univ, Tallahassee, FL; SR; BA; Englsh.

**FROGGE, JOHN B,** Middle Tn St Univ, Murfreesboro, TN; FR; BA; English; Publishing/Editing/Tech Writer.

**FROHNE, COURTNEY R,** Fl St Univ, Tallahassee, FL; JR; BA; Golden Key 90-; Humanities.

**FROM, JAMES T,** Andrew Coll, Cuthbert, GA; SO; AS; Phi Theta Kappa 90-; Biol; Envnmntl Sci.

**FRONCZAK, JOSEPH J,** Bryant Stratton Bus Inst Roch, Rochester, NY; AOS; Elctrncs Tech; Tech.

**FRONCZEK, LISA J,** S U N Y Coll At Fredonia, Fredonia, NY; JR; BA; Spanish Club V P 88-; Yrbk 88; Dorm Cncl Pres 89-90; Natl Spanish Hnr Soc 90-; Natl Pol Sci Hnr Soc; Res Asst; Semester Abroad Salamanca Spain 90; Pol Sci & Spanish; Law.

**FRONHEISER, DAWN,** Georgian Court Coll, Lakewood, NJ; FR.

**FRONISTA, LISA L,** Miami Jacobs Jr Coll Of Bus, Dayton, OH; GD; AS; Fashion Mrchndsng.

**FRONKOSKI, DORIS M,** Anne Arundel Comm Coll, Arnold, MD; SO; BA; Drama Clb 90-; Cmmnty Serv; Engl/Thtr; Educ.

**FRONTERA, JANET M,** Comm Coll Algny Co Algny Cmps, Pittsburgh, PA; FR; BSN; Stdnt Nrs Assn PA 90-; Phi Theta Kappa 90-; Acdmc Achvmnt 90-; Acdmc Schlrshp; Mktg Corp Essay Cntst Rnr-Up 90; Schl PTA 87-; Chrch Lctr 85-; Grp Hlth Ins Indstry 70-88; Nrsng; RN.

**FRONTERA, JOSE A,** Univ Of Sc At Columbia, Columbia, SC; SO; BA; Vrsty Tennis 89; Bsnss; Accntng.

**FRONTERA-MUNOZ, MARGARITA M,** Univ Of Pr At Rio Piedras, Rio Piedras, PR; SR; BED; Amer Inst Arch Stdnts Pres 87-; Arch Stdnt Cncl Vp 87-90; Ntl Clgte Arch/Dsgn Awd 90; Arch.

**FRONTZ, LEIGH A,** Defiance Coll, Defiance, OH; JR; BA; Amer Payroll Assoc 90; Controllers Asst 90; AAB Northwest Tech Clg 89; Acctg/Mgmt.

**FROOT, STEVEN E,** Nova Univ, Ft Lauderdale, FL; GD; MBA; Fnnce Scty 89; Phi Beta Lambda 89; Lambda Chi Alpha 89; BS Florida St Univ 89; Fnnce Bus; Cntrllr Accntg.

**FROSELL, ARNETT D,** Commonwealth Coll, Norfolk, VA; GD; Scrtrl Clb Pres 90; Prof Scrtrl Intl; Alpha Beta Gamma; Alpha Tau; Wrkstdy Acdmcs Dept; AAS Legal Offc Admn; Legal Offc; Prlgl.

**FROST, BETHANY A,** Liberty Univ, Lynchburg, VA; SO; BA; Big Bro Big Sis 90-; Kappa Pi Tres 90-; Art; Prof.

**FROST, DANIELLE J,** D Youville Coll, Buffalo, NY; SO; BAMA; Bsktbl Capt 89-; Phys Ther; Phys Ther/Sports Med.

**FROST, MELISSA L,** Atlantic Union Coll, S Lancaster, MA; JR; Soph Clss Offcr Sec 89-90; Jr Clss Lffcr Tres 90-; New Eng Yth Ensmbl 2nd Violin 88-; Deans B List 88-; Hnr Core Soc 88-; Nursing AS/MUSIC BA; Musical Nurse.**

**FROST, PATRICIA K,** Stetson Univ, Deland, FL; FR, BS; Cthlc Campus Mnstry 90-; X-Cntry 90; Biolgy; Phys Therpy.

**FROST, RICHARD D,** Albertus Magnus Coll, New Haven, CT; JR; BA; Pol Sci; Tchr.

**FROST, SHANNON D,** Radford Univ, Radford, VA; SO; BA; Nursing; MSN.

**FRUCHTENICHT, BJORN U,** Fl Atlantic Univ, Boca Raton, FL; SR; MBA; Alumni Assn; Pres Hon Soc 88-89; Phi Kappa Phi 87-89; Vrsty Tennis Tm 87-89; BBA; Intl Bus.**

**FRUCI, CONNIE,** Newbury Coll, Brookline, MA; JR; BLA; Deans List 89; Interior Design Internship; AS; Design/Liberalarts; Eng.

**FRUEH, CHARLES H,** Hudson Valley Comm Coll, Troy, NY; FR; BA; Archtctrl Dsgn; Archtct.

**FRUIN, KELLY J,** Teikyo Post Univ, Waterbury, CT; SO; BA; Choir 89-90; Stdnt Tchr Middlebury Sch Spec Ed; Modern Dance; AS; Elem Ed; Tchg.

**FRUSCIANO, LISA M,** Rutgers St Un At New Brunswick, New Brunswick, NJ; SO; BS; Ntl Athltc Trnrs Assoc 90-; Stu Athltc Trnr 90-; Lambda Kappa Sigma; Phrmcy.**

**FRY, AARON MARIE E,** Univ Of Ct, Storrs, CT; SR; Block/Bridle Clb 87-88; Ball Rm Dance Clb 89; Alpha Zeta 88-; Golden Key 89-; Gamma Sigma Delta 89-; Alpha Phi Omega Pr 87-; Carp Steel Tech Schlrshp 87-; U Of CT Alumni Assn Schlrshp 90-; Gov Foot Grd Schlrshp 89-90; BS; Vet.

**FRY, ADRIENNE L,** Univ Of Southern Ms, Hattiesburg, MS; FR; BA; Stdnt Alum Assoc 90-; Chi Omega; Chi O T's Girls Choir; Speech Cmmnctn; Pub Rltns.

**FRY, DANA C,** Univ Of Cincinnati-Clrmnt Coll, Batavia, OH; FR; BED; Miami Vly Cncl Natv Amer 90-; Math/Hstry; Tchng.

**FRY, GWEN K,** Indiana Univ Of Pa, Indiana, PA; FR; News Anchor For Campus Radio Statn 90; BA; BS; Cmnctns Mediz/Jrnlsm; Publc Rltns/Comm Corp.

**FRY, JENNIFER L,** Susquehanna Univ, Selinsgrove, PA; FR; BS; Bio Clb 90-; Big Bro/Sis 90-; Intl Clb 90-; Alpha Lambda Delta; Track/Field Vrsty; Bio; Vet.

**FRY, JENNIFER L,** John Carroll Univ, Cleveland, OH; FR; Commnctns; Pblc Rltns Spclst.

**FRY, JILL A,** Marshall University, Huntington, WV; SO; BA; Elem Ed; Tchr.

**FRY, JOANNE C,** Wv Univ, Morgantown, WV; JR; BS; AICE Treas 89-; Amrcn Chmcl Scty 87-89; Tau Beta Pi Sec 90-; Gldn Key 90-; Alpha Gamma Delta 88-; Internship FMC Copr 90-; CRC Press Frshmn Chmstry Awrd 88; Chmcl Eng; Eng Mrktng.

**FRY, JOHN A,** Middle Tn St Univ, Murfreesboro, TN; SR; BS; Flyng Raiders Pres 87-89; Flght Tm 87-; Alpha Eta Rho Pres 89-; Aerospc/Math; Eng.

**FRY, MARK E,** Oh St Univ At Marion, Marion, OH; SO; BA; Econ/Bsn Stdnt Soc; Bsn Admin; Rl Est/Urbn Anlys.

**FRY, SHERICE L,** Alcorn St Univ, Lorman, MS; JR; Pre-Law; Attny.

**FRY, THERESA M,** Mary Baldwin Coll, Staunton, VA; SO; BA; Outdr Prsts 90-; Alpha Lambda Delta 90-; Comm Invlvmnt 89-; Swm Tm 90-; Psychlgy/Educ; Mntl Hlth.

**FRY, YVONNE M,** Univ Of Southern Ms, Hattiesburg, MS; SR; BA; Stdnt Govt Exe Sec 90-; PRSSA Natl 90-; Amer Mktg Assn V P 90-; Gamma Beta Phi 90-; Amer Cancer Soc 88-89; Intrn Rgcy New Orleans; Pub Rltns; Politics.

**FRYDRYCHOWSKI, GAIL M,** Daemen Coll, Amherst, NY; JR; BS; Physical Thrpy.

**FRYE, ALLYSON PAIGE,** Univ Of Sc At Columbia, Columbia, SC; SO; BA; CES; Sierra Clb; EDF; EES; Pltcl Sci; Envrnmntl Law.

**FRYE, BENJAMIN D,** Middle Tn St Univ, Murfreesboro, TN; FR; BA; Ftbl; Sci; Phys Thrpy.

**FRYE, BEVERLY L,** Va Commonwealth Univ, Richmond, VA; SR; BS; Frmr Govt Serv Employee; Assoc 86; Educ.

**FRYE, JOHN R,** Marshall University, Huntington, WV; SR; BS; Data Prcsng Mgmt Assn 89-; USAF Cmmnctns Techncn/E-6 Tsgt/Hnrbl Dschrg; AAS Comm Coll Air Force 89; Cmptr Sci.

**FRYE, LUCY L,** Marshall University, Huntington, WV; SR; BA; Elem Ed.

**FRYE, PAMELA D,** Marshall University, Huntington, WV; JR; BBA; Acctg Clb; W Va Soc CPA; Gamma Beta Phi Soc 89-; Alpha Kappa Psi 90-; Delta Zeta; Acctg; CPA.

**FRYE, VERNON SCOTT,** Univ Of Tn At Martin, Martin, TN; FR; BS; Stdnt Govt Assn Elec Cmmsnr 90-; Intrfaith Cntr 90-; Hnrs Smnr 90-; Hnr Smnry Socty 90-; Mu Epsilon Delta 90-; Beta Beta Beta 90-; Dns Lst 90-; Biology; Chmstry; Medicine.

**FRYER, SUSAN T,** Univ Of South Al, Mobile, AL; SR; BA; Phi Theta Kappa 86-88; AA Faulkner State Jr Clg 88; AS Faulkner Stat Jr Clg 89; Spcl Ed Mntlly Rtrd/Mltpl Hndcppd; Tchg.

**FRYMAN, ALECIA M,** Northern Ky Univ, Highland Hts, KY; SR; BS; MAA 89-; Putnam Team 89-; Outstndg Sr Math 90-; Boy Scouts Amer Cub Sct Ldr 84-90; Mathematics; Secndry Educ.

**FRYSON, KENYA G,** Saint Pauls Coll, Lawrenceville, VA; SR; BS; SGA Pr 90-; NAACP 88-; Busn Admin/Mgmt; Mba.

**FU, LI KA,** Howard Univ, Washington, DC; JR; BA; Architecture.

**FUCCI, MICHAEL J,** Univ Of New England, Biddeford, ME; JR; BS; Lfe Sci Clb Pres 88-; Stdnt Intrnshp Frsbie Meml Hosp 90; Biol Fld Exp Intrnshp Clg Osteopthc Med 89; Med Biol; Med.

**FUCE, CARMELA A,** Fl A & M Univ, Tallahassee, FL; FR; BS; Eng Cncpt Inst 90; Hnr Roll 90; Rsdntl Assist; Deans Lst; Math; Indstrl Eng.

**FUCHIGAMI, YUKO,** Savannah Coll Of Art & Design, Savannah, GA; GD; MFA; Scnd Juried Exhbtn; M Curtis Propes Flwshp 89-; BFA Alchi Prfctrl Fine Art Univ 88; BS Kyushu Univ 84; Pntng; Artst.

**FUCHS, ALFREDO-LUIS C,** Fl International Univ, Miami, FL; SR; BA; Amer Mktg Assoc; Mktg-Intl Bsn.

**FUCHS, MARNIE R,** Yeshiva Univ, New York, NY; SR; Club Canada Pres 90-; Recylclng Comm 90; Fine Arts Soc 89-90; Deans Hon List; Sigma Delta Tho; Award For Creativity In Biolgcl Scis; AA; BA; Bio; Medcn.

**FUENTE, DANIELE N,** Fl A & M Univ, Tallahassee, FL; JR; BS; SNPHA 90-; Ladies Aux VFW 90-; Pres Schlrshp 87-88; AA Hillsborough Comm Coll 90; Phrmcy; Hosp Phrmcy.

**FUENTE, JOSEPH M,** Fl International Univ, Miami, FL; SR; BAT; Amer Inst Arch Stdnts 88-; Arch; Lnscp Arch.

**FUENTES ORTIZ, LEKNA M,** Inter Amer Univ Pr Barranquita, Barranquitas, PR; JR.

**FUENTES VASQUEZ, WILLIAM E,** Univ Of South Al, Mobile, AL; SR; BED; Latin Amer Wesley Fdtn Co-Fndr 90-; Latin Amer Stdnt Assoc Gen Coord 90-; Immigrant Yth Cnslg Pgm Co-Coord; Flwshp USIA Study USA; B Ed Inst Tech Santa Ana El Salvador 81; Ed; Spec Ed TMR.

**FUENTES, ANDREA E,** City Univ Of Ny La Guard Coll, Long Island Cty, NY; SR; Dns Lst 89-; Ofc Tech; Exec Sec.

**FUENTES, CARMEN L,** Univ Of Pr At Rio Piedras, Rio Piedras, PR; SR; Hnr Prgrm 88-; Comm Grps 87-88; Spnsh; Prof.

**FUENTES, DOMINGO,** Univ Politecnica De Pr, Hato Rey, PR; FR; Math; Engrg.

**FUENTES, ISHA M,** Inter Amer Univ Pr Hato Rey, Hato Rey, PR; FR; MBA; Assn Psychology 90-; Soc Serv; Psychology.

**FUENTES, JOSE ANDIES DE LEON,** Caribbean Center For Adv Stds, San Juan, PR; SR; PHD; Am Psychlgcl Assn; Natl Acad Neuropsychlgst; Psychlgy Dir Intern 89-90; BS 83; MS Caribbean Ctr Advance Studies 86; Psychlgy; Clncl Neuropsychlgst.

**FUENTES, JOSE ANDRES DE LEON,** Caribbean Center For Adv Stds, San Juan, PR; SR; Soc Psychlgy 89-; Amer Psychlgcl Assn 89-; All Amer Schlr 90-; Dstngshd Prfssr 87; Advncd Stdies Awrd 90; MS Cath Univ Ponce 86; BS Cath Univ Ponce 83; PhD Caribbean Cntr Advncd Stdies 90; Neuropsychlgy.

**FUENTES, YVETTE,** Barry Univ, Miami, FL; SR; BA; French Clb Secr 87-88; Spanish Clb 87-88; Clg Republs Secr 89-90; Phi Alpha Theta V P 89-; Pi Gamma Mu Pres 90-; Hstry; Tch.

**FUERST, STEVE A,** Gallaudet Univ, Washington, DC; FR; Class Govt 89-; Tower Clock Phtgrphy 89-; IM Bsktbl/Flg Ftbl/Sftbl 89-; Acctng; Bus Admin.

**FUGINI, MARCELLA L,** Slippery Rock Univ, Slippery Rock, PA; SR; BED; Amer Kinesiotherapy Assoc 90-; PA State HPERD 90-; Phi Epsilon Kappa; Phys Ed Mjr Kinesiotherapy.

**FUHR, LAURA J,** Univ Of Cincinnati, Cincinnati, OH; JR; BED; Spcl Edctn Mlt Hndcpd; Tchng.

**FUHR JR, RICHARD A,** Appalachian Bible Coll, Bradley, WV; SO; BA; Whitewtr Rftng Guide; Bible; Missnry.

**FUHRY, MARILYN T,** Kent St Univ Geauga Cmps, Burton Twp, OH; SO; MLS; Chrl Un; U S Army Rad Oper 86-90; Engl; Libr Sci.

**FUISTING, KIMBERLY L,** Castleton St Coll, Castleton, VT; SR; Mbr Castleton State Clge Alpine 87 88 90; Chorus 89; WIUV Radio 87-90; Running Team 87-89; Intrnshp & Producer/Dir Killington TV Killington VT 90; Communication Dept Awd 91; Communication.

**FUJIOKA, MISAO,** Methodist Coll, Fayetteville, NC; FR; MBA; Psychology; Cnslr.

**FUJISHIMA, IRENE Y,** Yale Univ, New Haven, CT; FR; BS; Math Hnr; Chem Engr.

**FUJITA, KAZUKO,** Northern Ky Univ, Highland Hts, KY; FR; BA; Intrntl Studies Bsnss; Trsm.

**FUJITA, SHINOBU,** Albertus Magnus Coll, New Haven, CT; JR; AA Chafu Gakuen Wmns Coll 90; Cmnctns.

**FUKASAWA, TAKESHI,** Univ Of South Al, Mobile, AL; FR; BA; Mgmt.

**FUKUSHIMA, SEIJI,** Wagner Coll, Staten Island, NY; JR; BA; BA Keio Univ 90; Art.

**FUKUYAMA, KUMIKO,** Barry Univ, Miami, FL; FR; BA; Mktg; Imprt/Exprt.

**FULCHER, ADRIENNE D,** Bloomfield Coll, Bloomfield, NJ; FR; African Am Assoc 90-; Eng; Prof.

**FULCHER, JENNIFER D,** Longwood Coll, Farmville, VA; FR; BS; Bapt Stdnt Un 90-; Nell Andersen Sprague Awd; Psych/Elem Educ; Tchr.

**FULCHER, MARTHA R,** Ms Univ For Women, Columbus, MS; SR; BS; Sigma Theta Tau; Rsrch Awd Sigma Theta Tau; Labor/Delivery Supvr; LPN/ADN 78; Cert 88; Nrsng; Masters Degree Mtrnl Chld.

**FULCO, FRANK A,** Wv Univ, Morgantown, WV; JR; BS; IM Scr 88-; Acdmy Stdnts Phrmcy 90-; Hnrs Pgm 88-; Hlvt Soph Hnry 89-90; Chimes Jrn Hnry 90-; Phi Kappa Phi; Pres Schlrshp 88; Orgnc Chmstry Stdnt Yr 89-90; Dns Lst 89-; Phrmcy; Med.

**FULFORD, LEIANE M,** Jacksonville Univ, Jacksonville, FL; SR; BSN; Rcrtmnt/Admsns Comm For Schl Of Nrsng; Curriculum Comm For Schl Of Nrsng 89-; Prcptrshp Intnsv Care Nrsng; Pres/Dns Lst 89-; Natl Coll Nrsng Awds 90-; Putnam Comm Hosp Rcrtmnt/Rtntn Comm; Emer Nrs; Nrsng; Critical Care.

**FULFORD, STEPHANIE S,** Fl St Univ, Tallahassee, FL; FR; BA; Cmpus Crsde Chrst 90-; Flyng High Circus 90-.

**FULGHAM, ROBYN R,** Univ Of Sc At Columbia, Columbia, SC; FR; BA; Educ; Tchr.

**FULK, KEVIN J,** Bowling Green St Univ, Bowling Green, OH; JR; BS; IM Bsktbl 87-; Frederick C Stone Memorial Schlrshp; Asst Estimator For Site Dvlpmnt Contractor 90; Asst Sanitary Engr Wood Cnty 90; Res Project Rep Abestos Tchn; Architecroal Envrmntl Design; Civil Engvmnt.

**FULK, TED S,** Kent St Univ Kent Cmps, Kent, OH; SR; Sinfonia 89-; Wind Ens 90-; Jazz Ens/Highest Praise 87-; Golden Key; Delta Omicron Treas 89-.

**FULKERSON, MICHAEL H,** Ky Wesleyan Coll, Owensboro, KY; SR; Psych Clb 89-; Green River Mental Health Vol Award 90; Ba; Crt Institute Reality Therapy; Psych; Certified Reality Therapist.

**FULKS, PAUL D,** Pellissippi St Tech Comm Coll, Knoxville, TN; SO; BS; Weight Lifting 89-; City Sftbl League 83-; Phi Tau Kappa 90-; Lambda Chi Alpha 86-87; Christian Church; Varsity Bsbl 85-86; Waiter 90-; Civil Engrg; Construction.

**FULKS, TIMOTHY W,** Univ Of Cincinnati, Cincinnati, OH; SO; AS; Sr Gnr/Tnk Cmndr U S Army 83-87; Ld Instlr; Pation Enclosures Inc 87-90; Cvl/Cnstrctn Engrg.

**FULLAM, KATHLEEN M,** Fordham Univ, Bronx, NY; JR; BS; Deans Lst 89-; Big Bro/Big Sis Xmas Cmpgn Drn Crdntr 90; All Amer Schlr Coll Awrd; All Conf Acdmc 89-; Var Crs Cntry Trck Tms 88-; Bus; Ads.

**FULLAM, TAMMY E,** Endicott Coll, Beverly, MA; FR; BS; Rtlng.

**FULLER, AMELIA R,** Univ Of Nc At Asheville, Asheville, NC; FR; BA; Seamstrs 80-; Psychlgy; Cnslng.

**FULLER, ANDREW B,** Tallahassee Comm Coll, Tallahassee, FL; SO; AA; Stdnt Govt 89; Phi Theta Kappa VP 89-90; Comptr Sci; Sys Anlyst.

**FULLER, ANTHONY C,** Univ Of Southern Ms, Hattiesburg, MS; FR; BBA; Shotokan Karate Clb 90-; Eagle Clb 90-; Phi Eta Sigma; Deans Lst 90-; Academic Schlrshp 90-; Marketing; Retailing.

**FULLER, BENJAMIN R,** Abraham Baldwin Agri Coll, Tifton, GA; JR; GA Colf Course Sprntdnt Assn; Golf Course Sprntdnt Assn; Pi Kappa Phi 87-89; Ornamental Horticulture; Gold Course Sprtndnt.

**FULLER, BETH C,** Univ Of Nh Plymouth St Coll, Plymouth, NH; SR; BS; Dean Lst; Pres Lst; Elem Educ; Tchr.

**FULLER, BRIAN M,** Univ Of Akron, Akron, OH; JR; BA; Deans Lst 89-90; US Army Reserves 86-; Ohio H S Ftbl Coaches Assoc 90-; Sec Educ Social Studies; Tchng Coaching.

**FULLER, CASSANDRA K,** Comm Coll Algny Co Algny Cmps, Pittsburgh, PA; SO; BA; Ornttn Peer Cnslr; Budget Conf; Mertrs Acdmc Achvmnt Awrd; AS; Sec Educ/Engl; Tchng.

**FULLER JR, CHARLES D,** Memphis St Univ, Memphis, TN; SR; BFA; Graphic Dsgn; Sls/Advtsng.

**FULLER, CHRISTOPHER S,** Truett Mc Connell Coll, Cleveland, GA; FR; BA; Wntrvle Bptst Chrch Dcn 79-; Pres Clb 90-; Hstry; Hstry Prfssr.

**FULLER, DAMON D,** Fl Atlantic Univ, Boca Raton, FL; JR; BA; AA Plm Bch Comm Clg 90; Acctg; CPA Law Enfrcmnt.**

**FULLER, DAVID,** Webber Coll, Babson Park, FL; SR; BS; SGA Csusj Drctr Arrfs 89-; Intrntnl Clb Trsr 86-89; Chmbr Cmmrc 90-; Tokoyo Jpn Exchng 87-88; AA Hartnell Cllg Calinas CA 89; Bsns Admn Mrktng; Bsns Mgmt.

**FULLER, DEVRIS L,** Morris Brown Coll, Atlanta, GA; SO; BA; Vars Ftbl; AS Cmptr Elect United Electronic Int 87-89; Mgmnt/Bus; Corp Mngr.

**FULLER, GREGORY M,** Interdenominational Theo Ctr, Atlanta, GA; GD; MDIV; BA Amer Bapt Clg 90; Theology; Tchr.

**FULLER, HEATHER L,** Christopher Newport Coll, Newport News, VA; JR; BS; Pol Sci; Law.

**FULLER, JACQUELINE A,** Sue Bennett Coll, London, KY; SO; BS; Sigma Nu; Phi Theta Kappa; Appalachian Cmptr Serv; Acctg.

**FULLER, JEAN E,** Alfred Univ, Alfred, NY; FR; BA; Bsn Adm; Bsn Tchg.

**FULLER, JENNIFER L,** Univ Of Sc At Columbia, Columbia, SC; FR; BA; Univ Nwspr Staff Writer 90-; Minority Assistance Peer Program 90-; Assoc For African Amer Stdnts 90-; Journalism; News Editorial Journalism.

**FULLER, KEVIN D,** Niagara Univ, Niagara Univ, NY; JR; BS; Blgy; Graduate Schl.

**FULLER, PATRICIA J,** Alfred Univ, Alfred, NY; JR; BA; Amercn Mktg Assoc 90-F Stdnt Sen 89-; Theta Theta Chi Secy 89-; Bus/Mktg.

**FULLER, RALPH F,** S U N Y Coll Of Tech At Delhi, Delhi, NY; SR; AOS; Auto Mechanics.

**FULLER, RENE M,** Cleveland Inst Of Art, Cleveland, OH; SR; BFA; Trnsfr Stdnt Schlrshp 88-89; Mrt Awd Schlrshp 89-; Spcs Nw Org Vsl Arts; Ohio Wms Cs Art; Hallinam Rlgs Shw; Hnrbl Mntn 90 Russell Juried Shw Bst Shw; Fine Arts/Mjr Gls; MFA/STD Art/Art Ed.

**FULLER, RUSSELL C,** Univ Of Al At Birmingham, Birmingham, AL; SO; Bovine Invstmnt Clb 87-; Pres Lst Jefferson State Jr Coll 86-88; Pres Lst 88-; Kodak Awd Hghst Acad Achvmnt; AS Jefferson State Comm Coll 88; AAS Jefferson State Comm Transfer Pgm; Radiography; Cardiac Cath Tech.

**FULLER, SCOTT W,** Glassboro St Coll, Glassboro, NJ; SR; BA; Coll Radio Sta 90-; Cmmnctns/Radio TV/FLM; Brdcstng.

**FULLER, SONYA C,** Juniata Coll, Huntingdon, PA; FR; BS; Cncrt Bnd 90-; Pep Bnd 90-; Jz Bnd; Rsrch/Marine Biolgy.

**FULLER, STACY L,** Univ Of Nc At Greensboro, Greensboro, NC; SR; BS; Comtng Stdnt Assn 87-; Intrnshp Bluford Elem Schl 90; Sthrn Elem Schl; Elem Ed; Schl Tchr.

**FULLER, WANDA C,** Univ Of Al At Birmingham, Birmingham, AL; JR; BA; BA Walker Clg 90; Elem Educ; Tchng.

**FULLER, WENDY K,** Lesley Coll, Cambridge, MA; SO; BA; Stdnt Govt Assoc Dir Of Pblcty 89-; SGA Pres; Orien Comm Pblcty Chr 90-; Elem Educ/Mod Spec Needs; Tchng.

**FULLER, WINNIFRED E,** Marshall University, Huntington, WV; SR; BA; Stdnts Christ Ldrshp Tm 88-; Opera Wrkshp 88-; Cmbr Choir 89-; Msc Edctrs Natl Cnfrnc 87-; Delta Omicron Dir Mscl Affrs 89-; Msc Ed; Pblc Schl Tchr.

**FULLINS, SUTANA,** Clark Atlanta Univ, Atlanta, GA; SR; Cmptr Sci Clb P 88-.

**FULLMER, TAMARA D,** Univ Of Nc At Charlotte, Charlotte, NC; JR; BS; Univ Prog Brd Chr 88-; SGA VP 89-; Alumni Ambsdr 90-; Golden Key Treas 90-; Omicron Delta Kappa; Pi Sigma Alpha 90-; Drctr Yr Univ Prog Brd 90-; Winningham Schrlshp; IM Bsktbl Co Rec Champs 88-; Bus/Pol Scie; Graduate Schl.

**FULLONE, JOSEPH S,** Saint John Fisher Coll, Rochester, NY; SR; Chem Clb Sec Fin Afrs 88-90; Orntn Stf 88-89; Undrgrd Rsrch Unv Rochester 90-; Natl Clgt Natl Sci Awrd 88; IM Sprts Sftbl Vlybl Flr Hcky Capt 87-90; BS/BA; Bio/Chem; Med Sch.**

**FULMER, ANGELA B,** Montclair St Coll, Upr Montclair, NJ; JR; BS; Chem Clb 88-; CHEERS VP 88-; IBM Rsrch 90; Merck/Co MCMD Intern; Chem/Edn; Tchr.**

**FULMER, DEIDRA L,** Brewer St Jr Coll, Fayette, AL; SO; BA; Phi Beta Lambda VP 90-; BAD; Phi Theta Kappa; ASINSC; Bus; Mgmt.

**FULMER, MARILYN H,** Truett Mc Connell Coll, Cleveland, GA; SO; Cntl Cmmnty Actn Tm Sec 89-; Tlcmmnctns Srvc Rep 79-; Bus.

**FULMER, MELISSA A,** Univ Of Sc At Columbia, Columbia, SC; FR; BA; Psychlgy.

**FULMER JR, MONROE E,** Univ Of Sc At Columbia, Columbia, SC; FR; BS; Mech Engr.

**FULMER, PAMELA A,** Memphis St Univ, Memphis, TN; JR; BLS; Legal/Engl/Soc; Law Schl.

**FULTON, BONNIE J,** East Carolina Univ, Greenville, NC; SR; ICF Worship Tm 87-; Wes Fel Chrstn Fllwshp Worship Ldr 88-; Ceramics Guild; Stdnt Show; Stdnt Tchg; Im Soccr Vlybl Asst Coach 87-90; Art Educ.

**FULTON, CYNTHIA E,** Livingston Univ, Livingston, AL; SR; Union Pgm Brd 86-87; Natrl Sci Math Clb 86-87; Phi Eta Sigma 86-; Delta Chi Little Sistr 87-88; Univ Schlrs Awd; Bsed; Bio; Tchg.

**FULTON, LYNN S,** Memphis St Univ, Memphis, TN; GD; BBA; Gamma Beta Phi; Le Bonheur Twiggs; VBS Dir; Rstrnt Mgr; BBA 82; Acctg.

**FULTON, MICHAEL G,** Nova Univ, Ft Lauderdale, FL; GD; MS; BA St Leo Clg 90; Hmn Res Mgmt; Mgmt Engr.

**FULTON, PAULA E,** Bowie St Univ, Bowie, MD; JR; BS; Ed Club; Kappa Delta Pi VP 90-; Sigma Tau Delta; Pres Schlrshp 90-F; English; Secdy Schl Tchr.

**FULTON, SHARON W,** Benedict Coll, Columbia, SC; GD; MBA; Day Stdt Org Treas; Delta Sigma Theta Secr; Jr Mssnry Sunday Schl Asst; Babysitter; Tutor; Dns Lst; Dr Gonzales Benedict Clg Intern; Publ Rels; Govt.

**FULTZ, DEBRA M,** Univ Of Tn At Knoxville, Knoxville, TN; JR; BS; Gamma Beta Phi 89-; Exec Undergrdts 88-; Beta Alpha Psi; Alpha Chi Omega Crspndng Sec 88-; Acctg/Bsn; CPA.

**FULTZ, DONALD P,** Capital Bible Seminary, Lanham, MD; GD; THM; BA Citadel Bible Clg 87; M Div 90; Theology; Foreign Missionary.

**FULWIDER, MICHELLE R,** The Johns Hopkins Univ, Baltimore, MD; SO; BA; NAACP 90-; Blck Stdnt Union; Univ Bible Flwshp; Chrsnt Flwshp; Alpha Kappa Alpha; Intrnshp Cncl On Hmsphrc Affrs; Intl Rel; Law.**

**FULWOOD, TERI A,** Fl A & M Univ, Tallahassee, FL; JR; Jazz Bnd 89-; Symph Bnd 89-; Concert Choir 89-90; Future FL Edctrs Amer 90-; Gwendolyn Sawyer Cherry Schlrshp Awd 90; Bnd Schlrshp 89-90; Vocal Schlrshp 89-90; AA 90; Elem Ed; Tchg.

**FUMERO CABAN, JOSE J,** Inter Amer Univ Pr Hato Rey, Hato Rey, PR; FR; Bio; Med Tech.

**FUNARI, SHARON K,** King Coll, Bristol, TN; JR; Flwshp Of Chrstn Athlts VP 89-; IM 89-; Kng Coll Ambsdr 89-90; Chrstn Outrch 89-; Res Asst 90-; NCCAA Schlr-Athlt 90-; Vrsty Vlybl Capt 89-; Psychlgy; Cnslng.

**FUNARO, JOSEPH A,** Wilmington Coll, New Castle, DE; SR; BS; Deans Lst 89-; Delta Epsilon Rho 90; Amer Soc Mltry Cmptrlrs; Cost Anlyst USAF; AAS 90; Bnkg.

**FUNCHES, MAURICE O,** Providence Coll, Providence, RI; FR; BS; Brd Minority Student Affairs Assist 90-; IM Bskbl 90-; Pre Engrg/Physics; Elec Engr.

**FUNCHESS, CHANT ANDREA L,** City Univ Of Ny City Coll, New York, NY; SR; BA; Newspapr Ed-In-Chief; Aspira 87-89; Mngng Edtr; Golden Key 90; Deans Lst; 1st Bapt Chrch Assist Scrtry; Fllwshps SS 87-90; Vlg Voice Intrn 90; Outstndng Acad Achvmnt Aspira Of Cty Clg NY 89-90; Cmmnctns Prnt Jrnlsm; Pblshng.

**FUNCHESS, EULA M,** Al St Univ, Montgomery, AL; FR; Ebony Clb Stdnt Cncl Com Ldr 88-; Bsktbl; Engl; Edn.

**FUNCHION, RANDY J,** Defiance Coll, Defiance, OH; JR; BA; ASA Sftbl Assoc; ASSOC Bus Admn 89-90; Bus Admn Mgt.

**FUNDERBURK, ANNE C,** Greenville Tech Coll, Greenville, SC; SR; ADN; SG Pres 89-; Nursing Adv Cmte 90-; Cert Red Cross Baby Sitting Inst 90-; Nursing.

**FUNDERBURK, JANE K,** Univ Of Ga, Athens, GA; GD; BS; GA Cncl Cnsmr Intrst Tnns; Cnsmr Ecnmcs; Sls.

**FUNDERBURK, VERNA,** Morris Brown Coll, Atlanta, GA; SR; BSN; Hon Clb 90-; Blck Nrs Assn VP 90-; Rgnts Of Nghtngle Cert 89; Chi Eta Phi Hon Schlrshp 90-; Nrsng.

**FUNG, ALICE,** City Univ Of Ny Baruch Coll, New York, NY; JR; BBA; Provost Schlrsph 90-; Fnnc; Bus.

**FUNG, HEI T,** Univ Of Rochester, Rochester, NY; JR; BS; Chns Chrstn Flwshp Dvtnl Ldr 90-; Tau Beta Pi 90-; Phi Beta Kappa 90-; Chu Schlrshp; Genesee Schlrhsp; Elect Eng.

**FUNG, RHONDA L,** Gallaudet Univ, Washington, DC; SR; BA; Asian-Pac Assoc Parlmntrn 87-; Stdnt Cncl Rep 88-89; Deans List Pres Schlrs 88-; Magna Cum Laude Hnr Grad; Natl Min Clge Awd; Delta Epsilon Corspndg Sec 89-; Psychology Awd; Schlr Exclnce Awd; Psychology Practicum Prog 90-; Psychology/Comm Arts; Clinical Psychology.

**FUNG-A-FAT, MARK A,** Coll Misericordia, Dallas, PA; SR; BS; Comp Sci Math Pres 89; Wght Lftng Clb Pres 90; Cmps Mnstry Brd Mmbr 90; Coll Msrcrdia Hnrs Scty 87-; Delta Sigma Epsilon; Kappa Gamma Pi; Cmps Mnstry; Pr Ttr; Rsdnt Asst; Rtry Yth Ldrshp Grp; Acad All Amer Awrd; Brd Of Trstees Awrd; Comp Sci And Math; Coll Tchng In Comps Math.

**FUNG-A-FAT, SHANE A,** Coll Misericordia, Dallas, PA; FR; BS; Cmptr Sci/Math Clb 90-; Hon Scty 90-; Cmptr Sci/Math; Eng.

**FUNK, BRYAN D,** Columbia Greene Comm Coll, Hudson, NY; SO; BS; Radio Clb Prgrm Dir; Forten Clb VP 90; Pres Schlr 90-; Regents Schlr 90-; Athltc Dir Awrd 90; Vrsty Bwlng Capt 90-; AS; Htl/Rest Mngt.

**FUNK, JENNIFER M,** Carson Newman Coll, Jefferson City, TN; FR; BS; Bapt Stdnt Un 90-; Stdnt Amb Assoc; Alpha Lamda Delta; Phi Eta Sigma; Fres Book Awd; Spec Educ; Teach.

**FUNK, NATALIE G,** Savannah Coll Of Art & Design, Savannah, GA; FR; BFA; SCAD Scty Of Illstrtrs Scrtry 90; Illstrtn; Bk Illstrtn.

**FUNK, THERESA M,** Columbia Greene Comm Coll, Hudson, NY; FR; SG; AS; Hmn Srv/Sub Abuse.

**FUNN, CAROLYN G,** Va Commonwealth Univ, Richmond, VA; SR; BS; Intshp Chstrfld Co Dpt Mntl Hlth/Mntl Rtdtn/Sub Abuse; Offndr Aid/Rstrtn 87-88; Dept Corr; AA Educ Reynolds Comm Clg 86; AS Lib Arts 86; Rehab Serv; Mntl Hlth.

**FUNYAK JR, JOHN P,** Comm Coll Algny Co Algny Cmps, Pittsburgh, PA; SO; Educ.

**FUQUA, MONICA D,** Al A & M Univ, Normal, AL; SO; BS; Acad Awd 90-; Acctg.

**FUQUA, SHARON E,** Univ Of Ga, Athens, GA; SR; BED; Chrldr Reinhardt Clg 87-89; Res Asst 88-89; Golden Key 90-; Dns Lst 90-; Psi Chi Omega Reinhardt Clg Secr 87-89; Assoc Arts/Sci Reinhardt Clg 89; Early Chldhd Ed; Tchg.

**FURANO, LU ANN,** Niagara Univ, Niagara Univ, NY; SR; BA; Exec Brd Orntn Brd 88-90; Sr Wk Com Mbr 90-; Frshmn Smnr Prog Tchr Asst 89; Phi Sigma Iota; Phi Alpha Theta; Pi Sigma Alpha; Study Abrd Seville Spain 90; Intl Studies.

**FURBEE, ELMER E,** Kent St Univ Kent Cmps, Kent, OH; SO; BA; Alpha Beta Gamma Hist 90-; Sftbl Coach 86-; Eagles Sec 90-; Acctg; CPA.

**FURBERT, ERICA R,** Howard Univ, Washington, DC; SR; BARCH; Bermuda Stdnts Assn Sec 88-; Curves Org Corr Sec 90-; Am Inst Architectural Stdnts; Tau Sigma Delta 89-; Gold Key 90-; Teach Asst Cmptr Appl 89-90; Am Inst Architects Cert Merit 89-90; Architecture; Lawyer.

**FURCON, THERESE C,** Wilkes Univ, Wilkes-Barre, PA; FR; BS; Wnd Ensmble 90-; Med Tech.

**FURDGE, CHERYL A,** Alcorn St Univ, Lorman, MS; SR; BS; Bio Club; AA Coahoma Jr Coll 89; Sci; Phys Thrpst.

**FUREDY, ALBERT D,** Comm Coll Algny Co Algny Cmps, Pittsburgh, PA; SO; BS; Future Engrs Club; Phi Theta Kappa 89-; Mech Engr Sci.

**FURER, JAMES L,** Oh St Univ At Marion, Marion, OH; JR; BA; Elem Ed; Tchr.

**FUREY, JULIE A,** Univ Of Nh Plymouth St Coll, Plymouth, NH; SR; BS; Erly Chldhd Club; Elem Edn; Day Care.

**FURINO, RAFFAELA,** City Univ Of Ny Baruch Coll, New York, NY; SO; BBA; Pub Admin; Law.

**FURKART, CHRISTINE C,** Bunker Hill Comm Coll, Boston, MA; SO; AS; Acctng.

**FURLOUGH, TERESA L,** Roanoke Bible Coll, Elizabeth Cy, NC; SO; Music; Music Drctr.

**FURLOW, STEPHANIE N,** Livingston Univ, Livingston, AL; SR; BS; Bapt Campus Mnstr BYW Pres 88-; Sngrs 88-; Choir 88-; Crdnl Key 90-; Alpha Chi 90-; Trustees Schlrshp 88-; Voice Schlrshp 88-; Music; Tch.

**FURMAN, ELLIOT M,** S U N Y At Buffalo, Buffalo, NY; SR; BSEE; IEEE Pres/Actvy Dir 90-; Seido Karate Clb 87-; Eta Kappa Nu 90-; Tau Beta Pi 90-; Rsrch/Indpndt Stdy; Flwshp; Elec Engr.

**FURMAN, LAURA F,** Univ Of Southern Ms, Hattiesburg, MS; SO; BS; Stdnt Eagle Clb; Stdnt Alumni Assn; Lambda Sigma Phi Eta Sigma Rtl Chr 90-; Alpha Lambda Delta; Phi Eta Sigma; Alpha Epsilon Delta; Pi Beta Phi Pldg Clss Ofcr 89-90; Gamma Beta Phi; Eagle Cnctn Stdnt Rcrtmnt Tm; Psych; Optmtry.

**FURMATO, MARY ANN,** Georgian Court Coll, Lakewood, NJ; SR; BS; Bio Res Undergrad 89-90; Dns Schlr; Intrnshp W Intl Flavr Frag 90-; Mbr St Peters PTA 85-; Nuclr Pwr Svcs 81-84; Bio; Tchng.

**FURNISS, JENNIFER B,** Kent St Univ Kent Cmps, Kent, OH; FR; BS; Hse Cncl Flr Rep 90-; Hon Coll 90-; Alpha Lambda Delta; Note-Tkr Dsabld Stdnt Serv; Finance.

**FURNO, LAURA A,** Univ Of South Fl, Tampa, FL; SR; BSN; Aid Assn Lthrns VP 90-; Clrwtr Fire Explrs Adlt Advsr 89-; Lthrn Chrl FL 89-; Seminole Fire Rescue Seminole FL; Nrsng Prcptrshp Srgcl Intnsv Cr Unt Bayfront Mdcl Cntr; Ctzn Ambsdr; Nrsng; Shnds Hsptl Srgcl Intnsv Cr Unt.

**FURR, KIMBERLY N,** Anderson Coll, Anderson, SC; SO; BS; Fin Mgmt; Anlyst.

**FURR, MELISSA D,** Methodist Coll, Fayetteville, NC; FR; BS; Bsktbl Sftbl 90-; Physcl Edctn; Tchr.

**FURST, TODD J,** East Stroudsburg Univ, E Stroudsburg, PA; JR; BA; Intr Vrsty Chrstn Fllwshp 89-; Mnre Rsdnce Hll Cncl Treas 90-; Flg Ftbl Sftbl Bsktbl 88-; Comp Sci.

**FURUYAMA, MANA,** Westminster Choir Coll, Princeton, NJ; SO; BM; Tchng Piano At Tokyo Christian Clg 88-89; BTH Tokyo Christian Clg 87; Church Music; Tchng.

**FURY, SHERRY S,** Cumberland Coll, Williamsburg, KY; FR; Bread World Fall 90-; Love In Action Tchr 90; Religion; Ministry.

**FUSARO, DANA C,** Univ Of Sc At Columbia, Columbia, SC; JR; BA; USTA 88-; Natl Audobon Soc 90-; Asst Benefit Hlth Dept 88-; Econ/Eng; Law Sch.

**FUSCO, JULIE ANN,** Notre Dame Coll, Cleveland, OH; JR; BA; Elem Ed; Tchr.

**FUSCO, RONALD C,** Middle Tn St Univ, Murfreesboro, TN; SR; BS; Bio; Envrnmntl Sci/Plltn Cntrl.

**FUSSELL, CANDACE E,** Dyersburg St Comm Coll, Dyersburg, TN; FR; Elem Educ; Tch.

**FUSZNER, LARA J,** Univ Of Southern Ms, Hattiesburg, MS; FR; Mrchng Bnd; Gamma Beta Phi 90-.

**FUTCH, MARIE-ELENA,** Hillsborough Comm Coll, Tampa, FL; FR; AS; AS Vet Tech St Ptrsbrg Jr Clg 86; Nrsng; RN.

**FUTCH, STACEY M,** Univ Of Al At Birmingham, Birmingham, AL; SR; BS; Womens Rec Cntr; Golf Team Capt 89-90; Soclgy; Resrch Or Cnclng.

**FUTCHER, HEATHER C,** Columbia Union Coll, Takoma Park, MD; JR; BS; Phi Eta Sigma; Bio; Veterinarian.**

**FUTRAL JR, CHARLES E,** Central Al Comm Coll, Alexander City, AL; SO; AS; Genl; Cmptr Tech.

**FUTRELL, MAYA C,** Concordia Coll, Selma, AL; FR; Psychlgy.

**FUTRELL-CAIN, ELVERNA DENISE,** Univ Of Tn At Martin, Martin, TN; SR; BS; Blck Stdnt Assn Pub Rel Dir 89-; SGA 89-90; Peer Enblng Pgm Pep Ldr 90-; Socl Wrk Clb 89-; Mnrty Stdnt Schlrshp 88-89; Delta Sigma Theta VP 89-90; Intrnshp Dept Yth Dev S W Regn; Univ Tenn Pacr Hostess 88-90; Socl Wrk; Ma Humn Res Mgmt.

**FYFE, SUSAN E,** Tuskegee Univ, Tuskegee Inst, AL; GD; DVM; Fndrsng Com 90-; Advrtsng Com Co Chrprsn 90-; Grnd Rnds Com Chrprsn 90-; Tau Delta Pres 90; IM Sftbl 90; BS VA Polytechnic Inst & St Univ 90; Vet Med; Vetrn.

**FYFFE, JULIET D,** Coppin St Coll, Baltimore, MD; SR; BS; Coppin Dancers Dncr 90; Gen Scnc Chem Emphasis; Pharmacy.

**FYFFE, MATTHEW J,** Univ Of Akron, Akron, OH; JR; BA; Ambssdrs Stdnt Advsry Cncl; Mu Kappa Tau; Gldn Ky; Pi Sigma Epsilon Pres 89-; Mktng; Sls/Mgmnt.

**FYKE, JANET L,** Volunteer St Comm Coll, Gallatin, TN; SO; BS; Rtrnng Wmns Orgnztn Sec Treas 90-; Gamma Beta Phi 90-; Gamma Beta Phi Schlrshp; Mgmt Mrktng; Mgmt.

**FYKE, KAREN L,** Anne Arundel Comm Coll, Arnold, MD; SO; BA; AA 88; Law.

# G

**GABIA, ANNE K,** S U N Y Coll Of Tech At Frmgdl, Farmingdale, NY; SR; AS; Sec; Cert Katharine Gibbs 86; Early Chldhd; Social Wrk.

**GABINETTI, PATRICIA A,** Bay Path Coll, Longmeadow, MA; FR; AS; Deans Lst; Accnts Pybl Rtlng; Fshn Mrchndsng; Clthng Byr.

**GABOR, TIMOTHY M,** Memphis St Univ, Memphis, TN; GD; MS; TN Acad Of Sce 90-; Amer Soc/Pammalogists; Wildlife Soc; Intrnshp WI Dept Of Natural Rsrcs 89; BS Univ Of WI 90; Biology; Acad/Rsrch.

**GABOUREL, ROSITA M,** Bloomfield Coll, Bloomfield, NJ; FR; BA; Cl Treas 90-; Sigma Gamma Rho Treas 90-; Accntng; CPA.

**GABRICH, DIANA M,** Univ Of South Al, Mobile, AL; SO; BA; Symphnc Bnd 89-90; Jr Pnhllnc Treas 90-; Food Srvc Comm 90-; Phi Chi Theta 90-; Alpha Gamma Delta 90-; VITA; St Marys Hm Tutr 90; Outstndg Pldg Alpha Gamma Delta; Bus Admin; Accntnt.

**GABRIELE, DANIELLE M,** Saint Johns Univ, Jamaica, NY; SR; BS; Educ N-6.

**GABRIELE, LINDA M,** Univ Of Ri, Kingston, RI; JR; BS; Sigma Theta Tau Delta Upsilon; Ntnl Cllgt Nrsng Awd; US Achvmnt Acad All Amrcn; Nrsng; RN.

**GABRIELE, ROSELLA,** Oh Coll Of Podiatric Med, Cleveland, OH; SO; DPM; Am Assoc Women Podiatrists 88-90; Pi Delta 90-; Pod Med Acdmc Schlrshp Rcpnt 90-; T V & Radio News Rprtr; BA Univ Akron Akron Oh 84; Pod Med; Pod Surgery.

**GADD, BRIAN D,** Kent St Univ Kent Cmps, Kent, OH; FR; BBA; New Stu Ornttn; Rcqtbl 90; Accntng; CPA.

**GADD, MARIE A,** Central St Univ, Wilberforce, OH; FR; Educ/Engl; H S Tchr.

**GADDIS, CHRISTOPHER P,** Alcorn St Univ, Lorman, MS; JR; BA; Alpha Phi Alpha 90; Alcorn A/M Marching Band 88-; Business Administration; Entreperuer.

**GADDY, ANGELA F,** Radford Univ, Radford, VA; JR; BA; Hnrs Prog 90-; Assoc Cntrl Va Vomm Coll 90; Phys Educ; Phys Thrpst.

**GADDY, LESLEY K,** Stillman Coll, Tuscaloosa, AL; SO; BA; Choir 89-; Bus Mngmnt; Bus Exec.

**GADDY, NANCY LYNN,** Coll Of Charleston, Charleston, SC; SO; MBA; Stdnt Alum Assn; Fellwshp Chrstn Athl 89-; Alpoha Delta Pi Tr 89-; Busn; Acctg/Finc.

**GADI, RENU,** Middlesex County Coll, Edison, NJ; SR; BA India 82; Blib India 83.

**GADIARE, HAROLD H,** City Univ Of Ny Baruch Coll, New York, NY; SR; BBA; Gldn Key; Beta Gamma Sigma; Dns Lst Kingsborough Cmnty Clge; Dns Lst Baruch Clge; AAS Kingsborough Cmnty Clge 88; Cmptr Info Systms; Elctrncs Tchnlgy/Elc Engr.

**GADSEY, DEA M,** Middle Tn St Univ, Murfreesboro, TN; SR; BS; Phi Epsilon Kappa 90-; Phys Ed-Sci; Tchg.

**GAEBEL, MILTON W,** S U N Y Coll Of Tech At Alfred, Alfred, NY; FR; Sigma Tau Epsilon Sec; Sftbl.

**GAETANO, DAVID A,** Oh Wesleyan Univ, Delaware, OH; FR; BA; OH Westeyan/Crestview Init Pgm; Phi Gamma Delta; IM Soccer/Sftbl; Pol Sci; Law.

**GAETANO, PATRICIA A,** Univ Of Ga, Athens, GA; SR; MED; Softball 87-; BSED UGA; Early Childhood/Reading; Elem Educ.

**GAFF, BETH A,** Kent St Univ Kent Cmps, Kent, OH; JR; BA; Golden Key; Bus Mgmt; Hotel/Rstrnt Mgmt.

**GAFFIN, NEIL,** Hahnemann Univ, Philadelphia, PA; SO; MD; William Goldman Schlrshp; BA Temple Univ 87; Med; Physcn.

**GAFFNEY, MARY E,** Comm Coll Algny Co Algny Cmps, Pittsburgh, PA; FR; BSN; Hairstylist 75-; Nursing.

**GAFFOS, KIMBERLY H,** Longwood Coll, Farmville, VA; SR; BS; NEA IM Intervrsty; Elem Educ; Tchr.

**GAFFRON, CHRISTIAN D,** Springfield Tech Comm Coll, Springfield, MA; SO; BA; Hon Pgm 89-; Actvts Nrsng Hms; AA; Ecnmcs; MBA.

**GAGE, ADAM F K,** Berkshire Comm Coll, Pittsfield, MA; FR; Vsl Arts; Mag Prod/Phtgrphy.

**GAGER, AMBER L,** Atlantic Comm Coll, Mays Landing, NJ; FR; Rtry Yth Ldr Assoc 89; Hnr Roll; Bsktbl Sftbl Var 86-90; Bsnss; Tchr.

**GAGIC, KSENIJA,** Columbia Univ, New York, NY; FR; BABS; Engl/Pre Med; Law/Med.

**GAGLIANO, JEFFREY R,** Cornell Univ Statutory College, Ithaca, NY; SO; Crnl Lacrosse Clb Strtg Mbr 90-; Phi Delta Theta; Wlk Amer 90; Hwrd Rsk Med Intrn 90; Orthpdc Srgn Intrn NY Univ Med Sch; Crnl Lacrosse 90-; Microbio; Med.

**GAGLIANO, MATTHEW V,** Manhattan Coll, Bronx, NY; FR; BS; Mnrty Un 90-; Crw Tm 90; Mchncl Eng.

**GAGLIARDO, MARIA,** Coll Of New Rochelle, New Rochelle, NY; SO; BA; Commnctn Arts; Brdcstng.

**GAGNE, REAL,** Asbury Theological Sem, Wilmore, KY; SR; MA; Intrntl Scty Theta Phi 90; MHR Free Meth Spcl Schlrshp 88; Dr Myron F Boyd Memrl Schlrshp 90; Free Meth Pstr 86-87; Bible Schl Stdnt 84-86; Cbnt Mkr 78-83; BA Spring Arbor Clg 89; Theology; Tchng.

**GAGNON, JEAN-PAUL E,** Saint Josephs Coll, Windham, ME; FR; BA; On Air Broadcaster; Cross Country; Communicatins; Journalism.

**GAGNON, RICHARD L,** Me Maritime Academy, Castine, ME; JR; BA; Reg Of Midshpmn Reg Cmndr; Deans Lst; Cmdnts Lst; Sftbl; ASSOC Southern ME Voc Tech Inst 84-86; Nuclear Engr.

**GAIA, AMEERA CELESTE,** Christian Brothers Univ, Memphis, TN; SR; BA; Zeta Tau Alpha 88-; Stdnt Govt Assn Senatr 90-; Frnch Clb 89-; Psi Chi Pres 87-; Deans Lst 87-; Acdmc Schlrshp 87-; Tau Kappa Epsilon Serv Chrprsn 87-; Intrnshp Schl For Grls; Psychlgy.

**GAIA, PATIENCE R,** Tallahassee Comm Coll, Tallahassee, FL; SO; BS; New Leaf Mkt Coop Treas 81-; Tallahassee Peace Coalition 82-; Kitchen Mgr 81-85; AA 90; Hlth Educ; Tchng.

**GAILEY JR, RICHARD M,** Waycross Coll, Waycross, GA; SO; BA; Stdnt Nwspr Waycross Clg Ed In Chf 90-; Otsdng Score/ Regents Exam; Pltcl Sci; Corp Law.

**GAILLARD, ULRICK,** City Univ Of Ny Baruch Coll, New York, NY; SR; BA; IDOF FDC Bd 90-; Bapt Ch 89; Commbd 90; Cellist Brooklyn Phil Orch; NYC Off Intrnshp Asst 89; NYS Assmbly Intrn Leg Asst 90; Baruch French Dept Hon; Cert Sch Cmptr Sci 84; Pltcl Sci; Law.

**GAINER, ANTHONY SCOTT,** Kent St Univ Kent Cmps, Kent, OH; SR; BBA; Acctg Assoc 89-; Natl Assoc Accnts 90-; Gldn Key 90-; Beta Alpha Psi 89-; Beta Gamma Sigma 90-; Intrnshp Arthur Andersen & Co; Acctg; CPA.

**GAINES, BRAD R,** Middle Tn St Univ, Murfreesboro, TN; SR; BBA; Gamma Iota Sigma 90-; Fnce; Ins.

**GAINES, CRAWFORD T,** Univ Of Fl, Gainesville, FL; FR; Microbio; Med.

**GAINES III, JOHN H,** Morehouse Coll, Atlanta, GA; FR; BA; Pre Law Soc/Campus 90-; All Star Chlnge Tm/Span Clb; Pltcl Sci Clb; Hon Prog Clb 90-; Suthrn Bell Intrnshp 89-; I M Bkbl 90-; Pltcl Sci; Astrolaw/Corp Law.

**GAINES JR, ROBERT K,** Middle Ga Coll, Cochran, GA; SO; BIE; Engineering Club V Pres 89-90; Chess & Checkers Club Pres 89-; Computer Club Pres 90; IM Council Treas 90-; Gamma Beta Phi Pres 90-; Res Hall Assistant 90-; Dorm Council Treas 89-90; AS; Indstrl Engrng.

**GAINES, TARRA T,** Eckerd Coll, St Petersburg, FL; SR; BA; Lit Magzn Lit Evltr 90-; AIDS Pmphlt Co-Wrtr; Spec Tlnt Schlrshp Awrd; Creatv Wrtng.

**GAINEY, ALKATRINIA C,** Fl A & M Univ, Tallahassee, FL; SO; BA; Cmptr Info Syst Clb Cmptrllr 90; Phi Eta Sigma 90; Intrnshp IBM 90; Intrnshp Eastman Kodak Co; Kodak Schlr; Cmptr Info Syst; Cmptr Prog/Bsnss Admin.

**GAINEY, ANN G,** Coker Coll, Hartsville, SC; JR; BA; Marshall 89-90; Alpha Beta Delta 89-90; Pr Lst 88-90; Phi Beta Lambda Hist 88-90; Educ Rsrces Fndtn Schlr 89-90; Stanley Tools Schlrshp 89; DAC Schlrshp 90-; Baptist Church S S Tchr 71-; Assc Degree 90; Cert; Acctng.**

**GAINEY, KATHY B,** Coker Coll, Hartsville, SC; SR; BA; Elem Ed; Tchr.

**GAINEY, MARIAN G,** Mount Olive Coll, Mount Olive, NC; SO; BS; Phi Beta Lambda 90-; Deans Lst 75-76; Pres Lst 90-; Acctg; CPA.

**GAINEY, SANDRA R,** Fl International Univ, Miami, FL; SR; AA Miami Dade Cmnty Clg 83; Educ; Elem Tchr.

**GAINZA, MARIA L,** Univ Of Miami, Coral Gables, FL; SR; BBA; SNET Pagng Inc 90; Powmn Ashe Schlrshp 88-90; Finc; Mgmt.

**GAIOLINI, STEVEN,** Savannah Coll Of Art & Design, Savannah, GA; JR; BA; Phto Grp 89-; Fiber Clb 90-; Phtgphy.

**GAISER, BETH A,** Indiana Univ Of Pa, Indiana, PA; SR; Dns Lst; BS 90; Elem Educ.

**GAITER, KATHY F,** Columbia Union Coll, Takoma Park, MD; SR; BA; The Silhouettes Corr Sec 89-; J & J Assn 85-; VP Pres Of K B Ent 81-85; Co-Owner Of Two Burger King Rest 89-; Bus Mngmnt; Law.

**GAL, DOV,** Talmudic Coll Of Fl, Miami Beach, FL; JR; BA; Scrd Soc/Relg Brl Svc 90-; Jwsh Bnvlnt Soc 90-; Tlmdc Law; Law.

**GALAMBOS, SHEILA M,** Glassboro St Coll, Glassboro, NJ; SO; BA; Psychlgy; Chld Psychlgsts.

**GALANDER, MOHMOND M,** Howard Univ, Washington, DC; GD; PHD; Jrnlst; Edtr 86-89; Afrcn Cncl Comm Edctn; MPA 86; Comm.

**GALANO, JULIE A,** Elms Coll, Chicopee, MA; JR; BA; Deans Lst 88-; Elem Ed; Elem Schl Tchr.

**GALANOS, KONSTANTINOS M,** Teikyo Post Univ, Waterbury, CT; JR; BA; Hist/Sociology/Pol Sci; Teach Law.**

**GALARCE, PABLO O,** Bunker Hill Comm Coll, Boston, MA; SO; BA; Intl Stu Clb 90-; Prguyn Govt Schlrshp; Pol Sci; Pblc Admin.

**GALARRAGA, OMAR,** Univ Of The Dist Of Columbia, Washington, DC; FR; MBA; Stdnt Govt Crse Pres Cls Rep 90; Tnns; Econs; Intl Econs.

**GALARZA, HERIBERTO,** Inter Amer Univ Pr Hato Rey, Hato Rey, PR; SO; PHD; Crp Vol Serv Coord 89-; Sldr Year 89; Acctng/Cmptrs; Avtn/Law.

**GALARZA, NITZA J,** Inter Amer Univ Pr Hato Rey, Hato Rey, PR; SR; BS; BS 85; Microbio; Mstr.

**GALAS, AMY C,** Indiana Univ Of Pa, Indiana, PA; JR; BED; Cncrt Dnc VP 89-; Beta Gamma Chptr Kappa Delta Pi 90-; Provost Schlr 89-; Hnr Comm Cllg 90-; Elem Ed; Tchr.

**GALASSO, RICHARD C,** Indiana Univ Of Pa, Indiana, PA; JR; BA; Coaching Elem Bsebl Hd Coach 85-87; Coach Elem Bsktbl Asst Coach; Coach Elem Instrctnl Bsktbl Pres/Head Coach; Provost Schlr 90; Deans Lst 90; Elem Edn; Teach K-6.

**GALAT JR, JAMES R,** Kent St Univ Kent Cmps, Kent, OH; SO; BA; Philosophy; Professor.

**GALAY, EVELYN,** City Univ Of Ny Hostos Coll, Bronx, NY; SO; AAS; Coll Dscvry 88-; Phi Theta Kappa 90-; Phi Theta Kappa 90-; Equtble Hspnc Schlrshp 89-; Incm Tax Asstnc Cert Awrd; AAS; Acctg; CPA.

**GALBAN, GEORGETTE,** Saint Thomas Univ, Miami, FL; SR; BA; S Dade Stdnt Assn Pres 89-90; Hmn Rsrcs; Law Sch.**

**GALBREATH, JACQUELINE E,** Tri County Tech Coll, Pendleton, SC; Offc Systms Tchnlgy.

**GALE, DOUGLAS A,** Univ Of Tn At Martin, Martin, TN; GD; MS; Bio.

**GALE, EMILY E,** Univ Of Sc At Columbia, Columbia, SC; Sailing Clb V P 87-89; Sailing/Racing Tm; Dns Lst 88-90; Golden Key 89-90; Pres Lst 90; Kappa Delta Epsilon 89-90; Kappa Delta Epsilon; BA Univ SC 90; Early Chldhd Ed; Tchr.

**GALE, GLORIA S,** Va Highlands Comm Coll, Abingdon, VA; GD; BA; Dns Lst 90; AS Acctng 85; Cert Sprvsn 84; Acctng/ Cmptr Info Sys; CPA Acctng.

**GALE, JUANITA T,** Chattahoochee Vly St Comm Coll, Phenix City, AL; SO; BA; Gamma Beta Phi, Art Schlrshp 90; Engl.

**GALE, NICOLE L,** Univ Of Md At Eastern Shore, Princess Anne, MD; SR; BS; Sys Cncl; Rehab Stdnt Assn Sec 90-; Natl Rehab Assn; Alpha Kappa Alpha VP 89-; Embssdrs Clb 88-; Peer Cnslrs 90-; Med Ctr Vol 87-90; H Frnkln Awd Excell; Otstdng Grk Awd 89-90; Sauk Clb; VFW Aux; Rehab Svcs; Grad Schl.

**GALE JR, RICHARD C,** Springfield Tech Comm Coll, Springfield, MA; SR; AS; Hm Bldrs Assoc 90-; Alpha Nu Omega 90-; MA Air Natl Grd Sr Airmn 89-; Airmn Of Yr 90; Base Fuels Airmn Of Yr 90; Air Force Achvmnt Mdl 89; Cvl Engr.

**GALE, TRICIA R,** Univ Of Southern Ms, Hattiesburg, MS; SR; BA; Rfrmd Univ Flwshp 89-; Lakeview Cntr Teen Help Line 88; Chmbr Orch 87-88; Gamma Beta Phi 90-; Gldn Key 90-; Psi Chi 90-; Pres Schlrshp Pensacola Jr Coll 87; Psychlgy.

**GALES, KEVIN D,** Hampton Univ, Hampton, VA; SO; BA; Class Comm Serv Proj 90-; Inroads/Columbus Inc Intrnshp Nationwide Ins Co 89-; Mrktng; Corp Law.**

**GALES, MICHAEL A,** Vance Granville Comm Coll, Henderson, NC; SO; Comm Coll Comp Clb 89-; USAF 88; Bus Comp Prog; Comp Prog.

**GALEY, DAVID E,** Owensboro Comm Coll, Owensboro, KY; FR; BA; Scty Of Physics Stdnts 90; Fnce/Pre-Med; Med.

**GALEY, JENNIFER ANN,** Memphis St Univ, Memphis, TN; JR; PHARM; Pre Phrmcy Clb 88-90; Stdnt Almn Assoc 88-90; Gamma Beta Phi 88-90; Dns Lst 88-90; Pre Phrmcy; Phrmcy.

**GALFANO, GREG T,** Middle Tn St Univ, Murfreesboro, TN; SR; BS; Natl Emer Numbrng Assn 88-; Kiwanis Clb Frankln 90-; Williamsn Cnty Ems/Ema 83-, EMT Ii 83; Aerospace Admin; Law/Govt Sci.

**GALIARDI, DANIEL G,** S U N Y At Buffalo, Buffalo, NY; SR; BS; UB Fncng Clb 87-88; Bus Admin/Mktg; BA Media Stdy Flm/Video.

**GALINDO, INOCENCIO E,** Georgetown Univ, Washington, DC; SO; BA; Grgtwns Puerto Rican Assn 89-; Grgtwns Latin Amer Stdnt Assn 89-90; Stdnt Tae Kwon Do; Deans Lst 90-; IM Sftbl; Bus/Law.

**GALIONE, WILLIAM P,** Univ Of Fl, Gainesville, FL; SR; BSBA; Bus Admin Coun Pres; Bus Peer Coun 90-; Philanthropy Proj Dir 90-; Dns Lst 90; Pres Hnr Rl 88; Mktng; Law.

**GALIOTTO, JOSHUA A,** Saint Vincents Coll & Seminary, Latrobe, PA; SO; BA; Engl/Philosophy.

**GALISKI, JOHN A,** S U N Y At Buffalo, Buffalo, NY; GD; MBA; Univ Rprtng Sec 90-; Intl Bus Clb; Natl Assoc Accnts 90-; Golden Key 90-; Beta Alpha Psi Pres; Grad Asstshp Cmptr Cnslnt 90-; BS; Acctg/Intl Mgmt; CPA.

**GALLAGHER, ANNE M,** Neumann Coll, Aston, PA; FR; BA; Vlybl Tm 90; Cmnctn Arts; Pblc Rltns.

**GALLAGHER, CHRIS W,** Merrimack Coll, North Andover, MA; SR; BA; Wrtng Cntr Tutor 88-; Nwsltr Edtr 89-; Pres Ldrshp Awd; Fr J Aherne Awd Engl; Engl; Tchng.

**GALLAGHER, DAVID T,** Duquesne Univ, Pittsburgh, PA; FR; MBA; Phi Eta Sgm; Vrsty Bsbl; Acctg; CPA.

**GALLAGHER, DEBRA LYNN,** Univ Of Sc At Columbia, Columbia, SC; SR; BA; Rsdnt Hl Assoc 88-89; Carolina Cqts 86-88; Delta Gamma Rtls Chrmn 88-89; Tau Beta Sigma 86-88; Resdnt Advsr 88-90; BA 90; Elem Ed; Tchg.

**GALLAGHER, ERIC D,** Duquesne Univ, Pittsburgh, PA; JR; BM; Lambda Sigma 89-90; All-Amer Schlrs; Sound Rec Tech/ Music.

**GALLAGHER, GRETA J,** Univ Of Ga, Athens, GA; SR; BLA; GA Stdnts Lndscpe Archtctr Pres 90-; Stdnt Afflt ASLA 90-; Goldn Key 90-; Sigma Lambda Alpha; Zeta Tau Alpha 87-89; Athns Area Hmlss Shltr 90; Lndscpe Archtctr.

**GALLAGHER, JADA S,** Immaculata Coll, Immaculata, PA; SO; BA; SGA Rep 89-; Class Sec; Hstry Cncl Chmn 90-; Phi Alpha Theta Vp 90-; Immaculata 90-; Env Clb Fndr 90-; Dns Lst 89-; Frdms Fndtn Pgm Ast 90-; Hstry/Eng; Grphy/Jrnlsm.

**GALLAGHER JR, JOHN L,** Wv Univ, Morgantown, WV; JR; BS; Amer Soc Mech Engrs VP 89-; Pi Tau Sigma Treas 89-; 3m Intrnshp; Mech Eng.

**GALLAGHER, JOSEPHINE B,** Univ Of Sc At Aiken, Aiken, SC; FR; BA; Aiken Womens Clb Schlrshp; Sls Sec Invntry Cntrl Clrk Accts Pybl Clrk; Psychlgy.

**GALLAGHER, KATHLEEN A,** Le Moyne Coll, Syracuse, NY; JR; BA; Indstrl Rels Clb 88-; Bsn Clb 88-; Creative Wrtg Clb 88-; Big Sis 88-89; Chldrns Aids Network Clg Pres 89-; Hosp Mnstry 89-; IM Vlybl 88-89; IM Soccer 88-; Indstrl Rels; MA.

**GALLAGHER, MAIGHREAD A,** Rivier Coll, Nashua, NH; Diploma Cork Univ; Intl Mktng; Mktng/Sales.

**GALLAGHER, MICHELLE L,** Hudson Valley Comm Coll, Troy, NY; FR; BA; Tutoring Pgm 90-; Deans Lst 90-; Pres Lst 90-; Bowling 90-; Elem Educ.

**GALLAGHER, NOREENE I,** Andover Coll, Portland, ME; GD; BA; Andvr Coll Pres Lst 89-; Emplyd Admin Asstnts Biomed Aplctns Prtlnd Me; AS; Acctg; Audit Mngr.

**GALLAGHER, PATRICIA S,** Lesley Coll, Cambridge, MA; SO; BA; Sgn Lang Crse 90; Deans Lst 88-; Hon Cert 90; Litrcy Cntr 89; Schl For Df 89; Proj Triangl Shltrd Wrkshp 89; Mlrse Mdl Schl 90; BA 90; Biolgcl Sci; Tchng.

**GALLAGHER, SCOTT F,** Oh Wesleyan Univ, Delaware, OH; SO; BA; Botany/Mgmnt Stdnt Bd 89-; Chem Clb 89-; Newman Comm 90-; Phi Eta Sigma 90-; Microbio Lab Asst 90-; IM; Pre-Profl Sports Med; Orthopaedics.

**GALLAGHER, THERESA R,** Hillsborough Comm Coll, Tampa, FL; SO; AA; Educf Erly Chldhd Tchr.

**GALLAGHER, THOMAS F,** Mount Saint Mary Coll, Newburgh, NY; JR; BA; Acad Achv Awd; AAS Orng Cnty Comm Clg 90; Law.

**GALLAHER, KIMBERLEY A,** John C Calhoun St Comm Coll, Decatur, AL; SO; BA; Warhawk Hsts 90-; Calhoun Theatre Co 90-; Hon Forum 89-; Phi Theta Kappa Treas 90-; Kellogg Beacon Kids Clg 90-; Top Ten Calhoun Stdnts 90-; Pres/Deans Lsts 89-; AS; Sec Ed Biology; Educ.**

**GALLAND, MICHELLE,** Springfield Tech Comm Coll, Springfield, MA; SO; AS; Acctg; Bus.

**GALLANT, ALICE M,** Wilmington Coll, New Castle, DE; JR; BSN; RN With Licenes In NJ/DE; Advnc Cardiac Life Support Certfd; Amercn Heart Assoc Advncd Cardiac Life Support Instrctr; ADN Brevard Cmnty Clg Cocoa FL 85; Nrsng; RN.

**GALLANT, DARLENE,** Newbury Coll, Brookline, MA; JR; Deans Lst; Intr Dsgn.

**GALLANT, LISA M,** Hilbert Coll, Hamburg, NY; SO; AAS; Lgl Asst.

**GALLANT, MELISSA A,** Western New England Coll, Springfield, MA; SR; BA; Bhvrl Scl Sci Clb 89; Yrbk Staff 90; Peer Tutor 90; Deans Lst 89; Cmmnty Rsrces For People Wth Autism Rspte Cre Prvdr 90; Psych; Neuropsychlgy.**

**GALLANTER, TISHA,** Le Moyne Coll, Syracuse, NY; SR; MD; Blgy Clb Sec 89-90-; Krt Clb; Sfty Cmmtt; Intrmrl Cmmtt; Intrmrl Vllybll; Intrml Sccrtri Beta 88-; Vol Fir Dpt Rsc Sqd 87-; Acdmc All Amrcn 87-; Jdeans Lst 87-; Vrsty SccBS Blgy Cum Laude; Med; Dctr.

**GALLARDO, CARMEN M,** Erie Comm Coll, Buffalo, NY; FR; Math Tutor; Comp Inf Sys; Assoc Degree CIS.

**GALLASPY, KIMBERLY S,** Univ Of Southern Ms, Hattiesburg, MS; JR; BS; Clg Repblcns Chrmn 88-; Almn Clb 90; Pnhllnc Cncl Hd Rsh Cnslr; Omicron Delta Kappa Pblc Rltns; Phi Delta Rho Vp; Golden Key Sec; Delta Delta Delta Vp 88-; Gamma Beta Phi 90; Intrn US Hse Reps 89; Poli Sci; Law.

**GALLATIN, MATTHEW S,** Allegheny Coll, Meadville, PA; JR; Econ Soc 90-; Republicans 90-; Sigma Alpha Epsilon Rsh Chrmn 88-; Alden Schlr 89-90; A G Edwarsd Invstmnt/Securites Intrnshp; Lacrosse 89-; Econ; Finance.

**GALLE, STEPHEN,** Embry Riddle Aeronautical Univ, Daytona Beach, FL; FR; AS; Rddle Plyrs Drama Clb Tchncl Dir 90; Scty Of Cmmrcl Aviation Tchncns 90; A E Crandall Hook/Lddr Co 87; Ownr/Opr Galles Garage 86-89; AOS Alfred State Clg 83-85; Aviation Maint Tchnlgy.

**GALLE, STEPHEN,** Univ Of Pittsburgh, Pittsburgh, PA; SO; BA; Allghny Cnty Fncng Assn 90-; Nplnc Scty Of N Amer 90-; Crwfrd Cnty Hstrcl Scty 89-; Allghny Cnty Hstrcl Scty 90-; Hstry And Archlgy; Tchng.

**GALLEGOS, CLAY W,** Salisbury St Univ, Salisbury, MD; SO; BS; Sigma Alpha Epsilon 90-; Cmctns; Pub Rels/Brdcstng.

**GALLEGOS, NENA ALYSSA,** Univ Of Ct, Storrs, CT; SR; BS; Dietetics.

**GALLEN, CORNELIA AGNES,** Neumann Coll, Aston, PA; FR; Rcyclng Comm 90-; Comm Cltrl Divsty 90-; Hons Prog 90-; Cmmnty Svc Prog 90-; Poli Sci; Law.

**GALLEN, MARY P,** Fl St Univ, Tallahassee, FL; SR; BS; Smnl Ambssdrs 89-; Cmps Ltrcy Allnc 90-; Alpha Scty; Alpha Delta Pi 88-; Rho Chi Pnhlnc Rsh Ldr; NBC TV NY NY Intern 90; Fredom Plz Life Care Retirement Cmmnty Intern; Cmmnctns; Mrktng.

**GALLERY, LAURA M,** Central Fl Comm Coll, Ocala, FL; SO; BA; Phi Theta Kappa 88-; AA 90; Elem Edctn; Tchr.

**GALLIANO, JASON A,** Middle Tn St Univ, Murfreesboro, TN; FR; BA; Spec Evnts Comm 90-; Dns Lst; Jubrn Judy Wakim Chem Schlrshp 90-; IM Sftbl Mgr 91; Prof Chem/Physcs/Math; Scient Res Devlpmnt.

**GALLIGAN, MARGARET M,** Central Fl Comm Coll, Ocala, FL; SO; AA; Spec Ed; Tchr.

**GALLIMORE, DIXIE L,** Univ Of Cincinnati-Clrmnt Coll, Batavia, OH; FR; Psych.

**GALLIMORE, KEVIN L,** Univ Of Tn At Martin, Martin, TN; SO; BS; BSA Asst Sctmstr 82-; Eagle Sct 89; Bapt Stdnt Un Chm 90; Bio; MD.

**GALLIMORE, TERESA E,** Radford Univ, Radford, VA; SO; Zeta Tau Alpha; Acctng.

**GALLINA, JILL,** City Univ Of Ny Baruch Coll, New York, NY; SR; BA; Vol Tutor 87-; Benefits Nrsg Homes 86-88; Kiwanis Sftbl 87-88; Natl Hnr Soc; Dns Lst 87-; Mktg Mgmt; Prod Mgmt.

**GALLINGER, SHELIA B,** Univ Of West Fl, Pensacola, FL; JR; BA; Pensacola Jr Clg SGA 88-89; UWF FCTM; FTP SNEA NCTM; Phi Theta Kappa 90-; PJC Milton Dept Schlr Lib Arts 88-89; Dept Schlrshp; Outstndng Chrprsn 90; AA Pensacola Jr Clg 90; Math/Sci Educ.

**GALLIPEAU, DAVID M,** Alfred Univ, Alfred, NY; SR; BS; IEEE Sec 89-; Tae Kwon Do 90-; Alpha Chi Rho 89-; Hons Fld Speclzn; Dns Lst 90; Elec Engr; Engr.

**GALLMON, TRACY M,** Fl A & M Univ, Tallahassee, FL; SR; BS; FL Stu Ldr Assn Tchr Educ 88-; NAACP 87-; Dean Lst 87-; Ele Educ; Tchr.

**GALLO FERNANDEZ, MIGUEL M,** Univ Politecnica De Pr, Hato Rey, PR; JR; Coin Cllctr 74-; Indl Engr.

**GALLO, MICHAEL C,** City Univ Of Ny Baruch Coll, New York, NY; JR; BBA; Humn Res Mgt Soc 90; Dns Lst 88-; Barch Pres Schlrshp 88-.

**GALLO, STEPHANIE M,** Washington & Jefferson Coll, Washington, PA; FR; BA; Lit Mag 90-; Kappa Alpha Theta 90-; Cncrng Yth Afrs Sprt Grp 90-; Engl; Pblc Opinion Rsrchr.

**GALLOP, RAECITA A,** Longwood Coll, Farmville, VA; SR; SGA Treas 87-88; Un Bd Blk Cltrl Enhncmnt Chrmn 88-89; Soc Wrkrs Fed Pres 90-; Lota Phi Lambda Pres 90; Assn Blk Stdnts Cmutyh Serv Chrmn 87-88; Prince Edward Cnty Ele Intrn 90; Va Bch Soc Svcs Intrn; Soph Yr 88-89; MSN/FAMILY/CHLDRN.

**GALLOWAY, AIMEE D,** Coker Coll, Hartsville, SC; FR; BA; Elem Ed; Ed.

**GALLOWAY, ANDREA K,** Memphis St Univ, Memphis, TN; JR; BS; BACCHUS/SADD Pres 89-90; Stdnt Activities Cncl Sec 89-90; Womens Panhellenic Cncl; Mortar Bord Pres 91-; Pha Kappa Phi V Pres; Omicron Delta Kappa V Pres; Alpha Epsilon Delta; Beta Beta Beta; Alpha Gmma Delta 90; Vlntr Med Hosp; Biology; Medicine.

**GALLOWAY, CHERIE L,** Univ Of Sc At Columbia, Columbia, SC; SO; BAIS; Army Rsrvs 90-; Ed/Psychlgy; Elem Ed.

**GALLOWAY, GREGORY L,** Western Carolina Univ, Cullowhee, NC; SR; BS; Stu Sntr; Wstrn Gld Rcrtrs; Bio Clb Oa Sec; BSA Asst Sctmstr; Hnrs Pro; Stu Rep Univ Comm; Ordr Arrow BSA; Alpha Lambda Delta Frshmn Hnr Soc 88-89; Phi Kappa Phi Sr Hnr Soc VP; Mrtr Brd Hnr Soc; Sctg/Chrch; Sr Rsrch Bio Indpndnt; Bio; Univ Fclty Rsrch.

**GALLOWAY, JOSEPH S,** Roane St Comm Coll, Harriman, TN; FR; Gamma Beta Phi; Pre Medicine; Physical Therapy.

**GALLOWAY, KELLY D,** Fl St Univ, Tallahassee, FL; JR; BA; Garnet Key; Magna Cum Laude 89; Schl Vol Vernon Elem Schl 90-; LVA Lit Vol; AA Gulf Coast Cmnty Clg 89; Elem Educ.

**GALLOWAY, LORI C,** Livingston Univ, Livingston, AL; SR; BA; Var Sftbl 88-; L Club 90; All Acad GSE Sftbl 88-; All Gulf So Cnfce 88-; IM89-; Phys Ed; Intercllgte Coach.

**GALLOWAY, MELISSA R,** Tri County Tech Coll, Pendleton, SC; FR; AA; Bus; Comp Prog.

**GALLOWAY, MONICA R,** Tougaloo Coll, Tougaloo, MS; SR; BA; Stdnt Govt Assn 88-89; T C Care 89-90; Stdnt Spprt Svcs 88-; Alpha Lambda Delta 87; Tri Hi Y 87; Smrty Pnts Inc 90; Inst Schlrshp 88-90; Acad Hnrs; Chrldr 87-88; Pcychlgst.

**GALLOWAY, TIMOTHY K,** Northeast State Tech Comm Coll, Blountville, TN; FR; CERT; Automtv Tchnlgy; Auto Rcng Mech.

**GALLOWAY JR, WILLIAM M,** Memphis St Univ, Memphis, TN; SO; BS; Pro Mbr SBCCI 85-; Windy Hill Vol Fire Dept Fire Inspctr; Fire Inspctr 85-; Fire Admin; Fire Serv.

**GALLUP, NANCY G,** Atlantic Comm Coll, Mays Landing, NJ; SO; BA; Bus.

**GALPER, STEVEN A,** Fl St Univ, Tallahassee, FL; SR; BA; Sigma Alpha Mu Pldge Trnr 90-; IM Fbtl 86-87; IM Bsktbl 87-; IM Sftbl 87-; IM Soccer/Tennis/Bwlng/Bllrds 90-; Finance; Bus Invstmnts.

**GALPIN, LETITIA M,** Teikyo Post Univ, Waterbury, CT; SO; Stdnt Govt Assoc Bus Sntr 90-; Soph VP 90-; Stdnt Amb 90-; Deans Lst 89-; Rose Traurig Feml Ath Schlrshp 91; Fash Mrchndsng.

**GALUCY, ANTHONY F,** Seton Hall Univ, South Orange, NJ; SO; BA; Bsbl 90; IM Hockey 90; Deans Lst 89-; Scndry Ed/Math; Math Tchr.

**GALUSKY, JEFFREY E,** Wv Univ, Morgantown, WV; JR; BS; ROTC 89-; Crew Team 90-; Phi Kappa Phi; Aero Engr; Engr/Med.

**GALVAM, DEREK C,** Bridgewater St Coll, Bridgewater, MA; SO; Phys Ed/Rcrtn.**

**GALVAN, WALTER,** Bloomfield Coll, Bloomfield, NJ; GD; DC; Stdnt Advsry Brd Chr 88-90; Alumni Assn 89-90; Intrntl Stdnts Clb 88-90; Pre-Chiro Clb 87-90; BA; Pre-Chiro.

**GALVEZ, JENNIFER A,** Comm Coll Algny Co Algny Cmps, Pittsburgh, PA; SR; MBA; Wmn Cncrnd Fr Unbrn Chld; CPR Parents League For Emotional Adj; Chld Psych; Wrk Wth Emtnlly Dstrbd Chldrn.

**GALVIN, ANNIE D,** Bloomfield Coll, Bloomfield, NJ; Nurs Aide; Cert Drakes Bus Clg 69; Nurs.

**GALVIN, GAIL A,** Memphis St Univ, Memphis, TN; JR; BBA; Peer Mentor Prog 88-89; Dyslexia Fdtn/Memphis 88-; Gamma Beta Phi 89-; Finance; Mgmnt.

**GALVIN, GERARD M,** Clarkson Univ, Potsdam, NY; BS; Soc Acctnts 90-; Phi Theta Kappa 89-; Natl Assoc Acctnts; Natl Rcyclng Cltn; Internatl Trd Rcyclbl Wsts; AAS SUNY Canton 90; Acctng; Envrnmntl Law.

**GALVIN, KIMBERLY M,** Western New England Coll, Springfield, MA; JR; BA; Stdnt Tchng Asst 90-; Pr Advsr 90-; Rsdnce Hll Assn Pres Frnkln Hll 89-; Bhvrl Scl Sci Clb 90-; Smmr Orntn Grp Ldr 90; Psi Chi; Intrnshp Brtsde Fr Chldrn; Dns Lst; IM Vlybl; Psychlgy; Cnslng Adlscnce And Chldrn.**

**GALVIN, MICHAEL R,** Univ Of Scranton, Scranton, PA; SR; BS; Acctng Soc/Fnce Clb/Bsn Clb 87-; Delta Mu Delta 90-; Dns Lst 87-90; Pres Schlp 89-; IM Bsktbl/Wlybl/Vlybl/Sftbl; Acctng.

**GALVIN, WENDY S,** Bay Path Coll, Longmeadow, MA; SO; BA; SG 90-; RA 90-; Deans Lst 90-91; Sftbl 90-; ASSOC; Psych.

**GALYON, MINNIE S,** Roane St Comm Coll, Harriman, TN; SO; AAS; June Laing Med Rec Schlrshp 90-; Med Rec Tech.

**GAMA, MARIA F,** City Univ Of Ny Baruch Coll, New York, NY; SO; BBA; Italian Scty 89; Golden Key; Irving Weinstein Trust Fund Schlrshp; Finance.

**GAMACHE, DONNA M,** Univ Of Ri, Kingston, RI; FR; BS; Pre Law Scty 90-; Mrchng Band Clrgrd Ramettes; Phi Eta Sigma 90-; Deans List 90-; Peer Tutor 90-; Hnrs Admin Intrnshp; IM Vllybl 90-; Bsn Admin; Intrntnl Corp Law.

**GAMACHE, MARGARET E,** Marywood Coll, Scranton, PA; FR; BS; Bio; Med.

**GAMACHE, MICHELLE S,** Univ Of Nh Plymouth St Coll, Plymouth, NH; SR; BS; Ftbl Chrldng Capt 87-90; Bsktbl Chrldng Capt 87-90; Dns Lst 89; Pres Lst 90; Elem Educ; Tchg.

**GAMALIER, MOTTA LOPEZ,** Bayamon Tech Univ Coll, Bayamon, PR; SR; BA; Intl Assn Stdnts In Econ/Mgmt 88; Dns Lst 88-; AS; Acctng; Finance.

**GAMBILL, DEANA M,** Memphis St Univ, Memphis, TN; SR; ISD 89-90; Mrktng/Fshn Mrchndsng; Buyr.

**GAMBILL, KAREN D,** Middle Tn St Univ, Murfreesboro, TN; JR; BED; Gamma Beta Phi 88-; Kappa Delti Pi 89-; Hghst GPA 88-91; Dean Lst 88-; Hnr Rll 88-; Erly Chldhd Educ; Tchng.**

**GAMBINO, GINA M,** Columbus Coll Of Art & Design, Columbus, OH; FR; BA; Tchrs Awrd Schlrshp; Ads; Illstrtn.

**GAMBINO, KATHRYN J,** Villanova Univ, Villanova, PA; SO; BA; Prjct Snshn 90-; Ecnmc Soc 90-; Kappa Kappa Gamma 90; IM 90-; Ecnmcs; Law.

**GAMBLE, JASON P,** Univ Of Al At Birmingham, Birmingham, AL; SO; Amer Chem Scty; Alph Lmbd Dlt; Erly Med Schl Acptnc Pgm Un AL Med Sch 89-; Bio/Pre Med; Phys Medcn.

**GAMBLE, MELISSA J,** Lenoir Rhyne Coll, Hickory, NC; SO; BA; Stu NC Assn Edctrs VP; Dean Lst 89-; Pres Lst 89; Stu Mrshl Grad; Mddl Grds Educ; Tchng.

**GAMBLE, MISTY L,** Gadsden St Comm Coll, Gadsden, AL; SO; BA; BCM Flwshp Chrprsn 89-; A Cappella Choir 89-90; Alpha Beta Gamma; Bus; Acctnt.**

**GAMBLE, ROBERT J,** Coll Of Charleston, Charleston, SC; JR; BA; Computer Clb 90-; IM Tennis 89; Marine Biology.

**GAMBLE, ROBERT L,** Roane St Comm Coll, Harriman, TN; GD; AAS 90; Plc Sci.

**GAMBLE, STACY DE ANN,** Roane St Comm Coll, Harriman, TN; SO; BA; Bapt Stdnt Union 90; SGA Electn Cmsn 90; Schlrshp/Fincl Aid Cmt 90; Deans List 89-90; IM Bkstbl 89-90; Eng; Indstrl Eng.

**GAMBLER, NEAL J,** Univ Of South Al, Mobile, AL; SR; BS; Boy Scts Sctmstr 88-; Jr Hgh Bnd Prnts Assn Pres 88-89; Ret M Sgt/USAF; Corp VP Ocean Lns Inc 90-; AA MS Gulf Cst Comm Coll 82; AAS Comm Coll AF 88; AA Allan Hancock Coll 74; Fnnc; Entrprnr.

**GAMBLIN, RANCE M,** Ms St Univ, Miss State, MS; GD; DVM; Amer Vet Med Assn Treas 90-; Amer Anml Hosp Assn 88-; Soc Thrgnlgy 89-; Phi Kappa Phi 87-; Phi Zeta; Alpha Psi 88-; Lambda Sigma Pres 86-87; Coll Vet Med Envoys Pres 89-90; IM 88-; BS SAME 88; Vet Med; Vet Spclst.

**GAMBLIN, SHERRI R,** Univ Of Ky, Lexington, KY; JR; BA; Phi Theta Kappa; Schlr Amer; Ele Educ/Soc Bhvrl Sci; Tch.

**GAMBOA, XINIA M,** Univ Of South Al, Mobile, AL; SR; BED; Latin Amer Stdnt Assoc 90-; Spcl Olympics 89-; Special Games; Spec Educ; Multihandicapped.

**GAMBON, MARY E,** Boston Univ, Boston, MA; FR; BS; Choral Union 90-; Chmpns 90-; St Josephs Chrch Choir 88-; Jrnlsm.

**GAMBRELL, BRIAN F,** Tri County Tech Coll, Pendleton, SC; SR; AS; Andrsn Cnty Vol Fire Fghtr 1st Lt; Elctrncs; Eng.

**GAMBRELL, CELESTINE L,** City Univ Of Ny Baruch Coll, New York, NY; JR; BBA; Pstl Clrk 83-; Acctg.

**GAMBRELL, MELISSA A,** Coll Of Charleston, Charleston, SC; SR; BA; French Clb Pres 88-; Faclty Hnr Scty 89-; Phi Kappa Phi 90-; Outstndng Std Frnch Dpt; BA; French; Tchr.

**GAMBRILL, VICKIE L,** Salisbury St Univ, Salisbury, MD; SR; BA; Phi Eta Sigma; Phi Alpha Theta Pres 90-; Pi Gamma Mu; Phi Kappa Phi; History; Law.

**GAMBY, JEANNE E,** Oh St Univ At Marion, Marion, OH; FR; BED; Griffin Soc 90; Smcndctr Assmblr; Heavy Fnshr 77-90; Math; Elem Tchr.

**GAMEL, JUDITH M,** D Youville Coll, Buffalo, NY; FR; BS; Cmps Mnstry 90-; Stdnt Nurses Assc 90-; Presdntl Honors Prgrm 90-; Nursing.

**GAMES, DANIEL K,** Univ Of Southern Ms, Hattiesburg, MS; SR; Stdnt Eagle Clb; Stdnt Alumni Assoc; Sports Offcl Assoc 89-; Deans Lst Schlr 90-; Congressional Intern Cong Mike Parker 90; AD Copiah Lincoln Comm Clg 89; Political Sci; Fedl Govt.

**GAMEZ, ALVARO E,** Boricua Coll, New York, NY; SR; Chrmn Elctn Com Stdt Govt Ofcr Chrmn 90; Columbia U Intrnshp; Rdlgy Dept Adm Aid 90; ALBO RADA Grp Hmstdrs Assn Pres 89-90.

**GAMILES, DONALD S,** Bristol Univ, Bristol, TN; GD; MBA; Gamma Phi Delta; Sigma Nu; Resrch Asst OH St Univ 85-87; Air Monitoring Coord; BS Univ Of OR 85; MS Mech Engr OH St Univ 87; Bus Mngmnt.

**GAMMARO, LORAINE,** Bloomfield Coll, Bloomfield, NJ; SR; BS; A T&t Ntwrk Sys Fin Plng Speclst; Cert Inst Paralegal Stdes 83; Acctg/CPA; A T & T.

**GAMMILL, ALAN W,** Ms St Univ, Miss State, MS; SR; BA; Psychlgy Clb; Stu Advsry Commtt; Psychlgy; Clncl Exprmntl Psychlgy.

**GAMMILL, RENEE,** Ms St Univ, Miss State, MS; JR; BS; Pi Omega Pi; Deans Schlr; AAS Wood Jr College; Bus Ed; Tchng.

**GAMMON, CAROL LYNN,** Univ Of Sc At Aiken, Aiken, SC; GD; BA; Spcl Olympics; BA.

**GAMMON, MYRA D,** Univ Of Tn At Martin, Martin, TN; Undrgdt Alumni Council Pres 88-; Student Govt Congress Spkr Pro Temp 86-90; Student TN Ed Assoc 87-; Trustees 89-90; Martin Alumni Council 90-; Chi Omega Comm Chr 86-; Pocer Awd Outstndng Ldrshp; Panhellenic Serv Awd 90; Tchr.

**GAMMON, RODNEY W,** Toccoa Falls Coll, Toccoa Falls, GA; SR; BA; Sdnt Gvrnmnt Assoc Treas 89-90; Class Of 91 VP 88-89; SOAR 89; Alpha Nu Omega 88; Outstdng Yng Men Of Amer 89-90; Toccoa Optmsts Clb; Ga Mntl Hlth Cnslrs Assoc; Christian/Mssnry Allnce; Campus Cmmnty Chrch Intrnshp Pstrl Intrn 90; Im; Pstrl Mnstries; Marriage/Fam Thrpy.

**GANCI, JODI L,** York Coll Of Pa, York, PA; FR; BED; Spartan Nwspr 90-; Girls Scts Asst Ldr 90-; Peer Cnslr; Deans Lst York Coll 90-; Scndry Ed/Biology; Hs/Coll Biology Tchr.

**GANDER, DEBORAH J,** Univ Of Miami, Coral Gables, FL; SR; BS; Literary Mag Edtrl Brd; Hnr Stdnts Assn; Phi Kappi Phi; Golden Key; Sigma Tau Delta; Intrn WJHG-TV-( Production Dept; AA Gulf Coast Comm Clge 89; Advertising/Eng Majors; Law.

**GANDHI, ASHESH J,** Mercer Univ Schl Of Pharm, Atlanta, GA; SR; PHARM; Amer Pharm Assoc 89-; Amer Soc/Hosp Pharm 90-; Rho Chi Hnr Soc/Gamma Lpha Chptr 91-; Sr Intrst Comm 89-; Vol Meals On Whls Prog 89-; Undrgrd Rsrch Schlrshp $3600; Top 20% Rnkng In Cls 89-; Dean List 89-; Pharmacy; Clinical/Grad Study.

**GANDHI, MD FALGUNI,** City Univ Of Ny City Coll, New York, NY; SO; BS; Cdcs Scty 90; N Stp Prjct Ornttn Ldr; Pr Acad Advsr Fr Acad Advsng; Fr Dns Rcptn 90-; Blgy Chem; Med.

**GANDHI, NINA M,** Univ Of Md Baltimore Prof Schl, Baltimore, MD; JR; BS; Lyla Cmmtrs Assn 90; Indn Clb 90; Amer Phrmctcl Assn 90-; Rho Chi Rcgntn Cert 90-; MD Dstngshd Hnr 88-; Vldctrn 88; Dns Lst 88-; Phrmcy.

**GANDOLFO, LUCILA,** The Boston Conservatory, Boston, MA; FR; CD; Intl Stdnt Clb 90-; Stge Mk-Up Artst 85-86; Musicl Theatr; Prfrmr.

**GANDY, JAMES R,** Wv Univ, Morgantown, WV; JR; BSEM; Scty Of Mng Eng Pres; Tau Kappa Epsilon Chpln; Mng Eng; Mng Eng.

**GANDZIARSKI, CATHERINE A,** Duquesne Univ, Pittsburgh, PA; SR; BSBA; AMA 89; Sharp Pgm Vol 87-89; Beta Alph Phi 89-; Alpha Mu Alpha; Alpha Sgm Tau Pldge Dir 90; Duquesne Univ Schlr 87-; IM Vlybl/Sftbl 90-; Mktg.

**GANESAN, SANDHYA,** Mercer County Comm Coll, Trenton, NJ; SO; AS; Hist Clb 90; Yoga Clb; Bus Admin; CPA.

**GANESHAN, VINAY S,** Howard Univ, Washington, DC; JR; BACH; Indian 87-88; Natl Assoc Org Free Hlth Central Georgetown Guyana S Amer; US Pirg Camp; Dipl Univ Guyana 88; Arch/Bldg Georgetown; Architecture; Designer.

**GANGADHAR, NARENDRA,** Univ Of The Dist Of Columbia, Washington, DC; JR; BBA; Amer Acctg Assoc 89-; Acctg Clb 90-; AA San Fernando Tech Inst Trinidad W I 87; AAT Assoc Acctg Tech London Engl 87; Acctg; CPA.

**GANGEMI, STEPHANIE L,** Bowling Green St Univ, Bowling Green, OH; SO; BFD; Sport Mgmt Alliance 90; Le Club 8 89-; Alpha Lamda Delta 89-; Sport Mgtm; Graduate Schl/Hosp Work.

**GANGI, KATHRYN E,** Fl International Univ, Miami, FL; FR; Cmptr Sci; Prog.

**GANGLOFF, MARYANN M,** S U N Y Coll At Fredonia, Fredonia, NY; JR; BA; Stdnt Libry Advsry Cncl; Uppr Cls Buddy 90-; Stdnt Emplyee Of Reed Libry 89-; Intrnshp Ofc Of Clg Afrs; Clg Ambsdr 90-; Engl; Publc Rltns Practitnr.

**GANGULY, SAMRAT,** Yale Univ, New Haven, CT; FR; BS; Scntfc Mgzn Pblshr 90-; New Haven Hosp Stdnt Vol Emrgncy Rm 90-; Frnds Israel 90-; Bsn/Econ Frm 90-; Smr Rsrch Pgm Yale Blgy; Intrnshp Rose Hse Hmls Shltr Vol Cord 85-; Yale Stdnt Vol Hnr; IM Tbl Tns 90-; Mlclr Biophys/Biochmstry; Rsrch.

**GANIM, GREGORY M,** Cornell Univ Statutory College, Ithaca, NY; SO; BS; Stdnt Hlth Alliance Comm Chrmn 89-; Res Hl Govt Sen 90-; Ho-Nun-De-Kah; Hlth Ctr Med Asst Stdnt Coord; EMS 90-; IBM Watson Mem Schlr 89-; Dns Lst; Bio/Pre-Med; Med.**

**GANN, JO ANN,** Northwest Al Comm Coll, Phil Campbell, AL.

**GANN, LESLIE A,** Itawamba Comm Coll, Fulton, MS; SO; BA; Elem Ed; Tchng.

**GANNON, ELLA A,** Oh Univ-Southern Cmps, Ironton, OH; GD; MBA; Prnt Advsry Com 89-90; Allied-Sgnl Sprvsr Acctg 80-; AS 85; BBA 90; Bus; Educ.

**GANNON JR, JAMES S,** Temple Univ, Philadelphia, PA; JR; BS; Pa Phrmctcl Assn 89-; Amer Phrmctcl Assn 90-; By Scts Asst Sctmstr 87-; Gamma Beta Phi 87-88; Phi Eta Sigma 87-88; Phrmcy.

**GANNON, KELLEY J,** Univ Of Ky, Lexington, KY; SR; BA; Outstndng Srvc Intrhshp Cert; Soc Wrk; Ph D/Scl Wrk.

**GANNON, RACHEL A,** Bunker Hill Comm Coll, Boston, MA; FR; BA; Hnrs Prgm; Hstry; Law.

**GANSAR, PHILIP A,** Fl International Univ, Miami, FL; SR; BED; Miami Mnrlgcl/Lpdry Gld 90-; LA Gem/Mnrl Socty 74-90; GPAA 89-; Elem Educ; Tchr.

**GANSMAN, LAURA A,** Memphis St Univ, Memphis, TN; SR; BA; Psychlgy.

**GANSTER, PETE E,** Wv Univ, Morgantown, WV; SR; BS; SAE 88-; ASME Treas 88-; Pi Tau Sigma 89-; Mech Eng; Auto Eng Fld.

**GANT, A ROBIN,** Anne Arundel Comm Coll, Arnold, MD; BA; Homeowners Assc Pres; Architecture/Intr Dsgn.

**GANT, HAZEL J,** Middle Tn St Univ, Murfreesboro, TN; SR; BS; Spec Educ; Tchr.

**GANT, TAMMY L,** Southern Coll Of Tech, Marietta, GA; JR; BS; Gspl Chr 88-89; Phi Theta Kappa 88-; AA 90; Civil Engnrng Tech.

**GANTT, AMY M,** Catawba Valley Comm Coll, Hickory, NC; SR; AAS; Coop Educ Pgm 90-; Mktg/Rtlng.

**GANTT JR, CHARLES E,** S U N Y Coll Of A & T Morrisvl, Morrisville, NY; SR; AAS; Deans Lst 90; Acad Achiev Cert; IM Bsktbl; Indvdl Stds; Psych.

**GANZ, JODI L,** Marywood Coll, Scranton, PA; GD; MSW; Natl Assn Soc Wrk 88-; Pi Gamma Mu 90-; Alpha Delta Mu Sec 90-; BSW 90; Awrd Excllnce/Soc Wrk Hon Mntn 90; Soc Wrk; Mntl Hlth Fld.

**GANZ, NANCY B,** Fl International Univ, Miami, FL; BS; AA Broward Comm Coll 85; Elem Ed.

**GANZAK, ANTHONY P,** Comm Coll Algny Co Algny Cmps, Pittsburgh, PA; SO; BS; SGA Pres 88-89; Bd Of Pblctn 88-89; Bd Of Athltcs 88-89; Westinghouse Bettis Plnt Cad Dsgnr; AS; Elec Engr; Engr/Politics.

**GARAY, MARIA C,** Caribbean Univ, Bayamon, PR; JR; BA; AS 83; Math; CPA.

**GARBER, BRUCE K,** Barry Univ, Miami, FL; Amblnc Svce Rescue/Tactcl Tm 86-88; Sigma Theta Tau; CPR Instrctr 83-89; Amer Heart Assn Advncd Crdc Lf Sprrt Crtfd 83-; BS Rcrtn IN Univ 76; IN Cert Prmdc Blmngtn Hosp 86-; BS Nrsng 90; RN.

**GARBER, LYNN R,** Muskingum Coll, New Concord, OH; FR; BED; Chrl Socty 90-; Cntrbd Coffeehouse 90; FAD Socl Clb; Muskingum Coll Vol 90; Schlrshp Day 1st Year Awd Dstngshd Schlr Limited To Highest 5%; Elem Educ.

**GARBER, MICHAEL A,** Bridgewater Coll, Bridgewater, VA; SO; BA; Swm Tm 89-; IM Ftbll Bsktbll Sftbll 89-; Acctg; CPA.

**GARBER-TOLLES, BETH A,** Defiance Coll, Defiance, OH; FR; MBA; Dean Lst 90-; Bus; Fnncl Advsr.

**GARBONOLA, LYNETTE A,** Univ Of New Haven, West Haven, CT; JR; BA; Sftbl 88-; Bus Admin; Law.

**GARCEAU, GRETCHEN,** Colby Sawyer Coll, New London, NH; SR; BS; RA 88-90; Athl Trng Intern 90; Athl Trnr 88-; Sport Sci; Athl Trng.

**GARCES, MONICA,** Univ Of Miami, Coral Gables, FL; JR; BS; Alpha Lambda Delta Phi Eta Sigma 89-90; Alpha Epsilon Delta 90-; Hnrs Students Assoc 89-; Provosts Hnr Roll 89-; Deans List 89-; Biology; Medicine.

**GARCIA BASSAT, JESSIKA,** Inter Amer Univ Pr San German, San German, PR; JR; Amer Mrktg Assc Vp 90-; Eta Gamma Delta; Acad Exclnc Awd Inter Amer Univ 89-90; Ovrll Outstndg Prfrmnc Awd 90-; Mrktg; Bus.**

**GARCIA CRUZ, VALERIE,** Inter Amer Univ Pr Hato Rey, Hato Rey, PR; JR; Grp Of Hnr 88-; Math/Biol.

**GARCIA ESPINOSA, FILIBERTO,** Inter Amer Univ Pr Hato Rey, Hato Rey, PR; FR; Med.

**GARCIA FLORES, MARGARITA,** Univ Del Turabo, Gurabo, PR; JR; Magna Cum Laude; Engl; Educ.

**GARCIA MARTINEZ, EDWIN JAVIER,** Univ Politecnica De Pr, Hato Rey, PR; FR; ASSO; Bayamon Minor Bsbl Lgs 87f Twins Bsbl Lgs 87f Vagueros Bsbl Tm; Phi Sigma Alfa 90; Trophys Most Valuable Plyr 87; Indtl Engrg 89; Math; Industrial Engrg.

**GARCIA ORENGO, CARMEN D,** Inter Amer Univ Pr San German, San German, PR; SR; Psychlgy Assn 90-; Yth Cntr Vol; Spec Acdmc Pre-Med Awrd 90-; Psychlgy.

**GARCIA RAMOS, FERDINAND D,** Univ Of Pr At Rio Piedras, Rio Piedras, PR; JR; Dancers Grp 90-; Voice Festival 90; Natl Collegiate Arch/Dsgn Awd; Architecture; Int Dsgn.**

**GARCIA ROSARIO, BRENDA Y,** Inter Amer Univ Pr Hato Rey, Hato Rey, PR; FR; Hstry/Engl/Spnsh/Sci; Pblcty.

**GARCIA ROSARIO, LUZ P,** Univ Of Pr Medical Sciences, San Juan, PR; GD; MBA; Messangers Christ Juvenil Assoc Latin AM Cncl 87-; NSSLHA 89-; Acdc Exln Cert 90; BA SLT 90; Spch Lang Pthlgy.**

**GARCIA SANCHEZ, HECTOR,** Univ Politecnica De Pr, Hato Rey, PR; SO; Zeta Phi Beta; Indus Eng.

**GARCIA, AGNELY M,** Univ Of Pr Medical Sciences, San Juan, PR; GD; BA; Rho Chi Gamma Eta Chptr; Cert Merit Phrmctcl Tech/Phar 86; Clg Phrmcts PR; Cert Merit Clncl Phrmcy Prctc 87; Bchlr Degree Phrmcy Hnr Enrlmnt Otstndng Stdnt 87; Enrlld Mstr Degree Tower Industrial Phrmcy Hghst Hnr Stdnt; Reg Phrmcst; Industrial Phrmcy; Phrmcy.**

**GARCIA, ALBA I,** Syracuse Univ, Syracuse, NY; SO; BA; Tnns Clb ; Peer Adv Pgm; Dns Lst; Fnce/Ecnmcs; MBA.**

**GARCIA, AMARILIS L,** Inter Amer Univ Pr Hato Rey, Hato Rey, PR; SR; BBABA; Ntl Assoc Of Accntnts 89; Rosa-Bell Alumni Assoc VP Treas 87; United Fnd Ways 88; MDA Clb 80; Tutor In Accntng For U Stdnts; Accntng/Fnce; CPA CMA MBA.

**GARCIA, ANNETTE L,** Midlands Tech Coll, Columbia, SC; JR; BA; Rsprtry Thrphy Clb; Pres Hnrs Rl 90; Dean Hnr Rl 89-; Amer Red Crss; Chldrns Hlth Fair Vol 90-; Rsprtry Trpy.

**GARCIA, ANTONIO P,** Commonwealth Coll, Norfolk, VA; AA; Kghts Columbus 2nd Deg 85-; Marine Corps Lgue Ouantico VA; Yng Marines Mcl Quantico Drl Inst 87-88; Fstr Prnts Chld Cr Brley Thompsn Inc; Ret Marine; Lgl Admn; Paralegl.

**GARCIA, ARLETTE I,** Univ Of Miami, Coral Gables, FL; SO; MBA; Hon Stdnts Assn 89-; Deans Lst 89-90; Pres Hon Roll 90-; Acctg.

**GARCIA, ARTHUR,** Glassboro St Coll, Glassboro, NJ; SR; BA; RCA Elec Engr 47-89; BSEE Kansas State Univ Manhattan Ks 47; Foreign Lang; Engr Abrd.

**GARCIA, BRENDA M,** Univ Of Pr At Rio Piedras, Rio Piedras, PR; FR; BA; Air Force ROTC; Stdnt/Work/Study Excell Certif; Engl; Nrs.

**GARCIA, CARLOS L,** Miami Dade Comm Coll South, Miami, FL; SO; Bus Admin; CPA.

**GARCIA, CARMEN E,** Georgetown Univ, Washington, DC; JR; BSBA; PR Stdnts Accn Sec 88-; Ltn Am Stdnt Assn 88-; Chn Am Stdnts Assn Pub Rel Rep 89-; Bus Adm Mntrs Prog Coord 90-; Awd Chs Mnhttn Bk Internshp; Dns Lst 89-90; 1st Hons 90; Fin/Intl Mgmt; Bnkg.

**GARCIA, CARMEN T,** Barry Univ, Miami, FL; SO; BA; Peace Studies Com Stdnt Rep 90-; Barry-Soviet Exchng Cncl Pres 90-; Hon Stdnts Assn Fresh Rep/Sec 90-; Sthrn Rgnl Hon Cncl Stdnt Rep; Phi Alpha Delta Scl Chr 90-; Cmps Mnstry-Echrstc Mnstr 90-; Peer Advsr; Intl Studies; Intl Law.

**GARCIA, DANA H,** Hillsborough Comm Coll, Tampa, FL; SR; ASN; Cmnty Scl Orgnztns; Sno; Cvl Srvc Brd Vc Chrmn 84-90; RE Brkr 74-; Nrsng; Msn.

**GARCIA, DONNA M,** Glassboro St Coll, Glassboro, NJ; JR; BA; Phi Theta Kappa 89-; Am Cancer Soc 87-; Perm Pres Lst 90; Pres Lst 88-90; Marlton Rec Cncl Soccer Coach 88; Rice Sch PTA 90-; Agent Phys Asst; AA Camden Cnty Coll 90; Hist/Edn; Tchr.

**GARCIA, ELSA,** City Univ Of Ny Baruch Coll, New York, NY; GD; MBA; Untd Mthdst Chrch; AA La Guardia C C 85; Intrnatl Fnce.

**GARCIA, FELIX,** City Univ Of Ny Bronx Comm Col, Bronx, NY; SR; BA; Dns Lst 88-91; Phi Theta Kappa 90-; 136th St Bsktbl Shootout; Vol Ref Svc 90; New York Esquires/Just Say No To Drugs Bsktbl Clinic 90; Bsn Admin.

**GARCIA, JENNIFER C,** Univ Of South Al, Mobile, AL; GD; BA; Zeta Tau Alpha Pres 87-; Educ/Erly Chldhd; Tchr.

**GARCIA, LEILA E,** Univ Of Pr At Rio Piedras, Rio Piedras, PR; SO; BED; Dfndrs Chrstn Faith Chrch; Tehilin; Indus Pharm.

**GARCIA, LINDA D,** Albertus Magnus Coll, New Haven, CT; SO; BA; Radio Sta Engr/DJ; Natl Dnc Exer Instrctr 90-; Trng Assn; Asst To Cntrlf Univ 90-; AA; Cmmnctns; Radio/TV.

**GARCIA, LOURDES M,** Inter Amer Univ Pr Hato Rey, Hato Rey, PR; SO; BBA; Assn Georgia Fos En Act 90-; Assn Est De Con 90-; Pgrm Hnr; Assn Impedides 90-; Accntng; Bsn Admin.

**GARCIA, LUIS H,** City Univ Of Ny City Coll, New York, NY; SO; BS; Aspr Hspnc Clb PR 89-; Cty Clg Gay Std Govt Sntr 90-; Aspr NY Awd; LPN USAF Schl; Nutrition.

**GARCIA, MARIA JOAO NOBRE LOPES,** Comm Coll Algny Co Algny Cmps, Pittsburgh, PA; AS; Librn Arqvst 85-88; Asst Pub Rel 88-90; Sec Educ 78; Gen Acctg Crs 84; Libry Docmntn Crs 85; Mktg Mgmt.

**GARCIA, MARIA P,** Allegheny Coll, Meadville, PA; SR; BA; Otng Clb 87-89; Union Latina Co Fndr Drctr Actvts Pblc Rltns 88-; Frnch Clb 87-; Phi Sigma Eta 90-; Eta Gamma Delta 89-; Alden Schlr 89-; Chmbr Commerce Paris France 89-; French Intrntnl Stds; Corp Law.

**GARCIA, MAYRA L,** Mount Holyoke Coll, South Hadley, MA; FR; MBA; Stdnt Govt Rep 90-; Law Soc/Mock Trial Tm Witness 90-; La Unidad 90-; Hamilton Lrng Ctr Tutor 90-; Intl Rel; Law.

**GARCIA, MELANIE,** City Univ Of Ny Baruch Coll, New York, NY; SO; Accntng Soc VP; Nrsng Hme; Accntncy.

**GARCIA, MELINDA,** Univ Of Miami, Coral Gables, FL; SR; BBA; Mrktng Bus.

**GARCIA, MERCEDES,** City Univ Of Ny Baruch Coll, New York, NY; SR; BBA; Gldn Key 90-; AS Hrtnl Clg 87; Cmptr Sci; Prgrmmr.

**GARCIA, MIGNON L,** Wagner Coll, Staten Island, NY; SO; BS; Un Asian Leo Clb Staten Isl V P 89-; Stdnt Actvts Bd 89-; Alethea 90-; Philippine Jr Sci League 88-89; Chem; Med.

**GARCIA, MIRELLA,** Fl International Univ, Miami, FL; SR; BA; Ele Educ; Ele Tchr.

**GARCIA, NELSON,** Univ Of Miami, Coral Gables, FL; SO; BS; Blgy Clb; Alpha Epsilon Delta Hstrn; Sigma Chi Phlnthrpy Chr 90; Cir K Internatl; Blgy; Med.

**GARCIA, RICARDO,** Univ Of Miami, Coral Gables, FL; SR; BFA; Intrnshp Chnl 10 WPLG ABC Miami; AA Miami Dade Comm Coll 88; Grphc Arts; Dsgnr.

**GARCIA, RICARDO L,** Univ Of Pr At Rio Piedras, Rio Piedras, PR; JR; MD; Hosp Vol; Clg Hon List; Sci; MD.

**GARCIA, ROXANNE KAYE,** City Univ Of Ny Baruch Coll, New York, NY; SR; BA; Deans List 90; Salvation Army Spnsr 88-; TA State Ed Dprtmnt 89-; Mrktng W/Spclztsm Advrtsng Sclgy Hmn Ed Tchrc.

**GARCIA, SAUDY E,** Univ Politecnica De Pr, Hato Rey, PR; FR; BA; Leos Club Sec 87-; Engr.

**GARCIA, SUSANA,** Saint Thomas Univ, Miami, FL; FR; BA; By Scts Am Treas 89-; Comm Mbr; Sci; Cvl Eng.**

**GARCIA, VIVIAN P,** Fl International Univ, Miami, FL; SR; BA; NAEYC 88-; Phi Kappa Phi 90-; Kappa Dlt Pi 90-; Emps Exclnc Mc Kngiht Schrlshp 88; Cert Achvmnt MDCC 88; Schlstc Achvmnt Erly Chldhd Ed 79; Bnkng Admn/Trng; Ownr Lrng Child Dvlpmnt Ctr 86-; Erly Chldhd Ed; Elem/Erly Chldhd Ed Tchr.**

**GARCIA, WILLIAM A,** Fayetteville St Univ, Fayetteville, NC; JR; BS; Phy Educ Mjrs Clb Pres 90-; U S Sccr Fdrtn Ref 85-; NC Athltc Offcls Assc Sr 85-; AAS Fayetteville Tech Cmnty Clg 87; Hlth/Phy Educ/Psychlgy; Tchg.

**GARCIA-DU QUESNE, ELENA M,** Fl International Univ, Miami, FL; SR; Chrldr 87; Math Educ; Teacher.

**GARCIA-MELENDEZ, JORGE L,** Univ Politecnica De Pr, Hato Rey, PR; SR; BA; Lnd Surv/Mapg; Bsn/Surv MA.

**GARD, CYNTHIA R,** Owensboro Comm Coll, Owensboro, KY; SO.

**GARDEN, TARA L,** Bethany Coll, Bethany, WV; FR; BA; Frnch Clb 90-; Soc Of Prfsnl Jrnlsts 90-; Englsh; Law Schl.

**GARDENHIRE, BARBARA ANNE,** Glassboro St Coll, Glassboro, NJ; JR; BA; Pol Sci Club Model UN 90-; NJPIRG Orgnzr 88-; Phi Theta Kappa 88-90; Pi Sigma Alpha; Amnsty Intrntl 90-; NAACP; Insprtnl Gospel Choir 90-; AA Cumbrland Cnty Clg 90; Pol Sci/Hon/Womens Studies; Law.**

**GARDENHOUR, KELLY A,** Fl International Univ, Miami, FL; SR; BS; Univ Cntrl Fla Mrchng Bnd 86-88; Ocptnl Thrpy Clb 89-; Pi Theta Epsilon Pres 90-; Phi Kappa Phi 90-; Omicron Delta Kappa; Cnvctn 86; AA Univ Cntrl Fla 88; BS; Hlth; Ocptnl Thrpy.

**GARDINER, BIRDETTE E,** Smith Coll, Northampton, MA; GD; MSW; Caduceus Soc City Clg NY 88-89; Psych Clb City Clg NY 88-89; Stdnt Org Trtmnt Seq Repr 90-; Search Comm City Clg NY 90; BA City Univ NY 90; Clncl Scl Wrk; DSW Scl Welfare/Resrchr.

**GARDINER, KAREN L,** City Univ Of Ny Baruch Coll, New York, NY; JR; BBA; Acctng; CPA.

**GARDINI, LYNN,** City Univ Of Ny City Coll, New York, NY; BA.

**GARDINO, DEIRDRE E,** Radford Univ, Radford, VA; SR; BBA; AMA; Phi Beta Lambda 88-90; Sigma Kappa Corres Sec 88-; Strtgc Plnng Comm Stdnt Rep Mrktng; Mrktng.

**GARDNER, ANNE E,** Univ Of Sc At Columbia, Columbia, SC; SO; BA; Sigma Tau Delta; NEA/SCEA; Engl/Scndry Educ; Adult Educ.

**GARDNER, ARIC B,** Fl A & M Univ, Tallahassee, FL; FR; BS; Epcn Fshn Exprnc 90-; NASA Schlrs Assoc 90-; Prsdntl Schlrs Assoc 90-; Phi Eta SigmaNASA Schlr Intern 90-; Vrsty Bsbll 90-; Physcks; Med.

**GARDNER, BLONDA C,** Bowie St Univ, Bowie, MD; SR; BS; Ed Clb 89-; Chr 89; Cncrt Bnd 89-90; Liason NAEO Hghr Ed 90; Ltr Rcgntn Acad Mrt 90; Elem Ed; Tchr.

**GARDNER, BRUCE W,** Univ Of Sc At Columbia, Columbia, SC; SO; BA; Natl Assn Advncmnt Of Colored People 89-; Phi Theta Kappa 86-; Deans Hon Lst 90; Religion; Ministry.

**GARDNER, CARLA D,** Fisk Univ, Nashville, TN; SO; BS; Hlth Car Clb Nwspr Stf Yrbk Stf; Cncrnd Stdnts Fisk Unvrsty NAACP; Track; Biology; Orthopedics.

**GARDNER, CARYN L,** Coll Of Charleston, Charleston, SC; SR; BS; Stdnt Cncl Excep Chldrn VP 89-; Kappa Alpha Theta 90-; Dist Fac Hnrs Lst 89-; Hnrs Lst 89-90; BS; Elem Educ.

**GARDNER, CHARLES A,** Morehouse Coll, Atlanta, GA; FR; BA; Pre-Law/Ecnmcs; Law.

**GARDNER, CHARRISA R,** Al St Univ, Montgomery, AL; SR; BS; SOAR 89-; Alpha Kappa Mu; Alpha Kappa Alpha 90-; Pres Schlrshp 88-; Schlrshp NEA; Erly Chldhd Educ; Day Care Cntr Ownr/Educ.

**GARDNER, DEANA L,** Univ Of Ky, Lexington, KY; JR; BA; Psi Chi VP; Alpha Lambda Delta 89-90; Rsrch Asst Psych; Psych; Cnslng.

**GARDNER, DENISE N,** Al St Univ, Montgomery, AL; FR; BS; Pre Med; Pediatrics.

**GARDNER, DIANE I,** S U N Y At Buffalo, Buffalo, NY; JR; BS; Phi Eta Sigma Pres 89-; Acctg Assoc 90-; Deans Lst 88-; 5 Yr MBA Pgm; Acctg; Private Acctg/Law/Taxes.

**GARDNER, ELIZABETH S,** Fayetteville St Univ, Fayetteville, NC; SR; BS; Alpha Kappa Mu 90-; Beta Kappa Chi; Delta Sigma Theta 67; Acad Schlrshp; Advsry Cncl Voc Ed Cumberland Co Comm Chr 87-; Mdtr Dispute Rsltn Ctr 90-; Drg/Alchl Cnslr Ft Bragg NC 76-; Clncl Psych.

**GARDNER, ETHEL R,** Nc Agri & Tech St Univ, Greensboro, NC; SO; BS; ALOBEAM Acctg Clb 90-; NABA 90-; Alpha Lambda Delta 90-; Delta Sigma Theta; Thurgood Marshall Schlrshp 89-; GAO Intern; Acctg.**

**GARDNER, FAITH H,** Mayland Comm Coll, Spruce Pine, NC; Early Chldhd; Day Cr Tchr.

**GARDNER, GIANNA S,** Univ Of Sc At Columbia, Columbia, SC; SO; BA; Minority Stdnt Org Secr 89-; Bsn Clb Secr 90-; SGA; Gamma Beta Phi; Myrick Law Firm Secr Awd; Ofc Adm; Secr Profiency.

**GARDNER, JAMES ERIC,** Univ Of Tn At Martin, Martin, TN; JR; BS; Hnrs Prog 88-89; Vrsty Gymnstcs Ltr 88-90; Chrldg 90; Chem; Med/Orthpdc Srgn.

**GARDNER, JAMES M,** Va Commonwealth Univ, Richmond, VA; GD; MD; Chrstn Med/Dntl Soc Exec Com 89-90; Am Acdmy Fmly Prctc; Am Med Assn; Appalachian Trail Cnfrnc; Prsbytrn Chr; Alpha Omega Alpha; Phi Beta Kappa; Robert C Bryan Prize; A H Robins Schlrshp; Sidney Barham Schlrshp; IM Bsktbl/Sftbl; Med.

**GARDNER, JEFFREY R,** Hartwick Coll, Oneonta, NY; JR; BA; SADD Pres 88-90; Bsktbl Statstcn Scr Kppr 88-; Play Fair 89-; Amer Cancer Soc 88-; Otsego Cnty Stop-DWI 88-; Natl Soccer Hall Of Fame Vol 88-; Mngmt Acctg; CPA.**

**GARDNER, JO ANNE,** Newbury Coll, Brookline, MA; FR; Med Nrsng.

**GARDNER, KRISTEN R,** Univ Of Akron, Akron, OH; JR; BED; Gldn Ky; Elem Educ; Tchng.**

**GARDNER, LANCE R,** Bethel Coll, Mckenzie, TN; JR; BS; Bus Clb 90-; Psychlgy Clb 88-90; Bob Hope Hon Schlrshp 88-; Bus Admin; Mktg.**

**GARDNER, LEO M,** Va St Univ, Petersburg, VA; FR; BA; Business; Marketing.

**GARDNER, MICHAEL J,** De Tech & Comm Coll At Dover, Dover, DE; SR; BA; Knghts Col 3rd Deg 90; Stdnt Sprt Svcs 88-; Humn Svc Org 89-; Quadrplgc Prshng B A Deg After Accdnt; Humn Svcs; Cnslng.

**GARDNER, MICHELLE A,** Western New England Coll, Springfield, MA; JR; BA; Behvrl Soc Sci Clb 88-; Unit/Mutually Equal Clb 88-; Peer Advsr; Summer Orntatn Grp Ldr 90; Stdnt Tchng Asst 90-91; K Gordon Awd 89-90; Psygy Mgmt; Human Rsrce Mgmt.**

**GARDNER, PEGGY L,** Georgetown Coll, Georgetown, KY; SR; BS; Beta Beta Beta Prsdnt 89-; Alpha Lambda Delta 88-; Beta Beta Beta Upsilon Chptr 88-89; Biology Dptmnt Otstndng 89-90; Biology.

**GARDNER, RANDI K,** Bethel Coll, Mckenzie, TN; SO; BA; Crtv Wrtng Intrst Leag 90-; Chess Clb 90-; Gamma Beta Phi 90-; Hnr Roll 90-; Deans Lst 89-90; Wrtng; Author.

**GARDNER, ROBIN E,** S U N Y Coll Of Tech At Alfred, Alfred, NY; FR; AAS; Nrsng Asst; RN.

**GARDNER JR, RONALD D,** Md Inst Coll Of Art, Baltimore, MD; SR; BFA; Photo Clb; BFA; Fine Arts; Illstrn Dsgn.

**GARDNER, ROSE A,** Univ Of Southern Ms, Hattiesburg, MS; JR; BA; Phi Theta Kappa; AA Jones Cnty Jr Clge 90; Science; Teach.

**GARDNER, SCOTT C,** Fayetteville St Univ, Fayetteville, NC; SR; BS; Magna Cum Laude; AAS Fayetteville Tech Comm Coll 89; Crmnl Jstce; Fed Law Enfrcmnt.

**GARDNER, STPEHEN D,** Va Commonwealth Univ, Richmond, VA; JR; BA; US Army Cavalry Sct; Csc 2nd Bn 1st Inf FC Ft Lewis WA 84-86; Englsh; Tchr.

**GARDNER, TARA L,** Cheyney Univ Of Pa, Cheyney, PA; JR; BA; Ambsdrs Clb 90; Alpha Kappa Mu Prsdnt; Deans Lst; Acadmc Exclnc; Mt Calvary Bptst Chrch Schlrshp; Accntng; CPA.

**GARDNER, TOBIAS J,** Morehouse Coll, Atlanta, GA; SR; BS; Math Clb Prmntl Dir 87-; Ntn Scty Blck Eng 87-; GM Tchncl Clb Fndr 90-; GM Corp Cntrl Fndry Div Advnc Mfg Eng 88-; Blue Crss Blue Shld Oprtns Adt; Math Nchncl Eng; Eng Ed.

**GARDNER-JOHNSON, ANGELA L,** Fayetteville St Univ, Fayetteville, NC; SR; BS; Crmnl Just Clb 90-; Alpha Kappa Mu Miss AKM 90-; Schlrshp Awd; Crmnl Just Acad Awd 90-; Acad Schlrshp 87-; Crmnl Just; Law.**

**GAREE, TRACY D,** Hiwassee Coll, Madisonville, TN; SO; BS; Drm Clb 89-; Coll Bwl 90-; Yrbk Stff 90-; Phi Theta Kappa 89-; Grl Scts Amrc Asst LdrAYSO Cch 88-89; AA; Sci; Scndry Ed.

**GARELLI, JOHANNA,** Fl International Univ, Miami, FL; JR; BS; Soc Wmn Engrs Secr 90-; Amer Soc Mech Engrs Treas 90-; FL Engr Soc V P-Elect 90-; Hospice Org Vol 89-; Early Admissions Broward Cmnty Clg 87-88; AA 89; Mech Engr.

**GAREY, RACHEL S,** Tn Temple Univ, Chattanooga, TN; JR.

**GARFIELD, KELLY A,** Teikyo Post Univ, Waterbury, CT; SR; BS; AMA 90; Mrktng.

**GARFIELD, SCOTT M,** Elmira Coll, Elmira, NY; SR; Dorm Council VP 89-90; Busn Club; Jaybird/Mais Incorp Sales/Mktng 89-90; Ice Hockey/Golf; MBA; Busn Mgt.

**GARFUNKEL, STEVEN F,** Barry Univ, Miami, FL; SO; BA; Brdcst Cmmnctn; Sprtscstr.

**GARGUILO, STEPHANIE F,** S U N Y Coll Of Tech At Frmgdl, Farmingdale, NY; FR; AS; Off Mngmnt; Bus.

**GARINO, ANNE BENEDICTE,** Christopher Newport Coll, Newport News, VA; SR; BA; Modrn Jazz Danc Paris Amstrdm Std 89-90; Assn Intl Stdnts Montplr 88-89; Tellr Banque Natl Paris 86-90; Cpy Wrtr Adv Agncy Paris 89; Copy Wrtr Jr Adv Mktg; BA 97; Busn; Advrtsng.

**GARLAND, ADAM LENEAR,** Southern Coll Of Tech, Marietta, GA; JR; SGA 89; Cmps Crsde Fr Chrst 89; Tau Alpha Pi 90-; Schlrshp Grn Vlly Glf Clb 88; Coop Sthrn Co Srvcs Inc 89-; Appld Comp Sci Math; Comp Prgrmmr.

**GARLAND, ANNE L,** Portland School Of Art, Portland, ME; JR; BEA; ME Rgstry Intrprtrs Df 85-; Natl Rgstry Intrprtrs Df 83-; Intrprtr Df-Slf Emplyd 83-; BS Univ ME Orono 73; AA Pima Coll Tucson AZ 82; Pntng; Artst/Pntr.

**GARLAND, BRETT R,** Va Highlands Comm Coll, Abingdon, VA; SO; BA; Clg Forum 90-; Stdnt Svcs Comm 90-; Intrntl Ed Comm 90-; Phi Theta Kappa 90-; Cnslr Projct Excel 90-; Rotar Act Club; AD; Ec/Acctng; Law.

**GARLAND, BRIAN L,** Univ Of Sc At Columbia, Columbia, SC; FR; Bapt Stdnt Union Outreach Ldr 90; Clg Hnrs 90; Carolina Schlr Fnlst 90; Dns Lst 90; Dean Schlrshp 90; Jrnlsm.

**GARLAND, CHAD E,** Oh Wesleyan Univ, Delaware, OH; FR; BA; Habitat Hmnty 90-; Drmtry Gvrng Brd Pres 90-; Phi Eta Sigma 90-; Chi Phi 90-; Zoolgy/Comp Sci; Marine Biolgy.

**GARLAND, CRISTINA M,** Notre Dame Coll, Cleveland, OH; SO; BA; Pall Mall; Lit Soc Staff; Class VP; Deans Lst; Communicorp Intrn; Ldrshp Awrd; Gold Medal Awrd; Engl; Publishing.

**GARLAND, GEORGE H,** Cumberland County Coll, Vineland, NJ; FR; BA; Stdnt Senate; Hist; Scndry Ed Hist Tchr.

**GARLAND, KIMBERLY S,** Casco Bay Coll, Portland, ME; SR; BA; Cert; Law.

**GARLAND, MELISSA A,** Va Commonwealth Univ, Richmond, VA; SR; BFA; Alt Flms Comm; Cmmnctns Arts/Dsgn; Grphc Dsgn.

**GARLAND, MICHAEL S,** Univ Of Rochester, Rochester, NY; JR; AS; Machinist/Tool Mkr; AS Tech Drftng/Dsgn Keene State Coll Keene NH 89; Apprntcshp Prog State Of NH; Mech Engr.

**GARLAND, VIRGNIA L,** Middle Tn St Univ, Murfreesboro, TN; FR; BS; Danc Clb 90-; Gamma Beta Phi; Ldrshp Perfrmc Schlrshp 90-; Dns Lst 90; Pub Rel.

**GARLING, KELLY J,** Bowling Green St Univ, Bowling Green, OH; FR; BA; Amer Inst Arch Std 90-; Phi Eta Sigma 90-; Achvmnt Schlp 90-; IM Sftbl 90-; Arch/Env Dsgn.

**GARMAN, ANDRA R,** Converse Coll, Spartanburg, SC; FR; BM; Sprtnbrg Symphny; Alpha Lambda Delta; Delta Omicron; Msc; Prfssr Ph D.

**GARMAN, JULIE A,** Wv Univ, Morgantown, WV; SR; BSN; Golden Key; Sigma Theta Tau; Schlrshp/Nason Hosp; Nrsg; Midwife.

**GARMAN, REBECCA L,** Univ Of Pittsburgh, Pittsburgh, PA; SO; BS; Rsdnt Stdnt Assn Chrprsn 90; Phi Eta Sigma 89-; Eng.

**GARMAN, SARAH,** Fl St Univ, Tallahassee, FL; SR; BS; Future Edctrs Amer 88-; Golden Key 90-; Kappa Delta Pi 90-; Sigma Pi 87-; Deans Lst 89-; AA 89; Elem Educ.

**GARMESTANI, SEYYEDEH SEDDIGHEH,** Fl A & M Univ, Tallahassee, FL; FR; Premed; Pharmacy.

**GARMON, ANGELENA S,** Univ Of Nc At Greensboro, Greensboro, NC; GD; BS; Inter Vars Chrstn Fllwshp 88-90; Dns Lst 90; Intrnshp 90; BS 90; NC Tchng Cert 90; Elem Educ; Tchng.

**GARMON, GERALD A,** Univ Of Nc At Charlotte, Charlotte, NC; SR; BS; Crim Just; Adult Prob Ofcr.

**GARMON JR, ROBERT L,** Walker Coll, Jasper, AL; SO; BA; Phi Theta Kappa 90-; Jrnlsm; Wrtr/Rprtr.

**GARMON, TRACEY L,** Valdosta St Coll, Valdosta, GA; FR; Stdnt Govt Assn Sntr 90-; Insght Ldr; Chrstn Otrch; Chi Omega Actvts Chrmn 90-; Erly Chldhd Educ; Tchr.

**GARNEAU, VERONICA S,** Savannah Coll Of Art & Design, Savannah, GA; JR; BFA; Fiber Arts.

**GARNEM, CLAUDETTE J,** Univ Of Al At Birmingham, Birmingham, AL; JR; BA; Natl Hnr Roll 88-; Golden Key; Phi Kappa Phi; Crawford & VIRGINIA Johnson Schlrshp; Business; Marketing.

**GARNER, ALISHA,** Cheyney Univ Of Pa, Cheyney, PA; SR; Rcrtn Club; Sigma Dove Pres; Rho Phi Lamda; Assist Cheerleading Coach Slghtn Schl; Dns Lst; Cheerleader Co-Capt; Therapeutic Rcrtn; Wrk Juvenile Dlqnts.

**GARNER, BRENDA H,** Waycross Coll, Waycross, GA; JR; BSBA; Ntnl Asso/Acctnts; Auburn Un/Montgomery Acctng Cl; Soph Schol; Cert/Achvmnt/Math/Natl Sci; Deans List 89-; Busn/Acctng; Acctnt.

**GARNER, CATHY L,** Univ Of Tn At Martin, Martin, TN; FR; Taekesondo 4th Stripe Ylw Belt USTA 90-; ATA Camobelt; Criminal Justice; Law Enfor.

**GARNER II, DAVID T,** Al A & M Univ, Normal, AL; FR; BS; Food Sci Clb Prjct Dir 90-; Food Sci Intrn 89-90; Food Sci; Rsrch Bio Chem.

**GARNER, DUANE L,** Coppin St Coll, Baltimore, MD; FR; BA; Ambssdrs Clb 90-; Hnrs Prog 90-; Hgh Acdmc Achvmnt 90-; Cmmnty Serv Awrd 90-; Cmptr Sci; Sys Anlyst/P C Mntnc.

**GARNER, EDITH M,** Univ Of Ga, Athens, GA; SR; BED; Wrldwd Dscplshp Assc 88-; Alph Dlt Pi 88-; Elem Ed; Tchr.

**GARNER, JAMES D,** Tri County Tech Coll, Pendleton, SC; IMT; Indstrl Mech Tech.

**GARNER, JASON A,** Wv Univ, Morgantown, WV; SR; SPE Pres 89-; Ptrlm Eng.

**GARNER, JASON P,** Univ Of Miami, Coral Gables, FL; JR; BM; Audio Engr Soc 89-; Phi Kappa Phi 90; Golden Key 90; Music Engr; Audio Engr.

**GARNER, JENNIFER A,** Liberty Univ, Lynchburg, VA; JR; BS; Clg Repblcns 88-; Actvts Cncl; Hon Prog 90; Acctg; Law.

**GARNER, JOHN T,** Univ Of Sc At Columbia, Columbia, SC; FR; BA; Seidkoan Aikedo Club Pres 90-; Marchng Bnd 90-; Kappa Kappa Psi 90-; Im Soccer 90; Mktg.

**GARNER, KATHERINE A,** Nc St Univ At Raleigh, Raleigh, NC; FR; BA; Pre-Vet Clb 90; Flwshp Chrstn Athls; Alpha Lambda Delta; Phi Eta Sigma; Schlrs Pgm; Zoology/Pre-Vet; Vet Med.

**GARNER, KELLY K,** Belmont Coll, Nashville, TN; SR; BM; Std Govt Pres 86-87; Phi Theta Kappa Chrmn 86-87; Pi Lambda Theta 88-; Delta Omcrn 88-; Cir K Intl Chrmn 85-87; The Messiah Alto Soloist; Benson Msc Grp; Pres Cup 87; AL Mst Outstdng Std Rnnr Up 87; Bllrds; AS 87; BS Ed; Comm Voice Perf; Sngr/Sngwrtr/Math Tchr.

**GARNER, KEVIN L,** Alcorn St Univ, Lorman, MS; SO; BS; Pre Law Clb 89-; Pre Law; Atty.

**GARNER, KIMBERLY A,** Comm Coll Algny Co Algny Cmps, Pittsburgh, PA; SO; ASSC; Bus; Mgmt.

**GARNER, KRISTI L,** Univ Of Tn At Knoxville, Knoxville, TN; SO; MBA; Alph Lmbd Dlt 89-; Phi Eta Sgm 89-; Bus; Fin.

**GARNER, MELISSA DIANNE,** Ms St Univ, Miss State, MS; JR; BA; Nwspr Feature Ed 90-; Campus Crusade Chrst 88-; Coll Rpblcns 88-89; Gamma Beta Phi 88-; Pi Sigma Alpha; Pres Schlr 88-; Deans Lst 88-; IMS 89-; Pol Sci; Jrnlsm.

**GARNER, MICHELE E,** Middle Tn St Univ, Murfreesboro, TN; SR; BA; Pre Law Soc 89-; Gamma Beta Phi 87-; Pi Gamma Mu 89-; Tau Omicron 89-; Alpha Gamma Rho 88-; Pre Law Intrnshp 90; Deans Lst 87-; Norman Parks Pol Sci Awd; Pol Sci; Law.

**GARNER, MONTE J,** Blue Mountain Coll, Blue Mountain, MS; JR; BS; Math Sci Clb; Cmmtr Clb; Phi Theta Kappa Almn; Euzelian Soc; Math; Tchr.

**GARNER, RENEE J,** Tuskegee Univ, Tuskegee Inst, AL; SR; BS; Psych Clb 89; Kappa Delta Pi; Hnr Roll; Psychlgy; Psychtry.

**GARNER, RONALD W,** Chattahoochee Vly St Comm Coll, Phenix City, AL; SO; School Play 90; Vrsty Bsbl 89-; Physical Educ Drama; Schl Tchr Coach.

**GARNER, SHAYNE M,** Washington State Comm Coll, Marietta, OH; FR; Diesel Mech.

**GARNER, SHELLY S,** Central Al Comm Coll, Alexander City, AL; SO; BA; Elem Ed; Tch.

**GARNER, VALORIE K,** Marshall University, Huntington, WV; SO; BA; Acctg Club Brd Dir 90-; Gamma Beta Phi 90-; Alpha Kappa Psi Treas 90-; Deans List 89-; Acctg; CPA.

**GARNER, VANESSA S,** Univ Of Tn At Martin, Martin, TN; SR; BS; Coll Dem Sec 85-86; STEA 90-; Econ Clb Fndng Mbr 87-88; Sovran Bank Intrnshp 88; BS Educ 90.

**GARNER-RICHARDSON, LORETTA FAYE,** Stillman Coll, Tuscaloosa, AL; SR; BS; Phi Theta Kappa 79; SSCC Pres Awd 79; Univ Wmn Org Univ AL Schlrshp; Missionary Helper; AS Shelton State Cmnty Clg 85; Certif Shelton State Cmnty Clg 85; Elem Ed; Tchr.

**GARNETT, CHRISTIAN F,** Univ Of Sc At Columbia, Columbia, SC; JR; BA; Carolina Cares Pblcty Chr; Jud Bd; Epworth Chldrns Home Tutor 89-; Golden Key 90-; Gamma Beta Phi; Alpha Delta Pi Schlrshp Chr; Deans List 89-; Redstone Arsenal Officers Wives Club Merit Awd 90; IM Fl Ftbl Soccer Sftbl; Pol Sci; Law Sch.

**GARNETT, RONALD EDWARD,** Univ Of Ky, Lexington, KY; JR; BS; Inst Elec/Elec Engrs 90-; Chrmn Engrs Wk; Eta Kappa Nu Pres 90-; Goldn Key 90-; Tau Beta Pi Ctlgr/Hstrn 90-; Rmnwtz Awrd Outstndng EE Jr; US Air Force 85-89; Eta Kappa Nu Awrd Outstndng EE Jr; Preprfsnl Intrnshp; ASEET Comm Coll Of AF 88; Elec Eng; Eng/Comp/Cntrls.

**GAROFALO, LAURA B,** Univ Of Miami, Coral Gables, FL; SR; Arch Assn In London 90-; Marshipping Line 87-; Arch Hnrs 87-90; 4th Yr Design Awd; Karate 88-90; Arch Art.

**GAROFALO, MARIA L,** Glassboro St Coll, Glassboro, NJ; SR; BA; Prjct Santa Fndrsng 87-88; Sec Crspndng Psychlgy Clb 90-; Yrbk Staff Sports Edtr 90-; Psi Chi; Gloucester Cty Comm Serv Sprvsr 8-89; Tutor 90-; The Bridge Cnslr; IM; Psychlgy; Grad Schl.

**GARRA, LISA M,** Marywood Coll, Scranton, PA; JR; BA; Data Entry Opr; AS Luzerne Cnty Cmmnty Clg 90; Soc Sci Mjr; Pblc Admin.

**GARRATY, CHRISTOPHER P,** Pa St Univ Delaware Cty Cmps, Media, PA; SO; MBA; Bsns; Mrktng.

**GARREN, PAULA M,** Thomas Coll, Thomasville, GA; FR; BA; Engl; Brdcst Jrnlsm.

**GARREN, REBECCA H,** Univ Of Nc At Asheville, Asheville, NC; SO; BA; Acctng; CPA.

**GARREN, TERESA A,** Longwood Coll, Farmville, VA; FR; BS; Hnr Stdnt; Lngwd Schlr; Occptnl Thrpy; Occptnl Thrpst Rgstrd.

**GARRETSON, SUSAN F,** S U N Y Coll At Fredonia, Fredonia, NY; JR; BM; Amer Strng Tchrs Assn VP 90-; MENC; Symphny Orch; Strng Qrtt; Pi Kappa Lambda; Strng Plyrs Schlrshp 89-; Schl Music Srvc Awrd 90-; Hnr Stu; Music; Educ.

**GARRETT, ANGELA L,** Fl Inst Of Tech, Melbourne, FL; FR; BA; Crs Cntry 90; Math Ed; Tchr.

**GARRETT, BANORO W,** Commonwealth Coll, Virginia Beach, VA; SO; Elecs Clb Pres 90-; NAACP; Dns Lst 90-; Elec Tech; Eng.

**GARRETT, BERNADINE C,** Central Al Comm Coll, Alexander City, AL; FR; BA; Bapt Chrch Yth Chr Dir; PTA Sec 90-; Sci; Phys Thrpy.

**GARRETT, BOBBI J,** Miami Jacobs Jr Coll Of Bus, Dayton, OH; SO; AS; Dayton Wms Bwlng Assoc Brd Dir 90-; Mktg; Bsn/Mktg.

**GARRETT, CAROL T,** Southern Coll Of Tech, Marietta, GA; SR; Bapt Stdnt Un 85-90; Tau Alpha Pi 89-90; Natl Coll Comp Sci Award 90.

**GARRETT, CHEERIE LEE,** Memphis St Univ, Memphis, TN; SR; BED; Elem Educ; Tchng.

**GARRETT, CHRISTOPHER S,** Oh Univ, Athens, OH; FR; BSEE; IEEE; IM Vlybl Brmbl Sftbl; Elect Engrng.

**GARRETT, DARIN S,** Oh Univ, Athens, OH; JR; BS; Inst Of Elctrcl/Elctrncs Engr 89-; Eta Kappa Nu; JAYCEE; Co-Op Ed Stdnt 89-; Elec Engr.

**GARRETT, JO ANN B,** Birmingham Southern Coll, Birmingham, AL; JR; BA; Pres Advsry Cncl 90-; Adlt Stds Rcrtr; Alpha Lambda Delta 89; Phi Eta Sigma 89; Alpha Sigma Lambda Treas 90-; Omicron Delta Kappa 90-; Mrtr Brd; Alpha Sigma Lambda Educ Hnr Scty Schlrshp Rcpnt 90-; Lgl Sec Fr Rives/Peterson 79-; Bus Mngmnt.

**GARRETT, JOHN M,** Union Univ, Jackson, TN; JR; BA; Bapt Stdnt Union; Relgn, Mnstry.

**GARRETT, KAREN L,** Univ Of Al At Birmingham, Birmingham, AL; SR; BS; UAB Blzr Pep Bnd 89-; UAB Wind Ensmble 89-; UAB Comm Bnd 88-; Omicron Delta Kappa 90-; Music Ed; Tchng.

**GARRETT, KATHLEEN A,** Saint Francis Coll, Loretto, PA; SR; BS; Psych Clb Pres 90-; Interfrtrnty Sorty Cncl 90-; Delta Epsilon Sigma; Hnr Soc; Theta Phi Alpha VP 89-; Psychlgy; Grdt Schl Occptnl Thrpy.

**GARRETT, KIMBERLEY D,** Southern Coll Of Tech, Marietta, GA; FR; BA; AIAS 90-; Arch.

**GARRETT, KIMBERLY R,** Marshall University, Huntington, WV; SR; BBA; Acctng Clb 89-; Gamma Beta Phi 87-89; Sigma Sigma Sigma Treas 89-; Deans Lst 87-; Business; Acctng.

**GARRETT, LINDA W,** Coll Of Charleston, Charleston, SC; SO; BA; Bus.

**GARRETT, LISA C,** Univ Of Southern Ms, Hattiesburg, MS; JR; BS; SGA Vp 88-90; Yrbk Stff 88-90; Glf Cst Rflctns Capt 88-90; VP Lst 88-90; Deans Lst; MCCCC Frndlst Grl 90; Psychlgy.

**GARRETT, MATTHEW L,** Fl St Univ, Tallahassee, FL; SO; BME; BOA 89-; CMENC 90-; Phi Eta Sigma 89-; Music; Choral Music Teacher.

**GARRETT, MITZI L,** Roane St Comm Coll, Harriman, TN; SO; AAS; Amer Phy Thrpy Assc 89-; Meth Med Ctr Oak Ridge 90; Oak Ridge Hlth Care Ctr 90; Knoxville Hlth Care Ctr; Phys Thrpy Asstnt; Phys Thrpy Asstnt.

**GARRETT, PATRICIA A,** Univ Of Tn At Knoxville, Knoxville, TN; SO; BA; Track Asst 90-; Gamma Beta Phi 90-; Phi Eta Sigma 89-; Fin; Invstmnt Prtflios.

**GARRETT, RANJI M,** Univ Of Sc At Aiken, Aiken, SC; JR; BA; Lit Mgzn Asst Edtr 90-; Stu Spprt Orgn 90-; Mentor 90; Gamma Beta Phi 90-; Sigma Tau Delta VP 90-; Wrtng Cntr Ttr 89-; Engl; Law.

**GARRETT, REBECCA L,** Radford Univ, Radford, VA; JR; BS; Kappa Delta Pi 89-; Erly/Mddl Educ; Teacher.

**GARRETT, RHONDA L,** Mayland Comm Coll, Spruce Pine, NC; SO; BA; Acctg/Comp Pgmg; CPA.

**GARRETT, ROBIN S,** West Liberty St Coll, West Liberty, WV; FR; BS; Clg Knshp; Crs Cntry; Psych.

**GARRETT, RODNEY G,** Univ Of Louisville, Louisville, KY; SR; MENG; BES; Elctrcl Eng; Eng.

**GARRETT, SARAH E,** Valdosta St Coll, Valdosta, GA; JR; Stdnt Govt 88-89; Chi Omega Grk Wk Chrmn 88-; Miss Valdosta St Clg 90-; Clndr Girl 88-90; Erly Chldhd Educ; Teach.

**GARRETT, SCOTT E,** Birmingham Southern Coll, Birmingham, AL; JR; Psychlgy.

**GARRETT, SHANNON M,** Univ Of Sc At Aiken, Aiken, SC; SR; BS; Baptst Stu Un Sec 88-89; Stu Pers Serv.

**GARRETT, SHERRY E,** Itawamba Comm Coll, Fulton, MS; FR; AAS; Phi Theta Kappa 90-; 90-; Phys Ther Asst.

**GARRETT, TONYA V,** Fayetteville St Univ, Fayetteville, NC; JR; BA; IBM Clb Rep 74-84; Kappa Delta Pi 90-; Orten Dyslxia Soc 90-; Hon Stdnt Cert Achvmnt 89-; Spec Olympcs Coach 85-86; Jr Achvmnt Advsr 87-88; IBM Trm Ls Anlyst 72-88; Psychlgy; Spec Ed/Lrning Dsblties.

**GARRETT, TYRONE R,** Clark Atlanta Univ, Atlanta, GA; JR; BA; Phi Beta Sigma Prlmntry; IM Bsktbl; Pltcl Sci; Pblc Plcy Mkng.

**GARRICK, VICTORIA ANNE,** Univ Of Tn At Martin, Martin, TN; JR; BA; Educ; Tchng.

**GARRIDO, HENRY A,** City Univ Of Ny City Coll, New York, NY; SO; NYPIRG 90-; Acdmclly Otstndng SEEK Stu 90-; Athltc Acdmc Hnr Rll 89-; Bsktbl 89-; Arch/Envrmntl.

**GARRIGAN, ANNA N,** Univ Of Tn At Martin, Martin, TN; SR; BS; Alpha Gamma Delta Crrspndng Sec 90-; Ggrphy Trl And Trsm; Trvl Indstry.

**GARRIGAN, JENNIFER L,** Memphis St Univ, Memphis, TN; SR; BA; Psych Clb 90-; Phi Eta Sigma 88; Chi Beta Phi 90-; Foerstner Schlrshp 88-; Schl Psych.

**GARRIS, LINDA D,** Fayetteville St Univ, Fayetteville, NC; SR; BS; Scty Advncmnt Mgt Sec 85-86; Fast Track Summer Intern; AAS Fayetteville Tech Comm Coll 86; Economics; Fed Economist.

**GARRISON, AMANDA ELLEN,** Univ Of Nc At Charlotte, Charlotte, NC; JR; BA; Res Hll Rep 88-89; Pre Law Soc 90-; Intern Attrny Shuster; Psych/Crmnl Jstc; Law.

**GARRISON, CHRISTOPHER A,** Tn Temple Univ, Chattanooga, TN; JR; BS; Choir 89-90; Univ Ens 89-90; Deans Lst 89-; Alpha Omega Delta Ath Dir 90-; Youth Pastoral Intern 88-89; Psych; Youth Pastor/Educ.

**GARRISON, CRYSTAL D,** Univ Of Sc At Columbia, Columbia, SC; FR; Science; Nursing.

**GARRISON, DEBORAH M,** Western Ky Univ, Bowling Green, KY; SR; MA; Fllwship Chrstn Athlts Ldrshp Fmly 88-; Kappa Delta Pi 90-; Phi Eta Sigma 87-88; Alpha Lambda Delta 87-88; Phi Kappa Phi 90-; Prsdnts Schlr 87-; Grad Asstnshp; Natl Coll Edctn Award; Grad Summa Cum Laude; BS; Spch Pthlgy; Pthlgst.

**GARRISON, GAY,** Elmira Coll, Elmira, NY; SR; BSN; Hon Schlr 89-90; Nrsng; Mdwfry.

**GARRISON, HEATHER A,** East Stroudsburg Univ, E Stroudsburg, PA; FR; BA; Hall Cnsl 90-; Womens Ctr Org 90-; IM Vlybl 90; Specl Educ Tchr.

**GARRISON, JEFF W,** Univ Of Nc At Asheville, Asheville, NC; SR; BS; Am Coll Hlthcare Exec; SAM 90-; Study Abrd Europe Hlth Admin; Hlth Care Admin Mgmnt; Sr Hlth Care Mgmnt.**

**GARRISON, JOHN C,** Univ Of Al At Huntsville, Huntsville, AL; SR; AIAA VP 89-90; Mech Engr.

**GARRISON, JOHN G,** Birmingham Southern Coll, Birmingham, AL; SR; BA; Blgy; Med.

**GARRISON, KATHY J,** Oh St Univ At Marion, Marion, OH; SO; BA; Alpha Lmbd Dlt 89-; Phi Eta Sgm 89-; Grfn Scty 90-; Summa Awrd 89; Engl; Elem Educ.

**GARRISON, KEITH P,** Western Piedmont Comm Coll, Morganton, NC; FR; AASC; Phi Theta Kappa; U S Navy 85-90; Cvl Engr Tech; Cvl Engr.

**GARRISON, M,** Western Ky Univ, Bowling Green, KY; SR; BS; Flwshp Chrstn Athlts Ldrshp Fmly 88-; Ntl Stdnt Spch-Lang-Hrng Assn 90-; Alpha Lambda Delta 88; Phi Eta Sigma 88; Phi Kappa Phi/Kappa Delta Pi 90-; NCEA Wnnr; Schlrshp Memphis State Univ Grad Asstshp; Pres Schlr 87-; IM Vlybl 88; Spch Pthlgy; MA.

**GARRISON, PAMELA J,** Brewer St Jr Coll, Fayette, AL; SO; MBA; Pres Lst 90-; Dns Lst 90-; Acctg; CPA.

**GARRISON, PHYLLIS A,** Western Ky Univ, Bowling Green, KY; JR; BSW; Soc Wrk/Psychology; Cnslgn/Soc Wrk Fld.

**GARRISON, ROBIN CAREY,** Tri County Tech Coll, Pendleton, SC; SR; AS; Phi Theta Kappa; Indstrl Elec Tech.

**GARRISON, TRENT G,** North Ga Coll, Dahlonega, GA; FR; BA; ROTC 90-; Hnr Scty; Ftbl Sftbl 90-; Personell Mgt; Soldier.

**GARRISON, VERENDA L,** Norfolk St Univ, Norfolk, VA; SO; Hume Soc 89-.

**GARRISON, WAYNE E,** Tn St Univ, Nashville, TN; JR; BA; Natl Soc Black Engrs; IEEE; Hon Stdnt; Tau Sigma Upsilon Pr 90-; Phi Beta Sigma 90-; Intrn Delco Elec 90-; Gen Motors Schlr 90-; Outstndng Jr Elec Engr; Math/Sci; Engr.

**GARRITY, JEFFREY A,** S U N Y Coll At Fredonia, Fredonia, NY; SR; BS; Res Asst 88-; Res Asst Advsry Brd Tres 89-; Mrktg Srvyr/Intrn Driene Lk Thm Pk 90; IM Sftbl/Bsktbl/Vlybl 87-; Bus Admin; Finance.

**GARRO, PATRICIA M,** Glassboro St Coll, Glassboro, NJ; GD; Biolgy Clb 89-90; Deans Lst; Ltl Feet Wldlf Refuge Vol 89; BS 90; Biolgy; Envrnmntl Speclst.

**GARRON, KEN N,** Cumberland County Coll, Vineland, NJ; SO; BA; Bsn Clb 90-; Pres Lst; AAS; Mrktg.

**GARRONE, CINDY R,** Bloomfield Coll, Bloomfield, NJ; JR; BS; Acctng; CPA.

**GARRONE, ROSALIE M,** Univ Of Med & Dentistry Of Nj, Newark, NJ; GD; Mid Atlantic Soc Txclgsts 89-90; MASOT; ASCP 87-; Clncl Exclnc Awd 90; Hackensack Med Ctr 86-; BS 90; Txclgy/Clncl Lab Sci.

**GARROTT, BENJAMIN E,** Union Univ, Jackson, TN; FR; BS; Sigma Alpha Epsilon IM Chrmn 90-; Acctg; CPA.

**GARROW, JANICE E,** Castleton St Coll, Castleton, VT; SR; BS; SEA 90-; Arthritis Fndtn; ACS; Restaurant Mngmnt; Childrens Literature; Elem Teacher.

**GARROW, TONYA A,** Johnson St Coll, Johnson, VT; FR; BA; Yth Grp 90-; Dnc Clb 90-; Elem Ed; Tchr.

**GARSIN, DANIELLE A,** Cornell Univ Statutory College, Ithaca, NY; FR; BA; Outing Clb 90-; Biol.

**GARSKE, ANGELA M,** Fl St Univ, Tallahassee, FL; SO; BA; Stu Gov Sntr 90-; Mdl UN Sec 90-; Crusade For Christ 89-90; Phi Eta Sigma; Pi Delta Phi; Sigma Kappa Actvs Chrwmn; Intl Afrs; Fed Gov.

**GARSKE, CHRISTINE L,** S U N Y Coll At Fredonia, Fredonia, NY; JR; BSED; Grl Sct Ldr 78-84; Rlgs Ed Catechist 84-89; Prnt Tchr Assc Sec 79-80; Elctn Inspctr Chautauqua Cty 86-88; Grl Sct Ldr 5 Yr Svc Rcgntn 83; Catechist/Rlgs Edctr Yr 87-88; Erly Chldhd Ed/Soc Wrk; Fld Tchng/Soc Wrk.

**GARSON, ADAM J,** Eckerd Coll, St Petersburg, FL; SO; BS; Pet Cncl 90-; Vrsty Crss-Cntry 89-; Psychlgy; Cnsmr Psychlgy.

**GARST, ELIZABETH A,** Northeast State Tech Comm Coll, Blountville, TN; FR; Amer Chem Scty; Sbls Sct PTA Treas 89-; Dn Ldr Hlstn Mddle Schl PTA Treas Bstrs 89; Chrldrs Plsant Hll Nrtre Chr 87-; Chrch Of The Brthrn Nrtre Camp Brd 90-; Cmp Plcs Dir Cnslr; Brthrn Cmp Brd Sec; Hmrmkrs Clb POW Chrprsn 89-; Co Mgr; Wtrss; Chem Tech; Lab Tech.

**GARTLAND, ANGELA Y,** Va Commonwealth Univ, Richmond, VA; SO; BS; Phi Eta Sigma; C L Ford Jwlrs 77-90; Acctng.

**GARTLAND, DWAYNE A,** Univ Of Louisville, Louisville, KY; JR; Cmptr Sci; Cmptr Anlys.

**GARTMAN, JIM,** Oh Univ, Athens, OH; JR; BS; IM Sports/Precision Flight Team 90; Aircraft Owners/Pilots 89; Alpha Eta Rho V P 89; Delta Upsilon 89-90; Ftbl/Sftbl/Brmbl/Vlybl/Bsktbl Coach 87; Airway Sci; Pilot.

**GARTMAN, SUSAN D,** Univ Of Sc At Spartanburg, Spartanburg, SC; JR; BA; Gamma Beta Phi; Deans Lst 88-90; Chnclrs Lst 90; Mgmt.

**GARTNER, GEOFFREY W,** Central Fl Comm Coll, Ocala, FL; ME; IM Sprts Pgm; Vartns 90; Phi Theta Kappa; IM Sprts; Mech Eng.

**GARTON, KEVIN E,** Glassboro St Coll, Glassboro, NJ; GD; Law Enfrcmnt Soc 89; Jvnl Conf Cmmtt 87-88; Vol Fir Co Lt 90-; Bptst Chrch Sec; Dean Lst 88-90; Magna Cum Laude 90; Pres Lst CCC 87; AS Camden Co Coll 87; BA Glassboro St Coll 90; Crmnl Jstc/Fire Serv.

**GARTUNG, MARK E,** S U N Y Coll Of Tech At Frmgdl, Farmingdale, NY; SR; IEEE; Deans List; Pres List; IM Sftbl Vlybl Ftbl; AAS 89; BET; Electrl Engrng Tchnlgy; Elec Engrng.

**GARVELLI, KEVIN C,** Wagner Coll, Staten Island, NY; SR; BS; Stdnt Gov Assn VP 90; Omicron Delta Kappa 89-; Delta Mu Delta VP; THETA Chi Treas 90; Schlstc All Amer 89; IM Sftbl/Hcky/Ftbl/Vlybl; Bus Admin.**

**GARVER, BRENDA L,** Univ Of Southern Ms, Hattiesburg, MS; SR; BS; Panhellnc Cncl Prsctr 89-90; Campus Crsde Chrst 88-89; Acdmc Cncl 90; Phi Mu; Lambda Sigma Omicron Delta Kappa; Order Of Omega Treas 90-; Phi Delta Rho VP 90; Beta Alpha Psi VP Intiates; Rho Chi 90; Acctg.

**GARVER, PATRICIA ANN,** Notre Dame Coll, Cleveland, OH; SR; Res Assn Brd Sec 90-; Cmps Actvt Brd Sec 88-; Clss Offcr Treas 88-90; Phi Alpha Theta VP 90-; United Way 88-89; Dean Lst 87-; Ldrshp Serv Awrds 88-; Mdl Arab Lea Rpprtr 90-; BA; Pol Sci; Paralegal.

**GARVEY, KARA L,** Bay Path Coll, Longmeadow, MA; SO; AD; Intshp Steigers; Fshn Merch; Buyer.

**GARVEY, LEANNE,** Merrimack Coll, North Andover, MA; JR; BA; Orient Coord 89-; Psych Club Treas 90-; MORE Retreat 90-; Psi Chi 89-; Sr Week Usher; Psych.

**GARVEY, PATRICK T,** Hillsborough Comm Coll, Tampa, FL; FR; BA; Science; Electrcl Engnrng.

**GARVIN, BARBARA A,** Univ Of Cincinnati, Cincinnati, OH; GD; MED; Assoc Dean Coll Educ Grad Asst 90-; BA-PSYCHLGY Edgecliff Coll 73; Long Dstnc Oper/Sub Tchr/Thrpst/Job Trng Cnslr; Dipl-Exec Sec Sci Fnshng Tchs Sec Schl; Elem Ed; Tch.

**GARVIN, ERIN G,** James Madison University, Harrisonburg, VA; FR; BA; Psychology Clb 90-; IM Vllybl 90-; BACCHUS 90-; Aniaml Rts Coalition 90-; Cncl Envir Officer 90-; IM Vllybl; Psychology.

**GARVIN, JOY NEWTON,** Coll Of Charleston, Charleston, SC; SR; BS; Elem Ed; Tchng.

**GARVIN, RAE LEIGH,** Univ Of Sc At Aiken, Aiken, SC; JR; BA; Gamma Beta Phi 89-; Yrbk Stf; Nwspr Stf 90; Gamma Beta Phi 89-; Grphc/Engl; Grphc Dsgnr/Phtgphr.

**GARVIN, SHONIA D,** Univ Of Sc At Aiken, Aiken, SC; JR; BS; Pacesetter 89-; Gamma Beta Phi 89-; Alpha Kappa Psi; Alpha Kappa Alpha; Army Rsrv 88-; Pres Hon Roll 89-90; D L Scurry Schlrshp 88-89; Acad Achvmnt Cert 90-; Bus Admn/Acctg; Acctnt.

**GARVIS, KIMBERLY A,** George Mason Univ, Fairfax, VA; FR; RSA Rep 90-; Dvsr; Bus.

**GARWOOD, DIANE R,** Glassboro St Coll, Glassboro, NJ; JR; BA; Stdnt Econ Soc 90-; Part-Time Pos Commerce Bnk 90-; Econ Studies; Bnkg.

**GARY, BRENDA J,** Univ Of Miami, Coral Gables, FL; SR; BSN; Blk Nrs Assoc Schlrshp 90; Blk Nrs Assoc; Flght Attndnt Pan Am; Hospice Inc; ASD Nrsng Miami Dade Comm Clg 83; Nursing; Educator.

**GARY, KENNETH A,** Norfolk St Univ, Norfolk, VA; SR; MA; Marching Spartan Legion Bnd 86-88; Speech Pathology Audiology Club Pres 89-90; Alpha Kappa Mu; African Amer Flwshp Memphis State Univ Audiology Memphis TN; Speech Pathology/Audiology BA; Audiology; Clinical Audiologist.

**GARY, LARRAINE V,** Johnson C Smith Univ, Charlotte, NC; JR; BS; Hist Club Secy; Model UN 90; Deans List 89-; Museum Rsrch Intrn; Hist; PhD.

**GARY, LISA A,** Pellissippi St Tech Comm Coll, Knoxville, TN; SO; BA; Sch Photographr; Deans List 89-; E Side/Union Cnty Nghbr 87-; Artcls/Layout/Design; ET Chldrns Hosp Telethon 90; Drkrm Wrk ET Chldrns Hosp 90; Pstr Artwrk/Bks A Million 90; Art Hist/Archaeology; Grad Schl.**

**GARY, SANDRA R,** Al A & M Univ, Normal, AL; JR; BS; Stdnts Free Enterprise; Fncl Mgmnt Assn; Finance; Fncl Cons.

**GARY, SEDONIA P,** Cheyney Univ Of Pa, Cheyney, PA; JR; BED; Fidelity Bnk/Customer Serv Generalist I; Elem Ed; Tchng.

**GARY, SONYA D,** Winthrop Coll, Rock Hill, SC; SO; BA; Abndnt Lf Chrst Bible Study Sec 90-; Stdnt Govt Assn Sntr; Assn Ebonites VP; Psi Chi Sec; PACE Clb 90-; Pres Host; Cltrl Dvrsty Fcltr; AOE Gspl Choir 89-; Psychlgy; Tchng.

**GARY, TINA R,** Ms St Univ, Miss State, MS; SR; BSED; Ladies Aux Gideons; Kappa Delta Phi; AA Itawamba Comm Colg 85; Elem Ed; Tch Gifted Stdnts.

**GASCHEL, REBECCA MONA,** Univ Of Hartford, West Hartford, CT; FR; BA; Envrnmntl Org 90-; Spec Ed/Erly Chldhd Ed.

**GASKIN, CHRISTINA L,** Coll Of Charleston, Charleston, SC; SR; LEADS 80-; Highly Dist Hons Lst; Alpha Delta Pi 88-; BS; Elem Tchr.

**GASKIN, ELIZABETH C,** Univ Of Sc At Salkehatchie, Allendale, SC; FR; BS; SG 90-; Gamma Beta Phi 90-; D L Scurry Schlrshp 90-; Yrbk Edtr Chf 90-; Blgy-Chem; RN.

**GASKIN, MANUELA I,** Itawamba Comm Coll, Fulton, MS; SO; All Amer Bnd Clrgrd Capt 89-; Choir 88-89; Stdnt Art League 89-; Kaleidoscope 88-; Graphics Comm; Graphic Arts.

**GASKIN, SHARON R,** Union Inst, Cincinnati, OH; SR; BA; Admin Blessed Sacrament Preschl 81; Erly Chldhd Ed; Chld Dvlpmnt.

**GASKINS, RENEE D,** Bristol Univ, Bristol, TN; SO; AAS; E Tenn Schl Taekwondo Karate 86-; Natl Spelgcl Soc 86-; Amer Cave Cons Assn 86-; Mtn Emp Grotto Tr; CAVES Reg Tr Sec 86-88; Kingsprt Legl Sec Assn Sec Yr 87; Kingsprt Legl Sec Assn Pr 86-88; Paralegl; Busn; Law/Paralgl.

**GASPARD, JOSEPH P,** Univ Of West Fl, Pensacola, FL; SR; BS; Assn Gen Cntrctrs 90-; Bsbl 85-88; AA Gulf Coast Comm Clg 87; Bldg Cnstrctn; Cnstrctn Mgmnt.

**GASPARDINO, ANDREA M,** Western New England Coll, Springfield, MA; JR; Peer Advsr 89-; RHA VP 90-; LA Std Tchrs 89-; Ambssdr 90-; Almn Awd Excllnc; Regstrtn Comm; Sblng Wknd Comm 90-; Plymouth Hall Cncl Rep 89; History; Mstrs Std Prsnnl Admn.

**GASPARI, MARK A,** Wilmington Coll, New Castle, DE; FR; BA; Sci; Eng.

**GASPARRI, ROSEMARIE,** Fl Atlantic Univ, Boca Raton, FL; SR; JD; Ldrs Prgm Sec 90-; Rsdnc Hll Assoc Sec 87-88; Dnc Tm 89-90; Phi Kappa Phi 90-; Beta Gamma Sigma 90-; Univ Schlr 89-90; BBA; Law.

**GASS, AMY L,** Saint Vincents Coll & Seminary, Latrobe, PA; SO; BA; Brdcstg Clb/Own Radio Shw 90-; Hsty Clb 90-; IM Vlybl Arbcs 89-; Cmmnctns; TV Dir/Prodctn.

**GASSEN, ESTHER C,** Ms St Univ, Miss State, MS; GD; DVM; SCAVMA 90-; Alpha Psi; Vet Med.

**GASSETTE, RENEICE,** Comm Coll Algny Co Algny Cmps, Pittsburgh, PA; JR; BA; Bus Adm.

**GASSLER, AMY K,** Daemen Coll, Amherst, NY; JR; BS; SG 88-89; Activities Board 88-89; Alumni Assc 88-89; Tutor Clb 88-89; Physcl Thrpy Clncl Intrn 90; Physcl Thrpy.

**GASSMAN, LISA J,** S U N Y At Buffalo, Buffalo, NY; SR; MS; Am Soc Civil Engrs 89-; Water Pollution Cntrl Fed; Gold Key 89-; Tau Beta Pi VP 89-; Chi Epsilon Sec 90-; Phi Eta Sigma 88-; Univ Pres Hon Schlr; Civil Eng Sr Flwshp 90-; Soc Military Engrs Schlrshp 90-; U B Chrldr Ftbl/Bsktbl; Civil Eng; Envrnmntl Eng.

**GASSNER, JOHN J,** Oh St Univ, Columbus, OH; SR; BS; Wldlfe Scty Treas 90-; Intrntl Scty Fr Endngrd Cats VP 89-; Gldn Ky; Phi Eta Sigma; Wldlfe Mgmt; Wldlfe Blgy.

**GAST, ERIK D,** Bethany Coll, Bethany, WV; SR; SIFE 88-; Soc Bsn Std 87-; BOG Rep 87-; Lit Mag 90; Beta Theta Pi Chrmn 88-; Hayes Pnkmyr Schlp 90-; Stfl Schlstc Schlp 87-; Dns Lst; All Conf 88; Acad Schlp 87-; Ice Hcky Clb Capt Pres 87-; Bsbl Tm Capt 87-; BA; Acctng; CPA.

**GASTEL, GARY,** Miami Dade Comm Coll North, Miami, FL; SO; BA; Clg Brd Otstndng Mnrty Grad 90; MDCC N Cmps Deans List 90-; AA 91; Fin Bus Admn; Fin.

**GASTER, DORIS S,** Williamsburg Tech Coll, Kingstree, SC; GD; Stdnt Govt VP 89-90; Phi Theta Kappa Tres 90; Deans List 89-90; AB.

**GASTON, JAMES V,** Howard Univ, Washington, DC; SR; BARCH; Archtctr/Plng Stdnt Assmbly Cls Rep 87-88; Gspl Choir Choir Rep 87-90; Vclst 87-90; AIA Beaux Arts Ball Plnng Com Asst 88-89; Smmr Intrnshp Bertram F Jones Archtct Drftsmn 89; Archtctr; Archtctr Intr Dsgn Set Dsgn.**

**GASTON, JEREMY S,** Univ Of Akron, Akron, OH; JR; BS; Amer Soc Cvl Engrs 88-; Phi Eta Sigma 87-; Goldn Key 89-; Phi Sigma Kappa Sntnl 87-; Natl Grk Mert Awrd 88; Eng Co-Op Prog 90-; Coll Engr Schlrshp 90-; Cvl Eng; Prof Engr.

**GASTON, MICHELLE L,** Duquesne Univ, Pittsburgh, PA; FR; BS; SHSRP Vol; Phi Eta Sigma; Lambda Sigma; Ebnsbrg Cntr; Pblctn Edtn Bklt; Phrmcy.

**GASTONGUAY, KRIS A,** Newbury Coll, Brookline, MA; FR; Appt Coord 86.

**GAT, ROTEM,** Fl International Univ, Miami, FL; FR; BA; Intl Stdnts Clb VP 90-; Hsptlty Mgmnt; Bus.

**GAT, RUTH,** Univ Of Sc At Coastal Carolina, Conway, SC; FR; BA; Israeli Army 84-86; Cert Univ Haifa 88; Psychlgy; Psychlgst.

**GATES, DUSTIN B,** Univ Of North Fl, Jacksonville, FL; JR; BA; AA 90; Fnnce; Insrnce.

**GATES, JANICE C,** Le Moyne Coll, Syracuse, NY; JR; BA; Socty Hmn Rsrc Mgmt Treas 90-; Indus Rel Socty 88-; Tour Guide Open Hse 88-; Intl Hse 88-; Dns Lst 88-; Indus Rel; Law.

**GATES, JULIA,** Boston Univ, Boston, MA; GD; MD; Stdnt Dir Edtr Pub 88-89; Cls Grp Photo Organ 89; Robbins Awd Chee Cls Rep 90; Cls Gift Comm; Alpha Omega Alpha 90; Mech E MIT 84; SM MIT 84; MS RPI 82; Med; Diagnostic Radiology Biomed Eng.

**GATES, ROBERT W,** Temple Univ, Philadelphia, PA; JR; BS; IEEE 90; Radio Stn Art Dir 84-88; Golden Key 89; Pres Awd; Schlstc Ntl Merit Schlrshp; Electrical Eng; Optical Forensics.

**GATEWOOD, JOSEPH C,** Univ Of Ms Medical Center, Jackson, MS; JR; DMD; Cls Ofcr Pres 88-; Deans Hon List; Beta Beta Beta 87; Amercn Chem Soc 87-88; Curriculum Comm Mbr 89; Outcome/Evaltns Comm 88-; Im Soccer 88-; Dentstry.

**GATEWOOD, SHERRY L,** Longwood Coll, Farmville, VA; SO; BA; Nwspr 89-; Peer Advsr 90-; Orntn Ldr; Alpha Lambda Delta VP 89-90; Clss Awd; Deans List 89; Yrbk Copy Ed 90-; Mrtl Arts Clb 90; Jr Buddy Prog Coord; English; FBI.

**GATHINGS, ANGELA G,** Wingate Coll, Wingate, NC; JR; BS; Psychlgy/Hmn Srvcw; Schl Psychlgst.**

**GATJE, JEAN C,** Mary Baldwin Coll, Staunton, VA; SO; BA; Stdnt Snte 89-90; Advsry Brd Of Vstrs Stdnt Rep 90f Extrcrrclr Actvtes Brd; Alpha Lambda Delta VP 90; Vol Wstrn State Hosp 89-90; Vol Staunton Corr Ctr 90; Prctcm Bessie Weller Elem 89; Golf Tennis 89; Sociolgy.

**GATLIN, TAMMY R,** Univ Of South Al, Mobile, AL; JR; BA; Phi Theta Kappa; Spec Ed; Cncl Retarded.

**GATLIN, VERONICA E,** Bethune Cookman Coll, Daytona Beach, FL; SR; MA; Wmns Senate Tres 90-; NAACP 90; Psi Chi Psychology Tres 90-; Intrnshp Prvt Indstry Cncl 90; Asstntshp Bwlng Green St Unv; BS.

**GATLING, JAMES M,** Coppin St Coll, Baltimore, MD; SR; Mgmt Sci.

**GATLING, RHONDA A,** Norfolk St Univ, Norfolk, VA; SO; IEEE 89-; Stu Assc 89-90; Spartan Alpha Tau 90-; Elect Eng.

**GATTI, MARK H,** Glassboro St Coll, Glassboro, NJ; SR; BA; Geography; Plng.

**GATTIS, BRENDA K,** Middle Tn St Univ, Murfreesboro, TN; SO; BA; Business; Mngmnt.

**GATTIS, ROBIN L,** Middle Tn St Univ, Murfreesboro, TN; SR; BS; STEA 89-; Yrbk 86-88; IM Sftbl Ftbl Vlybl Bsktbl 86-; Elem Ed; Teaching.

**GATTO, ANN-MARIE,** Newbury Coll, Brookline, MA; FR; BA; Crfts Precision Inc Payroll Admin 87-; Htl Mgmt; Hsptlty.

**GATTO, ANTONINE,** Saint Francis Coll, Loretto, PA; SR; BA; Peer Tutor 87; Math Clb Pres 87; Stdnt Activities Org Treas 89-90; Kappa Mu Epsilon VP 88; Hnr Soc; Delta Epsilon Sigma; Ntl Collgte Stdnt Govt Awd; James Lieb Math Awd 90; Math; Indstrl Eng.

**GATTON, PHIL J,** Univ Of Louisville, Louisville, KY; SO; MENG; Primatas 90-; Sword Pens Ltd 87-; De Paul Hon Grp 89-90; Chgo Hmls Hngr Cleanup; De Paul IMS; Elec Eng.

**GATTS, MARCY L,** Comm Coll Algny Co Algny Cmps, Pittsburgh, PA; FR; Nrsg Asst; Nrsg.

**GAUDIUSO, GIOIA,** Pa St Univ Delaware Cty Cmps, Media, PA; FR; SGA; Athl Assn 90-; Chrstn Flwshp 90-; Dns Lst 90-; Keystone; Bsktbl 90-; Sci/Psychlgy; Occup Thrpst.

**GAUG, PATRICIA L**, Anne Arundel Comm Coll, Arnold, MD; FR; BA; Bay Are Prlgl Assc 90-; Pblc Jstc Ctr Hay Advct; Cert Prlgl; Law.

**GAUGHAN, TINA M**, Daytona Beach Comm Coll, Daytona Beach, FL; FR; AS; Stdnt Resp Cr Assoc Sec 90-; Rsprtry Thrpy Tchnlgy.

**GAUL, RENE J**, Pa St Univ Delaware Cty Cmps, Media, PA; SO; BSN; Eberty Coll Sci Awd 90; Nrsng.

**GAULT, GREGORY T**, Univ Of Cincinnati, Cincinnati, OH; SO; BS; IEEE 89-; Alpha Lambda Delta 89-; Deans List 89-; Coop Job Cincinnati Gas Elect Co; Elect Engrng Tech.

**GAULT, NANCY S**, Coll Of Charleston, Charleston, SC; JR; BS; Kappa Alpha Sigma; Stdnt Marshall For Grad; Bsns Admn/Mth; Bsns Mgmt/Bnkng.

**GAULT, RONALD J**, Ms St Univ, Miss State, MS; JR; BA; Mortar Brd; Phi Theta Kappa Sec 89-90; Gamma Beta Phi; Pres Lst 90-; AA Meridian Cmnty Clg 90; Econs; Law.

**GAUSE, NORA E**, Goucher Coll, Towson, MD; JR; BA; Opn Cir Thtr SGA Rep 88-; SGA Rep 88-90; Crtcl Theory Grp 88-; Prfc Lit Mag; Rssn Clb Sec 90-; Isabelle Kellogg Thomas Awd Engl 88-; Phi Beta Kappa Awd 90-; Deans Schlr 88-; Engl/Rssn Lit Emphs; Acad Coll Tchng.

**GAUSE, PATRICIA E**, Christopher Newport Coll, Newport News, VA; SR; BSBA 90; Mgmt; Bus Mgmt.

**GAUTHIER, ROBERT R**, Unity Coll, Unity, ME; FR; BS; Wildlf Clb 90-; Deans Lst 90-; IM Vlybl 90-; Wildlife; Wildlife Mgt.

**GAUVIN, STEPHANE J**, Cornell Univ Statutory College, Ithaca, NY; JR; BS; Ath Actn 88-; Red Ky Soc; Drftd Winnipg Jets Natl Hcky Leag; Vars Ice Hcky; Educ; Tchr.

**GAVEL, KENNETH FRANKLIN**, Asbury Theological Sem, Wilmore, KY; JR; MDIV; Coun Pres 75-76; Theta Phi 90; BA Bethany Bible Coll Sussex N B Canada E0e 1p0 76; Theology; Pastor.

**GAVIN, ELLEN M**, Le Moyne Coll, Syracuse, NY; SR; BA; Wmns Bsktbl Tm Tri Cptn 87-; Vaules Comm 89-90; Math Clb Sec 88-; Pi Mu Epsilon 89-; Rcvd Leon J Maltby Mdl Math 91; Full Schlrshp Lemoyne Athletic & Acadmc 87-; Mmbr 1991 Gte Acdmc All Amrcn Tm 91; Math; Acturl Sciences.

**GAVIN, KIRK E**, Fl A & M Univ, Tallahassee, FL; SR; MED; Gldn Key; Hnr Rl; Dns Lst; Ecnmc Intshp; Prince Hl Master Msn Sec; St John M B Chrch Yth Dir 83-91; Cmptr Oper III; BS; AA Tall Comm Clg 86; Educ Ldrshp; Admn.

**GAVIN, M MEGHAN**, Central Fl Comm Coll, Ocala, FL; SO; Phi Theta Kappa 90-; Bus/Acctg; CPA.

**GAVIN, MARION V**, Eckerd Coll, St Petersburg, FL; SR; BA; Internatl Stdnt Assoc 87-; Internatl Bus Club 90-; Soc Advcmnt Of Mgmnt 90-; ELS Interaction Prog Dir 89-; Rotoract 87-88; Intrnshp Arts Mgmnt Bayfront Ctr; Hnrs Schlrshp 87-; Natl Clgte Social Sciences Awd; Internatl Bus; PR Or Arts Mgmnt.

**GAVIN, SARAH A**, Gallaudet Univ, Washington, DC; SR; BA; Nwspaper Rep 90-; Hnrs Org 90-; Never Too Late Clb Sec 90-; Phi Alpha Pi; Quota Intl Fellow 90-; Hnrs Assn Deaf 85-; Travis Cnty Cncl Deaf Sec 86-; Psych; Schl Psychgst/Profssr.

**GAVIN, STEPHEN M**, Tougaloo Coll, Tougaloo, MS; SR; BA; Hmn Svc Clb 90-; Sclgy Clb 90-; Hlth Promo Confo Intrnshp Stdnt Wrkr 90; Grntlgy Awd Intrnshp 90-; Deans Lst; BA; Sclgy/Gerntlgy Cert; Hmn Svc Dept.

**GAVINA, BEATRIMAR L**, Bloomfield Coll, Bloomfield, NJ; SR; BSN; Hi Hnrs 90; Deans Lst 90; Nrsg.

**GAVSIE, BRIAN J**, Univ Of Miami, Coral Gables, FL; SO; BA; Rthsklr Adv Brd Treas; Intfrat Cncl Chm 90-; Pres 100 90-; Orntn Asst 90; Asc Grk Ltrs Org; Hnrs Pgm 88-; Sigma Alpha Mu Chm; Ecnmcs; Law.

**GAW, PAMELA L**, Valdosta St Coll, Valdosta, GA; SR; BED; Delta Chi Ltl Sis 89-; Natl Stdnt Spch/Lang/Hrg Assoc 89-; Amer Spch/Hrg Assoc; Phi Mu Prlmntrn 89-90; Spch Lang Pthlgy; MA Med.

**GAWIN, AGNIESZKA M**, Peabody Inst Of J Hopkins Univ, Baltimore, MD; JR; BM; Music Clb 89-; Itzhak Perlman 90; The B Piesecka Johnson Fndtn Grant 90-; Polish Amer Heritage Leag Awd 90; Gove Fmly Mem Fndtn Trst Schlrshp 89-; Voice; Opera Singer.**

**GAWORECKI, JANSON J**, Niagara Univ, Niagara Univ, NY; FR.

**GAWORECKI, MARY C**, Volunteer St Comm Coll, Gallatin, TN; FR; Math; Tchr.

**GAY, CHARLOTTE K**, Univ Of Ky, Lexington, KY; GD; MD; Kappa Kappa Gamma Pldg Trnr 87-88; Madison Hse 86; Carden Jennings Pblshng Intern 88-Offc Mgr 89-90; BA Univ VA 89; Pre Med Engl Undrgrad; Med.

**GAY, DARLENE A**, Nyack Coll, Nyack, NY; JR; Gspl Tm 90-; Christie Hl Bible Stdy 90-; Deans Lst 90-; Hghr Educ Pro 88-; Wrk Stdy Dir Admsns Asst 90-; Psych; Marr/Fmly Cnslr.

**GAY, DAWNE M**, Fisk Univ, Nashville, TN; JR; Stndt Gov Assoc V Pres; Rept SGA 89-90; Newpr Entertnmnt 88-89; Mortar Brd; Alpha Kappa Alpha Philactor 90-; STEP Intern Prog; Montgomery Cnty Childrens Serv Inter 90; Tuition Schlrshp; English; Law.

**GAY, KIMBERLY D**, Castleton St Coll, Castleton, VT; FR; BAART; Prob Stat Tutor 90-; New Hall 90-; Sigma Delta Chi 90-; Castltn Schlr Schlrshp 90-; IM 90-; Tm Mgr 90-; Art/Comm; Adv Desgn.

**GAY, PATRICK C**, Univ Of Sc At Columbia, Columbia, SC; FR; MED; Voc Educ; Tchr.

**GAY, SANDRA J**, Univ Of Sc At Columbia, Columbia, SC; FR; Stdnt Nrs Assn 90-; Nrsng; Adn-RN.

**GAY, SONIA S**, William Paterson Coll, Wayne, NJ; GD; BA; Elem Educ Assn Clg Life Un Brd Cinema Comm; Psi Chi; Res Asst Prof Powel Boski; Dns Lst; Elem Educ/Psych; Tchr.

**GAY, TERRIOUS J**, Saint Pauls Coll, Lawrenceville, VA; SO; BS; NAACP 89-90; Wmn Cncl 89-90; Alpha Swthrt 89-90; Dns Lst; Alpha Kappa Alpha Asst Dn Intake Treas; Elem Ed; Tchr.

**GAYA-GONZALEZ, IVELISSE M**, Univ Of Pr At Mayaguez, Mayaguez, PR; GD; BS; AIESEC Pub Rel Offcr 89-90; Amer Mktg Assn 89-; Phi Kappa Phi 90-; Hnr Rl 88-; Prof Mdl Fontecha Acad 85-88; GMAC AACSB Mnrty Smr Inst Niv Of Mich Ann Arbor 90; Intrnshp Univ Wis-Milw 88; Mktg; Intl Bus.

**GAYFORD, JENNIFER E**, S U N Y Coll At Fredonia, Fredonia, NY; SR; BA; Teacher Ed Club 90; Kappa Delta Pi; Deans List 88; Elem Ed; Teacher.

**GAYLE, KEVIN A**, Univ Of Southern Ms, Hattiesburg, MS; SR; BS; Med Tech Clb Pres 90-; Mem Hosp Glfprt Auxlry Schlrshp Rcpnt 90-; BS MS Coll 89; Med Tech; Clncl Lab Scntst.

**GAYLOR, ANITA R**, Union Coll, Barbourville, KY; JR; Gamma Beta Phi 90-; Iota Sigma Nu; Pres Laureate; Psych Sclgy; Clncl Psych.

**GAYLORD, JEFFREY M**, Defiance Coll, Defiance, OH; JR; BS; Crmnl Just Soc VP 90-; Alpha Rho Lambda 89-; US Achvmnt Acdmy 90-; Co-Op Stdnt Gnrl Motors Corp Scrty Offcr 88-; Crmnl Just; Law Enfrcmnt.

**GAYNOR, JANET**, Providence Coll, Providence, RI; SR; BA; Theta Alpha Phi 90-; Phi Sigma Tau 90-; Trinity Rprty Co Intshp 90; Engl/Thetre Arts.

**GAYNOR, MICHELLE R**, Univ Of North Fl, Jacksonville, FL; SR; BA; Sawmill Slough 89; Psych Clb Pres 90; Psi Chi VP 90; Golden Key 89-; Phi Kappa Phi; Indpdnt Study/Resrch On Memory; Psych; Crim Just.

**GAYNOR, SHAWNA**, Fl Atlantic Univ, Boca Raton, FL; FR; BA; Phi Eta Sigma; Phi Kappa Phi; Bus; Acctg/CPA.

**GAZSO, KIMBERLY M**, Albertus Magnus Coll, New Haven, CT; SR; BA; Engl Club 90-; Philosphy Club 88-; Spanish Club 87-90; Intrnshp 89-; Varsity Sftbl Cptn 88-; Cmnctns.

**GAZTAMBIDE-FERNANDEZ, RUBEN A**, The Boston Conservatory, Boston, MA; SO; BM; Stdnt Govt Hse Of Rep; Intrnatl Stdnts Orgnztn Chr Prsn; Bsktbl Cch; Cnsrvtry Asstshp Wrk As Int Stdnt Advsr; Msc; Cmpsr And Tchr.

**GAZZARA, TRACY L**, Glassboro St Coll, Glassboro, NJ; JR; BA; Psychlgy Clb 88; Psychlgy.

**GDULA, KIMBERLY A**, Schenectady County Comm Coll, Schenectady, NY; SO; AS; Stdnt Govt Assn Pres 90-; Drama Clb Pres 89-; Stdnt Actvts Bd V P 90-; Faculty Stdnt Assn Bd Dir 90-; Ski Clb Pres 89-90; SGA Fresh Sntr 89-90; Miss Teen 4th Runrup 89; Miss Teen Ctes Amer Natl Pagnt Cntstnt 90; Stnt Vol Org; Prfrmng Arts.

**GEAGAN, PETER**, Becker Coll At Leicester, Leicester, MA; SO; Bsnss Staff Of Yrbk 90; Phi Theta Kappa 90; Intrnshp Bsnss Staff Of Yrbk 90; Deans Lst 90; Im Bsktbl 89; Bsnss Admin; Prchsng Agent.

**GEANS, BRENDA MARIE**, Univ Of Cin R Walters Coll, Blue Ash, OH; SO; AA; Dns Lst 90; Sec Wrkshp; Exec Sec; Bsn Admin; Mgmt.

**GEAR-STINE, SUE N**, Univ Of Cin R Walters Coll, Blue Ash, OH; FR; BS; Phi Theta Kappa; Mgng Dg/Ct Brdng Fclty 89-; Ntrl Sci; Hlth Srv.

**GEARHART, AMY M**, Meridian Comm Coll, Meridian, MS; SO; BS; Deans List 89-90; Presidents List 89-90; Phi Theta Kappa Brd Mbr 89-90; Sftbl 89-90; Medcl Serv Air Force Trng Schools 88-89; Spclst MSS; Served In Desert Storm 90-91; Pre Med; Medical Dr.

**GEARHART, JENNIFER H**, Wv Univ At Parkersburg, Parkersburg, WV; JR; BS; Tutor 90-; C P Telep W Vr Oprtr 88-; Math; Rsrch.

**GEARHART, SONYA L**, Duquesne Univ, Pittsburgh, PA; FR; BA; Phi Eta Sigma; Bus; Acctng/Finance.

**GEARY, LINDA M**, Union Univ, Jackson, TN; SR; BS; STEA 90-; Asst Math Dept 87-89; Alpha Chi 89-; Sigma Zeta 89-; Kappa Mu Epsilon 89-; Math; Hgh Schl Tchr.

**GEARY, THOMAS J**, City Univ Of Ny Queensbrough, New York, NY; SR; BBA; Stdnt Orien Ldr 89-; AAS; Cmptr Prgrmng.

**GEBBEN, VICKI A**, Univ Of Cincinnati, Cincinnati, OH; SR; Eunice Comles Cncl; Ohio Cncl Internatl Rdng Assoc; BS; Erly Chldhd Ed.

**GEBBIA, LUCIA**, Fl International Univ, Miami, FL; FR; Biolgy; Med.

**GEBERS, MARY PAT P**, Defiance Coll, Defiance, OH; SR; BS; Stdnt Body Organ 87; Alpha Chi; Northwest Ohio Hsng Coltn Bd Dir 90-; Inst Mngmnt Actnt 90-; Fiscal Dir First Call Help Inc 89-; AA N W Tech Coll 84-86; Acctg Mngmnt.

**GEBOSKIE, LARA J**, Springfield Tech Comm Coll, Springfield, MA; SO; AS; Radio Nws Dir; Deans Lst; Radio Intrn Bd Oprtr; Cable Vsn Intrn; Tlcmnctns; Advrtsng BA.

**GEDDES, VICKI L**, Hudson Valley Comm Coll, Troy, NY; SO; AAS; Capt/Conifer Pk Intern 89-; Hosp Rehab Vol 90-; NYFAC 90-; Human Serv; Soc Wrkr.

**GEDEON, KATHLEEN A**, Niagara Univ, Niagara Univ, NY; JR; BA; Orntn Exec Brd Chrprsn 89-; Prnts Wkend Dcmt 90-; Frshmn Yr Exprnc Cmt 90-; Dlt Epsln Sgm; Pi Lmbd Theta 90-; Awrd Exclnc Educ 89-90; Educ Fac Rep; Elem Educ/Engl; Tchng.

**GEE, CORINTHIA E**, Claflin Coll, Orangeburg, SC; JR; BS; SGA; Hon Pgm Schlr 88-; Alpha Kappa Alpha Pres; Miss Claflin Coll Attndnt; Bus Admin; Mgmt Cnsltng.

**GEE, DAVID A**, Richard Bland Coll, Petersburg, VA; SO; BA; Phi Beta Lamba Jrnlst 88-89; Pi Kappa Pi 90-; AS; Bus.

**GEE, DIANA**, City Univ Of Ny Baruch Coll, New York, NY; JR; BA; Mngmnt.

**GEE, ERICA J**, Tougaloo Coll, Tougaloo, MS; JR; BA; NAACP; Ed Club; Miss Oceanside 89; Miss Black/Gold; Elem Ed; Admn.

**GEE, GEORGE B**, Capitol Coll, Laurel, MD; JR; BS; AA 90; Cmptr Eng Tech; Cmptr Prgrmr.**

**GEE, HANNEY**, City Univ Of Ny Baruch Coll, New York, NY; JR; BBA; Varsty Bwlng Tm Capt 88-; Cmptr Pgrmg; Pgrmr Anlyst.

**GEE, JEFFRY T**, Ashland Comm Coll, Ashland, KY; SO; BA; Television Commercials Model 88-; College/High Schl Chem Tutor 89-; Dns Lst 89-; Health Careers Opportunity Prog Univ Of KY; Microbiology; Doctor Of Medicine.

**GEE, MEI-LOON**, Univ Of Ky, Lexington, KY; JR; BS; MSO 90-; AICHE 90-; Chem Engrng; Engrng.

**GEE, MICHAEL B**, Liberty Univ, Lynchburg, VA; SR; Prayer Ldr 89-90; Spiritual Life Dir 90-; Concert Choir 89-; Alpha Lambda Delta 88-; Chemist Intern 89-; Sacred Music/Cnslng; Music Minister.

**GEENTY, KELLI J**, Mount Saint Mary Coll, Newburgh, NY; JR; BACCHUS V P 88-; Gaelic Soc 88-; Hnrs Allinc 89-; Psych; Statcs.

**GEER, CHRISTINE M**, Newbury Coll, Brookline, MA; FR; AS; Paralegal; Law.

**GEER, MARY F**, Nova Univ, Ft Lauderdale, FL; GD; MBA; Southern Bell Tel/Tel Co Erv Manager; BS Nova Univ 89; AA Fla Comm Clg 77; Business; Teach.

**GEER, TECORA M**, Albany St Coll, Albany, GA; GD; BS; Kappa Delta Pi; Cum Laude Grad; AS 87; Diploma Tri-Cnty Tech Clg 77; Early Chldhd Ed; Masters.

**GEGENFURTNER, COLLEEN M**, S U N Y Coll Of Tech At Alfred, Alfred, NY; SO; AA; Outdoor Recr Clb Secr 90-; Invir Clb 90-; Soccer 89-90; Sch Mag 90-; Creative Wrtg 90-; IM Sftbl 89-90; Engl; Ed/Jrnlsm.

**GEH, TRACY L**, Indiana Univ Of Pa, Indiana, PA; SO; BA; Intrntl Stdnt Clb 90; Speech-Lang Pthlgy; Clncl Serv.

**GEHLFUSS, GINA M**, Notre Dame Coll, Cleveland, OH; JR; BA; Bus; Acctg.

**GEHLHAUSEN, PAMELA R**, Kent St Univ Kent Cmps, Kent, OH; FR; Alpha Lambda Delta; Delta Zeta Comm Chr 90-; Lang Transltn/Intl Mktg; Intl Bsn.

**GEHRIG, LINDA S**, Lansdale School Of Bus, North Wales, PA; SO; Lttr Crrier 88-; Wrd Prcssng; Bus.

**GEHRING, PATRICIA ANN**, Indiana Univ Of Pa, Indiana, PA; SR; BED; Math Clb 87-; Math; Eductn.

**GEHRLICH, ELLEN ELIZABETH**, Oh St Univ, Columbus, OH; JR; BS; Dstngshd Schlr Schlrshp 88-89; Joseph N Bradford Memrl Schlrshp; Archtctr; Archtct.

**GEIB, JENNIFER J**, The Johns Hopkins Univ, Baltimore, MD; JR; BS; Cncrt Bnd 89; Mrchng Bnd 89; Tri Beta 90; Uppr Alln Fre Dept 89-; Cnsrtm Awrd 91-; Nrsng; Prcttnr.

**GEIGER, CARLA G**, Univ Of Fl, Gainesville, FL; SR; Gator Mrchng Bnd Sec Ldr 86-90; Symphnc Cncrt Bkbl Bnds 87-90; Clgte Music Eductrs Natl Conf 89-; Tau Beta Sigma S E Dist Sec 86-; Pres Hon Rl; Natl Intrclgte Band; UF I M Co Ed Sftbl; BMM Ed; Music Educ; Band Dir.

**GEIGER, GREGORY J**, Temple Univ, Philadelphia, PA; SO; BS; Envir Eng Tech; Indstrl Envir Eng.

**GEIGER, JENNIFER L**, Univ Of Rochester, Rochester, NY; SO; Vrsty Bsktbl 89-; Bio.

**GEIGER-ADDISON, KIMMOALECA O**, Hood Coll, Frederick, MD; FR; BA; Blck Un 90; Vllybll 90; Blgy; Med.

**GEISEL, MARY B**, Northern Ky Univ, Highland Hts, KY; SR; BA; Lrng Asst Cntr 88-; LALINK VP 88; Assc Edtr Ky Stds 89; Assc Edtr Dept Publctn 88; Alpha Chi 90; Sigma Tau Delta 90; Kappa Delta Pi; PINNACLE Sec; Eng/Sec Educ; Tchng.

**GEISENDAFFER, CARLA M**, Longwood Coll, Farmville, VA; FR; BA; Assoc Cthlc Stdt Treas 90-; Bsn.

**GEISER, AIMEE L**, Univ Of Akron, Akron, OH; FR; BS; Hnrs Club Univ Of Akron; Phi Eta Sigma; Alpha Lambda Delta; Bus Mrktng Intl Bus; Mrktng/Ballet Dancer.

**GEISLER, DONNA JEAN**, Comm Coll Algny Co Algny Cmps, Pittsburgh, PA; FR; Drafting/Computer Aid; Eng.

**GEISLER, GAYLE L**, Indiana Univ Of Pa, Indiana, PA; SR; PSEA 89-; Stdnt Tchr-Franklin Rgnl Schl Dist; Pre-Stdnt Tchr-W A Mc Creery Schl 90; Asst Grp Sprvsr-IN Cnty Chld Day Cr Pgm Inc; BED.

**GEIST, KIMBERLY J**, Daytona Beach Comm Coll, Daytona Beach, FL; GD; AS; BA OH Univ 84; Graphic Design; Freelance Artist.

**GEIST, LA DIEH F,** Columbus Coll Of Art & Design, Columbus, OH; SO; BFA; Illstrn/Ad Dsng.

**GEIST, TIMOTHY S,** Embry Riddle Aeronautical Univ, Daytona Beach, FL; SR; BSABA; Im Sftbl; Aeronautical Sci/Aviation Bsnss; Prof Pilot.

**GEITHMANN, SUZANNA L,** Christopher Newport Coll, Newport News, VA; SR; Order Omega Pres 89; Gamma Phi Beta Pres 89-; Jr Achvmnt Bus Cons 88; Sailing Tm 86-90; BA; Intl Culture/Commerce; Bus Mgmnt.

**GELADE, MELISSA B,** Dickinson Coll, Carlisle, PA; FR; BA; Bl Lttl Prgm 90-; Envrnmntl Clb 90-; Hll Cncl Pblcty Chrwmn 90-; Alpha Lambda Delta; Bg Lttl Prgm 90; Dana Schlrshp Applcnt; Frnch.

**GELAUDE, ANNE E,** Miami Univ, Oxford, OH; SO; BS; Ctr For Cmnty Invlvmnt Adopt-A-Grandparent Prs 89-; Hall Govt Pres 90-; Skyscrapers Treas 89-90; Natl Res Hall Hnry Pres 90-; Deans Scholar 89; Business; Business Mgmnt.**

**GELCH, GARY D,** Univ Of Fl, Gainesville, FL; JR; BA; Phi Eta Sigma 88-; Golden Key 90-; Pi Lambda Phi Athltc Dir 89-90; IM Bsktbl/Sftbl/Vlybl/Bwlng89-90; Plyr/Coach All-Cmps Sftbl Tm; Mrktng; Law.

**GELINEAU, GINA M,** Western New England Coll, Springfield, MA; JR; BSW; Bhvrl Scl Sci Clb 89-; Stglss Plyrs 89-90; Alpn Ski Tm 88-89; Deans Lst 88-; Slc Wrk; Admn.

**GELLER, HAYLEY F,** Temple Univ, Philadelphia, PA; BS; Phrmctcl Assn 90-; BSW La Salle Univ 85; Sci; Phrmcy.**

**GELLMAN, DAVID M,** Yeshiva Univ, New York, NY; SR; BA; Yrbk Edtr In Chf 89-; Nwsppr Crdntg Edtr 88-; Dns Lst 87-; Ice Hockey Club; IM Hockey Capt 88-; Hstry; Law.

**GELLNER III, RICHARD E,** Truett Mc Connell Coll, Cleveland, GA; SO; BA; Boy Scouts/Life Scout 87; Pres Lst Georgia Military Clg 89-; Bsn Mgmt.

**GELMAN, NATALYA,** Cooper Union, New York, NY; SO; BE; KESHER 89-; SWE 89-90; Bowling 89-90; Elctrcl Engr.

**GELMAN, SUSAN E,** Fl International Univ, Miami, FL; SR; BS; Phi Theta Kappa; Hotel Sls/Mktg Assn Intl Gold Coast Chapt 82-86; AA Broward Comm Coll 90; Cmnctns; Publ Rel.

**GELOSE, CHRISTOPHER J,** Niagara Univ, Niagara Univ, NY; SR; BA; Cmps Mnstry 90-; Lit Sngrs 90-; Twn Plyrs Thtrcl Grp 79-; Brnch Lfe Mnstrs 88-; KC 87-; Dir Cmp Trnr Promo Video 88; VP Prof Video Grp 87-89; BA 89; Psy/Gdnc Cnslng; Schl Cnslr.

**GELPI, CAROL S,** William Carey Coll, Hattiesburg, MS; BSN; Sigma Sigma Sigma; Nurse; BS Loyola Univ 66; Nursing.

**GELPI, EDNA MARIE,** Central Fl Comm Coll, Ocala, FL; AA; Boys/Girls Clb Vol; Fla Soc Anesthesia Tech FSAT 90-; Ocala Ch God Mnstry; LPN; Nurs/Educ; Cert Reg Nurs Anesthetist.

**GELSTON, KELLY L,** Comm Coll Algny Co Algny Cmps, Pittsburgh, PA; SO; AA; Lib Art Sci.

**GEMBERLING, LAURA L,** Elmira Coll, Elmira, NY; SR; BS; Orchesis Treas 89-; Fin Brd Rep 90-; AS Cnty Clg Of Morris 89; Acctng; CPA.

**GEMMITI, JAMES A,** Portland School Of Art, Portland, ME; GD; BFA; Stdnt Govt Rep 88-89; Nwsppr Stf 89-90; Phtgrphy; Phtgrphr.

**GENAUER, ETZION I,** Yeshiva Univ, New York, NY.

**GENCO, ANDREW R,** Springfield Tech Comm Coll, Springfield, MA; SR; EDEL; Comps/Laser Optcs; Comp Tech.

**GENDRON, ELAINE C,** Johnson St Coll, Johnson, VT; JR; BA; Chsmr Hnr Soc; Grl Scts America Ldr 77-82; Elem Edctn; Tchr.

**GENDUSA, AMY E,** Univ Of Southern Ms, Hattiesburg, MS; SO; Stdnt Alumni Assoc; Campus United Way; Yng Republicans; Delta Delta Delta Hsng Chair 90-; Hist; Scndry Edn.

**GENERALOVICH, ALYSSA,** Univ Of Pittsburgh, Pittsburgh, PA; FR; BS; Lambda Sigma; Delta Delta Delta; Chrldr; Lib Arts; Phrmcy.

**GENERETT JR, WILLIAM O,** Morehouse Coll, Atlanta, GA; SO; BA; Pol Sci Soc Pres 90-; Stdnt Govt Assn Chair Pol Action Com; Pre Law Soc; Yth Mntrng Pgm 89-; Cngrsnl Blck Cacus Flwshp; Hon Roll 89-; Pol Sci/Spnsh; Law.

**GENETSKI, CHRISTIAN S,** Birmingham Southern Coll, Birmingham, AL; JR; BA; Stdnt Jdcry 902; Dns Advsry Comm 90-; Pub Bd 89-90; Intrfrtrnty Cncl 89-90; Race Rel Prtnrshp 90-; Tutoring Prog 90-; Mrtr Bd 90-; Phi Alpha Theta 90-; Alpha Lambda Delta 89-; Phi Eta Sigma 89-; Sigma Alpha Epsilon Rush Chrmn 88-; Hstry/Engl; Law.

**GENEVIEVE-TWEED, NICHOLAS,** Interdenominational Theo Ctr, Atlanta, GA; GD; MDIV; S H Giles Awd Acad Excl 90-; ITC Hon Rl/Dns Lst 90-; Asst Mnstr Big Bethel AME; BA Hons Mdlsx Polytech Ldn,Englnd 89; Thlgy.

**GENIER, JOSEPH P,** Cornell Univ Statutory College, Ithaca, NY; JR; BS; Prog Brd Chrmn 88; Daily Sun 89-90; Tae Kwon Doe Clb; Cmmnctns.

**GENNICK, RANDALL,** Chattanooga St Tech Comm Coll, Chattanooga, TN; SO; AS; Deans List; Misty Meadows SPA Chrch Schl Tchr; Info Systems.

**GENO, LAURIE L,** Johnson St Coll, Johnson, VT; SR; BA; Elem/Spec Educ; Tchr.

**GENOVESE, ALEXANDER V,** Bloomfield Coll, Bloomfield, NJ; FR; BA; Crmnl Jstce; Law Enfrcemnt.

**GENTEK, GREGORY A,** Glassboro St Coll, Glassboro, NJ; JR; BS; Ftbl 88-89; Ecnmcs; Stkbrkr.

**GENTHNER, BRENDA E,** S U N Y Coll At Fredonia, Fredonia, NY; SR; BSE; AASS Jamestown Comm Clg 89; Educ Erly Chldhd; Teacher.

**GENTILE, JOSEPH A,** S U N Y Coll At Fredonia, Fredonia, NY; JR; BS; Coll Audio Prod/Brdcstng Radio/TV; SCCC Deans Lst 87-90; Suffolk Cnty Comm Coll 90; Cmnctns/Radio/Audio Prod.

**GENTILE, LISA A,** Lesley Coll, Cambridge, MA; JR; BED; Early Chldhd Ed; Tch.

**GENTILE, RONALD P,** City Univ Of Ny Baruch Coll, New York, NY; JR; BBA; Baruch Schlr 88-; Amer Cancer 88-90; Leukemia 89-90; Baruch Pres Schlrshp 88-; NY State Regents Schlrshp 88-; Acctg; CPA.

**GENTILE, SHERI L,** Springfield Tech Comm Coll, Springfield, MA; SO.

**GENTLE, RAYMOND PATRICK,** Norwalk St Tech Coll, Norwalk, CT; SO; BS; Tutor Students; Phi Theta Kappa; Pres List; Stamford Teen Life Center 86-90; AS; Data Processing.

**GENTLES, MOUREEN M,** Coppin St Coll, Baltimore, MD; JR; BA; Nrsng.

**GENTRY, CHARLOTTE S,** Midlands Tech Coll, Columbia, SC; SR; AHS; Phi Theta Kappa; Natl Nurses Achvmnt Awrd; All Amer Achvmnt Awrd; Shandon Baptist Church; LPN; Nursing.

**GENTRY, CHERI L,** King Coll, Bristol, TN; SO; BA; Fllwshp Chrstn Athlts; Ambssdr King Coll; Vlybl Trnr; Bhvrl Sci; Elem Ed.

**GENTRY, CHRISTIE HOPE,** Univ Of Nc At Charlotte, Charlotte, NC; FR; Intrdscplnry Hnrs Assoc 90; Phi Eta Sigma; Sftbl Ims.

**GENTRY, KARMAN K,** Univ Of Montevallo, Montevallo, AL; SO; MD; Alpha Gamma Delta 90-; Awd Hnrs Day; Valedictorian Schlrshp 89; Psych.

**GENTRY, MELISSA D,** Madisonville Comm Coll, Madisonville, KY; JR; MA; Phi Beta Lambda 89-90; SIFE; Eastern Star; Acctng; CPA.

**GENTRY, MELISSA G,** Germanna Comm Coll, Locust Grove, VA; FR; BA; Psychlgy; Elem Educ.

**GENTRY, NIKI D,** Middle Tn St Univ, Murfreesboro, TN; JR; BS; Arspc Admn; USAF Offcr.

**GENTRY, REGINA M,** Jackson St Univ, Jackson, MS; SR; BBA; Dunbar Drmtc Gld 87-88; Phi Kappa Phi; Alph Kappa Mu 90-; Dlt Mu Dlt 89-; Zeta Phi Beta Pres; Intrnshp Shell Oil Co Houston Acctnt; Acctg; Tchng.

**GENTRY, SHERYL E,** Univ Of Tn At Chattanooga, Chattanooga, TN; FR; Marching Band 90-; Pep Bnd 90-; Bayside Christmas Pag 90; Christmas Concert 90; Bayside Baptist Church Orch 90-; Chem Engr.

**GENTRY, STEPHANIE L,** Snead St Jr Coll, Boaz, AL; JR; BS; Amrcn Mrktng Assoc 90-; Snd St Ambsdr 89-90; Omncrn Delta Kappa 90-; Delta Zeta 90-; Phi Beta Lambda 90-; As 90; Mrktng/Hmn Rsrc Mngmnt; Advrtsng.

**GENUNG, BARBARA,** Columbia Greene Comm Coll, Hudson, NY; FR; AAS; Bsnss; Accntng Bkkpng Payroll.

**GEOGHEGAN, EDWARD E,** Saint Josephs Coll Sufflk Cmps, Patchogue, NY; SO; BS; Nwspr 86-89; Yrbk 86-89; Cir K 89-; Bio Clb 89-; Hstry Clb 89-; Cmps Mnstry 89-; Spnsh Hnr Soc 88-89; Natl Themla Hnr Soc 88-89; Sigma Iota Chi 90-; Rlgn Tchr 84-; Euchrstc Mnstr 89-; Dns Lst 89-90; Bio; Doctor.**

**GEOGHEGAN, KATHERINE A,** Villanova Univ, Villanova, PA; JR; BA; Spcl Olympcs 90-; Stdnt Union 88-89; Pi Beta Phi Standards Brd 89-; Acdmc Achvmnt Awd; Deans Lst 90-; Englsh; Jrnlsm Pblc Rltns.

**GEORGAKAKIS, KALLIOPI,** Fl Atlantic Univ, Boca Raton, FL; FR; BA; Maids Athena Pres 86-; Phi Eta Sigma; Bus; Acctg.

**GEORGE, AIMEE B,** Indiana Univ Of Pa, Indiana, PA; JR; BA; Zeta Tau Alpha VP 89-; WIUP-TV 90-; ASTD 90-; Ordr Of Omega; Lit Corps 89; Outstndng Serv Awrd; Communcatns.

**GEORGE, BECKY D,** Univ Of Akron, Akron, OH; SR; BA; OSHA 89-; ASHA 87-; NSSLHA 87-; Golden Key 89-; Phi Eta Sigma 87-; Alpha Lambda Delta 87-; Food Kitchn Vol; Asstnt Tchr Untd Way 82-; Outstndng Stdnt OSHA 90; Kiwanis Award 90; Cmnctv Disrdrs; Spch/Lang Pathlgy.

**GEORGE, CARLOS E,** Univ Of Pr At Rio Piedras, Rio Piedras, PR; SO; BA; AIESEC; Fin/Acctg; Law.

**GEORGE, CARRIE A,** Mount Aloysius Jr Coll, Cresson, PA; FR; BED; Acctg.

**GEORGE, CARRIE E,** Columbia Greene Comm Coll, Hudson, NY; SO; AS; Phi Theta Kappa; Intl Schlstc Hon Soc 2 Yr Clgs; Assoc Sci/Nrsng; Nrsng.

**GEORGE, CHRISTOPHER L,** Samford Univ, Birmingham, AL; FR; JD; AICHE; Law Rvw; Chvrn USA Chvrn Chem; Hoechst Celanese; BA Chem Eng Auburn Un 81; Law; Envrnmntl/Intlctl Law.

**GEORGE, DOUGLAS M,** Defiance Coll, Defiance, OH; BS; Optimist Club 85-86; Athletic Boosters Treas 87-; Acctg & Finance Club 90-; Chmbr Comm Downtwn Revitalization Comm 87; Ins Acct Executive; BS 78; Marketing Accounting; CPA.

**GEORGE, JAMES E,** S U N Y Coll Of Tech At Alfred, Alfred, NY; SR; ASSOC; Sigma Tau Epsilon 89-; High Schlstc Hnrs; Acad Distinctn; Bldg Constr.

**GEORGE, MARIA A,** Savannah St Coll, Savannah, GA; SR; SGA 89-; Soph Cls Plnng Comm 88-89; Jr Cls Plnng Comm 89-90; Bus/Info Sys; Comptr Progrmmr.

**GEORGE, OMEGA D,** Univ Of South Al, Mobile, AL; FR; BED; Phi Eta Sigma; Phi Kappa Phi; Alpha Lambda Delta; Elem Ed; Tch.

**GEORGE, PATRICIA D,** Saint Francis Coll, Loretto, PA; FR; BS; Deans List 90-; Acctg.

**GEORGE, RAY A,** Univ Of The Virgin Islands, St Thomas, VI; SR; BA; Univ V Is V P 90-; Pres Clb Treas; Phi Theta Kappa; Lambda Nu Chapt; IM Bsebl/Bsktbl; AS Bronx Cmnty Clg CUNY 90; Acctg; Chartered Accnt.

**GEORGE, RICARDO,** Fl Atlantic Univ, Boca Raton, FL; SR; Intl Bus Clb 89-90; Beta Gamma Sigma 90; Phi Kappa Phi 90; U S Achvmnt Acad 90; All-Amer Schlrs 90; BSBA; Intl Bus; MBA.

**GEORGE, SEAN C,** Morehouse Coll, Atlanta, GA; JR; BA; Natl Blck Coll Allnc VP Prmtns 89-; Amer Cncr Soc 86-; Jr Achvmnt; Union Untd Mthdst Chrch Schlrshp 88; Reebok/Untd Negro Coll Fnd Schlrshp 89-; Reebok Intl LTD Intrnshp Prmtns Intrn 90; Mass Cmnctns/Pblc Rltns/Mktg; Entrtnmnt Lwyr.

**GEORGE, SEAN P S,** Univ Of Southern Ms, Hattiesburg, MS; SO; BA; Stdnt Alumni Assoc 90-; Gamma Beta Phi 89-; Lambda Sigma Edtr 90-; Delta Tau Delta Pldge Educ 89-; Pr Schlrshp; Natl Merit Schlrshp; Choral Perf Schlrshp; IM Ftbl/Bsktbl/Vlybl; Psych.

**GEORGE, STACY G,** Capitol Coll, Laurel, MD; SO; BA; Soc Tech Cmnctns 90-; Stdnt Gov Assn P/V P 89-; Soc Wmn Eng 89-; Pres Awd; Awds Ldrshp/Svc; Tech Cmnctns Tech Wrtng.

**GEORGE, STEPHANIE M,** City Univ Of Ny City Coll, New York, NY; SR; BS; Natl Soc Blck Engrs 84-87; Goldn Key Clb 90-; Comp Sci; Comp Prog.

**GEORGE, TARA D,** Fl A & M Univ, Tallahassee, FL; JR; BA; AA Santa Fe Comm Clg 90; Business Accounting.

**GEORGE, TERESSA C,** Northwest Al Comm Coll, Phil Campbell, AL; Med-Prctcl Nrsng; LPN.

**GEORGE, TERESSA R,** Univ Of Rochester, Rochester, NY; SR; BA; Black & Hispanic Alliance Apres 88-90; Black Stdnt Un; Grapevine Mag; Delta Sigma Theta V P 90-; Susan B Anthony Schlrshp 90-; Intern Statewide Yth Advcy 88-; Eng & African-Am Studies; Cmmnctns Mgmt.

**GEORGE, THOMAS A,** Clayton St Coll, Morrow, GA; SR; BBA; Soc Hmn Rsrc Mngmnt 90-; Amer Prod Inv Cntrl Soc 90-; Alumni Assoc; Deans List 90; IM Bdmntn Trnmnt Sngls/Dbls 87-90; AA 89; Human Rsrc Mgmnt; Admin.

**GEORGE, TRACEY L,** Volunteer St Comm Coll, Gallatin, TN; GD; AS; Allied Hlth; Med Rcrds.

**GEORGE, TRAVIS A,** Memphis St Univ, Memphis, TN; FR; BS; Elec Engrg; Engrg.

**GEORGE, VATTETHU C,** Nova Univ, Ft Lauderdale, FL; GD; MBA; Soc Svc Leag 89-91; Chrch Actvts Trust 88; Chemist; BS U C Clg Alwayc India 66; MS St Johns Clg Agra India 70; Chem; Dctrl Bus Mgmt.

**GEORGE, WILFRED I L,** Monroe Comm Coll, Rochester, NY; SO; BS MS; Govt Stdnt Senator 90; Senate Repr Brd Dir; Phi Theta Kappa 90-; SUNY State Minority Schlrshp 90; Talent Roster Distngshd Acdmc Perf; Genesee Vly Nurses Assoc; Nrsng; MSC MBA.

**GEORGE, WINIFRED L,** Anne Arundel Comm Coll, Arnold, MD; SO; BA; Phi Theta Kappa 90-; Dns Lst 88-; Bd Ed 87; PTO V P 86-87; CAC Pres 86-87; AA Suma Cum Laude; Early Chldhd Ed; Tchr.

**GEORGE-ROBERTS, JENNIFER L,** Southern Coll Of Tech, Marietta, GA; JR; BS; Log Stf; Alpha Delta Pi Rprtr/Stndrds Chrprsn 89; Co-Op Stdnt Atlanta Gas Light Co 89-; Dns Lst; Indus Engr Tech; Engr Corp Law.

**GEORGELOS, PANAGIOTIS,** Villanova Univ, Villanova, PA; FR; BA; Hosp Univ PA Vol; Plpnnsn Soc Schlp Awd; Bio; Med/Ped/Orthpdcs.

**GEORGES, ALBERT,** Univ Of Sc At Columbia, Columbia, SC; FR; BS; Southern Bell Co 89-; Crim Just; Ct Invstgtr.

**GEORGET, RACHEL R,** Coll Of Charleston, Charleston, SC; JR; BS/BA; Frnch Clb 89-; Fca 90-; Bsu 90-; Hnrs Prgrm 90-; Deans Lst 90-; Math/French.

**GEORGIOU, MARINA A,** City Univ Of Ny Baruch Coll, New York, NY; JR; BBA; Baruch Endwmnt Fund Prvsts Schlrshp 89-90; Acctg; MBA/FIN.

**GEORGITSOS, MARIA,** Univ Of Md Baltimore Prof Schl, Baltimore, MD; SR; BS; Sec Med Tchnlgy Sec 89-; Phi Kappa Phi; MD St Sntrl Schlrshp; Vlybl 90-; Med Tchnlgy.

**GEORGOULAKOS, VAHNI,** Univ Of Nc At Charlotte, Charlotte, NC; FR; BCA; Phi Eta Sigma 90-; Intrdscplnry; BA; English/Vsl Arts; Grpic/Cmrcl Art/Jrnlsm.

**GEOSITS, SCOTT J,** East Stroudsburg Univ, E Stroudsburg, PA; JR; BS; Chem Clb 90-; Chem/Eng; Comp Sci.

**GEOTZINGER, BECKY L,** Univ Of Ky, Lexington, KY; JR; BED; Advsry Cncl 89; Lambda Sigma 90; Epsilon Delta Membrshp 90; Cmmnty Serv; Tutor; Religious Ed Vol; Elem Ed Spanish; Tchr.

**GEPHART, CHRISTOPHER R,** Univ Of Sc At Columbia, Columbia, SC; SO; BS; Math Club Pres 89-; Piedmont Soc 81-; Gamma Beta Phi 89-90; Math.

**GERA, SANJAY,** City Univ Of Ny La Guard Coll, Long Island Cty, NY; SR; AS; Bus; Admnstrtr.

**GERACI, ANITA R,** Univ Of Miami, Coral Gables, FL; JR; BA; Pre Legal Soc 90-91; Rotaract 90-91; U S Sntr Robert Graham Intrn 91; Crmnl Juste; Law.

**GERAGOSIAN, AMY M,** S U N Y Coll At Fredonia, Fredonia, NY; SO; BS; Apld Cmnctns Assoc Crdntr 90-; Coll TV Sta Co Prod 89-90; Lacrosse Clb 89-; Cmnctns; Indstrl/Lbr Rltns.

**GERARDY, TONJA M,** Univ Of Nc At Charlotte, Charlotte, NC; SR; Phi Kappa Phi 89-; Golden Key 89-; Marshall At Graduation 90; BS; Religious Studies; Youth Ministry.

**GERCHAK, ROBERTA F,** Wilmington Coll, Wilmington, OH; GD; BA; Hnr Schlrshp 88-; Green Key Soc; Hosp Intrn; Acdmc Exclnc Awrd; Wrtg Awrd Jrnlstc Essay 89; Spcl Cntrbtr Wlmngtn Nws Jrnl 89-; AA 88; BA; Engl Cmnctns; Frlnc Feature Wrtg.

**GERCHICK, STUART CRAIG,** S U N Y At Binghamton, Binghamton, NY; JR; BS; Cir K Clb Dir Of Spr Dnce 88; Clg Yng Demcrts Treas 89; NYPIRG 89-90; Stdnts Prmtng Campus Unity Treas 89; Tchrs Asst In Fnce; Jr Accntng Stdnt Awd; BS; Accntng.

**GERDES, STEPHAN,** City Univ Of Ny Baruch Coll, New York, NY; JR; BBA; Beta Alpha Psi Treas; NABA 90-; VITA; Golden Key 89-; Beta Gamma Sigma; State Cmnts Aid Assoc Vol 90-; United Negro Coll Fund 90; AICPA Schrlshp 90-; Murray N Niedorf Schrlshp 90; Sponsors Educ Opport Intern; Accounting; CPA.

**GERDINE, CLINT A,** Fl A & M Univ, Tallahassee, FL; JR; BS; Stanfrd Blck Stdnt Un 88-; Natl Soc Blck Sci Engrs Soc Chr Of Lcl Chptr 88-; IEEE 88-; Elec Engr; Grad Sch Comm.

**GEREAU-SCHURER, THERESA L,** Univ Of Nc At Charlotte, Charlotte, NC; SR; BS; Magna Cum Laude 90; Rsrch Asstntshp 89-90; Hospice Vol 90-; Anml Hosp 88-; BA Univ WI Oshkosh 82; Psychlgy; Cnslng.

**GEREG, SAMUEL S,** Fl St Univ, Tallahassee, FL; JR; BA; Lamda Alpha Epsilon 90-; Law Enfrcmnt Intrn; Deans Lst 88-; Jvnl Jstc Awd Amrcn Crmnl Jstc Assn, IM Sftbl, AA Okaloosa Walton Comm Clg 90; Crmnlgy; Law Enfrcmnt.

**GEREN, LORI A,** Defiance Coll, Defiance, OH; SO; BED; Chrldr 90-; Gamma Omega Kappa 90-; Hndcppd Schl Vol 90-; Pres Hst 90-; Elem Educ; Tchr.

**GERENA, JORGE L,** Univ Of Pr At Rio Piedras, Rio Piedras, PR; JR; Chorus; Golden Key Pres 90-; Hnr Assoc 90-; Red Crss Lfgrd 90-; Frst Aid 90; CPR 90-; Hnr Stdnt 89; Hnr Stdnt Univ Interamericana 87; Swmmng Instrctr; Hstry/Educ; Law.

**GERENCSER, TRACI A,** Univ Of Akron, Akron, OH; JR; BA; Rho Lambda; Kappa Delta Pi; Alpha Phi Schlrshp Chrmn; Deans List 89; Elmntry Ed; Tchr.

**GERGES, BRENDA S,** Lansdale School Of Bus, North Wales, PA; SR; ASB; Prf Attdnc; ASB; Acctng.

**GERHART, BARBARA L,** De Tech & Comm Coll At Dover, Dover, DE; GD; AAS; Phi Theta Kappa 89-; Outstdng Std Nrsng Tech 90-; LPN; Nrsng; BSN.

**GERKEN, ESTHA,** Juniata Coll, Huntingdon, PA; SR; BS; Intl Clb; Biblestudy Grp; Bio; Gen Educ.

**GERKEN, MICHAEL D,** Lenoir Rhyne Coll, Hickory, NC; JR; MBA; Dns Lst; IM Tenns/Ftbl/Vlybl; Busn Admin.

**GERLACH, HEIDI E,** Columbia Greene Comm Coll, Hudson, NY; FR; Phi Theta Kappa; Nrsng; RN.

**GERLITZ, ELLEN M,** Portland School Of Art, Portland, ME; SR; BA; BA IN Univ 69; MA OH State Univ 71; Fine Art/ Paintng; Tchng/Free Lance Art Wrk.

**GERLOFF, STEVEN M,** Unity Coll, Unity, ME; JR; BS; Cnsrvtn Law Enfrcmnt Clb 88-89; AS Sci 90-; Cnsrvtn Law Enfrcmnt.

**GERMAN, ALICIA LYNN,** Fisk Univ, Nashville, TN; SO; BA; Cls Bus Mgr 90-; Fisk Clb Miss AL 89-; Intrnl Rvn Svc Co Op; Acctg.

**GERMAN, ANTHONY LAMAR,** Commonwealth Coll, Norfolk, VA; USN Avionics Elctrncs Tech 86; USN Intrmdte Lvl Maint EZ-C Arbrne Erly Wrng Syst; BS Tuskegee U 78; Cert US Dept Of Lbr Jrnymn Elctrncs Mchnc; Occptnl Stndrds; Own/Oprte As Avionics Rpr.

**GERMAN, JACQUELINE M,** Inter Amer Univ Pr Guayama, Guayama, PR; SR; BA; Scientfc Cir 89-90; Ed Clb 86-90; Hon Stdnt 86-; Biolgy; Physclgy.

**GERMAN, RONALD S,** Bristol Univ, Bristol, TN; GD; MBA; Medcl Grp Mgmt Assn; Amer Mgmt Assn; Amer Coll Medcl Grp Admin; TN Vly Prsnnl Assn Sec/Treas 88-89; Medcl Grp Mgmt Assn Pres 81; Knxvl Medcl Grp Mgmt Assn Pres; Admin Mgmt Assn Bd Dir 90; BS Univ TN 74; Mgmt; Mgmt-CEO.

**GERMANO, PEGGY L,** Hudson Valley Comm Coll, Troy, NY; SR; Pres Lst; Hist; Govt.

**GERMANO, SONYA,** Lancaster Bible Coll, Lancaster, PA; SO; BS; Varsty Clb 89-; TVFF VP 90-; Res Affrs Cncl; Chrldng 89; Bsktbl 89-91; Sftbl 90; Elem Educ; Tch.

**GERMANY, ALBERT T,** East Central Comm Coll, Decatur, MS; SO; Warrior Corp 90-; Pr Cncl 90-; Phi Theta Kappa 90-; Mu Alpha Theta 90-; Hall Of Fame; IM Ftbl/Bsktbl/Sftbl 90-; Med.

**GERMICK, EDWARD J,** Marywood Coll, Scranton, PA; JR; BA; Natl Grd Spclst E-4 88-; St Cecilias Msc Clb 89-; MENC 88-90; Socl Sci; Educ.

**GERNER, JUDITH L,** Glassboro St Coll, Glassboro, NJ; JR; Dns Lst; AA Gloucester Co Clge 76; Elem Ed/Sclgy; Tch/Lib Sci.

**GERNERT, AMY L,** Indiana Univ Of Pa, Indiana, PA; SR; Natl Cncl Tchrs Engl 90-; Penn Cncl Tchrs Engl 90-; Habit Humnty 89-; Engl Clb Tr 89-; Germn Clb 88-90; Alpha Xi Delta 89-; Dns Lst 90-; Waynsbrg Lads Aux; Schlrshp 87; Wallace Maxwl Mem Schlrshp 87; Delta Kappa Gamma Intl Grnt 90; Im 88; Sec Educ/ Engl; Tchng.

**GERO, MARLENE B,** Daytona Beach Comm Coll, Daytona Beach, FL; SO; BS; Phi Theta Kappa; Pres Lst 90-; Physcns Asst; Neontl Intnsv Cr.

**GEROLIMATOS, SAMANTHA E,** Clarkson Univ, Potsdam, NY; JR; BA; Stdnt Nwspr Arts/Entrtnmnt Edtr 90-; Acctg; Acctg/Law/Tchng.

**GEROMETTA, DAWN M,** Palm Beach Comm Coll, Lake Worth, FL; SO; BA; Phi Theta Kappa 90-; Awrd Acad Exclnc Achvmnts; AA; Sci; Psychlgy.**

**GEROSKI, ALISON K,** Garrett Comm Coll, Mchenry, MD; FR; BA; 4-H Hndcpd Riding; Sci; Phys Ther.

**GERRELL, REGINA K,** James Sprunt Comm Coll, Kenansville, NC; FR; BA; Deans List; Solvay Animal Hlth Schlrshp; Murphy Farms Inc Schlrshp; 105 Math Tutor; Agric Busn; Agric.

**GERRINGER, MELISSA R,** Volunteer St Comm Coll, Gallatin, TN; SO; AAS; Gamma Beta Phi 90-; St Conf 90-; Temprnc Hall Emmnl; Sunday Schl Tchr; APTA; Physcl Thrpy; LPT Assnt.

**GERRINGER, MICHAEL,** S U N Y At Stony Brook, Stony Brook, NY; GD; MD; Tau Beta Pi 83-84; Eta Kappa Nu 83-84; Hewltt Packrd Blood Drv Comm; Clarksn Univ Vrsty Bsbl; BS/ ELEC Engr/Clarksn Univ; Med; Cardlgy.

**GERRIS JR, FRANCIS C,** Glassboro St Coll, Glassboro, NJ; FR; BS; Cncl Off Cmps Lvng VP 90-; Waiter/Bartender; Cmptr Sci.

**GERRISH, KIMBERLY L,** Merrimack Coll, North Andover, MA; JR; BA; Psi Chi; Psychology; Phd Chld Psychlgy.

**GERSBERG, PABLO C,** Univ Of Fl, Gainesville, FL; JR; BS; Soc Engr Sci Pres 90-; Nwspr Edtr Chf 89-90; Mortr Brd 90-; Tau Beta Pi 89-; Phi Theta Kappa 87-; F Troop 88-; Comp Edge Pres Ldr 89-; FL Stdnt Yr Mntn 88-89; AA Broward Comm Clg 89; Engr.

**GERSHGORIN, IGOR,** Bunker Hill Comm Coll, Boston, MA; FR; Radiation Hlth Sci.

**GERSHON, MICHAEL K,** Hudson Valley Comm Coll, Troy, NY; FR; AS; Engrng/Indstrl Technlgs; Constrctn.

**GERSON, SHAWN M,** Union Univ, Jackson, TN; SO; BS; STEA; Bapt Stdnt Union; Chi Omega Asst V P; Math; Tch.

**GERTZ, CHRISTOPHER J,** Univ Of Miami, Coral Gables, FL; SO; Lacrosse Clb; Phi Eta Sigma 89-; Alpha Lambda Delta 90; Pi Kappa Alpha 90-; Lacrosse; Economics; Bus.

**GERTZ JR, RICHARD D,** Univ Of Miami, Coral Gables, FL; JR; BBA; Lacrosse Clb Pres 88-; Hon Stdnt Assn 88-; Hon Stdnt 88-; Frat Stndrds Comm 90-; Oltcl Sci; Bus.

**GERVAIS, PHILIP J,** De Vry Inst Of Tech, Columbus, OH; FR; BA; Elec Engr.

**GERVAS, SOFIA M,** Univ Of Sc At Columbia, Columbia, SC; JR; BS; Metro Conf Comm Lst 88-90; Var Golf Tm 88-; Math.

**GERVASI, JENNIFER LYNN,** Atlantic Comm Coll, Mays Landing, NJ; SO; Bus Admin; Entrpnr.

**GERVIN, MARION E,** Fl International Univ, Miami, FL; JR; BA; Phi Beta Lambda 89-; ACE; PETA; Grnpce; AA 90; Mrktng/ Mgmt; Entrprnrshp Publ/Priv Sectrs.

**GESELL, MELODY,** S U N Y Coll At Fredonia, Fredonia, NY; SR; BA; Art; Creative/Artistic Expression.

**GESSE, PAMELA J,** Fl International Univ, Miami, FL; SR; BS; Future Educ Of Amer 90-; Pi Kappa Pi; Kappa Delta Pi; Sabbath Schl Tchr; Mbr Miami Oratorio Soc Fncl Sec 85-89; PTA Mbr Sec 90; Acct Rcvbl Sprvsr 83-; AA Miami Dade Comm Coll 88; Elem Educ; Tchr.

**GESSNER, ANGELA J,** Juniata Coll, Huntingdon, PA; JR; BS; Scalpel/Probe 89-; Peer Advsng 90-; Beta Beta Beta 90-; HAC 90-; Mcrblgy Lab Asst 90-; Deans Lst 88-; Mdl Atlntc Cnfrnc Spg Acdmc Hon Rl-Trck 90; Trck/Fld 89-; Blgy; Med.

**GESWALDO, ANDREA M,** Le Moyne Coll, Syracuse, NY; SO; Natl Hnr Soc 90; Psych; Sports Sci.

**GETER, JACQUELINE J,** Clayton St Coll, Morrow, GA; SO; AD; Governors Intrnshp Prgrm 90; Deans List 88; Nrsng; Tchng.

**GETER, JACQULYN Y,** Univ Of Nc At Charlotte, Charlotte, NC; SO; Stdnt Ct Chief Jstce; Rsdnt Advsr; Emrgng Ldr Mntr; Phi Eta Sigma; Golden Key; Delta Sigma Theta VP.

**GETGEN, KIMBERLY M,** Radford Univ, Radford, VA; FR; BA; Stdnt Govt 90-; Co-Chair Academic Integrity Comm 90-; Ambassadors 90-; Alpha Sigma Alpha; Most Outstndg Pledge Awd; Pub Essay In Hnr Nwspr; Political Science; Envrmntl Law.

**GETHERS, FELICIA L,** Univ Of Sc At Columbia, Columbia, SC; JR; BA; AAAS S 88-; NAACP 88-; SG 90-; Crrclum Comm; Air Frc Jr ROTC T 88; Phi Beta Sigam Aux VP 88-89; Comm Svc Intrn; Cngrssnl Yth Ldrsh Conf 90; Rcrtng Hostess 90-; SG 87-88; Drama Clb 87-88; ROTC Pbl Affrs 87; Hon Grad 88; Psych/Crmnl Just; Cnslng Psych.

**GETROST, CHRISTINA D,** Kent St Univ Kent Cmps, Kent, OH; SR; BA; ACPB VP 90-; Coll Bowl Qz Tm Pres 87-; Omicron Delta Kappa 90-; Sigma Tau Delta 90-; Engl; Lbry Sci.

**GETSON, EILEEN C,** Fl St Univ, Tallahassee, FL; JR; BS; Rsdnt Asst Altrnt 90; Orntatn Ldr Applcnt 91; Smnl Ambsdr Applcnt 91; Phi Thete Kappa 88; Phi Sigma Kappa Lttl Sstr 89-; Wmn Cmmnctns Ntl Mmbr 91; Walt Disney Wrld Clg Prgrm Intrnshp 91; IM Flg Ftbl Sftbl 89-90; Gnrl Cmmnctns; Pblc Rltns Hmn Rsrcs.

**GETT, YVETTE G,** City Univ Of Ny Baruch Coll, New York, NY; SR; BA; Jrnlsm.

**GETZ, BRENDA S,** Liberty Univ, Lynchburg, VA; SR; Stdnt Govt 90-; Clg Rpblcns 89-; Pre Law Soc 89-; Hons Prog 89-90; Bptst Stdnt Union 90-; Deans List; Intrnshp Rutherford Inst; BS Liberty Univ; Cert Emmans Bible Clg 88; Govt; Law/Legal Asst.

**GETZ, JEFFREY E,** Asbury Theological Sem, Wilmore, KY; GD; MDIV; Stdnt Mnstrs Assn Pres 86-87; Coll Choir 83-87; Coll Clss 87 VP 83-87; Delta Epsilon Chi 87; Theta Pi 89-90; Coll Vldctrn 87; BA Gods Bible Coll 87-; Cincinnati Bible Smnry 88; Theo.

**GEVEDEN, KIMBALL G,** Ky St Univ, Frankfort, KY; JR; BA; Big Bro/Big Sis 88-89; Asst Ntl Rsrcs Envrnmntl Prtctn Abnts Lglstv Liaison 90; Intrnshp Son Wendell Fund Wash DC 81; Admin Asst Ntrl Rsrcs Env Prtctn Cabnt 88-; Lbrl Stds; Law-Pltcl Cnsltng.

**GEYSER, SANDRA M,** Duquesne Univ, Pittsburgh, PA; SR; BA; NARD; ASHP; AMER Pharm Assc 89-; Phi Eta Sigma 88-89; Lambda Sigma 88-89; PPA 89-; WPSHP 89-; Alpha Gamma Delta Rtvl 88-; Wstrn PA Hmne Scty 89-; ASHP Stdnt Ldrshp Awd; MS/BS Phrmclgy/Txclgy Prog 90-; Phrmcy Schlr 87-88; Phrmcy; Phrmclgy/Txclgy.

**GHALY, MAGDY A,** Bunker Hill Comm Coll, Boston, MA; JR; BA; Sporting Clb Alexandria Eqypt 77-88; Zamalik Clb Alexandria Egypt 77-88; Dns Lst; Army Svcs Alexandria Egypt Mjr 77-88; BA Alexandria Univ Egypt 89; Econ/Pol Sci; MA Econ.

**GHANSAH, AGNES,** Fisk Univ, Nashville, TN; SO; BSC; Cmptr Science Clb 90; Catholic Assc 89; Usher 90; Dubois Hnrs Prgrm 90, Deans List 90; Math/Cmptr Science; Tchng/Comp Engrng.

**GHANT, WALTER ALLEN,** Howard Univ, Washington, DC; GD; Student Council Howard Univ Schl Divinity Chr Worship Comm 90-; Spiritual Life Warner Pacific Clg Port Ore Dir 86-88; Student Life Warner Pacific Clg 85-88; Benjamin E Mays Schl 89-; Public Reltns/Pastor.

**GHANTA, MANMOHAN K,** Univ Of Al At Birmingham, Birmingham, AL; SO; BS; Phi Sigma 90-; ISA 90-; Alpha Lambda Delta Treas 90-; Alpha Epsln Delta 90-; Hosp Vol 90-; Rotary Intl Clb 90; Ldrshp Awd; Pres Hnrs 90-; Bio; Med.

**GHATANI, SHILLA S,** Yeshiva Univ, New York, NY; JR; BA; Math Clb 87-90; Chem Clb 88-90; Sehavadic Clb 88-; Louding Plaut Schlrshp Fnd 89-90; Max Yablick Mem Schlr 89-; Amer Chem Soc 88-; Amer Inst Chem Engrs 90-; Omid Org 89-; Intrnshp Mt Sinai Hosp 89-; Intrnshp Hoechst Celanese; Chem; Engr.

**GHAZNAVI, YASMEEN E,** Coll Misericordia, Dallas, PA; SO; BSN; Cert Phlbtmst Nrth Amrcn Blgcl Inc 89; Cert Mdcl Rcptnst 86; Nrsng; Ansthtst.

**GHEE, KAREN O,** Nc Central Univ, Durham, NC; GD; JD; Mnrty Cltrs Comm UVA 86-89; UAV Wmns Bsktbl Tm 86-; BA Unv VA 89; Law; Corp Law.

**GHEZZI, ANDREW T,** S U N Y At Binghamton, Binghamton, NY; SO; BS; Bnghmtn Tlvsn Mgr 89-; Acctng Mgmt Org 89-; Dns Lst; Bsn; Acctng.

**GHEZZI, PAUL E,** Fl St Univ, Tallahassee, FL; JR; BA; AA Valencia Cmnty Clg 90; Cmnctns; Law.

**GHIM, MIMI M,** Univ Of Rochester, Rochester, NY; SR; BA; Adpt A Grndprnt Pgm 90; Stdnt Piano 87-88; Phi Sigma Sigma 88-90; Intl Lvng Ctr 88-89; Im Socr 90; Psych; M D.

**GHIRGHI, NOEMI,** Fl St Univ, Tallahassee, FL; JR; BA; Mdl UN Sec; Stdy Abrd Prgrm; Hnrs Major; Intrntnl Affrs; Frgn Srvc.

**GHIRMAY, NEZANET,** Univ Of West Fl, Pensacola, FL; SO; Aerobic Club; Alpha Kappa Alpha; Tchng Strgs; Elem Edn.

**GHOLSON, GWYN R,** George Mason Univ, Fairfax, VA; JR; BS; Golden Key 90-; Alpha Chi 90-; Bus Mgmnt; Sprts Mgmnt.

**GHOLSTON, BRANDON E,** Morris Brown Coll, Atlanta, GA; JR; BA; Arch Clb Pres 89-; Natl Rog Minority Architects Pres 90-; Stdnt Spprt Serv 88-; Earth Parks Dsgn/Comm Pres 89-; Stdnt Judge 90-; Archtitecture/Math.

**GHOLSTON, TIFFANY L,** Chattanooga St Tech Comm Coll, Chattanooga, TN; SO; BS; Acctg Clb Media Nwltr 89-; Phi Theta Kappa 90-; Dns Lst 89-; Nom Econ Mrt Awd; AS; Acctg.

**GHOSSEIN, SAMAR J,** Daytona Beach Comm Coll, Daytona Beach, FL; SO; BA; Bus Admin.

**GIACALONE, VIRGINIA J,** Newbury Coll, Brookline, MA; SR; ASSOC; PAL 90; Fashion Design; Elem Teacher.

**GIACOBBI, THOMAS J,** Le Moyne Coll, Syracuse, NY; SR; BS; Nwspr Mgng Edtr 88-; Judicial Bd 88-; Yrbk Photo; Alpha Sigma Nu 90-; Beta Beta Beta 89-; Deans Lst; Human Serv Assn Treas 88-; Biology Clg Treas 88-; Wmns Food Mkts Schlrshp 87-; Biology; Dentistry.

**GIACOBONI, MARK J,** Fl St Univ, Tallahassee, FL; SO; BS; Phi Eta Sigma 90-; AA FSU; Engr.

**GIACONI, ANDREW G,** Univ Of Southern Ms, Hattiesburg, MS; SR; BA; Yng Dems; Psi Chi Pr 90-; Phi Kappa Phi; Gldn Key; Wlt Dsny Wrld Clg Pgm Spg 90; Zed Hstn Brns Undrgrad Psych Awd; Psych; Cnslr.

**GIAMBRA, JULIA A,** S U N Y Coll At Fredonia, Fredonia, NY; SO; BS; Chem Club Sec 89-; Stdnt Govt Rep 89-90; Dingledy Schlrshp; Fredonia Fndtn Schlrshp; Am Assn Of Univ Women Schlrshp; Chem & Bio; Biochem Or Genetics.

**GIAMBRONE, CARLA ANN,** S U N Y Coll At Fredonia, Fredonia, NY; SR; BA; Kappa Delta Pi; SPIE VP; Laura Foster Awd Excell 19th Centry Lit 90; Soph Ed Awd; Sec-Treas; Engl Ed; Secndry Tchng.

**GIAMBUSSO, GINA M,** Newbury Coll, Brookline, MA; SO; AS; Flr Mngr; Media Tech; BA.

**GIAMPILIS, MARLENA M,** Coll Of Saint Elizabeth, Convent Sta, NJ; SR; Math Clb 87-; Eliz Educ Assoc 87-; Cncl Excptnl Chldr 87-; NJ Educ Assoc 90-; NJ Cncl Scl Study 90-; BA; Educ; Tchr.**

**GIAMPORTONE, JOSEPH S,** Wagner Coll, Staten Island, NY; SR; BA; Stdnts 4 Planet Earth Fndr; Beta Beta Beta 89-; Projct Connct Fndr Coor 90-; Awardes An Asstntshp In Molecular Genetcs At Rutgers Univ PhD Candidate; New Sprngvl Ltl League Bsbl 88-; Staten Isl Ctzns For Clean Air 90-; Bio/Chem; Sci Cmnctn.

**GIAN, DIANA L,** D Youville Coll, Buffalo, NY; GD; BS; Bus Clb Pres 88-90; Nwspr 88; Kappa Gamma Pi; Sr Hon Soc 90; Vol Friends Night People; Intrn Mktg; Bus Mgmt/Mktg; Bus Fld/Mktg Wrk.

**GIANGRECO, TERRY A,** S U N Y At Buffalo, Buffalo, NY; SO; DDS; Lacrosse 86-89; Hon Soc 86-89; Delta Upsilon Rutgers Treas Scl Chrmn 86-89; Deans Lst Rutgers 87-89; Excllnc Oral Occlsn/Antmy Awd 90; Schlrshp Acdmc UB Dntl Schl 90-; BS Rutgers Univ 89; Art/Sci Undrgrad Dntstry UB; Oral Srgry.

**GIANGRESSO, MICHELE F,** Bloomfield Coll, Bloomfield, NJ; JR; BS; Mountain Side Hosp Class Ofcr/Nrsg Class; V P 87; Deans List 90-; Mountain Side Hosp Alum Asso; Cert Oncology; Cert CPR; RC Instr Cert 87-88; RN Mountainside Hosp Schl Nrsg/Montclair Colg 88; Sci-Biol; Med Phys.

**GIANNAKOPOULOS, IRENE K,** Savannah Coll Of Art & Design, Savannah, GA; SR; Fiber Arts Assoc 89-; Student Ambdr; Outsntng Student Fiber Arts 91; BFA 91; Fiber Arts; Textile Designer.

**GIANNANTONIO, JENNIFER A,** Salisbury St Univ, Salisbury, MD; SR; Cyclng Clb VP 89-; Ornttn Cnslr 89; Area Dir Srch Comm 89; Phi Eta Sigma; Phi Kappa Phi; Omcrn Delta Kappa VP 90-; Delta Mu Delta; Phi Beta Lambda VP 90-; Dns Lst 87-; Awd Serv/Dedictn; IM Vlybl/Flr Hcky; BS; Bsn Admn; Retail Buyer.

**GIANNET, LOULA D,** Univ Of South Fl, Tampa, FL; SO; BA; Intl Law Stdnt Assoc 90-; Intl Stdnt Mnstrs 90-; Acad Grievance Comm 90-; Pi Sigma Alpha 90-; Themis Hnr Soc 89-; Arts/Sci Hnr Soc 89-; Alpha Theta Lambda 89-; Red Cross Soc 89-; Church Choir 86-; Univ Acad Schlrshp 89-; Hnrs Convctn Awd 89-; Pol Sci; Law.**

**GIANNICO, ANGELA,** Ny Law School, New York, NY; GD; JD; Law Review Articles Edtr 90; Amer Jrsprdnce Awd 89; BBA Pace Univ 89; Law.

**GIANNONE, KIMBERLY A,** Christopher Newport Coll, Newport News, VA; FR; BS; Equestrn Clb; U S Air Force; Mgmt; Priv Busn.

**GIANNOPOULOS, EVANGELOS A,** City Univ Of Ny Baruch Coll, New York, NY; SR; BBA; AAS NYCT Clg 86; Human Res Mgmt; Mgt Lvl Postn In Dental Co.

**GIANNOZZI, ROBYN GIARLA,** Portland School Of Art, Portland, ME; SR; Studio Arts Intl 87-89; BFA.

**GIANOLA, TERRI A,** Columbia Greene Comm Coll, Hudson, NY; BA; AA; Anthrplgy; Wrtg.

**GIANOTTI, JENNIFER L,** Capital Univ, Columbus, OH; SO; BSN; Co-Op Pgm; Deans Lst Huntington Coll 89-90; Nrsng.

**GIANOUKAKIS, NICHOLAS,** City Univ Of Ny City Coll, New York, NY; SO; BS; Sndy Sch Tchr 89-; Deans List 89-; Medcn; Pedtrcn.

**GIAQUINTO, MAUREEN B,** Nova Univ, Ft Lauderdale, FL; SR; MBA; Pills/Quills 73-75; Amer Med Rcrd Assc 73-78; Tlphn Pnrs Amer Ftr Pnr Rep 86-87; Natl Assc Female Exec 87-; Mrktng Svc Cnsltnt 87-; AA Miami Dade Jr Coll 72; BS Univ Central FL 78; Bus; Telecomm/Adm.

**GIARDINA, TONI-ANNE,** Ramapo Coll Of Nj, Mahwah, NJ; SO; BA; Rsdnt Stdnts Assn Acctg Clb 90-; Deans Lst; IM Sports Sftbl 89-90; Acctg; CPA.

**GIARDINO, JOHN D,** Villanova Univ, Villanova, PA; FR; BS; Project Sunshine 90-; Chem; Health Field.

**GIARRATANA, GINA M,** Providence Coll, Providence, RI; JR; BS; AISEC; Pstrl Cncl; Bus Admn Clb; R I Spec Olympcs; Bd Of Prgrmrs; Cncl Excptnl Chldrn; Deans Lst 88-; 4.0 Smstr GPA; I M Sprts Ftns Cls 88-; Bus Admn; MBA/ENTREPRENEUR.

**GIBBIONS JR, JAMES V,** Nj Inst Of Tech, Newark, NJ; JR; BS; Chrch Choir 80-; Yth Org 80-; Natl Socty Blck Engrs 89-; Inst Hnr Socty 89-; Intrnshp G E Aerospace Elec Systs Div 90; Intrnshp Merck Co Inc; Chem Engr; Med Srgry.**

**GIBBONS, HOLLY J,** Kent St Univ Kent Cmps, Kent, OH; SR; BA; Judson Hills Bapt Cmp Brd Of Dir Chrprsn 89; Crmnl Jstce; Law/Crrctns.

**GIBBONS, JEAN G,** Smith Coll, Northampton, MA; JR; BA; Smth Ppl Chc Crdntr 90-; Wslyn Stdnts Rprdctv Chc Crdntr 89-; Cstmr; Prgm Sxl Hrssmntgym Plnng Cmmtt 89-; Intern Fmly Plnng Cncl 90; Intern Natl Abrtn Rghts Actn Lg 90; Crw 88-89; Amrcn Stds; Scl Srvc.

**GIBBONS, KENNETH M,** Bloomfield Coll, Bloomfield, NJ; SR; BS; Univ Mart Art Inst Tae Kwon Do/Hap Ki Do Green Belt 90-; Acctng; Bus/CPA.

**GIBBONS, MICHAEL S,** Old Dominion Univ, Norfolk, VA; SR; BS; IM Soccer; Elec Engr Tech.

**GIBBONS, MITZI RACHELLE,** Converse Coll, Spartanburg, SC; SO; BA; SAC; Alcohol/Drug Awareness Prvntn Team 90; Habitat Hmnty 90; Alpha Lambda Delta 90; Rgnl Med Ctr Intern 90; Dance Assemble 89-; Bio/Psych; Med.

**GIBBONS, NICOLE F,** Colby Sawyer Coll, New London, NH; JR; BSN; Stdnt Hlth Advsry Com Co-Chrmn 89-; Outing Clb; Deans Lst; Vrsty Sccr 88-; Nrsng; Rsrch.

**GIBBONS, SHANNON L,** Ky Wesleyan Coll, Owensboro, KY; JR; BA; Southern Crmnl Jstc Assn 89-; Alpha Chi 90-; Golden Heart Sigma Phi Epsilon 89-; Crmnl Jstc; Law.

**GIBBONS, SUSAN C,** Comm Coll Algny Co Algny Cmps, Pittsburgh, PA; FR; BA; Crsrds; Ed; Elem Tchr.

**GIBBS, ADRIANNE E,** Fl International Univ, Miami, FL; SO; BA; Mainstage 89-; Fclty Schlrs 89-; Dnc; Educ.

**GIBBS, CARI L,** Eckerd Coll, St Petersburg, FL; FR; Mdl UN; Intl Stdnts Assn; Scuba Clb; Spec Hon Prog; Biolgy; Med.

**GIBBS, CAROL ANNE WILLIAMS,** Va St Univ, Petersburg, VA; SR; VA Stdnt Educ Assoc 90-; Kappa Delta Pi; Cerf Of Achvmnt Otsdng Schlrshp; Church Choir; SS Teacher; Sub Teacher Dinwiddie Cnty; Elem Educ; Teacher.

**GIBBS, DARLENE J,** Mayland Comm Coll, Spruce Pine, NC; SO; AS; Outstndng Fresh Awd 90; 1st Bapt Chrch 73-; Damin Ofc Mgr 90-; Bus; Acctg.

**GIBBS, DEREK N,** Ms St Univ, Miss State, MS; JR; BA; New Man Clb 87-89; Yng Rep 88; Dns Lst 88-89; Pi Kappa Alpha Pldg Trnr 88-89; IBM Co Op; IM; Cmptr Systs/Bus; MA.

**GIBBS JR, FRANKLIN G,** Thomas Nelson Comm Coll, Hampton, VA; FR; BA; Bwlng Sec/Pres 89-; Peninsula Jr Clssc Scrtch League Tm Capt 89-90; Right Stuff Awrd Space Acdmy 88; Accntng; CPA.

**GIBBS, HEATHER G,** Va Commonwealth Univ, Richmond, VA; JR; BS; Psych/Ed EEI; Tchg.

**GIBBS, JAMES R,** Interdenominational Theo Ctr, Atlanta, GA; GD; MDIV; Univ S Car Sprtnbrg; SGA Rep 75; S Car All Black Stdnts 75-76; Phi Rho Psi 72; 12th Annual Speech Festvl Miami Dade Comm Clg 72; Hotel Restrnt Mngmt Inst Assoc 71-72; AA Miami-Dade Comm Clg 72; Thlgy; Minister.

**GIBBS, JONEE S,** Univ Of Nc At Charlotte, Charlotte, NC; SO; BA; Dnce Tm 89-; Dns Lst 89-; Phi Eta Sigma; Engl; Law.

**GIBBS, KEITH L,** Claflin Coll, Orangeburg, SC; SR; BA; Art Clb 89; Alpha RHO 89; Deans List; Art; Advrtsng/Cartooning.

**GIBBS, KENDRA S,** The Kings Coll, Briarclf Mnr, NY; FR; BA; Chrstn Svc Otrch Chldrns Mnstry; Grls Soccr 90-; Psych; Cnslng.

**GIBBS, LINDA K,** Abraham Baldwin Agri Coll, Tifton, GA; JR; BED; Prof Sec Intl Sec 86; Bldwn Wmns Clb Sec 84; Alpha Beta Gamma Sigma Sec 89; Sr Sec 86-; CPS 89; Math; Educator.

**GIBBS, LISA G,** Volunteer St Comm Coll, Gallatin, TN; SO; AAS; Tn Soc Radlgc Technlgsts 90-; Gamma Beta Phi 90-; St Thomas Hosp MRI Asst 90-; Radiolgc Technlgy; Radtn Thrpst.

**GIBBS, MICHAEL R,** Univ Of Sc At Coastal Carolina, Conway, SC; FR; BA; Kappa Delta Rho Alumni Penn St Behrend Cmps 88-; Acctg; CPA.

**GIBBS, NATALIE A,** Allegheny Coll, Meadville, PA; SR; BS; Orchesis Pres 90-; Orientation Advsr 90-; Tourguide 90-; Tutor 90-; Psychl TA 90-; CAB; Anbimal Ethics Comm; Lambda Sigma; Psi Chi; Phi Beta Kappa; Alpha Chi Omega Hstrn 87-88; Homecmg Queen 89; Rsch Flwshp Western Pscy Inst; Psychology; Ph D.

**GIBBS, PAULETTE,** Coppin St Coll, Baltimore, MD; SR; BS; Phi Theta Kappa 76; Cyttchnlgst; AA Comm Coll Baltimore 76; BS 80; Spec Educ; Lrnng Dsbld Indvdls.

**GIBBS, TONYA S,** Univ Of Tn At Martin, Martin, TN; FR; MBA; Rsdnc Assn Hall Sntr 90-; Walgreens 89-; Science; Pharmacy.

**GIBBY, NATALIE A,** Clayton St Coll, Morrow, GA; JR; MBA; AA; Jrnlsm; Jrnlst Rprtr.

**GIBERSON, JEANNIE J,** Fl International Univ, Miami, FL; JR; BSW; AA Polk Comm Cmps 90; Soc Wrk.

**GIBERSON, MONICA P,** Fl International Univ, Miami, FL; SR; JD; Ctr Ltn Am/Crbn 89-90; Phi Beta Kappa 87-88; Phi Kappa Phi 89-90; BA 90; ACLU Dade Cty Chptr 88-90; Yth Neoliberalism 84-87; Jdcl Intrnship Dade Cty Crct; Govt/Honrbl Michael Dalmon; IM 90; Intrntl Rltns/Pol Sci; Law.

**GIBERT, MARIA D,** Fl International Univ, Miami, FL; GD; MS; Psi Chi 88-; Kappa Delta Pi 89-; Big Bro/Big Sis 90-; BS 90; BA 90; Schl Psych.

**GIBLIN, DONNA M,** Univ Of Cincinnati-Clrmnt Coll, Batavia, OH; FR; BA; Liberal Arts; Bus.

**GIBLIN, THOMAS A,** Providence Coll, Providence, RI; SR; BA; Pi Sigma Alpha 87-; RI St Govt Intershp Pgm 89-90; S C Johnson Son Inc Smr Sls Intrn 87-; Vldctrn; IM Sprts; Pltcl Sci; Law Schl.

**GIBNEY, JULIE A,** Schenectady County Comm Coll, Schenectady, NY; FR; BA; Residential Nursing Home Activities Intern 90-; Human Services; Psychology.

**GIBSON, A CHRISTINE,** S U N Y Coll Of Tech At Alfred, Alfred, NY; Alfred Almond Bible Chrch Mbr 87-; GED 85; Medcl Hlth; Med Lab Tech.

**GIBSON, AMY K,** Middle Tn St Univ, Murfreesboro, TN; SR; MBA; Delta Zeta 89-; BS; Pub Hlth.

**GIBSON, ANN C,** Nc Agri & Tech St Univ, Greensboro, NC; JR; BS; Dgt Cir Sec; ACM; Chncllrs Exec Smnr; At/T Schlrshp/Intrnshp; William Penn Schlrshp; Altrusa Fndtn Schlrshp; Cmptr Sci; Ph D.

**GIBSON, ANN E,** Savannah Coll Of Art & Design, Savannah, GA; JR; BFA; Grphx Clb 89-; BACCHUS 89-90; Deans Lst 88-; Grphc Dsgn; Commrcl Art/Advtsng.

**GIBSON, BARBARA J,** Indiana Univ Of Pa, Indiana, PA; JR; BED; ACEI Mmbrshp Comm 90; Smth Mmrl Schlrshp; Elem Ed.

**GIBSON, BRETT B,** Univ Of Miami, Coral Gables, FL; FR; BA; Hnrs Stu Assc 90-; IM Sprts 90-; Alpha Lambda Delta 90-; Pres Hnr Rll; Intl Fnnc Mrktng; Law.

**GIBSON, BYRON W,** Morehouse Coll, Atlanta, GA; SR; BS; Mentoring Pgm 89-; Pre-Law Soc 89-; United Negro Clg Fund Intern 90-; Pol Sci/Psych; Law.

**GIBSON, CAROL A,** Rhodes Coll, Memphis, TN; FR; BA; Pep Bnd 90-; Bptst Stdnt Union Sec 90-; BACCHUS 90-; Chrstn Yth Fllwshp 87-; Pblcatns/The Sou Wester/Rhodes Today; Bio.

**GIBSON, CHARLES G,** Univ Of Sc At Columbia, Columbia, SC; JR; BA; Danville Clg All Stars Bsbl Tm 90; Gamma Beta Phi 88-; Alpha Lambda Delta 89-; Beta Gamma Sigma 90-; Delta Upsilon; Coach Ltl League 89-; Fund Rsr MD Assn 89-90; All Star Tennis Tm 89-90; Davis/Lavendar Law Firm 90; Pres List 88-90; IM Sports; Bus; Law.

**GIBSON, CYPRIANNA LILLIAN P,** Livingston Univ, Livingston, AL; SR; BA; Intl Stu Assoc; Pnhlnc Assoc 90-; Alpha Kappa Alpha Hstrn 90-; Cir K 88-89; AA 89; BA; Tchnlgy; Arch Engr.**

**GIBSON, DAVID M,** Christopher Newport Coll, Newport News, VA; JR; BSBA; Alpha Chi; Mgmt/Psych; Prsnl Mgmt.

**GIBSON, DONNA S,** Middle Tn St Univ, Murfreesboro, TN; SR; BS; Stdnt Tn Ed Assoc 90; Stdnt Hm Ec Assoc 88-90; Kappa Delta Pi 89; Gamma Beta Phi 89; Kappa Omicron Nu 89; Phi Kappa Phi 90; Wrk Schlrshp 90; Early Chldhd Ed; Tchr Kndrgrtn 1st Grde.

**GIBSON, GINGER M,** Winthrop Coll, Rock Hill, SC; SO; BA; Hl Cncl 90-; Res Assoc 90-; Hstry Clb 90-; Econ Clb 90-; Alpha Lambda Delta Hstrn 90-; Big Sis Pgm 90; Marshall; Pres Lst 89; Dns Lst 90; Hstry; Tch.

**GIBSON, GLADYS M,** Alice Lloyd Coll, Pippa Passes, KY; SR; BA; Dns Lst 88-; Floyd Cnty Hd Strt Prgrm Tchr Garrett Pgrm 79-81; AHS 77-79; Early Elem Educ; Tchng.

**GIBSON JR, JAMES P,** Catawba Valley Comm Coll, Hickory, NC; FR; Iredell Co Rescue Sqd 2nd Lt; EMS Vol Res 90-; Burlingtn Ind Kntting Mgr 78-; Emer Med Sci; Paramed/Nrsng.

**GIBSON, JENIFER L,** Ms St Univ, Miss State, MS; SO; BS; Gamma Beta Phi; Amer Cncr Socty; Pres Schlr; Med Tech; Medicine.

**GIBSON, KELLY R,** Univ Of Southern Ms, Hattiesburg, MS; JR; BA; CAID 90-; Signing Eagles 90; Phi Beta Gamma; Spec Ed.

**GIBSON, KENYA N,** Morgan St Univ, Baltimore, MD; JR; BS; Scl Wrk/Mntl Hlth Stdnt Org V P 90-; Peer Cnslr; Alpha Kappa Mu; Pi Gamma Mu; Alpha Nu Omega 90-; Gov Summer Intrnshp Prog 90; Social Work.

**GIBSON, LA VONDA S,** Oh Univ-Southern Cmps, Ironton, OH; JR; Bapt Chrch; Sals Rep Schl Tchr; Math; Educ.

**GIBSON, LINDA F,** Snead St Jr Coll, Boaz, AL; JR; AD; Deans List 90; Pres List 90; Nrsng; RN.

**GIBSON, MELANIE K,** Ky St Univ, Frankfort, KY; JR; BA; Cncer Chr; Vcl Ensmbls Sec Ldr 88-; Deans Lst 89-; Chr Schlrshp 88-; Chrldng; Chld Dvlpmnt Fmly Rltns Chld Cntrs Fmly Cnsln.

**GIBSON, MELINDA K,** Oh Wesleyan Univ, Delaware, OH; SO; BSN; Nrsg Stdnt Bd; Orientation Asst; Pi Beta Phi Heritage Chr 90-; Chi Phi Ltl Sis Chr 89-; Nrsg; RN.**

**GIBSON, MICHELE S,** Richard Bland Coll, Petersburg, VA; SO; BED; Stdnt Govt Assn VP 89-; Alchl Awrnss Com Chrprsn 90-; Comm Serv Com Chrprsn 90-; AA 90-; Elem Ed; Tchng/Chldhd Psychlgy.

**GIBSON, MICHELLE M,** Al A & M Univ, Normal, AL; SR; BS; Lambda Sigma Pi Math Clb VP; Dns Lst 87-; Acdmc Hnr Rll 87-; Math; Eng/Resrch.

**GIBSON, PHILLIP A,** Western Ky Univ, Bowling Green, KY; JR; BGS; Phi Beta Lambda 87-88; Phi Kappa Phi; Phi Theta Kappa 87-; Educ Schrshp 87; N Cntrl Ky Educ Fndtn Outstndg Achvmnt 88; Grad Hgh Distctn 88; Rtl Str Mgr; Prod Ln Supv; AA 88; Bus; Dir.

**GIBSON, RHONDA L,** Radford Univ, Radford, VA; JR; BS; SEA 90-; AS Wytheville Cmnty Clg 90; Inter Dscplnry Stds; Elem Tchr.

**GIBSON, ROBERT J,** Univ Of Sc At Columbia, Columbia, SC; SR; Amer Mrktg Assoc 90-; Gldn Key 90-; Alpha Phi Omega 87-; BA; Mrktg; Envrnmntl Cnsltg.

**GIBSON, SANDRA F,** Jackson St Univ, Jackson, MS; FR; BA; Hnrs Clg 90-; Alpha Lambda Delta 90-; Acad Schlrshp Rcpnt 90-; Acctg.

**GIBSON, SHONDA L,** Fl A & M Univ, Tallahassee, FL; FR; MBA; Pres Schlrs Assn 90-; Phi Eta Sigma; Pres Schlrs Awrd 90-; Acctng Schl Of Bus And Indstry; CPA.

**GIBSON, STACIE R,** Roane St Comm Coll, Harriman, TN; FR; BA; Computer Club; Harriman State Area Voc Tech Schl 90; Computer Science; Computer Programmer.

**GIBSON, STACY E,** Univ Of Ky, Lexington, KY; JR; BA; Yrbk Acdmcs Ed 90-; Bg Bddy Drp Ot Prvntn Prgm; Pi Sigma Alpha; Sigm Atau Delta 90-; Gldn Key 90-; Scts Pr Lghs; Deans Shclrshp; Acdmc Excllnc Schlrshp 90-; Engl; Pltcl Sci; Law.

**GIBSON, SUSE V,** Mary Holmes Coll, West Point, MS; SO; AA; Elem Educ; Tch.

**GIBSON, THERESA J,** Fl Atlantic Univ, Boca Raton, FL; JR; BBA; Finance; Invstmnts/Scrts.

**GIBSON, THERESA L,** Univ Of Sc At Columbia, Columbia, SC; SR; Intrnshp Ofc Of The Solicitor 2nd Jdcl Circt; Crmnl Jstc; Law.

**GIBSON, TODD ANDREW,** Memphis St Univ, Memphis, TN; SR; BA; Stdnt Govt Assoc; Gamma Beta Phi 90-; Philosophy; Law.

**GIBSON, TRACY L,** Northern Ky Univ, Highland Hts, KY; SR; BA; Elem Edctn; Tchng.

**GIBSON, TROY D,** Marshall University, Huntington, WV; SR; BA; Lambda Chi Alpha Sec 89; Amrcn Mrktng Assn VP Plcmnt 90-; Accntng Clb; Rugby Clb 88-; Marktng; Mstrs Degree.

**GIBSON, VICTORIA V,** Va St Univ, Petersburg, VA; SO; BS; Bus; Acctng.

**GIBSON, WENDY R,** Univ Of Sc At Spartanburg, Spartanburg, SC; SR; BA; Church Choir; Piedmont Soc 90-; Kappa Delta Pi 89-; Erly Chldhd Edctn; Tchng.

**GIBSON-HUBBARD, ELISHA M,** Bryant Stratton Bus Inst Roch, Rochester, NY; SO; AOS; Gods Healing Pwr Pryr Bnd Inc Vol; Yng Adlts Afltd With St Paul Hobiness Chrch; Cont Educ/Ernd BA Acctg; Cert RICE 89; Cert Cmptr Confdnc Trng Speclst 87; Acctg/Bus Admn; Acctg.

**GICK, LINUS E,** Allegheny Coll, Meadville, PA; JR; BA; Soc For Env Awarnss Pres 88-90; Aldn Schlr; Engl/Hstry.

**GIDDARIE, SUSAN A,** City Univ Of Ny Queensbrough, New York, NY; SO; Alpha Beta Gamma; Mgmt; Hotel Mgmt.

**GIDDENS, JOHN S,** Middle Ga Coll, Cochran, GA; SO; BBA; Phi Beta Lambda 90-; Newspaper Stf Wrtr 90-; Gamma Beta Phi; AS; Mrktng.

**GIDDENS, PAMELA S,** Abraham Baldwin Agri Coll, Tifton, GA; FR; AD; Nrsng/RN.

**GIDDINGS, SAMIA P,** Morris Brown Coll, Atlanta, GA; SR; JD; Crmnl Jstce Clb VP; Engl Clb; Mrrs Brwn Hnrs Clb; Gldn Ky; Alpha Kappa Delta; Pn Hllnc Cncl; US Prg; Cngrss Of Natl Blck Chrchs Instrctr; Chrstms Fr Chldrn Prog; US Dstr Ctrs Fed Prbtn Intrn; Odetta S Nelson Acad Awrd; Alpha Kappa Alpha; BA; Crmnl Jstce; Law.

**GIDGE, BRETT DAVID,** Salisbury St Univ, Salisbury, MD; SO; BS; Cumm Tutorng 88-89; Phi Eta Sigma 89-; Deans Lst 89-90; SSU Soccer 89-90; Engr; Engr/Bus.

**GIDUMAL, ROBBIN C,** Fayetteville St Univ, Fayetteville, NC; JR; BA; 2nd Bn 504 PIR Wives Org & Family Support Grp 89; 1st Bn 504 PIR Wives Org & Family Support Grp 89-; Psych; Edn/Work With Terminally Ill.

**GIECK, ELIZABETH D,** Univ Of Va, Charlottesville, VA; GD; Jr Vrsty Fld Hcky 86-88; Vrsty Olo 88-90; Big Sis 89-90; BS 90; Sprts Med; Phys Thrpy.

**GIEGER, MATTHEW J,** Defiance Coll, Defiance, OH; JR; SGT U S Army Mltry Intlgnc Elctrnc Wrfr 85-89; Hnr Grdt U S Army Intlgnc Ctr Schl 86; Math; Tchg.

**GIEK, PAULA J,** Unity Coll, Unity, ME; SR; BA; WEA; Wldrns Frst Rspndr 89-; Maine Trip Ldr 90; Stdnt Tchng Intrnshp 90-; Vlybl 89-90; Lbrl Arts; Educ.

**GIELAROWSKI, LORI A,** Comm Coll Algny Co Algny Cmps, Pittsburgh, PA; GD; Schlrshp Legal Sec; BA 89-; English; Law.

**GIELSTRA, CORNELIS SIEMON,** Univ Of Sc At Columbia, Columbia, SC; SR; BS; Cert HTS Leeuwarden Netherlands 61; Marine Sci; Geology.**

**GIERING, WENDY L,** Slippery Rock Univ, Slippery Rock, PA; FR; BA; HEPRD 90-; Phy Ed; Tchr.

**GIESE, NANCY J,** Broward Comm Coll, Ft Lauderdale, FL; SO; Phi Theta Kappa 90-; Asst Ofc Mgr Of New Car Dlrshp 84-; Lib Arts; Hlth/Med.

**GIESY, JEWEL J,** Hillsborough Comm Coll, Tampa, FL; SO; AA; Phi Theta Kappa 90-; Ntl Schlr Ath 90-; Vlybl Schlrshp Furman U; Vlybl All-Conf 89-91; Vlybl All-State Slctns; Sci/Chem/Bio/Phys; Sprts Med.

**GIFFORD, DARLA LYNN,** Univ Of Sc At Coastal Carolina, Conway, SC; JR; AD; SSGT/EMPLOYEE/GRAND Strand Gnrl Hosp Emergncy Room Registr; Ntnl Cllgt Nrsng Awrd; Nrsng; Midwife.

**GIFFORD, DARLENE L,** Comm Coll Algny Co Algny Cmps, Pittsburgh, PA; SO; ASSOC; Scl Wrk Clb 90-; Using Prsnl Ptntl Clb 90-; Amer Lgn Aux; Vet Frgn Wars Ladies Aux 84-; Vtnm Vet Ldrshp Pgm Exec Bd 87-; Serv Mltry Fmls/Vtrns Amer Red Crss 86-; Scl Wrk; Hmn Serv.

**GIFFORD, LYNN E,** Univ Of Akron, Akron, OH; JR; Un Marching Band 88-; Un Varsity Band 90-; Golden Key; 4-H Advisor 90-; Co 4-H Office Asst 89-; Elem Edn; Teach.**

**GIFFORD, TROY S,** Liberty Univ, Lynchburg, VA; JR; BA; Golf 88-89; Bus Mktg; Bus.

**GIGANTE, STEPHEN,** Ny Institute Of Tech Ny City, New York, NY; SR; BS; Dns Lst; Fld Engr IBM Corp; Engrg.

**GIGUERE, STACY L,** Saint Joseph Coll, West Hartford, CT; JR; BA; JASP Plbcty Mgr 88-89; Psychlgy Clb Pres 88-; Art Cnnctn Co Fndr 90-; Hnrs Sympsm; Deans Lst 88-; Psychlgy; Clncl Psychlgy.**

**GIKAS, CHRISTOPHER J,** City Univ Of Ny City Coll, New York, NY; GD; ASME Pres 89-90; Mech Undrgrad Com 89-90; AIAA; Pi Tau Sigma 89-90; Steinman Awd 89-90; ASME Awd 89-90; Bsbl 86-87; Wrstlng 87-88; BE 90; Mech Eng; Eng/MBA.

**GIL, ELENA M,** Miami Dade Comm Coll, Miami, FL; SO; Sec Stds.

**GIL, LISSETTE,** Fl International Univ, Miami, FL; SR; Fea 90-; Adolf Coors Ed Schlrshp; Minrty Transfr Cmnty Schlrshp; Spcl Educ.

**GIL, PATRICIA,** Univ Of South Fl, Tampa, FL; FR; MBA; Ltn Amrcn Stdnt Assoc 90-; Blgy; Med.

**GIL, TERESITA,** Fl International Univ, Miami, FL; FR; Phi Sgm Sgm 90-91; Bio; Medcn.

**GILABERT, MICHELE,** William Paterson Coll, Wayne, NJ; SR; Cncl Excptnl Chldrn 88-90; Spec Ed Clb 88-90.

**GILBERT, ADRIANNE P,** Wilberforce Univ, Wilberforce, OH; FR; BA; Acctng.

**GILBERT, ANDREE L,** Castleton St Coll, Castleton, VT; FR; BA; Stage Lft Sec 90-; Otstndng Fresh Thtr Dept 90-; Thtr Arts; Actng/Prfrmng.

**GILBERT, BARBARA L,** Sinclair Comm Coll, Dayton, OH; JR; Pioneers Of America 84-; Otstndng Mnrty Stdnts Tlnt Rstr 90-; Untd Negro Clg Fnd 90-; Dayton Urbanleg; OH Bell Employee 72-; Cmrcl Art Tchnlgy; Artst Cmmrcl Fine.

**GILBERT, BRENDA J,** Ashland Univ, Ashland, OH; FR; BS; Alpha Dlt Pi; Swm Tm 90-; Rcrtn Bus; Corprt Ftns.

**GILBERT, CHRISTOPHER S,** Elmira Coll, Elmira, NY; SR; BS; Bus Clb V P 89-; Natl Acctng Assn 90-; Natl Soc Pblc Acctnts 90-; Phi Eta Sigma 90-; Arctic League; NY State Soc CPA; Superiro Schlrshp; Acctng.

**GILBERT, DANIEL R,** S U N Y At Buffalo, Buffalo, NY; JR; BS; Skydvg Tm; IEEE 90-; Tau Beta Pi; Transfer Hnrs Schlr; AAS Broome Cmnty Clg 90; Elctrcl Engr.

**GILBERT, DWIGHT C,** Alcorn St Univ, Lorman, MS; FR; Phy Ed; Bsebl Coach.

**GILBERT, JOHAN B,** Univ Of Miami, Coral Gables, FL; JR; BA; Art Msm 90-; Dean Lst 89-; Schlrshp; AA Miami Dade Comm Coll 90; Art/Pntng; Prfssr/Pntr.

**GILBERT, KIMBERLY A,** Belmont Coll, Nashville, TN; JR; Psy Club 90-; Psy; Medical Schl Psyc.

**GILBERT, LYNDA RUTH,** Bishop St Comm Coll, Mobile, AL; SO; BA; Jazz Sngrs 89-90; Choir 89-; Phi Theta Kappa 89-; Pres Lst 88-; Perf Schlp 89-; Yoga Tchr 87-; Rlxtn Smnrs Perf Artsts; Comm Arts; Camera Work.

**GILBERT, MARC R,** Ga Inst Of Tech At Atlanta, Atlanta, GA; FR; BA; Prgrms Brd; Tech Tlvsn Ntwrk Chrmn; Frshmn Cncl 90-; Phi Eta Sigma; Lambda Sigma; Phi Gamma Delta 90-; Lambda Sigma; Army ROTC Schlrshp 90-94; Deans Lst; IM; Elctrcl Engnrng; Engnrng.

**GILBERT, MARK D,** Holyoke Comm Coll, Holyoke, MA; SO; BS; Air Ntl Grd 86-; AS Sec Admn Comm Clg AF; Crmnl Jstc; Law Enf.

**GILBERT, MATTHEW A,** Univ Of Hartford, West Hartford, CT; SO; BA; Pre Law Scty; Clg Rpblcns; Pltcl Science; Law.

**GILBERT, MICHAEL T,** Cornell Univ Statutory College, Ithaca, NY; JR; BS; Bio Sci; Law.

**GILBERT, MICHELE L,** Univ Of Sc At Coastal Carolina, Conway, SC; FR; BA; Sigma Delta Phi 90-; Bus.

**GILBERT, ROCHELLE M,** Drexel Univ, Philadelphia, PA; FR; Deans List; Art; Interier Design.

**GILBERT, STEVE A,** Broward Comm Coll, Ft Lauderdale, FL; SO; AA; Coll Rep 90-; Natl Assoc Pblc Accts 90-; USAF Scrty Plc; Pres Lst 90-; Deans Lst 88; Gd Cndct Mdl USAF Achvmnt Mdl USAF 90; Vol Spcl Olympcs 89; By Scts Fnd Rsrs 89; Offc Mgmt 90-; Cert Indstrl Scrty 87; Bus Mgmt.

**GILBERT, TINA M,** Univ Of Nc At Asheville, Asheville, NC; JR; BA; Sprts Med Clb; Fllwshp Chrstn Athl Pgm Coord 90-; Concrt Pep Bnd; Phi Eta Sigma; Stdnt Athl Trnr; Pres Hnr Rl Vlybl/Trck; Bio; Sprts Med Phy Thrpst.

**GILBEY, LISA R,** Wilmington Coll, New Castle, DE; JR; MBA; Deans List 90-; Sftbl First Team All Dist 88-; Bsn Mngmnt; Doctorate Tch Univ.

**GILBRAITH, KENNETH S,** Niagara Univ, Niagara Univ, NY; SR; BS; Mktg Club 90-; Columnst Univ Nwspaper 87-88; DJ Campus Radio Sta WRNU 87-89; Amercn Mktg Assoc 90-; Im Sports Ftbl/Bsktbl/Sftbl 87-; Mgt/Mktg; Adv/Sports Mktg.

**GILBRIDE, MAUREEN E,** Le Moyne Coll, Syracuse, NY; FR; BA; Schl Nwsppr 90; Cmps Mnstry 90; Swmmng 90; Pltcl Sci; Law.

**GILBRIDE, RITA M,** Marywood Coll, Scranton, PA; JR; BS; Psychlgy Clb; Phlsphy Clb; Delta Epsilon Sigma; Weavers Guild Boston; Psychlgy; Psychlgy-Clncl.

**GILCHER, JODY C,** Univ Of Cincinnati, Cincinnati, OH; SO; BM; Ohio Coll Mus Educ Assn Publicty 89-; Hon Prog 90-; Alpha Lambda Delta 90-; Sigma Alpha Iota; Music; Teaching/Educ.

**GILCHRIST, ADRIENNE M,** Coppin St Coll, Baltimore, MD; JR; Mgmnt Sci Soc; Eastern Hlth Educ Awareness Proj; Mgmnt Sci; Entrepreneur.

**GILCHRIST, JESSE R,** Univ Of Cincinnati-Clrmnt Coll, Batavia, OH; FR; Wldr At Ambssdr Heat Trnfr Co Cincinnati; Cmptrs; Cmptr Prog.

**GILES, ALAN W,** Meridian Comm Coll, Meridian, MS; SO; BED; JC Penney Sr Mrchndsr 79-90; Hstry; Tchr Elem Ed.

**GILES, AMELIA M,** Winthrop Coll, Rock Hill, SC; JR; BS; FCA 87-89; Vol Serv 87-89; Kappa Delta Pi 90-; Emntry Ed; Tch.

**GILES, ANGELA G,** Greenville Tech Coll, Greenville, SC; FR; Bk Of Math Clb; Dbledy Bk Clb; Cmptrs; Law Frm Or Drs Offce.

**GILES, CHISMA D,** Univ Of Pittsburgh, Pittsburgh, PA; FR; Soc Wmn Eng 90-; Schl Eng Ttr; Intern Duguesmelight Eng 90-; Eng; Elec Eng.

**GILES, ENRICO M,** Fl A & M Univ, Tallahassee, FL; FR; BA; NACME Schlr; Chem Eng.

**GILES, EVELYN J,** Memphis St Univ, Memphis, TN; SR; BS; Coop Educ Stu Malone/Hyde Co 87-88; Coop Stu St Tech Inst Memphis 86-87; Vol Intl Paper Co 88-; Acctg Clrk; Asstnt Bkkpr; Sec Intl Paper Co; AS 88; Acctg; CPA.

**GILES, GREGORY S,** West Liberty St Coll, West Liberty, WV; SO; BS; Hon Prog 90-; Grtr Stbnvl/Jfrsn Co Cmbr Comm 89-; Shp Frmn Pops Rdtr Serv 80-; Bus Mgmt.

**GILES, JANET R,** Hillsborough Comm Coll, Tampa, FL; FR; AS; Bsns Ed Lab Asst 90-; Envrnmntl Rgnl Srvc Prjct Sec; Aa Clntn Comm Coll 86; Scrtrl Mngmnt.

**GILES, JENNIFER A,** Univ Of Southern Ms, Hattiesburg, MS; SO; BS; Stdnt Alumni Assn 90-; Bacchus 90-; Alcohol Awrns Tsk Frc; Gamma Beta Phi 90-; Phi Chi Theta 90-; Chi Omega 89-; Bsns Mrktng; Sls.

**GILES, JOSEPH T,** Morehouse Coll, Atlanta, GA; SR; BA; Natl Assn Of Blck Accts 88-; Clss Sec 88; Bus Assn 87-; Gldn Ky 90-; Big Bro Big Sis Of Sgnw; Jr Achvmnt 90-; Dw Crng Intrnshps 89-; Shearson Lehman Hutton Intrnshp 88; Acctng; Tax Law.**

**GILES, KATHY,** Al St Univ, Montgomery, AL; FR; BA; Mrchng Hornets 90-; Symphnc Band; Law.

**GILES, KATHY TIPTON,** Watterson Coll, Louisville, KY; GD; ASSOC; DPMA Treas 89-; Pres Lst; Acctg.

**GILES, KELLI E,** Univ Of Cincinnati, Cincinnati, OH; SR; BS; Golden Key; Kappa Delta Pi; Elem Ed.

**GILES, LAURA CHRISTI,** Fl St Univ, Tallahassee, FL; SR; BS; Fllwshp Chrstn Athlts 87-89; Ctty Coll Dnc Rprtr 87-89; Prsdnts Lst 88-89; Kth Ellsn Mmrl Schlrshp; Deans Lst 90-; AA 89; AA 90; Cmmnctn Dsrdrs.

**GILES, LAURA L,** Fl A & M Univ, Tallahassee, FL; JR; BS; Pre Occptnl Thrpy Clb Pres; Gardner Eastern Star Schlrshp 89-; Gardner Masonic Schlr; AA Okaloosa Walton Cmmntycoll 90; Occptnl Thrpy.

**GILES, SHEILA D,** Middle Tn St Univ, Murfreesboro, TN; JR; BS; STEA Pres 90-; Kappa Delta Pi; Mbr House Rep; Kappa Delta Pi; Univ & Colleges; Hnr Roll; Deans List; Sub Tchrin Rutherford Cntyt Schools; Elem Ed; Elem Tchr.

**GILES, TANGLA A,** Fisk Univ, Nashville, TN; SO; BA; Fisk Black Mass Gospel Choir; Baptist Student Union; NAACP; Health Care Administration Prog Treas Of HCAP; Student Support Services; Deans List; Business Management; Hospital Administration.

**GILES-ALVERSON, CYNTHIA,** Univ Of Sc At Columbia, Columbia, SC; SR; BS; AS Spartanburg Meth Clg 87; Crmnl Just; Soc Wrkr.

**GILEVICH, DARLENE J,** West Liberty St Coll, West Liberty, WV; SR; BS; Mbr Emgncy Med Sqd 89-90; SADHA 88-90; Sadha 90-F Chi Beta Phi 90-; Theta Xi Strs Org VP 88-90; AS Dent Hyg 90; Dental Hygn/Scnc; Teaching.

**GILFOY, RACHEL M,** Lesley Coll, Cambridge, MA; JR; BA; AS Mass Bay Comm Coll 89; Educ.

**GILGHREST, LISA D,** Fl A & M Univ, Tallahassee, FL; SR; BS; Ftr FL Educrs Amer; Natl Collgt Educrs Awrd; All Amer Schlr; AA St Petrsbrg Jr Coll 89; Elem Ed; Tchng.

**GILKERSON, KIMBERLY LYNN,** Marshall University, Huntington, WV; SR; BS; Pks/Rec Org Stdnts Pres 90-; WVRPA Comm; WVRPA Cunningham Grant 90; MWR Rec Intrnshp US Navy Fallon Nvl Air Sta Fallon NV; Pks/Rec Lsr Svcs; MS.

**GILKESON, SHANNON E,** Ohio Valley Coll, Parkersburg, WV; FR; BA; Sigma Epsilon Chi; Chrldr; Stage Band; Co-Head 90-; Elem Ed.

**GILL, ALEX,** Mayland Comm Coll, Spruce Pine, NC.

**GILL, ALICIA M,** Univ Of South Al, Mobile, AL; JR; BA; Res Life Cncl Rep 90-; Elem Ed; Tchr.

**GILL, COLLEEN B,** S U N Y Coll At Fredonia, Fredonia, NY; JR; BS; Edctn Clb Sec 89-; Orchss 89-90; Lrng Cntr Math Ttr 90; Sphmr Edctn Awrd 89; Ed Math; Tchr Elem Jr Hgh Lvl.

**GILL, DOROTHY M,** Passaic County Comm Coll, Paterson, NJ; GD; AS; SNA 90-; LPN; Nrsng; Mtrnl Chld Hlth.

**GILL, FRANCES L,** Central Fl Comm Coll, Ocala, FL; FR; AA; Cls Rep; Comp Sci.

**GILL, GINNIE T,** Tougaloo Coll, Tougaloo, MS; JR; BA; Educ Clb 89-; Alpha Sweetheart 89; VP Lst 88-90; G S Ldr 87-; Nurses Asst 90-; Stdnt Natl Educ Assn 90-; IM 89-; NAACP 90-; Nurses Asast 90-; Elem Tchr.

**GILL, GRACIALA Y**, Saint Pauls Coll, Lawrenceville, VA; JR; BA; Phi Beta Lamdba Historian 89-; Class 1992 Pres 88-; SGA Repres 88-; Alpha Kappa Mu; Alpha Kappa Alpha Basileus 88-; NAACP Secty 89-; NASA United States Navy Summer Res Prog 90; Busn Admin; Entpr.

**GILL, JANET D**, King Coll, Bristol, TN; SO; SIFE Chr Ed Comm 90-; Kappa Epsilon 90-; Old Tstmnt Awd 89-90; Intrmdt Spnsh Awd 89-90; Bhvrl Sci/Elem Ed; Tch.

**GILL, JILLIAN GEMERLINE**, Univ Of The Dist Of Columbia, Washington, DC; SR; BA; Sr Class Pres; Mgmt Club Exec V P 90-; Econ Club V P 87; Stdnts Free Entrpse; Grievance Comm; J E Miller Chapman Schlrshp Awd 90; Acdmc Achvmnt Awd 90; Daug Un Vet Of Civil Awd Schlrshp Awd 90; Souran Bk Pro Tennis Trnmnt Vol 84-90; Bus Mgmt; Human Res Mgmt.

**GILL, JOHN R**, Univ Of Akron, Akron, OH; SR; BS; USAR Sgt/E5 89-; Actv Dty With US Army 87-89; AA; Mgmt/Info Sys; MBA In MIS.

**GILL, KEVIN MATTHEW**, Univ Of Nc At Charlotte, Charlotte, NC; SR; BA; Charlotte Music Clb Awrd 89-90; A J Fletcher Schlrshp 89-; Music; Architecture.

**GILL, MARGARET K**, Radford Univ, Radford, VA; JR; BS; AACD 90-; ASCA 90-; Pi Gamma Mu; Psych; Schl Cnslng.

**GILL, MARY E**, Vanderbilt Univ, Nashville, TN; SO; BS; Interhall Dorm Pres 90-; Hnr Cncl; Vu Cept; Arts/Sci Cncl Chm; Gamma Beta Phi 90-; Alpha Lambda Delta 90-; Phi Eta Sigma 90-; Kappa Alpha Theta Pldg Secr; Math; Law.

**GILL, MARY K**, Wright St Univ Lake Cmps, Celina, OH; SO; BS; SG VP 90-; Alpha Lambda Delta 90-; Bus.

**GILL, MICHELLE**, Univ Of Akron, Akron, OH; SR; BSBA; Clas Brd 90-; Program Brd Treas 87-; Hall Cncl VP 88-89; Orientation 86-87; NRHH PR Dir 90-; Pi Sigma Epsilon 88-89; Ldrs Cncl Vol 89-90; Homecoming Committee Vol Coord 89; Key Awrd; Deans Lst 89-90; Advertising/Mrktng; Layout Designer.

**GILL, PAUL M**, Le Moyne Coll, Syracuse, NY; JR; Dorm Cncl Rep 88-89; Swim Clb 89-; Psi Chi; Swim Tm Vrsty; Psychlgy/Spcl Ed Cert; Tch.

**GILL, SCOTT T**, Memphis St Univ, Memphis, TN; FR; BA; Baptist Stdnt Un; Ldrshp Schlrshp Pgm; Cmctn Arts; Ministry.

**GILL, SHAYNE H**, Univ Of Montevallo, Montevallo, AL; JR; Sntr Stdnt Govt 88-; Alpha Lambda Deltya 88; Omicronm Delta Kappa; Montevallo Mstrs 90-; Phi Alpha Theta Hstrn 90-; Alpha Tau Omega Sec 88-; Red Crs Vol 88-; Soc Sci; Govt Soc Sec.

**GILL, STEPHANIE L**, Univ Of Pa, Philadelphia, PA; SO; Arts Hse Dnce Co Pblcty Chr 90-; Whrtn Wmn 90-; Delta Delta Delta Phlnthrpy 90-; Vol Ronald Mc Donald Hse; Dns Lst 89-; Law Intrnshp; Acctng Fnnce; Law.**

**GILL, TRACY A**, Va Highlands Comm Coll, Abingdon, VA; SO; BS; SNAG; Phi Theta Kappa; Rtry Clb Schlr 81-90; Food Cntry Acctg/Bus Schlr 90-; Acctng; CPA.

**GILL-LA HAYE, KIM A**, Midway Coll, Midway, KY; SO; PHI Thea Kappa 89-; Emplyd Thrghbrd Indstry 73-; Equine Mgmt.

**GILLAIRD, KAREN J**, Strayer Coll, Washington, DC; GD; BS; Alpha Chi 90-; Strayer Schlrshp 90-; Washington Gas Light Co Progrmr; DPD Strayer Clg 89; AAS N VA Cmnty Clg 83; Info Syst; Pgm Cnsltnt.

**GILLAM, MARY E**, Oh Univ, Athens, OH; FR; The Movement Org V P; Dance; Performance.

**GILLAND, MICHAEL W**, Univ Of Cincinnati, Cincinnati, OH; FR; BA; Energy Cnsltnts Adv Mgr 82-86; Willis Music Co Retl Mgr 86-90; Elec Media; Audio Video Prod/Comm Adv.

**GILLEN, ELIZABETH M**, S U N Y Coll Of Tech At Frmgdl, Farmingdale, NY; SR; AS; SNA 88-; Nrsng.

**GILLEN, KEVIN ANDRES**, Southern Coll Of Tech, Marietta, GA; JR; AS; Sftbl Vllybl; Engr; Elec Engr.

**GILLENARDO, TODD A**, Univ Of Md At Eastern Shore, Princess Anne, MD; SO; BA; Certif Acad Achvmnt; Hnrs 89-; Cmnctns; Radio P D/Theatre.

**GILLENBERGER, CHRISTINE L**, Comm Coll Algny Co Algny Cmps, Pittsburgh, PA; SO; AS; Ultra Snd; Ultrsngrphr Tech.

**GILLENWATER, SHARON A**, Bluefield Coll, Bluefield, VA; SO; BA; VA Ed Assn 90-; Bapt Stdnt Union Rvivl Tm Ldr 90-; Bluefield Sngrs/Vrtns 89-; Alpha Phi Sigma 90-; Intrnshp; Music Ed.**

**GILLESPIE, ANNA M**, Marshall University, Huntington, WV; JR; BA; Amrcn Mrktng Assoc Pres Mmbrshp 90-; Mrktng.

**GILLESPIE, AUDRIA L**, Mayland Comm Coll, Spruce Pine, NC; JR; AAS; Bus Admnstrn.

**GILLESPIE, CHRISTY L**, Fayetteville St Univ, Fayetteville, NC; FR; BA; Futr Almn Assc Sec 90-; Gpsl Choir 90-; Fllwshp Chrstn Std 90-; Psychgy; Cnslng/Scl Wrk.

**GILLESPIE, ELIZABETH D**, Western Piedmont Comm Coll, Morganton, NC; SO; AAS; Phi Theta Kappa 90-; Recep NC Rehab 90; Assoc Mc Clelland Schlrshp; Intern Therapeutic Rec W/Nc Easter Seals Scty; Therapeutic Recre; Commty Recreationl.

**GILLESPIE, ILA**, Western Piedmont Comm Coll, Morganton, NC; FR; AN; Nrsng Clb 90-; BS Sir K P Cmmrc Coll India 85; Nrsng.

**GILLESPIE, JOHN A**, Roane St Comm Coll, Harriman, TN; FR; AAS; Gamma Beta Phi; Phys Therapy.

**GILLESPIE, KATHERINE R**, Univ Of Ga, Athens, GA; SR; MED; Gldn Ky 88-; Kappa Delta Pi 89-; Kappa Delta Epsilon 88-; Assoc Chldhd Educ Intl 89-; Kappa Kappa Gamma Phlnthrpy Chrmn 87-; B Ed; Educ; Tchr/Sch Media Spec.

**GILLESPIE, MICHELLE F**, Broward Comm Coll, Ft Lauderdale, FL; SO; BA; Phi Beta Lambda Secy 90-; Phi Theta Kappa 90-; AA; Bus Admin; Mgmnt/Mktng/Finance.

**GILLESPIE, ROBERT C**, Roane St Comm Coll, Harriman, TN; FR; BA; Educ; Tchr.

**GILLESPIE, SUSAN R**, Wilberforce Univ, Wilberforce, OH; SR; BA; Sigma Omega 89-; Delta Sigma Theta; Phi Eta Psi Emerald 89-; Stdnt Ambssdr Ramo T Menashe Israel 89; Golf 88-; Teach HS English; Liberal Studies; Teach.

**GILLESPIE, TIFFANY A**, Columbus Coll Of Art & Design, Columbus, OH; SR; Bible Stdy; Fshn Dsgn.

**GILLESPIE, YOLANDA MECHELLE**, Mary Holmes Coll, West Point, MS; SO; BS; Phi Theta Kappa 89-; BA; Edctn; Cmptr Sci.

**GILLETT, EMILIA M**, Univ Of North Fl, Jacksonville, FL; SR; BAED; Civitan Club Treas; Internal Stdnts Assoc 90-; Appeals Comm Undergrad Rep 90-; Assoc Sci St Johns College 74; Biology; Teaching.

**GILLETTE, MICHAEL J**, Columbus Coll Of Art & Design, Columbus, OH; FR; BA; Crrctns Offcr; Art Illstrtn; Illstrtr.

**GILLEY, BRUCE W**, Univ Of South Al, Mobile, AL; SR; BED; BA 86; Secondary Social Scncs; Scl Scie Tchr.

**GILLEY, SHANNON L**, Tn Temple Univ, Chattanooga, TN; SR; Floor Govt Sec 87-90; Alpha Epsilon Theta 87-; R A Torrey V P 89-90; Sr Prsnlty; BS TN Temple Univ 90; Bus; Office Admin.

**GILLGREN JR, JOHN S**, George Mason Univ, Fairfax, VA; SR; BS; Kappa Delta Pi 90-; Golden Key 90-; Otsdng Sr Phys Educ; Track Field 80-; Artcl Pub ICHPER; U S Army 66-79; Phys Educ/Hlth; Tch/Coach.

**GILLIAM, JULIE A**, Northern Ky Univ, Highland Hts, KY; SR; BS; Natl Assoc Of Acctnts; Tutor 90-; Alpha Chi 90-; Nu Kappa Alpha; Alpha Gamma Sigma 89; Deans List 90-; AS Miramar Coll 89; Cert 89; Acctng; CPA.**

**GILLIAM, LESLIE HOPE**, Univ Of Sc At Columbia, Columbia, SC; SO; BA; Delta Delta Delta 89-; Psychgy; Law/Forensic Psychlgy.

**GILLIAM, LINDA D**, Bishop St Comm Coll, Mobile, AL; JR; BA; Phi Theta Kappa; Hstry; Tchr.

**GILLIAM, MICHAEL R**, Univ Of Sc At Columbia, Columbia, SC; JR; BA; Tchr Of Yr Comm; Frnch Awd; Engl Awd; Tchr Of Yr; Comm; USC Hon Stdnt; Dns Lst 89-; Pol Sci/Engl; Pre Law.

**GILLIAM, VERONICA T**, Lincoln Univ, Lincoln Univ, PA; JR; BA; Big Bro/Sis; Alpha Chi; Alpha Mu Gamma; Dobro Solov; Acctng/Russian.

**GILLIAN, CATHERINE P**, Spartanburg Methodist Coll, Spartanburg, SC; FR; Psi Beta; Ed; Tchr.

**GILLIAN, MARCEY J**, James Madison University, Harrisonburg, VA; SR; Ctr Svc Lrng 89-; Bapt Stdnt Union 88-; Outing Clb 87-90; VA Tchg Schlrshp 89-90; BS; Spec Ed LD/MR; Spec Ed Tchr.

**GILLIES, CASEY A**, Western Carolina Univ, Cullowhee, NC; BS; Deans List; Sigma Kappa VP Mmbrshp 88-; NC Spcl Olympics 90; Intrnshp WWSB TV Station; Wstrn Tennis Tm; Radio-Tv; TV Brdcstng.

**GILLIES, MATTHEW A**, Univ Of Ky, Lexington, KY; FR; BS; Cvl Eng; Eng.

**GILLIHAN, REBECCA J**, Memphis St Univ, Memphis, TN; SR; BSN; Memphis Area Oncology Int Grp 89-; Oncology Nrsng Soc 83-90; Am Cancer Soc Serv Rehab Chm 83-90; Edn Comm Germantown Comm Hosp Prof Edn Comm; Oncology Nurse Cert 89-91; ONC Onclgy Nrsng Soc; RN St Jos Hosp Sch Of Nrsng 76; Nursing.

**GILLILAND, DELONA G**, Central Al Comm Coll, Alexander City, AL; SO; BS; Elem Educ; Tchr.

**GILLILAND, JOHN R**, Columbia Union Coll, Takoma Park, MD; SO; BS; ACM Pblc Rltns; Math/Chem; Math/Chem Eng.

**GILLIS, BONITA S**, Univ Of West Fl, Pensacola, FL; JR; BA; Depty Clrk Santa Rosa Cnty; Bus Admin.

**GILLIS, CARRIE M**, Auburn Univ At Auburn, Auburn, AL; JR; BA; Univ Pgm Cncl 88-89; Spikettes Trck Hostess 89-90; Ala Assn Yng Chldrn; Kappa Omicron Nu 90-; Delta Zeta Sor 88-; Proj Uplift Big Sistr Pgm 89-; Otstdng Achvmnt Awd; Fmly/Chld Dev; Tchng.

**GILLIS, CHRISTOPHER C**, Mt Saint Marys Coll & Seminary, Emmitsburg, MD; SO; Coll Nwspr 90-; Soc Prsrvtn Old Mills 89-; Frederick Cnty Hist Soc Mrylnd 89-; Soc Collegiate Jrnlsts 90-; AFS Belgium 88-89; Natl Endwmnt Hmnties Yngr Schlr; Alliance Francaise Cert Dexcellence; Intrntl Stud.

**GILLIS, JOSEPH P**, Wright St Univ Lake Cmps, Celina, OH; FR; BS; Bus; Fnnc.

**GILLIUM, GINGER A**, Walker Coll, Jasper, AL; FR; BA; Yrbk Stf; Stdnt Gvrnmnt Assn 90-; Schlrs Bwl Comm; Cnty Cnsrvncy; Biology; Med.

**GILLMAN, SHANNON A**, Fl St Univ, Tallahassee, FL; SR; BA; FL Acad Schlr 88-; FL Power Corp Intrn 89; Govs Press Ofc Intrn; Commctns.

**GILLSON, STACI L**, Valdosta St Coll, Valdosta, GA; SO; BFA; Art Stdnts League Secr/Treas 89-; ACES; Alpha Lambda Delta 89-90; Sigma Alpha Chi 90-; Kappa Delta V P Publ Rels 89-; Co-Op IBM; IM Ftbl/Vlybl 89-; Mst Outstndg Pldg Awd 90; Studio Art; Med Illustr.

**GILMAN, CARYN S**, Teikyo Post Univ, Waterbury, CT; JR; BA; Stdnt Govt Assn Asst Treas 89-90; Yrbk Chf Fin 89-90; Dns Lst Hgh Hnrs 90; First Annual Stdnt Pnl Dscsn 89; Amer Red Crs Vol 88-90; Opn Hse New Stdnt Gud 89; Amer Hrt Assn Vol 90; Amer Cncr Soc Vol; Desk Aid 90-; AS; Fshn Mrchndsng Rtlng; Fshn Buyer.

**GILMAN, MICHELE L**, Univ Of Sc At Spartanburg, Spartanburg, SC; FR; BS; Sci; Physcl Thrpst.

**GILMARTIN, ELIZABETH K**, Georgian Court Coll, Lakewood, NJ; SO; BA; Schl Nwsppr 90-; Cncrt Bnd 89-; Flte Ensmble 90-; Dns Lst 90; Engl.

**GILMER, AMANDA E**, Emory & Henry Coll, Emory, VA; SR; BA; Choir; Alpha Psi Omega Sec/Treas 88; Cardinal Key 89; Pi Gamma Mu; Sigma Upsilon Nu Pldgmstr 89; AT&T Intrnshp 90; Emory/Henry Schlr 89; Victor S Armbrister Schlrshp Rcpnt 90; Bsn Mgmt/Cmptr Infor.

**GILMER, CHERYL R**, Bridgewater Coll, Bridgewater, VA; FR; BA; Sales Clrk 89-; Psych; Elem Tchr.

**GILMER, DONNA L**, Middle Tn St Univ, Murfreesboro, TN; JR; Kappa Delta Pi 90-; Athl/Acad Schlrshp CSTOC 88-90; Vrsty Bsktbl CSTCC 88-90; BS Chattanooga State Tech Comm Coll 90; Elem Educ/Socl Sci; Tchr.

**GILMER, KARRIEM O**, Fl A & M Univ, Tallahassee, FL; FR; BS; CIS Clb 90-; Congrssnl Intern John Conyers Jr; Cmptr Infrmtns Sys; Sys Anlyst.

**GILMER, LESLIE S**, Univ Of Nc At Greensboro, Greensboro, NC; SR; BS; Intrntl Cmprshp YMCA NY Sthhmptn Eng Activities Dir 89; Emp Ellness Mose H Cone Hosp Intrn; Exercise Sci.

**GILMER, SCOTT W**, Univ Of Tn At Martin, Martin, TN; JR; BS; 4 H Rprtr 89-; Chrch Chrst Stdnt Cntr 89-; Peoples Law Schl 90; Phi Eta Sigma; Unv Schlrs Orgnztn 89-; Alpha Epsilon Rho Cnvtn Dlgt 89-; Sigma Delata Chi Tres 89-; Intrn TN Hs Spkr Jimmy Naifeh; Intrn WKRN RV Nshvl; Phi Kappa Phi 90; Cmmnctns; Brdcst Nws Mgmt.

**GILMORE, ANDRE A**, Morehouse Coll, Atlanta, GA; FR; BA; Natl Soc Blck Engrs 90-; Morehouse Pre-Alumni Assn 90-; Math; Elec Eng.

**GILMORE, ANGELA M**, Comm Coll Algny Co Algny Cmps, Pittsburgh, PA; SR; Soclgy Clb Sec 89; Scl Wrk Clb 90-; Soclgy Clb Vp; Cert Median Schl 121 9th St Pgh PA 15222 82.

**GILMORE, CAROLYN H**, Methodist Coll, Fayetteville, NC; FR; BS; Kelly Springfield Tire Co 81-; Psychology.

**GILMORE, CHRISTOPHER W**, Univ Of Southern Ms, Hattiesburg, MS; SO; BA; Newman Clb VP 90-; Symphnc Wnd Ensmbl; Jz Lb Bnd; Gamma Beta Phi; Music Educ; Prfrmr.

**GILMORE, CYNTHIA A**, Indiana Univ Of Pa, Indiana, PA; SR; BED; Math; Scndry Math Tchr.

**GILMORE, ERIKA J**, Howard Univ, Washington, DC; JR; BARCH; Am Inst Archit Stdnts Comm Chrmn 89-; Abslm Jns Stdnt Assn Epscpl Mnstry Pres 90-; Archt/Dsgnr.

**GILMORE III, JOHN**, Sc St Coll, Orangeburg, SC; FR; Bronze Mdlln; Cmptr Sci; Sys Anlyst.

**GILMORE, LISA A**, Alcorn St Univ, Lorman, MS; SO; BA; Govt 90-; Pre-Law.

**GILMORE, MARCIE A**, Columbus Coll Of Art & Design, Columbus, OH; FR; BFA; Illstrtn; Illstrtr.

**GILMORE, PATRICIA L**, Univ Of South Al, Mobile, AL; JR; BA; Sec Math Educ.

**GILMORE, RODNEY E**, Nc Agri & Tech St Univ, Greensboro, NC; SR; BS; Cncrt Choir VP 89-; Untd Chrstn Flwshp 87-; Phi Mu Alpha 90-; Res Asst 87-; Deans Lst 89-; Music; Tchr.

**GILMORE, SARAH E**, Neumann Coll, Aston, PA; FR; BA; Very Imp Vol For Admissions 90-; Prof Educ Soc 90-; Elem Educ; Tchng.

**GILMORE, STEPHANIE Y**, Alcorn St Univ, Lorman, MS; GD; BS; Home Econ Club 87-; Ms Hm Econ Assn; Kappa Omicron Nu Pres 88-; Alpha Kappa Alpha 90-; Asst; Food & Nutrition; Reg Dietician.

**GILMORE, TINA M**, Tallahassee Comm Coll, Tallahassee, FL; SR; AS; SADHA 89-; Comm Dntl Hlth Prjcts 90-; Dns Lst 89-; Prctr Gmble Dntl Hygnst Prfssnl; Awrd Prvntve Orl Hlth Care; Bapt Chrch 79-; ADHA 89-; Dntl Asst 83-; Cert Chipola Jr Coll 82; Prfssnl Hlth Care; Dntl Hygnst.

**GILMOUR, KELLY J**, Dowling Coll, Oakdale Li, NY; SR; BS; AA SUNY Ag/Tech 87-89; Ed; Tchng.

**GILMOUR JR, RONALD W**, Fl St Univ, Tallahassee, FL; JR; BA; Bio; Rsrch.

**GILPIN, DAVID G**, Univ Of Ky, Lexington, KY; SR; BA; Pi Mu Epsilon 90-; Sallie E Pence Awrd; Sci And Math Awrd S Bnntt Coll 89; Math Educ; Tchr.

**GILREATH, PAUL A**, Univ Of Cincinnati-Clrmnt Coll, Batavia, OH; JR; Comp Clb 88; Syst Mngr 90-; UCCC Comp Oper 89-90; Deans Lst Clermont Coll 89-90; Oracle Pgmr 88-; Natl Deans Lst 89-90; Mntr Schlrshp Syst Asst 89; AAB 90; Comp; Comp Pgmr/Syst Mngr.

**GILROY, BERNARD H P,** Catholic Univ Of America, Washington, DC; JR; BS; Undrgrad Stdnt Govt Jdcl Brnch Chr Cnsttn Rvsn 90-; Scty Of Physcs Stdnts Pres 88-; CUA Coll Bwl Tm 90-; Univ Hnrs Prog Univ Schlr Clsscl Phil 88-; Phi Eta Sigma 88-; Roy Bode Mem Awrd; CUA Dns Lst 88-; IM Vlybl Tm 90; Physcs; Prfssrshp In Physics.**

**GILROY, MICHAEL R,** Memphis St Univ, Memphis, TN; SO; Bus; Lgl Advsr.

**GILSTRAP, DEBRA L,** Queens Coll, Charlotte, NC; SR; BA; Art Club 87-; Amnisty Intl 89-; Soccer Tm 87-88; Asst Ath Trnr Hd Stdnt Trnr 89-; Studio Art; Masters In Art Thrpy.

**GILSTRAP, JODY E,** Birmingham Southern Coll, Birmingham, AL; SO; BS; Triangle Clb 90-; Phi Eta Sigma 89-; Alpha Lambda Delta 89-; Deans Lst; Alpha Epsilon Delta 90-; Theta Chi Corrspndg Sec 89-; Admn Intrn; Med Ctr Intrn; Urban Mnstres Tutor; Biology/Psychlgy; Med.

**GILSTRAP, ROBERT H,** Univ Of Tn At Knoxville, Knoxville, TN; FR; BA; Ggrphy.

**GILSTRAP, TRINA G,** North Ga Coll, Dahlonega, GA; FR; MBA; All Fresh Tm 90-; NAIA; Bsktbl; Phys Ed; H S Bsktbl Coach.

**GILYARD, TORR A,** Fl A & M Univ, Tallahassee, FL; FR; BS; Law Clb 90-; Fornscs/Dbte Tm Pres 90-; Pltcl Sci; Law.

**GIMPLIN, DEBORAH A,** Niagara Univ, Niagara Univ, NY; JR; BS; NSNA 88-; Clss Rep 90-; Clncl Rep 90-; Cncpts Rep 90-; LPN H B Ward Tech Ctr 88; Nrsng/Bio; Med Dr.

**GINAC, JOSEPH MICHEAL,** Hudson Valley Comm Coll, Troy, NY; SO; MS; Elec Eng.

**GINADER, JENNIFER L,** Longwood Coll, Farmville, VA; FR; BA; Alpha Lambda Delta 90-; Pltcl Sci.

**GINDHART, KAREN R,** Cumberland County Coll, Vineland, NJ; FR; AAS; Lgl Asst Assc VP 90-; Deans List; Vrsty Mock Trl Ld Atty 90; Cty Dmcrtc Cmt Sec 89-; Lgl Sec 88-; Lgl Asstnt Pgm; Law.

**GINES, MARIA DE L,** Univ Of Pr At Rio Piedras, Rio Piedras, PR; SR; Gldn Key; Assoc Acctg Stdnts; Acctg; Law.

**GINGRAS, RENEE M,** Univ Of Pa, Philadelphia, PA; FR; BA; Amnesty Internatl Philosophi Soc 90-; Tutorial Svc; Deans List; 1st Grp Schlr; Econ/Bus.

**GINGRICH, DAVID L,** Millersville Univ Of Pa, Millersville, PA; FR; BA; IM Vlybl/Sftbl/Bsktbl.

**GINN, BOBBIE D,** Univ Of Cincinnati-Clrmnt Coll, Batavia, OH; FR; BA; Monroe Twnshp Womens Aux Treas 91; Am Quarterhorse Assoc 69-; Media Dist Spvsr; Cert Natl Am Corres Sch Vet Asst 89; Comp Sci; Comp Engrng.

**GINN, CATHERINE MARIA,** Univ Of Southern Ms, Hattiesburg, MS; JR; BS; Alpha Omega 88-90; Phi Theta Kappa 88-90; Brookhavens Miss Hsptlty 90; Nrsng; Nrs Ansthtst.

**GINN, DAVID,** Western Carolina Univ, Cullowhee, NC; SO; BA; Hnr Stdnt; Stdnt Mrshll; Mscns Un Lcl; Intl Trmpt Gld; Trmpt Music Synths; Muscn Tchr.

**GINN JR, DONNIE H,** Univ Of Ky, Lexington, KY; SR; BSCE; Amer Scty Of Civil Eng; AS Morehead State Univ 90; Civil Eng; Eng.

**GINN, PARKER C,** Ms St Univ, Miss State, MS; JR; BA; Traffic Appeals Court 90-; Pi Kappa Alpha Pldg Edctr 89-90; IM Ftbl/Sftbl/Rqtbl; Mktg; Mktg Cnsltnt.

**GINN, WENDY FAYE,** Univ Of Southern Ms, Hattiesburg, MS; SR; BA; Am Bus Women Assn Bulletin Chm 86-; AAS Pearl River Jr Coll 80; Bus Admn; Phrmctcl Sales.

**GINNITY JR, JOHN F,** Clarkson Univ, Potsdam, NY; SR; Stdnt Sen Sentr/Publc Rltns 90-; Pre Law Soc Pres 90-; Psychlgy Club Treas 90-; Phi Kappa Sigma 90-; Trustees Schlrshp; Phalany Ldrshp Award; Weblows Hlpr; Fincl Mgt Assoc; Air Force 84-90; BS; Mgt/Psychlgy; MBA/LAW Sch.

**GINSBERG, CORRI J,** Fl Atlantic Univ, Boca Raton, FL; GD; MBA; B'nai Brith Women 88-89; Deans List 88-90; AA Broward Comm Coll 88; BA 90; Bus; Klaw.

**GINSBERG, PENINA,** Yeshiva Univ, New York, NY; GD; Stu Strggl Svt Jwry; Jnt Bus Soc; NYS Regents Schlrshp; Dean Lst 86-90; Erly Admssns; Magna Cum Laude; Tnns Tm 86-87; Bus.

**GINSBURG, ESTHER M,** Yeshiva Univ, New York, NY; SR; Stdnt Gvrnmnt Sec 88-89; Stdnt Gvrnmnt VP 89-90; Deans List 88-90; Acct/Pre/Law; CPA/LAW.

**GINYARD, GARRICK S,** Morehouse Coll, Atlanta, GA; JR; BA; Glee Clb 88-; Cls Treas 88-89; Calif Clb 88-; Hon Rl 90; Phi Mu Alpha 90; Orgnst 88-90; Panst Bible Way Ch 90; Music.

**GINZBURG, MARK Y,** Bunker Hill Comm Coll, Boston, MA; FR; BA; Hnr Bureau Jwsh Educ Grtr Boston; Engr.

**GIOIA, JANET E,** Schenectady County Comm Coll, Schenectady, NY; SR; Jurisprudence Clb VP 90-; AAS; Law.

**GIOIA, RONALD,** Wilmington Coll, New Castle, DE; SR; BS; Ind Eng Asst; AS Delaware Tech 86; Bus Mgmt.

**GIORDANO, GUIDO L,** Harvard Univ, Cambridge, MA; FR; BA; Athlts Cltrl Dvlpmnt Cmnty Fndr 90-; Scr 90-; Lcrs 90-; Govt; Law.

**GIORDANO III, HARRY,** Cumberland County Coll, Vineland, NJ; FR; BA; Wrkd Sales; Bus/Mrktng; Mrktng Mgt/Advrtsng.

**GIORDANO, MARC A,** Widener Univ, Chester, PA; SO; BA; Inst Mngmnt Accntnts 90-; Schl Mngmnt Hnrs; Accntng/Bus; CPA.

**GIORDANO, TRISHA M,** Fayetteville St Univ, Fayetteville, NC; SR; BS; Math/Cmptr Sci Clb; Cooprtv Educ; Kappa Delta Pi; Chnclrs Lst; IBM Inc; Nrthrn Telecom Inc; AS 85; Cmptr Sci; Sftwr Engr.

**GIORGI, MATTHEW J,** Le Moyne Coll, Syracuse, NY; SR; BS; Envrnmntl Cltn Pres 89; Symposium 90; Phi Sigma Tau 90; Chem Hnrs; Chem Awd; Phlsphy Awd; Phlsphy Chem; PHD Phlsphy.

**GIOSI, KENNETH J,** S U N Y Coll Of Tech At Frmgdl, Farmingdale, NY; JR; BA; Frgn Lang Club V P 89-90; Educ Of The Ftre Hd Advrtsng; Sigma Beta Strng Comm; Golden Key 90-; Sigma Beta 90-; Dns Lst 90-; Gymnastics; AAS 90; History; Tchng/Law.

**GIOTTA, RACHEL E,** Drew Univ, Madison, NJ; FR; BA; Scl Comm 90-; IM Sccr 90-; Univ Orchstra 90-; Beta Beta Beta 90-; Scl Comm 90-; Marine Bio.

**GIOTTI, ALBERT J,** Villanova Univ, Villanova, PA; JR; BS; Math; Actrl Sci.

**GIPSON, TRAVIS,** Univ Of Sc At Coastal Carolina, Conway, SC; FR; BS; Cmptr Sci.

**GIRARD, J ANDRE,** Univ Of Sc At Coastal Carolina, Conway, SC; SO; BA; Dns Lst; IM Ftbl 89; Coed Vlybl 90; Psych Mjr Phlsphy Mnr.

**GIRARD, JANET G,** Piedmont Tech Coll, Greenwood, SC; FR; AAS; Phi Beta Lmbd; Deans List; Kiwanis Clb Schlrshp; Dipl Rsprtry Thrpy Piedmont Tech Clg 79; Prnts Advsry Cncl SC Sch Deaf/Blind; Bus Emphs Acctg; Acctg.

**GIRARD, JOSEPH M,** Le Moyne Coll, Syracuse, NY; FR; BA; Bsktbl Rookie Of Yr; Bus.

**GIRARD, KIRSTEN J,** Colby Sawyer Coll, New London, NH; JR; BS; SGA Pres 90-; Key Assoc Co Actvts Pblcty Dir 88-; Deans List 90-; Brd Trs Rep 90-; Athlt Of Yr 90f Drtmth Mary Htchck Day Care Aide; Warner NH Simond Schl Ch/Rdng; Var Tennis/Bsktbl Capt MVP 88-; ; Warner NH Simond Schl Ch/Rdng; Chld Stdy/Psych, Teach MA.

**GIRARDI, MARIA T,** Manhattan Coll, Bronx, NY; SR; Epsln Sigma Pi 90-; Iou Beta Pi 89-; St La Salle Hnr Soc 87-; Eta Kappa Nu 89-; BSEF.

**GIROD, CARMEN C,** Catholic Univ Of Pr, Ponce, PR; GD; JD; Law Review 89-; Phi Alpha Delta 90-; ANED 88-; Amer Bar Assn 88-; Curriculum Comm 90-; BA 88.

**GIRONDA, JENNIFER K,** Indiana Univ Of Pa, Indiana, PA; GD; BS; Early Childhood Educ; Full Time Educator.

**GIROUX, LISA A,** Daemen Coll, Amherst, NY; SO; BS; Aerobics; Delta Phi Mu Sec; Vol Comm Svcs Leukemia Soc 90-; IM Vlbl Sftbl 90-; Phys Therapy.

**GIRTEN, MINDY M,** Colby Sawyer Coll, New London, NH; SR; BS; Res Hall RA 88-89; 14 Wk 15 Credit Intnshp/Maj Area/ Study Sport Sci; Intercllgte Vlybl/Bsktbl Capt 87-89; CNA Hillcrest Nrsg Home 86; Sport Sci; Exercise Specist; Prsnl Fitness.

**GIRTON, ROCHELLE M,** Memphis St Univ, Memphis, TN; FR; BS; Educ Sppt Prog 90-; Alpha Lambda Delta 90-; Biolgy; Med.

**GISELA, ALVAREZ PEREZ,** Caribbean Center For Adv Stds, San Juan, PR; GD; MS; Soc Human Rscrs Mngmnt P R 89-; Amer Assn Cnslng Dvlpmnt 89-; BA Cum Laude Univ Puerto Rico 89; Indstrl/Organ Psychlgy; P Hd I/O Psychlgy.

**GISH, JEFFREY A,** Middle Tn St Univ, Murfreesboro, TN; SO; BA; Pi Kappa Phi; TV Production; Director.

**GISI, TINA M,** Boston Univ, Boston, MA; SO; BA; Pre Med Soc 90-; Human Apld Physiology; Med.

**GISPAN, DINA,** Miami Dade Comm Coll, Miami, FL; SO; Cert Outstdng Acad Achvmnt 90-; Int Dsgn.

**GISSENDANNER, JULIE D,** Memphis St Univ, Memphis, TN; SO; BA; Pre Law Soc 89-; Alpha Lambda Delta 89-; Pi Beta Phi VP Mntl Advncmnt 89-; Englsh; Law.

**GITELMAN, LARRY R,** Comm Coll Algny Co Algny Cmps, Pittsburgh, PA; JR; MSN; Cmmnty Mntl Hlth Spclst 90; RN Shadyside Hosp 88; Scif Ansthtst.

**GITHIORA, CAROLINE W,** City Univ Of Ny City Coll, New York, NY; SR; BA; Kenya Stdnt Organ Sec 88-89; Natl Deans Lst; Golden Key 89-90; French Spanish; Intl Fld.

**GITMAN, LEDA V,** Fl International Univ, Miami, FL; FR; BFA; Faculty Schlr 90; Hons Prog 90; Visual Art; Pntng.

**GITNIK, LISA JILL,** Univ Of Rochester, Rochester, NY; JR; BA; Co Photo Edtr 88-90; Univ Roch Adm Intervwr 90-; Peer Ldr Amps Disc Grp Ldr; Dns Lst 88-; Delta Gamma Asst Rush Chrprsn 90-; Dist Attys Offc Intrn 90; Firm Solictrs Londn Eng Intrn; Pol Sci/Psych; Law/Psych Grad Schl.

**GITOMER, SCOTT H,** Atlantic Comm Coll, Mays Landing, NJ; FR; Clnry; Ownr.

**GITTENS, FELICIA C,** Borough Of Manhattan Comm Coll, New York, NY; SO; BBA; AAS; Accntng; CPA.

**GITTENS, JULIET M,** Elmira Coll, Elmira, NY; SR; BS; Internatl Clb VP 87-89; Nrsg Clb Sec 88-; Nrsg/Psychlgy.

**GIUFFRE, JOSEPH L,** Hudson Valley Comm Coll, Troy, NY; FR; CIS; Cmptr Inf Systms; Cmptr Pgmng.

**GIUNTA, JONATHAN P,** S U N Y Coll Of Tech At Delhi, Delhi, NY; FR; BA; Engl Elec.

**GIUNTA, STEPHANIE L,** Villanova Univ, Villanova, PA; SO; BS; Villanova Unvrsty Shop 89-; Deans Lst 89-; Hlth Sprts Stds; Physcl Thrpy.

**GIUNTA, VITA M,** Le Moyne Coll, Syracuse, NY; SO; BA; Psychology Club 89-; Health Services Club 89-90; Catholic Charities 90-; Psychology & French; Psychologist.

**GIUPPONI, LAURA C,** Western New England Coll, Springfield, MA; JR; BA; Mgmnt; Bus.

**GIVEN, JENNIFER A,** S U N Y Coll At Geneseo, Geneseo, NY; FR; BA; Inter Res Cncl Rep 90-; Cls Rep 90-; Hall Rep 90-; Anthropologist/Cultural.

**GIVEN, TONYA G,** Fairmont St Coll, Fairmont, WV; FR; MA; Crmnl Jstc Clb 90-; Pep Clb 90-; Phi Mu 90-; Kappa Delta Phi 90-; Stu Sec Tm Ldr 90-; Elem Educ; Tchr.

**GIVENS, MARY R,** Jacksonville St Univ, Jacksonville, AL; JR; BSN; ASN 81; Nurs.

**GIVENS, STEPHANIE L,** Univ Of Tn At Martin, Martin, TN; SO; BA; Primary Org Pr 90-; Single Adults Rep 88-90; Comp Sci.

**GIVENS, TONYA R,** Ky St Univ, Frankfort, KY; FR; MBA; Band 90-; Gospel Ensemble; Psychology.

**GIVHAN, MERCER A,** Morehouse Coll, Atlanta, GA; SR; ID; NAACP 87-; Amnesty Intl 87-; Big Brother/Big Sister Of Atlanta 87-; Golden Key 90-; Cum Laude; Deans List; Hnr Roll; BA; Law.

**GIVHAN, RASHARA N,** Tn St Univ, Nashville, TN; SO; BA; Physc Clb 90-; Bsktbl 89-90; SWE 90-; Univ Hon Pgm 89-; Achvmnt Awds 89-; Wght Trnr 90-; Eng; Elect Eng.

**GIZOWSKI, JOHN E,** Hilbert Coll, Hamburg, NY; SO; BA; Phi Beta Lambda VP; Bus Mgt.

**GJURICH, DANA C,** Saint Francis Coll, Loretto, PA; SR; BS; Math Clb; Hon Pgm 87-; Bio Clb VP 87-; Chem Clb 87-; Deans Lst 87-; Natl Catholic Hon Soc 90-; Hon Soc 90-; Beta Beta Beta 89-; Dorothy Day Ctr 87-88; Chem Awd 87-88; Pres Schlrshp 87-; Bio; Optometry.

**GLAAB, REBECCA A,** Univ Of Southern Ms, Hattiesburg, MS; SR; BS; Spch Cmnctn Assn PR Com 89-; Catholic Stdnt Assn Message Com Chrmn 88-; Stdnt Alumni Assn 89-; Lambda Pi Eta Booksale Chrmn 90-; Gamma Beta Phi 89-; Catholic Stdnt Assn 88-; Intrnshp MS Rpblcn Party 90-; Spch Cmnctns/Jrnlsm; Corp Cmnctns/PR.

**GLACKEN, KIMBERLY M,** Longwood Coll, Farmville, VA; SR; BS; Acctng Asc; VA Tax Asc Vol; Natl Asc Acctnts; Bsn Admn/ Acctng; CPA.

**GLADDEN, JULIE A,** Fl A & M Univ, Tallahassee, FL; JR; BS; Kappa Delta Big Evnts Chrmn 86-90; Garnet/Gold 87-90; Kappa Delta 86-90; BS FL State Univ 90; Phys Ther.

**GLADDEN, SHIKINA T,** Fl A & M Univ, Tallahassee, FL; JR; BS; Pre Phys Thrpy Clb; Phys Thrpy; Thrpst Neurlgy/Gerintrc.

**GLADDEN, TIFFANIE M,** Hampton Univ, Hampton, VA; FR; BS; Womens Sen 90-; Hon Roll 90-; Comptr Sci; Progrmmr.

**GLADDEN-LAMB, LA DONNA G,** Univ Of Sc At Columbia, Columbia, SC; SR; BA; Soup Ktchn; CSRA Fam Coun Cen Bd 87-; Alchol/Drub Rehab; Psych; MA.

**GLADFELTER JR, GARRISON E,** Indiana Univ Of Pa, Indiana, PA; Hstry Clb 89-; Clg Rpblcns 87-; PSEA/NEA 89-; Pi Gamma Mu 89-; Phi Alpha Theta 90-; Delta Sigma Phi 87-; Deans Lst 88-; Tnns 86-87; BED 90.**

**GLADMAN, PATRICIA A,** Muskingum Coll, New Concord, OH; SO; BA; Wind Ensmble 90-; March/Spirit Band 89-; Geology Clb 89-90; Alumni Awd 89; Sara Wilhelm Awd Engl; Engl; Editing Publshng.

**GLADNEY, MICHELLE,** Voorhees Coll, Denmark, SC; SR; BS; Pep Sqd; Dance Sqd; Alpha Chi 90-; Alpha Kappa Mu VP 89-; Delta Sigma Theta; Comptr Sci; Comptr Info Sys.

**GLADWELL, JERRARD M,** Marshall University, Huntington, WV; FR; BA; Crs Co Indr/Otdr Trck 90-91; Mrktng.

**GLANNON, ALLYSON L,** Marshall University, Huntington, WV; SR; BED; Gamma Beta Phi 90; Elem Educ; Tchng.

**GLANTZ, KAREN R,** Cornell Univ Statutory College, Ithaca, NY; JR; BS; Eclgy Hs 88-; Botany Inter Smithsonian Inst Msm Natrl Hstry 90; Plnt Sci; Ethnbtny.

**GLANTZ, NATALIE P,** Saint Josephs Univ, Philadelphia, PA; GD; Grad Hlth Admin Awrd; Bach Of Sci In Nrsng; BSN Widener Univ 82; MSHA; Hlth Admin; Devl Mnge Del Of Hlth Care Srvcs.

**GLAROS, MELISSA G,** Univ Of North Fl, Jacksonville, FL; JR; BA; Gldn Key 89-; Hndbll Chr 88-; AA UNF 89-90; Art Hstry; Hstrn.**

**GLAS, CATHRYN J,** Univ Of Sc At Columbia, Columbia, SC; SO; BBA; Sec 89; Bus.

**GLASER, BETH J,** Dowling Coll, Oakdale Li, NY; SR; BA; Alpha Chi 90-; Dns Lst 90-; Amer Assn Med Trnscrptn AAMA Chrprsn Mbrshp Comm 81; Med Trnscrptnst Rdlgy 73-; Elem Educ; Tchr.

**GLASER, ERIC B,** Univ Of Pittsburgh, Pittsburgh, PA; SO; Natl Hnr Soc 86-89; Mech Engr.

**GLASER, MICHAEL P,** Belmont Coll, Nashville, TN; JR; BA; Music; Commerical Music.

**GLASER, MICHAEL R,** S U N Y At Albany, Albany, NY; SO; BA; Peer Sxl Hrsmnt Awrvns Actr; Chinese Stu/Bus Admn; Intl Law.

**GLASGOW, CELESTE Y,** Univ Of Rochester, Rochester, NY; SR; STING Hmcmng Chr 90-; Gspl Chr 87-; Blck Stdnts Union 90-; Gft Drve Chllnge Tm Capt; Krdns Pres 90-; Rsdnt Advsr 88-; Prnt Ornttn Prog Chrprsn 89; Actvts Intrn 90; Prctr And Gmble Intrn Sales Rep 90; BA; Bus Cmmnctns PR.

**GLASGOW, CHRISTOPHER A,** Oh Univ, Athens, OH; SO; BFA; Costume Design 90-; Theatre; Costume Design.

**GLASGOW, MC GREGOR E M,** Central Al Comm Coll, Alexander City, AL; JR; Cncrt Bnd; Jazz/Show Bnd; Music Schlrshp; Allied Hlth; Phys Thrpy.

**GLASGOW, REGINA M,** Norfolk St Univ, Norfolk, VA; SO; Alpha Kappa Delta; Soc; Govt Work.

**GLASKER, ROBERT C,** Va St Univ, Petersburg, VA; JR; BA; Yth Dept Promise Lnd Bapt Chrch Pres 86-89; Mbr FBLA 86-88; Bsns Mgmt/Admn; Mgr/Admnstr.

**GLASMAN, ABRAHAM M,** Univ Of Rochester, Rochester, NY; SO; BA; Amer Isrl Pblc Afrs Cmt 90-; Intrntl Trade Rltns.

**GLASNAPP, ERIC O,** Univ Of North Fl, Jacksonville, FL; JR; BS; Statistcs Math Clb Hstrn 88-89; Actuarial Intern; AAF; Statistics; Actry.

**GLASPIE, CHRISTOPHER,** Fayetteville St Univ, Fayetteville, NC; GD; Soc Club 88-90; Criminal Justice Treas 88-90; N C St Schlrshp 87-88; N C T & T Schlrshp 84-85; N C Comm Coll Schlrshp 85-86; AAS James Sprunt Comm Coll 84-86; BS 87-90; Criminal Justice; Law Sch.

**GLASS, ELIZABETH A,** Middle Tn St Univ, Murfreesboro, TN; SR; BSN; Natl Flight Nrs Assoc; RN 79; AD Nrsg Austin Peay State Univ 79; Nrsg.

**GLASS, JAMES R,** Dyersburg St Comm Coll, Dyersburg, TN; FR; BA; Sci; Phys Ther.

**GLASS, MARIE C,** Univ Of West Fl, Pensacola, FL; SR; BS; Kappa Delta Pi 88-; Cub Scouts Boy Scouts Am Parent Vol 86-; Deans Lst 88-; PTA Parent Vol 84-; E Brent Bapt Ch Chldrns Div 85-; AS Pensacola Jr Coll 74; Elem Edn; Teach.

**GLASS, SHEILA L,** Clark Atlanta Univ, Atlanta, GA; SR; BSW; Org Scl Chng Pres 90-; Outstndng Stdnt; Atlanta Chldrns Shltr Intrn 90-; Chld Wlfr Schlrshp 89-90; Scl Wrk; MSW.

**GLASS, STEPHANIE A,** Pa St Univ Altoona Cmps, Altoona, PA; SO; BA; Unity Plyrs 89-; Cir K 90-; Lit Mag 90-; Poetry Awd; Dns Lst; NACA 90; Engl Lit; Law.**

**GLASSCOCK, AUDREY Y,** Longwood Coll, Farmville, VA; SR; BS; Stdnt Educ Assn 90-; Sigma Kappa Crspndg Sec 87-; Stdnt Tchr Grd 6 90; Elem Educ; Tchr.

**GLASSCOCK, KIMBERLY L,** Middle Tn St Univ, Murfreesboro, TN; SR; MED; Stdnt Govt Math Assoc 89-; Pi Gamma Mu 90-; Chi Omega 89-; AS Motlow St Cmnty Clg 89; BS MTSU; Ed.

**GLASSER, BURNITTA L,** Antonelli Inst Of Art & Photo, Cincinnati, OH; SR; ASSC; Alpha Betta Kappa 90-; Phtgrphy Pblsh Phtgrphrs Forum/Best Clg Phtgrphy; Received 3 Hnrbl Mentions 1 Awrd Achvmnt; PPO; Phtgrphy.

**GLASSER, EVE F,** Ny Univ, New York, NY; SR; Hillel Briar Birth Scl Dir 90-; Deans Cir; Alpha Phi Epsilon Prlmntrn 89-; Intrnshp Eurpn Prlmnt 90; Pltcs; Pre-Law.

**GLASSER, JOANNE,** Nova Univ, Ft Lauderdale, FL; GD; MBA; Delta Mu Delta; Delta Tau Alpha; Amer Inst Cert Pblc Acctnts; BA Adelphi U 86; AS Nassau Comm Coll 83.

**GLASSER, PAUL J,** Comm Coll Algny Co Algny Cmps, Pittsburgh, PA; FR; AS; Fire Dept Tres 81-86; Amblnc Srvc Prsdnt 81-82; US Air Force 75-79; EMT 82; Automotiv Tech; Engnrng.

**GLASSER, STEPHANIE W,** Allegheny Coll, Meadville, PA; JR; BS; Debate Tm 90-; Hillel V P 88-; MAA 90-; Alpha Gamma Delta V P Schlrshp 89-; Alden Schlr 88-90; Stdnt Orntatn Advsr; Math; Law.

**GLASSMAN, GREGORY A,** Univ Of Nc At Charlotte, Charlotte, NC; JR; BA; Pre-Law Soc 89-; Colg Demo 89-90; Chi-Rho 88-; Phi Alpha Theta 90; Pol Sci; Law.

**GLASSMEYER, SUSAN T,** Xavier Univ, Cincinnati, OH; SO; College Bowl 90-; Alchemist Clb Rep 89-; Yrbk 89-; Schlrs Cncl 90-; MORE 89-; Chemistry.**

**GLAST, VERONICA E,** Va Union Univ, Richmond, VA; FR; MBA; Vlybl 90-; Bus Inf Sys; Comp Tech.

**GLATT, MARSHA J,** Univ Of Sc At Spartanburg, Spartanburg, SC; FR; BSN; Nurs; RN.

**GLATT, RODERICK J,** Tn St Univ, Nashville, TN; SR; Aristcrt Bnds; Pol Sci Org Pres; TN Legsltv Intrn; Dns Lst; Grt Debate 2nd Finlst; Res Fndrs Dy Attnd Awd; Mason; NAACP; TN Legsltv Intrn; BS 90; Govt; Law.

**GLATT, RUTHANNE,** Univ Of Pittsburgh At Bradford, Bradford, PA; FR; BA; Pblc Rltns Clb Sec 90-; Pblc Rltns Spec.

**GLAZE, DAISY L,** Fl A & M Univ, Tallahassee, FL; SR; BS; Stdnt Natl Phrmctcl Assoc 86-88; Roche Phrmcy Cmnctn Awd; Phrmcy.

**GLAZE, KIMBERLY A,** Paine Coll, Augusta, GA; SO; BA; SGA 89-90; Alpha Swthrt Chpln 89-; Clg Hon Roll; Bus Admnstrtn/Comps.

**GLAZER, SHERYL,** Yeshiva Univ, New York, NY; JR; BS; Bd Mbr Sy Syms Sch Of Bus VP 90-; Stdnt Cncl; Nwspaper Proof/ Copy Edtr 89-90; Jacob Burns Schlr; Deans List 88-; Acctng Intrnshp; Acctng; CPA.

**GLEASON, ANGELA B,** Saint Josephs Coll, Windham, ME; FR; BS; Bsktbl/Vlybl/Sftbl 90-; Commctns; Foreign Corresp/T V News.

**GLEASON, JEFF S,** Thomas Nelson Comm Coll, Hampton, VA; SO; AAS; Rcqtbl Sccr Vllybl Phtgrphy; Upsilon Gamma Etta; Phtgrphy.

**GLEASON, LESLIE ANN,** Norfolk St Univ, Norfolk, VA; SR; BA; Spch Lang Pathology Clb Sec 89-; Olympian Hon Clb 87-89; Ambsdr 88-90; Alpha Kappa Mu 88-; Sigma Tau Delta 89-; Spartan Alpha Tau 87-; NSASHA 89-; Untd Way W W Houston Boys Clb Chmn 86-88; Astntshp 89-; Intrnshp VA Sch Deaf/ Blind; Spch Lang Pathology Audiology; Clncl Res.

**GLEASON, MARY M,** Oh Univ, Athens, OH; SO; AB; O V Alpine Clb 90; O V Tae Kwan Do Clb; Psych.

**GLEASON, PAMELA J,** Niagara Univ, Niagara Univ, NY; SR; BS; Amercn Mktg Assoc 89-; Niagara Univ Mktg Club 88-; Delta Epsilon Sigma 89-; Alpha Kappa Psi 89-; Intrnshp Gardenway Fmg Inc 89; Jr/Sr Awards For Exclnc In Comm; Pres Schlrshp; NCAA Div 1 Womens Bsktbl Cptn 87-; Comrc/Mktg/CIS; Bus.

**GLEASON, TINA L,** S U N Y Coll At Fredonia, Fredonia, NY; JR; BA; Psychlgy Clb 90; Asmnt Cmt Psychlgy Dept; Help Svc; Tchng Asstnt 90; Psychlgy; Cnslng.

**GLEBA, MICHAEL W,** Carnegie Mellon Univ, Pittsburgh, PA; GD; BA; IM; Beta Gamma Sigma; Indus Mgmt; JD Smba.

**GLEE, MELISSA R,** Howard Univ, Washington, DC; SR; NAACP 87-90; Educ Cncl; Kappa Delta Pi 90-; Dns Lst 90-; Trustee Schlp 90-; BA; Elem Ed.

**GLEIM, JULIE A,** Capital Univ, Columbus, OH; FR; BA; Educ Soc 90-; 94 Corp Cmte 90-; Stdnt Amb 90-; Phi Beta Co-Usher Chrmn; Clg Flwshp 90-; Engl; Sec Educ.

**GLEISSNER, DENNIS J,** Embry Riddle Aeronautical Univ, Daytona Beach, FL; JR; BA; Swim Meets 89-90; Clb Vlybl/ Rcktbl/Hcky; Aeronautical Scinc; Pilot.

**GLENCER, KATHLEEN T,** Birmingham Southern Coll, Birmingham, AL; FR; Wdnsdy Clg 90-; Phi Eta Sigma 90-; Alpha Lambda Delta 90-; Dns Lst 90-; Mntr New Adlt Wmn; Adlt Stds Adv Cncl 90-; Vol Ok Mtn Elem; PTA 90-; Den/Cmp Asst BSA 90-; Actv Prntng Asc 90-; Lib Arts.

**GLENN, CATHY D,** Univ Of Sc At Columbia, Columbia, SC; SR; BA; Empl Gov Offc 90-; Pltcl Scnc; Lw Schl.

**GLENN, CHRISTOPHER M,** David Lipscomb Univ, Nashville, TN; FR; BS; Frshmn Chorus 90-; Cncrt Band 90-; Clgt Msc Edctrs Natl Cnfrnc 90-; Msc Ed; Msc Tchng.

**GLENN, DE LONA G,** Central Al Comm Coll, Alexander City, AL; FR; Assembly Of God Prims Sponsor Daisey Sponsor 87-88; Head Room Mother Chelsea Elem 88-; Vol Fire & Rescue EMT 88-; Childrens Aid Soc Bham AL Family Care Worker 88-90; Shelby Co Dept Of Ed; English Science; Elem Ed.

**GLENN, LISA C,** Va Commonwealth Univ, Richmond, VA; SR; BA; Ntnl Hnr Scty 90-; Engl; Dir Cmmnctns.

**GLENN, MILES J,** Northwest Al Comm Coll, Phil Campbell, AL; FR; BS; Eng.

**GLENN, NANCY P ATKINS,** Saint Pauls Coll, Lawrenceville, VA; SO; BS; Nondonmnl Bible Stdy Grp Pr 89-; Stdnt Nwspr Edtr 90-; Alpha Kappa Mu; Dns Lst 90-; Woods Schlrshp; Cert Apprec Acad Achvmnt; Engl/Lit; Tchr.

**GLENN, ROBERT P,** Univ Of New England, Biddeford, ME; JR; BA; Scuba Clb Pres; Sailing Clb Pres; Earth Envrnmntl Cncrnd Org; Amer Red Crs Water Safety Instr; Maine Dept Marine Rsrs Asstshp; Prfsnl Assoc Dive Instr; Marine Biology; Grad Sch/Rsrch Tch.

**GLENN, ROSELYN BARTON,** Middle Ga Coll, Cochran, GA; SO; BS; AHEA 90; GHEA Treas 90; Gamma Beta Phi; Dieticns Assist; Vietnam Vet Of Amer; Ntrtn; Clncl Dietitian.

**GLENN, SCOTT A,** Anderson Coll, Anderson, SC; SO; BA; Church Vocations Pr 90-; Campus Ministries; Spanish Clb Pr 90; Achvmnt Awd; AA; Math Tchr.

**GLENN, STEPHANIE R,** Central St Univ, Wilberforce, OH; SO; BS; DAPP/PEER Cnslr 90-; Hall Govt Sec 89-90; PSI Chi; Deans Lst 89-; Alchl/Adult Child/Alchlcs/Stdnt Rschr; Min Rsch Apprntcshp Prog; Psych; Grad Schl/Child Psych.

**GLENN, THANE P,** Academy Of The New Church, Bryn Athyn, PA; FR; AA; Clg Mscl Ld; Ushr Dty 85-; Rlgs Intrnshp; Hmnts.

**GLENNON, GREGORY T,** S U N Y Coll Of Tech At Frmgdl, Farmingdale, NY; SO; BA; Hstry; Comm Pilot.

**GLENWRIGHT, BRIAN G,** Bowling Green St Univ, Bowling Green, OH; SR; Alpha Eta Rho 89-; Cert Instrmnt Flght Instr 90-; Am Legion Acad Excell; Crs Cntry/Track 87-88; BA; Aerotechnology; Prfl Pilot.

**GLESNER, DEBORA L,** Lasell Coll, Newton, MA; JR; BA; Assoc 90; Erly Chlhd Educ; Tchr.

**GLICK, DOV Y,** City Univ Of Ny Baruch Coll, New York, NY; SR; BBA; Hllel Clb Treas; Fnnce And Econs Scty 90; Gldn Ky; Prvst Schlr; Robert Demb Fnd Schlr; Fnnce; Invstmnt Bnkng.

**GLICK, HENRY E,** Southeastern Coll Of Hlth Sci, N Miami Beach, FL; GD; Am Pharmaceutical Assoc 87-89; FL Phrmcy Assoc 87-90; S FL Soc Hosp Phrmcts 87-90; Deans Awd 90; Golf 78-79; BBA FL Atlantic Univ 82; BS Pharm 90; Pharmacy.

**GLICKMAN, ERIC,** City Univ Of Ny Baruch Coll, New York, NY; SR; BBA; Gldn Key 90-; Alpha Phi Delta Treas 90-; Statstcs.

**GLIDDEN, JENNIFER L,** Northeastern Univ, Boston, MA; FR; JD; Fndng Sstr Sigma Sigma Sigma Sprt Chrwmn; Crmnl Jstc; Law.

**GLIDDEN, MARTHA R,** Univ Of Nh Plymouth St Coll, Plymouth, NH; JR; BA; Psi Chi 90-; Orttn Ldr; Prsdnts Lst; Psychlgy.

**GLOMBOSKI, DEBORAH A,** Niagara Univ, Niagara Univ, NY; SR; BS; IBS Sec; Chem Soc; Prnts Wknd Comm Chrprsn; Orientn; Aquarm Intrnshp; Biolgy; Biolgy Tchr.

**GLOSS, KATHLEEN L,** Univ Of Pittsburgh At Bradford, Bradford, PA; SO; Bus Mgmtf Acctnt.

**GLOSSEN, MARIE F,** Univ Of Akron, Akron, OH; SR; BA; Gldn Ky; Elem Educ/Concentration Psychology; Tchr.

**GLOVER, ALLISON L,** Allegheny Coll, Meadville, PA; JR; BA; Alden Schlr 89-90; Alpha Chi Omega 89-; Vars Sccr Capt; Hist; Law.

**GLOVER JR, DANNY R,** Cumberland Coll, Williamsburg, KY; JR; BS; Deans Lst 88-; Hi Hnr Awrd 89-; Hnr Awrd 88-90; Soph Rep Hmcmg Ct 89; Intrcoll Bsbl 89-; IM Ftbl/Bsktbl/Vlybl; Bus Admin; Intl Law.

**GLOVER, EDWARD J,** Claflin Coll, Orangeburg, SC; SO; BA; Soc Club 90-; Athlts/Action 88-89; Pan Hellenic Cncl; Kappa Alpha Psi Stgs SE Reg; Hnr Rl/Deans Lst; Bsktbl Francis Marion Clg 89; Soc/Comp Sci; Grad Schl.

**GLOVER, ERSKINE R,** Univ Of Sc At Columbia, Columbia, SC; SR; BS; NAACP V Pres 89-; Assoc Of African Amer Stdnts 87-; UMOJA Grand Minister 90-; Child Care Working With Nderpriveledged Youth 90-; Urban League Of Rochester; IM Bsktbl Ftbl 90-; Statistics/Bus Mktg; Ed Operate Mktg Agncy.**

**GLOVER, GIDGET S,** Hillsborough Comm Coll, Tampa, FL; FR; BS; Cert RT LRMC Schl Rdlgy 89; Sci Nrsng; Nrs Anthtstst.

**GLOVER, IRVING,** Fl International Univ, Miami, FL; SR; MASTE; Phi Lambda Hist; Amer Soc Ind Sec 85-88; Lions Clb Sec 85-86; Amer Soc Indstrl Sec 85-88; Lions Clb Sec 85-86; Sec Mngmnt; BS; AA 4as Miami Dade Comm Coll 70-88; Crim Just; Sec Mngmnt/Law.

**GLOVER, JULIE M,** Indiana Univ Of Pa, Indiana, PA; JR; BED; Assoc Chldhd Educ Intl 90-; Sign Lang Club 90-; Sim Vlybl Tm Co Cpt 89-90; Erly Chldhd Educ; Teacher.

**GLOVER, LISA M,** Georgetown Univ, Washington, DC; SR; BSBA; Trnsfr Stdnt Advsr 90-; Beta Gamma Sigma; Delta Sigma Pi VP Chptr Oprtns 88-; Kappa Delta Schlrshp Chrmn 87-89; Oxford Univ Cmprtv Bus Plcy Summer Prog 90; Intrnshp Bank IV Wichita 89; Finance/Intl Mgt; Cnsltng.

**GLOVER, LYNETTE B,** Wilberforce Univ, Wilberforce, OH; SR; BS; Alpha Kappa Mu; Alpha Kappa Alpha; Outstndng Bsn Stdnt Awards; Dns Lst; Bsn Mktg; Advrtsng Cnsltn.

**GLOVER, SARA J,** Owensboro Comm Coll, Owensboro, KY; FR; AAS; Hlth Srvcs; Physcl Thrpst.

**GLOVER, STEPHEN N,** Owensboro Comm Coll, Owensboro, KY; FR; MSEE; Scty Physcs Stdnts; Awrd Outstanding Achviement Physics; Awrd Acdmc Excllnc 84-86; AASEET ITT Tech Inst 86; Elec Eng.

**GLOW, CARLA J,** West Liberty St Coll, West Liberty, WV; GD; All Amer Schlrs 90; US Achvmnt Acad 90; BA W Liberty State Clg 90; Elem Educ.**

**GLOWACKI, AMY E,** Le Moyne Coll, Syracuse, NY; SR; BA; Varsity Sftbl Co Cptn 87-; Hist Acad 89-; Pi Gamma Mu; Phi Alpha Theta 89-; Alpha Gamma Iota Pres 89-; Hist; MA Publc Hist IN U Indianapolis.

**GLOWACKI, T J,** Univ Of South Fl, Tampa, FL; JR; BFA; Phi Kappa Phi; Music-Perf; Prof Muscn.

**GLOWASKI, CARRIE D,** Middle Tn St Univ, Murfreesboro, TN; SO; BFA; Deans Lst; Grphc Dsng; Advrtsng.

**GLOYER, KAREN A,** Memphis St Univ, Memphis, TN; SO; BA; Social Work.

**GLUCK, KAREN E,** Fl International Univ, Miami, FL; SR; BS; Phi Lambda 90-; Cthlc Cmps Mnstry Sec 88-89; Clnnd Htl Mgmt Trn; Ryl Crbbn Crs Lns; Deans Lst; BS; Hsptlty Mgmt; Trsm.

**GLUTH, DALE R,** Kent St Univ Kent Cmps, Kent, OH; SR; BA; Peer Awrns Wth Stdnts Ex Dir 90-; Knt Intrhl Cncl Hl Rep 88-89; Gldn Key 90-; Otstndng Yng Mn Amrca 90-; Omicron Delta Kappa; Alpha Kappa Delta; Pi Gamma Mu; Chmcl Abs Rdcd Thr Edctn Srvcs Smr Intrn 90; Ksu Psych Dept Rsrch Asst 90-; Psychlgy & Soclgy; Cnslng.

**GLUTZ, CHRISTINE M,** East Stroudsburg Univ, E Stroudsburg, PA; SO; BS; Econ/Mgmt Club; Bsn Mgmt; Acct.

**GLYMPH, TARA L,** Jackson St Univ, Jackson, MS; JR; BA; Cls Repr SGA 89-90; Legislative Cncl 89-90; Jr Recruiter 88-90; NAACP 89-90; Delta Mu Delta 90-; Alpha Kappa Mu; Phi Beta Lambda 89-; Fed Res Bk Kansas City; Intl Bsn Machines 90-; Finance; Analyst.

**GNAGE, PATRICK J,** Univ Of Rochester, Rochester, NY; SO; BM BA; Eastman Opera Thtr/Opera Thtr Rchstr 89-; Apld Music Perf/Voice; Prfrmnc/Rcrdng.**

**GNIADEK, ELIZABETH JEAN,** Birmingham Southern Coll, Birmingham, AL; FR; BS; Phi Eta Sigma; Alpha Lambda Delta; Beta Beta Beta 90-; Chi Omega Treas 90-; Alpha Phi Omega 90-; Claude S Lawson Schrlshp 90-; Recruiting Tm/Schl Hostess 90-; Math/Biology; Medicine.

**GOAD, BELITA A,** Western Ky Univ, Bowling Green, KY; JR; Wm Trnstn 89-; Eng/Psychlgy; Psychlgst/Attrny.

**GOAD, BONNIE J,** Beckley Coll, Beckley, WV; FR; Hnrs Clg; Edctn; Tchr.

**GOAD, DELANA R,** Roane St Comm Coll, Harriman, TN; SO; BA; Soc Sci; Cnslr.

**GOAD, JO E,** Western Ky Univ, Bowling Green, KY; SR; BA; Intl Assn Bus Cmmnctrs 89-; Vol St Amer Inst Bnkng Stdy Grp Pres 88; Phi Kappa Phi 89-; Natl Hnr Soc 89-; Intern 89-90; Vol St Comm Coll Vclty Awrd 89; Schlr; Amer Inst Bnkng Mrt Awrd 89; Intl Assn Bus Cmmn Schlr Awrd; Untd Wy; AS 89; Corp Orgn Cmmnctn.

**GOAD, KATRINA A,** Oh St Univ At Marion, Marion, OH; SO; Scty Creative Anachronisms Inc 90-; Phi Eta Sigma 90-; Alpha Lamda Delta 90-; History; Museum.

**GOAD, SHERRY LYNN,** Radford Univ, Radford, VA; JR; BA; SEA 90-; Ltry Grp 90-; Hon Pgm 90-; AAS New Rvr Comm Coll 90; Engl; Educ/Tchng.

**GOANS, PAULA P,** Roane St Comm Coll, Harriman, TN; SO; MBA; Early Ed/Spec Ed; Tchr/Spec Ed.**

**GOBBEL, AUDRA R,** Univ Of Sc At Columbia, Columbia, SC; FR; BA; Sociology; Personnel Mgmnt.

**GOBBLE, HEATHER,** Univ Of Tn At Martin, Martin, TN; FR; BS; Edcth; Psychlgy; Coun/Gdnce.

**GOBIN, BRYAN R,** Temple Univ, Philadelphia, PA; JR; BS; Kappa Psi V P 89-90; Pa Soc/Hosp Phmcst V P 89-90; Pa Phrmctcl Asso 89-; IM 89-; Phmcy; Phrmcst.

**GOBLE, CHANTAL D,** Wv Univ, Morgantown, WV; FR; BA; Ski Clb 90-; Mountaineer Cncl 90-; Kappa Delta 90-; Bus; Acctng.

**GOBLE, TAMARA A,** Ashland Comm Coll, Ashland, KY; SO; BA; History; Elem Ed.

**GOCHAKOWSKI, ROBIN M,** Bunker Hill Comm Coll, Boston, MA; FR; AS; Lgl Ofc Admn.

**GOCHENOUR, TRACEY L,** Marshall University, Huntington, WV; JR; BBA; Buskirk Res Hl Assn Pres 90-; Advsry Cncl V P 88-90; Inter Hall Govt Cncl Sec 88; Mrchng Band 88; Deans Lst 90; Fin/Bus Law; FBI.

**GODARD, MICHAEL P,** Methodist Coll, Fayetteville, NC; SO; BS; Natl Strngth/Condtng Assc 90-; Cmps Rcrtn IM Pgm Orgnzr Asstnt Dir 89-; Spec Olympcs 89-; Trck/Fld 89-; Exrcs Technlgy; Coach.

**GODBEE, FELICIA D,** Radford Univ, Radford, VA; SR; Pblc Rltns Clb 90-; BS; Pblc Rltns; Corp Rltns.

**GODBEE, JOY F,** Univ Of Sc At Columbia, Columbia, SC; SO; EE; USC AIKEN Eng Clb Pres 89-; Derby Day Com Chrwmn 90; USC-AIKEN Media Bd 90-; Gamma Beta Phi 89-; USC-AIKEN Pcsttr; USC-AIKEN Alumni Ambssdr; USC-AIKEN Eng Stdnt Yr 89-; Wstnghs Svnnh Rvr Co Smmr Intrnshp; Comp/Elect Eng; Eng.

**GODBEHERE, STEPHEN ANDREW,** Univ Of Tn At Chattanooga, Chattanooga, TN; SO; BA; Acad Schrlshp 89-; Physcs/Math; Eng.

**GODBEY, PATRICIA A,** Wv Univ At Parkersburg, Parkersburg, WV; SO; BSED; WV Stdnt Ed Assc 90-; Natl Ed Assc Stdnt Pgm 90-; Phi Theta Kappa 90-; Pres Schlr 88; Ntry Pblc 84-; US Pstl Svc 79-87; Elem Ed.

**GODDARD, BETH E,** Univ Of Ct, Storrs, CT; SR; BS; Nutritnl Sci Club Pres 90-; Food Drives/Deliveries To Needy; Im Soccer/Vlybl/Wtrpolo 87-; Nutritnl Sci; Regstrd Dietcn.

**GODDARD, DEBORAH J,** Comm Coll Algny Co Algny Cmps, Pittsburgh, PA; FR; AD; Med Rec Clb.

**GODEK, KIRSTEN MARIE,** Western New England Coll, Springfield, MA; SR; BSBA; Fnncl Mngmnt Assc Pres 90-; Ambssdr 90-; Career Fair Assc 90-; Delta Mu Delta 90-; Peer Ttr 88-90; Rep Brd Dir; Fnnc Intern; Ski Tm 87-; Fnnc; Bnkng.

**GODFRET, MARGAIRE LYNNE,** Norfolk St Univ, Norfolk, VA; SR; BS; Soc Human Rsrcs Mgmt 88-; Alpha Kappa Mu 88-; Beta Gamma Sigma 90-; Coop Army Intlgnc/Threat Anlys Ctr; Prsnl Indus Rltns; Rcrtmnt/Stfng.

**GODFREY, DONALD G,** S U N Y Coll Of Tech At Alfred, Alfred, NY; FR; AAS; Actvts Cncl Pres 90-; Rd Mgr; Eng.

**GODFREY, FELICIA M,** Fayetteville St Univ, Fayetteville, NC; FR; BA; Choir Univ/Chmbr 90-; Chncllrs Schlrshp 90-; Cmptr Sci; Program.

**GODFREY, IRENE C,** Air Force Inst Of Tech, Wrt-Ptrsn Afb, OH; GD; MS; Phi Kappa Phi; Beta Gamma Sigma; Alpha Chi; Sigma Iota Epsilon; Soc Of Cst Estmtng & Analsys; Amrcn Soc Mltry Cmptrlrs: Cost Analyst; Bba Nmsu 83; Mba Gldn Gt Univ 85; Cst Anlyst.

**GODFREY, MARY B,** Nova Univ, Ft Lauderdale, FL; GD; MBA; Schl Accntng Cncl Cls Rep 85; Beaty Twrs E Drmtry Flr Rep 84; Beta Alpha Psi 86; Alpha Lambda Delta 83-84; Deans Lst 83-86; Soph Hnrs Schlrshp 84-85; Tax Accntnt J M Fmly Entrprs Inc 87-; BS Accntng Unv FL; Bsns; Accntng.

**GODFREY, STEPHEN C,** Al A & M Univ, Normal, AL; SR; Omicron Hnry Acctg Clb; Natl Assoc Blck Accnts; Soc Residential Schlrs Pres 88-89; Alpha Kappa Mu; Delta Mu Delta; Phi Beta Lambda Asst Treas 89-90; Pres Lst; Acad Hnr Rl; Magna Cum Laude 90; BS 90; Acctg; CPA.

**GODFREY, TORRENE N,** Comm Coll Algny Co Algny Cmps, Pittsburgh, PA; SO; Deans Lst; Honrd Coll Brds; Coll Schlshp Svc; Pre-Hlth Prof.

**GODING, TERESA L,** Longwood Coll, Farmville, VA; FR; BFA; Acad Advsry Com 90-; Shw Chr 90-; Thtr 90-; Cltrl Unfctn Com 90-; Fr Hl Fm 90-; Awd Lngwd Math Lvl I 90; IM Bwlng 90; Msc Thtr; Perf/Educ.

**GODLEWSKI, MICHELE A,** Comm Coll Algny Co Algny Cmps, Pittsburgh, PA; SO; BA; Crmnl Juste Clb 90; Phi Theta Kappa; Corrections Admn; Parole Ofcr.

**GODOY, BIANCA D,** City Univ Of Ny La Guard Coll, Long Island Cty, NY; SO; BA; Prnts Assoc Sec 89-90; Prnts Clb 89-; PTA Sec; Deans Lst 89-; Hstry Awrd 90; Vassar Trnsfr Prog 90; Alumni Assoc Rsrch Awrd 89; Vldctrn 88; Tutor; Sec; AS; AAS 88; Engl; Tch.

**GODOY, JARBAS M,** Univ Of Miami, Coral Gables, FL; GD; MA; Psy Chi; Gldn Ky; AA Miami Dade Comm Coll 88; Psychlgy.

**GODOY, TERESITA,** Fl International Univ, Miami, FL; SR; BA; AA Miami Dade Comm Coll 85; Elem Edn.

**GODREAU, ISAR P,** Univ Of Pr At Rio Piedras, Rio Piedras, PR; SR; MA; Assoc Anthrplgy Stdnts 90-; Scl Sci Stdnt Cncl Rep 88-89; Assoc Sclgy Stdnts Pres; Hnr Cert Otstndng Acdmc Achvmnt 86; Schlrshp Exchange Prgm 89; Anthrplgy; Rsrchr.

**GODREAU, SHEILA M,** Univ Of Pr At Mayaguez, Mayaguez, PR; JR; BSBA; NAA 90-; Christian Assn 90-; Phi Kappa Phi; Bus Merit Awd 89-90; Ldrshp Awd 90-91; Bus Admin; Acctng.**

**GODSEY, DARLA L,** Ms Gulf Coast Comm Coll, Perkinston, MS; FR; BA; Sftbl 90-; Bsn; Acctg.

**GODSEY, JONATHAN D,** Northwest Al Comm Coll, Phil Campbell, AL; FR; Phi Theta Kappa 90-; Bus; Banking/Finance.

**GODSEY, LEAH L,** Univ Of Sc At Columbia, Columbia, SC; SR; BS; Marine Science Clb 87-90; Phi Eta Sigma; Rsrch Asstshp 90; Marine Science; Rsrch/Marine Blgcl.

**GODSHALL, KARIN L,** Liberty Univ, Lynchburg, VA; SO; BS; Libty Hmn Ecology Assoc 89-; Hmn Ecology/Fmly Commty Studies; Counseling.

**GODSHALL, KRISTIN M,** Marywood Coll, Scranton, PA; SO; BS; Tchrs Tomorrow 89-; Athltc Advsry Brd Rep 90-; AGAPE Co Dir 90-; Pres Schlr 89-; Vlybl 89-; Elem Ed; Tchr.

**GODSHALL, TIFFANIE R,** Bapt Bible Coll & Seminary, Clarks Summit, PA; JR; BA; Gr Clss Treas 90-; Chr; Chmbr Sngrs Sec 88-; Rsdnt Asst 90-; Hmncmng Qn 90-; Ed.**

**GODWIN, AGNES M,** Clark Atlanta Univ, Atlanta, GA; GD; BA; Fshn Clb Pres 88-90; NAACP 89-90; Asst Mngr 90-; Fshn Mrchndsg; MBA Mktg.

**GODWIN, ASHLEY D,** Univ Of Sc At Columbia, Columbia, SC; JR; BA; Hons Pgm Clb 88-; Alpha Mu Gamma; Phi Alpha Delta; Erth Envrnmntlst Soc 90; Coastl Carolina Schlr 88-; Dpndnt Schlrshp Tuition Awd 90; Deans/Pres Lst 90-; Poly Sci; Law/Scrty Plcy.

**GODWIN, CHRISTIE L,** Univ Of South Al, Mobile, AL; JR; BA; YMCA Actvts; Phi Mu 88; Bus Admin; Mgmt.

**GODWIN, HEATHER T,** Univ Of South Al, Mobile, AL; FR; MBA; Prsdnts Lst 90; Deans Lst 90; 2d Plc Bll Rghts Essy Cntst; USA Prsdnts Schlrs.

**GODWIN, KATHERINE CHOLLET,** Fl St Univ, Tallahassee, FL; JR; BS; Lady Sclphntrs Hs Rep 89-; Stdnt Alumni Fndtn 89-; Seminol Ambassdrs 89-; Phi Eta Sigma 88-; Gldn Ky 90-; Beta Kappa Alpha 89-; Pi Beta Phi VP 88-; Hmcmg Strng Comm 89; GCLC Banq Comm 90; Pi Beta Phi Hmcmng Svc Dy Chrmn 89; Bus Mktg; MBA/LAW.

**GODWIN, THERESA R,** Tougaloo Coll, Tougaloo, MS; SO; BA; SGA Treas 89-; Pltcl Sci Clb Treas 90-; Yng Demo Sec 90-; NAACP Sec 89-; Rsrch Prog; Pltcl Sci; Law.

**GODWIN, WENDY D,** Davis & Elkins Coll, Elkins, WV; JR; BA; SGA 90-; Stdnt Actvts Brd VP 89-; Stdnt Almn Cncl VP 89-; Phi Beta Lambda 90-; Natl Clgte Bsn Mrt Awd 90-; Tns; Trvl/Trsm/Rsrt/Htl Mgmt; Mgng Rsrt.**

**GODWIN-HILL, LAURA S,** Savannah Coll Of Art & Design, Savannah, GA; SR; BFA; Cert Merit Capitol Art Exhbt 88; Schlrsh Art/Dsgn Clg 87; Graphic Dsgn; Grphc Dsgnr.

**GOEDDE, CALLIE A,** Middle Tn St Univ, Murfreesboro, TN; SO; BS; Gamma Beta Phi 89-; Kappa Delta Pi 90-; Gamma Beta Phi 89-; Oklnds Kwns Schlrshp 89-; Ldrshp Prfrmnce Fll Schlrshp 89-; Elem Educ; Tchr.

**GOEDEKE, SHAWN M,** Roane St Comm Coll, Harriman, TN; FR; Mech Engr.

**GOEDEL, KATHLEEN E,** Northern Ky Univ, Highland Hts, KY; SR; BS; Pi Sigma Alpha; Delta Zeta 89; Cty Fin Intrn; Pblc Admin; Govt.

**GOEHNER, LISA N,** Longwood Coll, Farmville, VA; SO; BSBA; Intvars 89-; Ornttn Ldrs; Lds Sccr Tm 89-; Alpha Lambda Delta 90-; Sigma Kappa; Bsn; Acctng.

**GOEHRIG, SAMMYE L,** Fl St Univ, Tallahassee, FL; JR; BA; CMNEC 88-; Fl Flute Assoc 88-; Mrchg Chief 88-; Tau Beta Sigma 88-; Cert Music Prfmnc; Music Educ; Dir.**

**GOEHRING, TED C,** Columbia Greene Comm Coll, Hudson, NY; FR; Mental Hlth Assn; Psych; Cnslr.

**GOELLER, NANCY M,** Bryant Stratton Bus Inst Roch, Rochester, NY; SO; ASSOC; Cmptrs; Wrd Prcsg Sec.

**GOERGEN, BELINDA M,** Niagara Univ, Niagara Univ, NY; SR; BA; Clb Intrntl 88-; Phi Sigma Iota Pres 88-; Delta Epsilon Sigma 89-; Phi Alpha Theta 89-; Pi Sigma Alpha; Intrntl Stds/Frnch; Pblshng.

**GOERING, JULIA M,** S U N Y Coll Of A & T Morrisvl, Morrisville, NY; FR; AA; Lbrl Arts/Hmnts; Entrtnmnt.

**GOERLER, KAREN B,** Chatfield Coll, Saint Martin, OH; SO; BS; Commty Ed Comm; Sociology; Ecologist.

**GOERTZ, JENNIFER D,** Univ Of Sc At Columbia, Columbia, SC; FR; BA; Erly Chldhd Ed; Tchr.

**GOES, ERIK S,** Univ Of Ky, Lexington, KY; SR; BA; Amnsty Interntl 88-; Rep 87-; Golden Key 88-; Mortar Bd; Epsilon Delta VP 88-; Phi Sigma Alpha; Pi Kappa Alpha Risk Mngr 88-; Sal Army 88-; Ghostwrtrs Proj 90-; Deans List 87-; TM Soccer Co Capt 88-; His/P S; Eductn.

**GOETZ, ASHLEY K,** Memphis St Univ, Memphis, TN; JR; Alpha Lambda Delta 89-; Pi Beta Phi Treas 89-; Acad Excell Schlrshp; Fnc; Law.

**GOETZ, JEFFREY S,** Brescia Coll, Owensboro, KY; JR; BS; Sci Clb 89-; Phi Theta Kappa 89-90; Biol; Med.

**GOETZ, SUSAN E,** S U N Y Coll Of Tech At Alfred, Alfred, NY; SR; AAS; Offc Rprtng Tech Clb Trea 90-; Cncrt Bnd/Jzz Bnd Lbrrn 89-; Ambssdr; Tutor; Otstndng Wrd Prcssng Awrd; Ldrshp Awrd; Paul B Orvis Awrd; Wrd Prcssng; Scrtrl.

**GOFAS, DEBORAH,** Univ Of Rochester, Rochester, NY; SR; BS; Soc Wmn Engr 87; Bausch/Lomb Hnry Sci Award 87; Bausch/Lomb Schlrshp 87; Vars Wmsn Swmmng/Diving Team Co-Capt 87; Elctrcl Engr; Engr.

**GOFF, BARBARA J,** Castleton St Coll, Castleton, VT; JR; BA; AS Bay St Jr Coll 89; Educ; Elem Tchr.

**GOFF, CAROL A,** Univ Of Sc At Columbia, Columbia, SC; FR; BA; Phi Eta Sigma 90-; Erly Chldhd Educ; Tch.

**GOFF, CAROLYN M,** Columbia Union Coll, Takoma Park, MD; JR; BS; Rgstrd Ultrasngrphr; Hlth Care Admin.

**GOFF, JENNIFER L,** Fl St Univ, Tallahassee, FL; SR; BS; Natl Assoc For Edn Of Yng Chldrn Pres 89-; Yrbk Co-Edtr 88-89; Lady Scalphunters Booster Org 88-; Alpha Phi Omega 90-; Deans Adv Cncl 89-90; Admn Intrnshp; Child Dvlpmnt/Family Rltns; Dir Child Dev Ctr.

**GOFF, JOSEPH L,** Univ Of Ky, Lexington, KY; SR; BA; Acdmc Tm-UK 87; Pltcl Sci; Law.

**GOFF, LESLIE B,** Georgetown Coll, Georgetown, KY; JR; BA; Dbt Tm Capt 90-; SGA Prlmntrn 88-; Bptst Union 88-; Pi Kappa Delta Pres 89-; Kappa Delta VP 89-; Bd Trustees 90-; Belle Blue; Roger A Bailey Schlrshp 90-; Cmnctns/Pltcl Sci; TV Brdcstng/Law.

**GOFF, LINDA L,** Roane St Comm Coll, Harriman, TN; SO; BA; Otstndg Yng Womn Amer 88; By Scts Amer Dist 90-; AA 91; Acctg.

**GOFF, LYN M,** Oh Wesleyan Univ, Delaware, OH; FR; BA; Delta Gamma.

**GOFF, MARY J,** Madisonville Comm Coll, Madisonville, KY; SR; AS; Coll System 89-; Dns Lst 90; Math; Bus Mgmt.

**GOFF, MICHAEL E,** Univ Of Southern Ms, Hattiesburg, MS; SR; BS; Resdnt Asst 90; Jdcl Bd 89-; Logos Philsphy Club 89-; Hons Clg 89-; Pres Schlr 88-89; Acadmc Exclnc Schlr 90-; Engl; Profsr Of Engl.

**GOFF, S DENISE,** Memphis St Univ, Memphis, TN; SR; MRTC; Grad Magnum Cum Laude 77; Vol Wrld Plc/Fire Games; Vol MIFA-MEALS Whls; Vol Dixon Art Gllry-Hrtcltr; Pre-Med Rdlgc Tchnlgst; AS 77; Med.**

**GOFF, TIMOTHY A,** Columbia Union Coll, Takoma Park, MD; SR; Cmps Mnstrs Clg Sbbth Schl Dir 90-; Stdnt Mnstrl Assoc Sprtl VP 89-; Alpha Chi 90-; Cum Laude; Ba 91; Theology; Pastor/Teacher.

**GOFF, WINDELL H,** West Liberty St Coll, West Liberty, WV; FR; BA; Phys Tutor; Math Educ; Tchr.

**GOFFE, RACHEL,** Temple Univ, Philadelphia, PA; FR; BA; Arch.

**GOFORTH, CATHERINE E,** Ms St Univ, Miss State, MS; SO; BA; Cmps Actvts Brd 89-90; Fshn Focus 90-; Agrcltr Hm Ecnmcs Ambssdr; Gamma Beta Phi; Alpha Zeta; Frmhs Frtnty Lttl Sis 90-; 4-H Teen Ldr; 4-H All Strs Hstrn; D Dickens Schlrshp; Apprl Txtls Mrchndsng; Mrktng.

**GOFORTH, DEBORAH L SMITH,** Univ Of Fl, Gainesville, FL; SR; Phi Theta Kappa 87-88; Operations Mgr VP Operations; AA Santa Fe Comm Clg 88; Business.

**GOFORTH, EDWARD R,** Longwood Coll, Farmville, VA; SR; BS; Hampden Sydney Vol Fr Dept Sec 89-; Pi Mu Epsilon Sec Treas 90-; Phi Kappa Phi; Phi Theta Kappa 89-; Arts/Sci Hnrs Schlrshp 89-; SVCC Hnrs Pgm Schlrshp 88-89; AA S Southside Va Comm Clge 89; Math; Prfsr/Cmptr Sci.

**GOFORTH, MICHAEL K,** Christian Brothers Univ, Memphis, TN; JR; BA; AE Sta Tech Inst 82; Bus.

**GOFORTH, MICHELLE M,** Union Univ, Jackson, TN; SR; BS; Ambsdrs Chrstn Fllwshp Pres 86-88; Hlth Phys Soc; Univ Lovell Chptr Pres 86-88; Alpha Chi 90; Sigma Zeta 90; Natl Sci Fndtn; RA; Chem Physics; Navy/Nuclear Instr.

**GOFORTH, SANDRA D,** Meridian Comm Coll, Meridian, MS; GD; BSN; Organ Adv Assoc Degree Nrs 90-; Wmns Intl Bwling Congr 88-; Nursing.

**GOGICK, SUSAN L,** Univ Of Nc At Charlotte, Charlotte, NC; FR; BA; Stdnt Athl Bd 90-; Engl; Cmmnctns.

**GOGLIA, TRACY ANN,** Felician Coll, Lodi, NJ; SR; BA; Ed Clb; Psych Clb; Clg Hnrs 90; Dns Lst; Stdnt Tchg Internshps; Psych/Elem Ed; Psych Ph D.

**GOH, LYNETTE PIN-LIN,** City Univ Of Ny Baruch Coll, New York, NY; SR; BBA; Singapore Stdnts Assn VP 90; Untd Malaysian Stdnts Assn Pres; Asian Wk Plnng Com Exec Com; Beta Gamma Sigma; Engl Tutor Seek Dept Schl 90-; Deans Lst 89-90; Bus; Fin.

**GOHDE, KEVIN D,** S U N Y Coll Of Tech At Delhi, Delhi, NY; FR; AOS; Phi Theta Kappa; RSES; US Army 86-90; Rfrgrtn/Air Cndtng; Srv Mech.

**GOHEEN, MICHAEL W,** Fl Atlantic Univ, Boca Raton, FL; SR; MBA; AS Waubonsee Comm Coll 88; BA; Finance; Fncl Cnsltnt.**

**GOINES, LUGENIA,** Talladega Coll, Talladega, AL; FR; Choir Accmp 90-; Josephine Crawford Wilfred Haddock Schlrshp; Hamilton Weaver Awd; Alice W Holman Awd; Music Perf; Accmpnst.

**GOINES, SHANNON G,** Nc Agri & Tech St Univ, Greensboro, NC; JR; BS; Pi Omega Pi 90; Beta Gamma Sigma; Future Admnstrtv Exec Assn 90; Bus Ed; Ed/Pblc Serv.**

**GOING, CARMEN W,** Univ Of North Fl, Jacksonville, FL; JR; BA; Anthrplgcl Soc; Spnsh; Transltr.

**GOING, PAUL B,** Cooper Union, New York, NY; JR; BE; Cvl Eng; Trnsprttn Plnng.

**GOINS, HELEN F,** Union Coll, Barbourville, KY; BA; BLTN 88-; Cumberland River Comphrnsv Care Cnslr/Trnng 90-; Alochol/Drug Trtmnt Ctr; Art/Psychlgy/Soclgy; Cnslng Psychlgst.

**GOINS, JEFFREY L,** Radford Univ, Radford, VA; SO; SGA Clss Sec 90-; Hs Cncl VP Peery Hall VP 90-; Intrcllgt Crss Ctry 89-; Fin Bus; Corp Law.

**GOINS, KAREN E,** Univ Of Ky, Lexington, KY; FR; Math; Mddl Schl Ed.

**GOINS, KATHRYN L,** Johnson C Smith Univ, Charlotte, NC; JR; BA; Amer Fut Blck Exec Clb; Natl Assn Blck Acctnt Clb; Tau Beta Chi; Alpha Kappa Mu; Alpha Kappa Alpha Sor Dn Pledges 90-; Acctg.

**GOINS, ROGER E,** East Carolina Univ, Greenville, NC; BFA; BA Univ Richmond 75; Painting; Freelance Art/Tchng.

**GOINS, V MARIE,** Bristol Univ, Bristol, TN; JR; BA; March Dimes Walk Amer Tm Cptn; Heart Fund Cptn 90; Youth Counselor; Local Chrh Choir Church Pianist Youth Sponsor 87-; Holston Medl Grp; Busn Admin; Admin Office Superviosr.

**GOKEMEIJER, NILS J,** Franklin And Marshall Coll, Lancaster, PA; JR; BA; Crw Clb Equip Mgr 88-; Phi Kappa Psi 88-; John Kirschner Schlr Physcs; Hackman Schlr; Vrsty Crss Cntry 89; Phsycs.

**GOKUN, MARGARITA V,** Rivier Coll, Nashua, NH; JR; BS; Cert Pgmng Fortran Inst Oil/Gas Moscow USSR 86; Bio; Cancer Rsrch.

**GOLAY, YVETTE,** Endicott Coll, Beverly, MA; SO; ASSC; Class Offcr VP 90; Hall Cncl SGA VP 90; Bsn Clb 90; Hnr Dprtmnt/Advanced Clss 90; Phi Theta Kappa 90; Women Agnst Violence Cmmt; Nrsng Home Vltr 90; Law Offc INTER 90; Peer Tutor; Endiott Schlrshp Prom Tchrs Fclty 90; Political Science; Crmnl Prsctn.

**GOLD, ADAM,** City Univ Of Ny Baruch Coll, New York, NY; GD; BBA; Bskbl/Queens Clg 83-85; Acctng; CPA.

**GOLD, DAVID,** Miami Dade Comm Coll, Miami, FL; JR; Englsh; Wrtr.

**GOLD, GERALD C,** Oh Coll Of Podiatric Med, Cleveland, OH; JR; DPM; Amer Clg Foot Surgeons 90-; Pi Delta 90-; Mich Pharmaceutical Assn 78-; Pharmacist; BS Wayne State Univ 78; Podiatry.

**GOLD, MICHELLE H,** Cornell Univ Statutory College, Ithaca, NY; SO; BS; Ambssdr; Red Crpt Soc 89-90; Trdtn Fllwshp 89-; Alpha Epsilon Phi Treas; Admssns Off; Tech Asst Lbrry 89-90; Rsrch Asst; Indpndnt Stdy Dr Michael Walter; IM Sftbl; Thomas J Watson Mmrl Schlr 89-; Envrmntl Sys Tech; Envrmntl Eng.

**GOLD, TRACY L,** Univ Of Sc At Columbia, Columbia, SC; FR; BS; Rsdnc Hl Assoc Sntr 90-; Assoc Afrcn Amer Stdnts 90-; NAACP 90-; Intrnshp CIGNA; Sci/Math; Cmptr Sci.

**GOLDAU, ELIZABETH H,** Livingston Univ, Livingston, AL; JR; BS; Bio.

**GOLDBACH, JEANETTE M,** Daemen Coll, Amherst, NY; SR; BS; Bg R Bgr Beta 85-87; Delta Phi Mu Pres 88-; Phi Mu; Lambda Ta Pres 88-; Lkm Scty Wstrn NY 90-; Lambda Tau Hnrbl Mntn 90; Mdcl Tchnlgy; Gntcs.**

**GOLDBACH, OTTO P,** Abraham Baldwin Agri Coll, Tifton, GA; FR; BED; Horticulture Clb 90; Horticulture; Lndscpe Mgmnt.

**GOLDBERG, AMI B,** Fl St Univ, Tallahassee, FL; SO; BS; Radio Cmptrlr 90-; Phi Eta Sigma 89-90; Sigma Delta Tau; Advrtsg/Cmnctns; Advrtsg Agcy.

**GOLDBERG, ANDREW B,** Emory Univ, Atlanta, GA; JR; BBA; Clg Cncl Elctd Repr 88-89; Stdnt Concerns Com Chrprsn 90-; Emory Mrktg Assoc 90-; IM Sftbl 88-89; Mrktg; Bsn.

**GOLDBERG, CHARLES G,** Nova Univ, Ft Lauderdale, FL; GD; MBA; Phi Delta Theta Treas; Co-Op Educ-Tampa Elctrc Co; IEEE Comp Soc; Sftwr Engr; BET-BACH Eng Tchnlgy-Univ S FL 86; Comp Eng/Bus Mgmt; Eng Mgmt.

**GOLDBERG, DARCIE L,** Immaculata Coll, Immaculata, PA; JR; BA; Comm Mntl Hlth Serv Inc Brd Dir/Sec/Tres 88-; Cert Art Inst 79; Sclgy; Art Thrpy.

**GOLDBERG, ERICA L,** Nyack Coll, Nyack, NY; SO; BA; Manhattan Gspl Tm Sec 90-; Sec Ed/Eng; Eng Tchr.

**GOLDBERG, JESSICA R,** Ny Univ, New York, NY; FR; MBA; Rough Drft; Piano; Big Str; Dramatic Wrtr; Author.

**GOLDBERG, KAREN E,** Yeshiva Univ, New York, NY; SO; BA; Clss Advrtsng Mgr 88-89; Deans Lst 89; Vars Bsktbl; Fine Arts Jdc Stds; MA Art Ther.

**GOLDBERG, LOUIS,** Broward Comm Coll, Ft Lauderdale, FL; Scl Wrkr 80-87; MSW Wash Univ 80; BA Yeshiva Unv 76; Educ; Tch.

**GOLDBERG, MARJORIE L,** Yeshiva Univ, New York, NY; SR; SGA Sen 89-90; Sch Nwspaper Copy Edtr 90-; Sch Radio Sta DJ 89; Jewish Erly Chldhd Assoc Award 88; Ed Dept Award For Profsnl Grwth In Ed; BA; Ed/Judaic Studies; Erly Chldhd Tchr.

**GOLDBERG, MITCHELL,** City Univ Of Ny Baruch Coll, New York, NY; SO; BBA; Natl Assoc Sys; Prgrmrs; Cap Planner Sys Anlyst 87-; Acctg; EOP Audtng.

**GOLDBERG, THOMAS J,** Dowling Coll, Oakdale Li, NY; SR; BS; AOPA 88-; Lion Escadrille Pilot; Hnr Hl 89; Dns Lst 90-; US Nvl Res Aircrew Ordncmn Petty Ofcr 87-; AAS SUNY Farmingdale 90; Aerontcs; Prfsnl Pilot.

**GOLDBURN, GEORGIA M,** Albertus Magnus Coll, New Haven, CT; SO; BA; Best Buddies Orgnzr 89-; Cltn Cltrl Dvrsty; Mnrty Un; Spanish; Pblc Rltns.

**GOLDEN, DAPHNE E,** Abraham Baldwin Agri Coll, Tifton, GA; FR; BS; Baptist Std Union Scl Comm 90-; Phi Theat Kappa 90-; Hnr Std 90-; Hnr Std 90-; Pres Lst 90-; Dns Lst 90-; Secndry Ed/Math; Profssr.

**GOLDEN, GRACIE A,** Al St Univ, Montgomery, AL; FR; BA; Engl; Tchr.

**GOLDEN, HOLLEN M,** Univ Of North Fl, Jacksonville, FL; JR; BHS; Amer Coll Hlth Care Admin Stdnt 90-; Socty Right To Die 90-; Alzheimers Assn Vol 89-90; Phi Theta Kappa Acad 88-; Phi Theta Kappa Acad; Alzheimers Assn 89-90; Acad Schlrshp; AA Fla Comm Coll Jax 89; Hlth Sci; Nrsng Home Admin.

**GOLDEN, HOPE R,** Niagara Univ, Niagara Univ, NY; SO; Sftbl; Acctg; CPA.

**GOLDEN, JENNIFER L,** Univ Of Ga, Athens, GA; SO; PH D; Communiversity Big Bro/Big Sis V P 89-; Stdnt For Envrnmntl Awareness 90-; Pi Beta Phi 90-; Speech Path; Speech Thrpy.

**GOLDEN, KATHLEEN,** Le Moyne Coll, Syracuse, NY; SR; Newspapr Ed-In-Chief 87; Rsdnt Assist 89; Prjcts In Cmmnty Tutorng 87-88; Cmmnctns Offce Intrn 90; Alumni Brd Of Gvrnrs; BA; Engl/Cmmnctns; Jrnlsm.

**GOLDEN, LAURA L,** Middle Tn St Univ, Murfreesboro, TN; SR; BS; Kappa Delta Pi 90-; Deans Lst 89-90; Elen Educ; Tch.

**GOLDEN, LYNETTE,** Atlantic Comm Coll, Mays Landing, NJ; SO; BA; Arts; Grphc Dsgn.

**GOLDEN, PAUL C,** Bapt Bible Coll & Seminary, Clarks Summit, PA; SR; VP Jr Cls 89-90; IM Dir 89-90; Stdnt Msnry Flwshp Rep 87-88; Nrsng Hm 87; Abington Bsktbl League Coach 88-89; Chmbr Sngrs 87-88; BBC Alumni Schlrshp 89; Hoop It Up Dir 90-; BS Bible; Bible; Seminary.

**GOLDEN, SABRINA K,** Abraham Baldwin Agri Coll, Tifton, GA; FR; BS; Stdnt Bd For Arts; Phi Theta Kappa; Engl Lang Studies Ctr Tutor; Math; Elect Eng.

**GOLDEN, SHARON K,** Hillsborough Comm Coll, Tampa, FL; FR; AS; Nurs.

**GOLDEN, TIMOTHY C,** Hudson Valley Comm Coll, Troy, NY; SO; BED; Tamanack Outdrsmn Treas 87-; Mktg.

**GOLDEN, TRAVIS L,** Saint Pauls Coll, Lawrenceville, VA; FR; MBA; NAACP 90-; Bus; Acct.

**GOLDENBURG, ADOLPH W,** Valdosta St Coll, Valdosta, GA; FR; BA; Stdnts Agnst Vltng Envrnmnt; Amnsty Intl; Stdnt Govt; John Odum Schlr; Dbt Tm; Hstry; Cvl Rghts Actvst.

**GOLDFARB, HEIDI B,** William Paterson Coll, Wayne, NJ; SR; BA; Amrcn Math Scty; Assoc Wmn Math; Amrcn Sttstcl Assoc; Tky Awrd; Math.

**GOLDFARB, ZACHARY,** City Univ Of Ny La Guard Coll, Long Island Cty, NY; SO; Phi Theta Kappa; Deans Lst 90-; Adv Brd Fordham Univ EMS; EMS Chf Ofcr 87-; AS Cert 78; Mngmnt; EMS Mgmnt.

**GOLDFINCH, PATRICIA F,** Univ Of Sc At Coastal Carolina, Conway, SC; JR; Erly Chldhd Ed; Tchr.

**GOLDINA, IRINA A,** Bunker Hill Comm Coll, Boston, MA; SO; BA; Phi Theta Kappa; Bus Mgmnt.

**GOLDINGER, SEBRINA R,** Albany St Coll, Albany, GA; JR; BS; Alpha Beta Gamma 90-; Marine Crps Lgstc 87-; AS Darton Coll 89; Accntng.

**GOLDMAN, BARBARA BROFF,** Comm Coll Algny Co Algny Cmps, Pittsburgh, PA; AS; Phi Theta Kappa 88-; Dept Awd Art; Assoc 89.

**GOLDMAN, CHRISTIANNE,** Univ Of Sc At Coastal Carolina, Conway, SC; JR; BA; Ad Clb; Pi Kappa Phi 85; Myrtle Bch Jycs; Br Mgr Msns Srmr 90-; Stdio Art Grphcs; Grphc Art Dsgn.

**GOLDMAN, COREY EVE,** Univ Of Sc At Columbia, Columbia, SC; SO; Batgrl/Ad Clb; Dns Lst; Zeta Tau Alpha 90-; Carer Ctr Vol 90-; Dns Schlp; IM 90-; Adv/Pblc Rltns; Law Schl.

**GOLDMAN, DAVID M,** Saint Elizabeth Hosp Sch Nurs, Utica, NY; SR; AS; By Scts Amer Egl Sctmstr 81-; Centolella Mem Schlrshp 90; St Louis Schrec Mem Schlrshp 90; Lake Delta Vol Fire Dept 85-; U S Air Force Rsrvs 86-; AOS Mohawk Vly Cmnty Clge 83; Nrsg; Med.

**GOLDMAN, DAVID S,** Univ Of Rochester, Rochester, NY; SO; BS; IEEE 90-; IM Sccr Bsktbl 89-; Electrcl Engrng.

**GOLDMAN II, GEORGE E,** Harding Grad School Of Relig, Memphis, TN; GD; MDIV; BA David Lipscomb Unv 88; Bible; Prchng Tchng.

**GOLDMAN, JERRY L,** George Mason Univ, Fairfax, VA; JR; BA; Accntng Clb; Gldn Ky; AAS Camden Co Comm Coll 77; Mngrl Accntng.

**GOLDMAN, PETER C,** Miles Coll, Birmingham, AL; JR; Ushr Brd Pres; AS Lawson State Jr Clg 90; AS Bessanor State Tech Clg 82; Bus Admn; Frm Htl Mgmt.

**GOLDMAN, RICHARD J,** Bethany Coll, Bethany, WV; FR; BA; Amnesty Intl 90-; T V Stff 90-; Radio DJ 90-; Nwspr Stf Photog 90-; Film/Engl; Phtgrphy.

**GOLDMANN, JEFFREY D,** Univ Of Tn At Knoxville, Knoxville, TN; SO; BA; Gamma Iota Sigma; Im Bsktbl; Fin.**

**GOLDNER, ROBERT F,** Youngstown St Univ, Youngstown, OH; JR; BS; OH Soc Prof Eng 90-; Ntl Soc Prof Eng 90-; Eng/Math Mtrl Eng Plymr.

**GOLDRICK, MARY-LYNN,** Webber Coll, Babson Park, FL; SR; BS; Lake Wales Chmbr Commrce 87-; Altrusa Of Lake Wales; Offce Sprvsr 86-; AA St Petersburg Jr Coll 87; Bus Admin; Mgr Power Corp.

**GOLDSBY JR, WILMER D,** Wilberforce Univ, Wilberforce, OH; SO; BA; New Voices Praise Pres 90-; Stu Cncl VP 87-88; Chrstn Yth Org Pres 88-89; Boys Clb Tutor 88-90; Boys St Amer Legion Jr Cnslr 89-90; Deans Lst 89-90; William Scarborough Awrd Acdmcs; Mass Media Cmnctns; Mnstr.

**GOLDSCHMIDT, JEFFREY S,** Fordham Univ, Bronx, NY; SO; BA; Cltrl Affrs Pblcty Hd 89-90; 2 Mainstage Prod Bckstg Mgr 90-; Dns Lst 89-91; Engl/Theatre; Tchng.**

**GOLDSMITH, JOHN M,** Oh Wesleyan Univ, Delaware, OH; JR; BA; Cncl Stdnt Affairs Treas 89-; Stdnt Fndtn Tour Guide 90-; Mortar Bd; Campus Ctr Plng Com Stdnt Body Rep 90-; Omicron Delta Epsilon 90-; Intrnshp Customer Serv Rep Bnk NY Intern 90; Res Advsr Ohio Wesleyan Univ 90-; Econ; Analysist Auto Inds.

**GOLDSMITH, MARGO H,** Univ Of Nc At Asheville, Asheville, NC; SO; Science; Nrsng.

**GOLDSMITH, MICHELE E,** Anne Arundel Comm Coll, Arnold, MD; SO; BS; Res Mgr Grp Hm Mntlly Ret Adlts; Math; Tchr.

**GOLDSMITH, RHONDA L,** Watterson Coll, Louisville, KY; SR; AD; Acctng; Cpa.

**GOLDSTEIN, ALLISON J,** S U N Y At Stony Brook, Stony Brook, NY; JR; BA; Stdnt Alumni 88-; Icon Sci Conf Treas 88-; Sci Fictn Forum Secy 88-; Goldey Key 90-; Sigma Beta 88-; Psi Chi 89-; Pi Sigma Alpha 90-; SADD 88-; Deans List 88-; Rsrch Asst 88-; Hons Prog 88-; Vlg Of Islandia Histrn 88-; Pol Sci; Technlgy.**

**GOLDSTEIN, BENJAMIN E,** Yeshiva Univ, New York, NY; JR; BA; Secrty Comm Co Dir 90-; Nwspr; Trck; Econs; Law.

**GOLDSTEIN, BETTY F,** Bowie St Univ, Bowie, MD; JR; BA; Edn Clb 90-; Kappa Delta Pi Pres 89-; Hon Pgm; Marsha Blavett Schlrshp Edn Awd Wnr 88; Kappa Delta Pi Outstndg Serv Chapt 89-90; Elem Edn; Teach.

**GOLDSTEIN, CHANI B,** New Comm Coll Of Baltimore, Baltimore, MD; SO; BA; AA; Erly Chldhd Educ.

**GOLDSTEIN, IRA M,** Cornell Univ Statutory College, Ithaca, NY; SO; BS; Prspctve Exec Edit 89-; Stdnt Assmbly VP; Stdnt Hlth Allnce Chrmn PB 90-; Ho Nun De Kah; Emer Med Srvce 90-; Microblgy Gntcs; Med Prctce Rsrch.

**GOLDSTEIN, JOSHUA H,** Yeshiva Univ, New York, NY; JR; Chrty Fndrsng Jms Strr Schl 88-89; NYSPAC Jnr Asst Sct Mstr; Natl Hnr Scty Indct Crdkrt Tr Dj Systm; Pltcl Sci.

**GOLDSTEIN, KEITH A,** Univ Of Cincinnati, Cincinnati, OH; JR; BS; AS Cinn Tech Coll 81; AS 90; Arch Eng; Bldng Dsgn/Cnstrctn.

**GOLDSTEIN, ROBERT B,** Univ Of Fl, Gainesville, FL; JR; BHS; Stdnt Hnr Crt Assoc Jstc; Flrd Occptnl Thrpy Assoc Rep 90-; Amrcn Occptn Thry Assoc; Phi Kappa Phi 90-; Phi Alph A Theta 87-; Psi Chi 87-; Stdnt Occptnl Thrpy Assoc 90-; Vol Rsrch Asstnt 90; AA 89; Occptnl Thrpy.

**GOLDSTEIN, STEPHANIE L,** Fl International Univ, Miami, FL; JR; BA; WYUR DJ 88-89; Phi Lambda 90-; Tchr Jvnl Dlnqnts 90-; Tnns Tm 88-89; Spcl Edctn; Tchr.

**GOLDSTONE, RONDA M,** Univ Of Cin R Walters Coll, Blue Ash, OH; FR; ASSOC; Radiology Clb Tres 90-; Rdlgc Tchnlgy.

**GOLDTHWAIT, LEON W,** Worcester Poly Inst, Worcester, MA; FR; BA; Arspc; Eng.

**GOLDTHWAITE, MELISSA A,** Daemen Coll, Amherst, NY; JR; BA; Stdnt Amer Phys Thrpy Assn 90-; Phys Thrpy.

**GOLDWEBER, MICHAEL,** Comm Coll Algny Co Algny Cmps, Pittsburgh, PA; SO; AS; Phoenix Magazine/Newspaper Editor In Chf 90-; Gaming Assn Pres 89-; Stdnt Govt Senator 90; Alpha Mu Theta; Stdnt Affrs Comm Chrmn 90-; Bd Phy Dvlpmnt; Architecture/Soc Sci; Eng.

**GOLDWIRE, LISA M,** Savannah St Coll, Savannah, GA; SR; BA; Alpha Kappa Mu Sec 89-; Engl Lang/Lit; Law.

**GOLEBIEWSKI, THOMAS,** S U N Y Coll Of Tech At Frmgdl, Farmingdale, NY; AS; AS Nassau Cmnty Clg 86; BA C W Post Long Islnd Univ 89; Mortuary Sci; Funrl Dir.

**GOLEC, CHARLEEN A,** Saint Joseph Coll, West Hartford, CT; JR; BS; PALS Co-Chrprsn 88; Accntng Scty VP 89; Bsnss Scty 89; Deans Lst; Outstndng Jr Bsnss Stdnt 90; Bsnss Admin/Accntng; CPA.**

**GOLEMBIEWSKI, CHRISTENA L,** Gallaudet Univ, Washington, DC; JR; BS; Trng Co 90-; Apha Sigma Theta Sor Frst Pldg Cls 90-; Home Ec/Nutrtn/Food.

**GOLFIERI, TONI L,** Bay Path Coll, Longmeadow, MA; JR; BA; Yrbk Ed-Chf 90; Stdnt Govt; Cls Treas; Tutor; Maroon Key; Merril Lynch Intern; Assoc Lib Arts 90; Bsn; Acctg.

**GOLFINOPOULOS, CATHERINE,** Adelphi Univ, Garden City, NY; GD; MA; Hstry Hnr Scty St Jhns Univ 81; Ottle Hm Fr Chldrn 85; Dglstn Art Lgue; Arttngl Mchl Wmns Phlptchs 81-; POS Business School 63; Fne Arts; MFA Pntr Tchr.

**GOLIA, RACHEL D,** Gainesville Coll, Gainesville, GA; FR; BS; Hist; Law.

**GOLIGHTLY, SCOTT J,** Christopher Newport Coll, Newport News, VA; JR; BA; Acad Deans Lst 89-; Poli Sci; Law.

**GOLKAR, ROXANNE SHIRIN,** Univ Of Miami, Coral Gables, FL; GD; PHD; Pizzaz Dnc Clb 87-89; Rdrnnrs Clb 87-88; Phi Eta Sigma 87-; Alpha Lambda Delta 87-; Sigma Tau Delta 87-; BA; Engl; Law.

**GOLLIHUE, JEANI,** Marshall University, Huntington, WV; GD; MS; Phi Kappa Phi 86; Acad All Amrcn Sftbl 86; Morehead State Sftbl Capt 85-86; Natl Educ Assn 87-; HS Tchr 86-; BA Morehead State Univ 86; Math; Elctrcl Engr.

**GOLLMAR, HEATHER E,** Converse Coll, Spartanburg, SC; SR; PHD; Tarpan Shark Clb 88-; Stdnt Chrstn Assn 87-; SGA 87-; Habitat Humanity 90-; Phi Gamma Mu Alpha Lambda Delta 80-; Stdnt Vol Srvcs 88-; Hnr Schlrshp 87-; TA Penn State Univ; Swim Tm 88-; BA; Pol Sci.

**GOLTSCH, LOREN R,** City Univ Of Ny Queens Coll, Flushing, NY; SO; BA; St Bartholomews Parish CCD Pgm Asst Tchr 85-; Psychlgy; Elem Edn.

**GOLTZ, VICTORIA E,** Univ Of Miami, Coral Gables, FL; SR; DPM; Nrsng Assn VP 89; Mrsty Bwlng Tm Capt 88; Phi Theta Kappa 85; Pres Lst; Donna Murphy Schlrshp; Dupont Schlrshp; Hll Est Schlrshp; Dns Lst; Bwlng Tm 90; FL Nrsng Assn; RN BSN; BSN 89; BS; Pdtry.

**GOLUB, STACEY H,** Cornell Univ Statutory College, Ithaca, NY; SO; BS; Emer Med Srvce EMT Fnnce Offcr 89-; Ithaca Fire Dept EMT Firefghtr; Bllmre Mrrck Vol Amblnce Co EMT 88-; Crnll Vrsty Polo Tm Treas 89-; Anml Sci; Vet.

**GOLWAY, MICHAEL W,** Univ Of Louisville, Louisville, KY; SR; BS; Inst Of Ind Engrs 87-; Hon Order Of KY Colonels 85-; Soc For Mfg Engrs 87-; Alpha Pi Mu 90-; Intrnshp With Initial USA Textile Systms 90-; Asstshp For Facility Design Cnsltng 90; Ind Engr.

**GOMES, DENISE L,** Univ Of The Virgin Islands, St Thomas, VI; SR; BA; Stdnt Assc Tres 90; Phi Eta Sgm 89-; Dlt Mu Dlt 90-; FBLA 90-; Intrnshp Acctg Ofc; Erly Admsn Schlrshp 87-; Bus Admn/MGT; Entrprnr.

**GOMES, ERIC A,** Cornell Univ Statutory College, Ithaca, NY; SR; MD; Phi Kappa Phi 89-; Ho Nun De Kah 89-; Gldn Key 89-; Merrill Prsdntl Schlr; Alpha Zeta Key 88; Almn Schlstc Rcgntn Awrd; BS; Bio Chmstry; Med.

**GOMES, JENNIFER M,** Western New England Coll, Springfield, MA; FR; BSBA; Soccer Mgr 90-; Fin; Law.

**GOMEZ ACOSTA, FRANCISCO M,** Univ Politecnica De Pr, Hato Rey, PR; SO.

**GOMEZ, ADRIANA M,** City Univ Of Ny La Guard Coll, Long Island Cty, NY; SO; BBA; Phi Theta Kappa Recdng Secr Pres 90-; Soc Wrk Flshng Hosp 90-; Math Tutor 89-; Conslr Srvs Asst 90-; AS; Comp Bus; Mgmt Info Systs.

**GOMEZ, AILEEN,** Univ Of Pr At Rio Piedras, Rio Piedras, PR; SO; Invstgtn Sci Celular Moleulr; Frsmn Soph; Vol Chldrns Hosp; Mbrshp Hon Ltry Cntst; Natrl Sci; Medcn.

**GOMEZ, CONSTANZA,** Fl St Univ, Tallahassee, FL; SR; BA; Engl Assn; German/French/Spanish Clbs; Day Care Asst; Comparative Lit; Ph D/Prof.

**GOMEZ, FLOR M,** Univ Del Turabo, Gurabo, PR; GD; Hnr List 88-, Deans List 90-; Deaf Interp Assoc PR 89-F Psicology Student Assoc 89-; Hd Start San Lorenzo Vltr Wk 85-88; Deaf Interp 77-; Psicology; Counseling.

**GOMEZ, JANET,** Fl International Univ, Miami, FL; SR; BA; Ftr Ed Amrc 90-; Phi Kappa Phpi; Deans Lst 90-; AA 89; Elem Ed.

**GOMEZ, JOSE F,** Univ Of Pr At Mayaguez, Mayaguez, PR; JR; BA; KNAA VP 89-; Univ Puerto Rico 88-; Phi Alpha Delta 90-; Price Wtrhse Intshp 90-; Acctng; Law.

**GOMEZ, JUAN C,** Miami Dade Comm Coll North, Miami, FL; SO; Phi Theta Kappa 90-; Bus Amdn; Law.

**GOMEZ, LINDA R,** Daytona Beach Comm Coll, Daytona Beach, FL; SO; AS; CAD; Eng; Drftng/Dsgn.

**GOMEZ, MARIELA,** Fl International Univ, Miami, FL; JR; BBA; Mktg; MBA.

**GOMEZ, MARTA R,** Inter Amer Univ Pr Hato Rey, Hato Rey, PR; JR; BA; Cert Gabriela Mistral Schl 78; CERT Cmptr Inst 89; Mrktng; Prdct Mngr.

**GOMEZ, MARY C,** Saint Thomas Univ, Miami, FL; JR; BS; Poltcl Actn Clb 90-; Wstrn Cvlztn Hstry 90; NW Dade Comm Mntl Hlth Cntr Vol; AS FL Natl Coll 89; Poltcl Sci; Law.

**GOMEZ, MILAGROS,** Fl International Univ, Miami, FL; SO; BA; Fture Edctrs Of Amer 90-; AA Miami Dade Comm Coll 90; Elem Educ; Tchng.

**GOMEZ, NIURKA N,** Miami Dade Comm Coll South, Miami, FL; SR; BA; Phi Theta Kappa 89-; AA; Psych; Chld Psych.

**GOMEZ, OSCAR M,** Va St Univ, Petersburg, VA; FR; BA; Yrbk Stf Phtgrphr 90-; Psychlgy Clb 90-; Tchnlgy Clb 90-; Hnrs Coll 90; Tennis 90-; Mchncl Engnrng.

**GOMEZ, RENE F,** Miami Dade Comm Coll South, Miami, FL; SO; BA; Frst Bapt Chrch Hlh Sndy Schl Tchr; AA Miami Dade Comm Coll; Med; Phys Thrpy.

**GOMEZ, SUZANNE H,** Univ Of Ga, Athens, GA; SR; BSED; Mddl Sch Educ Clb 89-; Kappa Delta Epsilon 89-; Gldn Ky Hon Soc 88-; Kappa Delta Pi 89-; Mdl Sch Math Educ; Tchr.

**GOMEZ, ZACHARY A,** Fl St Univ, Tallahassee, FL; FR; BMED; Phi Eta Sigma 90-; Phi Kappa Tau 90-; Schlrshp Out Of St Wavr 90-; Music Educ; Perf/Tchr.

**GOMEZ-FERNANDEZ, CARMEN R,** Univ Of Miami, Coral Gables, FL; GD; Alpha Omega Alpha 90-; BA Univ Miami 87; MD Miami Sch Of Med; Med; Res In Pathlgy.

**GOMEZ-ROSADO, DAVID,** Columbia Greene Comm Coll, Hudson, NY; SO; Indstrl Dsgn; Prdct Dsgnr.

**GOMORY, WILLIAM PAUL,** Fl Atlantic Univ, Boca Raton, FL; JR; BA; Phi Kappa Phi; Dns Lst Miami Dade Com Coll 87-89; Cert Cmmndtn Spch Fstvl Miami Dade Impromptu 2nd Plc 90; Pres Lst Fl/Sprng 90-; Head Barman 86-; AA Miami Dade Comm Coll 90; Finance; Corp Finance/Mgmt.

**GONGOLA, JANET A,** Muskingum Coll, New Concord, OH; FR; BA; Yrbk 90; Amer Chem Soc 90-; Nwspr; Chi Alpha Nu; Chem; Prof.

**GONGORA, MICHAEL C,** Univ Of Miami, Coral Gables, FL; SR; BS; Cable News Anchor; Play Lead 88; AERHO; Brdcst Intrn WPLG-CHNNL 10 News 90; B Ashe A Schlrshp Rcpnt 87-; Screen Actors Guild 90-; Real Est Lcns B R Schl Real Est/State FL 90; Brdcstng; Law.

**GONOS, RENEE M,** Marywood Coll, Scranton, PA; SR; BA; AA Broome Comm Coll 87; Bus; Bus Mgmt.

**GONTESKI, JODI L,** Bloomfield Coll, Bloomfield, NJ; SO; BA; Chrprctc Clb Sec 90-; Hnrs Pgm 89-; Pre Chrprct Advsry Brd 90-; Chrprct.

**GONTKOVSKY, SAMUEL T,** Kent St Univ Kent Cmps, Kent, OH; JR; BGS; Arcrft Ownrs/Plts Assoc 87; Ntl Rifle Assoc 84; Golden Key; AA; Croatian Frat Union Of Amer 182 VP 79; Aux Plce; Pri Plts Lcnse 88; Amateur Radio Assoc Schlrshp 90; R J Wean Schlrshp; Law.

**GONYEA, KIRSTEN E,** Atlantic Comm Coll, Mays Landing, NJ; SO; AA; PETA; RAN; NRDC; Schlrshp Norway; Elem Ed; Scnd Grd Tchr.

**GONZAGA, MARIA F,** City Univ Of Ny Baruch Coll, New York, NY; SR; Acctg Soc 89-90; Beta Alpha Psi Assoc Mbr 89-90; BBA Baruch Clb; Acctg; CPA.

**GONZALES, DIANA M,** City Univ Of Ny Queensbrough, New York, NY; FR; Engl; Nvlst.

**GONZALES, FRANCOISE,** Palm Beach Comm Coll, Lake Worth, FL; ASSOC; Students Intl Udstndng Club 90-; Architrecture.

**GONZALES, JUAN C,** Fl International Univ, Miami, FL; SO; MBA; Math; Elect Eng.

**GONZALES, MICHELLE S,** Rivier Coll, Nashua, NH; SO; BS; Paralgl Soc 90-; Paralgl.**

**GONZALES, PATRICK,** Palm Beach Comm Coll, Lake Worth, FL; SR; Stdnt Intrntnl Undrstdng Clb 90-; Assc; Hosplty Mgmt.**

**GONZALES, SYLVETA A,** Coll Of New Rochelle, New Rochelle, NY; SR; Stdnt Cncl VP 89-90; Stdnt Cncl Pres 90-; Mentor Matilda Cumos Mntrng Prgrm 90-; Tutr Amrca Chldrn Soc 88-; Sojourneil Trth Srvc Awd 89; Grd Hnrs Summa Cum Laude; Certf Mrt Rcgntn Otstndng; Dom Srvc Offc Cncl Prsdnt Cty NY; Rlgn Mnr Psych; PHD Thlgy Wrk Wrld Cncl Chrc.

**GONZALEZ ALAMO, JANET,** Univ Del Turabo, Gurabo, PR; BA; Acctg.

**GONZALEZ COTTO, NORMA L,** Inter Amer Univ Pr Hato Rey, Hato Rey, PR; SR; Acctg Stdnts Assoc 87-89; Acctg; Law/CPA.

**GONZALEZ DIAZ, MARIDALI,** Univ Of Pr At Mayaguez, Mayaguez, PR; JR; BSIE; Tau Beta Pi; Alpha Pi Mu; Mu Alpha Phi; Engrg.

**GONZALEZ FIGUEROA, BENNY,** Univ Politecnica De Pr, Hato Rey, PR; FR; AF ROTC; Engr.

**GONZALEZ HENRIQUEZ, RAMON M,** Univ Politecnica De Pr, Hato Rey, PR; FR; Ingenieria Elec.

**GONZALEZ MATOS, LUIS A,** Univ Of Pr At Rio Piedras, Rio Piedras, PR; JR; BA; Acctg Stdnt Assoc 89-; Golden Key 90-; Acctg; CPA.

**GONZALEZ MONTES, HERIBERTO,** Inter Amer Univ Pr San German, San German, PR; SO; BS; AS RUM Univ PR 81; Cmptrs; MA Cmptr Sci.

**GONZALEZ MORENO, ROSA E,** Inter Amer Univ Pr San German, San German, PR; FR; BS; Blgy; Mcrblgst.

**GONZALEZ NEGRON, ERNESTO P,** Inter Amer Univ Pr Hato Rey, Hato Rey, PR; FR; Fash Show/Talen Show 89-90; Oratory 86-87; Theatre 88-90; Vets Hosp 89-90; Mssns Of Church 89; Acctg.

**GONZALEZ RIVERA, LIZA I,** Inter Amer Univ Pr Hato Rey, Hato Rey, PR; FR; BA 90-; Acctg.

**GONZALEZ ROSARIO, LUZ I,** Inter Amer Univ Pr Hato Rey, Hato Rey, PR; SR; BA; Spanishf Tchrs.

**GONZALEZ SOTO, MARIBEL,** Univ Politecnica De Pr, Hato Rey, PR; Magna Cum Laude 86-88; AS EDP Coll 86-88; Engineering.

**GONZALEZ, ADA R,** Univ Of The Virgin Islands, St Thomas, VI; SR; BA; Foreign Lang Clb VP 87-88; Catholic Clb 89-90; Pr Clb 90-; Psych Awrd 90-; Soc Sci; Psych/Med.

**GONZALEZ, ADILIA,** Univ Del Turabo, Gurabo, PR; SR; BA; Caribn Assoc TRIO Progs PR Virgin Isl 90-; Grad Cls Pres; Hon Brd 4 Cert Stdnts Achvmnts 87-; TESOL 89; NEA 89; Res Engl Tchr 84-90; Engl; Tchr.

**GONZALEZ, ALISA L,** Va Commonwealth Univ, Richmond, VA; JR; BSMA; Pre Physcl Thrpy Clb 88-; Stdnt Athltc Trainee 89-; Physcl Thrpy.

**GONZALEZ, BRENDA,** Univ Of Pr At Rio Piedras, Rio Piedras, PR; JR; Hnr Stdnts Pgrm 90-; Chrchs Chrs; Peer Cnslrs Pgrm; Adventist Fedrtn; Biology; Physlgcl Psyclgy.

**GONZALEZ, C JAVIER,** Northern Va Comm Coll, Annandale, VA; SO; BA; Stu Act Offc Spanish Tutor 89-91; Coll Bd Talnt Roster 90; Deans List 89; Psychology; Clincl Psych.

**GONZALEZ, CELIA I,** City Univ Of Ny Queensbrough, New York, NY; SO; BA; Am Occptnl Therapy Assn; Occptnl Therapy.

**GONZALEZ, CHARLENE,** Univ Of Pr At Mayaguez, Mayaguez, PR; SO; BA; Engr; Mech.

**GONZALEZ, DALIA M,** Fl International Univ, Miami, FL; SO; BA; Sigma Gamma Wmns Interest Grp Pres 90-; Phi Eta Sigma 90-; Engl/Philosophy; Law.

**GONZALEZ, DEBBIE,** Bayamon Central Univ, Bayamon, PR; JR; BA; Bed Electronic Colg/Cmptr Prog 87-88; Cmptrzd Sys; Phmcy.

**GONZALEZ, EILEEN L,** Fl St Univ, Tallahassee, FL; JR; BA; Seminole Ambsdrs; Lady Scalphunters; Lambda Pi Eta; PRSA; Gamma Phi Beta; Amer Soc On Aging Intrn; Cmunctns; Corp Pub Rltns.

**GONZALEZ, ELVIRA M,** Fl Atlantic Univ, Boca Raton, FL; SR; BA; Modern Music Masters Soc Pres 87-; Acctg Stdnts Assoc 90-; Phi Theta Kappa Secr 89-; Phi Kappa Phi; Schlrs Awd 89; AA Miami-Dade Cmnty Clg 89; Acctg; Law.

**GONZALEZ, EUSEBIO,** Barry Univ, Miami, FL; JR; BA; Phi Alpha Theta; Phi Alpha Delta Marshall 90-; Rugby Club 90-; Law.

**GONZALEZ, FELIX R,** Univ Politecnica De Pr, Hato Rey, PR; SO; BA; Phtgrphy Club & Visual Arts 88-89; Judo 88-89; Civil Engrng.

**GONZALEZ, GLADYMAR,** Inter Amer Univ Pr Hato Rey, Hato Rey, PR; JR; Mktg.

**GONZALEZ, GLADYS D,** Univ Of Pr At Mayaguez, Mayaguez, PR; SO; Cuadro Hnr Ingieneria Ind 90-; Indstrl; Engr.

**GONZALEZ, IDALMIS,** Fl International Univ, Miami, FL; JR; BA; AA 90; Math.

**GONZALEZ, IRIS M,** Univ Politecnica De Pr, Hato Rey, PR; FR; BIE; Ind Eng; Eng.

**GONZALEZ, IRIS N,** Seton Hall Univ, South Orange, NJ; JR; BSN; Nurses Stdnt Assoc 88-; Sigma Theta Tau; Chldrns Spec Hosp Nrs Asst Prog Summer; Nrsng.

**GONZALEZ, IRMA,** City Univ Of Ny City Coll, New York, NY; JR; BA; Orntn Pgm Coord 90-; Discp Comm 90; ASPIRA Sprt Svcs Coord 88-; Drg Alchl Pgm Res; Spec Pgms Co Cnslr 90; Wrtng Ctr Tutr 89-90; Rosnbrg Hmphry Pol Sci Intrn; Stdnt Affrs Cert Mrt 90; Psych; Ma Clin Psych.

**GONZALEZ, ISABEL CHRISTINA,** Fl International Univ, Miami, FL; SR; BA; Chi Alpha Theta Treas 89-90; Sigma Sigma Sigma 90-; St Frm Ins Co Mnrty Intrnshp Prog; Sftbl; Fin/Mrktng.**

**GONZALEZ, IVETTE,** Saint Thomas Univ, Miami, FL; JR; BA; Delta Epsilon Chi 89-90; Fshn Grp Intl Inc 90-; Fshn Intern Sks Ffth Ave 89; AA 90; Mrktng; Fshn Mrktng.

**GONZALEZ, JACQUELINE,** Inter Amer Univ Pr San Juan, Hato Rey, PR; SR; JD; SPELL Pres/Treas 90-; Amer Mrktng Assn VP Prmtns 87-; Hnrs Prog 87-; All Amer Schlr 87-; Hnrs Assn 87-; Magna Cum Laude; Bus Fnnc Medal; BA; Brd Elctns Stu Cncl 90-; Law.**

**GONZALEZ, JANINE M,** Wagner Coll, Staten Island, NY; SR; BED; Kappa Delta Pi 89-90; Grad Cum Laude 90; Educ; Tchr.

**GONZALEZ, JESUS C,** Nova Univ, Ft Lauderdale, FL; GD; MBA; Tlphn Pnrs Amer 80-; Jr Achvmnt Cnsltnt 89-; Mgr Southern Bell 71-; AA Miami Dade Cmnty Clge 80; BA Barry Univ Miami 88.

**GONZALEZ, JOEL,** Miami Dade Comm Coll South, Miami, FL; SO; AA; Eng.

**GONZALEZ, JOSE M,** Bunker Hill Comm Coll, Boston, MA; FR; HRM; Food Srvc 87-; Bar Mgmnt Bstn Brtndng Schl 88-89; Englsh; Rstrnt Mgmt.

**GONZALEZ, JUAN CARLOS LUGO,** Univ Of Pr At Mayaguez, Mayaguez, PR; SO; PHD; Phi Sigma Alpha 90-; Eng.

**GONZALEZ, JULIE A,** Univ Of Miami, Coral Gables, FL; SR; Panhellenic V P 90; Assn Greek Letter Org; Hnr Stdnt 88-; Beta Gamma Sigma 90-; Phi Kappa Phi 89-; Gldn Ky 89-; Rho Lambda Panhellenic Ldrshp Hnr Soc 90-; Alpha Epsilon Phi V P 89; Mobil Oil Corp Mktng Intrnshp 90; Stanford Schlrshp 88-; Intl Finance/Mktg; Law Schl.

**GONZALEZ, LEONOR M,** Inter Amer Univ Pr Fajardo, Fajardo, PR; SR; BA; Engl Mjrs Assc; Atbgrphy Cntst Lbry Week 90; Hnr Grad 74; PR Prfssnl Nrsng Assc 79; TESOL 90; RN 74; ASN Univ PR 74; Engl Ltrt; US TESOL.

**GONZALEZ, LOUIS O,** Univ Of Al At Birmingham, Birmingham, AL; SR; BS; Amer Soc Mechanical Engrs 89-; Golden Key; Outstanding Internatl Stdnt 89; Mechanical Engrng; Engrng.

**GONZALEZ, LUIS E,** Inter Amer Univ Pr Hato Rey, Hato Rey, PR; SR; Humacaco PR Mncpl Bnd 78-87; Sax Mscn; Cath Chrch Ldrshp Pgm Music Tchr 88-89; Pro Yr Squibb Mfg Inc 89; Cmptrzd Envrnmnt Sr Prgrmr/Anlyst; AS 81; Math/Cmptr Sci; Cmptrs Pro.

**GONZALEZ, MADELYN,** Fl International Univ, Miami, FL; SR; MA; St John Apstl Yth Grp Co-Coord 88-; Commnty Actn Agncy Treas 87-88; Stdnt Tchng; Natl Hon Roll; BS 89; AA Miami Dade Comm Coll 89; Elem Ed; Tchng.

**GONZALEZ, MARC D,** City Univ Of Ny Baruch Coll, New York, NY; SO; Bus/Fin; Invstmnt Bnkg.

**GONZALEZ, MARIA,** City Univ Of Ny Baruch Coll, New York, NY; SR; Frgn Trd Soc 90-; Amer Mktg Assn 90-; Gldn Key 89-; Deans Lst 88-; BBA; Provost Schlrshp 88-90; Intl Mktg.

**GONZALEZ, MARITZA VALERIE,** Fl International Univ, Miami, FL; JR; BA; FL Inter Amer Schlrshp Fndtn 89-; Asst Actnt-Aruba 84-89; Bus; Acctg.

**GONZALEZ, MARTHA R,** Fl International Univ, Miami, FL; JR; BS; IEEE 90-; SWE Pres 90-; Sci/Math; Elctrcl Engr.

**GONZALEZ, MAURA,** Fl International Univ, Miami, FL; GD; BSN; Phi Kappa Phi; Deans Honor Roll 89-; AA Miami Dade So Comm Clg 89; Cert Art Instruction Schl Minneap Mn 83; Nurse Practichenor.

**GONZALEZ, MAYTE TERESA,** Miami Dade Comm Coll, Miami, FL; JR; BA; Bus; Fin/Ecnmcs.

**GONZALEZ, NANETTE L,** Univ Of Pr At Rio Piedras, Rio Piedras, PR; SO; Bio; Medicine.

**GONZALEZ, NELSON J,** Inter Amer Univ Pr San German, San German, PR; FR; Cmptr Sci; Technen Cmptrs Cmptr Pgmng.

**GONZALEZ, NILDA S,** Barry Univ, Miami, FL; SR; BS; RN; ADN Miami Dade Comm Clg Med Ctr 87; Bio/Educ; H S Bio Tchr.

**GONZALEZ, PATRICIA D,** Univ Of Miami, Coral Gables, FL; JR; BM; Fl Chptr Of Music Edctrs Ntl Conf Treas; St Agatha Yng-Adlts Grp Pres; Golden Key 90; Bowman Ashe Acad Schlrshp 89-90; Music Ed.

**GONZALEZ, RALPH A,** City Univ Of Ny Baruch Coll, New York, NY; JR; BA; AAS Borough Manhattan Cmnty Clg 88; Cert Word Proc Robert Fiance Bsn Inst 85; Corp Cmnctn/Graphic Art; Publ Rels.

**GONZALEZ, RAMIA IDANIS,** Inter Amer Univ Pr Hato Rey, Hato Rey, PR; Bus; Mktg.

**GONZALEZ, RIGOBERTO,** Miami Dade Comm Coll North, Miami, FL; JR; BA; Am Mktg Assn 90; Coll Bds Coll Schlrshp Serv Dstngshd Acad Perf; Acctg.

**GONZALEZ, ROBIN A,** Owensboro Comm Coll, Owensboro, KY; FR; BED; Acctng.

**GONZALEZ JR, RUBEN L,** Fl International Univ, Miami, FL; FR; BS; FIV Cmps Cath Mnstry; Chem; Sci Educ Scndry.

**GONZALEZ, RUBY E,** Inter Amer Univ Pr San German, San German, PR; FR; Stdnt Cnsl; Srta Prpa 90-; Mu Alpha Phi; Ldrshp 90-; Mrthn Coqui Salinas 89; Bsn Admin/Fnce.

**GONZALEZ, SALVADOR A,** Mount Saint Mary Coll, Newburgh, NY; SO; BA; Yng Dmcrts Pres 89-; Stu Jdcl Brd Jstc; Elctn Cmmtt; Hspnc Agncy 90-; Co Op Evening News 90; Law Lbrry Clrk 89-90; YMCA Recrtnl Aide 90-; Crss Cntry Clb; Engl; Attrny.

**GONZALEZ, SAMUEL,** Fl International Univ, Miami, FL; SR; BSW; United Way Aspira 88-90; Deans Lst 88; Metro-Dade DHR AA NA Aids Ntwrk 87-90; AA Miami Dade Cmmnty Clg Miami Fl 87; Soc Wrk; PHD Soc Sci Or JD Civil Law.

**GONZALEZ, SHIELA N,** Univ Of Tn At Martin, Martin, TN; SO; Scty Hon Smnr Stdnt 90-; Phi Eta Sgm 90-; Bio; Dntstry.

**GONZALEZ, SONIA M,** Caribbean Center For Adv Stds, San Juan, PR; GD; MA; Soc Hmn Rsrc Mgmt 89-; All Amrcn Schlr; Delta Delta Delta 81-85; Indstrl Orgnztnl Psychology.

**GONZALEZ, SYLVIA B,** Fl International Univ, Miami, FL; FR; Engl; Jrnlst/Lwyr.

**GONZALEZ, VICTORIA B,** Fl International Univ, Miami, FL; SR; BA; Phi Lambda; AS Miami Dade Cmnty Clg 89; Emotional Disturbance; Tch.

**GONZALEZ, YAMILE,** Fl International Univ, Miami, FL; SR; BS; AA Miami Dade Cmuty Clg 89; Sec Math Educ; Tch Math Sec Level.

**GONZALEZ-BUXTON, CARLOS M,** Fl International Univ, Miami, FL; SR; BS; Amer Socty Mech Engr; Socty Physcs Stdnts; Alpha Omega Chi 89-90; Phi Eta Sigma; Phi Kappa Phi; Hnrs Cncl Rep 90-; Fclty Schlrs Schlrshp; Outstdng Acad Achvmnt 87; Sci; Engr/Physics.

**GONZALEZ-QUEVEDO, BELKYS C,** Fl International Univ, Miami, FL; FR; Spanish Club 90-; FBLA 90-; Art Club 90; Spanish Hnr Scty Pres 89-; Chi Alpha Theta 90-; Sftbl 90; Cert Robert Morgan Voctl Schl 87-88; Psy; Law.

**GOOCH, ANGELA K,** Middle Tn St Univ, Murfreesboro, TN; SR; BS; Natl Coll Allgnc Scrtrs; Stdnt Ed Assoc Sec 90-; Stdnt Ed Assoc Dlgt 91; AAS 85; Cert Bus Mgmt 85; Elem Ed.

**GOOCH, VERONICA,** Shaw Univ, Raleigh, NC; JR; BS; Ford Mtr Co Schlp 90-; Univ Gold Metal; SEANC 89-; IAPES 89-; Stats Rsch Asst Emplymnt Scrty Cmmssn NC Lbr Mkt Info Div; Bsn Mgmt; MBA.

**GOOD, ALICIA J,** Univ Of Cincinnati, Cincinnati, OH; SR; BA; Amer Gld Orgnsts Treas 88-; Golden Key 88-; Phi Eta Sigma 87-; Orgn Prfrmnc; Msc Dir/Law.**

**GOOD, CARIANNE G,** Univ Of Nh Plymouth St Coll, Plymouth, NH; SR; Karate Clb 87-88; Beta Sigma Omicron VP 86-87; IM 86-; Elem Ed; Tchr.

**GOOD, JEFFREY W,** U S Coast Guard Academy, New London, CT; SO; BS; Ftbl 89-; Cvl Engr; Cst Grd Ofcr.

**GOOD, LEAH D,** Indiana Univ Of Pa, Indiana, PA; SO; Delta Pi 90-; Gamma Sigma Sigma 90-; Deans Lst 89-; Stddabrd Englnd; Elem Ed.**

**GOOD, MISTY D,** Oh St Univ, Columbus, OH; FR; BA; Pre-Alld Med Prof Soc 90-; Block O 90; Phi Eta Sigma; Dns Lst 90-; Physcl Thrpy.

**GOOD, PATRICIA M,** Comm Coll Algny Co Algny Cmps, Pittsburgh, PA; FR; BA; Mrktng; Adv Exec.

**GOOD, SARA J CONE,** Memphis St Univ, Memphis, TN; GD; MFA; Art Assn 86; Art Assn Schlrshp UHCLC 86; Mar Jones Schlrshp 87; Behavioral Sci 87-; Dept Schlrshp; Grad Assist MSU 88-; Clg Comm/Fine Arts; BFA Cum Laude 90; Fine Art; Clg/Univ Fine Art.

**GOOD, STACEY L,** Indiana Univ Of Pa, Indiana, PA; SO; BA; WIUP T V 90-; I M Aerobics 89-; Sigma Sigma Sigma Lambda Chapt 90-; Cmunctns Media; Advtsng T V Film.

**GOOD, TRICIA L,** Univ Of Cincinnati, Cincinnati, OH; SR; BA; Phi Eta Sigma; Golden Key; Organ Performance.**

**GOODALL, ELIZABETH M,** Owensboro Jr Coll Of Bus, Owensboro, KY; GD; AS; Cert WP 88; Paralglsm; Law.

**GOODALL, SALLY E,** Univ Of Akron, Akron, OH; SR; BA; AAS 73; Commnctv Dsrdrs.

**GOODBODY, JOHN W,** Daemen Coll, Amherst, NY; SR; BS; Big Bro/Big Sis 89-90; Spec Olympics 90; Booga Booga Beta 87-90; Genesee Hosp 89; UCPA At Rochester 90; NW Hosp Rehab; Princeton Med Ctr; Sprts Thrpy Rehab; Physical Therapy; Chiropractic Phy Thrpy.

**GOODE, CARY R,** Piedmont Tech Coll, Greenwood, SC; SO; AS; Phi Theta Kappa 89-; Cub Scts Den Ldr 87-; Forstry Tech 77-; AS Abrhm Baldwn Agric Clg 77; Elec Eng Tech.

**GOODE, DARRELL T,** Piedmont Tech Coll, Greenwood, SC; SR; Natl Voc Hon Soc 89-90.

**GOODE, EMILY C,** Ms St Univ, Miss State, MS; JR; BS; Hme Ec Clb 89-; Stdnt Assoc Int Dsgnrs Secr 89-; Ambassadors; Gamma Beta Phi; Phi Eta Sigma; Alpha Zeta; Stdnt Correspndg; Amer Soc Int Dsgnrs; Kappa Delta Proj Excell Chrmn 88-90; Toys Tots 86-90; Palmer Hme Chldrn 87-90; Hme Ec; Int Design.

**GOODE, LELIA C,** Fayetteville St Univ, Fayetteville, NC; SR; BS; Natl NC LPN Assoc 88-; Alpha Kappa Mu; Cum Laude; Parnt/Tchr Assoc 89-; LPN Assoc 88-; US Army Sgt 1st Cls 78-; AA 84; LPN Lic NC Brd Nrsng 83; Psych; Cnslng/Nrsng.

**GOODE, MELINDA A,** Radford Univ, Radford, VA; FR; Cthlc Stdnt Assn 90-; X-Cntry 90-; Elem Ed; Tchng Spec Ed.

**GOODE, NATASHA P,** Morgan St Univ, Baltimore, MD; SO; BA; SGA Sentr; Phila Soc Treas; Alpha Lambda Delta VP; Phi Beta Kappa; Promthn Kappa Tau; Phila Exp Yth Assoc; Inroads Intern Arco Chem Co; Indoor Track Tm; Acctg; Fin Cnsultant.

**GOODE, PATRICK A,** Va St Univ, Petersburg, VA; SR; BS; Army ROTC SFC 87-90; Deans List 87-88/90-; Intrnshp Ptrsbr Plc Sta 90-; IM Flg Ftbl Plyr/Coach 87-; Admin Of Justice; FBI CIA Wrdn/Prison.

**GOODEN, HAZEL G,** Saint Josephs Coll New York, Brooklyn, NY; SR; BS; Amer Crdvsclr Tech 1st Assoc Tres 87-88; Aux Sndy Sch Tchr 85-88; EKG Tech Dir 73-88; AA 81; Cert 87; Hlth Care Admin; Hm Hlth Care Prvdr.

**GOODEN, KELLY L,** Howard Univ, Washington, DC; JR; BA; Kappa Delta Pi Pres; Deans Lst 89-; Trustee Schlrshp 90-; Ks Cty Tchr Tuition Asstnc Schlrshp; Elem Ed; Tchr.

**GOODENOW, STEPHEN G,** Indiana Univ Of Pa, Indiana, PA; SR; BS; Maranatha Clb Pres 87-89; Navigators Pres 87-89; Schlrsp 88; Phys Educ; Tch.

**GOODERMOTE, SANDRA M,** Saint Joseph Coll, West Hartford, CT; JR; BS; Blgy Clb Co Pres 90-; Chem Clb 89-; Drm Cncl 90-; Cmps Mnstry 89-; Rsdnt Asst 90-; Jvnle Dbts Fndtn Fllwshp 90; Pfzr Corp Smmr Rsrch Fllwshp; Amer Chem Scty Orgnc And Anlytcl Chem Awrds 90-; Chem.**

**GOODFELLOW, MATTHEW S,** Wv Northern Comm Coll, Wheeling, WV; FR; BA; Math/Sci; Engr.

**GOODFRED, WENDY D,** Middle Tn St Univ, Murfreesboro, TN; JR; BS; Hnr Soc 89-; Delta Zeta 89-; Elem Edctn; Tchr.

**GOODFRIEND, DAVID I,** Widener Univ, Chester, PA; JR; BS; Actvty Comm 89-; Omnicron Delta Omega 90-; Pi Gamma Mu 90-; Bsns; Mrktng.

**GOODHEART, JOHN E,** Univ Of New Haven, West Haven, CT; SR; BA; Day Stdnt Govt Sntr 88; Mrktng Awd 90; All-Amer Schlrs Cllgte Awd 90; Mens Trk Tm Capt 87; Mrktng; Mrktng Cnsltnt.

**GOODHUE, JODI A,** Merrimack Coll, North Andover, MA; SR; BA; SGA Judge 87-88; E Gloucester Vikings Yth Prog 90-; Phi Theta Kappa 87-; Merit Schlrshp Acad Excel 87; Zayre Corp Schlrshp 87; Gordon Grp Schlrshp 88; AS N Shore Comm Coll 89; Math; Actuary.

**GOODING, KARLENE A,** Borough Of Manhattan Comm Coll, New York, NY; GD; BA; Caribbean Stdnts Assn; Phi Theta Kappa 88; Teach Asst/Peer Cnslr Fr Pgm 89; Jrnlsm Engl.**

**GOODISON, JACQUELINE,** Medaille Coll, Buffalo, NY; FR; BA; Deans Lst; Chld Cr Coaltn; Lgl Asst/Sec 86-; Cert Bryant/Stratton 86; Hmn Rsrces; Lgl Admin.

**GOODLET, DEBORAH E,** Mercyhurst Coll, Erie, PA; GD; MS; Bd Mbr Eve Earn St Pgm; Intnsv Prbtn Offcr Eve Cnty Jvnl Prbtn; Gdnc/Cnslng Gannon Univ; Crmnl Juste Admin; Law Enfrcmnt.

**GOODLOE, TONI R,** Methodist Coll, Fayetteville, NC; SO; BS; Acctg.

**GOODMAN, CYNTHIA A,** Cumberland Coll, Williamsburg, KY; FR; BA; Chrl; Crl Ensmbl 90-; Appalachian Mnstrs 90-; Admssn Stff; Dean Lst 90-; Hnr Stu 90-; Achvmnt Acdmy; IM Tnns 90-; Psych; Chrstn Psych/PHD.

**GOODMAN, DEBORAH E,** William Paterson Coll, Wayne, NJ; SR; BA; Spec Ed Clb 88; Fmnst Collctv 88; Alpha Sigma Alpha; Spec Ed; Tchr.

**GOODMAN, HENRIETTA SPENCER,** Univ Of Nc At Charlotte, Charlotte, NC; SR; Lttry Edit CPCC Lttry Arts Mag 89; Asst Lttry Edit; Lttry Arts Mag; Natl Cllgte Lttry Arts Mag 90; Chrltte Wrtrs Grp; Zlgy; Btny Lab 88; Tchng Asst; Chrltte Mcklnbrg Pblc Schls 89; Srra Clb 89-; AA Central Piedmont Comm Coll; BA; Engl; Wrtr.

**GOODMAN, LORI S,** Univ Of Nc At Asheville, Asheville, NC; SO; BA; Flwshp Chrstn Athlts 90-; SNEA 89-; Tchng Flw 89-; Psychlgy; Tchr.

**GOODMAN, MIKO C,** Union Univ, Jackson, TN; SR; BA; Alpha Chi 90-; Sigma Alpha Iota Rcrdng Sec 90-; Sigma Tau Delta 90-; Deans Lst 88-; Engl/Music; Tchr.

**GOODMAN, PAULA L,** Univ Of Ms Main Cmps, University, MS; FR; BBA; Univ Ambassdrs 90-; Hons Pgm 90-; Alpha Lambda Delta Histrn 90-; Phi Eta Sigma 90-; Gamma Beta Phi 90-; Phi Beta Lambda Rprtr 90-; Hearin-Hess Bus Schlr; Bus Admin.

**GOODMAN JR, RONALD L,** Abraham Baldwin Agri Coll, Tifton, GA; GD; AA; Hnr Stdnt Art Show 89-; Pace Setter Awd 90-; Ga Artis With Disabilities 90-; Comm Ldrshp Cl; Artist; Art; Wildlife Cnsrvtn.

**GOODMAN, TONIA J,** Middle Tn St Univ, Murfreesboro, TN; JR; BS; Science; Medl Tchnlgy.

**GOODNER, DEADRA J,** Cleveland St Comm Coll, Cleveland, TN; FR; AAS; Nursing; Rn.

**GOODNIGHT, BETH A,** Bowling Green St Univ, Bowling Green, OH; JR; BS; Visual Comm Tech Org 90-; Stdnt Org Ldrshp Dvlpmnt 90-; Hnrs Stdnt Assn; Vars Trck/Fld Tm 88-89; Visual Comm Tech; Prntng.

**GOODNIGHT, STEPHANY L,** Memphis St Univ, Memphis, TN; SO; BBA; Gamma Beta Phi 90-; Bsn; Acctg.

**GOODNIGHT, SUSAN M,** Univ Of Miami, Coral Gables, FL; SO; BA; Pre Lgl Soc 90-; Hnr Stu; Henry King Stnfrd Schlrshp 89-; Deans Lst 90-; Fl Tuition Vchr 90-; Ecnmcs; Law.**

**GOODRICH, EDWARD C,** Univ Of Cincinnati, Cincinnati, OH; JR; BS; Archtctre.

**GOODRICH, JULIE L,** Fl St Univ, Tallahassee, FL; JR; BA; Cmmnctns; Sprts Info.

**GOODRICH, MARK D,** Cornell Univ, Ithaca, NY; FR; BS; Mdl Cngrss Clb Cmmtt Chrmn 90-; Cltn Life 90-; Cthlc Undrgrd Grp 90-; Alpha Phi Omega Almn Sec 90-; Red Crpt Soc 90-; Kodak Schlrshp Fnlst; Elect/Mech Eng; Eng.

**GOODRICH, SARAH J,** Castleton St Coll, Castleton, VT; SR; BS; Orntn Coord 89-; Vrsty Ath Clb Pres 87-; Hall Cncl Pres 89-; IM 87-; PE Clb 87-; Deans List 90; Mary Ellen Evans Awd; Caroline Woodruff Ldrshp Awd; Bsktbl Mgr 87-; Vrsty Fld Hcky Capt MVP 87-; Physical Educ; Teach.

**GOODRICH, SUSAN W,** Univ Of South Fl, Tampa, FL; GD; PHD; Amer Diabetes Assn 85-; Amer Assoc Diabetes Edctrs 89-; Amer Pblc Hlth Assn 84-; Delta Omega Soc 87-; US Pblc Hlth Trnshp 80-82; Pblc Hlth Grad Assist 87-89; BA Coll Charleston 82; MPH U Of SC 84; Comm Hlth Ed.

**GOODRICH, TASHA N,** Castleton St Coll, Castleton, VT; JR; BS; AS; Busn; Mktg.

**GOODROE, JAMIE R,** Middle Ga Coll, Cochran, GA; SO; BA; AA Scndry Ed; Math/Sci Edn; Educator.

**GOODSON, DEANNA J,** Univ Of Nc At Greensboro, Greensboro, NC; JR; BS; Holladay Hlthcare Pharmcy; Nutrition; Dietitian.

**GOODSON, LAURA A,** Univ Of Tn At Knoxville, Knoxville, TN; SR; BS; Stdnt Govt Intrnl Afrs Comm 89-90; Exec Undrgrad Bus Prog 87-; Goldn Key 89-90; Phi Eta Sigma 87-; Alpha Lambda Delta 87-; Beta Alpha Psi 89-; Phi Mu Ass Treas 88-; Acctg; CPA.

**GOODSON, MARGARET B,** Wallace St Comm Coll At Selma, Selma, AL; SO; BS; Cmnctn Skills Lab Tutor; Bus; Acctg.

**GOODSON, SHEILA A,** Fl St Univ, Tallahassee, FL; SR; BS; Phi Alpha 89-; Phi Theta Kappa 88-89; Mntl Hlth Serv Vol 89-; PATH Vol 89-90; Tallahassee Mem Psychitric Ctr Intern 90-; Cosmetologist/Assist Mgr 85-; AA Tallahassee Comm Clg 89; Schl Soc Wrk; Prof Soc Wrkr.

**GOODSON, WYNN L,** Fl A & M Univ, Tallahassee, FL; SR; BS; FSLATE 89-90; FFEA 90-; Tchg; Elem Ed; Tch.

**GOODSPEED, TERRIE M,** Hudson Valley Comm Coll, Troy, NY; GD; AA; Pres Lst 88-90; Grad W Hons; Grl Sct Ldr; Asst Coach Hudsn Vly Cncl For Lansngbrg Ltl League; Indv Stdies; Elem Educ/Hstry/Pol Sci.

**GOODWATER, TORRY F,** Johnson C Smith Univ, Charlotte, NC; FR; AFJROTC Cdt Grp Cmndr; Rtrd Ofcrs Assoc Awd Mdl; Air Frc Assoc Awd Mdl; Outstndng Cdt Awd Charleston Chptr; Drl Tm; Srv Hnr Rl; Alpha Lambda Delta Frshmn Hnr Soc; Dns Lst 90; SC Achvmnt Rbn; Acdmc Achvmnt; Elctrcl Engrg; Air Frc Ofcr/Engr.

**GOODWIN, ALISON R,** Memphis St Univ, Memphis, TN; SR; BA; Amer Soc Wm Actnts Schlrshp; St Peters Cath Chrch; Asst Fin Dir; Acctg; CPA.

**GOODWIN, DAVID E,** Livingston Univ, Livingston, AL; FR; ADN; Vet USN; Navy Combat Corpsman Hsptlmn Scnd Class; Nrsng.

**GOODWIN, EVERETT T,** Univ Of Sc At Columbia, Columbia, SC; FR; BS; Mech Eng.

**GOODWIN JR, GEORGE R,** Central St Univ, Wilberforce, OH; JR; BA; Chi Theta Pi Pres 88-; Stdnt Govt Assn Orgnztnl Rep 90; Rsrce Offcrs Trng Corps 88-; Chrstn Mnstrs 90; Emrgncy Med Srvce 89-; Acad Achvmnt Awrd 88-; Vlybl 89; Rsrve Offcrs Assn Awrd ROTC; Vets Frm WWII Krea And Vtnm Awrd 2 Tms ROTC 90-; Chem Pre Med Emphss; Med Dr.

**GOODWIN, JANA L,** Va Commonwealth Univ, Richmond, VA; FR; BA; Dns Lst 90-; Spec Ed; Tchg Lrng Disabled.

**GOODWIN, KENNETH A,** Johnson C Smith Univ, Charlotte, NC; FR; MBA; Liston Hl Cncl 90-; 2 Flr Northside Rep Of Liston Hl 90-; Concrt Choir Sect Ldr 90; Tutor At Double Oaks Aftr Sch Prog 90-; Asst Charlotte Soup Ktchn For Needy 90-; Bsns Mgmt; Corp Mgr/Stck Mrkt Anlst.

**GOODWIN, LADISSA R,** Ms Univ For Women, Columbus, MS; FR; BS; Dixie Belle Scl Clb Chpln/Sngldr 90-; Lntrn Hnry 90-; Elem Ed.

**GOODWIN, MARY E,** Univ Of Nc At Chapel Hill, Chapel Hill, NC; GD; JD; Phi Alpha Delta 90-; BA Barton Coll 87; MBA; Law; Tx Law/Acctg.

**GOODWIN, MELISSA A,** Rivier Coll, Nashua, NH; JR; BS; Comp Sci; Comp Prgrmmng.

**GOODWIN, MICHELE P,** Pa St Univ Delaware Cty Cmps, Media, PA; SR; BA; Cmps Ambsdr; Provident Natl Bank 83-89; Lbrl Arts; Intl Bus.

**GOODWIN, MINNIE S,** Univ Of Sc At Columbia, Columbia, SC; SO; BAS; Gamma Beta Phi 90-; Assn Hnrs Stdnts 89-; Chiu Omega 90-; Grtr Col Lit Cncl 90-; Intrnshp Ft Mill Times; Page S C St Hs Rep; Baccalrs Artm Sci; Wrtg.

**GOODWIN, PATRICIA M,** Va Commonwealth Univ, Richmond, VA; SR; BS; Mrktng Club 82-86; Latin Club 85-86; Educ Assoc 89-; Beta Beta Beta 89-; Lat Club Hnr Soc 89-; Phi Eta Sigma 83; NEA; Sigma Chi Aux; Summa Cum Laude 83; Phi Eta Sigma 83; Deans List 83; IM; Camp Co Dir 90; Ins Sls Repr 87-88; Elem Educa; Teacher.

**GOODWIN, QUENTIN W,** Coll Of Charleston, Charleston, SC; JR; BS; Interfrat Cncl Treas 89-; Stdnt Union Mnrty Affrs; SPECTRA Cnslr 88-; Outstndg Sigma Yr; Omicron Delta Kappa 90-; Phi Beta Sigma Pres 88-; Washington Ctr Intern/Acad Seminar; Bsn Adm; Mktg/Intl Bsn.

**GOODWIN, SYLVIA ALICA,** Bloomfield Coll, Bloomfield, NJ; GD; BS; Day Stdnt Govt Treas 90-; Yrbk Co Edtr 90-; Alpha Chi Stdnt Delegte 89-90; Alpha Kappa Psi Pres 90-; Acctg; Tax Accnt.

**GOODWIN, TAMMY M,** Univ Of Al At Birmingham, Birmingham, AL; JR; BA; ASSOC Shelton St Comm Clg; Cert UAB; Radiation Thrpy.

**GOODWIN, TIMOTHY T,** Middle Tn St Univ, Murfreesboro, TN; JR; BA; AS Columbia State Cmnty Clg 90; Bsn Mgmt; Bsn.

**GOODWIN, WENDY ELIZABETH,** Univ Of Sc At Columbia, Columbia, SC; JR; Rho Chi; Assoc Hnrs Stdnts 90-; Hnrs Clge 89-; Golden Key; Phi Beta Kappa 90-91; Gamma Beta Phi Social Chrmn 89-; Phi Eta Sigma 89-; Alpha Lambda Delta 89-; Zeta Tau Alpha Schlrshp Chrmn 88-; Stdnts Allied Green Earth 90-; Internatl Relations; Law.

**GOODYEAR, MELANIE,** Wellesley Coll, Wellesley, MA; SO; BA; Wellesley Envrnmntl 90-; Cntrl Amrcn Sldrty Assoc 90; Rlgn; Tchr.**

**GOOLSBY, KRISTI L,** Valdosta St Coll, Valdosta, GA; SO; BED; Spcl Edn; Teach.

**GOOLSBY, WILLISIA A,** Auburn Univ At Auburn, Auburn, AL; FR; BA; Phi Eta Sigma; Gamma Sigma Delta; Alpha Lambda Delta; Russell Schlr; Anamerle Arant Schlrshp; Apparel/Txtls; Apparel Dsgnr.

**GOOSHAW, JAMES G,** Hudson Valley Comm Coll, Troy, NY; JR; AA; Atmtv Tech; Engrng.

**GOOSLEY, LISA ANN,** Fayetteville St Univ, Fayetteville, NC; SR; Alpha Kappa Mu 90-; Dprtmnt Elmntry Ed Significant; Acdmc Achvmnt Awrd; Schl Ed Deans Awrd Acdmc Excllnc; Chancellrs List Deans List 88; Bchlr Scnc Elmntry Ed/Second Major Pltcl Scnc.

**GOPAL, SHIVANI,** Oh St Univ, Columbus, OH; SR; BS; Univ Hnr Soc 87-; Awrd Excell 90; Dns Lst 88-; OMA Schlrshp Excel 87-; Psychlgy; Clin Child Psych.

**GOPP, DONALD P,** Kent St Univ Stark Cmps, North Canton, OH; SR; BA; Alpha Phi Sigma; Lamba Alpha Epsilon; Cnty Coroners Offc Intrn Invstgtr; Police Offcr 84-; AA Kent State Univ 89; Crmnl Jstc Stds; MA CJST/LAW Enf Admin.

**GORAL, KARI J,** Susquehanna Univ, Selinsgrove, PA; FR; BS; Alpha Lambda Delta; Zeta Tau Alpha Asst Treas; Math; Scndry Ed.

**GORBATY, LEON J,** Univ Of Pittsburgh, Pittsburgh, PA; JR; BA; Golden Key 89; Ice Hcky 87; Eng.

**GORBEA PABON, LOURDES M,** Univ Of Pr At Rio Piedras, Rio Piedras, PR; SR; MA; Dsgn Comm Stdnt Rep 87-90; AIAS 86-89; BED 90; Architecture; Rmdlng.

**GORDICK, ROBERT A,** Thomas Nelson Comm Coll, Hampton, VA; SO; BA; Data Proc Mngmnt Assn Treas 90-; Upsilon Gamma Eta Chrprsn 87-; Data Proc Mngmnt Assn Schlrshp; AS Cmptr Sci Thomas Nelson Comm Coll 90; Cmptr Infor Sys; Cmptr Cnsltnt/Sys Anlyst.

**GORDISH, CHRISTA L,** Indiana Univ Of Pa, Indiana, PA; FR; Gamma Sigma Sigma Pledge Class Tr; Math Tchr.

**GORDON, ALISA L,** Univ Of Tn At Martin, Martin, TN; SO; PHARM; Amrcn Chmcl Scty 90-; Hnrs Smnr 89-; Phi Eta Sigma 90-; Alpha Omicron Pi Intrmrls Chr; Phrmcst.

**GORDON, ANGELIC,** Bloomfield Coll, Bloomfield, NJ; FR; BS; Sigma Gamma Rho; Deans Lst 90-; Acad Excel 90-; Nursing.

**GORDON JR, BENJAMIN W,** Samford Univ, Birmingham, AL; SR; JD; Amercns Untd For Seprtn Of Church/State Pres 89-90; Sr Trial Comptn Dir 89-90; Assoc Editr Cumberland Law Revw; Grad Cume Laude; JD 90; Law; Attrny.

**GORDON, BILLIE MAE,** Stonehill Coll, North Easton, MA; SR; BA; Advsry Comm 88-90; Beta Xi Tres 90-; Trnty Nrsry Sch Tres 84-90; Old Clny Hspc 89-; Amer Assoc Resp Care 77-; Resp Thrpst 78-; Asst Dept Mgr 85-; AS 78; Humanities; Smnry.

**GORDON, CHARWANDA M,** Alcorn St Univ, Lorman, MS; FR; Mrchng Bnd 90-; Wind Ensmbl 90-; Jazz Ensmbl 90-; Music Schlrshp 90-; Mus Educ; Prfrmng/Tch.

**GORDON, CHERYL A,** Hudson Valley Comm Coll, Troy, NY; SR; AA; LRC Math Tutor 89-90; Phi Theta Kappa 90-; Otto J Guenther Schlrshp; Acctg Clrk Garden Way Inc Troy NY 88-; Bsn; Acctg.

**GORDON, CHRISTINA M,** West Liberty St Coll, West Liberty, WV; SR; Chi Beta Phi; Bio/Chem; Envlr Blo.

**GORDON, DESMOND O N,** East Tn St Univ, Johnson City, TN; JR; BA; All-Amer Schlr; Natl Asc Accntnt Schlr; Blck Affrs; Beta Alpha Psi; Gamma Beta Phi; Omcrn Delta Kappa; Deacon Brstl SDA Chrch; Yng Adlt Instctr; Pblc Accntnt Cpa.

**GORDON, DIMITRA D,** Bennett Coll, Greensboro, NC; FR; Assoc Stdnt Bdy Sec; Untd Bro/Sis Sec; Ftr Bus Amer Treas; Yng People Dept Pres; Vol Illtrcy Pgm; Org Schlrshp Pgm Pres; MBRS Rsrchr; Trck; Blgy/Pre-Med; Obstrcn.

**GORDON, GLENN D,** Columbia Union Coll, Takoma Park, MD; JR; BS; Eng Tech U S Postal Serv Eng/Dvlpmtn Ctr Pres; AA Frederick Comm Clg 83; Org Mgmnt.

**GORDON, JASON A,** United States Naval Academy, Annapolis, MD; FR; BS; Pol Sci; U S Navy/Marines.

**GORDON, JILL D,** Univ Of Akron, Akron, OH; SR; BED; Cncl Ed Stdnts; Alpha Lambda Delta 88; Kappa Delta Pi 90-; Deans Lst 88-; IM 88-; Alpha Delta Pi Schlrshp Chr 90-; Rho Lambda Schlrshp Awd 88-; Elem Ed; Tchr.

**GORDON, JOHN C,** Memphis St Univ, Memphis, TN; SR; BA; Smpr Fidelis VP 88-; Navy ROTC Bttln Cmmndr 88-; Res Life 90; Trident 90; Phi Alpha Theta 89-; Mrtr Brd; Hstry Intern; U S Marine Corp Serg 84-88; Hstry; Cmmssnd Offc US Marine.

**GORDON, JOHNTHAN,** Univ Of Sc At Columbia, Columbia, SC; SO; BS; Sci Clb 89-; Bio Clb; Pacesttrs; Gamma Beta Phi 89-; Pres Hnr Rl 90; Dns Lst 89-90; Crtfct Achvmnt 87-90; Bio; Gentc Eng.

**GORDON, JUNIOR M,** Cheyney Univ Of Pa, Cheyney, PA; JR; BA; Internatl Stdnt Assc; Cert Mktg Clg Art Sci Technlgy Jr 86; Assc Degree Mktg Inst Mktg 87; Mktg Mgmt.

**GORDON, KAREN M,** Univ Of Sc At Columbia, Columbia, SC; FR; BA; Phi Eta Sigma; Dns Lst 90; Intrnatl Rltns; Trnsltr Govt Rltns.

**GORDON, KATHY A,** Edward Waters Coll, Jacksonville, FL; SR; BA; Farmer Aid Bnft Assn 89-; Clncl Lab Mgmt Assn 87-; AS Santa Fe Comm Coll 88; Admnstrtv Mngr-Shands Hosp Lab 80-; Bus Admin; Bus-Mgmt.

**GORDON, LEE ARLENE,** Ny Law School, New York, NY; GD; JD; Phi Alpha Delta 89-; Dns Schlp 87-; NY Law Schl Law Rvw Edtr 90-; Rsch Asst 90-; Amer Jrsprdnc Awd 88; Tchng Flwshp 88-90; Std Clrkshp 88-; BA Hollins Clg 71; Law.

**GORDON, LISA,** Johnson C Smith Univ, Charlotte, NC; SR; BA; Warner Cmnctn Inc Schlrshp Cmncnts Arts Acad Achvmnt Awd; Grad Cum Laude; Cmnctns/PR; Spch/Lang Pathologist.

**GORDON, MARLEEN K,** Fl International Univ, Miami, FL; JR; BA; PTA 84-; Norview Gdns Neighborhd Assoc Secr 79-85; Tech Word Process 85-90; AA Miami-Dade Cmnty Clg S 90; Elem Ed; Tchg.

**GORDON, MARY A,** Va Commonwealth Univ, Richmond, VA; SR; Stdnt Educ Assc 88-; Sigma Delta Pi 89-; Grl Scts Ldr 88-; Cbscts Comm Chrmn 88-; AS Miami Dade Cmnty Clg 77; BS Magna Cum Laude; Spnsh Scndry Educ; Guidnc/Cnslg Educ.

**GORDON, MICHAEL S,** Wallace St Comm Coll At Selma, Selma, AL; FR; MBA; Stdnt Govt Sen 90-; Phi Theta Kappa; Ambsdr 90-; Vars Tnns 90-; Math; HS Clg Instr.

**GORDON, MURRAY A,** Coll Of Charleston, Charleston, SC; SO; BA; FCA 89-; Delta Delta Delta Rec Corres Sec 89-; Elem Ed; Elem Tchr.

**GORDON, NINA CHE,** Clark Atlanta Univ, Atlanta, GA; JR; BA; Accntng Clb 90-; All Amer Schlr 90-; Acctng; CPA.

**GORDON, REBECCA L,** Rivier Coll, Nashua, NH; FR.

**GORDON, REGINA D,** Truett Mc Connell Coll, Cleveland, GA; JR; BBA; Mu Kappa Tau; Deans Lst 90; Cum Laude 90; Sftbl 88-90; AS 90; Mktg; Sls Advtsng.

**GORDON, RUTH ANN,** Georgetown Univ, Washington, DC; SO; Best Buddies Prog Coord 89-; Jr Class Commt; Swim Tm 89-; Phi Eta Sigma 89-; OCSA Outstndng Clg Student Amer 90-; Swim Tm 89-; Intl Busn/Finance; Law.

**GORDON, SCOTT B,** Univ Of Sc At Columbia, Columbia, SC; SO; BS; Mountaineering/Whitewater Clb; Geology.

**GORDON, SCOTT S,** Univ Of Ky, Lexington, KY; FR.

**GORDON, SHANNON L,** S U N Y Coll Of Tech At Delhi, Delhi, NY; SR; NYSAPEHRD Sen 90-; Phi Theta Kappa; Phys Edn; SUNY Cortland Athltc Trng Phys Ed.

**GORDON, STACY A,** City Univ Of Ny Baruch Coll, New York, NY; JR; BBA; Dipl Clg Arts Sci Tchnlgy 87; Intl Mrktng; Mgr.

**GORDON, STEVEN E,** Fl St Univ, Tallahassee, FL; JR; BS; Mktg; Prof Golf/Mktg Mgmt.

**GORDON, VICTORIA D,** Univ Of Sc At Columbia, Columbia, SC; FR; BA; Amer Hon Soc 90-; Hon Coll 90-; Mrchng Bnd 90-; Engl; Tchng.

**GORE, BARBARA L,** Memphis St Univ, Memphis, TN; FR; BA; Hnrs Prog; Para Profl 84-88; English; Secdy Ed English Tchr.

**GORE, HOLLY A,** James Madison University, Harrisonburg, VA; SR; BS; Assoc Educ Yng Chldrn 89-; Golden Key 90-; Kappa Delta Pi 90-; Zeta Tau Alpha Chpln 88-; Erly Chldhd Educ; Teacher.

**GORE, JOSEPHINE M,** Atlantic Comm Coll, Mays Landing, NJ; FR; AAS; Nrsng/Sci; Nrsng.

**GORE, JULIE M,** West Liberty St Coll, West Liberty, WV; JR; BS; Dns Lst 90; Delta Mu Delta; Smll Bus Inst; Bus Acctng; Acct.

**GORE, KATHERINE E,** Oh Univ-Southern Cmps, Ironton, OH; SR; BED; Gamma Pi Delta; Tchng.

**GORE, SANDRA F,** D Youville Coll, Buffalo, NY; SR; BS; Ftr Tchrs Educ Clb 89-90; AAS Trocaire Coll 88; Elem Educ; Tchr.

**GORETSKY, IVY M,** Barry Univ, Miami, FL; SR; BA; Danceline 88-89; Lit Mag 89-90; Folk Choir 88-; Vstng Hmless Shltr Camillus Hse 90-; Tutor Gratiny Elem 90-; Chapel Rnvtn Comm 89-; Stdnt Advsry Comm/Cmps Mnstry 90-; Hunger Clean-Up Core Tm 89-; Natl Hunger Clean-Up 88-89; Theology; Youth/Cmps Mnstry.

**GORETZKA, MICHAEL J,** Duquesne Univ, Pittsburgh, PA; JR; BS; Fnc; Invstmnt Bnkr.

**GOREY, JILL M,** Radford Univ, Radford, VA; SR; BSN; Stdnt Awds Comm Chr 88-90; Clss Hstrn 89-90; VA Stdnt Nrs Assn Treas 90-; Prgrssn Grad Ccomm Admssn 90-; Intrnshp Med Coll VA.

**GOREY, NICOLE M,** Alfred Univ, Alfred, NY; FR; BS; Sftbl; Alumni Assn; Hon Prog; Alpha Lambda Delta; Pres Schlrshpo; Ceramic Engr; Engr.

**GORHAM, DEBRA F,** Birmingham Southern Coll, Birmingham, AL; SR; BS; St Vncnts Hosp; AS Jfrsn St Jr Coll 83; Bus Admin/Finance; Hosp Admin.

**GORKA, KATHERINE A,** Univ Of Akron, Akron, OH; JR; BFA; Gldn Key; Grphc Dsgn.

**GORKA, KRISTANA M,** Immaculata Coll, Immaculata, PA; JR; BS; Chorale/Ensmbl Secy 88-; AHEA Pres 88-; Newspaper 88-89; SAM 90-; Hons Prog 88-; Kappa Omicron Nu 90-; Fash Merchndsng.

**GORMAN, ERIN E,** Nova Univ, Ft Lauderdale, FL; GD; MBA; Alpha Kappa Psi 84; HTE Applctn Spec; AA/BS Sthrn Ill Univ; Bsn Mgmt.

**GORMAN JR, GARY A,** Salisbury St Univ, Salisbury, MD; SO; BA; Surf Clb Treas 89-; Phi Eta Sigma; Frnklin Perdue Schlrshp; Bus Admin; Marine Corps Aviation Ofcr.

**GORMAN, JOHN V,** Villanova Univ, Villanova, PA; FR; Jazz Bnd; Pep Bnd; Marching Bnd; Blue Key Soc.

**GORMAN, KEVIN J,** Western New England Coll, Springfield, MA; SR; BSEE; ACM Tr 87-; IEEE 89-; Elec Engr.

**GORMAN, KIMBERLY A,** Elms Coll, Chicopee, MA; JR; BA; AA Holyoke Comm Clg 90; Early Chldhd/Elem Ed; Tch.

**GORMAN, LYNN M,** S U N Y Coll At Fredonia, Fredonia, NY; JR; BM; Music Educators Natl Conf 89-90; Am String Tchrs Assoc 89-; Am Harp Soc; Pi Kappa Lamda; Sigma Alpha Iota Chap; Music Perf-Harp; Perf Music/Teach/Harpist.

**GORMAN, MARJORIE E,** Univ Of Tn At Martin, Martin, TN; SO; BS; Amer Hm Econ Assn Chrprsn 90-; Bapt Stdnt Union 89-; Socty Hnrs Smnr Stdnts 89-90; Univ Schlrs 90-; Phi Eta Sigma 90-; Natl Alumni Schlrshp Vldctrn 89-90; Dietetics/Nutrition; Clin Dietician.

**GORMAN, TIMBER H,** Hahnemann Univ, Philadelphia, PA; GD; MD; Sigma Xi Assoc Mbr 87-; AOA; Orville George Schlrshp 88-; BS Univ VT 87; Med; Opthmlgy.

**GORMLEY, MARK A,** Columbus Coll Of Art & Design, Columbus, OH; FR; BFA; Adv Dsgn; Layout Artst.

**GORMONT, MARLENE K,** Edinboro Univ Of Pa, Edinboro, PA; FR; BS; IM Vllybl; Phi Eta Sigma; Vars Chrldr 90-; Ind Biochem; Med.

**GORNICKI, MICHELE A,** Daemen Coll, Amherst, NY; JR; BA; Spec Elec Educ; Tchng.

**GORNO, LORRI A,** Univ Of Toledo, Toledo, OH; GD; JD; Stdnt Bar Assoc 88-90; Gvrng Brd 88-; Peer Adv Pres 88; Deans Lst 88-; Westlaw Achvmnt Awrds 88-; Lawyers Coop Achvmnt Awrd 88-; Stdnt Mbr Amer Bar 88-; Law Review 89-; Delta Zeta 84-; Intrn-Sylvania Pros Ofc 90-; Law Review Edtr 89-; Law.

**GORODETSKY, SVETLANA,** Alfred Univ, Alfred, NY; JR; BA; SG Chrprsn 89-90; AMA VP Fndrsng; Deans Advsry Cncl 88-; Alpha Phi Omega; Mktg Rsrch Intrnshp/1st Fdrl Bnk 90; IM Vlybl 89-; Pltcl Sci/Mktg; Law.

**GORRELL, KIMBERLY A,** Spartanburg Methodist Coll, Spartanburg, SC; GD; AA; Criminal Justice Clb 88-90; Day Student Assoc Brd 88-90; AA 90; Criminal Justice; Security Consultant.

**GORSICH, MELISSA J,** Duquesne Univ, Pittsburgh, PA; FR; BS; Dnce Tm 90-; Phi Eta Sigma; Delta Zeta; Fndrs Schlrshp 90-; Phrmcy.

**GORSLINE, SARAH D,** Univ Of Rochester, Rochester, NY; JR; BA; Bllt Clb Sec 90-; Undrgrad Anthrplgy Cncl Treas 90-; Anthrplgy Rlgn Mnr; Prfssr.

**GORTHALA, RAVI,** Univ Of Ms Main Cmps, University, MS; GD; PHD; ASME 89-; Phi Kappa Phi 90-; Hnrs Fllwshp 86-; Deptmntl Asstntshp 86-; Grad Schl Achvmnt Awrd 90-; MS 87; Mech Engr.

**GORTNEY, JOSEPH D,** Central Al Comm Coll, Alexander City, AL; SO; BA; AL Army Natl Grd 87-; Lab Russell Corp Mill 4; Blgy; Physcl Thrpst.

**GORTON, ADRIAN A,** Kent St Univ Geauga Cmps, Burton Twp, OH; JR; BBA; Acctng; Law.

**GORTYCH, ADRIENNE R,** Wagner Coll, Staten Island, NY; JR; BA; Chrstn Cl 88-; Danceworks Dance Cl 88-89; Choir/Choir Tour; Omicron Delta Kappa; Alethea; Theatre Prod 90-; Solos Ensmb 90; Acctng Tutor 89-90; Antioch Yth Grp Tm Ldr/Spkr 87-89; Cath Yth Org 88-89; Hofstra Dance Schlrshp 88; Theatre/Spch/Busn.

**GORY, SONJA S,** Univ Of Sc At Columbia, Columbia, SC; FR; Gamma Beta Phi Hgh Hon; Acctg; CPA.

**GOSHCO, TARA J,** Boston Coll, Chestnut Hill, MA; FR; BS; Sccr Clb 90-; Mrktng; Entrpnr.

**GOSHIMA, ASAMI,** Comm Coll Algny Co Algny Cmps, Pittsburgh, PA; FR; AS; Deans Lst 90; Chld Dvlpmnt.

**GOSHORN, SARA B,** Ashland Comm Coll, Ashland, KY; SO; AAS; Computer Info Syst; Computer Prog Word Proc.

**GOSIAN, STEVEN M,** City Univ Of Ny Baruch Coll, New York, NY; SO; MBA; Baruch Schlrshp 89-; Acctg; CPA.

**GOSNELL, BEVERLY F,** Western Ky Univ, Bowling Green, KY; JR; Pres Schlr 88-; Otstndng Coll Stdnt 88-; BA; Hstry; Educ.

**GOSNELL, SHERRY ANN,** Beckley Coll, Beckley, WV; SO; BA; Comm Fd Bskt 83-; Postl Serv; SPN 74-; Inf Proc Cert 89; Soc Wrk; Occuptl Thrpst.

**GOSNEY, HEATHER L,** Duquesne Univ, Pittsburgh, PA; JR; BED; Nw Trnsfr Stdnt At Duquesne; Educ; Tchng Elem.

**GOSS, DEANNA L,** Univ Of Tn At Martin, Martin, TN; JR; BA; RA 89-; Phi Eta Sigma 88-; IM Activities 88-; Elem Specl Educ Tchr.

**GOSS, JAMES E,** Hudson Valley Comm Coll, Troy, NY; FR; BA; IM Lacrosse Indr Lacrosse Dfns 90-; Crmnl Juste; Law.

**GOSS, SHANA M,** Univ Of Southern Ms, Hattiesburg, MS; SR; BSW; Soc Wrk Club 90-; NASW 90-; Intrnshp The Arlington Convlscnt Hm 90; Intrnshp Blake Clinc For Handcpd Chldrn; Soc Wrk.**

**GOSSAGE, BRENDA S,** William Carey Coll, Hattiesburg, MS; SR; BA; Bptst Stdnt Un; Engl; Frgn Mssnry.

**GOSSELIN, LISA A,** Newbury Coll, Brookline, MA; SR; AS; Deans Lst 90-; Suma Cum Laude; Ed Acct Rep; Bus; BA.

**GOSSELIN, PETER J,** Bryant Coll Of Bus Admin, Smithfield, RI; FR; BA; Licensed Radio Disc Jcky; Outdoor Trck; Finance; Invstmnts/Securities.

**GOSSETT, DANA E,** Univ Of Sc At Spartanburg, Spartanburg, SC; JR; BS; Campus Crusade Christ Pblcty 88-; Psychlgy; Cnslng Screenprinting.

**GOSSETT, KATHERINE A,** Coll Of Charleston, Charleston, SC; SR; BS; Comm Excep Chldrn Treas 90-; Zeta Tau Alpha 86-; Educ; Spec Educ Tchr.

**GOSTON, GRETCHEN M,** Comm Coll Algny Co Algny Cmps, Pittsburgh, PA; JR; MLT; Bio; Lab Tech.

**GOSWAMI, DEBJANI,** Ms St Univ, Miss State, MS; SR; BA; Coll Rpblcns 88-; Jdcl Brd 89-; Trffc Appls Ct 90; Phi Kappa Phi; Mrtr Brd; Gamma Beta Phi 88-; Pi Sigma Alpha 90-; Drg Ed Vol 90; Lbrry Vol 88; Nrsng Hom Vol; Rgnts Coll Lndn Englnd Intrn; JC Stennis Schlr; Pol Sci; Law JD.

**GOTAY, BETZAIDA,** Catholic Univ Of Pr, Ponce, PR; JR.

**GOTJEN, DEIDRE L,** Anne Arundel Comm Coll, Arnold, MD; SO; AS; Psychlgy.

**GOTKIN, LISA M,** Univ Of Rochester, Rochester, NY; SR; BA; Radio Nwscstr 87-90; Wmns Caucus 87-90; Deans Lst 87-; Sigma Delta Tau Spirit Chrmn 88-; Hngr Cltn 88-89; Pblc Dfndrs Offc Intrnshp 89; Crmnl Law London Intrnshp 90; Anti Defamationleg Intrnshp 90; Pltcl Sci; Law Schl.

**GOTLOP, YVONNE,** Central St Univ, Wilberforce, OH; SO; BS; Fllwshp Chrstn Stdnts VP 89-90; Tnns; Wtr Rsrcs Mgmt.

**GOTTESMAN, BETH C,** Univ Of Miami, Coral Gables, FL; SR; Phi Beta Kappa; Gold Key 90-; Phi Kappa Phi 90-; Rho Lambda 90-; Delta Phi Epsilon Schlrshp Chmn 88-; Henry King Stanford Tuition Schlrshp 88-; Deans Mstr Tutor Hist 89-; Pnhlnc Hghst Grade Point Avg Awd 89; Hist; Law.

**GOTTESMAN, TODD J,** Cornell Univ Statutory College, Ithaca, NY; SR; MBA; Intl Bsns Assoc 90-; Bsns Opprtnties Clb 87-88; Desbook Chf Photo 87-89; Nwspr Photo Edtr 90-; Ski Clb 87-89; Yrbk 90-; Gldn Ky; Orntn Cnslr 89-90; Adv 89-90; 5 Yr Jnt Deg Prog; J Thomas Clark Schlr Entrprnrshp; Bsns; Mrktng.

**GOTTFRIED, SANDY K,** North Central Tech Coll, Mansfield, OH; SR; ADN; LPN Mid Ohio Prctcl Nurse Prog 72; Nrsng; RN.

**GOTTLIEB, BETTY ANNE,** Case Western Reserve Univ, Cleveland, OH; FR; Jwsh Stdnts Actvts Bd 90-; Phi Mu.

**GOTTLIEB, DAVID M,** Yeshiva Univ, New York, NY; GD; JD; Sr Cls Gov Brd Pres 89-90; Hrvrd Natl Mdl UN Delegate 88-89; Deans Lst 87-90; Vrsty Bsktbl Capt 89-90; BA 90; Law.

**GOTTLIEB, JORDAN S,** Oh Wesleyan Univ, Delaware, OH; FR; BS; Hillel 90-; Sfty Bd 90-; Botny/Micrblgy Bd 90-; Med Microblgy; Med.

**GOTTLIEB, STEVEN M,** Yeshiva Univ, New York, NY; SO; Acctg Soc 89-90; Gruss Schlr 90-; Deans Lst 89-90.

**GOTTSLEBEN, TREVOR LEE,** Fl St Univ, Tallahassee, FL; SO; BA; Pres Cabinet Spcl Prjcts 89-; Kellum Hl Rep 89-90; Sailing Clb 89-; Delta Sigma Phi; Natl Res Hl Hnry 90-; Stdnt Asst Kellum Hl 90-; Rep Yr Kellum Hl 89-90; Deans Lst 90; IM Ftbl/Bsktbl/Sftbl 89-90; AA FSU; Business/Mgmt; Mba.**

**GOTTUNG, GARY E,** Hudson Valley Comm Coll, Troy, NY; BA; Frnchs Asst Mgr; Bsn.

**GOUBEAUX, PAMELA K,** Univ Of Cincinnati, Cincinnati, OH; SR; NRSNG; Ntnl Stdnt Nrs Assn; BSN.

**GOUCHER, YVONNE L,** Western New England Coll, Springfield, MA; JR; BA; Stgls Plyrs Drama Pres Dir 88-; Mktg Assoc 88-; Mgmnt Assoc 88-90; Soup Ktchn Vol 86-; Intrn Stg West Mktg Intrn; Mktg; Ad.

**GOUDE, GINRI L,** Univ Of Sc At Columbia, Columbia, SC; FR; Math.

**GOUDLING, TERRANCE J,** Duquesne Univ, Pittsburgh, PA; SR; BA; Soc Hmn Rsrc Mgmt Pres 90-; Phi Mu Alpha 88-; Intrn Cnsldtn Coal Co Stu Anlyst 90; Bus Admin; Mgmt.

**GOUED NJAYIG, ALINE PASCALE,** City Univ Of Ny City Coll, New York, NY; GD; MBA; Nwspr Photogrphr 87-88; Cnslr Mntl Hlth Ctr 90; Mc Cabe Ralshon Oconnor Schlrshp 89-90; Deans Lst 89-90; Intern 89-90; Mktng/Advrtsng.

**GOUGE, WILLIAM PAUL,** Emory & Henry Coll, Emory, VA; SR; BA; Certifd Master Auto Hvy Trck Body Paint Tchncn; ASIA ASE Wrld Cls Tchncn; AA Wingate Clg 72; AAS Univ Techncl Inst 88; Religion Philosophy; Minister.

**GOUGH, CHARLENE E,** Univ Of Charleston, Charleston, WV; SR; Stdnt Edn Assn V P 89-; Frshmn Orntn Ldr 90-; Pi Gamma Mu; Chi Beta Phi 89-; Alpha Lambda Delta 88-; Theta Kappa Pi Treas 88-; Chrldng Co Capt 87-90.**

**GOUIN, MAY,** City Univ Of Ny City Coll, New York, NY; SO; Wrkshp Ldr Tutor 90-; Sci; Med.

**GOULART, RUI ALEXANDER S,** Radford Univ, Radford, VA; JR; BA; AA VA Western Cmnty Clg 90; Crim Just; Law.

**GOULD, HEATHER A,** Tn Temple Univ, Chattanooga, TN; FR; BS; Univ Choir; Bus; Office Admin.

**GOULD III, JOHN,** Norfolk St Univ, Norfolk, VA; JR; BS; Alpha Lambda Delta 88; OBT Tutor 90; Lockheed Eng/Sci Co Eng Aide 89; Mngmnt Cmptr Info Syst; Univ Prof.

**GOULD, KIMBERLY LYNN,** Western New England Coll, Springfield, MA; SR; BA; Pol Sci Clb VP 89-; Govt; Law.

**GOULD, LORETTA J,** Univ Of Southern Ms, Hattiesburg, MS; SR; BA; Eagle Clb 90-; Bptst Un 87-; Psi Chi 90-; Phi Delta Rho; Alpha Delta Pi Actvts Hnrs Stndrds Chrmn 88-; Deans Lst 89-; Psychology; Cnslng.

**GOULD, MELISSA A,** Davis & Elkins Coll, Elkins, WV; SR; BS; Stdnt Educ Assn VP 89-90; Amer Assn Univ Wmn Schlrshp; Cum Laude; Elem Educ; Tchr.

**GOULD, RACHEA K,** Univ Of Montevallo, Montevallo, AL; SR; BS; Stdnt AM Ed Assc Pres 90; AM Council Social Studies 90; Kappa Delta Pi 91; Elmntry/Early Chldhd Ed; Tchr.**

**GOULD, WILLIAM M,** Western New England Coll, Springfield, MA; JR; BS EE; Stdnt Senate VP 90-; Sigma Beta Tau; Stdnt Ambsdr; Elec/Cmptr Engr.

**GOULET, CELINE D,** Colby Sawyer Coll, New London, NH; FR; BFA; Otng Clb 90; Prz Art Shw; Art.

**GOULET, LORRAINE C,** City Univ Of Ny City Coll, New York, NY; SR; BS; Alpha Sigma Lamda; Deans Lst 86; QUIPP Comm Tchr Trng/Stff Dev 88-; UFT Del 87-89; Educ Assc Paraprfssnl 76-; Spcl Educ; Tchg.

**GOULETTE, KERRY A,** Castleton St Coll, Castleton, VT; SO; BA; Elem Educ; Tchng.

**GOULSTONE, ROBERTA J,** Marywood Coll, Scranton, PA; SO; Stdnt Dietetic Assc 90-; Omcrn Nu; Pres Schlr ; Dietary Mgr LCCC 90; Assc Sum Cum Laude; Human Eclgy; Dietetics.

**GOURDINE, TIMOTHY,** Norfolk St Univ, Norfolk, VA; SR; BS; Stdnts Advsry Comm/Schl Tech Pres; Stdnt Natl Tech Assn Parl 90-; NROTC Snr Chf 90; IM Vlybl Team 90-; US Navy 81-; Elctrnc Tech; Naval Officer.

**GOURLEY, JEREMY J,** Middle Tn St Univ, Murfreesboro, TN; SO; BBA; Blue Marching Band Concert Band Jazz Band 89-; Phi Mu Alpha Sinfonia 90-; Computer Inf Systems; Systems Analyst.

**GOUSSET, JAMES M,** Ms St Univ, Miss State, MS; FR; BS; Soc Of Physics Stdnts 90-; Gamers Assn 90-; Gamma Beta Phi; Pr Schlr 90-; Physics/Comp Sci.

**GOUTELL, CARL R,** Embry Riddle Aeronautical Univ, Daytona Beach, FL; SR; BS; Aeronautical Stdes; Aviation.

**GOVENER, DAVID L,** Nyack Coll, Nyack, NY; JR; Nyack Clg Bsktbl Tm Hgh Scorer 90-; Smmr Socthrpst 90-; Clg Bsktbl Tm 91-; Psych; Mrrge/Fmly Cnslr.

**GOVER, TARA L,** Northern Ky Univ, Highland Hts, KY; JR; BS; Social Wk; Therapist Counselor.

**GOVERNO, NICOLE,** Wagner Coll, Staten Island, NY; JR; BA; Piano Cnvctn 88-89; Omicron Delta Kappa 90-; Rlgs Instrctr Scrd Hrt Chrch 90; Piano Plyng Awrds 87-; Deans Lst 87-; Elem Ed; Edctr.

**GOVEY, SUZANNE J,** Univ Of Akron, Akron, OH; JR; BS; Coun/Edctn; Golden Key; Coach's Awd 90; Cnfce Acad Awd 89-90; All Cnfce 90; Var X Cntry 88-90; Var Track Co Capt 89-; Elem Edctn; Tch.

**GOWDA III, EDWARD B,** Md Coll Of Art & Design, Silver Spring, MD; FR; BA; Vsl Cmnctns; Illstrtn/Advrtsg.

**GOWENS, RACHEL R,** Voorhees Coll, Denmark, SC; JR; BS; Soph Cls Sec; Deans Lst 89-90; Alpha Kappa Mu VP; US Achvmnt Acad Acad All Amrcn 89-90; Cmptr Lab Asst; Cmptr Sci; Cmptr Prgrmmng.

**GOYAL, VIPIN K,** Villanova Univ, Villanova, PA; FR; BS; Stdnt Prgrmng Cncl 90-; PA St Spcl Olympics 90-; Abbot Northwestern Hosp Vol 90-; Comm Svc 87-; IM Ftbl/Sftbl 90-; Bilogy; Medicine.

**GOYCO RODRIGUEZ, OSVALDO,** Univ Of Pr At Mayaguez, Mayaguez, PR; JR; Deans Lst 90-; Vlybl/Bsktbl/Trk/Fld/Bsebl 88.

**GOYETTE, CARRIE A,** Syracuse Univ, Syracuse, NY; FR; BSN; Mrchng Bnd; Bsktbl Pep Bnd; Nrsng; Onclgy Nrsng.

**GOYTIA, ANGEL MANUEL,** Inter Amer Univ Pr Hato Rey, Hato Rey, PR; FR.

**GOZANSKY, WENDOLYN S,** Smith Coll, Northampton, MA; SR; BA; Pre Hlth Soc Co Chrmn 90-; Svc Org Smith 89-90; Hnrs Thesis 90-; Ballet Dncr 84-87; Wmns Stds; Med.

**GRAAS, JOSEPH A,** Univ Of Ky, Lexington, KY; JR; Tau Beta Pi; Pi Tau Sigma; Eng Hons Award Elizabethtown Clg 90; Otis A Singletary Schlrshp 90; Bus/Inds Schlrshp Elizabethtown Cmnty Clg; Eng Techn 85-88; Mech Engr.

**GRAB, JENNIFER L,** Duquesne Univ, Pittsburgh, PA; SR; BSBA; Fin Mgmt Assoc Pres 90-; Stdnt Adv Bd; Beta Alpha Phi 89-; Best Overall Stdnt B A P; Pittsburgh Chapt Cr Un 90; Youth Ambsdr; Duquesne Cmptv Schlrshp 87-; Harwood Rl Est Natl Awd 91; Rsrch Asst Westinghouse Corp 90-; P And C 89-; Fin/Acctng; Auditing/ Real Est/Ins.

**GRABBE, TIMMON J,** Memphis St Univ, Memphis, TN; JR; BSME; Cath Stdnt Orgnztn VP 88-; Gamma Beta Phi 90-; Mech Eng; Eng.

**GRABEEL, STEPHEN H,** Bridgewater Coll, Bridgewater, VA; JR; BS; Ftbll Tm; Bsbll Tm; Hlth Physcl Ed.

**GRABIEC, JENNIFER A,** Daemen Coll, Amherst, NY; SR; BS; Wings 89-; Delta Mu Delta Treas 89-; HEOP Tutor 89; Deans List 87-; Clge Schlshp 87-; Front Office Supervisor; Transptn Trvl Mgmnt; Hsptlty Indstry Bus.

**GRABILL, STEPHEN J,** Liberty Univ, Lynchburg, VA; SR; BA; German Clb 88-90; Hnrs Prog 87-; Phi Sigma Tau 88-; German Award 90; Philosphy Govt; Legal Consultant.

**GRABNER, REINHARD S,** Barry Univ, Miami, FL; SR; BPS; IEEE 87-; GI 84-90; Self-Emp 90-; Ee Fdrl Dept Engnrng Austria 82; Telecomm Rsrch Dvlpmt Syst Anlys Mrktng 78-90; Lib Arts/Bus; Arts/Bus/Intl Studies/Engnrng.

**GRABOWSKI, JENNIFER A,** Duquesne Univ, Pittsburgh, PA; JR; BSBA; Amrcn Mrktng Assn VP 91-92; Phi Sigma Epsilon; Duquesne Unvrsty Deans Lst; Mrktng; Sls.

**GRABOWSKI, JENNIFER M,** S U N Y Coll Of Tech At Frmgdl, Farmingdale, NY; FR; Bus Admin; CPA.

**GRABOWSKI, LEAH M,** Castleton St Coll, Castleton, VT; JR; BSEDU; Kappa Delta Pi; Awrd Acdmc Excllnc Sclgy Dept; Wtrss; Scl Sci; Tchng.

**GRABOWSKI, SIGRUN,** Strayer Coll, Washington, DC; SO; BS; Trnsltr 82-; Intl Frght Frwrdng 84-; Cert Wurzburger Dochetschersaule Fr G 82; Cmptr Info Sys/Acctg.

**GRABSKI, KRISTY L,** Duquesne Univ, Pittsburgh, PA; SO; BA; Phi Chi Theta 89-; IM 89-; Phi Eta Sigma 90-; Deans Lst 89-; Bus.

**GRACE, CATHY A,** Meridian Comm Coll, Meridian, MS; SO; BS; Clg Activities Brd 90; Schlrs Bowl Tm 90; Ed Clg Times; Assist Clg Times 90; Assist Video For Lady Eagles Sftbl 89-90; Eng.

**GRACE, JOAN,** Cumberland County Coll, Vineland, NJ; FR; AA; Comp Clb; Comp Info Systms.

**GRACE, THOMAS C,** Univ Of Louisville, Louisville, KY; JR; ASM VP 88-; Amer Scty Htng/Air Cndtng/Rfrgrtn Engnrs 88-; Amer Scty Mchncl Engnrs 88-; Amer Scty Metals 88-; Intrnshp Henry Vogt Mchn Co; Draftsman CAD; BA 87; Mechanical Engineering.

**GRACEY, TANYA N**, Ms St Univ, Miss State, MS; JR; BS; Bptst Stdnt Un; Blldg Hstss; Stdnt Smmr Mssns; Kappa Delta Pi; Prvt Schlrshp; Sci Ed; Tchng.

**GRACIANO RIOS, ANABELLE**, Inter Amer Univ Pr Hato Rey, Hato Rey, PR; Acctg Assn Sec 88-89; Eta Phi Zeta 88-; M D Fndrsr 87-; Cncr Soc; Chrch Yth Ldr 87-88; Mscl 89-; Did Maria Cadilla De Martinez 85; Acctg; Elem Ed.

**GRADISCHEK, MONICA L**, Ny Univ, New York, NY; FR; BFA; Clb Arts NYC 90-; Acting; Performing Arts.

**GRADL, SHANNON B**, Univ Of Ky, Lexington, KY; FR; Hall Cncl Sec 90-; Cmptr Clb 90-; Drama Clb 90-; Phi Beta Kambda 90-; Chi Omega 90-; Radio Soc 90-; Trck Cmptn 90-; Cmunctns/Psychology.

**GRADY, BENJAMIN M**, Old Dominion Univ, Norfolk, VA; JR; BS; Vol Fr Spcl Eng; Tau Alpha Pi Hnrs 90-; IEEE; Avncs Tech 87-90; AAS Elec Tech Cntrl VA Cmnty Clg 87; Elec Eng.

**GRADY, ERIC L**, Embry Riddle Aeronautical Univ, Daytona Beach, FL; FR; BS; Naval Avtn Clb 90; IM Vllybl Sftbl; Aeronautical Sci; Prof Plt.

**GRADY, HOWARD D**, Ms St Univ, Miss State, MS; SO; BME; Band 90; Msc Educ Natl Conf 90; Phi Mu Alpha Sinfonia 90; Msc Educ; Band Dir/Cmposer.

**GRADY, PHYLLIS D**, Fort Valley St Coll, Fort Valley, GA; SR; BA; GA Assn Stdnt Home Ec Hstrn 90-; Deans Lst 90-; AS South GA Clg 89; AAS Waycross Clg 88; Home Ec Educ; Prfssr.

**GRADY, SUSAN J**, Coll Of New Rochelle, New Rochelle, NY; FR; BA; Admssns Hsptlty Clb Exec Bd 90-; Hon Bd Fr Rep 90-; Vrsty Swmmg 90-; Hon Pgm Fr Rep 90-; James Madison Soc 90-; Harvard Model Untd Ntns; Swmmg-Vrsty 90-; Pltcl Sci; Pltcl Rsrchr.

**GRAEBER, JEREMY J**, Univ Of Sc At Columbia, Columbia, SC; FR; BS; Vrsty Soccr 90-; Mech Eng.

**GRAETZ, LAURIE J**, Univ Of Fl, Gainesville, FL; SR; BHS; Intervar Chrstn Flwshp 87-90; Stdnt Occptnl Thrpy Assn 89-; Phi Eta Sigma 87-; Alpha Lambda Delta 87-; Golden Key 89-; Intrnshp CPC Ft Lauderdale Hosp; Intnshp Sunrise Rehab; AA 89; Hlth Pffsns; Occptnl Thrpy.

**GRAF, JANICE CARYN**, Bethany Coll, Bethany, WV; JR; BA; Bd Gvrnrs Stdnt V P Rcrdng Sec 89-90; Kappa Mu Epsilon; Gamma Sigma Kappa; Kalon; Phi Mu Pnhllnc Pres; Bethany Clg Snack Bar Mgr; IM Ftbl/Vllybl/Sftbl 88-; Econ.

**GRAF, JASON D**, Univ Of Louisville, Louisville, KY; JR; BS; Phi Eta Sigma 87-88; Gldn Ky 90-; Kentucky Frd Chkn Hdqrtrs Intern; Cmptr Prgrmng.

**GRAF, PAUL E**, Providence Coll, Providence, RI; SR; PHD; Econ Clb 87-; Vrsty Hockey 87-89; IMS Hockey/Sftbl/Ftbl/Street Hockey 87-; Omicron Delta Epsilon 89-; Deans Lst 87-; Teach Asstntshp Penn State; Vrsty Hockey 87-89; BA; Math Econ.**

**GRAF-SIRAKAYA, BEATRICE**, Tri County Tech Coll, Pendleton, SC; FR; BA; Karate Clb 83-89; Horse Clb 80-89; Care Handcpd 85-89; Asst Arts/Sci Div; AB Ecole Benedict Swizerland 85; AA Tourism State Switzerland 89; Psychlgy; Rsrch.

**GRAFF, CARYN A**, Univ Of Rochester, Rochester, NY; SO; BA; IM Sprts; Psych/Hlth Soc.

**GRAFF, DARREN R**, Niagara Univ, Niagara Univ, NY; JR; BA; Acctg Soc; Delta Epsilon Sigma; Delta Epsilon Sigma Awd 90; Intrnshp Lawrence M Doherty CPA; Acctg; CPA.

**GRAFF, NATHANIEL C**, Salisbury St Univ, Salisbury, MD; JR; BSW; Scl Work Clb Pres; Phi Eta Sigma VP 90-; Phi Gamma Mu; Phi Alpha VP; Adult Med Day Cr 89; Slisbury Nsg Hm 90; Cross Cntry 88-89; Soc Wk; Msw Hosp Adm.

**GRAFF, TERESA M**, Genesee Comm Coll, Batavia, NY; FR; BA; Actvts Comm; Elem Edctn.

**GRAFFAGNINI, BONNIE T**, Ms St Univ, Miss State, MS; SO; BS; SAID 90-; Int Design.

**GRAFTON, NINA SUZANNE**, Univ Of Southern Ms, Hattiesburg, MS; SR; BA; Phi Kappa Phi; Gldn Ky 90-; Library Sci Assist; Amer Library Assn; AA Hinds Comm Clg 88; Library Sci.

**GRAFTON, RYAN S**, Bapt Bible Coll & Seminary, Clarks Summit, PA; Awn 90-; Cncrt Chr 90-; Artt 90-; Drm VP 90-; Pstrl Stds.**

**GRAGG, DEANNA E**, Lenoir Rhyne Coll, Hickory, NC; SR; BA; Intrn Great Lakes Carbon Corp; 90 Deans List; 88-89 Deans List Western Piedmont Comm; 87-88 Vivian G & J Alex Mull Fndtn Schlrshp; AA Western Piedmont Comm Coll 89; Bus Admn; Acctng Asst/Computers.

**GRAHAM, ADRIENNE S**, Univ Of Southern Ms, Hattiesburg, MS; SR; BS; Symphy Bnd 88-89; Schlrshp Musician; Lambda Pi Eta 89-90; Alpha Epslon Delta 86-87; English; Law.**

**GRAHAM, ALISON M**, Univ Of South Fl, Tampa, FL; GD; MSPH; Univ FL Psychlgy Clb 86-88; Pub Hlth Stdnt Assn Treas 90-; Crisis Cntr Vol 88; Vol W/AIDS Patients; US Pub Hlth Trneeshp 90-; Pub Hlth/Biostatstcs.

**GRAHAM, ANTHONY L**, Middle Tn St Univ, Murfreesboro, TN; JR; BA; Psychlgy; Gdnc Cnslr.

**GRAHAM, ARLENE A**, Fl International Univ, Miami, FL; SR; BA; Blck Stdnt Union 86-87; Beta Alpha Psi Secr 90-; Phi Beta Alpha Secr 90-; Broward Ctr Blind Vol; Broward United Way Ctr Cnslr; Golden Drum Awds 86-; Natl Assoc Blck Accts; Beta Alpha Psi Acad Schl; Acctg/Mgmt Info Syst; CPA.

**GRAHAM, CAROL D**, Vance Granville Comm Coll, Henderson, NC; GD; Csmtlgst; Csmtlgy.

**GRAHAM, CONSTANCE ANN**, Univ Of Sc At Coastal Carolina, Conway, SC; SR; BA; Phi Sigma Tau 89-90; Sigma Tau Delta 90; UN Daughter Confederacy Rprtr 77; Crafters Clb 77; ADA Cstl; Marion Mullins Vocational Ed Cntr 77; Engl; Masters Lngstc/Phlsfhy.

**GRAHAM, DAVID W**, Itawamba Comm Coll, Fulton, MS; SO; BA; Ftbl/Bsktbl/Bsebl 89-; Math; Eng.

**GRAHAM, DONNA J**, Comm Coll Algny Co Algny Cmps, Pittsburgh, PA; FR; BA; Comp Spclst.

**GRAHAM, ELIZABETH C**, Univ Of Ky, Lexington, KY; SO; BA; Emrgng Ldr Inst; Engl; Law.

**GRAHAM, ERICK D**, Morehouse Coll, Atlanta, GA; SO; BA; SGA 89-; Ala Club 89-; Psi Chi; Deans Lst 89-; Psychlgy.

**GRAHAM, GLADYS M**, Univ Of Cincinnati, Cincinnati, OH; SO; BED; Kappa Delta Pi; Schl Crtv Prfrmng Arts Chldrn Co Chr Prnt Comm 90-; Rsk Strng Cmm 90-Wrkd Instrctnl Asst Cn Pblc Schl Systm 89-; Sclgy.

**GRAHAM, HEATHER L**, Muskingum Coll, New Concord, OH; SO; BA; Frst Circle Edtr; Res Asst; Chi Alpha Nu Serv Chrprsn; Vrsty X-Cntry 90-; Engl; Poet.

**GRAHAM, JADE E**, Middle Tn St Univ, Murfreesboro, TN; FR; BA; Walter R Courtenay Eagle Scout Awd; Pol Sci; Govt.

**GRAHAM, JAMES K**, Hellenic Coll/Holy Cross, Brookline, MA; GD; MDIV; Holy Crs Chrch Pastroal Intrn 90; Ofc Comm Earchy Newton Edtrl Lutern; St George Melkite Grk Cath Chrch Prsh Coun Sacramento Ca Pres 85-87,Sec 81-85,87-88; Sys Intgrtrs Inc Pub Edtr Graph Sprvsr 80-89; BA Cowell Coll 71; MA Cal St Un 76; Theology; Prsthd Melkite Grk Cath Chrch.

**GRAHAM JR, JAMES L**, Univ Of Southern Ms, Hattiesburg, MS; SR; BS; Fncrs Clb 85-87; Col Rpblcns 85-87; Rho Epsilon Real Estate Frat 85-87; Pi Kappa Alpha Hs Mgr 83-85; Grk Acdmc Awrd Bnqt 84; Frmrly Emplyd Rtl Crdt Indstry; BBA 87; Scndry Educ; Scl Studies Educ.

**GRAHAM, JAMES W**, Fl Atlantic Univ, Boca Raton, FL; SR; BS; Drama Club 87-; Phi Kappa Phi 89-; Beta Gamma Sigma 89-; Pres List 89-90; Acctng; CPA.

**GRAHAM, JAMIE H**, Faulkner St Jr Coll, Bay Minette, AL; GD; AS; Mdcl.

**GRAHAM, JENNIFER**, Fl A & M Univ, Tallahassee, FL; JR; BA; Cmptr Info Syst Clb 90-; Dns Lst 90-; Hnr Rl 89-; Co-Op IBM Boulder CO; Cmptr Info Syst; Cmptr Pgmg.

**GRAHAM, JEREMY S**, Murray St Univ, Murray, KY; FR; BS; FFA State Treass 90-; Deans List 90; Alpha Gamma Rho; Agriculture; Vetry Medicinie.

**GRAHAM JR, JOHN F**, Comm Coll Algny Co Algny Cmps, Pittsburgh, PA; SR; Radiatior Oncology Soc; Grant 1st Stdnts Recieve Univ Radiotherapy Assoc Inc; AS Radiation Therapy; Radiation Therapy.

**GRAHAM, JULIE R**, Univ Of Nc At Charlotte, Charlotte, NC; SO; BA; Res Stdnt Assoc 90; Bapt Stdnt Union; Psych.

**GRAHAM, KAREN L**, Univ Of Akron, Akron, OH; FR; BFA; RHPB Pblcty Comm; Alpha Lambda Delta; Hnrs Pgm 90-; IM Ftbl 90; Grphc Dsgn/Illus.

**GRAHAM, KATHIE K**, Fl International Univ, Miami, FL; SO; BS; Outstdng Acad Achvmnt 90-; Wrld Wings Intl Inc 89-; Med/Lgl Sec 67-69; Pan Amer Wrld Airways Flght Attdnt Intl Qlfd Frnch 69-89; Cert Cert Sec Bryant/Stratton Bsn Inst 67; Dietetics/Nutrition; Doctor Pblc Hlth Intl.

**GRAHAM, KATHREEN V**, Univ Of Sc At Coastal Carolina, Conway, SC; SO.

**GRAHAM, KELLY E**, Univ Of Sc At Columbia, Columbia, SC; SR; BS; Comp Clb; Gamma Beta Phi VP 87-90; Gldn Key 88-90; Delta Sigma Pi VP Pldg Ed 88-90; Gamma Iota Sigma VP Pldg Ed 89-90; Clnl Lf Accdnt Schlrshp 89-90; Prsdnts Hnr Rll; Deans Lst 88-90; Bus Admn.

**GRAHAM, KRISTEN S**, Indiana Univ Of Pa, Indiana, PA; SR; Assn Chldhd Ed Intl 89-; PA Sci Tchrs Assn; PSEA; Phi Theta Kappa 87-; Vol Tutor Chevy Chase Comm Ctr; Grad Cum Laude; Deans List; Nmntd Outstndg Stdnt Tchr Yr; BS Elem Ed IN Univ PA; Elem Ed; Tch/Day Care.

**GRAHAM, KRISTIE Y**, Fayetteville St Univ, Fayetteville, NC; SR; Psychlgy Clb Pres 87-; Crmnl Jstce Clb 87-; IM Sprts 89-; BS; Psychlgy/Crmnl Jstce.

**GRAHAM, LEIGH A**, Univ Of Southern Ms, Hattiesburg, MS; FR; BS; Gamma Beta Phi; Med; Nrsg.

**GRAHAM, MELISSA**, Univ Of Nc At Charlotte, Charlotte, NC; SO; BS; Phase Four A Hall Cncl 89-; Stdnt Advsng Fresh Exclnc Cnslr; Interdsplnry; Phi Eta Sigma 89-; Biology; Med.

**GRAHAM, MERIDITH T**, Univ Of Sc At Columbia, Columbia, SC; FR; Stdnt Chrstn Flwshp 90-; Assoc Afrcn Amrcn Stdnts 90-; Naacp 90-; Mnrty Stdnt Hnr 90-; Mthmtcs; Edctn.

**GRAHAM, MICHAEL A**, Univ Of Sc At Sumter, Sumter, SC; SO; BS; Bsns Finance.

**GRAHAM, PATRICK K**, Nova Univ, Ft Lauderdale, FL; GD; MA; AA Brookdl Comm Clg 78; BA Montclr St Clg 80; Acctg.

**GRAHAM, PAUL C**, Univ Of Sc At Columbia, Columbia, SC; FR; BA; Stdnt Art Guild 90; Art Educ; Tchr.

**GRAHAM, R SCOTT**, Va Commonwealth Univ, Richmond, VA; GD; MD; Stdnt Govt Clss Rep 88-90; Athltc Advsry Comm 87; Symr Schtz Schlrshp 90-; Natl Coll Stdnt Govt Awrd 90; Wllm Mry Vrsty Swmmng Capt Rcrd Hldr 83-87; BS 87; Med.

**GRAHAM, RHONDA M**, Univ Of Montevallo, Montevallo, AL; SO; Hon Orgztn Stdng Cmtee 89-; Alpha Lambda Delta 89-90; Biology; Med.

**GRAHAM, ROGER R**, Univ Of Tn At Martin, Martin, TN; SR; BS; Ed Crtnst Nwspr 90-; Sigma Pi Tres 88-; Ed Crtn Awd; Prof Jrnlsts; Mrk Of Excllnc; Psych.

**GRAHAM, ROSEMARIE J**, Barry Univ, Miami, FL; SO; BA; Jmcn Assoc; Intl Stdnts Org; Comp Sci; Bus.

**GRAHAM, SHARON M**, Tuskegee Univ, Tuskegee Inst, AL; SO; BSN; Sigma Doues Chpln 88-F Stdnt Nrs Assn 87-88; Chi Eta Phi Sorty Inc Nrsng 90-; Nrsng; RN/BUS.

**GRAHAM, STACYE M**, Tri County Tech Coll, Pendleton, SC; FR; AB; Phi Theta Kappa; Dsk/Chr Video 89-; Acctg; Acctnt.

**GRAHAM, SUSAN L**, Memphis St Univ, Memphis, TN; SO; BS; Bacchus 90-; Gamma Beta Phi 90-; Phi Etta Sigma 90-; Drmsn Crss Aux 90-; Delta Gamma Rtls Chrmn 89-; Pnhllnc 3.50 Clb 90-; Oprylnd Intl Trvl-Trvl Asst; Bus; Trsm/Htl Ind.

**GRAHAM, SUSAN M**, Lexington Comm Coll, Lexington, KY; JR; AA; Dns Lst 87-; Prgm Dvlpmnt Comm Stdnt Mbr 88; Acctg.

**GRAHAM, TANYA R**, Thomas Nelson Comm Coll, Hampton, VA; FR; BA; INCC Nasa Lngly Rsrch Cntrs; Scrtrl Coop Ed Prgm; Psychlgy.

**GRAHAM, TOMMY D**, Livingston Univ, Livingston, AL; SR; Vrsty Bsebl Meridian Jr Clg; Troy State Univ; Hstry PE.

**GRAHAM, TONYA N**, Utica Jr Coll, Utica, MS; SO; AA; Stdnt Govt Org Pres 90-; Dstngshd Employees Awds Comm 90-; Dist Stdnt Affrs Comm 90-; Phi Theta Kappa 90-; Dns Lst 89-; Vol Wrkr Smith Robertson Museum 90-; Anncmnt Clrk Greater Mt Sinai M B Chrch 90-; Pres Hls Natchez Trace Hm Ownrs 89-; Crmnl Jstc; Law.

**GRAHAM, TRACEY L**, Santa Fe Comm Coll, Gainesville, FL; SO; AA; Cert Of Achvmnt; P S Pharmacy.

**GRAHAM, TROY A**, Kent St Univ Kent Cmps, Kent, OH; JR; BBA; Musselmn Hl Hse Cncl Wng Rep 90-, Golden Key, Jaycees Int VP 89-; Pres Lst 90-; Dns Lst 90-; State Univ Newark Golf Tm 89; U S Army 85-88; Cmptr Sci; Pub Acctnt.

**GRAHAM, WANDA F**, Univ Of Sc At Columbia, Columbia, SC; SR; BS; Psi Chi 90-; Dogwood Hill Baptist Church Tchr Mbr 77; Legal Asstnt For Law Firm 83-87; Sec Treas For Gen Cont Corp 87; AS Southerastern Cmnty Clge 83; Psychology; Probation/School Coubseling.

**GRAHAM, WENDY G**, Faulkner Univ, Montgomery, AL; GD; BA; Bg Sistr Pgm; Proj Lit Plus; Fla Real Est Lic; Law; Paralegal.

**GRAHAM, WILLIAM B**, Kent St Univ Kent Cmps, Kent, OH; SR; BA; Fncng Clb 89-90; Golden Key 89; Pi Gamma Mu 89; Pres Lst 88-90; Anthrplgy/Phlsphy; Anthrplgst/Clg Prof.

**GRAHAM-WARD, GEORGIA S**, George Washington Univ, Washington, DC; SO; BA; Geography; Envrnmtl Rsrc Plcy.**

**GRAJALES SOTO, MARIBEL**, Inter Amer Univ Pr Hato Rey, Hato Rey, PR; FR; Vlybl 87-90; Acctg.

**GRAJEWSKI, MARIA F**, Saint Vincents Coll & Seminary, Latrobe, PA; FR; BS; Crs Cntry; IM Vlybl 90-; Biology; Vet Med.

**GRAMLICH, STEPHEN PETER**, Glassboro St Coll, Glassboro, NJ; JR; BA; Stdnt Math Assoc 90-F WGLS 90-; Kappa Delta Pi 90-F Gamma Tau Sigma 90-; Tau Kappa Epsilon 89-; Hghst GPA Of All Frat Mbrs 89; Tau Kappa Epsilon Schlr Of The Yr 89-90; Im Indr Soccer/Hocky 88-; Math/Secndry Ed; HS Tchr.**

**GRAMM, ROGER A**, Univ Of Miami, Coral Gables, FL; SR; BARCH; Golden Key 1st V P 89-; Arch; Arch.

**GRAMMATICO, GARY S**, Univ Of New Haven, West Haven, CT; SO; BA; Glds Gym Pwrlftng Tm 89-; BAD 90-; Acctg; CPA.

**GRAMMATICO JR, JOSEPH N**, Quinnipiac Coll, Hamden, CT; FR; Acctg; CPA.

**GRAMOLINI, ANGELA L**, Elms Coll, Chicopee, MA; SO; BS; Ambssdrs 89-; Amer Chem Soc 89-; Stdnt Govt 90-; Show Dir 90-; Ldrshp Awd; Blgy/Med Tech.

**GRAN, KATHLEEN A**, Mount Saint Mary Coll, Newburgh, NY; SO; BA; Newspaper Writer; Chorus 90; Paragon Cable Intern; Communication Arts; Production.

**GRANADOS, AMPARO C**, Univ Of Miami, Coral Gables, FL; SO; BA; Sclgy; Law.

**GRANADOS, YSOMAR C**, Univ Of Miami, Coral Gables, FL; SO; BM; Natl Fed Msc Clbs 89; Piano Perfrmnc.

**GRANAT, DOUGLAS T**, Emory Univ, Atlanta, GA; SR; BBA; Beta Gamma Sigma; Fnncl Exectvs Instt Bus Schlr 90; All Amrcn Schlr Coll Awrd; Acctg.

**GRANATA, MICHAEL**, Salisbury St Univ, Salisbury, MD; SR; BFA; Advtsng Dsgn; Grphc Dsgnr.

**GRANATO, NANCY T**, Cumberland County Coll, Vineland, NJ; FR; Adult Ed Tchr-Slk Flwr Arrng Tchr; Ck Dec; Bty Prlr Oper/Mgr 78-; Csmtlgy Cert Bty Acad 76; Bus Adm; Spvr Rsrt/Mtl.

**GRANBERRY, JAMELL R**, Alcorn St Univ, Lorman, MS; SO; BA; Hnr Stdnt Orgnztn Senator 89-; Cls VP 89-; Yrbk Stf 90-; Acctg Clb 90-; Inroads Inc 87-; Intern Mark Twain Bancshares 89-90; Intern Metro Swr Distct; Acctng; CPA.

**GRANDA, EDUARDO**, Miami Dade Comm Coll South, Miami, FL; SO; BA; Commrcl Bnkr SE Bnk; Dplma Amer Inst Bnkng 86; Finance; Financl Serv.

**GRANDE, FEDERICO**, Univ Of Miami, Coral Gables, FL; FR; BA; IM Tennis 90-; Bio; Dntl Schl.

**GRANDE, JEFFREY,** Bapt Bible Coll & Seminary, Clarks Summit, PA; JR; BS; Marrd Stdnts Assn; RN Nrsng Sprvsr; Sharon Gen Hosp Schl Nrsng 81; Hm Mssns.

**GRANDERSON, BETTY L,** Memphis St Univ, Memphis, TN; JR; BA; Active Mbr Trvlrs Rest 1 Church 90-; Crcntl Offcr; US Air Force 79-87; Los Angeles Dpty Sheriff 88-90; Phy Ed; Phy Ed Tchr/Bsktbl Coach.

**GRANDERSON, KENNETH E,** Hampton Univ, Hampton, VA; JR; BARCH; Am Inst Architectural Stdnts Ofcr 89-; Deans Lst 88-; Omega Psi Phi Ofcr 90-; Outstndg Ch Serv Awd; Hon Architectural Dsgn; Architecture.**

**GRANDISON, CARMEN D,** Comm Coll Algny Co Algny Cmps, Pittsburgh, PA; SO; BA; Engl Comm; Jrnlsts.

**GRANDIZIO, STEVEN M,** Wilmington Coll, New Castle, DE; SO; BA; DE Cnty Semi-Pro Bsbl 89-; Leag/MD State Semi-Pro Leag; Deans Lst 89-90; Pres Lst 90-; Acdmc/Athltc H S 90; Pres Schlrshp; Food Serv Needy 87-; Natl Assn Intrclgt Athltcs 1st Tm All Dist All Rgn; Dello Semi-Pro Rookie Yr 90; Cmnctns; Grphc Dsgn Advrtsng.

**GRANDSTAFF, JAMES L,** Kent St Univ Kent Cmps, Kent, OH; SR; BA; Intrhl Cncl Flr Rep 88-89; Hist.

**GRANELL-ALONSO, IRMA A,** Univ Of Pr At Mayaguez, Mayaguez, PR; SR; BS; Natl Assoc Acctnts 90-; Beta Beta Beta 89; Psychlgy Stdnt Assoc AEPSIC 86-88; Phi Alpha Delta Treas 90-; Eta Gamma Delta 89-; Bus Adm Fclty Schlrshp 90; Delegate Natl Model United Nations 88; Collegiate Confrnc NY City 89; Bus Admin Acctng; MBA/LAW.

**GRANEY, SHARON E,** Gallaudet Univ, Washington, DC; GD; MS; Natl Stdnt Speech/Lang Hrng Assn 89-; Adrienne Kaplan Awd 90; Schl Of Comm Awd; BA Univ Delaware 85; Speech/ Lang Pthlgy; Pthlgst.

**GRANGER, JOHN J,** Univ Of North Fl, Jacksonville, FL; SR; BT; Phi Theta Kappa 86-87; Phi Kappa Phi 90-; AS FL Comm Coll 88; AA FL Comm Coll 88; Mnfctrn Tech; Mngmnt.

**GRANITTO, MATTHEW J,** Cleveland St Univ, Cleveland, OH; JR; BSEE; Eta Kappa Nu 90-; Mid Cont Univ All Acad 89-90; Vrsty Bsbl 87-; Elect/Cmptr Eng; Eng.**

**GRANIZO, DIEGO E,** Univ Of Pittsburgh, Pittsburgh, PA; JR; IIE 90-; Math; Engr.

**GRANJA, WILSON E,** Saint Thomas Univ, Miami, FL; JR; BA; Natl Clgt Business Merit Awds 90; Finannce/Mrktng; Mba.**

**GRANNAN, ELAINE C,** Ky Wesleyan Coll, Owensboro, KY; SO; FCA; John Graham Scty; Kappa Dlt Rcrdg Sec 90-; Substnc Abse Cmt; Resdnt Asstnt; KY Wesleyan Sftbl Tm; Phys Math; Rsrch Nuclear Physcs.

**GRANNAN, JENNIFER L,** Christian Brothers Univ, Memphis, TN; SO; BA; Tau Kappa Epsilon Ltl Sis 89-; Peer Cnslr 90-; Phi Alpha Theta; Zeta Tau Alpha Stndrds Chrprsn Rtl Chrprsn 89-; Hstry; Law.

**GRANT, ANDREA C,** Tri County Tech Coll, Pendleton, SC; FR; Stdnt Govt 90-; Alpha Zeta Beta 90-; Fncl Mgmt.

**GRANT, ANN,** Stockton St Coll, Pomona, NJ; FR; BA; Nwsppr Typesttr 90-; Ltrry Mag; Mntr Schlr Prog; Dns Lst; Literature; Athr Fctn Nvlst.

**GRANT, BARBARA G,** Va Highlands Comm Coll, Abingdon, VA; FR; AAS; Nrsng; Human Serv.

**GRANT, BETTY J,** Medaille Coll, Buffalo, NY; JR; BA; Humn Svc Clb; Act Brd; Orntn Comm; Hnrs Pgm 88-; Dns Lst 88-90; Brd Dir Crucl Humn Serv Agncy 89-; NAACP 86-; Mgr Deli Store 80-; Educ/Humn Svcs.

**GRANT, BRADLEY PICKETT,** Univ Of Ky, Lexington, KY; JR; BS; SMART; HCOP 90; Phi Theta Kappa 88-90; Clg Schlrs Amer 90-; Alpha Epsilon Delta Rptr 90-; Merit Awd 90; IM Ftbl 88-90; Biology; Med.

**GRANT, CAMESHA M,** Va St Univ, Petersburg, VA; SO; BA; Psych Clb 89-90; Deans List 89-; Big Bros/Strs Org 90-; Offc Asst 90-; Res Asst; Admin Of Justice; Law.

**GRANT, DARREL W,** Springfield Tech Comm Coll, Springfield, MA; SO; BA; Msspng 89-; Mercy Hosp 89-; Cmnctns; Advrtsng.

**GRANT, DARRON T,** Fl A & M Univ, Tallahassee, FL; JR; BA; AA Tallahassee Cmmnty Coll 90; Cvl Eng Tchnlgy.

**GRANT, DAVID S,** Univ Of Akron, Akron, OH; FR; BA; Hons Clb; Alpha Lambda Delta Phi Eta Sigma; Hons Stdnt Schlrshp; IM; Mech Eng.

**GRANT, DEBORAH K,** Coll Of Charleston, Charleston, SC; SR; Elem Ed; Tchr.

**GRANT, DONALD F,** S U N Y Coll Of A & T Morrisvl, Morrisville, NY; FR; AS; Phi Theta Kappa; Boy Scts Of Amer Sctmstr 85-; Eng Sci.

**GRANT, EDWARD A,** Norfolk St Univ, Norfolk, VA; SR; Stdnt Govt Assn Cls Ofcl 87-88; Am Assn Hlth Phy Ed Rec Dance Stdnt Ldr 86-; Majors Clb 86-; IM Bsktbl 89-; Vrsty Ftbl/Bsebl 87-89; BS; Cert Drivers Edn 90; Interdisciplinary Studies/Phy Edn; Med Field.

**GRANT, HEATHER L,** Univ Of Al At Birmingham, Birmingham, AL; FR; BS; Psychlgy Rsrch Asstnt; Prsdntl Hnr Rll 90; Psychlgy; Psychlgy Rsrch.

**GRANT, HILLARY S,** Endicott Coll, Beverly, MA; FR; Busn Clb 90-; Intrnshp Fdlty Inv; Busn Admin.

**GRANT, JARROD K,** Wilberforce Univ, Wilberforce, OH; SR; Stdnt Govt 2nd VP 90-; Vars Bsktbl Tm Capt 90-; Vars Bsktbl Mst Valbl Plyr Awd 90-; Pres Dns Lst; Alpha Phi Alpha; Blck Ml Coaltn Achvmnt Awd 90; Immnl Bapt Chrch; BA; Pol Sci; Law.**

**GRANT, JOHN R,** Univ Of Al At Huntsville, Huntsville, AL; SR; BSEE; Eta Kappa Nu 77-; IEEE Rgn 5 Stdnt Actvs Com Rep 74-78; Optmst Clb Madison 87-; Wyle Lab Huntsvl AL Sr Eng Spclst 87-; Ross Hill Cntrls Corp Houston TX Prjct Engr 80-87; Elect Eng; Sftwr Eng.

**GRANT, KAREN S,** Univ Of Miami, Coral Gables, FL; SR; BBA; Stdnt Govt Sen 89-90; Untd Blck Stdnts Tr 88-; Strctly Busn 89-; Rho Lambda Pr 90-; Alpha Kappa Alpha Pr 88-; Panhellnc Otstdng Womn 91; Mktg; Law.

**GRANT, KAYE-ANN E,** Univ Of Fl, Gainesville, FL; SR; BHS; Amercn Dietetic Assoc 88-; Broward Cnty Dietetic Assoc; Stdnt Dietetic Assoc Nwsltr Edtr 90-; Golden Key; Phi Theta Kappa 88-; Schlstc Achvmnt FA Atlntc U 89; Schlstc All Amercn Award 89; Clinical Dietetics.

**GRANT, KELLY T,** Univ Of South Al, Mobile, AL; SR; BED; Kappa Delta Pi; Alpha Chi; Pres Lst; Deans Lst; Elem Educ.

**GRANT, KIM DONNA M,** Strayer Coll, Washington, DC; JR; BA; Alpha Chi Hnrs Soc Schlrshp 90-; Acad Achvmnt Awd 90; Jr Anlyst Acctnt Busn; Assoc 90; Busn/Acctg; Buns.

**GRANT, KIMBERLY,** Bennett Coll, Greensboro, NC; SR; BA; Pre-Alumnae Cncl 89-; Pol Sci Clb Pres 88-90; Hstry Tutor 89-90; Pi Gamma Mu 88-; Bennett Schlrs 88-; Congressman Donald Payne Intern 90; Rsrch Pgm Univ NY Stony Brook RA 90; Legal Intern Attny Marquis D Street; Pol Sci; Law.

**GRANT, LATONIA M,** Saint Pauls Coll, Lawrenceville, VA; FR; BA; Dns Lst 90-; Engl; Tchr.

**GRANT, LEONE A,** Univ Of The Dist Of Columbia, Washington, DC; SR; BBA; Data Proc Mgmt Assn VP 88-89; Pr 89-; COBPM Undergrad Stdnt Adv Cncl Pr 90-; COBPM Blck Data Proc Assc; COBPM Epsilon Sigma Pr 90-; Amer Red Cross; Hm Nrsng Inst; Wall Street Jrnl Awd; Dns Lst; Grace Murray Hopper Awd; Cmptr Inf Syst Sci; Prgmg/Anlyst.

**GRANT, LINDA JO,** West Liberty St Coll, West Liberty, WV; SO; Alpha Xi Delta; Fshn Mrktng; Coor.

**GRANT, LISA M,** Castleton St Coll, Castleton, VT; SO; BA; Phys Educ; Tch.

**GRANT, MELISSA A,** Defiance Coll, Defiance, OH; SO; BA; Defender 89-; Oraculum Yrbk 90-; Campus Actvty Bd 90-; Beta Sigma Alumni Secr 90-; Engl/Hstry; Publ Svc.**

**GRANT, PAT L,** Defiance Coll, Defiance, OH; Law.

**GRANT, PATRICIA S,** Univ Of Sc At Columbia, Columbia, SC; SO; BA; Stdnt Govt Sec 90-; Rtrng Stdnt Assn Pres 90; Educ Clb SGA Sntr 89-90; Phi Eta Sigma 89-; Delta Iota Zeta; Cncrt Chr Schlrshp 89-90; Eastrn Star Ruth 89-; Omicron Delta Kappa Ldr Yr 90-; Early Chldhd Educ; Tchng.

**GRANT, PAUL M,** Salisbury St Univ, Salisbury, MD; SR; BS; Sigma Alpha Epsilon Eminent Deputy Treas; Inter Frat Cncl Cmnty Svc Chrmn; Delta Mu Delta; US Coast Guard Res 80; Salisbury Jr Chmbr Comm 90-; Mgmt; Law.

**GRANT JR, RICHARD N,** Northern Ky Univ, Highland Hts, KY; SR; BS; Physc Clb 89-; IM Sprts 87-; Physc/Math; Eng.

**GRANT, SHERRYCE A,** Univ Of Sc At Columbia, Columbia, SC; FR; BS; Bsktbll Sprt; Med Tech; Medicine.

**GRANT, SIMONE Y,** Va St Univ, Petersburg, VA; SR; BS; Big Brthrs Big Sstrs Orgnztn Tres 89-; Phtgrphy Clb 89-; Yrbk Stf 89-90; Mmbr NAACP Tres 89-; Rsdnt Asst 88-89; Jr Cls Tres 89; US Smmr Stdnt Prgrm 90-91; Mjr Bsns Admn Mnr Mgmt; Corp Mngr.

**GRANT, TRACY T,** Lasell Coll, Newton, MA; FR; AS; Hnrs Lst 90; Cmptr Book Awd; Crew 90-; Early Chldhd Educ; Chld Psychlgst.

**GRANT-LEVY, TATIA R,** Eckerd Coll, St Petersburg, FL; SR; BS; Pre Med Clb Pres 87-; Dive Clb V P 89-; Biol Clb 87-; Deans Lst 87-; Med Ctr Vol 88-89; Rsrch Inst Lab Asst 88-89; Hosp Nrsg Assist 89-; Rcktbl/Wndsrfng/Dvng 87-; Biol/Pre Med; Med Schl.

**GRANTHAM, CAROL A,** Liberty Univ, Lynchburg, VA; SR; BS; Yth Quest Mnstry Tm 90-; Pryr Grp Ldr 90; Dsclplshp Grp Ldr 90; LACT 90; Elem Ed; Tchr.

**GRANTHAM, KEVIN J,** Liberty Univ, Lynchburg, VA; SR; BA; Stdnt Senate 88-89; Tehlgl Soc 90-; Phi Sigma Tau 90-; Religion; Educ.

**GRANVILLE, DAVID F,** Niagara Univ, Niagara Univ, NY; JR; BFA; Theatre; Solidary Hmn Rghts; Frnds Crtn Sprtlby; Natl Hon Scty Cthlc Unv Dlt Epsln Sgm; St Vincent Schlrshp; Real Estate Agent; CERT D Couville Clg 85; Cert Holy Names Clg 87; Theatre; Drmtc Artst.

**GRAPER, THOMAS D,** Norfolk St Univ, Norfolk, VA; SR; BA; Frst Trmpt Va Bch Comm Orch 86-; Alfa Kappa Mu; Va Bch Arts Hum Comm; Mng Brd; Va Bch Comm Orch; Pub Rel/ Jrnlsm; Symph Orch Mgmt.

**GRAPHMAN, MARGARET M,** Columbus Coll Of Art & Design, Columbus, OH; FR; BA; Pres Lst 90-; Art; Comm Fine Art Phtgrphy.

**GRAPPONE, RACHELE K,** Le Moyne Coll, Syracuse, NY; JR; BA; Ski Clb; Deans Lst 89-90; Bsns Finance Accntng; Invstmnt Cnslr.

**GRASBERGER, MARIA,** Neumann Coll, Aston, PA; SO; BSN; Nurs; Nurs Pedatrcs.

**GRASMEHR, GAYLE M,** Ms St Univ, Miss State, MS; GD; DVM; Vet Coll Yrbk Ad Promoter 89-; Coll Vet Med Wildlife Assn Caretaker 89-; Vet Med Assn 89-; Clncl Dietician Awd Hls 88-89; BA Bio Univ San Diego 88; Vet Med.

**GRASS, LISA A,** Tougaloo Coll, Tougaloo, MS; SR; MBA; Bsn Clb 88; Frnch Clb Pblsh Newsltr Pres 90-; Outstndg Empl Awd Dept Labor 88; BA 90; Econ.

**GRASSO, ANTONIA M,** Middle Tn St Univ, Murfreesboro, TN; FR; BA; Spec Events Comm 90-.

**GRASSO, LAURA A,** Daytona Beach Comm Coll, Daytona Beach, FL; FR; Hnrs Prog 90-; Quanta Prog 90-; Psychlgy; Elem Educ.

**GRASSO, MOLLY A,** Indiana Univ Of Pa, Indiana, PA; SR; BS; Tele Sta 88-89; Amer Soc Trng Develpmnt 90-; Zeta Tau Alpha VP 87-; Comm Media; Pub Rel.

**GRASSO, ROBERT F,** Georgetown Univ, Washington, DC; SO; BS; Bus Admn Acctg Intl Bus.

**GRATER, PATRICIA L,** James Madison University, Harrisonburg, VA; SR; BS; Ntl Assn Educ Yng Chldn 88-; Mrchg Clr Grd 87-; Phi Kappa Phi 90-; Kappa Delta Pi 89-; E H Wigley Mmrl Schlrshp 90; Erly Chldhd Educ; Tchng Grds K-2.

**GRATTON, LARRY A,** Western Carolina Univ, Cullowhee, NC; JR; BS; Alpha Lambda Belta 89-; Intrn Natl Sci Fndtn Rsrch Exprnc Under Grad; Physics; Engr Rsrch.

**GRATZ, STEPHANIE L,** Pellissippi St Tech Comm Coll, Knoxville, TN; GD; AAS; Info Sys Tech Cert; Info Sys Tech; Word Prcssr.

**GRAU, CARLITA R,** Duquesne Univ, Pittsburgh, PA; GD; MA; Daughters Of St Paul Gen Councillor 77-89; Religious Sister Jobs Held Hd Edtl 72-77; Formation Mbrs 72-77; BA St Scholastics Clg Manila Philippines 58; MA English Catholic Amer Washington DC 60; Formative Spirituality.

**GRAUEL, JONATHAN P,** East Carolina Univ, Greenville, NC; SR; BFA; Inter Christian Cncl Pres 90-; Intervrsty Christian Fllwshp 89-; Phi Eta Sigma 88-; Pi Kappa Phi 89-; Hnr Stdnt 87-; Burroughs Welcome Purchase Awrd; 1 Pl Amateur Div State Fair Art 90; Painting; Serve God.

**GRAULAU SANTIAGO, JAIME A,** Univ Of Pr At Mayaguez, Mayaguez, PR; SO; Hon Soc Eng Stdnts; Eng.

**GRAVELLE, KRISTI J,** Univ Of Sc At Columbia, Columbia, SC; SR; BA; Yrbk Wrtr 85-87; Im Sprts 85-87; Piedmont Scty 89; Gamma Beta Phi 89; United Way Vol 89; Crtve Serv Intrnshp Lckwd Greene Eng 90; Accntnt 89; Engl/Jrnlsm; Bsnss Wrtng.

**GRAVEMAN, BRIAN A,** Univ Of Al At Birmingham, Birmingham, AL; SR; BS; Education Math; Secondary Schl Tchr.

**GRAVENSTINE, CLARE M,** Duquesne Univ, Pittsburgh, PA; SO; BS; Sign Waves Sec; Campus Mnstry; Phi Eta Sigma; Mu Phi Epsilon; Music Therapy.

**GRAVES, AMELIA S,** Memphis Academy Of The Arts, Memphis, TN; SO; BA; Illstrtn; Art.

**GRAVES, AMY S,** Radford Univ, Radford, VA; SR; BS; Radford Schlrshp 89-; Biology; Cardiology.**

**GRAVES, ANGLEA R,** Middle Tn St Univ, Murfreesboro, TN; JR; BS; Hon Roll 88-; Deans List 88-; Schlr/Athlete All Am 2nd Tm Bsktbl Vol State 90; Vol State Bsktbl IMS 89; Vol State Wmns Bsktbl Tm Grd 90; Elem Ed.

**GRAVES, CYNTHIA J,** Oh St Univ At Newark, Newark, OH; SO; BA; Phi Sigma 89-; Chrls Prsslr Hstry Awd 89; Gold Wrtng Awd 89-90; Binkovitz/Klein Schlp; Gnrl Acad Schlp; Engl/Hstry; MA Clg/Corp Lbrn.

**GRAVES, ELIZABETH A,** Ms St Univ, Miss State, MS; SR; BA; Stdnt Chptr NEA MEA VVP; Xi Kappa; Mrchng Bnd 88; Engl Ed.

**GRAVES, GEORGIA K,** Averett Coll, Danville, VA; SR; BA; Baptist Stdnt Un Fmly Grp Ldr 87-; Clg Activities Brd Scls Chair 87-; Stdnt Govt Assoc Pres 88-; Stdnt Fndtn 90-; Presidents Lst; Hmcmng Ct Queen 87-; Cougar Spirit Award 88-90; C L Davenport Awrd Genl Excllnc 90-; Psychology; Community Serv.

**GRAVES, GWENDOLYN M,** Cumberland Coll, Williamsburg, KY; FR; Var Bsktbl/Sftbl 90-; Elem Ed; Tchg.

**GRAVES, JENNIFER E,** Tri County Tech Coll, Pendleton, SC; FR; AS; Wrkng Intrnshp Clemsn Anml Hosp; Sci; Vet Tech.

**GRAVES, JEREMY B,** Univ Of Southern Ms, Hattiesburg, MS; FR; BS; Eagle Clb; Sigma Nu; Sim Sftbl Tns Bsktbl; Cmptr Sci.

**GRAVES, KATHALEEN C,** Univ Of Pittsburgh At Bradford, Bradford, PA; JR; Dns Lst; Bkkpr YWCA; Cert Wrk Wth Bttrd Wmn; Hmn Rels; Psych.

**GRAVES, KRISTYNA E,** Middle Tn St Univ, Murfreesboro, TN; SR; BA; Sigma Chi 88-; Delta Zeta Recrdng Sec 90-; Acad Schlrshp 87-; IM 87-; Engl Tchr.

**GRAVES, LEIGH T,** Coll Of Charleston, Charleston, SC; JR; BA; Finance.

**GRAVES, MITCHELL E,** Middle Tn St Univ, Murfreesboro, TN; FR; Fllwshp Chrstn Athlts 90-; Bptst Stdnt Un 90-; MTSU Wrk Schlrshp 90-; MTSU Ldrshp/Prfrmnce Schlrshp 90-; Pre-Phys Therpy; Sprts Phys Therpy.

**GRAVES, R TRENT,** Ky Christian Coll, Grayson, KY; FR; Yth Minister 90-; Bible/Chrstn Mnstrs; Ministry.

**GRAVES, SHERRY R,** Norfolk St Univ, Norfolk, VA; SR; BSW; Whitney Young Sch Soc Wrk Clb 89-; Natl Assn Soc Wrkrs 90-; Alpha Delta Mu 90-; Soc Wrk; MSW.

**GRAVES, TIFFANY L,** Al St Univ, Montgomery, AL; SO; BA; Montgomery Jazz Orchestra 90-; Music Media 89-; Academic Scholar 89-; Public Relations.

**GRAVES, VICTOR L,** Columbia Union Coll, Takoma Park, MD; SR; BS; Gamma Beta Phi 86; Alpha Chi 90; Dir Of Mrktng 87-; Bus Admn; Law Sch.

**GRAVISH, LORI A,** Pa St Univ Main Cmps, University Pk, PA; FR; BA; Bck Lions Clb; Hlth Fld; Physcl Thrpy.

**GRAVLIN, HEATHER L,** Univ Of Miami, Coral Gables, FL; SO; BFA; Flwshp Chrstn Athletes 89-; Alpha Lambda Delta 89-; Phi Eta Sigma 89-; Golden Cane Lvng Schlrshp 89-; Pres Hon Rl 90; Acad All Amer Swmng 89-90; Swim Tm 89-; Fine Arts/Paintr; Fine Artst/Art Tchr.

**GRAVLIN, VIRGNIA M,** Univ Of Miami, Coral Gables, FL; SO; BBA; Vrsty Swm Tm Acdmc Cptn 89-; Hnrs Stdnt Assn 90-; Flwshp Chrstn Athlts 89-; Alpha Lambda Delta 90-; Phi Eta Sigma 90-; Prsdnts Hnr Roll 89-; Henry King Stanford Schlrshp Awd 89-; Ed Fox Mmrl Schlrshp Awd 90-; Mgmnt Mrktng; Bsns Career.

**GRAY, ASHLEY L,** Univ Of South Al, Mobile, AL; SR; BS; Zeta Tau Alpha Svc Chmn 86-; Early Chldhd Edn; Teach.

**GRAY, BARRY S,** Southern Coll Of Tech, Marietta, GA; JR; BS; Campus Radio Sta Oper Mgr 86; Mech Engr Tech; Engr.

**GRAY, BRIAN Q,** Wv Northern Comm Coll, Wheeling, WV; SO; BA; Science; Engnrng.

**GRAY, CATHERINE G,** Mount Aloysius Jr Coll, Cresson, PA; SO; Occup Thrpy Assist; OTA.

**GRAY, CRAIG B,** Radford Univ, Radford, VA; SR; BBA; Act Budgt Comm 90-; Clg Rep 87-; Lead Tr 88-89; Alpha Lambda Delta 87-88; Delta Mu Delta 89-; Finc; Fincl Plng.

**GRAY, DANETTE L,** Murray St Univ, Murray, KY; FR; BA; Bapt Stdnt Un; Northsd Bapt Yth Grp; Elem Educ; Tchr.

**GRAY, DAVID S,** Central St Univ, Wilberforce, OH; JR; Dean Lsts; Bsnss Mngmnt.

**GRAY, DAWN-MARIE,** Howard Univ, Washington, DC; JR; BA; Intrn Gm Mngmt Oper Wash Bullets NBA 89-; Asst U Pres Intl Sports Wrtr 90-; Intrn-WTTG Fox Chanl 5 Sprts Dept; Bsktbl Howard Univ 88-89; Brdcst Jrnlsm.

**GRAY, DONNA-MARIE P,** Bloomfield Coll, Bloomfield, NJ; SO.

**GRAY, EILEEN J,** Christopher Newport Coll, Newport News, VA; SR; BSBA; Omicron Delta Epsilon; USA Vet; Finance; Mgmnt/Fin Serv.

**GRAY, HAROLD,** Bergen Comm Coll, Paramus, NJ; GD; AA; Phi Theta Kappa; Rd Tv Elec Sqr Clb Pres 62; Elec Rep Assoc Sr VP 69; Fght Sght; Elec Rep Assoc Indstrl Cmpnnts Div VP 67-68; Tchncl Elctrnc Dst Inc Pres 65-84; Fine Arts.

**GRAY, HOPE G,** Stillman Coll, Tuscaloosa, AL; FR; BS; Chrstn Stdnt Assoc; NAACP; Chr 90-; Gamma Lota Sigma; Dns Lst 90-; Pres Hnrs Pgm/Achvmnt Awd; Cmptr Sci; Cmptr Pgmr.

**GRAY, JAMES L,** West Liberty St Coll, West Liberty, WV; SO; BS; Natl Assoc Accntnts; Hnr Scty 90; Delta Sigma Pi VP Chapter Oper 90-; Co C 1092 Engr BN Spc E-4 89-; US Army Comba Infntry 11h Spc E4 85-89; Acctng; CPA/FEDL Serv.**

**GRAY, JAMES STANFIELD,** Univ Of Sc At Columbia, Columbia, SC; JR; BA; Stu Affrs Cmmtt 90-; Sigma Alpha Epsilon; Intern Liz Patterson Hse Rep DC; Ultmt Frsb 90-; Engl; PHD Col Prfssr.

**GRAY, JOHN E,** Western New England Coll, Springfield, MA; JR; BA; Bsbl; Law Enf.

**GRAY IV, JOHN W,** Central St Univ, Wilberforce, OH; SR; BS; Stdnt Govt Assoc Pn Hlnc Sntr 90; Fnce Invstmnt Scty 90; Mns Cncl Pres 89; Kappa Alpha Psi Prlmntrn 88-; Gen Mtrs Moraine Asmbly Plnt 90; CSU Schl Bsn Admin Acdmc Achvmnt Awd 90; Fnce/Acctng; Bkg Indstry.

**GRAY, JOSEPH P,** Temple Univ, Philadelphia, PA; FR; BS; EESA; Envrmntl Eng; Eng.

**GRAY, JULIA V,** Univ Of West Fl, Pensacola, FL; JR; BA; Pres Lst 89-; Deans Lst 88 90; Tchr Asst Rocky Bayou Chrstn Schl 85-88; Tchr 88-; Coach 86-; Elem Ed; Tchng/Coachg.

**GRAY, KEA M,** Univ Of Ga, Athens, GA; JR; BS; AA Gainesville Clg 90; Chld/Fmly Dev; Chld Life Spec.

**GRAY, LA VERNE,** Wilberforce Univ, Wilberforce, OH; SO; BA; Ill Pre Alumni; Class Fund Raising Public Rltns Comm 90-; Sigma Omega 90-; Tau Gamma Delta Schlrshp 90-; Rhbltn Chld Dvlpmnt.

**GRAY JR, LAYMON L,** Tallahassee Comm Coll, Tallahassee, FL; JR; BS; AA Bus Mngmnt; Cvl Engrng.

**GRAY, LISA,** Western Carolina Univ, Cullowhee, NC; SO; BS; Geography.

**GRAY, MEGAN M,** Bridgewater Coll, Bridgewater, VA; FR; BS; Stdnt Senate 90-; Choir; Tour Guide; Deputation Tms; Voice Stdnt; BSU 90-; Brethren Stdnt Fllwshp Histrn Outreach Chpsn 90-; Biol; Genetic Engrng.

**GRAY, MELISSA D,** Owensboro Comm Coll, Owensboro, KY; FR; BA; Jnr Achvmnt 86-90; Sprt Clb 86-87; Deans Lst 90-; Sps Abs Cntr Chld Cr 90-; Lgl Sec; Bus; Law.

**GRAY, MICHAEL J,** Univ Of Me At Augusta, Augusta, ME; FR; BA; Music Perf; Educ/Cmpstn.

**GRAY, MICHAEL KEVIN,** East Tn St Univ, Johnson City, TN; GD; MD; Appalachian Hstry Med Soc 87-; Alpha Omega Alpha Pres 90-; Phi Kappa Phi 86-87; Amer Fed Clin Res 90-; AOA Res Awd 88; Mc Graw Hill Awd 88; Summer Res Flwshp 88; Vars Rifle Tm 84-87; MD; BS Univ TN Martin 87; Med; Ophthalmology.

**GRAY, MICHAEL R,** Memphis St Univ, Memphis, TN; SR; BA; TN Shrfs Assc 88-; DMW Prnc Hall Grnd Ldg F&AM TN 83-; Amer Crctns Assc 89-; Crctnl Ofcr TN Dept Crtns 82-; Psychlgy; Clncl Psychlgy.

**GRAY, MICHELLE L,** Beckley Coll, Beckley, WV; SO; BA; Deans Lst; Bus; Acctng.

**GRAY, MICHELLE M,** Glassboro St Coll, Glassboro, NJ; SR; MA; Deans List 86-87; Cum Laude; BA Psychology; Psychology; Law School.

**GRAY, MISCHA K,** Union Univ, Jackson, TN; JR; BA; Elem Educ Kndrgrtn Endrsmnt; Tchng.

**GRAY, MISTY D,** East Tn St Univ, Johnson City, TN; FR; BS; Alpha Lambda Delta; Engl.

**GRAY, MOLLIE S,** Memphis St Univ, Memphis, TN; JR; BA; Boxer Clb AZ; Vol Obediance Assoc 90-; Trng/Competvly Showing Dogs Obedience 89-; Zeta Tau Alpha 87-; Philosophy.

**GRAY, NAOMI B,** Mary Washington Coll, Fredericksburg, VA; FR; BA; Piano Accmpnt Rctls 90-; Music/Pltcl Sci; Tch.

**GRAY, NYLES A,** Neumann Coll, Aston, PA; SR; BA; SGA Del Co Cmnty Clg Pres 84-85; Karate Clb Del Co Cmnty Clg Instr 84-85; Dns Lsts 90-; Cheyney Career Ctr Asstntshp; Karate Instr Phys Ed 90; Neighborhood Ctr Yth Dev Pres 83-; NCYD Karate Clb Instr; AS DE Co Cmnty Clg 89; Lib Studies/Sociology; Adult/Continuing Ed.

**GRAY, PAUL RAYN,** Marshall University, Huntington, WV; JR; Intl Finance.

**GRAY, RHONDA M,** Winthrop Coll, Rock Hill, SC; JR; BS; Beta Beta Beta 90-; Sigma Sigma Sigma 89-; Dance Tm Capt 88-; Biol; Phys Thrpy.**

**GRAY, ROXANNE T,** Felician Coll, Lodi, NJ; JR; BA; Educ Clb VP 88-; Hstry Clb 90-; Ssg 91; Kappa Sigma Xi; TA Tutor 91; Hstry; Professor.

**GRAY, SAMMIE J,** Univ Of Tn At Martin, Martin, TN; SO; BA; Hist; Tchng.

**GRAY, SHARON D,** Univ Of South Al, Mobile, AL; FR; Alpha Epsilon Delta 90; Phi Eta Sigma; Biomed Sci; Med.

**GRAY, SHERRI JEAN,** James Madison University, Harrisonburg, VA; JR; Cncl Excep Chldrn 89-; Frndshp Clb; Kappa Delta Pi 89-; Sigma Kappa 90-; Ctr Svc Lrng 90; Pres Lst 88-90; Erly Chldhd Educ; Tchg/Grad Schl.

**GRAY, TAMMY L,** Indiana Univ Of Pa, Indiana, PA; JR; BA; Stdnt Lgl Asst Pres 80-81; VP Chrch Yth Advsr 84-85; Dir Pine Sprgs Cmp Wk 86; Cmmnwlth Of PA Offc Atty Gen Clrk/Stno 81-90; AS Cntrl PA Bus Schl 81; Elem Educ; Teach.

**GRAY, TARA C,** Al A & M Univ, Normal, AL; SO; BS; Acctng Clb; MLK Srvce Orgnztn; Fr Hnr Stdnt; Hnr Stdnt; Acctng; Acctnt.

**GRAY, TAUNYA D,** Roane St Comm Coll, Harriman, TN; SO; BA; Stdnt Dentl Hygn Assoc; Dentl Hysn.

**GRAY, TAWANNA A,** Al A & M Univ, Normal, AL; SO; Dns Lst 90-; Acdmc Hnr Rl 89-; Kappa Delta Pi; Erly Chldhd Ed; Tchr.

**GRAY, THERESA M,** Kent St Univ Kent Cmps, Kent, OH; JR; BA; Chorale 86087; Pirates Pensance Choir 86; Golden Key; Deans List 86-; Pres List 90-; Eagle Awd 90; Canton Ballet 89; Plyrs Guild; G E Capital Bill Clctr 89-; Metro Ed/Entrtnmnt Telemrktng; Diploma John Robert Powers 89; Radio Prdctn; Msc Bus.

**GRAY, THOMAS E,** Memphis St Univ, Memphis, TN; JR; BSEE; IEEE 89-; SAE 90-; Tau Beta Pi; Stdnt Asst Rsrch Elec Eng; Electrical Eng; Comp Eng.

**GRAY, TWANA E,** Saint Pauls Coll, Lawrenceville, VA; FR; Bsn Mngmnt; Mngmnt.

**GRAYBEAL, DANIEL Y,** Emory & Henry Coll, Emory, VA; JR; BA; Math Assc Pres 88-; Cmps Govt; Wasp Radio 89-; Sigma Mu Pres; Blue Key VP 90; Alpha Phi Omega Sgt At Arms 90-; Fresh Math Awd 88; Victor S Armbrister Awd Acdmc Exc/Chrstn Chrctr; Math/Geography; Coll Tchr.

**GRAYBEAL, LAURA J,** Coll Of Charleston, Charleston, SC; FR; BS; Stdnt Alumni Assn 90-; Psych Clb 90-; 4 H; Biology; Med.

**GRAYBEAL, NANCY D,** Milligan Coll, Milligan Clg, TN; JR; BA; SACS 90-; Elem Ed; Tch.**

**GRAYBEAL, STUART C,** Univ Of Sc At Columbia, Columbia, SC; SO; BS; Crim Jstc Assoc 89-90; Alpha Lambda Delta 90; Crim Jstc; St Law Enfrcmnt Dvsn.

**GRAYBEAL, SUSAN E,** Northeast State Tech Comm Coll, Blountville, TN; FR; AAS; Mgmnt Info Sci; Cmptr Pgmmng.

**GRAYBOSCH, MARK R,** Univ Of Pa, Philadelphia, PA; FR; BA; Beta Theta Pi; Buisness.

**GRAYS, RONDA N,** Tougaloo Coll, Tougaloo, MS; FR; BA; Alpha Lambda Delta; Pres Schlr; IM Vlybl; Engl; Law.

**GRAYSON, BENITA M,** Tougaloo Coll, Tougaloo, MS; SO; BS; Alpha Kappa Alpha; Economics/Accntng; Accntnt.

**GRAYSON, CHRISTAL M,** Rust Coll, Holly Springs, MS; SO; NAACP Asst Treas 90-.

**GRAYSON, EDWARD V,** Nova Univ, Ft Lauderdale, FL; GD; Amer Clg Of Physcn Exec; Ntl Inst Of Hlth Fllwshp 72-74; BA Boston U 67; MD; Hlth Care Mngmnt; Hlthcre.

**GRAYSON, ETHAN T,** Anne Arundel Comm Coll, Arnold, MD; FR.

**GRAYSON, JO E,** Memphis St Univ, Memphis, TN; JR; BA; Rprtr For Tri-State Defender Nwsppr; Jrnlsm; Freelance Phtojrnlst.

**GRAYSON, JOHN M,** Univ Of Ky, Lexington, KY; SR; Rssn Clb 90-; BA; Pol Sci/Rssn Estrn Stdies; Govt/Bsns.

**GRAYSON, NIKOLE PHELICIA,** Fl International Univ, Miami, FL; SO; BA; Hosp Vol; Psychlgy.

**GRAZIANO, CHRISTINA M,** Philadelphia Coll Pharm & Sci, Philadelphia, PA; SR; BS; Sngrs Pres 86-; B A Frnd 86-; Nswppr Stf 88-; Pr Cnslng 88-; Wrtng Cntr Ttr 90; Advsry Brd 89; Deans Lst 86-; Nghbrs Htbr Schlrshp 86-90; Costep Indn Hlth Srvc 90; Im Vlybl Cpt 86-90; Pa Drma Gld/Acdmy Msc 87-; Pharmacy.

**GRAZIANO, JOSEPH A JR,** Kent St Univ Kent Cmps, Kent, OH; JR; BA; Gldn Ky; Alpha Phi Sigma; Dns Lst 89-90; Pres Lst 90-; IM Bsktbl 90-; Crim Just; Law.

**GRAZIANO, JOSEPH F,** Salisbury St Univ, Salisbury, MD; JR; BA; Clg Rpblns Pres 88-; Intrclg Stdsn Inst; Army ROTC Cadet 88-; Pi Lambda Upi Pres; Luis Luna For Congrewss Fld Dir 90; Pol Sci.

**GRAZIANO, LISA J,** Georgetown Univ, Washington, DC; SR; BSN; NSNA Cls Rep 89-; Psychlgy Clb 89-; Sigma Theta Tau 89-; Nrsg.

**GRAZIO, CHRISTINE G,** Rivier Coll, Nashua, NH; SO; BA; Stdnt Adm Com 89-; Stdnt Act Bd Sec 90-; Nwspr Stf Wrtr 90-; Spcl Pgrmng Com 90-; Rivier Fine Arts Scty 89-; Deans Lst 89-90; English; Grad Schl.**

**GRE GOIRE, VICTOR VITAL,** City Univ Of Ny Queensbrough, New York, NY; JR; ET.

**GREAR, MARILYN L,** Atlantic Comm Coll, Mays Landing, NJ; FR; Vrsty Archry; Comp Sci; Drftng.

**GREATHOUSE, EVA J,** Univ Of Akron, Akron, OH; JR; BS; Prsnl Dept; Elem Ed; Tchg.

**GREATHOUSE, MELISSA A,** Wv Univ At Parkersburg, Parkersburg, WV; FR; Phi Theta Kappa; Vol St Josephs Hosp 88-90; Med Lab Tech.

**GREATOREX, JAMES J,** Providence Coll, Providence, RI; JR; BS; Acctg Tutor Tchg Asstnt 90-; Acctg; Private.

**GREAUX, CHRISTOPHER G,** Univ Of Miami, Coral Gables, FL; SR; BSEE; Cmptr Eng; Eng.

**GREAVES, SHERRY R,** Ramapo Coll Of Nj, Mahwah, NJ; JR; BS; Stdtn Govt V P Fin 88-90; RSA Chrprsn 88-90; Allocations Comm 88-90; NRHH Pres 90-; Activities Award 90; Ldrshp Award 89; Oxford Hnrs Pgm; Lube/Unisys Schlrshp; Acad Achvmnt Schlrshp 88-; Cmptr Sci.

**GREBNER, LESLEY B,** Comm Coll Algny Co Algny Cmps, Pittsburgh, PA; Rgstrd Nrs; Nrsng.

**GRECH, AMY B,** York Coll Of Pa, York, PA; FR; BA; Jazz Ensmbl 90-; Lit Mag Stff 90-; Shrt Stry/Poem Pblshd Images; Engl/Wrtng; Authr/Tchr.

**GRECH, WILLIAM A,** Univ Of Sc At Columbia, Columbia, SC; FR; BA; Cmps Crsd Chrst 90-; Bsn; Econ/Stck Mkt.

**GRECKO, MATTHEW G,** Youngstown St Univ, Youngstown, OH; JR; BE; Cntrns 89-90; IEEE VP; Tau Beta Pi; Elec Engr.

**GRECO, JENNIFER J,** S U N Y Coll Of Tech At Frmgdl, Farmingdale, NY; SO; BS; Lbrl Arts Pres 90-; Lbrl Art Clb Sec 89-90; Radio Sec 89-90; Chrmn Awrd 90-; Bwlng Tm 90; AA; Lbrl Arts; Pharm.

**GRECO, NOELLE JANEANE,** Albertus Magnus Coll, New Haven, CT; SR; BA; Frnch Clb Treas 87-89; Frnch Allnce Of New Hvn 90; Phi Sigma Iota; Hghlnd Hts Vol 87-89; Soup Ktchn Vol 88; Scrd Hrt Schl Vol 90; Schlr Athlete Awd 88-89; Amity Clb Schlrshp 90; Tennis 87-88; Scl Sci; Ed.

**GRECO, SIMONE M,** Oh St Univ At Newark, Newark, OH; FR; BA; Engl; Wrtr/Author.

**GREDIG, ROBERT A,** Univ Of Cincinnati, Cincinnati, OH; SO; BS; Stdnt Ath Trnr Intrn 90-; Eta Sigma Gamma 90-; Helen M Fulton Schlrshp; Augustus T Ceclia J Welsh Schlrshp; IM Sftbl; Sprts Med; Sprts Physcl Thrpst.

**GREEAR II, JOSEPH P,** Northeast State Tech Comm Coll, Blountville, TN; FR.

**GREEAR, MARTY L,** Univ Of Va Clinch Valley Coll, Wise, VA; JR; BS; Darden Soc; Elec Tech Navy )-5 78-82; Elec Tech NASA Spce Prog 85-86; Psych; Psych/Lrng Res.

**GREEK, CINDY L,** Rochester Bus Inst, Rochester, NY; FR; BS; Estmn Kodak Coop 90; Comp Sci; Prgrmmr.

**GREEN BUCKLEY, JANICE M,** Univ Of Southern Ms, Hattiesburg, MS; SR; BS; Bptst Stdnt Union 87-; Phi Theta Kappa 88-90; AA Hind Comm Coll Raymond MS 89; Psychlgy.

**GREEN, ADAM L,** Ms St Univ, Miss State, MS; SR; BS; Amer Scty Svl Eng Chrmn; Photogrphr Univ Nwspr; Tau Beta Pi 90-; Chi Epsilon 90-; Phi Eta Sigam/Gamma Beta Phi; Schlrshp Dpt Dvl Eng 88-; Cvl Eng.

**GREEN, ALICIA E,** Central St Univ, Wilberforce, OH; FR; Frnch Clb Sec 90-; Var Chrldng Tm Capt 87-90.

**GREEN, ALLEN V,** Univ Of Sc At Aiken, Aiken, SC; SR; BA; Vocal Ensemble Pres/Mscl Dir 87-; Mnrty Affairs 87; Mnrty Acdmc Schlrshp 88-89; Sclgy; Optometrey.

**GREEN, AMY L,** Toccoa Falls Coll, Toccoa Falls, GA; SR; Dorm Cncl Flr Rep 87-88; Mstrs Soc VP 88-89; Deans Lst 87-; Erly Chldhd Ed; Pblc Schl Tchr.

**GREEN, ANGELA D,** Memphis St Univ, Memphis, TN; SO; BSET; Hl Assn 90; Gamma Beta Phi 90-; Blck Schlrs Unlmtd 90-; TN Lgsltv Intrn; Archtctrl Tchnlgy; Archtctr.

**GREEN, ANGELA M,** Indiana Univ Of Pa, Indiana, PA; SR; IUP Ldrshp Comm 89-90; Stdnt PSEA; Kappa Delta Pi 89-; Delta Zeta V P 88-; Summa Cum Laude; Greek Awrds; Deans List IUP 87-; BED; Elem Educ; Tchng.

**GREEN, BETSY J,** Central Pa Bus School, Summerdale, PA; SR; ASB; ASB; Acctg.

**GREEN, BEVERLY L,** Snead St Jr Coll, Boaz, AL; SO; BS; Phi Theta Kappa 89-; Alld Hlth Phys Thrpy; Phys Thrpst.

**GREEN, BRENDA CAROL,** Bethel Coll, Mckenzie, TN; FR; BS; Pt Pleasant Bptst Yng Wm; Prt Tm Sec Joe V Martin Mech Cntrctrs 90-; Elem Ed; Tchr.

**GREEN, BRENDA L,** Wv Northern Comm Coll, Wheeling, WV; GD; AAS; Phi Theta Kappa; Deans List; Theta Kappa 2 Yr Secretarial Awd; NAACP; Julilee Chrstn Flwshp Worship Team 88-; Supervisor Of Nursery; Secretarial Science; Child Psychology.

**GREEN, BRENDA S,** Alcorn St Univ, Lorman, MS; JR; BA; Pine Grove Bptst Chrch; BA Hinds Commnty Clg 89; Clncl Psychlgy.

**GREEN, CINDY M,** Kent St Univ Stark Cmps, North Canton, OH; FR; Cert Sec Studies Trumbull Bus Schl 76; Elem Educ; Teacher.

**GREEN, CONSTANCE L,** Univ Of Md At Eastern Shore, Princess Anne, MD; SR; MA; Ftr Bsn Ldrs Of Amer 90-; MD Bsn Educ Assn 89-90; Amer Clg Clgte Award 90; Hnr Soc 88; Amer Clg Clgte Award 89; AS Sec Sci/Bsn; BS Estrn Shore Cmnty Clg 74; Engl; Scndry Educ.

**GREEN, DIONNE NICOLE,** Harvard Univ, Cambridge, MA; SO; BS; Kuumba Sngrs 89-90; Expressions Dance Co 90-; Afro-Am Cultural Ctr 90; Eng Sci Mech; Engr.**

**GREEN, DONALD K,** Univ Of Nc At Charlotte, Charlotte, NC; JR; BA; AIAS 80; Phi Theta Kappa 89-; Alpha Sigma Phi V P; Deans Lst 88; AAS Northampton Co Area Comm Clgs 82-; AFA 90; AA 90; Arch/Bus; Arch.

**GREEN, DONNA B,** Middle Tn St Univ, Murfreesboro, TN; FR; Elem Ed; Tchng.

**GREEN, DONNA M,** Univ Of Cin R Walters Coll, Blue Ash, OH; FR; BED; Ntrlst-Tchr Cincinnati Pk Brd 73-77; Cincinnai Ntr Ctr 77-81; Russn Lang; Tchr.

**GREEN, ELLA M,** Coppin St Coll, Baltimore, MD; SR; BS; Ntnl Inst Drug Absrs Intrn 90; John Hpkns Prvntn Cntr; Hygiene Pblc Hlth; Psychology; Alcohol Sbstnc Abse; Pbhl Hlth Adm.

**GREEN, GABRIEL V,** Ms St Univ, Miss State, MS; SR; BA; AF Resrv Ofcr Training Corps Grp Exec Ofcr; Arnold Air Soc Publc Afrs Ofcr 89; BSA Order Of The Arrow Asst Scout Mstr/Ledge Chf 87; Gamma Beta Phi 88; Phi Kappa Phi; AF Sgts Assoc Outstndng Ldrshp Award 88; Cmnctn; AF Ofcr.

**GREEN, GARY L,** Harding Grad School Of Relig, Memphis, TN; GD; MAR; Phi Eta Sigma 81; Phi Kappa Phi 82-87; Amer Soc Anml Sci Ntl Sch 81-82; Amer Vet Med Assoc 87-; Amer Anml Hosp Assoc 87-89; Vet Sml Anml Med Exclsvly 87-89; BS 84; DVM 87; Religion; Msnry.

**GREEN, GENE E,** Christopher Newport Coll, Newport News, VA; JR; BS; Paramedic; Bio; Med Doctor.

**GREEN, GLORIA J,** Wv Univ At Parkersburg, Parkersburg, WV; SO; BA; Phi Theta Kappa 89-; ABA; Bus.

**GREEN JR, HAROLD M,** Embry Riddle Aeronautical Univ, Daytona Beach, FL; SR; BS; Aero Clbs; Nvl Nclr Rctr Operator; Flght Instrctr; Aerontcl Scnc; Airline Pilot.

**GREEN, HEATHER C,** Bunker Hill Comm Coll, Boston, MA; FR; BA; Clnry Arts; Pstry Chef.

**GREEN, JAMES W,** Allegheny Coll, Meadville, PA; SO; BA; Vrsty Sccr 89-; Stdnt Govt 89-; Stdnt Fac Acdmc Stndrds Com 89-; Ad Hoc Mltcltrl Com 89-; IM Bsbl/Bsktbl 89-; Lambda Sigma 90-; Alden Schlr 89-; Phi Delta Theta Treas 90-; Lambda Sigma 90-; K Norwood Schlrshps 90-; Ecnmcs/Pltcl Sci; Bus/Law Grad Schl.

**GREEN, JANET E,** City Univ Of Ny Hunter Coll, New York, NY; SR; MS; Natl Stdnt Spch Lang/Hrng Assc; Spch/Lang Path; BS Marquette Univ Milwaukee Wi 84; Comm Sci/Audlgy.

**GREEN, JANICE P,** Hudson Valley Comm Coll, Troy, NY; SR; BA; AAS; Finance; Insurance.

**GREEN, JENNIFER A,** Univ Of Cincinnati, Cincinnati, OH; SO; BA; Sigma Alpha Iota; Music Ed.

**GREEN, JENNIFER L,** Liberty Univ, Lynchburg, VA; SR; BS; Cir K Intl Sec 90-; LHEA 89-; Alpha Lambda Delta 88-; Intrnshp At Preschool; IM Tennis 87-90; Cmnty Studies; Early Educ.

**GREEN, JENNIFER LYNN,** Univ Of Nc At Wilmington, Wilmington, NC; FR; BSN; Nurs.

**GREEN, JONATHON SAMUEL,** Yeshiva Univ, New York, NY; SO; BA; Stdnts Strgl For Soviet Jews Secy 89-90; Natl Confrnc Of Synagog Youth Advsr; Econ; Bus Fin.

**GREEN, KAREN J,** Ga St Univ, Atlanta, GA; JR; BED; Kappa Delta Pi; Golden Key 89-; Early Chldhd Ed; Tchr.

**GREEN, KIMBERLY J,** Voorhees Coll, Denmark, SC; SR; BS; Yrbk Edtr 90-; Alpha Kappa Mu; Alpha Chi 90-; Sigma Gamma Rho; Vrsty Sftbl 88-; Cmptr Sci; Prgrmr.

**GREEN, LAJUANA,** Alcorn St Univ, Lorman, MS; SO; BS; Hnr Stdnt Org 89-; Tech Clb 89-; Hnr Stdnt Org 89-; Ordr Eastrn Str; Air Trffc Cntrl Intrnshp 90-; Elec Eng.

**GREEN, LAJUANA G,** Univ Of Al At Birmingham, Birmingham, AL; JR; MRA; Stdnt Govt Assn Senatr 90-; Med Rec Clb 90-; Amer Med Rec Assn 90-; US Jaycee Org Dir 89-90; Med Rec Dir Hosp 82-88; AS G C Wallace Comm Coll 90; Med Rec Sci; Cnsltnt.

**GREEN, LARRY S,** Univ Of West Fl, Pensacola, FL; SR; BA; AA Pensacola Jr Clg 89; Spec Educ/Lrng Dsblties.

**GREEN, LAURIE S,** Liberty Univ, Lynchburg, VA; FR; BA; Chi Alpha 90-; SGA 90-; Res Hall Ldrshp Prayer Ldr; Alpha Lambda Delta; Natl Merit Schlr 90-; Dns Lst 90-; Engl/Educ Mnstrs; Sec Ed Engl Tchr/Yth Wrk.

**GREEN, LEAH L,** Va St Univ, Petersburg, VA; SR; BS; Nw Gnrtn Campus Mnstries VP 87-; Acctg Clb Treas 88; Tdwtr Pre-Almni Assn 87; Deans Lst Prog 87-; Schlrshp 87; Natl Assn Blck Acctnt Schlrshp 90; Acctg; Auditng.

**GREEN, LESLIE K,** Univ Of Rochester, Rochester, NY; SO; BA; Kappa Delta 90-; Var Swm Tm 89-; Psych.

**GREEN, LESLIE M,** Lane Coll, Jackson, TN; SO; Ntl Hon Soc 89-; Habtat Hmnty; Spec Educ; Educ Instrtr.

**GREEN, LOREN R,** Fl Baptist Theological Coll, Graceville, FL; SR; BTH; Theol Clb; SGA Jr Cls Pres 89-90; Welder; Theol; Pstrl Mnstr.

**GREEN, MARCUS A,** Fl A & M Univ, Tallahassee, FL; JR; BA; Keynote Piano Guild Pr 90-; NAACP 80-; FMENC 90-; Hon Roll Deans Lst 88-; Music Educ/Perf.

**GREEN, MARGIE S,** Emory Univ, Atlanta, GA; JR; BBA; Vol Emory 88-90; Pre Law Soc; Beta Alpha Psi 90-; Vol Emory 88-90; Stdnt Asst Depty Dn Busn Schl 89-; Dns Lst 88-; Acad All Amer; Acctg; Law.

**GREEN, MARY CATHARINE,** Univ Of Tn At Knoxville, Knoxville, TN; SR; BS; Univ TN Advrtsng Clb 90-; Kappa Tau Alpha; Gamma Beta Phi; Gldn Key; Practicum Job Lamar Outdoor Advrtsng; Advrtsng; Creative/Rsrch.

**GREEN, MELISSA C,** Claflin Coll, Orangeburg, SC; SR; BS; Stdnt Govt Assoc VP 90; Yrbk Staff Ed 89-90; Alpha Kappa Mu Pres 90; Delta Sigma Theta Treas 89-90; Acad Schlrshp; Fllwshp At Indiana Univ; Intrn MIT; Chemistry; Clg Prof.

**GREEN, MELISSA M,** Central St Univ, Wilberforce, OH; JR; Clss Offr VP 90-; Stu Assn Chrmn Scl Cmmtt 89-; Hnr Rll 89-; Nrsng; RN.

**GREEN, MELVA I,** Johnson C Smith Univ, Charlotte, NC; FR; Gvrnmnt Assn 90-; Exctv Brd MS Frshmn 90-; Anl Stf R W Sprtl Chr 90-; Deans Lst 90-; Alpha Swthrt Crt 90-; Mst Otstndng Stdnt 90-; US Dptmnt Agrcltr; Intrnshp Blgcl Tchncn; Chmstry; Orthndst.

**GREEN, MICHAEL S,** Univ Of Tn At Martin, Martin, TN; SO; BED; Phi Sigma Kappa Pr; Red Cross 89-; Interfrat Cncl Tr 90; Math Educ; Tchg.

**GREEN, MICHELLE D,** Dowling Coll, Oakdale Li, NY; SO; BA; Big Brothers/Big Sisters; Tutor Connequot; Long Island Univ Awards Cnvctn 89; Cngrssnl Schlr 90; Natl Yng Ldrs Confer; Town Islips Yth Bureau Rcgntn Nght; Hstry; Law.

**GREEN, MOISETTE I,** Univ Of Sc At Columbia, Columbia, SC; FR; BS; Air Frc ROTC 90-; NAACP 90-; Afrcn Amer Assc 90-; Alpha Lambda Delta; Gamma Beta Phi; Phi Eta Sigma; Alpha Kappa Alpha; Air Frc Assc 90-; Arnold Air Scty 90-; Hnrs Clg; Cmptr Sci; Law.

**GREEN, NILA J,** Alcorn St Univ, Lorman, MS; SO; BS; Biolgy; Nrsng.

**GREEN JR, NOLTON M,** Va St Univ, Petersburg, VA; JR; BA; Big Bro Big Sis 90-; Chess Club 88-; Math Club 88-; Deans List 89; Phi Beta Sigma; Res Asst Head 89-; Elect Engrng Club Pres 89; Pres List 90; Va Tech Grad Prog Intern; Elect Engrng.**

**GREEN, NORMAN J,** Christian Brothers Univ, Memphis, TN; GD; MBA; Alpha Chi 90-; Alpha Phi Omega 66-68; Data Prcssng; Acctg; Ed.

**GREEN, PAMELA S,** Volunteer St Comm Coll, Gallatin, TN; GD; AS; Amrcn Physcl Thrpy Assoc 90-; Clss Pres 90-; Cert Excllnc Awrd 90-; Physcl Thrpy.

**GREEN, PATRICIA D,** Univ Of The Dist Of Columbia, Washington, DC; SR; Delta Mu Delta; Dns Lst 86-90; Fac Awd Chevron Schlrshp 87-89; Magna Cum Laude; Cmmnctns Anlyst; BBA; Bus; Law MIS.

**GREEN, PHILIP H,** Univ Of Al At Birmingham, Birmingham, AL; JR; BA; Jzz Ensmble 90-; Dns Lst 90-; Pres Hnrs 90; Hzz Hrtge Fndtn Bnd 82-; US Army 87; Dpty Shrff Jffrsn Cnty Shrffs Offce 88-; Crmnl Jstce; Law Enfrcmnt.

**GREEN, RETINA CELESTE,** Denmark Tech Coll, Denmark, SC; SR; BS; Stdnt Govt Assoc Pres 90-; Phi Theta Kappa 90-; Alpha Delta Omega 90-; Esq Swthrt XIII 90-; Bsktbl Co Capt 89-90; Psych.

**GREEN, RICHARD KENNETH,** Oh St Univ At Marion, Marion, OH; SR; BS; Bus; CPA.

**GREEN, ROBERT J,** Passaic County Comm Coll, Paterson, NJ; SR; AAS; Natl Stdnt Nrs Assc 90-; Haledon First Aid Squad 87-; Paramedic 86-91; Cert Davenport Coll Ctr StdyEMS 85; ACLS Wayne Gen Hosp 89; Nrsng; Bsn.

**GREEN, SCOTT R,** Itawamba Comm Coll, Fulton, MS; FR; AAS; Frnch Clb VP 90-; Phi Theta Kappa 90-; Pres Lst 90; Deans Lst; Nrsg; Psych.

**GREEN, SHARON L,** Middle Tn St Univ, Murfreesboro, TN; JR; BA; Gamma Beta Phi 88-; Gnrl Sci; Scndry Tchr.

**GREEN, SHAWNA ALEXA,** Norfolk St Univ, Norfolk, VA; SO; BA; Intrnatl Stdnts Orgnztn Sec 90-; Alpha Epsilon Rho 90-; Stdnt Ambssdr 90-; Spartan Alpha Tau 89-; Mss Cmmnctns Brdcst Mgmt; Exec Prdcr.

**GREEN, SHERRI L,** West Liberty St Coll, West Liberty, WV; JR; BA; SADHA Treas 90-; Ski Club 87-88; Theta Xi Little Sis 87-88; Greenpeace 88-; Dental Hygiene.

**GREEN, SHIREEN A,** Fl A & M Univ, Tallahassee, FL; FR; Big Bro/Big Sis 90-; Gospel Choir 90; NABA 90; Phi Eta Sigma 90; Acctg; Corp Law.

**GREEN, STACEY A,** Univ Of Akron, Akron, OH; SR; BSN; Nrsng; RN.

**GREEN, SUSAN B,** Beckley Coll, Beckley, WV; JR; BED; Gamma Beta Phi; MADD 83; AS Beckley Clg 74; Educ; Tch.

**GREEN, SUSAN C,** Univ Of Al At Huntsville, Huntsville, AL; SR; BSE; IEEE 88-; SWE 88-; Rowing Clb Treas 87-90; Tau Beta Pi 89-; Eta Kappa Nu Treas 89-90; UAW Overall Schlr Athlete 89-90; Crew Schlr Athlete 87-90; Coop Stdnt 88-; Crew Tm 87-90; Elec Eng.

**GREEN, TAMMY I,** Roane St Comm Coll, Harriman, TN; SO; Elem Ed; Tchr.

**GREEN, TERESA N,** Savannah Coll Of Art & Design, Savannah, GA; SO; BFA; GSA Gold Awd 89-; Illustration; Childrens Books.

**GREEN, TERRANCE D,** Bloomfield Coll, Bloomfield, NJ; FR; Criminal Justice.

**GREEN, TIMOTHY D,** Univ Of Sc At Columbia, Columbia, SC; SO; BA; History; Ed.

**GREEN, TINA E,** Univ Of Southern Ms, Hattiesburg, MS; JR; BS; Speech Path/Audio.

**GREEN, TODD H,** Birmingham Southern Coll, Birmingham, AL; FR; BA; Std Almni Asc 90-; Adlt Lit Pgm 90-; Phi Eta Sigma 90-; Alpha Tau Omega Sgt/Arms 90-; Engl; Tchng.

**GREEN, TRACI ANN,** Colby Sawyer Coll, New London, NH; FR; BSN; Std Almni Asc 90-; Nrs.

**GREEN, VERNITA A,** Alcorn St Univ, Lorman, MS; FR; MBA; All Amer Schlr; Engl Educ.

**GREEN, WAYNE R,** Stillman Coll, Tuscaloosa, AL; SR; BA; Dn Lst 90-; Hnry Treas Alabama 88; Un Pres 86-90; Bus Admin; Human Rsrc Mgr.

**GREEN, WILSON F,** Birmingham Southern Coll, Birmingham, AL; SR; BA; Concert Choir Pres 88-90; Phi Beta Kappa; Mortar Bd 90-; Chem Rubber Co Freshmn Award 89; Amercn Bible Soc Award; Relgn; Law.

**GREENAWALT, DALE W,** Youngstown St Univ, Youngstown, OH; SR; BE; IEEE Pres 89-; Engrs Stdnt Soc Cncl 89-90; Order Engr; Elec Eng.

**GREENAWALT, JANIS G,** Mount Aloysius Jr Coll, Cresson, PA; FR; AS; Med Asstnt Clb; Phi Theta Kappa; PTA VP 87-; Demo Comm 90-; Csmtlgst 80-; Med Asstnt.

**GREENAWAY, ERICA L,** Ms St Univ, Miss State, MS; FR; BA; Concert Band; Campus Crusade; Musicianshp Awd; Clncl Psychlgst.

**GREENBERG, DENA M,** Franklin And Marshall Coll, Lancaster, PA; SR; Tennis; Squash; Tour Guide; Orientation Advsr; Phi Beta Kappa; Alpha Phi; Cum Laude; Carl Hartzell Prize; John Kershner Schlr 90-; Ronald Stewart Prize; Math French.

**GREENBERG, GARY M,** Univ Of North Fl, Jacksonville, FL; JR; BA; SGA Advocate Comm; Pol Sci Soc 90-; Literacy Tutor 88-89; Amer Plng Assoc; Pol Sci/Publ Adm; MA Ph D Urban/Reg Plng.

**GREENBERG, LEON M,** Ny Law School, New York, NY; JR; JD; Stdnt Bar Assoc Senator 89-90; NY Law Sch Jrnl Intl/Comparitive Law 89; Deans Merit Schlrshp 88-; Law Clerk Tantleff Cohen PC; BS Empire State Coll 89; Law/Labor Studies.

**GREENBERG, SUSAN B,** Columbus Coll Of Art & Design, Columbus, OH; FR; Pntngs Stdnt Exhbtn.

**GREENBLATT, PERRI L,** S U N Y Coll Of Tech At Frmgdl, Farmingdale, NY; SO; AA; Tenns 90; Sclgy; Cnslng.

**GREENE, ALICE S,** Roane St Comm Coll, Harriman, TN; SO; BS; Acctng; CPA.

**GREENE, ANGELA M,** Fl International Univ, Miami, FL; JR; BA; Phi Kappa Phi; AA Broward Comm Coll 90; Psychlgy/Crmnl Jstc; Forensic Psychlgy.

**GREENE, ANSELIA S,** Newbury Coll, Brookline, MA; SR; Deans Lst; Intern Sharon Hosp; Intern Jewish Meml Hosp; Intern Downton Phys Therapy; Assoc Newbury Coll; CPR/1ST Aide Cert Red Cross; Phys Therapist Asst.

**GREENE, ARLICIA L,** Johnson C Smith Univ, Charlotte, NC; SO; BA; Fndrsng 90-; Cmmnctn Arts; TV Brdcstg.

**GREENE, ASHLEY Y,** Roane St Comm Coll, Harriman, TN; FR; BA; Vrsty Bsbl 90-; Sci; Physcn Asst.

**GREENE, BRENDA S,** Univ Of Cincinnati-Clrmnt Coll, Batavia, OH; SO; ECE; Dns Lst 90-; Pierce Elem Prnt Tchr Org Vol Coord Sec 89-; New Rchmnd Schl Dist Input Com; 1st Bptst Chrch Nw Rchmnd Asst Sec/Libr 73; Sndy Schl Tchr 73-; Eng/Chldrns Lit; Tchr Elem Educ.

**GREENE, BRIAN,** Brescia Coll, Owensboro, KY; SO; BA; Math Clb SGA Rep Intrclb Rep 90-; Ambssdr 90-; Hon Pgm 89-; Alpha Chi 90-; Deans Lst; All-Amer Schlr; Engl; Prfssr.

**GREENE, BRIAN J,** Dowling Coll, Oakdale Li, NY; SR; BA; Aero Clb 88; STAR 89; Chorus 87-; Aerontcs; Avation.

**GREENE, CAROL B,** Memphis St Univ, Memphis, TN; FR; BSN; Nrsng.

**GREENE, CHRISTINA L,** Marshall University, Huntington, WV; SR; Amer Mtkng Assoc 90-F Gamma Beta Phi 89; Delta Zeta 89; Mktng Intshp 90; Deans List 87-90; March Of Dimes Vltr 89-; Mktng; Sales/Mkt Research.

**GREENE, CHRISTOPHER M,** Univ Of Miami, Coral Gables, FL; SR; BARCH; Am Inst Archtctrl Stdnts 86-87; Sigma Phi Epsilon Asst Pledge Edctr 87-; Natl Clgt Archtctr/Dsgn Awd 90; Pres Hons 90; IM Rcqtbl; Archtctr.**

**GREENE, CRYSTAL AILENE,** Western Piedmont Comm Coll, Morganton, NC; SO; BA; Prlgl Assoc 90-; Prlgl Tchnlgy.

**GREENE, CYNTHIA A,** Christopher Newport Coll, Newport News, VA; JR; BS; Alpha Chi 90-; Hond Excell Schlrshp 90-; Deans Lst 88-; Sftbl MVP Capt 88-; Bio; Vet Med.

**GREENE, DANIEL J,** Marshall University, Huntington, WV; SO; BA; RHA Treas 89-; Dsbld Org 89-; Rcyclng Prog 89-; Acctg; CPA.

**GREENE, DARNANNE H,** Mobile Coll, Mobile, AL; JR; BSN; MCANS 90-; Nrsng.

**GREENE, DAWN W,** Montgomery Comm Coll, Troy, NC; SR; AD; SGA Rep 90-; Vol March Dms; Chld Care Cntr Ownr/Oprtr; AS; Erly Chldhd Educ; Chld Cr Cntr Ownr.

**GREENE, DEBORAH LYNN,** Emory Univ, Atlanta, GA; SR; BBA; Stdnt Progrmng Cncl Films Comm VP 89-; Beta Gamma Sigma; Delta Gamma 89-; Deans List; BBA.

**GREENE, DELORES J,** Kent St Univ Kent Cmps, Kent, OH; JR; BA; Gldn Key Tres; Kappa Omicron Nu; Alpha Kappa Mu; Mary Mcleod Bethune Awrd; Blck Unt Stu Awrd; Mntrg Mthrs Pro; Fmly/Indvdl Stdy; Scl Wrk.

**GREENE, EILEEN L,** Savannah Coll Of Art & Design, Savannah, GA; GD; MFA; Hortcltrst Asst 88; Fine Arts Dplm; Pnnslvn Acdmy Fine Arts 80; Pntng; Tchr.

**GREENE, ELIZABETH S,** Univ Of Miami, Coral Gables, FL; JR; BA; Psi Chi; Wm Dstrs; Rsrch Asst 90-; AA Broward Comm Clg 90; Psychlgy/Crim Jstc; Crim Psychlgst.

**GREENE, ERIC B,** Claflin Coll, Orangeburg, SC; FR; BA; Cncrt Chr Bssldr 90-; Stdtn Govt Assoc Rep 90-; Deans Lst Awrd 90-; Music Ed.

**GREENE, ERICA N,** Christopher Newport Coll, Newport News, VA; JR; BA; Deans List 90; Alpha Kappa Alpha Pres; Acctg.

**GREENE, GLORIA K,** Norfolk St Univ, Norfolk, VA; SO; BA; Army ROTC Rangr Cadt Stf Sgt 90-; Spartn Alpha Tau; Hlth; Nrsng.

**GREENE, GREG D,** S U N Y Coll Of Tech At Delhi, Delhi, NY; FR; Phi Theta Kappa 90; Ntl Eagle Scout Assoc 89; Ordr Of Arrow 86; BSA Assist Scout Mstr 82.

**GREENE, JAMES C,** Univ Of Tn At Martin, Martin, TN; JR; BS; Chrch Christ Stdnt Cntr; Wldlf Soc; Phi Theta Kappa 90-; IM Sftbl/Bsktbl; AS Jackson State Comm Coll; Wldlf Blgy; TN Wldlf Rsrcs Agncy.

**GREENE, JAMES R,** Mountain Empire Comm Coll, Big Stone Gap, VA; SO; AS; Envrnmntl Science Clb Pres 90-; Hazardous Waste Disposal Trngn; Plnng/Zoning Cmmt Chrmn 89; Cert 90; Science; Rep Cmmrcl Grnhouse Grower.

**GREENE, JAMIE J,** Univ Of Akron, Akron, OH; JR; BA; Goldn Key; Acctg.

**GREENE, JOHN E,** City Univ Of Ny La Guard Coll, Long Island Cty, NY; SO; AAS; Phi Theta Kappa 90-; Cmptr Prgrmng; Cpmtr Info Sys.

**GREENE, KAREN D,** Al A & M Univ, Normal, AL; JR; BSED; Elem/Early Chldhd Clb Sec/Treas 90-; Kappa Delta Pi; Acdmc Hon Roll 89-90; Pres Cup 90; BA Mt St Vincent Univ Nova Scotia 85; Early Chldhd Ed; Tch.**

**GREENE, KATHRYN,** Savannah Coll Of Art & Design, Savannah, GA; SO; Intereior Design.

**GREENE, KATHY T,** Univ Of Sc At Columbia, Columbia, SC; SR; BA; SGA Rep 89; Afro Amer Assc 87-89; Piedmont Scty 88-; Kappa Delta Pi 90-; Ldrshp Dvlpmnt Intern Salvation Army Latchkey Pgm 89-90; Elem Education; Teach.

**GREENE, KELLI K,** Indiana Univ Of Pa, Indiana, PA; SR; BED; Assn Fr Chldhd Educ Intrnatl Chrmn Fndrsng; PA St Educ Assn; Natl Sci Tchrs Assn; Phi Delta Kappa; Fr Ftd Frnds; Sndy Schl Tchng Asst; Nmntd Fr Wmns Ldrshp Awrd; Dns Lst; Sld Tckts At Ftbl Gms Bsktbl Gms; Educ; Tchng.

**GREENE, KIMBERLY M,** Shaw Univ, Raleigh, NC; SO; BA; Gospel Choir; Chorale Soc; Bus; Mktg.**

**GREENE, LAMAR DAVID,** Saint Pauls Coll, Lawrenceville, VA; SR; Natl Beta Bus Clb VP; Kappa Alpha Psi Polemarch; Keystone Clb Boys/Girls Clb Pres 87; Srvc Awd Safeway 87; Boy Of Yr Jellett Boys Clb; Paying/Rcvng Teller Riggs Bsnk; Bus Admin; MBA.

**GREENE, LYDA LIZ,** Univ Of Sc At Coastal Carolina, Conway, SC; SR; BS; Athnm Yrbk 90-; Phi Sigma Tau; Omicron Delta Kappa; Elctns Comm SGA 90-; Stu Govt Assoc 90-; Lcky Serv Awrd Fnlst 90-; Cnstutnl Rvsn Comm; Prof Yr Comm 90-; Campus Jdcl Brd Altrnt; Bk Exchng Comm SGA 90-; Psychlgy; Law.

**GREENE II, LYNDOL G,** Middle Tn St Univ, Murfreesboro, TN; FR; BS; Gamma Beta Phi; Rcdrng Indstry Mgmt.

**GREENE, MARSHA J,** Slippery Rock Univ, Slippery Rock, PA; JR; BS; Roclette Mrchng Rckts; Kineseotherapy Clb; Lambda Sigma; Phi Eta Sigma; Phi Epsilon Kappa; Deans Lst; Maree Mckay Schlrshp; Top Ten Major; Kinescothereapy; Phy Thrpy.

**GREENE, MELISSA M,** Longwood Coll, Farmville, VA; FR; BA; Rugby Ftbl Club; English; Elem Ed.

**GREENE, PAMELA E,** Winthrop Coll, Rock Hill, SC; SO; BS; Schl Of Bus Clb 89-; L Wckr Hll Cncl Rep 90; Dnce Thtr 90; Alpha Kappa Psi 90-; Dns Lst; Acctng.

**GREENE, ROBIN J,** Schenectady County Comm Coll, Schenectady, NY; FR; BS; Speclst Govt Acctg; Bus Admn; Corp Fin.

**GREENE, SHAUN Y,** Ky St Univ, Frankfort, KY; SO; BA; Lady Diamond Clb; Marching/Symph Bnd; Theatre Drama; Deans Lst Natl Hon Soc; Pres Schlr; Forensics Fest; 1st Pl Solo & Ens Bnd Fest; Pres Schlrshp; Highest GPA; St Univ Bnd; Engl Educ; Law.

**GREENE, SHERRI D,** Roane St Comm Coll, Harriman, TN; SO; AAS; Audubon Soc; Ofice Admnstrn; Word Processing.

**GREENE, SONJA A,** Johnson C Smith Univ, Charlotte, NC; SO; BS; NAACP 89-; Alpha Llamda Delta; Prjct Vote 90-; Delta Sigma Theta Fnr Wmnhd 88-89; JCSU Schlrshp Recpnt 90-; Acctg; CPA.

**GREENE, SYLVIA I,** Union Univ, Jackson, TN; SO; BS; Bapt Stdnt Un; Blck Chrstn Fllwshp; Elem Educ; Educ Law.

**GREENE, TAMIA D,** Duquesne Univ, Pittsburgh, PA; FR; BSED; Vldctrn Rcrtmnt Grp; Phi Eta Sigma; Chnclr Awrd; Educ; Tchr.

**GREENE, TRULAINE,** Tougaloo Coll, Tougaloo, MS; FR; BS; Pre Med Clb; Stdnt Spprt Svcs; Hgh Hnr Rl; Bio/Pre Med; Pedtrc Dr.

**GREENE, VALERIE M,** Univ Of Fl, Gainesville, FL; SR; BS; First Steps Fellowship Mbr 90-; Stdnt Assoc Physician Asstnts Mbr 89-; Fla Academy Physician Asstnts 89-; Amer Acdmy Phy Asstnts 89-; Medl Technologist 80-89; BS 80; Physician Assistant.

**GREENE, YOLANDA M,** Coppin St Coll, Baltimore, MD; JR; Psychlgy Clb 90-; Psychlgy.

**GREENE-HOFFMANN, SUSAN E,** Nova Univ, Ft Lauderdale, FL; GD; MBA; AA Broward Comm Coll 83; BA FLA Atlantic Univ 86; Bus; Mkgt.

**GREENER, THOMAS M,** Duquesne Univ, Pittsburgh, PA; GD; PHD; Methodist Youth Flwshp Pres 79-; Alpha Tau Omega Social Chrmn 83-86; Eta Sigma Phi 84-86; Cong Michael De Wine Intern 83; Sen Howard Baker Intern 83; Warren Dee Awd Chch Hstry 90; BA Vanderbilt Univ 86; M Div Garrett-Evngl Theo Sem; Formative Spirituality.

**GREENFIELD, COREY B,** Bradford Coll, Bradford, MA; FR; BA; Stdnt Senate 90; Radio Clb 90; Stdnt Actvts 90; Business.

**GREENFIELD, KIMBERLY R,** Univ Of Ky, Lexington, KY; SR; BS; Pi Sigma Alpha 89-; Golden Key 90-; Rsrch Asst For Dean Of Clg Of Arts/Sci 90-; Pol Sci/Hist; Law.

**GREENHALGE, ELAINE M,** Oh St Univ, Columbus, OH; GD; Phi Kappa Phi; Golden Key; Summa Awd 88; Excllnc Schlrshp Awd 90; Franklin Cty Wmns Golf Chmpn 73-86; BA OH State Univ 90; Psychlgy; Law/Psychlgy.

**GREENHAM, MARTHA R,** Bowling Green St Univ At Huron, Huron, OH; SR; AS; Phi Kappa Phi; Beta Beta Beta 70-73; Alpha Gamma Delta 70-73; Amer Assn Univ Wmn Mbrshp VP 85-; BS 73; Hlth Info Tech; Med Rcrds.

**GREENIDGE, DIANA S,** Suffolk Comm Coll Eastern Cmps, Riverhead, NY; JR; AS; Lib Arts; Psych.

**GREENLAND, DAVID W,** Univ Of Al At Birmingham, Birmingham, AL; GD; MED; Sigma Chi; Dean Lst; Pres Lst; BA; Elem Educ; PHD In ECE.

**GREENMAN, JULIE E,** Manhattan School Of Music, New York, NY; SO.

**GREENO JR, RICHARD L,** East Tn St Univ, Johnson City, TN; GD; MD; Phi Roho Sigma VP 88; Amer Clg Of Emer Physcns; Amer Acad Of Fmly Physcns 88; BS UC Davis 80; BSH Duke U 85; Med; Emer Med.**

**GREENSPAN, LEAH RUTH,** Fl International Univ, Miami, FL; JR; Dietetics Assn 90-; Class Govt 90-; Phi Kappa Phi; Tau Epsilon Phi 86-87; AA Miami Dade Comm Clg 89; Hlt/Nutrition/Dietetics; MSW.

**GREENSPAN, MELANIE B,** Hudson Valley Comm Coll, Troy, NY; CPA; BA St Univ NY Albany 84; Acctg.

**GREENSTEIN, JOETTE E,** Oh Univ, Athens, OH; GD; D O; Stdnt Osteopathic Med Assn V P 89-90; Undrgrdte Amer Acad Osteopathy 89-; Sports Med Club; Sigma Sigma Phi 90-; Delta Delta Delta Schlrshp Chrmn 87-; IM Vlybl; BS Ohio State Univ 88; Osteopathy; Physician.

**GREENUP, LYNN G,** Fayetteville St Univ, Fayetteville, NC; SR; BS; Non-Trad Soc 88-; Kappa Delti Pi 87-; Deans Awrd; Tutoring Achvmnt; Early Educ.

**GREENWAY, LORI J,** Coll Of Charleston, Charleston, SC; FR; BSN; Nrsg.

**GREENWAY, SCHOND L,** Fl A & M Univ, Tallahassee, FL; FR; BS; Comp Sci; Arfrc Offcr Govt Emply.

**GREENWOOD, KIMBERLY A,** Radford Univ, Radford, VA; SR; Tour Guides Radford Univ Co Coord 90-; Pblc Rltns Clb; SGA Chrmn 90; Quest Asstnt RV Stdnt Orntn 89; News Wrtr Univ Paper; Consultant Intern Delia Horwitz; BA; Communications; Bus Cnsltnt.

**GREENY, DEANNE B,** Mercer County Comm Coll, Trenton, NJ; FR; AAS; Lab Tech; Biolgcl/Chem Tech.

**GREER, DAYLAN K,** Va St Univ, Petersburg, VA; JR; BA; Bg Bro Bd Sistr Org 90-; Vir St Gospl Chr 88-; Conn Pre Alum 89; Hstry; Mnstry.

**GREER, DEANNA L,** Cornell Univ Statutory College, Ithaca, NY; SO; BS; IM Soccer/Sftbl 89-; Pre-Vet Clb 89-; Cornell Coll 4-H Pres 89-; Cornell Tradition 89-; Cornell Tradition Spcl Evnt Com 89-; Orntn Cnslr 90-; Cornell Coll 4-H Pres 89-; Thompkins Co Coop Ext GIAC 90-; Cornell Red Carpet 89-; Anmnl Sci; Vet.

**GREER, DELLA S,** Le Moyne Coll, Syracuse, NY; FR; BA; Stdnt Govt Mltcltrl Rep 90-; POWER 90-; Inrds Upstat NY 90-; Acctg.

**GREER JR, DORSEY E,** Tri County Tech Coll, Pendleton, SC; FR; AS; Intrntnl Mngmnt Cncl; Alice Manfctrng Supvsr; Txtl Techlgy.

**GREER, ERICK R,** Univ Of Nc At Charlotte, Charlotte, NC; GD; Pol Sci.

**GREER, GAYLE D,** Southern Coll Of Tech, Marietta, GA; SO; CPET; Fulton Co Sheriffs Dept/Reserve Sgt; Owner Gayles Groom Shop 79-89; Comp Engrng; Engrng/Electrical/Comp.

**GREER JR, JAMES N,** Univ Of Al At Birmingham, Birmingham, AL; SO; BS; AS Jefferson State Comm Coll; Alld Hlth; Rsprtry Thrpy.

**GREER, KENDALL L,** Tri County Tech Coll, Pendleton, SC; FR; BS; US Navy 1st Cls Petty Ofcr; Gas Turbine Elec Tech; Alpha Zeta Beta; GII Solutions Elctrncs Consultant/Troubleshooter; Engr; Elctrnc Circuit Design.

**GREER, LISA M,** Auburn Univ At Auburn, Auburn, AL; FR; BA; SGA Bld Dr Comm 90-; Mktg; Law.

**GREER JR, MURPHY R,** Tougaloo Coll, Tougaloo, MS; SO; BS; Pre Hlth 89-; Stdnt Govt 89-; Young Democrats 89-90; Day Stdnt Union 89-; Stdnt Spprt Serv 89-; Hmn Rghts/Coalition; Bowling; Biol, Med.

**GREER, NANCY K,** King Coll, Bristol, TN; SO; BS; Hlth Sci Clb; Stdnt Ambsdr 90-; Gen Chem Lab Asst 90-; Biology/Pre Med; Med/Surgery.

**GREER, RICHARD J,** Univ Of Ky, Lexington, KY; FR; BA; Mrching Bnd 90; Pep Bnd 90-; Alpha Lambda Delta; Kappa Kappa Psi 90-; IMS 90-; Pol Sci; Law.

**GREER, TA-TANISHA,** Lasell Coll, Newton, MA; FR; Acctng; Bus.

**GREER, THERESA D,** Univ Of Sc At Columbia, Columbia, SC; FR; BS; Concert Choir; Bus Admn.

**GREER, WENDY M,** Radford Univ, Radford, VA; SO; BA; Prfssnl Mscn Ply Bss Gtr And Sng In Bnd 82-; Comp Oprtr Frst Natl Bnk 90; Art Grphc Dsgn; Cmmrcl Artst.

**GREEVY, NICOLE L,** Ny Univ, New York, NY; FR; BFA; Drama/Actng; Theatr.

**GREGER, RICHARD J,** Atlantic Comm Coll, Mays Landing, NJ; FR; BA; Deans Lst 90-; Coach Tnshp Soccer Tm 88-90; Capenters Apprntc 87-90; Educ; Ele Educ.

**GREGG, DAWN M,** Saint Francis Coll, Loretto, PA; FR; BS; Red Key Club 90-; Cinema Showcase 90-; Pre-Law Club 90-; Theta Phi Alpha; Indoor/Outdoor Track & Field 90-; Acctng; Corp Law.

**GREGG, KARRI S,** Clarkson Univ, Potsdam, NY; JR; Amer Mktg Assn 90-; Fin Cmtee 90; Safety Escort Serv 89-90; Mktg; Advtsng/Retail Rsrch.

**GREGG, STEPHANIE M,** Northern Ky Univ, Highland Hts, KY; SO; BA; Commctns; Radio TV Flm.

**GREGG, WILLARD B,** Ms St Univ, Miss State, MS; SR; Frstry Clb VP 90-; Rfrmd Univ Fllwshp; Frst Rsrcs Dns Cncl SG Pres 90-; Blue Ky; Phi Kappa Phi; Xi Sigma Pi Assc Frstr 90-; Alpha Zeta; Kappa Alpha Ordr Asst Pldge Educ Offcr 90; Alpine Cmp Cnslr 90; Pres Schlr; Frst Mgmt; Envrnmntl Plcy Law.

**GREGGAINS, TAMRICA A,** Le Moyne Coll, Syracuse, NY; FR; Dwnhll Ski Clb 90-; IM Bsktbll 90-; Blgy Chmstry; Mdcl.

**GREGGS, KEVIN O,** Univ Of The Dist Of Columbia, Washington, DC; SR; BA; Sgn Of The Times Cultural Wrkshp/Gallery Vol 83-; Montgomery Clg Cable Access Chnl Intrnshp 88; Bell Atlantic Corp TV Intrnshp 88; AA Montgomery Clg 89; Cmnctns/TV; Film Prodcng.

**GREGOIRE, JANE F,** Hilbert Coll, Hamburg, NY; SR; AAS; AS Erie Cmuty Clg 85; BS 88; Legal Asst; Law.

**GREGOR, CHARLENE E,** Saint Josephs Coll, Windham, ME; FR; BA; Sprkds Phtgrphr; Pre Law Soc; Hll Cncl Pres; Stdnt Govt; Intrhl Cncl Treas; Hstry; Law.

**GREGORI, DINA J,** Widener Univ, Chester, PA; BA; Soc Advncmnt Mgt 90-; Mrktng/Mgt; MBA Mrktng.

**GREGORI, JEANLUCIE R,** Kent St Univ Kent Cmps, Kent, OH; JR; BBA; Natl Asc Acctnts 90-; Acctng Asc Chrp 89-; Stopher Hl Hse Cncl Treas 88-90; VITA; Natl Hnry Res Hl Serv Awd Treas 90; IRS Cert Apprctn; Acctng; CPA.

**GREGORIOU, CHRISTOS,** Long Island Univ C W Post Cntr, Greenvale, NY; SR; BFA; Hellenic Soc 90-; Intrnshp KODA Advtsng 90; HD Fredrk Plytchnc Univ Cyprus 89; Graphic Dsgn; Cmptr Graphics.

**GREGORY, BRENDA S,** Wv Univ, Morgantown, WV; SR; BSSW; Undrgrad Soc Wrk Stdnt Org 89-90; Natl Assoc Of Soc Wrkrs 90-; Soc Wrk.

**GREGORY, CHARLESTON,** Wilberforce Univ, Wilberforce, OH; FR; Blckml Cltn 90-; Pltcl Sci; Crprt Attrny.

**GREGORY, CHARLOTTE A,** Jackson St Univ, Jackson, MS; FR; BA; Pltcl Sci; Law.

**GREGORY, CYNTHIA L,** Northern Ky Univ, Highland Hts, KY; FR; PHD; Engl.

**GREGORY, DEANA M,** Christopher Newport Coll, Newport News, VA; JR; Sftbl; Mary Immaculate Hosp; Hidenwood Elem Schl; Psychlgy; Child Care.

**GREGORY, DENNIS F,** Oh Univ-Southern Cmps, Ironton, OH; SR; MS; Pres Lst 90; Perennial Deans St Crclevlle Bible Clg 84-87; Sigma Phi Sigma; Cert For Outstndng Acad Achievemnt Awd; Hnry Chpln At Miss State Lgsltre 88; BA 87; AAS 88; Kiwanis; Pstr 90; Grad Vldctrn 87; Morton Dorsey Expstry Sermon Awd; Cmmnctns; Pblc Rltns.

**GREGORY, GRETTA G,** Wv Univ At Parkersburg, Parkersburg, WV; JR; BED; Elem Educ; Tchr/Day Cr.

**GREGORY, JENNIFER N,** Clayton St Coll, Morrow, GA; SO; BBA; Acctg.

**GREGORY, KAREN R,** Pa St Univ Delaware Cty Cmps, Media, PA; SO; BS; H Leonard Krouse Schlrshp Acad Excell; Acctg.

**GREGORY, KAREN Y,** Inter Amer Univ Pr San German, San German, PR; SR; BS; Clb Robrac 88-; Blgy Clb 89-; Tri Beta Beta 90-; Eta Gamma Delta Sec 89-; Noche De Lugroi 90; Microblgy; Ma.

**GREGORY, KAUHNYA M,** Miami Jacobs Jr Coll Of Bus, Dayton, OH; FR; Medcl Ofc Asst; Wrk In Hosp.

**GREGORY, KEITH R,** Wagner Coll, Staten Island, NY; SR; MA; BA; Medieval History; Tch.

**GREGORY, LESA A,** Middle Tn St Univ, Murfreesboro, TN; SR; Dns Lst 87 90; BBA 90; Bsn Adm; Hmn Res Mgmt.

**GREGORY, MARK F,** Univ Of Louisville, Louisville, KY; SR; BS; Pgrmr Systms Dvlpmnt Intrnshp Humama Inc 90-; S E Chrstn Chrch; AS Jefferson Cmnty Clge 87; Cmptr Sci; Prgmr/Anlyst.

**GREGORY, MARTHA KAREN,** Univ Of Sc At Spartanburg, Spartanburg, SC; GD; ADN; Gamma Beta Phi 89-; Nrsng; RN.

**GREGORY, MELISSA E,** Middle Tn St Univ, Murfreesboro, TN; JR; BBA; Bookkeeper 87-; Acctg; CPA.

**GREGORY, MICHAEL RAY,** Middle Tn St Univ, Murfreesboro, TN; SR; BS; Intern Vanderblit Univ Med Ctr; Mid TN Region Amer Hrt Assc Co Chrmn 89-90; Brentwood Pks Rec Dept; Hlth Edu CPR Instr; AS St Tech Inst Memphis 80; Hlth Educ/Rec Thrpy; Rcrtn MS.

**GREGORY, PAMELA K,** Muskingum Coll, New Concord, OH; FR; Elem Ed; Tchr.

**GREGORY, TIMOTHY E,** Liberty Univ, Lynchburg, VA; SO; BA; Stdnt Sen Dorm Sen 90-; IM Sprts Sccr/Vlybl Plyr 89-F; Hist.

**GREIF, SANDRA NICOLE,** Georgian Court Coll, Lakewood, NJ; SO; BSW; Stdnt Ambsdr 90-; Soc Wrkrs Clb 89-; Court Page 90-; 90 Cnvoctn; Adad Schlrshp 89-; Soc Wrk; Alcohol Drg Coun.

**GREINER, BRETT R,** Univ Of Miami, Coral Gables, FL; SR; JDMBA; Bacchus Alchl Awrnss Pgm; Intrnshp Pgm 90-; Alum Mentr Pgm 90-; Alpha Kappa Psi 90-; Lambda Chi Alpha Soc Chrmn 87-; Spec Olympcs; Dns Lst 89-; Prvsts Hnr Rll 90-; Pres Hnr Rl 90-; BBA; Finc; Law.

**GREINER, LISA R,** Comm Coll Algny Co Algny Cmps, Pittsburgh, PA; FR; BSN; Data Entry Clrk/Bllng Clrk 81-; Assoc Art Inst 83; Nrsng.

**GREINER, NANCY A,** City Univ Of Ny Queensbrough, New York, NY; FR; BA; Evening Stdnts Humanites Clb VP; QCC Deans Lst 90-; Alpha Beta Gamma; Sec Sci Betty Owens Bus Sch 80; Bus; Cmptr Field.

**GREMMELS, ELIZABETH A,** Livingston Univ, Livingston, AL; JR; BS; Hstry Clb Sec 88-89; Frnds Lbry; Educ/Scl Sci; Tchng.

**GRENGBONDAI, JULES C,** Central St Univ, Wilberforce, OH; JR; BS; Schlrshp Stdnt Rsrch 90; Cmptr Sci/Math; Eng.

**GRENIER, SUSAN E,** Radford Univ, Radford, VA; JR; Hons Pgm; Acctg Soc VP 90-; Alpha Sigma Tau Chpln 89-; VITA; Rsng Sr Schlrshp Coll Bus/Econ; Schlrshp Awd; Acctg.

**GRENNAN, MICHELLE,** Portland School Of Art, Portland, ME; FR; BFA; Fdtn Pgm/Jewelrymaking; Jeweler.

**GRENNELL, RENZA F,** Alcorn St Univ, Lorman, MS; JR; BS; Agrnmy.

**GRESCHKE, JASON S,** Va Commonwealth Univ, Richmond, VA; FR; BS; Phi Eta Sigma; Math/Educ.

**GRESENS, KAREN M,** S U N Y Coll At Fredonia, Fredonia, NY; SO; BS; WCA Hm Vol 90; Intrn At Harris Moran Seed Co 90; Vllybl 90; Med Tchnlgy/Art; Med Illstrtn.

**GRESHA, MARILYN F,** Coastal Carolina Comm Coll, Jacksonville, NC; SO; BS/BA; Cert Hardbarger Bus Coll 74; AAS/AA; Bus Comp Pgmg; Scl Wrkr.

**GRESHAM, CYNTHIA M,** Johnson C Smith Univ, Charlotte, NC; SO; BS; Sci Clb Prlmntrn 89-90; R W Johnson Sprtl Choir Qn 90-; MBRS 89-90; MSAC 90-; Blgy/Pre-Med; Medcl Dctr.

**GRESHAM, ERIC D,** Fl International Univ, Miami, FL; FR; BS; Stdnt Chptr IEEE 90-; Electrncs Techncn In US Army 84-90; Elec Engrng.

**GRESHAM, MARIAN J,** Oh Dominican Coll, Columbus, OH; SO; BA; Rgstrd Nrse/State OH AASN Kent State Univ Ashtabula Campus 79; Cross/Dscplnary Cmmnctns Grntlgy; Hltcare Law.

**GRESIK, CAROLYN R,** Saint Francis Coll, Loretto, PA; SO; MMSC; Physician Assist Stdnt Soc Sec 90; Vol For Ntl Aids Quilt; Hnrs Prog; A Big Sis For Frshmn Hnrs Stdnt; Vol For The Plus-1 Prog At Our Dorothy Day Ctr; Physician Assist.

**GRESKO, JEANENE M,** Saint Francis Coll, Loretto, PA; JR; BA; Stdnt Actvties Org/Prnts Wknd Comm 88-; Educ Clb 90-; Grad Preprtn Stf 88-; Almni Wknd Stf 90; Frgn Lnguage Fstvl Jdg; IMS 88-; Engl/Sec Educ; Sec Educ/Pblsh.

**GRESKO, RAYMOND D,** Temple Univ, Philadelphia, PA; SR; BS; Phi Beta Kappa 87-89; Cmptr Sci; Sys Prog.

**GRESS II, WILLIAM J,** Capital Univ, Columbus, OH; JR; BA; Sigma Theta Tau; Nrsng; Nrsng Anesthesiology.

**GRESSER, VICTOR S,** Goucher Coll, Towson, MD; JR; BA; AIDS Awrnswk Exec Coord 90-; Theatre 89-; State Arts Cncl Intern Visual Arts Dir 90; Art/Theatre; Visual/Theatre Arts.

**GRESSETT, ANDRIA L,** Ms St Univ, Miss State, MS; FR; BA; Unvrsty Hnrs Cncl Sec 90-; 1st Bptst Chrch Unvrsty Sngrs 90-; Hall Cncl VP; Gamma Beta Phi; Alpha Lambda Delta; Phi Eta Sigma; Prsdnt Schlr 90-; Otstndng Hnrs Soph; Bsns.

**GRETCHEN, JANINE M,** West Liberty St Coll, West Liberty, WV; SR; BS; Delta Mu Delta; Delta Sigm Api Treas 90-; Bus Admn.

**GRETO, KRISTEN S,** Castleton St Coll, Castleton, VT; JR; BA; SEA 90-; Dean Lst 90; Vrsty Sccr 88-; IM Vllybll Sccr Hcky Sftbl 88-; Educ Erly Chldhd; Elem Tchr.

**GREULICH, THOMAS G,** Southern Coll Of Tech, Marietta, GA; FR; BS; U S Air Force 83-90; Instrctr Airborn Cmptr Dsply Main Tech; Physics; Eng.

**GREUTMAN, TIMOTHY A,** Defiance Coll, Defiance, OH; FR; BA; Mfg Eng 86-; Dns Lst 90-; Mfg Tech 87-; Sr Proc Eng Cooper Power Tools 82-; Bus Mngmnt.

**GREVE, MARK J,** Oh St Univ Lima Campus, Lima, OH; FR; BS; Ohio Natl Guard Nuclear Bio Chem Non Cmsnl Ofcr Chrg 89-; Intrnshp Study Physics Moscow Inst Physics 90; Astronomy Physics; Astrophysicist.

**GREWELL, GAIL E,** Kent St Univ Kent Cmps, Kent, OH; SO; BA; Stdnt Senate Stark Campus 90-; Global Affairs Clb Pres 89-90; Natl Pol Sci; Intrnshp City Canton OH Ofc Mayor Sam Persus; Paralegal Cert Am Inst Paralegal Studies 88; Pol Sci; Law.

**GRGAS, ROBERT,** City Univ Of Ny Baruch Coll, New York, NY; SO; BBA; Acctg.

**GRIBBIN, DOROTHY,** Muhlenberg Coll, Allentown, PA; SO; BA; Exec Cncl; Dance Clb Treas 90-; Engl Hon Soc; Dana Assoc 90-; Engl.**

**GRIBBON, ELIZABETH JANE,** Nova Univ, Ft Lauderdale, FL; GD; MPA; Frat Order Of Police Treas 80-; Police Benvlnt Assoc 82-; Police Offcr 80-; BA U Of Fla 77; Fla LEO Cert Broward Cnty Police Acad 80; Pub Admin; Law.

**GRICE, DAVID D,** S U N Y Coll Of Tech At Alfred, Alfred, NY; SO; AAS; Agrnmy Clb Treas 88-; Ag Ldrs Clb 89; Hosp Date Entry Oper 89-; Agrnmy; Agrnmst Cnsrvtnst.

**GRICE, DEWEY W,** Fl A & M Univ, Tallahassee, FL; SR; AA Chipola Jr Coll 89; Crmnl Jste; Lwyr.

**GRICE, MELISSA N,** William Carey Coll, Hattiesburg, MS; SR; BS; Alpha Psi Omega Sec 87-88; Elem Ed; Tch.

**GRICE, NELL H,** William Carey Coll, Hattiesburg, MS; SR; BA; Adlt Bible Stdy Tchr 58-; Elem Ed.

**GRICE, ROBERT D,** Old Dominion Univ, Norfolk, VA; FR; BSCE; Envrnmntl Cvl Eng; Eng.

**GRICKIS, KARIN L,** Teikyo Post Univ, Waterbury, CT; FR; BA; Fshn Mrchndsng; Fshn Dsgn.

**GRIDER, DONALD L,** Morehouse Coll, Atlanta, GA; JR; BS; Bnd 88-89; Stdnt Mnrty Acss Resrch Trnng; Crss Cntry/Trck 89-; Biology; Dntstry.**

**GRIEB, MARGIT,** Daytona Beach Comm Coll, Daytona Beach, FL; SO; BED; Lrng Supprt Cntr Tutr/Engl/Algbra/Frnch/Grmn 89-; Phi Theta Kappa Rpvsnl Membr 89-; Forgn Language; Educ.

**GRIER, MITZI A,** Commonwealth Coll, Virginia Beach, VA; GD; Clgte Secr Intl 90-; Secr Clb Treas 90-; Stdnt Govt Assoc Secr 90-; AAS; Bsn; Ofc Adm.**

**GRIER, TIMOTHY P,** Univ Of Scranton, Scranton, PA; SR; Boys Scouts Of Amer Asst Ascout Master; Omicron Delta Epsilon V Pres 90-; Delta Mu Delta; Pi Gamma Mu; GPPAW Memorial Schlrshp; Butler/Mc Crane Schlrshp; BS; Finance.

**GRIESCHE, DAVID W,** Unity Coll, Unity, ME; FR; BS; Deans Lst 90-; Stdnt Peer Cnslr; Fisheries Mgmnt; U S Fish/Wldlf Serv.

**GRIFFETH, LAURA A,** Ms St Univ, Miss State, MS; SR; MS; Livestock Judging Team 90; Metas Judging Team; Block & Bridle 88; Phi Kappa Phi 89-; Gamma Sigma Delta; Alpha Zeta 90-; Soc Animal Science 89-; Gamma Beta Phi 88-89; TX A&M Regents Flwshp; Pres Scholar Acdmc Schlrshp 87-; Summa Cum Laude; BS; Animal Science.

**GRIFFIN, ALEXIS K,** Univ Of Sc At Lancaster, Lancaster, SC; FR; BA; USC-L Stdnt Govt 90-; Dns Lst; Publ Rels-Cmnctns.

**GRIFFIN, ANDREW I,** Waycross Coll, Waycross, GA; FR; BSN; Nursing.

**GRIFFIN, ANNETTE C,** Univ Of Sc At Aiken, Aiken, SC; FR; ASN; Nrsng; RN.

**GRIFFIN, AUDRA R,** Indiana Univ Of Pa, Indiana, PA; JR; BA; Sign Lang Clb Pres 88-; Sign In 89-; Res Hall Assn 90-; Kappa Delta Pi 90-; Deans Lst 88-90; Res Asst 90-; IM Vlybl Mgr 88-90; Hrng Imprd Ed; Tchng.**

**GRIFFIN, CARLA R,** Alcorn St Univ, Lorman, MS; FR; Fr Cls Sntr 90-; Nrsg; RN.

**GRIFFIN, CONNIE E,** Columbia Greene Comm Coll, Hudson, NY; SO; AS; SAGE Clb Sec 90-; Nrsng Clb 90-; Prsdnts Lst 89-; Cub Sct Den Ldr 90-; PTA 90-; Nrsng Asst 87-; Nrsng; CPA.

**GRIFFIN, DAVID A,** Univ Of Ga, Athens, GA; JR; BLA; GA Soc Lndscp Archtcts 90-; Envrnmntl Awrnss 90-; Lndscp Archtctr.

**GRIFFIN, DEXTER K,** Jackson St Univ, Jackson, MS; JR; BA; Hnrs Clg 88-; Phi Beta Lambda Prsdnt; Coop Edctn Clb 89-; Delta Mu Delta 90-; Deans Lst Schlr 88-; Acd Schlrshp 88-; Allstate Ins Co Intrn 89-; Cntrl Intlgnc Agncy Intrn 90-; Finance; Fnncl Plnr Invstmnts.

**GRIFFIN, DIANA R,** Univ Of Sc At Columbia, Columbia, SC; SO; BS; EFNEP Adv Brd 87-; Natl Prnt Aide Assoc 88-; Prog Rec Mntr Clncl Cr; Psych; Cnslng.

**GRIFFIN, GEORGE B,** Abraham Baldwin Agri Coll, Tifton, GA; FR; AS; Hnrs Day 90-; Wldlf Tech; Wldlf Mgmt.

**GRIFFIN, GWENDOLYN S,** Western Ky Univ, Bowling Green, KY; SR; BA; Pi Mu Epsilon Exctv Cm Mmbr 90-; Gldn Key; Phi Kappa Phi; Mthmtcs; Tchr.

**GRIFFIN, JASON E,** Valdosta St Coll, Valdosta, GA; JR; BS; Phi Kappa Phi; Alpha Chi; Sigma Alpha Chi; Alpha Epsilon Delta; Freshman Schlr; Biology; Med.

**GRIFFIN, JEFFREY A,** S U N Y Coll Of Tech At Alfred, Alfred, NY; SR; AAS; Acctg Clb 90-; Acctg.

**GRIFFIN, JENNIFER M,** Univ Of Nc At Charlotte, Charlotte, NC; SR; BA; Pre Law Soc; Chi Rho Cath Stdnt Un; Chnclr Lst 89; Pltcl Sci; Law.

**GRIFFIN, JOHN W,** Liberty Univ, Lynchburg, VA; JR; BA; Librty Assn Chrstn Tchrs 91; Ythquest 89-91; Sprtl Lfe Dir 90-91; Soc Scif Educ.

**GRIFFIN, KAREN E,** Lesley Coll, Cambridge, MA; FR; BED; Cthlc Commnty Sec 90-; Emrld Key 90-; Acdmc Hon 90-; Elem Ed; Tchng.

**GRIFFIN, KAREN S,** Univ Of Miami, Coral Gables, FL; SR; BS; Gldn Key; Rosenstiel Schl Marine/Atmospheric Sci Flwshp 89; Singer Schlrshp; Pres List 89; Deans Lst 87; Blgy; Educ.

**GRIFFIN, KELLY M,** Univ Of Nc At Greensboro, Greensboro, NC; SR; MS; Food/Nutr Clb Treas 89-; Kappa Omicron Nu 89-; Tri Beta 90-; Golden Chain 89-; Tri Sigma Fndsrg Chr/Alumnae Rels 88-; Rev/Mrs G D Albanese Schlrshp 90; Outstndg Sr Awd; Jr Achvmnt Awd 90; BS; Nutr; Dietetics/Rsrch.

**GRIFFIN, KIM L,** East Central Comm Coll, Decatur, MS; FR; BS; Stu Bdy Assoc Tres; Cls Tres 90-; Drm Cncl Pres 90-; Bnd Cncl Pres 90-; Mu Alpha Theta 90-; Phi Theta Kappa VP 90-; Warrior Corps 90-; Pres Cncl 90-; Pres Lst 90-; Drum Mjr 90-; IM Sprts 90-; Phrmcy.

**GRIFFIN, KRISTI D,** Bridgewater Coll, Bridgewater, VA; FR; BA; Dorm Hall Rep 90-; Baptist Stdnt Union 90-; IM Vlybl; Engl; Secndry Educ.

**GRIFFIN, KRISTI L,** Anderson Coll, Anderson, SC; SO; PHARM; Stdnt Govt Comm Chrprsn 90-; Sci Clb Pres 90-; Stdnt Alumni Cncl Sec/Treas 90-; Campus Mnstries Otrch Ofcr 90-; Hons Prog Mbr 89-; Physcs Awd 90-; Biol Awd 89-90; AA Anderson Clg; Sci; Phrmcst.

**GRIFFIN, LA VADA M,** Univ Of Southern Ms, Hattiesburg, MS; JR; Afro Amer Stu Org; Love Slvtn/Dtrmntn Choir Tres; Elem Educ; Tchr.

**GRIFFIN, LISA A,** Mount Aloysius Jr Coll, Cresson, PA; FR; AS; OT Clb 90-F Phi Theta Kappa; Spec Olympics; Rlgs Educ Teacher 89-F; Occup Theray; COTA.

**GRIFFIN, LISA A,** Univ Of Sc At Spartanburg, Spartanburg, SC; SR; BA; Intl Clb 90; Most Outstdng Engl/Jrnlsm Mjr; Intshp WRET-ETV 90-; Sprts Clrk Grnvl News 89-; Engl; Tch.

**GRIFFIN, LISA D,** Memphis St Univ, Memphis, TN; SR; BBA; Beta Gamma Sigma; Phi Kappa Phi 90-; Mrtr Bd 90-; Gldn Ky 89-; Gamma Beta Phi Chrprsn Nwslttr Com 88-; Gldn Ky Ntl Hon Soc Schlrshp 89; Summa Cum Laude; Fin/Mgmt; Law.

**GRIFFIN, LYNN M,** S U N Y Coll Of Tech At Alfred, Alfred, NY; SO; MA; Cmmtr Cncl VP; ERGO Sec; Ttr Prjcts Dsbld Stdnts; Psychlgy; Cnslng.

**GRIFFIN, MARK C,** Vance Granville Comm Coll, Henderson, NC; SR; AAS; Phi Theta Kappa; Acdmc Schlrshp 90-; NC Ntl Assoc Ltr Carriers Pres 89-; Stem Comm Fire Dept Pres Brd Dir 90-; Ltr Carrier US Pstl Serv; Bus Admin.

**GRIFFIN, MARY M,** Auburn Univ At Auburn, Auburn, AL; JR; Trentan-Greshan Lctre Series; Vsl Intrnshp Wth Prsns; Deans Lst; Fshn Mrchndsng; Bsnss Ownr.

**GRIFFIN, MICHAEL J,** Western Carolina Univ, Cullowhee, NC; SR; BS; Bus Law Clb 88-90; Govt Legal Afrs V P 90-; Ski Clb 87-; FCA 90; SG; Lpi Gamma Mu 89-; Phi Alpha Delta Mrshl 87-; Pub Dfndrs Intrn; Var Ski 87; Pltcl Sci/Bus Law; Law.

**GRIFFIN, MICHELLE L,** Sage Jr Coll Of Albany, Albany, NY; FR; AAS; Bus Admnstrtn.

**GRIFFIN, MIRANDA D,** Fl A & M Univ, Tallahassee, FL; FR; BA; Phi Eta Sigma 90-; Engl; Engl Prof/Occptnl Thrpy.

**GRIFFIN, NORA M,** Western Piedmont Comm Coll, Morganton, NC; FR; AA; Phi Theta Kappa; Elem Ed.

**GRIFFIN, RAY S,** Univ Of Ky, Lexington, KY; SO; IM Bsktbl/Ftbl/Vlybl 90-; Blgy; Med Schl.

**GRIFFIN, RUBY D,** Univ Of North Fl, Jacksonville, FL; SR; BA; Phi Theta Kappa 86-88; Kappa Delta Pi; Gldn Ky 90-; Intern; AA FL Comm Coll Jax 88; Elem Educ; Tchr.

**GRIFFIN, SANDRA E WHITTAKER,** Ky Wesleyan Coll, Owensboro, KY; GD; MA; Bhvrl Sci Bd; Stdnt Actvts Prgmng Bd; Stdnt Govt Assc; Clg Nwspr; Psychlgy Clb Pres; Sclgy Clb Pres; Deans Lst 86-89; Sigma Kappa 86-; Crisis Lne Phn Cnslr Vol 87-89; Spse Abse Shltr Vol 88; BA 89; Psychlgy/Sclgy/Spnsh; Dpt Fr Scl Srvcs.**

**GRIFFIN, SANDRA L,** Hillsborough Comm Coll, Tampa, FL; GD; ADN; LPN 2 Yrs; LPN 89; ADN; Nursing; RN.

**GRIFFIN, SHARON A,** Merrimack Coll, North Andover, MA; JR; BA; Educ Clb; Outrch Retrts; Tutor 90-; Bg Srs 90-; IM Vllybl 90; Math; Sec Educ.

**GRIFFIN, SHARON D,** Voorhees Coll, Denmark, SC; SR; BS; Scl Clb Sec 89-; Kappa Dmnd 89-; Self Stdy Steerg Com 90-; Comp Sci Dvsnl Hon; Miss EIAC; Comp Sci; Comp Spclst.

**GRIFFIN, SUSAN E,** Southern Vt Coll, Bennington, VT; JR; BA; US Budokai Karate Assoc 88-; AAS Hudson Vly Comm Clg 83; AS Hudson Vly Comm Clg 89; Management Business; Consultant.

**GRIFFIN, TAMMY L,** Anne Arundel Comm Coll, Arnold, MD; FR; BA; Fltm Columbia Kitchens Of Md Inc Exec Sec 89-; Pol Sci; Law.

**GRIFFIN, TONYA V,** Clark Atlanta Univ, Atlanta, GA; SO; BA; Blck Natl Dance Clg Exchng Chf Org 90-; Stdt Govt Rep 90-; Pltcl Sci Clb VP 90-; Intrnshp Atlanta Govt Agencies; Tchr Asst Asst; Pltcl Sci; Law.**

**GRIFFIN, VALERIE R,** Alcorn St Univ, Lorman, MS; JR; Deans Lst 88-89; President Lst 90; Social Work; Mental Hlth Cnslr.**

**GRIFFITH, AMY,** Schenectady County Comm Coll, Schenectady, NY; FR; MBA; Dns Lst 90-; Math; Elem Tchr.

**GRIFFITH, AMY E,** Oh Wesleyan Univ, Delaware, OH; JR; BA; Pres Club VP 89-; WSF 89-; Sigma Tau Delta; Kappa Delta Pi; Engl; Secndry Ed.

**GRIFFITH, ANGELIA M,** Cumberland Coll, Williamsburg, KY; SO; BS; Cmptr/Bsn Adm; Mgmt.

**GRIFFITH, ANNE E,** Villanova Univ, Villanova, PA; JR; BA; Theatre Creative Brd 88-90; Resid Hall Council Pres 89-90; Musical Thtr Mbr 90-; Hnr Prog Hnrs Council Mau 89-; Campus Ministry Music Minister 88-89; Blue Key H Schl Rectmt 89; Faclty Flw 88-90; Peer Tutor Writing Ctr Conslt; English; Entertaiment Law/Perf.

**GRIFFITH, ANNE M,** Radford Univ, Radford, VA; JR; BA; Bptst Stdnt Union 88-90; Scl Wrk Clb 90; Phi Theta Kappa 89-90; Phi Sigma Pi; Schlrshp Danvl Comm Coll 88-90; Schlrshp DCC 90; IM 89-90; Assoc Lbrl Arts Danvl Comm Coll 90; Scl Wrk; Plnng/Admin.

**GRIFFITH, BARBARA A,** Indiana Univ Of Pa, Indiana, PA; SO; B ED; Elmntry Edctn; Spnsh.

**GRIFFITH, CATHY S,** Methodist Coll, Fayetteville, NC; SO; BA; Engl; Tchr.

**GRIFFITH, CHRISTOPHER D,** City Univ Of Ny City Coll, New York, NY; SO; BEE; Brklyn Tbrncl Dlvrnc Ctr Mnstr 87-88; Alpha Sigma Lambda; Com Ed Co; Electrical Eng.

**GRIFFITH, DAVID A,** Univ Of Akron, Akron, OH; SR; BS; Fncl Mgmt Assoc Cmnctns Coord 90; VP Pblc Rltns; VP Fnce; Beta Gamma Sigma; Golden Key; Fncl Mgmt Assoc Hnr Soc; Paine Weber Sec Inc Corp Intrn 89-90; Galen J Roush Mem Schlrshp; Edith Mae Eckler Schlrshp; Fnce.

**GRIFFITH, DREAMA S,** Univ Of Ky, Lexington, KY; SR; BA; KEA; NEA; Wesley Fndtn; Dns Lst; Eng; Sec Ed.**

**GRIFFITH III, EUGENE F,** Abraham Baldwin Agri Coll, Tifton, GA; SO; Horticulture Clb; Phi Theta Kappa 90; Pres Adv Brd 90; Exhcnage Clb; ELUS Clb; Gen Mgr Of Cntry Clbs; AA Brunswick Jr Clg 74; Club Mgmnt.

**GRIFFITH, GARRETH C,** Saint Andrews Presbytrn Coll, Laurinburg, NC; SO; BA; Actvts Union VP; Rgby Clb VP 90-; Hnrs; Nwspr Art Drctr 90-; Schlr Athlete; Trck MVP 89-; Cmptr Grphcs; Advrtsng.

**GRIFFITH, GLORIA J,** Nova Univ, Ft Lauderdale, FL; MBA; RN Nrsg Class Pres 80; Peer Tutor; Hlth Fair Coord; Phi Theta Kappa; Pinellas Point Crime Watch Coord; Wmns Chmbr Cmrce Pres; Lds Kiwanis Pres; Mound Prk Hosp Auxiliary/Clndr Girl; Stokley-Van Camp Best Cook Of The Week; Bsn; Insur/Hlth Care Plns.

**GRIFFITH, JAMES D,** Va Commonwealth Univ, Richmond, VA; SR; MS; Jrnymn Plmbr 77-86; Advrtsng/Cpywrtr 87-90; Pre-Physcl Thrpy; Physcl Thrpst.

**GRIFFITH, JEFFREY A,** Radford Univ, Radford, VA; JR; BA; Bus Mgmnt.

**GRIFFITH, JULIA G,** Radford Univ, Radford, VA; JR; BS; Kappa Delta Pi 90-; Phi Kappa Phi; Educ; Tch.

**GRIFFITH, JULIE M,** Christopher Newport Coll, Newport News, VA; SR; BA; YMCA Yth Dir 88-90; BA 88; Ele Educ; Tch.

**GRIFFITH, LINDA B,** S U N Y Coll Of Tech At Delhi, Delhi, NY; SO; BS; Std Prgmmng Brd Chrprsn 90-; Mddl States Comm Std Adv 90-; Wmn Color 89-90; Wrtng Cnslnt 90-; Peer Tutor 89-; RA 90-; AS; Bsn Admn; Bsn.

**GRIFFITH, MARY C,** Univ Of Southern Ms, Hattiesburg, MS; SO; BS; Hnrs Coll 89-; Hnrs Stu Assn Treas 89-; Almn Assn 90-; Phi Eta Sigma 90-; Alpha Lambda Delta 90-; Delta Gamma 90-; Mdl Pldg; Spch Pthlgy.

**GRIFFITH, REBA L,** Alice Lloyd Coll, Pippa Passes, KY; SR; BA; Kappa Delta Epsilon; Elem Educ; Tchr.

**GRIFFITH, TERESSA P,** Univ Of Nc At Greensboro, Greensboro, NC; SR; BS; NCCTM 90-; Unvrsty Mrshls 89-; Intrnshp; Mddl Grds Edctn; Tchr.

**GRIFFITH, TINA M,** Radford Univ, Radford, VA; SR; BS; Ntv Amer Hrtg Assoc Treas 88-; Athltc Prmtns Cmte 89-; Pi Gamma Mu 90-; Psi Chi 90-; Zeta Tau Alpha 88-90; BS; Psychlgy.

**GRIFFITHS, DANA L,** Duquesne Univ, Pittsburgh, PA; FR; MBA; Orentatn Stff Chrprsn 90-; Im Vybl; Biology; Phys Thrpy.

**GRIFFITHS, DAVID A,** Univ Of Ky, Lexington, KY; JR; BA; Allnc Frncs 90-; Mfrs Rep 82-90; Sls Eng 77-82; Frnch; Tchng.

**GRIFFITHS, KAREN D,** Univ Of Tn At Martin, Martin, TN; SO; BS; Chrch Chrst Stdnt Cntr 89-; Phi Chi Theta VP 90-; Acctg.

**GRIFFITHS, KIMBERLY P,** Fl St Univ, Tallahassee, FL; SR; MA; Phi Theta Kappa; Psi Beta; Psi Chi; Golden Key; Alumni Vlg Presch Tchr; AA 86; BA 89; Ele Educ; Tch Pre Sch.

**GRIFFITHS, MICHAEL C,** Elizabethtown Coll, Elizabethtown, PA; FR; BA; Actvties Plnng Brd Pblcty Chrmn 90-; Class Sec; Acdmc Hnr Scty 90-; Big Brthr 90-; Acdmc Schlrshp 90-; IM Bsktbll And Sftbll 90-; Math; Actrl Sci.

**GRIFFITHS, RICHARD A,** Univ Of Nc At Charlotte, Charlotte, NC; JR; BA; NC Mvrs Assoc 85-; VP Oprtns Armstrong Untd Van Lines 88-; AAS Clge Of Dupage 83; Crim Jstc.

**GRIFFITHS, SHARRONDA L,** Univ Of Sc At Columbia, Columbia, SC; SO; BS; SG Penn State 87-88; Union Brd Tr 87-88; Hnrs Pgm 87-; Guardn Ad Litem 90-; ACVI Leadrshp Conf 87; Chrldng 87-88; Sftbll 87-88; Psych; Clin Psych.

**GRIGAS, SHERRY A,** Duquesne Univ, Pittsburgh, PA; FR; Mntr Grp 90-; Chrch Lctr 88-; Hosp Vol 90-; IM Bsktbl; Phrmcy.

**GRIGG, CAROLYN W,** Emory Univ, Atlanta, GA; JR; BSN; Red Crs 88-; Critical Care Nurse.

**GRIGGS, ANDRE R,** Clark Atlanta Univ, Atlanta, GA; SO; BA; Psych; Clncl Psych.**

**GRIGGS, BARRY TODD,** Univ Of Tn At Martin, Martin, TN; SO; PE Majors Club Hstrn; Bsktbl/Ftbl Yth Coach; Phi Esplison Mu; Phys Educ.

**GRIGGS, CERETA J,** Univ Of Montevallo, Montevallo, AL; SR; BS; Orntn Ldr; Montevallo Master; Yrbk Stff; Sr Advsry Bd Schl Arts/Sci VP 90-; Phi Kappa Phi; Omicron Delta Kappa; Sigma Tau Delta; Kappa Delta P2; Lambda Sigma Pi; Phi Theta Kappa Treas; Chi Omega Scl Chrmn 90-; Pres Ldrshp Schlrshp; Deans Lst; Engl/Lang Arts; Scndry Educ.

**GRIGGS, MICHAEL L,** Univ Of Ky, Lexington, KY; FR; BS; Fed Cvl Svc DOD CBM Cmptr Ctr; AS Inst Elec Tech 83; Elec Eng.

**GRIGGS, PATTY L,** Southern Coll Of Tech, Marietta, GA; JR; BS; Lambda Chi Alpha 90-; Pres Lst; Dean Lst; IM Sftbl 90; Elect Eng.

**GRIGGS, TRICIA A,** Chattahoochee Vly St Comm Coll, Phenix City, AL; FR; BED; Pres List; Gamma Beta Phi Nominee; History/Gvrnmt; Law/Tchng.

**GRIGLIO, GINA,** Seton Hall Univ, South Orange, NJ; FR; BS; Nrsng.

**GRIGORACI, GINA V,** Marshall University, Huntington, WV; SR; BBA; Mgmt.

**GRIGSBY, AMY F,** Lexington Comm Coll, Lexington, KY; FR; BA; Biology.

**GRIGSBY, REBECCA D,** Union Coll, Barbourville, KY; SO; BS; Acctng; CPA.

**GRILLO, DEBORAH C,** City Univ Of Ny Brooklyn Coll, Brooklyn, NY; FR; BA; Newman Clb Treas; Elem Ed/Psych; Tchr.

**GRILLO, JEFFREY S,** Cayuga County Comm Coll, Auburn, NY; FR; BA; Phi Theta Kappa; Rgnts Schlrshp; Hnrs Schlrshp; Englsh; Tchr.

**GRILLO, MELISSA A,** Villanova Univ, Villanova, PA; SO; Alpha Chi Omega; Proj Sunshine Vol; Spec Olympics; Tennis; Gen Arts/Bsn/Pol Sci.

**GRIM, CHRISTOPHER J,** Univ Of Miami, Coral Gables, FL; JR; BS; Scuba Clb 90-; Marine Sci-Bio; Scientist.

**GRIM, DOREEN K,** S U N Y Coll Of Tech At Alfred, Alfred, NY; FR; AS; Sls/Office/Chldcr; Med/Sec Olean Bus Inst 85; Hmn Srvcs; Crmnl Jstc.

**GRIM, VALERIA R,** Univ Of Southern Ms, Hattiesburg, MS; SR; BS; Psychology/Soc Wrk; Grad Schl.

**GRIMALDI, DAWN M,** Edinboro Univ Of Pa, Edinboro, PA; FR; BS; Phi Eta Sigma 90-; Fr Hon Schlrshp 90-; Alumni Assoc Schlrshp 90-; Edinboro U Hon Pgm 90-; Bio; Marine Bio/Anml Behavior.

**GRIMALDI, FRANCES A,** Le Moyne Coll, Syracuse, NY; JR; BA; Pre Law Scty 88-; Pol Sci Acad VP 90-; Dns Lst 90-; Cnty Atts Offce Intrn; Pol Sci; Law.**

**GRIMALDI, FRANK,** Merrimack Coll, North Andover, MA; JR; BA; Psi Chi 90-; Psy; Pstrl Cnslng/Clncl Psy.

**GRIMARD, SALLY A,** Lesley Coll, Cambridge, MA; FR; BA; Emerld Key 90-; LINC 90-; Dns Lst 90-; Lesly Schlr 90-; Cambrd Pub Schl Vol 90-; Mentr Amer Chld Vol 90-; Undrgrad Schl Schlrhp 90-; Aerbocs 90-; Librl Arts; Elem Educ.

**GRIMAUD, REBECCA D,** Atlantic Union Coll, S Lancaster, MA; SO; BS; Blgy Clb/Cls Org Cls Sec 89-; Hnrs Cr; Dns Lst; NAIA 1st/2nd All Dstrct Tm 89-; Vlybl Schlrshp/Dept/Athltc; Vlybl/Bsktbl Co Capt 89-; Blgy; Med.

**GRIMES, ANGEL R,** Commonwealth Coll, Virginia Beach, VA; SO; Pres Med Clb 90-; Hstrn Med Clb 90; Intrnshp VA Beach Gen Hosp Lab; CPR 90; Pres List; Deans List 89-; Data Entry Tchncn; MAA AS 89-; Med; Cytlgst BA.

**GRIMES, CRAIG S,** Norfolk St Univ, Norfolk, VA; GD; BA; Pol Sci Assoc 86-90; Yng Democrats 90; Deans Lst 89-90; Hon Roll 88-89; Pol Sci; Tchng.

**GRIMES, DAVID E,** Univ Of Louisville, Louisville, KY; GD; MENG; Inst Elec/Elctrnc Eng; Stdnt Cncl Old Dominion U VP 88-89; Opn Hse Chr 88-89; ETI Exam 79; US Nvl Rsrvs Exec Ofcr 89-90; US Nvy Lt 83-87; BS 78; M Eng 79; Elec Eng.

**GRIMES, DEBORAH B,** Williamsburg Tech Coll, Kingstree, SC; SO; BS; Phi Theta Kappa; LPN 81; Sci.

**GRIMES, JAMITA L,** Wilberforce Univ, Wilberforce, OH; JR; Kappa Swthrt Org 89-; NAACP 89-; Kappa Theta Epsilon; Delta Sigma Theta Treas 90-; Cargill Incorp EEOC Endwmnt Schlrshp Awd; Mrktng Bus; Fshn Mrchndsng.

**GRIMES, JOANNE,** S U N Y Coll Of Tech At Delhi, Delhi, NY; SO; BA; Delhi Bus Assoc VP 90-; Stu Govt Ofcr 89-90; Exec Clb 89-90; Delhi Hlth Squad Crw Chf 89-; Dept Pblc Sfty Stu Cmnctr 90-; Admsns Ofc Tr Guide 90-; Tutrl Awrd 90; AAS; Bus Admin; Hosp.

**GRIMES, KELLI A,** Truett Mc Connell Coll, Cleveland, GA; FR; Church Christ; Media Paraprfsnl Lafayette High Schl 88-; Elem Ed; Tch.

**GRIMES, KYRA M,** Fisk Univ, Nashville, TN; SO; BA; Gospel Choir Sectn Ldr; NAACP; Alpha Kappa Alpha Chpln; Deans List; Engl; Publc Rltns.

**GRIMES, MINDY E,** Fl International Univ, Miami, FL; SR; BS; Bunche Park Elem Chptr I Para Prof Of Yr 89-90; Elem Educ Intrnshp 89-90; Elem Educ; Tchr.

**GRIMES, PAMELA,** Paine Coll, Augusta, GA; SR; BS; Presidential Lst 90; Edward C Davis Awrd 90; Math; Actuary/Teacher.

**GRIMES, PAULETTE H,** Univ Of The Dist Of Columbia, Washington, DC; SR; Acctng Clb Treas 88-89; Pre Alumni Assn 88-89; Prof Bkkg Assn 89-; Deans Lst 86-90; Pepco Schlrshp 88; Alton Wilson 88; Acctng Outstand Jr 89; Silver Medal Awd/Spcl Achvmnt Awd 85-87; Acad Achvmnt Awd 89; CERT 83; BBA 90; Acctng; Auditing.

**GRIMES, RHONDA SUE,** Univ Of Tn At Martin, Martin, TN; FR; Beta Clb VP; Sch Nwspr Asst Ed; Yrbk Stf; Eng.

**GRIMES, SHERRY L,** Salisbury St Univ, Salisbury, MD; FR; BA; SG 90-; Alpha Omega 90-; Alpha Sigma Tau VP 90; Biology; Marine Biological Rsrch.

**GRIMES, WILLIAM L,** Marshall University, Huntington, WV; FR; Cmmcrl Pilot Flght Instr; Chief Flght Instr Mntnr Srng Clb; 1st Offcr; Comm Sel Mel Inst Comari Avation Acdmy 90; Bus Admn/Mngmnt; Pilot/Airlne Mltry Corp.

**GRIMISON, MELINDA S,** Fl St Univ, Tallahassee, FL; SR; BA; FEA 90-; Phi Theta Kappa 89-; AA Brevard Cmnty Clg 87-89; Math Educ.

**GRIMM, DANIEL P,** Comm Coll Algny Co Algny Cmps, Pittsburgh, PA; SO; BA; Intl Bsn; Intl Law.

**GRIMM, LISA A,** Univ Of Nc At Greensboro, Greensboro, NC; SR; BM; Colligiate Music Edtrs NC 88-; Phi Kappa Lambda; Mu Phi Epsilon Treas 89-; Deans List 88-; Univ Marshal 89-; Katnarine Smith Reynolds Schlr 88-; Natl Merit Schlr 88-; Music Ed/Perfr; Tchng.

**GRIMM, MATHEW B,** Univ Of Ga, Athens, GA; SO; BS; Hnrs Prog 89; IM Ftbl Sftbl Bsktbl 90-F; Physics.

**GRIMM, MICHELLE E,** Univ Of Akron, Akron, OH; SR; BED; ACES 90; Golden Key 89; AS Kent State Tusc Campus 88; Elem Ed; Ed.

**GRIMM, ROBERT R,** Wv Univ At Parkersburg, Parkersburg, WV; SO; BA; Glenville State Ftbl Vrsty 88-89; Drafting Mason Co Voc 88; Drftng Tech; Eng.

**GRIMM, TINA D,** Marshall University, Huntington, WV; SR; BA; Acctg Clb 90-; Acctg.

**GRIMMER, JULIE A,** Lesley Coll, Cambridge, MA; FR; BA; Rep Govt Brd Cmtr Rep 90-; Aftrschl Prog 90-; Asst Dirc; Human Services; Psychology.

**GRIMMETT, DEBBY A,** Marshall University, Huntington, WV; FR; BA; Business; Accntng.

**GRIMMETTE, MACHELLE D,** Marshall University, Huntington, WV; JR; BA; Gamma Beta Phi; Ele Tchr.

**GRIMSLEY, JENNIFER B,** Univ Of Ky, Lexington, KY; FR; BA; Stdnt Actvts Bd 90-; Alpha Lambda Delta; Alpha Gamma Delta 90-; Acctg.

**GRIMSLEY, MELANIE D,** Univ Of Charleston, Charleston, WV; JR; BA; Bptst Campus Mnstrs Pres 89-; Pi Gamma Mu; Alpha Lambda Delta; Psi Chi Pres; Pi Delta Phi; Psychlgy; Cnslng.

**GRINE, KIMBERLEY A,** Oh Wesleyan Univ, Delaware, OH; FR; BA; Women In Sci 90-; Zoology; Med.

**GRINER, CHRIS S,** Valdosta St Coll, Valdosta, GA; JR; BBA; Alpha Epsln Alpha Pres; Phi Kappa Phi; Alpha Lambda Delta; Sigma Alpha Chi; Pres Schlr; Acctng.

**GRINNELL, JOSEPH N,** Univ Of New Haven, West Haven, CT; FR; BA; History; Tchng.

**GRINNELL, KATHLEEN L,** Elms Coll, Chicopee, MA; JR; BA; Jdcl Bd Chrprsn 90-; Pre-Law Intrnshp; Pre-Law; Law.

**GRINZAYD, ALEXANDER,** City Univ Of Ny Baruch Coll, New York, NY; SO; BS; French Clb; Russian Clb Moskva; Sigma Beta; Dns Lst 89-; Cmptr Sci; Grad/Law Sch.

**GRIPPO, JACQUELINE M,** Univ Of Med & Dentistry Of Nj, Newark, NJ; GD; MPT; Cls Rep 89-; BS Rutgers Univ 89; Phsy Thrpy.

**GRIPPO, TONY J,** Johnson And Wales Univ, Providence, RI; FR; BA; Clnry-Htl/Rest Mgmt; Own Bus.

**GRISAFE, LUANN MARIE,** Teikyo Post Univ, Waterbury, CT; SO; BS; Stdnt Govt Assn Sec 90-; Paralgl Clb VP; Entrtnmnt Com Sntr 90-; Deans List 90-; Hmlss Vol; Bld Drs; Paralgl; Law.

**GRISHAM, BRENDA F,** Univ Of Tn At Martin, Martin, TN; SR; BS; STEA 89-; Erly Chldhd Ed; Tchng/Cnslng.

**GRISSOM, BRYAN S,** Birmingham Southern Coll, Birmingham, AL; SR; MASTE; Bsbll 87-; Fllwshp Chrstn Athlts 87-; Schl Rcrtr 87-88; Hnrs Scty Jnr Coll 87-88; Psi Chi; Intern Fulton Police Dept 90-; Coll Bsbll 87-; Smmr Lg Bsbll Cch 89-; Plc Offcr Prt Tm 90-; BA; Mstrs; Sclty Psychlgy; Fdrl Law Enfrcmnt Spcl Agnt.

**GRIZZLE, DARYL K,** Ashland Comm Coll, Ashland, KY; SO; BBA; Phi Beta Lambda 90-; Voc Indus Clb Amer Treas 80-82; Tutor Stdnt Sprt Serv; Wrkshp Asst Admns 90-; Deans Lst 90-; VICA Ldr 82; Planetary Soc 90-; Cmptr Lab Instr 87 90; AA 90; AAS 91; Cmptr Info Sys; Cmptr Prgrmr/Sys Anlyst.

**GROBE, KATHERINE F,** Fl St Univ, Tallahassee, FL; FR; BMED; Collegiate Music Educ Natl Conf 90-; Sigma Alpha Iota; Music Educ.

**GROBELNY, CHRISTOPHER J,** Duquesne Univ, Pittsburgh, PA; SO; Fncl Mgmt Assc; Sigma Tau Gamma; IM Ftbl/Sftbl; Fnce; Invstmnt Bnkng.

**GROCE, PAMELA E,** Ms St Univ, Miss State, MS; FR; BPA; Acctg.

**GROCE, SHIRLEY,** Gadsden St Comm Coll, Gadsden, AL; SO; Chrch Chr; S S Tchr; Military Prsnnl Clrk.

**GROCHOWSKI, CHRISTINE K,** Univ Of Ga, Athens, GA; SR; BED; Communiv Tchr Asst 90-; Kappa Delta Epsilon 90-; Athens Tutorial Prog 89-; Erly Chldhd Edn.

**GRODEN, SUSAN VOIGHT,** Fl International Univ, Miami, FL; JR; BA; Stdnt Home Ec Assn Pres 90-; Ftr Edctrs Amer 90-; Deans Lst 90-; Jr Leag Miami 89-; Dade Hrtg Trust 85-; Miami Shores Elem Schl PTA 83-; New England Ins Agnt 88-; AA Miami-Dade Comm Coll 85; Home Ec Educ; Tch.

**GRODZICKI, ERIC R,** Western New England Coll, Springfield, MA; FR; BS; Comp Sci.

**GROFF, JENNIFER L,** Indiana Univ Of Pa, Indiana, PA; FR; BA; Cmnctns-Media; Brdcstng.

**GROFF, KYLA LORELEI,** Samford Univ, Birmingham, AL; GD; JD; Stdnt Bar Assn 90-; Amer Bar Assn 90-; AL Bar Assn 90-; Beta Alpha Phi 87-89; Alpha Theta Epsilon Corr Sec 86-90; Phi Delta Phi Clrk 90-; Cumberland Law Rvw; Deans Lst 90-; BS Univ New Orleans 90; Law.

**GROH, DIANE J,** Indiana Univ Of Pa, Indiana, PA; SR; Natl Hon Soc 88-; Cltn Chrstn Outrch 89-; Yth Ldr 89; Cross Cntry/Trck 87-.

**GROHMAN, CHRISTOPHER JOHN,** Lancaster Bible Coll, Lancaster, PA; JR; BS; Christian Cnslng Flwshp Pres 90-; Varsity Club 89-; Yth Ctr Day Camp Cnslr; S S Tchr 90-; Bsbl 90-; Bible; Guidance Cnslr/Yth Mnstr.

**GROHS JR, RICHARD L,** Univ Of Cin R Walters Coll, Blue Ash, OH; SO; AAB; ECM Specialist 86-; Ndustrial Management.

**GRONAU, DAPHNE MARIE,** Catholic Univ Of Pr, Ponce, PR; GD; JD; Stdnt Cncl Pres 88-89; Sr Clss Brd Dir Pub Chrmn 89-90; Phi Alpha Delta 88-; Mo Alpha Phi 85-; BA Univ Puerto Rico 88; Pol Sci.

**GRONE, CATHERINE R,** Wright St Univ Lake Cmps, Celina, OH; JR; BA; Bus Pro Amer 90-; Deans Lst 89-; Acctncy; CPA.

**GRONER, MARKUS DANIEL,** Univ Of Sc At Columbia, Columbia, SC; SO; BS; Mntnrng Whtwtr Clb 89-; IM Sccr; Chmstry.

**GRONER, MELANIE L,** Ms St Univ, Miss State, MS; SR; BS; Bptst Stdnt Union VP 88-; Mrtr Bd Hstrn; Phi Eta Sigma 88-; Gamma Beta Phi 88-; Kappa Delta Pi; Untd Way Cbnt Mbr 90-; Stdnt Spprt Serv Blnd; William Winter Schlrshp 90-; Acdmc Schlrshp 88-; IM Sports; Math Educ; Tch.

**GROOM, CHAD L,** Morehouse Coll, Atlanta, GA; JR; BS; Glee Clb; Bus Assn; Psychlgy Clb; Psychlgy Intern; Psychlgy; Advrtsng/Radio TV Flm.

**GROOM, MADONNA N,** Hilbert Coll, Hamburg, NY; FR; AAS; Prof Asst Clb 90-; Ofc Tech; Med.

**GROOMS, SHANNON R,** Pfeiffer Coll, Misenheimer, NC; FR; BA; Poll Sitter 90-; Pres Awd 90-; IM Vlybl 90-; Acctg; CPA.

**GROSE, JANET ELAINE,** Wv Northern Comm Coll, Wheeling, WV; FR; Marshall Conty Exec Comm Secy 89-; WV State Comm; PTA 80-88; Mgr Sounds Easy 82-85.

**GROSES, LORRAINE E,** Coll Of New Rochelle, New Rochelle, NY; JR; BS; Clss VP 89-90; Cnsl Stdnts 89-; Props/Paint Theatre Grp 88-90; Hnrs Prog 88-; Swmphny Coord 90-; Art Therapy.

**GROSNER, DAVID R,** Providence Coll, Providence, RI; SO; BA; Rsdnce Brd Pres 89-90; Rsdnce Exec Brd Treas 90; Deans Lst 89; Var Golf Tm 90; Hbtat For Hmnty 89-90; Big E Rght Grd Acad All-Star Tm 90; Flg Ftbl Ims 89; Bsnss Fnce; Stck Brkr.

**GROSPE, EDWIN B,** Fordham Univ, Bronx, NY; SO; CBA; IMS 89-; Cmnty Svc 89; Track/Field 89-; Finance; Lawyer.

**GROSS, ALLEN J,** Davis & Elkins Coll, Elkins, WV; SR; BS; Intl Std Org VP 89-; Physcl Ed Mjrs Clb Treas 89-; Spnsh Clb 87-; Alpha Phi Omega Sgt/Arms 89-; Tchng Asstshp; Std Tchng K-12 90; Bkstbl/Tnns 87-; Outstdng Physcl Ed Mjrs Year AAHPERD; Physcl Ed; Tchng/Athltc Admn/Coaching.

**GROSS, CORA J,** Union Coll, Barbourville, KY; JR; BS; Acad Tm 90-; Union News Editor 89-90; Baptist Union 88-90; Iota Sigma Nu 89-; Alpha Psi Omega Pres 89-; Judicial Bd 89-90; Beverly/Mossie Wilson Mem Awd; Engl/Biol; Tech Wrtr.

**GROSS, CYNTHIA M,** Kent St Univ Kent Cmps, Kent, OH; JR; BA; Acctg Assoc 90-; Beta Alpha Psi 90-; Acctg; CPA.

**GROSS, DANA L,** Comm Coll Algny Co Algny Cmps, Pittsburgh, PA; BA; Deans Lst 90-; Pltcl Sci; Dctrt/Tch.

**GROSS, IDITE P,** Fl Atlantic Univ, Boca Raton, FL; JR; BA; Act Std Asc; Act; CPA.

**GROSS, JAMIE K,** Va Highlands Comm Coll, Abingdon, VA; SO; Mthr Of 5; Peoples Inc Comm Actn Agncy; AS VHCC 90; Ed/Sci; RN.

**GROSS, JOHN DARREN,** Univ Of Tn At Martin, Martin, TN; SO; BS; Rsdnce Hll Assn Ellngtn Hll VP 90; Kappa Alpha Hstrn 89-; Spcl Ldrshp Schlrshp 89-; Stdnt Asst At Univ Of TN Med Cntr Knxvlle; Blgy; Med Dr Rdlgst.

**GROSS, LISA L,** Univ Of Pittsburgh, Pittsburgh, PA; SR; BS; ASME 88-90; Grmn Clb; Gldn Key 90-; Coop Pgm Wrkng Packard Electric 89-; Mchncl Engrg.

**GROSS, LOUISE,** Lees Coll, Jackson, KY; FR; RN.

**GROSS, M ASHLEY,** Converse Coll, Spartanburg, SC; FR; BA; SGA 90-; Coll Repub 90-; Alpha Lambda Delta 90-; Bst Camp Cnslr Awd 90; Bus Adm/Pltcl Sci.

**GROSS, MICHELE L,** S U N Y Coll At Fredonia, Fredonia, NY; SR; BS; Amer Mktg Assoc 90-; Bsn Clb 88-90; Undergrad Alumni Cncl 89-90; Fredonia State Ambsdr 89-; Sml Bsn Inst Spons Sml Bsn Adm; Bsn Adm; Mktg.

**GROSS, MIRIAM S,** Sue Bennett Coll, London, KY; SR; BA; Chrstn Serv Com 89-90; Schl Mssnry Cbnt 88-89; Chrstn Educ Intrnshp; Chrstn Educ Awd; AA 5Y Mtn Bible Coll 90; Chrstn Educ/Bible; Mssns/Edctnl Mnstry Lcl Ch.

**GROSS, NEIL O,** Bowie St Univ, Bowie, MD; JR; BA; Deacons/Brotherhood Clb Of G B W Church; Boys/Young Men Clb VP 89-90; Hons Pgm; Delta Mu Delta; Alpha Phi Alpha; Bus Admin; CPA.

**GROSS, PAULINE J,** Fisk Univ, Nashville, TN; FR; BS; Stdnt Gvt Rep 90-; Natl Assc For Advncmnt Clrd People 89-; Fisk Mdrn Blck Mass Chr; Hlth Careers Clb 90-; Utd Negro Coll Fund Premed Summner Inst; Biology; Medicine.

**GROSS, RANDY S,** Middle Tn St Univ, Murfreesboro, TN; SO; Aerospace; Pilot.

**GROSS, RANELLE D,** Univ Of Md At Eastern Shore, Princess Anne, MD; SO; BS; Pre Prfsnl Scty 90-; NAACP 90-; Athltc Trnr 90-; Acad Exclnc Awrd 9-; Mst Valbl Athltc Trnr; Phys Thrpy.

**GROSS, RENEE L,** Elmira Coll, Elmira, NY; JR; BA; Nwspr Copy Nws Edtrs 88-; Lit Mag Poetry Edtr 88-; Yrbk Phtgphr 89-; Phi Eta Sigma 90-; Publ Rel Asst Arnot Ogden Mem Hosp; Tutor; Hon/Pres Schlr 88-; Sarah L Tracy Prize; Bst Photgrphy Reg Art Exhbt Arnot Art Museum 90; Engl Lit.

**GROSS, RICHARD J,** West Chester Univ, West Chester, PA; GD; BS; Music Edn.

**GROSS, ROBERT C,** Univ Of Nc At Asheville, Asheville, NC; SR; BS; Hnrs Prog 90-; Celo Comm Inc 82-; Dsgnr/Bldr; Env Studies; Energy Mgmnt.

**GROSS, SHEILA A,** Memphis St Univ, Memphis, TN; FR; NW Airlines CSA 86-.

**GROSS, TAMARA B,** Yeshiva Univ, New York, NY; SR; BA; Prelaw Scty; Ttr Wrtng Cntrs 90-; Nwsppr Stff 90-; Psychlgy Clb 88-; Dns Lst 88-; Cum Laude; Pblc Dfndr Of Mmi Intrn 90; BA; AA; Psychlgy; Law.

**GROSSEN II, JOHN F,** Oh Univ, Athens, OH; FR; BA; Ecology Clb 90-; I M Sftbl Vybl Ftbl 90-; Fine Arts; Graphic Dsgn.

**GROSSENBACHER, KATHERINE A,** George Mason Univ, Fairfax, VA; SR; BS; SEA 89-; Golden Key 90-; Kappa Delta Pi 90-; Alpha Chi; Jr Lge Honolulu; AS Palomar Clg 88; Erly Chldhd Educ; Tchr.

**GROSSI, RICHARD B,** S U N Y Coll Of Tech At Frmgdl, Farmingdale, NY; FR; MBA; Farmngdl Firarms Sec 90-; Cmptr Sci; Prgmg.

**GROSSKOPF, BABETTE,** Va Commonwealth Univ, Richmond, VA; SR; SGA 87; Gold Key 90; Phi Kappa Phi; Phi Theta Kappa; Magna Cum Laude 87; BS Psychlgy Richard Bland Coll 87; Psychlgy.

**GROSSMAN, JEFFREY A,** Cornell Univ Statutory College, Ithaca, NY; FR; BS; Dns Lst 90-; Bsn.

**GROSSMAN, JORDAN P,** Oh Coll Of Podiatric Med, Cleveland, OH; SO; DPM; Amer Clg Of Ft Srgns Stdnt Chptr 90; Podiatric Med Stdnt Assoc 90; Sprts Med Clb 90; Alpha Gamma Kappa; Lambda Chi Alpha 88; Alpha Gamma Kappa Prk Ln Clinic 90; Alpha Gamma Kappa Cty Mssn Clinic 90; Alpha Gamma Kappa 1st Mthdst Clnc 90; BA 90; Podiatric Med; Dor Of Podiatric Med.

**GROSSMAN, MICHELE C,** Fl International Univ, Miami, FL; GD; Key Clb 84-85; Beta Psi Delta 87-88; BA 88; Engl; Writer.

**GROSSNICKLE, MICHELLE MARIE,** Fl St Univ, Tallahassee, FL; FR; BS; Hon Schlrs Pgm 90-; Peer Mentor; Phi Eta Sgm; Deans List 90; IM Vlybl 90; Chem Eng.

**GROSSNICKLE, ROBERT S,** Univ Of Md At College Park, College Park, MD; SR; IEEE 89-; Eta Kappa Nu Bridge Cor 90-; Tau Beta Pi 90-; Phi Kappa Phi 89-; Summa Cum Laude; BS; Elec Engineering; Professor.**

**GROTH, VICKI LYNN,** Bryant Stratton Bus Inst Roch, Rochester, NY; SR; AOS; Med Clb Treas 90-; Extrnshp 3 Mnth Prog; Med Asst; Med Fld.

**GROVE, CAROL A,** Saint Francis Coll, Loretto, PA; SO; BS; Physcn Asst Std Soc Rep 90-; Std Govt Asc 90-; Admssns/Stndrds Comm Fclty Snt Rep; Hnrs Pgm 89-; PA Pgm Rsch Asst 90-; Physcn Asst/Psy; Med Psy.

**GROVE, KELLY B,** Bridgewater Coll, Bridgewater, VA; JR; BS; Oratorio Chr; Concrt Chr; Lambda Soc; Psych; Chld/Fmly Cnslng.

**GROVE, NICOLE M,** Univ Of Miami, Coral Gables, FL; SO; BA; Cin Arts Comm Pub 90-; Cable 51 90-; Eatn Clg Cncl 89-90; Alpha Lambda Delta 89-; Sigma Tau Delta; Brdcstng/Engl; Wrtng Film T V.

**GROVE, SHARON M,** Mount Aloysius Jr Coll, Cresson, PA; FR; BSN; Phi Theta Kappa 89-90; Grl Sct Ldr 85-; Nrsng.

**GROVE, STEPHANIE M,** Duquesne Univ, Pittsburgh, PA; JR; BA; WTAE Explr Grp 88-89; Monroeville Mall Mnstry Tlk Shp 90-; Bus/Mngmnt Info Sys.

**GROVER, RACHEL L,** Cornell Univ Statutory College, Ithaca, NY; SO; BS; Cornell Chorus 89-; Cornell Frnscs Socty 89-; Most Outstdng New Mbr Cornell Forensics Socty; Hmn Dev/Fmly Stds; Clin Psychlgy.

**GROVES, BRENDA A,** Univ Of North Fl, Jacksonville, FL; SR; BA; Gldn Key 88-; Summa Awrd OSU; Psychlgy; Frfghtng.

**GROVES, JOHN EDWARD,** Tn Temple Univ, Chattanooga, TN; SR; BS; Old Stone Bptst Chrc Pstr; Chrstn Ed; Mnstry.

**GROVES, MARK A,** Temple Univ, Philadelphia, PA; JR; BS; Assoc Gen Cont Amer Sec 90-; Amer Soc Cvl Engrs 90-; Amer Concrt Inst 89-; Subrbn Cont Assoc Schlrshp; Asst Supt Trnee Gra Const Houston TX; AGS Montgomery Co Comm Clg 88; Cvl/Const Engr; Proj Mgmt.

**GROVES, MICHELLE D,** Coll Of Charleston, Charleston, SC; JR; BS; Bapt Stdnt Un 90-; Omicron Delta Kappa; Charlie Post Meml Schlrshp; Athletic Hon Roll Pfeiffer Coll 88-89; Highly Dstngshd Stdnt 90-; Athletic Trng Stdnt Intern 88-; Phys Edn/Athletic Trng.

**GROWDEN, LINDA M,** Duquesne Univ, Pittsburgh, PA; SO; BS; Phi Eta; Big Sis; Univ Schlr; Phrmcy.

**GRUBB, JULIA A,** Ashland Comm Coll, Ashland, KY; FR; BA; KY Cert Emergncy Med Tech 88-; Jrnyman Diesl Elec Mech 88-; Engrng.

**GRUBB, KEVIN C,** Allegheny Coll, Meadville, PA; SO; BA; Hnr Comm 90; ALLIES 89-90; Yng Repubs 89-90; Econ; MA.

**GRUBB, KRISTEN R,** Wv Univ, Morgantown, WV; SO; BS; Chem Engrng.

**GRUBB, PATRICIA L,** Cincinnati Metropolitan Coll, Cincinnati, OH; JR; AD; Med Asstg Prog Vp/Pres; Metro Mssg Nwspr Stf; Janis E Eiler MD Intrnshp Med Asst; CPR/EMRGNCY Frst Aid Cert; Electrcrdgrph Tech Cert; Sftbl/Vlybl; Hoxworth Dnr; Med Asst.

**GRUBB, REBECCA G,** East Tn St Univ, Johnson City, TN; JR; BBA; Amer Mktg Assn; Bapt Stdnt Union; Delta Sigma Pi Finance Chr 90-; Mktg; Advrtsng/Promotion.

**GRUBB, STACEY R,** Spartanburg Methodist Coll, Spartanburg, SC; FR; BA; Criminal Justice Club 90-; Day Student Assoc 90-; Criminal Justice; Counseling.

**GRUBBS, C AMY D,** Radford Univ, Radford, VA; FR; BSN; Radford Redcoats Equestrian Tm 90-; Alpha Lambda Delta 90-; Delta Zeta 90-; Nursing; Pediatric/Nurse/Clinical Spec.

**GRUBBS, DENISE A,** Univ Of Al At Birmingham, Birmingham, AL; BA; Alpha Lmbd Dlt; Cmnctns; Brdcst Jrnlst.

**GRUBBS, JEFFREY W,** Univ Of Ms Main Cmps, University, MS; GD; PH D; Assn Fr Comp Mchnry 89-; Upsilon Pi Epsilon Pres 89-; Theta Xi Pres 80; Tuition Schlrshp 89-; Achvmnt Awrd 90; BA Illinois Institute Of Tech 80; MS 90; Comp Sci; Sftwre Eng.

**GRUBBS, JULIA F,** Thomas Nelson Comm Coll, Hampton, VA; JR; AAS; Pblc Admin; Pblc Admnstrtr.

**GRUBBS, NORRIS C,** Union Univ, Jackson, TN; FR; BA; Alpha Tau Omega 90-; Math; Pastor.

**GRUBBS, REBEKAH SMITH,** Liberty Univ, Lynchburg, VA; SR; BS; Hlth Dimensions Mjrs Clb Treas 89-; Amer Hrt Assn Intrn; Comm Hlth; Hlth Educ.

**GRUBBS, TERRI P,** Univ Of Southern Ms, Hattiesburg, MS; JR; BA; Stdnt Govt VP; Mrchg Bnd Drm Mjr; Stdnt Almn Assoc; Phi Theta Kappa Sec; Alpha Delta Pi Treas; Acctng/Econ Awds; Hl Fm; Stdnt Egl Clb; AS SW Miss Cmnty Clge 90; Acctng; CPA.

**GRUBER, GEORGE D,** Ithaca Coll, Ithaca, NY; JR; BS; Pres Host 89-; AMA 90-; Tae Kwon Do 89-; IM Vlybl 89-90; Mktg; Law.**

**GRUBER, JODI,** Nova Univ, Ft Lauderdale, FL; GD; MIBA; Mrktng Rep Art Inst Of Ft Ldrdle; BPS Bany Univ 90; AA Indian River Comm Coll 82; Intrntl Bus; Intrntl Mrktng.

**GRUBMAN, SETH D,** Univ Of Miami, Coral Gables, FL; FR; MBA; Hnrs Stdnts Assoc 90; Alpha Lambda Delta 90; Deans List 90; Intl Finance.

**GRUENFELD, JUDITH B,** Georgian Court Coll, Lakewood, NJ; SR; BSW; Scl Wrk Clb 90-; Delta Tau Kappa; OCC Phi Theta Kappa; Steuben Awd 85; AA Ocean Cty Coll Toms Rvr 87; Sclgy/Scl Wrk.

**GRUETTER, DANA M,** Edmondson Coll, Chattanooga, TN; FR; Bsnss Admin; Bsnss Mngmnt/Ownrshp.

**GRUHLER, DIANE L,** East Stroudsburg Univ, E Stroudsburg, PA; JR; BS; Organic Chem Tutor 90-; Bio/Pre-Med; Vet Med.

**GRUM, ALEXANDER M,** Duquesne Univ, Pittsburgh, PA; JR; BS; SAA VP 90; Beta Alpha Phi 90; Alpha Phi Omega; Acct; MBA CPA.

**GRUMBINE, MICHAEL S,** Univ Of Pittsburgh, Pittsburgh, PA; FR; BS; Engnrng.

**GRUNDNER, CHRISTOPHER T,** S U N Y Coll At Fredonia, Fredonia, NY; JR; Summer League Sftbl 89-; Wgtlftng 88-; Bus Clb 89-; Phlsphy Clb; Delta Mu Delta 90; Omicron Delta Epsilon; Undrgrad Tchrs Asst Bus; Undrgrad Tchrs Asst Phlsphy; IM Ftbl 88-.

**GRUNDON, BRYAN K,** Savannah Coll Of Art & Design, Savannah, GA; BFA 90; Pntng; Art Ed.

**GRUNDSETH, MAYTE A,** Univ Of Nc At Greensboro, Greensboro, NC; SR; BS; Foods Ntrtn Clb 89-; Amrcn Dietic Assn 90-; Fds Ntrtn; Clncl Dietetics.

**GRUNDY, DAMON LEE,** Univ Of New Haven, West Haven, CT; GD; BSC; Sccr; Lacrosse; Enrld Englsh Hnrs Crs 90; HND Thms Vly Clg 86-89; Htl Mgmnt; Htl Ctrng Indstry.

**GRUNDY, GLENN T,** Muskingum Coll, New Concord, OH; SR; BS; Jazz Ensmbl Wind Ensmbl Pep Band Pit Band 87-; Talent Show Crdntr Parents Wkend 88-; Sr Honorary 90-; Acdmc Achvmnt 89-90; IM Bsbl 87-88; English & Music; Teaching/Writing.

**GRUNER, HOLLY B,** Glassboro St Coll, Glassboro, NJ; JR; BA; Nwspaper Photogrphy Edtr 89-90; Photogrphr 90-; Pres List 88-89; Deans List 90; Religious Newsletter Edtr 90; Photogrphy Spclst JCC Camp 90; AA Camden Cnty Clg 90; Cmnctns.

**GRUNIG, LAURA A,** Univ Of Southern Ms, Hattiesburg, MS; JR; BS; Alumni Assn Exec Brd 89; Panhellenic Cncl Treas 90; Eagle Club 90; Alpha Lambda Delta 89; Omicron Delta Kappa 90-92; Phi Delta Rho Sec; Gamma Alpha Epsilon 90; Beta Alpha Psi 90; Phi Kappa Phi 90; Phi Eta Sigma 89; Acctg; CPA.

**GRUNINGER, JOHN E,** Le Moyne Coll, Syracuse, NY; SR; BA; Acctng; Tax Career Plnng.

**GRUNOW, KIERSTAN L,** Oh Wesleyan Univ, Delaware, OH; FR; WCSA 90-; Proj Hope 90-; Wsf 90-; Phi Eta Sigma 90-; Delta Zeta Clnd Clb Chr 90-; Proj Hope; Vars Wmns Bsktbl 90-; Econ; Intrntl Bus.

**GRUSCHOW, KATHLEEN M,** D Youville Coll, Buffalo, NY; SO; MS; Stu Occptnl Thrpy Assoc 90-; Res Cncl Tres; Occptnl Thrpy.

**GRUWELL, PHILIP S,** Tomlinson Coll, Cleveland, TN; SO; BA; Prfsnl Sngng Grp 89-; Bsktbl 89-; AA; Bsn; CPA.

**GRYSKIEWICZ HAGERTY, FRANCINE M,** Univ Of West Fl, Pensacola, FL; SR; Stdnt Cncl Excptnl Chldrn 89-; Bptst Campus Mnstry 89-; AA Pnscola Jr Coll; BA; Spec Ed; Emtnlly Hndcpd.

**GRZESIK, NANCY T,** Anne Arundel Comm Coll, Arnold, MD; GD; CERT; MD Assoc Of CPAS; MED Suffolk Univ 75; BS Gwynedd Mercy Clg 70; Fin Acctng; CPA.

**GRZYB, ROSEMARY S,** Slippery Rock Univ, Slippery Rock, PA; SR; BA; Spnsh Clb 90; Sigma Delta Pi; Deans Lst 90; Spnsh; Tchr.

**GSCHIEL, KIMBERLY J,** Univ Of Ga, Athens, GA; SR; BSED; Newspaper Ed 89-90; Yrbk 86-87; Choir 87-89; Hnr Soc 89-; Engl Ed; Tch MS.

**GSELL, LILLIAN STARR,** Wilmington Coll, New Castle, DE; SR; BS; Delta Epsilon Rho 90-; Dns Ls T88-; Acctng; CPA.

**GUADAGNO, ALEXANDER L,** Clarkson Univ, Potsdam, NY; SR; BS; Rd Hst Clarkson Rd St DJ; Dns Lst 90; Fnce; Fncl Mgmt.

**GUADAGNO, SUSAN J,** Ga St Univ, Atlanta, GA; SR; BA 90; Early Chldhd Educ; Tchr.

**GUADALUPE, MYRNA LEE ALAMO,** Univ Of Pr Cayey Univ Coll, Cayey, PR; JR; Hon Soc; Ed/Spnsh/Espcl Ed; Law.

**GUAGLIARDO, PAIGE A,** Hillsborough Comm Coll, Tampa, FL; JR; Math Educ; Tch.

**GUALBERTI, JOANN,** Wagner Coll, Staten Island, NY; SR; BS; Alld Hlth Sci Clb 89-; Stu Plnt Earth 89-90; Wgnr Coll Ushr 88-90; Omicron Delta Kappa Hstrn 90-; Beta Beta Beta Hstrn 89-; Alethea Wmns Recog Soc 89-; EM Rm Vol SI Univ Hosp 88-89; Bio; Med.

**GUALBERTI, LISA,** Wagner Coll, Staten Island, NY; SR; BS; Allied Hlth Sci Sec 89-90; Stu Plnt Earth 89-90; Rsrch/Orgnc Synthesis 90-; Omicron Delta Kappa Tres 90-; Alethea Wmns Recog Soc 89-; Amer Chem Soc/Stu Aflt 88-90; EM Rm Vol SI Univ Hosp 88-89; Chem; Med.

**GUALTIERI, JENNIFER,** Fordham Univ, Bronx, NY; FR; BS; Psych Clb 90-; Stdnt Nwspr 90-; EPAC 90-; Tutor 90-; Give A Child A Xmas 90; Comm Svc Chldrns Halloween Prty Dorm Coord 90; Physics.

**GUAN, CHANG-QIAN,** S U N Y Maritime Coll, Bronx, NY; SR; MBA; Piano/Bl Plyr Maritime Clg Bnd 90-; Thrd Ofcr Gnrl Shps Ou Shun/Kin Wai 84-86; Yick Fung Shpng Co Hong Kong; Dipl Timer Mavigation Inst Fugian Pr China 83; BS SUNY Maritime Clg; Bus Admin/Marine Trans.

**GUARD-KESHUTA, ALISON M,** Immaculata Coll, Immaculata, PA; SO; BA; Acctng; CPA.

**GUARDA, MICHAEL E,** Ny Univ, New York, NY; SO; AA; SG 90-; Debte 89-; Karate Shotokan 87-; Horse Back Rdng Awds 87-; Sigma Phi Epsilon 89-; Unit Nations Dev Prog Jerusalem Israel Intrn; Pltcl Sci/Econ; Intl Rltns/Pub Afrs BA.

**GUARNIERI, MARGARET M,** Spalding Univ, Louisville, KY; SR; BS; Adlt Stdnts Org Pres 90-; Delta Epsilon Sigma; Grad Magna Cum Laude; Wmn In Cmnctn Inc 90-; Optmst Clb; Cmnctns/Psychlgy; Mktg/Dvlpmnt.

**GUASP FERNANDEZ, LIZA M,** Inter Amer Univ Pr Guayama, Guayama, PR; SR; BA; Theatrical Grp 87-; Sci Cir 90-; Mu Delta Sigma Pres; Biology; Tch.

**GUAY, THOMAS D,** Univ Of Al At Huntsville, Huntsville, AL; GD; MSE; Amer Soc Mech Engrs 89-; Amer Inst Aero/Astro 89-; Pi Tau Sigma 90-; Co-Op Pgm Teledyne Brown Engr Diploma 88-90, BSE 90, Mech Engr, Engr.

**GUBA, KURT V,** The Boston Conservatory, Boston, MA; FR; BFA; Mus Theatre.

**GUBERT, WENDY A,** Univ Of Southern Ms, Hattiesburg, MS; SO; BA; Army ROTC 89-; AROTC Rngr Co 89-; Dept Army Suprior Cadet Awrd 89-; Nrsng.

**GUBSER, JOSEPH E,** Northern Ky Univ, Highland Hts, KY; FR; BS; Bus.

**GUCCIONE, JOANNE M,** City Univ Of Ny Baruch Coll, New York, NY; SR; Italian Soc 87; Advertising Intrnshp; Mktg; Advrtsng Rsrch.

**GUDGER, DENISE M,** Univ Of Nc At Greensboro, Greensboro, NC; GD; Ordr Omega 890-90; Sigma Sigma Sigma Pldg Pres 89-90; BS 90; Early Chldhd Educ; Tchr.

**GUDYKA, MICHELE K,** Germanna Comm Coll, Locust Grove, VA; AAS; Gamma Chi V P 90-; Alpha Beta Gamma 87-; Lambda Alpha Epsilon 90-; AAS 90; Crmnl Justice; Law.

**GUEH, GBOR SOLOMON,** Interdenominational Theo Ctr, Atlanta, GA; GD; MDIV; Intl Stdnt Assn 89-; ITC Pres 89-; Lbrn Cmnty Assn GA V P 90-; Chrstn Educ Fndtn Liberia Pres 85; Intl Chrstn Fllwshp Mnstr Rel 90-; Edith Hines African Stdnt Award; Dipl Gbarnsa Schl Theology 77; BTH 87; Mnstry/Old Tstmnt; Minister.

**GUELCHER, KARYN R,** Oh St Univ, Columbus, OH; SR; BA; Crw Clb 87-89; Univ Hons Prgrm 87-; Yr-Long Co-Op; Arabic.

**GUENARD, LISA M,** Bunker Hill Comm Coll, Boston, MA; SO; BA; AA; Graphics/Visual Cmnctns; Illus.

**GUENTHER, JEAN M,** Westminster Coll, New Wilmingtn, PA; SO; BA; Deans Lst 89-; Spanish; Educ.

**GUERCIO, CHRISTINE E,** Indiana Univ Of Pa, Indiana, PA; SR; PSEA-NEA 89-90; Stdnt Tchng 90; BED 90; Elem Ed; Tchng.

**GUERCIO, KIMBERLY ANN,** Univ Of Akron, Akron, OH; SR; Akron Cncl Ed Stdnts 90-; Bapt Stdnt Union 90-; Sierra Clb 89-90; Deans Lst 88-90; Cleveland City Schls Vlntr 89-; Girl Sct Cncl Ldr 90-; Grn Vly Elem Sch Stdnt Tchr 90-; BS Ed; Tchng.

**GUERETTE, RANDALL T,** Univ Of Nh Plymouth St Coll, Plymouth, NH; SO; MBA; Stdnt Govt Frshmn Sntor 89-90; Plymouth St Hngldng Clb 89-90; Jdcl Brd 89-90; Rwng Clb Fndr/Pres 90-; Psi Chi; Scott Descoteux Schlrshp 90-; Bard Intvntnl Prdts 87-89; U S Navy USS Enterprise CVN 65 83-87; Bsn; Mktg.

**GUERIN, JULIE D,** Washington & Lee Univ, Lexington, VA; FR; Actvies Brd 90-; Orntn 90-; Chi Omega 90-.

**GUERIN, MARSHALL W,** Univ Of Toledo, Toledo, OH; GD; JD; BA Earlham Clg 89; Law.

**GUERIN, NATHALIE D,** Alcorn St Univ, Lorman, MS; SO; BS; Nrsng.

**GUERINO, ALISON C,** Univ Of Fl, Gainesville, FL; SR; BAE; Art Educ/Conc Prnt Mkng; Tchg.

**GUERNICA OYARZON, MAGDALENA M,** Inter Amer Univ Pr Hato Rey, Hato Rey, PR; FR; BA; Engl/Lit; Tch.

**GUERRA, BRIDGET M,** Newbury Coll, Brookline, MA; FR; BA; Cumberland Farms 87; Acct.

**GUERRA, TRACY A,** Endicott Coll, Beverly, MA; SO; BA; Shpmts 89-; Yrbk Lyout Edtr 90-; Orientation Ldr 90-; Actvties 90-; Dns Lst 89-; Phi Theta Kappa 90-; Chronicle Nwspr Glens Fall N Y Intrn 90; Lange Collyer Assoc Ad Agency Intrn; Advrtsng.

**GUERRERO DAVILA, YOLANDA,** Bayamon Central Univ, Bayamon, PR; SR; BA; Coll Sec Intl Assn 87-; Estudns 89-; Sec.

**GUERRERO, ESTHER M,** Fl International Univ, Miami, FL; JR; BA; Teacher Aide St Brendan Elem 90-; Elem Ed; Tchr.

**GUERRERO, JORGE,** Univ Politecnica De Pr, Hato Rey, PR; FR.

**GUERRERO, RICHARD,** Savannah Coll Of Art & Design, Savannah, GA; SO; BA; Grphc Dsgn.

**GUERRIER, ROCH ANTHONY,** Miami Dade Comm Coll North, Miami, FL; SO; AA; Blck Incentive Awd Schlrshp 89-; Psychlgy; Soc Wrk.

**GUERRIERO, FRANCO G,** Pa St Univ Delaware Cty Cmps, Media, PA; FR; BA; Bus; Acctng.

**GUERRIERO, MICHELLE M,** Mount Saint Mary Coll, Newburgh, NY; JR; BS; Stdnts Actvies Comm Sec 88-89; VP 89-90; Orntn Ldr; Co Chrmn Stdnt Tele Fnd; Phi Theta Kappa; Cls Agnt; Dns Lst Awd; Phi Theta Kappa; Roscoe Woodward Schlrshp; Peer Tutor; Tour Gde; Grl Sct Ldr Asst; Adpt A Trstee; Dn For Day; Grad Spkr; Soc Sci; Elem Educ Tchr.

**GUERRINI, JAMES G,** Boston Univ, Boston, MA; GD; MD; Amer Medl Schl Assoc 90-; Alpha Omega Alpha VP; Golden Key; Phi Delta Epsilon Secy; BA 88; Family Medicine.

**GUERRIOS, RICARDO MATOS,** Caribbean Univ, Bayamon, PR; SO; Fui Miembro De La Assoc De Est; De Admin De Empresas En La Univ; Del Sagrado Conazon; Math/Hstry; MBA/ADMIN Cmrcl.

**GUERTIN, CHRISTOPHER M,** Barry Univ, Miami, FL; SO; Amer Mktg Assn; Ecnmcs Clb 90-; Hon Stdnt Assn 89-90; Outstndng Fresh 89-90; Outstndng Soph 90-; Mktg.

**GUEST, GINA W,** Ms St Univ, Miss State, MS; SO; BVA; Hall Cncl; Stdnt Assn Fin Comm Sec; Gamma Beta Phi; Phi Eta Sigma; Chi Omega; Mgmt.

**GUEST, SCOTT H,** Ms St Univ, Miss State, MS; SO; BA; Kappa Alpha Alumni Chr 89; Cave/Curr Comm 89-; Trffc Appls 89-; Phi Eta Sigma 89-; Gamma Beta Phi 90-; Blue Key 90-; Beta Beta Beta 89-; Untd Way 89-; MD 89-; Bio Sci/Orient 90-; Schlrshp Recog Day/Pres Lst 90; IM Ftbl 89-; Micro; Med Field.

**GUET, SYLVAIN B,** Fl International Univ, Miami, FL; JR; Edit Mtrmrphsis Miami Dade Edit 90; Sigma Alpha Mu; Hsptlty Mgt; Law.**

**GUETERMAN, SCOTT A,** Univ Of Cincinnati, Cincinnati, OH; JR; BA; Audio Eng Scty 89; Prcssve Arts Scty 89; Brdcstng; Media Prdctn.

**GUEVARA, DIEGO GERMAN,** Meridian Comm Coll, Meridian, MS; MBA; HRM DECA Pres 89-; Red Cross WSI 90-; Life Gd 85-; Kitchen Mgr; Prod Sprvsr Hosp Dietary; AS Meridian Comm Coll 90; Math Mgmt Mkrg; Bus Admin Mgmt.

**GUEVARA, MANUEL A,** City Univ Of Ny La Guard Coll, Long Island Cty, NY; SR; Ecuador Scl Clb V P/Pres 89-; Cmptr Sci Engr.

**GUEVARA JR, MARTIN,** Univ Of Pr At Mayaguez, Mayaguez, PR; FR; AICHE 90-; IIQPR P R 90-; Soc Sci; Chem Engr.

**GUEVARA, MIRTHA M,** Fl International Univ, Miami, FL; SR; MAT; Phi Kappa Phi 90-; Tchr Atlantis Acad 90-; BA 87; Cert Educ 89-90; Spcl Educ; Mstrs.

**GUEVIN, LAURA M,** Univ Of New Haven, West Haven, CT; FR; BA; Schl Newspapr Wrtr 90; Hnrs Prog 90; Pres Schlrshp 90; Cmmnctns; Jrnlsm.

**GUFFEY, TERESA E,** Western Piedmont Comm Coll, Morganton, NC; FR; BA; Stdnt Govt Sntr 90-; Phi Theta Kappa; Bsn Cmptr Pgmg; Bsn.

**GUGLIOTTI, GIOVANNA E,** Teikyo Post Univ, Waterbury, CT; JR; BA; Fshn Merch; Buyer.

**GUGLIOTTI, JOHN E,** Mattatuck Comm Coll, Waterbury, CT; SO; AS; Boy Scts Egl Sct 86-; Police Explr Capt 87-; Criminal Justice; Police Ofcr.**

**GUHSE, LAURA K,** Anne Arundel Comm Coll, Arnold, MD; SO; BA; Psychlgy.**

**GUIA, BARBARA M,** Saint Thomas Univ, Miami, FL; SR; BA; Elem Educ.

**GUIBAL, S SABINE,** Ms St Univ, Miss State, MS; SR; BA; Vrsty Tns Tm 88-90; Spnsh Frnch Clb; Intrntnl Stdnts Clb; Prsdnts Schlr 89-; Frnch Hnr Soc; Athltc Schlrshp; Frgn Lang Trnsltn.

**GUIBERNAU, MARIANA,** Saint Thomas Univ, Miami, FL; SR; Pol Action Club VP 89-; Delta Epsilon Sigma Secy 90-; Delta Phi Epsilon 90-; Vol At Palm Spring Gen Hosp Bus Ofc; Acadmc Exclnc In Crmnl Jstc; BA; Crmn Jstc/Pol Sci; Law.**

**GUICE, JENNIFER N,** Univ Of Al At Huntsville, Huntsville, AL; FR; BA; Natl Scty Black Engrs; Black Stdnt Assoc VP 90-; Alpha Lambda Delta; Engrng; Optical.

**GUICE, VICTORIA L,** Alcorn St Univ, Lorman, MS; FR; Hstry; Econ.

**GUIDARELLI, PATRICIA A,** Schenectady County Comm Coll, Schenectady, NY; AAS; Cmptr Prgrmng.

**GUIDER, KATHY S,** Benedict Coll, Columbia, SC; SR; BS; MATE 88-90; NEA; Tchng Spl Ed 77; BS Of Front Cover; Spl Ed Minor Early Childhood; Ed Admin.**

**GUIDER, LORA C,** Pellissippi St Tech Comm Coll, Knoxville, TN; SO; AAS; Clgte Secr Intl V P 90-; Bsn.**

**GUIDICE, LAURA A,** Indiana Univ Of Pa, Indiana, PA; SR; BS; WIUP-TV Newswrtr Flr Dir 89-; Awrded Nwswrtr Awd WIUP-TV 90; Outstndng Mem Awd WIUP-TV 90; Cmnctns Media; Pblc Rltns.

**GUIDO, DINA M,** Fordham Univ, Bronx, NY; JR; BS; Frdhm Dnc Tm 89-90; Fnc Scty89-; Cmmnty Srvc Ttrng 89-; Fnc Internshp NBC 90; Dnc Tm 89-90; Bus Amdn Fnc.

**GUIDO, MAUREEN C,** Coll Misericordia, Dallas, PA; SR; BSA; Acctg Clb Pblcty 89-; Envrnmntl Clb Treas 89-; Ltrtr Clb Layout Stff 87-89; Bus/Acctg; Mngrl Acctg.

**GUIDRY, LISA MARIE,** Radford Univ, Radford, VA; FR; BS; Nwspr Wrtr 90-; Brdcstrs Gld 90-; Zeta Tau Alpha 90-; Spch; Pblc Rltns/Bsn.

**GUIDRY, MONA J,** Thomas Nelson Comm Coll, Hampton, VA; SO; AAS; Intrnshp Houston Color Dsgn/Mktg 90-; Cmmrcl Art; Cmmrcl Dsgn.

**GUIDRY, RUTH A,** Univ Of Southern Ms, Hattiesburg, MS; SO; Plymr Sci Clb Tresr 90; Pent Chrstn Fllwshp 90-; Hnr Std Assc 89-90; Alpha Epsilon Delta 89-90; Alpha Lambda Delta 90-; Gamma Beta Phi 90-; Prs Schlr 89-; Pre Med Std Yr 89-90; Dns Lst 90; Math; Scndry Ed.

**GUILARTE, VANESSA VINAS,** Fl International Univ, Miami, FL; SR; BA; AA Miami Dade Comm Clg 88; Engl Ed; Tchr.

**GUILBAUD, STANLEY,** Inter Amer Univ Pr Hato Rey, Hato Rey, PR; SO; Sccr 88-90; Judo 87-90; Alphbtztn Prgrm 89-90; Science 87-90; Math 87-90; Elctrncs; Engnrng.

**GUILBEAULT, MARYBETH C,** Daytona Beach Comm Coll, Daytona Beach, FL; SO; Phi Theta Kappa; Bus; Admn.

**GUILBERT, SHERRIE M,** Elmira Coll, Elmira, NY; FR; RI Hnr Soc 90; IM Sftbl 90-; Psy; Grntlgy.

**GUILFORD, WENDY CAROL,** Norfolk St Univ, Norfolk, VA; SR; BA; Naacp 86-88; Mass Commnctns Scty Assoc 88-; Intrnng Pblc Affrs Offc; Communications; Pblc Rltns.

**GUILFOYLE, PATRICIA A,** Va Commonwealth Univ, Richmond, VA; SR; BA; Engl; Prfsr.

**GUILIANELLI, AMY L,** Allegheny Coll, Meadville, PA; SO; BA; Alden Schlr 89-90; Kappa Alpha Theta 90-; Psychlgy/Elem Ed; Hgh Schl Gdnc Cnslr/Schl Ps.

**GUILLEMETTE, EVE-LYNE G,** Fl St Univ, Tallahassee, FL; SR; BA; Stdnt Govt/Nwspr Grphc Dsgnr 88-89; Intl Clb 87-88; Pi Delta Phi 90-; Art Awd 87-88; IM Sccr/Sftbl 88-89; Multi Lngl Multi Cltrl Educ; Tchng/Trnsltns.

**GUILLEN MARICHAL, IAN E,** Univ Of Pr Cayey Univ Coll, Cayey, PR; FR; Hnr Rl; Acctng; Law.

**GUILLEN, SUSANNE A,** Christopher Newport Coll, Newport News, VA; SR; BS; Aircraft Owners/Pilots Assn 87-; Amer Red Crs 86-; Mgt Flying Clb 87-89; FAA PPL Flight Intl/Fed Aviation Admin 89; Mgmt; Aviation.

**GUILLERMAIN, SUZANNE M,** Atlantic Comm Coll, Mays Landing, NJ; JR; BA; Dns Lst 90; AA 90; Bus; Acctng.

**GUILLERMO, CRISTINA A,** Brevard Coll, Brevard, NC; FR; BA; Cncrt Bnd; Woodwnd Ensmbl; Proj Inside-Out; Lang.

**GUILLORY, BRANT D,** Nc St Univ At Raleigh, Raleigh, NC; FR; BA; Cllgte Mscns Gld 90; Army ROTC 90; Army ROTC Schlrshp; Im Soccer 90; Engl Wrtng Edtng; Mltry Intllgnce Offcr.

**GUILLOT, LORI A,** Univ Of Southern Ms, Hattiesburg, MS; SO; BA; Jr Vrsty Chrldr/Sthrn Ms Dnc Tm/Stdnt Almn Assoc 89-; Lambda Sigma 89-; Gamma Beta Phi 89-; Chi Tau Epsilon 89-; Kappa Delta Prlmntrn 89-; Rs Mny Absd Chldrn 89-; Dns Lst/Dnc Schlrshps 89-; Dnc; Own Dnc Std/Ftns Ctr.

**GUIMOND, LORI A,** Western New England Coll, Springfield, MA; SO; BA; Acctg Assoc 89-; Mgmt Assoc 90-; Alpha Lambda Delta 89-; Stdnt Asst Acctg Dept 90-; Dns Lst 89-; Acctg; CPA.

**GUIMOND, SCOTT A,** Western New England Coll, Springfield, MA; FR; BA; Mngmnt; Bus.

**GUIMOND, TANIA A,** Merrimack Coll, North Andover, MA; SO; BA; Model Un 90-; Coll Lit Mag Edtr 90-; Ash Hl Cncl Pres 89-; Wrtng Ctr Peer Tutor 90-; Engl; Actng/Dir.

**GUIN, ELIZABETH S,** Northwest Al Comm Coll, Phil Campbell, AL; FR; Phi Theta Kappa 90; LPN 90; RN.

**GUIN, STEPHANIE D,** Itawamba Comm Coll, Fulton, MS; SO; Choir.

**GUION, STEVEN C,** Christopher Newport Coll, Newport News, VA; JR; BSBA; Cert ECPI 86; Mgmt; Bsn.

**GUIRGUIS, IRENE,** Radford Univ, Radford, VA; SR; Va Stdnt Educ Assn St V P 87-; Stdnt Life 87-; Kappa Delta Pi 89-; Zeta Tau Alpha Sec 88-; Remedl Acad Aid; BS; Erly/Mdl Educ; Tchr.

**GUISHARD, INGRID P,** Al A & M Univ, Normal, AL; SO; Stdnt Drg Tsk Frc Rsrch Cmt 90-; Intrntl Stds Assc Assc Edtr 90-; Bapt Stdnt Union; Deans List; Engl/Psychlgy Ed; Cnslng.

**GUIVEN-LOPEZ, ANNIE,** Univ Of Pr At Rio Piedras, Rio Piedras, PR; SO; Pre Med Stdnts Org; Hnr Lst Of Flcty Of Nat Sci; JMV Religious Socty Srvc VP 90-; Biology; Med.

**GULA, JOHN J,** Univ Of Pittsburgh, Pittsburgh, PA; SR; BS; ASCE 89-; Chi Epsilon 90-; Cvl Eng.

**GULAK, MICHELE J,** Lesley Coll, Cambridge, MA; SR; BS; Stdnt Govt VP 88-89; Humn Svcs/Spec Educ.

**GULAM, SANDRA D,** Saint Johns Univ, Jamaica, NY; FR; Crmnl Jstc.

**GULLA, NATALIE M,** Wv Northern Comm Coll, Wheeling, WV; AD; Stdnt Nrs Assoc; Nursing.

**GULLA, TIFFINY M,** Oh Univ, Athens, OH; FR; BA; Mvmnt Dance Orgnztn 90-; Envrmntl Clb Otrch Brnch 90-; Ntnl Rcyclng Ed Scty 90; Dance; Chrgrphy.

**GULLEDGE, MITCHEL R,** Coker Coll, Hartsville, SC; JR; BA; Deans Lst 88-; Top Ten Stdnt 88-; Eng Tchncn SC State Hwy Dept 89-; Educ.

**GULLEY, CLARA C,** Concordia Coll, Selma, AL; SO; AA; Cmmnty Cntr Orgr Pres 90-; Chrch Clrk; Bus Admn.

**GULLEY, ELIZABETH E,** Merrimack Coll, North Andover, MA; SR; BA; Intrfratnty Sorty Cncl Pres; Pi Theta Epsilon; Rites Of Christian Initiation For Adlts Prog; Rev Joseph A Flaherty Schlrshp; Upperclsmn Acadmc Schlrshp; Engl; Ed/HS Tchr.

**GULLINESE, PETER J,** Schenectady County Comm Coll, Schenectady, NY; SR; AAS; Crmnl Justc Club SCCC 90; Phi Theta Kappa 90; Pres Lst 89; NY State Sheriffs Assn Schlrshp Rcpnt 90; NYS Army Natl Guard 88; Crmnl Justc; Fdrl Law Enfrcmnt.

**GULLION, KEVIN L,** Shawnee St Univ, Portsmouth, OH; FR; BA; Psych Clb Treas; Elem Educ; Tchr.

**GULLO, KRISTY R,** Vanderbilt Univ, Nashville, TN; FR; BS MD; I M Sftbl 90-; Gamma Beta Phi; Phi Eta Sigma; Alpha Lambda Delta; Hosp Vol 90-91; Biology.

**GULVAS, VICKI L,** Indiana Univ Of Pa, Indiana, PA; SR; BA; Midget Ftbl Chrldng Advsr 87-88; Elem Ed; Tchr.

**GUMA, RICHARD J,** Ny Chiropractic Coll, Glen Head, NY; SR; DC; Mstr Of Ceremonies NYCC Talent Shw; BA Montclair St Clg 87; Chiroprctc.

**GUMAN, DENISE L,** Indiana Univ Of Pa, Indiana, PA; SR; BA; Easter Seals Soc Dir 87-90; Cncl Exptnl Chldrn 90-; Univ Chrs 89-90; Educ Excptnl Prsns/Spnsh; Tchr.

**GUMBS, ALICIA ANN,** Allen Univ, Columbia, SC; SR; BA; Stu Govt Assn Bus Mgr 88-89; NAACP 88-; Phi Beta Lambda 88-; Pan Hllnc Cncl Pres 90; Delta Sigma Theta Pres 89-; Trck Tm Capt 89-90; Bus Admnf Intl Trade.

**GUMBS, CARLEEN PATRICIA,** Paine Coll, Augusta, GA; JR; BA; Intrntl Stdnt Org 88-; Bptst Stdnt Union 88-; Hnr Scty 88-; Hnr Rl 89-; Deans Lst 89-90; Amer Acad Yrbk 89-90; Bus Admin; CPA.

**GUMBS, CEPHAS S,** Tuskegee Univ, Tuskegee Inst, AL; JR; BARCH; Internatl Stdnts Assoc; Caribbean Stdnts Assoc; Alpha Kappa Mu; Tau Sigma Delta; Architecture.

**GUMP JR, JAMES N,** Univ Of Akron, Akron, OH; JR; BA; Choral; Kappa Delta Pi; Acad Schlrshp 89-; Educ Ministry.

**GUMPERT, ALICIA M,** James Madison University, Harrisonburg, VA; JR; BSN; Nrsng VP; Stdnt Nrs Assn VA Sec; Stndt Affrs/Mktg Com; N VA Comm Coll 88; EMT/CCT N VA Comm Coll 88; Nrsng; Medcl Schl.

**GUNASEKARA, CHANAKA H,** City Univ Of Ny City Coll, New York, NY; SO; ASCE Stdnt Chptr 90-; Concrete Canoe Clb; Federick Douglass Dbtng Scty 90; Deans Lst; Intl Stdnt Assc; Tutor; GCE Advncd Lvl Royal Coll Sri Lanka 88; Engineering; Civil/Env Eng.

**GUNASEKARA, RUKMAL D,** Strayer Coll, Washington, DC; JR; BSC; Alpha Chi Awd Outstndng Jr Stdnt; Cnfdntl Sec 75-84; Accnts Asst 87-; Cert USDA Grad Schl 89; Acctng/Mgmt.

**GUNDLACH, ELLEN,** Fl St Univ, Tallahassee, FL; FR; Marchng Chiefs 90; Concert Band; Phi Eta Sigma 90-; Golden Key 90-; Chem Engrng.

**GUNN, ANDREA R,** Univ Of Al At Birmingham, Birmingham, AL; FR; BA; Pres Lst; Chrldr Capt 90-; Phys Thrpy; Sprts Med.

**GUNN, BRIDGETT L,** Al St Univ, Montgomery, AL; SO; Phi Eta Sigma 90-; Bus; Actnt.

**GUNN, CANDIE R,** Univ Of Nc At Charlotte, Charlotte, NC; SR; BA; Psych Clb 90-; Psych.

**GUNN, JONI OTT,** Faulkner St Jr Coll, Bay Minette, AL; SO; BA; Leisure Svcs; Rcrtnl Thrpy.

**GUNN, KAREN L,** Univ Of South Al, Mobile, AL; JR; BED; Stdt Govt/Senator/Educ Dept Sntr 83; Stdt Council Exceptional Children Sec; Our Lady Gulf Catholic Church Lector 90-; Special Education.

**GUNN, KATHERINE M,** Western New England Coll, Springfield, MA; SR; Math Clb Pres 90-; Peer Tutor; Lambda Delta; Intrnshp Mass Mutual Life Insur Co; Allen E Anderson Awrd.

**GUNN, LARRY DONNELL,** Piedmont Comm Coll, Roxboro, NC; FR; ADN; Peer Tutor; Nrsng.

**GUNNELL, SCOTT R,** Univ Of Cin R Walters Coll, Blue Ash, OH; SO; AS; Outstndng Achvmnts Computer Sci; Bowling Tm 89; Computer Sci; Programmer.

**GUNNELS III, ROBERT E,** Univ Of Sc At Columbia, Columbia, SC; JR; BIS; Nwspr Sprts Edtr 90-; Tau Kappa Epsilon Tres 89-; Sprtscstr Radio 90-; Samuel A Cothran Jrnlsm; IM Bsktbl 90-; Ftr Aiken Cnty Comm Chmbr Cmrc; Navy 84-88; Qualified Subs; Jrnlsm; Sprtswrtr.**

**GUNNOE, JUDY A,** Beckley Coll, Beckley, WV; BS; Transp Mgr 86-90; Sci; RN.

**GUNSCH, ALBERT W,** Middle Tn St Univ, Murfreesboro, TN; FR; BA; Jzz Prfrmnce; Stdio Mscn.

**GUNTER, EMILY K,** Gannon Univ, Erie, PA; FR; MBA; Tri-Beta Tr 90-; Soccer Tm 90-; Bio; Med.

**GUNTER, JEANA L,** Judson Coll, Marion, AL; SO; BS; Soc Cmts Frhsmn Rep 89-90; Judson Schlrs Hstrn 90- Pres; Educ; Elem Sch Tchr.

**GUNTER, JERRICKA L,** Univ Of Fl, Gainesville, FL; SO; BS; Pres Minority Schlr 89-; Minority Mentor 89-90; AS; Bsn; Mktg.**

**GUNTER, KIMBERLY K,** Middle Tn St Univ, Murfreesboro, TN; SR; BS; Lambda Org MTSU VP 89-; Tau Omicron; Gamma Beta Phi Sec 87-89; Sigma Tau Delta; Phi Kappa Phi; Peck Awd Engl Dept 90; Engl; Rsrch.

**GUNTER, KRISTI A,** Radford Univ, Radford, VA; JR; BS; SEA 90-; Baptist Union 90-; Kappa Delta Pi 90-; Chldhd Tchr.

**GUNTHARP, PAMELA M,** Itawamba Comm Coll, Fulton, MS; SO; BA; Eng Club Pres 90-; Spanish Club Pres 89-90; Bapt Stdnt Un Exec Cncl Mbr 90-; Phi Theta Kappa 90-; Eng; Teach.

**GUNTHER, DANIEL J,** Univ Of Rochester, Rochester, NY; SO; BA; Econ/Mktg; Prodct Mktg Mgr.

**GUNTIN, JOSE A,** Fl International Univ, Miami, FL; JR; BA; AA Miami Dade Cmnty Clge 88; Psychlgy; PHD.

**GUPTA, AMITABHA,** Hahnemann Univ, Philadelphia, PA; GD; MD; Med Stdnt Rsrch Clb 89-; Hmlss Clnc 90-; Ptnt Grntd Comp Ntwrk Protocols 90; Berman Schlrshp 90; Ludwig Fndtn Schlrshp 90-; Mc Graw Hill Bk Awd 90; IEEE 86-; Eng Mgr Bell Northern Rsrch 82-89; BSEE Mc Master Univ 82; Med; Clncl Prctc/Rsrch.

**GUPTA, RACHNA,** City Univ Of Ny Baruch Coll, New York, NY; SO; BBA; Acctg Soc Corres Sec; Walkamerica Vol; Acctg.

**GUPTA, RITU,** Univ Of Miami, Coral Gables, FL; FR; BSMD; Nwspr Stf 90-; IM Mgr 90-; Circle K 90-; Hnrs Stdnt Assoc 90-; Frshmn Hnr Scty 90-; Indian Stdnts Assoc 90-; Hnrs Prog Medicine 90-; Resident Asstnt; IM Vlbybl Sftbl Ftbl Sccr; Biology; Medicine.

**GUPTA, SAMEER,** Old Dominion Univ, Norfolk, VA; GD; PHD; Eta Kappa Nu 88-; Tau Beta Pi 88-; Alha Chi 89-; IEEE 89-; Dmn Schlr 87-90; Kvnr Schlr 89-90; Comp Eng Fclty Awrd 90; BS 90; Comp Eng.

**GUPTA, VIBHOOTI SURENDRA,** George Mason Univ, Fairfax, VA; FR; BABS; Assn Indian Stu; Psychlgy Experm; Bus Admn; Dcsn Sci.

**GURA, DAMON E,** Oh Univ, Athens, OH; FR; BSEE; Rugby; Delta Tau Delta; Elec Engrng; Rsrch.

**GURDISON, BRUCE R,** Bloomfield Coll, Bloomfield, NJ; JR; BA; Alpha Chi; Amer Soc Qlty Cntrl; Prod Mngmnt QC; AA Union Co Coll 76; Cert; Mtrls Mngmnt.

**GUREVICH, YELENA,** City Univ Of Ny Baruch Coll, New York, NY; JR; BBA; CSTEP Clb; Computer Clb; Cmptr Info Syst; Cmptr Pgmg.

**GUREVITZ, MICHAEL J,** Oh St Univ, Columbus, OH; SR; BA; Goldn Key 90-; Pi Sigma Alpha 90-; Arts Sci Awd Excell Schlrshp 90; Summa Awd 87; Pol Sci; U S Govt.

**GURGANUS, JILL R,** Radford Univ, Radford, VA; SR; BS; Intrnshp Montgomery Co Hosp; Hlth Educ; Hosp Admin.

**GURLEY, ANGELA R,** Va Highlands Comm Coll, Abingdon, VA; JR; BA; Cost Analyst 86-; Acctg/Cmptrs.

**GURLEY, CORETTA,** Al A & M Univ, Normal, AL; JR; Natl Soc Blck Engrs 90-; Sigma Tall Epsilon 89-; Drll Tm 88-90; Pres Schlr Lst 88-89; Boeing Co-Op Intrnshp; Comp Sci; Pgmr.**

**GURLEY JR, JAMES R,** Middle Ga Coll, Cochran, GA; JR; BA; Bapt Stdnt Un Hall Sect 89-; Dns Lst; AA 90; Publ Admin; Cnty/Cty Plnnr.

**GURLEY, STEVEN N,** Univ Of Tn At Martin, Martin, TN; FR; BS; SCA Pres 90-; Stdnt Affil Amer Chem Soc 90-; Martial Arts Clb 90-; Soc Hnrs Sem Stdnts VP 90-; Tri Beta 90-; CRC Prs Frshmn Chmstry Acvmnt Awd; Chmstry/Biology; Chem Biological Rsrch.

**GURLEY, TERESA R,** Mayland Comm Coll, Spruce Pine, NC; FR; Empl Amer Thread Co 84-87; Empl Outboard Marine Corp 87-90; Med/Admin Offc Tech.

**GUSLER, LENORA L,** Western Ky Univ, Bowling Green, KY; SO; BA; Alpha Sigma Lambda Eta Iota Chaptr 90-; Holy Trinity Luth Church S S 84-85; AAL 83-; Tm Leader Materials Lord Corp 88-90; Bus Mngmnt.

**GUST, ANDREW C,** Cooper Union, New York, NY; SR; JD; Amer Soc Mech Engrs 89-; Fl Schlrshp 87-; BE; Mech Engr; Patnt Law.

**GUST, TRACY L,** Univ Of Ky, Lexington, KY; SR; BS; Gldn Ky 90-; Comp Sci.

**GUSTAFSON, ERICA C,** Duquesne Univ, Pittsburgh, PA; FR.

**GUSTAFSON, MARY T,** Kent St Univ Kent Cmps, Kent, OH; JR; BA; Mktg; Tchng.

**GUSTAFSSON, HELENA M,** Oh Wesleyan Univ, Delaware, OH; JR; BA; Chrl Art Soc 88-89; Chmbr Sngrs 88-89; INTRNL; Phi Eta Sigma 89-; Phi Soc; Phi Sigma Iota; Sigma Iota Rho; Intrntnl Rltns Frnch.

**GUSTIN, KATHY S,** Oh Univ-Southern Cmps, Ironton, OH; FR; BBA; Bus.

**GUSTWILLER, DAVID P,** Bowling Green St Univ, Bowling Green, OH; BFA; Amer Ctr Dsgn 90-; Beta Theta Pi Schlrshp 87-; Grphc Dsgnr.

**GUTARRA, EDGAR N,** Univ Of Pr At Mayaguez, Mayaguez, PR; SO; Psychlgy; Chem Engr.**

**GUTARRA-NEGRON, MIGUEL,** Bayamon Central Univ, Bayamon, PR; JR; Pgm Srvc Apy Al Estdnt 90-; Cert De Prgrs 85-86; Bsbl 87-88; Mrcd; Dir.

**GUTCHES, MICHAEL,** Christopher Newport Coll, Newport News, VA; SO; BA; Paratrpr 82nd Arbrn Div 87-90; Bsn Mgmt; Fncl Mgmt.

**GUTELIUS, KENNETH E,** Univ Of Rochester, Rochester, NY; SR; BS; Amer Soc Mech Engr 89-; Sailing Team 88-90; Mech Engr.

**GUTERRES, KATHLEEN M,** Johnson St Coll, Johnson, VT; SR; Magna Cum Laude; BA; Education Spec Educ; Tchr.

**GUTFRIEND, THELMA R,** Nova Univ, Ft Lauderdale, FL; GD; MBA; Stdnts For Israel Pres 69-70; Jewish Culture Fndtn VP 69-70; Fndrs Day Hnrs 71; N Y Union Jewish Stdnt Co VP 69-70; Vassar Coll Dns Lst 68-69; Mntry Phs Condo Bd Treas 90-; BA NYU Wash Sq Coll 71,MPA Grd Schl Pub Admn 77; Bus; Acctng/Mngmnt Cnsltng.

**GUTHALS, MELISSA D,** Savannah Coll Of Art & Design, Savannah, GA; SO; BFA; Bapt Stdnt Un Pr 89-90; Hall Cncl; HOW 90-; Video; Corp Video.

**GUTHINGER, DENNIS J,** Western New England Coll, Springfield, MA; SO; BS; IM Athletes; Math Resrce Tutor 90-; Var Flbl 89-90; Govt; Law.

**GUTHMANN, ROBERT A,** Fl Atlantic Univ, Boca Raton, FL; JR; BBA; Stdnt Govt Rep 88-89; MDCC; Chi Phi Dir Food Serv 79-81; IM Ftbl U Of Ga 81; Greater Miami Chefs Assn Del 85-; Oprtns Rep For Raymond James & Assoc 89-; Mgmt; MBA Corp Gen Mgmt.

**GUTHRIE, BENJAMIN J,** Univ Of Southern Ms, Hattiesburg, MS; JR; BA; Hnrs Assc 90-; Phi Theta Kappa Almn 90-; Delta Sigma Pi; Phi Theta Kappa Schlrshp 90; Schlr Awd 90; AA Est Cntrl Cmnty Clg 90; Acctg; CPA.

**GUTHRIE, BEVERLY D,** Walker Coll, Jasper, AL; SO; MBS; Phi Theta Kappa; Pres Lst 89; Kawanis Schlrshp 90-; Psychology; Cnslng Psychology.**

**GUTHRIE, BRENDA K,** Coll Of Charleston, Charleston, SC; SR; BS; Omicron Delta Kappa 90-; Phi Kappa Phi; Psi Chi; Chi Phi Ltl Sr 87-88; Oglthrp Schlrs Awd 87-89; Lowry Schlrshp 87-89; IM Sccr Vllybl 88-89; Psych; Soc Wrkr/Psych.

**GUTHRIE, BRIAN K C,** Franklin And Marshall Coll, Lancaster, PA; SR; MPA; Hstry Clb Pres 89-; Rsdnt Asst 90-; Stdnt Congress Prog Review Comm 89-; Phi Beta Kappa; Pi Gamma Mu 90-; Phi Alpha Theta 90-; Rsrch Ast Hstry Dept 90; Econ Hnrs Thesis; BA; Econ; Intl Law/Econ.

**GUTHRIE, CHRISTINA R,** Central St Univ, Wilberforce, OH; BA; Williamson Hall Drm Cncl 3rd/4th Flr Reps 90; Blk Affairs Cmmttee 90; Bsnss Mrktng; Mrktng Advrtsng.

**GUTHRIE, CHRISTINE R,** Univ Of Ky, Lexington, KY; SO; PHD; Phrmcy Clb; Kappa Kappa Gamma; Phrmcy.

**GUTHRIE, DEBBIE M,** Sue Bennett Coll, London, KY; FR; AA; Flwshp Cntmpry Coll; Phi Beta Lambda; Phi Theta Kappa; Nrsng; RN.

**GUTHRIE, FRANCINE W,** Thomas Nelson Comm Coll, Hampton, VA; FR; AAS; Scnd Bptst; Bsn/Offc Sys Tech Exec Sec.

**GUTHRIE, HILLARY N,** Univ Of Southern Ms, Hattiesburg, MS; FR; Campus Crusd Chrst; Stdnt Almni Assn; Stdnt Eagle Clb; Lambda Sigma Sec; Alpha Lambda Delta; Phi Eta Sigma; Delta Delta Delta Phlnthrpy Chrmn; Lambda Sigma Sec; Biolgcl Sci/Pre-Dntstry; Orthdntcs.

**GUTHRIE JR, JERRY D,** Univ Of Tn At Knoxville, Knoxville, TN; FR; BS; Bptst Stdnt Un 90-; Alpha Lambda Delta 90-; IM Sprts 90-; Mdcn.

**GUTHRIE, JULIE D,** Ms St Univ, Miss State, MS; JR; BED; Farmhouse Frtrnty Ltl Sis; Bus Ed; Tchng.

**GUTHRIE, LINDA C,** Brewer St Jr Coll, Fayette, AL; SO; BS; Frst Natl Bnk Cust Serv Rep Bnk Tllr; Cert Freed Hardeman Univ 77; Elem Erly Chldhd Educ; Tchr.

**GUTHRIE, LYNNE J,** Greenville Tech Coll, Greenville, SC; SO; MET3; Women In Engrng Tech 89-; EGT 3; DCD7 90; Engrng.

**GUTHRIE, MICHELLE D,** Univ Of Southern Ms, Hattiesburg, MS; SO; BS; SG 90-; Alumni Assn 89-; Kappa Delta Assist Pldg 89-; Deans Lst 89-; Ftbl/Bsktbl Dance Tms 89-; Soc Rehab Serv; 7S Cnslng Psychology.

**GUTHRIE, PAMELA J,** Univ Of Nc At Asheville, Asheville, NC; FR; BA; Stdnt Hlth Advsry Cmmtt 87-88; Phi Eta Sigma 87-; Chncllrs Cllqm 87-90; Scty Of Prfssnl Jrnlsts Sec 88-; Mss Cmmnctn Dept Award 90; Mss Cmmnctn; Pblc Rltns Advrtsng.

**GUTHRIE, SHARON A,** Schenectady County Comm Coll, Schenectady, NY; FR; Pres Lst; Oper Mustard Seed/Desert Storm 90-; Ballston Spa Jr Bsebl Wmns Aux; Paralgl; Law.

**GUTHRIE, STEPHEN S,** Livingston Univ, Livingston, AL; SR; Res Asst 88-; Res Lf Asst 90-; Blue Ky; Psych Clb 90-; Tau Kappa Epsilon Treas 87-; Frst Bapt Chrch 87-; Campus Otrch 87-89; Psych Clb Adv 90-; Pres Lst; IM Ftbl Bsktbl; BS; Psych; Clncl Psych.

**GUTHRIE, TIMOTHY D,** Birmingham Southern Coll, Birmingham, AL; SR; BS; Mthdst Church; Masonic Lodge SPE; Cstmr Serv Mgr Vec Div Ryder Intl 90-; Bus.

**GUTHRIE, WALTER G,** Birmingham Southern Coll, Birmingham, AL; FR; Phi Eta Sigma 90-; Alpha Lambda Delta 90-; Sigma Alpha Epsilon 90-; Triangle Clb 90-; Biology; Medicine.

**GUTIERREZ, ANGELA G,** Middlesex County Coll, Edison, NJ; SR; BED; Hispaniic Clb; Alpha Mu Gamma/Natl Lang Hon Soc; Bus Admn; BA CPA.

**GUTIERREZ, ARLENE C,** Univ Of Pa, Philadelphia, PA; FR; BA; Ju-Jit-Su Clb; Alpha Chi Omega 90-; Intrnshp/Pblc Serv Elec/Gas; Finc; Corp Finc.

**GUTIERREZ, DANILVY,** Antillian Adventist University, Mayaguez, PR; GD; Stdnt Assn Sec 90; Sec Of Yr 90; BS 90; Offce Admin; Exec Sec.

**GUTIERREZ, DOMINIQUE C,** Memphis St Univ, Memphis, TN; JR; BA; Gldn Key 90; Phi Kappa Phi 90; Kappa Tau Alpha; REPC Narraca Bayonne 74; BACAS 78; Jrnlsm.

**GUTIERREZ, EDWARD,** Embry Riddle Aeronautical Univ, Daytona Beach, FL; SO; BS; Schl Surf Clb 90; AS Elec Don Bosco Tech Inst 89; Aeronautical Sci; Profl Pilot.**

**GUTIERREZ, JENNIFER L,** Hudson Valley Comm Coll, Troy, NY; SR; MA; Early Chldhd Clb; Spch Lang Pathology.

**GUTIERREZ, JUAN DIEGO L,** Univ Of Miami, Coral Gables, FL; FR; BA; Intrvar Chrstn Flwshp 90-; Cane Cmtr Org 90-; COLSA; Acdmc Deans Lst 90; Sprsprts 90; Music Engr; Snd Dsgn.

**GUTIERREZ, MARIA L,** Inter Amer Univ Pr Hato Rey, Hato Rey, PR; SR; BA; Lns Intrnatl Trnr 88; Amer Mrktng Assn; Hnr Lst 88-; Mgmt; MBA.

**GUTIERREZ, RAFAEL,** Univ Of Miami, Coral Gables, FL; SR; BBA; Econ; Bus.

**GUTIERREZ, RAMIRO L,** Cornell Univ, Ithaca, NY; FR; BAG; Portugean Stdnt Assc 90-; Red Crpt Scty 90-; Otng Clb 90-; Otdr Ed 90-; Single Lks Grotto 90-; Biology; Rsrch/Microblgst.

**GUTIERREZ, REBECA,** Fl International Univ, Miami, FL; JR; BA; IDA 90-; Intr Dsgn.

**GUTILLO, MICHAEL P,** S U N Y At Buffalo, Buffalo, NY; GD; JD; Grad Mgmt Assoc Dir Extrn Afrs 90-; Stu Rep; Gldn Key 88-; Intrnshp Del N Co 86-90; BS; MBA; Finance; Law.

**GUTSHALL, BETH C,** Radford Univ, Radford, VA; JR; BS; Stdnt Lf Mvs Cmmtt 90-; Alpha Phi Omega; Elem Ed.

**GUTSHALL, DELLA L,** Central Pa Bus School, Summerdale, PA; SR; ASB; Deans List 90-; Co-Ed Sftbl; Acctg.

**GUTSHALL, LEIGHA R,** Life Coll, Marietta, GA; GD; DC; Yrbk/Life Rflctns/Life Clg Assist Editor 90; SOT Club 90; Gonstead Club; Phi Theta Kappa 88; Acad Rcgntn Day GA State Lgsltre 87-88; Repr Gainesville Clg; Chiropractic Assist 90; BS Gainesville Clg 90; Chiropractic.

**GUTZMER, JUSTIN E,** Morehouse Coll, Atlanta, GA; JR; BA; Cole Bus Assn 88-; Mntrng Prog 90-; Jr Achvmnt/Morehse Bus Assn Golf Tm 90-; Hnr Rl 88-89; Bus; Law.

**GUY, BRYANT D,** Tn St Univ, Nashville, TN; JR; BS; Crmnl Jstc; Law.

**GUY, CHERYL A,** Univ Of Ky, Lexington, KY; FR; BA; Biology/Pre Med; Med.

**GUY, PAMELA D,** Univ Of Southern Ms, Hattiesburg, MS; JR; BA; SEA; Sub Teacher; Elem Educ.

**GUY, STEPHEN,** Lenoir Rhyne Coll, Hickory, NC; FR; Varsity Soccer; Fr Of Yr Coll/Conf All Dist.

**GUY, VERONICA,** Alcorn St Univ, Lorman, MS; FR; Med Fld; RN.

**GUY, VINCENT S,** California Univ Of Pa, California, PA; FR; BED; Art Ed; Tchr.

**GUYNES, SHARON V,** Univ Of South Al, Mobile, AL; JR; BS; Chi Omega; Ed Sprts Injry Mgmt/Phys Thrpy; Athltc Trnr.

**GUYNN, ANNA M,** East Tn St Univ, Johnson City, TN; JR; BBA; Alpha Lambda Delta 86-; Busn; Mgmnt.

**GUYNN, KAREN E,** Univ Of Ga, Athens, GA; JR; BED; Georgette Bnd 88-90; PES Clb 90-; Kappa Delta 88-; Communiv 90; Pre-Phys Thrpy.

**GUYNUP, SARAH J,** Tusculum Coll, Greeneville, TN; JR; BA; Stdnt Cncl Excptnl Chldrn Prsdnt 90; Day Stdnt Orgnztn 88; Oak Fstvl Stdnt Coordntr 89; Alphi Chi Sec; Edctn; Tchr.

**GUYTON, ELIZABETH H,** Ms St Univ, Miss State, MS; JR; BA; Famous Maroon Bnd 88; Clrnt Choir 88-89; Gamma Beta Phi 88-; Alpha Lambda Delta 88; Phi Kappa Phi; Math.

**GUYTON, KARLA M,** Norfolk St Univ, Norfolk, VA; JR; BA; MCSA 89-; Alpha Kappa Mu; Candis Fd Bnk 90-; Mrn Crps Act 79-81; Cert Det Busn Inst 78; Mass Comm; Brdcst Mgmt.

**GUYTON, RUSSELL B,** Brewer St Jr Coll, Fayette, AL; FR; BS; Phi Theta Kappa; Sci; Phrmcy.

**GUYTON, SHANNON R,** Univ Of Montevallo, Montevallo, AL; SO; BS; Chi Alpha; Pre Med; MD Rdlgst.

**GUZEK, EUGENE E,** S U N Y At Buffalo, Buffalo, NY; JR; BS; Dscvry Invstmnt Clb 81-86; Natl Assn Invstmnt Clbs 78-83; Alpha Sigma Lambda 90-; Deans Lst 87/89-; AAS SUNY; Bus Admin; Audtr/Cmptrllr.

**GUZMAN CAMACHO, ANGEL M,** Inter Amer Univ Pr San German, San German, PR; SR; BA; BED 81; Music; Educ.

**GUZMAN COLON, SILVIA ANNETTE,** Bayamon Central Univ, Bayamon, PR; SR; BA; Clg Sec Intl 90-; Cert Curso De Secretarial Esc Fernando Suria Chavez 89; Sec Sci.

**GUZMAN CRUZ, ROSA E,** Univ Of Pr At Mayaguez, Mayaguez, PR; JR; Natl Soc Pro Engrs; Inst Ind Engrs; Cthlc Apstlc Grp; Ind Eng Stdnt Hon Bd; Ind; Eng.

**GUZMAN, CLAUDIA P,** Fl International Univ, Miami, FL; JR; BBA; AA Intrntnl Fine Arts Clg 89; Bsns; Mrktng Intrntnl Bsns.

**GUZMAN, KARINA V,** Miami Dade Comm Coll, Miami, FL; FR; BA; Nwsppr Stff Wrtr; Drama Clb; Envrmnntl Clb; Phi Theta Kappa Spcl Evnts Actvts; Cmmnctns/Hstry; Telecmmnctns/Law.

**GUZMAN, MIRIAM,** Boricua Coll, New York, NY; SR; BS; PTA 89-; Vol Prnt; Elem Ed; Blngl Tchr.

**GUZMAN, PIEDAD J,** Miami Dade Comm Coll South, Miami, FL; SO; Sigma Phi Sigma 90-; Bptst Hosp Aux 90-; Dvn Ar Elem Vol; Outstndg Comm Coll Stdnt/Coll Schlrshp Svc 89-; AA; Psychlgy; Dntstry.

**GUZMAN, VIVIAN,** Univ Of Pr Medical Sciences, San Juan, PR; GD; MEHS; Puertorican Assn Of Water Resrcs; Deans Lst 87-88; BS 84.

**GUZMAN-SUAREZ, EDGARDO,** Inter Amer Univ Pr Hato Rey, Hato Rey, PR; JR; BA; Cmptr Stdnt Assoc; Puerto Rico Prfsnl Photo Assn 90-; BA 71-75; Assoc 77-78; Educ/Cmptr Prgrmr.

**GUZY, SUSAN A,** Kent St Univ Kent Cmps, Kent, OH; SO; BS; Srgcl Tech Clvlnd Clnc Fndtn 82-; BS 71-75; Assoc 80-82; Nrsg.

**GUZZETTI, DEONNA L,** Univ Of Nc At Greensboro, Greensboro, NC; FR; BSN; Sigma Theta Alpha; Inter-Var Christian Flwshp; SEAA; NCNA; Sigma Theta Alpha; Nursing.

**GUZZO, ROBERT F,** Teikyo Post Univ, Waterbury, CT; SO; BA; Psych; Thrpy.

**GWALTNEY, WENDY L,** Old Dominion Univ, Norfolk, VA, SR; BS; Alpha Phi Omega V P 90-; Soc Sec 88-89; Scndry Edn; Mrktng.

**GWIN, STANFORD G,** Univ Of Southern Ms, Hattiesburg, MS; SO; BS; Southern Expsure Show Grp; LDS Stdnt Assn; Pres LDS Stdnt Assoc; Hon Clg; Hon Stdnt Assn 87-; Pi Tau Chi; Spch Comm.

**GWIN, STEPHEN P,** Univ Of Southern Ms, Hattiesburg, MS; SO; Latter Day Saint Stdnt Assoc; Hnr Stdnt Assoc Pres 89-90; Hnrs Clg; Golden Key; Hnrs Schlrshp; Star Stdnt Schlrshp; ACT Schlrshp; Med.

**GWINN, DENNIS F,** Anne Arundel Comm Coll, Arnold, MD; SO; AA; Bay Area Prlgl Asc; Real Est Sls Agnt 76-80; HVAC Tst/Blnc Qlty Cntrl Mgr 80-89; Prlgl/Bsn; Law.

**GWOZDZIK, MARK W,** Springfield Tech Comm Coll, Springfield, MA; JR; BA; Dns Lst 88-90; Elctrnc Engr Tech; Optical Engr.

**GYGAX, JEFFREY S,** Castleton St Coll, Castleton, VT; SO; BS; Cls Pres 90-; Drm Cncl Comm Tres 90-; RA Slctn Comm 90-; Tutoring 90-; Deans Lst; Mass Media Cmnctns; TV Flm Prod.

**GYIMAH, MIRIAM C,** Univ Of Md At Eastern Shore, Princess Anne, MD; JR; Cmps Pals Orgnztns; Mass Media Cmmnctns Clb Pblc Rltns 89-; Alpha Kappa Alpha Bas Levs 90-; Tlcmmctns Hnr 90; Englsh Comm Poli Sci; Jrnlst.

# H

**HA, BINH T,** Bunker Hill Comm Coll, Boston, MA; FR; Eng.

**HA, DAC V,** Hillsborough Comm Coll, Tampa, FL; FR; BED; Eng.

**HA, HYO CHOL,** Va Commonwealth Univ, Richmond, VA; SR; BS; Korean Stdnt Assc; Sigma Zeta; Ntl Hnr Frtrnty; Univ Hnr Shlrshp; Pres Schlrshp; Philip Morris Schlrshp; Sci/Eng Rsrch Smstr Argonne Natl Lab; Asst Prssmn; Chem; Med.

**HA, JESSICA M,** Northern Va Comm Coll, Annandale, VA; SO; BA; Decision Sci; Mgmt Infor Sys.

**HA, TRANG XUAN,** Mercer Univ Schl Of Pharm, Atlanta, GA; JR; ASP 89-; APHA; Diabetes Comm 89-; Geriatric Comm 89-; Intl Stdnt Comm 90-; Phrmcy; Dr Phrmcy/Residency.

**HAACK, CARLTON L,** Old Dominion Univ, Norfolk, VA; SR; BS; Amrcn Scty Cvl Engnrs Pres 90-; Natl Scty Prfsnl Engnrs Pres; Tau Beta Pi; Chi Epsilon Tres 89-90; Cvl Engnrng Achvmnt Awrd 89; Wm J Thmpsn Mmrl Awrd; Cvl Engnrng; Prfsnl Engnr.

**HAAG, DANIEL E,** Carnegie Mellon Univ, Pittsburgh, PA; SR; BS; IM Bsktbl/Flr Hcky/Ultimate Frisbee 89-; Phi Alpha Theta; Hist; Teach.

**HAAG JR, DONALD A,** Univ Of Louisville, Louisville, KY; SR; ASME Vp 88-; Co-Op Intern Us Naval Ord Stn Louisville Ky 88-89; Sftbl/IM Sports 87-90; Mech Engrng.

**HAAGA, CHARLES K,** Univ Of Southern Ms, Hattiesburg, MS; JR; BS; Stdnt Sprts Medcne Assn 89-; Natl Athltc Trnrs Assn 90-; Alpha Tau Omega 89-; Exrcse Physlgy/Athltc Trning; Clncl Trnr.

**HAAGEN, JENNIFER J,** Suffolk Comm Coll Eastern Cmps, Riverhead, NY; SO; AS; Phi Alpha Sigma 4 GPA; Bsns; Intl Bsns/Mrktng.

**HAAKER, JENNIFER J,** Univ Of Nh Plymouth St Coll, Plymouth, NH; SO; Orntn Ldr 90; Soph Class Pres 90-; Stdnt Alum Assoc Chm 90-; Pres List 89-.

**HAAS, ANDREA I,** Atlantic Comm Coll, Mays Landing, NJ; FR; PHD; Sngl Prnts Grp 90-; Clncl Psychlgst.

**HAAS, ARCHIE J,** Fordham Univ, Bronx, NY; SO; Acctg.

**HAAS, CAROL A,** Saint Francis Coll, Loretto, PA; SR; BA; Radio Stn Exe Com 89-; Eng Clb Sec/Treas 90-; Loretto Stf Wrtr 89-; Hnr Soc; Delta Epsilon Sigma; Sigma Tau Delta 90-; Alpha Phi Omega Hstrn 89-90; Pblc Rltns Intrnshp 89-90; Flmd Fl Lngth Dcmntry Non Prft Org 89-90; Vlybl 87-88; Eng/Pblc Rltns; Mktg Rsrch/Anlys.

**HAAS, DENISE K,** Kent St Univ Kent Cmps, Kent, OH; JR; BA; Golden Key; Sigma Tau Delta; Eng; Grad Sch In English Or Law Sch.

**HAAS, DONALD C,** Franklin And Marshall Coll, Lancaster, PA; SR; MD; Rugby Clb 89-; ACS 89-; Lambda Phi Upsilon; Pi Lambda Phi VP 87-; Water Street Rescue Mssn 89-90; Isaac E Roberts Blgy Prz 88; Cum Laude; Vrsty Ftbl 87-88; Easter Seals 87-; Hosp ER Vol 89-; BA; Chmstry; Medicine.

**HAAS, GREGORY S,** Univ Of Pittsburgh, Pittsburgh, PA; SR; Glee Clb Pres 87-; Amer Socty Mech Engrs Treas 89-; Natl Socty Prof Engrs 90-; Tau Beta Pi 89-; Pi Tau Sigma 90-; Phi Eta Sigma 87-; Univ Schlr Awd 90; Univ Acad/Engr Hnr Socty 87-; Intrnshp Amer Elec Power Co Inc Cols Oh 90; Mech Engr.

**HAAS, JOHN B,** Allegheny Coll, Meadville, PA; SO; BA; Campus Newspaper Sports Editor 90-; Choir 89-; Frshmn Cls Pres 89-90; Lambda Sigma 90-; Delta Tau Delta 90-; Alden Scholar 89-90; English; Law.

**HAAS, PATRICIA J,** Kent St Univ Kent Cmps, Kent, OH; SR; BA; Res Hall Sdtnt Govt Pres 87-88; Alpah Phi Sigma 88-; Criminal Justice; Law.

**HAASE, ELIZABETH M,** Slippery Rock Univ, Slippery Rock, PA; SR; BED; Spanish Club Treas 87-89; Clothing Bank Co Fndr 90; SGA 90; Sigma Delta Pi V P 89-; Order Of Omega 90-; Alpha Xi Delta 88-; VP 90-; Deans List 90-; IM Vlybl Gym 89-; Spanish; Teaching.

**HAASE, GARY D,** Univ Of Sc At Columbia, Columbia, SC; FR; BS; Deans List Clg Of Eng USC; Elec/Comptr Engr.

**HAASE, JENNIFER L,** Univ Of Nc At Charlotte, Charlotte, NC; JR; BA; Psych Clb 88-; IM Vlybl And Sftbl Capt 89; Hall Pres 89; Dns Lst; Indvdl Stds Prog Asstd Rsrch Prjct Asst; Psych; Lwyr.

**HABAFY, NORA,** Univ Of Nh Plymouth St Coll, Plymouth, NH; JR; BA; Intl Stu Assc Sec 90-; Anthrplgy/Sclgy; Intl Law.

**HABEEB, LINDA F,** Cornell Univ Statutory College, Ithaca, NY; SR; MD; Foreign Lang Exchg Prog 88-; Tai Chi Chvan 90-; Cornell U Marching Band 87-88; Corells V's Cle Of Agrclture & Life Sci Hnr Soc VP 90-91; Alpha Phi Omega 88-90; Christn Spg Applachian Proj 88-89; Summer Internship @ Exxon Res & Engr Co 89-; Microbiology; Medicine.

**HABER, ANDREA L,** Comm Coll Algny Co Algny Cmps, Pittsburgh, PA; FR; Doris Dan Animal Lg 89-; Animal Advcts 89-; People/Ethical Trtmnt/Animals 89-; English; Teach.

**HABERHERN, JEAN A,** Kent St Univ Kent Cmps, Kent, OH; GD; Luthrn Brothrhd Ins Frat Comm Educ Ofc 87-; BS Concordia Clg Seward NE 70; MLS 90; Lib Sci/Educ; Sec Lib/Media Sp.

**HABERL, JOANNE M,** Middle Tn St Univ, Murfreesboro, TN; JR; BFA; Grphc Dsgn.

**HABERMAN, CHRISTOPHER E,** Coll Of Charleston, Charleston, SC; JR; BS; Delta Tau Delta 88-90; Bio; Med.

**HABERMANN, DENISE,** Fl International Univ, Miami, FL; GD; MED; Wnd Ens Rep 90-; Mrchng Bnd/Cncrt Bnd Lbrn 84-89; Snrs Drm/Bgl Crp 86-91; Mu Upsln Alpha Prlmtrn 85-88; BA Rtgrs Unv 89; Spec Ed; Tchr.

**HABERSHAM, TRACY D,** Clark Atlanta Univ, Atlanta, GA; JR; BA; Cmptr Scnc Clb; German Clb; Alpha Kappa Mu; All Amer Schlr; Cmptr Scnc; Syst Analyst.

**HABORAK, KEVIN G,** Coll Of Charleston, Charleston, SC; FR; BS; Island Scty; Hnrs Prog Stdnt 90-; Sigma Chi Pledge; Math Geology; Envrnmntl Law.

**HACHE, ROBERT R,** Univ Of Nh Plymouth St Coll, Plymouth, NH; JR; BA; Pemigewasset Choral Soc 89-; Hang Glide Cl 89-; Common Ground 90-; Philosphy.

**HACHEY, SUZANNE,** Oh Wesleyan Univ, Delaware, OH; JR; BA; Psi Chi; Pi Beta Phi Rsh Chrprsn 88-; Var Swmtm 88-; Ind Org Psysch.

**HACK, NANCY C,** Univ Of Miami, Coral Gables, FL; SR; DVM; Golden Key; Owned/Opertd Silkscreen Art Co; BSC; Vetrnry Medcn.

**HACKATHORN, TAMMIE L,** West Liberty St Coll, West Liberty, WV; JR; BS; Fshn Mrktng Clb 90-; Bus Admn.

**HACKER, DEBRA L,** Temple Univ, Philadelphia, PA; JR; U Schlrs Pgm Penn St U 83-85; Phi Delta Chi VP 89-; NPC Intrnshp Up John Co; P Fresh Awd/H G Huber Schlrshp/Kondde Fnd Schlrshp/W J Carnahan Almni Mem 83-85; PAPHRMACTCL Assn 89-; Amer Pharmactcl Assn 89-; Pharm; Pharmctcl Indust.

**HACKER, MAYNARD F,** Lexington Comm Coll, Lexington, KY; GD; AS; AIAS 89-; CSI 90-; Dean Lst 90; Appl Sci; Arch Tech/Eng Tech.

**HACKETT, AMY C,** Memphis St Univ, Memphis, TN; SR; BA; Vol Invlmnt Alnc V Chrprsn; Alpha Kappa Delta; Lit Cncl 90-; Hstry/Sclgy; Tch.

**HACKETT, EMILY,** Univ Of Rochester, Rochester, NY; FR; BS; Colac Dir 90-; Intl Living Ctr 90-; Amnesty Intl 90-; Hispanic Yth Tutorial Pgm; Mech Eng; Civil Engr.

**HACKETT, HARRY L,** Hamilton Coll, Clinton, NY; FR; BA; Hmltn Brss Chr 2nd Trmpt; Pres Of Clss Stdnt Govt Pres; Doers And Thnkrs Ltrry Scty; Theta Delta Chi; Hngr Cln Up Wrkr; Crss Cntry Intr Coll Hcky Sftbl JV Tm; Engl; Intrntl Bus.

**HACKNEY, THERESA S,** Atlantic Comm Coll, Mays Landing, NJ; SO; Amer Lgn Aux Post 430; Nrsng.

**HACKWORTH, PAUL K,** Univ Of Ky, Lexington, KY; SO; Poltcl Sci; Intl Rltns.

**HADAD, LINDA D,** Fl Inst Of Tech, Melbourne, FL; FR; BS; Tri Beta 90-; Fclty Merit Schlrshp; Acdmc Schlr Schlrshp; Pre Prof; Psychtrst.

**HADALA, MARK A,** Fl St Univ, Tallahassee, FL; JR; BS; Union Bd Chrmn 90-; Seminole Party Pres Campaign Advsr 88-; Prkg Violations Appeals Bd 90-; Phi Gamma Delta Hstrn 88-; Union Bd Schlrshp 90-; Sports Cmnctn; Publ Rels.

**HADDAD, BASSAM F,** Youngstown St Univ, Youngstown, OH; SO; BE; Lebanese Stdnt Assn Sec 90-; IEEE 90-; Dns Lst; Elec Eng; Eng.

**HADDAD, ELIZABETH M,** Cornell Univ Statutory College, Ithaca, NY; SO; BS; Kappa Delta Sor; Vol Good Sam Hosp Suffurn NY; Bio; Med.

**HADDAD, JACQUELINE M,** Univ Of Tn At Martin, Martin, TN; SO; BS; Undrgrad Almni Cncl; Fr Orientatn Ldr; Natl Assn Acctnts; Phi Eta Sigma; Pi Sigma Epsilon CEI/OFFCR Pldg Clss 90; Chi Omega Pldg Trnr; Phi Kappa Phi Hon 89-90; IM Ftbl/Vlybl/Sftbl; Acctg; CPA.

**HADDAD, RAEDAH S,** Worcester Poly Inst, Worcester, MA; FR; Church Yth Grp 88-; Sndy Schl Tchr 88-90; Ping Pong Tm 86-87; Natl Hnr Scty 88-90; High Hnrs 89-90; Hnr Roll 87-90; Comm Svc 89-90; Electrical Eng.

**HADDEN, DONNA S,** Univ Of Ga, Athens, GA; SR; BA; Engl Educ; Tch Engl/For Lang.

**HADDIX, STEPHANIE,** Lees Coll, Jackson, KY; SO; BA; Hlth Sci Clb 90-; Phi Theta Kappa 90-; Sci; Frstry/Agri.

**HADDOCK, AMY A,** Converse Coll, Spartanburg, SC; SO; BABFA; WISE Global Awrns Task Frc 90-; Stdnt Advsry Comm 89-; Chamber Orchstra 89-; Dns Lst 90-; Crescent 90-; Cmps Beautfctn Jr Rep; Trustee Hnr Schlrshp 89-; Barry M Goldwater Schlrshp; Stdnt Gallery Show 90; Biology/Art; Biological Illstrtr.

**HADDOCK, RACHAEL A,** Coll Of Charleston, Charleston, SC; FR; BS; Fclty Hon Lst 90-; Phrmcy.

**HADDON, GEORGIA W,** Norfolk St Univ, Norfolk, VA; JR; BS; Telephone Pioneers Am; Cncl Psychlgst.

**HADDOX, STACIE ALINE,** Univ Of Ms Medical Center, Jackson, MS; JR; BSN; MASN 90-; Nmmsh Clb Chrmn 87-89; Adv Cncl 87-88; Mdlng Brd 87-89; Hmcmng Comm Hsts 87-88; BSU 87-89; SG 87-88; Nrs Chrstn Flwshp Pres 90-; Med Ctr Intrn; IM Ftbl 90; Nrsng.

**HADEN, REBECCA R,** Nyack Coll, Nyack, NY; FR; BA; Chorale Pianist 90; Easter Bskt Comm Chrprsn; Elem Educ; Elem Schl Tchr.

**HADFIELD, CAROLYN M,** Coll Misericordia, Dallas, PA; JR; BS; Clown Mnstry Cmps Mnstry 88-; Pre Hon Clb 88-89; Alpha Delta Kappa Treas 90-; Sccr 89-90; Elem Ed W/Cert Early Chldhd; Tchng.

**HADJI, PATRICIA M,** City Univ Of Ny Queensbrough, New York, NY; GD; BA; Phi Theta Kappa 88-89; Alpha Sigma Lampa 90-; Berel & Mullen Esqs Office Mngr 72-; Law.

**HADJILOUCAS, CHRISTAKIS C,** City Univ Of Ny City Coll, New York, NY; JR; BE; Gldn Key; City Coll Schlrshp 88-92; Pope Evans/Robbins Schlrshp; Engr.

**HADLEY, JANA MICHELLE,** George Mason Univ, Fairfax, VA; JR; BS; SEA; Kappa Delta Pi; Alpha Chi; Goldne Key Secy; Elem Ed; Tch.

**HADLEY, NICOLE M,** Clark Atlanta Univ, Atlanta, GA; SR; BA; Fshn Clb Tres 88-90; Fshn Mrchndsng; Rtl.

**HADLEY, NINA P,** Univ Of Sc At Columbia, Columbia, SC; FR; BS; Scuba Clb 90-; Schlr Athl 90; Dns Lst 90; Friends Baruch Inst Undergrad Schlrshp; Interclgte Cross Country/Track 90-; Marine Sci; Coastal Mgmt.

**HADLEY, PAMELA A,** Middle Tn St Univ, Murfreesboro, TN; SR; BS; Stdnt Govt Assn Rep 83-85; Deans List 87 90-; Internship WKRN; Mass Comm; Brdcst Mgmnt.

**HADLEY, PAULA L,** Washington State Comm Coll, Marietta, OH; JR; AS; Bus Club; Phi Theta Kappa; Bus Mgmt; Bus Owner.

**HADSELL, SHARON J,** West Liberty St Coll, West Liberty, WV; SR; BA; Phi Theta Kappa; Chi Beta Phi; Kappa Delta Pi; Asst Ldr 4-H; AS WV N Cmnty Clg 87; Bio; Tch.

**HAEFNER, CARL J,** Cornell Univ Statutory College, Ithaca, NY; JR; BS; Cornell Catholic Comm 88-; Hortus Forum Pres 88-; Hurlburt Hse Ecological Awrns 89-; Floral Dsgn Teach Asstntshp 90; Planting Fields Arboretum Intrnshp; Horticulture.

**HAEGELE, DARLENE S,** Univ Of Miami, Coral Gables, FL; SR; Ad Grp 89-90; Orntn Asst 87; Goldn Key 90-; Phi Kappa Phi 90-; Crspn Prtr Adv Intrnshp 90; BS Comm 90; Adv/Pol Sci; Publ Rel.

**HAEUSSLER, ELIZABETH,** Univ Of Pr Medical Sciences, San Juan, PR; FR; MBA; BA Nrsng University Of Sacred Heart 88; Nrsng; Admin.

**HAFEMANN, GEORGE T M,** Fordham Univ, Bronx, NY; FR; BA; Hstry; Rlgs Voc.

**HAFF, GLORIA M,** S U N Y Coll Of Tech At Frmgdl, Farmingdale, NY; SO; AAS; Hortcltr Club Treas 88-; Phi Theta Kappa; Intrnshp 89-90; Blark Botncl Grdns Intrnshp; Mid Atlntc Stdnt Lndscp Fld Day; Ornamntl Horticltr.

**HAFF, LORI M,** Oh Univ, Athens, OH; SO; BFA; Stdnts Fr Rprdctv Choices 89-; Chrl Union 89; Brown Pickering Hl Cncl Flr Rep 89-90; Theatre/Actg; Actr/Flm Prdctns.

**HAFFNER, ANDREA M,** Fordham Univ, Bronx, NY; SO; BA; Comm Svc Tutor 90-; Acctg.

**HAFNER, SHARON J,** King Coll, Bristol, TN; FR; BA; Abrtn Altrntvs And Crss Prgnncy 90-; Dns Lst 90; Psychlgy; Chrstn Cnslr.

**HAFTMANN-MOSES, MARY E,** West Liberty St Coll, West Liberty, WV; SR; BA; Lic W VA Socl Wrkr 86-; Bd Of Dir Comm Chld Cr Cntr 88-; Asst Dir Dept Socl Mnstrs; Diocese Wheeling/Charleston; Rgnts Lib Arts; Socl Wrk.

**HAGA, SAKURA,** Savannah Coll Of Art & Design, Savannah, GA; FR; Intrntl Stdnt Assc 90-; ASID; Tnns 90-; Interior Dsgn; Interior Dsgnr.

**HAGAN, JOSEPH D,** Glassboro St Coll, Glassboro, NJ; SR; BA; Jr Clss Govt 89-; BACCHUS 90; Emrgncy Sqd 90; Cnty Jvnl Dtntn Cntr Intrn; Law Jstc.

**HAGAN, KEN A,** Oh St Univ, Columbus, OH; SO; BS; Waterski Clb; Amnesty Internatl 90-; Hnrs Prog 90-; OSPE 90-; Natl Ski Patrol 88-; Lau Div Lab Inten; Worthington Industries Lab Intern; Materials Sci; Engrng.

**HAGAN, LISA M,** Univ Of Md At Eastern Shore, Princess Anne, MD; SR; BS; Intl Food Serv Exec Assc 90-; Intl Assc Hsptlty Accntnts 90-; Olive Garden Intern; Hotel/Rest Mngmnt.

**HAGAN, MARK R,** Univ Of Miami, Coral Gables, FL; SR; BA; AIAS; Arch; Arch Dsgn.

**HAGAN, SAMUEL J,** Fl St Univ, Tallahassee, FL; JR; BA; Sftbl; Sailing; Golden Key; Poltcl Sci/Econ; Law.

**HAGAN, STEPHEN G,** Wallace St Comm Coll At Selma, Selma, AL; FR; BA; Navy/Nuclear Power Sch Orlando Fl; Math; Nuclear Engr.

**HAGEDORN, ANDY W,** Thomas Nelson Comm Coll, Hampton, VA; FR; AS; Drftng; Drftng Dsgn.

**HAGEL SR, RICHARD L,** Wilmington Coll, New Castle, DE; SR; BS; Dtctv Sgt Plc Dept 81-; AA Wor-Wic Tech Comm Coll 84; Law Enfrcmnt.

**HAGEN, LYNN A,** Providence Coll, Providence, RI; JR; BA; Deans List 88-90; Lrng Assist Ctr Corrd 89-; Aerobics Inst 89-; English.

**HAGEN, TAMMY L,** Va Commonwealth Univ, Richmond, VA; FR; MA; Bus; Acctg.**

**HAGENDORF, DANA B,** Cornell Univ Statutory College, Ithaca, NY; FR; BA; Coll Of Ag/Life Sci Ambsdr; Cls Cncl; Nws Rprtr WVBR Trainee Radio Sta; Sigma Delta Tau; Dns Lst; Cmmnctns; Law.

**HAGER, HEATHER E,** Bridgewater Coll, Bridgewater, VA; SO; BS; Oratorio Choir 89-; Lambda Soc 90-; Dns Lst 89-; Bridgewater Home 90-; Bsn; Florist.

**HAGER, KELLY L,** Birmingham Southern Coll, Birmingham, AL; FR; BA; Fr Ldrshp Cls; Sthrn Chrl; Tringl Clb; Phi Eta Sigma Vp; Alpha Lambda Delta; Alpha Chi Omega Chptr Rltns/Stndrds Brd Pldg Cls Sec; Hstry; Tchg Clg Lvl/Law.

**HAGER, MARY J,** Univ Of Cincinnati-Clrmnt Coll, Batavia, OH; FR; AS; Fmly Crisis Cntr; Psych; Cnslr.

**HAGER, ROBERT E,** Va Commonwealth Univ, Richmond, VA; SR; Econs Clb 87-89; Frgn Affrs Clb 87-89; Phi Sigma Kappa Schlrshp Chrmn 89-; Schlrshp Awd 90; Wghtlftng Cntst 89; BS; Fin; FBI.

**HAGER, TERESA J,** Univ Of Charleston, Charleston, WV; FR; BSN; Nrsng; Nrs Anstst.

**HAGERMAN, CATHY A,** Univ Of Cincinnati, Cincinnati, OH; SO; BED; Beechwoods Elem PTA Pres 88-90; Girl Sct Co-Ldr 87-; Spcl Ed; Tch.

**HAGERMAN, KAREN R,** Owensboro Comm Coll, Owensboro, KY; FR; MBA; Math; Edn.

**HAGERTY, MARY MARTHA,** Univ Of Nc At Charlotte, Charlotte, NC; GD; Student Govt Repr 88-89; Sanford Hall Cnsl Pres 88-89; Dept Of Correction Div Adult Probation Parole Intern 90; IM Ftbl Bsktbl Sftbl 87-90.

**HAGERTY, TRACEY R,** Anne Arundel Comm Coll, Arnold, MD; SO; Sclgy Cmps 90-; Intrn Cntr Stdy Lcl Issues 90-; Deans Lst 90-; Sclgyf Crmnlgy.

**HAGGARD, JAMES E,** Union Univ, Jackson, TN; FR; BS; Univ Sngrs 90-; Chem; Optometry.

**HAGGARD, STEPHANIA L,** Troy St Univ At Dothan, Dothan, AL; SR; BS; Stdnt Govt V P 90; Cnsrvtn Clb; Gamma Beta Phi Sec 90; Stdnt Afrs Cmtee Rep 90; Crmnl Juste; Law.

**HAGGERTY, JEAN M,** Cornell Univ Statutory College, Ithaca, NY; JR; BS; Hall Cncl Stdnt Govt Sec 90-; RA; CIVITAS 90-; Animal Sci; Vet Med/Nutrition.

**HAGGERTY, SHANON A,** Berkeley Coll Of Westchester, White Plains, NY; FR; AAS; Phi Theta Kappa; Delta Epsilon Chi; Fashion Merdng/Mktng Fashion; Merdng.

**HAGGETT, CANDACE L,** Castleton St Coll, Castleton, VT; SR; BED; SEA Sec 89-90; Spc Wknds Comm 90-; Ed; Tch.

**HAGGMARK, KELLY L,** S U N Y Coll At Fredonia, Fredonia, NY; JR; BS; AS Jamestown Comm Coll 88; AOS Jamestown Bus Coll 80; Acctng; Mgmt Acctng.

**HAGHNEGAHDAR, HAMID R,** Middle Tn St Univ, Murfreesboro, TN; JR; BS; Blgy Clb 88-89; Chmcl Scty VP 90-F Gamma Beta Phi 88-89; Phi Mu Delta Pres 90-; Sccr 88-89; Chmstry.

**HAGIHARA, YUKI,** White Pines Coll, Chester, NH; FR; AA; Gnrl Stds.

**HAGIN, CHRISTINE M,** Bloomfield Coll, Bloomfield, NJ; FR; BA; News Pblcn Co-Ed; Recog Awd 90-; Svc Awd; Engl Cmnctns; Jrnlsm.

**HAGINS, PATRICIA M,** Winthrop Coll, Rock Hill, SC; SO; MBA; Alpha Lambda Delta; Alpha Lambda Delta 89-; Elem Educ; Tchng.

**HAGLUND, ALICIA,** Allegheny Coll, Meadville, PA; SO; Nwspr Asst News Edtr; Panhellenic Cncl Pblc Rltns Chair; Lambda Sigma 90-; Kappa Alpha Theta Panhel Delegate 90-; Tchng Asst Chem Lab; Clb La Crosse 89-; BS; Bio/Chem; Med.

**HAGMANN, ERHARD,** Georgetown Univ, Washington, DC; SO; BA; Cnsltng Work Book; Intl Bus.

**HAGOPIAN, LISA A,** Atlantic Comm Coll, Mays Landing, NJ; SO; BS; Big Sis Phil; Biol/Sci; Educ Sec.

**HAGUE, JULIE-ANN,** Univ Of New England, Biddeford, ME; SO; BA; Theater Prod Play Schoolmaster From Flat Creek 89-90; Deans List 89-; Soup Kitchen 90-; Natl Hispanic Schlrshp Awd 90-; James Z Naurison Schlrshp 89-92; Elem Edn; Teach.

**HAHLEN, LAUREL DAWN,** Valdosta St Coll, Valdosta, GA; SR; BFA; Stu Govt Assoc Sntr 87; Nwspr Stf Rprtr 84-87; Art Stu League 88-; WVVS-FM DJ 88-89; Mstng Union Brd 86-87; Intrn 99 Ways/Multimedia Radio Ancr 87; Miss Image Alive 86; AA 87; Prfmnc Art.

**HAHM, MARK D,** Univ Of Rochester, Rochester, NY; SO; BS/MS; Elctrcl Engr; Engr.

**HAHN, DAVID G,** Duquesne Univ, Pittsburgh, PA; FR; MS; Boy Scouts Of Amer Asst Patrol Ldr 87; Confraternity Christian Doctrine 87-90; Zeta Beta Tau Sftbl Coach 90-; Orient Staff Co-Ldr; St Valentines Church Altar Boy; Deans List 1st & 2nd Sem Pharmacy; IM Ftbl Bsktbl Plyr Coach 90-; Health Sciences; Physical Therapy.

**HAHN, DE ANNA K,** Lenoir Rhyne Coll, Hickory, NC; JR; BA; Beartrckrs 90-; Sccr Cubs 88-; Theta Chi Aux 89-; Delta Zeta Chpln 89-; YMCA Ldrs Clb 82-; Pres Schlr 88-; Chrldng 88-; Bus Admin/Ecnmcs/Math.

**HAHN, ELIZABETH A,** S U N Y At Binghamton, Binghamton, NY; FR; BS; Bio; Tchg/Rsrch.

**HAHN, ERIN C,** Indiana Univ Of Pa, Indiana, PA; FR; BA; Aerobics; Alpha Beta Gamma; IM Vlybl 90; Math; Elem Tchr.

**HAHN, GREGORY R,** Univ Of Tn At Martin, Martin, TN; JR; BS; Non-Cmssn Offcrs Clb Pres; Gooch Schlrshp 88; Natl Grd Eng Co 80-; Bus Admin Mgmt.

**HAHN, J J,** Univ Of De, Newark, DE; JR; BA; Amer Chemcl Soc Treas 88-; Amer Inst Chem Engrs 88-; Philosophia; Tau Beta Pi 90-; Phi Sigma Pi; Golden Key 90-; Genrl Hnrs Cert 90; Engr Schlrs Summer Intrnshp 90; Bche; Chemcl Engrng & Philosophy.**

**HAHN, MELISSA L,** Indiana Univ Of Pa, Indiana, PA; JR; WIUP-TV Segment Producer 90-; Equestrian Team 89-90; Amnesty Internatl 88-89; Alpha Epsilan Rho 90-; Commonidations Media/Theatre; Acting.

**HAHN, SUSAN P,** Memphis St Univ, Memphis, TN; SR; BFA; Art; Drctr/Grphc Dsgn.

**HAHN, TONYA L,** Richard Bland Coll, Petersburg, VA; SO; BA; Sci; RN.

**HAID, PAUL R,** Mount Aloysius Jr Coll, Cresson, PA; SO; AS; Stdnt Govt Senate 88-; Theatr 90-; Intrprtr Clb; Deans Lst 88-; PTK 90-; Stdnt Serv Cncl 88-; Campus Mnstry Pres 88-; Circle K 89-90; Scndry Educ/Soc Sci; Intrprtng F/Deaf.

**HAIGHT RHODES, STEPHANIE,** Fl International Univ, Miami, FL; SR; BA; Phi Kappa Phi 90; Phi Lamda 90; AA Miami Dade Cmmnty Clg 89; Ed; Emtnlly Hndcpped Tchr.

**HAIGHT, DANA E,** S U N Y Coll At Oswego, Oswego, NY; FR; BA; Crw Rwng; Cmmnctns.

**HAIGLER, JOYCE,** Univ Of Sc At Columbia, Columbia, SC; SR; BS; Phi Beta Gamma 90-; Golden Key 89-; Ofc Admin Awd 90; Deans Lst 90; Natl Bus Educ Assc 90-; Upward Bound Sec 86-; AAS Midlands Tech Clg 88; Bus Educ; Scndry Bus Educ Tchr.

**HAIKAL, FADIA M,** Wv Univ, Morgantown, WV; SR; BS; Rho Chi 89-; Phrmcy.

**HAILE, LEMLEM,** Clark Atlanta Univ, Atlanta, GA; JR; BA; Wmns Rsrc Ctr 87-; Allied Hlth Prog 87-; Wrk Study Stdnt 87-90; Pre Prfsnl Hlth Sci Prog 86; Schlrshp 87-90; Med Tech; Pharm.

**HAILIS, STEFANOS C,** Univ Of Rochester, Rochester, NY; SO; BSC; Wrld Tae Kwon Do Brwn Blt 89-; Amdrst Schlrshp 89-; IM Soccr/Vllybl Capt 90-; Cmptrs Sci/Gentcs; Cmptr Med Res.

**HAIM, YITZHAK,** Broward Comm Coll, Ft Lauderdale, FL; FR; BSC; Phi Theta Kappa 90; Pres Lst; Cmptr Lang Math Chem; Cmptr Eng.

**HAIN, CRYSTAL M,** Central Pa Bus School, Summerdale, PA; GD; Natl Crt Rprtrs Assn 90-; Deans Lst 89-; Court Rprtng; Court Stenog.

**HAIN, STEPHANIE R,** Tn Temple Univ, Chattanooga, TN; SR; Alpha Epsilon Theta; Ladies Bsktbl Tm 87-88; BS 91; Psych; Cnslng.

**HAINES, DEBORAH R,** Central Fl Comm Coll, Ocala, FL; SO; BBA; ACTS 29 Adlt Chldrn Temp Shltrs Sec/Treas 82-; Phi Theta Kappa Pres 90-; Alpha Nu Rho Pres 90-; City Slckrs Yth Serv Clb VP 89-; Gov Ldrshp Awrd 87; Bus; Bus Mgmt.

**HAINES, DIANA J,** Georgian Court Coll, Lakewood, NJ; SO; BA; Cncl Exptnl Chldrn 90-; De La Salle Educ Clb 90-; Hnr Soc VP 90-; Spnsh/Sec Ed; Tchr/Spnsh.

**HAINES, KEITH R,** Merrimack Coll, North Andover, MA; SO; BS; Bus Fin.

**HAINES, MALINDA J,** Temple Univ, Philadelphia, PA; SR; BS; Golden Key 89-; Alpha Sigma Alpha Asst Treas 89-90; ; PSAHPERDS Violet Baumbardner Awd 90; Nate Garfinkel Awd Temple; Phy Educ; Tchg.

**HAINING JR, GEORGE A,** Hudson County Comm Coll, Jersey City, NJ; GD; AS; Achvmnt Awrd; Police Captain; BS Criminal Justice Jersey City St Clg 80; Legal Asstnc; Paralegal.

**HAINLEY, DANA M,** Bethel Coll, Mckenzie, TN; JR; BED; STEA 89-; Gamma Beta Phi 89-; Elem Educ; Teacher.

**HAINS, DECKER B,** U S Military Academy, West Point, NY; FR; BS; Im Bsktbl Sndhrst; Eng; US Army Offcr.

**HAIRE JR, LINDSEY,** Morehouse Coll, Atlanta, GA; SO; BA; Morehouse Bsn Assoc 90-; Stdnt Govt Scl Comm 90-; Bsn; Mktg.

**HAIRE, THOMAS SAMUEL,** Piedmont Tech Coll, Greenwood, SC; FR; ASSOC; VRW Oper Dsrt Shld/Strm; Auto Manuf Tech; Robotics.

**HAIRE, TINA L,** Univ Of Sc At Columbia, Columbia, SC; SR; BS; Mdl Untd Ntns 89-90; Gamma Beta Phi 88-; Gldn Key 88-; Alpha Lambda Delta Cncl 87-89; Merrill Lynch Intrnshp; Ecnmcs/Fin; Anlyst.

**HAIRELL, DONNA S,** Univ Of Al At Huntsville, Huntsville, AL; SR; BSEE; IEEE; Eta Kappa Nu Pres 90-; Tau Beta Pi; Electrcl Engrng.

**HAIRSTON, BRENDA G,** Va St Univ, Petersburg, VA; JR; Elem Educ; Tchr.

**HAIRSTON, HOPE D,** Univ Of Al At Birmingham, Birmingham, AL; FR; Dns Lst; Bsn; Acctg.

**HAIRSTON JR, JACK E,** Univ Of The Dist Of Columbia, Washington, DC; SR; AAS; Ltgtn Sprt Spclst Arnold/Porter Cmptrzd 90-; AB 82; Lgl Asstnt Tech; Law.

**HAJARI, CHETANA V,** Univ Of Sc At Columbia, Columbia, SC; JR; BA; Intl Stdnts Clb 88-; Amnesty Intl 88-; Indians Assn For Svc 87-; Rape Crisis Ntk 90; AA Resrch 90; Econ Inn 90-; Psych.

**HAJDU, STEVEN,** Christian Brothers Univ, Memphis, TN; JR; BA; Intl Paper Co; Sys Prog Ii; AS Comp Tech 83-85; Tlcmnctns; Info Src.

**HAJHOSSEIN, MAZHAR,** Fl St Univ, Tallahassee, FL; SR; BS; Amer Scty Civil Engrg Mbr 89-; Deans List 90; Shlrshp 90; Schlrshp 90/Assist; BS Georgia Southern Univ 86; Civil Engrg; Engrg.

**HAJJ-SHEHADEH, HAYTHAM N,** Univ Of Tn At Martin, Martin, TN; JR; BS; Stdnt Asst Math Lab 89-; Math; Biomed Engr.

**HAKES, CHRISTOPHER F,** S U N Y Coll Of Tech At Alfred, Alfred, NY; FR; AOS; Sigma Tau Epsilan; Bldg Trade; Constr.

**HAKES, JAHN K,** Univ Of Fl, Gainesville, FL; SR; PHD; Stdnt Hnrs Org 87-; Wrtrs Guild V P 88-; Phi Beta Kappa; Golden Key 88-; Omicron Delta Epsilon 88-; Undergrad Econ Soc 89-; Hnrs Mentor; Sigma Tau Sigma 88-; Pres Hnr Rl 87 89-; Dns Lst 87-; Grad Asst Duke U; Interclgte Bowling 88-90; Econ; Ed/Rsrch.**

**HAKIM, KABIR S,** Howard Univ, Washington, DC; SO; BA; Wmns Scr Tm Hd Coach 89-; Rdio Anncr 89-; Deans Hnr Rl 90-; Ged Usarmy 89; Gce Msly Schl Uk 83; Brdcst Prdctn; Radio.

**HALAC, MADELEINE,** Univ Of Rochester, Rochester, NY; SO; BA; Stdnts Ethcl Trtmnt Anmls; Anthroplgy.

**HALADA, JEANINE F,** Fl St Univ, Tallahassee, FL; FR; BA; MARS; Phi Eta Sigma; Bus/Fin Mktg; Law.

**HALADY, DAVID J,** S U N Y Coll Of Tech At Alfred, Alfred, NY; SR; BS; Air Cndtng Clb Pres 89-; Almni Asc 90-; Sigma Tau 89-90; BSA Eagle Sct 81-; Goergen Mackwirth Shtmtl Co 90-; Qcknbsh Co Inc Mech Cntrctr; Outstdng Snr Awd; Frfghtr; Red Crs Bld Donor 87-; AAS Alfred St Clg; Dsgn Engr.

**HALBIG, RANDAL L,** Brescia Coll, Owensboro, KY; SR; BA; IM Vlybl/Sftbl/Bsktbl; BA Art; BA Graphic Dsgn; Cmrcl Art; Advrtsng Art.

**HALCHAK, LITA B,** Central Fl Comm Coll, Ocala, FL; JR; AA; Wbl Sct Ldr 89-90; Chptr I Ad 85-; Elem Ed.

**HALCOMB, JOSEPH B,** Clark Atlanta Univ, Atlanta, GA; SO; BA; Univ Hstrcl Scty; Deans Lst; Intrnshp Lawson Thornton Attys At Law; Political Sci; Intl Law.

**HALDER, CRAIG G,** United States Naval Academy, Annapolis, MD; GD; MS; Phi Kappa Phi Pres 89-; Pi Tau Sigma Pres 88-; Tau Beta Pi; Cycling Team ACC Champion 89-; BSME; Mechl Engineering; USN Sub Serv.

**HALE, DARRELL R,** Capitol Coll, Laurel, MD; SR; BS; Tau Alpha Pi V P 89-; Alpha Chi 89-; IEEE 89-; Soc Amer Mil Engrs 87-; Avrum Gudelsky Schlrshp Awd 90-; Elctrcl Engr; Engr.

**HALE, DONALD R,** Marshall University, Huntington, WV; MS; Ky Colonel; Part-Time Instr For Ashland Cmmnty Clg; BA Morehead State U 75; Part-Time Instr For Ky Tech Vctnl Schl; Sfty Trng Sprvsr Ashland Ptrlm Co; Vol For Amer Red Cross; Occptnl Sfty/Hlth; Cnsltng For Indstrl Sfty.

**HALE, ELIZABETH EVA,** Bryant Stratton Bus Inst Roch, Rochester, NY; SO; AS; Rchstr Adlt Lrnr Schlrshp; Sec Lgl Asst; Paralegal.

**HALE, GLORIA C,** Le Moyne Coll, Syracuse, NY; SR; MPH; Sclgy Clb VP 89-90; Intrntl Sclgy Hnr Scty; Papr Prsntn At 15th Annl Undrgrad 90; Sclgcl Rsrch Conf; 1st Pl Le Moyne Clg Kirby Essay Cntst On Ecnmc Jstce 89; Tennis Tm 90; Sclgcl Prctce Assoc 89; AA Ohondaga Cmmnty Clg 88; Pbl Hlth; Pbl Hlth Prcttnr.

**HALE, HOLLY A,** Univ Of Ky, Lexington, KY; FR; BSN; NSNA 90-; Stndt Athltcs 90-; Deans Lst 90; Nsg.

**HALE, JACQUELINE TRACY,** Centenary Coll, Hackettstown, NJ; SR; BS; Bus Clb Phi Beta Chamda 90-; Acctg Clb Sec 90-; VITA; Alpha Chi Omega 90-; Deans Trphy; VITA Pgm; Pres Lst; BS; Acctg; Actnt CPA.

**HALE, KAREN A,** Schenectady County Comm Coll, Schenectady, NY; JR; AAS; Coll Wrk Prog Walt Disney Wrld Orlando Fl; Trvl/Trsm; Trvl Prof.

**HALE, KELLI M,** Ms St Univ, Miss State, MS; SO; BS; Pre Vet Clb 89-; Anml Sci; Vet Med.

**HALE, KRISTEN L,** Univ Of Akron, Akron, OH; SR; MA; Natl Stdnt Spch/Lang/Hrng Assn 89-; Deans Lst; BA; Cmnctv Dsrdrs; Spch/Lang Pthlgst.

**HALE, LISA G,** Univ Of Nc At Greensboro, Greensboro, NC; GD; MSN; Sigma Theta Tau 85-; Assc Mem AANA 90-; Grdtd Cum Laude BSN Degree; RN; BSN UNCG 85; Nurse Anthsia; Cert RN Ansthtst.

**HALE, MARJORIE L,** Providence Coll, Providence, RI; FR; BSW; Dns Lst; Hospce Vol 89-; Bddy Vol RI Prjct Aids 90-; Scl Wrk; Cnslng Prsns Wth Aids.

**HALE, PATTI R,** Univ Of Montevallo, Montevallo, AL; JR; BA; Phi Kappa Phi; Educ.

**HALE, SCOTT E,** Ashland Comm Coll, Ashland, KY; SO; BA; Spnsh Awd 90-; Phrmcy.

**HALE, STEPHEN D,** Univ Of Louisville, Louisville, KY; JR; BS; IM Vlybl Chmpnshp Capt 90; Sim Sftbl/Soccer Co Capt 90; Phi Eta Sigma 90-; Chem Engr.

**HALE, SUSAN B,** Fl International Univ, Miami, FL; SR; BED; Ftr Ed Amrc 90-; Phi Theta Kappa 88-89; Phi Kappa Phi 90-; Mmbr Brd Drctrs Assoc; AA 89; Erly Chldhd Spclst.

**HALE, SUZANNE P,** Univ Of West Fl, Pensacola, FL; SR; Deans Lst 89-; Prsdnts Lst; Stdnt Tchng; BA UNF; Spcl Edctn; Tchr.

**HALEKAKIS, COSMAS J,** Hellenic Coll/Holy Cross, Brookline, MA; SO; BA; Religious Studies; Psych.

**HALEMAN, TROY L,** Ky Wesleyan Coll, Owensboro, KY; SO; BS; SGA Soph/Jr Repr 90-; Stdnt Ambsdr 90-; Pre-Prof Soc 89-; Sigma Zeta V P; Sigma Phi Epsilon Secr; Owensboro Davies Co Hosp Vol; James Brown Schlrshp 89-; Westerfield Zoology Awd 90; Catholic Univ Amer Schlrshp 90; Bio; Med.

**HALEY, CHRISTOPHER B,** Northern Ky Univ, Highland Hts, KY; JR; BA; Clmnt Coll Drma Clb 90; AS Univ Of Cincinnati 90; Hstry; Lbrry Sci Ph D Hstry.

**HALEY, DAWN S,** Univ Of Fl, Gainesville, FL; JR; BS; Amer Acdmy Physcn Assts 90-; FL Acdmy Physcn Assts 90-; SAPA 90-; Pres Hon Rl-Univ FL 90; Emrgncy Nrs Assn 89-90; Crtfd Emrgncy Nrs 89-; AS FL Comm Coll Jcksnvll 86; Physcn Asst.

**HALEY, KATHERINE G,** Patrick Henry Comm Coll, Martinsville, VA; SR; AAS; Dns Lst; SNAV; CPR; Amer Red Crs 75-; Danville Comm Coll 74; Oper Rm Nrs; RN.

**HALEY, LAURIE A,** Northern Ky Univ, Highland Hts, KY; JR; BED; Spanish Clb 87-88; Clermont Educ Clb Sec 89-90; Clb Hispania; DAR 87-; NSDAR 87-; Lector St Louis Church 87-; Mntrng Schlrshp Educ Asst 89-90; Dns Lst UC Clermont Coll 89-; Sec Educ/Spnsh/Hstry; Sec Educ.

**HALEY, MICHAEL D,** Univ Of Louisville, Louisville, KY; JR; BSE; Golden Key 90-; Amateur Boxing 88-; IM Bsktbl; Profsnl Boxing; IM Handbl; Golden Key 90-; Tau Beta Pi; Krauth Elec Co Intern; Army Phys Fitness Badge 89; Mech Engr/Mgmt; Engr/Bsn.

**HALEY, RITA S,** Univ Of Cincinnati-Clrmnt Coll, Batavia, OH; SO; Acct Asst.

**HALEY, ROBERT JAMES,** Life Coll, Marietta, GA; GD; DC; Gonstead Study Clb 90-; Motion Palpation Clb 90-; Thompson Clb; Wrld All Around Weightlftng Chmp 80 Kilo Chmpion 89; Exectv Ftns Cntr Instrctr 89; Jersey City St Clg Hd Strngth Coach 88-; Frmr Wrstlr Montclair St Clg Cptn 82-; Chiropractic.

**HALEY, SANDRA L,** Averett Coll, Danville, VA; SR; BA; Alpha Chi 90-; Dns Lst 89-; Legal Aide 89-; AAS Patrick Henry Comm Coll 89; Engl/Hstry; Law.

**HALEY, SHEILA MAE,** Middle Tn St Univ, Murfreesboro, TN; SO; BS; Hon Soc 89-; Biolgy; Tchng.

**HALEY, SHENEEN M,** Tn St Univ, Nashville, TN; SR; JD; Stdnt Union Bd Gov 87-; Crim Just Org 87-; Chgo Clb Pres 87-; Lambda Tau Epsilon 88-; Stdnt Yr; Crim Just; Corp Attny.

**HALEY, VIVIEN T,** Hillsborough Comm Coll, Tampa, FL; SO; AA; Psych; Early Chldhd Ed.

**HALFON, AMIR,** Manhattan School Of Music, New York, NY; JR; BM; The Amer Israel Foundation Schlrshp Awd; Jazz Music.

**HALINSKI, ALEXANDRA,** City Univ Of Ny La Guard Coll, Long Island Cty, NY; SR; AAS; Nursing; Med Surg Nurse.

**HALL, ALEXANDER LYNN,** Johnson C Smith Univ, Charlotte, NC; SO; BA; Stdnt Affairs Com 90-; Kappa Alpha Psi 90-; MIAKA Pres 89-90; Deans List 90-; Engl/Hist; Law.

**HALL, ALLISON D,** Univ Of Al At Birmingham, Birmingham, AL; SO; ASSOC; Amer Occup Ther Assn 90-; AL Occup Ther Assn 90-; Stdnt Occup Ther Assn 90-; Pr Lst 90-; Asst Elsie Mc Kibbin Otr; Intrnshp Spain Rehab; TN Rehab; IM Sftbl; Occup Ther Asst.

**HALL, ALLISON DOWELL,** Brescia Coll, Owensboro, KY; SO; Stu Dvlpmnt Cncl; UK Mdl Sch Assoc 90; Lambda Sigma 89-; Phi Eta Sigma 89-; Epsilon Delta Educ Comm Chr 89-; Univ Ky Acdmc Sch 89-; Brescia Coll Acdmc Schlrshp; Coll Educ Deans Lst 89-; Lrng/Bhvr Dsordrs Educ; Spcl Ed Tchr.

**HALL, AMY E,** Memphis St Univ, Memphis, TN; JR; BA; Psychlgy.

**HALL, ANGELA D,** Lenoir Rhyne Coll, Hickory, NC; FR; BS; Ltrn Stdnt Mvmnt 90-; Cmps Mnstrs Frm; A Cpll Chr 90-; Eng.

**HALL, ANN M,** James Sprunt Comm Coll, Kenansville, NC; SR; AAS; Deans Lst; Rep Admnstrtv Offc Tchnlgy; AAS 90; AAS; Bus Admn.

**HALL, BARBARA G,** Middle Tn St Univ, Murfreesboro, TN; JR; BS; Stdnt Hm Econ Assn 90-; Intrnshp Castner Knott; Proj Affirm 90-; Fshn Mrchndsng; BA Meredith Coll 87; Fshn Mrchndsng; Buyer.

**HALL, BARBARA J,** Atlantic Comm Coll, Mays Landing, NJ; SO; AAS; Lgl Assts Assn 90-; Kappa Sigma Phi Trntn St 89-; BS Trntn St Coll 90; Prlgl Stds; Prlgl.

**HALL, CANDICE D,** Clark Atlanta Univ, Atlanta, GA; JR; BA; Stdnt Ga Assn Educ; Ntl Educ Assc; Kappa Delta Epsilom; Early Chldhd Educ; Tchng.

**HALL, CARA L,** Bridgewater Coll, Bridgewater, VA; SO; BA; Pinion Players 90; Albemarle Rifles Civil War Reactg Unit 88-; Lambda Soc 90-; Brdgwtr Coll Deans Lst 89-90; Hist; Histrc Prsrvtn.

**HALL, CELESTE V,** Johnson C Smith Univ, Charlotte, NC; SO; BA; Var Chrldng Cap 88-; Res Advisor; Delta Sigma Theta; Acctg.

**HALL, CELINA C,** City Univ Of Ny La Guard Coll, Long Island Cty, NY; SO; Deans Lst 90-; Amer Occptnl Thrpy Assn; Occptnl Thrpy.

**HALL II, CHARLES W,** Univ Of North Fl, Jacksonville, FL; SR; BS; Comp Sci; Sftwre Eng.

**HALL, CHERYL N,** Memphis St Univ, Memphis, TN; FR.

**HALL, CHRIS A,** Salisbury St Univ, Salisbury, MD; SO; BA; Bsbl; Acctng; CPA.

**HALL, CHRISTONIA U,** Abraham Baldwin Agri Coll, Tifton, GA; JR; BA; IM Bsktbl 87-88; Soc Wrk.

**HALL, CINDY L,** Southern Vt Coll, Bennington, VT; JR; MBA; Ownr Mgr Seafood Rstrnt; Real Est Sls; ASS Hudson Vly Comm Clg 89; Acctg; CPA.

**HALL, COURTNEY L,** Paine Coll, Augusta, GA; SO; Alpha Swthrts 90; Math Ttr 90; Math; Eng.

**HALL, CYNTHIA A,** Marshall University, Huntington, WV; SR; BBA; Hl Advsry Cncl Pres 86-88; Intr Hl Gov Cncl VP 87-88; Amer Mrktg Assoc 89-; Alpha Kappa Psi Pres Pldg Cls 90-; IM 86-; Oper Crdntr Intrmed Care Fclty 89-; Mrktg; Dvlpmntl Dsblty.

**HALL, CYNTHIA R,** Fl A & M Univ, Tallahassee, FL; SR; PHARM; Supreme Court Jstce Stdnt Govt; Alpha Kappa Mu VP; Gold Key; Kappa Epsilon Sec; Alpha Kappa Alpha; Rsrch Intern Upjohn Co 90; Rsrch Intern 3m; Pharmacy; Patent Law.

**HALL, DANIEL E,** Univ Of Cin R Walters Coll, Blue Ash, OH; SO; Philosophy Clb Treas 89-90; Chem Dept Awd Excnlce 90-; Chem; Pharm Rsrch.

**HALL, DANIEL J,** Defiance Coll, Defiance, OH; SR; BA; Ly Ldr/Trst Ney Untd Meth Chrch; PW Lg Bsbl Ch; Prdctn Plnr/ Frst Ln Sprvsr 78-; AA Defiance Clge 86; Bsn Mgmt; Bsn Admin.

**HALL, DANNA D,** Univ Of Akron, Akron, OH; JR; BA; ACES; Kappa Delta Pi; Elem Ed; Tchr.

**HALL, DAVID E,** Memphis St Univ, Memphis, TN; JR; BA; Univ Fla Nwspr 82-83; Nwspr 90-; AA St Petersburg Jr Coll 84; Multi Media Opertn Fnctn; Msc Bus/Pub Rel.

**HALL JR, DAVID T,** Wv Univ, Morgantown, WV; JR; BSW; Pi Kappa Phi Asst Treas 89-90-; Socl Wrk.

**HALL, DEBRA N,** Hillsborough Comm Coll, Tampa, FL; FR; Phi Theta Kappa 90; Bus Admin; Mgmt.

**HALL, DINA M,** Lane Coll, Jackson, TN; SR; BS; Drama Clb 88-; Peer Cnslr 88-; Delta Sigma Theta; Deans Lst 87-88; Hon Roll 88-; Chrldng Mgr 88-89; Bus; MBA.

**HALL, DONALD R,** Springfield Tech Comm Coll, Springfield, MA; GD; AS; Alpha Omega; Cert Bus Educ Inst 84; Cmptr Pgmng; Cmptr Pgmr.

**HALL, DONALD T,** Hahnemann Univ, Philadelphia, PA; GD; MD; BS 89; Medicine.

**HALL, DOROTHY E,** Central Fl Comm Coll, Ocala, FL; SR; ASN; Stdnt Nrses Assoc; Phi Theta Kappa 88; LPN Going For RN; Med Nrsng; CCRN Then BSN.

**HALL, DOROTHY K,** Roane St Comm Coll, Harriman, TN; FR; BA; Psychology; Prctng Psychologist.

**HALL, EDWARD L,** Savannah Coll Of Art & Design, Savannah, GA; SR; BFA; Photo Grp 89-; Outstndg Photo Stdnt; AA Santa Fe Comm Clg Gainesville Fl 86-88; Photogrphy.

**HALL, ELIZABETH,** Commonwealth Coll, Norfolk, VA; JR.

**HALL, ELIZABETH A,** S U N Y Coll At Fredonia, Fredonia, NY; JR; BA; Amnsty Intl 89-90; IM Vlybl Tnns 89-90; Hstry Hon Soc; Res Lf Asst 89-; Hstry-Educ; Scndry Educ.

**HALL, ERICA MONIQUE,** Ms Valley St Univ, Itta Bena, MS; SO; BS; Cmptr Sci/Math Clb Treas 90-; Alpha Chi Hon Soc Treas 91-; Delta Sigma Theta; Hon Stdnt 89-; Outstndg Cmptr Sci Stdnt 90-; Cmptr Sci/Math; Cmptr Prgrmmr.

**HALL, FLORENCE B,** Prince Georges Comm Coll, Largo, MD; FR; PHD; Drama Clb; AV Clb; Hgh Hon Rl; Theatr/Med Stdies; Dr/Actrss.

**HALL, GARRETT W,** Georgetown Univ, Washington, DC; SO; BSBA; Fnc.

**HALL, GEOFFREY C,** Memphis St Univ, Memphis, TN; SO; BS; By Scts Amer Egl Sct 84-90; Pre Med; Med.

**HALL, GLEN A,** Gaston Coll, Dallas, NC; SO; BA; AAS Cmnty Clge Air Force 90; Bsn Admin.

**HALL II, HARRY P,** Samford Univ, Birmingham, AL; GD; JD; Envlt Law Scty 90-; Inter Fraty Counsel Co Chrmn Awrns Comm 87-88f; Hnr Court Cumberland Schl Law 90-; Kappa Alpha Order Old South Chr 85-89; Judge J O Haley Fedl Trial Comptn 90; Dr Judge J O Haley Fedl Trial Comptn; Law; Litigation Practice.

**HALL, INGRID C,** Ny Univ, New York, NY; SO; BA; Blck Flm Mkrs Assc; NABA; Oxford Univ England Exchng; Ntry Pblc; Amer Scty Notrs; Incm Tx Prepr; Fin Analyst; Cert H/R Block 90; Cert Bronx Cmnty Clg 90; Acctg; CPA.

**HALL, IRENE DENISE,** Wilberforce Univ, Wilberforce, OH; JR; BS; Inrds NE OH Campus VP 88-; Sigma Omega Treas 90-; Alpha Kappa Mu 90-; Kappa Theta Epsilon; Delta Sigma Theta 90-; Intrn Wth BP Amer 88-; Acctg; Fin Conslt.

**HALL, JANET A,** Marshall University, Huntington, WV; SR; BBA; Gamma Beta Phi 89-; Phi Eta Sigma Treas 90-; Hall Advsry Cncl Rep 88-89; WMUL; Mktg/Advtsng.

**HALL, JEFF E,** Unity Coll, Unity, ME; FR; BA; Spnl Crd Soc Pres 87-.

**HALL, JENNA R,** Anne Arundel Comm Coll, Arnold, MD; FR; BS; Choir Wesly Chapl Meth Chrch 87-; Sub Tchr Wesley Chpl Meth Chrch 90; Tchrs Asst Hilltop Daycare 89-; Elem Educ; Tchr.

**HALL, JEREL,** Bloomfield Coll, Bloomfield, NJ; FR; IM Bsktbl 90-; Mntrshp Schlrs Prog 90; Cmnctns; Video Prdctn.

**HALL, JOHN C,** Univ Of Ga, Athens, GA; SO; BSED; PBA; NMPOA; Plc Hnr Grd; Plc Offce/Mntd Unit; Sci; Middle Schl Sci/Scl Sci.

**HALL, JON A,** Northeast State Tech Comm Coll, Blountville, TN; BS; Comp Engnrng Tech.

**HALL, JUDY E,** Univ Of Sc At Coastal Carolina, Conway, SC; JR; BS; Dns Lst 89-; Fnce.

**HALL, JUDY E,** Univ Of Sc At Columbia, Columbia, SC; JR; BA; Adm Asst Corp Bnkng; Finance; IRS Bnkng Invstmnt.

**HALL, JULIE A,** Univ Of Miami, Coral Gables, FL; SR; BS; Stdnt Repr Coord 90-; AJAS Mbr 87-; Golden Key; Delta Gamma 88-90; Highest GPA Arch Engr 89-; Bowman Ashe Schlrshp 88-; Asstnt To Instrctr; Blood Dr 90; Architecture/Engrng.

**HALL, JULIE ANN,** The Johns Hopkins Univ, Baltimore, MD; SR; BSN; BA Univ Of Minn 90; Nursing.

**HALL, JULIE C,** Longwood Coll, Farmville, VA; JR; Phy Educ Mjrs Clb VP 88-; IM Aerobics Inst 90-; Dns Lst; Delta Psi Kappa VP 90-; Delta Zeta Prlmntrn 89-; Spirit Awd 88-89; Gymnastics 88-89; Phy Educ; Corp Fitness.

**HALL, KENNETH R,** Northern Ky Univ, Highland Hts, KY; SO; BA; Psychlgy; Clncl Prctnr.

**HALL, KIMBERLY D,** Al A & M Univ, Normal, AL; SO; BA; Bsktbl Cnfrnc Acdmc Awd 90; Bsktbl Capt 89-; Fin; Fin Mngr.

**HALL, KRISTI L,** Univ Of Nc At Greensboro, Greensboro, NC; JR; BS; Ntnl Assc Social Workers Stdnt Orgnztn 90-; Social Work; Schl Cnslng.

**HALL, KRISTIN L,** Clark Atlanta Univ, Atlanta, GA; SR; JD; Bowdoin Clg African Amer Soc Treas 87-; Coalition Of Concerned Stdnts 90-; Deans Lst; Bowdoin Ass The Retarded Cmnty Coord 87-; Engl As A Scnd Lang Cert; Bowdoin Clg Cmncmnt Spkr; Smithsonian Intrnshp; Natl Trust For Hist Pres Intrnshp 90; Hist; Law.

**HALL, KRISTINA M,** Cumberland Coll, Williamsburg, KY; JR; BA; Fllwshp Chrstn Athlts 88-; Bptst Stdnt Un Vllybl 90-; Tns Co-Cptn 88-; Co-Ed Chrldng 89-90; Edctn; Elem Frnch Edctn.

**HALL, LAURA L,** Midlands Tech Coll, Columbia, SC; SR; Intl Stdnts Clb Ofcr; Stdnts Surg Assoc V P 90; Intl Clb Vlybl; Surg Tech; Surg Tech/Air Force.

**HALL, LAURIE L,** Middle Tn St Univ, Murfreesboro, TN; SO; BBA; Acctg.

**HALL, LEIGH ANN,** Univ Of Sc At Columbia, Columbia, SC; SO; BA; DECA Bus Stff 88; Spcl Olmpcs 88; Chld Lfe Vol 89-; Psych; Dev Psychs.

**HALL, LINDA F,** Va St Univ, Petersburg, VA; JR; BA; Scl Wrk Clb 90-; Chesterfield Voc Svcs 90-; AS John Tyler Cmnty Clg 87; Scl Wrk; Law.

**HALL, LISA ANN,** Ky St Univ, Frankfort, KY; SO; ADN; UMC Nrsng Techncn; Nrsng; Surgcl RN.

**HALL, LISA M,** Va Commonwealth Univ, Richmond, VA; SR; BS; Stdnt Ed Assoc; Cncl Of Excptnl Chldrn; Bapt Stdnt Union; Spec Ed; Tchng.

**HALL, LISA M,** Wv Univ, Morgantown, WV; JR; BA; NASW 90-; Natl Key 88-; Mon Co Prbtn Office Intern; Soc Work; MA Rehab & Cnslng.

**HALL, LISA R,** Averett Coll, Danville, VA; SR; BS; Alpha Chi; Acctg; CPA.

**HALL, LORI ANN,** Univ Of Ky, Lexington, KY; SR; BA; Am Psychlgcl Assn Affiliate 90-; Golden Key 90-; Psi Chi 90-; Pulaski Co Ed Schlrshp; Indl/Orgnztnl Psychlgst.

**HALL, LORI L,** Central Fl Comm Coll, Ocala, FL; FR; AA; Pharmacy.

**HALL, LYNN M,** Southern Vt Coll, Bennington, VT; SR; BSW; IM Sccr/Bsktbl/Sftbl/Ski Tm 87-88; Sci Fair Jdg 87-88; Vol Eldrly Comm; Fcltr Sbstnc Abuse Pro 90-; Intrn Vrmnt Cncl Aging Brttlboro Area Adlt Day Serv; Cnslg Serv Eden Pk Nrsg Hm Brattleboro Vt; Intl Corp 90-; Scl Wrk.

**HALL, MARCIA C,** Albany St Coll, Albany, GA; JR; BA; Rlgs Life Org; Std Govt Chrp 90-; Cncrt Choir; Alpha Kappa Mu; Hnrs Cncl; Tlnts Undgrad Mnrty Flwshp; Albny St Clg Pres Schlr; Fox 31 News Intshp; Engl; Tchng/Crtv Wrtng.

**HALL, MARCIA D,** Abraham Baldwin Agri Coll, Tifton, GA; FR; AD; Math; Tchng.

**HALL, MARCUS R,** Hillsborough Comm Coll, Tampa, FL; SO; AS; US Jaycees 90-; Constr Estimator; Nucl Med Tech.

**HALL, MARGARET TISH,** Univ Of Ky, Lexington, KY; FR; Cmps Crsde Fr Christ; Deans Lst; Poli Sci; Intrntl Law.

**HALL, MARIA L,** Memphis St Univ, Memphis, TN; JR; BA; Phi Eta Sigma 90-; Alpha Lambda Delta 90-; Theatre Cmmnctns; Chldrns Theatre.

**HALL, MARION J,** Southern Vt Coll, Bennington, VT; SR; MBA; Envrnmntl Assoc 88-89; Earth Day Comm Chrprsn 89-90; Envrnmntl Awrns 89-90; BA 90; Envrnmntl Plng; Rgnl Planner.

**HALL, MELANIE J,** Longwood Coll, Farmville, VA; SO; BS; Alpha Lambda Delta 89-90; Math Contest 89-90; Psych.

**HALL, MELISSA E,** Middle Tn St Univ, Murfreesboro, TN; FR; PHARM; Gamma Beta Phi 90-; Intl Ordr Rnbw Girls Grand Faith 84-; Ordr Eastern Star 90-; Annual Outstanding Honors Freshman Award; Pharmacist.

**HALL, MICHAEL J,** Kent St Univ Kent Cmps, Kent, OH; SR; BBA; Univ Accntng Assoc 89; Golden Key; Accntng Intrnshp Pckrd Electric; Im Bsktbl 89; Accntng; Accntng Or Tax Law.

**HALL, MICHELLE LEIGH,** Univ Of Sc At Columbia, Columbia, SC; SO; BA; Sftbl 89-; Early Chldhd Educ; 2nd Grd Tchr.

**HALL, MICHELLE R,** Ky St Univ, Frankfort, KY; SO; BA; Busn Mgmt; Hotl Mgr.

**HALL, MICHELLE T,** Univ Of Nc At Chapel Hill, Chapel Hill, NC; FR; BA; Stdnt TV 90-; Delta Zeta 90-; English/Drama.

**HALL, NAILAH O,** Temple Univ, Philadelphia, PA; SO; BEE; Natl Scty Of Blck Engs; IEEE; Dns Lst 90; Intrnshp Phldphia Elec Co Jr Tech Asst; Natl Sci Fndtn Schlrshp; Elec Eng; Eng Or Med.

**HALL, PAIGE B,** Va Commonwealth Univ, Richmond, VA; SR; BS; Psi Chi; Goldn Key 89-; Hon Prog 87-; Hon Psychlgy 90-; Psychlgy; Crmnlgy.

**HALL, PARNIECE C,** Spartanburg Methodist Coll, Spartanburg, SC; FR; Spprt Srvcs 90-; Phi Theta Kappa 90-; Psi Beta 90-; Ed; Tch.

**HALL, PAUL B,** Tuskegee Univ, Tuskegee Inst, AL; JR; BA; Mrchng Band 88-90; NAACP Chpln 88-; US Achvmnt Acad 86-87; Omega Psi Phi 90-; 3M 90; Intrnshp Honeywell; Merit Schlrshp; Mech Engr/Physics.

**HALL, PAULA D,** Al A & M Univ, Normal, AL; SO; BS; Natl Soc Blck Eng 89-90; Cmptr Sci; Spec.

**HALL, PAULA L,** City Univ Of Ny City Coll, New York, NY; JR; BA; Mellon Mnrty Undrgrad Fllwshp 90; Rosenberg/ Humphrey Intrnshp NY State Govt; Phlsphy; Prfssr.

**HALL, PHYLLIS B,** Livingston Univ, Livingston, AL; JR; BS; Elem Educ.

**HALL, PHYLLIS P,** Pellissippi St Tech Comm Coll, Knoxville, TN; FR; AAS; Smokey Mt Mnscrpt Clb 87-88; :Gpa Awrd Jwlry Sls 89-; Crctnl Ofcr 89; Bus Mgmt; Retail Mgmt.

**HALL, REBEKAH D,** Univ Of Montevallo, Montevallo, AL; JR; BA; Ed Hrng Impaired; Tchr.

**HALL, RION B,** Embry Riddle Aeronautical Univ, Daytona Beach, FL; FR; BS; Caribbean Assoc Asst Secy; Avionics; Elec Engrng.

**HALL, ROBERT D,** Ashland Comm Coll, Ashland, KY; SO; AASET; AS 90; Eng Tech; Elect.

**HALL, ROBIN A,** Snead St Jr Coll, Boaz, AL; SO; AAS; N Amer Vet Tech Assn 89-; Phi Theta Kappa 90-; Highest GPA; Schlrshp Iams Pet Food Prod 90; Pell City Animal Hosp 89; Vet Tech.

**HALL, ROBIN M,** Lincoln Univ, Lincoln Univ, PA; JR; BS; Chem Clb 89-; Grmn Clb Tres 90-; Jrnl Clb 90-; Beta Kappa Chi; Pre Alum Cncl; Howard Univ Rsrch Awd 90; Actvts Apprec Awd 90-; Chem; Pharmclgy.

**HALL, SANDRA K,** Bethel Coll, Mckenzie, TN; JR; BS; Gamma Beta Phi Hnr Soc Rec Sec 90-; Iota Alpha Omega Sor 90-; Bus Admn; Mrktng Exec.

**HALL, SANDY,** Savannah St Coll, Savannah, GA; JR; BA; Union Mission; Girls Home Savannah; AS Andrew Jr Clg 88; Scl Wrk.

**HALL, SARA J,** Bridgewater Coll, Bridgewater, VA; SR; BA; Hnr Cncl Chf Jstce 89-; Omicron Delta Kappa VP 90; Alpha Chi 90-; Lambda 89-; Blgy; Envrnmntl Sci.

**HALL, SARA L,** Univ Of Tn At Knoxville, Knoxville, TN; JR; BA; Pres Golden Key VP; Pre Law Soc; U Hons Comm; Undergrad Acad Cncl; TN Schlrs Jr Rep; Stdnt Affrs Cncl; Alpha Omicron Delta; Comm Head Stdnt Rghts/Rspnsblties Comm; Camp Crsd Christ; Gamma Sigma Sigma Svc Srty; Pltcl Sci/Cmnctns; Law Schl.

**HALL, SARAH S,** Montgomery Comm Coll, Troy, NC; JR; BS; Stdnt Govt Assc Rep 88-90; Crisis Cncl Montgomery Cnty Vol 90-; Sndy Schl Tchr Cornerstone Bptst Star NC 89-; Bus Admin; Asst Admnstr.

**HALL, SHANTAE D,** Memphis St Univ, Memphis, TN; FR; BA; Phi Eta Sigma; Alpha Lambda Delta; Math; Educ.

**HALL, SHEILA M,** Livingston Univ, Livingston, AL; JR; BS; Ordr Estrn Star Chpln 83-84; Dghtrs Nile Tres 89-90; Alfa Eta; AS 78; Erly Chldhd; Tch.

**HALL, SHERRY ANNE,** Al St Univ, Montgomery, AL; SO; Scl Wrk.

**HALL, STEVE M,** Univ Of Ky, Lexington, KY; SR; BA; Exec Cncl Baptist Stdnt Union Frshmn Cncl Pr 87-88; UK Chptr Hab For Hum Sec 89-; Frshmn Orient Ldr 89-; Amer Soc Of Civil Engs 90-; Civil Eng.

**HALL, SUSAN A,** Snead St Jr Coll, Boaz, AL; FR; BS; Bus; Fshn Mrchndsng.

**HALL, SUSAN J,** City Univ Of Ny City Coll, New York, NY; SR; BFA; Strn Afrcn Stdnts Org 87-; Outstdng Dnc Mjr Cty Coll Recog Ntl Dnc Assn; Dnc; Prfrm/Tch.

**HALL, SUSAN M,** Univ Of Sc At Columbia, Columbia, SC; SO; BA; Gamma Beta Phi 90-; Deans Lst 89-F Chancllrs Hon Roll 89-; Psych; Spch Ther/Audlgy.

**HALL, TALLEY C,** Christian Brothers Univ, Memphis, TN; FR; BA; Deans Lst 90-; U S Council Intl Bnkng 88-; Bank Ntwrk Admin; Telecomm; Intrl Bnkng.

**HALL, TAMMY G,** Old Dominion Univ, Norfolk, VA; SR; MBS; DECA 90; Deans Lst 89-90; Letter Accommodation/US Navy 87; Letter Of Appreciation/US Navy 90; IM Vlybl/Ftbl/Sftbl 87-88; BS 90; Mktg Edn.

**HALL, TAMRON K,** Spartanburg Methodist Coll, Spartanburg, SC; SO; BA; Stdnt Govt VP 89-; Yrbk Stff 90-; Phi Theta Kappa Pres 89-; Psi Beta Pres 90-; Jr Achvmnt Vol 90; Spcl Olympcs Vol 89-; Hbtt Fr Hmnty Vol; Bsktbl Chrldr Co Capt; AA; Elem Educ; Tchr.

**HALL, TERESA GAIL,** Univ Of Sc At Columbia, Columbia, SC; FR; BA; Gamma Beta Phi Sec; Phi Epsilon Sigma; Graphic Dsgn.

**HALL, TERRY R,** Univ Of Tn At Knoxville, Knoxville, TN; SO; BA; Bapt Stdnt Union 89-; Rpblcns 90-; Phi Eta Sgm 90-; Alpha Lmbd Dlt 90-; Gamma Beta Phi; Pi Kappa Phi 89-; Outstandng Soph; Water Ski Clb/Tm; Acctg; Law.

**HALL, TIM L,** Gordon Coll, Barnesville, GA; JR; BA; Stdnt Govt Assoc Senator 89-90; Stdnt Recrtmnt Tm VP 89-90; Stdnt Affairs Comm Stdnt Repr 89-90; Phi Theta Kappa; IM Bsktbl Sftbl 88-90; Riverside Uniform Rentals Rte Supv 84-88; AA Psychology 90; Psychology; Indstrl Psychlgy.

**HALL, VALERIA G,** Fl A & M Univ, Tallahassee, FL; FR; BS; Phi Eta Sigma 90-; Bus; Ed.

**HALL, VERONICA,** Fayetteville St Univ, Fayetteville, NC; JR; BA; Sci Clb VP 90; Res Assist 90; Alpha Kappa Mu 90; Biomed Rsrch 90; Chem; Rsrch.

**HALL, VICKI D,** Univ Of Va, Charlottesville, VA; SR; BED; NSSLHA 89-; ETHOS 89-; Golden Key 89-; Cmunctn Dsrdrs; Spch Path/Thrpy.

**HALL, VICTORIA E,** Univ Of Nc At Charlotte, Charlotte, NC; FR; BA; Bus; Law.

**HALL, YULANDA C,** Central St Univ, Wilberforce, OH; FR; Accntng; Bsns.

**HALL-GOLDMAN, ALISON J,** William Paterson Coll, Wayne, NJ; GD; Ft Lee HS Tchr Ft Lee NJ 86-; EdM 84; BA 83; Spcl Educ.

**HALL-NILSEN, ELIZABETH B,** Univ Of Nh Plymouth St Coll, Plymouth, NH; JR; BS; Prsdnts Lst; Achvmnt Schlrshp 90-; Grphc Dsgnr Archtctrl Srvy Drftng; Art Edctn; Art Edctn.

**HALLAHAN, PATRICK D,** Univ Of Ga, Athens, GA; SR; BLA; Hall VP 88-; Landscape Arch.

**HALLAM, ANN L,** Comm Coll Algny Co Algny Cmps, Pittsburgh, PA; SO; AS; Peer Nrsng Tutor 90-; Phi Theta Kappa 90-; Nrsng; RN.

**HALLE, APRIL I,** Univ Of Miami, Coral Gables, FL; JR; BA; Hillel 88-90; Bnai Brith Wmn; Earth Day 90; Hnr Stdnts Assoc 88-; Engl Hnr Soc 90-; Golden Key 90-; Hnr Soc Buddies 90-; Dns Lst 89; Provosts Hnr Rl 89-90; Univ Miami Pearson Schlrshp 88-; Master Tutor Pgm; IMS 88; Engl; Law.

**HALLE, ROSS P,** Univ Of Miami, Coral Gables, FL; SR; BA; Hillel 88-89; Deans Lst; Study Abrd Pgm Rome Italy; Brickell Bay Bridge Cmptn 90; Wmns Mem Arlington Natl Cmptn 89; Amer Inst Architecture Stdnt 89; IMS 87-88; Architecture.

**HALLEE, KATHERINE GROVER,** Andover Coll, Portland, ME; SR; AAS; Deans Lst 88-90; Pres Lst 90; Sec At Andover Coll; AAS 90; Acctg; Tch.

**HALLER, DARIN L,** Univ Of South Fl, Tampa, FL; GD; JD; Entertainment Arts/Sprts Law Soc 90-; Pre Law Soc 89-; BA 90; Sociology; Law.**

**HALLER, MAYA,** Centenary Coll, Hackettstown, NJ; FR; C T/Dressage Team 90-; Phi Theta Kappa; Acad Mntrshp 90-; Equestrian Sci; Bsn.

**HALLER III, WILLIAM N,** Birmingham Southern Coll, Birmingham, AL; SR; BS; Alpha Kappa Psi 89-; Alpha Epsilon Delta 89-; Kappa Mu Epsilon 89-; Theta Chi Natl Pldge 87-; IM Sprts Ftbl Bsktbl Sccr; Bus Mgmt; Med.

**HALLETT, MARY E,** Winthrop Coll, Rock Hill, SC; JR; BFA; Deans Lst 90-; Cmps Plnng/Dsgn Dept Winthrop Coll Stff Dsgnr; BFA Queens Coll Charlotte NC 89; Interior Dsgn.

**HALLEY, DEBORAH L,** S U N Y Coll Of Tech At Delhi, Delhi, NY; SO; BA; NY State Assn Vet Tech 89-; Phi Theta Kappa 89-; AAS; Vet Sci; Return To Sch.

**HALLGREN, SEAN J,** Kent St Univ Stark Cmps, North Canton, OH; SO; PHD; Cmptr Sci; Rsrch.

**HALLIBURTON, LORI TILLMAN,** Memphis St Univ, Memphis, TN; JR; BED; DECA 84-86; Frnch Clb; Dict Intl Biog 87; Elem Educ; Tchng.

**HALLMAN, JODIE C,** Appalachian St Univ, Boone, NC; FR; BED; Lsr Stds Assoc; RSA Flr Rep; Spnsh Scndry Ed; Spnsh Tchr.

**HALLMARK, CALLIE L,** Univ Of Montevallo, Montevallo, AL; FR; BA; IRO 90-; Alpha Lambda Delta 90-; Freshman Hnrs Schlrshp; Linly/Heflin Schrlshp; English; Teacher/Writer.

**HALLO DE WOLF, AXEL ANIBAL,** Univ Of Miami, Coral Gables, FL; SO; BSEE; EXCEL 90-; Deans Lst 89-; Hon Roll 90-; A Bacheller Schlrshp 89-; Elec Eng.

**HALLOCK MORRIS, MARY T,** Defiance Coll, Defiance, OH; SR; Cmps Nswppr Vwpnts Ed 88-; Frnds Of Th Hrt 88-; Beta Sigma Vp 89-; Cmnctn Arts; Jrnlsm.

**HALLOCK, CINDY BETH,** Miami Dade Comm Coll, Miami, FL; GD; JD; Miami Dade Cmmnty Awd 84-89; Acad Achvmnt Barry U Awd; Vol Grdn Ad Litem-Chld Advcy Prog 90; BLS Bach Lib Stdies Barry U; Law.

**HALLOCK, DOUGLAS J,** Univ Of Ky, Lexington, KY; SR; JD; Sigma Tau Delta 90-; Grad W/Hons; Deans Lst 89-; IM Ftbl 88-90; BA; Engl/Phlsphy; Law.

**HALLOCK, LOIS A,** Youngstown St Univ, Youngstown, OH; SR; BSN; Invitation To Nrsng Socty 91; Dist 3 Ohio Nrs Assn Outstdng Nurse In Cls; Hnr Grad/Dir Awd 83; 4 Yrs Active Duty Army; 2 1/2 Yrs Walter Reed Army Med Ctr 82-86; LPN Fitzsimons Army Med Cntr US Army 83; Nrsng; Mstrs In Nrsng.

**HALLOWELL, THOMAS ACE,** Bloomfield Coll, Bloomfield, NJ; JR; BS; Exec Offcr; NJ Natl Gd 84-; Dns Lst High Hnrs 90; NJ Natl Gd Offcrs Assn 88-; Employee Actvty Assn VP 89-; Offcr Cand Schl 87-88; Offcr Bsc Crs 88-89; Blood Drive Chrmn; Sprvsr Basf Corp 84; Pres Adv Clng Srvcs 90; Crmnl Jstc.

**HALMETT, MEREDITH P,** Radford Univ, Radford, VA; JR; BS; Stdnt Nwspr Rprtr 90-; Grk Lf Mag Chrprsn; Stdnt Lf Hs Cncl Treas 89-90, Univ Hon 89 ; Alpha Sigma Tau Fndrsg Chrmn; Intrnshp-Richmond Times Dsptch Rprtr 90; Pblc Rltns Intrnshp-Sthsd Elctrc Coop; Jrnslm-Pblc Rltns; Brdcst Jrnlsm.

**HALMRAST, KELLY A,** Univ Of Sc At Columbia, Columbia, SC; GD; BA 90; Engl; Prsnl.

**HALOVIAK, BRENT D,** Columbia Union Coll, Takoma Park, MD; JR; BA; Cmps Lfe Comm 88-89; Pro Msca 90-; Phi Eta Sigma 88-; Alpha Chi; Cmps Mnstrs Dir 89-; Cmmndtn Excllnc Math 88-; Rce Dir 90-; Math; Tchg.

**HALPER, LISA M,** Syracuse Univ, Syracuse, NY; JR; BSBA; Hall Cncl VP 89/Pres 90-; NACURH Rep; RHA Rep 89; Phi Eta Sigma Treas 90-; NRHH 90-; Gldn Key 90-; Beta Alpha Psi Pres Elect; Excel Ldrshp Wrkshps 88-90; Siver Ldrshp Series 90; Orien Advsr 90; Univ Tennis Clb 89-; Acctg; CPA.**

**HALPERT, ARIELLA Y,** Yeshiva Univ, New York, NY; MA; Sr Cls Govt Treas 89-90; Comm IM Bsktbl Comm 87-88; Deans Lst 88-90; Tchiya Mgr 88-90; Proj Ari 89-; Magna Cum Laude 90; Hist Awd 90; U S Pblc Hlth Serv Trnshp 90; Bsktbl 89-90; BA 89-90; Machon Gold Clg For Wmn 86-87; Hist; Prof History.

**HALPERT, GWEN E,** S U N Y At Buffalo, Buffalo, NY; SR; BS; IIE Treas; Chi Omega; Indl Engr.

**HALPIN, JEANNE M,** Duquesne Univ, Pittsburgh, PA; JR; BA; YMCA 88-; Lambda Sigma 89-90; Phi Eta Sigma 89-90; Mc Klowsky Svc Awd 90-; Sclgy.

**HALPIN, JEFFREY L,** Thomas Nelson Comm Coll, Hampton, VA; SO; BA; AAS Degree 90; Admn Jstc; Law Enfrcmnt.**

**HALPIN, MARY F,** Kent St Univ Kent Cmps, Kent, OH; JR; BA; Prgsv Std Ntwrk Chr 89; Alpha Phi Sigma 90-; Intshp Fed Prsn; Dns Lst 89-; Psy/Crmnl Jstc; Law/Crrctns.

**HALPIN, NANCY C,** The Kings Coll, Briarclf Mnr, NY; SR; BS; Stdnt Govt Treas 90; Theater Clb Chrgrphr 90-; Fut Chrstn Educ Pres 87-; Brandywine Mnstries Ldr 87-; Hmcmng Queen 90; Dns Lst; Trck Tm 89-90; Elem Educ; Tchr.

**HALSCHEIDT, HEIDI,** Univ Of Akron, Akron, OH; SR; BED; Natl Strngth/Cndtng Assn 90-; Natl Athl Trnrs Assn 90-; US Cycling Fed 90-; Gldn Key 89-; MS Bike Tour 89; Intrnshp Akron Univ Athl Trng Prog 90-; Natl City Corp Relay Triathalon 3rd 90; Lake Metroparks Biathalon 1st 90; Athl Trng/Hlth/Phys Educ; Trnr/Tchr.

**HALSETH, THOMAS R,** Gallaudet Univ, Washington, DC; SR; BA; Stdnt Res Asst 89-90; Univ Jdcl Bd 89-90; Stdnt Body Govt Elect Com Chrmn 87-89; Phi Alpha Pi 90-; Delta Sigma Phi; Govt.

**HALSEY, CATHY E,** Volunteer St Comm Coll, Gallatin, TN; SO; ASSOC; Med Rcrd Tchncn; Pre Allied Hlth Career.

**HALSEY II, PAUL D,** Eastern Ky Univ, Richmond, KY; FR; BA; Pre Law; Lawyr Attrny.

**HALSTEAD, JANDA KAY,** Appalachian Bible Coll, Bradley, WV; FR; BA; Choral; Gospel Heralds; Christian Svc Music Grp; Music.

**HALSTEAD, MARK W,** Wv Inst Of Tech, Montgomery, WV; JR; BS; Chemical Engrng; Dsgn Engrng.

**HALTER, MARIA K,** Daytona Beach Comm Coll, Daytona Beach, FL; FR; BA; Quanta 90-; Engl; Tchr.

**HALTHON, MEREDITH N,** Talladega Coll, Talladega, AL; FR; BS; Talladega Chr 90-; Bsns Mgmnt; Entreprnr.

**HALTIWANGER, GRADY B,** Univ Of Sc At Columbia, Columbia, SC; JR; BA; AA Piedmont Tech Clg 84; Hist; Secndry Ed.

**HALUM, MICHELLE C,** Univ Of Sc At Columbia, Columbia, SC; SO; BA; Chi Omega 89-; Jrnlsm/Mass Cmmnctns; Law Schl.

**HALUSKY, DONIA L,** Univ Of North Fl, Jacksonville, FL; FR; Communications; Broadcasting.

**HALUSZCZAK, TIMOTHY A,** Robert Morris Coll, Coraopolis, PA; FR; BA; AMA 90-; Lambda Sigma VP 90-; Vrsty Trck 90-; Bus Mgmt Mrktng; Own Bus.

**HALUSZKA, LISA,** Salisbury St Univ, Salisbury, MD; SO; BS; Scl Wrk Clb 90; Plnd Prnthd Vlntr 89-90; Phi Eta Sigma 90; Rsprtry Thrpy.

**HALVERSON, AMY L,** Crichton Coll, Memphis, TN; SO; BA; Drama Clb; Deans Lst; Cmmnty Schlrshp; Bsns.

**HALVORSEN, ANN KATHRIN,** Salem-Teikyo Univ, Salem, WV; SO; BS; Mentr Clb 90-; Intl Clb 89-; Gamma Beta Phi Treas 90-; Bus Admin; Bus/Mktg.

**HAM, GERMAN,** Univ Of Miami, Coral Gables, FL; JR; BS; IEEE 90-; Hon Stdnts Assn 90-; Natl Soc Pro Engrs; Eta Kappa Nu 90-; Phi Eta Sigma 90-; All-Amer Schlr; Natl Cllgt Eng Awd; Elect Eng Appld Physcs; Eng.

**HAM, JASON E,** Le Moyne Coll, Syracuse, NY; SO; BA; Model United Nations Clb Sec 90-; Intgrl Hon Pgm 90-; Martial Arts Scty 89-; Pol Sci; Law.

**HAM, SAMUEL E,** Univ Of Southern Ms, Hattiesburg, MS; SR; BA; Phi Theta Kappa 87-89; Schlrs Bowl Jr Clg Act 26; Full Schlrshp SMCC Act 26; GMAT 620; AA SW Ms Cmmnty Clg 89; Bsnss Admin Gnrl; Entrprnr Tchr.

**HAM, SOO-HYUN,** Cleveland Inst Of Art, Cleveland, OH; SO; BFA; Hon Schlrshp 90-; Fine Arts; Ind Design.

**HAMAD, JULIE A,** Kent St Univ Kent Cmps, Kent, OH; GD; Amer Mktg Assn 88-90; Mktg Assn 88-90; Goldn Key 90; Delta Sigma Pi 89-90; Pres Lst 89; Dns Lst; Sup Schlrshp Awd 90; BSBA 90.

**HAMAKER, LEAH D,** Va Commonwealth Univ, Richmond, VA; SR; BS; Friendlys Restaurant 86-; Golden Key; Alpha Phi Sigma; Internship; Field Hockey 86; Pre-Law/Justice-Risk Adm; Law.

**HAMANN, HOLLIE A,** S U N Y Coll At Fredonia, Fredonia, NY; SR; BS; Clncn Henry Youngerman Ctr 90-; Stdnt Tchng LDP N Tonawanda; Spch Lang Path/Audlgy.

**HAMANN, KAREN L,** Averett Coll, Danville, VA; SR; BA; BUS; Avrt Sngrs Cnctr 90-; Avrt Rngrs Cndctr 90-; Swn Msc Schlrshp 89-; Wlmsn Msc Schlrshp 89-; Msc Mnstry.

**HAMANN, THERESA M,** Adelphi Univ, Garden City, NY; FR; BS; Circle K Intrnatl 90-; Stdnt Actvts Brd 90-; Elem Educ Math; Tchr.

**HAMBLEN, CAROLYN L,** Allegheny Coll, Meadville, PA; SR; BS; Elem Tutr 89-; Alpha Chi Omega V P 89-; Doane Schlr 89-; Tchrs Asst 89-90; Crs Cntry 87-88; Psych; Phy Thrpy/M S.

**HAMBLEN, H DEAN,** Southside Va Comm Coll, Alberta, VA; GD; AAS; Phi Theta Kappa; Bus Mgmt.**

**HAMBLEN, TASHA L,** Greenville Tech Coll, Greenville, SC; FR; BS; Med Explorers 90; Southside Bapt Chrch 80-; Clg Trnsfr; Phys Thrpy.

**HAMBLIN, LEASA D,** Georgetown Coll, Georgetown, KY; FR; Band Bapt Stdnt Un; Alpha Lambda Delta; All Colligate Band.

**HAMBRICK, DEBRA L,** Ashland Comm Coll, Ashland, KY; SO; BA; Morehd Regnl Hnrs Schlrshp; Dns Lst 89-; Spec Ed; Tchng.

**HAMBRICK, LESLIE D,** Western Piedmont Comm Coll, Morganton, NC; SO; AA; Stdnt Govt Sen 89; Phi Theta Kappa 90-; Pres Schlrshp Lenoir Rhyne Hickory N C; Intrntl Bus; Law.

**HAMBY, A LYNETTE,** Roane St Comm Coll, Harriman, TN; SO; Elem Educ.

**HAMBY, BETTY C,** Roane St Comm Coll, Harriman, TN; SO; BS; Wmns Stdnt Orgn 89-; Gnrl; Elem Edctn.

**HAMBY, BEVERLY A,** Tn Tech Univ, Cookeville, TN; SR; BS; Wesly Fndtn 85-88; Kappa Omicron Nu 89-; Vanderbilt Chldrns Hosp Intern; Chld Dvlpmnt Fmly Sci; Chld Lf Spclst.

**HAMBY, CYNTHIANNA,** Central Fl Comm Coll, Ocala, FL; SO; AS; FSNA 89-; NSNA 90-; Phi Thet Akappa 89-; Nursing.

**HAMBY, DEBRA M,** Cumberland County Coll, Vineland, NJ; SO; BA; Lgl Asstnt Clb 90-; Phi Theta Kappa 79-; GSA Asstnt Ldr 80-89; Mck Trl Cmptn; Vice Chrmn Zng Bd Maurice River Twp 90-; Maurice Rwer Twp Demo Comm 90-; Mbr NJ Fded Plng Offc 90-; AA; Pol Sci; Mncpl.

**HAMBY, LINDA G,** Western Piedmont Comm Coll, Morganton, NC; FR; AS; Prlgl Assn Clb 90-; Admnstrtv Sec; Wrk Law Offc.

**HAMBY, LYNN B,** Clemson Univ, Clemson, SC; JR; BSN; Phillips Fibers Corp Seneca SC 76-88; Nrsng.

**HAMBY, PATRICIA L,** Western Piedmont Comm Coll, Morganton, NC; JR; AASC; Indstrl Mgmt; Qulty Cntrl Tchncn.

**HAMBY, PHILLIP H,** Winthrop Coll, Rock Hill, SC; SO; BA; BSU/GLEE Club 90-; FCA 90; Chorale; Dunlap Schlrshp Bnkng/Fnc; IM Sftbl/Sccr/Vlybl V Ball Tm Capt 90-; Bus Admin/Finance; Banking.

**HAMDAN-ROACH, AMIRA ELLEN,** Elms Coll, Chicopee, MA; SR; BA; Chrch Treas/Snday Schl Tchr/Yth Grp Mnstr 89-; Psychlgy Assn 89-; Psi Chi 89-; Deans Lst; Psychlgy; Mnstry.

**HAMEL, HEATHER D,** Indiana Univ Of Pa, Indiana, PA; FR; BS; Stdnts Anml Rights VP 90-; Engl Ed; Law.

**HAMEL, RENEE D,** Coker Coll, Hartsville, SC; FR; V P 90-; Drama Clb 90-; Dance Troupe 90-; Cultural Arts Comm 90-; Fencing Clb Secr/Treas 90-; Ecology Clb 90-; Poetry Publshd Old Hickory Review 90.

**HAMELIN, JENNIFER J,** Rivier Coll, Nashua, NH; SO; BA; Yrbk Stf 90-; Commuter Committee 90-; Nashua Soup Kitchen Vol 90-; Londonderry Baptist Soup Kitchen Vol 90-; Londonderry Presby Chrch Day Care Vol 90-; Acctng; CPA.

**HAMER, ALJANAL L,** Fayetteville St Univ, Fayetteville, NC; FR; Fut Alumni Assoc Treas 90-; Acctg.

**HAMER, CAROL A,** Liberty Univ, Lynchburg, VA; JR; BA; Soc Hmn Rsrc Mgt VP 90-; Mrktg Assoc 90-; Coll Rpblcns 88-; Bus; Mgt.

**HAMER, RACHEL S,** William Paterson Coll, Wayne, NJ; FR; BA; Math; Teach.

**HAMES, CARLOS E,** Univ Of Tn At Chattanooga, Chattanooga, TN; FR; BS; IM Bstkbl; Eng.

**HAMES, MELISSA B,** Univ Of Ga, Athens, GA; SR; BSED; Rcrtn Clb 89-; Yng Rpblcns 87-; Deans Lst; Delta Zeta Acdmcs Scl Rush 87-; Tau Kappa Epsilon Ltl Sis Pres 88-; IM Sccr Wtrpolo Tnns Vlybl Ftbl; Rcrtn/Lsr Studies; Physcl Thrpy.

**HAMILL, PHILIP J,** Indiana Univ Of Pa, Indiana, PA; SR; BED; Assc Rehab Advocates 89-; Alpha Chi Rho 89-; Rehab Education; Rehab Counselor.

**HAMILTON, AMANDA C,** Wallace St Comm Coll At Selma, Selma, AL; FR; BSN; Life Ins Cmsn Acctg Supv; Nrsg; RN.

**HAMILTON, ANNIE M,** Stillman Coll, Tuscaloosa, AL; SR; BA; Dns Lst; Natl Hnr Socty; AA Concordia Coll 87; Elem Ed; Tchng.

**HAMILTON, ANTHONY P,** De Tech & Comm Coll At Dover, Dover, DE; FR; AS; Voctnl Indstrl Clubs Of Amer 88-90; Natl Voctnl Tech Hon Soc 88-90; Elec/Elec Engr.

**HAMILTON, AQUAYA L,** Clark Atlanta Univ, Atlanta, GA; SO; Acctg; CPA.

**HAMILTON, BARBARA L,** Oh Univ, Athens, OH; JR; BFA; Intrntnl Amer Flwshp Grp Co Grp Ldr 89-91; Photgrphy.**

**HAMILTON, BETH A,** Liberty Univ, Lynchburg, VA; FR; BS; Chi Alpha 90-; Psych; Cnslg.

**HAMILTON, BRENDA G,** Abraham Baldwin Agri Coll, Tifton, GA; SO; BS; Pres List; Deans List; Rcgnzd Schls Hon Day; Tifton Sunbelt Running Clb; Sec Un GA Cstl Pln Expt Sta; Bio/Spnsh; Rsrch.

**HAMILTON, CARLETTA Y,** Tuskegee Univ, Tuskegee Inst, AL; SR; BS; OH Clb Secy 87-89; Pom Pom Squad 87-89; Kappa Delta Pi Secy 90-; Edctr Elmntry.

**HAMILTON, CHAD E,** Alice Lloyd Coll, Pippa Passes, KY; FR; BA; IMS 90-; Sci.

**HAMILTON, CHERYL L,** Belmont Coll, Nashville, TN; JR; BS; Gamma Beta Phi 89-; Kappa Delta Pi 90-; Elem Ed; Tch.

**HAMILTON, CYNTHIA A,** Univ Of Cincinnati, Cincinnati, OH; SR; BS; Kappa Delta Pi; Golden Key; Crim Just; Juv Corrs.

**HAMILTON, CYNTHIA L,** Oglethorpe Univ, Atlanta, GA; FR; BA; Sigma Sigma Sigma; Oglthrp Schlrs Awd; Bus/Bhvrl Sci; Mgmt.

**HAMILTON, DAVID J,** Ms St Univ, Miss State, MS; SR; BS; ASME 90-; Phi Kappa Phi 88-; Tau Beta Pi 88-; INPO Schlr; 89-; MS St Eng Hl Fame; GTE Achmc All Amer Bsbl; Vrsty Bsbl 87-; Mech Eng; Eng.

**HAMILTON, DONNA SIMONE,** City Univ Of Ny Baruch Coll, New York, NY; SR; BBA; Human Res Mgmt; Publshng.

**HAMILTON, EDWARD J,** Univ Of Rochester, Rochester, NY; SR; Undrgrad Coun Econ 87-; Wash Semester 90; Vol Awd 89; Intrns Law Pgrm 89; Economics; Pub Admin.

**HAMILTON JR, EUGENE R,** Manhattan Coll, Bronx, NY; FR; BA; Senate; St Thomas More Law Scty 90-; St De La Salle Hnr Scty 90; Deans Lst 90-; Cmps Mnstry Euchrstc Mnstr/Lctr; Philosophy; Law.

**HAMILTON, HEATHER D,** Miami Univ, Oxford, OH; JR; BA; Pre-Law Soc 90-; CSO Sntr 89-90; Stdnt Govt Sntr 89-90; Delta Phi Alpha 90-; Intl Studies; Law.

**HAMILTON, JACQUELINE M,** City Univ Of Ny City Coll, New York, NY; SR; B; Crbbn Clb 88-; Cty Coll Acad Pre Pro Pgm 90-; Golden Key 90-; Amer Inst Arch Stdnts 88-; Role Mdl Pgm Cltn 100 Blk Wmn 90-; Intrn NY Cty Dept Prsrvtn/Dvlpmnt 90; Intrn IBM Corp; Bnk Emplyee; Arch.**

**HAMILTON, JAMIL A,** Howard Univ, Washington, DC; JR; BS; AIAS 89-; Architecture/Plng Stdnt Assn 89-; Cmnty Outrch Dsadvntgd Chldrn 88; Cmnty Serv Awd Dsgn 90; Architecture/Plng; Cmrcl Architecture.

**HAMILTON, JEFFREY B,** Western Carolina Univ, Cullowhee, NC; SO; BS; Hnrs Pgm 89-90; Sigma Phi Epsilon 90-; IMS 89-; Cmptr Sci; Cmptr Dsgn Pgmg.

**HAMILTON III, JOHN F,** Slippery Rock Univ, Slippery Rock, PA; SO; BA; Hlth/Phys Educ.

**HAMILTON, JOSEPH C,** Md Coll Of Art & Design, Silver Spring, MD; SO; BA; One Man Art Show; Art Shw Awd; Congrssmn Art Contest Judge; Fine Arts.

**HAMILTON, KATHLEEN L,** Cumberland County Coll, Vineland, NJ; FR; AAS; Hortcltr Clb Sec; Pres Lst 90; PTA Pr 86-; Cub Sct Cnty PTA Trp Chrmn Pub Chr 90-; Meth Chrch Cls Sec 87-; Ornmntl Hortcltr; Landscp Dsgnr.

**HAMILTON, KATHY L,** Western Ky Univ, Bowling Green, KY; SR; BS; Women In Transition Pres 89-; Phi Eta Sigma: Phi Kappa Phi; Kappa Delta Pi; Elem Ed; Teaching.

**HAMILTON, KENNETH B,** Univ Of Ky, Lexington, KY; FR; Untd Meth Stdnt Ctr 90-; Hnrs Pgm 90-.

**HAMILTON, KIMBERLY A,** Webber Coll, Babson Park, FL; JR; BS; Mgmt-Bus; Mgmt.

**HAMILTON, LESLIE K,** Univ Of Sc At Columbia, Columbia, SC; JR; BA; Adv Clb 89-; PRSSA Natl Liasn Chrmn 90-; Gamecock TV Intrn Sentr Strom Thurmond; Gldn Ky; Outstndng Coll Stdfnt Of Amer; Dns Lst; Alpha Delta Pi; Specl Olympcs; Hungr Clean-Up; WIS-TV Promo Intrn; Columbia Metrpltn Mag Asst To Pblshr; BPME; Jrnlsm/Mass Comm; TV Promos.

**HAMILTON, MARK A,** Bapt Bible Coll & Seminary, Clarks Summit, PA; SO; BSM; Msc Intrst Flwshp 89-; Cncrt Chr/Trvlng Chr 89-; Scrd Msc; Msc Ed/Msc Mnstr.

**HAMILTON, MICHELLE M,** West Liberty St Coll, West Liberty, WV; GD; BA; WV Sci Tchrs Assn 89-; WV Mth Tchrs Assn 87-; Dns Lst 90-; OH Co Readng Tutr 89-; St Thomas Aquns Preschl Eductr 87-; Hmrm Mthr Chrmn 89-90; Cthlc Comm Chrmn 90-; W Lbrty Pck 40 Sec 90-; Hlpd Prepare/Name Pblshd/Exprmntl Physcs 2nd Ed 90; Elem Ed; Tchr.

**HAMILTON, NORMA JEAN,** Miami Jacobs Jr Coll Of Bus, Dayton, OH; SO; AS; Miami Vly Med Asst Assn 90-; Cert CPR/1ST Aid 90-; Dytn Antch Shrn Hlth Scrn 90-; Clncl; Med Asst.

**HAMILTON, ORLANDO N,** Coppin St Coll, Baltimore, MD; SR; BS; Chrstn Cncl Inc Pres 87-88; Jr Chmbr Of Comrc Jcs VP 90-; Psychlgy Clb Advsr 90-; Alpha Kappa Mu 90-; Deans Lst 87-; Th B Evngl Chrstn Univ 90; CCE Frlndia Inst 88; Psychlgy/Drg Alchl Cnslng.**

**HAMILTON, PEGGY P,** Central Fl Comm Coll, Ocala, FL; SO; AA; Mgmnt Info Sys/Dsrd Scncs; MIS.

**HAMILTON JR, RONALD N,** Northeastern Univ, Boston, MA; FR; MBA; NAACP 90-; NABA; Ralph Bunche Schlrshp 90-; Norma V Woods Awd; Deans Lst 90-; Busines Adm; Acctng.

**HAMILTON, ROSANNA L,** Marshall University, Huntington, WV; SO; BA; Bus; Fin.

**HAMILTON, SHANTEL T,** Vance Granville Comm Coll, Henderson, NC; SO; AS; Scif Recreation.

**HAMILTON, SHIRLEY J,** Al A & M Univ, Normal, AL; SO; BNS; Scottish Cntry Dancers/Hertitage Soc 90-; Acad Awd 90-; All Amer Awd 90-; Deans List 90-; Peace Corp Vol 87-89; Return Peace Corp Lctr 90-; Agribus; Grass Roots Dvlpr/3rd World.**

**HAMILTON, THERESA E,** Meridian Comm Coll, Meridian, MS; FR; Hrtcltr Clb Treas 90-; Hrtcltr; Lndscpng.

**HAMILTON, THOMAS B,** William Carey Coll, Hattiesburg, MS; FR; Phi Beta Lmbd 90-; Acctg.

**HAMILTON, TONYA A,** Alcorn St Univ, Lorman, MS; JR; BS; Alpha Swthrt Org Inc Sec 90-; USAA All Amer Schlr; Bus Admin; Exec Mgr.

**HAMILTON, TRACY A,** Fl St Univ, Tallahassee, FL; SR; BA; Seminole Scuba Club Treas 89-; Phi Eta Sigma 84-; Golden Key 89-; Phi Kappa Phi 90-; Magna Cum Laude 90; Cackpckng/Canoeing/Caving 82-89; AA 85; Studio Art; Grad Study.

**HAMILTON, VONDA DENISE,** Univ Of Sc At Columbia, Columbia, SC; JR; BA; Phi Alpha Theta Pres 90-; Phi Alpha Delta 90-; Phi Eta Sigma 88-; Chnclrs Lst 88-; Cstl Carolina Coll Chorus; Hon Clb 88-; Hstry Clb 88-; Omicron Delta Kappa; Grdn Ad Ltm; Hstry/Poltcl Sci; Law.

**HAMILTON, YOLANDE T,** Claflin Coll, Orangeburg, SC; FR; BS; Hnr Stdnt 90-; Grad Pred Rsrch Bowling Green State Univ; Math; Stats.

**HAMLET, BOBBY D,** Univ Of Nc At Greensboro, Greensboro, NC; FR; Otng Clb VP 90-; SGA Pres 90-; Gamma Beta Phi Pres 90-; Deans Lst 90-; Ttr 90-; ICS Lgl Asst Schl 90-; Law.

**HAMLET, STEPHEN DOUGLAS,** Newbury Coll, Brookline, MA; FR; BA; Branch Mgr 78-.

**HAMLETT, GAIL D,** Bloomfield Coll, Bloomfield, NJ; JR; BA; Sociology; Soc Wrk.

**HAMLETT, MEREDITH P,** Radford Univ, Radford, VA; JR; BS; Nwspr Rep 90-; Stdnt Hse Cncl Treas 89-90; Hons Prog 89-; Richmnd Times Dsptch Intrnshp Jrnlsm Intrnshp 90; Southside Elec Coop PR Intrnshp; Jrnlsm/Publ Rels; Brdcst Jrnlsm/Nws Anchr.

**HAMLIN, ELIZABETH A,** Allegheny Coll, Meadville, PA; SR; BA; ALLIES VP 90-; Admssns Trgd Stdnt Asst 88-; Lambda Sigma 88-89; Alpha Delta Pi Sec 89-; Art Hstry; Archtctrl Hstry.

**HAMLIN, ERIKA M,** Fl A & M Univ, Tallahassee, FL; SR; BS; NAACP 88-; Soph V Pres 88-89; Colleg Blck Archives Treas 88-89; Phi Eta Sigma 88-; Elem Educ; Tchng.

**HAMLIN, JON H,** Valdosta St Coll, Valdosta, GA; SO; BA; Assn Cmptng Mchnry 90-; Assn Coop Edctn Stdnts; Sigma Alpha Chi; Coop Edctn Stdnt Trainee 90-; Cmptr Sci; Sftwr Pblshng.

**HAMLIN, KASEY L,** Univ Of Sc At Columbia, Columbia, SC; JR; BS; Psi Chi 90-; Gamma Beta Phi 89-; Phi Beta Kappa; Intrnshp Western Psychiatric Inst Pittsburgh PA 91; Psychology; Psychologist.

**HAMLIN, PAULA A,** Univ Of Nc At Asheville, Asheville, NC; SO; BA; Hstry Assn; Edctn Clb; SNEA; Hnr Soc; Alpha Delta Pi MEVP; NC Tchng Fllws Schlrshp; Hstry; Tchng.

**HAMLIN, SEKINAH M,** Bennett Coll, Greensboro, NC; FR; Pol Sci Clb 90-; NAACP 90-; Stdnt Chrstn Flwshp 90-; Pres Schlrshp 90-; Pres Excell Awrd 90-; Pol Sci; Law.

**HAMM, CATHY L,** Middle Tn St Univ, Murfreesboro, TN; SR; BS; Stdnt Home Ecnmc Assc 89-90; Ntnl Assc Ed Young Chldrn 90-; Kappa Omicron Nu Treas 89-; Cum Laude; Erly Chldhd Ed; Tchng.

**HAMM, ELIZABETH C,** Univ Of Ky, Lexington, KY; SO; BS; SMART 89-90; Alpha Lambda Delta 90-; Prof Educ Prep Prog 89; Hlth Careers Opportunities Prog; Biol; Med.

**HAMM, ELLEN M,** D Youville Coll, Buffalo, NY; GD; BS/MS; Stdnt Occptnl Thrpy Assn 86-; N Y St Hlth Srvc Corps Schlrshp 89-; Occptnl Thrpy.

**HAMM, JANIE D,** Bethel Coll, Mckenzie, TN; SO; BED; STEA VP 90-; Cls VP 90-; Pep Clb Pres 90-; Gamma Beta Phi Corr Sec; Theta Psi 90-; Diakona 89-; Elem Ed; Tchng.**

**HAMM, LA SANDRA E,** Clark Atlanta Univ, Atlanta, GA; JR; BA; Acctg Clb 88; Finance Clb 89; Faith Choir; Carter Pres Ctr Intern; Achvmnt Awd; Bus Admin.

**HAMM, RENE L,** Vance Granville Comm Coll, Henderson, NC; SO; Phi Theta Kappa.

**HAMMACK, LONNIE P,** Albany St Coll, Albany, GA; JR; BA; Frat Ordr Frfghtrs 88-; USAF Rsrvs 402 Clss Robins AFB 89-; USAF 83-88; Albany Fire Dept 88-; ALS 87; AAS 87; Cmptr Sci; Prgmg.

**HAMMAR, JAROD R,** Southern Coll Of Tech, Marietta, GA; SR; BSMET; Natl Soc Prfsnl Engrs Brd 89-; Amer Soc Mchncl Engrs 90-; Rsdnc Hl Assoc Pres 89-90; Mchncl Engrg Tchnlgy; Engr.

**HAMMAR, SOFIA V,** Savannah Coll Of Art & Design, Savannah, GA; FR; BA; Grphc Dsgn; Advrtsng.

**HAMME II, ASHTON T,** Jackson St Univ, Jackson, MS; JR; BS; Chmsty Soc 88-; Hon Colg; Pres List; Deans List; Phi Kappa Phi; Beta Kappa Chi; Kappa Alpha Psi Treas 90-; Dow Chem Schlrshp; Chmsty Ph D.

**HAMMELL, TARA L,** Talladega Coll, Talladega, AL; FR; Adopt A Family Peer Totor 90-; Soc Work.

**HAMMER, AMY L,** Oh Univ, Athens, OH; FR; BBA; Hnrs Coll Advsry Cncl; Alpha Lambda Delta; Extern AM & G Accntng Firm; Copeland Schlr; Bus Mngmnt; Accntng.

**HAMMER, ANN M,** Villanova Univ, Villanova, PA; SO; BA; Spcl Olympcs Vol 89-90; Pi Beta Phi 90-; Prjct Sunshine Vol 90; Cmmnctns; Film Brdcstng.

**HAMMER, BETH A,** Muskingum Coll, New Concord, OH; JR; BA; Omicron Delta Kappa 89-; Phi Theta Beta; Muskingum Plyrs Drmtc Soc VP 88-; Sigma Alpha Iota Scl Chr 90-; FAD Scl Clb 89-; Agnes Moorehead Awd Thtr; Dept Schlrshps Music/Thtr 89-; Elem Ed Thtr.

**HAMMER, JOHN C,** Tn Tech Univ, Cookeville, TN; JR; BA; Soc Advncmnt/Fin/Ecnmcs; Intl Cncl Serv Chair 88-90; Stdnt Alumni Ambssdr 89; Mortar Brd; Omicoron Delta Kappa Nat Ledrshp Hnr Soc VP; Alpha Lambda Delta Treas 88-89; Sigma Iota Epsilon; Sigma Chi Annotator 88-; Finance; Consultant.

**HAMMER, JONATHAN AARON,** Univ Of Rochester, Rochester, NY; SO; BA; Radio 89-90; Cncrts 89-; Dorm Cncl Rep 89-90; U S Holocaust Mem Museum Intrn 90-; Psych/Pltcl Sci.

**HAMMER, KELLI R,** Eckerd Coll, St Petersburg, FL; SR; MS; Vars Chrldrs Capt 87-; Biol Clb 87-; Natl Sci Sen Rep 87-; Omicron Delta Kappa Pres 89-; Spec Olymp; Yth Motvtr; Save The Manatees; Pinellas Yth Serv; Res Intrn Sea Wrld Orlando 90; Hons Schlrshp 87-; Marine Env Sci; Envrn Assmnt.

**HAMMER, TRACY A,** Oh St Univ, Columbus, OH; SR; BA; Anthrplgy Clb 88-89; Gldn Key 90; Arts Scincs Awrd Acdmc Excllnc 90; Antrhplgy.

**HAMMERLE, ANGELA R,** Commonwealth Coll, Virginia Beach, VA; FR; AMA; Wives Clb-USS Eisnhwr Spprt Grp 90-; Welcome Hm Com 90-; Ntnwd Rcrtrs 90-; Medcl; Physcns.

**HAMMERSMITH, KIMBERLY L,** Pellissippi St Tech Comm Coll, Knoxville, TN; SO; BS; Amb 89; SGA Issues/Concrns Cmte Co Chrprsn 89; Vision Vol Network 89; The Pines Cmnty Dev Corp Treas 90; Corp Acctng.

**HAMMES, LOUISE V,** Coll Of Charleston, Charleston, SC; SR; BS; Psi Chi 89-; Psychology.

**HAMMETT, ANDREW C,** Clarkson Univ, Potsdam, NY; SO; Fin Mgmt Assn Sec 90-; Delta Sigma Phi Chpln 90-; Nwspr Sls Agnt 90-; Mgmt/Mktg; Bus.

**HAMMETT, BRENDA ELIZABETH,** Univ Of Southern Ms, Hattiesburg, MS; JR; BS; Pre Law Soc 87-90; Yng Rpblcns 87-; Pnhlnc Jdcl Cncl 90; Alpha Delta Pi Stndrds Chrmn 89; BAACHUS Alchl Awrns Tsk Frc 88-89; Rght Lf Pres 90-; EXPOW Schlrshp 87-; IM Vlybl/Bwlng Cpt 87-90; Econ/Intrnatl Bsn; Law.

**HAMMETT, KAREN L,** Wv Univ At Parkersburg, Parkersburg, WV; SO; AA; Stdnt Govt Rept 90-; Phi Theta Kappa VP 90-; Engl Tutor 90-; Engl; Engl Instrctr.

**HAMMETT, RICHARD D,** Thomas Nelson Comm Coll, Hampton, VA; SO; Newport News Shipyard Coop 90-.

**HAMMETTE, DEBRA S,** Univ Of North Fl, Jacksonville, FL; SR; BA; Cncl Excptnl Chldrn; Kappa Delta Pi Cmmnctns Offcr 90-; Prdntl Ins Co Sprvsr 70-85; Spcl Edctn; Tchng.

**HAMMOCK, DAVID L,** Gordon Coll, Barnesville, GA; JR; ABJ; Recrtmnt Tm 89-; Clg Rpblcns 90-; Phi Theta Kappa 89-90; T V Intrn; Deans Lst 88-; AA Gordon Clg 90; Brdcst Nws; Sprtscstng.

**HAMMOCK, LORIE E,** Volunteer St Comm Coll, Gallatin, TN; SO; BA; All Wstrn Div Bsktbl 90-; Deans List 90; Bsktbl Tm 89-; AS Volunteer St 91; Phy Ed/Sports Med; Tch/Coach/Thrpst.

**HAMMOND, ANDREA L,** Colby Sawyer Coll, New London, NH; FR; BED; Chld Stds; Chld Lf Spclst.

**HAMMOND, BERNADETTE C,** Bloomfield Coll, Bloomfield, NJ; SO; BA; Deans Lst High Hnrs 87-90; HAM Vlntr 82-; Bsns Admnstrtn; Mgmt.

**HAMMOND, CHRISTOPHER R,** Southern Coll Of Tech, Marietta, GA; SR; BS; Elec Engr Tech.

**HAMMOND, CLAIRE A,** Univ Of Sc At Columbia, Columbia, SC; FR; BS; PE Clb 90-; Phi Eta Sigma; Tns Tm 90; Psycl Educ; Mgmt.

**HAMMOND, CONNIE LEE,** Univ Of South Fl, Tampa, FL; SR; USF Karate Clb 75-77; Univ Comm Hosp Tampa Fl 83-; BA 79; Acctg Fin; Nrsng.

**HAMMOND, CRISTI L,** Univ Of Miami, Coral Gables, FL; FR; BA; SG Cmnty Affrs Chr 90-; Newspaper Lit Mag Asst Ed 90-; US Figure Skating Assoc; Hnr Assoc 90-; Alpha Lambda Delta; United Way Coord; Tutor; Vol Grp; IM Sftbl; IM Vlybl; Law/Med.

**HAMMOND III, J EMMETT,** Univ Of Miami, Coral Gables, FL; JR; BA; Earth Alert; Hnrs Stdnt Soc 88-; Sigma Chi Tribune 89-; Intrnshp La Salle Natl Bank; Fin; Invstmnt Bnkng/Portfolio Mgmt.

**HAMMOND, MELISSA K,** West Liberty St Coll, West Liberty, WV; SO; BA; Bsktbl/Sftbl Co Capt 89-90; Bus Admin.

**HAMMOND, MICHELLE L,** Univ Of Southern Ms, Hattiesburg, MS; JR; BS; The Exercise Physiology Club 90-; Hall Rep; Newman Club Social Chrprsn 90-; Alpha Lambda Delta; Gamma Beta Phi; Golden Key; Exercise Physiology.**

**HAMMOND, NINA S,** Barry Univ, Miami, FL; FR; BS; Pediatrics.

**HAMMOND, RICHARD E,** Univ Of Akron, Akron, OH; SR; BS; Krt Clb 87-90; Tau Kappa Epsilon Pres; Athltc Trng Sprts Med; Pdtry.

**HAMMOND, SHARON ANN,** Providence Coll, Providence, RI; JR; BA; Spnsh Clb/Yng Demo 89-; Commtr Clb/Pstrl Cncl 88-; AIESAC 88-90; Lbrl Arts Hnrs 88-; Phi Sigma Tau 90-; Teach ESL 89-; Progreso Latino; Humanities/Asian Stds; Intl Law.

**HAMMOND, TIFFANY Y,** Coll Of Charleston, Charleston, SC; JR; BA; Mnrty Affairs Bd 89-; Gospel Choir Pres 89-; Peer Mntr Assn 90; Omicron Delta Kappa; Hon Pgm Assn 89-; Zeta Phi Beta VP 90-; Rsrch Pgm Univ MD; Palmetto Schlr 89; Engl/Frnch; Intl Bus.

**HAMMOND, VIRGINIA P,** Fl St Univ, Tallahassee, FL; SR; Alpha Delta Pi Srrty Asst Schlrshp Chrmn 90; Hnrs And Schlrs; Fncng Clb; Phi Beta Kappa; Beta Kappa Alpha; Phi Kappa Phi; Gldn Ky; Dns Lst; Magna Cum Laude; IM Vlybl Bwlng; BA; Engl Bus; Law.

**HAMMOND, WAYNE D,** Meridian Comm Coll, Meridian, MS; FR; BA; Phi Theta Kappa; Dean Lst; Elect Eng.

**HAMMONDS, ERIC R,** Kent St Univ Kent Cmps, Kent, OH; SR; BA; AMA; Symphony Band 89-90; Deans Lst; IM Ice Hcky Ftbl Capt 87-; Mrktng; Business.

**HAMMONDS, JEANINE C,** Univ Of Cin R Walters Coll, Blue Ash, OH; FR; Tch Hnd Bll Chr St Mrys Lthrn Chrch 90-; Cert Acctng Live Oaks Vocational Schl 88; Cert Data Entry Live Oaks Vocational Schl; Bus.

**HAMMONDS, KATHLEEN L,** Fl A & M Univ, Tallahassee, FL; JR; BED; FFEA Exec Bd 90-; White/Gold Hnr Soc; AA St Petersburg Jr Clg 90; Elem Educ; Educ.

**HAMMONDS, MARGARET H,** Central Al Comm Coll, Alexander City, AL; SO; ASSOC; Nrsng.

**HAMMONS, ANGELA M,** Union Coll, Barbourville, KY; SR; BS; College Singers 88-; Iota Sigma Nu 90-; Gamma Beta Phi 88-; Elem Edctn; Tchng.

**HAMMONS, JENNIFER A,** Univ Of Ky, Lexington, KY; SO; BA; Bsbl Tm Bat Tirl 88-; Elem Ed; Tch.

**HAMMONS, LINDA A,** Brewer St Jr Coll, Fayette, AL; SO; BA; AS Walker Jr Clg 90; Med; Occup Ther.

**HAMMONS, SHANNON D,** Union Coll, Barbourville, KY; JR; BS; Iota Sigma Nu; Gamma Beta Phi 90-; Bus Admn; Persnl Mgt.

**HAMMONS, SHANNON R,** Memphis St Univ, Memphis, TN; SO; Math.

**HAMMONS, SUZANNE L,** Union Coll, Barbourville, KY; SO; BS; Commuter Council 90-; Deans Lst 89-; Gamma Beta Phi 90-; Early Acceptance Dental Schl; Biology; Dentistry.

**HAMMONS, TIMOTHY J,** Old Dominion Univ, Norfolk, VA; SR; BS; Elec Eng Tech.

**HAMP, MICHELE L,** Strayer Coll, Washington, DC; SR; BA; Alpha Chi; Astnt Ofc Mngr Actrl Rsrch Corp; Bsns Admnstrtn; Admnstrtv.

**HAMP, RONDA A,** Neumann Coll, Aston, PA; SO; BA; Stdnt Govt Assn VP 89-90; Actvty Cncl 90-; VIVA Org 89-; Schl Spnsr Wlk Amer 89-90; Educ.

**HAMPE JR, CHARLES R,** Comm Coll Algny Co Algny Cmps, Pittsburgh, PA; SO; BA; Army Fr Yrs; AS Sci; Eng; Elec Eng.

**HAMPSON, WENDY A,** Fl St Univ, Tallahassee, FL; SO; BA; Chi Omega; Englsh Crtv Wrtng; Frgn Crspndnt.

**HAMPTON, BOBBY J,** Winthrop Coll, Rock Hill, SC; SR; BS; Winthrop Ftnss Clb 88-; Ftnss Inst YMCA 88-; SC Assn Of Hlth/Phys Ed/Rec/Danc 90-; Delta Psi Kappa; Winthrp Dns Lst 90-; Pres Sprts Awrd In Ftnss; IM Ftbl/Vlybl 90-; AA Greenvll Tech Coll 89; Phys Ed; Cardc Rehab.

**HAMPTON, BUFFY S,** Roane St Comm Coll, Harriman, TN; SO; AAS; Off Admin; Exec Asst.

**HAMPTON, GARY W,** Marshall University, Huntington, WV; FR; BA; Black Un Stdnt 90-; Phi Eta Sigma 90-; IM Bsktbl 90-; Fincl Anal.

**HAMPTON, JAMES S,** Middle Ga Coll, Cochran, GA; FR; BA; Gamma Beta Phi; Eng; Cvl Eng.

**HAMPTON, JUDY A,** Livingston Univ, Livingston, AL; SO; BA; Elem Ed.

**HAMPTON, KELLY J,** Tallahassee Comm Coll, Tallahassee, FL; SO; BA; Sigma Alpha Epsilon 89-90; AA 90f; Bus; Hotel/Rest Mgmnt.

**HAMPTON, MARK A,** Middle Tn St Univ, Murfreesboro, TN; JR; BA; Gamma Beta Phi 90-; Phi Alpha Theta; Pi Gamma Mu 90-; Phi Kappa Phi; Schlrshp Hghst GPA; Hstry; Prfssr.

**HAMPTON, MARLEEN E,** Oh Univ, Athens, OH; JR; Resident Life Admin Res Asstnt 89-; Golden Key; Deans List 88-; Deans Schlrshp 89-; Special Educ.

**HAMPTON, RACHEL M,** Anderson Coll, Anderson, SC; SO; BMED; Choir; Dir Children & Youth Choirs Handbell Choir Musicals Trinity Un Meth Church; AA; Music Education; Teach.

**HAMRA, CHRISTA M,** Marshall University, Huntington, WV; JR; BA; Hall Advsry Cncl 88-; Marching Band 88-89; Alpha Kappa Psi Chrmn Prfsnl Comm 89-; Adopt A Hwy; Deans List 89-; IM Sports 88-; Mktg; Advertising Firm.

**HAMRA, JACQUELINE K,** Rhodes Coll, Memphis, TN; SO; BA; European Studies Prog; Habitat Hmnty 90-; FCA 89-; Jr Rtrn; Lambda Alpha Lambda; People People Russia Exchg 88; US Sen Danforth Intrn; US Cngrss Gephardt Intrn 90; Lgl Asst Intrn 89; Spirit Ldr 90-; Vrsty Tennis 89-; Intrntl Studies; Law.**

**HAMRICK, BENJAMIN R,** East Tn St Univ, Johnson City, TN; SO; BS; Cmptr Sci/Math; Cmptr Scientist.

**HAMRICK, KISTA R,** Wv Univ, Morgantown, WV; JR; BSN; Jr Cls Stdnt Govt Pres 90-; Sigma Theta Tau 90-; Hnrs Lst 88-90; Nrsng; Geriactric Nrs Prctnr.

**HAMRICK, LAURA J,** Univ Of Nc At Charlotte, Charlotte, NC; JR; BA; Baptist Union 88-90; Pep Band 88-90; Emerging Leaders 88-89; Engl; Tch.

**HAMRICK, W DAVID,** Bapt Bible Coll & Seminary, Clarks Summit, PA; FR; Linden Kiwanis Clb Pres 85-; Pres Beta Bkry Inc 83-90; Bible.

**HAMRYKA, RUSSELL A,** Southern Coll Of Tech, Marietta, GA; JR; BAET; Amer Inst Arch Stdnts 89-; Campus Crsde Chrst 89-; Bptst Stdnt Un 89-; SGA Judicry Comm 90-; Archtctrl Eng Tchnlgy.

**HAMS, MARY KAY K,** Fayetteville St Univ, Fayetteville, NC; SO; BS; Nrsg; RN.

**HAMSHAR, JASON A,** Schenectady County Comm Coll, Schenectady, NY; SO; BA; Phi Theta Kappa; Peer Tutor 90-F Cmptr Lab Monitor 90-; AS; Sci; Prgrmmng/Sftwr Dvlpmnt.

**HANAN, CHRISTOPHER C,** Georgetown Univ, Washington, DC; SO; BS; AIESEC 90-; Intrntl Rltns Clb 90-; 1st And 2nd Hnrs Dns Lst SBA 90-; Nestle Prdcts Scty Ky Acct Mgr; Nvce Crw 90; Fed Matura Gym 88; Intl Mgmt; Intl Bus.

**HANCE COLON, CARMEN IRIS,** Catholic Univ Of Pr, Ponce, PR; SO; DECA 87-90; Gen Elem Ed.

**HANCE, MARK S,** S U N Y Coll Of Tech At Delhi, Delhi, NY; SO; BA; Dorm Council V P; Construction Inspctr For NY State Dept Transp; IM Bsktbl 89-; AAS; Civil Engrng.

**HANCHAR, STACY M,** Central Fl Comm Coll, Ocala, FL; FR; AA; Hlth; Physcl Thrpy Pdtrcs.

**HANCOCK, AMY E,** Colby Sawyer Coll, New London, NH; SR; Student Acad Counselor Tutor 89-; Alpha Chi 89-; Deans List; Summa Cum Laude Grad; Amer Studies; Ed.

**HANCOCK, AMY K,** Kent St Univ Kent Cmps, Kent, OH; JR; BS; Stdnts Prof Nrsg 90-; Alpha Lamgda Delta 89; Golden Key; Pres Lst; Nrsg.

**HANCOCK, ANISSA R,** Va Western Comm Coll, Roanoke, VA; SO; Deans List Spring 90-; Outstndng Minority Student HNR; Cerfit Alliance Exce 90; General Studies; Psychology.

**HANCOCK, DAVID S,** Abraham Baldwin Agri Coll, Tifton, GA; SO; AAS; Hrtcltr Clb 89-; Dns Lst 90; Pres Lst 90; Glden Eagle Cntry Clb Intrnshp 90; Ornmntl Hrtcltr; Golf Clb Mgr.

**HANCOCK, DEBORAH B,** Coker Coll, Hartsville, SC; JR; BS; Dns Lst; Acctnt; AS Data Proc Florence-Darlington Tech Clg 82; AS Acctg 83; Bsn Adm.

**HANCOCK, DENAE H,** Defiance Coll, Defiance, OH; JR; BED; Pres Host 88-; Ed Soclgy/Psychlgy; Elem Tchr.

**HANCOCK, IRA A,** Mount Saint Mary Coll, Newburgh, NY; JR; BA; Psychiatric Tech Private Psychiatric Fac Upstate NY Co-Op Ednl Intern Psych Tech; AA W/Hon Dutchess Comm Coll 90; Psych/Elem Spec Ed; Clncl Psychlgy.

**HANCOCK, KRISTA M,** Owensboro Comm Coll, Owensboro, KY; SO; BA; Cllgt Sec Intl Pres 90-; Otstndng Achvmnt Offc Admn Awrd; Blue Grss Gms 90; AAS; Tlcmmnctns; TV Brdcstng.

**HANCOCK, MICHAEL,** Ramapo Coll Of Nj, Mahwah, NJ; SR; BSC; MENSA 87-; Prgrmmr/Sys Anlst/Databse Admin/Tech Spprt/Prjct Ldr 85-89; Cmptr Sci; Cmptr Rsrch.

**HANCOCK, MORGAN DAN,** Colby Sawyer Coll, New London, NH; FR; BA; Dns Lst; Vars Bsktbl Capt 90-; Sprts Mgmt; Athltc Admn.

**HANCOCK, TERRISA G,** Commonwealth Coll, Virginia Beach, VA; SO; AA; Acctg Clb 90-; Mu Alpha Theta 90; Dns Lst 90; Pres Lst 90-; Indvdl Rdy Rsrvst U S Nvl Rsrv 88-; Acctg.

**HANCZOR, JENNIFER C,** S U N Y Coll Of Tech At Frmgdl, Farmingdale, NY; FR; AAD; Clg Nwspr Lyt Edtr 90-; Art; Adv.

**HAND, MARGARET J,** Hillsborough Comm Coll, Tampa, FL; FR; ASN; SNO 90; Riverhills Elem Schl PTA Brd Hmrm Coord 90-; Brnie Troop Ldr 87-90; Nrsng.

**HAND, TAMMYE L,** Fl A & M Univ, Tallahassee, FL; FR; Natl Assoc Univ Wmn Debtnts Sec; Yng Pls Dept Pres 89; Alpha Phi Alpha Swthrt; FL A M Univ Gspl Chr; Brdcst Jrnlsm; Cmmnctns.

**HANDAL, JENNIFER,** Duke Univ, Durham, NC; FR; BA; Phi Eta Sigma 90-; Pi Beta Phi Asst Scl Chr 90-; Poly Sci; Intntl Bus.

**HANDBACK, LAWRENCE SCOTT,** Queens Coll, Charlotte, NC; SR; BA; Intrgrk Cncl Pres/Fndr 90-; Alumni Ambsdrs Pres/Fndr; Pres Cncl 89-; Mu Alpha Theta 89-90; Pi Kappa Phi Pres 89-; PUSH 89-; Asstnt Sprts Info Dir 90-; Asst Bsktbl Coach Myers Pk Hi Var Grls 89-90; Tns Tm 88-; Glf Tm 90-; Bus; Mrktg.

**HANDEL, SUSAN B,** Wagner Coll, Staten Island, NY; SR; Soclgy Clb; Alph Kappa Dlt; Meals On Whls; Deans List; BA; Intrnshp NYC Dept Ddprbtn/SI Alzhmrs; Soclgy; Law.

**HANDELSMAN, SHARON FRANCES,** Ny Univ, New York, NY; SO; BA; Bnai Brith Women Pres 75-85; Richmond Fmly Pl Pres 78; Asstnt To Dir Of Stdnt Svcx NY Univ; Gen Bus; Ed.

**HANDIBOE, THERESA L,** Anne Arundel Comm Coll, Arnold, MD; SO; Sclgy Clb 90; Engl; Tchng.

**HANDIEKAR, ANJALI U,** Univ Of Nc At Chapel Hill, Chapel Hill, NC; SR; BS; Amer Phrmctcl Assc 89-; Dean Lst 88-; Phrmcy.**

**HANDLEY, ELIZABETH A,** Univ Of Tn At Martin, Martin, TN; SO; Stu Aflts Amer Chem Soc 89-; Peer Enblmnt Pro 90-; Pom Pon Squad 90-; Mu Epsilon Delta 90-; Alpha Omicron Pi 89-; JV Pompon 89-90; Bio; Med.**

**HANDLEY, MISTY L,** Walker Coll, Jasper, AL; FR; BA; Elem Ed; Teaching.

**HANDLEY, TABATHA L,** Univ Of Al At Birmingham, Birmingham, AL; JR; BA; SGA Sec 87; SOTA Comm Serv Com 90; IM Sports 90; Phi Theta Kappa 87; Chldrns Hosp Vol 88-90; BS UAB 90; Occptnl Thrpy; Pdtrcs/Hnd Thrpy.

**HANDS, ARLYNE,** Miami Dade Comm Coll South, Miami, FL; SO; AD; Cert Talent Roster Dstngshd Acad Perf; Pageant 2nd Fnlst; Cmnctns.

**HANDS, JENNIFER LYNN,** Saint Andrews Presbytrn Coll, Laurinburg, NC; SR; Engl Clb/Wrtrs Forum; Theatr Grp; BA; Engl.

**HANDSFORD, IRENE E,** Fl Memorial Coll, Miami, FL; JR; BS; PTSA Sec Nrth Dade Mdl Schl Miami FL 89-; Mstrs Dgr In Mngmnt Fld; Bus Admin.

**HANDY, BUFFY S,** Kent St Univ Kent Cmps, Kent, OH; SO; BA; Gym Club; Camp Super Kids Gym Instr; Aerobic Club; Fl Reps Ldr; March Of Dimes Campaign; Scarlet & Gray Schlrshp; Sci; Nursing.

**HANDY, CHRISTOPHER M,** Georgetown Univ, Washington, DC; JR; BS; Blck Stdnt Alliance Treas 89-; Delta Sigma Pi; Arthur Andersen Intrnshp; IM Chmpn/All Star 90-; Acctng; Mgmnt.

**HANDY, DEREK EDISON,** Al St Univ, Montgomery, AL; FR; Symphnc Bnd 90-; Jzz Ensmbl; Music; Tchr Prfrmr.

**HANDY, ERIK S,** Hampton Univ, Hampton, VA; FR; BA; Chem Clb 90-; Ohio Pre-Alumni Clb 90-91; Afr Stu Clustr Mentrshp Prog Mntr 90-; Offc Nav Resrch Sems Prog; Pres Eminent Schlrs Awd 90-; 3m Co Schlrshp; Chemistry.

**HANDY, INGRID A,** Sinclair Comm Coll, Dayton, OH; SR; MAC Clb 88-; Cert Of Achvmnt 90-; Intrnshp Comm Srvcs Fr The Deaf 90-; Intrnshp Snclr Comm Coll 90-; AAS 90-; Mnl Cmmnctns; Intrprtr.

**HANDY, JEANNE M,** Providence Coll, Providence, RI; JR; BA; Fndr PC Envrnmntl/Wldlfe Clb Pres 90; Adlt Lit Tutor 88; Im Athletics 88; Phi Sigma Tau; Scl Actn Cmmttee 88; R I Rape Crisis Ctr Intrn; Phlsphy Mnr Bsnss Admin; Pblc Serv Law.

**HANDY, LUKE A,** Univ Of Rochester, Rochester, NY; SO; BS; BASIC 89-; Bio; Physcian.

**HANDY, TROBIE T,** Widener Univ, Chester, PA; SR; BS; AICE 90-; Widener Ambsdr 89-; SWE Treas 88-90; Tau Beta Pi 89-; Alpha Chi; Phi Kappa Phi; AICHE Natl Schlr; AICHE Awd Outstdng Achvmnt; ACS Awd Outstdng Perf Organic Chmstry; Natl Coll Engr Awd 89-; Chem Engr; Envrnmntl Engr.**

**HANE, TAMARA L,** Univ Of Tn At Martin, Martin, TN; JR; BS; Natl Assc Accntnts VP 90-; Phi Chi Theta 89-; Chi Omega Asst Treas 88-; Intern Attnry Gen Offc 90; Bus Admn/Accntng; CPA.

**HANES, KATHY J,** Fl International Univ, Miami, FL; JR; BA; AS Broward Comm Coll 90; Elem Educ; Tchr.

**HANES, LISA M,** S U N Y Coll Of Tech At Alfred, Alfred, NY; FR; AS; Bsns; Accntng.

**HANES, ROBERT M,** Cooper Union, New York, NY; SO; BA; Peer Tutoring 89-; Phi Theta Kappa 89-; Zeta Beta Tau 87-; Chem; Eng.

**HANEY, GARY CLAY,** Lexington Comm Coll, Lexington, KY; SO; BA; Bus; Finance.

**HANEY, JONATHAN MARK,** Univ Of Sc At Columbia, Columbia, SC; FR; BS; Elect Eng; Eng.

**HANEY, LARRY B,** Univ Of Sc At Columbia, Columbia, SC; FR; BS; William K Laughlin Memrl Schlrshp; Elect Eng.

**HANEY, LINDA SUE,** Marshall University, Huntington, WV; SR; BBA; Finf Fin/Bkng.

**HANEY, PATRICIA E,** Ms Univ For Women, Columbus, MS; FR; BS; Lantrn Tr; Fr Soph Math/Sci Hnry; Silhouette Socl Clb Alum Sec; Acctg.

**HANEY, PATRICIA E,** D Youville Coll, Buffalo, NY; JR; BSN; Stdnt Nurses Assn 88-89; Blue Masquers 58-59; Beta Sigma Phi; Boy Scts Cmte Chrmn 78-81; Girl Scts Brownie Ldr 81; Camp Fire Girls Grp Ldr 80-83; Cub Sct Awd 81; Young Prof Clb VP 66-68; Altar Rosary Soc VP 81-83; Nursing.

**HANEY, SHELLY A,** Oh Univ-Southern Cmps, Ironton, OH; SR; BCJ; WOW 90-; Intrnshp Lawrence Co Muni Court Probation Asst 89-; IM Vlybl Sftbl Golf Canoe Boating Archery 88-; Republican Club 89-; Womens Republican Club; Trail Riders Assoc 89-; Dpty Clerk Lawrence Co Mncpl Court; Criminal Justice; Public Admnstrn.

**HANEY, STEPHANIE M,** Radford Univ, Radford, VA; JR; BS; Stdnt Educ Assn 90-; Kappa Delta Pi 90-; Zeta Tau Alpha; Dns Lst; Educ; Tchng.

**HANEY, TAMMY D,** Ms Univ For Women, Columbus, MS; SR; BA; Miss Assn Edctrs 89-; Kappa Delta Epsilon Treas 89-; Troubadour Clb Rsh Chrmn 89-; Elem Educ; Tchr.

**HANFTWURZEL, ERICK,** Inter Amer Univ Pr Hato Rey, Hato Rey, PR; FR; BA; Engrng.

**HANG, MAUREEN,** City Univ Of Ny Baruch Coll, New York, NY; SR; BBA; Gldn Key 89-; Endowment Fund Provosts Schlrshp 88-89; Acctng.

**HANK, KELLY D,** Radford Univ, Radford, VA; SO; BA; Intrdscplnry Studies; Elem Ed.

**HANKIN, JONATHAN I,** Savannah Coll Of Art & Design, Savannah, GA; JR; BFA; U S Army 85-87; Illustrtn/Phtgrphy; Movie Prod/Freelnc.

**HANKINS, ANTHONY L,** Al A & M Univ, Normal, AL; JR; BS; NSBE 90-; Soc Of Pr Schlrs Pr 88-90; Hon Stdnt 88-; IM Sports; Comp Sci; Syst Pgm.

**HANKINS, CINDY L,** Northwest Al Comm Coll, Phil Campbell, AL; SO; BA; Sci; Tchr.

**HANKINS, DANIEL V,** Radford Univ, Radford, VA; SR; Amer Mktg Assn; Deans Lst; BBA; Bus Mktg; Sales.

**HANKINS, JODY M,** Ms Univ For Women, Columbus, MS; JR; BA; Ambssdrs 89-; SMAE 90-; Kappa Delta Epsilon 90-; Elem Ed; Tchr/Adlt Ed.

**HANKINS, SALLY J,** Oh Univ-Southern Cmps, Ironton, OH; FR; BA; Lrng Dsblties; Elem Ed.

**HANKINS, TAMARA P,** Spalding Univ, Louisville, KY; SR; BOSS Pres 90-; Delta Epsilon Sigma 90-; Two Plus Two Schlrshp 89-; BS; Bus Admin.

**HANKO, PAMELA S,** Pa St Univ Main Cmps, University Pk, PA; FR; Alpha Lambda Delta; Deans Lst 90; Bus; Mgmt.

**HANLEY, AMANDA L,** Roane St Comm Coll, Harriman, TN; FR; BS; Gamma Beta Phi; Dean Lst 90-; Math; Eng.

**HANLEY, DEIRDRE D,** Atlantic Comm Coll, Mays Landing, NJ; FR; Prfrmng Arts Clb; Intrnshp Atlantic Mntl Hlth; Psychlgy; Ocptnl Thrpy.

**HANLEY, DEIRDRE L,** Stonehill Coll, North Easton, MA; GD; BA; Stdnt Advsry Bd 89-90; Peer Cnslng 90-; Alpha Sigma Lambda VP 86-89; Thurston Mem Schlrshp 89; John Weihrer Awd; Stdnt Spkr ACHE Conf; Neponset Chrl Socty 83-84; RG 65-; AS RN Lasell Coll 65; Pol Sci/Psychlgy; Acad Cnslng.

**HANLEY, DOREEN A,** Coll Of Insurance, New York, NY; SO; BBA; Ins Club VP; Corp Spnsr Stdnt 90-; Profsnl Ins Whlslrs Assoc Schlrshp; Ins; Ins Profsnl.

**HANLEY, LAKEISHA,** Norfolk St Univ, Norfolk, VA; JR; BA; Alpha Epsilon Rao Sec 90-; Mass Comm Stdnt Assoc 89-; Stdnt Senate WNSB FM Stff Asst Dev Dir 90-; NACWC Schlrshp 89-90f; Mass Comm; Brdcst Mgmnt.

**HANLEY, SEAN A,** Al A & M Univ, Normal, AL; JR; BS; Crbbn Assn Mr CSA; Sccr Capt; Drg Tsk Mvmnt 90-; Medcl Tchnlgy; Med.

**HANLON, ANTHONY J,** Mount Aloysius Jr Coll, Cresson, PA; SO; BS; Deaf Club 89-90; Grad Magna Cum Laude 90; Vol At A State Prison 87-; Disabld Coal Mnr; AA 90; Chem Depndncy; Cnslr For Alchlc/Drug Adcts.

**HANLON, CARRI L,** Indiana Univ Of Pa, Indiana, PA; SR; Byd Schlrshp; Deans Lst; Ld Wrkr Clthng Cp Str; Magna Cum Laude; BS Elm Ed 90-; Instrctnl I; Elem Tchr.

**HANLON, KATHLEEN P,** Marywood Coll, Scranton, PA; FR; BS; Math Clb 90; Pres Schlr 90; Math; Ed.

**HANLON, STACY R,** Mount Aloysius Jr Coll, Cresson, PA; FR; BA; Deans List 90; Wrk Stdy Progrm Wrkng For Rsrs For The Deaf 90-; Law; Paralgl.

**HANLON, TERESA J,** Saint Francis Coll, Loretto, PA; FR; Bio Club 90-; Artists Series 90-; Pres Schlrshp 90-; Deans List 90-; Bio; Sci.

**HANN, WILLIAM E,** Le Moyne Coll, Syracuse, NY; SO; BA; Theatre Co 90; Chess Clb; Hnrs Prog 90; Prose Awd; Im Sftbl; Psychlgy.

**HANNA, CRAIG E,** Univ Of Sc At Columbia, Columbia, SC; JR; BA; Kung Fu Club; Kac-Kwon-Do Club; Hnrs Pgm; CPCC Radio Print Hndcpped; Phi Theta Kappa 88-; Gamma Beta Phi 90-; Betty Gragg Austin Schlrshp 89; USC Schlrshp 90; Store Cable Awards 86; AA Ctrl Piedmont Cmnty Clg 90; Film/Tv; Write/Direct Mtn Pctrs.

**HANNA, DAVID J,** Eckerd Coll, St Petersburg, FL; SR; BA; Stdnt Comm Serv Coord 89-90; Rec Gmrm Prog Coord 88-89; Cmncemnt Comm; Acdmc Hon Schlrshp 89-; Deans Lst 89-90; Chrst Prsbytrn Chrch Yth Advsr; FL Autsm Assn Cnslr; ASPEC Wrtng Awrd 90; IM Sprts 87-; Proj Success Vol 90-; Hmn Dvlpmnt Serv.

**HANNA, GEORGE N,** Wv Univ, Morgantown, WV; FR; BS; Engrg.

**HANNA, GEORGE T,** Ms St Univ, Miss State, MS; SR; VITA 88-89; Phi Kappa Phi 90-; Phi Beta Lambda 87-89; BBA; Bnkg; Fnce.

**HANNA JR, JOE N,** Memphis St Univ, Memphis, TN; FR; BA; Crmnl Juste; FBI Agent.

**HANNA, NICOLE,** Seton Hall Univ, South Orange, NJ; JR; BSN; Clncl I/II Intrn Rtatn; Deans Lst 88-90; Nrsng; RN.

**HANNA, REBECCA M,** Ms St Univ, Miss State, MS; JR; Rdrnr Stdnt Rcrtr 90-; Kappa Alph Sthrn Belles 89-; Stdnt Hl Cncl Flr Rep 88-89; Phi Kappa Phi 90-; Omcrn Dlt Kappa 90-; Gamma Alpha Epsln 90-; Kappa Dlt Pi 90-; Chi Omega 88-; Lambda Sgm 89-90; Crdnl Key 90-; Rep Stdnt Hsng Conf; Elem; Ed.

**HANNA, RONDA L,** Central Al Comm Coll, Alexander City, AL; SO; AS; Bus Mgmt.

**HANNA, STEPHANIE,** West Liberty St Coll, West Liberty, WV; SR; BS; Sch Nwspr Asst Edtr 89-; Prgmng 89-; Sigma Phi Alpha; AS 90; Dental Hygienist.

**HANNA, TROY E,** Ohio Valley Coll, Parkersburg, WV; FR; BA; Stdnt Govt Assn Fr Pr 90-; Mssns Clb V P 90-; TIE 90-; Delta Tr 90-; Ambssdr 90-; Bibl; Yth Mnstr.

**HANNAH, CAROLYN B,** Vance Granville Comm Coll, Henderson, NC; SO; AAS; Cmptr Clb Scl Cmte 89-90; Cr Dy Hsts; Phi Theta Kappa; Wlk Amer 85-89; Acdmc Achvmnt Schlrshp 90-; Wake Forest Chrch God Prphcy; Qlty Asrnc Inspectr; Elctrnc Engrg Tchnlgy; Elc Trnc Engrg.

**HANNAH, MELISSA A,** Univ Of Al At Birmingham, Birmingham, AL; JR; BA; Campus Crusade For Christ; Presidential Hnr Roll; Psychology; Occupational Therapist.

**HANNAH, RANCIE W,** Univ Of Ky, Lexington, KY; FR; BS; Untd Meth Stdnt Cntr; Phi Eta Sigma; Biology; Pre Med.

**HANNAH, WENDY A,** Auburn Univ At Auburn, Auburn, AL; GD; MA; Bapt Stdnt Union Purdue U Scl Chr 90-; Chrch Choir Purdue U 90-; Phi Kapp Aphi Auburn 90; Pi Lambda Theta 89-90; Zeta Tau Alpha 86-90; Proj Uplft Vlntr Big Bro/Sis Pgm Auburn 86-; Pres Awd 90; Intrn Mdsn Pk Hope Ctr 90; Spch-Lang Path; Path Multi Hndcpd Chldrn.

**HANNER, AMANDA L,** Central Fl Comm Coll, Ocala, FL; SO; AA; Inglis-Yankeetown Lioness; Yankeetown Vol Fire Dept; Business; Mngmnt.

**HANNIBAL, NEAVER L,** Ny Univ, New York, NY; JR; BA; Blck Stdnt Org Houghton Clg V P 87; Mentor Pgm; Fortune Soc Vol Tutor Svc Tutor; Wilbur Bill La Motta Msc Sch; Psych; Psych CSW.

**HANNIGAN, PATRICIA A,** Saint Francis Coll, Loretto, PA; JR; BS; Stdnt Actvts Org Treas 90-; Acctg Clb; Stdnt Actvtos Org Spec Evnts Chr 88-90; Intrn Cardiac Rehab Inst Acctg; Acctg; CPA.

**HANNING, JULIE L,** Hocking Tech Coll, Nelsonville, OH; JR; AA; Sec Sci Practcm; Dns Lst Hckng Clg 88-; Hckng Clg Bkstr Stdnt Clrk 88-; Peopls Bnk Schlrshp 88-89; AA Bsns Mgmt 90; Cert Persnnl Tech/Rtl Mgmt Tech 90; Bsns; Bsns/Mgmt.**

**HANNON, HILARY F,** Allegheny Coll, Meadville, PA; JR; BA; Admsns Tourguide 89-; VISK; Big Bro/Sis 90-; Ldrshp Grp Coord 90-; Psi Chi 89-; Alpha Delta Pi Jr Panhel Dlg 88-; Serv Ldrshp Com; Practicum Chld Life Dept The Cleveland Clinic Fndtn Ohio; Varsity Tennis 88-89; Psychlgy/Edn; Rehab Cnslng.

**HANNON, JANET L,** Blue Mountain Coll, Blue Mountain, MS; SR; BED; Tchr Asst Hrg Imprd Chld; Bed Northeast Cmnty Clg 86-88; Bed Blue Mtn 88-; Elem Ed; Tchg.

**HANNON, JOHN M,** Oh Univ, Athens, OH; JR; BA; SAM; Ohio Univ Barbell Clb; Ohio Univ Dns Lst 90-; Gldn Ky; Alpha Epsilon Rho; USAF Resrvs Sgt 89-; W Rvc AM/FM Radio Sta; OU Rugby Tm Cap 90-; USAF 86-; ASSO Degree Cntrl Tex Clg 90; Telecomm; Exec Mngmt.

**HANNON, SHARON L,** Le Moyne Coll, Syracuse, NY; SO; BA; Cllg Rpblcns Vice Chrmn 90-; Stdnt Senate Sntr 90-; Rsdnt Advsr Stf RA; Hnr Cls 89-; Cny Rpblcn Triad Srvc Comm 90-; Offrd Trip England Rcvng Rqrd Score Frgn Stdy Exam 90-; IM Hcky Vlybl 89-; Englsh Cmmnctns; Englsh Tchng.

**HANNON, VIVIAN N,** Univ Of Al At Huntsville, Huntsville, AL; JR; BSN; Cls Sec 90-; Alpha Lambda Delta 82; Omicron Delta Kappa; Sigma Theta Tau; Epsilon Sigma Alpha Jnql Grl 72-76; Boy Scts Amer Trp Ldr 80-88; Cb Scts Amer Dn Ldr 85-88; Grl Scts Amer Dn Ldr 74; Nrsg; Prctnr.

**HANNUM, JANINA,** Ny Univ, New York, NY; SO; AA; Architectural Draftswoman; Art.

**HANNUM, MARK O,** Tallahassee Comm Coll, Tallahassee, FL; FR; AA; Music.

**HANNY, BARBARA A,** Hilbert Coll, Hamburg, NY; SO; BS; Acctng Clb 88-; Alpha Beta Gamma 90-; Deans Lst 89-; All Saints Lutheran Church Secy 83-; AAS; Acctng.

**HANRAHAN, TRICIA E,** Iona College, New Rochelle, NY; FR; Hons Pgm 90-; Fll Schlrshp; Bus.

**HANRATTY, BARBARA A,** Univ Of West Fl, Pensacola, FL; JR; BA; Scuba Diving Club; Alpha Delta Pi Pres 88-; IM Sftbl/Vlybl 88-; Educ; Teacher.

**HANRIGHT JR, DAVID W,** Portland School Of Art, Portland, ME; SO; BFA; Runner 15th Annual PSA Auction 90; Baxter Furbish Schlrhsp Fnd 90; Payson Schlrshp Comp; Painting/Fine Art.

**HANSARD, EUNICE A,** Harrisburg Area Comm Coll, Harrisburg, PA; SO; BS; Blue Mntn Chptr Wmn Of The Yr 84; Amer Bus Wmns Assn Pres 84; Hmlck Grl Sct Cncl Trp Orgnzr Ldr 87-; Rtrd Hmn Rsrce Dev Spclst; Sclgy; Scl Wrk.

**HANSCOM, LAURA L,** Commonwealth Coll, Virginia Beach, VA; SO; AS; Off Admin Clb 90-; Bwlng League Capt 87-88; NCOA Aux 90-; PTA 87-88; Nghbrhd Wtch 87-88; Exec Off Admin; Exec Sec.

**HANSELL, HOWARD F,** Temple Univ, Philadelphia, PA; GD; PHD; Psychlgy; Clncl Psychlgy.

**HANSEN, CLARE M,** Ithaca Coll, Ithaca, NY; JR; BS; Pres Host Com 90-; Stdnt Physcl Thrpy Assn 88-; Physcl Thrpy.**

**HANSEN, DAVID P,** Westminster Coll, New Wilmingtn, PA; SO; BA; Crnrstn Pres 90-; Radio Cvnt Shw 90-; Clwng Svc Tm 89-; Hse Cncl Rep 89-; Lmbd Sgm 90-; Alph Phi Omega VP Svc 89-; Cncrt Chr 89-; Chpl Drama 89-; Pol Sci/Soclgy; Cnslng.

**HANSEN, ELAINE L,** Oh St Univ At Marion, Marion, OH; SR; OEA 89-; PTO Treas 85-; Elem Ed; Tchng.

**HANSEN, ERIC C,** Georgetown Univ, Washington, DC; JR; BSBA; Office Clerk Natl Acdmy Sci/Trnsprtn Rsrch Brd 89-; First Hons; Deans List 90; IM Ftbl/Bsktbl/Tennis/Sftbl 88-; Finance; Invstmnt Bnkng.

**HANSEN, HANNE,** Ny Univ, New York, NY; FR; BA; B Ed 67-86; Psych; Scl Wrk.

**HANSEN JR, HAROLD JAMES,** Bridgeport Engr Inst, Fairfield, CT; JR; BSEE; Tau Alpha Pi VP 88; ASNT; Ct Schl Of Elecs GPA Awrd 90; Dsgn Eng; Cert CT Schl Of Electronics 86; ASEE Greater New Haven St Tech 88; Eng.**

**HANSEN, HILLARY A,** Manhattanville Coll, Purchase, NY; SR; BA; Dnce/Theater Ensmbl Pres 90-; Clbs Cncl 89-; Quad Jam Hd Of Stg 88-89; Intrn Minot Snd Studio 89-90; Perf Arts Merit Schlrshp 87-; Snd Prod; Snd Engr.

**HANSEN, KARIN,** Fl International Univ, Miami, FL; SR; BA; AA Miami-Dade Cmnty Clg 88; Engl Lit; Engl Tchr.

**HANSEN, LEROY M,** Tri County Tech Coll, Pendleton, SC; SO; AS; Phi Theta Kappa; Amer Red Cross First Aid Inst 89-; IEEE 86-; Kendall Healthcare Prod Co Project Eng 81-; Math/Sci; Eng/Mgt.

**HANSEN, MARK KEITH,** Mercer Univ Schl Of Pharm, Atlanta, GA; GD; PHARM; Class Pres 88; Cncl Of Stdnts Pres 88; Chrstn Stdnt Union Treas 88; Rho Chi 89; Phi Lambda Sigma Scrtry 89; Deans Schlrshp 90; Searle Fllwshp In Phrmcy; Chrches Hm Fndtn Schlrshp 89-90; Merit Schlrshp 89; BA Carson Newman Clg 85; Pharmacy.**

**HANSEN, METTE V,** Ky St Univ, Frankfort, KY; FR; Pol Sci; Intl Dvlpmnt.

**HANSEN, MICHAEL R,** Glassboro St Coll, Glassboro, NJ; SR; Top Stdnt; BS; Cmptr Sci; Sys Sftwr Dvlpmnt.

**HANSEN, NAOMI RUTH Y,** Univ Of West Fl, Pensacola, FL; JR; Pensacola Jr Coll Hnr Cncl Brd Mmbr 87-89; Phi Theta Kappa 87-; Psi Beta 89-90; Alpha Beta Gamma Pres 88-90; NOW 88-; PTA Pres 82-; Srr Clb 90-; Sphmr Hnr Schlrshpnatl Cncl Tchrs Math; FL Tchng Prfssn; Natl Ed Assoc 90-; Vol Scts; AA Pnscl Coll; Mddl Schl Math Ci; Ed.

**HANSHAW, MICHELLE N,** Marshall University, Huntington, WV; SO; BBA; Ceredo Kenova Alumni Band 90-; Management Bsns.

**HANSHEW, CHRISTINA M,** Tn Temple Univ, Chattanooga, TN; JR; BSN; Wrd Life Sngrs/Actvties Tm 90-; Wrd Life Clb Cnslr 90-; Bible Study Tchr; Dns Lst; Lamba Delta Rho 90-; Bible Wrd Life Bible Inst 90; Nrsg/Missions; Nrs.

**HANSON, ANGELA M,** Endicott Coll, Beverly, MA; SR; Retail Store 90-; Phi Theta Kappa 90-; Yawkey Schlrshp 90-; Retail Dep Schlrshp 90; Fashion Merch; Retail Buyer.

**HANSON, COLEEN M,** Smith Coll, Northampton, MA; SO; BA; Russian Clb 89-; Frshmn Cls Rep 89-90; Acad Rep 90-; 1st Grp Schlr 90-; Hstry; Professor/Wrtr.

**HANSON, DAVID A,** Hudson Valley Comm Coll, Troy, NY; FR; AS; Peer Stdnt Tutor Pgm; Pres Lst 90; ASCAP; Claims Examiner; Cmptr Infor Sys.

**HANSON, DAVID W,** Volunteer St Comm Coll, Gallatin, TN; SO; AS; Gamma Beta Phi 88-89; Natl Collgt Math Awrd; Eng; Elec Engr.**

**HANSON, DAVID WINTHROP,** Oh Northern Univ, Ada, OH; GD; JD; Law Review Edtr; Moot Court Bd Advocates 90-; Moot Ct Comp; Sigma Phi Epsilon; Amer Jurisprudence Bk Awds 89-; BS Univ Tampa 89; Law.

**HANSON, JAMES R,** Univ Of Akron, Akron, OH; SR; BS; ASME AIAA; Golden Key; Phi Eta Sigma; Mech Engrng.

**HANSON, KAROLA E,** Springfield Tech Comm Coll, Springfield, MA; SO; BA; CRACK Organ Against Drgs; Psy Chi 90-; Dns Lst; Psychlgy; Chld/Psych/Psych Rsrch.

**HANSON, KATHRYN A,** Univ Of Southern Ms, Hattiesburg, MS; SO; BS; Yrbk Grk Ed 89-; Stdnt Almn Assoc 89-; Assoc Stdnt Bdy Exec Cbnt Ed 90-; Lambda Sigma 90-; Alpha Lambda Delta 89-; Phi Eta Sigma 89-; Delta Gamma Crspndng Sec 89-; Biochem; Med Rsrch.

**HANSON, KRISTEN S,** Allegheny Coll, Meadville, PA; SR; BA; Res Adv 89-80; D J Coll Radio 87-90; Allegheny Comm Exchange 87-89; Alpha Delta Pi Pldg Edn V P 87-; Vol Nursing Hm; Alden Schlr 89-90; Completed Sr Cmprhnsv Project; IM Spts 90-; Soc/Edn; Teach.

**HANSON, MARY ALEXANDRIA,** Springfield Tech Comm Coll, Springfield, MA; SR; BS; Biochemistry.

**HANSON, MICHELLE L,** Carnegie Mellon Univ, Pittsburgh, PA; SO; BS; Cmps Assn Reprdctv Rghts 90; Dns Lst 90-; Soc/Dcsn Sci; Acad Rsrch.

**HANSON, ROBERT D,** Univ Of Pittsburgh, Pittsburgh, PA; JR; BS; Intshp USS Divis USX; Published CALL APPLE Mag 83-84; Computer Sftwr Desgr 84-; AS Comm Clg Allegheny County 85; Infor Sci; MIS Mgr/Sftwr Design.

**HANSON, RODNEY D,** Memphis St Univ, Memphis, TN; SR; BA; Pi Sigma Epsilon 89-; Gamma Iotta; Risk Mmgmnt/Ins; Law.

**HANSON, SHANNON M,** Univ Of Sc At Beaufort, Beaufort, SC; SO; BED; AA; Erly Chldhd Ed; Tchg/Cnslng.

**HANSON, SHIRLEY R,** Savannah St Coll, Savannah, GA; SO; Inst Electrcl Elctrnc Eng 90-; Elctrnc Eng.

**HANSON, THOMAS W,** Univ Of Ga, Athens, GA; MA Lat Am Stdy American Univ 67; BS USMA W Point 56; Educ; Tchng Scndry.

**HANSON-BECKLES, CAROL A,** S U N Y Hlth Sci Cent Brooklyn, Brooklyn, NY; JR; BS; Nrsng Clb 86-87; Prfssnl Nrsng Srty VP 88-90; RN; AAS Kngsbrgh Cmmnty Clg 88; Nrsng.

**HANSTINE, KIMBERLY S,** Central Fl Comm Coll, Ocala, FL; SO; AA; Stdnt Govt Treas 90-; Phi Theta Kappa 90-; Math; Fin Anlst.

**HAPPEL, CYNTHIA R,** Univ Of Louisville, Louisville, KY; GD; MS; Subdvsn Homeowners Assoc Pres 86-; Oldham Co Metro United Way VCRC 88-; Mgr S Central Bell 76-90; AB Western Ky Univ 76; Computer Sci; Computer Sftwr Dlpmnt.

**HAQ, DANIEL N,** Univ Of Tn At Knoxville, Knoxville, TN; FR; BA; IM Bsktbl; Bsns.

**HARA, NOELLE M,** Savannah Coll Of Art & Design, Savannah, GA; SR; BFA; Alga 90-; Graph Grp 89-; 1st Pl Valentines Card Contest; Graphic Dsgn; Grphc Dsgnr.

**HARAHAN, PATRICIA A,** Immaculata Coll, Immaculata, PA; JR; BA; Vol Com Lionvl Elem Sch; Cb Sct Ldr; CCD Tchr; Acctg; Bus.

**HARAHAN, SONDRA S,** Univ Of Nc At Greensboro, Greensboro, NC; SR; Dean Lst 90; BS 90; Elem Educ.

**HARAN, MICHAEL J,** Univ Of Hartford, West Hartford, CT; JR; BSBA; Jdcl Brd Mmbr 90-; Mns Golf Tm 89-; Econ.

**HARATY, JONATHAN D,** Holyoke Comm Coll, Holyoke, MA; FR; AS; E Longmeadow Cnsrvtn Cmmssn; Envrmntl Sci; Envnmntl Law.

**HARAVITCH, HEIDI G,** Allegheny Coll, Meadville, PA; SR; BA; Creer Svcs 90-; SG 87-88; Psi Chi 89-; Alpha Chi Omega Rcrdng Sec 88-; Hosp Hmn Rsrcs Intrn 89-90; TA 89-90; Vars Sccr 87; Alden Schlr 89-90; Psych; Hosp Admin.

**HARAWAY, LEONARD MATTHEW,** Averett Coll, Danville, VA; SR; Stdnt Govt Rep 75-76; Honor Comm 79-81; Beta Beta Beta 90; All Amer Schlr Awd; Life Saving Crew 74-80; Police Aux 84-89; BS; Bio.

**HARB, BASSAM A,** Merrimack Coll, North Andover, MA; JR; IEEE 90-; Ferris II Schlrshp; Assoc Nthrn Essex Com Coll 90; Elec Eng.

**HARBERT-CHAPPEL, LENA,** Wv Northern Comm Coll, Wheeling, WV; GD; AS; Sec Clb 88-90; Hon Grad; Deans Lst; Hghr Educ Grnt; Csmtlgst 55-57; Real Est Jfrsn Tech Coll 78-79; Slsprsn OH Lcns; Sec Sci.

**HARBIN, BARRY S,** Tri County Tech Coll, Pendleton, SC; FR; AS; Indus Elec; Engr.

**HARBIN, BETSY L,** Comm Coll Algny Co Algny Cmps, Pittsburgh, PA; JR; ASSOC; Pedeology.

**HARBIN, ERIC SHANE,** East Tn St Univ, Johnson City, TN; JR; BA; Bus.

**HARBIN, JERAMIE JUDD,** Birmingham Southern Coll, Birmingham, AL; JR; BS; Res Hll Assn Pres 89-; Alpha Lambda Delta 89; Psi Chi; Mrtr Brd Sec; Asst Hse Dir; Asst To Dir Res Life 89-; Stu Opnn Srvy Asst To VP Stu Affrs 90-; Psychlgy; Stu Prsnnl Serv Hghr Educ.

**HARBIN, JERYL L,** Alcorn St Univ, Lorman, MS; JR; BS; Biol Modeling Clb Pres; Natl Panhellenic Cncl; Hnrs Clb; Hnrs Prog; Deans Lst; Delta Sigma Theta Exec Bd; Biol; Dentistry.

**HARBIN, LYDIA R,** Univ Of Nc At Asheville, Asheville, NC; SR; BA; Pep Bnd; Cmmnty Bnd; Phi Eta Sigma; Alpha Phi Omega Pres90; BSU Mssns Vol; Deans Lst 87-88; Hnrs Stdnt; Schlrshp; Musci; Grad Schl Orchstr.**

**HARBIN, REYNOLD M,** George Mason Univ, Fairfax, VA; JR; BS; Vrsty Tennis 88-; Bus.

**HARBIN, SONYA R,** Univ Of South Al, Mobile, AL; SR; Alpha Chi; Deans Lst; Pres Lst; Edn/Engl/Psychlgy; High Sch Engl/Tchr.

**HARBISON, JAMES E,** Beckley Coll, Beckley, WV; SO; BA; Busn Mgmt; Hotl Rsrt Mgmt.

**HARBOR, ELIZABETH L,** Walker Coll, Jasper, AL; FR; Bus; Acctng.

**HARBOR, MARY M,** Itawamba Comm Coll, Fulton, MS; SO; BA; Elem Educ; Tch.

**HARBOURI, DIANA L,** Defiance Coll, Defiance, OH; JR; BA; Cmmnty Bnd Lbrrn 90-; Church Choir; Cntrl Foundry/GM; AAP NW Tech Coll 90; Engl; Wrt/Tch.

**HARBUCK, DEBORAH C,** Savannah St Coll, Savannah, GA; FR; BA; Ltl Sis Sigma Alpha Epsln; Fncl Mgr Jones/Assoc Intrs 89-; Engl.

**HARCHFIELD, CHRISTY M,** Univ Of Tn At Martin, Martin, TN; JR; BS; Amer Hm Econ Assn 89-; Stdnt Sctn 89-90; Pi Sigma Epsilon Dir/Cmnctns 89-90; Alpha Delta Pi Rec Sec 88-; All Amer Schlr Collgt Awrd; Home Econ/Gnrl; Dsgn.

**HARCLEROAD, BARBARA L,** S U N Y Coll Of Tech At Alfred, Alfred, NY; SR; AAS; Lit Mag 90-; Nrsg Clb Sec 89-; Hnrs Pro 89-90; Nrsg.

**HARCOURT, WAYNE D,** Univ Of Cincinnati-Clrmnt Coll, Batavia, OH; SO; BSEE; Asst Engr Eng Firm 90-; US Army 84-86; US Army Res 86-; AS; Elec Eng.

**HARDBECK, CHRISTOPHER D,** Middle Ga Coll, Cochran, GA; SO; BS; SADD 89-F Drm Cncl Fr Hmcmng; IM Bsktbl Sftbl 89-; Blgy; Orthpdc Srgn.

**HARDCASTLE, EDGAR G,** Univ Of North Fl, Jacksonville, FL; SR; BA; Awd Outstndng Schlstc Prfrmnc Sclgy; AA Fl Cmnty Clge 86; Sclgy; Soc Srvc.

**HARDCASTLE, SHARON L,** Savannah Coll Of Art & Design, Savannah, GA; SO; BA; Painting.

**HARDEN, COLLEEN A,** Asbury Theological Sem, Wilmore, KY; GD; MDIV; Sigma Zeta 79-81; Alpha Chi 79-81; Biochem Rschr Lab Tech 81-89; BA Adrsn Coll 81; Biblcl Stds; Chrstn Mnstry.

**HARDEN, GREGORY M,** Alcorn St Univ, Lorman, MS; SR; BS; Animal Sci Clb 89-; Kappa Alpha Psi Strategus 89-; Ftbl Tm 87-; Animal Sci; Vet Med.

**HARDEN, KIMBERLY D,** Tuskegee Univ, Tuskegee Inst, AL; SO; Archtctr Dsgn Awrd 90-; Deans List 89-90; Archtctr Cnstrctn Sci Mgmt.

**HARDEN, MELINDA K,** Methodist Coll, Fayetteville, NC; JR; BS; Monarch Playmakers; Elizabeth Weaver Schlr 90; Female Theater Tchncnof The Year 90; AA North Seattle Comm Clg 88; Theater; Medicine.

**HARDEN, RICHARD L,** Eckerd Coll, St Petersburg, FL; SR; BA; ECOS Stdnt Govt Prlmntrn 87-; ASPEC Stdnt Liaison Tsk Frc 87-; Sigma Alpha Pi 88-; Omikron Delta Kappa 89-; Cir K Treas 87-89; Ford Apprntc Schlr 89-; Fr Grc Schlrshp 88; Spnsh/Frnch; Frgn Svc.

**HARDEN, ROBIN B,** Univ Of Nc At Greensboro, Greensboro, NC; SR; Stdnt NC SNCAE Assn Edctrs; Deberry Schlrshp; Roxie King Schlrshp; Escheats Schlrshp; BS 90; Edctn.

**HARDEN, SHANNON N,** Wilberforce Univ, Wilberforce, OH; JR; Newspapr Edtr 88; Radio News Mgr 90; Emplyee Of Mnth Tme Lfe Sls Rep 89; Chrldr 90; Jrnlsm; Prof.

**HARDEN, SHARON K,** Wilmington Coll, New Castle, DE; JR; BS; AS Un Dlwr 75; Hmn Rsrc Mgmt.

**HARDEN, TANIA DRIVER,** Middle Tn St Univ, Murfreesboro, TN; SO; BSN; Flag Corp 80; Sigma Phi Epsilon Gldn Hrt Sr 80-83; Dns Lst 83,90-; Advtsng Mgr 84-90; Co Fndr Amer Wild Trky Soc 90; BFA 84; Nrsng.**

**HARDER, NATASHA M,** Univ Of Tn At Martin, Martin, TN; FR; Mu Epsilon Delta Pledge 90; Bio; Int Med.

**HARDESTY, MELISSA D,** Wv Univ At Parkersburg, Parkersburg, WV; JR; AAS; Bsns Admn; Mgmt/Acctg.

**HARDESTY, SUSAN P,** Brescia Coll, Owensboro, KY; FR; BA; Asmblr/Mchn Oprtr 86-89; Graphic Dsgn/Photography.

**HARDICK, DAVID J,** Philadelphia Coll Pharm & Sci, Philadelphia, PA; SR; MPT; APTA 89-; Upsilon Sigma Phi 90-; Vllybl 90-; BS Wheaton Clg 87; Phy Thrpy.

**HARDIE, G ELLEN,** Patrick Henry Comm Coll, Martinsville, VA; FR; RNAD; Stdnt Nrs Assn; Phi Theta Kappa; SPIRE; LPN 80-; Ind Voc Tech Clg 76; Nrsng.

**HARDIE, ROBERT LEVON,** Nc Agri & Tech St Univ, Greensboro, NC; SR; BS; ACM 90-; Acad Achvmnt Awd 90-; Cmptr Sci; Sys Anlyst.

**HARDIGREE, SOPHIA D,** Univ Of Ga, Athens, GA; FR; BA; Acctng/Ins Agent 87-90; Socl Wrk.

**HARDIMAN, DAVID F,** Univ Of Al At Huntsville, Huntsville, AL; SR; BS; IEEE 90-; Bacchus 90-; Eta Kappa Nu 89-; Tau Beta Pi 90-; 3 M Schlrshp; All Amer Schlr 89-90; IM 87-88; Elec Eng.

**HARDIMAN, ROBERT D,** Central Fl Comm Coll, Ocala, FL; SO; ASDRN; Rgstrd Nrs.

**HARDIN, CYNTHIA P,** Gaston Coll, Dallas, NC; FR; G; Lgl; Paralgl.

**HARDIN, HEATHER M,** Winthrop Coll, Rock Hill, SC; JR; BS; Stdnt Govt Assn Sen 89-90; Stdnt Govt Assn Sec Treas 90-; Kappa Delta Pi 90-; Phelps Hall Coun Treas 89-90; Alpha Lambda Delta 89-; Chi Omega Treas 90-; Pres Lst 90; Stdnt Marshals 90-; Panhellenic Higest GPA 90-; Biology; Scndry Educ/Biology.

**HARDIN, LEIGH A,** Owensboro Comm Coll, Owensboro, KY; SO; AA; Psychlgy.

**HARDIN, MARTY R,** Univ Of Tn At Knoxville, Knoxville, TN; FR; BS; AF ROTC; Arnld Air Soc 2 Lt; Hnr Rl; Mech Engr.

**HARDIN, MICHELLE RENEE,** Owensboro Comm Coll, Owensboro, KY; SR; BA; Radlgy; Radlgc Technlgst.

**HARDIN, NANCY J,** New England Coll Of Optometry, Boston, MA; GD; OD; Beta Sigma Kappa 88-; BSC Univ Calgary 85; Optometry.**

**HARDIN, PATRICIA E,** Bellarmine Coll, Louisville, KY; SR; BA; MAA 90-; Delta Epsilon Sigma 90-; COMAP Math Model Contest Hnrbl Mntn 90; William M Mercer Inc Intern-Compensation Analyst 90-; Cross Country 87-89; Math/Cmptr Sci; Cmpnstn Analyst.

**HARDIN, PATSY ANN,** Univ Of Sc At Spartanburg, Spartanburg, SC; FR; BS; Amnesty Intl; Green Peace; Scty Free Thinkers 90-; Klear Knit Ind Clover SC 89-90; Psychology; Scl Wrk.

**HARDIN, RHONDA L,** Univ Of Sc At Columbia, Columbia, SC; SR; BS; Psychlgy Clb Sec 88-; Gamma Beta Phi Sec 88-; Pdmnt Scty 88-; Sthstrn Physchlgc Assocotstndng Psychlgy Stdnt; Deans Lst; Prsdnts Lst 88-; Psychlgy.

**HARDIN, RODNEY E,** Union Univ, Jackson, TN; SR; BA; N Amer Scty Aldrn Ssychlgy 90; Mnstrs Assc 88; Pstr Sthrn Bapt Chrch 86-; Natl Yng Ldrs Conf 87; Yth Ldrshp Awrd; Congrsnl Yth Ldrshp Cncl; Psychlgy Rlgn; Cnslng/Pstrng.

**HARDIN, SANDRA A,** Watterson Coll, Louisville, KY; GD; Deans Lst 89-; Pres Lst 89-; Cert Watterson Coll 89-; Word Prcssng.

**HARDIN, SARAH E,** Univ Of Southern Ms, Hattiesburg, MS; FR; Gamma Beta Phi; Phi Eta Sigma; Bsn; Acctng.

**HARDIN, SHANE K,** East Tn St Univ, Johnson City, TN; SO; BA; PBUS-ACCT.

**HARDIN, TRACEY M,** Univ Of Md At Eastern Shore, Princess Anne, MD; SR; BS; Gspl Choir 90-; Pep Clb 88-90; Pre Prof Soc 88-89; Tutorial Pro 90-91; Rehab; Phys Thrpy.

**HARDIN, WENDY T,** Methodist Coll, Fayetteville, NC; SR; Res Hall Govt Pres 88-89; IM Sports Tm Capt 88-89; BA U Of NC 89; Math.

**HARDING, BENJAMIN F,** Univ Of Al At Huntsville, Huntsville, AL; SR; BS; IEEE; Coop Prog; Eta Kappa Nu; Elect Engr Signal Procsng.

**HARDING, C DENISE,** Christopher Newport Coll, Newport News, VA; SR; BSBA; Child Nuture 86-89; Tennis 86; Marketing/Mgmnt; Personnel.

**HARDING, DAWN W,** City Univ Of Ny Baruch Coll, New York, NY; JR; BBA; Club Caricom Baruch Cllg 90-; Hmn Rsrc Mgmt; Prsnl Mgmnt.

**HARDING, DIANE E,** Central Fl Comm Coll, Ocala, FL; FR; BA; Math/Sci Hon Clb 90-; Phi Theta Kappa; Cmuty Schlr; I M Ftbl; Biology; Med.

**HARDING, GERALDINE H,** Winthrop Coll, Rock Hill, SC; SR; BED; Kappa Delta Psi 89-; Elem Educ.

**HARDING, KAREN L,** Va Commonwealth Univ, Richmond, VA; SR; BS; Cncl Excep Chldrn; Stdnt Educ Assn; Magna Cum Laude; Vir Tchr Schlrshp 90-; Golden Key 90-; Phi Eta Sigma 87-; Spec Educ/Lrng Dis; Tchng.

**HARDING, L RUSSELL,** Comm Coll Algny Co Algny Cmps, Pittsburgh, PA; GD; AS.

**HARDING, MARK H,** Radford Univ, Radford, VA; JR; BA; Stdnt Gvnmnt; SAM; Phi Sigma Kappa; Vrsty Bsbl 88-89; Bsns Mgmnt; CEO Mjr Orgnztn.

**HARDING, MIKEL B,** Univ Of Akron, Akron, OH; JR; BSA; Acctg Assn 90; Gldn Key 90-; Deans Lst 88-; Beta Alpha Psi; IM Ftbl Bsktbl/Sftbl 88-; Acctg; CPA.

**HARDING, RUBY J,** Hillsborough Comm Coll, Tampa, FL; SO; BA; Boy Scts Am Hndcppd Trp Com Chair 87-; Para Prfsnl Yr Doris Sanders Lrng Ctr 90-; Polk Cty Schl Brd 87-; Crtfd Sub Tchr; Spcl Ed; Tchr.

**HARDING, TRISCILLA M,** Central Fl Comm Coll, Ocala, FL; FR; BA; Phi Theta Kappa; Acctg.

**HARDISON, CHAD M,** Brescia Coll, Owensboro, KY; FR; BS; IM Sprts; Stu Ambssdr; Pres Awrd; Bsktbl; Accntng; Accntnt.

**HARDISON, JAY-CHRIS,** Savannah Coll Of Art & Design, Savannah, GA; JR; BA; Dns Lst 89-; RA 89-90; Graphc Desgn; Adv/Fashn Merch.

**HARDISON, JEFFREY A,** Gallaudet Univ, Washington, DC; GD; MA; Rgstry Of Intrprtrs Fr Df 87-; Pi Kappa Alpha Almns 87-; Pres Schlr 90-; BA Univ Of Florida 87; Lngstcs; Edctr.

**HARDISON, JOEL C,** Western Carolina Univ, Cullowhee, NC; JR; BS; Anthrplgy Clb Pr 90-; Pi Gamma Mu 90-; Undergrad Res Conf Pres Papr 90-; Canoe Tm 90-; AA Lenior Comm Clg 90; Anthrplgy/Archlgy; Archlgst.

**HARDISON, JOSEPH E,** Morris Brown Coll, Atlanta, GA; SO; Archtctr Clb Sec 89-; Hnr Stdnt 90; Kappa Alpha Psi; Earth Pk Clbrtn 89-90; Fndrsr Archtctr Clb 89-.

**HARDISON, LAURA D,** Middle Tn St Univ, Murfreesboro, TN; SO; BS; Stdnt Amb 90-; Mass Cmmnctns; Pub Rltns.

**HARDISON, TRESJE L,** Middle Tn St Univ, Murfreesboro, TN; FR; BS; Math Clb 90-; Dean Lst; Hnr Rll; Arspc Eng/Math; Arntcl Eng.

**HARDJONO, LISA I,** Brevard Comm Coll, Cocoa, FL; SO; AA; Arch.**

**HARDRICK, ANTHONY L,** Univ Of Al At Birmingham, Birmingham, AL; ASSOC; Pres Lst 89-90; Assoc Jefferson St Comm Coll 88-89; Cert 89-90; Elec/Biomed; Eng.**

**HARDRICK, RODNEY,** Coppin St Coll, Baltimore, MD; SR; BS; Stdnt Hnrs Assoc Treas 86-90; Cmptr Intllgnce Scty 90; Big Bro/Sis Prog; Yth/Yng Adlt Comm Membr 86-88; Math; Eng.

**HARDT, JOHN DAVID HINDLE,** Va Commonwealth Univ, Richmond, VA; SR; BA; Rep Natl Elctn Cmps Wrk 88; Prncmr Rdrs 89; Deans Lst 90-; Gldn Key; Intrn Lng Lgc Mth Systms 89; Lcrss Tm 89; Engl.**

**HARDWICK, ALEXANDER A,** Univ Of Sc At Columbia, Columbia, SC; SR; BS; SGA Leg Adv 89; Fin Mngmnt Assn; Am Mrktng Assn; Tau Kappa Epsilon Pldg Pres 87; Intrnshp Comp Grp Inc Sys Mngr 89; Im Bsktbl; Glf; Vlybl; Ftbl; Fin; Mrktng.**

**HARDWICK, SHERRON F,** Miles Coll, Birmingham, AL; SR; BS; Poltcl/Soc Sci Clb 90-; Natl Hon Comm 90-; CASA Vol 87-88; Hon Awrd Soc Wrk 88-89; Deans Lst Lawson St 88-89; Cert Awrd Gamma Phi Chptr 90-; Brownie Ldr 87-88; Spnsr Lady Phi Delta Sorority 86-87; AAS 89; Soc Sci; Soc Wrkr.

**HARDWICK, VALERIE P,** Univ Of North Fl, Jacksonville, FL; SR; BA; Psychlgy Clb Pres; Psi Chi 90-; Gldn Key 88-; Alph Lmbd Dlt 87-; Rsrch Asstnt; Suicide Prvntn Ctr Crsis Wrkr 90-; Intrnshp HRS Chld Prtctv Svc Asst Invstgtns; Clncl Psychlgy.

**HARDY, ANDREW J,** Old Dominion Univ, Norfolk, VA; SR; BSCE; Pres Chi Epsilon; ASCE; NSPE; Tau Beta Pi; Chi Epsilon Pres; Alpha Chi; Undergrad Eng Asst; Natl Coll Eng Awd Wnr 90; Civil Eng; Geological Eng.

**HARDY, BIANCA JUSELLE,** Tn St Univ, Nashville, TN; SO; Yrbk; Alpha Mu Gamma; Biology; Med Ob Gyn.

**HARDY, BRIAN E,** Alcorn St Univ, Lorman, MS; FR; BED; Hon Stdnt Orgnztn; Elem Ed; Tchr.

**HARDY, ELLSWORTH F,** Coppin St Coll, Baltimore, MD; JR; Newspr Rptr 90-; TV Sta Crew 90-.**

**HARDY, ERA D,** Bennett Coll, Greensboro, NC; JR; BA; Wmn In Comm Treas 90-; Peer Cnslr; Delta Sigma Theta Pres; Hmlss Shltr Chrstn Otrch Prog; Dns Lst; Bennett Schlr; Hon Lst; Sftbl 89-90; Comm/Bsns; MBA Fin.**

**HARDY, GALIENA E,** Western Carolina Univ, Cullowhee, NC; FR; BS; Res Hl Cnsl; Wstrn Gold 90-; Math; Bus.

**HARDY, JANICE E,** Norfolk St Univ, Norfolk, VA; JR; BA; Praise Flwshp 88-; Hnrs Cncl; Alpha Kappa Mu; Psi Chi; Psychlgy.

**HARDY, JEFFREY W,** Ms St Univ, Miss State, MS; SR; MS; Phi Kappa Phi 90-; Sigma Gamma Epsilon 90-; Pres Schlr; Magna Cum Laude; BS Miss State Univ; Geography; Climatology.

**HARDY, JENNIFER L,** Birmingham Southern Coll, Birmingham, AL; SR; Almn Assc 89-; Alpha Kappa Delta 89-; Sigma Tau Delta 89-; Alpha Omicron Pi Sec 87-; Intern Birmingham Magazine 87; Intern Birmingham Bus Jrnl 88; BA; Sclgy/Engl; Cnslng.

**HARDY, MARK A,** Univ Of Tn At Martin, Martin, TN; JR; BA; Wkly Cnty Drg Fr Allnc Cmmtt 88-; Deans Lst 88-; Phi Eta Sigma 89-; Phi Kappa Phi 89; Mu Epsilon Delta 89-; Beta Beta Beta 89-; Gch Acdmc Awrd; Krk H Grhm Acdmc Awrd; All Glf Sth Cnfrnc Acdmc Awrd; Vrsty Bsktbll; Blgy; Med.

**HARDY, MICHAEL,** Hudson Valley Comm Coll, Troy, NY; FR; BA; Dlvry Drvr; Acctg.

**HARDY, NEAL W,** Embry Riddle Aeronautical Univ, Daytona Beach, FL; JR; BA; Aerontcl Sci; Avatn.

**HARDY, PAMELA,** Bunker Hill Comm Coll, Boston, MA; FR; MBA; Asst Super Cstmr Acct Srvcs Prvte Bnk 87-; Fnnce; Fnncl Cnsltnt.

**HARDY, RICK L,** Anne Arundel Comm Coll, Arnold, MD; SO; AS; Bus.

**HARDY, SHERRIE L,** Va St Univ, Petersburg, VA; SO; BA; CSAP 89; Va Lst Dllr 89-90; Scl Wrk Hmnties.

**HARDY, STEPHANIE L,** Clark Atlanta Univ, Atlanta, GA; SO; BA; Insprtnl Vcs Of Fth Gspl Chr 89-; Comp Sci.

**HARDY, W SCOTT,** Allegheny Coll, Meadville, PA; SO; BA; Admin Asst Stu Gov; Allies 90-; Pre Lgl Soc; Alden Schlr 89-90; Larve Smith Endwmnt 90-; Ftbl 89-; Ecnmcs; Law.

**HARDY, YOLANDA L,** Al A & M Univ, Normal, AL; JR; BS; Mrcng Bnd 89-90; Kappa Delta Pi 90-; Delta Sigma Theta Miss 90-; Math Educ; Prfssr/Tchng.

**HARDY-VARNEY, JUNE A,** Univ Of Ky, Lexington, KY; SR; BA; Dns Lst 90-; Shriners Hosp Scl Wrkr; Jvnl Crt Intake 89-; Scl Wrk.

**HARDYK, RISE R,** Kent St Univ Kent Cmps, Kent, OH; SO; BA; Gym Clb IM 89-; Rsdnce Srvcs Offce 90-; Engl; Law.

**HARDYMAN III, CHARLES B,** Central Fl Comm Coll, Ocala, FL; FR; MED; Hist; Scndry Ed.

**HARE, TARA J,** Univ Of Nc At Charlotte, Charlotte, NC; FR; BA; Engl; Brdcstng.

**HAREWOOD, PAUL N,** Marywood Coll, Scranton, PA; SO; BSC; Interntl Clb 89-; Phlsophy Clb 90-; Math/Cmptr Sci; Oper Rsrch.

**HARFORD, KATHRYN G,** Belmont Coll, Nashville, TN; SR; BBA; Amer Mktg Assc 90-; Gspl Msc Assc Intrnshp 87-88; Mtkg.

**HARGEST, VICTORIA A,** Va Commonwealth Univ, Richmond, VA; GD; MD; Tri Beta Pres 84; MS Univ Of Maryland 88; BS Univ Of Richmond 84; Med.

**HARGETT, CEDRIC J,** Fayetteville St Univ, Fayetteville, NC; SO; BS; Phi Beta Sigma Asst Sec; Acad Hon 90-; Crmnl Justice.

**HARGETT, LAURA M,** Univ Of Tn At Martin, Martin, TN; SR; BS; SGA 90-; Undergrad Alumni Cncl 89-; Stdnt Amb 89-; Stdnt Tchr Educ Assoc 89-; Chi Omega Pub Rels 87-; Gooch Schlrshp 90-; Jr Aux Schlrshp 87-90; Chi Omega Most Imprvd GPA 89; Elem Educ.

**HARGETT, TARA Y,** Univ Of Tn At Martin, Martin, TN; SO; BA; SGA Chf Jstc; Sprt Stff 90-; Coll Repub Sec; Phi Eta Sigma; Hnrs Soc Soph Rep 90-; Chi Omega Cmmnt Serv 89-91; Alpha Pi Omega Almn Sec 90-; Project Rcycl; Undrgrad Almn Cncl; Cmmnctns.

**HARGIS, MARK W,** Lindsey Wilson Coll, Columbia, KY; SR; Phi Beta Lambda; Busn Admin Awd; BA Lindsey Wilsn Clg; AAS Somerst Comm Clg 88; Busn Admin; Sales/Mktg.**

**HARGRAVE, DOUGLAS M,** Glassboro St Coll, Glassboro, NJ; SR; BS; Bio Clb 89-; Pre Prof Soc VP 90-; Bureau Sci Org Sec; Bio Clb Mdln Awrd; Bio; Med.

**HARGRETT, BRIAN T,** Fl A & M Univ, Tallahassee, FL; FR; Phi Eta Sigma; Natl Soc Blck Eng; Natl Actn Cncl Minrts Eng; Ftbl/Trck Tm; Sci; Chem Eng.

**HARGROVE, DONALD C,** Univ Of Sc At Columbia, Columbia, SC; SR; BS; USC Scuba Clb 90-; Elctrn Home Remdlr 83-90; Glgy; Envrnmntl Glgy.

**HARGROVE, JENNIFER B,** Hillsborough Comm Coll, Tampa, FL; SO; AA; Psychlgy.

**HARGROVE, MELINDA F,** Middle Tn St Univ, Murfreesboro, TN; SO; BS; Engrng Tech; Electo Mech Engrng Tech.

**HARK, PATRICIA A,** Erie Comm Coll, Buffalo, NY; FR; ASSOC; Office Tech/Comp.

**HARKAVY, ARTHUR S,** Life Coll, Marietta, GA; GD; DC; Toftness Clb; SOT Clb; Activator Clb; Beth Jacob Congregation Atlanta GA; BS Biochem SUNY Binghamton 83; BA Clscl Cvlztn; Chiropractic Sci.

**HARKCOM, LAURA A,** Carnegie Mellon Univ, Pittsburgh, PA; SO; BA; Dancer's Symposium 89-; Deans List 90; Rsrch Asst/Prof; IM Wrstlg Stat 91; Engl/Drama; Wrtr.

**HARKEN, BRAD S,** Hampton Univ, Hampton, VA; FR; BS; NROTC 90-; Sftbl Tm 90-; Adpt/Schl 90-; Mltry Serv Mdl Oper Dsrt Shld/Strm 90-; Presb Chrch; Nclr Pwr Oper US Navy Nclr Pwr Trng Unt 89-90; Arway Sci Admn; US Nvl Pilot/NASA.

**HARKEN III, HAROLD D,** Air Force Inst Of Tech, Wrt-Ptrsn Afb, OH; GD; Tau Beta Pi 89-; USAF Dist Grad 89; USAF Capt 90-; BS Comp Engr 85; MS Comp Engr 89; Comp Engr; Continue USAF.

**HARKER, TERESA J,** Mount Aloysius Jr Coll, Cresson, PA; FR; Surg Tech Clb V P 90-; Surg Tech.

**HARKEY, LEAH D,** Fl St Univ, Tallahassee, FL; SR; BS; Renegade Yrbk Stf Sr Sctn Edtr 88-89; Assn Stdnt Socl Wrkrs 90-; Phi Alpha 90-; Rookie Of Yr Yrbk Stf Sr Section Edtr 88-89; Multidsplnry Cntr Intrnshp Socl Wrk; Socl Wrk; Med Socl Wrk Pediatrics.

**HARKEY, PAMELA D,** Shelton St Comm Coll, Tuscaloosa, AL; FR; BS; Phi Theta Kappa 90-; Acad Schlrshps 90-; Acctng; Acctnt/Tchr.

**HARKINS, JANINE M,** Univ Of Miami, Coral Gables, FL; JR; BA; Natl Press Phtgrphrs Assn Sec 90-; Gldn Key; Photocmmnctn Psychlgy; Psychlgst Cnslr.

**HARKINS, KIMBERLY A,** Point Park Coll, Pittsburgh, PA; SO; BA; Legal Sec U S Dept Of Justice 87-; Cert Acctng Bradford Schl Of Bus 86; Acctn; Law Enfrcmnt.

**HARKLESS, JOHN A W,** Morehouse Coll, Atlanta, GA; FR; BS; Mrchng Band 90-; Campus All Star Chlng 90-; Amoco Schlr 90-; William Penn Schlr 90-; Math/Chem; Rsrch.

**HARKNESS, CHRISTINE P,** S U N Y Coll At Geneseo, Geneseo, NY; FR; BA; Thtr 90-; Math Bus; Sttstcn.

**HARKNESS, MICHELLE D,** Muskingum Coll, New Concord, OH; SO; BA; Hnrbl Mntn Acdmc All Amer 90-; Wmn Bsktbl Tm 89-; Biol; Phys Thrpy.

**HARLAN, BRIAN J,** Univ Of Al At Huntsville, Huntsville, AL; SR; BS; Mech Eng.

**HARLAN, ELLEN B,** Salisbury St Univ, Salisbury, MD; JR; BSBA; Elem Edctn Cmmnctn Arts; Tchr.

**HARLAN, LORI A,** Ky St Univ, Frankfort, KY; JR; BA; Phi Theta Kappa 88-89; AA Madisonville Comm Colg 89; Acctng; CPA.

**HARLAN, LORRIE B,** Indiana Univ Of Pa, Indiana, PA; SR; Sigma Sigma Sigma 87-; Vybl Panhellenic Cncl; BS; Ele Educ.

**HARLE, CYNTHIA D,** Ky Wesleyan Coll, Owensboro, KY; JR; BA; Sigma Kappa Rgstr 89-; Vlybl Acdmc All Cnfrnc 90; Vlybl 88-90; Bus Admin; Entrprnrshp.

**HARLESS JR, CARL Y,** Roane St Comm Coll, Harriman, TN; SO; AS; Deans Lst 89-; Eng.**

**HARLESS, JUANITA L,** Roane St Comm Coll, Harriman, TN; SO; BS; Fee Bd 88-89; Tchr Aid 89-; Sub Tchr; Dns Lst 88-90; AS 90; Hm Econ Educ; Tchr.**

**HARLESS, NIKI L,** Edinboro Univ Of Pa, Edinboro, PA; FR; BFA; Frnch Clb 90-; Anthrplgy Clb 90-; Appld/Media Art; Art.

**HARLESS, ROGER EUGENE,** Wv Univ At Parkersburg, Parkersburg, WV; FR; AA; Acctg; Cnsltnt.

**HARLETT, VICTORIA J,** Kent St Univ Kent Cmps, Kent, OH; JR; BA; KSHA 88-89; Psych Cl 90-; Co-Ed Rec Vlybl Cl; Psi Chi 90-; Phi Beta Kappa; S J Luft Meml Awd 90-; Psychlgy; Adult Indv Coun.

**HARLEY, ALEXANDER,** Atlantic Comm Coll, Mays Landing, NJ; JR; BA; Peer Mntr; Deans Lst; Intrcllgt Bsktbl Capt; Phy Ed.

**HARLEY, MELISSA L,** Milligan Coll, Milligan Clg, TN; SR; BA; Dorm Council Treas 89-90; Annual Festival One Act Plays Stage Mgr 88-89; Intl Club 89-90; Delta Kappa 90; Spiritual Life Comm 90; Deans List 89-90; ACT/SAT Schlrshp 87-90; German Awd; Sweetheart Cand 89; Acctng Math.

**HARLEY, SHIRLEY S,** Univ Of Sc At Columbia, Columbia, SC; FR; Gamma Beta Phi; Acctg; CPA.

**HARLING, NANCY I,** Univ Of Sc At Columbia, Columbia, SC; FR; BS; Soc Wmn Eng 90-; Assn Hon Stdnts 90-; Chem Eng.

**HARLOW, DIANE J,** Central Me Medical Center, Lewiston, ME; SR; ADN; Grad Comm; Son Cntnl Comm; Dip 77; Nrsng; RN-BSN.

**HARLOW, TINA R,** Univ Of Sc At Aiken, Aiken, SC; SR; BS; Jr Achvmnt Bus Bascs Cnsltnt; Bus Admn; Indstrl Projct Mgt.**

**HARMAN, CHRISTOPHER M,** Oh Wesleyan Univ, Delaware, OH; FR; PHD; Big Pal Ltl Pal Prgrm 90-; Prsdnts Clb; Phi Eta Sigma 90-; Chi Phi 90-; Phi Eta Sigma 90-; Pldg Cls Prsdnts 90-; Psychlgy Phlsphy; Clncl Psychlgst.

**HARMAN, DANA M,** Lycoming Coll, Williamsport, PA; FR; Achvmnt Cert 90; Chrldr 90-; Blgy; Peds Dntst.

**HARMAN, JAMES T,** Radford Univ, Radford, VA; JR; BS; Art; Graphic Dsgn.

**HARMISON, LAURA L,** Wilmington Coll, Wilmington, OH; SR; BS; AS Owens Tchncl Clg 88; Agrcltr Bsns; Agrcltr Sls Srvc.

**HARMON JR, ARTHUR T,** Commonwealth Coll, Virginia Beach, VA; SO; Electrncs Techcn; Techcn.

**HARMON, CARLOS E,** Univ Of Tn At Knoxville, Knoxville, TN; FR; BA; Boy Scouts Amer Asst Sctmstr 90-; Alpha Lambda Delta; Tchng.

**HARMON, CINDY LYNN,** Univ Of Sc At Coastal Carolina, Conway, SC; FR; BA; Phi Eta Sigma; Social Work; Cnslng.

**HARMON, JOHN B,** Le Moyne Coll, Syracuse, NY; SR; Le Moyne Coll Vrsty Soccer NCAA Div 2 Capt Snr Yr 90; WLMU Coll Radio DJ 89; Newhouse Writing Awd Poetry; Two Time Coll Schlstc All-Am; BA; Engl Cmnctns; Jrnlsm TV Nwspr.

**HARMON, JUSTIN C,** Georgetown Univ, Washington, DC; FR; BA; NAACP 90-; Blck Stu Alnc 90-; Intl Rltns Clb 90-; Wrtr Lit Pblctn 90-; Intl Rltns; Frgn Serv Offce.

**HARMON, KEISHA M,** Va St Univ, Petersburg, VA; SO; BS; Accntng Clb 89; Blk Stdnts Agnst Drgs 90; Ntl Assoc Of Blk Accntnts Admin Sec 89; Tri-Cty Assoc Of Ed Offce Prsnnl Schlr; Larry J Saunders Schlr; Lela H Wms Schlr; Webster L Harris Schlr; Union Bapt Chrch Membr 81; Deans Lst 89; Accntng; CPA.

**HARMON, KIMBERLY K,** Marshall University, Huntington, WV; SO; BA; Majorette 90-; Educ; Tchr.

**HARMON, MELINDA R,** Saint Catharine Coll, St Catharine, KY; SO; BED; Phi Theta Kappa 90-; Hstry Tchr.

**HARMON, PAUL J,** Middle Tn St Univ, Murfreesboro, TN; SR; Sgm Iota Epsln; AA Brookhaven Comm Clg 86; BBA Mdl TN State Univ 91; Mgmt; Sales/Mktg.**

**HARMON, SARA JEANNE T,** Marshall University, Huntington, WV; GD; MA; HS Chrldr Spnsr 90-; Tchng 5th-Grd; Erly Chldhd Educ.

**HARMON, SHUNDERA L,** Alcorn St Univ, Lorman, MS; SO; Clgt Secty Intl Pres 90-; Busn Office Admin; Data/Word Proc.

**HARMON, SIDNEY S,** Samford Univ, Birmingham, AL; GD; JD; Hspnc Lang Clb 86-87; Rugby Clb 86-87; Moo Duk Kwan Tae Kwan Do Clb 83-84; Tau Kappa Epsilon Hyphpts 83-87; Trial Advcy Brd Cmbrlnd Sch Law; Intrshps Lgl Aid Soc Brmnghm; US Attrny/Circt Jd/Crmnl Court; BA 87; AA 85; Law.

**HARMON, TERRI L,** Univ Of Montevallo, Montevallo, AL; FR; BA; ARS 90-; Blue Cross Blue Shield Claims Processor 89-90; Educ; Teacher.

**HARMON, TIMOTHY D,** Embry Riddle Aeronautical Univ, Daytona Beach, FL; JR; BS; Amer Assn Airport Exec 90-; Aircraft Ownrs/Plts Assn 88-; Instrmnt Prv Pilot 87-; Arntcl Sci; Airline/Corp Pilot.

**HARMS, DAVID A,** Me Maritime Academy, Castine, ME; FR; BS; Vol Firemn/EMS 89-; Ftbl 90-; Eng.

**HARMS, KRISTIE A,** S U N Y Coll At Fredonia, Fredonia, NY; SO; BS; Deans Lst; Ice Sktng 89; Gntcs Blgy; Gntc Eng Rsrch.**

**HARNE, GEORGE ANTHONY,** Univ Of Southern Ms, Hattiesburg, MS; SO; BME; Phi Kappa Phi; Amnsty Intrntl 89-; Colloqm Bk Awd 89; Msc Educ.

**HARNER, RICHARD J,** Nyack Coll, Nyack, NY; JR; BA; Mnhttn Gspl Tm Pres 89-; Mtrpltn Dstrct Blb Qzzng Dir 89-; Alpha Chi 90-; Nnt Schl Dstrct Ch Wrstlng Vllybll Sftbll; Phlsphy.

**HARNESS, VICKI L,** Owensboro Jr Coll Of Bus, Owensboro, KY; GD; BA; Cum Laude; Progress Printing Co Cmptr Oper; AS SE IL Clg 86; Cmptr Studies; Pgm/Syst Analysis.

**HARNETTY, AMY E,** Oh Univ, Athens, OH; SR; BFA; OH U Tae Kwon Do 90-; Intrntl Stdnts Union; Art Hist; Crtr Art Gllry.

**HARNEY, CAROLINE L,** Hampton Univ, Hampton, VA; FR.**

**HARNISH-BECK, LESLIE A,** Washington State Comm Coll, Marietta, OH; FR; Scl Svcs.

**HAROOTUNIAN, RANDY A,** Emory Univ, Atlanta, GA; JR; BBA; Chi Phi Hs Mgr 88-; Pr Export Cncl Intrnshp; Deans Lst 90-; IM Ftbl/Bsktbl 88-; Bus Admin/Psych; Law.

**HARP, DEVONA N,** Middle Ga Coll, Cochran, GA; SO; BA; Blck Stdnt Clb Treas; Bapt Stdnt Union; Joyful Mnstrs; Nrsg; Dr.

**HARP, JONATHAN C,** Lexington Comm Coll, Lexington, KY; SO; BS; Science; Optometry.

**HARPER, AIMEE L,** Pellissippi St Tech Comm Coll, Knoxville, TN; FR; MS; Acdmc Wrk Schlrshp 90-; Eng/Sci; Eng/Chmcl.

**HARPER, AMY KATHLEEN,** Merrimack Coll, North Andover, MA; SO; BA; Psych Clb; Psych.

**HARPER, BETH A,** Glassboro St Coll, Glassboro, NJ; SO; BA; Activities Brd Exec Brd Comedy Clb Crdntr 90-; Peer Referal Orientn Stf; Communications; Public Relations.

**HARPER III, CHARLES E,** Ms St Univ, Miss State, MS; SO; BA; Rffmd Univ Flwshp; Cncrt Bnd; Psychlgy.

**HARPER, CHERYL L,** Al St Univ, Montgomery, AL; FR.

**HARPER, CYNTHIA ANN,** Ga St Univ, Atlanta, GA; SR; BA; Natl Cncl Tchrs Math; Gldn Key 89-; Kappa Delta Pi; Deans Key 90; Deans Lst 89-; Edctn Math/Scl Sci; Tchng.

**HARPER, DARLENE Y,** Fayetteville St Univ, Fayetteville, NC; SR; BS; Natl Stdnt Bus League Sec 89-90; Stdnt Acad Advsry Pgm 89-90; Sec Hood Hall Sec 88-90; Small Bus Tech Dvlpmnt Ctr Intrnshp 90; BS 90; Bus Admin.

**HARPER, DAWN M,** Wv Univ At Parkersburg, Parkersburg, WV; SO; BSN; Nurs.

**HARPER, GARY L,** Radford Univ, Radford, VA; JR; BS; Pol Sci Soc 89-; Pi Gamma Mu; Phi Kappa Phi; US Army Rsrv; US Army 85-89; AAS 88; Pol Sci; Law.

**HARPER, JANICE C,** Alcorn St Univ, Lorman, MS; SO; BA; Comm Clb; Dns Lst; Comm; Commentr.

**HARPER, JASON A,** Middle Tn St Univ, Murfreesboro, TN; JR; BS; Stdnt Orientation Ambsdr 89-; Bapt Stdnt Union 90-; Ext Sch Pgm Murfreesboro; Dns Lst; Vars Chrldr 88-; Aerosp Adm; Intl Rels.

**HARPER, JENNIFER L,** Univ Of Southern Ms, Hattiesburg, MS; JR; Elem Educ; Tch.

**HARPER, JULIE A,** Ohio Valley Coll, Parkersburg, WV; FR; AS; Dns Lst 90-; Theta VP 90-; Hd Rsdnt Asst; Sec Sci; Elem Educ.

**HARPER, KIMBERLY A,** Bennett Coll, Greensboro, NC; SO; BA; Afrcn Awrnss Assmbly P 90; Marshall Brd 90-; Bennett Plyrs 89-90; Hons Lst; Deans Lst; Pres Schlr; Engl; Law.

**HARPER, KIMBERLY L,** Univ Of Montevallo, Montevallo, AL; SR; BS; SGA Sentr 87-88; Cir K 86-87; Ocfcl Host Org WSCC 86-88; Ala Jr Ms Schlrsp 86-88; Deans List 89; Pres List 90; Elem Educ; Tchr.

**HARPER, LAURA S,** Lexington Comm Coll, Lexington, KY; SO; BA; Crmnl Jstc Orgnztn Pres 90-; Crmnl Jstc Orgnztn Tres 89-90; Scl Wrk/Lw Enfrcmnt; Wrk Wth Ppl.**

**HARPER, LAUREN B,** Elms Coll, Chicopee, MA; SR; BA; Fclty Commt Clgs Self Study Rept; Phi Alpha Theta; Delta Epsilon Sigma; Marie E Butler Awd History; Founders Gold Cross Sr Jr Acad Achievment; AB Paralegal 91; Ba History; Law.

**HARPER, LEE A,** Southern Coll Of Tech, Marietta, GA; GD; Ntl Scty Black Engnrs 89-; Instit Indstrl Engnrs 89-; US Army Reserves 87-; Intl Assoc Mach/Aerospace Wrkrs 87-; Intrnshp Ciba Vision Corp 90; Deans List; Awd Acad Achvmnt 90; BS; Industrical Engineering Technology.

**HARPER, LEILANI D,** Univ Of Sc At Columbia, Columbia, SC; SR; BA; Stdnt Govt Sntr 86-88; Gamma Beta Phi Pres 84-; Stdnt Yr 87-88; AA 87; Mst Vlbl Mbr 87-88; Byrne Miller Dance Theater Cmt 79-89; Admnst Spec 88-; Boy Scts Am Dist Trngn Chrmn 86-; Hist/Bus; Educ.

**HARPER, MARIE E,** Univ Of North Fl, Jacksonville, FL; SR; BSN; Sigma Theta Tau 90-; Gldn Key; Ptnt Edctn Assoc Sec; Eplpsy Fdtn; MD Assoc; Grl Scts Amrc; RN; Pdctrc Nrlgy Clncn; AS FL Comm Coll 73; Nrsng; MSN Pdtrc Nrs Prctnr.

**HARPER, MATTHEW D,** Univ Of Toledo, Toledo, OH; GD; JD; Law Rvw Mng Edtr; Tau Kappa Epsln Pres 88; Gamma Alpha Kappa; BA Ashland Univ 89; Crmnl Jstc; Law.

**HARPER, TAMARA DENISE,** Bowling Green St Univ, Bowling Green, OH; SO; BA; Stdnt Alumni Cncl Sec/Treas 89-90; Deans List Bowling Green State; Intl Bus.

**HARPER, TAMI R,** Kent St Univ Kent Cmps, Kent, OH; JR; BA; Acctng Asc 90-; Alpha Lambda Delta 89; Beta Alpha Psi 90-; Acctng; CPA.

**HARPER, TERRY T,** Univ Of South Fl, Tampa, FL; FR; BS; BSU 90-; SAMES/NSBE 90-; Stdnt Rcrtr 90-; Vstkn Inrds Clss Rep 90-; Cmptr Sci; Eng.

**HARPER, THOMAS W,** Univ Of Ky, Lexington, KY; FR; BS; Mrchng Bnd; Pep Bnd ; Hrnrs Prgm; Cmmnwlth Schlr; Chmcl Eng.

**HARPER, VESTA T,** Alcorn St Univ, Lorman, MS; SO; BS; Hnr Stu Org 89-; Alpha Kappa Alpha 90-; Acctg; CPA.

**HARPER, YVONNE C,** Volunteer St Comm Coll, Gallatin, TN; SO; BA; Black Stdnt Assoc Edtr 87-; New Stdnt Orientation Helper 90-; State Brd Of Regents Schlrshp 90; Human Services; Counselor.

**HARRAH, KENNETH D,** Cincinnati Bible Coll & Sem, Cincinnati, OH; GD; MA; Grad Assist 90; BA 89; Biblical Studies; Mnstry.

**HARREL, MITCHEL D,** Fl St Univ, Tallahassee, FL; SR; Stdnt Govt 83-84; Garnet Key 89-; Bay County Art Alliance; BS; Minor Art; Elem Educ; Ldrshp Educ.

**HARREL, RUTH A,** Norfolk St Univ, Norfolk, VA; SR; BA; Stdnt VA Ed Assoc 89-; Alpha Kappa Mu; Elem Ed; Educator.

**HARRELL, CARTER B,** Christopher Newport Coll, Newport News, VA; SR; BS; Commissioner Revenues Ofc Newport News Intern; Dns Lst; Purch Dept 83-90; Publ Mgmt; Govt.

**HARRELL, CORINA,** Commonwealth Coll, Virginia Beach, VA; FR; Lgl Offc Amdn; Prlgl Lawyer.

**HARRELL, DEBORAH L,** Univ Of Ga, Athens, GA; SO; BED; Wm Tate Socty Pres 90-; Union 89-90; Rcrtmnt Tm 89-; Alpha Lambda Delta 89-; Phi Eta Sigma 90-; Blue Key; Gamma Beta Phi 90-; Kappa Delta Epsilon Sec; Tchrs Asst 89-90; Gamma Sigma Sigma VP 90-; Coll Educ Schlrshp; Alumni Schlrshp 89-; Math Educ; Tchr.

**HARRELL, DONNA W,** Middle Ga Coll, Cochran, GA; SO; AS; Sociolgy Awrd; Deans Lst 90-; Sociolgy; Probtn Offcr.

**HARRELL, ERIC A,** Norfolk St Univ, Norfolk, VA; SO; BS; Hmpton Rds Blck Md Prfsnls 90-; Ms Cmnctns Stdnt Assoc 90-; NAACP Norfolk Yth Chptr Pres 89-; WNSB Jz Stn Ar Ancr; Spartan Alpha Tau 90-; Hnr Rl 89-90; Dns Lst 90-; Ms Cmnctns Dept Outstndng Acdmc Achvmnt Awd 90-; Ms Cmnctns; Prdcr/Dir Cmnctns Fld.

**HARRELL, JANIE L,** Northeast State Tech Comm Coll, Blountville, TN; SO; BA; BS E TN State Univ 76; Hlth Care.

**HARRELL, JEFFREY S,** Bellarmine Coll, Louisville, KY; JR; BA; Alpha Delta Gamma Sec 88-; Psychology Club V Pres 88-; Pre-Law Soc 90-; Delta Epsilon Sigma; Alpha Delta Gamma Sec 88-; KY Shakespeare Festival Intrnshp; IM Flashball Bsktbl Vlybl 88-; Psychology/Communications; Law.

**HARRELL, JENNIFER BETH,** Univ Of Tn At Martin, Martin, TN; JR; STEA Pres; Erly Chldhd Edn; Teach.

**HARRELL, KATINA R,** Alcorn St Univ, Lorman, MS; FR; BA; Psychlgy.

**HARRELL, LAURA E,** Greenville Tech Coll, Greenville, SC; SO; ASN; NSNA; Deans List 90; Hon Grad Med Clrcl Pgm; Cert MC; Nrsng; RN Neonatal Nrs Prctnr.

**HARRELL, LINDA KAREN,** Tn Wesleyan Coll, Athens, TN; JR; MSW; Alpha Chi 90-; Exclnc English Cmpsitn 86-87; Kiwanis Hgst GPA 87-88; Acad Schlrshp Awds 87-; Cntct Tle Hlp Line 89-; Mentl Hlth Adult Day Care 85-86; Cmptr Oprtr/Off; Factory Wrk; Human Serv/Psych; In Patient Psychiatric Care.

**HARRELL, NANCY L,** Wilmington Coll, New Castle, DE; SO; BSN; Assoc Fr Prctctnrs Infctn Cntrl 90-; NJ Emply Hlth Nrs Assoc 90-; Infctn Cntrl Emply Hlth Crdntr MHSC 90-; AAS Nrsng Cmbrlnd Coll 88; LPN Slm Coll 76; Mrsng; MSN.

**HARRELL, SHERRI G,** Troy St Univ At Dothan, Dothan, AL; SR; MED; AA Darton Clg 88; BS; Early Tchr.

**HARRELL, STACY R,** Radford Univ, Radford, VA; SR; BS; Stu VA Educ Assn Fndrsng Chrmn 90-; Erly Mddl Educ; Tch/Law.

**HARRELL, TYRONE,** Coppin St Coll, Baltimore, MD; SO; BS; Prjct Trnarnd Inc AA Dir 83-88; Lft Bank Jazz Mbr; Soc Sci.

**HARRELSON, AUDIE KIRK,** Piedmont Tech Coll, Greenwood, SC; SO; ABM; AVX Corp Myrtle Bch SC Prodct Engr Tecxhncn 87-89; AS Florence-Dasrlington Technel Clge 87; Math; Engr.

**HARRELSON, DANIELE L,** Univ Of Sc At Columbia, Columbia, SC; FR; BA; Bsn; Fin.

**HARRELSON, DANIELE L,** Univ Of Sc At Sumter, Sumter, SC; FR; BA; Bsn; Fin.

**HARRELSON, GREGORY A,** Univ Of Al At Birmingham, Birmingham, AL; JR; MBA; AL Soc Radiologic Tech; Sci; Mech Eng.

**HARRELSON JR, MICHAEL L,** Middle Ga Coll, Cochran, GA; SO; BA; Engr Clb 89-90; Bptst Std Un 89-; Joyfl Mnstrs 90-; Cmptr Engr.

**HARREN, JULIE C,** Tn Temple Univ, Chattanooga, TN; SR; BS; Stu Afrs Cncl Drm Rep 90-; Intrdrm Cncl VP 90-; Drm Pres 90-; Alpha Epsilon Theta 90-; Jdsn Soc; Ruby 3rd; Alpha Gamma Rho Pres 90-; Res Asstnt 88-90; Bus Mnstry 87-; Intrnshp; IM Vlybl/Bsktbl; Psych; Cnslg.

**HARRICK, KRISTEN A,** Ms St Univ, Miss State, MS; SO; BBA; Bapt Stdnt Union 89; Famous Maroon Mrchng Bnd 89; Campus Crusade For Chrst 90; Pres Lst 90; Deans Lst; Awrded Acad U Schlrshp 89; Im Co-Ed Sftbl Tm; Mrktng; Advrtsng Co.

**HARRIED, VELVEDA L,** Alcorn St Univ, Lorman, MS; FR; BS; Indus Tech Club; Hnrs Stdnt Org; Chem Engr.

**HARRIGAN, STEVEN,** Univ Of Fl, Gainesville, FL; SR; BS; AIAA VP 90-; Phi Theta Kappa VP 88-89; UF Manolin Human Pwrd Sbmrn Tm; IM Ftbl/Sftbl; AS Comm Clgair Force 87; AA Santa Fe Comm Clg 89; Aerospace Engr.

**HARRILL, DALLAS H,** Saint Andrews Presbytrn Coll, Laurinburg, NC; SO; BA; Board Cert Rgstrd Rsprtry 88; Thrpst Mbr Clvry Mem Chrch 78; Moore Rgnl Hosp 87; ASCD Sand Hills Cmnty Clg 88; Allied Health; Hlth Admin.

**HARRILL, ROBERT L,** Univ Of Tn At Knoxville, Knoxville, TN; SO; BA; Am Mktg Assn; Phi Eta Sigma 90-; Alpha Lambda Delta 90-; Gamma Beta Phi; Bus; Acctg.

**HARRIMAN, SUSAN G,** Springfield Tech Comm Coll, Springfield, MA; GD; Grad Cum Laude 90; Dns Lst 88-90; ANA 90-; Charge Nrs; ASN 90.

**HARRINGTON, AMY K,** Univ Of Nc At Greensboro, Greensboro, NC; JR; BS; Greater Greensboro Open Golf Trnmnt Hostess; Campus Tours Lead 89-90; SNCAE; Chi Omega Pres; Chi Omega Comm Serv Chr 90-; Tchng Intrnshp; Educ; Tchng.

**HARRINGTON, CAROL A,** Bunker Hill Comm Coll, Boston, MA; SO; Hsptlty Clb Clnry Arts Rstrnt Htl Mgmt VP 90-; Phi Theta Kappa VP Elect; Clnry Arts; Own Bd N Brkfst.

**HARRINGTON, CHRISTINE B,** Eckerd Coll, St Petersburg, FL; SO; BA; Crss Cntry 89-; Accntng; CPA.

**HARRINGTON, GREGORY M,** Clarkson Univ, Potsdam, NY; JR; BS; Nwspr Bsns Mngr 89-; Tlvsn Asst Exec Prdctn 88-; Soc Assntnts 88-90; Trustee Schlrshp 88-; Accntng Finance; CPA.

**HARRINGTON, JAMES P,** Liberty Univ, Lynchburg, VA; SO; Hon Prog; Bus/Mktg.

**HARRINGTON, JENNIFER E,** Bethany Coll, Bethany, WV; SO; BA; FAC 89-90; Adv Clb 90-; Lab Asst For Comms Dept 90-; Intrdsplnry Grphcs Dsgn; Grphc Dsgnr/Adv.

**HARRINGTON, JODIE M,** Univ Of Southern Ms, Hattiesburg, MS; SR; Cert Awrd Spnsh Cmptn JSU; BS; Psychlgy.

**HARRINGTON, KRISTEN D,** Wagner Coll, Staten Island, NY, SR; BA; Engl Clb; Chrldng Capt; Jazz Bnd/Flute Lssns; Aletha Womens Hnr Soc; Cmptr Ctr Assist; Fitness Ctr Assist; Engl; Bsnss.

**HARRINGTON, LISA H,** Catawba Valley Comm Coll, Hickory, NC; FR; AS; Gamma Beta Phi; Math; Secdry Ed.

**HARRINGTON, MILDRED L,** Fayetteville St Univ, Fayetteville, NC; SO; BS; DECA Pres 90-; ABLE Builds Ldrshp/Execl 90-; Univ Ambrd 90-; Alpha Kappa Alpha Sorority; Appointed Natl Brd Mbr Natl Brd Mnbr; Prestly Field Experience NASA Goddard Space Flight Ctr Greenbelt Maryland; Mktng Ed/Econ; NASA.

**HARRINGTON, STEFANIE A,** Glassboro St Coll, Glassboro, NJ; SO; BA; Kappa Lambda Psi Hstrn/Treas; Bio; Med.

**HARRINGTON, THOMAS A,** Georgetown Univ, Washington, DC; JR; BSBA; Acctg Soc Sec; Delta Sigma Pi; Acctg; Pub Acctg.

**HARRINGTON, YOLANDA DENISE,** Jackson St Univ, Jackson, MS; FR; BA; Deans Lst 90-; Alpha Lambda Delta 90-; Mgmnt; Bus.

**HARRION, MELANIE,** Jackson St Univ, Jackson, MS; SO; Alpha Lambda Delta; Mktg; Advrtsng.

**HARRIS, AILEEN L,** Stillman Coll, Tuscaloosa, AL; SO; BA; Nwspr 90-; Coll Cmnctns Assn 90-; Plyrs 90-; Gamma Iota Sigma; Cordell Wynn Hon Pgm; All-Amer Schlr; Deans Schlr; Cmnctns; Jrnlsm.

**HARRIS, ALBERT N,** Fl A & M Univ, Tallahassee, FL; SO; BS; Caribbean Stdnts Assn PR 89-; Chem Clb VP 90-; Marcus Garvey Clb 89-; Chem; Physician.

**HARRIS, ALDRIC D,** Vance Granville Comm Coll, Henderson, NC; SR; Comp Clb 90-; Usher Brd Pres; Choir Sec 90-; Phi Theta Kappa; Alpha Sigma Chi; Acdmc Schlrshp 90-; Hosiery Tech; AS Vance Granvl Comm Coll; Bus Comp Prog; Data Prcssng/Prog.

**HARRIS, ALETHEA G,** Talladega Coll, Talladega, AL; SO; Presdntl II Schlrshp 89-; Lettie Pate Whitehead Schlrshp 90-.

**HARRIS, ALFREADA S,** Bishop St Comm Coll, Mobile, AL; SO; ASSOC; Phi Theta Kappa; Acad Achvmnt Awd Sci/Math 90; Vol Cancer Soc; Amer Heart Assn; Vol Amer Red Crs; LPN; Dip S W State Tech Clg 81; Nurs; Nurs/Clncl Nurs Spec.

**HARRIS, ALISON L,** Univ Of West Fl, Pensacola, FL; SR; BA; AA Pensacola Jr Clg 87; Elem Edctn; Tchr.

**HARRIS, ALISON S,** Radford Univ, Radford, VA; SO; BA; X-Cntry 90-; Finance; Bnkng.

**HARRIS, ALLISON K,** Middle Tn St Univ, Murfreesboro, TN; JR; BS; Gamma Beta Phi 90-; Kappa Delta Pi 90-; Tau Omicron 90-; Work Schlrshp 89-; Psychlgy; PhD Psychlgy-Mrrg/Fmly Thrpst.

**HARRIS, ANDREA H,** Medical Coll Of Ga, Augusta, GA; SR; BSN; Nrsng.

**HARRIS, ANDREA M,** Cuyahoga Comm Coll, Cleveland, OH; JR; Mrktng Prmtn/Fndrsng Actvts Untd Black Fund Grtr Cleveland Inc/Salem Inc 84-; Deans List 84-89; Serv Actvts Trnsfgrtn Epscpl Church Hunger Ctr/Yth Grp/Sunday Schl 76-; Office Admnstrtn; Csmtlgy Franchise.

**HARRIS, ANDREA S,** Norfolk St Univ, Norfolk, VA; FR; BA; MCSA 90-; Mass Cmnctns; News/Publ Affairs.

**HARRIS, ANNETTE S,** Cheyney Univ Of Pa, Cheyney, PA; SR; BED; Video Club Secty; Hme Econ Ed Assoc; PSEA NEA; Kappa Omicron Nu Secty; Alpha Phi Sigma; Alice A Johnson Schlrshp Awd Hme Econ Assoc Philadelphia 90-; Acad Exce 88; Hme Econ Ed.

**HARRIS, ANTHONY R,** Univ Of Nh, Durham, NH; FR; BA; Univ Radio; Mask & Dagger-Little Shop Of Horrors.

**HARRIS, APRIL E,** Johnson And Wales Univ, Providence, RI; FR; VICA 90-; Slvr Key 90-; Clnry Arts; Rest Mgt.

**HARRIS, BENJAMINE D,** Tn St Univ, Nashville, TN; SR; BS; Chem.

**HARRIS, BRENDA B,** Sue Bennett Coll, London, KY; SO; BS; Psychology; Cnclng Psychology.

**HARRIS, BRENDA J,** Pellissippi St Tech Comm Coll, Knoxville, TN; SO; BS; Sga 90-; Im Comm; Phi Theta Kappa 90-; Dns Lst 90-; Acctg.

**HARRIS, BRENDA L,** Coll Of New Rochelle, New Rochelle, NY; GD; BA; Clg Human Serv Dean List 88; Brd Trustees Gtr Mt Plsnt BC Chrprsn 84-89; Yth Spprt Cncl Gtr Mt Plsnt Chrprsn 88; Yth Choir Gtr Mt Plsnt BC Asst Supvsr 75-79; Tenant Ldrshp Awd NYC Hsng Auth 89; YMCA Wom Of Yr 77; Mrkhm Gdns Tenant Assoc; Rlgs Stds; Mdiv.

**HARRIS, BRIAN P,** Spartanburg Methodist Coll, Spartanburg, SC; SO; BED; Phi Theta Kappa 89-; AA 89; Ed.

**HARRIS, BRIAN T,** Univ Of Sc At Columbia, Columbia, SC; SO; Stu Afrs Ofc Intrn 90-; AA ; AS; Math; Scndry Educ.

**HARRIS, CANDACE A,** Kent St Univ Kent Cmps, Kent, OH; JR; BS; Gldn Key 90-; Delta Zeta Pldg Pres 89-90; Pre Med/ Chmstry; Med Dctr.

**HARRIS JR, CARL E,** Thomas Nelson Comm Coll, Hampton, VA; FR; AS; Comp/Appld Math; Prog.

**HARRIS, CARL R,** Marshall University, Huntington, WV; SR; BBA; Natl Mgmt Assoc 90-; Natl Frnch Hnrry Scty 83-84; Phi Beta Lambda 86-88; 4H Clb 82-; Spcl Olympcs Vol 83-85; US Army Rsrv Athle Schlr Awrd 84-85; Hlth H Awrd 81; Bus Mgmt.

**HARRIS, CAROLYN S,** Bishop St Comm Coll, Mobile, AL; FR; AS; Phi Theta Kappa 90-; AAT Southwest Tech Clg 77; Bus Admin; Acctng.

**HARRIS, CHARLES R,** Saint Francis Coll, Loretto, PA; JR; BA; Indpndnt Stdy Prpsl Cmt 90-; Knghts Clmbs Clg Theater 88-; Phi Alpha Theta; Alpha Psi Omega; Dorothy Day Ctr 88-90; Cmps Mnstry 88-; Vrsty Crs Cntry Ltrmn 88; Sthrn Algncs Museum Art Intrnshp; Margaret M Tobin Archvs Ctr Intrnshp 90; IM 88-89; Hist; Bus.

**HARRIS, CHARLOTTE M,** Univ Of Sc At Columbia, Columbia, SC; SR; BS; Psi Chi 89-; Golden Key 90-; Psych; Grad Schl.

**HARRIS, CHARLOTTE M,** Al St Univ, Montgomery, AL; FR; BS; Psychlgy.

**HARRIS, CHARLTON J,** Johnson C Smith Univ, Charlotte, NC; JR; BS; NAACP 89-; Time Warner Inc Tutrng Prgrm Schls Coord 89-; Alpha Chi 90-; Tau Beta Chi 90-; Kappa Alpha Psi Rprtr; Hnrs Cllg 89-; Bsns Admnstrtn; Mngmnt.

**HARRIS, CHERYL D,** Longwood Coll, Farmville, VA; SR; BS; Delta Zeta; Elmntry Ed; Tchng NK4.

**HARRIS, CHRISTINE M,** Marist Coll, Poughkeepsie, NY; SO; BS; SG 90-; Commuter Union 90-; Tutor 90-; Deans Lst 90-; IM Prog 90-; Dollars For Schlrs Schlrshp; Comm Ctr Vol; Biol/ Psychology.**

**HARRIS, CHRISTINE R,** Western Piedmont Comm Coll, Morganton, NC; SO; BA; March Dimes 89-; Bus Mgmt.

**HARRIS, CHRISTOPHER G,** Barry Univ, Miami, FL; JR; BA; BEA; Phi Alpha Theta 90-; Hstry; Hgh Schl Tchr.

**HARRIS III, CURTIS W,** Va St Univ, Petersburg, VA; JR; BA; Bus Admnstrtn Clb Forum Com Chrmn; Tennis Clb 87-; Orientation Staff Grp Ldr; Southern Chrstn Ldrshp Chptr; Cmpgnd Douglas Wilder; All Acdmc Tm; Tennis Tm 87-; Bus Admnstrtn; Finance.

**HARRIS, CYNTHIA MCGEATHEY,** Medical Univ Of Sc, Charleston, SC; SR; BSN; Sigma Theta Tau; Homelss Clnc Nrs 90-; SCNA 90-; DHEC Chld Hlth Nrsng; Chldrns Hosp/Peds Nrsng; ASN Univ DC 85; BS Howard Univ 83; Nrsng; Pediatrc Nrs/MSN.

**HARRIS, DAMON F,** Univ Of Southern Ms, Hattiesburg, MS; SR; BA; Entrprnr; AA Prl Rvr Jr Coll 81; Bus Adm; Bus Dvlpmnt.

**HARRIS, DANA L,** Coll Of Charleston, Charleston, SC; JR; BS; Fllwshp Chrstn Athlts Offcr Stf 89-; IM Cptn 88-; Marine Biology; Rsrch.**

**HARRIS, DAWNLYN M,** Univ Of Southern Ms, Hattiesburg, MS; FR; BABA; Ofc Mgr/Lgl Scpst; Bus Adm; Law.

**HARRIS, DEBRA A,** Daytona Beach Comm Coll, Daytona Beach, FL; FR; BA; De Bary Chmbr Of Comm 90-; Citizens For De Bary 90-; Mary Kay Cosmetics Business/Good Life Enterprises 89-; Acctg/Computers; Bus Admnstrn.

**HARRIS, DEBRA K,** Memphis St Univ, Memphis, TN; SO; BA; Peer Mentor Prog; Alpha Lambda Delta Treas 90-; Phi Eta Sigma; Gamma Beta Phi; Pi Beta Phi; Bus; Acctng.

**HARRIS, DENISE T,** Jackson St Univ, Jackson, MS; JR; BS; Natl Assoc Blck Jrnlsts 90-; Emmanuel Clb 90-; Publ Rels Assoc MS 90-; Newspaper Stf Wrtr 89-; Yrbk Stf 89-; Hnrs Clg 89-; Mass Cmnctn; Publ Rels Prctnr.

**HARRIS, DONNA L,** Springfield Tech Comm Coll, Springfield, MA; JR; BA; Amer Red Crs Dstr Vol; Erly Chldhd Ed; Tchr.

**HARRIS, DONNA L,** Va Commonwealth Univ, Richmond, VA; SO; BS; Admin Justice; Law.

**HARRIS, ELKER L,** Bethune Cookman Coll, Daytona Beach, FL; JR; BA; Concert Chorale Stdnt Dir 89-; MENC Chaptr Pr 90-; Alpha Chi; United Negro Clg Fund Micheal Jackson Schlrshp 90-; Clg Merit Schlr 89-; Music; Opera.

**HARRIS, ELLEN A,** Bishop St Comm Coll, Mobile, AL; JR; Phi Theta Kappa; Acctng; Spec Educ; Tchng.

**HARRIS, EVERARD R,** Fayetteville St Univ, Fayetteville, NC; SO; BA; Piano Tchrs Assn; Piano Instr; Music; Professor/ Musician.

**HARRIS JR, FRANK W,** Cumberland County Coll, Vineland, NJ; SO; BA; Phi Theta Kappa 89-; Bus Admn; Frmng.

**HARRIS, FREDERICK J,** Wilberforce Univ, Wilberforce, OH; SR; BS; Bsktbl Tm Sr Capt 88-; Alpha Phi Alpha Sgt Arms 89-; Math; Engr.

**HARRIS, GAIL L,** Medical Coll Of Ga, Augusta, GA; JR; BSN; GA Stdnt Nrs Assc 90-; LPN Pediatric ICU Medical Clg Of GA 83-; Nrsg Pediactric ICU.

**HARRIS, GARY L,** Radford Univ, Radford, VA; JR; BS; US Army 81-85; AAS New River Comm Coll 90; Mktg; Advrtsng.

**HARRIS, GLORIA J,** Benedict Coll, Columbia, SC; SR; BA; Engl Clb 87-; Law Clerk Intrn; Chrldr 90; Nrsng Tech 86-; Engl; Law.

**HARRIS, JACQUELINE H,** Saint Pauls Coll, Lawrenceville, VA; SR; BA; Non-Dnmntnl Bible Stdy Grp 89-; Provost List 87-89; Alpha Kappa Mu Chpln 90-; Hons Day Com Ushrs Com 90-; Shorts Chpl RZUA Church Fincl Sec 89-; Mt Zion Yng Adult Choir Treas; Nwspr Stdnt Mnth; Lobbyist Gen Assem; Bus Ed; Admin Exec.**

**HARRIS, JAMES P,** Bellarmine Coll, Louisville, KY; JR; BA; Pre Law Soc 90-; Delta Epsilon Sigma; Intrnshp UPS Supervsr; Bus; Law.

**HARRIS, JAMES R,** Wv Univ, Morgantown, WV; JR; BSME; BSA Asst Scoutmstr 81-; March Band 89-90; Deans List 89-91; Tau Beta Pi; Proffsnl Engr Intnshp 90-; Eagle Scout 88; IM Bsktbl; Mech Engr; Engrng.

**HARRIS JR, JAMES R,** Abraham Baldwin Agri Coll, Tifton, GA; FR; BA; Radio Mngr 90-; Bapt Stdnt Un 90-; Phi Theta Kappa; Cmptr Sci; Eng Radio Brdcstng.

**HARRIS, JANICE L,** Savannah St Coll, Savannah, GA; SO; BS; Phase II 89-90; Phi Beta Lambda 90-; Savannah Hm Fr Grls Vol; Jr Wmmn Excllnc; Deans Lst; Hnrs Lst; Bus; Mngmnt Infrmtn Sys.

**HARRIS, JEANNIE M,** Va St Univ, Petersburg, VA; SO; BED; Hm Econ Educ; Educ/Zoology.

**HARRIS, JEFFREY S,** Ms St Univ, Miss State, MS; FR; BA; Professional Glf Mgmt Clb 90-; Bsn; Class A Glf Professional.

**HARRIS, JENNIFER J,** Univ Of Louisville, Louisville, KY; JR; MENG; Tau Beta Pi; Phi Eta Sigma; Amer Inst Chem Engrs Asst Sec 90-; Kodak Schlr; Chem Eng; Eng.

**HARRIS, JENNIFER M,** Va Commonwealth Univ, Richmond, VA; FR; BA; Art; Prntmkng.

**HARRIS, JOY M,** Univ Of Sc At Columbia, Columbia, SC; SR; Piedmont Scty 88-; Kappa Delta Pi 89-; Gamma Beta Phi Hstrn 90-.

**HARRIS I, KEITH W,** Suffolk Comm Coll Eastern Cmps, Riverhead, NY; SO; AS; Pi Alpha Sigma; Northfork Sccr Brd Dir 87-; Frmn Sprvsrs 86-; Bus Admn.

**HARRIS, KELLI L,** Univ Of Sc At Columbia, Columbia, SC; SR; BA; Elem Ed/Psychlgy; Tch.

**HARRIS, KENYANA L,** Hampton Univ, Hampton, VA; FR; Gospel Choir 90; Players/Company 90-; S C Pre-Alumni Asst Sec 90-; Spch Cmnctns; Entertainment Lawyer.

**HARRIS, KIMBERLY A,** Jackson St Univ, Jackson, MS; JR; Math Clb 89-; NAACP 89-90; Miss Pi Mu Epsln; Alpha Lambda Delta 90-; Pi Mu Epsln; Alpha Chi; Delta Sigma Theta Corr Sec; Bell Comm Rsch Intshp 90; AT/T Lab Intshp; Math; MBA.

**HARRIS, KIMBERLY K,** Salisbury St Univ, Salisbury, MD; SR; BA; Deans Lst; Bio; Optmtry Schl.

**HARRIS, KRISTEN E,** Columbus Coll Of Art & Design, Columbus, OH; SR; BFA; Bttclli Stdnt Ltrry Pblctn 90-; Rtl Advrtsng; Advrtsng Dsgn.

**HARRIS, LA MONICA M,** S U N Y Coll At Brockport, Brockport, NY; FR; BA; OSAD LDI SMART 90-; Spl Friend 90-; CJ Towers Inc 90-; History; Law.

**HARRIS, LANCE A,** Marshall University, Huntington, WV; JR; BBA; NMA V P Pub Rltns 90-; Deans Lst 88-; Var Track Crs Cntry Tms 88-; Mgmt; Bus Admn.

**HARRIS, LATICIA G,** Savannah St Coll, Savannah, GA; SO; BA; Mngmnt Finance.

**HARRIS, LAVETA D,** Lasell Coll, Newton, MA; SO; AA; Chrs 90-; Intl Clb 89-; Tour Gde 90-; Lib Arts; Tch Spec Ed.

**HARRIS, LEIGH ALLISON,** Memphis St Univ, Memphis, TN; JR; BA; British Lit/Engl.

**HARRIS, LEON XAVIER,** Alcorn St Univ, Lorman, MS; FR; BS; Combat Med Spclst U S Arm Frc; Biology; Med.

**HARRIS, LINDA A,** Alcorn St Univ, Lorman, MS; SO; MBA; Busn/Acctng.

**HARRIS, LINDA C,** Sue Bennett Coll, London, KY; SO; BA; Sigma Nu 89-; Creative Writing 89-90; Phi Theta Kappa 90-; Silver Medal/Gold Medal; Edctn/Elem; Spcl Ed; Tch.

**HARRIS, LINDA P,** Wilmington Coll, New Castle, DE; SR; BS; Delta Epsilon Rho 90; Forum To Advance Minorities In Eng Parent Com Treas 89-; BDEA 84-; Customer Serv Rep Du Pont Co; AAS Univ DE 75; Human Resource Mgmnt.

**HARRIS, LISA A,** Norfolk St Univ, Norfolk, VA; JR; French Clb 87-; Intl Clb 88-89; Engl/For Lang Majors Clb 89-; Alpha Kappa Mu 90-; Phi Theta Kappa 88-89; Hon Annual Awrds Convctn 90-; Deans Lst 87-; Easter Seal Soc Spcl Projs Coord 86-; Amer Inst For For Study Area Dir 87-; French Tchr.

**HARRIS, LIZETTE A,** Hofstra Univ, Hempstead, NY; FR; BA; African Pople Orgztn Nwsltr Edtr 90; Clgte Sci/Tech Entry Prog 90; J Rector Sci Clb 90; Pltcl Sci; Law.

**HARRIS, LORI A,** Univ Of South Al, Mobile, AL; SR; BED; Engl Clb; Lang Arts.

**HARRIS, LYNDA A,** Castleton St Coll, Castleton, VT; JR; BA; Art Stdnt Leag Sec; Art; Grad Schl/Tchng.

**HARRIS, MALENDA G,** Ms St Univ, Miss State, MS; SR; BA; Stdnt Assn Chrmn 89-90; Pnhllnc Jdcl Bd 90; Alpha Gamma Delta Alumni Chrmn 88-90; Pres Lst 88; Deans Lst 87 89-; Psychlgy; Law.

**HARRIS, MAQUILA CHUVETTE,** Al A & M Univ, Normal, AL; FR; BS; Acad Hon Rl 90-; Dns Lst 90-91; Comp Sci; Comp Prog.

**HARRIS, MAR SHON K,** Lane Coll, Jackson, TN; SO; Omega Psi Phi; Bsbl 90; Elem Ed.

**HARRIS, MARIO D,** Tougaloo Coll, Tougaloo, MS; JR; BS; SGA 90-; Chr 88-; Dnc Grp 89-; Dns Lst; Eng-Pre Law; Law.

**HARRIS, MARK C,** Longwood Coll, Farmville, VA; SO; BS; Co-Capt Wrstlng Tm/Acdmc All Amrcn Stheastrn Rgnl Chmpn Tm Rep Athltc Comm 90-; Bsns Admnstrtn; Sales Mngmnt.

**HARRIS, MARTHA G,** Tn Wesleyan Coll, Athens, TN; SR; Phi Theta Kappa 88-89; Alpha Chi 90-; Athens Area Chmbr Cmrc Awd; Kiwanis Clb Acdmc Awd 90-; Tn Wesleyan Acctng Awd; Tellico Plns Elem PTO 88-; AA Hiwassee Clge 89; BS; Acctng/ Bsn Mgmt; Acctnt/CPA.

**HARRIS, MARY H,** Va Commonwealth Univ, Richmond, VA; JR; BS; Phi Theta Kappa 84-85; Cum Laude Patric Henry Comm Coll 85; Rsrch Grant; Undergrad Rsrch Grant Prog Comm Richmond Mcv; AS Patrick Henry Comm Coll Martinsville Va 24112 85; Nursing.

**HARRIS, MEHGANN E,** Colby Sawyer Coll, New London, NH; SR; BS; Deans List 90; Varsity Lacrosse 87; Varsith Soccer 87-90; Sports Sci; Corp Fitness/Nrsng.

**HARRIS, MICHAEL D,** Livingston Univ, Livingston, AL; FR; BA; Mgmt.

**HARRIS, MICHAEL O,** Al A & M Univ, Normal, AL; FR; BA; Deans List 90; Pres Awrd 90; Math; Mech Eng.

**HARRIS, MICHELLE L,** Univ Of Nc At Greensboro, Greensboro, NC; SO; BS; SNCAE 89-; Deans Lst 90; Elem Ed; Tchng.

**HARRIS, MICHELLE RENEE,** Goucher Coll, Towson, MD; SR; BA; SGA 88-; Math/Comp Sci Clb Sec 87-; Soc Comm Hs Sec 88; Commnty Aux; C L Telinde Schlrshp 87-; MD Sentorl/ Gen St Schlrshp; Lothian Ruritan Schlrshp; Cls 1905 Flwshp; MD Schlr Athlt 87-; Soc Tchn Cmnctn Tech Rprt Awrd 90; Math/ Comp Sci; Sftwr Engr.

**HARRIS, PAMELA K,** Memphis St Univ, Memphis, TN; SO; BA; Blck Schlrs Unlmtd 90-; Blck Stdnt Assn 90-; Edctnl Spprt Pgm 89-; Blck Schlrs Unlmtd 90-; Zeta Phi Beta Sec 90-; Deans Lst; Ordr Omega Clb; Hghst GPA Pan-Hllnc Cncl; IM Bsktbl; Educ; Tchr.

**HARRIS, PAMELA S,** Univ Of Southern Ms, Hattiesburg, MS; JR; BA; Stdnt Spch Hrng Assc 90-; Cath Stdnt Assc 90-; Gamma Beta Phi 90; Spch Lang Pathlgy; Spch Thrpy.

**HARRIS, PATRICIA K,** Broward Comm Coll, Ft Lauderdale, FL; FR; AA; Phi Theta Kappa; Pres Lst; Frst Plc Ltrs Natl Lg Amer Pen Wm; Phrmcy; Nclr Phrmcy.

**HARRIS, PATSY J,** East Central Comm Coll, Decatur, MS; FR; BS; IM Ftbl/Bsktbl 90-; Phi Theta Kappa 90-; Mu Alpha Theta 90-; Math/Comp Sci; Bus.

**HARRIS, PEGGY L,** Norfolk St Univ, Norfolk, VA; SR; BA; Alpha Epsilon Rho; Brdcstng Soc; Alpha Kappa Mu 89; Spartan Alpha Tau 88-89; All Amer Schlr 89; Mass Cmmnctns; Telecmmnctns.

**HARRIS, PENNY J,** Univ Of Ga, Athens, GA; FR; BBA; Cmuty Serv Rep 90-; Acctg; Bus.

**HARRIS, PETER E,** Medical Coll Of Ga, Augusta, GA; FR; DMD; BS Univ Of GA 90; Dntstry.

**HARRIS, PHILIP T,** Southern Coll Of Tech, Marietta, GA; SR; Amer Assoc Text Colorist Chemist 87-; Co-Op Prog Thomaston Mills Inc 87-90; Apparel Foundation Schlrshp 87-; IM Sports 86-; BS; Apparel/Textile Engrg; Division Auality Coord.

**HARRIS, PHILIP W,** Va Highlands Comm Coll, Abingdon, VA; SO; BA; Eckerd Drug Store Mgr 85-; Bus Mgmt.

**HARRIS, PHYLLIS L,** Ms Univ For Women, Columbus, MS; JR; BS; SMAE 90-; Pres Lst 90; Kappa Delta Epsilon Pub Chrmn; Elem Tchr.

**HARRIS, RACHEL M,** Ms St Univ, Miss State, MS; FR; Comm 82; Phi Eta Sigma; Alpha Lambda Delta; Gamma Beta Phi; Blck Acdmc Awrd; Pres Schlr; Aerobics; Biol Sci; Ped.

**HARRIS, RAMONA HINES,** Phillips Jr Coll Charlotte, Charlotte, NC; GD; SGA 89-; Deans List Pres List 89-; Phi Beta Llambda; Sprngfst Vol 81-91; Jazz Charlotte/Westfest/Tutor/Corp Cup; Doc Cntrl Asst 79; AAS Phllps Jr Clg 90; Sec Scnc.

**HARRIS, RAYSHON E,** Howard Univ, Washington, DC; SO; BA; Hmcmg Strng Comm Var Show Coord 89-; Stdnt Ambssdr 89-; Undergrad Stdnt Assmbly Comm Rep 90-; Comm Stdnt Cncl Comm Otrch Dir 90-; BET D C T V Intrn Dir/Prodcr; WHMM Ch 32 Stdnt Trnee; Tele Prod; T V Wrtr/Prodcr/Dir.

**HARRIS, REBECCA A,** Ky St Univ, Frankfort, KY; FR; BA; Dns Lst; Lib Arts; Med Schl Psychtrst.

**HARRIS, RENEE,** Tougaloo Coll, Tougaloo, MS; SR; BS; Bible Study/Flwshp Pres 90-; Bio; Tch.

**HARRIS, RENEE J,** Longwood Coll, Farmville, VA; GD; Kappa Delta Pi; BS 90; Elem Ed; Tch N K-4.

**HARRIS SR, RICHARD J,** Mount Olive Coll, Mount Olive, NC; JR; BS; Psi Chi Treas; Phi Theta Kappa; Amer Mltry Scty; NAACP; USAF Rtrd 88; AA Wayne Comm Coll 90; Psych; Crr Cnslng.

**HARRIS, ROBIN L,** Fayetteville St Univ, Fayetteville, NC; JR; BA; Nwspapr Rprtr 88-89; Psych Clb Sec 90-; Hlth Svcs Clb 90-; Psych; Psych Res.

**HARRIS II, RONALD C,** Pa St Univ Delaware Cty Cmps, Media, PA; FR; BA; Bus Admin.

**HARRIS, ROY W,** Oh Univ, Athens, OH; GD; DO; Sprts Med/Atlas/ Fmly Med Clbs; IM Ftbl/Sftbl; Alpha Epsilon Delta; Phi Sigma Gamma; Sigma Sigma Phi; Deans Lst; Amer Ostpthc Assoc; Amer Med Assoc; Ohio Ostpthc Assoc; Ohio St Med Assoc; Stu Gov Athlts 90; ACGP; Med Ostpthc; Physcn.

**HARRIS, SALLIE L,** Ashland Comm Coll, Ashland, KY; SR; BSN; Deans Lst 74-75; Ashlnd Oil Inc Sbldgr Clrk; Crnr Tobacco Shp; Lbr CSX Rlrd; Scl Wrk; Drug Alcohol Rehab.

**HARRIS, SANDI J,** Univ Of Sc At Aiken, Aiken, SC; SR; BA; Pre Law Clb VP 90-; French Clb Pres 89-; Stdnt Alumni Ambssdrs 90-; Gamma Beta Phi 89-; Outstndng Stdnt Pltcl Sci Awd 89-90; Pres List 89-; Rsrch Asst 89-; Pltcl Sci; Govt Serv.

**HARRIS, SERITHA Y,** Middle Tn St Univ, Murfreesboro, TN; JR; BA; Adv Club 89-; Dance Tm/Pom Pon Squad 89-90; Vlybl Ftbl 88-90; Adv; Art Dir.

**HARRIS, SHANNON J,** Al A & M Univ, Normal, AL; JR; BA; Dnc Trp 88-89; Nwspr Typst 90; Kappa Swthrt 90-; Psychlgy; Lwyr.

**HARRIS, SHARON E,** Miami Jacobs Jr Coll Of Bus, Dayton, OH; SR; AA; PSI; Info Procsng; Medcl Fld.

**HARRIS, SHEILA K,** Ky St Univ, Frankfort, KY; SR; BA; Band 86-88; Choir/Gspl Ens Dir VP 86-; Std Govt Sntr/Pres 87-; Natl Hnry Bnd Sor Serv Org 90-; Natl Clgt Achvmnt Awd 90-; US Dpt Agri Coop; Sclgy; Educ Cnslng/Law.

**HARRIS, SHERRI L,** Liberty Univ, Lynchburg, VA; SR; BS; LACT 89; Kappa Delta Pi 90; Elem Ed; Tchr.

**HARRIS, SHERYL L,** Marywood Coll, Scranton, PA; JR; BA; Wrtng Clb VP 88-; Campus Mnstry Publ Chrprsn 88-; Lit Mag 90-; Lambda Iota Tau 90-; Delta Epsilon Sigma 90-; Engl; Wrtng.

**HARRIS, SHONDA LYNN,** Walker Coll, Jasper, AL; FR; BS; Stdt Gvt Assoc Sec 90-; Compass Clb 90-; Phi Theta Kappa Pres 90-; Hmcmng Ct 90-; Freshman Favorite 90-; Chemistry; Pharmacy.

**HARRIS, SONDRA T,** Univ Of Southern Ms, Hattiesburg, MS; JR; BSBA; Beta Gamma Sigma; Acctg Clerk/Prsnl Ofcrs Asst 87-90; Acctg; CPA.

**HARRIS, STEPHANIE M,** Longwood Coll, Farmville, VA; SR; Phys Educ Mjrs Clb 88-90; Delta Psi Kappa Pr 88-90; Acad Achvmnt Awrd 90; BS 90; Phys Educ Tchr.

**HARRIS, STEPHENIE G,** Univ Of Sc At Spartanburg, Spartanburg, SC; FR; BA; Sftbl 90-; Cmptr Sci; Cmptr Pgm.

**HARRIS, STERLING BARNARD,** Univ Of Sc At Columbia, Columbia, SC; SR; Mrchng Bnd/Pep Bnd Sqd Ldr 87-89; NAACP/SYMPHNC Bnd Sectn Ldr 88; Omcrn Dlta Kappa; Gspl Chr/Assn Of Afro Amer Stdnts Membrshp Comm 88-89; Omicron Delta Kappa; Gldn Ky; Dns Lst 87-89; Pres Hnr Lst; Kappa Kappa Psi; Alpha Phi Alpha Treas 89-90; Tch Band.

**HARRIS, SUNIL P,** Columbia Union Coll, Takoma Park, MD; JR; AA; Lttr Apprctn Washington Advntst Hosp Lab; Rsprtry Thrpy; Med.

**HARRIS, SUSAN L,** Salisbury St Univ, Salisbury, MD; SR; BA; Res Hall Cncl Pr 87-89; Flyr Nws Mag Ent Edtr 87-90; Clg Rep 88-; Phi Eta Sigma; Alpha Sigma Tau Hstrn 89-; Hnrs Grk Yr 90-; Alpha Sigma Tau Sr Yr 90-; Alpha Sigma Tau Otstdng Schlr Yr 90; Camps Life Awd 84-; IM Vlybl/Sftbl/F Hcky 87-; Comm/Pol Sci; Brdcst Jrnlsm.

**HARRIS, SUZANNE M,** Ms St Univ, Miss State, MS; JR; Arnold Air Soc Pldg Cmdr 88-89; Engl; Law.

**HARRIS JR, SYLVESTER J,** Alcorn St Univ, Lorman, MS; JR; BS; Stdnt Govt Chrmn; Indus Tech Clb Rep; Deans Lst; Merit Rl; Kappa Alpha Psi Hstrn; Golf Team Capt; Oasis Fox Masnc Ldg Deacon; Indus Tch Const; Arch.

**HARRIS, TAMARA L,** Univ Of Cincinnati-Clrmnt Coll, Batavia, OH; SO; ASSOC; Acctng Tech; Acct.

**HARRIS, TAMMARA T,** Le Moyne Owen Coll, Memphis, TN; SO; SGA Sen Athltc Affrs 90-; Pre Prfssnl Hlth Scty 89-; NAACP 90-; Prsdnts Schlr; Pr Cnslr 90-; Stdnt Cncrn Cmmtt 90-; Moses Julia Plough Schlrshp 89-; Clss Pres 90-; Blgy; RN.

**HARRIS, TAMMIE R,** Claflin Coll, Orangeburg, SC; SO; BA; Engl Clb Co Chr 90-; Tchrs Of The 21st Cntry Sec 90-; Alpha Kappa Alpha; Miss Hmcmng 90-; Miss Frshmn 89-90; Engl Educ.

**HARRIS, TANYA M,** Chattahoochee Vly St Comm Coll, Phenix City, AL; FR; AAS; Deans Lst 90-; Bus Mngmt.

**HARRIS, TANYA M,** Jackson St Univ, Jackson, MS; FR; BA; Alpha Lambda Delta 90-; Cmptr Sci; Cmptr Sales.

**HARRIS, TERESA L,** Fl St Univ, Tallahassee, FL; SR; BM; Tallahassee Symphny Orch 89-; Seminole Trchbearers; Glen Key 89-; Pi Kappa Lambda 90-; Sigma Alpha Iota Crspndng Sec 88-; Dns Lst 89; Music.

**HARRIS, TEREZ,** Faulkner Univ, Montgomery, AL; SO; Boys Club Of Amer; Natl Hnr Rl; Spnsh Hnr Socty; Sgnfcnt Achvmnt Awd 89; Best Def Bsktbl Player Of 89-90; Amy True Awd 90; Bsktbl; Sci/Math; Elec Engr.

**HARRIS, TERRI L,** Fl A & M Univ, Tallahassee, FL; SO; BA; VP Hatchett Pre/Law Clb VP 90; NAACP; Delta Signa Theta; Beta Alpha Chapter; Political Science/Minor Eng; Attend Law Schl.

**HARRIS, TERYL P,** Wallace St Comm Coll At Selma, Selma, AL; SO; Dns Lst 90-; Math.

**HARRIS, THELMA M,** Chattahoochee Vly St Comm Coll, Phenix City, AL; FR; Gamma Beta Phi; Off Admn; Bus; Word Proc.

**HARRIS IV, THOMAS Y,** Univ Of Ga, Athens, GA; GD; MED; Yrbk Phtgrphr 86; Coll Rpblcns 86; BA 90; Educ.

**HARRIS, TINA L,** Univ Of Montevallo, Montevallo, AL; GD; Stdnt Tchng 90; BA; Educ; Tch.

**HARRIS, TODD C,** The Kings Coll, Briarclf Mnr, NY; SR; BS; Intrnshp Hudson Heritage Grp Mktng Assist 90; Intrnshp MCI Telecomm Corp Mktg Assist; IM Ftbl/Hcky/Bsktbl; Bus Admin/Econ; Mktng.

**HARRIS, TRESSY R,** Univ Of Tn At Martin, Martin, TN; FR; Chi Omega 90-; Occptnl Thrpy.

**HARRIS, TYRONE,** Al A & M Univ, Normal, AL; SO; BS; Baptist Stdnt Union 90-; Drug Task Force 90-; NAACP 89-; Acctng; CPA.

**HARRIS, VICKIE L,** Al St Univ, Montgomery, AL; GD; BS; Mrhng Crimson Piper Bnd 83-86; Flag Corp/Co-Cptn 84-86f Song Ldr 84-85; Acad Hnr Roll Biology 90-; BS; Biology; Medl Assist.

**HARRIS, WENDY L,** North Greenville Coll, Tigerville, SC; SO; BS; Flwshp Chrstn Athls 89-; Cmps Ambsdrs 89-; Bptst Stdnt Un 89-; Stdnt Govt Soph Pres 90-; Am Lgn Awd 90-; AS; Educ; Tch Chldrn.

**HARRIS, WILLIAM D,** Anne Arundel Comm Coll, Arnold, MD; FR; AA; Eng.

**HARRIS, WILLIAM R,** David Lipscomb Univ, Nashville, TN; SO; BA; Intrnshp WLAC Radio; Spch Cmnctn; Brdcstng Mass Media.**

**HARRIS, YOLANDA A,** Al A & M Univ, Normal, AL; JR; BA; Telecomm Clb Sec 90-; SGA Jr Cls Rep 90-; Natl Asc Advncd Clrd People 89-; Co-Op Wrk Exp USDA Cntrctng Spec; Telecomm; Bus Lawyer.

**HARRIS, YOLANDA M,** Ms St Univ, Miss State, MS; FR; BS; Blk Awns Awd Outsntnd Achmt 90-; Pres Schlr 90; Deans List; Math; Secondary Ed.

**HARRIS, YOLANDA M,** Jackson St Univ, Jackson, MS; SO; BS; Alpha Lambda Delta Secr 89-; SG Asst Secr 90-; Chem Soc 89-; Alpha Lambda Delta Secr 89-; Minority Bio Med Rsrch Support 90-; Bio; Phrmcy.

**HARRIS-COLEMAN, JUDITH,** Atlantic Comm Coll, Mays Landing, NJ; SO; Registar 90; Nrsg; Psych Nrs.

**HARRISON, ADELIA H,** Univ Of Rochester, Rochester, NY; SO; BM; Estmn Sch Music Orntn Pres 89-90; Muisc Prfrmnc.

**HARRISON, AMY M,** Wv Univ At Parkersburg, Parkersburg, WV; FR; AAS; Data Proc; Cmptr Prog.

**HARRISON, ANDRE L,** Al St Univ, Montgomery, AL; JR; BED; Tutor Engl Math Cmptr Lab Asst; Engl/Lng Arts; Tch/Prfssr.

**HARRISON, ANGELA C,** Saint Pauls Coll, Lawrenceville, VA; SR; BA; NAACP; Alpha Kappa Mu; Alpha Kappa Alpha; English; Law.

**HARRISON, ANGELA K,** Walker Coll, Jasper, AL; SO; BS; SGA Rep 89-; Phi Theta Kappa 90-; Cir K 90-; Coll Pres Schlrhsp 89-; Big B Drugs Pharm Asst 90-; Stars/Bars Pgnt Altrnt 90-; Chem; Pharm.

**HARRISON, ANGELA L,** Vance Granville Comm Coll, Henderson, NC; Dns Lst; Csmtlgy.

**HARRISON, BELINDA J,** Univ Of South Al, Mobile, AL; FR; BS; Bus Acctg; CPA.

**HARRISON, BETH A,** Merrimack Coll, North Andover, MA; SR; BS; Stdnt Govt Rep 87-90; Orntn Coord 88-90; Amer Mktg Assoc; Alpha Mu Alpha; Pres Schlr; Coop Educ Stdnt 88-90; Stdy Abrd Paris France 90; Mrktg/Frnch; Sls.

**HARRISON, BETTY S,** Mayland Comm Coll, Spruce Pine, NC; FR; AS; Pres Lst; Bus; Mdcl Ofc Tech.

**HARRISON, BRENTON P,** Morgan St Univ, Baltimore, MD; SO; USAA All Am Schlrs; Natl Lib Med Undergrad Rsrch Study Pgm; Elec Eng.

**HARRISON, BRIAN N,** Bowie St Univ, Bowie, MD; SO; BA; Bus; Acctg.

**HARRISON, CAROL L,** Commonwealth Coll, Virginia Beach, VA; FR; MA; Mdcl.

**HARRISON, CHERYL A,** Duquesne Univ, Pittsburgh, PA; FR; BS; Pharm.

**HARRISON, CHERYL E,** Marshall University, Huntington, WV; GD; CERT; Alpha Xi Delta 68-71; BA 71; MA COGS 75; Preshcl Hndcpd.

**HARRISON, CHRISTA D,** Lenoir Rhyne Coll, Hickory, NC; SR; Intl Club VP 90-; Chi Beta Phi 90-; Mu Sigma Epsilon 90-; Alpha Lambda Delta 89-90; Biology Achvmnt Awrd 89; Biology; Optometry.

**HARRISON, CHRISTA D,** Volunteer St Comm Coll, Gallatin, TN; FR; BA; Elem Educ; Tchr.

**HARRISON, CHRISTOPHER J,** Hampshire Coll, Amherst, MA; SO; Aspen Substance Abuse Pgm; Writers Conf; Writing; Child Educ.

**HARRISON, CLARISSA C,** Volunteer St Comm Coll, Gallatin, TN; JR; AS; Acctg Clb; Oprylnd Htl-Nashvl TN; Acctg-Mcrcomp; Acctg.

**HARRISON, CLIFTON,** City Univ Of Ny Baruch Coll, New York, NY; GD; AAS NY City Tech Clg 87; Acctg; CPA.

**HARRISON, DANA L,** Longwood Coll, Farmville, VA; SO; MBA; Alpha Delta Pi; Psy/Spec Ed.

**HARRISON, DAWN M,** S U N Y Coll Of Tech At Frmgdl, Farmingdale, NY; SO; AAS; Aerobcs; Bwlng; Tnns; Deans Lst; Grphc Dsgn; Advrtsng Agncy.

**HARRISON, DEBORAH G,** Rivier Coll, Nashua, NH; SO; BA; Sunset Rivier Adptn Com Brd 89-; PTO Treas 88-90; Sun Schl Tchr 87-90; Secr 73-89; Diploma Chandler Schl Women 73; Psychlgy Sclgy.

**HARRISON, DONNA E,** Univ Of Montevallo, Montevallo, AL; SR; BS; Res Hall Assn Pres 89-90; Res Asst 89-; Kappa Delta Pi 89-; Sigma Alpha Pi 90-; Lambda Sigma Pi 90-; Vldctrn Schlrshp 88-; Deans Lst Pres Lst 88-90; J R Churchill Schlrshp Awd; Educ Hrng Imprd; Grad Sch.

**HARRISON, ELIZABETH A,** Univ Of Ms Main Cmps, University, MS; JR; BED; Schl Pblctn 88-; French Clb 88-90; Spnsh Clb 89-90; Golden Key; Pi Delta Phi; AA Itawamba Comm Clg 90; French/Spanish; Sec Educ.**

**HARRISON, FRANKLIN R,** Central St Univ, Wilberforce, OH; FR; FBLA 89-90; St Pauls Yth Grp 87-; Track/Cross Cntry Capt 88-90; Acctg; Fin Advsr.

**HARRISON, HELEN C,** Birmingham Southern Coll, Birmingham, AL; SO; BA; Zeta Tau Alpha Schlrshp Chrmn; John Franklin Locke Prize; Math; Med.

**HARRISON, IN-HYANG P,** Va Commonwealth Univ, Richmond, VA; SR; BA; AM Cntr For Design; Korean Clb; Cmmnctn Art/Dsgn Phtgrphy; Dsgnr.

**HARRISON, JAMES T,** Radford Univ, Radford, VA; SR; BS; Crmnl Justice Clb 89-90; Math Clb 87-88; Pi Gamma Mu 90-; Deans List 90; Crmnl Justice; Law.

**HARRISON, JANEEN M,** City Univ Of Ny Baruch Coll, New York, NY; SO; BA; Theatron Clb; Dance Clb Treas; Mgmnt.

**HARRISON, JENNIFER S,** Tallahassee Comm Coll, Tallahassee, FL; FR; AA; Hstry; Rsrch/Wrtg/Tchg.

**HARRISON, JERRE D,** Univ Of Nc At Greensboro, Greensboro, NC; SR; BS; Phi Theta Kappa 88-; Intrnshp 4th Gr Peck Elem; Deans List 90-; Teachers Asstnt; Early Childhood Educ; Teacher.

**HARRISON, JERRY M,** Middle Tn St Univ, Murfreesboro, TN; SR; BS; STEA 90-; Proj Help; Non Trad Stdnt Org 90-; Columbia St Comm Clg Deans List; Univ Deans List 90-; IM Bsktbl/Ftbl/Sftbl; Main Sprvsr Cty Of Columbia Prks/Rec Dept Columbia TN 78-84; Soc Stds/Hist; Sec Educ.

**HARRISON JR, JOHN A,** Ny Theological Seminary, New York, NY; SR; Harlem YMCA Krt Clb; Prnc Hll Mason Rec Sec; AIDS Inttv Prog 90; New Breed Dynamic Yth Inc 83-; Dcmntry Mother AME Zion Chrch 86; Dept Chrstn Educ; Assmbly Chrstn Edctrs; Yth Mnstr 86-; AA Fashion Inst Tech 77; BA; Thlgy; Pstrl Care/Smnry Prfssr.

**HARRISON, KAY A,** Comm Coll Algny Co Algny Cmps, Pittsburgh, PA; SO; CERT; Secretary 84-; Science; Medical Tech.

**HARRISON, LORI L,** Univ Of Montevallo, Montevallo, AL; FR; BBA; Accounting; Cpa.

**HARRISON, LORRIE L,** Kent St Univ Stark Cmps, North Canton, OH; FR; BA; Hstry; Scndry Educ Tchr-Hstry.

**HARRISON, MARGARET R,** Wv Inst Of Tech, Montgomery, WV; SR; BS; AICHE 89-; Tau Beta Pi 89-; Grl Scts 87-; Chem Eng.

**HARRISON, MARIE A,** Columbia Greene Comm Coll, Hudson, NY; SO; AAS; Head Strt Vol; Fctry Wrkr; Human Serv; Sbstnce Abuse Cnslng.

**HARRISON, MARY C,** Univ Of Nc At Charlotte, Charlotte, NC; SO; BA; Prod Asst Univ Times 89-90; Phi Eta Sigma; Kokenes Awd 90; Engl/French.

**HARRISON, MARY D,** Salisbury St Univ, Salisbury, MD; SO; BS; Deans Stdnt Advsry Bd Perdue Schl Bus; Acctg; CPA.

**HARRISON, MONICA P,** Longwood Coll, Farmville, VA; JR; Longwood Abmassdrs; Phi Beta Lambda Pres 90-; Phi Kappa Phi; Sigma Kappa Sis Act Chr; Winne Schlrshp; Bus; Mktg.

**HARRISON, NICOLA,** Tn St Univ, Nashville, TN; JR; BS; Martial Arts Tm 88-89; Biology; Med.

**HARRISON, REBECCA G,** Univ Of Va Clinch Valley Coll, Wise, VA; JR; Psych.

**HARRISON, ROBBIE B,** Univ Of South Al, Mobile, AL; JR; BS; Mgmt; Opertn Systms Mgr.

**HARRISON, ROBIN D,** Livingston Univ, Livingston, AL; SO; Hstrcl Scty 90-; Schlrshp; Bus; Admin Asst.

**HARRISON, SHARON A,** Univ Of Montevallo, Montevallo, AL; SR; BS; Deans Lst 89-; Pres Lst 90-; Kappa Delta Pi 90-; Lambda Sigma Pi; Val Schlrshp 88-; Chrldr 89-; Elem Educ; Tchr.

**HARRISON, TERESA D,** Norfolk St Univ, Norfolk, VA; SR; BA; Hm Ec Rltd Occptns 82-84; Future Bus Ldrs Amer 80-82; Judges Prstgs Awd 83-84; Ntl Yth Awd 83-84; Fash Dsgn Bus; Fine Arts Ed; Fash Dsgn/Merch.

**HARRISON, TERRY PATTERSON,** Piedmont Tech Coll, Greenwood, SC; FR; BA; Bus; Bankng.

**HARRISON, THADDEUS F,** Jackson St Univ, Jackson, MS; SO; BS; Alpha Lambda Delta; Pi Mu Epsilon; Eng Rsrch Cntr/ Comptnl Fld Sim; Dns Lst; Pres Lst; IM Bsktbl; Math; Rsrch Eng.

**HARRITON, FRANCIS W,** Mount Aloysius Jr Coll, Cresson, PA; FR; AD; Occptnl Thrpy Clb 90-; Phi Theta Kappa; Occptnl Thrpy.

**HARROD, BILLIE J,** Ky St Univ, Frankfort, KY; SO; ADN; Stdnt Govt Pres 90-; Natl Stdnt Nurses Assoc Inc 90-; Sot Of Nrsng Prfsnls; Whos Who In Am Nrsng; Hospice Vol 90-; Dir Of Work Activity Mentally & Phys Handicapped 86-89; Reg Nurse.

**HARROD, JERI R,** Ms St Univ, Miss State, MS; SR; Acctng Scty 89-90; Beta Alpha Psi 90-; Gamma Beta Phi 89-90; Acdmc Schlrshp 87-; Dance Tm 87-88; BPA; Acctng; Auditing.

**HARROLD, ANGELA M,** Fl A & M Univ, Tallahassee, FL; FR; BA; Phi Eta Sigma; Leander L Boykin Schlp; Univ Schlp; Elec Engr; Cmptr Engr.

**HARROLD, KAREN K,** Univ Of Miami, Coral Gables, FL; SR; BSC; Wmns Chrs 88-90; Alpha Epsilon Rho 89-; Phi Lambda Pi Chpln 88-; Pres Hon Roll; Deans List; Outstndng Brdcstng Sr; TV Intrn 90; Brdcstng/Msc.

**HARRY, DEAN R,** Nc Central Univ, Durham, NC; GD; JD; Pres Clsc Wnrs 87-; BA Wash Univ 73; Law.

**HARRY, NANCY S,** Bethany Coll, Bethany, WV; JR; BA; Natl Rehab Assn 82-; OH Rehab Assn Jb Plcmnt Dis Pres 89; OH Rehab Srvcs Cmmssn Voc Rehab Cnslr 83-; Psych.

**HARSA, SHARON R,** Univ Of Akron, Akron, OH; JR; BA; Beta Alpha Psi; Acdmc Schlrshp; Deans Lst; Accntng; Pblc Accntnt.

**HARSCH, CARL H,** Coll Of Charleston, Charleston, SC; FR; BA; Ret US Navy Mstr Chf Ptty Ofcr E9; Bsns; Fin.

**HARSCH JR, JOHN D,** S U N Y At Buffalo, Buffalo, NY; GD; MBA; Golden Key; M/T Intern; Mktg Cert; Written Skills Awrd; BS Univ Of Buffalo 90; Mktg/Bus/Mngmnt.

**HARSH, KIMBERLY A,** Comm Coll Algny Co Algny Cmps, Pittsburgh, PA; SO; MBA; Boys/Grls Clb Vol; Sec AP AR At Chujko Bros Inc 81; Engl; Elem Ed.

**HARSHAW, APRIL W,** Eckerd Coll, St Petersburg, FL; SR; BA; Cmps Tow Guide/Host 87-89; Pres Schlr 87-; Hnrs Schlr 87-; Yng Life Ldr 87-; Ford Apprentice Schlr 89-; Tennis Team 87-; Intl Stds; Intl Jrnlsm/Coll/Univ.

**HARSHMAN, AMY J,** Va Commonwealth Univ, Richmond, VA; SR; William Smith Sngrs 77-79; Peer Advsr 79-81; Jazz Ensemble 77-81; Deans List 79-81; Phi Beta Kappa; Magna Cum Laude; Phi Kappa Tau; BA William Smith Clg 81; Info Sys.

**HARSHMAN, MICHELLE D,** Bowling Green St Univ, Bowling Green, OH; FR; BA; Strdy Mrng Rec; Alpha Lambda Delta; Phi Eta Sigma; Ed; Tchng.

**HART, ANN L,** Christopher Newport Coll, Newport News, VA; JR; BA; Honda Exclnc Schlrshp Thomas Nelson Cmnty Clg 89-90; Co Rcpnt Pres Awd 90; Prsh Lfe Comm Chrmns 88-; Pstrl Cncl Rep 88-; Bkkpr Immaculate Conception Cath Chrch 90-; AS Thomas Nelson Cmnty Clg 90; Acctg; CPA.

**HART, CASSANDRA A,** Tougaloo Coll, Tougaloo, MS; JR; Acad Affairs Cncl 90-; Delta Sigma Theta; Econ; Law.

**HART, CHELSEA L,** Univ Of Nc At Greensboro, Greensboro, NC; JR; BS; Inter Advsry Comm 90-; Soc Work Clb 89-90; Alpha Delta Pi; Elderly Protective Servs; Marshal; Scholar 90-; Soc Work; Family Cnslng/Thrpy.

**HART, CHRISTOPHER E,** Greenville Tech Coll, Greenville, SC; FR; BS; Carl Hart Assoc VP; U S Navy VP Carl Hart Assoc; Elec Eng Tech.

**HART, DAVID P,** Northeast State Tech Comm Coll, Blountville, TN; SR; AAS; Mech Tech; Engr.

**HART, ELIZABETH H,** Univ Of Nc At Greensboro, Greensboro, NC; SR; BSN; Nrsng.

**HART, ERIKA E,** Talladega Coll, Talladega, AL; SR; BA; Soc Of Physics Stdnts 87; Stdnt Gvrnmnt Assoc Sntr 89-90; Pre-Alumni Cncl 87-99; Alpha Chi 89; Ntl Hnr Soc 89; Beta Kappa Chi 89; Alpha Kappa Alpha Pres 89; NAACP; US Envrnmntl Prot Agncy 90; Seven-Up Schlr 87; GEICO Schlr 87; Chrldr 89-; Physics; Eng.

**HART, FELICIA A,** Alcorn St Univ, Lorman, MS; FR; BA; ROTC; Gspl Choir; Bio Clb; Hmcmng Comm; Hnr Stdnt Org; Pres Schlr; IM Sftbl; Acctg; CPA.

**HART, GREGORY J,** Duquesne Univ, Pittsburgh, PA; JR; BS; Acctng; CPA.

**HART, JAMES A,** Alcorn St Univ, Lorman, MS; JR; BA; Hnr Stdnt Org 88-; Phi Beta Lambda 90-; Class V P; Alpha Kappa Mu 90-; Acctg.

**HART, JEFFREY T,** Barry Univ, Miami, FL; GD; BLS; Dns Lst; Busn/Soc Sci.

**HART, JEFFREY W,** Tallahassee Comm Coll, Tallahassee, FL; JR; AA; IM Bsktbl Vllybl Sftbl 88-90; Advrtsng Jrnlsm.

**HART, JIMMY D,** Anderson Coll, Anderson, SC; SO; BA; Corp Sprvsr; AS Tr Co Tech Coll 84; Relgn; Chrch Serv.

**HART, KAREN L,** Ms St Univ, Miss State, MS; JR; BBA; Stdnt Newspr 90; Stdnt Mag Exec Asst 90; Soc Adv Mngmt 90; Bus Mngmt.

**HART, KAREN L,** S U N Y Coll Of Tech At Frmgdl, Farmingdale, NY; GD; SADHA 88-90; ADHA; Cert St Of N J Dentistry 90; Den Tal Hygiene/Sci; Hygienist.

**HART, LA TONIA A,** Tougaloo Coll, Tougaloo, MS; FR; Bsn Adm.

**HART, MEGAN E,** Indiana Univ Of Pa, Indiana, PA; SO; BA; Res Hall Assoc VP 80; Jrnlsm; Pbl Rltns.

**HART, PATRICK E,** Longwood Coll, Farmville, VA; SR; Bio Club; Beta Beta Beta; Phi Kappa Phi; Bio; Med.

**HART, RAHMON S,** Slippery Rock Univ, Slippery Rock, PA; FR; BA; BAS 90-; Omega Psi Phi; Youth Home Vol 90-; Acadmc Schlrshp; Athltc Schlrshp 90-; SRU Man Of The Yr 90-; Varsty Ftbl 90-; Hlth Svc; Physcl Thrpy.

**HART, SHARON E,** Valdosta St Coll, Valdosta, GA; SR; SG Sen 90-; Rho Lambda 90-; Alpha Delta Pi Trnr 90-; BSED; Early Chldhd Ed; Tch.

**HART, SHARON L,** Univ Of Nc At Charlotte, Charlotte, NC; JR; BA; Tchng Flws; Delta Stdnt Chpt NCCTM Treas 90-; Gldn Ky; Phi Eta Sigma; Pi Mu Epsilon; Math; Educ.

**HART, STEPHANIE A,** Claflin Coll, Orangeburg, SC; SO; BA; Gospel Choir Pres 89-; Spanish Clb; Drama Clb; Hnr Prog; Alpha Kappa Alpha; NAACP; Stdt Support Serv Peer Cnslr 89-; Intrnshp Savannah River Site/Westinghouse; Math/Engrg Tech; Engrg.

**HART, STEPHANIE J,** Univ Of Southern Ms, Hattiesburg, MS; FR; BS; Mrchg Bnd; USM Cncrt Bnd; Hon Coll; Math; Tchng.

**HART, STEVEN D,** Lexington Comm Coll, Lexington, KY; FR.

**HART, TAMARA M,** Central Fl Comm Coll, Ocala, FL; SO; Hlth; Occupational Therapy.

**HART, TONYA F,** Savannah St Coll, Savannah, GA; JR; BSW; Baptist Stdnt Un V P Fnrsng 88-89; Soc Wrkrs 88-; Pi Gamma Mu 90; Big Brthers/Big Sisters; Rgnts Schlrshp; Pickens Cir Schlrshp 88; Soc Wrk; Crim Just.

**HARTEL, KIMBERLY,** Kent St Univ Kent Cmps, Kent, OH; SO; BA; Gerontology; Nrsng Hm Admin.

**HARTFORD, MICHAEL SEAN,** Radford Univ, Radford, VA; SR; BS; Univ Hnrs Pgm 90-; Acctg; Publ Acctg.

**HARTIG, JASON T,** Union Univ, Jackson, TN; JR; BA; Bapt Union; Mnstrl Assoc; SG 89-90; Sigma Tau Delta; Lit Publctn; Engl/Religion; Foreign Missions.

**HARTLEB, MARY BETH,** Upsala Coll, East Orange, NJ; GD; MS; AMMO P 87-88; Grad Asst Intrnshp 88; Deans Lst 87; SIOP 90-; SHRM 90-; 2 Yrs Prvs Exprnc HR Fld 88-90; BA 88; Hmn Rsrc Mgmt.

**HARTLEY, ADAM P,** Blue Mountain Coll, Blue Mountain, MS; FR; BA; Mnstrl Allnc; Bible; Pstrl.

**HARTLEY, ADONICIO H,** Morehouse Coll, Atlanta, GA; SO; BS; NSBE 90-; Endvr Spc Clb 90; Bys Grls Clb Mntr Tr; Gldn Key; NAACP Pblc Rltns Chr; Ronald E Mcnair Prjct Spc 89-; Amoco Schlr 89-90; IM Vllybll Capt 90; Eng; Law.

**HARTLEY, ALLEN D,** Univ Of Tn At Chattanooga, Chattanooga, TN; JR; BSE; Co-Op Sequoyah Nuclear PlantTVA; Elec Eng.

**HARTLEY, CHAD A,** Oh Univ, Athens, OH; FR; BA; Eng.

**HARTLEY, CHRISTINA A,** Toccoa Falls Coll, Toccoa Falls, GA; SR; BS; Music Educ Natl VP 90-; Concert Band Pres 90-; Music Schlrshp 87-; Music.

**HARTLEY, DAVID B,** Univ Of Al At Birmingham, Birmingham, AL; JR; BA; Ambsdrs; IFC Schlrshp Chmn; SG Srvcs Co Chmn; Lambda Chi Alpha VP 89-; Ambsdrs Schlrshp; Pres Hnrs; Dns Lst 89; Frat IM 89-; Hstry; Law.

**HARTLEY, DOUGLAS L,** Longwood Coll, Farmville, VA; SR; BS; Stdnt Edn Assn; Delta Sigma Phi Rush Chrmn Schlrshp Chmn 88-; Within Soc Frat 87-; Coll State Champ Wrstlng 87-88; Wrstlng Team Capt 88-89; Set Rec Most Wins Fr 87-88; Wrstlng State Champ/Stdnt Asst Coach 87-; Earth Sci; MS Admin.

**HARTLEY, ELIZABETH A,** Livingston Univ, Livingston, AL; SR; BED; Cmps Otrch Mnstry 87-; RA; IM Sftbl 87-88; Erly Chldhd Educf Tch/Cnslng.

**HARTLEY, HEIDI M,** Univ Of Pittsburgh At Bradford, Bradford, PA; JR; SGA 89-; Biology Clb 89-90; Stdnt Actvts 89-90; Amrcn Stds Clb; Alpha Lambda Delta 88-90; Zeta Alpha Chi 89-; Sftbl 89; Englsh.

**HARTLEY, JAHMAL D,** City Univ Of Ny City Coll, New York, NY; SO; BEE; Soc Blck Eng; Assc Cmptng Mach 89; Sony Music Enter Rec Oprtns; Wrstlng Tm 89-; Cntr Anlyss Strctrs Intrfc Rsrch Asst 90-; Elect Eng; Optic/Audio.**

**HARTLEY, JANET D,** Oh Univ, Athens, OH; SR; BM; Wind Symphny; Brass Choir; Trumpt Ensmbl; Univ Band; Choral Union; Jazz Band; Glee Club; OMEA Histrn 89-90; Sigma Alpha Iota Pres 89-90; Sigma Tau Alpha 89-90; Music Ed; HS Band Dir.

**HARTLEY, JOEL J,** Central Fl Comm Coll, Ocala, FL; FR; AA; Brain Bwl; Paper Spts Rep 90-; 2nd Pl Spts Nws 90-; 2nd Pl Sprts Feature In Patriot Prss 90-; IM; Bsns Admn; Acct/Sprtscstr.

**HARTLEY, MARK W,** Univ Of Sc At Spartanburg, Spartanburg, SC; JR; BS; Customer Svc Eng; Hist; Rsrch/Ed.

**HARTLEY, MARY PATRICIA,** Univ Of Sc At Columbia, Columbia, SC; SR; BA; Natl Educ Assn 90-91; Assn Continuing Higher Educ 89-; Stdnt Serv Spec 88-; Univ Of S Carolina 89; Comm On Military Educ 88-; History/Cnslng.

**HARTLEY, SCOTT M,** Bapt Bible Coll & Seminary, Clarks Summit, PA; FR; Bapt Bibl Indr Soccr Leag 90-; Soccr 90-; Elec Eng.

**HARTLEY, SHANE R,** Fl St Univ, Tallahassee, FL; JR; BA; Stdnt Sen Stdnt Govt 89-90; RA; Campus Crusade Christ 89-; IM Bsebl 90; Cmnctn; Ministry.

**HARTLEY, SHIRLEY L,** Wv Univ At Parkersburg, Parkersburg, WV; SO; AAS; Internatl Personnel Mgmnt Assoc 90-; Bus Admnstrn; Bus.

**HARTLEY, SUSAN R,** George Mason Univ, Fairfax, VA; SR; BS; Stu Educ Assc 89-; Gldn Ky 88-; Alpha Chi; Alpha Lambda Delta 87-; Kappa Delta Pi; Chi Omega 89-; Elem Educ; Tchng Admn.

**HARTLEY, WADE L,** Birmingham Southern Coll, Birmingham, AL; SR; BA; Pre Law Soc 89-; Dmcrts 89-; Mrtr Bd 90-; Orde Omega 90-; Chi Sigma Chi Pres 89-; Omicron Delta Kappa Treas 89-; Alpha Phi Omega 89-90; AA Jefferson Davis Jr Coll 89; Pltcl Sci/Hstry; Law.

**HARTLINE, SUSAN LAMAR,** Germanna Comm Coll, Locust Grove, VA; SO; AAS; Clg Nwspr 90; Phi Theta Kappa; Assn/ Prsrvtn VA Antiquities 88-; Docent Mary Ball Washington House 88-90; Gen Studies; Hstrc Prsrvtn/Ed.

**HARTMAN, ANNA L,** Univ Of Cin R Walters Coll, Blue Ash, OH; SO; ADN; Phi Theta Kappa; EMT 86-87; Payroll Adm 84-86; Nrsng/Wmns Studies; Ob/Emer Nrsng.

**HARTMAN, BILLIE S,** Bridgewater Coll, Bridgewater, VA; SR; BA; Foreign Lang Clb Pres 90-; MENC Treas 89-; Margie Ann Conner Schlrshp 87-; Accmpnst Chldrns Choir; Prince Wm Little Theatre 82-87; Bus Cmptrs Sales Recptnst 79-87; Assoc N VA Comm Clg 84; BA; Music; Tchr.

**HARTMAN, CHRISTINE A,** S U N Y Coll At Fredonia, Fredonia, NY; SR; BS; Msc Thrpy Clb VP 89-; Dnatl Assc Msc Thrpy Tres; Otstndng Frshmn 86-87; Hillman Schlrshp 86-87; Elizabeth Marsh Schlrshp 90-; Intrnshp Wassaic Dvlpmnt Ctr; Deans List; Msc Thrpy/Apld Voice.

**HARTMAN, CLIFFORD G,** S U N Y Coll Of Tech At Frmgdl, Farmingdale, NY; SO; BS; N Y Natl Guard 87-; AAS Suny Farmingdale; Indstrl Engr; Mgmt.

**HARTMAN, DEIRDRE A,** Univ Of Sc At Columbia, Columbia, SC; FR; BA; Stdnt Gov Fresh Cncl 90-; Carolina Pgm Union 90-F Sccr Clb 90-; Pltcl Sci.

**HARTMAN, ELIZABETH MERRY,** Marshall University, Huntington, WV; JR; BA; Res Hall Assn 89-; Res Advsr 90-; Prsbytrn Mnr Vol; Cnslng/Rehab.

**HARTMAN, HEATHER M,** Comm Coll Algny Co Algny Cmps, Pittsburgh, PA; SO; BA; Mktg; Advrtsg.

**HARTMAN, KEVIN M,** Le Moyne Coll, Syracuse, NY; JR; BA; Brockport Legal Inf Serv Legal Advsr 88-89; Young Democrats SUNY Brockport 88-89; Deans List Le Moyne Clge 90-91; KORE UPS Serv Comm Keeping Our Rep For Excl 90-91; Political Science; Law.

**HARTMAN, KRISTIE A,** Tn Temple Univ, Chattanooga, TN; FR; BS; Sigma Delta Rho; Coll Vlybl; Engl; Tchr.

**HARTMAN, MARK T,** Christopher Newport Coll, Newport News, VA; SO; BA; Psychlgy.

**HARTMAN, MICHAEL J,** Comm Coll Algny Co Algny Cmps, Pittsburgh, PA; SO; BA; VITA; Bus; Acctg.

**HARTMAN JR, RANDALL L,** Nova Univ, Ft Lauderdale, FL; MBA; Mech Eng Rckwll Int Cllns Ar Trnsprt Div 79-; BSME Le Tourneau Univ 79; Bus Admin; Mgmt.

**HARTMAN, TAMARA L,** Davis & Elkins Coll, Elkins, WV; SR; BS; Yrbk Staff Activ Commt Org Commt 87-89; Fashion Club VP 88-; Model; Hnr Prog 87-90; Hnrs Assoc 87-90f Phi Beta Lamdga 90-; Beta Alpha Beta 90-; Intshp Cato 285 Elkins 90; Fashion Merch/Mgt; Own Busn.

**HARTMAN, TIMOTHY W,** Central St Univ, Wilberforce, OH; FR; BS; ROTC 90-; US Army E-4 87-90; 62nd Army Bnd Ft Blss TX 87-90; Acctg/Bus Mgmt; Mltry Fnc/Acctg.

**HARTMANN, CHRISTOPHER M,** Western New England Coll, Springfield, MA; JR; BS; Cmptr Pgmr Intern 88-; Cmptr Sci; Cmptr Fld.

**HARTMANN II, RICHARD L,** Univ Of Akron, Akron, OH; JR; BSEE; IEEE 88-; Gldn Key; Elec Eng.

**HARTNER, ERIC M,** Univ Of Sc At Columbia, Columbia, SC; SO; BS; Cmptr Sci; Prgrmng.

**HARTNESS JR, CHARLES E,** Memphis St Univ, Memphis, TN; SR; BBA; Delta Sigma Pi VP Prof Actvties; Finance; Bus.

**HARTNETT, EILEEN BREGATTA,** Beaver Coll, Glenside, PA; GD; MED; Phi Delta Kappa; Tght Scndry Schls 73-83; BS 73; Ed.

**HARTNETT, WILLIAM J,** Coll Of Charleston, Charleston, SC; SR; BA; Hard Rock Miner; Logger; Commrcl Fishrmn; Constrctn Contrctr; Chem; Medcn.

**HARTSELL, JOEY S,** Life Coll, Marietta, GA; FR; CHRPR; Intrntn Chrprctc Assn 90-; Deans Lst; AS Physcl Sci NW CT Comm Clg 90; Chrprctc Sci.

**HARTSFIELD, LANCE A,** Tn Temple Univ, Chattanooga, TN; GD; M DIV; Singing Men 85-86; D L Moody Soc 85-89; Ordained Mnstr; Bible; Pstrt.

**HARTSOUGH, MELANIE T,** Juniata Coll, Huntingdon, PA; SR; BS; Choir/Choir Four 87-90; Soloist Handels Messiah 89; Madnigal Comm 89-90; Chem Club 87; Choreographer Musical 88; All Class Night 90; Honor Society 90; Amaco Fndtn Schlshp 87; Alumni Annual Sppt Schlrshp 87; Charles C Ellis Schlrshp 90; Chemistry; PHD/PHARMACOLOGY.

**HARTUNG, JEANNE M,** Allegheny Coll, Meadville, PA; SR; BS; Allegheny Chrstn Outrch Pblcty 87-; Hbt Hmnty Sec 89-; Wnd Symphny 87-; Lambda Sigma 88-89; Sp Ktchn 88-89; IM Vlybl 89-; Biolgy.

**HARTWELL, HEIDI L,** Schenectady County Comm Coll, Schenectady, NY; FR; Intrnshp Walt Disney World 91; Htl/Rstrnt Mgt; Rsrt Mgr.

**HARTWELL, THERESA A,** Radford Univ, Radford, VA; SR; Cathlc Stdnt Assoc Chrprsn 90-; Inst For Intrntl Econ Cpmpetvns Asst 88-90; Fld Hockey Team 87-88; BBA; Mktg; Sales.

**HARTWICK, GARY S,** George Mason Univ, Fairfax, VA; SR; Fncl Mgnt Assn; Finance Clb; Fncl Analyst; Finance.

**HARTWIG, DANIEL L,** S U N Y Coll Of Tech At Alfred, Alfred, NY; FR; BA; Otdr Rcrtn Clb 90-; Comp Grphcs Tech; Grphc Eng.

**HARTWIG, HANS G,** Norfolk St Univ, Norfolk, VA; SR; BS; NROTC Unit Hampton Roads Midn Batt Cor 87-; Alpha Kappa Mu 89-; Beta Gamma Sigma 90-, Acctg; Navy Pilot.**

**HARTWIGSEN, SUSAN B,** Coll Misericordia, Dallas, PA; SR; MS; Educ Club Treas 87; Camp Min Chldrns Parties Coord 88-90; Class Comm Rep 87-88; Elem Educ; Tchng.

**HARTWILL, ALBERTINE L,** Va St Univ, Petersburg, VA; JR; Gspl Ens 88-90; Pltcl Sci Assc 90-; Stdnt Un Actvts Bd 89-90; NAACP 90-; Glasgow Cncrnd Ctzns 89-; Pltcl Sci; Research.

**HARTZEL, GREGORY A,** S U N Y At Buffalo, Buffalo, NY; SR; BS; Nvgtrs Chrstn Fllwshp 87-; Inst Of Elec And Elecs Engs 89-; Ski Clb 87-; Dayton T Brown Eng Schlrshp; Grumman Eng Schlrshp; Elec Eng.

**HARTZFELD, ANITA E,** Nyack Coll, Nyack, NY; FR; BA; Vrsty Bsktbl 90; Engl Hstry; Clg Prfssr.

**HARTZOG, TIFARAH L,** Tougaloo Coll, Tougaloo, MS; SO; Stdnt Spprt Serv 89-; Spnsh Clb 90-; Bsktbl Tm 89-; Psychlgy; Nrsng.

**HARVATH, DAVID M,** Liberty Univ, Lynchburg, VA; SR; Fnncl Mgmt Assn 90-; Fnncl Advsry Srvcs Intrnshp 90-; Tutor; BS; Bus; Fnnce.

**HARVATIN, ROBERT M,** S U N Y Coll Of Tech At Alfred, Alfred, NY; SR; BTEET; Alfred St Clg Concrt Band 86-; Pres 89-90; Alfred St Clg Jazz Ensmbl 86-; Pres 90-; Xi Beta 90-; Door Guard 86; Resdnt Asstnt 87-89; Alumni Assoc Schrlshp 86 88; Matthew Burzycki Mem Schlrshp 88; Pres Ldrshp Cls Alfred St Clg 89; Elec Eng Tech.**

**HARVEL, STACEY A,** Radford Univ, Radford, VA; SR; BS; Pltcl Sci Clb 87-89; Qst Asst 90; Rsdnt Asst 88-89; Pi Gamma Mu Pres 90-; Alpha Sigma Tau Cmmtt Hd 89-; Pltcl Sci.

**HARVELL, LISA L,** Abraham Baldwin Agri Coll, Tifton, GA; FR; BA; Edctn; Scl Sci Tchr.

**HARVELL, ROBIN C,** Mount Olive Coll, Mount Olive, NC; SR; BS; Psychology Clb Pres 90-; Crim Just Publcst Clb 87-89; SCC; Psi Chi; Rescue Squad EMT 78-83; Honors Proj Peer Advisor 90-; TA 90-; AAS Sampson Comm Coll 89; Psychology; Probation/Parole Soc Srvc.

**HARVELL, THOMAS E,** Univ Of Nh Plymouth St Coll, Plymouth, NH; SO; BA; Snwbrdng Clb Co-Fdnr; Kappa Delta Phi; Thtr; Stage Dsgn.

**HARVERSON-PILECKAS, PATRICIA M,** Glassboro St Coll, Glassboro, NJ; JR; BA; Glassboro Parent Co Op Pres 90-; BOSO Pres 90-; Math; Ed.

**HARVEY, AUDELLE R,** Morgan St Univ, Baltimore, MD; FR; BS; Nwspr Rprtr 90-; Phi Eta Sigma 90-; Alpha Lambda Delta 90-; Deans List 90-; Promethean Kappa Tau 90-; Vlybl 90-; Bus Admn; Intl Bus Or Law.

**HARVEY, DIANE M,** Marywood Coll, Scranton, PA; SR; BS; Math Clb Pres 87-; TOT 88-; Kappa Mu Epsilon Pres 89-; Delta Epsilon Sigma 90-91; Act 101 Tutor 88-; Pres Schlr 87-; Math.

**HARVEY, DOUGLAS A,** Oh Wesleyan Univ, Delaware, OH; FR; BA; Phi Eta Sgm 90; Pre Med; Medcn.

**HARVEY, ELIZABETH A,** Ms St Univ, Miss State, MS; SR; BS; ACM Secty 90-; Hnrs Prog; Phi Kappa Phi; Upsilon Phi Epsilon; Computer Sci; System Analyst.

**HARVEY, ELLA J,** Bethany Coll, Bethany, WV; SR; MD; Amer Chem Soc Pres 87-; Physcl Life Sci Clb Sec 88-; Chrch Orgnst 87-; Gamma Sigma Kappa 90-; Gamma Sigma Epsilon 88-; Beta Beta Beta 88-; Amer Gld Orgnsts 87-; Kappa Delta Pblc Rltns 87-88; Biochemstry; Acdmc Med.

**HARVEY JR, GARY A,** Univ Of Va Clinch Valley Coll, Wise, VA; SR; Dean Lst; C Bascom Slemp Schlrshp; IM Sprts; BS; Bus Admn; Fnnc/Mngmnt.

**HARVEY, GILLIAN R,** Fl Coll, Temple Terrace, FL; SO; Chorus Trio 89-; Drama Prdctns Vrs Rls Props Mstrss 89-; Yng Wmns Trng Org 89-; Phi Theta Kappa 90-; ARETE 89-90; Alpha Clb 90-; Acdmc Achvmnt Awd 90-; Romine Schlrshp 89-90; Hon Rdng 89-; AA; Home Ec; Ntrtn.

**HARVEY, GREGOR R,** Fl St Univ, Tallahassee, FL; SR; BM; Ensembles; Pi Kappa Lambda; Music Awd; Music; Perf Cmptns.

**HARVEY, JESSICA L,** Vance Granville Comm Coll, Henderson, NC; SO; AAS; Bus Cmptr Prgrmng/Bus Admin.

**HARVEY, JOHN C,** Fl Atlantic Univ, Boca Raton, FL; SR; BS; Caribbean Cnnctn Cl 89-; ASME; Tau Beta Pi 89-; Phi Kappa Phi; IMPAC Awd 90-; Minority Edctnl Achvmnt Awd 88-; AA Broward Comm Colg 87; Engrng; Mechncl Engrr.

**HARVEY, JULIE A,** George Mason Univ, Fairfax, VA; SR; Decision Sci Clb; Soc Advncmnt Mgmt; Golden Key; United Way; Natl Merit Awd; Bread For Wrld Schlrshp; Deans Lst; BS 90; Info Sys; Cnsltnt.

**HARVEY, LISA A,** Va Commonwealth Univ, Richmond, VA; JR; Pub Rltns Stdnt Soc Amer 90-; Stf Wrtr Commwealth Times; Psi Beta 89-; Golden Key; Ordr Eastern Star Star Point 90-; Crowned Miss Richmond 90; Mass Comm; Pub Rltns Spclst Pltcs.

**HARVEY, MARK O,** Clarkson Univ, Potsdam, NY; SR; BA; Rangers Amer 87-; Captain U S Army; Mgmt; U S Army Ofcr.

**HARVEY, MARY ELLEN,** Univ Of Scranton, Scranton, PA; SO; BA; IM La Crosse; Mktg; Bus.

**HARVEY, MICHELLE ANN,** Notre Dame Coll, Cleveland, OH; SO; BA; Latin Clb 89; Crnt Afrs Frm 90; St Alexis 89; Cert Exclnc 89; Pall Mall Awrd; Engl Hist; Law.

**HARVEY, PHYLLIS J,** Schenectady County Comm Coll, Schenectady, NY; FR; Humanities; LPN.

**HARVEY, ROBERT E,** Bunker Hill Comm Coll, Boston, MA; FR; A; Crmnl Jstc; Law Enf.

**HARVEY, ROSA L,** Bloomfield Coll, Bloomfield, NJ; GD; BS; Ldrshp/Mntrng Prog 90-; Stch Comm 88-; Advsry Brd 88-89; Deans Lst 87-90; Alpha Kappa Psi Pblc Rltns Coord 90-; Srv Awd 90-; Ldrshp Awd; Trnsfr Orgn 88-89; AS Ntl Bus Clg 86; MA Educ.**

**HARVEY, SUSAN M,** Clarkson Univ, Potsdam, NY; FR; MBA; Fin; Corp Fin/Banking.

**HARVEY, TRACIE K,** Univ Of Sc At Columbia, Columbia, SC; JR; BA; FCA 89-90; Golden Key 90-; Kappa Delta Epsilon 90-; Gamma Beta Phi 90-; Early Chldhd Educ; Law.

**HARVEY, VANESSA,** Edward Waters Coll, Jacksonville, FL; GD; Omg Prl Sec 89; Deans List 89; Pres List 90; Bonwondie Tusculum Clg Sec 86; Estrn Star Pblc Rltns 90-; Omega Psi Phi Frat Inc Chi; Mst Achvd Intrn 90.

**HARVEY, VIRGINIA L,** Central Fl Comm Coll, Ocala, FL; SO; AS; Dean List 89-; LPN Tom Linson St Petersburg Fl 75; Business Management; Bus Admin.

**HARVEY, WENDELYN K,** Oh Univ-Southern Cmps, Ironton, OH; SO; BA; PTO; Bus Mgmnt; Bus; Mus Mgnt.

**HARVILL, JOYCE MICHELLE,** Commonwealth Coll, Virginia Beach, VA; SO; BA; ISIA; Arts.

**HARVLEY, PATRICIA L,** Hillsborough Comm Coll, Tampa, FL; SO; BSN; Tau Beta Sigma 88-90; Nurs.

**HARWELL, CHRISTINE A,** Salisbury St Univ, Salisbury, MD; JR; Elem Edn; Teach.

**HARWELL, EMILY R,** Middle Tn St Univ, Murfreesboro, TN; FR; BA; Lncln Co Hrsmns Assn; Crrge Hse Plyrs Thtr Co; Engl; Tchng.

**HARWELL, LISA A,** Middle Tn St Univ, Murfreesboro, TN; SR; BS; MSCC Psychlgy Clb 88-89; Gamma Beta Phi 88-90; AS Motlow State Comm Coll 89; Psychlgy; Therapist.

**HARWICK, RICHARD L,** Gallaudet Univ, Washington, DC; SR; BS; Phi Alpha Pi; Phi Kappa Psi 83-; IM Sftbl/Bwlng 89; Bus Admin; MBA.

**HARWOOD, ELIZABETH A,** Memphis St Univ, Memphis, TN; SR; BS; Kappa Omicron Nu 90-; USAA Natl Coll Ed Awrds; Home Econ.

**HARWOOD, MARY CHRISTINE,** Union Univ, Jackson, TN; JR; BA; Drama; Mission Tms; Alpha Psi Omega; Chi Omega VP; Phot Lab Wrkshpr; Elem Educ; Speech Path.

**HARWOOD, RUSSELL B,** Cleveland St Univ, Cleveland, OH; SR; BSET; FETS Tres 89-; SME Pres 89-89; Tau Alpha Pi; Engineers Wk Cntst Third Pl 89; Electronic Tech; Engineering.**

**HARWOOD, TRACIE A,** Univ Of Akron, Akron, OH; SR; BS; Kappa Delta Pi 90; Golden Key 90; Acad Schlrshp 88; Math Tutor 90; YWCA Instrctr 88; Elem Ed Math; Tchr.

**HARZEWSKI, ERICA M,** S U N Y At Buffalo, Buffalo, NY; SR; BS; IIE; ASQC; Alpha Pi Mu Treas 90-; Omega Rho; Golden Key; 1st Pl Tech Paper & Oral Prsntn At IIE Reg Conf Rochester N Y; Intren Rich Prod Corp; Ind Engrng.

**HASAN, SAIYID A,** Univ Of Ky, Lexington, KY; SR; BA; Alpha Epsilon Delta 88-; Clgns Acad Excllnc 88-; HPSAC 88-; Phi Beta Kappa; Mortar Brd 90-; Hngr Cln Up Comm 88-; Amer Hrt Assoc 88-; Orntn Ldr 88-; Hmstd Nrsng Hm 88-; Hmwrk Htln 88-; Mar Of Dms 88-; SMART 88-; Singletary Schlrshp; Hlth/Human Studies; Medicine.**

**HASAN, TANYA S,** Fl A & M Univ, Tallahassee, FL; SO; BS; IEEE; Islamic Assn; Phi Eta Sigma; USAA All Amer Schlr; Elec Eng Tech.

**HASEGAWA, YORIKO,** Central Fl Comm Coll, Ocala, FL; FR; AA; Dance Wrkshp 90-; Phi Theta Kappa 90-; Pub Rel; Brdcst Jrnlst.

**HASFJORD, KRISTIN A,** Emory Univ, Atlanta, GA; JR; BBA; AIESEC Local Comm Exchng Contrlr 90-; Emory Christn Flwshp Sml Grp Ldr 90-; Chi Omega Career Dev 90-; Bus Admn/Mktg; Mkt Rsrch/Prodct Dev.

**HASH, JAMES J,** Univ Of Ky, Lexington, KY; SO; BA; Yrbk Dsgn/Grphcs Edtr 89-; Frnch Clb; Stdt Affrs Div Nwsltr Asst Edtr; Pi Delta Phi VP; Phi Eta Sigma 89-; Yrbk Outstanding Male Staff Mmbr; Frnch/Psychlgy; Interpreter/Intl Cmmnctns.

**HASHIM, MUFADDAL M,** Oh St Univ, Columbus, OH; SR; BS; Pakistani Stdnt Assn 87-; Hon Soc 87-; Golden Key; Arts/Sci Awd Excell Schlrshp; Scarlet/Gray Schlrshp; Zoology; Med.

**HASHIM, SADIA,** Bloomfield Coll, Bloomfield, NJ; FR; BSC 86-87.

**HASHIMOTO, MICHIYO,** Univ Of Miami, Coral Gables, FL; SR; BS; Marine Sci; BS Tokai Univ Japan 89; Psych.

**HASIS, BARBARA J,** Comm Coll Algny Co Algny Cmps, Pittsburgh, PA; FR; AS; Res Advsr; BS Penn St 87; Radiatn Thrpy.

**HASKELL, ELLEN M,** Hudson Valley Comm Coll, Troy, NY; FR; BA; Troy Musical Arts Choral Scty; Psy; Psy/Nutrition Research.

**HASKEN, KATHRYN L,** Univ Of Southern Ms, Hattiesburg, MS; SR; BS; USM Sports Med Assc Lb Sec 90-; Natl Athltc Trnrs Assc; SE Athltc Trnrs Assc; Phi Theta Kappa; USM Stdnt Trnr Schlrsp; AA Patrick Henry St Jr Coll89; Coachng/Sprts Adm; Athltc Trng.

**HASKETT, SYLVIA D,** Va St Univ, Petersburg, VA; SR; BA; Big Bro/Sis Org 89-; Alpha Kappa Mu; Deans Lst 87-; AICPA Schlrshp 90-; NABA Schlrshp; G G Singleton Acctg Awd; Acctg.

**HASKIN, CRISTINA R C,** Fl International Univ, Miami, FL; SR; BA; Intl Engl Hnr Soc Mbr 90; Phi Lambda Mbr 90; Bk Fair 89; Chr Chrch Ltl Flwr 87; Swtchbrd Miami Inc Crisis Ln Blngl Vol 87-88; Deans Lst 89-90; Asstnc Dr FL Yudin Dept Mdrn Lang 89; AA 87; Engl; Wrtr Flm Mkr.**

**HASKINS, LISA R,** Anderson Coll, Anderson, SC; SO; BA; Hnrs Prog 90-; Phi Theta Kappa Secy 89-; Gamma Beta Phi 89-; AA Bus Admin; Mngmnt/Mrktng.

**HASKINS, MARY S,** Patrick Henry Comm Coll, Martinsville, VA; SO; AAS; Mbr NTSO 90-; Ridgeway Rescue Sqd Sqd Sgt Trng Ofcr 85-; Rookie Of Yr Rescue Sqd; Mbr Brd Dir Amer Heart Assoc Sec 89-; United Way Chrprsn; March Of Dimes Assoc; Spousal Abuse Vol Cnslr; Business; Sprts Mngmnt.

**HASLER, DORIS B,** Fayetteville St Univ, Fayetteville, NC; MA; Pol Sci Clb Pres 89; Kappa Delta Pi 90; BA 90; Scrty Mngmnt; Scrty Cnsltnt.

**HASLETT, KATRINA N,** Al A & M Univ, Normal, AL; JR; BS; Chrldr Capt 88-; Alabama Academy Of Sci 90-; Dns Lst 88-; Beta Kappa Chi 90-; MARC 90-; Princeton Univ Pgrm; Chrldng Capt 88-; Zoology; Doctor/Ob/Gyn.

**HASLETT, KRISTA,** Mount Saint Mary Coll, Newburgh, NY; SR; BS; Bicycle Clb VP 88-; Ceramic Clb 90-; Youth Soccer Coach 88; Sr Sales Assoc 88-; Bus Mgmt/Admin; MBA.

**HASNA, KHALID F,** Univ Of South Al, Mobile, AL; SR; MBA; Amrcl Soc Cvl Engnrs 82-; Intrntnl Clb Sec 87; Shr Tm 87; SOS Tm Mmbr 87; Ntnl Soc Prfsnl Engnrs; Cvl Engnr; Bsce; Bsns; Engnrng Mgmt.

**HASSA JR, GEORGE C,** Rensselaer Polytechnic Inst, Troy, NY; FR; BS; Space Soc 90-; Astrophysical Soc 90; Serv Frat Alpha Phi Omega 90; Elect Engr.

**HASSAMONTR, JARAMPORN,** Univ Of Pittsburgh, Pittsburgh, PA; FR; BS; Trm Hnr Lst; Deans Hnr Lst Schl Eng 90-; Schlrshp Ryl Thai Embssy 90-; Cert Triam Udom Suksa Schl Bangkok 89; Mech Eng.

**HASSAN, AMR A,** Cooper Union, New York, NY; SO; BENG; Mech Engr.

**HASSAN, AMV A,** Cooper Union, New York, NY; SO; BENG; Mech Engr.

**HASSAN, MARY B,** Point Park Coll, Pittsburgh, PA; SR; BS; AA Penn State Un 86; Acctg.

**HASSE, DEBRA E,** Saint Elizabeth Hosp Sch Nurs, Utica, NY; FR; AS; Spec Educ Teacher 75-90; BS Western Ill Univ 74; Nursing/Speech Path; Reg Nrs.

**HASSELBROOK, DAVID S,** Univ Of Pittsburgh, Pittsburgh, PA; JR; BS; Mosites Schlrshp 90-; Vars Gymnastics 87-; Cvl Engr.

**HASSELL, TRACY A,** Univ Of Tn At Martin, Martin, TN; FR; BS; Pre-Law Club 90-; Hnrs Soc 90-; Phi Alpha Delta 90-; Pol Sci; Corp Law.

**HASSEN, DEBORAH M,** Richard Bland Coll, Petersburg, VA; SO; BS; AS 90; Psychology; Marketing Human Resources.

**HASSENFRATZ, NICHOLE D,** City Univ Of Ny Queensbrough, New York, NY; FR; BA; Psychology; Child Psychologist.

**HASTIE, JAMES A,** Le Moyne Coll, Syracuse, NY; SR; Stdnt Govt 89-; Envrnmntl Coalition 89-; Acctg Soc 89-; Intrnshp Dean Witter Reynolds 89-; BS; Finance/Acctg.

**HASTIE, MARONDA LIZETTE,** Savannah St Coll, Savannah, GA; JR; BS; Intrntnl Frm 90-; Math Cmptr Sci; Analyst.

**HASTINGS, KERRI A,** Union Univ School Of Nursing, Memphis, TN; FR; Nrsng.

**HASTINGS, RICHARD D,** Ny Univ, New York, NY; AAS; Cntng Ed Schlr; Crtfctn High Prcntle Rnkng; Finances; Advncd Statstcl Anlys.

**HASTINGS, TARA K,** Jackson St Univ, Jackson, MS; SO; BS; Blue Wht Flsh Nwspr Nws Wrtr 90; Alpha Lambda Delta 90-; Bio; Med.

**HASTON, REGAS N,** Al A & M Univ, Normal, AL; SO; BA; Clss Offcr Pres 87-89; Chr Pres 89-90; Hnr Rll 87-90; Gamma Phi Kappa 89-; Bptst Stu Unn; Tnns Trck; Music Educ; Edctr.

**HATA, AYAKO,** Manhattanville Coll, Purchase, NY; SR; BA; Frnch Dept Hon; Frnch.

**HATALSKY, SUSAN,** Schenectady County Comm Coll, Schenectady, NY; FR; BA; Comm Serv Cntr Brd Membr; NY St Rstrnt Assn; Rstrnt Ownr 82-89; Bus/Ed; Tch.

**HATAWAY, LINDA MARIE,** Ms St Univ, Miss State, MS; FR; Pnhlnc; Hnrs Pro; Phi Eta Sigma; Gamma Beta Phi; Alpha Lambda Delta; Alpha Gamma Delta Pldg Cls Pres Rcrdg Sec 90-; Circle K; Acdmc/ACT Schlrshp; IM Ftbl/Vlybl; Acctg; CPA.

**HATCH, JULIA S,** Christopher Newport Coll, Newport News, VA; SR; BA; Alphia Chi 88-; Trng Jvnls; VA Tchrs Schlrshp 89-; Langley Research Smmr Schlr Rsrch; Dr W T Patrick Jr Schlrshp For Physics; Physcs; Tchr Mtrls Rsrch.

**HATCH, TERESA A,** Fl Atlantic Univ, Boca Raton, FL; JR; Acctg; CPA.

**HATCHELL, WILLIAM R,** Univ Of Sc At Columbia, Columbia, SC; FR; BS; Prbtn Parole Assoc; Phi Eta Sigma; Crmnl Justice; Law Enfrcmnt.

**HATCHER, CHRISTOPHER C,** Alcorn St Univ, Lorman, MS; SO; MBA; FFA; Agrnmy Clb Pres; Alpha Tau Alpha Vp; Outstndg Agrnmy Stdnt Of Yr; Ntl FFA Cnvntns Del; NTL ATA Cnclv Del; Ftbl; Agrnmy; Soil Scntst.

**HATCHER, HEATHER VICTORIA,** Middle Tn St Univ, Murfreesboro, TN; FR; BS; Psychlgy/Crmnl Jstce; Crmnl Psychlgy.

**HATCHER, KAREN A,** Wv Univ At Parkersburg, Parkersburg, WV; FR; AAS; Schl Vol Evns Elem 88; Nrsng; RN.

**HATCHER, LISA M,** Radford Univ, Radford, VA; SO; BED; Hs Cncl Treas 89; Elem Ed.

**HATCHER, MELISSA D,** Ms St Univ, Miss State, MS; JR; BA; Mu Alpha Theta 88-89; Stdnt Free Entrprse 89-90; Phi Theta Kappa Sec 89; Gamma Beta Phi 90-; Bptst Stdnt Un Pres 88-; AA E Cntrl Comm Coll 90; Bus; Mgmt.

**HATCHER, RICK A,** Glassboro St Coll, Glassboro, NJ; JR; BS; ACS 88-; Hnrs Pgrm 89-; Hnrs Clb 90-; Asst Wrdn Epscpl Chrch 89-; Diocese Dlgt; Gdn St Schlrshp; Chmstry; Chem Eng.

**HATCHER, ROBERT I,** Southern Coll Of Tech, Marietta, GA; SR; BS; Comp Sci; Sftwr Engr.

**HATCHER, RUFUS E,** Interdenominational Theo Ctr, Atlanta, GA; GD; MDIV; Johnson C Smith Smnry Fllwshp Chrprsn Social Action; Phi Mu Alpha 71; Ntnl Blck; Atlanta Chptr Blck Prsbytrn Caucus Smnrn Rep; BA Shaw Clg Detroit 76; Tchng Cert Univ Michigan 82; Pstrl Care Thlgy; Post Grad Studies.

**HATCHER, TERRY D,** Chesterfield Marlboro Coll, Cheraw, SC; FR; AD; Automatic Machine Oprtr; Engrng Graphics.

**HATCHETT, CARITA,** Morris Brown Coll, Atlanta, GA; SO; BA; Bsktbl 90-; AST; Hnr Rl 89-90; Mktg; Rsrchr.

**HATFIELD, CRAIG S,** Oh Univ, Athens, OH; FR; E Grn Cncl Rep 90-; Alcoa Fndtn Schlrshp 90-; Res Life Acad Achiev Awd; Coll Eng/Tech Acad Achiev Awd; Deans Lst 90.

**HATFIELD, DAVID W,** Oh St Univ At Marion, Marion, OH; SO; BA; Phi Eta Sigma 90-; Alpha Lambda Delta 90-; Hist Educ.

**HATFIELD, DEBORAH A,** Univ Of Ky, Lexington, KY; JR; BA; Ntl Ed Assoc 90; Red Cross Bld Dr 86; Cmmnwlth Schlrshp 88; Scndry Ed; Tchng Law.

**HATFIELD, ERIC J,** Brewer St Jr Coll, Fayette, AL; FR; Phi Beta Lambda; Advsry Com; Blgy; Med Or Optmtry.

**HATFIELD, JON H,** Marshall University, Huntington, WV; JR; BA; Assoc CPAS; Pi Kappa Alpha; Acctg.

**HATFIELD, KAREN J,** Liberty Univ, Lynchburg, VA; SR; BS; Cllg Rpblcns 87-88; Alpha Lambda Delta 87-; Kappa Delta Pi VP 88-; Sigma Tau Delta 89-; Scndry Edctn Awd; Hghst Acdmc Adhvmnt Englsh Edctn; Englsh Edctn.

**HATFIELD, KRISTIAN E,** Wallace St Comm Coll At Selma, Selma, AL; SO; Phi Theta Kappa; Ambassador; Early Chldhd Ed; Tch.

**HATFIELD, PATRICIA G,** Lincoln Memorial Univ, Harrogate, TN; SO; Science Biological; Nursing.

**HATFIELD, SONYA R,** Univ Of Sc At Columbia, Columbia, SC; FR; BS; Amer Chem Soc 90-; Chem; Med.

**HATHAWAY, LISA J,** Savannah Coll Of Art & Design, Savannah, GA; SR; Graphic Design Clb 90; Tennis 90; Irene Rousaris Summer Travel Schlrshp 90.

**HATHAWAY, POLLY CATHERINE,** Longwood Coll, Farmville, VA; SR; Alpha Gamma Delta Pres 88-; Ntl Ord Omega Sec 90-; Jdcl Bd Sec 89-90; Ortntn Ldr 88-; Stdnt Asst Grk Afrs Ofc 89-; Rush Cnslr 90-; Jdcry Stdnt Cnslnt 90-; Alchl Plcy Rev Com 90-; Rsh Rls Rev Com 90; Pres Rndtbl 89-; Lngwd Hon Symp Pnlst.

**HATHCOCK, ELIZABETH DENNISE,** Union Univ, Jackson, TN; JR; BS; Clsscl Piano 87-; Band 88-89; Pom Pom Squad 88-89; ACT Schlrsp 88-89; GPA Schlrshp 88-89; Chrch Schlrshp 90-; Psycl Thrpy Tchnn Mcnairy Co Gen Hsp 89-90; Phrmcy Tech 90-; Swim Clb; Cmstry; Dctr Phrmcy.

**HATHORNE, CORY D,** Univ Of Tn At Chattanooga, Chattanooga, TN; JR; BSE; Amer Soc Of Mchncl Eng; US Achievemnt Acad; Ntl Hnr Soc; Co-Op Stdnt Wth Saturn Corp; Mech Eng; Shp Bldg Prof Drag Race Cars.

**HATLER, SUSAN LYNNE,** Middle Tn St Univ, Murfreesboro, TN; JR; BS; Mass Cmnctns/Jrnlsm; Jrnlsm/Mag Wrtng.

**HATLEY, JAMEY M,** Univ Of Tn At Knoxville, Knoxville, TN; FR; BA; Phi Eta Sigma 90; Inroads; Bsn Admin; Mktg.

**HATLEY, MARY K,** Univ Of Tn At Martin, Martin, TN; JR; BA; STEA 90-; Alpha Omicron Pi Panhellenic 88-; Dns Lst 89-; Elem Educ; Tchr.

**HATTAWAY, SHANNON G,** Ashland Comm Coll, Ashland, KY; SO; BA; Soclyg; Socl Wrk.**

**HATTEN, JURINE D,** Spelman Coll, Atlanta, GA; FR; BA; Bio; Sports Med Doctor.

**HATTEN, MICHAEL E,** Marshall University, Huntington, WV; SO; BA; Bus; Mgmnt.

**HATTEN, WILLIAM L,** Watterson Coll, Louisville, KY; GD; BACH; Data Prcssng Mngrl Assn VP 89-; AAS IN Tchncl Clg 81-83; Cmptr Prgrmmng; Data Base Admn.

**HATTIANGADI, ANITA U,** Univ Of Rochester, Rochester, NY; SO; BA; Eqstrn Clb 90-; Symphny Orch 89-; Cmps Tms 89-90; Prtnrs Rdng 89-90; Ec.

**HATWELL, KAREN R,** Mary Washington Coll, Fredericksburg, VA; FR; BS; Hillel Intr Clb Assn Rep 90-; Pre-Med Clb 90-; Drama; Rugby 90-; Chem; Med.

**HATZFELD JR, MICHAEL J,** Duquesne Univ, Pittsburgh, PA; FR; MBA; Phi Eta Sigma 90-; Vlntr Prgrm DUV 90-; Bsns; CPA.

**HATZIGEORGIS, DROSOULA A,** Birmingham Southern Coll, Birmingham, AL; SR; BA; Phi Sigma Iota 90-; Alpha Lambda Delta 89-; Phi Eta Sigma 89-; Prs Hon Schlrshp 89-; Southrn Vol Serv Stdnt Coordntr 89; Spnsh; Tchng.

**HATZIRIGAS, EVANGELOS,** Youngstown St Univ, Youngstown, OH; JR; Hellenic Orthodox Assn VP 89-90; Youngstown State Univ Asstnshp 88-90; Elec Eng.

**HAUCK, BRAD E,** Univ Of Cincinnati, Cincinnati, OH; JR; BA; Soc Mnfctrng Engnrs Tres 89-; ASME; Gldn Key; Tau Alpha Pi; Alpha Lambda Delta; OH Vly Antique Mach Show Drctr 90-; Co-Op R A Jones Co; Engnrng; Mchncl Engnrng.

**HAUCK, DARRYL J,** Comm Coll Algny Co Algny Cmps, Pittsburgh, PA; SO; AA; Soc Scncs; Educ.

**HAUGHT, BRIAN A,** Wv Univ, Morgantown, WV; FR; BS; Chem Engrng; Engr.

**HAUGHT, CHRISTINE M,** Bethany Coll, Bethany, WV; SO; BA; Advrtsng Clb; BISONS 89-; Alpha Xi Delta Quill Chrmn 90-; Vrsty Trck 89-; Fine Arts; Grphc Dsgn.

**HAUGHT, ELNA RONILE,** Comm Coll Algny Co Algny Cmps, Pittsburgh, PA; SO; AS; Indochinese Mtl Astnc Assoc WPBA Pres 85-87; Rfg Rstlmnt Cnslt 80-; Cmptr Sci; Soc Wrk.

**HAUGHT, TINA M,** Longwood Coll, Farmville, VA; JR; BS; Longwd Ambssdr 89-; Phi Beta Lambda Pr 88-; Acctg Assn Pr 90-; Natl Sco Publ Acctnts 90-; Beckr Rep; Acctg/Busn.

**HAUKE, MELISSA A,** Univ Of Nc At Asheville, Asheville, NC; GD; CERT; Chi Omega Pldge Treas 84; Stdnt Ttr; Lbch Ltrcy Cncl 87; Cncnnti Zoo Vol 90; BA Univ Of Kentucky 84; Tchng.

**HAULK, KELLY L,** Univ Of Nc At Charlotte, Charlotte, NC; SO; BA; Asstnt Beauty Salon; English; Teacher.

**HAUN, DAVID E,** Univ Of Tn At Chattanooga, Chattanooga, TN; SR; BS; Tau Beta Pi; Golden Key; Alpha Scty; SGA Outstanding Sr Award; Ntl Collegiate Engineering Award; Engineering/Electrical.

**HAUPTFLEISCH, TANYA M,** Cornell Univ Statutory College, Ithaca, NY; SO; BS; Ho Nun De Kah; Mcrblgy; Rsrch.

**HAUPTMAN, BEVERLY H,** Elmira Coll, Elmira, NY; SR; MS; Alpha Sigma Lambda; Hm Hlth Cr Srvc Treas 86-; Hlth Cr Fncl Mgmt Assoc Advncd 68-; Cntrlrs Corning Hosp 80-; AAS Alfred St Clge 58; Soc Sci Emphs.

**HAUSER, ANGIE N,** Univ Of Sc At Columbia, Columbia, SC; SO; Columbia Ballet Schl 86-; Dns Lst 90-; SC Arts Cmmssn Intrnshp 90-; Art Histry; Tchng/Dance/Crrtr.

**HAUSER, ERIC R,** Duquesne Univ, Pittsburgh, PA; SO; BS; Intern Thrft Drg Co Inter 90-; CRC Pss Frshmn Chmstry Achvmnt Awrd; Phrmcy.

**HAUSER, FREDERIC R,** Cornell Univ Statutory College, Ithaca, NY; JR; BA; Amer Soc Landscpe Arch 88-; Landscape Arch.

**HAUSER, LISA A,** Cedar Crest Coll, Allentown, PA; FR; Foreign Lang.

**HAUSER, NOEL ALAN,** Western Ky Univ, Bowling Green, KY; SR; BS; Assoc Comp Mchnry 89-91; Gldn Key 90-; Phi Kappa Phi; Upsilon Pi Epsilon 90-; Comp Sci Awrd 89; Comp Sci.

**HAUSLER JR, RICHARD J,** Va Commonwealth Univ, Richmond, VA; JR; BA; Phi Eta Sigma 88-89; Pol Sci; Law.

**HAUSMAN, LISA L,** Columbia Greene Comm Coll, Hudson, NY; SO; AS; Sigma Delta Mu; Rape Crisis Cnslr 90-; Psych; Cnslr-Tns/Fam.

**HAUSMAN, MELODIE L,** Westminster Choir Coll, Princeton, NJ; SO; BM; Fresh Cls Std Govt Treas 90; MENC VP 89-; Wstmnstr Chrstn Flwshp; Dns Lst 90-; John Finley Williamson Schlp 89-; Mabel June/Arthur S Wagner Schlp 90-; Msc Ed/Chrch Msc; Msc Tchr/Chrl Cndctr.

**HAUSSMANN, JULIE A,** S U N Y Coll Of Tech At Frmgdl, Farmingdale, NY; SO; BA; Psych; Clncl Psych.

**HAUSSMANN, LEAH K,** Univ Of Nc At Charlotte, Charlotte, NC; JR; BCA; N C Youth Advcy & Invlvmnt Offices St Govt Intrnshp Prog Graphic Design; Art; Graphic Design.

**HAVELIN, JULIA,** Univ Of South Fl, Tampa, FL; GD; MPH; Tmpa Bay Ntwrk Fr Peace; Wmn Fr Guatemala; Phi Beta Kappa; Sigma Theta Tau; Pblc Hlth Srvc Trneeshp 89-90; Grdt Flwsp 90; Ba Grnl Coll 81; Bsn Univ Of Iowa 82; Epidemiology/Biostatistics; Professor.

**HAVER, CHRISTOPHER J,** Saint Francis Coll, Loretto, PA; JR; BS; Res Asst; Math/Comp Sci Clb V P 88-; Instrmntl Ensmbl V P 88-; Kappa Mu Epsilon 89-; Knights Columbus Mbrshp Dir 88-; Pres Upperclassman Schlrshp 89-; Math/Comp Sci; Syst Analyst.

**HAVERLY, ROBIN A,** Western New England Coll, Springfield, MA; JR; BSBA; Fin Mngmnt Assoc 90-; Pre-Law Soc 88-; Bowling Clb Pres 88-; Delta Mu Delta; Alpha Lambda Delta 89-; Deans Lst 88-; Stdnt Amb 90-; Acad All-Amer Bwlr 89-; Var Womens Bwlng Tm Capt 88-, Womans Var Soccer Tm 89-; Fin; Law.

**HAVERSTICK, HOLLY A,** George Washington Univ, Washington, DC; FR; BA; Univ Bnd 90; Hll Cncl Flr Rep 90; Stdnt Admssn Rep; Intl Affrs; Govt Srvc.

**HAVERSTICK, KRAIG L,** Univ Of Rochester, Rochester, NY; SO; BS; German Interest Floor; Joseph C Wilson Society; Chemical Engineering.

**HAVIOR, KENNETH B,** Jackson St Univ, Jackson, MS; SO; BA; Math Clb 89-; NSBE 90-; Alpha Lambda Delta 89-; Pi Mu Epsilon; Acdmc Schlrshp 89-; Deans Lst Schlr 89-; John A Peoples Dstngshd Awd; Math; Eng.

**HAVISON, SUSAN J,** Bloomfield Coll, Bloomfield, NJ; JR; BS; Asc Mngr AT&T Finance Systm Mgmt Orgnztn; Bsns Admn Cmptr Inf Systm.

**HAWA, GRACE A,** Marymount Manhattan Coll, New York, NY; SO; BA; Chldrn Of War Charity Pres 89; SG 90; Walk America 90; Pol Sci Award; Cntr For The Study Of The Presdncy Symposium; Pol Sci/Law.

**HAWARI, MAJID M,** Univ Of Southern Ms, Hattiesburg, MS; SR; BS; Natl Assoc Of Hm Bldrs; J D Coleman Arch & Plnr Intrnshp 89; AS Hillsborough Comm Coll 90; Arch Engrng Tech; Drftsmn/Arch Or Engr.

**HAWCK, TAMARA J,** Albertus Magnus Coll, New Haven, CT; SO; BA; Cst Mbr; Wrtr For Schl Newspapr; Egl; Mag Pblctn.

**HAWCROFT, BRAD B,** Ms St Univ, Miss State, MS; JR; BS; Hrtcltr Clb Pres 88-; Agrnmy Clb 88-89; Fshrs Clb 89-; Gamma Beta Phi 89-; Gamma Sigma Delta 90-; Phi Kappa Phi 90-; Alpha Zeta Pres 90-; Pi Alpha Xi Pres 90-; Amer Soc Hrtcltrl Sci Ntl Nwsltr Rptr 90-; Intl Prtnrs Pro 89-90; Ornmntl Hrtcltr.

**HAWES, TAMMI R,** Lincoln Univ, Lincoln Univ, PA; JR; BS; Educ Club Pres 89-; Forensic Soc 90; Dns Lst; Elem/Erly Chldhd Educ; Tch.

**HAWES, WARREN J,** Methodist Coll, Fayetteville, NC; JR; BS; Flwshp Chrstn Athlts 89-; Vrsty Tennis Tm 88-; Assoc Jstce Stdnt Judicial Ct 90-; Tennis Tm MVP 88-90; All Cnfrnce Slctn In Tennis; Bus Admin; Coachng Coll.

**HAWK, ALLYSON K,** Northeast State Tech Comm Coll, Blountville, TN; FR; BA; Bus Mgmt.

**HAWK, JAMES B,** Univ Of Nc At Asheville, Asheville, NC; SR; BS; BSU 90-; FCA 90-; Golf Team Altrnt 90-; Mgt; Fincl Plnnr.

**HAWK, JAMES D,** Cornell Univ Statutory College, Ithaca, NY; SR; Wildlife Scty 89-91; IM Ftbl/Sftbl/Bskbl/Tennis/Vlybl 87-; Biology; Grad Study.

**HAWK, PAMELA M,** Va Commonwealth Univ, Richmond, VA; SO; BSW; Bchlr Soc Work Assn 89-; Rsdnt Asst; Soc Work.

**HAWKER MALTZAN, CARRIE E,** Roanoke Bible Coll, Elizabeth Cy, NC; FR; Bible.

**HAWKER, PENNY J,** Radford Univ, Radford, VA; JR; BS; Phi Alpha 90-; Soc Wrk; Fmly Cnslr.

**HAWKES, LINDA S,** Tn Temple Univ, Chattanooga, TN; SR; BA; IM Vlybl/Bsktbl 87-89; Alpha Epsilon Theta Hnr Soc; Alpha Gamma Rho 90; Bus Mnstry 87-; Sch Choir 87-89; Choir Ensmbl Grp 88-89; Wmns Var Vlybl 87; Elem Educ; Tchg.**

**HAWKINS, ALANA U,** Clark Atlanta Univ, Atlanta, GA; SO; Mt Ephiram Bptst Church Chr 90-; Deans Lst 89-90; Business Adm; Mrktng.

**HAWKINS, AUDRA P,** Univ Of Md At Eastern Shore, Princess Anne, MD; SR; BS; Eta Rho Mu 88-; Alpha Kappa Mu 90-; Eta Sigma Delta 90-; Peomethean Kappa Tau 88-; Hotel/Rstrnt Mgmt; Hmn Rsrcs.

**HAWKINS, BENJAMIN,** Cheyney Univ Of Pa, Cheyney, PA; GD; MBA; PICPA Stdnt Of Yr; BS; Accntng; CPA.

**HAWKINS, CAROL R,** Ga St Univ, Atlanta, GA; JR; BSED; Golden Key 90; Kappa Delta Phi; Erly Chldhd Ed; Tchr.

**HAWKINS, CONSTANCE A,** Oh Dominican Coll, Columbus, OH; BA; Blck Achvmnts Adlt Vol 88-; Hlth Admin.

**HAWKINS, COREY D,** Al A & M Univ, Normal, AL; FR; BS; Physcl Ed; Cchng.

**HAWKINS, DONNA L,** Middle Tn St Univ, Murfreesboro, TN; FR; BA; Bus; Mgt.

**HAWKINS, ELVIN GABRIEL,** Fl A & M Univ, Tallahassee, FL; SR; Mktg Clb 85-87; Ml Clb VP 87-; Econ Clb 89-; Bg Brthrs/Bg Sistrs 90-; Cost Acctg Intrn 87; Sale Intrn 88; IM Bsbl 90; Econ; Entrprnrshp/Grad Schl.

**HAWKINS, FREDERICK L,** Univ Of Sc At Coastal Carolina, Conway, SC; FR; BS; Biology; Medicine Veterinary.

**HAWKINS, FREDRICK BRYAN,** Southern Coll Of Tech, Marietta, GA; JR; BS; Tau Alpha Pi 88; Instit Electricaland Elctrncs Engnrs Inc 90-; Assoc Cmptng Mach; Shop Foreman Architetural Millwork 88-; Elctrcl Engnrng Tech/Cmptr Scie; Engnrngfrm.

**HAWKINS, JACKIE L,** Athens St Coll, Athens, AL; JR; BS; Socrates Soc 88-; Cert Prof Sec 90; AS Calhoun Comm Coll 88; Bus; Edn.

**HAWKINS, KRISTY L,** Univ Of Tn At Martin, Martin, TN; JR; BMME; Bands 88-; Drum Major 88-; Phi Kappa Phi 90-; Phi Eta Sigma 89-; Order Omega Hon Pres 90-; Sigma Alpha Iota Pres 89-; Alpha Omicron Pi Pres 88-; Most Outstndg Fr Inst Music Major 88-89; Harriet Fulton Meml Schlrshp 90-; Music Edn; College Music Prfsr.

**HAWKINS, LEIGH K,** Tougaloo Coll, Tougaloo, MS; JR; BS; Pre Alumni Club Parl 90-; Pre Hlth Club 88-; Pan-Hellenic Cncl Pres 90-; Alpha Lambda Delta Sec 89; Alpha Kappa Alpha Pres 89; Bio; Rsrch.

**HAWKINS, MARVIN J,** Hampton Univ, Hampton, VA; SO; BS; Assoc Comptng Mchnry 90-; Hampton U Gspl Chr 89-; 2nd Plc ACM Exxon Prgmmng Cntst 90amercn Schlr Awrd 90; Comp Sci Awrd; Comp Sci; Systms Anlyst.**

**HAWKINS, MELISSA,** Middle Tn St Univ, Murfreesboro, TN; JR; BBA; Bus Admn.

**HAWKINS, MELISSA L,** Franklin And Marshall Coll, Lancaster, PA; SO; BA; Rsdnce Hll Assn Pres 89-; RA 90-; Nrsng Home Vol 89-; Bio Psych; Med.

**HAWKINS, MICHELLE L,** Bridgewater Coll, Bridgewater, VA; JR; BS; Pre Med Scty 89-; Blgy; Tchr.

**HAWKINS, PAMELA D,** Jackson St Univ, Jackson, MS; FR; Bsktbl 90-; Clncl Psychlgy; Acctg.

**HAWKINS, PAMELA S,** Georgetown Coll, Georgetown, KY; SR; BS; Elem Educ; Tchng.

**HAWKINS, ROBERT T,** George Mason Univ, Fairfax, VA; SR; BS; Alpha Chi; Golden Key 90; Asst VP Liberty Savngs Bnk 83-89; Mngmnt; Info Syst.

**HAWKINS, RONDA J,** Radford Univ, Radford, VA; SR; BS; Sclgy; Hmn Rsrc Dvlpmnt.

**HAWKINS, SCOTTY A,** Piedmont Comm Coll, Roxboro, NC; SR; AAS; Acad Exc Awd; Medical Tech.

**HAWKINS, SHANNON K,** Roane St Comm Coll, Harriman, TN; FR; AAS; Gamma Beta Phi; Radiology; Radiology Tech.

**HAWKINS, STACY L,** Jackson St Univ, Jackson, MS; SO; BS; Newspaper Stf; Natl Assoc Blck Jrnlsts; Bapt Stdnt Union; Sch Lib Arts Stdnt Advsry Cncl Secr; Alpha Lambda Delta; USA Today Intern; Arkansas Gazette Intern 90; Mass Cmnctns; Editor.

**HAWKINS, STEPHANIE C,** Ms St Univ, Miss State, MS; SR; BBA; Busn Ind Acad Stndrds Comm 90-; Gamma Beta Phi 89-; Alpha Lambda Delta; Phi Kappa Phi 89-; Phi Eta Sigma; Phi Mu 88-; Busn Mgmt; Persnl Mgmt.

**HAWKINS, STEVEN B,** Broward Comm Coll, Ft Lauderdale, FL; SO; BSME; Pres Lst 90-; Engr; Mech Engr.**

**HAWKINS, TASHA D,** Hillsborough Comm Coll, Tampa, FL; FR; BA; Church Chours; Inter City Youth Grp; Math; Sml Bus Mgr.

**HAWKINS, THOMAS C,** Va Commonwealth Univ, Richmond, VA; JR; Intl Stdnt Un Brd Mbr 88-89; Orthdx Chrcn Amrc 88-; Deans Lst 88-; Prdctn Oprtns Mgmt.

**HAWKINS, THOMAS L,** Tn Temple Univ, Chattanooga, TN; SR; BS; Univ Choir Ensmbl; Univ Choir Pres 89-90; Cls Ofcr Res Asst VP 90-; Sigma Chi Delta; IM; Scndry Edn/Soc Studies; Tchr/Admnstr.

**HAWKINS, TRAVIS M,** Univ Of South Al, Mobile, AL; SO; BA; Rec Sid Sue Magnes Schlrshp Busn; Finance.

**HAWKINS, UMIKI T,** Alcorn St Univ, Lorman, MS; SR; Bptst Stdnt Un; Choir; Irvin Johnson Awd Chr Mbr Yr; BS; Bus Adm.

**HAWKINSON, ALEXANDER L,** Carnegie Mellon Univ, Pittsburgh, PA; FR; BS; Explorers Clb 90-; Phi Kappa Theta; Research Asstnt Psychology TA; IM Tennis 90-; Cognitive Sci; Research Teaching.

**HAWKS, GREGARY LANE,** Univ Of Tn At Martin, Martin, TN; FR; BS; Agri; Bsn.

**HAWKS, JENNIFER A,** Ms St Univ, Miss State, MS; FR; BA; Inter Res Hl Cncl Pub Cmtee; Inter Res Hall Cncl Garner Hall Soc Chrmn; Refrmd Univ Flwshp; Lambda Sigma; Alpha Gamma Delta Alumne Chrm 90; Alpha Gamma Delta JDF; Otsdng Hall Cncl Mbr; Mst Otsdng Pldg Alpha Gamma Delta; Pltcl Sci.

**HAWKS, MARIE S,** Richard Bland Coll, Petersburg, VA; SO; BS; Spnsh Clb VP 90; Phi Theta Kappa Treas 90; Carson Untd Meth Chrch Treas; Bnkng Asst VP 69-89; Math; Tchr Sec Schl.

**HAWKS, SUSAN L,** Memphis St Univ, Memphis, TN; SR; Gldn Ky 89-; Phi Kappa Phi 90-; Nightingale Awrd 90; Dns Lst 85-; Assn Of Oprtng Rm Nrss 82-; Lcy Schl PTA Pres 88; Prprtve Nrs Lt US Nvy Rsrve; RN Baptist Memorial Hosp School Of Nursing 74; BNS 90.

**HAWKS, WILLIAM A,** William Carey Coll, Hattiesburg, MS; SR; BA; BSU Pres 87-88; SGA Pres 88-89; Rlgn; Mnstry.

**HAWTHORNE, PAMELA M,** Ms Univ For Women, Columbus, MS; SR; BS; Phi Kappa Phi; Nu Epsilon Delta-Prlgl 90-; Prlgl.

**HAY, ADRIENNE L,** Univ Of Cincinnati, Cincinnati, OH; SO; BA; Habitat Hmnty 90-; Pi Beta Phi Cnsr Asst Sec 88-; Alpha Phi Omega 89-90; IM Sports 88-; Spec Ed; Psychlgy.

**HAY, ANGELA R,** Middle Tn St Univ, Murfreesboro, TN; SR; BBA; Gamma Beta Phi 89; Beta Alpha Psi; CSCC Blgy Awrd 89; CSCC Wmns Bsktbl Tm 80; Frst Frmrs And Mrchnts Natl Bnk 81-; AS Summa Cum Laude Columbia St Comm Coll 89; Acctng; CPA.

**HAY, APRIL K,** Univ Of Va Clinch Valley Coll, Wise, VA; BA; Drug Alchl Wllness/Awrnss Comm 90-; SW VA Educ Assoc 90-; Clinch Vly Clg Lib Comm 90-; Pri Tchr Intrnshp 90-; Elem Educ; Tchr.

**HAY, KATHLEEN A,** The Kings Coll, Briarclf Mnr, NY; SR; BS; CSO 87-88; Ntl Hnr Soc; Robt A Cook Schlrshp 87; Elem Ed; Elem Schl Tchr.

**HAY, KAY M,** Central Al Comm Coll, Alexander City, AL; SO.

**HAYA, BECKY,** Fl International Univ, Miami, FL; SO; BA.

**HAYASHI, NAOKO,** D Youville Coll, Buffalo, NY; SO; BSN; Natl Student Nurses Assoc; Regist Nurse Tokyo Japan 87-89; Nurses Aid Ashland Ohio USA 90; Diploma N Japan Baptist Schl Nrsng 83-86; Nursing.

**HAYASHI, NORIKO,** Wv Northern Comm Coll, Wheeling, WV; FR; AA; ANA Hotel Kyoto Inc 88; Lbrl Arts; Blngl Educ.

**HAYASHI, SATOMI,** Brevard Coll, Brevard, NC; FR; BA; Phi Theta Kappa 90-; Cmnctn.

**HAYDEN, DAVID V,** Valdosta St Coll, Valdosta, GA; SO; BED; Stu Asst Cmptr Ed Lab; Knghts Of Columbus 85-; Lk Pk Auto Trck Plaza 80-; Mdl Chld Educ.

**HAYDEN, DENISE R,** Middle Tn St Univ, Murfreesboro, TN; JR; BBA; Alpha Mu Alpha; Gamma Beta Sigma; March Of Dimes Walk Amer Chrprsn; Acctg Clerk; Mktg.**

**HAYDEN, EMILY F,** Central Fl Comm Coll, Ocala, FL; JR; BA; SGA PTK Rep 90; Phi Thetta Kappa Recording Sec 90; AA 90; Elem Educ.

**HAYDEN, GAMBLE L,** Bennett Coll, Greensboro, NC; JR; BA; Sigma Tau Delta; Delta Sigma Theta; All Amer Schlr Cllgt Awd; Engl; Edtr-In-Chf.

**HAYDEN, JEFFREY M,** Onondaga Comm Coll, Syracuse, NY; FR; Bus Admin.

**HAYDEN, JULIE B,** Univ Of Ky, Lexington, KY; FR; BA; Psych; Law.

**HAYDEN, MAXINE A,** Al A & M Univ, Normal, AL; FR; Inst Asst Fr Day Care; Erly Chldhd Educ And Bus Admin; Day Care.

**HAYDEN, MICHAEL K,** Saint Catharine Coll, St Catharine, KY; SO; BA; Deans List 89-; Ag Sci; Rsrch.

**HAYDEN, MICHAEL P,** Western New England Coll, Springfield, MA; SO; AA Springfield Tech Comm Coll 81; AA Community Coll Air Force 86; Elec Eng; Eng.

**HAYDEN, RICHARD J,** Univ Of Ky, Lexington, KY; JR; Pi Kappa Alpha 89-; Phi Eta Sigma 88-; Pre-Phrmcy.

**HAYDEN, STUART W,** Georgian Court Coll, Lakewood, NJ; SO; BS; Amer Chem Soc; Res/Dev Recg Chemstry; Lonza Inc Stf Tech; Chem; Res/Dev.

**HAYDEN, TERRI L,** Liberty Univ, Lynchburg, VA; SR; BS; Light Clb 88-90; Engl Intern; US Govt Dept Defense 79-; AA 89; Engl; Tch Engl Overseas.

**HAYDEN, WILLIAM B,** Radford Univ, Radford, VA; SO; MBA; House Cncl VP 89-90; Judo Clb 90-; Rsdnt Asst 90-; Psychlgy/Sociology; Coll Admnstrtr.

**HAYDEN, YVONNE M,** Union Univ, Jackson, TN; JR; BSBA; AA Paducah Comm Clg 89; Accntng; CPA.

**HAYDIBELL, ORTIZ SERRA,** Bayamon Tech Univ Coll, Bayamon, PR; JR; MBA; BEA; Bus Admn; Fin.

**HAYEK, JEANINE,** William Paterson Coll, Wayne, NJ; SR; BA; Grk Senate Pres 89-90; People For Peace 87-88; Phi Alpha Theta; Gamma Chi VP 88-89; Alcohol/Drug Awrns Wk Comm 89-90; Orntn Pro Crdntr Fcltr Orntn Ldr 88-89; Dean Stu Awrd Campus Serv/Acdmc Achvmnt 88-89; Alumni Assoc Schlrshp 88-89; Hstry; Grad Sch.

**HAYES, ADRIAN B,** Morehouse Coll, Atlanta, GA; FR; BS; Hon Prg; Precalc II Awd; Bio; Med.

**HAYES, ALESIA L,** Va Commonwealth Univ, Richmond, VA; SO; BA; Phi Eta Sigma 89-90; Bus.

**HAYES, BENJAMIN B,** Davidson Coll, Davidson, NC; FR; BA; Kappa Alph 90-; Sccr Vrsty 90-; Engl; Medcn.

**HAYES, CANDY L,** Univ Of Nc At Greensboro, Greensboro, NC; SR; BMUS; MENC 88-; Intrvrsty Chrstn Flwshp 87-89; Pi Kappa Lambda; Mu Phi Epsilon Treas 88-; Compact Disc Rcrdng; Sketches By The UNC-G Prcsn Ensmbl; Music Educ; Tchr.

**HAYES, CAROL ANN,** Coppin St Coll, Baltimore, MD; SR; BS; Chrldng; Deans Lst 90; Parole/Prbtn Ofc Intern 90; Crmnl Justice/Scl Work; Counselor.

**HAYES, CHRISTA E,** Coker Coll, Hartsville, SC; SO; BS; Spirit Com 90-; Dnc Com 90-; Cmmssnrs Co-Head 90-; Sccr/Naia/Sc State 89-; Acctg; CPA.

**HAYES, CHRISTINA L,** Anne Arundel Comm Coll, Arnold, MD; FR; Biology/Pre Med; Med/Pediatricn.

**HAYES, CINDY JEAN,** Bishop St Comm Coll, Mobile, AL; SO; Cub Sct Ldr; Teachers Aid; Rgstrd Xray Tech Baptist Mem Schl Xray Tech 73; Deaf Interpreting/Education; Tchng.

**HAYES JR, CLIFFORD DAVID,** Central St Univ, Wilberforce, OH; JR; BED; Educ Soc 90-; DAPP Drg Achohol Prvntn Pgrm 90-; Tchrs Aide Clvlnd Bd Educ Smr Yth Pgrm 90; Elem Educ; Tchr.

**HAYES, CONNIE H,** Vance Granville Comm Coll, Henderson, NC; GD; AAS; Cmptr Clb Stu 89-; Govt Assoc; Phi Theta Kappa; Pres Mrt Awrd Schlrshp; Bus Cmptr Prgmg.

**HAYES, CYNTHIA D,** Edinboro Univ Of Pa, Edinboro, PA; FR; BED; Std Govt Asc Cngrs 90; Natl Hnr 90-; Phi Eta Sigma; Scndry Ed/Bio; Tchr.

**HAYES, CYNTHIA M,** Glassboro St Coll, Glassboro, NJ; SR; BA; Black Culture League 1st VP 89-90; Natl Assn Clrd Wmn Clbs 88-; Stdnt Govt Assn Sntr 88-89; Alpha Kappa Alpha 89-; Psychlgy.

**HAYES, DANA L,** Va Highlands Comm Coll, Abingdon, VA; SO; Pres Hons Lst 90-; Cosmtlgy 82; Pol Sci; Law Enf.

**HAYES, DAWN M,** Bennett Coll, Greensboro, NC; JR; BA; Engl Clb Tr 90-; Hl Cncl Sec 90-; Bnnt Schlrs; Sigma Tau Delta; Delta Sigma Theta; Engl; Law.

**HAYES, DAWN M,** Johnson St Coll, Johnson, VT; SR; BA; Kindergarten Intern 90; 2nd Grade Intern 90; Elem Ed; Tchr.

**HAYES, DEON L,** Jackson St Univ, Jackson, MS; FR; Jr Rcrtrs 90-; Fnce Clb 90-; NAACP 90-; Alpha Lambda Delta; Key Clb VP 89-; Dns Lst 90; Fnce/Cmptr Sci; Grdt Schl.

**HAYES, JAMES E,** Univ Of Pittsburgh, Pittsburgh, PA; JR; BS; Cert Gateway Tech Schl 83; Mech Engrg.

**HAYES, JEAN I,** Univ Of Ga, Athens, GA; JR; BA; RHA 90-; Tutor 90-; RA 90-; Physcl Ed Intern 90-; Erly Chldhd Ed; Teach.

**HAYES, JENNIFER E,** Coker Coll, Hartsville, SC; JR; BA; Elem Edn; Teach.

**HAYES, JOHN A,** Univ Of Sc At Columbia, Columbia, SC; SR; BA; Psych; Bsn.

**HAYES, JOHN J,** Univ Of Sc At Columbia, Columbia, SC; SO; BS; Natl Aquarium Intrn; Everglades Natl Park Intrn; Marine Bio.

**HAYES, JULIE F,** Bunker Hill Comm Coll, Boston, MA; SO; Psychlgy.

**HAYES, KIMBERLY M,** Allegheny Coll, Meadville, PA; JR; BS; Allghny Stdnt Gov Comm Hd 88-90; ALLIES 89-90; Panhel Sec 89-; Lambda Sigma Jr Advsr 89-90; Order Omega; Alden Schlr 88-; Psi Chi 89-; Kappa Alpha Theta Sec 89-; Lambda Sigma Jr Advsr 89-90; Psych/Bio; Dr Clncl Psych.**

**HAYES, LATISHA L,** Longwood Coll, Farmville, VA; SO; BA; Assoc For Retrded Citizens; Cncl For Exceptnl Chldrn; Alpha Lambda Delta; Psi Chi; Phi Kappa Phi; Zeta Tau Alpha Rush Asst 90-; Intrn 88-89; Specl Educ Tchr.

**HAYES, LENDOZIA F,** Clark Atlanta Univ, Atlanta, GA; SR; BS; Gspl Chr VP; NSBE; Math Clb; Beta Kappa Chi; Pi Mu Epilison 90-; Mstrs Inst Prgrm; Math; Engnrng.

**HAYES, LESLIE R,** Temple Univ, Philadelphia, PA; FR; Accntng.

**HAYES, MARGUERITE H,** Longwood Coll, Farmville, VA; SR; BS; IM Athltcs 89-; Psi Chi 89-; Phi Kappa Phi; Intrnshp Psychlgy; Psychologist.

**HAYES, MATTHEW,** S U N Y Coll Of Tech At Alfred, Alfred, NY; SR; BS; Assoc Gen Contractors Of Amer VP; Civil Engr.

**HAYES, PATRICK H,** Alfred Univ, Alfred, NY; SO; BS; Alph Lambd Dlt 89-; Prsdtnl Sclrshp 89-; IM Bsktbl 89-; Elect Eng; Eng.

**HAYES, SANDRA R,** Roane St Comm Coll, Harriman, TN; FR; AA; Business Mgmt/Sprvsn.

**HAYES, SHANNON L,** Fl A & M Univ, Tallahassee, FL; FR; MBA; Deans Lst; Hnr Rll 90; Hnr Cnvctn Hnr; Bus Admn; Bus.

**HAYES, SHARON MARIE,** Coker Coll, Hartsville, SC; JR; BS; Schlrshp; Stu Vol 90-; AS Central Tx Coll 88; Bus Mngmnt; Bus Admn.

**HAYES, SHERYL L,** Univ Of Sc At Aiken, Aiken, SC; FR; BA; Gamma Beta Phi; CPR Instr; Cert Rsprtry Thrpst; RN; AS Columbus St Comm Coll 83; AS 87; Biol; Med/Physcn.

**HAYES, SHONDRA M,** Union Univ, Jackson, TN; SR; BA; Hnrs Assc 88; Rutledge Hnry Hstry Clb 89; Focus 90; Alpha Chi 90; Alpha Psi Omego VP 90; Sigma Alpha Iota Sergeant At Arms 90; Sigma Tau Delta 90; Best Theatre Newcomer 88-89; Theatre; MA Drama.

**HAYES, STANLEY M,** Greenville Tech Coll, Greenville, SC; FR; AD; BEM 6; Indstrl Maint Tchnlgy.

**HAYES, STEPHANIE M,** Univ Of Nc At Charlotte, Charlotte, NC; SR; BA; Mountaineering Clb 90-; Exch Stdnt ENG 90-; Hstry; Intl Rel.

**HAYES, SUSAN J,** Carnegie Mellon Univ, Pittsburgh, PA; SR; BS; Assn Ind Mgmt/Ecnmcs Sec 89-90; Beta Gamma Sigma Co-Pres 90-; Clnt Serv Intrnshp-D F Nc Namee WCRS; Ind Mgmt; Mktg.

**HAYES, TABITHA,** Concordia Coll, Selma, AL; SO; BBA; AA 90; Bus Admin.

**HAYES, TAMMIE A,** Marshall University, Huntington, WV; SR; BBA; Natl Mgt Assn Treas 90-; Am Clg Hlghcr Exec; Phi Eta Sigma 90-; Mgt; Hosp Mgt/Admin.

**HAYES, TAMMY R,** Volunteer St Comm Coll, Gallatin, TN; SO; AAS; Blck Std Org 88-; Ad Hoc Comm; Gamma Beta Phi 89-; Admn Grant; Pres Schlp 88-89; Acad Schlp 88-89; St Brd Rgnts Schlp 89-; Mgmt; Hmn Rsc.

**HAYES, TARA LA SHAWN,** Alcorn St Univ, Lorman, MS; FR; Natl Hnr Soc; Acctg; Law.

**HAYES JR, TIMOTHY P,** East Stroudsburg Univ, E Stroudsburg, PA; FR; BA; Hnrs Prog 90-; Army ROTC Cdt 90-; Scl Sci; Law.

**HAYES, TIMOTHY SCOTT,** Spartanburg Methodist Coll, Spartanburg, SC; SO; Excellence Microecnmcs 90-; Most Imprvmnt Hist 90-; Pres Hon List 90-; AA; Hist; Law.

**HAYES, VIOLET V,** De Tech & Comm Coll At Dover, Dover, DE; BA; Wrk Sngls Chrch Dvrc Sngls Mnstr 87-89; Rcvry Emtnly Dstrbd Chldrn; Data Prcsng Accntng; CPA.

**HAYES, WILLIAM L,** Univ Of Cincinnati, Cincinnati, OH; JR; BMUS; Stdnt Govt Sntr 87-88; Mens Chorus Stdnt Dir 88-89; Music Educ; Music Mnstry/Educ.

**HAYGOOD, CARLTON L,** Livingston Univ, Livingston, AL; JR; Afrcn Amrcn Cltrl Assn Prsdnt 89-; Angelic Voices Faith Gspl Chr 89-.

**HAYGOOD, HEATHER L,** Univ Of Sc At Columbia, Columbia, SC; SR; MM; Mrchg Bnd 87-90; Concert Bnd 87-89; Chorus 88-89; Phi Kappa Lambda 90-; Golden Key 89-; Tau Beta Sigma Exec Cncl 88-89; D H Baldwin Flwshp; Certs Awd 89; Piano Studio Tchr; Tchr Certif Kindermusik; Piano Pedagogy; Tchr.

**HAYMAN, TRACY A,** Univ Of Md At Eastern Shore, Princess Anne, MD; JR; Salisbury Nrsng Home 88; Special Ed; Tch.

**HAYMES, JENNIFER R,** Alfred Univ, Alfred, NY; SR; BS; Ntl Assoc Accnts 89-; Ntl Career Womens Assoc 89-; Admiss Cmps Guide Hd Guide 88-; Rsdnt Asst Res Hall Stf 90; Delta Mu Delta Pres 90-; Beta Gamma Sigma 89-; Pacioli Scty 89-; Phi Kappa Phi 89-; Alpha Iota Delta 90-; A L Poryman Mem Schlshp; Business Administration; Law.**

**HAYNER, KRISTA A,** Univ Of Rochester, Rochester, NY; JR; BA; Prtnrs In Reading 88-90; RA; Stdy Awrd USSR 90; IM Sccr 88-; Psych.

**HAYNES, ARTYCE M,** Clark Atlanta Univ, Atlanta, GA; SO; BA; Mrchng Band; Symphonic Band; Symphonic Orch; Cmptr Sci Club; Hnr Pgm; Cmptr Sci.

**HAYNES, AVONELLE U,** Coll Of Insurance, New York, NY; JR; BBA; Preface Leader 90-; Insur Club 90; Insur.

**HAYNES, BRYANT L,** Memphis St Univ, Memphis, TN; SO; BA; Chrch Admn Brd 89-; Wsly Fndtn 90-; Rlft Rrl Mnstrs 87-; Applchn Srvc Prjct 86; Cmmnctns Brdcstng.

**HAYNES, CHARLOTTE D,** Edison Comm Coll, Fort Myers, FL; SO; BA; BSU; SGA; Otstndng Mnrty Stdnt; Hnr Roll; Vlybl; AA; Mass Cmmnctns; Brdcst Flm Prdctn.

**HAYNES, DIANNE,** City Univ Of Ny Baruch Coll, New York, NY; JR; BA; Biomed Soc; Bio; Med.

**HAYNES, DOLLY J,** Sinclair Comm Coll, Dayton, OH; AA; Cntrl Bptst Chrch Clrk 81-; Leag Wmn Vtrs 80-; Cvl Srvnt; Fine Arts Drwng.

**HAYNES, EBONI M,** Hampton Univ, Hampton, VA; FR; BS; Econs Clb; Hnr Cncl; Mrktng.

**HAYNES III, GEORGE W,** Middle Tn St Univ, Murfreesboro, TN; JR; BA; Sigma Alpha Epsilon; Val; Jennings/Ayers Fnrl Hm; Mortcn; AS J A Gupton Schl Mortry Sci 89; Bus; Morticn.

**HAYNES, HEATHER P,** Memphis St Univ, Memphis, TN; JR; BS; Chem Clb; Phi Eta Sigma; Alpha Lambda Delta; Gamma Beta Phi; Bptst Mem Hosp Vol Serv Emerg Dpt; Chem; Med.**

**HAYNES, KENNETH DREW,** Samford Univ, Birmingham, AL; GD; JD; Omicron Delta Kappa Louisiana St Univ 83-84; Alpha Gamma Rho LSU Pres 81-84; Henry Ypson Sims Moot Court Bd Assoc Jstc 89-; Cumiserland Trial Bd 89-; Canterbury United Meth Chrch; BS LSU 84; Law.

**HAYNES, KRISTA D,** Gaston Coll, Dallas, NC; FR; Deans List Gaston Clg; Bus; Admn Ofc Technlgy.

**HAYNES, PENELOPE S,** Univ Of Al At Birmingham, Birmingham, AL; SR; BS; Fclty Wmns Schlrshp 90-; BSA Woodbadge Crse Birmingham Area Cncl 89; By Scts Cbmstr Mbr Comm 79-; Grl Scts Trp Ldr 87-90; Comptr/Info Sci; Comptr Cnsltnt.

**HAYNES, PHILIP G,** Pellissippi St Tech Comm Coll, Knoxville, TN; ASSOC; DPMA; Phi Theta Kappa; NICET 84-; AS St Tech 84; Comp Sci; Res Tech.

**HAYNES, RANDY A,** Univ Of Al At Birmingham, Birmingham, AL; JR; ASSOC; Sntr Dgrphrs Prgm; Stdnt Gvrnmnt; AL Soc Rdlgc Tchnlgst; Rdgrphr; Rgstrd Rdlgc Tchnlgst.

**HAYNES, SEAN M,** Saint Andrews Presbytrn Coll, Laurinburg, NC; JR; BA; Wrld Culture Soc 88-89; Math/Cmptr Studies V P 89-; Film Club Soc 90-; Math; Info Sys Master.

**HAYNES, SHANETTI Y,** Alcorn St Univ, Lorman, MS; JR; Ordr Estrn Star 90-; NAACP 89-; 27th Ward Com 87-; Alpha Kappa Mu; Hon Stdnt Org 89-; Crss Cntry Tm 88-; Trck Tm 88-; Mrchng Bnd 89-90; Bus Admin; Fin Anlyst.

**HAYNES, SHEILA A,** Univ Of Tn At Knoxville, Knoxville, TN; FR; MBA; Humes Hl Res Assc 90-; Yrbk Rprtr 90-; Res Asst; Sigma Delta Pi; Pblc Rltns; PR Spclst.

**HAYNES, STEVEN F,** Univ Of Ky, Lexington, KY; JR; Pharmacy.

**HAYNES, TERRY L,** American Baptist Coll, Nashville, TN; FR; BA; Sprnghl Mssnry Bptst Chrch Pstr; Oprtn Outrch Mnstry Advsr; NAACP Pres; Thlgy/Psychlgy; Psychlgsts.

**HAYNES, WENDY L,** Univ Of Sc At Columbia, Columbia, SC; SO; BA; Gamma Beta Phi 89-; Business Accounting.

**HAYNIE JR, HAROLD,** Guilford Tech Comm Coll, Jamestown, NC; SR; AAS; Talent Roster Dstngshd Acad Perf; Fire Fighter II 85-; Fire Protection Tech; Fire Fighting.

**HAYNIE, LEEANN M,** Georgetown Coll, Georgetown, KY; JR; BA; Bapt Stdnt Un Puppet Tm 88-; Creative Ministries 90-; Frat Ltl Sr 90; Alpha Lambda Delta 89-90; Psi Chi VP; Psychology; Clin Psychology.

**HAYNIE, LINDA J,** Fl St Univ, Tallahassee, FL; JR; BS; Nutrtn Clb 89-; BACCHUS 89-; Seminole Prty; Hnrs/Schlrs Prog 88-89; 4 H Vol 89-; MDA Vol 89-; Tallahasee 10k Run; IM Sccr/Sftbl 89-90; AA Florida St Univ 90; Nutrtn/Ftnss; RS/MS.

**HAYNIE, SUSAN M,** Northeast State Tech Comm Coll, Blountville, TN; SO; AAS; Offce Syst Tech; Sec.

**HAYS, ANNA-MARIA A,** Emory & Henry Coll, Emory, VA; SO; BS/BA; Chapel Choir 90-; Chrstn Fllwshp 90-; Bio/Grmn; Envir/Sci.

**HAYS, GABRIELE E,** Lexington Comm Coll, Lexington, KY; FR; Dental Lab Techcn.

**HAYS, LAURA L,** Univ Of Al At Birmingham, Birmingham, AL; SO; BS; Ambassadors; Recruiter; Business; Law.

**HAYSLETTE, KIMBERLY D,** Marshall University, Huntington, WV; GD; MA; Gamma Beta Phi 84-87; Acad Schlrshp 83-87; Dns Lst 83-87; Cum Laude 87; Lic Ins Agnt; Offc Mgr; BA 87; Educ; Schl Cnslr.

**HAYTAIAN, PETER D,** Clarkson Univ, Potsdam, NY; SR; BS; Hcky Prog 87-90; Dean Lst 87-; Pres Lst 87-; Mrktng; Law.

**HAYTER, TRACY E,** Lesley Coll, Cambridge, MA; SR; Stdnt Alumni Assoc 87-89; Human Serv Stdnt Rep 90-; Dns Lst 87-; Northcambrdg Chldrns Ctr 87-88; Hastings Hse 88-89; Mc Leans Hosp 89-90; Samaritans Hotln 90-; Tch Asst Fr Human Serv 90; BA; Cnslng/Psych; Grad Sch.

**HAYWARD, DONNA L,** Smith Coll, Northampton, MA; SR; Serv Orgztn 90-; Glee Clb 87-; 1st Grp Schlr 90-; BA; Philosophy; Educ Law.

**HAYWARD, LARA J,** Univ Of Miami, Coral Gables, FL; JR; BA; AES 89-; Music Engrng; Rcrdng.**

**HAYWARD, RONDA C,** Benedict Coll, Columbia, SC; SR; BA; SC Natl Educ Assn 90-; Dns Lst 88-90; Alpha Kappa Alpha 89; Early Chldhd Educ.

**HAYWOOD, BARBARA S,** Alcorn St Univ, Lorman, MS; FR; Bapt Stdnt Union; Prayer Band; Bio; Phys Thrpst.

**HAYWOOD, MARY E,** Coll Of Charleston, Charleston, SC; SO; BA; Hnrs Prog 89; Alpha Delta Pi Asst Schlrshp; Cross Cntry 89; Accntng; Accntnt.

**HAYWOOD, SAVONI J,** Al A & M Univ, Normal, AL; SR; BA; Off Sys Mgmt Club 89-; Yth Mtvtn Task Force 89; NAACP 89; Hnr Roll 90-; Deans List 89-90; Delta Mu Delta Sec 89-; Tutor; AAB Youngstown St Univ 89; Bus; Comp Consultant.

**HAYWORTH, JULIE R,** Univ Of Nc At Charlotte, Charlotte, NC; FR; BA; Nwspr 90-; Engl/Comms; Publ Rels.

**HAZBUN, ALICE C,** Fl International Univ, Miami, FL; JR; BA; Finance/Intl Bus; Bnkng.

**HAZEL, ALLYSON A,** Lasell Coll, Newton, MA; JR; BS; Stdnt Govt Pres Rep 89-; High Hon 88-; Fshn/Retail Mgmnt; Corp Retail.

**HAZEL, MARGARET A,** Univ Of Sc At Columbia, Columbia, SC; JR; BA; Mrchng/Symphnc Bnd 86-87; Wmns Rugby 86-88; Psychlgy; Ed.

**HAZEL, ROBERT F,** Univ Of Pa, Philadelphia, PA; SR; BBA; Deans List 89-90; Bell Of PA 75-87; MISIAP Consultg; Consltnt Reohr Tech Svc Co Inc 87-; ABA Cum Laude 83; Mgmnt; Consltg.

**HAZELDEN, GREGORY B,** Savannah Coll Of Art & Design, Savannah, GA; GD; Stdnt Rpsrvtn Assn 90-; Bus Clb 90; Fllw Natl Trst Fr Hstrc Prsrvtn 90; Intrn Srtga Sprngs Prsrvtn Fndtn 90; Apprntce Archtctrl Crmcs 90; Intrn 89; BA Skidmore Coll Saratoga Springs NY 90; Hstrc Prsrvtn.

**HAZELRIGS, KRISTIE A,** Spartanburg Methodist Coll, Spartanburg, SC; SO; Yrbk 89-90; SADSAC 89-; Spprt Srvcs 89-90; Fstpch Sftbl 89-; AA; Bsns Mngmnt; Mngmnt.

**HAZELTON, AMY K,** Defiance Coll, Defiance, OH; JR; BS; Pres Hst 89; Inter Grk Cncl Co Pres 90; Inter Srrty Cncl Pres 90-; Sigma Phi Epsilon; Beta Sigma Rec Sec 89-; Robert O Bleeks Asst Physcl Ed; Chemcil Rubber Co Awrd 89; Stdnt Athltc Trner 88-; Wllnss Sprts Med; Athltc Trnng Physcl Thrpy.

**HAZELTON, CHERYL L,** Memphis St Univ, Memphis, TN; JR; BFA; Cltn Nnvlnt Soc Act Coord; Yrbk Phtgrphy Ed 90-; Gamma Beta Phi 90-; St Brd Rgnts Schlrshp 88-; Otstndng Stff Mmbr Awrd Phtgrphy 90; Art Educ; Tchng.

**HAZELTON, MADRINA D,** Ms St Univ, Miss State, MS; FR; BA; BARK 90-; Bapt Stdnt Union; Hnrs Prog; Gamma Beta Phi; Cmmnctns; Brdcst News Jrnlst.

**HAZELWOOD, JENNIFER LEE,** Roane St Comm Coll, Harriman, TN; FR; Psychlgy; Chld Psychlgst.

**HAZEN, STACY A,** Westminster Coll, New Wilmingtn, PA; SR; BS; Pub Cmtee Mgr 87-; Orntatn 89-90; SG 90-; Mrtr Bd Sec 90-; Pi Sigma Pi 90-; Biology Awd 87-; Biology; MS Physiolosy.

**HAZIMEH, IBA I,** Vance Granville Comm Coll, Henderson, NC; SO; Stdnt Govt Assoc Sec/Treas Rprtr 89-; Drama/Hist Clbs 90-; Deans List; Acad Achvmnt Schlrshp 90-.

**HAZIMEH, LAMA I,** Vance Granville Comm Coll, Henderson, NC; SR; BA; Sga 83-85; Deans Lst 89-; Business Adm.

**HAZLEHURST III, WILLIAM Y,** Tri County Tech Coll, Pendleton, SC; FR; AS; Habitat Hmnty; Nrsg.

**HAZLETT, AUDREY L,** East Stroudsburg Univ, E Stroudsburg, PA; SR; BS; Cir K 88-89; Hawthorn Hall Cncl 87-89; Lead Hawthrn Hall Aerobics 87-88; Intrnshp New Bolton Ctr Univ PA; Envrnmntl.

**HAZLETT, MICHELLE E,** Hiram Coll, Hiram, OH; FR; BA; Mdl Untd Ntns Brd 90-; Mdrgl Sngrs 90-; Alpha Lambda Delta; Delt Chi Lambda 90-; Music Prfrmnc.

**HAZLETT, ROBERT HENRY,** Univ Of South Al, Mobile, AL; SO; BA; Acctg; CPA.

**HAZLEWOOD, JULIE M,** Hinds Comm Coll, Raymond, MS; FR.

**HAZLIN, SARAH A,** Catholic Univ Of America, Washington, DC; JR; Judical Branch Stdnt Govt 88-90; Acad All Amer 89-90; Pres Chlr 88-; Var Swim Tm 88.

**HE, KATHERINE YIHUA,** Savannah Coll Of Art & Design, Savannah, GA; GD; MFA; Intl TV Assn 89-90; BS Nanjing Telecomm Inst China 82; Video Prod.

**HEAD, ANNETTE L,** Brescia Coll, Owensboro, KY; SO; BA; Stdnt Spprt Srvcs 90-; Alpha Chi 90-; Mddl Grd Ed.

**HEAD, ASHLEY E,** Univ Of Montevallo, Montevallo, AL; SO; BS; Erly Chldhd/Elem Educ; Tchng.

**HEAD, BRENDA L,** Bishop St Comm Coll, Mobile, AL; SO; ASS; Phi Theta Kappa V P 90-; MS Phi Theta Kappa 90-; Dlgte State Con 89-; Dlgte Natl 90-; Ldrshp Schlrshp 90-; Educ; Soc Work.

**HEAD, JOSEPH M,** Ky Wesleyan Coll, Owensboro, KY; GD; Psychlgy Clb VP 86-90; FCA 86-90; IM 86-90; Hon Mntn All Mid-South Conf 88; Best Linebacker 89; Varsity Ftbl Capt 86-89; BA 90; Psychlgy.

**HEAD, KAREN L,** Savannah St Coll, Savannah, GA; JR; BA; Smns Info Systms Awrd 90; AS 89; Hnrs; Info Systms.

**HEAD, LISA A,** Marshall University, Huntington, WV; SR; BA; MENC 90-; Music; Educ.

**HEAD, LISA F,** Univ Of Ky, Lexington, KY; JR; BS; Sci Asso 86; Alpha Chi 84-86; Lambda Kappa Sigma; Am Inst/Chem Awd 86; Owensboro Busn/Profssnl Wmn's Cl Schlrshp; BS Brescia Colg 86; Phmcy; Phmcy Prac.

**HEAD, MARLA J,** Memphis St Univ, Memphis, TN; SO; PHD; Pre-Pharmacy; Pharmacy.

**HEAD, SERITA F,** Madisonville Comm Coll, Madisonville, KY; FR; ACC; Acctg Tchnlgy.

**HEAD, ZACKERY,** Clark Atlanta Univ, Atlanta, GA; SO; BS; Hnrs Prgm 90-; Alld Hlth Scty 90-; Awrd Excllnc Math 90; Hlth Crrs Oopptrnty Prgm; Cmmnty Hlth Ed.

**HEADEN, GWENDOLYN C,** Mount Olive Coll, Mount Olive, NC; SR; BAS; Sec Sci Advsry Brd 89-; Alpha Phi Kappa 89; AAS Lenoir Comm Coll 89; Bus Mgmt.

**HEADLEY, CAMELE S,** Rutgers St Un At New Brunswick, New Brunswick, NJ; SO; BA; W Indian Stdnt Org 89-; Biomed Careers Prog; Bio; Med/Dr.**

**HEADLEY, LESLIE ANITA,** Columbia Union Coll, Takoma Park, MD; SR; BA; Stdnt Assoc Stdnt Govt Exec V Pres 90-; Theta Alpha Beta Womens Club Pres 89-90; Sigma Tau Delta Pres 90-; Alpha Chi 90-; Phi Eta Sigma 90-; English; Law.

**HEADLEY, VANDA VALERIE,** Univ Of The Dist Of Columbia, Washington, DC; GD; BBA; DPMA 88-; Marriott Schlp 89-90; Cmptr Sys Mgr Law Firm/Skadden ARPS 85-; Prgmmg/Sys Anlys Cmptr Lrng Ctrs 74; Cmptr Info Sys Sci; Law.

**HEADRICK, WILMA D,** Pellissippi St Tech Comm Coll, Knoxville, TN; SO; Info Syst Tech; Law.

**HEAGLER, SHELIA R,** Spartanburg Methodist Coll, Spartanburg, SC; FR; BA; Bsktbl 90-; Acctng.

**HEAL, MATTHEW E,** Wilmington Coll, New Castle, DE; FR; Yrbk; Bsktbl Tm; Crmnl Jstce; Law Scndry Educ.

**HEALD, BENJAMIN F,** Milligan Coll, Milligan Clg, TN; SO; BA; Concrt Comm Hse Chrmn 89-; Bible Stdy 89-; Alpha Omega 90-; Serv Seekrs Mus Dir 90-; Busn; Busn Mgmt.

**HEALEY, DIANE J,** Saint Josephs Coll New York, Brooklyn, NY; GD; BA; Deans Lst; J Hannan Schlrshp Awrd 79; Clncl Rcgntn In Psych 80; Grad W/Dstnctn 80; Hm/Hosp For Aged Vol 90-; N Y St Nrs Assn 86-90; RN; Qualty Ass Rvwr 87-90; AAS Nrsng 80; Cert 73/77; Hlth Admin; Qualty Ass Admin.

**HEALEY, LISA M,** Niagara Univ, Niagara Univ, NY; SR; BBA; Delta Epsilon Sigma 90-; Louis Genovese Schlrshp 90-; Acctg; CPA.

**HEALEY, THERESA V,** Georgian Court Coll, Lakewood, NJ; SR; BA; Comm Serv Hispanic Assn; Chrstn Org Non Profit Agencies; AA Ocean Cnty Coll 86; Humanities/Psychlgy.

**HEALY, DANA L,** Colby Sawyer Coll, New London, NH; FR; BA; SGA 90-; Eqstrn Tm Trck Fld Clb 90-; Biology; Medicine.

**HEALY, JENNIFER M,** Western New England Coll, Springfield, MA; SR; BA; Fundrsng Chrprsn Mktg Clb Fndrsng Chr 90; Dns Lst 89-90; Busn Digst Mag Intrnshp 90; Mktg; Grad Schl/Busn.

**HEALY, JO ANN D,** Western New England Coll, Springfield, MA; SO; BA; Economics; Law.

**HEALY, PETER R,** Daemen Coll, Amherst, NY; JR; BA; Bartenders Against Drunk Drivers 90-; Acctg; Law.

**HEARD, BRADLEY E,** Morehouse Coll, Atlanta, GA; JR; BA; Hnrs Prog Clb Pres 88-; Pol Sci Scty VP 89-; Mrhse Mntrng Prog 90-; Phi Beta Kappa; Gldn Ky; Mrhse Hnrs Prog 88-; Cngrssnl Intrn Sen W Fwlr And Rep O Pcktt 90; Pol Sci; Law Coll Tchng.

**HEARD, DARRYL,** Fl A & M Univ, Tallahassee, FL; SO; BA; Natl Assoc Blk Accntns 89-; WSBI Studios Dir 89-; SBI Trvl 89-90; Phi Eta Sigma 90-; Pres Schlrs Assoc 89-; Eastman Kodak Schlr Intrnshp 90-; Acctg; CPA.

**HEARD, DAVITA L,** Al A & M Univ, Normal, AL; SO; BS; Stdnt Drg Tsk Frce 89-; Alpha Kappa Alpha; M L King Serv Org; Acdmc Schlrshp 89-; Val 89; Deans Lst 89-; Med Technlgy; Dctr.

**HEARD, KIMMIERIA,** Nc Agri & Tech St Univ, Greensboro, NC; SO; Hampton Elem City Schls; AA Guilford Tech Cmnty Clg 89; Elem Educ; Tchr.

**HEARD, LA DONNA S,** East Tn St Univ, Johnson City, TN; SR; BBA; Phi Kappa Phi; Beta Gamma Sigma; Bus Support 80-; Human Rsrcs Mgmt/Bus; Rcrtng Mjr Co.

**HEARD, VALERIE L,** Al St Univ, Montgomery, AL; FR; Stingette 90-; Hon Soc/Roll 90-; Phi Mu Alpha Queen 90-; Bus Admin; Legal Sec.

**HEARD, WILLIAM T,** Southern Coll Of Tech, Marietta, GA; JR; BA; Deans Lst 90; Pres Cert Fr Acad Exclnc 90; Intrmrl Bllrds 87-90; IM Sftbl 87-89; ASSC Chem Floyd Clg Rome GA; Tau Alpha Pi 91; Indstrl/Cvl Eng.

**HEARN, GLORIA R,** Mary Baldwin Coll, Staunton, VA; SR; BA; Psychlgy; Tch.

**HEARN, HEATHER A,** Castleton St Coll, Castleton, VT; SO; BA; Yrbk Comm; Math Club; Phi Eta Sigma; Kiwanis Hnr Soc; Old Wall Hist Soc; Math; Actuarial.

**HEARN, JEAN M,** Univ Of Ga, Athens, GA; SR; EN Ltl Sis 88-; Communiversity Tutor 90-; Dns Lst 90-; No Harme Treas 90-; SEA 90-; Ed; Tch Primary/Cnsl.

**HEARTSFIELD, CHARLES C,** Nova Univ, Ft Lauderdale, FL; GD; MBA; Natl Univ Ldrshp Awrd Schlrshp 83; Travelers Outstndng Achvmnt Awrd 88; Dade Area Legal Assts Inc 89; Natl Black MBA Assoc Inc; BA Temple Univ 83; ABA Inst For Paralegal Trng 86; Real Est Dev/Mngmnt; Bus.

**HEARY, NICOLE A,** S U N Y At Buffalo, Buffalo, NY; FR; BA; Poly Sci; Law.

**HEASLEY, LINDA S,** Univ Of Sc At Columbia, Columbia, SC; SR; BA; Am Mrktg Assoc; Marketing.

**HEATH, CORLISS D,** Clark Atlanta Univ, Atlanta, GA; SO; BS; Natl Soc Blck Engrs 89-; Tour Gde/Orntn 89-; Gde Corp; Delta Sigma Theta Chpln; Deans List 90-; Dual Deg Hnr Rl UNCF FM 90-; ABWA Schlr Rcpnt 89-90; Physics/Elec Engr; Rsrch/Devl.

**HEATH, CRAIG A,** Union Coll, Barbourville, KY; GD; BA; ROTC Grad 88-90; IM Brd 85; Wldrns Clb; 1 Of Top 12 Campus Men 90-; Univ/Coll Otstndg Mrt/Acmplshmnt 90-; Coll Bsbl 85-88; BA; Bus Admin.

**HEATH, GAIL R,** James Sprunt Comm Coll, Kenansville, NC; FR; RN.

**HEATH, JOHN C,** Volunteer St Comm Coll, Gallatin, TN; SO; AS; Gamma Beta Phi 90-; TN Soc Rad Tech 90-; Rad Tech/Allied Hlth; Radiographer.

**HEATH, JULIE S,** Smith Coll, Northampton, MA; SO; BA; Scrd/Ltrgcl Dnc 89-; Deans Lst/Frst Grp Schlr 89-90; Chpl Intern 90-; Gen Assmbly Prsbytrn Chrch 90; Engl; Rlgn.

**HEATH, NORA G,** Univ Of Sc At Columbia, Columbia, SC; JR; BFA; Art Edctn; Edctn.

**HEATH, SANDRA L,** Va Highlands Comm Coll, Abingdon, VA; SO; BA; Deans Lst 89-; AA; Soc Wrk/Spec Ed; Soc Wrkr/Spec Ed Tchr.

**HEATH, SUSAN K,** Daemen Coll, Amherst, NY; SO; BS; IM Vlybl/Bsktbl 88-; Physcl Thrpy; Physcl Thrpst/Hlthtrama/Grtrcs.

**HEATH, SUSAN M,** Ms Univ For Women, Columbus, MS; Alumnae Assoc 90-; Lckhrt Soc Clb Hist 88-; SMAE Co Pres; Kappa Delta Epsilon Sec; Torch Hnry Clb 90-.

**HEATHER, MARGARET M,** Daemen Coll, Amherst, NY; JR; BA; AS Trocdire Coll 87; Phy Thrpy.

**HEATHER, SARAH L,** Central Fl Comm Coll, Ocala, FL; FR.

**HEATHERLY, NANCY M,** Spartanburg Methodist Coll, Spartanburg, SC; JR; BA; AS Spartanburg Meth 90; Finc; Bnkng.

**HEATHERLY, ROBERT C,** Univ Of Montevallo, Montevallo, AL; SR; BA; Math; Engrg.

**HEATHERTON, MICHELLE P,** Univ Of Cincinnati, Cincinnati, OH; SR; BFA; Stdnt Govt Publctns Comm Mbr 89-; Brdcst Tribunal Repr 88-90; Golden Key 89-; Stdnt Advising Advsr 88-89; Alpha Lambda Delta 88-; Alpha Epsilon Rho Repr 87-88; Natl Org Wmn 87-; Promotions Dept Intern 90; Miami Univ Mass Cmnctn Dept Asstntshp; Brdcstg; Mass Media Mgmt/Policy.

**HEATON, JIMMY W,** Roane St Comm Coll, Harriman, TN; SO; BA; Math; Eng.

**HEATON, JULIE S,** Indiana Univ Of Pa, Indiana, PA; JR; BS; Sgn Lng Clb 90-; Ed Clb 89-90; Cncrt Chr 89-90; Ed Hrng Imprd; Tchg.

**HEATON, KIM DE WAYNE,** Birmingham Southern Coll, Birmingham, AL; SR; BA; Cir K 73-74; Omicron Delta Kappa 90-; AA Walker Clge 71-74; Fnce; Law.

**HEATON, LISA A,** Bethel Coll, Mckenzie, TN; JR; BS; STEA Stdnt Govt Rep 89-; Yrbk Ed Chief 88-; Gamma Beta Phi State/Local Treas 89-; Soc Coll Jrnlsts 90-; Iota Alpha Omega 89-; Engl; Teach.

**HEATON, TODD M,** Savannah Coll Of Art & Design, Savannah, GA; SR; BFA; Photo Grp 89-; Pi Kappa Phi; Phtgrphy; Tchr.

**HEATWOLE, GLEN W,** Roane St Comm Coll, Harriman, TN; SO; BA; Bus; Law Sch.

**HEAVEN, PAULA M,** Fl A & M Univ, Tallahassee, FL; FR; BA; Nrsng; Rn.

**HEAVENER, LISA R,** Ms St Univ, Miss State, MS; FR; Rcrtr; Bptst Un 90-; Untd Way 90-; Phi Eta Sigma; Lambda Sigma VP; Delta Gamma 90-; Tupelo Ms Hsptlty; Cmnctns; Pblc Rltns.

**HEAVRIN, LAURA A,** Univ Of Sc At Columbia, Columbia, SC; SR; MBA; Amrcn Mrktng Assn 89-; Assn Hnr Stdnts 88-; Phi Beta Kappa 89-; Gamma Beta Sigma 89-; Gamma Beta Phi 88-; Intrn Columbia Sls Mrktng Exec Assn 90-; BA; Bsns; Mrktng.

**HEBER, KEVIN E,** Univ Of Miami, Coral Gables, FL; SR; BMU; Music Engrng Technology; Digital Design.

**HEBERLIG, ERIC S,** Franklin And Marshall Coll, Lancaster, PA; JR; BA; Sym Wnd Ens/Orch 88-; Env Actn Allnc 89-; Wldrns Clb Chr 88-; Pi Sigma Alpha; Mu Upsln Sigma Chr 90-; Pi Gamma Mu; Blck Prymd; Hnrs Lst 88-; Pol Rsch Mths Asst; NE Mdwst Cngrssnl Cltn Intshp; Govt; Acad.

**HEBERLING, THOMAS E,** Commonwealth Coll, Virginia Beach, VA; SR; Summa Cum Laude 89-; Pres Hon 89-; Electrnc Technlgy; Eng.

**HEBERT, BRIAN L,** Saint Francis Coll, Loretto, PA; SR; BA; NCAA Div III Ftbl 88; Math Comp Clb Treas 87-; Clss Offcr Pres 89; Kappa Mu Epsilon Math Treas 87-; Stdnts Actve In Ldrshp 89; Stndrd Stl Intrnshp 90; Dns Lst 90; Ftbl 88; Math Comp Sci; Comp Eng.

**HEBERT, MARGARET R,** Fl St Univ, Tallahassee, FL; SR; BA; Circle K 90-; Intl Affairs; Govt.

**HEBLER, GARY A,** Univ Of Southern Ms, Hattiesburg, MS; JR; BA; Annthro Cl 88-; Lambda Alpha 89-; Tau Kappa Epsilon Treas 90-; Anthro; Archeol.

**HECHT, ALAN C,** Valley Forge Christian Coll, Phoenixville, PA; JR; Tutor 87-; RA 88-90; Asst Dean Men Elim Bbl Inst 89-90; Valedictorian Elim Bbl Inst; Chldrns Mnstry Dir; Mngr Bicycle Shp 87-; ETTA Elim Bbl Inst 90; Bible; Pst Sec Tchng.

**HECHT, ERIK W,** Univ Of Sc At Columbia, Columbia, SC; FR; PHARD; Alpha Lambda Delta Cncl 90-; Phi Eta Sigma 90-; Gamma Beta Pi 90-; Phrmcy; Rsrch.

**HECHT, ROBERT L,** Ny Univ, New York, NY; GD; MBA; Econ.

**HECKATHORN, RHONDA L,** Daemen Coll, Amherst, NY; SO; BS; Comm Serv Vol Physcl Thrpy Dpts 88-89; AAS SUNY Delhi 86; PT.

**HECKMAN, CHRISTINE D,** Shippensburg Univ, Shippensburg, PA; SO; Mrchng Bnd 89-; Silk Squad 89-; Acctng/Finance Clb 90-; Phi Sigma Pi Treas; Acctng Internshp; Acctng; Chief Financial Officer.**

**HECKMAN, KATHRYN A,** Eastern Coll, Saint Davids, PA; FR; BA; Nwspaper/Litry Magzn 90-; Hons Prog 90-; Habitat For Humanity 90-; Engl; Creative Wrtng/Jrnlsm.

**HECKMANN, NATASCHA,** Miami Dade Comm Coll, Miami, FL; FR; BED; Phi Theta Kappa 90-; Bsn Admin.

**HECTOR, KENYATIA R,** Stillman Coll, Tuscaloosa, AL; FR; BA; Gamma Iowa Sigma 90-; Sociology.

**HECTOR, RON E,** Oh Univ, Athens, OH; FR; BA; Crmnl Jstce Clb 90; Alpha Almbda Delta 90; Chem Eng; Rsrch In Phrmctcls.

**HEDAYAT, NAZANIN M,** Savannah Coll Of Art & Design, Savannah, GA; FR; BFA; Deans Lst 90-; Intrnshp Weaving Tchr Kingswood Day Camp; Fiber Arts; Fabric Artist/Textile Dsgn Fshn.

**HEDETNIEMI, MEGAN C,** Anne Arundel Comm Coll, Arnold, MD; SO; BA; Stdnt Nwspr Edtr 88-; Fn Arts Lit Mag Mng Co Edtr 89-; Otstndng Stdnt Ldrshp Awd; 1st Annl AMARANTH Vllybl Tourn Co Org; AA; Engl/Jrnlsm; Jrnlst/Nws Reprtr.

**HEDGE, CHERYL L,** Univ Of Cin R Walters Coll, Blue Ash, OH; SO; AAS; Vtrnry Med; Tchncn.

**HEDGECOCK, AMY L,** Winthrop Coll, Rock Hill, SC; SO; BS; Alpha Lambda Delta; Winthrop Schlrs; Aerobics; Sci; Med Tech.

**HEDGECOCK, SUSAN R,** Patrick Henry Comm Coll, Martinsville, VA; SO; AS; Phi Theta Kappa 89-; Genl Studies; Nrsng Degree PHCC/RN.

**HEDGEPATH, KIMBERLY D,** Draughons Jr Coll Nashville, Nashville, TN; SO; AS; Pres Lst 90-F; Bus Mgmt.

**HEDGEPETH, CHRISTY L,** Univ Of Southern Ms, Hattiesburg, MS; SR; MBA; Stdnt Edn Assn 88-90; Alpha Lambda Delta Sec 87-89; Proj Wild Cert Instr 90; BA Elem Edn 90; Elem Edn.**

**HEDGES, SHAE B,** Central Fl Comm Coll, Ocala, FL; FR; AA; Schlrshp 90-; Nrsg.

**HEDIGER, KIM R,** Ny Chiropractic Coll, Glen Head, NY; GD; Talent Show Cmtee Stg Mgr; Deans Lst 88-; Hon Frat 89-; Acad Schlrshp 90-; BS Rutgers Univ 87; Chirprctc.

**HEDIN, DIANE MARIE,** George Mason Univ, Fairfax, VA; SR; BS; US Yth Natl Soccer Team 87; Kappa Delta Pi 87-; IM Bsktbl/Soccer Capt 86-89; Phys Educ/Hlth Ed; Mktg Rsrch.

**HEDLUND, KRISTIN B,** Bowling Green St Univ, Bowling Green, OH; SR; BED; Actvts Orgn 87-90; Alpha Lambda Delta 87-; Gldn Ky 89-; Phi Epsilon Omega 90-; Indpndnt Rsrch Stdy 90; Intern Health Pl 90; Arbcs Instr 90-; Sprt Mngmnt; Wlnss Corp Ftnss.

**HEDLUND, TANIA L,** Univ Of Rochester, Rochester, NY; SO; BA; Chmbr Sngrs 90-; Peer Asst Career Svcs/Plcmnt Ctr; Tieman Res Hall Rep 89-; Delta Gamma Sngldr 90-; Vars Vlybl Ltr 89-90; Psych; Scl Wrk/Prof.

**HEDMAN, STACEY A,** Fl Atlantic Univ, Boca Raton, FL; FR; BA; Phi Eta Sigma; Liberal Arts; Law.

**HEDRICK, BRENDA L,** Christopher Newport Coll, Newport News, VA; SR; BS; Aerbcs Instr; Lgl Sec 78-82; AAS Thomas Nelson Comm Coll 78; Phy Ed; Tchr.

**HEDRICK, KEITH,** Lenoir Rhyne Coll, Hickory, NC; JR; Mu Sigma Epsilon 90; Cmptr Prog.**

**HEDRICK, KIMBERLY A,** Gaston Coll, Dallas, NC; FR; Eastridge Mall Fashion Bd 90-; Deans Lst 90; Pr Lst; Gamma Beta Phi 90-; Schlstic Achvmnt Schlrshp Awd 90-; Bus/Real Est; Acctng.

**HEDRINGTON, PATRICE C,** Hampton Univ, Hampton, VA; FR; Intrntl Stdnts Assoc 90; Psych/Lrng Dsordrs; Spec Ed.

**HEDSTROM, DANIEL R,** Embry Riddle Aeronautical Univ, Daytona Beach, FL; SR; BA; Prcsn/Dmnstrtn Flght Tm 90-; USAF Mssl Mntnce Tech 85-90; Aerontcl Sci; Arln Pilot.

**HEEG, STEPHEN A,** Northern Ky Univ, Highland Hts, KY; JR; BA; Provident Bnkrs Assoc 90-; IM 89; Hstry; Law.

**HEEREN, EMILY D,** Mount Olive Coll, Mount Olive, NC; SO; BAS; Concert Choir 89-; Ldrs Schlr 89-; Choir Ldrshp Awd 89-; Music; Vocal Dir.

**HEESCH, J TODD,** Lexington Comm Coll, Lexington, KY; FR; BS; Bio; MD.

**HEFFER, ANGELA D,** Va Commonwealth Univ, Richmond, VA; SR; BA MT; Intl Stdnt Assc 88-89; Phi Eta Sigma; Sigma Delta Pi Tres; VA Tchr Schlrshp/Loan 90-; Paul Douglas Tchng Schlrshp 90-; Spanish/Education; Teaching.

**HEFFERN, PATRICIA A,** Hudson Valley Comm Coll, Troy, NY; SO; AAS; Human Svcs Clb 89-; Phi Theta Kappa 90-; Otto Gunther Schlrshp; Addie Timber Human Svcs Schlrshp; Soc Wk; Schl Soc Wk.

**HEFFERNAN, CATHERINE S,** Marywood Coll, Scranton, PA; FR; BFA; Intrntl Clb 90; Art.

**HEFFERNAN, KRISTIN M,** Niagara Univ, Niagara Univ, NY; JR; BA; Artn Exctv Brd Sec 89-; Prnts Wknd Cmmtt Chrprns 90-; Stdnt Govt Pblcty Chrprsn; Clncl Psychlgst.

**HEFFERNAN, ROBERT R,** Cornell Univ Statutory College, Ithaca, NY; FR; Navy ROTC; Bsn; Navy Ofcr.

**HEFFINGTON, TERESA K,** Volunteer St Comm Coll, Gallatin, TN; SO; BBA; Acctng Clb 90-; Beta Sigma Phi Treas 86-; Gamma Beta Phi 85; Admin Asstnt 85-88; Employee Commonwealth VA Dept Hlth 89-90; Bus; Acctng.

**HEFFRON, PATRICK J,** Bloomsburg Univ Of Pa, Bloomsburg, PA; FR; BA; Sci; Tchr.

**HEFLIN, JOHNNY L**, Univ Of Al At Huntsville, Huntsville, AL; SR; BS; Engrs Clb 88-89; Eta Kappa Nu 90-; Tau Betta Pi; Phi Theta Kappa 88-89; IEEE; Co-Op Stdnt NASA 90-; AS J C Calhoun St Jr Coll 89; Elect Engr.**

**HEFLIN, NECHELLE D**, Central St Univ, Wilberforce, OH; FR; BS; Hnr Stdnt; Cashier; Bsn; Fin.

**HEFNER, HOLLY L**, Longwood Coll, Farmville, VA; SR; NA; Stdnt Educ Assn 90-; Natl R Crs 87; Spec Olympcs Vol 87-; BS 90-; Ele Educ; Educ/Tch.

**HEFNER, KRISTI GREENE**, Univ Of Ga, Athens, GA; SO; BSFCS; Rcrtmnt Tm 89-; Htl/Rstrnt Adm; Corp Law.

**HEFNER, MARK E**, Clemson Univ, Clemson, SC; SO; BS; Calhoun Hnrs Coll 89-; Palmetto Fellow 89-; Computer Engineering.**

**HEGENBART III, JOSEPH JOHN**, Georgetown Univ, Washington, DC; SR; BA; Bus; CPA.

**HEGER, ALLYSON R**, Univ Of Cin R Walters Coll, Blue Ash, OH; SO; BS; Vrsty Dvng 90-; Bus; Law.

**HEGER, ELISE A**, Univ Of Nc At Greensboro, Greensboro, NC; JR; BS; Gama Beta Phi 89-90; Mrshls; Glfrd Mddle Intshp; Ed; Tch.

**HEGNER, PAUL A**, Fl International Univ, Miami, FL; SR; BS; Phi Kappa Phi 89-; Grad W/Hon 90; AA Miami Dade Comm Coll 85; Educ; Tchr.

**HEGSETH, JO DELL M**, Georgetown Univ, Washington, DC; SO; BSBA; Bus; Intl Bus.

**HEGWOOD, BARBARA L**, Univ Of Ga, Athens, GA; SR; BSED; AATSP; ACTFL; Goldn Key; Sigma Delta Pi; Kappa Delta Epsilon; Kappa Delta Pi; Mltry Fmly Spprt Grp; Tchrs Aide 80-88; Spnsh; Tchr.

**HEGWOOD, TRACY L**, Wallace St Comm Coll At Selma, Selma, AL; JR; BA; Edctn.

**HEIBERGER, JOSEPH D**, Univ Of Southern Ms, Hattiesburg, MS; JR; BA; USM Mrchng Bnd Sctn Ldr; St Louis Comm Coll Meramec Music Stdnt Yr; Music Educ; H S Bnd Dir.

**HEICHBERGER, LISA E**, S U N Y Coll At Fredonia, Fredonia, NY; FR; BS; Nwsltr Editor Dorm Cncl 90-; Biol/Pre Med; Med.

**HEID, CHRISTY A**, Westminster Coll, New Wilmingtn, PA; SR; BS; Soc Phys Stdnts 89-; Math Assn Amer VP 90-; Westminster Coll Orch Sectn Ldr 87-90; Kappa Mu Epsilon VP 89-; Pi Sigma Pi 90-; Mortar Brd 90-; Lambda Sigma 88-89; Omicron Delta Kappa 90-; Sigma Pi Sigma 90-; Kappa Delta Phlnthrpy 88-; Physcs/Mth; Grad Schl.

**HEID, LUCILLE P**, Schenectady County Comm Coll, Schenectady, NY; FR; Bus; MBA.

**HEIDE JR, HANS D**, S U N Y At Binghamton, Binghamton, NY; SR; BS; Clg Repubs 90-; Acctg Mgmt Org 87-; Round Hill Masons 89-; USAA All-Amer Schlr 90-; Dns Lst 90; Acctg/Hstry; Law CPA.

**HEIDENFELDT JR, DENNIS A**, Univ Of Sc At Sumter, Sumter, SC; SO; BS; Bio; Cytotech.

**HEIDENREICH, BETH E**, Anderson Coll, Anderson, SC; SO; Alumni Cncl Pres 89-; Gamma Beta Phi 89-; Hon Pgm 89-; Tutor 89-; Clg Bowl 90-; Intrntl Bus; Upr Mgmt Mltntl Corp.

**HEIDENREICH, MARYANNE**, Franklin And Marshall Coll, Lancaster, PA; SR; Bus Clb Pres 87-; Phi Betta Kappa 90; Pi Gamma Mu 90; Alpha Phi Schlrshp Chrmn 88-; Marketing Interns 88-90; Dana Schlr; Noel P Laird Prz; Mrktng.

**HEIER, ELIZABETH A**, Ga St Univ, Atlanta, GA; SO; BSE; Dns Schlrshp Key 89-90; Early Chldhd Educ; Tchr.

**HEIFNER JUNGE, SANDRA**, Brescia Coll, Owensboro, KY; SR; BS; NSSLHA Pres 90-; Alpha Chi; Dns Lst; Sec Worthington Steel Co 79-90; Cmntv Sci Dsrdrs; Spch Pthlgy.

**HEIGEL, KRISTIN M**, Duquesne Univ, Pittsburgh, PA; SO; BS; SNAP 90-; Lambda Sigma 90-; Phi Eta Sigma 90-; Pres Awd; Deans Lst; Nrsng.

**HEIGH, IRENE M**, Coppin St Coll, Baltimore, MD; SR; BS; Vd Prdctn Clb Cntnty Wrtr 89-; Arn Plyrs Cmmnty Thtr Hstrn 85-; Sigma Tau Delta 90-; Hnr Engl Md Arts Stdnt 90-; Gvrnrs Smmr Interh Pbl Rltns Offcr Intern; Prk Hghts Cmmnty Corp; Cncrnd Ctzns; Erly Chldhd Cert 87; AA Cmmnty Coll Baltimore; Gen Ed Erly Chldhd Engl; Pschlgy Thtr.

**HEIGHLEY, CATHY R**, Kent St Univ Stark Cmps, North Canton, OH; SO; BED; Alpha Lambda Delta 89; Scl Studies; Scndry Educ.

**HEIJNEN, JEROEN A**, Univ Of Akron, Akron, OH; SR; BA; Bsns Fin/Intl Bsns; Fin.

**HEIL, REBECCA M**, Univ Of Sc At Columbia, Columbia, SC; SO; BS; Assoc Hnrs Stdnts Secr 89-; Canterbury Clb 89-90; Beta Beta Beta 89-; Gamma Beta Phi 89-90; Kappa Kappa Gamma Schlrshp Chr 90-; Bio; Physician.

**HEILMAN, JEAN A**, Northern Ky Univ, Highland Hts, KY; SO; BFA; Baptist Stdt Union 89-; Chior 90-; Stdt Alumni Ambsdr 90-; Presdtl Ambsdr 90-; Art/Psychology; Art Therapy.

**HEILSHORN, SANDRA K**, Defiance Coll, Defiance, OH; JR; BS; Elem Ed.

**HEIM, ANN RENEE**, Longwood Coll, Farmville, VA; SO; BA; Dramatic Grp 89-; Forensics Tm; Delta Phi Alpha V P 90-; Rotunda Feature Columnist Sch Newsppr; Nancy Weir Waters Lyons Schlrshp; Engl; Newscaster/Jrnlst.

**HEIN, KARL S**, Unity Coll, Unity, ME; JR; BS; Soc Sci; BMA.

**HEINATZ, CHRISTINA M**, Christopher Newport Coll, Newport News, VA; JR; BA; Elem Tchr.

**HEINECK, PATRICIA E**, The Kings Coll, Briarclf Mnr, NY; FR; BA; Cmps Life Stff; Accntng.

**HEINEMANN, MARK G**, S U N Y Coll Of Tech At Alfred, Alfred, NY; SR; AAS; Soc Manuf Engrs Pres; Engr; Mltry Serv.

**HEINEN, AMY M**, Endicott Coll, Beverly, MA; SR; AS; Pres Bus Clb 89-; Stdnt Orien Ldr Shipmat 90-; Ambsdrs Prog; Phi Theta Kappa 89-; Acctng; CPA.

**HEINKE, TAMARA L**, Capital Univ, Columbus, OH; SR; BSN; Pi Phi Epsilon S 90-F SAFECO Stdnt Gov 90; Crclm Comm Jr Rep 90; Sigma Theta Tau; Ldrshp Achiev Awd; Nrsng.

**HEINLEIN, BONNIE J**, Indiana Univ Of Pa, Indiana, PA; JR; BED; PSEA 89-90; Alice Paul House Womns Shltr; Delta Gamma 90-; Speech Pathology Audiology; Speech Pathology.

**HEINLEIN, MELISSA A**, Duquesne Univ, Pittsburgh, PA; FR; BS; Ornttn Stff; Acad Of Stdnts Of Phrmcy 90-; Lambda Kappa Sigma 90-; Hosp Phrmcy.

**HEINO JR, WILLIAM J**, Molloy Coll, Rockville Ctr, NY; JR; BS; Std Govt Pres 89-90; Cmps Mnstrs 88-; Lit Mag Treas 90-; Delta Epsln Sigma; Omcrn Alpha Zeta; Chi Beta Phi; Lynbrook Aux Police 89-; KC 89-; Franklin Gen Hosp Intshp; Baseball 89-; Bio/Chem/Pol Sci; Med/Law.**

**HEINRICH, GRETCHEN A**, Mount Aloysius Jr Coll, Cresson, PA; SO; Vlybl Sftbl MVP Awd 90-; Cmptr Sci/Acctg.

**HEINRICHER, MICHAEL A**, Grove City Coll, Grove City, PA; FR; BS; Vrsty Bsbl; Vrsty Sccr; IM; Rndtble VP; Phi Tau Alpha; Intrntl Bus; Bus.

**HEINTZ, STEPHANIE M**, Univ Of Nc At Charlotte, Charlotte, NC; JR; BA; Bapt Stdnt Unn BSU Cncl Mssns Chrprsn Mnstry Chrprsn 89-; IM Ftbl Vlybl Bsktbl Sft; Chlrtte Chrle 89-; Phi Kappa Phi; Phi Eta Sigma 89-; Gldn Ky 90-; Vol Sr Gms; Bapt Stdnt Unn Cncl 89-; Colvard Schlrshp 88-; Offcl Of Ssn Sftbl Ftbl 90; Engl; Educ Scndry.

**HEINTZE, THERESA C**, Univ Of Pittsburgh, Pittsburgh, PA; SR; BASW; Cmpln Choir Comm 89-; Univ Info Chrctr 90-; Univ Schlr 90-; Dns Schlr Awd; MBR Hnrs Cnvct; BSC Monash Univ 85; Scl Wrk.

**HEINTZEL, LINDA K**, Indiana Univ Of Pa, Indiana, PA; SR; BED; Asn Chldhd Educ Intl; PA St Educ Asn 90-; Kappa Delta Pi 90-; Dns Lst 87-; Erly Chldhd Educ; Tchng/Admn.

**HEINZ, ERICH R**, United States Naval Academy, Annapolis, MD; SR; MD; FCA 88; Phi Alpha Theta; S Sch Tchr 90-; J V Wndsrfng 90; BS; Med; Fam Prctc Dctr.

**HEINZ, M MICHELE**, Univ Of Ky, Lexington, KY; JR; PHARM; KASP Tres; KAGE 85-90; Leg Wmn Vtrs Tres 88-90; PTA Chrmn Gftd Tlntd 89-90; Yth Sccr Asst Coach 88-89; BS Physics Unv Dayton 75; Pharmacy.

**HEINZ, ROBERT C**, Widener Univ, Chester, PA; JR; BS; Amer Inst Chem Engrs Stdnt Govt Assn Rep; Chem Eng.

**HEINZEN, DONNA M**, Hudson Valley Comm Coll, Troy, NY; FR; BA; Girl Scout Ldr 87-; PTA; Phi Theta Kappa; Liberal Arts.

**HEIOB, JOAN M**, Northern Ky Univ, Highland Hts, KY; SO; BA; Grphc Dsgn Art.

**HEIS, AMY K**, Univ Of Cincinnati, Cincinnati, OH; JR; Kappa Delta Pi 89-; Stdnt Cncl Excptnl Chldrn 89-; Drill Tm 88-89; Multihandicapped Edn; Tchr.

**HEISCHMAN, SUSANNAH L**, Kent St Univ Kent Cmps, Kent, OH; JR; BA; Fshn Stdnts Org 88-89; Alpha Lambda Delta 89-; Pres Lst 90; Anthrplgy/Hstry; Archlgy.

**HEISE, SCOTT R**, Air Force Inst Of Tech, Wrt-Ptrsn Afb, OH; GD; MSSM; Tau Beta Pi 85-; Eta Kappa Nu 85-; Sigma Iota Epsilon; Air Force 86-; Reliability Maintainability Eng 86-90; Ingrtd Logstcs Supp Mngr; BSEE Univ Tx Arlington 85; Bus Mngmnt.

**HEISE, SUSAN K**, Hillsborough Comm Coll, Tampa, FL; SR; RTT; Radiation Thrpy Clb 90-; Awd For Acad Excel 90-; ARRT 71-; Swfsrtt 81-; Morton Plnt Hosp Rad Thrpy; RT Morton Plant Hosp 71; Rad Thrpy.**

**HEISELBERG, ANN**, Lasell Coll, Newton, MA; SO; AA; High Hnrs 89-90; Liberal Arts.

**HEISER, CANDICE E**, Univ Of Akron, Akron, OH; FR; BS; Honors Program; Acctg; CPA.

**HEISER, TODD M**, Savannah Coll Of Art & Design, Savannah, GA; JR; Amer Assc Archtctr Stdnt 89-; ISID 89; Deans List 89-; Rsdnt Asstnt 90-; Actvts Cncl 89-90; NAAB Crd Inclsn; Frncs Mccommon Schlrshp 89-; Archtctr.

**HEISINGER, ELIZABETH**, Columbia Greene Comm Coll, Hudson, NY; NY; CAC; Drg/Alchlsm Grp Thrpst St Peters Adctn Rcvry Ctr; BA Suny New Paltz 90; Adctn Stds; Intrvntn Spclst.

**HEIST, HOLLY L**, Radford Univ, Radford, VA; SR; BS; Psychlgy Clb 90; Womens Rsrc Cntr Vlntr 90; IM Vllybll 87-88; Psychlgy; Industrial/Orgnztnl Psychlgy.

**HEISTER, ERIK D**, Fl International Univ, Miami, FL; SO; Chr 90-; Flr Govt 90-; Yga Clb 90-; Aikido Clb 90-; Pr Md Hnr Scty 90-; Phi Eta Sigma 90-; Hnrd Pnst; Engnrng; Mdcl.

**HEIT, ETHAN D**, Univ Of Miami, Coral Gables, FL; SO; BSEE; Hnrs Asc 89-; Jwsh Org 89-; Alpha Lambda Delta; Phi Eta Sigma; Alpha Epsln Pi 89-; Dns Lst 89-90; Pres Hnr Rl 90; Elec/Elec Engr 90-; Cmptr Engr; Med.

**HEITZ, BRIAN J**, Kent St Univ Kent Cmps, Kent, OH; JR; BS; Biology; Envrnmntl Serv.

**HELBERT, VALERIE M**, Bridgewater Coll, Bridgewater, VA; SO; BA; Pinion Plyrs 89-; Brthrn Stdnt Fllwshp Treas 89-; Intrdstrct Yth Cbnt Treas 90-; Lambda 90-; Lacrosse 89-; Hist/Pltcl Scnc; Elem Teach.

**HELD, AMY R**, Univ Of Akron, Akron, OH; SR; BA; Alpha Lambda Delta 87-; Golden Key 89-; Pi Mu Epsilon Sec 90-; Kappa Delta Pi 89-; Am Bus Machines Awd 90; Teaching Asst Calculus; Math/Bus; Scndry Edn.

**HELD, SARAH E**, Coll Of Charleston, Charleston, SC; SR; BS; Psychlgy Clb; Omicron Delta Kappa; Chi Omega Pnhlnc Dlgt 89-90; Deans Lst; Psychlgy/Sclgy; Cnslng/Tchng.

**HELEMAN, BETH S**, Rutgers St Un At New Brunswick, New Brunswick, NJ; SO; BA; Fr Cncl 89-; Soph Cncl Chrmn 90-; Chabad Hse 89-; Deans Lst; CHAIR; Econ/Pol Sci; Law.**

**HELF, JANICE D**, Borough Of Manhattan Comm Coll, New York, NY; SO; Deans Lst 90-; Grad Hnrs; AAS; Acctng; CPA.**

**HELFENSTEIN, MARY A**, Saint Francis Coll, Loretto, PA; JR; BS; Scl Wrk Clb VP 90; Rd Ky Clb Co Crdntr Spcl Evnts 88-; Vol 88-; Alpha Delta Mu; Scl Wrk.

**HELFER, LORI A**, Duquesne Univ, Pittsburgh, PA; SR; BA; Alpha Phi Pblc Rltns 88-89; Acctg Frm/Mktg Intrn; Mktg.

**HELFER, WENDY**, Ursinus Coll, Collegeville, PA; SR; BS; Phi Alpha Psi 88-; Psychlgy Clb 87-90; Phi Alpha Psi 88-; Spcl Olympcs 90-; Deans List 87-; Psychlgy; Tch.

**HELFGOTT, BATSHEVA**, Yeshiva Univ, New York, NY; GD; BA; Chem Clb 88-89; Cmptr Sci Clb 88-89; Drama Soc 88-89; Cum Laude 90; Dns Lst 87-88; Sigma Delta Rho 89; Hlth Career Oppor Pgm Rusk Inst 89; Bellvue Hosp Occup Thrpy Dept 89; Arts Crfts Tchr Syng 87-89; Hlth Sci; Occup Thrpy.

**HELFRICH, BRIAN R**, Niagara Univ, Niagara Univ, NY; SO; BBA; Acctg Scty Natl Assoc Acctnts 89-; Orttn Exec Brd; SGA Cmmtr Rep 89-; Econ Fnc Clb; Avtn Clb 90-F Alpha Kappa Psi 90-; IM Sftbll; IM Hcky; IM Ftbll 89-; Acctg Pol Sci; Law Pltcs.**

**HELFRICH, JENNIFER S**, Indiana Univ Of Pa, Indiana, PA; SR; PA St Educ Assn 88-; Assn Chldhd Ed Intl 89-; Intl Readng Assn 89-; Kystn St Readng Assn 89-; IN Readng Cncl 89-; PA Sci Tchrs Assn 89-; NEA 88-; Kappa Delta Pi 90-; Zeta Tau Alpha Rec Sec 86-90; Specolympcs 90; BS Elem Ed 90; Elem Ed; Tchr.

**HELFRICH, JOSEPH E**, Univ Of Miami, Coral Gables, FL; SO; BA; Lacrosse Clb VP 90; Alpha Lambda Delta; Ims 90; Econ CIS.

**HELLARD, KEITH A**, Ky St Univ, Frankfort, KY; SO; AS; Nwspr Dsgn Ed 90-; Press Assoc Humor Clmn Writing Cntst; Electronics.

**HELLEBUSCH, LORNA A**, Northern Ky Univ, Highland Hts, KY; SR; BA; Soc Wrk Clb 89-; Theta Phi Alpha V P 87-; Soc Wrk.

**HELLER, CARRIE J**, Univ Of Cincinnati, Cincinnati, OH; FR; BA; Sccm Ballet Ensemble 90-; Dance Major; Ballet Dncr/Dance Dept Hd.

**HELLER, DAVID M**, Univ Of Nc At Greensboro, Greensboro, NC; FR; BS; Prcssn Ensmbl 90; All Amer Schlr 90-; Physcs; Tchr.

**HELLER, KARENNA A**, Univ Of Fl, Gainesville, FL; SR; BA; Chmbr Sngrs VP 88-89; Chr 87-90; Phi Kappa Phi 90-; Golden Key 89-; Sigma Alpha Iota VP 88-; ACOA 90-; CMENC 87-; Intrnshp Pk Spgs Elem Music Tchr; Intrnshp Piper HS Muisc Tchr; Prfmd White House Wash DC 88; Music Ed; Prof.

**HELLER, KRISTEN LYNNE**, Lesley Coll, Cambridge, MA; JR; BA; Res Life Res Asst 90-; Daycare At Rsk Chldrn Intrnshp 88-89; Aid Inc Mthrs Int 89-90; Newtn Wellsly Hosp Intrnshp 90-; Humn Svcs; Chld Abuse Adv.

**HELLING, SCOTT**, Fl International Univ, Miami, FL; JR; BA; Phi Theta Kappa 89-; Kappa Delta Phi 90-; AS Cincinnati Tech Coll 81; AA Miami-Dade Comm Coll 89; Ed; Tch.

**HELLINGER, JULIE A**, Univ Of Nh Plymouth St Coll, Plymouth, NH; JR; BS; Schlrshp Awd Bsn Dept Scott Decoteux Concord Bank; Mktg; Bsn/Mktg.

**HELLMAN, DENISE K**, Univ Of Cin R Walters Coll, Blue Ash, OH; FR; BSN; Nrsng; Medwifery.

**HELM SMALLS, LESLIE M**, Ny Univ, New York, NY; SO; BA; Blue Cross Blue Shield; Bsn Mgmt.

**HELMICK, BARBARA A**, Averett Coll, Danville, VA; SR; BS; Newcomers Clb Mrtnsvl/Henry Cty Pres 74-80; SPIRE 90-; Hrns Schlrshp 89; Piedmont Yth Sccr Leg 79-; Mrtnsvl H S Parent Grp 89-; AAS Patrick Henry Comm Clg 87; Mgmnt.

**HELMICK, CYRSTAL L**, Wv Northern Comm Coll, Wheeling, WV; SO; AAF; Sec Sci; Offce Mgmt.

**HELMICK, JACKIE L**, Wv Northern Comm Coll, Wheeling, WV; SO; Phi Theta Kappa; AA WVNCC 91; Human Serv; Human Resource Mgt.

**HELMICK, WINDY G**, Univ Of Akron, Akron, OH; SR; BS; ACES 90-; Dns Lst 88-90; VFW Ladies Aux Post 7971 89-; Elem Ed; Ed.

**HELMS, COLIN S**, Indiana Univ Of Pa, Indiana, PA; SO; BS; Pblc Radio Assist Music Dir 89; Alpha Epsilon Rho 89-; Dns Lst 90; Cmnctns Media; Music Indus.

**HELMS, DEBORAH J**, Commonwealth Coll, Virginia Beach, VA; GD; AS; Lynnhaven Linc-Merc Data Engry Clrk 90-; Cmpr Sci.

**HELMS, JEFFREY L,** Greenville Tech Coll, Greenville, SC; SO; AA; Bio Clb 89-90; Psych; Cnslr.

**HELMS, KENNETH B,** Univ Of Nc At Charlotte, Charlotte, NC; SR; BS; Chem.

**HELMS, LORRETTA C,** Daytona Beach Comm Coll, Daytona Beach, FL; SO; Phi Theta Kappa Sec 90; Cmptr; Eng.

**HELMS, MELISSA DAWN,** Univ Of Nc At Charlotte, Charlotte, NC; JR; BA; Emrgng Ldrs Flctr 88-89; RA 90-; Orntn Tr Gde; Golden Key; NRHH; Clg Schlrs Amer; IM Vlybl/Sftbl Cpt 88-; BA UNC Charlotte; Bio/Educ; Tch.

**HELMS, RHONDA L,** Mercer Univ Schl Of Pharm, Atlanta, GA; JR; PHARM; ASP 90-; SNAPHA 90-; Cultural Div Comm 90-; Alpha Lambda Delta 87-88; Gamma Beta Phi 88-89; Kappa Epsilon Rec Sec; Merit Schlrshp Awd 90; Natl Coll Mnrty Ldrshp Awd; Deans List 87-; Pharmacy.

**HELMS, TIMOTHY A,** Methodist Coll, Fayetteville, NC; SR; BS; Bus; Mrktng.

**HELMUTH, MARK S,** Savannah Coll Of Art & Design, Savannah, GA; SO; BFA; Bapt Un 90-; Mry Whln Schlrshp 89-; Vd.

**HELTER, JAMES M,** Univ Of Akron, Akron, OH; SR; BA; Assoc Kent State 86; Hstry; Tchr.

**HELTON, JOHN D,** Univ Of Nc At Asheville, Asheville, NC; GD; BS; Baseball Schlrshp 86-; AS Montreat Anderson Clge 88; Bus Admnstrn; Business.

**HELTON, LAURA L,** Liberty Univ, Lynchburg, VA; JR; BS; Health Dimensions Clb Pres; Military Ministries; Dorm Prayer Ldr; Alpha Lambda Delta; Amer Alliance Hlth Physical Educ Recr Dance; Exercise Physiology Intrnshp 89; Yth Ministeries Intrnshp 90; Pediatric Rehbltn Int; Community Health; Health Psychology.

**HELTON, LINDA K,** Univ Of Southern Ms, Hattiesburg, MS; SR; BS; Big Crk Bapt Chrch Soso Ms; MANG 2nd Lt; Assoc Of Army Ntl Guard Nrses 90; Ms Nrses Assoc 88; Allnce Of Army Ntl Grd Hlth Care Prof 90; RN Chrge Nrse 88; AA Jones Cnty Jr Clg 88; Nrsng.

**HELTON, ROBERT T,** Indian River Comm Coll, Fort Pierce, FL; FR; AS; Sci; Radlgy.

**HELTON, SYDNEY A,** Univ Of Cincinnati-Clrmnt Coll, Batavia, OH; FR; AA; Deans Lst 90-; Bnkng 79-89; Lbrl Arts; Fctn Wrtng/Scl Wrk.

**HELTON, VICTORIA S,** Pellissippi St Tech Comm Coll, Knoxville, TN; SO; BSN; Sci; Nrsng.

**HELWIG, HARRY L,** Savannah Coll Of Art & Design, Savannah, GA; JR; BA; Arch.

**HEMANN, SUSAN J,** S U N Y Coll At Fredonia, Fredonia, NY; JR; MBA; Bus; Sigma Kappa 89-; Bus/Mktg.

**HEMBREE, BILLIE J,** Pellissippi St Tech Comm Coll, Knoxville, TN; SO; BS; Std Govt Sntr 90-; Phi Theta Kappa 90-; Scl Wrk; Chld/Fmly Serv.

**HEMBREE, SHERYL E,** Univ Of Sc At Columbia, Columbia, SC; SR; Erly Chldhd Edn; Teach.

**HEMBY, VIRGINIA,** Univ Of Southern Ms, Hattiesburg, MS; SR; BS; Pi Omega Pi 90-; Gldn Key 89-; Annelle Bonner Bsns Ed Schlrshp 89-; MS Bsns Edctn Awd Schlrshp 90-; Bsns Edctnf MED.

**HEMBY JR, WILLIAM E,** Va St Univ, Petersburg, VA; FR; BA; Mrchng Clb VP 90-; Drum Phi 90-; Pol Sci; Law.

**HEMMELGARN, JODY L,** Univ Of Cincinnati, Cincinnati, OH; JR; BA; SCEC 89-; Spec Educ; Tchr.

**HEMMER, ANTHONY R,** Univ Of Ky, Lexington, KY; JR; BS; 4 H St Tech Cncl 90; Alpha Epsilon Delta 88-; Yrbk Sctrn Edit 88-; Sftbl; Blgy; Med.

**HEMMER, PETER H,** Savannah Coll Of Art & Design, Savannah, GA; GD; MFA; BFA 87; Grphc Dsgn.

**HEMMINGS, HOWARD W,** Capitol Coll, Laurel, MD; SR; BS; Soccer Clb 90-; NSBE 89-; Alpha Chi 89-; Soccer Clb; Elec Engr.

**HEMOND, ROBYN M,** Fl St Univ, Tallahassee, FL; SR; MS; Phi Theta Kappa 88-89; BS; Lbry Sci; Childrens Media.

**HEMPFLING, LEIGH B,** Coll Of Charleston, Charleston, SC; SR; BS; Psych.

**HEMPHILL, SHANDA L,** Ms St Univ, Miss State, MS; FR; BA; Clg Repub 90-; Gamma Beta Phi 90-; Alpha Lambda Delta 90-; Phi Mu Kappa Alpha 90-; Deans Lst 90-; Occup Therapy.

**HEMSLEY, BONNIE J,** Ms St Univ, Miss State, MS; JR; BA; Alfa Romeo Owners Clb 86-; Sports Car Clb Am 86-; Gamma Beta Phi 88-; Phi Alpha Theta; Pi Sigma Alpha VP; ACT Schlrshp 88-; Pol Sci/Hist; Law.

**HENAGE, K DIANE,** Northern Ky Univ, Highland Hts, KY; SR; BA; Sec 84-90; Elem Tchr.

**HENCHEY, JEAN L,** Merrimack Coll, North Andover, MA; SO; BS; ACM Sec; Yrbk Layout Stf 90-; Corale 90-; Deans Lst 90; Muscn Merrimacks Collchrch 90-; Muscn St Theresas Chrch 85-; Atnd Ntl ACM Cont San Antonio Dlgt; Ergng Ldrs Conf; Cmptr Sci; Sys Anlyst.

**HENDERBERG, MARY,** Niagara Univ, Niagara Univ, NY; JR; BA; Stdnt Advsry Comm Dn Acdmc Explrtn 88-90; Internatl Hnr Soc Hstry; Natl Schlstc Hnr Soc; Big Bros/Big Sis 90-; NUCAP 88-89; Hnrs Ths Hstry; Hstry; Asian Stds.

**HENDERSON, ADAM WILLIAM,** Roanoke Bible Coll, Elizabeth Cy, NC; FR; BA; Bible/Theology; Chrstn Mnstry.

**HENDERSON, ADRIENNE V,** Clark Atlanta Univ, Atlanta, GA; SR; Alld Hlth Clb 87-; Carrier Thomas Jordan Schlrshp 89; BS; Comm Hlth Educ; Rehab Cnslr.

**HENDERSON, AMY MICHELE,** Univ Of Nc At Greensboro, Greensboro, NC; SR; BS; Deans Lst 88; Golden Chain 90; NAEYC 88; AEYC 88; NCAE 90; Erly Chldhd Ed; Tchr.**

**HENDERSON, ANN M,** Marshall University, Huntington, WV; FR; Bptst Campus Mnstries 90-; Mdl Lgue Arab States 90-; Phi Eta Sigma; Gamma Beta Phi; Comp/Bus Info Syst; Anlyst.

**HENDERSON, BETH A,** Univ Of Tn At Knoxville, Knoxville, TN; FR; BS; CHRA Exec Rep 90-; Crew 90-; Alpha Lambda Delta; Phi Eta Sigma; Pre Med; Occptnl Thrpst.

**HENDERSON, BRIAN J,** Fl A & M Univ, Tallahassee, FL; FR; BA; Theatre; Phi Eta Sigma; CIS; Computer Analyst.

**HENDERSON, CASSANDRA D,** Lane Coll, Jackson, TN; FR; BA; Blck Chrstn Fllwshp 90-; Acctng; CPA.

**HENDERSON, CHAD W,** Univ Of Sc At Columbia, Columbia, SC; SO; BA; Deans Lst 89; Pres Lst 90; Smmr Coop Prog Wth WABCO; AS USC Union; Eng.

**HENDERSON, CHERI A,** Fl St Univ, Tallahassee, FL; SO; MENSA 90-; Fut Educ Of Amer 90-; Phi Eta Sigma 89-; Cir K Dist Sec 90-; Otstndng Mbr FL Dist Of Cir K Intl 90-; Elem Educ; Tchr.

**HENDERSON, CHERYL L,** Coll Of William & Mary, Williamsburg, VA; FR; Stu Educ Assoc 90-; Psych Clb 90-; Educ Psychlgy; Tchg.

**HENDERSON, CHRISTOPHER SCOTT,** Me Maritime Academy, Castine, ME; SO; BA; Hockey 89-; Eng; Shppng.

**HENDERSON, CHRISTY HARRIS,** Emory & Henry Coll, Emory, VA; SO; Intrdscplnry Englsh; Elem Tchng.

**HENDERSON, CHRISTY M,** Univ Of Montevallo, Montevallo, AL; JR; BA; Stdnt Govt Sntr 88-90; Grmn Clb Pres 88-; Hon Clb 88-; Phi Alpha Theta Treas 90-; Omicron Delta Kappa 90-; Comm Cncl 88-89; Hon Advsry Bd 90-; Sr Advsry Bd 90-; Pres Lst 89-; Pltcl Sci; Frgn Serv.

**HENDERSON, DOUGLAS A,** Embry Riddle Aeronautical Univ, Daytona Beach, FL; FR; BS; Mgt Clb 90-; Scrmng Eagles Mdl Arpln Clb 90-; Deans Lst 90-; Aerontcl Sci; Prof Pilot.

**HENDERSON, DOUGLAS C,** Univ Of Nc At Charlotte, Charlotte, NC; SR; BA; Stu Govt 87-89; Rugby Clb 88-90; Intern Bureau Alchl Tbcco Frnrms; Chldr 89-; Crmnl Jstc; Fdrl Job.

**HENDERSON, EVALYN H,** Spelman Coll, Atlanta, GA; SO; BS; Natl Scty Of Blck Engs Fnncl Dir; CAU Physcs Clb Treas; Natl Scty Of Blck Physcts; Alpha Lambda Delta 89-; AT & T Schlr 89-; Coll Schlrs Of Amer; Otstndng Soph Dual Dgree; Math; Elec Eng.**

**HENDERSON, HOLLY J,** Samford Univ, Birmingham, AL; JR; BS; Dns Lst 89-; Otstndng Jr Elem Educ; Hgst Cls Hons Ruric E Wheeler Schlrshp Awd 90-; Elem Educ; Tchr.**

**HENDERSON, JAMES B,** Va Commonwealth Univ, Richmond, VA; SR; BA; Admnstrn Of Justice; Criminal Law.

**HENDERSON, JILL E,** Memphis St Univ, Memphis, TN; SR; BA; Alpha Lambda Delta/Phi Eta Sigma 88-90; Communications; Law.

**HENDERSON, JILL M,** Univ Of Akron, Akron, OH; SR; Gold Key 89-; Deans Lst 87-; Summa Cum Laude; BS; Elem Edn.

**HENDERSON, JOSEPH D,** James Sprunt Comm Coll, Kenansville, NC; JR; BS; Crmnl Jstc; Law.

**HENDERSON, JULIE A,** West Liberty St Coll, West Liberty, WV; GD; BA 90; Elem Ed.

**HENDERSON, KIMBERLY A,** Comm Coll Algny Co Algny Cmps, Pittsburgh, PA; SO; AS; SNAP 90-; Son/God Mnstry Evnglst; Nrsng.

**HENDERSON, LAURA L,** Averett Coll, Danville, VA; JR; BS; Deans Lst 89-; Grad Cum Laude; All Amer Schlrs; AS Danvl Comm Coll 90; Sclgy/Crmnl Juste; Prbtn Offcr Law.

**HENDERSON, M ELAINE SPEARS,** Univ Of Sc At Columbia, Columbia, SC; SR; BA; AA Midlands Tech Clg 81; Crmnl Jstc.

**HENDERSON, MARLOE Y,** Cheyney Univ Of Pa, Cheyney, PA; SR; BA; Fresh Orntatn Ldr 89-90; Nwspr 89; Video Prod Clb 90; Acad Exclnc 90; Deans Lst 90; Chrldrs Co Capt 88; Cmunctns.

**HENDERSON, MARY E,** Vt Law School, S Royalton, VT; GD; JD; Review Staff 90-; Review Note Editor; Am Jurisprudence Awd-Torts 89-90; Licensed Maine Real Estate Broker; BA Univ S Maine 80; Cert Univ S Maine 86; Law.

**HENDERSON, MARY M,** Western Piedmont Comm Coll, Morganton, NC; FR; Intrr Dsgn Clb 90-; Dns Lst; Intrr Dsgn.

**HENDERSON, MELISSA D,** Fl A & M Univ, Tallahassee, FL; SR; BS; Fl Physcl Thrpy Assn 89-; Amer Physcl Thrpy Assn 89-; Dean Lst 87-; Otstndng Vol Dept Hlth Rehab Serv; AA Fla Comm Coll Jacksonville 87; Physcl Thrpy; Reg Physcl Thrpst.

**HENDERSON, MICHELLE,** Miami Jacobs Jr Coll Of Bus, Dayton, OH; SO; AS; PTO 90-; AS 91; Comp Prgrmmg.

**HENDERSON, MICHELLE M,** Univ Of Miami, Coral Gables, FL; JR; BFA; Lcnsd Csmtlgst 82-; AA Miami Dade Cmmnty Clg 90; Grphc Dsgn/Illstrtn; Cmmrcl Artst.

**HENDERSON, NHYERE LYNN,** Central St Univ, Wilberforce, OH; SR; Prshng Rfls; Alpha And Omega; Spcl Olympcs 87-; Cmmssnd Offcr 2nd Lt US Army; ROTC; B Ed; Spcl Educ SBH DH LD; Tch.

**HENDERSON, PAULA EVETTE,** Central St Univ, Wilberforce, OH; SR; Pol Sci Assmbly; Alpha Kappa Mu; Hnr Stdnt; Alpha Kappa Alpha Sgt At Arms 90-; US Achvmnt Acad All Amer Schlr; Cllgte Awrd; CLEO Fllw; BA; Pol Sci Pre Law.

**HENDERSON, ROBERT M,** Chattahoochee Vly St Comm Coll, Phenix City, AL; SO; BSC; Bldg Sci; Cnstrctn Mgmt.

**HENDERSON, RODNEY L,** Birmingham Southern Coll, Birmingham, AL; FR; Ldrshp Cls 90-; Links Up 90-; Alpha Lambda Delta; Phi Eta Sigma; Kappa Alpha Order IM Chrmn.

**HENDERSON, SHARON M,** Radford Univ, Radford, VA; JR; BA; Intrvrsty Chrstn Fllwshp Grp Coord; Alpha Lambda Delta 89-; Psi Chi 90-; Phi Kappa Phi; Psych; Educ.

**HENDERSON, SONYA R,** Univ Of Sc At Columbia, Columbia, SC; SO; BA; Dance Co; French Clb; Deans Lst; French; Intl Bus.

**HENDERSON, STEPHANIE E,** Central St Univ, Wilberforce, OH; JR; BS; Kappa Pres 89-90; Natl Stdnt Bus League; Dns Lst; Bus Mgmt; Entrprnr.

**HENDERSON, VICKIE L,** Howard Univ, Washington, DC; FR; BBA; Columbia Lghthse For The Blind Vol; Ladies Of The Quad 90-; Bwlng Tm 90-; Bus Mngmnt; Corprte Law.

**HENDERSON, ZACHARY L,** Davis & Elkins Coll, Elkins, WV; FR; BA; Actvts Board Treas 90; Hnrs Assn 90; All Amer Schlr; IM Soccer; Outdoor Rcrtn; Outdoor Educ.

**HENDLEY, CHAD JONATHAN,** Univ Of Ga, Athens, GA; SO; BSED; GAHPERD/AAHPERD/PES Clb; Exrcs Sprt Sci; Phys Thrpsts.

**HENDLEY, CORRY L,** Univ Of Sc At Columbia, Columbia, SC; FR; BA; Assn Hon Stdnts 90-; Alpha Lambda Delta; Intl Stdies; Law.

**HENDLEY, GREGG L,** Livingston Univ, Livingston, AL; FR; BS; Pharmacy.

**HENDLEY, KEITH G,** Fl St Univ, Tallahassee, FL; SO; BS; Hons/Schlrs Pgm 90-; One Of Most Outstndng Frshmn Chem Stdnts 90-91; IM Ftbl 90; Elec Engr.

**HENDREICKS, MELISSA J,** Middle Tn St Univ, Murfreesboro, TN; JR; Anthrplgcl Scty 90-; Anthrplgy.

**HENDREN, MICHAEL A,** Murray St Univ, Murray, KY; JR; BME; Prcssn Ensmbl 90-; Mrchng Bnd 90; AS 89; Music Ed; Bnd Dir.**

**HENDREN, PENNIE J,** Dyersburg St Comm Coll, Dyersburg, TN; FR; Phi Theta Kappa; Psychology.

**HENDRICK, AMY D,** Western Ky Univ, Bowling Green, KY; FR; BA; Phi Eta Sigma; Elem Ed.

**HENDRICK, SHARON YVONNE,** Saint Pauls Coll, Lawrenceville, VA; SR; BED; Phi Beta Lambda Hstrn 90-; Natl Bus Educ Assn 90-; Mary Namlette Talley Mem Schlrshp; Ames Dept Store; Mecklenburg Cnty Schl Bd; Peebles Dept Store; AAS Data Prcsng SIDE VA Comm Coll 85; Bus Educ; Ph D Educ.

**HENDRICK, SUREYA Z,** Al St Univ, Montgomery, AL; FR; Phi Eta Sigma; Pres Schlrshp; Pol Sci; Corp Law.

**HENDRICKS, ANDREA L,** Univ Of Cincinnati, Cincinnati, OH; FR; BSN; Wash DC Schlrshp; Vol Amer Cncr Socty 9-; Vol Jewish Hosp; Lgl Sec 87-90; AAB 87; Nrsng.

**HENDRICKS, ERICA P,** Ky St Univ, Frankfort, KY; FR; BA; Deans Lst 90-; Sftbl Gldn Glv 90-; Comp Sci/Mth; Comp Tchncn.

**HENDRICKS, JUDITH M,** Bryant Stratton Bus Inst Roch, Rochester, NY; FR; AOS; Barbara J Nehrboss Schlrshp Awd 90; Comp Pgmg.

**HENDRICKS, MARY A,** Middle Tn St Univ, Murfreesboro, TN; SO; BED; Sec Metro Pblc Schls Nashville TN; Math/Elem Ed; Ed.

**HENDRICKS, RICHARD I,** Comm Coll Algny Co Algny Cmps, Pittsburgh, PA; FR; BA; USN; Archtctr.

**HENDRICKS, WENDY A,** Univ Of North Fl, Jacksonville, FL; SR; BA; Gldn Ky 90-; Kappa Delta Pi; AA Lake City Comm Coll 88; Elem Educ; Tchr.

**HENDRICKSON, JEAN M,** Schenectady County Comm Coll, Schenectady, NY; FR; Hmn Srvc Clb Pres 89-; Vol Eldry; By Clb Cb Scts; Hmn Srvcs; Engl.

**HENDRICKSON, LYNN M,** Comm Coll Algny Co Algny Cmps, Pittsburgh, PA; SO; ASSOC; Acctg; CPA.

**HENDRIX, C JENNIFER,** Fl St Univ, Tallahassee, FL; JR; BA; Grnt Key; Gym Coach Rec/Cmptv Lvl; Ownd Own Gym Prt Tm; AA 83; Elem Ed; Tchr.

**HENDRIX, DONALD K,** Univ Of Sc At Columbia, Columbia, SC; SO; BA; Acctg.

**HENDRIX, DUSTIN D,** Middle Tn St Univ, Murfreesboro, TN; SO; BA; Art; Cmmrcl Art.

**HENDRIX, TERRI L,** Appalachian St Univ, Boone, NC; SO; BA; Gamma Beta Phi; Bus; Acctng.

**HENDRIX, TODD A,** Middle Tn St Univ, Murfreesboro, TN; SR; BS; Aerspace; Airline Pilot.

**HENDRY, QUENTIN DONALD,** Clayton St Coll, Morrow, GA; JR; BBA; Sfty Escort Srvc Ariz State Univ; SGA Crdntr 85-87; Boy Scts Of Amer Asst Sr Ptrl Ldr 81-85; Order Of Arrow; Boy Scts; Robt Kalin Awd/Ldrshp/Rpnsblty 86; Sga Socty CPA'S Atlanta Chptr Test 3rd Plc 90; Mgmt Cmptrs; Mgr/Cnsltnt.

**HENDRY IV, WILLIAM C,** Old Dominion Univ, Norfolk, VA; SR; BS; VSE Proj Coord 89-; Golden Key 89; Tau Alpha Pi; Klinefelter Awd; U S Coast Gd 80-; AS Un/St N Y 88; Elec Engnrg/Tech.

**HENG, PO C,** Univ Of Al At Huntsville, Huntsville, AL; SR; BA; Eta Kappa Nu 89-; Tau Beta Pi 89-; Co-Op Intrnshp Boeing Comp Svcs Inc 88-; Elec Eng; Engrng.

**HENGBER, GREGORY P,** Stetson Univ, Deland, FL; JR; BA; Yth Mtvtrs 90-; Stdnt Ambssdr 90-; Mck Trl Tm 90-; Phi Alpha Delta VP 90-; Delta Sigma Phi 90-; Jdcl Intrshp Volusia Cnty Crthse; IM Athltcs 90-; AA Broward Comm Coll 90; Pol Sci; Law.**

**HENKE, DAVID THADDEUS,** Duquesne Univ, Pittsburgh, PA; FR.

**HENKE JR, ROBERT L,** Widener Univ, Chester, PA; GD; BS; IEEE 88-; SAE 89-; Tau Beta Pi; Elect Eng.

**HENKE, STEPHANIE J,** Univ Of Southern Ms, Hattiesburg, MS; SO; BSBED; Res Hall Assoc R A 90; Cnslr/Bilogy Lab Tchr Spcly Gftd Stdnts; Tau Beta Sigma Hstrn 89-90; Asst Biology Lab 90; Marine Bio/Educ; Tch Marine Mammal Stdy.**

**HENKEL, GREGORY M,** Univ Of Sc At Columbia, Columbia, SC; SR; BA; SCO 87-; Hbtt Hmnty; IM Bsktbl Sftbl 87-; Gldn Key 90; Emplyee Qrtr Bkstr 89; Mktg/Ins; Bus.

**HENKEL, ROBERT A,** Salisbury St Univ, Salisbury, MD; SO; BS; Math Assoc/Amer Pres; Phi Eta Sigma 89-; Cmptr Prg Intrnshp; Top 50% Ptnm Natl Comp; Meritorious Achvmnt Awd; Math/Physics.

**HENLEY, BRENDA K,** Winthrop Coll, Rock Hill, SC; SR; BED; Greeks Agnst Mismngmnt Alchl 90-; Kappa Delta Pi 89-; Delta Zeta Jdcl Brd 88-; Elem Ed; Ed.

**HENLEY, CYNTHIA D,** Valdosta St Coll, Valdosta, GA; SO; BSN; Mgr Nrdgnstc Lab 88-; Nrsng.

**HENLEY, ILENE JEWELL,** Livingston Univ, Livingston, AL; SR; BED; Alpha Chi; Alpha Upsilon Alpha VP; 7YSO-SCCR Tm Mthr; Tchr; Choir Dir-Meridian Ward-LDS Chrch; AA Music Educ Casper Coll 85; Educ; Tchng.

**HENLEY, KAREN,** Tougaloo Coll, Tougaloo, MS; SR; BA; Delta Sigma Theta Sgt At Arms 89-90; Economics; Tax Lawyer.

**HENLEY, KATHY M,** Roane St Comm Coll, Harriman, TN; SO; AAS; Cert Cmptr Oper Cahttanooga St Tech Comm Coll 82; Bus Mngd Tech; Bus/Insur.

**HENLEY, KRISTIN E,** Villanova Univ, Villanova, PA; SO; Spec Olympcs Buddy 89; Kappa Kappa Gamma 90-; Deans List 89-.

**HENLEY, LISA C,** Ms St Univ, Miss State, MS; FR; MPA; Stdnt Assoc Traff Appls Ct; Campus Crusade For Chrst 90; Gamma Beta Phi; Alpha Lambda Delta; Alpha Gamma Delta 90-; Pres Schlr 90; Pom Squad; Acctg.

**HENLEY, PATRICIA,** City Univ Of Ny City Coll, New York, NY; JR; BA; Debate Tm 89-90; Law Govt Scty 89-; Gldn Key 90-; Govt Rltns Intrn AAAS Wash Dc; CCNY Rosenberg Humphrey Intrn Nys Asmbly Albany NY; Comm Afrs Pdir Fndrsr 72-89; Natl Coalition 100 Black Wmn Pgm Comm 87-88 Cnvtn Mgr 87-88; Pblc Intrst Law/Pol Sci; U S Atty Fed Jdg.

**HENLEY, STEVE M,** International Bible Coll, Florence, AL; SR; MA; Stdnt Govt Drm Rep 88-89; Mssn Clb VP; Mt Plsnt Chrch ; Amrcn Rd Crss Instrctr 88-90mnstr 88-90; Engl.

**HENLEY, TANYA K,** Univ Of Nc At Charlotte, Charlotte, NC; SO; BS; Civitan Clb 89-; Bapt Un 90-; Beta Beta Beta 90-; Bio; Med.**

**HENLINE, TRACEY L,** Garrett Comm Coll, Mchenry, MD; SO; AA; Bsktbl Tm Co Cptn 89-; Hstry.

**HENN, JAMES E,** Ky St Univ, Frankfort, KY; SR; BA; U S Army 76; Non Commsnd Ofcrs Assn 80; AA Univ Mrylnd 86; Bus; Fin Cnsltnt.

**HENNE, ANNE K,** Allegheny Coll, Meadville, PA; JR; Orchss; Bible Stdy Ldr; Kappa Kappa Gamma; Psychlgy Math & Rel Stds; Bus.

**HENNE, CHRISTIAN L,** Oh St Univ At Newark, Newark, OH; SO; MBS; Schlrshp Bnqt 86-88; Ntl Hnr Scty 88-89; Newark Hnr Scty 90-; Acad Schlrshp 89-; Spcl Wrk Fr Pataskala Police Dpt; Glf/Tnns; ASA; Sci; Aerontcl Eng.

**HENNEBERRY, KRISTIN M,** Miami Univ, Oxford, OH; FR; BA; Sor ACEI; Hl Govt 90-; Dns Lst 90-; Phi Eta Sigma 90-; Alpha Lambda Dalta 90-; IM Sftbl 90-; Educ; Tchr.

**HENNEDY, MARY KATHRYN,** Providence Coll, Providence, RI; JR; BA; Pep Bnd 88-; Pep Bnd Pres 90-; Choir 88-; Choir Pres 89-; Jazz Bnd; Voice Lessons; Wnd Ensmbl 88-; Wnd Ensmbl Publcty Chr 90-; Lib Arts Hnrs Pgm 88-; Pastoral Cncl Lector 89-; Engl; Tchr/Wrtr.

**HENNEKES, LISA M,** Bellarmine Coll, Louisville, KY; SR; BA; Soc Hmn Rsrc Mgmt 90-; Econ Soc 89-; Orient Assist 89; Kappa Gamma Pi; Delta Epsilon Sigma 90-; Kappa Kappa Gamma 87-88; Habitats Hmnty 90-; St Vincent Depaul Soup Kitchen 89-90; IM Athl 89-90; Soccer Team 89-90; Bsn Admin/Econ; Mgmt.

**HENNEN, AMY E,** West Liberty St Coll, West Liberty, WV; JR; BS; Pnhlnc Cncl Dlgte; Delta Mu Delta; Alpha Xi Delta Treas; Bsn Admin; Mgmt.

**HENNESSEE, FRANKIE R G,** Middle Tn St Univ, Murfreesboro, TN; GD; Deans Lst 89-90; Boy Scouts Asst Ldr 90-; Sub Tchr; BS MTSU 90; Elem Edn; Teach.

**HENNESSEY, AMY L,** Manhattanville Coll, Purchase, NY; JR; BA; Econ/Mgmt Clb Pres 90-; Cmpus Radio Sta D J 88-; Alcohol Tsk Frc Rcgntn Wmn Soc 89; Res Asst 90-; Vol Ntwrk 90-; Tour Guide 89-; Gen Foods Intrn 90-; Mgmt; Human Rsrcs.

**HENNESSEY, DEBORAH A,** Temple Univ, Philadelphia, PA; JR; BSN; BS Duquesne Univ 88; Nrsng.

**HENNESSEY, LYNNE M,** Univ Of New Haven, West Haven, CT; SO; BBA; Cmmnctns; TV/RADIO.

**HENNESSY, REGINA L,** Bellarmine Coll, Louisville, KY; JR; BA; Ecnmcs Clb Pres 89-; Ecnmcs Jrnl Assoc Edtr 90-; Pres Schlrs 88-; Cmps Mnstry 90-; Pres Schlr 88-; Deans List 88; Lbtry Fund Cllqm 90; Economics; Govt.

**HENNIG, ARTHUR S,** Univ Of Hartford, West Hartford, CT; JR; BSBA; Stdnt Athletic Cncl Treas 90; N Athletic Conf All-Acad Tm 89; Div I Soccer 87; Mrktng; Sprts Med.

**HENNIGAN, TIMOTHY J,** S U N Y Coll At Fredonia, Fredonia, NY; SO; BA; WNYE Station; Asst Prdctn Mgr; Stdnt Assoc Rep 89-; Intern Applied Media Assoc; Cmmnctn; Dir.**

**HENNIGEN, CARL S,** Northern Ky Univ, Highland Hts, KY; FR; BA; Radio TV Film; Brdcstng Prgrmmng.

**HENNING, MARK J,** Cornell Univ Statutory College, Ithaca, NY; SO; BS; Stdnts Publ Serv Ctr 90-; Habitat Humanity; Protestant Coop Mnstry Co-Chair Pgm/Personell Comm/Chair Msns Comm 90; Crs Cntry Indoor Track 89-90; Plant Sci; Rsrch.

**HENNING JR, THOMAS L,** Bethel Coll, Mckenzie, TN; JR; BS; Stu Govt Assoc Sec Comm 90-; Food Comm 89-90; Blck Stu Union 89-90; Bsktbl Tm 90-; Chem Engr.

**HENNINGER, KATHERINE R,** Savannah Coll Of Art & Design, Savannah, GA; GD; MFA; Grad Stdnt Assn; Phi Beta Kappa 87-; Video Post Prod Proj Coord 86-; BA Univ PA 88; Photography; Teach.

**HENNINGS, JOY M,** Fl A & M Univ, Tallahassee, FL; FR; Actrl Sci; Actry.

**HENRARD, MARION B,** Manhattan Coll, Bronx, NY; JR; BE; Sngrs Clb Pres 89-; Plyrs Clb 89-; Math/Comp Sci Clb 89-; Pi Mu Epsilon 90-; Amer Inst Chem Engnrs 90-; Intern Exxon; Chem Engnrng.

**HENRIE, RACHNEE L,** Davis & Elkins Coll, Elkins, WV; SO; Art; Ed.

**HENRIKSON, DAN R,** Univ Of Sc At Columbia, Columbia, SC; SO; BA; Bus Admin; Entrprnr.

**HENRIQUES, CHRISTINA T,** Univ Of Miami, Coral Gables, FL; JR; BA; Soc Prof Jrnlsts Pres 90-; Dns Lst 88-; Hnrs Pgm 90-; MCA Rcrds Intshp PR 90; Jrnlsm Asstshp Clrcl 90; Jerry Bassin Adv Intshp 89; Jrnlsm; Law.

**HENRIQUEZ, CARLOS H,** Atlantic Union Coll, S Lancaster, MA; SR; BA; Theta Alpha Kappa; Scty Rlgs Studies Thlgy; AM Bible Scty Awrd; BA Columbia/European Clg 83; Religion/Thlgy; Thlgy.

**HENRIQUEZ, MISAEL,** Columbia Union Coll, Takoma Park, MD; SO; BS; ACM 89; Acctg Asstnt Intrn 90; Cmptr Sci/Acctg; Sftwr Eng.

**HENRY ANDINO, GEORGE MC D,** Univ Politecnica De Pr, Hato Rey, PR; FR; JR Achvmnt Qulty Cntrl Inspctr 88; Bsktbl Team 88-90; Cmptr Sci; Elctrcl Engr.

**HENRY, ANN L,** Neumann Coll, Aston, PA; SR; BS; Bus Clb Pres 89-; Intl Clb 87-89; Neumann Coll Comm Chorus 87-; Psi Chi 90-; Delta Epsilon Sigma 90-; Natl Coll Bus Merit Awd; Deans Lst 87-; Validictory Medal; Cert Coll So Quebec 87; Dip Antigua State Coll 83; Bus Admin/Acctg; Acctnt.

**HENRY, CHRISTINE R,** Comm Coll Algny Co Algny Cmps, Pittsburgh, PA; SR; AS; Tri State Radiation Oncology Scty 90; Radiation Therapy; RTT.

**HENRY, CYNTHIA L,** Hillsborough Comm Coll, Tampa, FL; SO; BED; SGA Sec 90-; Educ; Elem.

**HENRY, DOROTHY HOWARD,** Owensboro Comm Coll, Owensboro, KY; FR; ASN; Relgs Ed Tchr; Sci; RN.

**HENRY, ELAINE,** Paine Coll, Augusta, GA; SO; Psych; Schl Cnslr.

**HENRY JR, HUBERT,** S U N Y Coll Of Tech At Frmgdl, Farmingdale, NY; SO; AAS; Advrtsng Art/Dsgn; Grphc Dsgn.

**HENRY, JANET LYNN,** Millersville Univ Of Pa, Millersville, PA; SR; BSN; Comm Clincl Nrsng Perf Onclgy Nrsng Comm Mntl Hlth Nrsng 90-; Dipl R N Lancstr Gen Hosp Schl Nrsng; Sci Nrsng; Ger Nrsng.**

**HENRY, KANAN B,** Hampton Univ, Hampton, VA; SO; BBA; Stu Ldr 90-; Dance Co 89-; Bus Clb 90-; NAACP 90-; Fnnc; Law.**

**HENRY, KEIRA M,** Endicott Coll, Beverly, MA; SO; Bus Clb; Vars Clb; Tutr; Phi Theta Kappa P; Vlybl Capt; Sftbl Capt; Fash Merch.

**HENRY, LISA N R,** Medical Coll Of Ga, Augusta, GA; JR; BSN; Flwshp Chrstn Athletes 87-90; Cncrt Choir 86-87; Vanderbuddies 87-90; Chi Omega Chapln 87-90; Summer Pediatric Extrnshp; BS Vanderbilt Univ 90; Nurs; Pediatrics Nurs.

**HENRY, MELINDA S,** Univ Of Sc At Columbia, Columbia, SC; FR; BA; Math Clb; Intrmrl Offcl; Asst Coaching Chrch Team Vllybl 90-; Deans List 90-; Athltc Drctrs Hnr Roll 90-; Vlybll 90-; Mthmtcs; Engrng.

**HENRY, MICHAEL C,** Howard Univ, Washington, DC; GD; PHD; Nobche 89; Phi Theta Kappa 79; Jaycees; MS H V 85; BA Univ D C 82; Chemist.

**HENRY, PAMELA J,** Broward Comm Coll, Ft Lauderdale, FL; FR; AS; Phys Thrpst Asst Clb VP; Kappa Delta Pi 77-79; Davie Untd Meth Chrch 87-; BS Ed Ashland Univ 79; Phy Thrpy; Reg Physcl Thrpst.

**HENRY, REBECCA L,** Fl St Univ, Tallahassee, FL; JR; BME; Cmps Crsd Chrst 89-90; Pi Kappa Lmbd; Sgm Alph Iota Crspndc Sec 89-; Msc Educ.

**HENRY, RHONDA L,** Pellissippi St Tech Comm Coll, Knoxville, TN; SO; BS; Vsn Ntwrk 90-; Phi Theta Kappa 90-; Deans Lst 90-; Elem Ed; Tchr.

**HENRY, RONALD A,** City Univ Of Ny Lehman Coll, Bronx, NY; SR; BS; Gldn Ky Exec Comm Mbr 89-; CUNY Fndtn Schlrshp 89-; Pres Schlr 90-; Cmptng/Mgmnt; Prgrmng.

**HENRY, RUTH ANN,** Atlantic Comm Coll, Mays Landing, NJ; SO; BA; Cub Sct Den Mthr; Crisis Ln Vol; Utd Meth Wmn; Cert Medix Schl 78; Engl/Edctn; Tchr.

**HENRY, SHAWN M,** Fl International Univ, Miami, FL; JR; AA Miami Dade Comm Clg 90; Elem Educ/Erly Chldhd; Tchr.

**HENRY, TAMMY R,** Liberty Univ, Lynchburg, VA; JR; BS; SGA 90-; Pre Law Clb 90-; Econ; Law.

**HENRY, TODD G,** Univ Of Ky, Lexington, KY; FR; BARCH; Amer Inst Arch Stu 90-; Alpha Lambda Delta 90-; Phi Eta Sigma 90-; Arch/Cvl Eng; Cty Plnng Bldng Dsgn.

**HENRY, TRACY D,** Fayetteville St Univ, Fayetteville, NC; SO; BA; Std Gov Asc Sntr; Elem Ed/Sclgy; Tchr.

**HENRY, VIVA C,** Fl A & M Univ, Tallahassee, FL; JR; BA; FFEA 90-; BACCHUS 89-; White/Gold 90-; Beta Sigma Phi 87-; Elem Ed; Tchg.**

**HENRY-FORDE, VANESSA A,** City Univ Of Ny Med Evers Coll, Brooklyn, NY; SO; BS; Stdnt Gov Soph Rep; Tchr 84-84; Secretary; Business Adm; Mba.

**HENSHAW, BONNIE S,** Western Ky Univ, Bowling Green, KY; JR; BS; Phi Theta Kappa 90-F Phi Kappa Phi; Engl Award; Faculty Schlstc Award; Elem Ed; Ed.

**HENSHAW, JACQUELINE C,** Longwood Coll, Farmville, VA; SR; MA; Clg Rpblcns 87-; Mdrn Lang Clb 87-; Clg Radio DJ 88-90; Pi Delta Phi Pres 89-; Lambda Iota Tau 89-; French Bk Prize; BA; French.

**HENSLEY, ELIZABETH D,** Univ Of Ky, Lexington, KY; SR; Alpha Lambda Delta 88-89; Sigma Theta Tau 90-; Grad Dstnctn; BSN 90-; Nrsng; Ansthtst.

**HENSLEY, GEORGIA L,** Miami Chrisitian Coll, Miami, FL; SR; BS; Sr Cl V P 90-; Deans List 88-; Miami Chrstn Coll Schlr 88-; AA 90; Elem Edn; Teach.

**HENSLEY, JAMIE LUANNE,** Mercer Univ Schl Of Pharm, Atlanta, GA; SR; BPHAR; Amer Phrmctcl Assoc/Acdmy Stdnts Pharm Sec 87-88; Hyprtnsn Drg Abs Cmte ASP 87-89; Amer Soc Hosp Pharm 88-89; Red Crs CPR Lf Sfty Cert 87; Prtcptd Atlanta Hlth Fr 87-90; Kappa Epsilon Soc Chrm 87-; Kappa Psi 87-; Phrmcy.

**HENSLEY, JAN W,** Univ Of Tn At Martin, Martin, TN; SO; BBA; Alumni Council; Flwshp Of Chrstn Athletes; Pi Sigma Epsilon Pres 89-; Pi Kappa Alpha Treas 89-; Acctg; Law.

**HENSLEY, JENNIFER S,** Muskingum Coll, New Concord, OH; SR; Chrldr Capt 88-89; Stdnt Snte; Stdnt Fac Judcry Bd; Sr Hon; Phi Theta Beta 90-; Delta Gamma Theta Soc Chrmn 88-89; Chrldr Capt 88-90; Ele Educ.

**HENSLEY, MARY HELEN,** Coker Coll, Hartsville, SC; SR; Crew Tm Capt 88-; Chrldrs 88; Coker Singers 87-90; Commissioner 87-; Dns Lst; Fl Tme Practicum PWDE-TV 15 TV Grphcs Intern; Soccer 87-88; BA; Cmnctns; Grphc Art.

**HENSLEY, MIKE E,** Univ Of Sc At Columbia, Columbia, SC; FR; BA; Bus; Acctg/Mgmt.

**HENSON, AMANDA T,** Univ Of Sc At Spartanburg, Spartanburg, SC; FR; AD; Pclt Hls Bptst Chrch; Nrs; Neontl IC Nrs.

**HENSON, AUDREY R,** Western Carolina Univ, Cullowhee, NC; SR; BA; Stdnt Advsr Dean Arts/Sci 90-; Phi Gamma Mu 89-; Phi Kappa Phi 90-; Deans Lst 87-; Intrnshp Macon Cnty Mngrs Ofc; Pltcl Sci Merit Awd 89-; Pltcl Sci.

**HENSON, CAROL A,** Oh Univ-Southern Cmps, Ironton, OH; SO; BA; WOW Orgnztn 90-; Deans Lst 89-90; Baptist Church SS Tchr 90-; OA 90; Business.

**HENSON, CRISTINA L,** Livingston Univ, Livingston, AL; FR; Acctng.

**HENSON, JENNIFER K,** Coll Of Charleston, Charleston, SC; FR; BS; Blgy; Optmtrst.

**HENSON III, JOHN W,** Memphis St Univ, Memphis, TN; SR; BA; Cum Laude; Psychlgy; MA.

**HENSON, KEVIN T,** Univ Of Sc At Columbia, Columbia, SC; SR; BA; Skydvng Clb 88; Mountnr Whitewtr Clb; Kappa Psi 89-; Bio/Pre Phrmcy; Phrmcst.

**HENSON, MARSHA M,** East Carolina Univ, Greenville, NC; SR; BFA; Painting Guild; Gamma Beta Phi; Painting; Studio Artist.

**HENSON, MELISSA T,** Christian Brothers Univ, Memphis, TN; SO; BS; SHEA Organ Annual Stf 88-89; Dns Lst DSU CBU 88-; Tri Delta Sor Delta St Un 86-89; St Francis Hosp Vol Wk; Educ; Tchr.

**HENSON, MICHELLE A,** Univ Of Charleston, Charleston, WV; JR; BA; Intrng W/Ranson Ranson/Mc Henry Law Firm; Hdstrt Pgm Clssrm Vlntr 89-; Bnk Tllr; Indvdulzd/Scl Sci; Law.

**HENSON, NATALIE S,** Howard Univ, Washington, DC; JR; BA; Gldn Key 90-; Ntl Cmptv Schlrshp 88-; Elem Ed.

**HENSON, PATSY G,** Univ Of Tn At Martin, Martin, TN; SR; BS; Deans Lst 79-80; Vol Ltrcy Pgms; AA Jackson St Comm Coll 83; Engl; Educ.

**HENSON, RANDY W,** Newbury Coll, Brookline, MA; FR; AS; Culinary Arts.

**HENTGES, AMY L,** Georgetown Univ, Washington, DC; JR; BSBA; Yrbk Stff Asst Edtr 88-90; Cr Un Asst Treas 89-90; Bus Schl Advsr 89-90; Phi Eta Sigma; Phone Frnd 88-89; Stdy Abrd/ Austrlia 90-; Acctg; Pub Acctnt.

**HENTON, EULANDO D,** Bethel Coll, Mckenzie, TN; SO; BA; Rlgn; Clergy.**

**HEPBURN, GARRYE A,** Miami Dade Comm Coll North, Miami, FL; FR; MBA; Engrng; Aeronautical Admin Engr.

**HEPBURN, INGA A,** Barry Univ, Miami, FL; SR; BA; Stdnt Govt 87-; Bahamian Clb 87-; Pblc Rel Scty Amer 87-89; Deans Lst 88-; Intrnshp Bahamas Tourist Ofc Coral Gables FL; Pblc Rel; PR Cnsltnt.

**HEPLER, JENNIFER A,** Comm Coll Algny Co Algny Cmps, Pittsburgh, PA; FR; BA; Avtrs Clb 90-; Avtn; Pilot.

**HEPNER, AIMEE M,** Central Pa Bus School, Summerdale, PA; SR; ASB; SG 89-; DPMA Treas 90-; Deans Lst 90-; Comp Info Syst.

**HEPP, DAVID C,** Le Moyne Coll, Syracuse, NY; JR; BS; Delta Mu Delta 90-; Internal Auditors Amer Awd; Acctg; Law.

**HEPPENSTALL, JENNIFER N,** Univ Of Sc At Columbia, Columbia, SC; JR; BA; Crlna Cares; Chi Omega Treas; Deans Lst; Fshn Mrchndsg.

**HEPPNER, MICHELLE,** Univ Of Sc At Columbia, Columbia, SC; FR; IM Vlyb!/Flag Ftbl; Sci/Math; Pre Med.

**HEQUEMBOURG, AMY L,** S U N Y Coll At Fredonia, Fredonia, NY; JR; BA; Hlth Serv Admin Clb 88-; Robert Rie Schlrshp; Hlth Serv Admin; Grad Schl.

**HERBAGE, MONIQUE N,** Memphis St Univ, Memphis, TN; SR; BA; Stdnt Govt Assn Senate 89-; Bands 88-90; Saxophone Quartet 88-89; Res Hall Assn Pgmmng Chair 89-90; Gamma Beta Phi 88-; MSU Band Schlrshp 88-90; Deans Lst 88-; Pol Sci/ Philosophy; Law.

**HERBERS, JENNIFER A,** Univ Of Cincinnati, Cincinnati, OH; SR; BED; Ntl Assoc For The Ed Of Yng Chldrn; Kappa Delta Pi 90; Golden Key 89; Alpha Lambda Delta 87; Hons Schlrshp 90; Tchrs Clg Alumni Assoc Schlrshp 90; J J Rollman Schlrshp 89-90; Early Chldhd Ed; Tchr.

**HERBERT, CHRISTOPHER W,** Oh Coll Of Podiatric Med, Cleveland, OH; SO; DPM; Stdnt Govt Treas 90-; Podiatric Medical Resch Asstnt 90-; Deans List 89-90; Merit Schlrshp 90-; Medicine; Dr Of Podiatric Medicine.

**HERBERT JR, DAVID L,** Wv Univ, Morgantown, WV; JR; BA; Aerospace Engnrng.

**HERBERT, SUSAN L,** Oh Wesleyan Univ, Delaware, OH; FR; BA; Phi Eta Sigma; Hbtat Hmnty.

**HERBSMAN, EVAN,** Yeshiva Univ, New York, NY; SR; BA; Economics; Law.

**HERBST, CHRISTINE HEIDI,** Ny Univ, New York, NY; MS; Grmn Clb Pres 81-84; IM Sftbll; Vlntr Rehb Dpt 89-90; Untd Wy Allctns Brd Cmmtt Mmb; Asst Treas Mfg; BBA 85; Physcl Thrpy Physcl Thrpst.

**HERBST IV, EDWARD J,** Temple Univ, Philadelphia, PA; GD; MA; Phi Theta Kappa 88-; Phi Alpha Theta 90-; Gldn Ky 90-; AS Montgomery County Comm Coll 88; BA 90; Hstry; Law.

**HERBST, HOLLY M,** Univ Of Cincinnati, Cincinnati, OH; SO; BA; Educ; Math.

**HERBST, MICHAEL E,** S U N Y Coll Of Tech At Frmgdl, Farmingdale, NY; FR; IM Ftbl/Sftbl/Var Tennis/Bwlng Tm/Lib Arts Clb 90-; Math; Educ.

**HERBSTER, KEITH A,** Juniata Coll, Huntingdon, PA; SO; BA; Ftbl Team Help Out With Easter Seals 89-; Var Ftbl IM Sftbl Soccer 89-; Pre-Law History; Law Or Hist Ed.

**HERC, JOHN C,** Duquesne Univ, Pittsburgh, PA; FR; BS; Pres Awd 90-; Dns Lst 90-; Bsn Admn; MBA.

**HERCEG, ELIZABETH M,** Case Western Reserve Univ, Cleveland, OH; FR; BA; Alpha Chi Omega; Thtre; MFA Actng.

**HERCHENHAHN, JAY D,** Tn Temple Univ, Chattanooga, TN; SO; BS; Bsktbl 89-90; Phy Educ; Coachg.

**HEREDIA, YOLANDA,** Univ Of Pr At Rio Piedras, Rio Piedras, PR; FR; BA; Natl Sci; Medicine.

**HERELLE, SIMON R,** City Univ Of Ny Baruch Coll, New York, NY; JR; BA; Clb Caricom 89-90; Econ; Law.

**HERENDEEN, BETH LEE,** Oh Wesleyan Univ, Delaware, OH; SO; BM; Pk Ave Jaz Wnd Ens Cntrl Ohio Symph Orch Sectn Ldr 89-; Musc Educ Natl Cnf VP 89-; Bibl Stdy 89-; Phi Eta Sigma 89-90; Phi Soc 90-; Mu Phi Epsilon Sec; Big Ltl Pal 89-90; Proj Hope 90-; Musc Educ; Tchg Musc.

**HERFORTH, BRENDA K,** Elmira Coll, Elmira, NY; JR; BA; AS Comm Clge Finger Lakes 79; Howard Hanlon Elem Schl Prnt Fclty Org; B C Cate Elem Schl Prnt Fclty Org; Chrc Schdlr Ltrgcl Mnstrs; Sbst Lay Rdr; Sbst Echrstc Mnstry; Cargill Wms Cncl; Amer Cncr Soc Vol; Math/Ed; Engrg/Ed.

**HERHAL, DEBRA A,** Hillsborough Comm Coll, Tampa, FL; SO; BA; Stdnt Support Servs Prog 90-; Phi Theta Kappa 90-; Bnkng/Finance; AA; Hist/Hmnts; Tch/Rsrch.

**HERHOLZ, MICHAEL E,** Fayetteville St Univ, Fayetteville, NC; FR; BS; Westarea Vol Fire Dept Inc Dep Chf/Pres Bd 88-; Ret Firefighter Fayetteville; Aerosp Engr; Engr.

**HERING, DAVID C,** George Mason Univ, Fairfax, VA; SO; BS; Clg Repubs 89-; Bapt Stdnt Union 89-; Alpha Lambda Delta 90-; Bsn Adm.

**HERIVEAUX, HERVE,** Ny Univ, New York, NY; FR; BA; Apple Bank Svngs Cstmr Serv Rep; Hnrbl Dschrg US Naval Seabees 89; Bus Finance; Bus Mgt.

**HERKE, KEVIN M,** Univ Of Charleston, Charleston, WV; SO; BA; Alpha Lambda Delta; Bsns.

**HERKES, SCOTT M,** Nova Univ, Ft Lauderdale, FL; GD; MBA; Amer Soc For Quality Control 90-; Rockwell Graphic Systems Div 87-; AA Univ Of MD 81; BS Iowa State Univ 87; Business; Quality Management.

**HERMAN, ADAM J,** S U N Y At Buffalo, Buffalo, NY; SR; BS; Univ Buffalo Acctg Assoc 89-; Natl Acctg Assoc 89-; Dns Lst 88-90; Edwin Gould Fdtn Schlrshp 87-; Pi Sigma Epsilon Fndg Father 88-; Res Advsr 90-; Pi Lambda Phi Fndg Father/Secr 87-; Asst Acad Coord Clifford Furnas Ctr Ldrshp 88; Acctg/Fincl Analysis; CPA.

**HERMAN JR, DAVID,** Fl A & M Univ, Tallahassee, FL; SO; BA; Career Ctr Cncl Pr 88-89; VICA 87-89; Big Bro; Printing Mgmnt; CEO.

**HERMAN, GAIL L,** D Youville Coll, Buffalo, NY; JR; BS; Clg Hnr Soc; St Catherine Amelia Awd 90; Employed St Josephs Hosp 86-; Med Secy 86-; AA Erie Comm Clg 86; Spec Educ; Handicapped Tchr.

**HERMAN, JONATHAN D,** Juniata Coll, Huntingdon, PA; SO; IM Bsktbl/Sftbl/Vlybl 90-; Soc Sci/Scndry Ed/Hist; Ed.

**HERMAN, KENNETH STEVEN,** Broward Comm Coll, Ft Lauderdale, FL; SO; BA; Phi Theta Kappa 90-; Co Prsntr Rsrch Tchng Psy Conf; Co Prsntr Rsrch Frshmn Yr Exp Conf 90; Cnslr Drug Rehab Facility 88-; Psychology; Private Practice Cnslr.

**HERMAN, ROBERT G,** Liberty Univ, Lynchburg, VA; JR; BS; Clss Pres Rep 89; Phi Alpha Theta 90-; Sigma Tau Delta 90-; Acad Dns Lst 86; BA Arizona College Of The Bible 89; Cert Phoenix Coll 90; Phlsphy And Govt; Law.**

**HERMAN, STEVEN D,** Widener Univ, Chester, PA; JR; BA; Std Nwspr Edtr 89-; Std Radio Sta Ofc Mgr 89-; Std Actv Comm 89-; Bsn Mgmt; Adv.

**HERMANCE, CHRISTOPHER P,** Wilmington Coll, New Castle, DE; FR; BA; Dover Air Force Base Aero Clb Stdnts Pilot 90-; Comml Pilot; U S Air Force Active Srvd Oper Des Strm Dplyr Armn 1st Cls 89-; Aviation Mngmnt; Commercial.

**HERMANN, MARGARET R,** Ursinus Coll, Collegeville, PA; SR; BS; Nwspr Editor In Chf 87-; Whitians 90-; Kappa Mu Epsilon 89-; AWM 89-; Kappa Delta Kappa Treas 88-; Acad Schlrshp 87-; Robert Reid Assoc 89-90; Deans Lst 88-; Vars Trck 87-88; Math; Actuary.

**HERMES, SUSAN J,** George Mason Univ, Fairfax, VA; JR; BWS; Gldn Key 90; Soc Wrk.

**HERMIDA, JANETTE D,** Univ Of Miami, Coral Gables, FL; SO; BA; Cane Cmmtr Org V P 90-; Stdnt Govt Sen Chrprsn 90-; Fed Cubn Stdnts; Phi Eta Sigma Sec 90-; Alpha Lambda Delta; Orient Pgm Asst Pgm Coord Cmtr Stdnst; Comm Publ Rel Chrprsn S G; Adv Ldrshp Inst Grad; Ldrshp Inst Co Tchr; Soc/ Philsphy; Law Educ.**

**HERMIDA, TERESA E,** Smith Coll, Northampton, MA; SO; BA; Pre Health Soc 90; Soph Rep 90-; Hlth Rep; Girl Scouts Trp Ldr 90; Deans Lst 89; First Grp Schlr 90-; USF Rsrch Prog; .psych; Med.

**HERMSTEIN, SONJA S,** Fayetteville St Univ, Fayetteville, NC; SO; BA; Elem Educ; Tchng.

**HERN, LEIGH A,** Miami Jacobs Jr Coll Of Bus, Dayton, OH; FR; Business; Inf Systms Mgmnt.

**HERNANDES, JOSE LUIS CABAN,** Catholic Univ Of Pr, Ponce, PR; GD; JD; Delta Theta Phi 90; Knight Colombus 74; Scl Wrkr; BA Intr American Unvrsty 72; MBA Intr Amercn Unvrsty 77; Law.

**HERNANDEZ AYALA, CLARISSA,** Inter Amer Univ Pr Hato Rey, Hato Rey, PR; SR; BA; Stu Comm 87; Hnr 85-86; BA 90-; Spnsh.

**HERNANDEZ CARLO, MARANGELLI,** Inter Amer Univ Pr San German, San German, PR; SO; BA; Biomed Sci; Dr.**

**HERNANDEZ DELIZ, DORIS I,** Caribbean Univ, Bayamon, PR; GD; CERT; BS SUNY Oswego 65; MA Univ Bridgeport 78; Engl Tchng.

**HERNANDEZ FERNANDINI, SONIA N,** Inter Amer Univ Pr San German, San German, PR; GD; BA; Camara Jr Univ 89-; Assn Comp Achvmnt Sec 87-; Bud Kappa Lambda 89-; Hon Stdnt Univ 86-; BA; Comp Sci.

**HERNANDEZ REYES, MIGUEL A,** Univ Politecnica De Pr, Hato Rey, PR; FR; BA; Civil Air Patrol Cmmctns Asst 89-90; ARC Refuge Dir 89-90; Karate/Ftbl League 86-87; Mechanic,Engrng.

**HERNANDEZ RIVERA, JANETTE,** Inter Amer Univ Pr Hato Rey, Hato Rey, PR; SO; Lns Clb VP; Msclr Dstrfy Assoc; Crmnl Jstc.

**HERNANDEZ ROBLES, IVELISSE,** Inter Amer Univ Pr Hato Rey, Hato Rey, PR; SO; BA; Hnr Pgm; Acctng; Law.

**HERNANDEZ RODRIGUEZ, MARIA I,** Univ Of Pr At Mayaguez, Mayaguez, PR; SR; BA; AICE 90-; Chem Engr.**

**HERNANDEZ SALVA, NANCY J,** Caribbean Univ, Bayamon, PR; SR.

**HERNANDEZ SAURI, JAVIER,** Univ Politecnica De Pr, Hato Rey, PR; FR; BA; Math Hon Clb 90-; Vlybl Tm Capt 90-; Math; Eng.

**HERNANDEZ, ALBERTO,** Edison Comm Coll, Fort Myers, FL; SO; AA; Intervar Chrstn Flwshp 89-; Spec Serv Prog 90-; Otsdng Tlntd Mnrty Cmuty Clg Stdnt; Singles Mnstry Greeter 90-; Chrus 89; Music ; Mnstr Music/Voclst.

**HERNANDEZ, ALYNA L,** Va St Univ, Petersburg, VA; JR; Gspl Choir 89-; Photo Stf 90-; Big Sis Treas 89-; Acctng; CPA.

**HERNANDEZ, AMANDA M,** S U N Y Coll Of Tech At Frmgdl, Farmingdale, NY; SO; AS; Early Childhood Club Sec/ Hist 90-; Yourth Oportunities United 89-; Early Childhood Ed; Tchr/Adminstr.

**HERNANDEZ, AMRI I,** Univ Of Pr At Mayaguez, Mayaguez, PR; JR; EE BS; IEEE Stdnt Chptr Dir 90-; Tau Beta Pi; Elec Eng Dept Hnr Rll 88-; Elec Eng Elecs; Eng.

**HERNANDEZ, ANA MARIA,** Fl International Univ, Miami, FL; SR; BA; FEA 90-; Elem Educ.

**HERNANDEZ, AURA V,** Howard Univ, Washington, DC; JR; US Aid Schlrshp 89-; Archtctr/Plnng; Urbn Dsgn.

**HERNANDEZ, BARBARA R,** Liberty Univ, Lynchburg, VA; SR; BS; Assoc Chrstn Tchrs 88-89; Stdnts Amer 88-89; Urbn Outrch 88-90; Alpha Lambda Delta 89-90; Frshmn Math Awd 89-90; Math Ed; Tchg.

**HERNANDEZ, BLANCA N,** Univ Of Pr Medical Sciences, San Juan, PR; Bd Dir Prvntn Cmuty Prog Sec 86-; Exclnc Schlrshp/ Ldrshp Merit Cert; Grad Cert Med Sci Sch Gerontocogy; Clg Soc Wrkrs 69-; P R Gerontology Soc; MA Soc Wrk 69; BA 66; Soc Wrk.

**HERNANDEZ, CHERYL W,** Tri County Tech Coll, Pendleton, SC; FR; ADN; Sales; Nrsng.

**HERNANDEZ, DANESSA,** Caribbean Univ, Bayamon, PR; MBA; Tchrs Ftr Pres; Adlscnt Org Ldr 84-90; Hnr Stdnt 90-; Mdls Asstnc C Prtn 90-; BA; Ed; Dctrs Dgr.

**HERNANDEZ, DAVID A,** Barry Univ, Miami, FL; SO; BA; Spanish Clb 90-91; Biology; Dentist.

**HERNANDEZ, DAWN M,** Mount Saint Mary Coll, Newburgh, NY; SO; BA; Hnr Allnc 89-90; New Paltz Ladies Aux 90-; Hstry/ Elem Spc Educ; Tchr.

**HERNANDEZ, DRINA G,** Barry Univ, Miami, FL; JR; BA; Natl Stdnt Nrs Assn 88-; Bptst Hosp Summer Extrnshp Nrs Extern 90; South Miami Summer Extrnshp Hosp Nrs Extern; Schl Nrsng Sftbl/Vlybl Game Tm Mbr 89-90; Nrsng; Nrs Mdwfry.

**HERNANDEZ, EDDY A,** Univ Of Miami, Coral Gables, FL; SR; BA; Frnch Clb 88-; Italian Clb 90-; Pi Delta Phi 88-; Gldn Key 89-; Master Tutor 88-90; Frnch; Psychlgy.

**HERNANDEZ, EDUARDO J,** Univ Of Miami, Coral Gables, FL; JR; BA; Pre Legal Soc 90-; Bst Of Amer Says No; Mastes Tutor Pgm; Golden Key 90-; Alpha Lambda Delta Snr Advsr 89-; Phi Eta Sigma 89-; South Miami Affairs Schl Hse; Dns Lst 88-; Provosts Lst 90; Sclgy; Law.**

**HERNANDEZ, ELIZABETH,** Inter Amer Univ Pr Barranquita, Barranquitas, PR; BA; Dns Lst 89-90; Sec/Psychlgy.

**HERNANDEZ, ESTHER,** Fl International Univ, Miami, FL; SR; BA; Future Edctrs Am 90-; Phi Kappa Phi 90-; Chldrns Home Scty; Dns Lst Miami Dade Cmnty Clg 89-90; Dns Lst 90-; Ins Agnt 220-Lcnsd 85; AA Miami Dade Cmnty Clg 90; BA; Elem Ed; Tchr.

**HERNANDEZ, EUNICE,** Commonwealth Coll, Virginia Beach, VA; FR; Acctg Club 90-; Presidents List 90-; Nurses Aide Cert Rice Inst Of Nursing 85; Acctg; CPA.

**HERNANDEZ, GILBERT N,** Northern Va Comm Coll, Annandale, VA; SO; BA; Stdnt Gov Assn Sntr 90-; G Mason Univ French Clb 90-; Intl Stdnt Cncl Rep 90-; Cultural Assn Salvadorean Evts Sec 90-; Dean Lst 89; Hon Rl 89; Cmunctns; Brdcst Jrnslm.**

**HERNANDEZ, GUISELA M,** Adelphi Univ, Garden City, NY; FR; BA; Chrldng 90; Hons Pgm 90-; Bio; Med.

**HERNANDEZ, JOSE A,** Univ Politecnica De Pr, Hato Rey, PR; SO; BA; Army Vet Lab Tech Cert QC Inspctr; AS Univ Of P R 89; Elect Eng.

**HERNANDEZ, JOSE I,** Univ Of Pr Medical Sciences, San Juan, PR; GD; MS; Chrch Bnd 82-; Emerson Elctrc Co Schlrshp 86-90; Ecnmc Dvlpmnt Admin PR Schlrshp 90-; BS Univ PR Rio Piedras Cmps 90; Phrmcy; PhD/IND Phrmcy.

**HERNANDEZ, JOSE M RUIZ,** Caribbean Univ, Bayamon, PR; SO; BS; Mscn; Spnsr Wrld Vsn Pgm; Bio; Eng.

**HERNANDEZ JR, JUAN,** Valley Forge Christian Coll, Phoenixville, PA; SR; MDIV; Intrm Pstr 89-90; BSB Vly Frg Chrstn Clg; Pstrl Mnstry; Tchng.

**HERNANDEZ, JUANA E,** S U N Y At Stony Brook, Stony Brook, NY; FR; Intvars Chrstn Flwshp Ldr 90-; Med.

**HERNANDEZ, KAREN,** Fl International Univ, Miami, FL; JR; BA; Phi Lambda 90; Engl; Law.

**HERNANDEZ, KAREN C,** Bob Jones Univ, Greenville, SC; FR; BS; Theta Sigma Chi 90-; Elem Ed; Tchng.

**HERNANDEZ, KARITZMA,** Inter Amer Univ Pr San German, San German, PR; GD; BA; Cert Hon 89-90; BS Antillian Coll 89; Psychlgy.

**HERNANDEZ, LEANEL A,** Univ Of Pr Medical Sciences, San Juan, PR; GD; MS; Grad Stdnt Assc; Med Sci Cmps 90-; Mnrty Biochem Rsrch Schlrshp Prog; Colegio Tecnologos Medicos De Puerto Rico 80-; Prto Rcn Scty Microbio 90-; MT 80; Microbio.

**HERNANDEZ, LUCILA,** City Univ Of Ny Hostos Coll, Bronx, NY; SR; CD Prog Hon Stdnt.

**HERNANDEZ, LUCY,** Fl International Univ, Miami, FL; SR; Encrtro Jvnls Ldr 85-90; BS FIU; AA Miami-Dade Comm Clg 88; Elem Ed; Tchr.

**HERNANDEZ, MARIA EUGENIA,** Fl International Univ, Miami, FL; SR; PHD; Kappa Delta Pi Exec Bd Rcrdng Sec 90-; BA 90; Elem Ed.

**HERNANDEZ, MARIA L,** Inter Amer Univ Pr San German, San German, PR; FR; BA; Sci.

**HERNANDEZ, MARIAN YVONNE,** Gallaudet Univ, Washington, DC; SR; BA; SGA Cmmtt Actvty 89-; Coll Nwsppr Comp Typst 90-; Mdl Scndry Schl Df Egl Cntr Act Spabbys 89-90; Bus Admn.

**HERNANDEZ, MARIEL,** Univ Politecnica De Pr, Hato Rey, PR; FR; BSME; Math; Eng.

**HERNANDEZ, MARLENE,** Seton Hall Univ, South Orange, NJ; SO; BA; Kappa Delta Pi; Alpha Phi 90-; Elem Ed/Engl; Tchng.

**HERNANDEZ, MAYLENE B,** Fl International Univ, Miami, FL; JR; BA; Phi Sigma Sigma Pldg Mistress 89-; Retail Mgmt-Mktg.

**HERNANDEZ, MIGUEL,** Fl International Univ, Miami, FL; SR; BA; Aids Walk-A-Thon; Alpha Phi Sigma; St John Cath Ch Field 87-; Dade Co Jail Stockade ICDC & Womens Annex 89; Deans List; Exec Intrnshp 89; AA Miami Dade Co Coll 89; Crmnl Justice; Masters In Crmnl Just/Law Sch.

**HERNANDEZ, NESTOR H,** Bunker Hill Comm Coll, Boston, MA; GD; BA; Eng.

**HERNANDEZ, NOEL,** Edison Comm Coll, Fort Myers, FL; SO; Phi Theta Kappa 90-; Outstanding Minority Talent Roster 90-; All-American Scholar Collegiate Award 90-; Minority Scholar Award 90-; AA Edison Community College 89-.

**HERNANDEZ, NOEMA B,** Miami Dade Comm Coll, Miami, FL; SO; AA; Phi Theta Kappa 90-; AA; Bus Adm; MIS.

**HERNANDEZ, PATRICIA M,** Univ Of Miami, Coral Gables, FL; JR; BA; Fdrtn Cuban Stdnts 90; Hnr Stdnt Assn 90; Alpha Lambda Delta 90; Dns Lst 90; Pres Hnr Roll 90; All Amer Schlr 90; Poltcl Sci/Engl; Law.

**HERNANDEZ, PAUL M,** Univ Of Southern Ms, Hattiesburg, MS; JR; BS; SDA Pres 90-; SHEA 90-; ADA 90-; Kappa Omicron Nu; Dtcs; Rsrch.

**HERNANDEZ, RAFAEL A,** Rutgers St Univ At Newark, Newark, NJ; JR; BA; Spnsh Clb; Newspaper Ed 88-89; Publish Book Dir 86; HPA Pres; Observer Hlth/Sci Ed 89-; Dns Lst; Talent Rstr Certif Achvmnt 90; Chess Champ 90-; Hackensack Med Ctr Emerg Rm Vol 88-; Indst l Instrmntn Tech 83; Bio/Pre-Med; Med.

**HERNANDEZ, RAMON J,** Inter Amer Univ Pr Hato Rey, Hato Rey, PR; SO; Bus Admn.

**HERNANDEZ, RODO A,** Univ Of Pr At Rio Piedras, Rio Piedras, PR; SO; AIESEC; Natl Clgte Bsn Merit Awd NCBMA; All-Amer Schlr Clgte Awd; Acctg; Law.

**HERNANDEZ, ROGER I,** Columbia Union Coll, Takoma Park, MD; JR; BA; Stdnt Mnstrl Assn Pres 90-; Friends Christ Co-Ldr 90-; 7th Day Advntst Yth Cbnt Pres; Hon Roll 90-; Loaves/Fishes Asst 89-90; Rsdnt Asst RA 90-; Stdnt Chpln; Mnstry Intrnshp Capital Spanish Church DC Yth Pstr; Bsktbl/Soccer Vrsty 89-; Thlgy; Pstr.

**HERNANDEZ, ROSANNE P,** Fl Atlantic Univ, Boca Raton, FL; JR; BA; Cath Stdnt Union; Phi Kappa Phi; Phi Theta Kappa; Miami Rsc Msn; Ddeans List; AA AS Miami Dade Comm Clg 90; Otstndng Acad Achvmnt Miaim Dade Comm Clg 82-84; Cmptr Inf Systms; Prgmr/Anlyst.

**HERNANDEZ, SILVIA M,** Univ Of Miami, Coral Gables, FL; SR; BBA; Mgrl Fin Orgnztn 9-; Alph Kappa Psi 90-; Fin.

**HERNANDEZ, WANDA I,** Univ Of Pr At Mayaguez, Mayaguez, PR; JR; BA; Advntst Fed Of Univs 88-; Bus Admin; Acctng.

**HERNANDEZ, YOMARA HERMINIA,** City Univ Of Ny Baruch Coll, New York, NY; SR; Ntl Assn Blk Accts; BBA; Acctnt.

**HERNANDEZ, ZAHMARI M,** Barry Univ, Miami, FL; SR; BA; Span Clb V P 90-; Alpha Mu Gamma Pres 90-; Delta Epsilon Sigma 90; Lambda Iota Tau 90-; Pres Lst 88-; Deans Lst 88-; Vybl Sftbl Ims 89-; Spanish; Trnsltr Tch.

**HERNANDEZ-CAMARENO, JAVIER,** Univ Politecnica De Pr, Hato Rey, PR; FR; Chorus; Boy Scouts; Bsktbl/Vllybl; Math/Sci; Elec Eng.

**HERNANDEZ-LIZARDO, OMAYRA,** Miami Dade Comm Coll, Miami, FL; SO; AA; Elem; Tchr.

**HERNANDEZ-ROBLES, JAVIER F,** Univ Of Pr At Mayaguez, Mayaguez, PR; JR; BSCE; Eng.

**HERNDON, EMILY W,** Valdosta St Coll, Valdosta, GA; FR; BA; Ambsdr; Alpha Lambda Delta 90-; Chi Omega Asst Tres 90-; S Ga Cnsl Aging 90-; Hspc S Ga; Deans Lst; Hghst GPA 90-; IM Bsktbl/Vlybl/Sftbl 90-; Bio; Med.

**HERNDON, KIMBERLEY A,** West Liberty St Coll, West Liberty, WV; SR; BS; Gamma Beta Phi 87-; WV St Leg Intrn 86-87; Blmnt Cnty OH Pblc Dfdr Inv Intrn; Crmnl Dfns/Cvl Prvt Invstgtr/Phtgrphr; Crmnl Jstc; Law Schl.

**HERNDON, LORA A,** Valdosta St Coll, Valdosta, GA; JR; BS; Alpha Chi Pres; Ed; Tchg.

**HERNDON, MAKEBA R,** Fl A & M Univ, Tallahassee, FL; JR; BS; Cir K Intl 90-; Future Fl Edctrs Of Am 90-; Elem Edn.

**HEROD, CHRISTAL L,** Clark Atlanta Univ, Atlanta, GA; SO; Beta Psi Treas 90-; Acctng Clb 90-; Hnr Rl 89-90; Phi Beta Lambda 89-; Delta Sigma Theta Fin Secy; Bus/Acctng.**

**HEROLD, JOANNE,** Middle Tn St Univ, Murfreesboro, TN; FR; BA; Math Organ 90-; Gamma Beta Phi; Math; Tcher.

**HERON, KATHERINE A,** Duquesne Univ, Pittsburgh, PA; SO; BS; MENC 90-; Chmbr Sngrs 90-; Mu Phi Epsilon Chpln 90-; Music Educ Voice; Music Edctr Opera.

**HEROUX, MARK D,** Springfield Tech Comm Coll, Springfield, MA; GD; BA; Glf Tm 89; As 90; Accntng.

**HERR, ELIZABETH L,** Radford Univ, Radford, VA; FR; BMT; Cir K Sec; Mus Therapy Clb; Wesley Fdntn; Alpha Lamda Delta Sec; Hon Stu Assn; Music Therapy.

**HERREN, TAMMY M,** Clayton St Coll, Morrow, GA; SR; ADN; GA Assn Nrsng Stdnts 89-; Hons Assn 89-; Vlntr Amer Red Crss Hlth Fair; Ntl Coll Nrsng Awd Wnr; Nrsng; Crtcl Cr RN.

**HERRERA, ANNETTE M,** Fl International Univ, Miami, FL; JR; BA; AA Miami Dade Cmmt Clg 82; Engl Ed; Tchng.

**HERRERA, IWONNE E,** Methodist Coll, Fayetteville, NC; SR; BBA; Stdnt Gov Sen Drm Rep 88; Bus Clb 87-; Theta Capa Gama Rep 87-88; Outreach 91 Asst; Tch A Kid Asst 87-88; Food Ktchn Asst 87-88; Prof Intl Bus/Econ Asst 90-; Bus Adm; Personel Adm.**

**HERRERA, ROBERT R,** Fl International Univ, Miami, FL; SO; BA; Bus Admn; Mgmt.

**HERRERA, RODRIGO M,** Univ Of Miami, Coral Gables, FL; SO; BA; Archtctr.

**HERRERA, SHARON M,** Dowling Coll, Oakdale Li, NY; FR; Dns Lst 90; Hnr Rl 90; Vars Vlybl 90; Cmptr Sci.

**HERRERO ROMAN, GLORIMAR,** Inter Amer Univ Pr Hato Rey, Hato Rey, PR; FR; BA; Chmstry; Chemist.

**HERRERO, VIVIAN E,** Univ Of Pr At Mayaguez, Mayaguez, PR; GD; BS; Inst Ind Engrs 88-; Natl Soc Pro Engrs 89-; Soc Wmn Engrs 88-; Tau Beta Pi 89-; Alpha Pi Mu 89-; Hon Rl 86-; Hon Cert 86-; Ind Eng; Eng.

**HERREROS, MAURICIO,** Nova Univ, Ft Lauderdale, FL; GD; MBA; Y K Kim Tae Kwon Do Brown Belt 90-; Rutgers Univ Deans List 86-87; BA Rutgers Univ 87; Cert Universidao De Chile Chile 81; Intrntl Mktg.

**HERRICK, DIANE E,** Univ Of Ky, Lexington, KY; FR; BA; Scty Of Gvrnrs Schlrs 90; Hnrs Prog Stdnt Advsry Cncl Scl Chrmn; Alpha Lambda Delta; Psychlgy; Clncl Psychlgy.

**HERRICK, MURRAY H,** Newbury Coll, Brookline, MA; FR; AAS; Std Govt Org Rep 90-; Std Actv Comm Rep 90-; Peer Actv Ldr PAL 90-; RA; Acad Exclnc Awd; Std Life Awd; Intschlstc Vlybl 90-; Clnry Arts.

**HERRIMAN JR, ROBERT E,** Columbia Union Coll, Takoma Park, MD; SR; BS; Amrcn Mdcl Tchnlgsts 88-; Amrcn Scty Clncl Pthlgsts 88-; Med Lab Tech AF 82-; AAS 88; AGS 88; Hlth Care Admn.

**HERRIN, JANET L,** Univ Of Cincinnati-Clrmnt Coll, Batavia, OH; SO; BA; IM Tennis 89-90; Delta Gamma 89-; Accntng.

**HERRIN, KIMELA H,** Univ Of Southern Ms, Hattiesburg, MS; SR; BS; BS; Soc/Rehab Serv; Psychlgy.

**HERRIN, LINDA F,** Al A & M Univ, Normal, AL; SR; BA; N AL Dietetic Asso; AS John Calhoun Jr Colg 85; Cert Un AL 85; Fds/Nutrtn; Nrsg Home Dietcn.

**HERRING, ADAM J,** Fayetteville St Univ, Fayetteville, NC; SR; BA; Yth Motvtn Tsk Frc 87; Pol Sci Clb 89; AFROTC; Arnld Air; Cmbrlnd Cnty Medtr; BA; Pol Sci/Crim Just; Law.

**HERRING, CHRISTOPHER S,** Christian Brothers Univ, Memphis, TN; FR; BA; Pi Kappa Phi 90-; Psychlgy; Prfssnl Prctce.

**HERRING, DAVID A,** Memphis St Univ, Memphis, TN; FR; MBA; Phi Eta Sigma; Kappa Alpha Order 90-; Highst Pldg GPA Kappa Alpha Order 90; IM 90-; Acctg.

**HERRING, GLORIA J,** Alcorn St Univ, Lorman, MS; SR; NAACP Secy; Engl Clb 86-90; Dmcrtc Women Cmmt; BA Alcorn State Unic 90; Jrnlsm Retail.

**HERRING, JEFFREY G,** Mount Olive Coll, Mount Olive, NC; JR; BPSY; Psych Club 90-; Psi Chi; Phi Theta Kappa 88-; Hons Schlrshp 90-; Acad Schlrshp 88-90; AA Lenoir Cmnty Clg 90; Psych.

**HERRING JR, LEWIS N,** Univ Of Southern Ms, Hattiesburg, MS; BSN; Grdtn Boac Cptn 76-; BS 76; Nrsng.

**HERRING, MELISSA S,** Univ Of Al At Birmingham, Birmingham, AL; SO; BA; Med; Physician Asst.

**HERRING, PHILIP R,** Crichton Coll, Memphis, TN; SO; BA; Stdnt Govt Sphmr Rep 90-; Chr 89-; Egl Sct; Bus Admn.

**HERRING, TIRIA E,** Middle Tn St Univ, Murfreesboro, TN; GD; Prsbytrn Stdnt Flwshp Msc Dir 88-90; Kappa Delta Pi 89-90; Delta Omicron Asst Msc Dir/Chpln 87-90; BA Belmont Clge 80-84; BM 90; Msc; Tchr.

**HERRINGTON, ALEXIA Y,** Morris Brown Coll, Atlanta, GA; SR; BS; Mrchng Bnd Sctn Ldr; Concert Bnd; Therapeutic Rcrtn Club; Hnr Roll Stdnt 88-90; MISS Hper 89-90; Therapeutic Rcrtn; Actvty Thrpst.

**HERRINGTON, CYNTHIA L,** Univ Of Southern Ms, Hattiesburg, MS; SR; BS; Wmns Intrntl Bwlng Cngrss 86-; Hattiesburg Wmns Bwlng Assc 86-; Beta Alpha Psi 90-; Acctg; CPA.

**HERRINGTON, DEANNA L,** Allegheny Coll, Meadville, PA; JR; MBA; Wmns Trck/Cross Cntry 88-89; Cmps Newspr Wrtr/Typst 88-; SGA Hall Repr 88-90; Alden Schlr 88-; Kappa Alpha Theta 88; Hstss Prspctv Stdnts 88; Rush Cnslr 90; Mst Imprvd Plyrs Award 88-89; Vars Trck/Cross Cntry 88-89; Econ/German; Bsn Mgmt.

**HERRINGTON, LYNN E,** Duquesne Univ, Pittsburgh, PA; FR; BS BA; Japanese Clb Sec; Union Prog Bd Pub Rel Chr; Rsdnc Hl Rep; Lambda Sigma Sec; Duquesne Univ Vol; Cmps Mnstry/Choir; 3 Yr ROTC Schlrshp; Pres Awd; Econ/Business.

**HERRINGTON, TRINA R,** Chattahoochee Vly St Comm Coll, Phenix City, AL; SO; BED; Tuitn Schlrshp Grls Clb Colmbs GA 90-; Engl; Engl Tchr.

**HERRMAN, JOHN E,** Athens St Coll, Athens, AL; SR; BA; Lambda Alpha Epsilon 89-; Athn Hst 90-; Amrcn Psychlgcl Assoc; Amrcn Psychlgcl Scty; Psi Chi; Tau Kappa Epsilon VP 89-; Bradford Group Inc Internshp; Athens Counseling Center Internshp; Sclgy; Clncl Psychlgy.

**HERRMANN, CHERYL LYNN F,** Va Commonwealth Univ, Richmond, VA; SR; Alpha Sigma Alpha Fndrsng Chr Pblcty Chr 88-; Intrn Natl Geogrphc Soc Prmtn/Edctnl Serv Div 87-90; BFA; Cncpts/Dsgn Advrtsng.

**HERRMANN, JILL M,** Univ Of Fl, Gainesville, FL; JR; BHS; Mrchng Bnd 88-89; Newman Clb Pres 89-; St Augustines Chrch Choir 89-; Alpha Lambda Delta 89-; Phi Eta Sigma 89-; Prepro Serv Org 90-; Sigma Tau Sigma 90-; Hon Pgm 89-90; Gldn Key 90; Schlrsh Fund 88-; AA 90; Clncl Lab Sci; Med.

**HERRMANN, SUSAN M,** Southern Vt Coll, Bennington, VT; GD; BSN; Stdnt Nrs Assn Pres 89-90; LPN Thompson Sch Prctl Nrsng 75; Nrsng.

**HERRON, ANGELA D,** Coker Coll, Hartsville, SC; FR; BA; May Day Comm; BACCHUS; Socl Dnc Comm; Sec Class; Cmmsnr Org Hd Cmmnsnr; Fld Serv Exper; Endowment Schlrshp; Psychlgy/Cmptr Sci; Rsrch.

**HERRON, DAWN M,** S U N Y At Buffalo, Buffalo, NY; SO; BA; Stdnt Wide Judiciary Justice 89-; Univ Buffalo Acctg Assn 90-; Outdoor Adventure Clb 89-90; Chi Omega Grkwk Chrmn 89-; Town W Seneca Yth Ct 86-; Erie Cnty Sheriffs Dept Robert S Insalaco Yth Awd 90-; Dorothy Long Meml Schlrshp; Acctg; Law.

**HERRON, MARK E,** Comm Coll Algny Co Algny Cmps, Pittsburgh, PA; AS; Radiation Therapy Techlgt; BS.

**HERRON, TINA K,** Ashland Comm Coll, Ashland, KY; SO; BA; Am Govt; Law.

**HERRON, WENDY B,** Denmark Tech Coll, Denmark, SC; GD; Off Sys Tech.

**HERRY, LESLIE J,** Comm Coll Of Finger Lakes, Canandaigua, NY; FR; AAS; BASIC Ldr 90-; Walter And Mae Neenan Schlrshp; Nrsng.

**HERSEE, MARK D,** Erie Comm Coll South Cmps, Orchard Park, NY; SR; BA; Phi Theta Kappa; Ryl Rngrs Assmbly God 88-; Sctng Prog Scrb; Frcs Mntcm Wlfe 89-; AA; Soc Stu/Hstry Ed; Tchr.

**HERSEY, LISA M,** Wilmington Coll, Wilmington, OH; JR; BED; Commuter Concerns Secr/Treas 90-; Tutor; Elem Ed; Tchr.

**HERSEY, STEPHANIE M,** Univ Of Ri, Kingston, RI; FR; BS; Stdnt Alumni Assc; Elem Education; Teacher.

**HERSHENSON, TRENT M,** Univ Of Miami, Coral Gables, FL; FR; BA; Bowling Club VP 90-; SGA 90-; Org Of Jewish Stdnts 90-; Hon Stdnts 90-; Im Soccer Cptn 90-; Engl; Author.

**HERSHEY, ALISHA L,** Liberty Univ, Lynchburg, VA; SO; Alpha Lambda Delta 90-; Elem Ed; Tchr.

**HERSHEY, JENNIFER L,** Kent St Univ Kent Cmps, Kent, OH; SR; Music Educ Natl Conf 88-; Ohio Collegiate Music Educ Assn 88-; Golden Key 90-; Pi Kappa Lambda; Alpha Lambda Delta 88-; Delta Omicron Ec 89-; Schl Of Music Schlrshp 87-; Outstandng Future Music Educ Awd; Music Educ; Tchng.

**HERSHEY, MELANIE S,** Gettysburg Coll, Gettysburg, PA; FR; BS; Actvts Com 90-; GECO 90-; Pro Chce Orgnztn 90-; Gamma Phi Beta 90-; Big Sis 90-; Rotoract 90-; Intrntl Bus.

**HERSKOWITZ, MICHAEL V,** Case Western Reserve Univ, Cleveland, OH; FR; BA; Dean Lst 90-; Orntn Ldr 90-; Sci Olympiad 90-; Bdmntn Trnmnt 90-; Chmstry; Med/Pdtrcs.

**HERSMAN, CHERYL D,** Wv Univ At Parkersburg, Parkersburg, WV; SO; BA; Prnt Advsry Cncl-Cottagevl Elem Pres 90-; Educ.

**HERSMAN, CHERYL L,** Wv Univ At Parkersburg, Parkersburg, WV; FR; Mltree Hlth Cre Axlry Pres 89-; Rne Cnty Rpblcn Wmns Clb VP 87-; Fll Tme Emplyee WV Div Vets Affrs 86-; Admin.

**HERSTEIN, JENNIFER K,** Cornell Univ Statutory College, Ithaca, NY; FR; BS; Bus Mgt.

**HERSTINE, BRADLEY S,** Greenville Tech Coll, Greenville, SC; JR; AS; Prof Avtn Mntnc Assn; Natl Wld Trky Fdrtn; Natl Arbor Day Fndtn; Hnrs Grad US Army; Mdls Hghtst Sqt; Rcyclng Adpt Hwy; Table Rock St Pk Vol; Chdrns Bcycl Rodeo Vol; NCO US Army Ordnnc Co; PFC; Satellite Cmmnctns; Avtn Mntn Tech; BS Helicopters.

**HERTER, SAMANTHA G,** Univ Of Tn At Knoxville, Knoxville, TN; SO; BA; Financial Mgmt Assn Prsdnt; Bsns Stdnts Advsry Cncl Prsdnt 90-; Triathlon Clb; Alpha Lambda Delta; Phi Eta Sigma; Exectv Undrgrd Prgrm; Delta Zeta Pldg Cls Pres 89-90; Untd Armstrng Van Lines; Otstndng Delta Zeta Awd 90; Bsns; Finance Bnkng.

**HERTLING JR, ROBERT B,** Capitol Coll, Laurel, MD; SR; BS; Alpha Chi 90-; Tau Alpha Pi; USCG Chief Petty Ofcrs Assoc 85-; Active Duty With US Coast Guard 76-; AATET 90; Mgmnt Of Tele Cmnctns Systms; Degree.

**HERTZEL, LISA M,** Kent St Univ Kent Cmps, Kent, OH; SR; RA; KIC Asst Comm 87-88; KIC Hall Rep 87-89; RA; Crmnl Jstc/Sclgy; Law.

**HERVEY, BETHANN D,** Westminster Coll, New Wilmingtn, PA; SR; BA; Habta Hmnty; Hse Cncl Sec/VP; Mortar Brd Sclctn; Omicron Delta Kappa; Lambda Sigma; Kappa Delta Pi Pres; Pi Sigma Pi; Kappa Delta Pres; Estblshd Svc Tms Chr; Elem Ed; Tch K-6.

**HERVEY, CINDY L,** Savannah Coll Of Art & Design, Savannah, GA; FR; ISID 90; Interior/Fshn Dsgn.

**HERVEY, ROBERT M,** Nc St Univ At Raleigh, Raleigh, NC; FR; BS; Computer Engrg.

**HERVIG, DONOVAN H,** George Mason Univ, Fairfax, VA; FR; BS; Stdnt Fr Sen 90-; Stdnts/Objtvsm Sec 90-; Hervig Enterpr Pres Dsktp Pub Sl-Prop 90-; Stdnt Sen Proj Yr Free Spch Aly Chmn 90-; Cngrsnl Internshp Hon F Wolfe Intrn; Mason Schlr VA 90-; Rcqtbl; Psychlgy; Law.

**HERZIG, SUZAN M,** Univ Of West Fl, Pensacola, FL; JR; BA; Vlybl 90-; Bus Educ; Tchr.

**HERZOG, CHRISTOPHER D,** Coll Of Charleston, Charleston, SC; SO; BS; Peer Mentor Assoc; Psychlgy.

**HERZOG, CHRISTOPHER R,** Northern Ky Univ, Highland Hts, KY; SO; BA; Hons Prog 89-; Comp Sci; Prgrmr.

**HERZOG, MICHELLE S,** Flagler Coll, St Augustine, FL; SR; Alpha Chi 89-; BA; Scndry Educ Spnsh LAS; Spnsh Frnch ESOL Tch.**

**HESELTON, BENJAMIN E,** S U N Y Coll At Fredonia, Fredonia, NY; SO; BA; Income Tax Asst Pgm; Fclty/Stdnt Assoc Bd Secr 89-; Festival Chorus; Finance; Law.

**HESKETT, DEBORAH D,** Univ Of Tn At Martin, Martin, TN; SO; BA; Social Work Club; Laborer; Social Work; Substance Abuse Cnslr.

**HESLER, LILLIAN M,** Univ Of Cincinnati-Clrmnt Coll, Batavia, OH; BSN; RN 90; ADN; SW Virgia Cmmnty Clg 82; Nrsng; Nrsng Cmmnty Hlth.

**HESLER, VAGGELI J,** Univ Of Al, Tuscaloosa, AL; SO; BS; Cir K; AL Trngl Asc; Gamma Beta Phi 90-; Phi Eta Sigma 90-; Outstdng New Mbr; Dns Lst Awd; Sprts Ftns Mgmt.**

**HESLIN, MARY LOUISE,** Becker Coll At Leicester, Leicester, MA; SO; AS; Trvl Clb; Phi Theta Kappa Scrtry 89; Vldctrn; Trvl/Trsm.

**HESS, AUDRA L,** Comm Coll Algny Co Algny Cmps, Pittsburgh, PA; SO; AS; Scl Wrk Tech.

**HESS, BRENDA R,** Marywood Coll, Scranton, PA; FR; BA; Clss Offcr Sec 90-; Orntn Comm 90-; Res Repr 90-; Deans List 90-; Adpt A Grndprnt 90-; Fld Hcky 90-; Law.

**HESS, JENNIFER S,** Univ Of Sc At Aiken, Aiken, SC; FR; BA; Pcsttrs; Chld Psych.

**HESS, LAURA A,** Memphis St Univ, Memphis, TN; SR; BS; Deans List 90-; Otsdng Clg Stdnts 87-; Biology; Physical Thrpy.

**HESS, MICHELE A,** Comm Coll Algny Co Algny Cmps, Pittsburgh, PA; FR; BA; Sarah Heinz Hs 82-88; Natl Hnrs Scty Perry Trdtnl Acdmy 89-90; Sarah Heinz Hs 84-89; Cnslr Trng Heinz Hs Camp 86-87; Clss Valedictorian 90; Otstndng Mbr Sarah Heinz Hs; Rcrtn Lsr Psychlgy.

**HESS, PAMELA D,** Emory & Henry Coll, Emory, VA; SO; Stdnt Vir Educ Assn 89-; Alpha Phi Omega; Fr Honor Schlr 89-90; Elem Educ.

**HESS, PAUL R,** Ms St Univ, Miss State, MS; GD; DVM; SCAVMA 88-; Phi Zeta; Prsdnts Schlr 88-; Impromed Awrd; Phase Surgery Awrd; BA Rutgers Coll Rutgers Unit 82; BA Rutgers Coll 85; Vet Med; Vet.

**HESS, RICHARD B,** Savannah Coll Of Art & Design, Savannah, GA; SO; BARCH; Amer Inst Archtctr Stdnts 89-; Archtctr.

**HESSE, JENNIFER M,** Univ Of Cincinnati, Cincinnati, OH; JR; BS; AM Dietetic Assc 90-; Omicron Nu 90-; Alpha Phi Omega Sergeant Arms 90-; Dean List; Dietetics; Dietition.

**HESSELBART, DIANE L,** Kent St Univ Kent Cmps, Kent, OH; SO; BBA; Bus; Acctg.

**HESSEN, TAMMI L,** Mt Saint Marys Coll & Seminary, Emmitsburg, MD; FR; Ldrs Flwshp Earth Secr; Seminar Ldr; German Clb Co-Pres; Philosophy-German; Prfsr Philosphy.

**HESSIE, DAVID A,** Salisbury St Univ, Salisbury, MD; JR; BA; Phi Beta Lambda Treas; Fresh Hnr Soc 88-; IM Sftbl/Vlybl 86-; Bsn Mgmt.

**HESSLINK, WENDY L,** Oh Univ, Athens, OH; JR; BA; STYLE Com Hd/Fndng Mem; Art Hist/Sculpture.

**HESSON, LISA M,** Univ Of Tn At Martin, Martin, TN; GD; OD; Mu Epsilon Delta VP 89-90; Beta Beta Beta Sec 88-90; Phi Theta Epsilon 90; Biol; Optmtry.

**HESTER, ANGELA D,** Fl St Univ, Tallahassee, FL; SR; BS; Univ Mascot 88-89; FEA Pblcty Chrmn 90-; FCA 90-; Phi Eta Sigma; Kappa Delta Pi 90-; Intern Ruediger Elem Schl 5th Grd; No FL Fair Soloist; Elem Ed; Tchng.

**HESTER, GREGORY K,** Memphis St Univ, Memphis, TN; JR; BA; Prchs Awd Art Comp 87-88; AS Vol St Comm Clg 88; Phlsphy; Msc/Perf.**

**HESTER, JERA M,** Univ Of Tn At Martin, Martin, TN; SR; Park/Rcratn Admn; Pre Vet; Vet Med.

**HESTER, LINDA M,** Thomas Nelson Comm Coll, Hampton, VA; SO; Phi Theta Kappa Crrspndng Sec 89; Phi Beta Lambda; Canon Schlrshp 90-; Amrcn Ints Bnkng Vice Cnsl 86-; Admnstrtv Asst Ntns Bnk; AAS; Bsns Admn Accntng; CPA.

**HETCHLER, RICKY L,** Faulkner St Jr Coll, Bay Minette, AL; SO; Phi Theta Kappa; Mrtuary Sci.

**HETRICK, GEORGIA A,** Pa St Univ Altoona Cmps, Altoona, PA; FR; BSN; Sci; Nrsng.

**HETRICK, KATRIN L,** S U N Y Coll At Fredonia, Fredonia, NY; JR; Teacher Educ Club 90-; Alumni Hall Dorm Cncl 90-; Natl Educ Hnr Soc; Chrldng 87-88; Elem Educ; Teaching.

**HETTIARACHCHI, LAWRENCE PRADEEP,** Saint Thomas Univ, Miami, FL; SO; BA; Intrntl Stdnts Orgnztn 89-; Biochem; Med Tech.

**HETTICK, CINDY M,** Liberty Univ, Lynchburg, VA; SR; Lbrty Hmn Eclgy Assoc 89-; Fshn Mrchndsng Intrnshp.

**HETTINGER, MARY ANN,** Spalding Univ, Louisville, KY; SR; BS; Natl Educ Asc 90-; Delta Epsln Sigma 90-; Univ Hnrs 89-; Magna Cum Laude; Schlps 87-; Elem Ed; Tch.

**HETTMAN, JUDITH L,** Bunker Hill Comm Coll, Boston, MA; SO; BSBA; Blue Crs/Blue Shld; AA 80; Acctg; CPA.

**HETZEL, VIRGINIA M,** Slippery Rock Univ, Slippery Rock, PA; SR; BS; SLAHPERD Secr 90-; PAHPERD; H S Asst Trck Coach 89-; Kappa Delta Pi; PSEA 90-; Phi Epsilon Kappa 90-; Outstndg Exec Awd SRAHPERD; IM Vlybl; Hlth/Phys Ed; Educator/Coach.

**HEUER, JOHN A,** S U N Y Coll Of Tech At Frmgdl, Farmingdale, NY; SO; AS; Phi Theta Kappa 89-; U S Naval Res HM2 85-; Psych Attndnt 86-; Nursing.

**HEUERMAN, TAMMY M,** Defiance Coll, Defiance, OH; GD; BA; AS NW Tech Clg 86; Acctng.

**HEVERLY, PHYLLIS J,** Juniata Coll, Huntingdon, PA; JR; BA; Wom Rugby Clb Treas 88-90; Pblc Affrs Clb 88-; Prsnnl Evltn Comm 88-90; Jdcl Brd/Theatre Comm 90-; Juniata Clg Admin Assoc/Tour Gdng 90-; Pres Lf Stff 89-90; Fnd Rsng Comm Spec Evnts Hd 90-; Soc Dist Amer HS Stdnts 87-88; Acad/Amer 86-87; Pltcl Scnc; Law.

**HEWES, GREGORY B,** William Carey Coll, Hattiesburg, MS; SR; BS; Phillips Jr Coll Stdnt Cncl 87-88; Hon Soc 89-; Ntl Coll Bus Merit Awd 89-90; AS Phillips Jr Coll 88; Acctg.**

**HEWETT, ANGELA D,** Univ Of Cincinnati, Cincinnati, OH; FR; BA; Erly Chldhd Educ.

**HEWINS, KELLY L,** Clemson Univ, Clemson, SC; JR; BSN; Stdnt Nrs Assoc 1st VP 90-; Stdnt Nrs Assoc SC Cmt Nmntns Chrprsn; FCA 90-; Gldn Key 90-; Dns Lst 90-; Nrsg; NICU Nrs.

**HEWITT, CINDY R,** Wv Univ At Parkersburg, Parkersburg, WV; SO; BA; Phi Theta Kappa 90-; AA; Bus Adm; Corp Lawyer.

**HEWITT, ERIKA A,** Oh Wesleyan Univ, Delaware, OH; SO; Wmn Tsk Frc Pres 89-; Hbtt Hmnty Rep 89-; OWU Lit Mag Edtr 90-; Phi Eta Sigma 90-; Phi Soc; Mrtr Brd; Omcrn Delta Kappa; Pres Schlp 89-; WCSA Acad/Ldrshp Schlp; Psy Std Brd 90-.

**HEWITT, GREGORY A,** Marshall University, Huntington, WV; FR; MBA; Lambda Chi Alpha 90-; Business; Bus Mngmnt.

**HEWITT, GWENDOLYN D,** William Carey Coll, Hattiesburg, MS; JR; BA; Chrl Grp 90-; SMCC Mrchng 88-90; Stdnt Fndtn 90; AA 90; English; Scndry Tchng.

**HEWITT, SUSAN L,** Univ Of Southern Ms, Hattiesburg, MS; SR; BS; Cmps Nwspr Cpy Edtr 89-; Soc Prof Jrnlsts Pgrm Chr 89-; Gamma Beta Phi 90-; AA Hinds Comm Coll 89; Jrnlsm; Rptr.

**HEWITT, TIFFINY P,** Fl St Univ, Tallahassee, FL; JR; BA; AA Tallahassee Comm Coll 89; Art Educ; Elem Art Tchr.

**HEWLETT, KENNETH J,** Life Coll, Marietta, GA; GD; DC; BS State Univ NY Cortland 87; Chiropractic.

**HEXTALL, LLOYD S,** City Univ Of Ny Bronx Comm Col, Bronx, NY; SO; AAS; Chem Clb 89-; Phi Theta Kappa 89-; Talent Roster 90-; Pharm.

**HEYER, DEANNE L,** James Madison University, Harrisonburg, VA; SO; BS; Psychlyg Clb 89-; Psi Chi 90-; Alpha Chi Omega 90-; Hons Prog 89-; Psychlgy; Cnslng.

**HEYMAN, DENISE E,** Univ Of Miami, Coral Gables, FL; JR; BA; Scuba Club 87-88; Earth Alert 89-; Cir K 90-; Marine Afrs; Medcl Sch.

**HEYMAN, MICHAEL B,** Franklin And Marshall Coll, Lancaster, PA; JR; Jazz Ensemble; Symphnc Winds Ensemble Chmbr Wind Ens 88-; Bessie Smith Soc 89-; Prlg Lit Mag 89-90; Mu Upsilon Sigma VP 89-; Englsh.

**HEYN, SANDRA L,** Univ Of Sc At Aiken, Aiken, SC; JR; BIS; Indpndt Stdy Cty Coroner; Schlrshp Vlybl; Criminal Justice; PI/FBI.

**HEYNER, MATTHEW G,** Va Commonwealth Univ, Richmond, VA; FR; MBA; Arts/Sclptr; Altrctns.

**HEYNING, KIMBERLY ANN,** Memphis St Univ, Memphis, TN; JR; BSN; Phi Eta Sigma 89-; Beta Beta Beta 89-; Gamma Beta Phi; Mu Epsilon Delta 89-90; Alpha Phi Omega Treas 88-; Nrsng/Blgy; Nrsng.

**HEYSEK, PENNY J,** Edinboro Univ Of Pa, Edinboro, PA; JR; Psychlgy Clb; Phi Eta Sigma 90; Psi Chi; Psychlgy; Chld Psychlgst.

**HEYWARD, JOYCE ANN,** Univ Of Sc At Columbia, Columbia, SC; SO; BA; Chrch Yth Grp; Chrch Choir; Alpha Lambda Delta; Bsns; Acctg.

**HIBBERT, MATTHEW,** Bridgewater St Coll, Bridgewater, MA; SO; BS; Chem Club 89-90; Sci At Bridgewater 90; Recrtnl Swmmng 90; YMCA Lfgrd/Instrctr 90-; Chem; Chem Sls/Phrmsctcls.**

**HIBBITTS, LARRY E,** Univ Of Ky, Lexington, KY; FR; Stdnt Athls Cncl 90-; Sigma Gamma Sigma 90-; Gov Schlr Alumni Assoc; Chem Engr.

**HIBBS, MARK E,** Univ Of Tn At Chattanooga, Chattanooga, TN; SO; BSME; Amer Soc Of Mechanical Engrs 90-; Golden Key 90-; BS Buss Adm 87; Engineering.

**HIBBS, MARY LESA,** Western Ky Univ, Bowling Green, KY; SR; BA; Bellevue Bapt Church Chrmn Preschool Aged Chldrn; BA; Engl; Tchng.

**HIBLER, JESSICA L,** Anne Arundel Comm Coll, Arnold, MD; SO; BSRN; Nrsng.

**HICKENBOTTOM, THERESA L,** Ringling School Of Art, Sarasota, FL; JR; BFA; Amer Soc Intrer Dsgnrs Hstrn 89-; Bst Rnglng Stdnt Show; IBD Cir Charette 1st Pl; Pub Rngling Stdnt Mag, Interior Dsgn; Interior Dsgnr.

**HICKERSON, EMILY C,** Univ Of Tn At Martin, Martin, TN; SO; BS; Univ Schlrs Orgn 90-; Wldlfe Scty 90-; Rodeo Bstr; Outstndng Chem Stdnt Awd 90; Deans Lst Wth Hghst Hnrs 89-; Grl Scts Amer Area Orgnzr 87-89; Helpline Vol Tm Ldr 85-87; Wldlf Bio.

**HICKERSON, MECHELLE D,** Georgetown Coll, Georgetown, KY; SO; BS; Bapt Stdnt Unn 89-; Math Assn Of Amer VP 90-; Alpha Lambda Delta Sec 90-; Phi Beta Lambda 90-; Otstndng Stdnt 90; Spkr Cnfrnce Math Assn Of Amer; Math; Oprtns Rsrch.

**HICKEY, DAVID W,** Comm Coll Algny Co Algny Cmps, Pittsburgh, PA; SO; Cert Comm Coll North 82; Personnel Mngmnt; Bus Personnel.

**HICKEY, KAREN L,** S U N Y Coll At Fredonia, Fredonia, NY; SR; Spl Ed Intshp 91; Ms FSU Body 90; Building Contest; BA Spl Studies SUNY Fred 91; Ed; Tchr El Ed.

**HICKEY, MARY L,** Castleton St Coll, Castleton, VT; JR; BS; Non-Trdtnl Stdnts Clb Pres; Pblc Accss Cbl Advsry Bd; AS Comm Coll VT 86; Cmnctns; Media.

**HICKEY, MICHELE D,** Columbia Greene Comm Coll, Hudson, NY; FR; AA; Sccr/Sftbl 90-; Psy.

**HICKEY, PATRICK N,** Hudson Valley Comm Coll, Troy, NY; FR; Engr.

**HICKEY, TONI R,** Northern Ky Univ, Highland Hts, KY; JR; BA; Geography Union Nrthrn Kentucky 90; Phi Alpha Theta; Stdnt Sprt Srvc 88; Hstry/Geo; Clg Prof.

**HICKIN, JULIE M,** Univ Of Akron, Akron, OH; SR; BSED; ACES 90; Elem Ed; Tchr Prmry Grdes.

**HICKMAN, AMY S,** Goucher Coll, Towson, MD; SR; BA; Debate Clb Co Pres 87-; Nwspr Edtrls Edtr 89-; Literary Mag Poetry Edtr 87-; Phi Beta Kappa 90; Deans Scholor 87-; Reese Ptry Awd 90; Acad Amer Poets Prize 90-; Bucknell Younger Poets Fellowship; English; Teaching.

**HICKMAN, CHARLENE RENEE,** Univ Of Al At Birmingham, Birmingham, AL; SR; BS; Am Ocptnl Thrpy Assc 89; AL Ocptnl Thrpy Assc 89-; Phi Epsln Kappa 86-87; Stdnt Ocptnl Thrpy Assc Scrpbk Cmt Chrprsn; Pi Theta Epsln; IM Sftbl Vlybl 89-; Spec Olympcs Crdntr Hoover Cty Sch 88-; BS Auburn Un 87; Ocptnl Thrpy.

**HICKMAN, ELIZABETH J,** Ms St Univ, Miss State, MS; JR; BA; Bapt Stdnt Un 90-; Bapt Campus Mnstry Pensacola Jr Coll Pres 88-90; So Bapt Yth Ldr G A Camp Cnslr 88-; Gamma Beta Phi 90-; Kappa Delta Pi 90-; Phi Theta Kappa 89-90; BSU Stdnt Msnry Vancouver Canada/New Jersey; Pres Schlr 90-; Elem Edn; Teach.

**HICKMAN, GEORGIA E,** Cedarville Coll, Cedarville, OH; FR; BA; Chi Theta Pi 90-; Cedar Kids 90-; Dns Hnr Lst 90-; Bio; Peds.

**HICKMAN, HOLLY V,** Christian Brothers Univ, Memphis, TN; SR; BA; Pi Kappa Phi Ltl Sis 87-89; Wmns Assn Mtvt Sprt 87-; Vrsty Vlybl Capt 87-; Soc Cllgt Jrnlsts 87-; Zeta Tau Alpha VP 88-; Vol Usher Orphm Thtr 88-; Acdmc All-Amer NAIA 90-; All Dstrct 88-; All Cnfrnc 88-; Vlybl Capt 88-; Cmnctn Arts/Mktg Minor.

**HICKMAN, JULIA G,** City Univ Of Ny Baruch Coll, New York, NY; SR; Cmptr Clb; New Music Forum; Cmptr Cnsltnt; Sftwr Spec/Asset Prog Mgr; BBA Baruch Clg 90; Cmptr Info Sys.

**HICKMAN, SHERRI D,** Atlantic Comm Coll, Mays Landing, NJ; SO; AS; Bsktbl Stats 89-90; Corrections/Juvenile Jstce; Stf/Cnslr.

**HICKMAN, SONYA,** Comm Coll Algny Co Algny Cmps, Pittsburgh, PA; SO; Grl Sct Ldr; Cert Sawyer Sch 85; Hstry; Bsns/Publ Admn.

**HICKMAN, THOMAS J,** Nyack Coll, Nyack, NY; SR; BS; SGA Cls 90-; Alpha Chi 89-; Hnr Soc; Dept Asstnt Elem Educ 90-; Elem Educ; Tchr.

**HICKMAN, TRACEY D,** Benedict Coll, Columbia, SC; JR; BA; Stdnt Ed Assoc 90-; Early Chldhd Ed; Tchg.

**HICKMAN, TRACY D,** Fl A & M Univ, Tallahassee, FL; JR; BA; Phi Theta Kappa 89-; Tchng Asst; AA Lake City Comm Coll 87; Elem Educ; Tch Spcfc Lrng Dsbld.

**HICKMAN, TRICIA ANN,** Univ Of Sc At Coastal Carolina, Conway, SC; JR; BS; Blgy Clb 88-90; Acdmc Deans Lst 90-; Math; Envrnmntl Eng.

**HICKMON, SANDRA A,** Univ Of Sc At Columbia, Columbia, SC; JR; BA; Stu Affr Cmmtt Stu Govt 90-; Ass Afro Amer Stu 88-; Mnrty Asst Peer Cnslr 90-; Alpha Phi Sigma 90-; Richard T Greener Schlrshp 88-; Crmnl Jstc; Law.

**HICKOX, DEBORAH J,** Anne Arundel Comm Coll, Arnold, MD; SO; BS; AA Anne Arundel Cmmnty Clg; Accntng.

**HICKS, ANTERRIA L,** Fl A & M Univ, Tallahassee, FL; JR; BA; FFEA Capt 90-; SG; Alpha Swthrt Sec 88; Zeta Delta Pi Sec 88; Andy Ser Awrd 87-88; Ldrshp Awrd African Dscndnts Org 87-88; AS 88; Elem Ed; Tch.

**HICKS, CHARLES W,** Georgetown Coll, Georgetown, KY; JR; BA; SGA Cngrsnl Whp 89-; Psi Chi Pres 90-; Grmn Clb 89-; Alpha Lambda Delta 89-; Beta Beta Beta 90-; Pi Kappa Alpha Rsk Mgmt Crdntr; Outstndg Prfrmnc Undrclsmn Lwr Dvsn Phlsphy 90; Phlsphy/Blgy.

**HICKS, CHERISSE R,** Commonwealth Coll, Virginia Beach, VA; JR; AA; Paralgl.

**HICKS, CHRISTINA M,** Fl St Univ, Tallahassee, FL; JR; BA; AA Tallahassee Cmnty Clg 90; Engl; Tchr.

**HICKS, CHRISTY L,** Middle Tn St Univ, Murfreesboro, TN; FR; Science; Nrsng.

**HICKS, DANA L,** Winthrop Coll, Rock Hill, SC; SR; BS; Beta Beta Beta VP 88-; Kappa Delta Pi 88-; Phi Kappa Phi 89-; Mary Mildred Sullivan Schlrshp; Dns Lst; Pres Lst; Biol; Sec Biol Tchr.

**HICKS, DARRYL C,** Va St Univ, Petersburg, VA; JR; BA; Sprts Infr Asst 88-; Intern Weyerhaeuser Corp Fnnc Admn Asst; Accntng; Accntnt.

**HICKS, DEBORAH C,** Clayton St Coll, Morrow, GA; SO; BBA; Acctng; CPA.

**HICKS, DIANA L,** Roane St Comm Coll, Harriman, TN; FR; Hlth Phy Tech/Entrtnr/Dance Instrctr; Physics/Ind Mgmnt.

**HICKS, DIANNA L,** Va St Univ, Petersburg, VA; SO; BS; Bus Admin Clb 90-; NAACP 90-; Bus Admin.

**HICKS, ERIN KATHLEEN,** Mount Holyoke Coll, South Hadley, MA; FR; BA; Mt Hlyke Coll Stdnt Govt Sec Drm Sntr Co Chr Elctns 90-; Glee Chr; Cncrt Chr 90-; Atty Gen Of TX Intrn; Pol Sci; Law.

**HICKS, HEATHER A,** Alfred Univ, Alfred, NY; JR; BS; AMA VP Careers/Placement 90-; NCWA 90-; Chorus 89-90; Pres Schlrshp Alfred Univ; Regents Shlrshp; IM Athletic 88-89; Busn Adminf Mktng.

**HICKS, HOLLY H,** Memphis St Univ, Memphis, TN; SR; BBA; Stdnt Govt Assn Assoc Sec St 89-90; Spanish Clb 90-; Beta Gamma Sigma 90-; Gamma Beta Phi 89-; Phi Kappa Phi 89-; Gldn Ky 90-; Goldsmiths Schlrshp 88-91; Intrntl Bus/Spnsh; Bus.

**HICKS, JOHN W,** Univ Of Sc At Columbia, Columbia, SC; FR; BSN; Army ROTC; Alpha Lambda Delta; USN 84-90; Navy Rsrves 90; Nrsng.

**HICKS, KATHRYN A,** Miami Dade Comm Coll South, Miami, FL; SO; BA; Stdnt Bdgt Comm; Miambiance Lit Mag Essy Ed 89-; Phi Theta Kappa Pres 90-; Awd Excell Omicron Tau Chptr; Hons Dept Outstdng Stdnt Yr; Tlnt Rstr Outstndg Mnrty Comm Coll Grads; AA; Hist; Law.

**HICKS, KATHY SUE,** Bethel Coll, Mckenzie, TN; FR; BS; Retail Mgmt; Bus Admn; Cmptr Priority.

**HICKS, KELLEY F,** Becker Coll At Leicester, Leicester, MA; SO; BS; Std Govt Comm 90-; Yrbk Comm 89-90; Std Advsr 90; Phi Theta Kappa; Dns Lst 89-; Std Tutor 90-; Wmns Sccr Capt 89-; AS; Htl Rest Mgmt.

**HICKS, KELLI M,** Univ Of West Fl, Pensacola, FL; SR; BA; Alpha Sigma Lambda 90-; AA Lurleen B Wallace Jr Coll 89; Elem Educ; Tchr.

**HICKS, KIMBERLY B,** Univ Of Sc At Columbia, Columbia, SC; JR; BS; AS Acctg; Spartanburg Tech 90; Psy; CPA.

**HICKS, KYLE L,** Va St Univ, Petersburg, VA; FR; NAACP 90-; BSAD 90-; Urbn Plng Cncl Sec 90-; Trnsprtn Cty Plng; Envrnmntl Prot Agnt.

**HICKS, LORI A,** Ms St Univ, Miss State, MS; JR; BA; Psychology Club 90-; Stdnt Health Advsry Comm 90-; Gamma Beta Phi 89-; Psi Chi VP 89-; Zeta Tau Alpha Ritual Chrmn 89-; Friend On Campus 88-89; Psychology.

**HICKS, MARK RICHARD,** Univ Of Akron, Akron, OH; JR; BS; Natl Hnr Scty; Acctg.

**HICKS, RUDOLPH,** Lexington Comm Coll, Lexington, KY; FR; AS; Elctrcl Engrg.

**HICKS III, SAMMY,** Morehouse Coll, Atlanta, GA; SO; BA; Stdnt Govt Assn Chief Stf 90-; STARS Dir Rcrtmnt 90-; Graves Hall Dorm Cncl Pres 89-; Bus Assn 89-; NABA VP; Omega Psi Phi Kpr Finance; Oglethorpe Elem Sch Mntr/Hmwrk Asst 90-; NAACP; Acctg; Fncl Plnr.

**HICKS, SHEWONIA L,** Jackson St Univ, Jackson, MS; JR; BED; Pierian Lit Soc Asst Sec 89-90; Stdnt Natl Edn Assn 88-; Alpha Lambda Delta 89-; Alpha Mu Gamma 88-89; Deans Lst 88-; Smr Intern Fed State Pgms Clrk Senior 90; Elem Edn; Tchr.

**HICKS, TAMMY W,** Phillips Jr Coll Spartanburg, Spartanburg, SC; JR; AA; AA 90; AA 91; Med Admin Asst.

**HICKS, TERESA A,** Norfolk St Univ, Norfolk, VA; JR; BSW; Chrstn Org 89-90; Scl Wrk; Adoption Worker.

**HICKS, THERESE D,** Watterson Coll, Louisville, KY; GD.

**HICKS, THOMAS B,** Vance Granville Comm Coll, Henderson, NC; FR; AA; Stdnt Govtmnt Pres 90-; Phi Theta Kappa Fund Raising Chrmn 90-; History; Teach.

**HICKS, TINA M,** Dyersburg St Comm Coll, Dyersburg, TN; SO; Stdnt Govt Assn Pres; Bus Offc Assn Pres 90-; Data Proc Mgmt Assn 90-; Phi Theta Kappa 90-; Pblshd Short Stories Ltry Jrnl; Deans Lst 90-; Outstndng Stdnt 90-; Bonnie F Jones Memrl Schlrshp; Outstndng DSBOSA 90-; Offc Syst Tchnlgy; Law.

**HICKS, TONYA J,** Univ Of Tn At Martin, Martin, TN; SR; BS; Brdcstng Guild; Cmps Radio Station; Deans List 90; Cmnctns Brdcst; Radio Prgrmng.

**HICKS, VINCENT T,** Western Ky Univ, Bowling Green, KY; SO; BA; Black Student Alliance 89-90; Assoc Blk Student Achievers 89-90; Martin Luther King Meml Awd; Prestl Schl 90-; Intshp Bell South 89; Im Ftbl 89; Acctng; CPA.

**HICKS, VIRGINIA C,** Nc Agri & Tech St Univ, Greensboro, NC; JR; BS; Mrchng/Cncrt Bnd 88-; Mu Phi Epsilon Pres; Deans Lst 88-; Chncllrs Exec Smnr 90-; Asst Mscn Laughln Untd Mthdst Chrch Asst Mscn; Univ Bwlng Tm; Msc Educ; Msc Edctr.

**HICKS, WANDA J,** Va Commonwealth Univ, Richmond, VA; JR; BS; Pub Rels Stdnt Soc Of Amer 90-; Golden Key; Marsh/Mc Lennan; Desktop Publshng Intrn; Mass Cmctns; Pub Rels.

**HICKS, WILLENE A,** Georgetown Univ, Washington, DC; SR; BSBA; Gospel Choir; Move In Cmmt 88; DC Schools Prjt 89-; Delta Sigma Theta 90-; Soup Kitchens 89-; Deans List 88-; Acctng; Pblc Acctng.

**HICKS, WILLIAM D,** Univ Of Southern Ms, Hattiesburg, MS; SR; BS; Sign Lang Muscl Trpe; Phi Alpha Theta; History; Tch.

**HICKS, WILLIAM DAVID,** Liberty Univ, Lynchburg, VA; SR; College Republicans; Grad Magna Cum Laude.

**HICKSON, DANA L,** Volunteer St Comm Coll, Gallatin, TN; SO; BA; Elem Ed; Tchr.

**HICKSON, PRISCILLA R,** Hudson Valley Comm Coll, Troy, NY; JR.

**HIDALGO, CARMEN C,** City Univ Of Ny La Guard Coll, Long Island Cty, NY; SO; AAS; Trvl/Trsm Clb Pres 90 VP 89; Deans Lst; Intrn Pan Amer Airwys 90-; Trvl/Trsm.

**HIDALGO, MARISOL M,** Fl International Univ, Miami, FL; SR; BA; FEA 90-; Dns Lst 90-; Elem Educ; Elem Tchr.

**HIDALGO, MYRIAM C,** Univ Of Miami, Coral Gables, FL; SR; BBA; Mbr Univ MI Alumni Assoc 91-; Jury Serv Circuit Crt FL Dade Co Chrmn 91; Dns Lst 86-87; Otstndng Acad Achvmnt 87-88; Uppr Lvl Status Sch Bsns 89; Dns Lst Sch Bsns Admn Univ Miami 91; AA Miami-Dade Comm Clg 88; Bsns Mgmt/Org; Bsns.

**HIDALGO, YARICE A,** Boston Univ, Boston, MA; FR; Dean Lst 90-; Prt Rcn Awrnss Day Chrprsn; Cmmnctns; Pblc Rltns.

**HIDAY, TRACEY L,** Cumberland Coll, Williamsburg, KY; JR; BA; Sigma Tau Delta Pres; Newspapr Staff; Yrbk Staff Ed; Sigma Tau Delta; Virginia Lovett Engl Schlrshp; Engl; Pblshng/Wrtr.

**HIDINGER, JULIE A,** North Central Tech Coll, Mansfield, OH; SR; ASN; LPN 80-; Nrsng; CCU RN.

**HIDLE, LISA MICHELLE,** Fl A & M Univ, Tallahassee, FL; FR; BA; Dns Lst 90; Hnr Rll; Phrmcy; Retl Phrmcst.

**HIEBLER, CHARLOTTE M,** Univ Of Md Baltimore Prof Schl, Baltimore, MD; JR; BS; MD Soc Med Tech Stdnt Rep; Tutr Immnlgy U MD 90; Amer Soc Med Tech; Deans Lst U MD 89-; Med Tech; Med Schl.

**HIERS, YVONNE M,** Piedmont Tech Coll, Greenwood, SC; GD; AS; Cert 90; Indstrl Tchnlgy.

**HIGBY, MELANIE S,** Saint John Fisher Coll, Rochester, NY; JR; BS; Stdnt Govt Comm Acadamics 90-; Vol Coach Amer Youth Soc 89-90; Econ Tutor Acctng 90-; Financial Exec Inst Achvmnt Awd; Pres Schlrshp 88-; Regents Schlrshp 88-; IM Sftbl 88-90; Acctng; CPA.

**HIGBY, RALPH F,** S U N Y Coll Of Tech At Alfred, Alfred, NY; JR; BED; Chem Clb Treas 90-; Chemistry.

**HIGDON, MAURICE D,** Bishop St Comm Coll, Mobile, AL; SO; AAAS; Fnrl Svc Ed Clb Sgt Arms 89-90; Phi Theta Kappa 90-; Intrnshp Rogers-Northview Fnrl Hm; Fnrl Svc; Mrtcn.

**HIGGINBOTHAM, DEBRA L,** West Liberty St Coll, West Liberty, WV; SR; BA; Peer Tutor/Cnslr 89; Undgrad Acad Schlp 87-90; Natl Clgt Ed Awd 87-89; Kappa Delta Pi 89-; C/P Tlphn Co Schlp 88-89; Geirgia Haught Cochran Mem Awd 90; Doris Lake Jones Schlp 89-; Pres Lst 88-; Elem Ed; Tchr.**

**HIGGINBOTHAM, GINGER R,** Univ Of Ga, Athens, GA; JR; BSED; Stdnt Edctn Assn 89-90; NCAA Sccr Oglthrp Unv 89-90; Kappa Delta Epsilon; Sigma Sigma Sigma Msc Chrmn 88-89; Sccr 89-90; Scl Stds Spnsh; Tchr.

**HIGGINBOTHAM, HEATHER L,** Lenoir Rhyne Coll, Hickory, NC; SO; MBA; Hist; Preservationist/Archaeologist.

**HIGGINBOTHAM, JAMES W,** Marshall University, Huntington, WV; SO; BED; Elem Ed; Tchng Elem Stdnts.

**HIGGINBOTHAM, JEANETTE M,** Middle Tn St Univ, Murfreesboro, TN; JR; BS; Gamma Beta Phi; Phys Thrpy.

**HIGGINBOTHAM, JEFFREY L,** Wv Univ At Parkersburg, Parkersburg, WV; FR; BA; Real Estate 83-; Bsn Admin; Rl Estate Indus.

**HIGGINS, JACQUELINE R,** Cornell Univ Statutory College, Ithaca, NY; JR; BA; Pre-Vet Scty; Anml Sci; Vet.

**HIGGINS, JASON C,** Me Maritime Academy, Castine, ME; SR; Rugby Clb 87-; Cmpny Adjtnt 90-; Cdt Shppng Awd 90; Boiler Oprtrs Lic 90; US Nvl Frfghtng Certf 89; NAVI Opnwtr Certf 88; BS; Marine Pwr Engnrng.

**HIGGINS, JENNIFER M,** Univ Of North Fl, Jacksonville, FL; SR; Phi Kappa Phi 90-; Gldn Ky 90-; Dns Lst; BAE Univ Of North Florida; Elem Educ; Tchng.

**HIGGINS, JERRY L,** Univ Of Tn At Martin, Martin, TN; JR; BS; Elec Eng Tech.

**HIGGINS, JOEL M,** Wv Univ, Morgantown, WV; FR; BSCE; Civil Engr; Engr Cnsltn.

**HIGGINS, KRISTIN E,** Lesley Coll, Cambridge, MA; FR; Poetry/Creative Writing Clb VP 90-; Day Care Ldrshp/Soc Sci.

**HIGGINS, LINDA W,** Univ Of Pittsburgh, Pittsburgh, PA; GD; PHD; Nurses Org 86-; Sigma Theta Tau 82-; Lecturer Carlow Coll Pittsburgh Pa 88-; MSN 87; Bsn Duquesne Univ 82; Nursing Edn & Rsrch.

**HIGGINS, LISA A,** Eckerd Coll, St Petersburg, FL; SR; BA; Eckrd Clg Rep 87; Eckred Clg IM 87-; Vol Suncst Chldrns Make A Wish Fndtn 90; Vol Juv Diabetes 90; Law Intrnshp W St Attys Offc 90; Res Asst Asscmnt Offce 90-; Eckrd Clg Womns Sftbl 87-90; Soc/Crim Law; Law Schl.

**HIGGINS, MARY BETH,** Molloy Coll, Rockville Ctr, NY; JR; BSN; Nrsng Dept Crclm Comm 90-; Nrsng Clb 88-; Gaelc Soc 90-; Sigma Theta Tau 2nd VP; Delta Epsilon Sigma; Omicron Alpha Zeta; NLN Comm; Acdmc Brd Rep Nrsng; LI Jwsh Med Cntr Extrnshp; Nrsng; RN.

**HIGGINS, MARY ELLEN,** Pa St Univ Delaware Cty Cmps, Media, PA; SR; BA; Campus Ambsdrs 87-; Ogontz Dnce Co 88; Coll Hlth/Hmn Dvlpmnt Hon Soc 88; Keystn Soc Pres 87-88; Scnd Mile Frnds Prog; Deans Lst 87-90; Gen Arts/Sci; Soc Wrk/Educ.

**HIGGINS, PRISCILLA R,** West Liberty St Coll, West Liberty, WV; JR; BS; SEAC Pres; Chi Beta Phi Treas; Chem; PhD Chem.

**HIGGINS, QUIN M,** Univ Of South Fl, Tampa, FL; FR; Russian Clb Pres; USF Hnrs Prgrm 90-; Crck K Asst Treas 90- ; Admssn With Dstnctn USF 90; Frshmn Schlr Awd; FL Undrgrdt Schlr Awd; Math; Prfssrshp.

**HIGGINS, SUSAN L,** Radford Univ, Radford, VA; JR; BS; Quest Asst; Judicial Bd; Pi Gamma Mu V P Alumnae Affairs; Phi Sigma Sigma; Alison Horwitz Awd; Greek IMS 89-; Sclgy/Anthrplgy; Ph D/Professor.

**HIGGINS, WILLIAM L,** Savannah Coll Of Art & Design, Savannah, GA; FR; BFA; Campus Bible Study; Photography; Illustrator/Wildlife.

**HIGGLER, ANDREA E,** S U N Y Coll Of Tech At Frmgdl, Farmingdale, NY; SO; AS; Advrtsng Art.

**HIGGS, HOLLY L,** Coppin St Coll, Baltimore, MD; SO; BS; Feed Hmlss Vol 90-; Deans Lst 90-; Info Sys; Cmptr Sci.

**HIGGS, SHANNON M,** Fl International Univ, Miami, FL; SR; BS; Occup Ther Clb Pr 89-; Pi Theta Epsilon 90-; Phi Lambda 90-; Rehab Svc Admin Trainee 90-; AA Valencia Cmnty Clg 88; Hlth; Occup Ther.

**HIGGS, TRACY T,** Saint Thomas Univ, Miami, FL; SO; BA; Ftre Bus Ldrs Of Amer 89; Intr Dorm Cncl 90-; Chrldr 90; Comp Info Systms; Comp Prgrmmr.

**HIGH JR, CHESTER J,** Cleveland St Univ, Cleveland, OH; SO; BME; Natl Tech Assn Mbrshp Chrpr; Natl Soc Black Engs; Outstndng Soph Mech Eng Stdnt 90-; Deans List 89-; IM Ftbl/Bsktbl 90-; Mech Eng.**

**HIGH, DONALD R,** Univ Of Tn At Martin, Martin, TN; SO; BS; Phi Epsilon Mu 90-; Ldrs In Res 89-90; Dns Lst 90-; All Amer Schlr; Phy Educ/Hlth; Tchr/Coach.

**HIGH, ELIZABETH A,** Univ Of Tn At Martin, Martin, TN; SO; Stdnt Govt Stdnt Juste 90-; Pi Sigma Epsilon; Hl Assn 89-90; Phi Eta Sigma; Hon Smnr Pgm 89-; Pi Sigma Epsilon; Chi Omega Chrmn Fvrs Com 89-; Chrldr 89-90; Math; Actry.

**HIGH, HOLLY J,** James Madison University, Harrisonburg, VA; SR; BS; Psychology Clb Pres 88-; Hll Cncl Pblcty Chrmn 88-89; Ski Clb 88-90; Psi Chi; Gldn Key; Psychology; Cnslng.

**HIGH, JENNIFER L,** Middle Tn St Univ, Murfreesboro, TN; SO; BFD; Band Blue 89-90; Orchestra 89-; Residento Asst 90-; Bio; Tch Scrndry Schls.

**HIGH, KRISTEN L,** Fl St Univ, Tallahassee, FL; SR; BS; Grnt Gld Grls 87-; Smnl Ambssdrs Almn Rltns 87-; Almn Fndtn Rltns Offc 88-; Deans Lstkappa Delta; Kappa Alpha Lttl Sstr Rsc Crt Almn Rltns Treas 86-; Rep Coll Ed 89-; Cnvctn Comm 89-91; Erly Chldhd Ed.

**HIGHAM, JENNIFER L,** Fl St Univ, Tallahassee, FL; SO; Pnhllnc Jdcl Brd; Phi Eta Sigma 90-; Beta Kappa Alpha; Kappa Kappa Gamma Corr Sec; Wlt Dsney Wrld Coll Prog Intrnshp; Acctg; Law.

**HIGHFIELD, JENNIFER A,** Birmingham Southern Coll, Birmingham, AL; SO; Habitat Hmnty; Phi Sigma Iota; Alpha Chi Omega 89-; English/French; Photojrnlsm.

**HIGHFIELD, SHELLY A,** Ashland Comm Coll, Ashland, KY; JR; BA; Accntng; CPA.

**HIGHTOWER, BRETT C,** Life Coll, Marietta, GA; GD; DC; Gamma Beta Phi; BS 84; Chrprctc.

**HIGHTOWER, CRYSTAL D,** Gulf Coast Comm Coll, Panama City, FL; FR; AA; Blck Stdnt Un Chrprsn 90-; Hm Econ; Dttcs.

**HIGHTOWER, DANIELLE E,** Morris Coll, Sumter, SC; SR; BS; Alpha Kappa Mu 90-; Phi Beta Lambda Treas 90-; Eaton Corp Intrnshp 90; Acctg; CPA.

**HIGHTOWER, MARIA A,** Fl A & M Univ, Tallahassee, FL; SO; BED; Fl Fut Educ Amer; Elem Ed; Tchg.

**HIGHTOWER, WILLIAM PHILLIP,** Livingston Univ, Livingston, AL; FR; BS; Stdnt Govt; Bsn; Mgmt.

**HIGUERA, EVELYN LUCY,** Hilbert Coll, Hamburg, NY; SR; BA; Talent Roster Cert Achvmnt; Grad Hnrs; Hskpng Sprvsr 77-; Drctr Res Lf 83-87; Drctr Rec Ctr 87-89; Drctr Material Mgmt 89-; Crmnl Justice/Human Svcs; Wrk With Juveniles.

**HILAIRE, VIRGINIE,** Barry Univ, Miami, FL; SR; BSN; Lambda Chi 90-; Tutrshp Pgm Elem Schl Vol 90; Nrsng; Midwife.

**HILAL, FREDERIC,** Goucher Coll, Towson, MD; SO; BA; Tns 89-; MD Assoc Clgte Dir Athltcs; Math; Bsn.

**HILAL, RAOUF E,** Coll Of Charleston, Charleston, SC; JR; BS; Bard Scty Pres 89-90; Hnrs Prgm Std Assc 88-; Omicron Delta Kappa; Phi Kappa Phi; Alpha Chi Sigma Rprtr 89-; Alpha Epsilon Delta 89-; Med Unv SC Rsrch Asst Awd 90-; Hghly Dstngshd Std 89-; Bio Chem; Med.

**HILAND, LACEY D,** Toccoa Falls Coll, Toccoa Falls, GA; SR; Stephens Co Mntl Hlth Cntr Intrnshp 90-; Psychlgy; Med.

**HILBORN, CHRISTINE M,** Richard Bland Coll, Petersburg, VA; SO; Roteract Treas 90; Phi Theta Kappa 90; Accntng.

**HILBRECHT, MOLLY J,** S U N Y Coll At Fredonia, Fredonia, NY; SO; BA; Econ Clb Treas 90-; Omicrn Delta Epsilon Pres Elect; Econ; Plcy Mkng Advsr.

**HILBURGER, BARBARA J,** S U N Y At Buffalo, Buffalo, NY; SR; BS; Stdnt Assmbly Rep 89-; SGA Spkr Bureau Crdntr 89-90; Am Mrktng Assn 90-; Rlgs Ed Tchr 89-; Schussmeister Ski Clb; Mgt/Mktng; Sales Food Ind.

**HILBURN, MARK R,** Livingston Univ, Livingston, AL; FR; BA; Flwshp Chrstn Athls; Ftbl; Indstrl Tech; Drafter.

**HILDEBRAND, CHERYL L,** Oh St Univ At Marion, Marion, OH; JR; BA; Alpha Lambda Delta; Phi Eta Sigma; Golden Key; Phi Kappa Phi; Children Of Am Rev Pres Mingo Soc 90-; AA 90; Adv & Spanish.

**HILDEBRAND, GLORIA,** City Univ Of Ny City Coll, New York, NY; SR; BA; Bkbl 87-; Soc; Ph D Soc Prfsr.

**HILDEBRAND, KENT D,** Tallahassee Comm Coll, Tallahassee, FL; SO; BA; Srvce Mgr At Ppee RV Cntr 86-; Bus And Comp Sci; Strt My Own Bus.

**HILDERBRAND, CHARLOTTE R,** Univ Of Southern Ms, Hattiesburg, MS; SR; BS; Rsdnc Hall Assn; Educ Assn; Geographic Alliance; MS Asn Of Educatros; USM Hnrs Coll 87-90; USM Dns Lst 89-90; Educ/Socl Stds; Educator.**

**HILDERBRAND II, JOHN C,** Univ Of Pittsburgh, Pittsburgh, PA; SR; BS; Univ Schlr; Kiwanis; W Penn Pwr Scl Com Pres 90-; W Pen Pwr Co 85-; AS EE PA State Univ 85; Elctrcl Engrg.

**HILEMAN, RICKY L,** Univ Of Akron, Akron, OH; JR; BSA; Golden Key; IM; Acctng; CPA.

**HILER, CARI L,** Smith Coll, Northampton, MA; SO; BA; Pre-Hlth Soc 90-; Masspirg Envir Grp 89-90; First Grp Schlr; Hse Hlth Rep; Bio; Med.

**HILFER, AMY M,** Univ Of Akron, Akron, OH; JR; BED; Akron Coll Of Edn Stdnts 90-; Golden Key 90-; Kappa Delta Pi; Elem Edn; Teach.

**HILFERTY, JUNE J,** Temple Univ, Philadelphia, PA; JR; BA; Gld Key 90; Bllng Admnstrtr Drxlbrk Eng 90-; AA Bucks Cnty Comm Coll Newtown PA 87; Bus.

**HILGENBERG-NELSON, NINA A,** Univ Of North Fl, Jacksonville, FL; SR; BSN; AACN 86-; CCRN; RN/AAN 82-; AAN John C Calhoun Coll Clg 82; Nrsng; Mstrs Crtcl Care Nrsng.

**HILKER, MICHELLE L,** Radford Univ, Radford, VA; SO; BA; Rcratn Clb 89-; Therapeutic Rcrtn; Rcrtnl Thrpst.

**HILL, AGNELA C,** Univ Of Nc At Greensboro, Greensboro, NC; FR; BA; Intervarsity Chrstn Flwshp 90-; Alpha Lambda Delta 90-; Teaching Fellow; Elem Ed; Teaching.

**HILL, ANGELA S,** Catawba Valley Comm Coll, Hickory, NC; JR; AIM 90-; Cert Prfssnl Srvc Rep 90-; ASSC Western Piedmont Cmmnty Coll 85; Cmmrcl Art; Advrtsng.

**HILL, BARBARA T,** Lenoir Rhyne Coll, Hickory, NC; SO; BA; PTA V P 87-90; Hmownrs Bd Pres 88-; Ele Soccer Coach 86-90; Bnkg; Sec; Indus Engr; O B Plcmnt; Accnt Clrk; English; Educ.

**HILL, BARTON ERIC,** Univ Of Southern Ms, Hattiesburg, MS; SR; BA; Library Sci; Tchng.

**HILL II, BERTRAM A,** Bloomfield Coll, Bloomfield, NJ; SO; BA; Athltc Schlrshp; Bus Admin; Real Estate.

**HILL, BOBBIE L,** Univ Of North Fl, Jacksonville, FL; JR; BA; RA 89-90; Phi Eta Sigma 89-; Gldn Key VP; AA FL St Unv 90; Comm; Natl Park Serv.

**HILL, BRETT Z,** Oh Univ, Athens, OH; SO; BA; Film; Feature Film Dir.

**HILL, CARNELA R,** Nc Agri & Tech St Univ, Greensboro, NC; JR; BA; SCAC Pres 88-; ACM Sec 88-; Alpha Lambda Delta 88-89; Coop IBM; Cmptr Sci; Cmptr Prgrmngs.**

**HILL III, CHARLES E,** Georgetown Univ, Washington, DC; JR; Mktg Socty 90-; Vp Pldge Educ Delta Sigma Pi 89-; Dean Of Pldgs Alpha Phi Alpha 90-; Campus Pblcty Rep For Walt Disney, Touchstone, Hollywood Pictures; Mktg; Entertainment Mktg.

**HILL JR, CHARLIE ANDREW,** Univ Of Sc At Columbia, Columbia, SC; FR; BA; USAF E-4 88-; Bus.

**HILL, CHERYLEE B,** Spartanburg Methodist Coll, Spartanburg, SC; SO; MBA; Herodotus Pres 90-; Stdnt Govt Assn Sec/Treas 90-; ROTC 89-; Chrstn Mvmnt; Workstudy Tutor 90-; Cheerleading Co-Capt 89-; Hstry; Law.

**HILL, COLLEEN G,** Univ Of Miami, Coral Gables, FL; SR; BS; IEEE 89; Eng Scty 86; Eta Kappa Nu Pres 89; Golden Key 89; Phi Kappa Phi 89; Tau Beta Pi 89; LPN Fl 84; Elctrcl/Cmptr Eng.

**HILL, CONNIE L,** Cumberland Coll, Williamsburg, KY; SR; BS; Acctng; Bus.

**HILL, CRAIG S,** Clemson Univ, Clemson, SC; SR; Forestry Club 87-; Soc Of Amercn Foresters 87-; Xi Sigma Pi Secy/Fiscal Agnt 88-; Alpha Zeta 88-.

**HILL, CRYSTAL L,** Northeast State Tech Comm Coll, Blountville, TN; FR; Am Chem Soc Pres 90-; Stdnt Govt 90-; Chem; Eng.

**HILL, DARRELL F,** Al A & M Univ, Normal, AL; SR; Natl Soc Blck Engrs; TN Vly Chapt Am Def Preparedness Assoc Schlrshp; Deans Lst 87-90; Sigma Tau Epsilon; Alpha Phi Alpha; Ftbl; Bsebl; Track; Mech Engr/Drafting.

**HILL, DEBRA F,** Ms Valley St Univ, Itta Bena, MS; SR; BS; Sara White Angel Flight ROTC 83-86; Tchr; BS Crim Just 86; Educ Admin; Law.

**HILL, DENISE V,** Samford Univ, Birmingham, AL; JR; Stdnt Bar Assoc 90-; Deans List; Academic Schlrshp; RN; BS UAB Schl Nursing 83; Law.

**HILL, DONOVAN L,** Al A & M Univ, Normal, AL; SO; BS; Asst NASAS Salad Mach Pgm 90-; Hrtcltr.

**HILL, EDGAR L,** Birmingham Southern Coll, Birmingham, AL; JR; BS; Deans Lst 90-; NAA 90-; Acctg/Finance; Financl Serv.

**HILL, FRANCIS M,** Univ Of Montevallo, Montevallo, AL; JR; BA; Cmps Lvng Assc Rsdnt Asst 88-92; Montvallo Assc Hmn Svc 90-92; Dr Jan Eagles Schlrshp; Chld Care Ed/Dvlpmnt I/Ii 86-88; Soc Wrk/Csnlng/Guid; Cmbrlnd Law Sch.

**HILL, GENE G,** Univ Of Akron, Akron, OH; JR; MS; Stdnt Chptr Of Amercn Soc Of Cvl Engrs Pres; Golden Key 90-; Civil Engrng.

**HILL, GIDGET W,** Blue Mountain Coll, Blue Mountain, MS; SR; BS; MS Assc Edctrs Stdnt Pgm 90-; Pres Hon Roll 90-; Eunomian 90-; Elem Educ; Tchng.

**HILL, HELEN LOUISE,** Roane St Comm Coll, Harriman, TN; SO; BA; Blcks In Govt Sec 88; Tstmstrs Intnatl Admin VP 86; Prog Anlyst In Govt Inst; Bus Mgmt; Bus.

**HILL, JAMIE D,** Abraham Baldwin Agri Coll, Tifton, GA; SO; BS; Sci/Frstry; Tmbr Mgt.

**HILL, JAMIE T,** Univ Of West Fl, Pensacola, FL; SR; BA; SGA Educ Rep 90-; Alpha Sigma Lambda Pres 90-; AA Okaloosa Walton Jr Coll 88; Elem Educ; Tchr.

**HILL, JEAN E,** Coppin St Coll, Baltimore, MD; SR; BS; Arena Plyrs Coord/Corp Sec/Dir 89-90; Actor/John Waters Flms; Prnt Model; Rockshots NY NY; Comstock Reno Nevada; AA Comm Coll Of Balt 76; Spec Ed; Tchr/Actr/Modl.

**HILL JR, JENNINGS L,** Spartanburg Methodist Coll, Spartanburg, SC; SO; ACJ; Frat Ord Pol 88-; Phi Theta Kappa; Sec Mgr TW Servs Inc Spartanbrg SC; Crmnl Jstce; Corp Sec.

**HILL, JESSICA G,** Tn St Univ, Nashville, TN; GD; BS; Pep Clb; Natl Assc Yng Chldrn; Nashvl Assc Yng Chldrn; Phi Beta Lmbd; Zeta Phi Beta Pres 89-90; Ctr Exclnc Dvlpmnt Unit Aprctn Cert; Chld Dvlpmnt/Fmly Rltns; Spec Educ Tchr.

**HILL, JOHN R,** Temple Univ, Philadelphia, PA; SR; BARCH; Gldn Key 89; Exchng Clb 87-87; Slf Emplyd Prfssnl Phtgrphr 80-87; Archtctr.

**HILL, JOHN W,** Univ Of Akron, Akron, OH; SR; BSME; Soc Of Automotive Engrs 90-; Golden Key 90-; Oh Bd Of Regents Acdmc Schlrshp 87-; Stewart L-Catherine E Dow Mem Schlrshp 89-90; John F Good Mem Schlrshp 90-; Natl Coll Engrng Awds 90-; Deans List 87-; Mech Engrng.**

**HILL, JUAN D,** Memphis St Univ, Memphis, TN; JR; BS; Computer Engineering.

**HILL, JULIA M,** Alcorn St Univ, Lorman, MS; SO; BA; Wmn Lanier Hll Sec 90-; SNEA 90-; Dean Lst 90-; Math; Elem Educ.

**HILL, JULIE M,** Northern Ky Univ, Highland Hts, KY; JR; BA; SNEA; DEA; NKAR; Educ.

**HILL, KANTAYLIENIERE Y,** Le Moyne Owen Coll, Memphis, TN; SO; BS; Stdnt Govt Assoc Sen 90-; Peer Cnslr 90-; Cls VP 90-; Dubois Schlrs Prog; Tutor Cummngs Elem 90-; Dns Lst 89-; Pres Schlr 89-; Hgst GPA 90-; Elem Educ; Instr.

**HILL, KENDRA L,** Fl St Univ, Tallahassee, FL; SR; BS; Alpha Chi Omega Hse Mgr/Coll Rush Info Chr 87-; Chld Dvlpmnt; Ed.

**HILL, KEVIN J,** Cheyney Univ Of Pa, Cheyney, PA; FR; BA; Deans Lst; Educ; Tchng.

**HILL, KIMBERLY R,** Ms St Univ, Miss State, MS; SR; BS; MI Assn Chldrn Under Six Treas; Bptst Stdnt Union 90-; Alpha Beta Gamma 88-89; Kappa Delta Pi 90-; Pres Schlr 90-; AA Hinds Comm Coll 89; Elem Ed; Tchng.

**HILL, LA NEATA D,** Al St Univ, Montgomery, AL; JR; BS; Phi Eta Sigma 89-; Pi Mu Epsilon Sec 90-; Alpha Kappa Mu; Rsrch Linear Algebra; Institute Tech; Math/Engr.

**HILL, LAURETTA D,** Hampton Univ, Hampton, VA; SR; BS; Educ Clb 88-; SVEA 89-; Alpha Kappa Mu 90-; Dean Lst 87-; Educ Sch; Tch.

**HILL, LAVELLE,** Ny Univ, New York, NY; FR; BA; Acctnt 89-; Bus/Finance.

**HILL, LESLIE ANN,** Univ Of Tn At Knoxville, Knoxville, TN; FR; Choir 90-; Bus; Acctg.

**HILL, LISA L,** Univ Of Southern Ms, Hattiesburg, MS; SO; BS; Pgm Assist/Cnslng/Educ/Rsrcs For Stdnts 90; Panhellenic Cncl V P 90-; Judicial Bd Chrmn 90-; Stdnts Agnst Driving Drunk 90-; JR Panhellenic Cncl Advsr 90-; Alcohol Awareness Task Force 90-; Psych; Clncl Psych.

**HILL, MARCI D,** Univ Of Rochester, Rochester, NY; SO; BA; Sor Soc Com; Sor Hsng Com; Sigma Delta Tau Sor; Psychlgy; Law.

**HILL, MELISSA K,** Va Commonwealth Univ, Richmond, VA; SO; MED; Engl; Spcl Educ Tchr.

**HILL, MELISSA L,** Univ Of Ga, Athens, GA; SO; BS; Recr Mjrs Clb; Swim Clb 90; Kappa Delta Asst Pldg Edctr 89-; Communiversity; Recr/Leisure Studies; Pk Mgmt/YMCA Dir.

**HILL, MICHAEL R,** Univ Of Tn At Martin, Martin, TN; SR; BS; Sdtnt Govt Spkr 90-; Clg Rpblcns Chrmn 90-; Pre Legal Clb Pres 88-89; Phi Eta Sigma 87-; Phi Kappa Phi; Ord Of Omega; Phi Alpha Delta Pres 89-; Sigma Pi Pres 90-; Pol Sci; Law.

**HILL, MICHAEL T,** Belmont Coll, Nashville, TN; GD; BBA; Bus/Finance Assn 90-; Yng Rpblcns 84-; Beta Beta Beta 87-; Lambda Chi Alpha 84-; BS 88; Finance/MBA.

**HILL, PETER S,** Univ Of Nc At Asheville, Asheville, NC; FR; BA; 2MS Bsktbl Sftbl Ftbl; Envrnmntl Sci; Enrgy/Wst Mgmt.

**HILL, RAE A,** Wv Univ At Parkersburg, Parkersburg, WV; JR; C Edna Chptr 140 Ordr Estrn Star 90-; AA 90; AAS 90; Mgmt.

**HILL, ROGER J,** Univ Of West Fl, Pensacola, FL; JR; BS; US Air Force Non-Cmssnd Offcrs Assn 87-89; Tchnlgy Applctns 90-; AS UND 89; Elec Eng Technlgy; Appld Eng.

**HILL, RONALD L,** Univ Of Cin R Walters Coll, Blue Ash, OH; FR; Cgie; Math; Indus Mngmnt.

**HILL, RONNI L,** Va St Univ, Petersburg, VA; FR; BA; Hnrs Coll; Chrldg Squad; Bus Info; Cmptr Pro.

**HILL, SAMUEL E,** Savannah Coll Of Art & Design, Savannah, GA; SO; BA; Illustration.

**HILL, SCOTT A,** Ashland Comm Coll, Ashland, KY; SO; SG Rep 90-; Drug Info Unit Peer Edcatr 90-; AA; Police Admin; Law Enfrcmnt.

**HILL, SEAN L,** S U N Y Coll Of A & T Morrisvl, Morrisville, NY; SO; Vrsty Bsktbl MVP Capt 89-; Blck Stu Unn; Frairs Thtr Grp; Schl Mlrm; Intern Phys Ed Tchr; MAD Cmpgn; IM Bsktbl Sftbl; Crmnl Jstc; Soc Wrk.

**HILL, SHLITA MONIQUE,** Fl A & M Univ, Tallahassee, FL; FR; PHARM; Rose Buds 90-; Phi Eta Sigma; Hnr Roll 90-; Deans List 90; Pharmacy.

**HILL, STANLEY W,** Univ Of Ky, Lexington, KY; SR; MA; BA; History; Prfsr.

**HILL, STEPHANIE A,** Univ Of Tn At Martin, Martin, TN; JR; BA; Natl Assn Acctnts 90-; Pnhlnc Cncl Pres 89-; Phi Eta Sigma VP 90-; Order Omega; Phi Kappa Phi; Phi Chi Theta Rush Chrmn 90-; Zeta Tau Alpha Sr Pnhlnc; Univ Serv Awd; Most Outstndg Stdnt Bus Admin 90; Bus Admin; Acctg.

**HILL, STEPHANIE R,** Univ Of Md At Eastern Shore, Princess Anne, MD; SR; BS; Bsktbl Pep Club Sec 88-89; Soph Class Sec 88-89; Jr Class Sec 89-90; Acdmc Hnrs 89-; Edctnl Hnrs 90-; Kappa Delta Pi 90-; Elem Spec Edn.

**HILL, STEPHEN T,** Univ Of Ky, Lexington, KY; JR; BS; Tau Beta Pi 90-; Eta Kappa Nu 90-; Kodak Schlrshp 89-; IM Tennis 88-; Elec Engrng; Engrng.

**HILL, SUSAN Y,** Albany St Coll, Albany, GA; JR; BS; ROTC 87-; Phi Beta Lambda 90-; Delta Sigma Theta; Natl Sojourners Awd 90; Flag Corps Cptn 87-90; Business Mgt.

**HILL, SUZANNE C,** Univ Of Tn At Martin, Martin, TN; FR; BED; Rdgmnt PTA VP 75-; Grl Scts Ldr 80-; Art Edctn; Tchng.

**HILL, TAMMY L,** Spalding Univ, Louisville, KY; JR; BSN; NSA VP 90-F Sigma Theta Tau; Delta Epsilon Sigma; Nrsng.

**HILL III, THEODORE D,** Old Dominion Univ, Norfolk, VA; FR; BA; Wrstlng 90; Elctrcl Eng; Eng.

**HILL, THERESA F,** Alcorn St Univ, Lorman, MS; SO; Bus Admins; Mgmnt.**

**HILL, TIFFANI A,** Brewer St Jr Coll, Fayette, AL; FR; BA; Sftbl 90-; Jrnlsm.

**HILL, TONIA D,** Central Al Comm Coll, Alexander City, AL; FR; MBA; Phi Theta Kappa; Biology/Chmstry; Tchr.

**HILL, TONYA R,** Faulkner St Jr Coll, Bay Minette, AL; SO; BS; Phi Theta Kappa 90-; Acctg; Crtfd Mngrl Accnt.

**HILL JR, URAL H,** Interdenominational Theo Ctr, Atlanta, GA; GD; MDIV; Stdnt Govt V P 89-90; Natl Coll Black Caucus Chm/Founder 89-90; M L K Jr March Comm/Parate Grand Marshall 90-; K C's Banquet Chr 88; Omega Psi Phi Local Treas 83; Natl Coll Black Cacus Chm Fndr Adv Agt89-; Soc Of Rel; Pastor/Coll Prof.

**HILL, VICKI K,** Watterson Coll, Louisville, KY; SR; AD Wttrsn Clg 91; Bsns Admnstrtn.

**HILL, VIDA M,** Savannah St Coll, Savannah, GA; JR; BA; Fut Bus Ldrs Amer; Delta Sigma Pi; Alpha Kappa Alpha; Sarah Mills Hodge Acdmc Schlrshp 89-91; Rgnts Schlrshp 90; Acctg; CPA.

**HILL, VIRGINIA T,** Coker Coll, Hartsville, SC; SO; BA; Judicial Cncl; Behavioral Sci Clb; Stdnts Org To Protect Environment 90-; Adult Educ Tutor 90-; Psychology; Clinical Psychologist.

**HILL, YOLANDA A,** Clark Atlanta Univ, Atlanta, GA; SO; BA; Pblc Rltns; Advrtsng.

**HILLER, JOSEPH R,** Middle Ga Coll, Cochran, GA; FR; BS; Hghst Frshmn Avrg Awrd; Mrshl Grad; Bsbl; Sprts Sci; Coach.

**HILLIARD, CHERYL A,** Univ Of Nc At Charlotte, Charlotte, NC; FR; SGA Stdnt Affairs Comm 90-; Emerging Ldrs 90-; Progrmaming Board 90-; Phi Eta Sigma 90-; Inter Displinary Hnrs Prog; Zachs Frozen Yogurt; Recycling Educ Week; Intervarsity 90-; SGA Executive 90; Pre Business; Bus Mngmnt.

**HILLIARD, HIRAM SPENCER,** Vance Granville Comm Coll, Henderson, NC; AA; Phi Theta Kappa; NC Sfty/Scrty Hlth Care Cncl Pres 90-; Natl Ctr Missing Chldrn; Crime Prvntn Prctnr Duke Univ Pblc Sfty; New York Inst Phtgrphy 84; Crmnl Just; Hosp Scrty Cnsltnt.

**HILLIARD, KATRINA J,** Middle Ga Coll, Cochran, GA; JR; PHAMD; AS Mddl Coll; Phrmcy.

**HILLIARD, KIMBERLY,** Univ Of Ga, Athens, GA; SR; BSHE; Gldn Key 90; Phi Umicron 89; Zeta Tau Alpha Kappa Alpha Zeta Asst Pldg Tr Msc Crm 87; Prjt ARC Cln Cmmnty Cmmsn Special Olympics Vlnt 86; Miss Warner Robins 89; Miss Georgia 89; Top Ten/Miss Georgia Sprstr 89; Miss NE Georgia 90; Deans List 90; Chl Dvlpmnt; Pre/Schl Tchr.

**HILLIARD, SANDRA C,** Itawamba Comm Coll, Fulton, MS; BA; Univ Ml Cncrt Sngrs/Slst; Cncrt Sngrs Prfrmng Paris Frnc Lndn Englnd Notre Dame; Slst Tupelo MS Symphny; Natl Assn Tchrs Sngng St Comptn; Ldrshp Schlrshp; Won Sngr Yr Awd ICC; Smmr Mssnry Sacramento CA; Bptst Stdnt Union Actvts; Cntmpry Chrstn Music/Deaf Educ.

**HILLIARD, THEDA E,** Univ Of Sc At Columbia, Columbia, SC; FR; AS; Nursing.

**HILLMAN, KIMBERLY A,** Colby Sawyer Coll, New London, NH; FR; BA; AEYC; Child Study; Tchg/Daycare Mgmnt.

**HILLMAN, KIMBERLY J,** Va Commonwealth Univ, Richmond, VA; JR; BS; Rep J Sargeant Reynolds Ntnl Stdnt Symposium 89; Phi Theta Kappa 87-89; Hnrs Prgrm 90-; Rcpnt Deans Schlrshp 90-; Richmond Assctn Lgl Asst Schlrshp 88-89; Lgl Asstng Intrnshp Rappahannock Lgl Srvcs; Admn Jstc Intrnshp Monhollon/Monhollon; Adm Jstc; Law Schl.

**HILLMAN, LISA R,** Bowling Green St Univ, Bowling Green, OH; SR; BED; Sport Mgt Club 88-90; Phi Epsilon Omega; Phi Eta Sigma; Omicron Delta Kappa; Deans List 88-; Mid Amercn Confrnc Commsnrs Award; Acadmc Hons Stdnt 88-90; Mid Americn Donfrnc All Acadmc Team In Gymnstcs 88-90; Sport Mgt/Fitns Spclst; Hlth/Fitnsfld/Coachng.

**HILLMAN, MELISSA L,** East Central Comm Coll, Decatur, MS; SO; BS; Mu Alpha Theta; Phi Theta Kappa 90-; Adopt-A-Hwy 90-; Hnr Stdnt; Dns Schlr 89-; AA; Pre-Phys Ther; Phys Ther.

**HILLMANN, KELLY B,** Limestone Coll, Gaffney, SC; SR; BA; Comm Chorus 90-; Vocal Ensemble 90-; Music Edctrs Natl Cnfrnc 90-; Ldrshp Schlrshp 90-; Fine Arts Schlrshp 90-; Music Ed; Tchr.

**HILLMUTH, KIMBERLY S,** Salisbury St Univ, Salisbury, MD; JR; BSN; Stdnt Nrs Assoc; Phi Eta Sigma; Phi Kappa Phi; Zeta Tau Alpha Sec 90; MD St Nrsng Schlrshp 88-; SSU Pres Schlrshp 88-; Seiden Nrsng Schlrshp; Deans List 88-; Nursing; RN/MTRNL Chld Nrsng.

**HILLS-JOHNSON, SHARON L,** Bloomfield Coll, Bloomfield, NJ; GD; BA; Circus Troupe; Crmnl Jstce/Sociolgy Intrnshp Parole Offcr 90; AS Essex Co Coll 83; Fine Arts/Crmnl Jstce/Bus Admin/Mgmt.

**HILLSTEAD, RICHARD A,** Nova Univ, Ft Lauderdale, FL; GD; MBA; Amer Hmbrwrs Assn 90-; Peer Cnslr 75-76; MOCC Golf Tm Capt 74-76; Amer Hrt Assn 87-; Cncl On Clin Crdlgy; Cncl Crdvsclr Rdlgy; Laennec Socty; Amer Met Assn; Awd 8 US Patents/2 European Patent Pub; Bus/Mgmt; Medical Device R & D Mgt.

**HILMARSSON, HELGI HRAFN,** Embry Riddle Aeronautical Univ, Daytona Beach, FL; SO; BS; Deans List 90; Aviation Tech.

**HILTON, CANDIE J,** East Tn St Univ, Johnson City, TN; FR; Elem Education; Teach.

**HILTON, HAROLD T,** Wv Univ At Parkersburg, Parkersburg, WV; FR; CERT; Steelworkers Union; Indus Mech.

**HILTON, KRYSTAL M,** Norfolk St Univ, Norfolk, VA; SO; BS; Gospel Express 90-; Spartan Alpha Tau 90-; Med Soc 90-; Appld Sci Awd 90-; Hnr Rl 90; Medical Center Intern; Biology; MD OB Gyn.

**HILTON, PHOEBE A,** Denmark Tech Coll, Denmark, SC; GD; ASSOC; Pblc Policy Assist Secy 90-; Alpha Delta Omega; Phi Beta Lambda Treas/V P 89-; Criminal Justice; Pre Law.

**HILTON, SCOTT,** William Carey Coll, Hattiesburg, MS; SO; BSB; Bus Mgmt; Mnstry.

**HILTON, SHARON S,** Univ Of Nc At Greensboro, Greensboro, NC; SR; BED; AA Albany Jr Clg 83; Engl; Tch.

**HILTON, SHEILA Y,** Ny Univ, New York, NY; JR; BA; Data Entry Optr Sherman/Sterling; AA; Intl Studies; Intl Political Economist.

**HILTS, PAUL J,** Univ Of Pittsburgh, Pittsburgh, PA; FR; BS; Christian Outreach 90-; Engineering.

**HILTUNEN, SHAWN M,** Ms St Univ, Miss State, MS; JR; BBA; Scotchgrd Aux Sec/Tr 90-; Rice Hall Cncl VP 90-; Campus Crusade For Christ 88-89; Young Repubs 88-89; Alpha Lambda Delta 89-; Gamma Alpha Epsilon 89-; Gamma Beta Phi 89-; Pi Sigma Epsilon 90-; Alpha Gamma Delta Asst Tr 88-; Bus Info Syst; Mgmnt.

**HILTY, JULIA C,** Oh St Univ, Columbus, OH; FR; Ldrshp OH State 90-; Alpha Lambda Delta 90-; Phi Eta Sigma 90-; Mirrors 90-; Law.

**HILVERT, JOHN M,** Saint Francis Coll, Loretto, PA; SR; BS; Hon Pgm 87-; Coll Nwsppr Wrtr 88; Coll Hon Soc; Plus I Pgm-Big Bro; Bsktbl Capt 87-; Hlth Cr Admin; Physcl Thrpy.

**HILYER, JEFFERY P,** Northwest Al Comm Coll, Phil Campbell, AL; SR; AASD; Phi Theta Kappa; Drftng/Dsgn Tchnlgy.

**HILYER, NICOLE P,** Wallace St Comm Coll At Selma, Selma, AL; SO.

**HIMEL, STEPHANIE M,** Univ Of Miami, Coral Gables, FL; FR; BS; ROTC 90-; Delta Gamma 90-; Comp Sci; Comps.

**HIMES, JACQUELINE M,** Thomas Nelson Comm Coll, Hampton, VA; SO; AAS; Med/Dntl Adm Cert Arostotle Clg 86; Early Chldhd/Sci; Tchr/Dir.

**HIMES, PAMELA E,** Univ Of Nc At Greensboro, Greensboro, NC; SR; BSN; Trinity Chnancel Choir; NCMHCO Bd Of Dir 90; Field Rep For Duke Power Co 81-89; Nursing.

**HIMMELSBACH, LORI J,** Northern Ky Univ, Highland Hts, KY; SR; BA; Sigma Tau Delta Pr 90-; Lambda Chi 86-; Alpha Lambda Delta 88-; Alpha Xi Delta Pldg Pr 86-87; Dns Schlrshp 90-; Lit; Tch Coll Levl.

**HINCHCLIFFE, TAMMY M,** Western New England Coll, Springfield, MA; SO; BA; Peer Alchol Rsrce Team 89; Peer Review Board; Rsdnt Advisor 90; Tutor Central Hgh Sch; Psychlgy; Graduate Sch/Industrial Psy.

**HINCHEE, ROBERT A,** Wv Northern Comm Coll, Wheeling, WV; SR; BS; Firefighter Of The Year 78-82; Pub Serv Awd From Sec Of State WV 83; Humanitarian Serv Awd WV State EMS 85; Weirton Hts Vol Fire Dept Cptn 82-87; Weirton Area Amb & Rescue Sqd Asst Chf 88-; Weirton Firefighter & Fire Prev Ofcr 87; Fire Science; Fire Science Technology.

**HINCKS JR, WILLIAM G,** Univ Of Southern Ms, Hattiesburg, MS; JR; BA; Alpha Lambda Delta 89-; Lambda Sigma 89-; Mrchng Band Sqd Ldr 88-; Hon Cncl 89-90; Gamma Beta Phi 88-; Hon Stu Org 88-; Hon Coll Bk Awd 89; Poltcl Sci; Law.

**HINDAL, JODI L,** Bapt Bible Coll & Seminary, Clarks Summit, PA; FR; BA; Cncrt Choir 90-; Weekend Mnstry Tm 90-; Piano Tchng.

**HINDENLANG, SANDY,** Elmira Coll, Elmira, NY; FR; BS; IM Sftbl; Acctg; CPA.

**HINDMAN, AMY M,** Ms St Univ, Miss State, MS; JR; BA; Mrchng Bnd 88-90; Symphonic Suza Bnd 88-90; Flag Corps 88-90; Deans Lst 88-90; Presidents Lst 90-; Acdmc Schlrshp NE Comm Clg 88-90; Schlrshp Greater Amer Fedl Svngs Loan 88-90; AA 90; Acctng; CPA.

**HINDS JR, DONALD E,** Clarkson Univ, Potsdam, NY; SR; BA; Dorm Cncl V P 87-88; Beta Tau; JV Ice Hcky 87.

**HINDS, JENNIFER JOY,** Univ Of Tn At Martin, Martin, TN; FR; BS; Univ Schlrs Prog 90-; Geosci; Glgy.

**HINE, MELISSA J,** Cornell Univ Statutory College, Ithaca, NY; JR; BA; Wmns Rugby 90-; Stdnt Lvstck Show 90-; Deans List 90-; Animal Sci; Vet Sci.

**HINELINE, DAVID R,** Univ Of Tn At Knoxville, Knoxville, TN; JR; BS; Victory 88 George Bush Pres 88; Jerry Lewis Telvn 87-88; Phi Kappa Psi Scl Chrmn 89; SBE 90-; IMS Vlybl/Soccer/Ftbl/Flr Hockey 89-; Acctng Econ; Busn Consultant.

**HINES GANTT, LINDA,** Gaston Coll, Dallas, NC; GD; Gamma Beta Phi; Acctg.

**HINES, ALICIA D,** Central St Univ, Wilberforce, OH; SR; BA; Poltical Sci Assmby Pres 90-; African Awareness Committee 90-; Stdnt Govt Assoc Rec Secy 89-90; Alpha Kappa Mu 90-; Southern Chrstn Ldrshp Conf; Ohio Governors Hnrs Intrnshp Prog 90; Minority Fllwshp; Political Sci Pre Law; Hlth Serv Mngmnt.

**HINES, ANGELA M,** Tuskegee Univ, Tuskegee Inst, AL; SO; BED; Golden Voices Cncrt Choir; Elem Edn; Teach.

**HINES, ANNIE M,** Georgetown Coll, Georgetown, KY; SO; BS; Psi Chi 89-; Psychlgy/Biology; Medicine.

**HINES, CRAIG,** Va St Univ, Petersburg, VA; SR; Eng Tchnlgy Clb VP 90-; BS; Mech Eng Tchnlgy.

**HINES, EMILY R,** Winthrop Coll, Rock Hill, SC; SO; Cncl Excptnl Chldrn 90-; Baptist Std Union 90-; Spec Ed.

**HINES, EVA MARY,** Spring Hill Coll, Mobile, AL; FR; Prague Schl Of Econ 86; Engrnmntl Stds.

**HINES, JANICE M,** City Univ Of Ny City Coll, New York, NY; JR; BS; Cty Coll Biomdcl Sen VC 88-90; Thrd Wrld Org Pres 87-88; Stdnt Natl Mdcl Assoc; Gldn Key 90-; Yng Lds Axllry VP 86-; Hlpng Hnds Prgm Mem 88-90-; Otstndng Yng Wmn Amrc 90-; Cltn Blck Wmn Rl Mdl Awrd 89-90; Bio Mdlc Sci; Mdcl Dctr.

**HINES JR, KERMIT MAURICE,** Fayetteville St Univ, Fayetteville, NC; JR; Phi Beta Lambda 90-; Chrch Yth Drctr 90; Congrssnl Ad Internshp; Acctg; Law Cmmrcl.

**HINES III, MACK TORISE,** Voorhees Coll, Denmark, SC; SO; BA; Phi Beta Lambda Treas; Socl Stds; Law/Scl Cses.**

**HINES, MELISSA A,** Commonwealth Coll, Virginia Beach, VA; SO; AC; Acctg.

**HINES, MITZI L,** Univ Of Southern Ms, Hattiesburg, MS; JR; BA; Psy; Social/Rehb Serv.

**HINES, NICOLE J,** Eckerd Coll, St Petersburg, FL; SO; BA; Intl Stu Assoc 89-; Intl Bus Clb 89-; ELS Intl Pal Pro 89-; Ford Aprntc Schlr; Selby Schlr 90-; Aerobics IM Vlybl 89-; Intl Studies; Bus.

**HINES, TIMOTHY P,** Southern Coll Of Tech, Marietta, GA; SR; BS; IEEE 88-; NSPE 90-; Tau Alpha Pi 89-; Deans Awd/Excel; Elec Engrng Tech; Engrng.

**HINES, URHONDA RENE,** Morris Brown Coll, Atlanta, GA; JR; BS; Stdnt Support Serv 88-; Goldn Key; Pi Mu Epsilon; Hon Roll 88-; Outstndng Prfrmnce In Mathmtcs 90-; Mathmtcs; Educ/Statstcs.**

**HINES-JETER, MAUDE ELIZABETH,** City Univ Of Ny City Coll, New York, NY; JR; BA; Stdnt Advsry Com; Gldn Key 90-; Alpha Sigma Lambda; Fllwshp; Schlrshp; Day Stdnt Govt Achvmnt Awd; Untd Fdrtn Tchrs; NYC Bd Educ; Engl.

**HINKEL JR, JOHN C,** Univ Of Akron, Akron, OH; JR; BS; Natl Soc Pershing Rifles Actg Cmdr 90; AUSA 90; George C Marshall Awd 90; Cvl Engr; Engr.

**HINKELMAN, JEFFREY A,** Carnegie Mellon Univ, Pittsburgh, PA; SR; BS; Phi Alpha Theta; Hon Pgm 90-; Hist; Tchng.

**HINKEN, GLENN G,** Air Force Inst Of Tech, Wrt-Ptrsn Afb, OH; GD; MS; Sigma Iota Epsilon 90-; Alpha Chi 83-84; Otstndng Stdnt Phlsphy N Ky Univ 84; Otstndng Stdnt Jrnlsm N Ky Univ 84; USAF Cmmndtn Medal 90; USAF Defense Serv Medal; Air Force Assoc 85-; Capt USAF; BA N Ky Univ 84; BA N Ky Univ 87; Logistics Mgmt; Air Force Officer.

**HINKLE, BENJAMIN A,** Hillsborough Comm Coll, Tampa, FL; FR; BA; Faith Bible Chpl Sprvsr; AS PC Spec 90-; Comptr Engr; Systems Analyst.

**HINKLE, CHERYEL,** Fayetteville St Univ, Fayetteville, NC; JR; BS; SGA Stdnt Govt Rep 88; CJC Club 88-; Victims Rights Vol 89-90; Child Care Asst 88-; Math Hon Awrd 88; Chem Hon Awrd 88; Track/Cross Cntry 87-88; Crim Just; Law.

**HINKLE, JASON A,** Georgetown Univ, Washington, DC; FR; BSBA; Intl Bus/Finance.

**HINKLE, LYNDA L,** Glassboro St Coll, Glassboro, NJ; SO.

**HINKLE, SUSAN E,** Indiana Univ Of Pa, Indiana, PA; JR; Assc Rhbltn Advcts 90-; Rehbltn; Voctnl Evltr.

**HINKLE, TAMERA L,** Univ Of Nc At Greensboro, Greensboro, NC; JR; BS; Marshalls 90-; Chld Dvlpmnt; Yth Cnslng.

**HINKLEMAN, C AMY,** Wv Northern Comm Coll, Wheeling, WV; JR; BS; Pitt Prog 85; Quo Vadis 85; Phi Alpha Theta 87-88; Sigma Tau Delta 87-88; Phi Theta Kappa 84; Alpha Delta Pi 85-88; Biennial Intl Cnvntn; Victorian Wheeling Soc 90-; BA W Liberty State Clg 88 AA 84; Acctng.

**HINMAN, KATHY L,** Va Commonwealth Univ, Richmond, VA; SR; P E Majors Club 89-90; VAHPERD 89-90; AAHPER D 90-; Deans List 87-; Golden Key 90; BS; Sports Med; Physicians Asst.**

**HINNANT, LISA C,** Fayetteville St Univ, Fayetteville, NC; SR; BS; AAS Ctl Carolina Commty Clg 86; Busn Admin.

**HINSHAW, JAMES M,** Volunteer St Comm Coll, Gallatin, TN; SO; BA; Acctg.

**HINSON, ANNA LEE,** Univ Of Ga, Athens, GA; JR; BED; Cmpus Lfe Actvty Dir 89-; Deans Lst; Early Chldhd Educ; Tch.

**HINSON, BART E,** Univ Of North Fl, Jacksonville, FL; JR; BA; Bsn/Mktg; Entprnshp.

**HINSON, KIMBERLY ANN,** Winthrop Coll, Rock Hill, SC; SR; Palmetto St Tchr Assoc 90-; Deans Lst; Sndy Schl Tchr 90-; Tchr Intern 90-; Sub Tchr Lancaster Cty 89-; Bus Ed.

**HINSON, MARILYN C,** Fl St Univ, Tallahassee, FL; SR; BS; Mrchng Chfs 88-89; IM Sftbl 89-90; AA 90; Engl Ed.

**HINSON, NICOLE A,** Univ Of Md At Eastern Shore, Princess Anne, MD; SO; BA; Reg Reader Delta Sigma Theta 90-; Vol D C Dept Of Rcrtn 89-91; The Bronks Club; Natl Assn Of Negro Bus & Prof Womens Club Inc Presented As Debutante 90; Univ Of MD Estrn Shore; Intern Dept Of Eng & Lang/Mr Bernard P Mattei; Cmmnctns/Eng; Chldrns T V/Media Prod.

**HINSON, ROBERT H,** Spartanburg Methodist Coll, Spartanburg, SC; FR; AA; Criminal Justice Club 90-; Scuba Club 90-; Criminal Justice; Law.

**HINSON, SUSAN L,** Univ Of Ky, Lexington, KY; JR; PHARM; Ky Acdmy Stdnts Phrmcy 90-; Phi Delta Chi VP/RSH Chrmn Elct 90-; BS 78; Phrmcy.

**HINSON, TANYA S,** Ga St Univ, Atlanta, GA; SR; BA; SGAE 90-; Golden Key 90-; Kappa Delta Pi 90-; BA; Mdl Grds Educ; Tchr.

**HINSON, TRACY D,** Univ Of Tn At Martin, Martin, TN; JR; BED; Phi Theta Kappa 88-90; Math; Educ.

**HINTON, CAROLINE H,** Union Univ, Jackson, TN; JR; BS; Bapt Union 89-; Revival Tms 89-; Schlrs Excell 89-; Cmnctn Arts; Publ Rels.

**HINTON, DAVID A,** Univ Of Southern Ms, Hattiesburg, MS; JR; BA; Phi Theta Kappa 88-90; Beta Alpha Psi 90-; Act Schlrshp; M M King Schlrshp; Acdmc Achvmnt Awrd; AS Jones Co Jr Coll 90; Acctg.

**HINTON, ELIZABETH V,** Ga St Univ, Atlanta, GA; SR; Hnrs Prog 87-; Gldn Ky 90-; Alpha Lambda Delta; Phi Eta Sigma Sec 88-; Dean Ky 88-; BS; Erly Chldhd Educ; Tchr.

**HINTON JR, GARRY L,** Va St Univ, Petersburg, VA; SO; BS; Drftg Tech Clb Secr; Big Bro/Sis Org; Drftg Tech; Archt Engr.

**HINTON, JANET L,** Wv Northern Comm Coll, Wheeling, WV.

**HINTON, MARSHA A,** Jackson St Univ, Jackson, MS; JR; BS; Assoc For Comptng Mach 88-; Natl Soc Of Blck Engrs 89-; Comptr Sci Club 88-; Pi Mu Epsilon 89-; Alpha Gamma Mu 90-; Phi Kappa Phi 90-; Eastman Kodak Schlrshp 89-; Herrin-Hess Schlrshp 88-; Comptr Sci/Math; Sftwr Engr.

**HINTON, MERRI L,** Western Ky Univ, Bowling Green, KY; SO; Sewng; Elem Educ/Lbry Media; Tchg.

**HINTON, SHEILA D,** Univ Of Cincinnati, Cincinnati, OH; JR; BED; Yth Cllbrtv Tutor 88-90; Dir YMCA Chldcr Serv 90-; Soc Stu/Hstry; Elem Educ.

**HINTON, TIFFANY D,** Jones County Jr Coll, Ellisville, MS; FR; BA; Bus Admn; Bus Exectv Law.

**HINTON, VERNETTA L,** Va St Univ, Petersburg, VA; SR; Big Bro/Strs; Alpha Kappa Alpha 90-; Upward Bound 90-; Chldrn Bapt Hm 90-; Divne Bapt Ch Yng Voices Choir Pres 90-; Gantos Corp Intrn 90; BS; Fashion Buying.

**HINTON-JENKINS, KAREN A,** Hudson Valley Comm Coll, Troy, NY; FR; AA; Afrcn-Am Stdnt Allnc 90-, Tutor, USAF 78-82; Humn Svcs; Alchlsm Cnslr.

**HINTZ, JULIANNE E,** Kent St Univ Kent Cmps, Kent, OH; JR; BA; Acctg Assc; Stdnts Free Entrprs 90; Beta Alpha Psi; Acctg.

**HINTZ, MARIE E,** Univ Of Akron, Akron, OH; JR; Ujniv Prog Bd 89-90; Akron Cncl Of Edctn Stdnts 90-; BS Ed; Elem Edn; Teach/Writing.

**HINTZ, MICHELLE M,** Elmira Coll, Elmira, NY; SO; BA; Ski Clb 90-; Otng Clb 90-; Bus Admn.

**HINZMAN, WENDY D,** Appalachian Bible Coll, Bradley, WV; JR; BA; Class Sec 90-; Stdnt Cncl Treas 90-; RA 90-; Drama Tm Sec 89-; Bible; Elem Tchr.

**HIPP, MICHAEL L,** Univ Of Sc At Columbia, Columbia, SC; FR; BA; Naval ROTC 90-; Civil Eng; Naval Officer.

**HIPPELY, AMY L,** Kent St Univ Kent Cmps, Kent, OH; JR; BA; Am Mrktng Assoc 90-; Alpha Xi Delta 90-; Home Svgs Bank Of Kent; Mrktng/Mgmt; Hosp Admn.

**HIPPERT, GREGORY D,** Univ Of Nc At Charlotte, Charlotte, NC; JR; BS; AA Louisburg Coll 90; Envir Earth Sci; Prvt Bus.

**HIPPLE, MICHAEL J,** Savannah Coll Of Art & Design, Savannah, GA; JR; BFA; Phtogrp 90; Phtogrphy; Fshn Phtgrphr.

**HIPPOLYTE, LUANA S,** Saint Thomas Univ, Miami, FL; SO; BA; Intl Orgs; Delta Phi Epsilon; Frshmn Achvmnt Awd; Pol Sci/Hstry; MA.

**HIPPS, RENDELL L,** Univ Of Nc At Asheville, Asheville, NC; SO; BS; Phi Eta Sigma 90-; Elec Eng.

**HIRALDO HIRALDO, OLGA I,** Caribbean Univ, Bayamon, PR; BA; Cert 85; Secretarial.

**HIRE, TANYA G,** Oh Univ, Athens, OH; JR; BS; Indstrl/Systms Eng; Eng.

**HIROMATSU, TERUYO,** Georgian Court Coll, Lakewood, NJ; SR; BS; Trnsfr Clb 89-; Intl Clb 89-; Swmng Clb Kobe City Univ Foreign Stds 85-89; Dns Schlr 89-90; BA Kobe City Univ Foreign Stds Japan 89; Bus Admin; Prsnl Mgmt.

**HIRSCH, KRISTY E,** S U N Y Coll Of Tech At Alfred, Alfred, NY; FR; Pi Nu Epsilon Schlstc Advsr 90-; Door Guard Burdick Hall 90-.

**HIRSCH, MICHAEL,** S U N Y Coll Of Tech At Frmgdl, Farmingdale, NY; FR; BA; Lbrl Arts Clb 90; Forgn Lang Clb 90-; Bus; Mktg.

**HIRSCH, ROBERTA A,** Mount Saint Mary Coll, Newburgh, NY; SR; BA; Delta Mu Delta 90-; Chamber Of Commerce 90-; AAS O C Comm Clg 85; Business.

**HIRSCH, STEPHEN DAVID,** Salisbury St Univ, Salisbury, MD; GD; MBA; Dtbs Mgmt Clb 89-90; Outstndng Sr Awd MIS 90; Spec Schlrshp Rcpnt 90; Cndt Grd Asstntshp; Brd Amer Heart Assoc 89-; Orgn Prcrmnt Cmte 90-; Bsn; Tch/Info Systms.

**HIRSCHER, RANDY A,** Capital Bible Seminary, Lanham, MD; MDV; BA Univ Minnesota Minneapolis St Paul 86; BS Univ Minnesota Minneapolis St Paul 86; Biblical Greek/Hebrew; Pastor.

**HIRSHAUT, SHIRA Z,** Yeshiva Univ, New York, NY; GD; MA; Comp-Sci Clb Sec 89-90; Torah Act Cncl 88-90; Phi Sigma Omcrn; Comm Svc Pgm Jerusalem 87-88; Vldctrn Stern Coll Wmnyeshiva U; Levine Aws Excell Math; Rgnts Schlrshp; Max Stern Schlrshp; BA 90; Math/Comp Sci/Jwsh Stds; Ed.

**HIRSHON, BRAD B,** City Univ Of Ny Baruch Coll, New York, NY; GD; BA; Baruch Schlr; Fncng Team 87-88; Law.

**HIRST, SANDRA A,** Univ Of Pa, Philadelphia, PA; SR; BBA; Louis Rudolph CPA Acctg Award; Achvmnt Award ET Dupont Denemours 89; BS Biology Villanova Univ 84; Acctg.

**HIRT, ERIKA G,** Western Piedmont Comm Coll, Morganton, NC; FR; AAS; AAS United States Air Forece 81; Horticulture; Horticultural Sci.

**HIRT, JEFFREY A,** Kent St Univ Kent Cmps, Kent, OH; JR; BA; US Army ROTC Rngr Cmmndr 88-; Amrcn Lgn Awd Schlrshp; US ROTC 89; Ecnmcs; Bsns.

**HISE, RANDALL S,** Middle Tn St Univ, Murfreesboro, TN; JR; Law/Govt Clb; Art Clb; Outdoor/Sci Clb; Beta Gamma Sigma; Beta Alpha Psi; Phi Theta Kappa; Grad Top 10; AS Motlow State Comm Coll 90; Acctng; CPA/CMA.

**HISE, STEPHEN R,** S U N Y Coll Of Tech At Alfred, Alfred, NY; SO; BT; AS; Mechncl Engrng Tchnlgy.

**HISER, KIMBERLY M,** Oh St Univ At Newark, Newark, OH; JR; BSN; IM Spts/Co Ed Vlybl Sftbl Tennis Bsktbl; Vol Chldrns Hosp 90; Vol Univ Of Ky Hosp With Mnstry Tm From Asbury Coll 90; Vol Nursing Homes With Mnstry Tm From Cedarville Coll 89; Nurse Ped Unit Of Hosp.

**HISLER, TRACY L,** Barry Univ, Miami, FL; SR; BA; Ambssdr Clb Pres 89-; Pblc Rltns Stdnt Scty Amrc VP 89-; Intern WSVN 90; PRSSA Schlrshp Otstndng Achvmnt 90; Comm Arts.

**HISMAN, STACY L,** Le Moyne Coll, Syracuse, NY; FR; BS; Sprng Olympcs; IM Bsktbl; Wrk Stdy; Indstrl Rltns Hmn Rsrce Mgmt Mjr; Bus Law.

**HISSAM, LISA A,** Salem-Teikyo Univ, Salem, WV; SR; BS; SNEA 90-; Deans List 87-; Educ/Chem/Bio/Gen Sci; Eductr.**

**HITCH, NEAL V,** Oh St Univ, Columbus, OH; JR; BA; Amer Inst Arch Stdnts 90-; Golden Key 90-; Arch.

**HITCHCOCK, BRENDA J,** S U N Y Coll Of Tech At Alfred, Alfred, NY; FR; AAS; Cllgt Agrcltrl Ldrs 90-; Agrnmy Clb 90-; Dean Lst 90-; Peer Ttr 90-; Wrk Stdy Empl Yr 90-; Anml Hsbndry; Agrcltr Dry Frm Inspctr.

**HITCHCOCK, JANICE R,** Univ Of Al At Birmingham, Birmingham, AL; SR; BA.

**HITCHCOCK, RICHARD A,** Bryant Stratton Bus Inst Roch, Rochester, NY; SR; AOS; Elec Tech.

**HITCHCOCK, SHIRL L,** Becker Coll At Leicester, Leicester, MA; SO; SGA Pres 90-; Student Actity Pres 89-; Aerobics Club Yrbk VP 89-90; Phi Theta Kappa 90-; Resid Assist; Enegy Conserv Commt; Grad Commt; Intshp 90-; Soccer 89-90; Busn; Mtkng.

**HITCHCOCK, SUSAN M,** Hudson Valley Comm Coll, Troy, NY; FR; AAS; Early Childhd Clb; Asst Mgr Loews Theatres Mohawk Mall 85-; Nursery Schl Tchr.

**HITCHCOCK, TODD A,** Univ Of Rochester, Rochester, NY; SO; BA; J C Wilson Soc 89; Sigma Chi Tribune Soc Chrmn 89-; I M Bkbl 89; English/Hstry; Clg Prfsr English.

**HITCHCOCK JR, WILLIAM J,** S U N Y Coll Of Tech At Alfred, Alfred, NY; FR; AS; Acctg Clb 90-; IM Ftbl/Sftbl; Acctg; CPA.

**HITE, SIMONA GENENE,** Cheyney Univ Of Pa, Cheyney, PA; SR; BA; Natl Cncl Of Negro Wmn 88-; Inter Greek Cncl Sec 88-89; Sex/Bsn Club V P 89-90; Delta Sigma Meta Sorority Inc Pres 89-; Rsdnt Advsr 88-; CEL Ldrhsp Grp 88-; BA Cheyley Univ 91; Mktg.

**HITE, TINA M,** Bowling Green St Univ, Bowling Green, OH; SO; BA; United Karate Sys 89-90; Phi Eta Sigma 90-; Alpha Omicron Pi 90-; Visual Cmunctn Tech; Advtsng.

**HITE, TRACI L,** Univ Of Sc At Columbia, Columbia, SC; SR; BA; Phi Beta Kappa; Sociology; Soc Wrk.

**HITECHEW, CHRISTOPHER L,** Northeast State Tech Comm Coll, Blountville, TN; FR; AD; Carter Cnty Rescue Squad Capt/Dir 84-; Emerg Med Tech Instr; Emerg Med Tech 88-; BS E TN State Univ 90; Emerg Med Serv Mgmnt.

**HITER, AMY B,** Volunteer St Comm Coll, Gallatin, TN; FR; Vctnl Offc Ed Assoc 87-88; Bus Prfssnls Amrc Chptr Sec 88-89; Bus Cmmrc; Bus.**

**HITT, JEFFREY G,** East Central Comm Coll, Decatur, MS; SO; BA/M; LIFE 90-; Debate Team Pres 90-; Math Team; Stdnt Educ Assn; Players; Phi Theta Kappa 90-; Pres Lst 90-; Dns Lst 90-; Schlrs Bowl Team; Poltcl Sci; Educ/Politics.

**HITZEMAN, DARILYN R,** Savannah Coll Of Art & Design, Savannah, GA; FR; BARCH; Mary Rene Nellings Whelan Schlrshp; Archtctr; Archtctrl Dsgn.

**HITZHUSEN, GREGORY E,** Cornell Univ Statutory College, Ithaca, NY; JR; BS; Outdr Ed Progrm Instrctr 88-; Outing Club Fishing Chrmn 89; Wildrns Reflctns Guide Trnr 89-90; Pi Kappa Phi Warden/Fndng Father 89-; Habitat For Humnty Outrch Chrmn 90-; Natl Schlrs 88-; Pi Kappa Phi 90-; Crew 88; Biolgcl Sci; Envrnmntl Cmnctn.

**HIX, DENISE R,** Middle Tn St Univ, Murfreesboro, TN; FR; BA; Recording Industry Mgmt; Producer/Promoter.

**HIX, LISA M,** Va Commonwealth Univ, Richmond, VA; FR; BA; Business; Accounting.

**HIX, REBECCA K,** Tri County Tech Coll, Pendleton, SC; SO; Law.

**HIXSON-BEAR, JENNIFER A,** Palm Beach Comm Coll, Lake Worth, FL; SO; BA; Phi Alpha Theta; Acad Achvmnt 89-; Classic Golf Trnmnt Schlrshp 90; AA 90; History; Educ.**

**HLAVAC, GEORGE C,** Franklin And Marshall Coll, Lancaster, PA; SR; JD; Cls VP 87-90; Govt Clb/Clscs Clb Sec Gov Clb 87-; Stf Wrtr 87-; Tour Guide; Blck Pyrmd 90-; Pi Gamma Mu 89-; Pi Sigma Alpha 89-; Phi Beta Kappa 90-; Pi Lumbda Phi Scl Dir 90-; Thomas Apple Gilmore Prize 88; Clscs Dept Awrd 90; Govt; Law.

**HLYWA, GAYLE M,** Coll Misericordia, Dallas, PA; SO; BA; Stdnt Ocptnl Thrpy Assc 89-; Cmps Mnstry Chlndrns Parties 89-; Dadpt Grndprnt 89-90; Stdnt Hon Assc 89-; Ocptnl Thrpy.

**HO, APRIL,** City Univ Of Ny Baruch Coll, New York, NY; GD; Am Mktg Assn 89-90; Frgn Trd Soc; Intl Mktg; Mkgt/Mgmt.

**HO, DIANA TRAM MY,** Univ Of Md Baltimore Prof Schl, Baltimore, MD; JR; BS; Advnced Sci Incorp; Dept Antmy; Otstndg Prfmnc Awrd Montgomery Coll; Hnr Deans Lst 86; Dntl Hygiene.

**HO, KAH KIN,** S U N Y At Buffalo, Buffalo, NY; JR; BS; Psy Chi; IEEE; Victoria Inst Red Cross Soc Malaysia Mdcl Offcr 87-89; Intrnshp M&t Bnk Cmptr Applctn; Deans Lst 90-; Elctrcl Engnrng Psychlgy; Engnrng.

**HO, LAP,** Oh Univ, Athens, OH; JR; ECE; Micro Computer; Engrg.

**HO, LIH-YUN CAROLINE,** Fl International Univ, Miami, FL; SR; BA 90; Hosptlty Mgt; Hotel.

**HO, MARY,** City Univ Of Ny Baruch Coll, New York, NY; SO.

**HO, SELINA S,** City Univ Of Ny Baruch Coll, New York, NY; SR; BA; Acctg Soc 89-; Beta Alpha Psi; Beta Gamma Sigma; Vol Income Tax Assn; Actnt.

**HO-HIO-HEN, HELENE N,** Eckerd Coll, St Petersburg, FL; SR; BA; Intl Stu 88-; Stu Rep Bhvrl Sci Coll 90-; Stu Asstnt Mgmt Info Sys Cls 90-; Intl Stu Yr Mgmt; Mgmt; Bus.

**HOAK, BARBARA K,** Saint Vincents Coll & Seminary, Latrobe, PA; SR; BA; Bus; CPA.

**HOANG, TRINH LE,** Manhattan Coll, Bronx, NY; FR; BS; Chem; Engr.

**HOANG, XUYEN T,** S U N Y Coll Of Tech At Alfred, Alfred, NY; SR; Instrmnt Scty Amer VP 90-; Sgm Tau Epsln; AOS; Elec Mech Systm; Technlgst.

**HOAR, TERRI L,** Univ Of Al At Birmingham, Birmingham, AL; SR; BS; Psych Clb; Golden Key; Omicron Delta Kappa; Phi Kappa Phi; Psych; Clin Psych.

**HOBACK, SARA J,** Longwood Coll, Farmville, VA; SO; BS; Ctlns Synchrzd Swm Tm Pres 90-; Bio/Pre-Med; MD.

**HOBALES, SHANNON R,** Fl International Univ, Miami, FL; SR; Jackson Mem Hosp Breast Cancer Task Force Intern; Reg Dntl Hyg 88-; AS Miami Dade Cmnty Clg 88; BHSA; Hlth Svcs Adm; Law.

**HOBART II, CHARLES WILLIAM,** Middle Tn St Univ, Murfreesboro, TN; JR; BS; GORP 87-88; Biology Club 90-; Biology; Orthodontics.

**HOBART, DANIEL T,** Me Maritime Academy, Castine, ME; FR; BS; Pwr Eng Tech.

**HOBART, KRISTEN S,** Univ Of Rochester, Rochester, NY; SR; BA; Grssrts Envrnmntl Grp 88; Hngr Coaltn 88-; Oxfam Amre Rep 88; Deans Lst 90; Comm Serv Awrd 88-90; Psychlgy; Mntl Hlth Prfssn.

**HOBBS, APRIL V,** Chattahoochee Vly St Comm Coll, Phenix City, AL; FR; Sci; Med/Phrmcy.

**HOBBS, DEBRA M,** Oh St Univ At Newark, Newark, OH; FR; Aid Retarded Children Vltr; Parent To Parent Vltr; Biology; Med.

**HOBBS, GENA A,** Fl St Univ, Tallahassee, FL; SR; Wmn Cmnctn Inc 90-; FL Publ Interest Rsrch Grp 90-; Deans Lst; Cmnctn; Publ Rel.

**HOBBS, HEATHER L,** Livingston Univ, Livingston, AL; JR; BS; Engl Clb 89-; Hist Soc 89-; Nwspr Staff/Yrbk Staff 89-; Sigma Tau Delta 90-; Phi Eta Sigma 89-; Stdnts In Free Ent 90-; Tau Kappa Epsilon Little Sis Hist 89-90; Univ Envoy; Stdnt Spprt Svcs Tutor 90-; Deans Lst 89-; R W Gilbert Wrtng Awrd 89; Engl; Law.

**HOBBS, JENNIFER S,** Univ Of Sc At Columbia, Columbia, SC; SO; MBA; Fincl Aid Offc 89-; Alpha Chi Omega 90-; Bus; Acctg.

**HOBBS, JENNIFER S,** Nyack Coll, Nyack, NY; FR; ASBS; Deans Lst 90-; Wmns Vlybl 90-; Sci; Nrsng.

**HOBBS, KIMBERLY D,** Univ Of Nc At Greensboro, Greensboro, NC; SR; BS; Assn Educ 90-; Deans Lst 90-; Cum Laude Grad; Tchr Intrnshp; Stdnt Tchr; Elem Ed; Tchr.

**HOBBS, MICHAEL D,** Northeast State Tech Comm Coll, Blountville, TN; FR; AAS; IEEE; Elctrncs; Tchncn.

**HOBBS, PATRICIA M,** S U N Y Coll Of Tech At Delhi, Delhi, NY; JR; AOS; AC Refrig Elect Controls; Engrng.

**HOBERG, PAULA M,** Univ Of Cincinnati, Cincinnati, OH; SR; BED; Stdnt Alumni Cncl 90; Rsdnt Advsr 88; Tchrs Applyng Whle Lang 90; Kappa Delta Pi V P 89; Golden Key 90; Univ Dns Lst 88; Mst Dedicated Res Advsr 88-89; IM Ftbl/Sftbl Co-Capt 85-89; Elem Educ; Elem Sci Tchr.**

**HOBSON, BRIAN J,** Wilmington Coll, New Castle, DE; JR; MBA; Bus Crmnl Jstc.

**HOBSON, GLORIA J,** Jackson St Univ, Jackson, MS; SR; BA; Hist Clb Miss Hist 90-; Mass Cmnctns Clb 88-; Natl Assn Black Jrnlsts; Interned Miss 103 Rprtr 90; MS Edctnl TV Wrkd Prdctn; Mass Cmnctns/Jrnlsm; Law.

**HOBSON, KATHERINE J,** Univ Of Ga, Athens, GA; GD; Young Democrats Of Clarke Cnty; NCTE Annual Conf Comm 90; NCTE; GCTE; B Sed; Teaching Cert State Of GA; Engl Educ; Tchr.

**HOBSON, MELANIE D,** Univ Of Al At Birmingham, Birmingham, AL; SR; BS; Prsdntl Hnrs 90-; Deans Lst 90-; Spcl Ed Lrng Dsblts; Tch.

**HOBSON, REBECCA K,** Middle Tn St Univ, Murfreesboro, TN; SR; BS; Tau Omicron 88-; Gamma Beta Phi 89-; Kappa Delta Pi 89-; Chi Omega Sec 87-; Awd Grad Tchng Asstshp Elem Ed Dept; Elem Ed; Media Spclst.

**HOBSON, SHELIA C,** Alcorn St Univ, Lorman, MS; SO; BS; Deans Lst 89-; Acctg; CPA.**

**HOCH, JENNIFER LEE,** Daemen Coll, Amherst, NY; SR; Intrgrk Assc Rep 90; Stdnt Phy Thrpy Assc 90-; Sigma Omega Chi Sec 88-; Spcl Olympcs 89; IM Sccr 88; BS Phy Thrpy; Phy Thrpy.

**HOCH, MARK A,** Saint Thomas Univ, Miami, FL; JR; BA; Pltcl Actn Clb; AA Broward Comm Coll 88; Pltcl Sci; Gov Wrk.

**HOCHKRAUT, JOHN A,** Kent St Univ Kent Cmps, Kent, OH; SR; MBA; Magna Cum Laude; Grad Asstnshp; BBA; Fin; Cnsltng.

**HOCHMAN, DAVID P,** Ny Univ, New York, NY; SR; BA; Bus Systms Anlyst 82-; Ltrry Stds Bus Srvc.

**HOCHSTEAD, IAN,** Cooper Union, New York, NY; FR; BSE; Kesher 90-; Bwlng Tm 90-; Engnrng.

**HOCK, CHRISTOPHER MATTHEWS,** Saint Andrews Presbytrn Coll, Laurinburg, NC; JR; BA; Math/Cmptr Stds Clb Pres 90-; Coll Hnr Socty 90-; Alpha Chi 90-; Hnr Stdnt Assn 88-90; Math; Cmptr Prgrmng.

**HOCK, JULIE MARIE,** Mt Saint Marys Coll & Seminary, Emmitsburg, MD; JR; BS; Mnt Sngrs 90-; Chpl Chr 89; Wmns Lcrsse Clb 89-; Delta Mu Delta 90-; Acctng; CPA.

**HOCKENSMITH, KENNETH D,** Ky St Univ, Frankfort, KY; JR; BED; SNEA Treas 89-; Fllwshp Chrstn Athletes 89-; Masonic Lodge; Big Brother 87-; Legislative Rsrch Commission Comm Aide 88-; Hist Educ; Pblc Schl Tchr/Coach.

**HOCKER, JONATHAN E,** Univ Of Ky, Lexington, KY; FR; BSCE; Alpha Lambda Delta 90-; Phi Eta Sigma 90-; Civil Engr.

**HOCKMAN, SHARON L,** Middle Tn St Univ, Murfreesboro, TN; SR; JD; Stdnt Govt H Of Rep Cobol Prgmng Tm 90; Data Prcsng Mgt Assoc 88-90; Gamma Beta Phi 88-90; Raider Corps 86-88; Tau Omicron 88-90; Deans Cir 89-90; IM 86-90; AS Roane St Comm Coll 88; BBA Mid Tn St Univ 90; Comp Inf Sys; Law Sch.

**HOCKMAN, SUSAN N,** Memphis St Univ, Memphis, TN; SR; BA; Psychlgy Clb 89-90; Dorm Cnsl Treas 89-90; Scr Clb 89-90; Orchstr 88-90; Mortar Brd 90-; Alpha Lamda Delta 88-89; Chi Beta Phi 90-; TRIAD Hd Ldr 89-90; Upr Cmbrlnd Hndcp Outrch 89-90; Germantown Symphny Orchstr 88-89/90-; Scr 89-90; Psychlgy; Indstrl/Org Psychlgst.

**HOCTER, JENNIFER G,** Valdosta St Coll, Valdosta, GA; FR; BED; Hlthg; Tch.

**HODAPP, AMY E,** Marshall University, Huntington, WV; JR; BA; Mdl League Of Arab States Pres 89-; Mdl UN Treas 89-; Gamma Beta Phi 89-; Phi Eta Sigma 90-; Pi Sigma Alpha Treas 90-; Natl MLAS Hon Deleg 90-; Natl MUN Hnr Deleg; Maier Awd 90; Intl Affrs/Physics.**

**HODER, JANE S,** Univ Of Rochester, Rochester, NY; SR; BA; Adopt A Grndprnt Pgm 90; Intrn Memrl AA Gllry; IM Sccr 90; BA; Hstry; Msm Studies/Intr Dsgn.

**HODES, DEBORAH L,** Daemen Coll, Amherst, NY; SO; BS; Booga Booga Beta 89-; Admissions Asstnt 90-; Deans Lst 90-; Presidents Schlrshp 89-; Ski Clb Pres 89-; Physical Therapy; Medical Schl.

**HODGE, ANDREA B,** Northern Ky Univ, Highland Hts, KY; SO; BS; Stdnt Sprt Serv 90-; Psychology Clb 90-; Stdnt Govt Bk Fund Awd; Achvmnt Awd Stdnt Sprt Serv 90-; Deans Lst 90; Psychology; Psychology Doctorate.

**HODGE, CHRISTOPHER E,** Oh Univ, Athens, OH; SR; BS; Eta Kappa Nu 90-; Elec Engr; Engrg.

**HODGE, CONSUELA A,** Fayetteville St Univ, Fayetteville, NC; FR; Fayetteville State Chrldr; Peer Assist; Bus; Mktng/Fashion Merch.

**HODGE, DAMON C,** Morehouse Coll, Atlanta, GA; FR; BA; Bsn/Mrktg; Sports/Entertainment.

**HODGE, DAVID B,** Kent St Univ Kent Cmps, Kent, OH; FR; BA; COSO 90-; Math/Comp Sci; Eng.

**HODGE, DEXTER W,** Univ Of Rochester, Rochester, NY; JR; BS; Inter Varsity Christian Fellowship Univ Rochester Smll Grp Disc Ldr 88-; Superconducting Electronics Lab Univ Roch NY Rsrch Asst 90-; Univ Roch Track/Field Team 88-; Solid State Electrical Engineering.

**HODGE, DONNA J,** Univ Of Sc At Sumter, Sumter, SC; SR; BS; USA Pblc Rltns 89; Concert Choir 89-90; Bapt Stdnt Un Activ Ofcr 85-86; Alpha Kappa Mu 89-; Presidential Medallion 88-90; Deans Lst; AA; Educ; Teacher.

**HODGE, JENNIFER L,** Ms Gulf Coast Comm Coll, Perkinston, MS; FR; BS; Prk Plyrs 90-; Hnrs Prgm 90; VP Lst 90; Thtr.

**HODGE, KELLI M,** Univ Of Sc At Columbia, Columbia, SC; JR; BS; Pi Mu Epsilon 90-; Phi Beta Kappa; Gold Key 90-; Gamma Beta Phi 88-90; Deans Lst 88-; Pres Lst 88-; Math; Edn.

**HODGE, KRISTA L,** Ky Christian Coll, Grayson, KY; JR; BS; Ed Orgnztn VP 90-; PACK Crdntr 88-; Elem Ed K-4; Tchng.

**HODGE, LISA E,** Georgetown Univ, Washington, DC; SR; BSBA; Nwspr Asst Ad Mgr 87-89; Chinese Stdnt Org Pres 89-90; Stdnt Fed Cred Un Supv 88; IBM Mrktng Sls Asst 90-; Fin Intl Mgmt; Fin.

**HODGE, MARLENE K,** Central Al Comm Coll, Alexander City, AL; FR; Chrch Jesus Chrst Latter Day Sts 2nd Cnslr 90-; Estmtr; Engl; Cnstrctn Ofc Mgmt.

**HODGE, REDA J,** Wv Northern Comm Coll, Wheeling, WV; GD; AAAS; Lbrl Arts; Govt.

**HODGE, RICHARD S,** Marshall University, Huntington, WV; JR; BBA; Gamma Beta Phi 88-90; Phi Eta Sigma 90; Finance Bsns Law; Fncl Srvcs.

**HODGE JR, ROBERT D,** Commonwealth Coll, Virginia Beach, VA; BA; Phi Beta Lambda V P 90-; Alpha Beta Gamma; CITC Pres 90-; Pres Lst 89-; Dns Lst 89-; Met Life Ins Co Intern; Vlybl 90-; Tutor Elem Kids; US Navy 84-; AS; Bsn/Acctg-Cmptrs; Acctnt.

**HODGE, SHAWN B,** Hillsborough Comm Coll, Tampa, FL; FR; AA; Phi Theta Kappa; Med; Physcn.

**HODGE, SUZANNE S,** Univ Of Nc At Greensboro, Greensboro, NC; SR; BS; Stdnt Nrth Crlng Assn Of Edctrs VP 90-; Dns Lst; Elem Educ; Tchr.**

**HODGE, TIMOTHY D,** Ms St Univ, Miss State, MS; JR; DVM; Amrcn Anml Hosp Assoc; Wldlf Spprt Grp; Bapt Stdnt Un 89-990; Pre Vet Clb 89-; Otstndng Coll Stdnts Amrc 89-; Chrstn Vet Fllwshp; Tupelo Wmns Jr Axllry Schlsrhp 88; Lee Cnty Water Soil Cnsrvtn Scty Schlrshp 89-; Vet Med; Vet.

**HODGE JR, VERNE A,** Univ Of The Virgin Islands, St Thomas, VI; SR; BA; Afrcn Hrtg Comm; Pres Clb; Bache Schlrshp Awd; Barnett Frank Awd; Asst Fscl Ofcr; AA 90; Bus Mngmt; Law.

**HODGENS, HEATHER L,** Univ Of Sc At Coastal Carolina, Conway, SC; JR; BA; Internatl Club 90-; Fellowshp Of Christian Athlts 90.

**HODGES, AMY L,** Western Ky Univ, Bowling Green, KY; SO; Math; Actrl Sci/Insur.

**HODGES, ANGELA D,** Coker Coll, Hartsville, SC; SO; BA; Coker Sngrs 90-; SGA Chrprsn 90-; Commissioners 90-; Bacchus 90-; Chldrns Choir Dir 90; Top Ten 89-90; Music Educ; Educator.

**HODGES, CLIFFORD M,** Univ Of Ga, Athens, GA; SR; BSED; ROTC Capt 88-; Soc Sci Clb; Soc Sci Educ; Army.

**HODGES, DALE W,** Longwood Coll, Farmville, VA; GD; Biology Clb 88-90; Beta Beta Beta Hstrn 89-90; Alpha Phi Omega 90-; Public Schl Teacher; BS 90; Biology; Teaching.

**HODGES, DE ANNA L,** Fayetteville St Univ, Fayetteville, NC; GD; Drama Clb; Intrnshp TV Station Cohosted; Dance Elec Cohosted Anncd Hmcng Parade 89; BA 90; Cmmnctns; TV Prdctn.

**HODGES, DIEDRA L,** Univ Of Sc At Columbia, Columbia, SC; FR; BA; Elem Edn; Tchr.

**HODGES, ELIZABETH ANN,** Sinclair Comm Coll, Dayton, OH; SO; AS; AS 84; Nrsng.

**HODGES, JAMIE W,** Ms St Univ, Miss State, MS; SR; BA; Stdnt Hlth Advsy Comm Vc Chr 90-; Stdnt Asso Academic Afrs Comm 89-90; German Clb 89-90; Mortar Bd; Phi Kappa Phi 90-; Schlrs Arts Sci; Pres Schlr 88-; Alpha Gamma Delta Pearl Chr 89-; Rd Crs Hosp 90; Foreign Lang; Intrntl Bus.

**HODGES, KAREN M,** Bob Jones Univ, Greenville, SC; FR; BS; Theta Pi Delta; Elem Education; Teacher.

**HODGES, MELANIE C,** Chesterfield Marlboro Coll, Cheraw, SC; SO; BA; Presidents Lst; Assoc Sci; Science; Radiology.

**HODGES, PHILIP D,** Lancaster Bible Coll, Lancaster, PA; SO; BS; Intl Stdnt Flwshp Treas 90-; Drama Clb; Comp; Mnstry.

**HODGES, SANDI D,** Va Commonwealth Univ, Richmond, VA; SR; Alpha Chi 90-; Golden Key; Beta Gamma Sigma; Dns Lst Schlrshp 90-; Acad Schlrshp 87-90; BS; Bsn.

**HODGES, STEVEN S,** Birmingham Southern Coll, Birmingham, AL; JR; BS; Resident Advisor; Stdnt Nwspr Asstnt Edtr 90; Wind Ensemble Bras Quintet 88-; Mortor Board; Omicron Delta Kappa 90-; Kappa Mu Epsilon 89-; Sigma Nu Schrlshp Chr; Amnesty Intl; Hnrs Schlrshp; Math History; Law.

**HODGES, TODD L,** Univ Of Southern Ms, Hattiesburg, MS; FR; BS; Sci; Pharmacy.

**HODGETTS, KATHLEEN L,** Univ Of New England, Biddeford, ME; FR; BA; Andvr Coll Ntl Hnr Scty Treas 89-90; PROPS Plcy Cncl 89-; Lcl Hdstrt 89-90; Vol Brighton Mdcl Cntr Er Spcl Srvcs; AS Andover Coll Portland ME 90; Ndcl Blgy Pre Med; Med Dctr Ostpthy.

**HODGIN, AMY E,** Radford Univ, Radford, VA; JR; Stdnt Ed Asso 89-90; Phi Sigma Sigma Judcl Bd 89-; Socl Sci; Hmn Svc; Edctn.

**HODGINS, RAYMOND E,** Livingston Univ, Livingston, AL; SR; MA; BS Elem Ed; Ythmnstr Smnry.

**HODGSON, GILBERT P,** Le Moyne Coll, Syracuse, NY; FR; BA; Tae Kwon Do Clb 90-; Env Coaltn Treas; IM Sccr 90-; Biol; Env Law.

**HODNETT, CHARLES E,** Old Dominion Univ, Norfolk, VA; JR; BS; Golden Key; Soc Mfg Engrs; Tunstall Fire Dept; Dipl Danville Cmnty Clg 90; Engr Tech.

**HODNETT II, TYRONE M,** Fl A & M Univ, Tallahassee, FL; SO; Close-Up Org Mgr 90-; Phi Eta Sigma; Dns Lst 89-; Close-Up Mgr Of Yr 90-; Bsns Admn; Law Sch.

**HOEBICH, MARYANGELA,** Hillsborough Comm Coll, Tampa, FL; FR; BA; Hillsborough Comm Coll Vlybl 90; Lib Arts; Comm.

**HOECK, SUSAN G,** Salisbury St Univ, Salisbury, MD; JR; BA; Phi Alpha Theta; Pi Gamma Mu; Wicomico Cnty Wmns Clb Awd; Vlybl/Tnns 89-90; Eden Untd Mth Chrch; Wrkd Rdtn Ther Tech Peninsula Gen Hosp 82-; Cert Peninsula Gen Hosp Schl Rdlgc Tech 81; Cert Essex Comm Coll/John Hopkins Sch 82; Hist/Scndry Ed; Tchng.

**HOEFER, PAMELA R,** Eckerd Coll, St Petersburg, FL; JR; BSC; Psych Clb 90; Org Rape Awrns Wk; Vol Tutor 88-60; Vol Youth Mtvtr 89; Frshmn Ldrshp Awrd 88-89; Deans Lst 88-; Hnrs Schlrshp 88-; Athltc Trnr 88-; Psych; Lgsltn Educ.**

**HOEFLICH, PAULA A,** Univ Of Cincinnati-Clrmnt Coll, Batavia, OH; SO; BA; Makro Wrhse Clb; Mrchnds Asst; Asst Byr 88-90; AA; Mktg; Rtl Prchsng.

**HOEFLICH, SUSAN D,** Univ Of De, Newark, DE; FR; BS; Pre Physcl Thrpy; Physcl Thrpy.

**HOEHN, JENNIFER F,** Ky Mountain Bible Coll, Vancleve, KY; JR; BA; Cncl Sec 89-; Yrbk Stf Edtr 89-; Yth Tmprnc Cncl State Pres 88-; Rlgn/Bible; Chrstn Svc.

**HOEHN, KATHERINE I,** Newbury Coll, Brookline, MA; SR; ASSOC; Natl Socty Pub Acctnts; Alpha Beta Gamma; Phi Theta Kappa; Outstdng Acvhmnt; Merit Schlrshp; Acctng; CPA.

**HOEKSTRA, JUDD D,** Cornell Univ Statutory College, Ithaca, NY; JR; BA; Chrstn Flwshp Grp 89-; Delta Kappa Epsilon; Bro Nu 89-90; Ithaca Yth Bur One To One Big Bro 90-; Minn Twns Bsbl Clb Emplee 89-90; Hockey Tm 88-90; Bus Mgmt/Mktg; Small Bus Ownr.

**HOES, CHERYL R,** Fl St Univ, Tallahassee, FL; JR; MS; Natl Stdnt Spch Lng/Hrng Assoc 90-; Alpha Gamma Sigma 86-; Outstndng Undrgrdt Stdnt Cmnctn Dsrdrs 90-; Fl Dept Ed 88-; AA Fullerton Cmty Clge 86; Spch/Lng Pthlgy.

**HOETING, KATHLEEN M,** Univ Of Cincinnati, Cincinnati, OH; JR; BSN; Natl Stu Nrs Assn 90-; OH Nrsng Stu Assn 89-; US Achvmnt Acdmy 89-; Sigma Theta Tau; Mary Rowe Moore Admn Dist Awrd; Albert B Voorheis Hnr Schlrshp; Charles Fleischmann Schlrshp; Natl Coll Nrsng Awrd; Nrsng.

**HOEVERTSZ, SUSAN A,** Barry Univ, Miami, FL; SR; BPS; Ex-Canadian Airlines Intl Empl; Hmn Res Mgmt.

**HOFER, CYD C,** Kent St Univ Kent Cmps, Kent, OH; JR; BA; Camp Crsd Christ 89-; Bible Stdy 89-; Golden Key; Deans Lst 89-90; Crmntl Just; Crctns.

**HOFF, AIMEE J,** Cleveland St Univ, Cleveland, OH; SO; BEE; Soc Wmn Engrs Pres 90-; Jnt Engr Cncl; Elec Engr/Comp.**

**HOFF, MELISSA J,** Indiana Univ Of Pa, Indiana, PA; FR; BA; Cmnty Svcs 90-; Math Tchr.

**HOFF, NANCY E,** S U N Y Coll At Fredonia, Fredonia, NY; JR; BA; Elem Ed.

**HOFF, STEFFIE J,** Southeastern Coll Of Hlth Sci, N Miami Beach, FL; SR; Acdmy Stdnt Phrmcsts 89-; Alpha Zeta Omega 89; Resp Thrpst Rrt 75-87; AS SPJC 79; Pharmacy.

**HOFFER, JENNIFER A,** Temple Univ, Philadelphia, PA; JR; BA; Golden Key 89-; Vlybl Schlrshp 88-; Phys Educ; Exrcs Physgy.

**HOFFHINE III, CHARLES R,** Univ Of Sc At Sumter, Sumter, SC; SO; BS; Rcrtnl Sprts Clb 89-; Dns Lst 89-90; IM Actvts 89-; Phy Thrpy; Phy Thrpst.

**HOFFHINE, LISA M,** Univ Of Sc At Columbia, Columbia, SC; SR; BA; Stu Govt Sec 88; Gldn Ky 90; Gamma Beta Phi 90; Phi Alpha Delta 88-; AA Western Ok St Coll 88; Hstry; Mngmnt.

**HOFFHINES, PHILIP L,** City Univ Of Ny City Coll, New York, NY; SR; BA; The Joan Kelley Prize 90; Hist.

**HOFFMAN, AMY K,** Univ Of Ga, Athens, GA; JR; Young Life Mnstry 90-; Cmps Crusade Christ 90-; Ntl Stdt Spch/Lang/Hrng Assoc 90-; Alpha Delta Pi 89-; Stdt Vol Ser 88-; Habitat Humanity 88-F; Ommnctn Scie/Disorders; Spch Pathology.

**HOFFMAN, BETSY I,** Bergen Comm Coll, Paramus, NJ; AS; Stdnt Concerns Comm; Phi Theta Kappa; Dns Lst; Tutor; Big Sisters; NOW; PTA; Spec Educ; Social Services.

**HOFFMAN, CANDACE M,** Coker Coll, Hartsville, SC; SO; BA; Special Olympics Vol 90; Top Ten Frshmn/Soph Class 90-; College Deans List 89-; S C Education Excellence Team Special Ed; Sunday School Teacher 89-; Special Ed; Teacher.

**HOFFMAN, CATHERINE A,** Hudson Valley Comm Coll, Troy, NY; JR; BA; Phi Theta Kappa 90-; Mrktg; Ads.

**HOFFMAN, CRAIG M,** Duquesne Univ, Pittsburgh, PA; GD; MA; Psi Chi; AA 86; BA 90; Psychlgy; Mntl Hlth Serv.

**HOFFMAN, DANIEL W,** Union Coll, Barbourville, KY; FR; Eng.

**HOFFMAN, DAVID J,** Union Coll, Barbourville, KY; FR; BA; Chem Rubber Co Frshmn Chemistry Awd 90-; Eng; Civil Eng.

**HOFFMAN, DIANA K,** Endicott Coll, Beverly, MA; SR; AS; Stdnt Govt Exec Cncl Sec 90-; Yrbk Asst Pht Ed 90-; Ski Clb Co Pres; Envrmntl Ldrshp Clb 90-; Shpmts Fnd Rsng 90-; London Intrnshp Sablers Wells Thtr; Gen Ed; Lawyer.

**HOFFMAN, ERIC J,** Western New England Coll, Springfield, MA; SO; BS; Stdnt Snt Lgsltv Chrprsn 90-; Peer Advsng 91-; Pre-Law Soc 90-; Alpha Lambda Delta 90-; Phrmcy; Medcl Schl.

**HOFFMAN III, HARRY W,** Methodist Coll, Fayetteville, NC; SO; Acctg; Actnt Bsn.

**HOFFMAN, HEIDI A,** Franklin And Marshall Coll, Lancaster, PA; SR; BA; Frnkln Mrshll Orchstr Cncrt Mstrtss 87-; John Crrll Assoc Treas 89-90; Blck Pyrmd Snr Hnr Scty 90-; Phi Beta Kappa; Sigma Sigma Sigma Pres Sec Prlmntrn 88-; FM Vol Tr Gds Scl Chrman 88-; Hckmn Fllw Econ Rsrc; Theodore Wood Prize Econ; Econ; Cmmrcl Bnkng.

**HOFFMAN, HILARY S,** S U N Y Coll At New Paltz, New Paltz, NY; FR; Bus Stdnt Org VP Advrtsng 90-; Deans Lst 90-; Business Adm.

**HOFFMAN, JENNIFER MICHELLE,** Wv Northern Comm Coll, Wheeling, WV; FR.

**HOFFMAN, JILL M,** Indiana Univ Of Pa, Indiana, PA; SO; BED; Elem Educ.

**HOFFMAN, JOAN E,** Atlantic Comm Coll, Mays Landing, NJ; SO; AS; Egg Harbor Twp Republ Club Secty 88-F Bargaintown Vol Fire Co Ladies Aux Pres 83-90; Hswfe Mother 71-; NJ Forest Fire Serv Firefighter 85-; General.

**HOFFMAN, JODI I,** Dowling Coll, Oakdale Li, NY; SR; Deans Lst 90; Hghst GPA 90; BBA; Mrktng; Mrktng Rsrch Or Human Rsrces Advsr.

**HOFFMAN, JOHN W,** Alfred Univ, Alfred, NY; FR; BS; Univ Rescue Sqd 2nd Lt 90-; Securty Aide 90-; Alpha Lambda Delta 90-; Hons Prog 90-; Resdnt Asst 90-; Ceramic Engr.

**HOFFMAN, JULIE A,** D Youville Coll, Buffalo, NY; SR.

**HOFFMAN, LINDA S,** Glassboro St Coll, Glassboro, NJ; GD; Psychology Clb Sec 87-89; Parents Co Op Day Care 87-90; M L K Schlrs Achvmnt 87-90; Drug Abuse Cnslr 90-; BA 90; Psychology.

**HOFFMAN, MICHAEL,** Bristol Univ, Bristol, TN; GD; MBA; Cntrllr 86-; BS Oral Rbrts Univ 81.

**HOFFMAN, MICHELE L,** D Youville Coll, Buffalo, NY; SO; MS; Adopt A Grandprnt 89-; Stdnt Physcl Thrpy Assc 89-; Mvng Up Days Chrprsn 90-; Lambda Sigma 90-; Deans Lst 89-; Dvsn Rehab Schlrshp 89-; Physcl Thrpy.

**HOFFMAN, NICOLE P,** Univ Of South Al, Mobile, AL; SR; MA; Alph Chi 90; Phi Chi Theta 90; Pres Lst 90; BS 90; Mktng.

**HOFFMAN, PAUL,** Univ Of Rochester, Rochester, NY; JR; BA; Chess Clb Pres 88; Phi Theta Kappa 88-; Meliora Schlrshp 90-; Statstcs; Finance.

**HOFFMAN, RANDOL K,** Anne Arundel Comm Coll, Arnold, MD; SO; BS; Odenton Vol Fire Co Fire Fighter 88-; Air Force Srgnts Assn Trustee 87-; Engr Co Op; Joint Service Cmmndtn Mdl 90-; Meritorious Srvc Mdl Sgt; USAF 85-; AAS Comm Coll Of Air Force 90; Elec Engr.

**HOFFMAN III, RUSSELL O,** Univ Of Cincinnati, Cincinnati, OH; FR; BSN; Nrsng; Rsrch/PHD.

**HOFFMAN, SHANNON R,** Oh St Univ At Marion, Marion, OH; FR; BS; Alpha Lambda Delta 90-; Phi Eta Sigma 90-; Chem.

**HOFFMAN, SUNSHINE,** Central Pa Bus School, Summerdale, PA; FR; AA; Trvl/Trsm; Trvl.

**HOFFMAN, TAMERA LYNN,** Brescia Coll, Owensboro, KY; SR; BA; Ambssdr 86-; NEA 90-; Intrcollgt Athltc Advsry Comm 90-; Deans Lst 87-90; Juried Art Exhbt Merit Awrd 90-; Sr R I Golden Schlrshp Art Awrd 90-; IM Vlybl/Bsktbl 86-90; Grphcs/Art; Ed.

**HOFFMAN, THOMAS M,** Northern Ky Univ, Highland Hts, KY; JR; BA; Dixie Jaycees; Summer Sprts Intrn 700 WLW Radio; Cmmnctns; Radio Prsnlty.

**HOFFMAN, VINCENT E,** Middle Ga Coll, Cochran, GA; SO; BA; Blgy/Pre/Med; Mdcl Schl.

**HOFFMAN, WILLIAM F,** Univ Of Cincinnati, Cincinnati, OH; FR; MBA; Mech Eng.

**HOFFMANN, ANGELA J,** Mercer Univ Schl Of Pharm, Atlanta, GA; GD; PHARM; Chrstn Stdnt Union Sec 88-90; Fresh Lcss Rep 87-88; ASHP ASP ASHP 87-90; Rho Chi Co-Chr Prjcts 88-; Phi Beta Kappa 89-; New Zealand Intrntl Rtn Clrkshp 90; Phi Delta Chi Pharm Frat VP 87-; Parke-Davis Intrnshps 89; Meals On Whls 89; Dr Pharm Degree; Clncl Pharm.

**HOFFMANN, MICHAEL J,** Atlantic Comm Coll, Mays Landing, NJ; SO; AS; Bus; Accntng.

**HOFFMEIER, BRENT L,** Univ Of Louisville, Louisville, KY; JR; BA; Stdnt Govt 89-90; Kappa Sigma 88-; Chrldng 89-; Fnce; Invstmnt Bkg/Rl Est Fnce.**

**HOFFNAGLE, ERIC R,** Villanova Univ, Villanova, PA; JR; BA; Ecnmcs; Bus.

**HOFMANN, DIANA L,** Wv Univ At Parkersburg, Parkersburg, WV; SO; BA; Utd Natl Bank Cust Svc 89-; Free-Lance Make Up Artist; Business Adm; Mgmt.

**HOFMANN, GREGORY D,** S U N Y At Buffalo, Buffalo, NY; SR; BS; Accntng Assn 89-; NAA 89-; NSPA 90-; Phi Eta Sigma 88-; Golden Key 90-; Grace W Capen Mmrl Awd; Ntnl Scty Pblc Accntnts Schlrshp; Plbc Accntng Intrn; Accntng; CPA.

**HOFSTETTER, BONNIE L,** Univ Of Akron, Akron, OH; SR; BED; Phys Ed; Tchr.

**HOFSTETTER, BONNIE YODER,** Wilmington Coll, New Castle, DE; SR; BSN; Charles E Varney Awd-Nrsng Schl 75; Med Srgcl Nrsng Awd 75; Bd Of Dir Harrington Sr Cntr 87-88; Adv Bd Cert Occup Assts Prog 90-; Detech Comm Coll; Nrsng Sprvsr 88-; RN Milford Mem Hosp 75; Nrsng; MSN.

**HOFSTETTER, HOLLY L,** Univ Of Akron, Akron, OH; SO; BS; Chorus 1st Alto 90; Amer Inst Chem Engrs 90-; Phi Eta Sigma 90-; Alpha Lambda Delta 90-; Delta Gamma Song Mistress 89-; Pres Schlrshp 89-; Ohio Bd Regents Schlrshp 89-; Johnson Rubber Co Schlrshp 89-; IM Vlybl/Bsktbl 89-90; Chem Engr; Med Sch.

**HOGAN, CATHERINE A,** Smith Coll, Northampton, MA; SR; MSW; Spec Nds Comm 89-; Comm Lvng Vdeo Wrkshps 88-; Phi Beta Kappa; Psi Chi 88-; Dana Grant Awd Intrnshp W Spgfld MA 89; Cert Recog 89; Hampshr Comm Actn Comm Bd Dir 87-; Mayor Comm Handcpd Afrs 88-89; Fin Conslt; Psych; Soc Wrk.

**HOGAN, CHRISTOPHER LAMAR,** Central St Univ, Wilberforce, OH; FR; MBA; Bsn Admin/Cmptr Info; Entrprnr.

**HOGAN, DANA D,** Univ Of Tn At Martin, Martin, TN; SO; BA; Zeta Tau Alpha 90-; Biomedcl Engr.

**HOGAN JR, DAVID E,** Fl A & M Univ, Tallahassee, FL; FR; BSME; Std Govt Sntr 89-; Fresh Cls 89-90; NASA Schlrs Asc Clb Prlmtrn 89-; Phi Eta Sigma Prlmtrn 89-; Cir K 89-90; NASA Johnson Space Ctr Intshp 89-90; Cmps All-Star Chlng Natl Champ 89-90; IM Sftbl 89-90; Mech Engr; Engr/Astronaut.

**HOGAN, KATHERINE J,** Marywood Coll, Scranton, PA; SR; MA; Pugwash Prsdnt 90-; Phi Beta Lambda Sec 88-90; Mnstry 87-88; Delta Epsilon Sigma; Alpha Mu Gamma; BS; Intrntnl Dvlpmnt.

**HOGAN, KEITH J,** Univ Of Ky, Lexington, KY; SR; BA; KSPE NSPE ASCE 88-; Stdnts Ath Cncl; Chi Epsilon VP 89-; Tau Beta Pi 89-; Golden Key 91-; Sigma Pi 90-; Church Yth Grp 86-; GASC Schlrshp; Clg Of Engrng Schlrshp 90-; U Of KY Schlrshp 90-; IM Vlybl/Sftbl 89-; Engr.

**HOGAN, LINDA R,** Montgomery Comm Coll, Troy, NC; SO; AAS; Stdnt Govt Assn; Pres Lst; Bus Admn/Acctg.

**HOGEN, RICHARD,** City Univ Of Ny City Coll, New York, NY; SR; BS; Earth Sci Clb Sec 90-; Geosci Ctr; Physcs Rsch Asst; Gldn Key; Dns Lst; Earth/Atmsphrc Sci; Plntry Sci.

**HOGG, BARBARA E,** Va Commonwealth Univ, Richmond, VA; GD; MD; Medcl Stdnt Govt Pres 90-; AMA 89-; AMSA 90-; Southrn Medcl Assoc 89-; Phi Beta Kappa 88-; Alpha Epsilon Delta; Stdnts Tchng Aids To Stdnts Co Coor 89-; Amercn Jr League 88-89; A D Williams Summer Flwshp 90; Joh R Mc Cain Smr Flwshp 90; Medcn.

**HOGGLE, NINA C,** Livingston Univ, Livingston, AL; SR; Hstrcl Scty 89-; BS; Engl And Hstry; Grad Schl.

**HOGLE, CYNTHIA J,** Central Fl Comm Coll, Ocala, FL; SO; MBA; AS 82-83; Sci; Eng.

**HOGUE, BRENDA L,** Nyack Coll, Nyack, NY; FR; MBA; Sccr Clb Head Ref 90-; Bsktbl Vrsty Frshmn Of Yr 90-; Sftbl Vrsty 90-; Spec Olympcs 89-; NCAA Bsktbl Awrds Alnc Bsktbl Trny 90-; Psychlgy; Cnslng.

**HOGUE JR, CLARANCE N,** Norfolk St Univ, Norfolk, VA; SO; BS; Stdnt Ntl Tech Assc; Alpha Tau; Alpha Kappa Mu; U S Marine Crps 69-89; Elec Technlgy; Elec Crct Rpr.

**HOGUE, ETHEL LOUISE,** Talladega Coll, Talladega, AL; JR; BS; Soc Wrk Clb VP; Crimson Ambass 90-; Dns Lst 88; All Amer Schlr 90; Soc Wk; Admin.

**HOGUE, JOHN D,** Univ Of Cincinnati-Clrmnt Coll, Batavia, OH; SO; BA; Acctng; CPA.

**HOGUE, MATTHEW T,** Savannah Coll Of Art & Design, Savannah, GA; SO; BARCH; Am Inst Arch Stdnts; Phi Eta Sigma; Arch.

**HOHENBRINK, SHIRLEY J,** Defiance Coll, Defiance, OH; SO; BA; Ntl Assc Bnk Wmn Publcty Chrmn 76-90; Defiance Hsp Aux 85-90; Loan Offcr 76-90; Elem Educ; Tchng.

**HOHL, JEFFREY J,** Indiana Univ Of Pa, Indiana, PA; FR; BED; Elem Ed; Tchng.

**HOHMAN, CHARLES S,** Davis & Elkins Coll, Elkins, WV; SR; BS; Beta Alpha Beta Treas 89-; Alpha Chi; Hnry Schiev Awdc-Bus Admin 90; Hnry Achiev Awd Cmptr Sci 89; Acctg/Mgmt/Cmptr Sci Bus.

**HOILMAN, IVORY GAIL,** Mayland Comm Coll, Spruce Pine, NC; SO; SGA; AAS; Horticulture/Envrnmntl Stds; BAS.

**HOILMAN, MELINDA L,** Univ Of Nc At Greensboro, Greensboro, NC; SO; BA; Gateway Ed Ctr Vol; Social Work.

**HOITT, TRACY L,** Univ Of Sc At Columbia, Columbia, SC; FR; BS; Bsn Adm; Acctg.

**HOKE, KATRINA L,** Mansfield Univ, Mansfield, PA; FR; BA; Laurel Hl Cncl; Delta Zeta; Educ.

**HOLADAY, JOHN G,** Ms St Univ, Miss State, MS; SR; BA; Hnrs Prgm 87-88; Sigma Tau Delta 90-; Phi Alpha Theta 90-; Gamma Beta Phi 90-; Pres Lst 90; Engl; Law.

**HOLBEIN, AMY L,** Faulkner St Jr Coll, Bay Minette, AL; SO; ASSOC; Cheerleader Co-Capt 89-; Elem Educ; Tchr.

**HOLBERT, TRACY G,** Germanna Comm Coll, Locust Grove, VA; SO; BLS; Cum Laude Grad; AAS; Math/Sci; Envrmntl Sci.

**HOLBROOK, CONNIE,** Univ Of Ky, Lexington, KY; JR; Phi Theta Kappa 88-90; Epsilon Delta 90; Patterson Schlr 90; High Dstnctn 90; Lnsdwne Elem PTA 90; AA Prestonburg Cmmnty Clg 90; Schl Media Ed/Engl; Lbrn.

**HOLBROOK, DAVID M,** Ky Christian Coll, Grayson, KY; JR; BA; SG VP; England Intrn 90-; Sccr Tm Capt 90-; Crhstn Mnstrs.

**HOLBROOK, DONNA R,** Radford Univ, Radford, VA; JR; BFA; Draper Hall House Cncl 88-89; RA Muse 6-9 89-; Phi Sigma Sigma.

**HOLBROOK, ERIC H,** Cornell Univ Statutory College, Ithaca, NY; SR; MD; Phi Kappa Psi Crrspndng Sec 88-; Dns Lst Cum Laude; Fllw Awrd Schlrshp; Rsrch Asst Chrmn Nrlgy And Bhvr; Vrsty Hvywght Crw 87-; BS; Blgy; Med.

**HOLBROOK, MARGIE L,** Northern Ky Univ, Highland Hts, KY; SO; ADN; Tutrng Elem Lvl; LPM; LPN Nrthrn KY Hlth Occptns Cntr 85; Nrsng; Med/Surg Nrsng.

**HOLBROOK, PATRICK JOHN,** Patrick Henry Comm Coll, Martinsville, VA; SO; BA; Phi Theta Kappa 90-; Mgmt; Hmn Rsrcs Mgmt.

**HOLBROOK, VICKIE L,** Univ Of Tn At Memphis, Memphis, TN; GD; MSN; Blck Stdnt Assn 88-89; Natl Stdnt Nrs Assn 88-89; Lrds Tbrncl Holines Chrch 84-; NA Cnslr Teen Moms Sunrs Prog 89; AACN; BSN 90; Nrsng/Crtcl Cr; MA Crtcl Cr.

**HOLBROOKS, ERIC T,** Tri County Tech Coll, Pendleton, SC; SO; BA; Alpha Zeta Beta V P 90-; Copr Fin; Fin Mgmt.

**HOLBROOKS, WENDI A,** Tri County Tech Coll, Pendleton, SC; SO; Alpha Zeta Beta 90-; Anderson Cnty Republican Party 3rd V Chrmn Elect; Acctg.

**HOLCOMB, AMY C,** Cumberland Coll, Williamsburg, KY; SR; BS; Admsns Stf 87-90; Flwshp Chrstn Athlts Actvts Dir 88-; Natl Sci Tchrs Of Amer 89-; Sigma Tau Delta Sec 89-; Laubach Literacy Prog Tutor 87-88; Schlrshp 87-; Elem Educ; Tchng.

**HOLCOMB, JILL S,** Univ Of Akron, Akron, OH; JR; BA; Elmntry Ed; Tchng Day Care.

**HOLCOMB, KIMBERLY D,** Univ Of Sc At Sumter, Sumter, SC; SO; BS; Cir K Pres 89-; Pres Lst 90; Fnc.

**HOLCOMB, MATTHEW N,** Berry Coll, Rome, GA; FR; BA; Clg Bowl Tm 90-; Cncrt Choir 90-; 60 Mins 90-; Religion; Prof.

**HOLCOMB, PATTI M,** Blue Mountain Coll, Blue Mountain, MS; SR; BS; Bapt Stdnt Union Cncl 88-; MS Assoc Educators 89-; Psychology Club 89-; Bapt Stndt Union Ensbl 87-; Modenian Soc 89-; Acdmc Schlrshp 87-89; Presdntl Acdmc Schlrshp 89-90; Choir Schlrshp 87-89; Assoc Itawamba Cmnty Clge 89; Elem Ed.

**HOLCOMB, S JOYCE,** Itawamba Comm Coll, Fulton, MS; SO; AAS; PASTE BSU 88-; Deans Lst 88-; WMV Dir/Deacons Wife/VBS Dir; Chld Dvlpmnt.

**HOLCOMB, SHARI K,** Southern Junior Coll, Birmingham, AL; GD; AAS; Educ Dvlpmnt; Dean Lst; Pres Lst; Perseverence Awrd; GPA Awrd; Sec; Cmptr Infrmtn Systms; Prgrmmr.

**HOLCOMB, THOMAS L,** Christopher Newport Coll, Newport News, VA; SO; BA; DARE Drg Awrnss Prog 88; Deans Acad Hnr Lst; Fin; Invstmnt Bnkg.

**HOLCOMBE, CHARLES W RADER,** Univ Of Montevallo, Montevallo, AL; JR; BA; Alpha Lambda Delta 88-89; Lambda Chi Alpha Sec 90-; Hstry; Profssr.

**HOLCOMBE, LORI A,** Univ Of Nc At Asheville, Asheville, NC; JR; BA; M5c Serv Soc Clb Sec 89-90; Clncl Psychlgy.

**HOLDEN, BARBARA L,** Univ Of South Fl, Tampa, FL; SR; BS; Kappa Delta Phi; AA St Pete Jr Clg 87-; Educ; Tch.**

**HOLDEN, CYNETHA L,** Al A & M Univ, Normal, AL; SO; BA; Upward Bnd Prg Assist Of AL A & M Univ 89-; Pershing Rifle Swthrt 90-; Tutor 89-90; Vacation Bible Schl Tchr; Boys Trck Tm Mgr 89-90; Telecomm/Engl.

**HOLDEN, TRACIE M,** Nyack Coll, Nyack, NY; JR; BA; AA 90; Psych.

**HOLDER, CATHY M,** Midlands Tech Coll, Columbia, SC; SR; PTD; Advisement Cmte Vice Chrprsn; Deans Hon Rl; Walk Amer For March Of Dimes 89-; Pharm.

**HOLDER, CHERRY ANN M,** Morris Brown Coll, Atlanta, GA; SO; BA; Metro Atlnta Crcn Stdnts Assn Pblc Rltns Rep 90-; Intrntl Stdnts Org 89-; Hon Roll; Vlntr Cnslr Fmly Plng Cnslr 87-; Assn Trinidad/Tobgs 89; Cert John S Donaldson Tech Inst 84; Mass Cmnctn; Pblc Rltns.

**HOLDER, JANICE B,** Mayland Comm Coll, Spruce Pine, NC; SO; AAS; Alpha Pi Kappa Tr 90; Stdnt Mnth Aug Otstdng Fr Sec Fld 88-90; Prt Time Legl Sec Asst; Admin Offc Tech/Busn Admin; Legl Asst.**

**HOLDER, MELISSA C,** Ms St Univ, Miss State, MS; JR; BS; ECJC Plyrs 83-85; Phi Theta Kappa 84-85; Gamma Beta Pji; Jay Cees 88-; Pres Lst 90-; AA E Cntrl Comm Coll 85; Elem Ed; Tchng.

**HOLDER, MELISSA GUYNES,** Univ Of Southern Ms, Hattiesburg, MS; SR; Spirit Club 89-90; Dns Lst; Soc Prof Jrnlsts 90-; Kappa Delta; Kappa Sigma Little Sister Grp Chrprsn 86-90; Tutor 89-90; Walt Disney World Coop 88-; Intrnshp WLOX 13 Tv Rep/Prdcr; Sthrn News Jrnl Anchor 90-; Outstndng SR; Radio/Tv/Film; Broadcast Jrnlsm/News Anchor.

**HOLDER, REGINALD T,** Tn St Univ, Nashville, TN; SO; BS; Elec Engr.

**HOLDER, STEPHEN R,** Univ Of Sc At Columbia, Columbia, SC; SR.

**HOLDER, TESSA O,** City Univ Of Ny City Coll, New York, NY; SR; BA; Frederick Douglass Dbtng Socty 89-; Evng Stdnt Govt Nwsppr Stf Wrtr Mgr 90-; Caribbean Stdnt Org 88-; Blck Alumni Assn; Educ Alumni; Intrn Case Wrkr Offc Of Congrssmn Chas Rangel Intrn Case Wrkr; Pre Law/Pol Sci; Atty.

**HOLDERFIELD, KAREN L,** Spalding Univ, Louisville, KY; SR; BS; Ntnl Stdts Spch/Language/Hearing Ass 89-; The Fillies Inc 86-; Cmmunctv Dsrdrs; Spch/Language Pathologist.

**HOLDING, PATRICIA J,** Middle Tn St Univ, Murfreesboro, TN; GD; MBA; Psi Chi 90-; Gamma Beta Phi 88-; Tau Omicron 90-; Pi Gamma Mu; Soc Intrnshp Domestic Violnc Shltr; BS; Psych; Clin Psych.

**HOLDREN, BRET A,** Duquesne Univ, Pittsburgh, PA; SO; BA; Fncl Mgmt Assoc Sec 90-; Rpblcn Natl Comm; Sigma Tau Gamma VP Mmbrshp 89-; Prsndtl Schlrshp Awrd; Econ Acctg; Bus.

**HOLDREN, LANA E,** Middle Tn St Univ, Murfreesboro, TN; SO; BS; Gamma Beta Phi 90-; Env Sci.

**HOLDRIDGE, PATRICIA,** Columbia Greene Comm Coll, Hudson, NY; FR; BA; English; Elem Schl Tchr.

**HOLDSAMBECK, KIMBERLY R,** Univ Of Montevallo, Montevallo, AL; SR; Cmpss Clb 87; Stu Educ Assn 90; BS 90; Educ; Tchr.

**HOLECEK, PATRICIA A,** Kent St Univ Kent Cmps, Kent, OH; SR; BA; Cncl Fmly Rltns 89-; Vstng Nrs Assoc 89; Highland Hm Hlth Care; Residence/Cosmetology Intl Schl Of Csmthlgy 86; Ind/Famly Stds; Cnslng.

**HOLIDAY, ANGELA D,** Allen Univ, Columbia, SC; SO; Deans Lst 90-; John & Amy Northop Schlrshp; Awrd Asstnc Org Religious Pro; Chrldg Squad 89.

**HOLIHAN, MICHAEL P,** Bryant Stratton Bus Inst Roch, Rochester, NY; FR; ASC; Computer Prog; Computer Sci.

**HOLKA, RAMEE L,** Colby Sawyer Coll, New London, NH; FR; BA; Choices; Art Edn; Teach.

**HOLLA, JO ANN M,** D Youville Coll, Buffalo, NY; SO; BS; Yrbk Stf; Stdnt Phys Therapy Assn; Inglis Hse Phila PA; NYS Park Games Phys Chlngd; Newark Dvlpmnt Ctr Voc; Res Asst St Joes Univ; Tutor High Sch Stdnts Math; Phys Therapy.

**HOLLAHAN, KATHRYN L,** Memphis St Univ, Memphis, TN; SR; BS; NSNA; Beta Beta Beta 82; Grnpc/Mrch Dimes/Save Chldrn 90-; Natl Clgt Nrsg Awd; Slsprsn Photo Studio 85-; Nrsng; Gntc Cnslng.

**HOLLAND, ANGELA M,** Ms St Univ, Miss State, MS; JR; BA; Psychology.

**HOLLAND, DANIELLE M,** Allegheny Coll, Meadville, PA; SO; BA; Crss Cntry 89-; Trk 89-; Schlr Ath Awd 90-; Alden Schlr 90-; Pltcl Sci.

**HOLLAND JR, DAVID L,** Univ Of South Fl, Tampa, FL; JR; BA; Stdnt Govt V Pres 86-88; Circle K Internatl Treas 87-88; Phi Theta Kappa Pres 86-88; Inter Campus Corodntng Cncl Of Stdnts Sgt At Arms 87-88; Golden Key 89-90; Hillsborough Cmnty Clge Stdnt Serv Comm 87-88; Phi Theta Kappa Schlrshp 87-88; AA; Political Science; Teacher.**

**HOLLAND, DEIRDRE C,** Univ Of Sc At Columbia, Columbia, SC; SR; BS; CA Classics 88-90; Offc Admin; Off Mngmnt.

**HOLLAND, ELIZABETH Y,** Univ Of Sc At Columbia, Columbia, SC; GD; Beta Chi 88-90; Pres Lst 90; Dns Lst/Emory Univ 86; BS Furman Univ 90; Bio; Med.

**HOLLAND, EMILY T,** Clark Atlanta Univ, Atlanta, GA; SO; BA; Nws Anchr 90-; Nws Assgnmnt Edtr 90-; Crtv Optns Advsr 90-; Deans Lst 89-90; Delta Sigma Theta; Mass Cmnctns; Radio Flm/TV.

**HOLLAND, JENNIFER A,** Univ Of Ga, Athens, GA; SR; BED; Early Chldhd Educ; Teach K-4.

**HOLLAND, JOHN C,** Spalding Univ, Louisville, KY; JR; BA; United Way; Supv UPS; Asso Jefferson Comm 87; Commctn; Mgmnt UPS.

**HOLLAND, JULIE C,** Longwood Coll, Farmville, VA; SO; BS; Elem Ed; Tchng.

**HOLLAND, KAREN M,** Georgian Court Coll, Lakewood, NJ; SO; BS; Bsn Clb 89-; Pre-Law Soc Treas 90-; Pi Delta Phi 90-; Epsln Zeta; Natl Hnr Soc Bsn; Book Schlp Outstdng Soph 90; Bsn Admn; Corp Intl Trade/Law.

**HOLLAND, LAURA A,** Interdenominational Theo Ctr, Atlanta, GA; MDIV; Frst Presbytrn Chrch Qtmn GA Eldr 83; Prsbytrn Wmn Mnthly Hmls Prsbytrn Hm Pres; Jhnsn Smth Prsbytrn Fllwshp Clr 90-; Theta Phi 90; Amer Nrss Assn; BA Univ Of PA 57; RN Philadelphia Gen Hosp Schl Of Nrsng 49; Bblcl Stds; Prsh Mnstry.

**HOLLAND, LAURIE M,** Pellissippi St Tech Comm Coll, Knoxville, TN; FR; BA; Deans Hnr List 90; Nursing.

**HOLLAND, ONSLOW P,** Coppin St Coll, Baltimore, MD; FR; BA; Math; Elect Eng.

**HOLLAND, PATRICIA M,** Northwest Al Comm Coll, Phil Campbell, AL; Nrs Aide Coord; Nrsng.

**HOLLAND JR, ROBERT W,** Univ Of Tn At Martin, Martin, TN; SR; BA; Hsng Res Hall Assoc Advsr 90-; Block Bridle Clb 88-90; Coll 4-H Clb 88-; Alpha Zeta 90-; Phillip Morris Agric Ext Intrnshp; Natl Agri Awd 90-; Madge/Dave Harrison Agri Schlrshp 90-; Agri Bus.

**HOLLAND, ROMONA J,** Alcorn St Univ, Lorman, MS; SR; Cmptr Sci/Math Clb Sec 86-89; Yrbk Stf Typst/Lyot 86-; Rnld Mcnair Intrn Pro Flw 90; BS 86; Cmptr Sci; Tch.

**HOLLAND, SACHA B,** Fl Atlantic Univ, Boca Raton, FL; SR; BSME; ASM 90-; Engnrng Soc Advncd Mblty Lnd; Sea Air Space; Tau Beta Pi 90-; Englsh Police Offcr 85-87; Mchncl Engnrng; Engnrng.

**HOLLAND, SHAUNA S,** Bennett Coll, Greensboro, NC; SO; BS; Chem; Orthodontist.

**HOLLAND, SIA L,** Morris Brown Coll, Atlanta, GA; JR; Cncrt Chr 88-; Delta Omicron Pres 90-; Synfntte Scty 89-; Msc; Prfrmnce.

**HOLLAND, STACY Y,** Georgian Court Coll, Lakewood, NJ; FR; Bkbl Tm Capt 87-89; Bkbl Tm 89-; Pi Delta Phi 90-; White Mullane Schlrshp 90-; Blck Wmns Lgue 89-; BA; AA 88-89; French; NFO U S Navy.

**HOLLANDER, DAVID J,** Univ Of Rochester, Rochester, NY; SR; Phi Kappa Tau VP 90-; Senate Appropriations Com Cntrl 88-90; Sntr 87-88; Phi Kappa Tau VP 90-; Intern Publ Affairs Dept Guinnesss PLC London; Mktg Intern Xerox Rochester NY; Pol Sci; Bus.

**HOLLANDER-GOLDFARB, WERED A,** Yeshiva Univ, New York, NY; GD; MA; Bnei Alciva Yth Mvmnt Reg Dir 86; Cum Laude 89; Bible/Judaic Stdes; Tch.

**HOLLAR, DENISE C,** Univ Of Nc At Greensboro, Greensboro, NC; JR; BS; Watermark Press Editors Choice Awd For Poetry 90; Intrnshp Kindergarten Cls; Elme Educ; Tchr.

**HOLLEMAN, TERESA L,** Univ Of Nc At Charlotte, Charlotte, NC; SR; BA; AA 88; Psychlgy.

**HOLLENDER, VICTOR,** Case Western Reserve Univ, Cleveland, OH; FR; BA; Debate Soc VP 90-; Raheemya Intl Fndr 90-; K Lemmerman Essay Awrd; Phlsphy/Econ/Psychlgy.

**HOLLEY, CHAD A,** Ms St Univ, Miss State, MS; SO; Reformed Fllwshp; Phi Eta Sigma; Gamma Beta Phi; Pi Kappa Alpha; Schillig Schlrshp; Honors Prog; Philosophy.

**HOLLEY, CHERYL D,** Tn Temple Univ, Chattanooga, TN; SR; Alpha Epsilon Theta; BS; Music; Tchng.

**HOLLEY, KEVIN W,** Univ Of Sc At Columbia, Columbia, SC; SO; BS; Eng Clb 89-; Sci Educ Enrchmnt Day 90; Gamma Beta Phi 89-; Burger King Schlrshp 89; R E Phelon Co Schlrshp 90; USCA Eng Schlrshp; Frank B Herty Schlrshp; Mech Eng; Eng.

**HOLLEY, LA SHAUNN,** Tuskegee Univ, Tuskegee Inst, AL; SR; BA; Miss Ga Clb 88-89; Miss Shriner Clb 88-89; Delta Sigma Theta; Hnr Rl 89-90; Pres Essay Awd 89; Psychlgy; Spch Path.

**HOLLEY, NICHOLE R,** Va St Univ, Petersburg, VA; JR; BA; Pblc Admnstrtn Clb Prsdnt; Frshmn Cls VP 88-89; US Dpt Agrcltr Intrn; Prgrm Stdnts Enrld 1890 Lnd Grnt Inst 90-; Pblc Admnstrtn; Law.

**HOLLEY, PAMELA D,** Radford Univ, Radford, VA; JR; BMT; Music Thrpy Clb Scrtry 90; Sigma Alpha Iota; Music Thrpy.

**HOLLEY, SANDRA R,** Univ Of Tn At Martin, Martin, TN; SR; Phi Eta Sigma 89-; Soc Hnr Smnr Stu 88-; Phi Chi Theta Coor Sec 89-; Accntng.

**HOLLEY, SYLVIA S,** Univ Of South Al, Mobile, AL; SR; BS; Kappa Delta Pi; Elem Educ.

**HOLLEY-MOORE, AMANDA J,** Univ Of North Fl, Jacksonville, FL; JR; Elem Ed; Tchr.

**HOLLIDAY, DAWNEESE L,** Stillman Coll, Tuscaloosa, AL; FR; Sci Clb 90-; Sphstctn Unlmtd 90-; Alpha Swthrt Clb; Deans List 90; Stillman Schlr 90; All Am Schlr 90; Bio/Nrsng.

**HOLLIDAY, JOHN E,** Truett Mc Connell Coll, Cleveland, GA; SO; ASSOC; Jazz Bnd 89-; Cncrt Bnd 89-; Music.

**HOLLIDAY, KRISTINA L,** Univ Of Sc At Columbia, Columbia, SC; SO; BA; Aerobics Instrctr Univ Rec Ctr 90-; Educ; Tchng Elem.

**HOLLIDAY, TINA,** Northern Ky Univ, Highland Hts, KY; SO; Alpha Beta Phi; Dns Lst 90; Soc Stds/Sec Ed; Soc Stds Tchr H S.

**HOLLIE, JAMES A,** Stillman Coll, Tuscaloosa, AL; SO; BS; Gamma Iota Sigma 90-; Phi Beta Sigma 90-; Chem; Eng.

**HOLLIFIELD, CINDY L,** East Tn St Univ, Johnson City, TN; JR; BA; Prvw Ldr Fresh 90-; Pnhllnc Schlrshp Chr 90-; Pres Pride 90-; Alpha Lambda Delta 88-; Gamma Beta Phi 89-; Rho Lambda 90-; Kappa Delta Treas 88-; Ecnmcs; Law.

**HOLLIFIELD, DAVID L,** Northeast State Tech Comm Coll, Blountville, TN; SR; Amer Design Drafting Assoc V Pres 90-; Phi Theta Kappa; Deans List; Fred L Jones Schlrshp Recip; Assoc Degree Drafing Design; Drafting Design; Engrg Degree.

**HOLLIMAN, CHRISTMA Y,** Auburn Univ At Auburn, Auburn, AL; SO; Zeta Tau Alpha 89-; Natl Yth Ldrshp Cnfrnc 89; Natl Yth Cngrss 89-90; Clvry Assmbly; Arts Bus; Intr Dsgn.**

**HOLLIMON, DANA L,** Alcorn St Univ, Lorman, MS; SO; Eastern Star.

**HOLLIMON, JENNIE L,** Univ Of Southern Ms, Hattiesburg, MS; JR; BS/ED; Convention Amer Instr Of The Deaf 90-; Deaf Educ; Tch.

**HOLLIN, KIMBERLEY S,** Univ Of Akron, Akron, OH; JR; Deans Lst 87-; Firestone Park PTA; BA; Phys Educ Tchr.

**HOLLINGSWORTH, BRENDA B,** Fayetteville St Univ, Fayetteville, NC; JR; BS; AA James Sprunt Cmmnty Clg 90; Elem Ed; Mntl Hlth Spclst.

**HOLLINGSWORTH, CAROL L,** Univ Of Sc At Columbia, Columbia, SC; FR; ADN; Nursing.

**HOLLINGSWORTH JR, GARL L,** Al A & M Univ, Normal, AL; SO; BS; Cmptr Sci; Systms Anlys.

**HOLLINGSWORTH, JENNIFER A,** Memphis St Univ, Memphis, TN; SO; BBA; Alpha Lambda Delta; Phi Eta Simga; Pi Beta Phi VP; Bus Mgmt Info; Bus.

**HOLLINGSWORTH, NACHELLE L,** Alcorn St Univ, Lorman, MS; JR; BS; Deans List Schlr 88-; Alpha Kappa Alpha 90; Tau Beta Sigma 89; Beta Beta Beta; USDA Dairy Lab Asst; Marching Bnd 88-; Biology/Pre Med; Intl Med Phys.

**HOLLINGSWORTH, RHONDA L,** Univ Of Sc At Columbia, Columbia, SC; SR; BA; M Ed; Assoc Degree Spartanburg Meth Coll 79; Edn; Elem Sch Teacher.

**HOLLINGSWORTH, TWYLA E,** Alcorn St Univ, Lorman, MS; SO; BS; Deans List Sclr 89-; Alpha Kappa Alpha; Hnr Prog; Marching Bnd 89-; English.

**HOLLINS, CLARENCE D,** Fl A & M Univ, Tallahassee, FL; FR; IM Bsktbl Capt 90-; Pol Sci; Law.

**HOLLINS, JOHN S,** Univ Of Sc At Columbia, Columbia, SC; SO; BM; ACDA Vp 90-; Univ Deans Lst; Prsdnts Hnr Rll; Piano Prfrmnc.

**HOLLIS, CATHERLEEN,** Nova Univ, Ft Lauderdale, FL; MBA; Ntl Mgmt Assoc Richland Brd Mbr 85-; Tri City Voc Educ Brd 89-; Tri Cities WA Links Inc Pres 84-; In Plant Mgmt Assoc Prog Coord 90-; Complete Mba Prog/Career Corp Mgmt; BED Sav State Clg Sav Ga 71; Business Administration; Entrepeneur.

**HOLLIS III, CHARLES FRANKLIN,** Northern Ky Univ, Highland Hts, KY; SO; BA; Cmps Rpblcns Pub Rltns 89-; Phi Alpha Theta VP; Phi Alpha Theta VP; Hist/Pol Sci; Law/Hist.

**HOLLIS, GREGORY D,** Middle Tn St Univ, Murfreesboro, TN; SO; BA; Math Orgztn 90-; Rifle Tm 89-90; Gamma Beta Phi 90-; Pi Mu Epsilon; Kappa Sigma Frat Guard 89-; Deans Lst 90-; Rifle Tm 89-90; Math/Sci; Engr.

**HOLLIS, HAROLD A,** Gordon Coll, Barnesville, GA; JR; BSEE; VP Hollis TV Inc 88-; ISCET Cert Electronic Tchn 88-; Sr VCR Techn; AS 90; Cert Griffin Tech 82; Electrcl Engrng.

**HOLLIS, JEFFREY K,** Samford Univ, Birmingham, AL; GD; JD; Amer Jrnl Trial Advocacy Ed-Chf 90-; Legal Research/Wrtg Flwshp 89-90; Dns Lst; Amer Jurisprudence Awd; BS Univ S FL 88; Law.

**HOLLIS, KIMBERLY D,** Univ Of Sc At Columbia, Columbia, SC; JR; BA; Prt Tm Empl SC Crmnl Jstc Acad 89-; Poli Sci; Law.

**HOLLIS, LINDSEY M,** Norfolk St Univ, Norfolk, VA; SR; BA; Alpha Kapa Mu 90-; Erly Chldhd Ed.

**HOLLIS, ROBB A,** California Univ Of Pa, California, PA; FR; BS; Comp Sci; Prog.

**HOLLIS, RONALD E,** Al A & M Univ, Normal, AL; SR; BA; Tlcmnctns Clb 87-89; SIFE VP 89-90; Media Pllng Bd 87-89; Kappa Alpha Psi; Intrnd WFTS Chnnl 28 Tampa FL Assoc Prdcr 90; Intrnd Tlcmnctns Dept AL A/M Asst Cmrmn 90-; Tlcmnctns; Prdcr/Dir.

**HOLLIS, SANDRA D,** Middle Tn St Univ, Murfreesboro, TN; JR; All Sing Group Guide Reception Comm; Gamma Beta Phi 88-; Tau Omicron 90-; Indstrl Tchnlgy; Mchncl Engrng.

**HOLLISTER, CAROL ANN,** Hudson Valley Comm Coll, Troy, NY; GD; CERT; Vlntr Town Colonie EMT/PRMDC 90-; Emerg Med Svc Dept; Rsrch Tech Albany Med Coll; BA Bio SUNY Albany 90; Paramed; Tchng.

**HOLLOMAN, DONALD L,** Winthrop Coll, Rock Hill, SC; SR; BA; Wnthrp Orntn Prgm Stf Crdntr 88-90; Lappa Mu Epsilon Pres 89-; Omicron Delta Kappa Prgm Crdntr 89-; The Bk/Key; Pres Lst 87-; Tillman Awrd; Isshinryu Katate 88-; Math; Tchr.

**HOLLOMAN, LORI L,** Univ Of Nc At Asheville, Asheville, NC; JR; BA; Psi Chi; Phi Theta Kappa Psichi; Hnr Rll; Deans Lst; Psychlgy; Clncl Chld.**

**HOLLON, CHRISTOPHER J,** Ms St Univ, Miss State, MS; SO; BS; Prfssnl Glf Mgmt Clb 89-; Gamma Beta Phi; Bus.

**HOLLOS, KATE S,** Univ Of Rochester, Rochester, NY; SO; Undrgrad Cncl For Women; Delta Gamma 90-; Art Hist.

**HOLLOWAY, ANDREA L,** Memphis St Univ, Memphis, TN; FR; BA; Crmnl Jstce/Engl; Law.

**HOLLOWAY, ANGELA MARIE,** Chattanooga St Tech Comm Coll, Chattanooga, TN; SO; BS; Stdnt Ed Clb Pres 89-90; Chatt St Ambsdrs Sec 90-; Bptst Stdnt Un 89-; Phi Theta Kapp 89-; Miss Chat St 1 Runner Up 90; AS CSTCC; Elem Ed.

**HOLLOWAY, ANNE E,** Bridgewater Coll, Bridgewater, VA; JR; BA; Stdnt Cncl Rlgs Actvts VP 89-; Rsdnc Hall Cncl VP 90-; Rsdnt Cnslr 90-; Lambda Soc 89-; Alpha Chi 90-; Stdnt Orntatn Cnslr 89-; Psychology; Rsrch.

**HOLLOWAY, CATHERINE L,** Western Ky Univ, Bowling Green, KY; SO; SNEA 90-; Christian Flwshp 89-; Pr Schlr 89-.

**HOLLOWAY, CHRISTOPHER D,** Saint Pauls Coll, Lawrenceville, VA; JR; BS; Sec Jr Cls 90-; Gspl Choir Pianst Chpln 89-; Mth/Sci Clb Chpln 90-; Alpha Kappa Mu Chpln 91-; Stdnt Soc Intrv Prog 89-; Invncbls Awd 90-; Biol/Pre-Med; Physcn/Emerg Med.

**HOLLOWAY, KENNETH D,** Univ Of Sc At Columbia, Columbia, SC; FR; BA; Afro-Am Soc 90-; NAACP 90-; Finance.

**HOLLOWAY, KIMBERLY L,** Univ Of Ga, Athens, GA; JR; BS; CCI Pres; Hall Cncl Tres 90-; Big Sis; Delta Sigma Theta 90-; Intern Farmers Home Adm Cty Sprvsr Asst; Housing/Consumer Econ; Housing.

**HOLLOWAY, MICHAEL R,** Middle Tn St Univ, Murfreesboro, TN; FR; BS; Yth Christ Brd 90; Pastor Bptst Crch 90-; Sclgy; Chrch Mnstry.

**HOLLOWAY, SUSAN L,** Christian Brothers Univ, Memphis, TN; SR; BS; Magna Cum Laude State Tech Inst 86; MADD 89-; Sr Pgrmmr Fed Express Corp Memphis TN; AS State Tech Inst Memphis 86; Telecmnctns Info Sys Mgmnt; Proj Mgmnt Info.

**HOLLOWAY, THOMAS B,** Univ Of Sc At Spartanburg, Spartanburg, SC; FR; BA; Shoestring Plyrs Soc Free Thnkrs 90-; Psychlgy; Cnslng.

**HOLLOWELL, DENNIS R,** Norfolk St Univ, Norfolk, VA; SR; BS; Cncrt Chr; MENC; Alpha Kappa Mu; Chr Green Acrs Prsbytrn Chr; AA Tidewater Comm Coll 89; Vocal Music Educ; Chrstn Mnstry.

**HOLLOWELL, DONYA P,** Norfolk St Univ, Norfolk, VA; SO; PHD; Vrgn Hm Econ Assoc 89-; Sprtn Alpha Tau 89-; Hosp Cndystrppr 87-89; Hm Econ.

**HOLLOWELL, JENNIFER D,** Radford Univ, Radford, VA; JR; BS; House Cncl Sec/Dir Of Acdmc Intgrty 88-90; Stdnt Life-Comdy Clb/Psych Clb/Yrbk Stff; Univ Emergncy Med Serv 90-; Phys Ed/Sprtsmed; Phys Thrpy.

**HOLLOWELL, RALPH R,** Va St Univ, Petersburg, VA; JR; BS; Ag Sci Org VP 90-; W Point Turitans Pres 81-; Ftbll 57-60; Dem Comm Brd 83-89; Supvsr Lumber Indtry 62-; Aquatic Sci; Tchng.

**HOLLSTEGGE, SANDRA L,** Univ Of Cincinnati, Cincinnati, OH; JR; BED; Educ/Engl; Elem Educ.

**HOLLY, SCOTT A,** Gallaudet Univ, Washington, DC; SO; PHD; Honor Soc; Delta Sigma Phi; Psychology; Clinical Forensic Psychologist.

**HOLLYFIELD, SARAH E,** East Tn St Univ, Johnson City, TN; JR; BBA; Stu Govt Assn Sen Sec Tres 89-; Phi Beta Lambda 90-; Univ Chr 89-90; Pnhllnc Hstrn; Rho Lambda 90-; Omicron Delta Kappa 90-; Kappa Delta VP Schlrshp Chrmn 88-; Pres Pride 90-; Sentor Yr 90-; Fnnc; Fnncl Anlyst.

**HOLM, RAINA A,** Cornell Univ Statutory College, Ithaca, NY; SO; BS; Pre-Vet Soc 90-; Athls Action; Natl Schlr; Stolle Rsrch/Dev Intern; Polo Capt 89-; Animal Sci; Vet Sch.

**HOLM JR, ROBERT A,** Oh Wesleyan Univ, Delaware, OH; SR; BA; Vlybl; Intrntnl Assc Firefighter Pres 87-88; Frfghtr/Prmdc 82-; Cert Grant Hosp 84; Pre Prfsnl Zoology; Med Sch.

**HOLMAN, CHEKIBE C,** Al A & M Univ, Normal, AL; SO; Cls Pres 90-; NAACP Pres 90-; Circle K; Ldrshp Awd 90-; SROP Intrnshp Urb Chmpgn.

**HOLMAN, JANET A,** S U N Y Coll Of Tech At Frmgdl, Farmingdale, NY; JR; AS; Student Nrsng Assoc; Deans List 90-; Farmingdale PTA 90-; Brunswick Hosp; Nrsng; RN.

**HOLMAN JR, PETER,** Johnson C Smith Univ, Charlotte, NC; FR; BA; Westvaco Comp Explrs Post Pres 89-90; Alpha Lambda Delta; Johnson C Smith Univ Deans List; Johnson C Smith Univ Golf Tm 90-; Comp Sci.

**HOLMAN, ROY F,** Lexington Comm Coll, Lexington, KY; GD; AIAS Sec 89-90; Hbt Hmnty 89-90; Awd Burchfield Acdmic Schlrshp 89-90.

**HOLMAN, SHELLY D,** Faulkner St Jr Coll, Bay Minette, AL; SO; OAD.

**HOLMES, BRET P,** Fl St Univ, Tallahassee, FL; SR; JD; Finc Soc 90-; Golden Key 90-; BS; Finc; Law.

**HOLMES, CEYLON K,** Wilberforce Univ, Wilberforce, OH; SR; BA; Wmn Hldng Intrst Prfssnlsm Pres 88-90; Univ Schlrshp 87-90; Dean Lst 87-90; Prjct Ldrshp Advncs Dvlpmnt 90; Prjct LEAD; Rhbltn-Chld Dvlpmnt; Stdy Spec Ed/Grntlgy.**

**HOLMES, DANETTE L,** Clemson Univ, Clemson, SC; SO; BS; Univ Gspl Chr 89-; NAACP 89-; Stdnt Otrch Unty Lv; NSBE 90-; Blck Edctnl Spprt Tm Mntr 90-; Blck Stdnts Prms Awrd 89-; Elec Eng.**

**HOLMES, DANIEL K,** Ms St Univ, Miss State, MS; SO; BA; Bus Admn; Mktg.

**HOLMES, DEBRA Y,** Selma Univ, Selma, AL; SO; BS; Hnr Soc 90-; Phi Beta Lambda 89-; Magnu Cum Laude; AA; Bsn Adm; Bsn.

**HOLMES, GUSSIE R,** Memphis St Univ, Memphis, TN; SR; BSN; AAS Shelby State Commty Clg 82; Sci; Nrsng.

**HOLMES, HEIDEMARIE C,** Longwood Coll, Farmville, VA; SR; MA; Synchronized Swim 89-; BS Longwood Coll; Edn; Lib Sci; Tchr.

**HOLMES, JUDITH A,** Atlantic Comm Coll, Mays Landing, NJ; SR; AAS; Army Cmmndtn Mdl 89; Army Good Cndct Mdl 88; US Army 86-90; Harrahs Marina Casino Htl; Cert Cherry Hill Trvl Schl 85; Htl Mgmt; Entrtnmnt Dir.

**HOLMES, JUNE C,** Portland School Of Art, Portland, ME; GD; MA; YWCA Mbr; Jrd Show PSA 86 87 89; Art Show; Cape Elizabeth Cmnty Svcs Docent Portland Museum Of Art; Stitch Tech Pres Cape Elizabeth ME; BFA 90; Art; Ed.

**HOLMES, KANDY K,** Mount Aloysius Jr Coll, Cresson, PA; GD; Phi Theta Kappa 90-; Assoc Microcomp Sci.

**HOLMES, KRISTEN M,** Univ Of Ga, Athens, GA; JR; BED; Spec Ed-Mntl Retrdtn; Tchg.

**HOLMES, LA SHAWN R,** Univ Of Nc At Charlotte, Charlotte, NC; JR; BA; Nwspr Edtr 90; Feature Artcls/Poems 90; Delta Sigma Theta Comm 90-; Pres Elec Voter Reg Cnslr 88; Hmn Rsc Asst 90-; Engl/Comm; Law.

**HOLMES, LISA A,** Fl St Univ, Tallahassee, FL; JR; BED; Gldn Girls 89-; Phi Eta Sigma 89-; Beta Kappa Alpha; Kappa Delta Hstrn 89-; Dnc Instrctr UDA; Elem Ed; Tchr.

**HOLMES, LISA M,** Univ Of Sc At Coastal Carolina, Conway, SC; SR; BA; Ed Clb 89-90; Kappa Delta Pi; Conway Hosp 82-; Elem Ed.

**HOLMES, MIRANDA C,** Hilbert Coll, Hamburg, NY; FR; ASSOC; Rd Crs Brd Dir Brd Mbr; CPR/1ST Aid Instr; Wtrsfty Instr Lfgrd Inst 90-; Emer Med Tech 90; Lbrl Arts; Bio.

**HOLMES, NEIL D,** Coll Of Charleston, Charleston, SC; FR; BA; Hnr Board 90-; Faculty Hnrs Lst; Philosphy Political Sci; Law.

**HOLMES, PATRICK J,** Youngstown St Univ, Youngstown, OH; SR; BE; ASM 87-; SAMPE 87-; Mtrl Engnrng; Prfsnl Engnr.

**HOLMES, RHONDA F,** Fayetteville St Univ, Fayetteville, NC; SR; BS; Stdnts Free Entrprs Pres; Alpha Kappa Mu; Kappa Delta Pi; Sec/Bkkpr/Bus Mngr Mark II Entrprs; Bus Admin; Prtnrshp Acct/Fin.

**HOLMES, SAMANTHA K,** Middle Tn St Univ, Murfreesboro, TN; SO; BBA; Bapt Stdnt Union 89-90; Gamma Beta Phi 90-; Alpha Delta Pi 90-; Red Cross Blood Drive 90-; Rsng Money Ronald Mc Donald Hse 90; Dns Lst 89-; Hnr Roll 89-; Mgmt/Bsn Admin.

**HOLMES, STACEY L,** Lincoln Univ, Lincoln Univ, PA; SR; Sclgy Clb Chrprsn 90-; Spnsh Clb VP 89-; Thrgd Mrshl Law Soc 90-; Lady Bsktbl Mgr 88-; Phi Beta Sigma Frat Tres 89-; Intrn Phila Ct Cmn Pls PO Juvnl; BS; Crmnl Jstc; Sclgy.

**HOLMES, TINA V,** Al St Univ, Montgomery, AL; JR; BA; Erly Chldhd Ed; Tchr.

**HOLMES, VINCENT E,** Lincoln Univ, Lincoln Univ, PA; FR; Eng Clb Pres; Physc Clb VP; Japanese Clb; Rsrch Asst IA St U; Tnns Tm; Eng.

**HOLMSTOCK, JOEL M,** Univ Of Sc At Columbia, Columbia, SC; SR; BS; Bdybldng Club; Crmnl Justc Assn; AAS Gloucester Cnty Clg 87; Crmnl Justc; Law Enfor.

**HOLNBECK, JACK P,** S U N Y At Buffalo, Buffalo, NY; GD; Henry Adams Medal Highest GPA; Deans Lst 87-; Self Employed Dsgnr/Bldr 86-; Architecture; Tchng.

**HOLOBINKO, JOSEPH N,** Juniata Coll, Huntingdon, PA; JR; BS; Scalpel/Probe 90-; Wght Lftng Club 88-90; Beta Beta Beta 89-; Hershey Med Ctr Whitaker Schlrshp Award; Juniata Clg Merit Schlrshp 88; Ftbl 88-; Bio; Med.

**HOLSCLAW, SHARON L,** Univ Of Nc At Chapel Hill, Chapel Hill, NC; FR; BS; Pre Law Clb 90-; Carolina Fvr 90-; Carolina Athltc Assoc Hmcmg Dir; Drm Govt Pblcty Chr 90-; Carolina Athltc Assoc Make A Wish Fndtn Carolina Rd Rc; Pol Sci; Law.

**HOLSHOUSER, SUSAN E,** Peace Coll, Raleigh, NC; FR; AA; BACCHUS Task Force 90-; Loaves/Fishes Tutor Children 90-; Phi Theta Kappa 90-; Ldrshp Schlr 90-; Jones Schlr 90-; Student Assist Psy Dept 90-; Busn; Intl Relations.

**HOLSINGER, LANESSA,** Radford Univ, Radford, VA; JR; BS; Assoc Educ Yng Chldrn 90-; Ntl Educ Assoc 90-; Hs Cncl VP 90-; Elem Educ; Admin.

**HOLSONBACK, JENNIFER S,** Coll Of Charleston, Charleston, SC; SO; BA; Alpha Delta Pi Schlrshp Chrmn Elect; Bsns.**

**HOLSTEIN, DANIEL L,** Univ Of Charleston, Charleston, WV; JR; BA; Pol Sci Clb Pres 89-90; Nwsppr Stff 89-; Stu Govt Assn Sec Tres 90; Alpha Lambda Delta; Pi Gamma Mu Pres 90; Intern Leg Judith A Herndon; Intern U S Atrnys Offc Vctm Wtnss Asst 90; Fraisure Singleton Leg Prog 90; Pol Sci; Law/Pltcs.

**HOLT, ANNA M,** Roane St Comm Coll, Harriman, TN; SO; BS; Gamma Beta Phi; AS Roane St Comm Coll; Elementary Education.

**HOLT, ANNE E,** Univ Of Nc At Charlotte, Charlotte, NC; SR; BS; Soclgy; Cnsl Yth.

**HOLT, BENJAMIN A,** Germanna Comm Coll, Locust Grove, VA; AAS; Intr Vrsty Chrstn Fllwshp 89-91; Stffrd Hgh Schl Almn Bbl Stdy 90-; Ushr 90; Vol Data Entry 90-; Typst Mntl Hlth Assoc; Dean Lst 90-; Prsdnt Lst; Comp Sci; Mssnry.**

**HOLT, BRIAN C,** Forsyth Tech Comm Coll, Winston-Salem, NC; SO; BA; Asst Trust Offcr Wachovia Bnk NC; Acctng; CPA/FINANCIAL Anlyst.**

**HOLT, DANIEL F,** Richard Bland Coll, Petersburg, VA; JR; BSBA; Phi Theta Kapp Ofc Arms 89-; Deans List; Pres List; AS Richard Bland Clg 90; Bus Admn Fin; MBA.

**HOLT, FREDA K,** Univ Of Nc At Asheville, Asheville, NC; FR; BSED; Spch Hrng Dsrdrs.

**HOLT, HOLLY,** Univ Of Ky, Lexington, KY; SR; BED; Sigma Gamma Sigma Tr 90-; Epsilon Delta 89-; Goldn Key 89-; Elm Sch Buddy 90-; Elem Educ; Tchg.

**HOLT, KEIA K,** Jackson St Univ, Jackson, MS; FR; BS; Nwspaper 90; Alpha Lambda Delta 90-; Pr Lst 90; Jrnlsm; Brdcst Jrnlist.

**HOLT, KIMBERLY A,** Oh Univ-Southern Cmps, Ironton, OH; SR; BA; Deans Lst 89-; Goldn Key 89-; Kappa Delta 84-; Alpha Gamma Rho 83-; Chrch Lxngtn 85-; Ashlnd Plza 90-; Hudsn Entrprs 79-85; Lxngtn Mntssri Schl 85-87; Elem Ed.

**HOLT, MATTHEW R,** Univ Of Sc At Columbia, Columbia, SC; FR; Naval Rsrv Ofcr Trn Corps; Blue Gold Soc Pres; U S C Hnrs Coll 90-; Sons Amer Rev Ldrshp Awd; Spanish; Naval Ofcr.

**HOLT, PATSY M,** Sue Bennett Coll, London, KY; FR; AA; Phi Beta Lambda 90-; Bus.

**HOLT, ROBERT F,** Queens Coll, Charlotte, NC; FR; Drama; Flwshp Chrstn Athls; Pi Kappa Phi Chpln; PUSH; Soccer; Acctg; CPA.

**HOLT, TAMMY M,** Central Fl Comm Coll, Ocala, FL; FR; AS; Phi Theta Kappa; Legal Asstng; Paralegal.

**HOLT, TIMOTHY J,** Miami Univ, Oxford, OH; FR; BA; Hall Govt Pblcty 90-; Cmps Crsde For Chrst; Ski Clb; Deans Schlrshp 90; Intrntnl Studies.

**HOLT, VIRGINIA L,** Roane St Comm Coll, Harriman, TN; FR; AAS; Natl Envrnmntl Hlth Assoc; Gamma Beta Phi; Indstrl Hygiene Tchn.

**HOLTBY, KRISTA ANNE,** Niagara Univ, Niagara Univ, NY; SO; Ornttn; Ambssdr; Sftbll Schrlshp; Engl.

**HOLTERMAN, DENISE ELLEN STEWART,** Georgian Court Coll, Lakewood, NJ; JR; BA; Ltry Mgzn Edtr 86-88; Stf Wrtr Vkng Nws 85-87; Phi Theta Kappa 86-88; Sigma Tau Delta 90-; Drctr Bible Schl St Andrws Mthdst Chrch 87-; Codrctr Lvng Lst Supper 89-; Aa Ocean Cnty Coll 88; Elmntry Ed/Englsh; Tchng.

**HOLTHAUS, DEBORAH R,** Salisbury St Univ, Salisbury, MD; GD; MSW; Intrn Big Bros/Big Strs 87; Intern Estrn Shr Hosp Cntr 89-90; Grad Cum Laude 90; Soc Worker; BA Soc Wrk Salisbury St Univ 90; Soc Wrk/Clncl Cncntrtn.

**HOLTON, VICKIE A,** Abraham Baldwin Agri Coll, Tifton, GA; SO; AS; Alpha Beta Gamma Sec; Bus; Acctnt.

**HOLTSLANDER, ERNEST J,** Embry Riddle Aeronautical Univ, Daytona Beach, FL; JR; BA; Arntcl Sci; Airline Trnsprt Pilot.

**HOLTVLUWER, JOY,** Univ Of Miami, Coral Gables, FL; FR; BS; Marine Sci/Biol; Mar Biol.

**HOLTZ, AMU E,** Kent St Univ Kent Cmps, Kent, OH; SR; BA; Accntng Assoc; NAA; Golden Key; Beta Alpha Psi; Accntng Intrn; Accntng; Pblc Accntng.

**HOLTZ, BARBARA L,** Indiana Univ Of Pa, Indiana, PA; SO; BS; Sgn Lang Clb; Cncl Excep Chldrn 90; Phi Sigma Pi; Educ; Tchg.

**HOLTZ, DAVID PAUL,** S U N Y Coll At Fredonia, Fredonia, NY; SR; BED; Var Bsktbl 87-; Athlts Agnst Drugs/Alcohol 90-; Chldrns Fair; Res Asst 89-; Elem Ed; Tchr.

**HOLTZAPFEL, CHAD E,** Oh Univ-Southern Cmps, Ironton, OH; FR; BS; Deans Lst 90; Trumbo Fmly Schlrshp; Deans Lst Schlrshp D U Athens; IM Vlybl/Sftbl; Cvl Eng.

**HOLTZAPPLE, NINA L,** Fl St Univ, Tallahassee, FL; SO; BS; SGA 89-90; SAM 89-; Blgcl Sci; Gntc Engnrng.

**HOLTZCLAW, TERESA F,** Chattanooga St Tech Comm Coll, Chattanooga, TN; SO; BA; Natl Reg Interprts Deaf 90-; Singn Hnds Sign Chr 90-; Natl Assn Deaf 90-; Psi Beta 90-; Phi Theta Kappa 90-; Psych.

**HOLWAY, BETSY J,** Columbia Greene Comm Coll, Hudson, NY; FR; RN; Tutrg Nrsng Stdnts; Valatie Vol Rsce Sqd 90-; Exmnr/Phlbtnst Fr Ins Applcnts; AAS/MLT Nrth Cntry Cmmnty Clg 85; Math/Sci/Nrsg; Nrsg Amer Indian Rsrvtns.

**HOLYNSKI, DEBORA ANN,** Hilbert Coll, Hamburg, NY; SO; AAS; Bus Admin.

**HOLZ, NOEL R,** Univ Of Ky, Lexington, KY; FR; BA; Phi Eta Sigma; Lambda Sigma; W V Governor's Intnshp; Ntnl Merit Schol; Pres Schlrshp; English.

**HOLZAPFEL, JAYNE A,** Oh St Univ At Newark, Newark, OH; FR; BA; Hon Soc; Exmplry Wrtng Awd/Sprior Catgry; Tutr; Psych Lab Asst 90; Psych; Grad Sch Ph D.

**HOMA HODINKO, JOAN E,** Univ Of Pittsburgh, Pittsburgh, PA; GD; MSN; Sigma Theta Tau 89-; Natl Assc Pediatric Nrs Assc/Prac 90-; Nrs Prac Asc SW PA 90-; RN 79-; CRNP; BSN 79; MSN 90; Pediatric Nursing.

**HOMAN, RUSSELL J,** Univ Of Rochester, Rochester, NY; SR; BS; Im Bsktbl 90-; Im Ftbl 87-88; NROTC 87-; Optcl Soc Of Amer 87-; Optck Engrng.

**HOMAN, SHAUNNA L,** Univ Of Cin R Walters Coll, Blue Ash, OH; SO; BS; Science; Nrsng.

**HOMAYOUN, NIMA,** Old Dominion Univ, Norfolk, VA; SR; MS; Ambassdr Fndng Fthr 89-; RA 86-; Prvw Cnslr 88; Tau Beta Pi Pres 89; Eta Kappa Nu; Omicron Delta Kappa; NSPE Treas 90-; Olympcs Chr Prsn; Math Cnt Tstng Coor 90; Krover Schlrshp; Kaufman Awrd 90; Rsrch Asst 89; Vlybl 90; Elec Eng; Eng.

**HOMBERG, KIMBERLY A,** Anne Arundel Comm Coll, Arnold, MD; FR; BSN; Science; Nursing.

**HOMER, DOUGLAS ANTHONY,** Davis & Elkins Coll, Elkins, WV; SO; BA; Lit Mag Ed Chf 90-; Jennings Randolph Ldrshp Pgm Advsry Bd 90-; Vrsty Soccer Pgm Ath Rep 89-; Hon Assoc Acad Advsr 90-; Engl Dept Hon Assn Pres 90-; Randolph Cnty Bd Edn Fine Arts Instr 90-; Jennings Randolph Ldrshp Serv Org 90-; Music; Jazz Performance/Crmnl Law.

**HOMER, JILL M,** Birmingham Southern Coll, Birmingham, AL; FR; 1st Pl Alys Robinson Stephens Piano Comp; Piano.

**HOMER, JOHN B,** Univ Of Pittsburgh, Pittsburgh, PA; JR; BS; MENSA Scty 88-; ASME 89-; Tau Beta Pi 90-; Pi Tau Sigma Treas; Phi Eta Sigma 88-; Golden Key 89-; Intrnshp US Steel 90; Deans Lst 88-; Glf Clb 89-; Mech Eng; Eng/Law.

**HOMER, MELINDA S,** Univ Of Sc At Columbia, Columbia, SC; SR; BA; Secy 82-; AS 78; Early Chldhd Ed; Tchng.

**HOMESLEY, WILLIAM C,** Gaston Coll, Dallas, NC; SO; BS; High Hnrs Grad; Untd Prcl Srvc Mgmnt Oprtns Sprvsr 89-; AA; Accntng; UPS Accntng.

**HOMICK JR, PAUL S,** Saint Vincents Coll & Seminary, Latrobe, PA; SR; BA; St Vncnt Vol Fre Dept 1st Lt 89-; Otstndng Stdnt Almni Ldrshp Awrd; Coll Hnr Prog; Awrd Acad Excllnce Pol Sci; Dns Lst; St Vncnt Schlrshp; Bst Brf Awrd; Brd Of Educ; Yngst Grp Fclttr; Fre Ldrshp Rtrt; Stdnt Snte; Coor Big Bro Big Sis; Pol Sci; Law.

**HOMICZ, JULIE A,** Villanova Univ, Villanova, PA; FR; BA; French Clb 90-; French Hon Soc 90-; Tennis 90-; Intl Rels.

**HOMMEY, JAN F,** Kent St Univ Kent Cmps, Kent, OH; SR; BBA; Alpha Eta Rho 87-88; Org Continuence Of Aviation Educ Pbl Rltns 89-90; Beta Gamma Sigma 90-; Golden Key 90-; Internship Unite D Airlines 90; As Comm Clg Beaver Cnty 86-88; AS; Aviation; Prof Pilot.

**HOMSANY, SOPHIE,** Univ Of North Fl, Jacksonville, FL; JR; BA; Phi Theta Kappa 89; Gold Key; AA FL Comm Coll 89; Elem Edn; Teach.

**HOMSHER, SARAH E,** Univ Of Akron, Akron, OH; JR; BA; Campus Focus 90-; Kent State Univ Hnrs Bnd 87-88; Cedarville Clg Hnrs Bnd 87-88; Elem Educ; Elem Tchng/Tesol.

**HOMULKA, LISA R,** Saint Vincents Coll & Seminary, Latrobe, PA; FR; BA; Acntng; CPA.

**HONAN, CHRISTOPHER M,** Univ Of Ct, Storrs, CT; SR; BS; Triangle Frtrnty Sec 90-; CT Assc Avcltr 87-90; Patho Bio; Vet Schl.

**HONAN, KIM L,** Methodist Coll, Fayetteville, NC; JR; BS; Phi Theta Kappa VP 82-83; Grdn Et Litum Offcr Crt 90-; Ft Bragg Yth Sccr Coach; AS Grayson Coll 82-83; Scl Wrk/Sclgy.

**HONE, CAROL S,** Central Fl Comm Coll, Ocala, FL; GD; AS; Paramedic Amblnc 88-; AS CFCC; Emrgncy Med; Amb/Hlcptr Prmdc/Reg Nrs.

**HONECK, AMY L,** S U N Y Coll Of Tech At Alfred, Alfred, NY; SO; BA; Scl/Bhvrl Sci Clb 89-90; Drm Cncl 90-; Theatre 89-90; Hnr Soc 89-; Campus Tour Guide 90-; IM 89-; AA 89-; Hmn Dvlpmnt; Marr/Family Cnslg.

**HONEGGER, KELLY L,** Le Moyne Coll, Syracuse, NY; SO; BA; CAN Vol 90-; Intrmrl Sprts; Vllybll; Sccr; Bsktbll 89-; Bus Admn; Prlgl.

**HONESTY, TAMARA L,** Wilmington Coll, Wilmington, OH; SO; BA; Res Life Res Asst 90-; Stu Fndtn 89-; Ldr Schlrshp 89-; Miami Univ Smmr Thtr; Thtr; Grad Schl/Prof.**

**HONEY, SEAN R,** Georgetown Univ, Washington, DC; SO; BSBA; Lck/Chn 89-90; Sigma Chi; Intrn Trndl Amer Corp Asst Prj Mgr 90; 1st Union Ntl Bk Cnsmr Bnkg; Var Lacrosse 89-; Finance; Intl Bus.

**HONEYCUTT, AVERICE J,** Roane St Comm Coll, Harriman, TN; FR; SSAS; Soc Sci.

**HONEYCUTT, DEBRA D,** Central Al Comm Coll, Alexander City, AL; FR; Acdmc Tm; Pre Eng.

**HONEYCUTT JR, JOSEPH EUGENE,** Univ Of Al At Birmingham, Birmingham, AL; SR; BSME; Tau Beta Pi 84-; Beta Theta Pi; AL Emmaus/Kaivors Cmnty; Cahaba Hgt United Meth Church; Ath Assn; Mgr Prep/Support Engrng Drummond Co Inc; Mach Engr.

**HONEYCUTT, MELISSA S,** Livingston Univ, Livingston, AL; SR; BS; Acad/Ldrshp Schlrshp 90-; AS Brewer State Jr Coll 90; Math; Scndry Edn.

**HONEYWELL, MARLON S,** Fl A & M Univ, Tallahassee, FL; FR; MBA; Alpha Phi Omega 90-; Alpha Phi Omega 90-; Phrmcy; Obstrtcn.

**HONG, DAVID H,** Univ Of Southern Ms, Hattiesburg, MS; JR; BS; Almn Assc 89-; Mrchng Bnd 88-; Gldn Key 90-; Gamma Beta Phi 89-; Alpha Epsln Dlt 88-; Amer Chem Scty 89-; Alph Tau Omega Hstrn 88-; IM 88-; Chem; Medcn.

**HONG, GUANGZHI,** Ms St Univ, Miss State, MS; JR; BS; Gamma Beta Phi; Pres Schlr; Computer Sci.

**HONG, JUDY E,** Cornell Univ Statutory College, Ithaca, NY; FR; BS; Korean Soc Soc Chr; Korean Bible Study; Cmnctns; Bus.

**HONG, PATRICIA S,** City Univ Of Ny City Coll, New York, NY; SR; Korean Amer Fmly Svc Ctr Vol/Ofc Mgr; Ec Nwspr Cnsmr Rprtr Korea Exec Sec Nwspr Co; YWCA; St Lukes Hosp; Vol; Scl Wrkr; Korean Amer Svc Ctr; BA; Sclgy; Comm Cnslr Hmn Rltd Svc.

**HONIGFOD, MARIA L,** Central St Univ, Wilberforce, OH; JR; Student Assoc Seargent At Arms 90-; Nursing.

**HONKALA, SUSAN M,** Notre Dame Coll, Cleveland, OH; SR; BS; Notre Dame Ntrtn Assc 90-; Deans Lst; Amer Dietetic Assc 90-; Clevelnd Dietetic Assc 90-; Dietetics.

**HONSTED, JAMES D,** Tallahassee Comm Coll, Tallahassee, FL; JR; BA; Bus Mgmt.

**HOO, TRACIE E,** Univ Of Miami, Coral Gables, FL; SR; BBA; Org Jamaican Unty Treas 88-89; Carbbn Stdnts Assn; Pres 100 Rep 87; Hrrcn Glbrt Rlf Fnd 88; Intl Finance/Mktg; Cnsltnt.

**HOOD, BRENDAN,** Univ Of Rochester, Rochester, NY; JR; BA; Engl; Screenwriting/Dir.

**HOOD, DEANNA D,** Bowling Green St Univ, Bowling Green, OH; FR; BS; Alpha Lambda Delta 90-; Phi Eta Sigma 90-; Biochmstry; Medicine.

**HOOD, DEBORAH A,** Livingston Univ, Livingston, AL; SR; MA; Hstrcl Soc Treas 90-; Panhellenic Cncl 88-; Res Life Staff 89-; Omicron Delta Kappa 89-; Alpha Sigma Tau Pres 88-; Hmcmnc Ct 89; Ms LU 90; BA; Hist; Hstrn Archvst.

**HOOD, DOUGLAS R,** Univ Of Ky, Lexington, KY; SO; BEE; Elect Tech 82-; AAS 82; Elect Engr; Robotics Engr/Dsgn.

**HOOD, EDWAN HOOD M,** Memphis St Univ, Memphis, TN; FR; BSEE; Mrchng Bnd; Cncrt Bnd; Elect Eng; Bus.

**HOOD, EVAN C,** Comm Coll Algny Co Algny Cmps, Pittsburgh, PA.

**HOOD, GINA R,** Pellissippi St Tech Comm Coll, Knoxville, TN; SO; BSN; Deans Lst 90-; Sci.

**HOOD, GLADYS B,** Stillman Coll, Tuscaloosa, AL; JR; NAACP Asst Sec 90-; UNCF 88-; Players Drama Club 90-; Gordell Wynn Hnrs Prog 89-; Gamma Iota Sigma 89-; Epsilon Eta; Schlr 90-; All Amer Schlr 90-; Deans List 88-; Elem Ed; Teacher.**

**HOOD, JANA S,** Itawamba Comm Coll, Fulton, MS; FR; MBA; Acctg.

**HOOD, JOHNICA A,** Clark Atlanta Univ, Atlanta, GA; FR; Math Clb Sec 90-; Hon Soc 90-; Hon Rl 90-; Hon Mention Civil Rghts Essay Contest 90-; Math; Tchr.

**HOOD, KELLY W,** Univ Of Tn At Martin, Martin, TN; SR; BS; Tri-Beta 90-; Kappa Alpha Order 88-; Dept Bio Tchng Asst 90-; Bio; Med.

**HOOD, KIMBERLI D,** Blue Mountain Coll, Blue Mountain, MS; SR; BA; Bapt Stdnt Un State Sec 86-90; Miss Assoc Eductrs Stdnt Prog State Rep 88-90; Cntrestage V P 86-88; Alpha Psi Omega Pres 88-; Bapt Stdnt Un Summer Msnry 89; Creative Wrtng Awd 89-90; Spch/Drama Stdnt Yr 88-89; Puiser Spch Awd/Bst Actress; English; Sec Educ.

**HOOD, LOU ANN,** Ms St Univ, Miss State, MS; FR; Gamma Beta Phi; Lambda Sigma; Alpha Lambda Delta Treas; Phi Mu Treas; Bio; Phy Thrpy.

**HOOD, MARY K,** Ringling School Of Art, Sarasota, FL; SO; BA; Dsgnd Pstr Acfofest Milw WI 88; Lndscp Oil/Best Of Ringling; Art In The Park; AA Cmrcl Art MATC Milw WI 88; Fine Arts; Painting.

**HOOD, NICOLE R,** Va St Univ, Petersburg, VA; JR; BS; Data Prcssng Mgmt Assn; Blck Stdnts Agnst Drgs; NAACP; Bsns Infrmtn Systm; Cmptr Prgrmmng.

**HOOD, PAMELA D,** Univ Of Tn At Knoxville, Knoxville, TN; SR; BS; Exec Clb; Beta Gamma Sigma 89-; Phi Kappa Phi 90-; Acctg.

**HOOD, SARAH A,** Birmingham Southern Coll, Birmingham, AL; SO; BA; Clg Paper 89-; Habitat For Humanity 89-; Phi Eta Sigma 90-; Alpha Lambda Delta 90-; Hist.

**HOOD, SUE C,** Greenville Tech Coll, Greenville, SC; GD; AD; Phi Theta Kappa Prlmntrn 90; Beta Sigma Phi Pres 86-88; Paralegal; Law.

**HOOD, TAMARA DIANE,** Longwood Coll, Farmville, VA; SO; FSSW 89-; Alpha Delta Mu; Sigma Kappa Schlrshp Chrmn; Emrg Ldrs Conf 90; Coll Offcr Trnng Schl; Soc Wrk; Fstr Cr Crtv Arts Thrpy.

**HOOD, TED B,** Saint Catharine Coll, St Catharine, KY; SO; AS; Stdnt Sen Pres 90-; Intrntl Clb 90-; Sci Clb; Phi Theta Kappa 90-; WA Cnty Lit Pgm Vlntr 89-; Chem.

**HOOD, WILLIAM S,** Bristol Univ, Bristol, TN; JR; BS; Bus Admin; Mgmt.

**HOOIE, DEBORAH A,** Birmingham Southern Coll, Birmingham, AL; SO; BA; Bsn Mgmt; Mortgage Bkr.

**HOOKER, CYNTHIA L,** Fl St Univ, Tallahassee, FL; SR; BS; Alpha Tau Omega Little Sister 89-90; Intrnshp Sealey Elem Schl Tall; AA Cntrl Fl Comm Clg 89; Elem Educ; Teach/Principal.

**HOOKER, ELIZABETH D,** Univ Of Nc At Greensboro, Greensboro, NC; SR; BS; Alpha Stu Chap NCTM 90-; Univ Mrshls 89-; Deberry Schlrshp; AAS 74; Math.

**HOOKER, SARAH H,** Saint Joseph Coll, West Hartford, CT; SR; RA 90-; Schlr Athlt Awrd; Sister Maria Sullivan Fndrs Fnd Awrd Engl; Sftbl Co Capt 88-; BA; Engl; Tch.

**HOOKER, SOPHIE,** Jackson St Univ, Jackson, MS; FR; MD; Yrbk Stf; Alpha Lambda Delta; Biology; Pre Medicine.

**HOOKER, THOMAS F,** Villanova Univ, Villanova, PA; JR; BA; Villanova Chem Soc 88-; Stdnt Prgmng Cncl 88-; CRC Press Frshmn Chem Stdnt Of Yr At Villanova 89; Rsrch Chmst.

**HOOKOM, MELISSA P,** Univ Of Cincinnati-Clrmnt Coll, Batavia, OH; FR; BA; Art Educ; Tchg.

**HOOKS, CANDACE D,** Tomlinson Coll, Cleveland, TN; SO; Newspr 89-90; Chorale 89-; Drama Club V P 90; Phi Theta Kappa Treas 89; Soph Schlrshp Award 90; Pres Schlrshp 89-90; Math/Sci; Tch.

**HOOKS, DENISE R,** Jackson St Univ, Jackson, MS; SO; BS; Fr Clss Soph Clss VP 89-; Chem Scty; Stdnt Govt Jstce; Alpha Lambda Delta Edtr 90-; Beta Kappa Chi; Intrn At Upjhn; MBRS 90-; Marc Schlr; Chem; Med Schl.

**HOOKS, LORI M,** Cumberland County Coll, Vineland, NJ; FR; Nrsg; RN.

**HOOKS, PATRICIA L,** Valdosta St Coll, Valdosta, GA; JR; BA; Alpha Lambda Delta 89-; Phi Alpha Theta 90-; Sigma Alpha Chi 90-; Alpha Chi; Pi Gamma Mu; Phi Kappa Phi; Pres Schlr 88-89; Hstry; Law.

**HOOMES, DONNA S,** Univ Of Montevallo, Montevallo, AL; JR; BS; Phi Kappa Phi 89-; Kappa Delta Pi 90-; Lambda Sigma Pi 90-; Highest Hnrs Hnrs Day 89-; Elem Educ; Tchr.

**HOOP, KIMBERLY J,** Univ Of Fl, Gainesville, FL; SR; BA; AA Santa Fe Cmuty Clg 89; Art Educ; Educ/Fine Artist.

**HOOPER, CAROLYN Y,** Kent St Univ Kent Cmps, Kent, OH; JR; BA; Flr Rep 90f Kent Intrhll Cncl Rep 90; Psych Clb 90-; Psi Chi 90-; Ebony Ach Awd 88-; Fanny L Hamer Fresh Schlrshp Awd 89; Deans Lst 89-90; Pres Lst 90-; F E Davidson Awd; NSF-REU Intrnshp; Chld Psych.

**HOOPER, CHRIS AUDREY,** Medical Univ Of Sc, Charleston, SC; SR; Nurse Clinic Homeless 88-89; Sigma Theta Tau; BSN; Nursing.

**HOOPER, HALEY S,** Greenville Tech Coll, Greenville, SC; GD; ASSC; Comp Prgrmmng.

**HOOPER, KERRIE A,** Univ Of South Fl, Tampa, FL; FR; BA; Chorus Pres 86-; Chmbr Ensmbl 86-; Interact Serv Clb 87-90; Natl Hon Soc 89-90; Candte Themus Hon Soc 90; Musicnshp Awd 87-90; Sr Musicn Yr 90; Wmn NATS Rgnls; MBA; Voice Prfrmnc; Opera/Stage Singer.

**HOOPER, PAULA J,** Univ Of Tn At Martin, Martin, TN; SR; Stdnt Tchr Ed Assn 88-; Chi Omega Career Dvlpmnt 87-; Stdnt Tchr; BS; Elem Ed; Spch/Lang Path.

**HOOPER, SANDRA A,** Univ Of Sc At Sumter, Sumter, SC; SO; Afro Amer Scty; Chrch Choir; Ralph Canty Cmpgn; CERT NJ Rl Est Lcnse 89; Fin; Cnsltnt.

**HOOPER-GULLEY, LE VONNE L,** Middle Tn St Univ, Murfreesboro, TN; SR; BS; Stdnt Home Ec Assn 88-; Kappa Delta Pi 88-; Tau Omicron 88-; Gamma Beta Phi 89-; Kappa Omicron Nu 88-; Early Chldhd Ed; Tchr.

**HOOS, DAVID M,** Tallahassee Comm Coll, Tallahassee, FL; SO; BA; State Certif Bldg Contr 85-; Math; Elect Engrg.

**HOOSER, TERESA J,** Kent St Univ Kent Cmps, Kent, OH; SR; BBA; TIMS 89-; Grad Cum Laude; IM Sccr 89; Opers Res; Bsms Mgmt/Conslt.

**HOOTEN, CHRIS A,** Univ Of Al At Birmingham, Birmingham, AL; SR; BS; Omicron Delta Epsilon 90-; Golden Key 89-; Rho Epsilon; Tau Kappa Epsilon 86-; Birmingham Assoc Rltrs Schlrshp; Prestl Hnr Rll 88-; Tau Kappa Epsilon Top Schlr Awd 90-; Cum Laude; Rqt Ball Club; Finance; Law.

**HOOVER, ANGELA E,** West Chester Univ, West Chester, PA; JR; BED; Msc Edctr Natl Conf Treas 88-; W Chstr Unv Choir Sec 89-; WCU Opera Theatre Ens; Sigma Alpha Iota Pres 89-; Msc Educ/Voice.

**HOOVER, ANNALEE,** Ashland Univ, Ashland, OH; FR; BS; Hope Flwshp 90-; Flwshp Chrstn Athletes 90-; Cmnty Care 90-; Hope Flwshp Gospel Tm 90-; Bio/Religion; Medicine.

**HOOVER, BRIAN W,** Saint Thomas Univ, Miami, FL; SO; Wghtrm Mgr 89-90; Omailia Schlrshp; Sccr Clb Mgr 89-; Psychlgy; Clncl Psychlgst Ph D.

**HOOVER, CARLA L,** Hillsborough Comm Coll, Tampa, FL; SR; AS; Nwspr Stfr Wrtr 90-; Beta Phi Gamma; Certf Erwin Voc Tech Tampa FL 90-; WVNCC New Martinsville WV 85; Offc Systms Tchnlgy.

**HOOVER, CHRISTOPHER S,** Univ Of Nc At Greensboro, Greensboro, NC; SR; BA; Jr Wrld Tm Rep Pwrlftng; Phy Ed Mjrs Assoc Brd 89; Hnrs Prog 89; Hnrs Scty Pres; Serv Org Mrshll 88-89; Outstndng Exrcse/Sprt Sci Mjr; Inquiry Hnr Jrnl Cnsltng Ed; Susan Stout Mem Awd 90; Exercise Sci; MBA.

**HOOVER, CHRISTY LEE,** Oh Univ, Athens, OH; FR; BA; Newman Cath Yth Grp 90-; Sprts Info 90-; Deans Lst; Telecmunctns; Sprts Acctg/Fin.

**HOOVER, LIZBETH C,** Univ Of Akron, Akron, OH; JR; BA; Stdnt Activities Cncl Rep 83-84; Akron Cncl Of Ed Stdnts 90; Golden Key 90; Deans Lst 90; Vol Worley Elem Schl 89; Acad Schlrshps 82-85; Math Tutor Assistntshp 82-85; Cmptr Opr/Prog 85-88; Elem Ed; Tchr.

**HOOVER, TAMARA D,** Univ Of Al At Birmingham, Birmingham, AL; JR; OD; Phi Eta Sigma; Lances Jr Honorary; Gldn Key Ntnl Hnry; Omega Epsilon Phi; Delta Gamma Fndtns Chair Pldg Class 88-89; Optometry.

**HOPE, BARBARA G,** Norfolk St Univ, Norfolk, VA; SR; BS; Alpha Kappa Mu 90; Educ; Tchg/Spec Educ.

**HOPE, KAREN S,** Bellarmine Coll, Louisville, KY; SR; BA; Pres Ldrshp Soc 87-; Acctg Clb 87-; Acctg.

**HOPE II, MARION C,** Univ Of Sc At Columbia, Columbia, SC; SR; BS; AICHE; Tau Beta Pi VP; Ghents Brnch Baptst Church 79-; Co-Op With Savannah Rvr Plnt In Aiken SC 88-; Chem Engr; Indstrl Chem Prodctn.

**HOPE, TONYA M,** Va St Univ, Petersburg, VA; SO; BS; Pep Club 90; Hnrs Clg 90; Bsn Infor Sys; Cmptr Anlyst.

**HOPKINS, AMY MARIE,** Radford Univ, Radford, VA; JR; BS; Stdnt Educ Assn 90-; Alpha Lambda Delta 88-; Kappa Delta Pi 90-; Phi Kappa Phi; Erly Mddle Chldhd Educ; Tchng.

**HOPKINS, ANGELIA M,** Bluefield St Coll, Bluefield, WV; SO; BA; Dns Lst; Acctng.**

**HOPKINS, ANNE M,** Mount Saint Mary Coll, Newburgh, NY; FR; BS; Spcl Olympcs; Ldrshp Dev; Crss Cntry Clb; Vlybl Tm; Nrsg; Orthpdc Nrs.

**HOPKINS, CHRISTINE S,** Bethany Coll, Bethany, WV; FR; Kappa Delta; Edctn; Elem Tchr.

**HOPKINS, DAVID M,** Middle Tn St Univ, Murfreesboro, TN; SO; BA; Music.

**HOPKINS, JANNA A,** Liberty Univ, Lynchburg, VA; SO; BA; Piano 77-; Pryr Ldr 90-; Alpha Lambda Delta 90; Lingstcs; Trnsltn Wrk.

**HOPKINS, PAUL R,** Ms St Univ, Miss State, MS; SR; BPA; Arnld Ar Scty 88-90; Bl Knghts 88-89; Prsdntl Schlr; Deans Schlr 87-90; IM Sprts; Acctg.

**HOPKINS, ROSIE L,** Univ Of Sc At Columbia, Columbia, SC; SR; Univ SC Hmcmng Cmmssn 86-88; Alpha Kappa Alpha Prlmntrn 89-; Alpha Phi Omega Sgt ArmBS; Blgy; Hlth Srvcs Admn.

**HOPKINS, TINA JOE,** Saint Josephs Coll, Windham, ME; FR; BED; Stdnt Tchng; Elem Ed; Tchr.

**HOPKINS, TRAVIS D,** Temple Univ, Philadelphia, PA; SO; BS; Alpha Lambda Delta 89; Mech Eng.

**HOPKINS, TRICIA L,** Northern Ky Univ, Highland Hts, KY; FR; Accntng; CPA.

**HOPKINSON, SALLY K,** Univ Of West Fl, Pensacola, FL; SR; BA; Prod Mgr Software Co; GA Coll Of St Thomas 87; Elem Edn; Teach.

**HOPP, PHILIP H,** Liberty Univ, Lynchburg, VA; BS; Lght Clb 88-; Yth Qst Clb 88-; Pre Med Hnr Scty 90-; Alpha Lambda Delta 88-; Blgy Pre Med; Gen Srgn.

**HOPPE, ANDREAS,** Coll Of Charleston, Charleston, SC; SO; BA; Catholic Campus Clb; Foreign Lang; Clg Prfssr.

**HOPPE, ERIC P,** Oh St Univ At Newark, Newark, OH; SO; Hnr Soc VP 90-; Ntl Grd Srgt 89-; IM Vlybl; IM Sftbl; Mechanical Engrng.

**HOPPE, LYNN S,** Atlantic Comm Coll, Mays Landing, NJ; SO; BA; Stdnt Chptr Htl Sls Mrktng Assoc 89-90; Mmrl Schlrshp 90; Deans Lst 89-; Hsptlty Mgmt Crs Certs 89-; AAS; Htl Mgmt Bus; Hmn Rsrcs Pblc Rltns.

**HOPPE, SUSAN K,** Bethany Coll, Bethany, WV; JR; BS; Amer Chem Socty Stdnt Affl Stdnt Bd Of Gov Rep 90-; Biology; Medicine.

**HOPPER, ANDREA B,** Ms Univ For Women, Columbus, MS; SR; BA; Alpha Delta Psi 85-86; Chorus 84-86; Presidential Schlr 84-86; Presidents Lst; Legal Secy Ofc Mngr 89-; Acctng/ Paralegal; CPA Law.

**HOPPER, CANDIS D,** Volunteer St Comm Coll, Gallatin, TN; FR; MBA; Intrnshp Zenda Inc Museum Rsrch/Cnsltng Firm Cnsltnt 89-; Amer Assn State/Local Hstry 89-; Amer Assn Museums 89-; Hstry; Museum Dir/Educator.

**HOPPER, CATHERINE L,** Tri County Tech Coll, Pendleton, SC; FR; BS; Asst Advisor 90-; Mathematics; Clg Ed.

**HOPPER, DANIEL L,** Columbus Coll Of Art & Design, Columbus, OH; FR; BFA; Illstrtn/Advrtsng.

**HOPPER, DAPHNE L,** Va Commonwealth Univ, Richmond, VA; SR; BM; Symphnc Wnd Ens 87-; Orch 89-90; Pi Kappa Lambda; Schlp Awd 89; Music/Flute Perf.

**HOPPER, DIANE S,** Bishop St Comm Coll, Mobile, AL; SO; AAS; Phi Theta Kappa; Offc Admin; Secretarial.

**HOPPER, EARL RUSSELL,** Mount Saint Mary Coll, Newburgh, NY; SO; BA; Math; Tchr.

**HOPPER, ELAINE A,** Nova Univ, Ft Lauderdale, FL; GD; Phi Beta Lambda Rprtr 84-85; Phi Beta Kappa 85-86; Delta Sigma Pi Treas 86-88; Sigma Psi Alpha 87-; Spec Hon USM; BA 88; MBA 91; Acctg/Bus; Acctg.

**HOPPER, MICHELLE M,** Valdosta St Coll, Valdosta, GA; SR; BA; Sigma Alpha Chi 89; Phi Alpha Delta Co Chr Mbrshp Comm; Persnnl Rep; AA 90; Pol Sci; Law/Publc Admn.

**HOPPER, RONALD,** Pasco Hernando Comm Coll, Dade City, FL; GD; BA; Karate 87; Phi Theta Kappa 90; AA; High Finance.**

**HOPPER, ROY W,** Univ Of Tn At Martin, Martin, TN; FR; BS; Bio; Frnc Archlgst.

**HOPPER, SHANNON L,** Blue Mountain Coll, Blue Mountain, MS; SO; Acctg.

**HOPPER-BARNETTE, MARY ALICE,** Univ Of Sc At Columbia, Columbia, SC; SR; BAIS; AA FL Jr Clg 80; Soclgy; Soc Work.

**HOPPING, BARBARA L,** Univ Of Cin R Walters Coll, Blue Ash, OH; FR; ASSO; Rdlgy Clb Pres 90-; Grl Scts Chrmn 88-; Rdlgy Tech; Tchng.

**HOPPS, JILL E,** Tn Temple Univ, Chattanooga, TN; SR; BS; Elem Ed; Tchr.

**HOPSON, DEREK D,** Univ Of Southern Ms, Hattiesburg, MS; JR; BSBA; Assoc Stdnt Body Dir Stdnt Rltns 90-; Univ Div Rcrtnl Sprts Pblc Rltns Coord 90-; Stdnts Prmtng Ed/Empwrng Dvrsty 90-; Phi Chi Theta Beta Alpha Chptr 90-; Phi Eta Sigma 89-90; Alpha Lambda Delta 89-90; Gamma Beta Phi 89-90; Bus; Acctg/Law.

**HOPSON, MONICA A,** Norfolk St Univ, Norfolk, VA; SO; BA; SGA Asst Treas 89-90; Lershp Prog 89-; Spartan Alpha Tau 89-; Bus Mgmt/Info Sys; Sys Anlyst/Data Entry.

**HOPTON, ALISON C,** Savannah Coll Of Art & Design, Savannah, GA; GD; MFA; Grad Intr Dsgn Soc Pres 89-; Intl Soc Intr Dsgnrs Treas 89-; Pres Cncl 90-; Chi Omega Almna Assn; BA Belhvn Coll 82; Intr Dsgn.

**HOPWOOD, TRACY L,** Marshall University, Huntington, WV; SR; BBA; Im 87; Hall Advsry Cncl 88; Alpha Kappa Psi 90; Mngmnt; Hotel Mngmnt.

**HOR, IVAN K C,** Oh Univ, Athens, OH; JR; BS; Gldn Key; Tau Beta Pi 90-; Eta Kappa Nu 90-; Elect/Comp Eng; Eng.

**HORACE, L TONYA RHNEA,** Fl A & M Univ, Tallahassee, FL; FR; PHARM; Pharm.

**HORAJ, MARY A,** Strayer Coll, Washington, DC; SR; BS; Alpha Chi 90-; MADD 90-; Ntnl Audubon Soc 90-; AS Cerro Coso Cmmnty Clg Rdgcrst CA 88; Bsns Mgmnt.

**HORAN, SHANNON E,** Cornell Univ Statutory College, Ithaca, NY; JR; BS; Marine Bio.

**HORAN, STACY L,** Trenton St Coll, Trenton, NJ; FR; BA; Engl Club 90-; Engl/Scndry Educ; Tchr.

**HORAN, THOMAS MICHAEL,** Anne Arundel Comm Coll, Arnold, MD; AA; AF/AM Md Ldg 120 85-; Deans Lst 90; PK 707 Cub Scts PWD Comm 90; Cape St Clarie Lacross Prnt Asst; Lcmtv Engnr 76-; Cert CSXT Engnrs SC; Cert USAF Weapons Tech SC 69; Comm Arts Tech; Tv.

**HORATSCHKI, STEPHANIE I,** Kent St Univ Kent Cmps, Kent, OH; JR; BA; Acctg Assc 89-90; Golden Key 90-; Acctg.**

**HORD, AMY M,** Fl St Univ, Tallahassee, FL; JR; BA; Interhse Hon Coun; Choral Union 89-90; Intnl Affr; Intnl Law.

**HORD, MICHELLE D,** Howard Univ, Washington, DC; SR; BA; Mrchng Bnd Sctn Ldr 87-; Pep Bnd Sctn Ldr 88-90; Nwspr 88-90; Scty Prfsnl Jrnlsts 90-; Natl Assoc Blck Jrnlsts 90-; Alpha Kappa Alpha 90-; ABC Capital Cts Mnrty Trng Flw Hnr; NAACP Nws Tms Jrnlsm Schlrshp 87-89; Brdcst Jrnlsm/Eng; TV Jrnlsim/Prdctn.

**HORD, TINA R,** Roane St Comm Coll, Harriman, TN; FR; Biology; Radiology.

**HORD-MILLER, KAREN S,** Oh St Univ At Marion, Marion, OH; SR; Educ Soc 90-; Beta Sigma Phi Pres 79-83; Jr Serv Gld Brd 83-; Jaycees; Comm Thtr Grp Sec; BED.

**HORDATT, TABITHA T,** Fl International Univ, Miami, FL; JR; BS; Intl Clb; Dns Lst 88-; AS Peirce Jr Clg 88-90; Hosp Mgmt; Caterer/Hotel Mgr.

**HORDE, KRISTINA DANNELLE,** Univ Of Tn At Martin, Martin, TN; SR; BS; Psychology; Clncl Psychlgy.

**HORDESKY, MARY ANN M,** Marywood Coll, Scranton, PA; SO; BS; Dttcs; Prvte Prctce.

**HORDINES, HELENE M,** Ny Univ, New York, NY; FR; BA; Bio/Math; Optmtry.

**HORELICK, JULIE L,** Univ Of Rochester, Rochester, NY; JR; BA; Ecnmcs Cncl 88-; Twrs Dorm Cncl 90-; Hillel 88-; Deans List 88-; Sigma Delta Tau Exec VP 88-; Amer Cncr Soc Vol 89-; Mltpl Sclrs Soc 88-; Rgnts Schlrshp 88; Merrill Lynch Intrnshp 90-; Finance; Cnsltng.

**HORETH, NANCY E,** Niagara Univ, Niagara Univ, NY; JR; BA; Tactics ROTC Pres 89-; Advsry Cmtee 90-; Rangers 89-90; Delta Epsilon Sigma; Scabbard Blade 90-; Supr Cadet Awd 90; ROTC Schlrshp 89-; Rugby; Cmptr Sci; Army Active Duty.

**HORGAN, MARY A,** Rivier Coll, Nashua, NH; JR; BS; Projct HUG Buddy Progrm 89-; Commuter Comm 88-; Bus; Info Mgt.

**HORGER, JONATHAN T,** Univ Of Nh Plymouth St Coll, Plymouth, NH; FR; BS; Dorm Cmmttee 90; Im Soccer 90; Phy Ed Exrcse Sci; Sprts Med.

**HORMELL, PATRICIA A N,** Univ Of Nh Plymouth St Coll, Plymouth, NH; JR; BS; Girl Scouts Troop Ldr 87; Ashland Aftrschl Ctr Vol 87; Sndy Schl Tchr 87-; Elem Educ; Tchr.

**HORN, ARTEMUS A,** Stillman Coll, Tuscaloosa, AL; SR; Masonic Ldg 88-; US Army Transportation Corps 2nd Lieut 90-; IM Bskbl; Busn/Mktng.

**HORN, BOBBI J,** Oh Univ-Southern Cmps, Ironton, OH; GD; Stdnt Gvrnmnt 86-90 VP 89-90; OH HS Athltc Assn 86-89; Deans Lst; YMCA Crtfd Arbc Instrctr; Prncpl Awrd 90; Sttng Up Kids Sccs 90; Certf Mrt 90; Trck Evnts Sftbl Coach 90; Tchr Expctatns Stdnt Adhvmnt 90; Elem Tchr; 90-; Elem Edctn Englsh; Elem Cllg Cnslr.

**HORN, BONNIE S,** Univ Of Tn At Knoxville, Knoxville, TN; SO; BA; Am Mktg Assn Com Liason; Rec Com 90-; Snow Ski Clb 90-; Gamma Beta Psi; Alpha Kappa Psi Com Mktg/Soc 90-; Mktg/Advrtsng/Spanish; Intl Bus.

**HORN, CARLA A,** Marshall University, Huntington, WV; GD; MBA; Concord Clg Acctng Clb Cmte Chrmn 87-90; Cardinal Key 89-90; Gamma Beta Phi 88-90; Grad Asst/Marshall Univ Admin Dir Of MBA Pgms 90-; Outstndng Acctng Stdnt 90; Amer Red Cross Vol 84-; Amer Baptist Women Treas 79-; BS Concord Clg 90; Bus Admin; CPA.

**HORN, CHRISTOPHER D,** William Paterson Coll, Wayne, NJ; JR; BS; Math Club; Applied Math; Comp/Rsrch.

**HORN, JENNIFER L,** Rutgers St Un At New Brunswick, New Brunswick, NJ; FR; BS/BA; Ltrary Mag; Hll Govt; Phi Eta Sigma; Cir K; Comm Outr Ch Big Bddy Prgrm; Rtgrs Pres Schlr; Ed Bloustein Schlr; Bio/Psych; Psych.

**HORN, JULIA P,** Western Ky Univ, Bowling Green, KY; SR; BS; Phi Kappa Phi; AAS E Town Comm Coll 86; Spch Lngge Pthlgy.

**HORN, SHELIA D,** Al A & M Univ, Normal, AL; JR; BA; Mrchng Cncrt Bnd 88-; SGA Sec 90; Tau Beta Sigma Sec 90-; Dns Lst; Hnr Rll 88-; NAACP SCLS Rd Crss 87-; Srvce Cntr Cnslr 89-; Engl; Law.

**HORN, TINA L,** Bridgewater Coll, Bridgewater, VA; SO; Yrbk Stf 90-; Stdnt Athletic Trnr 90-; Hlth Sci.

**HORNBACH, JAMES T,** Univ Of Cin R Walters Coll, Blue Ash, OH; SO; Mc Micken Hnrs; Acctg.

**HORNBERGER, RITA L,** Glassboro St Coll, Glassboro, NJ; SR; BA; Stdnt Math Assn Pblc Rltns Chrprsn 90-; Math Scndry Edctn; HS Math Tchr.

**HORNBUCKLE, SCOTT D,** Morehouse Coll, Atlanta, GA; SR; MBA; Golden Key; Morehouse Bus Assn 89-; Morehouse Mentroing Pgm 90-; Deans Lst; Persnl Mngmnt Of GA Schlrshp; Jr Clg Bsktbl 87-88; BA; Mngmnt Info Syst.

**HORNE, AMANDA J,** Middle Ga Coll, Cochran, GA; FR; AA; Gamma Beta Phi; Deans Lst; GAP Awd; Psych; Yth Mnstry.

**HORNE, ELIZABETH R,** Mary Baldwin Coll, Staunton, VA; SO; BA; ACTS 89-; Yrbk 90-; Chr 89-; Alpha Lambda Delta; Hnrs Schlrs 89-; Hillhouse Schlr 90-; Marshal; Bailey Schlr 89-; Englsh.

**HORNE, ELLIOT M,** Fl A & M Univ, Tallahassee, FL; SO; BS; Phi Eta Sigma 89-; Cir Kapers 90-; Intrnshp Chevron USA Concord CA; IM Ftbl 90-; Acctg; Sole Prprtr.

**HORNE, FRANCES LANORA,** Tougaloo Coll, Tougaloo, MS; JR; BA; Stdnt Spprt Serv; Wadkazi; Psychlgy; Clncl Psychlgst.

**HORNE, GREGORY S,** Oh St Univ At Newark, Newark, OH; SO; BA; Chem Engr.

**HORNE, KEVIN C,** Univ Of Al At Birmingham, Birmingham, AL; SR; BS; Omega Chi 76-78; Sowers Club 76-78; Preacher Ch Of Christ 80-84; AA Fl Coll 80; Psych; Prosthetist.

**HORNE, KYLE D,** Univ Of Sc At Aiken, Aiken, SC; JR; BS; Outstndng Chem Awrd 89-90; Rich M Wallc Mem Schlrshp; Chem.

**HORNE, LINDA M,** Memphis St Univ, Memphis, TN; BSN; BA MSU Mphs Tn 71; MSSW U T Knoxville Tn 80; Nrsng; RN.

**HORNE, MICHELLE L,** Univ Of Nc At Charlotte, Charlotte, NC; FR; BA; Stdnt Govt Hall Cncl Rep 90-; Orientation Cnslr SOAR; IM Vlybl 90-; Clncl Psych/Soc Work.

**HORNE, ONEKA S,** City Univ Of Ny City Coll, New York, NY; SO; MARCH; Island Schlr St Vincent 89; Outstndng Scnd Yr Stdnt Arch; Netball 82-86; Architechture/Env Studies.

**HORNE, TERRI WALL,** Univ Of Sc At Columbia, Columbia, SC; SR; BA; Ed Mjrs Clb 90-; Gamma Beta Phi 88-; Erly Chldhd Ed.

**HORNER, GREGORY W,** Old Dominion Univ, Norfolk, VA; JR; BS; ASME 88-89; Ntnl Soc Prfsnl Engnrs; Mchncl Engnrng.

**HORNER, HOLLY A,** Beaver Coll, Glenside, PA; Phi Delta Kappa 90-; Alpha Xi Delta 80-; NEA/PSEA 86-; Montgomery Cty Sch Nurs Assn 86-; Natl Assoc Sch Nurs 86-; BSN BS 77-81; MA Educ; Sch Nurs/Pub Sch.

**HORNER, KAREN Y,** Univ Of Nc At Greensboro, Greensboro, NC; JR; BSN; Golden Chain 90-; Schlr 90-; Nrsg.

**HORNER, MICHELLE L,** Indiana Univ Of Pa, Indiana, PA; SR; BED; Pa St Edn Assoc V P 89-; Eng Club 88-; Sigma Tau Delta Pres 89-; Sigma Delta Pi 90-; Kappa Delta Pi 90-; Alpha Sigma Alpha Stndrds Chm 87-; Arin Adult Ltrcy Tutor 89; Paraprof Peer Tutor Staff 88-90; ARA Schlrsph 88; Mc Farland Schlrshp 88; Provost; Spanish/Eng Edn; Educator.

**HORNER, ROBIN M,** Birmingham Southern Coll, Birmingham, AL; JR; Vol Serv/Tutoring 89; Kappa Delta Epsilon VP 90-; Alpha Omicron Pi Asst Treas/Soc Chair; Lttle Sister Rose Awd; Educ Elem; Teach.

**HORNER, TONYA L,** Cumberland Coll, Williamsburg, KY; SR; BS; Amer Chem Scty 88-; Envir Awrnss Com 90-; House Cncl VP 90; Acad All Amer Schlr 90-; Envir Awrnss Com 90-; Love In Actn 89-; Mntn Otrch 90; Cumberland Coll Acad Schlrshp 89-; George I Aldan Schlrshp 89-; Chem; Eng.

**HORNICKEL, DANIEL P,** The Kings Coll, Briarclf Mnr, NY; FR; Stdnt Nwspaper Wrtr 90-; Hist; Law.

**HORNING, PHIL L,** Slippery Rock Univ, Slippery Rock, PA; SO; BED; Phys Ed Mjrs Club 90-; Ftbl 89-; Track 90-; Phys Ed; Tchr.

**HORNKOHL, JOLA,** Middle Tn St Univ, Murfreesboro, TN; SR; BS; Deans Lst 89-90; Hnr Rll 90-; Rsdnt Asst; Chrldr Mtlw St Cmmnty Coll 88-89; AS 89; Crmnl Jstc Admn.

**HORNSBY, LARRY R,** Cumberland Coll, Williamsburg, KY; JR; BS; Phi Alpah Theta Hstrn 89-; Sigma Tau Delta 90-; IM Bsktbl 89; Poli Sci; Law.

**HORNUNG, TONILYN,** The Boston Conservatory, Boston, MA; FR; BFA; Sngr Actr Dncr; Nrthwstrn Univ 89; Asst Dir St Cclia Acad Nshvlle TN 89; Frnscs Awrd 90; Mscl Thtre; Actrss.

**HORNYAK, DEBRA A,** Univ Of Pittsburgh, Pittsburgh, PA; GD; MSN; Stf Nrs Comm Chldrns Hosp Pgh Chrprsn 90-; Emer Dept Oper Comm Chldrns Hosp Pgh 88-; Nrs Rtn/Rcrmnt Comm 87-88; Sigma Theta Tau Inc 90-; Prcptr Nw Nrs 87-; Med Vol Pgh Mrthn 87-89; Instr Bcycl Sfty Bndm Ped Trauma Pro; CEN Status 87-; Nrsg.

**HORNYAK, ROBERT D,** Comm Coll Algny Co Algny Cmps, Pittsburgh, PA; SR; ASSOC; U Pitsbrgh Ski Clb Pres 88-90; Sigma Alpha Epsilon U Pgh Chr 88-; Avtn; BA Cmrcl Arln Pilot.

**HOROSCHAK, SIGRID,** Univ Of Rochester, Rochester, NY; JR; BS; Chrldr Ftbl Bkbl 89-90; Dandelion Orgztn 89-90; Soc Phys Stdnts 88-; Natl Audobon Soc 88-; Wrld Wildlfe Orgztn 88-; Rsrch Prog High Energy Phys; Phys/Astronomyf Astrophysics.

**HOROSZEWSKI, ROBERT W,** S U N Y Coll Of Tech At Frmgdl, Farmingdale, NY; SO; BA; Aaeronautics/Mngmnt; Pilot.

**HOROTN, JACQUELYN M,** Univ Of Tn At Martin, Martin, TN; SR; BSSW; Blck Stdnt Assoc; Dnc Schlrshp Rcpnt 88-89; Soc Wrk Clb 90-; Dns Lst 88-89; Ltl Str VP 87-88; Vol Wrkr 89-90; Porter Leath Chldrn Ctr Intrnshp; Memphis Vol Yth Cnslng Vol 88-89; Goodwill Hms Grp Ldr 90; BSSW; Soc Wrk; Cnslr.

**HOROVCHAK, DEBRA A,** Comm Coll Algny Co Algny Cmps, Pittsburgh, PA.

**HOROWITZ, ABRAHAM P,** Univ Of Miami, Coral Gables, FL; JR; BBA; Stdnt Govt Cabinet 88-89; Alpha Epsilon Pi Pres 90-; Finance; Law Invstmnt Bnkng.

**HORCWITZ, LISA A,** Yeshiva Univ, New York, NY; SR; SG Pres 88-; Class Pres; Secy; Psychology Clb VP 89-90; Deans Lst 87-; Remes Awrd; IM Bsktbl 88-89; BA; Psychology; Social Work Admin.

**HORRIED, RHONDA M,** Bennett Coll, Greensboro, NC; JR; BA; Maryland Stdnt Lgsltv Vice Chrprsn 89-90; NCCC Bd 88-; NBMCR Bd 86-89; Literacy Corps 90-; NBCDI Tutor 90-; Marshal Bd 90-; Bureau Of Afrcn Affrs Intrn; Wash Cntr Intrn; NAACP Essay Awd; Pol Sci; Theologian/Tchng/Missions.

**HORST, JAMES N,** Fl International Univ, Miami, FL; JR; BA; Pre Med Assc 90-; Psi Chi 91-; Phi Lambda 90-; Sgm Phi Epsln 89-; Ftbl/Bsktbl 89-; Masonic Lodge 308 91-; Psychology Pre Med; Medcn.

**HORSTMAN, KEVIN D,** Defiance Coll, Defiance, OH; FR; Sch Nwspaper Colmnst; Schlr Athlt; Track/Cross Cntry Ltr Winner; Math Ed; Tchr.

**HORSTMYER, JAMES J,** Neumann Coll, Aston, PA; JR; BA; Stdnt Nrs Assoc 90-; Male Nrsg Stdnts Clb 90-; Delta Epsilon Sigma; Curr Comm Nrsg 90-; Acad Grant; W W Smith Trust Awd; Nrsg.

**HORTIS, GREG EMMANUEL,** Univ Of Sc At Spartanburg, Spartanburg, SC; SR; BA; Psychlgy; Prsnnl Mgmt.

**HORTON, A LOUANNE,** Univ Of Sc At Lancaster, Lancaster, SC; FR; BA; Bptst Un 90-; Deans Lst 90-; Bus Admn; Mrktng Rl Est.

**HORTON, ANTHONY A,** Kent St Univ Kent Cmps, Kent, OH; JR; BS; Cmptr Clb; Gold Key; Pres Lst; Deans Lst; IM Flag Ftbl 1st Pl 87-; AS Kent State Stark; Cmptr Sci; Pgmmng.

**HORTON, BARBARA G,** Catawba Valley Comm Coll, Hickory, NC; FR; AS; BED Wstrn Carolina Univ 70; Furniture Dsgn/Dvlpmnt.

**HORTON, CATINA A,** Nc Agri & Tech St Univ, Greensboro, NC; FR; Elem Edct; Tchr.

**HORTON, CHERYL J,** Itawamba Comm Coll, Fulton, MS; SO; MPA; Phi Beta Lamda 89-; Stdnt/Free Enterprise Sec 90-; Yrbk Staff 89-; Phi Beta Kappa 90-; Pres List 89; Deans List 90; AA; Acctng; Corp Acctng.

**HORTON, DARLENE P,** Central St Univ, Wilberforce, OH; SR; BS; RN 81; AAS Ohio Univ 81; Cmnty Hlth; Nrsg.

**HORTON JR, ERWIN A,** Middle Tn St Univ, Murfreesboro, TN; JR; BA; Retired US Army 90; Hstry; Wrtr.

**HORTON, JEFFREY S,** Memphis St Univ, Memphis, TN; SO; BS; Cmptr Engr; Priv Entrprs.

**HORTON, KARI M,** Thomas Nelson Comm Coll, Hampton, VA; SO; AAS; Sailng Clb; Intrnsp James City Cnty Hmn Svcs Case Wrkr; US Army 81-86; Prsnl Mgmt Spec; Hmn Svcs/Scl Wrk; Case Mgr.

**HORTON, KEMPTON D,** Alcorn St Univ, Lorman, MS; SR; Animal Science Clb Reporter 87-88; FFA Treas 88-89; Alpha Tau Alpha Chaplin 88-89; IM Ftbl 86-87; Animal Sci; Soil Conservationist.

**HORTON, MICHAEL KEITH,** Tallahassee Comm Coll, Tallahassee, FL; SO; BS; Scnc/Medical; Hlth Care Spc.

**HORTON, MICHELLE D,** Univ Of Southern Ms, Hattiesburg, MS; GD; Lambda Pi Eta 89-; Sigma Delta Chi 89-; BA 90; Jrnlsm; Poetry Wrtr.

**HORTON, PATTY,** Columbia Coll, Columbia, SC; SO; BA; Dnce Co 89-; Dnce; Perf/Tchr.**

**HORTON, RAYMOND C G,** Univ Of Sc At Columbia, Columbia, SC; SO; BS; Stdnt Orient Ldr 90-; ROTC Color Guard Ldr 89-; Natl Stdnt Exch Rcpnt Univ MN 90-; Bio/Pre Med; Med.

**HORTON, RENNETTA SHIN A,** Wilberforce Univ, Wilberforce, OH; FR; BA; Acctg; CPA.

**HORTON, SANDRA J,** Syracuse Univ, Syracuse, NY; FR; BA; SOS 90-; Yth To Yth 86; NSNA 90-; Adult Vol Irving Mem Hosp 90-; Eastgreenwich Tsk Frc 89; Nurs.

**HORTON, SHAWN C,** Pellissippi St Tech Comm Coll, Knoxville, TN; FR; AS; Sciences; Engineering.

**HORTON, STORMY HEATHER,** Lasell Coll, Newton, MA; JR; BS; Res Assist 89-; Edtr/Chf Yrbk 89-; Sing Grp; Deans Lst 89-; Walt Disney Wrld Intrnshp; AS 90; Hotel Admin.

**HORTON, TELESHIA L,** Univ Of Ga, Athens, GA; SR; BSED; Girl Sct Ldr 90-; Athens Tutorial Prog Tutor 90; Res Hall Assn 88-89; Phi Beta Lambda 90-; Delta Sigma Theta Sec 89-90; Deans Lst 90; Delta Sigma Theta 90; Bus Educ; Tchr.

**HORTON JR, WILLIAM R,** S U N Y Coll Of Tech At Alfred, Alfred, NY; FR; AAS; Vet VIP Clb; Alfred Air Cndtng Clb; Co Rec Vlybl; Army 4 Yrs; Crpntr 2 Yrs; Mech Eng.

**HORVAT, KERI LYNDA,** Univ Of Miami, Coral Gables, FL; JR; BS; Offc Mngr/Legal Sec; Cmmnctns/Sclgy; Law.

**HORVATH, ANDREW R,** Cornell Univ, Ithaca, NY; FR; BA; Young Life 90-; Campus Crusade For Christ 90-; Vlybl Coach 90.

**HORVATH, ANNE T,** Univ Of Cincinnati, Cincinnati, OH; SO; BM; Music/Violin Perf; Violinist.

**HORVATH, BRIAN J,** Cornell Univ Statutory College, Ithaca, NY; FR; BS; Greens Clb 90-; Dean Lst 90-; Nuerobiol; Med.

**HORVATH, CHRISTINE L,** Boston Univ, Boston, MA; SR; MA; Stdnt Cncl Exec Brd Treas 89-; Occptnl Thrpy Clb Edtr/Pblcty 88-; Peer Cnslr/Big Sis 90-; Mortar Brd Hon Soc Treas 90-; Pi Theta Epsilon Treas 89-; Goldn Key 89-; Harold C Case Schlr 90; Hon Aux 90-; Grad Summa Cum Laude; Occptnl Thrpy; Pdtrc/Neontl Occptnl Thrpy.

**HORVATH, KENDRA J,** Univ Of Akron, Akron, OH; SO; BA; NSSLHA 90-; Phi Eta Sigma 90-; Alpha Lambda Delta 90-; Commctv Disorders; Speech Path.

**HORVATH, STAR M,** Salisbury St Univ, Salisbury, MD; SO; BA; Educ Assn 90; IM Sftbl 90; Vlybl 90; Elem Educ; Tchng.

**HORWATT, JOANNE M,** Duquesne Univ, Pittsburgh, PA; JR; BS; Omicron Delta Kappa 90-; Lambda Sigma 89; Phi Eta Sigma 88; Res Asst 90-; Intrn Revco Drug Co 90-; Rho Chi 90 Achvmnt Awrd; Atlntc 10 Acdmc All Conf Tm 89; Vlybl Tm 88-89; Phrmcy.

**HORWATT, KAREN L,** Duquesne Univ, Pittsburgh, PA; FR; BS; Phi Eta Sigma 90-; Lambda Sigma; Fndrs Awrd 90-; Schlrs Educ Awrd 90-; Crew 90; Math; Tchg.

**HORWEDEL, LON T,** Oh Univ, Athens, OH; SR; BFA; Stdnt Newpapr Phtgrphr 85-90; Trathln Fdrtn USA 90-; Biddefrd Jrnl-Trbne Intrn 85-; Cedar Pt Mktg Dept Intrn 86-88; Muskegon Chrncle 88-89; Colmbus Dsptch 89; Vsual Cmnctn; Phtjrnlst.

**HORWITZ, REBECCA A,** Fl International Univ, Miami, FL; GD; MPA; Sociology Anthropology Scty Jrnl Edtr 90-; Intrnshp City Lauderdale; Awrd Of Excellence In Fld; Top Crmnl Justice Stdnt 88; BA 90; Public Admin; Research Dvlp Prog.

**HOSACK, SUZANNE,** Lexington Comm Coll, Lexington, KY; FR; MBA; Upjohn Hlth Care Serv; Medcl; Physical Therapy.

**HOSIE, CHRISTINE M,** Comm Coll Algny Co Algny Cmps, Pittsburgh, PA; SO; AS; Criminal Justice Club Secty 90-; Phi Theta Kappa 89-; Correc Adminf Opng Grouphome Jurl Delinuents.

**HOSKINS, DANIEL NATE,** Univ Of Central Fl, Orlando, FL; SR; BA; Phi Kappa Phi; IFC Pnhlnc Awd Outstdng Schlr 89-90; Pi Sigma Alpha 90; Pi Kappa Alpha Chrmn 89-90; Pres Hnr Rl 89; Dns Lst 87-; Asst Coach 90-; Ftbl 87-; Bsn Law; Law.**

**HOSKINS, DIONNE LYNETTE,** Savannah St Coll, Savannah, GA; JR; BS; Chrldr Capt 88-; Nwspr Copy Edtr 90-; Mar Bio Clb Fndr 90; Delta Sigma Theta Pr 90-; Intrn Vir Inst Mar Sci 89-90; Walmrt Schlr 88; Porter Schlr 88-90; MARC Schlr 90-; Mar Bio; Res Scintst.

**HOSKINS, LISA R,** Hampton Univ, Hampton, VA; FR; BA; Bus; Acctg.

**HOSKINS, MELISSA S,** Union Coll, Barbourville, KY; JR; Sociology/Psychology; Soc Wrk.

**HOSKINS, NATISHA L,** Bennett Coll, Greensboro, NC; JR; SGA Tres; Stdnt Un Brd VP; Fd Srvc Comm Chrprsn; Alpha Kappa Alpha Tres; All Amrcn Schlr; Accntng; CPA.

**HOSMER, DAVID P,** D Youville Coll, Buffalo, NY; JR; BS; Ntnl Assc Accnts 90-; Clg Assc Accntnts Secy 90-; Bsn Clb 88-; Phlsphy Clb; John T Kennedy Memrl Awrd Winner 90-; Cert Acdmc Achvmnt 88-90; Deans List 89-90; Acctng.

**HOSNI, HOSNI,** Univ Of Med & Dentistry Of Nj, Newark, NJ; Veterinarian; BVSC U Of Vet Med Egypt 75.

**HOSSAIN, ANTASHA,** Edinboro Univ Of Pa, Edinboro, PA; SO; BSSB; Intl Stdnts Assoc 89-; Phi Eta Sigma; Beta Beta Beta; IM Bowling Champ 89; IM Vlybl 90; Bio/Math; Med.

**HOSTETLER, ALICIA A,** Converse Coll, Spartanburg, SC; JR; BM; Stdnt Fclty Rep 88-; Delta Omicron; Cncrt Cntst 90; Dnl Msc Schlrshp 88-; Music.

**HOTALING, SCOTT C,** Mohawk Valley Comm Coll, Utica, NY; FR; Vrsty Crss Cntry; Indr Otdr Trck 90-; Crmnl Jstc; Law.

**HOTARD, ALAN M,** Ms St Univ, Miss State, MS; SO; BPA; Lambda Sigma 90-; Gamma Beta Phi 90-; Phi Eta Sigma 90-; Catholic Stdnt Assoc Exec Cncl 89-; Hnrs Council Treas 90-; Outstanding Hnrs 90-; Pres List 89-90; Deans List; Acctg; CPA.

**HOTCHKIN-HEINLE, BARBARA A,** Univ Of Med & Dentistry Of Nj, Newark, NJ; GD; MPT; Orthpdcs Intrn; Chrldng 83-86; APTA; Ped; Phys Thrpy Aide 87-; BA NC St Univ 87; BS NC St Univ 87; Phys Thrpy.

**HOTELING, ANGELA LYNN,** S U N Y At Buffalo, Buffalo, NY; GD; JD; Prsnrs Logal Srvcs 90-; Stdnt Bar Assoc 90-; Assoc Wom Law Stdnts 90-; Phi Alpha Delta 89-; NY St Bar Assoc 90-; Law Schl Stdnt Brdgt Offc Offc Asst 90-; BS Niagara Univ 90; Law/Local/State Govt; Lawyr.

**HOTT, HOPE M,** George Mason Univ, Fairfax, VA; SR; BSW; Stdnt Scl Wrk Assos Secr 89-; Amer Mktg Assoc Adm; Candy Stripper 83-85; Yth Grp Ldr Bull Run Assembly God 87-88; LPN Monroe Vo-Tech 85-86; Assoc Sci NOVA 86-89; Scl Wrk; Fmly Ther-Clncl Cnslr.

**HOTT, REBEKAH E,** Wv Univ, Morgantown, WV; SR; BA; Kappa Psi; AASP; Rho Chi; Helvetia; Amer Inst Hstry Phrmcy Awd; Phrmcy.

**HOTTENROTT, DANIELLE M,** Barry Univ, Miami, FL; SR; BS; Stdnts Explrtn/Dvlpmnt Spc 85-; Assn Coll Engrprnrs 90-; Soc Advncmnt Mgmt Sec 87-88; Delta Mu Delta 90-; Vldctrn 87; DECA Achiev Awd 85-87; U Pres Lst 90-; Trade Cert Distr Ed Sthestrn Reg 87; Mgmt; Bus.

**HOU, YIWEI,** City Univ Of Ny City Coll, New York, NY; SR; PHD; Cty Clg NY Almn Assoc; Tau Beta Pi 90-; Eta Kappa Nu; Golden Key 90-; IEEE 90-; Dns Lst 88-; Stanley Katz Mem Awd 90; Heymann Awd; Engrng Almn Awd; Cty Clge Flwshps 88-; Schlrshps 89-; BE EE; Elctrcl Engrg; Eng.**

**HOUCHENS, MICHAEL E,** Western Ky Univ, Bowling Green, KY; SO; BS; Phi Eta Sigma 89-90; Geogrphy; Meteorlgy.

**HOUCK, HEATHER L,** Univ Of Southern Ms, Hattiesburg, MS; JR; BA; Stdnt Alumni Assn 90-; Elem Educ; Tchr.

**HOUCK, TODD E,** Wv Univ, Morgantown, WV; SO; Mech Eng.

**HOUGASIAN, ELIZABETH M,** Newbury Coll, Brookline, MA; Acctg.

**HOUGH, AMY D,** Univ Of Ga, Athens, GA; SR; Kappa Delta Pi 90-; Erly Chldhd Ed; Teaching.

**HOUGH, BRIAN A,** Christopher Newport Coll, Newport News, VA; FR; BA; Mgr 87-; Econ/Fin; Bkng/Bus.

**HOUGH, STACY L,** Commonwealth Coll, Virginia Beach, VA; SO; Acctg.

**HOUGH, SUSANNE L,** The Kings Coll, Briarclf Mnr, NY; SR; BS; Stdnt Govt Assn Soc Coord; Future Chrstn Edctrs Assn Pres 87-; Coll Concert Chr 88-; Elem Edn; Teach.

**HOUGHTON, KATHARINE A,** Western New England Coll, Springfield, MA; JR; BA; Outing Clb; Com Prgrmng/Entrtnmnt 88-90; Helping Hand Scty 90-; Intern Wistiarhurst Museum 90; History; Professor.

**HOUGHTON, RICHARD D,** Me Maritime Academy, Castine, ME; JR; BS; Prpllr Clb 89; Cadet Shppng Awd 90; Outstndng Sr Dck Cdt; Slng Intrn 90; Slng Tm 88-89; Marine Trnsprtn/Mngmnt; Mrchnt Marine.

**HOUK, WOODY G,** Catawba Valley Comm Coll, Hickory, NC; FR; ASSOC; Gamma Beta Phi VP; Apprntc For The Timken Co; Mech Engr.

**HOULE, JEFFREY J,** Hudson Valley Comm Coll, Troy, NY; FR; Ski Club 89-90; Tech Awd 88-90; Track 87; Rfrgtn Htng & A/C Mechanics; Tech/Engrng.

**HOULIHAN, KEVIN G,** Manhattan Coll, Bronx, NY; SR; BS; Amer Soc Mech Engrs 88-; IM Bsktbl Sftbl 86-; Mech Engr; Manuf Engr.

**HOUMERE, CYNTHIA R,** Newbury Coll, Brookline, MA; Armenian Assn; Empl Cred Un Brd Dir 90-; Acctnt; BBA Univ Mass Amhrst Ma 83.

**HOUPE, JEANNE D,** Lenoir Rhyne Coll, Hickory, NC; JR; Pol Sci Cl 88-; Literary Soc 88-90; SG Vice Deleg Chpsn 89-; Pi Sigma Alpha Pres 89-; SPJ; Delta Zeta V P 89-; Orntn; Ldrshp Prog 89-90; Lineberger Schlrshp; Nwspr Ed-Chf 88-; Dan Green/Congress Fld Coord/3 Coun 90; Pol Sci; Jrnlsm.

**HOURI, NICOLE M,** Ny Law School, New York, NY; GD; JD; Law Jrnl Editor 89-; Judge Jane Solomon Intern 90; BA Bryn Mawr Clg 86; Econ; Law.

**HOUSE, AMY E,** Sue Bennett Coll, London, KY; FR; BA; Acctng.

**HOUSE, KATHLEEN B,** Ms St Univ, Miss State, MS; SR; BS; Coll Rep 87; Rfrmd Univ Fllwshp 87-; Kappa Alpha Sthrn Blls Chpln 88-; Phi Meta Sigma 87-; Lambda Sigma 87-; Gamma Beta Phi 87-; Alph Aepsion Delta 90-; Chi Omega Chpln 87-; Prsdnt Lst 90; Gen Sci.

**HOUSE, KATHRYN L,** Ms St Univ, Miss State, MS; SR; Coll Rpblcns; Kappa Pi; Gamma Beta Phi; Lambda Sigma; Chi Omega; Intrnshp Dx Dlx Grphcs.

**HOUSE, KERRY C,** Univ Of Sc At Columbia, Columbia, SC; SR; BA; GAMA 87-89; Stdnts Agnst Vlnc 87-89; Stdnts Alld A Grnr Earth 88-90; Delta Delta Delta Trdnt Corrspdnt 87-; Media Arts; Phtgrphy.

**HOUSE, MARY D,** Univ Of Sc At Columbia, Columbia, SC; SO; BS; Phi Eta Sigma 89-; Pres Hnr Roll 89-; Mgmt; Systms Anlyst.

**HOUSE, MAXINE S,** Cecils Coll, Asheville, NC; SR; AAS; Med; Med Assistng.

**HOUSE, ROBERTA J,** Univ Of Tn At Knoxville, Knoxville, TN; JR; BS; Exec Undrgrdts 89-; Phi Eta Sigma 90-; Golden Key; Beta Gamma Sigma; Bsn Admin; Lgstcs.

**HOUSE, S DWANE,** Sue Bennett Coll, London, KY; SO; BA; SGA Activities Dir 90-; Language Club Treas 90-; Alumni Assc Activities Dir 90-; Pblc Relations Depart Asst 90-; Homecoming Cmmt Pblcty Activity Dir; Engl; Engl Literature Prffsr.

**HOUSE, TAMARA S,** John Carroll Univ, Cleveland, OH; FR; Psychlgy/Soclgy; Clinical Psychlgy.

**HOUSE, TAMMY A,** Owensboro Jr Coll Of Bus, Owensboro, KY; FR; AS; Indiana State Univ Terre Haute Sim Vlybl; Dorm Cncl; Flr Rep; Zeta Tau Alpha Indiana State Univ Crrspndg Sec 85; Brownie Ldr 88-90; Terra Haute Vol Of Mo 85; Vol Wrk Adult Day Care Ctr; Paralegal; Lgl Sec.

**HOUSENBOLD, JEFFREY T,** Carnegie Mellon Univ, Pittsburgh, PA; SR; BS; SAL 88-; Dean Srch Cmmt 90-; SDC 87-89; Lambda Sigma Chrmn Cmmnty Serv 88-89; Phi Eta Sigma Chrmn Social 87-88; Mortar Board 90-; Beta Gamma Sigma Pres 90-; Andrew Carnegie Scty Pres Schlr; Indstrl Mngmnt/Ecnmcs; Consulting.

**HOUSEND, LORI L,** Middle Ga Coll, Cochran, GA; JR; BS; Crmnl Just Clb; Psychlgy Clb; Psychlgy/Crmnl Just; Frnsc Psychlgy.

**HOUSER, ANGELA DAWN,** Univ Of Nc At Charlotte, Charlotte, NC; SO; BA; Intrntl Club 90-; Psychlgy Club 90-; Hmcmng Bd Comm 90-; Zeta Tau Alpha 90-; Vol At Broughton Hosp; Im 90-; Psyclhgy/MA Soc Wrk; Clincl Soc Wrkr.

**HOUSER, ANGELA F,** Wilson Coll, Chambersburg, PA; SO; MPT; Sci Clb 89-; Coll Sen 89; Mdrn Dnc Troupe 89; Dorthy Alcott Weeks Physics Prz; Maude Beatrice Wyman Awd 90-; Deans Lst 89-; Phys Ther.**

**HOUSER, AUDREY BAJERSKI,** Methodist Coll, Fayetteville, NC; SR; BS; Stdnt Cncl Excptnl Chldrn Pres 89-; Omicron Delta Kappa; Network Schlrshp; Spec Educ Parents Assn; Prof Chef 75-; AAS Suny 75; Spec Educ; Tchr.

**HOUSER, BRYAN G,** Hampton Univ, Hampton, VA; SO; BA; Am Inst Architecture Stdnts 89-; Dsgn Architect.**

**HOUSER, HANS S,** Indiana Univ Of Pa, Indiana, PA; SO; BS; Nrsg.

**HOUSER, JANET D,** Nova Univ, Ft Lauderdale, FL; GD; MBA; Stdnt Gov 61-62; OH State U; Alumnae Schlrshp Hse Alpha Sigma Eta OSU 61-63; Pres Spec Schlrshp Awd 63; Advsr Phi Beta Lambda Lamson Jr Coll 88-90; Instr Chrprs 87-; BS OH State U 66; Bus Admin; Tchng.

**HOUSER, KYLE D,** Central Fl Comm Coll, Ocala, FL; SO; BFA; Hnrble Mntn In Santa Fe Sprng Arts Fest; AA 90; Fine Art/Art Ed; Art Tchr/Artst.

**HOUSER, MARY L,** Univ Of Tn At Knoxville, Knoxville, TN; JR; BS; Ntl Deans Lst 89-90; 25 Yrs Tenn Vly Athrty; Acctg.

**HOUSER, TONYA L,** Coll Of Charleston, Charleston, SC; FR; BS; Chem.

**HOUSEWORTH, LINDA S,** Univ Of Nc At Greensboro, Greensboro, NC; FR; BS; Rcrtn/Lsr Studies; Lsr Serv/Trsm Mgmt.

**HOUSMAN, ERIC D,** Union Coll, Barbourville, KY; SO; BA; Stdnt Gvmnt Stdnt Rep; Wilnerss Clb; Envrnmntl Clb; Baseball; Wildlife Mgmt; Conservation Officer.

**HOUSMAN, JULIE A,** Union Coll, Barbourville, KY; SO; BS; Accntng Bsns Admnstrtn; Corp Accntnt CPA.

**HOUSTON, ANGELA A,** Western Carolina Univ, Cullowhee, NC; SR; BS; NASW; Pi Gamma Mu; Phi Kappa Phi; Phi Alpha Phi; Socl Wrk; Cnslr.

**HOUSTON, DEBORAH J,** James Sprunt Comm Coll, Kenansville, NC; SO; BA; Stdnt Govt Assoc Sntr 90; Deans Lst; Pres Lst; Ed; Elem Tchr.

**HOUSTON, ERICA L,** Al A & M Univ, Normal, AL; FR; AL A/M Gospel Chr 90-.

**HOUSTON, GINGER W,** Memphis St Univ, Memphis, TN; SR; BA; AA Sso Dalton Jr Coll 70; AS Chattanooga St 76; Home Econ.

**HOUSTON, JUDITH E,** Va Commonwealth Univ, Richmond, VA; SO; BS; Golden Key 90-; Pharmacy.

**HOUSTON, JULIA L,** East Tn St Univ, Johnson City, TN; SO; BS; Student Govt Fee Brd 89-90; Panhellenic Councial Serv Chm 90; Raider Corp 89-90; Gamma Beta Phi 90-; Alpha Delta Pi Jewelry Rep 90-; IM Girls Ftbl 90; Psy.

**HOUSTON, SARA R,** Birmingham Southern Coll, Birmingham, AL; FR; BS; Phi Eta Sigma; Alpha Lambda Delta; Phi Sigma Iota; Alpha Omicron Pi Pldg Cls Trs 90-; Habitat For Hmnty 90-; Alpha Omicron Pi Pldg Schlr; S Cntrl Bell Hnrs Tuition Schlr; Intrn 90-; Frnch Space Cmp 90; IM 90-; Chmstry/Math.

**HOUSTON, TODD E,** Ms St Univ, Miss State, MS; SR; AICHE 88-; Tchncl Assn Pupl & Papr Indstrs Tres 89-; IM Sprts; Bptst Stdnt Un 86-; Prsdnts Schlr 90-; Deans Schlr 86-89; Tau Beta Pi 90-; Omega Chi Epsilon 90-; Hnr Grad; Eagle Sct; God & Country Awd; BS; Chmcl Engnr; Engnr.

**HOUSTON, TRACEY M,** Fisk Univ, Nashville, TN; JR; BA; Deans List 88-90; PI Sigma Alpha; Delta Sigma Theta 89-; Polctl Sci; Intl Coop Lawyer.

**HOUSTON-LAY, SHERI DANIELLE,** Coll Of Boca Raton, Boca Raton, FL; SR; ITTA90-; IHMA Pres 89-; Eta Sigma Delta V P 89-; BS Bsn Adm AS Bsn Dm 90; AS Acctg AM Instit Bsn 83; Htl/Rstrnt Mmt.

**HOUT, MARY R,** Montgomery Comm Coll, Troy, NC; SR; BA; Techncn W/Centel 69-91; AA Mntgmry Tech Coll 90; Psychlgy.

**HOUZE, LATISHA P,** Rust Coll, Holly Springs, MS; JR; BS; Pre Med Cncl Pres 90-; A Cappella Choir Treas 90-; Pre Alumni Cncl; UNCF Dlgte; Alpha Kappa Mu Sec; Chi Beta Phi V P 90-; Delta Sigma Theta; MBRS Rsrch Stdnt; Tutor Cnslrl; HCOP 90-; Biology/Pre Med.

**HOVEKA, ERASTUS T,** Wilmington Coll, Wilmington, OH; SO; BA; Intl Clb Pres Elct; VP 90-; Acctg Clb; Ohio Soc CPAS; Acctg.

**HOVELL, RENEE CAMILLE,** Fisk Univ, Nashville, TN; GD; MPA; Pltcl Sci Clb 89-90; Lnks Inc 90; Clvlnd Fsk Alumni Clb Scrtry; Alpha Kappa Alpha Treas 89-90; Schlrshp 90; Asstntshp 90; BA Fisk U 90; Pblc Admin; Law.

**HOVEMEYER, ADRIENNE J,** S U N Y Coll At Fredonia, Fredonia, NY; JR; Chamber Plyrs; Symphony Cncrt Mstrs; Oll Clg Band; Seven Oclock; Jazz Tae Kwon Do; Erie Philharmonic Orch; Amer String Tchr Assn V P; Music Eductors; Sigma Alpha Iots Sgt At Arms: Trumpet Guild; Amer String Tchrs Assn V P 88; Music Educ; Ele Jr H Instrmntl Music.

**HOVEY, RICHARD L,** Germanna Comm Coll, Locust Grove, VA; SO; BA; Vlybl Bsktbl Wlybl IM; Soc Sci; Edn.

**HOVEY, ROBYN L,** Nyack Coll, Nyack, NY; SR; BS; Stdnt Govt Sec 90-; Sr Cls Ofcr Sec; Msns Comm VP; Alpha Chi 89-; Nyack Gspl Tm 88-90; Brklyn Gspl Tm 88-89; Dpt Asst Chrstn Educ 89-90; Yth Min Intrn 90-; Yth Mnstry.

**HOVIS, MARY C,** Univ Of Sc At Columbia, Columbia, SC; SR; BA; Engl; Pub Rltns/Comm.

**HOWARD, ALISHA A,** Ky St Univ, Frankfort, KY; SO; BA; Engl Clb; Delta Omicron; T Johnson Mus Awd 90; R Dixon Awd; Schlstc Cert; Music Educ; Music Thrpst/Accmpnst.

**HOWARD, ALLISON E,** Duquesne Univ, Pittsburgh, PA; FR; BS; IM Ftbl 90; Chem/Envr; Engr.

**HOWARD, ANDREA L,** Fl St Univ, Tallahassee, FL; SO; BS; Stdnt Govt 90-; US Army Reserve Offcr Trng Corps 90-; FSU Clg Dmcrts Pres 90-; Dubois Soc Sec 90-; Phi Theta Kappa 90-; Hons/Schlrs Cncl Incentive Rep 90-; US Senator Bob Graham; Ranger Prdctns Prmtns Chair; AA; Cmnctns/Pltcl Sci; Law.

**HOWARD, ANDREW C,** Al St Univ, Montgomery, AL; FR; BA; Busn; Hotel Mgt.

**HOWARD, ANGELA D,** Al St Univ, Montgomery, AL; SR; MBA; Alpha Kappa Mu 90; Alpha Kappa Alpha Inc 90; Wrks With Boys/Grl Clb Amer; Cont Grad Stdy; BED; Psych; Scl Wrk.

**HOWARD, ARNEIDA C,** Central St Univ, Wilberforce, OH; JR; AA Cuyahoga Cmnty Clg 90; Elem Educ.

**HOWARD, AUDREA S,** Alcorn St Univ, Lorman, MS; SO; Elem Educ; Tchng.

**HOWARD, BEVERLY J,** Univ Of Ky, Lexington, KY; FR; BS; Biochem.

**HOWARD, BONNIE S,** Atlantic Comm Coll, Mays Landing, NJ; SO; MBA; Bus Admin; Mgmt.

**HOWARD, CALVIN M,** Ashland Comm Coll, Ashland, KY; FR; APN; Acad Exclince Awd 90; Outstndng Acad Achievemnt Awd; Nrsng; Hlth Care Fld.

**HOWARD, CARLA B,** Univ Of The Dist Of Columbia, Washington, DC; JR; BA; Arts Assemble 88-90; Clg Paper Wrtr/Rep; Hnr Rl 88-; Dns Lst 88-; Washington Humane Soc Animal Contr Ofcr 86-; Inforces Animal Contr Laws; Theatre Arts/Actg; Perf Theatre.

**HOWARD, CHERYL DENICE,** Central Al Comm Coll, Alexander City, AL; SO; AIM Inmate Brd Of Dirs Sec 87-88; New Beginnings Sec 90-; Data Entry Oper AL Industries Of Corr 86-; AA; Psychology; Human Resource Counseling.

**HOWARD, CHRISTINE MARIE,** Univ Of Sc At Columbia, Columbia, SC; SR; BA; Trvl Tr Carolina Prgm Un Co Chrprsn 89-90; Appllt Crt Cmmtt 89-; Mdl UN; Intl Stdnts Assoc 90-; Gldn Key By Laws Cmmtt Gamma Beta Phi 89-90; Phi Beta Kappa; Sigma Iota Rho VP 90-; Alpha Lambda Delta Cncl 89-90; Evltn Tm GINT Dept 90-; Govt Intl Stds; Law.

**HOWARD, CHRISTOPHER A,** Christopher Newport Coll, Newport News, VA; SR; BA; Sigma Tau Delta 90-; Engl Lit; Tchng.

**HOWARD, CHRISTOPHER MARK,** Fl St Univ, Tallahassee, FL; JR; BA; Snr Clscl Leg Tres 89-; Clg Bwl 89-; Eta Sigma Phi VP 89-; Clsscs; Tchng.

**HOWARD, CLARISSA D,** Univ Of Sc At Columbia, Columbia, SC; SO; BA; Zeta Phi Beta Rspndnt Sec; Vol Int Nshp 90-; Vol Comm Serv Awd; Psychlgy; Chld Psychlgy.

**HOWARD, COLEMAN E,** New Comm Coll Of Baltimore, Baltimore, MD; SR; CIS; Stdnt Govt Slctv Brd 90-; NCCB 90-; Pres Cncl 90-; Cert PSI Inst Balto 88; Comp Sci.

**HOWARD, CRYSTAL COX,** Univ Of Sc At Columbia, Columbia, SC; BS; Natl Bus Educ Assc 90-; Cola Runnin Clb 88-; BS; Ofc Admn; Prsnl/Trng.

**HOWARD, CYNTHIA A,** Ms St Univ, Miss State, MS; FR; BA; Phi Beta Lambda Fund Raising Commt 90-; Mc Cool Busn Schl Peer Counselor 90-; Lamdba Sigma Ldrshp Scty; Hnrs Prog 90-; Gamma Phi Beta; Galpha Lambda Delta; Phi Eta Sigma; Econ; Law.

**HOWARD, DANIEL YOUNG,** Middle Ga Coll, Cochran, GA; SR; BBA; Phi Beta Kappa 90-; Valedictorian; Business Source Pres 88-; AS Middle GA Clge; AS Cmnty Clge Of The Air Force 85; Business; Business Law.

**HOWARD, DAVID R,** Middle Tn St Univ, Murfreesboro, TN; JR; BA; Judd Hall Cncl V P 89-; Hnrs Prog; Crmnl Just Admin; Writer.

**HOWARD, DENISE A,** Converse Coll, Spartanburg, SC; JR; BA; SC Stdnt Lglstr Chair 89-; Mdl Leag Arab States 90-; Cnvrs Hon Jdcl Bd V-Chair; Alpha Lambda Delta 89-; Mrtr Bd Schl Serv Chair; Cnvrs Jr Mrshll 90-; Stdnt Vol Serv 88-; All-Amer Schlr 88-90; Coll Schlrs Amer; Cnvrs Schlrs 90-; Pltcs/Engl/Hstry; Pltcs.

**HOWARD, DENISE M,** Roane St Comm Coll, Harriman, TN; FR; Nrsng.

**HOWARD, DEREK W,** Middle Tn St Univ, Murfreesboro, TN; SR; BS; Valiant Air Command Col; Experimental Aircraft Assoc 88-; Warbirds Amer 88-; TN Scenic Rvr Assoc 86-89; Amer Red Cross Life Svg-Lifeguard 86-; Dns Lst 87-; Tau Kappa Epsilon 89-; Intl Flight Ctr Intern; IM Sftbl/Flg Ftbl/Bsktbl/Golf; Aerosp; MA Cmrcl Pilot.

**HOWARD, ETHAN D,** Youngstown St Univ, Youngstown, OH; FR; BA; Dana Symph Orch; Dana Chmbr Orch; Nw Music Ensmbl; Strng Qrt; Nw Music Soc; Clscl Music Soc; Yngstwn Symph Orch; Howard Entrtnrs; Von Steuben Ensmbl; Dns Lst; Cls Hon; Music Perf/Violin; Perf Mjr Orch.

**HOWARD, GAIL L,** De Tech & Comm Coll At Dover, Dover, DE; FR; AA; SOSA 90; Girl Scouts Of America; Acctg; CPA.

**HOWARD, GLEN N,** Barry Univ, Miami, FL; JR; BS; Cmptr Sci; Cmptr Pgrmr.

**HOWARD, HEATHER A,** Hudson Valley Comm Coll, Troy, NY; FR; BA; Capt Chrldng Squad 90-; Bsktbl; Chrldr Ftbl; Elementary Educ; Grade School Teacher.

**HOWARD, HEATHER L,** Univ Of Al At Huntsville, Huntsville, AL; SR; BS; Eta Kappa Nu 89; Electrical Eng.

**HOWARD, HEATHER R,** Univ Of Nc At Charlotte, Charlotte, NC; JR; BS; Crmnl Jstc HS 90-; Psychlgy HS 90-; Deans List 90; Arson Task Frc Invstgns 90; Crmnl Jstc/Psychlgy; Spcl Agnt.

**HOWARD, JACQUELINE P,** Mount Olive Coll, Mount Olive, NC; SR; BAS; Psych Club 90-; PTA Pres 89-90; N C Edctnl Assoc Of Office Personnel 88-; Fin Asst City Schools 81-; AAS Sampson Comm Coll Exec Sec 79; AAS 85; Bus; Guidance/Edn Support Serv.

**HOWARD JR, JAMES B,** Thomas Nelson Comm Coll, Hampton, VA; SO; Boy Scts Am Sct Mstr 88-89; US Army Army Achvmnt Medal/Cert; Cer Machine Shop Tchnlgy New Horizon Tech Ctr 86 88; Htng/Air Cndtng; Mech Eng.

**HOWARD, JAMES W,** Embry Riddle Aeronautical Univ, Daytona Beach, FL; SO; BS; Daytona Bch Baptst Church 89-; Puppet Pals Puppet Team 87-; Aerontcl Sci; Bush Pilot.**

**HOWARD, JANE M,** Northern Ky Univ, Highland Hts, KY; SR; BA; Kappa Delta Pi; Pinnacle; Alpa Chi; Tsustee Cincinnati Boy Choir VCHRMN 87-; Englsh; Tchr.

**HOWARD, JENNIFER,** Howard Univ, Washington, DC; JR; BA; Alpha Sweetheart Court; Golden Key; Howard Newsvision; Assist Cmnctns Spec; Brdcst Jrnlsm; Cmnctns.

**HOWARD, JENNIFER K,** Radford Univ, Radford, VA; JR; BS; Var Crss Cntry 88-; IM Vlybl; Sigma Kappa Pnhllnc 90-; Comm Rec; Actvity Prog.

**HOWARD, JENNIFER L,** Univ Of Tn At Knoxville, Knoxville, TN; JR; BS; Exec Undergrads 90-; Stdnt Govt Assn 90-; Amer Mrktng Assn 90-; Gldn Ky; Omicron Delta Kappa; Alpha Omicron Pi VP Pldge Educ 88-; James Williamson Schlrshp; Natl Almni Schlrshp; Alpha Kappa Psi Schlrshp Rcgntn; Mgmt Prsnnl; Hmn Rsrcs.

**HOWARD, JEREMY C,** Academy Of The New Church, Bryn Athyn, PA; SO; MBA; Indstrl Dsgn.

**HOWARD, JOHN M,** Western Carolina Univ, Cullowhee, NC; FR; BS; Last Minute Prod 90-; Pre Med Clb 90-; Hon Prog 90-; Delta Chi Soc Chrmn 90-; Biology; Med.

**HOWARD, KENNETH M,** Southern Coll Of Tech, Marietta, GA; FR; BET; Hwy Cnstrctn 77-90; Cvl Eng Tech; Eng.

**HOWARD, KENNETH R,** Abraham Baldwin Agri Coll, Tifton, GA; SO; BS; Hrtcltr Clb 89-; Chr 90-; Dns Lst 89-; Pres Lst 90-; Sthrn Nrsrymns Assoc; Ornmntl Hrtcltr; Grnhsng Bsn.

**HOWARD, KRISTA M,** Oh St Univ, Columbus, OH; FR; Name/Seal Schlrshp, Scrlt/Gray Schlrshp 90-; Hstry; Elem Ed.

**HOWARD, LAURA A,** Roane St Comm Coll, Harriman, TN; SO; Annakusa Jr Womens Clb Schlrshp 88; Fifith Dist Vol Fire Dept Sec 90-; EMT Nrthlk Meth 82-89; Soc Sci; Alchl/Drg Trtmnt Cnslng.

**HOWARD, LAURA KAYE,** Western Ky Univ, Bowling Green, KY; JR; BA; The Herald Mng Ed Wstrn 90-; Rprtr 88-90; Phi Kappi Phi; Sigma Delta Chi; Kappa Tau Alpha; Wm Randolph Hearst Fndtn Jrnlsm Awds 90-; Intrnshps Cinn Entrprise/Anniston 90-; Pltcs/Jrnlsm Intrnshp Wash D C; Jrnlsm-Prnt; Nwspr.

**HOWARD, LAURA R,** Memphis St Univ, Memphis, TN; SO; Kappa Delta; Intl Bus/German.

**HOWARD, LESLIE J,** Univ Of Sc At Columbia, Columbia, SC; FR; BS; Acadmc Plnng Comm; Carolina For KIDS Frndr/Ldr 90-; Nuturng Ctr For Absd Chldrn 90-; Gamma Beta Phi; Hons Clg 90-; Carolina Schlr; Alpha Epsilon Delta 90-; Carolins Cares 90-; Ofc Of Cmnty Svc Intrn; Coca Cola Regnl Schlr; SC Acdmc Tm 90; Chem; Physcn.

**HOWARD, LINDA J,** Savannah St Coll, Savannah, GA; SR; BA; Savannah State Coll Hon Roll 72-89; Deans Lst 90; Intrnshp WHCJ FM Savannah GA; Asst Ed The Tigers Roar Savannah State Nwspr; At/T OSPS Op 75-; Mass Cmnctn/Bus; PR/TCHR.

**HOWARD, LISA ANNE,** Brescia Coll, Owensboro, KY; SR; BA; Chldrns Liturgist 90; Lit Cncl Publctn Dsgn 90; Court Referral Prog 90; Dsgn Pblshd Intl Bluegrass Music Assn 90; Bl; Graphic Dsgn; Clg Tchr.

**HOWARD, LORI D,** Univ Of Sc At Sumter, Sumter, SC; SO; AS; Circle K; Bus Fin; BS.

**HOWARD, MALISSA D,** Univ Of Tn At Martin, Martin, TN; SO; BS; Bnd Mrch 89-; Bnd Symphnc 89-; Jazz Bnd 89-; Hnr Smnr Schlrshp 89-; Bio; Gntc Engr.

**HOWARD, MARA,** Miami Dade Comm Coll, Miami, FL; SR; BA; Phi Theta Kappa 87-; Cert Of Appr Ctn 87; Otstndng Acdmc Achvmnt 90-; Camillus House Homeless Vol; Mc Claimore Ctr Abused Chldrn Vol; Music; Edn.

**HOWARD, MARGIE RENEE,** Alice Lloyd Coll, Pippa Passes, KY; GD; BA; Yrbk Stf; Phi Beta Lambda; Stdnts Btr Envrnmnt; Soc Stds; K-4 Tchr.

**HOWARD, MARIAN E,** Fl St Univ, Tallahassee, FL; SR; BS; SGA Sntr 88-89; Phi Theta Kappa 88-89; Mortar Brd 90-; Golden Key 90-; Phi Kappa Phi; Deans Awd Acdmc Exclnc 89; Soc Sci Awd 88; Summa Cum Laude 89; AA Lake Sumter Comm Clg 89; Pltcl Sci; Law.

**HOWARD, MARILYN R,** Owensboro Comm Coll, Owensboro, KY; GD; CERT; Srch Comm Owensboro Sch Supt Parent Rep; Estes Elem Sch PTA Pres 89-; Owensboro Comm Ctrs Adv Comm V Chm 90-; BA Bellarmine Coll 72; Elem Edn.

**HOWARD, MARTINE K,** Glassboro St Coll, Glassboro, NJ; SR; BA; French Clb Pres 89-; Phi Theta Kappa; Pi Delta Phi Pres 90-; Brd Alumni Camden Cty Clg; Dr Lawson J Brown Sr Schlrshp Awd; Florentino C Martinez French Awd; Grad Asstntshp Univ DE; AI Rites Belgium 79; French.

**HOWARD, MELISSA ANN,** Roane St Comm Coll, Harriman, TN; FR; RN; LPN St Area Voc Tech Schl 88.

**HOWARD, MELVA J,** Bishop St Comm Coll, Mobile, AL; SO; AAS; Acad Excell Awd 88-89; Offc Admin/Legal Optn; Paralegl.

**HOWARD, MENDY L,** Bridgewater Coll, Bridgewater, VA; FR; BA; Oratorio Choir 90; Hstry/Poltcl Sci; Law.

**HOWARD, MICHAEL H,** S U N Y Coll Of Tech At Alfred, Alfred, NY; FR; AAS; Class Rep; Sigma Tau Epsilon 90-; Elec; Techncn.

**HOWARD, MICHAEL T,** Univ Of Nc At Charlotte, Charlotte, NC; JR; Tree Spksprsn Edctn Comm; Gldn Key; Phlsphy; Prfsnl Schlrshp.

**HOWARD, MICHELE L,** Endicott Coll, Beverly, MA; SO; BS; The Saratoga Assc Intrnshp; Glenvle Tile/Desgn Cntr Intrn 90; Deans List 89; AS; Interior Dsgn.

**HOWARD, MICHELLE T,** Univ Of Ky, Lexington, KY; JR; Blck Stu Union 88-90; Stu Org Assoc BUS Rep 89-90; Deans Lst 90-; Alpha Kappa Alpha; GTE Intrn 89; Pblc Rltns; Law.

**HOWARD, MONICA E,** Tn St Univ, Nashville, TN; SR; BS; TSU Nwsppr Mtr Ftrs Edit 89; TSU Dns Lst 89; Phi Beta Lambda 87; Swthrt Of Alpha Phi Alpha Frat Inc 90; Intrn Scrptwrtr WTVF Ch 5 Tlk Of The Twn 89; Intrn Cptl Hll Rprtr Lgsltve Plza 91; Spch Cmmnctn And Thtre; Bcme A Jrnlst.

**HOWARD, NAOMI H,** Univ Of South Al, Mobile, AL; JR; BS; Phys Ed; Tchr.

**HOWARD, NATALIE K,** Anne Arundel Comm Coll, Arnold, MD; FR; Gen Stds; Psych.

**HOWARD, NICOLE L,** Tn St Univ, Nashville, TN; JR; BS; AECOMP 88-; Hnrs Prog 88-; Pom Pon Sqd 88-; Cmptr Sci; Systems Analysts.

**HOWARD, PATRICE P,** Fayetteville St Univ, Fayetteville, NC; JR; BS; Kappa Delta Pi; Booster Clb; Bapt Chrch; Elem Educ.

**HOWARD, R BRIAN,** Univ Of Sc At Aiken, Aiken, SC; FR; BA; Spnsrd Amateur Sktbrdr; R C Car Clb.

**HOWARD JR, ROBERT E,** Univ Of Sc At Columbia, Columbia, SC; FR; BA; Bus; Entrpnr.

**HOWARD, ROBERT L,** Morehouse Coll, Atlanta, GA; SO; BS; Stdtn Govt Assoc Stdnt Crt Jstc 89-; Cmps Crsd Chrst Bbl Stdy Lder 89-; Endvr Spc Clbmrhs Hnrs Prgm 89-; Ronald L Mc Nair Schlr NASA Intern 89-; Comp Sci Mst Otstndng Sphmr 90-; Comp Sci; Astrnt.**

**HOWARD, ROSEMARY M,** Alcorn St Univ, Lorman, MS; SR; BS; MB Chrch Chr Sec 87-; Hrns Jrch Crt 86-; Bus; Sctry.

**HOWARD, SEAN E,** Ky Wesleyan Coll, Owensboro, KY; SR; Alpha Chi 89-; Music Dept Awrd 90-; Music; Grad Schl.

**HOWARD, SELENA M,** Queens Coll, Charlotte, NC; JR; BA; Intl Clb 90-; Intrnshp Guardian Ad Litem 89; Intrnshp Georgetown Cnty Farm Bureau; Belk Awd 88-; Bus Admin.

**HOWARD, SHARON,** Univ Of Ky, Lexington, KY; SO; BSN; Phi Theta Kappa; AA Hazard Cmnty Clg 78; Nrsg.

**HOWARD, SHAWANA,** City Univ Of Ny Med Evers Coll, Brooklyn, NY; JR; BA; NY City Brd Of Ed An Eductional Assistant; Elem Ed.

**HOWARD, SHEILA G,** Brescia Coll, Owensboro, KY; SR; BS; NSSLHA S 90-; Cmnctn Sci/Dsrdrs; Clncl Spch-Lang Path.

**HOWARD, STEWART LYNN,** Univ Of West Fl, Pensacola, FL; JR; BA; Phi Theta Kappa 84-86 90; AS Drafting Okaloosa Walton Jr Clge 86; AA Okaloosa Walton Cmnty Clge 90; Education; Teach.

**HOWARD, TARA J,** Norfolk St Univ, Norfolk, VA; FR; BA; Stdnt Cncl Pres 89-90; Stdnts Agnst Drvng Drnk 89-90; Natl Hon Soc Sec; Pres Acdmc Ftnss Awrd; Govrs Citatn; Bus Mngmnt; Bnk Mngmnt.

**HOWARD, TARA L,** Nc Agri & Tech St Univ, Greensboro, NC; SO; BS; ASHRAE 89-; NSAE Tr 89-; Tau Beta Pi Sec 90-; Chem Eng.

**HOWARD, TIMOTHY W,** Va St Univ, Petersburg, VA; FR; BA; BIS; Cmptr Anlyst.

**HOWARD, TRACYE A,** Coppin St Coll, Baltimore, MD; SR; BS; Hstry Clb Pres; FTA; Phi Alpha Theta; Cert Strayer Bsn Clg 82; Hstry; Edctr.

**HOWARD, TREASA M,** Fl A & M Univ, Tallahassee, FL; FR; Phi Eta Sigma; Leander Boykin Awd Schlstc Excllnc; Agri Sci; Vet Med.

**HOWARD, TREVOR C,** Oh Univ, Athens, OH; SO; Ntl Hnr Scty 89-90; IM; Eng.

**HOWARD, TRINA R,** Newbury Coll, Brookline, MA; BS; Class Repr Sprng Semenster; Prlgl; Law.

**HOWARD III, WOODROW E,** Samford Univ, Birmingham, AL; GD; Univ Stdnt Senate Sntr 84-86; Pi Gamma Mu VP 84-86; Sigma Chi Frat Pi Chptr Ofcr 83-86; Cumberland Intl Moot Ct Tm Advct 88-89; Cumberland Natl Am Bar Assn Trial Tm Advct 89-90; Am Bar Assn AL Mbr 90; State Bar; Law.

**HOWARTH, RANDY M,** Hudson Valley Comm Coll, Troy, NY; FR; AAS; Tuoe Local 106 84-89; IEEE 90-; Firefighter Averill Pk Fire Dept 76-81; Presidents Lst 90; Maint Engr; AOS 75-76; Electrcl Tchnlgy Engrng; Dsgn Engr.

**HOWAT, VICKI A,** Univ Of Southern Ms, Hattiesburg, MS; JR; BSBA; Gamma Beta Pi 90-; Phi Chi Theta 90-; Golden Key 90-; Acctg; CPA.**

**HOWE, JADEANA K,** Volunteer St Comm Coll, Gallatin, TN; FR; AD; LPN 88-; LPN Schl Prctcl Nrsng 88; Nrsng.

**HOWE, JAMES A,** S U N Y Coll Of Tech At Alfred, Alfred, NY; SO; BED; Phi Theta Kappa; AOS 85; Hstry; Tchr.

**HOWE, MEGAN E,** Gaston Coll, Dallas, NC; FR; AS; Stdnt Govt; Deans Lst 90; Pres Lst 90; Math; Secndry Ed.

**HOWE, ROBERT B,** Oh Univ, Athens, OH; FR; BSEE; IM Bsktbll 90-; Tutor Prgrm; Elctrcl Engnr.

**HOWE, YVONNE E,** City Univ Of Ny City Coll, New York, NY; SR; BA; Aspiras Awd 88-90; Gold Key 89-; Manhattan Mntl Hlth Graham Windham Ctr; Chld Psychlgst.**

**HOWELL, ALLEN D,** Coker Coll, Hartsville, SC; JR; Dept Suprvsr; Bus Admn; Mgt.

**HOWELL, AMY L,** Va Commonwealth Univ, Richmond, VA; FR; BS; Psychlgy; Spcl Ed.

**HOWELL, BOBBI J,** Muskingum Coll, New Concord, OH; SO; BA; Elem Educ; Tchr.

**HOWELL, BRENDA R,** Western Piedmont Comm Coll, Morganton, NC; SR; AS Mc Dowell Tech Comm Coll; Comp Oprtns.

**HOWELL, CHANDA R,** Al A & M Univ, Normal, AL; SR; BS; Edtr Univ 90-; SGA 90-; Sec Media Plng Bd; VP Telecomm Clb; Alpha Kappa Mu; Drg Prvntn Tsk Frc; Natl Assn Blk Jrnlst; Dns Lst 89-90; WJAB Rd Sta Hntsvl Al; WAFF 48 NBC Affil Brdcstng Sta Hntsvl Al Intrnshp; Natl Enquire Mag 90-; Telecomm; Jrnlsm.

**HOWELL, DAWN L,** Cornell Univ Statutory College, Ithaca, NY; JR; BS; Block Bridle Clb 89-; Pre Vet Soc 88-89; Deans Lst; Contel Inc Cmmnty Actn Tm; Crew 88; Animal Sci; Med.

**HOWELL, FRANCES SHELLMAN,** Interdenominational Theo Ctr, Atlanta, GA; GD; MDIV; Gammon Stdnt Flwshp Treas 90-; Chrstns United Chrst Mnstry Assoc Dir 81-; Wmn Chrst Mnstry Natl Dir 78-; Rchng Out To Sr Adult ROSA Prog Crdntr 90-; Fncl Benefit Mnstry Fndr 90-; Dns Lst 4.0 Avg 90-; Pastoral Care; Cnslng.

**HOWELL, JANICE A,** Asnuntuck Comm Coll, Enfield, CT; CERT; AMVETS; Hallmark Cards Inc Enfield Dist Cen; 81-91; Busn Admin.

**HOWELL, JASON C,** Northwest Al Comm Coll, Phil Campbell, AL; SO; Phi Theta Kappa.

**HOWELL, JILL S,** Univ Of Ky, Lexington, KY; JR; BS; Stdnt Activ Bd; SAB Hmcmng Royalty Chrprsn 90-; Kappa Kappa Gamma Treas 90-; U K Water Ski Team Bd Of Dir 90-; Kappa Kappa Gamma Treas 90-; Vol Univ Hosp 90-; Intern Plant Path 89-; U S Water Ski Team Bd Of Dir 90-; Biol; Med.

**HOWELL, KENNETH B,** Univ Of Al At Birmingham, Birmingham, AL; JR; BS; AA Art Inst Atlanta 85; Finance; Law.

**HOWELL, KEVIN C,** Ms St Univ, Miss State, MS; FR; BS; IM Ftbl/Bsktbl/Bsbl 90-; Alpha Lambda Delta 90-; Phi Eta Sigma 90-; Pres Lst 90-; Deans Lst; Math; Engr.

**HOWELL, NORMA L,** Northwest Al Comm Coll, Phil Campbell, AL; JR; AS; Phi Theta Kappa 90-; Bus; Off Mgr.

**HOWELL, QUASI M,** Fort Valley St Coll, Fort Valley, GA; FR; BA; Agrnmy Clb Treas; Agrnmy.

**HOWELL, SHARON K,** Univ Of Southern Ms, Hattiesburg, MS; SR; BSBA; Alpha Delta Lambda 88; Delta Sigma Pi Pldg Educ 89-; Phi Beta Lambda 88-89; Ldrshp Schlrshp; Acctg.

**HOWELL, STEPHANIE R,** Radford Univ, Radford, VA; SO; BBA; SGA Off Cmps Stdnt Cncl Sec 90-; Acctg Soc 90-; Phi Beta Lambda Sec 90-; Scnd Place Acctg Phi Beta Lambda State Cmptn; Acctg.

**HOWELL, SUSAN C,** Northern Va Comm Coll, Annandale, VA; SO; AS; Psychology; BA/CORP Law.

**HOWELL JR, WALTER L,** Morehouse Coll, Atlanta, GA; JR; BA; NAACP 90-; Boys/Grls Clbs Metro Atlanta Bsktbl Coach/ Mntr W W Woolflk Clb; Hon Rl 89-; Deans Lst 90-; US Envrnmntl Prtctn Agncy Smmr Intrn Pgm 89-; Awd Outstndng Wrk Prfrmnc Smmr Intrn EPA 89; Pltcl Sci; Law.

**HOWELLS FRIAR, LINDA C,** Broward Comm Coll, Ft Lauderdale, FL; GD; BA; Hon Inst 90-; Phi Theta Kappa 90-; Deans Lst 90-; Hghst Hon; Deerfld Bch Bd Adjstmnts 90-; Deer Isle Hmownrs Assn VP/PRES 87-90; Cmnctns/Pltcl Sci; Law/ MBA.

**HOWELLS, JODI L,** Duquesne Univ, Pittsburgh, PA; SO; BA; Stdnt Nrs Assn PA 90-; Fresh Orntn Stff 90; Stdnt Rcrtmnt 89-90; Delta Zeta Corr Sec 90-; Nrsng.

**HOWELLS, KIMBERLEE A,** Longwood Coll, Farmville, VA; SR; Athltc Trnrs Clb Treas/Sec 88-89; Phy Ed Mjrs Clb 90; IM Athltcs 87-; Delta Psi Kappa 90-; Sigma Kappa 86-87; Intrcllgt Fld Hckry Pstn Goal Kpr 86-89; Phy Ed/Hlth; Tchr.

**HOWELLS II, RICHARD C,** Juniata Coll, Huntingdon, PA; JR; BS; Stdnt Hlth Advsry Comm Pres 89-; Scalpel Probe 89-; Hnr Soc; Tri Beta Pres; Whitaker Rsrch Schlrs Awd; Hnr Soc Schlrshp 89-; Fndrs Ward 88-; Ski Race 88-; Biology/Pre Med; Med.

**HOWERTON, TINA M,** Fayetteville St Univ, Fayetteville, NC; FR; BS; Math; Bsn/Acctg.

**HOWERY, MENDY L,** Emory & Henry Coll, Emory, VA; FR; Stdnt VA Edn Assn; IM Sftbl; Engl; Elem Edn.

**HOWES, ESTHER V,** Al A & M Univ, Normal, AL; JR; BS; Cncl Tres 90-; Kappa Omicron Nu; Food Ntrtn; Dietetics.

**HOWINGTON, STEPHANIE R,** Ms St Univ, Miss State, MS; JR; BS; Clg Rpblcns 88; Ms Assoc For Chldrn Undr Six 90; Alpha Tau Omega Swthrt 90; Gamma Beta Phi 89; Gamma Alpha Epsilon VP; Kappa Delta Pi; Alpha Gamma Delta 88; Pres Lst 88-90; Elem Ed; Tchr Prfssr.

**HOWISON, DUANE M,** Oh Wesleyan Univ, Delaware, OH; JR; BA; Circle K 89; Hl Treas 89-90; Wesleyan Stdnt Fndtn; Beta Theta Pi Sec 89-; Acctg/Math; Acturl.

**HOWITZ, LEO M,** Glassboro St Coll, Glassboro, NJ; SR; BA; Deans Lst 90; AA Phila Comm Coll 89; Math; Tchng.

**HOWLETT, DRIA S,** Edinboro Univ Of Pa, Edinboro, PA; SO; BS; Grd Appls Com 90-; Peace Clb 90-; Beta Beta Beta 90-; Phi Eta Sigma 90-; Fr Chem Stdnt Yr 89-90; Pres Stdy Abrd Hon Schlrshp 90; Pres Hon Schlrshp 89-90; Bio; Eclgy.

**HOWSER, SHANNON L,** Jamestown Comm Coll, Jamestown, NY; SO; Crmnl Jstc; Jvnl Prbtn.**

**HOWZE, CONSTANCE R,** Comm Coll Algny Co Algny Cmps, Pittsburgh, PA; JR; AS; Deans Lst 90-; Cert Comp Prog/Data Prcssng 78; Cert Nrs Aid/Unit Clrk 82; Comp Sci.

**HOWZE, GERALD L,** Al A & M Univ, Normal, AL; SO; BA; Telecmmnctns Clb 89-90; Judiciary Bd 89-90; Dns Lst 89-; Schl Of Arts/Sci 89-; Hnr Ro; Outstdng Future Blck Ldr Of Amer 89-90; Dorm Acad Awd; Telecomm/Mktg; Own Mktg Firm.

**HOYLE, ELIZABETH A,** Slippery Rock Univ, Slippery Rock, PA; FR; BED; Spcl Edn; Teach.

**HOYOS, BEATRIZ,** Miami Chrisitian Coll, Miami, FL; JR; BS; Cls Sec 90-; Vlybl 90; AA Miami Dade Comm Coll 89; Elem Educ; Tchr.

**HOYOS, ORLANDO,** Miami Dade Comm Coll, Miami, FL; GD; BA; Grad W/Hnrs; AA 90; Bsn/Acctg; CPA.

**HOYT, CAROLYN S,** Davis Coll, Toledo, OH; GD; Intrnshp TV; Cmrcl Art; Cmptr Graphic Dsgn.

**HOYT, DENISE I,** City Univ Of Ny Bronx Comm Col, Bronx, NY; SO; AAS; Sci Rsrch Clb 89-; Phi Theta Kappa Pres 89-; Deans Lst 89-90; Medcl Rsrch Intrn Mt Sinai Medcl Cntr-NY 89-90; Medcl Intrnshp Bronx Mncpl Hosp Cntr; Blgy; Physcn.

**HOYT, JOAN S,** East Stroudsburg Univ, E Stroudsburg, PA; SR; Soc Clb 90; IM Vlybl/Bsktbl/Sftbl 88-90; Cum Laude 90; Deans Lst 90; Intrnshp Middlesex Juv Shltr 90; BA 90; Soc/Crim Just; Elem Educ.

**HOYT, PHILIP A,** Broward Comm Coll, Ft Lauderdale, FL; SO; BS; Comp/Info Sci; Comp Prgrmr/Sys Analyst.

**HOYT, STUART T,** Univ Of Ky, Lexington, KY; JR; BSEE; Kntcky Cvl Ar Ptrl Lt Col 84-89; Prvt Plts Lcns 88; Phi Eta Sigma 89; Eta Kappa Nu Elec Eng Hnr; Ogdn Fndtn Sci Schlrshp 88-90; Elec Eng.

**HOYT, TAMMY L,** Colby Sawyer Coll, New London, NH; SR; BS; Cls V P 90-; Key Assoc 89-; Lacrosse Capt MVP 88-; Early Chldhd Ed; Tch.

**HRACH, RAYMOND E,** Comm Coll Algny Co Algny Cmps, Pittsburgh, PA; SO; BS; Avtrs VP 90-; Avtn; Pilot.

**HREHOCIK, JUDITH C,** Indiana Univ Of Pa, Indiana, PA; GD; Mktg Clb 86-88; Camp Cncl Cnsmr 86-88; Entrprnrs Clb 87-88; ARA Ctrng 88-90; State All Conf Tm Trk/Fld 86; Trk Tm 84-88; BS 88; Elem Ed; Cnsmr Affrs.

**HRISKO, PRESTON A,** Villanova Univ, Villanova, PA; JR; BA; Arts Sntr/Stdnt Govt Sntr; Finance Clb 89-90; Italian Clb 89-90; Sch Nwspr Stf Wrtr; Phi Kappa Phi; Omicron Delta Kappa; Phi Alpha Theta; Food Serv Attndt; Deans Lst 90-; Otstndg Coll Stdnts Am 89; Vrsty Ftbl Qrtrbck 88; IM Bsktbl 88-90; Hist Italian; Advrtsng.

**HROBAK, DAWN E,** Kent St Univ Trumbull Cmps, Warren, OH; SO; BBA; Acctng; Auditing.

**HRYHORENKO, ERIC A,** S U N Y Coll At Fredonia, Fredonia, NY; JR; BS; Wldrns Clb 90-; Cmptr Clb 88-89; Tri Beta 88-; Schlr Awd 90; Orgnc Chem Awd 90; Amer Chem Soc Awd 90; IM Ftbl 88-90; Gntcs; Rsch.

**HSIANG, LYNN LIN,** Barry Univ, Miami, FL; SO; BS; Org Chinese Amer Inc 88-; Chinese Cltrl Assn 89-; Busn Admin/Mktg; Mktg Mgmt.

**HSU, DANIEL P,** Univ Of Miami, Coral Gables, FL; JR; BA; Activities Fee Allocation Cmmttee; Orient Assist Coord; Hons Advsry Cmmttee; Golden Key; Alpha Epsilon Delta; Paideia; Lambda Chi Alpha Treas; Jr Var Chrldng; Chem; Med.

**HSU, YA-FENG BETTY,** Ny Univ, New York, NY; JR; BS; Acctg Scty 90; Mgmt Scty 90; Hrn Rll; Deans Lst 90; Lgl Sec; Acctg.

**HSU, YULING,** City Univ Of Ny Queensbrough, New York, NY; SO; BA; Lase/Photnic Clb Pres; Math Clb 89-; Orntn Ldrshp Clb; Phi Theta Kappa; Tau Alpha Pi; Tutor 90-; CRC Press Chem Achvmnt Awd 90; J N Eastham Awds; R Moncott Memrl Awd; Optc; Engnrng.

**HU, KATHARINE JIE,** City Univ Of Ny Baruch Coll, New York, NY; JR; MBA; STEP Clb V P; Golden Key 90-; Acctng.

**HUA, KIMBERLY KY,** City Univ Of Ny Baruch Coll, New York, NY; SR; BBA; Acctng Socty 90-; Comm Tae Aids Inc; Acctng; CPA.

**HUAM, EVELYN P,** Ms St Univ, Miss State, MS; JR; BA; Mktg.

**HUANG, CHIUNG TZU,** City Univ Of Ny La Guard Coll, Long Island Cty, NY; GD; AAS; Alpha Theta Phi 90; Deans Lst 90; AAS; Accntng.

**HUANG, DAVID A,** Savannah Coll Of Art & Design, Savannah, GA; SO; BFA; Chess Clb; Otstndng Frshmn 89-90; Video.

**HUANG, GIGI,** Univ Of Pa, Philadelphia, PA; SO; BA; Penn Dbt Tm 90-; Ntfctn Clrk Booth Mem Med Cntr 89-; Rsrch Tech 90-; Regents Schlrshp 89-; Chmstry; Med Law.

**HUANG, JIE,** City Univ Of Ny Baruch Coll, New York, NY; JR; BA; Actrl Sci Scty 90-; Dns Lst 90; Actrl Sci.

**HUANG, JUSTIN T,** Univ Of Pa, Philadelphia, PA; FR; BSEE; Bnd 90-; Elctrcl Engr; Law Sch.

**HUANG, YUHUI,** Howard Univ, Washington, DC; GD; PHD; Natl Clg Natrl Sci Awd; Resrch Asstnshp Laser Chem 89-; Tchr Asstntshp 90-; BS Beijing Univ 85; MS Inst Of Chem Acad Sinica China 88; Chem; Spectroscopist.

**HUBBARD, ADELE F,** Fayetteville St Univ, Fayetteville, NC; SR; BS; Crmnl Jstce VP; Sclgy Clb 90-; Alpha Kappa Mu Pres; Kappa Delta Pi 90-; Chncllrs Lst 90; Dean Jones Schlrshp 90; Hnr Stdnt; Cmbrlnd Cnty Dspte Mdtr 90-; Mrch Of Dms Spcl Olympcs Vol 90; Crmnl Jstce; Lwyr.

**HUBBARD, BETH O,** Holyoke Comm Coll, Holyoke, MA; FR; AS; Hnrs Rctl; Piano; Msc Educ/Prfmr.

**HUBBARD, JOHN C,** Asbury Theological Sem, Wilmore, KY; SR; MDIV; Theta Phi 90; Local Pstr 89-92; Pstrl Mnstry; BA Asbury Clg 88; Rlgn; Pstrl Mnstry.

**HUBBARD, JULIA J,** Christopher Newport Coll, Newport News, VA; JR; BSBA; Alpha Chi 90-; Ecnmcs/Mgmt; Bnkg Ind.

**HUBBARD, KIMBERLY E,** Radford Univ, Radford, VA; SO; BS; Zeta Tau Alpha Rtl Chrmn; Sclgy.

**HUBBARD, LALANIA L,** Columbus Coll Of Art & Design, Columbus, OH; JR; BA; Deans Lst 89; Fine Arts; Artist.

**HUBBARD, LELA J,** Jackson St Univ, Jackson, MS; SO; BA; Crml Jst Clb; NAACP; COGIC Clb; Dorm Cncl; SGA; Dunbar Drmtc Gld; Gspl Chr; Cls Parli 89-90; Alpha Lambda Delta Chpln 90-; Lambda Alpha Epsilon; Alpha Phi Alpha Sec 90-; Oper Shoestrng; Medger Evrs; Tn ASEP Prog; Jcksn Rec Svc; Crim Jstc; Juv Cnslr/Corrctns.

**HUBBARD, RANDY D,** Georgetown Coll, Georgetown, KY; SR; Ftbl Tm; Res Asst; Dorm Treas; NAIA Acad All-Am Ftbl 89; Tri Beta; U KY REU Rsrch Pgm 90; Ftbl; Bio/Chem; Educator.

**HUBBARD, SHELBA J,** West Liberty St Coll, West Liberty, WV; SR; BA; Kappa Delta Pi VP 89-90; Presbyterian Church Elder; Cert W VA Career Coll 76, Elem Educ; Tchr.

**HUBBARD, STEPHEN C,** Truett Mc Connell Coll, Cleveland, GA; SO; BA; Deans List 90-; Sci; Pre Med/Cardiology.

**HUBBARD, THOMAS J,** Bridgeport Engr Inst, Fairfield, CT; SO; BSEE; Elec Eng Asstnt Norden Sys Norwalk CT; Elec Engrng.

**HUBBELL, SARAH G,** Bridgewater Coll, Bridgewater, VA; FR; BA; Hl Repr 90-; Hstry/Pol Sci; Sec Tchr.

**HUBBS, AMY K,** Univ Of Tn At Knoxville, Knoxville, TN; FR; BS; Mktg.

**HUBBUCK, LISA B,** Univ Of Louisville, Louisville, KY; SR; Soc Wm Engrs Sec 87-89; AICHE 90-; Phi Eta Sigma 88-89; Dns Lst 87-88; Chem; Engrg.

**HUBER, ANNA K,** Univ Of Southern Ms, Hattiesburg, MS; SO; BS; Campus Crsde Chrst 90-; Stdnt Almni Assn 89-; Pi Tau Chi 90-; Alpha Epsilon Delta 90-; Delta Delta Delta Spnsrs Chr 89-; Hon Coll 89-90; Acdmc Schlrshp 89-; Psychlgy; Phys Thrpy.

**HUBER, DARIA R,** Georgian Court Coll, Lakewood, NJ; SR; BA; Phi Theta Kappa 85-86; Sigma Delta Mu 85-86; Sigma Tau Delta Sec 87-; AA Ocen Cnty Coll Toms River NJ 86; Engl; Grad Sch.

**HUBER, DOUGLAS A,** Univ Of Louisville, Louisville, KY; SR; BA; Computer Eng.

**HUBER, HOLLY A,** Midway Coll, Midway, KY; SR; BA; Stdnt Govt Clbs/Orgnztns Sntr 87-88; Am Bus Wmns Assn 90-; Nwspr Prdctn Offcr 89-90; Phi Theta Kappa 87-; Acdmc All Am 89-90; Intern Charles D Mitchell Co 88-89; Office Admnstrtn Awd 88-89; Vlybl Tm Capt 87-; AA; Bus Admnstrtn; Mrktng.

**HUBER, LYNNE M,** Coll Misericordia, Dallas, PA; JR; BS; CMSDTA 90; Pi Theta Epsilon 90; Tchng Assist In Occptnl Thrpy Dept; AOTA; AS Mt Aloysius Jr Clg 85; Occptnl Thrpy.

**HUBER, MATTHEW J,** Providence Coll, Providence, RI; SR; BS; Friars Clb Socl Srvc Org 88-; Smstr Abrd Florence Italy 90; Tau Pi Phi; Hnr Socty; Summer Intrshp Rsrchr Inc Mag 90; Bus Admin/Mktg; Entrprnrshp.

**HUBERT, AMY M,** Saint Josephs Coll, Windham, ME; SO; BS; Cmps Tour Guide 89-; Acad Hnrs Lst 89-90; Dns Lst 90-; US Achvmnt Acad; IM Aerobics; Bus Admin/Acctng; CPA.

**HUBERT, JEFFREY O,** Temple Univ, Philadelphia, PA; SR; Kappa Psi Treas 89-90; Amer Soc Hosp Phrmcsts 89-90; BS Univ Scrntn 78; MS 81; Phrmctcl Sci; Phar.

**HUBERT, JENNIFER D,** Univ Of Ga, Athens, GA; GD; MED; Math Educ Stdnt Assn 88-; Natl Cncl Tchrs Math 89-; Gldn Key Socty 89-; Kappa Delta Epsilon 89-90; Kappa Delta Pi 90-; Outstdng Coll Stdnts Of Amer 89-90; Asstshp 90-91; BSED Math 90; Math; Sec Educ.

**HUBERTY, ANDREA F,** Univ Of Rochester, Rochester, NY; JR; BS; Varsity Ftbl/Bsktbl Chrldr Capt 88-; Dlion 89-90; Natl Sci Fndtn; Bio; Teach/Rsrch.

**HUBIAK, ERIN M,** Duquesne Univ, Pittsburgh, PA; SO; BA; Busn Admin/Pre Law.

**HUBNER, KARL PHILLIP,** Middle Tn St Univ, Murfreesboro, TN; SR; BS; Audio Engrs Soc 90-; Psi Chi Secy 89-; Grad Asstntshp Spalding Univ Louisville KY 89-90; Cnslr In Prvt Psychtrc Fclty 87-89; BA Ohio State Univ 87; Recrdng Indstry Mgt; Audio Prodctn Engr.

**HUCKABA, JULIE A,** Memphis St Univ, Memphis, TN; SO; Amer Soc Civil Eng; Phi Eta Sigma 89-; Delta Gamma 90-; Angel Flight 90; Civil Eng; Envrnmnt.

**HUCKABY, DONNA GAIL,** Tri County Tech Coll, Pendleton, SC; SR; BA; Pi Sigma Phi Tres 78-79; US Vlybl Assn; Aahper; Acdmc Schlrshp 77; Vlybl Sftbl Mars Hill 77-79; Wldng Gnrl Elctrc; BS Mars Hill Clg 79; Certf Tri Cnty Tech 90; Welding; Gnrl Tchr.

**HUCKABY, JENNIFER A,** Anderson Coll, Anderson, SC; FR; BED; Deans Lst 90-; Elem Ed; Tchng.

**HUCKABY, MARK A,** Roane St Comm Coll, Harriman, TN; SO; AAS; Amer Cong Gov Indust Hygnsts 90-; Amer Inst Hygn Assn TV Vly Sctn; Amer Indust Hygn Assn 90-; Envrnmntl Hlth Tech; Indust Hygn.

**HUCKABY, TIMOTHY M,** Univ Of Sc At Columbia, Columbia, SC; SR; BA; Soc Clb Pr 89-90; Sci Clb 89-90; Omicron Delta Kappa 90-; Ldrshp Dev; AS N Greenville Clg 89; Psych; Ministry.

**HUCKINS, DAVID J,** Saint Josephs Coll, Windham, ME; SO; BA; Bsn Clb 90-; Bsn Admin; Acctg/CPA.

**HUCKINS, MICHAEL RICHARD,** Asbury Theological Sem, Wilmore, KY; GD; MDIV; BS Univ IL 78; Theology; Tchg.

**HUCKLEBERRY II, JAMES L,** Western Ky Univ, Bowling Green, KY; SR; BA; Cllg Dmcrts 88; Pi Sigma Alpha Prsdnt 90-; Phi Kappa Chi 90-; Phi Alpha Theta; Prsdntl 88-; Big Rvrs Elctrc Acdmc Schlrshp 88-; Intrn Ky Lgsltv Rsrch Cmmsn; Pltcl Sci; Gvrnmnt Srvc.

**HUCKS, JEFFREY M,** Univ Of Sc At Columbia, Columbia, SC; FR; MIB; Gamma Beta Phi; Alpha Lambda Delta; Bus; Intl Mktg Japan.

**HUCULAK, REIJA S,** Northern Ky Univ, Highland Hts, KY; SR; BSW; Scl Wrk Clb 90-; Intl Stdnt Org 90-; Alpha Chi 90; Scl Wrk; Scl Wrk Law.

**HUDAK, DANIEL M,** Columbus Coll Of Art & Design, Columbus, OH; FR; Illstrtn/Phtgrphy; Illstrtn.

**HUDAK, DONALD ANDREW,** Univ Of Nh Plymouth St Coll, Plymouth, NH; SO; BS; Fire Dept 87-; ASE Cert Mtr Tech/ Chvrlt Cert Mstr Tech; AAS NH Voc Tech Clg 86; Math Educ; Tch.

**HUDAK, TODD J,** Univ Of Sc At Columbia, Columbia, SC; SO; BA; Stdnt Govt Sntr; Clg Rpblcns 1st Vice Chrmn 90; Carolina Alive Show Choir 90; Phi Mu Alpha 90; Wm C Bochman Schlrshp; Appntd To SCFCR State Exec Cmmttee; Delegate To SC Fed Of Clg Rpblcns State Cnvtn 90; Jrnlsm; Law.

**HUDDLESTON, DENISE R,** Broward Comm Coll, Ft Lauderdale, FL; SO; AA; Phi Theta Kappa 90; AA; Accntng; CPA.

**HUDDLESTON III, EDWARD,** Univ Of Southern Ms, Hattiesburg, MS; SR; BS; African Am Stdnt Org 89-; Assoc Stdnt Body Dir Of Envrmntl Serv; Mnrty Stdnt Rltns Comm; Alpha Epsilon Delta 87-; Biological Sci; Med Dermatology.

**HUDDLESTON, SHEILA M,** Univ Of Charleston, Charleston, WV; JR; BA; Tchr Educ; Elem Tchr.

**HUDDLESTON, TIMOTHY L,** Chesterfield Marlboro Coll, Cheraw, SC; FR; Chrstms Aprl 90-; Engr Grphcs.

**HUDDLESTON, TJUANA P,** Clark Atlanta Univ, Atlanta, GA; SR; BA; Hons Pgm; Delta Sigma Theta Sgt-At-Arms 90-; Red Cross 89-; Mc Donnell Dgls Intrn 90; Deans Lst 90-; Comp Sci; MBA.

**HUDDLESTON, VINNIE D,** Union Coll, Barbourville, KY; SR; BA; Oxfrd Clb Asst Pres 89-90; Dns Lst 90-; Pastor Intrn; Wm Hugh Smith Awd; Relgn; Prof.

**HUDGINS, ANGELA E,** Western Piedmont Comm Coll, Morganton, NC; SO; BA; Schlrshp Burke Co Ed Ofc Prsnl; Acctng; CPA.

**HUDGINS, GILLIAN R,** Univ Of Al At Birmingham, Birmingham, AL; JR; BS; Secdy Ed; Counseling.

**HUDGINS, JOY A,** Old Dominion Univ, Norfolk, VA; SR; BS; Scty Wmn Eng Treas 89-; 4 H Ldr 86-87; Acdmc Hnr Sprgm 86-; Tau Beta Pi 89-; Pi Tau Sigma VP 89-; Natl Scty Prfssnl Eng; Coop Edctn 88-90; Mech Eng.

**HUDGINS, MARCIA A,** Univ Of Ga, Athens, GA; JR; BED; NSSHLA; Goldn Key; Kappa Delta Stndrds Rep 88-; Elem Schl Tutr; Spch/Lang Pthlgst.

**HUDGINS, SUSAN K,** Ms St Univ, Miss State, MS; SR; BBA; Cmps Actvs Bd 90-; Beta Gamma Sigma 90-; Gamma Beta Phi 87-; Mu Kappa Tau 90-; Phi Alpha Theta 90-; Phi Kappa Phi 90-; Kappa Delta 87-; Pres Schlr 89-90; Dns Schlr; Vrsty Chrldr 87-90.

**HUDNALL, CHRISTIE L,** Radford Univ, Radford, VA; JR; BBA; Phi Kappa Phi; Delta Mu Delta; Newcomers Club V P 88-; Infor Sys Fin Inst 83-91; Bsn Mgmt; Infor Sys.

**HUDNELL, DANIEL A,** Oh St Univ At Marion, Marion, OH; SO; BAS; USAF Sgt 82-88; Bsc Trng Hon Grad 82; Air Frc Achvmnt Mdl 84; Exprt Mrksmn 82-88; Grd Patrlmn Dsk Sgt Air Bse Grnd Dfndr 82-88; Cert Trng Lw Enf Spec Crs USAF Tech Trng Sch Lacklnd AFB TX 82; Crmnlgy/Crmnl Jstce; Law Enf.

**HUDOCK, DANIEL C,** Villanova Univ, Villanova, PA; FR; BA; Hstry; Law.

**HUDSMITH, PATRICIA H,** Memphis St Univ, Memphis, TN; SR; BSN; RN Lebonheur Chldrns Medcl Ctr; Dip Methodist Hosp Sch Of Nrsng 85; Nrsng.

**HUDSON, BRIAN D,** Cumberland Coll, Williamsburg, KY; FR; BS; Flwshp Chrstn Athlts 90-; Phlsphy Clb 90-; Mntn Outrch 90-; Hgh Hnrs Rcgntn 90-; Avtn.

**HUDSON, CARLA D,** Al A & M Univ, Normal, AL; JR; BS; Univ Marching Bnd 89-; Soc Pres Schlrs 89-; Tau Beta Sigma; Finance; Financial Advisor.

**HUDSON, CARMEN S,** Tn St Univ, Nashville, TN; JR; BS; Pep Clb 88-89; Michigan Clb 88-90; Thomas Edward Poag Plyrs Guild 90-; Gold Key 90-; Deans Lst 88-; Univ Hostess 90-; Spch Cmncntn/Theatre; Filmmaking.

**HUDSON, CHAD EBEN,** Spartanburg Methodist Coll, Spartanburg, SC; FR; BED; Elem Educ; Tchng.

**HUDSON, CHARLETTE Y,** Va St Univ, Petersburg, VA; SO; SGT US Army 85-90; Electronic Tech; Computer Tech.

**HUDSON, DEBORAH R,** Univ Of Southern Ms, Hattiesburg, MS; SO; BA; Paralgl.

**HUDSON, DEDRIC L,** Pa St Univ Gt Valley Grad Cntr, Malvern, PA; FR; Cmptr Sci.

**HUDSON, EMMA M,** Gaston Coll, Dallas, NC; FR; AS; Bus Mgmnt; Human Rel.

**HUDSON, ERIC W,** Univ Of Al At Birmingham, Birmingham, AL; JR; BS; Udrgdt Student Govt Assoc Prog Chr 90-; Acctng Studies Advisory Support Grp; Beta Alpha Psi; Deans List; Mensa; Acctng.

**HUDSON IV, FRANK W,** Univ Of Va Clinch Valley Coll, Wise, VA; JR; BA; Brd Sceaduland; Hstry; Law.**

**HUDSON, GERA L,** Ms St Univ, Miss State, MS; FR; PHARM; Phrmcy.

**HUDSON, JAMES D,** Univ Of Nc At Charlotte, Charlotte, NC; SR; MPA; NC Stdnt Legislature 89-; Pblc Admin.

**HUDSON, JAMES E,** Northern Ky Univ, Highland Hts, KY; SO; BA; Christian Stdnt Fllwshp 89; Clermont-Brown Yth Bsktbl League 88; Deans Lst 89; Golf 89-90; All-Acad Tm 89-90; Bsnss; Mrktng.

**HUDSON, JAMES R,** Univ Of Al At Huntsville, Huntsville, AL; JR; BS; BSU; Mech Eng.

**HUDSON, JILL L,** Radford Univ, Radford, VA; SR; BBA; Soc Advncmnt Mngmnt 89-; Bptst Stdnt Union 90-; Deans Lst 89-; Hnrs Prgrm; IM Vllybl; Bsns Mngmnt.

**HUDSON, JOHN KENNETH,** Middle Tn St Univ, Murfreesboro, TN; JR; BA; FCA; Beta Clb; By Scts Eagle Sct; Leo Clb; Gamma Beta Phi 89-; Egle Sct; Hstlmnt Awrd Bsbl 88; Assoc Motlow St Comm Coll 90; Bus Fnnce; Wrk In The Fld Of Fnnce.

**HUDSON, JOHN L,** Limestone Coll, Gaffney, SC; SR; BS; By Scts Egl Sct 87-; Vrsty Bsbll Tm Capt 89-; Physcl Ed.

**HUDSON, JOHN T,** City Univ Of Ny Baruch Coll, New York, NY; JR; US Navy Elctrnc Tech 83-88; Natl Assn Blck Accts 88-90; NAACP 90-; Golden Key; Sigma Alpha Delta; Aviation Warfare Spec US Navy 80-83; Surfare Warfare Spec US Navy 83-88; Jr Acct W/Chem Bnk 89-; Fin; MBA/CPA.

**HUDSON, KAREN L,** Wv Univ At Parkersburg, Parkersburg, WV; SO; AAS; Phi Theta Kappa 90-; Journalism.

**HUDSON, KATHERINE S,** Peace Coll, Raleigh, NC; FR; Tennis 90; Phi Theta Kappa 90-; Acdmc Exc Awd 90-; Deans Lst; Engl/Bus; Law.

**HUDSON, KENYATTA R,** Central St Univ, Wilberforce, OH; FR; BA; Engl; Law.

**HUDSON, KIMBERLY R,** Memphis St Univ, Memphis, TN; JR; BS; Pre-Pharm; Pharm.

**HUDSON, LAURA I,** Coll Of New Rochelle, New Rochelle, NY; SO; BA; Newspapr Layout Edtr 89-90; Lit Mag Layout Edtr 89-90; Hnrs Prog 89; Engl; Bkstre Mngmnt.

**HUDSON, LESLIE D,** West Liberty St Coll, West Liberty, WV; FR; BS; Newspaper Stf Wrtr 90-; Orientation Vol; Cmnctns; Jrnlsm.

**HUDSON, LISA R,** Al A & M Univ, Normal, AL; SO; BA; Hnr Rll Stdnt 90-; Dns Lst 89-; Arts And Scis; Ped Nrse.

**HUDSON, MELISSA D,** Univ Of Southern Ms, Hattiesburg, MS; SR; Outstdng Coll Stdnt Am; Gldn Ky; Beta Alpha Psi; Beta Gamma Sigm; Phi Kappa Phi VP 90-; Veta Alpha Psi; Beta Alpha Psi; Gldn Ky Soc; A/D Breland Schlrshp; MSCPA Schlrshp; W W King Awd; Beta Alpha Psi; Acctg Fac Awd; Acctg; CPA.

**HUDSON, MICHELE R,** Morgan St Univ, Baltimore, MD; JR; BS; Yng Womens Chrstn Assoc 89; Scty For Advncemnt Of Cmptr Sci 88; Prmthn Kappa Tau 88; Morgan State U Crrclm Bsed Hnr Stdnt 88; MSU Deans Lst 88; Smmr Inst In Cmptr Applctns 90; Cmptr Sci; Cmptr Progrmr Analyst.

**HUDSON, PATRICIA E,** Davis & Elkins Coll, Elkins, WV; FR; BA; Psychology.

**HUDSON JR, REAGAN B,** Hampton Univ, Hampton, VA; BA; Chrch Orgnst; Mnstr Music Chrch; Cert Clrcl Stds T N Comm Coll 81; Music/Orgn; Mnstr Music.

**HUDSON, REESHEMHA M,** Central Fl Comm Coll, Ocala, FL; SO; AA; Afrcn Amrcn Stdnt Un 90; Phi Theta Kappa; Edctn; Tchng.

**HUDSON, SHAWN P,** Averett Coll, Danville, VA; JR; BS; Cmmtr Lfe Exec Cmmttee 90; Bapt Chrch Sftbl Tm; Deans Lst; Pres Lst; Garland/Harriet Wyatt Schlrshp; Keegee Fnd; Accntng.

**HUDSON, STEVE A,** Mount Olive Coll, Mount Olive, NC; SR; BS; Fllwshp Chrstn Athlts 87-89; Stdnt Gvrnmnt Cls VP 90-; Bsbl Cptn 87-; Bsns.

**HUDSON, SUSAN J,** Salisbury St Univ, Salisbury, MD; SR; BSN; SNA VP 88-89; Phi Eta Sigma Phi Kappa Phi; Sigma Theta Tau; Nrsng.

**HUDSON, SUZANNE C,** Birmingham Southern Coll, Birmingham, AL; SR; BS; Lit Mag Poetry Edtr 89; Pres Serv Orgztn 90-; Peer Advsr 89-; Mrtr Bd 90-; Phi Beta Kappa 90-; Kappa Delta Epsilon Pres 89-; Omicron Delta Kappa; Alpha Phi Omega Pres 88-90; Cmpus Mnstres 88-89; Branscomb Awd 89-; DANA Intrn; Ele Educ; Tch.

**HUDSON, TIMOTHY M,** Providence Coll, Providence, RI; SO; BA; Radio 90-; Art Clb 90-; Thtr Wrkshp 90-; Pol Sci; Law.

**HUDSON, TINA M,** Volunteer St Comm Coll, Gallatin, TN; ASSOC; Dntl Asst.

**HUDSON, TRACI L,** Thiel Coll, Greenville, PA; FR; BA; Cmmtr Org Sec; Cmptr Sci.

**HUDSON, VENISSA J,** Bethel Coll, Mckenzie, TN; FR; BS; Vsprs Srvs; Frshmn Cls 90-; Deans Lst 90-; Hnr Rl 90-; Math; Educ.

**HUDSON JR, WALTER J,** Salisbury St Univ, Salisbury, MD; FR; BA; Frnch Clb 90-; Phi Eta Sigma 90-; Pres Schlrshp 90-; Seidel Educ Schlrshp 90-; Hstry; Educ.

**HUDSPETH, QUENTIN M,** Ms St Univ, Miss State, MS; SO; BS; Scty Physcs Stdnts 89-; Plntry Scty 89-; Schlrshp BASF 89-90; Acdmc Schlrshp 89-; Prsdnts Lst 90; Physcs.

**HUDSPETH, SCOTT G,** Cincinnati Bible Coll & Sem, Cincinnati, OH; GD; MADIV; Mission Trip Australia New Zealand Fiji 89; Grad Tchr Diploma Ev Tchr Trng Assoc 90; Ldrshp Schlrshp 84-86; Whos Who Am Chrstn Ldrshp 89; BA Fl Chrstn Coll 84; Ch Hstry/Theo Bblcl Studies; Tchr/Minister.**

**HUEBNER, JENNISON L,** Alfred Univ, Alfred, NY; FR; BA; Amer Mktg Assn; Tae Kwon Do Clb; Stdnt Snt; Alpha Lambda Delta; Var Swimming; Pol Sci; Law.

**HUELSMANN, MARTIN J,** Northern Ky Univ, Highland Hts, KY; JR; BA; Mud Clb; AFO; Studio Art; Art Therapy.

**HUEN, NELSON,** Georgetown Univ, Washington, DC; SR; BSBA; Stdnt Fdrl Crdt Union Treas Chf Fin Offcr 87-; Comm Tax Aid; Acctg/Intl Mgmt.

**HUENEFELD, AMY C,** Smith Coll, Northampton, MA; SO; BA; Ecnmcs.**

**HUERTA, CARLOS A,** Univ Of Miami, Coral Gables, FL; SR; BA; Join A Team Not A Gang Prog Miami Metro Dade Plce Dept 90-; Vrsty Ftbl Lttrmn 87-; Fnnce Acctng; Prfssnl Ftbl Bus Mgmt.

**HUERTAS, NATIVIDAD D,** City Univ Of Ny City Coll, New York, NY; JR; BE; Latin Engrs Amer Stdnt Assn Pub Rel 90-; Amer Inst Chem Engrs Pres 89-90; Swmng Tm 87-89; Tau Beta Pi; Gldn Key; Intrnshp Rohm/Haas; ASPIRA Acad Achvmnt Awd; Procter/Gamble Che Schlrshp; Chem Engr.

**HUERTAS-BERMUDEZ, ANTONIO F,** Univ Of Pr At Mayaguez, Mayaguez, PR; SO; BSCPE; Cmptr Eng Stdnt Assc 89-90; Cmptr Eng.**

**HUETTE, SCOTT E,** Oh Univ, Athens, OH; JR; BFA; Phtgrphy; Edctn.

**HUETWOHL, ROBERT V,** Meridian Comm Coll, Meridian, MS; FR; BA; Voc Ind Club Of Amer 90-; United Way 90-; Peavey Elect 90-; Hnrbly Dschrgd USMC 82-86; Elec; Engr.

**HUEY, MARY ALLISON,** Fl St Univ, Tallahassee, FL; SO; BA; Phi Eta Sigma; Delta Delta Delta Schlrshp Chrmn; IMS Sftbl/Bsktbl.

**HUFF II, CHARLES J,** Marshall University, Huntington, WV; GD; MBA; BBA Fin Marshall Univ 90-; Fin; Banking.

**HUFF, CHRISTOPHER BLANE,** Univ Of Sc At Columbia, Columbia, SC; SO; Advrtsng.

**HUFF, CYNTHIA R,** Hudson Valley Comm Coll, Troy, NY; SR; Early Chldhd Clb 89-; Coll/Career Clb 90-; Pres Lst 89-; Chldrns Chrch Tchr Dir 85-; Chrch Yth Ldr; Kingdom Prs Sec 88-; Saratoga Cnty Hm Bur Assn Schlrshp 90; Early Chldhd Fndtn Awd; AAS; Early Chldhd Educ.**

**HUFF, DEBORAH SUZAN,** Univ Of Ky, Lexington, KY; SR; BA; UK Mrchg Wldct Bnd/Pep/Cncrt Bnd 86-89; Tau Beta Sigma Actv 86-88; 1st Yr Arch Studio Dsgn Schlrshp 89-90; Accptd Archtctr Intrn Ntl Prks Serv; Archtctr.

**HUFF, ELLEN Q,** Univ Of Sc At Columbia, Columbia, SC; SR; BA; Educ Mjrs Clb 90-; Intl Reading Assn 89-; Natl Assn Educ Yng Chld 90-; Chrch Music Dir 87-; Sndy Schl Tchr 85-; Early Chldhd Educ; Tch.

**HUFF, GWYNNE G,** Greenville Tech Coll, Greenville, SC; SO; Sclgy; Educ.

**HUFF, J ADRIENNE,** Limestone Coll, Gaffney, SC; SO; BA; Ltrcy Mag 90-; Lmstn Clg Hon Pgm 89-; Psychlgy; Psychthrpy.

**HUFF, JACQUELINE D,** Middle Tn St Univ, Murfreesboro, TN; JR; BS; Kappa Delta Pi; Elem Ed; Tchng.

**HUFF, JULIE K,** Syracuse Univ, Syracuse, NY; JR; BSW; Undrgrad Scl Wrk Stu Org 90-; Ithaca Coll Spch Hrg/Lang Assoc 87-90; Scl Wrk.

**HUFF, KIMBERLY L,** Fl St Univ, Tallahassee, FL; FR; BED; Mrch Chfs 90-; Cncrt Bnc 90-; Brs Choir; Horn Choir; Wmns Glee 90-; Deans Lst 90-; Hon/Schlr Prog 90-; Sigma Alpha Iota; Sigma Alpha Iota Fresh Wmn Music Schlrshp 90; Mus Educ; Mus Prfrmnc/Educ.

**HUFF, LINDA V,** Hudson Valley Comm Coll, Troy, NY; FR; AAS; Phi Beta Kappa; Real Estate Rnvtn 87-90; Bsns; Fncl Mgmnt.

**HUFF, MARTHA K,** Bethany Coll, Bethany, WV; SR; BS; Pnhlnc Cncl VP 89-; Stdnt Ofr Sprt VP 89-; Stdnt Nwspr Sprts Ed 90; Phi Mu Pnhlnc 88-; Sr Flwshp Psychlgy 90-; Thomas H Briggs Awd Psychlgy; Dns Lst 87-; Vrsty Swmng 87-; Psychlgy; Cnslng.

**HUFF, MICHAEL R,** Ferrum Coll, Ferrum, VA; SO; BS; Hl Cncl Pres 89-; Clg Repubs Secr 89-; Ambsdr 90-; Lambda Sigma V P 90-; Phi Alpha Theta V P; Outstndg Stdnt Ldrshp Awd V P 89-90/Pres 90-; Hstry; Law.**

**HUFF, MICHELE M,** Central Pa Bus School, Summerdale, PA; SR; AS; Offc Cmnctns Big/Ltl Sis; CSI; Crss Cntry Tm Capt; Offc Cmnctns; Admnstrtv Asst.

**HUFF, SHARON D,** Union Coll, Barbourville, KY; FR; BS; Science; Nursing.

**HUFF, STEPHANIE A,** Blue Mountain Coll, Blue Mountain, MS; SR; Athltc Cncl Pres 90-; MAE Sp; Euzelian Scl Sor Pres 90-; Var Bsktbl Fl Schlrshp 87-; BS; Elem Ed.

**HUFF, TINA M,** Germanna Comm Coll, Locust Grove, VA; AS; Alpha Beta Gama 90; Mktg Mgmt; Mktg.

**HUFFARD, ELLIOTT CLAY,** Radford Univ, Radford, VA; FR; BSN; Ski Club Clge Republicans; Jse Cncl; Alpha Lampda Delta; CRNA.

**HUFFMAN, ANGELA B,** Catawba Valley Comm Coll, Hickory, NC; SO; Acctg.

**HUFFMAN, BRYAN C,** Lenoir Rhyne Coll, Hickory, NC; FR; AB; Cmptr Sci; Cmptr Bus.

**HUFFMAN, CHRISTY N,** Catawba Valley Comm Coll, Hickory, NC; FR; AAS; Hortcltr Tech; Grnhse Bsns.

**HUFFMAN, CRAIG K,** Morehouse Coll, Atlanta, GA; JR; Stdnt Gvrnmnt Assn Crrspndng; SGA Acdmc Affrs Comm Pblc Rltns 90-; MTC Entrprs Pstv Mssg Actv Wr Prsdnt 89-; Hnr Roll 90-; Deans Lst 91-; Sntr Paul Simon Wshgtn DC Offc Frgn Rel Int; Pltcl Sci Pre Law; Law Bsns Pltcs.

**HUFFMAN, DAVID L,** Univ Of Southern Ms, Hattiesburg, MS; JR; BA; Alpha Lambola Delta 89-; Golden Key 90-; Phi Alpha Theta; Gamma Beta Phi 89-; Pres Schlr 88-; Hon Coll 88-; History; Minstry.

**HUFFMAN, ELMER B,** Limestone Coll, Gaffney, SC; GD; BS; Retired Merchant; AAS Cecils Jr Clg 76; Busmgmt; Missions.

**HUFFMAN, FRANCES H,** Beckley Coll, Beckley, WV; SR; AS; Med Asstnt.

**HUFFMAN, GARY C,** Coppin St Coll, Baltimore, MD; SR; BS; Psychology Clb Sntr 90; Mgmt Sci/Psychology.

**HUFFMAN III, JAMES WYLIE,** Univ Of Sc At Columbia, Columbia, SC; FR; BA; Phi Eta Sigma; Coastl Carolina Bsbll Tm 90-; Engl/Pol Sci; Law.

**HUFFMAN, JASON A,** Christian Brothers Univ, Memphis, TN; SR; BS; SG Pres 89-; Nwspr 88-89; Chorale 88-; Alpha Chi 90-; Tau Beta Pi Sec 89-; IEEE V P 87-; Sigma Alpha Epsilon Chpln 88-; Bacchus Sec 89-90; Acad Peer Cnslng 89-; Outstanding Eng 89-; IM Bsktbl; Elect Eng; Law.

**HUFFMAN, JENNIFER KATE,** Lenoir Rhyne Coll, Hickory, NC; SR; BA; Phi Beta Lambda 90; Dns Lst 90; Bus Admin; Mgmt.

**HUFFMAN, LISA M,** Indiana Univ Of Pa, Indiana, PA; SR; BS; Big Brothers 89-90; ACEI 90-; PSEA 90-; IM Vlybl/Sftbl 87-89; Elem Educ; Tchr.

**HUFFMAN, PAMELA D,** Univ Of Pittsburgh, Pittsburgh, PA; JR; BSN; Med Sr Staff 90-; NSNA 89-; Stdnt Nrsng Assn PA 89-; Nrsng.

**HUFFMAN, THOMAS MARK,** Campbell Univ, Buies Creek, NC; FR; BS; Presdntl Schlrs; Phi Eta Sigma; Biology; Medicine.

**HUFFSTETLER, ELIZABETH D,** Valdosta St Coll, Valdosta, GA; JR; BSN; Ga Assoc Of Nrsng Stdnts 90-; Natl Assoc Of Nrsng Stdntds 90-; Former Tchr 85-90; BS Appalachian Std Univ 75; Nursing.

**HUFFSTETLER, MELODY R,** Clayton St Coll, Morrow, GA; JR; BS; Baptist Student Union; AS; Science; Pharmacy.

**HUFFSTUTLER, VINCENT E,** Univ Of Al At Birmingham, Birmingham, AL; SO; UAB Sch Hlth Rel Prof Stdnt Assoc Repr 90-; Stdnt Occup Ther Assoc 90-; AL Occup Ther Assoc 90-; Alpha Eta; Pres Lst; Natl Eagle Scout Assoc 81-; AA Walker Clg Jasper AL 86; AAS Jefferson State Jr Clg; Occup Ther Asst.

**HUFNAL, KATHERINE H,** De Tech & Comm Coll At Dover, Dover, DE; JR; BAAC; Stdnt Spprt Serv VP 89-90; Scty Of Stdnt Accntnts 89; Accntng; CPA.

**HUG, JAMES D,** Defiance Coll, Defiance, OH; SO; Chamber Singers 89-; Theatre Prod 89-90; Pi Kappa Delta 90-; Schlr Athlete Awd; Dorothy Houck Weaner Schlrshp 90-; Tennis Tm 2nd Singles 89-; Comm Arts; Coll Prof.

**HUG, LORI R,** Univ Of Ga, Athens, GA; JR; BS; SCEC 90-; SCOAR 89-90; Gldn Ky 90-; Delta Zeta Asst Pldg Educ 89-90; Spec Educ; Tchng.

**HUGENBERG, LARA E,** Univ Of Cincinnati, Cincinnati, OH; SO; BS; Asst Eqp Mgr 89-; Tau Alpha Pi 90-; OCAS Recy Cmte 89-; Archtre Tech.

**HUGGINS, ALICIA,** Strayer Coll, Washington, DC; JR; BS; Alpha Chi Sec; AA; Business Adm; Financial Svcs.

**HUGGINS, ANGELA R,** Livingston Univ, Livingston, AL; FR; BA; Phi Eta Sigma; Pres Lst; Dns Lst; Gilbert Wrtng Awrd; IM Sftbl; Nrsng.

**HUGGINS, ELIZABETH A,** Austin Peay St Univ, Clarksville, TN; FR; BA; Stdnt Govt Sentr 90-; Stdnt Almni Cncl; Gvnrs Frst Ldy; Alpha Delta Pi 90-; Cmps Cvtn 90-; Pres Emrgng Ldr 90-; Gvnrs Ambssdr 90-; Orntatn Ldr 90-; Vrsty Chrldr 90-; Ed; Elem Ed.

**HUGGINS, GWENDOLYN G,** Al A & M Univ, Normal, AL; SO; Psych Clb 89-; Stndt Drg Task Force 90-; Glenwood Mntl Hlth Svcs; Camp Sunshine Pgm; Camp Cnslr Chldrn; Psych; Rsch.

**HUGGINS, MARSHA A,** Univ Of Sc At Coastal Carolina, Conway, SC; JR; BS; Phys Ed; Tch.

**HUGGINS, SHANELL,** Alcorn St Univ, Lorman, MS; JR; NAACP 88-; Eng Clb Pres 90-; Pan Hllnc Cncl 90-; Delta Sigma Theta Pres 90-; Eng Educ Scndry; Tch.

**HUGGINS, STACY E,** Denmark Tech Coll, Denmark, SC; SO; AA; SGA 90-; Peer Cnslr 90-; Phi Theta Kappa; Esquire Swthrts Pres 90-; Stdnt Mrshl Commncemnt Exer 90; Wmns Bsktbl Mgr 90-; Ofc Syst Tech; Bsn Ed.

**HUGHART, SHERRI D,** Wv Univ, Morgantown, WV; SR; BS; Amrcn Phrmctcl Assoc 90-; Alpha Phi Omega 87-88; Prsdntl Schlrshp; Phrmcy.

**HUGHES SMITH, RUTH J,** Mayland Comm Coll, Spruce Pine, NC; FR; MBA; Phi Theta Kappa; Engl; Teach.

**HUGHES, AMANDA B,** Univ Of Ga, Athens, GA; SR; Bptst Stdnt Un 87-; Wsly Fndtn 87-; Gldn Key 90-; Stdnt Prfssnl Assoc GA Edctns 90-; GA Assoc Edctrs; Chi Omega 87-; Stdnt Tchng Grantham England; BSED; Erly Chldhd Ed; Tchng.

**HUGHES, AMANDA L,** Anderson Coll, Anderson, SC; FR; BA; Gamma Beta Phi 90-; Hons Pgm 90-; Art Awd For Three-Dim Design; Vlybl Tm 90-; Sftbl Tm 90-; Graphic Design; Arch.

**HUGHES, AQUILINA T,** Fl A & M Univ, Tallahassee, FL; FR; Phrmcy.

**HUGHES, ATTA KAKRA,** Central St Univ, Wilberforce, OH; SO; BSC; Flwshp Chrstn Std 89-; Intl Std Asc 89-; Grp Intl Std 90; Wtr Rscs Mgmt; Engr/Bsn.

**HUGHES, CATHY,** Alcorn St Univ, Lorman, MS; SR; M A; Engl Clb 89-; Cncrt Choir 89-90; Herald Rprtr 89-90; Alpha Kappa Alpha; Top Ten Outstndng Stdnts 90-; BA; Engl; Prfssr.

**HUGHES, COLETTE L,** Longwood Coll, Farmville, VA; SO; BS; Thrptc Rcrtn Clb; Brmda Spcl Olympcs 86-; St Brendans Psychtrc 83-; Thrptc Rcrtn.

**HUGHES, CURTIS G,** Al A & M Univ, Normal, AL; FR; BTS; AATE Drake St 80; PSB Metropolitan Coll 70; Technology; Staff Mbr Al A/M Univ.

**HUGHES, CYNTHIA A,** Beckley Coll, Beckley, WV; JR; BA; Deans Lst 89-; Aa; Blgy; Scndry Edctn.

**HUGHES, DANA A,** Univ Of Montevallo, Montevallo, AL; JR; BA; SGA Rep 89-; Cable News Anchor; College Night 88-; Deans Lst; Phi Mu PR/ALUMNI Rel 88-90; Chldrns Miracle Ntwrk Radioathon 90; IM Powder Puff Ftbl; Mass Cmnctns; Jrnlst.

**HUGHES, DARIN C,** Univ Of Nc At Charlotte, Charlotte, NC; GD; Pi Kappa Phi 85-; BA 90; Psych.

**HUGHES, DARLA G,** Mayland Comm Coll, Spruce Pine, NC; FR.

**HUGHES, DAVID C,** Univ Of Southern Ms, Hattiesburg, MS; JR; Actvts Cncl 89-; Fncng Clb 89-; Hnrs Assn 89-90; Soc Physcs Stdnts 89-; Physics; Tchr.

**HUGHES, DAWN R,** Mayland Comm Coll, Spruce Pine, NC; GD; DIP; Stdnt Of Mnth; Gen Offce Tech Spec; Scrtry.

**HUGHES, EDWARD L,** Al A & M Univ, Normal, AL; SR; NSBE GPA Awd 88-90; Peer Cnslr 89-90; Yth Svc 88-90; Chattanooga Chmbr Cmrc Schlrshp 88-90; CST Pres Comm Awd 88; Drug Tsk Frc 89-90; Dsgn Eng; AS Chattanooga St Tech 88; Mech Eng Tech.

**HUGHES, ERICA R,** Rollins Coll, Winter Park, FL; FR; BA; Chrl Soc 90-; Chpl Choir 90-; Hnrs Dgr Pgm 90-; Math/Msc; Sec Tchng.

**HUGHES, GREGORY J,** Univ Of Sc At Columbia, Columbia, SC; FR; MBA; Fllwshp Of Christian Athletes 90; Water Ski Tm 90; SC Clg 90; Accntng.

**HUGHES, J ALLEN,** Univ Of South Al, Mobile, AL; JR; BS; Acctng Club NAA Treas; Inst Internal Auditors; Beta Alpha Psi; AL Scty CPA Schlrshp; IM Ftbl/Bskbl 90-; Acctng; CPA.

**HUGHES JR, JAMES THERON,** Memphis St Univ, Memphis, TN; JR; BSET; Adult Stdnt Assoc 90-; US Navy Electrnc Tchncn 3 Cls 84-89; Elctrnc Tchnlgy Engrng.

**HUGHES, JARED B,** Wv Univ At Parkersburg, Parkersburg, WV; FR; State FFA VP 90-; Elem Ed; Elem Tchr Wrstlng Coach.

**HUGHES, JEANNE M,** Tusculum Coll, Greeneville, TN; JR; BA; Dir Sr High Yth 89-; Cmptr Info Sys.

**HUGHES, JEFF B,** Univ Of Sc At Columbia, Columbia, SC; FR; Elec Engr.

**HUGHES, KATHLEEN H,** Dowling Coll, Oakdale Li, NY; SR; BA; PTA 82-; Septa 86-; Sigma Tau Belta Pres; Alpha Chi; Kappa Delta Pi; Phi Theta Kappa 88-89; Phi Alpha Sigma 87-88; Racanelli Schlr 89-; Deans Lst SCC 87-89; Lbrl Arts Schlrshp SCCC 89; AA 89; Engl; Educ.

**HUGHES, KELLY S,** Westminster Coll, New Wilmingtn, PA; SO; BA; Almn Assc 89-; Math Clb 90-; Kappa Mu Epsilon; Math; Actry.

**HUGHES, KEVIN S,** Walker Coll, Jasper, AL; FR; BS; Stdnt Govt 90-; Phi Theta Kappa; Chem Awd; Pres Hnrs Lst 90; Eng; Mech Eng.

**HUGHES, LAURA M,** Northern Ky Univ, Highland Hts, KY; SO; BA; Elem Educ; Tchng.

**HUGHES, LINDA A,** Boston Univ, Boston, MA; MD; Cum Laude 85; Rsrch Asst MCP 87; Alpha Oemga Alpah 90; TA 84-86; Tutr 84-86; Rho Chi 86-; MAS Med Sco 87-; J F Lnage Flwshp 85-86; Glee Clb 81-85; Bradbury Scott Schlrshp 85; AM Chem Soc 82-85; Beta Beta Beta 83-85; Med.

**HUGHES, LISA MARIE,** Kennesaw St Coll, Marietta, GA; FR; BS; Kennesaw Frshmn Fndtn Schlrshp; Info Sys.

**HUGHES II, LLOYD W,** Wv Univ At Parkersburg, Parkersburg, WV; SO; BS; Bus Admin.

**HUGHES, MARY BETH,** Univ Of Cincinnati-Clrmnt Coll, Batavia, OH; FR; Psych; Soc Wrk.

**HUGHES, MARY S,** Va Commonwealth Univ, Richmond, VA; BS; IM Capt 88-90; Hll Cncl 88-90; Vol Actn Comm 88-89; Intrvrsty 88-90; Psych.

**HUGHES, MARYLU,** Wv Univ At Parkersburg, Parkersburg, WV; FR; VITA; Bsns; Mgmt.

**HUGHES, MEGAN R,** Hampton Univ, Hampton, VA; FR; BA; Pre Med 90-; Biol 90-; Ms Soph Exec Cncl; Natl Hnr Soc 90-; Hnr Rl 90-; Pres Emminent Schlrshps 90-; Biol; Med/Orthopedic Surgeon.

**HUGHES, MELISSA R,** Christopher Newport Coll, Newport News, VA; JR; BSA; Acctg.

**HUGHES, MELODY A,** Univ Of Ky, Lexington, KY; SR; PHAM; Clgns For Acad Excel 90-; Rho Chi Pharm 90-; Phi Lambda Sigma 90-; Sci Hon 89-90; Lambda Kappa Sigma 89-; Pharmacy.

**HUGHES, MERNA P,** City Univ Of Ny Med Evers Coll, Brooklyn, NY; SR; BA; Ed.

**HUGHES, MICHAEL HOWARD,** Glassboro St Coll, Glassboro, NJ; SR; BA; Radio T V Assoc 88-; Clb Italian Amer Obsrvnce 90-; Alpha Phi Delta Treas 87; T V Supvr Fld Exprnce; I M Sprts 87; Cmunctns; T V.

**HUGHES, MIRIAM W,** Nova Univ, Ft Lauderdale, FL; GD; MA; FICPA 87-; Acctnt 87-; BA Mt Holyoke Clg 69; Acctg; CPA.

**HUGHES, MONICA J,** Alcorn St Univ, Lorman, MS; JR; BS; Khem Clb; Hon Org; Pan-Hllnc Cncl; Alpha Kappa Mu; Delta Sigma Theta Sor Treas 90-; Natl Cnsrtm Grad Degrees Mnrts Eng/Sci Fellow; Shell Oil Co Intrn; Eastmn Kodak Intrn; US Achvmnt; Acdmy Natl Awd; Chem; Ind/Tchng.

**HUGHES, PANYIN A,** Central St Univ, Wilberforce, OH; SO; BS; Flwshp Chrstn Std Stf Lsn 90-; Engr.

**HUGHES, PATRICIA A,** Al A & M Univ, Normal, AL; SR; BSW; Soc Wrk Clb 90-; Soc Wrk.

**HUGHES, PATRICK B,** Bapt Bible Coll & Seminary, Clarks Summit, PA; SR; BS; Stdnt Govt 90-; Dorm Pres 90-F Wrstlng Capt 88-91; Soccer 87-88; Pstrl Stds; Mnstry.

**HUGHES, PATTYE L,** Jackson St Univ, Jackson, MS; JR; BBA; NAACP V P 90-; Acctng Soc Assist Secy; Delta Mu Delta 90-; Alpha Lambda Delta 89-; Inroads Of Wisc 90-; Acctng.

**HUGHES, ROBERT S,** Savannah Coll Of Art & Design, Savannah, GA; JR; BA; London Showing Cmptr Animation; Phtgrphy; Trvl/Tchr.

**HUGHES, SANDRA E,** George Mason Univ, Fairfax, VA; SO; BA; Acctg Clb 90-; AHSA Hrsbckrdng Assoc 85-; Alpha Lambda Delta Treas 89-; Peer Adv; Schlrshp Frm Robert Morris Assoc; Acctg.

**HUGHES, SANDRA L,** Univ Of Sc At Columbia, Columbia, SC; FR; BA; Elem Educ; Tchr.

**HUGHES, SANDRA S,** Ky Wesleyan Coll, Owensboro, KY; SR; MA; Parnassus Ltry Scty Pres 88-; Wslyn Plyrs Drama Scty Pres 89-; Brd Pblctns Chrprsn 89-90; Chpl Wrshp Ldr; Psychlgy Clb 88-; Stdy Sessn Ldr 88-; Jammes Graham Brown Schlrs 88-; Alpha Chi 90-; Alpha Psi Omega; Engl/Spnsh/Psychlgy; Lit Prof.

**HUGHES, SHANNON L,** Central Al Comm Coll, Alexander City, AL; SO; BS; Bapt Camps Minstrs V P 89-; Phi Theta Kappa 90-; Dns Lst 89-; Otstdng Stdnt Soc Sci; Grad Magna Cum Laude 90-; AS; Elem Educ; Jr High Tchr/Cnslr.

**HUGHES, SHARON S,** Univ Of Al At Birmingham, Birmingham, AL; JR; SO; BA; Southern Inst Pres List/Deans List 87-88; Deans List 88-; Techlgy Sci; Radiologic Techlgt.

**HUGHES, SHELLY M,** Univ Of North Fl, Jacksonville, FL; JR; BA; Phi Theta Kappa 88-; St Catherines Peace/Jstc Cmt Chrprsn 86-; Diocese St Augustine Cmsn Jstc/Peace Subcomm Chr 90-; AA St Johns River Comm Clg 90; Psychlgy; Cnslng/Soc Wrk.

**HUGHES, SONIA E,** Savannah St Coll, Savannah, GA; FR; BA; Cncrt Choir 90-; LLM; Scl Sci; Law.

**HUGHES, SONJA J,** Clemson Univ, Clemson, SC; SR; BS; Stdnt Nrs Assn 87-; Goldn Key 89-; Sigma Theta Tau 90-; Phi Kappa Phi Cert Merit; Deans Lst 87-; Pres Lst 87-; Magna Cum Laude; Nrsng.

**HUGHES, TAMMY L,** Schenectady County Comm Coll, Schenectady, NY; SO; BA; Senior Chorus 85-86; Yrbk Com 86-87; Ski Clb 85-90; Geriatric Aide Nrsng Hm; Bus/Acctg.

**HUGHES, THOMAS A,** Univ Of Rochester, Rochester, NY; SR; BA; Inter Var Ldr 89-; Band 89-; Psych; Vocal Perf.

**HUGHES, TIFFANY F,** Auburn Univ At Auburn, Auburn, AL; FR; BS BA; Univ Of South Cncrt Chr 90; Auburn Cncrt Chr; Church Pianist 89-; Wilkins Schlr 90; Comm Summer Bnd Pgm; Elderly Visit Pgm 90; Biochemistry/Religion; Lab Rsrch/Teaching.

**HUGHES, TRACY M,** Va Commonwealth Univ, Richmond, VA; JR; BS; Natl Stdnt Nurses Assoc; Stdnt Nurses Assoc Of VA Elect Historian; Leukemia Soc 89-; Chrstn Chldrns Fund Sponsor 90-; Selected Applicant Fuld Schlrshp; A D Williams Schlrshp From MCV 90-; River Rd United Meth Church 88-; Nursing; ICU Nursing.

**HUGHES, VIRGINIA D,** Memphis St Univ, Memphis, TN; JR; BFA; Grphc Dsgn; Art Dir.

**HUGHES, W PARKES,** Emory Univ, Atlanta, GA; SR; AA Oxford Clg 89; Bus.

**HUGHES, WENDY P,** Barry Univ, Miami, FL; SR; BSC; Jamaicn Assn 89-; Delta Mu Delta 90-; Golden Z Clb 90-; Mgmt Inf Syst; Inf Syst Analyst.

**HUGHES, WILLIAM S,** Middle Tn St Univ, Murfreesboro, TN; JR; BA; Stdnt Govt Assoc Sen 90-; Hstry.

**HUGHEY, JOANNA D,** William Carey Coll, Hattiesburg, MS; SO; BS; Math Stdnt Of Yr 89-90; Math/Eng; Scndry Teacher.

**HUGHEY, MARY RUTH,** Univ Of Sc At Columbia, Columbia, SC; FR; BA; Lf Grd 90-; Sci; Sprts Admn.

**HUGHEY, SHERONDA L,** Univ Of Tn At Martin, Martin, TN; SO; BA; BSA 89-90; Intrn Fed Exprs 89-; Acctng; CPA.

**HUGHLEY, JENNIFER,** Gallaudet Univ, Washington, DC; SO; German Clb 89-; Educ Clb 90-; Early Chldhd Educf Tchg.

**HUH, JOON J,** Kent St Univ Kent Cmps, Kent, OH; JR; BS; Tae Kwon Doe Clb 89-; Cmps Crsd Christ 89-; Sftbl Vlybl Bsktbl IMS 90-; Pre-Med; Med.

**HUHN, RICHARD M,** Neumann Coll, Aston, PA; JR; BA, Nwspr Stf Wrtr 89; Deans Lst 90; IM Ftbl 89-90; Mrktg; Ad.

**HUIE, EDWARD,** City Univ Of Ny Baruch Coll, New York, NY; JR; BBA; Dns Lst 90; Acctng; CPA.

**HUIE, JENNIFER E,** Univ Of Montevallo, Montevallo, AL; SR; BS; Campus Outrch 88-; Sci Club 87; Phi Kappa Phi; Pres List 88-; Deans List 88-; Kappa Delta Pi 88-F Chi Omega Publcty Chr 88-F Im Ftbl For Women 90-; Elem Erly Chldhd Ed.

**HUIE, NANCY,** City Univ Of Ny Baruch Coll, New York, NY; SO; MBA; Acctng.

**HUJSAK, ALLEN R,** Va Commonwealth Univ, Richmond, VA; FR; BFA; Rugby; Phi Eta Sigma; Illstrtn; Freelance Advrtsng Illstrtr.

**HULAN, CHRISTY A,** Univ Of Tn At Martin, Martin, TN; SO; PHARM; Phi Eta Sigma; Mu Epsilon Delta V P Pldg Cl 90; Stdnt Affairs Serv Awd; Pharmcy U T Memphis.

**HULEY, DENISE,** Jackson St Univ, Jackson, MS; SR; Phi Alpha 90-; AA Coahoma Comm Clg 89; Scl Wrk.

**HULGAN, TERI L,** Univ Of Montevallo, Montevallo, AL; FR; Bapt Cmps Mnstries 90; Pre Pharmacy; Phrmcy.

**HULL, AARON,** Hudson Valley Comm Coll, Troy, NY; FR; Crlng Clb; Pres Lst 90-; Bus; Acctg.

**HULL, AMY E,** Nc Agri & Tech St Univ, Greensboro, NC; GD; CERT; Child Dev 84-88; Sec 87-88; NAEYC 86-88; Girls In Action Ldr 88-90; Sndy Schl Tchr 91-; Choir 88-90; Daisy Scout Troup Ldr 90-91; Vol Spec Olympics Swim Coach 89-90; Full Time Nanny Summer Mnths 86-87; Spec Educ; Tchr.

**HULL, ANGELA R,** Alcorn St Univ, Lorman, MS; FR; BS; Nrsng; Anesthetist.

**HULL, ARMON W,** Athens St Coll, Athens, AL; SR; Sr Class Pres 90-; Tau Kappa Epsilon 89-; AS Bessemer State Tech Clg 88; Bus.

**HULL, DOROTHY S,** Tougaloo Coll, Tougaloo, MS; JR; BABED; Prnts Clb 90-; Intrn Allstate Ins Co 90-; Yng People Org; Ins Co Emplee; Econ/Bus Admn; Bus Stdes/Tch.

**HULL, JORY A,** Savannah Coll Of Art & Design, Savannah, GA; SO; BA; Photo Clb 90-; Grphc Art; Grphc Artst/Phtgrphr.

**HULL, JUANITA MARIE,** Savannah Coll Of Art & Design, Savannah, GA; GD; MFA; Grad Stdnt Assoc 90-; MOSS 90-; Wstrn MI Univ Dir Of Fun Actvies 73-77; Alpha Beta Epsilon Schlrshp 74-77; Dghtrs Of Amer Rev 73-; Bg Bro/Bg Srs Asst Dir Newagy Co 78-79; Sierra Clb 77-80; Int Guild Natl Sci 90-; Art; Univ Tchr.

**HULL, KEVIN C,** Savannah Coll Of Art & Design, Savannah, GA; JR; BA; Illustration; Freelance Illustrator.

**HULL, W DAVID,** Oh Wesleyan Univ, Delaware, OH; FR; BA; Nwspr Rprtr 90-; Strand Theatr 90-; People Fr Ethcl Anml Trtmnt 89-; Phi Eta Sigma 90-; Ntl Hnr Scty 88-; Envrnmntl/Wldlf Clb 90-; Deans Lst 90; Scripps Howard Schlrshp Awd 90; Engl/Jrnlsm; Wrtr.

**HULSE, DIANE C,** Marywood Coll, Scranton, PA; SO; Ele Educ; Tch.

**HULSE, RAYMOND BRIAN,** Coll Of Charleston, Charleston, SC; FR; BA; Gay/Lesbn Allnce VP 90-; Alpha Phi Omega Pres 90; Hghiy Dist Fac Hons Lst; Low Cntry Gay/Lesbn Allnce Charlestn SC Treas 90-; US Navy Vet; Engl; Jrnlsm.

**HULSEN, INGRID M,** Immaculata Coll, Immaculata, PA; FR; BS; SADD; AHEA Sec 90-; Dietetics.

**HULSEY, TINA L,** Univ Of Al At Birmingham, Birmingham, AL; SR; BA; Gomerata Stf Auburn Univ; Prog Cncl; Specl Events Committee; Amer Mrktng Assoc; Delta Zeta; Business; Marketing.

**HULTS, LYNN V,** Univ Of South Al, Mobile, AL; SO; BED; Spec Ed/Hndcpd.

**HUMAN, CRYSTAL L,** Roane St Comm Coll, Harriman, TN; SO; AAS; TN Soc 90-; Rgstrd Tchnlgst Rdlty; Alpha Delta Pi Sng Ldr 87-88; Rdlgc Tchnlgy; Bsns Mgmnt.

**HUMBER, TONI CHERYL,** Howard Univ, Washington, DC; GD; PH D; Prfssnl Afflitns; Spch Cmmnctn Assn; Natl Cncl Tchrs Of Engl; Co Chr Blck Hsty Mnth; Grad Asstshp Schl Of Cmmnctns 89; M Ed Loyola Marymount Univ Los Angeles 75; BA CALIFORNIA St Univ Los Angeles 67; Elem Crdntl CA St Univ LA 68; Cmmnctns Sclngstcs; Univ Crr In Tchr Trnng.

**HUMBERS, STELLA R,** Northwest Al Comm Coll, Phil Campbell, AL; GD; AS; LPN 90; Nrsng; RN.

**HUME, ANNA M,** Lexington Comm Coll, Lexington, KY; SO; ADN; Nurse Apprntcshp; Nrsng.

**HUMER, ANDREW R,** Univ Of Sc At Columbia, Columbia, SC; SO; BS; Hnrs Clg 90-; Alpha Tau Omega 89-; Carolina Tour Guide Pgm; Abney Schlrshp Schlr 90-; Bsn Finance/Ins.

**HUMFLEET, VENETIA,** Sue Bennett Coll, London, KY; FR; BED; Cold Hill Elem PTO VP 88-89; Elem Edctn.

**HUMIC, KAREN L,** Le Moyne Coll, Syracuse, NY; SR; Alpha Sigma Pnu 89-; Spnsh; Edctn.

**HUMMEL, KRISTIN J,** Vanderbilt Univ, Nashville, TN; FR; BA; Stdnt Host 90-; Med Cntr Vol 90-; Vucept; Phi Eta Sigma 90-; Alpha Lambda Delta 90-; Kappa Delta 90-; Dns Lst; Vndrblt Crw 90-; Molculr Bio; Med.

**HUMMER, KERRY A,** Bloomsburg Univ Of Pa, Bloomsburg, PA; FR; BED; Im Vlybl 90-; Amnesty Intrntl 90-; Elem Ed; Tch.

**HUMMONS, DEBORAH A,** Cincinnati Metropolitan Coll, Cincinnati, OH; SR; AS; Bus Admin Cmptr Hrdwr/Sftwr 82-; CERT Queen City Voc; Mrktg/Acctg; Bus Admin.

**HUMPHREY, JUNE E,** Univ Of Fl, Gainesville, FL; SR; BSN; Stdnt Nrs Action 88-89; Sgm Theta Tau; Vtrns Admn Lrng Oprtnty Rsdncy Valor 90-; AA Cntrl FL Comm Clg 89; Nrsng; Clncl Spcplst.

**HUMPHREY, KATHY S,** Fayetteville St Univ, Fayetteville, NC; JR; BA; Assc 90; Bus; Rnng Own Bus.

**HUMPHREY, KRISTAL K,** Campbell Univ, Buies Creek, NC; JR; BBA; SGA Treas 89-; SAM 90-; Pres Schlrshp 90-; Phi Kappa Phi 90-; Intrnshp 88-; Bus Mgmt; Banking.**

**HUMPHREY, KRISTEN M,** Westminster Coll, New Wilmingtn, PA; JR; BA; Sclgy Intrst Grp; Phi Mu Rtual Chrmn 90-; Allegheny Cty Dstrct Atty Ofc Intern; Sclgy; Law.

**HUMPHREY, KYLE L,** Christopher Newport Coll, Newport News, VA; SR; BA; The Nelsonite At Thomas Nelson Cmnty Clge Asstnt Edtr 83; Interned WTKR Chnl 13; Grad Acdmy Of Modeling; Sales Mgr Ramada Inn The Omni Hotel Managed Night Club 86; AS Deg Thomas Nelson Cmnty 86; Liberal Arts Clge; English Writing; News Reporter.

**HUMPHREY, LUCINDA LOUISE,** Castleton St Coll, Castleton, VT; SO; BSED; Achvmnt Awd 88; Swmng; Sftbl; AS Liberal Arts Hudson Vly Comm Coll 88; Foreign Lang/Edn; Teach.

**HUMPHREY, MICHAEL D,** Va Commonwealth Univ, Richmond, VA; SR; BS; REBOS; Gldn Key; Virginia Rehab Assoc 90-; Ntl Rehab Assoc 90-; Virginia Assoc Alcohol Drug Abuse Cnslrs; Intrnshp Mt Wood Hosp; AAS 88; Alcohol/Drug Rehab Cnslg.

**HUMPHREY, PATRICIA A,** Hudson Valley Comm Coll, Troy, NY; SR; AAS; Pres List; Cert NY St Schl Of Indstrl/Labor Relations 90; Acctng/Auditing.

**HUMPHREY, SHEILA E,** Belmont Coll, Nashville, TN; SR; BS; Scl Wrk Clb Dir Of Pblcty 90; Belmont Lit Theatre 89-90; Intrn At Tn State Legsltre; Plnnd Prnthd Vol; Tn State Intrn; Scl Wrk; Cnslng.

**HUMPHREY, STEPHANIE T,** Fl A & M Univ, Tallahassee, FL; FR; PHD; Pres Schlrs Prlmntrn 90-; NASA Schlrs Assn; Ntl Soc Blck Eng; Phi Eta Sigma Comm Chr; NASA Intrnshp; ALCOA Intrnshp 90; Elec Eng.

**HUMPHREY, SUSAN J,** Juniata Coll, Huntingdon, PA; SR; BS; Yrbk 89-90; Chem Clb 87-; Math Clb 89-; Dupont Awd 90; Phys Chem Intern 90; Varsity Swmng Capt 88-; Chem; Rsrch.

**HUMPHREY, TRACEY ESTELLE,** D Youville Coll, Buffalo, NY; SO; BA; SPTA 89-; Stdnt Flwshp 89-; Lambda Sigma Treas 90-; Campus Mnstry 89-; Foreign Lang Awd; Phys Thrpy; Private Prctc.

**HUMPHREY, VONDA L,** Fort Valley St Coll, Fort Valley, GA; JR; BA; Agri Dmc Frm 88-; FFA 90-; Coop Devel Enrgy Prog 89-; Alpha Kappa Mu Rprtr 90-; Delta Sigma Theta Pres 90-; Hnrs Cnvctn 89-; Ag Econs; Agribus.

**HUMPHREY, WENDY L,** Central St Univ, Wilberforce, OH; JR; BA; Ambssdr; Alpha Kappa Mu 89; Delta Sigma Theta Pres 90; Brd Of Trustees 90; J C Penney Intrn 90; SUNY Stoney Brk U Intrn; Deans Lst 88; Trk 88-89; Chrldng 89-90; Psychlgy; Psychtrst.

**HUMPHREYS, MICHAEL SHAWN,** Daytona Beach Comm Coll, Daytona Beach, FL; FR; BA; Phi Theta Kappa; Comnty Serv; Hnrs Prog 90-; Phi Theta Kappa; Presidents List; Bus Mgmnt.

**HUMPHREYS, MICHELLE D,** Merrimack Coll, North Andover, MA; SO; BA; Envrnmntl Clb; Sigma Phi Omega 90-; Coop Educ; Womens Var Soccer Tm 89-; Mktg; Adv.

**HUMPHRIES, GREGORY S,** Bridgeport Engr Inst, Fairfield, CT; FR; BSME; Outstndg Apprntc Awd 81; Metl Wrkg Trds Apprntc Compt Tool Die Mkr 76-; Manfctng Eng.

**HUMPHRIES, JOHN C,** Bellarmine Coll, Louisville, KY; JR; BA; ACM 88-; Delta Epsilon Sigma; Cmptr Sci/Math; Consltnt.

**HUMPHRIES, MARK C,** Middle Tn St Univ, Murfreesboro, TN; JR; BS; Sccr Clb 89-90; Sigma Alpha Epsilon 90-; Sccr 89-90; Aerspc; Pro Pilot.

**HUMPHRIES, SHERRY L,** Univ Of Sc At Columbia, Columbia, SC; SO; Bapt Stdnt Un Mbr 88-89; Bus Mgmt; Open Own Bus.

**HUMPHRIES, TAMMY D,** Spartanburg Methodist Coll, Spartanburg, SC; SO; BA; Day Stdnt Assc 89-; AA; Econ/ Finance; Bnkng.

**HUMPHRIES, TRACY L,** Univ Of Nc At Greensboro, Greensboro, NC; SR; BME; Msc Edctrs Natl Cnfrnc Treas 89-90; Mu Phi Epsilon VP 90; Msc Ed; Band Dir.

**HUND, THOMAS J,** Asbury Theological Sem, Wilmore, KY; GD; MDIV; Theta Phi 88-; Sem Bsktbl 90-; Yth Mnstr Southand Evnglcl Meth Ch Lexington KY 88-; Taught Math 85-87; AA Neosho Cnty Comm Coll 82; BS KS State Univ 85; Christianity/ Religious Studies; Mnstry.

**HUNDLEY, MARZELLA L,** Ms St Univ, Miss State, MS; FR; BA; Chorus 90-; English; Law.

**HUNDLEY, RACHEL A,** Memphis St Univ, Memphis, TN; SR.

**HUNDLEY, THELMA K,** Univ Of Tn At Martin, Martin, TN; FR; BS; Home Ec Educ.

**HUNEYCUTT, KORENA S,** Appalachian St Univ, Boone, NC; FR; BS; Stdnt Govt Assoc Sen; Bapt Stdnt Union 90-; BSU Choir/Focus Tm 90-; Gamma Beta Phi; NCAE 90-; Math; Ed.

**HUNG, HELEN L,** Berkeley Coll Of Westchester, White Plains, NY; SO; BA; Phi Theta Kappa 90-; AAS; Math; Edctn.

**HUNIGAN, JAMIE W,** East Tn St Univ, Johnson City, TN; SR; Elctrnc Engr Tech; Engr/Bsn Owner.

**HUNKELER, JUDITH A,** Fl International Univ, Miami, FL; JR; BS; Stdnt Dttc Assoc 90; Offcrs Wvs Clb 89-; BS Psychlgy 88; Ntrtn Dtcs.

**HUNNICUTT, ROBIN L,** Longwood Coll, Farmville, VA; SR; Bapt Stdnt Unn Pres; Pr Advsr; Sigma Alpha Iota Sec; Sprts Info Hd Stdnt Asst; BS Longwood Coll; Educ; Tchng.

**HUNSBERGER, ANN M,** Univ Of Sc At Columbia, Columbia, SC; FR; BA; Bus; Law.

**HUNSINGER, DAVID S,** Univ Of Nc At Charlotte, Charlotte, NC; FR; BS; Phi Eta Sigma; Acctg.

**HUNSUCKER, RANDY C,** Western Carolina Univ, Cullowhee, NC; JR; BS; Pi Gamma Mu; Phi Alpha Delta 90-; Pol Sci; Military/Clg Prfsr.

**HUNT, ANDREW D,** Morehouse Coll, Atlanta, GA; FR; BA; Stdnt Cncl Cls Chpln 90-; Wheat Street Bapt Ch Assoc Mnstr 90-; IM Bsktbl Tm Capt 90-; Acctg/Religion.

**HUNT, BRIDGET P,** Univ Of Nh Plymouth St Coll, Plymouth, NH; SR; Hstry; Tchg.

**HUNT, CAROLYN ANN,** Middle Tn St Univ, Murfreesboro, TN; JR; BA; STEA 89-; Kappa Delta Pi 89-; Elem Ed; Upper Elem Tchr.

**HUNT, CHAD E,** Columbus Coll Of Art & Design, Columbus, OH; FR; Adv; Tchr.

**HUNT, CHADWICK D,** Sue Bennett Coll, London, KY; FR; Bsktbll Tm Guard; Spch Path; Tchg/Coach.

**HUNT, CHARLES E,** Al A & M Univ, Normal, AL; SO; BA; Thspn Soc 90-; Exrcs Sci; Orthpdtry Srgn.

**HUNT JR, DANIEL L,** Jackson St Univ, Jackson, MS; SR; BS; Alpha Lambda Delta 88-89; Pi Mu Epsilon 90-; Math Awd 89-90; Math; Tch.

**HUNT, DERRYK D,** Fayetteville St Univ, Fayetteville, NC; SO; BS; Math/Comp Sci Clb 89-; Stdnt Aide 90-; Rsdnt Asst; Chncllrs Schlr 90-; Intrnshp Caltechs Cntr Rsrch Parallel Compttn; Math/ Comp Sci.

**HUNT, DIANA L,** Springfield Tech Comm Coll, Springfield, MA; SO; AS; Engr Clb Pres 89-; Alpha Nu Omega 90-; Hamilton Standrd Div Un Tech 87-89; Engr; Mech Engr; Engr.

**HUNT, ENA MICHELLE,** Al A & M Univ, Normal, AL; SO; BA; AL AEM Acdmc Schlrshp; Thurgood Marshall Schlrshp; Psychlgy; Prbtn Offcr.

**HUNT, HEATHER A,** George Mason Univ, Fairfax, VA; SR; BS; Gldn Ky James Madison Univ Chptr 89-; Beta Gamma Sigma 90-; Bus/Mktng; Mngmnt.

**HUNT, KIMBERELY M,** Middle Tn St Univ, Murfreesboro, TN; SO; BS; Biology; Lab Sci.

**HUNT, KIMBERLEY A,** Fl International Univ, Miami, FL; SR; BA; Phi Kappa Phi; BA FIU 85; Ed Sperific Lrngn Disblt; Teach.

**HUNT, LARA B,** Fl St Univ, Tallahassee, FL; FR; Fla PIRG; Phi Eta Sigma; Delta Delta Delta; Phi Eta Sigma; Fla Scad Schlrshp Awd; Fla State Undrgrad Schlrshp.

**HUNT, LAURIE L,** Emory Univ, Atlanta, GA; FR; BA; Cncl 90-; Sclgy; Pblc Plcy.

**HUNT, LEONEL A,** The Johns Hopkins Univ, Baltimore, MD; FR; BS; NSBE 90-; NAACP 90-; Bio Mdcl Eng; Eng.

**HUNT, LORRIE A,** Commonwealth Coll, Virginia Beach, VA; SO; MWR Pres; Hnr Rll; Pres Lst 90; Sct Ldr 88-89; ACC Offc 77-; Acc.

**HUNT, MARGARET M,** D Youville Coll, Buffalo, NY; SO; BS; Natl Assc Acctnts 90-; Anthone Furniture Co 89-; AOS Bryant/ Stratton Bus Inst 89; Acctg; CPA.

**HUNT, REBECCA L,** Samford Univ, Birmingham, AL; GD; JD; Old Dominion Soc 90-; Chrstn Lgl Soc 90-; Amer Jrnl Trial Advcy; BA 88; Law.

**HUNT, RITA R,** Univ Of Sc At Spartanburg, Spartanburg, SC; SR; BS; SMC 77; Magna Cum Laude; Cert Profsnl Sec 82; Voc Sch Advsry Cncl; Exe Sec 76-; AA Sec Sci 77; Bus Educ/Cnslr Ed; Tch/Guidance MAT.

**HUNT, ROBERT B,** Univ Of Sc At Columbia, Columbia, SC; SO; BA; IM Bsktbl/Sftbl 89-; Hstry/Pol Sci; Politics.

**HUNT, SHAWNA N,** Fl A & M Univ, Tallahassee, FL; JR; BS; Stdnt Soc Work Clb 90-; Psychlgy Clb 90-; Peer Cnslr 89-90; Schlrshp Delta Sigma Theta 88-89; Cert Rcgntn 88-89; Cert Apprctn 89-90; Psychlgy.

**HUNT, SHEILA A,** Winthrop Coll, Rock Hill, SC; SR; BS; Rfrmd Univ Fllwshp 89-; Cmps Bptst Yng Wmn 88-89; IM Sports 87-; CLUES 87-88; Kappa Delta Pi 90-; Natl Edctrs Assn 89-; Intrnshp Stdnt Tchng 90-; Deans Lst 89-90; Pres Lst; IM Sports Sftbl Bsktbl 87-; Elem Ed; Tch SC.

**HUNT, SHELBY R,** Christopher Newport Coll, Newport News, VA; FR; BA; Bptst Stdnt Union/Innr Vrsty 90-; Acctg; CPA.

**HUNT, SHIRLEY M,** Goucher Coll, Towson, MD; SR; BA; Ed Clb Co-Pres 89; Deans Schlr 89; Tutor For Ed Dept 89; Mntrshp Prog 89-90; Chldrns Dvlpmntl Clnc At Essex Comm Clg 90; Fdrl Govt 80-90; Ed; Tchr.

**HUNT, STACEY E,** Tuskegee Univ, Tuskegee Inst, AL; SO; Natl Scty Of Blck Engs Treas 90; Inst Of Elecs And Elec Engs 90-; NAACP 89-; Wlk Amer Hndcppd 90; IMB Coop Educ; GE Latimer Awrd; Trck Tm 90; Math And Sci; Elec Eng.

**HUNT, STACY L,** Thomas Nelson Comm Coll, Hampton, VA; SO; AS; Mchncl Engnrng.

**HUNT, STEVEN H,** Piedmont Tech Coll, Greenwood, SC; SO; AS; Dns Lst; Engr Grphcs Tech; Engr.

**HUNT, TRENT W,** Snead St Jr Coll, Boaz, AL; SR; BS; Cmptr Sci; Pgrmng.

**HUNT, VICKIE A,** Middle Tn St Univ, Murfreesboro, TN; FR; BA; Art; Grphc Dsgn.

**HUNT III, WILLIE G,** Fayetteville St Univ, Fayetteville, NC; FR; BA; Litercy Educ; Chancllrs Acad Schlrshp; Achvmnt Awd; Busn Admin.

**HUNTER HYLEN, JILL A,** Belmont Coll, Nashville, TN; SR; Wall Street Journal Awrd.

**HUNTER, BARRY A,** Marshall University, Huntington, WV; SR; Intern Ins Agnt; IMS 87-88; Fnc Ins Optn; Ins Sls.

**HUNTER, BRETT F,** Oh Univ, Athens, OH; SR; Alpha Eta Rho 87-; Gvrnrs Schlr Dir 90; Dns Lst 87-; Tau Beta Pi; Untd Airlns Intrn; Outstdng Grad Snr; Hnrs; IM Sftbl/Brmbl/Wtrskng 87-; AAS 89; Avtn; Pilot.

**HUNTER, BRIGITTE L,** Al A & M Univ, Normal, AL; SR; Stdnt Govt 85; Hist Award 85; Dance Team 85; Ballet 85; Tap 85; Jazz 85; Piano 85; Sr Red Cir Church Grp 85; Church Choir 85; Sundy Sch Asst Secy 85; Natl Hon Soc 85-87; Schlrs Cir 85-87; Hist Award Hghst Avrg Amercn Govt; Chem; Pharmcy.

**HUNTER, CAROLYN F,** Middle Tn St Univ, Murfreesboro, TN; JR; BS; Psi Chi 90-; Kappa Delta Pi 90-; Families Crisis 90-; Psych; Exper Psych.

**HUNTER, CAROLYN J,** S U N Y Coll Of A & T Morrisvl, Morrisville, NY; SR; BS; Phi Theta Kappa Secty 90-; Intshp Hmn Serv Vltr Oxford Primary Schl 90-; YMCA Instr; PTA; Boy Scouts Amer Den Ldr 90-; Vocatl Rehbtn Serv Coach 88-; AA; Elem Ed.

**HUNTER, CHAUNSEY Z,** Morehouse Coll, Atlanta, GA; SR; BA; Bsn Assoc 87-90; MO Clb 88-89; Pre Almn Assoc 88-89; Hnr Rl 89-90; Dns Lst 90; U S Army Rsrv Spec 4 86-; Smr Intrnshp CIGNA Co 90; Med Spec U S Army Acdmy Hlth Sci 87; Econ; Ed/Law.

**HUNTER, CHRISTOPHER J,** Wright St Univ Lake Cmps, Celina, OH; SO; BS; US Navy E-5 86-89; US Naval Rsrvs E-5 89-; Elctrcl Engr.

**HUNTER, DAVID E,** Cornell Univ Statutory College, Ithaca, NY; SR; BS; Outdoor Educ Instrctr 87-89; Dept Energy; Sers Flwshp; Dns Lst 89-; Cornell Biological Fld Sta Smn Intrn 89; Wrstlng 87-90; Nat Rsrcs; Envrnmntl Law.

**HUNTER, DEANA S,** Winthrop Coll, Rock Hill, SC; SR; BA; Commnctn Assoc 89-90; SPJ Secy 90-; Mass Cmmnctn Jrnlsm; Pblc Rltns Advrtsng.

**HUNTER, FREDA A,** Central Fl Comm Coll, Ocala, FL; FR; BA; Bus Admin; Acctg/Cmptrs.

**HUNTER, JENNIFER L,** Washington State Comm Coll, Marietta, OH; FR; AAB; Accntng Tech; Sales Mrktng.

**HUNTER, JENNIFER L,** Univ Of Ky, Lexington, KY; FR; Christian Stdnt Flwshp 90-; Alpha Lambda Delta; Phi Eta Sigma; Psych.

**HUNTER, JENNIFER L,** Univ Of South Al, Mobile, AL; SR; BA; Rsdnc Lf Cncl/Delta Area Cncl 90-; Beta Gamma Sigma; Alpha Chi; Pres Schlrshp 86-88; Acdmc Achvmnt Schlrshp; Fin; Fin/Law.

**HUNTER, KARRI ANNE,** Univ Of Al, Tuscaloosa, AL; FR; BA; Mjrt Univ Al; Phi Eta Sigma; Bus; Acctg.

**HUNTER, KAYLE M,** Hudson Valley Comm Coll, Troy, NY; SO; AAS; W P Cert Spencer Bus Inst 85; Cmptr Info Sys; Prgrmr.

**HUNTER, KEITH,** Claflin Coll, Orangeburg, SC; SO; BA; Oxford Clb 90-; Non Trdtnl Stdnt Clb 90-; NAACP 2nd V P 89-; Prince Hall Mason/Royal Arch Mason S W & Sec 87-; AS Williamsburg Tech Clg 85; Rlgn/Philosophy; Mnstry.

**HUNTER, KELLY A,** Univ Of Sc At Columbia, Columbia, SC; SR; BA; Natl Stdnt Exch Stdnt Treas; Sigma Alpha Mu Little Sister; Dns Lst Calif State Univ; AA 89; Bio; Genetic Rsrch.

**HUNTER, KERRY A,** Lesley Coll, Cambridge, MA; FR; BA; Emrld Ky; SOAR 90-; Lbrl Arts Lit; Tchng.

**HUNTER, LATECHA N,** Va St Univ, Petersburg, VA; FR; BA; Eng; Primary Sch Tchr.

**HUNTER, LAWRENCE D,** Memphis St Univ, Memphis, TN; SR; BA; AS State Tech Inst Memphis TN 72; Bus Mgmt; Mgmt.

**HUNTER, LINDA G,** Life Coll, Marietta, GA; Phi Theta Kappa VP 86-87; Phi Tau Delta 90; Alpha Delta Upsilon Pres 89-90; Beta Sigma Phi 2nd VP 90; Adults Lity Prog; Big Brothers/Big Sisters; BS Nutrition 90; Chiropractic.

**HUNTER, LISA E,** Alcorn St Univ, Lorman, MS; SR; BS; Hnrs Std Org Sntr 90-; Std Snt Sec 90-; Gspl Choir Treas 88-; Alpha Kappa Mu 89; Alpha Kappa Alpha Prlmtrn 90; SPIFFERS Sec 87-; Sthrn Rgnl Hnrs Cncl 87-; Pnhlnc Cncl 90-; Pol Sci Clb 87-; Yng Dmcrts 87-; Cmps Brdcstng Asc Fdn 90-; Pol Sci/Pre-Law.

**HUNTER, LISA J,** Becker Coll At Leicester, Leicester, MA; SO; BA; Hospitality Clb Pres 90-; Travel Clb V P 89-90; Trvl/Tourism Adm; Trvl Agcy/Airlines.

**HUNTER, LORI A,** Univ Of Al At Huntsville, Huntsville, AL; FR; BA; SWE; Alpha Lambda Delta; Kappa Delta Asst Mmbrshp 90-; Elctrcl Engnrng; Engnrng.

**HUNTER, MICHELLINA D,** City Univ Of Ny City Coll, New York, NY; SR; BA; Role Model Pgm 90; Gldn Key 89; Cmnctns; Pblc Rltns/Advrtsng.

**HUNTER, PHILIP R,** Le Moyne Coll, Syracuse, NY; SO; BA; Blgy Clb Treas 89-; Chrch Chrs 90-; Beta Beta Beta 90-; Mns Tnns Tm 89-; Blgy Pre Med; Dr Of Ostpthy.

**HUNTER, PRIDE,** Wilberforce Univ, Wilberforce, OH; FR; Deans Lst 90-; Blck Male Cltn 90-; IM Bsktbl; Bus; Entrprnr.

**HUNTER, RENEE A,** Cornell Univ Statutory College, Ithaca, NY; JR; BA; Pep Band 88-; Red Carpet Soc 88-; Alpha Phi Frat Ed/Schlrshp Comm 89-; Orientn Steering Comm 89-90; Suprvsry Orientn Cnslr; Orientn Cnslr 89; Sheila Turner Seed Mem Award; NY Press Assoc Schlrshp; Intrnshp Schlstc Inc; Cmnctns; Jrnlsm/ Law.

**HUNTER, ROBERT K,** Comm Coll Algny Co Algny Cmps, Pittsburgh, PA; JR; BA; Finance; Reast Est Invstng.

**HUNTER, ROSALIND Y,** Univ Of Southern Ms, Hattiesburg, MS; SR; BS; Grl Scts Ldr 89; Deans Lst 89-90; Psychlgy.

**HUNTER, SUZANNE E,** Volunteer St Comm Coll, Gallatin, TN; SO; BS; Gamma Beta Phi 90-; Vol Wrkr Psyiothrpy Assocs; Alld Hlth; Physcl Thrpy.

**HUNTER, TARA L,** Al A & M Univ, Normal, AL; JR; BSW; Soc Work Clb Rprtr 90-; Drug Task Force 89-; Pre Alumni; Soc Work.

**HUNTER, TRACEY L,** Al A & M Univ, Normal, AL; SO; BS; Chr 90-; Intr Drm Cncl 89-; Frds Schlrs Prgrm 89-; Elem Edctn; Tchng.

**HUNTER-ADAMS, KAREN S,** Owensboro Comm Coll, Owensboro, KY; SO; BA; Ocrncs Nwspr Stf/KIPA Awd Winr Rprtr/Clmnst 89-; AA; Eng/Jrnlsm.

**HUNTING, LYNN E,** Univ Of Sc At Coastal Carolina, Conway, SC; SO; Educ; Tchr.

**HUNTINGTON, TIMOTHY P,** Muskingum Coll, New Concord, OH; JR; BA; Jz Ensmbl/Drms 88-; Coll Radio DJ 89-90; Phi Kappa Tau 89-; Music; Bus.

**HUNTLEY, JAMES A,** Al A & M Univ, Normal, AL; SR; BA; Amer Mktg Assn; Phi Beta Lambda 87-; Gen Mtrs Intrn 88; Mktg; Corp Law.

**HUNTLEY, JILL E,** Juniata Coll, Huntingdon, PA; SO; BA; Psych Clb V P 89-; Yrbk Fac Edtr 89-90; Rugby Clb 90-; Cir K 89-90; Fndrs Schlrshp 89-; Psych; Clin Psych.

**HUNTLEY, MISTY D,** Al A & M Univ, Normal, AL; SR; BA; Telecomm Clb Sec 87-88; NAACP 88; Miss Soph Ct 87; WAAY-TV Intern; Telecomm; Ma.

**HUPKA, SHELLEY L,** West Liberty St Coll, West Liberty, WV; SO; Amnsty Intrntl.

**HUPP, ANGEL M,** Univ Of Cincinnati, Cincinnati, OH; SO; AS; Scl Comm 89-; Dpt Rep Std Govt 90-; Co-Op 90-; Chem Tech; Med.

**HUPPERT, LEO W,** Univ Of Miami, Coral Gables, FL; SR; MM; Essey Comm Clg Stdnt Fac Rltns Cmtee V P 78-; Phi Kappa Phi 91; Pi Kappa Lambda; Mst Otsdng Music Stdnt 78-79; Full Schlrshp Sch Music 90-; Pres Hon Rl 90-; Grad Asstshp 91; AA Essex Comm Clg 79; BM; Jazz Bass Prfrmnc; Prfrmng/Rcrd/ Tchng.

**HURCHIK, LISA M,** Pa St Univ Delaware Cty Cmps, Media, PA; SO; BA; Acctng; Tax Lawyer.

**HURD, JEREMY T,** Univ Of Rochester, Rochester, NY; SO; BA; Blck Stdnt Union 89-; Theta Delta Chi Acad Chr; Big Bro/Big Sis 89-; Tchrs Asst; Vars Ftbl 89-; Pol Sci; Law.

**HURD, PHILIP A,** Life Coll, Marietta, GA; GD; DC; Actvtr Mthds Clb Pres 88-; Intl Chrprctc Assn 89-; Amer Chrprctc Assn; BS W GA Coll 74; MA Univ NC Grnsbro 78; Chrprctc.

**HURKETT, CYNTHIA L,** Lasell Coll, Newton, MA; SO; ASSOC; Phys Ther Asst.

**HURLEY, BRENT W,** Juniata Coll, Huntingdon, PA; SO; BA; Concrt Choir 89-; Choral Un 89-; Cmnctns/Music.

**HURLEY, BRYAN R,** Salisbury St Univ, Salisbury, MD; SR; BA; MENC 90-; Pi Lambda Phi 87-; Psychlgy/Msc; Ph D.

**HURLEY, DONNA M,** The Johns Hopkins Univ, Baltimore, MD; JR; BSN; Mbrshp Prod Amer Legion Aux; Natl Assoc Dntl Assts; Dntl Asst Wrkng W/Parents; Nursing; Mstrs Deg/Nurse Prctnr.

**HURLEY, JENNIFER L,** Univ Of Ky, Lexington, KY; SR; BAEDU; Early Ele Educ; Tch.

**HURLEY, KIM M,** Le Moyne Coll, Syracuse, NY; JR; BS; Psych Clb Sec 89-; RA 90-; Cmps Mnstry Rtrts; Hnrs Prog 90-; Psy Chi; St Hnrs Smnr 90-; St Assmbly Intern 88-; Drug Trtmnt Cntr Intern; Dvlpmntlly Dsbld Clss Vol 90-; Schl Olympcs; IM Bsktbl Sccr Wllybl; Psych; PHD Clncl Psych.

**HURLEY, LAURIE K,** Defiance Coll, Defiance, OH; SR; BS; Bryan Area Rdng Coaltn 89-90; Williams Co YWCA Brd Of Dir 83-; Les Bas Bleus Gfts/Flwrs 87-; Soc Actvies Dir 81-86; GRI Univ AL 74; OCAD Owens Tech Clg 83; Elem Educ; Elem Educ Tchr.

**HURLEY, MELISSA K,** Middle Tn St Univ, Murfreesboro, TN; SR; BSE; Tau Omicron 90-; Kappa Delta Pi 90-; Elem Ed; Library Sci.**

**HURLEY, REBECCA L,** Schenectady County Comm Coll, Schenectady, NY; FR; Math; Phrmcy.

**HURM, SHARI A,** Mount Aloysius Jr Coll, Cresson, PA; FR; AAS; Natl Hon Soc; Phi Theta Kapa Chrmn Civic Litrcy; Law Ofcs Intrnshp; Legal Asstnt; Law.

**HURM, THOMAS J,** Wright St Univ Lake Cmps, Celina, OH; FR; BS; Chem; Med.

**HUROWITZ, BRIAN M,** Cornell Univ Statutory College, Ithaca, NY; SO; BA; I M Sprts Mgr 90-; Ho Nun De Kah; Tau Epsilon Phi Ordrng Stwrd; Apld Bus Mgmt/Mktg; Law.

**HURSEY, KRISTINA E,** Coll Of Charleston, Charleston, SC; JR; BA; Bus Admn; Mgt.

**HURST, ANGELA D,** Lincoln Univ, Lincoln Univ, PA; SR; BS; Health Physcl Ed & Rec Club Sec 90; Phi Beta Sigma Soul Auxillary Pres 89-; Adult Literacy Prog 89; Intrnshp Chestnut Hill Rehab Hsptl 90; BS; Therapeutic Recreation; Recreation Therapist.

**HURST, DENITA K,** Ky St Univ, Frankfort, KY; FR; Bsnss Admin; Accntng.

**HURST, DERRICK A,** Univ Of Nc At Asheville, Asheville, NC; FR; Schlrs Pgrm 90; Biology; Trauma Doctor.

**HURST, ERIK G,** Clarkson Univ, Potsdam, NY; SO; BA; Stdt Senate Cmptrllr; Acad Spprt Ctr Peer Tutor 90-; Schl Radio 89-; SOS 90-; Pres Schlr; Ilse J Shaw Otstndng Schl Mgmt Fresh 90-; Mcgill Awd Otstndng Soph Acad/Serv; IM Sftbl 89-; Economics/Finance; Law.

**HURST, MICHELE S,** Lexington Comm Coll, Lexington, KY; FR; ADN; Dns Lst 90; Nrsng.

**HURST, NATALIE D,** Oh Wesleyan Univ, Delaware, OH; JR; BA; Trnscrpt/Rep/Editor 89-90; Phi Soc 89-90; Phi Sigma Lota; Kappa Alpha Theta 90; Rsrch Assist; Jrnlsm/Frnch.

**HURST, RICHARD B,** Univ Of Cincinnati, Cincinnati, OH; SR; BA; Stdnt Cncl Excptnl Chldrn 87-; Aths For Bttrmnt Of Cinn 87-; Kappa Delta Pi; Jimmy Nippert Awd; Otstndng Sr Spec Educ; Trck/Fld Mvp 90-; Spec Educ; Comm Cnslr.

**HURST, RONA M,** Univ Of Rochester, Rochester, NY; SR; BA; Undrgrad Ecnmcs Cncl 87; Omicron Delta Epsilon; Adopt-A-Grndprnt 88-89; D'lions Org Assist R A 88-89; Ecnmcs; Accntng.

**HURST, YULONDA M,** Fort Valley St Coll, Fort Valley, GA; JR; BA; Nwspr Rprtr/Edtr 91-; Cncrt Chr; Mass Comm Clb Asst Sec; Amer Clgt Awd 88; Hnrs Cnvctn; WCLK 91.9 FM Stdnt Asst 89-90; Comm; Pblc Rltns.

**HURST-WOLKONOWSKI, ELIZABETH A,** Tn Tech Univ, Cookeville, TN; SR; BS; Food Ntrtn Dietetic Club Pres 88-; Kappa Omicron Nu 90-; Phi Gamma Nu 89-90; Dietetic Intrnshp Vanderbilt Univ Hosp; Barbour/Whitlow Schlrsph; HEC Dietetics; Reg Dietition.

**HURSTON, GINA R,** Morris Brown Coll, Atlanta, GA; SR; BA; Cncrt Choir 86-88; Dns Lst 89-90; Synfnt Dn Pldg 87-; Indctn Educ 90-; Erly Chldhd Ed; Tchr.

**HURT, ALEXANDER D,** Newbury Coll, Brookline, MA; FR; BA; Law.

**HURT, CATHERINE L,** Marshall University, Huntington, WV; SO; BA; Bsns Mngmnt; Htl Mngmnt.

**HURT, CINDEE M,** Methodist Coll, Fayetteville, NC; JR; BS; Yrbk 90; Marshall Grad 89; Psychlgy Clb 88; Alpha Epsilon Omega VP 89-90; Math; Grad Schl Acctg.

**HURT, KAREN LYNN,** Free Will Baptist Bible Coll, Nashville, TN; SR; BS; Foreign Missions Flwshp Treas 90-; Christiana Rossetti Soc 89-; ASN Polk Comm Coll 88; Bible; Nrsng.

**HURT, TRACEY M,** Ky St Univ, Frankfort, KY; SO; BA; Appld Math; Cvl Eng.

**HUSAIN, SYED F,** Oh Wesleyan Univ, Delaware, OH; SR; BA; Wesleyan Cncl Stdnt Affrs St Govt Acdmnc Affrs Comm Chrmn 89; Hrzns Intrntl Pres 87; Stdnt Cntr Entertainmnt Commt Pres 88-90; Sigma Lota Rho VP 90; Phi Alpha Theta 90; Citibank NA Karachi Pkstn Intrn 87; Exxon Chmcls Pkstn Intrn 89; Intrntnl Studies; Politics.

**HUSAIN, ZEESHAN S,** Ma Inst Of Tech, Cambridge, MA; FR; BS; Bngldsh Assoc; IM Ftbll Bsktbll Ultmt Sftbll Bdmntn Tbl Tnns Octthn; Zeta Beta Tau; Mdcl Cntr Fllwshp; IM Sprts; Chmstry; Med.

**HUSAREK, JAMES D,** Niagara Univ, Niagara Univ, NY; FR; Hon Pgm 90-; Cmptr Sci; Pgmmng.

**HUSBAND, MARY L,** Indiana Univ Of Pa, Indiana, PA; SR; BS; Kappa Mu Epsilon 90-; Kappa Delta Pi; Dstngshd Achvr Schlrshp 87-; Prvsts Schlr 89-90; Math Educ; Tchr.

**HUSBANDS, HARCOURT W,** Univ Of Rochester, Rochester, NY; JR; BA; N Shaolin Martial Arts Acdmy; Phi Theta Kappa; Sigma Nu; Phi Theta Kappa Schlrshp; Trnsfr Schlrshp; Ecnmcs; Mktg Intl.

**HUSE, CAROLINE R,** Fl International Univ, Miami, FL; SR; BED; Pep Bnd 87-90; Univ Wnd Ensmbl 87-90; Kappa Delta Pi 90-; Elem Educ Intern 89-; Mst Sprt Awrd Bnd; Elem Educ; Tchng/Cnslng/Admn.

**HUSEIN, IMAD F,** S U N Y At Buffalo, Buffalo, NY; SR; BS; Plstn Stdnt Assn Prsdnt 89-; Orgnztn Arab Stdnts Mmbr 88-; Gldn Key 90-; ETA Kappa Nu Mmbr Soc 90-; Elctrcl Engnrng.

**HUSEIN, SONYA T,** Kent St Univ Kent Cmps, Kent, OH; FR; BA; Scl Stds; Scndry Edctn.

**HUSI, COLLEEN D,** Hillsborough Comm Coll, Tampa, FL; FR; Stdnt Nrse Org Treas Elect; Phi Theta Kappa V Pres 90-; Banking 78-88; Nrsng.

**HUSKEY, JOY R,** Limestone Coll, Gaffney, SC; JR; BS; Stdnt Govt Assn Sec; Alpha Chi; Psychlgy/Cnslng.

**HUSS, BRENT H,** Western Piedmont Comm Coll, Morganton, NC; SO; Phi Theta Kappa; Math; Engr.

**HUSS, BRIAN R,** Fordham Univ, Bronx, NY; FR; BA; Rsdnc Hls Assn Sec/Treas Hall 90-; Univ Nwspr Ftrs Edtr 90-; Coll Bowl Capt 90-; Rose Hill Soc 90-; Engl; Jrnlsm/Tchng.

**HUSS, MARTHA J,** Univ Of Rochester, Rochester, NY; SO; BA; Sci Fctn Org Sec 89-; Engl Cncl 89-90; Deans Lst 89-; Xerox Schlrshp 89-; Engl/Hstry; Educ.

**HUSSAIN, SHAISTA,** Fl Atlantic Univ, Boca Raton, FL; SO; BA; Phi Eta Sigma; Fnc.

**HUSSAIN, SYED NAVEED,** Nova Univ, Ft Lauderdale, FL; FR; BS; Nova Intl Stdnt Assn 90; Cmptr Eng; Cvl Eng.

**HUSSAIN, ZEENAT A,** Univ Of Miami, Coral Gables, FL; JR; BS; Cncl Intrntnl Stdnts Assc 90; Phi Theta Kappa 89; Vlntr Corps Cmmty 88; Hghst Hnrs Distinction AA Degree 90; Clg Hnrs Prgrm Schlrshp 88-90; Pres Hnr Roll 90; AA Miami /Dade Cmmty Clg 90; Mngmnt Science; Info Systms Cnsltng.

**HUSSAR, JENNIFER L B,** Cornell Univ Statutory College, Ithaca, NY; FR; BS; Red Carpet Soc; IM Soccer; Orntn Cnslr; Cornell Gamelan; Cmnctns; Law.

**HUSSEIN, KHALIFA,** Jersey City St Coll, Jersey City, NJ; SO; BA; Soccer Team 89-; Comp Sci; Progrmmr.

**HUSSEY JR, THOMAS E,** Duquesne Univ, Pittsburgh, PA; SO; BA; Tutr 90; Mktg Intrn; IM 89-; Finance; Financl Cnsltnt.

**HUSTED, BOBBIE J,** Ithaca Coll, Ithaca, NY; FR; MS; Gymnstcs 90-; Physcl Thrpy.

**HUSTER, LORI A,** Southern Coll Of Tech, Marietta, GA; JR; BS; Inst/Indus Engr V P; Intl Org/Wmn Pilots 89-; Phi Theta Kappa; Indus Engrng.

**HUSTON, ALDYTH ROSELEE,** Lexington Comm Coll, Lexington, KY; FR; BA; Occptnl Thrpy.

**HUSTON, MARY E,** Allegheny Coll, Meadville, PA; SR; BA; Allghny Chrs 87-; Phi Sigma Iota; Alpha Gamma Delta VP 88-; Alpha Phi Omega VP 87-91; Aldn Schlr 87-; Dr J A H Stwrt Schlrshp Fnd; Env Stds/Germn; Educ.

**HUSTON, WENDY A,** Kent St Univ Kent Cmps, Kent, OH; JR; BS; USVBA Team 89; Golden Key; Presidents List 90; Pre-Med; MD.

**HUTCHENS, MICHELLE L,** Marshall University, Huntington, WV; FR; BA; RHA 90-; Phi Eta Sigma 90-; Deans Lst 90-; All Amer Schlr; Acctng; CPA.

**HUTCHENS, ROY S,** Pellissippi St Tech Comm Coll, Knoxville, TN; JR; AS; Phi Theta Kappa 89-; DPMA 89-; E Tn Cmptr Grp 89-; Comm Svc Comm; Phi Theta Kappa; Dns Lst 89-; Cmptr Sci; Softwr Devlpmnt.**

**HUTCHENS, TERI LYNETTE,** Univ Of Nc At Charlotte, Charlotte, NC; SO; BA; NC Cncl Tchrs Math 90-; Stdnt Natl Educ Assn 90-; Phi Eta Sigma 90-; Gldn Key; Tchnf Fellow 89; Dns Lst; Chnclrs Lst 90; Math; Educ.

**HUTCHERSON, FREDA M,** Univ Of Southern Ms, Hattiesburg, MS; SR; Nom Stdnt Tchr Of Yr 88-; Jones Jr Clg Acad Schlrshp 1600 Dlrs; Dns Lst; Pres Lst; Ltr J Awd Frm JCJC; Spec Olmpcs Hlpr; Hrt Fnd; Cncr Fnd; BS 90-; Elem Educ; Tchr.

**HUTCHERSON, PAMELA D,** Union Univ, Jackson, TN; SO; BS; Bsktbl; Comp Sci; Prgrmr.

**HUTCHERSON, PAULA E LAINE,** Union Univ, Jackson, TN; SO; BS; Baptist Stdnt Un 89-; Flwshp Of Christian Aths 89-; Sigma Delta 90-; Vol In Phys Rehab; U S Acad Achvmnt Acad 90-; IM Sftbl 89-; Var Bsktbl 89-; Psych; Phys Educ/Med.

**HUTCHESON, BETTY LEIGH,** Memphis St Univ, Memphis, TN; SR; BFA; Phtgrphc Soc Pres 89-90; Memphis Brooks Photgrphc Cir Brd Mbr; Polaroid Schlrshp; Dns Lst 89-; BA Univ FL 81; Art Phtgrphy; Commrcl Phtgrphy.

**HUTCHESON, BEVERLY LAUREN,** La Grange Coll, La Grange, GA; FR; BS; Clgte Sftbll 90-; Soccer/Chrldg; Math; Tchg.

**HUTCHESON, GIA ANGELINI,** Nova Univ, Ft Lauderdale, FL; GD; MBA; Tech Sales Spprt Rep Siemens Stronberg Carlson; BS Quinnipiar Coll 84.

**HUTCHESON, GINA M,** Central Fl Comm Coll, Ocala, FL; SO; BA; Phi Theta Kappa; Acdmc Exclnc Schlrshp; AA; Bus; Acctg.**

**HUTCHESON, MARK F,** Univ Of Rochester, Rochester, NY; GD; BS 90; Optcs; US Naval Offcr.

**HUTCHINGS, RITA A,** Memphis Academy Of The Arts, Memphis, TN; SO; BFA; Sr Cmptr Oprtr 78-; Fine Art/Paintng Sculpture; Clg Art Instr.

**HUTCHINS, PATRICE E,** White Pines Coll, Chester, NH; SR; AA; Deans List; Phi Theta Kappa Pres 90-; Photojournalism Intrnshp Bus Nh Mag; Cncl Friends Schrlshp; White Pines Clg Schrlshp; 25th Anniv Schrlshp; Mass Communications.

**HUTCHINS, SHEILA K,** Saint Catharine Coll, St Catharine, KY; FR; BA; Psych; Cnslng.

**HUTCHINS, TAMATHA Y,** Univ Of Ga, Athens, GA; FR; Res Hl Assoc 90-; Communiv Vol 90-; Big Bro/Big Sis Pgm 90-; Ed; Spec Ed.

**HUTCHINSON, CATHRYN A,** Va Commonwealth Univ, Richmond, VA; JR; BS; Fin Mgmt Assn 90-; Am Inst Bnkg 88-; Gldn Ky 90-; Mk-A-Wsh Fndtn; Vol Org 90-; Fin; Fin/Law.

**HUTCHINSON, DAWN B,** Nova Univ, Ft Lauderdale, FL; BA Univ Of The West Indies 66.

**HUTCHINSON, DONALD C,** East Tn St Univ, Johnson City, TN; FR; BA; Bptst Stdnt Union Pres Elect; Chrstn Stdnt Flwshp; Wrk Schlrshp Prog; Almn Schlrshp Prog; Acctg; Pstr.

**HUTCHINSON, HOLLY E,** Commonwealth Coll, Virginia Beach, VA; SO; BS; Frat Order Police Ladies Auxlry Sec 87-89; Alpha Chi 84-85; Pizza Hut 88-90; Allied Towing Corp 90-; Acctg Fld; Acctg/Bus.

**HUTCHINSON, JACQUELINE F,** Al A & M Univ, Normal, AL; SR; BS; Erly Chldhd Elem Ed Clb Pres 88-89; Zeta Phi Beta Pres 89; Membr Of U Echoes 89-90; Alpha Kappa Mu 89; Zeta Phi Beta Sigma Beta Chptr Pres 89; Erly Chldhd Ed; Degree In Chld Psychlgy.

**HUTCHINSON, JAMIE MALATACK,** Gordon Conwell Theol Sem, S Hamilton, MA; GD; MATS; BS Muhlenburg Clg 69; Cert U Of GA 71; Tchng/Theology; Writing.

**HUTCHINSON, JOHN D,** Univ Of Nh Plymouth St Coll, Plymouth, NH; SR; BABS; Forgn Lang Soc Pres; Phi Sigma Iota; Tchr Fllwshp 89-; Spanish; Busn Admin; Intnl Busn.

**HUTCHINSON, LISA A,** Univ Of Southern Ms, Hattiesburg, MS; FR; BA; Stdnts Against Rape Secr; Stdnt Alumni Assoc 90-; Alpha Lambda Delta; Phi Eta Sigma; Gamma Beta Phi; Pi Beta Phi Pldg Schlr 90-; Psych; Law.

**HUTCHINSON, PAMELA LYNNE,** Brewer St Jr Coll, Fayette, AL; SO; BA; Pscyhlgy; Crmnl Law.

**HUTCHINSON, PAMELA S,** Wv Univ, Morgantown, WV; SR; BS; Acad Stdnts Phrmcy 88-; Stdnt Comm Drg Abuse Educ 89-; Golden Key; Kappa Delta Tr 85-89; Phrmcy; Phrmcst Sales.

**HUTCHINSON, TONYA M,** Casco Bay Coll, Portland, ME; SR; BA; Cllgt Mrchndsng Assn Prsdnt 90-; Intrnshp Rtl Mgmnt Prts Brnswck; AS Mgmnt; Mgmt Fshn Mrchndsng.

**HUTCHISON, JAMES S,** Beckley Coll, Beckley, WV; SO; BA; Medieval Festival 90; Hnrs Clg 89-; Chrstn Witness Trp Pres 89-; Callway Hts Bptst Sndy Schl Tchr; Hnrs Clg Schlrshp 90-; Rep Fndtn For Independent Clgs; History; Educator.

**HUTCHISON, MELANIE A,** Alfred Univ, Alfred, NY; FR; BS; Eqstrn Tm 90-; Chrldng 90-; Hon Prog 90-; Pres Schlr 90-; Psychlgy; Law.

**HUTCHISON, NOAH T,** Central Fl Comm Coll, Ocala, FL; SO; MBA; Acctng; CPA.

**HUTMAKER, CHRISTOPHER A,** Columbia Univ, New York, NY; FR; Off Pub Info 90; Deans Lst 90; Bsbl Squad 90; Econ/Chem; Econ/Med.

**HUTSELL, LESLEA D,** Christopher Newport Coll, Newport News, VA; SO; BSN; Nrsng; RN.

**HUTSON, CHRISTOPHER M,** Clemson Univ, Clemson, SC; SO; BS; AIAS 90-; 2nd Yr Coll Archtrcr Fclty Awrd 90-; Dsgn Arch.**

**HUTSON, JANETTE L,** East Carolina Univ, Greenville, NC; SR; BFA; Phi Theta Kappa 85-86; Phi Kappa Phi 89-; AS Halfx Comm Coll 86; Art Educ; MFA Art Educ/Ph D Art Educ.

**HUTSON, JASON B,** Middle Tn St Univ, Murfreesboro, TN; JR; BA; ASB Hs Rep 90-; Fncl Mgmt Assoc; Kappa Alpha Ordr Treas 90-; Fnc; Stckbrkr.

**HUTSON, THOMAS E,** Oh Northern Univ, Ada, OH; JR; Ducks Unlmtd; Amer Chem Soc; Stdnt Plng Comm; Beta Beta Beta 89-; Rho Chi 89-; Phi Delta Chi 88-90; Sigma Phi Epsilon 88-; Instr Amer Red Crss; Dptmntl Hons; Rho Chi Achiev Awd; Deans Lst; IM Bsktbl/Swmng; Pharm-Bio; Med.**

**HUTT, CHERYL E,** Marshall University, Huntington, WV; JR; BA; Gamma Beta Phi 88-90; Ed/Spnsh; Tchr.

**HUTT, STEVEN C,** Villanova Univ, Villanova, PA; SO; BS; Vars Crew 89-; Bio; Phys Ther/Sports Med.

**HUTTER, DEBORAH A,** Immaculata Coll, Immaculata, PA; SO; BA; Biol/Chem Clbs 89-; Yrbk Edtr 89-; Acad Plcy Comm Stdt Rep 90-; Hnr Scty; Cmps Mnstry Sec 89-; So Seminole Comm Hsp Vol; Pres Schlrshp; Ntl Hnr Scty Schlrshp; Lifeguard 89-; Biology/Chemistry/Pre Medicine; Medicine.

**HUTTER, DOROTHY,** Immaculata Coll, Immaculata, PA; SO; BA; Biol/Chem Clb 89-; Soph Cls VP 90-; Yrbk Sect Edtr 89-; Immclt Clg Hnr Scty 90-; Cmps Mnstry 89-; Immclt Clg Childrens Theater 90-; Immaculate Coll Pres Scholarship; Biology; Research.

**HUTTO, MARSHELLE A,** Savannah Coll Of Art & Design, Savannah, GA; SO; BA; Grphc Dsgn Clb 90-; AIGA; Cmmrcl Advrtsng/Grphc Dsgn; Art Dir.

**HUTTO, SHANA C,** Univ Of Southern Ms, Hattiesburg, MS; SO; SAA 89-; ASB Spirit Com 89; ASB Elect Cmsnr 90-; Gamma Beta Phi 89-; Kappa Delta Sor Asstn Rush Chmn 89-; Prvntn Chld Abuse Vol 89-; Deans Lst 89-; Pi Kappa Alpha Lil Sis 90-; Mktg; Retail Mgmnt.

**HUTTO, SHARON F,** Midlands Tech Coll, Columbia, SC; FR; Deans Hon Roll 90; Med Lab Tech.

**HUTTON JR, DOYLE G,** Middle Tn St Univ, Murfreesboro, TN; SR; BA; Gamma Beta Phi 88-90; Sigma Tau Delta 90; Kappa Delta Pi; Mry Flrnc Bts Schlrshp; Englsh; Scndry Edctn.

**HUTTON, LISA A,** Neumann Coll, Aston, PA; SO; BS; VIVA 89; Cmps Mnstry 89-90; Bsktbl 89-90; Sftbl 89-90; Nrsg; Pediatric Nrsg.

**HUVER, WILLIAM D,** S U N Y Coll Of Tech At Alfred, Alfred, NY; FR; BS; Concrt Bnd Baritn Sctn Ldr 90-; Stsmn Jz Bnd 3rd Trmbn 90-; Coll Hon Prog 90-; Pres Hon Schlrs Prog 90-; Eagle Scout Awrd BSA; Elec Eng.

**HUXSOLL, DAVID B,** Wv Univ, Morgantown, WV; SR; MA; Radio/TV Nws Dir Assn Bd Of Dir 89-; Socty Prof Jrnlst 89-; Vrsty Mns Glee Clb 87-; Order Of Omega 89-; Phi Kappa Phi 89-; Gldn Key 89-; Tau Kappa Alpha 89-; Kappa Sigma Grnd Scribe 88-; Kearns Schlr ABC News 90; WVV Schl Of Jrnlsm 91; Pol Sci.**

**HUYKE-NICOLE, LOIS E,** Univ Of Pr At Mayaguez, Mayaguez, PR; SO; BE; Eta Gamma Delta 89-; Cvl Engr; Engr.

**HVARRE, KIMBERLY J,** Westminster Choir Coll, Princeton, NJ; SR; BM; Chrstn Flwshp Sec 88-; Yrbk Edtr; Msc Ed; Tchng.

**HVIZDAK, ROBERT J A,** Duquesne Univ, Pittsburgh, PA; SR; AMA VP 90-; Beta Alpha Phi 90-; Mktg Intrnshp 90-; Bernard Haldane Assoc Asst; Vol-Whales Tail Yth Shltr 90; BS; Mktg.

**HVIZDAK, TIMOTHY E,** Columbia Greene Comm Coll, Hudson, NY; FR; ASA; Sci Clb Pres 88-90; Cmptr Clb Secr 84 87-88; Boys Brigade Lt 85-; Joyful Noise 88-; Phi Theta Kappa 90-; Dns Lst; Regents Schlrshp; Pres Schlrshp; Boys State; Mscl Excell Awd; Soccer/Tennis Capt 85-90; Mech Engr/Cmptr Sci.

**HWANG, EDWARD,** Univ Of Al At Birmingham, Birmingham, AL; SR; BS; SGA; Tns Club; Drama Club; Gamma Beta Phi; Phi Kappa Phi; Golden Key; Phi Sigma; Delta Sigma Phi Secty 88-89; Biology; Med.

**HWANG, RICHARD F,** Univ Of Al At Birmingham, Birmingham, AL; SR; BS; Intrfrat Cncl; Tennis Clb; Gamma Beta Phi; Phi Kappa Phi; Gldn Key; Phi Sigma; Delta Upsilon Chptr Sec 88-89; Biology; Medicine.

**HWANG, SUNHA,** Kent St Univ Kent Cmps, Kent, OH; JR; BA; KOSAK 90-; Math; Eductng.

**HYATT, BOBBY K S,** East Tn St Univ, Johnson City, TN; SR; BBA; Accntng; Cpa; Law; Mba.

**HYATT, ELIZABETH A,** Spartanburg Methodist Coll, Spartanburg, SC; JR; Intl Clb 90-; Fllwshp Chrstn Athlts 90-; Grphc Cmnctn; Grphc Dsgn/Artst.

**HYATT, EMILIE P,** Univ Of Tn At Knoxville, Knoxville, TN; SO; MBA; Circle K 89-; Clement Hall Res Asso Flr Rep 89-; Phi Eta Sigma; Alpha Lambda Delta 89-; Gamma Beta Phi 89-; Phi Sigma Kappa Sweetheart 89-; Finance; Banking.

**HYATT, LORA R,** Univ Of Sc At Coastal Carolina, Conway, SC; SO; BA; Choir; All-Amer Schlr 89-90; Ntl Coll Ed Awd 90; Deans Lst 89-90; Elem Ed.

**HYATT, RUBY YOUNT,** Catawba Valley Comm Coll, Hickory, NC; FR; AAS; Indstrl Eng Tech; Eng.

**HYBL, RUEANNA M,** Methodist Coll, Fayetteville, NC; SO; BS; Show You Care Day; Share The Warmth Day; Special Olympics; Adopt A Hwy 89-90; Bsktbl 89-; Manager Womens Sftbl; Education; Teaching.

**HYCHE, WINNA I,** Tougaloo Coll, Tougaloo, MS; FR; Frshmn Showcase; Pol Sci; Law-Attny.

**HYCLAK, SANDRA A,** Oh Dominican Coll, Columbus, OH; JR; BA; Col Bar Assn Chrprsn 87-; Frnkln Cnty Libry Assn Pr 87-; Ohio Reg Assn Law Libr 89-; Matesck Schlrshp Mthrs; Mrgt Fldrs Schlrshp; Law Librn Legl Res; Libr Sci; Law Librn.

**HYDE, ALLISON J,** Univ Of Ga, Athens, GA; SR; BSED; Georgia Girl 90-; Big Bro Big Str Tutor 90; Deans Lst 90; Early Chldhd Educ; Tch.

**HYDE, CHRISTOPHER ALLEN,** Duquesne Univ, Pittsburgh, PA; SO; Hist Clb 90-; Hist; Profr.

**HYDE, JANE A,** Univ Of Nc At Asheville, Asheville, NC; SR; Spanish Clb Prsdnt 88; Spnsh Ntnl Hnr Soc; Intrprtr.

**HYDE, SUSAN B,** Univ Of Tn At Martin, Martin, TN; SR; Clg Rep 90; Phi Theta Kappa 88; Stdnt Tchr Educ Assn 90; Chi Omega Sec 90-; Taylor E Richardson Schlrshp 88; Damon R Headden Schlrshp 90-; Elem Educ.

**HYDE, THOMAS C,** Southern Coll Of Tech, Marietta, GA; JR; BSME; Mech Engr.

**HYDER, CHRISTOPHER L,** East Tn St Univ, Johnson City, TN; SO; BA; Bus; Acctng.

**HYDORN, SHAWN J,** Univ Of Nc At Charlotte, Charlotte, NC; JR; BA; Golden Key; Economics; Tchng.

**HYEON, HAE M,** Richard Bland Coll, Petersburg, VA; FR; Rotoract; Eng; Arospc Eng.

**HYER JR, WILLARD P,** Univ Of West Fl, Pensacola, FL; JR; BED; Stdnt Assn Math Tchrs VP; Stdnt Natl Edn Assn; NEA; NSTA; NCTM; FCTM; USN Mstr Trng Spclst 87; Fleet Res Assn Brnch 6 71-; Am Legion Post 340 70-; USN Retired 66-89; AA Pensacola Jr Coll 90; Math/Sci Middle Sch; Teach.

**HYERA, ASTERIA B,** Howard Univ, Washington, DC; FR; BA; Archtctr.

**HYKES, KATHI J,** Edinboro Univ Of Pa, Edinboro, PA; JR; BED; Ftr Elem Educ Club 88; Spirit Of Scots Mrchng Bnd 88; Phi Eta Sigma 88-89; Kappa Delta Pi 90; Sigma Pi 89-90; Univ Hnrs Pgm 88; Dns Lst 88; Elem/Erly Chldhd Educ.

**HYLAND, ANN-MARIE,** James Madison University, Harrisonburg, VA; SR; BA; Hall Cncl Pres 87-88; Sigma Eta; Golden Key; Cert U Of Paris 88-89; Frnch/Psychology; Advrtsng.

**HYLAND, LYNN A,** Univ Of Ga, Athens, GA; GD; MSW; Scl Wrk Clb 88-90; Hons Soc Macon Coll 85-88; Hons Pgm Macon Coll 85-88; Rgnts Schlrshp 86-87; GA Cncl Chld Abse 86-87; Prnts Annms 87-88; Crdt Intrnshps Elks-Aidmore Chldrns Ctr 90; Oconee Ctr Sbstnc Abuse Svcs 90; Scl Wrk; Sbstnc Abse Cnslr.

**HYLAND, STEPHEN J,** Univ Of Sc At Columbia, Columbia, SC; FR; BA; Intl Clb Secy; Hist/Govt; Tchng.

**HYLTON, DEANNA R,** Va Commonwealth Univ, Richmond, VA; FR; B; Hnrs Prog 90-; Psychlgy; Govt/Poli Wrk.

**HYLTON, JONATHAN M,** Nc St Univ At Raleigh, Raleigh, NC; FR; BS; Natl Order St Patrick 90-; IM Actvts 90-; Phys Sci; Mech Engr.

**HYLTON, KATHIE A,** Univ Of Sc At Sumter, Sumter, SC; JR; BA; Wargamers Clb Qrtrmstr 90-; Partisan Post Stff Wrtr 89-; Deans Lst 89-; Hubert Graham Osteen Schlrshp 89-; Deans Schlrshp; Partisan Post SCPA Awd 90; Hon Grad 90; IM Vlybl 90; AA Univ SC Sumter 90; Jrnlsm; Advrtsng.**

**HYLTON III, MORRIS U,** Univ Of Ky, Lexington, KY; SO; BARCH; Hmnts Adv Cncl 90; Kappa Sigma 89-90; Hmls Soup Kitchen 89-90; Rvrvw Mnr Nrsng Hm 89-90; Children 90-; Arch.

**HYLTON, WILLIAM A,** Liberty Univ, Lynchburg, VA; SR; MBA; Stdnt Gvrmnt 88-89; IM Sprts; BS; Finance.

**HYLTON, WILMA Y,** Radford Univ, Radford, VA; JR; BGS; Grl Scts Prnt Vol 90-; Ftr Pnrs Amer 89-90; Cert Cmptr Appl New Rvr Comm Clg 90; Cert Elec/Trnsfrm Thry 85; Bsn; Fncl Plnng.

**HYLTON-MARTIN, JEANNIE,** Patrick Henry Comm Coll, Martinsville, VA; SO; BA; Phi Theta Kappa; Edn; Tchr.

**HYMAN, BRUCE H,** Saint Thomas Univ, Miami, FL; SR; MED; Aikido Clb Barry Univ Sec 83-85; Jesuit Vol Assoc 85-88; Mst Otsdng Stdnt; Jesuit Prsthod; BA; Psych.

**HYMAN, DENISE R,** Wv Northern Comm Coll, Wheeling, WV; FR; A; Dns Lst; Lgl Sec Typstr Prntng Prs; Mail Carrier U S Pstl Svc; Appld Sci; Nrsng.

**HYNDMAN, JOSEPH E,** Anne Arundel Comm Coll, Arnold, MD; SO; BS; ASET Elctrncs Tech US Navy Schl 86; Mech Engr; Engr.

**HYNDMAN, NANCY F,** Asbury Theological Sem, Wilmore, KY; GD; MA; Delta Epsln Chi; Theta Phi; Earle/Ione Stine Chrstn Serv Awd 88; BA Vennard Clg 88; Chrstn Ed; Tch.

**HYNES, SUE F,** Newbury Coll, Brookline, MA; SR; Save Erth Comm 90-; Oxfam Amer 90-; Phi Theta Kappa; Wlk Hngr; Dept Awd; Merit Schlrshp 90; AA Clnry Arts 90; AA Htl/Res Mgmt; Clnry/Htl.

**HYNES, TERESA M,** City Univ Of Ny Queensbrough, New York, NY; SO; BA; Ftbl Clb Sec 89-90; Alpha Beta Gamma; Deans Lst 90-; Cert Real Estate Lic 90-; Dntl Nurse 86-; REL Lawrence High Sch 90; Acctg; CPA.

**HYORA, JENNIFER K,** Colby Sawyer Coll, New London, NH; JR; BED; Stdnt Peer Cnslr; Erly Chldhd Educ; Tchr.

**HYPES, GARY A,** West Liberty St Coll, West Liberty, WV; FR; BA; Tutor; Schlr Athelete 90-; Wrslng 90-; Acctg; CPA.

**HYPES, STACEY L,** Fl St Univ, Tallahassee, FL; FR; Delta Delta Delta Almnae Rltns Chrmn; Bus; Acctnt.

**HYRE, JEFFREY A,** Anne Arundel Comm Coll, Arnold, MD; SO; BA; Crmnl Jstc; Fdrl Agnt.

**HYSONG, SYLVIA J,** Univ Of Rochester, Rochester, NY; SR; BA; Sci Fiction Interest Grp Bsn Mgr 88-; Chamber Singers 88-; Vocal Point 90-; Natl Assoc Female Execs 90-; Family Svcs Intern 90; Mgmt Studies Certif; Indstrl/Org Psych.

# I

**IACARUSO, MICHELLE L,** Juniata Coll, Huntingdon, PA; SR; BS; Scalpel/Probe 87-; Stdnt Hlth Advsry Comm 87-; Hnr Socty; Dns Lst; Sim Vlybl 87-90; Pre Med/Biology; Med Schl.

**IACCARINO, GREGORY J,** Glassboro St Coll, Glassboro, NJ; JR; BA; Psych Club V P; Gamma Tau Sigma; Psi Chi; Essays Pblshd Wrtng Anthlgy 88; Psych; Cnslng Psychlgst.

**IACOBUCCI, STEVEN O,** Univ Of Cin R Walters Coll, Blue Ash, OH; JR; BS; Commercial Pilot 89-; Advanced Grnd Instrctr Flght Inst 89-; Cert Shields Aviation 89; Prfssnl Arntcs; Airline Trnsprt Pilot.

**IACONA, LEIGH M,** Saint Andrews Presbytrn Coll, Laurinburg, NC; FR; BA; Knghts Of Rnd Tbl Clb VP 90-; Japanese Ens 90-; Bgng Japanese Ens Tutor 90-; English; Author Horror Fiction.

**IACOVANGELO, ANTHONY B,** Niagara Univ, Niagara Univ, NY; SR; BS; Chrmn Prod Comm 90-; Stdnt Govt; Trip Coord Math Secy 90-; Stdnt Tchr 90; IM Ftbl 87-; Mgmnt/Commerce; Law.

**IACOVONE, STEVE C,** Glassboro St Coll, Glassboro, NJ; SR; BA; Crim Just Soc; Camden Cty Publ Defenders Ofc Invstgtr; Law/Just; MBA Crmnlgy.

**IADANZA, JOHN MICHAEL J,** Winthrop Coll, Rock Hill, SC; JR; BS; Newmn Cthlc Comm 88-; Alpha Lambda Delta 89-; Pres Lst 88; Deans Lst 89-; Sprngs Schlrshp 88-89; RHNB Blck-Dnlp Schlrshp; IM Soccr/Bsktbl/Sftbl 88-; Bus/Finance.

**IANARO, JENISE M,** Va Commonwealth Univ, Richmond, VA; JR; BSN; NSNA 90-; BS Juniata Clge 90; Nursing; RN.

**IANCHOVICHINA, ELENA IVANOVA,** Univ Of Sc At Columbia, Columbia, SC; JR; BA; Math/Mgmt; Mgmt Sci.

**IANNARELLI, JODI-LYNN,** Indiana Univ Of Pa, Indiana, PA; SR; Stdnt Gvrnmnt 88-89; Big Brothers Big Sisters Orgnztn 90-; Kappa Delta Pi 88-; Ordr Omega 89-; Alpha Gamma Delta Mmbrshp 88-; IUP Exclng Grk Awd; IUP Wmns Ldrshp Awd.

**IANNARELLI, NORMAN,** Alfred Univ, Alfred, NY; FR; BS; Stdnt Snt Stdnt Govt Rep; Stdnt Snt Fnc Cmmtt Intrn; Alph Alambda Delta; Mgmt.

**IANNONE, JERYL A,** Ms St Univ, Miss State, MS; GD; DVM; Alpha Psi Treas 90-; AVMA 90-; IM Vlybl 90-; BAAS Univ Delaware 86; Vet Med.

**IATOMASI, MARINA L,** Albertus Magnus Coll, New Haven, CT; SO; BA; Itln Clb; Leukemia Soc Vol; Psy; Clncl Psy.

**IBRAHIM, NOOR AZAH,** Univ Of South Al, Mobile, AL; SR; BS; Assoc Gen Stds IN U Purdue Indy 89; Bus Mgmt Fnc; Bnkg Exec.

**ICE, CAROL S,** Wv Univ At Parkersburg, Parkersburg, WV; SR; Alpha Beta Gama; Am Bus Wmns Assn; Norrell Employee Advsry Com; League Wmn Vtrs; Vienna Wmns Clb; YWCA; Prfsnl Wmns Assn; Parkersburg Lioness; AAS PCC 86; Bus.

**ICE, JODI L,** Marshall University, Huntington, WV; SR; BA; Campus Crus/Christ 90; Deans List 89-; Edctn; Tch.

**ICE, THOMAS W,** Univ Of Ky, Lexington, KY; FR; BS; Sigma Pi; Poli Sci; Law.

**IDDINGS, MARCIA L,** Univ Of Sc At Columbia, Columbia, SC; SO; BS; Vrsty Swim Tm 89-; Gamma Beta Phi 89; Alpha Chi Omega 90-; Blgy Psych; Physcl Thrpy.

**IDEN, MARY JO,** Univ Of Akron, Akron, OH; SR; BED; Coll Edn Schlrshp; Engl; Teach.

**IDO, MAKIKO,** Endicott Coll, Beverly, MA; SO; Horseback Rdg; AS; Int Dsgn.

**IEMMITI, LISA,** S U N Y Coll Of Tech At Frmgdl, Farmingdale, NY; SO; ASSOC; Acad Excell Awrd; Liberal Arts.

**IFFT, JOHN R,** Univ Of Va, Charlottesville, VA; FR; BA; Fllwshp Chrstn Athlts 90-; Echols Schlrs 90-; Dogwood Fstvl Sqsh Trmnt 90-; Sci/Math; Rsrch/Tchng.

**IFILL, AYANNA N,** Hampton Univ, Hampton, VA; SO; BS; IBM Intrn ; Dns Lst 89-; Acctng; Intl Auditor.**

**IFKOVICH, PATRICIA M,** Erie Comm Coll South Cmps, Orchard Park, NY; SR; Phi Theta Kappa 90-; Acdmc All Amer Nominee 90-; Otstndg Yng Wmn Amer; Empr Amer Rlty Crdt Corp; AAS; Ofc Tech; Sec.

**IGLESIAS PINERO, JOSE L,** Inter Amer Univ Pr San German, San German, PR; JR; BA; Ofc Clrk J N Cnstrctn Mayoguez Pr 90-; Acctg; CPA.

**IGLESIAS, CINDY A,** Nova Univ, Ft Lauderdale, FL; GD; Miami Dade Comm Coll Outstndng Acdmc Achvmnt Awrd 80-82; Sunday Schl Tchr 85-; BA 89; AA Miami Dade Comm Coll 83; Acctg; CPA.

**IGLESIAS, MARIVI,** Miami Dade Comm Coll South, Miami, FL; SO; BA; Hnrs Prgrm 89-90; Phi Theta Kappa Dir/Exec Brd Membr 89-90; Hnrs Prgrm Schlrshp 89-90; AA MDCC Sth Cmps; Art; Photo/Film.

**IGNATOWSKI, JENNIFER M,** Univ Of New Haven, West Haven, CT; SO; BS; Day Stdnt Govt Sntr; Accntng Clb 90; Rwng Clb 89-90; Accntng; CPA.

**IGNOTZ, LISA M,** Wv Northern Comm Coll, Wheeling, WV; JR; Delta Phi Epsln; Educ; Tchr.

**IGNOZZI, BRYAN K,** Allegheny Coll, Meadville, PA; SO; BA; Radio Station Finance Dir; Lambda Sigma; Alden Schlr; Delta Tau Delta 89-; IMS 89-; Econ; Law.

**IGWEBUIKE, ADAEZE R,** Kent St Univ Kent Cmps, Kent, OH; JR; BS/MD; Harambee Cult Organ Treas 89-; Mdlng Schl Fshn Kent State; Alpha Lambda Delta; Alpha Kapa Mu; Gldn Ky; Amer Rd Crs Vol; Stdnts King Kennedy Ctr Pres; Case Western Rsrv Med Pgrm; Awd Schlrshp; Helda Graham Academic Awd; Intgrd Lf Sci/Accel Premed; Med Doctor.

**IHDE, DAVID J,** Old Dominion Univ, Norfolk, VA; SO; CE; ASCE 89; Engr/Tech Dns Lst 90-; Cvl Engr; Hwy Engr.

**IHLENFELD, PAUL V,** Temple Univ, Philadelphia, PA; SO; BS; IEEE 90-; Plntry Soc 90-; Karate Orgn; AS Lehigh Co CC 90; PA Army Natl Grd; US Army 85-87; Elect Eng.

**IKER, JAMES L,** Univ Of Miami, Coral Gables, FL; FR; Psi Beta 90-; Army ROTC Cadet 90-; AED Pre-Med Hnr Soc 90-; Psychobio/Chem; Med.

**IKPOH, VINCENT A,** Springfield Tech Comm Coll, Springfield, MA; SO; BSC; Pblc Rltns Offcr Cmptr Clb; Hnr Awrd; Cmmt Ldrshp Awrd Pblc Rltns Ntnl Scty Engrs; Alpha Nu Omega; Ntnl Mnrty Clgt Ldrshp Awrd; NAACP; Peer Cnselr NE Univ; Former Peer Advsr STCC; Tutor Math/Physcs/Chmstry; Drctr Envrnmntl Ed; Chncl Engrng; Engr.

**ILARRAZA, EDWARD,** Inter Amer Univ Pr San German, San German, PR; JR; BMUSE; Jzz Bnd 88-; Prcssn Ensmbl 88-; Cncrt Bnd 88-; Poplr Musc Wrkshp 88-; Cncrt Chr 88-; Actv Srvc US Navy 81-87; Musc Educ; Prfssnl Muscn.

**ILES, JOSEPH D,** Allegheny Coll, Meadville, PA; JR; BA; Yrbk Copy Edtr 88-89; Theta Chi Pres; Humnts Awd 89; Psych Dept Stdnt Intrn; Psych Dept Techng Asst; IM 90-; Psychlgy.

**ILES, ROGER D,** Crichton Coll, Memphis, TN; JR; BS; Stdnt Govt 90-; Deans List 89-90; Naval Sea Cadet Corps Oper Offcr; USN Mstr Trng Spec 87-; Bptst Ch Deacon SS Dir 89-F NCOA Cnsllr 90-; Elctrncs Tech 69-89; AA Univ Of St NY Rgnts Cll 89; Bus; Voc Educ.

**ILLA, ALINA S,** Fl International Univ, Miami, FL; GD; Kappa Delta Pi Chrprsn Fndrsrs 89-; Deans List 89-; BA 90; Ed; Tch.**

**ILLERS, PATRICIA M,** Fl St Univ, Tallahassee, FL; JR; BA; Tallahassee Wmns Newcomers Clb VP 90; Grocery Procurement Wetterau Foods Inc Greenville KY 78-88; Elem Edn; Tchr.

**ILLICKAL, MANOJ,** City Univ Of Ny City Coll, New York, NY; JR; BS; Frederick Douglass Debating Soc Tm Capt 88-; Sci/Engl Tutor 89; Chess Clb 88-90; Natl Forensic League Judge 88-; Hstry; Scanlon Spch Awd 90; Citizens Advice Bureau S Bronx Cnslr-Trng 90-; Sci; Publ Sci.

**ILUNDAIN, SHEILA,** City Univ Of Ny Baruch Coll, New York, NY; SR; BBA; Human Rsrc Mgmt.

**IM, JI H,** Fl St Univ, Tallahassee, FL; SR; BFA; FSU Smnl Dv Clb 89-90; Psi Chi 90; Flm Psychlgy; Flm Prdctn.

**IMAM, SIMEE S,** Va Commonwealth Univ, Richmond, VA; SO; BS; PSA Treas 90-; Cvtn Clb 89-; Phi Eta Sigma 89-; RA; Bio; Med.

**IMBURGIA, KAREN EILEEN,** Atlantic Comm Coll, Mays Landing, NJ; SO; BA; Ntl Hon Soc Atlantic Act Mem/T Bnft 89-90; Snshn Fndtn Prtcpnt 87; Coachd Grls Sftbl 6th 8th Grd Coach 90; Co-Op Yr Fed Avtn Admin Co-Op Pgm Atlantic Comm Coll/Fed Avtn Admin 90; Info/Cmptr Sci.

**IMEOKPARIA, REMI L,** Univ Of South Fl, Tampa, FL; GD; Delta Omega 90-; Grad Asst 07 89; Grad Assoc 90-; MD Kharkov Univ USSR 74; MPH Univ Of Sydney, Astrla 82; Epdmlgy.

**IMHOF, KATHRYN A,** Liberty Univ, Lynchburg, VA; FR; BA; Acctg; CPA.

**IMHOFF, MICHELLE M,** Carnegie Mellon Univ, Pittsburgh, PA; JR; BS; Stndg Com Stdnt Aid 88-90; Allghny Rprtr Dnc 88-90; Orchs Dnc Co 88-90; Lambda Sigma 89-90; Mrtr Bd; Andrew Carnegie Schlr; Wqed Pllnd Gfts Intrn; Kappa Alpha Theta Frat Eeuc Chrprsn Stndrds Com 88-; Alden Schlr 89-90; Scl/Dcsn Sci; MBA/MHA.

**IMHOFF, NICOLE M,** Anne Arundel Comm Coll, Arnold, MD; FR; Envir Sci.

**IMONTI, CYNTHIA J,** Newbury Coll, Brookline, MA; FR; AA; Fshn Clb; Fshn Mrchndsng/Arts; Fshn Byng.

**IMOTO, KUMIKO,** Savannah Coll Of Art & Design, Savannah, GA; GD; MFA; Tchr Joshi Seigakuin Hgh Sch 82-87; BA Kyoritsu Wmns Un 82; BA Lagrange Clg 90; Grphc Dsgn.

**IMPAGLIAZZO, JOAN H,** Pa St Univ Delaware Cty Cmps, Media, PA; JR; BA; Adlt Stdnt Org VP/PRES Elect 90-; Kystone Soc VP 90-; Campus Ambsdr 89-; Deans Lst 89-; Awrd Coll Lbrl Arts; Penn St Delco Schlrshp; R Finueane Schlrshp 90-; L Burns Prz In Hmnties; Hmnties/Amer Stdies; Tch.

**IMPARATO, DAWN M,** Centenary Coll, Hackettstown, NJ; SO; BS; Fshn Grp Sec 89-; Brd Trsts Acdmc Afrs Cmte 89-; Phi Theta Kappa 90-; Arnold Ind Schlrshp; Amer Bsn Wms Assoc Schlrshp; Kiwanis Clb Hammonton Schlrshp; Cert Mrt Fshn Mrchndsng; Jane Barbara Thomas Schlrshp Mrchndsng; Ldrshp Awd 89-; Fshn Mrchndsng; Fshn Byng/Advrtsng.

**INCITTI, LISA M,** Univ Of Scranton, Scranton, PA; FR; BA; Cmps Mnstry Ltrgcl Mscn Pnst 90-; Tr Gde 90-; Circle K Clb Fndr And Pres 90-; Cllgte Vols 90-; Advcts Fr Df Awrnss VP 90-; Cmmnctns; Chldrns Tlvsn Brdcstng.

**INCORVAIA, DENISE,** Salisbury St Univ, Salisbury, MD; SR; WSUR Prsnnl Dir 87-; Phi Eta Sigma 88-; Pi Gamma Mu 90-; Phi Mu Pres 88-; Hon Pgm 87-; Cmps Lf Awd 88-90; Achvmnt Key Awd; BA Salisbury State; Cmnctns/Sclgy; Law Schl.

**INDILICATO, VICKI M,** Providence Coll, Providence, RI; SR; MBA; Pastoral Cncl 88-; Tau Pi Phi; Big Bro Big Sis 89-90; Grad Magna Cum Laude; Helderberg Womens Bus Assn Schlrshp 88; BS; Human Resources.

**INDORF, DIAN M,** Univ Of Akron, Akron, OH; JR; BA; ACES 89-; Gldn Ky 90-; Alpha Lambda Delta 88-; YWCA Chld Cr Employ 90-; Elem Educ/Engl; Elem Schl Tchr.

**INDRIOLO, JOSEPH,** Ny Univ, New York, NY; GD; DDS; Pace Chem Hnr Soc 85; Amer Chem Soc 85; BA 87; Med; Dntstry.

**INESTA, FLAVIA A,** Univ Of Pr At Mayaguez, Mayaguez, PR; SR; DPM; Beta Beta Beta Vocal 89-; Eta Gamma Delta Nwspr Comm 88-; Deans List 89-90; BS; Biology; Podiatric Med.**

**INFANTINO, DANIEL P,** Saint Andrews Presbytrn Coll, Laurinburg, NC; JR; BA; Guitar Instrctr Sandhills Comm Clg Pinehurst NC; Sngr Gtrst Entrtnr; AA Sandhills Comm Clg 90; Music; Music Prfsr.

**INFERRERA, LINDA M,** Atlantic Comm Coll, Mays Landing, NJ; GD; BA; St Joseph's Church; Phi Theta Kappa 90-; Law.

**INGBER, MARK I,** Erie Comm Coll, Buffalo, NY; SO; BACC; Norstar Bank NA Hd Tlr Supvr 88-; Barnett Bnk S FL NA Sr Trlr; AAS; Acctng.

**INGERMAN, IVAN W,** Fl St Univ, Tallahassee, FL; SR; Theatre Patrons Schlrshp 88; Pres Schlrshp 88; Tallahassee Theatre Gld Awd 88-89; Theatre/Cost Scn Dsgn; Theatre Flm Dsgn.

**INGERSON, JAMES W,** Northeastern Christian Jr Coll, Villanova, PA; JR; BSN; Sonrise Pblc Rltns Trvlg Bnd Drmr/Sngr 88-90; Acapplla Chrs Tnr 90; NCSC Sci Awd 89-90; AS 90; Nrsng; Trauma Nrs.

**INGHAM, DANA R,** Comm Coll Algny Co Algny Cmps, Pittsburgh, PA; FR; Assoc Art Inst Pitts 86; Fine Arts.

**INGHAM, MARY E,** Valdosta St Coll, Valdosta, GA; SO; BS; Hnrs Prog; Biology/Geography; Conservation.

**INGHAM, SUSAN A,** Davis & Elkins Coll, Elkins, WV; JR; BS; Acadmc All Amercn Schlr; Deans List 90-; Elem Ed; Tchng.

**INGLE, LEAH M,** Muskingum Coll, New Concord, OH; FR; BA; Tourgud; Vars Trck Tm 90-; Hlth/Phy Ed; Tchng.

**INGLE, MARBETH A,** Richard Bland Coll, Petersburg, VA; SO; BS; Stdnt Govt Rep 90-; Lgsltv/Jdcl Com Rep 90-; Stdnts Infree Entrps Sec 90-; Ms Richard Bland Clg/Miss Cngnlty 90-; Natl Tlnt Rstr 90-; ASB; Acctnt/Mgmt; Resort Hotel Mgr.

**INGLE, SHERI L,** Univ Of Montevallo, Montevallo, AL; JR; BA; Phys Educ Clb 87-; ASAHPERD 87-; Edythe Saylor Awd; Phys Ftns Instr 89-90; Hlth Ftns Prog Instr 90; Aerbc Cls Instr 90; IDEA Cert Amer Cncl Excrse; Phys Educ; Radilgy/Phys Thrpy Spts Med.

**INGLE, TAMELA L,** Northwest Al Comm Coll, Phil Campbell, AL; SO; AS; Phi Theta Kappa 90-; Dns Lst 89-; Elem Ed; Tchr.

**INGLES, MARK R,** Schenectady County Comm Coll, Schenectady, NY; BA; Ownr/Oper 79-; Engl; Tchng.

**INGLUT, GREGORY R,** S U N Y Coll Of Tech At Alfred, Alfred, NY; FR; AAS; Elctrcl Clb VP 90-; Sigma Tau Epsilon 90-; IM Ftbl/Sftbl; Cnstrctn Maint Elect; Tchng/Elect.

**INGOLD, ERIC A,** Va Commonwealth Univ, Richmond, VA; FR; Med Club 90-; Hnrs Prog 90-; Humanities & Sci Awd; Phi Eta Sigma; Provost Schlrshp 90-.

**INGOLDSBY, ROBYN T,** Univ Of North Fl, Jacksonville, FL; SO; BA; AS Daytona Bch Comm Coll 85; Dipl Word Of Life Bible Inst 87; Engl Lit.

**INGRAM, ALISA D,** Fl A & M Univ, Tallahassee, FL; FR; BA; Orchs Stdnt Cntmpry Dncrs; Prtty Psn Dncrs; Phi Eta Sigma; Summer Intrnshp Tanzania Africa Prjct HEAD; Agri-Bus; Bus.

**INGRAM, ANTHONY V K,** Wilmington Coll, New Castle, DE; SR; MBA; Stdnt Assc Amer Coll Hlthcr Exec 89-; Delta Epsilon Rho 90-; Hosp Adm 83-; Cmsnd 2ND Lt USAF; AAS Comm Coll Air Force 88; Busn/Hospital Mgt; Admin.

**INGRAM, CHRISTI E,** Univ Of Sc At Sumter, Sumter, SC; SO; BA; Bus Mgmt; Bus Fld.

**INGRAM, CYNTHIA R,** Middle Tn St Univ, Murfreesboro, TN; SR; BA; Stdnt Ambsdrs 89-; Cmpus Nwspr Stf Wrtr 90-; Gamma Beta Phi Soc Chrprsn 89; Rho Lambda; Tau Imicron 90; Soc Prfsnl Jrnslt; Alpha Delta Pi 90-; English; Tech Wrtr/Edtng.

**INGRAM, DEBRA L,** Milligan Coll, Milligan Clg, TN; FR; BA; Psych.

**INGRAM, JEANNETTE M,** Univ Of Southern Ms, Hattiesburg, MS; FR; BA; Stdnt Eagle Club 90-; Alpha Lambda Delta 90-; Chem; Medcl Rsrch.

**INGRAM, JEFFREY L,** Samford Univ, Birmingham, AL; GD; JD; Cumberland Law Review Rsrch/Projcts Edtr 90-; BS MIT 87; Law.

**INGRAM, JONATHAN W,** Univ Of Southern Ms, Hattiesburg, MS; JR; BA; Yrbk Copy Ed 88; Hnrs Stdnt Assoc 88; Psychology.

**INGRAM, LAURA M,** King Coll, Bristol, TN; FR; BA; Lit Mag Crative Svc; Newspaper Rprtr; World Christian Flwshp Pblcty Direc; Childrens Hm Mnsgry; Top Stdnt Soph Lit; Deans Lst; Enlglish/History; History Prof.

**INGRAM, LAURA M,** Univ Of Southern Ms, Hattiesburg, MS; SR; Opera Theatre; Soc Pro Musica; Sthrn Geo Soc; Phi Alpha Theta; Phi Delta Rho; Gamma Alpha Epsilon; Phi Eta Sigma; Alpha Lambda Delta; Golden Key; Hons Clg; Pi Beta Phi Sigma Nu Little Sis; Flwshp At Wake Forest Univ; Magna Cum Laude; BA 90; Hist; Museum Studies.

**INGRAM, M LYNN,** Univ Of Cin R Walters Coll, Blue Ash, OH; SO; BA; Prfsnl Scrtrs Intrntnl 88-; Bsns Mgmnt; Bsns.

**INGRAM, MARIA D,** Converse Coll, Spartanburg, SC; FR; BA; Stdnt Chrstn Assoc 90-; Bapt Stdnt Union Frshmn Repr 90-; Stdnt Admsns Bd 90-; Alpha Lambda Delta 90-; Crescent; Habitat Humanity 90-; Stdnt Vol Svcs 90-; Clown Mnstrs 90-; Psych/Deaf Ed; Phys Ther.

**INGRAM, REBA D,** Alcorn St Univ, Lorman, MS; SO; BS; Hnrs Students Organization 89-90; Appeared Schl Publ Cognita 90-; Biology Pre Med; Clg Instr.

**INGRAM, ROBERT R,** Chattahoochee Vly St Comm Coll, Phenix City, AL; SO; BA; Dipl Col Tech Inst Data Proc Tech 89; Cmptr Inf Mgmt; Syst Anlyst Pgrmr.

**INGRAM, ROBIN M,** Wv Univ At Parkersburg, Parkersburg, WV; FR; Gldn Grl; Bus; Invstmnt Brkr.

**INGRAM, SANDRA R,** Univ Of Rochester, Rochester, NY; SO; BA; Cmptr Intrst Flr Tres 89-; Scrty Escrt Serv; Ecnmcs; Actry.

**INGRAM, SHANTELL R,** Western New England Coll, Springfield, MA; SO; BS; Untd/Mtlly Equal VP 89-; Amer Pharm Assoc 90-; Pharmacy.**

**INGRAM II, VERNON D,** Hampton Univ, Hampton, VA; FR; BS; Naval ROTC 90-; Exec Cncl 90-; Stdnt Govt Assoc 90-; BOOST Prog; Naval ROTC Schlrshp No 1 Mdshpmn 90-; Ushered Ftbl Games 90-; Comp Sci; U S Navy.

**INGRAM, WENDY M,** Middle Tn St Univ, Murfreesboro, TN; SR; Chmstry.**

**INGRAM, WONDA L,** Nc Agri & Tech St Univ, Greensboro, NC; JR; SNEA; ACEI; Ambssdr; Alpha Kappa Alpha; Elem Educ; Cnslgn.

**INKS, ALLEN W,** Univ Of Toledo, Toledo, OH; GD; JD; Univ Toledo Law Revw Tech Edtr 90; Amer Bar Assn Law Stdnt Div 88-; Ohio Sta Bar Assn Assoc 88-; Golden Key 84-; Amer Jrsprdnc Awd Crmnl Law 89; Law Alumni Schlrshp 88-; Bishops Cmtee; Better Bus Bur Arbtrtr 87-; MSA; BET; Law; Patent Law.

**INMAN, CAROLYN C,** Volunteer St Comm Coll, Gallatin, TN; SO; BS; Bsn/Prof Wmns Org 88-89; Boy Scts Amer Cubmstr 88-89; Church Yng Wmns Pres 87-; Exec Secr/Admin Asst 86-; Info Syst Tech; Cmptr Pgm/Mgmt.

**INMAN, DANA L,** Brescia Coll, Owensboro, KY; SR; BS; KY Educ Assn Mbrshp Chrprsn 89-; Natl Educ Assn; Intl Rdng Assn; Alpha Chi 90-; Circle K 90-; KY Tchrs Schlrshp 90-; Educ; Elem Educ.

**INMAN, DENISE M,** Immaculata Coll, Immaculata, PA; FR; BS; Yrbk Staff 90-; Annual Art Show Vol 90-; Vlybl 90-; Bio; Vet Med.

**INMAN, ELIZABETH C,** Patrick Henry Comm Coll, Martinsville, VA; SR; Stdnt Nrs Assoc Va 89-; AAS P Henry Comm Clg; Nrsng; Emergency Rm.

**INMAN, JOHN M,** Univ Of Rochester, Rochester, NY; JR; BA; Vrsty Ftbll 89-; MBA; Hstry Pltcl Sci; Govt Agnt Lwyr.

**INMAN, KATHERINE N,** Oh Univ, Athens, OH; FR; BFA; Sigma Tau Alpha Treas; Theatre Arts; Stage Mgmnt.

**INMAN, KRISTY N,** Univ Of Tn At Martin, Martin, TN; SR; BS; Stdnt TN Educ Assn 90-; Phi Eta Sigma 89-; Phi Kappa Phi; Scty Hnrs Smnr Stdnts 88-; Scndry Educ Math; Tchng.

**INMAN, REBECCA L,** Savannah Coll Of Art & Design, Savannah, GA; GD; MFA; SCAD Grphcs Clb 87; Clg Art Assoc 90; BFA 89; BFA U Of Tn 90; Grphc Dsgn/Cmptr Grphcs; Grphc Dsgnr/Instr.

**INMAN, SUSAN M,** Le Moyne Coll, Syracuse, NY; SO; Nwspr Wrtr 90-; Engl Clb; Pre Law Soc; Work Study Prog Bishop Foery Yth Dir 89-; Cthlc Chrts 90-; Intrnshp Coolican-Le Mon Advrtsng Agency; Olympics 90-; Engl; Law.

**INMON, JENNIFER,** Ms St Univ, Miss State, MS; FR; AS; DECA Hstrn 89-90; FCA 87-90; Annl Stff Fnncl Bks 88-89; Kappa Delta 90-; Hrt Assn 86-89; Cncr Soc 86-89; Salvation Army Anchr Clb 87-89; Hostess 90; Cert Merit Art Exhb 89; Math; Accntng.

**INNISS, JOHN P,** Va St Univ, Petersburg, VA; SR; BS; Bsns Admn Dpt Clb 90-; Blck Stdnts Agnst Drgs Clb 90-; AS St Unv MY Frmngdale 89; Mgmnt Bsns; Bsns.

**INNISS, MARCIA F D,** Univ Of The Virgin Islands, St Thomas, VI; SR; BA; Pres Clb; Deans Lst 88-; Acctg.

**INNISS, MONIQUE A,** Benedict Coll, Columbia, SC; SR; BSC; Pre-Hlth Clb Treas 90-; Intlstdnts Assc 89-; Alpha Chi; Alpha Kappa Mu; MBRS 90-; AA Coll Bahamas 89; Intern Merch Sharpe Doehme Rsrch Lab Westpoint PA; Blgy; Fisheries/Marine Blgy.

**INOUE, MICHIRO,** A D Little Mgmt Educ Inst, Cambridge, MA; GD; MSN; Bus.

**INSCOE, ROBERT L,** Oh Univ-Southern Cmps, Ironton, OH; FR; BS; Data Prcssng Mngr 84-87; Data Base Consltnt 87-90; Sftwr Eng 90-; AS CS BA Huntington Jr Coll 84; Cmptr Sci; Sftwr Eng/Scntfc.

**INSINGA, JOHN F,** Radford Univ, Radford, VA; SO; BA; EMS; Gym 89-90; Biol; Med.

**INSLEY-CAREY, DAWN M,** Salisbury St Univ, Salisbury, MD; SO; BA; Amer Mktg Assn; Delta Theta Chi Ltl Sis; Mktg; Advrtsng.

**INSOCNA, APRIL A,** Schenectady County Comm Coll, Schenectady, NY; AAS; NYS Dept Of Socl Svcs 82-; Data Proc; Bus Syst.

**INSUA, STEPHANA T,** Hillsborough Comm Coll, Tampa, FL; AS.

**INTERLANDI, HELEN E,** S U N Y Coll Of Tech At Frmgdl, Farmingdale, NY; FR; AS; Busn Admin; Acctng.

**INTHAPANNHA, SOMNET,** Bridgeport Engr Inst, Fairfield, CT; JR; BS; Sr Data Comm Rpr Tech; Engr.

**INTINDOLA, MICHELE M,** Bloomfield Coll, Bloomfield, NJ; JR; Family Day Nursery; BA Bloomfield Clg; Psych.

**INYANG, BARBARA A,** Albany St Coll, Albany, GA; SR; MED; Nwspr Stf Writer 89-; Kappa Delta Pi Pres/Sec 89-; Upward Bnd Asst Treas 90-; Chld Care I Cert Albany Area Tech Inst 85; Edn Middle Grades; Tchr.

**INZERILLE, NOEL P,** Valdosta St Coll, Valdosta, GA; SR; BA; Tau Delta Phi 64-67; Police Assoc DC Fraternal Order Police; Fedl Enformnt Officer; Liet US Park Police; Public Admin; Crim Justice/Criminal Law.

**ION, PATRICIA M,** Duquesne Univ, Pittsburgh, PA; SR; BA; Rngr Clb Vrsty 87-; ROTC 87-; Army Rsrv 89-90; Phi Eta Sigma; Lambda Sigma; Mrtr Brd; Alpha Gamma Delta Mmbrshp Offcr 87-; Amer Lgn Aux 85-; Intern Cngrss William Coyne 90-; Intl Rel/Pol Sci; Fdrl Srvc.

**IONESCU, JULIANA,** City Univ Of Ny Queensbrough, New York, NY; SO; BS; Deans Lst 90-; Rose Mancott Memrl Awd; Comp Anlyst-Mc Graw Hill Inc 88-90; Sci; Pshycl Thrpy.

**IOVINE, NICOLE M,** City Univ Of Ny Baruch Coll, New York, NY; JR; BS; Bio Med Soc; Golden Key 90; Bio; Doctor Or Profsr.

**IPOCK, DORA A,** Madisonville Comm Coll, Madisonville, KY; SO; Ofc Adm.

**IPPOLITO, DANNY A,** Seton Hall Univ, South Orange, NJ; JR; BS; NAA 90-; Beta Gamma Sigma; Beta Alpha Psi 90-; Fox Lambrs CPA Rev Crs; Acctg.

**IPPOLITO, JEFFREY P,** Le Moyne Coll, Syracuse, NY; SO; BS; Acctg.

**IPPOLITO, KELLY A,** Jamestown Comm Coll, Jamestown, NY; FR; MBA; Acctg; CPA.

**IPSALE, KAREN,** Marywood Coll, Scranton, PA; FR; BS; Rstrnt/Flrl Dsgn Flds; Cmnctns Dsrdrs; Df Ed/Tchr.

**IRANI, ANITA A,** Univ Of Miami, Coral Gables, FL; SO; BS; HPME 88-; Alpha Epsilon Delta 90; Blgy; Med.

**IRANIPOUR, AFSANEH,** Hillsborough Comm Coll, Tampa, FL; FR; AS; Intl Clb 90; Vol Humana Hosp Physcl Thrpy; Alld Hlth; Ophthlmc Dspnsng Tech.

**IRBY, MELISSA R,** Univ Of Southern Ms, Hattiesburg, MS; GD; Amrcn Mrktng Assn; Alpha Lambda Delta; Phi Eta Sigma; Gamma Beta Phi; Alpha Mu Alpha; BSBA USM 90; Mrktng.

**IRBY, VESPER C,** Univ Of Nc At Charlotte, Charlotte, NC; SR; BA; Engl; Advrtsng/Wrtng.

**IRELAND, ANNE M,** Va Commonwealth Univ, Richmond, VA; SR; BS; Golden Key; Bus Admin; Human Resource Mgmnt.

**IRELAND, BETTY A,** Pamlico Comm Coll, Grantsboro, NC; SO; AAS; Phi Theta Kappa; Gen Ofc Tech.

**IRELAND, SHARON A,** The Kings Coll, Briarclf Mnr, NY; SO; Stdnt Msn Flwshp Tres 90-; Stdnt Gvrnmnt Tres; Schl Nwsppr Lay-Out Ed 89-90.

**IRENE-COLON, OMAYRA,** Bayamon Central Univ, Bayamon, PR; SO; BET; Tech Ed Assn 90-; Instrctnl Dsgn And Prdctn; Educ Tech.

**IRIARTE, JOSE PABLO,** Barry Univ, Miami, FL; SO; BA; Stdnt Nwspr Editor In Chief 89-; SGA Senator 89-; Hrn Stdnt Assoc VP 89-; Math English; Wrtng Tchng.

**IRICK, MATTHEW C,** Winthrop Coll, Rock Hill, SC; SO; BA; Pi Kappa Alpha Asst Treas 90-; IM 89-; Acctg; CPA.

**IRILLI, LISA M,** Kent St Univ Kent Cmps, Kent, OH; JR; BBA; AMA 90-; CPPC 90-; Intrhl Cncl Flr Rep 88-89; Golden Key; Delta Gamma Corrspndng Sec 88-; Kent Lions Clb 88-; Deans Lst 88-; Grk Hnrs Lst 88-; IM Aerbcs 88-; Indstrl Mrktng.

**IRIZARRY GARCIA, ROBERTO,** Inter Amer Univ Pr San German, San German, PR; SO; BA; Natl Hnr Soc PR Guanin Chptr Of Yauco 88-89; Bus Admin; CPA.

**IRIZARRY VELEZ, NORMAJAL,** Catholic Univ Of Pr, Ponce, PR; JR; Assoc Scl Wrks Stdnts 89; Coll Arts.

**IRIZARRY, AUDREY H,** Fl St Univ, Tallahassee, FL; JR; BA; Music Brd Advsrs 90-; MENC 89-; Mrchng Bnd 89-; Hons/Schlrs Pgm 88-; Golden Key; Simga Alpha Iota T; FSU Deans Lst 88-91; Music.

**IRIZARRY, CRISILDA,** Inter Amer Univ Pr San German, San German, PR; JR; BS; Chem Assn; Hon Stdnt; Chem; Med Schl.

**IRIZARRY, NEILA M,** Univ Of Pr At Rio Piedras, Rio Piedras, PR; SR; BA; Pre Med Stdnts Assn 89-; Microbiology Stdnts 90-; Nat Sci Fac Bd Hnr 89-; Sci; Med.**

**IRIZARRY, NITZA I,** Fl International Univ, Miami, FL; FR; BED; Elem Ed; Tchr.

**IRIZARRY, SALLY V,** Catholic Univ Of Pr, Ponce, PR; SO; Ponce Aero Trng; Museum Lab Conservation Asst Ponces Museum Art 90-; Museum Guide Vol 90-; Cmptr Data Sst; Mktg/Art Hstry; Merch/Museum.

**IRIZARRY, SHARON D,** Catholic Univ Of Pr, Ponce, PR; SR; Engl Tchr; ASS Deg Univ Hawaii 84; BSS; Engl; Mstr Degree.

**IRIZARRY, TOMMY,** Inter Amer Univ Pr San German, San German, PR; FR; BA; Sci; Eng.

**IRIZARRY, WALESKA I,** Inter Amer Univ Pr San German, San German, PR; JR; BBA; Amer Mrktng Assn 90-; Natl Assn Of Accts 89-; Ttr 87-; Mrktng; MBA Intrnatl Bus.

**IRIZARRY, YLCE,** Le Moyne Coll, Syracuse, NY; SO; BA; Radio DJ 89; Mrtl Arts Scty 89-; Prjcts In The Comm Tutor 90; Dns Lst 90; Inrds Intrnshp Coopers And Lybrand 90; Tae Kwon Do Tstng 90; Engl Lit.

**IRIZARY, SAMUEL,** Atlantic Comm Coll, Mays Landing, NJ; SO; MBA; Elec Engr.

**IRONS, CHARMAINE ANGELA,** Coll Of Insurance, New York, NY; SO; BS; Phtgrphy Clb 89-90; Wheatly Hl FLA A/M Univ VP 89; Bronze Schlrshp 89-90; Ldrshp Schlrshp 90-; Deans Lst 90; Actrl Sci.

**IRVIN, ELIZABETH A,** Marshall University, Huntington, WV; FR; BA; Engl/Math; Sec Ed.

**IRVIN, JOAN S,** Snead St Jr Coll, Boaz, AL; FR; BA; Math; Architecture.

**IRVIN, JONNA M,** Indiana Univ Of Pa, Indiana, PA; GD; Stdnt Teach Physically Hndcp/Lrng Disabilities; Cub Scouts/Cmnty Serv Adolescents; Spcl Edn.

**IRVIN, MARIA JOSE PERALTA,** Fl International Univ, Miami, FL; GD; MA; Psi Chi; BA FL Intl Univ 90; Psychlgy; Grntlgy.

**IRVINE, HOLLY E,** Colby Sawyer Coll, New London, NH; FR; BS; Vars Vlybl/Tennis 90-; Bsn Sports Mgmt.

**IRVINE, PAMELA R,** Albany St Coll, Albany, GA; SO; BS; Stdnt Govt Cngrss Mmbr 89-; Brd Mgrs 90-; Nwsppr Asst Bus Mgr 90-; Hnrs Cncl Rep 89-; Delta Sigma Theta; Bst Bdds Chptr Dir; Mrktng.

**IRVINE, THOMAS J,** Temple Univ, Philadelphia, PA; SR; BS; Golden Key 88-; Temple Univ Vars Crew Team 87-90; Exercise Sci.

**IRVING, JENNIFER ONA,** S U N Y Coll At Fredonia, Fredonia, NY; JR; BS; Tchr Ed Clb Treas 88-F Vlntr Tutrng Pgm Co-Coord 88-F Phi Mu Epsilon; Tchrs Asst Math 101; Math; Scndry Ed.

**IRVING, VALORIE J,** Bennett Coll, Greensboro, NC; JR; BS; Stdnt NC Assc Edctrs 90-; Deans Lst 90-; Zeta Phi Beta; AA Natl Bus Coll 78-80; Stdnt Crdntr Ltrcy Core; Edctn; Elem Ed.

**IRVIS, VALERIE,** Columbia Greene Comm Coll, Hudson, NY; FR; BA; Individual Studies; Elem Ed.

**IRWIN, CHRISTOPHER J,** S U N Y At Buffalo, Buffalo, NY; JR; BS; Natl Soc Prof Engrs IM Capt 89-; Gldn Ky 90-; Phi Eta Sigma 88-89; Tau Beta Pi 90-; IEEE 90-; Dunlop Tire Smmr Intrnshp 89; Suny Clncl Ctr Smmr Asst; Elec/Comp Engr; Engr.

**IRWIN, GERONA M,** Framingham St Coll, Framingham, MA; SR; BA; AS Fisher Jr Clg 63; Liberal.

**IRWIN, KIMBERLEE L,** Howard Univ, Washington, DC; GD; MA; Untd Blck Stdnt Assn 87-89; Assn Stdnt Oregon State Univ/ Spirit Club 89-90; Wmn Cmnctns Inc Repr 89-; Oregon St Univ Dns Lst 88-89; Dns Lst 90; Intrnshp Blck Entrtnmn Tlvsn 90-; Intrnshp W Usa-Cbs Chnnl 9 Wsh Dc 90; Mass Cmnctn Thry; Univ Tchng.

**IRWIN, KRISTEN E,** Ms St Univ, Miss State, MS; FR; Var Crs Cntry Tm 90-; Var Trkc Tm 90-; Alpha Lambda Delta; Cnsrvtn Grp 90-; Bio Sci; Marine.

**IRWIN, LYNDA L,** Coll Of Charleston, Charleston, SC; SR; BS; Beta Gamma Sigma; Phi Kappa Phi; Omicron Delta Kappa; Nghbrhd Wtch Capt; Sndy Schl Tchr Jr Hgh; BS; Bus Admin; Stds In Fnnce.

**IRWIN, MARCIA L,** Westminster Coll, New Wilmingtn, PA; SR; BA; Kappa Delta Pi 89-; Pi Sigma Pi 90-; Clara Cockerel Schlrshp 90; Elem Ed; Phd Erly Chldhd Dvlpmnt/Cnslng.

**IRWIN, PETER J,** Cornell Univ Statutory College, Ithaca, NY; SO; BS; Alpha Sigma Phi 90-; Apld Econ; Law.

**ISAAC, GINGER K,** Radford Univ, Radford, VA; JR; BS; Fshn Soc Dsgn/Mrchndsng 88-89; Alpha Sigma Tau Crrspndg Sec 90-; Fshn Mrchngsng; Rtl Byng/Mgmt.

**ISAAC, JACQUELINE P,** Coppin St Coll, Baltimore, MD; SR; BS; Psych Club V P; Caring Hearts Chrty Comm Pres; Video Club; Mcnair Schlr; Hrn Soc; Courier Newspr Edit; LMC Cmnty Ctr Vol; BS; Psych.

**ISAAC, REGINA E,** Al St Univ, Montgomery, AL; SO; Crmnl Jstc; Crctnl Ofcr.

**ISAAC, TAMMYRA Y,** Central St Univ, Wilberforce, OH; SR; BA; NABJ 90-; Alpha Kappa Aipha; Res Assntshp 90-; Dns Lst 88-; Engl Lit; Tchr.

**ISAACS, KEITH A,** Ky Christian Coll, Grayson, KY; SR; Tchr Educ Std Yr; Cum Laude; Bsktbl Coach Htchns Elem Schl 87-; Isaacs Rdtr Serv Ownr 85-; Mech/Hvy Eqpmnt Oper 82-; BS; Engl/Comm/Scl Stds; Tchr/Coach.

**ISAACS, KIMBERLY A,** Univ Of Sc At Columbia, Columbia, SC; FR; BA; SCC 90-; Lambda Chi Alpha-Ltl Sis; Spnsh/Comp; Comp Pgmr.

**ISAACSON JR, DONALD E,** Central Fl Comm Coll, Ocala, FL; FR; BS; Envrnmntl Clb 90-; Acctg; CPA.

**ISABELL, JOSEPH A,** Davis & Elkins Coll, Elkins, WV; SR; Lit Mag Edtr 88; Radio Prog Dir 89; BA; Engl Comp; Tchr.

**ISABELL, LEE J,** Norfolk St Univ, Norfolk, VA; FR; BA; Prs Flwshp Rlgs Grp; Spartan Alpha Tau/Local; Wrstlng; Bio-Pre-Med; Pyscn/Srgn.

**ISABELLE, DALE W,** Jackson St Univ, Jackson, MS; JR; BS; Bio Soc 88; Beta Kappa Chi; WEB Dubois Hnrs Clg 88; Bio; Med.

**ISALY, TINA M,** West Liberty St Coll, West Liberty, WV; JR; BA; Cert Recog Acad Perf 3rd Level Spanish; Speech Path/Audio.

**ISAULA, MARIA RAQUEL,** Univ Of Tn At Martin, Martin, TN; SR; BA; Agrnmy Clb Sec 89-90; Deans Lst; Sclgy Ag Sci.

**ISAVA, DUANE M,** Fl International Univ, Miami, FL; FR; BA; Tao Chuan Fa Kung Fu Clb 89; Gld Gym Hlth Clb 89-; IM Sccr Vice Capt 90; AA Cambridge Queens Royal Coll 89; Psych; Chld Psych.

**ISBELL, ROBERT E,** Bethel Coll, Mckenzie, TN; SR; MA; Psych Clb VP 89-; IM Bsktbl Ftbl Sftbl 88-; Intrnshp Bapt Mem Hosp Alchl And Drg; Pysch Unit Union Cty TN; Vrsty Bsbl 89; Cmmn Cause 90-; US Army 88; Rsdntl Cnslr; BS; Clncl Psych.

**ISEMAN, STEPHANIE A,** Rutgers St Univ At Camden, Camden, NJ; SR; BS; Acctng.

**ISENBERG, JOEL D,** Univ Of Sc At Columbia, Columbia, SC; FR; BAIS; Deacon 1st Bapt Chrch Grt Falls SC; US Nvy 80-89; Cmptrs Oper 89-; Phlsphy/Sclgy; Bapt Mnstr.

**ISER, MALINDA A,** Wv Univ, Morgantown, WV; SR; Pi Tau Sigma 90-; AAME 89; BSME 90; Mchncl Eng.

**ISKOWITZ, GILA M,** Yeshiva Univ, New York, NY; GD; Nwspr Edtr 88-89; Psych Jrnl Edtr 89-90; Fine Arts Jrnl; Beckin Schlr; Rsdnc Cncl Chrprsn 88-89; Jacob Bluttal Awrd 90; Rsrch Asstnt 89-; BA 90; AA 90; Psych; Clncl.

**ISKRA, FRANK,** Kent St Univ Kent Cmps, Kent, OH; SR; Finance Assn 90-; Fnncl Mgmnt Assn; Gldn Key 89-; Fnncl Mgmnt Assn Ntnl Hnr Soc; IM Bsktbl 89-; BBA; Finance; Mgmnt.

**ISLAM, FARHANA,** Saint Francis Coll, Loretto, PA; SO; BS; Cmptr Sci.

**ISLAM, MAHBUBUL,** City Univ Of Ny City Coll, New York, NY; JR; BS; Am Inst Chem Engrs 90-; Soc Profl Engrs 90-; Ronald Mcnair Schlrshp Rcpnt; Chem Eng.**

**ISLER, GLENDA R,** Tn Temple Univ, Chattanooga, TN; FR; BSN; Nursing.

**ISLER, JAMES CLARK,** Comm Coll Algny Co Algny Cmps, Pittsburgh, PA; SO; MED; Scty Fr Crtv Anchrnsms 86-; Envrnmntl Clb Pres Ad Hoc 88-; AA; Hstry; Tch Scndry Lvl.

**ISLEY, CAROL M,** Univ Of Al At Birmingham, Birmingham, AL; JR; BS; Pres Lst; Deans Lst; Frfghtr/EMT 89-; Amer Assoc Crtcl Care Nrs 84-; Hosp RN; ASN 83; Allied Hlth; Nrsg.

**ISNER, CYNTHIA A,** Univ Of Nc At Charlotte, Charlotte, NC; JR; BA; Gldn Key; Hstry; Tch Sec Ed.

**ISOM, ADRIAN J,** Albany St Coll, Albany, GA; SO; BA; Drm Clb 90-; Thtr Drm; Tchng.

**ISOM, CHERYL S,** Le Moyne Coll, Syracuse, NY; JR; BS; Joseph Cashier Medal 90; Anthony Henninger Medal; Indstrl Rel Rsrch Assn Schlrshp; Rest Mngmt; AS Onondage Comm Coll 89; Indstrl Rel; Coll Prfssr IR.

**ISOM, DIANNE D,** Fl A & M Univ, Tallahassee, FL; SR; PHD; Pres Schlrs Assn 87-; Comp Info Sys Clb 87-88; Phi Eta Sigma 87-; Wht/Gld Hon Soc 89-; Alpha Kappa Mu 89-; Gldn Ky 90-; Pres Schlrshp 87; Estmn Kodak Schlrshp Intrnshp 88-89; Prdntl Ins Co Intern 88; BS; Comp Info Sys; Sftwr Eng.

**ISON, BARBARA A,** Valdosta St Coll, Valdosta, GA; FR; BS; Alpha Lambda Delta 90-; Bio; Ntrtn.

**ISON, SUSAN Y,** Ashland Comm Coll, Ashland, KY; FR; Acctg.

**ISRAEL, ARI,** Yeshiva Univ, New York, NY; JR; NCSY 88-; Cmmtt Svst Jwry 90-; Capitol Hill Intern Cngrssmn 89; Biol Jwsh Hstry; Tchng.

**ISRAEL, BRENTLY D,** Univ Of Sc At Columbia, Columbia, SC; SO; BA; Pilot.

**ISRAEL, JASMINE C,** Columbia Union Coll, Takoma Park, MD; SR; BS; Pre-Law Clb 89-; Snte 90-; Cmps Soup Ktchn Vol 90-; Sabbath Schl Tchr 90-; Bsn Admn; Law.

**ISRAEL, JOANNE R,** Univ Of Rochester, Rochester, NY; JR; BA; Kappa Delta; Econ/Spnsh Minor; Finc.

**ISRAEL, JOSHUA J,** Yeshiva Univ, New York, NY; FR; BS; Cmptr Sci; Cmptr Prgmr.

**ISRAEL, SCOTT M,** Atlantic Comm Coll, Mays Landing, NJ; SO; BS; Jewish Stdnt Asso Pres 90-; Sci Cl SAA Treas 86-87; Virginia Mason Hosp Seattle Wa Cmte 88-89; Intnl Asso/ Hlthcare Cen Svc Mtl Mgmnt 88-; Cert/Reg Cen Svc Techn Atlantic City Med Cen 88-; Biol/Med; MD.

**ISSA, PAUL A,** Univ Of Miami, Coral Gables, FL; SR; BBA; Beta Gamma Sigma; Fin; Bus.

**ISTVANKO, LE ANNE M,** Memphis St Univ, Memphis, TN; JR; BED; SCEC Exec Brd 90-; Deans Lst 88-90; Spcl Educ; Tchg.

**ITO, KEIKO,** Broward Comm Coll, Ft Lauderdale, FL; SO; BS; Grad BCC With Highest Hons 90; AA; Math.

**ITO, MARI,** Savannah Coll Of Art & Design, Savannah, GA; SO; BFA; YMCA Athltc Clb 90-; Pc/Jstc; Asahi Chmcl Indstry; Internatl Cngrs Agt; Pntngf Artst.

**ITO, NAOMI,** Bay Path Coll, Longmeadow, MA; SO; AA; Glee Clb 89-90; Maroon Key 89-; Tutor Asst 90-; Lib Arts; Jrnlsm **

**ITOH, HIROE,** Newbury Coll, Brookline, MA; FR; AAS; Intrnl Stdnt Clb Sec 90-; Dns Lst 90; Trvl Trsm Mngmnt.

**ITOI, SAYOKO,** Fordham Univ, Bronx, NY; BA; Beta Gamma Sigma; Rntr Japan 87-90; Acctg; CPA.

**ITRO, MARGARET A,** Glassboro St Coll, Glassboro, NJ; SR; BA; PRSSA 89-; Newman Ctr 89; Cmnctns; Publc Rltns.

**ITZKOVITZ, ROBERT,** City Univ Of Ny City Coll, New York, NY; SR; BA; Frederick Douflas Debating Soc 90; Govt/Law Soc 90; Ec Soc 90; Golden Key 90; Felix S Cohen Prize; Summa Cum Laude; Deans List; Law.

**IULIUCCI, THERESA ROSE,** Fl International Univ, Miami, FL; SR; BS; Phys Edn Majors Club Fndng Sec; Varsity Bsktbl; AA Indian River Comm Coll 88; Phys Edn; Edn/Teach.

**IVANCICH, WANDA JEAN,** Coll Of New Rochelle, New Rochelle, NY; JR; BA; Hon Rep 90-; Bus Brd VP 90-; Hon Soc 89-90; Deans Lst 89-; Lndn Exchng; Cathlc Bg Sistrs 89-; Econ; Bus.

**IVELISSE, LOPEZ,** Univ Of Pr At Mayaguez, Mayaguez, PR; JR; BA; Yth Assn; BBB; Natl Collgt Natrl Sci Awrd; Hon Stdnt; Biolgy; Med.

**IVERSON, ANDA L,** Ms St Univ, Miss State, MS; SR; Dmnd Grl 90-; Sigma Chi Lil Sis 88-; Kappa Delta Pi 90-; Kappa Delta Sgt At Arms 88-; Chld Abse Fndtn; Dmn Grl; EED; Educ; Tchng.

**IVERSON, FRANCES A,** Wv Northern Comm Coll, Wheeling, WV; SO; BA; Phi Theta Kappa 90-; Pres Lst Achiev Awd 89; Deans Lst 90-; AS; Acctg Bus Admin; CPA.

**IVES, WILLIAM S,** Kent St Univ Kent Cmps, Kent, OH; SR; MBA; AIESEC Exec VP 88-; Stndt Credit Union Fndr 90-; Stdnt Senate Allocations 89-; Alpha Lambda Delta; Omicron Delta Kappa V P 90-; Gldn Ky 90-; Delta Sigma Pi 90-; Delta Chi V P 88-89; KSU Dist Schlrs Awd 87-; Mktng/Finance; Comm Bnkng.

**IVEY, CHRISTY A,** James Madison University, Harrisonburg, VA; FR; BA; Crs Cntry Tm 90-; Chld Psy.

**IVEY, DENISE M,** Univ Of Montevallo, Montevallo, AL; JR; BA; PTK-CACC 89-90; DKP-MONTEVALLO 90; Amer Lung Assoc Vol Cmmnty CP 87-88; A H Watwood Yrbk Advsr 88-89; Elem/Mddl Schl Sci; Tchr.

**IVEY JR, JAMES M,** Chesterfield Marlboro Coll, Cheraw, SC; FR; AA; Rnbw Dist Burlngtn NC Cand Distbtr; Alamance Comm Clg Haw Rvr NC Dip Digtl Elec 88-; Comp Sls/Serv; Law/Sls.

**IVEY, KIMBERLY R,** Fl International Univ, Miami, FL; JR; Elem Ed.

**IVEY, LEE S,** Gallaudet Univ, Washington, DC; JR; BA; Tchrs Ad; Std Art.

**IVEY, LESLIE A,** Middle Tn St Univ, Murfreesboro, TN; JR; BS; Crmnl Jstc Soc Chrmn Schlrshp Comm; Crmnl Jstc Admin/Psych; Law.

**IVEY, M TONYA,** Liberty Univ, Lynchburg, VA; JR; BA; Psy; Gdnc Cnslr.

**IVINS, PAMELA K,** Meridian Comm Coll, Meridian, MS; SO; BS; Phi Theta Kappa; Retail Mgt Administrative Assist; Busn Admin; Sales/Mktng.

**IVORY, REGINA C,** Fort Valley St Coll, Fort Valley, GA; FR; BA; Coop Dev Enrgy Prog; Hons Prog; Hons Convctn; Dns Lst; Hons Convctn Awd; Cis; Corp Acctg.

**IVY, N JUNE,** Meridian Comm Coll, Meridian, MS; FR; BSW; Lead Bspt Stu Union 90-; Stu Lit Corp Recog Pres Bush Point Of Lght 90-; Hnr Stu MSU 89-90; Psychl Scl Wrk

**IVY, STEPHEN D,** Itawamba Comm Coll, Fulton, MS; FR; BS; Pblctns Nwsppr Stff Wrtr 90-; Sftbll Mngr; Coachng Sprts Admn; Bsbll Frnt Offc Oper.

**IWAMOTO, HIROKO,** Cornell Univ, Ithaca, NY; FR; BA; Mrchng Bnd 90-; Pep Bnd 90-; Symphonic Bnd; Engl.

**IWATA, KEIKO,** S U N Y Coll At Fredonia, Fredonia, NY; JR; BA; Bus; Mktg.

**IWIG, CARA L,** Asbury Theological Sem, Wilmore, KY; GD; MDIV; Chrstn Srvc Mnstrs Pryr Coord 90-; Chrstns Biblcl Eqlty; Theta Phi 90-; Phi Kappa Phi 87-; Psi Chi 86-; Res Asst Psych Washbrn Univ 87-89; BA Washbrn Univ Topeka Ks 89; Theolgy; Pstrl Mnstry.

**IYAWE, CHRISTOPHER IGHARUOSA,** Tn St Univ, Nashville, TN; JR; BSC; Zeta Kappa Nu Zeta; Elec; Eng.

**IZAJ, CHRISTINE M,** Duquesne Univ, Pittsburgh, PA; JR; BA; Beta Alpha Phi Sec 90-; Stdnts Against Drunk Driving 88-; Schlrshp Acctng Assoc 90-; Schlrshp Citizens Fndtn 90-; Acctng/Human Res Mgmt; Law.

**IZCOA, CARMEN R,** Univ Of Pr At Rio Piedras, Rio Piedras, PR; JR; BA; AMA 89-; Intl Swmmng Fdrtn 75-; Key Gldn; Dean Lst 90-; Hrn Schlrshp 89-.

**IZQUIERDO JR, FILENO J,** Fl International Univ, Miami, FL; JR; BEE; Delta Chi 89-; Math/Sci; Engr.

**IZQUIERDO, GUILLERMO,** S U N Y At Buffalo, Buffalo, NY; JR; BA; Mag Advrtsng Exec Mngr 89-; Mngmnt; Law.

**IZQUIERDO, NELSON,** Saint Thomas Univ, Miami, FL; JR; Bsbl Team Capt; All Dstrct All Amer 89-90; Ed; Soc Stdies.

**IZQUIERDO, OTONIEL,** Nova Univ, Ft Lauderdale, FL; GD; Pres Hnr Lst 85; ASME 85-; Fla Prf Eng Intern; Deans Lst 85-876; Sftbl 85; BSME Fla State Univ 76; Mech Eng.

**IZUMI, JUNKO,** Newbury Coll, Brookline, MA; SO; IDA; Intnl Club; Interior Desgn Awd; FBA Kobe Kaisei Wmns Colg 88; Interior Dsgn; Archtctre.

**IZURIETA, WALTER E,** Nova Univ, Ft Lauderdale, FL; SR; MA; Natl Scty Pblc Acctnts 85; Asst Area Cntrlr 87-; BA Mercy Coll 81; Intl Bus; Doctorate Intern Bus.

**IZVORSKI, IVAILO V,** Univ Of Sc At Columbia, Columbia, SC; JR; BA; Econ Soc 90-; U S Info Agency Schlrshp 90-; Michael J Unngs Schlrshp 90-; Econs/Fin.

**IZZO, MARY ALICE M,** Neumann Coll, Aston, PA; JR; Educ Clb 88-; BA; Elem Ed; Tch.

# J

**JAAFAR, ABDELGHANI,** Southern Coll Of Tech, Marietta, GA; SO; MBA; US Sccr Assoc; Teach Frnch/Mddle Schl Pupils; Indoor Soccer; Elec Eng Tech/Math; Rsrch.

**JABLONSKI, JENNIFER L,** George Mason Univ, Fairfax, VA; JR; BS; Alpha Chi; Phi Mu P; Bus; Mktg.

**JABLONSKI, LINDA L,** Marywood Coll, Scranton, PA; SR; BS; Bio Clb Pres 87-; Chem Clb 87-90; Delta Epsilon Sigma 89-; All Amer Schlr Coll Awrd 89; Bio; Scndry Educ.

**JABLONSKI, MARK A,** Comm Coll Algny Co Algny Cmps, Pittsburgh, PA; SO; BA; Phi Theta Kappa; AS CCAC 90; Law.

**JABLONSKI, NANCY C,** Glassboro St Coll, Glassboro, NJ; JR; BS; Atlantic City/Cnty Bd Realtors Schlrshp 90; Natl Assoc Acctnts; AS Atlantic Comm Coll 90; Bus Admin; Acctg.

**JABLONSKI, VICTORIA M,** Castleton St Coll, Castleton, VT; SR; BS; Phi Eta Sigma 88; Dns Lst; Independent Study Personal Finance 90; Bsn Adm/Finance; Sales Asst-Investment Co.**

**JABLUNOVSKY, MARIANNE,** Indiana Univ Of Pa, Indiana, PA; SO; BA; Actvts Plnng Brd 89-90; Grmn Clb 90; PSEA 90-; Hbtt Hmnty 90-; Stu Lit Corp 90; Kappa Delta Pi 90-; VTA 90; Provost Schlr Hnr; Bus Tmrrw Conf; Rlgs Educ; Educ.

**JACHIMEK, DR GAIL A,** Life Coll, Marietta, GA; GD; DC; X Ray Dept VP 90-; Roentgenological Technlgcl Scty Sec 89-90; Chiropractic.

**JACHIMEK, DR RICHARD H,** Life Coll, Marietta, GA; GD; DC; Radiology Sec 89; Roentgenological/Tech Soc 89-90; Phi Theta Kappa 86-87; Army Helicopter Pilot 77-81; Cmrcl Pilot 81-82; AA Manatee Comm Clg 87; Chiropractic.

**JACHLEWSKI JR, TIMOTHY F,** S U N Y Coll Of Tech At Alfred, Alfred, NY; SO; AAS; Hrtcltr Clb 89-; Lndscp Coord Annl Hrtcltr Shw; Sigma Tau Epsilon 89-; Phi Theta Kappa; Prsdnts Hnrs Schlrshp 89-; Rgnts Schlrshp 89-; Deans Lst 89-; Lndscp Dsgn; Lndscp Archtctr.

**JACK, ALEX F,** Ky Christian Coll, Grayson, KY; JR; BA; Rlgn; Mnstry.

**JACK, DEBRA C,** Borough Of Manhattan Comm Coll, New York, NY; SO; BA; Dnc Clb 89-; AA; Math/Spnsh; Tchr/NYC Brd Ed.

**JACK, HOPETON L,** City Univ Of Ny City Coll, New York, NY; SO; BS; Sec 86-89; ASCAC; Hstry; Jrnlsm.

**JACK, JACK B,** Edward Waters Coll, Jacksonville, FL; SR; BA; Phi Theta Kappa 87-88; Magna Cum Laude; CERT Control Data Inst 83; AA FL Cmnty Clg Jacksonville 88; Mss Cmnctns; Jrnlsm.

**JACK, JENNIFER L,** Univ Of Southern Ms, Hattiesburg, MS; SO; BA; Stdnt Almn Assoc 89-; Gamma Beta Phi 90-; Hnrs Clge 89-; Eng; Grdt Schl.

**JACKEY, DAMON M,** Univ Of Ky, Lexington, KY; SR; BED; Middle Schl Assoc 90-; Deans Lst 90; Math/Socl Studies Tchr.

**JACKLET, JASON C,** Fl Coll, Temple Terrace, FL; FR; BS; Christians For Rsrch/Exmntn Of Sci/Tchnlgy 90; Orain Bowl 90; Phi Theta Kappa; ARETE 90; Electrical Eng; Eng.

**JACKMAN, JOHN R,** Univ Of Nh Plymouth St Coll, Plymouth, NH; SR; BS; I M Soccer; Bus/Acctg.**

**JACKMAN, LAURA AIMEE,** Commonwealth Coll, Virginia Beach, VA; FR; Acctg; CPA.

**JACKOVICH, KELLY R,** Univ Of Sc At Columbia, Columbia, SC; FR; BA; PUFF 90-; Friends Of Lexington Libry; Elem Educ.

**JACKSITS, JANICE C,** Coppin St Coll, Baltimore, MD; SR; BS; Phi Theta Kappa 82-; MSESC-NEA 85-; BACA/TABCO; Spec Ed Instnl; AA Essex Comm Clg 85; Spec Ed; Tchr.

**JACKSON THOMAS, CASSANDRA LYNN,** Al St Univ, Montgomery, AL; SO; BA; Chem; Biomed Rsrch.

**JACKSON, AKIBA N,** Miami Dade Comm Coll North, Miami, FL; SO; BA; Pan Afrcn Stdnt Cncl Brd Mbr 89-; Spch Tm 90-; Phi Rho Pi Pres 90-; Phi Rho Pi Flwshp Awd; AA; Econ/Poli Sci; Law.

**JACKSON, ALBERT E,** Univ Of Akron, Akron, OH; SR; BA; Gold Key 90-; Deans List 90; Dept Mngt 88; Lndscp Dsgnr/Excel Lndscpng; Assoc Deg Ohio St Univ 80; Acctg/Auditor.

**JACKSON, ALEXIS R,** Fayetteville St Univ, Fayetteville, NC; FR; BS; Phrmcst.

**JACKSON, ALLESA PAIGE,** Fl A & M Univ, Tallahassee, FL; JR; PHARM; SGA Sen 88-; White Gld Ky; Kappa Epsilon 88-; Alpha Kappa Alpha Schlrshp Cmmtt 89-; Intern Merck & Co NJ; Interm Cipa Geigy Corp NJ 90; Phrmctcl Sci; Phrmcst.

**JACKSON, AMY E,** Univ Of Tn At Martin, Martin, TN; SO; BS; Cstmr Serv Dept Avon Books/Hearst Pub NY 6 Yr; Geography; Lndscp Archtctr.

**JACKSON, ANGELA R,** Va St Univ, Petersburg, VA; SO; BA; Admn Jstc Clb Sec 89-; Dcrtng Cmmtt 89-; Gnrl Mbr; Sclgy Admn Jstc; Law.

**JACKSON, ANGELA S,** Univ Of Tn At Martin, Martin, TN; FR; BA; Hon Smnr 90-; Mu Epsilon Delta 90-; Alpha Gamma Delta; Biolgy; Med.

**JACKSON, ANISSA LEE,** Alcorn St Univ, Lorman, MS; SR; BS; NAACP Stdnt Snt; Sigma Stars Swthrt Clb Sec 88-; Cmps Radio Stdnt Emplyee; Psychlgy Clb Chpln; Hon Stdnt Org 87-; Alpha Kappa Mu 89-; Pres Schlr 89; Delta Sigma Theta 90; Vol Apprctn Awd 89; Psychlgy Intrnshp; Schl Psychlgst.

**JACKSON, ANNA S,** Ky Christian Coll, Grayson, KY; SO; BA; Work Childrens Yth Grp First Church Of Christ Grayson; Bible; Communication.

**JACKSON JR, ARTHUR C,** Jackson St Univ, Jackson, MS; SR; BA; Soc Advncmnt Mgmt; Amer Mktg Assn; Phi Beta Lambda; Alpha Chi; Delta Mu Delta; Bus; Htl/Mtl Mgmt.

**JACKSON, AYANNA M,** Bowie St Univ, Bowie, MD; FR; BA; Dns Lst; Accntg; CPA.

**JACKSON, BABA L,** Athens St Coll, Athens, AL; SR; Sigma Tau Delta 89-90; Magna Cum Laude 89-90; BA Athens St 90; Art/Engl; Mstrs Art Hstry.**

**JACKSON, BENNETTA R,** Va Union Univ, Richmond, VA; SR; BED; Stdnt Educ Assn 87-; NAACP Sec 89-90; Alpha Kappa Mu Sec 90-; Comm Schlrs Sec 87-90; Alpha Kappa Alpha Sec 90-; Richmond Area Redevel Hsng Auth Serv Awd 90; Stdnt Ldrshp Awd; Miss NAACP 89-90; Erly Childhd Educ; Admin/Dir Daycare Ctr.

**JACKSON, BRIAN A,** Haverford Coll, Haverford, PA; FR; BS; Clg Wspr Phtgrphr 90-; Big Bro/Sis Pgm; Fresh Chem Awd; Chem/Engl; Med.

**JACKSON, BRYAN C,** Ohio Valley Coll, Parkersburg, WV; FR; BA; Bus Finance; Law.

**JACKSON, BUFFY M,** Univ Of North Fl, Jacksonville, FL; SO; BA; Pol Sci; Law.

**JACKSON, CARLA D,** Univ Of Nc At Chapel Hill, Chapel Hill, NC; FR; BA; Glee Clb 90-; NC Tchng Flw 90-; IM Bsktbl 90-; IM Vlybl/Sftbl Champs 90-; Math; Scndry Ed.

**JACKSON, CAROLYN E,** Belmont Coll, Nashville, TN; SO; BA; Accntng; CPA.

**JACKSON, CHARLES A,** Western Piedmont Comm Coll, Morganton, NC; Doc Crctnl Srgnt Burke Cty Reserve Dpty Sheriff; AAS 82; Law Enfrcmnt Instrctr.

**JACKSON, CHRISTINE,** Allen Univ, Columbia, SC; FR; BA; Track; Bus Admn.

**JACKSON, CHRISTOPHER L,** Ms St Univ, Miss State, MS; FR; BS; Gamma Beta Phi 90-; Pre-Med/Blgy; Medcn.

**JACKSON, CLAY,** Union Univ, Jackson, TN; SO; BS; Cls 93 Pres 89-91; Stdnt Fndtns; Sigma Zeta 90-; CRC Fr Chem Awd 89-90; Un Univ Fr Bio Awd 89-90; Ntl Sci Alnc Rsrch; Chem/Bio; Envrnmntl Chem.

**JACKSON, CYNTHIA L,** Mount Olive Coll, Mount Olive, NC; FR; Clge Mrsh; Pres Lst; All Amer Schlr; Claude Moore Hstry Awd; Hstry; Law.

**JACKSON, DANIEL D,** Univ Of Sc At Columbia, Columbia, SC; SR; BS; Mktg Schlrs Pgm; Delta Sigma Pi VP Pldg Ed 89-; Glden Key 90-; IM Sftbl/Ftbl; Bsn Mktg.

**JACKSON, DANIELLE P,** Fl A & M Univ, Tallahassee, FL; FR; All-Star Clg Bwl Tm 90-; Phi Eta Sigma 90-; Psych/Biol; Psych.

**JACKSON, DAVID W,** Radford Univ, Radford, VA; JR; BA; Eng; Prfsnl Wrtr.

**JACKSON, DEBBIE A,** Univ Of Pa, Philadelphia, PA; SR; JD; Johnson/Johnson Cultural Awareness Cmmt 89-; Chi Alpha Phi; Johnson/Johnson Achtmt Awd; Robert L Mc Donald Spcl Achievt Awd; Legal Assist Intrshp Wintrhrop Stimson Putnam & Roberts; Acctng; Law.**

**JACKSON, DEBORAH A,** Univ Of Al At Birmingham, Birmingham, AL; SR; BA; CEC Lrning Dsablties 90-; Spec Ed; Tchng.

**JACKSON, DEBRA L,** Ms St Univ, Miss State, MS; GD; DVM; Amer Vet Med Assc Sec 88-; Zoo/Anran Assc 88-; Clg Vet Medcn Open Hose Chrprsn 88-; Natl Rsrcs Natl Hon Scty 81-; Stdnt Amer Vet Medcn Assc Sympsn Cmt Chrprsn 90-; CVM Wldlf Sprt Grp Pres 88-; Pfizer Vet Schlrshp; Audubon Schlrshp; MS 87; Vet Medcn; Endngrd Spcs Rsrch.

**JACKSON, DEDRIC N,** Norfolk St Univ, Norfolk, VA; FR; MBA; NROTC 90-; Spartan Alpha Tau 90-; IM Ftbl 90; Fnc; Rl Estate.

**JACKSON, DEIRDRE D,** Birmingham Southern Coll, Birmingham, AL; FR; Triangle Clb; Blck Stdnt Un 90-; Frmn Ldrshp Dvlpmnt 90-; Alpha Lambda Delta; Phi Eta Sigma; Pol Sci; Corp Law.

**JACKSON, DIANE B,** Limestone Coll, Gaffney, SC; SO; BS; Tchr Asst 4 Yrs; Elem Tchr.

**JACKSON, DIANE D,** Alcorn St Univ, Lorman, MS; JR; BA; Indstrl Tchnlgy Clb 89-; Hnr Rl Frshmn 88-89; Eastern Star Lvng Frndshp Chptr 90-; Vol Wrk Good Shepherd Cntr Tutor; Contract Stdnt Waterways Exprmnt Stat 90-; Engrng; Cvl Engr.

**JACKSON, DONNA W,** Blue Mountain Coll, Blue Mountain, MS; SR; BS; MAE SP 90-; Mdlng Sqd 83-86; Cmmtr Clb 90-; Elem Edctn; Tchr.

**JACKSON, DOROTHY CHERYL,** Middle Tn St Univ, Murfreesboro, TN; SR; BSW; Alpha Delta Mu 90-; Hospice Albuquerque NM 85; Crisis Intrvntn Cntr Phn Cnslr; Med Lab Tech 74-86; AS 74; Scl Wrk.

**JACKSON, ERIN L,** Union Univ, Jackson, TN; JR; BSBA; Chi Omega Asst Secy 88-; Fellowship Christian Athletes 90-; Baptist Stdnt Union 88-; Hnr Stdnt Assoc 88-89; Chi Omega Asst Secy 88-; Deans Lst; Economics Finance; Banking.

**JACKSON, ERVIN C,** International Bible Coll, Florence, AL; SO; BA; Church Of Christ Tuscumbia AL Asst Mnstr 90-; Bible; Full Time Mnstry.

**JACKSON, FELICIA R,** Fl A & M Univ, Tallahassee, FL; SO; PHD; Stdnt Govt Assoc 90-; Church Benevolent Wrkr 87-; Spnsh Interpreter 88-90; Med Ctr Needy Pgm Vol Singer 89-; Sub Tchr Bible Study 87-; Pres Schlr 89; Phrmcy.

**JACKSON, G FELICIA,** Saint Pauls Coll, Lawrenceville, VA; SO; BA; Wmns Council Org Pres 90-; Soph Class Exec Chpln 90-F St Pauls Clg Gospel Chr 89-; REACH Rsng Exp Achiev Thru Cmmty Help 90-; Sftbl 90; English; Criminal Lawyer.

**JACKSON, GENA N,** Al A & M Univ, Normal, AL; JR; BS; Maketing Club; Delta Mu Delta 90-; MI State Comp Schlrshp Awd; Amer Mktg Assoc; Bus Admnstrn; Corp Law/Mgmnt.

**JACKSON, GEORGE L,** Salisbury St Univ, Salisbury, MD; SO; Bushin Kai Karate; Phi Eta Sigma; Physics/Engrng.

**JACKSON, GERRY L,** Al A & M Univ, Normal, AL; JR; Stdnt In Free Entrprze 90-; Alpha Kappa Mu 90-; Kappa Alpha Psi 90-; Deans Lst 88-; Schlrshp Rcpnt 89-; Mktg.

**JACKSON, GLENDA E,** Norfolk St Univ, Norfolk, VA; JR; BS; Stdnt Govt Assn Grvncs Dir 90-; Facity/Stdnt Grvncs Ct 90-; Natl Assn Blck Acctnt 89-; Zeta Phi Beta Corr Sec 90-; Schlrshp Zeta Phi Beta; IM Bsktbll 89-; Cpa.

**JACKSON, GLENDA F,** Wallace St Comm Coll At Selma, Selma, AL; FR; BA; Spcl Educ; Spch Hrg Imprd.

**JACKSON, HEATHER M,** Kent St Univ Kent Cmps, Kent, OH; JR; BA; Busf Human Rsrc Mgmt.

**JACKSON, HOLLY L,** Fl International Univ, Miami, FL; GD; AA Broward Comm Clg 89; BS 90; Hspltlty Mgt; Htl/Rstrnt/Trvl Ind.

**JACKSON, JABARI A,** Morehouse Coll, Atlanta, GA; FR; Hnrs Prog Clb; Cmps All Str Chllnge Clb Treas 90-; Hnrs Prog; Inrds Intrn Chcgo 90-; Bus; Acctng; Bnkng.

**JACKSON, JACINTA B,** Comm Coll Algny Co Algny Cmps, Pittsburgh, PA; AS; Nrsng/BA.

**JACKSON, JACQUELINE A,** Univ Of Miami, Coral Gables, FL; SR; BA; Org Jamaican Unty Pr 89-; Carbbn Stdnts Assn Exec Offcr 87-89; Cncl Pres 89-90; Maranatha Yth Chr 87-; Maranatha 7 Day Advntst Chrch 87-; IM Soccr 87-90; Econ; Enterprnr.

**JACKSON, JAYSON M,** Va St Univ, Petersburg, VA; JR; BA; Perfrms Pres 88-; Student Govt VP; Pan Hellenic Council VP; Deans List; Kappa Alpha Psi Vice Polemarch; Congsl Intern D Major Owens; Sociology; Law.

**JACKSON, JERRY L,** Va St Univ, Petersburg, VA; SO; BA; IM Ftbl 90-; Acctng.

**JACKSON, JESSI J,** Oh Univ, Athens, OH; FR; BFA; Art Leag 90-; IM Spts 90-; Grphc Dsgn.

**JACKSON, JOHN D,** Coppin St Coll, Baltimore, MD; SR; BS; Crim Just Clb 89-; Ofcrs Clb 89-; AA Cmnty Clg 89; Crim Just.

**JACKSON, JULIA O,** Columbia Union Coll, Takoma Park, MD; SR; BS; Botsmota 86-87; Assoc Cmptr Pgmr 85; Bsn Admin; Cmptr Pgmr.

**JACKSON, JUSTIN W,** Memphis St Univ, Memphis, TN; SR; BS; IEE 88-; Tau Beta Pi Sec 89-; Phi Kappa Phi 90-; Gamma Beta Phi 88-; Gldn Key 89-; Memphis Jnt Eng Cncl; Gtrd Eng Stdnt 1st Pl Awd; Elect Eng; Eng.

**JACKSON, KAREN E,** Murray St Univ, Murray, KY; FR; BA; Frgn Lang Clb Spkr 90-; Crtcl Thnkg Forum Treas; Lab Asst Rsrch; Indus Psychlgst.

**JACKSON, KAREN ELLEN,** Nova Univ, Ft Lauderdale, FL; GD; MBA; DECA BCC 90-; Cactus Comm Action Cncl; Deans Ldrshp Conf 89; BA Tulane Univ 90; Bus; Corp Exec.

**JACKSON, KAREN P,** Univ Of Sc At Coastal Carolina, Conway, SC; JR; ASSC; Nrsng Dgree Sci.

**JACKSON, KARRIE A,** Wilmington Coll, Wilmington, OH; SO; BA; Hnr Schlrshp; Frnch; Intrntl Mrktng.

**JACKSON, KELLY A,** Northeast Ms Cc, Booneville, MS; FR; BA; Phi Theta Kappa; English Ed; Teaching.

**JACKSON, KELLY G,** Middle Tn St Univ, Murfreesboro, TN; SO; BA; US Achvmnt Acad; All-Am Schlr; Math/Comp Sci.

**JACKSON, KENDALLE,** Livingston Univ, Livingston, AL; SO; BA; SGA Repr 90-; Kappa Alpha Psi Rep 90-; Indus Tech; Indus Tech.

**JACKSON, KESHA D,** Al A & M Univ, Normal, AL; FR; BS; Frshmn Hnr Rll 90-; Acctg: CPA.

**JACKSON, KEVIN F,** Johnson C Smith Univ, Charlotte, NC; SO; BS; NAACP 89-; SGA 89-; Pan African Cncl 90-; Delta Gntlmn 89-; Inroads 90-; Wegmans Schlrshp 89-; Omega Psi Phi Schlrshp 89; Bsktbl Tm 89-; Bus Admnstrtn/Psychlgy; MBA.

**JACKSON, KIMBERLY A,** Ms St Univ, Miss State, MS; SR; BS; Kappa Delta Pi 90-; Gamma Beta Phi 90-; Phi Kappa Phi 90-; MAE NEA 90-; MACUS SACUS 90-; AA SW MS Comm Clg 89; Elem Educ; Tchr.

**JACKSON, KIMBERLY E,** Vance Granville Comm Coll, Henderson, NC; AAS; Henderson Jr Womans Club 2nd V P 89-; Corres Sec; Phi Theta Kappa; N C Assn Edctnl Office Personnel; Sec; Diploma Vance-Granville Comm Coll 88; Bus Admn.

**JACKSON, KIMBERLY R,** Dyersburg St Comm Coll, Dyersburg, TN; FR; BS; Ed; Tchng.

**JACKSON, LA SONYA A,** Meridian Comm Coll, Meridian, MS; FR; BS; Phi Theta Kappa 90-; Ambssdrs 90-; Med Lab Tech.

**JACKSON, LA TANDRA C,** Va St Univ, Petersburg, VA; FR; BS; Deans Lst 90-; Offcr Trng Yng Adlt Chr; Clrk Typst; Bus Info Systms; Bus Frm.

**JACKSON, LARRY W,** Watterson Coll, Louisville, KY; JR; Pres Lst.

**JACKSON, LAURA L,** Univ Of Tn At Martin, Martin, TN; GD; Mrchng Band Majrt Cap 87-; Zeta Tau Alpha 87-88; Band Schlrshp 87-; Chrldng Schlrshp 87-88; BS 90; Comm; Schl Tchr.

**JACKSON, LEAH E,** Univ Of Tn At Martin, Martin, TN; JR; BS; Obion Co Ltrcy Prog Tutr; Degr W Tn Bus Coll 87; Psychlgy; Cnslng.

**JACKSON, LESLIE V,** Fl International Univ, Miami, FL; SR; BA; Beta Gamma Sigma; Phi Kappa Phi; Cert Rcgntn Dept Dcsn Sci/Info Sys; South FL Hosp Info Mgt/Sys Soc 90-; Natl Assn Sgstn Sys 90-; Mgt Eng Cedars Med Ctr; Mgt Info Sys.

**JACKSON, LINDA J,** Univ Of West Fl, Pensacola, FL; GD; BA; Alpha Sigma Lambda 90-; Erly Chldhd/Elem Educ; Tchr.

**JACKSON, LORETTA L,** Harford Comm Coll, Bel Air, MD; FR; Nrsng; LPN.

**JACKSON, MALIKKA N,** Clark Atlanta Univ, Atlanta, GA; SO; BA; Acctng; CPA.

**JACKSON, MAMIE E,** Central St Univ, Wilberforce, OH; JR; Wright Patterson Air Force Base Gospel Choir; U S Air Force 79-84; Elem Edn; Tchr.

**JACKSON, MANOAH Z,** Talladega Coll, Talladega, AL; SR; BA; Math Clb 90-; Scty Physcs Stdnt Sec 87-; Beta Kappa Chi Sec 89-; Nal Hon Scty Chpln 87-; Wstnghse Elec Intrn Systms Anlyst 90; Eqtbl Intrn 88; Boeing Cmptr Svcs Intrn Systms Anlyst 89; Cmptr Sci; MIS.

**JACKSON, MARY ANNE C,** Seton Hall Univ, South Orange, NJ; JR; BS; Focus Fndng 90-; Rsdnt Stdnt Assn Pres 90-; Kappa Delta Pi 90-; Elem Ed/Psychlgy; Tchr.

**JACKSON, MAUDETTE M,** Univ Of Rochester, Rochester, NY; SR; BA; Phi Eta Sigma 87-; Phi Beta Kappa; Psychlgy/Wmns Studies; Clncl Psychlgst.

**JACKSON, MELANIE K,** Radford Univ, Radford, VA; JR; BS; Alpha Sigma Alpha; Erly Mddl Edctn; Tchng Mstrs Elem Cnslng.

**JACKSON, MERRILY J,** Univ Of Miami, Coral Gables, FL; SR; BM; Mss Univ Of Mmi 90; Dlgte To FL Stwde Cnfrnce Fr Vlntrsm 90; Grp Ldr Olympcs; Alpha Lambda Delta 89; Phi Eta Sigma 89; Delta Omicron Scl Chrmn 90; Alpha Phi Snglr; Invol ROTARACT 90; Otstndng Yng Wmn Of Amer; Sprtsfst Ftbl Sftbl; Msc Eng Tech; Msc Rcrdng.

**JACKSON, MICHAEL A,** Pa St Univ Main Cmps, University Pk, PA; FR; BS; Intrvrsty Chrstn Flwshp 90-; Outng Clb 90-; Allnc Chrstn Flwshp 90-; Phi Eta Sigma; Physics/Math; Rsrch Mysicst.

**JACKSON, MICHAEL A,** Tri County Tech Coll, Pendleton, SC; FR; BA; Bus Ldrs Tmrrw 90-; Mnrty Stdnt Assoc 90-; Chr VP 90-; Acctg.

**JACKSON, MICHAEL E,** Atlanta Christian Coll, East Point, GA; FR; Bible; Christian Ministry.

**JACKSON, MONICA C,** Fl A & M Univ, Tallahassee, FL; JR; BA; Phi Theta Kappa 89-90; Jr Coll; AA 90; Elem Ed; Tch.

**JACKSON, MONICA I,** Univ Of Ga, Athens, GA; GD; MSW; Band 86; Soc Wk Clb 88-90; Natl Assn Soc Wkrs 88-; Phi Theta Kappa 87; Gldn Ky 89-90; Gamma Sigma Sigma 89-90; UGA Marr Fmly Thrpy Cert Pgrm 90-; Hnrs Day Part 87-90; Dns Lst 87-90; Otstndng Bhvrl Sci Stdnt 88; AA 88; BSW 90; Clin Soc Wk; Fmly Thrpy/Sub Abuse Trtmnt.

**JACKSON, MONICA L,** Howard Univ, Washington, DC; GD; PHD; Orgnztn Grad Soclgsts Pres 89-; Pan/African Rsrch Cntr; Assoc Scl Behvrl Scints; Natl Mrt Schlr Scty; Intrnshp Natl Urban League 87; Minority Fllwshp 85-87; Afrcn Sis Sldrty Ntwrk 90-; Rsrch Assc; Natl Urbn Lg Rsrch Dept; MA Uv OK 87; BA; Soclgy/Rsrch Methdlgy/Stats; Tchng.

**JACKSON, NICOLE,** Davis & Elkins Coll, Elkins, WV; FR; BA; Hnrs Asc 90-; Schl Nwspr 90-; Jennings Randolph Ldrs Pgm 90-; Hnrs Pgm/Asc 90-; Jrnlsm/Engl; Jrnlst.

**JACKSON, NICOLE A,** Hampton Univ, Hampton, VA; SO; BA; SVEA 90-; Alumni Big Sis Prog 89-; Tutor; IM Bsktbl Capt 90-; Engl/Elec Educ; Teach.

**JACKSON, NITIKA B,** Morris Brown Coll, Atlanta, GA; SO; Commutr Stdnts Pgms 90-; Honor 89-90; Erly Chldhd Educ; Tchg.

**JACKSON, NORMA L,** Alcorn St Univ, Lorman, MS; FR; BA; Hnrs Prog; Cmptr Sci; Tech.

**JACKSON, NOVENE M,** Miles Coll, Birmingham, AL; SO; BA; Miles Hmnts Clb Chpln; Acad Achvmnt Cert; Deans List; AAS Lawson State Comm Clg 90; Cmnctns; Brdcst Jrnlsm; Jrnlsm.

**JACKSON, OLIVER R,** Abraham Baldwin Agri Coll, Tifton, GA; JR; BA; Tennis; Phi Theta Kappa; Clncl Psychlgy.

**JACKSON, PAMELA D,** Clark Atlanta Univ, Atlanta, GA; FR; BA; Highest Frshmn Avg; All Amer Schlr Awd; Bus; Bus Admin.

**JACKSON, PATRICIA A,** S U N Y Coll Of Tech At Alfred, Alfred, NY; FR; BA; Bsktbl/Sftbl; Lib Arts/Math/Sci; Phy Thrpy/Ed.

**JACKSON, PATRICIA J,** Eckerd Coll, St Petersburg, FL; SR; MS; Rsrch Grnt Kltnbrn Fndtn; Coll Hnrs Schlrshp; Chrty Dy Schlrshp; AA 89; Cmmnctn Phtrc.

**JACKSON, PAUL M,** Comm Coll Algny Co Algny Cmps, Pittsburgh, PA; SO; Pharmacology.

**JACKSON, R GENTRY,** Univ Of Tn At Martin, Martin, TN; SO; Inst Elctrcl Elctrncs Engnrs 89-; Ldrs Rsdnc 89-90; Hnrs Emnr 89-.

**JACKSON, RACHELLE M,** Comm Coll Algny Co Algny Cmps, Pittsburgh, PA; JR; BA; Natl Crt Rprtrs Assn 77-; Blck Alumni Assn 80-; Afrcn-Amer Schlstc Achvmnt Awd; AS 79; Rlgs Studies Bus Mgmt; Crt Rprtng/Mnstry.

**JACKSON, RANDOLPH T,** Valdosta St Coll, Valdosta, GA; FR; BS; Biol; Med.

**JACKSON, RAY L,** Al A & M Univ, Normal, AL; SO; BA; Agri; Agri Educ.

**JACKSON, RHONDA B,** Blue Mountain Coll, Blue Mountain, MS; JR; BS; Cmmtr Clb VP 90-; Phi Theta Kappa 88-90; Mdn Soc 90-; Prsdnts Lst 90-; AA Nrthest MS Cmmnty Clg Bnvl MS 90; Elem Edctn; Tchr.

**JACKSON, ROBBIN L,** Central St Univ, Wilberforce, OH; SR; BS; Mktg Clb Mbrshp Chr 88-; Chrldng Squad Co Capt 87-89; Mktg/Math; Mktg Mgr.

**JACKSON III, ROBERT A,** Howard Univ, Washington, DC; MA; Strng Island Prod Co Fndr 89-; Grad Cncl Edtr 90-; Grad Asstshp 90-; Hmn Cmmcntn Stds 90-; Blck Entrtnmt TV Intrn 90; BA Xavier Univ 87; Mass Comm; Media/Sprts/Entrtnmnt.

**JACKSON, ROBERT R,** The Kings Coll, Briarclf Mnr, NY; SO; BS; Spirtl Affrs Comm Sec 89-90; I Wtnss Tm 89; Dobbs Frry Chldrn Vlg 90; IM Ftbl 89; IM Bsktbl Co Capt 89; Liason NY St Soc CPA 89; Acctg; Bsns Admn/Chrch Agcy.

**JACKSON, ROBIN T,** Coppin St Coll, Baltimore, MD; SR; BA; Stdnt Hnrs Assoc 87-90; Chi Sigma Chi; Pi Gamma Mu 90; Alpha Kappa Mu; Ntl Cllgte Mnrty Awd 89-90; Scl Sci; Urbn Plnng.

**JACKSON, RODERICK D,** Jackson St Univ, Jackson, MS; SO; BS; Bio Club 89-; SGA 90-; Alpha Lambda Delta 90-; Deans Lst 89-; Bio; Pharm.

**JACKSON, RODNEY BERNARD,** Interdenominational Theo Ctr, Atlanta, GA; SR; MA; J W Anderson Fdtn Schlrshp 90; Asst Pastor Gospel Tabernacle 86-; BA Morehosue Clg 76; Chrstn Ed; Ministry.

**JACKSON, RONALD W,** Univ Of Ky, Lexington, KY; SR; BA; AIAS Treas 90; Book Awd For Outstndng Design 89-; Venetian Exchg Study Pgm; Arch.

**JACKSON, ROSALIND L,** Al A & M Univ, Normal, AL; FR; Tlcmmncns; TV Prdctn Movie Prdctn.

**JACKSON, ROSLYN M,** Tougaloo Coll, Tougaloo, MS; JR; BA; Political Science Clb 90; Wakadzi 90; Operation Shoestring 90; VP List 88-90; Political Science; Pblc Policy.

**JACKSON, RUSS A,** Savannah St Coll, Savannah, GA; SO; Mass Comm; Tlvsn Brdcstng.

**JACKSON, SELENA R,** Lincoln Univ, Lincoln Univ, PA; SR; BS; Bus Clb VP 89-; Frnch Clb Treas 89-; Natl Advncmnt Assoc Colored Peo 89-; Big Bro/Sis Pgm TIME 90-; Ldrshp Awd Bus/Econ Dept 90-; Deans Lst 89-; Bus Admin; Law Sch.

**JACKSON, SERRITTA G,** Ky St Univ, Frankfort, KY; FR; BA; Intr Stdnt Assc 90-; Sigma 87-; IM 90-; Fshn Mrchndsng/Spnsh; Retl Buyng/Pblc Reltns.

**JACKSON, SHANIA L,** Johnson C Smith Univ, Charlotte, NC; SR; Sprtl Chr 90; NAACP 90; Dke Hll Cncl Flr Rep 90-; Myrs Hll Cncl Sec Treas 88; Ira Aldrdge Drma Gld 88-; YMCA Big Sis Lil Sis Prog 90-; Alpha Psi Omega VP 90; Delta Sigma Theta 89-; Dke Univ Mrne Lab 90-; Sthrn Educ Fndtn Schlr 89; BS; Blgy; Hlth Fld.

**JACKSON, SHANNON E,** Univ Of Southern Ms, Hattiesburg, MS; JR; BA; SW MS Commclg Flg Corp 88; SW MS CC Dance Line 89; SW MS CC 88-89; Elem Edtn; Tchng.

**JACKSON, SHARITA Y,** Central St Univ, Wilberforce, OH; FR; Bus Prof Of Amer 88-90; Stdnt Cncl Treas 89-90; Data Proc Clss Pres 89-90; Kappa Swthrt; Perfect Attndnc 88-90; Merit/Hnr Rl Stdnt 88-90; Schlrshp 90-; Tennis Singles/Dbls Plyr 89-90; Psych; Industrial.

**JACKSON, SHARON L,** Al St Univ, Montgomery, AL; SO; Zeta Phi Beta; Acctg/Math; Accnt.

**JACKSON, SHEREE J,** Al St Univ, Montgomery, AL; JR; BA; Schl Nwspr; Stdnt Sen 90-; Univ Chr; Miss ASU Scnd Atndnt; Delta Omicron VP 90-; Cath Scl Svc/Mc Innis Adlt Ctr Vol; Ldrshp Schlrshp 90-; English/Comm; Law.

**JACKSON, SHERLYNN,** Wilmington Coll, New Castle, DE; FR; BA; RT 73; Deans Lst 90-; X-Ray Tech 73-; Amer Reg Rdgrphc Tech 71-; Natl Schl Bd Assc 87-; Marbrook Schl PTA VP 86-87; Red Clay Con Schl Bd Ed 87-; Tutor 90-; Woodcrest Cvc Assc 82-; Richardson Pk Comm Actn Pgm Fndrsr Chrprsn 84-86; Erly Chldhd/Elem Ed; Teacher.

**JACKSON, SHERRY T,** Fl A & M Univ, Tallahassee, FL; SR; BS; Epcrn Mdlng Trp Sec 87-; Hatchetts Pre-Law Clb 87-; Deans Lst; Alpha Kappa Alpha Corr Sec 87-; Pltcl Sci; MA/CRPRT Attrny.

**JACKSON, SHONNETT M,** Tougaloo Coll, Tougaloo, MS; JR; Edn Clb 90-; CWWW Asst Sec 90-; Elem Edn; Tchr.

**JACKSON, SONJA D,** Fayetteville St Univ, Fayetteville, NC; SR; BS; Psychlgy Clb Sec 87-90; Crmnl Jstce Clb 87-90; Intrnshp Fayetteville Police Dept 90; Ofc Asst Dean Edn Ofc 87-90; Ofc Asst Stdnt Govt Ofc 86; Psychlgy; Human Serv.

**JACKSON, STACI M,** Roane St Comm Coll, Harriman, TN; GD; Miss Roane State Schlrshp Pagent 90; Miss Congeniality; AAS 90.

**JACKSON, STACY R,** Okaloosa Walton Comm Coll, Niceville, FL; SO; BA; Phi Theta Kappa Sec 90-; Outstndng Mnrty Comm Coll Grad; AA; Business; Acctng.

**JACKSON, STEPHANIE L,** Birmingham Southern Coll, Birmingham, AL; SR; BS; Crisis Ctr Tele Cnslr 89-; Alpha Epsilon Delta; Beta Beta Beta; Kappa Mu Epsilon; Psi Ch Psychology; Pres Hon Schlrshp 88; Summer Schlr 87; Soc Distngshd Amer Clg Stdnts 89-; Biology/Psychology Indscplnry; Med.

**JACKSON, STEPHEN B,** Jackson St Univ, Jackson, MS; SO; BA; Chmstry Soc; Physc Soc; Mnrty Accss Rsrch/Careers; Alpha Almbda Delta; Beta Kappa Chi; Heisenberg Awd Wnnr; Dow Chem Schlr; Intrnshp Drackett Co; Chem; Med.

**JACKSON, SUSAN C,** Middle Tn St Univ, Murfreesboro, TN; SR; BS; Kappa Delta Pi 90-; Stdnt Tenn Educ Assn 89-; Marching Band 89; Data Proc Mngmnt Assn 87-89; Dns Lst 90; Elem Educ; Elem Schl Tchr.

**JACKSON, TABITHA L,** Clark Atlanta Univ, Atlanta, GA; JR; BA; Stdnt Georgia Assc Edctrs; Kappa Delta Epsilion; Band 89-90; Ed; Tchr/Cnslr.

**JACKSON, TAMARA D,** Roane St Comm Coll, Harriman, TN; FR; Psychology; Hlth Sci.

**JACKSON, TAMMY L,** Al St Univ, Montgomery, AL; SR; BS; Natl Assn Blck Acctnts 89-; Vol Income Tax Asst Prog; Natl Socty Pub Acctnts Mbr 89-; Delta Mu Delta Pres 90-; Actng; CPA.

**JACKSON, TEKESHA V,** Fl A & M Univ, Tallahassee, FL; FR; Utilis Matronae Debutante VP 88; VICA VP 88-89; Stdnt Govt 89-90; Phi Eta Sigma; Natl Hnr Socty 87; Beta Clb 88; DCT Schl/Wrk Prog 87-90; Math; Mktg/Engr.

**JACKSON III, TELLIS X,** Cheyney Univ Of Pa, Cheyney, PA; SO; BA; PLUS 90-; Deans List 90-; Var Ftbl 90-; Pol Scnc/Hist; Law.

**JACKSON, TERESA S,** Wv Northern Comm Coll, Wheeling, WV; FR; BED; Phi Theta Kappa Cmps Rep 91-; Pres Lst; Acdmc Schlrshp 90-; Science; Tchng.

**JACKSON, VALERIE B,** Va Commonwealth Univ, Richmond, VA; SO; Erly Chldhd Educ; Tchr.

**JACKSON, VERNA M,** Southern Junior Coll, Birmingham, AL; SR; SGA Pres 90-; Night Div.

**JACKSON, VICKI L,** Univ Of Cincinnati-Clrmnt Coll, Batavia, OH; BED; BA KY Chrstn Coll 71; Educ; Elem Ed.

**JACKSON, VICTORIA C,** Alcorn St Univ, Lorman, MS; JR; BA; Chrldr; Alpha Kappa Mu 90-; Acctg; CPA.**

**JACKSON III, WILLIAM M,** Savannah Coll Of Art & Design, Savannah, GA; SR; BFA; Grphc Dsgn; Advrtsng.

**JACKSON, WILLIE J,** Central St Univ, Wilberforce, OH; FR; Stdnt Govt Assoc Treas; AMORC 87-; IBM 90-; Bsn Admin/CIS/PHLSPHY; Mgmt CIS.

**JACKSON, WILLIE L,** American Baptist Coll, Nashville, TN; GD; THB; Minister Bapt Chrch Assoc Pstr 87-; Bible Stdy Tchr 88-90; BA 90; Thlgy/Psych; Cnslr/Mnstr.

**JACKSON, YOICHI N,** Alcorn St Univ, Lorman, MS; JR; BA; Phi Beta Lambda 89-; Hnrs Org 88-; Scl Sci Ed; Law.

**JACKSON, ZONDRA M,** Robert Morris Coll, Coraopolis, PA; FR; BA; Stdnt Govt; Bus; Admin Mgmt.

**JACKSON-WOODS, ZURI S,** City Univ Of Ny Med Evers Coll, Brooklyn, NY; MBA; Magna Cum Laude; Alpha Kappa Alpha; Deans Lst 86-; Teacher; BS; Elem Ed; Lawyer.

**JACOB, BETH-ANNE,** Howard Univ, Washington, DC; GD; MSW; Distinction On Sr Thesis 89; Grad Departmental Hnrs 89; BA Vassar Clge 89; Clinical Social Work.

**JACOB, JACQUELINE RENEE,** Univ Of Southern Ms, Hattiesburg, MS; SR; BS; Jr Pnhllnc P 88-89; Amer Soc Interior Dsgn S; Hon Soc 90; Delta Zeta 88-89; Untd Way 88-89; Baker Kanpp/Tubbs Houston TX; Ben Bio Grp Amer Inc Houston TX 89-; Hm Ec; Int Dsgn.

**JACOB, KATHRYN B,** Univ Of Sc At Columbia, Columbia, SC; SO; BAIS; VBS Dir; Chldrn Mnstrs; Edwards Mem ARP Chrch 87-90; Chldrns Choir Dir; PTA Exec Comm Homeroom Chrmn 87-; Dir Extnd Day Pgm 90-; Psych; Elem Educ.

**JACOB, MARTY,** Yeshiva Univ, New York, NY; SR; Englewood Vltnr Amb Corps 89-; Hebrew Tchr Jewish Yth Enctr Pgm 89-90; Yth Advsr Ntl Conf Snygge Yth 90-; BA; Bio; Med.

**JACOB, STEPHANIE M,** Univ Of Ga, Athens, GA; JR; BED; Sigma Kappa Upsilon Pres 89-90; Math Educ Stdnt Assn; Kappa Delta Pi; AS Young Harris Coll 90; Sec Math; Sec Educ.

**JACOB-RITCHIE, DOROTHY A,** Chatfield Coll, Saint Martin, OH; SO; AA; Commrcl Art/Graphc Dsgn/Illstrtn.

**JACOBS, BRUCE M,** Carnegie Mellon Univ, Pittsburgh, PA; GD; JD; Inter Frat Cncl Asst Rush 87; Untd Jwsh Fed Cmps Div Pittsburgh Co Chrmn 88; IM Sports Ftbl/Hcky/Sftbl/Bsktbl/Rcqtbl/Wrstlng 87-; Kappa Sigma VP; Am Jrsprdnc Awd; BS 90; Law.

**JACOBS, C DONALD,** S U N Y At Buffalo, Buffalo, NY; SR; BS; NFOA 87-; BSE Univ PA 84; Civil Eng.

**JACOBS, CHERYL L,** Duquesne Univ, Pittsburgh, PA; FR; Phi Eta Sigma; Deans Lst 90-; Pharmacy.

**JACOBS, CYNTHIA L,** Salisbury St Univ, Salisbury, MD; SO; BS; Phi Eta Sigma 90-; Bus/Finance; Invstmnt Bnkng.

**JACOBS, DE ANNA B,** Memphis St Univ, Memphis, TN; JR; BBA; ATM Netwrk Sttlmnt Coord 87-; Finance; Bnkng.

**JACOBS, DONNA A,** Georgian Court Coll, Lakewood, NJ; JR; BA; Psychlgy Clb Sec/Treas 89-90; Psi Chi Pres 90; Psychlgy; Advrtsng.

**JACOBS, GINA R,** Ga St Univ, Atlanta, GA; SO; Chemistry; Pharmacy.

**JACOBS JR, GRICE,** Univ Of Sc At Columbia, Columbia, SC; FR; BS; MAPP 90-; Opprtnty Schlrs Prgm; Comp Sci; Prgrmmng.

**JACOBS, JASON D,** Suny Health Sciences-Buffalo, Buffalo, NY; FR; BS; Univ Hnrs Prog; Chem; Eng.

**JACOBS, JAY D,** Univ Of Miami, Coral Gables, FL; JR; BSEE; IEEE Rec Sec 90-; Tau Beta Pi Rec Sec 90-; Eta Kappa Nu 90-; Natl Ocnc And Atmos Admin Intrn; Elec Eng; Comp Eng.

**JACOBS, JEFFREY J,** Northern Ky Univ, Highland Hts, KY; SR; Ofc Sys Tech; Comp Ctr Asst/Mgmt.

**JACOBS, JODIAH H,** Hudson Valley Comm Coll, Troy, NY; SO; Untd Brthrhd Carpenters Jrnymn 89-; Civil Engrng.

**JACOBS, KRISTALEAN R,** Univ Of Ky, Lexington, KY; SR; BARCH; Amer Inst Of Archtctre Stdnts 89-; Dns Lst Coll Of Archtctre Univ Of KY 90-; 1st Yr Dsgn Schlrshp 90; 2nd Yr Alumni Assn Schlrshp; Vrsty Tnns Tm 89; Archtctre.

**JACOBS, LAUNITA,** Tougaloo Coll, Tougaloo, MS; SO; BS; Chrldr; Cncrt Chr; Ebny Dncrs; Delta Sigma Theta Custdn; Grl Scts Lder; Ceon Acctg.**

**JACOBS, LESLIE J,** Saint Francis Coll, Loretto, PA; JR; BSN; Jr Nrsng Awd; Nrsng.

**JACOBS, MALCIA J,** Western New England Coll, Springfield, MA; FR; BA; Untd Mtlly Eql Sec; Mem Cmmnty Coll Org 90-; Mem DAACP; Elec Eng.

**JACOBS, MARY JO,** Mount Aloysius Jr Coll, Cresson, PA; SO; ASC; Stdnt Nrsng Orgnztn 89-; Nrsng; Hosp Admn.

**JACOBS, ROBERT E,** Toccoa Falls Coll, Toccoa Falls, GA; SR; BA; Music Evnglsm Tms Grp Ldr 88-; Asst Res Asst 89; Clg Choir/Cncrt Bnd Sctn Ldr 87-89; Intrnsp Elberta Chrstn/Mssnry Allnc Chrch Asst Pstr Yth/Music 89; Bsktbl Tm 87-88; Asst Intrnshp Cmps Comm Chrch Mnstr/Music 89; Intrnshp Fytvl Chrtn/Mss Alln Chrch; Bible/Theology; Pstrl Mnstry.

**JACOBS, SHANNON M,** Atlantic Comm Coll, Mays Landing, NJ; SO; BA; AA; Psychlgy.

**JACOBS, SHERRY HILLIS,** Middle Tn St Univ, Murfreesboro, TN; SR; BS; Edn; Teach Elem Edn.

**JACOBS, SHERYL L,** Germanna Comm Coll, Locust Grove, VA; FR.

**JACOBS, SILVERIA E,** Univ Of The Virgin Islands, St Thomas, VI; SR; BA; Vrsty Vllybl Tm Cptn 89-90; Stdnt Gvrnmnt Fd Comm Chrprsn 90-; Tlnt Clb 90-; Prsdnts Clb 90-; Vrsty Vlybl Tm Clb 87-; Elem Edctn Math Cncntrtn.

**JACOBS, SUSAN E,** Duquesne Univ, Pittsburgh, PA; FR; Duquesne Univ Orch 90-; Exterior Choir Perf; Chmbr Music Grp; Mu Phi Epsilon 90-; City Music Ctr Vol; Jewish Cmnty Orch; Music; College Lvl Teach Conducting.

**JACOBS, VINCENT E,** Norfolk St Univ, Norfolk, VA; SR; BA; Army ROTC Stf Sgt 86-88; By Scts Am PR Chrmn 90-; Comp Sftwr Ttrng Lab Asst 90-; Dns Lst; Hon Rl 90-; Ntl Yth Sprts Prg Cnslr 87; Eng/Lib Arts; Mgmt.

**JACOBSEN, JEANNE M,** Univ Of Md Baltimore Prof Schl, Baltimore, MD; SR; BSP; Phrmcsts Assc; Rho Chi Treas; Beta Beta Beta; Chrstn Chldrns Fnd Inc; Gradtd Wth Dstnctn; Amer Rgstry Radlgc Tech; Nclr Med Tech RT 84-; BA Bio Valparaiso Univ 83; CERT Nclr Med St Joseph Hsp Schl Nclr Med Tech 84; Hsp Phrmcy.

**JACOBSMEYER, RICHARD A,** Fayetteville St Univ, Fayetteville, NC; FR; BS; USMC 84-90; Hist; High Sch Tchr.

**JACOBSON, CHERYL F,** Cornell Univ Statutory College, Ithaca, NY; SR; Cls 91 Cncl VP 88-90; Clg Ag Lf Ambsdrs 87-; Phi Kappa Phi; Gamma Sigma Delta; Gldn Ky 90-; Psi Chi 90-; BS; Comm; Mgmt.

**JACOBSON, DARYL L,** Clarkson Univ, Potsdam, NY; SO; BS; Rcqtbl Clb 90; IM 89-; Pres Schlr 89-; Acdmc Stu Cntr Ttr 90-; Vrsty Tnns 90-; Accntng; Corp Fnnc.

**JACOBSON, JENNIFER E,** Fl St Univ, Tallahassee, FL; SR; Pre-Law Soc 90; FL Pblc Inrst Rsrch Grp 88-89; STU Govt GOTV Coord 90-; Lambda Pi Eta; BS; Cmmnctn; Law.

**JACOBSON, NEIL A,** Univ Of Rochester, Rochester, NY; JR; BS; Cmptr Sci/Appld Math; Cmptr Prgmng.

**JACOBSON, SABINE S,** Christopher Newport Coll, Newport News, VA; SR; BSIS; Alpha Chi; Info Sci.

**JACOBSON, WILLIAM J,** The Kings Coll, Briarclf Mnr, NY; JR; BA; Chrstn Srvc Org Chldrns Mnstry Co Ldr 90-; Crs Cntry/Trck 88-; Frnch; Tchr.

**JACOBUS, NATALIE J,** Oh Wesleyan Univ, Delaware, OH; JR; BA; Envrnmnt Wldlf Clb Treas 89-; Ad Hc Cmmtt Envrnmntl Cncrns Stdnt Rep 90-; Bg Pls Lttlhnrs Prgm 88-; Appls Crt Jstc 90-; Srtt Ntr Cntr Intrn Natrlst 90; Eqstrn Tm Treas 90; Grphy Envrnmntl Stds.

**JACOBY, JODY J,** Wright St Univ Lake Cmps, Celina, OH; FR; BS; Sec Educ/Soc Stds; Law.

**JACOBY, LORRAINE M,** Comm Coll Of Beaver County, Monaca, PA; GD; AAS; Tau Pi Rho; ADN Nrsg.

**JACOBY, TRACY A,** Longwood Coll, Farmville, VA; SR; Alpha Delta Mu; Ntl Scl Wrk Assoc; Intrnshp BSW DVI DAART Fairfax Co; BSW; Scl Wrk.

**JACOWAY, KAREN L,** Livingston Univ, Livingston, AL; SR; IM Sports 89-; Phi Mu/Pi Kappa Phi 89-; BS; Edn.

**JACOWAY, PAMELA S,** Univ Of Al At Birmingham, Birmingham, AL; SO; BS; Nrsng; Anesthesia.

**JACQUAYS, CONNIE L,** S U N Y Coll At Fredonia, Fredonia, NY; JR; BA; Amer Strng Tchrs Assn 89-; Music Educ Natl Conf Sec 88-; Educ Clb 90-; Schlrshp MENC Conf; Elem Educ/Music; Tchr.

**JACQUEMIN, PATRICK J,** Univ Of Miami, Coral Gables, FL; JR; BA; Alliance Fransaise Miami Dir; Soccer Clb Pres Capt 90-; Stdnt Govt Mktg Dir 89-90; Phi Theta Kappa Active Mbr 89; Hon Stdnt Assoc 90-; H K Stanford Schlrshp 90; Pres Hon Rl; Transfer Hon Prog Schlrshp; Tennis Tm 88-90; AA 90; Intl Fin/Mktg; Bus.

**JACQUES, JUDITH A,** Framingham St Coll, Framingham, MA; SR; BA; RN 64-; Admin Asst 87-; Liberal Studies.

**JACQUES, KEVIN W,** Monmouth Coll, W Long Branch, NJ; FR; Phi Eta Sigma; Deans Lst 90-; Bus; Acctnt.

**JACQUES, ROBERT M,** Western New England Coll, Springfield, MA; SR; BA; Pol Sci Clb; Lambda Delta; State Rep Paul Caron Stf Asst 87-; Govt.

**JACQUOT, AMY J,** Univ Of Bridgeport, Bridgeport, CT; SO, Bsc Stds Tutoring 90-; Phi Kappa Phi; Bpt Prsdntl Schlrshp; 3tstndng Englsh Achvmnt Awd; MBA; Englsh Lit; Edctn Wrtng.

**JADAV, ARPANA M,** Fl St Univ, Tallahassee, FL; SR; BA; Gldn Key 89-; Pre-Law Soc 88-90; Buddy Mckay Snt/Chiles Mckay Govt Org Head 88-90; Lib Stds Hnr Pgm Chr 88-; Pol Sci/Hstry; Law Schl.

**JADAVJI, SHAFIQ,** S U N Y At Buffalo, Buffalo, NY; JR; BA; Amer Mktg Assn VP Fin; Undrgrad Mngmnt Assn Sec; Fin Mngmnt Assn; Phi Theta Kappa; Delta Sigma Pi; Finlay Corp Schlrshp U B Hnrs Schlrshp; IM Spts Ftbl Sqsh; AS Monroe Comm Coll 90; Mngmnt; Fin Analyst.

**JAFARACE, LAURA E,** West Liberty St Coll, West Liberty, WV; GD; BA; Deans Lst WVNCC 85-87; Deans Lst 89; Ordr Eastern Star 81; AAS W Va Northern Comm Coll 87; Elem Educ; Sci.**

**JAFARJIAN, ALBERT,** S U N Y Coll At Fredonia, Fredonia, NY; JR; BA; Educ Clb 90-; Acctg Soc 89-90; Uppr Cls Bddy Prog 90 -; Omicron Delta Epsilon 90-; Phi Alpha Theta; Pheta Alpha Theta; Lit Vol Amer; Vol HS Tutor 90-; Bsktbl Lg 88-90; Hist/Sec Educ; Soc Studies Teacher.

**JAFFAR, MUHAMMED AMIN,** Fl International Univ, Miami, FL; JR; BS; FIU Hon Pre Med Scty 91-; Alpha Epsln Dlt 91-; Phi Kappa Phi 90-; AA Miami Dade Comm Clg 89; Bio; Medcn.

**JAFFE, JANA M,** Hudson Valley Comm Coll, Troy, NY; CAC; Addctd Wmn Recvry Conf; Psyco/Drama; Mgr Lavlers Stk/Seafd; BS Oswago State 85; Alchl/Sbstnc Abuse Cnslr.

**JAFFREY, LYNETTE M,** Liberty Univ, Lynchburg, VA; SR; BS; Assn Of Accts Treas 89-; Mrchng Bnd 88-; Cncrt Bnd 90; Alpha Lambda Delta 88-; Hrtge Bptst Chrch Chr 89-; Acctng; CPA.

**JAFFRI, ALI ABID,** S U N Y At Buffalo, Buffalo, NY; SR; Pakistani Stdnts Assoc 88-; Stdnt Assoc 88-; IEEE 89-; Mennen Med Instr Intern; Lab Tutor 89-; AA Engr Sci; Elctrcl/Cmptr Engr.

**JAFRI, AMIR A,** Allegheny Coll, Meadville, PA; SO; BS; Intl Clb 89-; Assn Cmptng Mach Sec 90-; Lambda Sigma 90-; Alden Schlr 89-90; Rugby 89; Cmptr Sci/Math; Sys Prgmng.

**JAGAN, JUDY N,** Barry Univ, Miami, FL; SR; BA; Jamaican Assn Pres 89- Treas 88-89; Acdmc Deans Lst 90; Mcromtc Simultn CEO 89; Mgmt Info Syst; MBA.

**JAGDEOSINGH, SITA,** Nova Univ, Ft Lauderdale, FL; GD; MBA; Propeller Clb U Of M 87; Chmbr Cmmrc 87; PIA Big I Spcl Insrnc Undrwrtr; BBA Unvr Miami 80-87; Finance; Intrntnl Trade.

**JAGER, BRENDA K,** Salisbury St Univ, Salisbury, MD; SO; Acctg; CPA/CNTRLLR.

**JAGGERS, BARBARA A,** Oh Univ-Southern Cmps, Ironton, OH; FR; BA; Chrch Pnst; SS Tchr; Jrnlsm; Wrtr/Tchr.

**JAGGERS, NEVIN C,** Marshall University, Huntington, WV; SR; BBA; Alpha Sigma Phi 87-; Econ; Mgmnt.

**JAHN, LISA M,** Brescia Coll, Owensboro, KY; JR; BS; SGA Tres 90-; Soph Pres 89-90; Jr Cls VP 90-; Lttl Thtr Trp; Alpha Chi Sec 90-; Hnrs Prog 88-; Phi Beta Lambda Pres 90-; Wall St Jrnl Achvmnt Awrd 88-; Dean Lst 88-; Chrldr 90-; 5th Pl Ecnmcs; 1st Pl Mrktng; Bus Admn/Mrktng; Mrktng/Mngmnt.

**JAHN, STEPHANIE L,** Towson St Univ, Baltimore, MD; FR; BFA; Performing Arts Lrngn Cntr Tap-Jazz Instrc 90-; Gerstung Intsprt Dance Instr; Dance Perfor/Ed; Dance Instrc.

**JAIN, ANNAT,** Savannah Coll Of Art & Design, Savannah, GA; BARCH; Intnl Stdnts Org Pres 90-; Am Inst Archt Stdnts 90-; Water Ski Tm 90-; Fndtn Wall/Ceiling Indstry Schlrshp 90; M R Nellings-Whelan Schlrshp 88-; Architct.

**JAIN, KALPANA,** Univ Of Al At Birmingham, Birmingham, AL; JR; Alpha Lambda Delta; Phi Sigma Phi; Gldn Ky; R Mcdonald Hse; Intrnshp Vdrblt Univ Nshvl TN 89; Stdnt Asstshp Phrmclgy UAB; Bio; Med.

**JAIN, MANISH VIMAL,** Univ Of Southern Ms, Hattiesburg, MS; SR; MBA; YMCA 88-; Intl Rel Clb 90-; Cricket Univ State 87-90; BSC Univ Of Pune 87-90.

**JAINCHILL, SUSAN Y,** Cornell Univ Statutory College, Ithaca, NY; JR; BS; Stdnt Chptr Of The Amercn Soc Of Landscp Arch 89-; Ho-Nun-De-Kah; Alpha Chi Omega Hsng Chr 88-90; Landscp Arch; Urban Plnng.

**JAIYESINMI, GANIAT M,** Clark Atlanta Univ, Atlanta, GA; SR; BS; Pre-Profl Hlth Careers Pgm 86-90; Chem Clb 86-; Intl Stdnts Org 88-90; Hon Pgm Chrmn Rsrch/Publcty 86-88; Am Red Crs 84-85; Spcl Schlrshp Clark Coll 86; Intrnshp GA Inst Tech Envrnmntl Eng Dept 90; Bio; Med.

**JAIYESINMI, MUFULIAT KEMI,** Clark Atlanta Univ, Atlanta, GA; SR; BS; Orntn Guide Corp 88-90; Pre-Profl Hlth Soc 87-; Vol Job Meharry Hosp 90; Cert Excell Math; Cert Cmpltn Smr Pgm 90; Bio; Obstetrician/Gynecologist.

**JAKI, TIMOTHY C,** Saint Vincents Coll & Seminary, Latrobe, PA; FR; BA; Soccer 90-; Math; Engrng.

**JAKLITSCH, JENNIE A,** Coll Of New Rochelle, New Rochelle, NY; JR; BS; Tri Beta 88-90; Sci/Math Clb 90-; Sci/Math Nwsltr 89-; Biology Bd 90-; Cmtr Cncl 88-90; Terence Cardinal Cooke Mem Schlrshp 88; Hnrs Stdnt 88-90; Westchster Chem Socty Awd Outstdng Schlstc Pwrf 1st Yr Chmstry 89; Biology; Grad Schl.

**JAKUBOWSKI, JENNIFER L,** S U N Y Coll Of Tech At Alfred, Alfred, NY; FR; MBA; Psychology; Clinical Physcologist.

**JAKUBOWSKI, TONIA S,** Columbus Coll Of Art & Design, Columbus, OH; JR; BFA; BFA Columbus Clg Art/Dsgn 90-; Advrsng Dsgn; Advrtsng/Cmrcl Artist.**

**JALALI, HAMID J,** Old Dominion Univ, Norfolk, VA; SO; BSCPE; Comp Eng.

**JALALI-BIDGOLI, HASSAN,** Univ Of Miami, Coral Gables, FL; SR; Frnch Clb 88-89; Ski Clb Tchr 87-89; Deans Lst 87-89; Stu Serv 87-88; Ski; BS; Const Mgt.

**JALOWITZ-THOM, EDWINA,** Cumberland County Coll, Vineland, NJ; SO; AA BA; Intrnshp Cmbrlnd Cnty Gdnc Cntr 90-; Symphny Chrs 87-; Sprt Grp Fclttr 87-; Prnts W/O Prtnrs 87-; Sngl Prnts Scty 87-; Crtfdpblc Mngrs 86-; Social Wrk/Hstry-Sclgy.

**JAMERSON, BENJAMIN S,** East Tn St Univ, Johnson City, TN; FR; BS; Alpha Lambda Delta 90; Electronics Eng Tech; Eng.

**JAMERSON, ROBIN R,** Longwood Coll, Farmville, VA; FR; Alpha Lambda Delta 90-; Hstry; Law.

**JAMES, AARON S,** Univ Of Charleston, Charleston, WV; FR; BA; Scrty Ofcr 88-; Cert Dret Sch 87; Gen; Law.

**JAMES, AINSWORTH,** City Univ Of Ny John Jay Coll, New York, NY; SR; BA; Caribbn Clb 88-; Lex Revw/Coll Nwspapr Stff Writr 89-; Triathln Clb Mem 90; Dns Lst 88-; Sccr Plyr 88-; Dept Fire Sfty Dir 89-; Fire Sfty Dir 90; Govt/Pblc Admin; Law/Poli.**

**JAMES, ALEXANDRA M,** Columbus Coll Of Art & Design, Columbus, OH; SO; BFA; Clr Whls Art Instrctr; Fine Arts; Art Thrpy.

**JAMES, BARBARA L,** Mount Olive Coll, Mount Olive, NC; SR; BS; Psi Chi; Protestant Wmn Chapel V P 83-84; Sub Tchr; AS 83; Psych; Cnslg.

**JAMES, BARBIE R,** Thomas Nelson Comm Coll, Hampton, VA; SO; BA/AS; Bapt Stdnt Union 90-; Rhodes-Johnson Assn Pres 89; Exch Stdnt Schlrshp Argentina 89; Spanish; Educ.

**JAMES, BERNADETTE R,** Columbia Union Coll, Takoma Park, MD; FR; BA; Fresh Cls Offcr Sgt Arms 90-; Gspl Choir Sgt/Arms 90-; Theta Alpha Beta 90-; Bsktbl 90-; Engl Ed; Tch.

**JAMES, BERNICE M,** Nyack Coll, Nyack, NY; SR; BMUS; Music Edtrs Natl Confr Pres 90-; ACDA Amer Choral Dir Assoc 87-; NYACK Clg Chorale; Ladies Glee Club 87-89; Food Serv Committe; Dept Assist Music Dept 90; Certif Merit 89-91; Music Ed; Music Ed/Singer.

**JAMES, CANDYCE L,** Paine Coll, Augusta, GA; SO; BS; Deans Lst 90-; Prgrm Asst Gnrl Edctn Srvcs Upswrd Bnd; Meadowbrook Elem PTA 90-; Biology; Diagnostic Mdcl Sngrphr.

**JAMES, CHANTICE D,** Va St Univ, Petersburg, VA; SO; BA; Bsns Admnstrtn Clb Chrprsn Actvts 90; English; Entrprnr.

**JAMES, CHARLENE CASSTEVENS,** Union Univ School Of Nursing, Memphis, TN; SR; BSN; Deans Lst; Natl Cllgt Nsg Awd; AORN; Baptist Mem Hosp East OR Stf Nrs 88-; ADN Wake Tech Comm Coll 74; PNE Wake Tech Comm Coll 72; Nursing.

**JAMES, CRYSTAL M,** Casco Bay Coll, Portland, ME; SR; AS; Sr Mntr Prog; AS; CERT; Acctg.

**JAMES, CYNTHIA A,** Cornell Univ Statutory College, Ithaca, NY; FR; BS; Mrchng Band 90-; Sage Chapel Choir; Stdnt Advsry Cmtee; Biology; Rsrch/Med.

**JAMES, CYNTHIA V,** Univ Of Tn At Martin, Martin, TN; SR; BA; Phi Theta Kappa 88-90; AS Dyersburg State Comm Clg 90; Mrktng; Sls.

**JAMES, DANA MARIE,** Va Commonwealth Univ, Richmond, VA; SR; BA; Gldn Key 90-; Deans Lt 90-; Natl Arts Scty 88-89; Fn Arts Shw 88; Jrd Andrsn Gllry Sh; Fin Arts.

**JAMES, DAVID BERLIN,** Middle Ga Coll, Cochran, GA; FR; BA; Engr.

**JAMES, DEBORAH RENEE,** King Coll, Bristol, TN; JR; BA; Stdnts Fr Enterprs 90-; Phi Theta Kappa 88-90; Otstdng Achvmnt Cntmpry Physcs 89-90; Econ/Busn.

**JAMES, DEIDRA M,** Commonwealth Coll, Virginia Beach, VA; SO; AAS; U S Navy 85-90; Bus; Acctg.

**JAMES, EDWARD J,** City Univ Of Ny Med Evers Coll, Brooklyn, NY; JR; BS; Caribbean Assn; AS 90; Bus Admin; MBA.

**JAMES, ELIZABETH A,** Christopher Newport Coll, Newport News, VA; JR; BS; Crcl K 88-89; Psychlgy.

**JAMES, ERIC M,** Univ Of Sc At Columbia, Columbia, SC; JR; BA; Graphic Dsgn; Corp/Freelance/Comm Dsgn.

**JAMES, FRANKIE E,** Central St Univ, Wilberforce, OH; SR; BSPSY; Psi Chi 90-; Air Force Sgts Assoc 86-; LSW OH Cnslr/Socl Wrk Brd 89-; Assoc Mental Hlth Tech 85; Assoc Early Childhd Educ 83; Psych.

**JAMES JR, FREDERICK E,** Old Dominion Univ, Norfolk, VA; SR; BS; Intrn 88; Intrn Va Dept Trnsprtatn 89-; Bkbl Golf 87-; Cvl Engr.

**JAMES, GEZELL A,** Norfolk St Univ, Norfolk, VA; SO; BA; Dozoretz Natl Inst 89-; Treas 90-; Spartan Alpha Tau 90-; Dozoretz Natl Inst Schlrshp 89-; Intern Natl Inst Of Hlth 90-; IM Aerobic Dancing 91; Math; Statistician/Actuary.

**JAMES, JAMIE G,** Tn St Univ, Nashville, TN; SR; BS; Amrcn Soc Cvl Engnrs 89-; Physics Clb 90-; Gldn Key 90-; Otstndng Cvl Engnrng Stdnt 90-; US Navy Oprtns Spclst Frst Cls 81-88; Cvl Engnrng; Engnrng.

**JAMES, JEANNINE M,** Temple Univ, Philadelphia, PA; SR; BS; IM Vlybl 89-90; Amer Phrmctcl Assn 88-; PA Phrmctcl Assn 88-; Rho Chi; Lambda Kappa Sigma Soc Chrmn 88-; Phrmcy.

**JAMES, JENNIFER J,** Fl International Univ, Miami, FL; JR; BS; AA Lake City Comm Clg 90; Nrsng; RN.

**JAMES, JOYCELYN T,** Columbia Union Coll, Takoma Park, MD; SO; BS; Acting Frnds Drama Clb 90-; Gspl Choir Treas 90-; Acctg.

**JAMES, KEVIN L,** Middle Tn St Univ, Murfreesboro, TN; SR; BBA; INROADS Nashvl; Beta Alpha Psi; Gamma Beta Phi; Alpha Kappa Psi Treas 89; Brandon Vw Brthrhd Assoc VP; Brandon Vw Yng Adlt/Yth Mnstries Pres 90-; Intrnshp Price Waterhse 87-90; Acctg; Acrdtr.

**JAMES, KIMBERLY D,** Al St Univ, Montgomery, AL; JR; BA; Art; Ed.

**JAMES, KWAME J,** Ms St Univ, Miss State, MS; SR; BA; African Stdnts Assc 90-; Econ Clb Pblcty Sec 90-; Hall Of Fame 90; Pres Schlr 90-; Outstndng Work In Econ 90-; Soccer 86-88; Economics; Mba.

**JAMES, LIV A,** Fl St Univ, Tallahassee, FL; SR; BS; Model UN 90-; Spanish Clb 86-88; Mjr Hnrs; WWU Crew 86-87; Intl Affairs/Spnsh; Clg Prfsr.

**JAMES, LORI A,** Northern Ky Univ, Highland Hts, KY; FR; BA; Chorus 89-90; Shared Life 89-90; Hnrs Lst 90-; Amer Private Enterprise 88-89; Hnr Roll/Attndnc/Various Cls Awds 87-90; Psychlgy.

**JAMES, MARLA J,** Wv Univ At Parkersburg, Parkersburg, WV; JR; Math; Post-Sec Educ.

**JAMES, MARY-MARGARET,** Mercer Univ Schl Of Pharm, Atlanta, GA; GD; PHD; Amer Soc Hosp Phrmcsts 88-; Acadmy Stdnts Phrmcy 88-; GA Soc Hosp Phrmcsts 88-; Rho Chi; MA Chmbrs Awrd 89; Mer Schlrshp 89-; BA Biolgy Univ Rchmnd 88; Phrmcy; Med.

**JAMES, MELANIE D,** Middle Tn St Univ, Murfreesboro, TN; SO; NAACP 89-90; Stdnt Prg Spec Evnts 90-; Flwshp Chrstn Ath 89-; BS; Bio; Med Tech.

**JAMES, ORLANDO M,** Richard Bland Coll, Petersburg, VA; FR; MBA; SGA; Fndtn Schlr; Dns Lst 90-.

**JAMES, PAUL M,** Coll Misericordia, Dallas, PA; FR; BS; Rho Tau Clb; Rdgrphy.

**JAMES, RHONDA A,** Univ Of Tn At Martin, Martin, TN; SO; Phi Eta Sigma; Honors Smnr Prgrm 89-; Ldr Rsdnc 89-90; Elem Edctn; Tchr.

**JAMES, ROBERT VINCENT,** S U N Y Coll Of Tech At Delhi, Delhi, NY; FR; Physic Show.

**JAMES, SHERRI J,** Va Commonwealth Univ, Richmond, VA; SR; BA; Clnl Hts Jaycees Cmnty Dev Dir 90-; Spcl Olympcs 89-90; Mrch Of Dms 87-; AS Richard Bland Clg 88; Psychlgy; Yth Srvcs.

**JAMES, SUSAN E,** Kent St Univ Kent Cmps, Kent, OH; JR; BA; Finance Assn 90-; Gldn Ky 90-; Alpha Lambda Delta 89-; Beta Gamma Sigma 90-; Natl Coll Bus Merit Awd 90-; IM Sftbl 89-90; Bus; Finance.

**JAMES, SUSAN R,** Furman Univ, Greenville, SC; FR; Flwshp Of Chrstn Athlts 90-; Sftbl 90-; Bio; Vet Med.

**JAMES, TAMMY L,** Univ Of Southern Ms, Hattiesburg, MS; JR; BS; Hnrs Coll; Psych; Physcl Thrpy.

**JAMES, TARA Y,** Alcorn St Univ, Lorman, MS; JR; Pol Sci 88-; Hnr Stdnts Org 89-F Delta Sigma Theta 90-; Congressman Mike Espys Cswrkr Intrn 90; Pol Sci Pre Law; Prac Law.

**JAMES, TERESA L,** Univ Of Sc At Columbia, Columbia, SC; SR; BSN; Baptist Stdnt Union 87-89; Singers 87-; Natl Stdnt Nurses Assn 90-; Adv Cncl 90-; Nurses Aid Cert 87; Valedictorian; NA Donaldson Career Ctr 87; Nursing.**

**JAMES, TOI A H,** Oh Wesleyan Univ, Delaware, OH; FR; Sisters United; Dormatory Governing Brd 90-; Womens Task Force 90-; Mary Mc Leod Bethune Deans Lst 90-.

**JAMES, TRACIE L,** Fl A & M Univ, Tallahassee, FL; SR; BA; Computer Info Systems Club 88-; Gulf Life Ins Co Intern 88-; Computer Scientist Trainee Navy Base; Computer Information Systems.

**JAMES, VALLIERY D,** Alcorn St Univ, Lorman, MS; JR; BA; Engl Clb; Alpha Kappa Mu; Alpha Mu Gamma; Hon Roll Cert; Deans Lst; Engl/Lit; Publ Rel.

**JAMES, VANDERIUS L,** Morehouse Coll, Atlanta, GA; FR; MBA; Glee Clb 90-; Jr Quartet Bass 90-; Prfsnl Ed Consltnt Southwestern Co; Vcl Perf Msc/Bsn Mgmt; Arts Mgmt.

**JAMES, WALTER J,** Tri County Tech Coll, Pendleton, SC; SR.

**JAMES, WON-YAU,** City Univ Of Ny City Coll, New York, NY; SR; ME; Cty Clg Alumni Assoc; Physcs Chem Lrng Ctr Phycs Tutor 86-87; Ortn Prog Grp Ldr 87; Cty Hons Prog 85-90; Tau Beta Pi 87-; Eta Kappa Nu 87-; Gldn Ky 87-; Summa Cum Laude; Dns Lst 86-; Pope Evans Robbins Schlrshp 88-89; Elec Engr/Lasers.**

**JAMES-SINGLETON, GWENDOLYN L,** Fl A & M Univ, Tallahassee, FL; SO; BA; Psychlgy/Biol; Psychtry/Med.

**JAMIESON, MATTHEW E,** S U N Y Coll Of Tech At Canton, Canton, NY; SR; AAS; Cthlc Yth Org 80-81; Futr Bus Ldrs Amer 81-82; Stdnt Cncl Cls Rep 79-80; Phi Theta Kappa 89-; Bsktbl 79; Trck 82; Elec Eng Tech.

**JAMIESON, MICHELLE L,** Valdosta St Coll, Valdosta, GA; SO; ECE; Educ; Tch Kdg.

**JAMIL, KHAN N,** Univ Of Akron, Akron, OH; SR; BS; Yth Cnslr 88-; Edtr Yth Nwsltr 88-; Deans List; Acctg; Fincl Analyst.

**JAMILOWSKI, LINDA A,** Western New England Coll, Springfield, MA; SR; BA; Summa Cum Laude 79; Acct; Admn Lf Ins Pensn Mgmt; AES Thomas Coll Waterville 79; Bus Admn; Bus.

**JAMISON, ALAN W,** Univ Of Cin R Walters Coll, Blue Ash, OH; GD; CERT; AA 68; BS 71; MS 75; Acctg; CPA.

**JAMISON, CHRISTINE E,** Hampton Univ, Hampton, VA; FR; BA; DE Pre-Alumni Clb 90-; Upward Bnd Tutrl Pgm 90-; Cls Cncl Com 90-; Inroads Intrnshp 90-; Spch Cmnctns; Hmn Rsrcs Mgmt.

**JAMISON, DANIEL M,** Voorhees Coll, Denmark, SC; SR; Bsns Clb 90; Deans Lst 88-; Bank Bsns Ofc Intrn 90-; Bsns Admnstrtn; Bnkng Finance.

**JAMISON, FRANCES V,** Middle Tn St Univ, Murfreesboro, TN; JR; Musc Mstrs Msc Str 88-; Pltcl Sci; Law.

**JAMMES, MIRIAM D,** Univ Of North Fl, Jacksonville, FL; JR; BA; Gldn Key; Phi Theta Kappa Co Chrmn Fndrsg 88-89; Coop Clay Cnty Crths Pro Mntr; AA 88-90; Psych.

**JAMROG, DIANE C,** Smith Coll, Northampton, MA; SO; BA; Skiing/Sailing/Fshng/Photog 89-; First Grp Hnrs 89-; Deans Lst 89-; Mass State Schlr 89-90; Smith Acdmy Schlr 89-; Tennis 90-; Math/Photo; Architect/Artist.

**JANAVA, MINDY B,** George Mason Univ, Fairfax, VA; FR; BS; Bus; Mgmt.

**JANCAY, JENNIFER LYNN,** Indiana Univ Of Pa, Indiana, PA; SR; PSEA 90-; PACTE; Zeta Tau Alpha 87-; Dns Lst 90-; Bed; Elem Educ; Tch.

**JANCHOSEK, DAWN M,** Univ Of Akron, Akron, OH; SR; BS; TAPPI Fresh Repr 85-86; MAPPS Assist Sec 86-87; Amer Diabetes Assn 89; Pi Sigma Epsilon 88-90; Co-Oped Jefferson Smurfit Tech 87; Rsrch Ctr 88; Mktg; Sales.

**JANCO, JULIE A,** Case Western Reserve Univ, Cleveland, OH; JR; BA; Mrchng Bnd 88-90; Case-Rsrve Assoc For Schl Sprt VP 88; Psych 89; Theater 89; Psi Chi Membrshp Chr 90; Mrtr Brd; Sigma Nu Lit Sis 88-89; Proj Step-Up Tutor 90; TGIF 90; Teen Inst Staff 88; Rsrch Assist 89; Deans Hnrs High Hnrs 89; Psych; Cnslng In Sbstnce Abse.**

**JANDECKA, DARLENE L,** Hillsborough Comm Coll, Tampa, FL; FR; BA; Phi Theta Kappa; Mktg.

**JANDELLI, BARBARA,** Ny Univ, New York, NY; JR; BA; AA 88; Psychlgy; MSW/PSYCHO Therpst.

**JANDL, FRANK N,** Va St Univ, Petersburg, VA; JR; BS; Engr Tech V P 90-; Mech Engr Tech; Space Rsrch/Dvlmnt.

**JANDRASITS, DIANNE M,** Saint Francis Coll, Loretto, PA; JR; BA; Cmps Mnstry 89-; Jr Cls Pres 90-; Cinema Shwcs 88-; Hnor Prog 88-; Plus 1 89-; Stdnt Active Ldrshp Pres 90-; Atletic Acad Hnr Rl 89-; Stdnt Mbr Indept Stdy Comm 90-; Philosophy/Psychology; Hmn Serv.

**JANECEK, MICHELLE M,** Belmont Coll, Nashville, TN; FR; BA; Stdnt Fndtn 90-; SG 90-; Pres Schlrshp 90-; Elem Educ/Psych; Tchr.

**JANECKA, BEATA M,** Univ Of Rochester, Rochester, NY; SO; BA; D Lion Org 90-; Psych; Bsn.

**JANER VILA, ZILKIA,** Univ Of Pr At Rio Piedras, Rio Piedras, PR; SR; BA; Hon Pgm 89-; Gldn Key; Crtfd Pro Actrss; Asst Pro Hstrns Rsrch Hstry Snt PR; Cmprtv Lit; Ph D.

**JANES, KIMBERLY A,** Unity Coll, Unity, ME; SO; BA; Wildlife Clb; Wrk Study Stdnt 89-; Wildlife Mngmnt.

**JANES, REBECCA N,** Le Moyne Coll, Syracuse, NY; SO; BS; Prgrmmng Brd Cmmtr Rep 89-; Firehouse Thtr 89-; Art Clb 89-90; Hnrs Prog 89-; Catholic Chrts 89-; Hmn Serv Assn 89-90; Vrsty Vllybl 89-; Sclgy/Crmnl Jstc; Hmn Serv/Law.

**JANG, HARRIET J,** Ms St Univ, Miss State, MS; SR; BA; Pi Sigma Epsilon 89-90; Bus; Mktg.

**JANG, TAMMY J,** Ms St Univ, Miss State, MS; JR; BA; Cmps Act Bd Flm Comm 89-90; IM Sprts Chrprsn 90; Lambda Sigma; Phi Eta Sigma; Alpha Lambda Delta; Pi Sigma Epsilon Asst VP Prsnl 89-; Soc Advncmnt Mngmnt 90-; Bus; Mktng.

**JANICKE, CAROLYN A,** Fl Atlantic Univ, Boca Raton, FL; JR; BSMBA; Cir K Clb 90-; Stdnt Assn Mgt/Prsnl Admin SAMPA 90-; Deans List 89-; St Ambrose Yth Grp 90-; Summer Intrnshp First Union Bnk Lighthouse Point FL; Bus; Corp Mgt.

**JANIK, SUSAN E,** D Youville Coll, Buffalo, NY; SO; BS; Com Stdnt Assn Com Mbr 90-; Peer Cnslr 90-; Nrsng; Dctr/Pdtrcn.

**JANISH, TIMOTHY D,** S U N Y At Buffalo, Buffalo, NY; SR; MS; IEEE Actv Chrmn 88-; Shussmstrs Ski Clb 87-; Pep Bnd 87-88; Alpha Sigma Phi Mrshl 87-; BS; Cmptr Engr.

**JANKOWSKI, JAMES C,** Coll Of Charleston, Charleston, SC; SO; BA; Clg Hon Bd 90-; Pre Law Soc 90-; Vol Wrk In Drug/Alcohol Rehab For Adlscnc 88-; Faclty Hons List 90-; Intrnshp W/Dept Of Jstc; Varsity Sailing Team Skipper 89-; Pol Sci; Law.

**JANNEY, JOEL OWEN,** Anne Arundel Comm Coll, Arnold, MD; SO; BS; Frfghtr-Anne Arundel Cnty Fire Dept 88-; Crtfd Emrgny Med Tchncn State Of MD 88-; Crtfd Advncd Rescue-AA Cnty Fire Dept 89-; Envrnmntl Eng.

**JANNICELLI, COLLEEN M,** Hudson Valley Comm Coll, Troy, NY; SO; AAS; Prog Aide NY State Dept Soc Serv 74; Acctng.

**JANOSIK, THOMAS L,** Va Commonwealth Univ, Richmond, VA; SR; BS; Hopewell Jycees Comm Dvlpmnt VP 86-; Knights Of Clmbs 90-; P Morris Schlrshp 86; Bus Admin/Mgmt; Bus Mgmt.

**JANOUS, KENNETH G,** Ms St Univ, Miss State, MS; JR; BS; Music Maker Productions Promo Dir 89-; The Reflector Staff Stndt Nwspr Ad Slmsm 90-; Phi Mu H Ouseboy Asstnt Head 89-90; Gamma Beta Phi 89-; Mu Kappa Tau; Deans List 89; Marketing/Transportation.

**JANOWSKY, KAREN B,** Fl St Univ, Tallahassee, FL; JR; BA; Mrchng Chfs 89; Hillel Fndtn 88-; Phi Eta Sigma 89-; Lambda Iota Tau; FL First Cst Wrtrs Fstvl Hon Mntn Ptry; Cody Harris Allen Wrtng Awdhon Mntn Ptry; Ruby Diamond Hillel Schlrshp88-89; English; Prof.

**JANRCZEK, FRANCIS JOSEPH,** Fl International Univ, Miami, FL; JR; BA; Coll Dmcrts Pres 88-; SGA Sen 89-; SGA Asst Chrmn Wy Mns Cmmtt 90; Cthlc Cmps Mnstry; Amnsty Intl; Dean Lst; FPIRG 89-; FRONTLASH Pres 90-; Pol Sci; Law.**

**JANSEN, JULIE M,** Univ Of Tn At Knoxville, Knoxville, TN; SO; BS; Carrick Hall Rsdnt Assn 89-90; Alpha Lambda Delta 90-; Gamma Beta Phi; Exec Undergrad Prog 90-; Bus; Acctng.

**JANSEN, KRISTA I,** S U N Y Coll Of Tech At Frmgdl, Farmingdale, NY; SR; AS; Nrsg.

**JANSEN, LESLIE A,** S U N Y At Buffalo, Buffalo, NY; SO; BA; Amer Gnrl Cntrctrs Clb 90-; Cvl Eng.

**JANSON, JILL,** Lehigh Univ, Bethlehem, PA; SO; BA; Gryphon Soc RA; Peer Cnslr Assoc Cnslr; Choir/Sml Grp Sch Bnd Concert Mgr 90-; Delta Zeta Pldg Cls Pres; Rutherford Amblnce Vol Corp Capt 87-90; Columbia U Jrnlsm Awd 89; Engl/Wrtg.

**JANSON, KARINA H,** Univ Of Miami, Coral Gables, FL; JR; BA; Var Sccr Brown Univ 87; Cmmnctn/Psychlgy; Intrspcs Cmmnctn Rsrchr.

**JANSSEN, SUSAN C,** Niagara Univ, Niagara Univ, NY; JR; BA; SWAC 88-89; Ttr; Ed Brd; Sigma Tau Delta 89-; Deans Lst 88-90; 2M Sftbll Tnns Skng; Engl.

**JANUCIK, MICHELLE L,** Smith Coll, Northampton, MA; JR; BA; AIESEC Corp Mktg Dir 89-; Deans Lst 89-; First Grp Schlr 90-; Govt.

**JANUSIK, SHARON L,** Kent St Univ Kent Cmps, Kent, OH; SO; BA; Hse Cncl Pres 90-; Stdnt Dietetic Assoc; IM Aerobics Clb 89-; Nutr/Dietetics.

**JANUZELLI, NEYSA M,** Villanova Univ, Villanova, PA; SO; BA; Bus Admn.

**JARAMILLO, DENEEN L,** Commonwealth Coll, Virginia Beach, VA; FR; AAS; Sec Intl 90-; Lgl Ofc Admin.

**JARAMILLO, MANUELA,** Univ Of Miami, Coral Gables, FL; JR; French And Spnsh.

**JARAMILLO, MARCELA M,** Newbury Coll, Brookline, MA; Cert Emplmnt Cnnctns Inc 89-; Pattermaking Textile; Fashion Dsgn.

**JARAN, JOY C,** Teikyo Post Univ, Waterbury, CT; JR; BS; Alpha Chi.

**JARBOE, NATHAN E,** Brescia Coll, Owensboro, KY; SO; BS; Res Life Assn; Cyclng Clb; Mail Carrier; Bio.

**JARBOE, SARAH E,** Furman Univ, Greenville, SC; FR; BA; Wrldwd Dscplshp Assc 90-; Symphny Orch 90-; Cllgt Educ Serv Corps 90-.

**JARDIN, NICOLE,** Wellesley Coll, Wellesley, MA; FR; BS; Bio Chem; Med Doc.

**JARDINES, ELIZABETH A,** City Univ Of Ny Queensbrough, New York, NY; SO; BA; NY Pblc Int Rsrch Grp 89-90; AA QCC; Zoology/Ecology.

**JAREMA, CHRISTINA MARIA,** Saint Johns Univ, Jamaica, NY; FR; BS; Amer Phrmctcl Assc Rep 90-; Ukrainian Clb 90-; CHAIKA Ukrainian Dnc Ens 89-; St Johns Univ Cath HS Schlrshp 90-; Pharmacology.

**JARKOVSKY, RENEE J,** Univ Of Rochester, Rochester, NY; SR; BA; Tae Kwon Do Karate Cl Busn Mgr 90-; Undergrad Psych Coun Publ Dir 90-; IM Sftbl; Psychlgy; Advtsg/Mrktg.

**JARMON, ELSIE R,** Va St Univ, Petersburg, VA; GD; JD; Ntl Hry S Trmn Schlr 88-; Gvrnrs Intrn Va Gnrl Asmbly 89; Bs 90; Law/Urbn & Rgnl Plnng; Law.

**JARMON, MARY L,** Univ Of Sc At Columbia, Columbia, SC; JR; BSN; Hon Grad USAF Flght Nrs Schl 78; RN 74-; US Air Frc Major 76-; RN Beth Israel Schl Nrsng NYC NY 74; Nrsng; Nrsng USAF.

**JARNICH, MATTHEW G,** Clarkson Univ, Potsdam, NY; FR; BS; Schl Nwspr 90-; Outing Clb 90-; ROTC 90-; CSA; Soccer/Ftbl 90-; Double May Finance/Acctg; Army/Bus.

**JAROLL, MICHELLE LYNN,** Univ Of Sc At Columbia, Columbia, SC; SO; BA; Psychlgy.

**JARRED, TERRY L,** Memphis St Univ, Memphis, TN; SO; BFA; Alpha Lmbd Dlt 90; Art; Grphc Dsgn.

**JARRELL, SUNDRA G,** Itawamba Comm Coll, Fulton, MS; SO; BA; Theatrical Soc 90-; Choir Band BSU 89-; Deans List 90-; Delta Psi Omega; Hnr Grad; Spirit Awd Choir; Best Actress So Pacific; IM Sftbl Vlybl 89-; AA; Jrnlsm.

**JARRELL, VALMORE W,** Guilford Tech Comm Coll, Jamestown, NC; SR; AAS; Talent Roster; Untd Way Carvsr 89; AT/T; Bus/Acct Exec.

**JARRELL-CAREY, FELICIA L,** City Univ Of Ny Baruch Coll, New York, NY; GD; BBA; AA New York City Tech Coll 86f; Hmn Rsrcs Mgmt.

**JARRETT, DELORES C,** Averett Coll, Danville, VA; JR; BS; Commuter Life Assoc 90-; Phi Theta Kappa 88-; SPIRE 90-, Sigma Lambda Epsilon; Deans List 89-90; Ridgeway Elem PTA Pres 90-; Sub Tchr 87-; ASS Patrick Henry Cmnty Clg 90; Math; Tchng.

**JARRETT, KAREN A,** Albany St Coll, Albany, GA; SO; BS; Sci Club Albany St Coll 90-; Alpha Eta Soc 90-; Sci Bowl Champ 90-; Kati Kati Cultural Ctr; Bio; Phys Thrpst.

**JARRETT, KAREN L,** Glassboro St Coll, Glassboro, NJ; JR; BA; Wmn Cmmnctns Inc 90-; Rdo/TV Assn 90; Hon Prog 90; Internshp WFMZ-TV 69; Sftbl 89; Comm/Radio/TV/FILM.

**JARRETT, RITA K,** Ashland Comm Coll, Ashland, KY; JR; AAS 90; Psych; Clncl Psych.

**JARRETTE, LE NAE T,** Hampton Univ, Hampton, VA; SR; MSW; Soc Wrk Clb VP 87-; Stdnt Asst Almn Afrs 90; Alpha Kappa Mu 89-; Soc Wrk Dept Awd 90-; Suma Cum Laude; BSW; Soc Wrk; Chld Wlfr Legsltr.

**JARVINA, AIMEE M,** City Univ Of Ny Baruch Coll, New York, NY; JR; BBA; Bsns; Accntng.

**JARVIS, DANA E,** Allegheny Coll, Meadville, PA; JR; SG Fnnc Cmmtt 90-; Dean Lst 88-89; Phi Gamma Delta 90-; Hntd Hse Lft O Thon 88-89; Alden Schlr 89-90; Yng Rpblcns 89-; John G Fulton Intern 90; Vrsty Wrsltng 89-90.

**JARVIS, DEBORAH L,** D Youville Coll, Buffalo, NY; JR; MS; Stdnt Occptnl Thrpy Assc; Cmps Mnstry; Buffalo Fndtn Schlrshp 88-89; Occptnl Thrpy; Pediatric Ot.

**JARVIS, GINGER L,** Univ Of Sc At Aiken, Aiken, SC; SO; BA; Psychology; Hmn Rltns.

**JARVIS, JANIS M,** Ga St Univ, Atlanta, GA; SR; BSED; SGAE 90-; Kappa Delta Pi 90-; Golden Key 89-; Deans Key 90-; Deans Plaque 90; Educ.

**JARVIS, KARMAN R,** Wilberforce Univ, Wilberforce, OH; SR; BS; Womn Hldng Int Prof Tr 90; Alpha Kappa Mu 90-; IBM Preprof Acctnt Intrn; Ohio CPA Brd Achvmnt Awd 90; Pres Awd 90; Acctg; Entrprnr.

**JARVIS, KIMBERLY D,** Johnson C Smith Univ, Charlotte, NC; JR; BA; Drill Tm 2nd Cmmndr 88-89; Englsh Clb 89-; Englsh; Law.

**JARVIS, SANDRA Y,** Univ Of South Al, Mobile, AL; FR; Scndry Educ; Tchg.

**JARVIS, ULRIC S,** Embry Riddle Aeronautical Univ, Daytona Beach, FL; SO; AMT; Crbn Assoc 90-; Islnd Vbrtns Bnd Ldr 90-; Avtn Mchncs; Arcrft Tech.

**JARY, FRANK J,** Cornell Univ, Ithaca, NY; FR; BS; Physics; Engineering.

**JASHINSKI, JODI E,** Davis & Elkins Coll, Elkins, WV; SR; BA; Almni Shwcse; Vars Bsktbl; AS Comm Clg Allegheny Co 90; Trvl/Toursm; Airlns.

**JASINSKI, JOSEPH M,** Univ Of De, Newark, DE; SO; BA; Bio; Medcn.**

**JASINSKI, MARK R,** Seton Hall Univ, South Orange, NJ; SR; IM Bsktbl/Sftbl/Ftbl Tm Cpt 87-; SHRM 90-; APICS Pres 90-; Beta Gamma Sigma 90-; Jr Sprts Leag Brick NJ Bsktbl Coach/Ref 87-; Dptmntl Hnrs Citn Mgmt/Indstrl Rltns; Deans Lst; IM Sprts 87-; BA; Bus Mngmnt.

**JASINSKI, MICHELLE A,** West Liberty St Coll, West Liberty, WV; SR; BA; Multicultural Edn 88-90; Kappa Delta Pi Pres 89-; Elem Edn; Tchr.

**JASKO, JOHN J,** Duquesne Univ, Pittsburgh, PA; SO; Drm Cncl 89-; Phi Eta Sigma 89-; Cmps Mnstry 90-; Hbt Hmnty 90; Frshmn Chmstry Hnrs; IM 89-; Blgy; Med.

**JASKOLKA, MELISSA M,** Niagara Univ, Niagara Univ, NY; SO; BA; Yrbk Stff Sprts Ed 90-F Orntn Tm Orntn Ldr; VITA Tax Svc; IM Bsktbl 89-; Acctg; Pblc Acctg/CPA.

**JASPER, LISA M,** Univ Of Sc At Columbia, Columbia, SC; JR; BA; Wrld Tae Kwon Do Clb VP/TREAS 88-; Mntnr Clb Pres 89-90; Gamma Beta Phi 90-; Gldn Key 90-; Assn Hon Stdnts 88-; Spec Olympcs Vol; SEEDS; 1st Annl Tae Kwon Do Trnmnt USC; Intl Studies/Psych; Intl Bus/Govt/Rsrch.

**JASPER JR, STERLING VICTOR,** Va St Univ, Petersburg, VA; JR; BA; Hotel/Rstrnt Mgr Clb Pres 89-; Alpha Phi Alpha; W Disney Wrld Clg Intrn Shift Mgr; W Disney World Mgr Prog Spvr 89; Ldrshp Awd; Hotel/Rstrnt Mgr; Hotel Mgr.

**JASSIN, BETH P,** Marymount Manhattan Coll, New York, NY; BA; Psi Chi 90-; Alpha Chi 90-; Covlenant Hse Cnslr 89-90; AA Amer Col Switzerland 75; Bellvue Hosp Chld Psychlgy Dept Rsrch Asst; Psych; Psychlgst.

**JASTREMSKI, KRISTEN E,** Le Moyne Coll, Syracuse, NY; JR; BA; Prtnrshp For Svc Lrng SD Prog; Engl Club; NIHIL Litry Magzn; Tutoring; Amnesty Interntl; Philsphy Sympsm; Phi Sigma Tau; Lake Effect Poetry Award; Deans List 90-; Engl Lit/Philosophy.

**JASTRZEMBSKI, IRENE M,** Univ Of Med & Dentistry Of Nj, Newark, NJ; SR; BA; Vlybl 86-87; USVBA Club Vlybl 87-90; Metpath Inc 90-; Stdnt Schlrshp; ASMT; NJSMT Stdnt Bowl; Clincl Lab Sci; Medcl Technlgy.

**JATTUSO, MIA L,** Univ Of Fl, Gainesville, FL; FR; BA; Stdnt Almn Assoc 90-; Intl Stdnts Assoc 90-; Hnrs Org 90-; Phi Eta Sigma 90-; IM Flg Ftbll 90-; Pltcl Sci; Law.

**JAUCH, JILL E,** Univ Of Sc At Columbia, Columbia, SC; FR; BA; DJ Radio Sta 90-; Cltrl Arts Comm Carolina 90-; Pgm Union/Emrgng Ldr Pgm; Soc Prof Jrnlsts; Jrnlsm.

**JAUCH, WENDY T,** Liberty Univ, Lynchburg, VA; SR; BA; Ythqust 88-90; Lib Assoc Chrstn Tchrs Dorm Rep 89-; AWANA Ldr 89-; Kappa Delta Pi Sec 89-; Elem Edn; Tchr Spcl Edn.

**JAUDON, CHRISTOPHER M,** Ms St Univ, Miss State, MS; FR; BS; ASME 90-; Campus Crusade 90-; Phi Eta Sigma; Mech Engr; Engr.

**JAUDON, RHONDA L,** Ms Univ For Women, Columbus, MS; SR; BS; Deans Lst 90; Night Auditor Ramada Inn; Bus Admin.

**JAVA, JOELLE ANNE,** Niagara Univ, Niagara Univ, NY; JR; BED; SG Cbnt S/Clss Rep 90-; Prnts Wkend Comm Chr 90-F Sigma Tau Delta; Hons Pgm 89-90; NUCAP 88-89; RA 90-; Engl/Ed; Elem Ed.

**JAVARONE, RICHARD J,** Life Coll, Marietta, GA; GD; DC; Thompson Club 87-90; Gonstead Club 87-90; Activator Club 87-90; Clinical Intrnshp 88-90; Drs Have A Hrt Prtcpnt 90; BS NY State Univ; Dr Chrprctcs; Chrprtcs.

**JAVIER, JOSE L,** Catholic Univ Of Pr, Ponce, PR; SR; BS; Pre Med Cr 90-; Beta Beta Beta Pres 90-; Alha Chi; Inst Hnr Pgm 90-; Deans Lst 89-; Blgy; Dntstry.

**JAVIER, PAGAN ROJAS,** Inter Amer Univ Pr San German, San German, PR; SR; BA; Elem Ed.

**JAVORSKY, CAROL A,** Univ Of Akron, Akron, OH; JR; BS; Rho Lambda 90-; Alpha Delta Pi 89-; Alpha Lambda Delta 89-; Phi Eta Sigma 89-; Goldn Key 90-; Mu Kappa Tau; Pi Sigma Epsilon 90-; Alpha Delta Pi Treas 88-; Circle K 89; Deans Lst 88-; Hon Schlrshp 88-; Intrnshp J M Smucker Co; Mktg.

**JAY, BRUCE A,** George Mason Univ, Fairfax, VA; SR; BIS; Deans Lst; AS N Va Cmuty Clg 81; Cmunctn/Info Rsrc Mgmt; Sftwre Cnslnt.

**JAY, JOHN R,** Livingston Univ, Livingston, AL; SR; AAS; Outstndg Tech Std 90-; Indstl Mantnc/Mngmnt

**JAYAKODY, UDITHA D,** Univ Of Sc At Columbia, Columbia, SC; FR; Elect Eng.

**JAYKO, KELLY A,** Pasco Hernando Comm Coll, Dade City, FL; FR; AA; Nrsg.

**JAYNES, ANGELA A,** Ms Univ For Women, Columbus, MS; SR; BS; Phi Beta Lambda VP 90-; DPMA 90-; Un Advsry 89; Rogue Soc Clb Sec/Treas 87-88; Bus Admin/Comp Info Syst.

**JAZMIN, ANNE MARIE O,** Ny Univ, New York, NY; SO; BA; Wrtng Tutr For Kds 89-90; Un Flpno Yth Cncl 90; Intl Assn Phlppne-Amer 90; Hosp Prog Vol; Psychlgy; Pre-Med.

**JEAN, MARJOLIE,** Central St Univ, Wilberforce, OH; JR; Natl Assn Ngro Bus/Prfssnl Wmns Clb Chpln 90-; Natl Stdnt Bus Lgue Pres 90-; Deans Lst 90-; Bus; Mktg.

**JEAN-BAPTISTE, CHARLYGORE,** City Univ Of Ny Kingsborough, Brooklyn, NY; SO; BA; Corp Careers Hnrs Club VP 90-; Haitian Club Advr 89-; Busn Admin; Hmn Res Mgt.

**JEAN-FRANCOIS, BEDA,** Fl International Univ, Miami, FL; SO; BA; Blck Union; Phi Lambda Sigma Secr 89-90; Phone Crisis Cnslr 90-; Psych; Clncl Psych.

**JEAN-LOUIS, MARIE JOSEE,** Barry Univ, Miami, FL; GD; BA; Demo Natl Pgrsv Sec 88-; Rally Of Haiti Pol Organ; Soc Psrvtn Haitan Cult 87-; Haitian Task Force Vol 89-90; Comm Invlvmnt Spclst 90-; Cert AA Miami Dade Comm Coll 89; Lib Arts Genl; Tchng.

**JEAN-PIERRE, JERRY,** Thomas Nelson Comm Coll, Hampton, VA; SO; BA; Airway Science.

**JEANOTTE, CRYSTELLE A,** Bryant Stratton Bus Inst Roch, Rochester, NY; Acctg Clb Treas 86-87; Bus Mgmt Clb Treas 89-; Stdnt Cncl Rep 90-; AOS; Acctg/Bus Mgmt; CMA.

**JEBB, CARROLL E,** Immaculata Coll, Immaculata, PA; FR; Community Theatre 81-; Admin Assist 81-.

**JEBB, MICHAEL E,** Barry Univ, Miami, FL; SO; BA; Cmptr Sci; Cmptr Dsgnr.

**JEFFCOAT, ANITA C,** Spartanburg Methodist Coll, Spartanburg, SC; FR; A; Lbrl Arts.

**JEFFERIES, ALEXA M,** East Tn St Univ, Johnson City, TN; SO; Bus; Mgmt.

**JEFFERS, KIMBERLY D,** Kent St Univ Kent Cmps, Kent, OH; SO; BBA; Alpha Lambda Delta 90-; Acctg.

**JEFFERS, MICHAEL D,** Georgetown Coll, Georgetown, KY; SR; BA; Anderson Hall Govt Pres 89-; Ftbl Tm 87-; Natl Assoc Intrclgte Athltcs Acdmc All Amer 89-90; John E Drake Acctg Schlrshp Awd 90; Mary Louise Fowt Acctg Schlrshp Awd 89; Mktg/Fnce; Acctg.

**JEFFERSON, BRIAN A,** Morehouse Coll, Atlanta, GA; FR; BA; Bio/Pre Med; Medcn.

**JEFFERSON, CHRISTIAN G,** Univ Of Sc At Columbia, Columbia, SC; SR; JDMBA; Fnncl Mgmt Assn Pres 90-; Acad Rspnsblty Com 89; Phi Beta Kappa 90-; Beta Gamma Sigma 90-; Alpha Lambda Delta 88-; Coll Of Bus Almni Schlrshp 90; SC Bnkrs Schl Schlrshp 90-; MBA Grad Asstshp; IM Athltcs 89-; BS; Finnce; Corp Law.

**JEFFERSON, EDDIE M,** Al A & M Univ, Normal, AL; JR; BS; Dns Lst 90-; Delta Mu Delta 90-; Chrstms Chrts 89-; Untd Way 76-83; AS Calhoun St Comm Clg 81; Bsn; Mgmt.

**JEFFERSON, KENNETH A,** Alcorn St Univ, Lorman, MS; SR; Comp Sci Clb Pr 86-90; Cntrct Waterways Experiment Sta 88-90; BA 90; Comp Sci; App Math.

**JEFFERSON, LORENA,** Fayetteville St Univ, Fayetteville, NC; SR; BA; Ms Rudolph Jones Stdnt Ctr 88-89; SGA 88-89; Future Almn 88-89; Soclgy; Cnslng.

**JEFFERSON, MICHAEL N,** United States Naval Academy, Annapolis, MD; FR; MBA; Chrstn Chr 90; Vrsty Ftbl 90-; Vrsty Trck 90-; Ecnmcs; Eng Bus Admn.

**JEFFERSON, SHEILAH M,** Howard Univ, Washington, DC; SR; BA; Educ Stdnt Cncl Pres 90-; Blck Nia FORCE Mbrshp 88-; Judcry Brd Howard Univ Stdnt Assoc; Kappa Delta Pi 90-; Elem Educ; Tchr.**

**JEFFERSON, YOLANDA T,** Talladega Coll, Talladega, AL; SO; BA; GA Sntr 89-90; Pre Law Scty 89-; Clge Chr 89-; Tutor Stdnt Sprt Srvc 90-; Pm Pn Sqd Capt 89-; Hstry/Pre Law; Law.

**JEFFORDS, PEARL F,** Coker Coll, Hartsville, SC; SR; BA; Chrprsn Evng Sch Cmt Chrprsn; Faclty Srch Cmt; Tsk Frc Edctnl Exclnc; Grl Scts Amer; PFA; Acad Booster Clb; Top Ten Cls Cmltv GPA 4.o 89-; Jr Cls Mrshl; Evng Sch Otstndg Stdnt Awrd; Asst Sun Sch Tchr; Asst Grl Sct Ldr; Intrprtr For Deaf; Excptnl Ed; Tchng.

**JEFFREY, CHARLES D,** Fayetteville St Univ, Fayetteville, NC; SR; BS; Delta Mu Delta; Proprietor SBS Systems Providing Bus Sserv To SE NC 87-; Bus Admn; Bus Cnsltng.

**JEFFREY, PAULA E,** Christopher Newport Coll, Newport News, VA; SR; BS; Blgy; Biotchnlgy; Biomdcl Rsrch.

**JEFFRIES, CARROL A,** Wright St Univ Lake Cmps, Celina, OH; FR; Elect Eng; Eng.

**JEFFRIES, D ANDREW,** Univ Of Sc At Columbia, Columbia, SC; SO; BA; USC Model United Ntns Clb Pres/VP 90; Head Delegate To Somalia At Ntl Cnvntn; United Way Big Bro; Naval Sea/Clg Prog 2nd Class Ptty Offcr; Govt/Intrntl Studies; Intrntl Bsnss.

**JEFFRIES, EDGAR W,** Commonwealth Coll, Virginia Beach, VA; SO; Acctng Clb Pres; Pres Lst 90; Hnr Rll; Lcl PTA 90-; Tchr Cmmnwlth Chldrns Coll 90-; BA Indiana Univ 76; Bus Mjr.

**JEFFRIES, HASAN K,** Morehouse Coll, Atlanta, GA; FR; BA; NY/NJ Clb 90-; Thurman Hl Step Tm; Morehouse Clg Mentoring Pgm 90-; Hnrs Rl 90-; Dns Lst; Hstry; Clg Professor.

**JEFFRIES, KATHRYN E,** Univ Of Sc At Columbia, Columbia, SC; SR; BA; The Gamcock Asst Features Edtr 86-89; The Navgtrs Bible Stdy Ldr 86-90; Carolna Cares Secy 86; Intrn The News/Courier 90; Intrn The Berkeley Democrat 89; Jrnlsm.

**JEFFRIES JR, WILLIAM H,** Univ Of Akron, Akron, OH; SO; BFA; Alpha Sgm Lmbd; Grphc Dsgn; Frlnc Dsgn.

**JEFFRIES-EL, JAMILLAH,** Howard Univ, Washington, DC; JR; BA; Vew Yrkrs Ltd 89; BIN 90; Brdcst Prdctn; Busn Comm.

**JEHLE, HANS CHRISTOPH,** Villanova Univ, Villanova, PA; JR; BA; Poltcl Clb 90-; Frnch Clb 90-; Francais Hon Soc 90; Frnch/Phlsphy/Arts/Sci; Coll Tchng.

**JEKABSONS, LAURA A,** Nova Univ, Ft Lauderdale, FL; GD; NAFE 90-; WWC 90-; Natl Hon Soc 79; NJ Girls State 79; At/T Ftr Pnr; Mc Graw-Hill Princeton NJ Acctg Intrn 84; Pgmr/Anlyst Fin Syst 84-; BA Georgian Ct Coll 84; BS 84; Math/Comp Sci/Bus Admin/Acctg; Fin/CPA.

**JELKOVAC, SANDRA L,** Indiana Univ Of Pa, Indiana, PA; JR; BA; JTS Hlth/Ftns 89-; Bkng 88-; Dns Lst 89-90; Elem Ed; Tchg Prfsn/Ph D.

**JELLICORSE, PATRICK M,** Pellissippi St Tech Comm Coll, Knoxville, TN; JR; BA; Comp Sci; Pgmr.

**JELLIE, CASEY J,** Longwood Coll, Farmville, VA; SO; MS; Deans Lst At Va Poly Inst/State U 84-85; Physcl Thrpy Dept Sthsde Cmmnty Hosp; Physcl Thrpy.

**JEMIELITA, CHRISTINE,** Yale Univ, New Haven, CT; FR; BS; Chldrns Thtr Wrkshps 90-; Blgy; Med.

**JEMISON, IRIS MARCIA,** Talladega Coll, Talladega, AL; FR; BA; Engl Mjrs Assn 90-; Dean Lst; Adpt Fmly Prog Ttr 90-; Grl Scts Amer Trp Ldr 89-90; Mrs R M Tenney Schlrshp Awrd; Engl; Tchr.

**JEMISON, LEDRA A,** Tuskegee Univ, Tuskegee Inst, AL; SR; SGA Pres 89-; Clg Democrats VP 90-; Lambda Lota Tau Pres 89-; Delta Sigma Theta Sec 90-; Tennis Team 88; BA Tuskegee Univ; English, Corporate Law.

**JEMMOTT, HENSLEY B,** Morehouse Coll, Atlanta, GA; FR; BA; Clg Bus Assoc 90-; Stripes 90-; Intrntl Studies; Invstmnt Bnkng.

**JEN, MIN-HSIU,** Univ Of Ga, Athens, GA; JR; Chinese Assn/Newslttr Editor 90; Quality Cntrl Foshing Airlines Taiwan 87-89; Cert Natl Pingtung Inst Of Agri 83; Food/Nutrition; Food Indus.

**JENDRISAK, DAVID J,** Kent St Univ Kent Cmps, Kent, OH; SR; BA; Undergrad Stdnt Sen Alctns Com; Sigma Alpha Epsilon Pldg Ed 88-; Vrsty Sccr 87; Outstndng Stdnt Svc Awd; Washington Pgm Natl Issues 90; Pltcl Sci; Grad Schl/Law.

**JENERETTE, COLLETTE R,** Benedict Coll, Columbia, SC; GD; MS; Crmnl Jstc Clb 89-90; Scl Wrk Clb 86-87; Delta Sigma Theta 88-; BS Benedict Clg 90; Crmnl Jstc; Cnslg.

**JENERETTE, CORETTA M,** Clemson Univ, Clemson, SC; SO; BS; SNA Sec; Natl Stdnt Nrs Assn; SC; Alpha Kappa Alpha Financl Sec; Deans Lst; Pres Lst; Clmsn Schlr; Blck Stdnt Of Promise; Bxtr Hlthcr Schlr; Nrsng; Anesthtst.

**JENERETTE, KEVIN M,** Univ Of Sc At Coastal Carolina, Conway, SC; JR; BS; Numbers/Bytes; ACM; Pi Mu Epsilon; Math/Cmptr Sci.

**JENIFER, SHADE L,** Hampton Univ, Hampton, VA; FR; BS; Pep Bnd 90-; March Bnd 90-; Cncrt Bnd; IM Bstkbl; Cmptr Scnc; Sftwr Engr.

**JENKENS, SHARON D,** Liberty Univ, Lynchburg, VA; SR; BS; TV Prod Mgr 89-; Alpha Lambda Delta 88-; TV Intern Wshington D C/Lynchburg VA; Video Prod; T V.

**JENKIN, DAWN S,** Georgian Court Coll, Lakewood, NJ; SR; BA; Ocean Cnty Coll Stdnt Govt Assn Stdnt Rep 89; Clionaes Soc 89-; Dns Schlr 90; Ocean Cnty Hist Museum 90-; Phi Alpha Theta Treas 90-; YMCA Asst Tchr 90-; Intrnshp Ocean Cnty Hist Museum 90; Saa Ocean Cnty Coll 89; Hist.

**JENKINS, AMANDA K,** Univ Of Tn At Martin, Martin, TN; FR; BS; Dnc Ensmbl 90; Sci; Phrmcy.

**JENKINS, AMY R,** Univ Of Sc At Columbia, Columbia, SC; FR; ASSOC; Acctng; Secy.

**JENKINS, ANDREA J,** Portland School Of Art, Portland, ME; JR; BFA; Professor Search Comm; Grphc Dsgn.

**JENKINS, ANGELA,** Le Moyne Owen Coll, Memphis, TN; SR; BS; Police Sci Assn Pres; Corrctnl Sci Assn; Stdnt Govt Bus Mgr; NAACP Ednl Chrmn; Phi Theta Kappa; Outstndg Stdnt Awd 87; Outstndg Grad Awd 88; TN Blcks Crmnl Jstce; TNOA; Police Ofcr; Pol Sci; Intl Law.

**JENKINS, ANGELA L,** Tn St Univ, Nashville, TN; SO; BA; Pltcl Sci Clb 89; Spnsh Clb 90-; Alpha Lambda Delta 90-; Hgh Hnrs Awrd; Pltcl Sci; Law.

**JENKINS, BEATRICE M,** Central St Univ, Wilberforce, OH; SR; Choir 87-; MENC NEA.**

**JENKINS, BRAD I,** Memphis St Univ, Memphis, TN; JR; BA; Communications; Film Production.

**JENKINS, CANDI J,** Ky Wesleyan Coll, Owensboro, KY; SR; BA; Phi Theta Kappa; Phi Beta Lmbd Pres 90; Deans List; Presdntl Schlrshp; U S Achvmnt Acad Mrt Awrd 89; Natl Assc Acctnt Awrd; AS U K Madisonvl Comm Clg 89; Acctnt; Pblc Acctng.

**JENKINS, CECILIA T,** Neumann Coll, Aston, PA; FR; BA; Actn Peace 90-; Cmps Mnstry 90-; Thtr Ensmbl 90-; Art.

**JENKINS, CHERYL D,** Univ Of Southern Ms, Hattiesburg, MS; FR; BA; Afro-Amer Stdnt Org; Engl; Law Schl.

**JENKINS, CINDY L,** Lenoir Rhyne Coll, Hickory, NC; JR; BA; Alpha Lambda Delta 88-; Mu Sigma Epsilon 90-; Phi Beta Lambda Hstrn 88-; Acctg; CPA.

**JENKINS, DAVID A,** Univ Of Tn At Knoxville, Knoxville, TN; FR; Singers 90-; Water Ski; Acctg; CPA.

**JENKINS, DEBRA P,** Teikyo Post Univ, Waterbury, CT; FR; BA; Max R Traurig Schlrshp; Pres Schlrshp; Intr Dsgn.

**JENKINS, DELILAH ANN,** Univ Of Tn At Martin, Martin, TN; JR; BA; Blck Stdnt Assoc 88-; Stdnt TN Edctrs Assoc; Early Chldhd Ed; Tch.

**JENKINS, DONNA K,** Univ Of Sc At Columbia, Columbia, SC; SR; BA 90; Elem Ed; Tchr.

**JENKINS, DOROTHY L,** Miami Jacobs Jr Coll Of Bus, Dayton, OH; FR; 4-H Advisor Sewing Clb 81-83; Dig Design Garden Clb 78-82; Clerk Typist; Teachers Aide 84-89; Vol Aide 81-84; Medl Transcription.

**JENKINS, ELAINE,** City Univ Of Ny La Guard Coll, Long Island Cty, NY; SO; BA; Tlnt Roaster; Englsh.

**JENKINS, ELOISE,** Concordia Coll, Selma, AL; JR; AA; Sunday Schl Tchr; Pres Of Missnry; Sec/Ushr Mt Olive Bptst; Schl/Comm Liaison Aid; Cnslr/Elem Ed.

**JENKINS, ERIC V,** Northeast State Tech Comm Coll, Blountville, TN; FR; AAS; Amer Chem Soc; Chemistry; Engr.

**JENKINS, FELICIA D,** Tougaloo Coll, Tougaloo, MS; SR; BA; Poltcl Sci; Pub Admin/Law.

**JENKINS, GABRIELLE,** Md Coll Of Art & Design, Silver Spring, MD; FR; AA; Stdnt Cncl Sec 90-; Vis Cmctns; Illust.

**JENKINS, JACQUELINE DARLING,** Nova Univ, Ft Lauderdale, FL; GD; MBA; Faith Mnstres S Sc Tchr 87-; Fl Jaycees Frfrtr Awd 84; Delta Sigma Theta 77-; Civic Lgue 90-; Fire Serv Admnstr Kennedy Sp Ctr Fla 85-; BA 84; FF EMT Brevard Comm Clg 79; Prsnl Human Rsrces; Pub Admn.

**JENKINS, JEFFREY K,** James Madison University, Harrisonburg, VA; SR; BS; SG 89-; Cntr Svc Lrng Vol 89-; Alpha Kappa Lambda Comm Svc Chrmn 87-; Psych; Rehab Cnslng.

**JENKINS, JEFFREY S,** Univ Of Nc At Charlotte, Charlotte, NC; GD; BA; Yng Almni Cncl 90-; Goldn Key 90-; Deans Lst 88-; Chnclrs Lst 89; Psychlgy.

**JENKINS, JERRY W,** Brewer St Jr Coll, Fayette, AL; FR; BA; Phi Theta Kappa; Science; Chmcl Engnrng.

**JENKINS, JILL A,** Tn Tech Univ, Cookeville, TN; SR; BS; Zeta Tau Alpha Schl Chm/Sec/VP/PRES 87-; Stdt Gvt Assoc Cmts Sntr 89-; Stdt Alumni Ambsdrs 90-; Phi Gamma Delta; Omicron Delta Kappa 90-; Zeta Tau Alpha Pres; Tn Tech Tennis Mst Valuable Plyr 88; Zeta Tau Alpha Bst Jr 90; Fashion Merchandising; Buyer.

**JENKINS, KAREN R,** Va Union Univ, Richmond, VA; SO; BA; Bus Admin; Own Bus.

**JENKINS, KENNETH MARK,** Middle Tn St Univ, Murfreesboro, TN; JR; BBA; FAA 89-90; Gamma Beta Phi Pblc Serv Chrmn 90-; Alpha Kappa Psi; Acctng; CPA.

**JENKINS, KIMBERLY A,** Valdosta St Coll, Valdosta, GA; JR; BSN; Nurs; RN Neo Natal Intsve Care Unit.

**JENKINS, LANTRINAE B,** Tuskegee Univ, Tuskegee Inst, AL; FR; Pol Sci; Corp Law.

**JENKINS, LISA G,** Univ Of Southern Ms, Hattiesburg, MS; SR; MS Nrs Assoc; Outstndng Stdnt 90-; RN; ADN Meridian Comm Clg 86; Nsrg; MS Cardiovsclr Nrsg.

**JENKINS, LISA G,** Meridian Comm Coll, Meridian, MS; GD; AA; Dstrbtv Edctn Clbs Amrca Rprtr 90-; Phi Theta Kappa 89; Mrktng & Dstrbtn; Sales.

**JENKINS, LISA J,** James Madison University, Harrisonburg, VA; JR; BS; Navgtrs VP 90-; Pres Lst 89-90; Erly Chldhd Educ; Tchr.

**JENKINS, LISA L,** Savannah St Coll, Savannah, GA; FR; BA.

**JENKINS, LORA A,** Wilmington Coll, New Castle, DE; JR; BA; Dlwre Tech Alumni Assoc 90; Deans Lst 90; Dlwre Hmn Rsrces Grp 88; AAS Dlwre Tchncl/Comm Clg 86; Hmn Rsrces Mngmnt; Uppr Lvl Mngmnt Career.

**JENKINS, LORRIE A,** Francis Marion Coll, Florence, SC; FR; BS; Yng Gftd; Black Chrs; Nrsng; RN.

**JENKINS, MAMIE D,** Univ Of Sc At Columbia, Columbia, SC; JR; BA; Gamma Beta Phi; Sub Tchr Estill Elem Schl; Vol Even Start Adlt Educ Pgm Estill SC; Assoc USC-AIKEN SC 90; Early Chldhd Educ; Tchng.

**JENKINS, MARGARET S,** Ms Gulf Coast Comm Coll, Perkinston, MS; SO; BS; Phi Theta Kappa 90-; Pres Lst; Gulfport Jr Aux 87-89; PTA; S S Tchr; Elem Educ; Tchr.

**JENKINS, MARK A,** Wilmington Coll, New Castle, DE; JR; BA; Elec Tech; AAS Delaware Tech/Comm Coll 90; AAS Delaware Tech Comm Coll 85; Bus Admin/Acctg; CPA.

**JENKINS, MARK B,** Univ Of Tn At Martin, Martin, TN; JR; Bptst Union 88; Scty Automotive Engrs 90; Ntnl FFA Alumni 88; Wilson Sprtng Goods Engr Intrn; IM; Elctrcl Engr Tech; Engr.

**JENKINS, MARSHELL C,** Coppin St Coll, Baltimore, MD; JR; BA; Sci Clb Sec 90-; Hon Prog; Prvt Donr Schlrshp; Sntrl Schlrshp; Dncrs; Biolgy; Med/Physcn.

**JENKINS, MEREDITH L,** Newbury Coll, Brookline, MA; AS; Magna Cum Laude; Comp Sci.

**JENKINS, MICHELLE L,** Edinboro Univ Of Pa, Edinboro, PA; FR; BA; Socl Wrk Clb 90-; Social Work.

**JENKINS, NICOLE L,** Hampton Univ, Hampton, VA; JR; BA; Tops Tutorial Pgm 88-89; Peer Cnslr Pgm Pres 89-; Psi Chi 90-; Tutor Wesley Church Org; Outstndng Peer Cnslr Awd; Psychology; Clncl Psychologist.

**JENKINS, PEGGY S,** Western Ky Univ, Bowling Green, KY; SO; BA; KMCA Dir 89-90; ICA; City Clrk; Acctg; Bsn.

**JENKINS, RUDA L,** Univ Of Ky, Lexington, KY; SO; BSN; Amer Nat Red Crs 90; Nrsng Stdnt Assn 90; Alpha Kappa Alpha; Dns Lst 90; Cncrt Bnd 89-; Mrchng Bnd 89-; Nrsng; Nrsng Anesthesia/Midwfry.

**JENKINS, SHAWN L,** Bluefield Coll, Bluefield, VA; JR; Varsity Bsktbl 88-; Alpha Phi Sigma 89-; Varsity Bsktbl 88-; Phrmcst.

**JENKINS, SONIQUE TEAKA,** Voorhees Coll, Denmark, SC; MSA; Cncrt Chr; Delta Sigma Theta Cstdn; Schlrshp SUNY; Bsns Admnstrtn.

**JENKINS, TAMMY L,** Bridgewater Coll, Bridgewater, VA; JR; BS; Flwshp Chrstn Athlts 90-; Pre-Med Soc 90-; Fld Hcky 88-; Blgy; Physcl Thrpy.

**JENKINS, TAMMY M,** Western Carolina Univ, Cullowhee, NC; FR; BS; Alpha Lambda Delta; Chmstry; Clncl Rsrch.

**JENKINS, TARA N,** Univ Of Ga, Athens, GA; SO; BS; SGA 90-; Zeta Tau Alpha 90-; World Carpts Schlrshp 89-; F E Kilgore Schlrshp 90-; Dns Lst/Hnrs Day; Educ; Tchg.

**JENKINS, TARI R,** Univ Of Akron, Akron, OH; SR; BSN; Nrsng Clb 89; Grad 1992 Class VP; Stdnt Tour Guide 87; Golden Key 89; Schlrshp 87; Prmtnl Video 90; Nrsng; Ped Nrse Prctnr.

**JENKINS, TASHA Y,** Hampton Univ, Hampton, VA; SR; BA; Stdnt Union Bd; Pre Med Club 87-; Biol Clb 87-; NAACP 87-; Alpha Kappa Mu 90-; Beta Kapap Chi 90-; Vet Admin Hosp Vol 90-; U S Army Reserves Cargo Spclst 88-; Deans Lst Hampton Univ 87-; Biol; Orthopedic Surgeon.

**JENKINS, TERESA A,** Birmingham Southern Coll, Birmingham, AL; SO; BA; Beta Beta Beta; Kappa Delta Schlrshp Chrmn; Southern Vol Serv 90-; Intrnshp Lab Asstnt Univ Ala Hosp; Diamond Girls Bsbl 89-; Biology; Medicine.

**JENKINS, TIFFANY R,** Fl A & M Univ, Tallahassee, FL; FR; BA; Bsn Invstmnt Fund 90-; WSBI 90; Phi Eta Sigma; Bsn Rcgntn Awrd; FL Academic Schlr 90-; FL A/M Presdntl Schlr 90-; Bsn Admin; Corp Law.

**JENKINS, TIVA D,** Va St Univ, Petersburg, VA; SO; BA; Intl Stu Clb Sec; Samuel Moak Schlrshp; Mrktg Mgmt.

**JENKINS, TRACY L,** Germanna Comm Coll, Locust Grove, VA; SO; BA; :Bed; Math; Ed.**

**JENKINS, TRAVIS S,** Univ Of Sc At Columbia, Columbia, SC; FR; MBS; Accntg; Bus.

**JENKINS, TREVA G,** Spartanburg Methodist Coll, Spartanburg, SC; FR; SG 90-; Crmnl Jstc Clb 90-; Hstry Clb 90-; Phi Theta Kappa 90-; Psi Beta 90-; Brd Trustee 90-; Outstdng Mnrty Comm Clg Grad 90-; Engl; Law.

**JENKINS, TRICIA L,** Kent St Univ Stark Cmps, North Canton, OH; FR; BFA; Centre Fash Brd 88-; Ballet Co 84-; Dance; Choreographer.

**JENKINS, TYRA D,** Johnson C Smith Univ, Charlotte, NC; FR; R W Johnson Spiritual Choir 90-; Stdnt Chrstn Assn; Shaki Models; Sec Dorms Hall Cncl; Alpha Lambda Delta; Engl; Mass Cmnctns.

**JENKINS, VANESSA M,** Queens Coll, Charlotte, NC; SO; BA; SBA Treas; NAA Sec And Treas 90-; Gspl Chr Treas; Alpha Kappa Alpha; Hbtt Fr Hmnty; OASIS 89-; Ernst & Young Acctng; Adtng Intrn; IM Bwlng 90-; Acctng; CPA.

**JENKINS, WILLIAM K,** Belmont Coll, Nashville, TN; JR; Bsbl; Assoc Aquinas Jr Coll 88-89; Exec Sci; Athltc Trnr.

**JENKS, RUTH E,** Toccoa Falls Coll, Toccoa Falls, GA; SR; BS; Atlnta St Min Ldr 89; ONU Wmns Sngng Grp 86-88; Cmps Hostess TFC 89-90; Chrtsn Cmp Sr Cnslr 89 Hskppr 90; Bible & Theology Schlrshp Nom; Cum Laude; Vlybl Ststcn 88-89; Cnslng.

**JENNE, BETTY J,** Nova Univ, Ft Lauderdale, FL; GD; MBA; BS Cntrl Washington Un 90; Bus Admn; Prsnl Mgmt.

**JENNINGS, ABIGAIL M,** Univ Of Nc At Charlotte, Charlotte, NC; BCA; Prnt/Drwng Soc 89-; Creatv Arts Lgue 89-90; Chnclrs Lst 87-90; Vsl Arts; Artst.

**JENNINGS, ALICIA M,** Howard Univ, Washington, DC; JR; BS; Howard Univ Rsdnc Hll Chr; Amrcn Chmcl Scty; Stdnt Afflts; Gldn Key; Beta Kappa Chi; All Amrcn Coll Schlr Awrd; Ford Motor Co Intern; IM Bwlng Lg Tm Capt 89-90; Chmstry; Med.**

**JENNINGS, ALMA L,** Al St Univ, Montgomery, AL; SO; BS; Phi Eta Sigma 90-; Amer Mktg Assoc Stdnt Clb; Delta Mu Delta; Cmptr Info Systms; Systm Anlyst.

**JENNINGS, BRANDIE J,** Univ Of Nc At Greensboro, Greensboro, NC; SR; Elem Ed; Tch.

**JENNINGS, BRYAN E,** Univ Of Sc At Columbia, Columbia, SC; SR; BS; Soc Undrwrtr Wrld 89; Delta Upsilon 86-89; IMS 86-89; Marine Sci; Envrnmntl Chemist.

**JENNINGS, CAROL S,** Univ Of Sc At Columbia, Columbia, SC; SR; BA; Psychlgy Clb 89-; Nwspr Edtr 73-74; Assc Wrtng Pgms 90-; Amer Psychlgcl Assc 90-; Sgm Tau Dlt 89-; Omcrn Dlt Kappa; Nancy Eller Mowry Acad Schlrhsp 90-; Poetry Awrd; PTO Pres 88-89; Ptry Mag Asstnt Ed 89-; Engl/Psychlgy; Educ/Mntl Hlth Svc.

**JENNINGS, JAMIE E,** Patrick Henry Comm Coll, Martinsville, VA; SO; Phi Theta Kappa 89-; Bus; CPA.

**JENNINGS, JAMIE L,** Univ Of Cincinnati, Cincinnati, OH; SR; BED; Kappa Delta Pi 89-; Elem Educ Sclgy; Tchr.

**JENNINGS, JOANNE,** Christopher Newport Coll, Newport News, VA; JR; AA Lib Arts 89; Poli Sci; Tch Elem Schl.

**JENNINGS, JOHN J,** Southern Coll Of Tech, Marietta, GA; SR; BS; Arbour Trace Hmeowners Assoc Treas 90-; IEEE 89-; Sigma Phi Epsilon 81-83; US Navy Nucl Plant Oper 83-89; Elctrcl Engr; Nucl Engr.

**JENNINGS, JONATHAN S,** Univ Of Miami, Coral Gables, FL; GD; BBA; Otdr Rcrtn Clb; Hnr Assn; Beta Gamma Sigma 89-; Phi Kappa Phi 89-; Phi Eta Sigma 87-; Alpha Lambda Delta 87-; Gnrl Unvrsty Hnrs 87-; Prsdnt Lst; Summa Cum Laude Candidate; USCG Cptn 89-; Certf Sea Schl Cptns Inst 89; Gnrl Bsns; Entrprnr Invstr.

**JENNINGS, JOSEPH J,** S U N Y Coll Of A & T Morrisvl, Morrisville, NY; SO; Rsdntl Asst 90-; All Rgn 90; AS; Phys Educ Tchr.

**JENNINGS, KEELAN B,** Morehouse Coll, Atlanta, GA; FR; BA; Endeavour Space Club Chrmn/Spc Ed Comm; Math Club; Mentoring Progrm 90-; Fredrick Douglass Tutorial Progrm; Ronald E Mc Nair Schlr 90-; Math/Elec Engr.

**JENNINGS, LAURA M,** Fayetteville St Univ, Fayetteville, NC; JR; BS; Geo Physics; Envrnmntl Rsrch.

**JENNINGS, MELISSA J,** Southern Coll Of Tech, Marietta, GA; JR; BA; Atlanta Gas Lght Co-Op 90-; Deans Lst 89-; Elect Eng Tchnlgy; Eng.

**JENNINGS, MICHAEL D,** Bristol Univ, Bristol, TN; GD; MBA; Dsgn Eng 87-; BSTE Univ Tenn 87; Exe Mngmnt; Eng Mngmnt.

**JENNINGS, PASCHAL S,** Univ Of Tn At Knoxville, Knoxville, TN; FR; Alpha Lambda Delta 90-; Math.

**JENNINGS, PATRICE M,** Norfolk St Univ, Norfolk, VA; SR; BA; ARK Prdctns Pres 87-; Galvus Perf Arts Grp Sec 86-87; Chr 87-; Radio Pgm Dir 90-; Radio Ancr 88-; Alpha Epsln Rho VP 90-; Fmly Chnl Cable Ntwrk Tech 90-; Intrnshp Dir/Video Tape Oper; Msc/Mass Cmncnts; Brdcstng/Cmpsng.

**JENNINGS, PAULA,** Voorhees Coll, Denmark, SC; GD; BS; Soc Sci Clb 90-; Drama Clb 88-89; Phi Beta Sigma Aux 88-; Cert Rcgntn SC Dept Soc Servs 90; Pres List 90; Deans List 88-90; Crmnl Justice; Soc Wrkr.

**JENNINGS, RICHARD H,** Univ Of Nc At Charlotte, Charlotte, NC; SR; MA; Pi Kappa Phi 88-; Park Rec Intern 90; Geography; Urban Planning.

**JENNINGS, RICHARD S,** Marshall University, Huntington, WV; SR; BA; Rugby Clb 89-; Financial Mgmt Assn 89-; Intrn Financl Cnsltnt 89-90; Financl Cnsltnt.

**JENNINGS, RICHARD T,** Northern Ky Univ, Highland Hts, KY; SR; BEDBA; Sierra Clb; River Plt 77-88; Engl Lit/Educ; Tch H Schl.

**JENNINGS, RODNEY D,** Norfolk St Univ, Norfolk, VA; JR; BA; SNTA Treas; Hon Rl Soc 89-; Kappa Alpha Psi; Randallstown Sr High Ftbl Tm 85-86; Cert RETS 88; Comp Engr.

**JENNINGS, SCOTT S,** Pace Univ At Pleasantville, Pleasantville, NY; FR; BBA; Rd Stn 90; Phi Eta Sigma; Alpha Phi Delta Histrn 90-; Deans Lst; Vllybll; Acctg; CPA.

**JENNINGS, STEPHEN A,** Johnson St Coll, Johnson, VT; FR; BA; Ims; Hist/Soclgy.

**JENNINGS, TONIA L,** Al A & M Univ, Normal, AL; SO; BS; Fin; Bus Admnstrtr.

**JENNINGS, TRACEY L,** Norfolk St Univ, Norfolk, VA; FR; BS; Pre Med Clb 90-; Spartan Alphsa Kappa Tau; Med Acdmc Advncmnt; Biology; Medicine.

**JENNINGS, WILLIAM RAY,** Old Dominion Univ, Norfolk, VA; BSET; Shpgldng Appren Schl Plnt Engbr NNS 75-; AAS Thomas Nelson Comm Clg 84; Apprntshp Shpbldng 75; Tech Oper; Plnt Engtr.

**JENSEN, BARBARA A,** Daytona Beach Comm Coll, Daytona Beach, FL; FR; AS; Pres Lst; Graphic Art Tech; Profl Illus.

**JENSEN, BERIT J,** Georgian Court Coll, Lakewood, NJ; SR; BED; Coun Excptnl Chlrn Sec 90-; Sibling Supp Grp; Dn Schlr 89-90; Peer Tutor Crit Thnkng Grnt; Spec Educ; Tchng.

**JENSEN, FINN OSCAR,** Le Moyne Coll, Syracuse, NY; JR; BS; Delta Mu Delta; Wmns Trnsprtn Clb Schlstc; UNYSCSA Acdmc Tm; Vrsty Swmmng Tm Cptn 90-; Bsns Admnstrtn Mrktng Op Mgmt.

**JENSEN, JENNIFER L,** Bowling Green St Univ At Huron, Huron, OH; JR; BLS; AA Lorain Cnty Comm Coll 90; Cmptr Prgrmng.

**JENSEN, KRISTIN NELDA,** Univ Of Nc At Greensboro, Greensboro, NC; FR; BS; Alpha Lamda Delta; Alpha Delta Pi; Chld Dvlpmnt; Chld Psychlgy.

**JENSEN, KRISTINA L,** Life Coll, Marietta, GA; FR; DC; Gnstd Clb; Mtn Plptn Clb; FA Clb; Alpha Zeta 87-, DB Univ FL 87; Chrprtc.

**JENSEN, MICHELLE L,** Georgetown Univ, Washington, DC; SO; BSBA; Georgetown Univ Womens Ctr Counselor 90-; Georgetown Univ Stdnt Federal Credit Union Accountant 90-; DC Schools Project Tutor 89-90; Acctg/Fine Arts Theatre; Criminal Law.

**JENSEN, REGAN E,** Univ Of Rochester, Rochester, NY; JR; BA; Phi Sigma Sigma 89-; Swm Tm; Engl Lit; Tchg.

**JENSEN JR, RONALD R,** Univ Of New Haven, West Haven, CT; JR; BS; Fire Science Clb 89-; RA 90-91; Cngrsnl Fire Srvcs Inst Intrn; Roosevelt Fire Dpt 85-; Arson Invstgtn Crmnl Justice; Fdrl St Lvl Inv.

**JENSEN, WENDY D,** Fl St Univ, Tallahassee, FL; SO; BA; Pre Law Soc; Tau Beta Sigma Treas 90-; Intrnshp At Atate Attrnys Ofc Sanford FL; Crmnlgy/Engl; Law/Attnd Law Sch.

**JENT, BRENDA K,** Alice Lloyd Coll, Pippa Passes, KY; SR; BA; Sr Wkr Stdy Awrd Wrkhd 90-; Presby Chrch; Estr Sls; Educ; Tch.

**JENTES, JILL E,** Oh St Univ, Columbus, OH; JR; BA; Alum Cncl 88-; Mtn Hnry Sec Elect; Office Asst 90-; Nat Rsrcs; Law.

**JEONG, KELLY C,** Univ Of Miami, Coral Gables, FL; FR; BA; Intrvarsity; Bio; Medcn.

**JERALD, ALLISON B,** Univ Of Fl, Gainesville, FL; SR; Art League Treas 87-89; Art Intern.

**JERBASI, CHRISTINE N,** Univ Of Sc At Columbia, Columbia, SC; JR; BA; Chester Ltl Leag 83-; Bus Mgmt; Real Estate.

**JEREMIE, DANIELLE,** Bunker Hill Comm Coll, Boston, MA; FR; BS; Lvng Wll 88-; Mbr Hygntre 87-; Tai-Chi Grp 89; Mbr Zen Soc 90-; WGBH Educ Fndtn 90-; Trustees Of Reserv 90-; Amer Natl Hygn Soc 90-; Spec Recog ABI 90; 2nd Pr Tbl Tnns Comp 88; Bst Crng Prsn L'arche De Jn Vnr 87; Acctg; Acctg/Natrpthc Med.

**JERKINS, JENNIFER K,** Troy St Univ At Troy, Troy, AL; FR; BS; Bsebl Trojan Hostess 90-; Campus Outreach; Alpha Lambda Delta 90-; Gamma Beta Phi; Phi Eta Sigma; Pres/Deans Lst 90-; Elem Edn.

**JERKO, SUSAN R,** Duquesne Univ, Pittsburgh, PA; SO; BSN; Stdnt Nrs Assn PA; Wtrss 87-; Nrsng; Mdwf.

**JERLES, CINDY L,** Converse Coll, Spartanburg, SC; JR; BA; Stdnt Christn Assoc Pres 88-; Art Clb/Yrbk Staff 88-; Cres Stdnt Adm Brd 89-; Alpha Lambda Delta Treas 89-90; Mortar Brd; Deans Lst; Art Educ; Tchr.

**JERNIGAN, CARISA C,** Univ Of Sc At Columbia, Columbia, SC; FR; BA; Elem Educ.

**JERNIGAN, GRACE E,** Auburn Univ At Auburn, Auburn, AL; GD; Erly Chldhd Ed Assn 90-; Phi Kappa Phi 90-; Pi Lambda Theta 90-; Mrtr Brd 90-; Smmrvlle Bapt Chr Clb Grds Dir 88-; St Mrk Free Wll Bapt Chrch Chldrns Chrch Ast Dir; Suma Cum Laude 90; Intrnshp Shrwd Elem AL 90; Univ Dns Lst 90; BED 90; Elry Chldhd Educ; Tchng K-3.

**JERNIGAN, JANET M,** Commonwealth Coll, Virginia Beach, VA; SO; AAS; Cmptr Clb Pres V Pres; Alpha Beta Gamma; Vybl; Emplee Bnkng Firm; Cmptr Lang; Cmptr.

**JERNIGAN, RICHARD CRAIG,** Fayetteville St Univ, Fayetteville, NC; JR; Kappa Delta Pi 89-; Art Clb; Hstry Clb; Rabbi Of Beth David Congregation; Alpha Kappa Mu 89-; Chnclrs Lst 89-; Spec Acad Awd; Cumberland Cnty Aids Tsk Frc; Natl Gay Tsk Frc; Gay Spkrs Gld; Senate Vote Crdntr Dem Prty; Chr; Art; Tchr.

**JEROLMON, LINNEA H,** Central Fl Comm Coll, Ocala, FL; JR; BE; Envrmntl Sci; Indstrl Cmplnc.

**JEROSKI, CARA A,** Saint Vincents Coll & Seminary, Latrobe, PA; FR; BA; In-Tch Clb; Tour Gud; Nwspr Advrtsng; Sprts Frndshp Day; Chrch Choir; Math; Tchr/Prfsr.

**JEROSZKO, ADRIENNE L,** Siena Coll, Loudonville, NY; FR; BA; Natl Soc Pub Acctnts; Acctg; CPA.

**JERRETT, TAMMY L,** Gallaudet Univ, Washington, DC; FR; Glldt Dnc Cmpny; Art; Bus Fshn Dsgns.

**JERRNIGAN, PATRICIA A,** Univ Of Montevallo, Montevallo, AL; JR; BA; Campus Cvtn Brd Drctrs; SGA Chpln; Alpha Lambda Delta 90-; Sigma Slpha Pi; Chi Omega Class Sprt 90-; Spch Pthlgy; Spch Thrpst/Clncn.

**JERRY BANDAN, SHARON E,** Lincoln Univ, Lincoln Univ, PA; SR; BA; Stdnt Ldr Ntwrk Assoc Scrtry 87-89; Pi Sigma Alpha VP 89; Alpha Mu Gamma 89; Alpha Chi; Delta Sigma Theta; Pblc Affrs; Pol Sci; Corp Law.

**JERZAK, PAGE A,** Univ Of Nc At Asheville, Asheville, NC; JR; BA; URPAC Undrgrad; Rsrch Prog Advsry Cncl; Jrnl Of Undrgrad Rsrch Co-Ed 90; UNCA Orient Ldr 8; Psi Chi Pres; Undrgrad Rsrch Fllwshp 88; Intrnshp At Jvnle Evltn Ctr 90; Intrnshp At Applchn Hall Pri Psych Hosp 89; Psych; PHD.

**JESCHELNIG, VIRGINIA E,** Kent St Univ Kent Cmps, Kent, OH; GD; Summa Cum Laude 74; Ohio Lib Assn 89-; Librarian Publ Lib 80-; Book Reviewer 89-; BA Ursuline Coll 74; MLS Kent State Univ 90.

**JESIONOWSKI, DOREEN M,** Univ Of New England, Biddeford, ME; FR; BA; Orth/Sprts Phys Thrpy 88-90; VNA Hmcre Hosp; Phys Thrpy Asst; AS Phys Thrpy Jr Clg 87-; Physical Thrpy.

**JESIONOWSKI, GARY A,** Univ Of Pittsburgh, Pittsburgh, PA; FR; BS; Math; Chem Engr.

**JESKE, ANNETTE C,** Alfred Univ, Alfred, NY; SR; BS; Natl Assoc Acctnts V P 89-; Natl Career Wmns Assoc 89-90; Income Tax Asst Pgm Vol; Pacioli Soc 89-; Alpha Iota Delta Pres 90-; Delta Mu Delta 90-; Adopt-A-Youth Pgm 89-; 1st Fed Bk Rochester NY Intern 90; Iota Nu Beta Schlrshp; Acctg; Publ Acctg.

**JESSAMY, DAVIAN S,** Marywood Coll, Scranton, PA; SO; BSC; Wght Lftng Clb Tres; Mltcltrl Clb 89-; Peer Ttr 89-; Mthmtcs; Sftwr Engnrng.**

**JESSE, DAVID A,** Bethel Coll, Mckenzie, TN; JR; BS; Math Clb Pres 89-; Psychlgy Clb 89-; Vrsty Bsktbll 88-; !gamma Beta Phi 89-; Phi Delta Sigma 89-; (AIA Natl Schlr Athlt 90-; Math.

**JESSER, NICOLE G,** Longwood Coll, Farmville, VA; JR; BS; Lngwd Ambsdrs 89-; Pr Hlprs 89-; GEIST; Ordr Omega; Alpha Delta Mu; Sigma Kappa Pnhlnc Dlgte 89-; Sprt Ldr 89; IM Indr Scr 89; Soc Wrk; Grdt Schl/Wrk Yth.

**JESSUP, JENNIFER L,** Univ Of Nc At Charlotte, Charlotte, NC; JR; BS; Allied Health Club 89; Bio Hnrs Pgm; Bio; Pharmacy.

**JESSUP, JUAQUIN F,** Capitol Coll, Laurel, MD; SR; BSET; Sr Elec Tech; AAET Prince Geo Comm Clg 81; Elec Engr Tech; RD.

**JESTER, CINDY L,** Wilmington Coll, New Castle, DE; SO; BSN; Amer Nphrlgy Nrs Asc; Nat Kdny Fdn; Amer/St Nrsg Asc; Stf Nrs; AA Wesley Clg 80; Nrsng.

**JESWALD JR, PATRICK J,** S U N Y At Buffalo, Buffalo, NY; JR; Acctg Assn 90-; Dns Lst 90; Beta Alpha Psi 90-; Acctg.

**JETER, ALISHA D,** Blue Mountain Coll, Blue Mountain, MS; JR; Soc Sci Pres 88-; Euzelian 88-; Spanish Awd 88-89; French Awd 90-; Pres Lst 89-; Soc Sci.

**JETER, BETH K,** Jackson St Univ, Jackson, MS; SR; BA; FLB Amer Sec; AAHPERD; Clgte Civitan; Sfbl; Vol Coach Cmunty Chldrn Sprts; Prod Asst/Dir; AA Holmes Cmuty Clg 72; Phys Educ; Doc Sprts Med.

**JETER, CHARLES E,** Univ Of Tn At Martin, Martin, TN; SR; Peer Enablng Prog VP 87-90; Undrgrad Alumni Cncl 89-90; Chrldr Co Capt 86-88; Kappa Alpha Order; Intrnshp Holiday Inn Wrldwde Ftnss Spec 90; Phys Educ; Yth Mnstry.

**JETER, TAMARA L,** Univ Of Akron, Akron, OH; SR; BSBA; Gldn Ky 89-; Mu Kappa Tau; Dns Lst 88-; Mrktng; MBA Mgmt.

**JETT, SHELIA L,** John C Calhoun St Comm Coll, Decatur, AL; SO; BS; Pres Ldrshp Schlrshp; Bsktbl 89-; AS; Hlth/Phy Ed/Blgy; Coach/Tch.**

**JETT, WILLIAM S,** Walker Coll, Jasper, AL; SO; BSEE; Phi Theta Kappa Pres 90-; Overall Highest GPA In Math; Best In Computer Sicence; Elec Engrng.

**JETTE, STEVEN M,** Ri Coll, Providence, RI; FR; BA; Stdnt Govt 90-; Acctg Assoc 90-; Dorm Stdnt Govt Treas 90-; Golf Clb V P; Soccer 90-; Acctg.

**JETTER, PATRICIA,** Univ Of Pr At Mayaguez, Mayaguez, PR; SR; BSBA; Acdmc Stdnt Sntr 89-; Stdnt Cncl 89-; Natl Assn Accnts VP 88-; Model UN Head Delegate 90-; Phi Kappa Phi 90-; Mu Alpha Phi Chrtbl Com Pres 87-; Am Cancer Soc Vol 87-90; Hon Roll Clg Bus Admnstrtn 88-; Hon Schlrshp 89-; Acctg; Pblc Acctg/Law.

**JETTON, MELISSA R,** Univ Of West Fl, Pensacola, FL; SR; BA; Stdnt Cncl Excptnl Chldrn Pltcl Actn Ntwrk Rep; AA Pensacola Jr Coll 89; Spec Ed-Mntl Rtrdtn; Spec Ed Tchr.

**JETTON, ROBERT H,** Univ Of Tn At Martin, Martin, TN; JR; BA; Older Stdnts Assoc Chrprsn 90-; UMC Mnstr; Soc Work/Sociology; Ministry.

**JEU, FAYE P,** Memphis St Univ, Memphis, TN; SR; BSN; Amer Assoc Neurlgcl Nrs; RN 82; Asst Nrs Mgr Neuro Trauma ICU Meth Hosp 88-; Dipl Meth Hosp Sch Nrsg 82; Nrsg.

**JEVARAJ, DAVID S,** Liberty Univ, Lynchburg, VA; JR; BSC; Liberty Prsn Mnstry 90-; Dip New Tribes Bible Inst 85-87; Dip Brtsh Careers Trng Coll 83; Cnslng; Overseas Tchr/Cnslr.

**JEWAN, CHETAN I,** Fl St Univ, Tallahassee, FL; JR; Elctrcl Engnrng.

**JEWELL, EDWARD A,** Ky St Univ, Frankfort, KY; FR; Bahai Clb Pres 90-; Hlth Clb 90-; Karate Clb 90-; Kentucky Colonels Colonel 85-; Red Crss; Bahai Fth Chrmn; 4h Adlt Cnslr 90-; Ruritan Clb; Kentucky Hed Injry; Acdmc Achvmnt Divsn Mthmtcs Sc; Cert Awrd Ltstndng Achvmnt Stdnt Sppt; Blgy/Psychgy; Med.

**JEWELL, ELONA Y,** Ky St Univ, Frankfort, KY; SR; BA; NAACP 87-89; Chrldrs Mss Chrldr 87-88; Chld Dvlpmnt/Fmly Rltns; Mrrge/Fmly Cnslg.

**JEWETT, AUBREY W,** Univ Of North Fl, Jacksonville, FL; JR; BA; Pres Envys; Phi Theta Kappa Pres 89-; Gldn Key; Phi Kappa Phi; Intrn Fl St Rep Joe Arnall; Intrn Terry Parker HS 90-; Intrn Fletcher Jr Hi; AA; Scndry Educ.

**JEWETT, DAWN M,** Colby Sawyer Coll, New London, NH; FR; BA; Yrbk 90-; Toys Tots 90-; Habitat Humanity 90-; IMS 90-; Chld Study/Psych; Tch/Psych.

**JEWETT, MEREDITH A,** Marywood Coll, Scranton, PA; SO; BS; Tchr Of Tmrrw Clb 89-90; Smmr Ornttn Chrprsn 90-; Vol Action 90-; Elem Educ; Tchng.

**JEWETT V, SHERMAN S,** Erie Comm Coll South Cmps, Orchard Park, NY; SO; BA; Hon Soc Actvts Coord 89-; Hstry; Law.

**JHANGIANI, SUNIL M,** City Univ Of Ny La Guard Coll, Long Island Cty, NY; GD; Phi Theta Kappa 89-; Bus; Whlsl Firm.

**JHEE, CATHERINE J,** Duke Univ, Durham, NC; FR; BA; Asian Std Asc Sec 90-; Nwspr 90-; Alpha Phi Omega 90-; Engl; Law.

**JIANG, XI,** Glassboro St Coll, Glassboro, NJ; FR; Stdnt Cltr Exchng Brd 90-; Physcs Clb Pres 87-88; Mth Clb 87-88; Chmstry Tchng Asst; Sccr Capt 87-88; Math Comp Sci.

**JIANG, YI,** City Univ Of Ny Baruch Coll, New York, NY; JR; BA; Acctg.

**JIANG, YIN,** Univ Of Tn At Memphis, Memphis, TN; SR; BSN; BM Shanghai Med Univ China 84; Nrsg.

**JIBRAN, JOSEPH A,** Embry Riddle Aeronautical Univ, Daytona Beach, FL; JR; BS; Aerontcl Sci; Aviatn.

**JIGGETTS, ALEXANDER H,** Coppin St Coll, Baltimore, MD; SR; BS; Mgmt Sci; Pblctn Dsgns.

**JILES, SCHERRILL D,** Concordia Coll, Selma, AL; SO; AA; Boy Scts Of Amer Clb Den Ldr/Coach 88-; Asst Super Chrch Schl 72-; Tchr Of Chrch Schl Primry 75-; Elem Ed; AA; Elem Ed.

**JIMENEZ CARDONA, MADELINE,** Inter Amer Univ Pr Hato Rey, Hato Rey, PR; Stu Assn Psychlgy PR 90-; Psych Law.

**JIMENEZ MARQUEZ, NELSON,** Univ Del Turabo, Gurabo, PR; GD; BA; E Commodore Users Club Fdr 86-88; ASECO Vocal 90-F Cuadro Hnr Acad 89-91; B; Computer Infor Syst; Prog.

**JIMENEZ MARTINEZ, MARISOL,** Univ Politecnica De Pr, Hato Rey, PR; SR; BS; Inst Ind Eng 89-; Indstrl Eng; Eng.

**JIMENEZ, CARLOS,** Univ Of Pr At Rio Piedras, Rio Piedras, PR; SR; BA; Econ Stdnts Assn 89-; Brazln Amer Cltrl Ctr 89-; Chrl Grp 89-; Interdomntl Chr 90; P R Econ Assn; Goldn Key 90; Civl Air Patrl Cadt Offcr 85-89; Mst Otstndg Stdnt Awd; Harry S Trumn Schlrshp 89; Stdnt Intrn Cty W Palm Bch Fla 90; Econ; Intl Busn.**

**JIMENEZ, DANIEL,** City Univ Of Ny Hostos Coll, Bronx, NY; GD; BS; Grvnc Comm Chrprsn 90; Dsclpnry Comm 90; Tlnt Rstr 90; Htl Emply 88-; AA; Physcns Asstnt; Med.

**JIMENEZ, EDWIN,** Univ Politecnica De Pr, Hato Rey, PR; FR; DPMA 90-; Alfa Kappa Omicron 90-; Hnr Mdl Acdm Advntst Sn Sbstn 88; CROEM Cedrt 90; CROEM Vlybll Tm 89-90; Eng.

**JIMENEZ, FERNANDO,** Fl International Univ, Miami, FL; FR; MBA; Math; Civil/Envrnmntl Eng.

**JIMENEZ, FRANCES,** Va St Univ, Petersburg, VA; FR; BA; Stdnt Natl Tech Assn; Summer Intrn Riverfront Recapture Inc; Ele Educ; Ele Tchr.

**JIMENEZ, FRANK P,** Univ Of Al At Birmingham, Birmingham, AL; SR; BS; Phi Theta Kappa 83; Intrntnl Stdnt Yr 83; US Army Vtrn 86-88; Army Achvmnt Mdls 87-88; Rsrch Engnrng Schl; Emplyd Allcl Engnrng Frm; AS Jfrsn St Jr Clg 83; Cvl Engnrng; Engnrng.

**JIMENEZ, GABRIELA,** Western New England Coll, Springfield, MA; FR; BA; United/Mtly Equ Clb; Pre Law Scty; Govt; Law.

**JIMENEZ, HECTOR R,** Univ Politecnica De Pr, Hato Rey, PR; FR.

**JIMENEZ, JACQUELINE,** Wagner Coll, Staten Island, NY; SR; Biology; Physcian Asst.

**JIMENEZ, JOSE L,** Bayamon Tech Univ Coll, Bayamon, PR; GD; MBA; Army ROTC 88-90; US Army Assn 89-; BBA 90; Acctg; Fncl Cnslng.

**JIMENEZ, JOSEPH ALBERTO,** Miami Dade Comm Coll, Miami, FL; SO; BA; Highst Hnrs; Cic K 89; Otstdng Achvmnt; Grad Highst Hnrs 91; Phlsphy/Soclgy/Anthrbio; Tchr/Doctr.

**JIMENEZ, JUDY L-MORIN,** Tri County Tech Coll, Pendleton, SC; SR; AS; Schlrshp; Bus/Acctng.

**JIMENEZ, NILDA M,** Univ Of Pr At Rio Piedras, Rio Piedras, PR; JR; Trck Fld; Biol; Zoologst.

**JIMENEZ, PABLO,** Methodist Coll, Fayetteville, NC; SO; BA; Acting Monarchs Clb; Deans Lst 90-; Soccer; Mass Media Cmnctns; Grad Sch.

**JIMENEZ, PEDRO A,** Fl International Univ, Miami, FL; SR; BA; Fncl Mgmt Asc Edtr 90-; Extra Curr Serv Awd 90-; Fnce; Law.

**JIMENEZ, SANDRA P,** Miami Dade Comm Coll, Miami, FL; SO; Schlrshp; YMCA 87-89; Natl Assn Of Soc Workers 88; Soc Worker 87; BA Soc Work Colegio Mayor De Cundinamarca Colombia 87; Soc Work.

**JIMENEZ, SYLVIA ENIT,** Univ Of Pr At Mayaguez, Mayaguez, PR; SO; Assn Anml Sci Dept; Vet Asst; Regnl Chem Comp In Pr; Sci Math Histry; Anml Sci Pre Vet; Vet Med.

**JIMENEZ, VILMA YANIRA,** Univ Of Pr At Rio Piedras, Rio Piedras, PR; SR; Indus/Orgztnl Psych.

**JIMENEZ-CALDERIN, EDGARDO R,** Inter Amer Univ Pr San Juan, Hato Rey, PR; GD; LLM; Amer Bar Assn 88-90; Fed Bar Assn; Colegio De Abogados 90-; BA Uvin PR 86; US Crt Of Appeals Frst Circuit; Suprm Crt PR Lwyr 90-; Fed Dst Crt Dstrct PR; JD Intramer PR 89; Eng/JD; Labor Law.

**JIMERSON, JASON E,** Va Commonwealth Univ, Richmond, VA; SO; BS; Chem.

**JIMERSON, TRACIE D,** Livingston Univ, Livingston, AL; SO; BS; Hstry; Ed.

**JIMISON, JOHN R,** Univ Of North Fl, Jacksonville, FL; SR; BA; AA FL Cmmnty Coll 89; Acctg; Bus Mgmt.

**JINDAL, ASHA R,** Vanderbilt Univ, Nashville, TN; FR; BA; Indian Stdnts Assc Co VP 90-; Nwspr Advrtsng Prdctn 90-; Radio Stn DJ 90-; Cmps Ldrshp Org 90-; Tutor 90-; Crclm Dvrsfctn Com 90-; Asstntshp Med Rsrch; Chem/Philosophy; Medicine.

**JINES, AMY R,** Kent St Univ Kent Cmps, Kent, OH; FR; BA; Habitat/Humnty P R 90-; Prog Stdnt Ntwrk 90-; Amnesty Intnl 90; Engl.

**JIRAU, INOEL,** Temple Univ, Philadelphia, PA; FR; BA; Music; Musician/Violinist.

**JIROUSEK, LORI M,** Univ Of Akron, Akron, OH; JR; BA; Neumann Cath Comm 88-; Frshmn Chorale/Univ Choral Union 88-89; Res Hl Prog Bd 89-90; Lit Gld 89-; Pub Rel Stdnts Of Amer 90-; Hnrs Clb 88-; Alpha Lambda Delta 88-; Phi Eta Sigma 88-; Phi Sigma Alpha 90-; Gldn Key 90; MS Socty Super Cities Walk 90; Engl; Coll Professor.

**JIVAN, DARLA K,** Univ Of Akron, Akron, OH; JR; Dns Lst 89-90; Akron Area Chrstn Frndshp Grp Sec 82-; ACC Yth Chr Pnst 88-90; E G Brkt Schlrshp 90-; Elem Educ.

**JIVIDEN, CARA L,** Univ Of Ky, Lexington, KY; SO; BS; Phi Eta Sigma; Lambda Sigma; Collgns Acad Excell 89-; Inco Allys Intrntl Intrn 90-; Emrgng Ldr Inst 90; Elec Eng Physics; Eng.

**JOBES, CHRISTOPHER A,** Memphis Academy Of The Arts, Memphis, TN; SR; BFA; Alliance Indpndnt Clg Arts New York Studio Prog; Mrytle Bowld Meml European Trvlng Flwshp; Alex Camp Meml Trvlng Flwshp Dmstc; AS Kwantlen Clg 87; Phtgrphy.

**JOE, DANIEL,** City Univ Of Ny Baruch Coll, New York, NY; SR; BBA; Korean Assoc VP 89; Frshmn Smnr Ldr 89; Golden Key 89; Deans Lst 88; Accntng; Law.

**JOERGER, JAMES A,** Elmira Coll, Elmira, NY; SO; BS; Outng Clb 90-; Bus Clb 90-; Res Asst 90-; Orient Ldr 90-; Vars Tnns Tm 89-90; Acctg; CPA.

**JOHANNESEN, JANET L,** S U N Y Coll At Plattsburgh, Plattsburgh, NY; JR; BA; Alpha Delta Theta Marshall; Elem Educ; Tch.**

**JOHANNINGMEIER, JENNIFER E,** Univ Of Southern Ms, Hattiesburg, MS; FR; BS; Stdnt Alumni Assn; Coll Rpblcns; Eagle Cnnctn Rcrtmnt; Lambda Sigma; Gamma Beta Phi; Pi Beta Phi VP Moral Advncmnt Pldg Cls 90-; Htl/Rstrnt/Trsm Mgmt; Htl Mgmt-Trsm Emphs.

**JOHANNIS, SUSAN A,** Newbury Coll, Brookline, MA; SO; ASSOC; Class Repres 88-; Outstndng Student Achiev Awd; Cum Laude; Scheduler Foxbozo Co; Busn Mgt.

**JOHANSEN, BARBARA J,** Anne Arundel Comm Coll, Arnold, MD; SO; AA; Computer Op Cert AACC 90; Buiness & Public Admnstrn; Acctg.

**JOHANSEN, J NETT,** Ny Univ, New York, NY; FR; BA; Psychology.

**JOHANSEN, KAREN S,** Teikyo Post Univ, Waterbury, CT; SO; AS; Occptnl Thrpy.

**JOHANSEN, KRISTEN M,** Alfred Univ, Alfred, NY; JR; BS; Bsn/Mktg.

**JOHANSSON, LARS,** Columbus Coll Of Art & Design, Columbus, OH; FR; BFAA; Graphic Dsgn; Advtsng.

**JOHENNING, LAURA R,** Georgetown Univ, Washington, DC; JR; BA; Stu Govt Cls Comm 89-90; Japan Clb 88-89; Hawaiian Clb 88-89; Buddy Sys Tutr 88-89; Bnk Tlr Crdt Union 90; Stdy Abrd Pro Tokoyo Japan; Finance; Jpns Asian Stdy.

**JOHN, AMANDA S,** Capital Univ, Columbus, OH; SO; Vrsty Sccr 90.

**JOHN, DEBORAH K,** Tusculum Coll, Greeneville, TN; SR; BA; Alpha Chi Sec/Treas 89-; Bus Admin/Acctng; MBA.

**JOHN, DESIREE C,** Va St Univ, Petersburg, VA; SR; BS; Hotel/Rest Mgmt Clb 88-; Dns Lst 90-; Natl Rest Assoc Santn Cert 90; Intrnshp Chart Hse Rest Dept Of Lbr; Hotel/Rest Mgmt; Hotel Mgmt/Genl Mgr.

**JOHN, SCOTT K,** Comm Coll Algny Co Algny Cmps, Pittsburgh, PA; SO; AS; Alcohol/Drug Care Vol 88-; Scl Wrk Tech Alcohol/Drug Cnslg; Sci/Engl; Alcohol/Drug Cnslr.

**JOHN, TIFFANY A,** Kent St Univ Kent Cmps, Kent, OH; FR; BS; House Cncl VP 90-; Soccer Clb 90-; Amb; Alpha Lambda Delta 90-.

**JOHNIKIN, MARITES MARIE,** Univ Of Sc At Columbia, Columbia, SC; SO; BA; Karate Clb 90; Sci; Admn.

**JOHNS, GREGORY C,** Fl St Univ, Tallahassee, FL; JR; BA; Mrchng Chfs Asst Drm Mjr 88-; Goldn Key 89-; Phi Eta Sigma 88-89; Phi Kappa Phi; Goldn Key Ldrshp Hon 89-; Natl Res Hall Hon 89-; Seminole Awrd; IM Ftbl/Soccr 88-90; Mortr Brd Cncl Of Hon; Psychlgy; Bus.**

**JOHNS, JENNIFER A,** Longwood Coll, Farmville, VA; SO; BA; Hall Cncl Sec 90-; Stdnt Educ Assn 90-; Concert Choir 89-; Kappa Delta Pi Sec; Alpha Chi Omega Sec 90-; Sprague Awd 90; Elem Tchr.

**JOHNS, JENNIFER E,** Oh Univ, Athens, OH; SO; BFA; STYLE; Phi Mu Delta Delta Art Chm Schlrshp Asst; Art Hist; Prof.

**JOHNS, KATHERINE S,** Georgetown Univ, Washington, DC; FR; BA; IMS 90-; CNG Trnsmsn Intrn; Tns Tm 90-; Acctg; Engr.

**JOHNS, KIMBERLY L,** Comm Coll Algny Co Algny Cmps, Pittsburgh, PA; FR; BA; Crmnl Admn; Law.

**JOHNS, LAURA L,** Coll Of Charleston, Charleston, SC; SR; BA; Pi Sigma Alpha 90-; Figg Amercnsm Schlrshp 88-89; Pol Sci; PhD.

**JOHNS, MARK L,** Univ Of Al At Birmingham, Birmingham, AL; JR; BS; Most Outstanding Criminal Justice Stdnt Jefferson State Cmnty Clge 90-; Criminal Just; Fed Prob & Parole Fed Law Enf.

**JOHNS, MARNEE L,** The Boston Conservatory, Boston, MA; SR; BM; Peer Support Aide; Sigma Alpha Iota; BM; Music/Opera; Perf.

**JOHNS, MELANIE D,** Wv Univ, Morgantown, WV; SR; BS; Acad Stdnts Phrmcy 88-90; Rho Chi Hist 89-91; Phi Kappa Phi 90; Gldn Key 89; Soph Org Chem Awd 88; Clncl Phrmcy.

**JOHNS, REBEKAH N,** Birmingham Southern Coll, Birmingham, AL; FR; BM; Jr Cvtns 90; Stdnt Govt Clss Sec 88; Natl Jr Hnr Scty 87; Natl Sr Hnr Scty 90; Sftbl 90; Fine Arts; Educ.

**JOHNS, SHERRY E,** Mount Aloysius Jr Coll, Cresson, PA; FR; AS; Occuptnl Thrpy Club 90-; Phi Theta Kappa; Girl Scouts Of Amer Talus Rock Cncl Asst Troop Ldr 89-90; Occuptnl Thrpy.

**JOHNS, VANESSA A,** Barry Univ, Miami, FL; SR; BSN; Nat Stdnt Nurses Assoc 89-; Sigma Theta Tau 90-; Presidents Lst; Deans Lst 89; Nursing; RN.

**JOHNSEN, ALLISON M,** City Univ Of Ny Baruch Coll, New York, NY; JR; BBA; Acctg Soc 89-; Golden Key; Baruch Clg Pres Schlrshp 88-; Baruch Clg Endwmnt Fund Provost Schlrshp 90; Acctg; CPA/LAWYER.

**JOHNSEN, JOHANNA,** Saint Josephs Coll New York, Brooklyn, NY; JR; BS; Phi Theta Kappa 88; Pres Awd Dist Schlp 89; Fmly Lit Comm 82-; Rlgs Ed Tchr 82-; Lector 82-; Home Schl Asc 82-; AAS Kngsbrgh Comm Clg 88; Bsn; Educ.

**JOHNSON CALIX, SHARON,** Nova Univ, Ft Lauderdale, FL; GD; MBA; Outstdng Yng Wmn 85; Delta Sigma Theta Chrtr Pres 84-85; Fall Minority Grad Schlrshp 6; B Sc Pemborke State Univ 85; Bus; Mgmnt Cnsltnt.

**JOHNSON, AARON S,** West Liberty St Coll, West Liberty, WV; JR; BS; Alpha Ilappa Psi Pres; Sml Bsns Inst; Usaf Rsrvs Sgt 89-; Usaf Actv Dty 85-89; Aas Comm Coll Of The Ar Frc 89; Bsns/Acctng; Cpa.

**JOHNSON, ABIGAIL,** Alcorn St Univ, Lorman, MS; SO; BA; Gspl Chr Mscn 89-90; Hon Stdnt Hon Pgm Mbr 89-90; Deans List 90; Fashion Mrchndsng; Fash Cnsltn/Crdntrn.

**JOHNSON, ALICIA M,** Converse Coll, Spartanburg, SC; SO; BA; Rsdntl Life Stf Comm Advsr 90-; Alpha Lambda Delta Treas 90-; Delta Omicron Musical Dir 90-; Music/Math; Professor/Performer.

**JOHNSON, ALICIA R,** Hampton Univ, Hampton, VA; SO; BA; Math Clb Sec 89-; Afrcn Stdies Clstrs 90-; Mntrshp Prog 90-; Physics Hon Soc; SEMS 89-; Physcs; Nuclear Physcs.

**JOHNSON, ALISHA L,** Alcorn St Univ, Lorman, MS; SR; BS; Gspl Choir Dir 86-; Alpha Kappa Mu; Delta Sigma Theta Chpln 90-; Chemstry; MD.

**JOHNSON, ALONDREA D,** Al St Univ, Montgomery, AL; SO; BA; Acctg.

**JOHNSON, ANDREA L,** Fl St Univ, Tallahassee, FL; SR; BA; SPJC Dance Repertory 88-89; Phi Theta Kappa 87-89; Golden Key; Tch Intrn; Ele Educ; Tch.

**JOHNSON, ANDREA P,** City Univ Of Ny City Coll, New York, NY; SR; BA; Golden Key 90-; Evans Securities Co Stckbrkr/Order Clrk 80-88; Psych.

**JOHNSON, ANGELA D,** Hampton Univ, Hampton, VA; FR; Sociology.

**JOHNSON, ANNETTE MESHELL,** Hampton Univ, Hampton, VA; FR; BA; ACM 90-; Cmptr Sci; Cmptr Analyst.

**JOHNSON, ANTONIETTE R,** Univ Of Tn At Martin, Martin, TN; FR; BA; Hon Seminar 90-; Bio; Optometry.

**JOHNSON, APRIL M,** Birmingham Southern Coll, Birmingham, AL, SO, BA, Tri Beta Club 90-; Conservancy 90; Float Bnnr Chrmn; Alpha Lambda Delta 90-; Phi Eta Sigma; Kappa Mu Epsilon; Alpha Epsilon Delta; Chi Omega VP; Kids On The Block; Biology; Med.

**JOHNSON, ASHLEY L,** Coll Of Charleston, Charleston, SC; FR; BA; Bsns.

**JOHNSON, AUDRA Y,** Clark Atlanta Univ, Atlanta, GA; SO; BA; Beta Psi Sec; Natl Assoc Of Black Accts 90-; Miss Acctng Clb 90-; Dorm Treas 89-90; Allstate Ins Co; Acad Achvmnt; Acctng.

**JOHNSON, BARBARA A,** Tougaloo Coll, Tougaloo, MS; FR; NAACP Math Cmptr Sci Clb 90-; Pol Sci; Law.

**JOHNSON, BASIL D,** Univ Of The Virgin Islands, St Thomas, VI; SR; BA; Prsdnts Clb 90; Ftr Bsns Ldrs America 89-; Caribbean Soc 90-; Cricket Tm Cptn; Certf St Kitts Nevis Tchr Trnng Clb 83; Bsns Admnstrtn; Corp Law.

**JOHNSON, BEVERLY H,** Western Piedmont Comm Coll, Morganton, NC; SO; ADN; Natl Stdnt Nrs Assoc; Phi Theta Kappa; AS 80; Nrsg.

**JOHNSON, BRENDA J,** Old Dominion Univ, Norfolk, VA; JR; BA; DPMA VP 89-; Alpha Chi 90-; Beta Gamma Sigma 90-; Bus Awd; AS Thomas Nelson Comm Coll 89; MIS; CIS.

**JOHNSON, BRENDA KAY,** Univ Of Al At Birmingham, Birmingham, AL; SR; BS; Kappa Delta Pi 90-; Phi Theta Kappa 87-89; Gldn Key 90-; Phi Kappa Phi; B'ham E Chrstn Wmns Clb 89-; Dns Schlrshp 90-; Elosie Bradshaw Crk Indn Schlshp 90-; Poarch Bnd Crk Indns Schlrshp 90-; Bptst Church 89-; LPN; Elem Ed; MS.

**JOHNSON, BRENDA M,** Univ Of Cincinnati, Cincinnati, OH; SR; BS; Gldn Key 89-; ASCD; Reading Cncl 90-; Kappa Delta Pi; Alpha Phi 79-; Cncr Soc 88-; Msclr Dystrophy Vol 88-; Hnrs Schlrshp 90-; Alumni Assn Schlrshp 90-; Deans Lst; Erly Chldhd Edctn; Primary Tchr.

**JOHNSON, BRETT A,** Univ Of Southern Ms, Hattiesburg, MS; SR; BED; Gulf Coast Comm Clg Nwspr Editor 88-; Engl; Law.

**JOHNSON, BRIAN A,** Savannah Coll Of Art & Design, Savannah, GA; JR; BA; Pntg Clb 89-; Paintng.

**JOHNSON, BRIAN K,** Univ Of Md At Eastern Shore, Princess Anne, MD; SR; BS; Crim Just Soc 89-90; Crim Just; FBI.**

**JOHNSON, BRIDGET L,** Fl A & M Univ, Tallahassee, FL; FR; BS; Phys Thrpy; Reg Phys Thrpst.

**JOHNSON, BRUCE A,** Univ Of Al At Birmingham, Birmingham, AL; JR; BED; Bnd 85-86; Crmnl Jst; Fed Law Enfrcmnt.

**JOHNSON, BRYAN S,** Univ Of Southern Ms, Hattiesburg, MS; SR; Spts Med Clb VP; Stdnt Trnr; Hlth/PE.

**JOHNSON, BRYCE A,** Abraham Baldwin Agri Coll, Tifton, GA; FR; Phi Theta Kappa 90-; Pol Sci; Law.

**JOHNSON, CANDACE L,** Univ Of Sc At Columbia, Columbia, SC; FR; BA; Nvgtrs 90-; Prsdnts Lst 90; Deans Lst 90; Acctg.

**JOHNSON, CAROLYN P,** Al St Univ, Montgomery, AL; SR; BS; Ntl Assoc Blck Accts 90-; COBA Invstmnt Clb VP 89-; Delta Mu Delta Sec 90-; VITA 90-; Smr Educ Enrchmnt Pro 90; Acctg; CPA.

**JOHNSON, CASSANDRA D,** Al St Univ, Montgomery, AL; FR; BS; AL State Univ Hornet Yrbk Asst Sec Edtr 90-; Acad Schlrshp 90-; Univ Hon Day Convocation Acad Achvmnt; Math/Ecnmcs/Sci; RN Bus Mgmt.

**JOHNSON, CATHRYNE ELIZABETH,** Fisk Univ, Nashville, TN; SR; SGA Bus Mgr 88-90; Natl Hlth Cr Assc 87-90; Hmcmng Comm 86-90; Acad Schlrshp 87-88; Kappa Alpha Psi Swthrt 87-90; Hubbard Hosp Vol 89-90; Pom Pon Squad 87-90; Men Bsktbl Stats 87-90; Blckexec Exch Pgm AT/T Intern 90; BS 90; Bus Mgmt; Mba/Mph.

**JOHNSON, CAZONDRA M,** Longwood Coll, Farmville, VA; JR; BA; Assn Of Blck Stdnts 90-; Ornttn Ldr; Blck Grk Cncl; Alpha Kappa Delta; Alpha Kappa Alpha Sec; Sclgy; Law.

**JOHNSON, CHADWICK L,** Livingston Univ, Livingston, AL; FR; BS; Delta Chi 90-; Comp Sci; Comp Prgrmr.

**JOHNSON, CHARLES SVEN,** Cleveland Inst Of Art, Cleveland, OH; SO; BFA; Cmndr Cleveland Nvl Rsrv Dtchmnt 89-; BS Univ Notre Dame 85; Indstrl Dsgn; Hgh Spd Trnsprtn Dsgn.

**JOHNSON, CHARLOTTE G,** Valdosta St Coll, Valdosta, GA; JR; BSN; Sigma Alpha Chi 90-; Stdnt Nurs Awd 90-; Nurs.**

**JOHNSON, CHERYL A,** Lurleen B Wallace St Jr Coll, Andalusia, AL; FR; AA BA; Math/Pre Law; Lawyer.

**JOHNSON, CHRIS A,** Anson Comm Coll, Ansonville, NC; GD; AAS; Eagle Scout; Bus Cmptr Programming; PC Specialist.

**JOHNSON, CHRISTINE A,** Marywood Coll, Scranton, PA; FR; Cmps Mnstry 90-; 1st Hnrs Dns Lst 90-; Clncl Psychlgy; Chld Psychlgst.

**JOHNSON, CONNIE L,** Mayland Comm Coll, Spruce Pine, NC; SO; BA; AAS 85; Dcsn Sci; Comp.

**JOHNSON, CORLISS A,** Stillman Coll, Tuscaloosa, AL; JR; Stdnt Al Ed Assoc Pres; BA; Elem Ed.

**JOHNSON, CORLISS A,** Fisk Univ, Nashville, TN; SO; BS; Ntl Org Prof Advncmnt Blck Chmsta/Chem Engrs VP 90-; Fisk Mdrn Blck Mass Choir 90-; Delta Sigma Theta; Deans Lst; Mass Inst Tchnlgy Mnrty Smr Rsrch Pro 90; Chem; Rsrch.

**JOHNSON, CORNELIA ANN,** Univ Of Southern Ms, Hattiesburg, MS; GD; MSW; Yth Clb 88-; NASW 90-; CASA 85-87; BS Univ Sthrn MS 90; Scl Wrk; Comm Wrk/Admn.

**JOHNSON, CORY C,** Thomas Nelson Comm Coll, Hampton, VA; FR; AS; Peninsula Amateur Radio Clb Novice; Phi Theta Kappa; SS Tchr 85-; Choir/Hand Bell Choir 85; Kngsml Rsrt/Conf Cntr 88-89; Busch Gradns 90-; Bus Admin; Mgmnt/Corp Bus.

**JOHNSON, CRAIG A,** Univ Of Southern Ms, Hattiesburg, MS; SR; BS; Deans Lst 89-90; Gamma Theta Upsilon 90-; Geography; Cartographer.

**JOHNSON, CRISTAL M,** Univ Of Nc At Greensboro, Greensboro, NC; FR; BA; Schl Human Env Sci Fresh Schlr Acdmc Exc; Crmnl Jstc-Sclgy/Spanish; Lawyer.

**JOHNSON, CURTIS M,** Pensacola Jr Coll, Pensacola, FL; SO; MS; Ntl Assoc Stu Engrs 90-; Ntl Bible Quizzing Assoc 88-; Hnr Soc 89-; Biomed Engr.

**JOHNSON, DALYCE G,** Va Commonwealth Univ, Richmond, VA; JR; BS; Afro-Amer Schlrs 90; Golden Key 90; Madison Temple Meth Chrch 88; AD W Va Inst Of Tech 75; Nrsng; RN.

**JOHNSON, DAMON S,** Fl A & M Univ, Tallahassee, FL; FR; BS; Mchncl Engrng.

**JOHNSON, DANA M,** Western Ky Univ, Bowling Green, KY; SO; BA; Phi Eta Sigma; Comp Info Syst; Oper/Anlyst.

**JOHNSON, DANIEL K,** City Univ Of Ny City Coll, New York, NY; SR; Jazz Clbs; Rock Clbs; BFA; Music; Jzz Perf/Tchng.

**JOHNSON, DARYL K,** Alcorn St Univ, Lorman, MS; SR; BS; Mrchg/Cncrt Bnd; Phi Beta Lambda; Bapt Stu Union; Omega Psi Phi Tres; Kappa Kappa Psi Hstrn; Bus Admin.**

**JOHNSON, DARYL LANCE,** Univ Of Ms Medical Center, Jackson, MS; FR; DMD; Alumni Publctn; Curr Cmtee; Beta Beta Beta 89; Alpha Epsilon Delta 87; Amer Stdnt Dental Assn 90-; Kappa Alpha; C M Gooch Schlrshp 86-; Acad Hon Schlrshp; J Sanders Schlrshp 87; BS 90; Dentistry.

**JOHNSON, DAVID H,** Md Coll Of Art & Design, Silver Spring, MD; FR; AA; Otdr Yoga Orgnztn; Awd Stdnt Show; Sclptr Art.

**JOHNSON, DAVID H,** Catawba Valley Comm Coll, Hickory, NC; FR; AA; Stu Nrs Assn Pres; Stu Affrs Cmmtt 90-; Mrshl 90-; BS Bob Jones Univ 76; Nrsng.

**JOHNSON, DAVID J,** Bellarmine Coll, Louisville, KY; JR; BA; Blgy Clb 90; IM Bsktbl 88-; Blgy; Med.

**JOHNSON, DAVID R,** Abraham Baldwin Agri Coll, Tifton, GA; SO; BA; Crmnl Juste; Law.

**JOHNSON, DEANNA D,** Wv Univ At Parkersburg, Parkersburg, WV; JR; AAS; Bus Admin.

**JOHNSON, DEBORAH,** Memphis St Univ, Memphis, TN; FR; BBA; Blck Schlrs Unlmted 90; Schlrshp Alpha Kappa Alpha 90; Bsnss Fnce; Corp Exctve.

**JOHNSON, DEBORAH A,** Phillips Jr Coll Spartanburg, Spartanburg, SC; FR; MBA; Campus Crusade Christ 90-; Sci.

**JOHNSON, DEBORAH L,** Belmont Coll, Nashville, TN; JR; BS; Psych Club Stdnt Cncl 90-; Soc Work Club 89-; Bapt Stdnt Un Comm 88-90; Crisis Intervention Ctr Vol 90-; Tn St Leg Intern; Mid Tn Mental Hlth Inst Admn Asst; Psych/Soc Work; Community Mental Hlth.

**JOHNSON, DEBORAH L,** Rensselaer Polytechnic Inst, Troy, NY; JR; BA; Yearbook Edtr In Chief; Stdnt Orient Steering Com 90-; Stdnt Orient Advsr 89-; Phi Sigma Sigma 90-; IM Sccr/Bsktbl 88-90; Comp/Systems Engineering; Sftwr Engineering.

**JOHNSON, DEBORAH P,** Fayetteville St Univ, Fayetteville, NC; GD; Kappa Delta Pi 89-90; Cncrnd Ctzns Harnett Cnty Chrprsn; BED; Hstry; Tchng.

**JOHNSON, DELLA E,** Univ Of Sc At Columbia, Columbia, SC; JR; BA; Erly Chldhd Ed; Teaching.

**JOHNSON, DENISE R,** Univ Of Al At Birmingham, Birmingham, AL; FR; Dean Lst 90-.

**JOHNSON, DENISE S,** Catawba Valley Comm Coll, Hickory, NC; JR; AASC; SGA Sntr 90; Gamma Beta Phi; Catawba Cnty Schls Vol 84; Mtn View Schl PTO Treas 87; Dplma Sec Sci Tchncl Clg 73; Cmmrcl Art/Advrtsng Dsgn; Grphc Dsgn.

**JOHNSON, DENNY N,** Al A & M Univ, Normal, AL; SR; BS; ECHOES Ldrshp Org Co-Cmps Spksmn 89-; Mnrts Agri Ntrl Rsrs/Rltd Sci Org Advsry Cncl 87-91; Tstmstrs Intl 90-; Alpha Zeta Sec 88-90; Alpha Phi Alpha Pres; Undrgrad Nrmlt Assn Soc 87-89; Agri Educ/Law; Law.

**JOHNSON, DEREK C,** Univ Of Tn At Martin, Martin, TN; SO; BA; Soc/Anthrplgy Club V P 90-; Poetry Reading; Sigma Tau Delta 90-; Otstndnt Stdnt In Arts Sci 90-; Pblshd Poetry In Campus Mag 90-; Hnrs Seminar 89; Soc; Pblshng.

**JOHNSON, DESMA Z,** Queens Coll, Charlotte, NC; JR; BA; Intntnl Clb; Rsdnt Assist; Chmbr Sngrs; Stdt Dvlpmnt Comm; Stdts Blck Awrnss; Spec Evts Comm VP; Delta Omicron 1st VP 90-; Mortar Board VP; Beta Beta Beta VP 90-; Geor Stegner Msc Schlr; Dana Schlr 89-; Soph/Jr Hnr Soc 90-; Spnsh/Msc; Grad Schl.

**JOHNSON, DEXTER C,** Clark Atlanta Univ, Atlanta, GA; SO; BS; Univ Chmstry Clb 90-; Natl Soc Blck Eng 89-; Cert Excl Math 90-; Chmstry/Chmcl Eng; Chmcl Eng.

**JOHNSON, DIANE E,** Comm Coll Algny Co Algny Cmps, Pittsburgh, PA; SO; ADN; Cert Med Asst Duffs Bsn Inst 85; Sci/Nrsng; RN.

**JOHNSON, DIANE R,** Univ Of West Fl, Pensacola, FL; JR; BA; Alpha Sigma Lambda; AA Bay De Noc Comm Coll 90; Erly Chldhd/Elem Educ; Tchng.

**JOHNSON, DIANNE E,** George Mason Univ, Fairfax, VA; SR; MBA; Deans Lst 86-; ASS Cum Laude; BS; ASS N VA Comm Coll 88; Ed; Tch.

**JOHNSON, DONNELL Z,** Johnson C Smith Univ, Charlotte, NC; JR; BA; Card Clb; IM Bsktbll Capt; Ftbl.

**JOHNSON, DWAYNE B,** Fl St Univ, Tallahassee, FL; SR; Symph Orch 87-90; AA Tallahassee Comm Coll 85-87; Music; Law.

**JOHNSON, DYNEESHA D,** Univ Of Md At Eastern Shore, Princess Anne, MD; JR; Preprofesssional Scty 89-; NAACP 89-; RA 89-; Delta Sigma Theta 90-; Sepums Research Prog 89; Nursing.

**JOHNSON, EARL F,** Memphis St Univ, Memphis, TN; SR; Psy Clb; Psychlgy; Law.

**JOHNSON, EARLINE,** Central St Univ, Wilberforce, OH; SO; Drama Organ Actor 89-; Aerobics 89-; Math; Spec Educ Teacher Handicapped Chldrn.

**JOHNSON, EDDIE J,** Alcorn St Univ, Lorman, MS; JR; BA; Deans Lst; Bus Admin; Fin.

**JOHNSON, EDWARD K,** Hofstra Univ, Hempstead, NY; FR; BA; Humor Mag Stf 90; Comedy Troupe 90-; Psychology; Wrtr.

**JOHNSON, ELATIO J,** Al A & M Univ, Normal, AL; JR; BS; Math Clb 88; Ntl Scty Of Blk Eng 89; Deans Lst 88; Alpha Kappa Alpha 89; Math; Bsnss.

**JOHNSON, ELISABETH A,** Univ Of Sc At Columbia, Columbia, SC; FR; Gamma Beta Phi; CRC Press Chmstry Achvmnt Awd; Phrmcy.

**JOHNSON, ELIZABETH L,** Old Dominion Univ, Norfolk, VA; JR; DECA; Intl Ordr Jobs Dghtrs Hon Qn 88-89; Deans Lst 90; Mktg Educ; Tch/Scndry Schl.

**JOHNSON, ERICA L,** Tougaloo Coll, Tougaloo, MS; SO; BS; Delta Sigma Theta 90-; Pr Schlr/Deans Lst 89-90; Bio/Pre Med; Hlth.

**JOHNSON, ESOPHIA J,** Al A & M Univ, Normal, AL; JR; BA; Psychlgy Clb Sec 87; WAS Peer Cnslr; Acad Hon Roll 87-; Psychlgy; Cnslng.

**JOHNSON, ESTHER R,** Marshall University, Huntington, WV; SR; BA; Hall Advsry Cncl 88-89; Bapt Campus Mnstrs 88-90; Intrnshp Seneca MH/MR Cncl Summersville WV 90; Cnslng/Rehab; Cnslr.

**JOHNSON, EUGENE M,** Savannah St Coll, Savannah, GA; JR; BA; Crmnal Jstc Clb 90-; Untd Way Cstl Empr; Frank Callens Boys Clb; US Air Frce Dis Vet 86-90; W Brd St YMCA; Crml Jstce; Law.

**JOHNSON, FELICIA M,** Richard Bland Coll, Petersburg, VA; FR; BS; Bus Info Sys; Cmptr Prgrmr/Anlyst.

**JOHNSON, GARRETT M,** Fl A & M Univ, Tallahassee, FL; FR; SGA Safe Tm 90; Phi Eta Sigma 90-; DC Metro Clb 90; Deans Lst 90; Hon Roll; Archtctrl Eng.

**JOHNSON II, GARY H,** Univ Of Sc At Columbia, Columbia, SC; JR; Omicron Delta Kappa; Order Of Omega; Delta Uspilon VP 89-; Hist; Law.

**JOHNSON, GAY A,** Hillsborough Comm Coll, Tampa, FL; SO; AA; Vol TAN; Exxon Co Drlng Supt 76-86; Tampa Tribune Crcltn Supv 87-89; Cmptr Engr.

**JOHNSON, GLADYS L,** Alcorn St Univ, Lorman, MS; JR; FFA Pres 90-; Animal Sci Clb 88-; Ms Agri Sci 90-; Alpha Tau Alpha 88-; Alpha Tau Alpha V P 90-; Soil Conserv Svc Stdnt Trainee Intern 89-; Animal Sci; Distr Cnsrvtnst.**

**JOHNSON, GLORIA G,** Memphis St Univ, Memphis, TN; SO; BS; Amer Hrt Asc 85-; Natl Brd Resp Care 90-; Resp Care Prctnr 80-; RRT Natl Brd Resp Care 90; Clncl Psy.

**JOHNSON, GLORY M,** Fl International Univ, Miami, FL; SR; BPA; Deans Lst 90; UPS Human Resources Dept 7 Yrs; Pblc Admnstrtn; Admnstrtrs/Gvrnmt Agncy.

**JOHNSON JR, GORDON LEE,** Pellissippi St Tech Comm Coll, Knoxville, TN; SO; AS; Pres Advsry Comm Chrmn 90-; Phi Theta Kappa; Tau Alpha Pi; Chem Engr; Chem/Envrnmntl Engr.

**JOHNSON, HAROLDEEN,** Morris Brown Coll, Atlanta, GA; SR; BA; Stdnt GA Assn Edctrs 89-; Ntnl Blck Chld Cvlpmnt Inst 90-; Ntnl Pltcl Cngrs Blck Wmn 87-; Pi Lambda Theta Mmbr 90-; Alpha Kappa Alpha Hodegus 90-; GA Tchr Crtfctn Tst Pssd; Erly Chldhd Edctn; Tchr Prncpl.

**JOHNSON, HEATHER K,** Bridgewater Coll, Bridgewater, VA; SR; BA; Coll Rpblcns Sec 87-; Frgn Lngge 90; Brdgwtr Intrnatl 90; Lambda Scty 88-; Alpha Chi 89-; Dns Lst 87-; Engl; Jrnlsm.**

**JOHNSON, HEATHER R,** Middle Tn St Univ, Murfreesboro, TN; SO; BS; Spec Evnts Comm 90-; ARMS 89-90; Rcrdng Indstry Mgmt.

**JOHNSON, HEIDI L,** Duquesne Univ, Pittsburgh, PA; FR; BA; Greek Sing; Tau Delta Tau; Pres Awd; Intl Soc Poets; Intl Bus; Lge Co Emplee.

**JOHNSON JR, HERBERT P,** Southern Coll Of Tech, Marietta, GA; JR; BS; Awrdd Mst Otstndng Stdnt In Math Flyd Coll 89; Nw Hrmny Bapt Chrch; Math Indstrl Eng; Prfssnl Eng.

**JOHNSON, HOLLY M,** Union Univ School Of Nursing, Memphis, TN; FR; BSN; Sci; RN.

**JOHNSON, HOLLY N,** Dartmouth Coll, Hanover, NH; JR; BA; NH Allnce Fr Chldrn And Yth; Stdnt Assmbly 90-; Hpkns Cntr Prfrmng Arts Ushr 88-; Univ Of Ednbrgh Sctlnd Frgn Stdy Prog 90; Kappa Alpha Theta; Big Bro Big Sis 88-; Gd Bgnngs 90-; Mry Htchck Mem Hosp 88; Helen & Louise Phillips Awrd; Hnrs Thss; Rlgn; Med.**

**JOHNSON, HOPE AZALEA,** Univ Of Sc At Columbia, Columbia, SC; JR; BA; Campus Un 88; Alfr Am 88-89; Kinston Lk Yng People Assn 87-89; Bnvlnce Cmtee 88-89; Practicum Tchr 89; Ele Educ; Tch.

**JOHNSON, INGA JO ANNE,** Embry Riddle Aeronautical Univ, Daytona Beach, FL; FR; BA; IM Tennis Tm; Aerntcl Sci/Math; Cmrcl Pilot.

**JOHNSON, IRMA S,** Ky St Univ, Frankfort, KY; BA; Natl Educ Assc 89-; Alpha Kappa Mu 90-; Otstndng Jr Educ Dept 90-; Erly Elem Educ; Tchng.

**JOHNSON, JAMERIA Y,** Al A & M Univ, Normal, AL; GD; Alpha Kappa Alpha Sec; Tau Beta Sigma Pres; Natl Soc Black Engrs Sec; Amer Soc Of Civil Engrs Sec; Sigma Tau Espilon; NAACP; James River Corp; BS AL A & M Univ 90; Civil Engrng.

**JOHNSON, JAMES B,** East Central Comm Coll, Decatur, MS; FR; BS; Sigma Sigma Mau Tau 90-; LIFE 90-; Phi Theta Kappa VP 90-; Acdmc All Am 90-; Chem Fclty Awd 90-; General Wilson Fclty Awd 90-; Sci; Nrsng.

**JOHNSON, JAMES M,** Morehouse Coll, Atlanta, GA; JR; BA; Amnesty Intl Pres 89-; NAACP; Morehouse Pre-Alumni Assoc; Jr Achvmnt Bsn Basics Pgm; Coleman A Young Schlrshp Awd 88-; Mays Schlrshp Awd 89; Econ; Law.**

**JOHNSON, JAMES W,** Ms St Univ, Miss State, MS; SR; BBA; MSU Amtr Radio Clb 88-90; Assn Cmptng Machnry 88-89; MSU Martial Arts Clb 90; Alpha Lambda Delta 86-90; Phi Heta Sigma 86-90; Tringl Frat Rcrdng Sec 88-; Magnolia Rptr Assn 89-90; BS 89; Mgmt Info Sys; Ntwrk Admin.

**JOHNSON, JAMEY C,** Fl A & M Univ, Tallahassee, FL; JR; BS; Chrstn Stdnts Assn VP 90-; Cmptr/Info Sys Clb 89-; FL A/M March 100 March Bnd 88; Cmptr/Info Sys.

**JOHNSON, JANET M,** Cumberland County Coll, Vineland, NJ; SO; BA; People For Ethical Trtmnt Of Anmls; ASPCA; Envirnmntl Sci; EPA/DEP Or Pvt Emplymnt.

**JOHNSON, JANET M,** Winthrop Coll, Rock Hill, SC; JR; BS; Assn Ebonites 88-89; PACE Awd; Elem Educ.

**JOHNSON, JANICE M,** Alcorn St Univ, Lorman, MS; FR; BS; Math; Bnkng/Fin.

**JOHNSON, JANNIFER J,** Mercer Univ Schl Of Pharm, Atlanta, GA; GD; PHARM; Amer Pharm Assc Acad Stdnt Pharm 90-; Cltrl Dvrsty Comm 90-; Stdnt Ntl Phrmctcl Assc 90-; Patnt Cnslg Stdtn Asst; Phi Beta Kappa; Phi Kappa Phi; Omicron Nu; Kappa Epsilon; Untd Wy Metro Atlanta Hlth Srvc Cncl 85-89; Phrmcy.

**JOHNSON, JAY A,** Univ Of North Fl, Jacksonville, FL; SR; BSN; Emerg Nrss Assn 88; Jcksnvlle Hosp Dsstr Cncl Pres 87; EMS Prvdrs Assn 89; Emerg And Crtcl Care Nrsng; Vrs Admin Pstns 81; AA Florida Comm Coll Jacksonville; AAS Delaware Tech And Comm Coll 77; Nrsng; Hlth Admin.

**JOHNSON, JEANNA C,** Univ Of Sc At Coastal Carolina, Conway, SC; JR.

**JOHNSON, JEFFREY L,** Northern Ky Univ, Highland Hts, KY; SO; BA; Music Performance; Music.

**JOHNSON, JENNIFER A,** Duquesne Univ, Pittsburgh, PA; FR; BS; Phi Eta Sigma; Sharp Vol 90-; Dir Cir 90-; Pharm.

**JOHNSON, JENNIFER A,** Univ Of Nc At Greensboro, Greensboro, NC; SR; BS; SNCAE 88-90; Jamison Hall Cncl Flr Rep 86-87; Wesley Luther House 86-90; Erly Chlhd Ed; K6 Cert.

**JOHNSON, JENNIFER D,** Ms St Univ, Miss State, MS; FR; Bus.

**JOHNSON, JENNIFER L,** Va Commonwealth Univ, Richmond, VA; SO; BS; Acctg Soc 90-; VITA; Phi Eta Sigma 89-; Golden Key 90-; Acctg Soc Dstngsht Mbr Awd 90-; Acctg; CPA.

**JOHNSON, JENNIFER L,** Itawamba Comm Coll, Fulton, MS; SO; BA; Stdnt Govt Rep 88-; Stdnt Scientists 88-89; Bapt Stdnt Un 90-; Wesley Fndtn 88-89; Cncrt/Symph/Jazz/Mrchng Bnds 88-; Wdwnd Ensmbl 90-; Bnd Secy/Treas 90-; French Clb 88-89; Orchestra; All State Band 90-; Psychology; Child Psychologist.

**JOHNSON, JENNIFER S,** Univ Of Ga, Athens, GA; SO; BED; Phi Eta Sigma 90-; Math Edn; Teach.

**JOHNSON, JENNY M,** Univ Of Sc At Columbia, Columbia, SC; FR; BA; Flwshp Chrstn Athl 90-; Alpha Lambda Delta 90-; Sclgy; Phys/Occup Ther.

**JOHNSON, JEREMI D,** Western Carolina Univ, Cullowhee, NC; FR; BA; Wstrn Gold 90-; Pre-Med Clb 90-; Alpha Lambda Delta; WCU Hons Pgm; Hon Mntn Fresh Math Awd WCU; Chem; Med.

**JOHNSON, JESSIE C,** Strayer Coll, Washington, DC; SR; BS; Alpha Chi 90-; OPSEC Prfsnl Soc; Dept Defense Cvln; Bus; MBA.

**JOHNSON, JESSIE L,** Union Univ, Jackson, TN; SR; BSBA; Chorus; Phi Beta Lambda 89; Epsilon Sigma Alpha; Summa Cum Laude 88; Pilot Clb; Bap Church; IRS; AS Jackson St Cmnty Clg 88; Paralegel 86; Bus; Mntmnt.

**JOHNSON, JILL CYNTHIA,** Memphis St Univ, Memphis, TN; FR; Deer Mntr Prgrm 90; Tutor Core 90; Alpha Lambda Delta; Phi Eta Sigma; Alpha Gamma Delta 90; Nrsng.

**JOHNSON, JOHANNA L,** Univ Of Ct, Storrs, CT; SR; BS; Ntrtnl Biochem; Rsrch.

**JOHNSON, JON F,** Emory & Henry Coll, Emory, VA; JR; Blue Key; Pi Gamma Mu; Pi Delta Chi 90-; Blue Gold Soc 90-.

**JOHNSON, JOSEPH E,** George Mason Univ, Fairfax, VA; SR; BS; Gldn Key 88; Physcl Educ; Tchr.

**JOHNSON, JOSEPH K,** Ms St Univ, Miss State, MS; FR; BM; Mrchng Band; Bapt Stdnt Union; Cncrt Choir; Univ Madrigal Sngrs.

**JOHNSON, JOSETTE E,** City Univ Of Ny Baruch Coll, New York, NY; JR; BBA; Fin/Ecnmc Soc; Frgn Trade Soc; Fin; Bnkg.

**JOHNSON, JOY L,** Wilberforce Univ, Wilberforce, OH; FR; BA; Ntl Soc Blck Eng P Brd Trstees; Deans Lst; Math; Mech Eng.

**JOHNSON, JUDITH E,** Liberty Univ, Lynchburg, VA; JR; BS; Librty Humn Eclgy Assn Sec 90-; Alpha Lamda Delta Mbr 89-; Humn Eclgy; Hm Econmst.

**JOHNSON, JULIANNE I,** Newbury Coll, Brookline, MA; SO; BM; Culinary Arts; Culinary Fld.

**JOHNSON, JULIE A,** Tn St Univ, Nashville, TN; JR; BSED; Citizen Action; Am Poetry Anthology 89-90; GA Nashville State Tech Inst 83; Art Edn; Free Lance Illustr.

**JOHNSON, JULIE E,** Richard Bland Coll, Petersburg, VA; FR; BED; Nwspr 90-; Math; Teach.

**JOHNSON, JULIE N,** Univ Of North Fl, Jacksonville, FL; SR; BA; Gldn Key; AA 89; Elem Ed; Tchr.

**JOHNSON, JULIET R,** Muskingum Coll, New Concord, OH; FR; BA; Muskingum Clge Cncrt Chr 90-; Cmnty Bnd; Asst Dir/Stg Mgr 90-; Stf Wrtr Schl Nwspr 90-; Ohio Clgte Msc Ed Assoc 90-; Hnrs Soc; Lambda Sigma Natl; Theta Phi Alpha; Muskingum Clge Pres Schlrshp 90-; Eng; Jrnlsm/Sec Tchg.

**JOHNSON, KAREN B,** Univ Of Sc At Coastal Carolina, Conway, SC; JR; BA; Elementary Education.

**JOHNSON, KAREN I,** Inter Amer Univ Pr San German, San German, PR; SO; BBA; Hnr Pgm 90-; Cert Acad Achvmnt 89-90; Mktg.

**JOHNSON, KAREN M,** Merrimack Coll, North Andover, MA; JR; BA; Cls Cncl Sec 91-; Stdnt Govt Rep 90; Yrbk 90; Math Ctr Tutr 90-; Math; Tchr Math.

**JOHNSON, KAREN MARIE,** Western Ky Univ, Bowling Green, KY; SR; BA; Pi Mu Epsilon Exec Comm 89-; Phi Kappa Phi 90-; Beta Beta Beta 90-; Kappa Pi Delta 89-; Golden Key 90-; Pres Schlr 89-91; 1st Chrstn Ch Deacon 90-; AAS Morehead St Univ 78; Math; Scndry Sch Teacher.

**JOHNSON, KARIN E,** Marymount Univ, Arlington, VA; FR; Nwspr Mgr 90-; Std Ldr 90-; Bsn/Nrsng.

**JOHNSON, KATHERINE J,** Abraham Baldwin Agri Coll, Tifton, GA; SO; BS; AS Sci; Hist; Law.

**JOHNSON, KATRINA B,** Howard Univ, Washington, DC; SR; BA; Rcgtn Achvmnt St Paul Untd Meth Chrch; Sprts Edtr Comm News 90-; Cert Rcgntn 85; Deans List Prince Georges Comm Clg 88; Comnctns Brdcst Jrnlsm; Pol Sci.

**JOHNSON, KATRINA L,** Alcorn St Univ, Lorman, MS; FR; BA; Pre-Med Clb 90-; Hon Clb 90-; Bio/Pre Med.

**JOHNSON, KELLI A,** Snead St Jr Coll, Boaz, AL; JR; BA; Ambsdr 88-90; Phi Theta Kappa 89; Pres Lst; Deans Lst; AS 90; Cmunctn.

**JOHNSON, KELLIE M,** Fl A & M Univ, Tallahassee, FL; SO; BS; Coutoure Models Inc 89-; Theatre 90-; Commodores Clb 90-; Pres Schlrs Assn 89-; Natl Socty Blck Engrs 89-; IM 90; Chem Engr; Biomed Engr.

**JOHNSON, KELLY A,** Univ Of Central Fl, Orlando, FL; SR; BSBA; Phi Eta Sigma 89-; Beta Gamma Sigma 90-; Gldn Key 90-; Phi Kappa Phi 90-; Fll Acdmc Schlrshp 87-; Univ Pres Hnr Rll 88; Univ Deans Lst 89-90; Acctg; CPA.**

**JOHNSON, KELLYE S,** East Tn St Univ, Johnson City, TN; SO; Dns Lst; Bus; Mgmt.

**JOHNSON II, KENNETH M,** Catawba Coll, Salisbury, NC; FR; BA; Ftbl; Mktg; Mktg Repr.

**JOHNSON, KERRY,** Elmira Coll, Elmira, NY; SR; BA; AAS 89; Elem Ed; Tchr.

**JOHNSON, KERRY S,** Univ Of Al At Birmingham, Birmingham, AL; JR; BS; ASME Chrmn; SWE; AL Scty Prof Eng; Mech Engineering.

**JOHNSON, KIMBERLY A,** Central Fl Comm Coll, Ocala, FL; SO; BA; United Way Loaned Exec Jr Achvmnt Cnsltnt; Cust Svc Supvsr 82-; Engl; Bus Mngmnt.

**JOHNSON, KIMBERLY DAWN,** Wilkes Comm Coll, Wilkesboro, NC; FR; BS; Bptst Std Un 90-; Elem Ed; Tchng.

**JOHNSON, KIMBERLY F,** Owensboro Comm Coll, Owensboro, KY; FR; AS; Hnrs Nominee Engl; Prntr Oper; DIPLOMA 85; Bus; Mgt.

**JOHNSON, KIMBERLY J,** Univ Of Nc At Greensboro, Greensboro, NC; FR; BM; Alpha Lamda Delta Chr Activ Comm 90-; Appalachian Svc Project 90; Deans Lst 90-; Mscl Thtr Natl Assc Tchrs Singing Mid Atlntc Rgn First Pl; Hnry Sec St NC 90; Alumni Schlr 90; Voice Perf; Stage/Screen Prfrmr.

**JOHNSON, KIMBERLY L,** Md Inst Coll Of Art, Baltimore, MD; FR; MBA; Art Clb 89-90; Natl Hon Soc 89-90; High Hon Roll 86-90; Mnrty Apprntcshp Pgm SUNY Ginghamton 90; Sculpture/Hist; Fine Artist.

**JOHNSON, KRISTA E,** Air Force Inst Of Tech, Wrt-Ptrsn Afb, OH; SR; PHD; Oprtns Rsrch Scty Amer Sec 90-; Math Assc Amer 84-; Scty Indstrl/Appld Math 90-; Tau Beta Pi 90-; Omega Rho 90-; Alpha Iota Delta 90-; Phi Kappa Phi 84-; BS Weber St Coll Ogden UT 84; MS 90; Oprtns Rsrch; US Air Force.

**JOHNSON, L TANYA,** Norfolk St Univ, Norfolk, VA; SO; BA; Army ROTC Cadet; Spartan Alpha Tau; Cert Gen Soc Of War 1812 Outstdng Stdnt Awd; W E B Dubois Citation Dept Pol Sci/Econ; Pol Sci/Pre Law.

**JOHNSON, LARISSA C,** Tuskegee Univ, Tuskegee Inst, AL; GD; DVM; Yrbk Comm 90-; Alpha Kappa Mu 89-90; Beta Kappa Chi 89-90; Vet Med.

**JOHNSON, LARRY A,** Hudson Valley Comm Coll, Troy, NY; SR; AAS; Laser Clb Pres 90-; Intl Elctrnc Elect Eng VP 90-; Deans Lst 90; Pres Lst; Laser Electro Optic Eng Tech; Rsrch/Dvlpmnt.

**JOHNSON II, LARRY J,** Univ Of Ky, Lexington, KY; FR; MBA; Alpha Almbda Delta; Bsnss Ecnmcs; Accntng.

**JOHNSON, LAURIE,** Univ Of Ga, Athens, GA; SR; BED; Wesley Fndtn Stdnt Cncl Bd Of Dir 87-; Comuniv Vol Org 87-88; Athens Urb Mnstry 90-; Athens Area Hmls Shltr Hsptlty Crdntr 89-; Chrtr Wnds Hosp Rec Thrpy; IMS 89-90; Educ Psychlgy; Educ Cnslng.

**JOHNSON, LEAH KELLY,** Univ Of Sc At Lancaster, Lancaster, SC; FR; MBA; Acctg.

**JOHNSON, LEIGH ANNE,** Kent St Univ Kent Cmps, Kent, OH; SO; BA; Schlr Rsdnc Schlrshp; Finance; Law.

**JOHNSON, LEIGH G,** Univ Of Nc At Asheville, Asheville, NC; SO; BA; Acctg; CPA.

**JOHNSON, LEMZEL B,** Tougaloo Coll, Tougaloo, MS; SO; Yng People Union Pres 89-90; State Holiness Brthrhd Corr Sect; Karate Clb Orgnzr 90-; NAACP; Caring-N-Sharing Tchr 90-; Gospel Choir Drummer 90-; Yth Yr 90-; Del State/Natl Congr 90-.

**JOHNSON, LENNELLE ARNICE,** Wilberforce Univ, Wilberforce, OH; SR; BS; Bio Mdcl Sci Clb 89-; Alpha Swthrt Org Sec 89-; Sigma Omega; Phrmcst Asst 87; Undr Grad Rsrch Asst; Hlth Crrs Enhncmnt Prgm Mnrtrs 89; Blgy Pre Med; Infnt Cr Physcn.

**JOHNSON, LEONARD W,** City Univ Of Ny City Coll, New York, NY; SO; BA; Lib Arts.

**JOHNSON, LETITIA D,** Alcorn St Univ, Lorman, MS; FR; BS; Eng; Tchg/Cmnctns.

**JOHNSON, LINDA G,** Univ Of Sc At Columbia, Columbia, SC; JR; BA; Elem Edctn; Tchng.

**JOHNSON, LINDA L,** Va St Univ, Petersburg, VA; SR; BS; Bus Adm Clb Sec 90-; Bsktbl Stats 87-90; Phi Beta Lambda 88-89; NJ Pre Alumni 87-; Whtng Hall Com VP 90-; Deans Lst 89-; Business Adm; Mgmt.

**JOHNSON, LISA A,** Methodist Coll, Fayetteville, NC; SR; BS; Chrldr; Acctg Clb; Phi-Sigma Iota; Pres Schlrshp 87-; Chrldng 88; BS Bus Admin; Assoc Frnch; Acctg.

**JOHNSON, LISA C,** Va St Univ, Petersburg, VA; SO; BA; Hotel Rstrnt Mgmt Clb Sec; Kappa Omicron Nu Pres; Hotel/Rstrnt Mgmt.

**JOHNSON, LISA D,** Pellissippi St Tech Comm Coll, Knoxville, TN; SO; AS; CSI VP 90-; Offce Systms Tech; Med Sec.

**JOHNSON, LISA M,** Kent St Univ Kent Cmps, Kent, OH; SR; BA; Indvdl/Fmly Studies; Fmly/Chldrn Cnslr.

**JOHNSON, LISA M,** Hampton Univ, Hampton, VA; SO; BA; Pre-Med Clb 90-; SGA 90-; Stdnt Un Brd 90-; Soph Senate 90-; Bg Brthr/Bg Sistr 90-; Biolgy/Pre-Med; Dntstry.

**JOHNSON, LOLITA R,** Alcorn St Univ, Lorman, MS; JR; Yrbk Stf; Agri Econ; Inspctr USDA.

**JOHNSON, LONNIE R,** Liberty Univ, Lynchburg, VA; FR; BA; Pastoral Ministries; Pastoral/Art.

**JOHNSON, LORETTA,** Lees Coll, Jackson, KY; FR; Nrsng.

**JOHNSON, LORRAINE,** Alcorn St Univ, Lorman, MS; SR; BA; Sociology Scl Wrk Clb Pres 89-90; Scl Sci Scty; Schlrshp Miss Concerned Citizen 86-; Intrnshp Miss State Hosp Scl Wrkr; BA; Sociology; Social Work.

**JOHNSON, LOUANNE M,** Univ Of Akron, Akron, OH; FR; BA; 4 H Pres; Ohio Wgn Trn Qn; Frm Br Pres; Hnrs Pgm; Acctg; Pblc.

**JOHNSON, LOUDENA J,** Wilmington Coll, New Castle, DE; SR; BN; Wilm Clg Hon Soc 89-; Delta Epsilon Ro 90-; Has CCRN; Nursing.

**JOHNSON, M GABRIELLA,** Columbia Union Coll, Takoma Park, MD; SO; BA; Cmps Mnstrs Chlrdn Cnntn 90-; Erly Chldhd Educ; Tchr.

**JOHNSON, MARC D,** Western New England Coll, Springfield, MA; SR; BA; AA Asnuntuck Comm Coll 89; Gen Bus.

**JOHNSON, MARCELLOUS,** Tusculum Coll, Greeneville, TN; GD; MA; Fllwshp Of Chrstn Athlts 90; Phi Beta Lambda 90; All Amer 88; Vrsty Ftbl Tm Capt 89; BS Cumberland Coll; Bus Admin; Educ Coach.

**JOHNSON, MARCIA J,** Fayetteville St Univ, Fayetteville, NC; SR; BA; Non Trad Clb; Kappa Delta Pi; Zeta Phi Beta; Chanclrs Lst 89; Deans Lst 89-90; Tchr.

**JOHNSON, MARCIA P,** Univ Of The Dist Of Columbia, Washington, DC; JR; BBA; Acctng Club; Acctng Clerk; Acctng; CPA.

**JOHNSON, MARILYN D,** Savannah St Coll, Savannah, GA; JR; BA; Blcks Amg Success Tres 88-90; ASSOC CS 87; Acc Cert 83; Acctg; CPA.

**JOHNSON, MARILYN P,** Univ Of The Virgin Islands, St Thomas, VI; SR; SGA Jr Sntr 90-; Acctng Assn Sec 90-; Advent Yth Flwshp Pres 89-; Pres Clb; Scndry Schl Tchr; Cert U Of West Indies; Acctng.

**JOHNSON, MARK A,** Oh Wesleyan Univ, Delaware, OH; SO; BFA; Art Ed.

**JOHNSON, MARK E,** Franklin And Marshall Coll, Lancaster, PA; JR; BA; Franklin Marshall Pres 90-; IFC; Natl Spnsh Hnr Soc Treas 90-; Pi Lambda Phi 88-; Dana Schlr 90-; ROTC Schlrshp 89-; Vars Ftbl 88-; Spnsh-Italian Ed; Tch.

**JOHNSON, MARLO D,** Alcorn St Univ, Lorman, MS; SO; STADIS 87-89; Beta Clb 83-85; Vlybl/Track/Bsktbl; Acctg; CPA.

**JOHNSON, MARY I,** Phillips Jr Coll Charlotte, Charlotte, NC; ASSC; Bapt Chrch; Bapt Chrch Sndy Schl Tchr; Ptnt Cre Coor Rdlgy; CNA II Central Piedmont Comm Coll 90; NA Central Piedmont Comm Coll 78; Med Offce Admin Asst; BS.

**JOHNSON, MARY TERESA,** Univ Of Southern Ms, Hattiesburg, MS; JR; BS; Almn Assoc; Gamma Beta Phi; Delta Zeta Schlrshp Chrprsn 90-; IM Sprts; Cmnctn.

**JOHNSON, MATT W,** Wv Univ, Morgantown, WV; SO; BS; IEEE; Pres Lst 90; Elec Eng.

**JOHNSON, MATTHEW L,** Ky St Univ, Frankfort, KY; GD; BA; Cncrt Choir/Trvlng Choir 86-; Sml Vocal Ensmble 90-; Alpha Kappa Mu 90-; Music; Opera Singing.

**JOHNSON, MATTHEW T,** Univ Of Nc At Asheville, Asheville, NC; SO; BS; Geography.

**JOHNSON, MELISSA F,** Roane St Comm Coll, Harriman, TN; SO; Stdnt; Choir; Nursing; Rn.

**JOHNSON, MELISSA K,** Indiana Univ Of Pa, Indiana, PA; SR; Big Bro/Big Sis; Sigma Kappa Exec Brd Reg 88-; Ed; Tchng.

**JOHNSON, MELISSA R,** Middle Tn St Univ, Murfreesboro, TN; SR; BBA; Alpha Kappa Psi Schlrshp Awrd; Ntl Assoc Acctnts Awrd; W Wallace Robertson Acctng Schlrshp; Bus; Acctg.

**JOHNSON, MERRI B,** Univ Of Tn At Memphis, Memphis, TN; GD; MACE; NCF 90; Bapt Stdnt Union Mexico Med Mission Team; BA Ed Clemson Univ 85; BSN 90; Chrstn Educ; Frgn Missions.

**JOHNSON, MICHAEL C,** Memphis St Univ, Memphis, TN; FR; BS; Mrchng Bnd; Cncrt Bnd; Med Tchnlgy.

**JOHNSON, MICHAEL K,** East Carolina Univ, Greenville, NC; SR; BM; Phi Mu Alpha Sinforia 90-; Opera Theatre 88-; Vocal Pedagody Intrn; Dns Lst; Univ Chr VP 90-; Concerto Awd; Msc/Vcl Pdgogy; Vcl Perf MA.

**JOHNSON, MICHAEL K,** Cumberland County Coll, Vineland, NJ; FR; AA; Deans List 90-; Engl Lit; Profsnl Wrtr.

**JOHNSON, MICHAEL R,** Catawba Valley Comm Coll, Hickory, NC; SO; BSEE; Gamma Beta Phi Hstrn 90-; Stu Mo; Grad Mrshl; Hnr Grad; AS; Elec Engr.**

**JOHNSON, MICHAEL S,** Univ Of Montevallo, Montevallo, AL; JR; BFA; AL Art Awrd; Art; Tchng.

**JOHNSON, MICHAEL T,** Al St Univ, Montgomery, AL; JR; BS; VITA; AL State Univ Hnr Stdnt 89-90; Clg Bsn Adm Hnr Stdnt 90-; IM Bsktbl/Ftbl 88-; Acctg.

**JOHNSON, MICHELLE D,** Oh Wesleyan Univ, Delaware, OH; SR; BSN; Nrsng Stdnt Bd Scl Chr 90-; Hon Soc Nrsng 90-; Nrsng Hon C.s Foot Clnc Hmlss Vol; Deans Lst 90-; Nrsng.

**JOHNSON, MICHELLE D,** Univ Of Al At Birmingham, Birmingham, AL; SR; MA; Alpha Kappa Alpha Grmmts 89-; BS; Crmnl Juste; Law.

**JOHNSON, MICHELLE M,** S U N Y Coll At Geneseo, Geneseo, NY; FR; BA; IM Ftbl 90; Bus; Acctng.

**JOHNSON, MICHELLE R,** Cincinnati Bible Coll & Sem, Cincinnati, OH; SO; BA; Schl Play; AA; Spch Pthlgy/Audlgy; Spch Thrpst/Audlgst.**

**JOHNSON, MICHELLE Y,** Fl St Univ, Tallahassee, FL; JR; BA; Engl; Publ Rels.

**JOHNSON, MONICA L,** Univ Of South Al, Mobile, AL; SR; BS; AS Mngmt/Sprvsn Tech Faulkner St Jr Clg; Thrptc Rec; Nrsg Hm.

**JOHNSON, MONICA L,** Cumberland Coll, Williamsburg, KY; SR; Amer Chem Soc 89-90; Std Admssns Stf 88-; Bio Clb 89-; Dns Lst 87-; BS Bio; Pharm Sales.

**JOHNSON, MONICA S,** Memphis St Univ, Memphis, TN; FR; BS; Pre Health Minority Assoc; Occupational Therapy/Pre Health.

**JOHNSON, MONIQUE LA SHAWN,** Lane Coll, Jackson, TN; JR; BS; Stdnt Govt 88-; Alpha Swthrt 90-; Miss Jr 90-; Rcrtn & Phys Edn & Elem Edn.

**JOHNSON, MYRA S,** Fl St Univ, Tallahassee, FL; JR; BA; Phi Theta Kappa 88-90; Byrd Duo Piano Comptn; FL Comm Clg Music Symposium; AA Manatee Comm Clg 90; Music; Therapy.

**JOHNSON, NANCY C,** Liberty Univ, Lynchburg, VA; SR; BS; Psychology; Marriage & Family Counseling.

**JOHNSON, NATHAN,** Atlantic Union Coll, S Lancaster, MA; SR; Stdnt Sen V P 87-88; Jr Cl Treas 89; BS 90; Bus Admn; Bus/Acctng.

**JOHNSON, NATSHAW L,** Va Union Univ, Richmond, VA; JR; Acctg Clb 88-; Acctg; CPA.**

**JOHNSON, NIKI M,** Radford Univ, Radford, VA; SO; BA; Camps Crsds Chrst 89-90; Bapt Stdnt Un 90-; Hnrs Pgm 89-; Im Socr 90-; Busn; Acctg.

**JOHNSON, OLA W,** Morehouse Coll, Atlanta, GA; SR; BA; Pre-Law Soc 88-; Poltcl Sci Soc 89-90; Gspl Choir 87-89; US Army ROTC Cadet SFC 89-90; Poltcl Sci; Urbn Plnr/Ed/Lwyr.

**JOHNSON, OLIVIA N,** Ma Inst Of Tech, Cambridge, MA; FR; BS; Army ROTC 90-; AIDS Rspns MIT Peer Edctr 90-; Alpha Chi Omega Schlrshp Chrmn 90-; IM Rsrch Trng Awd NIH 90-; IM Sccr/Tennis 90; Biology; Medicine.

**JOHNSON, PAMELA A,** Bay Path Coll, Longmeadow, MA; JR; BS; Yrbk Editor-In-Chf 90-; Phi Beta Lambda VP 90-; Maroon Key; Tutor Asst 90; Salutatorian; AS Acctng 90; Bus/Acctng; CPA.

**JOHNSON, PAMELA D,** Norfolk St Univ, Norfolk, VA; JR; BS; Math Cmptr Sci 90-; Cmptr Sci; Sys Analyst.

**JOHNSON, PAMELA E,** S U N Y Coll At Fredonia, Fredonia, NY; JR; BA; Ch Yth Tchr Dir; PTA; Sports Booster Clb; AS Jamestown Comm Coll 72; Bus Admin.

**JOHNSON, PAMELA MAILKI,** West Chester Univ, West Chester, PA; GD; Music Educators Natl Conf Sec 86-90; Marching Band Treas 89; Cavelcade Of Bands Schlrshp 86; MENC Ldrshp Awd 89; BS 90; Music Ed; Musician Teacher.**

**JOHNSON, PATCHES L,** Radford Univ, Radford, VA; SR; BS; Day Stdnt Cncl 87-88; Hon Prog 87-; Hon Stdnt Assn 87-90; Tri-M Math Clb 89-; Alpha Lambda Delta 87-89; Phi Kappa Phi 90-; Kappa Mu Epsilon Pres 89-; Rdfrd Univ Fndtn Schlr 87-88; Math Dept Curr Comm 90-; Cer Mem Schlrshp 90-; Math/Statstcs; MS Ph D Stat.

**JOHNSON, PATRICIA B,** Memphis St Univ, Memphis, TN; SR; BS; Bible Study Flwshp 87-90; Boy Sct Ldr 87-89; Sndy Schl Tchr 89-; Nrsng; Ped Nrs Prctnr.

**JOHNSON, PATRICIA G,** Univ Of Miami, Coral Gables, FL; SO; BA; AIAS 88-; Archtctrl Clb 89-; BA Univ CA; Archtctr.

**JOHNSON, PAUL B,** Morehouse Coll, Atlanta, GA; FR; BS; Computer Sci; Prgrmr.

**JOHNSON, PAUL F,** Univ Of Ky, Lexington, KY; SR; BASW; Sigma Phi Epsilon Pledge Trnr 86-89; Soccer Tm 86; Soc Work.

**JOHNSON, PEGGY D,** Le Moyne Owen Coll, Memphis, TN; JR; BED; Medl Stf Asstnt Regional Medl Ctr; Assoc Degree Shelby St Comm Clg 87; Certif Miller Hawkins Bus Clb 72; Elem Educ; Teach Certif.

**JOHNSON, PETER J,** Clarkson Univ, Potsdam, NY; SR; BA; Deans List Mbr 88-; Deans List 88-90; Clarkson Horkey 87-90; Busn Mgt/Tchl Comm; Indtl Mgt/Law.**

**JOHNSON, PETRO LEON,** Al A & M Univ, Normal, AL; JR; BS; FFA Pres 87-88; U S Army Reserve 87-; Masonic 88-; Soldier Of Yr 89; IM 89; Agribus Educ; Tchng.

**JOHNSON, PHILLIP A,** Va St Univ, Petersburg, VA; SR; ROTC 87-; SIFE 88-89; Deans Lst 89-90; VFW Medal 88-89; AUSA 89-90; AS Richard Bland Clg 89; BA; Hist/Intl Studies; Military.

**JOHNSON, PHYLLIS A,** Univ Of Montevallo, Montevallo, AL; JR; BS; Erly Chldhd Elem Ed; Tchr.

**JOHNSON, PHYLLIS DENISE,** Univ Of Sc At Coastal Carolina, Conway, SC; SR; AD; USAA All Amer Sclr 90-; LPN Conway Schl Prctcl Nrsg 86; BCLS Amer Heart Assoc 89; Nrsg; Ph D Nrsg.**

**JOHNSON, PLESHETTE G,** Va St Univ, Petersburg, VA; FR; Schl Bsns Hnrs Awdf Rsdnt Edctrs Hnrs Lst; VSU Deans Lst; Bsns; Corp Lawyer.

**JOHNSON, QUENTISHA L,** Tn St Univ, Nashville, TN; SO; BS; Chem Clb 90-; Gospel Choir Chpln 90-; Alpha Lambda Delta 89-; Chem; Phrmcy.

**JOHNSON, RAHSHAYLE R,** Tougaloo Coll, Tougaloo, MS; SO; BA; Pre-Health Cl 90-; NAACP 90-; Kappa Alpha Phi Aux Secy 89-90; Biol; O B.

**JOHNSON, RAQUEL M,** Wv Univ, Morgantown, WV; SO; BA; Tau Beta Pi; Dns Lst 90; Engr; Aerospc Engr/Pilot.

**JOHNSON, RAYMOND PATRICK,** Wv Univ, Morgantown, WV; FR; Pres Schlrshp; IM Wifflebl/Ftbl/Sftbl 90-; Chem Engr.

**JOHNSON, REGINALD,** Jackson St Univ, Jackson, MS; FR; Math; Eng.

**JOHNSON, RENEE E,** Duquesne Univ, Pittsburgh, PA; BA; Covenant Church Of Pittsburghs Hosanna House; Office Manager Auditor 84-; Pre-Law; Law.

**JOHNSON, RENEE S,** City Univ Of Ny City Coll, New York, NY; SR; BA; AAS Bronx Cmmnty Clg 87; Spcl Edctn.

**JOHNSON, RHONDA L,** Tuskegee Univ, Tuskegee Inst, AL; JR; BA; Cmps Dgst Edtr 90-; Pre-Law Soc Pres 90-; Lambda Iota Tau; Alpha Kappa Mu; Admsns Recruiter; Engl; Corp Law.

**JOHNSON, RIFE K,** Embry Riddle Aeronautical Univ, Daytona Beach, FL; SR; Mngmt Clb Pres 90-; Amer Assc Arprt Exec 89-; Stdnt Almn Assc 88-; Omicron Delta Kappa 90-; Amer Airlines Intrnshp; IM Ftbl/Sftbl 87-; Mngmt/Bus; Arlne Mgr.

**JOHNSON, RITA M,** Alcorn St Univ, Lorman, MS; SO; BA; Drill Tm Staff Sgt; Gospel Choir; Nursing Club; Persing Rifles Named Ms P/R; Tch Someone To Read; Nursing.

**JOHNSON, ROBERT A,** Univ Of Sc At Columbia, Columbia, SC; FR; BA; ARETE Hnrs Clb; Tom Mangum Schlrshp; Schl Brdcstng Schlrshp; Brdcstng; Law Brdcstng.

**JOHNSON, ROBERT W,** Winthrop Coll, Rock Hill, SC; JR; BA; Cls Pres 89-90; Hl Cncl Secr 90-; Res Stdnt Assoc Repr 90-; Kappa Delta Pi; AA East Coast Bible Clg 90; Hstry; Ed.

**JOHNSON, ROCHELLE L,** Gallaudet Univ, Washington, DC; JR; MA; Psychlgy; Chld Psychlgy.

**JOHNSON, ROMAINE F,** Lincoln Univ, Lincoln Univ, PA; SO; BA; Blk Stdnt Union 89-90; Stdnt Govt VP; Hahnemann Univ/Neurosci; Bio; Neurosci.

**JOHNSON, ROSALIND J,** Savannah St Coll, Savannah, GA; SO; BA; CPR Rgstrd; NAACP Membr; Para Prfssnl/Spec Educ Class; Soc Sci; Soc Wrk/Spec Educ.

**JOHNSON, ROSE M,** City Univ Of Ny La Guard Coll, Long Island Cty, NY; SR; AA; Hmn Serv Mntl Hlth; Scl Wrkr.

**JOHNSON, ROWENA,** Oh Dominican Coll, Columbus, OH; SR; BA; Ohio Grntolgcl Socty; Delta Epsilon Sigma; Courage Inc Volntr Wrk; SS Prtsmth Interst Bus Coll 57; Soc Sci.

**JOHNSON, RUSSELL SLOAN,** Union Univ, Jackson, TN; JR; BS; Baptist Stdnt Un 88-; Alpha Tau Omega 88-; Sclgy Clb 88-; United Way; IMS 88-; Cmmnctns/Sclgy; Phrmcdcl Sls.

**JOHNSON IV, SAMUEL QUINTON,** Salisbury St Univ, Salisbury, MD; GD; Rl Est Agnt; Ownr Vndng Co.

**JOHNSON, SARAH N,** Fl St Univ, Tallahassee, FL; FR; Phi Eta Sigma; Communications.

**JOHNSON, SEAN K,** Morehouse Coll, Atlanta, GA; FR; BS; Morehouse Bsn Assoc; Morehouse Pre-Alumni Assoc; Morehouse Prospective Stdnt Seminar Plng/Progmg Comm; Morehouse Schlstc Schlrshp; Delta Sigma Theta; Boeing Corp Awd; Pol Sci/Cmptr Sci; Corp Law.

**JOHNSON, SEDRIC L,** Pensacola Jr Coll, Pensacola, FL; SO; AA; GAB Prod; Clg Schlrshp Ach Awd 90-; P J C Academic Hons 90; Wrk Clothing Mfgr; Bus Admin; Law.

**JOHNSON, SHANNON L,** Radford Univ, Radford, VA; SR; Amer Mktg Asc 90-; BACCHUS 88-89; House Cncl Rep 87-89; Sigma Kappa Pres 88-; BBA; Mktg.

**JOHNSON, SHARON ALNITA,** Univ Of Sc At Columbia, Columbia, SC; SO; NAACP; Alpha Mambda Delta Phi Eta Sigma; Hnrs Clge; Major Criminal Justice Chem; Law Dea Lab.

**JOHNSON, SHARON C,** Miami Chrisitian Coll, Miami, FL; SR; BS; Psychlgy/Counseling.

**JOHNSON, SHARON J,** William Carey Coll, Hattiesburg, MS; JR; BSN; Intrnshp Wth All State Ins Co 89; Trck/Fld 82-86; BS U Of Oregon 89; Nrsng; Nrse Admin.

**JOHNSON, SHAWN K,** Univ Of Ky, Lexington, KY; SR; BA; Clge Rpblcns 87-; Stdnts Frdm Pres 88; Law Clb 90-; Assoc Prestonburg Comm Clge 87; Pltcl Sci/Sclgy; Law.

**JOHNSON, SHAWNDRA D,** Ky St Univ, Frankfort, KY; JR; AS; Pan Hellenic Cncl Rep Sec 90-; Dns Lst 90-; Zeta Phi Beta Pres 90-; MS Greek Of Yr 90-; Grk Female Most Comm Invlvmnt; Sftbl 87-90; Trck/Fld 88-89; Nrsng Grntlgy; RN.

**JOHNSON, SHAYLA R,** Univ Of Al At Birmingham, Birmingham, AL; FR; Elec Eng/Law.

**JOHNSON, SHELLEY R,** Univ Of Ky, Lexington, KY; FR; BA; PALS; Alpha Gamma Delta; Psych; Drug/Alch Rehab.

**JOHNSON, SHERRI E,** Volunteer St Comm Coll, Gallatin, TN; SO; BA; Allied Hlth; Physcl Thrpst.

**JOHNSON, SHERRI E,** Belmont Coll, Nashville, TN; JR; BS; Frnch Clb 89-90; Psychlgy; Nrsng Hm Admin.

**JOHNSON, SHERYLINE Y**, Bloomfield Coll, Bloomfield, NJ; FR; Delta Dorsch 87; Iota Phi Aux; Dns Lst 90-; Vrsty Vlybl; Acctg; Corp Attrny.

**JOHNSON, SHREASE H**, Univ Of Southern Ms, Hattiesburg, MS; JR; BFA; Chi Tau Epsilon VP 89-; Gamma Beta Phi 90-; Jim Clinton Schlrshp; Gnrl Schlrshp 88-; Amer Dnc Fstvl Schlrshp; Dnc; Dncr/Chrgrphr/Dnc Thrpy.**

**JOHNSON, SONJA M**, Univ Of Md At Eastern Shore, Princess Anne, MD; SR; MS; Blck Allnc Ntwrk; Univ MD Pom Sqd; Phi Beta Lambda; Alpha Phi Alpha; UMES Pom Sqd; BS Univ MD; Fmly Cnslg/Dvnty; Law/Psychlgy Deg.

**JOHNSON, SONYA L**, Bloomfield Coll, Bloomfield, NJ; FR; BA; Engl; Tchr/Writer.

**JOHNSON, STEPHANIE L**, Alcorn St Univ, Lorman, MS; SO; BS; Alcorn State Gospel Choir 89-; Baptist Stdnt Un 89-; Prayer Bnd 89-; Hnr Stdnt Org 89-; Deans Lst 89-; Acctng; CPA.**

**JOHNSON, STEPHANIE M**, Univ Of Md At Eastern Shore, Princess Anne, MD; SO; BS; Cert Acad Achvmnt 90; Hnrs Prog Schlrshp 90; Careers MARC Hnrs Undergrad Rsrch; Biol; Pediatrician.

**JOHNSON, STEPHANIE R**, Al A & M Univ, Normal, AL; SR; BS; French Clb/Bapt Stdnt Un; Math Assoc Amer 90; Math Clb Pres 90-; Alpha Kappa Mu 90; Tutrl Serv Math; Enrchmnt Ctr Yth Hon Bd Mbr; Math; Math/Engr.

**JOHNSON, STEPHEN E**, Ms St Univ, Miss State, MS; SO; BS; Biomedcl Engr Soc 90-; Natl Soc Of Profsnl Eng 90-; MS St Bioengr Soc 90-; Gamma Beta Phi 90-; Theta Tau 89-; Chem Engr.

**JOHNSON, STUART M**, Savannah Coll Of Art & Design, Savannah, GA; JR; BARCH; Amer Inst Archtctr Stdnts VP 89-; Archtctr; Archtctr/Urbn Plng.

**JOHNSON, SURBRENDA L**, Ky St Univ, Frankfort, KY; SO; BA; FBLA 88-89; Afro-Am Clb Sec 89; Grad Class Hon 89; Deans Lst 90-; Spcl Olympics Comm Vol 88; Neighborhd Clean-Up Pgm 89; Awd 2nd Rnr-Up Miss Black Shelbyville Smr Emplymnt Owens-IL 89-90; Bsktbl/Track; Bus/Acctg; CPA.

**JOHNSON, SUSAN L**, Winthrop Coll, Rock Hill, SC; JR; BS; Rfrmd Univ Flwshp; Elem Ed; Tchr.

**JOHNSON, SUSAN L**, Longwood Coll, Farmville, VA; SO; BS; Longwood Schlr 89-; Alpha Sigma Tau; Deans Lst 90; Elem Educ; Tchng.

**JOHNSON, SUSAN M**, Univ Of Nh Plymouth St Coll, Plymouth, NH; SR; BS; Hsng Assoc Treas 89-; Chi Alpha Sec 88-; NAA 89-; Acctg.

**JOHNSON, TALMADGE S W**, Spartanburg Methodist Coll, Spartanburg, SC; SO; AA; Stdnt Govt Assn Sntr; Dy Stdnt Assn Brd 90-; SC Yng Dems VP Stdnt Affrs 90-; Yng Dems Sec Pres 90-; Hstry Scndry Educ; Law Tch.

**JOHNSON, TAMMIE T**, Fl International Univ, Miami, FL; JR; BA; Std Govt Sec 90-; Pi Theta Epsln VP; AA Univ FL 89-90; Occptnl Thrpy; Pdtrcs.

**JOHNSON, TAMMY M**, Coll Of Charleston, Charleston, SC; SR; BED; Phi Kappa Phi; Ed; Tchng Career.

**JOHNSON, TAMMY T**, Johnson C Smith Univ, Charlotte, NC; JR; BS; Ntl Assoc Blck Acctnts 90-; Assoc Future Blck Exec 90-; BESI Mntr Pro 90; Acctg; Bus Law.

**JOHNSON, TASHA C**, Alcorn St Univ, Lorman, MS; SO; BS; Hnrs Org 89-; Gspl Choir 89-; Prews Schlr 90; Deans Schlr 89-; Acctg; Corporate.

**JOHNSON, TERESA A**, Hudson Valley Comm Coll, Troy, NY; FR; Cbl Splcng Tech; Pblc Hlth; Hlth Admin.

**JOHNSON, TERESA J**, Univ Of Ga, Athens, GA; SR; BSED; Athns Tutrl Prog 90-; Gldn Key 90-; Kappa Delta Epsilon 90-; Erly Chldhd; Tchr.

**JOHNSON, TERESA Y**, Wv Univ At Parkersburg, Parkersburg, WV; FR; BA; 4-H Ldr 89-; Bus; Bus Mgt.

**JOHNSON, TERRELL G**, Univ Of Md At Eastern Shore, Princess Anne, MD; JR; VFW Ladies Aux 87-; Intl Assn Hosp Actnts; AA Wor-Wic Tech Comm Coll 90.

**JOHNSON, TERRY WAYNE**, Radford Univ, Radford, VA; SR; Brdcstrs Gld VP 90-; WVRU Music Dir; Cmnctns; Flm Prod.

**JOHNSON, THOMAS D**, Univ Of Ky, Lexington, KY; SR; BS; Amer Scty Of Mech Eng; Mrqtte Univ Schlr Awrd 88; Robert C Mc Dowell Schlrshp Fnd 90; Natl Dns Lst Mltple Yr Awrd 89; Mrqtte Univ Trck And Fld 88; Mech Eng; Biomech Eng.

**JOHNSON, THOMAS E**, Middle Ga Coll, Cochran, GA; SO; BA; Pastor Assembly Of God Church; Istructor Risk Reduction Classes DUL; MINISTER; Cert Beulah Hgts Bible Clg 71; Psychology; Pastoring Ministry.

**JOHNSON, TIMOTHY L**, Columbia Greene Comm Coll, Hudson, NY; SO; BA; SAGE 90-; Radio Clb 88-90; Delaware/Otsego Coalition Peace; Poems Publshd; Subst Abuse/Alcoholism Cnslg Interns 89; Certif Subst Abuse Cnslg 89; AA; Psych/Letters; Hmn Svcs/Wrtg.

**JOHNSON, TIMOTHY W**, Ky Wesleyan Coll, Owensboro, KY; SO; BA; Acctg.

**JOHNSON, TONJA C**, Tougaloo Coll, Tougaloo, MS; FR; BA; Deans List; Bio; Nrsng.

**JOHNSON, TONYA G**, Ms Univ For Women, Columbus, MS; JR; BS; Bus Admin/Engl; MBA/LAW Schl.

**JOHNSON, TONYA R**, Univ Of Southern Ms, Hattiesburg, MS; JR; BS; Alpha Lambda Delta; Phi Eta Sigma; Phi Kappa Phi; Zeta Phi Beta; Bus; Acctg.

**JOHNSON, TONYA S**, Valdosta St Coll, Valdosta, GA; JR; BED; Mddl Grds Ed Math Sci; Tchr.

**JOHNSON, TORINCULE F**, Livingston Univ, Livingston, AL; SO; Alpha Kappa Alpha Phlctr 89-; Bus Admin; Mgmt.

**JOHNSON, TOYA J**, Hampton Univ, Hampton, VA; SR; BS; Amer Mktg Assn 88-; Univ Bnd 89-; Ohio Pre Alumni Assn Rep 87-; NAACP Chrmn 87-; Big Brother/Big Sis 88-; Intrnshp J C Penney Mgr 89; Mktg.**

**JOHNSON, TRACEY M**, Univ Of Cincinnati, Cincinnati, OH; JR; BS; Jdcl Cmmssn 88-89; Yoruba Sec 88-90; Stdnt Parlgl Assn 88-89; Alpha Kappa Alpha Corr Sec; Deans Lst 88-; Crmnl Jstce; Law Schl.

**JOHNSON, TRACY L**, Marshall University, Huntington, WV; JR; BA; Campus Crusade 89-; Gamma Beta Phi 88-89; Christ Cmnty Church 89-; Hosp Adlt Fitns Intrn; Fmly Fitness Ctr; Im; Adlt Fitns/Sports Sci; Christian Wrk.

**JOHNSON, TRACY S**, Sc St Coll, Orangeburg, SC; JR; BA; Agrbsnss Clb Pres 90-; Delta Mu Delta Tres; Alpha Kappa Alpha; USDA Schlrshp 88-89; USDA Smmr Intern Prog 90-; Pres Schlr 89-; Brnz Mdlln 89-; Agrbsnss/Ecnmcs; Ecnmst/USDA.

**JOHNSON, TREVA N**, Sinclair Comm Coll, Dayton, OH; SO; BA; Women Hlpng Women; Bus Admn; Comptr Sci.

**JOHNSON, URETTA**, Tougaloo Coll, Tougaloo, MS; SO; Biology; Pediat Dtr.

**JOHNSON, VALARIE Y**, Wilberforce Univ, Wilberforce, OH; SO; BA; Pre Law Club/Treas; Soph Class Sec; Stdnt Govt Sec; Alpha Kappa Alpha; Poltcl; Corp Lawyer.

**JOHNSON, VALERIE S**, Christopher Newport Coll, Newport News, VA; SO; BA; Gloucester Cmnty Educ Coor; Engl.

**JOHNSON, VANCE A**, Spartanburg Methodist Coll, Spartanburg, SC; SO; BS; Criminal Justice Clb 89-; Psi Beta 90-; AA; Criminal Justice; Law.

**JOHNSON JR, VAUGHN G**, Central Al Comm Coll, Alexander City, AL; FR; AA; Swords Of Hon Projcts Chrmn 90-; Choir 90-; Medcl Tech.

**JOHNSON, WANDA D**, Norfolk St Univ, Norfolk, VA; SO; BA; Mrchng Spartan Leg Bnd 88; Symp Wnd Ens 88-90; Norfolk State U Jazz Ens 88; Spartan Alpha Tau 90; Music Media; Prdcr In Music Indstry.

**JOHNSON, WENDIE A**, Colby Sawyer Coll, New London, NH; FR; BA; Choices Alcohol Awareness Org; Psych.

**JOHNSON, WENDY L**, Portland School Of Art, Portland, ME; SR; Interior Dsgn.

**JOHNSON, WENDY T**, Univ Of Tn At Martin, Martin, TN; SR; Social Wrk Clb 87; Dns Lst 87-90; Psychlgy; Educ Cnslng.

**JOHNSON, WILLETTA M**, Fort Valley St Coll, Fort Valley, GA; SR; BS; Agridemic Forum; Ag Ecnmc; Delta Sigma Theta Srnty; AF; Ag Ecnmcs; Mstrs In Bsnss.

**JOHNSON JR, WILLIAM C**, Longwood Coll, Farmville, VA; JR; BA; Orientn 89-90; Res Asst 89-90; Ldrshp Conf 89-90; ROTC 90-; Rugby Clb 89-; Delta Sigma Phi 89-; Adopt A Hwy 88-; Daughtr Vietnam War Awd; Wrstlng IM Athl 88-; Busn; Law.

**JOHNSON JR, WILLIAM H**, Fl International Univ, Miami, FL; FR; BA; Hist; Law.

**JOHNSON, WILLIAM O**, Nc Agri & Tech St Univ, Greensboro, NC; JR; BS; IEEE 90-; NSBE 90-; Xerox Xcel Intrn; Elec Engr.**

**JOHNSON, WINELL P**, Tallahassee Comm Coll, Tallahassee, FL; SO; AA; Nrsng; Fld Of Med Nrsng.

**JOHNSON, YOLANDA L**, Alcorn St Univ, Lorman, MS; JR; BA; Pol Sci; Corp Lwyr.

**JOHNSON-PALMER, VIRGINIA D**, Western Carolina Univ, Cullowhee, NC; JR; BS; Stdnt Govt Assn 88/89; Spnsh Club Treas 90-; Phi Theta Kappa 90-; Assoc Tri Cnty Cmnty Clg 90; Spnsh/Engl.

**JOHNSTON ALBERT, SUSAN MARIE**, Cheyney Univ Of Pa, Cheyney, PA; SR; BA; Ambsdr Corps; Rd Crss Instrctr; Intl Assn Wmn Police St Rep 86-89; Intl Nrctcs Offcrs Assn; VT St Troopr; Crmnl Jstce Plnr St Of DE; Cert Main Line Paralgl Inst 77; Soc Rltns/Crmnl Jstce; Law.

**JOHNSTON, AMY C**, George Mason Univ, Fairfax, VA; JR; BA; Educ; Tchr.

**JOHNSTON, BARBARA LYNN**, Indiana Univ Of Pa, Indiana, PA; SR; BED; Assctn Chldhd Edctn Intrntnl 89-; Cntstnt Miss IUP; Kappa Delta Pi 90-; Sigma Kappa 88-; Paul Douglas Tchrs Schlrshp 87-; Elem Edctn.

**JOHNSTON, BARRY A**, Owensboro Comm Coll, Owensboro, KY; FR; BA; BA Western KY Univ; Acctg.

**JOHNSTON, BERNADETTE A**, Univ Of Md Baltimore Prof Schl, Baltimore, MD; SR; DDS; Exam Critique Comm Chrmn 87-90; Stdnt Jdcl Bd 80-81; Stdnt Consmr Advcy Grp Chrmn 80-82; Gamma Pi Delta 89-; Phi Sigma 80-82; Acad Of Gen Dentstry 89-; Amercn Stdnt Dntl Assoc 90-; Psi Omega VP 88-; Dentstry.

**JOHNSTON, BRENDA K**, Wv Univ At Parkersburg, Parkersburg, WV; FR; BSN; LPN-OHIO Vly Hlth Cr; Nrsng.

**JOHNSTON, DAMIAN B**, Indiana Univ Of Pa, Indiana, PA; JR; BS; Sign Lang Clb 89-; Signin Asst Dir 89-; Alpha Phi Omega 89-; Head Res Asst 90-; Res Asst 89-; Educ Hearg Imprd; Stdnt Affrs.

**JOHNSTON, DAWN M**, Univ Of Miami, Coral Gables, FL; SR; BA; Anchr Prdcr 90-; Kappa Kappa Gamma 86; Intrnshp WTVJ Chnnl 4 Assc Prdcr 90-; Cmmnctns Pol Sci; Corp Tv.

**JOHNSTON, DEAN F**, Clarkson Univ, Potsdam, NY; SR; BA; Mln Ldg/Elles 1303 87-; Pres Schlr 90; Stf Acctnt Dragon Benware/Co Pc 88-89; IM Hcky 90-; AA SUNY Cntn Coll 87; Acctg; Fed Law Enfrcmnt.

**JOHNSTON, GREGORY M**, Christopher Newport Coll, Newport News, VA; FR; BS; ROTC 90-; Supr Cadet; ROTC Schlrshp; Biology; Med.

**JOHNSTON, GREGORY SCOTT**, Memphis St Univ, Memphis, TN; SR; Spnsh Clb Cnvrstn Grp; Dns Lst 89-90; Pres Lst 90; Univ Alicante Spain; Psychlgy; Adlscnt Psychlgst.

**JOHNSTON, GRETA L**, Kent St Univ Kent Cmps, Kent, OH; SO; BA; Fmly Stds/Grntlgy.

**JOHNSTON, HOLLY D**, Univ Of Cincinnati, Cincinnati, OH; JR; Cnstrctn Stdnts Assn VP 89-; Tau Alpha Pi 88-; Ntl Assn Wmn Cnstrctn Schlrshp 88-90; Hmbldrs Auxlry Grtr Cinn Schlrshp 88-90; Assn Gen Cntrctrs Schlrshp; OH Cntrctrs Assn Schlrshp; Cnstrctn Mgmt.

**JOHNSTON, JANET L**, Univ Of Ky, Lexington, KY; SR; Coll Dmcrts 88-89; Stdnts Dukakis Vtr Rgstrtn Chrprsn 88-89; Pi Sigma Alpha VP 90-; Intrnshp WA Offc Cngrssmn 89; Pltcl Sci; Pblc Admin.

**JOHNSTON, JANYNE M**, Asbury Theological Sem, Wilmore, KY; FR; MDIV; RN; BSN Univ IL Chgo 76; Bible; Tch/Mnstry.

**JOHNSTON, JEHANE C**, Hahnemann Univ, Philadelphia, PA; GD; MD; AAMC OSR Rep 90-; ASAPP 89-; BA Colby Colg Waterville Me 86; Med.

**JOHNSTON, JENNIFER E**, Georgetown Coll, Georgetown, KY; JR; BS; German Club 88-; Curriculum Comm 90-; Acctg Lab Dir 90-; Alpha Lambda Delta 89-90; Psi Chi; Phi Beta Lambda Hstrn 88-; A Hnr Roll 88-90; Dns Lst 90; Acctg.

**JOHNSTON, JESSICA L**, Univ Of Sc At Columbia, Columbia, SC; JR; BA; Hlth/Ftns.

**JOHNSTON, JOSEPH D**, Muskingum Coll, New Concord, OH; JR; BA; Vol East Ohio Reg Hosp Sec Offcr 88-; Stdnt Athl Trnr 88-89; Beta Beta Beta; Psi Chi; Stag Mens Clb Sgt Arms 89-90; Chem Acad Achvmnt Awd; Hlth/Phys Educ; Phy Thrpy.

**JOHNSTON JR, JOSEPH S**, Al A & M Univ, Normal, AL; SR; BS; Hntsvl Area Commodore Kmptr Socty Pres 90-; Huntsvl Opera Theatre VP/TECH Cir 83-84; Elec/Cmptr Maint 80-; Cmptr Maint Cert; Indus Tech Educ.

**JOHNSTON, KEVIN T**, Southern Coll Of Tech, Marietta, GA; JR; BS; Tau Alpha Pi; IEEE; U S Nvy Rsrvs 2nd Cls Pty Ofcr 90-; U S Nvy Arcrft Elctrcn 83-90; Elctrcl Engrg Tchnlgy; Plnt Engr.

**JOHNSTON, KIRSTEN A**, Cornell Univ Statutory College, Ithaca, NY; JR; BS; Ambssdrs Pres 89-; Ithaca Rap Crss Spkrs Bru 90-F Fncng Tm 88-90; Gldn Ky 90-; Mrtr Brd Treas; Ho Nun De Kak; Delta Delta Delta Educ Chrmn 89-; IM 88-; Natl Conv Land Grant Univ 90; ALS Brd Dir Stu Ldrshp Cmmtt 90-; Appld Ecnmcs/Bus Mgmt; Fnnc Mgmt Cnsltng.

**JOHNSTON, LAURA K**, Samford Univ, Birmingham, AL; GD; JD; Amrcnjrnl Trl Advcy Alumni Comm Chr; AL Stdnt Bar Assn; Chrstn Lgl Soc; Law Clrkshp Clrk Scott P C; BS Auburn Unvrsty 88; Law.

**JOHNSTON, PAIGE M**, Univ Of Al, Tuscaloosa, AL; FR; Pol Sci; Law.

**JOHNSTONE, REGINA W**, Univ Of Southern Ms, Hattiesburg, MS; JR; BA; Deans List 88-; Brock Schlrshp 88-89; Hnr Stdnt Schlrshp 90-; AA Sw Miss Comm Coll 90; Elem Edn.

**JOHNSTON, RONALD W**, Memphis St Univ, Memphis, TN; JR; BA; Exchng Stdnt Canada; Frnch; Intl Bus.

**JOHNSTON, RUSSELL HOLLIS**, Meridian Comm Coll, Meridian, MS; SO; BS; Clg Ambssdrs 90-; LEAD 90-; Bptst Stdnt Union 89-; Phi Theta Kappa 90-; Math/Cmptrs; Eng.

**JOHNSTON, SUSAN E**, Ms St Univ, Miss State, MS; SR; BS; Alpha Epsilon Delta 89-; Bioengr Socty 90-; Socty Wmn Engrs 90-; Tau Beta Pi 90-; Phi Kappa Phi 90-; Kappa Mu Epsilon 89-; Engr/Pre Med; Medicine.

**JOHNSTON, THOMAS R**, Comm Coll Algny Co Algny Cmps, Pittsburgh, PA; SO; AS; Lab Tech BASF Corp 89-; Obsrvr Allghny Obs 87-; BS La Roche Clg 88; Physcs; Engr.

**JOHNSTON, WENDY L**, Winthrop Coll, Rock Hill, SC; JR; BA; Interior Dsgn.

**JOHNSTON II, WILLIAM E**, Ms St Univ, Miss State, MS; SO; BS; MS State Bank; Choir; La Crosse Tm; Bioegrg Scty; Bioengineering/Pre Med; Med.

**JOHNSTONE, ROY O D**, Nova Univ, Ft Lauderdale, FL; GD; MBA; Comp Syst Anlyst; BC Univ Coll Galway 78; MS 79; Bus Admin/Mgmt.

**JOHNSTONE, WILLIAM W**, Montgomery Comm Coll, Troy, NC; SO; BS; NC Wldlf Rsrcs Cmmssn 84-; AAS 83; Fsh Wldlf Mgmt.

**JOHO, BRIAN C**, Upsala Coll, East Orange, NJ; SR; BA; Interfrat Cncl VP 89-; Rachel Carson Hlth/Ecology Clb VP 87-; Soc Of Dist Clg Amers 90-; Alpha Kappa Psi Sec 88-; Hons Pgm 87-; Cert Kansai Univ Of Foreign Studies Osaka Japan 89; Intl Bus.**

**JOINER, ALAN B**, Univ Of South Al, Mobile, AL; FR; MIS; EARTH Clb; Cmptr Sci; Law/Cmptr Prgrmmg.

**JOINER, ELLEN M,** Middle Ga Coll, Cochran, GA; FR; BA; Bus/Accntng.

**JOINER, JAMES JYM,** Savannah Coll Of Art & Design, Savannah, GA; JR; BS; BSIA Gen Mtrs Inst 82; Archt.

**JOINER, JESSICA ROSANNE,** Univ Of Sc At Columbia, Columbia, SC; SO; BA; Theatre Plyrs 89-; Plygrnd Plyrs 89-; Pcstrs 89-; Gamma Beta Phi 90-; Aikens Rep Ntl Youth Ldrshp Cnfrnc Coll Seminar Washington DC 90-; Merle P/Stephen D Mem Schlrshp 89; Aik Jr Wmns Clb Schlrshp; Theatre; Indstrl Cmnctns Anlyst.

**JOINER, LOTTIE L,** Jackson St Univ, Jackson, MS; FR; BS; Alpha Lambda Delta; Spnsh Hnr Scty; Nwscstr.

**JOINER, MICHAEL BURNETT,** Alcorn St Univ, Lorman, MS; JR; BS; Bible Stdy 89-; Bwlng; Mnrty Ldrshp Awrd 90-; Acdmc All Amer 89-; Alpha Kappa Mu; Alpha Mu Gamma Pres 90-; Deans Lst 87-88; Pres Lst 89-90; Bsbl/Trck 90-; Frnch Educ; Hgh Schl Frnch Tchr/Bsbl Coach.**

**JOINER, SHERRIE M,** Ga St Univ, Atlanta, GA; GD; Mrtr Bd 90-; Deans Lst 88-90; Magna Cum Lauda 90-; Pianst Bapt Msn 88-89; 1st Grade Tchr 90-; Early Chldhd Educ.

**JOINER V, WALTER S,** Univ Of Sc At Aiken, Aiken, SC; JR; BS; Math/Cmptr Sci Clb 90-; Gamma Beta Phi; Pres Hnr Rl 89-; Engr.

**JOINES, ANN E,** Western Carolina Univ, Cullowhee, NC; FR; BA; Westmnstr Flwshp 90-; Res Hall Cncl 90-; Western Gold 90-; Frshmn Collquy 90-; Dns Lst 90; Anthrpolgy; Law.

**JOISHER, MEENA M,** Ramapo Coll Of Nj, Mahwah, NJ; JR; BS; Intl Stdnt Orgztn 89-; Rtrng Stdnt Orgztn 89-; Acctg Clb 89-; Delta Mu Delta; Fndtn Ramapo Schlrshp; Tele Cmtee J Kilmer Sch Chrprsn 90-; Info Proc; MBA.

**JOKELA, CAROL J,** Univ Of West Fl, Pensacola, FL; SR; BA; Kappa Delta Pi 90-; Alpha Sigma Lambda 90-; Acdmc Schlrshp 89-; Pres Lst 89-; Deans Lst 89-; Csumma Cum Laude; Store Mngr Sears 78-89; AA N FL Jr Coll 81; Early Chldhd/Elem Ed; Tchng.

**JOLIVETTE, VINCENT D,** Oh Univ, Athens, OH; FR; BFA; Intra-Schl Yth Bible Stdy Clb; James Hall Rep W Grn Cncl; Deans Lst 90-; TV Sit-Com Audtn 90-; IM Bsktbl Bsbl Ftbl 90-; Thtr Arts Acting; Thtr Prfrmnc.

**JOLLAY III, LLOYD J,** Roane St Comm Coll, Harriman, TN; SO; AS; Natl Env Hlth Assoc; Eniv Hlth/Ind Hygiene; Industrial Hypienist.

**JOLLEY, WENDY R,** Converse Coll, Spartanburg, SC; SR; Stdnt Govt Assoc Treas 87-; Class Ofcr V P/Treas 87-; Stdnt Adm Brd 87-89; Pi Gamma Mu VP 90-; Crescent 88-89; Habitat For Humanity 90; Brd For World 89-; Natl Model League Of Arab States 90-; Deans Lst 89-; BA; Pol Sci; Religion.

**JOLLY, CAROLYN R,** Univ Of Sc At Spartanburg, Spartanburg, SC; JR; BED; Stdnt Govt Assoc Class Sntr 90; SC Stdnt Ed Pres 89; Yrbk Bsnss Ads Man 89; Kappa Delta Pi; Elem Ed; Tchng.

**JOLLY, JOYCE L,** Al St Univ, Montgomery, AL; SO; Hon Soc 90-; Acctg; CPA.

**JOLLY, TINA S,** Middle Ga Coll, Cochran, GA; SO; BSN; Stdnt Act Com 89-; GA Assn Nrsng Stdnts 90-; Bapt Stdnt Un 89-; PTO 88-; Deans Lst 89-90; DAR Hist Awd 90; Purchasing Expeditor 82-86; Customer Serv Rep 86-87; AAS 89; AS 90; OR Nurse.**

**JOLTES, VIVIAN A,** West Liberty St Coll, West Liberty, WV; JR; MSW; WV Soc Wrk Lic; Estrn Str; Bbl Schl Instr; Soc Wrkr 83-88; Nvgtn Prjct Asst 88 ; Cortc; Prchlgy; Cnslng.

**JON, ANAYS,** Fl International Univ, Miami, FL; SR; Amer Mktg Assc 90- Nwsltr Dcmt Prmtns Cmt; Phi Lmbd 90-; BBA; AA 89; Bus Admn; Mktg/Intrntl Bus.**

**JONA, MICHAL R,** Yeshiva Univ, New York, NY; SR; Sysms Schl Bus Stdnt Cncl Pres 89-; Stdnt Orientation Advsr 89-90; Hebrew Hnr Soc Pres 89-90; Bernard Brown Awd; BS; AA; Prudential Bache Securities Intern 89-90; Finance; Chem Bank.

**JONAS, ADAM H,** Boston Univ, Boston, MA; GD; MD; Daly Fr Prs Sci Edtr 88-90; STATS 88-89; Res Asst 88-; Gldn Key; Alpha Omega Alpha; BA; Med.

**JONAS, JONATHAN B,** Emory & Henry Coll, Emory, VA; SO; BA; Cncrt Choir 90-; Ortrio Choir 89-; Chrch Vctns Clb 90-; Blue Key; Im Ftbl/Bsktbl; Im Trck; Flwshp Chrstn Athlts 89-90; Coll Tr Gd Assoc 89-; Jn Emry Schlr 89-; Sigma Mu Frshmn Hnr Schlr 89-90; Marius Blesi Rdng Awrd 90-; Englsh/Phlsphy; Ordnd Mnstry.

**JONAS, RACHELLE C,** Clark Atlanta Univ, Atlanta, GA; SO; BA; Psych Clb 90-; Massachusetts Clb 89-90; Psych; Ph D.

**JONES II, AARON U,** Marshall University, Huntington, WV; SO; BBA; Natl Mgmt Assoc 90-; Amer Clg Hlthcre Exec 90-; Gamma Beta Phi 90-; Hlth Care Admn; Hlth Care Exec.

**JONES, ADAM T,** Coll Of Charleston, Charleston, SC; SO; Nwspaper; Hon Prog Stdnt Assn 90-; L M Harris Schlrshp; Engl.

**JONES JR, ALAN W,** Va Commonwealth Univ, Richmond, VA; SO; BS; J Sargeant Reynolds Comm Coll Brd Schlrshp 89-90; Accntng; CPA.

**JONES, AMI R,** Dyersburg St Comm Coll, Dyersburg, TN; FR; ASSOC; Phi Theta Kappa; MBA; Sci; Phrmcy.

**JONES, AMIRI L,** Fl A & M Univ, Tallahassee, FL; FR; BS; FAMU Essential Theatre 90-; Bond Elem Sch Spec Friends 90-; Phi Eta Sigma; Natl Soc Blck Engrs 90-; NASA Acad Schlrshp/ Intern 90-; FL Undergrad Schlrshp 90-; Thomas J Watson Mem Schlrshp 90-; Mech Engr; Engr Dsgn.

**JONES, AMY,** Bapt Bible Coll & Seminary, Clarks Summit, PA; SO; BED; Natl Right Lf Assn 89-; Music; Tchng Scndry.

**JONES, AMY E,** Univ Of New England, Biddeford, ME; JR; BA; Stdnt Advct Grp Dept Soc/Behav Sci Coord 89-; Psychlgy Clb 89-90; Stdnt Ldrs Org 90-; Wntr Trm Comm Rep 90-; Rsrch Asst 90-; Spec Stdnt Asst 89-; Univ Schlrs Prog 88-; Psychlgy; Chld Dvlpmnt/Fmly Stdies.

**JONES, AMY L,** Univ Of Nc At Greensboro, Greensboro, NC; SR; BS; Bptst Stdnt Un Cncl 89-; Stdnt NC Assc Edctrs 89-; Alpha Lambda Delta 88-; Gamma Sigma Sigma 88-; NC Tchng Flws Schlrshp 88-; Mdl Grades Ed; Tch/Law Schl.

**JONES, ANDRE L,** Fl Atlantic Univ, Boca Raton, FL; JR; BSC; Phi Theta Kappa 88-; AA Miami-Dade Comm Coll 90; Air Trffc Cntrl Trnsfprt Canada Trning Inst 85; Sci; Engrng.

**JONES, ANGELA B,** Al St Univ, Montgomery, AL; FR; Hnr Roll 90; Bsnss; Accntng.

**JONES, ANGELA C,** Longwood Coll, Farmville, VA; SO; BS; ABS Orgtn; Peer Advisor; Resid Assist; Gospel Choir; Minty Mnt Orient Ldr; Pres Fedtn Student Social Wrks; Alpha Lambda Delta; Social Wk.

**JONES, ANGELA D,** Univ Of Tn At Chattanooga, Chattanooga, TN; JR; BE; Soc Wmn Engrs 90-; Amer Soc Qulty Cntrl; US Achvmnt Acdmy Awrd Wnr; Qulty Engr Intrn; Qulty Engr.

**JONES, ANGELA G,** Fl St Univ, Tallahassee, FL; SR; BA; Chld Dev/Fmly Rel; Scl Wrk-Cnslr.

**JONES, ANGELYN SKELTON,** Univ Of South Al, Mobile, AL; JR; BED; Alpha Chi; Phi Theta Kappa 90-; Emplyee Rltns Mgr 79-87; Rl Est Slsprsn 77-79; AS Faulkner St Jr Coll 90; Lang Arts; Tchr/Gdnce Cnslr.

**JONES, ANTHONY E,** Temple Univ, Philadelphia, PA; SR; UPS Mgmnt Team; Business; UPS Mktg.

**JONES, ANTHONY L,** Catawba Valley Comm Coll, Hickory, NC; FR; Gamma Beta Phi, Sftbl; Mchnol Eng Tchnlgy; Fng.

**JONES, ANTOINETTE N,** Univ Of Ga, Athens, GA; JR; BS; Univ Cncl; Afro Amer Chrl Ensmbl 89-90; Delta Sigma Theta 90-; Home Econ Assn VP; Chld/Fmly Dev Assn VP; Chld/Fmly Dev; Chld Lf Spclst Chldrsn Hosp.

**JONES, ARCHIE L,** Morehouse Coll, Atlanta, GA; SO; BA; TX Clb Mr TX 89; Hbrt Hll Drmtry Cncl Pres 89-90; Clss Sen; Phi Gamma Nu; Frederick Douglas Ttrl Inst 89-; Deans Lst 90; Hnr Rlll 89-; Bus Admn Acctg; Law.

**JONES, ARNOLD E,** Hudson Valley Comm Coll, Troy, NY; BS Rehsselaer Polytechnic Inst 89; Acctg; CPA.

**JONES, BARBARA E,** Broward Comm Coll, Ft Lauderdale, FL; SO; BA; Broward Cmmnty Coll 89-90; Hnr Scty; Cmpltd Hnrs Prgm; Phi Theta Kappa 90; Bnk Offcr; AA Broward Cmmnty Coll 90; Bus; CPA.

**JONES, BEATRICE,** Al St Univ, Montgomery, AL; SO; BA; Phi Beta Lambda; AS Selma Univ 90; Bsn Ed; Tch.

**JONES II, BENNIE L,** Wilberforce Univ, Wilberforce, OH; SR; OH Pre-Almni Assn Pres 87-; Pres Cnsl; Nwspapr Staffwrtr 88-; Sr Of The Yr; BA; Cmnctns; Pub Rltns Cnsltnt.

**JONES, BERNADETTE W,** Al A & M Univ, Normal, AL; SR; BS; Phi Eta Sigma 88-; Alpha Kappa Mu 90-; Outstndg Schlr Awd; Pres Schlrshp 88-; Ford Schlr 89-; Acad Schlrshp 89-; Sec Edn/Engl Pol Sci.

**JONES, BETH R,** Mountain Empire Comm Coll, Big Stone Gap, VA; SR; Instrc Crrclm Cmmt 90-; Deans List 89-90; Drftng; Engrng.

**JONES, BETHANY P,** Oh Wesleyan Univ, Delaware, OH; FR; BA; Prjct Hope 90-; Phi Eta Sigma; Pre-Law; Law.

**JONES, BEVERLY,** Miami Jacobs Jr Coll Of Bus, Dayton, OH; FR; Bus Admn.

**JONES, BEVERLY D,** City Univ Of Ny Baruch Coll, New York, NY; JR; BA; Accntnt; CPA.

**JONES, BEVERLY F,** Bristol Univ, Bristol, TN; GD; Accnt Eng Div Martin Marietta Energy Sys; MBA Acctg 90; BUS Univ NM 87; Acctg.

**JONES, BILLY R,** Univ Of Al At Birmingham, Birmingham, AL; SR; Lions Club; Kiwanis Club; FNB Of Columbiana; BA; Elem Ed; Tchng.

**JONES, BRADLEY W,** Itawamba Comm Coll, Fulton, MS; FR; Phi Theta Kappa.

**JONES, BRANDI M,** Mary Baldwin Coll, Staunton, VA; FR; BA; Theatre Scnc/Mkup Artst 90-; Pool Sprvsr 90-; Cmnctns; Record Eng.

**JONES, BRENDA,** Memphis St Univ, Memphis, TN; FR; BBA; Peer Mentor Prog 90-; Blk Schlrs Unlimited 91; Bus/English; Bus Admn/Acctg.

**JONES, BRENDA J,** Catawba Valley Comm Coll, Hickory, NC; FR; BA; Unity Ctr Chrstnty Yth Ed Tchr 89-90; Brigade Of Light/Charlotte 90; Wrtrs Grp Express 90-; Fam Care Ctr Vol 90-; English/Psych; Wrtr/Substnc Abuse Cnslr.

**JONES, BRENDA L,** Marshall University, Huntington, WV; JR; BA; Alpha Kappa Psi 90-; Amrcn Mrktng Assoc 89-; Mrshl Intrnshp Prgrm 90-; Alpha Kappa Psi 90-; Deans Lst 88-; Instrnshp Shrsn Lhmn Bros Mkt Asst 90; Intrnshp Hntngtn Ml Mkt Intrn; Mrktng; Advrtsng/Mrktng Mngmnt.

**JONES, BRENDA S,** Univ Of West Fl, Pensacola, FL; JR; BA; CEC; Sub Tchr 90-; AA Okaloosa Walton Cmnty Clg 90; Spch Ed; Tchng.

**JONES, BRENDAL L S,** Univ Of Md At Eastern Shore, Princess Anne, MD; SR; BA; Rhbltn Svc Stdnt Assc Pres; Rhbltn Svc.

**JONES, BRUCE H,** Univ Of Sc At Columbia, Columbia, SC; SR; BA; RSA 87-88; Hall Cncl; Schl Bus Clb; 2 Cert Perf As Ofc Page 90; Ofc Page Sntr Sherry Martschinic SC St Senate; English; Coll Prof/Lit.

**JONES, BRYN A,** Kent St Univ Geauga Cmps, Burton Twp, OH; JR; BA; Law Office Mgr 85-88; Geog; Rsrc Mgmnt.

**JONES, CAROL K,** Union Coll, Barbourville, KY; FR; Tour Guide 90-; Bus; Corp Law.

**JONES, CAROL L,** Univ Of Cincinnati, Cincinnati, OH; JR; BA; PLTM Schl Progs Mgr Cinci Musmn Natrl Hist 78-90; Elem Educ; Tchr Sci.

**JONES, CAROL R,** Cumberland Coll, Williamsburg, KY; SR; BA; Elem Ed; Ed.

**JONES, CATHIE D,** East Central Comm Coll, Decatur, MS; FR; BA; Accnts 90-; Bnd 90-; Mu Alpha Theta 90-; Elem Ed; Tch.

**JONES, CATHY J,** Oh Dominican Coll, Columbus, OH; SR; BA; Judicial Board 88-90; Female Schlr Athlt Yr 90-; Otstndng Criminal Justice Major 90-; Acdmc VP Awrd Schlstc Achmnt Srs 90-; Lubrizol Awrd 87-88; Gary Dossin Schlshp 89-90; NAIA Acdmc All AM Fst Ptch Sfbl 90; Crmnl Justice; Fdrl Law Enfrcmnt.

**JONES, CENDA L,** Western Carolina Univ, Cullowhee, NC; SR; BA; Big Sis/Bro Org; Delta Zeta 88-; Co Red Vol 89-; Frmns Day Vol 90; Santa Pal 89-90; Grk Acad Achvmnt Awd; IM Bsktbl/ Sftbl 88-; Scl Wrk.

**JONES, CHANTA N,** Univ Of Sc At Columbia, Columbia, SC; FR; MBA; Bapt Stdnt Union 90-; Phi Eta Sigma; Alpha Lambda Delta; Nrsng; Peds.

**JONES, CHARISSA M,** Central St Univ, Wilberforce, OH; SO; BA; Chorus 89-; Hnrs Pgm 89-90; Cmptr Sci; Syst Analyst.

**JONES, CHARLENE W,** Tougaloo Coll, Tougaloo, MS; SR; Res Asst 89-; Stdnt English Litry Forum 0-; Yng Dmcrts 89-; All African Peoples Revlutnry 89-90; Stdnt Ldr 87-90; V Pres Schlr 89-91; Antioch Msnry Bapt Ch; BA; Spch Path Grad Sch.**

**JONES, CHARLES E,** Morehouse Coll, Atlanta, GA; SR; BS; Physcs Nclr Eng; Rctr Dsgn Eng.

**JONES, CHARLES L,** Oh Univ-Southern Cmps, Ironton, OH; JR; BA; Eagles 83-; VFW 90-; Millwright 81-; Math/Indus Arts; Math Tchr.

**JONES, CHARLES W,** Univ Of Sc At Columbia, Columbia, SC; SR; BS Psychlgy; Scl Srvcs.

**JONES, CHARLOTTE T,** Fl A & M Univ, Tallahassee, FL; SO; MBA; Playmkrs Build; Phi Eta Sigma 90-; Pres Schlr 89-; Acctg; CPA.

**JONES, CHARLOTTE T,** Univ Of Md Baltimore Prof Schl, Baltimore, MD; GD; MD/PH; Flwshp; Acdmc Awd; BA Oberlin Coll 86; Physcn Scntst.

**JONES, CHERYL L,** Clark Atlanta Univ, Atlanta, GA; SO; BA; Psych; Psych/Elem Ed Tchr.

**JONES, CHRISTA C,** Queens Coll, Charlotte, NC; SO; BA; Baptist Stdnt Union Pres 90-; Clge Union Brd Of Dir Sec; Admissions Core 90-; Communications & Development Internship Child Care Resources Inc; English.

**JONES, CHRISTINA R,** Univ Of Ga, Athens, GA; SR; BSHE; Phi Upsilon Omicron 90-; Deans Lst 90-; Intrnshps Mgmnt Training; Fshn Merch; Retail Mgmnt.

**JONES, CHRISTOPHER A,** Pellissippi St Tech Comm Coll, Knoxville, TN; FR; BFA; Media Arts; Advtsng.

**JONES, CHRISTOPHER A,** Fayetteville St Univ, Fayetteville, NC; SO; BA; IEEE 88-; Prsnl Cmptr Usrs Grp 85-; AAS 89-90; Cmptr Sci.

**JONES, CHRISTOPHER E,** Georgetown Univ, Washington, DC; SR; BSBA; Alpha Kappa Delta 89-; Delta Sigma Pi Chnclr 89-; Fnc/Intrntl Mgmt; Law.

**JONES, CHRISTOPHER E,** Univ Of Southern Ms, Hattiesburg, MS; JR; BS; Hall Scrtry 89-90; Alpha Lambda Alpha; Hnrs Clg 89-90; Argonne Ntl Lab Intrn; Chmstry; Rsrch.

**JONES, CHRISTOPHER J,** Syracuse Univ, Syracuse, NY; FR; BENG; Gn Sqd; Pr Advsr; Comp Eng.

**JONES, CHRISTOPHER L,** Spartanburg Methodist Coll, Spartanburg, SC; SO; BA; Stdnt Govt Assn Pres 90-; Blck Allnc 90-; Oln D Jhnstn Gd Ctznshp Awrd; Deans Lst 90-Bsktbll Acdmc Athltc Schlrshp Capt 90-; Sci.

**JONES, CHRISTOPHER R,** Volunteer St Comm Coll, Gallatin, TN; SO; AA; Coll Stdnt Nwspr Edtr In Chf 90-; Cncl Stdnt Ldrs; Deans List 90-; Hist; Jrnlst/Coll Prfsr.

**JONES, CHRISTY R,** Univ Of Tn At Martin, Martin, TN; FR; BSN; Nrsng.

**JONES JR, CLARENCE B,** Va Commonwealth Univ, Richmond, VA; JR; Jennings Scty 90-; Golden Key 90-; Omicron Delta Epsilon; Econ; Mgt/Fin.

**JONES, CLARENCE J,** Fayetteville St Univ, Fayetteville, NC; SR; BA; Pltcl Sci Clb Pres 89-; Groove Phi Pres 89-90; Nom Dlgt Model Untd Ntns 90; BS Pltcl Sci Intl Rltns Pblc Admin; Pltcl Sci; Grad Sch/Law Sch.

**JONES, COURTNEY G,** Nc Agri & Tech St Univ, Greensboro, NC; SR; BA; Std Natl Educ Asc 89-; Std Jdcry Cncl Rep 89-90; Tchr Educ Cncl Rep 89-; Alpha Kappa Alpha 90-; Elem Ed; Spch Pthlgy.

**JONES, CYNTHIA,** City Univ Of Ny City Coll, New York, NY; SR; BS; Tchr Ctzns Care Day Care Ctr III 76-; AA Bronx Comm Coll 74; Ed; Tchng.

**JONES, CYNTHIA L,** Clayton St Coll, Morrow, GA; SO; Stdt Gvt Assoc Pres 90-; Honors Assoc Pres 89-; Airport Rotary Schrlshp; Political Science/Business; Law.

**JONES, DALE G,** Univ Of Sc At Columbia, Columbia, SC; SR; Lung Asso Computerzd Bookpg Supv 81-90; BS Ed St Un/N Y 75; MS Ed Hofstra Un 77; Acctng.

**JONES, DALIAH N,** Va St Univ, Petersburg, VA; FR; BA; Business Adm.

**JONES, DANA R,** Bloomfield Coll, Bloomfield, NJ; SR; BA; ROTC 2nd Lt Army Natl Grd 87-; Sigma Phi Delta Sec; Sftbl 88-; Soclgy/Crim Jstc; DEA.

**JONES II, DANIEL D,** Roane St Comm Coll, Harriman, TN; FR; BS; Wild Life Biology.

**JONES, DAVID F,** Thomas Nelson Comm Coll, Hampton, VA; FR; BS; Eng.

**JONES, DAVID H,** Fl A & M Univ, Tallahassee, FL; SR; BS; Hspnc Clb VP 90-; IM Sccr 90-; Agribus; Agri Ecnmcs.

**JONES, DAVID R,** East Ms Comm Coll, Scooba, MS; FR; AAS; Yrbk Asst Edtr 90-; Ltry Mag Asst Edtr 90-; Coll Chr 90-; Sigma Phi Sigma 90-; Phillips Funeral Home Fnrl Drctr; Fnrl Srvce Ed; Emblmr.

**JONES, DAWN R,** Radford Univ, Radford, VA; FR; BS; Blck Stdnts Afrs Cncl Hstrn 90-; Un Ambsdr 90-; Blck Grk Cncl Hstrn; Alpha Lmbd Dlt 90-; Alpha Kappa Alpha Tres; Hghst GPA Mnrty Stdnt Frshmn Cls 90-; Psychlgy; Psychlgst.

**JONES, DEBORAH K,** Elon Coll, Elon, NC; SO; BA; Beta Beta Beta 90-; Bio; Vet.**

**JONES, DEBORAH K,** Al A & M Univ, Normal, AL; SR; BA; Kappa Delta Pi 89-; Pres Hon Soc 88-; Acdmc Schlrshp 88-; AA NE Jr Coll 87; AS NE Jr Coll 87; Sec Ed Eng/Frnch; Coll Instrctr.

**JONES, DEBORAH M,** Florida Christian Coll, Kissimmee, FL; SO; BA; Wvs Flwshp Pres 89-; Mssns Outrch Vctrious Evnglsm; Stdnts For Actn; Bookkeeper 84-88; Bible; Clncl Soc Wrk.

**JONES, DEBRA K,** Longwood Coll, Farmville, VA; JR; BSBA; Curry Hall Cncl Prsdnt 90-; Arts Sci Hnrs Prgrm 88-89; Bsns Admnstrtn; Systm Anlys.

**JONES, DEBRA Z,** Memphis St Univ, Memphis, TN; JR; BPS; AHTA 90-; Memphis Herb Soc 87-; Ernst/Young Publctns Coord 87; Thrpy/Psychlgy Rehab; Hort Thrpst.

**JONES, DEE J,** New Comm Coll Of Baltimore, Baltimore, MD; SR; Prsdnt Nrses Pinning Ceremony; Phi Theta Kappa; Nrsng Srvc Awd; Ntnl Cllgt Nrsng Awd; Nrsng.

**JONES, DENA G,** Henderson Comm Coll, Henderson, KY; FR; BA; Strgs Chmbr Of Cmmrce Schlrshp 90-; Sharon Caudill Schlrshp; Dns Lst 90; Bus; Acctng.

**JONES, DENISE L,** Newbury Coll, Brookline, MA.

**JONES, DENISE M,** Marshall University, Huntington, WV; JR; BA; Kappa Delta Pi; Sigma Tau Elta; Ruth Flowers Brown Schlrshp; Deans List Cert 88-; Educ.

**JONES JR, DENNIS G,** Gallaudet Univ, Washington, DC; SO; BA; Gymnastic Club; Newspr; Dns Lst; Pres Schlr; Hnr Pgm 90-; Ldrshp Award; Psych; Cnslng/Tchng/PHD.

**JONES, DOLLY G,** Radford Univ, Radford, VA; SO; BA; RA 90-; Accntng; CPA.

**JONES, DONNA J,** Wilmington Coll, New Castle, DE; GD; BS; Phi Theta Kappa 81-82; Deans Lst; Wrk Bnk Dlwr; AAS 82; Bnkng Fnc.

**JONES, DUTCHESS R,** Roane St Comm Coll, Harriman, TN; SO; BA; Tlnt Rstr Outstndng Mnrty Cmnty Clg Grdts; Psychlgy; Clncl Psychlgy/Ph D.

**JONES, EDDIE H,** Ky St Univ, Frankfort, KY; FR; BA; USDA Rsrc Clrk Intern; IM Bsktbl Ftbl; Bus; CPA.

**JONES, EDWARD T,** Claflin Coll, Orangeburg, SC; SO; BS; Air Force ROTC; NAACP 88-; Hnrs Prog Student 90-; NASA Hlth Montiroing Ct Inter; All Amer Schlr Clgt Awd 90-; Computer Sci; United States Air Force.

**JONES, ELIZABETH N,** Winthrop Coll, Rock Hill, SC; FR; BA; CLUES 90-; Schlr Schlrshp; Bus; Acctng.

**JONES, ELSWORTH S,** Union Coll, Barbourville, KY; FR; BA; ACE Clb U C 90-; Ftbl Tm/Swim Tm 90-; Union Clg Wgt Lftng Contest Helper 90-; Hist/Econs; Mktg/Fin.

**JONES, ERICKKA C,** Central St Univ, Wilberforce, OH; FR; BA; Afrcn Awrnss Comm; Pol Sci Clb; Pol Sci.

**JONES, ETHEL SIMPSON,** Ny Theological Seminary, New York, NY; SR; BA; Progrsve Ldes Ushers Bd Drill Mstrs 80; Urbanites Dup Bridge Clb Sec 75-81; Metropln Dup Clb Asst Sec 77-81; Abyssinian Bapt Ch Drill Mstrs 80-; Bell Sys Emplee6; Sec Cert; Psych/Soc Sci; Human Serv.

**JONES, EVELYN W,** Oh Wesleyan Univ, Delaware, OH; SR; BA; Wesleyan Coun Stdnt Afrs Cmps Chr 87-89; Pan Coun Pres 87-; Flwshp Chrstn Ath 90-; Phi Eta Sigma 88; Pi Sigma Alpha; Order Of Omega 89-; Kappa Alpha Theta VP 87-; Heritage Fndtn Intrnshp 90; Grk Wmn Yr 89; Otstndng Grk Schlrshp Ldrshp Ctznshp 90; Pol/Govt; Stdnt Adm Higher Educ.

**JONES, FELECIA S,** Al St Univ, Montgomery, AL; FR; Band 90-; Hons Prog 90-; Phi Eta Sigma 90-; Beau Monde Mdl Prdctn 90-; Crmnl Justice; Law/Dstrct Attrny.

**JONES III, FRANK C,** Tougaloo Coll, Tougaloo, MS; SR; BA; Yng Democrats; NAACP; Paer Helper; Omega Psi Phi Pres 90-; Intern Mbr Joint Legisl Staff MS Legist 90-; IM; English; Law/Policis/Ed.

**JONES JR, FRANK WESTON,** Md Inst Coll Of Art, Baltimore, MD; SR; BA; Fine Art; Cnsrvtnst.

**JONES, FULVIA MARISOL,** Middle Tn St Univ, Murfreesboro, TN; JR; BA; Phi Theta Kappa 89; Gamma Beta Phi; Tau Omicron; Alpha Mu Gamma; AA Copiah-Lincoln Comm Coll 90; Spnsh; Tchng.

**JONES, GERALDINE M F,** Catawba Valley Comm Coll, Hickory, NC; SO; BA; Psychlgy.

**JONES, GILLIAN CAMILLE,** Univ Of Miami, Coral Gables, FL; SO; BSC; Chemistry; Medicine.

**JONES, GLENDA L,** Chipola Jr Coll, Marianna, FL; SO; AA; Computer Sci; Comp Asstd Bkkpng.**

**JONES, GLORIA D,** Spartanburg Methodist Coll, Spartanburg, SC; SO; SGA Senator 89-; Drama Clb 89-90; Blck Alliance Clb Asst Secr 89-90; Phi Theta Kappa 89-; Psi Beta Secr 89-; Alpha Mu Gamma 90-; Spec Olympics 89-90; Soph Orientation Ldr 90-; Bsktbl Chrldr 89-90; AA; Elem Ed; Tchg.

**JONES, GWENDOLYN F,** Middle Tn St Univ, Murfreesboro, TN; SR; BA; Mass Comm; Brdcstng.

**JONES JR, HAROLD A,** Jackson St Univ, Jackson, MS; FR; BA; Dnce Ensmbl 90-; Hon Soc 90-; Ftbl 90-; Pol Sci; Law.

**JONES, HEATHER R,** Wv Univ At Parkersburg, Parkersburg, WV; FR; Assc Arts.

**JONES, HOLLY J,** Univ Of Cincinnati, Cincinnati, OH; SR; BSN; Dns Lst 90; Nrsng; MSN.

**JONES, HOPE L,** Edison Comm Coll, Fort Myers, FL; FR; AA; Blck Stdnt Unn 90-; Hnr Stdnt 90-; Math; Acct.

**JONES III, HORATIO C,** Univ Of Rochester, Rochester, NY; SR; BA; Ice Hcky 87-89; Bio; Medcl.

**JONES, HOWARD E,** Rensselaer Polytechnic Inst, Troy, NY; FR; BCHE; Rcqtbl Clb 90-; Vars Trck 90-; Chem Engr/Law.

**JONES, IMOGENE S,** Univ Of Fl, Gainesville, FL; GD; BFA; SOTA Peer Cnslr 88-90; Clgt Msc Edctrs Natl Cnfrnc Treas 88-90; Crdntr Concerto Cmptn 89; Golden Key 88-90; Phi Kappa Phi 90; Phi Delta Kappa 75; Spcl Citation FL Fed Wmns Clbs 88; Wmns Clb Pres 86-; ACDA 88-; FMEA 88-; FVA; Msc Ed; Thrpy/Cnslng/Guidance.

**JONES, JACK S,** Univ Of Akron, Akron, OH; SR; Fincl Mgmt Assn 89-; Fincl Mgmt Assn Natl Hnr Soc; Beta Gamma Sigma 90-; Gldn Key 89-; BS BA; Finc; Fincl Anlys.

**JONES, JAMES D,** Davis & Elkins Coll, Elkins, WV; SO; BA; Political Scie Clb 89-; Track Clb 90-; Political Science; Govt Service.

**JONES, JAMES V,** Union Univ, Jackson, TN; SR; BSBA; Delta Kappa Epsilon 82-; Chpt Sec 83-84; Intrntnl Cnvtn Sec 84; Leonard J Raymond Cllgt Echo Cmptn Prjct Coord; Golf Tm; Rtl Mgmnt; Automobile Sls Srvc Mgmt 84-90; Mrktng Mgmnt; Prdct Mgmnt.

**JONES, JANET L,** Univ Of Southern Ms, Hattiesburg, MS; SR; BS; Beta Alpha Psi 90-; AA Hinds Comm Clg 89; Acctg.

**JONES, JEFFORY VINCENT,** Coppin St Coll, Baltimore, MD; SR; BS; Hist Club Rec Sec 89-; Stdnt Sen Sen/Hstry 90-; Phi Alpha Theta; Cert Of Apprctn Exec Comm 90-; Cert Of Achvmnt Work Study; Natl Assn Of Black Accntnts 80-86; BS 90-; Hist; Curator/Teacher.

**JONES, JEFFREY M,** Oh St Univ At Newark, Newark, OH; SR; BS; Lttl Leag Brd Dir Chrmn 87-88; Asst Ftbl Coach 78-; Elem Educ; Tchr Coach.

**JONES, JEFFREY SCOTT,** Livingston Univ, Livingston, AL; SR; BS; Owned Bsn; Pstr Bptst Chrch; Scl Sci Cmprhsv; Tchr/Admnstr.

**JONES, JEFFREY T,** Alfred Univ, Alfred, NY; SR; BS; Amer Mrktng Assn Exec VP 88-; Intern John Hancock Fnncl Serv 90; Dean Lst 89-; Bus Admn; Mrktng Mngmnt.

**JONES, JENNIFER L,** Piedmont Coll, Demorest, GA; FR; BA; BSU Piedmont Schlrs Prog; Trustees Schlrshp; Psychology; Cnslr.

**JONES, JENNIFER L,** Ohio Valley Coll, Parkersburg, WV; FR; Singers 90-; Theta Psi Omega 90-.

**JONES, JENNIFER M,** Meridian Comm Coll, Meridian, MS; SO; BBA; Bus Admin; Law.

**JONES, JERRY ALLEN,** Wallace St Comm Coll At Dothan, Dothan, AL; SR; Yrbk Stf 87-88; ROTC 84-88; Outstndg Stdnt Electrcl 88-90; Spcl Schlstc Achv Electrcn 88-90; Elctrcn.**

**JONES JR, JERRY W,** Univ Of Sc At Sumter, Sumter, SC; FR; BA; SC Army Ntnl Grd C Btry 4th Bn 178 FA 87-; Westinghouse Elec Corp 88-; Accntng; CPA.

**JONES, JESSE M,** Thomas Nelson Comm Coll, Hampton, VA; AAS; Frbl Wrstlng Ftbl Cptn Ftbl Wrstlng 80-86; Emplyd Sntnl Sys AT&T Dstrbtr Sec Systm; Elctrncs; Elctrcl Engnrng.

**JONES, JESSE M,** Ky St Univ, Frankfort, KY; SR; BA; Scl Wrk Clb Sgt Arms 89-; Alpha Kappa Mu 90-; Frnkfort Hbltn Inc Intrshp; Hghst Achvmnt Stdnt Sprt Srvc 90; Dns Lst 89-; Scl Wrk Acdmc Achvmnt Awds; AA Murray St Univ 86; Scl Wrk.

**JONES, JILL A,** Tusculum Coll, Greeneville, TN; SO; BA; Stdnt Govt Assoc Soph Pres 90; Choir 89; Clg Plyrs 89; Pres Lst 89; Deans Lst 89; Chas Oliver Gray Schlr 90; Alpha Chi Acdmc Excllnce Awd 89-90; Ntl Anthem 89; Soloist Tms; Bio/Math; Genetic Rsrch.

**JONES, JODIE L,** Radford Univ, Radford, VA; JR; BSN; Sigma Theta Tau; Kappa Delta 87-; Methodist Chrch Chr 88-89; BS Clge William Mary 89; Nrsg.

**JONES JR, JODIE W,** Troy St Univ At Troy, Troy, AL; FR; BA; Alpha Lambda Delta; Lambda Alpha Epsilon V P; Lambda Chi Alpha High Sigma 90-; Crmnl Jstc; Law.

**JONES, JOEY S,** Kent St Univ Kent Cmps, Kent, OH; SR; Acctng Assoc 88-89; Delta Sigma Pi Pres 89-90; Bsn Pres Rndtbl 90; BBA 90; Acctng/Bsn Mgmt.

**JONES, JON M,** Va Commonwealth Univ, Richmond, VA; JR; BA; Golden Key; Bus Admin; Mgmt.

**JONES III, JOSEPH M,** Va Commonwealth Univ, Richmond, VA; FR; BA; Phi Eta Sigma; Hstry/Geo; Tchg.

**JONES, JOY A,** Northeastern Christian Jr Coll, Villanova, PA; FR; AS.

**JONES, JOYCE E,** Comm Coll Algny Co Algny Cmps, Pittsburgh, PA; FR; Surgeon.

**JONES, JUDY A,** Univ Of Sc At Coastal Carolina, Conway, SC; JR; BS; Alpha Mu Gamma; Phi Eta Sigma; Deans Lst; Phrmcy.

**JONES, JUDY M,** City Univ Of Ny Baruch Coll, New York, NY; GD; BBA; AAS Manhattan Comm Coll 81; Cmptr Infrm Systms; Systms Anlyst.

**JONES, JULIE L,** Union Univ, Jackson, TN; FR; Pre-Lgl Soc Sec/Treas 90-; Rtldg Hon Hstry Clb Asst Treas; Zeta Tau Alpha Schlstc Chrmn 90-; Math/Hstry; Law.

**JONES, JULIE SHARLEN,** Norfolk St Univ, Norfolk, VA; SO; BA; NABA; Acctg; CPA Law.

**JONES III, JULIUS TROY,** Gaston Coll, Dallas, NC; GD; BSEE; Mst Otstndg Grad; Softbl Tm; Vlybl Tm; AWWA; N C Cert Water Plnt Oper; N C Cert Lab Tech; N C Cert Waste Wtr Plnt Oper Grade II; Soc Amer Magcns; AS 84; Elec Eng; Publ Serv.

**JONES, JUSTIN B,** Univ Of Sc At Columbia, Columbia, SC; JR; BS; Clg Repblcns 88-90; Repblcn Party; Math Computer Sci; Computer Cnsltnt.

**JONES, KAREN,** Va St Univ, Petersburg, VA; SR; Mrchng Bnd Sctn Ldr 86-88; Pan Hllnc Cncl Del 88-; Sigma Gamma Rho Bsls 88-; Srrty NE Rgn Acdmc Awrd 88; BS; Bus Infrmtn Sys; Airline Infrmtn Sys.

**JONES, KAREN K,** Univ Of Ga, Athens, GA; JR; BED; CSD; Speech Pathlgy.

**JONES, KARIN M,** Hudson Valley Comm Coll, Troy, NY; SO; Erly Chldhd Clb 89-; Pres List 89-; Deans List 90; Otto Gunther Schlrhsp; AAS; Erly Chldhd; Spch Pathlgy/Adlgy.

**JONES, KATHERINE S,** Columbia Union Coll, Takoma Park, MD; JR; BS; RN 72-; Cert Cntrl Serv Tech 90-; AAS Washington Tech Inst 70; Hlth Cr Admin; Nrsng Hm Admnstrtr.

**JONES, KATHLEEN P,** Daytona Beach Comm Coll, Daytona Beach, FL; FR; AS; Sci; Nrsng.

**JONES, KEELAN DEREK,** Univ Of Sc At Columbia, Columbia, SC; FR; BA; Montaineering & Whitewater Club 90-; Canoe & Kayak Club 88-.

**JONES, KELLIE E,** Kent St Univ Kent Cmps, Kent, OH; SO; Hon Coll Schlrshp; Nutrition Dietetics; Registered Dietician.

**JONES, KELLY L,** Comm Coll Algny Co Algny Cmps, Pittsburgh, PA; SO; AS; Aviators Clb Treas 90-; Phi Theta Kappa 90-; Hons Schlrshp 89-; Flght Tech; Cmrcl Plt.

**JONES, KELLY-SNOW,** Salisbury St Univ, Salisbury, MD; JR; BA; Alpha Omega 89; Phi Eta Sigma 88; Beta Beta Beta Pres 90; Kappa Delta P; Blgy; Blgy Tchr.

**JONES, KEVIN H,** Va Commonwealth Univ, Richmond, VA; JR; BFA; Honrbl Mntn Virginia Museum; Flwshp Pgm; Painting/Prntmkng.

**JONES, KEVIN K,** Univ Of Sc At Columbia, Columbia, SC; FR; BS; Assoc Of Afro-Amer Stdnts 90; Acctng; Mngrl Accntnt.

**JONES, KEVIN L,** Tn Temple Univ, Chattanooga, TN; FR; BS; Contmpry Christian Bnd 90; Sigma Chi Delta 90; US Army Opr Dsrt Strm 88-90; Music; Cmpsr/Keybrdst.

**JONES, KEVIN M,** Liberty Univ, Lynchburg, VA; SR; BS; Mthmtcl Assc Amer 90-; Kappa Mu Epsilon 90-; Hnrs Pgm 87-; IM Ftbl/Bsktbl-Sftbl 87-; Math; Actuarial Sci.

**JONES, KEVIN R,** Vanderbilt Univ, Nashville, TN; FR; BM; Blr Hnr Schlrshp 90-; Music; Prfrmnc.

**JONES, KEVIN R,** Univ Of Louisville, Louisville, KY; GD; MENG; Speed Stdnt Cncl 89-; Assn Cmptng Mach Pres 90-; Tau Beta Pi 88-; Triangle 89-; Deans Schlr; BES 90; Eng Math/Cmptr Sci; Eng.

**JONES, KIMBERLY D,** Fl A & M Univ, Tallahassee, FL; SR; BS; Dvrsfd Labs Schl Bus Ind Ortrs Instr 89-90; Famuan Stff Wrtr 88-89; Stdnt Govt Assoc Sec Of Stdnt Wlfr 89-90; Hnr Soc; Golden Key; Pitney Bowes Inc Cr Corp Fin Anlyst 89; AAS Bus Comm Clg Of Phila 88f; Bus Educ; JD MBA Law Schl Beg 92.

**JONES, KIMBERLY M,** Auburn Univ At Auburn, Auburn, AL; JR; BA; Soc Dcrtv Dsgn 89-; Deans List 90; Clg Schlrs Am; Intr Dsgn.

**JONES, KIMBERLY S,** Hampton Univ, Hampton, VA; JR; BA; Psychlgy Clb 88-; Pr Cnlsr; Bg Brthrs Bg Sstrs Prgm 90-; Stdnt Un Brd 88-90; Ga Pre Almn Treas 88-; Alpha Kappa Mu 90-; Schl Cnslng Psychlgy.**

**JONES, KIMBERLYE E,** Central St Univ, Wilberforce, OH; SO; BA; AA Penn Valley Comm Coll 90; Cmmnctns Radio/TV; Grphcs.

**JONES, KIPLAN L,** Abraham Baldwin Agri Coll, Tifton, GA; SO; ACCT; Phi Theta Kappa 89-; Superior Hnr Stdnt 89-90; Dist Hnr Stdnt 90-; Acctng; CPA.**

**JONES, KISHA N,** Western New England Coll, Springfield, MA; FR; BA; United Mutually Equal 90-; Alpha Lambda Delta; English; Law.

**JONES, KRISTEN E,** Roane St Comm Coll, Harriman, TN; GD; AAS; Excell Typng 90; Ofc Admin Word Prcssng.**

**JONES, KRISTI A,** Radford Univ, Radford, VA; FR; Wmns Gym Tm Schrshp.

**JONES, KRISTI L,** Univ Of Nc At Greensboro, Greensboro, NC; SR; BSN; Natl Clgt Nrsng Awds 90-; Nursing.**

**JONES, KRISTIE A,** Univ Of Nc At Asheville, Asheville, NC; SO; BA; Drama; Tchng.

**JONES, LA TOYA S,** Central St Univ, Wilberforce, OH; FR; Pbtst Stu Unn 90; Drm Cncl Flr Rep 90; Eng.

**JONES, LA VITA D R,** Le Moyne Owen Coll, Memphis, TN; JR; BSW; Sigma Gamma Rho; Soc Wrk; Psychiatric Soc Wrk.

**JONES, LANDON A,** Stillman Coll, Tuscaloosa, AL; SO; BS; Untd Negro Clg Fnd Chrprsn 90-; NAACP Chrprsn 90-; Tutor; Deans List 90; All Amercn Schlr 90-; Track Team 90-; AA Electrncs Tech SW State Tech Clg 85; Math; Secndry Ed/ Banking.

**JONES, LARRY D,** Ky St Univ, Frankfort, KY; SR; BA; SG; Alumni; NAACP; Acctg Assoc; Cosmpoltn Clb; Yng Demo; Rotoract; Phi Beta Lamba Rep 88; Alpha Kappa Pi Treas 89; Bsns Hon Soc 89-; Bg Bros 88-90; USDA Forest Serv 90; Dns Lst 87-; Acad Awds 89-; Acctg/Bsns Admn; CPA.

**JONES III, LAURIE V,** Ms St Univ, Miss State, MS; JR; BARCH; Rfrmed Univ Fllwshp 88; Phi Eta Sigma 89; Tau Sigma Delta Treas 90; Gamma Beta Phi; Mortar Brd; Amer Inst Of Archtctre Stdnts Class Rep 88; Habitat For Hmnty Scrty 90; Schl Of Arch Fclty Book Awd 89; Deans Lst 88-90; Archtctre.

**JONES, LEIF A,** Univ Of Sc At Columbia, Columbia, SC; SR; MMA; LIFE Prgm Chrmn 89-90; Unv SC Aiken Band 87-88; Midland Vlly Lions Clb 88-; Media Arts; Corprt Media.

**JONES, LELA A,** Jackson St Univ, Jackson, MS; SO; BS; Baptist Union Rep 89-; Alpha Lambda Delta 90-; Dns Lst; Acad Schlrshp; Elem Ed; Tch.

**JONES, LEMUEL D,** Univ Of Nc At Asheville, Asheville, NC; JR; BA; Stdnt Prgmng Brd Spcl Events Chair 88-; Lit.

**JONES, LENDER R,** Meridian Comm Coll, Meridian, MS; FR; LPN Clb VP; VICA Comp Hlth Bwl Qz; Suprv; LPN.

**JONES, LEONIE M,** Fl International Univ, Miami, FL; SR; BA; Intl Stdnts Clb 89-; Asso Degr Bahamas Hotl Trng Clg 89; Hosp Mgmt; Rest Mgr.

**JONES, LESLIE D,** Hampton Univ, Hampton, VA; SO; BS; Stdnt Ldrs; Exec Cncl Mss Soph; NAACP; Alpha Kappa Mu; Acctng; CPA.

**JONES, LESLIE D,** Univ Of Ga, Athens, GA; SR; BAFCS; SPAGE; GAVC; SACUS; NAEYC; Hall Cncl Rep 88-89; Child Dvlpmnt Erly Chldhd Edn; Teach.

**JONES, LESLIE-ANN P,** Coppin St Coll, Baltimore, MD; SR; BS; Comp Sci Clb; Sport Clb Sec 89-; Coppin Hon Soc; AMA Cllgt Case Comp 90-; Mgmt Sci; Bus Mngr.

**JONES, LETHEA L,** Southern Junior Coll, Birmingham, AL; SO; Bsn Clb; Pres Lst/Dns Lst; USAR Spec E-4.

**JONES, LINDA D,** Comm Coll Algny Co Algny Cmps, Pittsburgh, PA; GD; MED; Sndy Shcl Tchr 86-; Vacation Bible Schl Tchr 87-90; Yth Fllwhship Advsr 89-90; BA Univ Pittsburgh 87; Elem Educ; Elem Tchng.

**JONES, LINDA M,** Al A & M Univ, Normal, AL; FR; Hon Roll; Deans List.

**JONES, LISA,** Univ Of Charleston, Charleston, WV; SR; BS; Cpto Assn Of Stdnt Nrss 90-; Nrsng Hnr Scty; Lgn Gen Hosp 82-; AA Southern WV Comm Coll 85; Nrsng; Crtcl Cre Nrse.

**JONES, LISA A,** Norfolk St Univ, Norfolk, VA; SO; BA; Sprtn Alpha Tau 90-; Nrflk St Hnrs Prgrm; Pres Va Colgt Hnrs Cncl Cnvntn; Pta Wrght Elem 87-; Englsh; Pblc Schl Lbrn.

**JONES, LISA M,** De Tech & Comm Coll At Dover, Dover, DE; FR; RNADN; Nrsng.

**JONES, LORI A,** George Mason Univ, Fairfax, VA; JR; BS; Arbcs Clb Pres 88-90; Gldn Ky VP; Zeta Tau Alpha Jdcl Chrmn 89-; Jon L Burleson Schlrshp; Bus Mngmnt; Rehab Cnslng.**

**JONES, LORI R,** Hillsborough Comm Coll, Tampa, FL; JR; BA; Stdnt Gov/Univ South FL Pres; Phi Theta Kappa; SCATT Univ South FL Strng Cmmt; Ed; Tchng.

**JONES, LYNETTE M,** Talladega Coll, Talladega, AL; SO; BS; Pre Alumni Cncl Sec 90-; Grmn Clb 90-; Biology Clb 90-; Bsns/ Ecnmcs Clb 90-; David Aronow Schlrshp Fnd; Deans Lst 90-; Biology Medicine; Neurosurgeon.

**JONES, MALLORY E,** Central Fl Comm Coll, Ocala, FL; SO; ADN; Natl Stdnt Nurses Assn 90-; Phi Theta Kappa; Central Fl Comm Coll 86; Phys Thrpy Intern; CMA Webster Coll 87; Reg Nurse; Nrsng Admn.

**JONES, MARCIA,** Coppin St Coll, Baltimore, MD; FR; BS; Sci Clb/Intrntl Stdnts Assoc; Hnrs Clb; Bio; Med.

**JONES, MARCIA Y,** Miami Dade Comm Coll North, Miami, FL; SO; Crcl K; Fshn Clb; Crrbn Clb; Acdmc Excllnc Awrd; Bus Admn.

**JONES, MARGARET A,** Coppin St Coll, Baltimore, MD; JR; BED; PTO Pres 89-90; Alpha Kappa Mu; Spec Ed; Tchr.

**JONES, MARGARET M,** Univ Of Ky, Lexington, KY; SR; Psi Chi Hnry 90-; Kappa Kappa Gamma VP 89-90; Clnc Asstnt PSC U Of Ky; BA; Psych; Grad Sch.

**JONES, MARIE F,** Kent St Univ Kent Cmps, Kent, OH; GD; MLS; Dionysia Lit/Vis Arts Mag Edtr 82-85; Chapel Choir 83-86; Phi Beta Mu 90 Lib Sci 90-; Kappa Alpha Phi 86-; Phi Beta 84-86; Grad Asst 90; Donnan Awrd Creative Wrtng 85; Outstndng Engl Maj Awrd 86; Amer Lib Assoc 90; Acad Lib Assoc Of OH Mbr 90; Acad Librarianship.

**JONES, MARIE-ANTOINETTE,** Jackson St Univ, Jackson, MS; JR; BS; Bptst Stdnt Un; Psych Clb; Wdwnd Ensbl; Les Exqsts A La Mode Mdlng Sqd; Psi Chi; Alpha Lambda Delta; SROP Stdnt Reschr 90; MARC Schlr 90-; MARC Intrnshp; WEB Du Bois Hon Coll 88; Outstdng Achvmnt Awd 90; Deans Lst 88-; Psych; Clncl Psychlgst.

**JONES, MARK T,** Northeast State Tech Comm Coll, Blountville, TN; SO; AAS; Automtv/Hvy Trck.

**JONES, MARY C,** Marywood Coll, Scranton, PA; SO; BFA; Camp Mnstry 90-; Vars Vlybl 89-; Vars Sftbl 89-; Camp Mnstry 90-; Coll Vlntrs 90-; IM Vlybl/Rqtbl 89-; Interior Dsgn.

**JONES, MARY L,** Univ Of Southern Ms, Hattiesburg, MS; JR; BS; NATA Stdnt Mbr 90-; SATA Stdnt Mbr 90-; Sprtsmed Clb 90-; Adopt A Hwy 90-; NMCC Athltc Schlrhp 89-90; Schlor Schlrshp 90-; Stdnt Athltc Trnr; AA NE MS Comm Coll 90; Amer Red Cross/CPR Inst 90-; Bsktbl/Sftbl 89-; Coaching/Sprts Adm; Athltc Trnr.

**JONES, MAX J,** Meridian Comm Coll, Meridian, MS; SO; MBA; Trnsfr Schlrshp Univ MS; Air Force 86-90; Bus; Corp Law.

**JONES, MC QUITA J,** Tn St Univ, Nashville, TN; SR; Pr Cnslr 87-; Kappa Omicron Nu Treas 89-; Intern Cprtv Extntn Prgm; Otstndng Coll Stdnts Amrc 88-89; Clthng Txtls.

**JONES, MELISSA HURST,** Univ Of Al At Birmingham, Birmingham, AL; SR; BA; Ambassador UAB 90-; Gldn Key 90-; Kappa Delta Pi 89-; Edctn; Elem Edctn Tchr.

**JONES, MELISSA K,** Middle Tn St Univ, Murfreesboro, TN; SR; BED; Soc Sci; Tchr.

**JONES, MELISSA R,** Fl A & M Univ, Tallahassee, FL; FR; BA; Natl Assn Blck Accntnts Sec 90-; SBI Invstmnt Fnds Tm Anylst 90-; Phi Eta Sigma; Cert Schlrshp; SBI Spec Recgntn Awrd; Math; Actrl Sci.

**JONES, MELVA E,** Central St Univ, Wilberforce, OH; GD; Eta Phi Beta 83; PTA Sprngfld Elem Pres 72; 4 H Prog Asst 76; Rcrtr Cnclr 85; Assc Chld Dev 80; Hstry Spcl Educ.

**JONES, MELVA O,** Univ Of Southern Ms, Hattiesburg, MS; JR; BSN; Stdnt Nrs Assn Sthrn MS; Gamma Beta Phi 89-; Bay Spgs Chruch Christ; Hlth/Hmn Sci; Nrsng.

**JONES, MICHAEL,** American Baptist Coll, Nashville, TN; SR; BSMS; BSU 90-; Alpha Phi Alpha 81-; Chicago Mnstr Cnfrnc; Chicago Yth Mnstr Cnfrnc; Chicago Police Dept Intrnshp 83; Pontiac Crctnl Ctr Intrnshp 86; SIU Vrsty Bsktbl 79-83; IL Dept Crctn Pontiac Crctnl Ctr 84-90; Crmnl Justice; Wrdn Crctnl Fclty/Pstr.

**JONES SR, MICHAEL A,** Alcorn St Univ, Lorman, MS; SR; Mbr High School Choir Pt Gibsn High 74-76; Mbr Blue Knights 75-76; Airmn Quartr U S Air Frc 78; Ind Tech; Eng/Constrctn.

**JONES, MICHAEL C,** Bridgewater Coll, Bridgewater, VA; JR; BA; Phi Beta Lambda 90-; Stdnt Cnslr 89-90; Dns Lst; W Shenandoah Ruritan Clb 87-; Bsn Adm; Bsn Sls/Mgmt/Mktg.

**JONES, MICHAEL D,** Va Commonwealth Univ, Richmond, VA; FR; PPL; Pre-Phrmcy Clb 90-; Chem; Phrmcst.

**JONES, MICHAEL E,** Barry Univ, Miami, FL; JR; BA; Scuba Clb; AA Martin Coll 88; Rcrtnl Dvng Mgmt; Scuba Educ.

**JONES, MICHAEL E,** Samford Univ, Birmingham, AL; JR; JD; FL Stdnt Bar Cumberland Sch Law 89-; Pre-Law Clb Oglethorpe U 86-89; Entrepreneurs Clb Oglethorpe U 85-89; Sigma Alpha Epsilon Oglethorpe U Treas 85-89; Walk-A-Thon March Dimes 85-89; Broad/Cassel Intern; Tobin/Miller Intern 90; IMS; Law.

**JONES, MICHAEL H,** Univ Of Nc At Asheville, Asheville, NC; SR; BS; Music Clb 89-; Studio Ensmble 89-; Hear Here Studio Intern 89; Upstream Intern 90; Dept Distinction Awd; Music; Audio Eng/Music Performance.

**JONES, MICHAEL S,** Univ Of Southern Ms, Hattiesburg, MS; FR; MD; Amer Chem Soc; Alumni Assn; SADD 90-; Lambda Sigma 90-; Phi Eta Sigma 90-; Beta Beta Beta 90-; Alpha Lambda Delta 90-; Gldn Key 90-; Gamma Beta Phi 90-; Outstndng Fresh 90-; Biochem; Physcn-Rsrch.

**JONES, MICHELE L,** Southern Coll Of Tech, Marietta, GA; SR; BS; Alpha Delta Pi Chpln 87-; Sftwr Eng.

**JONES, MICHELE L,** Northern Ky Univ, Highland Hts, KY; SO; BA; Soph Excllnce Schlrshp; Deans Lst; Hsng Schlrshp; Psych; Psychlgst.

**JONES, NANETTE,** Univ Of Ga, Athens, GA; SR; BSED; Bapt Stdnt Un 90-; Christian Assoc 88-90; Schlr 89-90; Phi Theta Kappa 89-90; Sigma Delta Mu 90; Kappa Delta Epsilon 90-; Kappa Delta Pi; Marshal 89-90; AA/AFAM Peace Clg 90; Early Educ.

**JONES, NATHAN R,** Providence Coll, Providence, RI; SO; BA; Weightlifting 89-; IMS 89-; Dns Lst 89-; Supersports 89-90; Ftbl 89-90; Finance; Bsn.

**JONES, NELDA C,** Jackson St Univ, Jackson, MS; SR; BS; Phi Kappa Phi 90-; Full Acad Schlrshp 88-; Dvlpmnt Schlrshp 86-88; Salutatorian 90-; Soc Studies; Scndry Tchr.

**JONES, NIKI A,** Union Univ, Jackson, TN; FR; BS; Stdnt TN Edctn Assoc VP 90-; Sigma Alpha Epsilon Lttl Sstr 90-; Elem Ed; Tch.

**JONES, OLIVER B,** Morris Brown Coll, Atlanta, GA; SO; BS; Mock Trl Tm 90-; Cls Offcr V P 90-; Pol Sci; Law.

**JONES, PAMELA,** Bryant Stratton Bus Inst Roch, Rochester, NY; FR.

**JONES, PAMELA L,** Pellissippi St Tech Comm Coll, Knoxville, TN; SO; AS; Otdrs Clb; Pre Pharmacy.

**JONES, PAMELA Y,** Va St Univ, Petersburg, VA; JR; Vets Of State Pres 90-; SEA 89-; Kappa Delta Pi 90-.

**JONES, PATRICIA L,** Univ Of Nc At Asheville, Asheville, NC; SO; BA; Psi Phi Pscyh Clb; Asst To Dr Nallan Rsrch Prjct In Psych; Glf; Cert Rsprtry Thrpst Univ Of New Mexico 85; Educ And Psych Mjr; Elem Tchr.

**JONES, POLLY D,** Univ Of Nh Plymouth St Coll, Plymouth, NH; SO; BS; Soc Wrk Clb Sec 90-; Pres Lst 89-; Dean Lst 90; Soc Wrk.

**JONES, PRISCILLA M,** Memphis St Univ, Memphis, TN; SR; BED; Phi Theta Kappa 90-; Kappa Delta Pi; Gibson Co Assoc Of EMT/PARAMEDIC 90-; Natl/St Of Stn Trauma Soc 90-; LPN/ PARAMEDIC; AAS Deg Jackson St Comm Clg 90; Prmdc Cerf 89; Educ Hlth/Safety; Emerg Med Serv.

**JONES, QUENDOLYN D,** Wilberforce Univ, Wilberforce, OH; GD; NAACP Rcrtr; Ntnl Stdnt Bsn League; Alpha Kappa Alpha Treas; John F Mrnng Bsn Awrd; OH Almn Schlrshp; Cert Apprctn Wright Patterson AFB Intrsh; BS 91; Acctng; Cert Pblc Acctn.

**JONES, RACHEL R,** Livingston Univ, Livingston, AL; SR; BED; Southern Busn Ed Assn; Phi Theta Kappa 89; Busn; Tchng.

**JONES JR, RALPH R,** Memphis St Univ, Memphis, TN; SO; BA; Hm Dsgnr Ralph Jones/Assoc; Frgn Lang/Clsscs; Tch/ Mnstry.

**JONES, RENEE L,** Marshall University, Huntington, WV; FR; BS; Blck Untd Stdnts 90-; Cmmtt Spprt Afrcn Amrcn Wmn Chrmn 90-; Inrds Intern 90-; Crss Cntry Indr Trck Otdr Trck; Bus Admn; Crprt Law.

**JONES, RENTA V,** Central St Univ, Wilberforce, OH; JR; BA; Acctg Clb; NAACP; Prshng Rfls; Alpha Kappa Mu; Acctg; CPA.

**JONES, RICHARD B,** Lenoir Rhyne Coll, Hickory, NC; JR; BS; Vrsty Ftbl 88-; FCA 88-; Chi Beta Phi Pres 90-; Tau Kappa Epsilon 88-; Acdmc All Cnfrnc 90; Acdmc Awd Ftbl 88-; Grk Athltc Awd; Blgy; Orthpdc Srgn.

**JONES, RICK E,** Northern Ky Univ, Highland Hts, KY; SR; BA; GUNK 90-; Phi Alpha Theta; IM Rcqtbl League; Soc Stdies; Prfssr.

**JONES, RITA K,** Livingston Univ, Livingston, AL; JR; BA; Elem Ed; Tchng.

**JONES, RITA M,** Thomas Coll, Thomasville, GA; FR; BSED; FBLA 67-68; 4 H 60-69; Tri Hi 4 66-69; Beta 67-68; DAR; PTO 78-; Sci Home Ec; Tchng.

**JONES, ROBERT,** Coppin St Coll, Baltimore, MD; SO; BA; Adptd Physcl Edctn Scty; Phi Beta Sigma; 5 Str Bsbll Cmp Bst Bsbll Plyrs; Bsbll; Adptd Physcl Edctn Phy Thpry.

**JONES, ROBERT C,** Univ Of Akron, Akron, OH; SO; BA; Mech Engr.

**JONES, ROBIN D,** Va St Univ, Petersburg, VA; FR; Bus.

**JONES, ROBIN W,** Livingston Univ, Livingston, AL; JR; BA; Band; Jazz Band; Choir; Phi Mu Alpha Sinfonia; Msc Prfrmnce; Tlnt Sct.

**JONES, ROSEMARY,** Univ Of Tn At Knoxville, Knoxville, TN; SR; DVM; Amer Vet Mdcl Assc; Amer Assc Quine Prctnrs Pres; Vet Bkstore Stdnt Co-Op Pres 90; Gamma Sigma Delta; Amer Assc Equine Prctnrs; US Dressage Fdrtn; BS Univ DE 73; MS Rugers Univ 75; Vet Medicine.

**JONES, SAMANTHA A,** College Of Mount St Joseph, Mt St Joseph, OH; FR; BA; Lit Mag Co Edtr 90-; Nwspr Assoc Edtr; Dns Lst 90-; Acad Achvmnt Awd; Engl; Jrnlsm/Tchng/Law.

**JONES, SANDRA MARIE,** Alcorn St Univ, Lorman, MS; SR; DDS; Stdnt Govt 88-89; NAACP 87-; Alpha Kappa Mu 89-90; Beta Kappa Chi 89-; Delta Sigma Theta 90-; Hon Grad; BS Degree Alcorn State Univ; Blgy; Dntstry.

**JONES, SARA E,** Wv Univ, Morgantown, WV; JR; BSN; Mntnr Amrcn Rd Crss Clb Bld Chrmn 88-89; Stdnt Nrss Assoc Rep 89-; Ordr Grl 90-; Natl Stdnt Nrss Asoc; Li Toon Awa Pres 89-90; Deans Lst 88-; Sigma Theta Tau; Kappa Kappa Gamma 89; Extrnshp Mdcl Instnsv Cr Unt Rby Mmrl Hosp; Vllybll Intrmrls 90; Nrsng.

**JONES, SARAH E,** Tusculum Coll, Greeneville, TN; GD; Stdnt Cncl Stdnts With Spec Abilities; Deans List 89-; Sr Key Hnr Awd Spec Ed 90; BS 90; Elem/Spec Edn; Teach.

**JONES, SCOTT W,** Univ Of Southern Ms, Hattiesburg, MS; SR; BS BA; Phi Theta Kappa 88-89; Bapt Stdnt Union Exec Cncl 88-; Eagle Clb/Alum Assn 90-; Bus Stdng Advsry Cncl Rep 90-; Miss BSU Msns Comm 90-; Outstdng Coll Stdnts Of Amer 89-90; Pres Lst 87-; Dns Lst 87-; Bnkng/Finance; Prfsr.

**JONES, SELINA C,** Middle Tn St Univ, Murfreesboro, TN; SO; STEA 90-; Ed; Kndrgrtn Tchr.

**JONES, SHAREN J,** Fl International Univ, Miami, FL; SR; BA; PTA 88-89; YMCA Cnslr 82-85; AA Miami Dade Comm Coll 87; Elem Ed; Tchr.

**JONES, SHARON E,** Bunker Hill Comm Coll, Boston, MA; FR; Engl; Cmptrs.

**JONES, SHARWANDA L,** Fl A & M Univ, Tallahassee, FL; JR; NAACP; White/Gold Hnr Soc; Phrmcy.

**JONES, SHAWNDELLE L,** Central St Univ, Wilberforce, OH; FR; BS; Chrch Sec 89-; Tutr High Schl/Coll Stdnts 90-; Cnslr Tnagrs In Pryr Mtngs 89-; All Amer Schlrshp Awrd; Natl Collgt Bus Mer Awrd; US Achvmnt Awrds 85; Acadmc Achvmnt Mer Awrd 90; Bus Admin/Comp Info Syst; Comp Sci.

**JONES, SHEILA Y,** Howard Univ, Washington, DC; GD; PHD; Grad Stdnts Clb 88-; SE Univ Grad Stdnt Cncl Pres 85-87; Alpha Kappa Delta 90-; St Augstn Hlth Mnstry Treas 84-; Natl Medcl Assn Intrn 85-87; Tchng Asst 90-; BS Howard Univ 77; MBA SE Univ 85; Med Sociolgy/Gerntlgy; Hlth Attrny.

**JONES, SHERRY J,** Dyersburg St Comm Coll, Dyersburg, TN; SO; ASBS; FHA 87; Art Clb 89; Sci Clb 88-89; Natl Hon Scty 90; Amer Chem Scty VP 90; Mu Alpha Theta 87-89; Dstngshd Yng Ldrshp Awrd 89-90; Bus Awrd 88; AS; Sci/Math; Optmtry.**

**JONES, SHERRY M,** Univ Of Rochester, Rochester, NY; SR; Blk Stdnt Union 86; Gospel Choir 86; Rho Rhose Swthrt To Sigma Phi Rho Frat Sec; Smmr Mngmnt Intrnshp At Sear/Roebuck 90; Pol Sci; Mgt Trng Prog.

**JONES, SHERYL L,** Truett Mc Connell Coll, Cleveland, GA; FR; BS; Bapt Un; Phi Theta Kappa; Sftbl; Med; Pharm.

**JONES, SHUNTE M,** Tougaloo Coll, Tougaloo, MS; SO; BS; Pre-Alumni Cncl; NAACP; Pre-Hlth Clb; Stdnt Support Svc; Chrldr 89-90; Miss UNCF 80-; Schlrshp; Fisk U Pre-Med Sci Pgm; Bio; Med Dr.

**JONES, SONIA M,** Ny Univ, New York, NY; SO; BA; Co Spnsr Drm Fndtn 89-; Mny Rsr Rbn Hd Chrty; Hstry.

**JONES, SONYA D,** Fayetteville St Univ, Fayetteville, NC; SO; BA; NCAE NEA 90-; Chnclrs Lst 90-; Elem Educ; Tchg.

**JONES, SOPHIA C,** Bennett Coll, Greensboro, NC; JR; BA; Poli Sci Clb Fndrsr 90-; Intresdnt Hse Cncl VP 90-; Drama Clb 89-90; Mdl UN; Wn Ctr Intern; Poli Sci; Law.

**JONES, STEPHANIE A,** Norfolk St Univ, Norfolk, VA; JR; BSW; Hnr Awd 90-; AA Tidewater Comm Clg 90; Soc Work.

**JONES, STEPHEN F,** Salisbury St Univ, Salisbury, MD; SR; BS; Geogrphc Soc 87-; Intl Geogrphc Hon Soc 89-; Henson Schl Sci Schlrshp 89-; IM Sftbl/Bsktbl; Geogrphy/Rgnl Plng.

**JONES, SUSAN E,** Middle Tn St Univ, Murfreesboro, TN; GD; MBA; Spcl Hnrs Grad Asst; Intl Stdnt Srvcs; Gamma Beta Phi 83; Alpha Kappa Psi 90-; Psi Alpha Srrty 84-86; Cert Scb Dvr 87-; BS 86; Mrktng.

**JONES, SUSAN E,** Liberty Univ, Lynchburg, VA; SR; BS; Actvties Dorm Dir 89-90; Urbn Outrch 89-90; Intl Schlrshp 90-; Fmly/Comm Stdies; Adlt Educr.

**JONES, SUSAN M,** Univ Of Tn At Knoxville, Knoxville, TN; SR; BS; Inter Vrsty Chrstn Flwshp 89-90; Golden Key 90-; Phi Eta Sigma 88-; Alpha Chi 89-; Beta Gamma Sigma 90-; Gamma Iota Sigma 89-90; John A Walker Bus Schlrshp 87-90; Mgt.

**JONES, SUSAN S,** Gaston Coll, Dallas, NC; FR; Gamma Beta Phi 90-; Rdlgy.

**JONES, TAMARA C,** Hillsborough Comm Coll, Tampa, FL; SR; BS; Phi Theta Kappa Sec 90; Kappa Delta Pi; Elem Ed; Tchng.

**JONES, TAMMY B,** Birmingham Southern Coll, Birmingham, AL; SO; BA; Acctng; CPA.

**JONES, TAMMY L,** Longwood Coll, Farmville, VA; SO; BS; Phi Kappa Phi 88-; Pharmacy.

**JONES, TAMMY R,** Lenoir Rhyne Coll, Hickory, NC; SR; BA; Coll Yrbk Ed 90-; Res Life Sr RA 89-90; Centennial Observance Com 90-; Mu Sigma Epsilon 90-; Omicron Delta Epsilon; Kappa Delta VP Membrshp 90-; Habitat For Humanity 88; Intl Bus; Banking.

**JONES, TAMMY R,** Phillips Jr Coll Spartanburg, Spartanburg, SC; FR; Nrsng; Rn/Bsn.

**JONES, TANGUELA D,** Univ Of Southern Ms, Hattiesburg, MS; SR; BA; Stdnt Almn Assc; Afro Amer Stdnt Orgnztn; IM Bsktbl; Kappa Mu Epsln; Phi Dlt Rho; Gamma Beta Phi Sec; Alph Lmbd Dlt; Phi Eta Sgm; Hon Stdnt Assc; Deans List 86-; Hercules Schlrshp Rcpnt Hon Clg Schlrshp 88-89; Afro Amer Stdnt Orgztn Schlstc Awrd; Math; Attnd Law Sch.

**JONES, TERESA B,** Univ Of Al At Birmingham, Birmingham, AL; SO; BS; Med Asst U S Army 84-87; Nrsng.

**JONES, TERESA L,** Concord Coll, Athens, WV; SR; BS; NBEA 90-; WVEA 90-; NEA 90-; Alpha Chi 89-; Kappa Delta Pi 89-; NBEA Awd Merit 91; Bus Educ Cmprhnsv; Bus Educ Tchr.

**JONES, TERESA L,** Univ Of Md At Eastern Shore, Princess Anne, MD; SR; MBA; Miss UMES SGA 90-; Ambr Club Yrbk; Nwprs Staff; Delta Sigma Theta Pres 90-; Chaplan 88-89; Dean Of Pledges 89-90; Peer Counselor; Acad Achiev Excellence; All Amer Schlr; Bowling League Chldr Pom Pom Sq; BA; Sociology/Pre Law.

**JONES, TERRELL E,** Univ Of Ms Medical Center, Jackson, MS; FR; Sigma Alpha Epsilon; Ph D Anatomy 84.

**JONES, TERRELL LA MAR,** Al St Univ, Montgomery, AL; SR; MBA; Drl Sgt Qlfd; Rngr Qlfd Ldrshp Rbns Rnk Stf Sgt; Stu Ldr Awrd; Psych; Kappa Alpha Psi VP 88-; Blck Union Pres 89-90; ASP 88-90; Spcl Olympcs 88-90; Untd Way 88-90; Pasadena Vol Yr 83; Bdy Bldg Awrds; BA; Cnslg; Prof.

**JONES, THOMAS E,** Univ Of Tn At Martin, Martin, TN; SR; BS; Eng Scty 88-; Psychlgy Clb 89-; Beta Beta Beta; Psi Chi; Tchg Asst Psychgy 90-; Sigma Xi Excel Undrgrdt Rsrch 90; Estes Kefauver Alumni Schlrshp 87-88; Bio/Psych; Med Dr.

**JONES, TIMOTHY J,** Fayetteville St Univ, Fayetteville, NC; SR; BS; Math/Cmptr Sci Clb 87; Stdnt Acad Advsr Univ Ambssdr 88; Yth Mtvtn Tsk Frce 90; Coop Ed 89; NC Intrnsh 90; CIAA Clg Ftbl 86; CIAA Clg Trck 87; Math/Cmptr Sci; Mstr In Cmptr Sci.

**JONES, TIMOTHY L,** Al A & M Univ, Normal, AL; FR; Masonic Clb; Stdnt Govt Assn; Videogrphrs Clb; Hon Roll 88; WALA TV Edtr/Intern 89; Cntntl Cablevsn Cameramn/Intern 90; WAFF TV Edtr/Empld; Tele Cmnctns; Brdcstng.**

**JONES, TINA D,** Ms St Univ, Miss State, MS; SR; BA; Real Est; Mrtg Finance.

**JONES, TODD P,** Univ Of Akron, Akron, OH; SO; BA; Art Schlp Comp; Grphc Dsgn.

**JONES, TOM S,** Spartanburg Methodist Coll, Spartanburg, SC; SO; BS; Crmnl Justc Club Pres; Stdnt Govt Sntr; Phi Theta Kappa; ASSOC; Crmnl Justc; Law.

**JONES, TRACEY T,** Va St Univ, Petersburg, VA; JR; Phi Alpha Theta; Pre Law Soc & Res Advsr 90-; Miss VSU Pageant; Deans List; Natl 4-H Schlrshp 89; Katherine T & Thomas Law Schlrshps; Natl 4-H Org 79-; NAACP 78-; Cir K Intl Org 88-90; Pub Spkng Amb 86-88; Sigma Xi Sci Rsrch Soc Awd; Hist/Intl Studies; Corp Law.

**JONES, TRACI L,** Valdosta St Coll, Valdosta, GA; JR; BED; NSSLHA 90-; Paul Douglas Tchr Schlrshp; Harold/Sara Whetherbee Fndtn Schlrshp; Assoc Spcl Edn Darton Coll 90; Spch/Lang Pathology.

**JONES, VICTORIA A,** Longwood Coll, Farmville, VA; SO; BS; Phi Kappa Phi 90-; Pharm.

**JONES, VICTORIA L,** Hampton Univ, Hampton, VA; FR; BA; Deans Lst 90-; Hon Coll 90-; Mass Media Arts/Jrnlsm; Print Jrnlsm.

**JONES, VINCENT G,** Norfolk St Univ, Norfolk, VA; FR; BA; Bus Mgmt; Bus Bkstre Ownr.

**JONES, WALTER C,** Greenville Tech Coll, Greenville, SC; SO; AS; Bsn Mgmt; Tch.

**JONES, WALTER W,** Wilmington Coll, New Castle, DE; SR; BS; Govrs Awd Emp Hndcpd 90; Ownr Athena Cmnctns; AAS Delaware Tch Comm Clge 89; Bhvr Sci; MA Nrsci/Tchg/Rsrch.

**JONES, WENDY R,** Converse Coll, Spartanburg, SC; JR; BA; Mdrn Lang Club VP 88-; Ecolgy Comm 90-; SC Stdnt Ed Assoc 89-; Day Stdnt Assoc 88-; Phi Sigma Iota VP 90-; Mortar Bd; Engl/Span; Tch On Secndry Lvl.

**JONES, WENDY S,** City Univ Of Ny City Coll, New York, NY; SR; BA; Mscl Dreams 87-89; Clb Fair Perf 89; Dns Lst 89; AA Borough Manhattan Cmnty Clg 89; Engl; Wrtg.

**JONES, WILLIAM,** Al St Univ, Montgomery, AL; FR; ETANI 90-; Vrsty Trck.

**JONES, WILLIAM A,** American Baptist Coll, Nashville, TN; SR; BA; Yrbk 90-; Nwspapr 90-; Chldrns Chrch Dir 88-; Vctry Bapt Chrch Assc Mnstr 88-; Bibl/Thlgy; Pastr.

**JONES, WILLIAM E,** Wv Northern Comm Coll, Wheeling, WV; JR; ASSOC; Vet Of Foreign Wars Blmnt Cnty Cncl Cmmdr 90; Cert Yth Serv Syst 90; Crmnl Jstce; Jvnle Prbtn.

**JONES, WILLIAM F,** Memphis St Univ, Memphis, TN; SR; BBA; US Navy Vet Rank E5 83-89; United Way Vol; AS Univ Of State Of (Y Regents 86; Fncl Cnsltnt.

**JONES, WILLIAM G,** Univ Of Fl, Gainesville, FL; JR; Golden Key; Deans Lst; Pres Lst; AA; Bsnss Admin-Mrktng; Med.

**JONES II, WILLIAM HOWARD,** Middle Tn St Univ, Murfreesboro, TN; SO; MBA; Deans Lst MTSU 90-; Wrk Stdy Bus/Econ Rsrch Ctr 90-.

**JONES, WILLIAM J,** Tougaloo Coll, Tougaloo, MS; SR; BA; Alpha Kappa Alpha 87-; Psychlgy.

**JONES, WILLIAM L,** Wv Northern Comm Coll, Wheeling, WV; SO; BS; Hnck Cnty 4h Jr Ldrs Pres 89-90; New Mnchstr Vol Fire Dept 89-; Drunk Drvng Comm Chrmn 89-90; I Dare You Awd/Jets Tm/Pres Ftnss Awd; Math; Elem Teacher.**

**JONES, WILLIE C,** Miami Jacobs Jr Coll Of Bus, Dayton, OH; FR; BA; US Army 68-; Bus Admin; Bus.

**JONES, WILMA I,** Madisonville Comm Coll, Madisonville, KY; JR; BA; Outstndng Stdnt Nmnee; AS 91; Acctg.

**JONES, YVONNE H,** Livingston Univ, Livingston, AL; JR; ADN; Gideons Auxiliary 88-; Asst Medl Tchn; Swmng/Water Sfty Instr 85-; AAS George C Wallace St Jr Clg 73; Nursing.

**JONSDOTTIR, KOLBRUN,** Atlantic Union Coll, S Lancaster, MA; SO; BS; Gymnstcs Clb Iceland Tchr/Coach 88-89; Aerosprts Tm So Lancaster Acad 87-88; Physical Therapy.

**JONSSON, EVA B,** Broward Comm Coll, Ft Lauderdale, FL; SO; AA; Frgn Lang; Intrprtr.

**JORDAN FORD, COLISTA E,** Jamestown Comm Coll, Jamestown, NY; GD; AAS; Hmn Services; Erly Ed Tchr.**

**JORDAN, AMY F,** Glassboro St Coll, Glassboro, NJ; SR; BS; Stdnt Govt Assn Rcrdng Sec 89-; Cncl Off-Cmps Lvng Sec/PR Dir 88-90; Bur Serv Org Sec 89-90; Gamma Tau Sigma 88-; 4-H Sec 87-89; Gvrnrs Tchng Schlr 87-; Grdn St Dstngshd Schlr 87-; Kynt Spkr 4-H Sr Nght 89; Physcl/Earth Sci; Educ.**

**JORDAN, C RUSSELL,** Piedmont Coll, Demorest, GA; JR; BS; Data Prcssng Asc 90-; Sci/Math Clb 90-; Alpha Chi Dlgt; Cmptr Sci/Math; Astronomy.

**JORDAN, CESAR A,** Univ Politecnica De Pr, Hato Rey, PR; Clb De Srvcs Cmnls Pnlns 90-.

**JORDAN, CHRISTINA L,** Univ Of Akron, Akron, OH; SR; BS; Accntg Asso 90-; Deans Advsy Coun; Ntnl Asso/Acctnts 90-; Golden Key 90-; Beta Alpha Psi V P/Admin 90-; Beta Gamma Sigma 90-; Intnshp/Acctng Coopers/Lybrand; Superior Contrbtn/Beta Psi; N B Becker Schlrshp; Acctng; CPA.

**JORDAN, CONNIE L,** Univ Of Tn At Martin, Martin, TN; FR; BS; Crmnl Just; Law.

**JORDAN, DANIEL M,** Memphis St Univ, Memphis, TN; JR; BA; Rifle Mrksmnshp Capt Fresh Tm 87-88; Wldlf/Fshrs; US Fish/Wldlf Offcr/FBI Agent.

**JORDAN, DANIEL N,** Saint Thomas Univ, Miami, FL; SR; BBA; Stdnt Govt Assoc VP 89-; Traffic Appeal Cmte 90-; Nwspr Writer 89-; Delta Epsilon Sigma 90-; Deans Lst 88-; Better Bus Bureau Of Miami 89; Cert Of Achvmnt 90; Bnkng Retail Mngmnt; Fin; Tchr.

**JORDAN, DEBORAH L,** Univ Of Sc At Columbia, Columbia, SC; SR; Dorm Govt; Clg Rpblcns; Grks Agnst Misuse Mgmt Alcohol; Stdnts Agnst Violnc/Crme; Soc Prfsnl Jrnlst 90-; Alpha Chi Omega 88; Rprtr Metuchen Edison Rvw 90; News Edtrl Jrnlsm; Jrnlsm/Rprtr.

**JORDAN, DEBRA A,** Elms Coll, Chicopee, MA; SR; BA; Paralegal/Psych.

**JORDAN, EDITH R,** Univ Of South Al, Mobile, AL; JR; BED; Elem Educ; Tchg.

**JORDAN, ERICA R,** Seton Hall Univ, South Orange, NJ; JR; Stdnt Nrss Assn 89-; Nrsng.

**JORDAN, EVELYN D,** Toccoa Falls Coll, Toccoa Falls, GA; GD; BA; AA 90-; Christian Educ; Teaching.

**JORDAN, GARY W,** Western Ky Univ, Bowling Green, KY; SR; BS; CSF 88; FCA 88; Phi Kappa Phi; Biology.

**JORDAN, HOLLY S,** Va Commonwealth Univ, Richmond, VA; SR; BME; Msc Edctrs Natl Cnfrnc 88-; Chamber Opera Co; Symphony Chorus; BM 88; Msc Ed/Choral; Tch.

**JORDAN, JANE MARIE,** Miami Univ, Oxford, OH; SO; BS; Assc Stdnt Govt Cmps Wd Elec Comm Co Chr Comm 90-; Legsltv Afrs Comm Ylw Rbn Proj 90; Rules/Review Comm Revw Stdnd Hndbk 90-; Omcrn Dlt Kappa; Kappa Dlt Pi 90-; Spers Co Chr 90-; Lmbd Sgm Scty 90-; Alph Lmbd Dlt/Phi Eta Sgm VP 90-; Scndry Ed Soc Stds/Pol Sci; Law.**

**JORDAN, JENNIFER S,** Va Polytechnic Inst & St Univ, Blacksburg, VA; SO; BS; Soc Wmn Eng 90-; Golden Key 90-; Garnet/Gold 90-; Coop Ed Stdnt Ashland Oil Inc Ashland KY 90-; Chem Eng.**

**JORDAN, JILL C,** Anne Arundel Comm Coll, Arnold, MD; FR; BS; Deans List 90; Bus Engrng; CPA/AERO Engr.

**JORDAN, JUANA R,** Johnson C Smith Univ, Charlotte, NC; SO; BA; Pan Africian Cncl 90-; Union Prog Brd/Acad Bowl Tm 90-; Rotaract Clb Brd Of Dir 90-; Alpha Lambda Delta 89-90; Awd Acad Tm 90-; Brrdcst/Jrnlsm.

**JORDAN, KAREN C,** Univ Of Sc At Columbia, Columbia, SC; JR; BA; Early Chldhd Ed; Tchr.

**JORDAN, KIMBERLY J,** Univ Of Nc At Charlotte, Charlotte, NC; SO; BSBA; Choir; Bus Admin; Finance.

**JORDAN, KIRSTEN I,** Coll Of Charleston, Charleston, SC; FR; BA; Phi Mu 90; Distgshd List; Flwshp Chrstn Athletics 90; Phys Therapy; Nursng.

**JORDAN, LISA A,** Germanna Comm Coll, Locust Grove, VA; FR; BA; Bus; CPA.

**JORDAN, LUCITA,** Inter Amer Univ Pr Hato Rey, Hato Rey, PR; JR.

**JORDAN, MARVIESTA A,** Middle Tn St Univ, Murfreesboro, TN; SR; BS; Natl Exch Clb Prev Child Abuse Vol; Gamma Beta Phi 87-; Psychology; Education.

**JORDAN, MELINDA KAY,** Univ Of Southern Ms, Hattiesburg, MS; SO; BA; Bapt Stdnt Un 89-; Right To Life 89-; Phi Eta Sigma 90-; Alpha Lambda Delta 90-; Engl/Jrnlsm; Jrnlst/Writer.

**JORDAN, MELINDA R,** Clark Atlanta Univ, Atlanta, GA; SR; BA; Stdnt Govt Assn 87-88; SGA Hghr Judcry 87-88; Psychlgy Clb 88-; Psi Chi; Delta Sigma Theta 88-; Rape Crisis Ctr Intrnshp; Psychlgy.

**JORDAN, MIKA R,** Middle Tn St Univ, Murfreesboro, TN; FR; BS; Specical Education; Teaching.

**JORDAN, MONICA C,** Fl St Univ, Tallahassee, FL; JR; Dubois Hnr Scty; Alpha Kappa Alpha 90-; Smithsonian Inst Internship 90; Radio Cert; Media Cmmnctn; Law.

**JORDAN, NICOLE D,** Hudson Valley Comm Coll, Troy, NY; FR; AA; Deans Lst 90-; Liberal Arts; Mktng.

**JORDAN, OLIVER R,** Univ Of Pittsburgh, Pittsburgh, PA; JR; BSN; Ski Clb 88-89; Wtr Ski Clb 88-89; Nrsng; Med.

**JORDAN, QUELINA M,** Central St Univ, Wilberforce, OH; JR; BS; Natl Techl Assoc Pres 89-90; Ed Scty Mbr 90-; Student Govt Assoc African Awns Mbr 90-; Alpha Kappa Mu Mbr 90-; Ohio State Univ Udgrte Research Asst; Math/Ed; Clg Prof.

**JORDAN, RAMONA L,** Georgetown Univ, Washington, DC; JR; BSN; Chrstn Flwshp; Sigma Theta Tau; Yth Stff 4th Presbyrn Chrch; Nrsng; Navy Nrs.

**JORDAN, ROBIN L,** Liberty Univ, Lynchburg, VA; SR; BS; RA 90-; Rsdnc Life Dept Top 12 90; Yth Quest 89-; Focused To Yth Mnstrs 89-; Urban Outrch Fcsd To Innr Cty Prog 89-90; Msns Trp To New York City 90; Chrstn Srvc Comm 89-; IM Sprts 89-90; Telecomm/Drama; TV/DIR/PRDCTN.

**JORDAN, RONALD K,** Southern Coll Of Tech, Marietta, GA; JR; BS; IEEE 90-; NSBE 90-; Tau Alpha Pi; Alpha Phi Omega 84-; Cmptr Eng Tech.

**JORDAN, SANDRA R,** Univ Of Sc At Spartanburg, Spartanburg, SC; FR; BA; Pep Bnd 90-; Pol Sci; Law.

**JORDAN, SHERITHA,** Univ Of Tn At Martin, Martin, TN; JR; BSN; Nrsng; RN Emergency Rm Nrs.

**JORDAN, SUSAN E,** Univ Of Ga, Athens, GA; SR; BSED; Newspr Floyd Clg Edtr 88-89; Golden Key 90; Ldrshp Award Floyd Clg 89; Erly Chldhd Educ.

**JORDAN, TAMMY L,** Univ Of Sc At Columbia, Columbia, SC; FR; BA.

**JORDAN, TONYA E,** Saint Andrews Presbytrn Coll, Laurinburg, NC; SR; Stdnt Govt Assn Sec 88-; St Andrws Hnr Soc 90-; Pi Gamma Mu 90-; Hnrs Pgm 87-88; Intrnshp Bennett Cardiac Ctr 88-89; Intrnshp Alex Chldrns Hm 90-; Ldr Cystic Fibrosis Aerbcs A Thon 87-89; Crs Cntry Tm 87-89; BA; BA; Psych/Phy Educ; Exer Physlgy.

**JORDAN, TRACIE D,** Asbury Theological Sem, Wilmore, KY; GD; MS; Natl Assoc Scl Wrk 88-90; Scl Wrk Clb 89-90; Wesley Fdtn 87-90; Central State Hosp Intern 89-90; Emergency Shelter 89-90; BSW Univ GA; Scl Wrk; Chrstn Svc-Missions.

**JORDAN, TRACIE M,** Univ Of Rochester, Rochester, NY; SO; BA; Alpha Phi Corres Sec 90-; Tiernan Proj; IM; Math.

**JORDAN, VICKI L,** Univ Of Charleston, Charleston, WV; JR; Music Edn; Teach Music.

**JORDAN, WENDY C,** Univ Of Tn At Martin, Martin, TN; SO; D PH; Mu Epsilon Delta 89-; Pre Pharmcy; Phrmcy.

**JORDAN-DAVIS, WYNN N,** Savannah St Coll, Savannah, GA; JR; BA; Acctnts Pblc Int Mbr; UPS Kore 89-; Clrk 88-; Acctgs.

**JORDON, ELIZABETH J,** Saint Catharine Coll, St Catharine, KY; FR; AA; Plcy Cncl Brd Hd Strt PTA Mmbr; Scl Sci; Cnslng.

**JORGE, HECTOR M,** City Univ Of Ny City Coll, New York, NY; SR; MA; Alcohol/Drug Prvtn Cmtee Tech Dept Rep 89; Golden Key 88; Deans Lst 89; Cum Laude; Hon Stdnt Awd; Yth Wrk Shop 81-; BS; Educ Tech; Admnstr.

**JORGE, SARAH E,** Newbury Coll, Brookline, MA; SO; AS; Sec Commonwealth Elect Co 90-; Comp Sci; Anlst.

**JORGENSEN, KIMBERLY E,** Dowling Coll, Oakdale Li, NY; JR; BA; Acctng Soc; Delta Mu Delta; Alpha Chi; Acctng.

**JORGENSEN, WILLIAM H,** Saint Andrews Presbytrn Coll, Laurinburg, NC; SR; BA; E Bullock Ed Schlrshp 90-; Vrsty Bsbl 86-88; Phys Ed.

**JORGENSON, KELLY J,** Radford Univ, Radford, VA; JR; BS; Pnhlnc Cncl Rep 90-; MD Asc Rep 89; Alchl/Hazing Comm 90; Sigma Sigma Sigma Rep 89-; Comm Serv Rep 89-; Fndrsng Comm Rep 89-; IMS 89-; Social Work/Psy.

**JOSE, CESAR A,** Saint Thomas Univ, Miami, FL; JR; BA; AS Miami Dade Cmnty Clg 89; AS Mgmt Miami Dade Cmnty Clg 90; Bsn Mgmt; Bsn Law.

**JOSE, PATRICIA L,** Endicott Coll, Beverly, MA; FR; Fitness Club Ldr 90-; Trexler Times Writer 90-; Orient Ldr; Intrnshp; Bio; Radiology.

**JOSE, RIVERA TORRES ARNALDO,** Bayamon Central Univ, Bayamon, PR; SO; Schl Miguel Melendez Munoz VP 85-86; DECA 84-85; Scntfc Fr 84.

**JOSEFIAK, GLENN R,** Univ Of Miami, Coral Gables, FL; SR; MS; Pep Band 87-; Tau Beta Pi; Eta Kappa Nu; Summa Cum Laude; Hon Schlr; BS Elec Eng SUNY Buffalo; Music Eng Tech.

**JOSEL, NANCI L,** Univ Of Ct, Storrs, CT; FR; Vet Tech 79-; Animal Sci.

**JOSEPH, ALICIA J C,** Bloomfield Coll, Bloomfield, NJ; FR; BS; Chem/Bio; Cyto Tech.

**JOSEPH, CAROL C,** George Mason Univ, Fairfax, VA; SR; BS ED; Gospel Choir 88-; Rcrdng Sec; Stdnt Educ Soc 87-90; Kappa Delta Pi 87-; Sigma Chi; Stdnt Emplee Yr Off Asst 90; Early Ele Educ; Early Ele Tchr.

**JOSEPH, CELIA M,** Univ Of The Virgin Islands, St Thomas, VI; SR; BA; Acctng Assc; Dominica Stdnt Assc Sec; Comp Org; Pres Clb; Deans Lst; Univ VI Acctng Ofc Bus Intern 90; Acctng; Cpa.

**JOSEPH, CHRISTOPHER F,** Temple Univ, Philadelphia, PA; JR; Alpha Phi Omega VP 88-89; Human Bio; Phys Therapy.**

**JOSEPH, CLAUDIA T,** City Univ Of Ny Med Evers Coll, Brooklyn, NY; JR; BA; Comp Pgmg Empire Tech Sch 84; Acctg; CPA.

**JOSEPH, DAVID E,** Morehouse Coll, Atlanta, GA; SR; BA; Morehouse Bus Assn 89-; Am Red Cross; Employed Part Time 89-; Summer Enrichment Edn Prog Hampton Univ; IM Bsktbl Vlybl 87-89; Mrktng; Sales/Distribution & Teaching.**

**JOSEPH, GARY T,** East Stroudsburg Univ, E Stroudsburg, PA; SR; BABS; Acad Achvmnt Awrd; AS Resprtry Thrpy 84; Psychlgy/Phys Educ; Prsng Mstrs Dctrl Degree.

**JOSEPH, GLENNIS-ANN L,** City Univ Of Ny Bronx Comm Col, Bronx, NY; JR; AAS; Dean List; Phi Theta Kappa; Educ; Tchng.

**JOSEPH, JUNE G,** Univ Of Ky, Lexington, KY; JR; BS; Yng Rpblcns Amer Dst Cptn 89-; Hlth Cr Oprtnty Pgm 90; Phi Theta Kappa 89-; Dns Lst 87-; AS Prestonsburg Cmnty Clge 90; Blgy; Med.

**JOSEPH, LAUREN M,** Duquesne Univ, Pittsburgh, PA; SR; BSN; Cls Pres 87-88; Sr Sld Shaw Comm Hd Of Comm; Lambda Sigma 88-; Alpha Tau Delta Hstrn 88-; Sigma Theta Tau 89-; Univ SHARP Vol 88-; Mercy Hosp Stdnt Nrs Extrn Prog 90-; Richard Behan Schlrshp; Mary Tobin Awd Excl Nr; Nrsng; RN.

**JOSEPH, LINDA A,** Al St Univ, Montgomery, AL; SO; Biol; Tch.

**JOSEPH, LISA,** Atlantic Union Coll, S Lancaster, MA; JR; BS; Stdnt Assn Exec Schlstc Sec 90-; Hmn Rltns Com 90-; Stdnt Assn Senate 90-; Asst Sabbath Schl Sprntndnt Church; Soc Work; Edctr/Clncl Psychlgst.

**JOSEPH, MERCY K,** Southeastern Coll Of Hlth Sci, N Miami Beach, FL; JR; PHARM; Intl Stdnts Assn 86-88; Amer Pharm Assn 89-90; Natl Assn Retail Druggist 90-; Dns Lst 89-; Phi Theta Kappa 87-88; Intrnshp Publix Pharm/Pharm Intern 90; AA Polk Cmnty Clg 88; Pharmacodynamics; Pharmacy.

**JOSEPH, MICHAEL H,** City Univ Of Ny City Coll, New York, NY; SR; BSC; ASCE 90; Tau Beta Pi 90; Cvl Engr; Envrnmtl Engr.

**JOSEPH, MOLVIE E L,** Univ Of The Virgin Islands, St Thomas, VI; JR; BA; Antiqua Assn Sec; Pres Clb; Phi Beta Lambda; Acctng; CPA.

**JOSEPH, OSWALD B,** Tuskegee Univ, Tuskegee Inst, AL; GD; BSC; Intl Stu Assoc 88-; Caribbean Stu Assn 88-; Alpha Kappa Mu; Jamma Sigma Delta; Pthfndrs Clb Instr; Prison Mnstry Ldr 88-; Dipo 82; Animal Sci; Educ Super.

**JOSEPH-CRAGG, PATRICIA,** Atlantic Union Coll, S Lancaster, MA; JR; BA; Soc Wrk Dept Pstr 88-89; S Lancaster Vlg Ch Tchr 89-90; Drftsmn 79-84; Arch Co; Soc Wrk/Crmnl Juste; Phys Thrpy/Dntsry.

**JOSHI, AJIT V,** Tufts Univ, Medford, MA; FR; BA; Sth Asns Assoc 90-; Tfts Flt Ensmbl 90-; Boston Cntr Intl Vstrs Prgmmr Intern; Intl Rltns Spnsh; Dplmcy Intl Law.

**JOSLYN, CHRISTOPHER E,** Northern Ky Univ, Highland Hts, KY; SR; BFA; Graphic Dsgn; Art Direction.**

**JOSSELYN, DAVID M,** Merrimack Coll, North Andover, MA; SO; BA; Nwspr Mgng Edtr 90-; Campus Mag Mgng Edtr 90-; The Writing Ctr Peer Tutor 90-; Engl; Creative Writing.

**JOST, DEBORAH M,** Memphis Academy Of The Arts, Memphis, TN; FR; BFA; Tunnel Ball; Prnt Mkng; H S Tchr/Art Thrpy.

**JOTKOWITZ, MICHAEL,** Yeshiva Univ, New York, NY; GD; Achy 87-90; Tech Org 89-90; IM Capt 87-88; Hstry; Hotl Mgmt.

**JOU, YI-CHUNG,** Univ Of Nc At Charlotte, Charlotte, NC; JR; Chinese Assoc 89-; Oriental Assoc Secty 89-90; Math; Actuary.

**JOU, YU SHAN,** Univ Of Nc At Charlotte, Charlotte, NC; JR; BCA; Orntl Stdnt Assc Edtr Chf 90; Intrntl Stdnt Assc 90-; Vsl Art/Cmptr Art/Grphc Dsgn/Cmptr Grphc Dsgn.

**JOURDAIN, RANDALL D,** Coll Of Charleston, Charleston, SC; JR; BS; Ind Psychology.

**JOURDAN, CATHERINE VIRGINIA,** Univ Of Ga, Athens, GA; JR; N GA Coll Stdnt Govt 89-90; Acad Advsmnt Comm 89; Kappa Delta Epsilon 90; Kappa Delta Pi 90; Kappa Delta 88-90; Amer Red Crs 88-; Math Educ; Tchng.

**JOURDAN, THOMAS B,** Univ Of Nc At Asheville, Asheville, NC; FR; BS; Phi Eta Sigma 90-; Crs Cntry/Track 90-; Bio; Dntstry.

**JOURNEY, ERICA C,** Tougaloo Coll, Tougaloo, MS; FR; Blgy/Pre Vet; Vet Med.

**JOVINGS, NICK A,** Univ Of Al At Birmingham, Birmingham, AL; JR; BS; SSA Rep Stdnt Govt; SSA/SGA Pres 90-; Coun SGA Pres 90-; Liason Comm 90-; Beta Theta Pi Auburn Univ; Ambsdr 87-88; Exchng Clb Stdnt Mnth Schlrshp; Med Rcrds Admin/Hlth Mngmnt.

**JOWETT, EDWARD S,** Temple Univ, Philadelphia, PA; SR; BS; Amer Soc Cvl Engrs 89-; Gen Bldg Contractors Assoc 90-; Dns Lst 90; Hnrbl Mntn ACI DE Vly Chapt Beam Competition 90; Wnr VICA Spons Evnt 83; Hnrbl Mntn State Competition; Temple Univ Cmptr Ctr Hd Cnsltnt/Lab Instr 88-; Engr/Cvl Structural.

**JOY, ARLENE C,** Univ Of Nc At Greensboro, Greensboro, NC; FR; BSN; Assc Nsg Stdnts 90-; Alpha Lambda Delta Chrprsn; Natl Clgt Nsg Awd 90-; Nsg/Art; Rn.

**JOY, JENNIFER L,** Univ Of Akron, Akron, OH; SO; BA; Akron Cncl Edctn Stdnts Drctr Pblc Rltns 90-; Phi Eta Sigma 89-; Alpha Lambda Delta 89-; Asst Hmn Dvlpmnt Lrng Prgrm Sml Grp Ldr 90-; Elem Edctn; Elem Tchr.

**JOY, SCARLETT PERSEPHONE,** Elmira Coll, Elmira, NY; SR; SCOPE VP 90-; Leg Brd 90-; Phi Eta Sigma 90-; Psi Chi 89-; Tchng 90; Asst Psych Nghbrhd Just Proj Intern; Chrldr 88-89; BA; Psych; Cnslr.

**JOY, SIRRETHA,** Southern Coll Of Tech, Marietta, GA; JR; BS; ACM 89; IEEE 90; AUSA 81; Natl Clgte Cmptr Sci Awd 90; U S Army 61-88; Cert U S Army Signal Sch 62; U S Army Adv Cmptr Sys Anlyst 73; Cmptr Sci Engr; Sys Prgrmr Fed Govt.**

**JOYCE, CHRISTINE A,** Univ Of Pittsburgh, Pittsburgh, PA; SO; BSN; Phi Eta Sigma 90-; Hnrs Convocation Tapee; Nrsg.

**JOYCE, COLLEEN A,** S U N Y At Buffalo, Buffalo, NY; SR; MBA; Golden Key 90-; Management; Accounting.

**JOYCE, DEBORAH E,** Memphis St Univ, Memphis, TN; SR; BED; Elem Edctn; Edctn.

**JOYCE, EDWARD S,** Univ Of Miami, Coral Gables, FL; JR; BA; AA FL State Univ 89; Video Film/Pol Sci; Motion Pictures.

**JOYCE, GRETCHEN M,** Univ Of Louisville, Louisville, KY; FR; IM Tnns; Chem Eng.

**JOYCE, HELEN M,** Univ Of Tn At Martin, Martin, TN; FR; BA; Hon Rl 90-; Phi Chi Theta 90-; Vlybl 90-; Bus; Fin.

**JOYCE, KATHLEEN M,** Kent St Univ Kent Cmps, Kent, OH; JR; BA; Cncl Fmly Rltns 90-; Hall Cncl 88-89; Dean List 90; Cath Chrts Vol; Chld Care Cnslr 90-; Ctr Hope Cswrkr; Indvdl Fmly Stds; Emply Asstnt.

**JOYCE, KATIE,** Univ Of Nc At Chapel Hill, Chapel Hill, NC; JR; BA; SOTA; Pi Delta Phi; Citibank Pblc Affrs 73-75; Assist To Dir Northrup Aviation Saudi Arabia 77-79; Frnch/Intl Studies.

**JOYCE, LAURA A,** William Paterson Coll, Wayne, NJ; SR; BA; NJ Edn Assoc 90-; CEC 89-91; WPC Spec Edn Club 88-91; Kappa Delta Pi; Mental Hlth Assoc Vol 90-; Spec Ed; Teach.

**JOYCE, LINDA C,** Va Commonwealth Univ, Richmond, VA; FR; BS; Pre Nrsng Clb 90-; Phi Eta Sgm 90-; Nrsng; Med Flght Nrsng.

**JOYCE, LORI A,** Patrick Henry Comm Coll, Martinsville, VA; SO; BA; Lbrl Arts; Ed.

**JOYCE JR, MICHAEL J,** Univ Of Pittsburgh, Pittsburgh, PA; FR; BA; Term Hnrs Lst 90-; Deans Lst; Electrcl Engrng.

**JOYCE, SHARON G,** Thomas Nelson Comm Coll, Hampton, VA; SO; AAS; DPMA 89-; Phi Theta Kappa; Cmptr Infrmtn Systms; Tchncl Sprt Bsns Infrmt.

**JOYCE, VALERIE J,** Asnuntuck Comm Coll, Enfield, CT; SO; BS; PTA 86-; Phi Theta Kappa; Am Cancer Soc Vol 86-; Psychtrc Aide 74-81; AS; Hlth Educ/Soc Wrk; Cancer Prog.

**JOYNER, DONALD T,** Christopher Newport Coll, Newport News, VA; FR; BSA; Bapt Stdnt Un 90-; Styron Schlr; Acctng; CPA.

**JOYNER, JANET L,** Mount Olive Coll, Mount Olive, NC; JR; BS; Sthrn Wayne Bus/Prfssnl Wmns Assc; Pres Lst; Acctg Sprvsr; AAS Acctg Wayne Cmnty Clg 89; Bus Admin/Acctg; CPA.

**JOYNER, JENNIFER CAROL,** Memphis St Univ, Memphis, TN; SR; BBA; Phi Kappa Phi; Beta Gamma Sigma; AAS 90; Acctg/Off Mgmt; Med Admn/Mgmt.

**JOYNER, LEDEAN R,** Fl St Univ, Tallahassee, FL; JR; BME; FL Unv Schl Msc Brd Advsrs Coord 90-; FL Undrgrd Schlrs Fnd Schlrshp Rcpnt 88-; Msc; Piano Pedagogy.

**JOYNER, PHILLIP E,** Univ Of Sc At Columbia, Columbia, SC; JR; BS; Campus Crusade For Christ 87-90; Amer Inst Chem Eng 90-; Chem Eng; Eng.

**JOYNER, SARA JANE,** Ms St Univ, Miss State, MS; FR; Grnr Hll Cncl 90-; Hll Rep 90-; Phi Eta Sigma; Alpha Lambda Delta; Gamma Beta Phi; Chi Omega Pres Pldg Clss 90-; Lambda Sigma; Pres Schlr 90; Deans Lst; Chmstry Pre Med.

**JOYNER, TRACEY L,** Univ Of Sc At Spartanburg, Spartanburg, SC; SO; BA; Amer Home Econ Assn 89-90; Amer Nrsng Assn; Dns Lst 89-90; Alpha Delta Pi Open Rush 87-90; Univ Of TN Schlrshp 87-88; Vlybl 87-88; Nrsng.

**JOYNT, TERENCE J,** Jersey City St Coll, Jersey City, NJ; SO; Stdnt Sntr 90-; Stdnt Govt Org 90-; Plng Dvlpmnt Bdgt Cmte Schl Snt 90-; IM Sftbl; Crim Jstc; Law Enfrcmnt.

**JOZWIAK, MARIESA A,** Marywood Coll, Scranton, PA; SO; BS; Class Stdnt Govt Crspndnc Sec 90-; Marywood Plyrs Drama Clb Treas 90-; Vols In Action 89-; Cmps Mnstry 89-; Tchrs Tomorrow 89-; Clgt Vols 89-; Spcl/Elem Ed; Tchr.

**JUAN-JUAN, PEDRO E,** Inter Amer Univ Pr San German, San German, PR; SO; Circulo De Recreo; Deans List; Hnr Stdnt; Pending; Bowling/Bsktbl/Tennis; Biology; Odontology.

**JUANES, MARLENE,** Fl International Univ, Miami, FL; JR; BA; FEA Pres Elect; Intl Club 89-90; Jesus Flwshp 89; Homeless Shelter 89; Childrens Hosp 90; E W Stirrup Elem Sch 88-89; Otstndng Cntrbtn Plaque 89-90; Hnr Roll Cert 88-; Elem Edn.

**JUDAH, JOSEPH,** City Univ Of Ny Baruch Coll, New York, NY; JR; BBA; Crw Cmmndr 81-84; Elctrcn Instrmntcn Plns; Isrl Dfnc Frc; Rsdntl Elctrcn 85-; Fnc.

**JUDAY, KENT L,** Liberty Univ, Lynchburg, VA; SR; BS; Alpha Lambda Delta; Elem Ed; Tch.

**JUDD, BEVERLY C,** Johnson St Coll, Johnson, VT; FR; ASMGT; Wrkg Practicum Ofc Mgmt Prog Asst Ofc Mgr; Chmbr Commerce; Cert Ofc Mgmt; Bsn Mgmt.

**JUDD, ELIZABETH A,** S U N Y Coll Of Tech At Delhi, Delhi, NY; SR; BA; Peer Tutor 89-; Grd Hnr; Prmsng Schlrs Schlp 89-; Bsn Admn.

**JUDD, SHERRI J,** Memphis St Univ, Memphis, TN; FR; BA; Maybelline Rep Voice Shades You 1-800 Number; Sr Secty/Mktng/Sales Opns Naybelle Inc; Econ/Intl Busn; Bnkng.

**JUDD, VIRGINIA A,** Schenectady County Comm Coll, Schenectady, NY; FR; AS; Cmptgr Output Microflm Sprvsr/Prgrmr 89-; Bus Admin; Mgmt.

**JUDD, WANDA J,** Middle Tn St Univ, Murfreesboro, TN; FR; BS; Aerospace.

**JUDGE, JASMEET,** Stillman Coll, Tuscaloosa, AL; JR; BS; Intl Intrcltrl Assoc 89-; Alpha Kappa Mu; Gamma Iota Sigma 90-; Crdll Wynn Hnrs 90-; Prsndts Schlr 89-; Deans Slt 89-; Eng.**

**JUDGE, JOHN W,** Univ Of Miami, Coral Gables, FL; JR; BA; Intl Bsn Assoc 90-; Golf Clb 90-; Golden Key 90-; Hnrs Pgm 87-; Phi Kappa Phi; Chamber Commerce Res Flwshp; Henry King Stanford Schlrshp 87-; Econ/Intl Studies.

**JUDGE, JULIA LAVON,** Univ Of Sc At Columbia, Columbia, SC; SR; MPER; NAACP 87-; SHRM 88-; Res Hall Govt Sec/Res Advsr; Natl Res Hl Hnry; Delta Sigma Pi 87-; Pres/Deans List; BS; Personnel Mgmnt; Corp Lawyer.

**JUDGE, MARY E,** Comm Coll Algny Co Algny Cmps, Pittsburgh, PA; FR; BED; Educ; Elem Educ.

**JUDGE, THOMAS P,** Kent St Univ Kent Cmps, Kent, OH; SR; BBA; Camp Crsd Christ 87-; Acctg Assn 89-; IM Sprts 87-; Acctg; Pblc Acctnt.

**JUDGE, VALERIE DAWN,** Univ Of Nc At Greensboro, Greensboro, NC; SO; BS; Inter Vrsty Chrstn Fllwshp 89-; Yng Wrld Day Cr Cntr 90-; Chld Dvlpmnt; Tchr.

**JUDKINS, FRANZETTA KAY,** Central Al Comm Coll, Alexander City, AL; SO; BS; Cmptr Sci.

**JUDON, THERESA L,** Livingston Univ, Livingston, AL; SO; BA; IM; Sci; Eng.

**JUDY, JACIE A,** Garrett Comm Coll, Mchenry, MD; SO; BA; Psych; Hmn Srvc.

**JUENGLING, CHRISTINE M,** Univ Of Cincinnati, Cincinnati, OH; GD; BS; Omicron Nu Sec 90-; Fund Rsng Com 90-; Deans List 90-; Nutrition/Dietetics.

**JUGDEESE, KARON E,** City Univ Of Ny City Coll, New York, NY; SR; BSN; Nrsng.

**JUHAS, STEFAN,** Salem-Teikyo Univ, Salem, WV; SO; BS; Med.

**JUHASZ, DONNA M,** Clarkson Univ, Potsdam, NY; SR; BS; Stdnt Law Scty 90-; Stdtn Ortn Srvcs 88-90; Omega Delta Phi Treas 89-; Acctg Fnc; MBA.

**JUHASZ, TRACY A,** Kent St Univ Geauga Cmps, Burton Twp, OH; SO; BA; Psychology; Chld Psychology.

**JUHNKE, CHRISTINE P,** Western Piedmont Comm Coll, Morganton, NC; FR; BA; Alpha Gamma Mu; English; Journalism.

**JUINIO, GEOFFREY T,** Univ Of Med & Dentistry Of Nj, Newark, NJ; SR; BS; Med Tech Soc Phlpns 85-88; Med Tech.

**JULES, ALBERT L,** City Univ Of Ny Baruch Coll, New York, NY; SR; MA; Golden Key 90-; Air Force Assoc 90-; Smithsonian Assoc; Vlybl; Amer Psych Assoc; United Fed Tchrs 78-; NY City Bd Ed 78-; BA Psych; Psych; Ed Psych.

**JULES, JULIENNE,** Ramapo Coll Of Nj, Mahwah, NJ; SR; BSW; Soc Wrk Clb 90-; Anisfield Schlrshp 90; Dns Lst 90; AAS In Med Lab Tech Queensbrgh Comm Clg 83; Soc Sci; MSW.

**JULIAN, MARIA J,** Hudson Valley Comm Coll, Troy, NY; FR; BA; Bus; Human Res.

**JULIAN, MELANIE B,** Univ Of Ky, Lexington, KY; FR; BA; Repr Cncl 90-; Kappa Kappa Gamma 90-; Fall Orientation Cnslr; Team Recruiting 90-; Hnrs Clb 90-; French Clb; Vol Home Abused Children 90; Rent A Greek; LKD GMAC Schrlshp; Intern Radio Station; English/Psychology/French.

**JULIAN, NATALIE,** Wv Univ, Morgantown, WV; SO; ACS 90-; AICHE 90-; Ord Grail Jr Hnry; Hnrs Prog 89-; Pi Mu Epsilon; Tau Beta Pi; Alpha Phi Omega Serv Comm 90-; Deans Lst 89-; Pres Awd 89-; Whitehill Chem Awd 90; Wimer Awd; Math/Sci; Chem Eng.

**JULIOUS, JEANNE,** Tougaloo Coll, Tougaloo, MS; FR; Math/Comp Sci; Comp Prgrmr.

**JULIUS, BARRY D,** Cornell Univ Statutory College, Ithaca, NY; FR; BS; Symph Bnd 90-; Alpha Epsilon Pi Schlrshp Chr; Bio Sci; Med.

**JULIUS, ULYN E,** Univ Of The Virgin Islands, St Thomas, VI; SR; BA; Crckt Clb Pres 90-; Trck Clb Coord 89-; Acctg Assn Chf Fndrsr 90-; Pres Clb Pres 90-; Cmptd Comp Grp 90-; Outstndng Acctg Stdnt 90-; Soccr/Crckt/Trck/Fld V Capt 90-; Acctg; Law/CPA.

**JUMPER, JENNIFER A,** Univ Of Sc At Aiken, Aiken, SC; JR; BA; Psychlgy Clb 90-; Psychlgy Hons Prog; CCAP 89; Psychlgy; Cnslng.

**JUNCO, JUDY L,** Hudson Valley Comm Coll, Troy, NY; SR; ASS; Pltcl Sci BA; Law.

**JUNEJA, TARUN K,** Columbia Union Coll, Takoma Park, MD; SR; BS; Bsn/Acctg; Tax Acctnt.

**JUNG, DAVID S,** Franklin And Marshall Coll, Lancaster, PA; FR; Vrsty Squash Tm; Pre Med/Engl; Medicine.

**JUNG, JOHN G,** Fl St Univ, Tallahassee, FL; JR; BA; Pre Law Soc 90; Phi Eta Sigma 89-; Sigma Iota Epsilon; IM Sftbl 89-; Bus; Law.

**JUNG, MING G,** Fl St Univ, Tallahassee, FL; SR; BA; Acctg Soc Chrprsn 89-; Pre Law Soc 89-; Phi Eta Sigma 89-; Beta Alpha Psi; Mrch Dimes; Mc Veigh Art Awd 88; Dns Lst 88-; Im Sftbl Capt 88-; Acctg; Law.

**JUNGHANS, SHEILA M,** Comm Coll Algny Co Algny Cmps, Pittsburgh, PA; JR; AS 88; AS 90; Scl Wrkr.

**JUNIOR, MAKEBA S,** Lincoln Univ, Lincoln Univ, PA; SR; BA; Acctg Clb 89-; Bsn Clb 88-; Chinese Clb 87-; Hnrs Pgm 87-; Acctg; Tax Accnt/Auditor.

**JUNKER JR, WILLIAM C,** Comm Coll Algny Co Algny Cmps, Pittsburgh, PA; SO; BA; Bsbl Tm Tm MVP All St All Rgn 90-; AAS; Bsns; Acct.

**JUNKIN, MARY ANN,** Univ Of Al, Tuscaloosa, AL; JR; BS; Gamma Beta Phi 88-; Acctng.**

**JURADO, RAQUEL A,** Inter Amer Univ Pr San Juan, Hato Rey, PR; GD; JD; BS Clg New Rochelle 89.

**JURASZEK, STEVEN J,** Univ Of Southern Ms, Hattiesburg, MS; JR; BS; Gamma Beta Phi; AA MI Gulf Cst Comm Coll 90; Medcl Tchnlgy.

**JURCZAK, DIANE M,** Le Moyne Coll, Syracuse, NY; JR; BS; AAS Cayuga Cmnty Clg 90; Acctg; CPA.

**JURECEK, CATHERINE E,** Winthrop Coll, Rock Hill, SC; SR; BFA; Amrcn Scty Intr Dsgnrs Sec 89-; Cmps Plnng Dsgn Dsgnr 89-; AA 88; Intr Dsgn.

**JURENA, JOHN S,** Saint Johns Univ, Jamaica, NY; FR; MBA; Bus; Finance.

**JURENKO, JENNIFER L,** S U N Y Coll At Fredonia, Fredonia, NY; JR; BED; Tchr Educ Clb 90-; Elem Educ; Grd Schl Tchr.

**JURIK, JOHN,** Embry Riddle Aeronautical Univ, Daytona Beach, FL; SR; MAS; Nvl Avtn Clb 87-88; BS; Avtn; Airline Pilot.

**JURIST, JONATHAN M,** Fl International Univ, Miami, FL; JR; BA; Sigma Tau Delta; Phi Lambda 90-; Prfsnl Mscn Cmpsr Audio Engnr 76-88; AA Reading Area Cmm Clg 89; Englsh; Tchng Scrnply Wrtng.

**JURKOSHEK, LORRI,** Kent St Univ Kent Cmps, Kent, OH; FR; BA; Trucking Co Sales Sprvsr 90-; Anthrplgy; Frnsc Anthrplgy.

**JURKOWSKI, MICHAEL M,** Western New England Coll, Springfield, MA; SR; BA; Excellence Hstry Awrd 90-; US Army 81-85; AA Holyoke Comm Clg 89; History.

**JUROS, KERRY S,** Boston Coll, Chestnut Hill, MA; JR; BA; Fstvl Frndshp 89; Gldn Key 90; Schl Ed Deans Lst 88-; Hmn Dvlpmnt Rlry Chldhd Ed; Chld Psychlgy.**

**JURS, SHARON LYNN,** Bryant Stratton Bus Inst Roch, Rochester, NY; FR.

**JURTA, STEPHANIE A,** Castleton St Coll, Castleton, VT; SR; BA; Alpha Phi Omega Pres 90-; Crmnl Jstce And Sclgy; Coll Instr Prctr; Intrn; Scrty Grd 89; MDA; VT Achvmnt Cntr; Fd Drve; Oprtn Snta Cls; Cath Chrts Vol; Rck A Thn; Rtrt Tm; Slvtn Army Vol; Dy Care Vol; Ltchky Prog Vol; Pres Of Srrty; Crmnl Jstce Sclgy; Frnsc Sci.

**JUSCZAK, CHERYL A,** Merrimack Coll, North Andover, MA; SO; BA; Cmmuter Cncl 89-; Coop Educ; Acctg; Accnt/CPA.

**JUSINO JIMENEZ, BELKY L,** Inter Amer Univ Pr San German, San German, PR; JR; BA; Rlztn Night 90-; Bsn Admn; Mgr.

**JUSINO LUGO, BRENDA J,** Inter Amer Univ Pr San German, San German, PR; SO; Hnr Prog 89-; Hnrs Rcgnt Nght 90-.

**JUSINO, ISMAEL E,** Catholic Univ Of Pr, Ponce, PR; SR; ABASD 89; Librl Arts Cncl V P 87-88; Puerto Rican Org 86-89; Law Rev Assc Ed 89-; Phi Alpha Delta 88-; Phi Eta Mu Ct Sec 88-; IM Bsktbl/Vlybl/Sftbl; BA Penns State Univ 88; Law.

**JUSTICE, COLETTE G,** Hillsborough Comm Coll, Tampa, FL; AS; Lcnsd Csmotolgst 74-89; Med; Ophthlmc Techncn.

**JUSTICE, DOLLY L,** Univ Of Sc At Columbia, Columbia, SC; FR; BA; Lambda Delta Gamba 90-; Gamma Beta Pi 90-; Pi Beta Phi 90-; Order Of Rainbow For Girls Worthy Advsr Grand Rel 86-; Senate Page 90-; Clncl Psychlgst.

**JUSTICE, FRANCES M,** Wv Univ At Parkersburg, Parkersburg, WV; FR; BA; St Hosp Psych Aide II; Psych.

**JUSTICE, NARCISSA D,** Univ Of Sc At Columbia, Columbia, SC; FR; BA; Alpha Lambda Delta; Tri Delta Pan Hellenic 90-; Htl Rstrnt Trsm Admnstrtn.

**JUSTICE, ROBIN E,** Western Piedmont Comm Coll, Morganton, NC; SO; Bus/Acctg; CPA.

**JUSTICE, SELENA GAIL,** Ashland Comm Coll, Ashland, KY; SO; PHD; Value City 89-; Coop Ed Prog; Chrstn Church 81; Deans List 90-; Tutoring Serv 90-; AB; M Ba; Indstrl Psychology.

**JUSTICE, TARA L,** Univ Of Charleston, Charleston, WV; FR; BA; Tlmrktng Fr Admssns 90-; Prlgl Intrnshp At Sts Atty Gen Offce; Prlgl; Lwyr.

**JUSTICE, WILMA L,** Ashland Comm Coll, Ashland, KY; SR; BSW; Stdnt Assc Soc Wrks 90-; Self Emplyd 84-; Soc Wrk.

**JUSTINIANO NEGRON, RUBEN,** Univ Politecnica De Pr, Hato Rey, PR; FR; Eng; Indstrl Engrg.

**JUSTINIANO JR, JORGE DANIEL,** Univ Of Southern Ms, Hattiesburg, MS; JR; BS; Comp Sci; Sftwr Eng.**

**JUSTINIANO, MARIA M,** Univ Of Pr Cayey Univ Coll, Cayey, PR; SO; BA; Rectors Hnr List; Cristians Students 90-; Math; Acctng.

**JUSTISS, SHELLEY J,** Memphis St Univ, Memphis, TN; FR; BA; Psych Rsrch Assistshp; Psych; Neuropsychlgst.

**JUSTOS, LESLIE M,** Liberty Univ, Lynchburg, VA; SO; BS; Clg Rpblcns 89-; Light Clb 89-; Bptst Stdnt Union 90-; Alpha Lambda Delta; Ed; Prfssr Mthmtcs.

**JUTSON, DANIEL J,** Fayetteville St Univ, Fayetteville, NC; SO; BA; Armed Forces Commun Elect Assn 87-; Indept Light Infntry 89-; U S Army 81-89; Elect Tech SRI Intl 89-; AGS Cntrl Tex Clg 88; Hist; Rsrch/Military Intllgnc.

**JUTTE, LYNN M,** Univ Of Akron, Akron, OH; SO; BA; Hon Prog 89-; Hon Clb 89-90; ACES 89-; Phi Eta Sigma 89-; Alpha Lambda Delta 89-; Pi Mu Epsilon 90-; Top Stdnt Atlete 89-; Var Crs Cntry Var Track 89-; Math/Cmptr Sci; Sec Educ.**

**JUUL-HANSEN, THOMAS,** Univ Of Miami, Coral Gables, FL; FR; BA; Alpha Lambda Delta; Architecture.

# K

**KAARI, JACQUELINE M,** Georgian Court Coll, Lakewood, NJ; JR; BS; Mndl Soc 88-; Re-Entry Wmn 88-89; Jrsy Shr Bio 89-; Dns Schlr 88-89; Ga Ct Coll Schlrshp 90-91; P Douglas Schlrshp 90-; Ocn Co G Sct Cncl Ldr 89-; Serv Unt Com; Assn Advcmnt Sci; Bio/Chem.

**KABIRU, J WANJIKU,** Central St Univ, Wilberforce, OH; SO; BS; Flwshp Christn Stu 89-; Biolgcl Soc VP 90-; Intl Stu Assn Treas 90-; Biology/Pre Med; Medicine.

**KACH, MONA B,** Bapt Bible Coll & Seminary, Clarks Summit, PA; GD; MSCSE; BA Bible Baptst Bible Clg Of PA 90; Elem Ed; Tchr/Missns.

**KACHANOVSKY, ASYA,** Berkeley School-New York, New York, NY; FR; BA; Engl; Acctng.

**KACHELE JR, LARRY S,** Thomas Nelson Comm Coll, Hampton, VA; FR; AS; U S Cst Grd; Mech Eng Tech; Navl Eng.

**KACHELMEYER, LORI LOJACONO,** S U N Y Coll At Fredonia, Fredonia, NY; SR; Ed Dev Pgm Peer Cnslr; Interclgte Capt Vlybl Tm 88-90; BS; Cmnctns; Video/Film Prod.

**KACPRZYK, HEATHER M,** Duquesne Univ, Pittsburgh, PA; JR; BS; Rho Chi Recog Cert 90; Dns Lst 89-; Intrnshp Med Shoppe; Pharm.

**KACZMARCZYK, CHRISTINE I,** Wilmington Coll, New Castle, DE; JR; BED; Trustees Awd 90; Diamond State Reading Assoc 89-; Natl Catholic Ed Assoc 87-; Spcl Reading Tchr Parochial Sch 83-; Cert DE Tech/Comm Coll 87; AS Early Ed 90; Lang Arts; Edn.

**KACZOR, SUSAN M,** Duquesne Univ, Pittsburgh, PA; GD; MBA; MBA Assn; Grad Asstshp; BSBA 90; Humn Res/Mgmt; Prod Mgmt.

**KACZYNSKI, MARY A,** Comm Coll Algny Co Algny Cmps, Pittsburgh, PA; JR; Univ Pgh Schlrshp; AA 90; Physics.

**KADIRI, AHMED Z,** Central St Univ, Wilberforce, OH; GD; MBA; Intl Stdnt Org Advsr 89-; Islamic Stdnt Org 90-; BS 87; Info Sys; MIS.

**KADLECIK, ROBERT M,** Bapt Bible Coll & Seminary, Clarks Summit, PA; SO; BS; Vrsty Soccr; Track; Bible; Yth Pstr.

**KAELBLE, CHRISTINE M,** Centenary Coll, Hackettstown, NJ; SO; BA; Equine Cl; Hunter Tm 90-; GSA; Inter Cllgte Riding Tm 89-; Equine Studies; Horse Trnr/Tch.

**KAELIN, AMY L,** Wv Univ, Morgantown, WV; SR; BS; NSNA 90-; Sigma Theta Tau 90-; Hall Assn 87-90; Nrsng.

**KAEPPLER, SUZANNE G,** Liberty Univ, Lynchburg, VA; SR; BS; Kappa Delta Pi 90-; LACT 90-; Elem Educ.

**KAGANOUSKY, ARKADY,** Ny Univ, New York, NY; JR; BS; Russian Amer Club Dom NYU Ex Vice Pres 90-; Acturial Societies; Deans Lst 90-; Award For Excellence 90-; AAS SCE NYU 90; Actuarial Sci; Business.

**KAGANSKY, DMITRY V,** Hofstra Univ, Hempstead, NY; FR; BBA; Org Cmmtr Stdnts 90-; Prog Bd 90-; Phi Alpha Delta; Kappa Sigma; Rugby Ftbl Tm 90-; Mktg.

**KAGEL, GEOFFREY A,** Case Western Reserve Univ, Cleveland, OH; SR; BA; Physics Clb Co-VP 87-; Debate Soc Sec 88-89; Philosophy Clb 88-89; Phi Beta Kappa; Deans Hon Awd 87-; Physics Schlrshp 87-89; Physics Intrnshp 89; Alumni Assn Schlrshp 89-; Deans High Hon Lst 87-88/90; Physics/Philosophy; Theoretical Physicist.**

**KAHALAS, STACY M,** Univ Of Rochester, Rochester, NY; JR; SWE 88-; Glee Clb Scl Chr 88-90; HILLEL 88-89; Deans Lst 88-; Phi Sigma Sigma Brsr 89-; Elec Eng.

**KAHILL, TERESA G,** Watterson Coll, Louisville, KY; GD; BA; Paralegal; Law.

**KAHL, JAMES DARRIN,** Univ Of Sc At Columbia, Columbia, SC; SR; BS; Crlna Cares 87; Beta Alpha Psi 89-; Deans Lst 87-90; Acctg; Sprts Fin Plnnr.

**KAHL, JOHN A,** Ms Gulf Coast Comm Coll, Perkinston, MS; JR; Math Club; Indtl Electn; Acctng/Math; Law Schl.

**KAHL, SHERYL L,** Univ Of Md Baltimore Prof Schl, Baltimore, MD; SR; BS; SADHA 90-; Pha Kappa Phi 90-; Nu Zeta Pi 90-; Dntl Hygn.

**KAHLE, GARY L,** Christian Brothers Univ, Memphis, TN; JR; BA; Current Emplymnt Pos Prgrmr Analyst; AA Lima Tech Coll 81; Mngmnt; Bus.

**KAHN, LARRY J,** Tri County Tech Coll, Pendleton, SC; SO; Bsns Ldrs Tomorrow; ASSOC Sci; Assoc EET; Sci/Comp.

**KAHN, MAZEEDA,** Manhattan Coll, Bronx, NY; FR; BS; Pres Schlp; Dns Lst; Sci/Cmptrs; Chem Engr.

**KAHN, STEPHEN N,** Bloomfield Coll, Bloomfield, NJ; SR; BS; Chrprctc Clb Pres 88-90; Class VP 90; Acad Jdcry Brd 90; Alpha Chi 90; Chi Beta Theta 90; Prof Bio; Medcl Gntst.

**KAHSAI, ELIZABETH,** Bunker Hill Comm Coll, Boston, MA; FR; AARTS; Sec Ethpn Arlns 86-87; Law Firm 87-90; Dplma Jnr Clg Cmmrc Addis Ababa Ethiopia 86; Lib Arts; Bsn Admn.

**KAIGHEN, PAMELA A,** Christopher Newport Coll, Newport News, VA; SO; BA; Grl Scts Amer 89-; Amer Red Crss 90-; Bus; Mktg.

**KAINAMURA, TOM K,** Teikyo Post Univ, Waterbury, CT; SO; BA; Stdnt Govt Assoc Rsdnt Sntr 90; Yrbk Clb Edtr In Chief 90; Stdnt Ambssdr 90; Accntng; CPA.

**KAISER, ANDREW T,** Univ Of Sc At Columbia, Columbia, SC; SO; BA; Model Un Natns VP; Stdnt Govt Comm Rep; Alpha Lambda Delta; Pres Hon Roll; Intl Stdies; Intl Bus.

**KAISER, DARRELL J,** Unity Coll, Unity, ME; SO; BS; Envrnmntl Awrness Clb 90-; Envmntl Sci/Soc Sci.

**KAISER, DRAKE H M,** Academy Of The New Church, Bryn Athyn, PA; FR; Curr Affairs Discn Grp; Muscl Prud; Ugher; LaCROSSE.

**KAISER, ERICH W,** Slippery Rock Univ, Slippery Rock, PA; SR; BA; Varsity Soccer Tm Cptn 87-90; Hlth/Physical Ed/Dance; Tchng.

**KAISER, MARIE A,** Indiana Univ Of Pa, Indiana, PA; JR; BS; Fast Food Mgr; AS Comm Clg Alleghny Cnty 90; Elem Educ; Tch.

**KAISER, RYAN P,** Belmont Coll, Nashville, TN; FR; BA; I M Bkbl; Bus.

**KALAFARSKI, DEBORA A,** Univ Of Rochester, Rochester, NY; JR; BA; Camp YMCA 89-; Omicron Delta Epsilon; Tutrng Pgm 90; L; Xerox Corp Intrnshp Bus Prcss Mgmt; Sftbl 90-; Econ; Bus/Fnc.

**KALAMA, LESLIE D,** Spartanburg Methodist Coll, Spartanburg, SC; FR; Sftbl 90-.

**KALAYIL, GEORGE V,** Univ Of Louisville, Louisville, KY; SO; BA; Geography Club 90-; Phi Eta Sigma 89-; Soc Porter Schlrs 89-; BS; Chemistry/Biology; Medicine.

**KALB, MARCIA R,** Univ Of Miami, Coral Gables, FL; JR; BA; Orntn Coord; Acctng Spvsr Commonwealth Mgmt & Dev Corp 88-; AA Edison Comm Coll 88; Intl Fin & Mrktng.

**KALBAUGH, TRACY A,** Radford Univ, Radford, VA; FR; BA; Alpha Lambda Delta 90-; Ryl Prstg Mktg Intrnshp; Bus.

**KALCHSTEIN, SCOTT,** Ramapo Coll Of Nj, Mahwah, NJ; SR; BA; Newspaper Ed-In-Chf 88-; Jewish Assoc 89-; Tutor 89-; Outstndg Tutor Awd 90; Dns Lst 89-; Dns Awd Except Svc; Ldrshp Awd 90; IM Ftbl/Hockey/Vlybl Champ 86-; Cmnctn Arts; Print Jrnlsm.

**KALE, ELAINE D,** Catawba Valley Comm Coll, Hickory, NC; FR; AAS; Acctng Club; Gamma Beta Phi 90-; Fire Dept Aux 90-; Acctng.

**KALE, VIJAY K,** Al A & M Univ, Normal, AL; FR; BS; Minority Rese Schlrshp Natl Instit Of Hlth 90; Molecular Biology; Biological Resec.

**KALEBIC, CHAD C,** Georgetown Univ, Washington, DC; SO; Invstmnt Allnce 89-90; Intl Bus Acctg, Bus Admn.

**KALEEL, JEHAD M,** Univ Of The Virgin Islands, St Thomas, VI; SR; BS; MBRS Rsrch Aide 88-; Prsdnt Clb; Chmstry Physcs; Medicine.

**KALFAS, MARINA E,** Northern Ky Univ, Highland Hts, KY; JR; BS; Pre Phys Thrpy.

**KALGREN, RAYMOND O,** Univ Of Tn At Knoxville, Knoxville, TN; SR; BS; Beta Gamma Sigma; Roddy Fdntn Schlr; Natl Brd Rsprtry Care 74-; Certfd Rsprtry Thrpy Techn 71-; Econ; Bkg.

**KALINDA, FLORENCE N,** Fl A & M Univ, Tallahassee, FL; SR; BS; SG Pres 87-89; Hnr Scty Pres 87-89; Big Sister 87-90; Vltr Yr; AA Peninsula Clg 88; Biology; Dr.

**KALINKIEWICZ, PATRICK J,** Bowling Green St Univ, Bowling Green, OH; SR; Stdnt Cnstrctn Mgmt Soc 86-; Cntrctrs Assn 88-; Natl Grd 86-; Beta Theta Pi 86-88; Cnstrctn Mgmt/Tech; Eng.

**KALINOSKI, SUZANNE M,** Mount Aloysius Jr Coll, Cresson, PA; SO; BA; Occuptnl Thrpy Clb 88-; Phi Theta Kappa 89-; Assc Sci; Sci; Occup Thrpst.

**KALINOWSKA, KATARZYNA A,** Univ Of Sc At Columbia, Columbia, SC; SR; BS; Eta Sigma Delta 90-; Appl Prffsnl Sci; Trsm.

**KALINOWSKI, ANDREW T,** Ms Univ For Women, Columbus, MS; SR; SGA Sntr 89-90; Data Prcsg Mgmt Treas 90-; Phi Beta Lambeda 90-; BS; Bus Admin; Cmptr Info Sys.

**KALINOWSKI, BRIAN H,** Teikyo Post Univ, Waterbury, CT; JR; BA; Alumni Schlrshp; Engl; Tchr/Writer.

**KALINOWSKI, WILLIAM S,** Univ Of New Haven, West Haven, CT; FR; BA; Acctg.

**KALKER, SUSAN MARIE,** Northern Ky Univ, Highland Hts, KY; SR; BA; Kappa Delta Tau 88; Newman Ctr; Ed Engl/Math; Ed Mdl Schl.

**KALLON, MARY H,** Columbia Union Coll, Takoma Park, MD; SR; MBA; Blue Cross Blue Shield Natl Capital Area 89-; BSC; Finance; Financial Consultant.

**KALLU, MATEWOS W,** S U N Y At Buffalo, Buffalo, NY; JR; BSEE; IEEE 90-; Natl Soc Blck Eng 89-; Eta Kappa Nu 90; Tau Beta Pi 90; Gldn Ky 90; Mnrty Rsrch Intern 89-; R Mcnair Achvmnt Prog; Elect/Cmptr Eng.

**KALMAN, MICHAEL D,** Brown Univ, Providence, RI; FR; BS; IM Strt Hcky; Comp Sci.

**KALMANSON, AMY J,** Univ Of Rochester, Rochester, NY; SR; BA; Psychlgy Cncl 89-; Hlth/Soc Cncl 89-; YMCA Bg Sistr/Bg Brthr Prog; Sigma Delta Tau Hstrn/Fndrsng Chrmn 87-; Adpt-Grndprnt Prog Pres 88-; Hlth/Soc Advsr 90-; Rsrch Asst 89-90; Intrnshp 90; Vrsty Tennis Team 87-89; Psychlgy/Hlth/Soc; MA.

**KALODNER, MELISSA F,** Atlantic Comm Coll, Mays Landing, NJ; GD; AA; Clg Radio Stdnt Govt Rep 89-; Stdnt Govt V P 90-; Envir Comm 89-; Pres List 90; Psychology; Clincial Wrk.

**KALOUDELIS, IOANNA,** Clark Univ, Worcester, MA; FR; BA; Maids Athena Sec 87-; George Javis Schlrshp 90-; Bus Mgt.

**KALP, LISA R,** Indiana Univ Of Pa, Indiana, PA; JR; BS; Bg Bros/Bs Strs 90-; Kappa Delta Pi 90-; Phi Sigma Pi 89-; Provost Schlr 90; Elem Educ; Tchr.

**KALTEN, WILLIAM A,** Hofstra Univ, Hempstead, NY; SR; BS; Kappa Mu Epsilon; Upsilon Pi Epsilon; Cmptr Sci; Law.**

**KALTENBAUGH, DAVID S,** Indiana Univ Of Pa, Indiana, PA; SR; BS; Alpha Phi Omega Almn Chrprsn 89-; Deans Lst 90-; Erth/Spc Sci Educ; Eductr.

**KALTER, STEWART M,** Widener Univ, Chester, PA; SO; BA; Deans Lst Stdnt 90; Acctg Soc 90-; Lambda Chi Alpha 90-; Spec Olympcs 89-; IM 89-; Acctg/Pre-Law; CPA/LAW.**

**KALTEYER, DONNA A,** Mayland Comm Coll, Spruce Pine, NC; FR; AAS; Phi Theta Kappa 90-; US Navy 82-88; Furniture Indstries 82-; Gen Educ; Syst Anlyst/Comp.

**KALWAYTIS, ELISA A,** Marywood Coll, Scranton, PA; FR; BSW; Soc Work; Corrctnl Faclty.

**KAM, MILTON H,** City Univ Of Ny City Coll, New York, NY; JR; BFA; Film/Video.

**KAM, SUETBEE,** Bowie St Univ, Bowie, MD; SR; BSEE; Intl Assoc 88-; Hon Pgm 88-; Elec Eng.**

**KAMADA, JUNKO,** Univ Of Tn At Martin, Martin, TN; FR; BA; Acctg; Acctnt.

**KAMADIA, SHAMSEH F,** Miami Dade Comm Coll, Miami, FL; FR; AA; Pkstn Assn; Phi Theta Kappa; Bus; Bus Admnstrtn.

**KAMAU, NJERI,** Pa St Univ Delaware Cty Cmps, Media, PA; SO; BA; Tn Vc Clb Pblc R Offcr 85-86; Intl Stdnts Assoc Fndr 90; Harambee Yth Sec 87-88; Swmmng Drm Sld Music Wn Trphs 79-86; Htl Mgmt; Bus Law.

**KAMBARA, EUNICE A,** Univ Of South Fl, Tampa, FL; SR; BA; Fine Arts Tlnt Grnt; Art.

**KAMEH, DARIAN S,** Univ Of Va, Charlottesville, VA; SR; Singer 87-90; Vlybl Clb 87; Pistol/Rifle Clb 88; Hosp Vol Hwu Madison Hse OR/ER 87-; BA; Bio; Med.**

**KAMENTZ, DIANE M,** Univ Of Miami, Coral Gables, FL; SR; BS; Assoc Teacher Internshp/Richmond Hghts Mddl Schl 90; BS 90; Biology; Educ.

**KAMER, JANET P,** Roane St Comm Coll, Harriman, TN; FR; AAS; Crnry Nrs Spclst 78-80; LPN 75; Spcl Ints Srgry/Ob Nwbrn Nrsg; Nrsg.

**KAMHOLZ, JENNIFER L,** Syracuse Univ, Syracuse, NY; SO; BS; Mrchng Bnd 89-91; Symphnic Bnd 89-90; Sgm Kappa 90-; Tau Beta Sgm Cmt Chrmn 89-; Deans List; Gymnstcs 89-90; Inf Stds/Ec; Fincl Plng.

**KAMINSKI, AARON M,** Hilbert Coll, Hamburg, NY; SO; AA; Psych/Lbrl Arts; Cnslng/Rsrch Psych.

**KAMINSKI, CHRISTINE R,** Comm Coll Algny Co Algny Cmps, Pittsburgh, PA; SO; AA; Phi Theta Kappa; Psych; Drug/Alcohol Cnslr Psych.

**KAMINSKI, JENNIFER L,** Savannah Coll Of Art & Design, Savannah, GA; FR; BFA; Deans Lst; Womens Soccer Tm; Art; Graphic Artist.

**KAMINSKI, KATHLEEN J,** Niagara Univ, Niagara Univ, NY; GD; Univ Plyrs Pres Emrts 90; Chpl Chr 90; Stdnt Advsry Cncl To Dn 90; Delta Epsilon Sigma 90; Sigma Alpha Sigma 90; BFA 90; Thtre; Dir Fr Thtre.

**KAMINSKI, KATHLEEN K,** Bethany Coll, Bethany, WV; SO; Stdnt Brd Govrnrs Rep 89-90; Fr Actvts Cncl Rep 89-90; Bthns Spprt Nw Stdnts Mbr 90-; Phi Mu Crrspndng Sec; Deans Lst 89-; Pltcl Sci.

**KAMINSKI, KATHLEEN M,** Coll Misericordia, Dallas, PA; JR; BA; Educ 90; AA Luzerne Cnty Comnty Clg 90; Elem Educ; Tch.

**KAMINSKI, KRISTEN D,** Dowling Coll, Oakdale Li, NY; SO; BBA; Acctng Scty 90-; Deans Lst 89-; Acctng; CPA.

**KAMINSKI, LYNNE M,** Medaille Coll, Buffalo, NY; SO; BED; Educ; Tchng.

**KAMINSKY, VERA M,** Georgetown Univ, Washington, DC; FR; BA; Credit Un Teller 90-; Yrbk Photogrphr 90-; Spirit Comm 90; Dorm Cncl 90-; Asst Career Eductr; Leavey Admn Info Dsk 90-; Im Vlybl; Intrntl Bus; Corp Bus.

**KAMMER III, CHARLES H,** Ms Coll, Clinton, MS; GD; JD; Alpha Tau Omega Alumni; Miss State Bar Assoc Pro Bono Proj 90; Deans Lst 90; Amer Jrsprdnce Awd 90; Tchng Assist Lgl Wrtng 90; BS La Tech U 89; Law.

**KAMPFER, PAULA J,** Univ Of North Fl, Jacksonville, FL; JR; BA; Phi Theta Kappa Chrmn Un Svc 90-; AA FL Comm Clg Jacksonville 89; Engl Ed; Tchr.

**KAMPHAUS, ROBERT A,** Univ Of Sc At Columbia, Columbia, SC; SO; BS; Carolina Alive Pop Chorus Sound Man 89-; Clg Work Stdy 89-; David Odum Underguard Schlrshp; Deans Hnr List 89-; Science; Phscl Ocngrphy.

**KAN, YU-HSIANG,** Univ Of Al At Huntsville, Huntsville, AL; JR; BA; Alpha Lambda Delta 90-; English; Tchr.**

**KANAGY, ROSALYNN J,** Livingston Univ, Livingston, AL; SO; BS; Mrchng Bnd 89-; Cncrt Bnd 89-; Alpha Phi Alpha Swthrt 89-; Delta Sigma Theta; Biol Sci; Med Schl/Pdtrcn.

**KANAKIS, ARIANA,** Saint Joseph Coll, West Hartford, CT; FR; BA; Best Buddies 90-; Spec Educ; Educ.

**KANDABAROW, ELIZABETH,** Cumberland County Coll, Vineland, NJ; SO; Ed/Cmptr Sci; Tch Elem.

**KANDARE, GLENN C,** Old Dominion Univ, Norfolk, VA; JR; BA; Tau Beta Pi Treas 90-; Pi Theta Kappa 86-87; Church Of Jesus Chrst Latterday Snts Eldr 87-; AS Tidewater Comm Coll 87; Mech Engr.

**KANDIE, KIGEN,** Embry Riddle Aeronautical Univ, Daytona Beach, FL; FR; BED; Elctrncs; Eng.

**KANDIES, ELIZABETH F,** Midlands Tech Coll, Columbia, SC; GD; Oper Rm Tech 90-; Assctn Srgcl Tech; ORT Tech; Oper Rm Tech; Nrs.

**KANE, BRODY N,** Middle Tn St Univ, Murfreesboro, TN; JR; BED; Pre-Law Soc 90-; Crim Just Soc 90-; Kappa Alpha 90-; Crim Just Adm; Law Sch.

**KANE, ERICA L,** Lesley Coll, Cambridge, MA; SO; BED; Emerald Key 89-; Pre Practicum Tchng 89-; Elem Educ; Tchr.

**KANE, KAREN KATHLEEN,** Bunker Hill Comm Coll, Boston, MA; FR; Harold K Mintz Spch Cmptn; Intl Hlth Nwtn Mass; Nrsg.

**KANE, KAREN R,** Univ Of Southern Ms, Hattiesburg, MS; JR.

**KANE, KATHLEEN P,** City Univ Of Ny Baruch Coll, New York, NY; SR; BA; St Johns Univ ROTC Trng/Oper Offcr 90; Tour Ldr 90-; Schlr 87-89; Engl; Military.

**KANE, NICOLE T,** Univ Of Rochester, Rochester, NY; SO; BA; Psychlgy; Ned.

**KANE, TERESA A,** Mount Saint Mary Coll, Newburgh, NY; SR; BA; Deans Lst 89-; Hnrs Alliance 89-; Alpha Chi 90-; Lds Aux BPOE Elks Clb 1977; Hstry; Scndry Edctn.

**KANE, TODD D,** Newbury Coll, Brookline, MA; FR; Med Disblty; Paralgl; Law.

**KANG, SANGHOON,** S U N Y At Buffalo, Buffalo, NY; GD; MARCH; Korean Stdnt Assns 87-90; BS Boston Univ 87; Archtctr.

**KANLONG, HENRY G,** Mount Saint Mary Coll, Newburgh, NY; FR; MBA; Admsns 90-; Specl Olympics 90-; Deans Lst; White Plains Hosp Vol 89-90; Human Svcs; Med.

**KANNE, ELIZABETH A,** Oh Wesleyan Univ, Delaware, OH; SO; BA; Le Bijou Yrbk Ed In Chief 89-90; Stdnt Hon Bd Stdnt Rep 90-; Econ Stdnt Bd Rep 90-; Phi Eta Sigma; Phi Sigma Iota; Phi Soc; Wesleyan Wnr; Stdnt Of Yr Awd; PICAS Flwshp Japanese Study; Jrnlsm/French/Econ Mgmt; Intl Sales.

**KANNING, JEANNIE R,** Spartanburg Methodist Coll, Spartanburg, SC; SO; Phi Beta Lambda; Jr Achvmnt 90; Phi Theta Kappa 90-; Acdmc Achvmnt Awrd; Pres Lst 89-; Bus Admin; Acctg.

**KANOFSKY, ALLISON,** Univ Of Rochester, Rochester, NY; SO; BA; Sigma Delta Tau Fndrsng Chrmn; Oper Desert Spprt; Dean Lst; Intern Clrk Michelle L Skalsky Esq; Pol Sci/Engl; Law.

**KANSAS, NICOLE M,** Savannah Coll Of Art & Design, Savannah, GA; SO; BFA; Fiber Arts Clb 90-; Grphc Dsgn; Advtsng/Dsgn.

**KANTARGIS, ANDREA A,** Univ Of Al At Birmingham, Birmingham, AL; SO; BA; Alpha Lambda Delta 90-; Alpha Gamma Delta Pub Chrmn 89-; English; Wrtr.

**KANTERMAN, ROBERT Y,** Univ Of Miami, Coral Gables, FL; GD; MD; Eastern Stdnt Rsrch Forum 90-; Alpha Omega Alpha; H Hughes Med Inst Rsrch Schlr Prog 88-90; BS 86; Med; Diagnostic Radiology.

**KANTOR, JOE R,** Livingston Univ, Livingston, AL; FR; Phi Eta Sigma 90-; Fr Of The Yr 90-; Tennis 1 Position 90-.

**KANTOR, STACEY L,** Univ Of Miami, Coral Gables, FL; SR; BA; Phi Sigma Sigma Bursar 89-90; Sociology/Educ; Early Chldhd/Preschool Educ.

**KANTOR, ZENA M,** Univ Of Miami, Coral Gables, FL; SR; BA; Funday 88-90; Hmcmng Com 90; Phi Sigma Sigma 89-90; Soclgy/Ed; Soc Wrkr/Diabetic Edctr.

**KANYA, DENISE L,** Oh Univ, Athens, OH; JR; BS; Soc For Women Engrs 89-; IIE 90-; Tau Beta Pi Rec Sec 90-; Alpha Pi Mu; IM Sftbl 89-; Engrng.

**KANYAN, JENNIFER L,** Indiana Univ Of Pa, Indiana, PA; SO; Elem Educ; Tchr.

**KANYI, GEORGE K,** Glassboro St Coll, Glassboro, NJ; SO; BS; Cmptr Sci.

**KAO, CHUNG-YING J,** Radford Univ, Radford, VA; FR; Asian Assoc VP; Human Rsrc Mgt; Bus.

**KAPELA, NICOLE D,** Univ Of Rochester, Rochester, NY; JR; BA; Drm Cncl Sec 88-90; Cmps Rep VP 90; Rsdntl Lf Advsry Comm 89-90; Alpha Phi Omega; Trn Prjct Sec 88-90; Stdnt Sprvsr; IM 88-; Engl.

**KAPELET, LAURIE A,** Valdosta St Coll, Valdosta, GA; SR; BED; Bapt Stdnt Un 90-; Stdnt Ga Assn Of Edctrs Sec; Prof Assn Of Ga Edctrs 90-; AA Clayton St Coll 89; Erly Chldhd Edn; Teach.

**KAPELL, LESLI R,** Union Inst, Cincinnati, OH; SR; BA; Wlmstwn Theatre Fstvl Asstnt Dir Adv Pblc Rltns 87; Hmn Rsrc Mgmt; Org Bhvr.

**KAPETANAKIS, KAREN,** Georgian Court Coll, Lakewood, NJ; JR; BA; Court Sngrs Sec 90-; Retail Sls; Hstry; Law.

**KAPILEVICH, MENDEL B,** Bunker Hill Comm Coll, Boston, MA; SO; Emplyee Of The USSR Estblshmnts Moscow 48-87; Engl/Comptr Progrmng Tech; Engr.

**KAPLAN, ANTHONY A,** Mount Saint Mary Coll, Newburgh, NY; JR; BA; Hnrs Allnc 89-; Bsktbll Mgr 90-; Stdnt Scrty 89-; Alpha Chi 89-; Delta Mu Delta; Aqns Schlr; Bus; Law.

**KAPLAN, CHERYL L,** Bay Path Coll, Longmeadow, MA; SO; ASSC; Dns Lst 90; Mrn Key And Pres Schlrshps; Spnsh Clb; WAPOR; SGCPO; Dns Lst 90-; Cert Ashuntuck Comm Coll 84; Prshnr All Snts Chrch; Attnd Univ Of CT; Trvld Crcs Vnzla Cnfrnce On Dem In Ltn Amer; Dscssd Pol Prblms Wth Dem Ldrs; Offce Admin; Exec Sec.

**KAPLAN, MICHAEL S,** Univ Of Miami, Coral Gables, FL; JR; BS; Chem Club; Psi Chi; Pre Med/Psy/Chem; Medcn.

**KAPLAN, PAUL M,** Yeshiva Univ, New York, NY; SR; BA; Coll Rpblcns Sec 88-89; Psychlgy Clb; Athltc Dept Asst Sprvsr 87-; Deans Lst 89-; I Tillem Prog Eldrly Schlr 89-; Orientatn Comm Stdnt Hst 87-88; Tennis MVP 90-; Tennis/Soccr Capt 87-; Psychlgy; Oral Srgry/Dntstry.

**KAPLAN, STEVEN L,** Cornell Univ Statutory College, Ithaca, NY; SR; BS; Bio Club Pres 88; Sci Fiction Assn V P Elect; Phi Theta Kappa 89; Gamma Sigma Delta; Kingsborough Pres Awd Dist Schlrshp 89; Bio Sci Awd 89; AS Kingsborough Comm Coll 88; Vet Med; DVM PHD.

**KAPLON, SUSAN M,** Indiana Univ Of Pa, Indiana, PA; SR; Outstndg Stdnt Tchr Awd; Dns Lst; BS; Sec Scl Studies Ed; Tch.

**KAPLUNOVICH, LANA S,** Cooper Union, New York, NY; SO; BSE; Kesher Jew Org 89-; Schlrshp Cooper Union 89-; Hmnty Essay Prize 89-90; Sci; Engr.

**KAPLYSZ, SCOTT H,** William Paterson Coll, Wayne, NJ; JR; Phlsphy; Phd Tchg.

**KAPOOR, ROSY,** City Univ Of Ny Baruch Coll, New York, NY; GD; BBA; Sigma Alpha Delta 90-; Alpha Beta Gamma QCC 87-89; Magna Cum Laude; Dns Hnr Lst 89-; Dns Hnr Lst QCC 86-88; AAS Queensborough Cmnt Clge 89; Bsn Mgmt/Mktg; Advrtsng Agcy.

**KAPOOR, SHAIWAL,** City Univ Of Ny Queensbrough, New York, NY; SO; BT; Tau Alpha Pi 90-; Vrsty Tnns 89; AAS; Elect Mech Tech; Eng.

**KAPOUSOUZ, MONIKA R,** Temple Univ, Philadelphia, PA; SR; BS; Jr Leag Rdng Inc Chr Pblcty Nom Asst Treas Plcmnt Audio Vsul All Brd Pstns 83-; Frnds Symph Brd 90-; Herb Soc Amer PA Hrtlnd Reg Annul Symp Chr Symph Bll 85-87; Golden Key; Fclty Awd; Hrtcltr; Own Bus/Cnsltng/Dsgng.

**KAPPAN, ANN MARIE,** Medaille Coll, Buffalo, NY; SO; BS; Soc Hmn Rsrc Mngmnt; Amer Soc Trng/Dev 89-; Hmn Rsrc Dev; Training.

**KAPPAS, BRETT M,** Northern Ky Univ, Highland Hts, KY; FR; BA; Hon Rl; Deans Lst; Acdmc Tm; Gvrnrs Schlr Cand; Hstry Bowl St Rep EKU; NKU Crtv Wrtng Comp Wnnr Fctn Shrt Stry Ctgry; Essay Wnnr 1st; Acdmc Dcthln Fnlst; Strght A Awd; Scl Stdies Awd; Pltcl Sci Awd; Engl Awd; NKU Deans Lst; NKU Hon Pgm; Hstry/Pltcl Sci; Law.

**KAPPES, JACQUELINE A,** Atlantic Comm Coll, Mays Landing, NJ; JR; BA; Psych Clb Pres; Psi Chi; Dns Lst 89-; Grad Wth Hons 90; AS Atlantic Comm Clg 90; Psych; MA.

**KAPSON, ELLEN L,** Elmira Coll, Elmira, NY; JR; BSN; Nrsng Club Pres 90-; Nrsng Exclnc Award Clncl Psychtrc Nrsng 87; Nrsng Exclnc Award Clncl Medcl Srgcl Nrsng 87; CPR Instrctr; AIDS Cnslr; Pres Geisinger WY Vly Medcl Ctr Sch Of Nrsng 86-87; Chrprsn Nrsng; Nwsltr Comm; Nrsng.

**KAPUSTKA, TACOMA S,** Univ Of Al At Huntsville, Huntsville, AL; SR; BS; Phi Kappa Phi; Ice Hcky 90; Elec Eng; Eng.

**KARABINUS, THERESA L,** Univ Of Akron, Akron, OH; FR; BED; Hnrs Clb 90; Akron Cncl Of Ed Stdnts 90; Rstrnt League Mixed Bwlng 90; Phi Eta Sigma 90; Alpha Lambda Delta 90; Hnrs Prog 90; Elem Ed; Tchr.

**KARADIMAS, IOANNIS,** City Univ Of Ny Baruch Coll, New York, NY; BBA; Hlnc Scty 88-90; Radio Stn Pgm Dir 88-90; Fnce/Ecnmcs Scty 88-90; Frgn Schlrshp 88-90; Fnce; Bnkg.

**KARAEFTHIMOGLU, ALEXIA,** Franklin And Marshall Coll, Lancaster, PA; SR; Hbtat Fr Hmnty 90-; FAMINE 89-; Elderlink 89-90; OCSA 89-; Phi Beta Kappa; Psi Chi 89-; Tutrg 90; Ord Ahepa Schlrshp/Plqe/Awd 85-86; Dghtrs Penelope Schlrshp/Awd 85-86; Cum Laude; BA; Frnch; Clncl Psychlgst.

**KARAGIANNIS, EVANGELOS C,** Duquesne Univ, Pittsburgh, PA; SR; JD; Greek Orthodox Church; Aderson/Frank/Steiner Intern 89-; Bs Admin Duquesme Univ 90-; Pre Law/Real Estate; Law.

**KARAM, KARA J,** Defiance Coll, Defiance, OH; SO; BA; Psych; Law.

**KARANZA, KARLA M,** Comm Coll Algny Co Algny Cmps, Pittsburgh, PA; SO; BA; Bus/Fin; Law.

**KARATEKIN, ERDEM,** Univ Of Louisville, Louisville, KY; FR; BS; Phi Eta Sigma; Deans Schlr; Swm Tm Athltc Schlrshp 90-; Chmcl Engnrng; Engnrng.

**KARAVA, KAREN M,** Fl Atlantic Univ, Boca Raton, FL; SR; BA; Phi Kappa Phi; Beta Alpha Si; Acctng Stdnts Assn VP 90-; Alpha Of FL Sec 90; Phi Theta Kappa Sec 89; Rcpnt Of Phi Theta Kappa Ttn Schlrshp 89-; AA 89; BA; Acctng Govt.

**KARCANES, JAMES A,** Univ Of Sc At Columbia, Columbia, SC; SO; BA; Flwshp Chrstn Ath 89-; Cmps Crsd Chrst 89-; Alpha Lamda Delta 89-; Pres Hnr Rl 89; Eta Sigma Theta 90-; Gamma Beta Phi 90-; Crs Cntry Trck Tms 89-; Psychlgy; Semnry/Pastorate.

**KARDOULIAS, TERESA A,** Marymount Manhattan Coll, New York, NY; JR; BA; Art; Med Illust/Comp Grphcs.

**KARELIS JR, THOMAS E,** Univ Of Ky, Lexington, KY; SR; BS; Shaolin Karate Clb Pres/Inst 88-; Ski Clb; Blgy; Med.

**KARIM, KANEEZA,** City Univ Of Ny Baruch Coll, New York, NY; JR; BBA; Helpline 87; Women Of Color Netwrk 90; Beta Gama Sigma; Weinstein Trst Fnd Schlr 88; Provost Schlrshp 88; Bank Clrk 75-86; Psych.

**KARIMI, KATAYOUN,** City Univ Of Ny Baruch Coll, New York, NY; SR; BBA; Goldn Key 90-; Beta Alpha Psi; Acctg.

**KARJALA, JUSTIN D,** Univ Of Miami, Coral Gables, FL; FR; BS; Boy Scouts Asst Sctmstr 90-; Eagle Scout; Biology; Medicine.

**KARKOS, MELANIE,** Univ Of Miami, Coral Gables, FL; SR; BBA; Hnr Stdnt Assoc 87-; Bnd Hr 87-88; Frshmn Ornttn Asst 89; Rtrct 88-89; IM Sprtsfst; Bwmn Ash Schlrshp 87-; Mrktng.

**KARL, DENNIS L,** S U N Y Coll Of Envr Sci & For, Syracuse, NY; JR; BS; SG; Frstry Eng Clb 90-; Sierra Clb 89-; NSPE 89-; Phi Eta Sigma 89-; Alpha Lambda Delta 89-; Stdnts Offrng Svc; OH Envrnmntl Cncl 89; Eng Grphcs TA 89-90; Alumni Assn Schlrshp 88-89; Chem Eng Schlrshp 89-90; Frstry Eng.

**KARL, JEFFERY A,** Oh Univ, Athens, OH; FR; BA; IM Ftbl Bsktbl; Elec Comp Eng; Eng.

**KARL, LORI A,** Duquesne Univ, Pittsburgh, PA; SR; BS; Univ Orntn 88; Mortor Brd 90-; Lambda Sigma Prlmntrn 88-89; Phi Eta Sigma 88-89; Alpha Phi Treas 89-; Pttsbrgh Proj Clean Up 89; Latch Key Prog Vol Coord 89-90; US Dept Cmmrc Stdnt Intrn; Harry S Mc Closkey Schlrshp 90; Univ Schlr 87-; Mrktng; Corp.

**KARL, MICHELLE R,** Methodist Coll, Fayetteville, NC; JR; BA; Actvts Cncl 90-; Sftbll Tm 88-; Sclgy.

**KARLEKAR, MOHANA B,** Cornell Univ Statutory College, Ithaca, NY; SR; Orntn Ldr Supvr Orntn Cnslr 87-88; Agri Ambsdr Sec 89-; Delta Phi 87-; Ithaca Yth Bureau Tutor; Stop Smoking Cnslr; Monroe Dvlpmntl Ctr Vol 87-; Civitas Vol Lrng Disabled Clsrm; Deans Lst 90-; IM Bsktbl 88; BS; Food Sci; Med Sch.

**KARLIN, JEFFREY S,** Cornell Univ Statutory College, Ithaca, NY; SO; Cncrt Commssn Asst Fin Dir 90-; Univ Newspr Ed 89-90; Agri/Lfe Sci Ambssdrs 90-; Lambda Chi Alpha Scl Dir Elect; A W Laubengayer Prz 90; Bio.

**KARLSEN, JOAN E,** Teikyo Post Univ, Waterbury, CT; SO; BA; Rs Trg Scty 90-; By Scts Amrca Cmmttee 89-; AS-THR; Hlth Cr.

**KARNES, RETHA E,** Univ Of South Al, Mobile, AL; SR; Dns Lst 89-90; Pres Lst 89; Fin.

**KARNILAW, MICHAEL L,** City Univ Of Ny City Coll, New York, NY; SR; BE; Amer Inst Chem Engr 85-; Emrld Soc NYC Plc Dept 88-; Pulaski Assoc Plc Dept 86-; AS 84; Chem Engr.

**KARP, JESSICA L,** Fl St Univ, Tallahassee, FL; SO; BM; Symphny Orch 90-; Tallahassee Orch 90-; Chmbr Orch; Music; Violinist.

**KARPF, MICHELLE B,** Nova Univ, Ft Lauderdale, FL; GD; MBA; Mrch Dimes Brth Dfcts Fndtn; BA Univ Fla 84; Busn Admin; Mgmt/Admin.

**KARPINSKI, JULIAN B,** Marshall University, Huntington, WV; SR; BBA; Upsilon Pi Epsilon 90-; Natl Collegiate Cmptr Sci Awd 89-90; U S Achvmnt Soc; Ashland Petroleum; Bus Info Sys.

**KARR, BETTY J,** Sue Bennett Coll, London, KY; FR; AA; Flwshp Cntmpry Clgns VP 90-; Phi Beta Lambda Sec 90; Phi Theta Kappa 90-; Silver Metal; Bus Admnstrtn.

**KARR, KIM L,** Univ Of Akron, Akron, OH; FR; BA; Bus Admin; CPA.

**KARR, KRISTINE S,** Univ Of Sc At Aiken, Aiken, SC; JR; BA; Deans Lst 89; Sftbl 90-; Psych.

**KARR, LUCIE,** Daytona Beach Comm Coll, Daytona Beach, FL; SO; MBA; Phi Theta Kappa Chrmn Acdmc Affrs 90-; Clb Richelein Wmn Dvsn Sec 85-86; Frnch Intrntl Clb; Ed/Frgn Lngs; Tchng Clg Level.

**KARR, MICHAEL E,** Kent St Univ Kent Cmps, Kent, OH; JR; BA; Dns Lst 90; IM Bsktbl 1st Plc; Bsn Mktg; Sports Mktg.

**KARR, SANDRA S,** Western Ky Univ, Bowling Green, KY; JR; BS; Phi Eta Sigma; Goldn Key; Phi Kappa Phi; Kappa Tau Alpha; Kappa Delta Sch Chrmn 89-; Mktg/Advrtsng.

**KARRICK, MARY M,** Univ Of Md Baltimore Prof Schl, Baltimore, MD; GD; MSW; Phi Kappa Phi; Sigma Theta Tau; BSN Amer Univ 83; Social Work.

**KARRMANN, KAREN L,** S U N Y Coll At Postdam, Potsdam, NY; JR; Alcohol/Drg Educ Prog 89-; Phi Eta Sigma 90-; Phi Alpha Eta 90-; Alpha Sigma Tau 90-; Pres Lst; V Swmng 89-90; Dev Psychlgy.**

**KARSHNER, KATHLEEN J,** Oh Univ, Athens, OH; SO; BFA; Education; Teach.

**KARST, LUCY P,** Miami Univ, Oxford, OH; FR; BA; Rcqtbll Clb 90; Appalachia Hnrs Com Scl Concerns; Hnrs Coll 90-; Kappa Alpha Theta 90-; IM Rcqtbll 90-; Zoology; Health.

**KARY, JENNIFER A,** Glassboro St Coll, Glassboro, NJ; JR; BED; AAE Gloucester Co Clg 90; Elem Educ; Tchr.

**KASAM, NASSEM I,** Union Univ School Of Nursing, Memphis, TN; SO; BSN; SG 77-78; Bombay Univ India Sec 78-79; Prfsnl Cooking 87; Cert Cordon Bleu Sch Cooking London 87; Nurs.

**KASARDA, LEE A,** Univ Of Akron, Akron, OH; JR; Natl Athltc Trnrs Assn 90; Sports Med-Athltc Trng; Crtfd Athltc Trnr.

**KASARI, MARK A,** Univ Of Sc At Columbia, Columbia, SC; SR; BS; Bio Clb; Repub Clb; Omicron Delta Kappa; Phi Eta Sigma; Sigma Phi Epsilon 88-; Roger L Moore Schlrshp; Chanclrs Lst; Outstndng Stdnt Awd Bio; Bio; Pharm/Toxicology.

**KASHEY, MELISSA J,** Bethany Coll, Bethany, WV; SO; BA; Psychology Clb 89-; German Clb 89-; Model U N 89-90; Kappa Delta 90-; Girl Scouts 89-; Registrars Office Asst 89-; Elem Educ; Cnslng.

**KASHIF, AKIN W,** Morgan St Univ, Baltimore, MD; FR; BSEE; Grant Brett Promethean Kappa Tau Frshmn 90-; Fl Hnrs Schlrshp 90-; Elec Engr.

**KASIN, BRYAN JAY,** S U N Y Coll Of Tech At Frmgdl, Farmingdale, NY; FR; AAS; Bus/Acctg; Accnt.

**KASKOW, ANDREA F,** Salisbury St Univ, Salisbury, MD; SO; Intl Assoc Bus Cmnctns 90-; Orntn Tchr New Stdnts 90-; Occptnl Thrpy.

**KASLANDER, EILEEN J,** Passaic County Comm Coll, Paterson, NJ; SR; ASSOC; LPN 74-; Nrsng; BSN.

**KASMAI, HOSSEIN F,** Fl International Univ, Miami, FL; SR; BSEE; IEEE 88-; Phdi Lmbd 90-; Elect Eng/Mcrcmptr Dsgn; Eng.

**KASMAUSKI, SUSAN M,** Commonwealth Coll, Virginia Beach, VA; JR; Electrncs Clb V P; Alpha Beta Gamma; Lic Alpha Omega Coll Real Est 88; Elec Eng.

**KASPAR, DAVID P,** William Paterson Coll, Wayne, NJ; JR; BA; Lit Clb Mag Staff 90-; Philosophy Clb 90-; English/Philosophy.

**KASPAREK, DORIGEN K,** Univ Of Sc At Columbia, Columbia, SC; SO; BS; Chi Omega Com Chr 89-; Frshmn Cncl 89-90; Carolina Cares 89-90; Gamma Beta Phi 90-; Hnrs College 89-; ASC 90-; Tchng Asstntshp 90-; IM Sprts 89-; Chemistry/Pre-Med; Med Schl.

**KASPER, ANDREA J,** Seton Hall Univ, South Orange, NJ; FR; BA; Vol N J Spec Olympcs 91 Spring Sprts Festvl; Economics Tutor; Deans Lst 90; Var Vybl NCAA Div I 90; Advtsng Art/Bus; Advtsng Art Dir.

**KASPER, BRENDA K,** Univ Of Cin R Walters Coll, Blue Ash, OH; SO; BS; Physics Clb 90-; Hnr Stu Yr 90-; Chem Awrd 89-90; Chem.

**KASPER, JEFFREY K,** Univ Of Akron, Akron, OH; JR; BS; Amer Inst Chem Engr 88-; Phi Eta Sigma 87-; Tau Kappa Epsilon 89-; Coop Educ W Cleuite Elastomers 90-; IM Sprts 87-; Chem Engr.

**KASPERSEN, ROSEMARIE BOREL,** Va Commonwealth Univ, Richmond, VA; JR; BFA; Golden Key; Dept Army Sustaine Superior Perfmnc 87; Deans Lst 89-; Juried Commnctn Arts Dsgn Show; Commnctn Arts Dsgn; Graphic Dsgn.

**KASPRZAK, LISA,** Indiana Univ Of Pa, Indiana, PA; JR; Proj Stride 90-; Habitat For Hum 90-; WIUP 88-89; Elem Educ.

**KASPRZYCKI, DEBORAH ANN,** Southern Ct St Univ, New Haven, CT; JR; BSN; Nursing.

**KASPUTIS, MARY LYNN,** Indiana Univ Of Pa, Indiana, PA; SR; Deans Lst; BS; Physics; Tchng.

**KASSNER, KAREN R,** Univ Of Southern Ms, Hattiesburg, MS; SR; BS; Psychology.

**KASTON, DEBORAH L,** S U N Y Coll Of A & T Morrisvl, Morrisville, NY; SO; ASSOC; Debate Tm 90-; Stdnt Tchg; Erly Chldhd Educ; Tchr.

**KASTORY, KIRSTEN L,** Clemson Univ, Clemson, SC; JR; BS; Clemsn Dncrs 87-88; GAMMA 89-; SC Rec/Parks Assoc 90-; Meetng Plnnrs Intl 90-; Snow Ski Clb 87-89; Hl Cncl 88-89; Alpha Delta Pi Spirit Chrmn 87-; Marriott Corp Intrn 90; Amelia Island Plantn Intrn; Prks/Rec/Toursm Mgmt; Meeting Plnng.

**KASYAN, MICHAEL S,** Comm Coll Algny Co Algny Cmps, Pittsburgh, PA; FR; AAS; Tandy Corp/Radio Shack; Nclr Med Tech.

**KASZA, KRISTEN A,** S U N Y Coll Of Tech At Delhi, Delhi, NY; SO; MBA; HSMA 89-; Htl Mgmt.

**KASZUPSKI, ROSE H,** Atlantic Comm Coll, Mays Landing, NJ; SO; BA; Phi Beta Lambda Treas 90-; Marriott Seaview Rsrt; Frnt Dsk Sprvsr 89-; Acctg; CPA.

**KATARIA, KAVITA K,** City Univ Of Ny Baruch Coll, New York, NY; JR; BBA; Intl Bnk; Fnce; Banking.

**KATHOLI, CONSTANCE D,** Snead St Jr Coll, Boaz, AL; SO; NAVTA 89-; Phi Theta Kappa; Science.

**KATRES, TANYA M,** Fl St Univ, Tallahassee, FL; SO; BA; NAEA; Phi Eta Sigma 90-; Gamma Phi Beta Hist 89-; PGA Bobbie Goodman Schlrshp; FL Acad Schlr 89-; IM Ftbl/Bsktbl 89-; So FL PGA Schlrshp 89-; Art Edn; Interior Dsgn.

**KATRIB, MONA,** Univ Of Charleston, Charleston, WV; SO; BS; Cmptr Info Syst.

**KATSARELIS, ANTHONY P,** Longwood Coll, Farmville, VA; GD; CERT; Pi Kappa Phi 88-90; BS 90; Math; Scndry Sch Tchr.

**KATSAVDAKIS, KOSTAS,** City Univ Of Ny Baruch Coll, New York, NY; SR; BA; Psychlgy Soc Pres 89-90; Psi Chi Pres 89-; Un Jwsh Fdrtn Chldrn/Fmly Serv Asst Tchr 87-88; Clncl Psychlgy; PhD.

**KATSIKAS, EPAMINONTAS G,** Strayer Coll, Washington, DC; JR; BA; Acctg Clb; Natl Assn Actnts; Alpha Chi; Acctg; Pblc Acctg.

**KATSIMATIDES, ANTHOUL,** City Univ Of Ny Baruch Coll, New York, NY; SO; BA; Baruch Law Soc 90-; Nisyrian Yth Org Gen Sec 86-; AHEPA 90-; Dns Lst 90; Mktg/Mgmt; Law.

**KATSKI, ROBERT T,** Anne Arundel Comm Coll, Arnold, MD; SO; BA; Atheletes Hnr Roll 90; La Crosse 90; Ecology.

**KATSTRA, DIRK P,** Univ Of Va, Charlottesville, VA; SR; Stdnt Athlt Mntr 90-; Mens Bsktbl Capt 90-; BS Ed 91; Sports Mgmt; Sports Admin.

**KATULIS, BRIAN M,** Villanova Univ, Villanova, PA; FR; BA; Project Sunshine 90-; Philadelphia Comm For Homeless 90-; Pre-Law Soc 90-; U S Govt Jr Flwshp Prog Mgmt Trainee 90-; Hist; Law.

**KATZ, DAVID B,** Oh Wesleyan Univ, Delaware, OH; FR; BM; Hillel 90-; Opera Wrkshp 90-; Chrl Art Soc 90-; Mu Phi Epsilon; Music; Univ Music Prfssr.

**KATZ, DAVID H,** Fl International Univ, Miami, FL; SR; BS; ASME 89-; Phi Et Sigma 88-; Alpha Omega Chi 90-; Phi Kappa Phi; Eng; Mech Eng.

**KATZ, ERIKA D,** Univ Of Nc At Charlotte, Charlotte, NC; JR; BA; Stdnt Alumni Amb; Phi Eta Sigma; Golden Key; Pi Sigma Alpha; Alpha Delta Pi 89-90; Pol Sci/Geography; Pub Admin.

**KATZ, JEANNE M,** City Univ Of Ny Queensbrough, New York, NY; SO; BA; Alpha Beta Gamma 88; Exec Secy AT & T 66-83; Custom Jwlry 84-86; Bus/W P Tech; Mgmt Secy/W P Div.

**KATZ, JENNIFER A,** Univ Of Miami, Coral Gables, FL; FR; BS; Insprtnl Cncrt Choir 90; Hons Stdnts Assoc 90; Deans Lst Pres Hon Roll 90; Psi Chi; Rsrch Assist Psych Prof; Psych; Clinical Psych.

**KATZ, MICHAEL S,** Temple Univ, Philadelphia, PA; JR; BA; Crmnl Justice Soc 90; Pre-Law Soc; Phi Eta Sigma Drexel Univ 88-89; Gldn Ky 90-; Dns Lst Drexel Univ/Temple Univ 88-; Crmnl Jstce; Law.

**KATZ, MITCHELL W,** City Univ Of Ny Baruch Coll, New York, NY; SR; BBA; Golden Key; Deans List; Cert Gemological Inst Of Amer 87; Cert Dale Carnegie Inst 88; Publc Acctng; Law.

**KATZ, SETH I,** Ny Univ, New York, NY; JR; BA; Pol Sci; Law.

**KATZ, STACEY A,** Fl St Univ, Tallahassee, FL; JR; IM Sftbl Ftbl Tns 88-; Tallahassee Cty Lg Sftbl 89-; Deans Lst 88-; Delta Zeta Sprt Chrmn 90-; Hmn Soc 91-.

**KATZ, STEVEN L,** Hillsborough Comm Coll, Tampa, FL; FR; AABSN; Pres Clb Awd; Otstdng New Accts Sls; Kinetic Concpts Inc 87-90; Ortho Tech Tampa Gen Hosp 85-87; USAFR Aermdcl Evac Sqd 80-86; Sci/Busn; Hosp Admin.

**KATZ, STEVEN M,** Ny Univ, New York, NY; GD; DDS; Jewish Clb V P 89-; Jewish Orgztn 89-; Dental Sch Asst 90-; Deans Lst 87-90; Alpha Omega; Intrn K B Y Sch Israel 86-87; Wrstlng/Swmng; Dentistry.

**KATZ JR, WILLIAM M,** Georgetown Univ, Washington, DC; SR; BSBA; Bsbl 87-88; Fnce/Internatl Mgmt; Law.

**KATZER, STACEY L,** Univ Of Ky, Lexington, KY; FR; Donovn Dorm V P 90-; Team U K 90-; Phi Eta Sigma 90-; Dns Lst 90-; Educ/Math; High Schl Tchr.

**KAUER, MICHAEL E,** Manhattanville Coll, Purchase, NY; FR; BS; Pre Law Soc 90-; D J For School Media Disc Jcky 90-; Pre Law; Lawyer.

**KAUFFMAN, DANIEL R,** Central Fl Comm Coll, Ocala, FL; SO; Fire Sci.

**KAUFFMAN, ROBIN L,** Comm Coll Algny Co Algny Cmps, Pittsburgh, PA; SO; Aviation Mngmnt Clb 90-; Child Care Clb 89-; CCAC Travelers Clb 90-; Deans Lst 89-; Pediatrics; Nurse/Phys.

**KAUFFMAN, SHELLEY J,** Juniata Coll, Huntingdon, PA; SR; BS; Geological Soc Pres 87-; Admsns Assoc 88-; Peer Advising Advsr 89; Hon Soc; Deans Lst 90-; Luthern Ch Retreat Cnslr 87-90; Environ Resources Intern 89-90; Lab Asst 89-90; Environmntl Geology; Cnsltng Firm.

**KAUFMAN, AMY L,** Slippery Rock Univ, Slippery Rock, PA; JR; BAMBA; Lambda Sigma Sec 89-90; Pa St Athletic Conf Schlr Ath Awd 90; Eastern Coll Champ Judo 145 Lbs 90; Judo 88-; Lifetime Fitness/Pre Phys Thrpy.

**KAUFMAN, BRAD M,** Middle Tn St Univ, Murfreesboro, TN; FR; BA; Bus.

**KAUFMAN, BRADLEY J,** Cornell Univ Statutory College, Ithaca, NY; SO; Emerg 90-; Medl Serv; Ski Club 90-; Delta Tau Delta 90-; Biological Sci; Medl.

**KAUFMAN, JAMES S,** Univ Of Fl, Gainesville, FL; SR; BA; Bd Coll Cncls; Bus Adm Coll Cncl; Phi Eta Sigma; Chi Phi VP 89; IM Ftbl/Sftbl; Gainesville Mntl Hlth Svc Vol; Shearson Lehman Bro 90-; Finance; Fncl Plng.

**KAUFMAN, JOANNE M,** Cornell Univ Statutory College, Ithaca, NY; SR; BS; Rotaract Clb Cmunctns Dir 87-88; Amnesty Intl 87-; Cncrt Cmsn 88-; Greenpeace 90; Ho Nun De Kah 89-; Phi Kappa Phi 89-; Gamma Sigma Delta 90-; Golden Key 89-; VIVITAS 88-89; Biology; Music.

**KAUFMAN, KARYN S,** Univ Of South Fl, Tampa, FL; SR; BA; Themis 89; Pi Gamma Mu 90-; Psychlgy.**

**KAUFMAN, KIMBERLEY B,** Kent St Univ Kent Cmps, Kent, OH; SO; Knt St Univ Amblnc Srvc 89-; Crmnl Jstc Studies; Spclztn In Ems Law.

**KAUFMAN, KIMBERLY A,** Univ Of Southern Ms, Hattiesburg, MS; SO; BED; Busn; Law.

**KAUFMAN, MARGOT A,** Goucher Coll, Towson, MD; SR; BA; Stdnt Govt Assn Chmn 90-; Schl Nwspr Nws/Features Ed 90-; Psychlgy Clb Co-Pres 90-; Psi Chi; Jewish Fmly Serv So NJ Vol 89-90; Deans Lst 89-90; Trustees/Pres Ldrshp Sem 90; Intrnshp Baltimore Evening Sun Rprtr/Rsrch Asst 89-; Psychlgy; Jrnlsm.

**KAUFMAN, MARLA L,** Lesley Coll, Cambridge, MA; JR; BA; Emrld Key 88-; Deans Lst 88-; Edc.

**KAUFMAN, SHAWN D,** Mount Aloysius Jr Coll, Cresson, PA; FR; AS; SG Pres; Bus Clb Pres; Theatre Grp 90-; Deans Lst; Bus; Mgmt.

**KAUTZ, MICHELLE P,** Duquesne Univ, Pittsburgh, PA; SO; BA; ACM 90-; Syrena Polish Folk Dancers 86-; Cmptr Sci; Cmptr Progmmng.

**KAVANAUGH, KAREN K,** Univ Of Ms Main Cmps, University, MS; FR; BSN; Kappa Kappa Gamma Sec Pldg Prsnl Com; Nrsng.

**KAVANSHANSKY, JOHN A,** Univ Of Akron, Akron, OH; SR; BS; Acctg; CPA.

**KAVESKI, LORA A,** Mount Aloysius Jr Coll, Cresson, PA; SO; AS; Bus Clb Sec 90-; Disciplinary Bd 90-; Phi Theta Kappa 90-; Meth Ch Auditor 90-; Cub Scout Den Ldr 90-; NAA; Bus Admin; Acctg.

**KAVIANI, KATAYOON,** Comm Coll Algny Co Algny Cmps, Pittsburgh, PA; FR; BA; Intl Club.

**KAVIC, STEPHEN M,** Univ Of Pa, Philadelphia, PA; SO; BA; PA Pol Union Vce Chr 90-; Undrgrad Chem Scty 90-; CRC Fr Chem Awrd 90; Chem; Physcn.**

**KAVULICH, MAUREEN A,** Villanova Univ, Villanova, PA; JR; BA; Yrbk 89-; Stdnt Un 88-90; Spcl Olym 88-; VIEW 89-90; Bln Day Com 88-; Pjct Snshn 89-; Cmps Mnstry 89-; IM Flg Ftbl Bsktbl Sftbl F Hcky Co-Cptn 88-; Poli Sci/Bus; Corp Lwyr/Tchr.

**KAW, SHEK-LIN,** Ms St Univ, Miss State, MS; SO; BS; Mlysn Stdnt Assn VP; Chns Stdnt Assn; Gamma Beta Phi; Phi Eta Sigma; Hall Cncl Rep 90; Comp Sci; Comp.

**KAWABATA, NOBUKO,** Endicott Coll, Beverly, MA; SO; AS; Fitness Clb 90-; Chrus Clb/Piano 90; Model UN; Intrnshp 89-90; AS; Hmnty.

**KAWABE, TOMOMI,** Elms Coll, Chicopee, MA; SR; Psy.

**KAWAHARA, KUNIKO,** Univ Of Tn At Knoxville, Knoxville, TN; JR; BA; Exec Prog 90-F Delta Nu Alpha; AA Wayo Wmns Jr Coll 83; Lgstcs/Trsnprtn.

**KAWANABA, YUKO,** Becker Coll At Leicester, Leicester, MA; SO; AA; Tutored Japanese Students 90; AA; Liberal Arts; Env Design.

**KAWARABAYASHI, THERESSE K,** Georgetown Univ, Washington, DC; FR; BA; Intl Rltns Clb Mdl Untd Ntns 90-; Jpn Clb 90-; Otdrs Clb 90-; Deans Lst 90-; IM Vllybll 90-; Intl Bus.

**KAWASAKI, YOSHIKO,** Newbury Coll, Brookline, MA; FR; AS; Trvl/Toursm Mgmt.

**KAWOHL, MICHAELA,** Coll Of Charleston, Charleston, SC; JR; SAA 89-; Adv Club 90-; Fin Club 90-; Running Club 90-; Phi Kappa Phi 90-; Omicron Delta Kappa 89-; Beta Gamma Sigma Pres 90-; All Amercn Schlr US Achvmnt Adadmy; Hghly Dstngshd Fclty Hons List 88-; Bus Admn; Mktg/Intrntl Bus.**

**KAWSKI, SCOTT A,** Niagara Univ, Niagara Univ, NY; JR; BS; Becceria 89-; Alpha Phi Sigma 90-; Schls Tutoring Dept 90-; Schls Sec Station Aid 90-; IM Bsktbl/Sftbl/Hcky; Crmnl Justice; Law.

**KAY, AMY H,** Cornell Univ Statutory College, Ithaca, NY; FR; BS; Publ Rel Stdnt Soc Amer 90-; Kappa Delta; Comms/Govt; Pol Publ Rel.

**KAY, DAVID J,** Yeshiva Univ, New York, NY; JR; BA; Clg Stdnt Cncl Pres; Clg Sen Chrmn 89-; Nwspr Sr Edtr 89-; Sigma Delta Rho Mbr 88-; Max Stern Div Commnl Serv Supv 88-; Dev Disbld Coord 88-; Blkin Schlr 88-; Fncng Capt 88-; Biol; Med.

**KAY, JENNIFER D,** Youngstown St Univ, Youngstown, OH; SR; Nutrition Scty 88-89; Deans Lst 87-; Honors Convocation 88; Presentor Wrtng Ctr Assoc 90; American Dietetic Assoc 88-; BS Youngstown St Univ; Food Nutrition; Dietitian Clncl Practice.

**KAY, KIRA,** Ny Univ, New York, NY; JR; BA; Scty Prfssnl Jrnlsts 90-; Schl Nwspr Edtr Rprtr 89-; Russian Clb 89-; Intrnshp ABC News Nghtln; Hnrbl Mntn Jessica Savitch Awd; Intrnshp Mag 89; Journalism; Broadcast Journalist.

**KAYAL, KIM R,** S U N Y Coll Of Tech At Frmgdl, Farmingdale, NY; SO; AS; Phi Theta Kappa 90-; Pres Lst 89-90; Med Technlgy.

**KAYATI, KIMBERLY M,** Atlantic Comm Coll, Mays Landing, NJ; JR; BA; Attndng Valdosta State Clg Valdosta Ga 90; Mrktng; Rsrch.

**KAYE, JENNIFER L,** Providence Coll, Providence, RI; SR; Cncl Excp Cldrn 90-.

**KAYE, MITCHELL M,** City Univ Of Ny Queensbrough, New York, NY; GD; BA; Phi Theta Kappa 88; Alpha Beta Gamma 88; Mngr Comp Opertns; Eng; Pre Law; Lawyer.

**KAYE, RACHEL P,** Univ Of Miami, Coral Gables, FL; SR; BBA; Finance Clb 90-; Delta Phi Epsilon Phlthrpc 87-89; Paine Webber Intrnshp 90-; Intl Finance/Mktng; Intl Law.

**KAYE, RICHARD,** S U N Y At Buffalo, Buffalo, NY; SR; MS; Stdnt Dorm Ptrl Prog 87-88; Jwsh Stdnt Un 87-; Phi Eta Sigma 88-; Tau Beta Pi 89-; Eta Kappa Nu 90-; NBC TV Ntwrk Intrnshp Prog; BS; Indstl Engr; Engr Mgmt.

**KAYLOR, LAURA M,** Coll Of Charleston, Charleston, SC; SO; BA; Hist; Secndry Tchng.

**KAYNAK, THOMAS J,** William Paterson Coll, Wayne, NJ; SR; BS; Stdnt Athltc Trnrs Clb Hd Stdnt Trnr 90-; Natl Athltc Trnrs Assn 90-; Pi Kappa Phi 86-88; Chrch Bd Trstees 90-; W Paterson Coll Schlrshp Acdmc Excllnc 90-; W Paterson Coll Alumni Schlrshp 90-; Outstndng Sr Awd Acdmc Achvmnt; Mvmnt Sci/Athltc Trng; Physcl Thrpy/Athltc Tr.

**KAYNE, MANUEL A,** Yale Univ, New Haven, CT; FR; Yale Pltcl Un 90-; Alpha Delta Phi 90-; Cngrsnl Intern Cong Mc Grath 89-; Yale La Crosse; Pltcl Sci; Law.

**KAYS, ELENA J,** Centenary Coll, Hackettstown, NJ; JR; BFA; ASID 90-; Alpha Chi; ASID Schrlshp; Interior Dsgn 85-90; AAS Chamberlayne Jr Clg Boston MA 87; Inter Dsgn; Prfssr.

**KAZOURIS JR, NIKITAS,** Emory Univ, Atlanta, GA; SR; Var Sccr 87-89; Vol Emory 87-; Gov Intrn 89-90; Beta Alpha Psi; Deans Lst; Mrktg Assoc Pres 90; Pi Kappa Alpha VP 87-; Food Dr Asst 88; Crdlgy Cntr Rsrch Asst; IM Vlybl/Sftbl/Ftbl 87-; BBA; Corp Finance; Corp Chem.

**KEA, DANIELLA F,** Middle Tn St Univ, Murfreesboro, TN; SR; BSN; Blgy Clb 85-87; Chem Clb 86-87; SOA 87-89; Rho Chi 87 89; Alpha Delta Pi Hsr Chrmn Rgstr 88; IM Flag Ftbl Sftbl Vlybl; Nrsng.

**KEA II, JOHN L,** Union Univ, Jackson, TN; SR; BS; Pre Legal Scty Pres 87-; Rutledge Hnry Hstry Clb VP 88-; Prexy Clb; Alpha Chi 89-; Hnr Stdt Assoc 88-; Phi Alpha Theta VP 89-; Pi Gamma Mu VP 89-; History; Law.

**KEAN, ERIC M,** Cornell Univ Statutory College, Ithaca, NY; SO; BS; Chmbr Orchstr Vlst 89-90; Actrl Clb Fndr; Mo Nun De Kah; Sttstcs; Actry.

**KEAN, JACK V,** Ms St Univ, Miss State, MS; GD; Pi Epsilon Tau Pres 89-90; Tau Beta Pi 90-; Alpha Lambda Delta Phi Eta Sigma 86-87; Soc Pet Engrs Proj Chrmn 89-90; Phi Gamma Delta 86-; Un Way Meals Whls 87; Jr Of Yr 88-89.

**KEANE, ELLEN,** Fl International Univ, Miami, FL; SR; BS; Phi Theta Kappa 87-88; Marriott Htl Schlrshp 88; Price Waterhse Admn Asst 80-; AAS Nassau Cmuty Clg 88; Hosptly Mgmt.

**KEANE, MICHAEL J,** Georgian Court Coll, Lakewood, NJ; SO; BA; Hmnts; Law.

**KEAR, DARLENE K,** Univ Of Akron, Akron, OH; JR; BS; Golden Key 90-; Elem Ed; Tchr.**

**KEARBY, COREY L,** Valdosta St Coll, Valdosta, GA; SO; Kappa Alpha 90-; Biol; Phrmcy.

**KEARLEY, FRANCINE H,** Livingston Univ, Livingston, AL; JR; BS; Coach Grls Sftbl Tm 88; Civiettes 87-90; AA Patrick Henry Jr Clg 90; Elem Ed Mddl Sch Cert; Tchr Lang Arts.

**KEARNEY, ANDREW W,** S U N Y Coll At Fredonia, Fredonia, NY; FR; BA; Stage Mngrs Anyms Mgr 90-; Hnrs Pgm Cmmtr 90-; Msc Ed; Band Dir.

**KEARNEY, ANN M,** Coll Misericordia, Dallas, PA; SR; Cnsl Excptnl Chldrn 88-; Assoc Rtrd Ctzns; BED.

**KEARNEY, ANNETTA L,** Univ Of Tn At Knoxville, Knoxville, TN; FR; CHRA 90; Nrsng; Nrsng Peds.

**KEARNEY, CYNTHIA L,** Radford Univ, Radford, VA; JR; BS; Univ Nwspr Wrt Hdlns/Laid Out Stories; Rho Lambda Sec; Zeta Tau Alpha Asst Treas; Cmncntns; Pblc Rltns.

**KEARNEY, DEBORAH E,** S U N Y Coll Of Tech At Delhi, Delhi, NY; SO; BS; Phi Theta Kappa 90-; Natl Scty Public Acctnts 90-; Bkkpg Serv 89-; AAS; Bus Econ; Acctng.

**KEARNEY, JENNIFER L,** Duquesne Univ, Pittsburgh, PA; FR; BA; Pre-Law Soc 90-; Phi Eta Sigma; Univ Vol 90-; Bsn/Adm; Law.

**KEARNEY, KAREN B,** Vance Granville Comm Coll, Henderson, NC; FR; AAS; Bus; Mgmt Entrprnr.

**KEARNEY, KIMBERLY ALICE,** Univ Of Sc At Columbia, Columbia, SC; SO; Alpha Chi Omega Sor 90-; Alpha Lambda Delta Frshmn 89-; Gamma Beta P Hi.

**KEARNEY, LENARD F,** Fl A & M Univ, Tallahassee, FL; SO; PHD; Pol Sci/Busn; Law.

**KEARNEY, TAMMI S,** Univ Of Va, Charlottesville, VA; SR; BSED; Natl Stdnts Speech Lang Hearing Assoc 90-; Peer Advisor 90-; Deans Lst 89-; Certificate Acdmc Excllnc 90; Grad With Honors; Cmmnctn Disorders; Speech Lang Pathologist.

**KEARNS, BRIAN P,** Va Commonwealth Univ, Richmond, VA; GD; MS; Wheelchr Wghtlftng 84-; Golden Key 88-; Alpha Phi Sigma 88-; Phi Kappa Phi 88-; Natl Private Invest Assn 85-; Vets Admin Vol 83-; P I; AS J S Reynolds Clg 88; BS VA Cmnwlth Univ 90; Law/Crim Just.

**KEARNS, EDWINA H,** Univ Of Nc At Charlotte, Charlotte, NC; SO; BA; NCCTM Sec 90-; Intrvrsty Chrstn Flwshp 89-; IM Ofcl 89-; Math; Educ.

**KEARNS, PAMELA R,** Univ Of Nc At Greensboro, Greensboro, NC; SR; Vol Srvcs To Eldrly; Pres Lst; Dns Lst; Hgh Pnt Jr Wmns Clb Schlrshp; Maggie Davis Schlrshp; Roxie King Schlrshp; Ornttn Asst; Pres NC Cncl Of Tchrs Math; BS 90; Mddle Schl Educ Math Sci; Tch.

**KEARNS, SADIE H,** Montgomery Comm Coll, Troy, NC; SO; SGA Rep 90-; Pres Lst 90-; Dns Lst 90-; Gnrl Ed; Tch.

**KEARNY, TOWANDA L,** Cumberland County Coll, Vineland, NJ; FR; Gospel Chr Sec; Latin Amer Clb; TV Rap Commcl; Dns Lst; Hnrs Course; Linguistics/Msc; Intrprtr/Mscn.

**KEARSE, LAURIE A,** Univ Of Sc At Columbia, Columbia, SC; FR; Blgy; Med.

**KEASLING, SHANNON D,** Middle Tn St Univ, Murfreesboro, TN; JR; BA; Clg Repubs 89-; TN Vol For Life Clg Chptr; Baptist Stdnt Union 89-; Pi Gamma Mu 90-; Hist; Phd In Hist.

**KEATING, AIMEE B,** Livingston Univ, Livingston, AL; SR; BS; Phi Mu Panhellenic Pres 88-89; Panhellinic VP 88-89; Delta Chi Little Sister 87-; Bus Admin/Computer Sci; Cmptr Programmer.

**KEATING, JAMES A,** Saint Vincents Coll & Seminary, Latrobe, PA; SR; MD; Blgy Clb; Chem Clb; Physics Clb; SR Clscl League 87-; Forbes Reg Hosp Vol 89; St Vincent Cmps Mnstry Guitarist 87-89; Orientation Com 89-; Vlybl Chmpnshp Tm 90; Mdcl Intern Monsour Mdcl Ctr 90; BS; Medicine.**

**KEATING, KARLA R,** Liberty Univ, Lynchburg, VA; SR; BS; Stdnt Govt Sntr 89-; Yth Quest Clb 88-89; Alpha Lambda Delta 89-; Kappa Delta Pi Senate Rep 90-; Elem Educ; Tch.

**KEATING, ROBYN,** Colby Sawyer Coll, New London, NH; SO; BA; Yrbk Stf 89-90; Key Assn 89-; Stdnt Alumnae Assn 89-; Early Chldhd Grp Natl Assoc Edn Yng Chldrn 89-; Deans Lst 89-; Vol Local Elem Sch 90-; Co-Chrmn Orgnzng Thanksgvng Bskts 90; Quilts Risk Babies; Chld Study; Tchr K-2.**

**KEATING, SHANE J,** Livingston Univ, Livingston, AL; SR; BS; Sports Med Cl V P 90-; L Club 87; Stdnt Athl Trnr/Yr 89; Head Stdnt Trnr 89-; Delta Chi 86-; EMT 88-; RA 90-; Phys Ed/Athl Trng; Athl Trnr.

**KEATING IV, WILLIAM B C,** Fl St Univ, Tallahassee, FL; JR; BS; Seminole Party Stdnt Govt 90; Fla Pub Intrst Rsrch Grp FPIRG 89; Goldenkey 90-; Alpha Kappa Psi; Lbrl Stdes Honprog 88-90; Deans Lst 89-; Univ Schlrshp 88-; I M Soccer 88-90; Multi Natl Bus/Mktg German; Intl Law.

**KEATING, WILLIAM J,** Eckerd Coll, St Petersburg, FL; JR; Chss Clb 88-; Dorm Pres 90; Math Clb 88-; By Scts 81-; John Knox Presb Chrch 84-; Egle Sct 88-; Chrch And Cmps Schlr 88-; Ordr Of The Arrw; Vrsty Sccr 88-; BS; Blgy; Rsrch Eclgy.

**KEATLEY, ROBERT LANCE,** Univ Of Tn At Chattanooga, Chattanooga, TN; FR; BSE; IM Bsktbl; Mech Eng.

**KEATON, DONALD ERIC,** Brevard Coll, Brevard, NC; SO; MBA; Chrstn Stu Fllwshp 89; Wsly Fllwshp 89; Phi Theta Kappa; Bus; Accntng.

**KEATON, EDWARD L,** Cleveland St Univ, Cleveland, OH; JR; ASCE 90-; Deans List 89-; Tau Beta Pi; Hnry Fenn Grant 90-; AS Lorain Cnty Comm Clg 89; Civil Engr; Strctrl.**

**KEATON, JODI W,** Valdosta St Coll, Valdosta, GA; SR; BSED; Stdnt GA Assc Edctrs Pres; Stdnt GA Assc Edctrs Vp 90-; Alpha Chi; Charlie Hicks Schlrshp; Educ/Math/Scl Stds.

**KEATON, SHARON A,** Anderson Coll, Anderson, SC; SO; MBA; Acdmc Advsry Cncl 90-; Phi Theta Kappa Treas 89-; Hon Pgm 90-; BA; Engl; Bus Wrtng.

**KEBERT, ELEISHA J,** Bethany Coll, Bethany, WV; SR; PHD; Amer Chem Soc Scl Dir 88-; Sftbl 87-90; Kalon Ldrshp Awd 87-; BS; Chem.

**KECK, ANNA L,** Savannah Coll Of Art & Design, Savannah, GA; SR; BFA; Fiber Arts 90-; Fiber Art; Weaving.

**KECK, FRIEDHELM R,** Eckerd Coll, St Petersburg, FL; SO; BA; Cert Germany 78; Mngmnt/Intl Bus; Arln Trnsprt Pilot.

**KECK, JAMES BRANDON,** Univ Of Ky, Lexington, KY; JR; BS; Mortar Bd 90-; Gldn Ky 90-; Gen Physics/Elect Eng.

**KECO, LAURIE A,** Miami Univ, Oxford, OH; SO; BS; Rght To Lfe 90-; Chrch Flwshp Grp 90-; Alpha Lambda Delta 90; Phi Eta Sigma 90; Sigma Sigma Sigma Educ Dir 90-; Prsh Vol 89-; Ohio Brd Rgnts Schlr 89; Deans Lst 89-; Dean Schlr; Pres Lst 90; Bus Mngmt; Law.**

**KEE, JEANINE C,** Columbia Union Coll, Takoma Park, MD; SR; BS; Assoc Telecmnctns Mgrs Treas 89-; Delta Sigma Theta; Asst Mgr 66-; Org Mgmt; Mgmt Cnsltnt.

**KEECH, SANDRA R,** West Liberty St Coll, West Liberty, WV; GD; BS; Busn Admin; Hosp Admin.

**KEEFAUVER, DAVID W,** Univ Of Tn At Knoxville, Knoxville, TN; FR; Exec Undgrad Pgm 90-; IM Athltcs; Alpha Lambda Delta; Sigma Phi Epsln Chrmn; Bsn; Sls Rep.

**KEEFE, ALISON M,** Univ Of West Fl, Pensacola, FL; FR; Kappa Alpha Order Little Sis 90-; IM 90-; Marine Biology.

**KEEFE, CATHERINE L,** Saint Francis Coll, Loretto, PA; JR; BA; Intrnshp-WTAJ-TV-10 Altoona PA; Cncl Prsn-Patton PA; Lctr/Euchrstc Mnstr/Rlgn Tchr St Marys Chrch; Engl/Cmnctns; News Rprtr.

**KEEFER, BRENT A,** S U N Y Coll At Fredonia, Fredonia, NY; JR; BS; All American Schlr; Acctg; CPA.

**KEEFER, MARY G,** Anne Arundel Comm Coll, Arnold, MD; FR; BS; Greater Severn Imprvmnt Assn Sec 90; Psychology.

**KEEFER, PHILIP A,** Univ Of Nc At Charlotte, Charlotte, NC; JR; BS/BA; German Club 89-; Cert Stdy Abroad Pgm; IM Sports 89; Mgmt Info Sys/Grmn; Cmptr Analyst.

**KEEFER, STEPHEN S,** Univ Of Sc At Columbia, Columbia, SC; JR; BA; Rsdnt Advsr 90-; Ldrshp Mntr; Grk Steerg Com; Sigma Chi 89-; Hstry; Tchr.

**KEEGAN, COLLEEN B,** Georgetown Univ, Washington, DC; SO; BBA; Cls Comm Stu Govt Tres 89-; Sthrn Soc Tres 90-; Acdmc Advsr; Amnsty Intl 89-90; Acctg.

**KEEGAN, WANDA J,** Winthrop Coll, Rock Hill, SC; SO; BFA; Alpha Lambda Delta; James V/Florence Bell Theodore Schlrshp; WV-AM Water Co 82-87; Intr Dsgn; Instnl Dsgn.

**KEEGAN, WILLIAM L,** Schenectady County Comm Coll, Schenectady, NY; FR; AD; Clnry Arts; Chef.

**KEEL, ALYCE N,** Univ Of Southern Ms, Hattiesburg, MS; SR; BS; Amer Soc Intr Dsgn 90-; Stdnt Home Ec Assn 90-; Pass Chrstn Hstrcl Soc 89-; Maricia Artigoes Intrs 89-; Intr Dsgn.

**KEEL, EDWARD D,** Univ Of Tn At Martin, Martin, TN; SR; Math/Comp Sci Clb Pres 88-; Stdnt Govt Assn Indpndnt Rep 89-; Martin Acdmc Tm 87-; Soc Hon Smnr Stdnts Nwsltr Edtr 88-; Bptst Stdnt Union Scl Chrmn 87-; Undrgrad Tchng Asst 89-; UT-MARTIN Math Awd; IM; Scndry Educ-Math; H S Math Tchr.

**KEEL, MITCHELL L,** Mount Olive Coll, Mount Olive, NC; SR; BS; Student Fovt 78-79; Bsktbl 78; Mgr Electric Systems; Aas Martin Cmnty Clge 77-79; Business Mgmnt.

**KEELE, RACHEL LYNNETTE,** Univ Of Tn At Martin, Martin, TN; SO; BS; Students For Life 89-; Overtime Ldrshp Committee 89-90; Campus Crusade 89-90; Bible Church Grp 89-; Honors Clg Az State 89-90; Deans Lst Az State 90; Deans Lst Univ Tenn 90; IM Bsktbl Sftbl Aerobics 89-; Sciences; Optometry.

**KEELER, MICHAEL P,** Fl International Univ, Miami, FL; JR; BS; Intern Univision Spanish Lang T V Network; AA Miami Dade Comm Coll 89; Cmmnctn; T V/Film Dir/Producer.

**KEELEY, KAREN M,** Wagner Coll, Staten Island, NY; SR; BS; SNA 87-; Sigma Theta Tau; Physical Ftns Trnr Parise Ftns Cntr 88-; Ice Hockey 87-; Nrsng; RN.

**KEELY, ALICIA J,** Union Coll, Barbourville, KY; FR; BS; Pzzzzrs Coll Dnc Tm 90-; Vet.

**KEELY, CATHERINE A,** Spalding Univ, Louisville, KY; SR; BSSW; Stdts Social Actn 89-; Ntnl Assoc Social Wrkrs 89-; Deans List 87-; Delta Epsilon Sigma 89-; Human Services; Social Work.

**KEEN, HENRY L,** Ms St Univ, Miss State, MS; SR; BS; IEEE 89-; Phi Kappa Phi 90-; Tau Beta Pi; Eta Kappa Nu 90-; Gamma Beta Pi 90-; Coll Serv Club 87-89; AA Holmes Comm Coll Ridgeland 89; Elect Engrng; Physiology.

**KEEN, JUNAID I,** Southern Coll Of Tech, Marietta, GA; SO; BED; Intl Stdnt Assoc VP 90-; RHA 90; IEEE 90-; Deans Lst 90-; Atlanta Pakistani Stdnt Assoc 89-; Stdnt Asst Hsng Offc 90-; Rsdnt Asst Sct Dorm Hll; Vllybll; Sccr; Fld Hcky; Elec Eng; Eng.

**KEEN, LISA L,** Middle Ga Coll, Cochran, GA; JR; BS; AA; Psychlgy; Crmnl Justice.

**KEEN, REGINA D,** Northern Ky Univ, Highland Hts, KY; SO; BA; Communications; Comm Advrtsng.

**KEENAN, ERICA E,** Georgetown Univ, Washington, DC; FR; BS; Spnsh Clb 90-; Intrntl Rltns Clb 90-; Envrnmntl Soc 90-; Intrntl Rltns.

**KEENAN, JOHN E,** Univ Of Cincinnati, Cincinnati, OH; Mscn/Music Tchr; AA 84; BM 90; Music.

**KEENAN, LADOSKA S,** Marshall University, Huntington, WV; JR; BA; Gamma Beta Phi 88-; Cnslng Rhbltatn; Fmly Cnslr.

**KEENE, AMY D,** Univ Of Southern Ms, Hattiesburg, MS; FR; Stdnt Alumni Assn 90-; Athltc Trnng Clb; Diamond Drlng Bsbl; Deans Lst 90-; Kappa Delta 90-; Athltc Trnng.

**KEENE, BEVERLY JO,** Mount Olive Coll, Mount Olive, NC; GD; Am Soc Military Cmptrlrs 89-; Civil Serv Fed Govt 71-.

**KEENE, HEATHER,** James Madison University, Harrisonburg, VA; SO; BS; Cncl Excptnl Chldrn 90-; Area J Spec Olmpcs 90-; Univ Prgmng Bd 90-; Ctr For Service Lrng Keister Elem 90-; Psyh; Spec Edn-Teach.

**KEENE, MATTHEW E,** Temple Univ, Philadelphia, PA; SO; BA; Pre-Law Soc 88; IM Sftbl 89-90; Tmple Univ Pres Awrd 88; H Treer Mem Schlrshp 89-90; Engl; Law.

**KEENER, BILLIE JO,** Lancaster Bible Coll, Lancaster, PA; SR; BS; Choir Sec; Stdnt Of The Yr; Stdnt Wrkr Of The Mnth; Bible/Music Educ.

**KEENER, DEBORAH FLATT,** Middle Tn St Univ, Murfreesboro, TN; SR; BSW; Deans Lst 90-; Intrnshp Cmbrlnd Mntl Hlth Cntr; Intrnshp Dept Of Hmn Serv 90; Soc Wrk.

**KEENER, WILLIAM T,** Univ Of Nc At Charlotte, Charlotte, NC; SR; BA; NC Cncl Teachers Math; Pi Mu Epsilon; Deans Lst; Chancellors Lst; Part Time Wrtr 89; Emrgncy Room Attndnt 80-89; Math; Computer Sci.

**KEENEY, KATHRYN I,** Elmira Coll, Elmira, NY; JR; BA; Caton Grange Sec 72-; Parnt Tchr Asst Tr 75-89; Catn Meth Chrch 77-; Grl Scts Ldr 76-89; Dir Pre Schl 86-; AA 90; Elem Educ; Tchr.

**KEENEY, MICHELLE M,** Salisbury St Univ, Salisbury, MD; SO; BA; Apprprtns Bd Chrprsn 90-; Stdnt Govt Ldrshp Conf Texas A/M Univ; Phi Eta Sigma 90-; Hnrs Prog Awd; Psychlgy; Vctm Advcy.

**KEENUM, SANDRA L,** Memphis St Univ, Memphis, TN; SR; BS; Jr Achvmnt; NCEA; Kappa Delta Pi; Elem Educ; Teacher.

**KEERY, TABOR L,** Concordia Coll, Bronxville, NY; FR; BS; Festvl Chorus 90-; Tour Choir 90-; Drama 90-; Soc Wrk Club 90-; Soc Wrk/Music.

**KEESLER, DOUGLAS R,** Cincinnati Bible Coll & Sem, Cincinnati, OH; GD; MDIV; BRE Gods Bible Clg 90; Blbcl Stds; Prfsrshp.

**KEESLER, LINDA K,** Central Fl Comm Coll, Ocala, FL; SO; AA; Accntng; CPA.

**KEETER, CARLA S,** Middle Tn St Univ, Murfreesboro, TN; JR; BS; Equestrian Tm PR Chmn 88-; Horsemans Assn 88-; Gamma Beta Phi 88-; Tau Omicron 90-; Ad Clb Nwsltr 90-; Am Advrtsng Fed 90-; Advrtsng Intrnshp; Wrk Schlrshp 88-; Creativity Awd; Advrtsng; Dsgn/Art.

**KEETER II, CHARLES R,** Chattahoochee Vly St Comm Coll, Phenix City, AL; FR; AA; Dns Lst Fall 90 Winter 91 90-; Busn; Acctg.

**KEETON II, CHARLES R,** Cornell Univ Statutory College, Ithaca, NY; FR; BA; Smphny Orchstra 90-; Pew Cnsrtn Physcs Lctr Demo Proj; Deans Lst 90-; Deans Schlrs 90-; Bst Fr Essay Awrd 90; Physcs; Sci Rsrch/Wrtng.

**KEETON, LORI B,** Middle Tn St Univ, Murfreesboro, TN; SR; BS; Chi Omega VP 87-; Pre Law Scty 87-89; Gamma Beta Phi 87-; Chi Omega VP 87-; Public Rltns.

**KEEVER, CAMILLA R,** Univ Of Sc At Columbia, Columbia, SC; JR; BMED; Mrchg Bnd 88-; Wnd Ensmbl 88-; Symphonic Bnd 89-; Orchestra 90-; Gldn Key 90-; Pi Kappa Lambda; Phi Beta Kappa; Music Educ.

**KEEZEL, PAMELA K,** Nova Univ, Ft Lauderdale, FL; GD; MBA; Phi Sigma Sigma Clss Pres 76-77; BS Univ IL 80; Acctg.

**KEFFER, SANDRA C,** Patrick Henry Comm Coll, Martinsville, VA; FR; AAS; NSAV 90-; Phi Theta Kappa; Nrsng; RN.

**KEGLEY, JENNY G,** Vance Granville Comm Coll, Henderson, NC; FR; Therapeutic Recreation.

**KEGLEY, TINA M,** Miami Jacobs Jr Coll Of Bus, Dayton, OH; FR; By Scts Dn Mthr; CPA.

**KEHOE, JENNIFER M,** James Madison University, Harrisonburg, VA; JR; BS; Psychol Clb; Ctr Serv Lrng 89-; Sigma Sigma Sigma Pblc Rltns 89-; Listening Ear Comm Hotline 90-; Pres List 90; IM Sccr/Sftbl 90-; Pscyhology/Hlth; MS.

**KEIDAN, JASEN L,** Gallaudet Univ, Washington, DC; GD; MA; Pierce Sgn Lang Clb Pres 84-87; Rsrch Asst 87-; Hotln Vol 84-89; Psi Chi 89-90; Alpha Gamma Sigma 84-87; Natl Assn Deaf 86-90; Grtr LA Cncl Dfnss 85-89; Cncllrs Awd Outstndng Stdnt Ldr 87; Chncllrs Dstngshd Hon Awd 86-87; Pres Awd 87; Mntl Hlth Cnslng; Psychlgy.

**KEIFER, SHELLY R,** West Liberty St Coll, West Liberty, WV; FR; BA; Egnl Educ; Hgh Sch Eng Tchr.

**KEIFLING, MICHAEL S,** Univ Of Cincinnati-Clrmnt Coll, Batavia, OH; FR; BARCH; Dsgn; Arch.

**KEIM, JENNI R,** Univ Of Sc At Columbia, Columbia, SC; FR; BA; Engl; Jrnlsm.

**KEIM, MICHELLE R,** Columbus Coll Of Art & Design, Columbus, OH; SO; Photography Fine Arts.

**KEIPER, ALINA E,** Glassboro St Coll, Glassboro, NJ; Stdnt Govt Assn Pblc Rltns Dir 88-89; Rsdnc Stdnt Assn Pblc Rltns Dir 87-88; BA 90.

**KEIPER, JOE B,** Bloomfield Coll, Bloomfield, NJ; SR; BS; Smithsonian Ntnl Assn 85-; Alpha Chi 89-; Untd States Achvmnt Acadamy 91; Deans Lst 89-; AS Raritan Vlly Comm Clg 89; Biology; Envrnmntl Scientist.

**KEIR, DAVID M,** Kent St Univ Kent Cmps, Kent, OH; SR; Kent Rcrtn Clb 89-; NRPA 90-; Golden Key; Rho Phi 89; G R Williams Awd; Leisure Stdes; Rcratn Admn.

**KEIS, ABDALLAH A,** Univ Of Cin R Walters Coll, Blue Ash, OH; SO; BA; Stdnt Day Host Nahf Vlg Isrl 84; Nahf Yth Clb Sccr; Bus; Acctg.

**KEISER, CHARLES M,** City Univ Of Ny Baruch Coll, New York, NY; JR; BBA; AAS Bsn New York Univ 87; Cmptr Sci; Tchg.

**KEISLER, DANA M,** Univ Of Sc At Columbia, Columbia, SC; FR; Nursing.

**KEISLER, RICHARD BERLIN,** Johnson C Smith Univ, Charlotte, NC; FR; BA; Pol Sci; Law.

**KEITER, MARY MARSHA,** Nova Univ, Ft Lauderdale, FL; GD; MBA; CPA Amer Inst; BA Univ S Flor 78; Bus Mngmnt; Auditing/Actng.

**KEITH, BETHANY D,** Greenville Tech Coll, Greenville, SC; SO; AA; Phi Theta Kappa; Tutr Litrcy Assn 90-; Cert Grphc Arts 88; Cert Fshn Merch 89; Elem Ed; Tchr.

**KEITH, CAROL LYNN,** Univ Of Southern Ms, Hattiesburg, MS; SR; BS; Paralegal Socty; Crim Just Assn; Paralegal Stud; Law.

**KEITH, ELIZABETH A,** Central Fl Comm Coll, Ocala, FL; SO; Firefghtr/Paramed.

**KEITH, GREGORY B,** Union Univ, Jackson, TN; SR; BA; Hon Stdnt Assn 87-; Sigma Tau Delta 88-; Deans Lst; Engl; Tchng.

**KEITH, HEATHER L,** Memphis St Univ, Memphis, TN; SO; BA; Stdnt Hall Coun; Phi Eta Sigma; Gamma Beta Phi; Psychlgy; Chld Psychlgst.

**KEITH, JENNIFER D,** Saint Francis Coll, Loretto, PA; FR; BS; Arts Sci.

**KEITH, LAURIE K,** Middle Tn St Univ, Murfreesboro, TN; SO; BBA; FAA Hstrn 89-90; Beta Alpha Psi; Gamma Beta Phi 89-; Acctg; CPA.

**KEITH, RICHARD B,** Vance Granville Comm Coll, Henderson, NC; SO; AAS; Crmnl Jstce Clb Pres 90-; NAACP; Knghts Of Pythgra; Frat Ord Of Mason Asst Sec 89-; Citznshp Awd; Acad Achvmnt Awd 90-; Bapt Chrch Brd Of Trstee; Choir; Empl By Dept Of Jstce Fed Bureau Of Prsns; AA Louisburg Jr Clg 84; Crmnlgy; US Marshall.

**KEITH, RUTH A,** City Univ Of Ny City Coll, New York, NY; JR; BS; Earth/Atmosphere Sci Clb Pres 90-; Asst Instr Scotland 79-81; BHSAI Fulmer Inst 79; Geology; Acad/Rsrch.

**KEITH, TEENA M,** Beckley Coll, Beckley, WV; SO; AKA Debutante 89; Crmnl Jstc; Law.

**KEITH, TONYA L,** Memphis St Univ, Memphis, TN; FR; BA; Bsn; Educ.

**KEIZER, JENNIFER L,** Bunker Hill Comm Coll, Boston, MA; SO; BA; Res Hall V P 90-; Cert Cmndtn Dept Army; Lbrl Arts; Marine Biology/Ecolgy.

**KEKESSIE, SETH C,** Teikyo Post Univ, Waterbury, CT; SO; BS; Intrntl Stdnts Clb VP; Phi Theta Kappa; Ldrshp Cert 90; Jdcl Brd 90; Cntng Ed Spclst Off Admsns 89-; Scr 89-; Mktg; Bsn.

**KELBERLAU, ELIZABETH A,** Univ Of Sc At Sumter, Sumter, SC; JR; BA; Pres Hon Rl 90; Amer Bnkrs Assn; S C Natl Bnk 88-; AAS 84; Bus; Acctg.

**KELCH, MICHAEL L,** Columbus Coll Of Art & Design, Columbus, OH; SR; BFA; Stdnt Hd Shamom Cls Treas 89-; Pres Lst; CSCA Awd 89-90; Sccr; 2 Show Fine Art Milan Italy Wnnr 90-; 2 Schlrshps Columbus Coll Art/Dsgn; Schlrshp CSCA; Phtgrphy/Fine Arts; Prfssr.

**KELCHLIN, ERIC P,** Unity Coll, Unity, ME; SR; MBS; Intrnshp Miles Wildlife Sanctuary 89; Wildlife Biol.

**KELIN, ALISA M,** Univ Of Cincinnati, Cincinnati, OH; SO; BFA; Mscl Theatre; Actress/Singer/Dancer.

**KELLAM, CATHERINE F,** Salisbury St Univ, Salisbury, MD; SR; MA; Psych Clb VP 90-; Ldrshp Wrkshp 90-; Psi Chi VP 90-; Rsrch Asst 90-; BA; Counseling Ed; Psychology.

**KELLAM, MONICA F,** Johnson C Smith Univ, Charlotte, NC; SR; BA; Union Prog Brd Pres 89-; Friends Ensemble Sec 89-90; Univ Choir Pres 90-; Deans List 89-; Alpha Phi Alpha 88-; G/C Pblc Rltns 90; Pblc Rltns; Promotion.**

**KELLEHER, CHRISTINE M,** Kent St Univ Kent Cmps, Kent, OH; FR; BSN; IM Bskbtll; Sftbll; Nrsng.

**KELLEHER, JOHN F,** Univ Of The Dist Of Columbia, Washington, DC; SO; BSW; Top Soph 90-; UDC Hons; Vol Cnslr Washington Free Clinic 89-; Socl Wrk.

**KELLEHER, PAMELA A,** Alfred Univ, Alfred, NY; JR; BA; Advsry Brd 88-; Delta Mu Delta; Sccr Tm 88-; Bus Admin; Mrktg/Hlth Plng Mgt.

**KELLEHER, PATRICIA M,** Alfred Univ, Alfred, NY; JR; BA; Vrsty Sccr 88; Bus Admin; Mrktg/Hlth Plng Mgt.

**KELLEHER, PATRICIA M,** Atlantic Comm Coll, Mays Landing, NJ; FR; AAS; Lcnsd Csmtlgst 89-; L; Act Ed.

**KELLEHER JR, ROBERT X,** Bloomfield Coll, Bloomfield, NJ; SR; BS; Mbr Alpha Chi; High Hnr Rl; Consolidated Edison Co 82-; Business/Acctng; Acctng/Finance.

**KELLEM, PAULA J,** Owensboro Jr Coll Of Bus, Owensboro, KY; SR; Bcus Off Spec Dip; Cmptrs.

**KELLER, CAROL G,** Valdosta St Coll, Valdosta, GA; JR; BS; Jnr Wmns Clb 88-90; Sigma Alpha Chi 90; Mattco Rltrs Mgt Dpt 85-; Math/Scl.

**KELLER, CHRISTINA A,** Shippensburg Univ, Shippensburg, PA; FR; BSED; Intrmrl Brd Dir 90-; Fshn Archvs Brd Stdnt Bdy Repr 90-; Math; Sec Ed.

**KELLER, CHRISTINE ANN,** Univ Of Akron, Akron, OH; SR; BED; Panhellenic Coun Pub Rltns; Order Of Omega VP; BACCHUS Sec; Gldn Ky; Mortar Bd Alumni Rltns; Rho Lambda VP 90-; Kappa Delta Pi; Kappa Kappa Gamma Pres 90-; Engl/Comm; Tchng/Admin.

**KELLER, CHRISTOPHER M,** Univ Of Tn At Knoxville, Knoxville, TN; FR; Bapt Stdnt Unn; Alpha Lambda Delta; Bus Admin.

**KELLER, ERIC J,** Saint Josephs Coll, Windham, ME; SO; BA; Mscns Clb 90-; IM Sftbl/Bsktbl/Vlybl 89-; Bus Admin.

**KELLER, HOLLY M,** Savannah Coll Of Art & Design, Savannah, GA; SO; Yrbk Co Edtr 88-89; Mu Alpha Theta 84-85; Dns Lst 90-; Grphc Dsgn.

**KELLER, JANET R,** Nova Univ, Ft Lauderdale, FL; GD; MS; Phi Theta Kappa 82-83; Grad St Leo Clg Magna Cum Laude 90; Scl Serv Crdntr 90-; AS Pasco Hernando Cmnty Clg 83; BS/HSA St Leo Clg St Leo FL 90; Hlth Serv Admin; Med Field.

**KELLER, KEVEN B,** Capitol Coll, Laurel, MD; SR; BS; Alpha Chi 89-; Tau Alpha Pi 90-; Telecmnctns Engr Tech; Satellite Cmnctns.

**KELLER, MEGAN R,** Univ Of Tn At Knoxville, Knoxville, TN; FR; BA; Alpha Lambda Delta 90-; Phi Eta Sigma 90-; Alpha Gamma Delta 90-; Bsn; Acctg.

**KELLER, MELISSA L,** Eckerd Coll, St Petersburg, FL; JR; BA; Srfce Wtr Imprvmnt/Mngmnt 89; Wrtng Excllnce; Clg Hnrs Schlrshp 90; Fl Pwr Corp 85-90; AA St Ptrsbrg Jr Clg 89; Hstry; Prof Clg Level Tchr.

**KELLER, MELISSA P,** Bridgewater Coll, Bridgewater, VA; SR; BS; Chorale 90-; Chr; Lambda Soc Stdnt Rep 88-; Grad Cum Laude; Math; Tchg/Res.

**KELLER, RANDY R,** Marshall University, Huntington, WV; GD; MS; Adjnct Prof; Amer Soc Sfty Engr 90-; Intl Soc Rsprtry Prtctn 90-; Union Carbide Copr Sfty Awrd Cmbstbl Gas Anlyzrs 90; MS 90; BA 76; Occptnl Sfty/Hlth.**

**KELLER, SUSAN G,** Miami Jacobs Jr Coll Of Bus, Dayton, OH; GD; BA; Stdnt Govt Sec 68; Bnd Sec 69; Bethel Tmple Assmbly Of God; CPS 86-; Exec Sec; Nrsg.

**KELLER, SUSAN S,** Howard Univ, Washington, DC; GD; MDIV; Theolgcl Consrtm Chr 90-; Peace Flwshp Co-Fndr 90-; Choir; Alpha Kappa Alpha 71-72; Benjamin E Mays Fellow 90-; D B Barton Awd; Ford Fdtn Flwshp; BA 72; Religio(; Mnstry.

**KELLER, TAMARA S,** Endicott Coll, Beverly, MA; FR; AS; Nwsppr 90-; Hnrs Prog 90-; Dns Lst 90-; Pub Affrs Intrn; Radio TV; Brdcst Jrnlsm.

**KELLER, TIM B,** Univ Of Ky, Lexington, KY; SR; BS; Rugby Clb Capt Treas 87-; Cath Newman Ctr 87-; Phi Beta Kappa; Hon Prog 87-89; Southern Hills Vol Life Sqd 90; Cmnwlth Schlrshp 87; Clg Agri Schlrshp 87; Hon Prog Wrtng Schlrshp 88; Biology; Med.

**KELLER, WILLIAM B,** Ms St Univ, Miss State, MS; SR; BS; Sigma Alpha Epsilon; Schlrshp Recognition Day Pres Schlr; Spec Olympics 89-; Phys Ed; Tchg/Coachg.

**KELLERMAN, STEPHANIE E,** Mount Saint Mary Coll, Newburgh, NY; JR; BED; Sprtndnt S S/Tchr 88-90; Girl Scts Aid 89-; Rdlgcl Techncn 72-74; AAS Broome Comm Coll 72; Educ/Socl Sci; Tchng.

**KELLETER, ARMIN K,** Va Commonwealth Univ, Richmond, VA; SR; BS; Altrntv Flm Comm 89-90; Mass Cmnctns; Video-Flm Artist.

**KELLEY, BENJAMIN W,** Univ Of Sc At Sumter, Sumter, SC; FR; IM Bsktbl/Ftbl; Bptst Stdnt Union.

**KELLEY, BETH D,** Salisbury St Univ, Salisbury, MD; SR; BED; Nwspr Ed 86-87; Advsry Brd Mbr 86-87; Elem Ed; Tch Schl 1-8.

**KELLEY, CAROL H,** Thomas Coll, Thomasville, GA; SO; BED; Stdnt Govt VP 90-; Merits Lst; Deans Lst 90-; Thomas Cnty Hist Soc 90; Chmbr Cmrce Tour Guide 90-; Colorguard Instr 90-; SEAA; Soc Sci; Tchr/Educator.

**KELLEY, CHARLES J,** Newbury Coll, Brookline, MA; SO; AS; Class Rep; USN Awds; Good Cndct Mdl Sea Serv/Bttle Effcncy Mdl; Nvy Ptty Offcr; Multicltrl Brd; Cmptr Sci; Prsnnl.

**KELLEY, CHRISTINE MARIE,** Central St Univ, Wilberforce, OH; GD; Mgt Club 89-90; Bus Award Schlrshp; BS 90; Mgt; Human Rsrcs Mgt/Fin.

**KELLEY, CLARA E,** Comm Coll Algny Co Algny Cmps, Pittsburgh, PA; SO; CERT; Psy.

**KELLEY, CORINNE M,** Univ Of Akron, Akron, OH; JR; BSN; Nrsng; Nrs Admin.

**KELLEY, CRISTINA M,** Christian Brothers Univ, Memphis, TN; SR; BS; Wmns Assn Motivate Spirit 87-89; Spnsh Clb 89-90; Delta Sigma Pi Prof Frat Hstrn 90; Intl Cmmnctns Schlrshp; Bd Of Trustees Schlrshp 87-; Tennis Tm 88-; Telecomm; Intl Bus/Grad Schl.

**KELLEY II, DALLAS K,** Marshall University, Huntington, WV; JR; MBA; Mrktng; Bsnss.

**KELLEY, ERIC,** Memphis St Univ, Memphis, TN; FR; BBA; Bptst Stu Un; Res Hll Assn; Stu Act Cncl Spcl Evnts Chrmn; Bus.

**KELLEY, GERALD P,** Bunker Hill Comm Coll, Boston, MA; SO; BS; US Army Natl Grd MA E 4 88-; Hcky Hkng Skiing Gtr; Phi Theta Kappa; Sci; Glgy.

**KELLEY, JENNIFER ANN,** D Youville Coll, Buffalo, NY; JR; BS; Physical Therapy; Sports Therapist.

**KELLEY, JOY H,** Univ Of Southern Ms, Hattiesburg, MS; SR; BS; Am Mrktng Assn 90-; Golden Key 90-; Civil Serv Overseas Comp/Acctg; Radio TV Film; Cmnctns/Mrktng.

**KELLEY, KEVIN T,** Asbury Theological Sem, Wilmore, KY; GD; MDIV; Cum Laude Grad; Cnslr Bethesda Msn 89-90; BA Messian Coll 89; Theology; Mnstr.

**KELLEY, LESLI A,** Oh Univ, Athens, OH; JR; BA; STYLE Arts Tres; Cnvrstn Prtnrs 90-; Hall Rep E Grn Hl Cncl 88-89; Fine Arts/Art Histy Grphc Dsgn; Art Hstrn.

**KELLEY, LORI A,** Oh Univ, Athens, OH; JR; BFA; Music Educ Assoc Treas 88-; Music Stdnt Adv Comm 90-; Athens Comm Music Sch Stdnt Dir 90-; Gldn Ky; Sigma Alpha Iota 90-; Mac S Bethel Schlrshp; Music; Music Educ.

**KELLEY, MARSHA C,** Jackson St Univ, Jackson, MS; FR; BED; Hnrs Clg 90-; Alpha Lambda Delta; Acctg.

**KELLEY, MONICA S,** Fl A & M Univ, Tallahassee, FL; FR; MBA; Sch Bus Indstry Svc Co; Bus Admn; Corprt Law.

**KELLEY, MONIQUE S,** Morris Brown Coll, Atlanta, GA; SO; BS; Acctg Clb 90-; Hnr Rl 89-; Alpha Kappa Alpha; Academic Schlr 89-; AICPA Schlrshp 90-; CSF; Acctg; CPA.

**KELLEY, PAMELA K,** Daytona Beach Comm Coll, Daytona Beach, FL; FR; AS; First Fl Bnk Loan Supr 89-90; Bus Admn Mgmt.

**KELLEY, ROWENA Y,** De St Coll, Dover, DE; SO; BSC; Wmns Sen Comm Gspl Choir 89-90; Grmn Clb Pres 90-; Biol Clb/Chem Clb Treas 90-; DE St Clg Hon Soc Mbr 89-; Mnrty Bio-Med Res Spprt Prog Mbr 90-; Mnrty Agric/Natl Res/Rel Sci Mbr 90-; Explrs Sec 89-; Career Enrchmnt Prog 89; Agri-Bsns/Chem; Res Sci.**

**KELLEY, SHARI L,** George Mason Univ, Fairfax, VA; SR; BS; Bus; Real Estate.

**KELLEY, SHARON B,** Asbury Theological Sem, Wilmore, KY; JR; MDIV; Chapel Choir 90-; Love Is Agless Coord; Chrstns For Biblical Equality; Pulaski Co Med Aux Dist Sec 87-2; Dist U M Women 87-89; Comm Status/Role Of Women; Ky Conf Dir Lay Spkng 89; Ky Conf Sch Dscplshp; Taught H S Eng/French 60-62; Theo Studies; Minister.

**KELLEY, SUSAN I,** Ashland Comm Coll, Ashland, KY; SO; BSN; Ins Agent Sec 79-89; Nrsng: RN.

**KELLEY, TARA LEA,** Liberty Univ, Lynchburg, VA; FR; BED; Ntnl Hnr Soc 89-91; Mu Alpha Theta; French Hnr Soc; Hnr Grd; Prsdntl Acdmc Ftns Awd; Elem Edctn.

**KELLEY, TERESA L,** Pikeville Coll, Pikeville, KY; FR; BA; Stdnt Govt 90-; St Awrd; Elem Educ; Educ.

**KELLEY, WAYNE DANIEL,** Bryant Stratton Bus Inst Roch, Rochester, NY; GD; Ski Clb 85-88; Electronics/Math; Eng.

**KELLEY JR, WILLIAM D,** Univ Of Nh, Durham, NH; SO; Mrchg Bnd Drum Mjr 89; Cool-Aid Promo Mgr 90-; Engl; Law.**

**KELLNER, ABBE H,** S U N Y At Buffalo, Buffalo, NY; GD; DDS; Dntl Stdnt Assc Cls 90-; Alpha Omega Fndrsr; Grad Hon 88; IM Sprts 90-; BA 88; Psychlgy; Dntstry.

**KELLOGG, AMY L,** Alfred Univ, Alfred, NY; SO; BA; Ntl Assn Acctnts 90-; Cmps Guide 90-; Alpha Iota Delta 90-; Acctng.

**KELLOGG, CAROLYN D,** Hillsborough Comm Coll, Tampa, FL; SR; AS; Radlgy Clb 89-; Hons Grad; Rdlgy.

**KELLOGG, SHERRI E,** Allegheny Coll, Meadville, PA; SO; Alden Schlr 88-90; Math.

**KELLOGG, SUSAN M,** Univ Of Southern Ms, Hattiesburg, MS; SR; BA; Pub Rel Stdnt Soc Of Amer Treas 89-90; Amer Mktg Assoc 89-; Golden Key 90-; Gamma Beta Phi 90-; Beta Gamma Sigma 90-; Phi Kappa Phi; Walt Disney Wrld 89; MS Power Co Mktg Faculty Acdmc Awd; Marketing; Advertising.

**KELLUM, MICHAEL DAVID,** Samford Univ, Birmingham, AL; GD; BS E TN Univ 81; Criminal Justice; Law.

**KELLUM, MONICA M,** Chatfield Coll, Saint Martin, OH; SO; BA; Bus/Crmnl Jstc; Law.

**KELLY, ANNE M,** Elms Coll, Chicopee, MA; SO; BS; Nrsng; Med.

**KELLY, BRIAN S,** Georgetown Univ, Washington, DC; JR; BA; Budget Advisory Committee 89-90; Student Senate Pres 89-90; Bskbl 88-92; Cincinnati Techl Clg 90; Busn Mgt.

**KELLY, BYRON L,** Paine Coll, Augusta, GA; SO; BA; Drama Clb Engl Clb Media Clb 89; Soph Class Pres 90; Cncrt Choir Chmbr Choir 89; Alpha Phi Alpha Treas 90; Hon Roll 90f Music Schlrshp 90; Drama Awd 89-90; Engl; Tchng.

**KELLY, CARLOS A,** Fl St Univ, Tallahassee, FL; JR; BA; Stu Govt Assn PR Chrmn 90; Stu Almn Fndtn; Gldn Ky; Delta Tau Delta Pldg Pres 90-; PUSH Peer Fcltr; Dean Lst 89-; Delta Tau Delta Pldg Schlr; Acdmc Schlrshp 88-; Cmmnctns; Pblc Srvc.

**KELLY, CAROL A,** Lexington Comm Coll, Lexington, KY; FR; AAS; Nursing; Emplymnt In Med Field.

**KELLY, CHARLANA M,** Central Fl Comm Coll, Ocala, FL; FR; Psy Beta Kappa 90-; Crdt Pros 90-; Untd Way; Fnc/Bnkng Indust; Jrnlsm/Cmnctns; Pblc Rltns.

**KELLY, CHARLOTTE C,** Western Carolina Univ, Cullowhee, NC; SR; BA; Pi Gamma Mu; Phi Theta Kappa; Outstndg Acad Achvmnt 89-90; Smoky Mntn Cnslng Serv; Bureau Indian Affairs Intrnshp; Cert Substance Abuse; Rader Inst Coord Fmly Pgm 89; Cedar Sprng Hosp Intrvntn Cnslr/Aftercare Coord 86-89; Soc Wrk.

**KELLY, CHRISTINE M,** Le Moyne Coll, Syracuse, NY; SO; BA; Acctng Socty 90-; Econ Clb 90-; IM Vlybl 89-; Acctng; CPA.

**KELLY, CHRISTINE MARIE,** Radford Univ, Radford, VA; JR; BHA; Acctg Scty 90-; Stdn Tlf Cmdy Clb Chrprns 60-; Bus Pr Advsr; Acctg.

**KELLY, COLLEEN J,** Fayetteville St Univ, Fayetteville, NC; SO; BS; Green Peace Intl 89-; Crmnl Jstc; Law.

**KELLY, COLLEEN L,** Western Carolina Univ, Cullowhee, NC; FR; Clg Democrts; Stdnts For Peace/Jstc Soc; Alpha Lambda Delta; Envrnmntl Hlth.

**KELLY, DEBORAH F,** Old Dominion Univ, Norfolk, VA; FR; BS; Tnns; Chmstry Blgy; Med.

**KELLY, DENISE C,** Kent St Univ Kent Cmps, Kent, OH; JR; BA; Fltchr Hall Wng Rep 88-89; Pnhllnc Cncl Treas 90-; Rho Chi 90; Rho Lambda 90-; Alpha Phi Pnhllnc Dlgt 87-; Senate Serv Awrd 89-90; Outstndng Ldrshp Awrd 89-90; Socilgy; Rsrch.

**KELLY, DINA K,** Marshall University, Huntington, WV; JR; BA; Sigma Tau Delta; Cnslng Rehab.

**KELLY, DOROTHY M,** Al St Univ, Montgomery, AL; SR; BA; Cert Hnr; St Stephens Bapt Chrch; AA 69; Hstry; Tch.

**KELLY, EDWARD,** Saint Thomas Univ, Miami, FL; JR; BA; Sftbl Coach 88-90; J C Penneys Asst Stckrm Mgr 87-90; AA Palm Bch Cmnty Clg 87; Sports Adm.

**KELLY, ELIZABETH A,** S U N Y Coll Of Tech At Alfred, Alfred, NY; FR; AS; Bio.

**KELLY, ERIC J,** Wv Univ, Morgantown, WV; FR; Army ROTC 90-; Engrng.

**KELLY, EVA M,** Garrett Comm Coll, Mchenry, MD; FR; BA; Acctg; CPA.

**KELLY, HEATHER A,** James Madison University, Harrisonburg, VA; JR; BA; Swmng Intr Mentally Retarted 89; Dir Study Literacy 91; Deans List 90-; Pres List; Psychology; Intl Orgtl Psy.

**KELLY SR, HENDERSON,** Tn St Univ, Nashville, TN; SR; Crmnl Jstc Clb 89-; Exec Bd Ctr Blck Fmly Lf 86-; Co Fndr 100 Blck Men Nshvl 88-; Cleveland Rec Ctr Dir 84-; St Ethnic Mnrty Sctn TRPA VP 89; Crmnl Sci; Pblc Adm.

**KELLY, IAN C,** Univ Of Rochester, Rochester, NY; SO; BA; Pol Sci/French; Intl Rel.

**KELLY, IRIS J,** Comm Coll Algny Co Algny Cmps, Pittsburgh, PA; BA; Bethleham Bpt Male Chr 89-; Bethelahm Bpt Sr Chr 89-; Bethleham Bpt Child Yth Chr; Natl Hnr Scty 90-; Afro Amer Achiev Awd 90-; Busn; Hmn Res Mgt.

**KELLY, JAMES P,** Saint Francis Coll, Loretto, PA; JR; BA; Chem Clb VP 90-; Knights Of Columbus 89-; Kappa Mu Epsilon 90-; Am Chem Soc 90-; Alpha Phi Omega VP 89-; CRC Fr Chem Awd 89; Math/Chem.

**KELLY JR, JAMES R,** Univ Of Southern Ms, Hattiesburg, MS; GD; BA; Hist Clb 90-; Phi Alph Tau 90-; Hstry; Ph D.

**KELLY, JARROD L,** Oh Univ, Athens, OH; FR; BA; Chrch Clg Grp 90; Res Life Pgmng; Apple Crk Dev Ctr Asst Dir 90-; Res Life Acad Achvmnt Awd 90-; Elec Eng; Power Syst Eng.

**KELLY, JEAN M,** Univ Of Rochester, Rochester, NY; JR; BA; Hlth/Scty Cncl 89-90; Prtnrs In Reading 89-90; Hlth/Scty; Hlth Care.

**KELLY, KAREN D,** Ramapo Coll Of Nj, Mahwah, NJ; SR; BA; Anthrplgy Scty 90-; Lit Clb 89-90; SHARE; Math Clb; Sigma Tau Delta Hstrn; Hnrs Pgm 90-; Schlrshps 90; Deans Lst 86-; Lit Hnr Scty Schlrshp 90; Lit/Psych.

**KELLY, KAREN M,** Univ Of Sc At Columbia, Columbia, SC; FR; BA; Bus Admin; CPA.

**KELLY, KAREN M,** Brewer St Jr Coll, Fayette, AL; SO; BS; Concert Band 89-; Phi Theta Kappa 89-; AS; Edn; Elem Tchr.**

**KELLY, KATHERINE E,** Winthrop Coll, Rock Hill, SC; SO; Coalition/Homeless 90-; Glee Club 90-; Circle K 90-; Alpha Delta Pi Pldg Cls Sngldr; Hmlss Shltr 90; Pres List Clemson Univ; English; Jrnlsm/Adv.

**KELLY, KERRY ERIN,** Wesleyan Univ, Middletown, CT; FR; BA; Assmbly/Coord Assmblmn 90-; Sub Cmmt; Mddltwn Tutoring Tutor 90-; Triannual Blood Dr 90-; Campus Cthlc Cmmty Serv 90-; Cocol Letters Lit-Hstry/Phlsphy; Thlgn.

**KELLY, KRISTINE M,** Fl Atlantic Univ, Boca Raton, FL; JR; BS; Amer Mktg Assn V P Pgms 88-; Intl Busn Clb V P 89-90; Mktg; Resrchr.

**KELLY, LA WANDRA D,** Alcorn St Univ, Lorman, MS; SO; Political Sci Club 89-; Inner Resid Hall Council 89-; Dormitory Officer Treas 89-90; USDA Forest Serv Assitshp 90-; IM 89-; Soc Sci; Poltl Sci.

**KELLY, LAURA A,** Longwood Coll, Farmville, VA; JR; BFA; Art Works Inc Pres 90; Stdnt Ed Assn 90-; Hons Prog 88-; Deans List; Art/Art Hist.

**KELLY, LORI J,** Univ Of Pittsburgh, Pittsburgh, PA; FR; BSN; Rsdnt Stdnt Assn 84-85; Undergrad Genetics Tchng Asst 86; Amer Redcrs CPR Instrctr Vol 86-; Prsbytrn Univ Hosp ER Vol 89-90; Rsrch Spclst 88-; BS 88; Nrsng; Trauma Nrs.

**KELLY, MARIAN A,** James Sprunt Comm Coll, Kenansville, NC; BA; Prks Rec Brd Sec 90-; Wallace Rosehill Bstr Clb Chrm Cncsns Comm 81-; Chrch Pianoist; Sunday Schl Tchr; 4 H Clb Ldr Ldr Yr 87; Tchr Schlrshp; Schl Imprvmnt Comm 90; Elem Ed Tchr.

**KELLY, MARY BRIDGET,** Univ Of Sc At Columbia, Columbia, SC; JR; BS; Math/Comp Sci Clb 90-; SC Cncl Tchrs Math 90-; Outstndng Stdnt 90-; Math Educ; Tchr.

**KELLY, MICHAEL A,** Univ Of Cincinnati, Cincinnati, OH; SO; BM; Ohio Collg Music Educ Assoc Comm Chrmn 90-; Clg Conserv Music Trib V Pres 90-; Editor Nwslttr 90-; Dns Lst; Wh Hse Pres Schlr Adv 89-; Ohio Bd Regnts Schlrshp 89-; Cincinnati Schlrshp Found Schlrshp 89-; Music Educ.

**KELLY, MICHAEL J,** Hudson Valley Comm Coll, Troy, NY; FR; ASSOC; BS Westfield State Clg 89; Mortuary Sci; Funeral Dir.

**KELLY, NOREEN T,** Univ Of Scranton, Scranton, PA; SO; Arts/Sci; Physcl Thrpy.

**KELLY, PATRICIA L,** Univ Of Ky, Lexington, KY; FR; BA; Pharmacy; Phrmcst.

**KELLY, PAULA J,** Christopher Newport Coll, Newport News, VA; SR; AS Bay Path Jr Clg 85; Elem Educ; Tchng.

**KELLY, REBECCA L,** Univ Of Md At Eastern Shore, Princess Anne, MD; SO; BS; Future Educs Of MD Pres; Newspr In Educ Coord The Daily Times 90-; Specl Educ.

**KELLY, ROSA E,** Univ Of Sc At Columbia, Columbia, SC; JR; BM; Chmbr Orchstra; Symphny Orchstra; Columbia Comm Orchstra; Full Msc Schlrshp 88-; Cndn Prfrmnc 90; Afrcn Mthdst Epscpl Cnfrnc Prfrmnc 88-; Msc; Educ.

**KELLY, RYAN PATRICK,** Comm Coll Algny Co Algny Cmps, Pittsburgh, PA; FR; MBA; Bus; Mktng.

**KELLY, SARAH ELAINE,** Fl St Univ, Tallahassee, FL; SR; Delta Zeta Sor Chr 88; Chappie James Schlrshp Loan 87; BS Fla State U 91; Elem Ed; Ed.

**KELLY, SEAN T,** Comm Coll Algny Co Algny Cmps, Pittsburgh, PA; FR; Pre Hlth Prof; Vet Med.

**KELLY, SELAH D,** Methodist Coll, Fayetteville, NC; JR; Natl Assc Accntnts 90-; Acctng Clb 88-; Acctng; Bus Law Atty.**

**KELLY, SHANNON R,** Winthrop Coll, Rock Hill, SC; SO; BA; Fshn Assn; Glee Clb 90-; Alpha Kappa Psi 90-; Bus; Fshn Mrchndsng.

**KELLY, SHARON J,** Bryant Stratton Bus Inst Roch, Rochester, NY; FR; ASS; Word Procsng/Secrtrl.

**KELLY, SHERRI J,** Atlanta Christian Coll, East Point, GA; FR; BA; Deans List 90-; Baptist Ch; Music; Compstn; Ch Minstry.

**KELLY, SIOBHAN N,** Villanova Univ, Villanova, PA; JR; BA; Cmps Mnstry 89-; Blue Key Soc; Spec Olymp 89-90; Stdnt Govt Cbnt-PR; Natl Hon Soc 87-88; Delta Delta Delta 89-; Pres Acdmc Ftnss Awd 88; Deans Lst; Acdmc All-Amer; Natl Scl Sci Awd; Cmnctns; Mktg.

**KELLY, SUSAN E,** Univ Of South Al, Mobile, AL; JR; Wallr Bros Sls; AD Ms Gulf Coast JR Coll 78; Mrktng Econ; Org Bus.

**KELLY, TAMMY V,** Univ Of Ky, Lexington, KY; SR; Mrchng Bnd 87-89; Amer Clsscl League; Goldn Key; Alpha Gamma Rho Ltl Sistr Sec 90; Deans Lst 89-90; Latin Prz 90-; Latin/Engl; Tchr.

**KELLY, TERESA C,** Fl St Univ, Tallahassee, FL; JR; BFA; Seminole Party 88-90; Amnsty Intl 88-90; Hnrs Schlrs Pblcty 88-; Phi Eta Sigma 88-; Peer Mentors; FLA Dept Educ Schlrshp 88-; London Stdy Prog; Film Prod.**

**KELLY, TERRI P,** Faulkner St Jr Coll, Bay Minette, AL; SO; BA; Pres List 90-; Deans List 90-; Elem Ed; Tchng.

**KELLY, TRACEY ANN,** Univ Of Nc At Charlotte, Charlotte, NC; JR; Wmns Iss Cncrns Cmps Assoc 89-90; Gldn Key 90-; Stdy Abrd Kngstn Plytchnc 90; Deans Lst 90; Chncllrs Lst 90-; Bsktbll; Engl.

**KELNER, SARAH E,** Bay Path Coll, Longmeadow, MA; SO; BS; Interfth Cncl VP 90-; Stdnt Govt 90-; Glee Clb 89-90; Law.

**KELSAY, ALFRED K,** Univ Of North Fl, Jacksonville, FL; JR; BA; Gld Key; PTA 81-; Flt Rsrv Assoc 88-; Nvl Srvc 68-88; AA FL Cmmnty Coll 90; EAWS US Nvy 86; Ed; Tchng.

**KELSCH, CHRISTINE A,** Pasco Hernando Comm Coll, Dade City, FL; SO; AA AS; SNO 89-; Phi Theta Kappa 90-; Amer Assn Of Crtcl Cre Nrss 90-; Nrsng.

**KELSER, DAVID A,** Salisbury St Univ, Salisbury, MD; JR; BA; Outdoor Clb 88-; Phlsphcl Soc 89-; Phi Kappa Phi 90-; Lambda Iota Tau 90-; Engl; Tch.

**KELSEY, COLLEEN D,** Oh Univ, Athens, OH; JR; BA; Natl Gld Orgnst 89-; Music Tchrs Natl Assoc 90-; Wsly Stdnt Cntr 88-; Uppr Clssmn Schlrshp 89-; Music Schlrshp 88-; Piano Perf Ped; Orgn Perf.**

**KELSEY, MAUREEN E,** Georgian Court Coll, Lakewood, NJ; GD; BA; Deans Schlr 86-; Applewood Mnr Nrsng Hm Freehold NJ Voc 87-88; Sunday Scl Tchr St Robert Bellarmine Chrch Freehold NJ; AA Bsns Brookdale Cmmnty Clg 86; Admnsrtn Lincroft NJ 86; Hmnts Bsns Admnstrtn.

**KELSICK, KEVIN H,** Saint Thomas Univ, Miami, FL; SR; BA; Commercial Art Awd 90; AA Intl Fine Arts Clg; Cmnctn Dsgn; Cmrcl Art.

**KELSO, ANGELA M,** Va Western Comm Coll, Roanoke, VA; SO; Stdnt Svc Stdnt Hlpr 90-; Tlnt Rstr 90-; Vol Berkshire Hlth Care Ctr 90-; Leann Whitlock Awrd 1st Rcpnt 90-; Cert Hon 89; MS; Gen Stds; Paralegal.

**KELSO, MICHAEL A,** Univ Of Tn At Knoxville, Knoxville, TN; SR; BS; Frshmn Advsry Brd 87; Beta Gamma Sigma 90-; Delta Tau Delta Scl Chrmn 87; Crew 90; Finance; Business.

**KELSO, PATRICIA A,** Univ Of New England, Biddeford, ME; SR; UNESOTA 89-; Grdtd Cum Laude; Intrnshp Miane Stay Nrsg Home 89-; Cerebral Palsy Ctr 89-; Med Ctr Hosp VT 89-; Sthrn ME Med Ctr 89-; BA; Occup Therapy; Occup Thrpst.

**KELTERBORN, NATALIE E,** Spartanburg Methodist Coll, Spartanburg, SC; FR; PPHYS; Ladys Sftbl Tm; Phy Educ; P E Tchr.

**KELTON, JERRY M,** Middle Tn St Univ, Murfreesboro, TN; SR; BS; Beta Beta Beta 89-90; Sigma Chi Treas 90-; Blgy/Chmstry; Med.**

**KELTON, KATHRYN E,** Univ Of Sc At Coastal Carolina, Conway, SC; JR; BA; AA Dutchess Comm Coll 90; Elem Education; Teaching Special Ed.

**KELTZ, BARBARA M,** The Johns Hopkins Univ, Baltimore, MD; SR; BSN; Nrsng Hon Soc; MS Dfns Intlgnc Clg 87; BA Penn State 74; Nrsng.

**KEMERER, TIMOTHY W,** Univ Of Miami, Coral Gables, FL; SO; BS; Scuba Club V P 89-; Hnr Stdnts Assn 89-90; Campus Wellness Comm 90-; Res Asst 90-; Marine Sci Flwshp; Bio/Marine Sci; Tchr/Prof.

**KEMME, SUSAN L,** Northern Ky Univ, Highland Hts, KY; SO; BA; Art/Graphic Dsgn.

**KEMMERLIN, STEFANIE G,** Coll Of Charleston, Charleston, SC; SR; Educ Clb; Flwshp Chrstn Athlts; BS; Elem Ed; Tchng.

**KEMMERLING, GLENDA M,** Duquesne Univ, Pittsburgh, PA; JR; BS; Vol Socty 90-; Cesta Assoc Tchng Alliance; Mrtr Bd 90-; Grtr Pgh Litrcy Cncl 90-; Duquesnes Dns Lst 90-; Bradley Res Grp Hm 88-; AS Chld Dev Allegheny Comm Coll 88-90; Elem/Spec Educ; Tchr.

**KEMP, CRYSTAL L,** S U N Y Coll Of Tech At Alfred, Alfred, NY; FR; Top Hat Clb VP 90-; Sigma Tau Epsion 90-; Natl Hnr Soc 76-80; Comstrock Food Cnny; Food Serv.

**KEMP, KIMBERLY J,** Oh Univ, Athens, OH; JR; BM; MENC V P/Pres 90-; Alpha Lambda Delta; Golden Key; Music Educ; Tchng.

**KEMP, MARILYN A,** Miami Jacobs Jr Coll Of Bus, Dayton, OH; FR.

**KEMP, RHONDA L,** Saint Francis Coll, Loretto, PA; SR; BA; Nwspr Copy Edtr 89-91; Radio PR Dir 89; Sigma Tau Delta 90-; Natl Cath Hnr Soc; Hnr Soc; Pen & Scribe Awd 90; Pub Rel Ofc Intern 90; Sftbl 87-; English/Communications.

**KEMPER, BETTY L,** Concord Coll, Athens, WV; GD; BS; Bs; Ed; Tchr.

**KEMPSON, JEANNIE C,** City Univ Of Ny City Coll, New York, NY; JR; BA; Sistars Inc Chrwmn 88-; NAACP; Estrn Strs Affl; Alpha Sigma Lambda; Vol Chprn/Orgnzr Actvty/Dance/Fld Trps Chldrn/Tngrs Harlem River Drive Hse Comm Cntr; Vol Fndrst Mem Baptist Church Dist Mary Kay; Fshn Cnsltnt; Entrtnmnt Orgnzr; Lib Arts; Chld Cr Wrkr.

**KENCHEN, RITA S,** Al St Univ, Montgomery, AL; FR; CIS.

**KENDALL, ARTEKA D,** Tn St Univ, Nashville, TN; SO; NAACP 90-; Michigan Club 89-; Deans List; Pharmacy; Pharmacist.

**KENDALL, CATHY L,** Univ Of Tn At Martin, Martin, TN; FR; BS; STEA 90-; Scndry Educ; Engl Tchr.

**KENDALL, ELLISA L,** Ms St Univ, Miss State, MS; SO; DVM; Vet Med.

**KENDALL, HOLLY S,** Wilmington Coll, Wilmington, OH; FR; Orgn Cmmtr Cncrns 90-; Math; Tchng.

**KENDALL, JENNIFER E,** Univ Of Ky, Lexington, KY; JR; Athltc Assn Drg Polcy Comm Stdnt Rep 90; Stdnt/Athlt NCAA Advsry Comm Rep 90-; Goldn Key 90-; Phi Eta Sigma 88-; Jr US Natl Trck Team 89; Vrsty Trck/X-Cntry 88-; Phrmcy.

**KENDALL, KIMBERLY W,** Univ Of Ky, Lexington, KY; SR; BSN; Homemakers V P 90-; ADS Maysville Comm Clg 83; ADN 86; Nrsng.

**KENDALL, KRISTINA L,** Univ Of South Al, Mobile, AL; FR; BA; Fab 50; Alpha Omicron Pi 90-; Pres Schlrshp; Bus.

**KENDRA, RACHEL A,** Neumann Coll, Aston, PA; SO; BS; Rptr Keystone Stdnt Nwspr 89-90; Stdnt Nurses Assn; Hon Pgm Kutztown Univ 89-90; RN/WRITER.

**KENDRICK, ALICIA M,** Jackson St Univ, Jackson, MS; FR; BS; Alpha Lambda Delta; Top Frshmn In Pi Mu Epsilon Math Comp; Math; Tchr.

**KENDRICK, BRIAN B,** Oh Univ, Athens, OH; FR; BSC; Cvl Engr; Golf Course Arch.

**KENDRICK, LA TRICIA MONA,** Central St Univ, Wilberforce, OH; SO; BA; Bus Mgmnt.

**KENERLEY, PHILIP M,** Glassboro St Coll, Glassboro, NJ; JR; DOCTO; Pres Lst; Deans Lst 87-; Human Serv Elderley 80-; Cmpn Elderley Need 80-; Hon Lstng; Pres Lst; Deans Lst 80-; Weight Lifting; AS Liberal Arts 90; Math; High Sch/Coll Math Profr.

**KENIA, KAREN L,** Marywood Coll, Scranton, PA; FR; BS; Bio Clb 90-; Bio; Vet.

**KENJARSKI II, THOMAS P,** Univ Of Rochester, Rochester, NY; SO; BA; RA 90-; Dorm Cncl 89-; Joseph C Wilson Soc 89-; Delta Upsilon VP-RUSH; Cmps YMCA 89-90; Frnds Strng Memrl Hosp 89-90; Clb Vlybl 89-; Blgy; Med.

**KENNARD, ELIZABETH M,** Barry Univ, Miami, FL; JR; BA; Res Hall Assn Sec 90-; Yrbkp Copyedtr 90-; Stdnt Actvty Advsry Bd 90-; Food Cmtee Bd; Res Life Advsry Bd 90-; Lambda Sigma 88-90; Res Advsr; Sociology.

**KENNEDY, ANISSA M,** Univ Of Nc At Asheville, Asheville, NC; JR; BA; Pltcl Sceince Assc 89-90; SGA Asst Prsctr 89-; Staff Frshmn Orntn 90-; Phi Alpha Delta Pres 89-; Kappa Phi 90-; Deans List; Intrnshp Dist Attrnys Off 90-; Pltcl Sceince; Law.

**KENNEDY, BRUCE ROBERT,** Univ Of New Haven, West Haven, CT; SR; BS; Crmnl Jstc Clb 88-; Ftbl 87-88; Crmnl Jstc; Fed Law Enfrcmnt.

**KENNEDY, CATHERINE,** Univ Of Nc At Charlotte, Charlotte, NC; SR; BA; Stdnt Cncl 86-87; Amer Inst Arch 88-90; Dns Lst 88-90; Arch; Lndscp Arch.

**KENNEDY, CATHEY L,** Middle Tn St Univ, Murfreesboro, TN; JR; BS; Stdnt TN Ed Assn 88-; Gamma Beta Phi 88-; AS Colmbia St Comm Coll 90; Ed; Tchr.

**KENNEDY, CERIECE M,** Al St Univ, Montgomery, AL; JR; BA; US Air Force Res Aeromed Tech 88-; Cmnctns; Radio TV/FILM.

**KENNEDY, DORIE L,** Comm Coll Algny Co Algny Cmps, Pittsburgh, PA; FR; Sci; Med Asst.

**KENNEDY, ELIZABETH D,** William Paterson Coll, Wayne, NJ; SO; BA; Hist; Museum Wrk.

**KENNEDY, FLORENCE M,** Bennett Coll, Greensboro, NC; SO; BA; Intl Stdnts Clb Bsns Clb Prlmntrn; Pltcl Sci Clb Tres; NCCIIE Dpty Sec Gnrl; Untd Sts Acdmy Schlr Awd; Schlrs Prgrm; Deans Lst; Hnrs Lst; Vllybl; Bsns Amnstrtn; Crp Lawyer.

**KENNEDY, GLORIA M,** Northwest Al Comm Coll, Phil Campbell, AL; FR; AS; Phi Theta Kappa 90-; Sci; Law/Parol Offcr.

**KENNEDY, HEATHER L,** Hudson Valley Comm Coll, Troy, NY; SO; AS; Accntng.

**KENNEDY, HOPE E,** Peace Coll, Raleigh, NC; FR; BS; Vol Chldcr Ltrcy Prog 90-; BACCHUS 90-; Phi Theta Kappa 90-; Acad Excllnc Awd; Amer Bus Wom Assoc Schlrshp 90-; Home Ec; Int Dsgn/Foods Nutrition.

**KENNEDY, JACKIE M,** Thomas Nelson Comm Coll, Hampton, VA; FR.

**KENNEDY, JENNIFER M,** Kent St Univ Kent Cmps, Kent, OH; SO; BA; Clsscl Leag Sec 89-; Hon Blltn 89-90; Alpha Lambda Delta 90-; Eta Sigma Phi; Deans Lst 89-90; Pres Lst 90; OH Clsscl Cnfrnc Schlrshp; Latin/Hist/Ed; Tch.

**KENNEDY, JOEL S,** Ms St Univ, Miss State, MS; JR; BA; Im Ofcl Stdnt Athltc Trnr; Physcl Ed; Sports Medcn.

**KENNEDY, JUANITA G,** East Central Comm Coll, Decatur, MS; SO; BED; Non-Trdtnl Stdnts Clb Treas 90; Bus; Tchr.

**KENNEDY, KAREN B,** Univ Of Southern Ms, Hattiesburg, MS; JR; BA; Phi Theta Kappa 89-90; Gamma Beta Phi; Psi Chi 90-; Psychlgy.

**KENNEDY, KATHLEEN M,** Bucks County Comm Coll, Newtown, PA; FR; BA; Nrsg.

**KENNEDY, KATHY,** Georgian Court Coll, Lakewood, NJ; SR; BA 90; Humanities; Mba.

**KENNEDY, KEVIN M,** James Madison University, Harrisonburg, VA; JR; BS; Psych Clb 90-; Skiing Clb 89; Alpha Epsilon Delta 90-; IM Tnns 88-; Psych; Med.

**KENNEDY, KEVIN S,** Univ Of Louisville, Louisville, KY; GD; MENG; ASME 87-; SAE 90-; Spd Std Cncl 90-; Wal Mart Fdn Schlr 86-88; KY Dst Schlr 86-88; GE Plstcs Dsgn Comp 90; BES 90; Mech Engr.

**KENNEDY, KEVIN T,** Cornell Univ, Ithaca, NY; FR; BA; Ski Tm 90-; Cmptr Sci; Programmer.

**KENNEDY, KYLE R,** Univ Of Rochester, Rochester, NY; JR, BA; Pol Sci; Law.

**KENNEDY, LAURA S,** Univ Of Cin R Walters Coll, Blue Ash, OH; SO; BA; Newspaper 90-; English; Law.

**KENNEDY, LESLIE E,** Tufts Univ, Medford, MA; FR; BA; Rcyclng Crdntr 90-; ESL 90-; Sailing Tm 90-.

**KENNEDY, MARGARET M,** D Youville Coll, Buffalo, NY; FR; MBA; Cmps Mnstry 90-; Clg Sfty Brd Comm; Physcl Thrpy.

**KENNEDY, MARIETTA,** Stillman Coll, Tuscaloosa, AL; SR; BS; Rotaract Clb Pres 90-; Cordell Wynn Hon Pgm; Stdnts Free Enterprise; Gamma Iota Sigma; Alpha Kappa Mu; Beta Kappa Chi; Phi Beta Lambda; Delta Sigma Theta; Smr Rsrch Apprentice Pgm Univ FL; Vlybl Capt 88-; Cmptr Sci; Sys Analyst.

**KENNEDY, MICHAEL G,** Kent St Univ Kent Cmps, Kent, OH; SR; BBA; Finance Assoc VP; IM 88-; Ftbl Stats 88; Deans Lst 89-90; Copr Finance.

**KENNEDY, MICHAEL K,** Old Dominion Univ, Norfolk, VA; GD; MSEE; Ski Clb 90-; Tau Beta Pi 89-; IEEE 88-; Rsrch Asstshp 90-; BSEE 90; Elect Eng.

**KENNEDY, MICHELLE L,** Union Univ, Jackson, TN; SR; Tn Edn Assn 90-; Stdnt Govt Assn 87-; Bapt Stdnt Un 87-; Chi Omega 87-89; BA; Elem Edn; Teach.

**KENNEDY, MICHELLE PORTER,** Univ Of Sc At Columbia, Columbia, SC; SR; BA; SCCTM; Protect Our Envrnmnt Pres 90-; Dns Lst 90-; Outstndg Stdnt Tchr; Pblshd Poetry/Amer Poetry Anthlgy 90; Sci Fair 1st Place Edctnl 90; Elem Educ; Tchr.

**KENNEDY, MICHELLE R,** S U N Y Coll Of Tech At Frmgdl, Farmingdale, NY; SO; BA; Nwspr Edtr 90-; Actvts Bd 90-; Radio DJ; Lbrl Arts Hon Soc; Acdmc Excllnc Awd; Engl; Educ/Jrnlsm.

**KENNEDY, MIRANDA L,** James Sprunt Comm Coll, Kenansville, NC; JR; AD; N Carolina Assn Nrsng Stdnts 90-; Natl Stdnt Nrs Assn 90-; Potters Hill Commony Vol Frmn Ladies Aux 89-; J Cameron R Smith Acad Schlrshp 89-90; Jim Mary E Albertson Acad Schlrshp 90-; Hlth/Sci; RN.

**KENNEDY, NATALIE M,** Univ Of Fl, Gainesville, FL; FR; Delta Gamma 90-91; Psych/Philo; Law.

**KENNEDY, PAMELA J,** Univ Of Nc At Charlotte, Charlotte, NC; JR; BA; Civilian Clb 88-; Psychology Clb; Lunch Buddy Pgrm; Psychology Hnr Soc; Civilian Clb 88-; Red Crs; Dns Lst; Psychology; Cnslr.

**KENNEDY, PATRICIA A,** Temple Univ, Philadelphia, PA; JR; BA; Prsh Ltrgy Cmmtt 84; Cert; Physcl Ed.

**KENNEDY, RACHELLE E,** Miami Univ, Oxford, OH; SO; BS; Radio 90-; Nws Rprtr 90-; WICI 90-; Alpha Epsilon Rho 90-; Delta Zeta 90-; Stdnt Fndtn Extrnshp 90; Mss Cmmnctns; Brdcst Jrnlsm.

**KENNEDY, ROBERT K,** Univ Of Sc At Columbia, Columbia, SC; SO; Arete 90-; Pres Hnr Rl; Mech 70-90; Voc Rehab.

**KENNEDY, ROBERT S,** George Mason Univ, Fairfax, VA; JR; BA; Sigma Phi Epsilon 88-; Fin; Invstmnts.

**KENNEDY, ROSEMARY O,** Beaver Coll, Glenside, PA; GD; Summa Cum Laude; Deans Lst Prof Hon Stdnt Tch Edn Dept Hon 85; Natl Cath Edn Assn 85-; Elem Edn Tchr; BS Elem Ed Gwynedd Mercy Coll 85; MED.

**KENNEDY, SHELBY J,** Providence Coll, Providence, RI; FR; English Club.

**KENNEDY, STEVEN D,** Hudson Valley Comm Coll, Troy, NY; FR; AS; USAF 83-87; Refrig/Htng/AC Mech.

**KENNEDY, SUSAN E,** Samford Univ, Birmingham, AL; GD; JD; Cumberland Law Review; Amer United Separation Church State Pres; Envi Law Scty; Deans List; Econ Hnry Scty; Delta Delta Delta Music Chr; Montage Club; Civitans; Legal Aid Scty; Assist Prof Cebala Em Univ; Law.

**KENNEDY, TARA C,** Western New England Coll, Springfield, MA; JR; BA; Pre Law Soc 90-; Phi Theta Kappa 89-90; Cmmnty Rltns Intern; AA Holyoke Comm Col 90; Engl/Cmmnctns; Pblc Rltns/Law.

**KENNEDY, TRAVIS D,** Univ Of Southern Ms, Hattiesburg, MS; SR; BS; Music Industry Assoc 89-90; Golden Key 90-; AA Pearl River Jr Clg 89; Electronics.

**KENNEMER, ANGELA,** Middle Tn St Univ, Murfreesboro, TN; SR; BS; Ed Clb 87-89; STEA 90-; AS Motlow State Comm Coll 89; Elem Ed; Tchr.

**KENNEY, CAROLE M,** Valdosta St Coll, Valdosta, GA; FR; BED; Cmps Otrch 90-; Bapt Stdnt Union 90-; Sgm Alph Chi 90-; Math; Scndry Math Ed.

**KENNEY, DAVID M,** Univ Of Va, Charlottesville, VA; SR; MS; Wsly Fndtn Msc Dir 87-; Univ Sngrs Lbrrn 90; Glee Clb 88; Dns Lst 90; US Achvmnt Acad 90; BS Educ; Spch Lngge Pthlgy; Spch Lngge Pthlgy Srvcs.

**KENNEY, JENIFER D,** Wv Univ, Morgantown, WV; FR; BSN; Nrsng; Nrsng Wth MA Ansthslgy.

**KENNEY, JOHN M,** Bloomfield Coll, Bloomfield, NJ; JR; BS; Serv Rep N J Bell Tele Co 88-; Cmptr Inf Syst/Acctg.

**KENNEY, KEVIN D,** Appalachian Bible Coll, Bradley, WV; GD; Dplm Grand Rapids Schl Bl/Msc 88; Bible; Msnry.

**KENNEY, LORI L,** Univ Of South Al, Mobile, AL; SR; BS; Alpha Lambda Delta Edtr 88; Beta Alpha Psi; Acctg; CMA Mgmnt.

**KENNEY, MICHELLE L,** Syracuse Univ, Syracuse, NY; SR; BARCH; ASO 87-, Peer Advsr 89 90; Peer Advsng Pgm Coord 90-; Deans Lst 89-; Meals On Wheels; Habitat For Humanity; Architecture.**

**KENNEY, STEVEN J,** Portland School Of Art, Portland, ME; JR; BFA; Hon Lst 89-; SMAC Stdnt Spkr 89; Endwmnt Woelfle/Scarvglni Mrt Schrlshp 90-; Stdnt Show Exhbtr 89-90; Fine Arts Sclptr Mjr; Wrk Art/Tch.**

**KENNEY, SUSAN M,** Univ Of Sc At Columbia, Columbia, SC; JR; BA; Rsdnc Hll Govt Sec 90-; Rsdnc Hll Govt Pres; Natl Yng Ldrs Cnfrnc 90; Spnsh Intl Stds; Intl Rltns.

**KENNEY, WALTER LAWRENCE,** Middle Ga Coll, Cochran, GA; FR; Bus; Bus/Mktg/Law.

**KENNISON, AARON E,** Oh Univ, Athens, OH; FR; BS; Air Force 86-90; Mech Eng; Rsrch Altrntv Energy.

**KENNY, ALISON M,** Seton Hall Univ, South Orange, NJ; FR; BSN; SHUFL 90-; Acad Schlrshp 90-; Comm Med Ctr Schlrshp 90-; Unit Sec Comm Med Ctr; Nrsng; Peds.

**KENNY, ANGELA J,** Radford Univ, Radford, VA; SR; BS; Amercn Soc Of Interior Dsgn 88-; Publc Rltns 90-; Lappa Omega Nu 89-; Pres 90-; AS VA Western Cmnty Clg 88; Interior Dsgn.

**KENNY, CATHLEEN L,** Univ Of Montevallo, Montevallo, AL; SR; BED; Phys Educ Clb Sec 88-; Delta Chi Ltl Str 88-; Alpha Delta Pi 87-; Alpha Delta Pi Pldg Eductr 87-; United Way 88-; M Mc Call Schlrshp 88 89; Hmcmng Actvts Vybl 87-; Phys Educ; Tch/Coach.

**KENNY, ELIZABETH A,** Wv Univ At Parkersburg, Parkersburg, WV; FR; FFA; 4-H Treas 85-90; Ofc Admin; Secretary.

**KENNY, GRETCHEN K,** Saint Francis Coll, Loretto, PA; SR; BSN; SNO 87; Stdnt Athltc Trnr 89; Nrs Extrn Chldrns Hsptl Phldph; IM; Nrsng; Pdtrc Ongclg Nrsng.

**KENNY, KATHLEEN B,** City Univ Of Ny Queensbrough, New York, NY; FR; BS; Dns Lst QCC 90-; Letters Cngrtltns Hnr Roll Frank Pavadan James H Scheuer 88; Pre-Physical Thrpy; Physical Ocptnl Thrpy.

**KENNY, LINDA J,** Saint Johns Univ, Jamaica, NY; SR; BS; Irsh Soc 87-; CAUSE Tr 88-89; Stdnt Un 88-89; Kappa Delta Pi 89-; Gldn Ky 88-; Kappa Delta Pi 89-; St Vncnt De Pl Soc Hstrn 89-; Cmps Mnstry 87-; Rev Breen Awd 90-; Dns Lst 88-; Educ; Tchng.**

**KENNY, PETER S,** Anne Arundel Comm Coll, Arnold, MD; FR; Clb Dead E Cst 88-; NORML 86-.

**KENNY, RANIER L,** Va St Univ, Petersburg, VA; JR; BS; Std Govt Asc VP 90-; Bltmr Pre-Almni Asc 87-89; Essnc Troy Dncrs Bnd Treas 88-; Alpha Mu Gamma Treas 89-; Alpha Kappa Phlctr 90-; Bsn Admn Mgmt; Grad Schl.

**KENNY, VALERIE E,** Fl Inst Of Tech, Melbourne, FL; FR; BS; SEA; FEA; Sci Educ; Tch.

**KENOSKY, LISA M,** Kent St Univ Kent Cmps, Kent, OH; SO; BA; Acctg; CPA.

**KENT, KATHERINE R,** Daytona Beach Comm Coll, Daytona Beach, FL; FR; AS; Voc Hon Schlrshp; Gifted Stdnt Schlrshp; Phtgrphy.

**KENT, M SUSAN,** Abraham Baldwin Agri Coll, Tifton, GA; FR; BA; Stdnt Govt Assoc Secy; Psychlgy.

**KENT, MARK G,** Birmingham Southern Coll, Birmingham, AL; SR; MD; SGA Snr Rep 90-; Stdnt Alumni Assn VP 87-; Rsdnt Advsr 90-; Phi Beta Kappa; Omicron Delta Kappa VP 90-; Kappa Mu Epsilon Prsdnt 89-; Phi Alpha Theta; Alpha Epsilon Delta 89-; Mortar Brd 90-; Kappa Alpha Schlrshp Chrmn 87-; Medicine.

**KENT, MARTINA B,** Lenoir Rhyne Coll, Hickory, NC; SR; BSN; Mu Sigma Epsilon; Sigma Theta Tau; Nursing; RN.

**KENT, MELINDA D,** Saint Thomas Univ, Miami, FL; SO; BA; Pltcl Sci; Corp Law.

**KENT, MELINDA S,** Birmingham Southern Coll, Birmingham, AL; SR; BS; Psi Chi; Alpha Phi Omega Rcrdg Sec 89-90; Psych; Scl Wrk.

**KENT, RUSSELL A,** Univ Of Southern Ms, Hattiesburg, MS; JR; BA; Stdnt Eagle Clb Pres; Exercise Physlgy Clb; Gamma Beta Phi; Phi Theta Kappa 90; Vol Wrk Athletic Dept; Intrnshp Sprts Info Dept; Im; Coaching/Sprts Admin; Sprts Mrktng/Mngmnt Frm.

**KENT, STACY M,** Endicott Coll, Beverly, MA; SO; BA; Varsty Club Spksprsn 89-; Clg Nwspaper Sports Wrtr 90-; Phi Theta Kappa Secy 89-; Intrnshp Evergreen Adv/Mktg Secy 90; Intrnshp Radio Statn Asst Promo Dir Sls Dept; Fld Hockey/Bsktbl/Sftbl Cptn 89-; AA; Adv; Mktg/Adv Exec.

**KENT, WALTER SCOTT,** Milligan Coll, Milligan Clg, TN; SR; BS; SGA; Pres Jr Cls; Treas Soph Cls; Rsdnt Asst 89-; Acctg; Big 6 Acctng Firm.

**KENTOURIS, KATHERINE,** City Univ Of Ny Baruch Coll, New York, NY; SR; BBA; Prtnrshp Prog Tm Ldr 88-89; Betas Gamma Sigma; Natl Hnr Roll 87; Golden Key; Mrktng; Intl Trade Operations.

**KENYON, FLOY C,** Univ Of Sc At Columbia, Columbia, SC; SO; BS; Kappa Delta 89-; Intl Stds; Law.

**KENZAKOSKI, CAROLYN M,** Marywood Coll, Scranton, PA; SR; BFA; St Lukes Art Soc 89; Delta Epsilon Sigma 90-; Kappa Pi Pres 90-; Peer Tutor 89-90; Tchrs Choice Art Award 89-90; Deans List 89-90; Adv Grphcs; Graphc Dsgn.

**KEOUGH, COLLEEN K,** Schenectady County Comm Coll, Schenectady, NY; FR; Trvl Tourism.

**KEOUGH, MARY E,** S U N Y Coll At Fredonia, Fredonia, NY; JR; BFA; AIGA; Fredonia Schlrs Awd/Deans Lst; Art; Grphc Dsgn.

**KEOWN JR, LARRY E,** Chattanooga St Tech Comm Coll, Chattanooga, TN; SO; AS; Amer Soc Cert Engr Tech 89-; Peer Cnslr 89-90; Phi Theta Kappa 90-; Deans Lst; Chem; Chem Tech.

**KEPECS, LAWRENCE ELIEZER,** Yeshiva Univ, New York, NY; JR; BABSE; Tns 88-; Pntng 88-; Karate Clb Pres 88-; Psychlgy Jwsh Hist Jwsh Stud; Canotr Opera.

**KEPHART, DAVID C,** Univ Of Tn At Martin, Martin, TN; JR; BS; Alpha Chi Lake Forest Coll; Park/Rec Adm Cmrcl Rec; Bicycle Touring Co.

**KEPHART, MICHELLE S,** Univ Of Sc At Columbia, Columbia, SC; FR; Hmcmng Cmmssn; Emrgng Ldrs; Delta Gamma; Exrcse Sci; Phys Thrpy.

**KEPHART, TIMOTHY A,** Univ Of Rochester, Rochester, NY; SR; Dorm Cncl Treas 89-90; Vrsty Bsbl Ltrmn 87-89; BA; Ecnmcs/Pltcl Sci.

**KEPICH, MARY J,** Univ Of North Fl, Jacksonville, FL; SO; BA; Deans Lst; X-Cntry/Trck 89-; Cmnctns; Engl.**

**KEREN, HADAR,** Univ Of South Al, Mobile, AL; FR; Young Judaea Zionist Mvmnt Mobile Chptr Ldr 90-.

**KERENICK, LAURA A,** Univ Of Sc At Columbia, Columbia, SC; JR; Early Chldhd Educ; Teach.

**KERFOOT, LYNN A,** Seton Hall Univ, South Orange, NJ; JR; BA; Nrsng; Admnstrtr.

**KERHOULAS-CREECH, ANDREA L,** Univ Of Nc At Greensboro, Greensboro, NC; SR; BS; Elliot U Cncl 85-86; Early Chldhd Ed; Tchr.

**KERKELA, RICHARD A,** Daytona Beach Comm Coll, Daytona Beach, FL; FR; AS; Wm C Butscher Jr Future Stds Schlrshp 80; AA Cntrl FL Comm Coll 80; Cmrcl/Indust Phtgrphy.**

**KERLEY, JEFFREY L,** Roane St Comm Coll, Harriman, TN; FR; Intl Soc Fire Serv Instctrs 88-; Prmdc Std Year; Snr Frfghtr/EMT Knxvl Fire Dpt 88-; EMT Cert State Tech Inst Knxvl 82; Fire Prtctn.

**KERLEY, KIMBERLY D,** Univ Of Tn At Martin, Martin, TN; JR; BSW; Scl Wrk Clb Chrmn Pblcty 88-; Alpha Gamma Delta VP 88-; Deans Lst 88-; Bst All Arnd Alpha Gam 88-; Intrmrl Sprts 88-; Scl Wrk Sclgy.

**KERLEY, PHYLLIS S,** Vance Granville Comm Coll, Henderson, NC; SO; AAS; SGA Soc Cmtee Chrm 90-; Beta Phi Upsilon Pres 90-; Phi Theta Kappa V P 90-; Ambsdr 90-; Sec Sci; Admn Asst.

**KERMISCH, JULIE M,** Lynchburg Coll, Lynchburg, VA; FR; BA; Stu Govt Assoc Splght/Trvl Comm; Fld Hcky/Lacrosse; Chld Psychlgst.

**KERN, ANGIE D,** Denison Univ, Granville, OH; FR; BA; Yrbk Stff 90-; COSEN 90-; Alpha Chi Omega 90-; Denison Comm Assn 90-; Univ Rcyclng Pgm 90-; Psych/Cmnctns.

**KERN, CHARLIE A,** Univ Of Ky, Lexington, KY; SR; Flwshp Chrstn Athlts; Omicron Delta Kappa; Phi Alpha Theta; Track/Fld Capt; Cross Cntry Capt; BA; Hist; Ed.

**KERN, DEBORAH,** Marywood Coll, Scranton, PA; SO; BA; St Lukes Art Clb 90-; Eucharistic Mnstr 89-90; Zigma Zigma 89-90; Tchrs Choice Exhbt 90-; Art; Illstrator.

**KERN, STACY J,** Fl St Univ, Tallahassee, FL; JR; BA; Elem Ed; Tchr.

**KERN, TRACY E,** Davis Coll, Toledo, OH; GD; AD; Intrnshp 90-; Water/Color Mem Parkview Hosp; Pres Lst; PTA; Prkvw Ostpthc Hosp 81-; LPN Nrthwstrn Ohio Prctcl Nrs Trng Ctr 81; Cmrcl Art; Advrtsng/Dsgn.

**KERNIK, TRAVIS L,** Univ Of Akron, Akron, OH; FR; MBA; Hnrs Club 90-; Phi Eta Sigma 90-; Deans List 90-; Chemistry; Engrng.

**KERNS, CHRISTINA L,** Brevard Coll, Brevard, NC; SO; BA; Ambssdr Admssns 90-; Res Asst 90-; AA; Psychlgy; Cnslr/Tchr.

**KERNS, JENNIFER D,** Wv Univ At Parkersburg, Parkersburg, WV; FR; AA; Den Mthr CSA 70; Vol Drvr Meals Whls; Slvtn Army 80-; Med Sec 70; Ownr/Mgr Rtl Frntr Str 80; Psych; Fmly Cnslg.

**KERNS, PETER M,** Kent St Univ Kent Cmps, Kent, OH; JR; BA; Macintosh Users Grp Pres; Acctg Assn 89-90; Acctg Assn Awd 90; Cmptr Sci; Sftware Engr.

**KERNS, TERRI L,** Oh St Univ At Marion, Marion, OH; JR; BSSW; Amer Psychlgcl Assn; Ohio Psychlgcl Assn; Natl Assn Scl Wrkrs; Griffin Hon Soc; Scl Wrk.

**KERNS, THOMAS K,** Southern Coll Of Tech, Marietta, GA; SR; BSEET; IEEE 90-; Co Op Stdnt Wth Atlnta Gas Lght Co 88-; Elec Eng; Eng.

**KERR, BRENDA L,** Meridian Comm Coll, Meridian, MS; SO; BA; Hstry/Scndry Educ.

**KERR, BRIAN D,** City Univ Of Ny Baruch Coll, New York, NY; SR; BBA; Debate Tm VP 89-; Stdnt Nwspapr Copy Edtr 90; Goldn Key 90-; Beta Alpha Psi 90-; Deloitte Haskins Sells Intrnshp 89; Clss Vldctrn; Acctg.

**KERR, CATHERINE A,** Medaille Coll, Buffalo, NY; FR; BS; Evening Stdnt Orientation Comm; Erie Co Industrial Dev Agcy Speaker; Comprehensive Empl Opport Support Ctr; Ofc Mgr Mgmt Cnsltg Firm 89-; Hmn Res Dev; Mgmt Cnsltg.

**KERR, COREY D,** Bethany Coll, Bethany, WV; JR; BA; Psychlgy Clb 90-; Rsdnt Asst 89-; BISONS Vol Grp Admsns 89-; Rnr Pgmng Brd 88-89; Alpha Beta Gamma Ed Treas 90-; Kalon Hnry 90-; Beta Theta Pi Sec 89-; Spec Olympcs Vol; Dns Lst 90-; Wrk Mntly Rtrd; Wm Baird Schlrshp; Vrsty Swmng; Psychlgy/Ed Interdscplnary; Tch.

**KERR, HEATHER ANN,** Univ Of Ky, Lexington, KY; SR; BA; AIAS 87-; Oper Frndshp Rgnl Rep/Delg 84-90; Ky Dsgn Asst Tm Ashland Ky 90; Tau Sigma Delta 89-; Monument/Counterpoint Comptn London Engl; Architecture.

**KERR, JEAN M,** Univ Of Akron, Akron, OH; JR; BA; Elem Educ.

**KERR, JENNIFER K,** Univ Of Miami, Coral Gables, FL; SR; BS; Univ Radio Gen Mgr 90-; Omicron Delta Kappa; Alpha Epsilon Rho; Intl Mag Prmtn; Brdcstng/Psychology; Music Indus.

**KERR, JENNIFER M,** Fl St Univ, Tallahassee, FL; JR; BA; FL Pub Rel Assoc 90-; Phi Kappa Phi; Intrnshp Tallahassee Cmnty Hosp Pub Rel Dir; AA 90; Communication; Law.

**KERR, KERRI A,** Univ Of Southern Ms, Hattiesburg, MS; JR; BS; Bethlehems Chldrns Hm 88-90; Hope Fndtn 88-90; Mentor Prog 89-90; Gamma Beta Phi; Phi Mu Scl Dir 88-; Nursing Biology Micro; Medicine.

**KERR, KRISTIE R,** Owensboro Comm Coll, Owensboro, KY; FR; Offce Admin.

**KERR, THOMAS K,** Wilmington Coll, New Castle, DE; GD; BS; Delta Epsilon Rho 89-; Sftbl Cch; Ky Wrkr Cmbnd Fer Cmpgn And AF Aid Scty; USAF; AAS CCAR 90; BS; Bus; AF Plt.

**KERR JR, WADE L,** Averett Coll, Danville, VA; SR; BS; ABB Pwr T/D Co Shop Sprvsr 70-91; AAS Durham Tech Inst 70; Mgmnt; Mfg Mgmnt.

**KERR, WILLIAM J,** East Tn St Univ, Johnson City, TN; SO; BA; Army Sgt 86-90; Cmptr Sci; Prgmng.

**KERR-HAISLIP, JUDITH D,** Va Commonwealth Univ, Richmond, VA; JR; BS; Natl Hmbldrs Assn 84-90; Girl Scts Asst Ldr 89-90; Estmtr Rsdntl Hm Bldr 78-89; Fnnc; Plnng.

**KERRICK, JOHN W,** Oh St Univ, Columbus, OH; SR; BM; German Clb Wittenberg U; Bnd Wittenberg U; Bnd Wittenberg U; Orch Wittenberg U; Lutheran Stdnt Assoc Wittenberg U; YMCA V P Wittenberg U 51-52; Stdnt Senate Wittenberg U 52-53; Religious Actvts Comm Chrmn Wittenberg U 52-53; Music Hstry; Grad Study-Wrtg/Tchg.

**KERRIDGE, JANE M,** Indiana Univ Of Pa, Indiana, PA; JR; BS; PSEA 90-; Prjct Strd 90; Sigma Sigma Sigma Fndrsr Chrmn 89-; Elem Ed.

**KERRIGAN, MICHELE A,** Marywood Coll, Scranton, PA; JR; BA; Marywood Chptr Amer Advrstng Pbl Rel Dir; TV Marywood Promo Dir; Dean Lst; PA Hmn Lf 84-; Credit Unn Yth Ambssdr; Intern Greater Wilkes Barre Prtnshp; Radio TV Advrtsng.

**KERSCHBAUM, WANDA F,** Memphis St Univ, Memphis, TN; JR; BED; March Of Dimes Vol 85-; Alumni Awrd Creative Ldrshp 77; Bike A Thon MCC Assoc Chrprsn 77; Educ; Bus Educ Trnr.

**KERSCHNER, TERRY L,** Salisbury St Univ, Salisbury, MD; SR; Psychlgy Clb Pres 88-; Pi Gamma Mu 90-; Psi Chi Pres 89-; Phi Eta Sigma 88-; Deans Lst 87-; BA; Psychlgy; PhD Chld Psychlgy.

**KERSHAW, DEBORAH M,** Norfolk St Univ, Norfolk, VA; SO; BA; Tchr Asst Emtnly Dstrbd Chldrn 89-90; Hsty Edctn; Tchr Grd 4.

**KERSHNER, TIFFANY L,** Univ Of Sc At Columbia, Columbia, SC; SO; BA; Intl Stdnts Assn 90-; Anthrplgy Stdnt Assn 90-; Mnstry Edtr Nwsltr Sec 89-; Gamma Beta Phi 89-; Phi Eta Sigma 89-; Alpha Lambda Delta 89-; Delta Gamma Sngldr 90-; Deans Lst 89-; Hon Coll 90-; Anthrplgy Frgn Lang; Frgn Serv.

**KERTON, CORA L,** Va St Univ, Petersburg, VA; JR; Mrktg Clb Sec; NJ Pre Alumni; Stu/Asst Clrk/Typst Mrktg Dept; Mrktg Mgr; Entrprnr.

**KERVICK, MIMI A,** East Tn St Univ, Johnson City, TN; FR; BA; Mass Cmnctns; Publc Rltns.

**KERVIN, SUSAN A,** Westminster Coll, New Wilmingtn, PA; SO; BA; Radio Stn News Dir 89-; TV Stn News Dir/Prdcr 89-; RA Res Lf Staff90-; Sigma Kappa Trngl Mag Crspndnt 90-; Inst Pltcl Jrnlsm Georgetown Univ 90; Intern States New Svc Wash DC 90; Intern News Rprtr WBBW YoungstownOH; Telecomm Jrnlsm; Jrnlst/Tv Radio.

**KERWIN, ELIZABETH A,** Limestone Coll, Gaffney, SC; JR; BA; Presby Woman Allison Creek Monorator 89-90; Acctnt Gold Bond Bldg Brod 78-; Business; Acctng.

**KESEL, SCOTT A,** S U N Y Coll Of Tech At Alfred, Alfred, NY; SR; BA; Lions Clb 90-; Amer Leg 90; Aviation Structural Mech 84-88; USMC 88; Psych.

**KESLER, HEIDI J,** Nyack Coll, Nyack, NY; SO; St Agathas Gspl Tm Sec 89-; Deans Lst; Scndry Educ Engl.

**KESLER, OLIVERA E,** Univ Of Pa, Philadelphia, PA; FR; BA; Envrnmntl/Rcyclng Grp 90; Cmmtr Org Scrtry 90; Ben Frnkln Schlr 90; Physcl Sci.

**KESOLITS, JENNIFER A,** William Paterson Coll, Wayne, NJ; JR; BA/MS; NJ Spch/Hrng Assn 89-; Natl Stdnt Spch Lang/Hrng Assn 90-; Rsdnt Asst William Paterson Coll Twrs 90-; Cmnctn Dsrdrs; Spch Pthlgy.**

**KESSELMAN, SCOTT L,** S U N Y At Buffalo, Buffalo, NY; GD; DDS; Cls Govt VP 90-; Amer Stdnt Dntl Assoc 89-; Dntl Stdnt Assoc 90-; Alpha Omega 89-; Tau Kappa Epsilon VP 83-87; William Tucker Schlrshp Awd 90-; Barrett Fndtn Schlrshp Awd 90-; IM 83-87; Dbrmn Pnchr Clb 90-; Dntl Med; Pst Dctrt Dgr Prsthdntcs.

**KESSINGER, MITCHELL W,** Richard Bland Coll, Petersburg, VA; SO; AS; Phi Theta Kappa; Sci/Math; Chem Engrng.**

**KESSLER, JEFF D,** Oh St Univ, Columbus, OH; SO; BS; Phi Kappa Phi 90-; Tau Kappa Epsilon 87-; Arch.

**KESSLER, JODI M,** Marywood Coll, Scranton, PA; SO; BFA; Graphic Dsgn; Artist.

**KESSLER, LISA C,** Ny Univ, New York, NY; FR; BSEE; Intl Brthrhd Of Electrcl Workers Founders Schlrshp Awd; Intl Brthrhd Of Elctrcl Workers Un Asst To Bus Mgr 89-; Elect Tech 79-; BS De Vry Tech Inst 79; Elect Engrng.

**KESSLER, SANDRA M,** Columbus Coll Of Art & Design, Columbus, OH; JR; BFA; Schlrshp Clmbs Coll Art Dsgn 90-; Fn Arts.

**KESSLER, VALERIE D,** Georgetown Coll, Georgetown, KY; SO; BA; Stdnt Govt Assn 89-; Alpha Lambda Delta Treas 89-; Sigma Gamma Sigma 89-; Phi Alpha Theta; Kappa Delta; Stdnt Rep Bd Trustees 90-; Engl/Hstry; Tchng.

**KESTEN, JOANNE S,** William Paterson Coll, Wayne, NJ; GD; MS; Kappa Delta Pi; Lakeland Coop Nrsry Schl Pres 90-; MADD VP 89-90; Bnfts Anlyst/Admn; BS St Univ NY 79; Spec Educ; Autistic Chldrn.

**KESTER, DAVID L,** Liberty Univ, Lynchburg, VA; JR; BS; Philosophy Club 89-; Debate Tm Varsity 88-; Phi Sigma Tau 89-; Inter Natl Ctr Public Policy Res 90; Philosophy; Law/Profr.

**KESTERSON, KYLE L,** Savannah Coll Of Art & Design, Savannah, GA; JR; BFA; Amer Soc Intr Dsgn; Intr Dsgn.

**KESTORY, ROBERT H,** Livingston Univ, Livingston, AL; JR; BS; Esquires 89-90; Bsbl 88-89; Physcl Ed/Soc Sci; Tchr.

**KETCH, WENDY S,** George Mason Univ, Fairfax, VA; FR; BS; Natl Hon Soc 88-; Bus; Acctg.

**KETCHIN, MARIKO J,** Castleton St Coll, Castleton, VT; SO; BA; Outing Clb 90-; Psychlgy; Cnslng.

**KETNER, JANICE S,** Pellissippi St Tech Comm Coll, Knoxville, TN; SO; BA; Own Bsnss; Cmptr Sci; Systms Prgrmmng.

**KETNER, LORI A,** Ashland Univ, Ashland, OH; JR; BA; Hope Flwshp 90-; Phi Mu; Bus Admnstrn; Hotel Mgr.**

**KETTELL, LISA L,** Boston Univ, Boston, MA; SR; BS; Occptnl Thrpy Clb 89-; Stu Cncl 89-90; Stu Unn 89-; Pi Theta Epsilon 90-; Empl New England Med Cntr 89-; Occptnl Thrpy.

**KETTENRING, YVONNE M,** Lexington Comm Coll, Lexington, KY; FR; Archtctrl Tech; Blue Print Drafting.

**KETTER, DEBORAH L,** Univ Of Nc At Greensboro, Greensboro, NC; SR; BSN; ANS 90-; Mrshls 90-; Sigma Theta Tau; Spec Olympics 90; Dns Lst 88-; All Amer Schlr Clgte Award 90; Natl Clgte Nrsg Award 90; Nrsg; RN.

**KETTERER, JAMES A,** Univ Of Akron, Akron, OH; SR; BS; Finance; Bnkng/Fincl Inst.

**KETTERMAN, CHRISTOPHE S,** Germanna Comm Coll, Locust Grove, VA; FR; BSE; Cert VA Emerg Med Tech; Eng.

**KETTLE, BARBARA Y,** East Stroudsburg Univ, E Stroudsburg, PA; JR; BA; Res Hall Assn Pres 88-90; Delta Phi Epsilon PR Asst Fund 89-; Stdnt Senate Corr Sec 88-90; Sigma Tau Delta; Delta Phi Epsilon Asst PR Frnrsr 90-; Natl Coll Stdnt Govt Awd 88; Spch Cmncnts; Publ Rel/Brdcstng.

**KETZ, STACEY L,** Le Moyne Coll, Syracuse, NY; FR; Chrl Scty 90f Theater Trpe 90; Hall Cncl Rep 90; Indstrl Rltns; Corp Law.

**KETZER, WILLIAM J,** Hudson Valley Comm Coll, Troy, NY; SR; ASSOC; Engl/Jrnlsm; Wrtr/Prfrmng Artist.

**KEUPER, KURT J,** Nova Univ, Ft Lauderdale, FL; GD; MBA; Cert Acad Achvmnt 90; Ftbl 74-76; Elder Our Svr Luth 87-; Prof Env Serv 90-; BSCE Vlprso Univ 76; Bsn Admn; Admn/Engr.

**KEVENEY, EMMET C,** Manhattan Coll, Bronx, NY; JR; BSCE; ASCE; Tau Beta Pi; Cvl Eng.

**KEY, AMANDA C,** Atlanta Christian Coll, East Point, GA; GD; MED; Sigma Iota Chi Sec/Treas 86-90; Engl Awd 90; Vars Capt 86-90; Erly Chldhd Ed; Tch.

**KEY, BRIAN M,** Old Dominion Univ, Norfolk, VA; SO; Amrcn Scty Cvl Eng Sec; Intern Balzer Assoc Archtcts Eng; Cvl Eng Tchnlgy; Eng.

**KEY, DENISE M,** Elmira Coll, Elmira, NY; SR; BS; Amer Cancer Soc; BS Niagara Univ 88; Speech/Hearing.

**KEY, EMMA B,** Memphis St Univ, Memphis, TN; SR; MBA; Easthaven Day Care Cntr Brd Of Dir Treas 90; TSEA TCSW 87; PTSO Germantown Hghlnd; Deans Lst 87; Intrnshp Shelby Cnty Jstce Cmplex; Positive Mntl Attitude Assoc; Richwoods Hm Ownrs Assoc; GS Prjct Chrmn 89-90; Sprvsr Tenn Dept Of Human Serv; Scl Wrk/Pblc Admin; Admin Scl Wrk.

**KEY, LISA C,** Ky Christian Coll, Grayson, KY; GD; Chrldng 86-88; Ldr Dcplshp Grp 89-90; Hon Rl; Chrstn Svc 86-90; IM Vlybl Cpt 88-90; BS 90; Elem Educ K-4; Tchng.

**KEY, PAUL M,** Dyersburg St Comm Coll, Dyersburg, TN; MFA; Jaycees VP 89; Wght Lftng Cmptn 1 Pl 90; Butcher Meat Mrkt Mgr 69-81; Bldg Trades Crew Ldr 81-; AS; Art; Psychology.

**KEY, SUSAN E,** Middle Tn St Univ, Murfreesboro, TN; SR; MSW; Social Work Stdnts Frm ASB Rep 88-; Anthrplgcl Scty; Project Help Intrn 90; Buddies Rutherford Cnty/Buddies Nshvll Intrn; Brd Dir Buddies Rutherford Cnty; BSW; Social Work; Admin Social Worker.

**KEY, VALERIE M,** Tuskegee Univ, Tuskegee Inst, AL; SR; BS; Stdnt Natl Ed Assoc Treas 89-; AL Assoc Yng Chldrn 90-; Early Chldhd Ed; Tchr.

**KEYACK, KIMBERLY A,** Salisbury St Univ, Salisbury, MD; SR; Vrsty Bsktbl 87-; Hstry; Tch/Gt Finncl Advsr Degr.

**KEYES JR, JERRY L,** Alcorn St Univ, Lorman, MS; SO; BS; Indus Tech Clb 89-; Hon Prog 89-; Alpha Phi Omega; Exe Sec 90-; Elect/Cmptr Tech.

**KEYES, LISA M,** Juniata Coll, Huntingdon, PA; SR; BS; Stdnt Govt Cmtee 87-90; Admsns Assoc 89-90; Res Hall Assoc 87-90; Hon Soc; Phi Chi Theta Gen Mgmt Co Chrprsn 89-; Tau Pi Phi 90-; Spec Olympcs 89-90; Gen Mgmt; Bus.

**KEYES, MELISSA L,** Univ Of Ga, Athens, GA; SR; BSED; Mdl Sch Educ Clb 88-; Educ; Mdl Schl Scl Tchr.

**KEYHANI, ROYA AMANDA,** Oh St Univ, Columbus, OH; SR; BS; Std Cncl 86-87; Sktng Clb 88; Amer Clg Swtzrlnd Grk Clb 88-89; ACS Yr Bk Clb; ACS Arbc Clb; Grmn Clb 89; Gldn Key 88-89; Alpha Epsln Delta 89-90; Phi Kappa Phi 89-90; Helix 89-; Phi Beta Kappa 90-; Summa Awd 86-87; Schlp Awd 90; Biochem; Med.

**KEYLON, DANA L,** Roane St Comm Coll, Harriman, TN; SO; AAS; CSI 90-; Outstndng Achvmnt Awd; Offc Admin; Mgmt.

**KEYLON, GARY W,** Univ Of Tn At Chattanooga, Chattanooga, TN; SR; BSE; IEEE VP 90-; Stdnt Govt Sntr 90-; Tau Beta Pi Pres 90-; Coop Prog Bllsth 87-; SGA Sr Mrt Awrd; OCSA; IM Ftbl And Wghtlftng 89; Elec Eng PE.

**KEYS, EVELYN B,** Oh Wesleyan Univ, Delaware, OH; SO; SETA; Delta Delta Delta; Bld Drv.

**KEYSER, AMANDA K,** Radford Univ, Radford, VA; SO; Scl Wrk; Cnslg.

**KEYSER, DAVID A,** Oh St Univ, Columbus, OH; SR; BS; Gold Key; Scarlet/Gray Schlrshp 90-; Architecture.

**KEYSER, NANCY L,** Hillsborough Comm Coll, Tampa, FL; SR; BS; Tabernacle Bptst Church Tchr/Choir 73-; Rdng Tutor 90-; Hnrs Cnvctn; SNO 90-; LPN; RN Cardiac Prgrsv Care; Cert St Joseph Hosp; Nrsng Sci; Nrsng Ed/Clncl Nrs/Cardiac Nrsng.

**KEYTON, ELIZABETH G,** Univ Of Al At Birmingham, Birmingham, AL; SR; BSN; Nrsng Stdnt Govt Assn Clss Rep; Natl Stdnt Nrsng Assn; AL Stdnt Nrsng Assn; Delta Delta Delta Treas 76; Univ AL Assn Of Nrsng Stdnts Sec; Pres Lst; IM Sftbl; Amer Spch Lngge Hrng Assn; BS Auburn Univ Auburn AL 77; MS Univ Of AL Tuscaloosa; Nrsng; Nntl Intnsve Cre Nrsng Ped Nrse Prctnr.

**KHADIRI, REZA,** George Mason Univ, Fairfax, VA; JR; BS; Alfa Chi Rho 88-; Ski Clb; Bsktbl/Karate/Rcktbl; Hlth Sci; Phys Thrpy.

**KHALAF, RANDY S,** Univ Of Southern Ms, Hattiesburg, MS; SR; BS; Stdnt Eagle Clb 90-; Dns Lst 90; Pres Lst; Therptc Rec; Phys Thrpy.

**KHALDI, OMAR R,** Schenectady County Comm Coll, Schenectady, NY; SO; AS; BSA Cmmdr 88; Math/Sci; Med.

**KHALID, HUMAYUN,** City Univ Of Ny City Coll, New York, NY; SR; BE; Pakistn Stdnts Org 89; Fresh Comm Advsr 90; Cltrl Soc Spec Rep; Golden Key; IEEP IEEE; SSC Brd Scndry Ed Karaeli 83; FSC Brd Hghr Scndry Ed Karaelin 85; Elec Eng.

**KHALIL, MEHNOOR M,** Univ Of Sc At Aiken, Aiken, SC; FR; BED; Educ Mjrs Clb; St Mrys Schl Of Hndcppd Chldrn 83; Awrdd Akn Dbtnte Scty Schlrshp; B Com Univ Of Poona India 86; Eled Educ; Tchng.

**KHALIL, WESAM N,** Al A & M Univ, Normal, AL; SO; BS; MSA Sec 89-; MAYA 89-; Tau Alpha Pi; Elec Engr.

**KHALILI, MARYAM,** Comm Coll Algny Co Algny Cmps, Pittsburgh, PA; SR; AS; Nrsng; RN.

**KHALIMSKY, OLGA R,** Wright St Univ, Dayton, OH; FR; BA; Hons Prog 90-; Alumni Assoc 90-; Alpha Lambda Delta; Dns Lst 90-; Phych; Med.

**KHAN, AFZAL,** Pellissippi St Tech Comm Coll, Knoxville, TN; SO; BS; Intl Students Club 89-; MCK 90-; Pell Grant 90-; FSC Shipowners Clg Pakistan 87; HSC Happy Dale Schl Pakistan 85; Elec Engrg; Engrg.

**KHAN, AISHA RAIS,** Univ Of Al At Birmingham, Birmingham, AL; FR; BS; Alpha Lambda Delta; Acctng; Author.

**KHAN, ANWARUL K,** Atlanta Metropolitan Coll, Atlanta, GA; FR; Bangladesh Stdnt Assoc 89-; Bangladesh Assoc 89-90; Dhaka Univ Chess Clb; Cmptr Sci; Syst Analyst.**

**KHAN, AZRA J,** Elmira Coll, Elmira, NY; SR; BS; Stdnt Actvts Bd 89-90; Amnesty Intl 89-; Publ Defenders Ofc Intern; Arnot Art Museum; IM Vlybl/Sftbl 88-90; BS; Pol Sci; Law.

**KHAN, BERNINE I,** Univ Of Miami, Coral Gables, FL; SR; BFA; Cncl Intl Std Org Dir 83-85; Shprd Intl; Undgrad Std Body Govt 83-84; Std Art Show 90; Intrn Intl Corp Serv; Amer Inst Grphc Arts 89; Manking Wlkthn 87; BSC 87; Art; Txtl Dsgnr.

**KHAN, IMRAN H,** Oh Wesleyan Univ, Delaware, OH; FR; Tauheed.

**KHAN, IMRAN M,** Univ Of South Al, Mobile, AL; SO; BS; Phi Eta Sigma; BA Univ Punja Lahore Pakistan 88; Mrktng; Bsns Mgmt.

**KHAN, MAHSIUL I,** City Univ Of Ny La Guard Coll, Long Island Cty, NY; SO; BSEE; Club Student Assoc Bangladesh 89-90, Elec Engrg.

**KHAN, MOHAMMAD ALI,** Univ Of The Dist Of Columbia, Washington, DC; SO; BBA; Phi Beta Lambda Treas; Strght A Stdnt; HSE Notre Dame Clg 87; Acctg; CPA.

**KHAN, NALENE N,** City Univ Of Ny Baruch Coll, New York, NY; JR; BA; Actuarial Sci; Gldn Ky 90-; Sigma Alpha Delta 89-; Acturial Sci; Cnsltng Actuary.

**KHANDAKAR, SAZZAD,** City Univ Of Ny City Coll, New York, NY; SO; BS; Bangldsh Stdnts Assn V P 89-; Untd Stdnts Bangldsh Exec Dir; Forgn Stdnts Schlrshps 90; Cmptr Sci/Eng.

**KHANDAKER, SHAHIDULLAH B I,** Livingston Univ, Livingston, AL; FR; Fr Chem Achvmnt Awrd 90-; Chem.

**KHANDELWAL, SORABH,** Oh St Univ, Columbus, OH; SR; BS; Stu Jud Bd 87-90; Hon Peer Sup Prog 88; Alpha Epsilon Delta 87-90; Alpha Lambda Delta/Phi Eta Sigma 88-; Phi Kappa Phi 89-; Hon Com Assn Ser Cmmtte 88; Vol Goodwl Rehab Cntr Asst Coord 90-; Vol Hosp 87-90; Arts Sci Awd Schlrshp; Biochemistry; Med.

**KHANI, PAYAM,** City Univ Of Ny Baruch Coll, New York, NY; SR; BBA; N Y St Assn CPA Cand 89-; Gldn Ky 89-; Dns Lst 86-; Baruch Endwmnt Fund Mrt Awd Schlrshp 87-88; Acctng; Acctnt CPA/RL Est Invstr.**

**KHANNA, SAMTA,** Elms Coll, Chicopee, MA; SO; BA; Intl Clb Mbr 89-; Drama Clb 89-; Stdnt Rep In Curriculum Cmte 90-; Choir Clb 89-90; Mbr Of Accred Cmte 90-; Soph Show Script Wrtr 90; Jud Brd Mbr 90-; Art Dept Nwsltr; Design Cards/Pgm Cvrs For Clg; Campus Ministry Mbr 89-; Lit Dancer 90-; Speech Awrd; Elem Tchr; Comrcl Art.

**KHANNA, SITA,** Elms Coll, Chicopee, MA; SR; MA; Intl Clb Treas 90-; Drmtc/Elctn Clb Ldng Rls 89-; Yrbk Com; Ambsdr; Orntn; RA 90-; Kappa Gamma Pi; Ltrgcl Dnc Grp; Elms Chr 89-; Cmps Mnstry 89-; Soup Kit Vol; TV Intern; AAS Loreto Coll Calcutta India 85; Educ; Schl Adm.

**KHAROD, AMIT S,** Franklin And Marshall Coll, Lancaster, PA; JR; BA; Res Hl Assoc Sec 88-; Intl Clb 88-; Stu Hlth Advsry Comm Tres 89-90; Ntl Res Hl Hnry Pres 89-; Hosp Vol Pro 90-; Charles A Daub Schlrshp 90-; IM 90-; Bio; Med.

**KHAROUFEH, JEFFREY P,** Oh Univ, Athens, OH; FR; BS; Indstrl/Syst Eng; Eng.

**KHATIWALA, BHARAT KUMAR A,** Widener Univ, Chester, PA; SR; BSEE; IEEE 89-; Intl Clb Treas 88-89; Tnns Tm 87-88; Fdrl Avtn Admin Elect Engr 90-; DELCORA Elect Engr 88-89; Vlybl IM 87-88; Elect Engr/Comp Sci; MBA/MSTRS Elect Engr.

**KHAW, ENG SIN,** Memphis St Univ, Memphis, TN; SR; MS; BSC Univ Sains Malayesia 88; Comp Sci; Bus.

**KHAW, LI KI,** Saint Andrews Presbytrn Coll, Laurinburg, NC; SR; BA; Wrld Cultr Soc V P 88-; Chrl Chmbr Sngrs Accpnst 88-; Busn Clb 89-; Hnrs 88-90; Alpha Chi; Intrnshp Libby Owns Ford Co; Music/Busn/Econ; Humn Resrcs.

**KHAYAT, VICTOR RUDOLPH,** Washington & Lee Univ, Lexington, VA; FR; BA; Model UN; Grmn Clb; Outdrsmn Clb VP; Phi Gamma Delta; Trky Trot Rn For Chrty; Vol Fire Fghtr; EMT; Biolgy; Med.

**KHAZAMIPOUR, SHILA,** Hillsborough Comm Coll, Tampa, FL; FR; BS; AS Roodaky Inst Iran 88; Scif Dntstry.

**KHODABAKHSH, SHOHREH,** Strayer Coll, Washington, DC; SR; BS; Cum Laud 86-; Cmptr Info Sys; Cmptr Prgmmr.

**KHOKHAR, TEHSEEN,** Howard Univ, Washington, DC; GD; MS; Amer Soc Cvl Eng 89-; Pkstn Eng Cncl 89-; Nigrn Eng Cncl 86-89; Tchng Asstshp 89-90; Rsrch Asstshp; BE ABU Nigeria 88; Envrnmntl Eng.

**KHOLODNAYA, ASYA,** Bunker Hill Comm Coll, Boston, MA; SO; BA; Tchr; Bed USSR Odessa Pedgcl Inst 49; Engl; Tchg.

**KHONYONGWA, GIGI R,** Univ Of Al At Birmingham, Birmingham, AL; JR; BS; Tuskegee Univ Escrt Chpln 89-90; ROTC Squad Ldr 88-89; Inner City Ministry; Deans Lst 90; Occup Ther.

**KHOO, KONG-WEE,** Oh Univ, Athens, OH; FR; BS; Malaysia Stdnts Assn OH Univ Treas; Eng.

**KHOSHGAVAR, PEYMAN,** Edinboro Univ Of Pa, Edinboro, PA; JR; BS; SGA Cngrssmn 90f Amnsty Intrnatl USA 90-; Phlsphy Clb VP 90-; Univ Hnrs Prog 89-; Blgy Hnr Scty 90-; Sccr Clb 90; Chss Clb 90; Intrnatl Stdts Assn 89-; Intrnatl Nwsppr Fcs 89-; Blgy; Med.

**KHOSHNOOD, NAYSON NAJAF,** Univ Of Louisville, Louisville, KY; SR; MENG; IEEE 88-; Cricket Clb Capt 89-; Soccer Tm Capt 89-; B Sc 90; Math/Physics/Cmptr Sci; Elec Eng.

**KHOUZAM, MARIE-JOELLE C,** Univ Of Toledo, Toledo, OH; GD; JD; Law Revw 89-; Gvrng Brd 90-; Moot Ct Brd; Natl Trial Tm 90-; Phi Alpha Delta VJ 90-; Natl Assn Of Women Lawyers; Outstndng Grad Awrd; IM Sftbl; BA Bowling Green St Univ 85; Law.

**KHUU, HUA M,** Univ Of Cincinnati, Cincinnati, OH; SO; BSEE; Elec Engr.

**KI, TSANG YEE,** Univ Of Tn At Knoxville, Knoxville, TN; JR; BA; Hong Kong Std Asc Sec; Panmac Jaycee Asn 90-; Acct.

**KIBBE, CAROLYN L,** Smith Coll, Northampton, MA; FR; BA; Smth Coll Chr Omega 90-; Art Hstry.

**KIBLER, KATHRYN D,** Kent St Univ Kent Cmps, Kent, OH; GD; MLS; Beta Phi Mu; Chldrns Librarian; BS Ed Kent State Univ 81; Childrens Librarian.

**KIBRIYE, SHIFERAW,** City Univ Of Ny City Coll, New York, NY; JR; BS; CCAP 89-; PPS 89-; Psychlgy; Medicine.

**KICINSKI, CHRISTINE A,** Immaculata Coll, Immaculata, PA, FR; BA; Cue Crtn Plyrs Ldng Rl 90-; Chrl Slst 90-; Awrd Dlta Psi Chptr Pi Kappa Lambda; Intern Frnkfrd Styl Rv; Music Vc Prfrmnc.

**KICK, ELLEN K,** Oh Wesleyan Univ, Delaware, OH; SO; BA; Flwshp Chrstn Ath 89-; Stdnt Fndtn 90-; Phi Eta Sigma 90-; Pi Soc; Delta Zeta Hs Mgr 89-; Intrnshp Davidson Coll PEW Grnt; Chem Rbr Co Awd; Vars Vlybl 89-; Chem; Biochem Rsrch.

**KICKEY, DANA D L,** Univ Of Sc At Columbia, Columbia, SC; FR; BA; Kappa Kappa Gamma 90-; Publ Spec Univ Hsg Svcs 90-; Engl; Professor.

**KICKLIGHER, MELANIE C,** Waycross Coll, Waycross, GA; FR; BA; Phi Theta Kappa 90-; Frshmn Schlr 90-; Deans Lst 90-; Presidents Lst; Math; Teach.

**KICKLIGHTER, CYNTHIA E,** Univ Of Miami, Coral Gables, FL; FR; BA; Earth Alert 90-; Hnrs Stdnt Assoc 90-; Marine Sci/Bio; Tch.

**KICOS, JOSEPH L,** Embry Riddle Aeronautical Univ, Daytona Beach, FL; GD; BA; Golf Clb/Mgmnt Clb; Aeronautical Science.

**KICZKOWSKI, SPRING,** Univ Of Sc At Columbia, Columbia, SC; SO; Mntnrng Clb/Rftng 90-; Alpha Phi 89-90; Sociolgy/Envrnmntl Stdies; Crmnl Law.

**KIDD, CAROLINE D,** Memphis St Univ, Memphis, TN; SR; BA; Yrbk Copy Edtr 88-89 Acdmcs Edtr 89-90; Pub Rltns Stdnt Soc Amer Treas 90-; Dfnse Depot Memphs Intrnshp 88; Jrnlsm/Pub Rltn; Cnsltng.

**KIDD, CHERYL D,** Univ Of Nc At Greensboro, Greensboro, NC; SR; Vet Of Us Navy 74-78; Nursing.

**KIDD, CHERYL K,** King Coll, Bristol, TN; FR.

**KIDD, JOANNA A,** Al A & M Univ, Normal, AL.

**KIDD, KIRSTIN E,** James Madison University, Harrisonburg, VA; JR; BS; Assc Educ Yng Chldrn 90-; Stdnty Cnrns Cmt; Gldn Key 90; Order Omega; Kappa Dlt Pi 90-; Alph Chi Omega Prsnl Dvlpmnt 89-; Ctr Svc Lnrng 88-90; Mortar Bd; Erly Chdlhd Educ; Tchng.

**KIDD, LERAY,** Alcorn St Univ, Lorman, MS; SR; BS; ROTC Capt 90; Bus Clb 90; Acctg Clb 89-90; ROTC Hon Stdtn 90; Distngshd Mltry Stdnt 90; Deans Lst 90; 2 Mile Clb 90; Bus Admn; Mltry Ofcr Corps.

**KIDD, MARTHA J,** Univ Of Southern Ms, Hattiesburg, MS; SR; BS; Ntl Educ Assn 89-; Gamma Beta Phi 90-; Stdnt Tchr Shdy Grv Elem; Elem Educ.

**KIDD, PHILLIP R,** Univ Of South Al, Mobile, AL; GD; Am Mktg Assn Exec VP 89-90; Pres Lst 89-90; Bus Frat 90-; Lambda Chi Alpha 81-83; Ntl Ldrshp Awd; Prof Mktg Assn 89-90; USMC 84-88; BS 90; Mktg; Distrt Mgr CCI Cntrl Fla.

**KIDD, RICHARD W,** Erie Comm Coll South Cmps, Orchard Park, NY; SO; Hnrs Clb 89; Hnrs Scty 89; Phi Theta Kappa; Bwlng 89-90; Psychlgy/Engl; Law Psychtry.

**KIDD, RONALD P,** Hillsborough Comm Coll, Tampa, FL; AA; US Navy Rsrv E3 87-; Rstrnt Mgr 89-; Chmstry; Med Schl.

**KIDD, WANDA L,** Al St Univ, Montgomery, AL; FR; BA; Accntng; CPA.

**KIDDER, PAMELA G,** Wv Univ At Parkersburg, Parkersburg, WV; JR; BS; Bus; Acctg.

**KIDDER, SARAH E,** Colby Sawyer Coll, New London, NH; JR; BS; Bus.

**KIDSTON, KAREN J,** Univ Of Rochester, Rochester, NY; SO; BA; AA Hartford Coll For Wmn 90; Psychlgy; Schl Cnslr.

**KIDWELL, MELISSA A,** Univ Of Cincinnati-Clrmnt Coll, Batavia, OH; SO; BA; Ednl Clb; Phi Theta Kappa; Sndy Sch Tchr; Tutor Clermont Cnty Crisis Ctr; Yth Grp Spnsr; Tchr New World Child Care 89-; Elem Edn/Psychlgy; Tchr.

**KIEFER, ANDREW J,** Saint Vincents Coll & Seminary, Latrobe, PA; SR; BS; Psychology Clb Co Chr 87-; I M Bkbl Tm Capt 88-; Orntatn Cmtee 88-; Clg Dean Lst; Campus Mnstry 87-; Acad Schlrshp 87-; Psychology; Soc Wrk/Rehab Cnslng.**

**KIEFER, CELIA S,** Ky Christian Coll, Grayson, KY; SR; BS; Msn Intrnshp Piedras Negras Mex 87-90; Caracas Venezuela 87; Indian Msn Az 90; PACK Ldr 88; KCC Cncrt Choir 88-; Adult Choir Dir 87; Yth Deaf Sign Choir 89; Taught Sign Lang MTH Classes 89-90; Jr Ch Song Ldr; Carter Co Spec Olymp Vol; Bible/Elem Ed Eng Soc Studies; Teach.

**KIEFER, SHAUNA M,** Atlantic Comm Coll, Mays Landing, NJ; FR; Cmnctn Prtnr; Physcl Therpy.

**KIEFER, STEPHEN M,** Northern Ky Univ, Highland Hts, KY; SR; BA; Cum Laude; Elem Educ; Tchr.

**KIEFFER, CHRISTOPHER M,** Boston Univ, Boston, MA; FR; BS; Coll Eng Deans Lst; Mchncl Eng; Eng.

**KIEFFER, SCOTT M,** Oh Univ, Athens, OH; SO; AF ROTC 89-; AFROTC Drill Tm Commander 89-; Arnold Air Scty Dir Oper Cmptrlr 90-; Cadet Of Command 89-90; Electrcl Computer Engrng; AF Ofcr.

**KIEFFER, SUZANNE C,** Univ Of Rochester, Rochester, NY; JR; BA; Yrbk Interpres Edr-In-Chief 88; Psy Chi; Alpha Phi 90; Circle-K VP 88; Psychlgy/Pol Sci; Tchng.

**KIEHL, ERIN M,** Wellesley Coll, Wellesley, MA; FR; BA; Fgre Sktng 87-; Hse Govt VP; Sftbl Clb 90-; Crss Cntry 90-; Chem; Med.

**KIEHL, SANDRA M,** Univ Of Akron, Akron, OH; JR; BS; Goldn Key 89-; Kappa Delta Pi; Elem Educ; Tch.

**KIEL, ROBERT M,** Defiance Coll, Defiance, OH; SR; BSBA; Weston Ldg 560 F AM; Toledo Scottish Rite Zenobia Shrine; Ohio Arch Soc; Maumee Grain Oper Mngr; Bus Admin.

**KIELCZYNSKI, ELIZABETH C,** Seton Hall Univ, South Orange, NJ; SR; BSNRN; Cmps Mnstry; Awrds Cmt; Stdnt Nrs Assc; Deans List; Nrsng; Admn Nrsng.

**KIELY, DANIELE J,** Muhlenberg Coll, Allentown, PA; FR; BA; Thtre Assn 90-; Envir Actn Clb; Actvts Cncl; Dns Lst; Thtre Psychlgy.

**KIERENIA, LINDA IRENE,** Fordham Univ, Bronx, NY; JR; BA; Cultrl Affrs 88-89; Math Clb Tr 89-90/Pr 90-; Phi Beta Kappa 90-; Matteo Ricci Soc 88-; Phi Kappa Phi 89-; Deans Lst 88-; Pr Schlrshp 88-; Intrnshp Metro Life Ins Co 90-; Math; Actuarial Sci.**

**KIERNAN, KATHLEEN J,** Dowling Coll, Oakdale Li, NY; JR; BA; Crew 88-90; Social Science; Elem Ed.

**KIERNAN, THERESA Z,** Fl International Univ, Miami, FL; SR; BA; Occup Ther Clb 89-90; Phi Theta Epsilon Tr 90-; Deans Lst 90; Occup Ther.

**KIERON, WENDY,** Saint Josephs Coll, Windham, ME; FR; BA; Yrbk 90-; Lit Magzne 90-; Nwspapr 90; Engl; Pblshng.

**KIFUS, JACQUELINE,** Radford Univ, Radford, VA; SR; BS; Zeta Tau Alpha VP 90; SPICE Stdnts Participating Cmmnty Enrichment; ZTA/RHO Chi/Pledge Mother VP 90; Otstndng Pledge 89; Otstndng Mbr 89; Ed; Tchr.

**KIGHT, LAWRENCE EDWARD,** Univ Of Ga, Athens, GA; SR; BED; BED; Engl; Educ.

**KIGHT, R CARSON,** Medical Univ Of Sc, Charleston, SC; SR; DMD; Amer Stdnt Dntl Assoc Features Ed 89-; Cls V P 89-; Dns Lst 83-; Psi Omega 86-; Oral/Maxillofacial Surg Emory Univ Extrnshp 90; SC Dntl Hyg Assoc 84-; Acad Gen Dntstry 88-; AS Med Clg GA 84; Dntstry; Priv Pract-Gen Dntstry.

**KIHALI, ELEKIAH ANDAGO,** Hellenic Coll/Holy Cross, Brookline, MA; GD; MDIV; Mssn Comm 90-; Pro Life Comm 90-; Rep Patriarchate Alexandria WCC Thessalaniki Greece 88; Stdnt Makarios Patriachal Orthodox Smnry 87-89; 4 Schlrshp Stdy Hly Crs 90-; Theology Hstry Bbick Ptrstc Stds; Pstrl Psych.

**KIHLMIRE, KELLY A,** Mount Saint Mary Coll, Newburgh, NY; SO; BA; Pres Comm Cncl Pres; Newspr Edtr 90; Hnrs Alliance 89-90; NYS Regnts Dipl 89; VFW Eastr Fair; Asst Sftbl Coach 90; Hudsn Vly Knghts Athl Mgr; Interdisp; Law.

**KIHM, JACQUELYN ANNE,** Temple Univ, Philadelphia, PA; JR; BA; TASA Stdnt Rep 90-; AIA RUDAT Prog To Stdy Urban Hsng Proj N Phila 90; Arch; Arch Dsgn/Plnng.

**KIIDER, MELISSA M,** S U N Y Coll Of Tech At Frmgdl, Farmingdale, NY; SO; ASSOC.

**KIIO, DANIEL M,** Bunker Hill Comm Coll, Boston, MA; JR; BA; Mbmt; Conslnt.

**KIJEWSKI, LINDA E,** Ursinus Coll, Collegeville, PA; SR; Rgstrd Crtcl Cre Nrs; AAS Reading Area Comm College 86; Blgy; Med Or Phrmctcl Rsrch.

**KIKER, DAVID S,** Univ Of Sc At Columbia, Columbia, SC; JR; BA; Gldn Key; Beta Gamma Sigma; Univ Schlrshp; Acctg; Coll Tchng.

**KILBURN, CAROL L,** Middle Tn St Univ, Murfreesboro, TN; JR; BA; Bus Mngmnt.

**KILBURN-PATTERSON, MARY K,** Sue Bennett Coll, London, KY; SO; BA; Sigma Nu; Bus; Accntnt/Cmptr Oper.

**KILCULLEN, ROBERT M,** Hudson County Comm Coll, Jersey City, NJ; SO.

**KILDAY, TONY B,** Tusculum Coll, Greeneville, TN; JR; BS; Deans Lst; Chrls Olvr Gry Schlr; Bus Admn.

**KILDOW, BARBARA A,** Wv Northern Comm Coll, Wheeling, WV; FR; AAS; Sci; Nrsng.

**KILDUFF, DIANE E,** Southeastern Ma Univ, N Dartmouth, MA; SR; BSN; Natl Stdnt Nrs Assoc Msschstts Stdnt Nrs Assoc 88-; Sigma Theta Tau 90-; Mr M Hwrd Schlrshp 89; Sigm Atheta Tau Stdnt Achvmnt Awrd; Wnmt Blffs Assoc 68-; Lgl Sec 75-; BA 75; Nrsng.

**KILE, ELLEN M,** Wv Univ, Morgantown, WV; SO; BS; 4-H 89-; Mech Engr; Biomedcl Engr.

**KILFEATHER, LISA M,** City Univ Of Ny La Guard Coll, Long Island Cty, NY; SO; AAS; Phi Theta Kappa; Intrnshp Pfizer Inc; Offc Tchnlgy; Bus.

**KILGO, KATHY Y,** Fl Coll, Temple Terrace, FL; SO; BED; Yng Wmns Trng Org 89-; Soc Arete 89-; Phi Theta Kappa 90-; Educ; Tchg.

**KILGORE, C DENISE,** Univ Of Ga, Athens, GA; SR; BSHE; Redcoat Band/Flagline 86-90; Bapt Stdnt Union 85-90; Tvlng Vocal Ensemble 86-87; Chld Dvlpmnt/Erly Chldhd Educ; Tchng.

**KILGORE, TAWANA S,** Walker Coll, Jasper, AL; FR; MBA; Psychlgy; Psychlgst.

**KILGORE, VICKI A,** Tri County Tech Coll, Pendleton, SC; JR; AB; Secretarial Science.

**KILIAN, KARIN ALISON,** Walters St Comm Coll, Morristown, TN; FR; Elm Edn.

**KILIRU, DAWN M,** City Univ Of Ny City Coll, New York, NY; SR; BFA; Dance Clb VP 90; Snt Lukes Schl Dnce Tchr 86-; BA The Legat School Of Classical Ballet 86; A Levels Legat School Of Clsscl Ballet; Dnce Thtre; Dnce Instrctr Actrss.

**KILLEBREW, JULIE ELIZABETH,** Univ Of South Al, Mobile, AL; SO; BS; Baptist Campus Ministries 8 9-; Church Activities; Alpha Lambda Delta 90-; Phi Eta Sigma 90-; Alpha Gamma Delta 89-; Panhellenic Outstndng Schlrshp 90; Deans Lst 89-; Presidents Lst 89-; Business; Marketing.

**KILLEBREW JR, KERRY S,** Univ Of Tn At Martin, Martin, TN; SO; BS; Clg Democrats 89-; Pi Kappa Alpha Sprts Chrmn 90-; Biology; Optometry.

**KILLEN, AMY DENISE,** Univ Of Tn At Martin, Martin, TN; SO; BA; Natl Wldlf Soc 90-; Alpha Phi Sigma 89-; Bsktbl Tm 89-; Biolgy/Chem; Pre-Med.

**KILLEN, THOMAS B,** John C Calhoun St Comm Coll, Decatur, AL; FR; Medical; Resp Therapy.

**KILLIAN, BRUCE A,** Univ Of Sc At Coastal Carolina, Conway, SC; JR; BA; Natl Assc Accntnts 90-; IM Ftbl Bsktbl Sftbl 88-; Accntng; CPA.

**KILLIAN, ELENA S,** Chattanooga St Tech Comm Coll, Chattanooga, TN; JR; Ed Club 89-90; Art Club 89-; Phi Theta Kappa 89-90; Chattanooga Cmnty Kitchn Cook 89-; Tlnt Rstr Of Outstndng Mnrty Clg Grads 90-91; Blue Rbns In Flrl Dsgn/Pntng Grdn Clubs Stdnt Jdg 80-90; TOS 88-; Spanish Lit; Tchng Clg.

**KILLIAN, LEONA M,** Saint Josephs Univ, Philadelphia, PA; GD; MS; APTA 81-; Arthritis Fndtn Spkrs Bureau; Gerontology Awd; Hahnemann Univ Hnrs 81; Hosp Stf Phys Thrpst 88-; BS Bilogy Chestnut Hill Coll 77; Cert Hahnemann Univ 81; Gerontological Srvcs.

**KILLIAN, LINDA S,** Piedmont Tech Coll, Greenwood, SC; GD; AAS; Phi Theta Kappa; Nrsng Hlth Sci; Nrsng.

**KILLIAN, MICHELLE L,** S U N Y Coll At Fredonia, Fredonia, NY; SO; BED; Elem Educ; Tchr/Sch Admn.

**KILLIAN, VIVIA L,** Univ Of Nc At Greensboro, Greensboro, NC; SR; Stdnt Assoc Ed 90-; Assoc Ed Yng Chldrn 90-; Dlvrnc Flwshp 87-; Alpha Lambda Delta 87-; Univ Mrshls 87-; Dns Lst 87-; Mnrty Pr Mntr 90-; BS; Elem Ed; Tchg K 6.

**KILLIANY, KRISTINA M,** Univ Of Scranton, Scranton, PA; JR; BS; Vrsty Tnns 88-; Bus Clb 89-; APIC 88-; Delta Mu Delta; Wmns Bus Hon Soc; Bus Mgmt; Mgmt.

**KILLINGSWORTH, GINA M,** Univ Of Montevallo, Montevallo, AL; JR; BA; Hnrs Pro 88-90; Psych Clb 90-; Props Crw Coll Nght Anl Drama Cmptn 90-; Psi Chi 90-; Amnsty Intl 90-; Bonnie Strcklnd Awrd Psych; Pres Awrd Exclnc Wrtg 90; Stu Asst Acdmc Rsrch Ofc; Psych; Cnslg.

**KILLION, MARK C,** Le Moyne Coll, Syracuse, NY; FR; BA; Le Moyne Krt Clb 90-; Frshmn Ldrshp Cmmtt 90-; Coll Intgrl Hnrs 90-; Hstry; Muscn.

**KILLOUGH, WENDI D,** Univ Of Sc At Columbia, Columbia, SC; SO; Gamma; FCS; Deans Hnr Rl; Zeta Tau Alpha Prog Cncl Rsh Comm; Bus; Fin/Mrktng.

**KILMER, GREGORY R,** West Chester Univ, West Chester, PA; SO; BS; RHA 91-; Cmpus Crsde 89-; I M Flr Hockey Bkbl 89-; Phi Epsilon Kappa 90-; Deans Lst 89-; Mgr Ftbl Tm; Phys Educ; Instr.

**KILMER, JANE M,** Miami Jacobs Jr Coll Of Bus, Dayton, OH; SR; AS; Brdcstng Indstry 86-; Mktg.

**KILMER, SANDRA E,** Marywood Coll, Scranton, PA; SO; BA; Ingl/Sec Ed; Tch.

**KILPATRICK, ASHLEY D,** Ms Univ For Women, Columbus, MS; JR; BS; Stdnt Govt Assn Sen 89-90; Hnrs Prog 88-; Art Stdnts League 89-; Torch; Sigma Tau Delta Treas 90-; Silhouette Hstrn 88-; Alcohol Awrnss Comm 89-90; Eng/Art; Higher Edn.**

**KILPATRICK, BRIAN M,** Univ Of Al At Birmingham, Birmingham, AL; SR; BA; Pol Sci; Law.

**KILPATRICK, JARRET L,** Memphis St Univ, Memphis, TN; JR; Athletic 3.5 Clb 90-; Bsbl 88-; Econ; Pilot.

**KILPATRICK, MELISSA D,** Central Al Comm Coll, Alexander City, AL; SO; BA; Stdnt Govt Sntr 90-; Co-Op Edn 88-; Act Com 90-; Phi Theta Kappa Pres 89-; Red Crs 89-90; Lake Martin Episcopal Retreat 89-; Ourtown Fire Dept Fndrsr 88-89; Outstndg Stdnt Coll Awd State Cmptn 90-; Sntr James B Allen Awd 90-; AS 90-; Info Sys; Sys Analyst.**

**KILROY, RENE C,** Wilmington Coll, New Castle, DE; SR; BS; Delaware Society Respiratory Care; National Board Respiratory Care; AAS Delaware Tech 83; Business Administration.

**KIM, ALICE H,** Yale Univ, New Haven, CT; FR; BA; Tchng.

**KIM, ALICIA ANN,** City Univ Of Ny Baruch Coll, New York, NY; SO; BA; Engl Jrnlsm.

**KIM, BANG HEE,** Univ Of Md Baltimore Prof Schl, Baltimore, MD; SR; BS; Rho Chi Pres 90-; Cls 91 VP 89-; SGA VP 90-; Lambda Kappa Sigma 89-; Stdnt Comm Drug Abuse Educ 89-; Acdmy Stdnts Pharmacy 88-; Honors Seminar 89-90; Plough Schrlshp 88-; Pharmacy.

**KIM, CHAN,** Asbury Theological Sem, Wilmore, KY; JR; M DIV; BPA Seoul City Univ 81; Theology.

**KIM, CHIN-SUN J,** Southern Coll Of Seventh Day, Collegedale, TN; FR; BS; Stdnt Assn Sntr 90-; Hon Roll 90-; Soccer/Vlybl/Bsktbl 90-; Nrsng; Pediatric Doctor.

**KIM, DO H,** Harvard Univ, Cambridge, MA; SO; BA; East Coast Asian Union New England Exec; Model UN Dir Comm Narcotic Drugs 90; Ford Undergrad Rsrch Flwshp; BA Harvard Univ; Sociology Afro Amer Stds.**

**KIM, EUI JUN,** City Univ Of Ny City Coll, New York, NY; JR; BE; AICHE 89-; Tau Beta Pi 90-; Dns Lst 88-; Schrl 87-90; Exxon Engr Intrn 90-; Chem Engr.

**KIM, EUN-MI,** Manhattan School Of Music, New York, NY; GD; MSTRS; Korean Stdnt Clb 87-; All Amer Schlr Clgt Awd; Piano/Classic; Concertpianist.

**KIM, EUNYOUNG,** Seton Hall Univ, South Orange, NJ; SO; Dns Lst; Nrsng.

**KIM, GEORGE J,** Ny Univ, New York, NY; SO; BS; Debate Scty 90; Asian Bsnss Assoc 90; Korean Stdnt Assoc 89; Grad Cmmncmnt Trnsltr; Orient Ldr Co-Dir 90; Scl Wrk/Pltcs/Cmptr; Lwry Or Jdge.**

**KIM, GEORGE S,** Dartmouth Coll, Hanover, NH; FR; BA; Daniel Webster Legal Soc 90-; Rpblcns 90-; Outing Clb Envrnmntl Studies Div 90-; Econ Stdnt Org 90-; Korean Am Stdnts Assn 90-; IM Ftbl/Soccer/Bsktbl; Tutor Clearinghse 90-; Hon Ceremony/Recpt 90-; Magna Cum Laude 90-; Hist/Econ; Law/Bus.

**KIM, GUNYONG JAMES,** Gordon Conwell Theol Sem, S Hamilton, MA; GD; MDIV; Wrld Chrstn Fllwshp 90-; Estmn Kodak Co Summer Intrnshp 81; Annual Ping Pong Chmpn 90-; Hm Chrch Clvry Korean Chrch SI NY 84-90; Korean Cmps Crsd NYC 87-90; Cmptr Systs Spec 84-90; BS Univ Of Rchstr 83; Mssnry.

**KIM, HELEN H,** City Univ Of Ny Baruch Coll, New York, NY; Advrtsng Soc 89-90; Beta Gamma Sigma.

**KIM, HI JOUNG,** Univ Of Tn At Martin, Martin, TN; SR; Ecnmc Asst Dr Davis Williams Assoc Prfsr Unv TN Martin 90-; Econ Finance; College Prfsr.

**KIM, HOON S,** Old Dominion Univ, Norfolk, VA; SO; Rugby Clb 90-; Elec Engr.

**KIM, HYUNGSUK,** Univ Of Tn At Martin, Martin, TN; GD; Svp Univ Korean Assn VP 89-90; Korean Prsbytrn Assn Pres 90; Econ/Int Bus; MBA.

**KIM, JAE W,** Nyack Coll, Nyack, NY; SO; BA; Bible; Msnry.

**KIM, JIYOUNG,** Va Commonwealth Univ, Richmond, VA; SR; MFA; Nova Korean Stdnt Assoc 87-88; Korean Stdnt Assoc 89-; Korean Chrstn Flwshp 89-; Korean Artists Assoc 90; Golden Key 89; Art Stdnt Mag 88; Paintg Exhib Carillon Museum; Printg Exhib Med Clg VA; AA N VA Cmnty Clg 87-89; Fine Arts; Prof Painter/Clg Prfsr.

**KIM, JOMI,** Bloomfield Coll, Bloomfield, NJ; SO; BA; Nrsng.

**KIM, JOONG Y,** Atlantic Comm Coll, Mays Landing, NJ; SO; Boy Sct 87-89; Bsktbl Clb; Tens Clb 88-89; Bsbl Clb Tbl Tens Clb 90-; Wk Intl Clb ACC; Finc.

**KIM, LEILANI P,** Endicott Coll, Beverly, MA; FR; Internship NW Airlines Guam Resvrtns Agent; Vlybl 90; Travel Tourism; Passenger Serv Agent.

**KIM, MIA C,** Princeton Univ, Princeton, NJ; FR; BA; Novice Crew 90-.

**KIM, MOON H,** Harding Grad School Of Relig, Memphis, TN; GD; MDIV; BS Hangug Univ Foreign Studies 85; BA St Paul Theolgcl Semnry 87; Bible; Prfsr/Mnstr.

**KIM, NYUK-KING T,** Al A & M Univ, Normal, AL; SO; BSC; Mgr Popeyes Fried Chicken; Sci; Elect Engr.

**KIM, SHA RAN,** Borough Of Manhattan Comm Coll, New York, NY; SO; Engl; Tchng.

**KIM, SHARON,** City Univ Of Ny Baruch Coll, New York, NY; SR; BBA; Bus To Bus Mrktng Soc VP 90-; Rtl Trade Soc 90-; Mrktng Mngmnt; Mrktng.

**KIM, SOO H,** Felician Coll, Lodi, NJ; SR; BA; Science Clb VP 90-; Art Clb Prsdnt 86-88; Nwspr Rprtr 85-86; Deans Lst 89-; Biology; PHD.

**KIM, SUN-JIN,** Radford Univ, Radford, VA; JR; BS; Intl Stdnts Clb; Art; Jewlry Dsgnr.

**KIM, TAE-HUI,** Harvard Univ, Cambridge, MA; SO; BA; Korean Mag Edtr 89-; Pltcl Rvw Stff Wrtr 89-90; Flk Arts Grp 90-; Hmlss Cmmtt 90-; Fefugee Yth Smmr Enrchmnt ESL Tchr; Elisabeth Agassiz Schlr 89-; Detur Prz 89-90; Wendell Schlrshp 89-90; IM Vllybl 89; Soc Stu; Law.**

**KIM, YOUNG-A,** Duquesne Univ, Pittsburgh, PA; FR; BA; Music Perfor.

**KIMAIYO, PIUS KIPCHUMBA,** Central St Univ, Wilberforce, OH; FR; BS; Cmptr Sci.

**KIMBALL, BEVERLY J,** Wilmington Coll, Wilmington, OH; FR; BS; Chemistry; Medical Research.

**KIMBALL, CHRISTINE J,** Gordon Conwell Theol Sem, S Hamilton, MA; GD; MDV; Prtnrs Fr Biblcl Eqlty 90-; BA Univ Pennsylvania 76; Biblcl Stds; Mnstry.

**KIMBALL, JENNIFER M,** Endicott Coll, Beverly, MA; FR; AS; Intrnshp Rock 101 WGIR-FM Promo Dept; Work/Study Endicott Clg 90-; Adv; Mktg.

**KIMBEL, ERICSON P,** Methodist Coll, Fayetteville, NC; JR; BA; Dbt Tm Cptn 90-; Dns Lst 89-; Marie C Fox Phlsphy Awd; Eng/Wrtng/Phlsphy; Law Schl.

**KIMBEL, STEFENIE K,** Univ Of Tn At Martin, Martin, TN; FR; Zeta Tau Alpha 90-91; RN.

**KIMBERLIN, BRENDA S,** Lenoir Rhyne Coll, Hickory, NC; SR; BA; SNCAE 89-; Sci Clb VP 88-89; NCCTM; Phi Theta Kappa Pres 88-89; Otstndng Stu Tchr; Paul Douglas Tchng Schlrshp 89-; Otstndng Trnsfr Stu Awrd 88; BA; AA AS Caldwell Community Coll 89; Math Sec; Tchr.

**KIMBLE, FREDERICK A,** Glassboro St Coll, Glassboro, NJ; FR; BA; Radio/TV Film Assoc Treas; Comm; Newsscaster.

**KIMBRELL, BURTEEN HORSLEY,** Birmingham Southern Coll, Birmingham, AL; SR; BS; Kappa Delta Epsilon 88-90; Adlt Lrng Cntr Tutor 79-; Bkkpr 73-90; Elem Ed; Tch.

**KIMBROUGH, AMY V,** Univ Of Tn At Martin, Martin, TN; SO; BA; Bptst Stdnt Union Pblcty Commt 89; Mu Epsilon Delta Sec 89; Occptnl Thrpy Clb; Hnrs Seminar Wrkshp Schlrshp 90; Psychlgy; Occupationa Therapist.

**KIMBROUGH, BENITA L,** Al A & M Univ, Normal, AL; SO; BS; Baptist Stdnt Union 89-; Acad Hnr Rl 89-; Deans Lst 89-; Bus Mgmnt.

**KIMBROUGH, ROSALIND A,** Univ Of Ga, Athens, GA; GD; MSW; Prof Blck Soc Wrkrs Assn Tr 89-; NASW 89-; IM Vlybl 90; BSW 90; Soc Wrk.

**KIMBROUGH, TANYA L,** Clark Atlanta Univ, Atlanta, GA; JR; BA; SGA Treas; Acctg Clb; Alpha Kappa Mu; Beta Gamma Sigma; Delta Sigma Theta Treas; Deloitte-Touche Intrnshp; Bsktbl Mgr 88-89; Acctg; CPA.

**KIME JR, EDWARD J,** Delaware Cnty Comm Coll, Media, PA; SO; BA; Peer Cnclng 90; AA; Psychology; MED.

**KIMMEL, MARY G,** Indiana Univ Of Pa, Indiana, PA; GD; Habitat For Hmnty Brd; Thrptc Actvy Aide IN Co Gdnce Ctr; BS Ed 86; Educ Exptnl.

**KIMMEL, WILLIAM B,** Hahnemann Univ, Philadelphia, PA; GD; MD; Rdng Blnd 90; Dean Lst Haheman Unv Schl Med 90-; Augustana Clg Aristea Hnr 84-88; Tri Beta Blgcl Hnr Soc 84-88; Phi Omega Phi Rck Islnd IL; Rufus B Weaver Schlrshp; Hnrs Antmc Pthlgy Lab Med Phrmclgy Ob/Gyn Srgcl Pthlgy 90-; Med; Srgcl Pthlgy Dgnstc Rdlgy.

**KIMMELL, JARRETT A,** Brevard Coll, Brevard, NC; SO; BA; Phi Theta Kappa; Math Tutor; Eng; Envrnmntl Eng.

**KIMMER, MARTHA L,** Univ Of Sc At Union, Union, SC; SO; ADN; Womens Aglow Worship Ldr; Correctional Ofcr Cross Anchr Corr Inst; RN.

**KIMMERLY, CASSANDRA W,** Univ Of Sc At Aiken, Aiken, SC; SO; BS; Deans List; Gamma Beta Phi Mbr; Bio/Art Studio; Med Illstrtn.

**KIMMERLY, WILLIAM M,** Univ Of Sc At Aiken, Aiken, SC; FR; BFA; Pres List; Deans List; Gamma Beta Phi; Art/Fshn; Fshn Dsgnr.

**KIMMONS, KYLE K,** Ms St Univ, Miss State, MS; SR; BS; AICHE 88; Azeotrope Soc 90-; Co-Op Dupont Delisle MSIM Vlybl 87-; Chem Engr.

**KIMOCK, JOHN T,** Embry Riddle Aeronautical Univ, Daytona Beach, FL; SR; BS; Aerontcl Sci; Airline Trnsprt Plt.

**KIMPTON, DAVID J,** Youngstown St Univ, Youngstown, OH; SO; BS; Biology/Pre Med; Physician.**

**KIMREY, CRISTAL D,** S U N Y Coll At Fredonia, Fredonia, NY; SR; Phi Alpha Theta 90-; Delta Phi Epsilon Actg Pres 87-; Deans Lst 88-90; BA; Scl Stdy; Tchg.**

**KIMULI, CONSTANTINOS MAGIMBI,** Hellenic Coll/Holy Cross, Brookline, MA; SR; BA; Uganda Orthodox Yth Assn Treas Amer 88-90; Bsktbl/Soccer; Cer Engl Lang Ctr 88; CHWA Ii Memorial Clg 86; Hstry; Theology.

**KIMURA, NAMI,** Christopher Newport Coll, Newport News, VA; SO; BS; Intl Stu Assc Tres 90-; Biol; Vet.

**KINAL, KATHLEEN,** S U N Y At Buffalo, Buffalo, NY; JR; BA; Cntrbtg Wrtr Fr Generation Mag 90-; Univ Poetry Rdgs 90-; Beta Sigma Phi 90-; AA Family Radio Bible Clg; Engl; Avnt Grde Poet/Flm Noir Crtc.

**KINARD, CLINT E,** Ms St Univ, Miss State, MS; SR; BBA; Phi Theta Kappa 87-88; Dns Sclhr 88-; Pres Schlr 87-90; Bsns Mgmt.

**KINARD, KATHRYN L,** Univ Of Sc At Columbia, Columbia, SC; SO; BA; Chmbr Of Cmmrce 90; Elem Ed; Tchr.

**KINCADE, TESSA A,** Univ Of Sc At Columbia, Columbia, SC; JR; BS; Cmps Actvts Cncl 88-90; Wmns Stdnt Assc; Beta Beta Beta 88-; Phi Eta Sigma; Alpha Lambda Delta 89-; Alpha Delta Pi 90-; Acdmc Cncl 89-90; Biology; Medicine.

**KINCAID, ALICIA D,** Univ Of Cincinnati, Cincinnati, OH; SO; BS; Kappa Delta Schlrshp 90-; Bio; Physician.

**KINCAID, ELIHU E,** Salisbury St Univ, Salisbury, MD; SR; BS; 25 Stdnt Union VP; Kappa Delta Pi; T J Caruthers Awrd; U S Navy; Elem Tchr.

**KINCAID, JANET K,** Univ Of Sc At Columbia, Columbia, SC; GD; MSW; Psi Chi; Schlrshp; M Kershaw Walsh Awd; Med Asst; Ntrl Image; Diploma Huntington Clg Bus 73; CPR Redd Cross; Psychlgy/Soc Work.

**KINCAID, JEANNE E,** Wilmington Coll, Wilmington, OH; SO; BA; Hourglass Cmps Nwspr Wrtr 89-; Caroline Amory Black Coffee; Stdnt Foundtn; Alpha Phi Kappa Pblc Rltns 90-; Math/Hist.

**KINCAID, LISA M,** Tougaloo Coll, Tougaloo, MS; GD; BA; Elem Education; Teacher.

**KINCAID, MELISSA D,** Beckley Coll, Beckley, WV; FR; Nrsng/Sci.

**KINCAID, PRISCILLA K,** Univ Of Charleston, Charleston, WV; FR; BSN; Nrsng.

**KINCAID, RABECCA ANN,** Bluefield Coll, Bluefield, VA; JR; BA; Bapt Stdnt Un 88-; SGA Sec; Lambda Alpha Epsilon VP 89-; Phi Mu Delta Lil Sis 88-; Asstntshp Fac Advsry Com Corriculum Stdnt Life 89; Crmnl Jstce; State Police Invstgtn.

**KINCH, KIM A,** Inter Amer Univ Pr San German, San German, PR; BA; Drma Clb 82-83; Frgn Lng Clb 82-87; Alnc Frncs 87-89; Carbn Exmns Cncl 89; Univ Cambrdg 89; Psych; Psychologist.

**KINDER, ANGELA M,** Radford Univ, Radford, VA; FR; Bus; Mgt.

**KINDNESS, MICHAEL G,** Springfield Tech Comm Coll, Springfield, MA; SR; BA; Graphic Arts Clb Yrbk Stf 90-; Theater Grp Treas 88-89; Alpha Nu Omega 89-90; AS; Art; Graphic Dsgn Advertising.

**KING, ALLISON M,** Lesley Coll, Cambridge, MA; JR; Class Brd Pblcty 90-; Orientation Com 89-; Elem Ed; Tchng.

**KING, AMY T,** Univ Of Ky, Lexington, KY; SR; PALS 90-; Psi Chi 90-; Spec Popultns Swim Prog Dir 90-; Deans List; BA; Psychologyf PHD.

**KING, ANDREA D,** Daytona Beach Comm Coll, Daytona Beach, FL; SO; BA; Soc Of Ourselves 89-; Quanta 89-; Handicapped Serv; Teacher Aide Silver Sands Jr High 90-; English; Envrmntl Law.

**KING, ANGELA L,** Univ Of Tn At Martin, Martin, TN; JR; BS; Pre-Phys Therapy Clb 90-; Bio; Phys Therapy.

**KING, ANGELA L,** Alcorn St Univ, Lorman, MS; SR; BA; Music Edctrs Ntnl Cfrnce Pres 90; Alcorn State Univ Senate Mbr; Alpha Kappa Mu; Presser Schrlshp Winner 90; Music Ed; Educator.

**KING, ANGELA M,** Univ Of Southern Ms, Hattiesburg, MS; FR; BS; Stdnt Alumni Assn 90-; Stdnt Eagle Clb Phi Mu Rep 90-; Plymer Sci Clb 90-; Lambda Sigma; Phi Eta Sigma; Alpha Lambda Delta; Gamma Betga Phi; Phi Mu Chpln 90-; RUF 90-; Polymer Sci; Sls/Rsrch.

**KING, ANGELA P,** Piedmont Coll, Demorest, GA; JR; BED; Stdnt GA Assc Of Edctrs 90-; Natl Ed Assc 90-; Friends For Lf Pres 88-90; AS Emmanuel Coll 90; Early Chldhd Ed; Teaching.

**KING, ANITA A,** Livingston Univ, Livingston, AL; FR; BA; Ofc Mgr/Sec Springdale Lnd Mgmt 90-; Elem Ed; Tchg.

**KING, ANNETTE M,** Roane St Comm Coll, Harriman, TN; SR; BS; Phrmcy Tech 78-; AS 90; Early Chldhd Edn.**

**KING, ANTOINETTE,** Univ Of Md At Eastern Shore, Princess Anne, MD; SO; BA; Cmps Pal 90-; Stdnt Acvtvy Bd 90-; NAACP VP 89-; Airway Sci; Air Trfc Cmptrlr.

**KING, ARIAIL E,** Univ Of Sc At Columbia, Columbia, SC; JR; BA; Psi Chi Hnr; Golden Key; Gamma Beta Phi; Alpha Delta Pi 88-; Psychology; Law.

**KING, BARBARA A,** Univ Of Tn At Martin, Martin, TN; JR; BS; Math Assoc Of Amer; Univ Schlrs Org VP 88-90; Phi Eta Sigma; Phi Kappa Phi; Phi Chi Sigma Treas 89-90; Secndry Ed/Math; Tchng.

**KING, BETH ANNE,** Univ Of Miami, Coral Gables, FL; SO; MBA; Hnr Stdnt Assoc 89-90; Alpha Lambda Delta 90-; RA 90-; Henry King Stanford Schlrshp 89-; FL Undergrad Schlrshp 89-; Pres Hnr Rl 89; Provosts Hnr Rl 90-; Bsn; Acctg.

**KING, BOBBY L,** Univ Of Sc At Columbia, Columbia, SC; JR; BS; NROTC; USN Enl Cmmsng Prog; Sftbl E-5 82-; Math; History; Naval Offcr; Tchr.

**KING, BRENDA K,** Wv Univ At Parkersburg, Parkersburg, WV; FR; BA; Phi Theta Kappa 90-; Nrsng.

**KING, BRENNAN M,** Univ Of Fl, Gainesville, FL; SR; BA; Fncl Mgmt Assoc 90; Bsn Adm Clg Cncl 90; Omicron Delta Upsilon 90; Finance Intern Clerk Coast Fed S & L 90; Finance; Fncl Mgr.

**KING, BRIAN S,** Ga Inst Of Tech At Atlanta, Atlanta, GA; FR; BEE; Acad Tm 90-; Pres Mrt Schlp 90-; Gvrnrs Schlp 90-; Natl Mrt Schlr 90; Elec Engr; Mscl Elctrncs.

**KING, BRIDGET M,** Tn St Univ, Nashville, TN; JR; BS; INROADS 86-; Hnrs Clb 88-; Intrnshp Rlstn Prna Co 88-; Mjrtte Capt 88-; Chem.

**KING, CAROLYN K,** Fayetteville St Univ, Fayetteville, NC; GD; BS; NC Soclgcl Assn 90; Chnclrs Lst 89; Alpha Kappa Delta 90; NC Hdstrt Assn 87-90; Cert Soc Wrk; Soc Wrk.

**KING, CATHERINE L,** Radford Univ, Radford, VA; SR; Std Govt 90-; Intl Gvrn 90-; Elec Brd Chrp 90-; Exec Cncl Univ Pres 89-; BBA; Mktg; Corp Sls.

**KING, CHRISTOPHER E,** Univ Of Nh, Durham, NH; FR; BA; Cmps Rd Sttn 90-; Mrn Mml Strndng Tm 90-; Hll Govt Flr Rep 90-; Pltcl Sci; Law Govt.

**KING, CURTIS R,** City Univ Of Ny Queensbrough, New York, NY; GD; German Clb 89; Govt 87-89; Natl Bus Hon Soc; Alpha Sigma Lamda; Sls Rep; Us Army Vet; Gallo Wine Distr Inc 89; AAS; Bus Mgt.

**KING, DARREL T,** Fl International Univ, Miami, FL; JR; BA; Blck Union Pres 89-; Unrepr Peoples Pol Action Cncl 87-; NAACP 88-; Yth/Law Advocacy Intern; Ralph Burche Pol Sci Schlr 90; AOP Schlrshp 88-; Pol Sci; Corp Law.

**KING, DAVID A,** Middle Tn St Univ, Murfreesboro, TN; SR; BS; German Clb 88-89; Amer Chem Scty 89-90; Math Clb 90-; Fclty Achvmnt Awrd Physics; Deans Lst 90-; Ftbl 86-89; Physics; Research.

**KING, DEVA P,** S U N Y Coll Of A & T Morrisvl, Morrisville, NY; JR; ASUBA 89-; Ed; Tchr.

**KING, DOROTHY J,** Roane St Comm Coll, Harriman, TN; FR; BA; Math/Cmptrs; Educ.

**KING JR, ECKEL RAY,** Fayetteville St Univ, Fayetteville, NC; SO; BA; Psych Clb 90-; Self Help Thrpy Area Chair 88-; Quest Lctr/Asst/Crmnl Jstc Dept; Substance Abuse Cls ; Ay Trech Comm Clg; Univ Bowlng Trnmnt 1st; Vets Admin Vol 88-; HVAC Fyttvll Tech Inst 75; Cert NC Sbstnc Abuse Cnslr; Psych; Substance Abuse Cnslr.

**KING, EFFIE M,** Lincoln Univ, Lincoln Univ, PA; JR; BA; Natl Assn Blcks Crmnl Jstc Sec; Sclgy Clb; Crmnl Jstc/Sclgy; Law.

**KING, ELLIE M,** Albany St Coll, Albany, GA; SR; MBA; Std Govt 90-; Crmnl Jstc Clb 90-; AA Bainbridge Cllg; BS; Crmnl Jstc; Law.

**KING, ERIKA R,** Hampton Univ, Hampton, VA; SO; Psych Clb 89-; Mntrshp Big Bro/Str 90-; NAACP 90-; Hnr Stdnt 89-; Deans List 89-; Psychiatrist.

**KING, ESTHER R,** Central Fl Comm Coll, Ocala, FL; GD; BS; Interior Dsgn Clb 90-; Phi Theta Kappa 90-; Scl Serv Christ Cntr Wmns Pregncy Ctr; Interior Dsgn.

**KING, GLENN D,** Memphis St Univ, Memphis, TN; FR; BA; Pres Island Ind Assn VP 89-; Quality Assurance Mgr 86-; Bus; Bus Mngmnt.

**KING, HEATHER L,** Univ Of Ga, Athens, GA; FR; BSN; Hosp Vsttn; Phi Eta Sigma 90-; Stu Cncrn W/Sexual Awrnss 90-; Dean Lst 90-; Hnrs Day Rcpnt; Nrsng; Nrsng Spclst.

**KING III, HERBERT W,** Univ Of Nc At Charlotte, Charlotte, NC; SO; Dean Lst; Mech Eng; Eng.

**KING, IRENE E,** Tn Tech Univ, Cookeville, TN; SR; BS; Kappa Omicron Nu Sec 89-; Fd Ntrtn Diettcs Clb 89-; Tnsee Tch Hm Ecnmcs Assn 89-; Phi Kappa Phi; Insttnl Whlsl Co Schlrshp 90-; Whitlw Schlrshp 89-90; Uppr Cmbrlnd Diettc Assn 89-; Fd Ntrtn Diettcs; Admnstrtv Diettcs.

**KING, JAMES R,** Univ Of Sc At Columbia, Columbia, SC; SO; BS; Pres List 90-; Deans List 90-; Mech Eng.

**KING, JANICE N,** Jackson St Univ, Jackson, MS; FR; BA; Alpha Lambda Delta; Bsn; Acctng.

**KING, JASON C,** Univ Of Sc At Columbia, Columbia, SC; SO; BS; Racquetbl Clb 89-90; Phi Eta Sigma; Pres Lst 90; IM 89-90; Biology; Med.

**KING, JEANNE A,** Immaculata Coll, Immaculata, PA; JR; BMVS; Music Tchr 76-; Music Thrpy; MVS Thrpy.

**KING, JENNIFER E,** Univ Of Rochester, Rochester, NY; SR; BA; Glee Clb Pres 87-; SAVE; Schl Psych.

**KING, JENNIFER P,** Fl St Univ, Tallahassee, FL; SO; MBA; Phi Eta Sigma 89-90; Acctg; CPA.

**KING, JIMMY W,** Univ Of Al At Birmingham, Birmingham, AL; SO; BA; Clg Rpblcns 89-; Hmcmng Comm 90-; Alpha Lambda Delta Natl Delg 90-; Tau Kappa Epsilon VP; Campus Civitan 89-; Spec Awd Hnrs Convctn; Ldrshp Awd 90; Ambassador; IM Rec IM Sprts 89-; Acctg; CPA.

**KING, JOHN C,** Old Dominion Univ, Norfolk, VA; SO; BA; Hon Cncl; Bus; Law.

**KING, JOHN P,** Hudson Valley Comm Coll, Troy, NY; SR; ASSOC; Bus.

**KING, JON T,** Lincoln Univ, Lincoln Univ, PA; BA; Bsns Clb 89-; Spnsh Clb Tutor 88-; IM Ftbl 87-; Econs; Bsns Mgmt.

**KING, JONATHAN D,** Memphis St Univ, Memphis, TN; SO; BS; Stdnt Actvts Cncl Rcrtn Com 90-; Phi Eta Sigma 89-; Elect Eng.

**KING, JONATHAN E,** Bryant Stratton Bus Inst Roch, Rochester, NY; FR; AOS; Radio Station Vol 89-; Brdcstg Engr/Elctrnc Tech.

**KING, JULIA R,** Georgetown Coll, Georgetown, KY; SR; SGA 89-90; Sigma Delta Pi; Phi Mu IM Chpsn 88-; IM Bsktbl/Sftbl/Vlybl 87-; Elem Ed; Spanish; Tch.

**KING, KEITH A,** Middle Ga Coll, Cochran, GA; FR; AS; Engr Tech; Engr.

**KING, KEITH A,** Wv Univ, Morgantown, WV; JR; BS; ROTA 89-; IEEE 90-; Tau Beta Pi 90-; Eta Kappa Nu; Dns Hnr Lst 90; AF ROTC Schlp 9-; Educ Achv Awd USAF 89; IM Flg Ftbl 90; Srfsd Vol Rsc Sqd 88; USAF Ntns Sys Spec 85-89; AS Comm Clg AF 88; Elec Engr; Mltry Offcr/Elec Engr.

**KING, KELLY J,** Clark Atlanta Univ, Atlanta, GA; SO; BA; Engl Clb Sec 89-90; Coord Engl Clb Caribbean Evening 90; Hostess/Coord Engl Clb Retreat 89; Delta Sigma Theta Sec 90-; Vol Big Bethel AME Church Welcome Table 89-; Engl; Clg Prof.

**KING, LA TONYA C,** Tougaloo Coll, Tougaloo, MS; FR; BA; Stdnt Spprt Svcs 90; Pres Jdsn Crs Hl 90; Ldy Blk/Gld 90; Bsktbl 90; Eng; Law.

**KING, LAURA E,** East Tn St Univ, Johnson City, TN; SR; BS; Design Perspectives Treas 89-; Stdnt Advsry Cncl Sch Appl Sci/Tech 90-; Kappa Omicron Nu Pres 89-; Alpha Lambda Delta Secr 88-; Gamma Beta Phi 90-; Omicron Delta Kappa 90-; Phi Kappa Phi 90-; Vivian Rockwood Outstndg Jr Hm Ec 89-90; Hm Ec-Int Dsgn.

**KING, LUANNE,** Georgian Court Coll, Lakewood, NJ; SR; BS; Club Soccer 87-88; Womens Var Sftbl 87-; Sigma Phi Sigma 89-; Delta Mu Delta 90-; Cap Womens Var Sftbl; All Dist All Conf Sftbl; MVP Sftbl Team; MVP Dist 31 Trnmnt Sftbl 89-90; Var Sftbl 87-; BS; Bus Admnstrn Mktg Concernation; Marketing.

**KING, MARGARET W,** Univ Of Sc At Columbia, Columbia, SC; SO; Wrtng Awd 90; Litrcy Assn; Bio; Med.

**KING, MARIA P,** Univ Of North Fl, Jacksonville, FL; SO; MBA; MANA; NAPD; SPE; Indstrl Mtrls Slsprns VP; Mrktng.

**KING, MARIFRANCES,** Georgian Court Coll, Lakewood, NJ; SR; Club Soccer 87-88; Delta Mu Delta 90-; Rookie Yr Awd Varsity Sftbl 87-88; Sftbl 87-; BS, Busn Admin; Mktng Entertainment Ind.

**KING, MARK R,** Univ Of Miami, Coral Gables, FL; SR; BA; Brdcstng/Engl; Brdcstng.

**KING, MARSIE,** Watterson Coll, Louisville, KY; GD; DMA; Externship Imm Care Cntr; Licenses Reg Nurse By 1995; Medical-DMA; Medical-RN.

**KING, MARTHA J,** Univ Of Nc At Charlotte, Charlotte, NC; JR; BA; Math Tchrs 90-; NCCTM 90-; MAA 90-; Phi Eta Sigma 89-; Golden Key; Pi Mu Epsilon; Outstndg Coll Stdnts Of Am 89-; Math; Secondary Edn.**

**KING, MARTHA L,** Portland School Of Art, Portland, ME; SR; BFA; SG 86-90; Harley Flaws Schlrshp; Gen Hnr Schlrshp; Florence Lief Schlrshp; Painting.

**KING, MARVIN L,** Talladega Coll, Talladega, AL; FR; Spprt Srvcs 90-; Dean Lst; All Amrcn Schlrs; Bsbll Tm; Engl.

**KING, MARY E,** Univ Of Nc At Charlotte, Charlotte, NC; FR; BED; Intrvrsty Chrstn Fllwshp 90; Cvtns 90; Spns Chpl UCC Yth Fllwshp 89; Phi Eta Sigma 90; Deans Lst 90; Im Vllybl 90; Elem Ed; Tchr.

**KING, MEGAN T,** Kent St Univ Kent Cmps, Kent, OH; SO; BA; Deans List 90-; Marketing; Law.

**KING, MICHAEL D,** Univ Of Akron, Akron, OH; JR; BA; Sigma Iota Epsilon; Delta Sigma Pi Pledge Class Pres; Deans List 90; Tch Clg Deans List 88-89; Indstrl Mngmt; Bsn.

**KING, MICHAEL S,** Ms St Univ, Miss State, MS; GD; MBA; BA 90; Bus Admin.

**KING, MONA L,** Al St Univ, Montgomery, AL; JR; BS; Ele Educ; Tch.

**KING, MONICA A,** Memphis St Univ, Memphis, TN; JR; BA; Crmnl Jstc Clb 88-89; Drama Clb 88-89; Stdnt Prog Brd 88-89; Gamma Beta Phi 89-; Cmptr Sci; Systems Analyst.

**KING, NICHOLE M,** East Tn St Univ, Johnson City, TN; SO; BSN; Bio/Engl; Med.**

**KING, NICOLE MARIA,** Wilberforce Univ, Wilberforce, OH; SR; BS; Natl Stdnt Bsn League Mbrshp Chr 90-; Natl Assoc Blck Accntnts Pres 90-; Vogue Phi Vogue 2nd V P 90-; Alpha Kappa Mu; Eta Phi Beta; Delta Sigma Theta; Ashland Oil Inc UNCF Schlrshp; GM Schlrshp; NABA Schlrshp; AICPA Schlrshp; Acctg; Asst Auditor.

**KING, PAMELA J,** City Univ Of Ny Baruch Coll, New York, NY; JR; BBA; Dnce Clb 89; Acctng; Real Est.

**KING, PETER I,** Univ Of South Fl, Tampa, FL; SR; BSN; Fla Coll Indr Scr Tm 87-88; Martial Art Tae Kwon Do Rd Blt 88-; VA Hosp; Sigma Theta Tau Inc 90-; Valor Nrsng Stdnt Tampa 90-; BSN; Nrsng.

**KING, RICHARD E,** Western New England Coll, Springfield, MA; SR; BA; Pre-Law Soc Pres 88-; Pol Sci Clb; Intrnshp Springfld Dist Crts Clerks Ofc 90; Govt; Law.

**KING, RICHARD P,** Temple Univ, Philadelphia, PA; SR; BARCH; Tenapue Assn Stdnt Architects 90-; Rural/Urban Dvlpmnt Asst Tm Phila 90; Asstntshp Architecture Dsgn Studio; Res Asst Temple Univ 89-90; Architecture.

**KING JR, RICHARD W,** Old Dominion Univ, Norfolk, VA; SO; BS; Newport Nws Shpbldng Dsgnr 84-85; Marinette Marine Corp De Operator 85-88; Diversified Tech 88-; Assoc Triangle Inst Tech Pittsburgh Pa 83; Mech Eng.

**KING, ROBERT H,** Univ Of Miami, Coral Gables, FL; SO; Golf Club 89-; Chess Club 90-; Alpha Lambda Delta 89-90; Phi Eta Sigma 89-90; IM Golf Sftbl Ftbl 89-; Econ/Fin; Bus.

**KING, ROBIN E,** Rivier Coll, Nashua, NH; SR; BA; Comm Srvce Orgnztn 88-; Phi Sigma Rho Mrshll 88-; Elem Educ; Tchng.

**KING, ROY C,** Memphis St Univ, Memphis, TN; SO; BA; Univ Hon Prog; US Navy Vet 69-74; Sales Rep Comp Indstry Svc Tech 70-88; Fin/Real Estate; MBA.

**KING, SAMANTHA K,** Radford Univ, Radford, VA; JR; BS; Geoloical Socty Treas 90-; Sigma Gamma Epsilon Pres 90-; Assn Engr Geologist VP; Geology; Hydrlgst/Environmntlst.

**KING, SCOTT D,** Bethany Coll, Bethany, WV; FR; BS; Stdnt Brd Gvnrs Rep 90-; Frshm Actvts Cncl 90-; Amnesty Internatl 90-; Kalon Ldrshp Soc 90-; Appalachia Workcamps 86-; Amnesty Internatl 90-; Betany Clg Recycling Cordntr 90-; Kalon Ldrshp Schlrshp 90-; Var Crs Cntry Trk 90-; Econ Poltcl Sci; Internatl Relations.

**KING, SCOTT D,** Savannah Coll Of Art & Design, Savannah, GA; FR; BFA; Soc Of Illus 90-; Soccer 90-; Graphic Dsgn/Illus; Advrtsg/Grphc Dsgn.

**KING, SERREDA R,** Univ Of Nc At Charlotte, Charlotte, NC; SR; BS; Phi Beta Sigma Aux P 88-90; ABLE 89-90; NAACP 89-90; Pblc Sfty Intrn 89; Pblc Dfndrs Ofc Intrn 90-; IM Vlybl 87; Crmnl Just.

**KING, SOPHIA LAFRANCE,** Al A & M Univ, Normal, AL; SR; BA; Kappa Kappa Mu 90; Acctg Clb 89-; Delta Sigma Theta 89-; Acctg.

**KING, STEPHANIE S,** Univ Of Sc At Lancaster, Lancaster, SC; FR; BSN; Pres List 90; Nursing; Comm Hlth.

**KING, STEPHEN B,** Western Carolina Univ, Cullowhee, NC; SR; Blgy Clb Sec 90-; Prepro VP Pblc Affrs 88-; Advsry Com 90-; WESC 90-; Phi Kappa Phi 90-; Alpha Lambda Delta 87-; Pi Kappa Phi; Merit Awd; Schlrshp 89; BS; Blgy; Vet.

**KING, STEVEN W,** Univ Of Pittsburgh At Bradford, Bradford, PA; FR; BS; Stdnt Govt Assn Foods Com Chrmn 90; Radio Clb DJ Msc Mgr 90; Aviation Sci; Pilot.

**KING, TAWN K,** Tougaloo Coll, Tougaloo, MS; FR; BS; Msssspp Sthrn Bnk; Blgy.

**KING, TERI C,** Bethel Coll, Mckenzie, TN; SO; Bethel Bsn Clb Treas; Bethel Sci Clb 90-; Beta Sigma Phi Pres; Henry Cty Chmbr Comm Intern; Bsn Adm/Acctg.

**KING JR, THOMAS L,** Univ Of Al At Birmingham, Birmingham, AL; JR; BS; Stndt Occupational Therapy Assoc 90-; AS John C Calhoun Cmnty State Cmnt Clge 90; Occupational Therapy.

**KING, TONYA JEAN,** Owensboro Jr Coll Of Bus, Owensboro, KY; SR; ASSOC; Cmptrzd Ofc; Htl/Rstrnt Mgr.

**KING, VINCENT E,** Morehouse Coll, Atlanta, GA; FR; BA; Atlanta Univ Ctr Art Clb 90-; Morehouse Clg Hnrs Prog Clb Publ Comm Chr 90-; W E B Dubois Hl Clb Hmcmg Comm Chr 90; Engl; Nvlst.

**KING, WILLIAM K,** Wilmington Coll, New Castle, DE; SR; BS; Soc Cable Tele Eng 84-; Tech Mgr 84-; AA Delaware Tech Comm Clg 78; Busn Mgmt.

**KING-OGG, CHERYL LYN,** Univ Of Tn At Martin, Martin, TN; SR; BA; History.

**KING-SMITH, HEATHER E,** Westminster Coll, New Wilmingtn, PA; SR; BA; Stdnt Govt Assn 90-; Serv Tm 90-; Psi Chi VP 89-; Omicron Delta Kappa 90-; Pi Sigma Pi 90-; Rsdnt Dir 90-; Henrietta Lee Schlrshp 90-; Mdwstrn Psychlgcl Assn Cnfrnc; IM Sftbl/Ski Clb 90-; Psychlgy; Med.

**KINGDON, ALICIA D,** Univ Of Miami, Coral Gables, FL; SO; BA; Earth Alert 89; Amnesty Intrntnl 89; Henry King Stanford Half Tuition Schlrshp; Anthropology; Research Anthropologist.

**KINGERY, JAMES C,** Western Ky Univ, Bowling Green, KY; SR; Wstrn KY Mddl Sch Assoc 90-91; Dns Schlr 87-88; Pres Schlr 89-; B Ed 91; Mddl Grds Educ; Tchr.

**KINGERY, TRACEY L,** Marshall University, Huntington, WV; FR; BA; Rsdnc Hll Assoc 90-; Fnc.

**KINGHORN, JULIE A,** S U N Y Coll At Fredonia, Fredonia, NY; SR; BS; Snd Serv Treas 89-90; Audio Engr 89-; Snd Tech.

**KINGMAN, CHRISTINE,** Atlantic Comm Coll, Mays Landing, NJ; SO; Art Clb; Charles Dooner Awd; Hghst Grd Pnt Avrg; Dr David Cooper Awd; S Shr Fndtn; Nrs Ad; LPN Atlantic Co Voc Tech N J St Brd Nrsg 87; AAS 90; Nrsg; RN.

**KINGSBURY JR, ROBERT N,** Coker Coll, Hartsville, SC; SR; BA; Alumni Trophy; Magna Cum Laude; U S Army 74-; AA Columbia Clge Columbia MO 88; Social Science/Psychology; Teaching.

**KINGSLEY, CHRISTOPHER,** Hudson Valley Comm Coll, Troy, NY; SR; AAS; Cmptr Drafter; Indus Tech Mgmt; Cmptr Aided Drftng.

**KINGSLEY, URSULA R,** D Youville Coll, Buffalo, NY; SO; BS; Bsn Clb Sec; Bsn Ed; Scndry Ed.

**KINGSTON, DOROTHY,** Hudson Valley Comm Coll, Troy, NY; FR; ASSC; Dntl Asst 90; Nrsng; Mstrs In Nrsng.

**KINGSTON, JEANETTE F,** Slippery Rock Univ, Slippery Rock, PA; JR; BA; IM Sprts 88-; House Cncl 88-89; Phi Eta Sigma 88-89; Phi Epsilon Kappa 88-89; Deans Lst 88-; Phy Ed; Phy Thrpy.

**KINGSTON, JONATHAN,** City Univ Of Ny Baruch Coll, New York, NY; JR; BA; Aux Plc Offcr 109 Pct Ptrlmn 90-; Lt WHVRS Qns Cnty Fld Spvsr 88-; Deans Lst 89-; Chf Amblnc Oprtns 89-; Fresh Mdws Vol Amblnc Chf; Rpblcn Clb 25th AD 90-; Intrn US Rep Scheuer Dist Offc Asst 88; Intrn NYS Assmblymn D Prescott 90-; Pltcl Sci; Law.

**KINLAW, TODD A,** James Sprunt Comm Coll, Kenansville, NC; SO; AS; Gold Tm Richard Bland Coll VA 88-89; Comp Bus Info Syst.

**KINMAN, JOY K,** Cumberland Coll, Williamsburg, KY; FR; BME; Bapt Stu Union 90-; Flwshp Athlts 90-; Mu Phi Epsilon; Vlybl; Music Educ; HS Choral/Bnd Dir.

**KINN, ANNMARIE,** Alfred Univ, Alfred, NY; JR; BA; Stdnts Free Enterprise 89-90; Delta Mu Delta; Tennis 90-; Bus Admin; Advrtsng.

**KINNAN, STEVEN V,** Nova Univ, Ft Lauderdale, FL; GD; MBA; Institute Intrnl Adtrs 90; Intrnl Adtr 85; BA Wstrn State Clg CO 82; Bnkng.

**KINNE, LYNETTE M,** Bapt Bible Coll & Seminary, Clarks Summit, PA; SO; BA; Elem Ed.

**KINNEY, ALLISON A,** Duquesne Univ, Pittsburgh, PA; FR; BA; Stdnt Advsry Cmtee Fresh Rep 90-; Orntatn Stf Co Ldr; Fresh Ldr 90-; Dealta Sigma Pi Prfsnl Co Ed Bus V P; DUV Awd Duquesne V Vol 90; Intl Bus/Fin Japan; Bus.

**KINNEY, MELANIE D,** Chattahoochee Vly St Comm Coll, Phenix City, AL; SO; BA; SGA Sec 90-; Bsns/Music; Int Dectr.

**KINNON, ALFREDA L,** Fl A & M Univ, Tallahassee, FL; FR; PHARM; Phi Eta Sigma; Schlstc Achvmnt Awd; Phrmcy.

**KINSELLA, DEBORAH L,** Saint John Fisher Coll, Rochester, NY; JR; BA; Acdmc Achvmnt Awd 88-89; AS Monroe Comm Coll 90; Comm/Jrnlsm.

**KINSELLA, SUSAN B,** City Univ Of Ny Queensbrough, New York, NY; SO; AAS; Phi Theta Kappa; Tau Alpha Pi; Mech Engr.

**KINSERVIK, FRAN B,** Valdosta St Coll, Valdosta, GA; JR; BA; Sclgy/Anthrplgy/Crmnl Jstc Clb 89-; Alpha Chi; Alpha Kappa Delta; Pi Gamma Mu; Lowndes Advcy Rsc Ctr Intshp; Jnr Wmns Clb 90-; Park Ave Untd Meth Chrch 86-; Sclgy; Mrrg/Fmly Thrpy.

**KINSEY JR, BILLY W,** Va Commonwealth Univ, Richmond, VA; JR; BA; Jennings Soc VP 90-; Hons Prog 89-; Phi Eta Sigma Sec 90-; Gldn Ky VP; Lib Dir Srch Comm Rep 90-; Econs; Tchr.

**KINSEY, GEOFFREY H,** Savannah Coll Of Art & Design, Savannah, GA; JR; MFA; Scad Crw 89-90; Eng Tutr 90; Soc Canottieri; Dns Lst 90; Intrnshp Mktg Gen Inc 90; Intrnshp Ntl Geo Soc Wash DC; Smstr Flrnc Italy/Syrcs Univ; Fn Arts; Illstr.

**KINSEY, KAREN J,** Indiana Univ Of Pa, Indiana, PA; SR; Orientation 87-88; RHA 86-88; Hist Club 89-90; Alpha Xi Delta 89-90; Deans List 89-90; Stdnt Tchng 90; BSED 90; Soc Studies Ed; Tchng.

**KINSEY, TAMMY L,** Marshall University, Huntington, WV; JR; BBA; Hl Advsry Comm 88-89; IMS Tm Rep 89-90; Pnhlnc Cncl Treas Elect; Alpha Chi Omega Publctns Chr Elect; HELP Pgm Tutor 89-; Bsn Mgmt; Corp Bsn.

**KINSINGER, JACQUELINE C,** Prince Georges Comm Coll, Largo, MD; SO; BA; Deans Lst 89-90; Sftbl 89-90; Bwlng 90-; Business Adm.**

**KINSLEY, DAVID J,** George Mason Univ, Fairfax, VA; JR; BS; US Marine 84-90; Fin; Cert Fincl Plnnr.

**KINSLEY, KATHLEEN,** S U N Y At Binghamton, Binghamton, NY; SR; BS; Rogues 89; Intrnshp Emplyee Asst Pgm; Dnc Hrt Amer Hrt Assn; Bus Mgmt-Hmn Rsrcs.

**KINSLEY, PETER D,** Univ Of New Haven, West Haven, CT; JR; BS; Harvard Natl Model Untd Ntns 90; Alpha Lambda Delta; CT Dept Crctns Vol; Mktg Analyst; Pblc Admin/Hlthcre Cntrtn; Hlth Care Indus.

**KINSMAN, CICI,** City Univ Of Ny Grad School, New York, NY; SR; BS; Tchr Karate Self Defense Chldrn Adlts Cntr Anti Vlnc Ed Brklyn NY 86; Grphc Arts Prfssnl 84; Consciousnss Social Chng; Intrntl Wmns Dvlpt.

**KINTISCH, JEAN M,** Cornell Univ Statutory College, Ithaca, NY; JR; BS; PRSSA Pres 88-; Delta Delta Delta Phlnthrpy Chr 88-; Publ Rels Intern; Pgm Asst 90-; Cmnctn; Mktg Cmnctns.

**KINTNER, PAUL W,** Bapt Bible Coll & Seminary, Clarks Summit, PA; GD; M MIN; Msnry Bptst Mid Msns S A; TH B Baptist Bible Seminary 65; Mnstry/Msns.

**KINZELER III, C WILLIAM,** Univ Of Dayton, Dayton, OH; FR; Var Bsbl; Engr.

**KINZER, KEVIN W,** Columbus Coll Of Art & Design, Columbus, OH; JR; BFA; Sndy Schl Tchr 82-; Gertrude Gibbons Mem Schlp 90-; Fine Arts; Painter.

**KINZLER, GEORGE P,** Old Dominion Univ, Norfolk, VA; JR; BSED; Ralph C Dumack P E/ASSOC Strctrl Engrs 88-90; AMET 90; Cvl Engr Tchnlgy; Strctrl.

**KIPPERMAN, GIDEON,** City Univ Of Ny City Coll, New York, NY; JR; DBA; Archt.

**KIPPLE, DWAYNE W,** Me Maritime Academy, Castine, ME; JR; BS; US Naval Inst 83; US Navy League 86; Rsdnt Assist NROTC Fnce Offcr; Alpha Phi Omega 88; Trng Rate TV State Of Me; Nautical Sci; Naval Offcr.

**KIPUST, JOANNE S,** Yeshiva Univ, New York, NY; SR; BA; Obsrvr Lyout Cpy Edit 89-; Ltrry Pblctns Edit 88; Intrnshp Lbcm Advrtsng 89; Engl Cmmnctns; Pblshng.

**KIRBY, AMIE M,** Union Univ, Jackson, TN; SO; BSBA; Bapt Stu Union 89-; Flwshp Chrstn Athlts 89-; Hnr Stu Assoc 89-; Chi Omega 89-; Spcl Olympics Jcksn Tn 89-; Acctg; CPA.

**KIRBY, ANITA K,** Middle Tn St Univ, Murfreesboro, TN; SR; BS; Boy Scouts Com Mem 89-; Early Chldhd Edn; Teach.

**KIRBY, ANN L,** S U N Y Coll At Fredonia, Fredonia, NY; JR; BS; Elem Ed; Elem Schl Tchr.

**KIRBY, DARRELL H,** Univ Of Louisville, Louisville, KY; JR; MENG; Am Soc Mech Engrs 90-; Occidental Chem Corp Intern; Mech Eng.

**KIRBY, JACQUELINE,** Atlantic Comm Coll, Mays Landing, NJ; SO; BA; Phi Beta Lambda 88-90; AAS 91; Acctg; CPA.

**KIRBY, JEREMY P,** Ma Inst Of Tech, Cambridge, MA; JR; BS; Stdnt Govt VP 91-; UA Alchl Pol Comm Chrmn 90-; MIT Collqm Comm Mbr 90-; Alpha Delta Phi VP 89-90; Sen Gore Intrn 90; Securd Motorcd Drvr Mandella US Tour Wash DC 90; Wm L Stewart Jr Awd; Pol Sci; Law/Pol.**

**KIRBY, JOYCE H,** Liberty Univ, Lynchburg, VA; SO; Alpha Lambda Delta 89-; Deans Lst 90; Engl; Scndry Educ.

**KIRBY, MICHAEL W,** Univ Of Louisville, Louisville, KY; SR; MENG; BA Morehead St Univ 87; Cvl Engr; Army Corps Engrs.

**KIRBY, SCOTTY L,** Life Coll, Marietta, GA; FR; DC; Chrprctr.

**KIRBY, THOMAS SHANE,** Bethel Coll, Mckenzie, TN; SO; BS; Var Bsktbl 89-; Math Clb Tr 90-; Gamma Beta Phi Tr 90-; Math/Chem; Eng.

**KIRCHER, EVELYN,** Lexington Comm Coll, Lexington, KY; SO; BED; Hndcpd Stdnt Org Treas 90-; Dns Lst 90-; Elem Ed; Tchg.

**KIRCHMYER, MATTHEW J,** Fl St Univ, Tallahassee, FL; JR; BA; African Drumming Ens; Viola De Casba Ens; Mortar Brd; Music.

**KIRCHNER, JENINE G,** Mount Aloysius Jr Coll, Cresson, PA; FR; AA; Mountebank Plyrs Amature Theatre; Commuter Asst Ofc Stdnt Srvcs 90-; Liberal Arts; Tchng/Cnslng.

**KIRCHOFF JR, EDWARD,** Tomlinson Coll, Cleveland, TN; SO; BA; Chorales 89-90; AS; English Writing.

**KIRGAN, DAVID M,** Liberty Univ, Lynchburg, VA; FR; BS; Govt; Law.

**KIRIBAMUNE, NAVINCHANDRA B,** Oh Wesleyan Univ, Delaware, OH; SO; BS; Horizons Intrntl 89; Scty Of Physics Stdnts; Pi Mu Epsilon; Sigma Pi Sigma; Phi Eta Sigma Phi Scty 90; Florence Leas Prze For Excllnce 90; Pre-Eng/Physics; Eng.

**KIRK, DAVID R,** Univ Of Al At Huntsville, Huntsville, AL; JR; BA; Elec Tech Tow II Missl 90; Elec Engr; Photo Optcs/Commnctn.

**KIRK, DEBORAH L,** Va Commonwealth Univ, Richmond, VA; SR; Amer Mrktng Assoc 90; Golde Key 90; Intrnshp With The Va Opera; Mrktng; Sales.

**KIRK, JERRY L,** Memphis St Univ, Memphis, TN; SR; BS; IEEE; AOPA; Gamma Beta Phi; Tau Beta Pi; Elctrcl Engr.

**KIRK, KRISTEN M,** Savannah Coll Of Art & Design, Savannah, GA; SR.

**KIRK, LARRY T,** Univ Of South Fl, Tampa, FL; SO; BA; Hspce Hllsbrgh Fmly Vol 89-; Music/Voice; Msc/Entrtnmnt.

**KIRK, LISA M,** Fl St Univ, Tallahassee, FL; FR; BA; Lady Scalphntrs Spirit Hnry 90; Phi Eta Sigma 90; Cmmnctns.

**KIRK, LORETTA L,** Central Al Comm Coll, Alexander City, AL; SO; ASBS; Bsns Admn; Comp Prog/Acctg.**

**KIRK, LYDIA K,** Middle Tn St Univ, Murfreesboro, TN; SR; Peer Cnlslr 88-89; STEA 89-; Deans Lt 88-; AS Columbia State Comm Coll 89; BS; Elem Sbjcts; Elem Ed.

**KIRK, NIPHON J,** Hampton Univ, Hampton, VA; SR; BS; Students VA Education Assoc SVEA 88-; CEC Summer Peer Counsel Pres 88-; Deans List; Special Ed; Bilmgual Spl Ed.

**KIRK, REBECCA L,** Radford Univ, Radford, VA; FR; BA; Wesly Fndtn Stdnt Cncl Nwsltr Edtr; Radford Hillel Exec Mbr 90-; Wesly Fndtn Clwn Trp 90-; Univ Hnrs Pgm 90-; Phi Sigma Pi; Hnrs Pgm Nwsltr Wrtr; Otdr Rec; Chld Psych.

**KIRK, TARA B,** Univ Of Charleston, Charleston, WV; FR; Vlybl Tm; Psych.

**KIRK, WENDY D,** Univ Of Tn At Martin, Martin, TN; SR; BS; Crmnl Jstc Soc Tres 90-; Ellngtn Hl Rep; Rsdnt Hl Assn; Deans Lst 90-; Phi Alpha Delta 89-; Amnsty Intrntnl 90-; Chrch Chrst Stdnt Cntr 88-; Crmnl Jstc; Law.

**KIRK, WENDY E,** Northeast Ms Cc, Booneville, MS; SO; BA; Ftre Bus Ldrs Amrca 90-; Orientation Cnslr 90-; Frshmn Class Fvrite 89-90; Frshmn Hmcmng Maid 89-90; Sphmore Class Fvrite 90-; Sphmore Hmcmng Maid 90-; Tlnt Rstr Cert Achvmnt Distngshd Acdmc Prfrmnce; AA; Bus Admn; Lwyer.

**KIRKBRIDE, JODI A,** Washington State Comm Coll, Marietta, OH; FR; BA; Phi Theta Kappa; Acctg.

**KIRKENDOLL, LELAND K,** Lane Coll, Jackson, TN; JR; Soph Cls VP 89-90; Jr Clss Pr 90-; Alpha Phi Alpha VP 89-; Chrstn Yth Flwshp 87-88; Chrch Choir 87-; NAACP 90-; Bsktbl 88-89; Cmptr Sci.

**KIRKER, KERRI A,** George Mason Univ, Fairfax, VA; JR; BA; Golden Key 90-; Alpha Chi; Gamma Phi Beta Stndrds 90-; Elem Educ.

**KIRKHAM, KRISTY L,** Birmingham Southern Coll, Birmingham, AL; SO; BS; Pre-Law Soc 89-; Jazz Bnd 90; Phi Eta Sigma 90-; Alpha Lambda Delta 90-; Zeta Tau Alpha Schlrshp Chrprsn 89-; IM Ftbl/Sftbl 89-; Pol Sci; Law.

**KIRKLAND, BARBARA H,** Piedmont Tech Coll, Greenwood, SC; SR; NVTHS 90-; Deans Lst; Atmtd Ofc.

**KIRKLAND, CHRISTIANA R,** Strayer Coll, Washington, DC; JR; AA; Entrprnr Csmtc Corp 90-; Dns Lst 89-; Pres Lst 89-; Natl Assoc Fml Exec; Admin Asst Law Frm/Goal Admin Attrny; Bsn Admin; BA/ADMIN/LAW.**

**KIRKLAND, DAWN R,** Livingston Univ, Livingston, AL; SO; BS; Cncrt Bnd 89-; Amer Chemcl Soc 90-; Alpha Sigma Tau Rcrdng Sec 89-; Chmstry.

**KIRKLAND, DONNA MICHELLE,** Coppin St Coll, Baltimore, MD; FR; Chemf Chem Engr.

**KIRKLAND, ERICKA A,** Fl A & M Univ, Tallahassee, FL; FR; BS; Comp Info Sys Nwsppr Rprtr; Pres Schlrs Assn Co Chrprsn; Fam Gspl Chr Ms Pres SchlrsPHI Eta Sigma; Lfe Gt Bttr Schlr; Pres Schlrs Assn; Intrnshp IDS Corp; Cath Yth Orgnztn; Comp Info Systs; Syst Anlyst Mgmt.

**KIRKLAND, LINDA K,** Roane St Comm Coll, Harriman, TN; FR; Radiology.

**KIRKLAND, SHERRY R,** Piedmont Tech Coll, Greenwood, SC; SO; AS; Phi Beta Lambda VP 90-; Phi Theta Kappa 90-; Bus; Acctng.

**KIRKLAND, THADDEUS,** Cheyney Univ Of Pa, Cheyney, PA; SR; BA; Toast Mstrs Intl 89-; Dns Lst 90; Wine Psi Phi 73-; Comm; Cnslng.

**KIRKLIN, PERCY L,** Tuskegee Univ, Tuskegee Inst, AL; SO; BS; Track; Aeronautical Engr; MS.

**KIRKMAN, LAURA L,** Univ Of Nc At Greensboro, Greensboro, NC; SO; BS; Bapt Stdnt Union Cncl; Elem Educ; Tchng.

**KIRKMAN, TRACEY L,** Univ Of Va, Charlottesville, VA; FR; BA; Blck Stndt Allnc 90-; Blck Voices 90-; Economics; Corp Law.

**KIRKPATRICK, AMY MICHELE,** Ringling School Of Art, Sarasota, FL; SR; BA; Printing Monotype Intern; AA Fla Comm Clg 89; Printmaking; Fine Arts/Mstr Prntr.

**KIRKPATRICK, GERALD C,** Univ Of Nh Plymouth St Coll, Plymouth, NH; SO; BS; Pemi-Baker Emer Hmls Shltr Brd Chr 89-90; Pblc Mgmt.

**KIRKPATRICK, HOBERT B,** Va Highlands Comm Coll, Abingdon, VA; SO; AAS; Law Enf Clb 90; Army Natl Guard 89; Phi Theta Kappa; Police Sci; Law Enf.

**KIRKPATRICK, KIMBERLY A,** Gallaudet Univ, Washington, DC; JR; BA; Swim Tm 88; Recycling Com 90; Dns Lst 90; Psych; Ed/Cnslg.

**KIRKPATRICK, LENA G,** Middle Ga Coll, Cochran, GA; SO; BS; Bptst Union VP 89-; Nwspr Staff Wrtr 90-; Geolgy.

**KIRKPATRICK, RONALD G,** Nova Univ, Ft Lauderdale, FL; GD; MBA; Magna Cum Laude 65; Natl Sci Fdtn Assis 65-66; Mngr/Advnc Plnng/G E Govt Servs; BA Okla City Univ 65; Mgmnt; Tech.

**KIRKPATRICK, STEVEN L,** Palm Beach Comm Coll, Lake Worth, FL; SO; AA; Deans Lst 89-; Chmstry; Medicine.**

**KIRKPATRICK, THOMAS KEITH,** Roane St Comm Coll, Harriman, TN; SO; SGA Sntr; Std Mrshl 90; Clg Tutor; High GPA; Alma Nelson Mem Schlp; TN Brd Rgnts Wrk Schlp; Tnns 89; Mech Engr.

**KIRKSEY, APRIL D,** Southeastern Comm Coll, Whiteville, NC; SO; ASSOC; Stu Nrs Assoc; Coll Brd Tlnt Rstr Otstndg Mnrty Comm Coll Grads; Mrshl For Grdtn 90; Nrsg; RN.

**KIRKWOOD, LARRY J,** Jackson St Univ, Jackson, MS; FR; BS; Hnrs Clg; Math; Engr.

**KIRKWOOD, YVETTE R,** Fl A & M Univ, Tallahassee, FL; SR; BA; White/Gold 90; FAMU Crny Org 90; Hnywl Bull Bstn Intrn 87; Ptny Bwls Stnfrd Ct Intrn 88; Prdntl Ins Intrn 89; Bus Admin; Law Sch.

**KIRMSE, KRISTINA J,** Carnegie Mellon Univ, Pittsburgh, PA; SR; BS; Grphc Cmnctn Mgmt 89; Stdnt Org; Chi Omega Rush/ Prsnl 86; Indus Mgmt/Grphc Cmnctns; Prntng Mgmt.

**KIRNES, ANDRE C,** Middle Tn St Univ, Murfreesboro, TN; SR; MBA; Cross Sabers 81-83; Alpha Phi Alpha 82-; NCAA Track All-Am 80/83; Dstngshd Military Grad 83; Track Tm 79-83; US Army Capt 86-; BS Bio 83; Bus Admin; US Army Ofcr.

**KIRSCH, WILLIAM P,** Eckerd Coll, St Petersburg, FL; JR; BS; Fla Natl Gd Offcr Cand Schl; Cmptr Sci; Engr.

**KIRSCH, WILLIAM R,** Univ Of West Fl, Pensacola, FL; SR; BA; Crtfd Gmlgst Amrcn Gem Soc 86; Jwlr 79-; BS 74; Edctn; Tchng.

**KIRSCHMAN, REBECCA A,** S U N Y Coll At Fredonia, Fredonia, NY; JR; BA; Assoc Jamestown Cmnty Clg 89; Art; Grphc Dsgn.

**KIRSCHSTEIN, MARGARET A,** City Univ Of Ny Baruch Coll, New York, NY; JR; BA; Coll Chorus 88-; Gold Key 90-; Deans Lst 89-; Intrnshp Times Nwswkly 90-; Jrnlsm; Sports Rprtng/PR.

**KIRSH, KATHLEEN E,** Oh Univ, Athens, OH; SO; BFA; The Slcng Edge Msc Jrnl Art Drctr 90-; Graphic Dsgn/Illstrn.

**KISER, ANNETT,** Johnson C Smith Univ, Charlotte, NC; JR; Royal Ins Intrn; Bus; Mktg.**

**KISER, DAVID M,** Nc St Univ At Raleigh, Raleigh, NC; SO; BA; Amer Hlcptr Soc 89-; Metcalf Lvng Lrng Pgm UCA 89-; Aerspc Eng; Eng.**

**KISER, KATHLEEN D,** James Madison University, Harrisonburg, VA; SR; BS; Stdnt Nrs Assn 89-; Nrsng Hnr Soc Sec 89-; Golden Key 89-; Phi Kappa Phi; Natl Coll Nrsng Awd 89-; Nrsng; RN.**

**KISER, NATHAN A,** King Coll, Bristol, TN; SO; BS; Physics/ Math; Physicist.

**KISER, ROBERT BLANE,** Saint Andrews Presbytrn Coll, Laurinburg, NC; JR; Stdnt Senate; Dorm Pres; Honor Soc; Bus Admin; Private Business.

**KISER, TRINA R,** Marshall University, Huntington, WV; GD; Sigma Tau Delta 87-; Rosanna Blake Schlp 90-; Tech Asst 89-90; Frnch Instctr Comm Adlt Educ Pgm 88-; BA 87; AS 84; Engl; Prfssr.

**KISH, BARBARA M,** S U N Y Coll At Postdam, Potsdam, NY; SR; BM; Intrntl Hrn Scty 88-90; Kappa Delta Pi 89-; Musc Educ/ Spcl Educ Musc; Tchg.

**KISHI, KOUICHIRO,** Salem-Teikyo Univ, Salem, WV; FR; BA; Newspaper; Stdnt Hndbk Comm; Res Life; Stdnt Fclty Conduct Comm; Gov Acad Ldrshp; Intl Cmnctns.

**KISIN, NATHAN,** Ny Univ, New York, NY; JR; BS; Chmbr Dpts 88-89; Econ Clb 90-; Econ/Intrntl Bus; Anlyst/Cnsltnt.

**KISS, CLARISSA C,** Wheeling Jesuit Coll, Wheeling, WV; FR; BA; Pr Ttrng; Deans Lst 90-; Hlth Sci; Rsprtry Thrpy.

**KISSELL, KAMILLA DACIA,** Univ Of Ma At Amherst, Amherst, MA; TTRA 87-; SEEP; CIEE 88; Intrnshp Slm Cmbr Cmmrc Adim Intrn; BS Leisure Stds/Rsrcs Univ Mass; Trvl Trsm/Spnsh; Trvl Admin.

**KITAJIMA, CHIZUKO,** Bay Path Coll, Longmeadow, MA; SO; AS; Gldn Clb Treas 89-; Maroon Key Pres Schlshp 90-; Ryvo Travel Serv 79-89; AA Tokyo Womens Jr Clg 76; Mrktng; Hotel Mngr.

**KITANI, MASAMI,** Albertus Magnus Coll, New Haven, CT; SR; BA; Tau Pi Phi 91-; Kappa Gamma Pi 91-; Admn Asst CEO Japan 81-89; Bus Econ/Fin; Bus.

**KITCHEN, KIMBERLY S,** Univ Of Ky, Lexington, KY; SR; BA; Delta Zeta 89-; Elem Edn; Teach.

**KITCHENS, DANA L,** Itawamba Comm Coll, Fulton, MS; FR; Hstry; Elem Educ.

**KITCHENS, JOHN F,** Middle Ga Coll, Cochran, GA; SO; BA; Bapt Stdt Union 88-90; AA; Bsnss Admin; Law.

**KITCHENS, STACI J,** Western Ky Univ, Bowling Green, KY; SO; AB; SGA Jr Cls Svp 90-; Univ Hnrs Prog 89-90; Panhellenic Assn Hstrn 90-; Phi Eta Sigma 90-; Pi Mu Epsilon 90-; Phi Kappa Phi; Alpha Delta Pi VP 89-; Math/Econ; Actuary.

**KITE, SALLY L A,** Middle Tn St Univ, Murfreesboro, TN; SR; BA; Band Of Blue 84-90; Jazz Ensmbl Sec 85-87; Clrnt Choir 84-89; Band Blue Schlrshp 84-90; Otsdng Concrt Bnd Awd 89; Clarinet Awd 88; Instrmntl Mus Educ; Band Dir.

**KITSOS, LINDA W,** Greenville Tech Coll, Greenville, SC; GD; CERT; Med Machine Trncrptn.

**KITTEL, VICKY L,** Comm Coll Algny Co Algny Cmps, Pittsburgh, PA; FR; Acctg.

**KITTLE, KATHERINE M,** Univ Of South Al, Mobile, AL; SO; Beta/Gamma Area Cncl Gamma Area Rep 90; Grtr Gulf Literacy Cncl Tutor; Soccer; Early Childhood Educ; Educ Teaching.

**KITTLER, ERICKA M,** Western New England Coll, Springfield, MA; JR; BA; Pre-Law Soc 90-; Pol Sci Clb 90-; ALA Brkshr Comm Clg 88-90; Pol Sci; Law Schl.

**KITTLESON, ANDREW P,** Univ Of Rochester, Rochester, NY; JR; BS; Roberts Wesleyan Clg Stdnt Assc Dir Stdnt Fin 89-90; ASME 90-; Alph Kappa Sgm; Mech Eng.

**KITTRELL, ANNIE B,** Vance Granville Comm Coll, Henderson, NC; GD; Voctnl Clb Advsry Comm.

**KITTRELL, LISA MICHELLE,** Middle Tn St Univ, Murfreesboro, TN; SR; BA; Gamma Beta Phi 88-; Alpha Kappa Psi V P 90; Busn Mgmt.

**KITZMAN, STEVEN K,** Univ Of Rochester, Rochester, NY; JR; BS; Amer Scty Mech Eng 89-; Audio Prdctn Eng 90-; Tau Beta Pi Treas 90-; Mech Eng.

**KIUCHI, SHIZUKO,** Albertus Magnus Coll, New Haven, CT; SR; BA; Athletic Assn Treas 89-90; Acad Deans List 90-; Schlr Athl Awd 90-; Vlybl/Capt/Swmng/Sftbal 87-; Communications; Advrtsng.

**KIVEL, BRIAN W,** Western New England Coll, Springfield, MA; SR; BA; Karate Clb 87-89; Amer Hapkido Assc 89-; Psych Intrnshp 90; James Z Navrison Schlrshp 88; Cert Real Est St MA 90; Psych; Bus/Sales.

**KIVI, MARK J,** Belmont Coll, Nashville, TN; JR; BBA; Audio Eng Soc; Prod Publ Intrn Rt 66 Music; Belmnt Golf Tm 90; Music Busn; Law Schl.

**KIYAGA, MICHAEL,** Stockton St Coll, Pomona, NJ; SO; BA; Chrstn Un Treas 88-89; Fnce/Acctng.

**KIZART, ETTA M,** Alcorn St Univ, Lorman, MS; SO; BA; Res Hall Cncl 89-90; Cmptr Sci/Appld Math; Prgrmr.

**KIZELNIK, YOSEFA D,** Yeshiva Univ, New York, NY; SR; BA; Club Canada Sec 89-; Stdnt Cncl Treas 90-; Deans Lst 88-; Psychology; Speech Path/Audiology.

**KIZER, BRIAN S,** Univ Of Sc At Columbia, Columbia, SC; SR; BA; Stdnt Govt Rep 88-89; Hist; Scndry Edn.

**KIZZIAH, KRISTIE G,** Univ Of Nc At Greensboro, Greensboro, NC; SO; BS; Intrvrsty Chrstn Flwshp 89-; Psychlgy Indpndnt Stdy; Soc Wrk; Schl Soc Wrkr.

**KIZZIRE, MICHAEL D,** Central Al Comm Coll, Alexander City, AL; FR; MBA; Bsbl Schlrshp 90-; Math; CPA.

**KJEER, BRIAN C,** Hillsborough Comm Coll, Tampa, FL; FR; AA; Gnrl; Law.

**KJEER, DAVID C,** Hillsborough Comm Coll, Tampa, FL; JR; BA; Busn; Acctg.

**KJELLERUP, BINE,** Univ Of Miami, Coral Gables, FL; FR; BFA; Fine Art; Grphc Dsgn.

**KLABEN, JASON D,** Le Moyne Coll, Syracuse, NY; SR; Rgby Clb 88; Delta Mu Delta Sr Mem 90-; Acctng Intrnshp Aloha Lsng 89-; Exec Fnncl Inst Mdl; IM Bsktbl Tm Capt 87-; BS; Acctng; Pblc Acctng.

**KLARE, JULIE L,** Univ Of Cincinnati, Cincinnati, OH; JR; BS; Vlybl Tm 90-; Stdnt Paralegal Assn 88; Fld Plcmnt Law Offc; AAS 90; Crmnl Jstc Paralegal.

**KLASMEYER JR, RONALD M,** Anne Arundel Comm Coll, Arnold, MD; SO; BSBA; Phi Theta Kappa 90-; Intl Bsn; Bsn.

**KLAUDA, KATHERINE A,** Columbia Greene Comm Coll, Hudson, NY; SO; Phi Thetta Kappa Treas 89-; Bus Div Awrd; Chrch Mouse Nrsry Schl Pres Treas 88-; AAS; Accntng.

**KLAUS, MICHAEL G,** Atlanta Christian Coll, East Point, GA; SR; B TH; Families Of Atlanta Chrstn Coll Stdnt Rep 90-; Ramser Schlrshp Atlanta Chrstn Coll; Pres Schlrshp 89; Yth Mnstr Intern S W Chrstn Ch 90-; Yth Cnslr Teenage Runaway Shl; AA Santa Fe Comm Coll 83; BS Fl St Univ 88; Theo; Ministry.

**KLAYMAN, ELISA R,** Bunker Hill Comm Coll, Boston, MA; SO; AD; Deans Lst; Nrsng; BSN.

**KLEAR, JOYCE A,** Defiance Coll, Defiance, OH; SR; BSW; Stu Soc Wrk Orgn 89-; Tchng Rlgn MR Stu Prmry 90; Jr Intern Wmn Fmly Serv 89; Sr Intern Coping Cntr Defiance Hosp; Soc Wrk; Gdnc Cnslr H S.

**KLEBAUR, SARAH J,** Castleton St Coll, Castleton, VT; SO; BA; Intl Clb Treas 90-; Deans Lst; Pres Schlrshp 89; Spnsh/Bus; Intl Rel/Bus.

**KLEE, ERIC A,** S U N Y Coll At Brockport, Brockport, NY; JR; Alpha Chi Treas; Sngl Rpnt Mag Hnr; Engl; Wrtng.**

**KLEEHAMMER, ELISSA R,** Fl St Univ, Tallahassee, FL; JR; BS; Golden Key 90f Psi Chi 90; Deans Lst 88; Outstndng Soph 90; Oustndng Jr 91; Phi Kappa Phi Chptr Hnrs 89-90; Psychlgy; Studies.**

**KLEIN, BETHEL J,** Teikyo Post Univ, Waterbury, CT; FR; BA; Interior Dsgn; Hstrcl Dcrtn.

**KLEIN, BRIDGET M,** Univ Of Cincinnati, Cincinnati, OH; JR; BM; Chrl Prgm Pres 85-89; Drm Clb 85-89; Delta Epsilon Sigma 87-89; Stdy Abrd Schlrshp; Chrl Prgm Schlrshp 85-89; CCM Tlnt Schlrshp 89-; Wrnr Schlrshp 90-; BA 85; Vc Prfrmnc.

**KLEIN, CHRISTINA L,** Wagner Coll, Staten Island, NY; SO; BA; Allied Hlth Pre Med 90-; Stdnt Art League 90-; Italian Club 90-; Althea 90-; Deans Lst 90-; Amer Red Cross 87-; Dental Asst 87-; IM Vlybl; Art/Bio; Dentistry.

**KLEIN, DAVID P,** Univ Of Southern Ms, Hattiesburg, MS; FR; BS; Am Chem Soc 90-; Gamma Beta Phi 90-; Deans List 90; PADI Cert Scuba Diver Adv Open Water With Night Diving Speciality 90; Marine Bio/Forenbsic Sci; Aquacltr Fish Frmng.

**KLEIN, DONALD J,** Tri County Tech Coll, Pendleton, SC; FR; AS; AS Tri County Tech Coll 88; Math; Engrng Elctrncs.

**KLEIN, ERIC J,** Stevens Inst Of Tech, Hoboken, NJ; FR; BE; Jazz Ensmbl 90-; Stvns Acad Fllwshp 90-; Chem Engr.

**KLEIN, JULIE B,** West Liberty St Coll, West Liberty, WV; SR; BS; Stdt Env Actn Cltn Fndr/Pres 90-; Chi Beta Phi Pres 90-; Soc Ethel Trtmnt Anmls 89-; Rgn Educ Serv Asc; Schlp 89-90; AS Ventura Clg 89; Bio/Chem.

**KLEIN, MICHELLE A,** Univ Of De, Newark, DE; FR; BA; Theatre Pub Chrmn 90-; Galadrim Sci Fictn Clb Socl Chr 90-; Engl; Film.

**KLEIN, MITCHELL J,** Fl Atlantic Univ, Boca Raton, FL; SR; BS; Nihon Takai Yama Karateo Do 85; AA Catonsville Cmmnty Clg 87; Cmptr Info; Cmptr Sci.

**KLEIN, SEAN J,** Georgetown Univ, Washington, DC; JR; BSBA; Admsns Ambsdr Prog 88-90; Sch Bus Admn 90-; Deans Lst 89-; Delta Sigma Pi 89-; Intrn Cngrsmn Geo Hochbrueckner; Acctlg; Law.

**KLEIN, SUSANNA B,** Va Commonwealth Univ, Richmond, VA; SO; BMUS; Orchstra Msc Ensmbls Cncrt Mstrss 89-; Hon Pgm; Pres Schlr; Pres Schlrshp; Msc Schlrshp; Hon Schlrshp; Msc Prfrmnc; Orchstrl Pro Mscn.

**KLEINER, PENNY P,** Mount Aloysius Jr Coll, Cresson, PA; GD; BA; Phi Theta Kappa 89-; AS; Sci; Medcl Lab Techncn.

**KLEINMAN, MONICA A,** City Univ Of Ny Baruch Coll, New York, NY; GD; MBA; Mgmt Hsptl Admn.

**KLEINSCHMIDT, HEIDI M,** Kent St Univ Kent Cmps, Kent, OH; JR; BA; Univ Sclrshp 90-; Ind Fmly Studies; Chld Life Spclst.

**KLEINSTUBER, ELLEN L,** Elizabethtown Coll, Elizabethtown, PA; JR; BS; Math Clb V P 89-; Cncrt Bnd 89-; Alpha Lambda Delta Pres 89-; Pi Mu Epsilon 90-; Delphi Sec; Mathmtcs; Actrl Cnsltnt.**

**KLEMIC, GEORGE G,** Case Western Reserve Univ, Cleveland, OH; FR; BS; Chs Clb Sec 90-; Symphnc Winds 90-; Prsdntl Schlrshp; IM Rcqtbl; Math; Acdmc.

**KLEMPA, BRYAN T,** S U N Y Coll Of Tech At Delhi, Delhi, NY; SO; Assoc Genl Cntrctrs Am 90-; Peer Tutor 90-; US Army Res Pfc; AS; Math/Sci; Eng Mgmnt.

**KLEMPNER, MICHAEL M,** City Univ Of Ny Baruch Coll, New York, NY; JR; BBA; Baruch Schlr; Finance/Invstmnts.

**KLEMS, KATHRYN M,** Univ Of Cincinnati, Cincinnati, OH; JR; BED; Acdmc Tutor 90-; Rsrrctn Schl PTO Pres 87-88; Co Pres 90-; Erly Chldhd Ed; Tchr.

**KLENZ, SARA A,** S U N Y Coll At Geneseo, Geneseo, NY; FR; BA; Ski Clb; Spnsh Clb; Almn Assc; Spnsh; Pblshng.

**KLEPIC, ANTHONY R,** Emory & Henry Coll, Emory, VA; SR; BA; SVEA 88-90; Phi Gamma Phi Pres 86-90; Vars Ftbl 86-89; Hist; Tchr.

**KLEPPER, SONYA C,** Univ Of Nc At Asheville, Asheville, NC; JR; BA; Sierra Clb; Hiking/Snow Skiing UNCA Outing Clb; Mass Communication/Lit; Advrtsng/Jrnlsm.

**KLESSEN, MARTHA A,** S U N Y At Buffalo, Buffalo, NY; JR; BS; Recrtnl Sftbl 89-90; Ski Club 89-; Anti Rape Tsk Frc 89-; Golden Key 90-; Bus Admn; Fin.

**KLETNICKS, CAROLYN G,** Radford Univ, Radford, VA; JR; AS Canton Coll Of Tech 85; Gen Studs.

**KLIBER, ALLISON A,** Duquesne Univ, Pittsburgh, PA; SO; BS; Univ Vol 89-; Campus Mnstry 89-; Pre-Hlth Prfsns Soc 90-; Lambda Sigma 90-; SHARP 89-; Bio/Pre-Med; Med.

**KLICKA, THERESA K,** De Tech & Comm Coll At Dover, Dover, DE; BAS; Phi Thetta Kappa V Pres 89-90; Non Traditional Oneer Schlrshp 88-89; Kent General Hospital 89-; AAS; Architecture; Engineering.

**KLIEBER, BONNIE R,** Fl St Univ, Tallahassee, FL; JR; BME; Tau Beta Sigma; CMENC 90-; FMENC St Rcrtmnt Chr; AA New Wrld Schl Arts 90; Music Educ-Gnrl; Tch/Elem Schl.

**KLIGMAN, JOSEPH F,** Univ Of Sc At Columbia, Columbia, SC; SR; BS; Eta Sigma Delta; Alpha Epsilon Pi; Pres Hnr Lst; Dns Hnr Lst; Rugby Clb; Hotel Rest Toursm Admin; Hosp Ind.

**KLIMA, WILLIAM C,** Roane St Comm Coll, Harriman, TN; SO; AA; Singers 89-; Music.

**KLIMEK, PAUL E,** Davis Coll, Toledo, OH; SO; AS; Fctry 76-82; Sm Trctr Trlr Drvr 82-; Avtn Admn.

**KLIMKEWICZ, LYN A,** Le Moyne Coll, Syracuse, NY; JR; BA; Indstrl Rel Clb; Soc Human Res Mgmnt; Bus Clb; IRL Clb; Deans Lst; Big Sis; Dorothy Day Vol; Food Drives; Vlybl/Wlybl/ Indoor Soccer; Indstrl Labor Rel; Law.

**KLIMUSZKO, JOAN M,** Fl St Univ, Tallahassee, FL; JR; BA; Acctng Scty; Hnrs/Schlrs Pgm; Gldn Key; Deans Lst 89-; Bus/ Acctng; Cpa.

**KLINE, CHERYL L,** Univ Of Cincinnati, Cincinnati, OH; SO; ASSOC; Coop Educ Wrk At Cincinnati Gas/Elec Co; Chem Tchnlgy; Chmstry.

**KLINE, DONNA M,** Allentown Coll Of St Francis, Center Valley, PA; FR; BSN; Stdnt Nrs Orgnztn Cmtr 90-; Nwspr Frmt Edtr 90-; Dance Instrctr 85-; Aerobics Cls 90-; Nrsng; Crtcl/ Emerg Care Nrsng.

**KLINE, FRANCIS D,** Atlantic Comm Coll, Mays Landing, NJ; SR; AAS; Prof Chefs Assn 90; Prfct Attndnce Award; Silver Medalist; Culinary Arts; Chef.

**KLINE, JENNIFER D,** Glassboro St Coll, Glassboro, NJ; JR; BA; Pblc Rltns Stdnt Soc Of Amer Assist To The Treas 90; Women In Cmmnctns Inc 89-90; Deans Lst 88-90; Cmmnctns/ Pblc Rltns; Pblc Rltns Prctnr.

**KLINE, MARY E,** Kent St Univ Geauga Cmps, Burton Twp, OH; FR; AA; Vietanm Vets Amer Assoc 88-; Qlty Cntrl Inspctr 83-89; Nrsng; RN Trauma Tm.

**KLINE, STEPHANIE GWEN,** Univ Of Rochester, Rochester, NY; JR; BA; Panhellenic Cncl Pres 89-90; Meridian Soc; Hmn Rltns Advocate; Order Of Omega 90-; Sigma Delta Tau Pledge Class Offcr 88-; Cmps Y 88-89; Prtnrs Rdng 89-90; Intrnshp Arthritis Fndtn; Intrnshp Vietnamese Refugee Ctr; Psychlgy/Pltcl Sci.

**KLINEDINST, DAVID M,** Central Pa Bus School, Summerdale, PA; FR; BA; Pathfndrs Cnslr 90-; Busn; Humn Res/Finc.

**KLINGBEIL, LISA M,** Univ Of Cincinnati, Cincinnati, OH; JR; BSED; AFB Sec 90-; Radio DJ/FCC Lcns 89-90; CPR Crtfctn 90; IDEA Fndtn Arbcs Instrctr Crtfctn 90; Crew; Hlth Prmtn/ Crdvsclr Ftnss; Exrcs Physlgy.

**KLINGELSMITH, SHELLEY L,** Oh Univ, Athens, OH; JR; BFA; IM Spts 89-90; Dns Lst 88-; Graphic Dsgn/Illstrn; Ilslstr/ Grphc Dsgnr.

**KLINGENBERG, TERESA L,** Washington State Comm Coll, Marietta, OH; GD; AA; Stdnt Govt V P 89-90; Phi Theta Kappa 89-; Walt Disney World Clg Intern 90; AA Brdcstg; Sls/Mktg.

**KLINGENBERG, VICTORIA A,** Univ Of Toledo, Toledo, OH; FR; Flag Corps; Bsktbl; Band; Kappa Kappa Psi; Dance Productions; Hnrs Pgm; Church Choir Duets; Outstndg Flg Corps Perf; Antrhrplgy/Biolgy; Genetics.

**KLINGER, MARK E,** Alfred Univ, Alfred, NY; FR; Alpha Lambda Delta; Klan Alpine; Deans Lst 90-; Var Ftbl 90; Bus; Acctg/Law.

**KLINGINSMITH, LAURA R,** Univ Of Akron, Akron, OH; SR; BS; Am Inst Chem Engr 87-; Outstdg Clg Std Am 87-; Gdyr Tire/Rubber Co Intrn 87-90; Coop 90-; Chem Engr.

**KLINGLER, KATHRYN DIANE,** Oh St Univ At Newark, Newark, OH; FR; BS; Wmn Eng 90-; Alpha Lambda Delta 90-; Phi Eta Sigma 90-; Habitat Hmnty 89-; Eng; Ind/Syst Eng.

**KLINK, MICHAEL C,** Univ Of Ct, Storrs, CT; SR; BS; Plnt Sci/Horticulutre.

**KLINKLER, CHRISTY L,** West Liberty St Coll, West Liberty, WV; JR; BS; Chi Beta Phi Pres; Little Sis Gamma Sigma Tau 89; NASA Tchstn Rsrch Labs; Biol/Chem; Rsrch.**

**KLITCH, JENNIFER L,** Oh St Univ, Columbus, OH; SR; BA; Co-Dir Sr Clss Gft Comm; Hons Stdnt/Cmpltd Hons Cntrct 87-90; Phi Beta Kappa/Phi Kappa Phi 90-; Prtcptd Fndrsng Cystic Fbrsis/Hrt Assn/M S 83-; Phi Kappa Phi Grad Flwshp; Pro Tnns Plyr Num 50 Wrld 82-88; Psych; Law.

**KLITZKE, HUGH P,** Glassboro St Coll, Glassboro, NJ; SO; BED; Cncrt Bnd; Cncrt Chr; Jazz/Lab Bnd; Lab Thtr; Orch; Cntmpry Msc Ens; Trmbn Quartet; Artists Ed Rghts; Orch Librarian 90-; Deans Lst; Music Ed/Composition; Composer.

**KLOC, DAWN M,** D Youville Coll, Buffalo, NY; FR; SOTA 90-; Cmps Mnstry 90-; Lambda Sigma; Cthlc Chrch Lector 90-; Deans List 90-; Occptnl Thrpy; Hlthfld.

**KLODZINSKI, KRISTI MICHELLE,** Memphis St Univ, Memphis, TN; SR; BA; Mrchng Bnd 86-88; Var Bnd 86-88; Flag Rifle Corp 86-; Psychology; MA Psychology.

**KLOEK, ANDREW P,** Western Ky Univ, Bowling Green, KY; SR; BS; Sci/Recmbnt Genetics; MS.

**KLOEKER, D ANNA M,** Northern Ky Univ, Highland Hts, KY; SR; BA; Elem Educ; Tchr.

**KLOHE, WILLIAM F,** Hudson Valley Comm Coll, Troy, NY; FR; BA; Elec Cnstrctn/Maintenance; Elctrcn.

**KLOMP, SARAH A,** Allegheny Coll, Meadville, PA; JR; BA; Rsdnt Advsr 90-; ALLIES Schlrshp Wknd Coor 89-; Lambda Sigma Fndrsng Chrmn 89-; Kappa Alpha Theta Pres 91-; Alden Schlr 88-; Dstngshd Alden Schlr; Doane Schlr 88-; Theta Phila Almne Schlrshp; Mu Chptr Schlrshp Rng 89; Hstry Engl; Pblshng.

**KLONOWSKA, EWA A,** City Univ Of Ny Baruch Coll, New York, NY; JR; BBA; Gldn Key 90-; Bus; Law.

**KLOPCIC, REBECCA S,** Franklin And Marshall Coll, Lancaster, PA; FR; Comm Orchestra; Pre Hlg Arts Clb; Michael A Lewis Physics Awrd; CRC Press Chem Achvmnt Awrd; Sccr 90; Trck; Med.

**KLOPFENSTEIN, MARY K,** Univ Of Tn At Martin, Martin, TN; SR; BS; Psi Chi 88; Deans Lst Hon Rl 86-; Psychology/ Philosophy; Cnslr.

**KLOPP, BETHANY L,** Univ Of Cincinnati, Cincinnati, OH; FR; BED; Chi Alpha 90-; Piano Rectl Accomp 90-; Sigma Alpha Iota; Musc Schlrshp 90-; Hnrs Thry/Musc Cours 90-; Musc Ed; Prof Muscn/Tchr.

**KLOSINSKI, JEAN M,** Univ Of Pittsburgh, Pittsburgh, PA; SO; BSN; Alpha Tau Delta Crrspndng Sec 89-; NSNA 90-; SNAP 89-; Hartford Hosp Intrn Clncl Nrsng Asst 90; Nrsng; Srgcl MSN.

**KLOSNER, JOHN D,** Fl A & M Univ, Tallahassee, FL; SR; BS; AGC; AIAS 86-87; Jaycees 88; Engr Tech; Bsn/Urban Plng MS.

**KLOSS, BRIAN L,** Univ Of Scranton, Scranton, PA; JR; BS; Acctng Soc 88-; Bus Club 88-; Phi Alpha Theta 90-; Natl Collgt Bus Merit Awrds 88-; PICPA 90-; Natl Assoc Of Acctnts 90-; Im 88-; Acctng; Law.

**KLOSSING, KIMBERLI K,** Univ Of Tn At Martin, Martin, TN; SO; BED; Edn; High Sch Engl Tchr.

**KLOSTERMAN, KATHLEEN A,** Univ Of Cincinnati, Cincinnati, OH; JR; BMED; Flying Clb Pres 87-; Cncrt Orchestra 90-; Northern Ky Msc Soc 90-; Msc Educ/Violin Cncntrtn; Orchstra Tchr/Tchr.

**KLOTZ, MAUREEN A,** Niagara Univ, Niagara Univ, NY; JR; BA; Stdnt Govt V P; Acctg Soc 90-; Stdnt Advsr - Dn Bsn; Dns Lst 90-; IM Vlybl 88-; Alpha Kappa Psi Chr Fndrsg 89-; Cherry City Vol Fire Co Helper-Spec Events 86-; Polish Falcons Amer Asst Elder; IM Wallybl 88-; Acctg; CPA.

**KLUG, CHRISTIE M,** Seton Hall Univ, South Orange, NJ; FR; BSN; SHUFL 90-; Pr Advsr; Vrsty Swm Tm 90-; Nrsng.

**KLUGE, MATTHEW B,** Emory Univ, Atlanta, GA; SR; BBA; Fin Clb 90-; Invstmnt Clb 90-; USAA All Amer Schlr Clgt Awrd; Beta Gamma Sgm; BBA; Fin.

**KLUMP, SARA E,** Christian Brothers Univ, Memphis, TN; FR; BA; Wmns Assn Mtvt Spirit Phlnthrpst 90-; Vrsty Vlybl 90-; Sci/ Physcl Thrpy.

**KLUNK, PATRICIA E,** Asnuntuck Comm Coll, Enfield, CT; AS; Acctg-Word Prcssg/Admnstrtv.

**KLUNK, WENDY L,** Franklin And Marshall Coll, Lancaster, PA; SR; Engl Clb Pres 88-; Wrtng Ctr Tutor 90-; Phi Beta Kappa; SAMS Vice Chrprsn 87-90; Env Actn Allnce 90-; Hackmn Schlr Intrnshp 88-90; BA; Engl; Law.

**KLUSMAN, KAREN M,** Univ Of Ky, Lexington, KY; FR.

**KLYMOK, THEODORE W B,** Tomlinson Coll, Cleveland, TN; SR; BA; SFL 89-; HOME 90-; Alpha Chi; All Amdricn Schlrs; Phi Theta Kappa 89-90; Fire Escp Mninstrs Dir 89-; Pres List 89-; Msns Schlrshp Chrch Of God Of Prphcy 89-; Tennis/Rollr Sktng/ Team Sprts; APFGGA 83-; CSME 83-; Mech Engr; BA; Minstry; Engr.

**KMECZA, KATHRYN N,** Univ Of Nc At Asheville, Asheville, NC; SO; BS; Envrmntl Stds.

**KMETZ, DANA J,** Western New England Coll, Springfield, MA; SO; BA; COPE 90-; Acctg.

**KMIEC, CAMILLA,** City Univ Of Ny Baruch Coll, New York, NY; JR; BBA; Acctncy; CPA.

**KNABLE, SHEILA R,** Owensboro Comm Coll, Owensboro, KY; FR; BA; Hist; Scndry Ed.

**KNAGGS, MARY E,** Bergen Comm Coll, Paramus, NJ; SO; MS; Phi Theta Kappa 90-; Cmmnctn Scie/Disorders; Speech Pathologist.

**KNAPINSKI, GREGORY J,** Kent St Univ Kent Cmps, Kent, OH; JR; BS; Pre Med Assn 90-; Inter Hall Cncl 88-89; IM Bsktbl/Wrstlng 88-; Biol/Pre Med; Med Schl.

**KNAPKA, MARY E,** Smith Coll, Northampton, MA; JR; Cmps Crsd Chrst 88-; Chr 88-89; Frnch Horn Piano Lsns 88-89; Amer Stds; Rsrch Advcy.

**KNAPP, DAVID A,** Elmira Coll, Elmira, NY; SO; Psychotherapist.

**KNAPP, MELISSA A,** Univ Of Rochester, Rochester, NY; SR; BS; SWE P 88-; Vars Tnns 87-90; Elec Eng.

**KNAPP, MICHAEL S,** Allegheny Coll, Meadville, PA; SR; BA; French Tutor 90; Doane Scholar 89-90; Phi Sigma Iota; French; French Professor.

**KNAPP, STEVAN A,** Castleton St Coll, Castleton, VT; SO; BA; Stdnt Gov S 90-; Math Clb P 90-; Coll Rpblcns VP 89-90; Phi Eta Sigma 89-90; Math; Eng.

**KNARR, TRACY L,** Indiana Univ Of Pa, Indiana, PA; JR; BS; Elem Educ; Tchng.

**KNAUB, KAREN E,** Indiana Univ Of Pa, Indiana, PA; SR; RHA 87-; Natl Res Hall Hon; Cncl Excptnl Chldrn 89-; PSEA 90-; Vrsty Vlybl 87-; BED; Ed Excptnl Prsns; Tchng.

**KNAUF, WENDY L,** Youngstown St Univ, Youngstown, OH; FR; BED; Cntrns; Deans Lst; Foundation Schlrshp; Math; Tchr.

**KNAUPP, ROBERT E,** Hudson Valley Comm Coll, Troy, NY; SO; AS; Business; Administration.

**KNAUSS, JULIE A,** Univ Of Akron, Akron, OH; SO; BA; Rsdnc Hall Cncl RHC Rep 90-; Prog Brd Mjr Evnts Com 90-; Rsdnt Asst; Natl Rsdnc Hall; Hons Prog 89-; IM Sports 89-; Mrktng.

**KNAZOVICH, GEORGIA G,** Pellissippi St Tech Comm Coll, Knoxville, TN; SO; Pellissippi Prlgl Assc 90-; Deans List; Cert Trvl Cnslr; BA San Jose State Univ 70; Legal Assist Technlgy; Law.

**KNEBEL, CONSTANCE A,** Broward Comm Coll, Ft Lauderdale, FL; JR; MBA; Violin Schlrshp 75-77; Amer Penn Wmns League Schlrshp; Art Museum Of Ft Laud; Art Contempories Of FL; Stk Brkr; Art; Educ.

**KNEDLIK, HEIDI J,** Converse Coll, Spartanburg, SC; SR; BA; Stdnt Faclty Rltns Cmtee 89-90; S G 88-90; Palmetto Plyrs 88-; Alpha Lamda Delta 88-89; Alpha Psi Omega 88-; Delta Omicron 89-; Hospice Vol 89-; Cir K 89-90; Marshall 89-90; Cnvrse Schlr V P 89-; Ldrshp Schlrsp 87-; Biology/French; Intl Hlth.

**KNEECE, JOSHUA F,** North Greenville Coll, Tigerville, SC; SO; BA; Baptst Stdnt Un 89; Joyful Sound; FCA; Campus Ambsdrs; Bio Club; Pep Club; Inner Missn Christn Drama Team; Rec Club; Engl; Baptst Mnstr.

**KNEELAND, CHRISTINE M,** Elms Coll, Chicopee, MA; JR; BSN; Stdnt Nrss Assoc 90-; Nrsng.

**KNEIS, HEIDI A,** Catholic Univ Of America, Washington, DC; JR; BA; Undrgrad Stdnt Govt/Legslatv Brnch Drm Rep 90-; Res Hall Cncl VP 89-90; IM Vlybl Capt 88-90; Elem Ed; Tchng.

**KNEISEL, JAMES A,** Bentley Coll, Waltham, MA; SO; BA; Ski Team 89-90; Emerging Ldrs Prog 90-; Deans Lst 89-; Ski Team 89-90; Acctng; CPA.**

**KNEPFLER, KRISTINA M,** S U N Y Coll Of Tech At Alfred, Alfred, NY; FR; ASSC; Outdoor Rcrtn Clb 90-; Confrmtn Mtngs 90-; IM Sccr Sftbl 90-; Math Sci; Phys Thrpy.

**KNEPP, CATHY L,** Marywood Coll, Scranton, PA; JR; BS; Cncl Excptnl Chldrn Pan Crdntr 88-; PA Assoc Rtrd Ctzns 88-; Tchrs Tomorrow 89-90; Educ; Tchr.

**KNEPPER, KIRBY S,** Duquesne Univ, Pittsburgh, PA; FR; BS; Mentor Pgm 90-; Untd Meth Chrch Chr/Pianist 83-; 4h Lvstck Clb 81-; Phi Eta Sgm 90-; Deans List 90-; IM Vlybl Bsktbl 90-; Pharm.

**KNERLY, VICKY W,** Fl International Univ, Miami, FL; SO; BA; Bus/Prfssnl Wmns Clb Pres 86-; Compas Proj Inc 88-89; Natl Assn Fmale Exec 89-; Lgl Sec/Eng Sec/Psnn Tech/Sls Admin/Sr Admin Aide 81-; AOS Cntrl City Bus Inst 84; Engl/Wrtng Cncntrtn; Admin.

**KNERR, MARCIE E,** Lehigh County Comm Coll, Schnecksville, PA; FR; ASSOC; Deans Lst 90-; Phi Theta Kappa 90-; Ofc Tech/ Legal Asst; Paralegal.

**KNESHTEL, MICHELLE R,** Univ Of Montevallo, Montevallo, AL; FR; Alpha Lmbd Dlt; Lbrl Arts.

**KNIBB, ROBERT B,** City Univ Of Ny City Coll, New York, NY; SR; BA; Jr Vrsty Bsktbl 81-82; Natl Bsktbl Assn Leag Offc 82-; Sclgy; Law.

**KNICK, MELISSA D,** Tn Temple Univ, Chattanooga, TN; SO; BS; Athltc Dir Coach 90-; Vrsty Vlybl/Bsktbl Capt 89-; Scndry Educ/Phy Ed; Coach/Tch HS.

**KNIER, L DONALD,** Appalachian Bible Coll, Bradley, WV; GD; MA; Sprtl Life Comm 86-90; Prayer Warriors Pres 87-90; Mission Conf Comm 87-90; Class Pres 88-90; Stdnt Cncl Rep 87-90; Contact 85; We Can 89-90; Soccer Co Cap 87-; BA 90; Biblical Cnslng.

**KNIGHT, AMANDA S,** Hillsborough Comm Coll, Tampa, FL; FR; AA; Eng; Ms Cmnctns.

**KNIGHT, BONNIE P,** Univ Of Sc At Columbia, Columbia, SC; SO; Stdnt Govt Assoc Pres 90; Otstndng Stdnt 90; Bthl Untd Mthd Chrch Chr; AS 91; Appld Math.

**KNIGHT, BRIAN D,** Western Carolina Univ, Cullowhee, NC; JR; BS; Stdnt Advsry Comm 90-; Deans Lst 90-; Comp Sci; Prog.

**KNIGHT, CHERYL B,** Univ Of Sc At Sumter, Sumter, SC; JR; BA; Sumter Ed Assc 89-; Dept Awd Div Humanaties Ed-Scl Sci 89; AA 90; Edctn; Erly Chldhd Ed.

**KNIGHT, CHERYL B,** Univ Of Sc At Sumter, Sumter, SC; JR; BA; SCEA 88-; Hmnts Scl Sci Ed Awrd 89; AA 90; Ed.

**KNIGHT, CRYSTAL A,** Fl A & M Univ, Tallahassee, FL; SO; BSW; Phi Eta Sigma; Social Welfare; Social Work.**

**KNIGHT, CYNTHIA A,** Univ Of Ky, Lexington, KY; SR; BA; Bapt Stdnt Union Frshmn Cncl Sec 87-; Clvry Bapt Chrch Coll Ldrshp Tm Wlcm 87-; Phi Alpha Theta 90-; Hstry; Educ.

**KNIGHT, DAPHNE D,** Norfolk St Univ, Norfolk, VA; SO; BA; SGA Cnrns/Grvncs Dir 90; Soc Clb 90; Soc; Law.

**KNIGHT, DARRYL LEE,** Crichton Coll, Memphis, TN; JR; BS; Biolgy; Tchr.

**KNIGHT, DENA L,** Meridian Comm Coll, Meridian, MS; SO; AA; Bus Admin.

**KNIGHT, FREDERICK C,** Morehouse Coll, Atlanta, GA; JR; BA; Phi Beta Kappa; Phi Alpha Theta; Kappa Alpha Psi; Schlrs Pgm 90-; Dana Schlrs/Apprntcs Pgm 90-; Hstry; Prfssrshp.

**KNIGHT, GAIL J,** Norfolk St Univ, Norfolk, VA; SR; BS; Nghbrhd Wtch Chr Prsn 90-; Adopt A Scchl Tutor 90-; Toys Tots Vol 90-; VITA 89-; Elec Instrctr Fleet Trng Ctr; U S Navy/Elec Tech 1st Cls 81-; Elec Tech; Eng.

**KNIGHT, JOHN M D,** Westminster Coll, New Wilmingtn, PA; SR; BA; IFC Repr 89-; Theta Chi Mrshl/Chrmn 90-; Hbt For Hmnty 86-91; Reg II Conf Chrmn; Asst Cnslr Educ Cnsltnt; BA Pblc Rltns; Pblc Rltns; Cnsltng.

**KNIGHT, LAWANA K,** Middle Tn St Univ, Murfreesboro, TN; FR; BA; Acctng; CPA.

**KNIGHT, LISA R,** Univ Of Sc At Columbia, Columbia, SC; SO; BAIS; Stu Govt Hl Rep 89-; Intl Ordr Rnbw Grls Faith 85-; Ordr Estrn Str Ruth 89-; Sftbl League; Lbrl Arts; Educ.

**KNIGHT, MARACHEL L,** Fl St Univ, Tallahassee, FL; FR; BS; Blk Stdnt Union 90-; Pratt/Whitney Intrn 90-; Outstndng Fresh Chem; Elec Eng; Cmptr Eng.

**KNIGHT, MONIQUE S,** Hampton Univ, Hampton, VA; JR; BS; NABA; Bus Clb; Alpha Kappa Mu; Acctg; CPA.

**KNIGHT, PAUL T,** Methodist Coll, Fayetteville, NC; FR; BS; Pi Kappa Phi 90; Vrsty Bsebl 90; Cmptr Sci.

**KNIGHT, PAULA L,** Univ Of Sc At Columbia, Columbia, SC; JR; BS; Stdnt Govt Senator 88-89; Colg Republicans 88-89; German Clb 90-; Bio; Phys Therapy.

**KNIGHT, STEPHANIE A,** Univ Of Southern Ms, Hattiesburg, MS; SR; BS; Farm Bur Yng Frmr/Rnchr Org; English; Teach/Soc Servs.

**KNIGHT, TIFFANY M,** Andrew Coll, Cuthbert, GA; SO; AA; Visit Nrsng Hms 90; Hdstrt Pgm 90-; Grk Cncl Sec 90-; Phi Theta Kappa Treas 89-; Zeta Delta Pi Pres 90-; Andrew Ambssdr 90-; Phi Theta Kappa Stdnt Schlr; Sccr 89-90; Hstry; Lwyr/Jdg.

**KNIGHT, TIMOTHY C,** Daemen Coll, Amherst, NY; FR.

**KNIGHT, TRACY M,** Tn St Univ, Nashville, TN; JR; BA; Order Estrn Star; Spch Lang Pathology.

**KNIGHT, WENDY M,** Univ Of Southern Ms, Hattiesburg, MS; JR; BS; Phi Theta Kappa 88-90; Hl Of Fm 89-90; Ms Glf Rsrch Lbrtry 88-89; Blgy; Blgst.

**KNIGHT, WILLIAM K,** Radford Univ, Radford, VA; JR; BA; BA; Fin; Fin Plnnr/Stck Brkr.

**KNIGHTES, CHRISTOPHER D,** Univ Of Rochester, Rochester, NY; JR; BS; COPA Secy 88-; Gymnstcs Club 88-; Drama House 89-; Alpha Psi Omega; Delta Upsilon 90-; Physics; Medcn.

**KNIGHTON, CADESIA G,** Fl A & M Univ, Tallahassee, FL; FR; BS; Mrchng Bnd 90-; Symphnc Bnd 90-; Chem Clb 90-; Eastman Kodak Schlrs; Chem.

**KNIPPEL, KURT C,** Central Fl Comm Coll, Ocala, FL; SO; BA; Music; Music Ed.

**KNIPPER, SHARON J,** Northern Ky Univ, Highland Hts, KY; SR; BS; AAS; Office Sys Tech/Office Admin.

**KNITE, CHRISTIN E,** Univ Of Tn At Knoxville, Knoxville, TN; SR; BA; Co-Op With IBM 89-90; Acctg; Public Acctg.

**KNIZAK, LOUISE,** City Univ Of Ny Grad School, New York, NY; SR; BA; Actd Chkhs Three Siss Hntr Coll; Natl Orgnztn Fr Wmn NOW; EDIT; Engl; Wrtr Plywrtng.

**KNODLER, NANCY J,** Schenectady County Comm Coll, Schenectady, NY; SO; BA; Homeroom Mother 90-; Cmptr Sci; Pgmmng.

**KNOLLINGER, CONSTANCE M,** Wv Univ At Parkersburg, Parkersburg, WV; SR; BA; Soc Humn Rsrce Prfsnl; Mngr Hmn Rsrcs; Bsns; Hmn Rsrcs.

**KNOP, MARGARITA,** Nyack Coll, Nyack, NY; SO; BS; Ele Educ Span; Tch.

**KNOPF, MARGARET A,** Xavier Univ, Cincinnati, OH; FR; BA; Coll Frnds Big Sis; The Anthenaeum 90-; Englsh Clb; Blgy Clb; Pre Med Scty; Schlr Athletes Mentor Pgm 90-; Enlgish; Pblshng.

**KNOPKA, MICHELLE C,** Atlantic Comm Coll, Mays Landing, NJ; FR; MBA; Nrsng.

**KNOTT, BRUCE T,** Piedmont Comm Coll, Roxboro, NC; Pres Lst; Deans Lst; Stdnt Mnth Clb; PCC Schlrshp; NCDCC Schlrshp; Stdnt Mnth Schlrshp; Elec; Elec Tech.

**KNOTT, DIANA L,** Wv Univ, Morgantown, WV; GD; MS; Kappa Tau Alpha; Pblc Tv Vol; Natl Small Flows Clrnghse; BSJ Cum Laude 85; Jrnlsm/Cmnctn Stds; Tchng/Rsrch.

**KNOTT, ENA C,** Jackson St Univ, Jackson, MS; SO; BS; Baptist Stdnt Union 89-; Psychology Clb 89-; Alpha Lambda Delta 89-; Alpha Mu Gamma; Psi Chi; MARC; Clncl Psychlgy.

**KNOTT, JOE A,** Tougaloo Coll, Tougaloo, MS; SR; BA; Clg Book Review Series 89-90; Stdnt Pan Afrcn Educ Ntwrk Repr 88-; Big Bro BSA 89-; Kappa Alpha Psi Hist/Rprtr; Intrn Jackson Advct Ed Artist 90; Art/Jrnlsm.

**KNOTT, ROGER R,** City Univ Of Ny Med Evers Coll, Brooklyn, NY; SO; BA; Caribbean Stdnt Assn 90; M Evers Theoritical Assn 90; Bus Admn; Acctg.

**KNOTT, ROTA L,** Salisbury St Univ, Salisbury, MD; JR; BA; Phi Theta Kappa 90-; Intrnshp Salisbury Dly Tms; AA Frederick Comm Clg 90; Comm Art/Engl; Jrnlsm.**

**KNOTT, TOBY M,** Univ Of Ky, Lexington, KY; FR; BSCE; Alpha Lambda Delta Pres; Phi Eta Sigma; Sigma Pi VP; Dns Lst 90-; IM Sftbl/Bkstbl; Cvl Engr.

**KNOTTS, BETH ANN,** Wv Univ At Parkersburg, Parkersburg, WV; FR; AAS; Offc Admnstrtn; Scrtrl.

**KNOTTS, DIANE M,** Univ Of Louisville, Louisville, KY; GD; IEEE; Natl Soc Prfssnl Engrs; Goldn Key; Zeta Tau Alpha Pnhllnc Rep; Intrnshp S Cntrl Bell 88-90; Natl Collgt Eng Awrd 89-90; IN Univ Almni Assn; BS 90; BS IN Univ 83; Elec Eng.

**KNOTTS, MELISSA M,** Univ Of Sc At Sumter, Sumter, SC; JR; BA; Oreintation Ldr 89; Stdnt Govt Assn Clss Rep 90-; Gamecock Ambssdr 90-; SEA 89-; Stdnt Liassn Rep 89; Pres Medaln 89; AA 90; Elem Educ; Tchr.

**KNOTTS, ZOE L,** Univ Of North Fl, Jacksonville, FL; SO; BA; Jazz Ensmbl 89-; Cncrt Bnd 89-; Bst Mscn 90-; Music Educ; Bnd Dir.

**KNOWLES, ARLENE D M,** Hampton Univ, Hampton, VA; BA; Track & Field; Biology; Med Dr.

**KNOWLES, JOYCE A,** Valdosta St Coll, Valdosta, GA; FR; BS; Cmptr Sci; Prgmng.

**KNOWLES, KELLY L,** Middle Tn St Univ, Murfreesboro, TN; SR; BBA; Assoc Stdnt Body Gen Sessions Cart Chf Jstc 87-; Prsbyterian Stdnt Fllwshp 87-; Beta Gamma Sigma; Gamma Bta Phi 87-; Tau Omicron Wom VP 89-; Beta Gamma Sigma; Gamma Omicron Delta Treas/Sec 88-90; Deans List/Hnr Rl 87-; Mgmnt; Corp Cnslting.

**KNOWLES, MELANIE D,** Abraham Baldwin Agri Coll, Tifton, GA; SO; BA; Coll Ambsdr 90; Cncrt Bnd 89; Stfwrtr/Advrtsng Dir 89-; Stdnt Nwsppr; Dstngshd Achvmnt Lst 90; Dns Hnr Lst; Hnr Stdnt 89-90; Jrnlsm; Advrtsng/Pub Rel.

**KNOWLTON, AARON W,** Univ Of Sc At Columbia, Columbia, SC; SO; Del Interfrat Cncl; Gamma Beta Phi; Sigma Phi Epsilon Hd Im 90-; Rec Acad Excell; IM Ftbl/Tenns/Sftbl/Flrhcky.

**KNOX, ANGELA L,** Paine Coll, Augusta, GA; SO; BA; NAACP 90-; Cncrt Choir Treas 90-; Meth Stdnt Assn 89-; Hon Soc VP 90-; Lina H Mc Cord Intrn 90-; Pres Schlr 89-90; Neal Schlr Awd 89-90; Bsktbl Chrldr 89-90; Mass Cmmnctns; TV Brdcstr.

**KNOX, ANNETTE DENISE,** Shaw Univ, Raleigh, NC; JR; BS; Stdnt Govt Sec Elect; Schlstc All Am Clgt Prog 90-; US Army Spec 4 76-79; AA Appl Sci Cape Fear Cmnty Clg 84; AA BA Cape Fear Cmty Clg 86; Bsn Mgmt; Hmn Rsrc Mgmt.

**KNOX, DEBORAH L,** Francis Marion Coll, Florence, SC; FR; BS; Bapt Stdnt Un; Alpha Delta Pi; Pre-Pharmacy; Pharmacy.

**KNOX, DEBORAH L,** Pellissippi St Tech Comm Coll, Knoxville, TN; SO; IEEE Sec 89-90; Boy Scts Of Amer Ldr/Cub Scts 90-; Electrncs; Engrng.

**KNOX, GUIQNOL,** Stillman Coll, Tuscaloosa, AL; GD; SG UNCF 84; Sclgy Clb Psychlgy Clb Treas 87-; Hon Rl 84; Psychlgy Clb; P E Clb Clss Sec Grls Scts 4-H Clss Treas 83-84; Eastrn Star; Sigma Dove; Fld Plcmnt 84-90; BA 90; Sclgy/Psychlgy; Scl Wrkr.

**KNOX, KANDACE L,** Castleton St Coll, Castleton, VT; SO; BS; Phi Eta Sigma; Pres Schlrshp; Bus Mgmt/Comp Info Syst.

**KNOX, MARY C,** Livingston Univ, Livingston, AL; SR; BS; AA East MS Jr Coll 83; Spcl Edn/Lrng Disabilites; Teach.

**KNOX, WYVITRA GE LINTE,** Paine Coll, Augusta, GA; SO; BS; Blgy Clb Pres 90-; Soph Clss VP 90-; NAACP Sec 90-; Natl Hon Soc 90-; Ms Ervin Hall 90-; Delta Sigma Theta; Medcl Coll GA Seep Smmr Pgm 89-90; Blgy; Pdtrcn.

**KNUCKLES, RAY E,** Union Coll, Barbourville, KY; JR; BA; IM; Hist; Resrchr.

**KNUDSEN, HAROLD S,** Neumann Coll, Aston, PA; JR; BA; Psi Chi 89-; Deans Lst 89-; Coop Educ Ireland Alchlc Thrp 90; Psychlgy; Cnslg.

**KNUDSEN, INGRID K,** Glassboro St Coll, Glassboro, NJ; SR; BA; Psych; Hmn Res.

**KNUDSEN, THOMAS E,** The Kings Coll, Briarclf Mnr, NY; SR; Psych Clb 88-; Clg Chr 88-90; Stdnt Chpln 90-; Res Asst 89-90; Mntl Hlth Intrn 90; Lehmn Strs Expstry Prchng Awd 90-; IM Ftbl; Psych; Clin Psych.

**KNYSZEK, LINDA A,** Oh St Univ, Columbus, OH; SR; BS; Wildlife Scty 88-; Literary Mag Art Edtr 88-89; ISEC 88-90; Mtn Hnry 89-; Gamma Sigma Delta 90-; US All-Amer Schlr; Teater Schlrshp; Wildlife Mgt; Ntl Resource/Envtl.

**KO, JOESON CHO-SHUN,** Newbury Coll, Brookline, MA; FR; Sccr 90; Bdmntn Tm Englnd 90-; Fshn; Fshn Indstrs.

**KOBASKO, KIMBERLY L,** West Liberty St Coll, West Liberty, WV; SO; BS; Hnrs Pgm Comm; Cmnctns; Publ Rels.

**KOBER, SUSAN L,** Indiana Univ Of Pa, Indiana, PA; SR; BED; YWCA 80-90; Beta Gamma 89-90; Mellon Secrties 78-89; Elem Ed; Tchng.

**KOBERT, LINDA J,** Univ Of Pittsburgh, Pittsburgh, PA; GD; MSN; Grad Stdnt Nrs Org 89-; Sigma Theta Tau 83-; PA Nrs Assoc Schlrshp Dist 6 90; PA Nrs Assoc Dist 6 87-; ASPO Certfd Chldbrth Eductr 88-; Pittsburgh Waldorf Sch Initv Treas 90-; BSN La Roche Clg 84; RN 77; Nrsng.

**KOBLENZER, ANDREW S,** Me Maritime Academy, Castine, ME; SO; BS; Sailing Tm; Marine Transp/Nautical Sci; Maritime Inds.

**KOBYLAR, SAMUEL S,** Hudson Valley Comm Coll, Troy, NY; SR; Albny Intrntl Mnnds NY; Rfrgrtn Htng Ar Cndtng.

**KOBYLYANSKY, ANNA,** Univ Of Rochester, Rochester, NY; SO; BS; Optics; Eng.

**KOCH, CHRISTINE E,** Johnson St Coll, Johnson, VT; SO; BA; Psych; Indstl Psych.

**KOCH, DONA L,** Univ Of Cin R Walters Coll, Blue Ash, OH; FR; AA; Dntl Hygn Fresh Cls Pres 90-; SADHA; Blgy Tutor 90-; Wrtng Lab Tutor 90-; RN Dplma Jwsh Hosp Schl Nrsng 68; Dntl Hygn.

**KOCH, JO ANN M,** S U N Y Coll Of A & T Morrisvl, Morrisville, NY; FR; AS; Phi Theta Kappa; Pre-Law/Ecology; Envrnmntl Lawyer.

**KOCH, KILLY A,** Brescia Coll, Owensboro, KY; FR; BA; Scl Sci Clb Pres 90-; Cmps Mnstry Assc 90-; Ambssdr; Hnrs Cllquy 90-; Owensboro Wmn Wk Essyst; Asst Statstcn Bsktbl 90-; Soclgy/Psychlgy; Nrsg Hm Admin.

**KOCH, LISA A,** Fl International Univ, Miami, FL; SO; BS; Phi Kappa Phi; Fclty Schlrs 90-; Occptnl Thrpy; Private Practice.

**KOCH, MARCI A,** Anne Arundel Comm Coll, Arnold, MD; SO; MBA; Art; Educ.

**KOCH, MARGARET A,** Radford Univ, Radford, VA; JR; BS; NEA; Aerobcs Clb 88-; Dnce Clb 88-89; Phi Sigma Sigma Rsh Chrmn 90-; Erly/Mddl Educ.

**KOCH, RANDALL G,** William Paterson Coll, Wayne, NJ; JR; BA; SGA V P 88-; Outdoors Clb 90-; Alpha Sigma Phi 90-; Notary Public; Deans Lst 90; Alumni Schlrshp 90-; Pol Sci; Law.**

**KOCH, RICHARD A,** Univ Of Md Baltimore Prof Schl, Baltimore, MD; GD; MSW; Phi Kappa Phi 90-; Cmmndtn Otstndng Srvce 90; Natl Assn Rtrdd Ctzns; NASW; Tchng Exprnce; Pst Prncpl; Sndy Schl Admin 90; CA Hebrew University Baltimore 81; BA Univ Of MD 86; Clcnl Admin Scl Wrk; Scl Wrk.

**KOCHANOWSKI, GREGORY T,** Temple Univ, Philadelphia, PA; JR; Archtrl Stdnts Assn 90-; Intrnshp-PDE Assoc 87-89; Archtctr.

**KOCHEM, SUSAN M,** Schenectady County Comm Coll, Schenectady, NY; FR; AAS; Phi Theta Kappa 90-; Info Rsrcs Supv 90-; Bus Prog Sys; Progrmmng.

**KOCHENSPARGER, CHRISTOPHER H,** Radford Univ, Radford, VA; JR; BS; Soc Clgt Jrnlst Pres 90-; Pblc Rltns Clb; Frshmn Rcrd Edtr; Jrnlsm/Engl; PR Prctnr.

**KOCHER, CINDY A,** West Liberty St Coll, West Liberty, WV; SR; BA; Kappa Delta Pi Hstrn 90-; Sigma Tau Delta 90-; Nomnee Ed Mjr; Summa Cum Laude Grad; AA WV Nrthrn 89; Engl; Tchng.

**KOCHIS, LISA M,** Hillsborough Comm Coll, Tampa, FL; SO; AA AS; Psych; Med Radiation Thrpy.

**KOCHIS, RAYMOND C,** Nyack Coll, Nyack, NY; SR; BA; RA 88; Clss Offcr; Jdcry Brd 90-; Deans Lst 89-90; Pi Upsilon Pi 87-89; Hstry Asst; Bsbll 90-; Hstry.

**KOCHMAN, DEBORAH A,** Daytona Beach Comm Coll, Daytona Beach, FL; BS; Natl Assoc Legal Assts 90-; Prlgl Stds; Assist.

**KOCIANIC, MICHAEL A,** Univ Of Akron, Akron, OH; SR; BA; APICS; Sigma Iota Epsilon; IM Bsktbl 90-; Bus Mgmt/Qlty Cntrl.

**KOCIK, STEPHANIE A,** Kent St Univ Kent Cmps, Kent, OH; FR; Busn; Mktng.

**KOCIMSKI, MARIBETH C,** Savannah Coll Of Art & Design, Savannah, GA; JR; BFA; YMCA; Video/Pntg; Prodcr/Dir/Scrptwrt Pntr.

**KOCSIS, DANIELLE D,** Kent St Univ Kent Cmps, Kent, OH; FR; BA; Kent Interhall Cncl; Olson Hse Cncl; Psych; Law.

**KOCSIS, ROLAND A,** Univ Of Cincinnati-Clrmnt Coll, Batavia, OH; FR; AA; Bus; Mgmnt.

**KODOSKY, DINA,** Indiana Univ Of Pa, Indiana, PA; SO; BS; NSSLHA Pres 89-; Sign Lang Clb 90-; Vlybl 89-; Swmng 90-; Spch Pathology/Audiology.

**KOEBLER, GABRIELE,** Univ Of Sc At Columbia, Columbia, SC; SO; BA; Tau Beta Sigma; Bus Admin; Intrntl Bus.

**KOEDAM, CYNTHIA L,** Midway Coll, Midway, KY; SO; AA; Stdnt Govt VP 90-; Phi Theta Kappa 89-; Hmnts; Acctg.

**KOEDAM, SHARON L,** Univ Of Fl, Gainesville, FL; JR; BA; Hlth Rltd Prof Coll Cncl Pres 90-; Brd Coll Cncls; Assoc Hlth Cntr Coll Cncls; Gldn Key 90-; Mrtr Brd Hnr Soc; Stu Occptnl Thrpy Assoc 90-; Stu Mbr Amer Occptnl Thrpy Assoc 90-; Kiwanis Fndtn Schlrshp 88-; Pres Sprng Awrd; Occptnl Thrpy.

**KOEHLER, JULIE A,** Notre Dame Coll, Cleveland, OH; SO; BA; Stdnt Un/Stdnt Govt Treas 90-; Crnt Afrs Frm Pltcl Sci Clb Sec/Treas 89-; Orntn Tm 89-; Cmps Ambsdr 89-; IM Clge Vlybl 90-; Pltcl Sci/Cmnctns; Law.

**KOEHLER, JULIE A,** S U N Y Coll Of Tech At Delhi, Delhi, NY; SR; AAS; NY Assn Of Vet Techs 89-; Sci; Vet Med.

**KOEHNLEIN, SUSAN J,** Miami Univ, Oxford, OH; FR; BS; Phi Eta Sigma; Alpha Lambda Delta 90-; Pres Lst; Deans Lst 90-; Delta Sigma Pi Serv Cmtee 90-; Delta Zeta 90-; Bus Admn; Acctg.

**KOELLE, SHARON M,** Middle Tn St Univ, Murfreesboro, TN; SR; BS; Fine Arts Comm 87-90; Gamma Beta Phi 88-; Tau Omicron 89-; Pub Rel Std Soc Amer 90-; Nashvl Radio Sta; Pub Rel.

**KOELLING, DWAYNE D,** Univ Of Tn At Martin, Martin, TN; FR; BS; Blck Brdl Clb 90-; Bptst Chr 90-; Hnrs Smnr 90-; Scty Hnrs Smnr Stdnts 90-; Bptst Stdnt Un Cncl 90-; Acdmc Mrt Awrd 90-; IM 90-; Anml Btchnlgy.

**KOENIG, JEFFREY C,** Univ Of Miami, Coral Gables, FL; SO; BMA; Hurricane Prod 90-; Alpha Lambda Delta 90-; Gen/Music Sch Hon Prog; Piano Tchr/Prfsnl Artst Mgr; Music; Prfsnl Muscn.

**KOENIG II, JERRY L,** Fl St Univ, Tallahassee, FL; SR; BS; Elec Eng.

**KOENIG, KELLY K,** Southern Coll Of Tech, Marietta, GA; SO; BA; Comp Sci; Sftwre Eng.

**KOENIG, SUSAN L,** Christopher Newport Coll, Newport News, VA; SR; CERT; Sociology/Soc Wk Clb 90-; Peninsula Agency Agng Cs Mngr; BA; Sociology.

**KOEPFINGER JR, LEROY R,** West Liberty St Coll, West Liberty, WV; FR; BS; Catholic Campus Ministry Prog Comm 90; Eldehrostel Prog; Hnrs Prog; Acad Schlrshp; AS Nashville Auto Diesel Clg 90; Spec Educ/Visual Hndcps; Educ Spclst.

**KOERBER, JOHN W,** West Liberty St Coll, West Liberty, WV; SR; Paden Cty Hgh Schl Almn Assoc Pres 89-; Vol Fir Comp Capt Trng Offcr 69-; Alpha Kappa Psi; By Scts Amrc Unit Cmmssnr 87; Lttl Lg Cch 80-87; Vet Vtnm War Fndr; WA Univ Fir Srvc Extnsn Instrctr 78-; Stat Frfghtrs Assoc 69-; Mgmt Psychlgy; Hmn Rsrcs Fr Srvc Law.

**KOERBER, KATHLEEN A,** Villanova Univ, Villanova, PA; SO; Spec Olymp 90-; Acdmc Awd 89-; Deans Lst 90-; Vrsty Swmmg 89-; Cmprhnsv Sci; Rsrch.

**KOERNER, MARK E,** Columbus Coll Of Art & Design, Columbus, OH; FR; BA; Art; Industrial Design.

**KOESTEL, ISABELLE Y,** Suffolk Comm Coll Eastern Cmps, Riverhead, NY; GD; Cert; Trvl/Trsm.

**KOESTER, AUDREY F,** Northern Ky Univ, Highland Hts, KY; SR; BABS; Math Clb 90-; Stdnt Sprt Tutor 89-; Lrng Asstnc Tutor 89-; Alph Chi; Brd Adjstmnts Chrprsn 88-; Plng Zoning 88-; AS Thomas More Clg 74; Acctg/Math; Math Grad Sch.

**KOESTER, CATHY M,** Bellarmine Coll, Louisville, KY; SR; BA; Ariel Pres 89-; Std Nwspr Edtr 87-90; Kappa Gammu Pi; Crdnl Sctns; St Vncnt De Paul; Mthr Teresas Mssnrs Chrty Smmr Cmp 88; Engl Spkng Un Schlp 90; In Veritatis Amore Awd 90; Lenihan Mem Awd 89; Engl/Cmmnctns; Clg Prfssr Engl.

**KOESTRING, WILLIAM E,** Daytona Beach Comm Coll, Daytona Beach, FL; FR; BS; Automotive; Tchncn.

**KOEVAL, JENNIFER J,** Fl St Univ, Tallahassee, FL; JR; BS; Phi Eta Sigma 88-89; Beta Kappa Alpha 90-; Kappa Delta 89-; Hghst Pldg GPA 89; Dnc Tm Sec 88-; Nrsg.

**KOEWLER, JACQUIE R,** Oh St Univ, Columbus, OH; SR; WAR 90-; Univ Stdnt Cncl 86-87; Alpha Lambda Delta 87-88; Phi Kappa Phi; Alpha Epsilon Delta 86-88; Grp Fcltr Natl Anrxc Aid Soc; IM Soccer 88; BS OH State Univ 90; Psychlgy.

**KOGEN, ZEEV M,** Yeshiva Univ, New York, NY; SO; BS; Jwsh Comm Cncl Of Wash Hgts 89-; Plnthrpc Socty; Biology; Biomed Rsrch/Med.

**KOGER JR, EDWARD W,** Clark Atlanta Univ, Atlanta, GA; JR; Fin Clb 89-; Entrepreneurs Clb 89; Deans Lst 90; Ch God In Christ Usher Bd Male Chorus; N Thomas Schlrshp Fund 90-; United Negro Clg Fund 88-; I M Bkbl Coach Plyr 90-; Bus Admn/Fin; Fin Cnsultnt.

**KOGER, RITA VANESIA,** Roane St Comm Coll, Harriman, TN; SO; AD; Stdnt Nrs Assoc 89-90; UT Nrsng Apprntshp Prog 90; Nrsng; Onclgy Nrsng.

**KOGGE, LAUREN M,** Johnson St Coll, Johnson, VT; GD; BA; Educ Dpt Awd Acad Achvmnt Jsc; Tchr; AA Ocean Cnty Clg 86; Elem Ed; Tchng.

**KOHAN JR, GEORGE F,** Barry Univ, Miami, FL; SR; BA; Engl; Educ.

**KOHL, KAREN P,** Atlantic Comm Coll, Mays Landing, NJ; SO; BA; Wrtng Tutr 90-; Educ; Tchr.

**KOHL, LYNDA S,** Allegheny Coll, Meadville, PA; SR; BS; Res Advsr 90-; VISA 87-89; Lambda Sigma 88-89; Intercoll Crs Cntry Trck/Fld Co Capt 87-; Bio; Phy Thrpy.

**KOHL, WALDEMAR R,** Georgetown Univ, Washington, DC; FR; BA; AISEC 90-; Chrstn Fllwshp Yth Grp 90-; Chr 90; Trd Blnd Fllw Stdnt 90-; Deans Lst; Bus; Intl Bus.

**KOHLER, JANIS C,** Cornell Univ Statutory College, Ithaca, NY; SR; SCA 87-; CUSFA 87-; Red Carept Scty Host 87-89; Orientation Cnsl 89; Deans Lst 88-.

**KOHLER, JOHN E,** Bridgeport Engr Inst, Fairfield, CT; JR; BSME; Amer Soc Plmbng Engrs 90-; Plmbg/Fire Prot Engr Fltchr Thmpsn 83-; Mech Engr; Fire Prot Engr.

**KOHLER, SAM G,** Va Commonwealth Univ, Richmond, VA; JR; BS; Bus Fnc; Bus Avtn.

**KOHLS, ERIC J,** Univ Of Cincinnati, Cincinnati, OH; SO; BS; Cnstrctn Mgmt; Proj Mgr.

**KOHN, CARYL A,** Nova Univ, Ft Lauderdale, FL; GD; MBA; NE Univ 81; BA 78; Hosp Admin.

**KOHN, DEENA R,** Yeshiva Univ, New York, NY; SR; BA; Pre-Law Soc VP 90-; Psychlgy Clb 89-; Yrbk Features Ed 90-; Deans Lst; Magna Cum Laude; SSSJ; Psychlgy; Law Sch.

**KOHRS, GAIL L,** Columbia Greene Comm Coll, Hudson, NY; SR; BS; Sbstnc Abse Clb 89-; Intl Clb 89; Vol Hdsn Corr Fclty 90; Cnslng; Scl Work.

**KOIDE, KANA,** Tougaloo Coll, Tougaloo, MS; FR; Intl Stdnts Assn 82-85; Exc Prog 90-; Hmnty Awd; Japan Africa Frndshp Assn 88-90; ORIX Inc 86-87; ECC For Lang Inst Tchr 87-90; BA Kobe College Japan 86; Interdspnry Career Orien Hmnty.

**KOIVISTO, REQUEL A,** Notre Dame Coll, Cleveland, OH; SO; BA; Coop/Vector Mktg Corp Asst Dist Mgr/Fld Sls Mgr 90-; D Connollay Bus Schlrshp; Dns Lst; Fst-Ptch Sftbl; Hmn Rsrc Mgmt/MIS; HRM Cnsltnt.

**KOJIMA, YOSHIMITSU,** Comm Coll Algny Co Algny Cmps, Pittsburgh, PA; JR; BA; BA Waseda Univ 88-; Jrnlsm; Advrtsng Agnt.

**KOKERAM, ASHRAM,** Embry Riddle Aeronautical Univ, Daytona Beach, FL; JR; BSC; Avncs Hnr Scty; Engrg Tchnlgsts Hnr Scty; Avncs Engrg Tchnlgy; Engrg.

**KOKIN, ELLADA,** City Univ Of Ny Baruch Coll, New York, NY; SR; BBA; Beta Gamma Sigma 90; Golden Key 89; Deans Lst 89; Cmptr Info Sys; Cmptr Prgrmng/Anlys.**

**KOKOTOWSKI, CAROLE A,** Bloomfield Coll, Bloomfield, NJ; SR; BA; Intl Stdnts Clb Sec 85-88; Chrs Handbll 84-; Evng Stdnt Govt Sec 85-86; Stdnt Cncl Pr 89-; MTA Clb Tr 90-; Alpha Sigma Lambda Sec 85-88/Pr 88-; Alpha Chi 88-; Handbell Awd; Serv Awd; Fine Arts; Graphc Arts/Cmptr Desk.

**KOLAKOWSKI, STEPHEN,** Lock Haven Univ, Lock Haven, PA; BS; Sprts Med Clb 90-; Alpha Chi Rho; IM Sccr; WRSTLNG 90; Sprts Med; Dctr.

**KOLASIENSKI, AEMON J,** Schenectady County Comm Coll, Schenectady, NY; SO; AA; Stdnt Govt Sntr 90-; Peer Tutor Pgm 90-; Pres Lst 90-; Pltcl Sci; Law/Educ.

**KOLAWOLE, KEHINDE,** Hiwassee Coll, Madisonville, TN; SO; BA; Phi Theta Kappa VP; Bsktbl; Acctg.

**KOLB, ERIK P,** City Univ Of Ny Baruch Coll, New York, NY; SO; BBA; Baruch Schlr Adv Bd 89-; Baruch Schlr Nwsltr 89-; Die Erstse Gottscheer Tonzgruppe 90-; Baruch Sachlr 89-; Acctng.

**KOLB, MARY J,** Univ Of West Fl, Pensacola, FL; SR; BA; AA Okaloosa Walton Comm Coll 89; Elem Ed/Early Chldhd; Tchng.

**KOLB, NEAL F,** Widener Univ, Chester, PA; SR; BS; Amer Soc Cvl Eng VP 90-; Intrntl Trns Eng; Cvl Eng.

**KOLB, TRACY M,** Coll Of Charleston, Charleston, SC; SO; BA; Dead Pts Scty; Brd Scty; HPSA Fcta; Hnrs Prgrm; Deans Lst; Engl; Ed.

**KOLCHARNO, MARIA,** Marywood Coll, Scranton, PA; SR; BSW; Caritas Club 87-; VIA 89-90; Pi Gamma Mu 90-; NASW 87-; Pratcicum 1st Hosp Wyoming Vly Wilkes Barre PA 90; Soc Wrk.

**KOLCZUN, PAMELA D,** Bowling Green St Univ At Huron, Huron, OH; JR; BLS; Lbrl Stds.

**KOLCZUN, TODD E,** Fordham Univ, Bronx, NY; SR; Fordham Fed Cr Union Sec 90-; Stdnt Nwsppr Sprts Phtgrphr 90-; Alli Schl Vlybl Trnmnt Chrmn 90-; Alpha Lambda Delta 88; Phi Beta Lambda 88-89; Delta Tau Delta Prlmntrn 87-89; Prdntl Scrts/Brkrs Asst 90-; Bus Finance; Law.

**KOLDYS, GREGORY R,** Univ Of Miami, Coral Gables, FL; SR; MA; Std Amer Advsr 88-; Intl Bsn Asc 89-; IM Sccr Capt 87-; BA 90; Intl Affrs; Foreign Serv.

**KOLEFAS, CAROL A,** Univ Of West Fl, Pensacola, FL; SR; BA; CEC 89-; Kappa Delta Pi 90-; Phi Theta Kappa 88-89; Alpha Sigma Lambda 90-; Arts/Dsgn Soc 83-84; AA Okaloosa Walton Comm Coll 89; Lrning Dsblty Ed.

**KOLESNIK, KAREN A,** Bryant Stratton Bus Inst Roch, Rochester, NY; FR; BA; Acctg; Acctnt.

**KOLIBABA, DANA M,** Cumberland County Coll, Vineland, NJ; SO; Wind Symphony; Nwspr; Tutor; Phi Theta Kappa 90-; Miss Holly City 88-89; Math Educ; Tch Guidance Cnslr.

**KOLIPINSKI, SHARON A,** Daemen Coll, Amherst, NY; JR; BSN; AACN 90-; NAACOG 90-; Pi Nu Epsilon 73-74; Boy Scts Dnldr 88-; RN 83-; AAS Niagara Cty Comm Coll 83; Nrsng-Hstry/Govt; Nrsng Mtrnl Hlth.

**KOLLAR, WILLIAM J,** Gallaudet Univ, Washington, DC; JR; BA; Hon Stdnts; Alpha Omega Spiritual Life Dir 87-88; Deans Lst 87-88; Soc Hon Stdnts 90-; Pres Schlr 90-; AA Univ Akron 88; Hist; Archeology.

**KOLLER, DOUGLAS S,** Univ Of Cincinnati, Cincinnati, OH; FR; BS; Cmptr Clb IEEE Phtgrphy 90-; Deans Lst 90-; Elctrcl Engnrng; Engnrng.

**KOLLER, KATHLEEN A,** Antonelli Inst Of Art & Photo, Cincinnati, OH; SR; ASSOC; Alpha Beta Kappa; Phtgrphy; Fshn Phtgrphr.

**KOLLER, SUSAN LYNNE,** Spartanburg Methodist Coll, Spartanburg, SC; FR; AA; Day Std Asc 90-; Phi Theta Kappa 90-; Psy; Educ.

**KOLLING, NICOLE,** Comm Coll Algny Co Algny Cmps, Pittsburgh, PA; SO; Accntng; CPA.

**KOLODZIEJ, KARYN M,** D Youville Coll, Buffalo, NY; JR; BS; Natl Hon Soc; Cmps Mnstry; Intrnshp WCA Hosp Jamestown; Medcl Tchnlgy; ASCP.

**KOLODZIK, MARTHA J,** Univ Of Cincinnati-Clrmnt Coll, Batavia, OH; SO; BBA; Frst Bptst Chrch Of Amzia 82-; Phi Theta Kappa; Acctng; CPA.

**KOLTAS, DAVID M,** Carnegie Mellon Univ, Pittsburgh, PA; JR; BS; Visual Cmnctns Clb; Arch Clb; Grphc Cmnctns Mgmt; Bsn.

**KOMAREK, CATHERINE M,** Dowling Coll, Oakdale Li, NY; SR; BA; Phi Theta Kappa; Pi Alpha Sigma; Acctg.

**KOMINEK, ANACKA K,** Univ Of Sc At Columbia, Columbia, SC; SR; BA; Grmn Clb 87-; Chrldng Ftbl/Bsktbl 88-89; Stdnt Cncl 87-89; Alpha Mu Gamma 88-; Sigma Iotr Rho; United Way 89-; United Negro Coll Fnd 89-; Nom Outstdng Sr Awd; Rgnts Schlrshp CLU 87-89; Intl Stds.

**KOMNIEY JR, ANDREW ROBERT,** Greenville Tech Coll, Greenville, SC; GD; Cert TV Trng Inst 79; Elctrncs Cmptrs; Emplymnt/Serv/Cstmrs.

**KOMPALLA, SHARON L,** Univ Of Miami, Coral Gables, FL; SR; BS; Hurrican Honeys 89-90; Sgm Alph Mu Aux 89-90; Pblc Rltns; Entrtnmnt.

**KONDILAS, KATHLEEN C,** Memphis St Univ, Memphis, TN; JR; BA; TN Water Color Soc Dir 89-90; Sea Isle Sch Instr 88-89; Courtroom Artist; Fine Art; Prof Sculptor/Artist.

**KONDROSKI, ALISON C,** Daytona Beach Comm Coll, Daytona Beach, FL; SO; AS; Law; Paralegal.

**KONECNY, JOSEPH W,** S U N Y Coll Of Tech At Delhi, Delhi, NY; FR; AOS; Natl Hot Rod Assn 89-; Cert Auto Tech; Auto Mech; Race Car Mech.

**KONEYAK, SHERRIE A,** Coppin St Coll, Baltimore, MD; SR; BS; AA Dundalk Comm Clg 85; BS; Spcl Edctn; Tchng.

**KONG, CHIONG BING,** Univ Of South Al, Mobile, AL; SR; MBA; Asean Stdnta Assn Actvts Coordntr Orgnzr Chinese New Yr Clbrtns 89-; IM Vlybl Cptn 89-; Vrsty Intrnshp Prgrm Stdnts Mngr 89-; BSC USA; Gnrl MBA; Bsns.

**KONG, ISABELLA,** S U N Y At Buffalo, Buffalo, NY; SO; BS; Acctg.

**KONG, KELLY,** City Univ Of Ny Baruch Coll, New York, NY; SO; BA; Acctng.

**KONG, MIN HAE,** Columbus Coll Of Art & Design, Columbus, OH; FR.

**KONG, RAYMOND,** S U N Y At Buffalo, Buffalo, NY; SR; BS; Natl Assn Accntnts 90-; Univ Buffalo Accntng Assn 90-; Beta Alpha Psi 89-; Beta Gamma Sigma 90-; Dean Lst; Accntng/Fnncl Anlys/Mngmnt Infr Sys; CPA.

**KONG, WING H,** City Univ Of Ny Baruch Coll, New York, NY; SR; BBA; Gldn Key; Auditor Trnee 87-88; Cstmr Sev Offcr Dragon Airline 86-87; Acctng; CPA.

**KONIG, LISA K,** Middle Tn St Univ, Murfreesboro, TN; GD; Stdnt Tchr Ed Assn; Engl Clb; Gamma Beta Phi; Sigma Tau Delta; BS Univ Of N Alabama 89; Engl; 2ndry Ed.

**KONSTANT, MARY P,** George Mason Univ, Fairfax, VA; SR; BED; Greek Club 88-90; Elem Edn; Teach.

**KOO, JUDITH M,** Memphis St Univ, Memphis, TN; SR; BA; Phi Kappa Phi; BA Univ Of NSW Australia 71; Psychlgy; Law.

**KOODERINGS-CLEMENS, CHRISTINE M,** Christopher Newport Coll, Newport News, VA; FR; BSA; German Clb; Acntng; CPA.

**KOOMEN, ERIC R,** S U N Y At Buffalo, Buffalo, NY; SO; BA; IM Soccer/Flr Hockey/Bsktbl 89-; Asst Soccer Coach; Frshmn Soccer Awd 89; J V/Vars Soccer 89-90; Mgmt.

**KOON, GEORGINA C,** Carnegie Mellon Univ, Pittsburgh, PA; FR; Nwspr Stf Wrtr 90-; Lambda Sigma; Carnegie Trdtn Awd 90-; Eng/Prfsnl Wrtng; Law.

**KOON, LAURA R,** Coker Coll, Hartsville, SC; FR; BA; Baccus 90-; Sprt Com 90-; Cmsnrs; Elem Educ; Schl Tchr.

**KOON, LAURIE L,** Univ Of Sc At Columbia, Columbia, SC; FR; Wmn Stdnt Assc 90-; Chi Omega 90-; Psychlgy.

**KOONS, LORI L,** Cumberland Coll, Williamsburg, KY; JR; BS; Cncrt Bnd/Mrchg Bnd 88-90; Psychlgy Clb Pres 89-; Psychlgy.

**KOONS, ROBERT S,** Nova Univ, Ft Lauderdale, FL; GD; MBA; Bell South Golf League Dir 89-90; Amer Inst Of Archtcts 75-78; Psi Upsilon Pi 72-76; Bell South Pnrs 88; Reg Archtct Ohio/Fla 79-82; BA 76; Real Estate/Dvlpmnt; Bsnss.

**KOONS, SUSAN E,** Savannah Coll Of Art & Design, Savannah, GA; SR; BFA; Prfsnl Phtgrphrs Assn 88-89; Phtgrphr 87-89; AA Harrisburg Area Comm Coll 78; Phtgrphy.

**KOONTZ, BONJANETTE J,** Kent St Univ Kent Cmps, Kent, OH; SR; BS; Stdnt Adv Comm 89-90; Cur Comm Clg Arts & Sci 89-90; Pi Mu Epsilon Treas 90-; Gldn Ky 90-; Alpha Lambda Delta 88-; Hnrs Schlrshp 87-; Grad Cum Laude; Math; Actuary.

**KOONTZ, GRETCHEN A,** Kent St Univ Kent Cmps, Kent, OH; SO; BS; Kent St Mrchg Bnd 89-; Alpha Lambda Delta 89-90; Tau Beta Sigma Prlmntrn 90-; Grmn.

**KOONTZ III, JACKSON W,** Central Fl Comm Coll, Ocala, FL; SO; BA; Intl Club Treas 89-90; BSA Eagle Sct 79-; Aletheia Stdnt Outreach 87-; Phi Beta Lamda 89-90; Intern Grace Presby PCA Vol 89-; Sports Contests Vlybl; AA; Intersisciplinary Studies; Yth Mnstry W/M Div.

**KOONTZ, JULIE L,** Wv Univ At Parkersburg, Parkersburg, WV; SO.

**KOOP, ANTHONY L,** Fl International Univ, Miami, FL; JR; BS; FL Pblc Intrst Rsrch Grp Rep Bd Drctrs 90-; Scty Envrnmntl Actn; Blgy.

**KOPA, ANGELIQUE M,** Duquesne Univ, Pittsburgh, PA; SO; BA; Hstry; Law.

**KOPAS, ANN R,** Indiana Univ Of Pa, Indiana, PA; SR; BSED; PA State Educ Assn 90-; Natl Cncl Tchrs Of Math 90-; Natl Educ Assn 90-; Kappa Mu Epsilon 90-; Cum Laude; Scndry Math Educ; Tchr.

**KOPECKY, KRISTINE A,** Embry Riddle Aeronautical Univ, Daytona Beach, FL; SO; BS; Half The Sky-Womens Org; I-CARE Vlntr; Deans List 89-; Aeronautical Science; Airline Piloting.

**KOPER, SHARON,** Duquesne Univ, Pittsburgh, PA; SR; BS; Amer Mktg Asc 90-; Zeta Tau Alpha Chr 90-; Dnc Mrthn 89-; Drby Dys/Grk Sng/Srnvl 88-; Intrl US Dpt Cmmrc Intl Trd Admn; Mktg; Sales.

**KOPESTONSKY, LARISSA A,** Kent St Univ Kent Cmps, Kent, OH; SO; BA; St Nicholas Russn Yth Dncrs 87-; St Nicholas Balalaika Orch 87-90; Natl Rec/Prk Assc 90-; Sierra Clb 90-; Wrld Wldlfe Fnd 90-; Leisure Srvcs Mngmnt; Recrtn/Rsrt Mngmnt.

**KOPF, VICKI R,** Allegheny Coll, Meadville, PA; JR; BS; LIFT 89-; Chemii 90; Amnsty Intl 88-; Lambda Sigma 89-90; ACE 88-89; Aldn Schlr 89 ; Biochem; Med.

**KOPLAN, ANDREW B,** Birmingham Southern Coll, Birmingham, AL; SO; BA; Tri Clb; Pre Law Soc; Cnsrvncy; Admn Intern; Alpha Lambda Delta; Phi Eta Sigma; Theta Chi; Bus; Law.

**KOPP, JO ANN E,** Methodist Coll, Fayetteville, NC; SO; BS; Chrstn Life Cncl Sec 90-; Kanona 89-; Alpha Epsilon Omega Sec 89-; Spcl Edn; Tchr.

**KOPP, KATHLEEN A,** Villanova Univ, Villanova, PA; SO; BA; Hse Cncl Wg Repr 89-; Pi Beta Phi Rsh Prty Chrpsn 90-; Proj Snshn Vol 90-; IM Sccr 90-; Lbrl Arts.

**KOPRIVA, LAURA M,** Univ Of Pittsburgh, Pittsburgh, PA; SR; BS; Chld Dvlpmnt Assn Stdnt Exec Cncl Rep 89-; Gldn Key 90-; Chld Dvlpmnt/Chld Cr; Chld Dvlpmnt Spclst.

**KOPSAK, DAVID P,** Kent St Univ Kent Cmps, Kent, OH; JR; BA; Gldn Key; Econ.

**KOPSER, CHRISTINE M,** Univ Of Ky, Lexington, KY; JR; BA; SAC 89-; Bus.

**KOPYTO, SONIA,** Ms St Univ, Miss State, MS; FR; BS; Gama Beta Phi; Phi Delta Phi; All-Amer Schlr; Pres Lst; Deans Lst; Wmns Tnns Tm 90-; Frgn Lang/Geogrphy; Intl Bus.

**KORCAK, JOHN M,** George Mason Univ, Fairfax, VA; SR; BS; Dbt Tm 87-89; Bus; Htl Mgmt.

**KORDANA, JODY A,** Berkshire Comm Coll, Pittsfield, MA; FR; AS; Ofc Mgmt; Bus.

**KORDELSKI, CYNTHIA A,** Kent St Univ Kent Cmps, Kent, OH; SR; BS; Animal Protecltion League Vol; Pre-Imed; Physician.

**KORDONSKY, ALEXANDER,** Ny Univ, New York, NY; GD; DDS; Chess Clb Pres 90-; Sch Scrd Arts Admin Dir 86-88; BA 86; Dntstry; Oral Hlth Care/Rsrch/Educ.

**KORECKO, MARK H,** Kent St Univ Kent Cmps, Kent, OH; JR; BA; Bus Mgmnt.

**KORHONEN, JARKKO P,** Averett Coll, Danville, VA; JR; BS; Intrnatl Clb 90; Alpha Chi; Bus Admn/Mgmt Sci.

**KORINCHAK, SANDRA M,** Westminster Coll, New Wilmingtn, PA; SO; BA; Engl; Publ.

**KORKORIAN, AHMADREZA,** Univ Of Akron, Akron, OH; $500 Acad Schlrshp 88; Swimming; Mech Engr.

**KORMELINK, AMY L,** Owensboro Comm Coll, Owensboro, KY; SO; BA; DPMA; Comp Sci; Sys Analyst.

**KORMICK, GERARD,** Comm Coll Algny Co Algny Cmps, Pittsburgh, PA; SO; Deans List; Hgh Sch Ftbl Dfns End 84; Vanevin Catholic Hgh Schl 88; Bsn Mngmnt; Office Or Firm Mngr.

**KORN, MALKIE,** Yeshiva Univ, New York, NY; JR; BS; Charity Cmmttee 90; Peer Advsr 90; Regstrtn Aid 90; Deans Hon 89-90; Stephen Klein Mem Awd 89-90; Accntng.

**KORNACKI, JULIE A,** Daemen Coll, Amherst, NY; JR; BA; Htlh Fld; Phys Ther.

**KORNEGAY, TERESA G,** Central Al Comm Coll, Alexander City, AL; SO; BS; Natl Hnr Soc 89-; Chi Omega 89-90; Sci; Phy Thrpy.

**KORNEGAY, THOMAS R,** Savannah Coll Of Art & Design, Savannah, GA; FR; Bapt Stdnt Unn 90-; Grphc Dsgn Clb 90-; Hlpng Or Wrld Envrnmntl Grp 90-; Grphc Dsgn; Advrtsng.

**KORNOWSKI, DEBRA L,** Bethany Coll, Bethany, WV; SO; BA; Stdnt Brd Govnr Hsng Rep 89-; Nwspr Prod Mgr 89-; Spnsh Clb 89-; Phdi Mu Fndrsng 90-; Kalon Ldrshp Awrd 89; Swim Tm 89; Intrntl Mktg.

**KOROGI, TODD M,** Univ Of Akron, Akron, OH; SO; BS; Amer Scty Mechncl Eng 89-; Mech Eng.

**KORONA, KAREN A,** Schenectady County Comm Coll, Schenectady, NY; JR; BS; Pres Lst 90; Exec Sec Lbrty Ent 85-; Gen Mgr A & F Prprty Mgmt Inc 86-; AOS Hghst Hnrs Albany Bus Coll 84; Bus Admin; Mrktng.

**KOROSEC, SHARON L,** Tri County Tech Coll, Pendleton, SC; GD; CERT; Cls Pres; Assn Surg Tech; Surg Tech; Nurs.

**KORPIEL, JOHN A,** Univ Of Pittsburgh, Pittsburgh, PA; FR; BS; Jazz Ensmbl Drmr 90-; Cvl Engr.

**KORT, KENNETH W,** Hudson Valley Comm Coll, Troy, NY; FR; AAS; Mrtry Sci Clb 90-; Brd Educ 88-; Police Bnvlnt Assc Trstee 79-; Police Serg 79-; Mrtry Sci; Fnrl Drctng.

**KORTREY, KERRY L,** Liberty Univ, Lynchburg, VA; SO; BA; Human Eclgy Assn 89-; Assn Chrstn Tchrs 89-; Alpha Lambda Delta 90-; Home Econ; Tch.

**KORUTZ, TANYA H,** Duquesne Univ, Pittsburgh, PA; FR; BBA; Sharp; Japanese Clb; Union Prog Bd Un Rltns Chr; Frshman Ldr 90-; Intl Bus; Int Mktng/Finance.

**KORYAKOVA, SVETLANA,** City Univ Of Ny Baruch Coll, New York, NY; JR; BA; Russian Clb V P 90-; Hebrew Clb 89-90; Hns Soc 88-; Cmnty Elderly Vol 88-90; Tutor 90-; Ballet Clb 90-; Cmnctns; Jrnlsm.

**KOSAKOWSKI, LEE A,** Saint Vincents Coll & Seminary, Latrobe, PA; FR; BA; Hist Clb 90; Pre Law Soc 90; Deans Lst 90; Hist Mjr Engl Mnr; Law.

**KOSCHMANN, FAITH L,** Oh Wesleyan Univ, Delaware, OH; FR; BA; OH Wesleyan Deans Lst 90-; Florence Leas Prz; Wmns Indr Trck/Wmns Outdr Trck 90-.

**KOSEK, TERESA J,** Columbia Union Coll, Takoma Park, MD; SR; BS; Alpha Chi; AORN 87-; Full Time Asst Ptnt Care Mgr 89-; RN Med Schl Nrs Poland 68; Hlth Care Admn; Mgr.

**KOSIER, ALLISON M,** Niagara Univ, Niagara Univ, NY; SO; Ntl Mktg Assn Pres 89-90; Ambssdrs 89-; Dorm Cncl 89-; NUCAP 90-; Bus; Advrtsng.

**KOSINSKY, TINA A,** Bryant Stratton Bus Inst Roch, Rochester, NY; GD; Fshn Mgmt Club 90-91; Stdnt Govt Repr; Dns Lst; Wegmans Schlrshp Work Rltd 89-91; Mktg; Cmnctn.

**KOSKI, CHRISTOPHER H,** Nova Univ, Ft Lauderdale, FL; MBA; Prof Med Rescue Assn Pres 79-84; Intrntl Assn Of Fire Fghtrs 75; BS Nova U 90; AS Broward Cmmnty Clg 81; Sprvsr Emer Serv Div 75; Bsnss Admin; EMS.

**KOSKI, JENNIFER L,** Indiana Univ Of Pa, Indiana, PA; FR; BED; Elem Educ; Tchr.

**KOSKINEN, KIRSTEN M,** Goucher Coll, Towson, MD; SR; BS; Gchr Crw Clb Pres 89-; Psychlgy Clb 89-; Intrnshp St Vncnts Chldrns Hm; Psychlgy; Nrsng Infnt Crtcl Cr.

**KOSLOSKI, STEPHANIE A,** Neumann Coll, Aston, PA; SO; BS; Nurs; Pediatric Nurs.

**KOSOWSKI, KRISTINA M,** Georgian Court Coll, Lakewood, NJ; SR; BA; Cncl Excptnl Chldrn 89-; Deans Lst 89-; Sr Stdnt Tchng; Jr Prctcm 90; Sophmore Experience; Spcl Edctn; Cnslng MA.

**KOSSOFF, ERIC H,** Cornell Univ Statutory College, Ithaca, NY; SR; MD; Sci Fctn Assn Treas 88-; Crrclm Com Rep 90-; Natrl Hstry Scty 88 ; Alpha Epsilon Delta VP 88-, Tau Kappa Epsilon Sec 89-; Grad In 3 Yrs; Dns Lst; Tchng Asst; BS; Blgy; Med.

**KOST, HELEN E,** Mount Aloysius Jr Coll, Cresson, PA; GD; ADN; Stdnt Nrsng Org Treas 89-90; Career Day Chrmn 89-90; Phi Theta Kappa; Nrsng; Nrsng Crtcl Cr Units.

**KOST, JAY S,** Oh Univ, Athens, OH; FR; BS; Rgby Clb 90-; Bbll Clb 90-; AFROTC Drll Tm Comp Srvc Offcr 90-; Delta Tau Delta; Elec Eng.

**KOST, JOHN R,** Radford Univ, Radford, VA; SR; BS; House Cncl Flr Rep 87-88; Radford Role Plyrs Guild 89-; Cmptr Clb Treas 90-; Hal Smith Schlrshp Awd 90; Eagle Scout 86; Cmptr Sci; Sftwr Eng/Ntwrkng.

**KOST, TAMARA M,** Univ Of Akron, Akron, OH; SR; BA; Elem Ed.

**KOSTAKOS, CASS C,** Fl International Univ, Miami, FL; SO; BA; Political Theory; Professor.

**KOSTAS, DEBORAH D,** Glassboro St Coll, Glassboro, NJ; FR; BA; Chrstn Fllwshp 90-; Stdnt Bible Mnstry Co Fndr Sec; Psychology.

**KOSTIVAL, ANN M,** Pa St Univ Main Cmps, University Pk, PA; FR; BAE; Arch Engr.

**KOSTKA, JUNE E,** East Stroudsburg Univ, E Stroudsburg, PA; SR; BA; Ambssdr 89-; Rsdnt Advsr 89-; Rsdnce Hll Assn 89-; Lrl Hll Cncl 90-; Omicron Delta Kappa VP 89-; Phi Alpha Theta 90-; Pi Sigma Alpha 90-; Intrnshp Prbtn Intrn Mrrs Cnty Prbtn Dept 90; Parents Assn Schlrshp 90-; Pol Sci Hstry; Law Or Grad Schl.

**KOSTMAYER, AIWEN L,** Univ Of South Al, Mobile, AL; SR; BS; Deans Lst; BA Guangzhou Tchrs Clg Guangzhou China 87; Accntng.

**KOSTOFF, DEBORAH K,** North Central Tech Coll, Mansfield, OH; SR; AS; Amer Soc Rdlgc Tchrs; Appld Sci; RN ICU.

**KOSTURA III, JAMES,** Temple Univ, Philadelphia, PA; JR; BS; IEEE 88-; Elect Engr; Engr.

**KOSTURKO, MICHAEL P,** Bloomfield Coll, Bloomfield, NJ; FR; BA; Bus Admn; Cmptr Info Sys.

**KOSZTYO, DAVID L,** Cornell Univ Statutory College, Ithaca, NY; JR; BS; Vrsty Ftbll 88-89; Ag Bus; Bus.

**KOSZUTA, DANETTE,** Allegheny Coll, Meadville, PA; SR; BA; SG 87-88; Alpha Chi Omega 87-; Allies 90-; Prac Atty Intrn 90; Pol Sci; Law.

**KOSZYCKI, TERESA E,** Lansdale School Of Bus, North Wales, PA; SR; BA; Persnl Achvmnt Awd; Stdnt Of Mnth; BED; Mgmt; Acctg.

**KOT, DENISE,** Indiana Univ Of Pa, Indiana, PA; JR; BA; Chrldr 89-90; Elem Ed.

**KOTA, JAMIE M,** Lock Haven Univ, Lock Haven, PA; FR; BA; Hlth Phys Educ Clb 90-; Wrstlng 90-; Hlth Psys Educ; Tchr/Coach.

**KOTANSKY, SUZANNE G,** Niagara Univ, Niagara Univ, NY; JR; BS; Cmps Mnstry 88-; Yrbk Stf 88-89; Phi Sigma Iota 90-; Delta Epsilon Sigma 90-; Pi Lambda Theta 90-; Deans Lst 88-; French; Edctn.

**KOTLER, BRADLEY L,** Emory Univ, Atlanta, GA; JR; BBA; Stdnt Slumni Assoc Secy/Treas 90-; Comm Of Clg Cncl 90-; Alpha Epsilon Pi 89-; Intrnshp For US Sentr Howard Metzenbaum Washington DC 90; Bus; Law.

**KOTRABA, KIRSTEN,** Mount Saint Mary Coll, Newburgh, NY; FR; BA; Acctg.

**KOTWICA, RONALD M,** Slippery Rock Univ, Slippery Rock, PA; FR; BED; Sccr; Hlth; Thrpy.

**KOUCHE III, EDWARD A,** Oh Wesleyan Univ, Delaware, OH; SO; BA; Prsdnts Clb 89-; Acdmc Status Comm Mmbr 90-; Phi Eta Sigma 90; Phi Soc Vlntr Comm 89-90; Flrnc Leas 2nd Prz Math 90; IM Sccr Bsktbl 89; Accntng; Bsns.

**KOUCOULIS, OURANIA,** City Univ Of Ny Baruch Coll, New York, NY; SO; BBA; Acctg; CPA.

**KOUNS, COSETTA G,** Ashland Comm Coll, Ashland, KY; FR; AAS; BS 89; Irnvl Indpt Bptst Chrch; GS Ldr 85-90 Asst Ldr 85-90; Bsn; Acctnt.

**KOUNS, STEPHANIE DIAN,** Univ Of Cin R Walters Coll, Blue Ash, OH; JR; BA; Natl Assc Secrty Dlrs; Lcnsd Prprty/Cslty Ins Agnt; Lcnsd Lf/Hlth Ins Agnt; Paul Revere Ins Grp Cincinnati OH Sr Custmr Svc Rep; Bus Mgmt.

**KOURAFALOS, PETER H,** Bunker Hill Comm Coll, Boston, MA; FR; BD; Music; Snd Rcrdng Engnr.

**KOURY, LOUIS ELIAS,** Hudson Valley Comm Coll, Troy, NY; GD; Chrstn Stdnts Assn Pres; Deans Lst 90-; Cohoes Comm Rsdnce Intrnshp Res Cnslr 90; Assn Rtrded Ctzns Intrnshp Res Cnslr; Wrshp Ldr 90-; New Lf Assmbly God Ss Tchr 90-; Pres Mns Flwshp 90-; Music Ldr 90-; Mnstrl Bible Coll 83; Tchng Dgree 88; Hmn Serv; Soc Wrkr.

**KOURY, PATRICIA,** Georgian Court Coll, Lakewood, NJ; SO; Deans List; Math.

**KOUSIS, KYRIACOS P,** City Univ Of Ny Baruch Coll, New York, NY; JR; BBA; Pncyprn Assoc 90; Intl Mrktng.

**KOUTLA, ANGELIKI,** Bethany Coll, Bethany, WV; FR; BA; Faith Srng Grp; Chpl Grp; Intl Stdnt Assn 90-; Multi-Cltrl Awrnss Clb 90-; SIFE; Mdwk 90-; Deans Lst 90-; Kappa Delta; Tnns 90-; Ecnmcs/Bus; Mgmt/Admin Bnk.

**KOUTRAKOS, MARY G,** Mount Saint Mary Coll, Newburgh, NY; SO; BS; Srch Comm Drctr Athltc 90; Hsng Coord 90-; Rsdnt Asst; Smmr Asstnt Drctr Rsdnc Lf 90; Accntng; Pblc Accntng.

**KOUWENHOVEN, BRIAN D,** S U N Y Coll Of Tech At Frmgdl, Farmingdale, NY; JR; BA; Tmplt Mkr Grmn Arcrft Syst 85-; Assoc 89; Mfg Eng Tech.

**KOVACH, KIMBERLY A,** Wagner Coll, Staten Island, NY; SO; BS; Intervarsity Chrstn Flwshp Sec/Treas 90-; Deans Merit Schlr; Elem Edn/Psychlgy; Spcl Edn.

**KOVACH, TERRI E,** Wv Northern Comm Coll, Wheeling, WV; SR; RN; Outstndng Nrsng Stdnt Of Yr; IAFF 85; CPR Instr 89; Cty Firefghtr; LPN Jffrsn Cnty Tech Inst 75; Nrsng; Firefghtng/Nrsng.

**KOVACIK, TISA N,** Oh St Univ, Columbus, OH; SR; BS; IDSA 88-; Phi Eta Sigma 88-; Alpha Lambda Delta 88-; Phi Kappa Phi 90-; OH Schlr; Vsl Cmmnctns; Grphc Dsgnr.

**KOVAL, SUSAN M,** Mount Aloysius Jr Coll, Cresson, PA; FR; AS; Med Asst Clb Sec; Med Asst; Med.

**KOVALCHIK, JOHN S,** Western New England Coll, Springfield, MA; SR; BS; YMCA Intrn; All-Conf Ftbl 90; WNEC Outstndng Lineman Awd 90; Var Ftbl 87-90; Psych.

**KOVATS JR, KENNETH R,** Univ Of Akron, Akron, OH; JR; BSN; US Army James A Garfield Co Pres 90-; Gldn Key 90-; US Army ROTC 3 Yr Schlrshp; Nrsng; US Army Nrs Corps Offcr.

**KOVELL, MICHELLE L,** Westminster Coll, New Wilmingtn, PA; SR; BA; Stdnt Admssns V P 89-; Frshmn Orient Org Tm 88-90; Res Ife Staff 89-90; Pi Delta Phi Pres 88-; Mortar Bd Alumni Chr 90-; Omicron Delta Kappa 90-; Sigma Kappa Corr Sec 88-; Vol Serv Of Amer 87-89; Learing Ctr Assist 89; French/Spanish; Tchng.

**KOVER, JANICE S,** Univ Of Akron, Akron, OH; JR; BA; Gold Key; Scndry Edn/Math/Hst; Tchr.

**KOVICK, CHAD O,** Kent St Univ Kent Cmps, Kent, OH; JR; BA; Acctng; CPA.

**KOWAL, MATTHEW A,** Univ Of Sc At Columbia, Columbia, SC; FR; MBA; Crln Prgm Un 90; Swm Tm 90; Intl Stds.

**KOWALEWSKI, SHARON M,** Boston Univ, Boston, MA; FR; BA; Serv Clb 90; SG 90-; Phys Therapy; Pediatric Phys Therapy.

**KOWALEWSKI, TERRI J,** Radford Univ, Radford, VA; SO; BS; Stdnt Ed Assn 90; Ed; Child Psychlgy.

**KOWALSKI, DAVID A,** Univ Of Akron, Akron, OH; SO; BA; Intrntnl Bsns Clb; Bsns Admnstrtn Accntng; Lawyr.

**KOWALSKI, DENISE M,** Life Coll, Marietta, GA; GD; DC; Sr X-Ray Intrn Pgm Pres 88-90; Thompson Tech Clb 87-; Mtn Palptn Clb 87-; BS Bio Farleigh Dickinson U 87; Chiro.

**KOWALSKI, JENNIFER A,** Juniata Coll, Huntingdon, PA; SO; BS; Chem Clb Treas; Admssns Assn 90-; Hon Soc; Beta Beta Beta 90-; Cir K VP 89-90; Fresh Chem Awd 90; Biochem; Med Rsrch.

**KOWALSKI, LYNETTE E,** Lorain County Comm Coll, Elyria, OH; FR; BED; Erly Chldhd Educ; Educ.

**KOWANICK, MARY M,** Marywood Coll, Scranton, PA; JR; BM; Delta Epsilon Sigma 90-; Pi Kappa Lambda; Music Perf; Priv Msc Tchr.

**KOWATCH, PATRICIA L,** Saint Vincents Coll & Seminary, Latrobe, PA; JR; BS; Alpha Sigma Lambda; Rsrch Assist 90-; Amer Occptnl Thrpy Assn 74-; Blrsvl Borough Reclyling 90-; AS Mt Aloysius Jr Clg 74; Bus Admin/Mgmnt; Ind Mgmnt.

**KOZAK, RENATA K,** Saint Joseph Coll, West Hartford, CT; FR; BSN; Nrsng.

**KOZAK, TRACI A,** S U N Y Coll At Fredonia, Fredonia, NY; SR; BS; BCIC 89-90; Delta Kappa Pi 89; Soph Ed Awd 88; Elem Ed; MS In Spec Ed.

**KOZAK, W MIKE,** Clarkson Univ, Potsdam, NY; SR; BS; Fran Neragin Awd; Vrsty Hcky 87-; Mktng; Mngmnt.

**KOZEL, PHILIP M,** Oh St Univ, Columbus, OH; SR; BA; Arts Scis Awrd Fr Exclnce In Schlrshp 90; Hstry Intrnatl Stds; Intnatl Dev Plnng.

**KOZIOL, CYNTHIA A,** Dyke Coll, Cleveland, OH; JR; BS; Paralegal Assn V P; Paralegal; Law.

**KOZLICKI, LAURIE VANESSA,** Radford Univ, Radford, VA; FR; BA; Stdnt Life Committee 90-; Alpha Lambda Delta; Psychology/Educ; Child Psychlgst/Elem Educ.

**KOZLIN, DAVID D,** Fl Atlantic Univ, Boca Raton, FL; SR; BBA; AA Palm Bch Cmmnty Clg 88; Fnce.

**KOZLOSKI, MICHAEL L,** Western New England Coll, Springfield, MA; JR; Rsrch With Prof In Accident Reconstrctn/ Investgtn Training 90-; Ftbl 87-88; Montague Police Spcl Ofcr 88-89; Psych; Grad Schl.

**KOZLOSKY, KIMBERLY S,** Marywood Coll, Scranton, PA; SO; Elem Ed; Tch.

**KOZMINSKI, KIRK D,** Univ Of Pittsburgh At Bradford, Bradford, PA; FR; BS; Alpha Lambda Delta; Chem.

**KOZMINSKI, MICHAEL J,** Univ Of Pittsburgh At Bradford, Bradford, PA; SR; BS; Amer Chem Soc 88-; Alpha Lambda Delta; Alpha Phi Omega 89-; NSF Intshp 90; Natl Sci Awd; Chem; Industry.

**KOZUMPLIK, A C,** Fl St Univ, Tallahassee, FL; SR; BS; People Like Us VP 85-88; FSU Cave Clb 88-; Musical Trio 88-; Undrgrad Rsrch Assist Dr J Carbonell Dept Of Psych FSU 87-88; Cpr; Ntrtn; Dietetics.

**KOZUSKO, GEORGEANNE L,** Comm Coll Algny Co Algny Cmps, Pittsburgh, PA; FR; Swmg; Chrch Fnctns; Nrsg Asst 82-84; Tchr.

**KRAEBEL, KIMBERLY S,** Edinboro Univ Of Pa, Edinboro, PA; SR; BA; Chrstn Flwshp Sec 87-; Psy Clb 87-; Phi Eta Sigma 87-; Alpha Chi 89-; Psi Chi 88-; Hnrs Schlp 87-88; Crowe Hnrs Schlp 88-90; Milles Psy Hnrs Awd 89-; APSCUF Schlp 88-; Crs Cntry/ Indr Trck/Outdr Trck 87-88; Psy; Exprmntl Psy.

**KRAEHMER, DAVID C,** Memphis St Univ, Memphis, TN; FR; BS; Phi Eta Sigma; Phi Gamma Delta Schlrshp Chrmn; Elec Eng.

**KRAEMER, DENISE S,** Hudson Valley Comm Coll, Troy, NY; SO; AAS; AS Ulster Cnty Comm Clg 90; Exec Ofc Asst.

**KRAEMER, LYNN A,** Georgian Court Coll, Lakewood, NJ; SO; Engl.

**KRAEUTLER, MELISSA A,** Univ Of Sc At Columbia, Columbia, SC; JR; BA; Advrtsng Clb; Frat Aux; Advrtsng/Mktg; Acct Mgr.

**KRAFT, HEATHERLYN A,** Univ Of Rochester, Rochester, NY; SO; Cmps Rd Pblc Srvc Dir; Cmmtt Prfrmng Arts Tchnl Offcr B; Alpha Psi Omega; Alpha Phi; Intern Crtvty Rsrch 90; Engl; Scndry Tchr.

**KRAFT, LYNN D,** Mount Aloysius Jr Coll, Cresson, PA; FR; AAS; S Alleghanies Reg VP 89-; Msm Avas Axlry; YWCA 89-; Mercy Hosp Gld 89-; Comm Arts Ctr 89-; Jycs 90-; Phi Theta Kappa 90-; Occup Therapy.

**KRAFT, STEPHANIE,** Univ Of Cin R Walters Coll, Blue Ash, OH; FR; AAS; Cert Inst Of Med/Dntl Tech 88-89; Dental Hygienist.

**KRAFTY, THOMAS J,** Bowling Green St Univ At Huron, Huron, OH; FR; AAS; Respiratory Care Club 90-; Ame Assoc For Respiratory Care 91-; Holy Angels Parish Council 85-87; Respiratory Therapy.

**KRAHAM, ALEXANDRA,** Univ Of Southern Ms, Hattiesburg, MS; SO; BA; Coll Rpblcns 90-; Stdnt Eagle Clb 90-; Gamma Alpha Epsilon 90-; Gamma Beta Phi 90-; Delta Delta Delta IM 90-; Sigma Alpha Epsilon Ltl Sis 90-; IM Flg Ftbll/Sftbll 90-; Env Biology; Law.

**KRAHN, SUSAN,** Ny Univ, New York, NY; FR; AAS; Bsn.

**KRAIZMAN, MICHAEL,** City Univ Of Ny Baruch Coll, New York, NY; SR; BBA; Beta Gamma Sigma 90; Gldn Key 89-; Sigma Alpha Delta 88-89; Untd Career Cntrs NY NY 85-89; Actncy; Acctg/Fin.

**KRAJCIRIK, BILL T,** Kent St Univ Geauga Cmps, Burton Twp, OH; JR; BA; Bus; Mrktg.

**KRAJEWSKI-ZIELINSKI, SUSAN M,** Univ Of Scranton, Scranton, PA; JR; MS; Delta Epsilon Pres; Delta Mu Dlta; Phi Beta Kappa; Phi Beta Lambda; Pre Law Socite; Pres List; Prelaw/ Econ/Finance/Minor History; Law Corp.

**KRAK, KEVIN R,** S U N Y At Buffalo, Buffalo, NY; JR; BA; Golden Key; Mktg; MBA.

**KRAKOVSKY, DAWN M,** Comm Coll Algny Co Algny Cmps, Pittsburgh, PA; JR; BA; Anml Shltr Vol; Pre-Vet; Vet Med.

**KRALL, DEBRA L,** Susquehanna Univ, Selinsgrove, PA; FR; BA; Mrchng/Symp Bnd 90; Alpha Lambda Delta; Sigma Alpha Iota; Hnrs Prog 90; Math; Actrl Sci.

**KRALY-MORRISON, VERONICA M,** Beaver Coll, Glenside, PA; GD; PHD; Phi Beta Kappa 86-; Kappa Delta Pi 85-; Tchng Asstshp 88-90; Grad Asstshp 86-90; Rsrch Asstshp 89-90; NCTE; Tchr Engl 88-; MA 90; 2 Certs 86; Engl; Ed.

**KRAMCZYNSKI, JOHN J,** Western New England Coll, Springfield, MA; SO; BS; Accntng Assn VP 90-; NAA Actvts Prsdnt; Vrsty Bwlng Cptn 89-; Alpha Lambda Delta; Deans Lst Stdnt 89-; Alpha Lambda Delta 89-; Tutor 89-; Accntng; CPA.

**KRAMER, BRIAN J,** Rutgers St Un At New Brunswick, New Brunswick, NJ; FR; BS; Comp Sci/Math; Sftwr Engr.

**KRAMER, DANIEL J,** Oh Univ, Athens, OH; GD; DO; SOMA 89-; Sprts Med Clb 90-; Fmly Prctc Clb 89-; Sigma Sigma Phi 90-; Rsrch Flwshp 90; BS Youngstown St Univ 88; Ostpthc Med; Med.

**KRAMER, GAIL H,** City Univ Of Ny City Coll, New York, NY; JR; BA; Amnsty Intl 88-; Grnpce 88-; NYPIRG 90-; City Coll Fllwshp; Engl; Prof.

**KRAMER, GLENN D,** Duquesne Univ, Pittsburgh, PA; SR; BA; Sftbl; Cmmtr Cncl; Dns Lst; Acct; Law.

**KRAMER, JOYCE C,** Univ Of Md Baltimore Prof Schl, Baltimore, MD; SR; Intrnshp NIMH 86; Intrnshp Returning Stdtns Porg 86-87; Natl Assn Soc Wrkrs 90-; BA U Of MD 88; MSW; Clinical Soc Wrk.

**KRAMER, KELLI R,** Univ Of Cin R Walters Coll, Blue Ash, OH; FR; AS; Nrsng.

**KRAMER, MELISSA T,** Glassboro St Coll, Glassboro, NJ; JR; BA; Literary Forum 90; Engl Hnr Scty; Engl; High Schl Engl Tchr.

**KRAMER, MICHELLE M,** Radford Univ, Radford, VA; FR; Sftbl 90-; IM Bsktbl 90-; Alpha Sigma Tau.

**KRAMER, SHANNON L,** Univ Of Akron, Akron, OH; JR; Rsdnce Hall Pblcty 89-90; Golden Key 90; Phi Eta Sigma 89; Alpha Lambda Delta 89; Athletic Trnr Sprvsr; Akron Womens Trk Tm; Westerville Physcl Thrpy Clnc; Im Trnr 89; Athletic Trng Physcl Thrpy; Physcl Thrpst.

**KRAMER, TARA E,** Loyola Coll In Md, Baltimore, MD; FR; BA; Wmns Lacrosse Tm Div I NCAA Vrsty; Comm Serv; Lacrosse-Vrsty; Elem Ed; Tchng Coachg Cnsltng.

**KRAMP, NANCY E,** Univ Of Cincinnati, Cincinnati, OH; SR; BSN; Sub S S Tchr; Sigma Theta Tau; NCNA Awrd; Gldn Ky; USAA; Valor Prog; Hnrd Div Undrgrad Stu Affrs; Nrsng/Hlth; Intnsv Care Nrsng CRNA.

**KRAMPF, CARRIE R,** Belmont Coll, Nashville, TN; FR; BBA; Music Bsns; A/R Publ Music.

**KRANE, JAMES M J,** City Univ Of Ny City Coll, New York, NY; SR; Intl Studies Clb 88-; Golden Key 90-; BA; Intl Studies/ Pol Sci; Jrnlsm.

**KRANER, TODD H,** Wilmington Coll, Wilmington, OH; JR; BA; SGA Pres 89-; Res Life Res Dir 89-; Stu Fndtns 89-; Mrktng/Mngmnt/Acct.

**KRANINGER, DANIEL J,** Villanova Univ, Villanova, PA; SO; BA; Sigma Phi Epsilon 89-90; Prjct Snshn 89-90; Cmmtt Hmlss 89; IM 89-90; Ecnmcs; Law.

**KRANJAC, JULIETTE E,** Fordham Univ, Bronx, NY; JR; BS; Vol Tax Asst Prog; Phi Kappa Phi 90-; Beta Gamma Sigma; Beta Alpha Psi; Schlstc Schlrshp 88-; Amer Soc Wmn Accntnts Schlrshp; Dean Lst 88-90; Accntng; CPA.

**KRANKEY, KIM M,** Ms St Univ, Miss State, MS; JR; BED; IM Sprts; Cath Stdnt Assoc; Phi Kappa Phi; Kappa Delta Pi Hist Elec; Sigma Tau Delta; Pres Schlr 88-; Sec Educ/English; Clg Prof.

**KRANSTEUBER, AMY S,** Univ Of Al At Huntsville, Huntsville, AL; SR; BSE; Crew Team 89-90; Alpha Lambda Delta 86-; Tau Beta Pi 88-; Eta Kappa Nu 88-; Phi Kappa Phi 88-; Elec Eng; Optics/Eng.

**KRANTZ, BRAD T,** Savannah Coll Of Art & Design, Savannah, GA; SR; BA; Am Soc Intr Dsgnrs; Hmncs Clb High Point Clg 88; Deans List 88 90-; Intr Dsgn.

**KRAPF, ALFRED T,** Providence Coll, Providence, RI; FR; BA; Lit Magazine; Englsh; Tchng.

**KRASNJANSKI, MOISHE A,** Central Yeshiva Tomchei Tmimim, Brooklyn, NY; GD; Talmudic Law Jrnl Chf Ed 87-89; Stdnt Union Pres 88-89; Talmudic Law Pt Lecturer 88-89; BA 89; Jewish Law.

**KRASNOFF, LISA ANNETTE,** Fl International Univ, Miami, FL; SR; BS; Htl Fd Trvl Assoc; Phi Lambda Chi Natl Hnrs Scty; Rstrnt Mgmt Intrn; IM Sftbll; Hsptlty Mgmt.

**KRASNOSKY, ROBERT C,** Fl St Univ, Tallahassee, FL; SR; BS; Amer Soc Cvl Engr Secr 89-; Natl Soc Prof Engrs 86-88; Engr Soc 86-88; FAMU PSU Clg Engr 89-; Phi Kappa Theta 86-88; IM Ftbl/Sftbl/Soccer Coach 89-; Cvl Engr; Engr.

**KRASOWSKI, MITCHELL J,** Coll Of Charleston, Charleston, SC; SO; BS; Comp Sci; Comp Mtrlgy/Astrnmy.

**KRASS, JEFFREY M,** Comm Coll Algny Co Algny Cmps, Pittsburgh, PA; FR; Theatre Prdctn Actor 89-90; Dfrnt Drummer Poetry Mag Staff Wrtr 90-; Deans List 89-; Dfrnt Drummer Mag Awd Staff Wrtr 90; Acctg/Clnry Arts.

**KRASUCKI, JANELLE,** Univ Of Rochester, Rochester, NY; SR; BA; D Lion Orgnztn 88-89; Dlt Gamma Anchr PR 89-; Chldrns Ctr Pgm Crdntr Intrn 90-; Engl; Educ Guidnc Cnslng.

**KRASZNAI, LESLIE K,** Middlesex County Coll, Edison, NJ; FR; AA; Dentl Asst 86-; Sci; Dentl Hygnst.

**KRATSMAN, FLORENCIA K,** Univ Of Pr At Rio Piedras, Rio Piedras, PR; SO; Arch.

**KRATTS, JULIE A,** Western Ky Univ, Bowling Green, KY; SR; BS; Phi Kappa Phi; Alpha Sigma Lamada; Fntn Sq Chrch Chldrns Chrch Dir 87-; Chrprsn Open Hnd Comm; Soc Diag Med Sonogrphr; Soc Varclr Tech; Reg Vasclr Tech; Reg Rad Tech; Reg Diag Med Songrphr; Reg Diag Cardc Songrphr; AAS Trocar Clg N Y 81; Alld Hlth Educ; Med Ultrsnd Tech Edctr.

**KRATZ, LA MAR R,** Lansdale School Of Bus, North Wales, PA; ASB; Deans Lst 89-; Am Vacuum Soc 90-; Manuf Prod Supvr 80-; Cert LSB; Ofc Mgmnt.

**KRATZER, MICHELE L,** Kent St Univ Kent Cmps, Kent, OH; JR; BS; Deans List; Pre Med; Physician.

**KRATZER, VINCENT X,** Glassboro St Coll, Glassboro, NJ; SR; BS; Intrnshp Salem Cnty Juvnl Prbtn Dept Salem Nj 90; AAS Salem Comm Coll 89; Law/Justice.

**KRAUS, TINA M,** Radford Univ, Radford, VA; SR; BS; LEAD Pres 89-90; Essay Schlrshp; Cmmnctns; Law.

**KRAUS-KOPF, KRISTINE M,** Wagner Coll, Staten Island, NY; SR; Tri-Beta Treas 87-88; Omicron Delta Kappa 89-; Hon Roll 87-; Schlrshp 87-; BS; Bio; Lab/Tchng.

**KRAUSE, CANDICE A,** Fl St Univ, Tallahassee, FL; SR; BS; Women In Cmmnctns Treas 89f Mrchng Chiefs 87-88; Fla Pblc Rltns Assoc 89-90; Phi Eta Sigma 87; Wesley Fndtn Cmmttee Chr 87-90; Summa Cum Laude; Deans Lst 87; Tchng Assist Cmptrs For Comn; Acmmnctns; Prsnnl.

**KRAUSE, CONSTANCE J,** Fl International Univ, Miami, FL; SR; BS; Stdnt Occuptnl Thrpy Assoc; Pi Theta Epsilon; Phi Kappa Phi; Occuptnl Thrpy.

**KRAUSE, DORIAN K,** Univ Of West Fl, Pensacola, FL; JR; BA; Phi Beta Lambda; AA Pensacola Jr Clg 81; Bus Tchr Ed; Tchr/Fed Govt.

**KRAUSE, KAREN D,** S U N Y Coll At Fredonia, Fredonia, NY; SR; BED; Kappa Dlt Pi; El Ed/En Endrsmnt.

**KRAUSE, KENT W,** Univ Of Miami, Coral Gables, FL; SR; BS; SGA Sen 89-90; Intrfrat Cncl Sec 881-89; Assn Greek Ltr Org Sec 88-89; Order Omega 90-; Omicron Delta Kappa 90-; Sigma Chi Pres 87-; Awd Excell Stdnt Indmnt; Marine Sci/Bio.

**KRAUSS, ALETA A,** Wilmington Coll, New Castle, DE; JR; BA; Phi Theta Kappa; BSA Comm Treas; AAS Del Tech 90; Acctng; Tch.

**KRAUZA, PAULA M,** Allegheny Coll, Meadville, PA; SR; BA; Radio Disc Jcky; Alpha Gamma Delta Recdng Sec; Fam Plng Serv Intrn; Alden Schlr; Sociology Art; Admsns Cnslr.

**KRAWCZYK, JOYCE A,** Le Moyne Coll, Syracuse, NY; SO; BA; Bus Admin.

**KRAWIEC, LORI J,** Atlantic Comm Coll, Mays Landing, NJ; FR; Cert DA Ocean Cnty Voctnl Tech Sch 85; Physcl Sci; Thrpst.

**KRAZINSKY, VICKI A,** Stockton St Coll, Pomona, NJ; JR; Tltn Athltc Clb; Cntrl; Acctg; CPA.

**KREBS, JEANNIE M,** Northern Ky Univ, Highland Hts, KY; SO; AD; Bsn Mngmnt; Avtn Admin.

**KREBS, KATHY LYNN,** Spalding Univ, Louisville, KY; SR; BED; NSSHLA 89-; AS Jefferson Community Clg 89; Speech Pathology; Teaching.

**KREBS, PATRICIA R,** Radford Univ, Radford, VA; SO; BS; Cntrl UMC Admin Bd 87-; New River Vly Hospice Assist Dir 87-89; Nrsng.

**KREBS, STEPHANIE K,** Oh Univ, Athens, OH; FR; BFA; Newman Clb 90-; I M Sftbl; Art.

**KREBS, SUSAN E,** Radford Univ, Radford, VA; SR; MA; Stdnt Rep Frgn Lang Crclm 89-90; Eta Sigma Phi Pres 90-; Pi Gamma Mu 90-; Tutor 90-; Deans Lst 89 91; BA; Latin; Grad Sch.

**KREGER, LISA A,** Duquesne Univ, Pittsburgh, PA; SR; BS; Folk Grp 87-89; IDEAS 88-89; Food Serv Review Com 90-; Lambda Sigma 88-89; Rho Chi Co-Chair Tutor 90-; Phi Kappa Phi; Rifle Tm Schlrshp 90-; IM Vlybl Champ 89; Deans Lst; Rifle Tm 89-; Instnl Phrmcy.**

**KREIDER, DOREEN M,** Lancaster Bible Coll, Lancaster, PA; FR; AS; Stdnt Govt Asst Sec; Class Sec; Cnslng.

**KREIDL, OLIVIER P,** George Mason Univ, Fairfax, VA; SO; BS; IEEE; AFCEA; Alpha Lambda Delta; Elec Comp Eng; Eng.**

**KREIGER, AMY R,** Cleveland Inst Of Art, Cleveland, OH; FR; Stdnt Cncl Cleve Inst Art Rep 90-; Schlrshp Awrd 90-; Cnslr Grl Scts 84-87; Grnbriar Comm Theatr 88-89; Art Educ.

**KREIN, CHRISTINE M,** Marist Coll, Poughkeepsie, NY; SO; BS; Sigma Zeta; Bausch/Lomb Sci Awd; Chem; Chem Engnr/Coll Prof.

**KREIS, KATHERINE M,** Le Moyne Coll, Syracuse, NY; SO; BA; Ins Claim Spclst 88-; Acctg; CPA.

**KREIS II, STEVEN D,** Univ Of Ky, Lexington, KY; FR; MSE; Engrng; Mng/Agri Engr.

**KREISBERG, JOHN A,** Fl St Univ, Tallahassee, FL; FR; BS; Phi Eta Sigma 90-; Math; Aerospce Eng.

**KREISEL, RUDOLPH K,** Nova Univ, Ft Lauderdale, FL; GD; MBA; Spnsh Rvr Chrch; AA Cvnnt Clg 82; BA Mgmt Sci/Sys 84; Mgmt Serv; Serv Mgmt.

**KREISLE, MARSHA R,** Univ Of Sc At Columbia, Columbia, SC; SO; BS; Moore & Springer Schlrshp Deans & Pres List 89-; Burroughs Foundn Schlrshp 90-; Biology; Medicine.**

**KREITZ, ANN M,** Oh Wesleyan Univ, Delaware, OH; JR; BFA; Stdnt Fdn; Big Pal Little Pal 90-; Cir K 89-90; Crss Cntry/Track Var 88-90; Fine Arts.

**KREITZER, DALE W,** Wv Northern Comm Coll, Wheeling, WV; GD; AAS; DPMA 90-; Data Prcssng Mgr 78-; Cmptr Infor Prcssng.

**KREITZER, JONAS J,** East Stroudsburg Univ, E Stroudsburg, PA; SO; BA; Hll Cncl 90; Res Hll Cmtt 90-; Dnng Hll Comm 90; Pblcty Trp Cmtt 90; Dean Lst 89-; Pres Lst 89-; IM Ftbl Sftbl Tm Capt 89-; Biol; Med.

**KREIZMAN, ISAAC J,** Yeshiva Univ, New York, NY; SR; BA; Jrnl Sci Resrch Abstracts Ed-In-Chf 90-; Russian Clb Pres 89-; Psych V P 90-; Powerhouse Weightlftg/Fitness Clb V P 89-90; Sci Resrch Hnr Soc V P 90-; Hebrew Hnr Soc 88-; Dns Lst 90; Toro Do Jo Karate Clb 3 Belts 88-; Bio/Psych; Med.

**KREMER, AMY L,** Georgetown Coll, Georgetown, KY; SO; BS; SGA 90; Alpha Lambda Delta 90; Envrnmntl Actn Grp 89; Rsdnt Assist 90; Dist 32 Schlr Athlete 90; Vllybl 89; Phy Ed; Tchr.

**KREMER, KEITH J,** Widener Univ, Chester, PA; SO; Track/Cross Cntry; Nwspr Ftr Edtr; Radio Sta DJ; Deans Lst; Acdmc Schlrshp.

**KRENTA, KAREN S,** Jersey City St Coll, Jersey City, NJ; SR; BSN; BA 83; Nursing.

**KRENTZ, TAMARA S,** Auburn Univ At Auburn, Auburn, AL; JR; BA; Hrtcltre Frm Sec 90-; UPC Flms Com 90; Pnhllnc Cncl 90-; Alpha Lambda Delta 89-; Phi Eta Sigma 89-; Omicron Delta Kappa; Pi Alpha Xi VP; Kappa Alpha Theta Pres 88-; Phi Kappa Phi 89; Gamma Sigma Delta 89-; Lncstr Almnae Pnhllnc Rcgntn Awrd 90-; Hrtcltre; Coll Prfssr.**

**KRENZER, BARBARA J,** S U N Y Coll Of Tech At Alfred, Alfred, NY; FR; PPGA; Flrcltr Prdctn.

**KRESCANKO, CYNTHIA A,** Univ Of Pittsburgh, Pittsburgh, PA; JR; BSN; U Schlr; AD Delaware Co Cmnty Clge 88; Nrsg; RN.**

**KRESS, BRADLEY A,** Savannah Coll Of Art & Design, Savannah, GA; JR; MBA; Photo/Hstry Prsrvtn; Arch Photo.

**KRESS, JUDY L,** Wilmington Coll, Wilmington, OH; SR; Commuter Clb 90-; Green Key; Magnu Cum Laude; BA; AA Southern St Comm Clg 89; Elem Educ; Teach.

**KRESSE, KENNETH A,** D Youville Coll, Buffalo, NY; JR; BA; Kappa Delta Pres 90-; Nwspr 90-; Hon Pgm 88-; Deans Lst 88-; Hist; Intelligence Wrk FBI/CIA.

**KRETOW, TAMARA M,** Univ Of Rochester, Rochester, NY; SR; BA; Yrbk Ed 87-; IM Flr Hcky Capt 87-; Deans Lst 88-; Certs; Math: Actrl Sci.

**KRETZ, CURTIS M,** S U N Y Coll Of Tech At Delhi, Delhi, NY; SR; BAS; NYSAVT 89-; David Cross Meml Awd; AAS; Vet Sci.

**KREUER, KENT A,** Nova Univ, Ft Lauderdale, FL; GD; MBA; Dist Sales Mngr; BBA Iowa St Univ 83.

**KREUTZ, MATTHEW P,** Cornell Univ, Ithaca, NY; FR; BA; Intr Frat Cncl Pres Of Jr Intr Frat Cncl; Sigma Phi Epsilon Socl Comm; Asst Tomkins Cnty Offc Agng; Vol Wrk Tompkins Cnty Hosp; Chmstry/Pre Med; Med Dr.

**KREUTZBERG, THOMAS J,** Anne Arundel Comm Coll, Arnold, MD; SO; BSEE; Elec Engr; Engr.

**KREUZER, TIMOTHY M,** Univ Of New Haven, West Haven, CT; SR; BS; Air Trans Mngmnt.

**KREVOKUCH, KRISTI L,** Indiana Univ Of Pa, Indiana, PA; FR; BS; Secondary Math Ed; Tch.

**KRIEG, JENNIFER K,** Teikyo Post Univ, Waterbury, CT; JR; BS; Stdnt Govt Assn Treas 90; Dorm Cncl Pres 88-90; Amer Mktng Assn Treas 88-90; Edwin H Angevire Schlrshp; Trustees Schlrshp 90-; Outstanding Ldrshp Awds 88-; Soccer Tm Athltc Schlrshp 88; Acctng.

**KRIEG, JENNIFER L,** Hillsborough Comm Coll, Tampa, FL; FR; AA; PAWS; Bus Admn/Acctg; Fin Mgmt.

**KRIEGER, KATHRYN M,** Defiance Coll, Defiance, OH; SR; BSW; Stdnt Soc Work Org 87-; Tau Mu 90-; OH Regents Flwshp; Soc Wrk.

**KRIER, VICKI M,** Commonwealth Coll, Virginia Beach, VA; SO; Law; Paralgl.

**KRIEVARS, ULDIS,** Univ Of Ct, Storrs, CT; FR; Franternitas Mtrpltn; Agri Economics; Economics.

**KRIMAS, DARCIE M,** Univ Of Akron, Akron, OH; FR; BA; Hstry.

**KRIMMER, KATHIE A,** Univ Of Cincinnati, Cincinnati, OH; JR; BA; Head Athltc Trainer At Turpin HS 90-; Hlth Ed/Sports Medcn; Athltc Trnng/Tch.

**KRISNANTO, ION,** Duquesne Univ, Pittsburgh, PA; Intl Stdtns Org Treas 89-; Finance; Banking.

**KRISS, SCOTT A,** Bethany Coll, Bethany, WV; SR; BA; Stdnt Brd Gov Asst Tr 89-90; Stdnts Fr Entrprs Sec 88-90; Schl Nwspr Asst Bs Mgr 89; Gamma Sigma Kappa 90-; Omicion Delta Epsilon 90-; Gamma Rho Imicron 90-; Kalon; Beta Theta Pi Sec 88-; Sr Felw Econ Busn Dept 90-; Outstdng Sr Busn; IM; Acctg.

**KRISTOFIK, KIRSTEN R,** Duquesne Univ, Pittsburgh, PA; SR; BS; Deans Lst; Lukemia Soc PA 90; DDF/M Advrtsng Mktg Intern 90; Mktg.

**KRITKAUSKY, KRISTINA A,** Bucknell Univ, Lewisburg, PA; JR; BA; Dnc Tm Capt 88-90; Frnch Clb 88-90; Kappa Kappa Gamma 89-; Intrnshp Amnsty Intl Geneva Switzrlnd 90; Intl Rltns French; IGO/NGO.

**KRIVIAN, KATALIN,** Hillsborough Comm Coll, Tampa, FL; SO; A; Wild Life Socty Hungary 82; Hnrd Nrs Hungary 82-83; Snasa Planetary Inst Houston Int; Nrsng License Hungary; Rgstrd Nurs Drenes Laszlo Debreccu Hungary 82; Blgy Physcs; Doctorate Genetics.

**KRIZANIC, SHARON R,** Comm Coll Algny Co Algny Cmps, Pittsburgh, PA; FR; AS; Math; Mtrlgy.

**KROEKER, KAREN J,** Emory & Henry Coll, Emory, VA; SO; BA; Stdnt VA Educ Assoc 89-; Phi Sigma Iota Pres; Emory/Henry Schlr; Engl; Elem Tchr.

**KROESSER, DAVE A,** Oh Univ, Athens, OH; JR; BA; Stdnt Govt 89-90; Flying Bobcats Coach 90-; Alpha Eta Rho 89-; Soccer 89; Airway Sci; Aviation.

**KROGER, DIANA L,** Univ Of Cincinnati, Cincinnati, OH; JR; BA; Guard Lt 88-; Varsity Band 88-; Alpha Lambda Delta 88-; Tau Beta Sigma 88-; Gold Key; Kappa Delta Pi 89-; Voorheis Schlrshp; Elem Edn; Tchr.

**KROK, PETER P,** Bridgeport Engr Inst, Fairfield, CT; SO; BS; D J Diasio Sr Schlrshp; Eng.

**KROL, CHRISTINE A,** Elms Coll, Chicopee, MA; FR; BA; Stdnt Act Com 90-; Stdnt Ambsdr 90-; St Agnes Yth Grp VP 88-90; Alpine Ski Team 87-90; Bus; Acctg.

**KROLL, HEIDI L,** Smith Coll, Northampton, MA; JR; BS; Hse Cncl 90-; Econs.

**KROLL, TRACIE A,** Fl St Univ, Tallahassee, FL; JR; BA; D J Radio; Intrn Record Bar 90; Bus Cmunctns; Music Shop Ownr.

**KROMA, THOMAS B,** Bowling Green St Univ, Bowling Green, OH; SR; BS; Construction Mngrs Scty 90-; Phi Theta Kappa 87-89; Epsilon Pi Tau; Pi Kappa Phi 87-89; Home Bldrs Assoc Schlrshp 90; Assoc Univ Toledo 86-89; Construction; Mngmnt.

**KROMASH, SELIENA P,** King Coll, Bristol, TN; SO; Pltcl Sci Clb 90-; RHA Sctn Rep 89-90; Ornttn Advsr; Delta Zeta 90-; Amblnc Crps Vol; Deans Lst 90-; IM Vllybll 89; Pltcl Sci.

**KROMER, JEFFERY L,** Savannah Coll Of Art & Design, Savannah, GA; SR; BFA; Pntng/Fine Arts; Prfssr.

**KROMIS, SHARON M,** Gaston Coll, Dallas, NC; FR; AAS; Gamma Beta Phi Pres 85-86; Acctg.

**KROMMIDAS, MARIA LO,** City Univ Of Ny La Guard Coll, Long Island Cty, NY; JR; Womens Clb; Phi Theta Kappa 89-; Deans Lst; Comp Sci.

**KRON, ALLEN L,** Ms St Univ, Miss State, MS; SR; BED; Jr Coll Ftbl Co Tm Capt 88; AA East Central Comm Coll 88; Tchng Cchng; Cch.

**KRONAUER, ELIZABETH J,** Univ Of Louisville, Louisville, KY; JR; MENG; IEEE 90-; Golden Key; Ntl Hon Roll 89-; NCEA; St Barnabas Cochng Stf 5/6 Coch 90; S Ctrl Bell Co-Op Ntwrk Oper; Schlrshp KY Soc Pro Eng 90; IM Bsktbl/Vlybl/Sccr Capt 88-; Elec Eng.

**KRONENBERGER, CRAIG A,** Univ Of Cincinnati, Cincinnati, OH; SO; BFA; News Record; AERHO; Broadcasting; Law.

**KRONER, CHRISTINE M,** Univ Of Cincinnati, Cincinnati, OH; SR; BS; St Catharine PTA Brd; Auction Co-Chr; Yth Mnstry; Westwood Cvc Assn; Ed-Hist.

**KRONER, JOHAN C,** Rutgers St Univ At Camden, Camden, NJ; SR; BABS; Stdnt Cngrss Rep 89-90; Intl Soc Treas 89; Athenaeum Camden Hon Soc; Omicron Delta Epsilon; Phi Kappa Sigma Comm Serv Chrmn 90-; Swim Tm Capt 88-; Bus/Ecnmcs; MBA.

**KRONFLE, HENRY F,** Univ Of Miami, Coral Gables, FL; FR; BED; Mech Eng; Eng.

**KRONZ, JUDITH A,** Comm Coll Algny Co Algny Cmps, Pittsburgh, PA; SO; BS; Ntnl Hon Soc; Pittsburgh Branch Fedl Rsve Bk/Cleveland 80-; Busn Mgmnt.

**KROPP, CHRISTINA M,** Marywood Coll, Scranton, PA; JR; BFA; Zeta Omnicron Stdnt Chapt Pres; Amer Soc Intror Dsgnrs Marywood Coll; Stdnt Gov Pres 88-89; Zeta Omnicron Pres; Delta Epsilon Sigma Cath Coll Mem 90-; Amer Soc Int Dsgnrs Pres; Vlntrs Actn/Coll Vlntrs 88-90; Ldrshp Schlrshp 88-; Int Dsgn.

**KROPP, EVELYN P,** Schenectady County Comm Coll, Schenectady, NY; FR; Zonta Clb 82-84; LPN 85-; Nrsng; RN.

**KROTZ, KRISTINA D,** Temple Univ, Philadelphia, PA; JR; BA; Beta Gamma Sigma; Mgmt And Fnnce; Corp Law Bnkng.

**KROWICKI, CATHY,** William Paterson Coll, Wayne, NJ; SO; BA; Grp Math; Stdnt Govt Assn; Delta Phi Epsilon Fndrsng Chr 90-; Vlybl Sftbl; Tutor Cmps Academic Sprt Cntr; Governors Tchng Schlr N J; Math; Tchr.

**KRUCIK, TRACY A,** Duquesne Univ, Pittsburgh, PA; SR; BS; Mgmt Info Syst; Comp Pgmg.

**KRUEGER, ROBERT V,** Old Dominion Univ, Norfolk, VA; JR; BS; Alpha Chi 90-; Rsrch Asst Fluid Mchncs Prfssr Selby Mem Dept; Mech Eng; Rsrch Eng.

**KRUEGER, SHERRI L,** Ms St Univ, Miss State, MS; SR; BBA; Prsdnts Schlr 89; 7SU Athltc Depot Blldg Hnr Rll 89; Sthstrn Cnfrnc Schlr 89; Msssppi St Ldys Gol Tm 86-90; Bus.

**KRUG, ANGELA R,** Christopher Newport Coll, Newport News, VA; SO; BA; Army ROTC Cdt; Sprr Cdt Dcrtn Awrd Fr Acad Yr 90; Pol Sci; Law US Army Offcr.

**KRUG, ROBERT L,** Oh Univ, Athens, OH; SO; Elec Engr.

**KRUGER, MARK J,** The Johns Hopkins Univ, Baltimore, MD; FR.

**KRULL, JAMES C,** Georgetown Univ, Washington, DC; FR; BA; Chrstn Fllwshp 90-; Biology/Pre Med; Doctor.

**KRULL, REBECCA J,** Comm Coll Algny Co Algny Cmps, Pittsburgh, PA; SO; BS; Mktg; Advrtsng.

**KRUMHANSL, ROBERT P,** Christian Brothers Univ, Memphis, TN; JR; Peer Cnslr 89-; Stdnt Ambssdr 90-; Tau Kappa Epsilon 88-; BS; Tele Cmmnctns Info Systm Mgmt.

**KRUMHOLTZ, JUSTIN M,** Central Fl Comm Coll, Ocala, FL; SR; AA; Cir K Suny Clg At Farmingdale Pres 73-75; Inverness Motorcycle Club Pres 88-; Suny Clg Buffalo Spartans 75-76; Inverness Downtown Deveplt Comm 88-; Med Elect Techn; AAS Suny Clg Farmingdale 76; BS Suny Clg Buffalo 81; Elec Tech; Tchng.

**KRUPA, STACY Y,** Oh Wesleyan Univ, Delaware, OH; FR; BA; Amnsty Intl 90-; Envrnmnt/Wldlf Clb 90-; Phi Eta Sigma 90-; Pres Schlrshp 90-; Stdnt Orientatn Asst 90-; IM Vlybl 90-; Chem; Eng.

**KRUPP, LISA P,** Univ Of Sc At Columbia, Columbia, SC; BSN; X-Ray Tech; RT Cert US Army 83; Nursing.

**KRUSE, SUSAN J,** D Youville Coll, Buffalo, NY; SO; BSPAC; Emer Squad 88-; Steelwrkr Outokumpu Amer Brs; Emer Erie Comm Clg 89; Med Tech; Med; Phy Asst.

**KRUSZEWSKI, KEVIN M,** Duquesne Univ, Pittsburgh, PA; JR; BA; Big Bro/Sis Pgm 90-; Deans Lst 88-; Phi Delta Chi 90-; St Vincent Hlth Ctr Intern 90-; Ftbl 88-89; Phrmcy.

**KRUT, CHRISTINA L,** Allegheny Coll, Meadville, PA; JR; RA 90-; Hon Cmtee 90-; Newman Clb 88-90; Alden Schlr 88-90; Lambda Sigma Sec 89-90; Big Bro Str 90-; Orthopedic Surg Intrn 90-; Cardiology Intrn; Biological Rsrch; I M Sprts 88-90; Biology; Med.**

**KRUTKO, SUSAN A,** Kent St Univ Kent Cmps, Kent, OH; JR; BSN; SPN 90-; Gldn Ky; Nrsng.

**KRUZELNICK, LINDA M,** William Paterson Coll, Wayne, NJ; GD; MA; Summa Cum Laude 83; BA Wm Paterson Clg 70; MA Fairleigh Dcknsn Unv 83; Tchng HS.

**KRZNARIC, SNEZANA,** Stockton St Coll, Pomona, NJ; SO; BS; Soc Physcs Stdnts Treas 90-; Sigma Pi Sigma; Physcs; Eng.**

**KU, NANCY B,** Duquesne Univ, Pittsburgh, PA; FR; BA; Phrmcy.

**KU, TSUNG-HUNG,** Memphis St Univ, Memphis, TN; JR; BS; Chinese Assoc 90-; Elctrcl Engrg.

**KU, YAN YAN,** Fl International Univ, Miami, FL; FR; BA; Asian Stdnts Interact Assoc Treas 90-; Bsn/Adm; Finance.

**KUBAITIS, CYNTHIA A,** Georgian Court Coll, Lakewood, NJ; SR; BA; Psychology Elem Ed; Tchr.

**KUBALA, KAREN M,** Univ Of Fl, Gainesville, FL; JR; Stdnt Govt Cmuty Afrs Cabnt 90-; Panhellenic Schlrshp Cmtee 88-90; Phi Eta Sigma 88-; Fin Mgmt Assoc 89-; Phi Sigma Sigma Schlrshp 88-; Amer Cancer Soc Vol 90-; Mktg Intrn; AA 90; Fin; Law.

**KUBICEK, EMILY A,** Univ Of Rochester, Rochester, NY; SR; BS; Blug Light Sec 88f Tau Beta Pi 90-; Deans List 87-; Mgmnt Cert; Optical Engr.

**KUBIDA, KRISTIN A,** East Stroudsburg Univ, E Stroudsburg, PA; FR; BS; Univ/Cmnty Concert Bnd 90-; Res Hl Cncl 90-; Hosptlty Mgmt Clb 90-; Hosptlty Mgmt; Rstrnt Mgmt.

**KUBINSKY, LAURIE S,** Indiana Univ Of Pa, Indiana, PA; FR; BED; Bg Brthrs/Bg Sistrs 90-; Spec Olympcs; Kappa Delta Pi; Ed Hrng Imprd; Tchr.

**KUBIS, JANEL J,** Wilmington Coll, New Castle, DE; SR; BA; Deans Lst 87-89; Deans Lst Wilm Clg 90-; Property Mgr/Bkkpr; AAS Delawae Tech Cmut Clg 88; Acctg.

**KUBOTA, MITSUHO,** Spartanburg Methodist Coll, Spartanburg, SC; SO; Vlybl Mgr 90; AS 89; Engl; Tchr.

**KUCEJ, KARINE I,** Valdosta St Coll, Valdosta, GA; SO; BS ED; Sprts Med; Prfsnl Athletic Trnr.

**KUCERA, SHEILA D,** Univ Of South Al, Mobile, AL; SR; BA; Psi Chi 88-; Engl/Psych; Sec Educ.

**KUCERA-HOWARD, SHEILA D,** Univ Of South Al, Mobile, AL; SR; BA; Psi Chi; Engl/Psych; Scndry Educ.

**KUCHENBROD, WADE,** Old Dominion Univ, Norfolk, VA; FR; BSME; Aerospace Eng.

**KUCHINSKI, REBECCA FAUST,** Va Commonwealth Univ, Richmond, VA; SR; BA; SVEA 90-; Golden Key 90-; Phi Kappa Phi 90-; BS Penn State Univ 85; Engl; MA.

**KUCZARSKI, ERIC J,** Western New England Coll, Springfield, MA; FR; BENGR; Fr Acad Awd 90-; IM Flr Hcky 90-; Mech Eng.

**KUDER, KAREN M,** Wagner Coll, Staten Island, NY; FR; BA; Ltry Mgzn Edtrl Stf 90-; Choir 90-; Im Bsktbl & Sftbl Tm Cpt 90-; Music & Hstry.

**KUDERER, LISA M,** Univ Of Cincinnati, Cincinnati, OH; JR; BSN; Curriculum Com 90-; Sigma Theta Tau; Bethesda Oak Extern Prog; Air Force Natl Grd 84-; Stdnt Loan Clerk/Mort Loan Clerk/Elctrcns Hlpr; Nrsng; Mgr.

**KUDLA, JOLANTA V,** Utica Coll Of Syracuse Univ, Utica, NY; SR; Math; Tch.

**KUDLESS, ALISON M,** Marywood Coll, Scranton, PA; SO; BS; Comm Ornttn Co-Chr; Kidstuff; Crspdng Sec; Spch Lang/Pthlgy.

**KUEBBING, SHARYN LEE,** Comm Coll Algny Co Algny Cmps, Pittsburgh, PA; FR; Scl Wrk Clb Sec 89-; Vol Allghny Gen Hosp 90-; Scl Wrk.

**KUEBLER, KAREN M,** Salem-Teikyo Univ, Salem, WV; SR; BS; Stent Admn V P 90-; Gamma Beta Phi 89-; Deans List 88-; Delta Mu Sor V P 89-; AA 90; Acctng/Bus Mgmt.

**KUEHL-STREET, SUSAN A,** George Mason Univ, Fairfax, VA; SR; BS; Stdnt Govt Judcl Bd Chrprsn 77-78; Charms Choir 78; Co Currclr Cncl Rep 77-78; Phi Theta Kappa 78; Sigma Tau Sigma 78; Alpha Theta Zeta 78; Cmpus Keys 77-78; Pres Awd Schlrshp Serv 78; Retail Buyer 78-90; AA Marymount Univ 78; Bus Mgmt; Assoc Mgmt.

**KUEHN, PAUL T,** Fl St Univ, Tallahassee, FL; SR; BSME; Amer Soc Of Mech Engrs Treas 89-; Golden Key; Outstndng Clg Stdnts Of Amer; Alfred I Dupont Schlrshp; Space Resrch; U S Army 84-87; U S Amry Resrve 87-; Mech Engr.

**KUEHN, REBECCA A,** Univ Of Rochester, Rochester, NY; SO; BA; Ballet 90-; Newman Cmnty Sundy Sch Tchr 90-F; Bio; Tchng.

**KUEHN, RICHARD J,** Hudson Valley Comm Coll, Troy, NY; FR; AAS; Capitol Dist Amiga Users Grp Computer Clb 90-; Fleet Maint Supv NYS Thruway 88-; Cmptr Info Syst; Pgmr/Analyst.

**KUELL, CAROL A,** Hilbert Coll, Hamburg, NY; SO; AAS; Prfssnl Assts Club 90-; Sectrl Sci/Med; Admin Asst.

**KUERZDOERFER, BETH A,** Daemen Coll, Amherst, NY; SO; BA; Twn Of Cheektowaga Admnstrtv Asstnt To Cnclman Andrew A Kulyk 90-; AAS Erie Cmnty Clg South Campus 90; Hist/Govt; Soc Studies Tchr.

**KUERZDOERFER, DAVID N,** Daemen Coll, Amherst, NY; JR; BA; Kappa Delta Pi; AA Erie Cmnty Clge 90; History & Govt Teachers Certification; Teach.

**KUETHE, JEFFREY T,** Middle Tn St Univ, Murfreesboro, TN; JR; BS; Chem Clb 90-; Amer Chem Soc; Chem; Orgnc Synths.

**KUGLER, MARILYN,** Barry Univ, Miami, FL; SR; BS; AA Miami-Dade Comm Clg 88; Acctg.

**KUH, LAWRENCE H,** Kent St Univ Kent Cmps, Kent, OH; JR; BS; Tr Guides Trnr 89-; Intrhl Cncl 88-89; Rec Clb/Vlybl/Ski Clb 88-90; Mrtr Brd VP; Phi Epsilon Kappa; Rho Phi Lambda; Alpha Epsilon Pi VP 89-; Ambsdr; Walt Disney Wrld Coll Pro; Lacrosse Clb Hd Coach 89-; Leisure Stdy; Rsrt Mgt.

**KUHL, JENNIFER L,** William Carey Coll, Hattiesburg, MS; SO; BLS; SGA Ed 90; Schl Newspapr Ed 90; Hnrs; Soccer 90; Psych/Bsnss.

**KUHLHOFF, JON-PIERRE,** Fl St Univ, Tallahassee, FL; JR; BS; ASME Design Coord 90-; NRA 88-; AA Tallahassee Comm Clg 85; Mechanical Aerospace Engrng.

**KUHN, CHARLENE M,** De Vry Inst Of Tech, Columbus, OH; FR; BA; Peer Advsrt Prgrm Peer Advsr; Deans Lst; Prsdnt Lst; Deans Lst; Prsdnts Lst; Cmptr Infrmtn Systm; Prgrmmng Mngr.

**KUHN, GERRILYN A,** S U N Y At Buffalo, Buffalo, NY; JR; BA; Under Grad Mgmt Assoc Sec 90-; Phi Eta Sigma 88-89; Delta Sigma Pi Cmmnty Srvc Chrm; IM Sccr 89-; IM Vllybll 88-89; Bus Fnc Mrktng; Fncl Mgmt.

**KUHN, JODIELYNN,** East Stroudsburg Univ, E Stroudsburg, PA; SO; BA; Adult Lit Pgm 90-; Friend Of The Pike Cnty Library 83-; Tutoring; Philosophy; Professor.

**KUHN, MICHAEL G,** Niagara Univ, Niagara Univ, NY; BA; GCE Un/London Schl Exam Bd 89; Engl Cmmctn; Cmmctn.

**KUHN, SHERI R,** Mt Saint Marys Coll & Seminary, Emmitsburg, MD; SR; Yrbk Cmmtt 90-; BA; Fn Arts; Grphc Dsgn.

**KUHN, THOMAS L,** Duquesne Univ, Pittsburgh, PA; FR; BA; Bus.

**KUHNER, REBECCA L,** Miami Jacobs Jr Coll Of Bus, Dayton, OH; FR; AA; Acctg.

**KUHNERT, GABRIELA A,** Anne Arundel Comm Coll, Arnold, MD; FR; ASSOC; Alpha Beta Kappa 86; Dns Lst 86; Sec Kerr Co 87; Cstmr Serv Rep Encore Nc 87-89; Sec Trammell Crow Rsdntl 89-90; Sec Riggs Bnk 90; Sec Interyacht 90-; Sec Fleet Bus Schl 86; Lib Arts; Dsgn Commnctns.

**KUHNS, JILL E,** Univ Of Nc At Charlotte, Charlotte, NC; SO; BA; Sanford Hall Cncl Suite Rep 90-.

**KUJAWA, DAVID A,** Univ Of Miami, Coral Gables, FL; JR; BA; Sprts Fest Comm; Mahoney Prgmng Cncl; Gldn Key 90-; Sigma Alpha Epsilon; Ecnmcs; Bnkg.

**KUJAWA, EDWARD J,** Bryant Stratton Bus Inst Roch, Rochester, NY; GD; AOS; Cad Civil Mr Patrol 83-; Amer Legion 82-; Natl Warbirds 84-; Elec Tchgly; Elec Engrg Later.

**KUJAWSKI, EDWARD T,** Univ Of Al At Birmingham, Birmingham, AL; SO; IEEE Mnl Sls 90-; Hnrs Pgm Cmptr Cmte Co Chr 89-; Hnrs Pgm 89-; Engrg.

**KUKODA, DAVID M,** Cooper Union, New York, NY; JR; BE; Amer Soc Cvl Engrs Treas 89-; Tau Beta Pi; Chi Epsilon; IM Sftbl Capt 88-; Cvl Eng; Pilot.

**KUKOLECA, MICHELLE,** Niagara Univ, Niagara Univ, NY; JR; BA; Resdnt Asstnt 89-; Pol Sci Forum Treas 88-; Progrmng Bd 90; Cmnty Actn Prog 88-; Dept Hons Prog Pol Sci; Rugby 90-; Pol Sci; PhD.

**KUKTA, ROBERT V,** Univ Of Pittsburgh, Pittsburgh, PA; SO; BA; W Penn Tstg Labs Intrshp 90; Westghse Elec Coop; IM Scr; Mech Engrng; Engrng.

**KULA, THEODORE J,** Bethany Coll, Bethany, WV; FR; BS; Phi Kappa Tau; Comp Sci.

**KULAKOWSKI, LAURA L,** Newbury Coll, Brookline, MA; SO; Corr Spec 88-; Acctg.

**KULAS, DIANE M,** Comm Coll Algny Co Algny Cmps, Pittsburgh, PA; FR; Nrsg.

**KULBURG, DEAN,** Bloomfield Coll, Bloomfield, NJ; SO; BA; Crim Just; Law.

**KULCSAR, ATTILA,** City Univ Of Ny Queensbrough, New York, NY; SO; Natl Bsn Hnr Scty; Soccer; Tennis; Bsn/Mrktg Rsrch; Intrntl Bsn.

**KULDANEK, LORRAINE M,** Glassboro St Coll, Glassboro, NJ; JR; BA; Advrtsng Clb; Deans Lst 90-; Cmmnctns Advrtsng.

**KULESA, PATRICK,** Mt Saint Marys Coll & Seminary, Emmitsburg, MD; SO; BS; Clg Nwspr Edtr-In-Chf Elect; Campus Ministry-Lector 90-; G H Miles Hon Soc Sec; Psi Chi; Soc For Clg Jrnlsts; Msgr Hugh J Phillips Prize 90; E Ryan Mem Prize; 3rd Pl In Soc For Clg Jrnlst Comp; Psych.

**KULESZA, SANDRA L,** Teikyo Post Univ, Waterbury, CT; JR; BS; Marketing; Rsrch.

**KULICHIK, GREGORY A,** Le Moyne Coll, Syracuse, NY; JR; BS; Mktg Clb 90-; Bsn Clb 90-; Ornttn Comm; Delta Mu Delta 90-; Visa/Mstrcrd Ad Cmpgn; Bsn; Mktg.

**KULICK, DALE I,** Carnegie Mellon Univ, Pittsburgh, PA; JR; BA; Psych Cl 90-; Hillel 88-; A Carnegie Schol 90-; United Jewish Fed Fund Raiser 88-; Intnshp Clin Psychlgy/W Psychiatric Inst Clin Asst Rsrch; Sr Hon T Hesis Prog 91-92; Clin Psychlgy; Coun.

**KULINA, JOSEPH S,** Univ Of Md At Eastern Shore, Princess Anne, MD; SR; BS; Engrng Scty Ofcr Secy 90-; AA Frederick Comm Clg 89; Electrcl Engrng.

**KULLING JR, DAVID K,** Pa St Univ Erie-Behrend Coll, Erie, PA; FR; BA; Business; Mgmt Info Syst.

**KULLMAN, ANGELA S,** Oh Univ, Athens, OH; SO; BSEE; Elect Eng; Cmmnctns.

**KULLMAN JR, CLYDE RONALD,** S U N Y Coll At Fredonia, Fredonia, NY; SR; Bus Clb; Delta Mu Delta; Omicron Delta Epsilon; Kappa Kappa Psi; Bus Finance; MBA.

**KULON, DARLA A,** Univ Of Akron, Akron, OH; SR; BS; Snr Cls Brd Chrp 89-90; Stf Wrtr Res Hl Nwspr 88-89; Res Hl Floor Rep 88-89; IM Ftbl/Vlybl 88-89; Bsn Admn; Mktg.

**KULP, KIMBERLY H,** Immaculata Coll, Immaculata, PA; GD; BSN; RN Clb 87-; ANA; AHNA; Psych/Mntl Hlth Certif 88-; Psych Nrs; Nrsg.

**KULTON, KELLIE L,** Va Commonwealth Univ, Richmond, VA; SR; BFA; Stdnt Art Space Cmmttee 90; Phi Kappa Phi; Awd For Pntg In Annl Stdnt Exhib; AA U Of Md Munich Campus W Grmny 86; Pntng/Prntmkng; Prof Artst.

**KULYESHIE, JOSEPH A,** Univ Of Miami, Coral Gables, FL; FR; BS; Pres Hon Rl 90-; Comp Sci; Pgmr.

**KULYS, TADAS R,** City Univ Of Ny Baruch Coll, New York, NY; SR; BBA; Gldn Key; Awrd Prvsts Schlrshp; Fnc.

**KUMARADITYA, VIJAYADITYA P,** City Univ Of Ny Baruch Coll, New York, NY; SR; BA; Brd Dir/Clg Asc 90-; Std Govt Pres 89-90; Acctng Soc Treas 88-89; Beta Gamma Sigma 90-; Comm Brd 87-88; Mgr NY Allstars Crckt Clb 90-; Stf Acctnt Goldman Sachs Co 87-; Corp Law.

**KUMBATOVIC, JOHN L,** Saint Johns Univ, Jamaica, NY; FR; BA; Bsn Adm-Acctg; Acctnt.

**KUMBATOVIC, ROBERT J,** Ny Univ, New York, NY; SR; Stdnt Cncl; Omicron Delta Epsilon Int Hnr Soc Econ; NY U Hnrs Schlr; Lgl Intrn Cty Cncl; BA; Econ; Law.**

**KUMLER, KELLIE A,** Oh St Univ, Columbus, OH; JR; BSLA; Lndscp Archtctr.

**KUMMER, MAUREEN L,** Indiana Univ Of Pa, Indiana, PA; SR; BED; PA St Educ Asn 89-; Natl Educ Asn 89-; Upsln Psi Pres 89-; Tutor Intshp; IM Vlybl 87-88; Elem Educ; Tch.

**KUNC, CHRISTINA J,** The Kings Coll, Briarclf Mnr, NY; FR; BA; Yrbk; Acad Schlrshp 90-; Pres Schlrshp 90-; Dns Lst; Rsh; Math; Sec Lvl Tchng.

**KUNDMAN, STEPHEN ANTHONY,** Pittsburgh Tech Inst, Pittsburgh, PA; GD; Engr Drftsmn; Mech Engr.

**KUNG, LAP CHUNG,** City Univ Of Ny Baruch Coll, New York, NY; JR; BBA; Retail Trade Socty 90; Phtgrphy Clb 89; Gldn Key; Oper Mgmt.

**KUNG, LO-TIN,** Cornell Univ Statutory College, Ithaca, NY; SO; BA; Animal Sci; Vet.

**KUNIAK, DEBBIE A,** Indiana Univ Of Pa, Indiana, PA; SR; BED; Univ Chorus 89-90; Proj STRIDE 88-89; Elem Educ; Tchr.

**KUNICKI, DAVID J,** The Kings Coll, Briarclf Mnr, NY; SR; BA; Std Mssns Flwshp 88-89; Sprtwngs Drama Clb Dir 89; Std Govt Asc 90-; Rsch Asst Sclgy Dpt 88-; Rsch Assc Intrn 90; C Reg Fordham Unv 90; Sclgy; Prfssr.

**KUNIS, ROBERT S,** Nova Univ, Ft Lauderdale, FL; GD; MBA; Am Mrktg Assoc; Gldn Key; Mu Kappa Tau Pres 84-85; Betta Gama Sigma; Pi Sigma Epsilon VP Mrktg 84-85; Muscular Dystrphy Assoc; Exclnc Mrktg Awd; Lewis F Gordon Mrktg Schlrshp Awd 84-85; Chmbr Cmmrc; Pharm Rep Slvy Pharm BBA 85; Mktg; Mgmt.

**KUNKEL, MICHAEL S,** Fayetteville St Univ, Fayetteville, NC; SO; BA; Air Force REOTC 90-; Math Cmptr Science Clb 90-; Sls Repsntv JVC Co America 89-; Elctrcl Engnr.

**KUNKLE, LINDA S,** Indiana Univ Of Pa, Indiana, PA; SR; BED 90.

**KUNKLEMAN, CHRISTINE A,** Tn Temple Univ, Chattanooga, TN; FR; BA; Zeta Nu Rho; English.

**KUNKLER, CATHLEEN E,** Elmira Coll, Elmira, NY; SR; BSN; New Author Awd; Orthpdc Nurs 87; Naon Schlrshp 89; Nurs Div Mgr 84-; Tioga Hls Hrmny Intl Chorus Bd Dir 86-87; Cltbls Quartet; ONC 88; Nurs; Nurs Admn.**

**KUNNEMANN, HEATHER K,** Fl St Univ, Tallahassee, FL; JR; BS; Telphne Cnslng/Rfrl Serv; Psi Chi; AS Lake City Comm Coll 90.

**KUNSELMAN, CHERYL A,** Indiana Univ Of Pa, Indiana, PA; JR; BED; NSSLHA 90-; Rsdnc Hl Assn 90; Delta Kappa Gamma Schlrshp; Speech Path/Audiology.

**KUNTUPIS, CONSTANCE R,** West Liberty St Coll, West Liberty, WV; SR; Prsdnts Lst; Deans Lst; Tchng; BA; Dntl Hygiene.

**KUNTZ, KIMBERLY A,** Unity Coll, Unity, ME; FR; BS; SG; Fitnss Clb Pres 90-; Radio Clb 90-; Alpine Clb 90-; Mtn Bike Clb 90-; Dns Lst Hghst Hons 90-; Comm Halloween Prty Vol 90; Grl Sct Lrng Day Vol; Aerobcs Inst 90-; IM Flr Hcky; Envrnmntl Educ; Tchr.

**KUNZE, PETER G,** Univ Of Akron, Akron, OH; SO; AICHE; Coop Pstn Dow Chmcl; Chmcl Eng; Eng.

**KUNZINGER, LESLEE F,** Kent St Univ Kent Cmps, Kent, OH; SR; BA; Mrchng Band Flg Corp 90-; Amer Scty Intr Dsgnrs 90-; Gldn Key; Kappa Omicron Nu; Tau Beta Sigma 90-; Deans Lst 88-90; Prctcm Deitrick/Assc Inc; Intr Dsgn.

**KUO, KUAN-SHIU,** Univ Of Sc At Aiken, Aiken, SC; FR; Indstl Engr; Engr.

**KUPEC, MARGARET E,** Western New England Coll, Springfield, MA; JR; BS; Deans Lst 89-90; Bus Mngmt.

**KUPFER, JENNIFER E,** Indiana Univ Of Pa, Indiana, PA; SR; BA; SADD 90-; Paraprfsnl Tutor Math 89-; Dns Lst; Sec Math Ed; Tch.

**KUPIEC, JOHN E,** Alfred Univ, Alfred, NY; JR; BS; Alfred Systems Grp 89-; Cmps Gui 89-; Ntl Assc Actnts 89-; Alpha Lambda Delta VP 89-; Alpha Iota Delta 90-; Beta Gamma Sigma 90-; Delta Mu Delta 90-; Pacioli Scty 90-; Finan Mgmt Assc VP 90-; Hghst Index Awd 89-; Accounting; Business Consulting.

**KUPISZEWSKI, JOSEPH ANDREW,** Fl St Univ, Tallahassee, FL; SR; BS; Scalp Hntrs 89-90; Smnle Ambssdrs 89; Stdnt Alumni Fndtn 89; Deans Lst 90; Phi Kappa Tau 87; Membrshp Orient Offcr 89; Schlrshp Chrmn 89; Fnd Rsng Chrmn 89; Mchncl Eng/Spnsh; Law/Eng.

**KUPRIANOV, ROSE E,** Atlantic Comm Coll, Mays Landing, NJ; FR; Sndy Schl Tchr 1st Untd Mthdst Chrch Wldwd Crest NJ 90-; Rgstrd X-Ray Tech; Pre-Law; Law.

**KURELICH JR, JOHN R,** George Mason Univ, Fairfax, VA; GD; MD; Pred Mdcl Clb 90-; Amrcn Hrt Assoc 87; Frfx Cnty Ftbll Bsktbll 87-90; Tau Kappa Epsilon Srgnt Arms 87-; Intern Orpdc Srgry Sprts Med Assoc 90; Mmrl Cdmc Schlrshp 90; 2M Ftbll Vllybll Bsktbll Sftbll 87-90; BS 90; Pre Mdcl Sci.

**KURENSZKI, LORI A,** West Liberty St Coll, West Liberty, WV; SO; BS; Bsn; Pharm Sls.

**KURI, YAMIL G,** Fl International Univ, Miami, FL; SR; BSCE; ASCE; ASME; Alpha Omega Chi; Phi Kappa Phi; BSME Univ Miami 86; Cvl Engr; Engr.

**KURIAN, PRIYA,** City Univ Of Ny Baruch Coll, New York, NY; SO; BA; Comp Info Systms.

**KURIGER, REX J,** Oh Univ, Athens, OH; FR.

**KURJIAKA, PAULA LOUISE,** Castleton St Coll, Castleton, VT; SO; ASN; SNA 89-; Deans List 90-; Nursing.

**KURKA, STACY B,** Lancaster Bible Coll, Lancaster, PA; FR; Deans Lst; Bsktbl/Sftbl; Bible/Elem Educ.

**KURLAND, MICHAEL D,** Pa St Univ Delaware Cty Cmps, Media, PA; SO; Camara Clb Tres 89-90; SADD 90-; Acctg; CPA.

**KURLANDER, LISA J,** Univ Of Rochester, Rochester, NY; SO; BA; Horseback Rdng Clb; SUBS; Deans List; Bio; Tchr.

**KURNICK, FRANCESCA,** S U N Y At Buffalo, Buffalo, NY; JR; BA; Dns Lst 88-; Alpha Sigma Lambda; Buffalo Psychiatric Cntr Vol Dept 90-; Psychlgy/Hlth/Hmn Srvcs; Cnslng/Educ Psychlgy.

**KURPISZ, PATRICIA L,** S U N Y At Buffalo, Buffalo, NY; SR; BS; Am Mktg Assoc Profl Activities Com 90-; Albright Knox Art Gallery 88-; Natl Org Women 90-; Golden Key 90-; Delta Sigma Pi Chrwmn Of Schlrshp Com 87-; Am Bus Womens Assoc 90-; Bus Admin.

**KURSCHNER, HOLGAR E,** S U N Y Coll Of Tech At Alfred, Alfred, NY; FR; BSME; Scty Atmtv Eng 90-; Atmtv Mchnst Mchnc 82-89; Cert 83; Intl Cmbstn Eng; Atmtv Eng.

**KURTANSKY, REGINA L,** Central Pa Bus School, Summerdale, PA; SR; ASB; Vlybl 89-90; Sm Bus Mgmnt.

**KURTYKA, SUZANNE M,** Seton Hall Univ, South Orange, NJ; BSN; Prsh Cncl Sec 90-; Piano Sng; Nrsng.

**KURTZ, ARTHUR LOUIS,** Longwood Coll, Farmville, VA; FR; BS; Stdtn Cncl Rep; Alph Lmbd Dlt; Bio; Marine Biologist.

**KURTZ II, CHARLES L,** Williams Coll, Williamstown, MA; FR; BA; X Cntry; Indr Trck; Otdr Trck Tm 90-; Hstry.

**KURTZ, JAMES I,** Kutztown University Of Penna, Kutztown, PA; JR; BFA; Cmnctn Dsgn; Illustrator.**

**KURTZ, JOLIE L,** Methodist Coll, Fayetteville, NC; JR; BS; Sclgy/Scl Wrk Clb Pres 90-; Yrbk Sprts Edtr 90-; Chrstn Life Comm; Psych Clb 89; Sigma Omega Chi VP 90-; Hnrs Acdmc Pro 89-, Coll Tutor 90-; Deans Lst 89 ; Pres Lst 90; 2M Vlybl/Trck/ Crs Cntry/Sftbl 89-90; Sclgy; Hspc Cnslr.

**KURTZ, LYNNE M,** Fl St Univ, Tallahassee, FL; SR; BS; Cmps Mnstry Bd Of Dir 87-; Phi Beta Kappa 89-; Psi Chi 89-; Phi Eta Sigma Pres 87-89; Lib Stds Hnrs Stdnt 87-; Univ Schlr 87-; Fla Acad Schlr 87-; Psychlgy.

**KURTZ, ROBERT D,** Broward Comm Coll, Ft Lauderdale, FL; SO; BA; Phi Theta Kappa 90-; Hnrs Inst 89-; Schlrs Awd 89-; Charles David Landscaping Inc 84-88; Comp Inf; Bus Systems Analyst.

**KURTZ, SYLVIA L,** Juniata Coll, Huntingdon, PA; FR; BA; Hnr Soc Schlrshp Acad Excell; Engl Secnd Lang Instrctr 89-90; Data Type Svcs 86-90; Engl/Secd Educ; Tch.

**KURUC, DAVID J,** East Stroudsburg Univ, E Stroudsburg, PA; SR; Ims Sftbl Bsktbl Flg Ftbl 87; Pi Sigma Alpha 90; Magna Cum Laude; Deas Lst 89; Var Bsebl Lttr 88-90; BA; Pol Sci; Law.

**KURZ, ROBERT S,** Univ Of Cincinnati, Cincinnati, OH; SR; BM; Muc Prfrmnc; Symphony Orch.

**KUS, MARY ANDREA,** Western Ky Univ, Bowling Green, KY; SR; BS; Soc Physc Stu Pres 89-; Pi Mu Epsilon 89-; Beta Beta Beta 88-90; Phi Kappa Phi; Sci Eng Rsrch Sem 90; Intern Eckenfelder Inc; Physc/Math; Envrmntl Eng.

**KUSEL, AMY B,** Cornell Univ Statutory College, Ithaca, NY; JR; DVM; Red Carpet Soc Chair 88-; Pre-Vet Soc 89-90; Ambassador 89-; Natl Schlr Sec 88-; Alpha Phi Omega 89-; Teach Asst 90-; Days Mgr 89-; BS; Bio/Cmnctns; Vet Med.

**KUSHIHASHI, PEGGY,** Univ Of Miami, Coral Gables, FL; JR; BA; Cinematics Art Commission 89-90; Msc; MA.

**KUSHIN, HEATHER E,** Univ Of Miami, Coral Gables, FL; SR; BA; A F ROTC Grp Cmndr 87-; Pre Law Soc 87-; Sigma Tau Delta Treas 89; Arnold Air Soc Dir 88; Golden Key 89-; Phi Kappa Phi 90-; Cir K Intl 87-89; Crew Team 87-88; English/Pltcs; Law.

**KUSHNER, JEREMY A,** Univ Of South Fl, Tampa, FL; JR; BM; Wnd Ens Symph Orch 90-; Mrimba Percsn Ens; Jazz Chbr Ens; Phi Mu Alpha Sinfonia 92; Dns Hnr; Music; Symph Orch.

**KUSHNER, PAMELA P,** Univ Of South Fl, Tampa, FL; JR; BA; Fine Arts.

**KUSHNICK, ADAM J,** S U N Y At Buffalo, Buffalo, NY; JR; BS; Stu Assoc 89; Sigma Alpha Mu Rcrdr 88-; Bus Admin; Mrktg.

**KUSS, JOHN KENNETH,** Daemen Coll, Amherst, NY; JR; BS; Am Phys Therapy Assn 90-; Deans Lst 90-; Alexandria Hosp 90; VA Hosp Syracuse NY; Phys Therapy.

**KUSSELL, LAURA J,** Univ Of Ga, Athens, GA; JR; BA; Erly Chldhd Educ; Tchr.

**KUSTER, JENNIFER E,** Oh St Univ At Newark, Newark, OH; SO; BS; Blck O OSU Ftbl 90-; Phi Sigma 89-90; OSU-N 89-90; Alpha Lambda Delta/Phi Eta Sigma 90-; Chimes Jr Clss Hnry; Pi Beta Phi Srorty 90-; Math; MBA-BUS.

**KUSTERMANN, GLEA B,** Fl St Univ, Tallahassee, FL; SR; BA; AA Palm Beach Comm Clge 85; Elem Ed; Elem Tchr.

**KUSY, VINCENT J,** S U N Y Coll Of Tech At Frmgdl, Farmingdale, NY; SO; MBA; Bsbl/Tennis; Acctng; CPA.

**KUTCHENRITER, JON V,** Marshall University, Huntington, WV; FR; BBA; Lambda Chi Alpha 90-; Econ; Bnkg/Finc.

**KUTLESIC, SVETLANA,** Kent St Univ Kent Cmps, Kent, OH; JR; BA; SIFE 90; Gldn Key 90-; Dns Lst 89-90; Mktg/Adv; Adv.

**KUTNER, EMILY D,** Univ Of Rochester, Rochester, NY; SO; BA; Gamma Phi Beta 90-; Pltcl Sci.

**KUTRZYBA III, EDWARD M,** Wv Univ, Morgantown, WV; JR; BS; Golden Key 90-; Tau Beta Pi 90-; Eta Kappa Nu 90-; Phi Sigma Pi 90-; Schlrshp 88-89; Elect Eng.

**KUTSKO, KENNETH A,** Univ Of Ga, Athens, GA; JR; BS; Htl/Rstrnt Assn Treas 90-; Cndct Rvw Bd Juste 90-; Cthlc Stdnt Flwshp 90-; Intrnshp-Holiday Inn Singer Islnd FL; Prtl Schlrshp Berry Coll 88-89; Htl Mgmt; Risk Mgmt/Ins.

**KUTTER, ANGELIA M,** Miami Jacobs Jr Coll Of Bus, Dayton, OH; SO; AA; CSI 90; Bus; Exec Sec.

**KUTZ III, WILLIAM A,** Furman Univ, Greenville, SC; FR; BS; Clgte Educ Serv Corp 90-; Alpha Epsilon Delta 90-; Deans Lst 90-; Biology/Pre Med; Med Sch/Duke Univ.

**KUWAMURA, MANAMI,** Ny Univ, New York, NY; FR; AA; Hakuhodo Advtsng Intrn; Cosmetic Fashion Indus 80-90; Bus/ Mktg; Mktg.

**KUYKENDALL, DAVID M,** Commonwealth Coll, Virginia Beach, VA; FR; Cmptr Scnc; Cmptr Prog/Analyst.

**KUZEL, IRENE N,** Univ Of Rochester, Rochester, NY; JR; BA; Stu Sen Edtr Nwslttr 89-90; Tutor 90; Phi Theta Kappa 90-; Phlsphy Awrd 90; Lit Awrd 89; Cmpr Vol 87; AS Monroe Comm Coll 90; Engl; PHD/TCH.

**KUZINA, LYNN M,** S U N Y At Buffalo, Buffalo, NY; JR; BS; Scssmstrs Ski Clb 89-; Gldn Key 90-; Delta Sigma Pi 90-; Bus Admn.

**KUZNIEWSKI, MARY,** Georgian Court Coll, Lakewood, NJ; SR; BA; BA; Cert; Psychlgy; Tch Elem Schl/Cnslng.

**KVEENE, DOUGLAS A,** Air Force Inst Of Tech, Wrt-Ptrsn Afb, OH; GD; MS; Sigma Iota Epsilon; MA Webster Univ 90; BA Univ Of MD 81; Info Resrce Mngmnt.

**KVYAT, BUSYA,** Bunker Hill Comm Coll, Boston, MA; FR; Wrkmns Cir 88-90; W Fens Snrs Clb 90-; USSR; Mech Engr; BS Mech Engr 46-50; MS Mech Engr 53-58; Cnsltng Engr Co 59-86; Dsgnr HVAC 53 59; Fld Supv 50-53; Engl; Art/Engr

**KWAISER, JENNIFER M,** Indiana Univ Of Pa, Indiana, PA; SO; Cncl Excptnl Chldrn Sec 89-; Prvst Schlr 90-; Delta Phi Epsilon Pres Pldg Cls; Educ; Spec Edctr.

**KWAN, KAREN,** Univ Of Akron, Akron, OH; SR; BS; FMA Sec 90-; Tstmstrs 90-; Bus Admin/Finance; Prof/Ph D.

**KWAN, KWOK-YUNG,** S U N Y At Buffalo, Buffalo, NY; SO; BS; IEEE 90-; Elec Eng.

**KWAN, MILDRED,** Cornell Univ Statutory College, Ithaca, NY; FR; BS; Asian Amer Coalition Publ Ofcr 90-; Symph Orch 90-; Bio; Genetics Rsrch.

**KWARTLER, JENNIFER E,** Univ Of North Fl, Jacksonville, FL; SO; BA; Stdnt Govt Seminole Party; Methodist Yth Grp Cnslr; Zeta Tau Alpha Pldg Cls Treas; Deans Lst 90-; FLA Undergraduate Schlrs Fund 89-; Intern Yth Dir 90-; AA; Political Sci/Art History; Intl Business.

**KWATENG, AKUA N,** Howard Univ, Washington, DC; SR; BSC; Apothcry Nwslttr Assoc Edtr 89-; Rho Chi 88-; Gldn Ky 89-; Kappa Epsilon 90-; Old Achmtns Assoc 88-; Natl Cncl Negro Wmn 87-88; Dns Hon Rl 88-; Phrmcy; Hosp Phrmcst.

**KWATERSKI, MELISSA L,** Catholic Univ Of America, Washington, DC; SO; BA; Org Amer States Chrprsn 89-; UN; Mnrty Tutrng; Pltcs; Frgn Serv.

**KWETKOWSKI, BRIAN G,** Providence Coll, Providence, RI; SR; MD; Dns Lst 89-; BS; Blgy; Med Dr.

**KWIATKOWSKI, BARBARA A,** Schenectady County Comm Coll, Schenectady, NY; SR; AAS; Bus Clb 89-; Phi Theta Kappa; SCCC Faclty Schlrshp Awd 90; Ntl Assn Acctnts; Acctng; Mgr Acctg.

**KWITKOSKI, DAWN M,** Seton Hall Univ, South Orange, NJ; JR; BA; Natl Nrs Assn 88-; Seton Hall Nrs Assn 88-; Deans List 88-; Roberwood Johnson Extern Nrsng Prog; CPR St Peters Med Ctr 89; Pediatric Nrs.

**KWOK, EILEEN Y,** Va Commonwealth Univ, Richmond, VA; JR; BS; DPMA Treas 90-; Acctg Soc; Gldn Key; DPMA Schlrshp 90; Bus; Acctg.

**KWOK, TSZ TING BENEDICT,** Muskingum Coll, New Concord, OH; SO; BA BS; Kappa Mu Epsilon 90-; Chem Asst 90; Physcs Asst And Ttr 90-; Physcs And Math; Phys Elec Eng.

**KWOKA, JOHN C,** Wilmington Coll, New Castle, DE; JR; BA; Bsbl 88; Acctng; CPA.

**KWON, JIMMY Y,** Ma Inst Of Tech, Cambridge, MA; SO; BS; Elctrncs Rsrch Soc 89-; Concert Bnd 89-; Lab Asst 90; Elctrcl Engr.**

**KWON, SUNG Y,** Carnegie Mellon Univ, Pittsburgh, PA; JR; BS; AIESEC VP/FIN 89-; Fndtn Stdnt Cmnctn Inc Crrspndt 89-; Korean Stdnt Assns; Deans Lst 90-; Intrnshp Recrt Ltd 90; Natl Cllgt Bus Merit Awds; Vrsty Lttrs Wrstlnb 85-88; Wrstlng Clb; Ind Mgmt/Ecnmcs; Invstmnt Bnkg/Cnlstng.

**KWONG, GILBERT C,** Jersey City St Coll, Jersey City, NJ; JR; BA; Chnse Clb; Photo Clb; Art Assn; Media Arts Phtgrphy; Dir Of Phtgrphy.

**KYLE, MITZI H,** Blue Mountain Coll, Blue Mountain, MS; JR; BS; Elem Ed.

**KYLE, WILLIAM J,** Ms St Univ, Miss State, MS; FR; Ruf Mrchng Bnd; Cncrt Bnd; Bskrbl Pep Bnd; Phi Mu Alpha Sinfonia; Cmptr Sci; Cmptr Spclst.

**KYPER, SANDRA E,** George Mason Univ, Fairfax, VA; JR; BS; Amrcn Mrktng Assoc 90-; Gldn Key 90-; Hnr Scty 88-; Alpha Chi 90-; Mrktng.

**KYRIAKIDES, LAKIS C,** City Univ Of Ny City Coll, New York, NY; GD; MBA; Pi Tau Sigma 89-; Dns Lst; ASME 89-; Almni Assn; Bnkng Fnncng; Eng.

**KYSER, SHARON R,** Christian Brothers Univ, Memphis, TN; SO; BS; Economics; Health Care Adm.

**KYZER, STEVEN J,** Wallace St Comm Coll At Selma, Selma, AL; Deans Lst; Bus; Actnt.

# L

**L ESPERANCE, MARK EDWARD,** Univ Of Nc At Greensboro, Greensboro, NC; SR; Asst Coach Var Bkstbl 90-; Cnslr Yth Care Psych Hosp 89-; Tchr.

**L HOMMEDIEU, DAVID M,** S U N Y Coll Of A & T Morrisvl, Morrisville, NY; SO; MBA; Ftbl/Wgtlftng; Math; Tchng.

**LA BANCA, PATRICIA ANNE,** Western New England Coll, Springfield, MA; JR; BA; Res Hl Repr 88-90; Stdnt Lit Corps Tutor 89-; Psych; Chld Psych.

**LA BARBARA, ANTHONY J,** Atlantic Comm Coll, Mays Landing, NJ; SO; AAS; Prfsnl Chefs Assn South Jersey Pres Jr 90-; Clnry Stdnt Assn Rep 90-; Stdnt Govt Rep 90-; Extrnshp Showboat Htl/Casino Atlantic City; Clnry Arts; Chef.

**LA BARBERA, MARC T,** Bryant Stratton Bus Inst Roch, Rochester, NY; GD; BA; AOS; Acctg.

**LA BELLA, ANTHONY J,** Temple Univ, Philadelphia, PA; SR; BBA; Bus Golf Leag 90-; Beta Gamma Sgm; Pres Schlr Awrd; Eng Unisys Corp; Fld Svc Eng File Net Corp 88-89; Diploma EET RETES Elctrnc Schls 84; Mktg; Tech Sls Fin Anlyst.

**LA BELLE, AMY LYN,** Western New England Coll, Springfield, MA; SO; MBA; Pre-Law Soc 90-; Math Ttr; Engl/Bus; Corp Law.

**LA BELLE, ROBERT M,** Columbia Greene Comm Coll, Hudson, NY; SO; BS; Phi Theta Kappa 90-; Pres Lst 90-; Engr; Elctrcl Engr.

**LA BONTE, CHARLES J,** Wv Northern Comm Coll, Wheeling, WV; SO; AD; Phi Theta Kappa 90-; US Navy; Bus.

**LA BOSSIERE, LUCRECE,** Teikyo Post Univ, Waterbury, CT; FR; Legal Clb Treas 90-; Liberal Arts; Law.

**LA BUE, BRAD A,** Life Coll, Marietta, GA; GD; DC; Intrntnl Chrprctrs Assn 90-; Mtn Palpation Clb Tchnique 90; Chi Rho 90-; Vlntr Wrk Cllg Clnc X Ray Dpt; Deans Lst 89-; Chrprct; Chiropractor.

**LA CARRUBBA, LISA,** Villanova Univ, Villanova, PA; SO; BS; Dnc Ens Sec 89-; Dnc Mrthn Chrprsn 90-; Phi Kappa Phi; Alpha Epsilon Delta; Uinv Med Dnstry Grad Schl Undrgrdt Prog; Biol; Med.

**LA CASSE, TINA M,** Springfield Tech Comm Coll, Springfield, MA; SR; AD; Math; Actuarial Sci.

**LA CHALL, DENISE,** Widener Univ, Chester, PA; SR; BS; Alpha Chi; Acctng; CPA.

**LA CHANCE, KIMBERLY A,** Christopher Newport Coll, Newport News, VA; SO; BSA; Amnsty Intl 90-; Deans Lst 90; Acctg; CPA.

**LA COE, JEAN A,** Univ Of Pittsburgh At Bradford, Bradford, PA; SO; BA; Jazz Bnd 89-90; Pblc Rltns Clb 90-; Wrtng; Career Wrtng Pblc Rltns.

**LA CORTE, JEROME J,** Kent St Univ Kent Cmps, Kent, OH; SO; BA; Prcssn Clb 90-; Music; Prfrm.

**LA COSTE, PATRICIA LAUREN,** Univ Of Sc At Columbia, Columbia, SC; SO; BA; AHS 89-; Zeta Tau Alpha Sor Cncl Del 89-; Pres Schlr 89-; Jr Achvmnt USC Bus Schlr 89-90; Bus Adm; Acctg.

**LA COUNT, JANET LOUISE,** Univ Of Ga, Athens, GA; GD; BSW; Ntnl Asso/Scl Wrkrs 90-; Scl Work; Scl Wrkr.

**LA CROSS, RICHARD E,** Western New England Coll, Springfield, MA; SR; BSBA; Acctng; CPA.

**LA DUKE JR, GILBERT H,** S U N Y Coll Of Tech At Canton, Canton, NY; SR; AS; Stdnt Fac Jud Bd 90-; Tau Alpha Pi; Phi Theta Kappa 90-; Delta Kappa Sigma 90-; Cert GPA; GPA Delta Kappa Sigma 90-91; Constrctn Engr Tech; Engrng.

**LA FARGE, MELBA R,** Univ Of Cin R Walters Coll, Blue Ash, OH; FR; BS; Scis; Dr Of Chrprctcs.

**LA FAVE, KELLY M,** Middle Tn St Univ, Murfreesboro, TN; FR; BA; Gamma Beta Phi; Kappa Delta Asst Schlrshp 90-; Mass Comnctns Pblc Rltns.

**LA FERRIERE, MARY JANE MARIE,** Elms Coll, Chicopee, MA; JR; BA; Res Cncl Pres 88-90; Res Adv 90-; Stdnt Ambsdr 88-90; Campus Mnstry 89-; Elms Ldrshp Awd 90; La Crsse 89-90; Spnsh/Educ; Tchr.

**LA FEVER, TAMMY R,** Univ Of Fl, Gainesville, FL; JR; BSN; FL Stdnt Nrs Assoc 90-; Golden Key; SFCC Hons Soc 89-89; Pres Hon Roll 90; Fawcett Schlrshp; Helene Field Crtcl Care Nrsng Flwshp 90; VA Valor Hons Prog; Deans List; AA Santa Fe Cmnty Clg 89; Nrsng; Critcl Care.

**LA FLEUR, MARKUS H,** Middle Ga Coll, Cochran, GA; SO; MIE; Middle Ga Plyrs VP 89-; Rotrct Clb 90-; Eng Clb 90-; Stdnt Act Comm 90-; Stdnt Adv Cncl Brd Rgnts Sec Stdnt Life Chr 90-; Dns Lst 90-; Oscar Bst Actr 90-; Ind Eng.

**LA FOREST, ROBBIE M,** Chattanooga St Tech Comm Coll, Chattanooga, TN; FR; AS; Acctg/Pre-Law; Acctnt.**

**LA FORTUNE, NATACHA,** Bloomfield Coll, Bloomfield, NJ; FR; Caribbean Stdnt Assn Sec; Iota Phi Theta Swthrts Pres; Sci; Nrsng.

**LA FOUNTAIN, SONIA A,** Elmira Coll, Elmira, NY; FR; BA; Pres Schlrshp; Intl Stds/Spnsh; Govt Srvc.

**LA FRENNIE, LORI L,** Atlantic Comm Coll, Mays Landing, NJ; FR; BA; Art Clb 90; Mentor 90; SGA 90; Single Parents Support Grp 90; Art Ed; Tchr.

**LA GAMBINA, JOSEPHINE,** S U N Y At Buffalo, Buffalo, NY; JR; BS; Acctg Assc 90-; Natl Assc Acctnt 90-; Gldn Key Tres 90-; Beta Alpha Psi; John T Kennedy Mem Awrd; Acctg.

**LA GRECA, SCOTT A,** Cornell Univ Statutory College, Ithaca, NY; SR; PHD; Red Crpt Soc 88-; Karate Clb 88-89; Peer Cnslr 90-; Smithsonian Inst Natl Museum; BS; Botany; Univ Prfssr/Msm Crtr.

**LA GROTTE, JEFFREY A,** Univ Of New Haven, West Haven, CT; SO; BS; Intra Frat Sor Cncl 90-; Alpha Lambda Delta 90-; Delta Sigma Alpha Rush Chrmn 90-; Intr Sftbl 90-; Fin Accntng.

**LA HOOD, SARA F,** Univ Of North Fl, Jacksonville, FL; JR; BA; Cncl Excptnl Childrn 90-; Golden Key 90-; Kappa Delta Pi 90-; BSA Cub Sct Den Ldr; AA Fla Comm Clg Jcksnvl; Spec Educ; Teach Deaf Educ.

**LA JEUNESSE, DAVID C,** Fl St Univ, Tallahassee, FL; SO; BME; Univ Sngrs 90-; Madrigal Sngrs 90; Phi Theta Kappa 89-90; Delta Psi Omega 90; Delta Chi 90-; AA Okaloosa-Walton Comm Coll 90; Mus; Mus Edctr.

**LA LANDE, GWENDOLYN LOUISE,** Interdenominational Theo Ctr, Atlanta, GA; SR; M DIV; Strs Faith 89-; Eastern Star; Pres Lst; Deans Lst; Hon Lst 89-; Elder 86; B E Mays UNCF Schlr 90; Ship/Wrtr Awd; YWCA Cnslr 89-90; Bus Rep N Y Tel Co M9-88; H S Eng Tchr 90-; BS Oh Cntrl Sta Univ 70; Pstrl Care/Cnslng Sys Theology; Hosp Chplncy.

**LA MONACA, VINCENT A,** Villanova Univ, Villanova, PA; JR; BA; Stdnt Musical Theatre VP 90; Campus Mnstry Music Coord 88; Law Schl Crt Jesters 89; Psi Chi NHS; Project Sunshine 88-89; Special Olympcs 88-89; Psychlgy; Cnslng.

**LA MOUNTAIN, KELLY J,** S U N Y At Albany, Albany, NY; FR; BED; Soc Stdies/Elem Ed.

**LA NEVE, ANDREA C,** Salisbury St Univ, Salisbury, MD; SR; BS; Res Hl Cncl Pres 89-; Dns Lst 90-; Elem Educ.

**LA PALME, LINDA E,** Bloomfield Coll, Bloomfield, NJ; FR; BSRN; Nrsng; Emrgncy Nrsng.

**LA PATTA, KRISTIN M,** Georgian Court Coll, Lakewood, NJ; JR; BED; Cncl Excep Chldrn Pres 90-; Spec Olympcs 90-; Crit Thnkg Peer Tutr; Sblng Spprt Grp; Dean Schlr 89-; Spec Educ; Tchr.

**LA PLACA, DOMINICK,** City Univ Of Ny Baruch Coll, New York, NY; SR; BBA; Golden Key; Alpha Iota Delta; Technician; Mgmnt.

**LA PLACA, KAREN,** Jersey City St Coll, Jersey City, NJ; SO; BSN; Crtcl Cr RN; Dplma RN Mntnsd Hosp Schl Nrsng 85; ACLS Amer Hrt Assn 89-; Nrsng.

**LA PLANTE, MARY BETH,** Western New England Coll, Springfield, MA; FR; BS; COPE 90-; Alpha Lambda Delta; Gen Bus; MBA.

**LA POINT, SCOTT F,** Univ Of Rochester, Rochester, NY; JR; BA; Ultmt Frisbee Clb 88-; Radio Station Disc Jcky 88-90; Tau Kappa Epsilon 89-; Psych; Med.

**LA POLT, CHRISTINE L,** Siena Coll, Loudonville, NY; SR; BBA; Acctg Clb NAA 88-; Ambsdrs Clb 87-90; Ldrs Soc 90-; Delta Sigma Pi 88-; Camps Mnstry Sp Ktchn 88-89; Bg Sis Proj Chlng 88-90; NYS Sls Tx Intrn 90-; Acctg.

**LA PORTE, JAMES K,** Univ Of South Al, Mobile, AL; SO; BA; Prsdnts Lst 90-; Deans Lst; Psychology; Clncl Psychology.

**LA ROCCA, TERESA E,** Jersey City St Coll, Jersey City, NJ; SR; MS; Comm Cmpnions Prog; Bayonne Hosp Intrnshp; Deans Lst 89-; NJ Soc Pub Hlth Ed 89-; Admin Asst 83-89; Legal Sec 89-90; BS; Hlth; Hosp Admin.

**LA ROCQUE, MICHELLE M,** Castleton St Coll, Castleton, VT; JR; BA; Psychlgy Clb Treas 90-; Exec Plng Comm Spec Wkends Chr 88-89; Phi Eta Sigma Pres 90-; Stdnt Orientation Stf Coord 89-; Frshmn Yr Awd 89; Presdntl Schlrshp 90; Dns Lst 88; Pres Lst 90; IM Vlybl/IM Sftbl 88-; Forensic Psychlgy; Law/Juv Dfns.

**LA ROCQUE, PAMELA A,** Commonwealth Coll, Virginia Beach, VA; GD; AS; Med Clb 89-90; Exp Med Care MAA; Baysd Med Ctr 90; Headstrt Pgm Seatck V Chr 89; Med Asst Gyn; Med Admin Asst.

**LA ROSA, BRIDGET,** Ny Univ, New York, NY; FR; BA; Appleton/Rice/Perrin Lgl Asst/Offc Mgr 83-; Paralgl Cert Baruch Coll 86; Bus; Law/Finance.

**LA ROSA, LISA A,** Merrimack Coll, North Andover, MA; SO; BS; Acctng; Bsn.

**LA ROSE, ELIZABETH A,** Rivier Coll, Nashua, NH; SO; BA; Nwspr Stf Wrtr; WICI; New Hampshire Pblc Radio WEVO 90-; Media Cmnctns.

**LA ROSE, NICOLE,** Unity Coll, Unity, ME; SR; BA; Educ.

**LA ROSE II, RAYMOND N,** Univ Of Nh Plymouth St Coll, Plymouth, NH; SO; BA; Hl Cncl VP 89-90; IM Sccr Indr Co Capt 89-90; Mrktng; Adv/Comp Prog.

**LA ROSE, SHERRY L,** Castleton St Coll, Castleton, VT; SO; BA; Sei Assn Sec 89-; Art Stdnts Leg 90-; Science Workshop Scndry Stdnts Ldr Orgnzr 90-; Phi Eta Sigma 90-; Ntrl Sci Art; Edctn.

**LA RUE, BARBARA E,** Va Commonwealth Univ, Richmond, VA; SR; BA; Sym Wind Ens 88-; Wdwnd Ens 89-; Bsktbl Pep Bnd 90-; Gldn Key VP 90-; Phi Kappa Phi; Hnrs Pgm 87-; Hnrs Pgm Comm; Magna Cum Laude; Engl/Psy; Tch.

**LA RUE, JUDY A,** Daemen Coll, Amherst, NY; FR; BS; Cmnty Svc Vol 90-; Phys Ther.

**LA RUE, LAURA E,** Va Commonwealth Univ, Richmond, VA; SR; BS; Gldn Key 90-; Phi Theta Kappa; CPR Instrctr-Amer Hrt Assn; Crtfd Chmthrpy Nrs; ENA 90-; Fries Frmns Ladies Aux; Ladies Moose; Emrgncy Dept Chrg Nrs; Srgcl Flr Chrg Nrs; Rcvry Rm Hm Hlth Physcns Offc; Nrsng.

**LA RUE, PAUL MICHAEL G,** Memphis St Univ, Memphis, TN; JR; BA; Beta Theta Pi 88-89; Anthropology; Commercial Pilot.

**LA RUE, S RENEE,** Embry Riddle Aeronautical Univ, Daytona Beach, FL; SR; AS; Aerospace Scty 89-90; Avion Nwspr 89-; Drama Clb 89-90; Litle Sigma Of Sigma Chi 90-; Aviation Bus Admin.**

**LA RUSSO, SHARON A,** Miami Dade Comm Coll, Miami, FL; GD; BA; Italians Fndtn; Cntrlr Birkowitz Dev Grp; Acctng; CPA.

**LA SALA, DEANA M,** Saint Johns Univ, Jamaica, NY; SR; BS; Educ Clb 89-; Coll Rep 90-; Jewish Stdnts Assn Asst To Pres 60-; Gldn Key 90-; Kappa Delta Pi 90-; Sigma Delta Pi 88-; Dns Hnr Lst 88-; Cert Acad Merit 90; Lt Joseph A Cestare Awd; Cert Appreciation; Substance Prev; Elem Educ; Tchr.

**LA SALLE, VICTORIA H,** Univ Of Miami, Coral Gables, FL; JR; BA; Frnch Clb 89-90; Gldn Key 90; Stdy Abroad In Paris Frnc; Frnch; Intl Bus/Law.

**LA SASSA, JENNIFER,** Glassboro St Coll, Glassboro, NJ; BA; Pr Rfrrl And Ornttn Stff 90; Jdcl Hrng Brd 89; Intnatl Sclgcl Hnr Scty 90; Rlgs Educ Tchr 89-; Scl Wrkr Grnbrr Nrsng Cntr 90-; BA 90; Elem Educ; Tchng.

**LA SELVA, SUSAN E,** Dowling Coll, Oakdale Li, NY; SO; BS; Psychlgy.

**LA SPINA, KAY K,** Bristol Univ, Bristol, TN; SR; AD; Assoc Lgl Student Pres 89-; Paralegal; Law.

**LA TONA, DOMINIQUE M,** D Youville Coll, Buffalo, NY; JR; BS; Bsns Mgmt; Mrktng.

**LA TORRE, KEZIAH L,** Pa St Univ Hazleton Cmps, Hazleton, PA; SO; BA; Multi Cultural Clb Pres 90-; Proj Dir Big Bro/Big Sis 90-; Gamma Sigma Sigma 89-90; Lions Awd Highest GPA; Engl; Tchr.**

**LA VALLEE, HEATHER A,** Saint Joseph Coll, West Hartford, CT; SO; BS; Biology Clb Prsdnt 90-; Stdnt Gvmnt 89-; Ntnl Chmstry Cnvtn 89; Deans Lst 89-; Deans Schlrshp 89-; Hnrs Smnr 89; Blood Dr 89-; Biology Chmstry; Med.**

**LA VALLEE, MICHELLE A,** Columbia Greene Comm Coll, Hudson, NY; FR; AAS; Den Ldr Fr The BSA Pck 58 Com Chr 89-; Crmnl Jstce; Law.

**LA VERDA, JAMES,** City Univ Of Ny Baruch Coll, New York, NY; SR; BBA; Golden Key 89-; Beta Gamma Sigma; Baruch Schlr 87-; Parish Youth Ldr 88-; Acctng.

**LA VIGNE, SHANNON K,** Hillsborough Comm Coll, Tampa, FL; SO; BS; Phi Theta Kapa 90-; AA Mott Comm Coll 90; Elem Ed; Tchr.

**LA VISTA, MICHAEL J,** Bloomfield Coll, Bloomfield, NJ; FR; BA; Proc Cntrlr Midlantic Natl Bk; Bus Admn.

**LA ZAROU, GEORGIOS Y,** City Univ Of Ny City Coll, New York, NY; JR; BE; Grk Clb 89-; Tau Beta Pi; Phi Theta Kappa 88-89; Elec Engr.

**LA ZETTE, PEGGY S,** Davis Coll, Toledo, OH; GD; Word Proc; Acctg.

**LA, YEN T,** Univ Of Tn At Martin, Martin, TN; JR; BS; ACM VP 90-F IEEE 90; NW Tn Macintosh Uder Grp 90-; Phi Eta Sigma 91; Chrh Christ Student Ctr 89-90; Faculty Wmns Club Schlrshp; Ldrshp Schlrshp 89; Gooch Schlrshp 90; Computer Sci; Opertng Syst Analyst Stwy.

**LAAKSO, TARJA M,** Broward Comm Coll, Ft Lauderdale, FL; GD; AS; Intl Clb 88-91; DECA 89-; Phi Beta Lambda 90-; Stdnt Ambssdrs 90-; Mrktng.

**LAB, KIMBERLY L,** Muskingum Coll, New Concord, OH; SO; BS; Phi Alpha Theta History Hnry 90-; 2nd Yr Schlrshp Awd; History/Polic Sci; Law.

**LABADIE, ANTHONY L,** S U N Y Coll Of Tech At Frmgdl, Farmingdale, NY; SO; BA; Alpha Beta Gamma 90-; Bsn.

**LABADIE, KELLY R,** Fayetteville St Univ, Fayetteville, NC; FR; BA; Coll Music Edctrs Natl Conf Sec 90-; Concert Choir 90-; Chamber Choir 90-; Deans List; Erly Chldhd Edn/Psych; Tch Pub Sch/Day Care.

**LABAHN, KATHY D,** Univ Of West Fl, Pensacola, FL; SR; BED; Schl Vol Ferry Pass Elem/Middle 89-; Erly Chldhd/Elem Educ; Teacher.

**LABAN, CHRISTIE A,** Alfred Univ, Alfred, NY; SO; BA; Stdnt Sen Fin Comm Chrmn; Alpha Lambda Delta 90-; Acctng; CPA.

**LABAN, MARGUERITE P,** Richard Bland Coll, Petersburg, VA; FR; AS; Alpha Beta Psi Hstrn 90-; Sci.

**LABBE, JAMES M,** Univ Of Akron, Akron, OH; JR; BA; Golden Key 90-; Deans Lst 88-; Bus Admin; Indstrl Mngmnt.

**LABO, JACQUELINE R,** Wright St Univ Lake Cmps, Celina, OH; FR; Acctng.

**LABONTE, LISA M,** Elms Coll, Chicopee, MA; JR; BA; Stdnt Scl Wrk Org Secr 88-; Scl Wrk Advsry Bd Jr Repr 90-; Dns Lst 90; Stdnt Admissions Org 88-89; Nrsg Home Companion 90-; Respite 89-90; Cmnty/Clg Actress 88-; Advocate Devlpmntly Delayed Adolescent 89-; Scl Wrk; Adjstmnt Cnslr.

**LABONTE, PATRICIA L,** Wv Northern Comm Coll, Wheeling, WV; SO; ADN; SNA 89-; Phi Theta Kappa 90-; Nrsng; Oncology.

**LABOSSIERE, HELEN D,** Springfield Coll, Springfield, MA; FR; Class Corr Sec 90-; Child Psych.

**LABOY, PEDRO Y,** Fayetteville St Univ, Fayetteville, NC; SR; BS; Pol Sci Clb 90-; Scty Fr Advncmnt Of Mgmt Treas 90-; Phi Beta Lambda Treas 90-; AA 90; Econs.

**LABRADA, LUIDMILA,** Miami Dade Comm Coll, Miami, FL; FR; Dns Lst 89-; Med Sci; Dntstry.

**LABUT, CHRISTINE A,** Univ Of Akron, Akron, OH; JR; BS; Am Inst/Chem Engr; Resd Hall Prog Bd 90; Alpha Lambda Delta 89; Phi Eta Sigma 89; Pres Schlrshp 89-90; Ntnl Collgte Engrng Awd; Co-Oping/Machi-1 Indus 90-; Chem Engr; Engrng.

**LACAYO, EDUARDO RAFAEL,** Miami Dade Comm Coll, Miami, FL; SO; AA; Archtctr.

**LACEDONIA, NANCY A,** Elms Coll, Chicopee, MA; SR; BED; Delta Epsln Sigma; Trp Ldr Pioneer Vly Grl Scts 90-; AS Sprngfld Tech Comm Clg 85; Elem Ed; Tchr.

**LACEK, SANDRA L,** Comm Coll Algny Co Algny Cmps, Pittsburgh, PA; SR; AS; Sec Treas Dept Fed Govt; Bus Mgmt.

**LACERENZA, RENEE M,** Saint Leo Coll, Saint Leo, FL; SR; BA; Psych Clb VP 89; Edtr Paper; Hnrs Prgrm Cncl 90; Delta Epsilon Sigma VP; Sigma Tau Delta; Hnrs Prgrm 89-; Alpha Xi Omega VP 89; Ambssdr; Emrgng Ldrs 90; Dns Lst 88-; Bat Girl Bsbll Tm 89; Engl; Advrtsng/Mrktng.**

**LACERENZA, WENDY M,** Elmira Coll, Elmira, NY; JR; BS; Amnsty Intl Sec 90-; Phi Eta Sigma; Hnrs Schlr; Crmnl Jstc.

**LACEWELL, ALAN CARLOS,** Fayetteville St Univ, Fayetteville, NC; JR; BS; Campus All-Star Chllnge 89; Stdnt Ctr Advsry Brd 89; Im Bwlng Champ Tm Capt 88; Pol Sci; Law Schl.

**LACEWELL, TAMMIE V,** City Univ Of Ny City Coll, New York, NY; JR; BA; Nwspr Ftrs Edtr; Gldn Key; Deans Lst 88-; Phi Beta Kappa; Engl; Wrtg.

**LACEY, ERIN L,** Univ Of Nc At Charlotte, Charlotte, NC; SR; BA; Blgy; Medcl Tchnlgy.

**LACEY, TIFFANY J,** Ms St Univ, Miss State, MS; SO; Fshn Brd 89-; Lambda Sigma 90-; Alpha Lambda Delta 90-; Phi Eta Sigma; Delta Gamma; Compass Clb 90-; Acctg.

**LACHANCE, KRISTAN A,** Gallaudet Univ, Washington, DC; GD; MA; Pres Schlr 90-; BSE Westfield State Clg 89; MA; Educ Deaf; Tch Deaf.

**LACHANCE, MARIE-PIERRE C,** Clarkson Univ, Potsdam, NY; SO; BA; Pres Schlr 90; Smstr Indstry IBM Fall Smstr; Acctg/Fnce; CPA.

**LACHLER, WENDY A,** Univ Of Miami, Coral Gables, FL; FR; BS; Air Force ROTC Clss Ldr 90; Angle Flght Slvr Wngs Pldge Trnng Offcr; Dist GMC; GMC Warrior Athlt; Amer Legion Mil Excl Awrd; Trck Tm Capt; Cmptr Sci; Air Force Offcr.

**LACHMAN, KAREY L,** Commonwealth Coll, Virginia Beach, VA; SR; BSN; Med; RN.

**LACHMAN-MILITELLO, HOLLY F,** Saint Thomas Univ, Miami, FL; JR; BA; Cncl Frtrnl Orgnztns Sec 78-79; Delta Omega Sorority Prsdnt 77-80; Rcrdr US Senate Comm Aging; FL Soc Rsprtry Care Actv Mmbr 82-; Amrcn Assn Resprtry Care Actvmmbr 82-; Rsprtry Thrpst 82-; AA Miami Dade Comm Clg; Psychology; PHD Clncl Psychlgy.

**LACHNICHT, DANA M,** Bloomfield Coll, Bloomfield, NJ; JR; BA; Bsn Clb 89; Phi Theta Kappa VP 89-90; AS Union Cnty Clg 90; Bsn.

**LACHTER, DEBRA S,** Fl St Univ, Tallahassee, FL; SR; Early Chldhd Rep 89-; Educ To Faculty; Phi Theta Kappa 88; Gldn Key 90; Tallahassee Chmbr Commerce 84-; Brd Membr High Schl Dance Tm 88-; BS; Early Educ; Tchr.

**LACKARD, ANGELA L,** Bay Path Coll, Longmeadow, MA; SO; BA; Goldn Z VP; SGA; Maroon Key; Slutatry Awrd; Lgl Stdies; Law Schl.

**LACKEY, MATTHEW S,** Miami Univ, Oxford, OH; FR; BA; Engl.

**LACKO, JOSEPH J,** Indiana Univ Of Pa, Indiana, PA; FR; BA; Engl; Tchng.

**LACNY, ANNE M,** Kent St Univ Geauga Cmps, Burton Twp, OH; SO; BED; Engl.

**LACOGNATA, JOHN T,** Life Coll, Marietta, GA; GD; DC; Motion Plptn Clb 90-; Gonstead Stdy Clb 90-; SOT Clb 90-; Intrntl Chiro Assc; Sftbl/Ftbl; BA Brklyn Coll 87; Chiropractic.

**LACOMA, NATHALIE A,** Manhattan Coll, Bronx, NY; JR; BS; AICE Treas 89; Drama Clb 89; Schl Newspapr 88-90; Omega Chi Epsilon 90; Crystllgrphy Rsrch Assist 89; Lederle Labs Eng Smmr Intrhshp; Chmcl Eng.**

**LACOMBE, DONALD J,** Central Fl Comm Coll, Ocala, FL; SO; AA; Dns Lst 90; Math; Rsrch/Tch.

**LACY, GLORIA M,** Milligan Coll, Milligan Clg, TN; SO; BSN; Cncrt Chr 89-; Chmbr Sngrs 89-; Drm Cmpny 89-; Symphny Slst; Deans Lst 89-; Nrsng.

**LACY, JENNIFER E,** Univ Of Tn At Martin, Martin, TN; FR; Mu Epsilon Dela Tres; Pre Physical Therapy.

**LACY, JOHN A,** Univ Of Miami, Coral Gables, FL; FR; BA; Gen Hons Prog 90-; Lambda Chi Alpha 90-; AF ROTC 90-; Arch; AF Ofcr.

**LACY, KENNETH B,** Fl International Univ, Miami, FL; JR; BA; Trinity Church Choir 90-; Mc Lamore Ctr Child Abuse Vol 89-; Dns Lsts 87-; Cross Country 87-89; AA Essex Cmnty Clg 89; Spec Ed; Tchr.

**LACY, RICHARD C,** Univ Of Sc At Columbia, Columbia, SC; SO; BA; Bus Admin; Finance.

**LACY, RONDA A,** Webber Coll, Babson Park, FL; SR; BA; Phi Theta Kappa 88; Vol Pblc Schl 88-; AA Polk Cmmnty Coll 88f; Bus Acctg.

**LACY, VALERIE A,** Univ Of Al At Birmingham, Birmingham, AL; FR; BA; Stdnts Bttr Erth 90-; Dmnd Drlngs; Alpha Lambda Delta; Alpha Omicron Pi 90-; Blzr Crw; Hon Schlrshp 90-; IM Sprts 90-; Educ/Pre-Phscl Thrpy; Physcl Thrpy.

**LACY, WALTER M,** Al A & M Univ, Normal, AL; SR; Natl Soc Blck Eng; Alpha Kappa Mu Pres 90-; Sigma Tau Epsilon; Alpha Phi Alpha; Deans Lst 89-; Hnr Rl 89-90; Bsktbl/All Acad Awd 89-90; Internshp Miller Brewing 90; Bsktbl; Mech Drftng/Eng; Dsgnr Eng.

**LADAS II, LUDWIG NICHOLAS,** Barry Univ, Miami, FL; GD; JD; Pres Lst 90-; Summa Cum Laude; Lw Enfrcmnt 75-; Law; Lawyer.

**LADBROOK, WARREN D,** Univ Of Tn At Chattanooga, Chattanooga, TN; SO; BSE; Mlr Lt Rgby Clb Chattanooga 90-; Yng Life Vol Ldr 90-; Assoc Hnrs Flw 90-; Phi Eta Sigma 90-; Amer Soc Cvl Engr Stu Chptr Tres 90-; Chattanooga Engrs Clb Schlrshp Rcpnt; New Zealand Lnds/Survy Dept 82-83; Cvl Engr; Strctrl.

**LADD, LOURDES J,** Marshall University, Huntington, WV; GD; MAT; Sigma Delta Pi 90-; Delta Zeta 69-73; Tchng Part-Time Spnsh 90 91; BBA 73; Spnsh, Tchr.

**LADD, MARGARET E,** Univ Of Nc At Asheville, Asheville, NC; JR; BA; SNEA V P 88-; Phi Eta Sigma 88; Kappa Phi Pres 89-; Rsrch Assist/Dr Gene Arnold 90; Psych; Tchng.

**LADEMANN, CHRISTINE A,** Ramapo Coll Of Nj, Mahwah, NJ; JR; BA; Pol Sci Clb; Pol Sci; Law.

**LADEWIG, RAGNA I,** Bergen Comm Coll, Paramus, NJ; GD; ASN; Phi Theta Kappa; Deans List 90; Nursing Mobility Award; Feminist Schlrshp 90; Church Choir; Wmns Mnstrs Pres 82-; Hosp Lpn 83-; Nursing; RN/CARDIAC Care.

**LADIPO, KATHY O,** Jackson St Univ, Jackson, MS; SR; BS; Dunbar Dramatic Gld; One Wmn Shw; Bus Law; Alpha Mu Gamma; Phi Kappa Phi; Chi Alpha Chi; Highes Dptmntl GPA; Mass Comm; Law.

**LADNER, AARON J,** Univ Of Southern Ms, Hattiesburg, MS; SO; BS; Vetrn US Cst Grd; Ectrnc Eng Tech.**

**LADNER, LELA A,** East Central Comm Coll, Decatur, MS; FR; BS; SEA VP 90-; Mu Alpha Theta 90-; Phi Theta Kappa 90-; Warrior Corps 90-91; Elem Ed; Tchr.

**LADNIER, THERESA G,** Livingston Univ, Livingston, AL; JR; BA; Sngrs 89-; Choir 89-; Phi Eta Sigma 89-; Alpha Chi 90-; Crdnl Key 90-; Music Educ.

**LADOUCEUR, KAREN M,** Salisbury St Univ, Salisbury, MD; JR; BS; Mrtl Arts Clb Treas VP 88-; Otdr Clb 90; NAA 90; IRS Crtfd Tx Advsr; VITA; IM Mrtl Arts 90; Acctng; CPA.

**LADUEW, JAMES M,** Troy St Univ At Dothan, Dothan, AL; SR; MS; Gamma Phi Beta 90; AS 88; BS 90; Comp Sci Hstry; Nclr Fld US Nvy.

**LADYGA, AMY B,** Muskingum Coll, New Concord, OH; JR; BA; Hmcmng Commtt Cmps; Stu Act Plnng Commtt 88-89; Res Asst 90-; Cmps Tr Gde 90-; Lambda Sigma 89-90; Omicron Delta Kappa 90-; Psi Chi 90-; Cmps Vol 88-; Psych; Clncl Psych.

**LAFEVERS, VALERIE M,** Univ Of Tn At Martin, Martin, TN; JR; BA; Sigma Tau Delta; Eng.

**LAFFERTY, KAREN M,** Daemen Coll, Amherst, NY; SO; BA; Rsdnt Asst; Physcl Thrpy.

**LAFFERTY, KEITH A,** Embry Riddle Aeronautical Univ, Daytona Beach, FL; SO; BA; Skydvg Clb Pres; Soc Cmrcl Aviation Tech; Aviation.

**LAFFERTY, MARY K,** Beckley Coll, Beckley, WV; SO; BED; Spcl Ed; Tchr/Law JD.

**LAFFITTE, LATONYA D,** Univ Of South Al, Mobile, AL; SO; BED; Blck Stdnt Union; Abeneefoo Kuo 90-; Alpha Lambda 90-; Phi Eta Sigma 90-; Alpha Kappa Alpha; Spch Pthlgy.**

**LAFLEUR, DAVID S,** Ms Gulf Coast Comm Coll, Perkinston, MS; SO; AA; Bus Admn; Gen Option.**

**LAFLEUR, JASON C,** Teikyo Post Univ, Waterbury, CT; SO; BA; Rqtbl; Smmng; Intr Dsgn.

**LAFLEUR, MICHAEL T,** Western New England Coll, Springfield, MA; JR; BA; Acctg Assn VP 89-; Stdnt Sen; Alpha Lambda Delta 89-; Delta Mu Delta; Vlntr Income Tax Asst 89-; Stdnt Ambss; Karate Tm 88-89; Pblc Acctg CPA.

**LAFON, CHARLES W,** Emory & Henry Coll, Emory, VA; JR; BA; Alpha Phi Omega 90-; Clg Repblcns 88; Stdnts For Peace/Envrnmntl Concrns 90; Pi Gamma Mu; Sigma Mu; Alpha Phi Omega 90-; Schlr Award 88-; Snavely Award 90-; Edgar Bingham Eareth Sci Schlrshp; Geo; Prof Geogrphy.

**LAFON, STEPHANE CHRISTIAN,** Fl International Univ, Miami, FL; JR; BS; Liaison Vineyard Christian Flwshp/Haitian Commty; Intev English Prog Univ Miami 89; DEUG LEA Univ De Nice 86-89; Hospitality Mgt.

**LAGACY, DANIEL A,** Univ Of Cincinnati, Cincinnati, OH; SO; BA; Msc Violin Perf; Orchestra Mscn.

**LAGASCA, RONALD JUDE S,** Fordham Univ, Bronx, NY; SO; BS; Filipino Amer Clb Sec Tr 89-90; Model U N Clb 90-; IM Sftb/Bsktbl 89-; Bio; Med.**

**LAGEMAN, TIBOR J,** Anne Arundel Comm Coll, Arnold, MD; FR; Air Force; AAS Com Clg Air Force 90.

**LAGERGREN, MARK E,** Columbus Coll Of Art & Design, Columbus, OH; SO.

**LAGEUUX, KIMBERLY B,** Castleton St Coll, Castleton, VT; SO; Castleton Schlr 89; Vrsty Soccer 90-; IM Sprts 90-; Sci; Lab Techncn.

**LAGREE, ROBERT,** Middlesex County Coll, Edison, NJ; FR.

**LAGROON, ROBERT J,** Medical Coll Of Ga, Augusta, GA; GD; DMD; Natl Brd Resp Care RRT 87-; SC Brd Med Exmnrs RCP 88; AS 86; BS 88; Dntstry.**

**LAGUERRE, GRACE D,** Univ Politecnica De Pr, Hato Rey, PR; FR; BIEE; Stdnt Cncl VP 89-90; Untd Ntns Cncl Rep 88-89; Ind Engnr; Engnrng.

**LAH, JOSEPH F,** Univ Of Akron, Akron, OH; SR; Delta Gamma Sigma; Sigma Iota Epsilon; APICS.

**LAHAR, KIM M,** Wv Northern Comm Coll, Wheeling, WV; FR; AD; Cmptrs; Cmptr Pgm.

**LAHAV, AMIT,** Cooper Union, New York, NY; FR; Elctrcl Engnrng; Engnrng.

**LAHEY, KAREN E,** Saint Joseph Coll, West Hartford, CT; SO; BA; Prsnl Admsns Liason Trgd 90-; Stu Nwspr 90-; Amnsty 90-; Pol Sci; Law.

**LAHR, SONYA A,** Bowling Green St Univ At Huron, Huron, OH; JR; ASSO; AMRA; OMRA; Med Records Techn.

**LAHRMAN, ROBERT F,** Pa St Univ Delaware Cty Cmps, Media, PA; SO; BA; Stdnt Ath Assn Pr 90-; Stdnt Govt Assn Exec Bd 90-; Penn State Keystone Soc 90-; Var Bsbl Capt 89-; Acctng; Bus Law.

**LAHTI, ANDREA M,** Univ Of Sc At Columbia, Columbia, SC; SR; BA; Phtgrphy Clb Chrprsn 88-89; Mtn Clb 89-; Innvtrs Clb 89; Grnwd Gntc Cnt Intern 90; Kdck Mdlln Excllnc 87; Phylsphy.

**LAI, CHI-WANG ALBERT,** Univ Of Miami, Coral Gables, FL; SO; BSEE; Hong Kong Stdnts Assn Pres 90-; Deans Lst 89-; IEEE 89-; Comp Eng/Comp Sci; Eng.

**LAI, CHRISTINE R,** Philadelphia Coll Pharm & Sci, Philadelphia, PA; SR; BS; Acad Stdnts Pharm APHA Stdnt Chap 87-; Agape Chrstn Flwshp 86-90; Orntl Stdnts Assn Treas 87-89; Adopt A Grnprnt Prog 86-88; Amer Chinese Pharm Assn 86-88; Penn Pharm Assn 90-; Deans Lst; Schlrshp; I M Vybl; Pharmacist.

**LAI, CHUNG L,** City Univ Of Ny Baruch Coll, New York, NY; SR; BBA; Golden Key 90; Beta Gamma Sigma; Fnc.

**LAI, JEAN SUONG,** Ms St Univ, Miss State, MS; JR; BS; Amer Soc Mech Eng 90-; Phi Kappa Phi; Bst Fr Chmstry 90; Schlrshp Rcngtns; Pres Schlr 90; Mech Eng.

**LAI, JUDY J,** Univ Of Ky, Lexington, KY; FR; BS; Stdnt Assoc 90-; Hnrs Pgm Secr; Sigma Gamma Sigma 90-; Alpha Lambda Delta; Sigma Alpha Iota Treas; Bio; Med.

**LAI, KEVIN YINGKEI,** S U N Y At Binghamton, Binghamton, NY; SR; MS; Intrntl Stdnt Assc 89-; Intrntl Stdnt Orgnztn 87-89; Sccr Tm 87-89; Pres List 87-89; Deans Hon List 89-; Phi Theta Kappa 87-; IEEE 89-; Tau Beta Tau 89-; Tau Beta Pi; Peer Tutoring 88-89; Tchng Asstnt; Frank G Paul Schlrshp 89-; BS; Elect Eng.**

**LAI, KOON-KEUNG,** Univ Of Rochester, Rochester, NY; JR; BS; Phi Beta Kappa 90-; Genesee Schlrshp 88-; Elec Engr.

**LAI, MEE-MEE,** Univ Of Rochester, Rochester, NY; SR; MSEE; Chinese Stdnt Assn 88-; Badmtn Soc 88-; IEEE 89-; Tchg Asst 90-; BSEE; Elec Eng; Grad Schl.

**LAI, YAN H,** City Univ Of Ny Baruch Coll, New York, NY; SO; BBA; Hong Kong Std Asc Sec; Acctng.

**LAIDLAW, ALAN W,** Academy Of The New Church, Bryn Athyn, PA; GD; Univ Edinburgh Stf Clb 90-; Beng 90; Elec Eng.

**LAIDLAW, BETH,** Academy Of The New Church, Bryn Athyn, PA; JR; BS; Educ; Elem Schl Tchr.

**LAIDLAW, PATRICK K,** Westminster Coll, New Wilmingtn, PA; SO; BS; Ski Clb; Hs Cncl Tres 90-; IM Bstkbl/Sftbl; Lambda Sigma Tres 90-; Kappa Mu Epsilon; Sigma Pi Sigma; Sigma Phi Epsilon 90-; Trustee Schlrshp 89-; Albright Schlrshp 89-; Var Sccr 89-; Physics; Engr.

**LAIDLOW-HARRIS, LYDIA L,** City Univ Of Ny Med Evers Coll, Brooklyn, NY; BSCED; Erly Chldhd Ed; Tchng.

**LAIL, MARINA G,** Saint Andrews Presbytrn Coll, Laurinburg, NC; SR; BA; Chrl 86-; Alpha Chi 89-; Pi Gamma Mu 88-; Univ Hon Soc 88-; Stdnt Tchr Yr; Paul Douglas Schlr 87-; Exchng Stdnt-Beijing China 89; Hstry/Mddl Grd Educ; Educ.

**LAIN, ALLEN W,** Bridgeport Engr Inst, Fairfield, CT; SR; BS; Amer Hlcptr Soc 84; Aviation Wk Tech Advsry Bd 90-; Rlblty/Maintblty Engr Sikorsky Aircraft 80; Mech Engr.

**LAIN, ANTHONY S,** Univ Of Tn At Martin, Martin, TN; FR; MBA; IM Sftbl; Econ Finance; Law.

**LAINHART, SARA A,** Northern Ky Univ, Highland Hts, KY; SO; BEDBA; Biolgcl Soc 90-; Chem Soc Sec; Biolgy/Ed; Lab Tech/Tchng.**

**LAINHART, TRINITY S,** Univ Of Tn At Knoxville, Knoxville, TN; FR; BS; Gamma Beta Phi; Anml Sci; Vetrnry Medcn.

**LAINIOTIS, GEORGIA ISMINI,** Smith Coll, Northampton, MA; GD; AISEC 86-87; Hse Soc Chrmn 85-86; Intl Stdnts Soc 85-90; 1st Grp Schlr 89-90; Dns Lst 88-90; Dghtrs Penelpe Reg Mbr CA 90-; Morgan Stanley Res Asst 89; Agric Bnk Greece Res Asst 87; Smith Clg Japanese Lang Tchr Asst/Tutor 89-90.

**LAIRD, KENNETH W,** Memphis Academy Of The Arts, Memphis, TN; JR; BFA; Soc Of Illus 89; Millington Art League 90-; Med Illus Intrnshp; School Graphics Design Agency; Illus.

**LAITY, NATASHA L,** Univ Of Cincinnati, Cincinnati, OH; FR; BFA; Animal Rights Cmnty 90-; UC Thespian Soc 90-; Cincinnati Vegetarian Soc; Hnrs Prog 90-; Shop Assistant 90-; Theatrical Design & Production; Makeup.

**LAJEWSKI, SANDRA J,** Western New England Coll, Springfield, MA; FR; BA; Mech Engr.

**LAJOIE, CHRISTINE ELLEN,** Andover Coll, Portland, ME; SR; AS; Intrnshp NESA; Bkkpr 91; Acctg.

**LAK, CYNTHIA J,** Gaston Coll, Dallas, NC; SO; BABS; Outstndg Stu Year 90; PTA Gr Par Chrmn 83-; Un Arts Cncl Comm 86-; Accntnt 85-; Bus Adminstrtn; Sales/Mrktng.

**LAKE, DAVID D,** Univ Of Cincinnati, Cincinnati, OH; JR; BA; Assoc MET UC; Eng.

**LAKE, KELLY JO,** Liberty Univ, Lynchburg, VA; JR; BS; SG; Dorm Pryr Ldr; SGA; Hnrs Lst; IM Vlybl; Bus Mgmnt.

**LAKE, STUART D,** Univ Of Sc At Salkehatchie, Allendale, SC; SO; BA; Gamma Beta Phi 90-; Newberry Coll Indian Bsebl 89-90; Bsebl 90-; Cmnty Ctr 89-; Phys Edn; Teach/Coach.

**LAKES, DEA L,** Sue Bennett Coll, London, KY; SO; BA; Am Colg Schol; Phi Theta Kapa V P 90-; Silver Medal Awd; Elem Ed.

**LAKES, SUZANNE K,** James Madison University, Harrisonburg, VA; SO; BS; Campus Crusade Christ 89-; Cntr Serv Lrng 90-; Campus Newspr 89-90; Pres Lst 90; Deans Lst 89-; IM Bsktbl/Indr Sccr 89-; Psych; Chld.

**LAKEY, ANGELA L,** Univ Of Nc At Greensboro, Greensboro, NC; FR; BS; Frshmn Schlr; Kappa Omicron Nu; Soc Wrk.

**LAKHMAN, MARIA,** Bunker Hill Comm Coll, Boston, MA; CERT; Dean Lst; Lbrry Lrnng Aid 89-90; Cert Tech Schl Moscow Russia 71; Offc Applctns; Wrd Prcssng.

**LAKIS JR, WILLIAM E,** Ny Law School, New York, NY; GD; JD; Law Rvw 90-; Amer Jrsprdnce Awrds; Amer Soc Mechncl Engrs 87-; Sr Engr Amer Bureau Shppng 85-; BS US Mrchnt Marine Acdmy 85; Admrlty Law.

**LAKOMY, RENEE A,** Duquesne Univ, Pittsburgh, PA; SR; Cls Sec 89-; BSN; Nrsng; Crdvsclr Thoracic.

**LAKY, TERESA L,** Valdosta St Coll, Valdosta, GA; SO; MBA; Marching Band 90-; Alpha Sigma Chi; Frshmn Schlr 89-90; Erly Chldhd Ed; Tchng.

**LALANCETTE, MICHELLE R,** Western New England Coll, Springfield, MA; SO; BA; Peer Advsr 90-; Ambsdr; Mgmnt Assn Sec 90-; Human Res Mgmnt; Mgr.

**LALIBERTE, JOANNE M,** Teikyo Post Univ, Waterbury, CT; GD; BS; Ambsdr Teikyo Pot Admsns Offc; Treas Stdnt Govt 89-90; Alpha Chi 89-; Alpha Gamma Delta 87-88; March Of Dimes 88-89; United Way; Intrnshp United Way; Co Op Budwitz/Meyerjack CPA Firm 89-91; Work Stdy/Stpu Bookstore; Acctng; CPA.

**LALIBERTE, MICHELLE S,** Newbury Coll, Brookline, MA; FR; AS; Art; Interior Dsgn/Arch.

**LALL, PRATIMA,** City Univ Of Ny Baruch Coll, New York, NY; JR; BBA; Golden Key; Mentoring Prog/Counsellor Tutor; Deans List; AICPA Schlrshp; Schlrshp; Acctng; Taxation CPA.

**LALLY, ELIZABETH M,** Bellarmine Coll, Louisville, KY; SR; Stdnt Cncl Exptnl Chldrn Pres 88-; Natl Educ Assn 88-; Undergrad Advsry Bd 89-90; Delta Epsilon Sigma 90-; Kappa Gamma Pi 90-; Kappa Delta 86-88; SGA Ldrshp Awd 90; Outstndg Stdnt CEC Awd 90-; BA; Spec Educ; Lrng Dsblty Tchr.

**LALLY, MARY R,** Teikyo Post Univ, Waterbury, CT; JR; Drug/Alchol Tsk Frc 90-; Church Org/Drama 87-; Hosp Vol 87-88; Psychlgy; Clncl Psychlgst.

**LALLY, ROBERT M,** Bunker Hill Comm Coll, Boston, MA; FR; AS; Alliance House; Cnslr; Crmnl Jstc; Law.

**LALONDE, LISA M,** Univ Of Ky, Lexington, KY; JR; Flwshp Chrstn Athlts 89-; SGA Hmcmng Comm 90-; IM Bsktbl/Sftbl 89-; Deans Lst 89-; Kappa Alpha Theta 90-; Goodwill Collctr 89-90; Blood Donr 90-; CASA 90-; Natl Acdmy Gym Dir 89-90.

**LALOR, TIMOTHY J,** Hudson Valley Comm Coll, Troy, NY; FR; Church Worship Tm 89-; Physics; Teach.

**LAM, ANGELA MARIE,** Bellarmine Coll, Louisville, KY; SR; BA; Deans Lst Jefferson Comm Coll; ASSOC Jefferson Comm Coll 89; Mgmt; Own Bus.

**LAM, ANMAY,** Ny Univ, New York, NY; FR; BA; Alpha Upsilon Pi 90-; Nwspr Stf 90-; Peers Ears 90-; Trustee Schlr 90-; Law.

**LAM, DONALD M,** City Univ Of Ny City Coll, New York, NY; SO; BS; Elec Eng.

**LAM, JUDE K,** Univ Of Tn At Knoxville, Knoxville, TN; SR; BS; Hong Kong Stdnt Assoc Pres 89-90; Knoxville Chinese Nw Yr Fstvl Chf Co Org 90; Golden Key; Beta Gamma Sigma; Phi Kappa Phi; Beta Alpha Psi; Sprng Internshp Siegiel Bible CPA Knoxville; Dupont Acctg Schlrshp 90; Acctg; Info Cnsltnt/CPA.

**LAM, KHON THIEU,** Bunker Hill Comm Coll, Boston, MA; FR; Acctg.

**LAM, MAN Y,** City Univ Of Ny Baruch Coll, New York, NY; SR; BBA; Hng Kng Clb 87-88; Beta Gamma Sigma; Accntng.

**LAM, STEPHEN W,** City Univ Of Ny La Guard Coll, Long Island Cty, NY; JR; BBA; Comp Bsbl Clb Pres 89-90; Phi Theta Kappa 90; Comp Info Syst; Syst Anlyst.

**LAM, STEPHEN W,** Univ Of Va Clinch Valley Coll, Wise, VA; SO; BA; Telemrktng For Coll; Dns Lst 90; Vice Chncllrs Awrd; IM Hlpr 90; Engl Cmmnctns BUAD; Sprts Brdcstng.

**LAM, TUAN QUANG,** Howard Univ, Washington, DC; SR; BA; Pharmacy.

**LAMA, GEORGE S,** Fl International Univ, Miami, FL; SR; BS; Stdnt Govt 88; Future Educ Amer 88-89; Sigma Alpha Mu Philanthropy Chrmn 88-90; Greek Wk 89-90; Educ/Excptnl Stdnt Ed; Educ/Tch.

**LAMANEC, STEPHANIE J,** Schenectady County Comm Coll, Schenectady, NY; SO; BS; Engr Tech New York State DOT 88-; Cmptr Sci; Engr.

**LAMANNA, LINDA J,** S U N Y Coll At Fredonia, Fredonia, NY; JR; BS; AAS Canton ATC 85; Spch Path/Audiology.

**LAMANNA, MARTHA B,** Kent St Univ Kent Cmps, Kent, OH; SR; BA; Golden Key; Humane Assn 85-86; Cust Serv Supv 86-89; Mortgage Broker 83-86; Ofc Mngr 81-83; Operations Supv 78-81; Teller 72-78; Escrow Assn 86-89; Psychology Humanitios; Financial Institution.

**LAMANTEER, MICHAEL J,** Villanova Univ, Villanova, PA; JR; BS; Alpha Epsilon Delta 89; Deans Lst 88-; Biology; Med.

**LAMAR, ADRIENNE K,** Cumberland County Coll, Vineland, NJ; SO; African Amer Cultural Clb 89-; Phi Theta Kappa 90-; Drug Elimination Pgm 90-; AAS; Cmnty Svc; Social Wrk.

**LAMAR, VERNA L,** Clark Atlanta Univ, Atlanta, GA; SR; BS; Mat Club Pres 88-; Hons Progrm 88-; Pi Mu Epsilon Secy 89-; Beta Kappa Chi Secy 90-; Alpha Kappa Mu; Upward Bound Tutor/Cnslr 88-; Outrch Progrm Tutor 89-90; UNCF/GTE Summer Intrnshp Prog 90; Math; Rsrch/Devlpmnt.

**LAMARCHE, ROSEMARIE N,** Fl International Univ, Miami, FL; SR; BA; Soc Wk; Law.

**LAMARRE, GILBERT J,** Merrimack Coll, North Andover, MA; SO; Prog Brd 89-90; Deans Lst 90; Nu Phi Kappa 90; Res Assist; Walt Dsny Wrld Clg Prog; Mngmnt.

**LAMB, DAVID R,** Northern Ky Univ, Highland Hts, KY; FR; BA; Hstry Pol Sci; Law.

**LAMB, DONNA M,** Univ Of Ky, Lexington, KY; SO; BA; Hnrs Pgm; Hnrs Pgm Schlrshp; Amnesty Intl; OPFF Res Cncl V P; Hstry; Law Sch.

**LAMB, EILEEN T,** S U N Y Coll At Fredonia, Fredonia, NY; SR; BS; Radio Dir 87-; Amnsty Intl 88-89; Alpha Epsln Rho 88; Arlie Muller Parks Awd 88; WBAB Intshp 88; Indpt Label Allnc Intshp 89; Comm/Media; Msc Indstry/Rcrdng.**

**LAMB, JESSICA M,** Indiana Univ Of Pa, Indiana, PA; SR; BA; Delta Zeta Pres 90-; Geog; Dvlpng.

**LAMB, KERRI L,** Univ Of Tn At Martin, Martin, TN; FR; BS; Coll FFA VP 90-; Agrnmy Clb 90-; Blck/Brdl 90-; Chrl Soc 90-; Coll Soil Jdgng Tm 90-; Frm Bur Ag Plcy Dbt; St FFA Sec 90-; Agrctr/Plnt/Sl Sci; Soil Csrvtn.

**LAMB, LINDA D,** Johnson St Coll, Johnson, VT; JR; BS; USAF ROTC 88-89; Arnld Air Soc 88-89; Deans Lst 90; Pres List 90; All-Am Schlr; Var Sftbl 90; Bio; Wldlf Mgmt.

**LAMB, MARIA C,** Fl St Univ, Tallahassee, FL; JR; BA; Latin Club 89-90; Tele Cnslng Rfrl Svc 90-; Psych/Scl Wrk; MSW.

**LAMB, PEARLIE M,** Al A & M Univ, Normal, AL; SO; BS; Army ROTC 89-; Kappa Delta Pi; Bsktbll 89-90; Lgstcs; Army.

**LAMB, ROBERTA Y,** Owensboro Comm Coll, Owensboro, KY; FR; AS; Nrs.

**LAMB, SHARON M,** Univ Of Sc At Columbia, Columbia, SC; GD; BS; YWCA; Amercn Soc For Quality Cntrl; Obtain The Certfd Quality Engr Sztatus; ASS Univ Of SC 86; Fin; Bus Mgt.

**LAMBERG, STEVEN K,** S U N Y Coll Of Tech At Frmgdl, Farmingdale, NY; JR; BA; Restrnt Mgmt Assn P 88-90; Boy Scts Eag; Led Dames Descdffier Schlrshp 89; AAS SUNY Farmingdale 90; Rest/Inst Mgmt; Corp Dng.

**LAMBERSON, NANCY L,** Memphis St Univ, Memphis, TN; GD; Phi Kappa 89; Pi Delta Phi 85; Sigma Elta Pi Ntnl; Liberal Arts 90; Gldn Key 87; Summa Cum Laude; BA; French/Spanish; Graduate Schl.

**LAMBERT FAULKENBERRY, LORI L,** Middle Tn St Univ, Murfreesboro, TN; FR; MBA; Law.

**LAMBERT, BRADLEY W,** Univ Of Sc At Columbia, Columbia, SC; SO; BA; Gamma Beta Phi 89-; RA; Engl/Poli Sci; Law.

**LAMBERT, BRIAN W,** Spartanburg Methodist Coll, Spartanburg, SC; FR; BS; Cub/Boy Scts Lf Sct 79-90; Beta Clb; Schlrshp; Acdmc Athlt Yr; Sccr Capt 77-; Math/Sci; Eng.

**LAMBERT, BRIDGET C,** Ms St Univ, Miss State, MS; SR; BBA; Gamma Beta Phi 88; Mu Kappa Tau 88-; Pi Sigma Epsilon 89-; Zeta Tau Alpha Grp Ldr 88-; IM Flg Ftbl Sftbl 87-; BBA; Mrktng; Phrmctcl Sls.

**LAMBERT, DAVID L,** Nc Central Univ, Durham, NC; SR; JD; Delta Tau Delta 84-88; CHANCE 87-88; Squash Tm; BA Duke Univ 88; Law.

**LAMBERT, ERIC M,** Marshall University, Huntington, WV; SR; BA; Otstndg Coll Stu Amer 89-; Gamma Beta Phi 88-90; Fruth Phrmcy Schlr; Chmst Yr 88-89; Mgt; Phrmcst.

**LAMBERT, ERIC S,** Univ Of Rochester, Rochester, NY; JR; BA; Mgmt Stds Cncl Co Pres 90-; Glee Clb Bus Mgr 88-; Acapella Jazz Grp Pblcty Mgr 90-; Omicron Delta Epsilon; Econ; Law.

**LAMBERT II, FRANKLIN R,** Wv Univ, Morgantown, WV; FR; BA; IM Sftbl; Accntng; Corp Law.

**LAMBERT, JACKIE L,** Ashland Comm Coll, Ashland, KY; FR; BA; Bapt Cmps Mnstrs 90-; Alderson-Broaddus Clg 90-; ABN Wrk Stdy Pgm; Nrsg.

**LAMBERT, JEANNE M,** Elmira Coll, Elmira, NY; JR; BS; Theatre 88-; SCOPE VP 90-; CARE Pgm Intern; Intern Mary Dalpe Dir Human Serv Marlboro Mass; Psychlgy; Fmly Cnslng.

**LAMBERT, JEFFERY R,** Winthrop Coll, Rock Hill, SC; JR; BS; Acctg Clb VP 90-; Natl Assn Accttnts 90-; Tax Deferred Spec Old Stone Bank 88-89; Cpa.

**LAMBERT, JEFFREY A,** Duquesne Univ, Pittsburgh, PA; JR; BA; Ski Clb 90-; Socty Hmn Rsrc Mgmt Treas 90-; Hmn Rsrc Mgmt; Business.

**LAMBERT, JERRY A,** Valdosta St Coll, Valdosta, GA; SO; BA; Bst Rsrch Paper Written Sectn Engl 102 90; State Music Com Ch God So GA 90-; Mnstr 89-; Pre-Med; Med Doc.

**LAMBERT, JEWEL DALE,** Univ Of Miami, Coral Gables, FL; FR; BS; Jugglng Clb; Phys/Math; Appld Phys.

**LAMBERT, JOHN H,** Western Piedmont Comm Coll, Morganton, NC; SO; AAS; Western Piedmont Comm Clg Crim Justice Club 88-; Phi Theta Kappa/Alpha Gamma Mu; Burke County Law Enfor Off Assoc 83-; NC Law Enfor Offic Assoc 83-; NC Law Enfor Trng Instr 90-; US Dept Justice/Crim Just Resec Serv 89-; Crim Just.

**LAMBERT, JUDY L,** Fayetteville St Univ, Fayetteville, NC; SO; MBA; Pres Lst 89-; NC Rltrs/Brbrs; Own Optr Hrstylg Salon; MS 79; Educ; Tchr.

**LAMBERT, KELLY L,** Univ Of Ct, Storrs, CT; FR; BA; I M Soccer; Bus Mktg.

**LAMBERT, LIONEL,** City Univ Of Ny Queensbrough, New York, NY; SO; BS; Phi Theta Kappa 89; Elctrnc Tech 83-; AS 83; Cmptr Sci.

**LAMBERT, MARSHAL D,** Univ Of Sc At Columbia, Columbia, SC; FR; BS; Mechanical Engineering.

**LAMBERT, MARY M,** Wv Univ At Parkersburg, Parkersburg, WV; Assoc Appld Sci; Ofc Admin; Sec.

**LAMBERT, MICHAEL J,** Glassboro St Coll, Glassboro, NJ; GD; BA 90; Math; Math/Chem Engr.

**LAMBERT, NATALIE ANN,** Castleton St Coll, Castleton, VT; JR; BS; Chrstn Fllwshp 88-; Phi Eta Sigma 88-; Delta Kappa Pi 90-; Lacrosse 89; Fld Hcky 88-; Elem Edctn; Kndrgrtn Tchr.

**LAMBERT, SANDRA L,** Ms St Univ, Miss State, MS; SR; BBA; Phi Kappa Phi 89-; Pi Sigma Epsilon 89-; Delta Delta Delta Fndrsng Chmn 87-; Gamma Beta Phi 87-; MS St Univ Pnhllnc Rsh Cnslr 90; Bus; Mrktng Rep.

**LAMBERT, SHEILA C,** Radford Univ, Radford, VA; JR; Accntng Soc 90-; Accntng; Accntnt.

**LAMBERT, STEVEN E,** Univ Of Al At Huntsville, Huntsville, AL; SO; BSE; Hnrs Pgm; Dns Lst Hnr Schlr 90; Mech Engr.

**LAMBERT, SUSAN C,** Univ Of Montevallo, Montevallo, AL; SR; BA; Coll Nght Cbnt; Ttr Fr Hrbrt Wrtng Cntr And Stdnt Spprt Srvcs; Phi Theta Kappa; Phi Kappa Phi; Omicron Delta Kappa; Lambda Sigma Pi; Sigma Tau Delta; Chi Omega; Hrbrt Wrtng Cntr Intrn; Engl Elite; Cnfrnce Ldr At SWCA; Sigma Tau Delta Bk Awrd; Engl; Educ.

**LAMBERT, TODD J,** Niagara Univ, Niagara Univ, NY; SR; BS; Ec Fin Clb VP 89-; Lacrosse Tm VP 87-; Avtn Clb Mktg Clb Psychlgy Clb 90-; Intrnshp Carborundum Abrsvs Co Prsnl Dept; Lacrosse VP 87-; Hmn Rsrc Mgmt Psychlgy.

**LAMBERT-NEIDIGH, PAULA J,** Univ Of Al At Birmingham, Birmingham, AL; JR; BA; Juried Stdnt Art Exhibition 90-; Sigma Tau Delta VP 90-; Golden Key; Presidential Hnrs 90-; Deans Lst 89-90; English; Professor.

**LAMBERTA, LYNNETTE B,** S U N Y Coll Of Tech At Frmgdl, Farmingdale, NY; SO; BA; Sec Purchsng Agt 89-; Liberal Arts Sci; Tchr Elem Lvl.

**LAMBETH, JAMES H,** Pellissippi St Tech Comm Coll, Knoxville, TN; SO; EET; IEEE; Phi Theata Kapa 89-; Tau Alpha Phi; Electrncs.

**LAMBETH, JAMES M,** Tn Temple Univ, Chattanooga, TN; JR; BS; Jr Boys Clb Ldr 88-90; Pryr Grp Ldr 89-90; Wesley Soc 88-; IM Soccer 88-; Zeta Chi Delta 88-; Acctg.

**LAMBIASE, CHRISTINA M,** Dowling Coll, Oakdale Li, NY; JR; BA; Tutor Stdnts Lvng Hmlss Shltr Edctnl Advct 89-90; Educ; Tchr.

**LAMBO, ALLYSON M,** Radford Univ, Radford, VA; FR; BA; House Cncl Comm 90; Hnrs Pgm 90-; Dns Lst 90; Educ; Elem Schl Tchr.

**LAMBO, ANN M,** Alfred Univ, Alfred, NY; JR; BA; Natl Career Wmns Assn 89-; Am Hlth Care Exec; Sftbl Clb; Tour Guide 90-; Stdnt Lrng Asstnc Prog Cnslr 90-; Bristol Myers Awd; Deans List 89-; Summer Intrnshp Strong Meml Hosp; Hlth Plng/Mng/Bus Adm; Hosp Admin.

**LAMBOUSES, EFTECHIOS H,** Western New England Coll, Springfield, MA; FR; MBA; Elect Engr; Elect Engr.

**LAMBOY, JEFFREY M,** City Univ Of Ny Baruch Coll, New York, NY; SO; BBA; Finance; Bnkng.

**LAMBRIGHT, NSOMBI A,** Tougaloo Coll, Tougaloo, MS; FR; BA; Newspaper Rep 90-; Ladies Blck/Gold; Engl/Jrnlsm; Law.

**LAMENDOLA, VICKI ANN,** Univ Of South Al, Mobile, AL; SR; BS; Phi Kappa Phi; Beta Gamma Sigma 89-; Acdmc Schlrshp; ABWA Cmmtt Chrmn 88-; Cthlc Chrch Prsh Cncl VP 89-; Oper Sys Mngmnt.

**LAMM, ANASTASIA M,** Kent St Univ Kent Cmps, Kent, OH; SR; BA; Soc Creative Anchrnsm VP 89; French; Lbry Sci.

**LAMM, DAVID W,** Christopher Newport Coll, Newport News, VA; SO; BA; Cross Cntry 89-90; Indr Trck/Trck/Fld 89-90; Busn Admin.

**LAMM, TAMARA L,** Tallahassee Comm Coll, Tallahassee, FL; SO; AA; Fam Enrchmnt Prog; Sub Tchr Taylor County; Elem Ed/Mntl Hlth Coun; Tchr.

**LAMME, JENNIFER A,** Albertus Magnus Coll, New Haven, CT; SR; BA; Deans Lst; Asst Prdctn Mjr Mkt Radio Pgm Wkci Intrn 90; Stone Soup Rnng Race Area Soup Ktchns 89; Cmnctns; TV Prdctn/Advrtsng.

**LAMMERS, CHARLENE R,** Memphis St Univ, Memphis, TN; SO; BA; Schlrshp Fclty Wives Clb; Jrnlsm; Public Rltns.

**LAMMERS, ERIC D,** Georgetown Univ, Washington, DC; FR; Intrntl Rltns Clb; The Exlctc Mnthly Commntry Edit; Delta Sigma Pi Schlrshp Chrmn; Intrnshp Arts Cncl; Bus.

**LAMON III, JOHN F,** Univ Of Ky, Lexington, KY; FR; BA; Phi Eta Sigma; Alpha Tau Omega Mbrshp Educ Chrmn 90-; Blgy.

**LAMON, MICHAEL D,** Univ Of Tn At Chattanooga, Chattanooga, TN; FR; BSE; Chem Engr.

**LAMONTAGNE, KARA L,** Univ Of Nh Plymouth St Coll, Plymouth, NH; SR; BS; Pace 89-90; Pres Lst 89-90; Elem Educ; Tchr.

**LAMOUREUX, DONNA R,** Fl St Univ, Tallahassee, FL; SO; BA; BACCHUS 90-; Phi Eta Sigma Cmmtt Chrmn 90-; 2M Sftbll; Cmmnctns.

**LAMOUREUX, LORI A,** Western New England Coll, Springfield, MA; SR; BA; Natl Assn Of Accts; Bus; Acctng.

**LAMP, MICHELLE L,** West Liberty St Coll, West Liberty, WV; SO; BS; Dns Lst; Acctg.

**LAMP, SCOTT M,** Wv Univ, Morgantown, WV; SR; BS; ASP 89-; Rho Chi 90-; Kappa Psi 89-; Dns Lst 87; Pharm.

**LAMPASONA, PETER C,** Mount Saint Mary Coll, Newburgh, NY; JR; BA; Dns Lst 90-; Alpha Chi 90-; AS Dutchess Cmnty Clg 90; Bsn Mgmt; Mgmt.

**LAMPE, SCOTT K,** Appalachian St Univ, Boone, NC; FR; BS; Intl Rltns Assn V P 90-; Gamma Beta Phi 90-; Alpha Phi Eta 90-; Acctng.

**LAMPE, TERESA L,** Bristol Univ, Bristol, TN; GD; MBA; Amer Prchsng Socty 89-; NAPM; AS Breward Comm Coll 76; BS 90; Bus; Prchsng.

**LAMPERT, ROGER A,** Fl International Univ, Miami, FL; SR; Phi Sigma Tau Treas; Bldrs Lic St FL 71; Pilots Lic Sngl Eng Fxd Wng 86; Lib Stdies/Philo/Anthplgy; Law.

**LAMPI, DOROTHY L,** Mount Saint Mary Coll, Newburgh, NY; GD; BED; Idea 85-; Town Recr Dir 81-82; Prog Coord 82-84; Fitness Dance Owner Dir 85-89; BS 81; BPS 81; Dance Recreation; Elem Schl Tchr.

**LAMPKE, JANE G,** Northern Ky Univ, Highland Hts, KY; SR; BS; Amer Mktg Assn VP 90-; Big Bro/Sis 89-; Alpha Chi 89-; Intrnshp Cinn Bell Info Sys 89-; Mktg; Law.

**LAMPKIN JR, ROBERT E,** Alcorn St Univ, Lorman, MS; JR; BS; Chmstry Clb 88; Hnrs Org 88; NAACP 90; Army ROTC Schlrshp 89; Chmstry; Offcr US Army.

**LAMPO, STEVEN J,** Grove City Coll, Grove City, PA; FR; BS; Cmptr Assoc 90-; Flwshp Chrstn Athletes 90-; Rndtbl; Delta Iota Kappa Brthrhd; Pres Athletic Conf All Conf Tm; Clg Schlr Athlete 90 91; Var Crs Cntry Trck/Fld; Cmptr Sys/Math; Sys Anlys.

**LAMPO, VALERIE J,** Comm Coll Algny Co Algny Cmps, Pittsburgh, PA; SO; BA; Den Ldr Asst Cub Scuts 90-; Genesis/Pittsburgh Pres 84-87; Acctg.

**LAMPON, SANTIAGO F,** Inter Amer Univ Pr San Juan, Hato Rey, PR; GD; JD; Law Review Editor In Chief 90; Amer Bar Assn 87-; Dns Lst 88; Tau Kappa Epsilon 80; Boy Scouts; TA; Natl Confer Law Rvws; Acct V P 87; BBA Sacred Heart Univ 83; Litigation; Law.

**LAMPSON, DAMON KE,** Atlantic Comm Coll, Mays Landing, NJ; SO; AAS; Tbl Tnns Clb Vp 90-; Radio Clb 90-; Mcrcmptr Rpr/Mntnce.

**LAMSON JR, RICHARD THOMAS,** Belmont Coll, Nashville, TN; SO.

**LANAM, PEGGY L,** Radford Univ, Radford, VA; SO; House Cncl VP 89-90; Rsdnt Asst 90-; Natl Rsdnc Hall; Alpha Lambda Delta 90-; Acdmc Exclnc Awd 90-; Deans List 89-; Outstndng Stdnt 89-; Bus Mgt; Bnkng.

**LANCASTER, ANTHONY E,** Univ Of Ky, Lexington, KY; JR; BA; Hosp Anesthesia Asst 87-; Sociology; Ph D.

**LANCASTER, CHRISTY E,** Univ Of Ga, Athens, GA; SR; BSED; Math Educ Std Asc 89-; Diamond Darlings 87-88; IMS Pgm 87-; Gldn Key 90-; Zeta Tau Alpha Chrmn 87-; Joseph R Hooten Awd; Math; Tch.

**LANCASTER, ELIZABETH A,** Southern St Comm Coll, Sardinia, OH; FR; MBA; Stdnt Govt 90-; Stdnt Ambsdr 90-; Trustee Acad Schlrshp; Sclgy; Psych.

**LANCASTER, JOSHUA W,** Ms St Univ, Miss State, MS; SO; BBA; Bapt Stu Union 89-90; Dorm Hl Cncl Rep 89-90; Pres Lst 89-; Bus; Mgmt.

**LANCASTER, KENSLEY C,** Peace Coll, Raleigh, NC; SO; Rec Assoc Pres 90-; SGA 90-; Hnr Ct 90-; Sigma Delta Mu 89-; Otstndg Soph 90-; May Queen 90-; AA; Engl; Law.

**LANCASTER, LAURIELYN,** Tn St Univ, Nashville, TN; JR; BA; Gldn Key; Spnsh Clb; Sigma Delta Pi; Alpha Mu Gamma; Sec; Legal Exec Sec; Spnsh.

**LANCE, JACQUELINE M,** Fl St Univ, Tallahassee, FL; JR; BA; Psi Chi 90-; DIS Rsrch Asst FL St Hosp; AA Tallahassee Comm Coll 89; Psychlgy.

**LANCE, PHOEBIE E,** Cumberland Coll, Williamsburg, KY; FR; BA; Lv In Actn 90-; Bapt Stu Union 90-; Flwshp Chrstn Athlts 90-; Coll Sngrs Wmns Chorus 90-; Chorale 90-; Mu Phi Epsilon 90-; Spcl Ed; Music Thrpy.

**LANCELLOTTI, JENIFER,** Villanova Univ, Villanova, PA; SO; PHD; Proj Snshn Tutrng 89-90; Alpha Phi Asst Msc Chr 90-; CYO Yth Advsr 89-; Deans Lst 89-; Elem Ed; Clncl Chld Psychlgy.

**LANCHONEY, THOMAS FRANCIS,** Cornell Univ Statutory College, Ithaca, NY; JR; BS; Ambrs Alumni Liason 89-; Ldrshp Commt 89-; Ski Club 89-; Natl Schlrs 88-; Ho Nun De Kah Social Chrmn 89-; Golden Key 90-; Catholic Commty 88-; Hlth Adts 90-; IN Sfrbl/Ftbl; Biology; Med.

**LANCIE, MARK E,** Comm Coll Algny Co Algny Cmps, Pittsburgh, PA; FR; BS; Allghny Airshow 90, High Hnrs 90-; Cmptr Sys Supv Dial America; AS 90; Mech Engr.

**LANCIN, MELISSA L,** Univ Of Tn At Martin, Martin, TN; FR; BSN; SGA; Alpha Delta Pi Clss Svc Chr 90-; Hons Smnr Schlrshp 90-; UTM Merit Schlrshp 90-; UT Alumni Schlrshp 90-; Nrsg; Dr Ansthslgy.

**LAND, DEAN P,** Univ Of Rochester, Rochester, NY; SR; BA; Campus Envnmntl Org 88-89; Intn/Cmmssn/Racial Eqlty London UK 90; Ski Tm Co-Capt 88-; Intnl Rltns Cmte; Pol Sci.

**LAND, LEORA LIGHT,** Bowling Green St Univ At Huron, Huron, OH; SO; AS; Soc Wrk.

**LANDAN, CLARA ORTA,** Caribbean Univ, Bayamon, PR; GD; BA.

**LANDENBERG, KEITH R,** Chattahoochee Vly St Comm Coll, Phenix City, AL; SO; BE; Intrntnl Assn Idntfctn; Frtrnl Ordr Police; US Army; Muscogee Cnty Ga Sheriff Dpt; Crmnl Jstc; Law Enfrcmnt.

**LANDER, MARY V,** Fl St Univ, Tallahassee, FL; SR; BA; Bay Pnt Wmns Clb 81-; Phi Theta Kappa 86; Garnet Kay 88; Gldn Key 89; Phi Kappa Phi 90; AS Drftng Doxiadis Tech Coll Athens Greece 72; AAS Drftng G C Wallace St Comm Coll Selma AL 81; Intl Affrs.

**LANDER-LUTZ, PEDRO J,** Nova Univ, Ft Lauderdale, FL; GD; MBA; International Business.

**LANDERS JR, ALBERT L,** Memphis St Univ, Memphis, TN; SR; BA; Phi Kappa Phi; Kappa Alpha 87-; Deans Lst 89-; Inter Frat Cncls 88-; Intrnshp 89-; IM 88-; Bus/Fin.

**LANDERS, ANDREA L,** Univ Of Nc At Charlotte, Charlotte, NC; FR; BA; Phi Etta Sigma.

**LANDERS, ROXCENA B,** Atlantic Comm Coll, Mays Landing, NJ; FR; AAS; Clnry Arts; Bus.

**LANDERS, TIMOTHY RAY,** Middle Tn St Univ, Murfreesboro, TN; SO; BS; Gamma Beta Phi; Mass Comm; Rcrdng Ind Mgmnt.

**LANDERS, WILLIAM P,** Kent St Univ Kent Cmps, Kent, OH; FR; Sci; Med.

**LANDES, MARGARET A,** Bridgewater Coll, Bridgewater, VA; JR; Campus Stdnt Cnslr 88-; Alpha Chi 89-; Lambda Soc 90-; Soc/Edn; Guidance Cnslr.

**LANDIN, PAUL A,** Ny Univ, New York, NY; SO; Praxis; Schl Children St Edwards Church Dallas; Sci Place Mus/Dallas Mus Natl History; Theatre Three/Talent Express; Film; Prod/Dir/Actor Film Industry.

**LANDING, STEPHANIE M,** Columbia Union Coll, Takoma Park, MD; FR; BA; Drama Clb Stg Mgr 90-; Stdnt Snte Sntr 90-; Phi Eta Sigma; Tch A Kid Tutr 90-; Soup Ktchn/Loaves/Fishes 90-; Engl; Law.

**LANDINO, LINDA M,** Bucknell Univ, Lewisburg, PA; FR; BA; Emrgncy Serv Tm 90-; Emrgng Ldrs 90-; Alpha Lambda Delta 90-; Phi Eta Sigma 90-; Delta Gamma; Alpha Phi Omega Com Chrprsn 90-; Extrnshp Polyclnc Hosp Harrisbrg PA; Blgy; Med/Dctr.

**LANDIS, EVELYN H,** Univ Of Nc At Greensboro, Greensboro, NC; JR; BM; Univ Orchestra Cncrtmstr 88-; Symphnc Chorus 88-; Collegium Musicum 90-; Pi Kappa Lambda; Alpha Lambda Delta 88-; Mu Phi Epsilon Alumni 90-; Dr Elizabeth Conling Msc Schlrshp 88-; Pi Kappa Lambda Schlrshp; Msc Prfrmnc; Prfsnl Vlnst/Msc Lbrn.

**LANDIS, KIMBERLY D,** Marshall University, Huntington, WV; FR; Cabell County Jr Fair Board Sec; Cabell County Fair Board Jr Bd Rep; Maier Freshman Essay Schlrshp Contest 6th Place.

**LANDIS, KIRSTEN L,** Coll Misericordia, Dallas, PA; SO; BS; CMSOTA 89-; Occup Ther.

**LANDIS, MICHAEL J,** Univ Of Miami, Coral Gables, FL; JR; BBA; Gldn Key 90-; Beta Gamma Sigma; Babe Ruth Baseball Umpire; Hnrs Prog 89-; Provosts Lst 89-; Dns Lst 89-; Sprtsfst 90-; Finance/Lgl Stds; Prsnl Invstng Law.

**LANDRETH, CHERYL A,** Univ Of Tn At Martin, Martin, TN; SO; MBA; Sigma Alpha Epsilon 90-; Alpha Omicron Pi Pldg Treas 89-90; Hnrs Seminar Ldrshp/Wrkshp Schlrshp 89-; Bsn Mgmt/Adm Svcs; Ofc Mgmt.

**LANDREVILLE, JOHN A,** Daytona Beach Comm Coll, Daytona Beach, FL; FR; PHD; Eastrn Srfng Assn 82-86; Good Cndct Mdl US Navy 88; Expdtns Mdl US Navy 89; Exprt Rflmn/Expct Pstlsht Mdls 88; Cryptgrphc Tech/Cmnctn Sup US Navy 84-90; Engl/Elect Eng; Elect Eng/Crtv Wrtng.

**LANDRUM, JENIFER D,** Northern Ky Univ, Highland Hts, KY; FR; Bapt Stdnt Un 90-; Hrtg Fllwshp Sth Yth Grp 86-; Edctn.

**LANDRUM, MELINDA K,** Christian Brothers Univ, Memphis, TN; SO; BS; Univ Hnrs Prog 89-; Alpha Sigma Alpha Pres 89-; S Cntl Bell Schlrshp/Intshp 89-; Elec Engrg; Engr.

**LANDRUM, MELISSA J C,** Samford Univ, Birmingham, AL; JR; BS; Alpha Lambda Delta 90-; Phi Kappa Phi; Alpha Epsilon Delta VP; Sanford Social Action 90-; Hosp Vol; Wheeler Howley Frnch Awd; Biologh/Chmstry; Medicine Biology Rsrch.**

**LANDRUM, RAYMOND G,** Anne Arundel Comm Coll, Arnold, MD; SR; AA; Tau Alpha Pi; Eng/Tech Div Outstndng Stdnt; BS US Naval Acad 58; MS US Naval Postgrad Schl 65; Architectural Tech.

**LANDRUM, SUSAN D,** Univ Of Sc At Columbia, Columbia, SC; JR; BA; Bapt Union 88-89; Dorm Govt Treas 89; Geography Bowl 90; Golden Key 90-; Phi Eta Sigma 89; Dns Lst 88; Hstry/Geography; Tch.

**LANDRY, ERIN RAE,** Univ Of Southern Ms, Hattiesburg, MS; SO; Tri Delta 89-; Gldn Grl 90-; Stu Alumni Acs 89; Gamma Beta Phi 89; Vol Phys Thrpy; Sigma Chi Ltl Sis; Sci; Phys Thrpy.

**LANDRY, KRISTIN R,** Ms St Univ, Miss State, MS; SR; MED; Spcl Olympcs 87-; Intrnshp Fr Crdc Rehab At Oschner Hrt And Vsclr Inst; Grad Asstshp To MSU In Exrcse Physlgy; BS; Exrcse Physlgy; Crdc Rehab.

**LANDRY, LINDA H,** Univ Of Ga, Athens, GA; GD; MSW; Goldn Key; NASW; BSW 90; Clncl Soc Wrk/Mntl Hlth.

**LANDRY, MICHAEL R,** Vance Granville Comm Coll, Henderson, NC; SO; AAS; Indstrl Mgmt; Eng.

**LANDRY, RHONDA M,** Newbury Coll, Brookline, MA; SO; BED; Cls Repr 90-; Paralegal Intrnshp Westboro D Crt; Law.

**LANE JR, ANDREW P,** Middle Tn St Univ, Murfreesboro, TN; JR; BS; Aerospace; Aerospace Techlgy.**

**LANE, BELINDA D,** Alcorn St Univ, Lorman, MS; SO; BA; SNEA Vice Pres; Deans Lst; Ed; Tchr.

**LANE, BRIAN T,** Roane St Comm Coll, Harriman, TN; SO; BA; Baptist Stdnt Union Sports Dir 89-; Elec Comm Stdng Govnmnt Chrprsn 89-; IM Ftbl Sftbl 89-; Gamma Beta Hi 90-; Boeing Schlr 89-; Estes Kefauver Schlr 89; Chem Engr; Engrng.

**LANE, DARLYNN M,** Valdosta St Coll, Valdosta, GA; SR; Phi Kappa Phi; Schlr; BA; Engl/Ed.

**LANE, KAI T,** Tn St Univ, Nashville, TN; FR; BS; Amer Soc Cvl Engrs Secr 90-; Natl Soc Blck Engrs 90-; Hnrs Pgm 90-; Engr Pre-Clg Pgms Cnslr 90-; Cvl Engr; Engr.

**LANE, KAREN G,** Salisbury St Univ, Salisbury, MD; JR; BA; Hnrs Pgm 89-; French Club 90-; French Soc 90-; Phi Eta Sigma 90-; French.

**LANE, LAWRENCE W,** Duquesne Univ, Pittsburgh, PA; SO; BSBA; Fncl Mgmt Assoc 90-; Rsdnt Asst 90-; Intrnshp Fdrtd Invstrs 90-; IM; Fnc.

**LANE, LISA M,** Comm Coll Algny Co Algny Cmps, Pittsburgh, PA; FR; Resp Ther Tech.

**LANE, LLOYD R,** Birmingham Southern Coll, Birmingham, AL; FR; BA; Natl Rifle Assoc 87-; Nmarine Corps Assoc 86-88; Corporal U S Marine Corps 86-; Bus Admnstrn Mgmnt.

**LANE, MARINA B,** Piedmont Tech Coll, Greenwood, SC; SO; APS; Psi Beta 90-; Gleaams Headstart 90; Brdgway Brdng Home; Laurens Cnty M R Bd; AC Foothills Career Coll 82; Psychlgy; Mntl Hlth.

**LANE, MELANIE A,** Univ Of Southern Ms, Hattiesburg, MS; FR; BA; Wesley Fndtn 90; Hon Stdnt Assn 90-; Res Hall Cncl RH Assoc Flr Rep 90-; Hist; Sci Writer.

**LANE, MELANIE M,** Ms St Univ, Miss State, MS; JR; Sigma Nu White Rose Court 89-; Gamma Beta Phi 90-; Phi Eta Sigma 90-; US Achvmnt Acad Ldrshp Awd; Acdmc Schlrshp 88-; Physcl Thrpy.

**LANE, MELISSA A,** Univ Of Tn At Knoxville, Knoxville, TN; SO; Pep Club 89-90; Phi Eta Sigma 89-90; Alpha Kappa Psi 90-; IMS; Acctng; Law.**

**LANE, MIHARU Q,** East Stroudsburg Univ, E Stroudsburg, PA; SR; BA; Intl Womens Yr Awd 75; 12 Solo Shows-Israel/US; Print Clctn; MOMA Brooklyn Bot Grdn; Monroe Cnty Arts Cncl 84-; Artt Stdnts League 71; CA Clg Of Arts/Crafts 69; MD Inst Of Art 68-69; VA Cmnwlth Univ 67-68; Art.

**LANE, MOLLY P,** Nova Univ, Ft Lauderdale, FL; GD; MBA; Schlrshp Mutual Security 87; Trust Co Finance Co 89-; Assist V P Manufactures Merchant Bank Ltd; BSC Mgmnt U Of West Indies 82-87; Finance/Mktg; Intl Finance.

**LANE, PATTI M,** Middle Tn St Univ, Murfreesboro, TN; JR; BBA; Gamma Beta Phi 88-90; Beta Alpha Psi Sec; Acctg; CPA.

**LANE, SANDRA L,** Queens Coll, Charlotte, NC; JR; Un Brd VP 89-; Music Thrpy Clb Pres 88-; BSU Chr 89-; Mrtr Brd; Delta Imicron Musicdeans Lst; Fltchr Music Schlr; Music.

**LANE, STEVEN K,** East Tn St Univ, Johnson City, TN; BSMS; Aviatn Arlne Plt/Flght Instr; Alpha Eta Rho Flght Tm 84-86; Arlne Plts Assoc Cmmttee; Arlne Plt; AAS Tx State Tchncl Inst 86; Aviatn/Aerospace Eng; Arlne Plt.

**LANE, THEODORE,** Alcorn St Univ, Lorman, MS; SR; BS; Natl Assn Industrial T Ech; Industrial Tech Clb; Jazz Bnd; Interfaith Gospel Chr; Dns Lst; Indstrl Tech Dept Achvmnt Awd; Indstrl Tech; Elec Eng.

**LANE, TISHA R,** Wilberforce Univ, Wilberforce, OH; SO; BS; Debtate Tm Ohio Pre Alum 90-; Radio D J 90-; VP 90-; Med Clb Nwspr 90-; Silhouettes Pr 90-; Var Trck; Bio; Physcn.

**LANE, VALERIE J,** East Tn St Univ, Johnson City, TN; FR; Pscyh; Psychlgst.

**LANEY, MICHELLE R,** Western Piedmont Comm Coll, Morganton, NC; SO; BS; AA; Envrnmntl Sci.

**LANEY, TERRI L,** Marshall University, Huntington, WV; SR; BA; WVEA 87-89; Chi Beta Pi 87-89; Math Hlth; Edctn.

**LANFORD, CATHERINE H,** Fayetteville St Univ, Fayetteville, NC; SO; BS; Frmly Spprt Grp Co Rep/Cntct Prsn 87-; Tchr Ast Algier B Wilkens Elem Schl 88-90; NC Assc Tchr Assts 88-90; Elem Educ; Tchg.

**LANG, BETH A,** Univ Of Akron, Akron, OH; SR; BS; Prgrmmr Anlyst 86-; AS Stark Technical Coll 84; Bus; Mgmt Data Prcssng.

**LANG, CHUCK C,** Univ Of Cin R Walters Coll, Blue Ash, OH; FR; BBA; Bus.

**LANG, COLLEEN,** City Univ Of Ny La Guard Coll, Long Island Cty, NY; SR; Phi Theta Kappa 88-; Glendale Vol Amb Corps Long Term Dir 77-; New Evergreen Block Assoc Pres 89-; AAS; Acctg.

**LANG, DAVID A,** Fl St Univ, Tallahassee, FL; GD; Cmps Crsd Chrst 87-; Hnrs/Schlrs 87-; Phi Beta Kappa 90-; Phi Kappa Phi 90; Golden Key 89; Phi Eta Sigma 87-; Kings Daughters Schlrshp Award 89; IM 89; Religion; Chrstn Mnstry.

**LANG, DIANA K,** S U N Y Coll Of Tech At Frmgdl, Farmingdale, NY; GD; BA; AS Bus Admin; Mktg; Bus.

**LANG, DONOVAN M,** Tougaloo Coll, Tougaloo, MS; JR; BA; Pre-Law Pltcl Sci Pres 90-; Stdnt Govt Assn; NAACP 90-; Pan-Afrcn Edctnl Ntwrk 89-; Vrsty Bsktbl Tm 90-; Pltcl Sci; Law.

**LANG, DOUGLAS E,** Univ Of Nc At Charlotte, Charlotte, NC; SR; BA; Tour Guide 90-; Hall Cncl 87-90; Radio Intern 90; Sanskrit Mag Phtgrph Awd; IM Sports 87-; Engl; Cmnctns/Media.

**LANG, JENNIFER CHRISTIAN,** Endicott Coll, Beverly, MA; FR; BA; Drama Co 90-; Intrnshp New Eng Scientific Assoc Salem N H; Mrktng; Mgmt.

**LANG, JESSE A,** Oh St Univ At Newark, Newark, OH; FR; Newark Cmps Stdnt Senate; IM Vlybl; Newark Hnrs Socty; Aeronautical/Astrntcl Engr.

**LANG, LAURA P,** Christopher Newport Coll, Newport News, VA; SR; BA; Alpha Kappa Delta; Kappa Alpha Theta 66-67; Sociology Rsrch Asst; Sociology; Social Wrk.

**LANG, LORI A,** Comm Coll Algny Co Algny Cmps, Pittsburgh, PA; GD; BS; Dns Lst; Amer Assoc Med Asstnts 89-; Mbr Natl Local Arthrts Fndtn; Cert Med Asst; AD Comm Clg Allegheny Cnty 90; Sci; Hlth Sci.**

**LANG, MARIANNE E,** Glassboro St Coll, Glassboro, NJ; JR; Pro Life; Neuman Cntr; Legion Of Mary VP 87-89; Tennis Tm Frth Sngls 87-89; Sociology.

**LANG, MELLISA S,** Lenoir Rhyne Coll, Hickory, NC; FR; BA; Thtr Cmpny 90-; Amnsty Intl 90-; Prsdntl Schlr 90-; Mx Hwrd Mgcns Intrn 90-; Thtr Arts.

**LANG, OLGA M,** S U N Y Coll Of Tech At Alfred, Alfred, NY; SR; AS; Pol Sci; Law.

**LANG, PETER F,** Univ Of Pa, Philadelphia, PA; FR; BA; Univ Of PA Crw Fr Frst Bt 90-; Hstry; Law.

**LANG, RICHARD R,** Univ Of New Haven, West Haven, CT; SR; BS; Am Soc Civil Engrs; Tutor; Phi Theta Kappa; Chi Epsilon; Clarence Dunham Dana Wiggin Drazio Di Mauro Schlrshps Outstndg Stdnt; AS Housatonic Comm Coll 88; Civil Eng.

**LANG, ROBERT J,** Univ Of Sc At Columbia, Columbia, SC; JR; BA; Campus Crusade For Christ 90-; Lacrosse Clb 90-; Wtr Ski Tm 90-; Ecnmcs; Bus Admin.

**LANG, SUSAN A,** Daemen Coll, Amherst, NY; JR; BED; Hrvrd Model Un; Hstry/Sci; Elem Tchr.

**LANG-THORBS, KATHI D,** Bishop St Comm Coll, Mobile, AL; JR; BS; Yrbk Edtr 90; Phi Theta Kappa 90; Otstndng Stdnt Hmnts Div 90; Otstndng Stdnt Yrbk; Pres List 89-90; Deans List 90; Hnr Roll 90-; 1st Pl Creative Writing Contest; Ldrshp Schlrshp Yrbk Edtr 90; Coast Guard Officers Wivees Club Schlrshp 90; Pol Sci; Paralegal Work/Law.

**LANGAN, SHERYL N,** Faulkner St Jr Coll, Bay Minette, AL; FR; BA; Phi Theta Kappa; Dns Lst; Pres Lst; Nrsng; Hlth Serv.

**LANGE, ALEC C,** Hudson Valley Comm Coll, Troy, NY; JR; BA; Sigma Lambda Sigma; Intrnshp N Greenbush Plc Dept 90-; AAS; Crim Jstc; Fed Lvl Law Enfrcmnt.

**LANGE, APRIL D,** Liberty Bible Coll, Pensacola, FL; FR; BA; AAS Sthrn Jr Coll 89; Chrstn Cnslng.

**LANGE, BARBARA J,** Brunswick Coll, Brunswick, GA; SO; BED; Phi Theta Kappa 90-; Soc Sci Awd; Deans Lst 89-; Pres Lst 90; Vars Sftbl 89-; Early Chldhd Educ; Tchr.**

**LANGE, CHARLES W,** Embry Riddle Aeronautical Univ, Daytona Beach, FL; JR; BS; NC World Trade Asc 88-; Natl Cstm Brkr/Frght Frwrdsr Assc 88-; Offc Mgr Al Smith CBI 88-; BA Miami U 86; Avtn.

**LANGE, CHRISTOPHER L,** Ms St Univ, Miss State, MS; SO; BS; Dggr Hll Cncl Treas 90; Scty Of Amer Mil Engs Pres 90-; ROTC Army; Alpha Lambda Delta 90; Gamma Beta Phi 90-; Scbbrd And Blde 90-; Sprr Cdt 89-; IM Sftbl; Biochem Mlclr Blgy; Med.

**LANGE, DAMON F,** Univ Of Louisville, Louisville, KY; FR; MB A; Engr/Math/Cmptr Sci; Engr Cmptr Sci.

**LANGE, DONNA A,** Univ Of South Al, Mobile, AL; SR; BS; Ntnl Assc Acctnts 89-; Beta Gamma Sigma 89-; Alpha Chi 89-; Beta Alpha Psi 90-; Sunday Schl Tchr Forest Prk Bible Chrch 84-; AA Grace Bible Clg 83; Acct; CPA.

**LANGE, LEANNE M,** S U N Y Coll At Fredonia, Fredonia, NY; SR; BS; Bus Clb 89-90; Invstmnt Clb 89; Delta Mu Delta; Omicron Delta Epsilon; IM Vllybll Wtrpl; Bus Econ.

**LANGE, SUSAN S,** Rivier Coll, Nashua, NH; SR; BS; AS Colby-Sawyer College 77; Biology; Education.

**LANGENBACKER, MARY E,** Ms Coll, Clinton, MS; GD; JD; Hon Ct Chf Juste 90-; Assoc Juste 90-; Moot Ct Bd 90-; Phi Delta Phi; Local Bar Assn; Cert Acad Avge; Acctg Lawyers; Deans Lst; Appellate Advcy Cmptn; BA 88.

**LANGENDORFER, SCOTT H,** Radford Univ, Radford, VA; JR; BA; Phi Beta Lambda 88-90; IM; AS Wytheville Cmnty Clg 90; Mktg; Bus Admin.

**LANGENFELD, AMY JO D,** Kent St Univ Kent Cmps, Kent, OH; JR; BBA; Mktg/Spnsh.

**LANGER, DARLENE J,** Castleton St Coll, Castleton, VT; SR; BSW; Outing Clb Publ Rels 88-89; Spartan Newspaper Chf Typestr 88-89; Scl Issues Clb 88-; Phi Eta Sigma 88; Dns Lst 88; Addison Co Parent/Chld Ctr Intern 90-; Wmns Soccer 89; Scl Wrk; Scl Svcs.

**LANGEVIN, BEVERLY C,** Philadelphia Coll Pharm & Sci, Philadelphia, PA; FR; NJ Pharmctcl Assoc 90-; Amer Phrmctcl Assoc Acad Of Stdnts Of Pharmcy 90-; Dns Lst 90-; Pres Schlrshp 90-; Citzns Schlrshp Fndtn Pol/Frmns Ins Assoc Awd 90-; IM Vllybl 90-; Phrmcy.

**LANGFORD, CAROLYN G,** North Ga Coll, Dahlonega, GA; SO; Acctg 85; Data Entry 86; Hstry; Rsrch.

**LANGFORD, LEONARDO D,** Strayer Coll, Washington, DC; SR; BS; Alpha Chi; Omega Psi Phi; Offcr US Nvy; BS Math Univ AL 73; MBA Gldn Gt Univ 86; Acctg; CPA.

**LANGFORD, PATRICIA PEACOCK,** Univ Of North Fl, Jacksonville, FL; SR; BA; Yrbk Stff 86-87; Ldrshp Clb 86-87; Gldn Key 90-; Pre Internship Emma Love Hardee 89; Pre Internship Yulee Elem 90; Internship Atlantic Elem; Assoc Arts 89; Elem Ed; Tch.

**LANGFORD, RHONDA M,** Morris Coll, Sumter, SC; JR; BA; Yrbk Co-Ed; All Amer Schlr; Ntl Coll Mnrty Ldr; Ntl Coll Ed Awd; O R Ruebe Schlr; Deans Lst; Omega Essence 90-; IM Vlybl; Sclgy; Scl Wrkr.

**LANGFORD, WILLIAM E,** Univ Of Tn At Martin, Martin, TN; SO; BA; Phi Alpha Delta 89-; Pre-Law Clb 89-; Tn St Legsltr Intrn 91; Poli Sci; Law.

**LANGHAM, ANGELA L,** Univ Of South Al, Mobile, AL; SR; BA; VITA 90; Bsn Admin; Fin.

**LANGHAM, ANITA C,** Bunker Hill Comm Coll, Boston, MA; FR.

**LANGHAM, CARVINE,** Stillman Coll, Tuscaloosa, AL; SO; BA; Stdnt Govt Assoc Treas 90-; Gamma Iota Sigma Hnr Soc; Cordell Wynn Hnrs Pgm; Alpha Kappa Alpha Treas; NAACP; Dns Schlr; Dns Lst; Chrldr Treas 90-; Eng/Hstry; Law.

**LANGHORNE, GERALD S,** Va St Univ, Petersburg, VA; SR; BS; Bus Adm Clb 90-; Mrktng Clb 90-; Phi Beta Lambda 88-89; Bus Adm; Mrktng/Sls Mgmt.

**LANGHORNE, SHERRY ANN,** Thomas Nelson Comm Coll, Hampton, VA; FR; AAS; Stu Govt Assn 90-; Erly Chldhd Educ; Tch.

**LANGLEY III, GEORGE G,** U S Coast Guard Academy, New London, CT; FR; BS; Acad Gld Str 90-; 3rd Clss Erpn Crse 90-; Applchn Srvce Prjct 90-; Chem Eng; Eng.

**LANGLEY, JOYCE D,** Widener Univ, Chester, PA; JR; BA; Soc Advncmnt Mgmt; Hnrs Pgm Gen Ed 90-; Big Bro/Big Sis Assoc Vol 87-; March Dimes Walker/Coord 76-; Boeing Helicopters 78-89; Reuben H Donnelley Corp 73-78; Mgmt-Hmn Res.

**LANGLEY, MELISSA D,** Roane St Comm Coll, Harriman, TN; SO; AS; Gamma Beta Phi; Med Radlgy.

**LANGLEY, RAHNA M,** Kent St Univ Kent Cmps, Kent, OH; GD; Intrnshp Portage Co Btrd Wms Shltr; BA 90; Indvdl/Fmly Cnsmr Stds; Soc Srvc Admin.

**LANGLEY, SHELLY J,** Univ Of Southern Ms, Hattiesburg, MS; SO; BA; Alum Assn 89-; Eagle Clb 89-; Alpha Lambda Delta Sec 90; Phi Eta Sigma; Gamma Beta Phi; Alpha Epsilon Delta; Pi Beta Phi Hrsng Chrmn 89-; Val Schlrshp 89; Mus Schlrshp 89; Intrm Ftbl/Sftbl 89-90; Biology; Medical.

**LANGLITZ III, GEORGE,** Springfield Tech Comm Coll, Springfield, MA; GD; AA Spgfld Tech Comm Coll; Pre-Med; Chiropractic Physician.

**LANGLOIS, MONICA E,** Fl St Univ, Tallahassee, FL; JR; Intrvrsty Chrstn Flwshp Mtng Coord 90-; Undershepherd Flwshp Bptst Chrch 90-; Ltl Sis Phi Sigma Kappa 90; Spec Olympcs Serv Prjcts Cmnctns Coord 89-90; Art; Grphc Dsgn.

**LANGMAN, JAMES H,** Columbus Coll Of Art & Design, Columbus, OH; FR; BFA; Cmmrcl Art/Dsgn.

**LANGO, THERESA L,** Teikyo Post Univ, Waterbury, CT; FR; Wrld Wild Lf Fdrtn 87; Frstry Assc 88; Humane Scty 86; Dns List; Envrmntl Sci.

**LANGONI, JEFFREY A,** Indiana Univ Of Pa, Indiana, PA; FR; BA; Prof Pilot; Airline Plt.

**LANGPAP, GRETA L,** Univ Of Ga, Athens, GA; SR; BSED; Cncrt Bnd 85-88/90; Symphnc Bnd 87; Delta Phi Alpha 88-; German Ed; Tchr.

**LANGSTON, AMANDA D,** Univ Of Sc At Columbia, Columbia, SC; SO; BMA; Carolina Pgm Un 89-; Columbia Film Soc 89-; Amnsty Intl 89-90; WOLO Tv Intshp Promo Asst; Media Arts; Film.

**LANGSTON, CATHERINE E,** Univ Of Sc At Columbia, Columbia, SC; SR; Kappa Epsilon Secy 87-; SC Scty Hosp Pharmacists 90-; ASHP 90-; Outstndng Clg Stdnts Amer 89; BS Zoology Clemson Univ 86; BS Pharmacy 90; Clinical Pharmacy.**

**LANGSTON, DIANE K,** Univ Of Sc At Columbia, Columbia, SC; JR; BS; Mrchg Bnd 88-89; Gldn Ky 90-; Alpha Epsilon Delta 90-; Tau Beta Sigma 88-; Kappa Alpha Theta 89-; Psychlgy; Optmtrst.

**LANGSTON, ELIZABETH A,** Anne Arundel Comm Coll, Arnold, MD; SO; BA; US Army 81-86; Ed; Tch.

**LANGSTON, GUY K,** International Bible Coll, Florence, AL; JR; BA; SGA VP 90-; Hghst Grd Pnt Avrg Clss 89-; Bbl Rlgs Ed.

**LANGSTON, HILARY E,** Univ Of Sc At Columbia, Columbia, SC; JR; BA; Sndy Schl; Clbrtn Sngrs; Red Cross; Mxmlln La Borde Schlrshp; German Schlrshp; Trustees Schlrshp; Engl; Tech Wrtr.

**LANGSTON, LACEY L,** Univ Of Al At Birmingham, Birmingham, AL; SO; BS; Blzr Crw; Ambsdr; Alpha Lambda Delta; Alpha Omicron Pi Mbrshp Ed Chrmn 90-; Hnrs Pgm 90-; EMSAP 90-; Ireland Pres Schlrshp 89-; Blgy; Med.

**LANGSTON, MARK A,** Memphis St Univ, Memphis, TN; JR; BPS; Phi Theta Kappa 76-77; Univ Coll Almn; AA Copiah Lincoln Jr Coll 82; Cmmrcl Avtn; Avtn Psychlgy.

**LANGSTON, MATTHEW D,** Univ Of Ga, Athens, GA; JR; BLA; GSLA 90-; Mrchng Bnd 89-; Lndscp Arch.

**LANGSTON, MONIQUE Y,** Oh Univ, Athens, OH; SO; PO; Stdnt Cncl Gov Sec 90-; Stdnt Ntl Med Assn 89-; Chrstn Med Soc 89-; IM Tnns 90-; BS Towson St U 88; Osteo Med.

**LANGSTON, NICOLE E,** James Sprunt Comm Coll, Kenansville, NC; FR; AAS; Bus.

**LANGSTON, THERESA J,** Commonwealth Coll, Virginia Beach, VA; GD; AS; Acctg Clb 89-90; AIPB; Acctg; CPA.

**LANGTON, MELANIE A,** Elmira Coll, Elmira, NY; SR; BS; Orchesis 87-89; Ldrshp Awd; Athltc Awd; Lowman Awd; Chrldng Vrsty Cptn 87-; Elemntry Edctn; Tchr.

**LANGWIELER, KERSTIN,** Univ Of Sc At Columbia, Columbia, SC; SR; BA; Phi Eta Sigma 88-; Sigma Iota Rho 88-; Pi Delta Phi 88-; Gamma Beta Phi 89-; Gldn Key 90-F Frnch Lit Awd 90-; Cert Pratique Frnch Bus Lang Dip; Intl Stds/Frnch; Intl Pol.

**LANHAM, KATHY J,** Watterson Coll, Louisville, KY; SR; Math; Med Asst.

**LANIER, ALISA A,** James Sprunt Comm Coll, Kenansville, NC; FR.

**LANIER, ANNETTE L,** Central St Univ, Wilberforce, OH; FR; BA; Yearbk Asst Edtr 90-; Audio/Visual Intrctnl Svcs 90-; Clg Hnrs 90-; Comm Radio-T V.

**LANIER, JAMES Q,** East Carolina Univ, Greenville, NC; SO; BFA; ECHO VP 89-; NC Tchng Flws 89-; Art Ed; Tchr.

**LANIER, JULIE A,** Fl A & M Univ, Tallahassee, FL; JR; BSN; Clss VP; Stdnt Nrs Assn; Blue/White; Nrsng.

**LANIER, SHELLY W,** Univ Of Nc At Greensboro, Greensboro, NC; SR; BS; Deans Lst 89-; Elem Educ; Tchg.

**LANIER, TRACY L,** Al A & M Univ, Normal, AL; JR; BS; Phi Beta Lambda Mr Phi Beta Lambda 88-; Msnc Ordr 89-; Lgstcs/ Prcrmnt; 2nd Lt US Army.

**LANIGAN III, WILLIAM ALFRED,** Ms Coll, Clinton, MS; GD; JD; Law Stdnt Bar Assn Sntr Lrg 88-; Envir Law Assn Fndg Mbr 89-; Mbr Exec Bd; Chrmn Rcyclg Comm; Phi Delta Phi 89-; Amer Bar Assn Stdnt Div 88-; BA Univ Sthwstrn Louisiana 87; JD Mississippi Clg; Law; Prctc Law.

**LANKFORD, DAWN A,** Cumberland Coll, Williamsburg, KY; SO; BS; Acctg; Financial Planner.

**LANKFORD, RANI D,** Radford Univ, Radford, VA; SR; BS; Art Exhbtns Cmte Pres; Rd Cmps Brdcstng; Eng; Tchg Sec.

**LANKFORD JR, ROBERT L,** Western Ky Univ, Bowling Green, KY; FR; Math; Clg Prfsr.

**LANKS, LEESA SUZANNE,** Anne Arundel Comm Coll, Arnold, MD; SO; BSN; Scuba Club 90-; Senatorical Schlrshp 89-; MD Nursing Schlrshp; Vlybl Team Stdnt Athletic Trainer 89-90; Nursing Asst Certificate 89; Nursing; Shock Trauma Nurse.

**LANNO, FRANK T,** S U N Y Coll Of Tech At Alfred, Alfred, NY; SO; BS; Karate Club Instr & Treas; AAS; Electro-Mechanical Engrng; Engrng.

**LANOTTE, JANINE,** Manhattanville Coll, Purchase, NY; FR; BFA; Art Wrk Stu Hndbk; Fine Art; Illstrtr.

**LANOUE, MARY D,** James Madison University, Harrisonburg, VA; JR; BS; SEA 90-; NEA 90-; Erly Chldhd Educ; Educ.

**LANSDOWN, JOHN,** Al A & M Univ, Normal, AL; SO; BS; Nrthrns Clb 90-; SPS 90-; Rsrch Intrn; Unvrsty Wscn; Ntnl Science Fndtn Fllwshp 90; Appld Physcs; Mtrls Science.

**LANSING, JEFFERY SCOTT,** Univ Of Southern Ms, Hattiesburg, MS; SR; Chi Alpha Pres 89-; Stdnt Sprts Med Assc VP 90-; Exercise Physlgy Clb 89-; Athltc Schlrshp 89-; Athltc Trnr 88-; MS Athltc Trnrs Assc 89-; NATA 89-; Sprts Med/ Athltc Trng; Clncl Stng/Yth Pastor.

**LANTER, APRIL R,** Northern Ky Univ, Highland Hts, KY; JR; BA; Alpha Chi 90-; Sigma Tau Delta 90-; Hon Prog 89-; Deans Lst 88-90; Engl; Grad Schl.**

**LANTER, GAYLE S,** Univ Of Al At Huntsville, Huntsville, AL; SR; BS; ASCE Pres 90-; Forstry 81-; BS Auburn Univ 81; Cvl Engr; Envrmntl Engr.

**LANTERMAN, HAROLD B,** Univ Of Akron, Akron, OH; SR; BS; Amer Inst Chem Engrs Pres 90-; Gldn Key 89-; Alpha Lambda Delta 87-; Phi Eta Simga 87-; Clmn J Mjr Awrd; Chem Engr.

**LANTHIER, JOHN D,** Oh Coll Of Podiatric Med, Cleveland, OH; JR; DPM; OCPM Pres 89-; Sports Med Clb 88-89; Dns Lst 88-; Pi Delta; Hockey Clb 88-; Cleveland Clinic Intern; Ontario Nrs Assoc 86-; LPN; RN 87-88; BSC Laurentian Univ 86; Podiatric Med.

**LANTZ, GARY S,** Univ Of Louisville, Louisville, KY; FR; MA; Chem Eng.

**LANTZ, JOSEPH R,** Duquesne Univ, Pittsburgh, PA; SO; BSBA; Japan Lang Clb 90-; I M Ftbl Bkbl 89-; Bus/Fin.

**LANTZ, MELINDA S,** Thomas Nelson Comm Coll, Hampton, VA; SO; Psychlgy; Elem Sch Tchr.

**LANTZ, RONALD L,** Univ Of Akron, Akron, OH; JR; Elem Ed; Tch.

**LANYI-JOHNSON, TERESA ELIZABETH,** Marshall University, Huntington, WV; JR; Deans Lst; Bus.

**LANZANO, JAMES GASPAR,** City Univ Of Ny Queensbrough, New York, NY; FR; AA; Psychlgy; Hlth/Ed.

**LANZARA JR, RONALD F,** Spartanburg Methodist Coll, Spartanburg, SC; SO; FSCO 90-; CSG 90-; Deans List N H Clg 89-90; Pres List Sprtnbrg Meth Coll 90-; Chir; Dr Chrprctc.

**LANZELOTTI, MARY ANN L,** Temple Univ, Philadelphia, PA; JR; BS; Pi Theta Epsilon 90-; Deans Lst 88-; Occptnl Thrpy; Thrpst.

**LANZILOTTI, JAMES M,** Hudson Valley Comm Coll, Troy, NY; SO; BA; Phi Theta Kappa 90-; Tennis 90-; AS; Mgmnt; Entrpnr.

**LAO, LAI I,** Middle Tn St Univ, Murfreesboro, TN; FR; BBA; Cis.

**LAO, LIXING,** Univ Of Md Baltimore Prof Schl, Baltimore, MD; GD; PRD; IADR Neuroscience Grp 87-; Amer Assn Accpnctr/ Orien Med 89-; MD Acupnctr Socty 89-; Grad Schl Merit Awd 87-89; NIH Rsrch Astshp 88-; Tchng Tai Chi Instrctr 89-; Phslgy; Med Sci.

**LAPE, RANDY L,** Hillsborough Comm Coll, Tampa, FL; FR; SGA VP 87-88; Phi Theta Kappa 90-; Asst Coach Wrstlng.

**LAPENA, AMELIA M,** Ma Inst Of Tech, Cambridge, MA; FR; BS; Drmtry Flr Rep Co Chrprsn; Chns Stdnt Clb 90-; Chmstry; Med.

**LAPID, RONALD ALLAN,** Duke Univ, Durham, NC; FR; BA; Asian Stdnt Assoc 90; Phi Eta Sigma; Deans Lst 90; Im Bsktbl 90; Intrntl Drctry Of Dstngshed Ldrshp 90; Cmprtve Area Stdies; Law/Govt.

**LAPIDUS, CELIA D,** Samford Univ, Birmingham, AL; GD; JD; Omicron Nu 87-89; BS U Of Md 89; Law.

**LAPINSKI, PAUL V,** Univ Of North Fl, Jacksonville, FL; FR; BS; Band 90-; Math; Tchr.

**LAPP, CHRISTOPHER R,** S U N Y Coll At Oswego, Oswego, NY; FR; BS; Chem Clb 90; Amer Chmcl Scty 90; Cncrt Bnd 90; Hnrs Prog 90; Pres Lst; Bio Chem; Med.

**LAPP, DAWN M,** Lancaster Bible Coll, Lancaster, PA; JR; BS; Married Cples Flwshp Socl Chm; Bsktbl 90-; Cnslng-Pastoral Studies; Biblical Cnslgn.

**LAPP, DEANNA J,** Hillsborough Comm Coll, Tampa, FL; SO; AA 90; Emtnl Hndcpd Chldrn; Tchng.

**LAPP, MARLON J,** Villanova Univ, Villanova, PA; SO; BA; Navy ROTC 89-; Alpha Tau Omega 90-; Hstry; Nvl Ofcr.

**LAPP, RENEE L,** West Chester Univ, West Chester, PA; SR; BM; SALT 87-88; Oper Mblztn 89; Hons Pgm; Pi Kappa Lambda; Miriam S Gottlieb Schlrshp 87; Swope Schlrshp 90; Piano Solo Orch 90; Aerobics 90-; Music; Profssr.

**LAPPING, SHERRYL L,** Fl A & M Univ, Tallahassee, FL; SR; BA; Psi Theta Kappa 88-90; Tallahassee Comm Coll Mag Edtr 90; FL A/M Univ Mag Edtr; Intrn Plc Chf Mag Tallahassee Dmcrt; AA Tallahassee Comm Coll 90; Jrnlsm; Jrnlst.

**LAPRAD, VALERIE J,** Middle Tn St Univ, Murfreesboro, TN; SR; BS; Stdnt Govt Sntr; Coll Nwspr Edtr; Pi Gamma Mu 90-; Gamma Beta Phi 86-; Schl Spirt Awd 87; AS Vol St Comm Coll 87; Sclgy; Rsrch.

**LARA, DEBORAH S,** Univ Of Rochester, Rochester, NY; JR; BS; Comp Interest Flr 88-; Undergrad Soc Geology Stdnts 89-; Univ Symphony Orchestra 88-; Stdnts Active Vol Entrprs; Bio/Geology; Rsrch.

**LARACH, MIGUEL A,** Clarkson Univ, Potsdam, NY; FR; Chmbr Cmrce Assoc 88-89; Soc Wrk Pres.

**LARCARA, MARIE,** D Youville Coll, Buffalo, NY; JR; BA; Equestrian Tm Delhi 79; Drill Tm Delhi 78-79; Deans Lst 77-79; Chorus; Swm Tm; Diving Tm; Bahai Comm Sec 88-90; Wrkd Anml Hosp NY/NJ 87-90; AAS Anml Sci SU NY Delhi 80; Scndry Edn Engl; Teach.

**LARCOM JR, JAMES R,** Davis Coll, Toledo, OH; SO; Stdnt Advsry Brd Avtn Rep 90-; Scrty Sprvsr 90-; Avtn Admn.

**LARDANI, GINA M,** Salisbury St Univ, Salisbury, MD; GD; IM Sports 87-; Phi Alpha Theta; Pi Lambda Phi Ltl Sis 87-88; BA 90; Lbrl Studies Hstry Psychlgy.

**LARDNER, JEANNE,** Hudson Valley Comm Coll, Troy, NY; FR; BS; Norrell Hm Hlth Serv; Tri-Cities Nrsng Serv; Nrsng/Med.

**LARESE, JENNIFER R,** Bethany Coll, Bethany, WV; FR; BA; FAC 90-; Multicultural Awareness Clb; Swm Tm 90-; Phi Mu; BISONS 90-; Engl; Educator.

**LARGE, BARSHA P,** Eckerd Coll, St Petersburg, FL; SO; Televsn Tech Dir 89-; Art Stdnts Assn 89-90.

**LARGE, CATHERINE C,** Emory & Henry Coll, Emory, VA; SR; BME; AAS VA Highlands Comm Coll 86; Math Physics; Eng.

**LARGE, DANNY H,** Pellissippi St Tech Comm Coll, Knoxville, TN; JR; AAS; Management; Prsnl Mgt.

**LARGESSE, CARA L,** Univ Of Miami, Coral Gables, FL; FR; BS; Cir K Vp Elect 90-; Hmcmng Exec Sbcmmtt 90; Rsdnt Asst; Alpha Lambda Delta; Phi Eta Sigma; IM Co Rec Sftbl 90-; Systms Anlyss.

**LARIA, MARIE ELANA,** Le Moyne Coll, Syracuse, NY; SO; Pol Sci Acad 89-; Pre Law Soc 89-; Math Clb 89-; WLMU Dsk Jcky 90-; Caftria Wrkr 90-; Pol Sci; Law.

**LARKIN, COLLEEN R,** Hillsborough Comm Coll, Tampa, FL; SO; BA; AA 90; Pol Sci; Law.

**LARKIN JR, DENNIS J,** The Boston Conservatory, Boston, MA; SR; BFA; AAS Westchester Comm Clg 85; Musicl Theatre; Film TV Video.

**LARKIN, INGRID R,** Tougaloo Coll, Tougaloo, MS; FR; Hnr Rl 90-; Art/Graphics Design.

**LARKIN, JOHN C,** Univ Of Tn At Martin, Martin, TN; FR; PHARM; Pharm.

**LARKIN, KRISTINE A,** Endicott Coll, Beverly, MA; JR; BA; Intrnshp At Bluesteins Ofc Spply 89; ASSOC 90; Interior Design.

**LARKIN, LAURA A,** Anne Arundel Comm Coll, Arnold, MD; FR; Bus Admin; Acctnt.

**LARKIN II, STEPHEN W,** Slippery Rock Univ, Slippery Rock, PA; FR; BA; Lambda Sigma; Phi Sigma Pi; Phi Kappa Theta 90-; Phy Educ; Tchg.

**LARKIN, SUSAN,** Newbury Coll, Brookline, MA; AAS; Phi Theta Kappa; Newbury Coll Acad Awd 90-; Fclty Awd Clnry; AFS Ntl Rest Assn 89; Clnry Arts; Pstry Chef.

**LARKIN, SUSAN M,** Wv Univ, Morgantown, WV; FR; Mrchng Bnd 90-; Eng; Mech Eng.

**LARKIN, TERESA E,** Marywood Coll, Scranton, PA; JR; BS; Math Clb Sec 88-; Stdnt Govt Commtr Rep 90-; Orchstra 88-; Kappa Mu Epsilon 90-; Delta Epsilon Sigma 90-; Math.

**LARKIN, VERONIA R,** Central St Univ, Wilberforce, OH; JR; Stdnt Govt Assn Silma Univ VP 89-90; Jackson Wilson Hall Selma Univ Pres 89-90; Chorus 90-; Edn Soc Cntrl State 90-; AA Selma Univ 90; Elem Edn; Tchr.

**LAROUNIS, JAMES J,** Fl International Univ, Miami, FL; SR; BS; Phi Lambda 90; AOS Clnry Inst Of Amer 89; Hosp Mngmnt.

**LARRABEE, KIMBERLY A,** White Pines Coll, Chester, NH; SR; AS; Yrbk Phtgrphr 89-; Clss P 89-90; Phi Theta Kappa VP 89-90; Rainbow 89-; Vars Trck 89-90; Phtgrphy; Pro Studio.

**LARRAGOITY, JASON,** City Univ Of Ny City Coll, New York, NY; SO; BA; Rgnts Schlrshp Awd; Pltcl Sci; Law.

**LARRAIN, CLAUDIA M,** Fl International Univ, Miami, FL; JR; BA; Neuropsychology Tstng/Data Cllctn Intern; AA Miami Dade Comm Clg 90; Psychology; Neuropsychology.

**LARRAIN, FLORENCE Q,** Miami Dade Comm Coll, Miami, FL; SO; AA; Phi Theta Kappa 90-; Dns Lst 90-; STO Miami Dade Cmnty Clge; Psychlgy.

**LARRAZABAL, MARIA B,** Southern Coll Of Tech, Marietta, GA; JR; BS; Vnzueln Golf Team Chmpnshp 87; Wrld Amatr Golf Team Chmpnshp 88; Apparel Eng Technlgy.

**LARRIEUX, JEAN R,** Daytona Beach Comm Coll, Daytona Beach, FL; SO; BA; Cert Act Trvl Schl 86; Intr Dsgn.

**LARRIMORE, JONATHAN W,** Livingston Univ, Livingston, AL; JR; BS; Acctg Clb V P 90-; Alpha Chi; Natl Hnr Rl 89-; Pres Lst 89-; Dns Lst 89-; Acctg; CPA.

**LARSEN, JENNIFER C L,** George Mason Univ, Fairfax, VA; SR; BS; Erly Chldhd Ed; Tchr.

**LARSEN, KAREN E,** Daytona Beach Comm Coll, Daytona Beach, FL; FR; BA; Paralegal/Attorney Law; Law.

**LARSEN, KATHY L,** Allegheny Coll, Meadville, PA; JR; BA; Allegheny Repertory Dnc 89-90; Phi Eta Sigma 88-89; Elem Tutor 90-; Dns Lst 88-89; Alden Schlr 89-90; Engl/Educ; Professor.

**LARSEN, LONNI L,** Elmira Coll, Elmira, NY; FR; BA; Judicial Bd Rep 90-; Iterm Leg Bd Rep; Valedictorian Schlrshp 90-; IM Sftbl; Law.

**LARSEN, PAULA A,** Radford Univ, Radford, VA; FR; BS; Psychlgy.

**LARSEN, REX HENRY,** Univ Of Sc At Spartanburg, Spartanburg, SC; FR; BA; Pep Bnd 90-; Spnsh Clb 90-; Intl Bus; Trnsltr.

**LARSEN, TANYA A,** Univ Of Nh Plymouth St Coll, Plymouth, NH; SO; AA; Retail Mgmt 86-; Lgl Sec 81-86; Sci; Phys Thrpst.

**LARSON, CYNTHIA S,** Univ Of Sc At Columbia, Columbia, SC; SO; BA; Alpha Lambda Delta; Deans Lst 89-90; Pres Lst 90; Engl/Hist; Coll Profsr.

**LARSON, ERIK N,** Liberty Univ, Lynchburg, VA; JR; BS; Stdnt Govt Assn Sntr Chrmn Snt Univ Lf Com 90-; Dbt Tm 89; Cncrt Choir 90-; Alpha Lambda Delta Pres Jr Advsr 89-; Phi Sigma Tau Natl Hon Soc Phlsphy 89-; Prelaw Soc 88-; Urban Outrch 88-89; Rutherford Inst Rsrch Asst; IM Bsktbl Coach 89-; Pltcl Sci; Cnstttnl Law.

**LARSON, JULIE A,** Univ Of New Haven, West Haven, CT; SO; BS; Fire Sci Clb 90-; Res Hll Cncl Sec 90-; Htl Rest Soc 89-90; Eta Sigma Delta 90-; AAS New Hampshire Coll 89; Htl Rest Mngmnt; Sfty Main Eng.

**LARSON, JULIE N,** Ms St Univ, Miss State, MS; JR; BBA; Rsdnc Hall Cncl Flr Rep 88-; Phtgrphr Schl Nwspr; Phi Eta Sigma 90-; Gamma Beta Phi 90-; Alpha Gamma Delta Phlnthrpy 90; Circle K Sec; Deans Lst; Prdnts Lst; Bsns Mgmt; Mgmt Crprtn.

**LARSON, MARY C,** Va Commonwealth Univ, Richmond, VA; JR; BS; BS VA Tech 89; Nrsng.

**LARSON, SARAH B,** Lesley Coll, Cambridge, MA; JR; Lrng Nghbrng Comm 90; Tennis Clb Sec 89; Schlrs 88-.

**LARSON, SARAH J,** Va Commonwealth Univ, Richmond, VA; JR; BFA; Grphc Artst 79-89; Pntng/Psy/Sclptr/Art Hstry; Art Thrpy.

**LARSON, TERRI L,** Univ Of Cin R Walters Coll, Blue Ash, OH; FR; BA; Sci; Tchr.

**LARSON, TRUDY J,** Indiana Univ Of Pa, Indiana, PA; SR; BS; Penn State Educ Assc 90-; Assc Chldhd Ed Intr Cmt 88-; Deans List Otstndng Stdnt 90-; Tchr Dawrd Intrnshp STRIDE 89-90; BS Ed; Elem Ed; Tchng.

**LARSSON, LISA DORA,** Castleton St Coll, Castleton, VT; JR; BED; Elementary Education; Speech Pathology.

**LARTZ, DOUGLAS J,** Memphis St Univ, Memphis, TN; SR; BSME; Meth Cntr; Phi Kappa Phi; Tau Beta Pi; Pi Tau Sigma; Gamma Beta Phi; AS Sauk Vly Comm Coll 88; Mech Eng.

**LARY, MONIQUE S,** Memphis St Univ, Memphis, TN; FR; BS; Deans Lst 90; Blgy/Chem; Scntfc Rsrch.

**LARYEA, JOHN A,** City Univ Of Ny La Guard Coll, Long Island Cty, NY; SR; AA; Law Clb 90-; Psychlgy Clb; Chrstn Clb; Dean Lst 90-; Talent Rstr 90; Coll Schlrshp Brd 90; Lib Arts; Law.

**LASCELLE, KRISTIN A,** Glassboro St Coll, Glassboro, NJ; SR; BA; AMA VP 90; PRSSA 89-90; Ltrcy Vol; Bsnss Ldrshp Awd 90; Cum Laude 90; Im 90; AA Raritan Vlly Cmmnty Clg 88; Cmmnctns; Pblc Rltns.

**LASCELLE, LANCE D,** Niagara Univ, Niagara Univ, NY; JR; BA; Philosophy; Tchr.

**LASCOLA, MATTHEW A,** Youngstown St Univ, Youngstown, OH; JR; BE; Alpha Lambda Delta 88; Gldn Ky 90-; Phi Kappa Tau 88-; Civil Eng.

**LASETER, ELLEN L,** Longwood Coll, Farmville, VA; JR; BS; Psych Clb 90-; Phi Theta Kappa Cookbk Chrmn 89-; Fed Stdnt Soc Wrkrs 90-; Grapevine Nwslttr Asst Ed 86-88; Entertng Tps Wrkshp Southside Comm Clg Tchr 89-90; Chrch Org/Pianst/Yth Ldr; Hons Prog Grad 90; Wmns Mssnry Un Concord Bapt Dir 87-; Soc Wrk; Cnslr/Thrpst.

**LASHINSKY, CHARESE S,** Slippery Rock Univ, Slippery Rock, PA; GD; MASTE; BS Gannon Univ Erie PA 87; Exercise Physiology.

**LASHLEY, JAMES E,** Univ Of Ga, Athens, GA; JR; PHARM; ASP; Rho Chi Awrd; Phrmcy; Phrmcy Prctce And Admin.

**LASHLEY, JAN R,** Univ Of Akron, Akron, OH; SO; BS; Mchncl Eng.

**LASHLEY, WENDY S,** Kent St Univ Kent Cmps, Kent, OH; SR; BA; Kent Cncl Family Rltns 89-; Vlntr Plnnd Prnthd 88; Deans Lst 87-; Fmly Indvdl Stds; Cnclng.

**LASKOWSKI, CHRISTINE,** Glassboro St Coll, Glassboro, NJ; JR; BA; Spanish Clb 90-; Orchid Fndtn; Asstshp Hogar Escuela Armando Rosemberg Dom Repub; Spanish; Intrntl Bus.

**LASLIE, CHRISTOPHER L,** Fl St Univ, Tallahassee, FL; SR; MPA; Phi Kappa Phi; Gldn Key 90-; Pi Sigma Alpha V P 90-; Gamma Theta Upsilon 90-; Pi Gamma Mu 90-; Phi Theta Kappa 87-88; J M Olin Pol Econ Intrnshp 90; Fla Sen Maj Offc; Summa Cum Laude 90; AA 88; BS 90; Publ Admin; Loc Govt Mgmt.

**LASSAN, JANET A,** Indiana Univ Of Pa, Indiana, PA; FR; BA; Fndtn Of Dstngshd Achvrs Schlrshp 90-; Robert Byrd Schlrshp 90; Frank N Zito Jr Mem Schlr Athlte Awrd 90-; Vlybl Vrsty 90; Engl; Prfssr.

**LASSETER, AMY E,** Samford Univ, Birmingham, AL; GD; Amer Jrnl Of Trl Advccy Artcls Edit 90-; Amer Jrsprdnce Bk Awrd Lgl Prcss 88; Bus Orgnztns Bst Memo Awrd 88; Acad And Ldrshp Schlrshp 90; JD Cumberland Schl Of Law Samford Univ; Law.

**LASSITER, JENNIE B,** Vance Granville Comm Coll, Henderson, NC; FR; AA; Educ Assn Clb Sec 90-; Phi Theta Kappa 90-; Ambssbrs Clb; Hnr Stu 90-; Educ.

**LASSITER, JERRY L,** Fl St Univ, Tallahassee, FL; JR; BA; Garnet Key 90-; City Rec Brd Chrprsn 88-; FOP Ldg 130 88-; Corp Polce Dept 77-; AA Glf Cst Comm Coll 90; Math Educ; Tchr.

**LASTER, ERIC D,** Albany St Coll, Albany, GA; SR; BA; Natl Scty Of Blck Engs; Chss Clb 89; Hnrs Cncl 88-; Dns Lst 88-; Hghst GPA Eng Prog; Math; Eng.

**LASTER, GWENDOLYN C,** Winthrop Coll, Rock Hill, SC; FR; Res Hall Cncl Hall Rep 90-; Frshmn Orientation Asst; Cir K Intl 90-; Bio.

**LASTER, JEWELL S,** Ky St Univ, Frankfort, KY; GD; MBA; Minority Adult Stdnt Assn Tsk Frc 87-88; Gspl Ensemble Campus Choir 88-90; Combs Hall Dorm Treas 89-90; Govt Commodities Prog 84-85; God Pantry Homeless 87-88; B A Degree Grad Stdnt 90-; BA 90; Educ; Tchr.

**LASTER, JONATHAN E,** Cumberland Coll, Williamsburg, KY; SR; BS; Stdnt Gvrnmnt Assn VP 88-; Stdnt Nwspr Edtr 88-90; Stdnt Alumni Rltns Cncl 87-90; Sigma Tau Delta VP 89-; T E Mohan Awd 90; Pblshd Artcl Jrnl Cmps Chptr Phi Alpha Theta 90; Englsh Dept Crtcl Wrtng Awd 91; Pltcl Sci Englsh; Law.

**LASTER, LOUIS,** Jackson St Univ, Jackson, MS; FR; BS; MI Clb 90-; GM Endwd Awd 90-; Indl Eng.

**LASTER, PAULINE H,** Gallaudet Univ, Washington, DC; SO; Natl Df Wmns Bwlng Assoc Pres 87-; Stdnt Bdy Govt Prlmntry 89-90; Deans Lst; Natl Vctms Asst Intern 90; Ldrshp Endowmnt 90; Df Ed Govt.

**LASUSKY, EDWARD C,** Cumberland County Coll, Vineland, NJ; SO; AAS; Stdnt Sen Repr 90; Phi Theta Kappa 90-; Catherine J Arpino Schlrshp 90-; Shore Mem Hosp Flwshp; Bd Chrstn Ed Chrmn 85-; Diag Radiography; Allied Med Svcs.

**LATA, JENNIFER L,** Univ Of Rochester, Rochester, NY; SO; BA; Nwspr News Editor 90-; D Lion 90-; Sigma Delta Tau 90-; Pol Sci/Jrnlsm.

**LATEN, MARLA K,** Middle Tn St Univ, Murfreesboro, TN; FR; BA; Gamma Beta Phi 90-; Psychlgy; Psychlgy Prfssr.

**LATHAM, CHRISTOPHER M O,** Allegheny Coll, Meadville, PA; JR; BA; Phi Kappa Psi Pres; Clg Republicans VP Brd 88-; Alden Scholar 88-; Attended Janus Panmonius Univ Hungary 90; History Political Sci; Law.**

**LATHAM, RAMONA S,** Alcorn St Univ, Lorman, MS; JR; BA; Alpha Beta Gamma 88-89; Ordr Eastrn Star Sec/Treas 89-; Exchng Clb Vcksbrg Chld Abs Prvntn Cntr-Prnt-Aide Vol 86-; AA Hinds Comm Coll Raymond MS 90; Bus Admin; Day Care.

**LATHAM, TERRIE E,** Univ Of Sc At Union, Union, SC; JR; BA; Prtnrshp Drug Free Amer 89-; Teach Paraprof Educ Mntlly Hndcppd 7/8th Grds; Psych; Counsel High Risk Adlscnts.**

**LATHAM, WILLIAM D,** Univ Of Sc At Union, Union, SC; JR; BA; Phi Beta Lambda 88-89; Help Restrctr Bk On USCU Policies/Rules 89-90; VITA 88-89; Deans List 87-90; AA Spartanburg Techncl Sch 87-89; ABA Spartanburg Techncl Sch 87-89; Bus Admn/Comptrs; Open Of Bus.**

**LATHAN II, JOHN D,** Spartanburg Methodist Coll, Spartanburg, SC; FR; BS; Coll Chrstn Mvmnt; Otstndng Comp Sci Stdnt; Comp Sci; Comp Anlyst Progrmmr.

**LATHBURY, KIMBERLY J,** Coll Of Charleston, Charleston, SC; JR; BA; Advertising Club 90-; Natl Stdnt Advertising Competition 90-; Advertising Rep Clge Nwspr; Intrnshp WXLY Radio Adv Copywriter 90-; WXTC 90-; Bus Admn; Advertising.

**LATHEM, KIMBERLY A,** Univ Of Montevallo, Montevallo, AL; JR; BA; Stdnt Pblctn Columnist; Intrnshp AL Symph Orch 90; Engl/Communications; Editing/Pblshng/Wrtng.

**LATHEM, KIMBERLY M,** Truett Mc Connell Coll, Cleveland, GA; GD; BA; Bapt Stu Union 88-90; Phi Theta Kappa Hnrs 88-90; AA 90; Psychlgy.

**LATHEY, SHIRLEY A,** Wv Univ At Parkersburg, Parkersburg, WV; FR; BA; AS 80; Bsns Admn Mgmt.

**LATHROP, CAMERON R,** Univ Of Pittsburgh At Bradford, Bradford, PA; SO; BS; Beta Beta Beta; Delta Omega Phi 90-; Bio/Chem; Med.

**LATIF, YAHYA A,** City Univ Of Ny Baruch Coll, New York, NY; SR; Intl Stdnt Clb 89-; Beta Gama Sigma Ind 91; Winner A Van Biema; Essay Contest; ASSOC Laguardia Comm Clg Cuny 88; BBA; Inv Banker/Finc Anlyst.

**LATIMER, STACEY S,** Piedmont Tech Coll, Greenwood, SC; SR; Stdnt Govt; Smll Bus Assn; Tlnt Rstr; Deans Lst; Alpha Phi Alpha; Cert Achvmnt Coll Bds; Coll Schlrshp Serv Acdmc Prfrmnc; Bus Mgmt; Mgmt.

**LATIMER, TONYA S,** Clark Atlanta Univ, Atlanta, GA; JR; BA; Stdnt Govt Rep 87-88; Hlms Hll Sec 87-89; Atlnt Assoc Blck Jrnlsts 90-; Grg Dept Ed Intern 90; Atlnt Vc Asst 88-89; Alx Hly Wrnr Comm Schlrsnp 90-; Mass Commnctns.

**LATIMORE, TRACY A,** City Univ Of Ny Baruch Coll, New York, NY; SR; BBA; NABA 90-; Acctg; CPA.

**LATINA, RAENA ALEXIS,** Univ Of Miami, Coral Gables, FL; BS; Staff Wrtr Miami Hurricane 90-; Fndy Spec Olympcs Grp Ldr; IM Tm Mngr Cpt 90-; Hnrs Stdnts Assoc 89-; Deans List 89-; Alpha Lambda Delta 89-; Phi Eta Sigma 89-; Pi Delta Phi; Hecht Stdnt Ldrs 90-; Pres 100 89-; Photocommunication/French; Photojournalist.

**LATORRE, AIDA I,** Fl International Univ, Miami, FL; FR; BA; Arch; Dom Arch Dsgn.

**LATORRE, EMILY M,** Daytona Beach Comm Coll, Daytona Beach, FL; FR; AS; Cmptr Sci; Analysis/Prog.

**LATORTUE, ROLAND,** Inter Amer Univ Pr San German, San German, PR; SR; BA; Camara Jr Rafael A Quinones C J 90-; Math/Cmptr; Engr.

**LATOUR, ROBERT J,** Western New England Coll, Springfield, MA; FR; BS; Math Ctr Tutor; Alpha Lambda Delta; Math; Envrnmntl Studies.

**LATSHA, LAURA ANN,** Univ Of Nh Plymouth St Coll, Plymouth, NH; SR; BS; Var Ftbl Chrldr/Bsktbl Chrldr 86-90; Stdnt Wrkr 86-90; Pres List 90; Ntnl Busn Tch/Am 90; Derry Chrldr Head Coach 89-90; Salem HS Head Coach; Busn Ed; Tch.

**LATTA, WENDY A,** Boston Univ, Boston, MA; SR; BS; Intrnshps Physcl Thrpy PT 90-; IM Vlybl/Brmbl 89-; Physcl Thrpy.

**LATTAKER, CHARLES D,** Catawba Valley Comm Coll, Hickory, NC; Artist; Gourmet Chef; Garnisher; Htng/Air Cond Central Piedmont Cmnty Clg 88-89; Quality Cooking Central Piedmont Cmnty Clg 90; Cooking/Furniture Wrk.

**LATTARI, KENNETH A,** Long Island Coll Hosp Of Nrsng, Brooklyn, NY; FR; ASSOC; Brooklyn Clb 87-88; Chmbr Comm 87-88; Mgmt Clb 87-88; Life Ins Agnt Lic 89-; Acct Rep 83-90; Nrsng; Instr.

**LATTIBOUDERE, RENNAE S,** Univ Of Miami, Coral Gables, FL; SR; BS; United Blck Stdnts V P 90-; Microbio; Hnrs Assoc; Golden Key; Omicron Delta Kappa; Phi Kappa Phi; Alpha Kappa Alpha; Microbio; Med Dr.

**LATTIMER, JEFFREY H,** S U N Y At Buffalo, Buffalo, NY; JR; BS; Beta Alpha Psi; Acdmc All Amer 90; AAS 90; Acctg; CPA.

**LATTIMORE, DEBBY L,** Univ Of Sc At Sumter, Sumter, SC; FR; BA; Statistics.

**LATTIN, LISA B,** Daytona Beach Comm Coll, Daytona Beach, FL; FR; AS; Best 3d Dsgn SCC Annual Stdnt Exhbt 88; Art Clb Schlrshp Awd 89; Art Exhbtn Studio Gallery 89; Grphc Dsgn; Grphc Dsgnr/Tchncl Illstrtr.

**LATTOMAS, AARON D,** Atlantic Comm Coll, Mays Landing, NJ; SO; Crtv Wrtng Clb; Assoc 90; Jrnlsm.

**LATTRELL, JODY A,** Mount Saint Mary Coll, Newburgh, NY; SR; BA; Hon Allnc Dfnt Stgs Bcchs; Edtr Chf Nwspr 90-; Dns Lst 88-; Aquinas Schlr; Alpha Chi; Asst Sr Pblc 90; Info Spclst; Eng; Mgmt.

**LAU, ANNA,** City Univ Of Ny Baruch Coll, New York, NY; SR; BBA; Beta Alpha Psi Tutrng Coord 90-; Gldn Ky; Acctg.

**LAU, JINYUM,** City Univ Of Ny Baruch Coll, New York, NY; JR; BBA; Acctg; CPA.

**LAU, STEVAN,** Univ Of Tn At Martin, Martin, TN; SR; BA; Bus Mgmt.

**LAU, WENDY,** City Univ Of Ny Baruch Coll, New York, NY; SO; BA; Deans List 90; Acctng; Acctny.

**LAU, YAU H,** City Univ Of Ny Baruch Coll, New York, NY; JR; BBA; Fin & Econ Soc; Intl Trade Soc; Golden Key; New York Telephone Minority Schlrshp; Baruch Endwmnt Fund Provosts Schlrshps; Fin; Bnkng & Invstmnt.

**LAU-HANSEN, SONIA,** Va Commonwealth Univ, Richmond, VA; SR; Soc Human Resources Mgmt; Cum Laude Hnr Rl.

**LAUB, STEVEN S,** Bergen Comm Coll, Paramus, NJ; SO; BS; Phi Theta Kappa Soc 90-; AAS 91; Acctng.

**LAUBENTHAL, LISA E,** Univ Of South Al, Mobile, AL; SR; BS; AS Faulkner St Junior Clg 88; Elem Educ.

**LAUBER, JORDANA,** Univ Of Toledo, Toledo, OH; FR; BS; Med Tech.

**LAUBER, SHANNON R,** Clarkson Univ, Potsdam, NY; JR; BS; Busing Coord 90-; Phi Kappa Phi; Indstrl Mngmnt; Mnfctrng.

**LAUCIRICA, ANNETTE,** Fl International Univ, Miami, FL; JR; BA; Surg/Obstetrcl Tech; ORT 86; Ele Educ; Educ.

**LAUDER, JAMES P,** Univ Of South Al, Mobile, AL; JR; BS; Eqstrn Clb 90-; Vlybl; Csmc Charlies Envrmnmtl Org Pres 90-; Dns Lst 90-; Pres Lst 90-; Lcrs 88-89; Fnce; Invstmnt Bkr.

**LAUDER, RICHARD A,** S U N Y Coll Of Tech At Frmgdl, Farmingdale, NY; FR; BS; Resident Advisor; Alpha Beta Gamma; Deans Lst 90; Mngmnt Info Systems; Computers Mngmnt.

**LAUDERDALE, PAMELA S,** Blue Mountain Coll, Blue Mountain, MS; JR; BS; Phi Beta Kappa 89-; AA NE Cmmnty Coll 90; Elem Ed; Tchng.

**LAUDICK, B ELAINE,** Northern Ky Univ, Highland Hts, KY; FR; BA; Psychlgy; Chld Psychlgst.

**LAUER, MARIAN K,** Piedmont Tech Coll, Greenwood, SC; SO; LPN 90; Nrsg.

**LAUFER, DANIEL M,** S U N Y At Buffalo, Buffalo, NY; SR; Beta Gamma Sigma 89-; Beta Alpha Psi 90-; NY State Soc Cert Pblc Acctnts Awd Outstndng Svc 90; Grad Hons Hghst Distnctn Summa Cum Laude; Buffalo Bureau Jwsh Ed 88-; Acctg.

**LAUFMAN, DARMA,** Miami Dade Comm Coll North, Miami, FL; SO.

**LAUGEL, DENVIA E,** Vanderbilt Univ, Nashville, TN; FR; BE; March Band 90; Bsktbl Band 90-; Wind Ensmbl; Am Inst Chem Engrs 90-; Chem Eng.

**LAUGHERY, SHELLEY L,** Fl St Univ, Tallahassee, FL; JR; BA; Shwchr 90; Phi Beta Kappa; FL Undrgrad Schlrshp 88-; Lbrl Studies Hon Pgm Cmpltn 90; Hon Mjr; IM Ftbl/Sftbl 90-; Engl; Law.

**LAUGHLIN, CHRISTOPHER DALE,** Univ Of Al At Birmingham, Birmingham, AL; SO; BS; Alpha Lambda Delta 90-; Engrng.

**LAUGHLIN, KATHLEEN M,** Elms Coll, Chicopee, MA; SR; BSN; Pgm Brchr Com; Stdnt Nrs Assn; Deans Lst; Eqstrn; Nrsng.

**LAUGHLIN, LISA D,** Univ Of Sc At Coastal Carolina, Conway, SC; FR; BA; Long Bay Slng Assoc 88-; Phi Eta Sigma; Mngr 89-; Educ; Teacher/Elem.

**LAUGHLIN, MARIA P,** Smith Coll, Northampton, MA; SO; BA; 1st Grp Schlr 89-; Deans Lst 89-; Ethel Olin Corbin Prize 90; Mrs Montagu Prize; Thomas Corwin Mendenhall Prize; Engl; Profsr.

**LAUGHLIN, MICHELLE A,** Free Will Baptist Bible Coll, Nashville, TN; SO; BA; Lmn Stff Asst Ed 90-; Ls Mae Alctt Ltry Sec 89-; Scty Sftbll Vllybll 89-; Engl.

**LAUGHORN, STEVE R,** Univ Of Akron, Akron, OH; JR; BSBA; Golden Key 90-; Beta Gamma Sigma 90-; Dns Lst 88-; IM Bsktbl 90-; Finance; Corp Finance.

**LAUGHREY, CHARLES A,** Univ Of Akron, Akron, OH; SO; BS; Phi Eta Sigma 89-90; Sci; Cvl Engr.

**LAUGHTER, KRISTI D,** Univ Of Nc At Asheville, Asheville, NC; JR; BA; SNEA; Alpha Xi Delta Asst Treas; Chnclrs Hnr Lst; Dns Lst; Natl Merit Schlr; Weizenblatt Endwmnt Schlrshp; IM; Math; Tchr.

**LAUGHTON, CHRISTOPHER A,** Cornell Univ Statutory College, Ithaca, NY; SO; BS; Jos J Yedouitz Sr Mem Awd 90; Crew 89-; Horticulture; Nursery Mgmnt.

**LAUGHTON, RALPH B,** Barry Univ, Miami, FL; SO; BA; Amer Civil Lbrties Union; Amer Mgmt Assoc 87; ACLU/NAACP; Rtl Mgmt; Bsnss; Law.

**LAUGLHIN, MARIA P,** Smith Coll, Northampton, MA; SO; BA; Frst Grp Schlr 89-90; Engl/Clsscs; Coll Prfssr.

**LAUL, CHRISTOPHER R,** Saint Francis Coll, Brooklyn, NY; FR; Asstntshp Downtown Brklyn Law Firm Beck/Iannuzzi PC 90-; Waterpolo/Swim 90-; Law.

**LAUREANO, EDUARDO,** Cumberland County Coll, Vineland, NJ; SO; Stdnt Snt 90-; Stdnt Actvts Brd 90-; Cmptr Clb; Phi Theta Kappa 90-.

**LAUREDO, MARIA E,** Univ Of Miami, Coral Gables, FL; JR; BA; Cne Cmmtr Orgnztn Nwslttr Edit 90-; Ded Of Dbn Stdnts 90-; Ornttn Asst Mmi Hrrcne; Sigma Tau Delta Pres; Phi Beta Kappa; Phi Kappa Phi; Phi Eta Sigma; Gldn Ky; Psi Chi; Dix Schl Of Arts & Sci Schlrshp 90-; Pres Hnr Rll 89; Prvsts Hnr Rll 90-; Engl Psychlgy; Law.

**LAURENCEAU, ANTONINA GERALDINE,** City Univ Of Ny Baruch Coll, New York, NY; SO; BBA; Bus; Acctng.

**LAURENT, NICOLE,** Lesley Coll, Cambridge, MA; JR; Fresh Orient 90-; Transfer Panel; Early Childhood/Daycare; Teacher.

**LAURIANO, CHRISTINE M,** Mount Saint Mary Coll, Newburgh, NY; JR; BSN; GTE Ldrshp Pgm Mt St Mary Clge 89-90; Dns Lst; Hnrs Allnc Clb 88-; Sigma Theta Tau; Beta Beta Beta 88-; Msn Wk Holly Cross Chrch; Bwl Kds Sk Big Bros/Sis 88; Phnthn Cptn Mt St Mary Clge 89-90; Nrsg.

**LAURIANO, LISA M,** Mount Saint Mary Coll, Newburgh, NY; SO; Nrsng Stdnt Un 89-; Hons Alliance 90-; Beta Beta Beta Bio Soc 89-; Nursing.

**LAURIE, LISAROSE,** Holyoke Comm Coll, Holyoke, MA; FR; BA; Blandford Fire Dept 84-87; Nursea Aide 75-84; Adm Sec 87-90; Reg Nurse.

**LAURILLA, KRISTEN E,** Longwood Coll, Farmville, VA; SR; BS; Kappa Delta Pi 90-; Phi Kappa Phi; Elem Educ; Tchr.

**LAURIN, DWAYNE E,** Hudson Valley Comm Coll, Troy, NY; SR; Presidents List 88-; Electrical Construction & Maintenance.

**LAURINO, JUAN C,** Hillsborough Comm Coll, Tampa, FL; FR; AA; Sci; Eng.

**LAURISTON, LINA M,** Miami Dade Comm Coll North, Miami, FL; GD; BA; BA 90; Engl; Bus.

**LAURITO, DAVID M,** Le Moyne Coll, Syracuse, NY; JR; BS; Mktg Clb Chrprsn 90-; Econ Clb 88-89; Yrbk Stf 90-; Delta Epsilon Chptr Delta Mu Delta; IM Sprts 88-; Bus Admin; Bnkng/Finance.

**LAURY, AQUALYN Y,** Spelman Coll, Atlanta, GA; FR; BS; Hnrs Pgm Assoc Secr 90-; Math.

**LAUSCH JR, LARRY LEE,** Life Coll, Marietta, GA; GD; DC; Biomechanics Clb; Gonstead Clb; Motion Plptn; IM; BA Gettysburg Coll 86; Chiropratic.

**LAUT, LOREN A,** Daytona Beach Comm Coll, Daytona Beach, FL; SO; BMED; Show/Conct Choir 90-; Cuyahoga Comm Colg Choir 89-90; Music Ed; Schl Choral Dir.

**LAUW, NICO J,** Fl International Univ, Miami, FL; JR; BA; Phi Theta Kappa 89-; Deans Lst 89-; Scty Mfg Eng Chptr Chrmn 83-; Mchnst CNC Cnvntl; AA Miami Dade Cmmnty Coll 90; Inddstrl Systms Eng.

**LAUX, MICHAEL R,** Northern Ky Univ, Highland Hts, KY; SR; BS; ACM 90-; Univ Hnrs Prog 89-; Alpha Chi 88-; At&t Bell Lab 90; Cmptr Sci; MS.

**LAUX, STEVEN A,** Saint Johns Univ, Jamaica, NY; FR; BS; Tlvsn Clb Prdctn Sec; Deans Lst 90-; Cmmnctns; Tlvsn Prdctn.

**LAUZURIQUE, ELIZABETH A,** Univ Politecnica De Pr, Hato Rey, PR; SR; IIE 87-; Cert Academic Achvmnt 90; AA Univ Fla 86; Eng; Indstrl Eng.

**LAVALLEE, KATHLEEN A,** S U N Y Coll Of Tech At Alfred, Alfred, NY; FR; AAS; Ct Rprtng.

**LAVANDERA, DUNIA,** Miami Dade Comm Coll, Miami, FL; SO; Talnt Rstr Mnrty Stdnt 89-; Bus Admn; Fin.

**LAVAS, MICHELE,** City Univ Of Ny Coll Staten Is, Staten Island, NY; SR; BA; Baccalaureate Pgm 87-; Dns Lst 87-; Elem Ed; Tchr.**

**LAVELLE, BRIAN C,** Providence Coll, Providence, RI; SO; BS; IM Ice Hcky 89-; Acctg; CPA.

**LAVENDER, BARBARA A,** Univ Of Toledo, Toledo, OH; GD; JD; Stdnt Bar Assn Rep 90-; SBA Schlrsh Slctn Cmtee; Mrtr Bd Hon Soc 90-; Deans Lst; Pres Hon Lst 88-; ABW Schlrshp 88-90; Admn Asst 78-; Bedford Twp Lbry Advsry Bd Treas 88-90; Organizer Fstvl 87-; BA 90; Law.

**LAVENDER, CHARLES L,** Nova Univ, Ft Lauderdale, FL; GD; MS; Frtrnl Ordr Eagles 90-; Bnvlnt/Prtctv Ordr Elks 90-; Deans Lst Seminole Comm 72; Chld Abs Prvntn Inc Osceola Cnty Exec Com 90-; Deans Lst Polk Comm 75; Deans Lst Rollins Coll 80; Mssng Chldrn Bllbd Cmpgn Exec Com 90-; Ldrshp Osceola 90; Hmn Serv; Law Enfrcmnt Mgmt.

**LAVENDER, KARA L,** Duke Univ, Durham, NC; FR; BS; Pi Beta Phi; Math.

**LAVENDER, LAURIE A,** Emory Univ, Atlanta, GA; JR; BBA; Beta Alphi Psi; All Amer Clgte Schlr Awd 90-; Acctg; CPA.

**LAVENDER, LAURIE W,** Univ Of Southern Ms, Hattiesburg, MS; SR; BS; Gamma Eta Phi; Phi Theta Kappa VP 89-90; Prknstn Cmps Awrd Wrld Hist 87-88; Hall Fame/Academic Achvmnt Awrd 89-90; AA MS Glf Coast Comm Clg 90; Bio; Sci Educ Instrctr.

**LAVENDER-LE CATES, LORRAINE D,** Wilmington Coll, New Castle, DE; JR; BSN; Reg Nrs Med Cntr Del; ADN Delaware Tech Comm Coll 88; Nrsng.

**LAVERDE, JOSE DAVID,** Nova Univ, Ft Lauderdale, FL; GD; MBA; Alumni Assoc 89-; Bus Mngr Sheridan Voc Tech Cntr 89-; Bus Cnsltnt Natl Serv Lrng Sena Bogota Colombia 78-84; BBA Acctg FL Atlntc Univ 89; BA Ecnmcs Indesco Coop Univ 80; Business.

**LAVERDIERE, AMY M,** Providence Coll, Providence, RI; FR; BS; Elem/Spec Ed; Tchng.

**LAVERGE FRANQUI, ALBA L,** Inter Amer Univ Pr San German, San German, PR; BS; Cmptr; Engr.

**LAVERGNE, MARIE L,** Inter Amer Univ Pr Hato Rey, Hato Rey, PR; SO; BA; Acctg Stdnts Assn 89-; Hon Lst 89-; BED Mnpwr Bus Trning Inst 78; Acctg; CPA.

**LAVERS, JASON R,** Me Maritime Academy, Castine, ME; SO; Co Yeomn 89-90; Reg Oper Ofcrs Yeomn 90-; Deans Lst 89-; Cmdnts Lst 89-.

**LAVEY, JOYCE M,** Newbury Coll, Brookline, MA; FR; AA; Dns Lst 90; Frshm Awd Acct 90; Acct; CPA.

**LAVIAN, AMOS,** City Univ Of Ny Baruch Coll, New York, NY; GD; Amrcn Mrktng Assoc VP 88-89; Jwsh Stdnt Cncl Clb Pres 89-90; Frgn Trd Scty 88-89; Ylnd Bnsn Hnr Scty; BBA 90; Intl Mrktng.

**LAVOI, IVETTE C,** Miami Dade Comm Coll South, Miami, FL; SO; BA; AA; AS; Elem Ed.

**LAVOIE, RENEE J,** Saint Joseph Coll, West Hartford, CT; SO; BA; Choir Sec 90-; Nwspr Asst Edtr; Tutor Logic 90; Pres Schlrshp; Engl/Philo; Law.

**LAVOIE-GRIFFIN, JENNIFER S,** Lesley Coll, Cambridge, MA; JR; BS; Commuter Club 88-; Academic Hnrs 89-; Elem Ed; Teacher.

**LAVON, LIORA,** William Paterson Coll, Wayne, NJ; SR; Orntatn Ldr Frshmns; Delta Psi Omega Lttl Sstr 88-89; Nu Theta Chi Scl Chrmn 89-90; Camp YMCA Snr Cnslr; Sbst Tchr Shomray Tora; Elem Soc; Tchng.**

**LAVRIN, ALEX,** Wv Univ, Morgantown, WV; JR; BSME; Mrchng Bnd 88-; Am Soc Mchncl Engr 89-; Soc Auto Engr 90-; Gldn Ky 90-; Tau Beta Pi Treas; Mech Engr.

**LAW, BRENDA W,** Roane St Comm Coll, Harriman, TN; SO; AAS; Gamma Beta Phi 90-; Blntmmrl Hosp Schlrshp; Amrcn Physcl Thrpy Assoc 90; Physcl Thrpst Asstnc.

**LAW, CASSANDRA M,** Clark Atlanta Univ, Atlanta, GA; SO; BA; Buffalo C/C Intern 88-; Busn Admin; Mgmnt.

**LAW, CHARLES W,** Pellissippi St Tech Comm Coll, Knoxville, TN; SO; AAS; Fclty Cncl Schlrshp Awd 89; Crpntr; Cmnctns Grphcs; Grphc Dsgn.

**LAW, CHRISTINA G,** Wv Univ At Parkersburg, Parkersburg, WV; FR; BA; Jrnlsm; Phtgrphy.

**LAW, DAVID,** Saint Andrews Presbytrn Coll, Laurinburg, NC; JR; BA; Rugby Clb 90-; Busn.

**LAW, ELIZABETH A,** Radford Univ, Radford, VA; JR; BS; Literary Arts Pblctn 90-; Circle K 89-90; Cmnty Hlth.

**LAW, JENNIFER A,** King Coll, Bristol, TN; FR; BA; SGA Clss Rep; Drma; Bible Rlgn; Yth Mnstry.

**LAW, JESSICA J,** Savannah Coll Of Art & Design, Savannah, GA; JR; BFA; Intl TV Assn; Video; TV Prod.

**LAW, KAM FAN,** East Tn St Univ, Johnson City, TN; BA; Chinese Assoc 78-81; Beta Gamma Sigma 83-; Cumlaude Hnr 81; Restaurant Gen Mgr 85-; BA Utah State Univ 81; MBA E Carolina Univ 83; Cmptr Info Sci; Prgrmmr.

**LAW, LINDA LOU,** Beckley Coll, Beckley, WV; FR; BED; History.

**LAW, SUZANNE D,** Atlantic Comm Coll, Mays Landing, NJ; SO; Culinary Stdnts Assoc SGA Stdnt Rep 89-; Prof Chefs Assoc S J 89-; Hotel Sls/Mktg Assoc Intern 89-90; Pres Lst 89-; Prof Chefs Assoc Schlr 90-; BBA Hofstra Univ 85; Culinary Arts; Pastry Chef.

**LAW, SUZANNE E,** Glassboro St Coll, Glassboro, NJ; FR; Engl; Law.

**LAW-MILLER, LISA A,** Glassboro St Coll, Glassboro, NJ; SR; BA; Dr James M Shafer Math Award 90-; Math/Cmnctns; Actuarial Sci.

**LAWES, ELIZABETH A,** Birmingham Southern Coll, Birmingham, AL; JR; BS; Orientation Stf 90-; Pre Law Scty 89-; Global Studies Assoc 90-; Psi Chi 90-; Chi Omega Secy 88-; Southern Vol Serv Links Up 90-; Kids On The Block; Clinical Psychology Intrnshp Fmly Chld Dvlpmnt Ctr; Psychology; Law.

**LAWHON, REBECCA L,** Fl St Univ, Tallahassee, FL; SR; BS; Deans 88; Elem Edctn; Tchr Prmry Grds.

**LAWHORN, GLENDA F,** Central Fl Comm Coll, Ocala, FL; SO; BA; AA; Cmnctns; Mktg-Advrtsg.

**LAWLER, DARREN A,** Univ Of Tn At Martin, Martin, TN; SR; Vrsty Bsktbl 89-; Deans Lst 90; All Glf S Cnfrnce Acdmc Team 90; Stdnt Tchr; AA Brevard Jr Coll 87-89; Scndry Bus Educ; Tch/Coach.

**LAWLER, KATHRYN A,** Univ Of Tn At Martin, Martin, TN; JR; BS; Phi Eta Sigma 90-; Hm Ec-Dietetcs; Dietician.

**LAWLER, REBECCA D,** Univ Of Montevallo, Montevallo, AL; SR; MA; Assn Hmn Serv; Alpha Lambda Delta; Phi Alpha Theta; Sclgy Clb; Alpha Gamma Delta VP 90; Sr Elite Sclgy; BS; Hstry/Sclgy; PHD.

**LAWLESS, KEITH MARTIN,** Univ Of South Fl, Tampa, FL; FR; BA; Mass Cmnctns; TV Producer.

**LAWLESS, KIMBERLY R,** Univ Of Sc At Aiken, Aiken, SC; SO; BA; Psych Clb Pres 89-; Hmecmg Queen; Cmnty Companion; Gamma Beta Phi 90-; Phi Mu V P 90-; Towler Schlrshp; Dept Schlrshp 90-; Vicki E Phillips Mem Schlrshp 89-90; Chld Psych.

**LAWLESS, MAUREEN E,** Villanova Univ, Villanova, PA; FR; Spec Olympics; Balloon Day Vol; Delta Delta Delta; Poltcl Sci; Law.

**LAWLESS, MELANIE D,** Univ Of Nc At Charlotte, Charlotte, NC; JR; BA; Yng Lf Ldr Vol 90-; Intervrsty Chrstn Flwshp 88-90; Gldn Key; Delta Zeta VP Pldg Ed 89-90; Intrnshp WBTV TV Stn Prmtns Dept 90; Outstndng Jr Province Delta Zeta; Outstndng Stndrds Chrmn Province 90; Eng; Pblc Rltns.

**LAWLOR, JOSEPHINE M,** City Univ Of Ny Baruch Coll, New York, NY; JR; BBA; Ntnl Yngldrs Cnfce 88-90; Schol 88-; Golden Key 90-; Deans List 90; Acctng.

**LAWLOR, KARIS L,** Bapt Bible Coll & Seminary, Clarks Summit, PA; SO; BA; Cncrt Choir 89-; Bptst Chrch Music 89-; Acdmc Schlrshp 90-; Deans Lst 89-; Scndry Educ Engl/Grmn; Tch.

**LAWLOR, RICHARD J,** Life Coll, Marietta, GA; SR; BS; S W Univ 87.

**LAWRENCE, ALLISON D,** Wallace St Comm Coll At Selma, Selma, AL; SO; BS; Pres Lst 90-; Acdmc Schlrshp; Math; Sec Ed.

**LAWRENCE, AMANDA L,** James Madison University, Harrisonburg, VA; SR; BS; Class V P 87-88; Alpha Sigma Alpha V P 88-; Ord Of Omega Schlrshp 89-; Lambda Chi Alpha Aux 89-; Info/Techn Cmptr Assist 88-; Presby Hndbll Choir 89-; Early Chldhd Educ; Tchr.

**LAWRENCE, BENITA C,** Univ Of Nc At Greensboro, Greensboro, NC; SR; MED; Stdnt Ldrs Cncl 89-90; SNCEA 89-90; Uiv Marshals Chf 89-90; Gldn Chain 87-90; UNCG Stdnt Excllnc Awd 90; NCEA 90-; BS 90; AAS Rcknghm Comm Clg 74; Elem Educ; Tchg/Admin.**

**LAWRENCE, BRADLEY V,** Ms St Univ, Miss State, MS; JR; BS; Capiah Lincoln Cmnty Clge Trail Blazers 88-90; Block & Bridle Treas 90-; Meat Judging Team 90- Alpha Omega 88-90; FFA; Vol Fir Dept; Amer Soc Of Animal Sci Schlrshp Awd; Dixie Natl Livestock Show Schlrshp; AA 90; Animal Science; Animal Nutrition Research.

**LAWRENCE, CAROLYN C,** Christopher Newport Coll, Newport News, VA; SR; BS; Ware Jr Wmns Clb V P Sec 89-; Bus Mgmt.

**LAWRENCE, DAVID L,** Lexington Comm Coll, Lexington, KY; SO; BA; Miksatnic Stdnt Union 89-; Ntl Eagle Sct Assn 86-; Boy Scts Amer Jr Sctmstr 86-; Eagle Sct 86; Histy/Poli Sci; Gov.**

**LAWRENCE, DONNA-MARIE E,** Miami Dade Comm Coll North, Miami, FL; SO; BA; Hnrs Prog; Bus Admin.

**LAWRENCE, FAITH W,** Univ Of Sc At Columbia, Columbia, SC; SO; BS; Stdnt Govt Assn Stdnt Senatr 89-; Mnrty Asstnce Peer Tm Comm Chr 90-; Emrgng Ldrs Prog Mentr 90; Omicron Delta Kappa; Phi Eta Sigma 90-; Deans Lst 90-; Alpha Lambda Delta 90-; Gamma Beta Phi 90-; Mnrty Soph/Jr Hghst GPR 90-; Biolgy; Med.

**LAWRENCE, GWENDOLYN,** Tuskegee Univ, Tuskegee Inst, AL; JR; BS; Fnce Clb 90-; Thtr Gld 88-; Delta Mu Delta 90-; Alpha Kappa Mu; Intern AC Rochester 90; Intern GE; Finance; Mba/Jd.

**LAWRENCE JR, HAROLD P,** Bethune Cookman Coll, Daytona Beach, FL; SR; BA; Pre Alumni Cncl Prlmntrn 87-; Bus Hon Scty 89-; Inroads 89-; Trck Capt 87-89; Bus Mgmt; Fin Idstry.

**LAWRENCE, IMANI S,** Tallahassee Comm Coll, Tallahassee, FL; SO; BA; Blck Stdnt Union 90-; NAACP Univ FL 88-89; Advsry Comm Allen Park Cls Repr 80-81; Zeta Phi Beta 83-85; Trck/Vlybl/Sftbl/Bsktbl Capt 87-88; Bsn Adm; Ofc Mgr.

**LAWRENCE, JOAN P,** Bloomfield Coll, Bloomfield, NJ; SO; BA; Customer Svc Admin 90-; Psych; Ind Psych.

**LAWRENCE, JODI L,** Gaston Coll, Dallas, NC; FR; AAS; Med Offc Tech; Med Sec.

**LAWRENCE, KATRINA,** Saint Pauls Coll, Lawrenceville, VA; FR; Math/Sci Clb; Campus Btfctn Clb; Sci/Math; Cmptr Anlyst.

**LAWRENCE, LEVONIE Z,** City Univ Of Ny Lehman Coll, Bronx, NY; SR; BA; Golden Key 90-; BS Univ West Indies 82; Acctg; Acctg/Bsn Mgmt.

**LAWRENCE, LISA D,** Berkeley Coll Of Westchester, White Plains, NY; SO; BA; Sr Stdnt Govt Treas 87; Intrn At Sportsmedcn Rehabltn 89; Walk America 88; Bus Admn; Mktg.

**LAWRENCE, MARGARET C B,** Portland School Of Art, Portland, ME; SO; BFA; Hospice Vol 82-88; RN 79-84; BS U Of PA 78; Painting

**LAWRENCE, MARVA S,** City Univ Of Ny Med Evers Coll, Brooklyn, NY; JR; BS; Elem Ed; Tchg.

**LAWRENCE, MONICA A,** Va St Univ, Petersburg, VA; SR; BA; Urbn Plnnng Cnsl Sec 88-90; Sigam Gamma Rho Pres 89-; Bptst Chrch Sr Ctzn 89-90; Oak Ridge Crrctn Cntr 89-90; March Dimes Pres 89; Mrchng Bnd 87-89; Ushr Brd Pres; Sclgy; Pblc Rltns.

**LAWRENCE, NANCY R,** Memphis St Univ, Memphis, TN; JR; BPS; Bsbl Treas 86-90; Phi Kappa Phi; Rl Est Agnt 83-85; AS Tulsa Jr Coll 89; Law.

**LAWRENCE, REGINA L,** Spartanburg Methodist Coll, Spartanburg, SC; FR; Day Stu Assoc Brd Mbr 90-; Phi Theta Kappa 90-; Phi Beta 90-; Jr Achvmnt Cnsltnt 90-; Bsktbl Chrldr 90-; Psych; Scndry Educ.

**LAWRENCE, RETA J,** Christopher Newport Coll, Newport News, VA; SR; BA; Ofcrs Wives Clb; Kappa Del Phi; L.

**LAWRENCE, SANDRA K,** East Tn St Univ, Johnson City, TN; GD; MA; MSGA 87-; AMA 87-; Am Med Wmns Assn Pres 87-; Alpha Lambda Delta 75; Alpha Omega Alpha 90; Phi Rho Sigma; Deans Lst 88-; J Glasgw Awrd; ASCP 79-; P Mcclain Rsrch Awrd 89; Fmly Prctce Rsrch Awrd 88; BS Univ TN 79; Med; MD/RADIOLGY.

**LAWRENCE, VICKIE M,** Va Union Univ, Richmond, VA; JR; BS; VA Union U Mrchgn Bnd 89-; Bapt Stdnt Union 88-89; Gospel Choir 88-89; Beta Kappa Chi 90-; Cmnty Schlrs 89-; Math; Eng.

**LAWRENCE, WADE D,** Southern Vt Coll, Bennington, VT, SO, BA; Stdnt Assoc Pres; Envrnmntl Actn Assoc 89; Clg Hnrs Prog Stdnt Rep; Vrsty Bsebl 90; Envrnmntl Studies; Law Ed.

**LAWRENCE-WEBB, CLAUDIA,** Howard Univ, Washington, DC; GD; PHD; Zeta Phi Beta 90-; Trustees Schlrshp 90; Mayors Cncl Infants/Toddlers 90-91; AAMFT/NASW; Univ Trainer; Soc Wrkr; Cons; Cert Marital/Fmly Therapist; BSW Univ MD Baltimore Co 78; MSW Howard Univ 84; Soc Wrk.

**LAWRIE, JODI L,** Hilbert Coll, Hamburg, NY; FR; BA; Rzepka Fncl Acdmc Sppt; Acctng.

**LAWRIE, SHARON J,** Univ Of Sc At Columbia, Columbia, SC; SR; MS; Pi Mu Epsilon 90; Golden Key 90; Delta Zeta Prlmntrn 86; BS; FRIENDS Of Baruch Schlrshp 90; Marine Sci; Rsrch/Tchr.

**LAWRITSON, CYNTHIA L,** Fl St Univ, Tallahassee, FL; SR; JD; Pnhllnc Coms 87-; Pre Law Scty 90; Frnscs 90-; Lambda Pi Eta 90-; Chi Omega Treas 87-; SHARE Tm PR Chrmn 90; Law.

**LAWRY, AMANDA J,** Roane St Comm Coll, Harriman, TN; GD; AAS; Deans Lst 90-; Exclnc Word Prcsg Awrd 90-; Ofc Admin; Mgmt.

**LAWRY, SHERRIE L,** Roane St Comm Coll, Harriman, TN; SO; AAS; Deans Lst; U S Army Spec 4th Clss 83-86; Bus; Admin.**

**LAWS, GARY SCOTT,** Brevard Coll, Brevard, NC; FR; BS; Phi Theta Kappa; Schlrshp; Track 90-; Natl Jr Coll Ath Assn Cross Cntry Chmpnshp 90-; Math Engrng.

**LAWS, JENNIFER D,** Univ Of Ky, Lexington, KY; JR; BED; Res Hl Govt/Res Hl Assoc Clerk/Stdnt Advsry Cncl/Epsilon Delta/Golden Key 90-; Elem Ed Spec Lang/Wrtng; Teach.

**LAWS, KIMBERLY N,** Hampton Univ, Hampton, VA; SR; Stdnts Vl Ed Assc Hstrn 87-; Alpha Kappa Mu 89-; Ed Clb 87-; Pittsbrgh Cty Schls Mnrty Rcrtmnt Prgrm Tchr; BS; Erly Chldhd Ed Nk8 Endrsmnt; Tchng.

**LAWSON, ANDREA L,** Roane St Comm Coll, Harriman, TN; SO; AD; NBRC 88-; St Marys Hosptl 88-; RCP 90-; Cert Mt Empire Comm Cllg 84-85; Resprtry Thrpy.

**LAWSON, ANGELIA D,** Middle Ga Coll, Cochran, GA; SO; Phi Beta Lambda 90-; Hnrs; Wrd Prcsg Cert 89; Bus Admin.

**LAWSON, BRENDA K,** Roane St Comm Coll, Harriman, TN; FR; AD; Med Cntr Nrs Extrn Prog; Elks Clb Nrsng Schlrshp; Nrsng.

**LAWSON, CARY B,** Fayetteville St Univ, Fayetteville, NC; SO; BBA; Vars Bsktbl Point Guard 88-; Bus Mgnt/Math; Sales.

**LAWSON, CATHERINE A,** Saint John Fisher Coll, Rochester, NY; GD; Delta Mu Gamma 88-90; Delta Epsilon Sigma 89-90; St John Fisher Trustees Schlrshp 87-; St John Fisher Frgn Lang Schlrshp 87; Spnsh; Interpreter.

**LAWSON, EDWARD D,** Univ Of Rochester, Rochester, NY; SO; BA; Satire Hmr Mag 89-; Undrgrad Hstry Cncl 90-; Nvl ROTC Bnd 89-; J S Wilsn Soc 89-; Sigma Nu 90-; Hstry; Miltry.

**LAWSON, GORDON S,** Univ Of Sc At Spartanburg, Spartanburg, SC; SR; BA; Pltcl Sci-Pblc Admn; State/Fed Gvt-Pblc Rltns.

**LAWSON, JAMES A,** Univ Of Miami, Coral Gables, FL; SR; BARCH; Prgrm Cncl Chrmn 87-89; Rthsklr Advsry Brd 87-88; Alpha Sigma Phi Frat Sec 87-90; SG 89-; Archtctr.

**LAWSON, JOSEPH A,** Va Commonwealth Univ, Richmond, VA; JR; BS; Hon Pgm 90-91; Vet USAF 823rd Ceshr 85-89; AAS New River Comm Coll 90; Psychlgy; Fed Law Enfrcmnt.

**LAWSON, JUDY C,** Pellissippi St Tech Comm Coll, Knoxville, TN; SO; BA; Drama; Hmn Ecolgy; Chld/Fmly Stdies.

**LAWSON, JUDY L,** Oh St Univ At Marion, Marion, OH; JR; BED; Engl; Elem Tchr.

**LAWSON, KEVIN W,** Radford Univ, Radford, VA; FR; BBA; Acctg; CPA

**LAWSON, LA TONYA A,** Nc Agri & Tech St Univ, Greensboro, NC; JR; BS; SNEA 89-; Wmns Clb 87-88; Chnclrs Exctv Smnr; ATT Schlrshp; Delta Sigma Theta Schlrshp 87; Elem Edctn; Tchr.

**LAWSON, LISA C,** Marshall University, Huntington, WV; SR; BA; Amrcn Mrktng Assoc VP 89-; Stdnt Govt Chrprsn 89-90; IM Mgr 87-88; Asstd Dsbld Stdnintrnshp Mrrll Lynch; Mrktg.

**LAWSON, MARSHAE D,** Lincoln Univ, Lincoln Univ, PA; SO; Chns Clb 89-; Hnrs Prgm; Schlrshp Acdmc Achvmnt; Hnrs Schlrshp; Bus Amdn; Bus.**

**LAWSON, MARY P,** Indiana Univ Of Pa, Indiana, PA; SR; BED; Univ Stdnts Chldrns Cntr Sec 89-90; Evergreen Mthrs Twins Clb VP 85-; PTA 87-; Sci; Tchng Jr/Sr High Stdnts.

**LAWSON, MOLLIE C,** Tusculum Coll, Greeneville, TN; JR; BA; CHOICE Vol Asstg Illtrt/At Rsk Hgh Schl Stdnts; Tusculum Clg Sftbl Tm 88-90; Educ.

**LAWSON IV, ROBERT E,** Life Coll, Marietta, GA; GD; Extrmts Clb; Thmpsn Clb; Gnstd Clb; Almn Assoc; Mtn Plptn Clb; Actvtr Clb; Deans Lst; Acdmc Schlrshp; Rgby 87; Amrcn Chrprctc Assoc; Clrd Chrprctrs Assoc; Intl Chrprctrs Assoc; Amrcn Chrprctc Sprts Cncl; AA 86; BS 90; BA; Blgy Chrprctc.

**LAWSON, SARA,** Colby Sawyer Coll, New London, NH; JR; BA; Erly Chldhd Clb 89-; Erly Chldhd Educ; Tch.

**LAWSON, SHANNON L,** Marshall University, Huntington, WV; GD; MAT; Afrcn Lit Assoc 87-88; Grad Asst HELP 90-; BA Univ Witwatersrand 88; Engl; Educ.

**LAWSON, SHERRY L,** Roane St Comm Coll, Harriman, TN; SO; BMAS; Hlthcr Financl Mgmt 85-89; E TN Users Grp 89-; Amer Bus Wmns Assn Treas 85-; ABWA Wmn Of The Yr; Amer Bus Wmns Assn; Cmbrlnd Med Cntr Dir/Data Syst.

**LAWSON, STACEY A,** Northeastern Univ, Boston, MA; SO; BA; Phys Ther Clb 89-; Dns Lst 89-; Hnrs Pgm 89-; Charles Irwin Travelli Schlrshp 89-90; Crew Tm 89-90; Phys Ther.**

**LAWSON, SUSIE J,** Northern Ky Univ, Highland Hts, KY; SO; BA; Biology Pre Physcl Thrpy; Physcl Thrpst.

**LAWSON, TAMMY S,** Garrett Comm Coll, Mchenry, MD; SO; AA; Mst Otsdng Wrk Study Awd; Soc Behvr Sci; Soc Wrk.

**LAWSON, TRACEY L,** Lincoln Univ, Lincoln Univ, PA; SR; Educ Clb Pres 89-90; Delta Sigma Theta Soc Actns Chrprsn 90; BS; Elem Educ; Prncpl.

**LAWTON, KAREN I,** Cumberland County Coll, Vineland, NJ; FR; Bus; Prsnnl Mgmnt.

**LAWVER, KIMBERLY D,** Univ Of Akron, Akron, OH; SR; MBA; Deans Lst 89; BA; Dnc; Instr.

**LAWWELL, TAMMY E,** Middle Tn St Univ, Murfreesboro, TN; JR; BS; Gamma Beta Phi 88-89; Kappa Delta Pi Secr 88-; Acad Schlrshp 88-; TN Tchr Trng Schlrshp 88-; Early Chldhd Ed; Tchr.

**LAWWILL, BEVERLY S,** Univ Of Cincinnati-Clrmnt Coll, Batavia, OH; SO; BS; Educ Clb; Deans Lst; Clermont Cost Excllnc Educ Fund; English; Teach Elem Educ.

**LAWYER II, ANDREW,** Fl St Univ, Tallahassee, FL; SR; BS; Mrchng Bnd 87-90; NSBE 88-90; Prsdntl Schlr Assn 87-89; Prsdntl Mrt Schlr 87-; IM Bsktbl Blrds 88-90; Elctrcl Engnrng; Engnrng.

**LAWYER, RENEE M,** Columbia Greene Comm Coll, Hudson, NY; SO; BA; Phi Theta Kappa 90-; Bskbtll; Sccr; Sftbll Capt 89-; Assoc; Math Sci; Eng.

**LAY, BEVERLY F,** Middle Ga Coll, Cochran, GA; SO; BSN; Golden Key; Easter Star; Nrsng; BSN/MA In Nrsng.

**LAY JR, HAROLD A,** Roane St Comm Coll, Harriman, TN; SO; AS; Gamma Beta Phi TN State Sec 90-; Literary Club Ast Edtr 90-; Campus Nwspr; Cmptr Sci; Cmptr Prgrmng.**

**LAY II, JAMES F,** Fayetteville St Univ, Fayetteville, NC; SO; BA; Fytvl Pol Dpt Vol Aux Offcr; Sprts Ctr Trvlng Rcqtbl Tm Co-Capt 88-; Cmbrlnd Cnty Schl Bus Drvr 90-; Pol Intrn Fytvl Pol Dpt; Pol Sci/Law.

**LAY, LARRY TRAVIS,** Univ Of Ky, Lexington, KY; JR; BARCH; AIAS 88-; Golden Key 90-; Tau Sigma Delta; Lyndon B Johnson Cong Intrnshp 87; Govs Cntr Excllnc Rsrch Fllow Univ TN 87; Pr Lb Tech Univ KY Ntrtn/Fd Sci 87-; BS Cumberland Clg Williamsburg KY 87; Architecture.

**LAY, ROBERT T,** Union Univ, Jackson, TN; JR; BS; Alpha Chi; Kappa Mu Epsilon; AS Jcksn St Comm Coll 75; Mathmtcs; Tch Sec Ed.

**LAYDEN, LISA D,** Marshall University, Huntington, WV; JR; BBA; Amer Mrktng Assoc Activities Co-Chrprsn 90; Deans Lst 88; Prt Tme Wrk Wth Summit Corp Assoc At Scribbles 668 89; Mrktng; Mrktng Mngmnt Buying.

**LAYELL, KIMBERLY I,** Va Commonwealth Univ, Richmond, VA; FR; MA; Lddr Success 90-; Univ Bnd; Hnvr Comm Bnd; Lbrty Christn; Bpst Stu Unions; Yth Grp Nw Stu Orntn; Intr Var Christian Flwshp; Phi Eta Sigma; Hnvr Comm Bnd 87-; Lbrty Chrstn Yth Grp 87-; Math; Educ.

**LAYER, DEBORAH L,** Christopher Newport Coll, Newport News, VA; JR; BA; Alpha Delta Pi Socl Chmn 85-88; Dir Ext Care Prog Waslingham Acad 90-; Asst Buyer 88-89; BS Longwood Colg 88; Elem Edctn.

**LAYFIELD, AMY G,** Wv Univ At Parkersburg, Parkersburg, WV; FR; BS; Bus Admin; Fnncl Mgr.

**LAYMAN, JACQUELINE R,** Radford Univ, Radford, VA; JR; BS; Early Educ.

**LAYMON, CONSTANCE A,** Schenectady County Comm Coll, Schenectady, NY; SO; BA; Engl; Law.

**LAYNE, KRISTI L,** Oh Univ, Athens, OH; SO; BA; Marching Band 89; Wind Symphony 89; Band 89; Music Educ Natl Confer Hstrn 89-91; Tau Beta Sigma 89; Sigma Alpha Tota; Dns Lst; Physics; Tch.

**LAYNE, LISA W,** Bridgewater Coll, Bridgewater, VA; JR; BS; Bapt Stdnt Union 88-; Oratorio Choir 89-; Dns Lst 90-; Coll Swtchbd Oper 90-; Coll Pool Rm Attndnt 90-; Bus; Acctnt.

**LAYNE, MELISSA D,** Chattanooga St Tech Comm Coll, Chattanooga, TN; SO; BS; Phi Theta Kappa 89-90; Edctrs Clb 89-90; Elem Educ; Tchr.**

**LAYNE, PAUL J,** Univ Of Miami, Coral Gables, FL; SR; JD; Rdio Dsc Jcky Nwscstr 90-; Mtrpls Nws Stf Wrtr; Phi Kappa Phi 90-; Beta Gamma Sigma 90-; Phi Theta Kappa Pres 87-; Jms W Mclmr Cntr Absd Chldrn 88-89; Nrctcs Unit St Attrnys Offc Law Clrk 90; Otstndng Grdtng Sr; Hnrs Prgrm Schlrshp; Ecnmcs/Bsns Admin; Law.

**LAYNE, TANYA S,** City Univ Of Ny Baruch Coll, New York, NY; JR; Flynn Book Scty VP 88-90; SGA Upper Cncl; Beta Gamma Sigma; Acctng; Law.

**LAYOG, MARIA LEONORA R,** Mobile Coll, Mobile, AL; GD; MBA; Intrntl Stdnts Org Rep 90-; Hnr Scty 82-86; Arthur Andersen Co; BSCS De La Salle Univ Manila Philippines 86; Bus/Cmptr Sci.

**LAYTON, JENNIFER M,** Livingston Univ, Livingston, AL; SR; Delta Durlins 90-; RA 88-; Tau Kappa Epsilon Lil Sis 87-88; Alpha Sigma Tau Sec 88-; L U Envoy 90-; IM 90; BS; Soc Wrk; History.

**LAYTON, LISA D,** Univ Of Al At Birmingham, Birmingham, AL; GD; BS; Cyttchnlgy Hsttchnlgy; Med.

**LAYTON, ROBYN M,** Livingston Univ, Livingston, AL; FR; Envoy.

**LAYTON, SHERYLL K,** Saint Francis Coll, Loretto, PA; SR; BS; Invstmnt Clb; Hnr Scty; Wll St Jrnl Stdnt Achvmnt Awrd; Delta Epsilon Sigma; Grad Summa Cum Laude; ASB 88; Bus Admn.

**LAYTON, SUSAN L,** Univ Of South Al, Mobile, AL; JR; BED; Southern Little League Brd Dir Chrmn 89-90; Elem Educ; Teaching.

**LAZA, DAYANA,** Fl International Univ, Miami, FL; FR; MBA; Phi Sigma Sigma Sprt Chr 90-; Crmnlgy; Law.

**LAZAR, SEAN W,** Comm Coll Algny Co Algny Cmps, Pittsburgh, PA; FR; RN; Anl 4 July Fstvl Comm; Dns Lst; Rdlgy Tech; RT R Presby Hosp Schl Rdlgc Tech 90; Sci; RN.

**LAZARIDES, ANASTASSIS A,** City Univ Of Ny City Coll, New York, NY; SR; IEEE; Tau Beta Pi Assn; Eta Kappa Nu Assn; Golden Key; Natl Engr; Dns Lst 90.**

**LAZARTO, FRANK R,** City Univ Of Ny Baruch Coll, New York, NY; JR; BBA; Corp Fnce.

**LAZEAR, LORI J,** Longwood Coll, Farmville, VA; SO; BA; Std Ed Asc Pblcty 89-; Alpha Phi Omega Chr 90-; Emrgng Ldr Awd 89-90; Invlmnt/Ldrshp Actv Awd 89-90; Cthrn Mrrwthr Sct/Paul Douglas Schlp 89-; Eqstrn Tm 89-; Elem Ed.

**LAZELLE, ALICIA ANN,** Northern Ky Univ, Highland Hts, KY; JR; BA; Hmn Srvc Clb 90-; Delta Zeta VP 87-; Yth Sccr Cch 88-; Spcl Olympcs 90-; Chldrns Hsptl Intrn 89-90; Hgh Schl Sccr Cch Intrn 90; IM Indr Sccr; AS Nrthrn Kntcky Univ 90; Hmn Srvc; Mntl Hlth; Wrk Wth Chldrn.

**LAZENBY, RITA Y,** Atlantic Comm Coll, Mays Landing, NJ; SO; ASSOC; Deans Lst 90; Nrsg; Pediatrics.

**LAZENBY, TAWANNA M,** Middle Tn St Univ, Murfreesboro, TN; SR; BBA; Drll Tm Spply Srgnt 90-; Rcrdng Indstry Mgmt; Mrktng.

**LAZO, ALFREDO,** Fl St Univ, Tallahassee, FL; SR; BA; Gldn Ky; Dns Lst 90; Pol Sci; Law.

**LAZORE, LISA C,** Saint Francis Coll, Loretto, PA; FR; BS; Math; Sec Educ.

**LAZORICK, CHARLENE M,** Temple Univ, Philadelphia, PA; JR; BA; Assn Stdtns Phrmcy 90-; Orientation Ldr 89-; Res Hall Senate 89-90; Newman Clb 89-90; Phrmcy.

**LAZZARO, ANDREW S,** Univ Of Miami, Coral Gables, FL; SO; BS; Crew Team Novice Capt 89-90; Res Asst 90-; Pres 100 Assn; Alpha Lambda Delta 89-90; Phi Eta Sigma 89-90; Alpha Epsilon Delta 89-; Anthrplgy.

**LE BAR, AIMEE L,** S U N Y Coll At Fredonia, Fredonia, NY; SO; BA; Math Clb 89-90; IM Bsktbl 89-90; Tutor; Pi Mu Epsilon; Tchg Asst; Math; Tchg.

**LE BAR, MICHELLE M,** S U N Y Coll At Fredonia, Fredonia, NY; SR; BS; Tchr Edn Clb 88-90; Tutor 88-90; Kappa Delta Pi 90-; Soph Edn Awd 89; IM Bsktbl 90; Elem Edn; Tchr.

**LE BARON, CAROL H,** Univ Of North Fl, Jacksonville, FL; SO; BA; Alpha Sigma Pi; Pilot Clb Of Jcksnvlle Pres 80; Cmpfre Of NE FL Pres 79; Acctng; CPA.

**LE BARON, PAIGE E,** Ms St Univ, Miss State, MS; FR; BS; Bapt Stdnt Union 90-; Gamma Beta Phi; Phi Eta Sigma; Med Tech.

**LE BEAU, CAROLE M,** Univ Of Akron, Akron, OH; JR; BA; Mjr Events 89-90; Hall Govt Rep 89-90; Humn Deveplt/Lrng Small Grp Ldr 90-; Comprehensive Social Studies; Tchng.

**LE BLANC, CATHERINE ANNE,** Ny Univ, New York, NY; SR; MA; Mntr Prog 87-; Deans Lst 87-; Natl Hon Soc 87-; Alpha Sigma Lambda 87-; Intrnshp Covnant House 90; Trtl Bay Assn Vol 88-; Chld Care Wrkr; AA Amer Acdmy Drmtc Arts 84; Psychlgy; Chld Psychlgst.

**LE BLANC, DARYL L,** Univ Of Miami, Coral Gables, FL; JR; BARCH; IM Ftbl 87; IM 3 On 3 Bsktbl 87-88; Archtctr.

**LE BLANC, JENNIFER E,** Lasell Coll, Newton, MA; SR; BA; Tchng Intrnshp W/Infants/Preschlrs 90-; Hnrs 90; High Hnrs 90; Vlybl 89; Sftbl 90; AS; Early Chldhd Educ; Infnt Tchr.

**LE BLANC, LISA M,** Western New England Coll, Springfield, MA; JR; BS; AS Asnuntuck Comm Clg 90; Acctg; CPA.

**LE BLANC, REE M,** Hampton Univ, Hampton, VA; JR; BA; CA Pre-Almni Pres 89-; Pre-Almni Cncl VP 90-; Stdnt Rcrtmnt Team 90-; Psi Chi 90-; Alpha Kappa Mu 90-; Psychlgy; Cnslng Psychlgy.

**LE BOULCH, THIERRY R,** Strayer Coll, Washington, DC; SO; BA; Deans List 90; Pres List 90-; Bus; Civil Engrng.

**LE BOVITCH, ROBERT,** Ny Univ, New York, NY; FR; BA; Biology; Med.

**LE BRUN, CLAIRE M,** Fl International Univ, Miami, FL; GD; MPH; Publ Hlth Stdnt Alumni Assoc 89-; ADA; Reg Dietitian; BS Univ FL 86; Hlth Prom3; Reg Dietitian.

**LE CLAIR, CHRISTINE MAY,** Univ Of Nh Plymouth St Coll, Plymouth, NH; SR; BS; Ntl Assoc Acctnts Tres 89-90; Phi Kappa Phi 90-; Gov Success Grnt 88; Awrd Cntrbtn NAA 89-90; Acctg; CPA.

**LE COINTE, DONNA A,** Lincoln Univ, Lincoln Univ, PA; GD; Acctng Clb Pres 89-90; Intl Clb; Acctg Ttr; W W Smith Schlrshp Ldrshp Awd; BS Lincoln Univ; Acctg; Pblc Acctnt.**

**LE COLE MILLER, TASHA,** Jackson St Univ, Jackson, MS; FR; Alpha Lambda Delta 90-; Math; Acctng.

**LE CUYER, MONIQUE A,** Hudson Valley Comm Coll, Troy, NY; SO; BS; Acctg.

**LE DOUX, BRANDIE J,** Emmanuel Coll Schl Chrstn Min, Franklin Sprg, GA; SR; Chrstn Srv Org 88-; Almn Assn 89-; Rebecca Clark Schrlshp 89-90; Bill De Lay Schlrshp 89-90; W G Drum Awd 90-; Asst Pstr/Msc Dir Elberton Pntcstl Hlns Chrch 89-; AA Emmanel Clge 89; Rlgn; Pstrl Mnstry Fld.

**LE DUC, CHARLES M,** Me Maritime Academy, Castine, ME; FR; BA; Pwr Eng; Eng.

**LE FILES, JEFFREY H,** Univ Of West Fl, Pensacola, FL; JR; BS; IEEE; Eagle Sct Boy Scts Amer 81; Dstngshd Grad Tctcl Stllt 88; Mcrwv Rpr US Army; AA Pensacola Jr Coll 86; Elect Eng; Eng.

**LE GARDYE, TIANNA J,** Wilberforce Univ, Wilberforce, OH; SO; Alpha Angls Soc Clb Sec 90-; Ldies Of Crt VP 90-; Campus Radio DJ 90-; Sigma Omega VP; O Walker Schlrshp; Cmnctns; Jrnlst.

**LE GRETT, MARK A,** S U N Y At Buffalo, Buffalo, NY; SR; BS; IIE 89-; ASQC 90-; SME 90-; Harrison Div Gen Mtrs Ergnmcs/Hmn Prod Intrn 90-; Welch Allyn Inc Indst Div 90; Med Div 89; Ind Engr; Manuf Engr.

**LE JEUNE, KEITH E,** Univ Of Pittsburgh, Pittsburgh, PA; FR; BA; E Township Athltc Assn 82-; Natl Hnr Scty 90; Rtrn Clb Stdnt Of The Mnth 90; Sci; Eng.

**LE MAIRE, MARK DOUGLAS,** Broward Comm Coll, Ft Lauderdale, FL; FR; BA; Phi Theta Kappa; Pres Lst; Thlgy; Chrch Mnstrs.

**LE MASTERS, LARRY E,** Univ Of Nc At Asheville, Asheville, NC; JR; BA; Future Wrtrs Assoc 90; Cntrbtng Poet Schl Papr 90; Theta Chi; Big Bro; Article Poet Mag; Tennis 90; Licnsed By NC Pri Prtctve Serv 90; Law Schl Then Career As Attrny/Athr; Paralegal Cert Denver Paralegal Inst 84; Lit; Law/Wrtng.

**LE MAY, RICHARD J,** Newbury Coll, Brookline, MA; SR; PTA; BA Univ Lowell 89; Phy Thrpy.

**LE MENA, JOHN A,** Univ Of Miami, Coral Gables, FL; SR; BM; Yng Dmcrts 89-90; Stdnt Music Cncl 90-; AS Schenectady Cty Comm Clg 87; Music Ind/Media; Mba.

**LE MIRE, JANICE L,** Endicott Coll, Beverly, MA; SO; B; Hse Cncl Rogers Hall Pres 89-90; VP Stdnt Govt Sr Cls VP 90-; Edn Psychlgy; Teach Author.

**LE PAGE, EMILY K,** Hobart And William Smith Coll, Geneva, NY; FR; BA; Soccer Coach 90-; HS Soccer Clinic Tchr 90-; Sftbl Coach 90-; Big Sistr 90-; Soccer Coaches Award 90; JV Varsity Soccer 90; Soviet Studies/Spanish; Tch.

**LE PAGE, JOY E,** Univ Of Sc At Columbia, Columbia, SC; SO; BA; Mrchng Band 86; NCNB Ntnl Bank 87-88; First Svngs Bank 90-; AA Usc Sumter; Eng Lit; Tchng.

**LE PAGE, JOY E,** Univ Of Sc At Sumter, Sumter, SC; SO; BA; Mrchng Bnd 86; NCNB Ntl Bnk 87-88; 1st Svg Bnk 90-; Assoc Arts; Engl Lit; Tchr HS/COLL.

**LE PAGE, LISA M,** Western New England Coll, Springfield, MA; SR; Behavioral Social Science Ofc Off Campus Red 89-; Graduation Comm; Marketing Club 87-88; Deans List 90-; Vlntr Springfield Soup Kitchen; BA; Psychology/Bussiness; Personnel.

**LE PAGE, SHERI A,** Indiana Univ Of Pa, Indiana, PA; SO; BA; Provst Schlr; All Amer Schlr; Trck/Fld/Crs Cntry 89-; Educ; Spch Path.

**LE PONT-CHERRY, JEANNETTE L,** Greenville Tech Coll, Greenville, SC; FR; BS; Math/Chem/Sci; Chem Eng.

**LE ROY, DONNA K,** Central St Univ, Wilberforce, OH; SR; BS; NEA Dea Schl Nrs Assoc; Tchrs Asoc; Nrs 81-; RN 69; Hlth.

**LE ROY, TIFFANY M,** Al St Univ, Montgomery, AL; SO; Nwspr Feature/Ent Ed 90-; Hon Stdnt; Pol Sci; Law.

**LE STAGE, PAUL J,** Castleton St Coll, Castleton, VT; SR; BS; Assoc Ftns/Bus Clb VP 90-; AAHPERD 88-90; VAHPERD 90-; Hlth/Rcqut Clb Ftns Instr Itrn; Phys Educ.

**LE VARDI, LISA A,** Western New England Coll, Springfield, MA; SR; Pre Law Scty 90; Crmnl Jstce Clb BCC 88; Prbtn Intrn; BS; AS Berkshire Comm Coll 88; Crmnl Jstce Psych; Law.**

**LE VIEN, DOUGLAS A,** La Salle Univ, Philadelphia, PA; FR; Rsrv Offcr Trng Corps ROTC Rnk Corprl 90-; Comm Seventy Pltcl Wtchdg Grp 90-; Stdnt Pltcl Awrns Assn; Cvnnt Hse Sprt Grp Chrmn 90-; Hmls Soup Ktchn 90-; La Salle Superior Athlt Awd; Sons American Rvltn Awd; Bsbl Cntr Fldr; Pltcl Sci; Law.

**LE VINE, MARK A,** City Univ Of Ny Grad School, New York, NY; GD; MA; Amnsty Intrntl 87-; Amer Peace Now NY Strng Comm Lctr 88-; Phi Beta Kappa; Summa Cum Laude 90; Hons Rlg Pinhas Mem 90; Blumberg Awd 90; Acad Achiev Awd 90; BA Hunter Coll 90; Mdl Estrn Stds; Dplnry Cnflct Rsltn.

**LE, CHIBAO N,** Univ Of Nc At Charlotte, Charlotte, NC; JR; BS; OSA 89-90; Gldn Key; Phi Eta Sigma 89; Chmcl Engnrng.

**LE, HUY X P,** Ma Inst Of Tech, Cambridge, MA; FR; NBA; Vietnamese Stdnt Assn; Spec Olympic; Pi Lambda Phi Athl Chrmn; IM Soccer/Vlbl/Sftbl; Elctrcl Engr.

**LE, JACQUELINE Y,** Univ Of Rochester, Rochester, NY; JR; BS; Charles Drew Premed Soc Intrnshp Smr Pgm Chrmn; Vietnamese Stdnt Assoc VP 89-90; Canoe/Kayak Clb; Asstnts Med Vol Hosp 88-89; NIH Smr IM Rsrch Awd Pgm; Smr Rsrch Flwshp SURF Pgm 90; Mulecular Genetics; Med.

**LE, KHA VAN,** Broward Comm Coll, Ft Lauderdale, FL; SO; BS; Electrcl Engrng.

**LE, NGHIEM VAN,** Bunker Hill Comm Coll, Boston, MA.

**LE, QUAN,** Univ Of Miami, Coral Gables, FL; FR; BA; Vlby Bl Clb 89-; IM Ftbl/Vlbl/Bsktbl; Pr Cnslr 90-; Rsdnt Asst; Crmnl Jstc; Law.

**LE, TAM H,** Hillsborough Comm Coll, Tampa, FL; FR; BS; Chess Club; Flying Club; Phi Theta Kappa; American Red Cross; Chem/Bio; Med.

**LE, THANH T,** Va Commonwealth Univ, Richmond, VA; FR; Vtnms Std Asc 90-; Phi Eta Sigma 90-; Vlybl IMS 90-; Bio/Chem; Med.

**LE, THANH-HA M,** Georgetown Univ, Washington, DC; JR; BA; Vietnms Stdnt Assn; Frnch Clb; Intl Mgmt; Bus.

**LE, TRAM Q,** Memphis St Univ, Memphis, TN; FR; Phi Eta Sigma 90; Pre-Med.

**LE, TRUNG X,** Muhlenberg Coll, Allentown, PA; FR; BS; Deans Lst 90; Koehler Awd 90; I M Soccer Vybl 90; Biology.

**LE, TRUONGAN T,** Univ Of Southern Ms, Hattiesburg, MS; FR; BA; Bus; Acctg.

**LEA, DAWN E,** Va Commonwealth Univ, Richmond, VA; SR; BFA; Phi Sigma Kappa Aux 88-89; Art/Pantg Prnt; Art Tch.

**LEA, KAJ N,** Univ Of Fl, Gainesville, FL; JR; BA; FMA; Prelgl Hnrry Scty; Gldn Ky; Pblc Dfndrs Intrn 90; AA 90; Bus Fnnce Rl Est.

**LEA, MARY S,** Univ Of Tn At Martin, Martin, TN; SR; BS; Stdnt Govt 88-89; Soc Wrk V Pres/Pres 87-; Ord Of Omega 89-; Alpha Delta Mu 89-; Chi Omega V P 87-; Intrnshp Dept Human Serv; Soc Wrk.

**LEA III, ROBERT L,** Averett Coll, Danville, VA; SR; CERT; Alpha Chi 87-; Sigma Lambda Epsilon 90-; Natl Ed Assc 90-; Bethanie Evan Mission Haiti Inc Pres/Fndr 87-; BA 88; Scl Sci/Hstry/Ed; Tchr Scndry Scl Studies.

**LEA, YOLANDA R,** Saint Andrews Presbytrn Coll, Laurinburg, NC; FR; BS; Blck Unn 90-; CAOS 90-; Chrstn Srvce Orgnztn 90-; Biochem; Med Scntst.

**LEABO, KIM E,** Anne Arundel Comm Coll, Arnold, MD; SO; BA; Otstndng Stdnt Awrd 90-; Cmmrcl Arts.

**LEACH, ANGELA G,** Roane St Comm Coll, Harriman, TN; FR; BS; Talnt Roster Of Outstndng Minrty Cmnty Clg Grads; Bus; Acctng.

**LEACH, BETH A,** Marshall University, Huntington, WV; JR; BBA; MU Accntng Club 89-; WV Soc CPA 89-; Koinonia Chrstn Fllwshp 89-; Cmps Crusade Chrst 88-; Accntng; CPA.

**LEACH, MARCUS A,** Fl A & M Univ, Tallahassee, FL; FR; BS; Pre Phy Thrpy Clb 90-; Phi Eta Sigma Hnr Soc 90-; Phi Eta Sigma 90-; FAMU Sprts Med Stf; Pre Phy Thrpy; Sprts Med.

**LEACH, NEREYDA,** Kent St Univ Kent Cmps, Kent, OH; JR; Student Yr Trumull Campus 89-90; Parttime Packard Elec Div Gen Motors 86-; AAB Kent State Univ 90; Acctng.

**LEACH, SHANNON K,** Univ Of Ky, Lexington, KY; JR; BA; Phi Eta Sigma; Gold Key; Psi Chi; Alpha Epsilon Delta; Psychlgy Res Asst; Psychlgy/Pre Med.

**LEACHMAN, MICHELLE R,** Faulkner St Jr Coll, Bay Minette, AL; SO; BA; Pow Wow Ldrshp Soc 88-90; Phi Theta Kappa 88-90; Sftbl/Bsktbl 88-90; Assoc 90; Psycl Thrpy; Psycl Thrpst.

**LEACHMAN, TAMARA S,** Wv Univ At Parkersburg, Parkersburg, WV; SO; AAS; Ofc Admin; Sec.

**LEADBETTER, FREDERICK E,** Univ Of Tn At Martin, Martin, TN; JR; Hrtcltr Clb 88-90; Amer Assn Actnts 90-; Chldrn Amer Rvltn Pres 90-; Epscpl Coll Flwshp 89-; Bus; Actnt.

**LEADER, BARBARA B,** Va Commonwealth Univ, Richmond, VA; SR; BFA; MCV Brd Wrks Paper Exhbtn 90; Andrsn Gllry Jrd Stdnt Show; Sr Exhbtn; BA Mrcr Unvrsty 85; Painting Prntmkng.

**LEADER, ERIC M J,** Life Coll, Marietta, GA; FR; DC; Jvnl Hcky 87-88; Almn Entrnc Schlrshp 86-87; Sci/Chem Univ Winnipeg 90; Chrprctc.

**LEADER, WALLACE G,** Univ Of Ky, Lexington, KY; GD; PHARM; Phi Kappa Phi 86-; Rho Chi 85-; Phi Eta Sigma 83-; Smith/Kline/Frnch Clncl Pharm Awd 86; ASHP 90-; KSHP 90-; BS NE LA U 86; Pharm Acdma/Rsrch.

**LEADHOLM, RONDA J,** Univ Of Fl, Gainesville, FL; SR; Deans Lst Smnle Cmmnty Clg 87-88; Shnds Tchng Hosp Med Tchnlgst Schlrshp 90; Sandra L Bullock Outstndng Sr Awd; AA Smnle Cmmnty Clg 88; BHS-MT; Med Lab Sci; Med Tchnlgst.

**LEADINGHAM, D PAT,** Union Coll, Barbourville, KY; FR; Bsbl Tm; Deans Lst; Law Enfrcmnt/Invstgtns; FBI.

**LEAF, ELLEN H,** Oh Univ, Athens, OH; SR; BA; Fred Waring US Chorus 86-90; Studio Lirico Stdnt 90; Alpha Omicron Pi Pres Pldg Cls 88-89; Ramseyer Schlrshp Canton Civicopera 87; Opera Theatre 87-; Vcl Perf; Opera.

**LEAHEY, EILEEN M,** City Univ Of Ny Baruch Coll, New York, NY; JR; BBA; Accntng Soc 90-; Golden Key 90-; Pub Acctg; Accnt.

**LEAHY, KAREN PATRICIA,** Providence Coll, Providence, RI; SO; BS; Music Mnstry 89-90; Envrnmntl Clb Vol Serv Animals 90-; Yng Rpblcns Clb 89-; Vol Hosp Med Rcrds Off Summer Vol 90-; Ltrcy Vol 90-; Karate Clb; I M Sftbl 90-; Hlth Plcy/Mgmt Humanities Hlth Admn.

**LEAHY, MARY C,** Bunker Hill Comm Coll, Boston, MA; FR; BA; Audio Vsl Asstnt; Cmmnctns; Media Brdcstng.

**LEAIR, SUE L,** Cleveland Inst Of Art, Cleveland, OH; SR; BFA; Art Illstrtn; Illstrtn.**

**LEAK, ANDREW N D,** S U N Y Coll Of Tech At Canton, Canton, NY; SO; AAS; Stdnt Aid Tansprt 89-; Eng Sci Clb 90-; Phi Theta Kappa 90-; Eng.

**LEAK, HELENA F,** Claflin Coll, Orangeburg, SC; SO; ROTC 90-; Hrns Prgm 89-; John M Shuler Schlp 90; Engl; Educ.

**LEAK, JAMES G,** Saint Pauls Coll, Lawrenceville, VA; SO; Stdnt Govt Rep 90-; Non Dnmntnl Bible Stdy Grp VP 89-; Gspl Choir Chpln 89-90; Mass Media; Mgr.

**LEAK, TANYA CHRISTINA,** Univ Of Med & Dentistry Of Nj, Newark, NJ; SR; Educ Opp Fnd Pgm 89-; Chmpn Schlp Acad Exclnc; Cert; Rdgrphy; Tch.

**LEAKE, AMANDA E,** Union Univ, Jackson, TN; SO; BS; Coll Yrbk 89-90; BSU/FCA 89-90; Natl Hnr Socty 87-89; Rutledge Hnr Hstry Clb 90-; Alpha Tau Omega 90-; Key Clb 87-89; Lake Cnty High Schl Valedctrn 89; Math; H S Tchr.**

**LEAKE, ROBERT W,** Univ Of New Haven, West Haven, CT; JR; BA; Acctng Club 90-; Fincl Acctng; Bus Or Law.

**LEAKS, TRACEY D,** Jackson St Univ, Jackson, MS; FR; BA; Hons Clg 90-; Bus Admnstrtn; Bus/Ind/Govt.

**LEAL, ANDREA M,** Fl International Univ, Miami, FL; JR; BA; Aftr Schl House Vol 89-; Bnkg; AA Miami Dade Comm Clg 90; Elem Educ; Tchg.

**LEAL, MONICA B,** Univ Of Miami, Coral Gables, FL; JR; BS; Bowman Ashe Schlrshp 88-; WHFS FM Intrnshp; Moak Schlrshp 90-; Jrnlsm/Engl; Cmmnctns.

**LEAMON, CAREN A,** Elmira Coll, Elmira, NY; SO; BA; Dorm Cncl Treas 89-90; Big Events Comm 90-; Orntn; Phi Eta Sigma 90-; Hnr Schlr 89-; Iris Ldrshp Awd 89-; Untd Crbrl Plsy Vol; Speech/Hearing; Deaf Educ.

**LEAMON, LORI J,** Univ Of Tn At Knoxville, Knoxville, TN; SR; TSCPA Stdnt Mbr 90-; Natl Assoc Acctnts Stdnt Mbr 90-; Beta Alpha Psi 90-; Exec Undergrad Clb 90-; Tech Cert Pract Nrsg IN Voc Tech Clg 83; BSBA.

**LEANZA, ANTHONY T,** Columbus Coll Of Art & Design, Columbus, OH; SR; BA; US Fencing Assoc 90-; NRA 88-; Republican Natl Comm 89-; Art Dir Frank Lerner Assoc 86-89; ASSOC Art Inst Seattle 86; Advertising Dsgn; Law.

**LEAPHART II, MARION E,** Univ Of Sc At Columbia, Columbia, SC; SO; BS; Phi Eta Sigma 90-; Alpha Lambda Delta 90-; Hnrs Clg 89-; Deans List; Chemical Engrng.

**LEARD, LINDA E,** Univ Of Southern Ms, Hattiesburg, MS; JR; BSN; Stdnt Nrs Assn; Phi Theta Kappa 74-75; Psi Chi 76-77; Rsrch Asstshp Geolgy 84-86; AL Geologcl Soc 84-; Amer Assn Petrlm Geolgsts 85-88; Psychlgst 77-80; BA Psychlgy 77; BS Geolgy 84; Nrsng.

**LEARDI, MARYEILEEN M,** Immaculata Coll, Immaculata, PA; JR; BA; Mdrn Frgn Lang Asc Sec 88-; Educ Clb Sec Treas VP 88-; Orntn Cnslr; Sigma Delta Pi Treas 89-; Bsktbl 88; Spnsh/Frnch/Sec Ed; Tchr.

**LEARY, ANDREW W,** Providence Coll, Providence, RI; FR; BA; WDOM-FM Radio Wkly Sprtscsts/Hocky Gm Prodcr/Color Man For Bsbl Brdcsts 90-; Im Flag Ftbl 90-; Cmnctns/Ed/Jrnlsm/Law.

**LEARY, KAREN M,** Liberty Univ, Lynchburg, VA; JR; Stdnt Gvrnmnt Assn Sntr 89-90; Clg Rep Mmbr 88-; Rsdnt Asst; Alpha Lambda Delta 89-; Kappa Delta Pi 89-; Urbn Otrch 89-; Denas Lst 88-; Gvrnmnt; Pltcl Orgnztn.

**LEAS, MICHELLE T,** Elms Coll, Chicopee, MA; SO; BSN; SNA 89; Nrsng; OR Nrse Crtcl Care.

**LEAS, NOEL,** Marywood Coll, Scranton, PA; SR; BFA; Mmbr Hnrs Prgrm 87-; Delta Epsilon Sigma; Two Tchrs Chc Exhbtn 88-89; BA BFA Candidate Exhbtn; Art; Illstrtn Chldrns Bks.

**LEASURE, MARY L,** Hillsborough Comm Coll, Tampa, FL; FR; BS; Elem Tchr.

**LEASURE, TASHA R,** Jefferson Tech Coll, Steubenville, OH; SO; Acctg.**

**LEATHERMAN, BRAD E,** Kent St Univ Kent Cmps, Kent, OH; JR; BA; IFSEA Sec 90-; Delta Upsilon Rsh Chrmn 89-90; Pldg Educ 90-; Intrnshp Marinrs Inn Res Lnge Mgr Bev Cntrlr 90; Hilton Hd Island SC Asst Bev Mgr; Hosp Fd Serv Mgmt.

**LEATHERMAN, BRYAN D,** Ms St Univ, Miss State, MS; SO; BA; Cir K Intntl Serv Club Chptr Pres 90-; Sigma Chi Plede Trnr; Microbiology; Medl Schl.

**LEATHERWOOD, DALE P,** Coker Coll, Hartsville, SC; JR; BA; Jdcl Brd 90-; Tchr Candidate Intrvw Brd 88-91; Natl Hon Scty 85-88; Vrsty Bkstbl 88-; Chrstms April Pgm 89-; Intrnshp Sonoco Prod Co 89-90; Otstndng Bus Stdnt 90-; Deans List 88-; Mktg/Sls.

**LEAUMONT, ANN K,** Univ Of Southern Ms, Hattiesburg, MS; SO; BA; Stdnt Alum Assc 90-; Stdnt Body Sntr Rules Chr; Coll Rpblcns; Annualorg Edtr; Alpha Lambda Delta 89-; Phi Eta Sigma 89-; Lambda Sigma; Gamma Beta Phi; Delta Gamma Sprt Chr 89-; Top 5 Outstdng Fresh Wmn 89-90; Rush Cnslr90-; Pltcl Sci; Law.

**LEAVELLE JR, ANDREW G,** Volunteer St Comm Coll, Gallatin, TN; SO; AAS; Rtrd Mltry; Rdlgy; Tchncn.

**LEBATO, SHIRLEY BLACK,** Nova Univ, Ft Lauderdale, FL; GD; MBA; Scty Of Nva Hosp Prfssnls Sec 90-; AA Brandywine Coll Of Widener Univ 69; BS 90.

**LEBBY, KIMBERLY A,** Hampton Univ, Hampton, VA; JR; BA; Sclgy Clb 88-; Sclgy; Edctn.**

**LEBENA, ADRIAN,** Fl International Univ, Miami, FL; SR; BS; AA Miami Dade Community Coll 87; Elec Eng; Eng.

**LEBID, DAWN M,** Temple Univ, Philadelphia, PA; JR; BSN; Alpha Lambda Delta 89-; Gldn Ky 90-; Nrs Extrn Tmpl Univ Hosp; Nrsng; Med.

**LEBKICHER, ELIZA A,** Juniata Coll, Huntingdon, PA; SO; BA; Nill Set Math Clb 90-; Std Stds; Wmns Spprt Grp; Intshp Prbtn/Prl Offc Juniata Cty; Math Asst Math Cmptcy Exms; Thrtcl Math; Lawyer.

**LEBO, TODD W,** Liberty Univ, Lynchburg, VA; SR; BS; Liberty Mktng Assn Pres; Bus; Mktng.

**LEBRECK, DAWN M,** Colby Sawyer Coll, New London, NH; SR; BS; Ky Assn 89-90; Stdnt Athltc Trnr Hd 89-90; Intern Stdnt Athlc Trnr Harvd Univ 90-; Stdnt Athltc Trnr Yr Awd Hd SAT 89-90; 3x Reg X Intercoll Eqstrn Tm Champ 87-90; Co-Ntl Intercoll Eqstrn Crtr Tm Mbr 89-90; CSC Alpn Ski Tm 87-88; CSC Eqstrn Tm; Sprts Med/Athltc Trng; Physcl Thrpy.

**LEBRON NIEVES, GLORIA L,** Inter Amer Univ Pr San Juan, Hato Rey, PR; GD; Law Rvw Edtr 90-; Aa Univ Of PR 85; BA Univ PR 88; Cvl Law.

**LEBRON, CAROL J,** Caribbean Center For Adv Stds, San Juan, PR; GD; PHD; Scty Hmn Res Mgt St Ch VP; SHRM 90-; BA Univ Puerto Rico 88; Psy; Indtl/Orgtl Psychology.

**LEBRON, KAREN,** Univ Of Pr At Rio Piedras, Rio Piedras, PR; JR; BA; Gldn Key; Exclnc Prz NSF Mnrty Grad Flwshp 90; Frnch; Frnch Prfssr.

**LEBRON, MARIBEL,** Univ Of Pr At Rio Piedras, Rio Piedras, PR; JR; BA; Envrnmntl Sci Stdnt Assn Sec 90; Am Chem Assn State Grp; Pre-Med Stdnts Assn; Nat Sci; Med Doctor.

**LEBRON-SANGUINETTI, KARMEN E,** Univ Of Pr Cayey Univ Coll, Cayey, PR; JR; BBA; Acctg; CPA.

**LECAKES, CARRIE,** Dowling Coll, Oakdale Li, NY; SR; BA; Sigma Tau Delta Pres; Comm Anml Shltr Vol; Engl/Spnsh; Educ.

**LECHMAN, ERIC R,** Allegheny Coll, Meadville, PA; SR; BS; Rugby Clb 87-88; Delta Tau Delta 87; Alden Schlr 89-90; Bio; Biotchnlgy.

**LECHNER, WENDY S,** Indiana Univ Of Pa, Indiana, PA; JR; BS; Deans Lst; NSSLA; Crisis Intrvntn Cnslr; Spch Path/Audio; Therapist.

**LECIEJEWSKI, BRIGITTE,** Piedmont Comm Coll, Roxboro, NC; GD; AAS; Stdnt Gov Treas 90; Gama Beta Phi 89; Phi Beta Lambda VP 89-; AAS; Bus Cmptr Prgrmng.**

**LEDBETTER, MELISSA A,** Univ Of Ky, Lexington, KY; BA; Phi Eta Sigma 90-; Acctng.

**LEDBETTER, MELISSA ELAINE,** Univ Of Montevallo, Montevallo, AL; FR; BS; Elem/Erly Chldhd Edn; Teach.

**LEDFORD, BEVERLY E,** Catawba Valley Comm Coll, Hickory, NC; Acctg Clb 84-85; Gamma Beta Phi 90; N C Luth Hm Vol; AAS 84; AAS 85; Cert Bus Cmptr Progrmng 90.

**LEDFORD, D KEITH,** Univ Of Ky, Lexington, KY; SR; Delta Tau Delta 86-88; Deans List 90; REU Program In Aquatic Ecology 90; BA 90; Biology.

**LEDFORD JR, DENNIS E,** Northeast State Tech Comm Coll, Blountville, TN; SR; AAS; Diesel Mech; Welding; Heavy Truck Mtce.

**LEDFORD, KATHIA N,** Southeastern Coll Of Hlth Sci, N Miami Beach, FL; GD; BPHAR; Acad Stdnts Of Pharmacy 89-; Stdnt Govt 90-; Alpha Kappa Alpha; Intern Walgreens; BS U Of FL 88; Pharmacy.

**LEDFORD, LAURA E,** Georgetown Coll, Georgetown, KY; SO; BS; Maskrafters 90-; Fllwshp Chrtn Athlts 89-; Campus Crsd Chrst 89-; Phi Eta Sigma 89-90; Otstndg Band Membr 90-; KY All Cllgt Band 90-; Psychlgy.

**LEDFORD, MELISSA A,** Univ Of Nc At Greensboro, Greensboro, NC; JR; BS; Bptst Un Comm Membr 88-; SNCAE 89-; Hall Cncl Sec 88-; Alpha Lambda Delta 88-; Mrshls 90-; All Amer Schlr 90-; Coll Schlrs Of Amer 90-; Elem Ed; Tch.

**LEDFORD, MICHELLE E,** Niagara Univ, Niagara Univ, NY; SR; MS; Alpha Phi Sigma VP 89-; Metro Atlantic Ath Conf 90-; Grad Asst Indian Univ Of PA; Prison Literate Tutor Intrnshp 90-; NY State Attny Gen Intrnshp 89-90; Div I NCAA Swimming Schlrshp Capt 90-; BS; Crim Just; Admin.

**LEDFORD, RICHARD S,** Central Al Comm Coll, Alexander City, AL; FR; BA; Elect 85-; Math; Elect Eng.

**LEDFORD, TAMMY D,** Western Carolina Univ, Cullowhee, NC; SR; MSW; Socl Wrk Clb Pres 89-; Dns Stdnt Advsry Comm 90-; IM Sprts 88-90; Pi Gamma Mu 89-; Phi Alpha 90-; NASW 90-; BSW 90; Socl Wrk.**

**LEDFORD, TIFFANY L,** Sue Bennett Coll, London, KY; SO; AA; SGA Pres 90-; NEA Pres 90-; Jdcl Cncl Chrprn 90-; KEA 90-; Phonthon 90-; Wells Schlr Prog 89-; IM Tnns 90-; Engl; Tchr.

**LEDFORD, TRACY RENEE,** Mayland Comm Coll, Spruce Pine, NC; GD; BA; SGA 87-90; Natl Hnr Soc 87; Dns Lst 87-90; Cmptr Oper Assist 88-89; Bsn; Kennel Mgmt/MBA.

**LEDFORD, TRAVIS K,** Western Carolina Univ, Cullowhee, NC; FR; Lst Min Prdctns 90-; Fr Chem Awd; Pre Eng; Mech Eng.

**LEDOUX, JULIE A,** Univ Of New England, Biddeford, ME; JR; BS; Vars Vlybl Capt 88-; Vars Bsktbl 88-89; Life Sci Club 88-; Vars Sftbl Capt 89; Alpha Chi Pres 91; Tutor 89-; Stdnt Jdcl Brd 91-; RA Comm 90; IM Bsktbl 90; Med Bio; Med Schl.

**LEE, ADINA L,** Univ Of Ct, Storrs, CT; SO; BS; Art Cnsltnt; Ntrtnl Sci.

**LEE, AMY E,** Hudson Valley Comm Coll, Troy, NY; SR; BA; Mentr Prog; Samaritan Hosp Sch Nrsng; SGA VP; Samaritan Sch Of Nrsng VP; Grad With Acad Hons From Sam Hosp Sch Of Nrsg; AS Samaritan Hosp Sch Nrsng; Nrsg; Crtcl Cr Nrsg.

**LEE, ANA,** City Univ Of Ny Baruch Coll, New York, NY; SR; BBA; Baruch Schlr 87-; Deans Lst 87-; Fnc; Invstmtn/Fncl Anlyst.

**LEE, ANDREW,** Cornell Univ Statutory College, Ithaca, NY; FR; Chinese Stu Assn; Arista; Bus Mngmnt; Bus.

**LEE, ANDREW K,** Carnegie Mellon Univ, Pittsburgh, PA; SO; BA; AIESEC 90-; Vars Tnns MVP 89-; Dns Lst 90; Std Amb Hong Kong 88; Ecnmcs/Ind Mgmt; Ecnmst.

**LEE, ANDREW M,** Salem-Teikyo Univ, Salem, WV; FR; BS; Schl Paper Prod Mgr 90-; Radio 90-; Gamma Beta Phi 90-; Cmptr Sci/Math; Cmptr Prgrmr.

**LEE, ANN MARIE,** Saint Peters Coll, Jersey City, NJ; SO; BA; Edn Teach; Sci Tchr.**

**LEE, ANNE M,** Providence Coll, Providence, RI; JR; BA; The Coul Edtrl Ed; Stdnts For Gndr Eqlty VP; Pstrl Cncl-Soc Actns Comm; Nom Truman Schlrshp; Lbrl Arts Hnrs Scty; Ims; Pol Sci; Jrnlsm.

**LEE, BARBARA D,** Memphis St Univ, Memphis, TN; FR; BA; Natl Assoc Of Legal Assistants; TN Paralegal Assoc Second V P; CLA Natl Assoc Of Legal Assistants 89; Pol Science; Law.

**LEE, CARL,** Hillsborough Comm Coll, Tampa, FL; FR; BA; Cmptrs; Cmptr Eng.

**LEE, CECELIA E,** Waycross Coll, Waycross, GA; SO; BED; Phi Theta Kappa 90-; AS; Tchr Educ.

**LEE, CHA HWA,** City Univ Of Ny Bronx Comm Col, Bronx, NY; SO; BA; Chem Clb 89-; Phi Theta Kappa 90-; Dns Lst 89-; AAS; Indl Pharm.**

**LEE, CHIH-CHEN SOPHIA,** Oh Univ, Athens, OH; SO; BM; Music Therapy; Performer.

**LEE, CHOR J,** Franklin And Marshall Coll, Lancaster, PA; SO; BA; Wldnss Clb Rckclmbn Instr 90-; Mensa Intl 89; Hnrs Lst 90; Dean Lst; Yth Exec Cmmtt; Cntr Creative Cmmty Intern 87; Dana Intern 90-; IM Coor 90-; Vrsty Swmmng 90-; Natl Soc Pblc Accntnts; Mltry Serv Singapore 88-; JB 88; Accntng; Intl Bus.

**LEE, CHRISTINA E,** Memphis St Univ, Memphis, TN; FR; BFA; Art; Bk Illstrtn.

**LEE, CHRISTINE A,** City Univ Of Ny Baruch Coll, New York, NY; JR; BBA; Acctng Soc; Saks 5th Ave Intrnshp; Acctng; CPA.

**LEE, CHRISTINE D,** Duke Univ, Durham, NC; FR; BA; Schl Ppr Mgng Ed 89-90; Hbt Hmnty 90-; Grn Erth Gng 90-; Natl Hnr Scty; Hsop Vol 90-; Chester P Middlesworth Awrd Mnscrpt Rsrch Hnrbl Mntn; Engl Blgy; Med.

**LEE, CHRISTOPHER A,** Villanova Univ, Villanova, PA; FR; BA; Bsktbl Clb 90-; Mnstry Sngr 90-; Math; Tch/Wrtng.

**LEE III, CHRISTOPHER J,** Columbia Union Coll, Takoma Park, MD; FR; BS; Cls Ofcr Treas 90-; Stdnt Sen Comm Sen; Pre-Med Soc 90-; Phi Eta Sigma 90-; Alpha Sigma Beta 90-; Fed Jr Fllwshp Prog 90-; Crss Co Tnns 90-; Bsns; Med.

**LEE, CHRISTOPHER S,** Univ Of Sc At Columbia, Columbia, SC; SR; The Outsider Mgr 89-90; Worked 89-; Gamma Iota Sigma; Tau Kappa Epsilon Pledge 88-; Natl Yth Sports Pgm Lifegrd 90; Stdnt Rep At Risk/Insur Mngmnt Soc 90; IM Ftbl/Bsktbl/Sftbl 88-; Insur/Real Est.

**LEE, CHRISTOPHER YUNG LING,** Belmont Coll, Nashville, TN; SR; BS; Intl Stdnt Assoc Pres; Stdnt Phys Soc Sec; Campus Kaledscp; Blue Ky Gamma Beta Phi; Intl Stdnt Awd; Math/Phys; Engr.**

**LEE, CHRISTY L,** Univ Of Sc At Columbia, Columbia, SC; SO; BAIS; Erly Chldhd Educ; Tchng.

**LEE, CRANSTENIA M,** Claflin Coll, Orangeburg, SC; SR; BS; Biology Clb 87-88; Hnr Soc 87-90; Deans Lst 90-; Chmstry; Rsrch.

**LEE, DANA J,** Pellissippi St Tech Comm Coll, Knoxville, TN; SO; ASS; Student Govt Asst Secty 89; Phi Theta Kappa 90; Office Syst Techlgy; Word Proc.

**LEE, DANNY L,** Univ Of Rochester, Rochester, NY; JR; BS; SG Secy 89-90; Goler Hs Dorm Cncl SG 90-; Asian Amercn Assoc Secy 90; Delta Upsilon VP 89-; Photochem Ctr Intrnshp 90-; Chem Award 89; Svc Award 90; Physic; Tchng/Rsrch.

**LEE, DAPHNE P,** Va St Univ, Petersburg, VA; SO; BS; Bsns Admn; Comptrlr/Fin Mgmt.

**LEE, DATHY M,** Univ Of Southern Ms, Hattiesburg, MS; FR; Phi Eta Sigma; Nrsng.

**LEE, DAVID A,** Duquesne Univ, Pittsburgh, PA; GD; MA; Res Hl Assoc IUP 87-89; Ecnmcs Clb 87-89; Cum Laude MBA; Ordr Omega 88-; Phi Kappa Psi Sec 86-; Nw Stu Asst Ortn Pro 87-88; Grad Rsrch/Tchg Asstntshp 90-; Ecnmc Clb Ptsbrgh 90-; BA 89; Ecnmcs; Mgmt Trng.

**LEE, DEBORAH M,** Oh St Univ, Columbus, OH; FR; BS; Univ Hnr Scty 90; Alpha Epsilon Delta 90-; Hsptls Vol Prog; Biology; Pre-Med.

**LEE, DENNIS H,** Ny Univ, New York, NY; JR; DDS; ASDA 88-; Dns Lst 88-; Xsi Psi Phi 90-; BS Albright Coll 88; Dntstry.

**LEE, DESIREE M,** Univ Of Sc At Columbia, Columbia, SC; FR; MBA; Carolina Prgrm Un Cltrl Arts Contmpry Snds Comm Wmns Chr 90-; Deans Lst; Fncng Clb 90-; Library Science Infrmtn; Lbrn.

**LEE, DONNA D,** Georgetown Coll, Georgetown, KY; FR; Bapt Stdnt Un 90-.

**LEE, ELIZABETH M,** Dutchess Comm Coll, Poughkeepsie, NY; SO; MBA; BA Mt Saint Mary Coll 85; Bus Adm/Eng.

**LEE, EMILY J,** Northern Ky Univ, Highland Hts, KY; FR; BA; Nrsng; RN.

**LEE, FLORA MIULING,** City Univ Of Ny Baruch Coll, New York, NY; SR; BBA; Administrator 85-; AAS New York City Tech Clg 85-; Acctng.

**LEE, FUNG B,** City Univ Of Ny Baruch Coll, New York, NY; SR; Frgn Trde Scty 89-; Hng Kng Stdnts Assn 90-; BBA; Mrktng Advrtsng.

**LEE, GRACE Y,** Univ Of Pa, Philadelphia, PA; JR; BA; Cnsltnt 84-; Mktg/Mgmt; Bus.

**LEE, HA YOUNG,** Union Univ, Jackson, TN; SO; BS; Art/Computer Sci; Computer Art.

**LEE, HAZLE J,** Alcorn St Univ, Lorman, MS; SO; BA; Pol Soc Pre Law Clb 90-; Hnr Stu Org 89-; Pre Law.

**LEE, HO S,** Va Commonwealth Univ, Richmond, VA; GD; MD; AMA 89-90; AMSA 89-; Tau Beta Pi 83-85; Alpha Epsln Delta 83-85; Korean Asc VP 81-86; BA Univ VA 86; Med.

**LEE, HOOVER K,** Cumberland Coll, Williamsburg, KY; SR; BS; Bapt Stdnt Union Cncl 87-; Stdnt Admsns Stf 88-; Frshmn Orien Ldr 90-; J T Vallandingham Hnr Socty; Cmptr Info Systs; Chrstn Mnstry.

**LEE, JAE S,** Middle Tn St Univ, Murfreesboro, TN; JR; BS; Mthmtcl Orgnztn 89-; Intrntl Stdnt Orgnztn 89-; Pi Mu Epsilon 89-; Abstrct Algb Awd; Tommy Renolds Schlrshp 90-; Tom Vickery Prjct Awrd; 76 Cert Prtc Mstr Tech 88; Mathematics; Cmptr Related Mthmtcl Rsrch.

**LEE, JAMIE,** Drew Univ, Madison, NJ; FR; Cmps Ppr Nws Rprtr 90-; Engl Ttr 90-; Asn Stdnts Amrc Assoc Pblc Rltns 90-; Cmps Lit Mag 90-; DEAL 90- ; Lvng Cncl 90-; Cntr Scl Otrch 90-; Deans Lst 90-; Engl Econ; Pblshng Jrnlsm.

**LEE, JANET LOUISE,** Univ Of Sc At Columbia, Columbia, SC; SR; BS; Tau Beta Phi; Eta Kappa Nu; Prsdnts Lst; Elctrcl Engnr.

**LEE, JANET P,** Defiance Coll, Defiance, OH; FR; BA; Chld Psych.

**LEE, JEANNE E,** Valdosta St Coll, Valdosta, GA; JR; BS; ACS Stdnt Affiliate 90-; Blazer Girls; Chemistry; Harmacology.

**LEE, JENNIFER A,** Fl St Univ, Tallahassee, FL; JR; BS; Univ Advrtsng Clb VP Elect; Kappa Alpha Theta 88-; Fla Assn Brdcstrs Intrnshp; Media Comm; Brdcstng.

**LEE, JENNIFER A,** Bethel Coll, Mckenzie, TN; JR; BS; Bus Clb VP 89-; Psych Clb Sec 89-; Stu Govt 90-; Iota Alpha Omega Tres 88-; Tennis Tm 90-; Bus Admin; Mgmt.

**LEE, JENNIFER J,** Univ Of Ga, Athens, GA; SR; BSED; Army ROTC; Silver Stars Pres 87-; Stdnt Govt Univ Cncl 90-; Ldrshp UGA; Alpha Gamma Delta 88-; Cmnvrsty Big Sis Pgm 88-; Athens Tutor Pgm 88-; Army ROTC Superior Ct; Early Chldhd Edn.

**LEE, JOE,** City Univ Of Ny Baruch Coll, New York, NY; SR; BBA; Cmptr Socty 90-; Cmptr Info Systs.

**LEE JR, JOHN C,** Univ Of Me, Orono, ME; FR; BS; Stdnt Snte 90-; Bsn; Law.

**LEE, JOO H,** Coll Of William & Mary, Williamsburg, VA; FR; Impact Org Intervarsity Christian 90-; Flwshp Wm/Mary Chorus Korean Clb; Korean Christian Flwshp Hosp Vol; Reg Rec Sports Im Vlybl Ping-Pong Trnmnt 90-; Chem; Med.

**LEE, JOONG H,** Univ Of Southern Ms, Hattiesburg, MS; SO; Gamma Beta Phi 90-; Comp Sci; Pgmr.

**LEE, JOYCE M,** Alcorn St Univ, Lorman, MS; GD; Nrsng; Bsn.

**LEE, JULIE A,** Limestone Coll, Gaffney, SC; JR; BA; Pep Clb 88; Snte VP 90; Stdnt Govt Assn Treas; Coll Hnrs Prog 88-; Kappa Delta Kappa Treas 89-; Rsdnt Asst 90-; Ornttn Com 90-; Psych Cnslng; Psych.

**LEE, JULIE H,** Kent St Univ Kent Cmps, Kent, OH; FR; Sherri Jo Luft Mem Awd; Hnrs Clg Schlp 90-; Val Schlp 90-.

**LEE, KATHLEEN L,** Univ Of Sc At Columbia, Columbia, SC; SR; BA; Wrtrs Cir 90-; Sigma Tau Delta 90-; Devils Millhopper Edtrl Asst 90-; Terr Grdn Clb 89-; Augusta Geneological Soc; Engl; Wrtng Rsrch.

**LEE, KATHRYN S,** Savannah Coll Of Art & Design, Savannah, GA; JR; BFA; Jewelry Clb Sec 89-90; Tchrs Workshop Forum 90-; Jewelry Tutor 89-90; Painting; Jeweler.

**LEE, KATHY T,** Tougaloo Coll, Tougaloo, MS; FR; Bio; Medcn.

**LEE, KEIN C,** City Univ Of Ny Queensbrough, New York, NY; SO; BSC; Asn Clb 88-90; Tnns Vrsty 88-90; Lsr Fbr Optc Scty 90; Lsr Fbr Optcs Tchnlgy; Eng.

**LEE, KENLOY E,** Barry Univ, Miami, FL; SR; BA; Economics Clb; Marketing Clb; Intl Stdt Organ; Tourism Tour Organiz 88-; Soccer Team 87-; Finance; Bank Manager.

**LEE, KENNETH D,** Al St Univ, Montgomery, AL; SO; Hon Soc 90-; Ftbl Plyr 89-; Math; Eng.

**LEE, KENNETH J H,** Duke Univ, Durham, NC; FR; BA; Asian Stdnts Assoc 89-; Assoc Clg Entreprnrs 89-; Phi Eta Sigma 89-; Habitat Humanity 90-; Undergrad Admsns Intern 90; Intervars Chrstn Flwshp 89-; Cancer Drug Scrng Rsrch Asst 90; Microbio/Immunlgy Intern; Med.

**LEE, KIENTO,** City Univ Of Ny City Coll, New York, NY; GD; Chns Elect Eng Stdnt Assn Sec 89-90; Gldn Key 89-; BE Elect Eng.

**LEE, KIM E,** Univ Of Pittsburgh, Pittsburgh, PA; SR; Golden Key 88-89; Sigma Theta Tau 90-; Memorial Hosp Bedford Co 85-; Hm Nrsg Agncy; AD Mt Aloysius Jr Clge 85; BSN 90; Nrsg.

**LEE, KIMBERLY C,** Rust Coll, Holly Springs, MS; SO; BS; Crmsn Schlr Assc; MAE; NAACP; Delta Sigma Theta; Ldrshp Awds; Elem Educ; Edctr/Adminstrtr.

**LEE, KIMBERLY FOUNTAIN,** Univ Of Montevallo, Montevallo, AL; GD; MED; Delta Zeta 87-88; BS 90; Elem/Early Chldhd Ed; Tch.

**LEE, KIMBERLY W,** Troy St Univ At Dothan, Dothan, AL; SR; MS; Stdnt AL Ed Assn Sec 89-; AL Ed Assn 89-; Natl Ed Assn 89-; Comm Bnd 90; Dothan Hgh Schl Intrnshp; Nrthview Hgh Schl Intrnshp; BS Ed; AA G C Wallace St Comm Coll 89; Engl/Biolgy; Biolgst/Tchr.

**LEE, KRISTINA R,** Johnson Bible Coll, Knoxville, TN; JR; BS; Bible.**

**LEE, KYUNG MUK,** Univ Of North Fl, Jacksonville, FL; JR; BA; US Army FL Ntnl Grd 89-; US Army 71g Mdcl Admn Spclst; Schl Hnr Grad Acdmy Hlth Sci Ft Sam Houston TX Deans Lst 90 UNF 90-; Dmptr Sci; Engnrng.

**LEE, LANNOR,** City Univ Of Ny Baruch Coll, New York, NY; SR; BBA; Offc Tchnlgy/Admin.

**LEE, LAUREEN M,** Broward Comm Coll, Ft Lauderdale, FL; SO; AA; Campus Advnc; Phi Theta Kappa; Hnrs Inst 89-; Deans Lst 89; Pres Lst 90; Psychology; Neuropsy Rsrch.

**LEE, LAURI E,** City Univ Of Ny City Coll, New York, NY; JR; BA; Psych Stdnts Assoc 89-; Psy Chi 90-; Fllw Rep 89-; Clncl Psych/Prof.

**LEE, LILIA M,** Univ Of Med & Dentistry Of Nj, Newark, NJ; JR; BS; Intrntl Stdnts Assn Asst VP 89-90; Mem Yr Awrd Intrntl Stdnts 89-90; Swm Tm 88-90; Phys Ther.

**LEE, LINDA,** City Univ Of Ny Queensbrough, New York, NY; FR; AAS; Hrsng; Gntc Rsrch.

**LEE, LISA G,** Queens Coll, Charlotte, NC; SR; BA; Holiday Committee; Social Activities; Queens Clg Republicans Chrmn 89-90; NC Federation Clg Repblcns 89-90; Deans Lst; All Amer Schlr; Elem Educ.**

**LEE, LOREN G,** Univ Of Miami, Coral Gables, FL; JR; BARCH; Archtct.

**LEE, LORETTA S,** S U N Y At Binghamton, Binghamton, NY; FR; BS; Acctg; Bsn.

**LEE, LYDIA LURENE,** Univ Of Akron, Akron, OH; JR; B ED; Deans Lst 89-90; Mnr Care-Nrsng Cntr Vol 87-; Elmntry Ed/Psychlgy; Elmntry Tchr.

**LEE, MARK E,** Wallace St Comm Coll At Selma, Selma, AL; FR; Phi Theta Kappa 90-; Computer Sci; Mechncl Engrng.

**LEE, MARK V,** Averett Coll, Danville, VA; SR; BS; AS VA Wstrn Comm Clg 73; Hmn Rsrc Dvlpmnt.

**LEE, MARVIN H,** Univ Of Miami, Coral Gables, FL; JR; BS; Alumni Awd Painting; 12th Annual Lanes Film Fstvl Awd Docmntry; US Achvmnt Acad Natl Coll Archtctr Dsgn Awd 90; Motion Pictures; Motion Picture Prod.

**LEE, MELINDA J,** Roane St Comm Coll, Harriman, TN; SO; BFA; Art Comp Mrt Awd; Chrch Orgnst/Asst Pnst 80-; Sndy Schl Tchr 86-; Clng/Carpet Care Bsn; AS 75; LPN State Area Voc-Tech Schl 77; Grphc Dsgn/Art Ed.

**LEE, MICHAEL A,** Fl St Univ, Tallahassee, FL; JR; BA; Golden Key 90-; Engl Lit; Tchg/Wrtg.

**LEE, MICHAEL D,** Univ Of Sc At Columbia, Columbia, SC; SO; BA; Acdmc Tm Hstrn Nwspr Stff Edtr 87-89; Math Tm Gvrnrs Schl Schlr; Ntnl Hnr Soc 87-89; Phi Beta Capa 87-; Deans Lst; Walmart Schlrshp; Prsdnt Schlrshp; James F Byrns Sch; Chsn 1 Of 4 Stdnts Spnd Yr Englnd; Page At SC St House 89-90; Hstry; Career FBI.

**LEE JR, MICHAEL G,** Citadel Military Coll Of Sc, Charleston, SC; FR; Crew Team; Air Soc AFROTC; Bus Admin; Acctnt.

**LEE, MICHAEL J,** Ms St Univ, Miss State, MS; SR; BA; Poultry Sci Hnr Club; Pres List 90-; Deans List; IM Bsbl/Ftbl/Sftbl/Bskbl; Co-Op Mc Curty Farms; Poultry Sci.

**LEE, MICHELE S,** Univ Of Miami, Coral Gables, FL; JR; BS; Stdnt Govt Senate 88-89; Caribbean Stdnts Assn Exec Offcr 89-90; Alpha Lambda Delta; Goldn Key; RAMP Schlrshp Prog; Biolgy; Med.

**LEE, NICOLE D,** Fl A & M Univ, Tallahassee, FL; SR; BA; ASCE 90-; NAACP 89-; Fed Hwy Admn Intrnshp 90; Cvl Engr Tech.

**LEE, ON HUNG ANDREW,** Univ Of Louisville, Louisville, KY; SR; BEE; AM Intrntl Rltnshp Clb 88-; Bptst Union 88-; Phi Eta Sigma 88 Pi Mu Epsilon 89; Gldn Key; Elctcl Engr; Engrng.

**LEE, PATRICIA A,** Alcorn St Univ, Lorman, MS; FR; Biol; Chldrns Nurse.

**LEE, PATRICK A,** Middle Tn St Univ, Murfreesboro, TN; JR; BS; AS N VI Cmnty Clg 90; Rec Ind Mgmt; Msc Ind Prof.

**LEE, PEI-LUN,** Wagner Coll, Staten Island, NY; SR; BA; Choir; Arnold Rng Meml Awd 90; Music; Pianist.

**LEE, PEI-YEE,** Manhattan School Of Music, New York, NY; FR; Piano; Tchr.

**LEE, PENNY L,** Anson Comm Coll, Ansonville, NC; GD; SSA; Scl Srvcs; Psychlgst.

**LEE, PETER P,** Univ Of Miami, Coral Gables, FL; SO; BA; Edtrl Brd Campus Lit Mag 90; Intrcllgte Debate Tm 90; Speech Cmmnctn/Engl; Grad Schl Then Law.

**LEE, POHKHIONG,** Radford Univ, Radford, VA; JR; BBA; Fnce; Fncl Anlys.

**LEE, ROBERT R,** Air Force Inst Of Tech, Wrt-Ptrsn Afb, OH; MS; Sigma Iota Epsilon; Logistics Offcr USAF; BS Ariz State Univ 86; MS Troy State Univ 88; Logistics Mgmt; Bus Mgmt.

**LEE, ROBIN E,** Al A & M Univ, Normal, AL; JR; BA; Assoc Columbia Coll; Bus Admin; Prcrmnt Mgr.

**LEE, SANDRA F,** Univ Of Sc At Columbia, Columbia, SC; FR; BS; Alpha Lambda Delta Cncl; Phi Eta Sigma; Gamma Beta Phi; Engrg.

**LEE, SANDRA F,** Le Moyne Owen Coll, Memphis, TN; SO; BA; Engl.

**LEE, SANDRA I,** Marymount Manhattan Coll, New York, NY; SO; BFA; Dance Co 90; Dns Lst; BFA Dance Schlrshp 89-93; Dns Schlrshp 89-93; Orig Cst Prof Jazz/Mdrn Piece Urban Dnc 89; Danc Dept Stdnt Chrgrphr/Prfrmr; Dance.

**LEE, SAU M,** City Univ Of Ny Baruch Coll, New York, NY; SR; Beta Alpha Psi; Beta Gamma Sigma; Vol Incm Tx Asst; Acctng; CPA.

**LEE, SHANNON M,** Northern Ky Univ, Highland Hts, KY; SO; BA; Human Serv; Early Chldhd Dvlpmnt.

**LEE, SHARON P,** Univ Of Tn At Martin, Martin, TN; GD; BA; STEA Secy 88-89; Alpha Delta Pi 82-87; March Band Drum Maj 82-88; Beauty Pageant Coord 89-90; Engl Edctn; Instr.

**LEE, SHEILA M,** Univ Of Akron, Akron, OH; SR; BA; Cmps Focus Pres 90-; Gldn Key 89-; Dns Lst 88-; IM Ftbl/Water Polo/Vlybl; Elem Educ.

**LEE, SHIRLEY H,** Owensboro Jr Coll Of Bus, Owensboro, KY; GD; AS; SGA 90; Bapt Chrch Chr Tchr Sec; Med.

**LEE, SHIRLEY S,** City Univ Of Ny Baruch Coll, New York, NY; JR; BBA; Gldn Key 90-; Acctg; CPA.

**LEE, SONYA N,** Univ Of Southern Ms, Hattiesburg, MS; JR; BS; Natl Collgt Nrsng Awrd; Nrsng.

**LEE, SOUL,** Anne Arundel Comm Coll, Arnold, MD; FR; Intl Stu Clb; Gen Stu; Jrnlst.

**LEE, STACY R,** Gordon Coll, Barnesville, GA; JR; BS; Occuptnl Thrpy Clb 90-; Phi Theta Kappa 89-90; Acad Recog Awd 90; Summa Cum Laude 90; AA Psych 90; AS 90; Occup Thrpy.

**LEE, STEPHANIE C,** Univ Of Sc At Columbia, Columbia, SC; FR; BS; Ntl Soc Blck Eng Treas 90-; Camp Crscd Christ 90-; Emrgng Ldrs Clss; Alpha Lambda Delta; Cmnty Svc Comm; Eng Chem; Rsrch Sci.

**LEE, STEPHEN B,** Univ Of Tn At Martin, Martin, TN; SR; BA; Sigma Pi Pres 89-90; Outstndng Serv Stdnt Affrs 89; Bsbl 86; Elem Ed; Tch/Coach.

**LEE, SUSAN A,** Southeastern Coll Of Hlth Sci, N Miami Beach, FL; JR; Acad Stdnts Phrmcy Treas 90-; Rho Pi Phi Scribe 90-; Miami Chldrns Hosp Intern 90-; AA Miami Dade Comm Coll 88; Bio; Phrmcy.

**LEE, SUZANNE,** Univ Of Miami, Coral Gables, FL; JR; BS; Bptst Cmps Mnstry Pres; Gldn Key 90-; Phi Kappa Phi; Hnrs Stdnts Assc 88-; IM/SPORTS Fest 88-; Advrtsng Comm.

**LEE, TAMMY,** Tusculum Coll, Greeneville, TN; SO; BA; Alpha Chi; Alpha Chi Frshmn Awd 88-89; EH Sargent Sci Awd; Blgy; Medicine.

**LEE, THERESA,** Edinboro Univ Of Pa, Edinboro, PA; JR; BS/BA; Phi Eta Sgm; Physcs BS/MATH BA.

**LEE, TYLER P,** Piedmont Coll, Demorest, GA; SO; BS; Trustee Schlrshp; Bio; Med.

**LEE, TYRONE M,** Hampton Univ, Hampton, VA; FR; BA; Stdnt Mntrshp Pgm 90-; Mech Eng.

**LEE, VONCELLE L,** Tuskegee Univ, Tuskegee Inst, AL; SR; BA; AISS Treas 90-; NAACP 90-; SGA Dir; Alpha Kappa Mu 90-; Beta Kappa Chi 90-; Mcdnnll Dgls Corp 90; Mss AIAA 90-; Arspce Eng; Eng.

**LEE, WAI HON,** City Univ Of Ny City Coll, New York, NY; GD; MS; Am Soc Mech Eng 87-; Pi Tau Sigma; Tau Beta Pi; Gldn Ky; Cty Coll Flwshp 88-90; BEME Cty Coll NY; Mech Eng; Engrng.

**LEE, WAI MING,** City Univ Of Ny Baruch Coll, New York, NY; GD; MBA; Finc Econ Soc Sec 89-90; Money Fincl Inv Assn Tr 89-90; Acctg Soc 90; Beta Gamma Sigma 90; Goldn Key 89-90; Omicron Delta Epsilon 90; Baruch Clg Dns Lst 88-90; Barch Endwmnt Fnd Provsts Schlrshp 88-90; BBA 91; Acctg.

**LEE, WAI-SHAN,** City Univ Of Ny City Coll, New York, NY; SR; BS; Han Wave Std Asc 89-90; Chns Elec Engr Std Asc VP 89-; Hnrs Pgm 88-; Dns Lst 89-; Intl Std Schlp 89-; Intshps Asst Engr; Elec Engr.

**LEE, WANHSIN,** Gallaudet Univ, Washington, DC; SR; BS; Gymnastic Clb 86-89; Acctng Tutor 89; Dance Co 90; Internship Amtrak Hmn Resource Plng Affrmtv Actn; Natl Cllgt Minority Ldrshp; Bus Admin Acctng.

**LEE, WILLIAM BARRY,** Univ Of Ky, Lexington, KY; FR; BA; Flwshp Christian Athletes; Crusades Christ; Sigma Nu Pledge Treas; Deans Lst; Ftbl/Bsktbl/Sftbl IMS; Chem; Dntstry.

**LEE, WOO J,** Cornell Univ Statutory College, Ithaca, NY; SO; BA; Korean Soc 90-; Entrepreneurs Club 90-; Tchrs Asst For Statistics Cls; Soccer 89-90; Statistics/Math; Cnsltng/Actuarial Sci.

**LEE, YONGHWA,** City Univ Of Ny Queensbrough, New York, NY; SO; Korean Clb 90-; Bull Invstmnt Clb Pres 90-.

**LEECH, STEPHEN J,** Spartanburg Methodist Coll, Spartanburg, SC; FR; PHD; School Newspaper Writer 90; Best Short Story Literar Magazine Illusions; Var Soccer 90; English; Journalism.

**LEEDER, DONNA J,** Glassboro St Coll, Glassboro, NJ; SR; Crmnl Jstc Clb Tres 87-89; Alph Dlt Epsln; Arbcs; BA; AAS; Law/Jstc; Tchng.

**LEEDY, MARVIN R,** Radford Univ, Radford, VA; SR; BS; Res Life RA 88-90; Soc Sci; Tchr.

**LEEK, KRISTY A,** Memphis St Univ, Memphis, TN; SO; BSN; Optemist Youth Fndtn 89-; Marty Hart Mem Schlrshp 89-; Top 10 Pct Cls 90-; Sci; Nrsng.

**LEESMAN, ROBERT G,** Univ Of Cincinnati, Cincinnati, OH; FR; BA; Tau Alpha Pi; Gamma Alpha; Elect Engrng.

**LEFAVOUR, JAMES A,** Hudson Valley Comm Coll, Troy, NY; FR; Presidents Lst 89-; Genl Laborer Factory Work 85-89; Electrical Technlgy Elctrncs; Engrng.

**LEFELD, DENNIS V,** Wright St Univ Lake Cmps, Celina, OH; FR; MIS; Bsktbll; Bus; Mgmt.

**LEFEVER, STEVEN E,** Oh St Univ At Newark, Newark, OH; FR; BS; Chem; Pharm.

**LEFEVER-GARBER, CHANDA P,** Coll Of Charleston, Charleston, SC; FR; BED; Early Chldnd Dev Ctr Vol; Col Actvts Bd 90; Dstngshd Hnr Rl 90-; Elem Educ; Tchr.

**LEFEVRE, SEBASTIEN N A,** Savannah Coll Of Art & Design, Savannah, GA; FR; BA; Architecture.

**LEFFEL, CHRISTINE E,** Univ Of Akron, Akron, OH; SR; BS; Alpha Lambda Delta 87-88; Phi Eta Sigma 87-88; Kappa Delta Pi 90-; Summa Cum Laude; Numerous Schlrshps 87-; Elem Educ.

**LEFFEL, TAMRA J,** Kent St Univ Kent Cmps, Kent, OH; SR; BA; SHRM Pres 90-; Orientation 88; SG Allctns Dept; Delta Sigma Pi V P 88-; Mgmt; Hmn Res Exec.

**LEFFINGWELL, JONATHAN R,** Memphis St Univ, Memphis, TN; FR; BS; TN Brd Of Rgnts Schlrshp; IM Sprts.

**LEFFLER, DARLENE J,** Richard Bland Coll, Petersburg, VA; JR; BFA; Honor Ct Chrprsn 89-90; Stdnt Gov Assoc 89-90; Nwspr Editor 89-90; Alpha Beta Psi V Pres 89-90; Gamma Psi Ltl Sistr 89-90; Comm Serv Commttee 89-90; Leg Rules Comm 89-90; Entrtnmnt Comm 89-90; Campus Most Notbl 89-90; Theatre Arts; Educ.

**LEFLER, MARK T,** Univ Of Tn At Knoxville, Knoxville, TN; FR; CPA; Young Life; Bus; Law.

**LEFLORE, AMY E,** Ms St Univ, Miss State, MS; JR; BS; Band 87-88; Bio Engr Soc 90; SWE 90; Gamma Beta Phi 88; Delta Delta Delta Exec V P 87; Bio Engr.

**LEFTWICH, KEVIN N,** Univ Of Nc At Asheville, Asheville, NC; SR; MS; Sigma Xi Sci Rsrch Soc; Phi Theta Kappa 87; Envrnmntl Sci Dstnctn Awd; US Forest Serv; Natl Pk Serv; AAS Haywood Comm Coll 87; BS 1NCA; Blgy; Blgst.**

**LEGAGNEUR, PIERRE L,** City Univ Of Ny City Coll, New York, NY; SO; BS; Haitian Stdnt Assc; Haitian Eng Stdnt Assc; Comp Sci; Eng/Business.**

**LEGER, JUDITH,** City Univ Of Ny City Coll, New York, NY; SR; BS; Educ Clb 89-90; Tutored 88-90; Gymnstc Tm 87; Elem Educ; Teacher.

**LEGER, MC KANDY,** Fl International Univ, Miami, FL; JR; BPA; Invtnl Schlr 88-; Pblc Admn; Fdrl Govt.

**LEGERE, JEFFREY J,** Me Maritime Academy, Castine, ME; FR; BA; Var Bsktbl Tm 90; Eng.

**LEGG, JENNY L,** Memphis St Univ, Memphis, TN; SR; BED; Zeta Tau Alpha 87-90; Natl Cllgt Educ Awrd; Elem Educ; Tchr.

**LEGGETT, AIMEE MICHELE M,** Univ Of Tn At Knoxville, Knoxville, TN; SO; Zeta Tau Alpha Pldg Cls Chpln 89-90.

**LEGGETT, LEIGH A,** Memphis St Univ, Memphis, TN; SR; BS; Esprit Corps Stdnt/Alumni Bd VP 89-; Actvts Cncl 88-89; Hon Stdnt Assn 87; Gldn Key Pres 89-; Phi Kappa Phi 90-; Omicron Delta Kappa 90-; Phi Eta Sigma 87; Chi Beta Phi Sec 88-; Phi Kappa Phi Schlrshp 90; Outstndg Stdnt; Comp Sci; Cnsltnt.

**LEGGETT, MATTHEW D,** Columbia Greene Comm Coll, Hudson, NY; SO; BA; Who Who Coll Stdnts 89-; AA; Psychlgcl Cnslng; Drg Cnslr Prbtn Offcr.

**LEGGIN, PATRICIA,** Coll Misericordia, Dallas, PA; SR; OD; Biolgcl Soc Pub 90-; Almni Assn Hon; Delta Epsilon Sigma; Kappa Gamma Pi; Grad Hon Soc; Campus Mnstry 90-; Tutrl Serv 90-; Dr Petrychenko Awrd Biolgy; Vldctrn Awrd; BS Coll Misericordia; Optmtry.

**LEGNARO, ILARIA M,** Univ Of Miami, Coral Gables, FL; JR; BA; Finance Clb 90-; Prsdnt 100 Intrntnl 90-; Mntr Prgrm 90-; Intrntnl Finance Mrktng; Finance.

**LEGOTT, ELIZABETH J,** Niagara Univ, Niagara Univ, NY; FR; BA; NUTHRA 90-; Rest Mgmt.

**LEGREE, KEILA M,** Univ Of Sc At Columbia, Columbia, SC; SO; BA; Stdnt Govt Dir Of Inst Affrs 90; Alumni Assoc 90; Assoc Of Hnrs Stdnt 90; Alpha Lambda Delta; Gamma Beta Phi; Phi Eta Sigma; Mnrty Assist Peer Prog 90; Pres Endwmnt Intrn SCETV; Stdnt Assist; Engl; Law.

**LEGROS, RICHARD L,** Indiana Univ Of Pa, Indiana, PA; JR; BED; Asst Hgh Schl Grls Vlybl Coach; Elem Ed; Tchng/Coaching.

**LEGUIZAMO, JORGE P,** Le Moyne Coll, Syracuse, NY; SR; MD; Vrsty Clb Crdntr 90-; Blgy Clb 87-; Hmn Srvcs Assoc 89-; Tri Beta Treas 88-; Ppl Actn 89-; Deans Lst 88-; Vrsty Tnns Tm Capt 87-; Blgy; Med.

**LEGUIZAMON, WENDY S,** Fl International Univ, Miami, FL; FR; BA; Elem Edn; Tchr.

**LEHMAN, ANGELA L,** S U N Y At Buffalo, Buffalo, NY; FR; DDS; DSA Stdnt Govt Rep 90-; Hmn Serv Assn Treas 89-90; Beta Beta Beta 88-; BS Blgy Lemoyne Coll; Dntstry.

**LEHMAN, APRIL E,** Lebanon Valley Coll, Annville, PA; FR; BS; Newspr Rep 90-; Delta Tau Chi; Pres Ldrshp Award 90-; Math; Tchng.

**LEHMAN, DEBORAH M,** Univ Of Akron, Akron, OH; SR; BED; Akron Cncl Edn Stdnts; Alpha Lambda Delta; Kappa Delta Pi; Elem Edn; Teach.

**LEHMAN, DIANE M,** Fl Atlantic Univ, Boca Raton, FL; JR; BA; Fnce; Law.

**LEHMAN JR, HAROLD HANS,** Daytona Beach Comm Coll, Daytona Beach, FL; FR; BA; Raquetbl 90-; Pres Lst 90; Raqtbll 90-; Pol Sci; Law Enfrcmnt/Publ Admin.

**LEHMAN, JEFFREY D,** Bowling Green St Univ, Bowling Green, OH; SO; BED; Sprt Mgmt Alnc 89-; Alph Lmbd Dlt 90-; Phi Eta Sgm 90-; Sprt Mgmt; Dathltc Admnstrtn.

**LEHMAN, LYNN M,** Converse Coll, Spartanburg, SC; FR; Alpha Lamba Delta.

**LEHMAN, MOLLY P,** Coll Misericordia, Dallas, PA; JR; BS; Pa Inst Of CPA'S; Acctng Club Sec 88-; Hnrs Prog 88-; Independent Study In Gvmntl Auditing; Acctng; CPA.**

**LEHMAN, THOMAS K,** Villanova Univ, Villanova, PA; FR; BA; Football; Communications/Psychology; Sports Mgmt.

**LEHMANN, MARGARET J,** George Mason Univ, Fairfax, VA; SR; BA; Stdnt Educ Assn 89-; Erly Elem Educ; Tchr.

**LEHMANN, PATRICIA A,** Univ Of Akron, Akron, OH; SR; BS; Natl Assn Acctg 89-; Gldn Key 87-; Alpha Lambda Delta 87-; Phi Eta Sigma 87-; Beta Gamma Sigma 89-; Pres Schlr 87-; Dns Lst 87-; Acctg; Ind Acctg.

**LEHNEMAN, PAMELA J,** Bay Path Coll, Longmeadow, MA; SO; Karate 89-90; Sftbl 89; Interior Dsgn.

**LEHNER, JASON R,** Cornell Univ Statutory College, Ithaca, NY; SR; BS; Phi Sigma Kappa Treas 89-; Rcvd Hellinger Awd From Cornell Univ Prsnl Entrprs Prog; Rsrch Intrn US Securities/Exch Comm 90; Bus Mgmt; Law.

**LEHNERT, BARBARA C,** Spalding Univ, Louisville, KY; SR; BS; Ntl Ed Assoc 89; La Assoc On Chldrn Undr 6 Stdnt Rep 90; Delta Epsilon Sigma Delta Iota Chptr Pres; Ky Ctr Of Arts Vol Organ 90; AAS 89; Free Lance Erly Chldhd Cnsltnt Wrtr Trnr; Ed; Tchr.

**LEHNERT, JENNIFER LYNN,** Univ Of Sc At Columbia, Columbia, SC; SO; PHARM; Baker Rsdnt Hl Govt Vp 90-; Gamma Beta Phi 90-; Nesbit Memrl Hsp Phrmcy Intrn; Deans Lst 89-; Clncl Phrm.

**LEHNERT, RICHARD L,** Univ Of Sc At Columbia, Columbia, SC; JR; PHARM; Golden Key 89-; Gamma Beta Phi; Intrnshp Nesbitt Mem Hsp Phrmcy; Deans Lst 88-; Phrmcy.

**LEHR, COLLEEN E,** Commonwealth Coll, Virginia Beach, VA; FR; AAS; Acctg.

**LEHRFIELD, LEORA,** Boston Univ, Boston, MA; SR; BS; Deans Host For Sargent Coll 88-90; Big Sis 89-90; Bnai Brith Hillel 87-; Golden Key 90-; Phys Thrpy: Thrpst.

**LEHTO, JASON A,** Univ Of Sc At Columbia, Columbia, SC; SO; BS; Socty Undersea World 89-90; Biology Clb 89-90; Sigma Phi Epsilon Acad Chr 89-90; Marine Sci; Rsrch Teach.

**LEIBER, RISA P,** Georgian Court Coll, Lakewood, NJ; SR; BS; Deans Schlr 88-; Acctg; CPA.

**LEIBERMAN, GENNADY,** City Univ Of Ny Baruch Coll, New York, NY; SR; BBA; Humn Resrc Mgt; Labr Rltns.

**LEIBOLD, JILL E,** Cumberland Coll, Williamsburg, KY; SO; BS; Lv Actn 90-; Blgy; Rsrch.

**LEIBOWITZ, HOWARD,** Fl International Univ, Miami, FL; GD; BS; AA Miami Dade Cmnty Clg 88; Crim Just; Govt Invest.

**LEICHER, ROBERT K,** Comm Coll Algny Co Algny Cmps, Pittsburgh, PA; FR; Lbrl Arts.

**LEICKLY, LINDA K,** Columbus Coll Of Art & Design, Columbus, OH; FR; Art; Advrtsng.

**LEIDER, PAUL R,** Carnegie Mellon Univ, Pittsburgh, PA; SR; BS; AIESEC 88-90; Deans Lst 90; ; Im Bsktbl/Flr Hcky Capt 88-; Ind Mgmnt; Finance.

**LEIFER, STEFANIE J,** Cornell Univ Statutory College, Ithaca, NY; JR; BS; Stdnt Advsr 90-; Panhlnc Grk Wk Comm 89-90; Ambsdrs 90-; Alpha Omicron Pi V P 88-; Newsday Cmnty Affrs Intern 89; NY Hosp Facilities Dev Intern; Bsn Mgmt/Mktg; Bsn Mgmt.

**LEIGERS, GIDGET A,** Bridgewater Coll, Bridgewater, VA; FR; BA; BSU 90-; Brethren Stdnt Fllwshp 90-; Busn.

**LEIGH, DAVID J,** Univ Of Akron, Akron, OH; SR; BSBA; Beta Gamma Sigma 89-; Mu Kappa Tau 89-; Pi Sigma Epsilon 89-; Beacon Jrnl Wrtng Cntst; Mrktng; Sales.

**LEIGH, GARY,** Univ Of Sc At Columbia, Columbia, SC; JR; BA; Naval ROTC Supply Ofcr; Deans Hnr Lst; US Naval Institute 85-; Fleet Reserve Assoc 89; Actv Duty US Navy Slctd Ofcr Slctn Prog 89-; AA City Clg Of Chicago 89; History; Naval Officer.

**LEIGH, JEANINE A,** Univ Of Med & Dentistry Of Nj, Newark, NJ; SR; RTR; EMS 84-87; Radlgc Tech; Rdlgst.

**LEIGHTON, ERNESTINE S,** Andover Coll, Portland, ME; GD; AS; Ins 87-88; City Clerks Office 88-; Bus Admin; Mgmnt.

**LEIMER, SHARON F,** William Carey Coll, Hattiesburg, MS; JR; BSN; Stdnt Nrs Assc 89-; LPN Indiana Area Voc Tech 83; Nrsng; Pblc Hlth.

**LEIMKUHLER, MATTHEW P,** Oh Univ, Athens, OH; FR; BA; Vrsty Swmng; Mech Eng; Eng.

**LEINBAUGH, MELISSA J,** Univ Of Southern Ms, Hattiesburg, MS; SO; BS; Hnr Stdnt Assn 90-; Wk Theatre Dept 90; Phi Eta Sigma; Alpha Lambda Delta; Gamma Beta Phi; Prsdntl Schlrshp 90-; Psychlgy; Clin Psychlgst.

**LEINBERGER, JENNIFER A,** Univ Of Cincinnati, Cincinnati, OH; FR; BFA; Dnce Ensmbl; Hnrs Schlrshp Cinti Clg Cnsrvtry Msc 90-; Ballt Solo Chicinnati Pops Orch; Dance; Prfssnl Ballt.

**LEINDECKER, JAN R,** Kent St Univ Kent Cmps, Kent, OH; SO; BS; Cmps Crsds Chrst Org 90-; IM Vllybll Bsktbll 89-91; Alpha Lambda Delta Sec 90; Bbl Stdy Grp 90; Bus Admn.**

**LEINWEBER, GREG D,** Glassboro St Coll, Glassboro, NJ; JR; Actvts Brd 84-85 90; Biol Clb 90-; Pineland Inst Instr 90-; BS Glassboro St 85; Biol/Chmstry; Envrnmntl Sci.

**LEIPOLD, ANTHONY J,** Univ Of Akron, Akron, OH; FR; BA; Am Socty Of Mech Engr; Hnrs Prgrm; Mech Engr.

**LEIRER, JUDI M,** Univ Of Montevallo, Montevallo, AL; SR; BS; Psych.

**LEIS, GINA M,** Juniata Coll, Huntingdon, PA; JR; BA; Vlybl Tm All-Cnfrnc Slctn 87-; Stdnts Stdnts Com; IM Vlybl/Bsktbl; Nwspr Clssfd Edtr; Vlybl Announcer; Sftbl Vlybl 87-; Engl/Cmnctns; Sports Jrnlsm.

**LEISSE, JAMES T,** Duquesne Univ, Pittsburgh, PA; FR; IM Ftbl Bsktbl Sftbl Vlybl; Phi Eta Sgm Tres; Lambda Sgm Hse Chrmn; Fndrs Schlrshp 90-; Bus Incntv Grnt 90-; Bus; Intrntl Bus.

**LEISTER, MICHELLE L,** Susquehanna Univ, Selinsgrove, PA; FR; BA; Stdnt Actvts Cmmtt; Orttn Plnng Cmmtt 90-; Crsdr Nwsppr Stff 90-; Wmns Chr; Stdnt Advsr 90; Natl Bg Brthr Bg Sstr Prgm 90-; Psychlgy; Scl Wrk.

**LEISTER, SCOTT B,** Temple Univ, Philadelphia, PA; SR; BS; Amer Socty Cvl Engr 88-; Gnrl Bldg Cntrctrs Assn 89-; Amer Concrete Inst 88-; Cvl/Cnstrctn Engr Tech; Proj Mgmt/Eng Dsgn.

**LEISURE, SHARON ADKINS,** Owensboro Comm Coll, Owensboro, KY; JR; BSN; Amer Assoc Crtcl Cr Nrs; Gldn Ky 90-; Hgst Acad Hons Grad Owensboro Voc Sch 87; RN Daviess Co Hosp Int Cr Unit; LPN 87; Assoc Western KY Univ 89; Nrsng.

**LEITER, ROBERT A,** S U N Y Coll At Fredonia, Fredonia, NY; SR; BS; Psychology Clb 89-; Bsns Clb 89-; Sclgy Clb 90-; Stdnts Stdnts 89-; Psychology Intrnshp Mntly Rtrd Emtnly Dstrbd Adlts Acdmc Schlrshp New England Clg 88; IM Vlybl Bsktbl 88-89; Psychology; Chld Psychlgst.

**LEITNER, BOBBIE D,** Univ Of Cin R Walters Coll, Blue Ash, OH; FR; BED; Natl Cncl Jwsh Wm 83-; Hdsh 89-; Bl Ash Elem Schl PTA Exec Brd 90-; Dns Lst Univ Cincinnati 90-; Untd Ord Tr Strs 83-; Wlns Cmnty; Rockdale Tmpl Strhd Brd PR Chrmn 89-90; Jewish Hosp Axlry; Eng.

**LEITNER, DEBRA A,** Univ Of Ky, Lexington, KY; SR; PHARM; Actvts Board 86-88; Org Assmbly 86-87; KY Acad Stdnts Pharm Pgm Chrmn 88-; Rho Chi Hstrn 90-; Alpha Lambda Delta 86-87; Lambda Sigma 88; Lances 88-89; Lambda Kappa Sigma V P 88-; Alpha Gamma Delta V P Schlrshp 86-90; COSTEP 90; Clinical Pharmacy.

**LEITNER, VALARIE A,** Comm Coll Algny Co Algny Cmps, Pittsburgh, PA; FR; BA; Bsnss; Accntng.

**LEIVNE, SETH A,** Univ Of Miami, Coral Gables, FL; JR; BBA; Hnr Std Assoc 88-; Sigma Phi Epsilon 89-; Intrnshp Paine Webber; Finnc; Law.

**LEJA, BERNARD S,** Comm Coll Algny Co Algny Cmps, Pittsburgh, PA; SO; BSBA; Phi Theta Kappa 90; Pi Kappa Alpha Sec 70; AS; Acctng.**

**LELE, AKSHAY M,** Fl International Univ, Miami, FL; JR; BA; Intl Assoc 88-; IM Sccr Ftbll 90; Mchncl Eng.

**LELIEVRE, AMY M,** Providence Coll, Providence, RI; FR; BA; Pastrl Cncl 90-; Lib Arts Hons 90-; Math Educ; Tchr.

**LELWIS, SHANE T,** East Tn St Univ, Johnson City, TN; JR; BS; Acctg Soc VP; Beta Gamma Sigma; Acctg.

**LEM, ANTHONY J,** Newbury Coll, Brookline, MA; FR; AS; Phys Thrpy.

**LEMAIRE, NANCY S,** Christopher Newport Coll, Newport News, VA; SR; BA; Acapella Choir-Lngwd Coll 40; Fine Arts Soc 90-; Alpha Sigma Tau Lngwd Coll 40-; Rdrs Dgst Schlrshp Lngwd Coll 39-40; AIG Sec 64-65; CWI 70; Amer Bus Wmns Assn Sec 70; Cmmssry Com LAFB VI 50; FBI 42-44; Bnkg Career 63-84; Fine/Prfrmng Arts; Art.

**LEMANSKI, JANET M,** Howard Comm Coll, Columbia, MD; JR; BS; Cltrl Clb 90-; Alph Alph Sgm 88-; Bsktbl Games; AA; Gen Stds; Natrl Rsrc Mgmt.**

**LEMBO, DIANA S,** William Paterson Coll, Wayne, NJ; JR; BA; Spcl Educ Clb 89-; CEC 89-; NJEA 89-; Dns Lst; Spcl Educ; Tchr.

**LEMIEUX, LUCKY L,** Fl International Univ, Miami, FL; GD; MPH; Publ Hlth Stdnt/Alumni Assoc; Phi Kappa Phi; Grad Asstshp 90-; AA Miami-Dade Cmnty Clg 86; BHSA; Publ Hlth-Envir Hlth.

**LEMKE, CHRISTINA,** Mount Saint Mary Coll, Newburgh, NY; SO; BA; Drama Clb 89-; Engl/Elem Ed; Tch.

**LEMKER, JANE V,** Univ Of Cincinnati, Cincinnati, OH; GD; Golden Key 89-; Kappa Delta Pi 88-; Outstndng Scndry Ed Grad; Ed Alumni Schlrshp 90; Magna Cum Laude; PTA 87; Symphony Orch Brd Sec 87; Wolf Den Ldr Boy Scts 88-; BS Ed Univ Cincinnati; Engl; Tchr Scndry.

**LEMKO, MAUREEN,** Long Island Coll Hosp Of Nrsng, Brooklyn, NY; FR; AD; Nrsg; BSN/MS.

**LEMME, TARA A,** Georgian Court Coll, Lakewood, NJ; JR; Art Hstry.

**LEMMO, ANNEMARIE,** Bunker Hill Comm Coll, Boston, MA; FR; BA; Hosp Vol; Secr Certif Burdett Bsn Sch 87; Acctg; Coopers-Lybrand.

**LEMMON, CHRISTINE ALLYSON,** Univ Of Nh Plymouth St Coll, Plymouth, NH; JR; BA; Almni Assn 82-; Oprtn Dsrt Strm Sergnt 84-; Pi Gamma Mu 90-; Phi Kappa Phi; USAR/ARMY Sergnt 84-; PSC Hstry Intrn 90-; Hstry; Law.

**LEMMONS, ANISSA M,** Univ Of Sc At Columbia, Columbia, SC; SO; BA; Lit Mag Art Edtr 90-; Shoestrng Players Prod Stf 90; Engl; Tchng.

**LEMOINE, DIANNE L,** Univ Of New England, Biddeford, ME; SR; BS; Non Trad Stdnts Org 89-90; Alpha Chi 90-; Dns Lst 88-; Trusts Schlrshp; APTA 89-; BA Bio Colby Clg Watrvl ME 84; Phy Thrpy.

**LEMOINE, KAREN H,** Western New England Coll, Springfield, MA; JR; PHRMD; Acdmy Stdnt Phrmcsts Co Leader 90-; Alpha Lambda Delta 90-; Phrmcy; Clinical Phrmcy.

**LEMON, JULI A,** Columbia Union Coll, Takoma Park, MD; JR; BA; Alpha Chi 89-; Psi Chi; Sports Acrobatics 89-; Psychlgy; Crmnl Anlst.

**LEMON, KIMBERLY A,** Memphis St Univ, Memphis, TN; JR; BA; Var Vlybl Schlrshp 88-; Ambas 89-; Metro Cnfce Cmmsnr List 89-; Tiger Acad List 89-; Spcl Olym 89-90; Elem Ed; Tch/Coach.

**LEMON, MARVETTA,** Wilmington Coll, New Castle, DE; SR; BS; Wilmington Police 89; Rooki Yr; DE Chamber Comm 90-; NAACP; Persl Coord; Behavioral Sci; Psychologist MS.

**LEMONS, LORILEE J,** Univ Of Tn At Martin, Martin, TN; JR; Alpha Delta Pi Corrspndnt 90-; Med Technlgy.

**LENA, KELLEY J,** Univ Of Southern Ms, Hattiesburg, MS; SO; BA; CCD Tchr St Thomas Chr 88-90; Scrd Hrt Chr 90-; Ldrshp Schlrshp 89; Pearl Reynolds Lch Schlrshp 90-; Pres List; Deans List; Elem Educ; Tchr.

**LENAHAN, JEFFERY M,** Brewer St Jr Coll, Fayette, AL; SO; BS; Phi Theta Kappa 90-; Outstndng Psychlgy Stdnt 89-90; Blgy; Optmtry.

**LENDERMAN, CAROL P,** Florida Christian Coll, Kissimmee, FL; FR; Drama Stdnts For Action Tm Ldr 90-; Choir/Voices Of Praise/New Life; Make A Wish Fndtn Prog; Vlybl Sftbl; Chrstn Edn; Teach.

**LENDOSKY, KIMBERLY J,** Marywood Coll, Scranton, PA; SR; BS; Phi Beta Lambda 90-; AS Lacawanna Jr Coll Scr PA 89; Admin/Mgmt.

**LENG, SEYLA,** Bunker Hill Comm Coll, Boston, MA; GD; BA; Assessmnt Cntr Tst Asst 90-; Math; Acctg.

**LENGA, SAMARA D,** Carnegie Mellon Univ, Pittsburgh, PA; JR; BS; Lambda Sigma 90; Study Abd London Schl Ecnmcs 90; Sccr 89-; Ind Mgmt; Bus.

**LENGAUER, ALLISON L,** Allegheny Coll, Meadville, PA; SO; BA; Hnr Comm 90-; Wnd Symphny 89-; Lift 90-; Tourguide 90-; Psi Chi 90-; Lambda Sigma 90-; Kappa Kappa Gamma 90-; Doane Dist Schlr 90-; Dist Alden Schlr 90-; Psych; Clncl.

**LENGAUER, KELLY A,** Allegheny Coll, Meadville, PA; SR; BA; IMS; Kappa Kappa Gamma; Baldwin-Reynolds Hse Museum Crawford Cnty Hstrcl Scty Intrnshp; BA; Art Hstry; Museum Area.

**LENHAM, MICHELLE A,** Anne Arundel Comm Coll, Arnold, MD; FR; BA; Bus Mngmnt; Law.

**LENHARDT, GARY A,** Hudson Valley Comm Coll, Troy, NY; FR; AOS; Ski Clb 88-89/91; Clss Pres 90-; AOS Elec Constr/Maint HVCC 88-89; Htng/Air Cond/Refrgtn.

**LENHART, CYNTHIA B,** Oh Univ, Athens, OH; FR; BS; Alpine Clb; IMS; Alpha Lambda Delta; Physics; Astronomy.

**LENHART, KRISTINE M,** Defiance Coll, Defiance, OH; JR; BS; Alpha Chi 90-; American Heart Assoc Event Chrwoman 89-; Outstanding Stdnt 90-; Bus Administration & Psychology.

**LENHART, SARAH A,** Allegheny Coll, Meadville, PA; SO; BA; Habitat For Humanity; Kappa Kappa Gamma 90-; Doane Schlr 90; Distinq Alden Schlr 90; Var Tnns 89-; Econ/Math; Bus.

**LENHOFF, DIANE B,** Webber Coll, Babson Park, FL; JR; BS; SGA Treas 90-; Intr Orgnztl Cncl 90-; Green Ky Ambsdrs; Mrktg; Adv.

**LENNEX, PATRICIA L,** Roane St Comm Coll, Harriman, TN; SO; AS; Gamma Beta Phi Rprtr; Bus Admn; CPA/GOVT Acctg.

**LENNON, BRIAN D,** Widener Univ, Chester, PA; JR; BS; Pi Gamma Mu; Mngmnt; Law.

**LENNON, SHANNON L,** Univ Of Ct, Storrs, CT; SO; BA; Captains Cncl 90-; Cross Country; Indoor/Outdoor Track Co-Capt 89-; Nutr; Dietician.

**LENNOX, MARYBETH S,** S U N Y At Binghamton, Binghamton, NY; FR; MBA; Soccer 90; Acctg.

**LENNOX, WILLIAM J,** S U N Y Coll At Fredonia, Fredonia, NY; JR; BS; Lacrss Clb Tm 89-; Eng Soc Scl Chr 89; Dorm Res Asst; Eng/Bus Admin.

**LENOIR, RONDA L,** Alcorn St Univ, Lorman, MS; JR; BS; OES; Bio; Med.

**LENOX, BOBBY L,** Faulkner St Jr Coll, Bay Minette, AL; SO; BSEE; Phi Theta Kappa; U S Air Force 86-90; AS 90-; Elec Eng.

**LENOX, KIMBERLY J,** Widener Univ, Chester, PA; FR; Cmmtr Stdnt Orgnztn 90-; Coop Edctn 90-; Accntng; Accntng CPA.

**LENTINI, GREGORY J,** Boston Univ, Boston, MA; FR; Coll Rpblcns 90-; Pres Rsdnc Hl; Cls Treas; IM 90-; Finance; Law Sch.

**LENTZ, CHARLES W,** Indiana Univ Of Pa, Indiana, PA; FR; BED; Bg Brthr Bg Sstr Org 90-; Chrst Chrch Yth Grp 90-; IUP Tr Gd 90-; Dstngshd Achvr Awr; Elem Ed; Tchng.

**LENTZ, HEATHER M,** Cornell Univ Statutory College, Ithaca, NY; SO; IM Hcky Clb 90-; Work Study Job 89-; Natl Schlrs 89-; Alpha Phi; One-To-One Prog 90-; Crew Tm 89-90; Scndry Ed.

**LENTZ, SHERRY A,** Itawamba Comm Coll, Fulton, MS; GD; Hnrs Grad; Office Adm Dept Awd; AAS.

**LENTZ, TARA L,** Clemson Univ, Clemson, SC; JR; BS; Tiger Band 88-; Reformed Univ Fllwshp 88-; SC Recr Parks Assoc 90-; Calhoun Schlr 89-; Golden Key 90-; Rho Phi Lambda 90-; G R Mac Donald Schlrshp 89-; Parks Recr Tourism Mngmnt; Christian Recrtn.

**LENZ, EDWARD W,** Saint Francis Coll, Loretto, PA; BA Frnkln/Mrshll Clg 72; Math/Educ; Rsrch.

**LENZ, SCOTT W,** Valdosta St Coll, Valdosta, GA; SR; BBA; VSC Recyclng Proj Budgt Comm Stdnt Chrmn 90-; Alpha Chi; Beta Gamma Sigma; Outstndng Econ Stdnt 90-; Hons Day; Econ.

**LENZ JR, SEYMOUR S,** Fl International Univ, Miami, FL; JR; BA; BACCHUS VP 90; CMAA; Theta Chi; Chldrns Thtr Deaf Vol 90; AA Univ FL 90; Htl/Clb Mgmt; Hsptlty.

**LEO, LISA ANN,** Univ Of Rochester, Rochester, NY; SR; BS; Undrgrad Eng Cncl Pres 89-; Soc Wmn Engrs 90-; Amer Soc Mech Engrs 90-; Phi Beta Kappa 90-; Tau Beta Pi Pblcty Offcr 89-; Univ Deans Lst 87-; Gnrl Mtrs Schlrs 89-; Bausch/Lomb Schlr 87-; Mech Eng.

**LEOCANI, LETIZIA M,** Eckerd Coll, St Petersburg, FL; SR; MA; Mln Slng Clb 88-; APS Wshngton; Pre Med Clb 90-; Med.

**LEON SANCHEZ, FRANCISCO M,** Catholic Univ Of Pr, Ponce, PR; GD; Cls Pres; Fclty Std Rep; Nwspr Edtr; Phi Alpha Delta 89-; BA Magna Cum Laude 89; Law Schl.

**LEON, ANGELA L,** Univ Of Pr Cayey Univ Coll, Cayey, PR; GD; BA; Cath Un Comm 89-; Deans List 89-; Soc Sci; Law.

**LEON, BARBARA C,** Univ Of Miami, Coral Gables, FL; GD; FL Nrs Assoc; RN AS Miami Dade Cmnty Clg 88; BSN 90; Nrsg; Nrs Anesth CRNA.

**LEON, CECILIA M,** Miami Dade Comm Coll, Miami, FL; SO; Book Fair Vol; IM Sports Tm-Tnns; Bus; Acctg.

**LEON, ERNESTO GABRIEL,** Univ Of Miami, Coral Gables, FL; JR; BSEE; FES 89-; NSPE 89-; IEEE 90-; Mathcounts 89; Math Team 89; Coll Bd Cert Of Achvmnt For Acdmc Perf 90; IM Rcqtbl; AA MDCC 90; Elect Engrng; MBA.**

**LEON, FRANCES R,** Univ Of Pr Cayey Univ Coll, Cayey, PR; SR; BBA; Mgmt; MBA.

**LEON, SONIA M,** City Univ Of Ny La Guard Coll, Long Island Cty, NY; SO; AAS; Phi Theta Kappa; Cmptr Tech; Elect Eng.

**LEON, YESENIA,** Fl International Univ, Miami, FL; SO; BS; Sci Educ.

**LEONARD, ALMA M,** Nc Central Univ, Durham, NC; FR; FBLA 88-89; HOSA 89-90; Chrldr 87-88; Chemistry.

**LEONARD, ANTHONY S,** Univ Of Nc At Charlotte, Charlotte, NC; JR; BS; Ald Hlth Clb 88-; IM Sftbl Bsktbl 90-; Pharm; Comm Hosp Phrmcst.

**LEONARD, CARLA YOUNGBLOOD,** Birmingham Southern Coll, Birmingham, AL; SO; BA; Almn Jr Achvmnt; Accntng; Acctg; Adtng Govt.

**LEONARD, CATHERINE E,** Univ Of Nc At Greensboro, Greensboro, NC; JR; BS; Natl Assn Educ Yng Chldrn Treas 88-; Amer Hm Ec Assn Fnd Rsr 89-; Wesley Luther Hse 88-; Univ Marshl 89-; Gamma Sigma Sigma 89-; Deans Lst; Fam Lfe Cncl Greensboro 90-; Humn Envrnmntl Sci Schlr 88; Chld Dev; Day Care Dir.

**LEONARD, ERIC MICHAEL,** Springfield Tech Comm Coll, Springfield, MA; GD; BSBA; Comp Sys Clb Pres 88-90; Alpha Nu Omega 88-90; AS Springfld Tech Cmnty Clg 90; Mis; Comp Pgm/Cnslt.

**LEONARD, HENRY L,** Talladega Coll, Talladega, AL; JR; BA; Stdnt Gov 4 Assc Jr Cl Sntr 90-; SIFE Co-Cptn 90-; All Amer Schlr; Bus/Econ Kennon Invstmnt Grptreas 89-; Crimson Ambsdr 90-; Assc Ameractng Assc; Alpha Phi Alpha Pres 89; NAACP; Big Brthr/Big Str 90; Adopt A Fmly; Acctng; Cpa.

**LEONARD, JACQUELINE A,** Dowling Coll, Oakdale Li, NY; JR; BSPLS; Homemakers Cncl Prog Dir 85-89; Suffold Cnty Police Explorers VP 73-76; Alpha Chi Pres; Deans Lst 89-; Deans Lst 75-76; PTA Connetquot Elem 87-; Girl Scts Co Ldr 89-; AS Criminal Justice 76; Spec Educ/Elem Educ; Occupational Therapist.**

**LEONARD, JOAN E,** Va Highlands Comm Coll, Abingdon, VA; GD; Police Bnvlnt Assn 90-; Frtrnl Ordr Police; Police Offcr 80-; Crmnl Jstc; Law Enfrcmnt.

**LEONARD, JULIA E,** Emory Univ, Atlanta, GA; GD; MN; Amer Nrs Assn Ana/Gna 84-87; Natl Assn Neonstal Nurse 89-; Res Thrgh Shrng Cnslr; Rainbows For All Gods Chldrn; Dipl R N G A Bapt Hosp Schl Or Nrsng 84; Nrsng/Neonatal Perintl.

**LEONARD, KAREN L,** Davis & Elkins Coll, Elkins, WV; SR; BS; Stdnt Ed Assoc 89-; Deans List 90; BS; Elem Ed; Tchr.

**LEONARD, KEM S,** Al St Univ, Montgomery, AL; SR; Whitney Young Scl Wrk Clb V P; Yng Clg Demos; Stdnt Alumni Assoc; Jr Cls Queen; Vol Cnslr Camp Sunshine.

**LEONARD, LEIGH A,** S U N Y Coll At Geneseo, Geneseo, NY; FR; BS; Biol/Zool.

**LEONARD, LINDA F,** Tusculum Coll, Greeneville, TN; FR; BA; Stu Ambsdrs 90-; Actvs Comm 90-; Flwshps Chrstn Athlts 90-; Deans Lst 90; Crs Cntry Mgr 90-; Bus; Law.

**LEONARD, LISA ANN,** Univ Of Southern Ms, Hattiesburg, MS; SR; BA; Latter Day St Stdnt Assoc 89-; Spch Cmnctn Assoc 90-; Intrntl Rltns Club; Phi Theta Kappa 85-86; Forrest Cnty Humane Soc 89-90; Im Sftbl 89-; AA Gulf Cst Jr Clg Jackson Cnty 86; Spch Cmnctn/Psychlgy; Grad Sch.

**LEONARD, PAMELA S,** Marshall University, Huntington, WV; GD; Chi Sigma Iota 90-; Dns Lst 88-; Crr Plnng Plcmnt Cnslr; Voc Rehab Cnslr 89; Acad Advsng; Rsdnce Life; NASPA 90-; AACD 90-; ACPA; WVACD 90-; WVCDA 90-; MA; BA 89; Cnslng; Stdnt Affrs.

**LEONARD, REBECCA S,** Univ Of Akron, Akron, OH; SR; BED; Campus Focus 87; ACES; Golden Key 90; Kappa Delta Pi; Deans Schlr 87-88; Deans Lst 89; Sec Ed/Soc Studies Comp; Tchr HS.

**LEONARD, ROBERT,** Univ Of Cincinnati, Cincinnati, OH; JR; BS; Wis Scty Fire Serv Instrctrs; Wis Scty Arson Invstgtrs; Firefighter City Brookfield Fire Dept; Assoc Fire Sci Tchnlgy; Fire Invstgtn.

**LEONARD, RON MATTHEW,** Univ Of Nc At Greensboro, Greensboro, NC; FR; BM; Clge Evnglstc Tm Msc Dir 90-; Symphnc Chrs 90-; Mns Gle Clb 90; Music Ed; Music Mnstr.

**LEONARD, SELICIA M,** Al A & M Univ, Normal, AL; SR; BA; Stdnt Clstr Org 90-; Chr 89-; Alpha Kappa Mu 89-; Sigma Tau Epsilon 90-; Ben Macarto Clb 89-; Intrnshp Ala Dept Yth Srvcs Trckng Mntr 90-; Sclgy; Law/Soc Svcs.

**LEONARD, SUSAN WENRICK,** Glassboro St Coll, Glassboro, NJ; JR; BA; Mrch Of Dimes Wlk Amer Vol 88-90; Spec Olympcs Vol 88-90; AA Pa State Univ 86; Cmmnctns; Tchncl Wrtng.

**LEONARD, WENDY ANN,** Univ Of Cincinnati-Clrmnt Coll, Batavia, OH; SO; BA; Prsnnl Admin Wth Rbbns Inc Manuf Of Hrdwd Flrng; Bus; Mrktng.

**LEONARDIS, PETER J,** Life Coll, Marietta, GA; JR; DC; BS Chem Richard Stockton State Clg 85; Chrprctc.

**LEONARDO, MARK A,** Univ Of Rochester, Rochester, NY; SO; BA; Delta Kappa Epsilon Tres 89-; Links; Var Ftbl Tm 89-; Ecnmcs; Acctg.

**LEONARDO, MONICA,** City Univ Of Ny City Coll, New York, NY; JR; Sci; Nrsng.**

**LEONARDO, ROBERT,** Georgetown Univ, Washington, DC; JR; BA; Georgetown Rugby Clb 88-; Theology; Law.**

**LEONE, DENNIS D,** Univ Of Miami, Coral Gables, FL; JR; BBA; Deans Lst 90-; La Cross Clb; Mgmt; Sports Law.

**LEONE, PHILIP D,** Erie Comm Coll, Buffalo, NY; SO; AAS; Paralegal Club Treas 90-; Phi Theta Kappa VP 90-; Outstanding Club Mbr 90-; Presidents Ldrshp Awd 90-; Denas List 90-; Paralega Paul William Beltz PC; Cert Sales Assoc Jones Real Estate Clge 87; Personal Injury Attorney.

**LEONG, CHAO HA,** Fl A & M Univ, Tallahassee, FL; JR; BPHAR; Intern Upjohn Phrmctcl Comp; AA Broward Comm Coll 90; Phrmcy; Hosp Phrmcy.

**LEONG, JOHNNY,** City Univ Of Ny Baruch Coll, New York, NY; SR; BBA; Hmn Rsrc Mngmnt.**

**LEONG, NGAN H,** Fl A & M Univ, Tallahassee, FL; FR; CIS Clb; Intl Stdnt Conf; Deans Lst 90-; Cmptr; Comp Pgrmr.

**LEONHARDSON, PEGGY J,** Defiance Coll, Defiance, OH; SR; BS; Def Clg Womn Comm 86-; Alpha Chi 89-; Tol Musm Art Tol Ohio Intrnshp 89; ADN Ill Ctrl Coll E Peo Ill 777; Fine Arts.

**LEONHARDT, TODD D,** Univ Of South Fl, Tampa, FL; FR; BA; Rho Oemga Zeta 90-; Astrnmy Obsrvtn Ssns Instrctr 90-; New Coll Fsbll Trnmnt 90-; Physcs; Grad Stdy.

**LEONHART, ANDREW S,** Marshall University, Huntington, WV; SR; BBA; Gamma Beta Phi Hon Scty 87-90; Pi Kappa Alpha 90-; Vrsty Chrldr 88-; Fin; Fed Bureau Invstgtn.

**LEOPARD, TORIE F,** Winthrop Coll, Rock Hill, SC; JR; BS; Kappa Delta Pi; Tchng Intern; AS Anderson Coll 79; Lic Ahirstyle Inst 82; Spec Educ; TMH; Tch.

**LEPINE, CHRISTOPHER W,** Univ Of Sc At Columbia, Columbia, SC; FR; BA; Bdybldg Clb; Sigma Chi 90-; Medicine.

**LEPKOWSKI III, BERNARD T,** Univ Of Akron, Akron, OH; JR; Gldn Ky; Phi Gamma Delta Awrds Chrmn 90; Amer Cncr Scty; Rd Crss; Dns Lst; IM; Acctng; CPA.

**LEPLEY, HEATHER M,** Liberty Univ, Lynchburg, VA; SO; Spiritual Life Dir 90; Alpha Lamda Delta 90; Psych; Cnslng.

**LEPORE, MICHAEL J,** Univ Of Rochester, Rochester, NY; SO; BA; Sailing Club 89-; Rcqtbl Club 89-90; Tulane Univ Prison Educ Prjct 89-90; Econ/Bio; MD.

**LERI, KRISTIN L,** Indiana Univ Of Pa, Indiana, PA; SO; BS; CEC Spec Olympics; Deans Lst 89-; Educ; Tchr.

**LERNER, JAY L,** Bloomfield Coll, Bloomfield, NJ; JR; BS; Pre-Chiro Clb Treas 89-; SUAB Rsng Star Prdctns U AZ 84-86; Zeta Bata Tau Fndng Fthr/Sec/Rsh Chr 82-86; Chiro Asst; IM Ruby Clb Mnclr 82-; Step Two Promos Advrtsng 88-; Chiro DC.

**LERVIK, ELAINE MARIE,** Nyack Coll, Nyack, NY; JR; BME; Chrl 88-; Orchstr 88-; Hndbls 88-; Msc Educ Natl Conf Treas/Sec 88-; Msc Dpt Ast 90-; Tutor 89-; Msc Dpt Asst 90-; Snr Rctl; Msc Ed; Tch.

**LESCALLEET, SCOTT F,** Bridgewater Coll, Bridgewater, VA; FR; BS; Ski/Otdr Clb Pres; Hnr Schlrshp; Biology; Medicine/Vet.

**LESCARBEAU, MICHAEL P,** Western New England Coll, Springfield, MA; SO; BS; Amer Scty Mechl Engrs 90-; Mechl Engrg; Engrg.**

**LESCODY, CHRISTOPHER L,** Oh Univ, Athens, OH; FR; BA; Cvl Eng; Eng.

**LESH, BRUCE A,** Salisbury St Univ, Salisbury, MD; SR; BA; Pi Gamma Mu; Phi Alpha Theta; Kappa Delta Pi; Vrsty Ftbl Capt 87-; Hstry/Pltcl Sci; Tch/Coach.

**LESHKIVICH, KAREN S,** Univ Of Tn At Knoxville, Knoxville, TN; GD; DVM; Amer Vet Med Assoc 90-; Cat Clb; Amer Bloodhound Clb; Keramos; Phi Kappa Phi; Amer Ceramic Soc; Magna Cum Laude; Iams Schlrshp; Ceramic Rsrch/Dev Engr; Ph D Alfred Univ 90; BS BA 77; Vet Med; Bioceramic Engr.

**LESHNOWER, ADINA M,** Univ Of Hartford, West Hartford, CT; FR; BS; Hillel Org 90-; Res Hll Assn Exec Fnc Sec; Redcaps Orent Pgm Stdnt Advsr; Acctg.

**LESHNOWER, MICHAEL D,** American Univ, Washington, DC; SO; BA; Rsdnce Hall Assn VP 90-; Coll Rpblcns; Alpha Lambda Delta; Intrnshp Cngrssmn C W Stenholm; IM Bsktbl Vlybl Ftbl Sccr; Pol Sci; Law.**

**LESHO, CHERYL L,** Oh Wesleyan Univ, Delaware, OH; FR; BA; Chem Club 90-; Women In Sci 90-; Phi Eta Sigma; Chem/Botny.

**LESICA, DIANE L,** City Univ Of Ny Baruch Coll, New York, NY; GD; Busn To Busn Mktng Scty Secty 89-90; Cum Laude; Busn To Busn Mktng Scty Awdf; BBA Baruch Clg 90; Indtl Mktng.

**LESICKI, ROBERT J,** Temple Univ, Philadelphia, PA; SR; BS; Am Phrmctcl Assn 88-; PA Phrmctcl Assn 88-; Acad Stdnts Phrmcy 88-; Rho Chi 90-; Am Soc Hosp Phrmcsts 88-; Drexel Bio Soc Treas 83-84; Deans Lst; BS Bio Drexel Univ 86; Indstrl Phrmcy.

**LESKO, JOSEPH R,** Saint Peters Coll, Jersey City, NJ; SO; BS; Cmptr Sci; Cmptrs.**

**LESLEY, ALTHEIA,** Univ Of Sc At Columbia, Columbia, SC; SR; Delta Sigma Theta; Council Schlrshp Chrprsn 90-; Phi Eta Sigma; Alpha Lambda Delta; BA.

**LESLEY, MELINDA H,** Tri County Tech Coll, Pendleton, SC; SR; AB; D C Garrsion Schlrshp 88-89; SC St Brd Nrsng RN 74-; Frst Fptst Chrch 87-; Grl Scout Ldr 81 90; AS Grnvle Tech Coll 74; Bus/Off Syst Tech; Sec.

**LESLIE, JILL MARIE,** Kent St Univ Kent Cmps, Kent, OH; SR; BA; Sprtn Hghlghts Dance Tm Cofndr 88-; Host Prgrm 88-; Phi Eta Sigma Pres 88-; Gldn Key 91; Delta Zeta Sngchrmn 89-; Advsr Aurora HS Advsr 90-; Highlights Drll Tm OH St Chmpns 91 Pom & Kick Dvsns; AA Unv Tampa 89; Psychology.

**LESLIE, KERRY L,** Union Univ School Of Nursing, Memphis, TN; FR; BA; Sci; Nrsng.

**LESLIE JR, LARRY F,** Fayetteville St Univ, Fayetteville, NC; NAACP 87; NAACP Fashion Shows Model 86-87; Cmnctns Clb 88; Drama Guild 89; Landsman-Webster Cmnctns Music Dir/Air Prsnlty 86-89; Hot Trax 89; Disc Jockey 84-; Camus Radio Sta Intern 87; Stereo Slsmn NWS Electronics 85-87; Bus Boy 84-85; Spch/Theatre; TV Entrtnmnt.

**LESLIE, LAURA,** Univ Of Sc At Columbia, Columbia, SC; SR; 1st Annl Intrntnl Cnfrnce Sprts Bus USC 90; 2nd Annl Int Cnfrnce Sprts Bus USC; Stdnt Prsdr; Nom Otstndng Sr Awd USC; Asst Dir Facility Plnng Evnt Mgmt 90; USC Sr Ring Recpnt; USC Lttrmn Assn Intrnshp Glbl Bsktbl Assn; Jr Vrsty Chrldr 87; Sprt Admnstrtr; Coll Athltcs.

**LESLIE, MICHAEL A,** Bethel Coll, Mckenzie, TN; SO; BA; Diakonoi VP 90-; Psychlgy Clb Stdnt Govt Rep; CIO Fndr/Pres 90-; Gamma Beta Phi Hstrn; Phi Delta Sigma Sec/Treas; Hendrix Schlr 89-; Psychlgy.

**LESLIE, NEVILLE M,** Univ Of Miami, Coral Gables, FL; FR; BA; Hnrs Soc; Crmnl Jstc; Law.

**LESLIE, PHYLLIS M,** Hillsborough Comm Coll, Tampa, FL; GD; AS; LPN Cert Erwin Voctnl Technel Ctr 84; Nrsng.

**LESLIE, STEVE E,** Christian Brothers Univ, Memphis, TN; JR; BS; Jr Achvmnt Clssrm Cnsltnt 88-; Intrntnl Pjct Mngr 88-; Mrktng; Mrktng Promotions/Rsrch.

**LESMES, KIMBERLY S,** S U N Y Coll At Fredonia, Fredonia, NY; JR; BA; SPIE; Cmptv Rnr; Erly Chldhd Ed; Tch.

**LESNAK, JOAN A,** Mount Aloysius Jr Coll, Cresson, PA; SO; OTA; Occptnl Thrpy Clb Edctnl Chrprsn 90-; Stdnt Rep-Cmmssn Educ POTA 90-; Stdnt Rep-Mt Aloysius Occptnl Thrpy Advsry Bd 90-; Spec Olymp Vol 82-; Fclty Sprvsr Intrmdt Cr Fclty Mntlly Rtrd Adlts 82-; Occptnl Thrpy; Occptnl Thrpy Asst.

**LESNETT, BRENDA R,** Slippery Rock Univ, Slippery Rock, PA; FR; BA; Phy Ed; Tchr.

**LESPERANCE, BRENDA R,** Comm Coll Algny Co Algny Cmps, Pittsburgh, PA; FR; ASSOC; Am Chem Soc 90-; PIAA Soccer Official Assn; Chemist; BA Potsdam St Univ 85; Nursing.

**LESSARD, JEANNE M,** Newbury Coll, Brookline, MA; BA; Sectl Legal; Legal Secty Tchng.

**LESSARD, PAMELA M,** Springfield Tech Comm Coll, Springfield, MA; JR; Cmptr Infrm Sys; Prgrmmng.

**LESSER, N TODD,** Bethany Coll, Bethany, WV; FR; BA; Bd Governors 90-; Radio DJ 90-; Newspaper Rep; Hnrs Engl 90; Amnesty Intl 90-; Cmnctns; Print Jrnlsm.

**LESSER, SARI J,** City Univ Of Ny Baruch Coll, New York, NY; SR; BBA; Lit Clb Treas 88-89; Golden Key 90-; Mgt; Hmn Rsrcs.

**LESSIG, MICHAEL D,** Saint Andrews Presbytrn Coll, Laurinburg, NC; FR; BA; Math/Sci/Cmptr Sci; Eng.

**LESSMAN, ERIK P,** Ms St Univ, Miss State, MS; FR; BS; Bio Engrs Soc 90-; Hons Cncl 90-; Gamma Beta Phi; Alpha Delta Lambda; Phi Eta Sigma; Resrch Asst To Chem Dept Head; Bio Engr/Chem; Med.

**LESTAGE, JULIET M,** Norfolk St Univ, Norfolk, VA; SR; BA; Engl-Lbry Media; Med Lbrn.

**LESTARDO, MELISSA A,** Neumann Coll, Aston, PA; JR; BA; Pol Sci; Govt/Bus.

**LESTER, DONNA M,** North Ga Coll, Dahlonega, GA; JR; BA; Stdnt Gvrnmnt Assn Frshmn Cls Rep 88-89; Bptst Stdnt Un 88-; Spctr Stf Wrtr; Phi Eta Sigma; Pi Sigma Alpha 90-; Phi Kappa Phi; Deans Lst NGC 88-; Acdmc Schlrshp NGC 88-; Sntr Sam Nunn Intrnshp; Pltcl Sci Ecnmcs; M Plbc Admnstrtn.**

**LESTER, JEANNIE L,** Owensboro Jr Coll Of Bus, Owensboro, KY; GD; DIP; Stdnt Govt Sec 90-; Ind Yth Scr Assn S Spencer Coach 89-90; Pres Lst 89-90; Hnrs Lst 90-; Lady Mercy Hosp Vol; Amer Hrt Assn Teleparty Vol 90; Contractor Pyrl Mgr 87-89; Med Ofc Asst.

**LESTER, JUSTIN B,** Marshall University, Huntington, WV; SR; BA; Mgmt.

**LESTER, KASSIE B,** Miami Jacobs Jr Coll Of Bus, Dayton, OH; FR; Accntng Tutor; Hghr Accntng; CPA.

**LESTER, KIMETHA L,** Cumberland Coll, Williamsburg, KY; JR; BS; Acctng.

**LESTER, LANYA L,** Christian Brothers Univ, Memphis, TN; SR; BS; Chmcl Soc 87-89; BSA 88; Alpha Kappa Alpha 89; Acdmc Schlrshp 87-89; Hnrbl Mntn; TN Acad Sci; W TN Rgnl Clgt Mtng; Chmstry; Lab Rsrch Analysis.

**LESTER, LISA F,** Clayton St Coll, Morrow, GA; SO; Comp Info Syst; Bus.

**LESTER, RONALD A,** Morehouse Coll, Atlanta, GA; SO; BS; Hlth Careers Soc 89-; Glee Clb 89; Deans Lst 89-; Biology; Physician.

**LESTER, ROSE M,** Defiance Coll, Defiance, OH; JR; BS; VFW Auxlry 71-; Vol For Filling Mem Home Of Mercy 82-84; ITT Higbie Mach Oper 72-; Soc Wrk; Drg/Alcohol Cnslng.

**LESTER, SHANNON D,** Univ Of Nc At Charlotte, Charlotte, NC; JR; BS; Gldn Key 90-; Chrlt Polo Clb; Stock Brkrs Lic 87 89; Prdntl Bache Sec Dean Wttr Scrts Mdlng; Crmnl Jstc Sclgy; JD MS.

**LESTER, SIMON N,** Georgetown Univ, Washington, DC; SO; BA; Law Soc Pres 90-; AIESEC Treas 90-; Invstmnt Allnc 89-; Tutor 90-; Std Advsr 90-; Intl Ecnmcs; Law.

**LESTER, THAD B,** Lexington Comm Coll, Lexington, KY; SO; BA; Poli Sci Tutr 90-; Bus.

**LESTER JR, THOMAS A,** Radford Univ, Radford, VA; JR; BS; Coll Rep 88-; Pltcl Sci Scty VP 90-; Phi Kappa Phi 90-; Ctzns Arts 86-; Pltcl Sci.

**LESTER III, WILLIAM M,** King Coll, Bristol, TN; SO; PA; Health Sciences Soc 89-90; Biology Assoc 90-; Chem Stdnt Of The Year 89-90; IM Sports 89-; Biology; Medicine.**

**LESTINGI, KERI A,** City Univ Of Ny Baruch Coll, New York, NY; SO; BBA; Finance.

**LETAIF, AIDA F,** George Mason Univ, Fairfax, VA; JR; B; Bus Admin; Fnnce.

**LETANOSKY, STEFANIE A,** Univ Of Montevallo, Montevallo, AL; JR; BA; Omicron Delta Kappa; Sigma Tau Delta 90-; Kappa Delta Pi; Alpha Gamma Delta VP 88-; Pres Awd Excel Wrtng 89; Univ Hnrs Prog 88-89; Engl; Tchng.

**LETCHER, HEATHER K,** Saint Francis Coll, Loretto, PA; SR; BS; Deans Lst 89-; Elem Ed.

**LETELLIER, KIMBERLY C,** George Mason Univ, Fairfax, VA; SR; Gldn Key 90; Alpha Cmi; BSED; Erly Chldhd Ed.

**LETENDRE, MARC L,** Springfield Tech Comm Coll, Springfield, MA; SO; BA; Noon Rprt Cmps Edtr; Video Clb 89-; Intrnshps Chnl 22 Wwlp-Sprngfld 90-; Communications; Vdeogrphr/Prdcr.

**LETO, BINMAR F,** S U N Y Coll Of Tech At Delhi, Delhi, NY; SR; BA; AIAS Pres 90-; Architecture.

**LETOURNEAU, MARIA LYNN,** Univ Of Md Baltimore Prof Schl, Baltimore, MD; SR; BS; Stdt Amer Dntl Hygnst Assoc Social Comm 90-; Phi Kappa Phi; Orthdntic Clrkshp 90-; Dental Hygiene.

**LETOURNEAU, MICHAEL H,** Bentley Coll, Waltham, MA; JR; BS; Acctng Socty Treas 88-; Math Clb Treas; Acctng; CPA.**

**LETSIE, MASEKHONYANA H,** Strayer Coll, Washington, DC; SR; BS; Lerothol Polytech Maseru Lesotho 87; Comp Info Syst.

**LETT, CHRISTI L,** Pellissippi St Tech Comm Coll, Knoxville, TN; AS; Mktg; Advrtsng.

**LETT, MICHAEL L,** Univ Of Tn At Knoxville, Knoxville, TN; SO; BA; Exec Undrgrad Prog 89; Phi Eta Sigma 89; Gamma Beta Phi 90; Tn Schlr Schlrshp; Fnce; Govt Serv.

**LETT, TAWANA M,** Concordia Coll, Selma, AL; SO; Soph Clb Sec 90-; Phi Theta Kappa Pblc Rltns 90; Deans Lst; Trphy PTK; Cert Ward Otstndg Acmplshmnts PTK; AA; Math.

**LETTA, JOELLE M,** The Boston Conservatory, Boston, MA; JR; BFA; Mdrn Dnc Co U Ok 87-89; Dns Lst 88-89; Barnett Schlrshp; Dns Lst 89-; Dnc Schlrshp; Vclst St Jsphs Cthlc Church; Tour Japan Mdrn Dnc Co 88; Concerts Mscl Thtr Prod; Lyric Thtr Ok Ensmbl 90; Show Chr Cmps Am Chrgrpr; Intrntl Tour Chrs Line; Dance/Musical Theatre; Performer.

**LETTERMAN, BEVERLY L,** De Tech & Comm Coll At Dover, Dover, DE; FR; LPN; Capping Ceremny Comm; Nrsng; RN.

**LETTMAN, DEBRA-ANNE J,** Fl International Univ, Miami, FL; JR; BS; SGA Pres 89-90; SAFE Pub Rels 89-90; WISA Pub Rels 90-; Phi Theta Kappa 89-90; Miami Resc Msn 90-; Hl Fm Stdnt Govt Assn 89-90; Pres Awd 89-90; AA Miami-Dade 90; Hosptlty Mgmt; Htl Mgmt.

**LETTS, ANTHONY D,** Liberty Univ, Lynchburg, VA; SO; BS; Kappa Mu Epsilon; Math; Actry.

**LETTSOME, NYDIA A,** Univ Of Md At Eastern Shore, Princess Anne, MD; SR; BS; Acctg Clb 88-; Crbbn Clb P 88-90; IM Sftbl/Vlybl 88-90; Acctg; CPA.

**LETTSOME, TRACY L,** Univ Of The Virgin Islands, St Thomas, VI; SR; Pre Law Assn 90-; Clss Sec 90-; VI Stdnt Assn Pres 90-; Pres Clb; Bus; Law.

**LETZ, KEITH D,** Univ Of Akron, Akron, OH; JR; BA; Hnrs Pro 88-; Deans Lst 88-; Sci; Mech Engr.

**LEUNG, ANGELA P,** Bloomfield Coll, Bloomfield, NJ; SO; BA; Sigma Phi Delta 90-; Bus; Mgmnt.

**LEUNG, BIK FUNG,** City Univ Of Ny Baruch Coll, New York, NY; JR; BBA; Acctng.

**LEUNG, ELINA,** City Univ Of Ny City Coll, New York, NY; JR; Hong Kong Clb Sec 90-; Metro Museum/Art 90-; Golden Key 90-; Deans List 90-; Art/Math; Adv Dsgn/Teach.**

**LEUNG, FUNG KUEN CAROL,** Univ Of South Al, Mobile, AL; JR.

**LEUNG, JENNIFER Y,** City Univ Of Ny Baruch Coll, New York, NY; JR; BBA; Acctg.

**LEUNG, LAI-SHAN C,** Middle Tn St Univ, Murfreesboro, TN; JR; BBA; Intrnatl Stdnts Clb MTSU 90-; Chnse Stdnts Assn MTSU 89-; AS Grantham Coll Of Education Hong Kong 89; Acctng.

**LEUNG, SHEUNG Y,** City Univ Of Ny City Coll, New York, NY; SR; BA; Cmmnctns Wrkrs Amrc 89-; Econ; Cmmnctns Mgmt.

**LEUNG, SHUK-DUEN,** City Univ Of Ny Baruch Coll, New York, NY; SR; BBA; Acctng Soc 88; Beta Alpha Psi; Ernest/Whinney Account Assist 82-85; AAS New York Tech Clg 89; Acctng; CPA.

**LEUNG, SUZANNE T,** Comm Coll Algny Co Algny Cmps, Pittsburgh, PA; FR; AD; Asst Brwne Ldr 90-; Sci; RN.

**LEUNG, WAI HO,** City Univ Of Ny City Coll, New York, NY; JR; BE; Chinese Stdnt Engr Soc 90-; Hong Kong Stdnt Engr Clb 90-; Elctrcl Engr; Engr.

**LEVAY, JENNIFER L,** Mattatuck Comm Coll, Waterbury, CT; FR; AS; Hm Ec Ed; Tchr.

**LEVEE, MICHELLE R,** Univ Of Sc At Columbia, Columbia, SC; FR; BA; Bsn Mgmt; Cmptr Rltd.

**LEVEILLE, PATRICIA A,** Univ Of South Al, Mobile, AL; SR; BS; Rsrv Offcrs Assoc 86-; Mrch Dimes Wlkamer Tm Capt; Amer Hrt Assoc Dnc For Hrt; Army Achvmnt Mdl 90; Army Serv Ribbon 87; Parachutst Bdg 86; US Army Rsrvs 87-; Aerobics/Ftns Instr 88-; BS 87; Phys Ed; Exrcs Physlgst.

**LEVENGOOD, JULIE V,** Wittenberg Univ, Springfield, OH; FR; BS; Rsdnce Hall Assn Dorm Sec 90; Nwspr Staff Writer 90; Alpha Lambda Delta 90; Gamma Phi Beta Assist Treas 90; Bio; Med.

**LEVENGOOD, LAURIE L,** Univ Of Sc At Columbia, Columbia, SC; FR; MBA; Srty Cncl 90-; Alpha Lambda Delta 90-; Alpha Delta Pi Asst Treas; Internshp Crawford Ftng Co; Dns Schlrshp; Jrnlsm; Brdcstng.

**LEVENSON, YVONNE T,** Oh Wesleyan Univ, Delaware, OH; FR; AIESEC-UB VP; Amnsty Intl; Ecnmcs-Intl Bus; Intl Law/Bus.

**LEVENTER, DAVID B,** Yeshiva Univ, New York, NY; SR; Clg Nwspr Phto/Art 89-; Belkin Schlr 89-; Deans Lst 89-; Max Stern Div Bd Mbr Yth Dir 89-; Sephardic Frnds Of Naimonides Hsp 84-; Cncl Rescue Strian Jews Bd 90-; IM Hcky 90-; BA; Hist/Pre Hlth; Med.

**LEVENTHAL, DANIELLE M,** Oh Univ, Athens, OH; FR; Ecology Clb 90-; Fine Arts.

**LEVENTRY, DAWN M,** Indiana Univ Of Pa, Indiana, PA; SR; PSEA 88-; NEA 88-; Oprtn Uplft Dir Crdntr 88-90; Intern Prjct Strd 88-90; Cum LaudeBS; Elem Ed; Tcher.

**LEVERETT, HAZEL G,** Bristol Univ, Bristol, TN; JR; BA; Opt Clb; NAACP Knoxville Branch Sec 90-; Exec Mngmnt.

**LEVERETTE, GLYNIS C,** Central Fl Comm Coll, Ocala, FL; JR; Chld Care; AA Cntrl FL Comm Clg 89; Elem Chld Care Mgmnt; Chld Care Tchr.

**LEVESQUE, NICOLE M,** Stonehill Coll, North Easton, MA; FR; MBA; Cmmtr Clb; Hnrs Schlr; Elem Ed; Tchr.

**LEVI, CHAVEVAH,** Fayetteville St Univ, Fayetteville, NC; GD; MS; Speech Clb; Wrtrs Clb VP 88-90; Drama Clb; Alpha Kappa Mu; Alpha Epsilon RHO Brklyn Clg VP; SE NC Radio Rdng Srvc 87-90; Intrn Invstgtv News Grp Geraldo Show Intrn; BA 90; Tlvsn Radio; Tlvsn Flm Prdctn.

**LEVI, DONNA J,** Univ Of Ky, Lexington, KY; FR; BA; Hd Start Hm Vstr 87-90; CDA Morehead Univ 89; Elem Ed; Tchr.

**LEVI, EMMA GAME,** James Sprunt Comm Coll, Kenansville, NC; FR; Adult Girl Scouting Brownee Troop Ldr 87-; Nrsg.

**LEVI, KERRI P,** James Madison University, Harrisonburg, VA; JR; BS; SEA 88-90; AEYC 89-; Kappa Delta Pi; Circle K 89-90; Early Chldhd Ed; Tch.

**LEVIN, DANIEL A,** Univ Of Pittsburgh, Pittsburgh, PA; FR; BS; Phi Eta Sigma; Mechl Engrg; Engrg.

**LEVIN, DAVID,** Southern Vt Coll, Bennington, VT; SR; BA; Appilacian Mountain Club 86; Maine Island Trail Assn 89; Capt Mens Vars Soccer; ASS Sci Quinsigamond Cmnty Clg 89; Bsn Mgmt; Bsn Owner.**

**LEVIN, JILL R,** Temple Univ, Philadelphia, PA; SR; BA; Bsn Mnmnt/Human Resource Admin; Hmn Resources.

**LEVIN, JILL S,** Univ Of Tn At Knoxville, Knoxville, TN; SR; BS; Gldn Key 89-; Phi Kappa Phi 90-; Beta Gamma Sigma 90-; F M Rodoy Schlrshp 89-90; Knoxvl Bd Rltrs; Knxvl Apt Cncl; Lic Rl Estate Brkr 82-; AS Roane St Com Coll 88; Acctg; Music Mgmt.

**LEVIN, JUDITH,** Radford Univ, Radford, VA; JR; BA; Envrnmntl Action Grp 90-; Pi Gamma Mu; Cnsrvtn Intern New England Aquarium; Geography/Envrnmntl Studies; Cnsrvtn Policy.

**LEVINE, ABBEY E,** Univ Of Miami, Coral Gables, FL; FR; Disc Jockey Campus Pub 90-; Rathskeller Advsry Brd; Campus Work Stdy; Hnrs Prog 90-; IM Sftbl 90-; Broadcasting Psychology.

**LEVINE, ALIZA R,** Yeshiva Univ, New York, NY; SR; BS; Acctg Soc 88-; Eta Beta Rho 89-90; Deans Lst 88-; Wall St Jrnl Awd Excllnc Ecnmcs; Acctg.

**LEVINE, BONNIE K,** Eckerd Coll, St Petersburg, FL; SO; BA; Theatre Prod 89-; Ford Schlrs Prgrm; Prsdntl Schlr Eckerd Clg; Religious Studies; Prfssr Rlgs Stdys.

**LEVINE III, HYMAN M,** Birmingham Southern Coll, Birmingham, AL; SR; BS; Pep Bnd; Jzz Bnd; Wnd Ensmbl; Jzz Combo Com Mbr 87-; Stdnt Nwspr Advrtsng Mngr 89-90; Stdnt Nwspr Clmnst; Peer Advsr 89-90; Food Serv Com 89-90; Pblcty Chrmn Hmcmng 90; Alpha Kappa Psi VP; Mall Mgmt Intrnshp Eastwd Mall 89-90; Bus Admin; Mall Mgmt.

**LEVINE, JOSHUA BRADFORD,** Univ Of Rochester, Rochester, NY; SO; BA; Cmmtt Prfrmn Arts 89-; Engl.

**LEVINE, JOSHUA N,** Cornell Univ Statutory College, Ithaca, NY; SR; Writer Candid Courses 89-; Ho-Non-Da-Kah 89-; Publ Affairs Mgmnt; Law.

**LEVISON, JODY A,** Univ Of Rochester, Rochester, NY; SR; BA; Psychlgy Cncl 89; Trnsfr Pr Advsr 89; Dlt Phi Epsln 87; Tchng Asstnt Intrdctn Psychlgy 90; Rsrch Asstnt Dept Psychlgy 90-; Psychlgy; Cert Soc Wrkr.

**LEVOS, MICHELLE M,** Defiance Coll, Defiance, OH; SR; BS; Deans Lst 90; 4 H Advsr 90-; Frst Chrstn Chrch 76; Crdt Cllctns Lndr Trnsprt 89; Offc Admn Pnsk Trck Lnsng 86-89; AAS 82; Acctg.

**LEVRAEA JR, VINCENT J,** Air Force Inst Of Tech, Wrt-Ptrsn Afb, OH; GD; ASME; AIAA; Pi Tau Sigma; Tau Beta Pi; Dstngsh Grad; Acdmc Achvmnt Awd; Capt USAF; BSME LA State Univ 83; MSAE 89.

**LEVY, ADA,** City Univ Of Ny Baruch Coll, New York, NY; SR; Alpha Betha Zigmo; BA; Psychology.

**LEVY, KIMBERLY,** Norfolk St Univ, Norfolk, VA; JR; BS; Med Rcd Admin; Reg Rcd Admin.

**LEVY, LYNETTE,** Barry Univ, Miami, FL; JR; BA; Hnr Soc 88-; Pi Gamma Mu 90-; Psi Chi; Psychlgy; Clincl Psychlgy.

**LEVY, VERA A,** S U N Y At Buffalo, Buffalo, NY; JR; BS; FMA; Alpha Epsilon Phi Treas 88-; Dean Witter Financial Servs Grp; Alpha Epsilon Phi 88-; Finance.

**LEW, LAI PING,** City Univ Of Ny City Coll, New York, NY; SO; Bio Med Stds; Medcn.

**LEWALLEN, CHRISTI L,** Piedmont Coll, Demorest, GA; JR; BA; AA Gainesville Coll 90; Acctng.

**LEWANDOWSKI, BRIAN S,** Univ Of Md At College Park, College Park, MD; FR; BS; Math/Sci; Civil Eng.

**LEWANDOWSKI, DENISE A,** Va Commonwealth Univ, Richmond, VA; SO; BFA; Visual Arts.

**LEWANDOWSKI, JENNIFER J,** Niagara Univ, Niagara Univ, NY; SO; BS; Ski Clb; Aviation Clb; Amer Inst Biological Sci; Amer Chem Scty; Dorm Cncl; Biology; Orthodontist.

**LEWANDOWSKI, ROBERT E,** Glassboro St Coll, Glassboro, NJ; SO; BA; Std Govt Chr 89-; NJ Pblc Intst Rsch Grp 90-; Std Rghts Cltn 90-; NAACP 90-; Pol Sci Asc 89-90; Dns Lst 89-; Hstry; Pol Phlsphy.

**LEWANE, JENNIFER ELIZABETH,** Notre Dame Coll, Cleveland, OH; JR; BS; ACS Pres 88-; Nu Delta Mu Sec 90-; Iota Sigma Pi; Coll Wooster Intern 90; Amer Chmcl Soc 89-; Chmstry.

**LEWELLEN, JOHN E,** Tn Temple Univ, Chattanooga, TN; SO; BA; Campus Quest; Stdnt Missions Flwshp; Vlybl Clb; Sigma Chi Delta Pr; Christian Svc; Outstndng Christian Svc Man Of Yr 90-; Math/Sci; Bible/Ministry.

**LEWELLEN, TONYA K,** Univ Of Sc At Columbia, Columbia, SC; SR; BA; Baptist Student Union 88-89; Golden Key 89-; Dir Youth Ministry 90-; Acteens Leader 87-90; Tutor Elem & H S Stdnts 87-; AS USC Lancaster 89; Elem Ed; Teaching/Guidance Counselor.

**LEWIS MAYMO, LE ROY,** Inter Amer Univ Pr San Juan, Hato Rey, PR; GD; JD; Gldn Key 88; Hghst Hnrs 89; BBA Unvrsty PR 89; Corp Law.

**LEWIS, ABIGAIL,** Manhattanville Coll, Purchase, NY; SR; Tri Beta 85-86; STEP Prog 89-90; Superior Portfolio; Intrnshp Historic Hudson Vly; Dept Dist Art Hist; Vrsty Fld Hcky 85/89-90; Biology/Art History; DVM.

**LEWIS, ADA H,** Albany St Coll, Albany, GA; SR; BS; Kappa Delta Pi.

**LEWIS IV, ALBERT M,** Fl St Univ, Tallahassee, FL; SO; BA; Communications; Creative Media Prods.

**LEWIS, ALCORNELIUS,** Birmingham Southern Coll, Birmingham, AL; SR; BS; Phi Eta Sigma; Alpha Lambda Delta; Blue Blazer Intern Southtrust Bk; Comp Info Syst; Info Proc/Mgmt.

**LEWIS, AMANDA C,** S U N Y Coll At Fredonia, Fredonia, NY; JR; BA; Trumpet Guild V Pres 90-; MENC Pres 90-; Service Awd 90-; Taught Marching Band & Winter Guards Union Endicott Jordan Elbridge 87-89; Taught Troopers Drum & Bugle Corps Casper WY 89-; LAAA Broome Cmnty Clge 85; Music Ed; Teach.

**LEWIS, AMY C,** Univ Of Cincinnati, Cincinnati, OH; SO; BFA; Theatr Dsgn/Prod; Stge Mgmt.

**LEWIS, ANDREA C,** Fl St Univ, Tallahassee, FL; SO; BA; Psychlgy; Law.

**LEWIS, ANDREW P,** Wilmington Coll, Wilmington, OH; FR; BA; Fresh Cls Rep Stdnt Govt; Ldrshp Schlrshp Recpnt; Bsbl; Hstry; Educ.

**LEWIS, ANTOINETTE D,** Coppin St Coll, Baltimore, MD; SR; B ED; Aa Essex Comm Coll 89; Erly Chldhd Edctn.

**LEWIS, ARDIAN M,** Tn St Univ, Nashville, TN; JR; BS; Cls Pres 90-; Campus Tr Guide 90-; Pr Cnslr; Alpha Mu Gamma 90-; Deans Lst 89-; Rnld Mcnair Post Bclurt Achrmnt Pro; Pol Sci; Law.

**LEWIS, ARLEATHIA L,** Al St Univ, Montgomery, AL; FR; BA; Hon Stu; Math; Engg.

**LEWIS JR, ARNOLD CHRISTOPHER,** Fl A & M Univ, Tallahassee, FL; SO; BS; Phi Eta Sigma 90-; Pres Schrls Assoc 89-; Access Enhanced Prog Univ Mo; IM Football; Political Science; Analyst/Professor.

**LEWIS, BARBARA A,** Morris Coll, Sumter, SC; SR; BA; Gspl Choir 87-89; Jdcry Comm 90; Army ROTC Cdt Cpt 87-; Deans Lst 87-; O R Ruben Schlr 88-; ROTC Schlrshp 88-; Alpha Kappa Alpah Schlrshp 90; Sftbl 88; Poli Sci; US Army/Law.

**LEWIS, BECKY J,** Milligan Coll, Milligan Clg, TN; JR; BS; Kappa Delta; Soc Affrs; Clss Offcr Tres; Rlgs Affrs; Pres Schlrshp; Bus Admn; Advrtsng.

**LEWIS, BETH A,** Oh Univ-Southern Cmps, Ironton, OH; SR; BED; Elem Tchr.

**LEWIS, BRAD L,** Morehouse Coll, Atlanta, GA; FR; BA; TX Clb 90-; Mss Cmmnctns Clb 90-; TX Estrn Prdcts Ppln Cmpny Asstntshp 90-; Ftbll; Bsktbll 90-; Engl; Mss Cmmnctns.

**LEWIS, BRADLEY S,** Univ Of Tn At Knoxville, Knoxville, TN; FR; BA; Young Life 90; North Carrick Flr Repr 90; Gamma Beta Phi; Bsn; Law.

**LEWIS, BRENDA M,** Hudson Valley Comm Coll, Troy, NY; SR; AA; Phtgrphy/Lbrl Stds.

**LEWIS JR, CARL D,** Univ Of Sc At Columbia, Columbia, SC; JR; BS; Food Lion Inc Mngmnt Lvl 82-89; Hardware Whlslrs Inc 89-; Bus Mngmnt; Ownr Bus.

**LEWIS III, CARL E,** Ms St Univ, Miss State, MS; JR; BA; Amer Inst Of Arntcs And Astrnts Pres; Sigma Gamma Tau Chrmn 90-; Rd Crss; Eng Asst US Army 89-; Arspce Eng; Ph D Eng And Bus.

**LEWIS, CARL P,** Brescia Coll, Owensboro, KY; SR; BS; Stu Govt EVP 89-; Sr Cls Jr Cls VP 89-; Pres Schlrshp 90-; US Achvmnt Acdmy; Annl Almn Awrd 90-; IM Vllybl; BS; Biol; Phrmcy.

**LEWIS, CARLA A,** Miami Univ, Oxford, OH; FR; BA; Stdnt Govt 90-; Keys Chr Fndrsng 90-; Sen Fin Comm; Democrts 90-; Intrn ERA Real Est Ofc 90; Acctg Mgr Miami Bus Enterprs 90-; Brmbl/Wlybl/Vlybl/Sftbl 90-; Fin; Law.

**LEWIS, CAROLINE E,** Dalton Coll, Dalton, GA; FR; BBA; Phi Theta Kappa; Math; Eng.

**LEWIS, CATHERINE L,** Univ Of Ga, Athens, GA; SR; BSED; Zeta Tau Alpha Jdcl Chrmn 89-90; Evltn/Review Brd/Pnhllnc Cncl Chrprsn 89-90; Math Ed Stdnt Assn; Deans Lst; Cmmnvrsty; Diamond Chllnge Chrmn 89-90; Stdnt Tchr Brookwood HS; Sftbl Bsktbl Bwlng Coach 87; Adv Lfesvng Athens YMCA 89; Math; HS Math Tchr.

**LEWIS, CAYA B,** Spelman Coll, Atlanta, GA; FR; Dance Thtre 90-; Stdnt Admssns Orgnztn 90-; Smmr Intrnshp Hwrd Cnty Pblc Schl Systm; Engl; Educ.

**LEWIS, CELITA M,** Univ Of The Dist Of Columbia, Washington, DC; FR; BS; Stdnt Natl Edctn Assoc; Mth Clb; Systmtc Tchr Prp Prgrm; Yth Engnrng Prgrm Asst; Mthmtcs; Tchng.

**LEWIS, CHARITY E,** Fayetteville St Univ, Fayetteville, NC; JR; BS; Phi Eta Sigma; Coors Vet Mem Schlp; Ausa Schlp; Chnclrs Lst; Mktg; Mktg Rsch Anlyst.

**LEWIS, CHERYL L,** Beckley Coll, Beckley, WV; FR; Ptcl Sci; Crmnl Cncl.

**LEWIS, CHRISTINA,** Al St Univ, Montgomery, AL; SO; BA; Bus Mgmt.

**LEWIS, CHRISTOPHER W,** Abraham Baldwin Agri Coll, Tifton, GA; SO; AS; Aet Clb 88-; Hortcltr Clb 90-; Deans List; AS 90-; AS 90; Glf Turf Mgmt; Glf Clb Mgr.

**LEWIS III, CORNELIUS F,** Univ Of Sc At Columbia, Columbia, SC; SO; BA; Scty Of Prfssnl Jrnlsts 90-; USMC Vet EAS Crprl 87; Jrnslm; Law.

**LEWIS, CYNTHIA V,** Univ Of Sc At Columbia, Columbia, SC; JR; BA; Stdnt Govt Assoc Repr Cmps Un 87-90-; Cmps Un Co Ord 88-; Internatl Clb Pblc Rltns Ofcr 90-; Cmps Un Pblc Rltns Ofcr 90-; Kappa Delta Pi; Omicron Delta Kappa; SACS Prps Comm 89-90; Acdmc Afrs Comm 88-89; Erly Chldhd Ed/Spch; Tch.

**LEWIS, DALE M,** Portland School Of Art, Portland, ME; SR; BFA; BA Univ NH 79; MA Univ Chicago 80; Grphc Dsgn; Fn Art.

**LEWIS, DEAN EDWARD,** Hocking Tech Coll, Nelsonville, OH; SO; ASSOC; Outdr Clb 89-; Intrn Pte Mouillee-State Game Area; Wldlf Mgmt; MI DNR.**

**LEWIS, DEBBIE-ANN C,** Bloomfield Coll, Bloomfield, NJ; SR; BS; Chr 89-; Alpha Chi 90-; Acctg.

**LEWIS, DEBORAH L,** Tomlinson Coll, Cleveland, TN; SR; Sldrs Undr Const Chldrns Mnstry Pres 90-; Sch Paper Edtr 88; Wrtr 87-; Phi Theta Kappa 87-; Alpha Chi 90-; Schrlshp With Spirit Awrd 89-; Sr Mnstry Awrd; Sr Cls Rep 90-; Grad Cls Top Hnr; AS 89; BS; Chrstn Educ; Tchg.

**LEWIS, DEENA N,** Va St Univ, Petersburg, VA; JR; Admn Jstc Clb 89-; Nrthrn VA Pre-Almni Clb 90-; Gspl Choir 88-89; Admn Jstc; Law.

**LEWIS, DEIRDRE M,** Fl A & M Univ, Tallahassee, FL; SO; BS; Phi Eta Sigma 89-; Deans List 89-; Hist Ed; Tchng/Law.

**LEWIS, DONNA F,** Univ Of South Al, Mobile, AL; SR; BS; Beta Alpha Psi 89-; Dns Lst 86-; Pres Lst 88-; Acctg; CPA.

**LEWIS, EARLEAN D,** Clark Atlanta Univ, Atlanta, GA; SO; BS; Pre-Prfsnl Hlth Scty 89-; Hnrs Prgrm 89-; Hwrd Hghs Schlrshp 89-; United Negro Coll Fund Pre-Med Schlrshp 90; Macedonia Bptst Chrch Schlrshp; Blgy; Medicine.

**LEWIS, EFFIE L,** Tn St Univ, Nashville, TN; JR; BA; Pol Sci Club 89-; Forensics Tm 90-; Sen Comm Spkr Of Com 90-; Deans List 89-; Hnrs Prog 89-; Alpha Phi Alpha Schlrshp 89-90; Alpha Kappa Alpha Schlrshp 90-; IM Track & Field 89-90; Pol Sci; Crmnl Lawyer.

**LEWIS, ELLEN M,** Univ Of Ky, Lexington, KY; JR; BA; Cath Newman Ctr; Tchr Educ Prog U K; Tchr Schlrshp 91-93; Middle Educ; Tch.

**LEWIS, ERIC J,** Memphis St Univ, Memphis, TN; FR; Marchng Bnd; Schlrshp; Comm Music; Busn/Acctnt/Lawyr.

**LEWIS, ERICA L,** Morgan St Univ, Baltimore, MD; SO; BA; Peer Cnslr 90-; Telecmctns Soc 89-; Promethean Kappa Tau; Alpha Delta Lambda; Phi Eta Sigma; Minority Stdnt Intrnshp DENORTH Co Inc; Telecmctns/Mktg; Pub Rels.

**LEWIS, ERIKA,** Univ Of Miami, Coral Gables, FL; SR; BBA; Cnsltnts Human Undrstndng Mngmnt 90-; Gldn Ky 89-; Phi Kappa Rhi 90-; Padeia 90-; Sigma Delta Tau VP 87-; Honoree Mktng Dept; Price Waterhouse Mktng Intrnshp 88; Mktng; Mktng Rsrch Sales.

**LEWIS, ERIKA D,** Hampton Univ, Hampton, VA; JR; Bus Clb 88-; NC Pre Alumni 89-90; NAACP 89-90; Alpha Kappa Mu 90-; Alpha Kappa Alpha 90-; Inroads (C Triangle 88-; Mktng; Pharm Sls.

**LEWIS, F MORRIS,** Belmont Coll, Nashville, TN; GD; BS; Tn Chess Assoc 89-90; Natl Schlstcs Tourney Dir 90; Computer Programmer Analyst Equinox Info Syst; Computer Sci.

**LEWIS III, FRANK C,** Embry Riddle Aeronautical Univ, Daytona Beach, FL; SO; BS; Swm Tm 90-; Arntcl Sci; Prfssnl Plt.

**LEWIS, GARNET A,** City Univ Of Ny City Coll, New York, NY; GD; MPA; Econ Soc; Omicron Delta Epsilon; Third Wrld Trade Intrnshp, Labor Studies Prog Intern, OM Endowment Schlr, Sol Chaiken Awd Labor Studies; IM Rec; BA 90; Econ/Mgmnt; Pblc Serv.

**LEWIS JR, GEORGE E,** Norfolk St Univ, Norfolk, VA; JR; BS; Norfolk Naval Shipyard Apprentice Assn Presdnt 83-84; Alpha Kappa Mu; Hnr Grad Norfolk Vnl Shpyard NNSY Apprntcshp; Elctrn; Elctrncs Tchnlgy; Cvl Srvnt.

**LEWIS, GINA M,** Western New England Coll, Springfield, MA; JR; BA; Mrktng Assoc; Stageless Plyrs Pres 90-; WNEK-FM; Delta Mu Delta Pres; Alpha Lambda Delta; Alpha Kappa Psi; RJR Nabisco Intrn; Res Adv; Mrktng/Comms.

**LEWIS, HAROLD D,** Interdenominational Theo Ctr, Atlanta, GA; GD; MDIV; Gammon Thlgcl Smnry Fllwshp Pres 90; Kappa Alpha Psi 80; Prnce Hall Afflted Mason MS Jrdctn 3rd Degree 80; Rise/Shine Hmless Mnstry Coord 90; Up/Out Of Pvrty Now Org; Peoples Inst For Srvl Bynd Undng Racism 90; BA 83; Biblical Studies; Prof Of Old Tstmnt.

**LEWIS, JAMELLE K,** George Mason Univ, Fairfax, VA; SR; BSED; Erly Chldhd Educ; Teacher.

**LEWIS III, JAMES G,** Old Dominion Univ, Norfolk, VA; SO; BS; Naval ROTC 88-; IM Bsktbl Soccer 89-; Elec Engrng Tchnlgy; Naval Ofcr Aviation.

**LEWIS, JAMES H,** Widener Univ, Chester, PA; JR; BS; Alpha Chi; Acctg; CPA.

**LEWIS, JAMES R,** Vance Granville Comm Coll, Henderson, NC; Vocational Clb Pres 90-; Elect Rep Stdnt Govt 90-; Grivernce Comm Stdnt Govt Rep 90-; Stdnt Of Qtr 89-90; Cert Calculating Ind Math; Elect Instlltn; Elctrcn.

**LEWIS, JANICE M,** Davis & Elkins Coll, Elkins, WV; AS; Psychlgy/Human Svc; Svc Wrkr.

**LEWIS, JENNIFER A,** Univ Of Tn At Martin, Martin, TN; SO; BA; Elctn Cmmssn-Stdnt Govt 90-; Zeta Tau Alpha 90-; Scndry Educ; Geogrphy Tchr.**

**LEWIS, JENNIFER C,** Fl St Univ, Tallahassee, FL; JR; BA; Mbr NSHLA/ASHA; Amer Speech/Hrng Assoc; Cmctn Disorders; Speech Path.

**LEWIS, JENNIFER L,** Univ Of Nc At Greensboro, Greensboro, NC; SR; BSN; Actvs Brd 87-89; Res Asstnt 89-90; Assoc Nrsg Stu 88-; Otstndg Col Stu Amer 87-; US Ntl Nrsg Assoc; Assoc Nrsg Stu 88-; Cngrsnl Youth Ldrshp Conf 90; Nrsg; Ped.

**LEWIS, JOHN M,** Middle Ga Coll, Cochran, GA; SO; SGA Pres 90-; Prsdnt Sclb VP 90-; Hrrs Hll Drmtry Cncl Treas 90-; Gamma Beta Phi 90lambda Chi Alpha Scl Chrmn 89; Deans Lst 89-; Mchnl Eng.

**LEWIS, JONATHAN G,** Memphis St Univ, Memphis, TN; FR; BBA; Phi Eta Sigma; Alpha Lambda Delta; Black Schlrs Unlmtd; Acctg; CPA.

**LEWIS, JOSEPH M,** Catawba Valley Comm Coll, Hickory, NC; FR; BA; Stdnt Cncl Sec/Treas 79-81; U S Air Force Staff Sgt Explsv Ord Dspsl 82-88; Dist Grad U S 21st Air Force Ldrshp Sch Dover AFB Delaware 86; Bus Admn; Mgmt Trucking Industry.

**LEWIS, JULIE R,** Univ Of Toledo, Toledo, OH; GD; JD; APICS VP 89-90; Kappa Delta Chrprsn 88-90; Brmbl Co Capt 89; BS Miami Univ 90; Law.

**LEWIS, KATHLEEN M,** Univ Of New Haven, West Haven, CT; JR; BA; Day Stdnt Govt Sntr; Grad Cmmttee 90; Pres Slctn Commttee U Pres 90; Rsdnt Assist For Rsdntl Lfe 90; Deans Lst 90; Ntl Kitchen/Bath Schlrshp; Soccer 90; Mgr Co Ed Im Sftbl 90; Intr Dsgn/Pre-Archtctre.

**LEWIS, KATHRYN M,** Univ Of Ky, Lexington, KY; JR; BS; Natl Socty Of Blck Engr Sec 89-; Untd Cmps Mnstry 89-; Math Clb 88-; Lances 90-; Gldn Ky 90-; Pi Mu Epsilon 90-; Habtat For Humnty; Collegns For Acdmc Excllnc 90-; Math Rsrch; Hnr Socty Schlrshp 90; Otis A Singltry Schlrshp 88-; Math; Comp.

**LEWIS, KEITH A,** Va Commonwealth Univ, Richmond, VA; JR; BFA; Commctn Arts/Design; Illus.

**LEWIS, KELLI A,** Univ Of Miami, Coral Gables, FL; JR; BA; Jazz Vocal Ensmbl Singers 87-; Choir 87-89; Sigma Kappa Psi Sec/Treas 87-89; Alumni Assoc Schlrshp 90-; Music Schlrshp 87-; Acad Schlrshp 87-; AA BCC 89; Studio Music/Jazz Vocal; Singer.**

**LEWIS, KEMIKO Y,** City Univ Of Ny Baruch Coll, New York, NY; SR; BBA; Phi Theta Kappa 85; AAS Borough Of Manhattan Comm Clg 86.

**LEWIS, KIMBERLY A,** Elmira Coll, Elmira, NY; SR; BS; Almni Cncl SUNY Brd 87-88; Ski Clb 88-89; Bus Clb 90-; Deans Lst 88-; Bus Inst Intrn 90-; Acctg.

**LEWIS, KIMBERLY L,** Talladega Coll, Talladega, AL; SO; BA; Alpha Phi Alpha Aux 89-90; Bsn Econ Club 89-90; VITA 90; Bsn Admin; Bnkng/Fin.

**LEWIS, KRISTIN M,** Kent St Univ Kent Cmps, Kent, OH; JR; BS; Fnce Assoc Treas 90-; Alpha Lambda Delta 89-; Gldn Key; Delta Sigma Pi Treas 89-; Fnce/Mgmt; Fncl Anlyst.

**LEWIS JR, LARRY A,** Univ Of Tn At Martin, Martin, TN; SO; BS; Phi Sigma Kappa House Mgr 89-; Biology; Medl Schl/Phar Macy Schl.

**LEWIS, LASHINA,** Ky St Univ, Frankfort, KY; SO; Pre Hlth Prfsns Clb Sec Tres; Stdnt Alumni Assn Prsdnt; Zeta Phi Beta Tres; Stdnt Ambsdrs Assn; Pres Schlrshp; Deans Lst; Biology Pre Med; Mdcl Schl Neural Srgn.

**LEWIS, LEE MICHELLE,** Univ Of Ga, Athens, GA; JR; BSED; Band Choreogrphr 88-; Golden Key 90-; Outstndg Clg Stdnts Amer 88-; Dns Lst 88-; Early Chldhd Ed; Tchg.

**LEWIS, LEONTYE L,** Coppin St Coll, Baltimore, MD, SR, BS, Ftr Tchrs MD 88-90; Stdnt Snt 89-90; Cls VP 90-; Alpha Kappa Mu; Chi Sigma Chi; Crcls Schlrm; Natl Blck Chld Dvlpmnt Inst; Hon Soc Pen-Pal Clb 88-89; Mc Nair Schlr 89-; Elem Ed; Tchng.

**LEWIS, LESLIE R,** Clark Atlanta Univ, Atlanta, GA; JR; MSW; Org Scl Change V P 90-; Alpha Kappa Mu; Delta Sigma Theta Chr; Families First Agcy Cnslr 89-90; Atlanta Chldrns Shelter Vol 89-90; UNCF 89-; Hnr Rl 88-; Dns Lst 90-; Scl Wrk; Hmn Res-Mgmt.

**LEWIS, LINDA L,** Anne Arundel Comm Coll, Arnold, MD; SO; BSW; Phi Theta Kappa; Summa Cum Laude; Scl Wrk; MSW/ LCNSD Clncl Scl Wrkr.

**LEWIS, LISA J,** Muskingum Coll, New Concord, OH; SO; BA; Flwshp Chrstn Athls; Phi Sigma Iota V P; Lambda Sigma Chrprsn; Econ Hnr; Delta Gamma Theta Pldg Mistress; Res Asst; Distngshd Schlr; Spch Schlrshp; Vars Vlybl; Spnsh-Intl Bsn; Intl Bsn.

**LEWIS, LORI D,** Southeast Comm Coll, Cumberland, KY; SO; BS; Phi Theta Kappa Scrty 90; AA; Accntng; CPA.**

**LEWIS, LORI J,** Vt Law School, S Royalton, VT; GD; JD; BA Williams Clg 84; Law; Envrnmntl Law.

**LEWIS, LOWELL G,** Coll Of Charleston, Charleston, SC; JR; BS; Im Bsktbl 88-90; Cmptr Sci; MS.

**LEWIS, MARK C,** Crichton Coll, Memphis, TN; SR; BS; Schl Ensmbl Schlrshp; Wrshp Ldr Coord 88-; Zeta Chi 88-89; US Army Pro Mscn Sgt; Hon Rl Deans Lst Elctd Mr Crichton 90-; Hmcmng King 89-90; Coll Stdnts VP Advncmnt Awd; Bd Mbr Hrvst Chrstn Mssns; Chrch Mnstrs/Bible Thlgy; Mnstry/Educ.

**LEWIS, MARK D,** Fl A & M Univ, Tallahassee, FL; JR; BA; NOMA 89-; BSU 88; IFC 87-88; Kappa Alpha Psi Strtgs 87; Archtctr.

**LEWIS, MELANIE F,** Fayetteville St Univ, Fayetteville, NC; FR; Bowling Trnmnt; Waitress 89-; Elem Edn; Teach.

**LEWIS, MONICA L,** Columbus Coll Of Art & Design, Columbus, OH; SR; Pres 89-; ASID; Art Schlrshp; Intr Dsgn Dept Schlrshp; Int Dsgn.

**LEWIS, MONIQUE Y,** Va St Univ, Petersburg, VA; SO; BA; Accntng.

**LEWIS, NADINE C,** City Univ Of Ny Queensbrough, New York, NY; FR; BA; QCC Writing Cntr Tutor 90; Psychlgy; Cnslng.

**LEWIS III, OLIVER J,** Morehouse Coll, Atlanta, GA; JR; BA; Spelman Pre-Law Soc 88-; Bsebl Clb; Orion Pictures Assn Local Filming Proj; Bus Admin/Mktg; Film Dir/Fshn Dsr Entrernr.

**LEWIS, PHILLIP R,** Beckley Coll, Beckley, WV; FR; BA; Chrch Yth Grp Asst Ldr; Phys Therapy.

**LEWIS, PRISCILLA L,** Vance Granville Comm Coll, Henderson, NC; BA; Bus; Cmptr Prgrmmng.

**LEWIS, RAQUEL L,** Univ Of Ga, Athens, GA; GD; Blck Afrs Cncl 86-87; Yng Dmcrt Assoc 87-89; Amer Fdrtn Tchrs; Dns Lst 90-; Stdnt Intrn AFL CIO 88-89; Intrn Amer Fdrtn Tchrs; BSED 90; Erly Chldhd Ed; Edctr.

**LEWIS, REBECCA R,** Marshall University, Huntington, WV; SR; BA; Phi Mu Phi Dir 88-; Spcl Educ; Tchr.

**LEWIS, ROSELINE KAGONYA,** Univ Of Ms Medical Center, Jackson, MS; JR; BSN; MS Stdnt Nrs Assc; NSNA Cnvntn Del; Stdnt Nrs Extern Adult Emer Rm UMC; Dip Bayridge Christian Coll 80; Mdcl Asst Cert Coastal Trng Inst 89; Nursing; Critical Care Nurse.

**LEWIS, ROY C,** Old Dominion Univ, Norfolk, VA; SR; BS; Nuclear Proj Eng 78-; AAS Broome Comm Clg 77; Mech Eng.

**LEWIS, SABRINA C,** Coppin St Coll, Baltimore, MD; SR; BS; NASW; CASA; BS; Scl Wrk.

**LEWIS, SABRINA L,** Middle Tn St Univ, Murfreesboro, TN; SO; BA; Kappa Delta Prsnl Enrchmnt Prog Chrmn 90-; Pol Sci; Law.

**LEWIS, SANDRA G,** Lenoir Rhyne Coll, Hickory, NC; SR; BSN; Lenoir Rhyne Nurses Assn 89-; Mu Sigma Epsilon 90-; LR Stdnt Nrs Assoc Awd 90; Hlth Care Tec I; AS Wstrn Piedmnt Comm Coll 86; AA 89; Nrsng; ICU Nurse VA Hosp.**

**LEWIS, SANDRA J,** Middle Tn St Univ, Murfreesboro, TN; JR; BA; Assoc Stdt Body Rep 89-90; Forensics Tm 89-; Stdt Envrmntl Action 89-; Alpha Delta Pi Scl Chrmn 89-90; Habitat Hmnty Pres 90-; Internship 90; Engl/Speech Cmnctn; Tchg.

**LEWIS, SANDRA L,** Commonwealth Coll, Virginia Beach, VA; GD; AAS; Perfect Attendence; Presidents Lst; Deans Lst; Medl Computer Specialist ECPI 89; Medl Ofc Mngmnt.

**LEWIS, SCOTT J,** S U N Y Coll Of Tech At Frmgdl, Farmingdale, NY; SO; BA; Acctg Soc 89-; Natl Assn Actnts; Acctng; Law.

**LEWIS, SHARON KATHRYN,** Va Highlands Comm Coll, Abingdon, VA; BA; Stdnt Govt Pres 90-; Law Enfrcmnt Clb 89-; Phi Thetta Kappa 90-; Stdnt Actn Cmmtt; Prsdnt Hnr Rll Smstr 90-; Prsdntl Schlrshp; AAS; Cert; Pltcl Sci; Law Enfrcmnt Cnslng.

**LEWIS, SHARON M,** Fayetteville St Univ, Fayetteville, NC; SO; BS; Tlephone Oprtr; Psychology; Clncl Psychlgst.

**LEWIS, SHERRI D,** Univ Of Fl, Gainesville, FL; SR; BS; Natl Stdnt Nrs Assn 90-; Goldn Key 90-; Phi Theta Kappa 88-; Pres Hon Roll 88-; AA Cntrl FL Comm Coll 89; Nrsng; Med/ Pediatrcs.

**LEWIS, SONYA L,** Oh Univ-Southern Cmps, Ironton, OH; SR; Phi Kappa Phi 90-; Kappa Delta Phi 89-; Mntrshp Prog Tutor 89; Data Entry Operator & Comp Operator 71 87; BS 90; Elem Edn.

**LEWIS, STACY R,** Oh Univ-Southern Cmps, Ironton, OH; FR; BA; Elem Edn Sci.

**LEWIS, STEPHANIE A,** Bowling Green St Univ, Bowling Green, OH; SO; VCTO 91; Phtgrphr Cmps Nwspr 90-; Alpha Lambda Delta 90-; Schlrshp Frst Ntnl Bnk OH 89-; Bk Schlrshp 90-; Vsl Cmmnctns; Phtgrphr.

**LEWIS, STEPHEN G,** Lexington Comm Coll, Lexington, KY; FR; Freelance Artist 85-90; Art.

**LEWIS, STEVE C,** Fl Memorial Coll, Miami, FL; SR; BBA; Acctng Club; Alpha Pha Alpha; AA Miami Dade North 88; Acctng; Auditing.

**LEWIS, STEVEN M,** Hudson Valley Comm Coll, Troy, NY; FR; AAS; Acct; Certified Pblc Acct.

**LEWIS, SUZANNE E,** Niagara Univ, Niagara Univ, NY; FR; BA; Acctg.

**LEWIS, TANGELA N,** Al A & M Univ, Normal, AL; SO; BS; SGA Comm Spcl Evnts 90; Tutor LL Btlr Pro 90-; Amer Rd Crs; Med Tech; Pblc Hlth.

**LEWIS, TERESA A,** Dyersburg St Comm Coll, Dyersburg, TN; SO; BA; Bapt Stdnt Un; Phi Theta Kappa; Math; Socl Work.

**LEWIS, TERESA L,** Blue Mountain Coll, Blue Mountain, MS; JR; BS; Cmmtr Clb 90-; Elem Educ; Tchr.

**LEWIS, TERESA R,** Al A & M Univ, Normal, AL; FR; BA; Deans Lst; Clncl Psychlgy.

**LEWIS, THOMAS L,** Northeast State Tech Comm Coll, Blountville, TN; FR; Math Lab Tutor 90-; Math; Cmptr Eng.

**LEWIS, TIREESE D,** Va St Univ, Petersburg, VA; FR; VEA Schlrshp 90-; Electrncs Ed; Engr.

**LEWIS, TONY L,** Memphis St Univ, Memphis, TN; SO; BSME; Ed Support Pgm 89-; Peer 89-; Gamma Beta Phi 90-; Mech Engr.

**LEWIS, TONYA R,** Alcorn St Univ, Lorman, MS; FR; Fshn Merch; Own Chain Clthng Stores.

**LEWIS, TRACI N,** Va St Univ, Petersburg, VA; FR; Engl; H S Tchr.

**LEWIS, VALENCIA Y,** Al A & M Univ, Normal, AL; SO; BA; Spch Pthlgy; Tchr.

**LEWIS, VICTORIA A,** Cumberland County Coll, Vineland, NJ; SO; BA; Phi Theta Kappa 89-; Prsdnt Slst; Ed.

**LEWIS, WANDA M,** Univ Of Cin R Walters Coll, Blue Ash, OH; JR; BS; Miami Syst Corp Prog; AAB S State Cmmnty Clg 89; Info Prcssng; Syst Analyst.

**LEWIS, WAYNE,** Nova Univ, Ft Lauderdale, FL; GD; MACC; BBA Unv N FL 76; Accntg; Govt Serv.

**LEWIS, WENDY D,** Univ Of Sc At Columbia, Columbia, SC; SO; BS; African-Amer Assoc Treas 89-; Stdnt Govt Assoc Senator 89-; Univ Bus Soc; Piedmont Soc 89-; Gamma Beta Phi Soc 90-; Piedmont Schlr 89-; Deans List; Pres List; Omicron Delta Kappa Frshmn/Soph Ldrshp Awd 90-; Awards Day Fclty Marshall 90; Business-Acctg.

**LEWIS, WENDY MARIE,** Longwood Coll, Farmville, VA; SR; BA; Intrvrsty Chrstn Fllwshp 90-; AA J Sargeant Reynolds Comm Coll 89; Hstry; Tchr.

**LEWIS, WILLIAM K,** Univ Of Southern Ms, Hattiesburg, MS; SR; BA; Yng Dplmts Rprtr 83; AA Pearl Rvr Cmnty Clg 83; Psychlgy; Cnslng.

**LEWIS JR, WILLIAM R,** Bowling Green St Univ At Huron, Huron, OH; FR; BGA; Alpha Lambda Delta; Sci-Math; Elect Eng.

**LEWIS-HARTMAN, LORI M,** Daytona Beach Comm Coll, Daytona Beach, FL; SO; MBA; Standardbred Horsewomen Fla Reg Rep 89-; Sch Part Time; CPA.

**LEWIS-WILLIAMS, DELVENNA S,** Savannah St Coll, Savannah, GA; SR; MPA; Stdnt Scl Wrkrs Assoc 89; Pntcstl Mrcle Dlvrnce Sistrhd Scty Pres 88; Cmmnty Serv Dvlpmnt Intrshp Wth EOA; Appnted Mnstr Of Ed At PMDC Mnstries 90; My Essence Poetry Cllctn Pblshed 89; BSW; Ntl Assoc Of Scl Wrkrs 90; Scl Wrk; Pblc Admin.

**LEWTER, JOHN A,** Univ Of Tn At Martin, Martin, TN; FR; BA; Stdnt Govt Assn 90-; Undergrad Almuni Cncl 90-; Peer Enabling Prog Ldr; Phi Alpha Delta V P 90-; Alpha Tau Omega 90-; Pol Sci; Law.

**LEX, RENEE E,** Schenectady County Comm Coll, Schenectady, NY; JR; Outstndng Sec Intern Of Leg Session 86; American Payroll Assoc 89-; Jardine Ins Brokers Inc 87-; Bus Admin; Human Res.

**LEYDEN, ERIN S,** Univ Of Akron, Akron, OH; SR; MFA; Ldrshp Seminar 90; Golden Key 90-; Phi Eta Sigma 89; Alpha Lambda Delta 89; BFA; Dance; Prfsnl Dncr/Tchr.

**LEYDEN, TARA E,** Ms St Univ, Miss State, MS; SR; BA; Alumni Deleg VP Of Pub Rel; Bnd; Gamma Beta Phi; Sigma Alpha Iota; Delta Gamma; Stdnt Sprt Srvcs Vol; WST Outstdng Soph Stdnt; Cmmnctns; Cnslng Ed.

**LEYVA, EMILIA,** Fl International Univ, Miami, FL; SR; BED; Stdnt Govt Assn Scrb 87-90; Ftr Edctrs Amer 88-90; Pnhllnc Cncl Pres 88-89; Phi Sigma Sigma Pres 86-; Outstndng Stdnt Awd 89-90; Educ; Elem Tchr.

**LI, CHIH-CHAO,** Oh Univ, Athens, OH; JR; BS; Dns Lt; Gldn Key; Dns Schlp; Chem Engr.

**LI, CONWAY,** Davis & Elkins Coll, Elkins, WV; FR; BA; Hnrs Assn; Intl Org 90-; Newspr; Alpha Phi Omega 91; Busn.

**LI, ELIZABETH M,** Boston Univ, Boston, MA; FR; BA; Stdnt Govt Flr Rep 90-; Chorus 90-; AMSA 90-; The League Siblings Pgm 90-; Marine Bio/Engl; Med.

**LI, FAI,** Univ Of Rochester, Rochester, NY; SR; BS; Chnse Stdnt Assn 87-; Optcl Soc Of Amer 87-; IEEE 87-; Tau Beta Pi 89-; Phi Beta Kappa 89-; C W Chu Fndtn Schlrshp 87-; Genesee Schlrshp 87-; Elec Eng/Optics.

**LI, FRANK KAM,** S U N Y At Buffalo, Buffalo, NY; SR; BS; Dean Hnr Lst 89-; 1st Prz Math 87; Hghr Cert Hong Kong Polytechnic 88; Dipl 87; Elect Eng/Cmptr Scif Cmptr Eng Scntst.

**LI, JING,** Univ Of Cincinnati, Cincinnati, OH; FR; BA; Deans Lst; Hnrs Schlrshp; Iano; Cncrt Pianst.

**LI, KELLY M,** Teikyo Post Univ, Waterbury, CT; GD; MBA; AMA Auxlry 85-89; Univ Hons Prog Unif Of NE 86-88; Post Clg Award Excelnc In Chem 90; Deans List 85-90; Magna Cum Laude 90; Mgt.

**LI, KETTY,** Pace Univ At Ny, New York, NY; FR; BBA; Chrstn Clb 90-; Asian Clb 90-; Cmptr Sci; Acctg Inf Systms.

**LI, LIANG,** City Univ Of Ny Baruch Coll, New York, NY; JR; BA; Mktg.

**LI, LICHAO,** City Univ Of Ny Baruch Coll, New York, NY; SO; BA; Intl Mrktng; Intl Bus.

**LI, RAYMOND K,** Temple Univ, Philadelphia, PA; JR; BS; Rho Chi Scty 90-; Am Phrmctcl Assoc 89-; Duty Flight Oper Ofcr 75-81; Sta Mgr Transit Railways Corp 81-86; Pharmacy.

**LI, SHAO J,** Cooper Union, New York, NY; JR; BE; CSA 89-; OCM 90-; ASCE 90-; Chi Epsilon.

**LI, SHU B,** City Univ Of Ny Baruch Coll, New York, NY; JR; BBA; Acctg.

**LI, SUK-HAN,** Howard Univ, Washington, DC; GD; BSW; NASW 89-90; Orgnztn Chinese American Wmn 90-; Bilingual Counselor 89-; MSW Univ Ala 88; MA Univ District Columbia 90; Social Work; Teach.

**LI, WEN TONG,** Saint Vincents Coll & Seminary, Latrobe, PA; SR; SVC Intl Clb Fndr/Pres 89-90; SVC Yrbk Clb 88-90; Amer Econ Assoc 88-90; Leland Smith Mem Schlrshp Summer Intrnshp 88-89; Acad Merit Schlrshp/Intl Stdnt Schlrshp 88-90; SVC Awd Excl Math/Econs 90-; BS 91; Econs/Math; Fin.**

**LI, XIN YU,** City Univ Of Ny Baruch Coll, New York, NY; SO; BA; Acctg Soc 90-; Blue Blet World Karate 89; CPR Cert 89-; Swmng Instr 90-; Math Asst; Acctg; CPA.

**LI, XUE TING,** City Univ Of Ny Baruch Coll, New York, NY; JR; Acctg.

**LI, YING-SHI,** City Univ Of Ny La Guard Coll, Long Island Cty, NY; SO; AAS; Phi Theta Kappa Soc Natl; CLS Guangzhou Sch Judicature China 85; Acctg/Data Process; CPA.

**LI, ZHAN QIN,** Palm Beach Comm Coll, Lake Worth, FL; JR; Bus Admin; Acctng.**

**LIAN, CINDY H T,** Radford Univ, Radford, VA; SO; BS; Intl Clb; Chorus; Chmbr Orch; Wrk Schlrshp; ATCL 89; Music Thrpy; Psychlgst.

**LIAN, JILL M,** Univ Of Nc At Charlotte, Charlotte, NC; SO; BA; Peer Educator; ICF; Lang Cnvrstn Prtnr; Engl; Tch.

**LIANG, CHIHONG,** City Univ Of Ny City Coll, New York, NY; JR; BS; ACM 87-; Gldn Key 90-; Mina Shaughnessy Oxford Univ Press Awd 90; Cmptr Sci; Cmptr Imgng/Pgm.

**LIANG, JIAN GUANG,** City Univ Of Ny Baruch Coll, New York, NY; JR; BA; Acctg; Banks/CPA Firm.

**LIANG, RONGXIN,** Fordham Univ, Bronx, NY; SO; BS; MIS; ASM; Asian Clb; Mgmt Info Systms; Mgmt.

**LIANOS, ATHANASIA D,** Athens St Coll, Athens, AL; SR; Otsdng Cmprhnsve Sci Awd; Cum Laude; BED; Cmprhnsve Sci Sec Educ.

**LIAUGAUDAS, VYDA G,** City Univ Of Ny City Coll, New York, NY; SR; BA; Gldn Key; Day Care Tchr; Educ.

**LIBBEY, CLARK A,** Oh Wesleyan Univ, Delaware, OH; FR; Fac Schlrshp 91-.

**LIBER, LIZA L,** Fl International Univ, Miami, FL; FR; MBA; Faculty Schlr 90-; FL Acad Schlr 90; Acctg; Tax Attny.

**LIBERA, ANNETTE,** Western New England Coll, Springfield, MA; FR; Plsh Natl Allnce 78-; Lfegrd Prog 87; Cnnd Fd Drve 90; Dns Lst 90-; Vol Ushr At Prmnt Thtre 90; Dept Of Scl Srvcs 90; Gen Bus; Bus.

**LIBERANTE, WENDY L,** Teikyo Post Univ, Waterbury, CT; GD; BS; Wmns Sccr Capt 88-90; Amer Mrktng Assoc Sec 90-; IM 89-90; Intrcultrl Trng Cert; NAIA Schlr Ath Top 10 89; AMA Achvmnt Awd; Schlr Ath 88-; Sccr Capt 88-90; AS; Cert; Mgmt; Htl/Rest.

**LIBERATORE, ADRIAN J,** Duquesne Univ, Pittsburgh, PA; JR; BED; Elem Ed; Law.

**LIBERMAN, GALINA,** Bunker Hill Comm Coll, Boston, MA; FR; Engl; Music.

**LIBERTI, TRICIA,** S U N Y Coll At Oneonta, Oneonta, NY; FR; BS; Stdnt Dtc Assoc; Amer Hm Ec Assoc; Otng Clb; Ldrshp Cnfrnc; Dns Lst Oneonta; CROP Wlkthn; Ntrtn; Dtn.

**LIBERTO JR, LARRY J,** Wv Northern Comm Coll, Wheeling, WV; JR; AAS; Phi Theta Kappa; Pres Lst 89-; Stdnt Of Yr 90-; CERT Rosedale Tech Inst 89; Comp Sci/Eng; BS Mech Eng.

**LIBERTY, RICHARD A,** Schenectady County Comm Coll, Schenectady, NY; SR; AAS; Elec Tech Clb Pres 90; Radio Clb Treas 90; Phi Theta Kappa; Elec Tech; Masters Elec Engr.

**LIBRIZZI, CHARLES M,** City Univ Of Ny La Guard Coll, Long Island Cty, NY; SO; MBA; Psychlgy Clb Sec 90; Acctg Clb 89; Phi Beta Kappa 89-; Data Base Mgmnt Intern 89-; Engl; Scndry Edn.

**LICARI, ANTONELLA,** Marist Coll, Poughkeepsie, NY; FR; BA; SGA Exctv Asst Pblc Rltns Dir 90-; Thtr Grp Pblcty Dir 90-; TV Clb 90-; Intern Cngrssmn Fhs Cswrkr; Awrd Ddctn Stdnt Bdy; Jrnymns Thtr; Mddl Sts Evltn Cm Mrst; Cmmnctns Pblc Rltns Trck; Advrtsng.

**LICARI, DEBRA R,** Slippery Rock Univ, Slippery Rock, PA; SO; Exrcs Physlgy.

**LICARI, MARIA GIOVANNA,** Marist Coll, Poughkeepsie, NY; SO; BA; Coll Cncl Thtr Arts Sec; Stdnt Govt Cmmtr Union Pres 90-; SGA Sec; Various Thtr Awds 89-; Coll Ltl Peopls Smmr Wrkshp Sr Cnslr; Engl/Scndry Educ; Tchng.**

**LICHTENFELS, KERI A,** Indiana Univ Of Pa, Indiana, PA; SR; PSEA 89-90; Dns Lst 88-90; Hnr Grdt Cum Laude 90; BED 90; Elem Ed; Elem Tchr.

**LICHTER, JONATHAN A,** William Paterson Coll, Wayne, NJ; JR; BA; Deans List 89; Schlrshp The NJ Assoc Public Accountants; Collegiate Investment Challenge A T & T; Alumni Assoc Schlrshp Acdmc Exc 88-89; Accounting.

**LICHTEY, LAURA A,** Bergen Comm Coll, Paramus, NJ; SO; BA; Phi Theta Kappa 90-; Rcpnt Highest Schlstc Avg Awd; AA; Psychlgy.

**LIDDELL, DRUMMOND M,** Univ Of Al At Birmingham, Birmingham, AL; JR; BS; FOP Lodge 88-; Dpty Shrf Jfrsn Co Shrfs Dept 88-; Crmnl Jstc; Law Enf.

**LIDDELL, TERRENCE T,** Morehouse Coll, Atlanta, GA; JR; BS; STRIPES 88-90; Frederick Douglass Tutrl Prog 88-; Hnrs Prog Clb Pub Dir 88-; Phi Beta Kappa; Pre Dctrl Intrnshp UNC Chapel Hill; UMARC Asstshp 90-; Top 40 Stdnts Morehouse Clg; Psychlgy; Indstrl Psy/Cnsltng.

**LIDDLE, DAVID E,** Nova Univ, Ft Lauderdale, FL; GD; MBA.

**LIDDLE, SARAH L,** Anne Arundel Comm Coll, Arnold, MD; SO; BA; Edctn; Psychlgy; Elem Schl Tchr.

**LIDDY, DAVID W,** Univ Of Sc At Columbia, Columbia, SC; SO; EE; Navy ROTC; IEEE; Stu Govt Rep Penn St Univ; Mltry Ordr W W Awrd; IM Ftbl Vllybl Hcky Sftbl Capt; Enlstd Cmmssn Prog; US Navy E-6 Offc Cand; Elect Eng; Eng/Nvl Offcr.

**LIDONNICE, JOHN M,** Saint Francis Coll, Loretto, PA; JR; BS; Yrbk Stf Bsn Mgr 90-; Hnrs Pgm Nwsltr Stf Edtr 90-; Bsktbl Tm Stats 89-; Hnrs Pgm Comm Chrmn 89-; KC Rcdr 90-; Dns Lst 88-; Natl Clgt Hnrs Cncl Conf 90; Pblctns Ntl Hnrs Rpt 90; Fncl Mgmt; Invstmnt Bnkng.

**LIDONNICE, JULIE A,** Saint Francis Coll, Loretto, PA; FR; BA; Engl; Tchr.

**LIEB, JUSTIN G,** George Mason Univ, Fairfax, VA; FR; BS; Scty Intrntl Stds 90-; Acad Actvts Cnsl Rep 90-; Rsdnt Stdnt Assc Rep 90-; Pre Bus; Law.

**LIEB, KEVIN E,** Univ Of Cincinnati, Cincinnati, OH; JR; BM; Pianist For Wnd Symphny 90; Accmpnst For Chrle/For Chmbr Sngrs 90; Hon Stdnt Assoc 88; Krefting Schlrshp 88-89; Perfrmd Live 90; Piano Perf; Cncrtzng Tchr At U.

**LIEB, LAURIE A,** Indiana Univ Of Pa, Indiana, PA; SR; BS; PA St Educ Assn 90-; Chld Cre Vol Fr Cntr Fr Imprvmnt Of Fam Life Inc 90-; Vol Offcl Fr Spcl Olympcs; Educ; Elem Educ.

**LIEB, MATTHEW C,** Georgetown Univ, Washington, DC; SO; ROTC 89-; Sccr Vrsty Lttr 89-90.

**LIEBOLD, SUSANNE M,** City Univ Of Ny Baruch Coll, New York, NY; SR; MBA; Itln Soc 87-89; Gldn Key 88-; Beta Gamma Sigma; BBA; Intl Mktg.

**LIEBROSS, IRA D,** Coll Of Health Sci Stony Brook, Stony Brook, NY; GD; MD; Stony Brook; BA Amherst Co 89.

**LIEGEL, KEVIN R,** Southern Coll Of Tech, Marietta, GA; GD.

**LIEN, CHIUNG Y,** Univ Of Nc At Charlotte, Charlotte, NC; SO; BA; Intl Clb; Chns Assn; Bio; Med Tech.

**LIEN, PATRICK L,** Univ Of Miami, Coral Gables, FL; JR; BS; Tau Kappa Epsilon; Intern JSB Cnsltng Engrs 89; Deans List U Of Miami 90-; Music Engrng; Recording Eng Music Ind.

**LIEN, STEVEN K,** Georgetown Univ, Washington, DC; SO; BA; Rd Stn Bus Mgr 89-; Chmbr Music Grp Brd Dir 89-; Mck Bnbl Drmtc Scty 89-; Sphmr Clss Comm Spcl Evnts Org 90-; Nw Stdnt Orrtn; Wrk Wd Mllr Assoc Intern 89-; Econ.

**LIESMAN, JESSICA L,** Immaculata Coll, Immaculata, PA; SR; BA; Edn Club 87-; Stdnt Un Rep 88-90; Chester Co Reading Assn 88-90; Coll Hnr Soc; Deans List 90-; Eng; Elem Tchr.

**LIEUW, JOAN M,** Fl International Univ, Miami, FL; SR; BA; Sigma Tau Delta Sec 90-; Phi Lambda Hstrn 90-; Phi Kappa Phi; Engl.

**LIFF, JOE A,** Washington State Comm Coll, Marietta, OH; FR; AAS; Auto Diesel Tech; Automotive Tchncn.

**LIFSEY, PAMELA KAY,** Middle Tn St Univ, Murfreesboro, TN; JR; BA; BA Nashvl Tech 90; Busn Mgmt; Insurnce.

**LIGA, STEVEN G,** Villanova Univ, Villanova, PA; SR; BA; Phldlphia Hmlss Strng Comm 88-; Stdnt Soc Actn/Awrnss Ntwrk Strng Comm 89-90; Stdnts Tgthr In Cmmnty Serv Rep 89-90; Phi Kappa Phi 90-; Merton/Day Awrd 90-; Acdmc Schlrshp 88-; Deans Lst 88-; IM Ftbl Capt 88-89; Engl.

**LIGGETT, CHARLES RICHARD,** Fl A & M Univ, Tallahassee, FL; SO; BS; Hist Educ; Tchng.

**LIGGON, RUSSELL D,** Fayetteville St Univ, Fayetteville, NC; SO; BA; US Army Spc 87-89; Dns Lst 89-90; Good Conduct Medal/Achvmnt Medal 89; Econ; Stockbroker.**

**LIGHT, AMY E,** The Kings Coll, Briarclf Mnr, NY; JR; Cheerleading Captn 88-90; Acctg.

**LIGHT, ERIC L,** East Tn St Univ, Johnson City, TN; JR; BS; Dietetics; RD Sports Nutrition.

**LIGHT, KATHERINE M,** Univ Of Cincinnati, Cincinnati, OH; SR; BFA; Nvgtrs Treas 89-; Cmps Crsd Chrst 88-89; Cincinnati Chldrns Thtr 89-90; Natl Key; Drmtc Prfrmnc; Acting/Cmnctn.

**LIGHT, PAMELA K,** Muskingum Coll, New Concord, OH; GD; Wmns Inst V P 89-; Stdnt Jdcl Brd 89-90; All Cmps Jdcl Brd 90-; Phi Alpha Theta 90-; Phi Theta Beta; Circ Omicron Delta Kappa 90-; Theta Phi Alpha V P 88-; Odyssey Of The Mind Coach/Jdge 90-; Natl Prsbytrn Schlrshp; Dns Lst; BA; Elem Educ; Tchr.

**LIGHT, ROBIN C,** Univ Of Cincinnati-Clrmnt Coll, Batavia, OH; SO; BA; Big Bro/Big Sis Org 89-90; Nrsng Assn 89-90; Choir; Sndy Schl Tchr 90; Psychlgy; Scl Wrk.

**LIGHTBOURNE, MARVIN R,** Benedict Coll, Columbia, SC; SO; BSC; Stdnt Rlgs Awrns Org Chpln 90-; Pr Hlth Clb; Intl Stdnts Assoc; Hnrs Stdnt Assoc 90-; Blgy.

**LIGHTFOOT, CAROLYN G,** Fl International Univ, Miami, FL; JR; BA; Psychlgy; Voc Cnslr.

**LIGHTFORD, WILLIE P,** Al A & M Univ, Normal, AL; SR; BA; Union Chpl Prog Matrons VP 89-; Mgt Assoc 84-; Certif C U Exec 90-; Mgr/Treas 84-; Certif Mc Kenzie Busn Schl 65; Busn Mgt; Small Busn Owner.

**LIGHTNER, SHARON R,** Milligan Coll, Milligan Clg, TN; JR; BED; Student Natl Edtl Assoc 90-; Elem Ed; Tchng.

**LIGHTSEY, ANTHONY KYLE,** Univ Of Southern Ms, Hattiesburg, MS; SR; BS; Polymer Sci Clb 90-; Amrcn Chmcl Soc 90-; Plstcs Engnrng Soc 90-; Polymer Rsrch; Polymer Sci; Rsrch.

**LIGHTSEY, BRIAN D,** Univ Of North Fl, Jacksonville, FL; JR; BA; Student Affiliate Amer Psy Scty; Phi Theta Kappa Publns Coord 89-90; Golden Key; Resrch Assitshp/Dr Jurek Karylowski UNF; AA FL Community Clg 90; Psy; Research Psy.

**LIGOURI, FRANK,** Comm Coll Algny Co Algny Cmps, Pittsburgh, PA; SO; BA; US Army Sgt Sqd Ldr 85-89; Rsrv US Army; Pol Sci; Law.

**LIKENS, ANN M,** Univ Of Tn At Martin, Martin, TN; SR; BSD; Earth Day Comm 89-90; Beta Beta Beta Pres 88-; Phi Kappa Phi; Mu Epsilon Delta 86-89; Sigma Kappa Hs Mngr 86-87; Biology; Microbiologist/Rsrch.

**LIKIN JR, RICHARD O,** Bridgewater Coll, Bridgewater, VA; SO; BS; Circle K VP 89-90; Stdnt Senate 90-; Ecnmcs Clb 90-; Chem; Rsrch/Doctorate.

**LIKUS, KRISTIN E,** Colby Sawyer Coll, New London, NH; JR; BFA; Equestrian Tm 88-; Art Stdnts League 90-; Acad Schlr Awd; Photo/Fine Arts.

**LILBURN, JAN MARIE,** William Paterson Coll, Wayne, NJ; SR; BA; Boonton Twnshp Brd Educ VP 85-; Deans List 86-; Math; Tchng.

**LILE, VIRGINIA R,** Georgetown Coll, Georgetown, KY; SR; SGA Rep 90-; Stdnt Fndtn 90-; Eta Delta Phi 90-; Delta Omicron 88-; Sigma Kappa Corr Sec 89-; BM; Chrch Music; Mnstr Of Msuic.

**LILES, JOYCE TARA,** Univ Of Sc At Coastal Carolina, Conway, SC; SR; BA; Erly Chldhd Ed; Tch.

**LILES, KENNETH R,** Univ Of Al At Huntsville, Huntsville, AL; GD; Swm Tm Parents Assoc Asst Distr Rep 90-; Certif US Swim Ofcl 90-; Certif Natl Radio Inst 82; Engr; Elctrcl Engr.

**LILJEBLAD, KIM M,** Univ Of Sc At Coastal Carolina, Conway, SC; FR; Cross Cntry 90-; Psychology.

**LILL, JOSEPH E,** S U N Y At Buffalo, Buffalo, NY; JR; BS; AICHE; Gldn Key; Tau Beta Pi; Phi Eta Sigma; Intern Eastman Kodak; IM Vllybll; Chmcl Eng; Eng.

**LILLARD, NYLEVE A,** Nc Agri & Tech St Univ, Greensboro, NC; JR; BS; Choir Sec 90-; Spnsh Clb Pres; La Mesa Espanola; Alpha Mu Gamma Sec 90-; NCATSU Chnclrs Exec Smnr 90-; Tnns 90-; Spnsh; Tchng.

**LILLEBERG, TODD C,** Univ Of Miami, Coral Gables, FL; FR; BA; JFW Pearson Schlrshp 90-; Fll Schlrshp Vrsty Trck Crss Cntry 90-; Pltcl Sci Engl; Law.

**LILLEY, LAURIE A,** Univ Of South Al, Mobile, AL; SR; BS; Phi Mu Sec 89-90; Pres Lst 89; Dns Lst 89; Elem Educ; Tchng.

**LILLIS, CHRISTINE ANN,** William Paterson Coll, Wayne, NJ; SR; CEC 88-90; Kappa Delta Pi; Zeta Alpha 90-; BA; Spec Ed; Schl Psychology.

**LILLY, ANNA M,** Beckley Coll, Beckley, WV; FR; BA; Sci; Nrsng.

**LILLY, AWKIE L,** Beckley Coll, Beckley, WV; SO; BA; Mem Bapt Chrch Cldrns Chrch Dir 77-; Busn; Mktg.

**LILLY, JERRY A,** Marshall University, Huntington, WV; JR; BS; Cmptr Sci/Info Sys; Sys Anlst/Dsgn.

**LILLY, MICHAEL J,** Univ Of Nc At Charlotte, Charlotte, NC; SO; BA; Chnclrs Cmmndtn; Im Vllybl/Soccer 90; Archtctre; Archtct/Edctr.

**LILLY, TAMARA Y,** Beckley Coll, Beckley, WV; FR; ASSOC; Cmptr Infrmtn Systm; Data Entry Oprtr.

**LIM, AMY F,** Queens Coll, Charlotte, NC; SO; BA; Intl Club Pres 89-; Union Brd Treas 90-; Learning Scty; Peer Advsr; SGA 90-; Janusian Order Secy Treas 90-; Hnr Rl 90; Dana Scholar 89-90; Art Communication; Advertising.

**LIM, BEE-CHENG,** Strayer Coll, Washington, DC; SR; BA; Alpha Chi; Acctg.

**LIM, CHAEHONG,** S U N Y At Buffalo, Buffalo, NY; SR; BS; Buffalo Korean Presb Church Clg Grp Pres 90-; Inst Elctrcl Elctrnc Engrs; Tau Beta Pi 89-; Golden Key 90-; David Smyth Langell Mem Flwshp 90; Elctrcl/Cmptr Engr.

**LIM, CHONG C,** City Univ Of Ny Baruch Coll, New York, NY; SR; BBA; Bdy Bldng Clb VP 90; Gldn Key; Beta Gamma Sigma; Omicron Delta Epsln; Untd Malaysian Stdnts Assn VP 89; Deans Lst 84-90; Finance Invstmnts; MBA.

**LIM, GEOK LIAN,** Memphis St Univ, Memphis, TN; SR; BA; Intl Stdnt Assc 87-; Malaysian Stdnt Soc 87-; Beta Gamma Sigma; Phi Kappa Phi; Gldn Key 90-; Finance; Fncl Analysis.**

**LIM, HUA H,** City Univ Of Ny Baruch Coll, New York, NY; SO; BBA; Acctg.

**LIM, IVY F,** Queens Coll, Charlotte, NC; SR; BA; Clg Un Brd Sec 89-90; Internatl Clb 88-; Peer Advsr 89-90; Admsns Core 89-; Yrbk Stdnt Life Ed 89-; Mortar Brd 89-; Amnesty Internatl Treas 88-89; Smr Abrd Flwshp 90; Dana Schlr 89-90; Eng/Cmnctn; Ed.

**LIM, JUAT-KEOW LYDIA,** Radford Univ, Radford, VA; SR; Fncl Mgmt Assoc 89-90; Phi Beta Lambda 89; Asian Culture Assoc 89-90; Delta Mu Delta 89-90; Hnr Stdnts Assoc 89-90; BBA Radford Univ; Finance; Bnkg.

**LIM, JUDY C,** City Univ Of Ny Baruch Coll, New York, NY; JR; BBA; Acctng.

**LIM, KAREN G,** Boston Coll, Chestnut Hill, MA; FR; BA; Hall Cncl 90-; Wrld Hngr Comm 90-; IM Sftball 90; Psychlgy; Clncl Psychlgy.

**LIM, KWAI FATT,** City Univ Of Ny La Guard Coll, Long Island Cty, NY; Acctg Clb; Hng Kng Clb Treas 90; Phi Theta Kappa; Ambsdr Fd Serv Asst Mgr 90-; Dept Comptrlr NYC Cntrct Adm Clrk; LCCI London Cmbr Comm Indstrl 88; Acctg; CPA.

**LIM, LEAN N,** City Univ Of Ny Baruch Coll, New York, NY; SR; BBA; Acctg Soc; Beta Alpha Psi; Beta Gamma Sigma; Goldn Key; Acctg.

**LIM, LEONG LINK,** Univ Of Ky, Lexington, KY; SO; BS; Computer Science; Computer Scientist.

**LIM, LOIS,** Nyack Coll, Nyack, NY; SO; BA; Yrbk Stf Art Ed 88; HEOP Rep 89-90; Korean Flwshp Pgm 89-; Law/Hon 86-89; Chld Edn; Foreign Msnry Chld Edn.

**LIM, RAMONA M,** Univ Of Miami, Coral Gables, FL; SR; BS; Carni Gras; Pblcty Comm; Cooking Excl 90-; Funday Comm Grp Ldr; Psychblgy Clb; Phi Eta Sigma ; Alpha Epsilon Delta; Alpha Lambda Delta; Deans Mstr Tutors; Kappa Alpha Psi Aux 89-90; Deans Lst 89-90; Biology; Medicine.

**LIM, SEOW F,** Univ Of Al At Huntsville, Huntsville, AL; GD; BED; IEEE Assc; Eta Kappa Nu 90-; Tau Beta Pi 90-; Elect Eng.

**LIM, STEPHEN S,** Tn Temple Univ, Chattanooga, TN; SO; BSC; Comp Sci; Comp.

**LIM, WAICHOO,** Radford Univ, Radford, VA; SO; BBA; Finance; Fnancl Anlyst.

**LIMA, AVELINO F,** Wv Univ At Parkersburg, Parkersburg, WV; BA; Country Soccer League Coach 90-; Scty Plastics Engrg; Chemist Techlg Attributions; BS Univ De Sao Pauls 72-75; English/German; Psychology.

**LIMA, JUAN CARLOS,** City Univ Of Ny City Coll, New York, NY; SO; BA; Amer Inst Arch Stdnts 88-90; Han Wave 90-; Bycle Rcng; Tennis; Cmunctns/Advtsng Dsgn; Advtsng.

**LIMA, JULIE A,** Colby Sawyer Coll, New London, NH; FR; Pres Fr Clss; Exec Brd; Stend Rep Ed Stndrd Comm; All Amer Schlr Awrd; Vrsty Soccr.

**LIMARDO, ABNER,** Univ Of Pr At Rio Piedras, Rio Piedras, PR; SR; BA; Pre-Med Std Asc 88-; Mcrblgy Std Asc 90-; Ntrl Sci Hnr Brd 89-; Ntrl Sci; Med.

**LIMING, MARY E,** Oh Wesleyan Univ, Delaware, OH; FR; BA; Stdnt Fndtn 90; Phi Eta Sigma 90; Circle K 90; Psychlgy.

**LIMONCELLI, SUSAN L,** Providence Coll, Providence, RI; JR; IM Sftbl/Vlybl.

**LIMONE, HELENA A,** William Paterson Coll, Wayne, NJ; GD; MA; Phi Sigma Iota 68-; Pi Lambda Theta; Spnsh Frnch Tchr 84-; BA OH Univ 68; Gdnc Cnslng; Bi Lngl Gdnc Cnslr.

**LIMRICK, BETH A,** Savannah Coll Of Art & Design, Savannah, GA; FR; BFA; Grphc Dsgn/Ill; Cmrcl Art.

**LIN, ADA TINA,** Harvard Univ, Cambridge, MA; FR; BA; Drma Clb Asst Stg Mngr 90-; Asn Amrcn Assoc; Vln Lssns 90-; Vrsty Lcrss; Hstry/Scnc; Mdcn.

**LIN, CECILIA KING-CHUNG,** Muskingum Coll, New Concord, OH; FR; Intl Stdnst Org 90-; Lambda Sigma; Sigma Alpha Iota; Music.

**LIN, DAVID A,** Cornell Univ Statutory College, Ithaca, NY; FR; BS; Bible Study 90-; Bible Study Choir 90-; Donald L Shapiro Stdnt Schlrshp U Rochester; IM Vlybl 90-; Bio Sci; Med.

**LIN, DAWEI,** S U N Y At Binghamton, Binghamton, NY; SO; BS; Acctg/Mgmt Org 90-; Bsn Mgmt; Finance.

**LIN, GEBI,** Christopher Newport Coll, Newport News, VA; SR; BS; Data Proc Mgmnt Assoc Treas 90-; Deans List 89-; Magna Gum Laude; Intrnshp CEBAF 90-; Cert Count Holyoke Clg 88-89; BA Beijang Normal Univ 84-88; Cmptr Scnc; System Analyst.

**LIN, HSUEH-JUNG CHRIS,** Memphis St Univ, Memphis, TN; JR; BA; Sales Assist Intl Paper Taiwan Ltd 85-90; Assoc Degree Ming Chuan Clg 78-83; Busn; Computer Progr.

**LIN, JIA L,** City Univ Of Ny Baruch Coll, New York, NY; SR; BBA; Finance/Ecnmc Soc 88-; Finance; Analysis.

**LIN, LIN,** Univ Of Cincinnati, Cincinnati, OH; JR; BM; Artsts Prgrm 89-; Otstndng Cllg Stdnts America 90; Gldn Key; Yng Keybrd Artists Assn 89; Intrntnl Piano Cmptition Orlando FL; Yng Mscns Cmpetition Lima Oh; Piano; Musician.

**LIN, SHIOU-HER,** Wagner Coll, Staten Island, NY; SO; Chinese Stdnt Assc 90-; Intl Stdnt Assc 90-; Art; Bus.

**LIN, SUSIE S,** Univ Of Rochester, Rochester, NY; SO; BA; Asian Amrcn Assn 90; Chinese Stdnts Assn 90; Psychlgy; Clncl Psychlgst.

**LIN, TSAN HSIANG,** Gallaudet Univ, Washington, DC; FR; BA; Twn Sgn Lng Cert; Intl Clb 89-90; Jpns Sgn Lng Certf Am Sgn Lng Cert; Yth Cmp Intrprtmdl Stdnt Awrd; Deans Lst 89-90; Bus Admn.

**LINARES, HADA E,** Chattahoochee Vly St Comm Coll, Phenix City, AL; SO; Gamma Beta Phi; Chrch Comm Srvc 89-; Bsns; Ad Mngmnt.

**LINARES, NILBA,** Fl International Univ, Miami, FL; JR; BA; FEA 90-; Phi Delta Kappa Schlrshp 90-; AA Miami Dade Cmnty Clge 90; Elem Ed/Spnsh.

**LINAUGH, PHILIP J,** Univ Of Sc At Columbia, Columbia, SC; SR; BA; Coll Young Rep 87-90; Sigma Nu 87-9-; Rugby Tm 87; Bus Sales.

**LINCOLN, BROOKE A,** Univ Of Ga, Athens, GA; SO; BED; Food/Ntrtn Assn 90-; Stdnt Home Ec Assn 90-; Pi Beta Phi 90-; Home Ec Educ; Tchng.

**LINCOLN, CHRISTINE F,** Univ Of Sc At Columbia, Columbia, SC; SR; BS; Acdmc Rspnsblty Cmmtt 90; WSI 81; Cert Scuba Dvr 83-; Triathelete 1st Pl 89-; Nrtrng Cntr Vol; Midland Cntr Vol 86; Athlete Schlrshp 83-87; All Amer; Psych; Educ MS.

**LINCOLN, KADE P,** Tn St Univ, Nashville, TN; SO; BS; Cmptr Sci Clb 89-; Deans Lst 89; Lab Asst; Acad Cmptng; Rsrch Asst 90-; Pub Prgrmr Intrn; Cert Booker Wash Inst 87; Cert W African Cmptr 88; Cmptr Sci; Sys Snlyst/Sftware Spec.

**LINCOLN, ROBIN L,** Hillsborough Comm Coll, Tampa, FL; SR; AS; Eastrn Star 79-; Calvry Chrch; LPN 79-; Med; Nrsng.

**LINCOLN, STEPHANIE J,** Univ Of Charleston, Charleston, WV; SO; ADN; Capito Assn Nrsng Stdnts 90-; Alpha Lambda Delta 90-; Jr League 90-; Nurse Extern; EMT Durham Comm Clg 85; Nrsng.

**LINDAHL, JAMI L,** Longwood Coll, Farmville, VA; JR; BS; Ambassadors 89-; Stdnt Ed Assc Treas 89-; Concert Choir 89-; Kappa Delta Pi Treas 90-; Math; Ed.

**LINDAHL, JESSICA K,** Indiana Univ Of Pa, Indiana, PA; JR; BSED; Stdnt Govt Comm Affrs Chmn 88-89; Sigma Tau Delta Sec; Prvsts Schlr 89-; Engl Ed.**

**LINDAMOOD, JEANIE M,** Radford Univ, Radford, VA; SR; BS; Pi Gamma Mu 90-; Fmly Rsrc Ctr Vol 90-; AAS Wytheville Cmnty Clg 88; Soclgy; Human Svcs.

**LINDAUER, KATHLEEN DEMETRA,** Ms St Univ, Miss State, MS; SR; BS; Cmps Phrmcy Tchncn; Scndry Ed; Tch.

**LINDAUER JR, ROBERT G,** Queens Coll, Charlotte, NC; JR; BA; Vars Bsktbl NCAA Div II 89-; Bsn; Sml Bsn Mgmt.

**LINDBERG, HELEN L,** Va Commonwealth Univ, Richmond, VA; SR; BFA; Theatre; Acting.

**LINDBLAD JR, JOHN E,** Va Commonwealth Univ, Richmond, VA; SO; BA; Cmnctn Art/Dsgn; Graphic Dsgnr.

**LINDBLAD, MARGRETTA E,** Merrimack Coll, North Andover, MA; FR; BS; Clss Cncl 90-; Hall Cncl 90-; Psych Clb 90-; Psych.

**LINDEMEIER, ELLEN B,** Savannah Coll Of Art & Design, Savannah, GA; JR; BFA; Pms Pblshd In Schl Ltrry Mag; Fndd Wrte The Vewfndr Vdeo Stdnt Pblctn; Spk Flnt Grmn; Art Hstry; Grad Schl Fr MFA.

**LINDER, KENNETH C,** Wv Univ At Parkersburg, Parkersburg, WV; SO; MBA; Wood Co Emerg Serv Res Sqd Sgt 86-; Instr CPR Bsc Rescr Instr 89-; Wood Co Shrfs Dept Intrnshp 90-; Crmnl Jstce/Bsns; IRS/FBI/DEA.

**LINDERMAN, MARIA L,** Univ Of Pr At Rio Piedras, Rio Piedras, PR; SO; Natl Clgt Bsns Merit Awd 90-; All Amer Schlr Clgt Awd 90-; Hon Regstrn 90-; Comp Inf Sys; Comp Prog.

**LINDGREN, KIM,** Wagner Coll, Staten Island, NY; SR; BSE; Yearbook 89-; Stage & Pep Bands 88-90; Chrstn Flwshp 90-; Kappa Delta I 89-; Omicron Delta Kappa 89-; Alethea 89-; Epsilon Delta Omicron 90-; Bethel Evangelical Free Church Sunday School Vac Bible Schl Tchr 87-; Elem Ed; Teaching.

**LINDH, TINA E,** Queens Coll, Charlotte, NC; SO; BA; Stdnt Gvrnmnt Soph Cls VP 90-; Admsns Care; Clg Un Brd Drctrs Chrprsn CEC 90-; Mrshl Hghst Cls Qpa 90-; Dana Schlr Ldrshp Acdmcs 90-; Psychology Spnsh; Cnslng.

**LINDHEIMER, MARY ALICE,** Hudson Valley Comm Coll, Troy, NY; FR; BA; Erly Chldhd Clb 90-; Prsdnts Lst 90; Deans Lst, Nrsry Schl Ta 90-, Edctn, Tchng Elem Edctn.

**LINDHURST, JEFFREY C,** Oh Univ, Athens, OH; JR; BSEE; Ski Clb 88-89; Eta Kappa Nu; Deans Schlrhsp 89-90; Elect Eng.

**LINDLEY, ANGELA S,** Walker Coll, Jasper, AL; SO; Cmps Clb 90-; Phrmcy.**

**LINDLEY, WENDY L,** Univ Of Al At Birmingham, Birmingham, AL; JR; BS; Golden Key; Friends Anmls 89-; FHA Invstr Rprtr Southtrust Mort 87-; AS Rets Inst 85; Crmnl Just; Frnsc Evdnc.

**LINDMAN, LINDA S,** Univ Of South Al, Mobile, AL; BSE; Exec Sec; Srvc Crdntr; Eng; Tchg.

**LINDO-THOMAS, PAMELA A,** Fl International Univ, Miami, FL; BA; Price Waterhouse Ja W I 83-85; Air Jamaica Ltd Ja W I 85-88 & Summers 90891 Miami Fl; AA Miami Dade Comm Coll 8 2; Lib Studies; Edctr.

**LINDOR JACKSON, MARIE U,** Inter Amer Univ Pr San German, San German, PR; GD; BA; Spnsh Ttr; Assoc Psychlgy Stdnts; Intl Stdnts Org; Phi Beta Chi; BA 88-; Psychlgy Elem Ed.

**LINDOR, EDDY J,** City Univ Of Ny Baruch Coll, New York, NY; SR; BBA; Gldn Key; Beta Gamma Sigma; Acntncy.

**LINDOR, ODINE,** Fl International Univ, Miami, FL; JR; BA; AS Miami Dade Comm Clge 88; Soc Wrk; Fed Prbtn Off.

**LINDQUIST, CAROLE ANNE,** Liberty Univ, Lynchburg, VA; JR; BS; Prayer Ldr; Tutor; Math Clb 90-; Splunking 90-; Alpha Lambda Delta 89-; Kappa Mu Epsilon; Hon Pgm 89-; Deans Lst 89-; Math; Actuarial.

**LINDQUIST, ROBERT ARTHUR,** George Mason Univ, Fairfax, VA; SR; BS; Golden Key; Alpha Chi; Omicron Delta Epsilon; Beta Gamma Sigma; Summa Cum Laude 89; AS Northern Va Comm Clg 89; Fin; Intl Fin Mgmt.

**LINDSAY, BRIDGET A,** Univ Of Cincinnati-Clrmnt Coll, Batavia, OH; JR; MBA; Theta Phi Alpha; Busn; Mktg.

**LINDSAY, HOPE D,** Coll Of Charleston, Charleston, SC; FR; MBA; Phi Theta Sorority Sen Executive Cncl 88-; CALF Charleston Animal Liberty Fund 90-; Work For The Prevention Of Cruelty To Animals & A Meat Free America; English; Photo Journalism.

**LINDSAY, JENNIFER F,** Univ Of South Al, Mobile, AL; FR; BA; English; Teaching.

**LINDSAY, JONATHON M,** Bridgewater Coll, Bridgewater, VA; JR; BS; Hlth Sci; Allied Hlth Field.

**LINDSAY, ROBERT F,** Oh Univ, Athens, OH; GD; DO; Chrstn Med Dntl Soc VP 90-; SOMA 90-; AMSA 90-; Phi Kappa Phi 87-; Gamma Sigma Delta 87-; Sigma Sigma Phi; BS Ohio St U 78; Ostpthc Med; Fmly Prctc Med.

**LINDSAY, SUSAN H,** Longwood Coll, Farmville, VA; SO; BS; Fld Hcky Var 89-90; Lacrosse Var; Sigma Sigma Sigma; Reach 89-90; Elem Ed; Tchr.

**LINDSEY, ALAN M,** Tn St Univ, Nashville, TN; JR; BS; NAACP Pres; Cmptr Sci Clb 88-; Assn Excllnc Cmptr Sci Math Physics 82-; TN Nature Cnsrvncy Inter; Cmptr Sci; Cmptr Eng.

**LINDSEY, BILLIE A,** S U N Y Coll At Fredonia, Fredonia, NY; JR; BA; Dorm Cncl VP 89-; Kappa Delta Pi; Edctn Englsh; Rsrch Lbrn.

**LINDSEY, BRENDA L,** Itawamba Comm Coll, Fulton, MS; FR; AD; Stdnt Nrs Assn 90-; Nrsng.

**LINDSEY JR, DAVID A,** Memphis St Univ, Memphis, TN; SR; BBA; Gamma Beta Phi Hon Soc 88-; Mortar Brd 90-; Amer Mktg Hon Soc; Delta Nu Alpha 90-; Deans Lst 89-; Grad Cum Laude 90-; Transp Logistics.

**LINDSEY, FELISA M,** Tallahassee Comm Coll, Tallahassee, FL; SO; AA; Deans Lst 90-; Mc Knight Achievers Soc Mother/ Spnsr; Limited Surety Agent 90-; AS FL Tech Coll Of Jax 87; Cmptr Info Sys; CIS Sys Analysts.

**LINDSEY, GINA D,** Winthrop Coll, Rock Hill, SC; JR; BA; Cncl Excptnl Chldrn 89-90; Kappa Delta Pi Hstrn/Pres 90-; Phi Kappa Phi 90-; Stdnt Mrshl 89-90; Pres Lst 89-; Deans Lst 88; Early Chldhd Ed; Tchr.

**LINDSEY, JANELL I,** Fisk Univ, Nashville, TN; BA; Bptst Stdnt Un VP 88-; Unvrsty Ushr Prsdnt 88-; Rsdnt Asstnt 89-; Deans Lst; Delta Sigma Theta; Alumni Ldrshp Awd; Hstry; Intrntnl Rltns.

**LINDSEY, JOY D,** Jackson St Univ, Jackson, MS; JR; BS; Amer Mktg Assc VP Fin; Mass Comm Clb; Alpha Lmbd Dlt 89-; Goodwin Grp Intrnshp Jackson MS; Mass Cmnctns; Advrtsng.

**LINDSEY, KATHY R,** Benedict Coll, Columbia, SC; SNEA 86-90; SCNEA 90-; NEA 90-; PEE DEE Intrntl Rdng Assn 90-; Alpha Kappa Mu 88-90; Alpha Chi 88-90; Alpha Kappa Alpah Chpln 89-; Tchr; BS Benedict Coll 90; Elem Ed; Tchr.

**LINDSEY, LINDA L,** Comm Coll Algny Co Algny Cmps, Pittsburgh, PA; SR; AS; Alta Hlth Strtgs-Cstmr Serv; Comp Info; Comp.

**LINDSEY, MARY L,** Univ Of South Al, Mobile, AL; FR; BS; Physics; Ind Rsrch & Dvlpmnt.

**LINDSEY, PAMELA M,** Phillips Jr Coll Charlotte, Charlotte, NC; GD; Peer Counselor 90; Prsdnt Lst 89-90; Deans Lst 89-90; Achvrs Pin; AS 89-90; Rutledge Clg; Cmptrs.

**LINDSEY, SHAWNDA R,** Univ Of Tn At Martin, Martin, TN; JR; BS; Un City Jcetts Chpln 88-; Elem Ed; Tch Spec Ed.

**LINDSEY, TINA M,** Teikyo Post Univ, Waterbury, CT; SO; BFA; Intr Dsgn Clb 89-; Phi Theta Kappa 90-; Big Bro/Big Sis 89-90; AS; Intr Dsgn; Arch Dsgn.

**LINDSEY, TONYA L,** Al St Univ, Montgomery, AL; SR; BS; WEB Dubois E Frnkln Frazier; Soc Clb VP 89-; Alpha Kappa Alpha Phlctr 89-; Bkkpng Acctg Carver St Tech Clg 86; Soc/Crim Just; Atty.

**LINDSEY, TRACY M,** Longwood Coll, Farmville, VA; JR; BS; Exctv Sec VA Dpt St Police Richmond VA 82-90; Clrcl Stds Southside VA Cmmnty Clg 81-82; Certf John H Daniel Camps Keysville VA; Bsns; Infrmtn Systm.

**LINDSLEY, WENDY E,** Georgian Court Coll, Lakewood, NJ; SR; BA; Delta Mu Delta 90-; Assoc Sci 89; Bus Acctg.

**LINDSTROM, GUSTAV H,** Mt Saint Marys Coll & Seminary, Emmitsburg, MD; BA; Intl Stdns Assoc 89-; George Henry Miles Hnr Soc 89-; Var Tennis 89-; Political Scnc; Civil Servi.

**LINDSTROM, KIRSTEN ELISE,** Endicott Coll, Beverly, MA; FR; BA; Academic Support; Comm Art.

**LINDSTROM, THERESE E,** Univ Of South Al, Mobile, AL; JR; BA; SGA 86-; European Assoc 86-; Jaguar Productions; Mkrtng Assoc; Phi Eta Sigma 86-87; Cert Phillips Clg 90; Bus Mrktng; Mrktng Promotions.

**LINEBERRY, AMANDA L,** Univ Of Al At Huntsville, Huntsville, AL; JR; BS; German Stdnt Orgnztn 90-; Soc Wmn Engnrs 88-; Tau Beta Pi; Pi Kappa Phi; Fllwshp Mcrgrvty 89; 3m Schlrshp; Hnr Schlr 88-90; Mchncl Engnrng.

**LINENBERGER, STEVEN C,** Univ Of Sc At Columbia, Columbia, SC; FR; BA; Tnns Tm 90; Engl; Film Wrtr/Dir.

**LING, KAY Y,** Univ Of Rochester, Rochester, NY; JR; BA; Asian Amer Assn 88-; Chinese Stdnt Assn 88-; Deans Lst 88-; Sigma Delta Tau 88-90; Econ/Japanese; Intrntl Bus.

**LINGER, DANIEL E,** Univ Of Akron, Akron, OH; SR; BS; Ski Cl V P 89-; Sigma Iota Epsilon; Var Ftbl 89-90; Indus Mgmnt; Prsnnl; Hmn Rsce Mgmnt.

**LINGER, HERBERT T,** Washington State Comm Coll, Marietta, OH; FR; AD; Mech; Crpntry/Mech.

**LINGIS, STEVEN S,** Faulkner St Jr Coll, Bay Minette, AL; SR; BS; Baldwin Cnty Mntl Hlth Ctr Mnstr 89-; So Baldwin Cnty Ltrcy Cncl 88-; AA; AS; Rel; Chrch Mnstrs.

**LINGLE, JAMI S,** Univ Of Md Baltimore Prof Schl, Baltimore, MD; SR; PHARM; Stdnt Com On Drg Abse; Amer Phrmctcl Assn; MD Phmrcsts Assn; Rho Chi; Phi Kappa Phi; Omicron Delta Kappa; Psi Chi; Phi Eta Sigma; Phi Sigma; Alpha Lambda Sigma; Phi Delta Chi Pres 90; Capa Schlr; TPA Schlr; BS Univ Of MD Coll Park 86; Phrmcy; Clncl Phrmcy.

**LINHARDT, SCOTT E,** S U N Y Coll Of Tech At Alfred, Alfred, NY; SR; AOS; Rsdnce Hall Drm Cncl V P 87-88; Stdnt Staff Trng Comm 89-90; Excel Tchng Comm; Rsdnt Assist 89-; Peer Tutor 90-; Tour Guide 90-; Dns Lst 88; AS 91; Bldng/Constr; Constr Mgmt.

**LINHART, STEVEN D,** Anne Arundel Comm Coll, Arnold, MD; SO; BS; Summa Cum Laude; Geogrphy; Trnsprtatn Plnnr/ Lnd Mgmt.

**LINHOLM, RHONDA D,** Univ Of Al At Birmingham, Birmingham, AL; SO; BS; The Peer Cnnctn 90; Im Sftbl.

**LINK, CARLA J,** Wv Northern Comm Coll, Wheeling, WV; FR; ADN; LPN BM Spurr Schl/Prctcl Nrsng/Glendale WV 77; Nrsng; RN.

**LINK, JEAN A,** Comm Coll Algny Co Algny Cmps, Pittsburgh, PA; FR; BS; Sci; Nrsng.

**LINK, KARLA S,** De St Coll, Dover, DE; SR; BED; Pres Hnrs Awd; BS; Fshrs/Wldlf Mgmt; Aquacltr.**

**LINK, KIMBERLY R,** Cincinnati Bible Coll & Sem, Cincinnati, OH; FR; BA; Pro Life; Chrch Msc; Mnstry.

**LINK, TERESA G,** Radford Univ, Radford, VA; FR; BBA; Alton Bapt Chrch Acteens Pres 89-; Alpha Lambda Delta; Acctg; Law.

**LINKENHOKER, CAROLE L,** Wv Northern Comm Coll, Wheeling, WV; FR; ASD; Nursng.

**LINKER, MARCI J,** Boston Univ, Boston, MA; SR; BS; Pi Theta Epsilon 90-; Alpha Chi 88-89; V A Schlrshp 90-; Karen Jacobs Schlrshp MAOT 90-; Occptnl Thrpy; Therapist.

**LINKESH, JOSEPH M,** West Liberty St Coll, West Liberty, WV; SO; BS; Wrstlng 90-; Business.

**LINKOUS, ALLISON L,** Fl St Univ, Tallahassee, FL; FR; MBA; Phi Eta Sigma 90-; Hnrs Schlrs Peer Mntr 90-; Bsn; Fnce/ Ecnmcs.

**LINKOUS, MICHELLE NICOLLE,** New River Comm Coll, Dublin, VA; FR; MBA; SGA Sntr 90-; Vlybl 90-; Engl; Cmmnctns.

**LINN, DAVIS E,** Ms St Univ, Miss State, MS; SR; Coll Bus Indstry Stdnt Cncl Sec VP 89-90; Acdmc Affrs Co; Univ Schlrshp Co; Inter Schl Cncl; Gamma Beta Phi; Deans Lst Schlr; Fncl Mgmt Assoc; Kappa Sigma Treas; ACT Hnrs Schlrshp; BA; Fnc; Corp Fnc Fncl Cnsltng.

**LINN, MARGARET E,** Middle Tn St Univ, Murfreesboro, TN; FR; BS; Stdnt For Env Action; Biology.

**LINN, SHANNON N,** Clemson Univ, Clemson, SC; FR; BS; Kappa Alpha Theta 90-; IM Tennis 90-; Indstrl Engnrng; Engnrng.

**LINNEAN, REBECCA J,** Univ Of Toledo, Toledo, OH; FR; Resdnc Hall Actvts Cncl 90-; Physical Therapy.

**LINNETZ, ERIC H,** Cornell Univ Statutory College, Ithaca, NY; FR; BS; Glee Clb; Biol; Vet Med.

**LINS, JENNIFER C,** Salisbury St Univ, Salisbury, MD; SO; BS; Phi Eta Sigma; Math.

**LINSER, SONYA A,** Watterson Coll, Louisville, KY; Pres Lst 90-; Intrn W/Ott Comm Inc; Diploma; Cmmrcl Srt.

**LINSKEY, VERNA J,** Savannah St Coll, Savannah, GA; GD; Asbus Ad Univ Southern Maine 82; Acctng; Certif Public Account.

**LINSTER, SHAUN M,** Thomas Nelson Comm Coll, Hampton, VA; FR; BA; Mars Con Staff; Hist/Engrng; Nasa.

**LINTON, AMY M,** Philadelphia Coll Tex & Sci, Philadelphia, PA; FR; BA; Chrl Scty Radio Station DJ Yrbk Co Edtr 90-; Amnsty Intrntl 90-; Costume Dsgn.

**LINTON, ANNIE J,** Talladega Coll, Talladega, AL; FR; BA; Cmptr Sci; Pgrmmr.

**LINTON, BRIAN R,** Allegheny Coll, Meadville, PA; SR; BA; Jzz Bnd Stdnt Dir VP 87-; Cmps Nwsppr Edit Brd 90; H Hghs Smmr Fllwshp 89; Schlr; Vrsty Tnns; Intrcllgte Clb Vlybl; Msc And Chem.

**LINTON, JULIA L,** Livingston Univ, Livingston, AL; SR; BS; Lttrmns Clb 89-; Orntn Intrn 88; FCA 87-; Phi Mu VP 88-89; Pi Kappa Phi Ltlt Sis 89-; Envoy 88-; Vars Chrldr/Coach 89-; Physlgy/Nutrition.

**LINTON, KATHYE J,** Meridian Comm Coll, Meridian, MS; SO; MRT; Sftbl; Med; Med Rcds Tech.

**LINTON II, OWEN BRUCE,** Univ Of South Al, Mobile, AL; SR; BS; Jgr Prdctns Asst Fn Drctr 88-; Phi Eta Sigma VP 88-89; Alpha Lambda Delta Treas 88-; Prsdntl Schrlshp 87-; Acctg.

**LINTZ, WAYNE J,** Fort Valley St Coll, Fort Valley, GA; SR; MA; Engl Club 89-; Natl Hist Hon Soc; Natl Foreign Lang/Hon Soc 90-; Clg Self-Study Edtrl Bd 89-90; Sous Chef; BA; Cmctns; Film/TV.

**LINYEAR, DERRON B,** Morehouse Coll, Atlanta, GA; JR; BA; Kappa Kappa Psi 89-; Frst Un Natl Bank GA Intern; Urban Bnkrs Wl Schlr 90; Inroads Wl Inc Outstndng Total Perf 90; Banking/Finance; Security Trdng/Bnkng.

**LINZELL, THOMAS J,** Oh St Univ, Columbus, OH; SR; BS; Golden Key 90-; H S Phillian Schlrshp Awd 90; Clg Engr Hon Stdnt 87-; Sch Arch Hon Stdnt 87-; I M Ftbl Bkbl Sftbl Soccer 87-; Arch.

**LINZER, MENACHEM M,** Yeshiva Univ, New York, NY; SO; BA; Deans Lst 89-90; Bsktbl; Math; Engr.

**LINZEY, DONNA N,** Univ Of South Al, Mobile, AL; SR; BS; Ele Educ.

**LIOTT, JAMES E,** Wilmington Coll, New Castle, DE; JR; BA; Blmbrg Univ Delta Omega Chi 85-88; Wrstlng 85-88; Cmmtr Srvc Admn Dept Of Trnsptn 89; Bus.

**LIPA, DANIEL J,** Le Moyne Coll, Syracuse, NY; JR; BS; Phi Theta Kappa 89-90; AA Broome Cmnty Clge 90; Business; Acctg.

**LIPARI, NICK S,** Oh St Univ, Columbus, OH; SR; BS; Hon Prog 87-; Excllnce Schlrshp Awrd; OH Hs Of Rep Cmmndtn; IM Soccr Chmpn 89; Psychlgy; Cnsltng.

**LIPCHIK, GAY L,** Edinboro Univ Of Pa, Edinboro, PA; SR; Psychlgy Clb 89-; Cmmtr Clb 89-90; Stdnts Wmns Equality 90-; Alpha Chi; Psi Chi; Dr Julia Marshall Bhvrl Sci Awd; Dr John Schell Bhvrl Sci Awd 90; Pres Hon Study Abroad Schlrshp; Grace A Crowe Hon Schlrshp 90; Cert Excell Rsrch; Psychlgy Clncl.

**LIPINSKI, LEANE E,** Coll Misericordia, Dallas, PA; SO; BS; Educ Clb 89-; Hnr Soc 89-; All Amer Schlr Clgt Awd 90-; Natl Clgt Bus Merit Awds 90-; Pres Schlrshp 89-; Elem Educ; Daycare Cntr/Psychology.

**LIPMAN, ANDREW A,** Univ Of Miami, Coral Gables, FL; SR; Pre-Law Soc 87-; Fnc Clb; Deans Lst 89-; BA Bus 90; BA Fnc; BA Rl Est; Fnc; Sprts Law.**

**LIPP, KATHLEEN S,** Capital Univ, Columbus, OH; SR; BSN; Kappa Alpha Pi; Dns Lst 89-; Reg Day Care Provdr 83-89; Nrsng; RN Onclgy.

**LIPP, STEPHANIE N,** Memphis St Univ, Memphis, TN; SR; STEA 89-; Kappa Delta Pi 87-; Elem Educ; Tchng.

**LIPPERT, CARRIE A,** Oh Wesleyan Univ, Delaware, OH; FR; BA; Symphny Orchstr 90-; Pres Clb 90-; Stdent Fndtn; Phi Eta Sigma 90-; Delta Zeta Pldg Cls Sec 90-; Psychlgy; Clinical Psychlgst.

**LIPPERT, MELANIE A,** Middle Tn St Univ, Murfreesboro, TN; SR; BA; Engl; Scndry Ed.

**LIPPIN, DANELLE L,** James Madison University, Harrisonburg, VA; SR; BS; SEA 89-90; Pres List; Early Chlhd Ed; Tch.

**LIPPS, DANIEL R,** Univ Of Cin R Walters Coll, Blue Ash, OH; SO; BA; R Walters Bus Clb VP 89-90; Acctg; CPA.

**LIPSCOMB, BRYAN J,** West Liberty St Coll, West Liberty, WV; FR; BA; Kappa Delta Rho; Bus Admin.

**LIPSCOMB, CHRISTINE E,** Univ Of Nc At Charlotte, Charlotte, NC; FR; BA; Bapt Un 90-; Chr Mnstry Tm 90-; Phi Eta Sigma 90-; Math.

**LIPSCOMB, DEANNA J,** Univ Of Tn At Knoxville, Knoxville, TN; JR; MBA; Gamma Sigma Sigma 89-; Tenn Trokette 89-; Exec Undgrad Bus Prog 89-; Phi Kappa Phi Gamma Beta Phi 86-; Golden Key 90; Delta Sigma Pi 89-; Beta Alpha Psi 90-; Accnt; CPA.

**LIPSCOMB, DEBORAH A,** Va St Univ, Petersburg, VA; SR; BA; Accntng Clb 89-; Vet Clb 89-; Non Trad Stu Clb 89-; Phi Beta Lamda 90-; Pres Lst 89; Dean Lst 89-90; Nghbrhd Wtch Jdg Advct 87-; Woodson Prnt Advsry Cncl 89-; AAS AS John Tyler Comm Coll 89; Accntng/Bus Admn; Accntng.

**LIPSCOMB, MELISSA G,** Birmingham Southern Coll, Birmingham, AL; JR; Prtnrshp 90; Sigma Tau Delta 90-; Alpha Si Omega; Thtr; Dir.

**LIPSCOMB II, RICHARD L,** Saint Thomas Univ, Miami, FL; SR; BA; Delta Tau Delta Alumni Rltns 87-90; TX Rngrs Bsbl Clb Intrnshp; Bus.

**LIPSCOMB, TIFFANY C,** Spelman Coll, Atlanta, GA; FR; BS; Grndghtrs Clb 90; Drm Step Tm 90; Alpha Lambda Delta 90; Ext Afrs Bd 90; Mary Alice English Knight Math Awd 90; Bkstbll 90; Math; Patent Law.

**LIPSEY, JESSICA E,** Johnson St Coll, Johnson, VT; SO; BA; Bhvrl Sci Clb Pres 89-90; Radio 89-90; Vol Serv 89-90; Dns Lst 89-90; Pres Lst 90; Frnsc Psychlgy.

**LIPSKY, JASON M,** Providence Coll, Providence, RI; FR; BA; Pre-Law Clb 90-; Vars Hcky Tm Mgr 90-; Hist; Law.

**LIPSY, JANET S,** S U N Y At Binghamton, Binghamton, NY; SR; BS; SUNNY Binghamton Mktg Assoc VP 90-; Im Sports 87-; Clairol Mkt Rsrch Intrn 90; Jewish Cmnty Center Intrn 90; Mgt; Mktg.

**LIPTAK, AMY R,** Barry Univ, Miami, FL; FR; BA; SG 90-; Ambassadors 90-; Cmnctns; Publ Rels.

**LIPTAK, KAREN M,** Kent St Univ Stark Cmps, North Canton, OH; FR; BS; KSSEA Treas 90-; OH Ed Assc; NEA; Alpha Lambda Delta; Paul Douglas Tchrs Schlrshp; Erly Chldhd Ed; Tchr.

**LIPTON, MARK DREW,** Barry Univ, Miami, FL; SO; BA; Scuba Diving/Camping/Water Sfty Instr; Lifeguard/Swim Instr; Fraternal Order Disposaliers; US Naval Special Warfare Group II; Navy Achtvt Awd Bravery/Letter Commdtn Secty Navy 3rd Class Petty Officer; Recreational Diving Mgt; Tchng Scuba.

**LIPTRAP, JOYCE LAW,** Mary Baldwin Coll, Staunton, VA; JR; BA; Stdnt Rels Cmte 90-; Alum Assoc Brd 90-; Sigma Tau Delta VP; VAEG 87-; Bethel Presby Church VP Womens Cir; Intl Womens AGLOW; Qual Of Educ Cmte 89; Poem Pub In Anthology Of Mod Wrters Author; AAS E Brant Schl Bus 67; Engl; Wrtng/Illus.

**LIRAG, MANOLITO R,** Bloomfield Coll, Bloomfield, NJ; JR; BS; Tae Kwon Do; Assc Indpndnt Clgs/Sch; Hon Grad Bus Cmptr Prgmng 85; Data Dictnry Spclst; Cert Cmptr Prgmng Sch Bus Machines 85; Cmptr Inf Systms; MIS.

**LIRIO, ROY R,** Franklin And Marshall Coll, Lancaster, PA; JR; BA; Intrntl Clb 89; Orchsta 88; Hnrs Lst; Dns Lst; Dana Corp Intrn 90; Physcs Acctng; Acctng.

**LIRO, MARY E,** Hillsborough Comm Coll, Tampa, FL; JR; BA; Phi Alpha Theta; AA Hllsbrgh Comm Clg 90; History; Edctn.**

**LIS, STEPHEN EDWARD,** Temple Univ, Philadelphia, PA; SO; BA; TASA 89-90; Archtctre.

**LIS, SUZANNE M,** Smith Coll, Northampton, MA; BA; Pnr Dvlpmntl Srvds Inc Cmpn 90-; Frst Grp Schlr 90-; Clncl Psychlgy.

**LISCIO, TINA M,** Univ Of Sc At Columbia, Columbia, SC; SR; BA; Gamma Beta Phi 89-; Golden Key 89-; Psi Chi Mbrshp Chrmn 89-; Zeta Tau Alpha Pldg Clss Treas 88-; Psych/Soc Work Law.

**LISENBY, ROD S,** City Univ Of Ny City Coll, New York, NY; JR; Deans Lst; Sociology; Bus Ownr/Architect.

**LISHINSKY JR, DAVID M,** Univ Of Pittsburgh, Pittsburgh, PA; SR; BS; Amer Phy Thrpy Assoc 89-; Phi Eta Sigma 87-; IMS 87-; Phy Thrpy.**

**LISICA, IGOR,** City Univ Of Ny City Coll, New York, NY; SO; BE; Deans Lst 90; Math Physics Tutor 90-; Elect Engr; Engr.

**LISK, THOMAS J,** Le Moyne Coll, Syracuse, NY; JR; BS; Choral Scty Secy 88-; Biology Clb 88-; IM Bsktbl 88-; Tri Beta 89-; PIC 90-; Tompkins Cnty Hosp Aux 89-; Cornell Sprts Info Sprts Wrtng Intrnshp 89; IMS 88-; Biology; Physical Therapy.

**LISOWSKI, GARY H,** Niagara Univ, Niagara Univ, NY; GD; Math Clb 88-90; Delta Epsilon Sigma 88-90; Kappa Mu Epsilon 89-90; Delta Epsilon Sigma Ntrl Science 89-90; George B Banks Memorial Awrd 90; Vrsty Golf 86-87; Law.

**LISOWSKI, MICHAEL F,** Glassboro St Coll, Glassboro, NJ; FR; PHD; Bwlng 88-; Bllrds 88-; Physcs; Astrphyscst.

**LISSNER, JANE M,** D Youville Coll, Buffalo, NY; SR; BS; Std Occptnl Thrpy Asc 89-; Amer Occptnl Thrpy Asc 88-; Snr Hnr Soc 89-; Dns Lst 89-; BA St Univ NY Buffalo 88; Occptnl Thrpy; Rehab/Head Injury.

**LISTER, BREWER S,** Clarkson Univ, Potsdam, NY; SO; BS; Spctrm Treas 89-; Phi Kappa Sigma 90-; Deans Lst 89; Prsdntl Schlr 90; Schlstc Achvmnt 90; 2M Sccr Bsktbll Brmbll 89-; Mrktng Econ.

**LISTER, DONNA M,** North Greenville Coll, Tigerville, SC; SO; AS; Bptst Stdnt Un 88-; Religion Vctn; Christian Cnslng.

**LISTER, ELINOR V,** Univ Of Sc At Columbia, Columbia, SC; JR; BA; Radio Nws Brdcstr 90-; SPJ VP Pgmng; Alpha Epsilon Rho 90-; Kappa Delta Chrmn Prjt Exclnc 88-; SC Snt Pg; Jrnlsm; Law.

**LISTER, ELIZABETH A,** Atlantic Comm Coll, Mays Landing, NJ; SO; AA; Educ; Psych.

**LISTER, KAREN ELIZABETH,** Univ Of South Al, Mobile, AL; SR; BS; Amer Mktg Assn Liaison 88-90; Hmecmng Comm 88; Propeller Club 88-90; Delta Nu Alpha 89-90; Alpha Omicron Pi Treas 85-90; Mktg; Pblc Rltns.

**LISTER, KELLI A,** Univ Of Sc At Columbia, Columbia, SC; SO; BA; Stdnt Sen Sec Mnrty Affairs; Coll Rpblcns Chm; Stdnt Leg 89-; Gamma Betga Phi 89-; Alpha Lambda Delta 89-90; Page For Sen H Samuel Stilwell; Pol Sci; Law.

**LISTER, MARGARET L,** Wilmington Coll, New Castle, DE; SR; BSN; Hon Soc; Instrctr Breast Self Exmntn Amer Cncr Soc; Spk Chllngs Nrsng Bd Exec Dir; RN Medcl Cntr DE Nrs Prcptr; BSN; Assoc Nrsg DE Tech/Comm Coll 85; Nrsng.

**LISTER, NATHAN A,** Thomas Nelson Comm Coll, Hampton, VA; FR; Elect Tech Advsr; Htng/Air Cond/Rfrg.

**LISTON, DARIN M,** United States Naval Academy, Annapolis, MD; SR; BS; Spanish Clb 89-; Photo Club 89-90; Phi Kappa Phi Treas 89-; Phi Sigma Iota 89-; Hist Hnr Soc 90-; Tutor 89-90; Dsgntd Faclty Cndt 90-; Olmstead Schlr 90-; Navy Burke Schlrshp 90-; Harry E Ward Mdl 90-; Slng Tm 87-88; Oceanography/Spanish; Naval Aviator.

**LISZCZ, LYDIA I,** West Chester Univ, West Chester, PA; SO; BS; Opera Soc; Cmnty Music Sch; Sigma Alpha Iota Treas; Sigma Alpha Iota Exclnc Schlrshp; Music Ed; Tchr.

**LITFIN, MATTHEW A,** Univ Of Tn At Knoxville, Knoxville, TN; SO; BS; Stdnt Gov Intrnl Affrs Comm 90-; Intrfrt Cncl Jdcl Brd 90-F Phi Eta Sigma Treas 90-; TN Schlrs; Exec Undrgrad; Phi Gamma Delta Scl Chr 89-; Grk Soph Awd; IFC Fresh Awd; Phi Gamma Delta Intrnshp; Memphis Cty Gov; Acctg 90; Fnc; Bus.

**LITKENHAUS, COLLEEN J,** Univ Of Ky, Lexington, KY; FR; Stdnt Actvts Brd; Rsn Clb Cls Rep; Phi Eta Sigma; Alpha Lambda Delta; Lambda Sigma; Big Lunch Buddy Prgrm; Pltcl Sci Rssn.

**LITRA, AMY E,** Winthrop Coll, Rock Hill, SC; SR; BA; SGA Artist Series Com 89-90; Greek Pres 90-; Chi Omega 87-; Chi Omega Pres 90-; Intern The Light Fctry Photo Ctr 90; Prof Photography Asst 90; Art/Comm; Museum Curator.

**LITTELL, MARIE A,** Marywood Coll, Scranton, PA; BA; Lgl Sec Scranton; Sec Dgr Lackawanna Bus Coll Scranton 66; Psychlgy/Clincl Pract.

**LITTEN, CRAIG G,** Daytona Beach Comm Coll, Daytona Beach, FL; SO; AS; BCM Chrstn Grwth Ofcr 90-; Photo; Photo.

**LITTLE, ALICE J,** Univ Of Al At Birmingham, Birmingham, AL; SO; AAS; Stdnt Phys Ther Org 90-; Amer Phys Ther Assoc 90-; Phi Theta Kappa 90-; Phys Ther.

**LITTLE, AMANDA S,** Univ Of Nc At Greensboro, Greensboro, NC; FR; BA; Stdnt NC Assn Edctrs 90-; Hall Cncl VP 90-; Vrsty Chrldng Squad 90-; Mdl Schl Ed/Engl; Tch.

**LITTLE, ANDREA M,** Tuskegee Univ, Tuskegee Inst, AL; FR; BS; Golden Voices Concert Chr; Gospel Ensemble Public Reltns 90-; Zeta Phi Beta; Elec Engrg; Profl Engr Tchng.

**LITTLE, BETTY S,** Liberty Univ, Lynchburg, VA; FR; Yth Qst Clb 90-; Chi Alpha 90-; Sndy Schl Asst Tchr; Chrstn Elem Prmry Educ; Open A Pre Schl.

**LITTLE, CHAD B,** Univ Of Pittsburgh At Bradford, Bradford, PA; FR; BA; Eng Clb 90-; Tau Epsilon Phi Hist 90; IM Bsktbl 90-; Elec Eng.

**LITTLE, CHAD D,** S U N Y Coll Of Tech At Alfred, Alfred, NY; SO; Sigma Tau Epsilon 89-; IM Ftbl 89-; AOS; Drftg; Drftg Engr.

**LITTLE, CRISTINA E,** Goucher Coll, Towson, MD; SO; BA; Chem Clb Sec 89-; SGA; Deans Stdnt 89-; Clara Claasen Chem Schlrshp 90-; Chem; Rsrch Chem Eng.

**LITTLE, ERIC S,** Lexington Comm Coll, Lexington, KY; FR; BA; Rls Cmmtt Stdnt Rep 90-; Deans Lst; Bus.

**LITTLE JR, JAMES H,** Univ Of Tn At Chattanooga, Chattanooga, TN; SR; BS; IEEE 90; Pi Mu Epsilon 87; Ntl Cllgte Eng Awd; Outstndng Clg Stdnts Of Amer 89; Pi Mu Epsilon Natl Math Soc; Eng Electrical.

**LITTLE, LAURA J,** Fl International Univ, Miami, FL; JR; BA; Natl Hnr Soc; Dns Lst; Kappa Delta Phi; AA Broward Cmnty Clg 90; Ed; Spec Ed Tchr.

**LITTLE, LYNELLE M,** Manor Jr Coll, Jenkintown, PA; SO; AS; Yearbook; Alpha Beta Gamma; Henry Lewandowski Memorial Schlrshp Extrnshp Paralegal; Paralegal.

**LITTLE, MATTHEW A,** Muskingum Coll, New Concord, OH; SO; BA; News Edtr Nwspr 90-; IM Bsktbl; Engl; Adv/Jrnlsm.

**LITTLE, MICHAEL L,** Univ Of Sc At Spartanburg, Spartanburg, SC; SR; BA; Offc B A Mikulski US Senator Intern; Offc B B Byron US Rep Intern; Supreme Crt US Mssngr; Pol Sci; Law Pltcs.

**LITTLE, NANCY E,** Fl St Univ, Tallahassee, FL; SO; BS; Gnss Ldrshp Prog 89-90; Wmns Ldrshp Conf 90; Omicron Delta Kappa; Phi Eta Sigma 90-; Intl Ordr Rnbw Grls Grnd Rep Ne/Fl 84-; Omicron Delta Kappa Hon Bnqt; Dns Lst 89-; Elec Engr.

**LITTLE II, REUBEN R,** Al A & M Univ, Normal, AL; JR; BS; Stdnt Cncl Fr Rep 88-89; Judcry Brd 88-89; Kappa Alpha Psi Rep 90-; Capston Smmr Hnrs Pgm 88; Zoolgy/Chem; Dntl Schl/Orthdntry.

**LITTLE JR, RICHARD J,** Western New England Coll, Springfield, MA; FR; BS; Cross Country 90; Engr.

**LITTLE, ROY L,** Univ Of Pittsburgh, Pittsburgh, PA; SO; BA; Wghtlftng; Elect Eng.

**LITTLE, SHERRY E,** Univ Of Southern Ms, Hattiesburg, MS; SO; BA; Stu Govt Chrmn Lgl Serv; ASB Ambssdr 90-; Gamma Beta Phi 89-; Psi Chi 90-; Kappa Delta VP 89-; Asst Cnslng Ed Rsrc 90-; Peer Cnslr; Amnsty Intl Sec 89-; Ornttn Fclttr 90-; Alpha Tau Omega Swthrt 90-; Psych/Pre Law; Law.

**LITTLE, TYRA J,** City Univ Of Ny La Guard Coll, Long Island Cty, NY; JR; Secr Sci/Adm Asst; Bsn Sch Tchr.

**LITTLE, WESLEY L,** East Carolina Univ, Greenville, NC; JR; BM; Stdnt Forum 90-; Phi Eta Sigma 89-; Phi Mu Alpha 89-90; Pi Kappa Lambda Cert Hon 89-90; Msc; Prfsnl Mscn.

**LITTLEFIELD, SHERRIE K,** Univ Of Montevallo, Montevallo, AL; JR; Tchr.

**LITTLEJOHN, DAWN R,** Norfolk St Univ, Norfolk, VA; JR; BA; MCSO 90-; Alpha Kappa Alpha 89-; Mass Comm; New Anchr/Sls/Brdcst.

**LITTLEJOHN, DEBORAH K,** Western Carolina Univ, Cullowhee, NC; SR; BFA; Arts Stdnt League 90-; Dsgn Art Stdnt Leag Tres 90-; Phi Eta Sigma 89-; AAS Wake Tchncl Comm Clg 89; Grphc Dsgn; Dsgn Illstrtn.

**LITTLEJOHN JR, GEORGE F,** Univ Of Sc At Columbia, Columbia, SC; SR; BS; Pcsttrs/Stdnt Orntn Grp; Gamma Beta Phi; Alpha Kappa Psi Tres 90-; Phi Kappa Psi Tgrbrn Chmn 80-84; Smmr Intrnsshp/Ecnmc Entrps Inst/Svnnh Rvr Site Tech Trnsfrs; Acctg; Clg Teach/Cnsltng.

**LITTLEJOHN, LORI KAI,** Fl A & M Univ, Tallahassee, FL; SO; Orchs 89-; Pres Schlrs Asc 89-; SBI Brnz Schlr Awd 89-90; Pres Schlr Awd 89-; Bsn Admn; Fnce/Law.

**LITTLEJOHN III, PAUL X,** Central Al Comm Coll, Alexander City, AL; FR; MBA; SGA Pres 90-; Dbt Tm Dbt Ldr 90-; Stdnt Tutrl Org Coord; Deans Lst 90-; Assn Dstngshd Stdnts Chrprsn 90-; Laubach Way Rdng Instr 89-; GED Instr State AL Crtfd Inst 87-; Cert Rcgntn RNEMA Bible Coll 87-; Math; Acctg.

**LITTLEPAGE, BRENT N,** Southern Coll Of Tech, Marietta, GA; SO; EET; BBA Univ Of Oklahoma 81; Elec Eng Tech; Eng.

**LITTLES-CAMPBELL, NORMA J,** Fayetteville St Univ, Fayetteville, NC; JR; BS; SGA Sntr At Lrg 91-; Pol Sci Clb 90-; Stu Free Entrprs 90-; Fellow NC Inst Pol Ldrshp 89; NS Rural Ldrs Pro 89; AS 87; Bus Admin; US State Dept.

**LITTLETON, ALICIA K,** Roane St Comm Coll, Harriman, TN; FR; AS; Gamma Beta Phi Tres; Acctg; CPA.

**LITTMAN, EVA D,** Duke Univ, Durham, NC; FR; BS; BSA 90-; Pre Hlth Org Frshmn Liason 90-; Dncng Dvls 90-; Howard Hughes Schlr 90-; Prjct Bld 90; Biology/Pre Med; Doctor.

**LITTON, BYRAN K,** Marshall University, Huntington, WV; JR; BA; Cmps Chrstn Ctr Cncl 88-; Eagles Nest 90-; Deans List 88-90; Vrsty Ftbl 88-; All Sthrn Conf Acad Tm 90; Bus.

**LITTS, BARBARA L,** Anne Arundel Comm Coll, Arnold, MD; FR; BA; Corp Spclst Rlty Co 90-; Bus Pblc Admn; Acctg CPA.

**LITWIN, TIMOTHY A,** Ky Wesleyan Coll, Owensboro, KY; SO; BA; Deans Lst 89-90; Dstngshd Schlr 90-; Vrsty Bsbl 89-; Sprts Med; Athltc Trnr Physcl Thrpst.

**LITZ, CRYSTAL M,** Northern Ky Univ, Highland Hts, KY; JR; BA; Yng Dem VP 89-; Speech Team Debate Team 90-; TV News Anchr 90-; Cmmnctns; TV Prod.

**LITZAU, JONATHAN J,** Liberty Univ, Lynchburg, VA; FR; BS; Alpha Lambda Delta; Dns Lst 90-; Chnclrs Schlrshp 90-; IM Vlybl/Sftbl 90-; Chmstry; Chem Engr.

**LITZENBERG, LORI L,** Muskingum Coll, New Concord, OH; FR; BA; Parents Weekend Com 90-; Lambda Sigma; Theta Phi Alpha; Muskingum Coll Tourguide; Schlrshp Day Hostess 90-; IM Vlybl 90-; Acctg.

**LITZINGER, LEE A,** Ms St Univ, Miss State, MS; FR; BA; Rfrmd Univ Flwshp 90-; Habitat Hmnty 90-; IM Sftbl 90-; Physics; Physicist.

**LIU, CHING CHEN,** City Univ Of Ny City Coll, New York, NY; SR; BE; IEEE; Chnse Stdnt Assn Stff; Goldn Key; Tau Beta Pi 90; Deans Lst 88-89; Calculus Awrd 87; Intrnshp Gen Motrs; Hon Cnvctn Cert; Elec Eng.

**LIU, CHING-HSIU M,** William Paterson Coll, Wayne, NJ; SO; BS; Chnse Clb Vp 90-; Chem Clb Co-Treas 90-; Galen Scty 89-; Sino Chnse Cltr Exc Scty 90-; NY Jpnse Cltr Exc Scty 90-; Cngrssnl Yth Ldrshp 90; Chem; Dctr.

**LIU, DONG-PING,** City Univ Of Ny Baruch Coll, New York, NY; JR; BBA; Cmptr Clb 90-; Rsrch Asstntshp Ststcs Oprtns Rsrch Dept 90-; Bdmtn Clb 89-90; Cmptr Sci; Cmptr Engrg.

**LIU, FLORENCE L,** City Univ Of Ny Baruch Coll, New York, NY; SR; BBA; Acctg Soc; Beta Alpha Psi; Beta Gamma Sigma; Baruch Provosts Schlrshp; Deans Lst 89-90; Acctg; CPA.

**LIU, HONG,** Va Commonwealth Univ, Richmond, VA; SR; PHD; BS Shanghai Jiaotung Univ 82-86; MA Shanghai Inst Of Mech Engrng 86-88; Phrmclgy; Scientific Rsrchr.

**LIU, HONG,** Converse Coll, Spartanburg, SC; SR; BM; Music; Performing.

**LIU, HSUEH M,** City Univ Of Ny Baruch Coll, New York, NY; SO; BBA; Econs.

**LIU, HUA,** City Univ Of Ny La Guard Coll, Long Island Cty, NY; SO; AAS; Acctng.

**LIU, LAURIE-ANN H,** Franklin And Marshall Coll, Lancaster, PA; SR; Porter Scntfc Soc 89-; Entrtnmnt Cmmtt 89-90; Healing Art Clb 89-90; Intl Clb 87-89; Phi Beta Kappa 90-; Stu Agnst Mltpl Sclrss 87-90; Amnsty Intl 89-90; Cum Laude; BA; Biol; Optmtry.

**LIU, LI LI,** Atlantic Comm Coll, Mays Landing, NJ; FR; Yth Summr Drwng Cntst 88-89; Chinese Essay Cntst 87; Math Hon Soc 87-88; Immgrtn Assn Sec 90; Law Frm Intrnshp Dir Asst 90; Law.

**LIU, LINDA L,** Belmont Coll, Nashville, TN; SR; BS; Psychology.

**LIU, LISA YU,** City Univ Of Ny Baruch Coll, New York, NY; JR; BBA; Acctng; Gldn Ky; Beta Gamma Sigma; Baruch Endwmnt Fnd; Provosts Schlrshp; Darmstaedter Fund Schlrshp; Acctng; CPA.

**LIU, QIANYE,** Cornell Univ Statutory College, Ithaca, NY; JR; BS; Intl Stdnt Prog Bd 90-91; Bd Govnrs 91; Goldenkey 90-91; Hughes Hon Prog 90-; Summer Med/Rsrch Trng Prog 91; Biology; Mee Rsrchs.

**LIU, QUN,** Teikyo Post Univ, Waterbury, CT; JR; BS; Culture Recrn Clb Dir 84-; Intl Clb 89-; Alpha Chi; Acad Schlrshp 89-; Bus Intrn Japan Schlrshp; Instr Tchr Clg China 86-; AA 86; Mgmt Info Sys.

**LIU, SAIRONG,** Middle Tn St Univ, Murfreesboro, TN; JR; BA; Univ Stdnts Assn; Wmns Clb Soc; Tri-Vly Chinese Bible Ch Dublin CA; Smng Clb; Acctg; Bus.

**LIU, SU HUA WOO,** City Univ Of Ny La Guard Coll, Long Island Cty, NY; JR; Acctg.

**LIU, XI S,** City Univ Of Ny Baruch Coll, New York, NY; SO; BS; Chinese Stdnt Assoc 88; Chrstn Fllwshp 89; Scnd Wnnr Of Tble Tennis SUNY Albny 90; Accntng; Accntnt.

**LIU, YIMING,** Savannah Coll Of Art & Design, Savannah, GA; GD; MFA; BA Textile Dsgn China; MA Fasion Dsgn China; Fiber Arts; Professor.

**LIU, ZHIQUN,** Univ Of Louisville, Louisville, KY; SO; Elec Engrg.

**LIVELY, ALAN DAVID,** Roane St Comm Coll, Harriman, TN; SO; AAS; Gamma Beta Phi; Deans Lst; Envrnmntl Hlth Tchnlgs; Hlth Physcs.

**LIVELY, JULIE A,** Univ Of Ky, Lexington, KY; JR; BA; Gamma Beta Phi 88-89; Acad Exclnc Schlrshp 90-; Marshall Univ Tuition Waiver; Psychology; Occuptnl Thrpy.

**LIVEOAK, JENIFER G,** Univ Of Montevallo, Montevallo, AL; SO; BS; Elem Ed; Network Mktg.

**LIVEOAK, WILLIAM T,** Univ Of Al At Birmingham, Birmingham, AL; SR; BSME; Tau Beta Pi; Mech Eng.

**LIVERMORE, AMY M,** Elmira Coll, Elmira, NY; SO; BA; Baroque Ensembles; Phi Eta Sigma; Blossburg Elem Schl Vlntr; Academic Tutor; English/French; Education.

**LIVERMORE, CRAIG W,** Franklin And Marshall Coll, Lancaster, PA; SR; BA; Habitat Humanity 87-89; Amnesty Intl 87-90; Phi Beta Kappa; Hackman Schlrshp 90; Magna Cum Laude; John Kershner Schlrshp Math 90-; Rev Arthur Barley Prize; IM Bsktbl/Sftbl/Vlybl/Ftbl Capt 87-; Religion; Clg Prfsr.

**LIVERMORE, DEBRA L,** Fl St Univ, Tallahassee, FL; JR; BA; Golden Key 90; Biology; Phys Thrpy/Occptnl Thrpy.

**LIVERSEDGE, KELLY-ANN,** Mount Olive Coll, Mount Olive, NC; SR; BS; Phi Beta Lambda 89-; Gym Sprts Acad Ownr 88-; Schlr 90-; Phi Beta Lambda 89-; Deans Lst 88-; Grad W/Hons 90; Assoc Gen Ed Johnston Comm Coll 90; Bus Admin; Bnkdr/Fncl Plnr.

**LIVERY, CANDICE L,** Kent St Univ Kent Cmps, Kent, OH; SO; BA; Math Tutor Lrng Dvlpmnt Ctr 90-; Alpha Lmbd Dlt 90-; Alpha Phi 90-; Acctg; CPA.

**LIVESEY, SARAH T,** Boston Univ, Boston, MA; SR; BS; NE Rehab Intrn; Hosp Intrn; Pblc Schl Intrn; Geriatric Occup Thrpst.

**LIVEZEY, AMY T,** Temple Univ, Philadelphia, PA; JR; BARCH; Arch Stdnts Assc 89-; Arch.

**LIVINGSTON, ALLEN P,** Meridian Comm Coll, Meridian, MS; SO; BA; USN 81-; Elctrncs.

**LIVINGSTON, ALYSSA A,** Univ Of Med & Dentistry Of Nj, Newark, NJ; SR; BS; APTA 89-; Bio Club 87-90; Pre Phys Thrpy Club 87-90; Natl Hnr Soc 87-; Clinical Exclnc Awd; Wheelchair Bsktbl Benefit Game 90-91; BS Minor Bio Kean Coll; Cert Phys Thrpy UMDNJ; Phys Thrpy; Mulenberg Hosp PT.

**LIVINGSTON, AMY G,** Tufts Univ, Medford, MA; FR; BA; Env Consciousness Otrch; Tufts Rcycling; Intern New England Env Mgmt Ctr; Environmental Study; Env Engineering.

**LIVINGSTON, DI ANN H,** Univ Of Sc At Columbia, Columbia, SC; SR; BS; Eta Sigma Delta; Phi Beta Kappa; B Riley HRTA Schlrshp; Hotel/Restrnt/Tourism Admn; Nrsg Hme Adm.

**LIVINGSTON, DONA L,** Memphis St Univ, Memphis, TN; JR; BA; Psy.

**LIVINGSTON, ELIZABETH A,** Howard Univ, Washington, DC; JR; BS; Schl Ed Stdnt Cncl Sec 89-; Under Grad Assmbly Rep; Ttr Meyer Elem Schl 89-90; Kappa Delta Pi 90-; NAACP 88-90; Mss Schl Ed 90-; Intern Univ CA 90; Elem Ed; Tchr.

**LIVINGSTON, FRANKLIN M,** Ky St Univ, Frankfort, KY; SR; Stdnt Body Rep 88-89; Model Il Govt State Sntr 88-89; Chorus 88-89; Phi Beta Lambda 87-89; Assoc Of US Army 90-; 22nd Sup Com Assoc; Explorers Scouts Of Amer Advsr 87-89; VFW; Tennis 89-90; Phys Educ; US Army.

**LIVINGSTON, JEFFREY O,** Wilmington Coll, New Castle, DE; SR; BS; Pol Crmnl Invest 85-; AA Wor-Wic Comm Colg 84; Crmnl Jstce; Law Enfcmnt Tch.

**LIVINGSTON, KURTIS ROBERT,** Univ Of Cincinnati, Cincinnati, OH; JR; BS; Amer Inst Archtctrl Stdns VP 90-; Amer Inst Cnstrctrs 88-; Photo Clb 88-; Lambda Chi Alpha Sec 84-87; William Mc Masters Schlrshp 89-; IM Bsktbl/Sftbl 88-; Assoc Apld Sci Archtctrl Tchnlgy/Cvl/Cnstrctn Engrg Tchnlgy Prfsnl Prctc Cert; Archtctrl Engrg Tchnlgy; Rsdntl/Cmrcl Arch.

**LIVINGSTON, LANETTE,** Dyersburg St Comm Coll, Dyersburg, TN; FR; BA; Phi Theta Kappa; Acctg.

**LIVINGSTON JR, MARTIN L,** Univ Of The Virgin Islands, St Thomas, VI; SR; BA; Pre-Lw Assoc Pres 89-; Prsdnts Clb Vp; Thtre Prdctn 89-90; Intl Smr Schl Schlrshp 90; Jane E Tuitt Schlr 87-; Chrls Trnbl Awrd Hstry 90; Social Sciences Hstry; Law.

**LIVINGSTON, REBECCA A,** Univ Of Sc At Columbia, Columbia, SC; SR; BA; Educ Majors Clb Sec Tres 90; Elem Educ; Tch Sch.

**LIVINGSTON II, ROBERT W,** Georgetown Univ, Washington, DC; SR; BA; Georgetown Invstmnt Allnce 90; Mrktng Soc 90; Saxa Sundries Drgstre 89; Delta Sigma Pi Chrmn Of Spirit Cmmttee 88; Bnk Of NY Intrn 89; Im S Capt 87-; Intrntl Mngmnt; Fnce.

**LIVINGSTON, SAMUEL T,** Univ Of Sc At Columbia, Columbia, SC; SR; BA; Assn Afrcn Amer Stdnts Com Chrmn 90-; NAACP 88-; AFROTC Chf Oper Cadet Capt 89-90; Psychlgy Hon Soc; Psi-Chi; Intrn Offc Comm Serv; Rsdnt Advsr 89-; Air Frc ROTC Ldrshp Awd 89; Mnrty Hon Awd 87-; AF Hon Soc 89-; Sftbl IM 89-; Psychlgy.

**LIVINGSTON, WILLIAM E,** Salisbury St Univ, Salisbury, MD; GD; MA; Psi Chi 90-; Phi Alpha Theta 90-; Grad Asst Psy 90-; Std Afflt APA 90-; BA Psy 90; Psy; PHD Scntst Prctnr.

**LIVSTONE, MICHAEL S,** Yale Univ, New Haven, CT; FR; BS; Humor Mag 90-; Prcsn Mrchng Bnd 90-; Coll Bowl Clb 90-; Charles M Runk Prize; Math/Molecular Biophys/Biochem.

**LIZAK, BONNIE J,** Springfield Tech Comm Coll, Springfield, MA; GD; BSN; Baystate Med Cntr RN; Nrse Ansthst; AS; Nrsng.

**LIZARDO, PAOLO V,** Fl International Univ, Miami, FL; FR; BA; Hnrs Prog 90-; Fclty Schlr 90-; Fla Undergrad Schlr 90-; Chmstry; Medicine.

**LIZOTTE, LINDA M,** Teikyo Post Univ, Waterbury, CT; SO; BA; Rose Traurig Schlrs 89-; Jdcry Com 90-; Morris Fndtn 87-; Psychlgy.

**LLACA, MARIANGELES,** Miami Dade Comm Coll South, Miami, FL; SO; MBA; Phi Theta Kappa 89-; Intl Schlstchnr Scty 89-; Phi Theta Kappa 89-; Grdtd Hghst Hnrs; Tltn Rstr Achvmnt 90-; Brds Schlrshp Srvc; Certs Otstndng Achvmnt Deans Lst Cert 90-; Fnc; Law.

**LLANA, ORESTES,** Univ Of Miami, Coral Gables, FL; GD; BS; FL Nrs Assn 86-90; Amer Nrs Assn 86-90; AA Miami-Dad Comm Coll 82; Dip Nrsg Jackson Memrl Hosp Schl Nrsng 86; Nrsng.

**LLANERAS, MARTHA,** Miami Dade Comm Coll, Miami, FL; FR; BA; Educ; Tchg.

**LLANOS QUIDGLEY, JOED,** Caribbean Univ, Bayamon, PR; SO; AS; Bus Admin; Mgmnt.

**LLANOS-QUINTERO, EDGAR O,** City Univ Of Ny La Guard Coll, Long Island Cty, NY; GD; AAS; Phi Theta Kappan 90; Univ Del Valle Intrnshp 70; Univ Santiago Schlrshp 73-77; Univ Of Puerto Rico Rio Piedras TA 78-80; Hon Stdnt 89; ACS 83; Intl Free Lance Photo Org; AA Univ Del Valle Colombia 70; BA 77; Cmrcl Photo.

**LLARYORA, ALBERTO L,** Univ Of New Haven, West Haven, CT; SO; BS; Intrntnl Assn Pblc Rltns Offcr 90-; Bsns Cmmnctn; Pblshng.

**LLEONART, GILBERTO R,** Fl International Univ, Miami, FL; SR; BA; Delta Five Hstrn 87; WERM Pldg 89; Sls; AA Miami Dade Com Clg 87; Scl Stds Educ; Tchr.

**LLEWELLYN, CRAIG J,** Salisbury St Univ, Salisbury, MD; SR; BA; Dns Lst 89-; Psy.

**LLEWELLYN, DEOBRAH A,** S U N Y Coll Of Tech At Frmgdl, Farmingdale, NY; SO; AAS; SADHA Pres 90-; Deans List 89-; Dental Hygiene; Dental Schl.

**LLEWELLYN, GENEVA A,** Tn Temple Univ, Chattanooga, TN; JR; BS; Weigle Cncrt Choir 89-; Class Pianist 89-90; Voices Triumph Prog Crdntr 90; RA 90-; Msc/Bible; Tchng/Chrstn Mnstry.

**LLEWELLYN, JACQUELINE D,** Coll Misericordia, Dallas, PA; SR; BS; Stdnt Peer Cnslr 87-89; Campus Trgd 87-89; Nw Stdnt Orientn Ldr 87-89; Deans Lst 87-; Acdmc Prfrmnce Awrd 89-90; AS Penn St Univ 87-89; Lbrl Stdies/Psychlgy; Psychlgy/Cnslng.

**LLINAS BETANCOURT, JOSE,** Univ Politecnica De Pr, Hato Rey, PR; GD; BDEE; Elec Eng Clb; IEEE Vcl 90.

**LLINAS, ISABEL,** Nova Univ, Ft Lauderdale, FL; GD; MBA; Alpha Chi 86; Centro Campesino Farmworker Ctr Inc Dir Of Dvlpmnt; BPS Barry Univ 86; Bus; Admn.

**LLOBERA, JEANETTE,** Fl International Univ, Miami, FL; SR; BS; Ftr Educ 90; Psi Chi; BS 90; Educ; MS.

**LLOMPART-ZENO, ISABEL,** Inter Amer Univ Pr San Juan, Hato Rey, PR; GD; JD.

**LLOVET, AMANDA,** City Univ Of Ny City Coll, New York, NY; SR; BS; Reserve Officer Training Corp Commision 2 Lt 87-; Elementary Education; Teacher.

**LLOYD, CAROLYN S,** Longwood Coll, Farmville, VA; SR; BS; Ntnl Hnr Scty 90; Otstndng Serv Awrd 89-90; Study Prgrm; Psychlgy; Cnslng.

**LLOYD, CATRIN M,** Univ Of Rochester, Rochester, NY; JR; Psychology.

**LLOYD, DEBORAH L,** George Mason Univ, Fairfax, VA; JR; MSED; Phi Mu 90-; Middle Education; Teach.

**LLOYD, FONDA MARIE,** Ny Univ, New York, NY; SR; Mnrty Jrnlst Soc 89-; PA Daily Nws Smmr Intrn; Times Picayune NO LA Smmr Intr 90; Record Hackensck NJ Smmr Intr 89; NY Assoc Blck Jrnlsts 89-; Prof Bttr Tmrrw 89-; Carreer Chg From Sec To Nwspr Rep 91; BA 91; Jrnlsm.

**LLOYD, LARA JEAN,** Middle Tn St Univ, Murfreesboro, TN; SR; Advtsng Clb Art Clb Sec 89-; Kappa Alpha Southern Belle Srvc Chrmn 88-; Dns Lst 89-; Alpha Hnr Soc 89-; Alpha Delta Pi Rptr 87-; Intrnshp Smyrna Twn Cntr Adv Asst 90-; BS; Advtsng/Graphic Dsgn; Advtsng/Cmptr Graphics.

**LLOYD, MELISSA E,** Univ Of Miami, Coral Gables, FL; JR; BA; Earth Alert Ecology Club Co Pres 89-; Stdnt Gove Cab 88-89; Omicron Delta Kappa Sec; Mortar Bd; Rho Rho Rho; Link Vol Serv Org Chp For Envrnmnt 89-90; Wellnesc Comm 89-; Res Asst 89-; Marine Affairs; Pub Serv.

**LLOYD, MINDY I,** Anderson Coll, Anderson, SC; SO; BS; SCA Sec 89-; Scl Brd 89-; Vars Athltcs Vllybl/Sftbl 89-; Hnrs Prg Advsy Comm 89-; Gamma Beta Phi Tresr 90-; Vllybl; Sftbl; AA; Pre Phrmcy.

**LLOYD, ROY M,** Strayer Coll, Washington, DC; SR; Pres Lst 90-; Deans Lst 90-; Mktg W/Times Jrnl 76-87; Logistics With The Defense Ind 88-90; BS; Comp Info Syst.

**LLOYD, STEVIE L,** Tougaloo Coll, Tougaloo, MS; SO; Pol/Sci Clb 90-.

**LLOYD, VALERIE E,** Anne Arundel Comm Coll, Arnold, MD; SO; BA; Cmmnctns; Grphc Arts.

**LLUVERAS-GARCIA, IRIS I,** Evangelical Semimary Of P R, Hato Rey, PR; JR; MBA; Club Ellas 90-; Natl Clg Min Ldrshp Awrds; World Vision 90-; Cum Laude 84; Dept Of Inst Publica De P R Junta Rep De La Iglesia Cristiana; BA Univ Of P R 74; MBA Univ Of P R 84; Socl Sci; Religion.

**LO CURTO, LESLIE M,** Univ Of Nh Plymouth St Coll, Plymouth, NH; SR; BS; Natl Acctg Assc 89-90; Phi Kappa Phi; Acctg; CPA.

**LO PARRINO, JOSEPH C,** S U N Y Coll Of Tech At Frmgdl, Farmingdale, NY; FR; BA; Acdmc Achvmnt Awrd; Pltcl Sci.

**LO PINTO, DIANE A,** City Univ Of Ny City Coll, New York, NY; SO.

**LO PRESTI, EDUARDO O,** Manhattan Coll, Bronx, NY; SO; BS; Elctncs Clb Pres 90; IEEF; Etta Kappa Ku; Tau Poeta Pi; Putnam Awrd 90; Elctcl Engrng; Engrng.

**LO PRESTI, NICOLE M,** Oh Wesleyan Univ, Delaware, OH; JR; BA; Choral Art Soc 89-; Wesleyan Plyrs 89-; Phi Eta Sigma 89-; Phi Soc 90-; Omicron Delta Kappa; Phi Sigma Iota; Deans Lst 88-; Rcgntn Awrd 90; Theatr/Frnch.

**LO PRESTI, VINCENT J,** Dowling Coll, Oakdale Li, NY; SR; Alpha Chi VP; Kappa Delta Pi Newslttr Ed; BA; Scl Sci; Ed.

**LO VERDE, THOMAS J,** S U N Y Coll Of Tech At Frmgdl, Farmingdale, NY; SO; AS; Intrvrsty Chrstn Flwshp Treas 89-; Crim Just Clb Treas 89-; Natl Hnr Soc 90-; Crim Just; Law Enfrcmnt.

**LO, SAI Y,** S U N Y Maritime Coll, Bronx, NY; FR; Crew 90-; Marine Eng.

**LO, SUK FUN,** Va Commonwealth Univ, Richmond, VA; FR; BA; Bus Admn; Bus.

**LOAIZA, MARIA TERESA,** City Univ Of Ny La Guard Coll, Long Island Cty, NY; SR; BA; Aristrain Intl Inc Adm Asst 86-; Acctg/Data Proc; CPA Econ.

**LOAKNATH, KHUSHDYALL B,** City Univ Of Ny La Guard Coll, Long Island Cty, NY; GD; BA; Acad Achvmnt Hnr; AS; Acctng.

**LOBACZ, JENNIFER A,** S U N Y Coll Of Tech At Frmgdl, Farmingdale, NY; FR; BA; Dns Lst; Good Samaritan Hosp; Acad Excel Award 90; Dns Lst; Elem Educ; Tchng.

**LOBATO JR, FLAVIO A,** Univ Of Miami, Coral Gables, FL; SR; BA; Alumni Mentor Pgm 90-; Beta Gamma Sigma; Golden Key 90-; Alpha Kappa Psi 90-; Zeta Beta Tau 87-; Pres 100 90-; Pres Hnr Rl 89; Provost Hnr Rl 90; Dns Lst 88-90; Finance/Mktg; Cnsltg/Bnkg.

**LOBB, DANIEL J,** Univ Of Tn At Martin, Martin, TN; FR; BA; Vrsty 90-; Bsns; Corp Bsns.

**LOBB, MELISSA B,** Daemen Coll, Amherst, NY; JR; BA; Ski Club 88-89; AS Jamestown Cmnty Clg 90; Bus Admin/Mktg.

**LOBBAN, MELINDA L,** Mary Baldwin Coll, Staunton, VA; JR; BA; Stdnt Snt 89-90; Yng Dmcrts 88-90; 4-H 88-; Bus Admin/Comp Sci; Law.

**LOBEL, DARLENE A,** Duke Univ, Durham, NC; SO; MD; Chance 90-; Tutor H S Stdnts 90-; Fresh Advsry Cnslr 90-; Hosp Vol Pediatrics 90; Hosp Vol Pschiatry; Psychoology; Med.**

**LOBEL, KEITH D,** Univ Of Pittsburgh, Pittsburgh, PA; SO; Casting Clb 90-; IM Soccer 90-; Dns Hnr Lst 89-; Engr.

**LOBERGER, LESLIE L,** Georgetown Coll, Georgetown, KY; JR; BS; Sigma Gamma Sigma Pres 88-; Amer Chem Soc VP 89-; Admsns/Schlrshp/Fncl Aid Comm Rep 90-; Alpha Lambda Delta Hstrn 88-90; Eta Delta Phi; Beta Beta Beta 90-; Pi Kappa Alpha Ltl Sis Comm Chrmn 89-; Chem.

**LOBMEYER, SUSAN D,** Providence Coll, Providence, RI; FR; BA; Radio Sta 90-; Pstrl Cncl 90-.

**LOBO, LYGIA BRUNO,** Miami Dade Comm Coll, Miami, FL; SO; BA; Phi Theta Kappa 89-; Hon Stdnts Advsry Com 90-; Schl Nwspr Wrtr; Outstndng Frgn Lang Stdnt Awd; Outstndng Hon Grad Awd; Vol Tutor 90-; Miami Bk Fair Intl 89-90; Henry King Stanford Schlrshp; Deans Lst 89-; Ecnmcs/Frgn Lang; Tch Univ.

**LOBO, MERVYN ANTHONY,** Al A & M Univ, Normal, AL; GD; Intrnatl Assn PR Offcr 90; Delta Mu Delta 90; Acctncy.

**LOCASCIO, MICHAEL J,** Ny Univ, New York, NY; SO; BS; Stdnt Gvrnmnt; Dns List 89-; Ups Mgmt Tm 90-; Acctng; Intnl Acctng.

**LOCASHIO, LAURIE A,** Univ Of Nh Plymouth St Coll, Plymouth, NH; FR; BS; Vol NH Humn Scty; Blgy; Wldlf Mgmt Cr.

**LOCHRIDGE, LAURIE B,** Ms St Univ, Miss State, MS; FR; Mdrgl Sngrs 90-; Rfrmd Univ Flwshp 90-; Bptst Stdnt Un90-; Lambda Sigma 90-; Gamma Beta Phi 90-; Phi Eta Sigma 90-; Alpha Lambda Delta 90-; Delta Delta Delta Phlnthrpy 90-; Msu Arbcs Clb 90-9-; Elem Ed; Tchr.

**LOCK, J JERRY,** Memphis St Univ, Memphis, TN; SR; Peer Monitor Prgrm 88-; Gamma Beta Phi 89-; Beta Gamma Sigma 90-; Phi Eta Sigma 89-; Merrill Lynch Intrnshp; Bus/Fin; Fin Plnr.

**LOCKABY, STANLEY M,** Piedmont Tech Coll, Greenwood, SC; FR; AAS; Phi Theta Kappa 90-; Engrng Graphics; Engr Graphic Designs.

**LOCKARD, MELISSA K,** Campbell Univ, Buies Creek, NC; FR; BS; Pres Schlrs Scty 90-; Phi Eta Sigma Tres; Elem Ed; Teacher.

**LOCKE, ALISON B,** Univ Of De, Newark, DE; FR; BS; Athltc Trnrs Clb 90-; Physcl Ed Clb 90-; Gamma Sigma Sigma 90-; Dns Lst; IM Bsktbl Offcl; Phys Ed ; Phys Thrpst/Athltc Trnr.

**LOCKE, CAROL D,** Faulkner St Jr Coll, Bay Minette, AL; SO; Pow Wow Ldrshp Soc 90-; Phi Beta Lambda 89-90; Acctng; CPA.

**LOCKE, DENISE NICOLE,** Wv Northern Comm Coll, Wheeling, WV; FR; AAS; Sec Sci; Secretary.

**LOCKE, DONNA R,** Univ Of Sc At Columbia, Columbia, SC; SR; BA; Gamma Beta Phi 89-; Dir Dycre And Kndrgrtn; Assoc Greenville Tech Coll 73; Psychlgy.

**LOCKE, FRIEDA G,** O'more School Of Design, Franklin, TN; SR; BA; ASID; Williamson Cnty Medl Aux Pres 90-; DAR; BS 75; Interior Design.

**LOCKE, KAREN A,** Gordon Coll, Barnesville, GA; JR; BA; Grffn Rnng Clb VP 89-; Sls Mngr 87-89; Mngr Mtyrls Prcng; Bsns; Mgmnt.

**LOCKE, KATHI E,** Johnson St Coll, Johnson, VT; SR; BA; Chesamore 89-; Phych; Cnslng/Clncl Psych.

**LOCKER, ROSEANNE L,** S U N Y Coll Of Tech At Frmgdl, Farmingdale, NY; SR; BSN; Stdnt Nurse Assoc 89-; Pres List 89; Deans List 89-90; PTA; AAS; Nursing.

**LOCKETT, CHRISTOPHER R,** Stillman Coll, Tuscaloosa, AL; SO; Phi Beta Sigma; Electrical Engineering.

**LOCKETT, DAVID A,** Kent St Univ Kent Cmps, Kent, OH; SR; BA; Fnnc Clb 90-; Delta Tau Delta Hse Mgr 88-; IM Ftbl Sftbl Glf 88-; Fnnc/Mngmnt; Fnnc.

**LOCKETT, KENDRICK R,** Univ Of Louisville, Louisville, KY; JR; MENG; Inst Elec Elctrnc Engr 90-; Deans Lst 90-; AAS 89; Elec Engr; Rsrch/Dsgn.

**LOCKHART, FELECIA A,** Jackson St Univ, Jackson, MS; SR; BA; Stdnt Govt Assn Jstce 90-; Jr Cls Chpln 89-90; Soph Cls Prlmntrn 88-89; Alpha Lambda Delta 88; Alpha Chi 90; Lambda Alpha Epsilon 88-89; Project VOTE 89; MS State Senate Intern; Pol Sci; Corp Lawyer.

**LOCKHART, LESLIE J,** Univ Of Sc At Columbia, Columbia, SC; JR; BS; Coll Rep; Phi Beta Lambda; Kappa Kappa Gamma; Carolina Cares; Chair Tchr Of Yr Comm For Coll Appl Prof Sci; Rtl Mgmt; Fshn Buyer/Phrmctcl Sls.

**LOCKHART, NATASHA K,** Memphis St Univ, Memphis, TN; FR; BBA; Stdnt Act Coun 90-; Tutor Core 90-; Peer Mentor Pgrm 90-; Acctng; Intrnl Auditing.

**LOCKHART III, ROBERT F,** Old Dominion Univ, Norfolk, VA; JR; BS; Sigma Phi Sigma; Physcs; Atomic/Nuc Physcs.

**LOCKHART, STEPHANIE Y,** Clark Atlanta Univ, Atlanta, GA; SO; BA; Spnsh Clb; Acctg Clb; Ntl Assn Blck Accts; Mst Outstndg Frshmn Stdnt 90; Hon Stdnt 89-; Schlrshp NABA 90; Acctg; CPA.

**LOCKHART, TAMERA H,** Oh Wesleyan Univ, Delaware, OH; SR; BA; Oh Wesleyan Lit Mag Edtr 89-; Stdnt Eng Bd Chr 90-; Wordworks Lit Mag Edtr 89-90; Sigma Tau Delta 90-; Phi Beta Kappa; Eng/Humanities-Classics; Pblshng.

**LOCKHART, WANDA F,** Al A & M Univ, Normal, AL; SO; BS; Cmptr Sci; Cmptr Eng.

**LOCKLAIR, STEVEN L,** Fl Coll, Temple Terrace, FL; GD; CERT; Sowers Clb; ARETE; Sftbl IM; BS Nora Univ 90; Bible; Mnstr.

**LOCKLEAR, ARLANA C,** Fayetteville St Univ, Fayetteville, NC; SO; BS; Biology; Educ Biology.

**LOCKMAN JR, HARRY E,** Univ Of Sc At Columbia, Columbia, SC; FR; Mrchng Bnd 86-90; Beta Clb Prsdnt 88-90; Prsdntl Acdmc Ftns Awd 90; Hnr Grad 90; Elctrcl Engnrng; Med.

**LOCKRIDGE, KIMBERLY N,** Hudson Valley Comm Coll, Troy, NY; SR; AAS; Erly Chldhd Clb 89-; Mnrty Mntrng Prog 90-; Mastrangelo Arnold Schlrshp 90; Bus Prfssnl Wmns Assn Schlrshp 90; Delta Sigma Theta Schlrshp 90; Sci Jstce Cltt 90-, Prnt Frnds Orgnztn Chldrns Schl 90-; Erly Chldhd Educ; Tchr.

**LOCKRIDGE, MARY ELAINE,** Jacksonville St Univ, Jacksonville, AL; SR; BSN; JANS 90-; ASNA 90-; AANS 90-; Omicron Delta Kappa 90-; George Gibbins Schlrshp 90-; Jcksonville Hsptl Nrsng Schlrshp 89-; Alabama St Nrsng Schlrshp 90-; Assembly Of God; LPN 87-; Nrsng.

**LOCKRIDGE, RANDOLPH J,** Fl A & M Univ, Tallahassee, FL; FR; History; HS Teacher.

**LOCKWOOD BENET, EDUARDO A,** Univ Politecnica De Pr, Hato Rey, PR; JR; BSME; Sci; Mech Eng.

**LOCKWOOD, KELLIE L,** Dowling Coll, Oakdale Li, NY; SR; BS; Nassau Cnty Assn Educ Yng Chldrn 87-; Dns Lst SUNY Farmingdale 87-89; Dns Lst 89-; Academic Hnr Schlrshp Pgrm 89-; AS SUNY Farmingdale N Y 89; Elem Educ; Tchr.

**LOCKWOOD, MARIA H,** Longwood Coll, Farmville, VA; SO; BA; LURE 90-; Intl Cir 90-; Educ; Tchng.

**LOCKWOOD, MATHEW J,** Duquesne Univ, Pittsburgh, PA; JR; BA; Intl Bsn Assoc 89-; German Clb 89-90; Beta Alpha Phi 89-; Pi Sigma Epsilon V P Pers; Alpha Phi Omega; Vol 90-; Intl Bsn; Intl Mktg.

**LODDO, CHRISTINE S,** Univ Of Akron, Akron, OH; JR; Ntl Stdnt Speech Lang Hrng Assoc 90; Golden Key 90; Longwood YMCA Yth Sprts Dir 89; Cmmnctve Dsordrs; Speech Pthlgy/Adlgy.

**LODGE, ALETHEA B,** City Univ Of Ny City Coll, New York, NY; SO; BA; Nwsppr Cmps Edtr 90-; Intl Stu Clb 90-; Engl Tutor 90-; Intern UAFUNIF; Intl Stu/Frnch; Frgn Affrs/Dplmcy.

**LODGE, MELANIE A,** Oh Univ, Athens, OH; SO; BA; SATO 89-; Sigma Kappa Hstrn Lbrrn 89-; Chld Psych/Art Thrpy.

**LOEB, BART D,** Univ Of Miami, Coral Gables, FL; SR; MS; ACM; TA; Cmptr Sls 83-85; Sftwr Dvlpr 86-90; BS; AA Broward Comm Clg 89; Cmptr Sci.

**LOEB, SUSAN B,** Beaver Coll, Glenside, PA; SR; BA; BAFA 89-90; Intrct 88; Engl Clb; Alchl Awrnss 89; Lambda Delta Alpha; Cert Of Ldrshp Rcgntn; Cmmnty Intrn 90; Sclgy; MSW.**

**LOESCH, SARAH J,** Northern Ky Univ, Highland Hts, KY; SR; Stdnt Govt 85-86; Kappa Kappa Gamma Treas 86-89; BBA Univ Cincinnati 89; Elem Educ; Teacher.

**LOESER, MARK B,** S U N Y At Buffalo, Buffalo, NY; SR; BS; Elect/Cmptr Eng.

**LOETHEN, JEFFREY E,** Oh St Univ, Columbus, OH; FR; BSBA; Ski Clb 90-; OH St Hnrs Scty 90-; IM Sprts 90-; Bus.

**LOEWENSTERN, LISA H,** Fl St Univ, Tallahassee, FL; SR; BS; Sprts Hghlghts Show 90; Cmps Radio 89; Jazz Pop Ensemble 88-; Gldn Key 89-; Delta Chi Lttl Sstr Tres 88-90; Big Brthrs Big Sstrs 88-89; Lbrl Stds Hnrs Prgrm 88-89; Deans Lst 89-; Chi Delphia 89; IM Ftbl 88-89; Media Prdctn; Scrnwrtr.

**LOEWI, RIVKA C,** City Univ Of Ny City Coll, New York, NY; GD; Scty Sigma Xi; Phi Beta Kappa Awrd; City Clg Schlr Awrd; Chemistry Alumni Awrd; S Fla Alumni Chapter Schlr Awrd; Hnrsm Chemistry; Biochemistry; Law.

**LOFARO, KRISTIN M,** Colby Sawyer Coll, New London, NH; JR; BFA; Alpha Chi; Art/Prnmkng; Scntfc Illstrtr.

**LOFFERT, REBECCA J,** Saint Andrews Presbytrn Coll, Laurinburg, NC; JR; BA; Hist Clb 89-; ECO Action 90-; Alpha Chi 90-; CSU 90-; Sage Tutor PSYC TA 89-90; Trck,Crs Cntry,Scr,Equestrian Tm 88-; Hist.

**LOFFREDA, RENATO,** Univ Of Pittsburgh, Pittsburgh, PA; SR; MS; Shotokan Karate Blue Belt; Eta Kappa Nu; Golden Key; Kappa Delta Rho Fnd Fthr 89; BS EE 90; Elec Eng.

**LOFLIN, KIMBERLY D,** Western Carolina Univ, Cullowhee, NC; SR; BA; Wstn Gld 88; Chncllrs Ambsdr 90; Engl Clb 90; Alpha Lambda Delta 89-90; Mortar Board 90-; Sigma Tau Delta 90-; Crum Schlrshp; Deans List 88; Engl; Tchng.

**LOFTERS, CAMILLE R,** Columbia Union Coll, Takoma Park, MD; FR; BA; Theta Alpha Beta 90-; Engl/Jrnlsm; Publshg/Wrtg.

**LOFTIN, ANDREA M,** Middle Tn St Univ, Murfreesboro, TN; SO; BA; Bus Admin; Mgmt.

**LOFTIN, DAVIS K,** Univ Of Sc At Columbia, Columbia, SC; JR; BS; WUSC FM Announcer 91; Pres Lst 89-90; Deans Lst; Bus; Law.

**LOFTIN, IVAN F,** Lenoir Rhyne Coll, Hickory, NC; JR; BA; Capela Chr 90-; FCA Fllwshp Chrstn Athlts 85-; LSM Lthrn Stdnt Mvmnt; Lenior Rhynean Schl Nwspr 88; Alpha Lambda Delta 89-; Broyhill Mntrs Ldrshp Prgrm 89-; Chpl Cncl 88-89; Wshngtn Vntr Hmls Shltr Lthr Pl; Mscchrstn Edctn.

**LOFTIS, KEVIN M,** Univ Of Fl, Gainesville, FL; SR; BS; Bsns Admn Cncl 90-; Gldn Ky 89-; Beta Gamma Sigma; Delta Sigma Pi 89-; Fin.

**LOFTIS, SHEILA E,** Middle Tn St Univ, Murfreesboro, TN; GD; STFA 89-90; SHEA 88-90; Spcl Evnts 86-89; Ko Phi 89-90; Kappa Delta Pi 89-90; Erly Chldhd Ed; Tchr.

**LOFTON, CASSANDRA P,** Albany St Coll, Albany, GA; SR; BA; Army ROTC Cdt 89-90; NODS 85-87; Zeta Phi Beta Parlmnt 90-; Catl Christies RAPP Grp 84-; Cathl Charities Spkprn 85-87; TV Nwsctr Intern 90-; Sr Awd Acad Achvmnt 90-; Speech/Theatre; Grad Schl.

**LOFTON JR, LIONEL S,** Univ Of Sc At Columbia, Columbia, SC; JR; BS; Crmnl Jstc Assoc 90-; Amer Hrt Assoc Instr 87-; Charleston Co EMS EMT/DIVER 87-; USC Police Dept State Constable 90-; USC Hlth Ctr Medic 89-; EMT Certif Trident Tech Clg 87-90; Crmnl Jstc; Law Enfrcmnt-Drugs.

**LOFTON, MICHELE D,** Univ Of South Al, Mobile, AL; JR; BS; Rd Crss Vol; Lbrry Clrk 87-; Elem Ed.

**LOFTON, SANDRENA S,** Alcorn St Univ, Lorman, MS; FR; MBA; Pres Fres Clss 90-; Amry ROTC Srgnt 90-; Dvsttn Drll Tm; Dean Lst 90-; Pre Law; Corp Lwyr.

**LOFTON, SUSAN L,** William Carey Coll, Hattiesburg, MS; SR; BMED; SGA VP 88-90; Rcrtng Team 89-90; Madrgl Sngrs 87-89; Pres Assn 89-90; MTNA 87-; Chorale Pres 87-90; Alpha Chi 90-; Omicron Delta Kappa 89-; Delta Omicron VP 88-; MENC Pres 88-90; MPE 90-; Pres Schlr 87-; Sr Music Awrd; Almni Assn Sprt Awrd; Music Educ; Music.

**LOFTUS, KRISTEN L,** Liberty Univ, Lynchburg, VA; SR; Youth Quest 87-89; Assn Christian Tchrs 88-; Kappa Delta Phi 90-; Urban Outreach Ministry 87-88; Deans Lst; Elem Educ.

**LOFTUS, SUZANNE E,** Temple Univ, Philadelphia, PA; JR; BA; Golden Key 90-; Assoc Montgomery Cnty Cmnty Clg 89; Clinical Psych.

**LOGA, SHARI A,** Ms St Univ, Miss State, MS; SR; Circle K Orgnztn 87-88; Catholic Stdnt Assoc; Miss Assoc Edctrs; Gamma Beta Phi 88-89; Phi Kappa Phi 89-; Magna Cum Laude; BS; Elem Educ; Teach.

**LOGAN, ANN K,** Defiance Coll, Defiance, OH; SR; BA; Communications Club Sec 90-; Ohio Univ Judicial Brd 88-90; Presidents Host 90-; Phi Mu Ohio Univ 88-90; Inter WOUB TV 89; Intern Duraline Medl Prod 90; Intern Defiance Clg Dvlpmnt Ofc Mgr; IM Bowling; Communication; Consulting.

**LOGAN, DANA N,** Roanoke Coll, Salem, VA; FR; BS; Rsdnt Hll Cncl Rep 90-; Erthbnd 90; Phn Thn 90-; Roanoke Coll Hnrs Prgm 90-; Stdnt Asst 90-; Math.

**LOGAN, ELAINE,** Stillman Coll, Tuscaloosa, AL; SR; BA; Phi Beta Lambda Sec 89-90; Stu Spprt Serv Sec 88-90; Kappa Alpha Psi Pres 89-; Dean Lst 89-; Sigma Gamma Iota 90-; Delta Sigma Theta; Bus Admn.

**LOGAN, JASON O,** Fl A & M Univ, Tallahassee, FL; JR; BA; Blck Stdnt Assn Sec Maryvl Clg 89-90; Hrld Sara Wetherbee Fndtn Grnt 88-; Pol Sci; Law.

**LOGAN, KAREN N,** Norfolk St Univ, Norfolk, VA; FR; BA; Bus Mgmt; Rtl Sls Mgr.

**LOGAN, KARNA E,** Bennett Coll, Greensboro, NC; JR; BA; Bus/Acctng Clb; NAACP Treas 90-; Delta Sigma Theta Treas 91-; Bus Admin/Acctng; Financial Cnsltnt.**

**LOGAN, MELINDA B,** Western Piedmont Comm Coll, Morganton, NC; SO; ASN; SUC Soc Hndcpd Adlts Rcrtnl Act Spec Olympics Grp Hms Chrch Act 86-; Phi Theta Kappa 90; Schl Act 72-86; Hlp Elderly 72-; CNA Mc Dowell Tech 89; EMT Mc Dowell Tech 82; Nrsng; RN.

**LOGAN, SHERRI L,** Lincoln Univ, Lincoln Univ, PA; JR; BS; Natl Blcks Crim Jstc; Sclgy Clb; Alpha Kappa Delta; Crim Jstc; Prbtn Ofcr.

**LOGAN, STEVE L,** Lexington Comm Coll, Lexington, KY; JR; BA; Dns Lst; Bsn; Bsn Mgmt.

**LOGAN, SUZANNE E,** Norfolk St Univ, Norfolk, VA; SO; BSN; Spartan Alpha Tau 90-F Commanc Ombudsman 87-89; Beth Shalom Hm 90-; Nrsng; Medicine.

**LOGAR, MONICA M,** Glassboro St Coll, Glassboro, NJ; SR; BA; Wmns Athltc Assn VP 87-90; Math Clb 90-; Vrsty Lcrss Capt 87-90; Math; Educ.

**LOGHRY, STEPHEN L,** Univ Of Tn At Chattanooga, Chattanooga, TN; SR; BSE; Stdnt Govt Assoc 88-89; Honor Ct; Student Orientation Brd; Tau Beta Pi Engr 89-; Mortar Brd; Golden Key 89-; Kappa Sigma Pres 87-; Lab Asstnt 90; Kappa Sigma Schlrshp; Ldrshp Awrd; IM Sftbl Bsktbl 87-; Chem Engrng.

**LOGIUDICE, DAWN M,** Memphis St Univ, Memphis, TN; JR; BBA; Navy Wires Clb Amer Corres Sec 90-; Homemaker Mother; Business Mgmt; Human Resources.

**LOGSDON, SUSAN E,** Univ Of Louisville, Louisville, KY; SO; BS; Soc Of Women Engrs 90-; Am Inst Of Chem Engrs 90-; Phi Eta Sigma 90-; Intrnshp 90; Chem Engrng.

**LOGUE, DONALD A,** Embry Riddle Aeronautical Univ, Daytona Beach, FL; SR; BA; A/P Mech; Prvt Pilot; Sftbl; Avtn Tchnlgy; Cmmrcl Pilot.

**LOGUE, JEFFREY S,** Embry Riddle Aeronautical Univ, Daytona Beach, FL; SO; BS; USAF 84-88; Aerospace Engr.

**LOH, CHRISTINE,** City Univ Of Ny Baruch Coll, New York, NY; SR; BA; Chnese Stdnt Assn 87-88; Stdnt Govt Cmnctn Brd 88-90; Vrsty Vlybl 88-90; Deans Lst 89-; Pub Rltns Intrnshp 90; Bus Cmnctn; Advtsng/Mktg.

**LOH, HAI KUNG,** Central Fl Comm Coll, Ocala, FL; SO; AS; Amrcn Nclr Scty 89-; Amrcn Tbl Tnns Assoc Natl Umpr 87-; Tbl Tnns Clb Cch 87; Phi Theta Kappa Vol Ttr Mth Physcs Chmstry 90; Schssw Schlrshps 90; Cert 65-70; Chmstry Rdtn Prtctn.

**LOHBERG, BIRGIT,** Fl Atlantic Univ, Boca Raton, FL; SO; BA; German Natl Swim Tm 83-89; Olympic Games Seoul Korea 88; Mdlst European Chmpnshps Bonn 89; Bus; Acctng.

**LOHMAN, JANINE,** Univ Of South Fl, Tampa, FL; FR; BA; CMENC; MENC; ACDA; Themis; Deans Lst; Msc Educ/Vcl Prfrmnc; Tchr.

**LOHMANN, ERICA M,** Fl St Univ, Tallahassee, FL; FR; BME; Hall Govt Sec 90-; Glee Clb; Comm Chorus 90; Hon/Schlrs Pgm 90-; Coll Music Ed Natl Conf 90-; Music Edn/Hist; Chorus Dir.

**LOHMEYER, DAVID C,** Fl Atlantic Univ, Boca Raton, FL; SR; BBA; Intrntl Bus Clb; Dns Lst 90-; BCC Glf Tm Co Capt 88; AA Broward Comm Coll 88; Bus Mgmt.

**LOHR, CONNIE R,** Nova Univ, Ft Lauderdale, FL; MBA; BS 89; Prsnnl Mgmt; DIBA/INTL Bus.

**LOHR II, ROBERT J,** Bridgeport Engr Inst, Fairfield, CT; GD; JD; Mech Eng Clb Pres 89-90; ASME 87-; SAE 88-90; BSME 90; Law.

**LOHRET, TIMOTHY A,** Siena Coll, Loudonville, NY; SR; BS; Biology Club 87-; Math Tutor 87-88; IM Bskbl/Ftbl 87-; Alpha Kappa Alpha; Prestl Schlr 87-; IM Sports 87-; Biology; Medl Schl.

**LOIACONO, MARY E,** Cornell Univ Statutory College, Ithaca, NY; JR; BS; Orntatn Cnslr 89-; Cath Choir 89-; Daily Sun; News Serv Intrn 90; Sci Comm; Jrnlsmn.

**LOICHINGER, MICHELE D,** Comm Coll Algny Co Algny Cmps, Pittsburgh, PA; FR; Gen Stds Pre Nrsng; RN.

**LOINES, SHARON M,** Daytona Beach Comm Coll, Daytona Beach, FL; FR; AA; Phi Theta Kappa 90-; Dean Lst 90-; Educ; Elem Schl Tchr.

**LOKEY, NICOLE E,** Univ Of Md At Eastern Shore, Princess Anne, MD; SO; Sclgy; Law.

**LOLLAR, DEBRA S,** Memphis St Univ, Memphis, TN; JR; BPS; Soc Resptry Cr Pres Elect; Amer Assoc Resp Cr; Amer Hrt Assoc Instr/Trnr CPR; AS Jackson St Comm Clg 81; Hlth Admn.

**LOLLATHIN, DANIEL C,** Salem-Teikyo Univ, Salem, WV; SR; BA; Res Asst 89-; Dns Lst 89-; Bsbl 88-; Ind Educ; Tchg.

**LOMASKY, TROY S,** Ny Chiropractic Coll, Glen Head, NY; GD; DC; Phi Chi Omega; BS Brklyn Coll; Chrprctc.

**LOMASTRO, JENNIFER L,** Univ Of Ct, Storrs, CT; SO; BS; Stdnts Fr Prvntn Of Scde 90; Pre Vet Clb Pres 89-; Pre Vet Clb VP; Dns Lst; Otstndng Stdnt Ldrshp Awrd Coll Of Ag 90-; Indpndnt Stdy In Lyme Dis; IM Sccr Vlybl Bsktbl Indr Sccr 90-; Pathoblgy; Vet Med Rsrch.

**LOMAURO, LYNNE P,** Trenton St Coll, Trenton, NJ; FR; BS; CEC 90-; Frndshp Day Comm Spec Ed Serv 90-; Sign Lang Club 90-; Spec Edn; Erly Intrvntn Thrpy.

**LOMAX, VALESKA L,** Ky St Univ, Frankfort, KY; FR; MBA; Clss VP/ Stdnt Cncl/Chrldr/Chr 90; Hnr Rll; Math.

**LOMBARDI, ATHENA C,** Marywood Coll, Scranton, PA; FR; BA; Psych Clb 90-; Psych.

**LOMBARDI, CAROL A,** Berkeley Coll Of Westchester, White Plains, NY; GD; High Hon; Bus.

**LOMBARDI, ROBERT A,** Dowling Coll, Oakdale Li, NY; GD; BS; Arntcs Clb 90; Alpha Eta Rho Asst Pldgmstr 90; Arntcs And Mgmt; Ar Trffc Cntrl Spclst.

**LOMBARDO, ANGELINA L,** Univ Of Akron, Akron, OH; SR; MBA; Acctg Assn 89-90; AUSA Treas 88-89; Italian Clb Treas 87-89; Rngrs Sqdldr 87-88; Goldn Key 89-90; Mortr Brd 89-90; Beta Alpha Psi 90; Delta Sigma Pi 88-89; Acdmc Awrd; IM Water Polo; BS Univ Akron 90; Acctg.

**LOMBARDO, ANGELO,** Georgetown Univ, Washington, DC; SO; BA; Itln Clb 90-; Chr; Hstry.

**LOMBARDO, MICHELLE A,** Univ Of Sc At Columbia, Columbia, SC; FR; BA; Alpha Lambda Delta; Kappa Alpha Theta Alumnae Rltns 90; Bsnss; Law.

**LOMORIELLO, JO-ANN L,** Manhattan Coll, Bronx, NY; JR; BSME; ASME 90-; Sae 90-; Tau Beta Pi 90-; Pi Tau Sigma 90-; Chldrns Choir Dir 84-90; Flk Grp 84-; Mech Engr.

**LONCAR, SUSAN M,** Kent St Univ Geauga Cmps, Burton Twp, OH; SO; BBA; Bus Mgmt; Indus Mgmt.

**LONCHER, KAREN M,** Kent St Univ Kent Cmps, Kent, OH; SO; BBA; Aerobics 89-; Stdnt Govt Hse Cncl 89-; Natl Alpha Lambda Delta; Finance; Govt Wrk.

**LONDON, BRENT S,** Univ Of North Fl, Jacksonville, FL; SR; BA; Stdnt Natl Ed Assoc Treas 90-; FL Stdnt Ldrs Tchr Ed 90-; Intl Scty Tchnlgy Ed; Phi Kappa Phi; Gldn Key; Pi Kappa Alpha 81-; Intern San Pablo Elem Schl 90; Intern Ponte Vedra Palm Valley Elem; Rsrt Mgmt 81-89; AA Cntrl FL Cmmnty Coll 79; Elem Ed; Elem Schl Tchnlgy Spclst.

**LONDON, JENNIFER F,** Bloomfield Coll, Bloomfield, NJ; FR; BSC; Nrsng; Pdtrc Nrs Spclst.

**LONDON JR, JOHNNY T,** Western Ky Univ, Bowling Green, KY; JR; BS; Amer Scty Mech Engnrs 90-; Inst Elctrcl/Elctrncs Engnrs Inc 90-; Phi Theta Kappa 89-; Vhcl Sprt GM Spnsrd Solar Race 90; Vldctrn; GM Ldrshp Awd 90; Intern GM Milford Prvng Grnds Dsgn Engr Trainee 90; AS Nashville Tech Inst 90; Electro-Mech Engrng; Racing Engrng.

**LONES, MARY R,** Hiwassee Coll, Madisonville, TN; SO; BSN; Phi Theta Kappa 90-; Magna Cum Laude; GSA Asst Ldr 79-; LPN Athens Comm Hosp 81-; LPN Superior Hm Hlth; AA; LPN 81; Psychlgy; RN.

**LONETTO, SHERRY G,** Dowling Coll, Oakdale Li, NY; SO; BS; Acdmc Achvmnt Awrd Town Of Islip Dept Of Humn Srvcs; Elem Ed; Tchng.

**LONEY, CHRISTOPHER G,** Atlantic Comm Coll, Mays Landing, NJ; FR; BS; Tau Kappa Epsilon 89-; Dns Lst 90; Peer Mentor Trng Candidate; Acctg.

**LONG, ANGEL R,** Northern Ky Univ, Highland Hts, KY; FR; Psychlgy.

**LONG, BARBARA A,** City Univ Of Ny City Coll, New York, NY; JR; BA; U S Army NATO Sp4; Cert NY Schl For Med Asst 73; Cert U S Signal Ctr 79; Anthropology.

**LONG, BENJAMIN F,** Rutgers St Univ At Camden, Camden, NJ; SR; BS; Rssn Clb 89-90; Acctg Clb 90-; Deans Lst 89-; AS 89; Acctg; Pblc Acctg.

**LONG, BETTYE LEE,** Athens St Coll, Athens, AL; SR; MS; Hnrs Forum 87-89; Scty Physics Stndts; Math/Comp Sci Clb Sec 90-; Phi Theta Kappa 87-89; AS John C Calhoun St Com Coll 89; BS Athens St Coll; Schlrshps; Dns/Pres Lst; Summa Cum Laude; Outstndng Psych Stdnt 89; Mathematics.**

**LONG, BRADLEY S,** Ms St Univ, Miss State, MS; JR; MBA; Phi Theta Kappa; Beta Alpha Si; Acad Schlrshp 88-; Phi Theta Kappa Schlrshp 90-; Assoc Degree NE Comm Clg Acctg; Acctg; CPA.

**LONG, CHRISTINA E,** Roane St Comm Coll, Harriman, TN; SO; BA; AS; Business; Med Records Admin.

**LONG, CHRISTINA M,** Kent St Univ Kent Cmps, Kent, OH; SR; BA; Gen Stds; Air Trffc Cntrllr.

**LONG, CHRISTY M,** Univ Of Ky, Lexington, KY; FR; BA; PALS; Alpha Lambda Delta; Psych.

**LONG, DALE A,** Columbia Union Coll, Takoma Park, MD; GD; BA; Stu Mnstrl Assn 86-; Thlgy; Pstr.

**LONG, DAVE S,** Northeast State Tech Comm Coll, Blountville, TN; SO; AAS; Automtv Svc Tech; Restrtn.

**LONG, DEANNA L,** Valdosta St Coll, Valdosta, GA; JR; BA; JANS Jacksnvl Assoc Nrsg Stu 88-89; Nrs Ambsdr Jcksnvl St Univ 88-89; Spkr Amer Cncr Soc Annistor Al 88-89; Nrsg; Ansthtst.

**LONG, DEBORAH R,** Radford Univ, Radford, VA; JR; BS; Sigma Kappa Natl Nwsltr Corres; Intrnshp Prog Comm Assist 90; Psychology.

**LONG, DENISE E,** Birmingham Southern Coll, Birmingham, AL; SO; BS; Concert Pep Bnd 90-; Zeta Tau Alpha Actvts Chrmn 89-; Alpha Phi Omega 90-; Cmptr Sci; Prgrmmng.

**LONG, DONNA M,** Snead St Jr Coll, Boaz, AL; FR; BS; Elctrcl Engr.

**LONG, DORENA K,** Elmira Coll, Elmira, NY; SO; BS; Vars Chrldr 89-90; Phi Eta Sigma 90-; Phi Beta Kappa Awd Wnr; Intrntl Bus.

**LONG, FREDRICK J,** Asbury Theological Sem, Wilmore, KY; GD; MDIV; Nvgtrs Chrstn Fllwshp 84-86; SGA Class Chpln 88-90; Inter Var Chrstn Fllwshp 86-87; Orient Mssn Scty Colombia S A 89; Yth Cnslr 84; Bsebl 89-90; BS U Of Ill 88; New Tstmnt Studies; Mssnry/Prof.

**LONG, HILLARY C,** Univ Of Richmond, Richmond, VA; FR; BA; Stdnt Educ Assn Pub Chrmn; Episcopal Yth Flwshp 90-; Richmond Hl/Hsng Assn Dorm Pr; Phi Eta Sigma; Alpha Chi Omega Cult Chrmn; Intrn U S Senator Charles S Robb 90; Womens Studies; Elem Educ.

**LONG, JACQUELINE M,** Tn St Univ, Nashville, TN; SR; Crim Just Org 89-; Socl Wrk Clb 90-; Crim Just Hons Outstanding Sr 90; Deans Lst 88-; Vol TN Prison For Women 89-; Vol Crim Just Ctr 89-; Cnslr For A/D Treatment Ctr 89-90; Juv Ct Employee 90-; BA; Crim Just.

**LONG, JAMES R,** Salisbury St Univ, Salisbury, MD; SR; MA; Martl Arts Clb 88-89; Hstry Clb Tr 88-89; Phi Alpha Theta; Pi Gamma Mu; Kappa Delta Pi; Dns Lst 88-90; BA 90; Hstry/ Antrhplgy; Archlgy.

**LONG, JANIE E,** Univ Of Southern Ms, Hattiesburg, MS; SR; BS; Gamma Beta Phi 90-; High Hnrs; RN; AA Nrsg Jones Co Jr Clg 82; Nrsg.

**LONG, JENNIFER L,** De St Coll, Dover, DE; SO; BS; Psychlgy Clb 89-; Mnrty Biomed Rsrch Sprt Prog Lab 90-; Rsrch Asst; Psychlgy; Ph D Cli Psychlgy.**

**LONG, JEROD F,** Wv Univ, Morgantown, WV; JR; BS; Inst Indus Engrs 90-; Alpha Pi Mu 90-; Pi Kappa Phi IFC Rep 88-; Indus Engr.

**LONG, JOHN STEPHEN,** Memphis St Univ, Memphis, TN; SR; BS; SGA Chf Juste 83-85; Interhall Cncl V P 82-84; Chf Estmtr Henders Boiler/Tank Co 86-; Mech Engr.

**LONG, KAYE S,** Univ Of Al At Birmingham, Birmingham, AL; SR; CERT; Amer Assoc Med Assistnts 90-; Phi Mu 69-; Medical Assisting.

**LONG, KENNETH K,** Univ Of North Fl, Jacksonville, FL; SR; BS; Blgcl Sci Chem; Vet Schl.

**LONG, KEVIN E,** Kent St Univ Kent Cmps, Kent, OH; SR; BA; Vars Bsbl 88-; Bsns Mgmt; Bsns.

**LONG, KEVIN M,** George Mason Univ, Fairfax, VA; JR; BA; Vars Soccer 88-; AAHPERD; PR Intern 90; Hlth Ed; Tch H S.

**LONG, KIMBERLY D,** Wv Univ At Parkersburg, Parkersburg, WV; SO; BS; Sci; Physcl Thrpy.

**LONG, KRAIG B,** Temple Univ, Philadelphia, PA; JR; BA; Afrcn Amer Entrpnr And Invstmnt Scty Fndr Co Chrmn 88; Intrnatl Bus Scty 90-; Dns Lst 89-; Intrnatl Bus; Invstmnt Bnkng.

**LONG, KRISTIE L,** Radford Univ, Radford, VA; FR; BS; Hon Soc; Nrsng/Bio.

**LONG, KRISTINE L,** Norfolk St Univ, Norfolk, VA; JR; BA; Engl Forgn Lang Majrs Clb Pr 90-; Yng Dems 90-; Sigma Tau Delta; Engl; Tchng.

**LONG, LINDA A,** Univ Of Ga, Athens, GA; SR; BSED; Big Brother/Big Sister Orgnztn 87-; Rsdnt Housing Assc Psychlgy Clb 88-; Chld Family Dvlpmnt Assc Chrtr Member; Delta Siama Theta Hnr; Deans List 90-; Nrsng Home Vol; Athens Mentle Hlth Assc; Stdnt Affl AM Psychlgl Assc; Ed/Psychlgy; Graduate Schl Cnslng Psy.

**LONG, MARA J,** Univ Of Sc At Columbia, Columbia, SC; JR; BAIS; Angl Flght Vce Cmmndr 89-; Area Rgn Cnclve Co Cmmndr 90-; Elem Educ Psych; Tchng Cnslr.

**LONG, MARK OLIN,** Lenoir Rhyne Coll, Hickory, NC; JR; BS; Alpha Delta Lambda 90-; Mu Sigma Epsilon; Chi Beta Phi; Marshal 89; Bsbl Ctchr 88-; Chem; Chem Eng.

**LONG, MARY E,** Central Al Comm Coll, Alexander City, AL; FR; Phi Theta Kappa.

**LONG, MATRECIA S,** Fl A & M Univ, Tallahassee, FL; SO; BA; Compass Clb Sec 89-90; Blck Stdnt Un 89-90; Phi Theta Kappa 89-; Mu Alpha Theta 89-; Chrch Choir Pianst; SS Stdnt Sec; Bsns Admn; Corp Law.

**LONG, MAUREEN A,** Southeastern Ma Univ, N Dartmouth, MA; GD; Mass Std Nsg Asc 88-90; Onclgy Nrsng Soc 90-; Natl Hnr Soc 88-90; Brghm/Wmns Clncl Asc Intshp 88-; New Engl Dcns Hosp Nrs Intshp 90; RN New Eng Dcns Hosp 90-.**

**LONG, MELANIE E,** Saint Andrews Presbytrn Coll, Laurinburg, NC; FR; BM; Chmbr Singrs 90-; Moore Co Chorl Soc 90-; Theatre Lead 90-; Music; Vocl Prfrmr.

**LONG, MELISSA A,** Valdosta St Coll, Valdosta, GA; FR; BA; Natl Assc Female Exec 90-; Buyer; Purch Mgmt Amer Mgmt Assc; Mgmt; Prchsng.

**LONG, NWADIKI D,** City Univ Of Ny Baruch Coll, New York, NY; SR; BBA; Helpline; Golden Key; Economics; Prof Ecnmst.

**LONG, PATRICK K,** Univ Of Ga, Athens, GA; SR; BLA; GSLA 90-; Bsbl 86-; AS Dekalb Clg; Landscape Arch.

**LONG, PAULA T,** Univ Of South Al, Mobile, AL; SO; B ED; Glgy Clb; Phi Thetta Kappa; Prsdntl Schlrshp; Bptst Chrch Tchr; Mrn Crps; Spcl Edctn; Tchr.

**LONG, R AARON,** Gordon Coll, Barnesville, GA; JR; MBA; Church Yth Ldr; Phi Theta Kappa VP 89-90; Rcqtbl; AA 90; Real Est License GA Real Est Commission 90; Pltcl Sci/Cmnctns; Law/Pltcs.

**LONG, R ETHAN,** Ringling School Of Art, Sarasota, FL; JR; BFA; Artst/Spkr S Cnty Yth Cntr Bradenton FL 90; Artst/Spkr Bascis Pls Elem Sch 90; People Wtch 91 Gulf Cst Mag Naples FL; Soc Ill Stdnt Schlrshp NY NY; Art Coll Exchng Trvlng Exhbtn 90; Head Instr Yth Pgm Ringling Schl Art/Desgn 88-90; Art/Lbrl Arts; Frlnc Ill-Tch.

**LONG JR, RICHARD P,** Univ Of Ky, Lexington, KY; SR; AICHE VP 86-; Omega Chi Epsilon; Otstndng AICHE Jr 90; IM Bsktbl Vllybl Sccr 87-.

**LONG, SABRINA M,** Sinclair Comm Coll, Dayton, OH; GD; Stdnt Govt 88-90; Peer Hlpr 89-90; Future Leader Awd; Mgt Pos; AAS Sinclair Cmcnty Clg 90; Mngmnt.

**LONG, SHANNON D,** Univ Of Ky, Lexington, KY; SO; BA; Hons Prog 89-; Phi Eta Sigma 89-; Deans List 89-; Acadmc Exclnc Recpnt 89-; Hist; Law.

**LONG, SHERYL A,** Univ Of West Fl, Pensacola, FL; JR; BA; Elem Educ; Tchng.

**LONG, SOPHIE M,** Davis & Elkins Coll, Elkins, WV; JR; BS; Chi Beta Phi Hstrn 90-; Biology Clb 89-; Alpha Chi VP; Hnrs Prgrm 89-; Hnrs Assn VP 89-; Purdum Goddin Awd 90-; Acdmc Achvmnt Awd 89-; Envrnmntl Sci; Biology.

**LONG, STACY L,** Univ Of Tn At Martin, Martin, TN; SO; BA; Yrbk 90-; Radio Sta; Newspr Stf Wrtr 90-; Alpha Epsilon Rho; Alpha Gamma Delta Phlntrypy 89-; Cmnctns; Brdcst Jrnlsm.

**LONG, STEVEN RAY,** Pellissippi St Tech Comm Coll, Knoxville, TN; SO; AS; IEEE Pres Elect; Math; Elec Eng.**

**LONG, THERESA K,** Central Fl Comm Coll, Ocala, FL; FR; AS; Phi Theta Kappa 90-; Phi Beta Lambda Hstrn 90-; Bsns Admn/Mgmt; Indstry.

**LONG, TIMOTHY R,** Me Maritime Academy, Castine, ME; SO; BS; Wrstld Coll William/Mary 85; Nutcl Sci; Maritime Indstry.

**LONG, TONYA J,** Univ Of Tn At Martin, Martin, TN; JR; BS; SGA Spkr Congress 88-; TN Intercollegiate State Legislature 89-; Stdnt Ambsdr 89-; Pi Sigma Alpha 90-; Phi Alpha Delta; Assist Hall Dir 90-; TN Advsry Comm Intrgvtmntl Intern 90-; Pol Sci; Educ Admin.

**LONG, TRACEY M,** East Stroudsburg Univ, E Stroudsburg, PA; JR; BA; Progmng Cncl 90-; Mgmt.

**LONG, TRICIA A,** Loyola Coll In Md, Baltimore, MD; JR; BS; Engrs Intelligence 90-; Intervrsty Flwshp 88-90; Tri-Beta 89-; Eta Sigma Phi Sec 88-; Tri-Beta Tutor 90-; Chem Achvmnt Awd 88-89; Latin Achvmnt Awd 88-89; Smr Flwshp Univ MD Med Sch; IM Sftbl 89-90; Bio/Chem; Med.**

**LONG, VICTORIA L,** Univ Of South Al, Mobile, AL; SR; BS; Kappa Delta Pi; Pres Lst; Dns Lst; Sec Ed/Lng Arts; Tchr.

**LONGA, MIRIAM I,** Antillian Adventist University, Mayaguez, PR; GD; BS; Nrsg Clb VP 90-; Univ Rlgs Actvts VP 85-86; Kappa Nu Epsilon Atlantic Clg 87-88; Nrsg.

**LONGACHER, JOSHUA W,** Old Dominion Univ, Norfolk, VA; JR; Pi Tau Sigma; Soc Auto Engr Chrmn 89-; Mech Engr; Prof Engr.

**LONGAZEL, TINA M,** Mount Aloysius Jr Coll, Cresson, PA; FR; ADN; Nrsg; RN.

**LONGHI, DEBRA A,** Greensboro Coll, Greensboro, NC; SO; BS; Math.**

**LONGIELIERE, TERESA J,** Valdosta St Coll, Valdosta, GA; SR; BS; Ambsdrs Sec 88-; Insght Ldr; IMS; Alpha Lambda Delta; Sigma Alpha Chi; Omicron Delta Kappa; Ordr Omega; Rho Lambda; Chi Omega VP 88-; Deans Lst; PEO Soc Schlrshp; Hnrs Pro; Otstndg Coll Stu Amer; Ntl Coll Ntl Sci Awrd; Bio; Marine Vet.

**LONGINO, SILENDA DUVELL,** Univ Of Southern Ms, Hattiesburg, MS; SO; BS; Gamma Beta Phi; Alpha Epsilon Delta; Career Images Ltd; Afro Amer Acad Awd; F J Walker Awds; Bio/Pre Med; Obstet/Gynclgy.

**LONGINOTTI FELER, LAURIE,** Memphis St Univ, Memphis, TN; Law Review 88-90; Stdnt ABA 87-89; Valedictorian 90; Corpus Juris Sec Awd 89; Law Alumni Schlrshp 90; RN 84-; BSN Vanderbilt 84; Law.

**LONGLEY, DIANE M,** George Mason Univ, Fairfax, VA; SO; BS; Alpha Lambda Delta 90-; Bus Acctg.

**LONGNO, NELL B,** Midlands Tech Coll, Columbia, SC; JR; ADN; Stdnt Nrs Assn By Laws Comm 90; Phi Theta Kappa; Pres Dns Lst 89-; Outstdng Nrsg Stdnt 90-; Stdnt Tech Bapt Med Ctr 90-; Mother Of 4; Hairdrsr 65-70; Nrsng; BS/MA Nrsng.

**LONGO, DIEGO M,** Barry Univ, Miami, FL; JR; Soccer; Acctg.

**LONGO, JULIE L,** Univ Of Miami, Coral Gables, FL; JR; BBA; Wlcm Wk Staff 89; Sdlns Sprt Org Comm Chrmn 88-89; Beta Gamma Sigma; Gamma Beta Phi 89-; Alpha Lambda Delta 88-; Delta Sigma Pi VP Prof Affrs 90-; Beta Beta Alpha 89-; Alpha Delta Pi Pldg Brd 88-; Bowman Ashe Schlrshp; Acctg.

**LONGO, LISA MARIE,** William Paterson Coll, Wayne, NJ; SR; BA; Bus Assoc 90-; Acctg Scty Brd Mbr 90-; Jr Yr Abrd Prgm 89-90; Deans Lst 90-; Achvmnt Awrd; Sq Corp 86-; Acctg.

**LONGO, MARK D,** Univ Of Rochester, Rochester, NY; SO; Sigma Alpha Mu 89; Tiernan Spec Intrst Hsng/Cmmnty Serv 89-90.

**LONGSON, LISA K,** West Liberty St Coll, West Liberty, WV; SO; BA; Mngr Wtrhds Etc 90-; Pre Law; Law.

**LONGSTAR, SANDRA J,** Columbia Greene Comm Coll, Hudson, NY; FR; AA; SAGE; VISTA 77-84; Empire Drvng Clb 77-; BITS 88; Hrsbck Rdng Instr Hndcppd; Cnstrctn Wrkr 84-86; Psychlgy; Fmly Cnslng.

**LONGSTREET, YOLANDA D,** Fayetteville St Univ, Fayetteville, NC; JR; BS; AA Gen Educ 90; Clncl Psychlgst.

**LONGSTRETH, JASON S,** Fl Coll, Temple Terrace, FL; FR; AA; CREST Club; ARETE 90-; Bible; Prchng.

**LONIA, SUZANNE M,** Glassboro St Coll, Glassboro, NJ; SR; BA; Cert Of Acdmc Achvmnt In Mjr/Soclgy Field Exprnc/Div Of Yth-Fmly Serv Glcstr Co NJ; Soclgy; Tchng/Secndry Ed.

**LONSKI, NYLEEN C,** De Tech & Comm Coll At Dover, Dover, DE; FR; AA; Humn Svcs Org; Phi Theta Kappa; Humn Svcs.

**LONSTEIN, CLIVE,** Univ Of Miami, Coral Gables, FL; FR; BA; HILLEL; Arch.

**LONSTEIN, LIANNE,** Univ Of Miami, Coral Gables, FL; JR; BA; HILLEL; Itln Soc; TABS; Phi Kappa Phi; USAA All-Amer Schlr; Dba U Witwaters Rand Johannesburg 89; Poly Sci; Law.

**LONZENSKI, JEANINE,** Southern Ct St Univ, New Haven, CT; SR; BSN; Sigma Theta Tau 90-; Zeta Delta Epsilon 88-; Cum Laude; Nursing; RN.

**LOO, JENNIFER I,** Oh Wesleyan Univ, Delaware, OH; JR; BA; Univ Film Series Sec 88-; Phi Eta Sigma VP 89-90; Phi Soc Sec 90-; Omicron Delta Epsilon; Pres Schlr; Acctg/Ecnmc Mgmt; Pblc Acctg.

**LOOBY III, JOHN J,** Western New England Coll, Springfield, MA; FR; BA; Peer Review Board; Alpha Lambda Delta 90-; History; Law.

**LOOMIS, LAURIE L,** Vt Coll, Montpelier, VT; FR; BARC; Blue/Gold Key 90-; Am Inst Architecture Stdnts 90-; Choraleers 90-; Architecture.

**LOONEY, BRIAN D,** Cumberland Coll, Williamsburg, KY; JR; BS; Outdoor Adventure Clb 89-; Am Chem Soc 90-; Tchrs Asst 90-; Rsdnts Asst; Ftbl 88-89; Chem; Optmtry.

**LOONEY, MELANIE L,** Birmingham Southern Coll, Birmingham, AL; JR; BA; SGA Spirit Com Chrmn 90-; Model Senate Advsr 88-; Clg Rpblcns 88-; Omicron Delta Kappa Pres 90-; Order Omega; Pi Sigma Alpha; Pre-Law Soc 88-; Chi Omega Sec 88-; Links Up Fndng Crdntr 88-90; General Motors Co-Op 89-; Pltcl Sci/Bus Admnstrtn; Law/Bus.

**LOONEY, TIMOTHY L,** Middle Tn St Univ, Murfreesboro, TN; SR; BS; Scty Mfg Eng 88-; Gamma Beta Phi 87-; Deans Lst 88-; Hnr Roll 89-; Early Adm To Coll; Engineering Tech; Prdct Dsgn Eng.

**LOOPER, JANICE MICHELLE,** Tri County Tech Coll, Pendleton, SC; FR; BA; Phi Theta Kappa; Sftbl; Math: Elem Ed.

**LOOS, KARLA LOUISE,** S U N Y Coll Of Optometry, New York, NY; JR; OD; VOSH 88-; Optmtrc Srvds Hmnty; Lmb Cntr Vsn Scrnng 89-; Beta Sigma Kappa Pres 90-; Mensa 85-; BS 88; Optmtry.

**LOOS JR, RALPH W,** Western New England Coll, Springfield, MA; SR; MBA; IM Bsktbl Hcky 87-90; Peer Tutor 90-; Vrsty Glf Tm 87-89; BSBA Wstrn New England Clg; Mtkg; Prfsr.

**LOPATOWSKI, STEVE,** City Univ Of Ny La Guard Coll, Long Island Cty, NY; GD; AAS; Srgnt US Army 84-88; Nrsng.

**LOPES, GRACE C,** Newbury Coll, Brookline, MA; FR; BA; T J Maxx Corp; Vendor Rltns Coord; Acctng.

**LOPES, JEFFREY C,** Norfolk St Univ, Norfolk, VA; FR; BA; Spartan Alpha Tau; Biol; Tchng.

**LOPES, TERESE M,** George Mason Univ, Fairfax, VA; SR; BS; Accntng Clb Scrtry 90; Accntng Hnr Scty; Ntnl Key Hnr Scty 90; LDS Chrch Chrstr 90; AA NVCC Alex Va 89; Accntng; Accntng CPA Tax.

**LOPEZ ACEVEDO, OMAYRA,** Inter Amer Univ Pr Hato Rey, Hato Rey, PR; SR; BA; Curso Intensillo De Ingles 1st Sch For Career 89; Math/Engl; Acctg.

**LOPEZ ARROYO, EMILIO JOSE,** Inter Amer Univ Pr San German, San German, PR; SO; BA; Civil Eng.

**LOPEZ CARRASQUILLO, RUBEN,** Univ Of Pr Humacao Univ Coll, Humacao, PR; SO; Hnrs Sch 90-; Cert 90-; Accnt Ecnmy; Accntnt.

**LOPEZ DEL VALLE, LYDIA M,** Univ Of Pr Medical Sciences, San Juan, PR; GD; MPH; Clg Of Dentstry PR 81-; Amercn Dentl Assoc 87-; PR Sch Of Dentrstry Fac Assoc 83-; BS Univ Of PR 77; DMD Univ Of PR Sch Of Dentstry 81; Dentstry/Biostatstcs.

**LOPEZ ECHEGARAY, ALEX J,** Inter Amer Univ Pr San German, San German, PR; FR; BA; Interamer Univ Choir 90-; Music.

**LOPEZ LOPEZ, MILAGROS,** Inter Amer Univ Pr Barranquita, Barranquitas, PR; BA; Ftr Sec Assn 87-; Comm Serv Cntr Vol 87-88; Magna Cum Laude; Sec Sci.

**LOPEZ NEGRONI, RAFAEL,** Inter Amer Univ Pr San Juan, Hato Rey, PR; SO; SGA Pres 90-; Acadmc Sen Interamercn Univ Sentr Elect; Young Legsltv Cncl Pres 89-; Natl Beta Club Pres 88-89; Pontivical Mission Aid Soc Sub Coor 87-.**

**LOPEZ OCASIO, DARIEN,** Inter Amer Univ Pr San German, San German, PR; SO; MBA; Qlty Gym 88-; Fontecha Acad 87-; Army ROTC 89-90; Natl Hon Soc 87-89; Virgin Mary Lgn 87; Acad Achvmnt 87; Bio; Genetics.

**LOPEZ ORTIZ, ANA D,** Inter Amer Univ Pr Hato Rey, Hato Rey, PR; SR; BA; Hon Stdnt; Sec Sci; Exec Sec.

**LOPEZ RAMOS, VANESSA Y,** Inter Amer Univ Pr Hato Rey, Hato Rey, PR; FR; Univ Hnr Scty 90-; Ed; Pre Schl Tchr.

**LOPEZ RIVERA, ISABEL,** Univ Of Pr At Rio Piedras, Rio Piedras, PR; SR; Pltcs; Law.

**LOPEZ ROCHE, LAURA LIS,** Univ Of Pr At Rio Piedras, Rio Piedras, PR; SR; BA; Gldn Key; DAAD Smmr Stds Germany 90; Frgn Lang Grmn.

**LOPEZ, ALEJANDRO PAUL,** Miami Dade Comm Coll, Miami, FL; FR; BA; Math/Physics; Engr.

**LOPEZ, ANNETTE M,** Univ Of Miami, Coral Gables, FL; SR; BA; Biology; Physcl Thrpy.

**LOPEZ, BARBARA I,** Miami Dade Comm Coll South, Miami, FL; SO; BA; Tchrs Aide Vol 90-; Hnrs Clb 89-; Vol Tchrs Aide Vol 90-; Tlnt Rstr 89-; AA MDCC South; Engl Educ; Scndry Tchr.

**LOPEZ, CARLOS R,** Nova Univ, Ft Lauderdale, FL; JR; BA; Alpha Chi; Fdtn C D Aguila 88-; Green Peace Actvst; Dns Lst 89-; Nova Univ Most Imprvd Cross Country Awd; Savings Amer Half-Marathon 90; Cross Country 90-; Finance/Econ; Bsn Adm.**

**LOPEZ, CRISTINA M,** Univ Of Miami, Coral Gables, FL; JR; BARCH; Archtctrl Clb Of Miami 89-; Tchng Asst 90; Archtctrl Eng Dsgn 90; Smmr Tchng Asst 90; Archtctre; MA Cert Archtct.

**LOPEZ, DAMON,** Chesterfield Marlboro Coll, Cheraw, SC; FR; MBA.

**LOPEZ, DENISE A,** Judson Coll, Marion, AL; JR; BA; Campus Ministries 89-; Jr Soph Cls Sec 90-; Schlrs Sec 90-; PLUS; IM Bsktbl,Sftbl,Fld Hcky,Hcky Capt 90; Psychology; Spec Educ.

**LOPEZ, EDITH Z,** Univ Of Pr Medical Sciences, San Juan, PR; JR; BS; APHA Stdnt Org 87-; Rho Chi; Natural Science/Chemistry; Pharmacy.

**LOPEZ, ELBA N,** Bayamon Central Univ, Bayamon, PR; SO; BA; St Peter Apostle Ch; Rlgus Instr Catechist 85-86; Hon Medal; Cert 4 Pt 89-90; Word Proc; Legal Wrk; AAS N Y City Comm Clg 68; Sec; Exec Sec.

**LOPEZ, EMILIA F,** City Univ Of Ny City Coll, New York, NY; SR; Aspira Clb; Chrch Grp Yth Tmro; Yng Dmncn Grp; ESL Cntst Awrd 87; Aspira Spprt Serv Awrds Acdmc Wrk 90-.

**LOPEZ, FRANCIS E,** Inter Amer Univ Pr Hato Rey, Hato Rey, PR; JR; BA; Amer Mrktng Assoc Exec VP 90-; Hon Prog Stdnt Assoc 90-; Mrktng; Bsns Admn.

**LOPEZ, HECTOR J,** Univ Of Miami, Coral Gables, FL; FR; BMUS; Sch Music Shlrshp 90-; Theory; Cmrcl Music.

**LOPEZ, HELEN M,** Georgetown Univ, Washington, DC; SR; BSBA; Stdt Fed Crdt Union 88-; Yrbk Stff 90-; Stdt Assc Spirit Comm 90-; Ntl Statistics Comm 90-; Bookshop 88-; Intl Mgmt/Marketing; Business.

**LOPEZ, JOSE JAVIER,** Univ Of Pr At Rio Piedras, Rio Piedras, PR; SR; MA; Geogr Stu Assn 90-; Gldn Ky 89-; Mnrty Asst; BA; Geogr; Prffsr.

**LOPEZ, LOURDES A,** Fl International Univ, Miami, FL; SR; BA; AA Miami Dade Comm Clg 89; Elem Ed.

**LOPEZ, LOYDA R,** Bayamon Tech Univ Coll, Bayamon, PR; GD; UM Yng Ppl Pres 90-; Summa Cum Laude 88; Magna Cum Laude 90; AS Univ Or P R 88; BS Univ P R 90; Cmptr Sci; Mstrs.

**LOPEZ, MARGORIE M,** Inter Amer Univ Pr Hato Rey, Hato Rey, PR; JR; BA; Swmng 90-; Econ; Syst Analyst.

**LOPEZ, MARIA F,** Fl International Univ, Miami, FL; SO; BS; Suicide Prvntn Tlks; Psych; Clncl.

**LOPEZ, MARIA G,** Fl International Univ, Miami, FL; SO; BA; Ed; Elem Ed.

**LOPEZ, MARIBEL,** Univ Of Pr Cayey Univ Coll, Cayey, PR; BA; Acctng Stdnts Assn 89-; Ping Pong; Acctng; CPA.

**LOPEZ, MAYTE,** Univ Of Miami, Coral Gables, FL; FR; BS; Pre Med Hon Soc; Biology; Med Doc.

**LOPEZ, NORAYMA,** Univ Politecnica De Pr, Hato Rey, PR; FR; BEE; Elctrcl Engnrng; Engnrng.

**LOPEZ, RICHARD A,** S U N Y Coll Of Tech At Frmgdl, Farmingdale, NY; SO; AAS; Stdnts Spcl Cncrns Com 90-; Estrn Prlyzd Vets Assn 87-; AMVETS 84-; US Army 82; Apple Scis; BS Cvl Eng.

**LOPEZ, ROSA H,** Inter Amer Univ Pr San German, San German, PR; FR; BA; Eng.

**LOPEZ, SAJID,** Miami Dade Comm Coll South, Miami, FL; SO; BA; Delta Phi Omega 89-90; Engl; Law.

**LOPEZ, SANDRA J,** Fl International Univ, Miami, FL; SR; BA 90; Elem Educ; Elem Tchr.

**LOPEZ, SANDRA L,** Univ Of Miami, Coral Gables, FL; SO; Mscl Theater Unv Singers 90-; Delta Gamma; Music Schlrshp; Msc Thrpy; Msc Theatr.

**LOPEZ, SUSY,** Fl International Univ, Miami, FL; SR; BA; Phi Kappa Phi 89-; Finance; Law.**

**LOPEZ, VANESSA,** Univ Of Pr At Rio Piedras, Rio Piedras, PR; JR; BBA; Acctg Stdnts Assn 90-; Gldn Ky; Hnr Rl 89-; Natl Coll Bus Awd 90-91; Bus Admin; Acctg/Cmptrs.

**LOPEZ-BURGOS, ROBERTO J,** Inter Amer Univ Pr Hato Rey, Hato Rey, PR; FR; BS; Chemsitry; Engrng.

**LOPEZ-CANDO, ANTHONY J,** Barry Univ, Miami, FL; SR; BS; Univ Pres Lst; AS Miami-Dade Comm Coll 81; AA Miami-Dade Comm Coll 90; Comp Info Syst; Masters Degree.

**LOPEZ-CEPERO, WANDA HEREDIA,** Bayamon Tech Univ Coll, Bayamon, PR; GD; Acctng Assoc 90-; Hon Soc 86-; Lions Clb Awrd; BA Univ Of P R 86; Acctgn; CPA.

**LOPEZ-FERNANDEZ, GERARDO L,** Central Fl Comm Coll, Ocala, FL; FR; BS; Spprt Stdnt Serv 90; Phi Theta Kappa; Cmptrs; Eng.

**LOPEZ-JIMENEZ, CARLOS J,** Inter Amer Univ Pr San Juan, Hato Rey, PR; GD; JD; Sch Of Law Hnrs Stndts Grp 90-; BA Communications 89; Juris Doctor/Generald; J D Degree.

**LOPEZ-RODRIGUEZ, JANICE S,** Univ Politecnica De Pr, Hato Rey, PR; FR; BA; Ind Eng; Eng.

**LOPEZ-ROSADO, NILSA H,** Univ Of Pr Medical Sciences, San Juan, PR; GD; MPHE; BA 80; Envrnmntl Hlth; Law.

**LOPEZ-SIERRA, HECTOR E,** Evangelical Semimary Of P R, Hato Rey, PR; GD; MDIV; Hspnc Schlr 89; Bapt Mnstr; BBAS 87; Thlgy.

**LOPORACARO, FRANCESCA M,** Saint John Fisher Coll, Rochester, NY; FR; BA; Psych; Psychtry.

**LOPRESTO, MARGARET A,** Saint Johns Univ, Jamaica, NY; SR; BA; Italian Cltrl Soc; Kappa Delta Pi; AS St Johns Unv 90; Edctn Spch Hrng; Tchr Spch Pthlgst.

**LORA, SONIA,** Miami Dade Comm Coll, Miami, FL; Phi Theta Kappa 79; Course OST 2311 Lotus 123 90; Plnnd Cert Mid Mgt In Acctng 79.

**LORANCE, LISA M,** Middle Tn St Univ, Murfreesboro, TN; JR; BS; Chem Clb 90-; Chem; Rsrch.

**LORD, DAVID W,** Univ Of Fl, Gainesville, FL; SR; BS; Rho Epsilon 88-; Undergrad Econ Soc 90-; Bus Admin Clg Cncl 90-; Fin/Mngmnt Assoc Hon Soc 89-; Golden Key 90-; Omicron Delta Epsilon 90-; Fin/Real Est; Intl Bus.

**LORD, GREGORY R,** Unity Coll, Unity, ME; JR; BS; Hallowell Consrvtn Commsn 88-; Wildlf/Frstry; Wldlf Biolgst; Forstr.

**LORD, KATHRYN E,** Atlantic Comm Coll, Mays Landing, NJ; SO; Girl Scouts Asst Ldr 85-; Art Awds 83-84; Freelance Artist.

**LORD, LORI J,** Univ Of New England, Biddeford, ME; SO; BS; Physcl Thrpy Clb 90-; Phi Eta Sigma 87-; Gldn Key 89-; Unv Rhode Islnd; Eqstrn Tm 88-90; Physcl Thrpy.

**LORDI, SANDRA S,** Asnuntuck Comm Coll, Enfield, CT; GD; Drama Club 89; Phi Theta Kappa 89-; AS; Bus; Gen Studies.

**LORE, PETER L,** S U N Y Coll Of Tech At Frmgdl, Farmingdale, NY; SO; MBA; Acctng.

**LOREE, GHISLAINE A,** Md Inst Coll Of Art, Baltimore, MD; SR; BFA; Fine Arts; Designer/Film Maker.

**LORENTE, MATEO,** Manhattan School Of Music, New York, NY; SR; BMA; Deans Lst; Piano.

**LORENTZ, CAROLYN S,** Gaston Coll, Dallas, NC; GD; Slippery Rock Univ HPER; IN Univ PA Scndry Educ/Sclgy; Slippery Rock Univ 80; Sclgy/Minor Hlth; Scndry Educ.

**LORENTZEN, JILL H,** Glassboro St Coll, Glassboro, NJ; SO; BA; NJPIRG 89-90; Venue Mag Prod 90-; Commctns; Adv.

**LORENZ, ERIC J,** Univ Of Nc At Charlotte, Charlotte, NC; JR; BA; TREE 90-; Am Inst Architecture Stdnts 90-; Natl Coll Architecture/Dsgn Awds 90-; Gold Key 90-; Club De Vieux Manor 89; Architecture.

**LORENZ, LORETTA J,** Bethany Coll, Bethany, WV; SO; BS; Stdnt Brd Of Govs Rep; Amer Chem Scty VP; Tri Beta Blgy; Dns Lst; Rynlds Mem Hosp Aux Hosp Vol; Chem Biochem; Med MD With Ph D In Biochem.

**LORENZ, MICHAEL A,** Columbus Coll Of Art & Design, Columbus, OH; SR; BFA; IDSA 87-; Natl Hon Soc 85; Crtv Serv Intrn 88; Mrt Awd IDSA; Ind Dsgn; Corp Dsgn Cnsltng.

**LORENZO, LOURDES M,** Univ Of Pr At Rio Piedras, Rio Piedras, PR; JR; BSPH; Amer Phrmctcl Assc 90-; Ntrl Sci/Pharmacy.

**LORETO, RICHARD J,** Manhattan Coll, Bronx, NY; JR; BE; ASME 89-; SAE 89-; Coop Educ Int 91-; Lederle Lab Mech Engr; Mech Engr.

**LORICCHIO, JAMES D,** Villanova Univ, Villanova, PA; JR; BS; Alpha Phi Delta Scl Chrprsn 89-90; Sci.

**LORINC, MARY K,** Smith Coll, Northampton, MA; SO; BA; Rugby Ftbo Clb; Hbbrd Hse Cncl Chr; Dns Lst/Frst Grp Schlrs 90-; Pblshng/Studio Intrn; Msc Cmpstn.

**LORINCZ, PETER,** Embry Riddle Aeronautical Univ, Daytona Beach, FL; SR; BS; Rsrv Ofcrs Assoc 88-; Assoc U S Army 88-; AOPA 88-; Crn Mnstres Co Ldr; Army ROTC Schlrshp; Rm/Bd Schlrshp; PTA Schlrshp; I M Vybl Capt 90; Aeronautical Sci; Miltry Aviation/Army.

**LORUSSO, NICOLE A,** Teikyo Post Univ, Waterbury, CT; JR; BS; Alpha Chi; Acctng; Account CPA.**

**LOSCAR, ANGELIQUE M,** Cornell Univ Statutory College, Ithaca, NY; SO; BS; Crnll Frnscs Scty Sec 89-; Stdnt Advsr; Ambssdr; Walt Disney Smmr Coll Prgm; Deans Lst; Blgy; Bus.

**LOSCH, BRETON E,** Wv Univ, Morgantown, WV; SO; BS; Lzr Tag 89-; Grotto 89-; Cmptr Soc Edtr 90-; IEE 90-; Phi Kappa Phi Schlr 89-90; Elec/Cmptr Engr.

**LOSEY, DONNA M,** Georgian Court Coll, Lakewood, NJ; FR; BA; Spec Educ; Tchng.

**LOSEY, SHERRI A,** Roane St Comm Coll, Harriman, TN; SO; BS; Spl Ed; Spl Ed Tchr.

**LOSIAO, YOUNGN,** City Univ Of Ny Baruch Coll, New York, NY; GD; BBA; Cptr/Quantitative Methods Scty Secty 90-; Beta Gamma Sigma 90; Natl Golden Key; Cis/Opr; Cptr Infor.

**LOSSI, JEANINE M,** Castleton St Coll, Castleton, VT; JR; BSPED; Phy Educ Majors Clb 88-; Womns Var Athl Clb 88-; Vermont Assn Hlth; Phy Educ; Recreatn; Dance 88-; Womns Var Sftbl Asst Coach Stdnt Tchg; Phy Educ; Tch.

**LOSTY, GRETCHEN A,** Immaculata Coll, Immaculata, PA; JR; BA; CUP 90-; ADA; PDA; Suburbn Gen Hosp 90-; AS Montgmry Cty Comm Clg 80; Clin Dietcs; Reg Dietcn.

**LOTA, JAMES V,** City Univ Of Ny Baruch Coll, New York, NY; SR; BS; BOSS Cl; Acctng Soc; Pres Hon 87-88; AA Sacramento City Colg 89; Busn Admin; CPA.

**LOTITO, ELIZABETH-ANNE L,** Villanova Univ, Villanova, PA; JR; BA; Stdnt Prgmg Cncl Pblc Rltns Ed 88-; Italian Clb Cls Repr 88-; Grphc Soc; Phi Kappa Phi; Pi Sigma Alpha VP; Phi Sigma Tau; Assoc Cmptng Mchnry VP; Tutor; Pltcl Sci; Law.

**LOTITO, JOSEPH G,** Fl Atlantic Univ, Boca Raton, FL; JR; BA; Masons 90-; Ch Christ Diaconate Cmtee 87; Karate Assn 90; Delta Sigma Pi; Big Bros; Bus Mgmt; Bus.

**LOTT, ANGELA J,** Owensboro Jr Coll Of Bus, Owensboro, KY; SO; AS; 2 Hon Awards 90; Pres Award; Comp Bus; Office Mngmnt.

**LOTT, JONATHAN T,** Ky St Univ, Frankfort, KY; JR; 300 Club; Music Educ.

**LOTT, SHERI L,** Univ Of Ga, Athens, GA; SO; BS; Bapt Un 89-90; Hall Cncl 89-; Alpha Lambda Delta 90-; Early Chldhd Educ; Tch.

**LOTT, VIRGINIA G,** Converse Coll, Spartanburg, SC; JR; BA; SAB 89-; SCACUS 88-; SCSEA 89-; Trstee Hon Schlrshp 88-; Early Chldhd/Elem Ed; Tchr.

**LOUDD, ALBA E,** Fl A & M Univ, Tallahassee, FL; SO; MBA; Pres Schlr 89-; Swim Tm 89-90; Busn Admin; Law.

**LOUDENSLAGER, SUSAN R,** Duquesne Univ, Pittsburgh, PA; JR; BS; Stdnt Acctng Assn Pres 90-; Yrbk Sect Ldr 89-; Beta Alpah Phi; Bus/Acctng; CPA.

**LOUDERBACK, HARRY F,** Bridgewater Coll, Bridgewater, VA; SR; BS; Math Cmptr Sci Clb VP 90-; Physics Clb; Day Stu Org 89-; Debate Tm 90; ABS; Math; Cmptr Pro.

**LOUDERBACK, MONICA R,** Alice Lloyd Coll, Pippa Passes, KY; SR; BA; Stdnts Actvties Brd 89-; Yrbk Stf 89-90; Drg Tsk Frce 89-; Alpha Chi Treas 90-; Kappa Delta Epsilon Treas 90-; A Lloyd Col Wrk Stdy Awrd 89-90; Outstndng Achvmnt Kappa Delta Epsilon 90-; Early Elem Ed; Tchng.

**LOUDERBACK, TAMMY S,** Madisonville Comm Coll, Madisonville, KY; FR; BA; Acctng; CPA.

**LOUDERMILL, LURETHA MOORE,** Fayetteville St Univ, Fayetteville, NC; GD; MA; Soc Assn 90-; ANEP 88-; Alpha Kappa Delta 89-90; PTA 88-; IRS; Sociology; Law.

**LOUDIN, SARAH A,** Univ Of Sc At Coastal Carolina, Conway, SC; FR; BA; Theatre Clb Sec 90-; Stdnt Gov Rep 90-; Stdnt Nwspr Asst Ed 90-; Hnrs Prgm 90-; Delta Iota Zeta 90-; Engl; Ed Ptry Magazine.

**LOUGH, DANIEL L,** Va Polytechnic Inst & St Univ, Blacksburg, VA; SO; BS; Amiga Usrs Grp; Cmptr Engrg; Engr.**

**LOUGH, KIMBERLEY A,** Western Carolina Univ, Cullowhee, NC; SO; BA; Baptist Stdnt Unin Internation Chrmn 89-; Creative Ministries Ldr; Alpha Lambda Delta 90-; Gamma Beta Phi; Stdnt Summer Missions 90-; Science Undergraduate Research Flwshp 89-90; History; Seminary.

**LOUGH, MARIEN YVETTE,** Univ Of North Fl, Jacksonville, FL; JR; BA; Gldn Key; Phi Theta Kappa 89-90; Frst Tchncn 78-; Asst Forest Tech Abraham Baldwin; Asst Lib Arts Lake City Cmmnty Coll 89; Elem Ed; Tch.

**LOUGH, MICHAEL B,** Oh Univ, Athens, OH; SO; BS; Elec Eng.

**LOUGHERY, SRILAKSHMI F,** Radford Univ, Radford, VA; JR; BSN; Sigma Theta Tau 90-; Sales; Wk Nursing Home; AA Southern Sem Jr Clg 87; BA Wash/Lee Univ 88; Nursing; Doctorate.

**LOUGHLIN, COLLEEN P,** City Univ Of Ny Queensbrough, New York, NY; SO; BA; AS Queensborough Comm Clg; Design/Computer Art.

**LOUGHLIN, HEATHER A,** S U N Y Coll Of Tech At Alfred, Alfred, NY; SR; AAS; Soc Of Mfg Engrs Treas/Sec 90-; Tau Alpha Pi; Phi Theta Kappa; Pres Schlrshp 89-; Prod/Mach Design; Engr.

**LOUGHRAN, JENNIFER A,** Merrimack Coll, North Andover, MA; FR; Psychlgy; Chld Psychlgst.

**LOUGHRAN, MONICA H,** Comm Coll Algny Co Algny Cmps, Pittsburgh, PA; FR; Secretary; Bus Mgmnt; Bnk Mngr.

**LOUGHREY, MARY ELLEN,** Niagara Univ, Niagara Univ, NY; SR; BS; Delta Epsilon Sigma; Dist Stdnt Awd; AA Jmstwn Comm Clg 89; Biology; Optometry.

**LOUGHRY, HOLLY A,** Oh Univ, Athens, OH; FR; BA; Stdnts Untd Life VP/PRES Elect 90-; Chrstn Org Cofndr/Treas 90-; Stdnt Gov Hll/Grn Cncls Rep Svrl Comm 90-; Deans Lst; Chrch 7-10 Yrs Old Tchr 90-; Intrn Marietta Times Rprtr; Tchng Asst Stats; 7 Schlrshps 90-; Jrnlsm; Nws/Mag Wrtng/Edtng.

**LOUIE, DAVID,** Fordham Univ, Bronx, NY; SO; BA; Repub Clb; Bsn Law Clb; Acctg Frat; Acctg; Acctg/Law.

**LOUIE, JOAN,** City Univ Of Ny Baruch Coll, New York, NY; JR; Gldn Key 90-; Accntng.

**LOUIE, STEVEN TON GEIN,** Appalachian Bible Coll, Bradley, WV; GD; BA; Stdnt Serv Dorm Res Asst 90-; Mssnry Conf Fllwup Comm Stdnt Chrmn 90-; Ushr Comm Mbr 89-; Awana Clb Mt Tabor Bapt Chrch Pal Ldr 90-; Pryr Wrrs 89-90; Bckly Chld Care Cntr Adlscnt Grp Ldr 89-; Bible; Pastoral.

**LOUIS, JEAN BERNARD,** Hudson County Comm Coll, Jersey City, NJ; GD; BS; Cvl Engr Inst Superior Tech Haiti 78-82; Cmptr Sci; Engr.

**LOUIS, LOUISE GINA,** Bunker Hill Comm Coll, Boston, MA; Engl; Nrsng/Phrmcy.

**LOUIS, MARSHA A,** East Tn St Univ, Johnson City, TN; SO; Prsdnts Prd Orgnztn 90-; Prvw Ornttn Ldr; Alpha Lambda Delta 89-; Vlntr Etsu Srvc Orgnztn 89-; Im Arbcs 90-; Bsns Fnc & Acctng; Crprt Law Or Cpa.

**LOUIS, WAYNE R,** Dowling Coll, Oakdale Li, NY; GD; MBA; Delta Mu Delta 89-; Cum Laude 90; Contracts Admnstrn Gumman Aerospace Corp; AS Suffolk Cnty Cmnty Clge 88; BBA Dowling Clge 90; Gnrl Mgmnt; Law.

**LOUKAS, PENNY,** Univ Of Nc At Asheville, Asheville, NC; SO; PH D; Hlth Occptns Stdnts Amer 89; Prstg HOSA 89; Blgy; Pre-Med.

**LOUKEDIS, ALEXANDER L,** Villanova Univ, Villanova, PA; JR; BA; V W Club Of Am 90-; Econ Soc 90-; IM Flag Ftbl 90-; Am Cancer Soc 87-; Econ; Law.

**LOUNSBURY, TOMI G,** Univ Of Ky, Lexington, KY; SR; BA; Commonwealth Of Ky St Govt 78-88; BS 78; Edn; Middle Sch Tchr.

**LOURY, MELISSA D,** Brevard Comm Coll, Cocoa, FL; FR; BA; Acdmc Schlrshp 90-; Psych; Mntl Hlth Tech.

**LOUTER, MICHAEL J S,** Brevard Coll, Brevard, NC; FR; BA; Sccr; Med; Phys Ther.

**LOVE, ALICE R,** Tougaloo Coll, Tougaloo, MS; FR; BA; Computer Sci.

**LOVE, COREY A,** Jackson St Univ, Jackson, MS; FR; Poltcl Sci Clb 90-; Deans Lst 90-; Mltry Sci Achvmnt 90-; Poltcl Sci; Law Schl.

**LOVE, CYNTHIA J,** Memphis St Univ, Memphis, TN; FR; BSCE; Ambsdr; Hon Assn; ASCE 90-; Alpha Lambda Delta; Delta Gamma 90-; Gamma Beta Phi; Cvl Engr.

**LOVE, DUSTIN L,** Univ Of Ky, Lexington, KY; FR; BS; Ecnmcs; Stck Brkr.

**LOVE, ELIZABETH STIFF,** Birmingham Southern Coll, Birmingham, AL; SR; BA; Campus Lit Mag Edtr 85-86; Campus Nwspr Stf Wrtr 84-86; Publ Brd 85-86; Zeta Tau Alpha Standrds Chr 82-86; Zeta Tau Alpha Alumnea Clb Gen Adv AN Chp 86-; So Vol 84-86; Pres Stdnt Serv Org 85-86; Asst Spec Evnts Coord 84-86; Hstry; Law.

**LOVE, HEATHER P,** Univ Of Sc At Columbia, Columbia, SC; FR; BS; Phi Eta Sigma; Gamma Beta Phi; Bio; Optometry.

**LOVE, JEFFREY I,** Cornell Univ Statutory College, Ithaca, NY; SR; BS; Dairy Sci Clb 90-; Mann Libr Stdnt Fclty Comm 90-; Alpha Gamma Rho 90-; Cargill/Nutrena Feeds Div Mktg Intern; Amer Agri Schlrshp Recip 90-; AAS SUNY 90; Animal Sci/Ag Econ; Mktg/Agri Finance.

**LOVE, KAREN J,** Ohio Valley Coll, Parkersburg, WV; SO; BA; Yrbk Clb 89-; Head RA 90-; Alpha Delta Chi 89-; Engl; Law.

**LOVE, KAREN L,** Univ Of Ct, Storrs, CT; SO; BS; Pre Vet Clb 89-; Goldn Ky; Gamma Sigma Delta; Alpha Zeta; Pathbiol; Vet Med.

**LOVE, MARTIN E,** Univ Of Ms Medical Center, Jackson, MS; SR; BS; Phi Theta Kappa 86; Sigma Theta Tau; Valor Pgm VAMC 90; Nrsng.

**LOVE, MELISSA K,** Ga Southern Univ, Statesboro, GA; FR; BS; Kapp Delta Hstrn/I M 90-; IM Bsktbl/Sftbl/Sccr 90-; Hlth/Phy Ed/Sprts Med; Coach-Ath Trnr.

**LOVE, REBA A,** Middle Tn St Univ, Murfreesboro, TN; SR; Kappa Delta Pi 90-; BS 90; Elem Ed; Tchng.

**LOVE, SYLVESTER,** Univ Of Southern Ms, Hattiesburg, MS; SR; Bsbl 87-88; Milwkee Brwrs Pro Bsbl Clb 88-90; Hlth; Occptnl Thrpst.

**LOVE, TATANISHA KWATIKI,** Norfolk St Univ, Norfolk, VA; SO; BA; Spartan Alpha Tau; Engl; Law.

**LOVE, TERESA M,** Al St Univ, Montgomery, AL; SO; Ed; Elem Schl Tchr.

**LOVE, TONI T,** Stillman Coll, Tuscaloosa, AL; JR; BA; Phi Beta Lambda; Yrbk Stf Pres 90-; Army ROTC Cdt; Dns Lst; Chnclrt; Cert Hair Dsgn Acdmy 89; Bsn Mgmt; Mgr/Gen Mgmt.

**LOVE, WANNETTA S,** Immaculata Coll, Immaculata, PA; FR; BSN; Phnxvl Hosp ICU/CCU Stf Nrs 77-; Hdlbrg Chrch Brd Chrstn Educ Sec; Nrsg Dplma 77; Nrsg.

**LOVEJOY, BARBARA J,** Univ Of Nh Plymouth St Coll, Plymouth, NH; JR; BS; Hngldng Clb Sec 90-; AS Sec Sci; Bsns Mgmt; Bsns Fld.

**LOVEJOY, ERIC V,** Univ Of Nh Plymouth St Coll, Plymouth, NH; JR; BS; Stdnt Govt V P 88-90; Nwspr Photo/Wrtr 88-90; Common Grand 89-90; Otng Clb 88-89; Cmunctsn Cmtee Co Chr 88-90; Library Cmtee 88-89; Chi Alpha 90-; Semester At Sea 90; Serv Cmuty Day; Ctznshp Promotn; Amer Govt Semester Prog; Bus/Pltcl Sci.

**LOVEJOY, ROBERT A,** Marshall University, Huntington, WV; SR; BBA; Mktng.

**LOVELACE, AMY M,** Fayetteville St Univ, Fayetteville, NC; SO; BS; Chncllrs Lst 90; Phrmcy.

**LOVELACE, ERICKA,** Morris Brown Coll, Atlanta, GA; SO; BA; Morris Brwn Clg Hnr Stdnt 89-90; Cmptr Sci; Cmptr Prgrmmr.

**LOVELACE III, GLEN C,** Univ Of De, Newark, DE; SO; BCE; Coll Bowl 90-; Tetratech Richardson Awd; Civil Eng/History.

**LOVELACE, LAURIE A,** Univ Of Montevallo, Montevallo, AL; JR; BA; Homecoming Cabinet Asst Dir 90; Lambda Sigma Pi Pres; Omicron Delta Kappa 90-; Phi Kappa Phi; Alpha Lambda Delta 88-; Sigma Tau Delta 89-; Alpha Gamma Delta Philanthropy Chrmn 88-; Deans List/Pres List 88-; Schrlshp; English/Political Science; Law.

**LOVELACE, SHARON P,** Al A & M Univ, Normal, AL; SO; BS; Mgmt.

**LOVELAND, ANDREW D,** Univ Of Miami, Coral Gables, FL; SR; BA; Vrsty Crew Capt 87-; Dean Lst 87-; Hnrs Stu Assn 87-88; Marine Afrs; Otdr Educ.

**LOVELESS, DANA KIMBERLY,** Fl International Univ, Miami, FL; GD; MBA; FEA 88-89; BS In Elem Ed 90; Ed; Tchr.

**LOVELESS, MARTHA T,** Western Ky Univ, Bowling Green, KY; SR; Phi Kappa Phi 90-; Wmns Chmbr Cmmrce Of KY; BA 90; Psychlgy/Engl; Scl Srvc/Prsnnl.

**LOVELESS, TERESA L,** Watterson Coll, Louisville, KY; FR; Hd Rec Clrk Furrow Bldg Material 85-90; Comp Progrmmr.

**LOVELETT, ANGELA M,** Mount Saint Mary Coll, Newburgh, NY; SR; BA; SG Treas 87-89; RA 88-; Drama 89-90; Alpha Chi 87-; Ralph Scholr 87-; Sguinus Sch; Deans List; Pres Schlr; Ambsdr Club 88-; Orientation Ldr 88-; Chrldng 87-88; Engl; Elem Tchr.

**LOVELL, AMY B,** Western New England Coll, Springfield, MA; SR; Intrnshp Sprngfld Day Nursry 90-; BSW; Soc Wrk; Elem Educ.

**LOVELL, BARBARA ANN,** Muskingum Coll, New Concord, OH; SR; Vrsty Bsktbl Chrldr 87-88; Stdnt Snt Repr 88-89; Vol Pgm 87-88; Lambda Sigma 88-89; Phi Beta Theta 90-; Hnry; Chi Alpha Nu Flt Chrmn/Rsh Chrmn 88-; Hbt Hmnty 90-; Helen De Jong Mem Schlrshp 90-; BA; Elem Ed; Tchg/Gdnc Cnsl/Admin.

**LOVELL, BARBARA M,** Barry Univ, Miami, FL; SO; BA; Yng Ptrnsses Of Opera Treas 89-90; Amer Bsnss Womens Assoc Pres 80-81; Scl Wlfre; Scl Wlfre Cnslr.

**LOVELL, CLAIRE,** Springfield Tech Comm Coll, Springfield, MA; SR.

**LOVELL, DONALD EDWARD,** Al A & M Univ, Normal, AL; SR; Natl Eng Hon Soc; IEEE; Asst Elec Engr NASA Microgravity Crystal Grwth Lab; Elec Eng.

**LOVELL, JACKIE A,** Southern Junior Coll, Birmingham, AL; GD; Perf Attndnc; HGST GPA; Stdnt Of Month.

**LOVELL, MARIE ANNE E,** Central Fl Comm Coll, Ocala, FL; SO; AA; Phi Theta Kappa 90; Thomas Jefferson Awd; Hist; Ins.

**LOVELL, PAMELA ANN,** Pellissippi St Tech Comm Coll, Knoxville, TN; SO; ASSC; IEEE 90-; ASOC; Cert Tech State Of TN 83; Cert ASOC 89; Elec Eng; Med Instrmnttn.

**LOVELL, SUSANNE G,** Univ Of Charleston, Charleston, WV; SO; BA; Intr Dsgn.

**LOVERDI, ROSEMARY J,** Rutgers St Univ At Camden, Camden, NJ; GD; JD; Acct Soc V P 88-90; Athenaeum 89-90; Phi Eta Sigma 86-90; Acctg Fac Awd 90-; Peat Marwick Main Schlrshp Awd 89-; Zonta Clb Schlrshp Awd 89-; BS Rutgers Univ 90-; Acctg; Law.

**LOVERIN, ROBERT ALFRED,** Univ Of Sc At Columbia, Columbia, SC; JR; BA; Engl/Scndry Edn; Tchr.

**LOVETT, BRIDGET L,** Central Fl Comm Coll, Ocala, FL; FR; Educ.

**LOVETT, GARY W,** Univ Of Tn At Martin, Martin, TN; JR; BS; Natl Wildlf Socty 88-; Crockett Cnty Focus Comm; 4h Vol; Wldlf Biology.

**LOVETT, LAURA J,** Univ Of Tn At Martin, Martin, TN; SO; BSW; Scl Wrk Clb 90-; Scl Wrk Crmnl Just.

**LOVETT, LONNA K,** Univ Of Tn At Martin, Martin, TN; SO; BS; Ch Of Christ Stdnt Ctr 89-; Coll 4-H Club Sec 89-; Tn 4-H Alum Assoc 89-; Alpha Zeta 90-; 4-H Golightly Extnsn Serv Intrnshp 90; Agri Dept Workstudy 89-; Animal Sci/Food Tech; Food Rsrch.

**LOVETT, LUTIE A,** Middle Tn St Univ, Murfreesboro, TN; SO; Engl; Ed.

**LOVETT, W NIGUEL,** Vance Granville Comm Coll, Henderson, NC; SO; BA; Wrtrs Cir; Engl; Prof Wrtng.

**LOVETTE, LUCIRIA LUCKEY,** Savannah St Coll, Savannah, GA; SO; BSN; Psychlgy Club 89-; Coastal Future Pioneers; Amercn Bus Women Assoc Mbrshp Chr; St Peters AME Church Youth Dept Youth Dir 90-; Coastal Utilities Inc Oper Svcs; Psychlgy; Nrsng.

**LOVING, FELICIA NICOLE,** Va Commonwealth Univ, Richmond, VA; SR; BS; VA Comm Museum Fine Arts Cmnctns Oper 90-; Adm Jstc; Law.

**LOVING, MARQUISE L,** Jackson St Univ, Jackson, MS; SO; BS; Alpha Lambda Delta 90-; Pres Schlr 89-; Ordr Of Eastrn Str 90-; NAACP 88-; Chrldng 89-90; Prncng J-Sette 90-; Bus/Acctg.**

**LOVINSKI, MEGHAN M,** West Liberty St Coll, West Liberty, WV; JR; BS; Clg Nwspr Edtr 88-; Outstdng Rptr Awd 90; Theater Intshp Dir Pblcty 90; Sftbl 88-90; Cmmctns.

**LOVIO, JESSICA B,** Fl International Univ, Miami, FL; JR; BA; Acctng Assn 90-; Phi Eta Sigma 90-; Phi Lambda 90-; Phi Kappa Phi; Deans Lst 89-; High Hnrs Phi Lambda 90-; Bus; CPA.**

**LOVIUS, CHERINANDE,** Bloomfield Coll, Bloomfield, NJ; FR; BS; Caribbean Stdnts Assn 90-; Commuter Stdnt Assn 90-; Iota Phi Theta Swthrt 90-; Tutor 90-; Vlybl; Nrsng.

**LOW, JEFFREY K,** Univ Of Ky, Lexington, KY; FR; PHD; Pre-Prhmcy Clb 90-; Alpha Lambda Delta 90-; Phrmcy.

**LOWE, ALESIA A,** Spartanburg Methodist Coll, Spartanburg, SC; FR; AS; Socr Tm 90-; Crim Just; Law.

**LOWE, ALICE F,** Alice Lloyd Coll, Pippa Passes, KY; FR; BS; Work Study Awd 90-; Bio; Dctr.

**LOWE, ANNE L,** Manor Jr Coll, Jenkintown, PA; SO; BS; Asst Mgr Bell PA; Bus Admin; Mgmt.

**LOWE, CHUCK S,** Univ Of Al At Birmingham, Birmingham, AL; JR; Bus Clb Pres 90-; Bptst Cmps Mnstrs 89-; Rho Epsion VP 90-; AL Real Est Schlrshp; Fnnc/Real Est Invstmnt; Securities Brkr.

**LOWE, CYNTHIA M,** Univ Of Ky, Lexington, KY; SO; BA; Arts Sci/Hlth Flds; Occptnl Thrpy.

**LOWE, EARNEST F,** Morris Brown Coll, Atlanta, GA; SO; BACHE; DOI Stdnt NSBE Mbr; Hnr Rl; Hnywl Intrnshp, Math, Eng.

**LOWE, HEATHER S,** Univ Of Sc At Columbia, Columbia, SC; SO; BA; Soc Of Profsnl Jrnlsts 89-; Gamecock TV; Gamma Beta Phi; Intrnshp WCSC Chnl 5 Charleston; SC Brdcstrs Assoc Schlrshp; Intrnshp WLTR Radio 90; Telecmnctns; Brdcst Jrnlst.

**LOWE, JENNIFER A,** Bridgewater Coll, Bridgewater, VA; FR; BS; Bapt Stdnt Union 90-; Stdnt Sen 90-; Cncl Rlgs Act; Sclgy; Scl Wrk.

**LOWE, JOHN ROBERT,** East Carolina Univ, Greenville, NC; SO; BM; Phi Eta Sigma 90-; Cert Hon Pi Kappa Lambda 90-; Music Ed-Tombone; Secndry Ed.

**LOWE, KAREN L,** Faulkner St Jr Coll, Bay Minette, AL; SO; BS; Phi Theta Kappa 89-90; Pi Psi 89-90; Bnkng Finance 8087; Elem Educ.

**LOWE, LAURIE L,** Anderson Coll, Anderson, SC; SO; BA; Gamma Beta Phi 90-; Deans Lst 90; Elem Educ; Teacher.

**LOWE, LORI A,** Oh Univ, Athens, OH; SR; BMUS; Cmpus Crsde Chrst 87-; Phi Eta Sigma 87; Pi Kappa Lambda; Sigma Alpha Iota Chpln 90; Music; Educ.

**LOWE, MAGDALYN J,** Johnson C Smith Univ, Charlotte, NC; JR; BA; Hon Soc; Soc/Crmnl Juste; Crmnl Juste/Jvnle Delnqncy.

**LOWE, MARK A,** Old Dominion Univ, Norfolk, VA; JR; BSMBA; Clb Lacrsse Co Capt 90-; Amer Mrktng Assoc 90-; Dev/Comm Rels Intrnshp; Mrktng Mgmt Intrnshp 90; Mrktng Asst 90; Mrktng Educ/Trng Spec; Intl Bsns.

**LOWE, MARNIE L,** Marshall University, Huntington, WV; JR; BBA; Rsdnc Hl Assoc 89-; Gamma Beta Phi90; Ygr Schlr 89-; Hlth Cr Mngmnt; Hsptl Admnstrtn.

**LOWE, MELVIN L,** Al St Univ, Montgomery, AL; FR; Bsn.

**LOWE, MICHAEL A,** Univ Of Southern Ms, Hattiesburg, MS; SR; BA; Gamma Beta Phi 90-; AA Pearl River Comm Coll 89; Psych; Rsrch.

**LOWE, NANCY S,** Nova Univ, Ft Lauderdale, FL; GD; MBA; Gldn Key Trea 86-88; Alpha Epsilon Delta Med Scty VP 86-88; Kappa Delta Delta Tau Delta Social Chrmn 86-88; Prffsnl Serv Org 84-88; EFA Corp Member 90; Phrmctcl Sales Rep 89; BS Univ Of FL 88.

**LOWE, PAIGE A,** Univ Of Nc At Charlotte, Charlotte, NC; JR; BA; Mag Edit 89-90; TX Wslyn Univ; AD 2 Adv Clb; Art/Studio Emphasis; Free-Lance Adv/Illstrtn.

**LOWE, RICARDO,** Alfred Univ, Alfred, NY; SR; BS; Amer Mktng Assn 90-; ROTC Pltn Ldr 89-; Deans Lst; Bus Admin.

**LOWE, ROBERT E,** Univ Of South Al, Mobile, AL; JR; BA; League Pickers Treas 90-; Bsn; Finance.

**LOWE, TIEN S,** Univ Of Miami, Coral Gables, FL; FR; BBA; Inf Res Cmptng Fac Payrl Mgr 91; Alpha Lambda Delta; Hnrs Pgm 90-; Miami Commtmnt Awd Acad Achvmnt; Busn Admin; Intl Finc/Mgmt.

**LOWE, TONIA J,** Roane St Comm Coll, Harriman, TN; SO; BA; Acctng.**

**LOWELL, CARLOS E,** Univ Of Miami, Coral Gables, FL; FR; BA; Hnrs Pgm 90-; Mech Engr; Patent Law.

**LOWENKRON, ROSEMARY,** Univ Of Miami, Coral Gables, FL; FR; Pre-Legal Soc 90-; Hons Assoc 90-; Alpha Lambda Delta 90-; Hist/Pol Sci; Law.

**LOWENSTEIN, LORIE S,** Dowling Coll, Oakdale Li, NY; SO; Dwlng Chrldng Sqd 89-; Pep Clb 89-; Elem Educ/Psych; Elem Sch Tchr.

**LOWERY, ANGELA K,** Walker Coll, Jasper, AL; FR; BA; Dns Lst 90-; Int Design.

**LOWERY, APRIL A,** Glassboro St Coll, Glassboro, NJ; FR; BS; Hnrs Prgrm 90-; Advncd Beta Grp Stdy; SICO Fndtn Schlrshp 90-; Phi Delta Kappa 90-; Mrtn Lthr King Jr Schlrshp 90-; Elks Schlrshp Awd 90-; Trustees Schlrs Schlrshp 90-; Edward J Bloustein Awd 90-; Blgcl Sci; Tchng.

**LOWERY, GRAFTON L,** Rust Coll, Holly Springs, MS; FR; NAACP 90-; HCOP 90-; Alpha Phi Omega 90-; Bsktbl.

**LOWERY, LONNIE M,** Kent St Univ Kent Cmps, Kent, OH; SR; MA; Tae Kwon Do 87-; Motor-Leisure Skls Pgm 89-; Bodybldr/Trnr 87-; Golden Key 89-; Dns Lst 87-; Acad Congrtltry Ltr 87-; BA Kent State Univ; Exer Physlgy; Rsrch/Clnc/Gym Owner-Trnr.

**LOWERY, PATRICK W,** John Wesley Coll, High Point, NC; GD; BA; Cls Pres 90; Psy; Cnslng.

**LOWERY, TAMMY T,** Univ Of Montevallo, Montevallo, AL; SR; BS; Stf Wrtr U M Nwspr 91; Kappa Pi 90-; Art; Photo.

**LOWERY, TERRI J,** Mary Holmes Coll, West Point, MS; SO; BS; Stdnt Ttrl Cnslr 90-; Hd Srtr Vlntr; Sprtsmnshp Awd Otstndng Schlr Caset; Acadmc Achvmnt Awd Amng Athlts; Cptn Sftbl Tm; AS; History; Scndry Instrctr.

**LOWIE, BRETT A,** Christian Brothers Univ, Memphis, TN; SR; BS; Sprvsr; Econ; Law.

**LOWMAN, GAIL B,** Western Piedmont Comm Coll, Morganton, NC; GD; CMA; Amer Assoc Med Asstnts 90-; Tom Chpmns Ladies Bowling League Tres 88-90; Catawba Vly NC Wmns Bwlg Assoc 80-; Admin Clncl Lab Stdy; Med Asstng.

**LOWMAN, MELISSA J,** Vt Law School, S Royalton, VT; GD; JD; Fclty Hrng Com Intrvwr 90-; Law Soc Jrnl Athr 90-; Amer Jrsprdnc Awd Cntrcts 90; BA Mddlbry Coll 87; MS; Law/Envrnmntl Law.

**LOWRANCE, SHEILA A,** Memphis St Univ, Memphis, TN; SR; BS; Girl Scouts Of Amer 90-; Vlntr Gir Scout Of Amer 90-; Tchr Of Teenage Sun Schl Class; Bookkeeper Internal Med Clinic Dyersbury; AS Dyersburg State Cmnty Clge 88; Elem Ed; Teach Elem Schl.**

**LOWRIMORE, MACHILLE D,** Commonwealth Coll, Virginia Beach, VA; SO; LOA; Lgl Asst; Prlgl.

**LOWRY, BOYD A,** Va Commonwealth Univ, Richmond, VA; SR; BSHRI; Rmpgs Yrbk Com Edit In Chf 88-; USMC Corp 86; Hmn Rsrce Mgmt; Mgmt Prfssr.

**LOWRY, SHAUN D,** Embry Riddle Aeronautical Univ, Daytona Beach, FL; FR; BA; Aviation Bsn Mgmt; Corp/Cmrcl Pilot.

**LOWTHER, GAYLA L,** Washington State Comm Coll, Marietta, OH; GD; BMT; Amer Lgn 84-; Pres Lst 90; DPC Wash Cnty Career Ctr 83; ATC Wash Cty Career Ctr 83; Bsn Mgmt/Acctng; Acctnt/Mgr.

**LOWY, KENNETH M,** City Univ Of Ny John Jay Coll, New York, NY; JR; BA; Psi Chi 88; Hnr Prog 88-; Amer Pscyh Assn 88-; Plce Dept Intrn 88; Dept Of Yth Intrn; Cert US Secret Service 90; Cert Federal Law Enforcement Training Center 90; Frnsc Psych; Law Enfrcmnt.**

**LOY, BETH A,** Wv Northern Comm Coll, Wheeling, WV; FR; BED; Optometric Tech 80-84 90-; Sci; Educ.

**LOY, CONNIE G,** Roane St Comm Coll, Harriman, TN; JR; BS; Stdnt Govt 72-73; AS Roane State Cmmnty Clg 73; Scl Sci; Scndry Ed Instr.

**LOYD, DAVID P,** Univ Of Sc At Sumter, Sumter, SC; FR; BS; Air Frc Assn; US Ar Frc 86-; Elect Eng; Eng.

**LOYD, MELANIE R,** Univ Of Tn At Martin, Martin, TN; FR; BS; Schlrs Org; Schlrs Prog; Bio/Chem; Med Sch.

**LOYD, TIFFANY ANTONIA,** Meridian Comm Coll, Meridian, MS; SO; AA; Nswppr Stff Rprtr; Bapt Stdnt Unn; Prlgl Lgl Stds.

**LOZADA, ALEJANDRO L,** Cincinnati Bible Coll & Sem, Cincinnati, OH; GD; MA; Stdnt Cncl Pres 86-89; Homelietics Awrd 89; BA 89; Hstry; Tchng.

**LOZADA, BRENELLY,** Univ Of Pr Cayey Univ Coll, Cayey, PR; FR; Chem Clb 90-; Hnr Scty 90-; Natural Sci/Chemistry; Medicine.

**LOZANO, SANDRA,** Edison Comm Coll, Fort Myers, FL; SO; BA; Outstndng Mnrty Stdnt; Math; Ed.

**LOZEAU, CATHLEEN T,** Castleton St Coll, Castleton, VT; SO; BSEDU; Rdng & Spcl Edctn; Tchng Elmntry.

**LU, ANA I,** Wagner Coll, Staten Island, NY; SR; Intl Clb Treas 87-88; Spnsh Clb VP 89-90; Soc Clb 89-90; Sociology.

**LUAYON, JOSEPH P,** Univ Of Miami, Coral Gables, FL; SO; BS; Alpha Epsilon Delta; Biology; Medicine.

**LUBANA, MOHANJIT,** Springfield Tech Comm Coll, Springfield, MA; SO; BA; Indian Assn Grtr Spngfld STEE Bus Clb Comm 89-; Alpha Nu Omega; VITA; Acctg; CPA.

**LUBANSKI, MICHAEL S,** Embry Riddle Aeronautical Univ, Daytona Beach, FL; FR; BA; Riddle Riders Mtr Cycle Clb Prsdnt 90-; Soc Cmmrcl Avtn Tchncns 90; US Army Spclst 84-88; FL Army Ntnl Grd 88-89; Avionics Tchnlgy; Tchncl Rep.

**LUBBERT, JILL E,** The Kings Coll, Briarclf Mnr, NY; JR; BA; Yrbk 88-89; Bible Stdy 88-; Biblical Stds/Elem Educ; Tchr.

**LUBER, JOHN R,** Niagara Univ, Niagara Univ, NY; SO; BBA; Karate Clb Pres 89-; Alpha Kappa Psi Treas 90-; Hnrs Prog 89-; Acctng; CPA/MBA.

**LUBETSKI, SHAUL,** Yeshiva Univ, New York, NY; GD; JD; Bsktbl IM Cmmssnr 88-90; Tlk Shw Hst Sprts Rap 90; Stff Wrtr Cmmntr Offcl Undrgrd Nwsppr 89-90; Stdnt Struggle/Soviet Jewry 88-90; BA; Economics; Law.

**LUBIN, LISA G,** Univ Of Sc At Columbia, Columbia, SC; FR; BA; Newspapr Phtgrphr 90; Scuba Clb 90; Carolina Prog Union 90; TV 90; Mass Cmmnctns; Brdcstng.

**LUBINIECKI, GREGORY M,** Ma Inst Of Tech, Cambridge, MA; FR; BS; Stdnt Gvmt 90-; Church Lectoring 90-; Frshmn Hvywght Crew Coxswain 90-; Biology; Medicine/Oncology.

**LUBINSKY, LUBI DENNIS S,** Alfred Univ, Alfred, NY; JR; Sccr 88-; Vrsty Glf; Amer Mktg Assc/Fin Mgmt Assc Pres; Fin Mgmt Assc Pres; Dlt Mu Dlt.

**LUBKOWSKI, DANIEL J F,** Strayer Coll, Washington, DC; JR; BS; NRA IWLA; Database Admnstrtr AT&T 89-; AAS Erie Comm Coll 80; Cmptr Infrmtn Sys; Admn.

**LUBY, KELLY E,** Bay Path Coll, Longmeadow, MA; FR; AS; Deans Lst 90-; Fashion Merc; Retail.

**LUCA, MARIA,** Borough Of Manhattan Comm Coll, New York, NY; JR; BA; Frnch.

**LUCADANO, JEANETTE C,** Liberty Univ, Lynchburg, VA; JR; BS; Acctg Clb 90-; Pre Law Soc 90-; Wms Chrs 89-90; Hnrs Pgm 89-; Alpha Lambda Delta 89-; Interclgte Univ Dbt Tm Nvc Jr V 89-; Frnsc Trnmts Jdg 90-; Chrch Yth Grp Ldr Sngr 89-90; Intrn Sec WBL Inc Pres Sec 89; Govt/Pre Law; Corp Law.

**LUCARELLI, DEAN M,** Wv Northern Comm Coll, Wheeling, WV; FR; BS; ASMT; Phi Theta Kappa; WVNCC Acdmc Schlrshp; Mdcl Lab Med; Mdcl Tchnlgst.

**LUCARELLI, LINDA,** Greenville Tech Coll, Greenville, SC; SO; Advsry Cncl 90-; Phi Theta Kappa; SPCA 87-; Sierra Clb 89-; Nom B S Goldwater Schlrshp 90; Blgy; Phd Blgy/Rsrch Envrnmntl Issues.

**LUCAS, ANDREA L,** Lenoir Rhyne Coll, Hickory, NC; SR; BA; Psych/Soc Clb 90-; Mu Sigma Epsilon; Delta Zeta Acdmcs Chrprsn 90-; Wmns Bsktbl 87-; Hnrs Thesis Psych 90-; Psych; Exprmntl Psych.

**LUCAS, ANGELA L,** Garrett Comm Coll, Mchenry, MD; SO; BS; AA Allegany Comm Clg 78; Earth Sci; Educ.

**LUCAS, GEORGINA,** Allegheny Coll, Meadville, PA; SR; BS; Panhellenic Cncl Treas 89-; Orientation 89-90; BACCHUS 88-89; Ldrshp Tm 88-90; VISA Tourguide 88-89; ALLIES 89-; Spec Events Ofc Asst 88-89; Dns Ofc Asst 89-; Alpha Delta Pi Schlrshp Chr 88-89; Alden Schlr 89-90; Frank Wilbur Main Schlrshp 90-; Econ/Math; MS Stats.

**LUCAS, JUDITH G,** Christopher Newport Coll, Newport News, VA; SR; Phys Educ Mjrs Clb 90-; Bapt Stdnt Un 88-89; Deans Lst 88-; Cum Laude; Var Grls Sftbl Tm 88-89; Wmn Sftbl City Lgue 85-; BS; Phys Educ; Tch.

**LUCAS, KELLY A,** Union Univ, Jackson, TN; SO; BS; Elem Educ Tchr.

**LUCAS, KRISTEN,** Radford Univ, Radford, VA; JR; BA; Poltcl Sci Soc Sec/Tres 90-; Crmnl Justc Club 90-; Sec Summer Achvmnt Prg Dept Energy 90-; Crmnl Justc/Poltcl Sci; Fdrl Invstgtn.

**LUCAS, KRYSTAL T,** Fayetteville St Univ, Fayetteville, NC; JR; BA; Soc Club; Clgt Sec Of Amer 89-90; Chanclr Schlr Tutor; Yth Motivtn Task Force 89; Soc; Soc Wrkr.

**LUCAS, RALPH P,** Coppin St Coll, Baltimore, MD; SR; BS; Psych.

**LUCAS, ROBERT D,** Manhattan Coll, Bronx, NY; FR; MBA; St De Lasalle Hnr Soc 90; Grdn State Dist Schlr Award 90; IM Sftbl/Vlybl 90; Chem Engr; Engr/Bsn.

**LUCAS, STEVE C,** Piedmont Bible Coll, Winston-Salem, NC; JR; BA; SGA Pres; Piedmont Prchrs Fllwshp Sec Tres 90-; USA All Amer Schlrs; Chi Sigma Delta 88-; Intern Pstr New Life Mnstrs 90-; Bblcl Stu; Pstr.**

**LUCAS, TAMMY LYNN,** Univ Of Charleston, Charleston, WV; SO; AA; Alpha Lambda Delta; Prlgl Intrnshp Rnsn Rnsn Mchnry; Otstndg Stu Prlgl Pro; AA; Law.

**LUCAS, WILLIAM D,** Piedmont Tech Coll, Greenwood, SC; SO; BS; Phi Theta Kappa; Whos Who; Eng.

**LUCCA, LEILANI M,** Utica Coll Of Syracuse Univ, Utica, NY; FR; BA; Thtr Ensmbl; Beta Sigma Phi; Deans Acdmc Schlrshp 90-; Engl; Tchng.

**LUCCA, TODD M,** Alfred Univ, Alfred, NY; FR; BS; Alpha Chi Rho; Dns Lst 90; IM Bsktbl; Engr; Crmc Engr.

**LUCCANI, LUIS D,** Columbia Union Coll, Takoma Park, MD; SR; BA; Bnkr Sctn Sprvsr 88; AA Mntgmry Clg 88; Mngmnt; Bsnss Admin.

**LUCE, AMY E,** Univ Of Cincinnati, Cincinnati, OH; SO; BFA; Show Ensmbl Pres 85-88; Muscls/Prod; Schlrshp 85-88; ASSOC Macomb Comm Clg 89; Muscl Theatre.

**LUCE, KEVIN P,** Milligan Coll, Milligan Clg, TN; FR; BS; Drama 90-; Choir Shmbr Sngrs Asst Dir 90-; Arts Cncl; Serv Skrs; IM Vlybl/Ftbl 90-; Heritage Pub Rltns Grp; Biolgy; Dctr/Mssnry.

**LUCENTE, CRYSTAL E,** Fl International Univ, Miami, FL; FR; Math; Tchr.

**LUCES, RICARDO MANUEL,** Fl International Univ, Miami, FL; SR; Sigma Phi Alpha 89-; Phi Lambda 89-; Outstndg Acad Achvmnt; Intrnshp Dade Cnty Publ Defenders Ofc; Pier Supvr Dolphin Cruiselines Seabreeze 88-; AA Miami Dade Comm Coll 89; BS 90; Crmnl Justice/Psychology; Law.

**LUCHINI, SHERI,** Central Fl Comm Coll, Ocala, FL; SO; BA; Elem Educ; Tch.

**LUCIA, JOHN ALLEN,** Univ Of Louisville, Louisville, KY; SR; BS; Data Proc Mgmt Assoc 90-; BA Univ State NY Regents Extern Degree Prog 82; Info Sci/Data Proc; Progmg.

**LUCIANO RAMIREZ, HECTOR I,** Univ Of Pr At Mayaguez, Mayaguez, PR; SO; BS; IEEE 89-; Engrng Hon Stdnt 89-; Natl Hispanic Schlr 90-; Deans Lst 89-90; Elec Engr; Master Engrng/Law.

**LUCIANO, BEVERLY,** Passaic County Comm Coll, Paterson, NJ; SR; AD; Natl Stdnt Nrs Assn Inc 90-; Sen Lewisham Hosp London U K 81; Nrsng; RN.

**LUCIANO, LISA,** City Univ Of Ny Bronx Comm Col, Bronx, NY; SO; BA; Mnrty Hon Pgm 89-; Phi Theta Kappa 90-; Intrnshp Brkhvn Natl Lab 90; Cmptr Pgmmng.

**LUCIDO, GAYLE M,** Lasell Coll, Newton, MA; FR; BA; Business Hnrs; Deans Lst; Business; Hotel Mngmnt.

**LUCIO-ZAVALETA, EGLANTINA,** Oh Wesleyan Univ, Delaware, OH; SO; BA; Phi Eta Sigma; Phi Soc; Botony/Picrobio Sequence In Genetics.

**LUCIUS, SHARON G,** Itawamba Comm Coll, Fulton, MS; FR; BA; Phi Theta Kappa; Old Union Bptst Church; Library Sci.

**LUCK III, LEON ELBERT,** Univ Of Southern Ms, Hattiesburg, MS; SR; ROTC 2ND Lt 85-87; Natl Gd 87-; Amry Avtn Assc 88-; BS 90; Elec Engnrng Tech.

**LUCKEN, MARK T,** S U N Y Coll Of Tech At Frmgdl, Farmingdale, NY; FR; Constr; Exrcse Physlgst.

**LUCKETT, ANGELA M,** Middle Tn St Univ, Murfreesboro, TN; SR; Pi Sigma Epsilon Pres 89-; Hon Stdnt 90-; Gamma Beta Phi 87-89; Mu Kappa Tau 90-; Hons Grad Cum Laude; Bus; Mrktng.**

**LUCKETT, ELLEN E,** Univ Of Louisville, Louisville, KY; SO; MBA; Math Comp Sci; Eng.

**LUCKETT JR, JAMES N,** Ky Wesleyan Coll, Owensboro, KY; JR; BS; Weslyn Pep Bnd 88; Jms Grhm Brwn Soc 88-; Sigma Zeta; Pre Prof Soc Pres 89-90; Sigma Phi Epsilon Sec 90; J Grhm Brwn Schlr 88-; Sumr Res Intrnshp Vndrblt Univ; Bio/Chem/Frnch; Medicn.

**LUCKEY, TINA C,** Ms St Univ, Miss State, MS; FR; BA; Soc Wmn Eng; Phi Eta Sigma; Med; Physcl Thrpy.

**LUCKHAM, JOAN C,** Broward Comm Coll, Ft Lauderdale, FL; JR; BA; French Club 89-90; Plus Tutor 89-90; AA 90; Pol Sci; Govt MPA.

**LUCKS, THOMAS E,** Univ Of Pittsburgh At Bradford, Bradford, PA; SR; BS; Judicial Review Brd 88; Tutor 88-89; Alpha Lambda Delta Awd 87; Univ Schlr 89-90; Fed Bureau Of Prsns Procuremnt Intrn; Pres Schlrshp 87; Bsnss Mngmnt; Fncl Serv.**

**LUCKY, DELICIA D,** Clark Atlanta Univ, Atlanta, GA; JR; BS; Orien Guide Corp; Alpha Kappa Mu; Inroads; GPA Awd; AT/T Network Syst Intern; Deans List/Hnr Rl; Assist Sports Infor Dir; Computer Sci; Computer Syst Analyst.**

**LUCUS, SHELLEY P,** Livingston Univ, Livingston, AL; FR; BA; Phi Eta Sigma; IM Sftbl; Math; Eng.

**LUDERITZ, RICHARD P,** Atlantic Comm Coll, Mays Landing, NJ; GD; BA; Phi Beta Lambda 89-; PBL Ntnl Awd Wnnr 90; PBL NJ State Awd Wnnr Mktg 90; PBL NJ State Awd Wnnr Bsn Prncpls/Mgmt 90; Rvrview Vlg Hmowners Asc V P; Mbl Int Care Paramed Atlantic/Cape May MICU Cnsrtm 84-; History/Pltcl Sci; Ed.

**LUDGOOD, DESI L,** Ms Gulf Coast Comm Coll, Perkinston, MS; SO; Natl Beta Clb 89-90; Afro-Amer Cltr Clb 89-90; Sci; Occptnl Thrpy.

**LUDLOW, LAURAL B,** Univ Of Rochester, Rochester, NY; JR; BS; Vocal Point Womns A Capella Sngn Grp Busn Mgr 88-; Tchng Asst Bio Dept; Biochem; Pharmctcls.

**LUDLUM, HOLLY D,** Troy St Univ At Troy, Troy, AL; FR; BS; Marching Band 90-; Symphony Band; Concert Band 90-; Gamma Beta Phi; Tau Beta Sigma Dist/Chapter Coord 90-; Flute Instr 90-; IM Sftbl; Instl Music Ed.

**LUDOLF, TAMMY J,** Itawamba Comm Coll, Fulton, MS; SO; Neumo Tai; AARC; CNA Holmes Cmnty Clg 90; Rsprtry Thrpy.

**LUDWIG, DENNIS J,** Nova Univ, Ft Lauderdale, FL; GD; MBA; Iowa Scty Of CPAS Ntnl Assoc Of Accntnts; Ntnl Cntrct Mngmnt Assoc Treas 90; CPA State Of Iowa; BS Mt Mercy Clg 76; Bsnss.

**LUDWIG, JULIE L,** D Youville Coll, Buffalo, NY; SO; BSN; Med Asstnt Chldrns Hosp 90; ASSC Gannon Univ 88; Sci; Nrsng.

**LUDWIG, PAMELA A,** Hillsborough Comm Coll, Tampa, FL; GD; AS; Rdtn Thrpy Tech Clb Pres 90-; W FL Scty Of Rdtn Thrpy Tech 90-; RT Ldrshp Awrd 90-; Prfrmcne Awrd 90-; Psco Arts Cntr 89; Rdlgy Assn Bllng Clr 89; Rdtn Thrpy Tech.

**LUE FOOK SANG, ANDRE S,** City Univ Of Ny City Coll, New York, NY; JR; BS; EMET 90-; IEEE 87-88; CBS/SONY Schlrshp 90-; AAS Queensborough Comm Coll 89; Elec Engr; Rsrch/Devlpmnt.

**LUEDDE, MICHELLE C,** Hillsborough Comm Coll, Tampa, FL; FR; AS; Stdnt Govt; Sonography Clb VP 90-; Diagnostic Med Sonography.

**LUEDERS, G SPENCER,** Univ Of Sc At Columbia, Columbia, SC; JR; BS; Stdnt Alumni Assn 90; Omicron Delta Kappa Fclty Cmtee; Gamma Beta Phi; Tau Beta Pi; Pres Lst 88-90; Deans Lst; Var Soccer 88-; Mech Engr; Engr.

**LUEHRS, JENNIFER MARIE,** Saint Thomas Univ, Miami, FL; JR; BA; The Infrmr Cntrbtng Edtr; Deans List 89-; Cmmnctns; Pblc Rltns.

**LUGGEN, WILLIAM W,** Union Inst, Cincinnati, OH; SR; BS; GENCA Chrmn; AAS Univ Cincinnati 72; Indl Mgt.

**LUGO RODRIGUEZ, WALDEMAR,** Inter Amer Univ Pr San German, San German, PR; FR; BA; Clb Rancho Deportivo 87-89; Wstnghs Sftbl Tm 89-; Inter Act 87-88; Math; Eng.

**LUGO RODRIGUEZ, WINDA I,** Inter Amer Univ Pr San German, San German, PR; FR; BA; Math.

**LUGO, CARLOS G,** Univ Of Pr At Rio Piedras, Rio Piedras, PR; SR; BA; Stdnt Cncl Schl Arch Pr 89-; Gen Stdnt Cncl Mbr 90-; Amer Inst Arch Stdnts Mbr 89-90; Env Desgn; Arch.

**LUGO, HELEN,** Inter Amer Univ Pr San German, San German, PR; JR; BA; Coll Sec Intl; Intr Amer Univ San Grmn PR; Nu Delta Iota Sor Pres 77; Admin Asstnt; Sec Sci; Admin Position.

**LUGO, JAMIE V C,** Rutgers St Un At New Brunswick, New Brunswick, NJ; FR; Hspnc Cltr Clb 90-; LIFFE 90-; Bio; Dr.

**LUGO, LOIMAR G,** Inter Amer Univ Pr San German, San German, PR; FR; BS; Gym Clb Msc Grp 90-; Chld Abse Cntrbtr Vlstry; Slvr Mdl Vlybl Tm; Intr Amer Univ; Mss Clgio 90; Sr Clss Qn Crclde Rcreo 87; Vlybl; Tlnt Shw Sngr 90; Blgy; Phys Thrpy.

**LUGO, MAYRA L,** Univ Of Pr At Rio Piedras, Rio Piedras, PR; SR; BA; Acctg Stu Assoc 87-; Cmptr Sci Stu Assoc 87-; Ntl Stu Exchng 88; Gldn Key 89-; All Amer Schlr Coll Awrd; Ntl Coll Bus Merit Awrd; Hnr Tuition; Acctg.

**LUGO, PEDRO A,** Univ Politecnica De Pr, Hato Rey, PR; SR; BSEE; City Hon Soc; FEMA Map Rdr 89-; Myrs Dplma Excellence; Bsktbl; Elec Engr; MBA/MSEE.

**LUGO-RUIZ, MARNIE,** Univ Of Pr At Mayaguez, Mayaguez, PR; SO; MBA; Mu Alpha Phi; Tns Plyr Vrsty; Mktg; Law.

**LUGOVOY, TAMAR M,** Neumann Coll, Aston, PA; SR; BA; Cmnctns Clb Treas 89-; VIVA 87-; Delta Epsilon Sigma 89-; Deans List 89-90; Intrnshp W/ Dupont 89; John Cacenda Schlrshp 90-; Sftbl/Chrldng/Vlybl Cptn 87-; Tech Degr For GA Howard Career Ctr 87; Cmnctns; Mgt/Publc Affrs.

**LUGTHART, ANNE-MARIE,** Le Moyne Coll, Syracuse, NY; JR; Yr Rnd Emplmnt Lyndon Pediatrics 89-; C E Mc Avoy Awd Soph Lbr Arts 90-; English; Grad Sch/Ph D English.

**LUK, WAI-TAT,** City Univ Of Ny Baruch Coll, New York, NY; SO; BA; Hong Kong; Asian Cltrl Un 89-90; OE Limage DJ Msc Ent Fndr 85-; Dns Lst 87-88; Davis Polk Wardwell Lbry 88-; AOS State Univ Delhi NY 86-88; Cmptr Info Sys; Mgr.

**LUK, WINNIE L,** S U N Y At Buffalo, Buffalo, NY; SR; BS; Asian Clb Pres 88-89; Acctg Assn 89-; Beta Alpha Psi 90; AS Monroe Cmuty Clb 89; Acctg; CPA.

**LUKA, AGNES K,** Daemen Coll, Amherst, NY; SR; BSN; Wstrn NY Emer Nrs Assc Crspndng Sec; RN Emer Rm; AAS Trocaire Clg 82; Nrsng; Nrsng Career.

**LUKAS, MARLO A,** Coll Misericordia, Dallas, PA; JR; Acctg Clb 90-; AICPA; Deans Lst 88-; Bus; CPA.**

**LUKCSO, DAVID G,** Coll Of Health Sci Stony Brook, Stony Brook, NY; GD; MD; Alpha Omega Alpha; Amer Med Assn 87-90; Med Socty Of State Of NY 87-; The Feld Ballet 81-86; BA Adelphi Univ 79; Med.

**LUKE, AMY E,** Alfred Univ, Alfred, NY; SO; BS; NCWA 90-; ACHE 90-; Alph Lmbd Dlt 89-90; Alph Iota Dlt 90-; Presdntl Schlrshp 89-; Hlth Plng/Admn/Bus; Nrsng Home Admnstr.

**LUKE, DANIELLE M,** Alfred Univ, Alfred, NY; SR; BS; Stdnt Alumni Assn Pres 87-90; Natl Careere Wmns Assn Hstrn 87-; Soc Wmn Eng 87-; Keramos 88-; Tau Beta Pi; Alpha Lambda Delta 87-88; Sigma Chi Nu 87-; Deans Lst; Pres Schlrshp 86-90; Wmn In Eng Schlrshps; Math; Ceramic Eng.

**LUKE, EDWARD D,** Pa St Univ Fayette Cmps, Uniontown, PA; FR; AE; Arch; Engr.

**LUKE, KATHY R,** Abraham Baldwin Agri Coll, Tifton, GA; SO; BSED; Ftre Sec Of Amer Rcrdng Sec 87; Cllgte Sec Intrnatl VP 88; C & S Natl Bnk 88-; AAS 88; Mddle Chldhd Educ Math; Tch.

**LUKE, THOMAS C,** Livingston Univ, Livingston, AL; SR; BS; Acctg Clb 88-; Bsn; Acctg.

**LUKINICH, JOHN R,** Comm Coll Algny Co Algny Cmps, Pittsburgh, PA; Bsnss Mngmnt; Own Bsnss.

**LUKS, HEATHER L,** Castleton St Coll, Castleton, VT; FR; Swmng 90-; Nurs; Neonatal Nurse/Mdwfe.

**LUMLEY, TIA L,** Roane St Comm Coll, Harriman, TN; FR; BFA; Norris Vol Fire Dept Trn; Vtrn US Air Force 87-90; Art; Psychlgy/Art Thrpy.

**LUMPKIN, CATHERINE LAURA,** Bennett Coll, Greensboro, NC; SR; Bennett Schlrs 88-; Miss Sophomore 88-89; Utd Negro Coll Fund 87-88.

**LUMPKIN, LA VARON L,** Ky St Univ, Frankfort, KY; SO; BS; Deans List; Alpha Phi Alpha; Ftbl 89-; Computer Sci; Computer Analyst.**

**LUMSDEN, JACQUELINE B,** Ms St Univ, Miss State, MS; SO; FM; Outdr Soc 90-; Frst Mgmt.

**LUMSDEN, LAREEN ANN,** Univ Of Miami, Coral Gables, FL; SO; BA; Peer Cnslr; Phi Eta Sigma 90-; Provosts List; Deans List; Math; Ed.

**LUNA, GIANCARLO,** Miami Dade Comm Coll South, Miami, FL; SO; BA; IM Bsktbl/Sftbl 89-90; AA; Acctg; CPA.

**LUNA, JOSEFINA A,** City Univ Of Ny La Guard Coll, Long Island Cty, NY; SR; AAS; Physcl Thrpy Clb SAC Repr 90-; MD Univ Autonomy Santo Domingo 81; Hmn Anatomy; BA Physical Thrpy.

**LUNA, JUNE ANNETTE,** John C Calhoun St Comm Coll, Decatur, AL; SR; Phi Theta Kappa 89-; Art; Phtgrphy Grphc Artc Dsgn.**

**LUNA, MINERVA,** Catholic Univ Of Pr, Ponce, PR; SR; BA; Amer Mrktng Assoc 88; Accntng Stdnts Assc Vcl 88; ECOS Stdnt Advsry Cmmttee 88; Hnrs Prog 90; Ntl Bsnss Hnr Scty VP 90; Accntng; CPA.

**LUNA, TATIANA M,** City Univ Of Ny City Coll, New York, NY; GD; BA; Bilingual Volunteers Of Amer 88-89; Dominican Rpblc Exprt Prmtns Ctr Intern 89; Israel E Drabkin Award 90; Econ; Econ Dvlpmnt.

**LUND, CHRISTOPHER A,** Alfred Univ, Alfred, NY; SR; Sigma Alpha Mu 88-; Amer Mrktng Assoc VP/PROGRMMG 90-; Delta Mu Delta; Alpha Ioa Delta; Magna Cum Laude; IM Athltcs; BS; Finance; Mgmnt.

**LUND, CINDY BRIGGS,** Ky Christian Coll, Grayson, KY; SR; BS; Psi Sigma Chi Psych Clb; Dns Lst 87-; Misns Intrnshp Austrlia 90-; Vlybl Intercoll Vrsty Capt 89-; Psych/Bibl; Missns/Psych.

**LUND, JENNIFER L,** Manhattanville Coll, Purchase, NY; JR; BA; Class Stdnt Govt VP 90; Vrsty Soccer 88-90; Intrmlrs Stdnt Dir 90; Instr 90; Amer Schlr 90f; Hstry/Amer Studies; Prof.

**LUND, LARS H,** Coll Of Charleston, Charleston, SC; SR; BS; Vars Tnns Capt 86-; Vars Crs Cntry 89-; Phi Kappa Phi 88-; Beta Gamma Sigma 89-; Omicron Delta Kappa 89-; Sigma Alpha Phi 90-; Bus/Econ.

**LUNDBERG, LENA M,** Univ Of New England, Biddeford, ME; JR; IM Vlybl 88-89; UNESOTA 90-; Alpha Chi 90-.

**LUNDBORG, LORRAINE L,** Central Fl Comm Coll, Ocala, FL; SO; AS; Asst Ldr Yth Frst Asmbly Gd Chrch; Nrsng.

**LUNDE, MARI E,** Univ Of Cincinnati, Cincinnati, OH; SR; BM; Philharmonia Orchstr Cncrtmstr 90-; 18th Cntry Msc Ensmbl Soloist 88-; Concerto Comp 90; Werner Schlrshp 89-; Starling Schlrshp 88-; Music; Musician.

**LUNDER, TERJE A,** Fl International Univ, Miami, FL; SR; BA; Hotel Sls/Mktg Assoc 89-90; Norway Exch 89-; SGA Norwegian Clg Hosptlty Mgmt Acctg Exec 88-89; Computer Expert Syst; Asst Tchr Hotel Cmptr Info Syst 89-; AS Norwegian Sch Mgmt 86; Htl/Fd Svc Adm; Htl Adm MS.

**LUNDIN, WENDY S,** Savannah Coll Of Art & Design, Savannah, GA; FR; BFA; Jbs Dghtrs Hnrd Qn 86-; Art; Ilstrtn.

**LUNDQUIST, KATARINA L,** Emory & Henry Coll, Emory, VA; SR; BA; Phi Gamma Mu; Phi Sigma Iota; French Drill Inst 90-; Bus Mngmnt.

**LUNDY, DOUG A,** Ms St Univ, Miss State, MS; FR; BA; Hstry; Coll Prfssr.

**LUNDY, KAREN N,** Univ Of South Al, Mobile, AL; FR; BS; Univ Symph Bnd 90; Bsn.

**LUNGARINI, DAVID G,** Providence Coll, Providence, RI; JR; BS; Yng Rpblcns 88-; Mstng Cr Clb 85-; Bus; Mrktng Mngr.

**LUNIEWSKI, RENEE M,** Hilbert Coll, Hamburg, NY; FR; Voston Patrts L L Ftbl Assoc Head Coach 84-90; Sec; Off Tech; Exec.

**LUNK, JENNIFER J,** Kennesaw St Coll, Marietta, GA; SO; BED; SOAR 90-; Phi Eta Sigma 89-; Math; Tchr.**

**LUNN, JEFFREY G,** Rensselaer Polytechnic Inst, Troy, NY; SO; BS; Pep Band 89-; Sympnc Band 90-; Dns Lst 89-; IM Sftbl/Bsktbl 90-; Cmptr Sci; Sftwr Engr.**

**LUNNEMANN, PEGGY M,** Northern Ky Univ, Highland Hts, KY; FR.

**LUNSFORD, LINDA C,** Union Univ, Jackson, TN; JR; BSBA; Acctng Clb 88-; Internship Parsons Sports Ctr 90-; Acctng Mngmnt Mrktng; CPA.

**LUNSFORD, LISA FRANCIS,** Va Commonwealth Univ, Richmond, VA; SR; BSN; Girl Scouts Amer Vol 90-; PTA 90-; Amer Heart Assn CPR Instr 88-; VA Full Schlrshp 86-88; RN 88; Nurs.

**LUNSTRUM, MAJ-STINA N,** Cornell Univ Statutory College, Ithaca, NY; SR; Phi Kappa Phi 88-; Gold Key 88-; Omicron Nu 88-; Hon Pgm Rsrch 89-; BS W/Hon Dstnctn; Deans Lst 88-; Eleanor Roosevelt Grant 88; Flora Rose Grant 89-; Human Dvlpmnt/Fmly Studies; Med.**

**LUNT, MARK A,** Univ Of Rochester, Rochester, NY; SO; BA; Eagle Scout Assn Fndrs/Pres 90; Stdnts Assn Senate Sntr 89-90; Acad Affrs Comm Chrmn 89-90; Sigma Phi Epsilon Jdcl Comm 89-; Eagle Scout Assn; Ultimate Frisbee 89-; Pol Sci/Intl Rel; Law.

**LUO, WEINA SHI,** Palm Beach Comm Coll, Lake Worth, FL; JR; BA; Tlnt Rstr Cert Achvmnt; Comp Sci; Sftwr Eng.

**LUONGO, NANCY-ANN,** City Univ Of Ny Lehman Coll, Bronx, NY; JR; BA; Ntl Hon Soc 58-59; Psychlgy/Educ; Tchng.

**LUPINO, NICOLE,** Embry Riddle Aeronautical Univ, Daytona Beach, FL; JR; Activities 90-; Aero Sci; Commercial Airline Pilot.

**LUPO, LORA L,** Hudson Valley Comm Coll, Troy, NY; SO; AAS; Cert Edctnl Opprtnty Cntr-Coll Prep 90; Crmnl Juste; Law Enfrcmnt.

**LUPOLI, DANA J,** Newbury Coll, Brookline, MA; FR; Sailing Boatng; Bus Mngt; Drftng/Bldn Cnstrctn.

**LURIE, JACQUELINE K,** Cornell Univ Statutory College, Ithaca, NY; SO; BS; EARS 89-; Ornttn Stff 90-; ALERT; Ho Nun De Kah; Chi Omega Asst Trea 90-; Dean Lst; Intern NY Hosp Pblc Affrs; Cmmnctns/Bus; Pblc Rltns/Advrtsng.

**LUSAN, MONIQUE D,** Univ Of Miami, Coral Gables, FL; SR; BA; Award Acad Excel 88; AA Miami Dade Cmnty Clg 88; Psych.

**LUSARDI, LUCA H,** Univ Of Miami, Coral Gables, FL; GD; PHD; Math Hnr Soc UM; Gldn Key; Grad Schlrshp Math Asstntshp; BS 90-; Math.

**LUSBY, ALLISON P,** Morehead St Univ, Morehead, KY; SR; BA; Blue Key 87; Chi Omega 88-; Walt Disney Intern; Radio-TV/STUDIO Art.**

**LUSBY, JENNY B,** Lexington Comm Coll, Lexington, KY; FR; MBA; Edctn; Schl Admnstrtn.

**LUSBY, TONETTE M,** Univ Of Akron, Akron, OH; JR; BA; Advtsng Clb; Gldn Key; Busn Admin; Mktg/Advrtsng.

**LUSHER, ANNA L,** Marshall University, Huntington, WV; SO; BBA; Barboursville Acad Boosters Clb Treas 90-; Acctng.**

**LUSHER, GARY L,** Marshall University, Huntington, WV; SO; Msnc Ldg Cubell Ldg 152 3 Dgr; Jrnymn Irnwkrs; Schl Bus Opr; Sfty Tech; Sfty Eng.

**LUSK, PATTI M,** Tri County Tech Coll, Pendleton, SC; SO; ASSOC; Bus Ldrs Tmrw; Cert 89; Cmptr Tech; Progrmg.

**LUSK, SCOTT H,** Ms St Univ, Miss State, MS; SO; BA; Pre-Law Soc 89-; Phi Eta Sigma; Pres Lst 90; Hon Schlrshp Recgntn Day; Poli Sci; Law.

**LUSSIER, LAURIE J,** Merrimack Coll, North Andover, MA; FR; BA; Asst Daycare Tchr 90-; Religous Yth Grp Retreats 90-; Math/Sec Educ; H S Tchr.

**LUST, JONATHAN EVAN,** Methodist Coll, Fayetteville, NC; JR; BS; Phi Eta Sigma 89-; Alpha Chi; Bus; Law.

**LUST, MATTHEW D,** Univ Of Sc At Columbia, Columbia, SC; FR; BA; Campus Crusade 90-; Crosswell Baptist Sftbl Team; Deans List 90; Presidential Hnr Roll 90; Computer Science; Programming.

**LUSTE, KIMBERLY C,** Columbia Union Coll, Takoma Park, MD; FR; BA; Phi Eta Sigma 90-; Theta Alpha Beta 90-; Bsktbl 90-; Engl; Invstgtv Rprtr.

**LUSTER, ELIZABETH M,** Salisbury St Univ, Salisbury, MD; JR; BSW; Vital Connection Clb; Socl Wrk Clb 90-; Socl Wrk; Fmly/Chldrn Socl Srvcs.

**LUTCH, DARLENE A,** Mount Aloysius Jr Coll, Cresson, PA; SO; AS; Mdcl Asstnt.

**LUTCHI, DOINA P,** Fl International Univ, Miami, FL; GD; Sen Schl Arts Sci 89; Wmn Cmmnctns Inc VP 87-88; Otstndng Advrtsng Stu 90; Schlrshp Greater Miami Ad Fed 89; BS 90.

**LUTE, TERESITA B,** Commonwealth Coll, Virginia Beach, VA; FR.

**LUTHER, MATTHEW D,** Indiana Univ Of Pa, Indiana, PA; SR; BA; Assn Rhbltn Advcts V P 90; Provost Schlr 90; Dns Lst 87-; Rhbltn Educ; Rhbltn Cnslr.**

**LUTHER, NANCY S,** Fl St Univ, Tallahassee, FL; SR; BS; SAACURH 80; Garnet Key 90-; Corrs/Prob/Parole Intrn 89-90; Acad Ldrshp Awrd; Waitress 88-; AA Gulf Coast Cmnty Clg 90; Crim Just.

**LUTHER, SANDRA L,** Kent St Univ Kent Cmps, Kent, OH; JR; BA; ETC 88-; Envrnmtl Clb KSU Trmbl 89-90; Gldn Key; Cir K; Acdmc Schlrshp ETC 89-90; Univ Schlrshp 90-; Deans Lst; Pres Lst 87-; Rac Actvty Crdntr; Grntlgy; Nrsg Hm Admin.

**LUTHRINGER, PETER JOSEPH,** Oh Coll Of Podiatric Med, Cleveland, OH; GD; DPM; BSN D'youville Coll 85; Alumni Assc Acad Schlrshp 90; Dstngshd Svc Awd OPMSA 90-; OH Pdtrc Mdcl Stdnt Assc 88-; Amer Col! Foot Srgns 90-; OCPM Adm Com Stdnt Rep 90-; Pi Delta; Sigma Theta Tau; Lambda Kappa; Alpha Gamma Kappa Pres 90-; Podiatry; Doctor.

**LUTON, MICHAEL P,** Univ Of Southern Ms, Hattiesburg, MS; FR; BA; Music; Cmptr Comm.

**LUTTRELL, BESSIE K,** Ky Wesleyan Coll, Owensboro, KY; SR; BA; Poltcl Sci Clb; Acdmy Crmnl Jstce Sci; Crmnl Jstce Soc 87-; Crmnl Jstce; Law.

**LUTTRELL, KATHY M,** Georgetown Coll, Georgetown, KY; SO; BS; Bptst Stdnt Union; Alpha Lambda Delta; Phi Mu; Comp Sci.

**LUTTRELL, TERESA S,** Union Coll, Barbourville, KY; JR; BA; Wmns Clb Sec 88; Gamma Beta Phi 90-; Fam Spprt Rep 89-; Army Comm Srvce; Almni Schlrshp; Dr LA Geiss Comp Awrd 90-; Dns Lst Pres Lrte 87-; Athltc Trnr 88; Mrktng Rep Admin Asst; Comp Info Systms Bus Admin; Systms Anlyst Mar.

**LUTTRINGER, ERIC J,** Duquesne Univ, Pittsburgh, PA; FR; MBA; Alpha Phi Omega 90-; Bus.

**LUTY, JOSEPH M,** Columbia Univ, New York, NY; FR; BS; Kandel Engr Almn Assoc Sec; Wolfon Schlr 90-; Chem Engr.

**LUTZ, CARRIE A,** Univ Of Charleston, Charleston, WV; JR; BS; BACCUS 89-; Alpha Lambda Delta 88-; Chi Beta Phi 89-; Kappa Tau Epsilon 90-; Deans Lst; Prtl Acad Schlrshp Univ Chrlstn 88-; Sccr Grnt 88-; Vars Sccr 88-; Bio; Med Schl.

**LUTZ, CATHLEEN E,** S U N Y Coll Of Tech At Frmgdl, Farmingdale, NY; SO; Early Chldhd; Tchng.

**LUTZ, KELLY J,** Valdosta St Coll, Valdosta, GA; JR; BA; Civiton Camp Big Heart For Mently Hndcpd; Medcl Nrsng Duties; LPN Maytzie Tech 78; EMT Valdosta Tech 86; Soclgy/Anthrplgy/Biolgy; Medcl Law.

**LUTZ, MARK M,** Pittsburgh Tech Inst, Pittsburgh, PA; GD; AST; Cmptr Aid Drftng/Desgn.

**LUTZ, MELISSA W,** Lexington Comm Coll, Lexington, KY; SO; BA; Bookpr Food Dist; Acctg.

**LUTZ, NANCY J,** S U N Y Coll Of Tech At Delhi, Delhi, NY; FR; AAS; Natl Hnr Scty 90-; DE Cty Amer Dairy Assc Sec 90-; Utd Meth Wmn 88-90; Hidden Inn Rest Inc Bkpr/Sec 90-; Business; Acctnt.

**LUTZ, RACHEL Y,** Northwest Ms Comm Coll, Senatobia, MS; FR; BS; Phi Theta Kappa 90-; All Amer Schlr Clgte Awd; Blgy; Physcl Thrpy.

**LUTZ, SHARON M,** Univ Of Scranton, Scranton, PA; FR; BA; Phy Ther Clb 90-; Pax Christi 90-; Camp Mnstry 92-; Stdnts Life 90-; Svc Orintd Stdnts 90-; Phys Ther.

**LUTZ, SHERYL B,** Thomas Nelson Comm Coll, Hampton, VA; SO; AS; Baptist Stdnt Un 89-; Phi Theta Kappa 89-; Intrnshp Sentars Nrsng Ctr 90-; Soc Wrk.

**LUTZ-THOMAS, MARIA KAY,** Western Ky Univ, Bowling Green, KY; SR; Gldn Ky; Kappa Delta Pi; Phi Kappa Phi; Phi Theta Kappa; Vokurka Mem Schlrshp 90-; Sas Elizabethtown Comm Coll 90; Elem Educ.

**LUU, DUC D,** George Mason Univ, Fairfax, VA; SO; Alpha Lambda Delta 90-91; Busn; Mgmt.

**LUU, PHUONG M,** Temple Univ, Philadelphia, PA; JR; RPH; PSHP 89-90; Viet Clb VP 89-90; BA Univ Penn 88; Phrmcy.

**LUU, SYDNEY D,** Widener Univ, Chester, PA; JR; BSEE; Dns Lst 89; W W Smith Schlrshps 88-89; Cum Laude Temple U 90; BS Temple U 89; Elctrcl Engr; MS Cmptr Engr/Ph D Microwv Eng.

**LUYENDYK, STEVEN R,** Ramapo Coll Of Nj, Mahwah, NJ; SR; BA; Literature; Educ.

**LUYSTER, DAVID J,** Oh Univ, Athens, OH; SO; BA; Breeders Assn 87-; Chrch Chrst 89-; Comm Bld Pgm 87-; Art Educ; Tchr.

**LUZAK, HEATHER R,** Neumann Coll, Aston, PA; FR; BS; Biol; Lab/Rscrch.

**LUZARDO, DORINDA,** Fl International Univ, Miami, FL; GD; Kappa Delta Pi Pgm Chr 90-; Phi Kappa Phi 90-; Metannia 88-; Ford Fndtn Clin Supvrsn Intrn 90-; BS; AA In Ed Miami Dade Comm Coll 86; Elem Educ.

**LUZUM, SUSAN L,** Nova Univ, Ft Lauderdale, FL; GD; MBA; Phi Alpha Theta 68-70; Pub Library Bd Sec 79-; Alumni Parent Rltns Stf; BA Luther Coll 70; Hist; Bus,Tchng.

**LUZWICK, CONNIE M,** Memphis St Univ, Memphis, TN; SR; Phi Kappa Phi; Block Chrmn Sprnghl Hmownrs Assn 90-; AA William Rainey Harper Coll Palatine Il 87; Acntng; Tch/Cnslr.

**LY, CU,** Bunker Hill Comm Coll, Boston, MA; FR; Philippine Refugee Prcsng Ctr Cnslr Sabang Morong Bataan Phillipines 89-90; Walter E Fernald St Sch; BD Vietnam Bapt Theo Seminary 72; Vo Tanh H S 62; Mnstr Bay Hien Bapt Ch Sg Vn 72-75; Macrobiotics Acupuncture 70-72; Boat Person 88; Eng; Rel & Psych.

**LY, DANITH,** Ga Inst Of Tech At Atlanta, Atlanta, GA; SO; BA; Cambodian Ed Yth Clb Pres 88-; Vlybl Clb Cptn 89-; Chem Engr Chmstry/Phlsphy; Engr Sci.

**LY, HOA NGOC,** City Univ Of Ny La Guard Coll, Long Island Cty, NY; SR; BA; La Grdn Stdnt Assn; 2( ('& 90-; Comp/Sci; Law.

**LY, KHANH N,** Hillsborough Comm Coll, Tampa, FL; FR.

**LY, NU T,** Univ Of Tn At Martin, Martin, TN; FR; Acctg.

**LY, SATTHYA,** Harrisburg Area Comm Coll, Harrisburg, PA; FR; BA; Cambodian Comm 90-; Elec Engr.

**LY, TAI K,** Bunker Hill Comm Coll, Boston, MA; FR; AS; Catholic Ofc Emerg Relief/Refugees; Philippine Refugee Process Ctr; Intl Catholic Migration Commission; Certif Recog; Med Interpretor; Physicians Asst; ESL Tchr; UN Vol; Lib Arts; Med Radgrphy.

**LYBA, MARC A,** Anne Arundel Comm Coll, Arnold, MD; SO; BA; Scuba Clb 90; Hstry; Scndry Educ.

**LYBRAND, DENISE B,** Univ Of Al At Birmingham, Birmingham, AL; JR; BA; Phi Theta Kappa 89-90; AS Jefferson St 90; Elem Educ; Tchr.

**LYDON, BRIAN P,** Duquesne Univ, Pittsburgh, PA; JR; BA; Phi Eta Sigma Pres 89-90; Lambda Sigma 89-90; KDKA TV Intern; Swim 88-; Brdcst Jrnlsm; Reporting.

**LYDON, MARY Y,** Christopher Newport Coll, Newport News, VA; SO; BS; Bio Clb 89-; Bio; Doctor.

**LYLE, BEVERLY K,** Belmont Coll, Nashville, TN; FR; BBA; Bsn; Office Admin.

**LYLE, DIANNA P,** Kent St Univ Kent Cmps, Kent, OH; SR; BS; Delta Omicron 88-; Elem Edctn; Tchng.

**LYLE, JERRI S,** Western Ky Univ, Bowling Green, KY; JR; BA; Deans Lst 89-; Prsdnts Lst 89-; Pre-Schl Tchr Asst 90-; Elmntry Edctn; Tchr.

**LYLE, ROBERT MONROE,** Memphis St Univ, Memphis, TN; SR; Navy ROTC Exec Offcr 87-; Trident Pres 87-; Magna Cum Laude; IM Bsktbl Capt 87-; BA; Bus-Mrktng; Naval Supply Corp Officer.

**LYLES, ANGELA M,** Al St Univ, Montgomery, AL; FR; BA; Comp Inf Sys; Comp Anlyst.

**LYLES, MONICA,** Alcorn St Univ, Lorman, MS; JR; BA; Bowling 89-; Modeling Squad 90-; Alpha Phi Alpha Swthrt 89-; Dns Lst 89-; Bsn Adm; Mktg.

**LYLES, PHILLIP V,** Wilberforce Univ, Wilberforce, OH; JR; BS; Natl Assn Blck Accntnts; Natl Stdnt Bus Leag; Cargill Acad Excell Schlrshp; Alpha Pi Alpha Schlrshp; Bus/Finance; Plnnr.

**LYLES, TREMEKA D,** Alcorn St Univ, Lorman, MS; SR; BS; Deans Lst; Sec Sci; Exec.

**LYMAN, LOIS E,** Kent St Univ Kent Cmps, Kent, OH; SR; BBA; Pi Kappa Delta Pres 89-; Gldn Ky 89-; Beta Gamma Sigma 90-; Beta Gamma Sigma Otstndng Jr Awd 90; Ohio Bd Rgnts Grad Flwshp; Pi Kappa Delta Individual Evnts Natl Qulfr 90; Bus/Human Resource Mngmnt; Prsnl Trng Dvlpmnt.

**LYMBURNER, BARBARA E,** Niagara Univ, Niagara Univ, NY; SR; BSN; NSANYS; Delta Epsilon Sigma 89-; Sigma Theta Tau 90-; PTA; Assmbly God Nrsry Chr Dir 89-90; Choir Sec 87-; AARP Schlrshp 89-90; Delta Epsilon Sigma Awd Exclnc 88-; Deans List 88-; Nrsng Awds 88-; Nrsng.

**LYMON, JUANDALYNN W,** Tougaloo Coll, Tougaloo, MS; JR; BA; Alpha Kappa Alpha VP 90; Ecnmcs; Acctg.

**LYN, JANICE A,** City Univ Of Ny Baruch Coll, New York, NY; SR; BA; H P Van Sickle Mem Awrd; AAS Botough Manhattan Comm Coll 89; Acctg.

**LYNAH, ANGELA L,** Claflin Coll, Orangeburg, SC; JR; BA; NEA Ntl Educ Assoc 88-; NAACP; Zeta Phi Beta; Cert Mrt Hnr Rl 89-90; Div Educ Awrd Otstndg Tchr Educ Mjr 90-; Elem Educ; Tchr.

**LYNCH, BRIDGET M,** Fl St Univ, Tallahassee, FL; JR; BA; Psi Chi; FPIRG 90-; Ind Stdy; AA St Petersbrg Jr Clg 90; Psych.

**LYNCH, CHRIS J,** Univ Of Fl, Gainesville, FL; SR; Amer Mktg Assoc V P Rec 88-; Mktg Resrch Comm; Acad/Profsnl Comm; Svc Comm; Career/Intern Comm; Amer Mktg Assoc Svc Comm 88-; Big Bro/Big Sis; Berger/Roed Advrtsg Inc Asst Acct Exec 89; J C Penney Co Inc Retail Mgr Intern 90; Mktg; Mktg Mgmt.

**LYNCH, CHRISTINE D,** Georgetown Univ, Washington, DC; SR; BSBA; Envrnmntl Soc 88-; Comm Action Coalition 88-89; Big Bro Big Str Prog 88-89; Fin Mgmt Assoc Hon Soc; Intrn Cngrsmn G Solomon 90-; Intrn N Y State Snte Fin Cmtee; Fin; Law.

**LYNCH, CHRISTOPHER J,** City Univ Of Ny Baruch Coll, New York, NY; SR; BBA; Phi Alpha Alpha; Aron Zweifach Mem Awd; Pub Admin; Mgmt.

**LYNCH, DANIEL P,** Slippery Rock Univ, Slippery Rock, PA; SR; BA; Rugby Ftbl Clb 90-; Phi Eta Sigma 87-; Pi Kappa Phi; Outstndng Cntrbtn Awd; Intrnshp Butler VAMC; Trck/Fld; PE Kinesiotherapy; Physcl Thrpy.

**LYNCH, DAVID M,** Medical Coll Of Ga, Augusta, GA; SR; BSN; Amer Assn Crtcl Cre Nrss; ANA 88-; GA Nrss Assn 88-; Sigma Phi Epsilon 84; RN; ASN Brunswick Coll 88; Nrsng; Nrse Ansthsia.

**LYNCH, DIANE M,** Coll Of New Rochelle, New Rochelle, NY; SO; BS; Sci Math Scty 89-; St Bndcts Ff Drm Tchr 79-; Cmmtr Cncl Rep 89-; Hnrs Lst 90-; Blgy Ed.

**LYNCH, DONALD F,** Alfred Univ, Alfred, NY; JR; Rescue Sqd Co Cap 88-; Jazz Bnd 88-; Tau Beta Pi 90-; Security Shft Sprvsr 89-; Co-Op The Carborundum Co; Co-Op M S Flynn Inc 90; Var Cross Cntry 8-; Ind Engr; Cnsltng Firm.

**LYNCH, ELFRIEDE M,** Univ Of Miami, Coral Gables, FL; FR; BA, IM Occr 90-, Intl Finance; Imprt/Enprt.

**LYNCH, JAMES R,** Atlantic Comm Coll, Mays Landing, NJ; FR; AAS; Clnry Stdnt Assoc Cls Repr 90-; Fd Srvc Sntn Cert Natl Rstrnt Assoc 90; Clnry Arts.

**LYNCH, JOHN C,** Widener Univ, Chester, PA; FR; BA; Acctng Scty 90-; Deans Lst 90-; Fnlst Mc Swmng Chmpnshps 90-; Intr Colgt Swm; Scl Rcrd Hldr Swmng90-; Accntng; Cpa.

**LYNCH JR, JOHN G,** Ny Law School, New York, NY; JD; NYLS Law Review Candidacy; BA Boston Univ 89; Criminal Law.

**LYNCH, KATHLEEN M,** Marywood Coll, Scranton, PA; SR; BA; Phi Beta Lambda Parlmntrn; Ski Clb; Hlth Svcs Adm Clb; Delta Epsilon Sigma; Acad Intrnshp Alld Svcs; Hmn Res Dept; Pres Schlrshp 87-; Wnr Jrdn Medal; Hlth Svcs; Hosp Admin.

**LYNCH, LA RISA R,** Cheyney Univ Of Pa, Cheyney, PA; JR; BA; Nwspr 88-90; Alumni Rltns 90; Chplns Office Vol 90; Alpah Kappa Mu 90; Notre Dame Univ Grads Studies Prog 90-; Jrnlsm; Novelist.

**LYNCH, MAYO,** Miami Jacobs Jr Coll Of Bus, Dayton, OH; FR; Diploma/Cert Nurses Asst; AS Cert S W Va Comm Coll 76; Med Office Asstng; Med Asst.

**LYNCH, MICHAEL B,** Widener Univ, Chester, PA; JR; BA; Acctg Soc 88-; Phi Eta Sigma Secy 90; Lambda Chi Alpha Treas 90; Sun Refining/Mrktg Clerk 89; E I Du Pont Nemours Asst; Swmg Capt 90; Acctg.

**LYNCH, ROBERT S,** Valdosta St Coll, Valdosta, GA; FR; BA; CAB 90-; Wsly Fdn 90-; IM Vlybl/Sftbl 90-; Bsn Admn.

**LYNCH, TRACEY A,** S U N Y Coll At Fredonia, Fredonia, NY; SR; BS; Hlth Serv Admn Club Rep 89-; Yrbk Staff; WCA Hosp Intern Asst To Hosp Adm; Hlth Serv Adm; Hosp Hlth Adm.

**LYNDE, JENNIFER E,** Teikyo Post Univ, Waterbury, CT; SO; BA; Interclgt Eqstrn Tm 90-; AS Eqstrn Studies; Equine Studies Cert; Engl; Wrtr.

**LYNK, LESLIE E,** George Mason Univ, Fairfax, VA; SO; BSED; Phys Ed; Tchr.

**LYNN, DAVID MICHAEL,** Univ Of Sc At Columbia, Columbia, SC; FR; BA; Res Hl Govt Repr 90-; Gamma Beta Phi 90-; Alpha Lambda Delta 90-; Bio; Med Rsrch.

**LYNN, REGINA M,** Morgan St Univ, Baltimore, MD; SO; BS; SGA Pres; Yrbk Phtgrphr 90-; African Act Pres 89-; Phi Eta Sigma; Mntoring Pgrm; Promethean Kappa Tau; Alpha Lambda Delta; Delta Sigma Theta Parlmntrn 90-; Inrds Intrn 90-; Dns Lst; Math; Tch.

**LYNN, SHARON A,** Memphis St Univ, Memphis, TN; GD; Deans Lst; Paralegal Cert; Law.

**LYNN, TRACY L,** Hiwassee Coll, Madisonville, TN; FR; AAS; Phi Theta Kappa Sec; Med Sec Tech.

**LYON, AMMEE R,** Univ Of Ga, Athens, GA; FR; BSED; Alpha Lambda Delta; Hlth Promo; Training.

**LYON, JENNIFER M,** Kent St Univ Kent Cmps, Kent, OH; FR; BA; CBC 90-; Deans List 90; Bus; Acctng.

**LYON, MONICA S,** Oh St Univ At Marion, Marion, OH; SR; BA; Gldn Key; Sec Engl Educ; H S Engl Tchr.

**LYONS, ALICIA C,** Christopher Newport Coll, Newport News, VA; SO; BS; Spcl Olym 88-; Living Museum 89-; Biol; Envnmntl Sci.

**LYONS, AMY L,** Newbury Coll, Brookline, MA; FR; ASSC; Arbcs Clb 90-; Fash Mrchndsng; Bus.

**LYONS, ANNE E,** Christopher Newport Coll, Newport News, VA; SR; MA; Lit Mag Clb 86-88; Bptst Std Un 88-90; Spnsh Clb 88-90; Intl Std Asc 88-90; Frnch Clb Sec 90; Alpha Chi 89-; Intshp Tchng Asst Frnch Mddle Schls 87-88; Fncng Clb 86-88; BA 90; Frnch; Clg Tchr.

**LYONS, BRENDA M,** Oh St Univ, Columbus, OH; FR; MD; Soc Of Women Engrs; Circle K; Vol OSU Hosp; Pre Med/Mech Engr; Cardiolgst.

**LYONS, CHRISTOPHER D,** Va Commonwealth Univ, Richmond, VA; SO; BS; Am Chem Soc 90-; Chem; Med Sch.

**LYONS, EBONY S,** Al St Univ, Montgomery, AL; FR; BA; Vllybl Tm 90-; Psych; Law.

**LYONS, KATHY L,** Kent St Univ Kent Cmps, Kent, OH; SO; BS; May 4tgh Task Force 89; Rainbows 85; Deans List 90; Interior Dsgn.

**LYONS, KATRINA L,** Univ Of Nc At Asheville, Asheville, NC; SR; BA; Natl Psy Chi 90-; Lab Asst 90-; Psychlgy; Phd Clncl Psychlgy.

**LYONS, KELLY R,** Stillman Coll, Tuscaloosa, AL; SR; BS; Cardell Wynn Hrs Soc; Beta Kappa Chi; Alpha Kappa Mu; Delta Sigma Theta; Cmptr Sci; Prgrmmr/Anlyst.

**LYONS, KENNETH P,** Univ Of Tn At Martin, Martin, TN; SR; BA; Engl Soc VP 89-; Engl.

**LYONS, KIMBERLY M,** Univ Of Ky, Lexington, KY; SR; BA; Rsdnce Hall Assn 87-; Pre Law Club Mbrshp Com 90; Stdnts Agnst Vltn Envrnmnt 90-; Dns Lst 90; Hnr Roll 87-; Blndng Twr Flag Ftbl Co-Capt 87-88; Hstry/Soc Stds; Law Schl.

**LYONS, MICHAEL D,** Univ Of Cincinnati-Clrmnt Coll, Batavia, OH; FR; BA; Bus; Opertns Mngmnt.

**LYONS, PAMELA S,** Indiana Univ Of Pa, Indiana, PA; FR; B; Ed; Elem Tchr.

**LYONS, PATRICK A,** Fl A & M Univ, Tallahassee, FL; FR; BS; Nvl ROTC Admn Chf; Math Clb 90-; Mdshpmn Mo; Actrl Sci/Math; Actry.

**LYONS JR, ROGER I,** Johnson C Smith Univ, Charlotte, NC; SO; BA; NAACP Pres 89-; Stdnt Orntn Ldr 90-; Comp Sci Clb; Alpha Phi Alpha Sec; Comp Sci/Info Syst; Sftwr Dsgn.**

**LYONS, SHAWN L,** Lincoln Univ, Lincoln Univ, PA; JR; BA; Acctng Clb; Chinese Clb; Pan Hellinic Cncl Sec 90-; Alpha Chi; Delta Sigma Pr; Fannie Mae Intrnshp; Red Lobster Acad Schlrshp; Hum Schlrshp; Acctng; CPA.

**LYONS, THEADORE,** Jackson St Univ, Jackson, MS; FR; BS; Yng Scientists Pgm; Alpha Delta Lambda; Chem; Phrmcy.

**LYONS III, THOMAS J,** Temple Univ, Philadelphia, PA; SR; BS; Golden Key 89-; Good Cndct Mdl US Nvy; Sea Svc Rbn US Nvy; 3 Lttrs Cmndtn US Nvy; Darby Fire Co No 1 Eng Asst 90-; Vet US Nvy Submarn Frc; Elctrcns Mate 1st Cll Nuc Pwr 81-88; AS St U NY 88; Elect Eng Tech; FBI Eng.

**LYSINGER, DENISE M,** Mount Aloysius Jr Coll, Cresson, PA; GD; BS; Accntng Clb 88-90; Ttr 88-90; Accntng; CPA.

**LYSIUK, LANCE C,** Embry Riddle Aeronautical Univ, Daytona Beach, FL; FR; BS; Aeronautical Sci; Prfsnl Pilot.

**LYSTER, CAROL L,** Daytona Beach Comm Coll, Daytona Beach, FL; FR; VICA; Prof Dsgnr; IE Wallace St Comm Clg 89; Int Dsgn/Uphlstry.

**LYTLE, FRANCES A,** Univ Of Miami, Coral Gables, FL; SR; Phi Kappa Phi; Phi Theta Kappa 83; Unit Nurse Of Yr 90-; FL Nurses Assn; Med/Surgical Cert Am Nurses Assn 90; AS Miami Dade Comm Coll 86; AA Miami Dade Comm Coll 83; Nrsng.

**LYTLE, JOSEPH M,** Cheyney Univ Of Pa, Cheyney, PA; SR; BS; DEX Bus Clb 90-; NAACP 90-; Acdmc Rcgntn Lst 87-; IM Bsktbl 87-88; Bus Admin; Acctnt.**

**LYTLE, KRISTA R,** Marshall University, Huntington, WV; JR; BA; NSSLHA 90-; Phi Eta Sigma 88-; Speech Path.

**LYTLE, TRACY B,** Union Univ School Of Nursing, Memphis, TN; SR; BSN; Stdnt Govt Pres 90-; Alpha Chi 89-; Sigma Theta Tau; Chge RN Lbnhr Chldrns Med Cntr 87-; Baptist Memorial Hosp School Of Nursing 87; Nrsng; MSN.

**LYTTLE, DEBORAH R,** Roane St Comm Coll, Harriman, TN; JR; AS; Bapt Stdnt Union; Hlth; Phys Ther.

# M

**MA GUIRK, CHRISTY E,** Univ Of Tn At Martin, Martin, TN; SO; BS; Wildlife Biology; Ornithology.

**MA MBEMBA, MAHUNGU JEFF,** Shaw Univ, Raleigh, NC; SO; Tennis Clb 90-; Bus Clb 90-; Hnr Stdnt 89-; Acad Achvmnt Cert 89-; Business Adm Mgt; Law.**

**MA, MAN L,** City Univ Of Ny Baruch Coll, New York, NY; SR; BBA; Beta Alpha Psi VP; Beta Gamma Sigma; Accntncy; Accntng.

**MA, SOPHIA S,** Ny Univ, New York, NY; SO; AA; New Apstlc Chrch 90-; Dns Lst 90-; Acctng.

**MAAG, JEFFERY R,** Defiance Coll, Defiance, OH; JR; BS; Wrestling Ofcl 84-; Basebl-Sftbl Umpire 90-; Umpire; OHSAA Ofcl; Computer Operator; AAB NW Techncl Clge 84; Bus Mgmnt Admnstrn; Data Processing.

**MAAG, SHERYL J,** Defiance Coll, Defiance, OH; JR; BA; Cmnctn Clb 90-; Ney Oil Co Cmptr Oper; Cmnctns Arts/Engl Ed; Tchg.

**MAAS, CAROLYN C,** Kent St Univ Stark Cmps, North Canton, OH; JR; BED; Engl; Tchng.

**MAAS, PIERRE F,** Miami Dade Comm Coll, Miami, FL; SO; BA; Boxing-US Marine Corps Cntndr 89; US Marine Corps Rsrv L Cpl 89-; Wackenhut Corp Scrty Gd 89-; Cert Tax Preparer H R Block 88; Acctg; CPA.

**MAASTRICHT, KARI L,** Coll Of Charleston, Charleston, SC; JR; BS; Soccer Tm 90-; Educ; Tchr.

**MABE, ELIZABETH A,** Va Commonwealth Univ, Richmond, VA; JR; BS; Bapt Stdnt Union 88-90; Math/Elem Ed; Elem Schl Tchr.

**MABE, JACQUELYN NICOLE,** Univ Of Sc At Columbia, Columbia, SC; FR; BS; Delta Zeta; Deans Lst 90-; Engr.

**MABE, KIMBERLY D,** Va Polytechnic Inst & St Univ, Blacksburg, VA; FR; BA; Lbrl Arts Sci.

**MABE, TINA R,** Univ Of Nc At Charlotte, Charlotte, NC; GD; Psych Clb 88-90; IM Sprts; BA 90; Psych.

**MABEE, FRANK P,** Pellissippi St Tech Comm Coll, Knoxville, TN; FR; AS; Phi Theta Kappa; Grphc Dsgn; Illustration/Music.

**MABEUS, DANA L,** Anne Arundel Comm Coll, Arnold, MD; SO; Phi Theta Kappa; Bay Area Prlgl Assoc; Law.

**MABINUORI, KEHINDE OLA,** City Univ Of Ny Baruch Coll, New York, NY; GD; Deans Lst 89-90; Alpha Iota Delta 89-90; BBA 90.

**MABOKELA, REITUMETSE O,** Oh Wesleyan Univ, Delaware, OH; JR; BA; Stndts Against Aprthd Mbr 89; Rafiki/Wa-Afrika VP 90; Womens Tsk Force Mbr 89; Mostar Brd Mbr; Stdnt Mntr Vstn Guide Mntr/Guide 90; Cyclng Team 90; Cross Cntry 89; Ecomonics/Mngmnt; Clg Prfsr.

**MABREY, MEREDITH I,** Judson Coll, Marion, AL; FR; Sci Club; Amb Sch Hostess; SGA Dorm Rep 90-; Schlrs; Beta Beta Beta; Awd Highest Grade In Chem; Highest GPA Frshmn Class; Deans List; Pre Med/Chem/Bio; Med.

**MABRY, COREY V,** Greenville Tech Coll, Greenville, SC; SO; BS; Im Sftbl 89-; Mthmtcs; Elctrcl Engnrng.

**MABRY, HEATHER L,** Central St Univ, Wilberforce, OH; JR; BS; Flwshp Chrstn Stdnts 90-; Ohio Stdnt Educ Assn 90-; Alpha Kappa Alpha; Acdmc Achvmnt Coll Educ 89-90; Schlstc Excllnc 89-90; Elem Ed; Tchng.

**MABRY, LINDA G,** Furman Univ, Greenville, SC; FR; Coll Ed Srvc Corp 90-; Intvrsty; Dnng Hl Ed Crrclm Lab 90-; Elem/Engl Educ; Tchng/Wrtng.

**MABRY, OTHA E,** Univ Of Tn At Martin, Martin, TN; FR; PHD; Philoghy Club Congressman SGA Dorm Rep Publiest 90-; Busn Rep Student Justice 90-; BSA Exec Assoc Pres 90-; Alpha Phi Alpha Histian 90-; Intshp Federal Express 90-; Outstndng Freshman BSA 90-; Finance/Econ; Tch Finance Historial Blk Clg.

**MABUNTANA, LINDELWA,** Glassboro St Coll, Glassboro, NJ; SO; BA; Stdnt Cltrl Exchnge Brd 89-; Ggrphy Clb 89-; Bsktbl 90; Ggrphy; Urbn Rgnl Plnng.

**MAC ARTHUR, STACEY L,** Western New England Coll, Springfield, MA; JR; BA; COPE 88-89; Fnncl Mngmnt Assc 89-; Alpha Kappa Psi Del 89-; Resource Intermediaries Inc Intern; Vrsty Sftbl; Fnnc; Bnkng.

**MAC BAIN, ELIZABETH,** Glassboro St Coll, Glassboro, NJ; SR; BA; Math.

**MAC CALLUM, VIRGINIA E,** Va Commonwealth Univ, Richmond, VA; SO; BFA; Modern Dance; Choreography.

**MAC CAUGHELTY, MICHAEL C,** Furman Univ, Greenville, SC; FR; BA; Stdnt Actvts Brd; Fllwshp Of Chrstn Athlts; IMS.

**MAC COY, SHARON D,** Nova Univ, Ft Lauderdale, FL; GD; MBA; Assn Fml Excutng; Mngng Coor Prudential Insu Amer; BS 90; Bus.

**MAC DONALD, BRETT W,** Salem-Teikyo Univ, Salem, WV; FR; BA; Rsdnt Asst; Gamma Beta Phi; Crmnl Jstc; Corp Law.

**MAC DONALD, CARRIE A,** Lasell Coll, Newton, MA; FR; BA; Erly Chldhd Educ; Tchr.

**MAC DONALD, DEVIN J,** Georgetown Univ, Washington, DC; JR; BA; Vrsty Ftbl 89; Zff Dvs Pblshng Co Ld Prspctr; All IMS 88-; Bus; Fnnce.

**MAC DONALD, JOHN E,** Embry Riddle Aeronautical Univ, Daytona Beach, FL; FR; BA; Scrmng Eagles Mdl Airplne Clb; Civl Air Ptrl Cadet Cmndr 87-; Seronautical Sci; Airline Pilot.

**MAC DONALD, MARY E,** Univ Of Rochester, Rochester, NY; FR; Psych.

**MAC DONALD, MELANIE L,** Nc Agri & Tech St Univ, Greensboro, NC; JR; BS; Stdnt Natl Ed Assn Publcty 89; Rfrmd Chrch Chrst Chrstn Ed Ldr 84-85; Henas Cnvctn 89-; Biolgcl Sci Tchng Asst; MARC Assoc; Diamnd Cntr 88-; Biolgy; PhD Tchng/Rsrch.

**MAC DONALD, MICHAEL J,** Barry Univ, Miami, FL; SO; Lib Arts.

**MAC DONALD, PATRICIA B,** S U N Y Coll Of Tech At Alfred, Alfred, NY; FR; AAS; Concert Bnd 89-; Stdnt Theater Prod 90-; Kanakadea Chorale 90-; Delta Psi Omega Dram Hnr Soc 90-; Agrcltrl Biotchngy; Brdcstng.

**MAC DONALD JR, PHILIP J,** Clarkson Univ, Potsdam, NY; SR; BS; Amer Prdctn Invntry Cntrl Soc Treas 89-; Trst Schlrshp 87-; Indstrl Mgmt; Mfg Plng/Sprvsr.

**MAC DONALD, RYAN S,** S U N Y Coll Of Tech At Alfred, Alfred, NY; SR; BS; Chem Club Treas 89-; Am Chem Soc; Sigma Tau Epsilon 89-91; Chem; Engrng.

**MAC DONALD-CRONLEY, CYNTHIA D,** Christopher Newport Coll, Newport News, VA; SR; BSBA; Bsn; Ecnmcs.

**MAC DONNELL, MARGARET J,** Loyola Coll In Md, Baltimore, MD; FR; BA; Russian Club 90-; Envrnmntl Club 90-; Tai Kwan Do 90-.

**MAC DOWALL, HEATHER E,** Fl St Univ, Tallahassee, FL; JR; BS; Scuba Dive Clb 90-; Indstrl Psych; Hmn Res Mgmt.

**MAC DOWELL, MERCY V,** Fl International Univ, Miami, FL; SR; BA; FEA 90-; Deans Lst 89-; Pan Am Airlines 88-; Kinloch Elem 88-; AA Miami Dade Cmmnty Clg 89; Elem Edctn; Tchrs.

**MAC EACHRON, SONYA A,** Radford Univ, Radford, VA; FR; BA; Rdfrd Ar Envrnmntl Actn Grp 90; Jd Clb; Symphny Orchstr; Intl Stds.

**MAC ENTEE, NANCY H,** Clarkson Univ, Potsdam, NY; JR; BS; Clarkson Soc Accntnts Pres 90-; Alpha Delta Kappa Tres 89-; James L Dohr Schlr; Accntng Fnnc; CPA.

**MAC EYRAS, RAMON A,** Nova Univ, Ft Lauderdale, FL; GD; MBA; Ame Soc Mech Eng 86-; Sr Process Eng/Prod Spvsr 87-; BSME U Of S Fla 87; Eng Mgmnt.

**MAC FADYEN, MARGARET A,** Georgian Court Coll, Lakewood, NJ; JR; BA; Amer Diabs Assoc 78-; Sigma Tau Delta 90-; John F Murray Schlrshps 88-; Engl/Elem Educ; Elem Tchr.

**MAC GABHANN, KEVIN L,** Davis & Elkins Coll, Elkins, WV; SO; Sntr Nwspr Prsnl Mngr 90-; Radio DJ Intl Org Pres 90-; Dbt Soc Phnx Allnc; Sccr 90-; Hon Pgm/Assn Cltrl Com 90-; Phi Beta Lambda 90-; Deans Lst; Acdmc Achvmnt Awd; Sccr-Schlrshp; Intl Bus.

**MAC GREGOR, MEGAN M,** Oh Univ, Athens, OH; SO; BSE; Amer Soc Chmcl Engnrs 90-; Soc Wm Engrs 90-; Chem Engrg; Bio Med.

**MAC GREGOR, NANCY E,** Coll Of New Rochelle, New Rochelle, NY; SR; BSN; Stdnt Nrs Assn Treas 87-; Vllybl 87-; Drama; Sigma Theta Tau; Deans Hnr Lst 87-; Pres Schlrshp 87-; Lndphny 87-; Vllybl 88-; Nrsng; RN.

**MAC HATTIE, STEPHEN R,** Hudson Valley Comm Coll, Troy, NY; SO; AAS; Acctnt 89-; U S Marines 82-86; Acctng.

**MAC ISAAC, SEAN M,** Daemen Coll, Amherst, NY; SO; BS; I M Ftbl Bkbl 89-90; Phys Thrpy.

**MAC KAY, MICHELLE L,** Univ Of Southern Ms, Hattiesburg, MS; JR; BS; Phys Ed Club; Varsity Sftbl/Soccer Club 88-; Phy Ed; Tch.

**MAC KENN, CHRISTINE ELIZABETH,** Radford Univ, Radford, VA; JR; BS; Kappa Mu Epsilon Sec/Treas; Co Ed Water Polo 2M 89; Math.

**MAC KINNON, KATHERINE I,** Saint Josephs Coll, Windham, ME; SR; BS; Soc Comm Co Chrprsn 89-90; Elem Ed Clb 89-90; Stdnt Govt 89-90; Delta Epsilon Sigma; Tchr Intrn 87-; Exchng Stdnt 90; Magna Cum Laude; Chrldr Cptn 87-; Elem Ed.

**MAC KINNON, SHERRY A,** Univ Of New England, Biddeford, ME; SO; BS; VNESOTA 89-; Annl Almni Tlthn Vol; Med; Occptnl Thrpy.

**MAC LEAN, JULIANNE,** Daytona Beach Comm Coll, Daytona Beach, FL; SO; AA; AS 90; Inter Dsgn; Psych.

**MAC LELLAN, CHRISTOPHER S,** Northeastern Univ, Boston, MA; FR; BS; Hons Pgm 90-; Elec Eng.

**MAC MELVILLE, SUZANNE,** Molloy Coll, Rockville Ctr, NY; JR; BA; Stdnt Govt 88f Math Clb Ed Clb 88f Gaelic Soc Campus Ministries 88; Mu Sigma Mu VP 90; Omicron Alpha Zeta 90; Delta Epsilon Sigma 90; Schlr Awd 88; St Thomas Aquinas Prog Tutoring 88; Math; Elem Ed.

**MAC MILLAN, CHRISTINE A,** Franklin And Marshall Coll, Lancaster, PA; SR; Chrl Scty Chmbr Sngrs Co Pres 88-; FM Plyrs Vcl Dir 89; Grn Rm Thtr Stg Mgr 87-; Phi Beta Kappa; Alpha Phi Music Dir 88-; Excllnc Music Awrd; Music.

**MAC MILLAN JR, JOHN F,** Mt Saint Marys Coll & Seminary, Emmitsburg, MD; SR; BS; Res Asst 88-; Phi Beta Delta Treas 87-; Geo Henry Miles 87-; Beta Beta Beta 90-; Hlth/Wlns Comm 87-89; Lab Asst Bio/Chem 89-; Vars Bsbl Capt 87-; Bio; Med.

**MAC MONIGLE, SHARON E,** Manhattan Coll, Bronx, NY; FR; BS; Chmcl Eng.

**MAC NEEL, DAVID N,** Univ Of Cincinnati, Cincinnati, OH; JR; BS; Cnstrctn Stdnt Assn; Cnstrctn Spec Inst 90-; Co-Op Stdnt Centex-Rooney Cnstr Co 90-; Co-Op Stdnt Wyco Eng 89-90; AAS 90; Cnstrctn Mngmnt; Cnstrctn Eng.

**MAC PHAIL, MARIE G,** Southern Vt Coll, Bennington, VT; GD; AD 90; Nrsng.

**MAC PHEE, SHERRY L,** Univ Of Sc At Columbia, Columbia, SC; JR; ADN; Nrsg.

**MAC PHERSON, BONITA L,** Southern Coll Of Tech, Marietta, GA; JR; BSEET; IEEE 84-86; Dgwd Mtng Sbstnc Abuse/Rehab Tres 90-; Rep Dklb Tech Inst Elctrncs 85-86; Engr Pro Advsry Comm; ASEET 86; Elec Engr Tech.

**MAC PHERSON, DORIS A,** Univ Of Miami, Coral Gables, FL; SR; BS; Wmn Cmmnctns 90-; Eye To Eye News Prgrm 90-; AERHO; WCIX TV Chnl 6 Miami Fl Intrnshp Rex Pompadour Awd Srvc Cbl Statn UM 90-; Brdcst Jrnlsm Sclgy; Tlvsn Brdcstng Nws.

**MAC PHERSON, DOUGLAS J,** Springfield Tech Comm Coll, Springfield, MA; SR; AS; Alpha Nu Omega 90-; Dns Lst 89-; Mech Tchnlgy/Drftg/Dsgn Tech; Engrg Tech.

**MAC WILLIAMS, AMY K,** Salisbury St Univ, Salisbury, MD; JR; BA; Poltcl Sci Clb Sec 89-90; Coll Rpblcns 89-; Phi Sigma Alpha; Poltcl Sci/Hstry; Intl Govt Dlngs.

**MACALUSO, JAMES R,** Bryant Stratton Bus Inst Roch, Rochester, NY; GD; Electronic Tech Clb Treas; Radiofrequency Technican.

**MACALUSO, MARY ELLEN,** Fl Atlantic Univ, Boca Raton, FL; JR; BS; Chrmn Fshn Shw Fndrsr Chrmn; Prmntl Cord Lvtz Frntr Corp 82-90; Comp Info Systms; Systms Anlyst.

**MACALUSO, MIA L,** George Mason Univ, Fairfax, VA; JR; BS; Alpha Chi 90-; Deans Lst 88-89; Wrk Rehab Ctr Mt Vernon Hosp Intrn 90; Comm Hlth; Corp Wllnss.

**MACARI, MICHAEL,** Boston Univ, Boston, MA; GD; Alpha Omega Alpah 1st VP 89-; Natl Pre Med Hnr Soc 86; Merck Manual Awrd; Gorman Awrd; MD Magna Cum Laude; BA Cum Laude 87; Med; Dgnstc Rdlgy.

**MACAULAY, HELENMARIE,** Towson St Univ, Baltimore, MD; JR; BS; Fllwshp Chrstn Athlts 90-; Merit Awd 89; Game Evnt Stf-Athl Dpt 90-; AAS Rochester Inst Tech 90; Spts Mgmt/Adm; Athl Dir.**

**MACAULAY, HENRIETTA O,** City Univ Of Ny City Coll, New York, NY; SR; BSC; Mth Clb 89-; Assc Cmptng Mchns 87-89; Golden Key 87-; Math; Actrl.

**MACCA, JEFFREY A,** Western New England Coll, Springfield, MA; JR; BA; Sftbl Ftbl Bsktbl Hcky 88-; Sftbl Marathn 88-; Comp Inf Sys.

**MACCHETTO, CLAUDIO F,** Georgetown Univ, Washington, DC; SR; BSBA; Mrktng Clb 90-; Beta Gamma Sigma; D C Schools Projects; Mrktng Intl Mngmnt; Intl Business.

**MACCHIO, LANCE F,** Dowling Coll, Oakdale Li, NY; SO; BS; Aeronautics; Pilot.

**MACE, ROBIN L,** Wv Univ At Parkersburg, Parkersburg, WV; JR; BA; Sec 87-90; Mlt Sbjcts Ed; Tchr.

**MACE, SHELLY A,** Wv Univ At Parkersburg, Parkersburg, WV; FR; MBA; Phi Theta Kappa; Elem Educ; Elem Tchr.

**MACEJKA, SHARON L,** Hudson Valley Comm Coll, Troy, NY; JR; CERT; Pres Lst 88-; Deans Lst 88; Cptl Dist Soc Rdlgc Tchnlgsts 88-89; Soc Dgnstc Medcl Sngrphrs 90-; Sngrphrs Cntng Educ 90-; AAS Rdlgc Tech 89; St Clares Hosp Schenectady NY 87-88; Vtrns Admin Medcl Cntr 88-89; Dgnstc Medcl Sngrphy.

**MACEY, VIRGINIA R,** Castleton St Coll, Castleton, VT; JR; BSW; Phi Eta Sigma 88; Acad Excell Awd; Mt Holly Comm Assn Sec 89; Belmnt Comm Coop 89; Soc Wrk/Sec Ed Hstry/Geo; Tchng/Cnslr.

**MACGREGOR, JENNIFER ROBIN,** Georgian Court Coll, Lakewood, NJ; JR; BA; Ntl Soc Pblc Acctnts 90-; Deans Lst Ocena Cnty Coll 88-90; Tau Iota OCC 89-90; AS Bus Admin Ocean Cnty Coll 90; Acctg; CPA.

**MACHADO, MELANIE M,** Hillsborough Comm Coll, Tampa, FL; SO; Sftbll Tm Cptn; Deans List; Sftbl Team Cptn; AA HCC; Elmntry Ed.

**MACHADO, RONALD L,** Fl St Univ, Tallahassee, FL; JR; BS; Landis Hl Gvrnmnt Prsdnt 88-90; Mrchng Chiefs Row Ldr 90-; Phi Eta Sigma 89-; Phi Beta Kappa 90-; FL Clg Stdnt Yr Rnnr Up 90; IM Ftbl Bsktbl Sftbl; Biochemistry; Medicine.

**MACHANIC, STEVEN,** Ny Institute Of Tech Ny City, New York, NY; SR; BT; Fclty Awd; Elec Eng Tech; TV Eng.

**MACHART, THEODORE D,** Tn Temple Univ, Chattanooga, TN; JR; BA; Mgr Mc Dnlds; 2nd Educ/Engl; Mssnry.

**MACHATTIE, MATTHEW S,** Schenectady County Comm Coll, Schenectady, NY; FR; AA; Hotel/Restaurant Mgmnt; Restaurant Bus.

**MACHERONE, CHRISTINE M,** Schenectady County Comm Coll, Schenectady, NY; FR; Intrnshp With The Marriot On Marco Islnd FL 90-; Culinary Arts; Chef Or Restrnt Mgt.**

**MACHESKI, HELEN P,** Castleton St Coll, Castleton, VT; JR; BA; Elem Ed; Tchng.

**MACHI, ANTHONY MARIO,** Duquesne Univ, Pittsburgh, PA; GD; MBA; Fincl Mgt Assn 88-; Mstr Bus Admin Assn; Deans List 86-; Beta Alpha Phi; Phi Chi Theta Crspndng Sec 89-90; Grad Asst; BSBA 90; Acctg/Finance.

**MACHIDA, KOJI,** Atlantic Comm Coll, Mays Landing, NJ; FR; Intl Clb; Bus Admin; Mngr.

**MACHMER, CHRISTOPHER M,** Clarion Univ Of Pa, Clarion, PA; SO; BA; Frnch Clb 89; Ambssrs Prog 89; Lambda Sigma Rcrdng Sec 89; Alpha Mu Gamma; Frnch; Lbrnshp.**

**MACHOBANE, NOLIWE B,** Jackson St Univ, Jackson, MS; SR; Pierian Lit Soc VP Sec 889-; NAACP; Drmtc Guild; Sigma Tau Delta VP 90-; Alpha Mu Gamma; All Amer Schlr Awrd; Pres Lst Schlr; Dean Lst Schlr; Acdmc Schlrshp; BA; Engl Lit; Media.

**MACHUGA, SHELLY L,** Erie Comm Coll South Cmps, Orchard Park, NY; SO; BED; Hnrs Clb 89; NJCAA Bwlng All Amer 90; Bwlng 89; AA; Elem Ed; Elem Schl Tchr.

**MACIA, JOSEPH J,** Barry Univ, Miami, FL; JR; BA; Future Tchrs Of Amer; Sigma Tau Delta; Pres Schlrshp 90; Engl; Tchng.

**MACIAG, NANCY E,** City Univ Of Ny Baruch Coll, New York, NY; JR; BBA; The Retail Trade Soc Ad Mgr; AMA Mbr; The Golden Key Mbr 90; Beta Gamms Sigtma Mbr; Resch Asstnt Dr Claytone Majete Dept Of Sociology; Advertising; Pub Rel.

**MACIAS, ELISEO RAMIRO,** Univ Of Tn At Martin, Martin, TN; SO; BS; IM Vlybl/Soccr 89-90; Mech Engr.

**MACIAS, JUANA I,** Al A & M Univ, Normal, AL; JR; BS; Intl Stdnts Assoc Sec 89-; Fd Ntrtn.

**MACIASZEK, ANDREW S,** New England Coll Of Optometry, Boston, MA; SR; OD; AOSA 88-; Beta Sigma Kappa 89-; VOSH; BS Univ Of MA 87; Optometry.

**MACK, ANTOINETTE,** Nc Agri & Tech St Univ, Greensboro, NC; SR; Digit Cir Math Clb; New Generation Cmps Ministries 88-; William Penn Stdnt Mentor; BS; Math/Prof; Oper Rsrch Analyst.

**MACK, ARTRELLA L,** Columbia Union Coll, Takoma Park, MD; BS; Outstndng US Army Rsrv Instrctr SFC 87; Org Mgmt; Phd Psychlgy.

**MACK, BELINDA D,** Bloomfield Coll, Bloomfield, NJ; JR; BSN; New Spirit Yth Grp V P 85; PCBC Usher Bd Pres 89-; Pstrs Aide Cmtee Sec 89; Ldrshp Prog 89-90; Rutgers Univ Rsrch Conf 90; Stdnt Advsry Bd 89-90; Soph Cls Rep 89-90; NAACP; Chem Awd 85; Miss Black Marianna 83-84; Exclnce Schlr; Nurs.**

**MACK, CHERYL L,** S U N Y Coll Of Tech At Alfred, Alfred, NY; SR; AAS; Drm Cncl Pres 89-90; Med Lab Tech Clb 89-; Phi Theta Kappa VP; Res Asst 90-; Med Lab Tech.

**MACK, DAVID W,** Northern Ky Univ, Highland Hts, KY; FR; BFA; Karate Trnmnt; Art; Pro Artst/Wrtr.

**MACK, DONALD J,** Mount Aloysius Jr Coll, Cresson, PA; FR; AD; Deans Lst 90; Nrsng; RN.

**MACK, JOANNE A,** Miami Dade Comm Coll North, Miami, FL; GD; BA; Cmptr Sci 89-90; OES PHA Sec/Treas 88; Cmptr Sci; Mngmnt Info Syst.

**MACK, JOHN C,** Univ Of Sc At Columbia, Columbia, SC; JR; BED; Stdt Govt Sntr 88-89; VP 89-90; Gamma Beta Phi 88-90; Allendale Psychlgy Awd 89; AS Assoc USC Salkahatchie 90; Physical Ed; Clge Ftbl Coach.

**MACK, LA JUANE D,** Fl Memorial Coll, Miami, FL; FR; BA; SGA VP; Poetry Club Pres 90-; Kappa Alpha Psi Treas; Clg Math Tutor 90-; Intshp Spring 90 Arts Great Rochester Acctng Assist 90; IM Guard; Acctng/Mktng; MBA CPA.

**MACK, LARRY K,** Al St Univ, Montgomery, AL; SO; BA; Gldn Ambssdr 90-; SG 88-89; Hon Soc 88-89; Natl Beta Clb Treas 88-89; Gift Lf 90-; Optmst Clb 88-89; M Cleland Awd 88-89; Optmst Awd 88; Co-Capt Vrsty Bsktbl Tm 88-89; Pltcl Sci; Attnry.

**MACK, REGINA,** Spartanburg Methodist Coll, Spartanburg, SC; SO; AA; Glee Club 90-; Black Alliance Sec 90-; Yrbk Staff/Club; Psi Beta V P 90-; Tutor 90-; Eng/Comp; Jrnlsm.

**MACK, REID,** Univ Of Miami, Coral Gables, FL; SR; BA; SGA Supreme 88; Econ; Bus.**

**MACK, SHERRI R,** Univ Of South Al, Mobile, AL; SR; BS; Bsns Mgmt; Bsns/Prsnl Mgmt.

**MACK, STEPHANIE V,** Johnson C Smith Univ, Charlotte, NC; SR; BA; Hl Cncl 87-88; Pi Gamma Mu 90-; Natl Hnr Soc 86-87; Delta Sigma Theta; Phi Beta Sigma Aux; Coconut Grove Cares; Silver Knight Awd 86-87; Sftbl Capt 87-90; Vlybl; Chrldg 87-89; Sclgy; MA.

**MACK, VALERIE L,** Concord Coll, Athens, WV; SR; BS; Dns Lst 87-; Elem Ed/Spec Ed; Tchng.

**MACK, VICKI RENEE,** Clark Atlanta Univ, Atlanta, GA; JR; BA; Psychlgy Clb; Psi Chi; Alpha Kappa Mu; ADAMHA-MARC Rsrch Prog; Ronald Mc Nair Fllwshp Prog; Psychlgy; Dvlpmntl Psychlgst.

**MACK, VOTURA H,** Miles Coll, Birmingham, AL; JR; BS; Stdnts In Free Enterprise Rpes 90-; Honors Club 90-; Presidential Scholar 90-; Sertoma Brd 90-; Assoc Lawson State Jr Clge 90; Business.

**MACK, YOLANDA C,** Miami Dade Comm Coll South, Miami, FL; SO; BA; Talent Roster Of Outstndng Minority Stdnts; Acctng; Comp Info Sys.

**MACK-BEY, HERBERT L,** Coppin St Coll, Baltimore, MD; GD; BS; Dns Lst 90-; Mgmt Sci; Mgr.

**MACKALL IV, DOUGLASS S,** Duquesne Univ, Pittsburgh, PA; GD; MA; Phi Theta Kappa V P 83-84; Alpha Chi; Sigma Phi Epsilon Treas 83-84; Acad Schlrshps 83-86; C P Minnick Awd; AA BA Ferrum Clg 86; Psych; Cnslg.

**MACKE, DANIEL J,** Colby Sawyer Coll, New London, NH; FR; Vrsty Bsktbl Capt/MVP 90-; Amer Stdies/Poltcl Sci; Law.

**MACKEL, YVETTE D,** Tougaloo Coll, Tougaloo, MS; JR; Chgo Elite Prlmntrn 89-; Kappa Alpha Psi Tres 89-; Hon Roll 90; IM Bwlng Tm Co Capt; Pol Sci; Law/Mortuary Sci.**

**MACKERT, CYNTHIA E,** Anne Arundel Comm Coll, Arnold, MD; SO; Dept Defense; Early Chldhd Ed; Tch.

**MACKESY, SANDRA D,** Miami Dade Comm Coll South, Miami, FL; SO; BA; AA; Engl; Intl Affrs/Brdcstng.

**MACKEY, JOHNNY WESLEY,** Lane Coll, Jackson, TN; SR; BA; Soclgy Clb 88-; Natl Summer Yth Prog Cnslr; Sprts Cmplx Smr Prog Cnslr 90-; Cnty Juv Crt Srvcs Mntr 89-; Hlpng Hnds Org Intrnshp 90-; Proj HOPE; Ftbl MVP 90; AA Mt San Jacinto Comm Coll 87; Soclgy; Correc Offcr Cnslr.

**MACKEY, LAQUETTA,** Cheyney Univ Of Pa, Cheyney, PA; FR; Pm Pm Grl Bnd 90-; Gspl Cncrt Chr 90-; Educ Clb 90-; Stndt Tchr Frnds Chld Care; Chr Mt Enon Bptst Ch Pres 76-; Ushr Pres 86-; Ed; Tchr.

**MACKEY, LAURA Y,** Univ Of Charleston, Charleston, WV; JR; BA; SGA Cncl Sec 90-; Admssns Ambsdr Trgd 90-; BACCHUS Sec 89-; Deans Lst 89-; Nwspaper Editr In Chf 90; Alpha Lambda Delta; Green Peace 90-; Amer Cretacn Soc; CRC Press Fr Chem Achvmnt Awrd 90; Vrsty Tennis 89; Biolgy/Chem; Med Schl.

**MACKEY, MICHAEL A,** Nc Agri & Tech St Univ, Greensboro, NC; SR; BS; Natl Soc Blck Engrs 88-; Bg Brthrs Grnsbro 89-; Dsabld Amer Vtrns 90-; Elec Eng; Eng.

**MACKEY, ROSEMARY K,** Tri County Tech Coll, Pendleton, SC; JR; AA.

**MACKIE, JENNIFER S,** Wilmington Coll, New Castle, DE; FR; BA; DE Assc Police Pshmbl; Derby Jr Com; Beta Sigma Phi; Deans Lst; Bnkng/Finance.

**MACKIE, TONJA L,** Univ Of Nh Plymouth St Coll, Plymouth, NH; FR; BS; PACE Music Prdctns Cmmttee 90; Accntng; Bsnss.

**MACKLAND, LAURA B,** Univ Of Southern Ms, Hattiesburg, MS; JR; BA; Univ Actvts Cncl Var Chrmn 90-; Hon Coll 89-; Hl Cncl 89-; Gama Bete Phi 90-; Pres Lst 90; RA 90-; Soc Stds; Tchng.

**MACKLER, NIKLAS J,** Univ Of Rochester, Rochester, NY; SO; BA; Nordic Ski Tm Bus Mngr 89-; Prtnrs In Rdng 89-; Outsde Spkrs Comm 90-; Ldrship Acknwgmnt; Comm Ser Awd; Biology.

**MACKLIN, YOLANDA A,** Wilberforce Univ, Wilberforce, OH; FR; BS; Choir Drctrss/Membr; Pres Awd Ntrl Sci Dvsn; D Ormonde Walker Schlrshp; Sci Math; Med OBGYN.

**MACLIN, LORI L,** Dyersburg St Comm Coll, Dyersburg, TN; SO; Data Proc Mgmt Assn 89-; Phi Theta Kappa; Alpha Delta Kappa 87-88; Computers; Data Proc.

**MACOMBER, KEVIN D,** S U N Y Coll Of Tech At Alfred, Alfred, NY; FR; BA; Natl Ski Patrol 88-; 2M Soccer/Vlybl/Lacrosse 90-; Archtctr.

**MACRI, JOSEPH A,** Hudson Valley Comm Coll, Troy, NY; FR; MBA; Fin Svcs.

**MACRI, MELISSA L,** Western New England Coll, Springfield, MA; SR; Res Hall Assn 87-89; Res Adv 88; Acctng Peer Tutor 89-; Psych Intrnshp 90-; Sftbl 87-88; Psych; Mngmnt.

**MACROGIANIS, KAREN E,** Newbury Coll, Brookline, MA; FR; AAS; Marco Polo Clb Treas 90; Aerobics Clb 90-; Drama Club; Travel/Tourism Mgmnt.

**MACY, LISA J,** Hillsborough Comm Coll, Tampa, FL; FR; AS; Ofcrs Wvs Clb Angel Vol Reg Coord 87-; Prog Coord Tinker AFB Okla Cord 88; Ofcrs Wives Clb Angel Vol Coord 89-; Ofcrs Wves Clb 7th Ave Arts/Crfts 89; Phi Theta Kappa; Fla Legal Assts; Asst Ch Panst 87-; Ch Cmuty Ldr 89-90; Law; Legal Asst.

**MACY, SARAH J,** Ky Christian Coll, Grayson, KY; SR; BS; Class Offcr VP 88-90; Chrldng Capt 86-90; Elem Ed; Elem Tchng.

**MADAN, NILIA M,** Nova Univ, Ft Lauderdale, FL; GD; MBA; Amer Soc Clncl Pathlgst; HRS Lic Spvr Clncl Lab 85-90; AA 73; BS 76; Human Rsrce Spec; Mgmt.

**MADAN, RUCHIKA,** Portland School Of Art, Portland, ME; SO; BFA; Stdnt Rep Assoc Cls Rep 89; Ceramics.

**MADDALONI, MARIA E,** Western New England Coll, Springfield, MA; SR; BA; Stdnt Snt Pres 87-90; Yrbk Edtr 88-; WNEK-FM Exec Bd 87-90; Alpha Almbda Delta 90-; Pltcl Sci Clb Tres 90-; St Rep Lgsltv Intrn 90; Govt/Cmmnctns; Edctn.

**MADDEN, AARON J,** Duquesne Univ, Pittsburgh, PA; SO; BBA; SGA; Amnesty Intl 89-; Delta Sigma Pi V P 90-; Pres/Caddie Schlrshp 90-; IM Bsktbl; Acctg; Bsn Law.

**MADDEN, CAROLYN L,** Univ Of Miami, Coral Gables, FL; SO; BS; Choir 90; Trck 90; Cmptr Sci.

**MADDEN, CHRISTOPHER D,** Shawnee St Univ, Portsmouth, OH; FR; BA; Phi Theta Kappa 90-; Math; Chmcl Eng.

**MADDEN, CHRISTOPHER W,** Merrimack Coll, North Andover, MA; JR; Hmcmng Com; IM Sports; Fin; Hlth Admnstr.

**MADDEN, KRISTIN M,** Univ Of Sc At Columbia, Columbia, SC; JR; BS; Stdnt Ed Assoc; Sec Ed; Tchg Bio H S.

**MADDEN, MICHAEL JAMES,** Western Carolina Univ, Cullowhee, NC; JR; BS; Pi Gamma Mu; Anthrplgy/Crmnl Jstc; Archlgy.

**MADDEN, NICOLA A C,** Fl International Univ, Miami, FL; SR; W Indn Std Asc VP 90-; Phi Kappa Phi; BSC; Hosp Mgmt; Hotel/Rest Mgmt.

**MADDEN, TAMMY L,** Hudson Valley Comm Coll, Troy, NY; FR; AS; Vol Fire Dept VP 89-90; Yth Cmmssn; NY Cert Emer Med Tch 88; Bkkpr 84; Mrktng; Bsnss.

**MADDEN, TIFFANY A,** Liberty Univ, Lynchburg, VA; FR; BA; Liberators Life; IM Bsktbl; Scndry Edn; Teach.

**MADDOCK, JENNIFER M,** Academy Of The New Church, Bryn Athyn, PA; SO; BS; Vol Grls Sftbl Cch 89; Otng Clb 89; Grl Of Yr Awrd 90; Intrcllgte Vlybl All Str 90; Dns Lst 90; Intrcllgte Vlybl 90; Eng; Arspce Eng.

**MADDOX, AARON L,** Univ Of Tn At Knoxville, Knoxville, TN; FR; BS; Alpha Lambda Delta 90; Phi Eta Sigma 90; Bus/Mktg.

**MADDOX, GREGORY THOMAS,** Kent St Univ Kent Cmps, Kent, OH; GD; Rugby Clb 86-87; Sigma Alpha Epsilon Pres 88-89; USS Vol Awrd; Cooperative Japanese Bus And Scty; IGPB Outstndng Schlstc Achvmnt Awrd; BBA 90; Finance; Public Serv.

**MADDOX, KAREN D,** East Tn St Univ, Johnson City, TN; SR; BBA; Beta Gamma Sigma 89-; Phi Kappa Phi 90-; Alpha Delta Pi 87-90; Outstndg Mgmt Sr Awd 90-; All-Amer Schlr Awd 90-; Mgmt.

**MADDOX, LOUIS L,** Middle Tn St Univ, Murfreesboro, TN; SR; BS; Vol TV Sta 89-90; Intrnshp WSMV-TV Nashvl TN 892-; Vol WMBT-FM Sports 89-90; Mass Cmnctns; Radio/TV Prod.

**MADDOX, MARY K,** Univ Of Montevallo, Montevallo, AL; FR; BS; Cmps Outrch 90-; Hnrs Clb; Cvtn Clb; Ldrshp Schlrshp 90-; Elem Ed; Tchr.

**MADDOX, MELINDA L,** Samford Univ, Birmingham, AL; JR; JD; FL Std Bar 89-90; Cmbrlnd Wmn Law 89-90; Psi Chi 88-; Wmns Hnrs Pgm 83-87; Mllt Assmbly 84-87; Phi Delta Phi 89-; Asst 87-89; Almni Hnrs Schlp 83-85; Cmptr Bsd Hnrs Pgm 83-84; BS Univ AL 87; Law.

**MADDOX, REBECCA F,** Emory Univ, Atlanta, GA; GD; Sigma Theta Tau 90-; Amer Assc Crtcl Cre Nrs 84-; Alpha Gamma Delta; Rome Srvc Leag 89; Crtcl Cre Nrs; BSN Med Clg GA 82; AD Sci Floyd Clg 80; Nrsg; Crtcl Cre.

**MADER, FRED H,** Elmira Coll, Elmira, NY; JR; Boy Scts Amer Asst Sctmstr 88-; Bus Admin; Oper Mngmnt.

**MADER, JEFFREY A,** Univ Of Tn At Knoxville, Knoxville, TN; FR; BA; Phi Eta Sigma; Alph Lambda Delta; Bus.

**MADER, THOMAS W,** Salisbury St Univ, Salisbury, MD; SR; BS; Physcs/Mech Eng.

**MADERA LOPEZ, AGNES EILEEN,** Catholic Univ Of Pr, Ponce, PR; GD; GCED 90-; PIBY 89-90; ICD 90-; Recepcionist Alcaldia Yauco PR 84; Ed.

**MADERA, MERILEE,** Duquesne Univ, Pittsburgh, PA; FR; BS; Phi Eta Sigma; Busn; Finance.

**MADERO, ANA M,** Fl International Univ, Miami, FL; JR; BS; Spnsh Cthlc Chrch Vol Sec 87-89; Acdmc Schlrshp Jr Achvmnt 83-86; AA Miami Dade Comm Coll 86; Educ; Tchr.

**MADEWELL, JAMES T,** Volunteer St Comm Coll, Gallatin, TN; FR; BS; Eng.

**MADHAVAN, LATHA,** Christian Brothers Univ, Memphis, TN; FR; BS; Poetry Scty Tn; Cstngs CBU Literary Mag Stf; Namaste Clb Promote Cltrl Awrnss; Beta Beta Beta; Rd Crss Vol Mid So Hrt Instit; Wrld Ptry Grt Ptry Ctst Hnrble Mntn; Ptry Scty Tn Eye Poem Cntst Hnrble Mntn; Biology; Medicine.

**MADIGAN, PATRICK J,** Univ Of Akron, Akron, OH; SR; BS; IM Sprts 87-; Res Hall Flr Rep 87-88; Beta Gamma Sigma 89-; Golden Key 90-; Fnc Intrn Ltl Tikes Co 89-; Acctg; MBA CMA.

**MADISON, ERIC D,** Univ Of Nc At Asheville, Asheville, NC; FR; BS; Chrstn Actn Flwshp 90-; Chi Alpha 90-; Eng; Cmptr Eng.

**MADISON, LISA A,** Glassboro St Coll, Glassboro, NJ; JR; BA; Schlrshp Assoc Degree; Lgl Sec 85-; AAS Cmbrlnd Cnty Coll 80; Elem Erly Chlhd Ed; Tchng.

**MADISON, WANDA K,** Univ Of Al At Birmingham, Birmingham, AL; SR; BSW; Stdnt Scl Wrk Assn 90-; Prsdnts Lst 90-; Deans Lst 90-; Evenflo Cor&oration 84-90; ASLA Wlke Clg 78-; Scl Wrk; Grd Schl Clncl Scl Wrkr.

**MADOLE, GRETCHEN E,** Univ Of Ct, Storrs, CT; JR; BS; Avry Pt Schlrshp Awd 89-90; Ntr Cnsrvncy Vol 88; Vet Tech 89-; Pathbio; Rsrch.

**MADRAZO, STEVE D,** S U N Y Coll Of Tech At Frmgdl, Farmingdale, NY; SR; ASS; Dean Slist 88-; Phi Theta Kappa; Zeta Beta Tau; NY Nurserymans Assoc Schlrshp; AA Nassau Cmnty Clg 89; Landscp Mgt; Lndscp Dsgn.

**MADRID, ALEJANDRO L,** The Boston Conservatory, Boston, MA; JR; BM; Bstn Clsscl Gtr Scty 90-; Intrnatl Stdnts Orgnztn 90-; Bstn Cnsrvtry Schlrshp 90-; Clsscl Gtr.

**MADRIGAL, ENRIQUE A,** Univ Of Sc At Sumter, Sumter, SC; FR; ASSOC; Stu Govt Assoc Frshmn Rep 90-; Intl Stu Org 90-; Campus Actvs Brd 90-; Deans Lst 90-; Sccr Cmp Instrctr; IM Sccr/Vlybl/Bsktbl/Bsbl/Flg Ftbl; Bus Admin; Intl Bnkg.

**MADRY JR, EURAL W,** Al A & M Univ, Normal, AL; FR; BS; Hosptlty Mgmr.

**MADSEN, DEBBIE E,** Carnegie Mellon Univ, Pittsburgh, PA; JR; BS; Pinrs Treas 88-; Phi Eta Sigma 89-90; Lambda Sigma 89-90; Mrtr Brd; Deans Lst 88; Andrw Crng Rcgntn Awrd 88-89; Andrw Crng Scty Schlr; Swm Tm 88-89; Sw Tm 88-; Econ.

**MADSEN, LYNETTE,** Comm Coll Algny Co Algny Cmps, Pittsburgh, PA; SR; ASSOC; Nuclr Med Tech; Hlth Pyscst.

**MADSEN, MARY W,** Newbury Coll, Brookline, MA; SR; AAS; Stdnt Optical Socty Pres 89-90; Alpha Beta Gamma 88-; Opthlmc Dspnsg.

**MADZIA, WENDY L,** Wv Northern Comm Coll, Wheeling, WV; FR; AAS; Nrsng; RN.

**MAES, DANIEL P,** Tallahassee Comm Coll, Tallahassee, FL; SO; AA; UNS; History.

**MAESSEN, SHEILA A,** Radford Univ, Radford, VA; SO; MBA; Nmntd Radford Un Otstndng Stdnt Awrd 89-90; Radford Un Gymnstc Tm 89-; Acctg; CPA.

**MAESTRE, OSMEL R,** Nova Univ, Ft Lauderdale, FL; GD; MBA; Univ Miami Alumni Assc Member 83-; United Way 83-; Inst Indstrl Engrs 81-; Awrd Corp Rcgntn Awrd Instrmntl Support Implmntn Elect Meter Rdng Prjct FPL Co 86; Recd Awrd Sppt Deming Awrd Audit FPL Co 89; Inst Indstrl Engrs 81-; BSIE 83; Engrng Fclts Operations Mngmnt.

**MAGALHAES, PAULO T,** Manhattan Coll, Bronx, NY; FR; BA; De La Salle 89-90; Engrg; Archtct/Cvl Engr.

**MAGALLANES, ERBA N,** Liberty Univ, Lynchburg, VA; FR; Pre-Med Clb 90-; Sci Clb Cnsltnt 90-; Pre-Med Hnr Soc; Chrch Serv Chldcr; Chrstn Serv Museum 90-; Schlp; TAG Schlp; Grade Schlp; Chem; Bio; Med Doctor.

**MAGARO, STEPHANIE A,** Indiana Univ Of Pa, Indiana, PA; SR; BSE; Bio Clb Tres 89-90; Univ Choir 88; Phi Sigma Pi Fndr 89-90; Dist Achvmnt Schlr 87-; Res Asst 89-; Hnrs Convocation Recip 89-; Deans Lst 87-; Biology Ed.

**MAGDZIAK JR, EDWARD J,** William Paterson Coll, Wayne, NJ; GD; Ba; Engl; Publshng.

**MAGEAU, DIANE M,** Anne Arundel Comm Coll, Arnold, MD; JR; BA; Vol Dr Comm 90-; AA 90; Bus Admin; Hosp.

**MAGEE, CLAYTON C,** Univ Of Southern Ms, Hattiesburg, MS; SR; Chorale; USM Oratorio Chorus; PRC Rvr Rd Shw Chr Rvr Mgc Ensmbl Pres; PRC Sngrs; Delta Psi Omega; PRC Pres List; Deans List; USM Pres; Assoc Degree Music Educ; Assoc Degree Business; Music Educ; Schl Tchng/Church Music.

**MAGEE, DAVID KEVIN,** Ms St Univ, Miss State, MS; SR; BS; Amercn Radio Relay League 80-; Baptst Stdnt Un 90-; Soc For Advncd Mgt 90-; Data Base Mgt Assoc; MSU Deans List; Deans List 89-90; Im Bsktbl; Bus Info Sys; Sys Anlyst.

**MAGEE, DONNA M,** Jackson St Univ, Jackson, MS; SO; BA; Acctg Soc Bus Mgr; Alpha Lambda Delta; Acctg.

**MAGEE JR, JAMES R,** Univ Of Ms Medical Center, Jackson, MS; FR; DMD; Acad Gen Dntstry; Am Phrmctcl Assc 85-88; Am Stdnt Dntl Assc 90-; Kappa Psi Chpln 85-88; Kappa Epsln Big Bro; Acad Exclnc Schlrshp 85-88; BS Pharm 88; Jr Clg Schlrs Bowl Awrd 85-86; IM Ftbl Sftbl Bsktbl; Dntstry; Orthdrtc.

**MAGEE, JAMIE G,** Alcorn St Univ, Lorman, MS; JR; BA; Intfth Choir 89-; ASU Deans List Schlr; Delta Sigma Theta Sorority Inc; Assist Dean Of Acad Affairs 1; Assist Library 2; Busn; Mgt.**

**MAGEE, KIMBERLY R,** Ms St Univ, Miss State, MS; SO; BS; GAMMA ASB Spirit Comm 88-89; Chi Omega 88-89; Nrsng; RN.

**MAGEE, MELODY R,** Ms Gulf Coast Comm Coll, Perkinston, MS; FR; Microcmptr Spec; Cmptrs; Microcmptrs Spec.

**MAGEE, NITA A,** Alcorn St Univ, Lorman, MS; SO; Pre Nrsg Clb Pres 90-; Nrsg; RN.

**MAGEE, NORMAN P,** City Univ Of Ny City Coll, New York, NY; SR; BS; Soccer V Cptn 88-90; Chemical Engrng.

**MAGEE, PAMELA L,** Fl International Univ, Miami, FL; FR; BS; Univ Hnrs Pgrm 90-; Phi Lambda Beta 90-; Faculty Schlr 90-; FL Undrgrad Schlr 90-; Intrntl Rel; Govt.

**MAGEE, SHARON A,** Livingston Univ, Livingston, AL; SR; BS; IMS 87-; Phi Mu Treas 88-; Spec Educ; Tchr Disabled.

**MAGER, MARLOWE G,** Saint Andrews Presbytrn Coll, Laurinburg, NC; JR; BA; Psych Clb Pres 88-; Wrtrs Forum Dir 88-; Radio Mtl Dir 88-90; Hons Stdnts Assn Flwshp Chr 88-; Hons Pgm 88-F Alpha Chi 90-; Achiev Schlrshp 89-; Deans Lst 88-; Psych/Engl; Rsrch.

**MAGERS, KEVIN L,** Itawamba Comm Coll, Fulton, MS; SO; BA; Phi Theta Kappa 89-; Bsbl 89-; Engrng; Elec Eng.

**MAGGARD, LORNA A,** Morehead St Univ, Morehead, KY; JR; BBA; Acad Hon Awd 90-; Acctg.

**MAGGIO, DEBORAH J,** Univ Of Ga, Athens, GA; SR; BSHE; Im Sftbl 90; Chld/Fmly Dvlpmnt; Fmly Thrpy/Scl Wrk.

**MAGGS, JENNIFER L,** Duquesne Univ, Pittsburgh, PA; SO; BA; Law.

**MAGID, MASON L,** Anne Arundel Comm Coll, Arnold, MD; FR; BEE; IEEE; Math Elec Eng.

**MAGID, MICHELLE,** Ny Univ, New York, NY; GD; DDS; Amer Student Dental Assoc 88-; Elistachius Pres 87-88; Hippocratic Scty 87; Student Coucil; Fauchardian Pres 87-88; Phi Beta Kappa Repres; Schlrs; Deans List 87-; Maurice Saklad Awd 88; Founders Day Awd 89; Alumni Club Schlrshp 89; Dentistry.**

**MAGIE, MARLENE R,** Nova Univ, Ft Lauderdale, FL; GD; MBA; Navy Achvmnt 81; Navy Cmndtn 83; FL Pblc Hlth Assc; St Patrick Catholic Chrch; USN Chief Hosp Corpmen; BS Vaverne Univ 83; Bus Hlth Care; Hlth Care Mgmt.

**MAGILL, BETH ANN,** Indiana Univ Of Pa, Indiana, PA; SR; BED; Oremus Contmpry Chrstn Show Choir 87-; Alph Phi Omega 88-; Educ Hrng Imprd; Educ.

**MAGILL, LUCY E,** Columbia Union Coll, Takoma Park, MD; SR; BS; Phi Theta Kappa 81-82; Phi Beta Lambda 81-82; Cncrnd Wmn Amer Lbbyst 85-86; Metro E Ply Lrn Cntr Bd Dir 90-; Dgtl Equip Corp Mrktng Prncpl Spec 88-; Bus Admn; Bus Mngmnt/Tchng.

**MAGLIACANE, ANGELA E,** Saint Vincents Coll & Seminary, Latrobe, PA; FR; BA; Stdnt Govt/Clss Offcr Sec 90-; STARS 90-; Grass Roots Rlgs Comm Org/Pnst 90-; Deans List 90-; Aerobics 90; English; Prfssr/Lwyr.

**MAGLIO, FRANK J,** Seton Hall Univ, South Orange, NJ; SR; BSB; Beta Gamma Sigma; National Honor Society Of Financial Management Association; Summa Cum Lade; Departmental Honors Citation In Finance; Financial; Fncl Cnsltnt.

**MAGLIONE, LOUIS D,** Univ Of Akron, Akron, OH; SR; BS; Hons Prog 87-; Golden Key 88-; Phi Eta Sigma 88-; Beta Gamma Sigma 90-; Optmst Intl 86-; Euchrstc Mnstr 86-; Yth Bsbl Coach 86-; Galen Roush Meml Schlrshp 88-; Hetnick/Apple/Co James Kausch Meml Schlrshp 90; Acctg/Bus Admin; CPA.

**MAGLOIRE, JOEL G,** Univ Of Rochester, Rochester, NY; SO; BA; Spnsh/Ltn Stdnts Assn Scl Chr 89-90; Delta Upsilon Hsng Mgr 89-; Lngustcs; Univ Prof.

**MAGNAGHI, TAMI A,** Roane St Comm Coll, Harriman, TN; SO; BS; AS 90; Txtls/Apprl Merch; Fash Byr/Merchndsr.

**MAGNER, THERESA M,** Limestone Coll, Gaffney, SC; SR; BS; Crntly Emplyd Trngtn Union SC OPT Anlyst 88-; Assoc 90; Bus Admin; Prod Mgt.

**MAGNES, JACQUELINE Y,** Univ Of Md Baltimore Prof Schl, Baltimore, MD; JR; BS; ASCP 89-; Phi Theta Kappa 89-90; Grad Hnrs Villa Jolie 90; Deans Lst 88-; AA MLT Villa Julie Clg 90; Mdcl Rsrch Tchnlgy.

**MAGNET, MARCUS,** City Univ Of Ny City Coll, New York, NY; JR; BS; Caudeuceaus Scty 88-; Amer Museum Natl History Assoc Mbr; Acad Pref Prep 88-; MBRS Resch Assist 90-; Biology; Med.

**MAGNUSEN, MARGARET A,** Wilmington Coll, New Castle, DE; JR; BS; Delta Epsilon Rho 89-90; Bsn Admin; Info Systms.

**MAGNUSON, KARIN L,** Brown Univ, Providence, RI; FR; BSE; Film Scty 90-; Bruin Clb 90-; Biomedical Engineering.

**MAGOON, INDU,** Georgetown Univ, Washington, DC; JR; BSBA; Acctng Soc; Intl Rels Clb; South Asian Clb; Phi Eta Sigma; Inst On Comp Pol/Econ Systems; Acctng; Law.

**MAGOON, SANJEEV,** Georgetown Univ, Washington, DC; FR; BSBA; Acctng Scty 90-; S Asian Clb 90-; Indian Chrch 90-; Acctng; Business Adm.

**MAGOS, ZENY C,** Glassboro St Coll, Glassboro, NJ; JR; Stdnt Govt 88-90; Res Asst 90-; Actvts Bd 88-; Deans List 88-; Lib Arts; Jrnlsm.

**MAGOWAN, BARTON J,** Memphis St Univ, Memphis, TN; FR; BA; Phi Eta Sigma; Mktng; Pub Rltns.

**MAGOWITZ, BETH E,** Juniata Coll, Huntingdon, PA; SO; BSW; Outrch 89-; Big Bro/Sis; Adopt-A-Grandparent; Sociology; Social Wrkr.

**MAGRATH, JULIE E,** Oh Wesleyan Univ, Delaware, OH; JR; BA; Kappa Alpha Theta Prchsng 90; Intrnatl Stdnt Abrd Ireland 90; Sclgy Hist; Crmnl Soc Wrk.

**MAGRINI JR, THOMAS W,** Capitol Coll, Laurel, MD; SR; BSEE; Math/Elctrncs Tutor 89-90; Alpha Chi 89-; Tau Alpha Pi 89-; MCI Schlrshp 90-; MD Schlrshp 89-; Outstdng Stdnt Emp Awd 89-90; IEEE 90-; Stst Engnr 90-; AAEET Capitol Coll 88; Elctrcl Engnrng; Cnsltng.**

**MAGTIRA-LOPEZ, MARJORIE A,** Fl International Univ, Miami, FL; GD; FTA 89-90; BS 90.

**MAGUIRE, JANET C,** George Mason Univ, Fairfax, VA; SR; BS; Kappa Delta Pi 90-; Assoc For Chldhd Ed Intrntls Confrnc Presntr 90; Early Ed.

**MAGUIRE, KEVIN C,** Belmont Coll, Nashville, TN; SR; BBA; Aquinas Jr Coll SGA VP 89-90; Intl Stdnt Assn Lgsltv Rep 90-; Phi Theta Kappa Pres 89-; Tennis Team 90-; Bus Mgmt; Intl Mgmt.

**MAGUIRE, KEVIN P,** Merrimack Coll, North Andover, MA; JR; BA; Vrsty Ftbl 88-89; Spec Nds Cmp 90-; Bsn/Fnce; Fncl Anlyst.

**MAGUIRE, KRISTINE A,** Pa St Univ Delaware Cty Cmps, Media, PA; FR; Business; Mrktng.

**MAGUIRE, MARY E,** Wv Northern Comm Coll, Wheeling, WV; FR; CERT; Ordr Of Estrn Str Esthr Ada 83-; Dghtrs Of Nile 89-; PTA Pkvw Elem Schl Pres 78; Whlng Rnbw Advsry Brd Awrds Chrmn 86-; Amer Rd Crss VIP Bld Dnr 88-; WV St Life PTA 77-; Ohio Cnty Life PTA 77-; Srgcl Tech; Physcns Asst Cert.

**MAGUIRE, NANCY J,** Mount Saint Mary Coll, Newburgh, NY; JR; BA; Psych/Engl; Fmly Cnslng.

**MAGUIRE, SARAH E,** Univ Of Vt & St Agri Coll, Burlington, VT; FR; BS; Res Hl Govt Treas 90-; Phi Eta Sigma; Dns Lst; IM Vlybl; Bsn Admn; Hmn Rsc/Acctng.

**MAGYAR, CATHRYN A,** Mount Aloysius Jr Coll, Cresson, PA; SO; AS; Medical Asstnt Club Rec Sec 89-; Madrigal Singers 89-; Specl Olympics Chrprsn 89-; Medical Assistant.

**MAHADEO, HARNARINE,** De Tech & Comm Coll At Dover, Dover, DE; FR; Deltech Ambassador 90-; Trinidad Fiobag Air Traffic Contrlrs Assn 88; Intl Fed Air Traffic Cntrllrs Assn 88; Elect Tech 88-; Cert Air Trffc Serv Scl 79; Cert John Donaldson Tech Inst 88.

**MAHADEVAN, KARTHIKEYAN,** Univ Of Ms Main Cmps, University, MS; GD; PHD; Phi Kappa Phi 88-; Sigma Xi 88-; IEEE Stdt 88-; Fllwshp Univ Mssppi 86-; BE Univ Madras India 80; MS Indian Insit Tech Madras India 83; Electrical Engnrng; Research/Educator.

**MAHAFFEY, JANET E,** Univ Of Sc At Columbia, Columbia, SC; FR; BA; Theatre; Kappa Kappa Gamma Cncl Dlgt; Arts/Crafts Hildrns Home; Deans Lst; Theatre/Broadcast Jrnlsm.

**MAHAFFEY, LINDA SUE,** Univ Of Nc At Asheville, Asheville, NC; FR; BS; Phi Eta Sigma; IM Sftbl; Indus Dsgn.

**MAHAFFEY, RUSSELL K,** Univ Of Sc At Spartanburg, Spartanburg, SC; JR; BA; Hist Clb; New Prospect Baptist Church; Ftbl Coach; Hist/Scndry Educ; Tchng/Coaching.

**MAHAFFEY, SYLVIA A,** Indiana Univ Of Pa, Indiana, PA; SO; BED; Educ; Sec Engl Tchr.

**MAHAN, FOREST EDWARD,** Coll Of Charleston, Charleston, SC; SO; BA; Drug Awrnss 90-; FCA 90-; Sprts Wrtr Nwspr 90-; Big Bro 89-; Statstcn Vlybl 90-; Hstry; Prfssr/Lwyr.

**MAHAN, KAREN E,** Union Coll, Barbourville, KY; JR; BA; BLTN 89-; Gamma Beta Phi 90-; Iota Sigma Nu 90-; Prnt Mdl 85-87; Admin Asst The Holder Grp Tampa Fl 85-86; Barnett Bnk Of Tampa 81-85; ACTG/BUAD/CIS; CPA.

**MAHAN, KIMBERLY K,** Providence Coll, Providence, RI; SO; BA; Ski Clb 89-; Sprts Eqpmnt Mngr 89-; Vol Lctr Cmps Chpl 89-; Deans Lst 89-; Pres Cert; Vrsty Sftbl 89-; Acctg; CPA/LAW.

**MAHAN, SHARON A,** Mobile Coll, Mobile, AL; JR; BS; AAYC; Outstanding Student; Bible Drill Leader Smithtown Baptist Church; Sunday School Teacher 88-; Educ Elem/Early Childhood; Teaching.

**MAHAN, STANLEY P,** Va Commonwealth Univ, Richmond, VA; SR; BS; Grad Cum Laude; Study Abrd Pgm-Univ London; Bus Admin/Mgmt.

**MAHAN, WILLIAM C,** Univ Of Sc At Columbia, Columbia, SC; FR; Drm Rsdnc Hl Gov 2nd Fl Pres 90-; Wuse Radio Sta DJ Wrtr Stu Nwspr 90-; Pr Cndct Brd.

**MAHANEY, TRACY L,** Ringling School Of Art, Sarasota, FL; SO; BFA; Am Soc Intr Dsgnrs Sec 90-; Intr Dsgn; Intr Archtctrl Dsgn.

**MAHAR, JOHN P,** Clarkson Univ, Potsdam, NY; FR; BS; Engr/Mngmnt.

**MAHARAJ, ANTHONY K,** Broward Comm Coll, Ft Lauderdale, FL; JR; DPM; Intrntnl Clb 89-; Wght Lftng Clb 88-; Spnch Clb 88-; Phi Theta Kappa Pblc Rltns 90-; Math Sci Acdmc Awd 89-; Prsdnt Lst Awd 88-; Broward Cllg Sccr 90-; AA Broward Comm Clg 90; Podiatric Med.

**MAHARAJ, JOHN,** Univ Of Miami, Coral Gables, FL; SO; LDP; Alpha Chi Rho Soc Coord 85-87; Intrnshp/Langan Eng Fld Inspctr 88-90; Lnd Plning/Dvlpmnt.

**MAHARAJ, RAVITA,** Howard Univ, Washington, DC; SR; BSW; AFSW Pres 90-; Golden Key; Achvmnt Acad; Dns Hnr Lst 89-; D C Hotline Vol 90-; H S Tchr 85-89; Residential Cnslr 90-; BA Univ Manitoba Winnipeg 84; S W Cert Univ West Indies Trinidad 89; Scl Wrk.

**MAHARAJ, ROGER W,** Broward Comm Coll, Ft Lauderdale, FL; GD; BS; Frnch Clb Le Cercle Defrancais VP 90-; Chlng Yth Mntr 90-; Phi Theta Pblc Rltns 90; AA 90; Sciences; Physical Thrpst.

**MAHATEKAR, PARAG A,** Birmingham Southern Coll, Birmingham, AL; SO; BS; Triangle Club 90-; Alpha Lambda Delta 90-; Phi Eta Sigma 90-; Chi Sigma Chi 90-; IM Ftbl Sccr Bsktbl Sftbl 90-; EMT Basic 90; Pre Med Science; Medicine MD.

**MAHAVADI, SRIKANTH,** Univ Of The Dist Of Columbia, Washington, DC; JR; BS; NSS Mbr 85-86; Beta Kappa Chi Mbr 90-; Natl Sci Fndtn 90-; Bio Rscrh Asst 90-; B Sc Kakatiya Univ 83-86; Med.

**MAHER, BRIAN D,** Le Moyne Coll, Syracuse, NY; JR; BA; Fndr Pres Vlybl Clb; Wrtr Nwsppr; Stdnt Cncl Fr Hrng Fclty; Phi Alpha Theta; USAA All Amer Schlr Awrd 90-; Vlybl; Hstry.

**MAHER, CANDACE CHRISTINE,** Univ Of Sc At Columbia, Columbia, SC; SO; BA; Cmps Cltn Lit 90-; Hmcmng Comm 89-90; Scuba Clb 89-; Kappa Alpha Theta 90-; Finance; Bnkng/Invstmnt.

**MAHER, CHRISTINA E,** Marshall University, Huntington, WV; JR; MBA; Gamma Beta Ofc Rtl 89-; Elem Edctn; Spcl Edctn.

**MAHER, COLLEEN M,** Radford Univ, Radford, VA; SR; BS; Catholic Stdnt Assn 87-; Soc Collegiate Jrnlsts 89-90; Sr Cllng Cmpgn Cls Agnt; Alpha Phi Omega Pldgmstr 87-; Jrnlsm.

**MAHER, MAUREEN E,** City Univ Of Ny Baruch Coll, New York, NY; SR; BBA Baruch Coll 91; Adv Major/Intl Mrktng Minor; Adv Field.

**MAHER, MIRIAM R,** Coll Of Health Sci Stony Brook, Stony Brook, NY; GD; MD; Med Stdnts ACT Edctr 90-; Rehab Vol Long Island Coll Hosp 87-88; BS 90; Saul Lyons Mem Schlrshp Gisses Awd 88-; Magna Cum Laude CUNY BA Dns List; Brklyn Coll Cls 33 Schlrshp Otstndng Acad Achvmnt; IM Sftbl; Prof Mdrn Dncr 80-85; Med/Orthpdcs.

**MAHER, PAUL M,** Rutgers St Univ At Camden, Camden, NJ; GD; BS; Mgmt; Sls.

**MAHER, TREVOR ANDREW,** Westminster Coll, New Wilmingtn, PA; SO; BA; Rpblcns Tres 90-; Sgm Phi Epsln Chpln 90-; Fin; Fincl Cnsltnt.

**MAHESH, GAYATHRI,** Sinclair Comm Coll, Dayton, OH; JR; BS; Hindu Cmnty Orgnztn 86-; Pel Grants Ohio Schlrshp Grant; Fed Asain Indians Orgnztn 89-; Scty Bank N A Cstmr Serv Rep; B A English U Madras India 86; A A Cmptr 89; Finance; Banking.

**MAHESWARI, SUNITA,** Fl Atlantic Univ, Boca Raton, FL; GD; MBA; Proj Intern NIIT India Spprt Fclty 88-89; Grad Tch Rsrch Asst Mktg Fla Univ 90-; BSC Physica Univ Of Calcutta 87; Diplma Systms Mgt NIIT 89.

**MAHLE, CHARLOTTE A,** Va Commonwealth Univ, Richmond, VA; SO; BS; Golden Key; Clg Of Hmnties Sci Awd; Parhamcy; Phrmcst.

**MAHLER, CHRISTOPHER D,** Union Coll, Barbourville, KY; JR; Deans Lst; Acctg Awrd; Physcs Awrd; Ftbll; Acctg Comp; CPA Comp Prgrmmr.

**MAHLER, GENE G,** Saint Elizabeth Hosp Sch Nurs, Utica, NY; SR; AAS; Chors/Fdltns 79-81; NYSAT NYS Anrml Tech 79-81; Nrs Asst Cert; AAS Eqn Stds; AAS Anml Hlth Tech; EMT Bsc; Nrs Asst; AAS Cazenaia Coll 79; AAS SUNY Delhi 81; Nrsng RN; BA.

**MAHLER, SAMANTHA A,** Univ Of Southern Ms, Hattiesburg, MS; JR; BA; Newman Clb; Alpha Lamda Delta; Phi Eta Sigma; Fine Arts/Graph Comm; Illustrator.

**MAHMOOD, AKHTAR H,** Edinboro Univ Of Pa, Edinboro, PA; SO; Cmptr Sci; Physcs; Phlsphy; Intl Std Asc; ACM; Stf Wrtr Edtr; Radio Show; Intl Comm Actv; Work Stdy; Cert Spr Acad Achv; Sccr/Png Png/Chs/Crckt; Cmptr Sci/Math/Physcs; Tch.

**MAHMOOD, NASIR,** City Univ Of Ny Baruch Coll, New York, NY; MBA; Intl Bus 77-85; Finance/Intl Bus.

**MAHMUD, MALEEHA,** George Mason Univ, Fairfax, VA; JR; BA; Mktg; Bsn.

**MAHOLMES, MAVIS Y,** Paine Coll, Augusta, GA; SR; Psychology Clb 89-90; Intrn Cmmnty Mntl Hlth Cntr 90; Mngr Meris Wmns Bsktbl 86-88; BA Paine Clg 90; Psychology; Chld Psychlgst.

**MAHON, CARRIE J,** Western New England Coll, Springfield, MA; SR; Schl Art/Lit Mag Art Editor 88-; Sprngfld Schl Vol Tutor 88-90; Dns Lst 87; Skookum Award Acad Stndrs/Cmnty Svc 90; Outstndng Cover Award 90; Review Amer Schlstc Press Assn 90; Intrnshp Chldrns Stdy Home; BA; Psych; Art Educ.

**MAHON, REBECCA L,** Strayer Coll, Washington, DC; JR; BS; Cert; Info Syst; Cmptr Trnng.

**MAHONE, REBECCA F,** Va Commonwealth Univ, Richmond, VA; FR; BA; Awana Leader 86; Phi Eta Sigma: Pres Schlrshp; Engl; Scndry Educ.

**MAHONE, TONYA DIANE,** Tougaloo Coll, Tougaloo, MS; FR; Gospel Choir 90-; Alpha Lambda Delta; CBS Schlr; Engl; Law/Coll Prof.

**MAHONEY, BRIAN S,** Duke Univ, Durham, NC; FR; Navy ROTC 90-; Dorm Cncl Prog Chrmn 90-; Phi Delta Theta; IM Sftbl And Vlybl 90-; Blgy; Mlclr Blgst.

**MAHONEY, KEITH M,** Oh Univ, Athens, OH; JR; IEEE; IM Ftbl/Vlybl/Sftbl; Alpha Lambda Delta 88-; Tau Beta Pi; Golden Key; Elec Eng.

**MAHONEY, KEITH P,** Manhattan Coll, Bronx, NY; SR; MS; Wtr Plltn Cntrl Fed 89-; ASCE 89-90; Phi Rho Pi 88-; BS; Envrnmntl Eng.

**MAHONEY, PATRICIA L,** Newbury Coll, Brookline, MA; FR; BA; Fund Raiser Am Lung Assoc 90; Vol Braintree Hosp 89-90; Underwriter Ins Co 70-84; Aerobic Instr Webbs Pro Fitness Norwell Ma 83-; Paralegal; Law.

**MAHONEY, RONDA M,** Univ Of Sc At Columbia, Columbia, SC; JR; BA; DSS Child Care; Outstndng Scrty Prsnl Desk Asst Cert Apprctn; Soclgy; Soc Work.

**MAHONY, MELISA A,** Lesley Coll, Cambridge, MA; SO; BED; Erly Chldhd Educ; Teaching.

**MAHOOD, PATRICIA K,** Coll Of New Rochelle, New Rochelle, NY; FR; BA; Hosptlty Clb 90-; Elem/Spec Educ; Tchng.

**MAHURIN, JENNIFER A,** Marshall University, Huntington, WV; JR; BBA; WV Scty CPAS; Acctg Clb 90-; Pnhllnc Treas 88-90; Gamma Beta Phi 89; Alpha Xi Delta Treas 88-90; Acctg.

**MAI, FRANK C,** Northeastern Univ, Boston, MA; JR; BA; Cncl For Univ Pgms-Lectures Cmte Chrprsn 88-; Hons Pgm 87-; Beta Gamma Sigma; Pr Awd; Beta Gamma Sigma Awd 89; Bus Mgmnt.**

**MAI, HUE-PHUONG,** Al A & M Univ, Normal, AL; JR; Bus.

**MAI, LAN T,** Columbus Coll Of Art & Design, Columbus, OH; JR; BFA; Capt Sftbl Team; Ilstrtn; Commrcl Artst.

**MAIBACH, MARK W,** Univ Of Akron, Akron, OH; SR; BSA; Gold Key; Beta Gamma Sigma; Acctg.

**MAICHLE, DEBORAH A,** Wilmington Coll, New Castle, DE; SR; BSN; Amer Nrs Assoc; Amer Soc Hypertension; Assoc Clncl Pharmclgy; Dipl Nrsg Sch Wilmington 72; Nrsg; Psych.

**MAIDEN, AKEBA HASANI,** Kent St Univ Geauga Cmps, Burton Twp, OH; JR; BS; UNCF Fnd Rsr 86-; Cncr Soc 86-; Lthrn Wmns Mssnry Leg Vol 86-; Ebony Achvmnt Awd 89-; Deans Lst 90; NAACP; NCNW; Leg Wmn Vtrs; Rstrnt Asst Mgr 88-89; Nghtclb Admnstrtr 86-89; Wtrs 84-86; Flght Attndnt 70-81; Scl Sciences; Cnslng Psychlgst.

**MAIER, DAVID W,** James Madison University, Harrisonburg, VA; SR; BS; Golden Key 89-; Deans Schlr Awd 90; Cert Of Rcgntn 90-; AS No VA Comm Coll 86; Psychology.

**MAIER, NATALIE J,** Western Ky Univ, Bowling Green, KY; JR; BS; Univ Cntr Brd Cncrt Comm Co Chrmn 88-; Grls Clb Vol 88-; Phi Eta Sigma 88-; Beta Gamma Sigma; Phi Kappa Phi; Beta Alpa Psi Pldg Ed 90-; Chi Omega Pres 88-; Internshp 88-; Prsdnts Schlr 88-; Acctg Bus; CPA.

**MAIER JR, ROBERT WILLARD,** Wv Univ, Morgantown, WV; SO; BA; US Chss Assoc; Frmnt Chss Clb; Hnrs Prgm; Umpr Lttl Lg 87-; Cheat Lake Bsktbll Sckprhgh Scr SAT ACT 90; Math Fld Dy; Cty Math 90; John Hopkins Math Awrds 90; Chmcl Eng.

**MAIER, SHEILA M,** Tuskegee Univ, Tuskegee Inst, AL; GD; DVM; Amer Animal Hosp 87-; Amer Vet Med Assoc 87-; Amer Assoc Bovine Practnrs Secr 87-; Phi Zeta 90-; Merk Awd 90-; Dns Lst 88-; IM Sftbl; BA Glassboro State Clg 86; AAS Gloucester Co Clg 84; Vet Med; Vet Dr.

**MAIGE, LOUIS A,** Central Fl Comm Coll, Ocala, FL; FR; AA; Prof Fir Fghtrs VP 87; Fire Dept Lt 87-; Fire Sci.

**MAIGNAN, MURIEL,** Georgetown Univ, Washington, DC; JR; Lctre Fnd 89-; Crrbn Cltre Cir VP 90; Mrktng Scty 90-; Fndtn Ttrng Prog 90; Inrds Intrn At Chbb And Sn Co 90-; Intrnatl Mgmt; Mrktng.

**MAIKOWSKI, SHEILA CARROLL,** S U N Y Coll Of Tech At Frmgdl, Farmingdale, NY; Part Time Matriculated Stdnt Inerly Chldhd Ed; Cert Miller Schl Secretarial 58; Erly Chldhd; Work Pre-School Envrmnt.

**MAILHOT, ROSE E,** Albertus Magnus Coll, New Haven, CT; SR; BA; Spnsh Clb Pres 89-; Engls Clb 90-; Sigma Delta Pi 90-; Phi Sigma Iota; Chthlc Coll Ntnl Hnr Scty; Intrnshp Yl Nw Hvn Hsptl; Englsh; Wrtng/Pblc Rltns.

**MAILLET, CHRISTY L,** Saint Josephs Coll, Windham, ME; FR; BA; Drama 90-; Stdnt Gov Hall Cncl Rep 90-; Spr Kds 90-; Sndy Schl Tchr 90-; Engl Awd; Hist; Law.

**MAILLOUX, JASON R,** Coll Of Charleston, Charleston, SC; SO; BS; Sigma Chi 90-; Sccr Leag 89-; Hons 89-; Deans Lst 89-; IM Sprts 89-; Pharm.

**MAIMONE, SANDRA M,** Castleton St Coll, Castleton, VT; SO; BS; Theater Dept Prod Our Town; Cmnctns/Mass Media; TV Film Dir.

**MAIN, TINA M,** Univ Of Southern Ms, Hattiesburg, MS; FR; BA; Dixie Darlins 90-; Gamma Beta Phi 90-; Dns Lst 90-; Micro Bio; Pediatrican.

**MAINA, DANIELA,** Univ Of Ct, Storrs, CT; SO; BS; Dorm Treas 90-; UCONN Ag Recgntyn Awrd 90-; Amer Soc Animal Sci Schlrshp 90-; IM Sports 89-; Animal Sci; Research.

**MAINA, MICHAEL P,** Slippery Rock Univ, Slippery Rock, PA; SR; BS; Pa HPERD 89-; Delta Psi Kappa 91-; Res Advsr 90-; Asst Lfgurd Instr; Var Ftbl/Clb Lacrosse 87-; Cert 89; Cert 90; Phys Educ/Hlth; Tch.

**MAINE, CANUTE O,** City Univ Of Ny Baruch Coll, New York, NY; SR; Bus Cncl 89; Beta Gamma Sigma; AAS Kingsborough Cmnty Clg 89; Fin Inv; CFO.

**MAINER, STACEY A,** Southern Coll Of Tech, Marietta, GA; SR; BS; Pr Fcltr 90-; Rd Dsc Jcky 88; NSBE 86-88; Alpha Phi Alpha Ax 88-; Indstrl Eng Tchnlgy.

**MAINES, LISA A,** Oh Dominican Coll, Columbus, OH; JR; BA; UFACW 89-90; Dns Lst 88-; Guide Prspctv Stdnts Ohio Dominican 89-90; ODC Acad Schlrshp 88-91; Engl/Humanities Tutor Dev Cntr; Engl; Mstrs Degree Educ.

**MAINHART, LORENA S,** Mount Aloysius Jr Coll, Cresson, PA; FR; OTA; Occup Ther.

**MAINIERI, MARIETTA,** Univ Of Miami, Coral Gables, FL; SR; BA; Goldn Key 90-; All Amer Schlr; Poltcl Sci/Art Hstry; Law.

**MAINOR, BRIAN A,** Valdosta St Coll, Valdosta, GA; JR; BED; Erly Chldhd; Educ Admn.

**MAINOR, MARY S,** Tuskegee Univ, Tuskegee Inst, AL; SO; BS; Soc Wrk Alnc Orgnztn 89-; Georgia Clb 90-; Hon Roll 89-90; Soc Wrk Sc Wrkr Jvnl Stng.

**MAINS, TAMMI A,** Univ Of Cincinnati, Cincinnati, OH; SR; BA; Natl Sci Tchrs Assn 90-; Cmprhnsve Comm Chld Cr 89-; Ed; Tchr.

**MAINVILLE, TAMARA E,** Longwood Coll, Farmville, VA; SR; BS; VEA; Sigma Sigma Sigma 88-; IM Bsktbl 87-88; Earth Sci/Geog; Tchr.

**MAIROSE, MARY A,** Northern Ky Univ, Highland Hts, KY; SR; BA; Phi Alpha Theta Sec 90-; Outstndg Wmn Grad; History; Tchng.

**MAISONET, LADDY M,** Columbus Coll Of Art & Design, Columbus, OH; SO; BA; Chrch Grp Ldr 90-; Schlrshp; Vsl Arts; Ilstrtn.

**MAITA, DENISE A,** Glassboro St Coll, Glassboro, NJ; JR; BA; La Crosse 89-; Mgr Bsktbl 90-; Jstc; Law.

**MAITA, RICHARD J,** Univ Of Miami, Coral Gables, FL; JR; BBA; Pre Lega Soc 88-; Stu Amer; Sprtsfst 88-; Bus Law; Law.

**MAITE, CASAIDEIRO STELLA,** Inter Amer Univ Pr Hato Rey, Hato Rey, PR; GD; BA; Ftr Scl Wrk Org 89-90; Pres Clsrm Yng Bus 86; Ortega/Gasset Ex Alumni 89-; Assoc Scrd Hrt Prsh Org Pres 83-88; Hon Soc; Scl Wrk; Pblc Adm.

**MAITER, MICHAEL R,** Ny Univ, New York, NY; FR; BS; NYNEX Cstmr Serv Rep; NY Univ Cert Prcssr; Acctng.

**MAITLAND, AMY R,** Lesley Coll, Cambridge, MA; FR; Commuter Club; Edn.

**MAITLAND, ANGELA S,** Christopher Newport Coll, Newport News, VA; SR; BA; Psychlgy.

**MAITLAND, STEPHEN R,** Mt Saint Marys Coll & Seminary, Emmitsburg, MD; SR; BA; Amrcn Pltcl Sci Assoc 89-; Grg Hnry Mls 89-; Pi Sigma Alpha 90-; Plntry Scty 88-; Amrcn Assoc Advncmnt Sci 88-; Poltcl Sci.

**MAJ, AGNIESZKA A,** Christopher Newport Coll, Newport News, VA; JR; BA; Frnch.

**MAJBOOR, BELQIS M,** Fl International Univ, Miami, FL; JR; BS; Phi Theta Kappa 87-88; AA MDCC 88; Structrs Auto CAD/ENBRNMNT; Engr.

**MAJCHRZAK, LISA MARIE,** Bryant Stratton Bus Inst Roch, Rochester, NY; FR; Bryant/Stratton Med Clb; Ogisto 86-; Native Amer Culturl Ctr 86-; Med Asst.

**MAJERIK, THERESA J,** Faulkner St Jr Coll, Bay Minette, AL; FR; BA; Phi Theta Kappa 90; Proprietor Res/Cmrcl Clng Serv 86-; Bus Admn.

**MAJETT, VERONDA D,** Comm Coll Of Philadelphia, Philadelphia, PA; FR; Sec Sci/Bus Educ; Tchr.

**MAJEWSKI, KARI A,** Bethany Coll, Bethany, WV; FR; BA; Discpls Stdnt Fllwshp 90-; Vars Swm Tm 90-; Res Asst 90-; Phi Mu; Dscpl Stdnt Fllwshp; Swm Tm; Relg Stdies; Intl Mssnry Wrk.

**MAJID, ANEESA S,** Univ Of Rochester, Rochester, NY; JR; BA; Meridn Soc; Adm Intrn Stdnt Intrwr; All Camps Jdcl Cncl Chf Just 90-; Rel/Bio; Med.

**MAJIED, CHRISTINE T,** Va Western Comm Coll, Roanoke, VA; GD; AAS; Alliance Exclnc Acad Exclnc Awd 90; Tlnt Rstr; Tns Bwlng Cptn 90; Comp Prgrmmg; Comp Info Syst; Syst Anlyst.

**MAJOR, ISHMEAL,** Univ Of Sc At Columbia, Columbia, SC; FR; Gamma Beta Phi Soc 90-; Blgy; Med.

**MAJOR, JOHN D,** S U N Y Coll At Fredonia, Fredonia, NY; SR; Econ Clb 90; IMS 88-; Dns Lst; Lacrosse Capt 88-; BS; Bsn Adm; Mgmt.

**MAJOR, STEVEN,** Yeshiva Univ, New York, NY; GD; MBA; Undrgrad Nwspr Sr Ed 87-90; Sigma Delta Rho 87-89; Alpha Epsilon Delta Sec 87-89; Engl Hons Soc Sigma Tau Delta 88-90; Deans Lst 87-90; Roosevelt Flwshp Hebrew U Jerusalem 89; IM Bsktbl 87-88; Fncl Anlyst 90-; Engl BA; Invstmnt Bnkg/Grad Schl.

**MAJORS, CHARLES E,** Duquesne Univ, Pittsburgh, PA; FR; BA; Math Clb 90-; Math.

**MAJORS, JOHN M,** Univ Of Tn At Knoxville, Knoxville, TN; SR; BS; Sigma Mu Alpha Stat Soc 89-; E T Chptr Amer Stat Assn 89-; Beta Gamma Sigma 89-; Gamma Beta Phi 89-; Phi Kappa Phi; Torchbr; Natl Alum Assn Schlrshp Stat 87-; Dept Schlrshp; M A Hanna Corp Schlrshp 90; IM Ftbl/Bsktbl; Stat/Math; Actrl Sci.

**MAJORS, LEAH W,** Memphis St Univ, Memphis, TN; SR; BA; Nwsppr Frlnce Rprtr 87; Nws Edit 89; Cpy Edit 89-; Svnnh Crr Intrn; Jrnlsm.

**MAJORS, SUSAN L,** Univ Of Cin R Walters Coll, Blue Ash, OH; SO; Phi Theta Kappa; Radiologic Tchnolgies; Ultra Snd Tchncn.

**MAK, GRACE C,** Bloomfield Coll, Bloomfield, NJ; FR; BA; Bus Admn.

**MAK, JEFFREY P,** City Univ Of Ny Baruch Coll, New York, NY; SR; BBA; Bus To Bus Mktg Soc Pres 89-; Amer Mktg Assn; Beta Gamma Sigma 90-; Mktg.

**MAK, PO H,** S U N Y Coll Of Tech At Frmgdl, Farmingdale, NY; SO; AAS; Advrtsng Art/Dsgn; Pblshng/Grphc Dsgn/Photo.

**MAK, SO HAN,** Fl International Univ, Miami, FL; JR; BA; AA Miami-Dade Comm Coll 90; Acctng.

**MAKAR, ANTHONY JOHN,** Univ Of Sc At Columbia, Columbia, SC; SR; BA; Rugby Clb 87-; Pi Kappa Phi Pldg Cls Pres 87-88; Vice Archn VP 90; PUSCH Play Units Svrly Hndcpd 87-; Indpndt Stdy Asstntshp 89-90; Indstrl Psychlgst.

**MAKAR, JOHN W,** Fordham Univ, Bronx, NY; FR; BA; Ukrainian Clb Pres 89-; Ukr Amrcn Yth Assn Sec 90-; Ukr Stdnts Assn Mykola Mikhonousky VP 89-; Smmr Cmp Cnslr Scnd Cmmnd 88-; Nwsppr Intrn 89-90; Viceo Prdctns Asst Mgr Intrn 90-; Jrnlsm.

**MAKAR, TAMALA S,** Georgian Court Coll, Lakewood, NJ; JR; BA; SG 87-89; Psych Cl 90; Phi Theta Kappa 87-; Sigma Delta Mu 88-; Psi Chi 90-; AA Hon Ocean County Colg 89; Psych; Elem Ed; Elem Schl Tchr.

**MAKATURA, TINA M,** Marywood Coll, Scranton, PA; FR; BFA; St Lukes Art Soc Clb 90-; Art Illustr.

**MAKAY, CHERIE D,** Univ Of Nc At Charlotte, Charlotte, NC; JR; BA; Psychlgy Clb; Crim Just Assn; Psi Chi; Sigma Kappa Corr Sec 90-; Rel Inc; Psychlgy; Crim Psychlgy.

**MAKHULI, MARK J,** Univ Of Rochester, Rochester, NY; SR; Soc For Undergrad Microbio 90-; Frshmn Comndtn List 87-88; Deans List 88-; Sigma Alpha Mu 89-; Varsty Bsktbl 88-; BS; Microbio; Medcn Medcl Sch At NYU.

**MAKINEN, ERIC W,** Univ Of Rochester, Rochester, NY; SO; BA; Std Govt 90-; Army ROC 89-; Rugby 90-; Pol Sci; Pol Anlys.

**MAKOUS, ELIZABETH ANN,** Univ Of Fl, Gainesville, FL; GD; BS; Preprofessnl Serv Orgntzn 84-87; Alpha Epsilon Delta 85-87; Pi Beta Phi 84; BS Univ FL 87; MESS Univ FL 90; Neurobilgl Sciences/Exercise Physlgy; Phy Trpy.

**MAKOWIEC, WILLIAM E,** Springfield Tech Comm Coll, Springfield, MA; SO; BSME; Fclty Awrd 90; Drftsmn Tell Tool; Assc; Mech Eng.

**MAKRANIN, MELISSA M,** Comm Coll Algny Co Algny Cmps, Pittsburgh, PA; JR; BED; Day Care Cntr 89; Abuse Cntr Wmn/Chldrn 90; Chld Dvlpmnt; Tchg.

**MAKRIS, GERASIMOS,** Hellenic Coll/Holy Cross, Brookline, MA; GD; MDIV; BA Forham U 89; Theo; Wrk Chrch.

**MAKRIS, HARRY,** City Univ Of Ny Baruch Coll, New York, NY; SO; BBA; Accntng.

**MAKUCH, LAURA L,** Univ Of Med & Dentistry Of Nj, Newark, NJ; GD; MS; BS Rutgers Univ 86; Phys Therapy.

**MAKUPSON JR, LEMUEL B,** Central St Univ, Wilberforce, OH; JR; Deans Lst 89-; Cub/Boy Scouts Comm; Miami Vly Cnsl Chrmn 88-; Real Esteate Brkr 89-; Quality Assurance Evaluator; AAS Sinclair Comm Clg 89; Pol Sci/Pblc Admn; Law Schl.

**MALANGA, DONNA M,** George Mason Univ, Fairfax, VA; SR; BA; Early Educ; Teach.

**MALATESTA, ANGELA M,** Kent St Univ Stark Cmps, North Canton, OH; FR; BA; Hons Clg 90-.

**MALAVE, BRENDA L,** Univ Of Pr Cayey Univ Coll, Cayey, PR; JR; BA; Bsn Adm; Law.

**MALAVE, MARIA G,** Inter Amer Univ Pr Barranquita, Barranquitas, PR; JR; Consejo De Estdnts Vcl 90-; Cmt Mdl St Assn Rep 90-; Prtncnte Al Cuadro De Hon 90-; Prmr Prmo Fstvl De Las Flores 84-90; Prmr Prmo Coop San Jose Fstvl De Chiringas 90.

**MALBURG, MICHELLE M,** Eckerd Coll, St Petersburg, FL; SR; Dorm Pres-Gov Rep 89-90; Nu Liasion To Admnstrn Rep 90-; Academic Afrs Comm Mbr 90-; Pinellas Cnty Schl Vlntr 87-88; Jordan Park Vlntr 88-90; Intern To Youth & Family Connection 90-; BA; Human Dvlpmnt Serv; Counseling Psychology.

**MALCOLM, DENIS M,** Hillsborough Comm Coll, Tampa, FL; SR; AS; Nuclr Med Clb VP 89-; Comp Cnsltnt 85-89; BA Fordhm Univ 72; Nuclr Med Tech.

**MALCOLM, FREDERICK,** Univ Of The Dist Of Columbia, Washington, DC; JR; AA; Lgl Asst.

**MALCOLM, KENNETH D,** Christopher Newport Coll, Newport News, VA; SO; Blgy.

**MALCOLM, LISA E,** Limestone Coll, Gaffney, SC; FR; BA; U S Achvmnt Acad; Assn Of Legal Sec 90-; Legal Asst 86-; Bus Mngmnt.

**MALCOLM, RONALD I,** Gallaudet Univ, Washington, DC; GD; Cncl Excptnl Chldrn Pres 89-; Kns Cmsn Fr Df Vc Chrmn 90-; Rly Cntr Fr Df Chrmn 90-; Prsdntl Schlr 89-; Kappa Delta Pi 90-; Ntl Assoc Fstr Prnts 87-; Amrcn Soc Df Chldrn 86-; A G Bl Assoc 86-; Rsrch Grnt 90-; Tchr Of Th Yr Cec 90-; Cnslng & Gdnc; Spcl Edctn Admnstrtn.

**MALDONADO CORTES, LENORA,** Caribbean Univ, Bayamon, PR; SR; BA; Clb Marriage Sec 88-89; AD Exe Sec 79; Cmrcl Ed; MBA.

**MALDONADO RIVERA, ANA L,** Inter Amer Univ Pr Hato Rey, Hato Rey, PR; SR; BA; History Asso; Chrstn Asso V P 89-; Hon Prog 90-; History.

**MALDONADO RUIZ, ELIZABETH M,** Inter Amer Univ Pr Hato Rey, Hato Rey, PR; JR; Bus Admn; Mrktng.

**MALDONADO SANCHEZ, REINALDO,** Univ Politecnica De Pr, Hato Rey, PR; GD; BSCE; Cvl Eng Inst 88-; Zeta Phi Beta Cncllr 89-; Asst Eng Eng Offc 88-; Cvl Eng; Cnsltng Engrs.

**MALDONADO VEGA, MIRNA,** Univ Of Pr Medical Sciences, San Juan, PR; SR; BA; Acad Of Stdnts Of Phrmcy 90-; Rho Chi Scty Of Phrmcy 90-; Magna Cum Laude On Bchlr In Phrmcy 90-; ADS UPR College Of Arecibo 88; Scis Of Phrmcy; Phrmcy.

**MALDONADO, BRENDA M,** Univ Of Pr At Mayaguez, Mayaguez, PR; SO; AICHE 89-; PRE Jac Dirigente 85-; Hijas De Maria 85-; Boca Por Natl Hspnc Schlrshp Fund 90-.**

**MALDONADO, CARMELO,** Univ Politecnica De Pr, Hato Rey, PR; SO; BSEE; 4-H Clb 88-90; Math; Engnrng.**

**MALDONADO, JAIME O,** Univ Politecnica De Pr, Hato Rey, PR; SR; BSEE; IEEE Student 89-; Mc Graw Hill Book Club; Elec/Elec Engrg; Engrg.

**MALDONADO, JANICE M,** Univ Of Pr At Mayaguez, Mayaguez, PR; JR; BS; IEEE 89-; ACS 89-90; SWE 90-; Tau Beta Pi; Kodak Internship 90-; Elctrcl Engr.

**MALDONADO, LAUTARO ALEX,** Savannah Coll Of Art & Design, Savannah, GA; GD; MBA; Natl Trst Hstrc; Pres Mbr 88-; Intl Stdnt Assn Mbr 90-; Intrnshp Proj Juletts; Low Gordn Hse Savannh Ga Plnr 90-; Tenns; Inst Arch Brd Mbr 77-; Chbr Bldrs 77-; Arch Bldr Desgnr 75-; BA Cuenco St Univ 75; Hstrc Pres; Arch Pres.

**MALDONADO, LUIS A,** Univ Politecnica De Pr, Hato Rey, PR; FR; Elec Engr.

**MALDONADO, LUZ JANETTE ORTIZ,** Inter Amer Univ Pr Barranquita, Barranquitas, PR; JR; Conf Natl Govt Juv; Stdnt Hnr; Certif Pgm Svc Ed Univ Intl VIPR; Grp Imp Stdnt S U Sen Oncous 85-86; Assoc Future Comm Amer 87-89; Pard Cons Stdnt Univ Interamer PR 90-; Assoc Stdnt Orientation 89-; Psych/Orientation/Ph D Ed.

**MALDONADO, MARCO A,** Hilbert Coll, Hamburg, NY; FR; AA; Hon Lst 90-; Soccer 90-; Lib Arts; Intl Rels/Pol.

**MALDONADO, MARLA A,** Univ Of Al At Birmingham, Birmingham, AL; JR; BA; Phi Kappa Phi; Deans Lst; Pres Lst 89-; I M Flag Ftbl; Bus; Acctg.

**MALDONADO, ROBERTO E,** Inter Amer Univ Pr Hato Rey, Hato Rey, PR; JR; BA; Hnr Lst 89-90; Dns Lst 89-90; Hnr Assn 90-; Tutor 90-; Chmpn Frst Math Olympiad 89; Chmstry; Odontology.

**MALDONADO, VIVIAN B,** Catholic Univ Of Pr, Ponce, PR; GD; Future Tchrs AM 88-90; Stdnt Delegate Ed Dprtmnt 89-90; Yng Chrstn Stdnts Treas 75-76; Cnfrtrnty Chrstn Dctrn 74-76; Provoc 90-; Deans List 89-90; Tchng Pre Kngr/Kndr CUPR 90; Acdmc Exclnc Awrd Ed 90; BA 90; Pursue MA Degree Cnsllng.

**MALDONADO-SERRANO, MARIA A,** Univ Of Pr At Rio Piedras, Rio Piedras, PR; GD; ED D; Mst Outstndng Grdt Stdnt Ed Rsrch 90-; Amer Assoc Wm Cmnty/Jr Clge 84-85; Natl Cncl Tchrs Math 85-; Assoc Sprvsn/Crclm Dvlpmnt 85-; Math Tchr/Sec Lvl 69-79; Assoc Prof 79-; Assoc Dn Acdmc Afrs 86-89; BA Univ Sacred Heart Math Hnr 69; Crclm/Tchng Math.

**MALDONADO-SUAREZ, PEDRO J,** Inter Amer Univ Pr Hato Rey, Hato Rey, PR; JR; BA; Elec Eng Tchnlgy Assn; Intrntnl Brthrhd Elctrcl Wrkrs 79-; Elctrncs Tchncn 89-; Elctrncs; Elctrncs Engnrng Tchnlgy.

**MALDONY, CHRISTOPHER M,** Andrew Coll, Cuthbert, GA; SO; AS; IM Ftbl; IM Sftbl 90; Phi Theta Kappa 90-; Bsbl 89-; Marine Sci.

**MALEC, JEFFREY L,** S U N Y Coll At Fredonia, Fredonia, NY; SO; BA; AM/FM Cmnty Affrs Dir 90-; TV 89-90; Ldrshp Dev Pgm 90-; Hnrs Pgm; Cmnctns; Mktg/Promos Media.

**MALECKI, CRYSTAL L,** Univ Of Al At Birmingham, Birmingham, AL; SO; BSN; Ntnl Stdnt Nrs Assn 90-; Nrsng.

**MALEK, BASSEM ADEL,** Asbury Theological Sem, Wilmore, KY; SR; MDIV; BS 84; Thlgy.

**MALEKI, SOHEILA J,** Univ Of Tn At Martin, Martin, TN; SR; BS; Envrnmntl Prtctn Scty VP 88-; Chem Scty Am Sec 89-; Chem; Bio Chem MS.

**MALER, MARILYN M,** Fl Atlantic Univ, Boca Raton, FL; JR; BBA; FAU Deans List 88-; Bus Mgmt; Law Sch.

**MALERBA, RICHARD J,** Wagner Coll, Staten Island, NY; SO; BA; Soclgy Clb 90; Psych Clb; Psych; Psychlgst.

**MALESKY, PAULA S,** Indiana Univ Of Pa, Indiana, PA; JR; Delta Gamma Scl Chr 90-; Educ; Elem Tchr.

**MALETTA, MICHELLE,** City Univ Of Ny Baruch Coll, New York, NY; SR; Trvl Clb 89-90.

**MALETTE, GREGORY M,** Syracuse Univ, Syracuse, NY; FR; BARCH; Amer Inst Arch Stdnts Mbr 90-; ASO Mbr 90-; Tenns Clb Mbr 90-; Kappa Delta Rho Mbr 90-; Arch; Archtct.

**MALEY II, JIMIE G,** Embry Riddle Aeronautical Univ, Daytona Beach, FL; FR; BS; SCAT; Dns Lst; Jrnymn Elctrcn 82-90; Priv Pilots Certif; Aviation Tech/Flight; Cmrcl/Corp Pilot.

**MALFA, FRANCES,** City Univ Of Ny Baruch Coll, New York, NY; SR; BBA; Gldn Ky 88-; Dns Lst 88; Prvst Schlrshp 89-; Mrktng; Law.**

**MALIKOWSKI, LISA M,** Marywood Coll, Scranton, PA; SR; BFA; Delg Ntnl Clgt; Hnrs Cncl Cnfrncs 88-; Ntl Clg Hnrs Cncl 90; Delta Epsilon Sigma Tres 89-; Kappa Gamma Pi; Kappa Pi 89-; Prsdntl Schlr 87-; Deans Lst Hnrs 87-; Edtr ARS Mag; Grphc Dsgn.

**MALINOSKI, DANIEL J,** Franklin And Marshall Coll, Lancaster, PA; JR; BA; F M Plyrs 90-; Col Dmcrts 88-; Psi Chi 90-; Psych/Drama; Psych.

**MALINOWSKI, CATHIE JO,** S U N Y Coll At Geneseo, Geneseo, NY; FR; Orgn Hrng Imprd; Chrl Chrstrs 90-; Spch Pthlgy/Adlgy; Spch Pthlgst.

**MALINOWSKI, KAREN A,** Niagara Univ, Niagara Univ, NY; SO; BA; Cmps Radio Station Sec 89-90; Ed Hon Soc; Tutoring; Elem Ed; Tch.

**MALINOWSKI, LAURA A,** Saint Andrews Presbytrn Coll, Laurinburg, NC; SO; BA; Judicial Comm Attny Gen; Cabinet; Class Hnrs; French/Politics; Foreign Rltns.

**MALINOWSKI, SCOTT P,** Castleton St Coll, Castleton, VT; JR; BA; Math Club Pres 90-; Computer Club Pres 90-; Pi Mu Epsilon 90-; Bronze US Congressional Awd 87; Red Cross Gallon Bld Dnr; Math/Computer Sci; Engrg/Sftwr.

**MALINOWSKI, TIMOTHY J,** Niagara Univ, Niagara Univ, NY; JR; BA; Acctg.

**MALINOWSKI, TRACY D,** Marywood Coll, Scranton, PA; JR; BA; Wght Trng Clb; Scrblrs Clb 90-; Lambda Iota Tau 88-; Deans Lst 88-; Scuba-Instrctr; Engl; Jrnlsm.

**MALINSKI, MARY ANN E,** Marywood Coll, Scranton, PA; SR; BS; Delta Epsilon Sigma 89-; Pres Schlrshp 87-; PICPA Sr Awrd; All Amer Schlr Cllgte Awrd 90; Acctng.

**MALISKA, JEFFREY F,** U S Military Academy, West Point, NY; FR; IM Ftbl/Sftbl 90-; Mchncl Engr.

**MALJIAN, MEROUJAN A,** Rutgers St Univ At Newark, Newark, NJ; FR; BS; Chmstry; Med.

**MALLACE, FRANK T,** Univ Of Sc At Columbia, Columbia, SC; JR; BM; Mrchng Bnd 88-; Big Bnd 88-; Music; Jzz Mscn/Chrstn Mssnry.

**MALLARD, HEIDI C,** Fl International Univ, Miami, FL; SR; BG; Future Edctrs Amer 90-; Intrn Coral Reef Elem Schl Asst Clssrm Tchr PTA 89-91; Elem Educ; Tchr.

**MALLARD, TODD S,** Saint Pauls Coll, Lawrenceville, VA; JR; BA; Deans List 88-89; Acctng; Tax Acctng.

**MALLAST, GERALDINE,** Commonwealth Coll, Virginia Beach, VA; JR; ASS; Electrncs 90-; Cmptr Sci 90-; Alpha Beta Gamma Sec 90-; Phi Beta Lambda; Electrn Cmptr Sci Stdes; Cert Natl Trng 88; Cert Maritime Trng 89; Electrn/Cmptr Sci; Engr.

**MALLET, MARIE A,** Anne Arundel Comm Coll, Arnold, MD; SO; AA; EDU 123; Erly Chldhd Edn; Day Care.

**MALLETT, BENJAMIN C,** Oh Univ, Athens, OH; FR; BFA; Navgtrs Alpn Clb 90-; Grphc Dsgn; Advrtsng.

**MALLETTE, SHERYL L,** S U N Y Coll At Fredonia, Fredonia, NY; JR; BA; BACCHUS Pres 90-; Bus Clb; Acctg Soc; Mgt Acctg/Mnfctrng.

**MALLETTE, STACEY D,** Univ Of Rochester, Rochester, NY; SR; BA; Hlth/Soc Cncl VP 88-; Dorm Cncl Rep 89-90; Strng Memrl Hosp Vol 89; Hlth/Soc; Hlth Cr Admin.

**MALLICK, JENNIFER L,** Central Pa Bus School, Summerdale, PA; SR; SLA 89-; Scnd Mi Harrisburg 90; Intrnshp Law Frm; Statstcn Bys Bsktbl 89-; Asbs; Lgl Scrtrl; Law/Rl Est.

**MALLNER, AMELIA A,** Mount Saint Mary Coll, Newburgh, NY; SO; BSN; Theatre 89-; Clg Reps V P 90-; Nrsng Stdnt Un 90-; Beta Beta Beta 89-; Dns Lst 90; Nrsng; Crit Care Nrsng.

**MALLO, TIM A,** Univ Of Akron, Akron, OH; SR; Phi Eta Sigma 88; Alpha Lambda Delta 88; Gldn Key 88; Pi Mu Epsilon 90-; Tau Beta I 90-; Vrsty Crss Cntry/Trck Capt 87-; Chmcl Engr.

**MALLON, KIMBERLY A,** Univ Of Sc At Coastal Carolina, Conway, SC; GD; CERIT; Sigma Phi Delta 86-87; Deans List 90; Varsity Soccer Co Cptn 88-89; YMCA Pre Schl/Child Care Tchr; BA Psych Univ Maryland Clg Pk 90; Early Childhood Ed; Ed Guidance Counseling.

**MALLORY, JENNIFER L,** Univ Of Sc At Columbia, Columbia, SC; SO; BAIS; Frshmn Cncl 89-90; SG Cmpgn Mgr; Frgn Affrs Frm; Gamma Beta Phi 89-; Alpha Hnr Scty; Alpha Delta Pi Pldg Schlrshp Chr; Crln Crs; Prsdnts Lst 90; Deans Lst 89-; Frnch Govt Intl Stds; Pblc Rltns.

**MALLORY, MONICA L,** Lincoln Univ, Lincoln Univ, PA; FR; BA; Chem; Med.

**MALLORY, RAE A,** Univ Of Charleston, Charleston, WV; FR; BS; Sprts Med.

**MALLORY, SHARON RENEE,** Univ Of Southern Ms, Hattiesburg, MS; FR; BS; Egl Clb 90-; Hl Cncl Treas; Gamma Beta Phi Hstrn; Alpha Lambda Delta Treas; Phi Eta Sigma; Gamma Beta Phi Hstrn; Acctg; CPA.

**MALLORY, SHERRI M,** Univ Of Ky, Lexington, KY; SR; BASW; Soc Wrk; Soc Serv Del.

**MALLORY, STANLEY A,** Merrimack Coll, North Andover, MA; FR; Nu Phi Kappa; Pgm Brd Pres 90-; Benzene Ring 90-; Stop/Shop; Dept Mgr Bradlees 86-90; Chem; Tchng.

**MALLORY, ZANDRA Y,** Fl A & M Univ, Tallahassee, FL; SR; PHARM; 5th Yr Phrmcy Cls Cncl Pres 90-; Coll Phrmcy Crt Sch Qn 89-90; Deans Stdnt Cncl 90-; Rho Chi Hon Soc 89-; Beta Kappa Chi 90-; Amer Hrt Assn Comm Rep 83-86; Mltpl Sclrs Comm Rep 83-86; White Hs Sci Intv Stdnt Awd 88-89; Phrmcy; Clncl Phrmcy.

**MALLOY, KELLY A,** Villanova Univ, Villanova, PA; SO; BS; Alpha Epsilon Delta; Phi Sigma; Deans Lst 90-; Biochem Lab Asst-USDA ERRC; Blgy; Med.

**MALLOY, KIM M,** Savannah St Coll, Savannah, GA; SR; BA; Psychlgy Clb; Pol Sci Clb; Model UN Clb; Pi Gamma Mu; Trck Tm; Pol Sci; Corp Law.

**MALLOY, REBECCA L,** Comm Coll Algny Co Algny Cmps, Pittsburgh, PA; FR; BED; Pdlgy Clb 90-; Educ; Spcl Ed.

**MALLOY SR, ROBERT L,** Daytona Beach Comm Coll, Daytona Beach, FL; SO; BA; Retired USA 1st Sg 69-90; Engl; Lang; Arts; Tchr.

**MALLOZZI, LAURA A,** Widener Univ, Chester, PA; JR; BA; Acctg Soc V P 90-; Delta Phi Epsilon 89-; Deans Lst 88-; Pres Schlrshp 88-; Deloitte & Touche Intrnshp; Fin Exec Inst Awd; Acctg/Minor Spanish; Taxes.**

**MALMQUIST, JANET L,** Roane St Comm Coll, Harriman, TN; SO; BS; Asst Ed Dir TN Sch Of Beauty Knoxville 86-; Dip TN Sch Of Beauty Oak Rdg TN 84; Acctng; Law.

**MALONE, ALTHEA H,** Fl International Univ, Miami, FL; JR; BSW; Miami Bch Sr Ctr; Scl Svcs Dept; Scl Wrk.

**MALONE, ANGELA D,** Wilberforce Univ, Wilberforce, OH; JR; Alpha Phi Alpha Swt Hrt Sec 90-; Ntl Stdnt Bus Leag 90-; Ambssdr; Bus Mgmt.

**MALONE, CANDICE M,** Mary Washington Coll, Fredericksburg, VA; FR; Fld Hcky 90; Hstry/Bsnss; Law.

**MALONE, CAROL A,** Bethany Coll, Bethany, WV; FR; Amnesty Intl; TV Prod Tech 90-; Rainbow Grand Serv 85-; Delta Chi Sigma Treas 90-; Kappa Delta; IM Vlybl Sftbl Bsktbl 90-; Psychlgy/Cmnctns; Publ Rel/Psychlgy.

**MALONE, CATHY J,** Draughons Jr Coll Johnson City, Johnson City, TN; GD; ABS; Lib Sci Clb 90-; Pres Lst 89-; Dns Lst 89-; Stdnt Of Qrtr 90; Corp Csmtlgy; Chrch Choir 90-; UMYF Pres 90-; Comm Nrsng Home; AAS Asst; Sec.**

**MALONE, CHARLOTTE COPE,** Memphis St Univ, Memphis, TN; SO; BA; Engl; Wrtng.

**MALONE, CHRISTOPHER S,** Comm Coll Algny Co Algny Cmps, Pittsburgh, PA; SO; BS; Phi Theta Kappa; Sci/Math; Elec Engr.

**MALONE, EMILY C,** Free Will Baptist Bible Coll, Nashville, TN; GD; BS; Drama Clb; Louisa Mae Alcott Soc; BA 85; Elem Tchr.

**MALONE, JOHN P,** Bridgewater Coll, Bridgewater, VA; SO; BA; Nwsppr Rprtr 90-; Lit Mag Poet; Engl.

**MALONE, KELLEY K,** Salisbury St Univ, Salisbury, MD; SR; BED; Engl.

**MALONE, KIMBERLY,** Georgian Court Coll, Lakewood, NJ; JR; BS; Bus Club; Deans List; Varsty Soccer Team; Acctng.

**MALONE, LUETTE A,** Univ Of The Virgin Islands, St Thomas, VI; SR; BA; FBLA; Phi Beta Lambda; Acctng Assn; Virgin Islands Assn; Prsdnts Clb; Dns Lst; Barnett Frank Class Awd Female Frshmn 87-88; Intrnshp Andreas Esberg & Co 90; Acctng; CPA.

**MALONE, MARK J,** S U N Y Coll At Fredonia, Fredonia, NY; SR; MM; Clssc Gtr Awrd; C Arnold Strng Schlrshp; Marvel Awrd; Asstshp U Of Akron; BM; Music; Tchng/Prfrmng.

**MALONE, MOLLIE D,** Univ Of South Al, Mobile, AL; SR; BS; Stdnt Sportsmedicine Assoc Pres 89-; Natl Athl Trnrs Assoc Stdnt Mbr 89-; Stdnt Stdnt Athl Trnr 88-; Sprts Injury Mgmt; Athl Trng.

**MALONE, PATRICK SEAN,** Memphis St Univ, Memphis, TN; FR; MBA; Gamma Beta Phi; Fnncl Srvcs Invstmnts.

**MALONE, SHARON E,** Ms St Univ, Miss State, MS; JR; BBA; Samford Univ Rcrtr 89-90; Yng Lf Ldr 89-90; MS State Univ Orntn Ldr 90-; Kappa Omicron Nu 89-; Phi Mu 88-; Acdmc Hon Rl 88-89; Coll Schlrs Amer 90-; MSU Pres Schlr; Mktg; Mktg Rep.

**MALONE, SUE,** Univ Of North Fl, Jacksonville, FL; JR; BED; UNF NEA Stdnt Prog Mmbrshp Chr 90-; Phi Theta Kappa; Gldn Ky; AA Florida Comm College At Jacksonville 90; Engl; Scndry Engl Tchr.

**MALONEY, CHRISTINE L,** Georgian Court Coll, Lakewood, NJ; SR; BA; SG Treas 89-; Math Assoc 90-; Ed Clb 88-; Pi Mu Epsilon Sec 89-; Sigma Phi Sigma 89-; Tutor 88-; Govnrs Tchg Schlr 87-; Math; Ed.

**MALONEY, GREGORY P,** Glassboro St Coll, Glassboro, NJ; JR; BA; Life Sci; Ph D Bio.

**MALONEY, HEATHER M,** Wagner Coll, Staten Island, NY; SO; BA; Usher 90-; Alithea; Zeta Delta Alpha Pres 91-; Deans Lst 89-; French Awd 89-90; Educ/French; Tch.

**MALONEY, JEAN M,** Bucknell Univ, Lewisburg, PA; FR; BS; Alpha Lambda Delta 90-; Kappa Kappa Gamma 90-; Water Polo Rgby 90-; Math; Tchng.

**MALONEY, JOSEPH TED,** Old Dominion Univ, Norfolk, VA; SR; BS; Radio Oper Mgr 87-; Constr Specifctns Inst 89-; Assoc Gen Contr 90-; Prfsnl Brdcstr 88-; Cvl Engr; Engr Media.

**MALONEY, LISA A,** Cornell Univ Statutory College, Ithaca, NY; JR; BS; Crnl Grns Rcyclng Coord 89-; Eclgy Hse Treas/Sec 88-; Stdnts Ethcl Trtmnt Anmls Sec 88-90; Ntrl Rsrcs; Envir Ed.

**MALONEY, LORA LEE,** Univ Of Ky, Lexington, KY; JR; BA; Hmcmg Comm 88; Mrtr Brd Pres; Chi Omega Exec Cncl Sec 88-; Gld Bg Cln Up Comm 90; Spch Pthlgy; MBA.

**MALONEY, WALTER B,** Methodist Coll, Fayetteville, NC; SO; BS; Res Advsr; Fllwshp Christian Athletes; Deans Lst 90-; Vrsty Bsbl 89-90; CPR Certif Red Cross 90; Crmnlgy Sclgy; Law Enfrcmnt.

**MALOOF, CYNTHIA A,** William Paterson Coll, Wayne, NJ; GD; MED; Kappa Delta Pi; Rdgwd Cncrt Bnd 87-; MENC 85-; NEA 87-; NJEA 87-; BCEA 87-; Instrmntl Msc Tchr 88-; BA Rtgrs Unv Douglas Cllg 86; Schl Guid Cnslr; Msc.

**MALOOF, LINDA E,** Western New England Coll, Springfield, MA; FR; Cmmnctns.

**MALOSH, GREGORY P,** Duquesne Univ, Pittsburgh, PA; SR; BS; Deans Lst; IM Capt; Bus.

**MALOTT, BRITTON K,** Univ Of Sc At Columbia, Columbia, SC; Vrsty Trck 87-; Deans Lst 87-; Mrn Sci Sclrshp 90; Sclr/Athlt 87-; Vrsty Trck 87-; Mrn Sci; Envrnmntl Prtctn.

**MALOY, TWINKLE F,** Nova Univ, Ft Lauderdale, FL; GD; MBA; Phi Beta Kappa 55-; Telephone Pioneers Amer Lcl Chptr Sec 85-; Asst Mngr 64-; Human Resource; Teaching.

**MALSKIS, TERESA,** S U N Y Coll Of Tech At Frmgdl, Farmingdale, NY; SO; Cpr Instrctr Amrcn Rd Crs 87; Med Tch/Med Asst Mnhttn Mdcl 68/87; Nrsng; Nrs Prctnr.

**MALSMAN, JUDITH N,** Bloomfield Coll, Bloomfield, NJ; FR.

**MALTBA, DERRICK C,** Univ Of Nc At Charlotte, Charlotte, NC; JR; BA; Golden Key; Human Serv; Cnslng.

**MALTBA, ROBERT E,** Western Piedmont Comm Coll, Morganton, NC; FR; U S Army Infntry Sgt 86-89; Nursng; Trauma Flght Nrs.

**MALTEMPO, PATRICIA L,** Hillsborough Comm Coll, Tampa, FL; SO; AS; Comp Eng Tech; Comp.

**MALTES, CLAUDIA M,** Fl International Univ, Miami, FL; SR; BA; AA Assoc Arts Miami Dade Comm Clg 89; Mgmnt Mrktng; Assc Mrktng Mgmnt.

**MALTON, POLLY MILLIKEN,** George Mason Univ, Fairfax, VA; SR; BSED; VEA-SEA 88-; Kappa Delta Pi 88-; Golden Key 89-; Methodist Church S S Tchr; Middle Tchr.

**MALVEIRA, DARLENE J,** Newbury Coll, Brookline, MA; SR; BA; Sptlghtrs Lynnfield Cmnty Thtr 81-; Mktg; Advrtsng/Mktg/Cmnctns.

**MALWITZ, MERRILLEE,** Ringling School Of Art, Sarasota, FL; SR; BFA; Art In Prk 89-; Juried Shw 90; Tampa Bay Prfrmng Arts Cntr Hot Artst 90-; Portfolio Schlrshp 89-; Pres Lst 90-; Cmstlgst 86-; AA Univ S FLA 85; Fine Arts; Gllrs Msms.**

**MALY, LESLIE L,** Fl St Univ, Tallahassee, FL; JR; BA; Hall Govt Rep 88-89; Natl Stdnt Spch Lang Hear Assn 90-; Hon Schlrs Pgm 88-89; Very Spcl Arts; Cmnty Serv Org 88-89; Hon Cmnctns Awd; Cmnctn Disorders; Spch Lang Pathology.

**MAMAKOS, CONSTANCE M,** Wv Univ, Morgantown, WV; JR; BS; Mds Athena Cvnr 87-89; Dns Lst; Alpha Phi Chr 89-90; Ruby Mem Hosp Nrs Extshp 90; Nrs.

**MAMBRETTI, MICHELLE R,** Mount Saint Mary Coll, Newburgh, NY; JR; BA; Explrs Post 1224 80-; English; Elem Educ.

**MAMBUCA, NANCY ANN,** Saint Johns Univ, Jamaica, NY; SR; BA; Educ Clb 88-; Chrldng Coach 88-; Golden Key 90-; Kappa Delta Pi 88-; Deans Lst 88; Silver Medal. Per Acad Achvmnt 90; Grad Schlrshp; Acad Grant 89-; NHSF 90-; Tcher.

**MAMELA, JONATHAN C,** Bethany Coll, Bethany, WV; FR; BA; Soc Physics Stdnts; Amer Chem Soc; Alpha Sigma Phi; Soccer; PA Conf; Chem Engr.

**MAMMA, CONSTANCE M,** Norfolk St Univ, Norfolk, VA; SR; BA; Stdnt Va Educ Assn 90-; Natl Educ Assn 90-; Coun Excptl Chldrn 89-; Pershing Angels Sec 77; AROTC Rifle Comp 1st Plc 77; Sub Tchr 84-; Stdnt Prnt Tchr Assn 87-; Spec Educ Mntl Rtrdtn/Lrng Dsblty; Tchng.

**MAMUN, SHAHRIAR A,** Coppin St Coll, Baltimore, MD; SO; Sci Clb; Ambsdrs Clb 89-; Coppin Courier Sprts Rprtr 89-; Intl Assn Pres; Hon Assn 89-; SIFE; Vrsty Tennis 89-; Math/Eng; Acad/Admin Rsrch Teach Eng.

**MAMUYA, WILFRED S,** Boston Univ, Boston, MA; GD; MDPHD; Phi Beta Kappa 85-; Alpha Omicron Alpha; H Hughes Pre-Doctoral Fellow 88-; BA 86; Med/Biochmsty; Sci.

**MANAFI, SEPIDEH,** Univ Of Sc At Columbia, Columbia, SC; SO; BS; Mdl Untd Ntns 90-; Intrntnl Stdnt Assn Sec; Hmcmng Cmmsn; Gamma Beta Phi; Artschlstc Awrds; Phrmcy.

**MANAGBANAG, LEOBERT P,** Asbury Theological Sem, Wilmore, KY; GD; M DIV; Scrblrs Chpln 89; Sprtl Lfe Com Stdnt Rep 88; Alpha Kappa Sigma 89; Coll Acad Envir Cntr Ttr 89; Stdnt Mnstry Grps To Chrchs Sngr 89; Coll Div Schlr 89; Wlsn Kng Awrd 89; Grad Magna Cum Laude 89; BA Greenville Coll 89; Phlsphy Thlgy; Educ Rlgs Mnstry.

**MANCE, MICHELLE DIANNE,** Smith Coll, Northampton, MA; GD; Blk Students Alliance Chr 88-89; NE Blk Students Allianace Conf Fdr Chr 87-88-; Admis Office Open Campus Panelist 89-90; Deans List 89-90; First Grp Schlr 89-90; Washington DC City Admin Offic Intern 88; Aetna Life/Casualty Sumner Intshp Pro 89; Econf Law Public Policy.

**MANCELL, JIMMIE,** Univ Of Tn At Martin, Martin, TN; GD; MD; Amrcn Mdcl Assoc Vc Chrprsn; Mdcl Schl Clss Offcr Scl Chrprsn; Mu Epsilon Delta; Alpha Tau Omega Hs Mgr 89-90; Mdcl Clss 94; BS; Med.

**MANCHIN, JEANNE E,** Univ Of Miami, Coral Gables, FL; FR; BS; Marne Blgy; Rsrch Mrne Blgst.

**MANCINI, CHRIS M,** Duquesne Univ, Pittsburgh, PA; FR; Radio DJ 90-; Drama Clb Sec 90-; Schlr Fndrs 90-; Schlrshp 90-; Deans Lst; Clncl Phrmcst.

**MANCINI, LAWRENCE M,** S U N Y Coll Of Tech At Frmgdl, Farmingdale, NY; SO; AS; NY Zlgcl Scty 88-; Deans List 90; Sprvsr Cstmr Serv; Bsn; Corp Finance Custom Relations.

**MANCINI, MARA L,** Bay Path Coll, Longmeadow, MA; SR; AS; Thtr 89-; Dnc Co 90-; Acad Tutor 90-; Intshp Aetna Lf/Cslty; Ofc Adm; Exec Sec.

**MANCINI, MARIA A,** Widener Univ, Chester, PA; SR; BS; IEEE 90; Tau Phi Delta 87; Head Teller 89; Elec Engr.

**MANCINI, MARIA PIA,** Jersey City St Coll, Jersey City, NJ; SR; Class VP 90-; Finance Clb Pblc Rel Office 90-; SGO Elctns/Crdntls Com 89-; NJ Fed Bus/Prfsnl Wmn Clbs Schlrshp 89.

**MANCUSO, ANTHONY J,** Appalachian St Univ, Boone, NC; SO; BS; WASU News Bureau 90-; ASU Musical Revue; Phi Eta Sigma 90-; ASU Hnrs Prog 91; Bus Hnrs Prog; IM Sprts 89-; Economics; Intl Ecnmc Frcstng.**

**MANCUSO, EDA-MARIE,** William Paterson Coll, Wayne, NJ; GD; Sunshn Fnd 90-; Elem Ed Scty 87-88; Flr Plnng Cmmtt 87-88; Alpha Kappa Delta 90-; BA Elem Ed Sclgy; Elem Ed; Sclgy; Tchr.

**MANCUSO, JAMES P,** Hofstra Univ, Hempstead, NY; JR; BS; Phi Beta Kappa; Kappa Mu Epsilon; Deans Lst 88-90; Provosts Lst 89-; Math; Actuarial Sci.**

**MANCUSO, MICHAEL,** Dickinson School Of Law, Carlisle, PA; SO; Intl Clb Pres 88; BA Kutztown U 89; Pol Sci; Intl Law.

**MANCUSO, RICHARD G,** Manhattan Coll, Bronx, NY; JR; BSEE; IEEE; Engrs Cncl; Tau Beta Pi Pres 90-; Eta Kappa Nu Treas 90-; Elec Engr; Cmptr Engr.

**MANDEL, JOANNE ELIZABETH,** George Mason Univ, Fairfax, VA; SR; BS; Robert F Allen Mem Schlrshp 90; Intern The Pragma Corp; Amer Pblc Hlth Assn; Pblc Hlth; Cnsltnt Intl Hlth.

**MANDEL, SARA B,** City Univ Of Ny Baruch Coll, New York, NY; GD; Adv Soc 89-90; Beta Gamma Sigma 89-; Golden Key 89-; BBA 90; Mrktng; Adv.

**MANDEL, TERI,** Univ Of Pittsburgh At Bradford, Bradford, PA; JR; BSC; Biology 90-; Biology; Phy Thrpy.

**MANDELL, MORDY,** Yeshiva Univ, New York, NY; GD; Jnt Bus Soc 88-89; Sigma Delta Rho 88-; Deans Lst 87-90; Cum Laude; Sam G Rothman Mem Awd Talmud; Trk Tm 88-89; Econ; Law.

**MANDERS, PAMELA L,** Univ Of South Al, Mobile, AL; SR; Pres Lst; Dns Lst; Elem Educ.

**MANDEVILLE, KIMBERLY J,** Beckley Coll, Beckley, WV; FR; BA; Acctg.

**MANDIA, THOMAS R,** Washington & Lee Univ, Lexington, VA; FR; BS; Univ Chrs 90-; Phi Gamma Delta Pldg Eductr 90-; Ftbl/Trck Lttrmn 90-; Bio; Med.

**MANDRELL, KAREN N,** Union Univ, Jackson, TN; SR; BS; Alpha Chi 89-; Sigma Zeta VP 89-; Kappa Mu Epsilon VP 89-; Alpha Tau Omega Swthrt 89-; Chem; Indstrl Rsrch.

**MANENTE, CARA A,** Niagara Univ, Niagara Univ, NY; SR; BA; Crmnl Jstc Soc; Niagara Fls Pol Dept Intshp 87-88; AAS Niagara Fls Comm Clg 88; Crmnl Jstc; Law.

**MANER, CATHERINE SUZANNE,** Univ Of Sc At Columbia, Columbia, SC; SO; BS; GAMMA Pres; Phi Eta Sigma 90-; Kappa Delta Asst Pledge Trainer; IM Bsktbl; Biology; Medicine.

**MANES, GAIL L,** Commonwealth Coll, Virginia Beach, VA; GD; Accntng Clb Pres 90; Boy Scts Of Amrca Tres 89-; Aas; Accounting; Cpa.

**MANES, JEAN E,** Liberty Univ, Lynchburg, VA; JR; Vybl Clb Asst Coach 89; Clg Repblcn 88-; Mission Trip France 90-; Snte Fregn Rltns Cmtee Inern 90-; Vybl Tm 89; Govt/Foreign Afrs.

**MANES, MONICA L,** Duquesne Univ, Pittsburgh, PA; JR; BM; Univ Choir 88-; Music Schlrshp 88-; Schlrs Awd 88-; Deans List 89-; Music; Perf.

**MANESS, DIANE S,** Montgomery Comm Coll, Troy, NC; SO; AS; Wom Clb Pres; SG Bus Repr 90-; Ind Sprvsn Advsry Tm 89-90; Intl Bluegrass Music; Cnty Demo Wom; Sprvsr Clayson Knttg Co 70-; Bus Admin; Mgmnt.

**MANESS, HANNAH L,** The Boston Conservatory, Boston, MA; JR; BFA; Theater.

**MANESS, LISA M,** Memphis St Univ, Memphis, TN; FR; BA; Gamma Beta Phi 90-; Chi Alpha 90-; Engl; Sec Educ.

**MANESS, LORI J,** Cornell Univ Statutory College, Ithaca, NY; SO; BS; Orchstr 89-90; JV Sccr 90-; Bio Chem; Mdcl Dctr.

**MANESS, MARY A,** Ms St Univ, Miss State, MS; JR; Cmps Crsde For Chrst 90-; Elem Ed; Tchr.

**MANESS, TRACY L,** Methodist Coll, Fayetteville, NC; SO; BS; Stdnt Govt VP 89-; Activities Cncl 89-; Monarch Plymkrs; Tour Guide 89-; All Acad Conf Tm 90; All Conf Tennis Tm 90-; Outstndg Stdnt Athlete 89-90; Deans Lst; Pres Lst; Tennis Tm Lettered 89-; Bus Admin; Finance.

**MANEY, MARY ELIZABETH,** Volunteer St Comm Coll, Gallatin, TN; SO; MBA; Gamma Beta Phi 90-; Acctg.

**MANFERDINI, DAVID G,** Western New England Coll, Springfield, MA; JR; BSBA; Acad Acievement Awd; Alumni Schlrshp 89-90; Dr Lawrence H Nath Awd; Mgt.

**MANFRA, DONNA M,** Newbury Coll, Brookline, MA; FR; AS; Clss Intro Parlgl; Clss Lgl Ofc Prcdr; Asst Oper Mgr; Prlgl; Law.

**MANFRED, TIANA L,** S U N Y At Binghamton, Binghamton, NY; SO; Stdnt Govt; English Lit/Span; Law.**

**MANFREDI, CAROL A,** Comm Coll Algny Co Algny Cmps, Pittsburgh, PA; FR; BA; Nrsng.

**MANGANELLO SR, DAVID J,** Albany St Coll, Albany, GA; SR; MBA; Mgt Clb 90-; Alpha Beta Gamma 88-; Intrnshp Delco Remy Div GMC; DEANS Lst Summa Cum Laude 89-; Dept Hon 89-; Mgt Trainee WTM Div Burlington Motor Carriers Albany GA; AA Darton Coll 89; Bus; Edn.

**MANGANO, ALEX S,** S U N Y Coll Of Tech At Frmgdl, Farmingdale, NY; SO; MBA; Liberal Arts; Business.

**MANGELS, JAMES R,** Lenoir Rhyne Coll, Hickory, NC; GD; IFC 89-90; Pi Kappa Phi Archn 89-90; Deans Lst 90; Sccr 86; BS 90; Bigy Ed.

**MANGES, LYNN E,** Ky Christian Coll, Grayson, KY; SR; BS; Stdnt Cncl Soc Comm Chr 89-; Matheteo Soc V P 89-; Missionary Intrn Spain/Costa Rica; Acad All Amer 90; NCAA Natl Chmpnshp 89; Wmsn Bsktbl Capt MVP 87-90f; Acad All A; Math/Phy Sci; Tch.

**MANGIN, STEVEN T,** Alfred Univ, Alfred, NY; FR; BS; Hall Coun Pres; Cmptg Asst; Ntnl Merit Schol; Ceramic Engr.

**MANGIONE, BETH A,** Hudson Valley Comm Coll, Troy, NY; SR; AAS; Dns Lst 89-90; Pres Lst 90-; Nrsng.

**MANGIONE, MICHAEL J,** Manhattan Coll, Bronx, NY; SR; BS; Am Soc Civil Engs VP 88-; Soc Auto Engs 90-; Chi Epsilon 89-; Deans List 87-; Boy Scouts Am Asst Sctmstr 87-; Tutor 87-90; Eagle Scout 87; IM Sftbl/Ftbl/Bsktbl Capt 87-; Civil Eng; Mstrs.

**MANGIONE, NAOMI A,** East Stroudsburg Univ, E Stroudsburg, PA; SR; BA; Phi Theta Kappa 88; Acad Schlrshp 88; Intrnshp Latin Evangelical Outrch Mssn; Soclgy; Cnslng.

**MANGLA, NEERAJ K,** Cornell Univ Statutory College, Ithaca, NY; JR; BS; Hlth Allnce At Crnll 89-90; Cncrt Cmmssn 90; Golden Key; EMS Drvr 89; Deans Lst 90; Bio Sci; Med.

**MANGOLD, JULIANNE,** Niagara Univ, Niagara Univ, NY; SR; BSN; Delta Epsilon Sigma; Nrsng.

**MANGOLD, MARCELLA M,** Anne Arundel Comm Coll, Arnold, MD; SO; BA; Handcp Sch Aide 90; AA Anne Arundle Cmnty Clg; Elem Ed/Chld Physclgy; Tchr.

**MANGRUM, GARNER E,** Middle Tn St Univ, Murfreesboro, TN; FR; BS; Cmptr Scnc/Math; Rsrch.

**MANGRUM, MICHAEL N,** Va Highlands Comm Coll, Abingdon, VA; FR; AAS; Hstry/Govt; Tch.

**MANGUAL, DAMARIS,** Univ Of Pr At Mayaguez, Mayaguez, PR; SR; MD; Indstrl Mcrblgy Soc 90-; Phi Kappa Phi 89-; Hnr Brd 87-; Magna Cum Laude; BS; Blgy; Med.

**MANGUM, TENA S,** Snead St Jr Coll, Boaz, AL; SO; AAS; Phi Theta Kappa 81-; Comp Prgrmmng; Eng.

**MANIBO, MARLENE B,** Immaculata Coll, Immaculata, PA; FR; BA; Hmn Corps CA State Univ; Deans Lst; Hstry/Intl Studies; Intl Pltcs.

**MANIER, SUSAN C,** Miami Jacobs Jr Coll Of Bus, Dayton, OH; SO; Cub Scouts Miami Dist Pack 82 Cubmstr Cmtee Mbr 90-; Bus Admn; Small Bus Owner.

**MANIGAUIT, LORRAINE YVONNE,** Coll Of New Rochelle, New Rochelle, NY; SR; BA; Nat Council Negro Wmn 87-; Eastern Star 87-; Deans List 87-; Hptl Imptnt Conslng 87-; Tutor 87-; Essay Awds 88-89; Postal Serv Achiev Awd 87; Pass Profile Asses Hnr 87; Sr Citizen Vol 87-; Psychology; Social Wrk.

**MANIKTALA, ANITA,** Univ Of Rochester, Rochester, NY; SR; BA; Crew 88; Tae Kwon Do 90-; Phi Sigma Sigma Jud Bd 88-; Circle K 87-90; Hon Thesis; Bio; Med.

**MANIS, PETER,** Va Commonwealth Univ, Richmond, VA; FR; BS; IM Sftbl Capt; Phi Eta Sigma; Bio; Med.

**MANISCALCO, ALBERT M,** Wagner Coll, Staten Island, NY; FR; Bsktbl 90-; Engr.

**MANISCALCO, DENISE,** S U N Y Coll Of Tech At Frmgdl, Farmingdale, NY; SO; Bowling; Acdmc Excllnc Awrd Lbrl Arts/ Sciences; Cert Merit Deans List; Bowling; Liberal Arts.

**MANISCALCO, FRANK S,** Western New England Coll, Springfield, MA; SO; SGA 90; Pre Law Soc 90; Hall Govt; Natl Hnrs Soc; IM Sports; Tech Mgmt; Law.

**MANKINS, CHAD D,** Liberty Univ, Lynchburg, VA; SR; BA; LU Hispanic Clb Treas 90-; Otstndng Acdmc Achvmnt Awrd/ Spnsh; Lngstcs/Mdrn Lngs; Trnsltn/Intrprtn Ovrs.

**MANKOFF, GERI L,** Univ Of Sc At Columbia, Columbia, SC; FR; MBA; Sftbl.

**MANLEY, JAMES S,** Piedmont Tech Coll, Greenwood, SC; FR; ASSOC; Phi Theta Kappa 90; Deans Lst 90-; Machine Tool Tech.

**MANLEY, JULIE MONTEIL,** Livingston Univ, Livingston, AL; JR; BSED; Ldrshp Schlrshp 90-; Pres List 90; Deans List 90-; Elem Edn; Teach.

**MANLEY, KARA A,** Norfolk St Univ, Norfolk, VA; JR; BS; SG 89-; DNIMAS 88-; Hosp Vol 90-; Univ Of Ill At Chic Intrn 89; Biology; Pediatrician.

**MANLEY, KELLY SHANNON,** Bridgewater Coll, Bridgewater, VA; SR; BA; Frgn Lang Club Sec/Treas 89; Yng Dmcrts Club Pres 88; Lambda Soc 88; Blue Ridge Svcs Intern 90; Sclgy/ Phlsphy; Law.

**MANLEY, KRISTIN L,** Univ Of Pittsburgh, Pittsburgh, PA; SO; MBA; Billiards Clb 90-; Sigma Dove Treas 90-; Hstry; Crim Lawyer.

**MANLEY, PATRICIA C,** Medaille Coll, Buffalo, NY; JR; BSHRD; Darien Lake Theme Pk Prsnnl Intshp; AAS 90; Hmn Rsc Dvlp/Bsn; Dir HRD.

**MANLEY, RACHEL T,** S U N Y Coll At Fredonia, Fredonia, NY; SO; BA; Ethos New Music Clb 89-; Hnrs Prog 89-; Music Cmpstn; Prfssr.

**MANN, AMBER R,** Univ Of Southern Ms, Hattiesburg, MS; JR; Future Tchrs Amrca 89-90; Englsh Clb 88-90; Phi Theta Kappa 88-90; Prsdnts Lst 88-; Phi Theta Kappa 90; Cmmnty Coll Prsdntl Awd 90; Jr Coll Achvmnt Awd 90; BA Co-Lin Comm Coll 90; Elmntry Ed; Tch.**

**MANN, CATHY D,** Wilmington Coll, New Castle, DE; SO; BA; Marriott Corp 87-; Cmptr Syst Spprt Spec; Busn Admin; Self Emplyd.

**MANN, DARREN W,** Mayland Comm Coll, Spruce Pine, NC; SO; BS; SGA Snt; Bus; Mgmt.

**MANN, DAWN M,** Fl Atlantic Univ, Boca Raton, FL; JR; BA; Pre Law Scty; Chmbr Cmmrc Vol; Phi Kappa Phi; Prlgl 88-90; AS 84; AA 88; Acctg; Law.

**MANN, GEORGE E,** Hillsborough Comm Coll, Tampa, FL; FR; AA; Librl Arts.

**MANN, JONATHAN R,** Syracuse Univ, Syracuse, NY; SR; BARCH; Arch Stdnt Assoc 87-; Arch.

**MANN, JOSHUA R,** Ms Gulf Coast Comm Coll, Perkinston, MS; JR; BS; Assoc Baptist Stdnts 88-90; Phi Theta Kappa 89-90; Resrch Asst Med Clg Georgia; Hall Fame 88-; Chem; Med.

**MANN, JOYCE A,** Clark Atlanta Univ, Atlanta, GA; SR; BA; Stdnt Govt 88; NAACP 90-; Dsgnrs Frm Asst Dsgnr 90; Natl Hnr Scty Treas 85; Big Sis Prog; Alpha Angel 88; Fnnce; Stck Brkr.

**MANN, KAROL M,** Barry Univ, Miami, FL; FR; BA; Acctg.

**MANN, KIMBERLY D,** Western Carolina Univ, Cullowhee, NC; JR; BA; Engl Clb 90-; Frnch Clb 90-; Sigma Tau Delta; Mortar Brd; Delta Zeta; Deans Lst 89-; Engl; Pub Rltns/Law.

**MANN, KRISTIN,** S U N Y Coll Of Tech At Frmgdl, Farmingdale, NY; SO; BA; Spec Olympcs/Asst Handcpd Chdrn; Bus; Advtsng/Cpywrtr.

**MANN, MICHELLE R,** Univ Of Ky, Lexington, KY; JR; BS; U Of Ky Mrchng Bnd 88; Tau Beta Sigma Treas 90; AICE 90; Alpha Lambda Delta 88-90; Lambda Sigma 88-90; Chem Eng; Eng.

**MANN, SHARRON C,** Nc Central Univ, Durham, NC; GD; JD; Law Week Comm 90-; Chrstn Lgl Soc 90-; Phi Beta Kappa 88-; Law Jrnl Candidate 90-; Phi Delta Phi 89-; Deans Lst 89-; BA U NC Greensboro 89; Law.

**MANN, STACEY J,** City Univ Of Ny Queensbrough, New York, NY; SR; Sctrl Hon Scty 88-89; Cooperative Educ 90; AAS; Wrd Prcsng; Bus; Cmptrs.

**MANN, TODD AARON,** Brevard Coll, Brevard, NC; FR; AFA; Music/Prcssn; Prfrmr.

**MANN, VICTORIA L,** Saint Francis Coll, Loretto, PA; SO; BS; Hstrns Rndtble/Socratic Clb Pres 89-; Physicians Asst Soc 90-; Phi Delta Kappa 90-; Newspaper Stf Wrtr 89-; Hnrs Pgm Stdnt Repr 89-; S Alleghenies Museum Art Intern 90-; Physcns Asst; Orthopdc Surg.**

**MANNA, TINA M,** Teikyo Post Univ, Waterbury, CT; SR; BA; Drama Club Box Off Mgr 88-90; Jud Bd 89-; Acctng.

**MANNARA, TRACY M,** S U N Y Coll Of Tech At Alfred, Alfred, NY; FR; AAS; IM Sftbl; Bus Admin; Mgmt.

**MANNING, CHRISTINA J,** Oh St Univ At Newark, Newark, OH; SO; BSN; Pblshd Wrtngs Acrss Crrclm OSUN Pblctn; Nrsng; Med Schl.

**MANNING, DEBORAH L,** Anne Arundel Comm Coll, Arnold, MD; SO; Educ Cmtee St Andrews Ch Chrmn; Ordr Eastern Star 78-; Amer Inst Prof Bkkpprs 89-; Promtnl Alyst Foodserv; AA; Bus Admn; Bus/Cmptr Alyst.

**MANNING, DEBRA C,** Tn Temple Univ, Chattanooga, TN; SR; BS; Flour Hse Zeta Tau Rho Treas 90-; Moody Soc PR 89-90; Fall 90 Tmpl Plyrs 90; Pres Hnr Rl 87-; Elem Educ.**

**MANNING, ERICKA S,** Norfolk St Univ, Norfolk, VA; JR; BA; Young Democrats SGA; NAACP Activities Dir Chrmn Mbrshp 89-; Mattie E Coleman Cir; Choir St John CME Church Sec Treas 87-; Hnr Rl; Deans Lst; Vlybl; Business Finance; Real Estate.

**MANNING, JOHN S,** Spartanburg Methodist Coll, Spartanburg, SC; SO; AA; Phi Theta Kappa 89-91; Phi Beta Lambda State Pres 89-90; Jr Achvmnt; Bus Stdnt Of Year; JA Ldrshp Awd; PBL 1st Place Economics 2nd Place Impro Spkng; Bus Economics; Invstmnt Banking.

**MANNING, KAREN G,** Cumberland Coll, Williamsburg, KY; FR; BA; Engl Assist; Engl; Scndry Educ.

**MANNING, KAREN M,** Cumberland Coll, Williamsburg, KY; SO; BA; Amer Chem Scty; Love In Action; Baptist Stdnt Union; Schl Nwspr Staff; Narrator TV Prod Of Christmas Specl 90; Summer Mssnry Orlando Fla; Deans Lst; Hnr Rl; Academic Schlrshps 89-; Architecture.

**MANNING, MELISSA D,** Univ Of Tn At Martin, Martin, TN; FR; Phys Thrpy Clb 90-; Tae Kwon Do 90-; Alpha Gamma Delta Ritual Chrmn 90-; Phys Thrpy Psychlgy.

**MANNING, MICHELLE M,** Wv Northern Comm Coll, Wheeling, WV; SO; AAS; Phi Theta Kappa; Sci.

**MANNING, NANCY YOUNG,** Piedmont Tech Coll, Greenwood, SC; SO; AA; Stdnt Peer Advsr 90-; Crisis Preg Cntr; Ofc Sys Tech Advsry Comm; Bsns Ofc Sys Tchnlgy; BS.

**MANNING, PATRICIA L,** Brescia Coll, Owensboro, KY; SO; BS; Phi Beta Lambda Historian 89-; Pep Clb Pres 90-; Alpha Chi 90-; Chrldr 89-; Acctng; CPA.

**MANNING, PAUL F,** Chattahoochee Vly St Comm Coll, Phenix City, AL; SO; BS; VFW; Amer Lgn; Engl/Ecnmcs.

**MANNING JR, PAUL R,** Ashland Comm Coll, Ashland, KY; FR; AA; Law Enfor.

**MANNING, RITCHIE L,** Memphis St Univ, Memphis, TN; SR; BS; AS Dyersburg State Cmnty Clg 88; Mech Engr; Engr.

**MANNINO, JOANNE R,** Glassboro St Coll, Glassboro, NJ; SR; BA; Stu Govt Brandywine Coll 88-89; Vllybll Tm 87-89; Dean Lst Brandywine 87-88; Zeta Mu Epsilon Asst Pldg Mstrss 88-; AS Brandywine Coll 89; Cmptr Sci.

**MANNO, MARY E,** Hudson County Comm Coll, Jersey City, NJ; SO; BA; Accntng; CPA.

**MANNON, KELLI Y,** S U N Y Coll Of Tech At Alfred, Alfred, NY; FR; AS; Stu Ambssdr; Ornttn Asst; Res Asst; Hmn Serv; Blngl Elem Educ.

**MANNS, COURTNEY K,** Comm Coll Algny Co Algny Cmps, Pittsburgh, PA; FR; BED; Edctn; Tchng Elem.

**MANNUCCIA, CHRISTINA M,** City Univ Of Ny Baruch Coll, New York, NY; JR; BBA; NY State Rgnts Schlrshp 88-; Barveh Schlrshp 88-; Indus/Org Psychlgy.

**MANO, SAMUEL A,** Marshall University, Huntington, WV; FR; BA; Res Hl Asc Rep 90-; Alpha Sigma Phi VP 90; Sprts Mgmt/Mktg; Law.

**MANOLAKES, LUCINDA A,** S U N Y At Stony Brook, Stony Brook, NY; FR; Sigma Beta.

**MANRIQUE, CARMEN IBERIA,** Bunker Hill Comm Coll, Boston, MA; SO; BA; Spnsh Clb Pres 90-; Stdnt Cncl 90-; Schl Nwsppr Stff 89-; Phi Theta Kappa 90-; Alpha Kappa Mu; Coll Brd Otstndng Mnrty Cmmnt Coll 90-; Hnrs Prgm 90-; Ttrs Smnr; Acdmc Excllnc Schlrshp Sprng Rcpnt; Cmm Dept Awrd 90-; Mass Cmmnctn; Brdcst Prnt Jrnlsm.

**MANSEAU, TRACY L,** Westfield St Coll, Westfield, MA; FR; Mass Comm Clb 90-; Tlvsn Prod 90-; Work Study Rcptnst 90-; Comm; Tlvsn Brdcstr.

**MANSFIELD, JON B,** Univ Of Louisville, Louisville, KY; FR; BCHE; Speed Sch; Chem Eng.

**MANSFIELD, JULIE A,** Middle Tn St Univ, Murfreesboro, TN; JR; MBA; Rho Lambda 90-; Chi Omega Ltl Sistrs 88-; Bus Admin; Finance.

**MANSFIELD, RICHARD J,** Coll Of William & Mary, Williamsburg, VA; FR; PHD; Cmps Crsd Chrst 90-; Phi Eta Sigma 90-; Alpha Lambda Delta 90-; Psi Upsilon 90-; Acdmc All Armcn 90-; Vrsty Gymnstcs 90-; Blgy; Med.

**MANSOUR, STEPHAN I,** Hudson Valley Comm Coll, Troy, NY; FR; AAS; Intnl Cl Sec 90-; Pres List 90-; Intnshp M Bender/Co Cmptr Info Svcs Cept 90-; Cmptr Instr E Jerusalem 86-89; Cmptr Info Sys; Prog.

**MANSOURIAN, AMIR,** Hudson Valley Comm Coll, Troy, NY; SO; AS; Bus; Mgmt.

**MANTAS, ANGELIKI,** Univ Of South Fl, Tampa, FL; JR; BA; Fine Arts; Archtctr.

**MANTEL, AARON J,** Bowling Green St Univ, Bowling Green, OH; JR; BS; Hnrs Assn 87-; Alpha Lambda Delta 87-88; Mich Intercoll Bwlng Conf 90-; Var Bwlng Capt 90-; Cmptr Sci; Cmptr/Elec Eng.

**MANTEL, DIANNE S,** Univ Of Toledo, Toledo, OH; FR; JD; Wmns Law Assn; Zonta Sec; League Wmn Vtrs; BA 90; Law.

**MANTEL, HEATHER A,** Univ Of Rochester, Rochester, NY; SO; BA; Dorm Cncl Rep D Lion Org 89-90; Asst RA 90-; Sftbl Tm 90-; Intrnshp St Rep 90-; Intrnshp Mbr Hse Commns London; Tnns Sftbl 89-; Pol Sci/Psych; Law/Govt.

**MANTELLO, MELINDA A,** Salisbury St Univ, Salisbury, MD; JR; BS; Med Careers Clb 89- VP 90-91; Yng Demo 89- Sec 90-91; Admsns Tour Guide 89-; Phi Eta Sgm 89-; Beta Beta Beta 90-; Ldr St Francis Jr High Cyo Ldr 89-; Algnqn Wldrns Orntn Cnslr 90; Presdntl Henson Schlrshp 89-; Sntrl Schlrshp 89-; Bio Pre Med; Doctor/Pedtrcn.

**MANTILLA, RENE,** Fl International Univ, Miami, FL; SR; BA; Future Educ Of Amer VP 90-; Kappa Delta Pi Pres Elect 90-; Phi Kappa Phi 91-; Alpha Phi Alpha 88-; Tchr Asst Prof E Joseph Kaplan; AA Fla State Univ 89; Educ Sec Soc Stds; H S Tchr.

**MANTILLA, SARA L G,** Fl International Univ, Miami, FL; SR; BA; FEA VP Membrshp 90; Kappa Delta Pi Histrn 90; Phi Lambda 90; AA Miami Dade Cmmnty Clg N 90; Sec Soc Studies Ed; Tchr.

**MANTLE, KEVANN S,** Ashland Comm Coll, Ashland, KY; FR; BS; Pharm Tech 89-; Med; Nrs.

**MANTLER, GORDON K,** Univ Of Sc At Columbia, Columbia, SC; FR; BA; Newspr Staff Writer 90-; Assist News Editor; Mdl Untd Ntns/Yng Dmcrts 90-; IM Tennis 90; Poltcl Sci; Jrnlsm.

**MANTSCH, JOHN R,** Allegheny Coll, Meadville, PA; SO; BA; Psi Chi 90-; Delta Tau Delta 89-; Alden Schlr 89-90; Cologne Exchng Prog; Crs Cntry Vrsty Ltr 90; Psychlgy/Grmn; Soc Wrk/Psychtry.

**MANU, SAMUEL O,** Asbury Theological Sem, Wilmore, KY; GD; MDIV; Campus Prsn Mnstry Co-Ldr 90; Prsn Fllwshp; Smrtn Hse 89; Intrn As Assist To Pstr; Smnry Bsktbl/Ims 90; Deaf Fllwshp 90; Ichthus Chrstn Yth Cnslr; BS Cmptr Sci Cal Poly-San Luis Obispo 88; Chrstn Mnstry; Pstr.

**MANUEL, CHRISTOPHER N,** Tn St Univ, Nashville, TN; SR; BS; Sclgy Clb 89-90; Campus Mnstry 89-90; Cum Laude 90-; Sociology; Teach.

**MANUEL, DEMETRIA F,** Fort Valley St Coll, Fort Valley, GA; FR; BA; March Band 90-; Bus Admin.

**MANUEL, LAINIE M,** Winthrop Coll, Rock Hill, SC; JR; BA; BA; Hist.

**MANVILLE, MELISSA J B,** Univ Of Nh Plymouth St Coll, Plymouth, NH; SR; BA; Kapa Delta Pi 90-; Phi Kappa Ohi 89-; Instr Aerob 89-; S S Tchr; Manual Intrptr/Tutor/Hearing Imprd Stdnts 84-88; Cert Claremont Vctnl Tech Colg 84; Elem Edctn; Tch.

**MANWARING, LORETTA M,** Elmira Coll, Elmira, NY; SO; BA; Amer Rgstry Rdlgc Tech 76-; Amer Socty Rdlgc Tech 76-; Rgstry Disg Med Sngrphrs 81-; X Ray Ultrasound/Nuclear Med Proc; St Josephs Schl 76; Math/Sec Educ; Math Instrctr.

**MANY, DANIELLE BETH,** George Washington Univ, Washington, DC; FR; BBA; Hl Cncl Sec 90-; AIESEC; Univ Bnd 90-; Intl Busn; Busn.

**MANYFIELD, CAROLYN J,** Tougaloo Coll, Tougaloo, MS; SO; BA; NAACP Treas 90-; Math/Cmptr Sci; Econ/Acctng; CPA.

**MANZANO, HELEN S,** West Chester Univ, West Chester, PA; SR; BS; Prcssn Ensmbl Pres 87-; Music Edctrs Natl Cnfrnc Sec 89-; Wnd Ensmbl Prncpl Plyr 88-; Sigma Alpha Iota 89-; Music Educ; Tchr.

**MANZARI, MARIA L,** Elmira Coll, Elmira, NY; SR; Orien Com 88-90; LISP 87-; ESL 89-; PAL 88-89; Soc Pltcl Un 89-; BS Elmira Coll NY; Deaf Educ.

**MANZI, MARY JO,** Niagara Univ, Niagara Univ, NY; FR; BA; Psych Club Mtg/Dxcssn 90-; Psych/Major Crmnl Jstc/Minor; Law.

**MANZOLILLO, LOUIS,** Ny Chiropractic Coll, Glen Head, NY; GD; Gnstd Clb 87-; Chi Phi Omega; NYCC Rsdncy Srvc Awrd; DC; Chrprctc.

**MAPA, MARIA H C,** Univ Of South Fl, Tampa, FL; FR; BA; Envrnmnt Cnscnc Grp 90-; Blgy; Mdcl Cr.

**MAPEL, WILLIAM B,** Cornell Univ, Ithaca, NY; SO; BS; Coll Repblcns Actvts Chrmn 90; Intrvrsty Chrstn Fllwshp; Indstrl/Lbr Relatns.

**MAPHIS, CHARLES SCOTT,** Old Dominion Univ, Norfolk, VA; JR; BS; Phi Kappa Phi 90-; Goldn Key 90-; Tau Alpha Pi 90-; Vol Spec Engrng Chrmn; Elec Engrng Tech.

**MAPLE, JOY,** Univ Of Ga, Athens, GA; SR; BSED; Rsdnt Asst Myrs Comm RA 89-; Rsdnc Hall Assn RHA Rep Mmbr 87-; Comm Hmcmng Com; Tch America 90-; Prjct LEAD 90-; Amrcn Asn Mntl Rtrdtn 88-; IM Sftbl Ftbl 87-; Erly Chldhd Edctn; Tchr Admnstrtr.

**MAPLE, TERRI JO,** Davis Coll, Toledo, OH; GD; AS; Acctng/Bus Mgmt; Corp Finance BA.

**MAPLES, BLAINE NUTTALL,** Saint Andrews Presbytrn Coll, Laurinburg, NC; SR; BA; Hnr Soc; Alpha Chi 90; Math; Tchr.

**MAPP, BRENDA C,** Univ Of The Dist Of Columbia, Washington, DC; SR; BA; Schltstc Achvmnt Awd 90-; William A Carroll Schlrshp Awd 90-; Fclty Schlrshp Awd Bus Dpt 89-; Adminstrv Sec US Postal Srvc Law Dpt Hdqrtrs; SCRTRL Sci Cortez W Peters Bus Clg 69; Bus Mngmnt.

**MAPPUS, STEVEN L,** Western New England Coll, Springfield, MA; JR; BSEE; AS Springfield Technel Cmnty Clg 89; Elec Engrs; Dsgn Engr.

**MAR, YEE MON,** Barry Univ, Miami, FL; FR; BA; Blgy; Med.

**MARAGH, CHANDU INSHAN,** Broward Comm Coll, Ft Lauderdale, FL; FR; Bio; Med.

**MARAGH, RAMESH C,** Tuskegee Univ, Tuskegee Inst, AL; SO; BA; Amer Inst Chem Eng 90-; Proctor/Gamble Awd; AD Clg Of Bahamas 87-89; Chem Eng.

**MARAIA, MARK,** Manhattan Coll, Bronx, NY; SR; ME; Amer Soc Cvl Engrs; Wtr Plltn Cntrl Fed; Chi Epsln Treas; Tau Beta Pi; Epsln Sigma Pi; Clcl Tutor Stds; Dns Lst; Env Engr Schlp; IM; BEC; Engr.

**MARANDINO, SARINA L,** Cumberland County Coll, Vineland, NJ; FR; Phi Theta Kappa 90; Radiography; Nuclear Med/Radiation Thrpy.

**MARANDO, JOHN M,** S U N Y Coll Of Tech At Alfred, Alfred, NY; FR; BA; Elec Engr.

**MARANDO, ROSANNA,** Univ Of Miami, Coral Gables, FL; SR; Future Edctrs Amer 90-; Tchg Intern Sunset Elem 90-; BA; Ed/Hstry; Tchg.

**MARANGONI, JANINE A,** Northern Ky Univ, Highland Hts, KY; JR; BA; Schl Nwspr Photo 88-89; Actvts Prog Brd 89-90; Alpha Chi 90-; Kappa Delta Pi; Osyssey Of The Mind Gftd Stdnts; Sky Blgrss Awd 90-; IM Aerobics Instr 91; Elem Educ/English; Pblc Schl Teacher.

**MARANO, EUGENIA T,** S U N Y Coll Of Tech At Frmgdl, Farmingdale, NY; GD; Hrtcltr Clb Sec 89-; Canine Soc Blnd Fnd Rsg Hndcpd 89-90; Hrtcltr; Flrl Dsgnr Shp Ownr.

**MARANO, LOUISE,** Bloomfield Coll, Bloomfield, NJ; SO; BA; Crmnl Justice/Pre Law; Atty At Law.

**MARANO, MARISA D,** Manhattanville Coll, Purchase, NY; SR; BA; Pre-Law Soc 89-90; Pre-Law Review Co-Ed 89-90; Sr Cls Comm 90-; Sftbl 90; Pol Sci; Law.

**MARASCO, PETER L,** Univ Of Rochester, Rochester, NY; SR; BS; Optical Soc Am 89-; Laser Emerg Lab Tech 89-; IM Bsktbl/Vlybl 89-; Optics; Eng.

**MARBERRY, ANDREA L,** Union Univ, Jackson, TN; JR; BS; Psych.

**MARBUARY, LA TONIA A,** Clark Atlanta Univ, Atlanta, GA; JR; BA; Erly Chld Educ; Tch.

**MARBURY NICHOLS, LEIGH B,** Univ Of Southern Ms, Hattiesburg, MS; SR; BS; NEA; Natl Cncl Tchrs Math; Kappa Mu Epsln; Gamma Beta Phi; Coop Bell South Svc 88; Math/Scnd Educ.

**MARBURY, GERALD D,** Univ Of Al At Birmingham, Birmingham, AL; FR; NSBE Prlmntrn; Elctrcl; Eng.

**MARBUT, HOWARD A,** Norfolk St Univ, Norfolk, VA; SO; MBA; Army ROTC 89-; Army ROTC 4 Yr Schlrshp 89-; Sclgy; Commission Army/Law Enfrcmnt.

**MARCA, MYRNA Y,** Univ Of Ky, Lexington, KY; JR; BA; Vlntr Intrnshp UK Med Hsptl; Estrn St Hsp 90; Englsh; Med.

**MARCANO, DEBBIE LEE,** Inter Amer Univ Pr Hato Rey, Hato Rey, PR; FR; Coro UPR.

**MARCANTONIO, MICHAEL H,** Meridian Comm Coll, Meridian, MS; SO; AA; Phi Theta Kappa 90-; Basebal 89-; English; Education.

**MARCARIO, MELISSA,** Alvernia Coll, Reading, PA; FR; BA; Pres Schlrshp 90-; Psychlgy.

**MARCARIO, ROBERT J,** Eckerd Coll, St Petersburg, FL; GD; BA; Psychlgy Clb 88-90; College Radio 87-90; Itln Clb 87; Spec Tlnt Awrds 87-; Psychlgy.

**MARCEAU, ROSEMARY D,** Springfield Tech Comm Coll, Springfield, MA; GD; BA; NALS Treas 87-90; CSI 88-90; AS 90; Sci-Offc Admin-Legal; Law.

**MARCELLA, DAWN R,** Univ Of Sc At Columbia, Columbia, SC; SO; BA; Schlrshps 88; Dns Lst 89-; Bsn.

**MARCELLO, JOSEPH C,** Cumberland County Coll, Vineland, NJ; SO; AA; Stdnt Snte Chrprsn 90; Cmptr Clb; Gospel Choir; Cntrbtng Ed For Schl Papr; Hons Schlrs Rsrch 89; Pres Lst 89; Phi Theta Kappa 90; Cult Dvrsty Cmmttee; Stdnt Advsry Brd; Snte Schlrshp; Al Biondi Schlrshp; Cmmnctns; Law.

**MARCENGILL, CYNTHIA L,** Coll Of Charleston, Charleston, SC; SO; Wesley Fndtn Pub Chrmn 90-; Alpha Delta Pi Hons Chrmn 90/Diamonds Dec Chrmn; Pr Lst Dist 90; IM Ftbl/Bsktbl/Vlybl/Sftbl 89-; Bus Admin; Bnking.

**MARCH, KELLY J,** Fl International Univ, Miami, FL; JR; BSW; West Indian Stdtns Assn Hstrn 90-; Cir K 86-87; Blck Hstry Month Chrprsn; AA Sociology Clg Bahamas 88; AA; Soc Wrk; Cnslr.

**MARCH, MARCUS U,** Univ Of Tn At Chattanooga, Chattanooga, TN; FR; MBA; Ntl Soc Blck Engr 90-; Blck Stu Assoc 90-; Intrn S Cntrl Bell 90-; IM Bsktbl/Ftbl 90-; Engr; Mech.

**MARCH, MONICA A,** Norfolk St Univ, Norfolk, VA; FR; BA; WG-9 Nuclear Marine Painter 82-90; Comptl 4yr Painter Apprenticeshp 82-86; Cert Tidewater Commty Clg 85; Fine Artsf Grphic Design.

**MARCHAND, BLANCHARD J,** Univ Of Sc At Columbia, Columbia, SC; FR; BA; Gamma Beta Phi 90-; Media Arts; Media Eng.

**MARCHAND, BRETT G,** Me Maritime Academy, Castine, ME; FR; BA; Eng.

**MARCHAND, SANDRA P,** Fl International Univ, Miami, FL; SR; BS; Dns Lst 90-; Royal Caribbean Cruises Tcktg Agt Intern; AS Daytona Bch Cmnty Clg 90; Hosptlty Mgmt; Bsn Mgmt.

**MARCHANT, LEWIS K,** Boston Univ, Boston, MA; GD; BA; Mass Med Soc Edtr 89-; AMA 89-; AMSA 89-; Alpha Omega Alpha; Golden Key 90-; Phi Delta Epsilon 89-; Lange Med Pblicatns Awd 90; Mc Graw Hill Awd Acad Excllnc 89; Dist Soph Awd 87; Med; MD.

**MARCHANT, NICOLE M,** Daytona Beach Comm Coll, Daytona Beach, FL; SO; AA; Otstndng Mrt Accmplshmnt Bus; Bus Admin; Cmptrzd Acctg.

**MARCHANY JUSTINIANO, MARIA L,** Univ Of Pr At Mayaguez, Mayaguez, PR; SR; BA; Pol Sci Stdnt Assoc Vcl 87-; Hnr Bd Art/Sci Fclty 90-; Phi Alpha Delta 89-; Pol Sci; Publ Adm.**

**MARCHBANKS, AMBER M,** Memphis St Univ, Memphis, TN; SO; Campus Crsde Chrst 89; Mst Imprvd Chrldr 89-90; Hghst GPA Awrd 90-; Natl Coll Prtnr Stnt Competitn 90-; Chrldr 89-; Psychlgy; Radiolgy/Ultrasnd.

**MARCHETTA, RYAN A,** Christian Brothers Univ, Memphis, TN; FR; MBA; Mech Engr.

**MARCHETTI, LAUREN,** Univ Of Med & Dentistry Of Nj, Newark, NJ; GD; Admssn Lsn Prog Clss Rep 87-89; Valedictorian 90; BS Thomas Jefferson Univ 89; RT 89; RMS Univ Med 90; Dgnstc Med Sngrphy; Ultrsngrphr.

**MARCHETTO, DANIEL P,** Comm Coll Algny Co Algny Cmps, Pittsburgh, PA; FR; BA; United Electricians Union 90-; Assoc US Army 85-; Bsn; Mgmt.

**MARCHIANO JR, JOSEPH E,** Unity Coll, Unity, ME; JR; BS; Assoc Sci 91; Consrvtn Law Enfrcmnt; Law Enfrcmnt.

**MARCHIONDA, CYNTHIA J,** Univ Of Cincinnati, Cincinnati, OH; SR; BFA; Southeast Theatre Conf 88-; Vocalist Vine Street Veterans Hosp; Comm/Univ Productions 88-91; Musical Theatre; Broadway.

**MARCIANO, LAWRENCE J,** Univ Of Rochester, Rochester, NY; SR; BA; Transfer Orntn 88-90; Pltcl Sci Cncl 88-89; Clg Republicans 88-89; Intrnshp Mrktng Coord Lakeside Meml 90-; Political Sci; Aviation Bus Admin.

**MARCIN, RIKKI,** Elmira Coll, Elmira, NY; SR; MAMS; BA; FLFR.

**MARCINIAK, SHEILA J,** D Youville Coll, Buffalo, NY; SO; Taught Kndrgdn Chldrn Spnsh For Spnsh Mnr; Spec Educ Vsly Imprd Cert; Mjr Opthmlgy.

**MARCINIAK, STEPHEN M,** Univ Of Rochester, Rochester, NY; JR; BA; Psychology; US Naval Serv.

**MARCINO, STEPHEN A,** Temple Univ, Philadelphia, PA; SR; BS; ASCE 88-; IM Vlybl/Sftbl/Ftbl; Civl Engr.

**MARCO, PATRICIA A,** Castleton St Coll, Castleton, VT; SR; BS; Clg Stdnt Assc Sec 90-; Stdnt Chptr Assc Fitns Bus Tres 90-; SADD Advrtsng Div 90-; Deer Ed Grp Co Orgntr 90-; Assc Hlth Phys Ed Pres 90-; Vol Amblnc Corp 84-; AA Orange Cnty Comm Clg 88; AS Orange Cnty Comm Clg 89; Phys Educ; Exrcs Physlgst.

**MARCONI, MICHAEL R,** Alfred Univ, Alfred, NY; FR; BA; AMA 90-; SAA 90-; Alpha Lambda Delta; Dns Lst 90-; Highest Index 90-; Acctng; Tx Attrny.

**MARCONI, MICHELLE M,** Indiana Univ Of Pa, Indiana, PA; SO; BA; Ed; Tchr.

**MARCONI, TRACEY A,** Mount Aloysius Jr Coll, Cresson, PA; GD; AS; Phi Theta Kappa 89-90; Legal Asst.

**MARCOS, GLENN,** Fl International Univ, Miami, FL; GD; MBA; Alpha Phi Sigma Prvsnl 90-; Phi Lambda 90-; Spcl Olympcs; AA Miami Dade Cmmnty Clg 89; BS 90; Crmnl Jstc; Law Schl.

**MARCOTTE, DEBORAH K,** Chattahoochee Vly St Comm Coll, Phenix City, AL; SO; AAS; Gamma Beta Phi; Crim Just; Law.

**MARCOTTE, KATHY M,** Castleton St Coll, Castleton, VT; SR; AS; Nwsppr Stff Wrtr 89-; Smmr Ornttn Stff Cnslr 90; Amer Coll Thtr Fest 90-; Phi Eta Sigma 90-; Advrtsng Slsprsn 87-89; Cmmnctns; Nwsppr Rptr/Edtr.

**MARCOUX, ALEXIA K,** Md Inst Coll Of Art, Baltimore, MD; SR; MFA; Dramatrgy Intrnshp Alley Theater 90; Schlrshp 87; ARTS Awd 87; Musicfst 87; BFA; Pntng/Flm; Tchr/Wrtr.

**MARCOUX, SUZY,** Western New England Coll, Springfield, MA; SR; BSBA; Acctg Assn VP Mem 90-; Delta Mu Delta 90-; BSBA; AS Holyoke Comm Coll 89; Acctg.

**MARCUCCI, JACQUELINE,** Univ Of Ga, Athens, GA; SR; Physcl Ed/Exrcs/Sprts Sci 90; Mjrs Clb; Communiv; Big Bro/Sis; Amer Clg Sprts Med; Alpha Lambda Delta; Gldn Key; BSED 90; Exrcs/Sprts Sci; Chrprctc.

**MARCUM, BETINA K,** Marshall University, Huntington, WV; SR; Deans List; Mason County Fair Brd; Ed; Elem Ed Tchr.

**MARCUM, KATHY ROSE,** Roane St Comm Coll, Harriman, TN; Police Sci.

**MARCUM, PAMELA J,** Lexington Comm Coll, Lexington, KY; SO; BA; Horse Trnr; Blgy; Med.

**MARCUM, STACY R,** Oh Wesleyan Univ, Delaware, OH; SO; BM; Stdnt Fdtn Tr Gd 90; MENC Trd Ed 89-; Phi Eta Sigma 89-90; Phi Scty 90; Mu Phi Epsilon 90; Pi Beta Phi Corres Sec 89-; Pi Beta Phi Phlnthrps Comm 90; Grk Schlrshp Awrd 89-; Music.

**MARCUM, TINA R,** Miami Jacobs Jr Coll Of Bus, Dayton, OH; FR; Typing Awd; Travel/Trsm.

**MARCUM, WILMA C,** Ashland Comm Coll, Ashland, KY; FR; MBA; Psy; Cnslng.

**MARCUS, JAAN S,** Univ Of Montevallo, Montevallo, AL; SO; BA; Bapt Campus Mnstrs 89-; Hnrs Clb 89-; Frshmn Acad Schlrshp 89-; Bsn; Acctg.

**MARCUS, JEFFREY F,** Univ Of Rochester, Rochester, NY; SO; BA; Gymnstcs Clb 89-; Stg Cmbt 90-; D Lion 90-; Tiernan Drm 89-; IM Cpt 89-; Psychlgy.

**MARCUS, KENYA M,** Al St Univ, Montgomery, AL; JR; BS; Frnch Clb VP 90-; Stdnt Orttn Assnce Rep Sec 89-; Biomed Sci Clb VP; Phi Eta Sigma 89-; Alpha Kappa Mu 90-; Beta Kappa Chi; Stdnt Of The Yr 90; Dns Awrd 90-; Hghst Rnkng Jr 90-; Blgy; Biomed Rsrch Med.

**MARCUS, MARY J,** Anderson Coll, Anderson, SC; SO; BS; Mgr Trng Brks Fash Intrnshp Merchdsng 90; Merchndsng; Corp Buyer.

**MARCY, DOUGLAS COLES,** Coll Of Charleston, Charleston, SC; SO; BS; Mens Glee Clb 90-; Geology Clb 90-; IM Bsktbl Bsbl; Geology; Grad Schl.

**MARCY, LESLIE A,** Rivier Coll, Nashua, NH; SR; Stdnt Govt Assn Corr Sec 89; Adpt A Grndprnt 90-; NH DWI Prvntn Cncl Exec Brd Sec; Intrnshp Excllnce In Exrcse Pr Wk Asst; BA; PR.

**MARDALES ESCANELLAS, MARIA M,** Univ Politecnica De Pr, Hato Rey, PR; FR; Indstl Engr.

**MARDERIAN, RICHARD V,** Broome Comm Coll, Binghamton, NY; FR; BA; Phi Theta Kappa; Pres List 90-; Frgn Lang; Trnsltn.

**MARDIS, PATRICK O,** Univ Of Southern Ms, Hattiesburg, MS; JR; Phi Theta Kappa Pres 89-90; Bus Adm Awd 89-90; Phi Theta Kappa Schlrshp 89-90; Jr Coll Achvmnt Schlrshp 89-90; Bus; Adm.

**MARENUS, PATTI R,** Univ Of Fl, Gainesville, FL; GD; Wmns Chorale V P 85-86; Florida Clgte Music Educ; Sigma Alpha Iota Vp 86-88; NATS 89; Florida Music Educ Assn/Florida Vocal Assn; CO Tchrs Assn; Florida Arts Clbrtn; BM Univ Florida 90; Music/Vocal/Cndctng; Tch.

**MARGARITIS, JILL L,** Wilmington Coll, Wilmington, OH; JR; BA; Stdnt Govt Bdgt Cmmtt 90-; Grk Cncl 90-; Grk Jdcl Brd 90-; Deans Lst 89-; Stdnts Fr Entrprs 89-; Mrktng Clb 90; Phi Alpha Psi Pres Elect; Cmps Ortn Ldr 88-; Cmps Tr Gd 88-; Cmps Hstss; Ttr; Mrktng Intern; Ftbll; Bstktll Chrldr Capt 88-; Econ Bus Mgmt.**

**MARGARUCCI, LISA MARIE,** S U N Y Coll At Fredonia, Fredonia, NY; SR; BED; Tchr Ed Clb/Amnsty Intl 89-91; Stdnt Govt 87-88; IMS 87-90; Ed Hon Soc 90-; Kappa Delta Pi Hstrn 89-; Pres Awrd 87-88; Erly Chldhd Ed; Tchr.

**MARGITA, STEPHEN A,** Duquesne Univ, Pittsburgh, PA; FR; BA; Music; Audio Engr.

**MARGOLIUS, LAURA M,** Univ Of Rochester, Rochester, NY; JR; BA; Grassroots 89-; Amnesty Intrntl 89-90; Sigma Delta Tau 88-; Intrn Aesthetic Ed Inst Rsrchr/Wrtr 90-; Rsrchr For Eductnl Settings 90-; Im Flr Hockey 89-; Engl/Psychlgy; Profsr Of Engl.

**MARGRAF, NATALIE M,** Kent St Univ Kent Cmps, Kent, OH; SR; BS; Pre Med Clb 89-; Alpha Lambda Delta 87-; Gldn Key; Mrchng Bnd 87-88; Pre Med; Med.

**MARGULIS, MARK,** Bunker Hill Comm Coll, Boston, MA; SO; BA; Jrnlst; Bed USSR Beltry Gym 40; Engl.

**MARGUSH, JEFFREY D,** Columbus Coll Of Art & Design, Columbus, OH; SO; BA; IDSA 90-; Amer Rcng Whl Dsgn Awrd 90; Sccr Tm 90-; Indstrl Dsgn; Trnsprttn/Prdct Dsgn.

**MARHATTA, JOSEPH ROBERT,** Bryant Stratton Bus Inst Roch, Rochester, NY; GD; BA; ADS 90; Elec Technlgy; Engrng.

**MARHSALL, JOHN W,** Univ Of Ky, Lexington, KY; GD; MD; Chrstn Medcl/Dntl Soc VP 89-; Chem Clb 87-88; Army ROTC 84-87; Univ Miami FL Hon Soc 84-85; Ldr Yng Adlt Grp Blvd SDA Chrch Asst Ldr 87-89; Ldr Yng Adlt Grp Lane Allen SDA Chrch Asst Ldr 89-; Asstshp Fmly Med 89; Med; Fmly Med.

**MARIANARO, PHILLIP A,** Univ Of Ky, Lexington, KY; SR; BSW; Amer Red Crss/Blue Grss Chptr Cnslr; Lxngtn Hbtat For Humnty Co-Coord; Prof Bldr/Marinaro Remodlng; Socl Wrk; Chld/Fmly Cnslr.

**MARIANETTI, ELIM Z,** Hudson Valley Comm Coll, Troy, NY; SR; Internatl Stdnt Clb 90-; Alpha Xi Sigma; Phi Theta Kappa; Tutor Watervliet Elem Schl 90-; Lght Wrld Chrstn Chrch 89-; Internatl Bsn.

**MARIANI, ALEC D,** Schenectady County Comm Coll, Schenectady, NY; SO; AS; Jzz Ensmbl-SCCC 90-; Chorus 87-; Symphny Orchstr 90-; Union Coll Chmbr Orchstra 90-; Music Cert 90; Music Educ.

**MARIANI, THERESA M,** Hilbert Coll, Hamburg, NY; AAS; Prlgl Clb :Vp 89-; Sftbll 81-; Deans Lst 89-; Lgl Asst Intern 90-; Sftbll 89; Prlgl Lgl Asst; Law.

**MARIANO, DENISE A,** Glassboro St Coll, Glassboro, NJ; SO; BA; RSA Pres 90-; Psychology; Psychlgst/Cnslr Thrpst.

**MARIBONA, PATRICIA M,** Fl International Univ, Miami, FL; JR; BS; Law Assoc; Phi Kappa Phi; Xi Delta 90-; Exec Ofc Pres/Ofc Adm/Publ Svc Intern; Intl Rels/Finance; Law.

**MARIEA, CHERISE R,** Bowling Green St Univ, Bowling Green, OH; FR; BS; Alpha Lambda Delta; Phi Eta Sigma; Hmls Awrns 90-; NARAL Ohio 90-; Dns Lst 90-; Ftwl Lab 90-; Bio/Pre-Med; Med Doctor.

**MARIEN, ANGELA NOELLE,** Ramapo Coll Of Nj, Mahwah, NJ; SR; BA; Spec Educ Orien Panel 89-90; Unity Week Solo Sngr 90; Theater 88-91; Prof Sngr 88-; Rcrdng Artist; Cmmnctns/Theater; Prof Sngr.

**MARIN MERINO, FRANCISCO E,** Inter Amer Univ Pr Hato Rey, Hato Rey, PR; SO; Honor Assn 90-; All Amer Schlrshp 90; Adm Cmptr Info Syst/Law; BS Adm Cmptr; Law.

**MARIN, LUIS A,** Alfred Univ, Alfred, NY; JR; BS; Inst Indstrl Eng Sec 88-; Tau Beta Pi 90-; Alpha Phi Iota; Indstrl Eng Awrd; Indstrl Eng; Eng.

**MARIN, OCTAVIO R,** Fl International Univ, Miami, FL; JR; BS; AA Miami Dade Comm Clg 89; Env; Cvl Eng.

**MARIN, YVETTE,** Embry Riddle Aeronautical Univ, Daytona Beach, FL; SO; BA; Brothers Of Wind 89-90; Arntcl Sci; Ar Trfc Cntrlr.

**MARIN-ALICEA, MANUAL,** Bayamon Central Univ, Bayamon, PR; SO; Entrp Mngmnt Assn.

**MARINA, VICTOR G,** Fl International Univ, Miami, FL; SR; BS; BS Elec Eng 89; Civil Engrng-Structures.

**MARINACCIO, ANGELA,** S U N Y Coll Of Tech At Frmgdl, Farmingdale, NY; SO; AS; Stdnt Amer Dntl Hygiensts Assoc 89; AA Nassau Cmmnty Clg 89; Dntl Hygiene.

**MARINARO, THERESA A,** Bunker Hill Comm Coll, Boston, MA; JR; MBA; Phi Theta Kappa 90; Hnrs Cert In Recgntn Acad Excllnc; AS; Rest Mgmnt.**

**MARINAS, BRIAN C,** Liberty Univ, Lynchburg, VA; SR; BS; Stdnt Bdy Treas Cabinet 89-90; Coll Rpblcns 88-90; Alpha Lambda Delta 88-; Hon Schlr 89-; GPA Schlrshp 89-; Summa Cum Laude 90-; Math; Prof Of Math.

**MARINELLI, PAULA E,** Savannah Coll Of Art & Design, Savannah, GA; GD; Cum Laude 88; Hghst GPA 88; IM Bsktbl 90; BA Providence Coll 88; MFA 90; Fine Art/Pntng/Illstrn; Instr.

**MARINER, FREDERICK L,** Fl A & M Univ, Tallahassee, FL; FR; MBA; Pres Spcl Schlrs Awd; Cmptr Sci; Sys Analysis.

**MARINEY, GLENDA,** Univ Of Sc At Aiken, Aiken, SC; SR; BS; Accs Chncllr; Dean Stdnts Srch; Comm Martin Luther King Plnng; Comm Treas Alpha Kappa Psi 90-; Recrtrs Schlrshp 89; Accntng; CPA.

**MARINICH, MARY CATHERINE,** Fayetteville St Univ, Fayetteville, NC; JR; Fmly Spprt Grp For Unit On Ft Bragg Drng Dsrt Strm Chrmn 90; Elem Ed; Tchr.

**MARINO, ANTHONY J,** Le Moyne Coll, Syracuse, NY; SO; BA; Radio Sta 89-; Nwsppr 90; Thtr Hse 89-; Le Moyne Acdmc Schlrhsp 89-; Dean Lst 90-; Cmmnty Nwspprs Intern; Engl/Cmmnctns.

**MARINO, BRENDA A,** Univ Of Ma At Amherst, Amherst, MA; FR; BA; Spnsh; Scdndry Ed.

**MARINO, DAVID W,** Coll Of Insurance, New York, NY; SR; BBA; Student Cncl Pres 87-90; Young Insurance Prfssnls Netwrk 90-; Corporate Sponsor Program; Ralph Bell Schlrshp; Sftbl Mgr 89-; Property Liability Ins.

**MARINO, JOSEPH J,** Bergen Comm Coll, Paramus, NJ; SR; AA; Radiogrphy Club 89-; Phi Theta Kappa 90-; NJ Soc Of Radiolgc Technlgsts 90-; BA Univ Of San Diego 71; Radiogrphc Sci; Nuclr Medcn.

**MARINO, KRISTA,** Univ Of Med & Dentistry Of Nj, Newark, NJ; SR; AS Farleigh Dickinson Univ 89; Diag Med Sono.

**MARINO, LISA A,** Westminster Coll, New Wilmingtn, PA; SR; BA; Kappa Delta Pi 90-; Srvc Tm Yth Dvlpmnt Cntr 87-88; Clara E Cockerille Schlrshp 90; Edctnl Intrnshp 90; BA; Elem Edctn; Elem Tchr.

**MARINO, LOUIS A,** Glassboro St Coll, Glassboro, NJ; GD; Vol Of Amer 88; Cert Acad Outstdng Achvmnt 89-; EOF Prog Awd; NJ Assn Stdnt Fncl Aid Admin Inc Awd 89-90; Gen Assmbly Of State Of NJ 88-89; Cert Cmmndtn 88-89; Auto Mech Cert Gloucester Vol Tech Schl 90; Psychlgy.

**MARINO, MONICA L,** Liberty Univ, Lynchburg, VA; FR; Spnsh Clb Pblcty Hd 90; Spnsh; Tchr.

**MARINO, ROSEANN,** Duquesne Univ, Pittsburgh, PA; FR; Lbrl Arts.

**MARINO, SUZANNA I,** Indiana Univ Of Pa, Indiana, PA; SR; BS; Biology Clb 88-90; Kappa Delta Pi 89-; Provost Schlr 89-; Biology; Tchng.

**MARINO, THERESA A,** Indiana Univ Of Pa, Indiana, PA; JR; BED; IM Bsktbl; Elem Educ.

**MARINO-HARGADON, LAURAL L,** Anne Arundel Comm Coll, Arnold, MD; SO; BA; Jaycees Of Glen Burnie 89-90; Ch 24 WHSW Intrnshp Brdcstr 90-; Mass Cmnctns; Brdcst Jrnlsm.

**MARION, SONYA D,** Univ Of Tn At Martin, Martin, TN; FR; BSA Choir Treas 90-; Mc Cord Hall Pres 90-; Electn Cmsnr Rep 90-; Black Stdnt Assoc 90-; IM Vlybl/Bsktbl 90-; Nursing.

**MARION, TONYA L,** Univ Of Tn At Martin, Martin, TN; FR; Stdnt Gvmt Fresh Rep 90-; NAACP Sec 90-; BSA Insprtnl Chr Sec 90-; BSA 90-91; Pre/Med; Dr.

**MARIUS, MELISSA MARIE,** Muskingum Coll, New Concord, OH; SO; BA; Ohio Collegiate Music Educators Assn VP 89-90; Concert Chr Chmber Sngrs 89-; Prnts Wkend Comm Tal Shw Chrprsn 89-; Stdnt Act Grp Sprt Bnd Wnd Ensem 89-; Lambda Sigma Zeta; Psi Chi; Omicron Delta Kappa; Sigma Alpha Iota; Theta Phi Alpha; Psychology/Msc; Msc Thrpy.

**MARIZAN, RICHARD A,** Talmudic Coll Of Fl, Miami Beach, FL; GD; MBA; Stdnt Govt Pres 90-; Schl Camp Drctr; 2 Yrs Jnt Israel Prgrm 87-89; Schl Frst Aid Instrctr 89-; Koske Drctr 89-; Ntnl Cnfrnc Synagogue Yth Ldr 87-; Bsbl Bsktbl 87-; BRE Talmudic Univ FL; Bsnss Mngmnt; Bsnss Ownr.

**MARJANOVIC, SVETLANA,** Bunker Hill Comm Coll, Boston, MA; FR; BA; Lbrl Arts; Foreign Lang/Mgmt.

**MARK, CHRISTINE A,** City Univ Of Ny City Coll, New York, NY; SR; Stdnts Art Media/Educ 90; NY Assn Blck Jrnlst 90-; WABC-TV Intrnshp 90; Role Model 90; BA.

**MARK, DONNA A,** Cumberland County Coll, Vineland, NJ; SO; AA; Tutor Algbr/Statstcs; Elem Ed; Algbr Tchr.

**MARK, GIOVANNA W,** Dekalb Coll, Decatur, GA; FR.

**MARK, JAMEELA A,** Clark Atlanta Univ, Atlanta, GA; FR; BA; Dns Lst 90-; Acctng; CPA.

**MARK, SANDRA B,** Duquesne Univ, Pittsburgh, PA; SO; BA; Spec/Elem Ed; Special Ed Teacher.

**MARKEL, JANET L,** Hillsborough Comm Coll, Tampa, FL; SO; BS; Cmptr Oprtr 87-; Cmptr/Math; Eng.

**MARKER, SEAN P,** Univ Of Pa, Philadelphia, PA; FR; BA; Acad Peer Advsr; 1st Yr Asst Res; Campus Crusade Christ; Pennlincs Sci Mntr; Deans Lst; Psychlgy/Bio Basis Bhvr/Math; Medicine.

**MARKER, SHUANA L,** De Tech & Comm Coll At Dover, Dover, DE; FR; Acctg; CPA.

**MARKER, STACEY M,** Lebanon Valley Coll, Annville, PA; JR; BS; Cmptr Clb 87-; Math Clb Quiz Bwl Co Orgztnr 88-; Cmptr Sci/Math.**

**MARKETTE, RICHARD R,** Savannah Coll Of Art & Design, Savannah, GA; SO; BFA; Intrmrl Bsktbll 89-90; Illstrntn.**

**MARKEY, AMY,** Immaculata Coll, Immaculata, PA; SR; BA; Sigma Zeta Sec 90-; Rsrch Intrnshp 90; Grad Flwshp; Molecular Bio.

**MARKEY, REBECCA S,** Union Coll, Barbourville, KY; FR; BA; Stdnt Govt Sntr 90-; Pizzazzers 90-; Flwshp Chrstn Athlts 90-; Sftbl 91; Acctng; CPA.

**MARKGRAF, SAMANTHA,** S U N Y Coll Of Tech At Frmgdl, Farmingdale, NY; SR; AA; Liberal Arts; Educ.

**MARKHAM, GLYNIS CHAMBERS,** Univ Of South Al, Mobile, AL; SR; BS; Mrtr Brd; Pres List 90-; Spec Olympics Vol Wrkr 89-90; Sprng Hl Bpst Chrc 87; Tutor Biloxi Cty Schl Systm 85-87; Elem Educ; Teach.**

**MARKHAM, HOUSTON L,** Al St Univ, Montgomery, AL; FR; BA; Bsbl; Math; Engr.

**MARKHAM, LARRY W,** Belmont Coll, Nashville, TN; JR; BS; Gamma Beta Phi 88-; Chemistry Awd 89; Cross Cntry 88; Chem Math; Medicine.

**MARKHAM, ROY MICHAEL,** Cumberland Coll, Williamsburg, KY; FR; BS; FRIENDS Sec 90-; Math Clb 90-; Eldrly Mnstrs 90-; U S Navy Nclr Mech 84-90; Math/Physcs/Sec Ed; Tch.

**MARKLAND, STACY R,** James Madison University, Harrisonburg, VA; JR; BS; Psychlgy Clb; Compeer 90-; Psi Chi 90-; Gldn Key Natl Hon Scty 90-; Deans List 89-; Pres List 90-; GMU Pres/Deans List 88-89; Pychlgy; Clncl/Cnslng Psychtrst.

**MARKLEY, DREW R,** Kent St Univ Kent Cmps, Kent, OH; JR; BA; Golden Key; Bus Mat/Mktg; Corp Law.

**MARKO, CYNTHIA M,** Duquesne Univ, Pittsburgh, PA; SO; BSBA; Frnch Clb 89-90; Phi Eta Sigma Treas 90-; Lambda Sigma 90-; Hnrs Pgm 89-90; IM Sftbl/Vlybl/Bsktbl 89-; Intl Bsn.

**MARKO, JENNIFER S,** Univ Of Akron, Akron, OH; FR; BS; Hnrs Coll 90-; Alpha Delta Pi Pldg Cls Soc Chr 90-; Dance Tm Capt 90-; Eng; Elec Eng.

**MARKOPOULOS, DAFNI,** S U N Y Coll Of Tech At Frmgdl, Farmingdale, NY; FR; BA; Crim Jstc; Plc Ofcr.

**MARKOU, AFRODITE,** City Univ Of Ny Baruch Coll, New York, NY; SR; BBA; Beta Gamma Sigma 90-; Goldn Key 89-; Coll Incntv Awrd 87-88; Deans Lst 88-; Endwmnt Fnd Prvsts Schlrshp 89-90; Acctg; CPA/GRAD Stdies.

**MARKOVICH, CHAD L,** Oh Univ, Athens, OH; FR; Elec Engr.

**MARKOWITZ, RACHEL,** Yeshiva Univ, New York, NY; SR; Observer Sch Ppr Bsn Mgr 89-; Acctg Soc 88-; NYSIPAC; BS; Acctg.

**MARKOWSKI, MARLA A,** Smith Coll, Northampton, MA; SR; MS; Crmcs Clb 90-; Crmcs Frng/Kiln Wrkshp; Cnfrnc Vol Escrt Envrnmnt; Math Liaison 89-90; Dorm Rcyclng Co-Chr 89-90; Fin Aid Liaison 89-90; Deans Lst 88-; 1st Grp Schlr 89-90; Univ MA Envrnmntl Eng Intrn 89; Dana Grant Intrnshp 89; Fin Aidofeice Intrn 88-90; Ntrl Rsrcl Ecnmcs; Cnsrvtn/Envrnmntl Pub Plcy.

**MARKOWSKI, TINA ROSE,** Elmira Coll, Elmira, NY; SR; Ed.

**MARKOWSKI, TRISHA D,** Embry Riddle Aeronautical Univ, Daytona Beach, FL; JR; BA; SGA 90-; Future Prfsnl Wmn Aviation Prsdnt 89-; Entrtnmnt Comm 89-; Deans Lst; Ldrshp Prgrm; IM Vlybl Cptn 90-; Arntcl Science Aviation; Pilot.

**MARKOZEN, GENE E,** Univ Of Louisville, Louisville, KY; SO; BA; IEEE 90-; Electrcl Engrng.

**MARKS, DALLAS J,** Univ Of Cincinnati, Cincinnati, OH; SR; BS; IEEE Brnch Chrmn 90-; Nwslttr Edtr 90-; Stu Tribunal 89-; Cert; Benjamin Pilhashy Mem Schlrshp 90-; Elect Eng Tech; Grad Schl Cmptr Eng.**

**MARKS, DAVID B,** Gordon Coll, Barnesville, GA; JR; BA; Glbl Encntr Org Stdnts; IM Sccr; Engl.

**MARKS, ELIZABETH A,** Belmont Coll, Nashville, TN; FR; BM; Chrstn Musc Soc; Choir; Music; Perf/Tchg.

**MARKS JR, RONALD P,** S U N Y Coll Of Tech At Delhi, Delhi, NY; FR; Elctrcl Contr.

**MARKS, THERESA A,** Univ Of Fl, Gainesville, FL; SR; BS; Occptnl Thrpy Assoc 89; Pi Kappa Phi Lit Sis 88; Occptnl Thrpy.

**MARKS, THERESA M,** Tuskegee Univ, Tuskegee Inst, AL; GD; DYM; Pre-Vet Clb Cook Coll Rtgrs U 85-87; Ham Radio Clb 76-90; SCAVMA 90-; IM Sftbl 90-; BA Douglass Coll Rtgrs U 88; Vet Med.

**MARKUSICH, HEATHER A,** Univ Of Va Clinch Valley Coll, Wise, VA; SR; MA; Intl Clb 88-; Dns Lst 89-; Phi Upsilon Omega Pres Elect; Hstry; Law Sch/Prac Intl Law.

**MARKWARDT, MARIE,** Immaculata Coll, Immaculata, PA; SR; BA; Psychlgy Clb Treas 90-; Fall Mscl Vrty Shows/Chrl 87-; Educ Clb 89-; Psi Chi Treas 90-; Kappa Gamma Pi-Delta Epsilon Sigma; Res Asst Stff 89-90; Tutor Spnsh-Spkng Chldrn/Coll Stdnts 88-90; Cert Elem Ed/Spnsh; Psychlgy; Educ/Psychlgy.

**MARLER, JAMES P,** Memphis St Univ, Memphis, TN; SO; Cmptr/Engr Technlgy.

**MARLEWSKI, MARIA K,** Kent St Univ Kent Cmps, Kent, OH; SR; BA; Psych Clb 90; Golden Key 90-; Dns Lst 86-90; Pres Lst 90; Psych; Adolescents Therapist.

**MARLEY, JOE B,** Middle Tn St Univ, Murfreesboro, TN; SR; BS; Farrier; Social Studies; Teacher.

**MARLEY IV, JOHN T,** S U N Y At Buffalo, Buffalo, NY; GD; DDS; Delta Sigma Delta 90-; Amer Dental Stdnt Assoc 90-; Army Hlth Prof Schlrshp; BS Cameron Univ 80; Dental Med.

**MARLIN, MELINDA JO,** Univ Of Ga, Athens, GA; SR; BSED; RHA 87-88; Hl V P 87-88; UGA Wmns Soccer Clb 87-; Early Chldhd Ed; Tchr.

**MARLING, SHERIE L,** Univ Of West Fl, Pensacola, FL; FR; AA; Wesley Fndtn 90-; Phi Eta Sigma 90-; Publshd Poetry In Intl Publctns; Elem Tchr.

**MARLOWE, DEBRA A,** Wv Univ, Morgantown, WV; SR; BSN; Natl Stdnt Nurses Assoc 88-; Sigma Theta Tau 90-; Golden Key 90-; Vetrns Admn Schlrshp 90-; NSNA Fndtn Schlrshp 90; Rstrnt Owner 84-86; RN.

**MARLOWE, KATHRYN R,** Univ Of Ga, Athens, GA; JR; BED; SCEC; IM Sftbl; Special Ed; Teaching.

**MARLOWE, LISA A,** Broward Comm Coll, Ft Lauderdale, FL; JR; AS; Phi Theta Kappa 86-88; Phi Theta Kappa 87-88; Otstndng Acdmc Achvmnt 86-88; ARRT Asrt Fl Scty Rd Tch; AAAS 86-88; Ultrsnd.

**MARLOWE, MARK E,** Western Piedmont Comm Coll, Morganton, NC; SO; AAS; Bsn Admn; Mgmt.

**MARLOWE, SHANNON D,** Univ Of Nc At Asheville, Asheville, NC; SO; BA; Spnsh; Elem Edctn.

**MARNELL, ELAINE A,** Juniata Coll, Huntingdon, PA; JR; BA; Intl Clb 88-89; Brmbgh-Ellis Pres Schlrshp; Gtwy Trvl Frgn Lang Schlrshp; Spnsh; Univ Tchng/Grad Study.

**MAROCCO, MICHELLE L,** Univ Of Rochester, Rochester, NY; SO; BS; Com On Prfrmng Arts Actng In 6 Plys 89-; BASS 7 Dnce Grp 90-; Dns Lst; Vol Hst Fr Prspctve Stdnts 89-; Alpha Psi Omega; Cmps Y 5 K Run; IM Sprts Sccr Flr Hcky 90; Pol Sci; Jrnslm Wrtng.

**MAROLF, NICOLE K,** Univ Of Fl, Gainesville, FL; JR; BS; Hmcmng Stf 88-90; Stdnt Occptnl Therpy Assn Comm Chrmn 90-; Career Expo Stf 88-89; Goldn Key 90-; Alpha Lambda Delta 88-; Amer Occptnl Therpy Assn 90-; Chi Omega 88-; IM Sftbl/ Vlybl 89-; FL Acdmc Schlr 88-; Pnhllnc Schlr Rcgntn 90-; AA 90; Occptnl Therpy; Pediatrc Therpy.

**MAROLI, KAREN E,** Cornell Univ Statutory College, Ithaca, NY; JR; BS; Orientation Cnslr 89; Peer Acad Advsr 90-; Red Carpet Soc 88-; Ambsdr 88-; Publ Rels Stdnt Soc Amer 90-; Friends Joe King Schlr 89-; Athl Schlr 89-; Walter H Forisch Schlrshp; Vars Bsktbl 88-; Bsn/Mktg Mgmt; Advrtsg.

**MARON, GERARD P,** Providence Coll, Providence, RI; SR; Acctg Assoc Exec VP 90-; Fin Clb 87-; Ski Clb 87-; Tau Pi Phi; Intrn J P Morgan Bnk Acctg Anlys 89; Intrn Twnsnd Entrpr 89; Intrn J P Morgan Fin Rep 90; BS; Acctg.

**MARON, SUSAN M,** Georgian Court Coll, Lakewood, NJ; SR; BA; Psychlgy Clb 90; Prnt Invlvmnt Prgrm; Prnt Advsry Brd; Psi Chi 90; Rn 76; Cert St Frncs Hsptl Schl Nrsng 76; Psychlgy; Clncl Psychlgy Or Cnslng.

**MARONE, MICHAEL L,** Georgetown Univ, Washington, DC; SR; BSBA; Mktg Scty; Grmn Clb Tres 90-; Invstmnt Alnc; Beta Gamma Sgm; Tutor 89-90; Fincl Acctg Intrn OPIC; Intrnl Mgmt Fin; JD/MBA.

**MARONI, BOBBIE J,** Oh Dominican Coll, Columbus, OH; FR; BA; Amer Intl Mbrshp 90-; Hnrs Cls Essay/Rsrch 90-; Ohio Dominian Coll Acad Schlrshp 90-; Cmmnctns; TV/PUB Rel.

**MARONSKI, VINCENT P,** S U N Y Coll Of A & T Morrisvl, Morrisville, NY; FR; AS; SADD; Rsdnt Asst; Pltcs/Hstry; Corp/ Envir Law.

**MAROON, LENORA A,** West Liberty St Coll, West Liberty, WV; SR; BS; Acad Appls Comm; Delta Mu Delta; Deans Lst; Wall St Jrnl Awd; U S Small Bus Admin Cert Of Merit; Mgmnt.

**MAROSI, SUZANNA E,** Univ Of Akron, Akron, OH; SR; BA; Flr Cncl 87; Stdnts Missn Flwshp 88; Litry Soc 89-90; Lang Prtnr 90; Educ; Tch Engl.

**MAROTTA, JANINE,** William Paterson Coll, Wayne, NJ; SR; BA; Med Asst Berdan Inst 85-86; Elem Ed/Sclgy; Tchr/Mntl Hlth.

**MAROTTA, MICHAEL A,** S U N Y Coll At Fredonia, Fredonia, NY; JR; BS; Deans List; Horace A Lanza Mem Schlrshp 88; Anthony J Patti Mem Schlrshp 90-; NYS Regnts Schlrshp 88-; NCAA Ice Hcky 88; IM Rcqtbl; Tlcmmnctns/ Ecnmcs Soc; Mngr.

**MAROTTA-ESPINOSA, AILEEN,** Inter Amer Univ Pr Hato Rey, Hato Rey, PR; SR; BA; Hstry Assn Sec 88-89 VP 89-90; Hstry; Law/MA/PHD.

**MARPLE, DOUGLAS W,** Wv Univ, Morgantown, WV; JR; BSME; SAE 89; ASME 89; ESWP 89; Golden Key 90; Deans Lst 89-90; Mchncl Eng; Eng.

**MARQUARDT, DEBRA A,** Univ Of Akron, Akron, OH; JR; BED; Sports Med Staff Sprvsr 88; Sunday Schl Tchr 88; Phi Eta Sigma 89; Alpha Lambda Delta 89; Gldn Key 90; Sprts Med Spclsts Intrn; Ctcntr Athl Clb Intrn; Dodge Middle Schl TA 90-; Sports Med/Athltc Trng Hlth Ed.

**MARQUES, DENIZE,** Comm Coll Algny Co Algny Cmps, Pittsburgh, PA; FR; AD; Adtr Coopers Lybrand Brazil 86-90; BS Unv Sao Paulo Brzl 88; Accntng; MBA Adtng.

**MARQUES, ISABEL D,** Georgian Court Coll, Lakewood, NJ; SO; Mendel Soc 89-; Deans Schlr 89-90; Biology; Medicine.

**MARQUEZ, ANNA K,** Ms St Univ, Miss State, MS; FR; BFA; Baptist Stdnt Un; Univ Hons Prog; Refrmd Univ Fellowshp; Alpha Lambda Delta; Lambda Sigma; Gamma Beta Phi; Deans Schlr; Pres Schlr; Art; Graphic Dsgn.

**MARQUEZ, DIANA N,** Univ Of Ga, Athens, GA; SR; Phi Beta Lambda Sec 88-90; Phi Sigma Sigma Prlmntrn 84-90; Boy Sct Explrs Trp Vol 90; Deans List 89-90; Coca-Cola Acdmc Schlrshp 84; BS Ed 90; Bus Ed; Tchr.

**MARQUEZ-MORALES, ALFREDO,** Inter Amer Univ Pr San Juan, Hato Rey, PR; GD; JD; Assn Nacl Estdnts De Drcho; Comingo Toledo Alamo Chptr PR Bar; Intr Amer Unvi Law Rvw 89-; BA University Of PR Rio Piedras Cmps 88.

**MARQUEZ-SCOTT, EMMA G,** Methodist Coll, Fayetteville, NC; GD; BS; Psych Clb 87-; Socl Wrk Clb 89-; Dns Lst 90-; U S Army Sgt 73-87; Mil Ldrshp Schl Grad 84; Yth Exp Arts Pres 89; 700 Clb CBN 87; Cert Persnl Admin Schl 82; Soc/Socl Wrk; Gerntlgy.

**MARQUIS, MARIA L,** Rivier Coll, Nashua, NH; GD; MSW; Dorm Pres 85-86; Dorm Snack Bar Mgr 85-86; Phi Nu 85-86; Intrn Hdstart Family Worker 90-; Intrn Mem Hosp 89-90; BSW; Soc Work.

**MARRA, ANNAMARIE,** Temple Univ, Philadelphia, PA; SR; BBA; Mktg; Mgmt.

**MARRA, MICHAEL J,** Indiana Univ Of Pa, Indiana, PA; SR; ROTC Cmmndoes 87; Alpha Psi Omega VP 90; Cmnctns/Thtr; Offcr Candidate Schl-USMC.

**MARRA, STEVEN P,** Univ Of Pittsburgh, Pittsburgh, PA; SO; BS; Mrchng Band Sqd Ldr 89-; Jazz Ensmbl 89-; Christn Outrch 90-; Iota Beta Kappa Pres 90-; Univ Acadmc Schlrshp 89-; Sch Of Engrs Schlrshp 89-; GM Schlrshp; Engrng; Mech Engr.

**MARRALE, MARIA C,** Univ Of Ky, Lexington, KY; SO; BS; SADD 90-; Sigma Delta Pi; Spnsh/Blgy/Psychlgy; Physcns Asst.

**MARRANGONI, NICK J,** Duquesne Univ, Pittsburgh, PA; JR; BA; Fnncl Mngmnt Assn 90-; Beta Alpha Phi 90-; Sigma Tau Gamma VP Fnnc 88-; IM Bsktbl Vllybl 88-; Fnnc; Bus.

**MARRAZZO, KIM M,** Barry Univ, Miami, FL; FR; BA; Ambssdr Clb 90-; Deans Lst 90-; Stdnt Colloquium 90-; Pres Schlr 90-; Engl; Tch.

**MARRELL, CLARICE,** Univ Of Southern Ms, Hattiesburg, MS; JR; BS; Soc Clinical Pathology 80-; Reg Lab Tech 80-; AA Med Lab Tech 80; Med Tech.

**MARRELLI, MARIETTA F,** Univ Of Nc At Asheville, Asheville, NC; SO; Catholic Org 89-90; Phi Eta Sigma 89-; Hnr Stdnt 89-; Bio; Med.

**MARREN, DAVID G,** Univ Of Ma At Amherst, Amherst, MA; SR; BS; AAS Esse Ag Techncl Inst 86; Urban Forestry.

**MARRERO BENSON, NILDA L,** Catholic Univ Of Pr, Ponce, PR; FR; BA; Deans Lst; Bus; Mgmt/Mrktng.

**MARRERO MARRERO, DAMARIS,** Univ Of Pr At Mayaguez, Mayaguez, PR; JR; Cuadro De Hon 88-89; Eng.

**MARRERO, ALMA V,** Inter Amer Univ Pr Hato Rey, Hato Rey, PR; SR; BA; Futr Tchrs Assn 89-90; BA Engl Lit; Engl; Tchr/Jrnlsm.

**MARRERO, CARLOS C,** Univ Of Pr Medical Sciences, San Juan, PR; SR; MD; Amrcn Acdmy Fmly Physcn; Amrcn Grtrc Scty; MD Fmly Prctc Spclst; Grntlgy; Fmly Med; Grntlgy.

**MARRERO, FELIX R,** Inter Amer Univ Pr Barranquita, Barranquitas, PR; SO; Cmmrcl Admin Stdnt Assn 90-; Sftbl; Rcrtnl Assn Plo Hncdo 89-; Cmmrcl Admin Accntg; Law.

**MARRERO, JASON C,** City Univ Of Ny Lehman Coll, Bronx, NY; FR; BS; Physics; Physics/Engr.

**MARRERO, JAVIER A,** Univ Politecnica De Pr, Hato Rey, PR; FR; Math; Eng.

**MARRERO, JERRY L,** Inter Amer Univ Pr San Juan, Hato Rey, PR; GD; JD; Caguas Cyclng Tm 89-90; Tabl Tnns Clb W Germny 8th Inf Div Capt 87-89; Tbl Tns Capt; Dns Lst Univ Of Purto Rico 89-90; Dns Lst 90-; US Army Rsrv Frcs Stff Srgnt 89-; Hnr Grad Univ Of Purto Rico 89-90; Army Commendtn Medl SSG 88; Achvmnt Mdl SGT 87; Constitutnl Law; Jurs Dr.

**MARRERO, MARCELINO N,** Univ Of Miami, Coral Gables, FL; JR; BA; Arch; Law.

**MARRERO, MIGDALIA,** Univ Of Pr Medical Sciences, San Juan, PR; SR; CG; Amer Eval Assc 87-; PR Inst Rsrch Assc 88-; Rsrch Asstntshp 83-85; Pblc Hlth Flwshp 82-84; MS 86; BA Univ PR 82; Gerontology.

**MARRERO, SHIRLEY A,** Columbia Greene Comm Coll, Hudson, NY; FR; AS; Jr Clvrbds 4-H Clb Co Ldr 90-; WILPF 87-89; Phi Theta Kappa; AS S Clg Lake Wrth FL 89; EMT NY EMT Trng 90; Nrsng; Mdwfry.

**MARRERO, WANDA I,** Univ Of Pr Medical Sciences, San Juan, PR; GD; MS; The Rho Chi; BS Ph 85; Indstrl Phrmcy.

**MARRERO, WENDY J,** Univ Politecnica De Pr, Hato Rey, PR; SO; BSME; Mech Engnrng Stdnt Chptr 90-; Puerto Rico Tchrs Fed 88-; Tchr PR Dept Ed 83-; BS Univ Puerto Rico 82; Mech Engnrng.

**MARRERO-ORTIZ, SANDRA ENID,** Univ Central Del Caribe, Cayey, PR; JR; MD; Sophy Zanphiorenzo Dance Grp 84-; San Juan Cyclist 87-88; Microbiol V P 84-88; Amer Med Assn 84-; Class Rank 3/64; Lifeguard Coast Gd 84; Med; Thoracic Srgry.

**MARRERO-ORTIZ, WANDA S,** Univ Of Pr At Rio Piedras, Rio Piedras, PR; JR; Golden Key; Natural Sci Fac Hon Rl 89-; Chem; Animal Hlth Tech.

**MARRINAN, SEAN W,** Rutgers St Un At New Brunswick, New Brunswick, NJ; FR; BS; Eng Govrng Cncl Rep 90-; Nw Stdnt Orttn Cmmtt; Hll Govt 90-; Deans Lst Coll Eng 90-; IM Bsbll 90-; Elec Eng; Comp Eng.

**MARRIOTT, KAREN M,** Bryant Stratton Bus Inst Roch, Rochester, NY; JR; AS; SG Sec 90-F Dns Lst 90-; Prof Sec; Intl Schlrshp; Sec/Engl Cmptrs; Sec Wrd Prcsng.

**MARRON, CHRISTINE M,** Siena Coll, Loudonville, NY; SR; BA; Econ Clb 90-; Stdnts Btr Wrld 90-; Yrbk Staff 88-90; Engl Hnrs Prgm 88-; Intrn Nys Ofc St Cmptrlr 90; Eqstrn Tm 89-90; Econ; Bus/Educ.

**MARRONE, MICHAEL V,** Fl Inst Of Tech, Melbourne, FL; FR; Stdnt Govt Sen; Res Life Cncl Bldg Rep 90-; Soc Sci Fiction/ Fantasy 90-; Co-Op Harris Corp; Cmptr Engr.

**MARRONGELLI, SANDRA E,** Bapt Bible Coll & Seminary, Clarks Summit, PA; SO; BS; Nwspr 89-90; Trck/Fld 90-; Vars Bsktbl 89-90; Crss Cntry 89-90; Bible/Engl; Engl Tchr.

**MARRONI, SALLY,** Univ Of Pittsburgh At Bradford, Bradford, PA; FR; AS; Nrsng.

**MARROQUIN, DEBORAH ANN,** Hillsborough Comm Coll, Tampa, FL; FR; AS; Computer Programming Analysis.

**MARROW, GREGORY J,** Univ Of New England, Biddeford, ME; JR; BS; P R Rep Stdnt Sen; Alpha Chi V P; Tau Epsilon Phi Sec 85; Asstshp Cons Bio 90; Otstndng Stdnt Div Of Life Sci 90-; Otstndng Undergrad Univ Of New Eng 90-; Marine Bio; Grad Work In Mar Bio Or Optmtry.

**MARRUS, MALIKAH A,** Fisk Univ, Nashville, TN; JR; BA; NAACP V Chr 89-; Kaleidoscope Strng Comm 88-90; Orientn 89-90; Mortr Brd; Dbois Hnrs Pgm Pr 89-90; So Reg Hnrs Conf Stdnt Rep 90-; Alpha Kappa Alpha 90-; Theo S Currior Excell Hstry; Agnes Jones Jacksn Schlr 90-; Roy Wilkns Schlr 88-90; Hstry; Tch.

**MARRY, RICHARD D,** Bridgeport Engr Inst, Fairfield, CT; JR; BSEE; Tau Alpha Pi 87-89; R&d Labs 87-; AS Norwalk St Tech Coll 89; Elec Eng.

**MARS, SABRINA S,** City Univ Of Ny Queensbrough, New York, NY; JR.

**MARS, WILLIAM V,** Univ Of Akron, Akron, OH; SO; BSME; Hons Prog 88-; Mech Eng.

**MARSALA, JENNIFER BROOKE,** Radford Univ, Radford, VA; JR; BBA; Amer Mktg Assn 90-; Stdnt Life 89-90; Sigma Kappa Hsng Chrmn 90-; Mktg/Advrtsng; Mktg Analyst.

**MARSCH, LISA A,** Univ Of Md Baltimore Prof Schl, Baltimore, MD; FR; BS; Disadvantaged Chldrn Grp Cnslr 90-; Dns Lst 90-; Psych/Indstrl Rels; Indstrl Psych.

**MARSCHALL, MELISSA J,** Fl St Univ, Tallahassee, FL; SR; Intnl Affrs Scty; Big Brother/Big Sister; Phi Eta Sigma; Golden Key; Chi Omega VP 87-; Cum Laude Graduate; IM Tennis/Soccer; BA; Intl Affairs/German; Graduate School.

**MARSDEN, JEFFREY C,** Univ Of Rochester, Rochester, NY; JR; BS; Amer Soc Mech Engrs 90-; Soc Actvtes Bd 89-90; Newman Cmunty 89-; Bausch/Lomb Schlr 88-; Deans Lst 89-; Mech Engdr.**

**MARSH, AILEEN U,** Franklin And Marshall Coll, Lancaster, PA; SO; BA; Amnesty Intl 89-; Intl Clb; Franklin Marshall Pre-Admission Tour Vol 90-; Franklin Marshall Summer Foreign Trvl Awd; Natl Coors Schlr 90-; German/Govt.

**MARSH, CYNTHIA A,** Duquesne Univ, Pittsburgh, PA; FR; BA; Union Prog Brd 90-; Lambda Sigma Soc; Deans List First Hons 90-; Law/Tchng.

**MARSH, DRENDA G,** Coker Coll, Hartsville, SC; SR; BED; BBA U Of Ga 78; Elem Ed.

**MARSH, HEATHER D,** Duquesne Univ, Pittsburgh, PA; FR; MBA; Japanese Lang Clb; Sigma Lambda Phi; Deans Lst; Crew Tm; Intrntnl Bsns Corp Law; Intrntnl Corp Lawyer.

**MARSH, JENNIFER M,** Liberty Univ, Lynchburg, VA; FR; BS; Clg Rpblcns 90-; Deans List 90-; Comm Hlth; Phys Thrpy.

**MARSH, LEO M,** Va Commonwealth Univ, Richmond, VA; JR; ROTC 88-89; Hon Soc 90-; Golden Key; Amer Crim Just Assoc Sec; Deans Lst 89-; Admin Just; Law.

**MARSH, RICALDO F,** City Univ Of Ny City Coll, New York, NY; SR; BED; Goldn Key 88-; Alpha Sigma Lambda 88; UFT 90-; Foreman 84-89; Cert Mico Tchrs Clg Kngstn Jam 75; Cert Voc Trng Dev Illust 83; Tech Educ; Tchr.

**MARSH, ROBERT G,** S U N Y Coll Of Tech At Alfred, Alfred, NY; SR; BS; AWANA Clbs Ldr 89-; AS; Aerospce Eng.

**MARSH, SHEILA M,** Central St Univ, Wilberforce, OH; SR; BS; Jr Achvmnt Advis 84-; Deans List SCC 84-; Deans List 89-; Manicurist 88-; Mgmt Dvlpmnt Assoc 89-; Intl Toastmistress Clb Srgnt/Arms 78-; Cost/Price Analyst Cntrctng/Prdctn Directorate 86-; AS Snclr Comm Coll 86; Mgmt Bus Admin; Contracting/Production.

**MARSH, STACY J,** Northeast State Tech Comm Coll, Blountville, TN; SO; AAS; Chem Soc Stdnt Gvrnmnt Rep 90; Phi Theta Kappa 90; Tutor 90; Kodak Chem Technlgy Schlrshp 89; Trnmnt Bsktbl Champs; Chem Technlgy; Chem Techncn.**

**MARSH, TODD A,** S U N Y At Buffalo, Buffalo, NY; GD; MARCH; Amer Inst Arch Stdnts; Phi Eta Sigma; Gldn Ky; Dsgn Fndtns Tchng Asstshp; BPS 90; Arch.

**MARSH, TODD D,** Defiance Coll, Defiance, OH; JR; BCS; Acctg Fin Clb Defiance Coll Sec Treas 89-; Incm Tx Prpr 89-; Spt Mngmnt Clb Bwlng Grn St Univ 90-; IM D C Bsktbl Vlybl 88-90; IM Bsktbl Vlybl BGSU 90-; Spt Mngmnt; Exercise Physiologist.

**MARSH, VALERIE A,** Morehead St Univ, Morehead, KY; FR; BA; Ashland Oil Intrn 91; Fine Arts; Photography.

**MARSHALIK, RON P,** Wv Univ, Morgantown, WV; JR; BS; Amer Inst Chem Engrs 89-; Chem Engr.

**MARSHALL, C YVONNE,** Wilmington Coll, New Castle, DE; BA; Dns Lst; Delaware Hosp Chronically Ill; Behav Sci.

**MARSHALL, CALVIN L,** Alcorn St Univ, Lorman, MS; FR; BS; Cmctns; Plywrght/Lyrcst.

**MARSHALL, CHAD E,** Southern Coll Of Tech, Marietta, GA; FR; BS; Dns Lst 90-; Cmptr Eng Tech; Hrdwr Sftwr Mfg.

**MARSHALL, CHARLES R,** Jackson St Univ, Jackson, MS; JR; BS; Natl Scty Blck Eng 89-; Chmstry Scty Prlmntrn 88-; Mr Jr 90-; Beta Kappa Chi; Alpha Chi; Alpha Lambda Delta; Mnrty Accss Rsrch Crrs 90; Drcktt Co Intrnshp; IM Bsktbll 88-; Chmstry Eng.

**MARSHALL, CYNTHIA D,** Univ Of Nc At Greensboro, Greensboro, NC; SR; BS; Bpt Student Union Prog Dir 89-90; Assoc Ed Young Children 88; IM Sftbl Vlybl 88-90; Elem Ed; Tch Public Schl System.**

**MARSHALL, DAVID T,** Benedict Coll, Columbia, SC; JR; BA; Benedict Clg Choir Cncrt 87-90; Snd Engrng Schl Plays 90-; Vol Yth Grp Dir 89-; Yth Grp At Church; Brdcstng/Jrnlsm; Audio Engr.

**MARSHALL, DAWN L,** Midway Coll, Midway, KY; SR; BSN; Salm Meth Chrch Sndy Schl Super; ADN 83; EMT Cntrl Ky Vo Tech 86; Nrsng.

**MARSHALL, DAWN MICHELLE,** Salisbury St Univ, Salisbury, MD; SR; MA; Psych Clb 90; Phi Alpha Theta 90; Pi Gamma Mu 90; BA 90; Psych.

**MARSHALL, ERIC C,** Morehouse Coll, Atlanta, GA; FR; MBA; Hubert Hall Dorm Cncl Treas 90-; Morehouse Hnrs Prog Club 90-; Hlth Careers Soc 90-; Bio; Psych.

**MARSHALL, GEOFFREY,** Me Maritime Academy, Castine, ME; SR; AS; Soc Nvl Archtcts/Mrne Engrs Sec 90-; BA Wash Coll 86; Nvl Archtctr.

**MARSHALL, JANICE S,** Va Commonwealth Univ, Richmond, VA; SR; BS; Amer Assn Crtcl-Cr Nrs 85-; AD Wstrn KY Univ 72; CCRN AACN 86; Nrsng.

**MARSHALL, JEFFREY G,** Germanna Comm Coll, Locust Grove, VA; FR; BS; Prvt Pilot Cert; IM Pocket Bllrds; Physcs/Eng; Pro Pilot.

**MARSHALL, JOAN MEDLOCK,** Univ Of Sc At Aiken, Aiken, SC; JR; ASN; Gamma Beta Phi 89-; Stdnt Nrs Assn 89-; Nrsng.

**MARSHALL, KENT S,** Ms St Univ, Miss State, MS; JR; BBA; Bapt Student Union Pres 88-; Student Recruiter; Gen Busn Admin; Busn Career.

**MARSHALL, KIMBERLY A,** Univ Of Southern Ms, Hattiesburg, MS; SR; BS; Am Advtsng Fed 89-; Pan Hellenic 89-90; Ordr Omega 90-; Delta Zeta VP 87-; Frst Gen Mktg Advtsng Intern; Advtsng; Copywrtr.

**MARSHALL, KIRK S,** Bridgewater St Coll, Bridgewater, MA; FR; BS; Math; Tchng.

**MARSHALL, KRISTEN R,** Univ Of Ky, Lexington, KY; SO; BS; Rsdnc Hl Govt Treas 89-90; Phi Eta Sigma 89-; Pres Schlrshp; Lady Wildcat Sftbl 90-; Biology; Medicine.

**MARSHALL, LISA A,** Columbia St Comm Coll, Columbia, TN; SO; AS; Stdnt Gov; Pltcl Science; Law.**

**MARSHALL, LLOYD A,** S U N Y Coll At Fredonia, Fredonia, NY; SO; MBA; Jazz Ensmbl 89-; Hispanic Soc 90-; Inter Var Chrstn Flwshp Otrch Event Coor; Span Sec Educ; Tech.

**MARSHALL, MICHAEL D,** S U N Y At Buffalo, Buffalo, NY; GD; DDS; IM 85-89; Alpha Epsilon Delta 87-89; Alpha Epsilon Delta 87-89; Wm Tuckr Schlrshp 90-; Orl Srgry Extrnshp; Mens Tenns Tm 85-89; BS J Carroll Univ 85-89; Dentstry.

**MARSHALL, PAULA R,** Univ Of Pittsburgh, Pittsburgh, PA; JR; BSN; Sigma Theta Tau; Extnshp Shadyside Hosp; Nrsng; Neurosci.

**MARSHALL, RONNIE DARYL,** Morgan St Univ, Baltimore, MD; SO; BS; NSBE 90-; IIE 90-; French Clb 90-; Promethean Kappa Tau 90-; Alpha Mu Gamma 90-; Bacchus 90-; Deans Lst 89; Curriculum Schlrshp 89-; Wal Mart Fndtn Schlrshp 89; I M Bkbl 90; Indus Engr/Cmptr Sci; Engr.

**MARSHALL, SHEILA A,** Lane Coll, Jackson, TN; SR; BS; E Ed; Tch Schl.

**MARSHALL, SOPHIA S L,** Jackson St Univ, Jackson, MS; SR; BS; Stdnt Natl Educ Assn VP 90-; Bptst Stdnt Union St Treas 88-89; Alpha Chi; Alpha Kappa Mu; Pi Lambda Theta VP 89-; Flwshp Univ KS 90; Lottie Thorntons Tchr Incntv Awd 90; Elem Ed.

**MARSHALL, TAMMY R,** Houghton Coll, Houghton, NY; SO; BA; Flr Bible Stdy Ldr 90-; Yth Grp Ldr 90-; Psychology; Counseling.

**MARSHALL, TAMMY S,** Radford Univ, Radford, VA; JR; BBA; Acctg Soc; Acctg; CPA.

**MARSHALL, TANA M,** Valdosta St Coll, Valdosta, GA; FR; BS; Biol; MD.

**MARSHALL, TRICHITA,** Southern Coll Of Tech, Marietta, GA; SR; BEE; IM Sftbl; Atlanta Youth At Risk Org Vol 90-; Elect Eng.

**MARSHALL, TROY E,** Blue Mountain Coll, Blue Mountain, MS; SR; 2BAS; SG Rule Comm 86-87; Music Club Pres 90-; MENC Pres 87-88; Alpha Psi Omega Points Keeper 86-; Alpha Phi Omega 88-; Kappa Kappa Psi Sec 87-; Otsdn Music Fres 85-86; Otsdng French Stdnt 89-90; Music Perf/Bible; Professor.

**MARSHALL, TWAYNA J,** Rust Coll, Holly Springs, MS; JR; BA; NAACP 88-; Ms Jr 90-; Sr Cls Secr; Sigma Tau Delta Treas 90-; Alpha Kappa Mu; Gamma Sigma Sigma Treas 88-; Eng/Jrnlsim; Tchr/Jrnlst.

**MARSHALL, VALERIE J,** Georgian Court Coll, Lakewood, NJ; JR; BA; Psych Clb 90-; Alliance Francais 90-; Psi Chi; Utd St Figure Sktng Assc 68-; Chrnc Fatigue Syndrm Assc 88-; Humane Scty US 90-; RN 80-; AA/AAS Ocean Cty Coll 81; RN St NJ 82; Psychlgy.

**MARSHAM, CORENE C,** Univ Of The Dist Of Columbia, Washington, DC; SR; BA; Choir 87-; Hon Pgm 88-; Deans Lst 88-; Alpha Kappa Alpha Pres 90-; CBS-TV Prmtns Intrn 90; Alumni Schlrshp 90-; Mass Media-TV Prod; Prdcr/Dir.

**MARSICO, MARY P,** Kent St Univ Kent Cmps, Kent, OH; SR; BS; USA Karate Fdrtns 89-; Natl Key 89-; Mktg; Med Sales.

**MARSILLO, ANNA L,** Univ Of Akron, Akron, OH; SO; BS; Amer Scty Mechanical Engrs 89-; Mechncl Engrng.

**MARSTON, LORRAINE,** Wilmington Coll, New Castle, DE; SR; BS; Du Pont Co Bnfts Admin Area Mgr 88-; AS Godley Beacom Clg 82; Human Resources Mgmt; Mgmt Corp Trainer.

**MARSTON, MARK W,** Duquesne Univ, Pittsburgh, PA; SO; BA; Guitar Assoc VP DUGA 90-; Cert 88; Music Prmnc.

**MARSTON, STEPHEN C,** U S Coast Guard Academy, New London, CT; SO; BS; Hmn Rltns Rep; Drll Crmns Stff; Inter Cmpny Sftbll Hndbll; Clr Grd; Gdn Cmpny; NCAA Bskbtll; Comp Math; Systms Anlyss.

**MARSTON, THERESA M,** Middle Tn St Univ, Murfreesboro, TN; SR; BS; AS Columbia St Comm Coll; Elem Ed; Tch.

**MARTE, JACQUELINE,** City Univ Of Ny Baruch Coll, New York, NY; SO; BBA; Bus Mgmt; Ind Psychlgst.

**MARTEL, LISA A,** Fairfield Univ, Fairfield, CT; SR; BSN; Stdnt Nrs Assn 87-; Fresh Orntn Stdnt Advsr 89-90; Mrsng Stdnt Tutor 90-; Nrsng Hon Soc 90-; Norwalk Hosp Florence Hightingale Awd; Nrsng/Psychlgy; RN.

**MARTEL, SYLVIA S,** Miami Dade Comm Coll North, Miami, FL; SR; BA; Co-Op Intern; IMS Grnblt Judo 90-; Part-Time Job Tchr Sub; AA; Spcl Edn; Tchr.

**MARTELL RIVERA, WILMER I,** Inter Amer Univ Pr San German, San German, PR; SO; BA; Mgt; Admnstrtr.

**MARTELL, CRISTINA M,** Univ Of Miami, Coral Gables, FL; SR; BBA; Roadrnrs Cmutr Clb 87-89; Golden Key 89-; Beta Gamma Sigma 91-; Beta Alpha Psi 90-; Acctg.

**MARTELL, MARK E,** Nova Univ, Ft Lauderdale, FL; GD; Mbr Amer Mrkting Assoc 90-; BS Univ Of Lowell Lowell MA 71; MBA.

**MARTELL, SUSAN M,** Fl International Univ, Miami, FL; GD; Phi Kappa Phi; Grad Hnrs; NAEYC 88-; Wk Chldrn Adlscnts Emotnl Prob 79-; AA Miami Dade Comm Coll South 88; BS; Elem Educ; Erly Chldhd Educ.

**MARTELLI, SUSAN,** Comm Coll Algny Co Algny Cmps, Pittsburgh, PA; BA; Bsn; Ins Underwriter.

**MARTENEY, GREGG S,** Kent St Univ Stark Cmps, North Canton, OH; FR; BA; Cmptr Sci; Prgrmr.

**MARTENS, JILL E,** Univ Of Miami, Coral Gables, FL; SR; MSPT; Std Athltc Trnr 88-; Delta Gamma 88-; BHS 86-; Pre-Physcl Thrpy.

**MARTHEY, CHERIE L,** Slippery Rock Univ, Slippery Rock, PA; JR; BED; Phi Eta Sigma 89-; Phi Epsilon Kappa 90-; Sftbl Capt 89-; Phys Ed; Tchg/Coach.

**MARTI, MARLA C,** Inter Amer Univ Pr San Juan, Hato Rey, PR; SO; BA; UN Clb 87-88; Clgrphy Clb 87-; JA 87-88; Univ Hnrs Pgm 89-; Engnrng.

**MARTICH, SANDRA E,** Dowling Coll, Oakdale Li, NY; JR; BS; VITA; Acdmc Schlrshp; AAS Briarcliffe Coll 89; Prfssnl/Lbrl Stdies; Bus Admin.

**MARTICORENA FLORES, CESAR O,** Newbury Coll, Brookline, MA; SR; AS; Intrntl Stdnt Organ Pres 90-; Dns Lst 90-; Stdnt Lf Awd; Intrnshp Four Seasons Hotel Boston; Engl; Htl Rest Mngmnt.

**MARTIN, AKESHIA R,** James Madison University, Harrisonburg, VA; SR; MS; Stdnt Of Mnrty Outrch 89; Blk Stdnt Allnce 87; Cntmpry Gspl Sngrs 87; Alpha Kappa Alpha Srty; Deans Lst 89; Pres Lst; BS; Cnslng Psychlgy; Cnslng Psychlgst.

**MARTIN, ALICE A,** Al A & M Univ, Normal, AL; SR; BTS; Grvtts Chpl AME Chrch Sec 89-; Intrgrph 83-; AA Arapahoe Comm Clg 71; Bsn Mgmt.

**MARTIN, ALICIA M,** Piedmont Tech Coll, Greenwood, SC; GD; Acad Advtg 89-90; Sngl Prnt Org 89-90; Dns Lst; Clncl Stdnt Yr 90; JTPA Stdnt 90; Dplm; Med; Rsprtry Thrpst.

**MARTIN, ALYSON H,** Univ Of Sc At Columbia, Columbia, SC; SR; BA; March Band 87-89; Tau Bta Sigma 87-89; Fllwshp Hull Univ England Jr Yr Abroad 89-90; History.

**MARTIN, AMANDA E,** The Boston Conservatory, Boston, MA; SR; MFA; Berkshire Ballet Soloist 89; North Atlantic Ballet 90; BFA.

**MARTIN, AMY J,** Middle Tn St Univ, Murfreesboro, TN; JR; BA; Baptist Student Union Sec 89-90; Chrstn Music Soc; Gamma Bet Phi Sec 89-90; AA Motlow State Cmnty Clge 90; Office Mgmnt.

**MARTIN, AMY S,** Vance Granville Comm Coll, Henderson, NC; SR; ADN; SGA 89-; Phi Theta Kappa; Pres Awd 90; Phi Theta Kappa; Un Meth Women; OB Nursing.

**MARTIN, ANDREA L,** Ga Southern Univ, Statesboro, GA; SO; BED; Brn Flwshp Assoc 87-88; Tau Sigma 87-88; ATEA VP 89-90; Zeta Tau Alpha Crspndng Sec 87-; Clayton Co Rotary Clb Schlrshp 89-90; Arprt Rotary GOAL 89; Dns Lst 87-90; Brenau Pres Schlrshp 87; Stdnt Qrtr 90; Spec Ed.

**MARTIN, ANDREA M,** Daemen Coll, Amherst, NY; JR; BS; Trvl Trsm Clb Treas; Delta Mu Delta; Delta Phi Mu 89-; Trvl Trsm Mgmt; Mtng Plnng.

**MARTIN, ANGELA C,** Univ Of Southern Ms, Hattiesburg, MS; SR; BSBA; Bus; Acctg.

**MARTIN, ANGELA KAYE,** Univ Of Ky, Lexington, KY; SR; BA; WS Webb Archlgcl Soc 90-; Oswld Awrd; Sr Rsrch Anlyst 89-; Anthrplgy.

**MARTIN, AUDREY M,** Univ Of Southern Ms, Hattiesburg, MS; SR; BS; Stdnt Nrs Assoc 89-; LPN 75-90; LPN Methdst Hsp Schl Prctcl Nrsng 75; Nrsng; Gerntlgcl.

**MARTIN, BARBARA A,** Univ Of Al At Birmingham, Birmingham, AL; SO; BS; Pi Eta Sigma 89-90; ; Alpha Lambda Delta Auburn 89-90; Pi Sigma Epsilon; Intrnshp Chenoweth & Assoc CPA 90-; Acctng; CPA.

**MARTIN, BARBARA H,** Livingston Univ, Livingston, AL; SR; BA; Delta Sigma Pi 89-; Alpha Kappa Alpha; Ordr Estr Star 90-; Elem/Erly Chldhd Educ.

**MARTIN, BARRY W,** Univ Of Sc At Columbia, Columbia, SC; FR; PHARM; Diploma Instrmntn Tech 84; Pharmacy.

**MARTIN, BRIAN A,** Western Carolina Univ, Cullowhee, NC; JR; BS; Stdnt Assn Govt/Lgl Affrs 88-; C Carpenter Pre-Law Soc 88-; Stdnt Govt Stdnt Crt Jdg 89; Dbt Tm 90-; Mrtr Bd; Pi Gamma Mau; Phi Alpha Theta; Phi Alpha Delta Pres 89-; Pi Kappa Delta Pres 90-; Sigma Nu VP 88-; IM 88-; Pltcl Sci; Law.

**MARTIN, CALVIN R,** Morehouse Coll, Atlanta, GA; JR; BA; MSCC Inc Exec Chr; Morehouse Bsn Assoc 89-; Jr Achvmnt Cnsltnt; MI Bell Schlrshp Intern 88-; Gen Motors Schlrshp 90-; Hublein Inc Schlrshp; Dns Lst 90-; Hnr Rl 88-; Acolyte Guild Pres 88-; Church Choir 90-; Pageant Dir 90-; Bsn Adm; Mktg/Prod Mgmt.**

**MARTIN, CARLISS P,** Paine Coll, Augusta, GA; JR; Hon Roll 90; Dlt Sgm Theta.

**MARTIN, CARLOS L,** Fl St Univ, Tallahassee, FL; SR; BS; IEEE; Eng Hon Soc; Deans Lst 90; Elec Eng; Energy Sys/Cntrl.

**MARTIN, CATHERINE A,** Univ Of Sc At Columbia, Columbia, SC; SR; Hmcmng Commssn 88-89; Stdnts Agnst Violnce; Dept Yth Serv Vol; Mortr Brd 89-; Grk Ldrshp Trning Prsntr; Phi Beta Kappa 86-; Omicron Delta Kappa 86-; Goldn Key; Gamma Beta Phi; Order Of Omega; Zeta Tau Alpha Pres 87-; Pres Lst; BAIS 90; Elem Ed; Tchng.

**MARTIN, CHAD A,** Univ Of Ky, Lexington, KY; SO; BA; Soc Concrnd Stdnts Pres 89-; Stdnts Agnst Violtn Of Envrnmnt 89-; Media Clb 89-; Hstry; Wrtr/Tchr.

**MARTIN, CHARLA L,** Middle Tn St Univ, Murfreesboro, TN; SO; BA; Gamma Beta Phi 89-; Hnr Rl 89-; Dns Lst 89-; Nrsg; Obs Nrs.**

**MARTIN, CHERYL J,** Nazareth Coll Of Rochester, Rochester, NY; FR; BA; Campus Mnstries 90-; SADD 90-; Nazrth Schlr 90-; Soclgy/Elem Educ; Tchr.

**MARTIN, CHRIS D,** Midlands Tech Coll, Columbia, SC; SR; Grad With Hons; Pharm Tech.

**MARTIN, CHRISTA W,** Savannah Coll Of Art & Design, Savannah, GA; GD; MFA; Scl Com Asst Scl Hd 88; Phi Alpha Eta 88-90; Cogswell Art Awd 90; Vrsty Crss-Cntry Trck 86-88; BA Principia Coll 90; Studio; Artst Dsgnr.

**MARTIN, CHRISTINE E,** Georgian Court Coll, Lakewood, NJ; SO; BED; SGA Cl Pres 89-; Stdnt/Socl Actn 89-; Sigma Phi Sigma 90-; Natl Stdnt Cmpgn/Hunger Homelessness; Natl Campgn Disarmnt/El Salvarod; Hstry; Scndry Ed; Tch.

**MARTIN, CHRISTOPHER A,** Anderson Coll, Anderson, SC; FR; Biolgcl Sci; Med Fld.

**MARTIN, CHRISTOPHER S,** Northern Ky Univ, Highland Hts, KY; JR; BA; Bsktbl Coach 89-; Pblc Admin; Bus/Pblc Srvc.

**MARTIN, CHUCK P,** Abraham Baldwin Agri Coll, Tifton, GA; GD; AS; Frstry/Wldlf Clb Proj Chrmn 89-; David Mullis Meml Schlrshp 90; AS Wldlf Tech; Natl Sci; Wldlf Mgmt.

**MARTIN, COLIN H,** Middle Tn St Univ, Murfreesboro, TN; SO; BA; Deans Lst; Acctng; CPA.

**MARTIN, CYNTHIA D,** Univ Of Tn At Martin, Martin, TN; FR; BSN; Ntl Stdnt Nrsng Assoc; Pre-Prof Med Pldge Class Pres; Nrsng; Neonatal Nrse.

**MARTIN, DAMIEN J,** Western New England Coll, Springfield, MA; SO; BA; Alpha Lamda Delta; Lamda Delta 90; Pre Law Scty 89; Gov; Law.**

**MARTIN, DANIEL J,** Life Coll, Marietta, GA; SR; Rntgnlgcl And Tech Assn; DC 90; Chrprctc.

**MARTIN, DANIEL P,** Wv Univ At Parkersburg, Parkersburg, WV; JR; BA; Pstr Cairo United Meth Charge; UM Conf Of WV; Jrynmn Elec Lcl 968 IBEW WV Mstr Elec; Apprntc Cmpltn Natl Joint App Comm NECA IBEW 82; Appr Comp US Dept Of Labor 82; Bd Of Rgnts; Mdiv/Pstrng.

**MARTIN II, DANIEL W,** Wv Univ, Morgantown, WV; SO; BS; Mech Eng; Eng.

**MARTIN, DAPHNE E,** Medical Coll Of Ga, Augusta, GA; SR; BSN; SGA 89-; GANS V P 89-; Kappa Delta 88-; Sigma Chi Ltl Sis 89-; Nrsg; Neurology Nrsg.

**MARTIN, DAVID W,** Univ Of Cincinnati, Cincinnati, OH; JR; BA; Amer Inst Constrctrs 90-; Gldn Ky 90-; Butler Cnty Eng Coop 88-89; Goettle Cnstrctn Coop 89-90; Paul Hemmer Cnstrctn Coop 90-; Assn Cincinnati Tech Coll 89; Cnstrctn Mngmnt; Bus Admin.

**MARTIN, DEAN D,** Southern Coll Of Tech, Marietta, GA; SR; BS; Amer Inst Undus Engrs 89-; AAS Elect Tech De Kalb Clg 88; Indus Engr Tech; Engr.

**MARTIN, DEANNA C,** Va Commonwealth Univ, Richmond, VA; JR; BS; Bio; Phys Thrpy.

**MARTIN, DEBORAH S,** Tri County Tech Coll, Pendleton, SC; FR; AS; Acctg.

**MARTIN, DENISE M,** Oh St Univ At Marion, Marion, OH; FR; BA; Griffins 90-; Pol Sci; Law.

**MARTIN, DENISE M,** Williamsburg Tech Coll, Kingstree, SC; SO; AA; Phi Theta Kappa; Psych.

**MARTIN, DENISE M,** Neumann Coll, Aston, PA; JR; BA; Educ Clb 89-; PA St Educ Assn; Elem/Early Chldhd Educ; Tchng.

**MARTIN, DENISE M,** Fl A & M Univ, Tallahassee, FL; SO; BS; Jrnlsm; Writer.

**MARTIN, DOUGLAS J,** Coker Coll, Hartsville, SC; SR; BS; US Army Assn 85-; Non-Comm Offcr Assn 88-; US Army Ft Jackson Drll Sgt 88-90; Training NCO 90-; Soclgy; Ed/Law Enfrcmnt.

**MARTIN, DWAYNE M,** Patrick Henry Comm Coll, Martinsville, VA; FR; BS; Patrick Henry Amateur Radio Clb 89-; Am Radio Relay League 90-; Cert Achvmnt Exclnc Acdmc Merit Navy Tech Trng Ctr Orlando FL 79; Intl Soc Crtfd Elctrnc Tchncns; Diploma Cleveland Inst Elctrncs 89; Elctrncs; Aerospace Eng.

**MARTIN, EDWARD F,** Union Coll, Schenectady, NY; JR; Wght Lftg 88-; IM 88-; Invstmnt Clb 90-; Deans Lst 90-; GE Intrn Finance Anlyst 90-; Key Bk Schlrshp 88-; Union Coll Schlrshp Acdmc 88-; Ftbl Div Iii 88-89; Mngrl Ecnmcs; Bus.**

**MARTIN, ELIZABETH M,** Kent St Univ Kent Cmps, Kent, OH; JR; BA; Intrhll Cncl Prog Dir 90; Untd Chrstn Mnstrs 89-; Mdl NATO Tm; Natl Rsdnce Hll 90-; Pol Sci; Mrtr Brd Treas; Ldrshp Awrd 90; Intrhll Cncl Dir Of Dstnctn 90; Otstndng Ldr Awrd 89; Intrntl Rltns; Law.

**MARTIN, ERIN M,** Bay Path Coll, Longmeadow, MA; JR; BA; Deans List 89; Maroon Key 89; Bottaro/Kolnick/Interiors 90; AS 90; Bsn/Intr Dsgn; Intr Dsngr.

**MARTIN JR, GARY D,** Salem-Teikyo Univ, Salem, WV; FR; BED; Gamma Beta Phi 90-; ESL 90; Foundation Schlrshp 90-; Computer Science; Computer Programmer.

**MARTIN, GINGER F,** Tougaloo Coll, Tougaloo, MS; SR; BA; Pltcl Sci Clb; Delt Sigma Theta; Dckns/Swt Law Intrn; Pltcl Sci; Law.

**MARTIN, GINGER R,** Duquesne Univ, Pittsburgh, PA; FR; BA; Ele Educ; Tchng.

**MARTIN, GREGORY,** Morehouse Coll, Atlanta, GA; SO; Bus Assoc 89-; Deans Lst; Hnr Rl; Bnk 1 Inrds Intrn 90-; Bus Admin; Law.

**MARTIN, GREGORY A,** Utica Coll Of Syracuse Univ, Utica, NY; JR; BS; Griffiss AFB Frfghtr Bnvlnt Assn VP 90-; NY St Emrgncy Mdcl Tchncn Lvl II 88-; US Air Force Frghtr 83-; AS Cmmnty Clg Air Force 90; Bsns Admnstrtn.

**MARTIN, GREGORY R,** Nova Univ, Ft Lauderdale, FL; GD; MBA; Hnrs 71; Amer Inst Cpa 75-; Fla Inst Cpa 75-; BS Univ Fla 71; BA Busn Admin 73; Busn; Chf Fincl Offcr.

**MARTIN, GREGORY S,** Duquesne Univ, Pittsburgh, PA; JR; PH D; Chap Amer Chem Soc Stdnt Affltes Pres/Stdnt Affltе Mbr 89; Sigma Xi 89; Intrnshp Univ Chemistry Rsrch; Chem.

**MARTIN, JACQUELINE R,** Univ Of The Virgin Islands, St Thomas, VI; SR; BA; Stdnt Gvrnmt Exctv Secy 88; Dbtng Clb Secy 89; UVI Flk Sngrs 90-; Pres Clb; Future Bsn Ldrs AM/PHI Beta Lamda; Dr Janet Stanley Marcano Ldrshp Awrd; Frank Barnett Awrd 89; RA Year; IM 90; Bsn; Hmn Rsrcs Mngmnt.

**MARTIN, JANET C,** Northern Ky Univ, Highland Hts, KY; SR; BA; Phi Beta Lambda 81-83; Admnstratr 83-90; BBA Arknsas Univ 83; Ed; Elem Tchr.

**MARTIN, JANET L,** Univ Of Akron, Akron, OH; SR; BA; Unv Accntng Assn 89-; Ntnl Assn Accntnts; Gldn Key 90-; Beta Alpha Psi; Intrnshp Rdwy Lgstcs; Accntncy.

**MARTIN, JASON K,** Union Univ, Jackson, TN; SR; BS; Focus; Pacers; Church Related Vocations; BSU; Alcohol Drug Educ Comm; Alpha Chi; Carl Perkins Child Abuse Ctr; Deans Lst; IM Bsktbl; Economics; Ministry.

**MARTIN, JEFFREY A,** United States Naval Academy, Annapolis, MD; SR; MS; Brigade Ldrshp Orgn Dptry Brg Cmmndr 90; Grmn Clb Trea 88-; Tau Beta Pi Pres 89-; Intern Los Alanos Natl Lab 90; Elect Eng; Naval Offcr.

**MARTIN, JEFFREY L,** Tri County Tech Coll, Pendleton, SC; Phi Theta Kappa; Bosch Appntcshp Prog 89-; Ind Tech; Eng.

**MARTIN, JEFFREY S,** Univ Of Cincinnati, Cincinnati, OH; JR; BFA; Mountaineering Clb 89-; Recommended To/Hired By Radio Sta 90-; Brdcstng; Audio Rcrdng.

**MARTIN, JEFFREY S,** Temple Univ, Philadelphia, PA; SO; BA; Fin; Invstmnt Bnkr.

**MARTIN, JEFFREY S,** S U N Y Coll Of Tech At Delhi, Delhi, NY; FR; Aircond/Refrig; Engr.

**MARTIN, JENNIFER M,** S U N Y At Buffalo, Buffalo, NY; SR; BS; Alpha Pi Mu; Tau Beta Pi; Fredonia Wmns Sccr Tm 86-89; BS St Univ NY Fredonia 86-90; Indstrl Engr.

**MARTIN, JENNIFER S,** Univ Of Akron, Akron, OH; FR; BA; Mrchng Bnd 90-; Univ Pgm Brd 90-; Natl Mrt Schlr; Hstry/Ecnmcs.

**MARTIN, JILL M,** Point Park Coll, Pittsburgh, PA; JR; Grtr Pitt Ltrcy Cncl Pttsbrgh Tutor 88-; Sr Fin Coord 86-; Cert ICM Schl Bus 86; Bus Mgmt/Mktg; Mktg.

**MARTIN, JILL S,** Univ Of Al At Birmingham, Birmingham, AL; SR; BA; Alpha Delta Pi Chlrshp Chrmn; Educ/Math; Tch Math.

**MARTIN, JOAN K,** Univ Of Nc At Asheville, Asheville, NC; JR; BA; Phi Eta Sigma 90-; Awd German 89-90; Schlrshp Awd AAUW; Philosophy; Clg Prfsr.

**MARTIN, JOHN J,** Ursinus Coll, Collegeville, PA; SR; BS; Soc Physcs Stdnts Pr 90-; Intrvrsty Chrstn Fllwshp Grp Ldr 88-; Cub Key 90-; Sigma Pi Sigma; Var X Cntry Trck/Fld Capt 87-; Physcs; Educ/Tchg.

**MARTIN, JON P,** S U N Y Coll At Fredonia, Fredonia, NY; SO; BA; Writers Guild 90-; Stdnts Against Racism & Prejudice VP 90-; Specturm Stdnt Org Actv 89-90; Hispanic Soc 90-; Deans List 89-; Alpha Phi Omega 89-; School Paper 89-90; English; Teaching/Writer.

**MARTIN, JOSEPH C,** Fl St Univ, Tallahassee, FL; SR; BS; Smnl Coll Assn Leisure Pro SCALP VP; Stdnt Rep Leisure Svcs/Stds Sr Clss 90-; Amer Assn Mntl Rtrdtn AAMR T 90; Rho Phi Lambda 90-; Spec Olmpcs Coach 82-; AA Suffolk Cnty Comm Coll 89; Therptc Rcrtn; Rhbltn.

**MARTIN, JOSEPHINA ANASTASIA,** Cumberland County Coll, Vineland, NJ; SR; GCE Ghana Africa 89; Acctg.

**MARTIN, KATHERINE A,** Middle Tn St Univ, Murfreesboro, TN; JR; BA; Aerosp Adm; Cmrcl Pilot-Priv Jets.

**MARTIN, KEITH R,** Kent St Univ Kent Cmps, Kent, OH; GD; MA; Soviet Stdnt Exchng Prog Host/Rmmate 90; Intrntl Club 85-87; Elem Schl French Instrctr Vol 86; Pi Delta Phi Pres 85-87; Schrlshp Recpnt 90; Miami Univ Alumni Acadmc Schlrshp 85-86; Educ.

**MARTIN, KELLEY R,** Univ Of Tn At Martin, Martin, TN; FR; BS; STEA; Educ; Teach.

**MARTIN, KELLI R,** Longwood Coll, Farmville, VA; SO; BS; Alpha Lambda Delta 90; Pi Mu Epsilon Pres; Delta Zeta Grk Cncl Rep 90-; Ambssdrs Tres; Dean Lst 89-; IM Sftbl 89-; Math; Tchng.

**MARTIN, KINGSLEY S,** Univ Of Ky, Lexington, KY; SR; BA; Delta Kappa Epsilon; Econ.

**MARTIN, LAURA L,** Faulkner Univ, Montgomery, AL; SO; BA; Sociology/Minor Computers; Counseling.

**MARTIN, LAURA M,** Birmingham Southern Coll, Birmingham, AL; SO; Alpha Lambda Delta 89-; Phi Eta Sigma 89-; Alpha Omicron Pi IM Chr 90-; Hbt Hmnty 89-; Urbn Mnstrs Tutor 89-90; Chldrns Hosp Vol 90-.

**MARTIN, LESLIE C,** Air Force Inst Of Tech, Wrt-Ptrsn Afb, OH; GD; MS; Sigma Iota Epsilon 90-; BS Ind Eng MS State Univ 81; Eng.

**MARTIN, LESLIE D,** Valdosta St Coll, Valdosta, GA; SR; MS; Phi Mu Schlrshp Chrmn 89-90; Virginia Gaskins Nrsng Schlrshp 90-; BS; Nrsng Ansthslgy; RN.

**MARTIN, LINDA S,** Univ Of Tn At Martin, Martin, TN; SO; BS; Oldr Stdnts Assn Sec 88-; GEO Clb 88-90; Phi Eta Sigma; Chi Omega Awrd 89-; Hon Roll 89-; Geosci; Geolgy.

**MARTIN III, LINUS B,** Univ Of Southern Ms, Hattiesburg, MS; SO; BS; Hnr Stdnt Assc 90-; Gamma Beta Phi 90-; Hnrs Coll 89-; Alpha Epsilon Delta; F J Walker Schlrshp; Intrmrl Ftbl; Microblgy; Med Biomed.

**MARTIN, LORI D,** Wv Inst Of Tech, Montgomery, WV; SO; BS; Ambssdrs; Amer Inst Chmcl Eng; Stu Govt Assn Sen; Alpha Sigma Tau Tres 90-; Intern Union Carbide 90-; Union Carbide Fr Schlrshp 89-90; Vldctrn Schlrshp 89-; Chem Eng; Prdctn Eng.

**MARTIN, LORI E,** Kent St Univ Kent Cmps, Kent, OH; SR; BA; Sclgy Clb Treas 89-; Amnsty Intl 90; Alpha Kappa Delta; Pi Gamma Mu; Intrnshp Akron Gnrl Medcl Cntr-Dept Scl Wrk; Sclgy/Mnrty Studies; Scl Wrk.

**MARTIN, LORI J,** Indiana Univ Of Pa, Indiana, PA; SR; BS; PA State Educ Assoc/Natl Educ Assn; Grad Cum Laude; Outstndng Stdnt Tchr 90; Elem Tchr.

**MARTIN, LOWELL D,** Univ Of Ky, Lexington, KY; SR; BA; ASCE 90-; Chi Epsilon 90-; Civil Eng; Eng.

**MARTIN, M ROMAYNE,** Edinboro Univ Of Pa, Edinboro, PA; SR; BED; Scndry Edn Assoc 88-; Univ Hon Pgm 88-; Phi Eta Sigma 88-; Alpha Chi 90-; Grace Crowe Schlrshp 88-89; Deans Lst 87-; Erie Co Diabetes Assoc 90-; Lic Cosmetology Tchr 72-; Cert Electrologist Kree Intl NY 84-; Cert Chrstn Edn; Dual Cert Engl/Spnsh; Grad Sch/MBA Read.

**MARTIN, MARK A,** Southern Coll Of Tech, Marietta, GA; SR; BSEET; Inst Elec/Electr Eng Inc 90-; Ntl Soc Arch Eng 90-; ROTC Stdnt 87-89; Army Schlrshp 87-89; Elec Dsgnr 88-; Elec Eng; Elec Dsgn Pwr Dstrbutn.

**MARTIN, MARY ANNE,** Kent St Univ Kent Cmps, Kent, OH; JR; BA; Sigma Tau Delta 90-; Gldn Ky 90-; Engl; Ed.

**MARTIN, MARY S,** Marshall University, Huntington, WV; BS; Dttcs Stdnt Advsry Brd 89-; Oldr Amrcns Hlth Fr 90; Cr Day 90; Kappa Omicron Nu 90-; Gamma Beta Phi 89-; Deans Lst 87-; Otstndng Coll Stdnts Amrc 89-90; Dttcs.**

**MARTIN, MELBA C,** Mary Baldwin Coll, Staunton, VA; SR; BA; Omicron Delta Epsilon 89; Omicron Delta Kappa 90; Hnr Stdnt 87; Magna Cum Laude; Bsnss Admin.

**MARTIN, MICHAEL E,** Itawamba Comm Coll, Fulton, MS; SO; MBA; Bptst Union 89-; SIFE 90-; Pres Lst 90-; Dns Lst; Acctg.

**MARTIN, MICHAEL R,** Piedmont Tech Coll, Greenwood, SC; SO; AS; Indstrl Elec.

**MARTIN, NATHANIEL,** Univ Of Tn At Martin, Martin, TN; SO; BA; Agrcltr; Agr Bus.

**MARTIN, NICOLE M,** Univ Of Akron, Akron, OH; FR; BA; Phi Eta Sigma; Alpha Lambda Delta; Univ Hon Pgm; Acctg; Corp Law.

**MARTIN, NICOLE R,** Clark Atlanta Univ, Atlanta, GA; SO; Publc Rltns Stdnts Soc Of Amer Public Rltns Dir; The New Englnd Club VP 90-; Emmanuel Baptst Church Choir Pres 85-89; Inroads/Boston 89-; 4 Yr Intrnshp At The New England 89-; BA; Mass Media Arts; Corp Cmnctns.

**MARTIN, ODESHA PATRISE,** Al St Univ, Montgomery, AL; SO; Gspl Tbrncle Choir Dir; Ntnl Art Hnr Treas.

**MARTIN, PAMELA ANN,** Middle Tn St Univ, Murfreesboro, TN; SR; BBA; Ftr Acct Amer Treas/Sec 89; Bill Taylors Bushido Krt Clb 87-89; Gamma Beta Phi 87-; Tau Omcrn 89-90; Dns Cir 90; Beta Alpha Psi 90-; Coop Std Wnnt Asc 90-; Dns Lst 87-; Acct; Pblc Acct.

**MARTIN, PAMELA L,** Va Commonwealth Univ, Richmond, VA; MD; Amrcn Mdcl Assn 88-; Alpha Omega Alpha; Alpha Epsilon Delta Prgrms Lead 86-88; Garnet & Gold 86-88; Gamma Beta Phi 86-88; Ch Omega Scl Chrmn 86-88; Sftbl Vllybl 88-; BS VA Tchncl 88; Medicine.

**MARTIN, PATRICIA D,** Wv Univ At Parkersburg, Parkersburg, WV; SO; RBAAA; Phi Beta Lambda Sec 90-; Phi Theta Kappa 90-; Cntrlr Keene Corp Vienna W V; Acctg; Mngmnt.

**MARTIN, PATRICIA J,** Schenectady County Comm Coll, Schenectady, NY; SO; BA; Leg Wmn Vtrs; Keybrd Spclst Dpt Trnsprtn; AA; Englsh.

**MARTIN, PATRICK J,** Univ Of Cincinnati, Cincinnati, OH; SO; BFA; Brdcstng; Music.

**MARTIN, PAUL C,** Youngstown St Univ, Youngstown, OH; SR; BE; AAS Kent State Univ 83; Cvl Eng.

**MARTIN, PHYLIS A,** Owensboro Jr Coll Of Bus, Owensboro, KY; FR; AS; Pres List 90; Deans List 90; Perfect Attndnc 90; Cmptrs; Cmptr Oper.

**MARTIN, RAMONA G,** Memphis St Univ, Memphis, TN; Adtr IRS 88-; BA Chrstn Bro Coll 82; Acctg.

**MARTIN, RAMONA LEA,** Middle Tn St Univ, Murfreesboro, TN; JR; BA; Accntng; Accntnt.

**MARTIN, RENE D,** Livingston Univ, Livingston, AL; JR; BS; Elem Ed; Scl Studies Tchr.

**MARTIN, ROBERT E,** Univ Of Tn At Martin, Martin, TN; SO; BMME; Mrchng Bnd 89-; Symphnc Bnd 89-; Jazz Bnd 89-; Phi Mu Alpha Sinfonia Tres; Msc Schlrshp 89-; Bnd Schlrshp 89-; Msc Edctn; Bnd Drctr.

**MARTIN JR, ROBERT R,** Wv Univ, Morgantown, WV; SO; BS; Elec Eng.

**MARTIN, RUBY J,** Benedict Coll, Columbia, SC; GD; Alpha Kappa Mu 87-; Alpha Chi 87-; SC Sbstnc Abuse Rsrch Asst 89-90; Multi Comm Cntr Prsdnt 87-; Outreach Prsn Mnstrs 89-; Employee Srvcs Inc SC Dpt Crrctn 87-; BA 90.

**MARTIN JR, SAMUEL A,** Duquesne Univ, Pittsburgh, PA; SO; Bsn.

**MARTIN, SANDRA N,** Univ Of New England, Biddeford, ME; FR; BA; Yrbk Clb 90-; Hstry; Elem Educ.

**MARTIN, SHANNON D,** Radford Univ, Radford, VA; SR; BS; Stdnt Ed Assoc 89-90; Early Mdl Chldhd Ed; Elem Sch Tchr.

**MARTIN, SHAWN M,** Youngstown St Univ, Youngstown, OH; JR; BE; Lttl Leag Bsbl Coach 87-; Dean Lst 89-90; Fndtn Schlrshp 88-; IM Fltbll 88-89; IM Sftbll 88; Svl Eng; Strctrl Eng.

**MARTIN, SHERRY E,** Abraham Baldwin Agri Coll, Tifton, GA; GD; AA; Tftn Mntl Hlth Cntr 90; Hd Strt Cntr Vol; Prprfssnl M PM Clss; Scl Wrk; Educ.

**MARTIN, SONJA A,** Univ Of Fl, Gainesville, FL; SR; BA; Pre Legal Scty Pres 89-; Cndct Brd Chrmn 88-; Finance; Law.

**MARTIN, SONYA D,** Roane St Comm Coll, Harriman, TN; FR; MBA; Gamma Beta Phi 90-; Bus Acctg; CPA.

**MARTIN, STEVEN C,** Hillsborough Comm Coll, Tampa, FL; SO; AA; Phi Theta Kappa 90-; Mensa 85-91; Chem; Med.

**MARTIN, SUE ELLEN,** Columbia Greene Comm Coll, Hudson, NY; SO; ASSOC; Phi Theta Kappa; Deans List; Pres List; Spcl Ed; Tch Lrng Disabled.

**MARTIN, TALMAHJIA L,** Univ Of Sc At Columbia, Columbia, SC; JR; BS; NAACP 88-89; Delta Sigma Theta Rcrdng Sect 89-; Deans Lst 88-89; Deans Lst 90; Pharmacy; Rgstrd Phrmcst.

**MARTIN, TANYA L,** Bridgewater Coll, Bridgewater, VA; SR; Brthrn Stdnt Fllwshp 89; Stdnt Educ Assn 89-; Lambda Scty 89-; Alpha Chi 89-; BA; Engl; Tchncl Wrtr PR.

**MARTIN, TERESA R,** Va Commonwealth Univ, Richmond, VA; SR; MSW; Golden Key 90; Phi Kappa Phi; Richmond Pbl Schls 90; BSW; Dept Of Mntl Hlth Rtrdtn Hmlss Serv 90; Soc Wrk; Mstrs Of Soc Wrk.

**MARTIN, TERRY L,** Phillips Jr Coll Spartanburg, Spartanburg, SC; GD; BA; Data Processing Clb VP 89-; Teachers Aide 90-; Deans List 89-; College Work/Study Finance Clerk 89-; AAS Phillips Jr Clg; Data Processing; Teaching.

**MARTIN, THOMAS A,** Oh Wesleyan Univ, Delaware, OH; SR; BA; Karate 90-; Kappa Delta Pi 90-; Jvnl Crt Tutr 90-; Biology Rsrch 89-90; HS T A 90-; Ftbl Vrsty Cptn; Biology Scndry Edctn; MS Envrnmntl Sci Txclg.

**MARTIN, THOMAS C,** Glassboro St Coll, Glassboro, NJ; SR; BA; Res Stdnt Assoc Willow Hall Pres 90; SGN Class Sntr 89; Radio TV Assoc 88; Gamma Tau Sigma 90; Intrnshp Orbis Cmmnctns NY 90; Intrnshp WAQX-FM Syracuse 89; Cmmnctns Radio TV Flm; TV Prog.

**MARTIN, TIMOTHY W,** Univ Of Pittsburgh, Pittsburgh, PA; SR; BS; Golden Key 90; Elec Engr.

**MARTIN, TREVOR J,** Spartanburg Methodist Coll, Spartanburg, SC; FR; BA; Crmnl Jstc Clb 90-; Stdnt Spprt Srvcs Awrd 90-; Bsktbll 90-; Crmnl Jstc; Bus Admn.

**MARTIN, VERA J,** Wv Northern Comm Coll, Wheeling, WV; FR; New Cumberland Church Of Nazarene Pianist 84-; Secy Sci; Legal Secy.

**MARTIN JR, VIRGIL LEE,** Appalachian Bible Coll, Bradley, WV; SO; BA; Var Bsktbl 89-90; Bible.

**MARTIN, VIRGINIA R,** S U N Y Coll At Fredonia, Fredonia, NY; JR; BA; Coll Nwspr Edtr Chf 84-86; Yrbk Copy Edtr 85-86; Stu Govt Asmbly Rep 85-86; Drm Cncl Rep 84-85; Media Brd Mbr 85-86; Media Cncl Exec 85-86; Oper/Procdrs Comm Mbr 85-86; Fredonia Crspndt Jmstwn Post Jrnl 90-; Engl; Jrnlsm.

**MARTIN, WANDA Y,** Saint Pauls Coll, Lawrenceville, VA; SR; BA; NAACP 90-; Dr Frances A Thruman Awd 90-; Sclgy; MA.

**MARTIN-DUARTE, IGNACIO,** Univ Of Miami, Coral Gables, FL; SO; Intl Fin/Mktg; Stck Brkr.

**MARTIN-PLAYER, SARAH E,** Univ Of Sc At Beaufort, Beaufort, SC; FR; BAIS; Zonta Clb Beaufort Pres 89-90; Zonta Clb Beaufort VP 88-89; SC Crdt Un Mgrs Assoc; Fncl Indstry; Mdl Schl Lvl Hstry Tchr; Hstry; Tchg.

**MARTINEAU, GREGORY LEO,** Johnson St Coll, Johnson, VT; SO; BAEED; Rsdnt Asstnt; Sccr; Elem Educ; Tchr.

**MARTINEAU, JOHN H,** Univ Of Southern Ms, Hattiesburg, MS; SR; BM; Pi Kappa Lambda; Phi Mu Alpha 89-; Chrch Msc.

**MARTINEK, GREGORY S,** Juniata Coll, Huntingdon, PA; JR; BS; Scpl Probe 88-; Beta Beta Beta Bio 89-; Intrnshp Fmly Physcn; IM Vlybl/Sftbl 88-; Bio; Physcn.

**MARTINELLE, BETTY M,** Dowling Coll, Oakdale Li, NY; SR; BS; Dean Lst 89-90; Acdmc Schlrshp 89-90; Dean Lst FIT 73-75; Clinton Ave PTA 88-; Cub Scts 89-; AAS Fashion Inst Of Tech 75; Educ; Doc Educ.

**MARTINELLI, LINDA A,** Centenary Coll, Hackettstown, NJ; FR; BFA; ASID VP 90-; Pres Lst 90; Exec Sec Fortune 500 Co; Paralegal Coll Felician Coll Lodi NJ 80; Interior Dsgn; Own Firm.

**MARTINEZ CASTILLO, ZARAHI,** Univ Of Pr At Mayaguez, Mayaguez, PR; SR; BA; Soc Hon Coll Admn Emprs 89-90; Bus Admn; Acctng.

**MARTINEZ GARCIA, MERCEDES,** Inter Amer Univ Pr Barranquita, Barranquitas, PR; SO; BA; IMS; Hnrs Assoc Repr 90-; Disciples Christ Yth Grp Pres 90-; Dns Lst; Schlstc Awd; Hnr Rl; Vlybl; Bsn Adm; Acctg.

**MARTINEZ LOPEZ, DESIREE M,** Univ Of Pr At Mayaguez, Mayaguez, PR; SR; Mc Graw Hill Bk Clb 90-; Tau Beta Pi; Univ Hnr Lst 87-; Dns Lst 87-; AICE 90-; Engrg; Chmcl Engrg.

**MARTINEZ OLIVIERI, ROSELYNN L,** Univ Of Pr At Rio Piedras, Rio Piedras, PR; SR; Golden Key; Bio; Med.

**MARTINEZ RODRIGUEZ, CYNTHIA,** Univ Politecnica De Pr, Hato Rey, PR; FR; BBA; Indus Eng.

**MARTINEZ ROSA, CELSO,** Univ Of Pr At Mayaguez, Mayaguez, PR; SO; Chmstry; Engnrng.

**MARTINEZ SILVESTRIN, JULIO A,** Univ Of Pr Cayey Univ Coll, Cayey, PR; FR; Wghtlftng Assoc; Cagey U Clg Hnr Soc; PR Ntl Wghtlftng Ntl Tngr Rcrd Hldr 90; Bio; Med.

**MARTINEZ, ABBY,** Fl International Univ, Miami, FL; SO; BS; Mass Commtns; Advtng.

**MARTINEZ, ANA I,** Univ Of Miami, Coral Gables, FL; FR; BA; Union Of Cuban Stdnts; Alpha Lambda Delta; Dns Lst; Pres Hnr Rl; Pol Sci; Law.

**MARTINEZ, ANNA JEANETTE,** Midlands Tech Coll, Columbia, SC; SR; Ambsdr 89-90; Phi Theta Kappa; Amer Red Cross; Grdn Ad Liter.

**MARTINEZ, ANNE E,** Fl International Univ, Miami, FL; SR; BA; Ftr Edctrs Amrc 89-; Edctn; Tchr.

**MARTINEZ, CARLOS A,** Central Fl Comm Coll, Ocala, FL; SO; BS; Chem; Med-Rdlgy.

**MARTINEZ, CARLOS I,** Univ Of Pr At Rio Piedras, Rio Piedras, PR; SO; Pastoral Juvenil Vlybl 90; Bsebl; ACS; Yth Mnstry 89-; Hon Entrance 89; Chem.

**MARTINEZ, CARLOS M,** Inter Amer Univ Pr Hato Rey, Hato Rey, PR; GD; BA; Beta Bta Beta 90-; Ldrshp Acknldgmnt 90-; Biology; Pblc Hlth.

**MARTINEZ, CARLOS O,** Univ Of Miami, Coral Gables, FL; SO; BS; Alpha Lambda Delta; Phi Eta Sigma; Alpha Epsilom Delta; Provsts Hnr Rl; Bio; Med Doctr.

**MARTINEZ, CARMELO,** Univ Of Pr Medical Sciences, San Juan, PR; GD; MSW; Soc Sci Stdnt Assn 87-88; Stdnt Assn Human Wlfre V P 88-90; BA U P R Rio Piedras Campus 90; Soc Wrk.

**MARTINEZ, DAVID,** City Univ Of Ny La Guard Coll, Long Island Cty, NY; SO; AS; Deaf Awareness VP 90-; Cmptr Sci; Pgrmmr.

**MARTINEZ, DORIS M,** Inter Amer Univ Pr Hato Rey, Hato Rey, PR; JR; BA; Socl Wrk; Law.

**MARTINEZ, EDGARDO,** City Univ Of Ny Baruch Coll, New York, NY; SO; BBA; Ltn Amer Stu Org 90-; Bdybldg Clb 90-; Bus; CPA.

**MARTINEZ, EILEEN,** Temple Univ, Philadelphia, PA; FR; BA; Sci; Ped Nrsg.

**MARTINEZ, ERIC F,** Inter Amer Univ Pr Hato Rey, Hato Rey, PR; JR; BA; Boys Scouts Of Amer Asst Sct Mstr 70-75; Cath Act Yth Pres 75-78; Natl Rif Assn 90-; El Verde Res Assn 87-; Metmor Fin Inv Rep Acct Pres; Coll/Forecls Mortgage Bnkr Sch; Taxes/Ins 88; Accntng; CPA/MBA.

**MARTINEZ, GLADYS M,** Univ Of Pr At Mayaguez, Mayaguez, PR; JR; BCHE; Amer Inst Chem Eng 90-; IIQPR 90-; All Amer Schlrs Coll Pgrm; Chem Eng.**

**MARTINEZ, GUSTAVO A TRISTANI,** Catholic Univ Of Pr, Ponce, PR; GD; JD; ROTC Cmmsnd 2lt PLT Ldr 87-88; Army Rsrvst 2nd Lt Enlisted 85-; Airborne Qualified US Army; Mltry Order Wrld Wars 90; Mbr UCPR Law Schl Law Review Writer 90; Judo Team Mbr UPR Mayaguez PR 86-87; LLM Crmnl Law.

**MARTINEZ, IBIS C,** City Univ Of Ny City Coll, New York, NY; SO; BA; Early Chldhd Educ; Tchr.

**MARTINEZ, JAVIER J,** Brescia Coll, Owensboro, KY; JR; BA; Dorm Govt 90-; Ambssdr 90-; Alpha Chi 88-89; RA; IM Vlybl; IM Indr Soccr; Hispnc Soc; Tutor; Famly Weekend King; Owensboro Yth Soccr Coach; Pres Schlrshp; Dns Lst Sev Times; Var Soccr; Chem/Math; Med Schl.

**MARTINEZ, JOSE I,** Univ Politecnica De Pr, Hato Rey, PR; FR; Mech; Engr.

**MARTINEZ, JOSE M,** Miami Dade Comm Coll South, Miami, FL; SO; BA; Chmstry; Mdcn.

**MARTINEZ, JOSE S,** Univ Of Med & Dentistry Of Nj, Newark, NJ; GD; RT; AARC 90-; Amer Hrt Assn 90-; Money Mkt Trdr; Asst Purchsng Mgr; Resp Thrpst; Resp Thrpy.

**MARTINEZ, LILLIAM I,** Inter Amer Univ Pr Hato Rey, Hato Rey, PR; FR.

**MARTINEZ, MARIEL ZORY,** Inter Amer Univ Pr San German, San German, PR; FR; BBA; Accntng; CPA.

**MARTINEZ, MARILU,** Inter Amer Univ Pr Hato Rey, Hato Rey, PR; FR; BBA; Bus Admin; Mktg.

**MARTINEZ, MARY L,** Va Commonwealth Univ, Richmond, VA; SR; BS; Bus Admin; Human Res/Indust Rels.

**MARTINEZ, MICHAEL A,** George Mason Univ, Fairfax, VA; JR; BS; Acctg Clb; Golden Key; Acctg.

**MARTINEZ, MIRTA IDALIA,** Manna Bible Inst, Philadelphia, PA; JR; BA; Sndy Sch Tchr Teens; Yth Ldr Hd Ldr; Stu Bdy Tres; Cmptr Prog Data Engry Oprtr; Cert Cmptr Sci; Cert Trvl Indstry; Chrstn Educ; Rlgn.

**MARTINEZ, RICHARD D,** Fl International Univ, Miami, FL; JR; BS; Stdnt Mbr Am Chem Soc 89-; Stdnt Mbr Assn Cmptng Mchnry; Comp Sci.

**MARTINEZ, ROBERTO L,** Univ Of Pr At Mayaguez, Mayaguez, PR; SO; BS; Cmptr Sci; Cmptr Eng.**

**MARTINEZ, ROSALIA A,** Wilmington Coll, New Castle, DE; JR; MBA; Latin Amercn Club Pres 87; Spanish Amercn Club Secy 87-89; Calvary Christn Acadmy; CAG Tchng 89-; Elem Ed; Tchng.

**MARTINEZ-VELKY, DEBORAH J,** Dutchess Comm Coll, Poughkeepsie, NY; SO; BA; Dnc Clb 88-; Actv Pacr Prgrm 88-; Schlrshp Vsr Clg Smmr Enrchmnt Prgrm 89-; Otstndng Mnrty Comm Clg Grad; Fndr Adtng Mmbr Beekman Food Coop 88-; Vlntr Excsng Care Tmbr Wolf Red Wolf Adbn Soc; Fndr Tonches Exprsns Unlmtd 88-; Dsgn; Dsgnr.

**MARTINI, KRISTA D,** Indiana Univ Of Pa, Indiana, PA; JR; BS; Delta Gamma Asst Treas 90-; Provost Schlr 89-; Cmnctns Media; Publ Rel.

**MARTINKO, DAVID J,** Anne Arundel Comm Coll, Arnold, MD; FR; AA; Sccr 89-; Eng.

**MARTINKO, NICOLE M,** Univ Of North Fl, Jacksonville, FL; JR; Kappa Alpha Frat Ltl Sis; Undrwrtng Asst State Farm Ins Co 87-; AS Univ Of Fla 88; Bus; Mgmt.

**MARTINO, ANGELINA,** Seton Hall Univ, South Orange, NJ; SR; BED; Eliz Ann Stn Educ Assn Sec 89-; Univ Chrs 88; Kappa Delta Pi 89-; Alpha Phi Chrtr Mmbr Phlnthrpy Chr Sprt Chr 87-; Stdnt NJ Educ Assn 87-; Vol NJ Spcl Olympcs 90-; Vldctn Of Coll Of Educ; Elem Educ Hnrs Cttn; Elem Educ And Engl; Tchng.

**MARTINO, ANNAMARIE,** Seton Hall Univ, South Orange, NJ; JR; BS; Eliz Ann Seton Educ Assoc 88-91; Kappa Delta Pi 89-; Teaching Intrnshp 88-; Elem Educ/Psych.

**MARTINO, JOAN J,** Univ Of Pa, Philadelphia, PA; SR; BBA; Brodo/Paoloni Mem Awd; Bucks Co Music Edctrs Assn; NEA/PSEA; Instrmntl Music Tchr/Cncl Rock Schls; B Music Ed Temple U 75; M Music Ed Beaver Coll 77; Accntcy; CPA.

**MARTINO, JOHN N,** Nova Univ, Ft Lauderdale, FL; GD; MBA; SFMA 90-; APICS 90-; Sr MFG Engnr; BSE Unv Cntrl FL 85; Intrntnl Bsns; Mgmt Cnsltnt.

**MARTINO, REBECCA S,** Univ Of Southern Ms, Hattiesburg, MS; SR; BSN; Gnrl Chem Awd; Chldrns Coord/Choir Dir-Collins Untd Mthdst Chrch; BS/ACCTG Univ S AL 80; Nrsng; Midwf.

**MARTINS, CHRISTOPHER J,** Merrimack Coll, North Andover, MA; FR; Pgm Brd; Nu Phi Kappa VP Pldg Cls; Emrg Stdnt Ldrs Cnfrnc Rtrt Wknd; Crs Cntry Rng; Acctg; CPA.

**MARTINSON, KRISTIAN L,** Notre Dame Coll, Cleveland, OH; JR; BS; Rsdnts Assoc Brd Sec; Edctn Advsry Cncl 90-; Clss Offcr Treas 90-; Pi Lambda Theta; Alpha Phi Omega 88-89; Elem Ed.

**MARTIOSKI, LORI J,** Framingham St Coll, Framingham, MA; FR; BA; Yrbk 90-; SVAB 90-; Chmstry.

**MARTIR, NOEL,** Inter Amer Univ Pr San German, San German, PR; FR.

**MARTONE, NICHOLAS J,** Georgetown Univ, Washington, DC; JR; MBA; Amnsty Intrntnl 90-; Envrnmntl Soc 90-; Accntng; CPA.

**MARTORANA, MELANIE L,** Marywood Coll, Scranton, PA; FR; BA; Lit Mag Art/Wrtr 90-; Peer Tutors 90-; Engl; Second Tchr.

**MARTUCCIO, ANN,** John Carroll Univ, Cleveland, OH; FR; MBA; Psych; Psychlgst.

**MARTY LOPEZ, MARIA DEL PILAR,** Inter Amer Univ Pr San German, San German, PR; GD; BA; Trpl Beta Beta Beta Beta 89-; Bio; Med.

**MARTYN, KATRINA M,** Defiance Coll, Defiance, OH; FR; BS; Acctng.

**MARTYN, THOMAS C,** Fordham Univ, Bronx, NY; SR; Fnnce Scty 89; Acctng Scty 89-; Cmmtrs Assn 89-; Dns Lst 89-; Beta Alpha Psi 89-; Bsktbl Clnc Grmmr Schl Orgnzr Coach 87-; Prsh Lctr 90-; Intrnshp Lgl Asst 90-; Fnnce Acctng; Law.

**MARTYNICK, VERA C,** City Univ Of Ny La Guard Coll, Long Island Cty, NY; SR; AS; Alpha Theta Phi 90-; Polish/Slavic Ctr Inc 86-; Not For Profit 86-; Spvsry Bkkpr 90-; Bus Admin; Acctng.

**MARTYNIUK, IRENE A,** Kent St Univ Kent Cmps, Kent, OH; SR; BA; Amnsty Intl 87; Phi Beta Kappa 90-; Goldn Key 90-; Alpha Lambda Delta 88-; Sigma Tau Delta 90-; Engl; Lit.

**MARUCCI, JOSEPH P,** Glassboro St Coll, Glassboro, NJ; SR; BA; Var Ftbl 87-90; Math; Syst Analyst.

**MARUSCHAK, MARTIN J,** Seton Hall Univ, South Orange, NJ; JR; BSE; Math Clb 90-F Kappa Delta Pi; Math Sec Educ; Tchng.

**MARUYAMA, MIHO,** Immaculata Coll, Immaculata, PA; FR; BA; Office Work; Sociology.

**MARVIN, CYNTHIA M,** S U N Y Coll Of Tech At Alfred, Alfred, NY; FR; AS; Hmn Svcs Clb 90-; SICA; Sch Bd 89-; PTSA Treas 90-; Alumni Assoc Secr 90-; Hmn Svcs; Ed.

**MARVIN, KATHARINE A,** Vt Law School, S Royalton, VT; GD; JD; VT Law Rvw; SB MA Inst Tchnlgy 83; Law/Envrnmntl Law.

**MARX, CLAUDIA M,** Glassboro St Coll, Glassboro, NJ; JR; BA; SCEB VP 90-; Intrnshp At FL Studio Theatre 88; Cmnctns/Radio TV Film; Brdcstng.

**MARX, JEFFREY A,** Hudson Valley Comm Coll, Troy, NY; SR; ASSOC; Civil Engr Tech; Engrg.

**MARX, LISA G,** Fl International Univ, Miami, FL; SR; BA; Ftr Edctrs Amrc 89-; Yth Crm Wtch 86-90; Bys Clb Amrc 89-; AA MDCC 89; Elem Ed; Tchng.

**MARX, MARGARET A,** Central Fl Comm Coll, Ocala, FL; FR; Ocala Fire Dept Frefghtr EMT 85-; Emerg Med; Continue Career.

**MARX, STACEY A,** Univ Of Louisville, Louisville, KY; SO; BA; Amer Inst Of Chem Engrng 90-; Soc Of Women Engrs 90-; U Of L Jazz Ens 89-90; Co-Op At Gen Elec Scl Dir Co-Op Brd; U Of L Mud Vlybl 89; Chem; Chem Engr.

**MARX, STEPHANIE J,** S U N Y At Buffalo, Buffalo, NY; SR; BS; Wmn Mgmt Treas 88-89; Gnrtn Bus/Advrtsng Mngr 88-89; Radio Bus Dir 90; Gnrl Assmbly 88-90; Acdmc Schlrshp 88-89; Bus Admi(; Altrntv Bus.

**MARZELLA, LAURA,** Kent St Univ Kent Cmps, Kent, OH; JR; BBA; Intnl Soccer Club Sec 89-; Karate Club 89; Gldn Key; Delta Sigma Pi 89-; Otstndng Intl Stdnt 89; Finance; Intl Bus.

**MARZILLI, DENEANE,** Univ Of Ri, Kingston, RI; FR; BABS; Proj Fitnss 90-; Phi Eta Sigma 90-; Dns Lst 90-; Educ/Psych; Tchr.

**MARZO, BRIAN A,** Atlantic Comm Coll, Mays Landing, NJ; JR; BS; Phi Beta Lombda V P 90; Phi Kappa Sigma V P; Outstndng Mbr Award Phi Beta Lambda 90; Street Hockey Capt 90; Assoc Atlantic Cmnty Clg 90; Acctg.

**MARZOLA, TARA J,** East Stroudsburg Univ, E Stroudsburg, PA; SR; BA; Spch Comm Org 88-; Spch Comm Assc PA 89-; Sigma Tau Delta 90-; Deans Lst 89-90; Intern WNEP-TV Nwswtch 16; Spch Comm; Pblc Rltns/Brdcstng.

**MARZOLF, BRADLEY J,** S U N Y Coll Of Tech At Alfred, Alfred, NY; SR; BS; Rescue Tm Capt 90-; Ag Ldrs Clb 88-; Pi Rho Zeta 90-; AAS SUNY Alfred 90; Dairy Sci; Nutrition.

**MARZOUCA, SHELLY MAE,** Univ Of Miami, Coral Gables, FL; SR.

**MARZUKI, MARIA,** Univ Of Rochester, Rochester, NY; SO; BSC; Math Clb; Math/Comp Sci; Prof.

**MARZULLO, MICHELLE L,** Pa St Univ Worthington Cmps, Dunmore, PA; FR; Orientation Comm Incmng Frshmn; Bu; Mrktng.

**MASADEH, LANA B,** Univ Of Cincinnati-Clrmnt Coll, Batavia, OH; FR; BFA; Phi Theta Kappa; Theater Design/Prod.

**MASAOKA, FUMIE,** Wagner Coll, Staten Island, NY; SR; BA; Cmptr; Eng.

**MASCARENHAS, ANJALI M,** Univ Of Miami, Coral Gables, FL; JR; BA; Arbcs Clb Instrctr 88-90; Karate Clb 88-90; Chmstry Clb 88-90; Wmn Dstrss 90-; Kids Dstrss 90-; Fllwshp Amrcn Cncr Scty Rsrch Asst 90-; Intern Univ Miami Med Schl; Sclgy; Mdcl Dctr.

**MASEFIELD, SUSAN B,** Western Piedmont Comm Coll, Morganton, NC; FR; ADN; Table Rock Optimist Club Treas 88-; Phi Theta Kappa 90-; BA Appalachian State Univ 83; Nursing/RN; BSN Graduation.

**MASELLA, LISA M,** Saint Vincents Coll & Seminary, Latrobe, PA; JR; BA; Dns List 88-90; Acdmc Schlrshp 88-; Aerobithon; Cmptng/Info Sci; Syst Analyst.

**MASELLI, CHRISTOPHER B,** Suffolk Univ, Boston, MA; FR; BA; Radio DJ 90-; Pre Law Assc 90-; Tau Kappa Epsln Pblc Rltns Chr 90-; All IM Sprts 90-; Crmnl Jstc; Law.

**MASH, LISA A,** Oh Dominican Coll, Columbus, OH; SO; BA; Invntry Cntrl Crdntr; Bus Admn.

**MASHBURN, DAVID T,** Middle Ga Coll, Cochran, GA; FR; PA Bsbl; Bsns.

**MASHBURN JR, WILLIAM E,** Central Fl Comm Coll, Ocala, FL; FR; BS; SGA Vp; Phi Theta Kappa 90-; AS 90; Ed.

**MASHETT, MARY E,** Univ Of Sc At Columbia, Columbia, SC; SR; BS; Beta Gamma Sigma 90-; Bruner/Wadell Bus Schlrshp 90-; Pres Lst 89-90; Deans Lst; Intern Pitman Moore Brazil Sao Paulo Brazil 90; IBM Stdnt Rep Pgm Tm Ldr 89-; Mgmt Info Systems; Systems Analyst.

**MASKALENKO, ERIC P,** Univ Of Sc At Columbia, Columbia, SC; JR; BS; Phi Beta Kappa; Golden Key; Mngr Marriott Educ Serv; AA Midland Tech Clg 88; AS 89; Chem Engr; Mgmnt Pstn/Engr.

**MASKASKY, HOPE E,** Univ Of Rochester, Rochester, NY; SR; BA; Yng Rpblcns 87; Tae Kwn Do 87; Dbte Clb 87; Psi Chi 88-; Delta Zeta Acad Chr 89-; Tchng Asst Intro To Psychlgy 89; Psychlgy; Bus Admin.

**MASKEW, CARRIE R,** Duquesne Univ, Pittsburgh, PA; JR; BA; Cmmtr Cncl 89-90; Delta Sigma Pi 90-; Acctg-Bus; CPA.

**MASLAK, JOSEPH W,** Le Moyne Coll, Syracuse, NY; SR; MD; Biol Clb 87-88; Fine Art Clb 7-88; Tutor 90-; RA 90-; Beta Beta Beta 88-; Hmn Srv Assn 88-; Intl Hse 89-90; Dean Lst 88-; Acdmc Schlrshp 90-; Cum Laude; Bsktbl Vllybl Ftbll Sftbl 87-; BS; Vol Wrk Hosp 90-; Biol/Chmstry; Mdcl Schl.

**MASLANKA, KRISTOF,** Me Maritime Academy, Castine, ME; JR; BS; Marine Engnrng Tchnlgy; Maritime Engnrng Offc.

**MASLANKA, SANDRA K,** Comm Coll Algny Co Algny Cmps, Pittsburgh, PA; SO; AS; Couples Vllybll League 90; Phi Theta Kappa; Pedlogy: Bsn Psychlgy MSW Social Work.

**MASLIAH, LILIAN R,** Fl International Univ, Miami, FL; JR; BS; Southern Crs Astrnmcl Soc Miami; Otsdng Yng Wmn Amer 91; AA Miami Dade Cmuty Clg; Physics; Physics/Engr.**

**MASON, ALLISON L,** Va St Univ, Petersburg, VA; SO; BS; Little Zion Baptist Church; Business Acctg; Auditing Tax Consultant.

**MASON, CARL D,** Nova Univ, Ft Lauderdale, FL; GD; MBA; Central Dist Pharmacy Assoc; Pharmaceutical Repr; BS Fla Southern Clg 86; Business.

**MASON, CORINNE K,** Univ Of Tn At Martin, Martin, TN; FR; BS; Ldrs In Res; Soc Of Hons 90-; Phys Thrpy.

**MASON, ENDIA V,** Tn St Univ, Nashville, TN; SO; BA; Scl Wrk Clb VP 89; NAACP Cmmttee Chrprsn 89; Red Cross 90; Access Enhncemnt Prog; Ped Scl Wrk; MSW.

**MASON, ERIC F,** Union Univ, Jackson, TN; SR; BA; Fllwshp Chrstn Athlts Pres 87-; Bptst Stdnt Un Cncl 87-; Schl Nwspr Edtr 87-; Alpha Chi 89-; Prexy Clb 89-; Sigma Delta Pres 88-90; Lambda Chi Alpha 87-89; Stdnt Fndtn 88-89; Peer Cnslr 89; Alcohol Drug Prvntn Comm 89-90; Rlgn Cmnnctn Arts; Chrstn Mnstry.

**MASON III, EUGENE,** Tuskegee Univ, Tuskegee Inst, AL; JR; BA; Amer Inst Of Archtct Stdnts 90-; Natl Orgnztn Of Mnrty Archtcts 90-; Tau Sigma Delta; Brwn And Mmn Asscts Intrnshp; Blck Entrtnmnt TV; Stdnt Athlte Of Wk 89; Vrsty Bsktbl Tm 88-; Archtctre Cnstrctn Mgr.**

**MASON III, FRANK HOUSTON,** Univ Of Tn At Knoxville, Knoxville, TN; FR; BA; Alpha Lambda Delta; Phi Eta Sigma; Deans List 90; Bus Admnstrn; Finance.

**MASON, FRANKLIN B,** Tallahassee Comm Coll, Tallahassee, FL; SO; BA; Educ.

**MASON, GARY A,** Fl St Univ, Tallahassee, FL; FR; Phi Eta Sigma; IM Ftbl/Bsktbl 90-.

**MASON, GARY W,** Asbury Theological Sem, Wilmore, KY; GD; M DIV; J Wesley Seminary Fndtn Stdnt Cncl Pres 89-; Asbury Semnry Prsn Mnstry Dir 89; Intrn Prison Flwshp; Free Meth Ch Mnstrl Candte 88; Admsns Rep 86-88; B A Greenville Clg 86; Divinity; Navy Chplncy/Clg Prfsr.

**MASON, GERARD T,** Seton Hall Univ, South Orange, NJ; JR; BSE; Hlth/Phys Ed Clb; Campus Mnstry 89-; Vol Spcl Olympics 88-; Kappa Dleta Pi; Deans Lst 88-; Pal Coach Ftbl Yth 87-; HS Var Bsktbl/Sccr 82-84; AAS 87; Hlth.**

**MASON, GINA C,** Atlantic Comm Coll, Mays Landing, NJ; SO; AAS; Vol For SPCA 85-; Elem Ed; Tch.

**MASON, HELEN M,** Allegheny Coll, Meadville, PA; SO; BA; Interclg Deb Co Capt 90; Womns Ens 89-; Coll Chr; Lambda Sigma 90-; Alpha Delta Pi Mem Educ V P 90-; Cmptr Sci TA 90-; RA; Pol Sci; Pol Anlys.

**MASON, JEFFREY T,** Howard Univ, Washington, DC; SR; Sch Of Arch/Plnng Stdnt Assmbly Rep 89-90; Undergrad Stdnt Assmbly Rep 90-; Amercn Inst Of Arch Stdnts 87-; US Armamnt Rsrch Dev Eng Ctr Intrn Eng Asst 89-90; Im Lacrosse Team 89-90; BA; Arch; MBA.

**MASON, JENA W,** Univ Of Sc At Columbia, Columbia, SC; SO; BA; Legal Sec 87-; Engl; Ed.

**MASON, JULIENNE M,** Fl St Univ, Tallahassee, FL; SR; BAMS; Art Hist; Admn.

**MASON, KAREN A,** Lenoir Rhyne Coll, Hickory, NC; SR; BA; Amnesty Intl 88-; Chpl Cncl 88-89; Baptist Stdnt Union 87-88; Mu Sigma Epsilon 90-; LRC Habitat Hmnty 87-90; Intern Ten Broeck Psychtrc Hosp; Soclgy; Clncl Psychlgst.

**MASON, KAREN A,** Castleton St Coll, Castleton, VT; SO; BA; Psych.

**MASON, KELLY J,** Western Ky Univ, Bowling Green, KY; SR; BS; Fllwshp Chrstn Athl 88-; Bapt Stdnt Union 88-90; Natl Stdnt Spch/Lang/Hrng Assn 89-; Alpha Lambda Delta 88-89; Phi Kappa Phi 90-; Natl Hnr Soc 85-; Sigma Kappa 89-; A Hnr Roll Georgetown Clg 88-89; Wstrn KY Univ Pres Lst 89-; Cmnctn Disorders; Speech/Lang Pathology.**

**MASON, KEVIN A,** Wv Univ At Parkersburg, Parkersburg, WV; FR; AAS; Wldng Tech.

**MASON, LEA A,** Bridgewater Coll, Bridgewater, VA; SR; BA; Dbt Pres 89-; Coll Rpblcns 87-89; Cncrt Bnd Scl Chrmn 87-; Deans Lst 88-; Intern Wdrw Wlsn Brthplc 90; BA 91; Hstry Pltcl Sci.

**MASON, LESLIE L,** Mary Baldwin Coll, Staunton, VA; SR; BA; Soclgy Clb Pres 90-; Circle K 88-; Socl Comm 88-89; Soclgy/Educ; Tchr.

**MASON, LYNN E,** Indiana Univ Of Pa, Indiana, PA; SO; BS; Mrchng Bnd 89-; Bsktbl Pep Bnd 89-; Elem Ed; Tchng Chld Psychlgy.

**MASON, MARCUS E,** Univ Of Miami, Coral Gables, FL; SO; BA; Intervarsity Chrstn Flwshp 89-; Untd Black Stdnts 89-; Orntn Asst 90-; Hnrs Stdnts Assoc 89-90; Hnrs Prog 89-; Mahoney Prog Cncl 89-90; Cert Of Apprctn Hnrs Stdnts Assn 89-90; Cert Of Achvmnt Hlth Careers Prog; Sptsfst; Bio; Med/Sci.

**MASON, MARIA,** Al A & M Univ, Normal, AL; SO; BS; Medcl Tchnlgy.

**MASON, MARK E,** Ohio Valley Coll, Parkersburg, WV; SR; MA; Delta Soc Clb 90-; Timthy Clb 90-; Sigma Zeta 89; J Walter Malone Schlr Malone Clg 87-89; Mnstrs Endwmnt Schlrshp 90-; Intrclgt Bsktbl Malone Clg 87-89; BA Malone Clg 89; Old Testmnt; Mnstry/Bible Prof.

**MASON, MICHAEL S,** Cape Fear Comm Coll, Wilmington, NC; SO; BA; Stdnt Govt Sntr 89; Crmnl Jstce; Law Enf State/Fdrl.

**MASON, PATRICIA L,** James Madison University, Harrisonburg, VA; SR; BSN; VA Nrsng Std Asc Chr 90-; Chptr VNSA Treas 90-; Dpt Nrsng Hnr Soc Treas 89-; Phi Kappa Phi 90-; Gldn Key 89-; Mrtr Brd 90-; Comm Invlmnt/Ldrshp Actv 89-; VA Hlth Prof Schlp 89-; Nrsng; Dctrl Degree Nrsg.

**MASON, PAULA A,** Andover Coll, Portland, ME; GD; Natl Hnr Soc Pres 89-90; Hnr Soc Pres 90; Assc 90; Busn Admin; Life Ins.

**MASON, PENNY A,** Georgetown Coll, Georgetown, KY; SO; BS; Beta Beta Beta Hstrn; Prsdnts House Assn Little Sis; Chrch Yth Choir Drctr; IM; Blgy; Medicine.

**MASON, REGINA A,** Univ Of Cincinnati, Cincinnati, OH; JR; BM; Sigma Delta Tau; Vln Prfrmnce; Emplymnt In Orchstra.

**MASON, RENEE M,** Elms Coll, Chicopee, MA; SR; BA; Ftr Tchrs Assc 88-89; Ambsdrs 88-89; Phi Alpha Theta 90; Thtr 90; Hist Scndry Ed; Hgh Schl Hist Tchr.

**MASON, ROBERT J,** Univ Of Tn At Knoxville, Knoxville, TN; GD; DVM; Student Chpt Amer Vety Mdl Assoc 90-; Penn State Pre Vet Club Treas 86-90; Gamma Sigma Delta 90-; Alpha Zeta 90-; BS PA Univ 90; Vety Med; Veterianarian.

**MASON, ROBYN L,** Comm Coll Algny Co Algny Cmps, Pittsburgh, PA; FR; MSN; Nrsng; MS Anstsia.

**MASON, SUSAN R,** Snead St Jr Coll, Boaz, AL; SO; BSED; Phi Theta Kappa Treas 90; Otstndng Engl Awrd 90; Grad Summa Cum Laude 90; AS 90; Scndry Educ; Tchr Engl And Econs.

**MASON, TAMMY M,** Greenville Tech Coll, Greenville, SC; SO; BS; Nurs.

**MASON, TERRY L,** Ms Univ For Women, Columbus, MS; FR; BS; SGA Sntr 90-; Hnrs Prog 90-; Slhtte Scl Clb Intrclb Dlgte; Hbtt Fr Hmnty 90-; Acctng; Tx Attrny.

**MASON, WENDY BETH,** Northern Ky Univ, Highland Hts, KY; SO; AD; Phi Sigma Sigma 89; Nrsng.

**MASON, WILLIAM D,** Univ Of Sc At Columbia, Columbia, SC; SR; BS; Buss Soc 87-89; Bsn Admn.

**MASSAFRA, PASQUALE F,** Manhattan Coll, Bronx, NY; SR; BSEE; Elect Eng.

**MASSAKOWSKI, CAROLYN J,** Temple Univ, Philadelphia, PA; SR; BS; Amer Pharmaceutical Assoc 89-; PA Pharmaceutical Assoc 89-; Rho Chi; Pharmacy; Pharmaceutical Chemistry.

**MASSAQUOI, EDWARD M,** Strayer Coll, Washington, DC; SO; AA; Comp Info Prcssng Sr Comp Oprtd Super 88; Comp Data Info Prcssng 88; Diploma Computer Information Systems; Comp Systms; Comp Data Prcssng.

**MASSARI, LILLIAN R,** Inter Amer Univ Pr Hato Rey, Hato Rey, PR; SR; BA; AIESEC; Sci Avtn.

**MASSARO, ANDREA K,** Kent St Univ Kent Cmps, Kent, OH; SR; BA; Fletcher Hall Hs Cncl 89-90; Alpha Phi Treas 87-; Alpha Phi Pi Club 88; Deans Lst; Finance.

**MASSE, KEVIN M,** Castleton St Coll, Castleton, VT; JR; BA; History Clb 89; Rugby Clb; I M Sprts 88-; History/Sec Educ; Tch.

**MASSEE, JUDITH H,** Piedmont Coll, Demorest, GA; JR; BA; Psychlgy Clb Sec 90-; Amer Psychlgy Assoc; Sthstrn Assoc Bhvr Anlys; Trch Clb; Psi Chi; Frnds Mntns; Psychlgy; Thrpst.

**MASSENGALE, KATHRYN A,** Auburn Univ At Auburn, Auburn, AL; GD; Phi Kappa Phi; Sigma Tau Delta; Pi Lambda Theta VP 90-; Auburn Untd Meth Chrch; AL Ed Assn; Ntl Cncl Tchrs Engl; Bnkg 73-90.

**MASSENGALE, TIM A,** Faulkner Univ, Montgomery, AL; JR; BS; Cystic Fibrosis Coordntr Fnd Rsr 90; Rookie League Bsbl Dir; Bsbl Team 90-; Sports Mgt.

**MASSEY, ANITA F,** Memphis St Univ, Memphis, TN; JR; BSN; Deans Lst; BS 87; Nrsng.

**MASSEY, DEBORAH D,** Hudson Valley Comm Coll, Troy, NY; SR; AA; Pres Lst; Hmn Srvc; Soc Wrk.

**MASSEY, DIANNE R,** Vance Granville Comm Coll, Henderson, NC; SO.

**MASSEY, DONNA HAMMERSLEY,** Western Piedmont Comm Coll, Morganton, NC; SO; AA; Phi Theta Kappa 90-; Liberal Arts; Socl Wrk.

**MASSEY III, HEZEKIAH,** Fayetteville St Univ, Fayetteville, NC; FR; BA; Chncllrs Schlrshp Prgm; LEAP Trng Prgm; Ftbll Tm; Psychlgy.

**MASSEY, JOHN G,** Middle Tn St Univ, Murfreesboro, TN; SO; BS; Gamma Beta Phi 90-; Physcs/Math.

**MASSEY, KATHERINE D,** Univ Of Southern Ms, Hattiesburg, MS; JR; Kappa Delta Chpln; Alchl Awrnss Chrmn; Sigma Chi Aux Pres; Fmly Lf Stdies/Chld Lf Dvlpmnt.

**MASSEY, KENT R,** Va Commonwealth Univ, Richmond, VA; GD; CERT; Orntl Rug Imprtr; Rltr; BS 74; Hstry Scl Sci Ed.

**MASSEY, KRYSTAL K,** Univ Of Southern Ms, Hattiesburg, MS; SR; Amer Adv Fed Rsrch Dir 90; Stdnt Alumni Assoc; Delta Delta Delta 89; Wesley Fdn; Dixie Darlings 87-90; So Misses 86-89; Intrn Maris West/Baker 89; Greenpeace; BS 90; Adv; Sales/Mgmnt.

**MASSEY, STEPHANIE F,** Coll Of Charleston, Charleston, SC; B; Flwshp Chrstn Athlts; Pschlgy; Cnslr.

**MASSEY, STEVEN M,** Limestone Coll, Gaffney, SC; SO; BS; Bus Mgt.

**MASSEY, TONYA E,** Univ Of North Fl, Jacksonville, FL; JR; BED; Phi Theta Kappa 87-88; Awana Ldr 88-90; Deans Lst 89-; Math Edn; Tchr.**

**MASSEY, VELVITHRA L,** Univ Of Ga, Athens, GA; SR; BED; Athltc Cncl 89-; Natl Athltc Trnrs Assn Asstshp 90-; Delta Sigma Theta Schlrs Clb 90-; Stdnt Trnr Wmns Sports 88-; MA/EDUC Admin PhD.

**MASSI, GIULIANA M,** Bryant Coll Of Bus Admin, Smithfield, RI; FR; BA; Res Asst; Acctg; Law.

**MASSI JR, JOHN J,** Pa St Univ Delaware Cty Cmps, Media, PA; FR; BA; Hnrs Cnvct Awd; Anml Biosci; Anml Rschr.

**MASSIC, TAMARA S,** Kent St Univ Kent Cmps, Kent, OH; JR; BA; Deans List 87; Family Comsumer Studies; Social Work/ Cnslng.**

**MASSICOTTE, KIMBERLY C,** Coppin St Coll, Baltimore, MD; SO; Cmptr Sci; Cmptr Systs Analyst.

**MASSIE, ETHELIA C,** Comm Coll Algny Co Algny Cmps, Pittsburgh, PA; FR; MBA; Certif Bradford Bus Schl 88; Acctng Spclst; CPA.

**MASSIE, ROBYN G,** Marshall University, Huntington, WV; SO; Acctng; CPA.

**MASSIE, VERONICA DEE,** Marshall University, Huntington, WV; SR; BA; MENC Treas 87-; Stdnts For Chrst 87-90; Big Green Mrchng Machne 87-; Marshall Univ Wnd Symphny 87-; MU Symphnc Bnd; Brs Ensmbl 87-; Jazz Ensmbl 87-; Delta Omicron Treas 88-; Music Educ.

**MASSING, CATHERINE ANN,** Glassboro St Coll, Glassboro, NJ; GD; Law Enforment Scty Secty 87-88; Adptn Daughter Rachael Massing Pre Se 90; Race Cuse 5k Run Breast Calker Foundation Runner; Spring Semester 87f Deans List 88; Summer Computer Camp Kids 90; Law/Justice; Law Schl.

**MASSING, CYNTHIA L,** Allegheny Coll, Meadville, PA; SO; BA; IM Vlybl Bsktbl Sftbl 89-; Alpha Chi Omega; All American Schlrs; Alden Schlr 89-90; Vrsty Sccr 89-; Poltical Sci Math; Schl Public Admin.

**MASSING, DANA L,** Edinboro Univ Of Pa, Edinboro, PA; JR; BA; Nwspaper Nws Edtr 90-; Engl/Wrtng.

**MASSINOPLE, WILHELMINA H,** Univ Of Nc At Asheville, Asheville, NC; SR; BA; Phi Alpha Theta Sec 90-; Phi Eta Sigma; Deans Lst; Chancellors Lst; Dstnctn Hist; Cum Laude; Hist.

**MASSON, JOSHUA J,** Univ Of Rochester, Rochester, NY; SO.

**MASSON, JUDITH A,** Schenectady County Comm Coll, Schenectady, NY; SO; AS; Spnsh Clb 90; Intrnshp Fndrsng Endwmnt Fund Comm Ctr 90; Arts/Crfts Coord Yth Free Lance Artist; Hmn Svcs; Act Dir/Rec Ther.

**MASSUCCI, LINDA M,** Teikyo Post Univ, Waterbury, CT; SO; AS; Erly Chldhd Educ; BS Chld Stdy.

**MAST, BRIAN E,** Temple Univ, Philadelphia, PA; SR; BS; Messiah Coll Soc Engrs VP 89; Am Soc Mech Engrs 89-; Messiah Cntry 87-89; Mech Eng; Rsrch/Dvlpmnt.

**MAST, DARCY A,** S U N Y Coll At Fredonia, Fredonia, NY; JR; BS; Villa Plyrs 88-90; Dns Lst 89-90; Fncl Wmn Intl 90; Pres Schlp 90; Buffalo/Niagira Sls/Mktg Exec 90; J C Penney Co Intrn 90; AAS Villa Maria Clg Bflo; Bsn Admn; Fnce.

**MASTANDREA, PABLO A,** Fl International Univ, Miami, FL; FR.

**MASTELE, SUSAN E,** Comm Coll Algny Co Algny Cmps, Pittsburgh, PA; FR; RN; Chld Dvlpmnt Club Pres 90-91; Phlsphy Club; RSA Club; Ftrs Editor; Allegheny View Newspr; Parent Of The Year Award/Chld Dvlpmtn 89-90; Nrsg; BSN/MSTRS/ TECH.

**MASTELLONE, SUSAN M,** Wagner Coll, Staten Island, NY; SR; BS; Alld Hlth Sci Org 88-; Irn Hls Cvc Assn 88-; Sl Swmmng Dvng Assn 78-; Omicron Delta Kappa 89-; Beta Beta Beta Sec 88-; Bio; Med.

**MASTER, WILLIAM L,** Duquesne Univ, Pittsburgh, PA; GD; MBA; Fncl Mgmt Assoc Pres 89-90; Intl Bsn Assoc Treas 90; Stdnt Advsry Comm Advsr-Dean 89-90; Red Masquers Theatre Assoc Actor 89-90; Commodities/Options 90; Pittsburgh Soc Fncl Analysts 89-90; 501 Clb; Intl Bsn.

**MASTERS, AMY N,** Oh Univ, Athens, OH; FR; BA; Mntl Hlth Ctr Vol 90; Aeronautical Eng; Eng.

**MASTERS, BRIAN S,** Univ Of Ky, Lexington, KY; SO; BS; Stdnt Govt Assoc Hndcp Serv Comm 90-; IM Cncl 90-; Lances Jr Mns Hnr Soc; Kappa Sigma; Hlth Crs Oprtnty Pgm/Med Intrnshp; Tns/Sftbl/Tbl Tns/Bsktbl/Scr/Vlybl 89-; Blgy; Med Schl.

**MASTERS, JULIE C,** Univ Of Rochester, Rochester, NY; FR; BS; IM Indoor/Spring Soccer 90-; Optics; Engr.

**MASTERS, KARIE M,** Columbus Coll Of Art & Design, Columbus, OH; FR; BFA; Adv Dsgn; Comm Art.

**MASTERS, MARGARET M,** Saint Francis Coll, Loretto, PA; SR; BA; Schl Nwsppr Edtr-Chf 87-; Pre-Law Clb/Orntn Asst 87-; Phlsphy Clb Pres 89-; Hon Pgm 87-; Gamma Sigma Sigma Pres 87-; Sftbl; Phlsphy/Pre-Law; Law.

**MASTERS, MELANIE C,** Oh Univ, Athens, OH; FR; BED; Thtr Wrk 90-; Thespians 87-; IM Ftbl 90-; Thtr Arts-Cstmng; Cstmr Thtr Prdctns.

**MASTERS, MILDRED V,** Univ Of North Fl, Jacksonville, FL; JR; BA; Golden Key; Assoc In Arts St Johns River Cmnty Clge; AA 89; Psychology; Counselor.

**MASTERSON, ALISA A,** Commonwealth Coll, Virginia Beach, VA; SO; AS; Med Offc Mgmt.

**MASTERSON, DEBORAH L,** Methodist Coll, Fayetteville, NC; JR; BM; Methdst Coll Chorus 89-; Rnbws End Ensmbl 89-; Hon Soc 89-90; Faymont Baptst Chrsh Pianst 90-; Music Educ; Music Tchr.

**MASTERSON, GEORGE A,** Atlantic Comm Coll, Mays Landing, NJ; SO; Bus Admin.

**MASTERSON, MARY M,** Saint Francis Coll, Loretto, PA; SO; BS; Actvs Org 89-; Bio/Math Clb 89-; Stu Gov Sntr; SAIL 90-; Beta Beta Beta; Phi Delta Kappa; Sftbl 90; Bio; Med.

**MASTERSON, MARY S,** Newbury Coll, Brookline, MA; FR; AAS; Lgl Sec Sci.

**MASTERSON, MELISSA A,** Seton Hall Univ, South Orange, NJ; JR; BA; Educ Assc/Elizabeth Seton 90-; Deans Lst 87-; IM Flg Ftbl 88-; Elem Educ/Cmmnctns; Tchr Dy Care.

**MASTERSON, PAT H,** Embry Riddle Aeronautical Univ, Daytona Beach, FL; FR; BA; Vlybl; Arntcl Stds; Arlne Plt.

**MASTIN, KAREN F,** Al A & M Univ, Normal, AL; JR; BS; Dns Lst Jr Coll; AA Queensborough Comm Coll 79; Offc Systs Mgmt; Exec Sec/Bus Ed.

**MASTORS, ANDREW J,** Univ Of Nc At Charlotte, Charlotte, NC; FR; BA; Stdnt Govt Intern 90-; Kappa Alpha Order Inter Frat Cncl Rep; Crmnl Jstce/Spanish; Crmnl Law.

**MASTRO, MARIO S,** Radford Univ, Radford, VA; JR; BA; Richard Bland Clg Clg William/Mary SIFE Tm Tri Ldr 89-90; SAM 90-; Omicron Delta Epsilon 90-; Hnrs Prog 90-; SIFE Semi Ntl Tri Ldr 90; Conf Busn Econ Hnrd Richard Bland Found Final Econ Essay 90; Hmn Res Econ; Mgt/Hmn Res Consulting.

**MASTRO, WENDY D,** Radford Univ, Radford, VA; JR; BBA; Deans Lst; Finance; Mngmnt.

**MASTROBERTI, JESSICA BROWN,** Univ Of Sc At Coastal Carolina, Conway, SC; SR; BA; Untd Mthdst Acad Schlp 86; D L Scurry Fdn Schlp; Pol Sci; Law Sch/PHD.

**MASTROIANNI, PETER,** Glassboro St Coll, Glassboro, NJ; SR; BA; Rdio Tv Assn; The Jhn Bntng Shw Prdcr; Dns Lst 90; MTV Intrn; Natl Assn Of Tv Prdcrs And Execs Cnvntn Intrn; Vrsty Ftbl; Cmmnctn; Tv Prdctn.**

**MASTROIANNI, VICTOR,** Glassboro St Coll, Glassboro, NJ; FR; BA; Stu Govt 90-; IM Vlybl/Sccr/Ftbl Tms 90-; Music; Vcl Prfmnc.

**MASTROMARINO, MELISSA ANNE,** Ny Univ, New York, NY; FR; BA; Hstry; Law.

**MASUKAWA, MASAKO,** Savannah Coll Of Art & Design, Savannah, GA; JR; Schlstc Art Awd; Gold Keys Hnrbl Mtn; Schlp 90-; Vlybl; Illstrtn; Art/Trnsltr.

**MATA, CARLOS E,** Univ Of Tn At Martin, Martin, TN; SR; BS; SIFE Proj Dir 89-90; Econ Clb 90-; Phi Kappa Phi; Vrsty Bsbl 87-89; Econ Finance; Fncl Plng/Analysis.

**MATCHETT, JANEA D,** Johnson C Smith Univ, Charlotte, NC; JR; BA; NABA Treas 89-; Christn Assoc 88-; Amercn Future Black Exec 90-; Tau Beta Chi 90-; Hons Clg 88-; Pres Schlrshp; AICPA Schlrshp; Charles Blackwell CPA Intrn 89-; Bus Admn; Acctng.

**MATEER, MELINDA L,** Univ Of Nc At Greensboro, Greensboro, NC; SR; BS; VP Stdnt Govt SFCC Sec 85-86; Sigma Sigma Sigma VP 88-; Elem Educ; Tchr.

**MATEN, DONNA L,** Livingston Univ, Livingston, AL; JR; BA; SGA V Pres 87-89; Annual Staff Co Edtr 88-89; SADD 87-89; Beta Club Pres 87-89; Acctg; Accountant CPA.**

**MATEO, MAGNOLIA,** Boricua Coll, New York, NY; GD; BA; Al Anon Cnslg Mnhst NY 88-; GSA Trps Cnslg Grt Nck NY 88-90; Bst Ldr 90; Chldrns Museum Mnhtn Best Attndnc Intrnshp 90-; Archtct 84; Engl; Engr Archtct.

**MATEO-MALDONADO, ADRIANA,** Catholic Univ Of Pr, Ponce, PR; SR; Mrktng.

**MATESHA, ROSE SECUNDA,** Immaculata Coll, Immaculata, PA; SR; Gospel Choir 87-; Vol Strs Infirmary 87-88; Blck Cultural Soc 87-; Cert Machakos Tchrs Clg Kenya 76-78; Sociologyf Tch/ Cnsl.

**MATHAM, SAMUEL WILFRED,** Capital Bible Seminary, Lanham, MD; GD; Ordnd Mnstr Rlgn Chrmn Dnmntns Exec Cncl 85-87; Chrstn Mnstry Pstrl Chrch-Plntng Bible Tchng 72-89; Thelogy; Lecturer Bible Coll.

**MATHASON, RACHEL D,** Univ Of Miami, Coral Gables, FL; FR; BFA; Cbl TV Stn Prdcr 90-; Nwspr Asst Nws Ed 90; Hnr Soc 90-; Intrhshp Chnl 25 TV 89-; Fl Prs Clb Schlrshp; Brdcst Jrnlsm/Pltcs; Law.

**MATHENY, BRYAN D,** Western Carolina Univ, Cullowhee, NC; SR; BA; Phi Alpha Theta; AA Isothermal Comm Coll 87; Hstry.

**MATHENY, EMILY C,** Univ Of Southern Ms, Hattiesburg, MS; FR; BA; Alpha Lambda Delta; Pltcl Sci; Law Schl.

**MATHENY, JERRIE J,** Univ Of Tn At Martin, Martin, TN; SR; BA; AS 84; Anml Sci.

**MATHER, ROBERT B,** Southern Vt Coll, Bennington, VT; SO; BA; Crmnl Jstc Asc 90-; INS Intshp; Bsbl; Crmnl Jstc; Fed Law Enf.

**MATHER, SUSAN M,** Kent St Univ Stark Cmps, North Canton, OH; SO; BA; Awana Yth Clb; Bapt Chrch Vol; Engl Psych/Sec Educ; Tchr/Publctns.

**MATHERLY, KELLY J,** Beckley Coll, Beckley, WV; SO; BA; Prlgl; Law.

**MATHERNE, MARCUS M,** Oh Univ, Athens, OH; JR; BS; Eta Kappa Nu Rcrdg Sec; Dns Lst; Elctrcl/Cmptr Engrg.

**MATHERNE, THERESA S,** Wv Northern Comm Coll, Wheeling, WV; FR; AA; Field Plcmnt Touchstones Drug/Alcohol Trtmnt Ctr; Mntl Hlth Inpatient 82-87; Drug/Alcohol Hlfwy Hses Trtmnt Ctr 90-; Hmn Svcs; Addiction Cnslng.

**MATHERS, JULIE,** Wv Univ At Parkersburg, Parkersburg, WV; AAS; Phi Theta Kappa 90-; Bus/Comp; Data Proc.

**MATHERS, LINDA C,** Wv Univ At Parkersburg, Parkersburg, WV; FR; Computer Science.

**MATHESON, DONNA M,** Wagner Coll, Staten Island, NY; JR; BSE; Sngfst Com; Kappa Delta Pi; Phi Beta Sigma Star Pres 90-; Educ; Law Schl.

**MATHEUS, FRANCINE M,** Univ Of Sc At Columbia, Columbia, SC; SR; BA; Dns Lst 88-; Swmnt Tm 88-90; Finance/ Owner Mgmt; Intl Finance.

**MATHEUS, JEAN D,** City Univ Of Ny Queensbrough, New York, NY; FR; AAS; Mech Engrg.

**MATHEWS, JAMES D,** Manhattan Coll, Bronx, NY; SO; BA; IM Bsktbl/Sftbl; Cls VP; Pres Schlrshp; IM; Elect Engrg; Engr.

**MATHEWS, JULIE C,** Univ Of Ga, Athens, GA; SO; BSED; Wrdlwd Dscplshp Assc; Deans Lst; Educ; Spch Pthlgy.

**MATHEWS, MARLA G,** Glassboro St Coll, Glassboro, NJ; JR; BA; SGA Rep 89-90; Psychology; Juvenile Cnslng.

**MATHEWS, MICHELLE A,** S U N Y Coll At Fredonia, Fredonia, NY; JR; BS; Reed Lib Stdnt Advsry Com Chrmn 88-; TV Nws Anchr/Telethon Host 88-; Alpha Epsilon Rho VP 88-; Hon Pgm 88-; Arlie Muller Parks Cmnctns Awd 88-89; Louis Adler Broadcast Jrnlsm Schlrshp 89-90; Arthur Maytum Cmnctns Schlrshp 90-; Cmnctns/Media Brdcstng; Brdcst Jrnlsm.

**MATHEWS, SARAH D,** Western New England Coll, Springfield, MA; SO; BA; COPE Tr 90-; Stdnt Snt Class Rep 90-; Bio Clb Co Chrprsn 90-; WNEK-FM Springfield D J 90-; PART 90-; Bio.

**MATHEWS, TRACY L,** Savannah Coll Of Art & Design, Savannah, GA; JR; BA; Architectivre; Architect.

**MATHEWSON III, PAUL,** Univ Of Nc At Charlotte, Charlotte, NC; BA; Finalist Trvlng Fllwshp Awrd Architecture; IM Soccer 87-; Architecture.

**MATHEWSON, THOMAS G E,** Schenectady County Comm Coll, Schenectady, NY; SO; BA; CAPTAIN Of Shenendehowa; Engl; Law.

**MATHEY, DAVID A,** Univ Of Akron, Akron, OH; JR; BS; Boy Scts-Sctmstr 90-; Gldn Key; Sigma Alpha Mu 88-; Fin.

**MATHIAS, CHRISTOPHER P,** Johnson And Wales Univ, Providence, RI; FR; BA; Hon 90-; Hotel/Restaurant Mgmnt.

**MATHIAS, DONNA L,** James Madison University, Harrisonburg, VA; SR; BA; Gldn Ky 90-; Elem Ed/Office Admin; Educ/Bus Fld.

**MATHIAS, MELISSA A,** Univ Of Sc At Columbia, Columbia, SC; JR; BA; Educ/Math; Elem Tchr.

**MATHIESEN, DANA L,** Univ Of Nc At Charlotte, Charlotte, NC; FR; BA; Phi Eta Sigma 90-; Psychlgy.

**MATHIEU, RHONDA L,** Newbury Coll, Brookline, MA; FR; BA; Exprsns Clb; Fshn Shw; Intr Dsgn.

**MATHIS, ANGELA D,** Univ Of Tn At Martin, Martin, TN; FR; MAC; Acctng.

**MATHIS, BETH L,** Saint Andrews Presbytrn Coll, Laurinburg, NC; SR; BA; Coll Chrstn Un Sec 89-90; Chrstn Serv Org Sec 90-; Coll Chorale 88-; Pi Gamma Mu; Cnslng Intrn 90; Psychlgy; Cnslng.

**MATHIS, BRADFORD K,** Univ Of Sc At Columbia, Columbia, SC; SR; BS; Admin Intrnshp Pres Offc 90-; Admin Intrnshp Athl Dept; IM Ftbl/Bsktbl/Sftbl; Sprt Admin; Clgte Athl Admin.

**MATHIS, BRIAN N,** Jackson St Univ, Jackson, MS; FR; Cmptr Sci.

**MATHIS, CORA LEE,** Barry Univ, Miami, FL; LA; Deans Lst Miami Dade Cmmnty Clg 90; Deans Lst; Mt Carmel Mssnry Bapt Chrch GEMS; Miami Brdge Ctr Vol; AA Miami Dade Cmmnty Clg N 90; Soc Wrk.

**MATHIS, GENEVA S,** Owensboro Comm Coll, Owensboro, KY; FR; AS; Sci; RN.

**MATHIS, J CHRISTOPHER,** Christian Brothers Univ, Memphis, TN; GD; MBA; Inst Mngmnt Actnts; Stf Actnt; BA 77; Acctg.

**MATHIS, KELLY R,** Univ Of Southern Ms, Hattiesburg, MS; SO; BED; Wind Ensmbl; Mrchng Band; Dimnd Darlngs; History; Tchng.

**MATHIS, KENNETH O,** Univ Of Sc At Columbia, Columbia, SC; FR; BS; NSBE; AFRO; NAACP; MAP; Intrnshp Union Carbide Chem & Plastics W Va; Chemical Engineering.

**MATHIS, LOYCE J,** Clayton St Coll, Morrow, GA; SO; BA; Music Clb Soc Chrmn 89-; Chrldr 90-; Choir/Music Theatr; Music; Mnstr Of Music/Ed.

**MATHIS, MARJORIE M,** Fl St Univ, Tallahassee, FL; JR; BA; Natl Stu Spch Lang Hrng Assn 90-; Stu Govt Assn 89-; Phi Theta Kappa 87-; AA Gulf Coast Comm Col 89; Cmmnctn Dsrdrs; Spch Pthlgy.

**MATHIS, PERRY T,** Univ Of Sc At Columbia, Columbia, SC; JR; BS; Palmetto Paddlers 90-; Fin/Org Mgmnt; Banking.

**MATHIS, SANDRA L,** Middle Tn St Univ, Murfreesboro, TN; SR; BS; SGA Jstc 88-89; Kappa Nu Chptr Phi Mu 88-89; Pol Sci; Paralgl Law.

**MATHIS, STEPHEN M,** Middle Tn St Univ, Murfreesboro, TN; JR; BA; Anthrpgcl Soc 90-; Anthropology.

**MATHIS, TINA E,** Univ Of Nc At Asheville, Asheville, NC; FR; BA; Flwshp Chrstn Athlts VP 90-; Chrldng; Univ Ambsdr 90-; Tchng Flws Schlp 90-; Frnch; Tchng.

**MATHIS, WILLIAM C,** Univ Of Tn At Chattanooga, Chattanooga, TN; FR; BA; Assn Camps Entertnmnt; SGA Elec Comm; SRA Sec 90-; Bad Pool Plyrs Guild Pr; Phi Eta Sigma V P; Alpha Lambda Delta V P; Univ Hnrs Fellow 90-; Cath Stdnt Ctr; Engl/Sec Educ; Tchng/Clergy.

**MATHISEN, MELVIN H,** Columbia Greene Comm Coll, Hudson, NY; FR; AAS; SAGE 90-; Fire Co Vol 81-; Acctg; CPA.

**MATHUR, BINDU,** George Mason Univ, Fairfax, VA; JR; BS; Acctg Clb 90-; Alpha Lambda Delta 89-; Beta Alpha Psi; Intrnshps Atlntc Rsrch Corp 88-89; Cntl Serv Corp 90; Deans Lst; Acctg; Auditor.

**MATIAS-DEL TORO, IVETTE,** Univ Of Pr At Mayaguez, Mayaguez, PR; SR; BSCE; Comp Engr Assn 89-; Tau Beta Pi 90-; Bellcr Internshp 90; Mtrl Internshp; Comp Engr.

**MATIJEVICH, GEORGEEN L,** Ms St Univ, Miss State, MS; FR; BH; Guardian Angel Prog; Alpha Lambda Delta 90; Angl Flght Cmptrllr; Deans Schlr; Im Sprts Vllybl Flgftbl Sccr Ping-Pong 90; Elem Ed; Tchr Own Day Care.

**MATISKO, GAIL J,** Marywood Coll, Scranton, PA; JR; BSN; Stdnt Nrs Assoc; Nrsg Hnr Soc; LPN Cmnty Med Ctr Peds 76-; LPN Lackawanna Area Vo Tech Schl 76; Nrsg; Hlth Care Admin.

**MATKOWSKY, DAVID E,** Yeshiva Univ, New York, NY; SR; BA; Phlsphy Soc Pres 89-; Coll Senate 90-; Mdl UN For Hgh Schl Stdnts Chf Of Stf 90-; Wrtng Cntr Tutr 89-90; SSSJ 89-; SAEJ 89-; Deans Schlrshp 89-; Belkin Schlrshp 89-; Phlsphy; Archtctr/Org Psychlgy.

**MATLAK, ANNA K,** Univ Of Sc At Columbia, Columbia, SC; JR; BA; Engl.

**MATLOCK, ELYSE NICOLE,** Vanderbilt Univ, Nashville, TN; SO; BMU; Sewanee Summer Music Fstvl 90; Eastrn Music Fstvl; Gamma Beta Phi 89-; Alpha Lambda Delta 89-90; Phi Eta Sigma 89-90; Vanderbuddies 89-; Music Prfrmnc/Oboe; Orchstrl Mscn/Oboe.

**MATLOCK, JANE P,** Jacksonville St Univ, Jacksonville, AL; JR; BSN; JANS; Phi Theta Kappa Chpln; Sigma Theta Tau; Dean Lst 90-; Al St Nrsng Schlrshp; Geoge Gibbins Schlrshp; Hosp Mdcl Cntr Wrk; Nrsng.**

**MATNEY, JANET S,** Fayetteville St Univ, Fayetteville, NC; JR; BS; AA Cntrl Oregon Comm Coll 90; Bus Admin; Mgmnt.

**MATNEY, MARGARET L,** Alice Lloyd Coll, Pippa Passes, KY; FR; Dstngshd Deans Lst 90-; Spch Thrpy Lw.

**MATNEY, MICHELLE J,** Coll Of Charleston, Charleston, SC; SO; BA; Hnrs Prgrm; Englsh; Wrtng.

**MATOS CACERES, SILVIA,** Univ Del Turabo, Gurabo, PR; GD; SGA; Hnr Soc.

**MATOS PEREZ, LISSETTE,** Inter Amer Univ Pr Arecibo Un, Arecibo, PR; FR; BED; Ele Educ.

**MATOS, DIANA,** Inter Amer Univ Pr San German, San German, PR; FR; BA; Vlybl 89-90; Bio/Hstry/Spnsh; Bio.

**MATOS, LUIS A GONZALEZ,** Univ Of Pr At Rio Piedras, Rio Piedras, PR; SR; BA; Acctg Stdnt Assoc 89-; Golden Key 90-; Acctg; CPA.**

**MATOS, LYDIA E,** Caribbean Univ, Bayamon, PR; SO; Engl; Bus Admin.

**MATOS, NATIVIDAD C,** Univ Of The Sacred Heart, Santurce, PR; FR; Jrnlsm Assn 90-; Cmmnctns; Jrnlsm.

**MATOS, YARITZA,** Inter Amer Univ Pr Arecibo Un, Arecibo, PR; FR; BED; Ele Educ.

**MATOTT, AMY S,** S U N Y Coll Of Tech At Delhi, Delhi, NY; SR; BA; Hotel Sales & Mrktng Assn 89-90; Phi Theta Kappa 89-; Home Bureau Schlrshp 90-; AAS Delhi Coll Of Tech; Hotel/Bus Mgt; Hospitality Field.

**MATOVELLE, ANNETTE M,** Fl International Univ, Miami, FL; JR; BA; FL Intl Univ Accntng Assc; Phi Theta Kappa 89-90; AA Miami Dade Comm Coll 90; Bus Admn; Accntng.

**MATOWE, DORCAS K,** Bennett Coll, Greensboro, NC; SO; BA; Intrntl Stdnts Org Vp 90-; Hm Econ Clb Vp 90-; Schlrs; Tnns Tm 89-; Bus/Fshn; Law.

**MATRISCIANI, JUDY,** Wagner Coll, Staten Island, NY; JR; BA; Psych Clb 89-; Dns Lst 89-; Psych; Cnslg.

**MATSON, ADAM P,** Univ Of Ct, Storrs, CT; SO; BA; Pre Vet Clb 90-; Deans Lst 89-; Vet Assist 90; Hartt Music Schlrshp 89-90; Pathobiol; Vet Med.

**MATSON, GLORIA E,** Castleton St Coll, Castleton, VT; JR; BS; SG Exe V P 90-; Var Athl Clb Treas 89-; P E Clb Treas; Phi Eta Sigma; Kappa Delta Pi; Var Soccer 88; Phys Educ; Educ.

**MATSUBAYASHI, TETSUJI,** Andrew Coll, Cuthbert, GA; FR; MA; Phi Theta Kappa; Ms Mda Commctn; Intl Commctn.

**MATSUMOTO, TAI,** Fl International Univ, Miami, FL; JR; BD; AIA Brd Of Dirs 90-; Arch.

**MATSUTANI, TOMOKO,** Endicott Coll, Beverly, MA; SR; AS; Admn Asst.

**MATSUURA, YUKI,** Oh Wesleyan Univ, Delaware, OH; FR; BA; Horizon Intl 90; Japan Club 90; Dns Lst 90; Engl.

**MATTA, DORIS H SANTIAGO,** Caribbean Univ, Bayamon, PR; GD; Pres Awrds Sci Dept Ints Pub; BA UPR Rio Piedras 82; Educ Elem Math; M A Orient.

**MATTA, LORI L,** Bethany Coll, Bethany, WV; SO; BA; Nwspaper Reprtr 90-; TV Music Notes Prodcr/Anchr 90-; Soc Of Colgt Jrnlsts VP; Sigma Delta Chi 90-; Alpha Xi Delta Purlcty Chr; Intrnshp Tri Cnty News; Cmnctns; Print Jrnlsm.

**MATTE, GRACE E,** Salem-Teikyo Univ, Salem, WV; SR; BA; Image Mag Mgr Ed 88-90; SG Org Rep 89-; Morrisville Horse Cl/Eqstrn Cl Pres 89-; Phi Theta Kappa 89-90; Gamma Beta Phi; 4-H Horse Cl 88-89; Intnshp/Mendon Cen Honeoye Falls N Y 89/Stables Asst Mgr 90-; AAS Jrnlsm Sunny 90; Commctns/Eqstrn Edctn; Freelance Jrnslt/Photo.

**MATTE, LISA M,** Hudson Valley Comm Coll, Troy, NY; SO; AAS; Asst Rstrnt Mgr 88-; Engl; Tchr Jrnlst.

**MATTEN, PAMELA S,** Franklin And Marshall Coll, Lancaster, PA; SR; Prhtng Arts Clb Rep 90-; Ornttn Advsr 90; Blck Prymd; Chi Omega Chr 89-; John Mrshl Schlr 88-; Dana Schlr; Hckmn Schlr Rsch Flwshp; Crs Cntry/Trck Fld; Chem; Med Schl.

**MATTER, COLLEEN A,** Daemen Coll, Amherst, NY; FR; BA; Psychlgy; Clin Psychlgst.

**MATTERSON, ANITA R,** Ny Univ, New York, NY; SO; BA; SCE Degree Stdnt Cncl VP 90-; Our Neighbors Vol 89-; Mgng Law Clrk; Intrntl Stds; Law.

**MATTES, RAYMOND ALAN,** Duquesne Univ, Pittsburgh, PA; JR; BA; Sclgy Clb Pres 90-; Alpha Kappa Delta Chptr Pred; Deans Lst; Grntlgy; Nrsg Hm Admin.

**MATTESON, JOHANNA M,** Elmira Coll, Elmira, NY; SO; BA; Amnesty Intl 89-; Hnrs Schlr 89-; Natl Yng Ldrs Conf 89; Scndry Educ/Engl; Tch.

**MATTESON, LYNNE P,** Univ Of New Haven, West Haven, CT; SR; BS; Chem Clb P 89-; Frnsc Sci Sco P 89-; Chem Lab Asst 90-; Alpha Lambda Delta 89-; Vlntr Amb Assn EMT-A 83-; AS Tunxis Comm Coll 86; Cert Tunxis Comm Coll 86; Chem/Frnsc Sci; Ph D Chem.

**MATTESON, THERESE H,** Elmira Coll, Elmira, NY; SR; MSED; Alpha Sigma Lambda; Embroidrs Glb Of Amer Chemung Vly Pres 82-90; NE St Rdng Assoc; AS Mth/Sci Corning Comm Clg 74; B Ed; Rdng/Elem Educ; Tchr.

**MATTHESS, MARY R,** Wv Northern Comm Coll, Wheeling, WV; GD; Cert Nrs Asst; Schl Fall LPN; LPN.

**MATTHEW, ANNE M,** Wv Northern Comm Coll, Wheeling, WV; JR; Sec Sci Clb Treas 90-; Deans Lst 90.

**MATTHEW, FRANCENE M,** Paine Coll, Augusta, GA; SO; BA; Omega Pearl Orga Dean Pldg 89-90; Stdnt Sprt Serv; Stdnt Natl Educ Ass 90; Deans Lst; Educ; Tch.

**MATTHEW, GINA C,** Fl International Univ, Miami, FL; JR; BA; SAFE; Stdnts For Hmn Rghts; AA Miami-Dade Comm Coll 90; Hsptlty Mgmt; Trvl/Trsm.

**MATTHEW, LETT R,** Univ Of The Virgin Islands, St Thomas, VI; SR; BA; Stdnt Lit Clb Pres 90-; Spnsh Clb Sec 88-89; VI Assn; Pres Clb 90-; Ebenezer Mem Bapt Chrch Yth Grp 87-; Independent Citizens Movement 90-; Jrnlsm; News Brdcstr/Lawyer.

**MATTHEW, MYRNA G,** City Univ Of Ny Bronx Comm Col, Bronx, NY; SO; AS; Phi Theta Kappa Sec; London City Coll England 87; Acctg; CPA.

**MATTHEW, YEISAN P,** Fl A & M Univ, Tallahassee, FL; SO; BS; Chmst.

**MATTHEWS JR, BOBBY,** Methodist Coll, Fayetteville, NC; GD; BS; Marshall 88-89; AWANA Ldr 88-89; Sndy Schl Tchr 86-; Stdnt Tchr 90-; Educ/Mddl Schl; Tch.**

**MATTHEWS, DEAN R,** Nc Agri & Tech St Univ, Greensboro, NC; SR; Natl Soc Of Black Engrs 87-89; Tau Beta Pi 87-89; FUSS 87-; Natl Clg Awrd; GEM Flwshp; Resrch UC Berkeley; BS 87-; Elec Engr.

**MATTHEWS, IVY S,** Lincoln Univ, Lincoln Univ, PA; FR; BA; Ntnl Assn Advncmnt Clrd People 90-; Mathf Actry.

**MATTHEWS, JAMES G,** Univ Of Nc At Charlotte, Charlotte, NC; JR; BS; Allied Hlth Clb 90-; Bible Stdy 89-90; IM Ftbl/Sftbl 89-90; Blgy; Med.

**MATTHEWS, JEANNINE F,** Western New England Coll, Springfield, MA; FR; BS; Comm Prgmmng Ent Sec; Behav/Scl Sci Clb 90-; Alpha Lambda Delta Hstrn; Scl Wrk.

**MATTHEWS, JENNIFER L,** Oh Univ, Athens, OH; FR; BS; Ecology Clb 90-; Elec Eng.

**MATTHEWS, JOSEPH R,** Defiance Coll, Defiance, OH; SR; BA; Cmctn Clb VP Fund Raising 90-; Ftbl Capt 87-90; Bus Admin/Cmctns.

**MATTHEWS, KENITH W,** Tougaloo Coll, Tougaloo, MS; FR; BA; Pre-Hlth Clb; Hstry Clb V P 90-; Hstry/Econ/Acctg; Lawyer/Prfsr.

**MATTHEWS, KIZZIE A,** Ga St Univ, Atlanta, GA; JR; BSED; Comm Life; Kappa Delta Pi; Mu Rho Sigma; AA Clayton St Coll 90; Erly Chldhd Ed; Tchng.

**MATTHEWS, LESLEE R,** Christopher Newport Coll, Newport News, VA; SO; BS; Psychlgy Clb 90-; Hstry Ttr 90-; Volntr 90-; Dns Lst 89-; Govt Adm; Env/Intl Law.

**MATTHEWS, MARK G,** Univ Of Hartford, West Hartford, CT; JR; BA; Capt; Bsktbl; Bus; Htl Mgmt.

**MATTHEWS, MELISSA A,** Bapt Bible Coll & Seminary, Clarks Summit, PA; FR; BS; Chstn Schl Flwshp 90-; Tutoring 90-; Evnglsm Tm 90; Thomson Dorm 90-; Tchng Sunday Sch Chldrns Chrch; Acpmnst Chrch Sngng Chrcn 90-; Deans List 90; Clg Rcrtmnt Vol Work; Elem Educ Bible; Tchng.

**MATTHEWS, NEAL R,** Schenectady County Comm Coll, Schenectady, NY; SO; US Air Force Actv Dty Rsrvs 85-; Telecomm; Comm.

**MATTHEWS, PAMELA K,** Univ Of Sc At Columbia, Columbia, SC; SO; BS; Psi Chi 90-; Psy; Scl Wrk.

**MATTHEWS, RENE K,** Univ Of Ky, Lexington, KY; SR; BA; Symphonic Bnd 89; KY Kernel Stf Wrtr 88; Baptist Stdnt Union Frshmn Cncl 88-89; Alpha Lambda Delta 89-; Phi Eta Sigma 89-; Clg Educ Stdnt Dvlpmnt Cncl; Stdnt Ldr 89; Baptist Sdtnt Un Smmr Missnry 89; Deans Lst 88-; Engl; Tchng.

**MATTHEWS, ROBIN G,** East Central Comm Coll, Decatur, MS; SO; AAS; Phi Theta Kappa 90-; Awrd Fr Otstndng Achvmnt; Chld Cr Sprvsn; Drctr & Tchr Preschl.

**MATTHEWS, STEPHANIE J,** Univ Of South Al, Mobile, AL; JR; BED; Pow Wow Ldrshp Soc Faulkner State 89-90; Phi Theta Kappa Faulkner St Jr Coll 89-90; Alpha Chi USA; Math; SCNDRY Ed.

**MATTHEWS, TAMMY A,** Gordon Coll, Barnesville, GA; JR; BA; Phi Theta Kappa 89-; Bus; Acctntng.

**MATTHEWS, TIFFANY L,** Norfolk St Univ, Norfolk, VA; FR; BA; Spartan Alpha Tau; Jrnlsm; Pblc Rltns.

**MATTHEWS, VANESSA M,** Fayetteville St Univ, Fayetteville, NC; SO; BA; Arnold Air Soc Cmmndr; AFROTC Schlrshp AAS Cmmndr Mjr; Deans Lst 89-90; Chncllrs Lst 90; Bus; Crprt Lwyr.

**MATTHEWS, VERONICA L,** Howard Univ, Washington, DC; SR; BBA; Soc Advcmnt Mgmt VP 89-; St Cyprian Gspl Choir 90-; Gldn Key 88-; Fed Rsv Brd Gvrnrs Intshp; Johnson/Higgins Intshp 90; Bsn Mgmt; Entpnr.**

**MATTHEWS, WENDY L,** Univ Of Akron, Akron, OH; JR; BFA; Stdnt Art League Pr 90-; Golden Key 90-; Deans Lst 89-; 3rd Pl Schlrshp Show 90; 6th Pl Art Schlrshp Show; Art-Metalsmithing; Jewelry Designing.

**MATTHIS, ANTOINETTE M,** Morris Coll, Sumter, SC; SR; BS; Bio Clb 87-90; Schlrs Bwl Tm Cpt 87; Clg Bwl 90; Alpha Kappa Mu Mss AKM 89-90; Alpha Kappa Alpha Pres 90; Natl Sci Fndtn Smmr Schlr AL Univ Huntsville 88; UNCF Pre Med Smmr Schlr Fisk Univ 89; Chrldr Sec 89; Bio; Rsrch Scintst.

**MATTICE, PAUL F,** Schenectady County Comm Coll, Schenectady, NY; GD; Htl Tech/Clnry Arts; Food Svc.

**MATTIMORE, GARY R,** S U N Y Coll Of Tech At Canton, Canton, NY; SO; AAS; Crim Jstc Stdnts Clb Pres 90-; Phi Theta Kappa 90-; Wtr Sfty Instrtr; Intrnshp Shrfs Dept 90; Crim Jstc; Law Enfrcmnt.

**MATTINGLY JR, FRANCIS DARRELL,** Univ Of Ky, Lexington, KY; FR; BS; Emrgng Ldr Inst; Alpha Lambda Delta; Comptr Sci; Sftwr Dsgn.

**MATTINGLY, JOHN F,** Saint Catharine Coll, St Catharine, KY; FR; BA; Phi Theta Kappa Hist 90-; Art/Indstrl Dsgn.

**MATTINGLY, KIMBERLY A,** Saint Catharine Coll, St Catharine, KY; SO; SGA 89-90; Phi Theta Kappa 89-; Deans List 89-; Grad High Dstnctn 90-; Schlrshp 90-; AS; Office Admnstrtn.

**MATTINGLY, MICHAEL D,** Univ Of Ky, Lexington, KY; FR; PHD; Amrcn Scty Cvl Eng 90-; Phi Eta Sigma 90-; Sigma Pi Pldg Clss Pres 90-; Cvl Eng.

**MATTISON, EDDIE B,** Hampton Univ, Hampton, VA; FR; BA; US Army Med Spec; Svc Ribbon; Over Seas Ribbon; Natl Defense Ribbon; Price Club Warehouse; Bsn; Acctg.

**MATTLE, DEBRA L,** Atlantic Comm Coll, Mays Landing, NJ; SO; AAS 91; Accounting/Finance; CPA.

**MATTNER, DONNA M,** Nyack Coll, Nyack, NY; SR; BA; Qns Gspl Tm 87-88; St Agathas Gspl Tm VP 88-; Mssnry Com; Cum Laude; Engl; Tchng Engl Overseas.

**MATTOCKS, CRAIG D,** Hudson Valley Comm Coll, Troy, NY; SR; AS; 2EEE; Phi Theta Kappa Sec 90-; Tau Alpha Pi 90-; Stdnt Tutoring 90-; Elec Engr.

**MATTONE, JANE KRISTIE,** S U N Y Coll Of Tech At Frmgdl, Farmingdale, NY; JR; AS; Elychnd Club 90-; Early Chdhd; Preschl Ectr.

**MATTOS, JOHN L,** Univ Of Rochester, Rochester, NY; JR; BS; Taekwon Do Clb Offcr 88-; V R Judo Clb 89-; Delta Upsilon Fndrsng Chrmn 89-; Tiernan Dorm Dorm Cncl 88-; IM Sprts; Mchncl Engnrng; Engnrng.

**MATTOX, JENNIFER L,** Coll Of Charleston, Charleston, SC; SO; BS; Appl Math Cmptr Sci.

**MATTOX, LISA F,** Univ Of Nc At Asheville, Asheville, NC; SO; Art Clb.

**MATTOX, ROBBIE R,** Draughons Jr Coll Nashville, Nashville, TN; FR; AS; Acctng/Bsn Mgmt; Acctnt/Tch.

**MATTOX, THOMAS F,** Univ Of Sc At Columbia, Columbia, SC; SR; BS; NIGP; AS Univ Sc Beaufort 90; Business Mgmt; Public Procurement.

**MATTRESS, ANDREA L,** Univ Of Sc At Columbia, Columbia, SC; SR; BAIS; Assc African Amer Stdnts 88-; Gamma Beta Phi 88-; Kappa Delta Epsilon 90-; Cecil Self Schlrshp; Interdisciplinary Studies Elem Ed; Teacher.

**MATULA, KARIANNE,** Marywood Coll, Scranton, PA; JR; BFA; SG Rep 89-; Clwn Mnstry 89-; Nwspr Edtr 89-; Delta Epsln Sigma 90-; Tchrs Choice Art Exhbt 89-90; IM Vlybl; Adv Grphcs.

**MATURA, AMY L,** S U N Y Coll Of Tech At Delhi, Delhi, NY; SO; BS; Intercoll Soccer 90-; AAS; Vet Tech; BS Cornell Anml Sci.

**MATUSICK, MICHELLE M,** Hilbert Coll, Hamburg, NY; SO; BA; AA; Engl/Comm; Jrnlsm.

**MATUSKEY, MICHAEL G,** Central Fl Comm Coll, Ocala, FL; SO; BA; Phi Theta Kappa 89-; AA; Certif St Pete Vo-Tech 88; Sci; Optometry.**

**MATUSZEWSKI, CHRISTINE M,** Manhattan Coll, Bronx, NY; SR; BSEE; IEEE 87-; Soc Wmn Eng 87-; Soc Automotive Eng 89-; Tau Beta Pi 89-; Eta Kappa Nu VP 89-; Epsilon Sigma Pi 90-; Elec Eng.

**MATUSZNY, LISA M,** Univ Of Akron, Akron, OH; SR; BS; Acctg Assn 90-; Alpha Lambda Delta 88-; Goldn Key 89-; Alpha Gamma Delta Treas 88-; Acctg.

**MATUSZWSKI, MELINDA L,** Kent St Univ Kent Cmps, Kent, OH; FR; Ldrshp Dvlpmnt Brd Wrkshp Chair 90-; Clg Democrates Treas 90-; Activities Ldrshp Awrd; Serv Awrd.

**MATVEY, VINCENT C,** Duquesne Univ, Pittsburgh, PA; FR; Bus; Accntng/Fnnc.

**MATVEYEVA, POLINA,** Yeshiva Univ, New York, NY; JR; BA; Jazz Band 89-; Karate Clb 89-; Chem; Med.

**MATZAL, STEFAN C,** Bapt Bible Coll & Seminary, Clarks Summit, PA; GD; THM; Stdnt Assoc; BA Bucknell Univ 88; Old Testament; Translation.

**MAUAD, RAYSA I SANTOS,** City Univ Of Ny City Coll, New York, NY; GD; BARCH; AIAS 85-; HAFE; Fntnblu Alumni 89-; CCAC 89-; Ntnl Hspnc Schlrshp 86-; Gnrl Mtrs Schlrshp 86-; Deans Lst 86-; Vrsty Tm 85-88; BS 90; Arch.

**MAUCK, ROBERT W,** Bridgewater Coll, Bridgewater, VA; SR; BS; Phys Clb Pres 87-; Boeing Cmptr Serv Intrn 89-90; Soccer 89-; Math Cmptr Sci Physics; Space Explrtn.

**MAUD, SANDRA J,** Teikyo Post Univ, Waterbury, CT; SO; BA; Intr Dsgn; Archtct/Intr Dsgnr.

**MAUE, THERESA P,** Union Inst, Cincinnati, OH; JR; BA; Dscvry Cntr Tchr 88-; Imago Eclgy Orgnztn 89-; Cmmnctns Spclst 84-; AS Xavier Univ 85; Cmmnctns; Wrtng Tchng.

**MAUGER, AMY M,** Atlantic Comm Coll, Mays Landing, NJ; JR; BA; Elem Ed Psch Mjr; Elem Ed Tchr.

**MAUGHERMAN, ALAN S,** Milligan Coll, Milligan Clg, TN; SO; MA; Stdnt Govt Assn Jr Rep 89-; Mssn To Homless Pres 90-; Deans Lst 89-; Pi Rho Delta 90-; Hunger Comm 90-; Host/Hostss Prog Prspctv Stdnts 90-; Slf-Stdy Comm 90-; USVBA Vlybl Team; Psychlgy; Phd.

**MAUGHON, SONYA M,** Mobile Coll, Mobile, AL; JR; BA; Touring Choir 88-; Campus Bapt Yng Wmn V P 90-; Dorm Cncl Repr 90-; Alpha Chi 90-; Music Schlrshp 88-; Valedictorian Schlrshp 88-; Charles Arendall Schlrshp 88-; Music; Tchr.

**MAULDIN, DAVID C,** Milligan Coll, Milligan Clg, TN; SO; BA; Phi Sigma Tau 90-; Chrstn Educ; Mnstr Of Educ/Wrtr.

**MAULDIN, LINDA L,** Univ Of Tn At Martin, Martin, TN; SR; BS; Stdnt Rsrch Gulf Coast Rsrch Lab 90-; Phi Eta Sigma 88; Mu Epsilon Delta 87-90; Stdnt Assn Amer Chem Soc 87-88; Mu Epsilon Delta Vlntr Gen Hosp; Bio/Pre-Med Tech; Med Tech.

**MAULL, MARIE E,** Fayetteville St Univ, Fayetteville, NC; SO; BS; Chem; Engrng.

**MAULT, KELLY A,** S U N Y Coll At Fredonia, Fredonia, NY; SR; BA; Gvrnr Athlts Agnst Drnk Drvng 89-; VITA 89-; Deans Lst 89; All Trnmnt Tm 90; Bsktbll Capt 87-; Bus Admn; Fnc.

**MAULTSBY, MICHAEL D,** Nc Central Univ, Durham, NC; GD; JD; Law Jrnl 90-; Pi Sigma Alpha 89; All Amercn Schlrs; Lyndon B Johnson Intrnshp In The Ofc Of Cngrsmn Charlie Rose 88; Rsrch Asst To Dean Janice Mills 90-; BA Univ Of NC Wilmington 89; Law; Attrny.

**MAUMUS, ETIENNE C F N,** Catholic Univ Of America, Washington, DC; JR; BA; Pi Sigma Alpha; Pi Gamm Mu; Phi Alpha Delta; Pltcl Sci; Law.**

**MAUNG, KYAW N,** City Univ Of Ny La Guard Coll, Long Island Cty, NY; FR; AS; Librl Arts/Sci; Engr.

**MAUPIN, MITZI M,** Dyersburg St Comm Coll, Dyersburg, TN; FR; BED; Elem Educ; Kndrgrtn Tchr.

**MAURER, BRETT P,** Oh Univ, Athens, OH; SO; BS; Alpine Club 89-; Deans List; Elect Engrng.

**MAURER III, FRANK H,** Wilmington Coll, New Castle, DE; JR; BBM; Natl Assoc Realtors 90-; AS Salem Cmnty Clg 90; Bsn; Bsn/Cmptr.

**MAURER, LAREN J,** Univ Of Miami, Coral Gables, FL; SR; BM; Mrchng Bnd Hour 86-88; Symphnc Bnd 87-89; Cncrt Bnd 86-89; Bptst Cmps Mnstry 87-; H K Stanford Schlrshp 86-90; FL Hon Schlrshp 86-90; Amer Buswmns Assn Schlrshp 86-87; Music Ind; Mgmt.

**MAURER, SCOTT R,** Va Commonwealth Univ, Richmond, VA; SO; BA; Human Rels Cmte 90-; Hist; Foreign Affrs.

**MAURICE, JANICE L,** Schenectady County Comm Coll, Schenectady, NY; Scl Juste Cntr Albany NY Waitt Hs Inc; Chld Cr Wrkr/Hs Mngr Waitt Hs Inc; Lbrl Arts.

**MAURICE, KYLE F,** Fl A & M Univ, Tallahassee, FL; FR; BA; NASA Schlrs Assn 90; Phi Eta Sigma 90-; NASA Rsrch Jet Propalsion Lab Intern; Elctrcl Engr; Engr.

**MAURIELLO, AMY C,** Schenectady County Comm Coll, Schenectady, NY; FR; Juris-Prdnc Law Clb 90-; Bus Adm/ Acctng.

**MAURO, CATHERINE,** S U N Y Coll Of Optometry, New York, NY; GD; OD; Optometrc Svcs 87-; Make A Wish 89-; Beta Sigma Kappa Pr 88-; Amer Opto Assn 87-; BS Cornl Univ 85; Optmtry.

**MAURYA, ALPA,** Temple Univ, Philadelphia, PA; SO; MBA; INDO US; OAS Actvts Spksprsn; Chr; Dns Lst; Blgy Hnr Scty; Phi Sigma Pi; Cndystrpr; Smrpn Indn Assn; Hnrs Prog; Rcrtr; Tmple And Enstn Hosps; Vlybl; Med; Dr.

**MAUSBACH, HEIDI E,** Univ Of Cincinnati, Cincinnati, OH; SO; BM; Prncpl Cellist 90; Cello Perf; Prof Mscns/Orch Mbr.

**MAVROMIHALIS, ANGELINE H,** Univ Of South Al, Mobile, AL; GD; BS; Deans Lst; Dean Hnr Lst; Pres Lst; Cum Laude; Eastern Star; Elem Educ; Tch.

**MAVROS, GEORGE S,** Nova Univ, Ft Lauderdale, FL; GD; MBA; Labor Mgr Admin/Techl Dir 88; Amer Scty Micrblgy; Fl Scty Med Techlgy; Clin Labty Mgt Assoc; Amer Mgt Assoc; Hospt Corp Amer Good Govt Group; Ba Univ S Florida Tampa 79; MS Univ S Florida Tampa 87; Hlth Serv Admin; Hlth Care Admin.**

**MAWDSLEY, JONATHAN R,** Harvard Univ, Cambridge, MA; FR; BS; Cambridge Entmlgcl Clb Secr 90-; Stdnt Conductg Orch 90-; Harvard Gilbert/Sullivan Players Orch 90-; Fclty Aide Dr J M Carpenter 90-; Bio; Entmlgy.

**MAWHINNEY, SUSAN M,** Wv Univ, Morgantown, WV; FR; Cqstrn Tm 90.

**MAWILMADA, NAYANA N,** Hampton Univ, Hampton, VA; FR; BARC; Amer Inst Arch Std 90-; Intl Std Asc PR Offcr; Studio High Achv Awd; Hnr Rl; Arch.

**MAX, BARBARA E,** Univ Of Miami, Coral Gables, FL; JR; CADX; Advrtsg/Engl; Lawyer.

**MAXEY, KIMBERLY A,** Radford Univ, Radford, VA; JR; BA; Univ Chorus 88-; Univ Radio DJ; Hse Cncl Flr Rep 90-; Brdcstrs Guild 90-; Alpha Epsilon Rho Pres; VA Assn Brdcstrs Intrshp WTVR Ch 6 Richmond VA Prod Asst 90; Spch/Radio/T V Brdcstng; TV Prdctn.

**MAXIE, JULIE I,** Radford Univ, Radford, VA; SR; AA BS; Kentucky Educ Assn Pres 87-; Vir Educ Assn 89-; 4h Clb; Phi Theta Kappa 87-; Whos Who; Deans Lst; Stdnt Tchng; Pres Awd 89; Summa Cum Laude 89; Vybl 87-; Early Middle Educ; Tch.**

**MAXIE, SELENA C,** Catawba Valley Comm Coll, Hickory, NC; FR; St NC Notary 90-; Humn Res/Mgmt; Bsns.

**MAXIM JR, DAVID E,** Univ Of Hartford, West Hartford, CT; FR; Cross Country/Track 90-; Art; Illustr/Animation.

**MAXIME, HILDA N,** Columbia Union Coll, Takoma Park, MD; SR; BS; ACE Drctr 90-; Mrktng Stdnt Yr 90-; Mrktng; Mrktng Rsrch.

**MAXIMIEK, JEFFREY F,** S U N Y Coll At Fredonia, Fredonia, NY; JR; BA; SUNY Fredonia Hon Pgm Lbrl Educ; Bus Admin Mktg Cnctrtn; MBA.

**MAXIMOV, JANE B,** Va Commonwealth Univ, Richmond, VA; SR; BA; AA Un Maryland 88; Engl; Evnrmntl Law.

**MAXSON, GEORGE F,** Mount Saint Mary Coll, Newburgh, NY; SO; BA; Cobocery Mgr; Busn Admin; MBA.

**MAXSON, JOEL E,** S U N Y Coll At Fredonia, Fredonia, NY; JR; BS; Acctng Scty Treas 89-; Invstmnt Clb; Comp Sci Clb; Delta Mu Delta; Bus Admin Intrn; IM Sprts; Acctng And Comp Sci; Prgrmmr.

**MAXSON, MICHELLE M,** Nc St Univ At Raleigh, Raleigh, NC; FR; Cmps Crsd Chrst 90-; Anml Sci Clb 90; Aquinus House 90-; Zlgy; Med.

**MAXSTADT, JAMES E,** Columbia Greene Comm Coll, Hudson, NY; FR; BA; Upstate Hptlgcl Scty; Rptle Prsnttns Fr Lcl Schls 90-; Blgy; Tchng Zoo Crtr.

**MAXWELL, DANIEL D,** Free Will Baptist Bible Coll, Nashville, TN; FR; BS; Math; Tch Math HS.

**MAXWELL, DAVID M,** Univ Of Nc At Charlotte, Charlotte, NC; SR; BA; Vrsty Tnns Capt 88-; Ptry Pblshd Rdngs; Mu Alpha Chi Pres 88-; Dns Lst; Otstndng Sr Awrd; Cert Of Mrt Sn Blt Confrnce; Psych; MFA Crtve Wrtng Prffssnl Tnns.

**MAXWELL, JANE,** City Univ Of Ny La Guard Coll, Long Island Cty, NY; SO; AAS; Nsng; RN.

**MAXWELL, JENNIFER A,** Old Dominion Univ, Norfolk, VA; SR; BS; Am Mktg Assn 90; Juvnl AIDS Vol 90-; Hosp Mktg Intern 89-90; Mktg Educ; Hosp Mktg/Pub Rltns.

**MAXWELL III, JOHN E,** Livingston Univ, Livingston, AL; SR; BS; Acctg Clb 89-; Intl Stdnts Assn 90-; Delta Sigma Pi Treas 89-; Deans Lst 88-89; VITA 89-; Acctg; CPA.

**MAXWELL, JOYCE A,** Univ Of Md At Eastern Shore, Princess Anne, MD; SO; BS; Hnrs Prgrm 90; Academic Hnr Awrd 89; Most Improved Athletic Awrd 89-90; Track/Field 89-90; Crimnal Justice; Law.

**MAXWELL, JULIE A,** Wv Univ, Morgantown, WV; FR; BS; Engrng; Chem.

**MAXWELL, MATTHEW B,** Anne Arundel Comm Coll, Arnold, MD; SO; AA; Law Enfrcmnt; US Marshall Serv.

**MAXWELL, NORMAN A,** Univ Of Tn At Martin, Martin, TN; SR; BS; ACM Sec/Treas 90-; Schlrs Org 87-89; Phi Kappa Phi 90-; Cmptr Sci; Prgrmr.

**MAXWELL, RAUDY G,** Univ Of Montevallo, Montevallo, AL; FR; BA; Bapt Stdnt Mnstrs; Alpha Lambda Delta 90-; Hnr Day Otstndg Ldrshp Acdmc Ablts; Pre Med; Csmtc Plstc Srgn.

**MAXWELL, SHARON D,** Benedict Coll, Columbia, SC; GD; BS; SGA V P 89-90 Treas 87-88; Alpha Kappa Alpha 90; Natl Cncl Negro Wmn 90; Bsktbl Hmcmng Queen 87-88; Elem Educ; Tchr.

**MAXWELL, STACEY M,** Atlantic Comm Coll, Mays Landing, NJ; FR; AS; Gen Stds.

**MAXWELL, SUSANNAH F,** Truett Mc Connell Coll, Cleveland, GA; SO; BED; Baptist Church 69-; Drag Racer 89-; TNS Mills Employee; Biol; Tchng.

**MAXWELL, TONYA P,** Alcorn St Univ, Lorman, MS; SO; BA; Nwsppr Edtr 90-; Nrsng Clb VP 90-; Ntnl Hnr Soc; US Achvmnt Acad Awd; Alpha Kappa Alpha; Biology; Nrsng.

**MAY, BRENDA L,** Central Fl Comm Coll, Ocala, FL; SO; MED; Phi Theta Kappa Mrshl 90-; Grad Hnrs 90; Bapt Chrch Grl Scts Ldr 89-90; Subs Tchr 90-; AA Cntrl Fla Comm Clg 90; Spec Educ.

**MAY, BRYAN W,** Methodist Coll, Fayetteville, NC; SO; BS; Ldrshp Cncl 89-90; Jr Dir Admissions 89-; Pi Kappa Phi Pres 89-; Vars Tennis 89-; Bsn Adm/Chem/Physics; Tch.

**MAY, CHARLES T,** S U N Y Coll Of Tech At Frmgdl, Farmingdale, NY; FR; BA; Waterbury Walk-A-Thon; Dns Lst; Engl; Sec Educ.

**MAY, CHRISTOPHER C,** Oh Univ, Athens, OH; FR; BS; ACACIA Human Serv 90-; Deans Lst 90-; Chem Engr.

**MAY, DEBORAH J,** Univ Of Southern Ms, Hattiesburg, MS; SR; BS; Psi Chi 90-; Lgl Fld 88-; Psychlgy; Law.

**MAY, DONNA L,** Brewer St Jr Coll, Fayette, AL; SO; BA; SGA Rep 90-; Acad Affrs Comm 90-; Brewer Cmps Mnstrs; Phi Theta Kappa 89-; Bapt Acteens Cls Asst 89-; Early Admsns To Auburn Schl Of Phrmcy; Phrmcy.

**MAY, DOROTHY L,** Defiance Coll, Defiance, OH; FR; Hons List For Part Time Stdnts; Elem Ed; Tchng.

**MAY, ERIC D,** Univ Of Rochester, Rochester, NY; JR; BA; COPA 88-; Drama Hse Res 89-; Psych; Rsrch.

**MAY, ESTEFANIA,** Univ Of Southern Ms, Hattiesburg, MS; SO; BS; Chmstry Clb 89-90; Theatre 90; Wrld Cltrs Soc 89-90; Vrsty Tns 89; Biochemistry; Rsrch.

**MAY, FAITH E,** Coll Of Charleston, Charleston, SC; SO; BS; SG 89-; Ldrshp Ed 89-; Highly Distnguishd Dns Lst; Chi Omega Hstrn 90-; Hosp Emerg Rm PRN; Washington DC Alcohol/Drug Conf 90; Biochem; Med.

**MAY, GRACE Y,** Gordon Conwell Theol Sem, S Hamilton, MA; GD; Partnrs Biblicl Equalty Chrmn 89-90; Exec Mbr 90-; Phi Alpha Chi; BA Yale Univ 86; Engl; Campus Mnstr.

**MAY, HOPE E,** William Paterson Coll, Wayne, NJ; JR; BA; Phlshy Clb Pres 90-; Ltrry Mg Sec 90-; Hlsphy; Prffsr.

**MAY, IRIS V,** Thomas Nelson Comm Coll, Hampton, VA; SO; AAS; Phi Sigma Of Phi Theta Kappa 90; PCBVI Corr Sec 88; Dip Clg Of Hmptn Rds 64-66; Wrd Prcssng; Secrtrl Wrd Prcssng.**

**MAY, JACQUELYN A,** Ashland Comm Coll, Ashland, KY; SR; AA; Comp Infrmtn Systms; Comp Prog.

**MAY, JENNIFER R,** Univ Of Rochester, Rochester, NY; JR; BA; Drm Cncl Sec 88-89; Stdy Abrd Pr Advsr; Trnn Scty 89-; Pychlgy Rsrch Internship; Mdcl Schl; Psychlgy; Clncl Psychlgy.

**MAY, KEVIN T,** Univ Of Sc At Columbia, Columbia, SC; SO; BSBA; Gamma Beta Phi; IM Sprts 90-; Accntng; CPA/TX Accntnt.

**MAY, KIMBERLY A,** Hudson Valley Comm Coll, Troy, NY; FR; AAS; Phi Theta Kappa 90-; John O Amstuz Schlrshp 90-; Pres Lst 90-; Enx Yth Shltr 90; Arlns Mgr 87-89; Hmn Srvc; Tech Cmnctns.

**MAY, LAURA M,** Coker Coll, Hartsville, SC; SR; BA; AGS IN Univ SE 83; Cmnctns; Pub Rltns.

**MAY, MARC R,** West Ga Coll, Carrollton, GA; FR; BA; Chmbr Sngrs 90-; Choir 90-; Opera Dept 90-; Service Awd 90-; Envrnmntl Design; Lndscpe Archtcture.

**MAY, MARGARET M,** Ky St Univ, Frankfort, KY; SR; BSBA 82; Nrsng.

**MAY, MELISSA R,** Memphis St Univ, Memphis, TN; GD; MS; Psych Clb Chr 90; Spnsh Clb 88; Suicide/Crisis Ctr Vol; Deans Hon Lst 90; Cum Laude 90; BA 90; Cnslng/Psych; Alcohol/Drug Abuse Cnslr.

**MAY, PATRICIA G,** Ashland Comm Coll, Ashland, KY; SO; BED; Scl Sci; Tchng.

**MAY, PHILLIP L,** Ms St Univ, Miss State, MS; SO; Govnmntl Affrs Comm MSU SGA 89-90; Stdnts MI Fndng Comm SGA 89-90; Phi Gamma Delta 89-; Deans Lst 89-; IM Flag Ftbl Vlybl Sftbl; Bnkng/Fin; Fin Invstgtn.

**MAY, SARAH V,** Alcorn St Univ, Lorman, MS; SR; BED; Stu Free Entrprs 90-; Prof Sec Intl Sec 90-; Nwsppr Cmps Edtr 90-; Alpha Kappa Mu 89-; Dean Lst 87-; Bus Educ; Tchr.

**MAY, SCOTT B,** Memphis St Univ, Memphis, TN; SR; BSET; U S Marine Crps Res Sgt 85-; Oper Desert Storm 90-; AAS Clevelnd St Comm Clg 87; Arch; Prop Develpmnt.

**MAY, STACEY L,** Hartwick Coll, Oneonta, NY; FR; SADD 90-; Hll Cncl 90-; Phnthn 90-.

**MAY, STEVEN P,** Columbia Union Coll, Takoma Park, MD; FR; BA; Scl Fr Stdnt Assn VP; Yrbk Lyout Edtr 90-; Pre Med Clb 90-; Phi Eta Sigma Hstrn; Engl Pre Med; Med.

**MAY, SUSANNE B,** Radford Univ, Radford, VA; JR; BA; Nwspr Stf Wrtr; Phi Theta Kappa 89-; Phi Sigma Pi Histrn; AA Northern VA Cmnty Clg 90; Jrnlsm; Writer.

**MAY, TIMOTHY L,** Lexington Comm Coll, Lexington, KY; FR; AAS; Non-Commisnd Ofcrs Assoc 82-; US Field Artillery Assoc 88-; US Army Active Fld Artillery 79-89; Nucl Med; Rsrch.

**MAY JR, WILLIAM B,** Ms St Univ, Miss State, MS; JR; BS; Forestry Club 89-; SAF 90-; Xi Sigma Pi; Sharp Forestry Schlrshp 90; J S Therrell Schlrshp 90-; Deans Schlr; IM; Forestry; Mgt.

**MAY, ZOE R,** Ms St Univ, Miss State, MS; SO; BS; Gamma Beta Phi Natl 90-; Beta Beta Beta 90-; 4-H Youth Org 90-; Zoolgy; Envrnmntl Protctn Agncy Biolgst.

**MAYA, ANA,** Fl International Univ, Miami, FL; SO; BS; Eng.

**MAYAZI, NEMA B,** Lincoln Univ, Lincoln Univ, PA; FR; Educ Clb Sntr 90-; Std Govt Chr Sntr 90-; Wrkstudy Pgm 90-; Tchr Asst; Elem Ed; Prncpl.

**MAYBERRY, SARAH A,** Syracuse Univ, Syracuse, NY; SR; BARCH; Stdnt Senate Senator 87-88; Archtctrl Stdnt Orgnztn Sec Treas 90-; Architecture/Religion; Arch History.

**MAYBURY, MELANIE E,** Wilmington Coll, Wilmington, OH; SO; BA; Chorale 90-; Prcsn Ensmbl 90-; Coll Musicum Rnsnc Ensmbl 90-; Music Educ; Thrpy.

**MAYE, ALICHA D,** Univ Of Southern Ms, Hattiesburg, MS; SO; BS; Stdnt Alumni Assoc; Stdnt Hl Cncl; Gamma Beta Phi; Afro Amer Schlstc Awd; Soc Sci; RN.

**MAYE, APRIL,** Al St Univ, Montgomery, AL; FR; Erly Chldhd Educ; Open Day Care.

**MAYE, SANDRA L,** Miami Jacobs Jr Coll Of Bus, Dayton, OH; FR; AA; Coll Sec Intl 90-; Drctrs Lst 90; Bapt Chrch 89-; Lgl Offc Admn; Jdcl.

**MAYE, WARRICK E,** Al St Univ, Montgomery, AL; SR; BA; Drmtc Gill Chpln; Bptst Cmps Mnstry; Phi Theta Kappa; Hstry; Educ.

**MAYER, BRIAN M,** Univ Of Cincinnati-Clrmnt Coll, Batavia, OH; SO; BS; Liberal Arts; Envir Rsrch.

**MAYER, JOSEPH F,** Univ Of Tn At Martin, Martin, TN; SO; BFA; Soc Crtv Anchrnsms 90-; Tae Kwondo 90-; Art.

**MAYER, KEIRA L,** Mercer Univ Schl Of Pharm, Atlanta, GA; GD; PHARM; Acad Of Stdnts Of Pharm 89-; Amer Pharm Assn 89-; Rho Chi 90-; Kappa Epsilon 90-; Pharmacy.

**MAYER, ROGER W,** Nova Univ, Ft Lauderdale, FL; GD; MBA; Diag Sls Rep For Vitek Systems; BS UN State New York 84; Mgmt Sls Mktg.

**MAYER, STEPHANIE L,** Muskingum Coll, New Concord, OH; FR; Spec Evnts Comm; Tour Guide Admssns Ofcr; Lambda Sigma; Trk; Elem Ed/Erth Sci/Scndry Cert; Edctr.

**MAYER, TIFFANY W,** Palm Beach Comm Coll, Lake Worth, FL; SO; BA; Engl; Scndry Ed.**

**MAYERS JR, CHALMERS W,** Jackson St Univ, Jackson, MS; SO; BA; Marchng Bnd 89-; Art Clb 90-; Alpha Lambda Delta 90-; IM Bsktbl 89-90; Art.

**MAYERS, JORDAN E,** Univ Of Fl, Gainesville, FL; JR; BS; Bus Admin Pr Cnslr; Pi Kappa Phi Asst Tres 89-; Orlando Magic NBA Intrn; Pres Hnr Lr; Fl Acdmc Schlrshp 88-; IM Ftbl; Finance; Plng.

**MAYES, AMY E,** Volunteer St Comm Coll, Gallatin, TN; FR; MBA; Nrsng; Spclzd RN.

**MAYES, ERNEST M,** Morehouse Coll, Atlanta, GA; SO; BA; Atlanta Un Ctr Ill Clb Soc Afrs Mctee Mbr 90-; Graphic Artist Mag; English; Advtsng/Flm Mkng Law.

**MAYES, RACHEL A L,** Christopher Newport Coll, Newport News, VA; JR; BA; Grk Cncl 90-; Pnhllnc Cncl VP 90-; Phi Mu Pnhllnc Rep 90-; Vrsty Fld Hcky Mary Baldwin Coll 88-90; Art.

**MAYES, WILLIAM D,** Univ Of Sc At Columbia, Columbia, SC; JR; BA; SG 88-89; Clge Rpblcns Pres 88-90; Golden Key 90-; Pol Sci; Law.

**MAYFIELD, LAQUANTA J,** Univ Of Tn At Martin, Martin, TN; SO; BA; Spanish Clb; Alpha Gamma Rho Little Sister; Cmmnctns; TV Broadcastingg.

**MAYFIELD, MELANIE ANNE,** Univ Of Ga, Athens, GA; JR; BSED; Clg Repubs Dalton Clg Pres 88-90; Kappa Delta Epsilon Pres-Elect; Phi Beta Lambda State Hstrn; Kappa Delta Pi; Phi Beta Lambda; Photographers Intern; ASBA Dalton Clg 90; Bsn Ed; Instr.

**MAYFIELD, TERESA K,** Western Piedmont Comm Coll, Morganton, NC; SO; AAS; Phi Theta Kappa 90-; Outstanding Sngl Prnt Voc Prg Awd 89-90; Cert Kings Clg 81; Cert 90; Cmptr Prog/Oper.

**MAYFIELD, WANDA L,** Savannah St Coll, Savannah, GA; SO; Math Clb; Cls V P 89-90; Dns Lst.

**MAYGER, MICHELE L,** Duquesne Univ, Pittsburgh, PA; FR; BA; Yrbk Edtr 90-; Ski Club 90-; Alpha Gamma Delta 90-; Cmmnctns; Print Jrnlsm.

**MAYHEW, FRITZ H,** Univ Of The Dist Of Columbia, Washington, DC; JR; BBA; Hgh Hon 89; Mgmt Intrn DC Enrgy Offc 89-90; Prvt Scrty Pro 90-; AAS 90; Inspctr Police Jamaica Cnstblry Frc 72-86; Prlgl Cert Amer Inst Bus/Tech 87; Mgmt; Law/MBA.

**MAYHUGH, DAWN M,** George Mason Univ, Fairfax, VA; SO; BA; Cir K 89-90; Phy Ed; Corp Ftnss.

**MAYHUGH, LINDA J,** Univ Of Cincinnati-Clrmnt Coll, Batavia, OH; FR; MENSA; Phi Theta Kappa; All Am Schlr; Envrnmntl Sci.

**MAYID, PRAMOJAYA,** S U N Y Coll Of Tech At Frmgdl, Farmingdale, NY; SO; ASS; Cub Sct Bsbl; Oper Eng; Eng.

**MAYKUT, MARK T,** Fl A & M Univ, Tallahassee, FL; JR; BS; Hnr Stdnt Deans Lst 90; Lndscpe Dsgn/Mngmnt.

**MAYLE, ROGER L,** Wv Univ At Parkersburg, Parkersburg, WV; SR; BS; Cmptr Cl 90-; Soc/Indus Engr 90-; Phi Theta Kappa 90; BA Marietta Colg; Engrng.

**MAYNARD, ANNETTE K,** Western Piedmont Comm Coll, Morganton, NC; FR; BS; Phi Thea Kappa; Pro Ballet Dncr Ballet IA Co/Tivoli Pntmn Thtr-Copehagen Dk 83-90; Sci; Physcl Thrpy.

**MAYNARD, BOBBI JO,** Univ Of New England, Biddeford, ME; FR; OTR; NOVI Drg Prvntn 90-; Frnds Hlpng Undrprvlgd Spksprsn 90-; Rrl Hlth Prjcts Intern 90; Vrsty Sccr 90-; Occptnl Thrpy.

**MAYNARD, BRET K,** Owensboro Comm Coll, Owensboro, KY; FR; AS; Academically/Clncly; Radiography.

**MAYNARD, DEBORAH A,** Radford Univ, Radford, VA; FR; BA; Ch Ldr 88-; Alpha Lambda Delta VP; Cmnctn Sci/Disorders; Spch Pathologist.

**MAYNARD, HEIDI L,** S U N Y Coll Of Tech At Delhi, Delhi, NY; SR; BAS; NYSAVT 89-; AALAS 89-; AAS; Vet Sci; PHD Vet Sci.

**MAYNARD, JEFFERY S,** Oh St Univ At Marion, Marion, OH; FR; BA; Acad Skill Ctr Lab Asst; Crimnlgy/Crim Just; Parole Offcr/Beh Sci.

**MAYNARD, LYNN A,** Northeastern Christian Jr Coll, Villanova, PA; SO; BA; Std Govt Asc VP; Gamma Delta Gamma; AA; Psy.

**MAYNARD, MARILYN L,** Clark Atlanta Univ, Atlanta, GA; SR; BA; Msc Edctrs Ntnl Cnfrnc; GA Msc Edctrs Assn Prsdnt ; Mrchng Symphnc Bnds Tres 89-; KAPPA Delta; Zeta Phi Beta; Msc Tchrs Ntnl Assn; GA Msc Tchrs Assn; Tchncl Wrtr IBM Corp 77-; Msc Edctn; Piano Pedagogy.

**MAYNARD, MARY T,** Marshall University, Huntington, WV; JR; BA; Lang Arts/Eng.

**MAYNARD, PRISCA,** Univ Of The Virgin Islands, St Thomas, VI; SR; BS; Frnch Clb 87-89; Pre-Profl Clb 87-; Explorers Clb 87-89; Am Lung Assn Vol 90-; Adult Swmng Cls Vol Hlpr 88-89; Bio; Doctor Med.

**MAYNE, DEBBIE K,** Troy St Univ At Dothan, Dothan, AL; SO; Acctng.

**MAYNOR, JANET L,** Al A & M Univ, Normal, AL; SO; BA; Bsktbl 89-; Mchncl Engrg/Mchncl Drftng Tchnlgy.

**MAYO, BETHANY L,** Univ Of Tn At Martin, Martin, TN; JR; BS; Phi Eta Sigma 90-; Beta Beta Beta 90-; Bio; Med Doc.

**MAYO, CORINA A,** Univ Of Cincinnati, Cincinnati, OH; SR; BSN; Untd Blck Assoc; Mnrty Hll Govt Advsr 87-88; SNA 87-88; Blck Stdnt Nrs Actn 89-; RA 90-; Army ROTC Schlrshp; Nrs Trng Prgm; Nellie Franz Schlrshp 87-88; Queen City Medical Auxillary Schlrshp 87-; IM Ftbll 90; Cert; Cpry Frst Ad 90; Nrsng; RN.

**MAYO, GWENDIA-LYNN,** Ashland Comm Coll, Ashland, KY; SO; BA; Brthrhd Of Lcmtve Engs 80-; Lcmtve Eng 86; Pol Sci; Law.

**MAYO, KATHERINE B,** Christopher Newport Coll, Newport News, VA; SR; BA; Alpha Sigma Tau 88-90; Sentara Hampton Hlth & Fitness Ctr 90; Leisure Studies/Rec Mgmt.

**MAYO, KERRI L,** Alfred Univ, Alfred, NY; FR; BS; Ldrshp; Acctng.

**MAYO, KIMBERLY M,** Univ Of Ky, Lexington, KY; JR; BA; Emerging Ldrs Inst 90; Black Stdnt Union 89-; Residence Hall Assoc Res Advsr 90-; Deans Lst; Alpha Kappa Alpha VP 90-; Voluntees For Shriners 90-; Deans Lst 90; Spanish Dept Awrd 90; Spanish; Intl Diplomacy.

**MAYO, TRACY LYNN,** Delta St Univ, Cleveland, MS; FR; BA; Acctng; CPA.

**MAYOL MASS, EDITH,** Inter Amer Univ Pr Hato Rey, Hato Rey, PR; GD; BED Santiago Veve Calzada HS 74; Cert Sec Post Scndry Degree Tarardo PR.

**MAYOR, JANET,** Univ Of Pr Medical Sciences, San Juan, PR; SR; DMD; Omicron Kappa Upsilon 90-; Bio; Pdodncs/Dnstry.

**MAYOR, STEPHANIE A,** Wv Univ, Morgantown, WV; FR; BS; Aerospc Eng; Astrntcs.

**MAYS, BRYCE C,** Univ Of Tn At Martin, Martin, TN; SR; BS; SAACS VP 89-; Phi Eta Sigma 88-; Phi Kappa Phi 90-; Beta Beta Beta 89-; Mu Epsilon Delta 89-; Chem Lab TA 90-; IM Sftbl Bsktbl Vlybl 87-; Blgy/Chem; Medcl Sch.

**MAYS, CARYN A,** Al St Univ, Montgomery, AL; JR; BS; Gldn Ambssdr; Intrn At Chldrns Cntr For Multi-Hndcppd 90-; Psych Asstntshp; Psych; Clncl Psych.

**MAYS JR, CHARLES I,** Pittsburgh Tech Inst, Pittsburgh, PA; SO; AS; Technlgy; Mech Engr.

**MAYS, ERICA L,** Fl A & M Univ, Tallahassee, FL; FR; BPHAR; Phi Eta Sigmaf Kappa Epsilon Rosebud; Prmclgy.

**MAYS, KENNETH E,** Christian Brothers Univ, Memphis, TN; SR; BS; Cmptr Sci; Ind Eng/Data Mgmt.

**MAYS, KENNETHA MARIE,** Tuskegee Univ, Tuskegee Inst, AL; FR; BS; Blgy Clb; Tuskegge ENHANCES Schrlshp; Natl Assc For Advncmnt Clrd People; Schlrshp Utd Negro Coll Fund Pre Med Summer Inst Fisk Univ; Biology; Research Scientist.

**MAYS, MELISSA R MALONE,** Oh Univ-Southern Cmps, Ironton, OH; JR; BS ED; Phi Kappa Phi 90; Math/Soc Stdes; Sec Tchr/Clg Prfsr.

**MAYS, MICHAEL E,** Tn Temple Univ, Chattanooga, TN; FR; BA; Weigle Cncrt Whoic; Cls Offcr Chorister; Acctng; Contmpry Gspl Music.

**MAYS, MIMI P,** The Johns Hopkins Univ, Baltimore, MD; SR; BSN; Mrsng Hon Soc; Tchr Elem Ed 75-83; Sls Assoc-Real Estate 83-89; BS Troys State Univ 75; Nrsng.

**MAYS, ROBIN A,** Coker Coll, Hartsville, SC; SR; BA; Biol Clb; Acdmc Awrd 90-; Educ; Tch.

**MAYS, TROY,** Central St Univ, Wilberforce, OH; JR; BA; Sci; Eng.

**MAYSEY III, EVERETT LEWIS,** Cincinnati Bible Coll & Sem, Cincinnati, OH; GD; MA; Eta Beta Rho Sec 89-; Sr Mnstr 90-; BA Roanoke Bible Clg 84; MA Cincin Bible Clg/Sem; Theogoly/NT Studies; Preaching Ministry.

**MAYSONET, WAYNE,** City Univ Of Ny La Guard Coll, Long Island Cty, NY; SR; Coll Phys Thrpy Clb; Am Phys Thrpy Assn; Dns Lst; AAS; Phys Thrpy; Licnsd Phys Thrpst.

**MAYTON, HILARY S,** Cornell Univ Statutory College, Ithaca, NY; JR; BS; Phi Theta Kappa 90; Sftbl Tm; AS Tompkins Cortland Comm Coll 90; SCAS; Rsrch.

**MAZANY, GLORIA J,** Comm Coll Algny Co Algny Cmps, Pittsburgh, PA; FR; St Bernards CCD Pgm Instr 87-90; Nrsg; Sci; Med.

**MAZE, BRIAN L,** Univ Of Al At Huntsville, Huntsville, AL; FR; BA; Elec Eng.

**MAZE, JENNIFER L,** Abraham Baldwin Agri Coll, Tifton, GA; SO; Phi Theta Kappa.

**MAZE, KENDALL S,** Univ Of Tn At Knoxville, Knoxville, TN; JR; BSSW; Stdnt Govt; Gamma Beta Phi 89-; Soc Wrk Org Mbr 90-; Soc Sci Stdnt Yr 90; Hghst Hons UT 90; Deans List Roane St 88-89; Gulfwood Swim Tm Brd 88-89; NASW; Utlty Employee 79-85; Soc Work; Plcy Frmtn Soc Wlfr.

**MAZE, SUSAN D,** Wv Univ At Parkersburg, Parkersburg, WV; SO; BA; Psych; Cnslng.

**MAZE, THOMAS C,** Methodist Coll, Fayetteville, NC; SO; BS; Ldrshp Cncl 89-90; Cmps Tours 89-; Pi Kappa Phi Scl Chrmn 90-; Intrn Breenbrier Rsrt; Bus Admin; Sports Wrld Bus.

**MAZGAJEWSKI, PATRICIA A,** Daemen Coll, Amherst, NY; JR; BSN; Lcky Nmbrs Lnchn Chrmn 89; Invst Clb Pres 90-; Frndly 48 Bwlng Leag VP 90-; ABQAURP 88-; Erie Co Mntl Hlth Assoc; AAS Trocaire Clg 76; Nrsng; Admn.

**MAZIN, MICHELE L,** Fl International Univ, Miami, FL; SR; BA; BA 91; Elem Educ; Tchng.

**MAZINANI, ALI,** Fl International Univ, Miami, FL; SR; BS; Mdl Labty Students Assoc Pres 90-; FL Meml Clg Hnr Student 85-87; AMI Hptl Kendall Regional Ctr Vltr; Bapt Hspt Miami Mdl Lab Techlgt; BS FIU; Medl Lab Sci; Pharmacy.

**MAZINSKI, JASON C,** Pa St Univ Beaver Cmps, Monaca, PA; FR; MBA; Matyh; Fncl Advsr.

**MAZUR, CHRISTOPHER J,** Coll Misericordia, Dallas, PA; FR; BS; Auto Sls Rep 88; Ocuptnl Thrpy.

**MAZUR, LAURIE A,** Salem-Teikyo Univ, Salem, WV; FR; BA; Tns Tm 90-; Bus.

**MAZUR, MICHELLE L,** Newbury Coll, Brookline, MA; FR; ASSOC; Aerobics Clb; Extrnshp At Glly Htch Rstrnt; Deans Lst 90; Vrsty Capt Sftbl; Clnry Arts; Chef.

**MAZUR, NICOLE R,** Bethany Coll, Bethany, WV; FR; BA; SADD 90; Circle K 90; Phi Mu; Rookie Of The Year 90; Vars Sftbl/Pac-First Team 90-; Math.

**MAZUR, SARA J,** Fl International Univ, Miami, FL; JR; BSW; Am Red Crs 89-; Cthlc Wmn Chpl 84-; Dns Lst Miami Dade Comm Coll 89-90; Soc Wrk; Clncl Soc Wrk.

**MAZUREK, DONNA J,** Cumberland County Coll, Vineland, NJ; FR; AA; Nrs Clb 90-; Nrs Intrn Burdette Tomlin Mem Hosp; Tutor Rdg/Mth; Sub Tchr; BA Riden Clge 71; Nrsg; RN.

**MAZURICK, TINA M,** Coll Misericordia, Dallas, PA; SR; Stdnts Occptnl Thrpy Assc 87-; Cmps Mnstry Exec Brd 88-; Love A Nun Prog Co Crdntr 88-; Pi Theta Epsilon Sec 89-; Hnrs Prog 87-; Appalachia Prjct 88-; Soup Ktchn Vol 87-; Clg Kids Prog 88-; Norristown St Hsp Intrn; Occptnl Thrpy.

**MAZYCK, WARREN,** Claflin Coll, Orangeburg, SC; FR; BS; JPTA Outstndng Achvmnt Coll Cnctn Pgm Awd 90; Bus Adm; Acctng.

**MAZZA, CLAUDIA,** Nyack Coll, Nyack, NY; FR; BA; Drama Ensmbl 90-; Acdmnc Affrs Commt Secy 90-; Hispanic Heritage Scty 90-; Engl; High Schl Tchr.

**MAZZA, DIANE M,** Comm Coll Algny Co Algny Cmps, Pittsburgh, PA; FR; BA; Bus Mgmnt.

**MAZZAGATTI, JANET M,** Rutgers St Univ At Camden, Camden, NJ; SR; BS; Alpha Gamma Delta VP Ed 83-84; Zeta Mu; Acctg; Law Schl.

**MAZZALONI, JACQUELYN,** Felician Coll, Lodi, NJ; SR; BA; Std Govt Pres 89-90; Tutor 87-; Zeta Alpha Zeta 89-; Cmps Mnstry 87-; Vldctrn; Math Awd; Sftbl 90-; Math; Tchng.

**MAZZARELLA, CAROL T,** Georgian Court Coll, Lakewood, NJ; SR; BS; Delta Mu Delta Sec 89-90; Admn Asst Of Visiting Nurse Serv; Bus Admn; Exec.

**MAZZARELLA, CHRISTIAN PETER,** Georgian Court Coll, Lakewood, NJ; SR; BS; Bus Clb 90-; Evening Advsry Brd; Ntry Pblc; Acctg.

**MAZZARIELLO, ANTHONY P,** Castleton St Coll, Castleton, VT; SO; BA; Assn Coll Entrepreneurs Pres 90-; Coll Republican Clb 90-; Nwspr 90-; Mktg; Sales.

**MAZZEI, FRANCO,** Villanova Univ, Villanova, PA; SO; BA; Hall House Council Secty/Treas 89-; Italian Club 89-; Villanova Orient Prog Admin; Villanova Peace/Justice; Deans List 90-; Awd Partial Schlrshp Columbians; IM Sftbl/Ftbl; Political Sci; Law.

**MAZZEO III, HENRY R,** Elon Coll, Elon, NC; SO; BS; Flwshp Chrstn Athletes 89-; Lit Tutor 90-; Writing Cntr Tutor 90; Ldrshp Flw 89-; Deans Lst 89-90; IM 89-; Soccer Mgr 89; Hlth Phys Edn Leisure; Athletic Dir.**

**MAZZOTTA, MELISSA C,** Univ Of Miami, Coral Gables, FL; FR; BHS; Tennis 90-; Health Science; Medical Schl.

**MAZZULLO JR, ANTHONY J,** Hillsborough Comm Coll, Tampa, FL; SO; AA Hillsborough Community Clg; Medicine; Radiology.

**MAZZURCO, PHILIP A,** Manhattan Coll, Bronx, NY; FR; Vrsty Wrstlng Tm; Asstntshp PASNY; Sci; Elect Eng.

**MBAH, CHRISTOPHER O,** Howard Univ, Washington, DC; SR; PHARM; ASP; Premed Assoc Howard Univ VP 87; Rho Chi 90; Dns Hnr Rl; Snaph 90; Amer Phrmctcl Assoc; Wash Hosp Ctr Phrmcy Tech 90-; Med Asst Zacheus Med Clnc Lb Prsnl 87; Walter Reed Army Med Ctr EKG Tech 86; Phrmcy.

**MBAH, SIDNEY C,** Cheyney Univ Of Pa, Cheyney, PA; SR; BA; International Stdnt Orgnization 88-; Bta Kappa Chi 89-; ACS Awrd; Deans List 90-; Acad Hon 89-; Chem; Medn.

**MBOGHO, JULIA W,** City Univ Of Ny City Coll, New York, NY; SR; BS; ACM 90-; Cmptr Sci; Prfssrshp.

**MBOW, PHILI I,** Central St Univ, Wilberforce, OH; SO; Intrntl Assoc 90; Muslim Assoc; Mrktng; Bsnss Admin.

**MBRAMOS, JOANNA,** Univ Of Miami, Coral Gables, FL; FR; Snstns Dance Tm 90-; Carni Gras Exec Comm 90-; Alpha Lambda Delta 90-.

**MBUAKOTO, NAMANGA C,** Univ Of Med & Dentistry Of Nj, Newark, NJ; SR; Cmrn Stdnts Assoc (J Chptr 90-; CAMSA NJ Fin Comm; EOFSA 90-; EOF Prof Assoc Acad Achvmnt Awd 91; Dean List Schl Of Hlth Rltd Prof 90-91; AS Essex Cnty Clg Newark Cmps 12/88; Radiography; Hlth Admin/Mgnt.

**MBUANOBE, NKENGASU OLIVIA,** Univ Of The Dist Of Columbia, Washington, DC; SR; BA; DPMC; Deans Lst 89-; Chrch Actvts 89-; Hndbll; Prgrmmr.

**MC ABEE, MELISSA D,** Clemson Univ, Clemson, SC; JR; BS; Snow Ski Clb 90-; Soc Wmn Engrs 90-; Hon Frat 88-90; Gamma Sigma Sigma 90-; Comp Sci Awrd 90; Achvmnt Awrd 90; Deans Lst/Pres Lst 88-90; Chrldr 88-90; AS Sprtnbrg Mthdst Coll 90; Indstrl Eng.

**MC ADAM, DENISE E,** Thomas Nelson Comm Coll, Hampton, VA; FR; Psychlgy; Chld Psychlgy.

**MC ADAMS JR, JAMES E,** Univ Of Nc At Charlotte, Charlotte, NC; SR; BCA; Creative Arts League 90-; Class Cncl 90; TV Intern Graphic Artist; Visual Arts; Graphic Artist.

**MC ADAMS, PATRICIA M,** Pa St Univ Delaware Cty Cmps, Media, PA; SR; BA; Adult Stdnt Organ Pres 90; Adult Stdnt News Edtr 90; Campus Nwsltr Edtr 89; Campus Nwspr Stf 90; Golden Key Penn State Brnch 89; Otstndng Adlt Hgr Ed; Pa Dept Ed Pa Assn Adlts Cont Educ; Otstndng Adlt Gen Arts Sci 90; Soc Tech Comm 90; Envrnmntl Comm; Sci.

**MC ADOO, LORRIE L,** Univ Of Nc At Charlotte, Charlotte, NC; SR; BA; Emrgng Ldrs 87; Pre Law Soc 87-88; Psychlgy Clb 88-89; Omega Essence Pres 88-; Intl Cnvrstns; Chldrn Sun Cltrl Chr 87-88; Delta Sigma Theta Pre Schl Rdng 90; Alex Mc Millian Intrnshp 90; IM Vlbyl/Bsktbl/Sftbl 87-.

**MC ADOO, MASSIE F,** Tuskegee Univ, Tuskegee Inst, AL; SR; BS; Tuskegee Chptr NAACP 89-90; Pi Mu Epsilon Sec 88-; Alpha Kappa Mu 89-; Beta Kappa Chi 89-; Untd Ngr Clge Fnd 21st Cntry Schlr 88-; Tuskegee U Hnr Rl Stdnt Dstngshd Schlr 87-; Joseph D Fuller Math Awd 88-89; Math; Mstrs Dgr/Phd.

**MC ADORY, DENIS D,** Tuskegee Univ, Tuskegee Inst, AL; SR; BS; Amer Soc Of Mchncl Eng; Pi Tau Sigma 90; Ctrpllr Co-Op 88-90; Delco Prods Intrn 90; Gem Fllw Timken Co; Mchncl Eng; Eng.

**MC ADOW, LINDA J,** Ashland Comm Coll, Ashland, KY; SO; BSN; AS; Nrsg/Sci.

**MC AFEE, CHARLES H,** Univ Of Sc At Columbia, Columbia, SC; FR; BA; Intrntl Bus; Law.

**MC AFEE, TANYA R,** Memphis St Univ, Memphis, TN; JR; BSET; Delta Zeta Athltc Dir 89-90; Arch Tech; Arch.

**MC AFOOS, TINA M,** Indiana Univ Of Pa, Indiana, PA; JR; PA State Educ Assoc 90-; Assoc For Chldhd Educ Intl 90-; Provost Schlr; Elem Tchr.

**MC ALEXANDER, MARY A,** Patrick Henry Comm Coll, Martinsville, VA; Pioneers Chrst 87-88; Phi Theta Kappa 90; AAS Ed Danville Comm Clg 90; AAS Lbrl Arts Danville Comm Clg 90; Cert Theater Arts; Ed Mnr Spnsh/Cmnctns/Theatr; Tchr.

**MC ALEXANDER, MICHAEL A,** Nc St Univ At Raleigh, Raleigh, NC; FR; BS; Stdnt Govt Rep; Bio Club; Coll Rpblcns 90; Tau Kappa Epsilon Chpln 90-; IM Bsktbl Tennis Vlybl; Biochem; Genetic Rsrch.

**MC ALEXANDER, ROBIN P,** Radford Univ, Radford, VA; SR; Sigma Kappa Exec Cncl 88-; Stdnt Ed Assoc 90-; Panhlnc Jdcl Bd 89; Pi Gamma Mu 90-; Tau Kappa Epsilon 89-; Stdnt Tchng Intrnshp; BA; BS; Soc Sci/Ed; Pol Sci Profsr.

**MC ALHANY, DONNA M,** Univ Of Sc At Columbia, Columbia, SC; SO; BA; Coll Repblcns 90-F Flwshp Chrstn Ath 89-; Phi Eta Sigma 89-90; Gamma Beta Phi 89-; Delta Gamma; IM Sprts 89-90; Acctg/Org Mgt.

**MC ALISTER, DARRELL S,** Old Dominion Univ, Norfolk, VA; JR; BS; Amer Soc Mech Engrs 89-90; Pi Tau Sigma 90-; Mech Eng.

**MC ALISTER, DAVID W,** Middle Tn St Univ, Murfreesboro, TN; SR; BS; ARMS 86-89; AES 88-; Intrnship Jin Owens/Assoc Fld Video Prod 89; Rcrdng Indstry Mgmt; Audio Engr/Prdcr.

**MC ALISTER, GLORIA R,** Winthrop Coll, Rock Hill, SC; JR; BA; Pi Delta Phi VP 90-; Frnch; Intrprtr.

**MC ALISTER, JAMES T,** Manhattan Coll, Bronx, NY; JR; BE; Amer Soc Mech Engrs 89-; Vygrs Clb 88-; IM Vlybl/Sftbl 88-; Mech Eng.

**MC ALLISTER, DAWN L,** Katherine Gibbs School, Providence, RI; FR; Yrbk Stff; Cls Rep; Cert Sec Awd; Bsns/Sec; Admn Asst.

**MC ALLISTER, DEBORAH A,** Troy St Univ At Dothan, Dothan, AL; SR; Pres Schlrshp; Pres Lst; Bapt Chrch And Assctnl Wrk; Chrch Stff; Stff Wrk; AA Enterprise St Junior Coll 73; Psych; Educ.

**MC ALLISTER, DIANA A,** Univ Of Southern Ms, Hattiesburg, MS; JR; BA; Stdnt Eagle Clb 90-; Stdnt Alumni Assn 90-; AA MS Gulf Coast Comm Coll 90; Therptc Rcrtn.

**MC ALLISTER, KATHERINE H,** Gaston Coll, Dallas, NC; SO; AAS; Phi Beta Lambda Vp 90; Prsdnts Lst 89-; Crtfct Bsc Cmptr Prgrmng 85; Bsns Admnstrtn; Bsns Mngr.

**MC ALLISTER II, LONNIE J,** Hampton Univ, Hampton, VA; FR; BA; Radio Clb; Mens Assc; ROTC Army Rdr Co; Live Sprts Tm; Newsbeat Stf; Amer Legn Mdl Schlstc Excl; Army ROTC Ldrshp Awd; Mass Media Arts; Brdcst Jrnlsm.

**MC ALLISTER, RONALD DEAN,** Lenoir Rhyne Coll, Hickory, NC; SR; BA; Alpha Lambda Delta 89-; Mu Sigma Epsilon 90-; SNCAE 90-; Hattie R Fowler Meml Awd Schlrshp; Elem Ed; Schl Admin.

**MC ALONEY, KAREN D,** Coll Of Charleston, Charleston, SC; JR; BS; Bapt Stdnt Union Comm Chr 89; Biology Clb 89-; Alpha Kappa Gamma; Biology Clb; Schlrshp 88-; C G Fuller Schlrshp 88-; Biology/Minor Educ; Bioloty Tchr.

**MC ALPIN, REBECCA L,** Crichton Coll, Memphis, TN; JR; BS; Yrbk Stf 88-90; Delta Kappa Chi 88-89; Ed; Tchg.

**MC ALPINE, KECIA L,** Talladega Coll, Talladega, AL; SO; BA; Stdnt Govt Assn VP; Cls Pres 90-; Engl Majors Assn Sec 90-; Choir; Natl Hon Soc 90-; Pre Alumni Cncl 90-; All Am Schlr 90-; Stone Schlrshp Fund; Am Mnrty Schlrshp 90-; Engl; Atty At Law.

**MC ANALLY, AMANDA L,** Roane St Comm Coll, Harriman, TN; SO; BA; Scndry Educ/Engl; Tch.**

**MC ANALLY, MARY E,** Union Univ, Jackson, TN; SR; BED; STEA 89-; Deans Lst 89-; Elem Ed; Kndrgrtn Tchr.**

**MC ANDREW, PAUL M,** Savannah Coll Of Art & Design, Savannah, GA; SR; Stdnt Prsrvtn Assn Treas 89-; Dns Lst; Hnr Rl; Pres Schlrshp 87-; Natl Trust 87-; Georgia Trust 87-; BFA; Hstrc Prsrvtn Archtctr.

**MC ARDLE, BRYAN M,** Bowling Green St Univ, Bowling Green, OH; SR; BS; Visual Comm Tech Org Tr 89-; Ski Clb V P 89-90; Epsilon Pi Tau; Phi Beta Lambda 90-; SFC Graphcs Inc 89; Fleming Foods Inc 88-90; Visual Comm Tech; Prnt Graphc Arts Ind.

**MC ARTHUR, JENNIFER O,** Univ Of Sc At Columbia, Columbia, SC; SO; BA; Philosophy; Tchg.

**MC ARTHUR, JUANA C,** Comm Coll Algny Co Algny Cmps, Pittsburgh, PA; SO; BA; Bus Mngmnt.

**MC ARTHUR, LINDA B,** Univ Of West Fl, Pensacola, FL; SR; BS; Lgl Asst Assoc 86-87; Boy Scts Comm 88-90; AS Pensacola Jr Coll 85; Elem Educ; Tchng.

**MC ATEE, BRIAN W,** Univ Of Sc At Columbia, Columbia, SC; SR; BA; Bapt Stdnt Union Prog Co Chm 88-89; Bapt Stdnt Union Msns 89-90; Bapt Stdnt Union Msnry S Korea; Phi Beta Kappa; Alpha Lambda Delta; Phi Eta Sigma 88; Gamma Beta Phi 88; Gldn Key 89; Outstdng Coll Stdnts Of Amer 89; Dns Lst; Psychlgy; Cnslng.

**MC ATEE, CARRIE L,** Univ Of Ga, Athens, GA; JR; BS; Kappa Delta Epsilon 90-; Early Chldhd Ed; Rdg Speclst.

**MC ATEE, CHRYSTAL G,** Univ Of Akron, Akron, OH; SO; BA; Dnc Tm; Deans Lst 89-; Nmrs Chldrn Shws; Nmrs Sr Ctzns; Asst Tchr; Stu Yr; Dance; Instr.

**MC ATEE, GARY A,** Nova Univ, Ft Lauderdale, FL; GD; MBA; NCMA Sec 87; NPMA; Delta Chi; Contracts/Procurement Mgr Resrch Prod Prchsng; BBA ID State Univ 72; Bus Admin.

**MC ATEE, MINDI L,** Univ Of Tn At Martin, Martin, TN; SR; BA; Stdnt Tn Edn Assoc; Alpha Gamma Delta Treas 89-; AS Dyersburg St Comm Coll 89; Scndry Edn/Math; Teach.

**MC ATEE, RICHARD E,** Unity Coll, Unity, ME; SO; BS; Cnsrvtn Law Enfrcmnt Clb 89-90; Cnsrvtn Law Enfrcmnt; Forest Ranger.

**MC ATEER, ANNETTE L,** Comm Coll Algny Co Algny Cmps, Pittsburgh, PA; FR; BA; Sci.

**MC BEAN, ROSEMARIE C,** Columbia Union Coll, Takoma Park, MD; SR; BS; Columbia Jrnl Sch Nwspr Prod Mgr 89-; Advntst Comm Eqlty Dir 90-; Alph Sgm Beta 90-; All Amer Schlr 90-; Cmnctns; Hmn Rsrc Mgmt.

**MC BEE, HEATHER S,** Belmont Coll, Nashville, TN; SO; BBA; Gamma Beta Phi 90-; Music Bus; Pblsg Prmtn.

**MC BEE, NORWOOD M,** Clemson Univ, Clemson, SC; SR; BS; NSNA; SNA Treas 90-; Sigma Theta Tau; Stdnt Exclnc Nrsg Awd; BA Chmstry Citadel 79; Nrsg; Med Schl.

**MC BEE, PAULA L,** Univ Of Sc At Columbia, Columbia, SC; FR; BA; Elem Educ; Tchg.

**MC BRAYER, CINDY L,** Daytona Beach Comm Coll, Daytona Beach, FL; SO; AS; Acdmcn Achvmnt/Rsdntl/Cmrcl Crpntry; Brwn Grl Scts Trp 619 90-; Cnstrctn; Cntrctng.

**MC BRAYER, LISA R,** Tusculum Coll, Greeneville, TN; SO; Bstkbl Tm 89-; Acad Hon 89-90.

**MC BREEN, DANIEL C,** Univ Of Cincinnati, Cincinnati, OH; FR; Stu Sntr Univ Cinn 90-; Nrsg Trbnl Mbr 90-; Envrnmntl Comm; Alpha Lambda Delta 90-; Stu Senate 90-; Nrsg; Admin.

**MC BRIDE, ANGELA D,** Tuskegee Univ, Tuskegee Inst, AL; SR; BA; NSBE 87-89; SWE 90-; Miss Russell Hl Drm Queen 87-88; Coop Stu GMC 90; Hnr Rl 89-; Deans Lst 89-; Elec Engr; Mgmt.

**MC BRIDE, BRIAN C,** Univ Of Rochester, Rochester, NY; JR; MBAJD; Alpha Phi Omega 91; Flr Hcky 89-91; Ecnmcs; Corp Law.

**MC BRIDE, CHRISTINE M,** Indiana Univ Of Pa, Indiana, PA; SR; BS; Judo Clb 87; ACEI 89-90; Outstndng Clge Stdnt 89; Outstndng Stdnt Tchr; Elem Ed; Tch Elem Grds.

**MC BRIDE, DAVID A,** Kent St Univ Kent Cmps, Kent, OH; SO; BBA; Acctng.

**MC BRIDE, DELORIS CHANEL,** Al St Univ, Montgomery, AL; SO.

**MC BRIDE JR, JOSEPH TERRY,** Queens Coll, Charlotte, NC; JR; BA; Stu Gov Assn Pres 88-; Admn Core 89-; Justinian Treas 89-90; Ord Of Omega Treas 90-; Janusian Ord Pres 89-; Mortar Bd; Pi Kappa Phi Treas 89-; OASIS 90-; Pres Schlr 88-; Intrnshp Dist Attrnys Ofc 90; Acctng/Poltcl Sci; CPA; Law.

**MC BRIDE, LATICE R,** Central Fl Comm Coll, Ocala, FL; SO; AA; Phi Theta Kappa Crrspndng Secy; Peer Advsr/Fund Rsrs-Dlgt To State Cnvnt Tutor; Bsn; Intrntl Affrs.

**MC BRIDE, RITA FRANCES,** Lansdale School Of Bus, North Wales, PA; AS; Med Clrcl; Wrkng In Hosp Wth Ptnts Or Thr Inf.

**MC BRIDE, RONALD J,** Fayetteville St Univ, Fayetteville, NC; SR; BS; Sigma Tau Delta; English Tchng; Tchng.

**MC BRIDE, SCOTT D,** Oh Wesleyan Univ, Delaware, OH; SO; BA; Pres Clb Sec 89-F Wesleyan Stdnt Fndtn Tr Guide 89-; Chrl Arts Soc 89-; Phi Eta Sigma Treas 89-; Phi Soc 90-; Order Omega 90-; Chi Phi Pldg Edctr 89-; Amer Cancer Soc 89-F Ntl Mlpl Sckrns Soc 90-; M D Assn 89-; Ed OH Weleyan Plbtn 90-; Pblc Rltns; Pltcl Sci.

**MC BRIDE, TIMOTHY J,** Juniata Coll, Huntingdon, PA; SR; BGA; Judo Clb 87-90; Wrtrs Grp 89-90; Creative Wrtng; Nvlst.

**MC BRIDE, WILLIAM A,** Samford Univ, Birmingham, AL; GD; JD; Parham Wms Trl Cmptn; Cmbrlnd Law Rvw; Pres Schlrshp Outstndng Acdmc Achvmnt 90-; Am Jr Bk Awd Cvl Prcdr 90; Dns Lst 90; BA Univ Miss 89; Law.

**MC CABE, CHRISTOPHER J,** Hudson Valley Comm Coll, Troy, NY; SR; BA; Im Bsktbl; Pres Lst; Deans Lst; All-Rgn Acad Tm For Tennis; Mens Tennis; SUNY Pltsbrgh Pres Schlrshp; Elem Ed; Elem Ed Psych.**

**MC CABE, CYNTHIA F,** Univ Of Sc At Sumter, Sumter, SC; SO; Dan E Turbevll Schlrshp 90-.

**MC CABE, SCOTT M,** Wright St Univ Lake Cmps, Celina, OH; FR; AAS; Frat Ord Eagles Aerie 767 86-; Amer Lgn Post 444; Vet U S Navy Lab Tech Hosp Corps 86-90; Elec Eng.

**MC CAFFERY, MARY G,** Ms St Univ, Miss State, MS; JR; BBA; Hall Cncl 88-89; Rfrmd Univ Flwshp 88-; Gamma Beta Phi 88-; SAM VP; CHI Omega Pblcty Comm 89-; ACT Acad Schlrshp 88-; Summers Schlrshp 88-; IM Flg Ftbl 89; Mktg; Sls.

**MC CAFFERY, MICHAEL H,** Bloomfield Coll, Bloomfield, NJ; SO; BA; Sierra Clb 86-; Taylor Inst Schlrshp 83; AS Taylor Inst 84; Accntng; CPA.

**MC CAIG, ANITA D,** Union Univ, Jackson, TN; SR; BA; Stdnt Gov Sen 90-; Linguae Mundi Pres 87-; Prexy Clb 90-; Hons Stdnt Assn Sen 87-; Ruthledge Hnry Hist Clb 88-; Sigma Tau Delta Engl 88-; Alpha Chi Delg Ntl Cnvntn 89-; Phi Sigma Iota Frgn Lang 90-; Honduras Bapt Med/Dntl Mssn Intrprtr; IM Sprts; Engl; Wrk Sclly Ntv/Ltn Amer.

**MC CAIG, JOSEPH J,** William Paterson Coll, Wayne, NJ; SR; BA; Engl Educ.

**MC CAIN III, JOHN NOLAN,** Univ Of South Al, Mobile, AL; SR; Beta Gamma Sigma 89-; Beta Alpha Psi 89-; Kappa Alpha Sec 84-87; BS; Acctg.

**MC CAIN, JOHN S,** Livingston Univ, Livingston, AL; SR; BS; AAHPERD 90-; Spec Olympcs 90-; Phy Educ; Tchr/Coach.

**MC CAIN, MICHELLE D,** John C Calhoun St Comm Coll, Decatur, AL; SR; BS; Psi Chi 90-; Psychlgy/Sociology.**

**MC CALL, CARLA D,** Hillsborough Comm Coll, Tampa, FL; FR; AA; Lbrl Arts.

**MC CALL, DANA ANN,** Neumann Coll, Aston, PA; SO; PH D; Wmns Bkbl 89-; Psychology; Clncl Psychlgst.

**MC CALL, DANIEL H,** Piedmont Tech Coll, Greenwood, SC; FR; Bsnss Mngmnt; Bsnss.

**MC CALL II, HOMER L,** Morehouse Coll, Atlanta, GA; SO; BS; Hlth Careers Soc 89-; Mu Alpha Theta 88-89; Bio; Med Cardiology.

**MC CALL, LEIGH A,** Univ Of Nc At Charlotte, Charlotte, NC; SO; BS; Biology; Tchr.

**MC CALL, LISA L,** Univ Of Sc At Columbia, Columbia, SC; FR; BA; Stdnt Govt Assn Exec Sec 90-; Gamma Beta Phi 90-; Eductnl Task Force LEAP; Journlsm; Wrtng.

**MC CALL, STACEY A,** Eckerd Coll, St Petersburg, FL; SO; BS; Anthrplgy Clb 90; Dance Cncrts; Dcrtn Com 89-90; Deans List 89-; Intrnshp Western Psychtrc Mntl Hlth Wrkr 90; Pressley Ridge Schls 89-90; IM Sports 89-; Clncl Psychlgst.

**MC CALLISTER, DONALD E,** Univ Of Akron, Akron, OH; JR; BA; Deans Lst 88-; Gldn Key 89-; Canton Plyrs Gld 87-; Elem Ed.

**MC CALLISTER, SHERI K,** Cumberland Coll, Williamsburg, KY; JR; Love In Action Tm Ldr 88-; Stdnt Adm Staff 89-90; Outdoor Adv Club V P 88-90; Mountain Outreach 89-90; Deans Liszt 88-; Elem Edn; Teach.

**MC CALLUM, OZE H,** Southern Coll Of Tech, Marietta, GA; SO; BSEE; Math; Eng.

**MC CALLUM JR, RODNEY A,** Tusculum Coll, Greeneville, TN; SO; BA; Scrtry Treas Of Kthrne Hall; Soccer Tm MVP 89-90; Bsnss/Cmptrs; Lwyr.

**MC CALMONT, ROBERT B,** Westminster Coll, New Wilmingtn, PA; SR; BA; Golf Tm 88-90; Bus Admin; Fncl Indstry.

**MC CAMPBELL, BRANDY R,** Univ Of Tn At Martin, Martin, TN; SO; Univ Schlrs Org 89-; Math Assn Amer 90-; Phi Eta Sigma 90-; Scndry Ed/Math.

**MC CAMPBELL, EMILY T,** Trinity Coll, Hartford, CT; FR; Fld Hockey/Skiing/La Crosse; Econs; Bus.

**MC CANE JR, HOWARD L,** Al A & M Univ, Normal, AL; SO; BS; Acad Dns Lst 89-90; Chem; Pharmctcls.

**MC CANLESS, KEITH A,** Univ Of Tn At Knoxville, Knoxville, TN; SO; BA; Rlgs Studies; Tchng.

**MC CANLESS, MARY H,** Dyersburg St Comm Coll, Dyersburg, TN; SO; BA; PTK; Sci; Elem Educ.

**MC CANN, ALEISE M,** Dartmouth Coll, Hanover, NH; FR; BA; Gl Clb; Admssns Offc Grtr; Math Anthrplgy; Law.

**MC CANN, CHRISTINE M,** Univ Of Rochester, Rochester, NY; SR; PHD; Nwspr Feat Edtr 87-; Admsn Cncl Ovrnght Visit Crdntr 87-88; Engl Clb 87-; Intrn Rchstr Hstrcl Soc; Engl; Tch.

**MC CANN, HOLLY LYNN,** Univ Of Ga, Athens, GA; SR; BED; Clg Bowl 90; Jeopardy Clg Tournmnt Contstnt; Phi Eta Sigma 88-; Frgn Lang Ed; Tchng/Wrkng Overseas.

**MC CANN, JASON K,** S U N Y Coll Of A & T Morrisvl, Morrisville, NY; SO; BA; Phlsphy; Wrtng.

**MC CANN, JEANNE M,** Cumberland County Coll, Vineland, NJ; SO; BA; Stdnt Senate 90-; Phi Theta Kappa 89-; Mu Alpha Theta; Math/Physics; Aerospace Eng.

**MC CANN, JOHN D,** Providence Coll, Providence, RI; JR; BA; Phi Mu Epsilon 90-; Math/Cmptr Sci.

**MC CANN, KEVIN M,** Temple Univ, Philadelphia, PA; SR; BA Temple Univ Ambler Campus; Mktg; Sales.

**MC CANN, MARIA DEL P,** Marshall University, Huntington, WV; SR; BA; Mrktng.

**MC CANN, MARY C,** Georgetown Univ, Washington, DC; JR; BA; Clss Comm 89-; Prgm Brd Mrktg Comm 90-; Deans Lst; Mrktg.

**MC CANN, TAMRA L,** Newbury Coll, Brookline, MA; BA; Hosp Ptnt Accts Crdt/Cllctns Coord; Med Asst; Hlth Admn.

**MC CANNADY, SARA,** Fayetteville St Univ, Fayetteville, NC; JR; Kappa Delta Pi; Elem Ed; Tchr.

**MC CANTS, KIMBERLY M,** Va St Univ, Petersburg, VA; JR; BA; Gspl Choir 88-89; Urbn Plng Clb 88-89; Admin Jstc Clb 90-; Admin Jsct; Law.

**MC CANTS, LA SHAWN M,** Lincoln Univ, Lincoln Univ, PA; SR; BS; Spnsh Clb 87-88; Bus Clb 88-; NAACP 89-; Acctg Clb Sen 89-; W H Madella Prz 90-; Floyd/Estelle Mourning Schlrshp 90-; Bus Adm; Fin Anlyst.**

**MC CANTS, SEAN A,** Cheyney Univ Of Pa, Cheyney, PA; SR; Psy Clb; Choir; Gspl Choir; ROTC; Kappa Alpha Psi Pres; Plque Red Crs Bld Dr; Dns Lst.

**MC CARDLE, JENNIFER K,** Indiana Univ Of Pa, Indiana, PA; FR; Erth/Spac Sci Educ; Tchr/Clg Prof.

**MC CARGO, ALEC K,** Va St Univ, Petersburg, VA; SO; BA; Bus Admin Clb 89-90; Acad Achvmnt Awd 90-; Bus Admin; Mgmt.

**MC CARGO, K,** Va St Univ, Petersburg, VA; SO; BA; BAD Clb 89-; Acad Achvmnt Awd 91; Bus; Mgmt.

**MC CARLEY, ELIZABETH T,** Univ Of Sc At Columbia, Columbia, SC; SR; BA; Cheerldr 86; BA Univ S C Sprtnbrg 91; Erly Chldhd Educ; Erly Chldhd Educ; Schl Tchr.

**MC CARRON, DOUGLAS J,** Fl St Univ, Tallahassee, FL; SO; BA; Phi Eta Sigma; Ftbl/Bsktbl/Vlybl/Sftbl; Bus; Law.

**MC CART, CHRISTINA B,** Univ Of Ga, Athens, GA; JR; BED; Kappa Delta Epsilon; Erly Chldhd Educ; Tchr.

**MC CARTER, SHANA M,** Roanoke Bible Coll, Elizabeth Cy, NC; SO; BS; Mssns Awrnss Tm Res Asst 89-; Deans Lst 89-; Deaf Studies; ASL Intprtr.

**MC CARTHY, ANNE M,** James Madison University, Harrisonburg, VA; SO; BS; Psychlgy Clb 90-; Amnesty Intl 89-; Cntr Serv Lrng 90-; Hmls Shltr Vol 89-90; Cntr Serv Lrng 90-; Deans Lst Univ Richmnd 90; Pres Lst; IM Soccer/Vlybl 90; Psychlgy; Fmly Physician.

**MC CARTHY, BLANE G,** Stetson Univ, Deland, FL; JR; BBA; Yng Lf W Volusia Vol Ldr 88-90; Greenfeather Fndrsng Cmt Crnvl Co Chr 90; Phi Eta Sgm 88-; Mrtr Brd Tres; Phi Alph Dlt Rsh Chrmn 90; Prsdntl Schlrshp 88-; Lmbd Chi Alph Schlrshp Chrmn 89-; Intrnshp Pblc Dfndrs Ofc Deland; IM Sccr 90-; Gen Bus Admn; Law.**

**MC CARTHY, CLAIRE R,** Georgian Court Coll, Lakewood, NJ; SR; BS; Brthrght Dir 83-; Exec Sec 70-78; Bus Admin; Mgmt.

**MC CARTHY, DYAN M,** Georgian Court Coll, Lakewood, NJ; SO; BA; Exec Sec 85-; Taylor Bus Inst 85; Acctng.

**MC CARTHY, EDIE B,** Univ Of North Fl, Jacksonville, FL; SR; BA; Alpha Sigma Pi; Gldn Key 90-; Phi Kappa Phi; Inst Mgmt Acctnts 90-; PTA 90-; Acctg; Pblc Acctg.

**MC CARTHY, EDWARD R,** Syracuse Univ, Syracuse, NY; FR; BA; IM Vlybl/Bsktbl; Sigma Phi Epsilon Intr Frtrnty Cncl Repr; Pre Med.

**MC CARTHY, GUY B,** Fl A & M Univ, Tallahassee, FL; JR; BS; Wrtr Fla Flambeau 90-; Media Lkwrtng Cmptitn; Vision Quest; Otwrd Bound Instr; Jrnlsm.

**MC CARTHY, JANET L,** Southern Vt Coll, Bennington, VT; JR; BA; Tutrng 89-; Prspct Schl Intrn 90-; AMTA; Certfd Msg Thrpst/Kripak Yoga Tchr 85-; Cert Bncrft Schl Msg Thrpy 85; Envrnmntl Stdies; Eductr.

**MC CARTHY, JENNIFER B,** Univ Of Sc At Columbia, Columbia, SC; JR; BA; Almni Asc; Order Omega; Ldrshp Mntr; Pnhlnc Pres Brd; Phi Beta Lambda; Pnhlnc Best Pldge 89; Zeta Tau Alpha VP 89 Serv Chrmn 90 Pres; Asc Merch Corp Intsp; Crwn Dvlpmnt Trust Fnd Schlp; IMS 89-; Rtlng/Fshn Merch; Corp Buyer/Display.

**MC CARTHY, JENNIFER L,** Univ Of North Fl, Jacksonville, FL; SR; BA; Frnch Clb 88-; Frnch Frgn Lngge Stdy Prog Univ Of Paris 89; Kappa Alpha Theta 90; Intrnshp William Cook Agncy; AA Florida State Univ 90; Cmmnctns; Advrtsng.

**MC CARTHY, JOHN FRANCIS,** Middle Tn St Univ, Murfreesboro, TN; SR; BS; Charter Mbr Aerospace Mntnc Club Wrenching Raiders; Mbr Hnrs Prog; Licensed Aircraft & Powerplant Mechanic 90; AS Clayton State Coll Morrow Ga 90; Aerspace Mntnc Mgmt; Aircraft Mntnc Mgmt.

**MC CARTHY, KRISTIN E,** William Paterson Coll, Wayne, NJ; JR; Alpha Kappa Delta; Sclgy; Crim Jstc.

**MC CARTHY, LINDA J,** Niagara Univ, Niagara Univ, NY; SO; BA; Vce Lssns In Thtr Dept 89-; Dns Lst 89-; Psi Chi; Cmpr Div Of Mntl Hlth Assn 89-; Psych; Psychthrpy.

**MC CARTHY, MARTHA J,** Waycross Coll, Waycross, GA; SO; Stdnt Govt Assn Rep 90-; Bus Clb Sec 90-; Phi Theta Kappa 90-; Labor Rel; Law.

**MC CARTHY, PATSY A,** Draughons Jr Coll Johnson City, Johnson City, TN; SO; AD; Dns Lst; Pres Lst; Cmptr Pgmng.**

**MC CARTHY, SHANNON K,** Providence Coll, Providence, RI; FR; BA; Hist; Law.

**MC CARTHY, STACEY M,** Univ Of Montevallo, Montevallo, AL; SO; Hnrs Prgrm 89-; Clg Nght 89-; Wnd Jazz Ensmblrs 89-; Alpha Lambda Delta 89-; Alpha Gamma Delta 89-; Msc; Msc Thrpy.

**MC CARTHY, THOMAS W,** Comm Coll Algny Co Algny Cmps, Pittsburgh, PA; SO; AS; Phi Theta Kappa 90-; Acctg; CPA.

**MC CARTNEY, BRENDAN F,** Hudson Valley Comm Coll, Troy, NY; BS; CCRN Cert 90; RN; AAS Kingsborough Cmnty Clg; Nsg/Bio; Medcl Fld Nrs Anesthtst.

**MC CARTNEY, JOANN M,** Salisbury St Univ, Salisbury, MD; SR; BA; Stdnt Nwspr Edtr In Chf 87-90; Stdnt Regent 90-; Omicron Delta Kappa Treas 90-; Phi Kappa Phi 90-; Phi Eta Sigma 87-; Comm Arts; Law.

**MC CARTNEY, KELLY L,** Indiana Univ Of Pa, Indiana, PA; FR; Sign Lang Clb 90; IM Vlybl 90; Educ Hrng Imprd; Tchg.

**MC CARTNEY, MELINDA S,** Comm Coll Algny Co Algny Cmps, Pittsburgh, PA; SO; BSN; Actv Prnt Tchrs Guild Chldrns Schl; Nrsg Assist Lcl Hosp; Nrsg; RN.

**MC CARTY, ANGELA K,** Univ Of Sc At Columbia, Columbia, SC; JR; BS; Office Adm; Management.

**MC CARTY, DOUGLAS A,** Livingston Univ, Livingston, AL; FR; BS; Stdnt Gov Rep; Math/Sci Clb; Pi Kappa Phi; Deans Lst; Bio; Optmtry.

**MC CARTY, JIM W,** Savannah Coll Of Art & Design, Savannah, GA; SO; BA; Rsdnt Asst RA Mnth 90-; Bsbl; Ilstrtn.

**MC CARTY, MAUREEN M,** Univ Of Fl, Gainesville, FL; SR; BS; Stdnt Occupational Therapy Assoc 89-; Sigma Tau Sigma 88-; Presidential Awrd 88; Deans Lst 88; IM Sftbl Vlybl Co Rec Flg Ftbl Bsktbl Sftbl; Occupational Therapy.

**MC CARTY JR, RICHARD E,** Salisbury St Univ, Salisbury, MD; JR; BS; Dns Stdnt Advsry Comm 90-; Phi Kappa Phi; Henson Sch Sci Schlrshp 90-; Physics/Elctrncs.

**MC CARTY, TIMOTHY P,** Cumberland Coll, Williamsburg, KY; GD; MA; Sigma Tau Delta 86; Phi Theta Kappa 86; Natl Cncl Of Tchrs Of Engl; Circle K 86; Shnr Chrch Of Christ 89-; Sub Tchr City Schl 90-; Apprl Mgr Kmrt Corp; A Of Arts Shawnee St Univ 84; BA David Lipscomb Univ 86; Engl; Tchr.

**MC CARY, HAROLD S,** Univ Of Al At Birmingham, Birmingham, AL; SO; Employed As Firefighter/EMT-HOOVER Fire Dept; Emergncy Med Serv; Career Firefgtr/Paramedic.

**MC CASKEY, BRUCE H A,** Erie Comm Coll, Buffalo, NY; JR; AAS; NY Fed Alchl Chmcl Dpndncy Cnslrs; Alchlms Cnslng; Psychthrpy.

**MC CASKILL, JEAN D,** Lenoir Rhyne Coll, Hickory, NC; SO; AB; Wmns Ccs 90-; Phi Beta Lambda 90-; Bus Admn.

**MC CASKILL, KIMBERLY A,** Mount Olive Coll, Mount Olive, NC; SO; BA; N Carolina Hnrs Schlrshp 89-; Acctng; CPA.

**MC CASKILL, LUTHER D,** Jackson St Univ, Jackson, MS; SO; BA; Blgy Clb 90-; NAACP 90-; Stdnt Govt Leg Cncl 90-; Alpha Lambda Delta; IM Bsktbl; Blgy; Phrmcy Schl.

**MC CASLAND, L PAIGE,** Univ Of Tn At Martin, Martin, TN; JR; BS; Alpha Gamma Rho Little Sister; Alpha Delta Pi Jr Mbr At Lrg; Communications; Public Rltns.

**MC CASLIN, JULIE D,** Memphis St Univ, Memphis, TN; FR; BA; Pi Beta Phi Alumni 85-86; Merle Norman Csmtcs Mngr 82-.

**MC CASLIN, LORNA M,** Capital Univ, Columbus, OH; SO; BSN; Cap Chorale Chorus 89-; Nursing.**

**MC CATHERN, MYRA A,** American Baptist Coll, Nashville, TN; JR; BA; Zeta Phi Beta Sec 90-; T B Boyd Educ Schlrshp; Social Sci.

**MC CAUGHEY, ANNE F,** City Univ Of Ny Baruch Coll, New York, NY; GD; BBA; Bsn To Bsn Mktg Club 90; Mktg/Mgmt; Law.

**MC CAULEY, APRIL L,** Lexington Comm Coll, Lexington, KY; FR; BA; Accntng; CPA.

**MC CAULEY, CANDACE R,** Univ Of Sc At Columbia, Columbia, SC; FR; NAACP Mnrty Asst Peer Prog; Vol Natl Yth Sprts Prog 90-; Alpha Lambda Delta Treas/Sec; Dns Lst 90-; Mnrty Stdnt Affrs Cert Of Recog 90-; IM Soccer Tm 90; IM Bsktbl Tm; Bus Admin; Intl Bus.

**MC CAULEY, JANE V,** Radford Univ, Radford, VA; JR; BS; SGA Jr Cls Sec 90; Sr Cls VP; Crmnl Jstce Clb Univ Affrs Cncl Rep 90; Cir K Intl 90-; Sen Rep For SGA Cls Ofc 90; Crmnl Jstce Intrnshps; IMS 90-; Crmnl Jstce; Law/Fed Govt.

**MC CAULEY, JOHN J,** Radford Univ, Radford, VA; SR; BS; Pol Sci Soc 90-; Geology Soc 90-; Pi Gamma Mu; Pol Sci; Cartography.

**MC CAULEY, KAREN M,** Fayetteville St Univ, Fayetteville, NC; FR; BA; Acctng.

**MC CAULEY, LEISA C,** Univ Of Sc At Columbia, Columbia, SC; SR; Gldn Key; BAIS 90; Elem Edctn; Tchng.

**MC CAULLA, PAUL M,** Memphis St Univ, Memphis, TN; SO; BSME; Gamma Beta Phi; Mech Eng.

**MC CAUSLAND, LINDA P,** Univ Of Cin R Walters Coll, Blue Ash, OH; FR; Gllry Asst Vol Cntmpry Art Ctr 87; BS Syracuse Univ 65; MS SUNY At Buffalo 80; Cmmrcl Art; Freelance Artist.

**MC CAY, MARY CAROLE,** Comm Coll Algny Co Algny Cmps, Pittsburgh, PA; SO; BA; Scl Wrk Clb 90; Admssns Asst 90; Nrsng Hm; Scl Wrk; Grtrc.

**MC CAY, MARY T,** Hillsborough Comm Coll, Tampa, FL; FR; AA; Phi Theta Kappa; Awds Convocation Creative Wrtng; Psychlgy.

**MC CHESNEY JR, DAVID C,** Cedarville Coll, Cedarville, OH; FR; BSE; Soc Automotive Engs 90-; Pres Schlr 90-; IM Bsktbl/Sftbl/Ftbl 90-; Eng/Chem; Rsrch.

**MC CHRYSTAL, JILL M,** Univ Of Akron, Akron, OH; JR; Gldn Ky; Delta Gamma Asst Schlrshp; Spch Pathlgy/Audlgy.

**MC CLAFFERTY, BRIAN W,** Univ Of Pittsburgh, Pittsburgh, PA; JR; MBA; IEEE 90-; Engr Hnrs 88-; Gldn Key 89-; Eta Kappa Nu 90-; Elec Engr.

**MC CLAIN, ANJALI M,** Central St Univ, Wilberforce, OH; SR; BA; Natl Assn Blck Jrnlsts 90-; Cntrl Belle Dncr 88-; Alpha Phi Alpha 89-; Hon Pgm 87-; Alpha Kappa Alpha 90-; Blck Achvrs Yth Achvr 85-89; Intrn-Natl Afro-Amer Museum 90; Intrn-WKRC Chnnl 12 Cincinnati 90; IM Vlybl 87-88; Cmnctns-TV/RADIO; TV Tlnt.

**MC CLAIN, M ANTHONY,** Southern Coll Of Tech, Marietta, GA; SR; CET; Amer Soc Cvl Engr 89-; Amer Cncrt Inst 88-; Tau Alpha Pi 90-; Jaycee's 88-; BA Berry Clg 84; Civil Engr.

**MC CLAIN, MARGARET E,** Univ Of Sc At Columbia, Columbia, SC; FR; Scuba Clb 90-; Girls Soccr 90-; Watr Hcky 90-; Soccr/Waterhcky/Scuba; Bio; Pre Med.

**MC CLAIN, PATRICK D,** Morehouse Coll, Atlanta, GA; SO; BS; Hlth Crs Soc 90-; Tenn Clb 89-; Bio; Psychn.

**MC CLAIN, STELIA K,** Blue Mountain Coll, Blue Mountain, MS; SR; Bapt Stdnt Union CBYW Pres 89; Sci Math Clb 88; Cmmtr Clb 90; Koinonia 89-; Sigma Sigma Gamma 89-; Alpha Psi Omega 89; Madenian Scty 90-; Mntnr Bus Mgnr 90-; IM Sprts 89-; BA; Bible Hstry.**

**MC CLAIN, STELLA D,** Nc Agri & Tech St Univ, Greensboro, NC; FR; NC Tchg Fellow 90-; Math Ed; Educator.

**MC CLANAHAN, BRENT M,** Marshall University, Huntington, WV; SR; Alpha Kappa Psi VP Ledge Cls 88-90; BBA Mngmnt 90; Mntmnt; Sales Eng.

**MC CLANAHAN, JUNE M,** Roane St Comm Coll, Harriman, TN; SO; ASBA; Blcks In Govt; Waste Mngmnt/Eng; Envrnmntl/Eng.

**MC CLANAHAN, SUSAN D,** Pellissippi St Tech Comm Coll, Knoxville, TN; SO; BA; Phi Theta Kappa 90-; Eng; Teach.

**MC CLARAN, JAMES CLYDE,** Middle Tn St Univ, Murfreesboro, TN; SO; BBA; Chess Clb; Presbyterian Stdnt Flwshp; Alpha Kappa Psi; Omicron Delta Sigma; Deans Lst 89-90; Econ/Finance; Analysis/Plnr Real Estate.

**MC CLARAN, MELISSA C,** Middle Tn St Univ, Murfreesboro, TN; SR; MBE; Natl Bus Educ Assc; STEA; Kappa Delta Pi; Bus Educ; Tchr.

**MC CLARD, MELISSA J,** Univ Of Sc At Columbia, Columbia, SC; FR; BA; Campus Crussade Christ; Poltcl Sci; Politics.

**MC CLARNON, MAUREEN T,** Oh St Univ, Columbus, OH; SR; BA; Radio Sta Prog Dir 87-90; Columbus Aids Tsk Frce 90-; Ntl Mrt Schlr 87-; Awd Fr Exclnc Arts/Sci 90; Scarlet/Gray Schlrshp 87-88; Cinmtgrphy; MA.

**MC CLASKEY, STEWART W,** Embry Riddle Aeronautical Univ, Daytona Beach, FL; JR; BS; Aernautcl Sci; Corp Aviatn.

**MC CLEAN, JOMO L,** City Univ Of Ny City Coll, New York, NY; JR; BE; NSBE; Amrcn Cncrt Inst; ASCE; CS; Phi Eta Sigma; Tau Beta Pi; Donald Griff Schlrshp; Big Engnrng Schlrshp Prgrm; IM Sftbl; Cvl Engnrng; Engnrng.

**MC CLEAN, TARA K,** Albertus Magnus Coll, New Haven, CT; SO; BA; Acctng Clb 90-; Dns Lst 89-90; Acctng; CPA.

**MC CLEANAHAN, RHONDA S,** Jackson St Univ, Jackson, MS; SO; BS; Alpha Lambda Delta; Elem Ed/Math/Engl; Tch.

**MC CLEARY, SUE D,** Clayton St Coll, Morrow, GA; SO; ADN; Assoc Degree Nrsg Secr 90-; CPIW IIA CPCU GA Assoc Ind Ins Agents 79-89; Insurance 62-89; CPCU Soc CPCU Malvern PA 80; Nrsg.

**MC CLEERY, MICHAEL A,** Liberty Univ, Lynchburg, VA; SO; Hnrs Prgm; Math.

**MC CLEESE, MELISSA F,** Radford Univ, Radford, VA; SR; BS; Political Science Club 89-90; Political Science/English.

**MC CLELLAN, BRENDA K,** Univ Of Tn At Chattanooga, Chattanooga, TN; FR; BS; Grl Scouts Of Amer Pln Brd Sec 79-; Alpha Lambda Delta 90-; Phi Eta Sigma 90-; Sci; Elect Eng.

**MC CLELLAN, DEBRA L,** Mount Aloysius Jr Coll, Cresson, PA; SO; AS; Phi Theta Kappa 88-89; Spec Olympics 90; Phi Theta Kappa 88-89; Girl Scouts 88-; Intrnshp Shoneys 90-; Restaurant Mgmnt.

**MC CLELLAN, JACLYN D,** Johnson C Smith Univ, Charlotte, NC; JR; BA; History Clb VP; Pan African Cncl; Alpha Sweetheart Orgnztn; Certif Apprctn Fedl Govt; Outstndng Prtcptn City Cerritos; Political Sci; Attorney.

**MC CLELLAN, JANCY L,** Columbus Coll Of Art & Design, Columbus, OH; FR; BA; Fine Arts; Art Therapy.

**MC CLELLAN, KATHLEEN D,** Hillsborough Comm Coll, Tampa, FL; SO; AS; Clncl Exclnc Sonogrphy 90-; Dgnstc Mdcl Sngrphy Tchnlgy; Ultrasound.

**MC CLELLAN, LAWANDA DENISE,** Middle Tn St Univ, Murfreesboro, TN; FR; BA; Grphc Dsgn; Cmmrcl Art/Advstng.

**MC CLELLAN, RANDALL D,** Birmingham Southern Coll, Birmingham, AL; JR; BS; Flwshp Chrstn Athlts; Hmcmng Com 89-; IM Bsktbl Vlybl Sftbl 88-; Mrtr Bd; Alpha Lambda Delta 88-; Phi Eta Sigma 88-; Alpha Epsilon Delta 90-; Theta Chi 88-; Kappa Mu Epsilon 90-; Beta Beta Beta; Birmingham Jycs; Pres Stdnt Serv Org; Math; Med.

**MC CLELLAN, SARAH W,** Fl St Univ, Tallahassee, FL; GD; BS; AA Tallahassee Comm Coll 89; Early Chldhd Educ; Tch.

**MC CLELLAN, TERRY L,** Chattahoochee Vly St Comm Coll, Phenix City, AL; GD; AS; Cmptr Inf Sys.

**MC CLELLAND, BRIAN T,** Pellissippi St Tech Comm Coll, Knoxville, TN; SO; PHD; Phi Theta Kappa; Phi Theta Kappa; Med; Genetics/Virology.

**MC CLENDON, BRENDA R,** Univ Of Akron, Akron, OH; SR; BS; Careers Clb 75-80; Gspl Choir 84-86; Bapt Choir/Ensmbl 74-; Delta Nu Alpha 78-80; Cert Barberton Schl Of Comm 68; AS Univ Akron 80; Elem Engl; Tchr Spec Educ.

**MC CLENDON, DARBY LEE,** Birmingham Southern Coll, Birmingham, AL; SR; BA; Trngl Clb Pres 88-89; Prs Stdnts Srvc Org 89-; Alpha Lambda Delta VP 89-90; Phi Eta Sigma 89-90; Phi Beta Kappa 89-; Mrtr Brd Pres 90; Omicron Delta Kappa; Kappa Delta Epsilon Sec Treas 90; Phi Alpha Theta; Pi Sigma Alpha; Alpha Chi Omega; Hstry Pltcl Sci Scndry Ed.

**MC CLENDON, ERNEST JAMES,** Lexington Comm Coll, Lexington, KY; SO; Psychlgy; Med.

**MC CLENDON, JERUSHA R,** Snead St Jr Coll, Boaz, AL; FR; Jazz Bnd 90; Phi Theta Kappa; Music Schlr Awd; Music Jrnlsm.

**MC CLENDON, RHONDA A,** Al St Univ, Montgomery, AL; SO; BS; Pres Schlrshp 89-; Acctg.

**MC CLENDON, TRICIA A,** Clark Atlanta Univ, Atlanta, GA; SR; BA; Engl Clb Pres 89-90; Sigma Tau Belta 90-; Delta Sigma Theta Prlmtrn 90-; BA 90-; Engl; Law.

**MC CLING, KATHRYN L,** Univ Of Al At Birmingham, Birmingham, AL; SO; AAS; Deans Lst; Radiography.

**MC CLINTICK, MELISSA A,** Univ Of Akron, Akron, OH; JR; BA; ACES 90; Proj PANDA; Math; Elem Educ.

**MC CLINTON JR, JAMES,** Fayetteville St Univ, Fayetteville, NC; SR; BA; Physchology Clb 89-; Boy Scouts Cmmssnr 75-; Ph D Boy Scouts 88; Psychology Cnslng; Soc Wrk.

**MC CLINTON, MALANA R,** Bloomfield Coll, Bloomfield, NJ; FR; BSN; Nrsng; Nrs Prctcnt.

**MC CLINTON II, ROBERT L,** Al St Univ, Montgomery, AL; FR; BA; Acctng; Lwyr.

**MC CLOSKEY, ANITA V,** S U N Y Coll Of Tech At Canton, Canton, NY; GD; BA; Phi Theta Kappa 90; Omega Alpha 89-; Ofc Tchnlgy Clb VP 89-; Hon Cnvctn 89-; Bus; Acctnt.

**MC CLOSKEY, JEANETTE M,** Saint Francis Coll, Loretto, PA; SO; BA; SG 90-; Stdnt Activ Org 90-; Pre Law/Current Affairs Clb 89-; New Theater 89-; Deans Lst 89-; Pres Schlrshp; Engl Mgmnt; Corp Law.

**MC CLOSKEY, ROBERT T,** Bloomfield Coll, Bloomfield, NJ; GD; MBA; Alpha Chi 90-; Jersey Judo Karate Acad Blck Blt 87-; Amer Prod Inv Contrl Soc 86-; Matrls Admn Smiths Indstries Aerspce Defnse 85-; AS Co Clg Morris 87; Bsns.

**MC CLOUD, AMY M,** Anne Arundel Comm Coll, Arnold, MD; SO.

**MC CLOUD, RODERICA A,** Va St Univ, Petersburg, VA; SO; BS; TAMM; Co-Coord Fshn Show; Alumni Schlrshp 90; Edward Gillis Schlrshp 90; Fshn Dsgn/Mss Cmnctns; Costume Dsgnr/Fshn Rep.

**MC CLOUD, WILLIAM A,** Marshall University, Huntington, WV; JR; BA; Educ; Teacher.

**MC CLUNEY, MILLARD M,** Univ Of Sc At Columbia, Columbia, SC; SR; BS; Stdnt Govt Assoc Sntr 89-; Psych Clb Pblc Rltns 89-; Gspl Choir 89-; Omicron Delta Kappa; Peer Eductrs 89-; Lifeline 89-90; Afrcn Amer Assoc 89-; S E Psych Assoc; SC Real Est 84-; SEG Spartanburg Tech Clg 80; Psych; Teach.

**MC CLUNG, DOUGLAS W,** Marshall University, Huntington, WV; JR; BBA; Accntng Clb Tutor 90; Bapt Campus Mnstries 90; Food Cmmttee Rep 88-89; Gamma Beta Phi 89; Deans Lst 88; RHA Flag Ftbl 88; Accntng; CPA.

**MC CLUNG, SHERRY A,** Lincoln Memorial Univ, Harrogate, TN; SO; AS; Whitaker Snyder Music Awd; Stdnt Nrs Assn; Nrsng; Grntlgy/Nrsng.

**MC CLURE, BRENDA G,** Western Ky Univ, Bowling Green, KY; GD; Phi Theta Kappa 87-90; M Mitchell Schl/Owensboro Ky; BS 90; Elem Ed; Tch.

**MC CLURE, DANA L,** Medical Coll Of Ga, Augusta, GA; JR; BA; Alpha Chi Omega Pblcty Chrmn 88-; GA Assn Nrsng Stdnts 90-; Natl Stdnt Nrs Assn 90-; Nrsng; Midwife.

**MC CLURE JR, DAVID J,** Bapt Bible Coll & Seminary, Clarks Summit, PA; SR; BS; Assoc Stdnt Cncl 90-; Ridley Dorm Pres 90-; Alpha Gamma Epsilon 90; Track/Field 88-89; Bible; Yth Pstr.

**MC CLURE, DEBRA A,** Univ Of South Al, Mobile, AL; SR; Educ; Tch.

**MC CLURE, JAMES P,** Va Commonwealth Univ, Richmond, VA; FR; Pltcl Sci Soc; Asst Edtr Nwsltr; Deans Lst; Pltcl Sci; Law Sch/Clg Level Educ.

**MC CLURE, JASON R,** Marshall University, Huntington, WV; JR; BBA; Acctg Clb VP 90-,Pres Elec; W Vir Soc CPA'S; Dns Lst; VITA; ACCTG Clb Vol Tutoring Svc; Intrnshp Steel W Vir; Acctg; CPA.

**MC CLURE, KATHY B,** Emory & Henry Coll, Emory, VA; JR; BA; Alpha Phi Omega Advsr 89-; Cncl Stdnt Affrs 85-; Hstry; Educ.

**MC CLURE, KEVIN R,** Univ Of Al At Huntsville, Huntsville, AL; SR; BSE; Eta Kappa Nu 89-; Omicron Delta Kappa VP 90-; Lapha Tau Omega VP 88-; IM 88-; Grk Schlrshp Awrd; Deans Lst 88-89; Elec Eng; Eng.

**MC CLURE, LAURIE,** S U N Y Coll At Fredonia, Fredonia, NY; SR; BS; Drm Cncl Rep 87-88; Hlth Serv Admn Assoc Res Dir 89-; Dns Lst 89-; Hlth Serv Admn Intrnshp 90-; Tnns Tm 87; Hlth Serv Admn; Admn.

**MC CLURE, MELISSA M,** Meridian Comm Coll, Meridian, MS; GD; Phi Beta Lambda 89-90; Schlrshp MS Assn Rehab Sec; Cert Bus/Ofc Tech 90; Sec Meridiah Comm Coll.

**MC CLURE, MICHAEL EDWIN,** Univ Of Al At Huntsville, Huntsville, AL; SR; BSE; IEEE 89-; Eta Kappa Nu 89-; Coop Educ Prog Elec Eng 89-; IM Flg Ftbl Sftbl Flr Hcky 90; Elec Eng; Eng.

**MC CLURE, MOLLIE ANN,** Univ Of Ky, Lexington, KY; SR; BA; Arts Sci Dns Schlrshp; Acdmc Exclnc Schlrshp; St Lukes Church Comm Serv Vol; Lone Oak Cntry Clb Tns Org; Eng; Prof Lit.

**MC CLURE, NANCY D,** Univ Of Charleston, Charleston, WV; FR; BS; Biology; Med.

**MC CLURE, PHYLLIS G,** Saint Josephs Coll New York, Brooklyn, NY; SR; BS; Deans Lst 90; NAACP 90; Med Sec 81-F AAS NYC Tech Coll 81; Hlth Admin; Publ Hlth.

**MC CLURE, SHERRI J,** Truett Mc Connell Coll, Cleveland, GA; SO; BED; Paraprofessional Gilmer Co School System 87-; Early Childhood Education; Teaching.

**MC CLURE, THIRZIE L,** Middle Tn St Univ, Murfreesboro, TN; SO; BS; Stdnt Ambsdr Bd Mbr 90-; Gamma Beta Phi 90-; Tau Omicron; Mass Comm; Brdcst Jrnlst TV.

**MC CLURE, TRINA R,** Middle Tn St Univ, Murfreesboro, TN; FR; BS; Stdnt Tenn Educ Assn 90-; Gamma Beta Phi 90; Elem Educ.

**MC CLUSKEY, CHRISTINE A,** Saint Vincents Coll & Seminary, Latrobe, PA; SO; BA; Cmps Mnstry 89-; IM Vlybll 90-; English.

**MC CLUSKEY JR, DAVID M,** Embry Riddle Aeronautical Univ, Daytona Beach, FL; JR; BS; Avnrs Clb 90-; Arcrft Elctrncs Assoc 90-; Cncl Mtrsprts Clb 90-; Psi Omega Pi 89-; Sigma Tau Delta 89-; Cmptr Lab Asst 88-; Outstndng Srv Awd Shoneys Rstrnt 90; IM Sftbl/Ftbl; Avnc Engrg Tech; Avnc Engr.

**MC CLUSKEY, FRANK N,** Univ Of Tn At Martin, Martin, TN; FR; BA; Tennis 90.

**MC CLUSKEY, LEE D,** West Liberty St Coll, West Liberty, WV; GD; Delta Mu Delta; Phi Alpha Theta; BS 85.

**MC CLUSKEY, MALIK D,** Morehouse Coll, Atlanta, GA; SO; BA; Mrhse Coll SGA Stdnt Cncrns Com Co Chr; Pol Sci Scty 90-; Mrn Tgr Nwsppr Edtrlst 90; Gldn Ky 90-; MPGRE Vstng Schlr Univ Of NC; Phlsphy Pol Sci; Coll Tchng.

**MC COLE, BERNADETTE M,** Saint Francis Coll, Loretto, PA; SO; Stdnt Actvts Org Pblc Rltns 90-; Pre Law Clb 90-; Theta Phi Alpha Sgt At Arms 90-; Soccer NCAA 90-; Ecnmcs; Law.

**MC COLLEY JR, JOSEPH V,** Villanova Univ, Villanova, PA; SR; BA; Res Hall Pres 87; Econ Soc 90-; Ftbl/Bsktbl/Sftbl 87-90; Phi Kappa Phi; Omicron Delta Epsilon 90-; Pi Sigma Alpha 90-; Econ Rsrch Asst 90-; Econ; Bus.

**MC COLLEY, KAREN K,** Wilmington Coll, New Castle, DE; JR; BA; New Century Clb 88-; Eliz Cir 90-; Pltry Grwr; Cnslt Skin Care Co 82-; Mngmnt Mrktng; Bus.

**MC COLLOUGH, LORI J,** Slippery Rock Univ, Slippery Rock, PA; FR; BA; Phi Sigma Pi 90-; IM Vllybll; IM Bsktbll 90-; Sprts Mgmt.

**MC COLLUM, KEVIN L,** Univ Of Tn At Knoxville, Knoxville, TN; SO; BS; Acctg; CPA.

**MC COLLUM, MICHAEL J,** Eckerd Coll, St Petersburg, FL; JR; BS; Blgy Clb 88-; Pre Med Clb 89; Vrsty Sccr 88-; Blgy; Med.

**MC COLLUM, RAYMOND E,** Fayetteville St Univ, Fayetteville, NC; JR; BA; Art Clb 90-; AAS Fytvl Tech Comm Coll 90; Vis Arts; Tchr/Instrctr.

**MC COMAS, MICHAEL T,** Univ Of Akron, Akron, OH; JR; BS; Electrical Engineering; Engineering.

**MC COMAS-STAATS, ANGELA F,** Wv Univ, Morgantown, WV; SO; BS; Scty Atmtv Eng 90-; Amrcn Scty Mchncl 90-; Presdntl Schlrshp; Grnt Exxn; Mchncl Eng.

**MC COMBIE, DANIEL T,** Mount Aloysius Jr Coll, Cresson, PA; FR; BA; O T Clb 90-; Phi Theta Kappa 90-; Home Bldrs Assn; Ltl Leag Bsbl Coach; Cert Wllmsprt Area Comm Coll 72-74; Occptnl Thrpy.

**MC COMBIE, MICHELLE A,** Indiana Univ Of Pa, Indiana, PA; FR; BED; Elem Educf Tchng/Wrtng.

**MC COMBS, LISA A,** Western Ky Univ, Bowling Green, KY; SO; AS; Hlthcare Info Systms Ldrshp Awrd 90; HCIS Class Pres 90; AMRA; Hlthcare InfoStstms; ART.

**MC COMMON, MONICA L,** Memphis St Univ, Memphis, TN; FR; BBA; Bus; Hmn Rsrces Mgmt.

**MC COMMON, SANDRA B,** Memphis St Univ, Memphis, TN; SR; Scty Advncmnt Mgmt Pres 90-; Scty Human Rsrc Mgmt; BBA Memphis St Univ.

**MC CONAHA, CAROLYN A,** Wv Univ At Parkersburg, Parkersburg, WV; SO; Comp Sci.

**MC CONAUGHY, LORRAINE L,** Northern Ky Univ, Highland Hts, KY; SO; BA; Educ; Elem/Mddl Sch Engl.

**MC CONAUGHY, MELANIE S,** Oh Coll Of Podiatric Med, Cleveland, OH; SO; DPM; Amer Coll Foot Srgns; OH Pdtrc Med Stdnt Assn 89-; Alpha Gamma Kappa Sec; Deans Lst 90-; BS OH St U 89; Pdtry.

**MC CONCHIE, LISA A,** James Madison University, Harrisonburg, VA; SR; BS; Vol Tutor 90-; Vol Crs Htln 90-; Prctcm Stdnt Frst Stp 90-; Psychlgy; Schl Cnslng.

**MC CONELL, SUMMER L,** Ms St Univ, Miss State, MS; SO; BA; Univ Hon Choir 89-; Hall Cncl Soc Progrmr 89-; Phi Eta Sigma; Jrnlsm; Publc Rltns Profsnl.

**MC CONICO, LA TONYA R,** Radford Univ, Radford, VA; JR; BA; Std Govt Asc Coord; Intl Acad Mgmt/Mktg VP; Delta Mu Delta 90-; Bsktbl Tm 88-; Sml Bsn Mgmt/Engl; Entpnr.**

**MC CONICO, VERONICA ANGELITA,** Univ Of South Al, Mobile, AL; SR; Stdnt Govt Assoc 90-; Blck Stdnt Un 87-; Shr Tm 88-; Abeneefuo Kuo 90; Yth Outrch Mnstrs 90-; Yth Cmnty Pres 88-; Tlntd Undrgrdt Mnrty Flwshp 90; Spcl Ed/Lrng Dsblts.

**MC CONKEY III, ROBERT C,** East Tn St Univ, Johnson City, TN; SO; BBA; Track/Field 90; Meth Clg Fresh Ldrshp Cncl 90-; Gamma Beta Phi 91-; Bus/Fin; Law.

**MC CONNAUGHEY, LISA J,** Wilmington Coll, Wilmington, OH; SO; BA; Ent; Teach Scndry Edn.

**MC CONNELL, ALISON L,** Le Moyne Coll, Syracuse, NY; FR; BS; Intl House 90-; Vrsty Tennis; Biology Pre Med; Medicine.

**MC CONNELL, ANGELA L,** Univ Of Nc At Greensboro, Greensboro, NC; JR; BSN; Chi Omega 87-; Nrsg; CRNA.

**MC CONNELL, BONNIE S,** Wv Northern Comm Coll, Wheeling, WV; FR.

**MC CONNELL, DEBRA A,** Central Fl Comm Coll, Ocala, FL; GD; BA; Deans Lst 89-; NAFE; Hosp Admn Coord 88-; Cert Brooks Clg 78; Bus Admn; Hlth Care.

**MC CONNELL, FELICE S,** Univ Of Nc At Charlotte, Charlotte, NC; SR; BS; Omicron Delta Kappa Pres 90-; Gldn Ky 89-; Phi Eta Sigma 88-; Odr Omega; Alpha Kappa Alpha VP 90-; Blck Stu Unn; NAACP; Stu Crt Jus; Acdmci Mrt Awrd; Dean Lst 87-; Schlrshps; Omicron Delta Kappa; Otstndng Awrd; Pre Law Soc; Crmnl Jus; Law.

**MC CONNELL, LESLIE A,** Indiana Univ Of Pa, Indiana, PA; SR; BS; Elem Educ.

**MC CONNELL, STEPHEN B,** Univ Of Tn At Martin, Martin, TN; FR; BSN; US Army Natl Grd Stf Sgt 90-; Nrsng.

**MC CONVILLE, JEANETTE B,** Central Va Comm Coll, Lynchburg, VA; FR; AA; Gen Stds; Bsn.

**MC CORD, BRIAN L,** Savannah St Coll, Savannah, GA; SR; Bus Acctg.

**MC CORD, HELEN MAE,** Middle Tn St Univ, Murfreesboro, TN; SR; BSN; ANTS 89-; Gamma Beta Phi 87-88; Kappa Delta Pi 90-; MTSU Nrsng Hon Soc Sec 90-; Phi Kappa Phi; Tau Omicron 90-; Magna Cum Laude; CRC Press Frsh Chem Achvmnt Awd; Math/Sci Awd VSCC 88-89; TN LPN Assoc 85-; Dodson Chapel UMC 88-; Hosp ICU Nrs; Nrsng.

**MC CORD, JENNIFER ANN,** Kennesaw St Coll, Marietta, GA; FR; BED; Bible Sch/Chldrn Choir; Elem Ed; Tchg.

**MC CORKLE, RICHARD C,** Unity Coll, Unity, ME; SR; La Crosse Clb 88-90; Intrnshp US Fish/Wldlf Serv 89-90; BS 90; Wldlf Mgmt; US Fsh Wlflf Serv.

**MC CORKLE, STEPHANIE L,** Memphis St Univ, Memphis, TN; SR; BS; Cir K; Chrldr; AS Pre Phys Thrpy 88-90; AS Sec Educ; Phys Thrpy; Med.

**MC CORKLE, VALLERY,** Comm Coll Algny Co Algny Cmps, Pittsburgh, PA; JR; AS; Chrch Clrk St James Bapt Chrch 7800 Bennett St Pgh PA 15208 88-; Sclgy.

**MC CORKLE, WAYNE D,** Univ Of Md At Eastern Shore, Princess Anne, MD; SR; BS; Outstanding Physical Therapy Senior; American Physical Therapy Assoc 89-; AA Harrisburg Area Comm Clg 89; Physical Theraphy.

**MC CORMACK, CHARLOTTE A,** Itawamba Comm Coll, Fulton, MS; FR; BA; Spnsh Clb Sec 90-; Ensmbl; Phi Theta Kappa 90-; Indn Dlgtn 90; Frgn Lng.

**MC CORMACK, JENNIFER A,** Oh Univ, Athens, OH; SR; BS; Amer Soc Mech Eng Sec 89-; Ntl Soc Pro Eng 90-; Paul/Irene Black Mecn Eng Schlrshp; Mach Dsgn Awd; Eng Intrn Donohue/Assoc Inc 90; Vars Ftbl Mgr 87-90; Mech Eng.

**MC CORMACK, JOANNA S,** Memphis St Univ, Memphis, TN; FR; BS; SAC Pblcty Comm 90; Gamma Beta Phi; Angl Flght/Slvr Wngs Dir Of Oprtns 90-; Bio; Med.

**MC CORMACK, SALLY A,** Univ Of New England, Biddeford, ME; SO; Varsity Soccer Tm 89-; Fr Cls Ofcr VP 89-90; Smr Intrnshp Maine Vet Home 90; Varsity Soccer 89-; Phys Therapy.

**MC CORMICK, ADRIENNE L,** Queens Coll, Charlotte, NC; SR; Phi Mu Rush Dir 89-; Cool It Natl Wildlife Federation; Signet Literary Magazine 89-; Mortar Brd Pres 90-; Phi Alpha Theta 88-; Sigma Upsilon 88-; NOW 89-; Intern Queens Wrtng Ctr; Fllwshp Exeter Clg Oxford 90; BA; English Drama; Professor.

**MC CORMICK, ANDREA D,** Univ Of Sc At Sumter, Sumter, SC; JR; BA; SEA Sec 89-; AA 90; Erly Chldhd Ed; Tchng.

**MC CORMICK, ANDREA M,** Union Univ, Jackson, TN; FR; BA; Bptst Un 90-; Rtldg Hon Hst Clb 90-; Kappa Delta Effc Chrm 90-; Poli Sci/Intl Stds; Govt Svc.

**MC CORMICK, ANNA A,** Fl St Univ, Tallahassee, FL; SO; MBA; Hl Govt 89-; Hnrs/Schlrs Pgm 89-; Fnce; Bkg.

**MC CORMICK, DAVID B,** Air Force Inst Of Tech, Wrt-Ptrsn Afb, OH; GD; MSEM; Sigma Iota Epsilon 90-; Soc Amer Mil Eng 90-; Dist Grad 90; Air Frc Comm Mdl 85-89; Air Frc; Capt U S Air Frc; Bsme Miss St Univ 81; Mech Eng; Air Force.

**MC CORMICK, ELIZABETH C,** Univ Of Al At Birmingham, Birmingham, AL; JR; BS; AL Amer Occ Ther Assns 90-; Stdnt OT Assn Rcrdng Sec 90-; Hosp/Spec Eqstrns; Delta Zeta Rfrnc Chr 84-85; Recog Sprior Perf 87; Delgt ASCOTA 90-; IM Sprts; Lab Asst 88-; BS Math 86; Occ Ther.

**MC CORMICK, JAMIE L,** Longwood Coll, Farmville, VA; JR; BS; Bus Admin; Mktg.

**MC CORMICK, JASON T,** Clarkson Univ, Potsdam, NY; FR; Outting Clg; Env Engr.

**MC CORMICK, JOHN,** Fl A & M Univ, Tallahassee, FL; SR; BA; Gldn Key 89-; Pharmacy.

**MC CORMICK, JULIE C,** Univ Of Rochester, Rochester, NY; JR; BA; Alpha Phi Pres Elect; La Crosse 88-90; English; Tech Edtr/Wrtr.

**MC CORMICK, PATRICIA A,** Columbus Coll, Columbus, GA; GD; BA; Stdnt Govt 69-71; Choir/Ensemble 69-71; Sigma Beta Sigma 69-71; PS Psychlgy 76; Art.

**MC CORMICK, SARAH A,** Univ Of Southern Ms, Hattiesburg, MS; SR; BA; Criminal Justice Assoc 87-; Gamma Beta Phi 89-; Letter J Award 89; Police Operations Award 89; Criminal Justice; Law.

**MC CORMICK, TERESA MARIE,** Ramapo Coll Of Nj, Mahwah, NJ; JR; BA; Deans Lst 89-; Delta Mu Delta 90-; Kodalux Proc Svcs 90-F; Fnc/Acctg; Fncl Mgr.

**MC CORQUODALE, MARY J,** Univ Of Sc At Columbia, Columbia, SC; SO; BA; Psychlgy; Rsrch/Psychlgy.

**MC COWEN, LINDA K,** Ringling School Of Art, Sarasota, FL; SR; BA; Inner City Big Sis; Campus Mnstry Bd 90-; Ringling Orntn 90; Prs List 89; Alpha Omicron Pi 88-89; St Petersburg Times Corp Art Intern 90-; Graphic Design Awd; Nelson Poynter Schlrshp Rcpnt 90-; RINGLING Sch Of Art & Design; Graphic Design.

**MC COWIN, GAYLE E,** Oh Univ, Athens, OH; SO; BS; ROTC 89-; Natl Soc Prshng Rifles 89-; Disc Jcky Radio; Alpha Omicron Pi 90-; Acad Achvmnt Award 89-; Civil Engr.

**MC COWN, ROBERT E,** Fl St Univ, Tallahassee, FL; SR; BS; IEEE 89-; Phi Kappa Phi 89-; Gldn Key 89-; Tau Beta Pi 90-; FAMU/FSU; Gldn Key; Tallahassee Trnmnt Drts Leag; Frmr US Nvy Sbmrn Svc 81-87; Elect Eng; Eng.**

**MC COWN, SYDNEY L,** Mary Baldwin Coll, Staunton, VA; SO; Freshman Hnr Soc 90-; Scholar Athelete Awd 90-; Var Lacrosse 90-; Psychology.

**MC COY, CASSANDRA A,** Savannah Coll Of Art & Design, Savannah, GA; SR; BA; BA 90; Fibr Arts/Txtls; Dsgn Txtls.

**MC COY, CHRISTY A,** Fl International Univ, Miami, FL; FR; BS; Baptist Campus Ministry Mission Cncl; Engl Educ; Engl Tchr.

**MC COY, DOUGLAS R,** Middle Tn St Univ, Murfreesboro, TN; SR; BUS; Univ Studies; Bus.

**MC COY, ELAINE M,** Univ Of Akron, Akron, OH; SO; BNS; AA VA Intermont Clg 68; Nrsg.

**MC COY, FRANK,** Marshall University, Huntington, WV; SO; BA; Gamma Beta Phi; Acctg.

**MC COY, JANICE A,** Comm Coll Of Beaver County, Monaca, PA; SR; AD; Tau Pi Rho; Cert Surgical Tech; Nrsng; RN.

**MC COY, JENNIFER KELLY,** Ga St Univ, Atlanta, GA; SR; BS; Pres Plaque Awd; Op Mgr Temporary Plcmnt Serv 87-89; AA Montgomery Coll 85; Early Chldhd Edn; Tchr.

**MC COY, JENNIFER L,** Memphis St Univ, Memphis, TN; GD; BA; MSU Vlybl Tm 88-90; Miami Dade S Vlybl Tm 86-88; Fl PIRG; Vol MCCA 89; AA 88; Art; Grphc Dsgnr.

**MC COY, JOHN PAUL,** Ms St Univ, Miss State, MS; SO; BS; Bapt Stdnt Un 89-; Hbt Hmnty; IM Ftbll Bsktbll Vllybll 90-; Mech Eng.

**MC COY, KATE P,** Colby Sawyer Coll, New London, NH; SR; BS; Cls Ofcr Pres 90-; Stdnt Govt Pres 89-90; All Amer Schlr Clgte Awd; Lacrosse Tm Mbr 88-; Nordic Ski Tm Capt 90-; Child Study; Early Chldhd Educ/Tch.

**MC COY, KENNETH C,** Miami Dade Comm Coll, Miami, FL; JR; Metro-Dade Cnty Risk Mgt; Busn; Law.

**MC COY, LENA V,** Chesterfield Marlboro Coll, Cheraw, SC; SO; BA; Alpha Beta Delta 90-; Phi Theta Kappa 90-; Outstndg Minority Cmnty Clg Grad 90-; SC Tech Ed Assoc Treas-Elect 90-; SC State Empl Assoc Bd Mbr 75-; Sr Acctnt CM Tech Clg; Assoc Arts; Mgmt.

**MC COY, LESLIE M,** Western Carolina Univ, Cullowhee, NC; JR; BED; Stdnt Natl Educ Assoc 90-; Stdnt Cncl Exceptl Cldrn Treas; Mrching Band 88; Hnrs Prog 88-; Outstndng Clg Stdnts Of Amer 88-89; Spec Educ Comm 90; Spec Educc; Tchr.**

**MC COY, MARY W T,** Univ Of Md Baltimore Prof Schl, Baltimore, MD; JR; BA; Veterinary Techn Hematology Labty; AA Essex Community Clg 83; Sci; Mdl Technology.

**MC COY, SHANTE J,** Alcorn St Univ, Lorman, MS; FR; BS; Psych.

**MC COY, SHARON L,** Univ Of Nc At Charlotte, Charlotte, NC; JR; BS; Deans Lst 90; Biol/Scdnry Educ; HS Tchr.

**MC COY, SUSIE Y,** Johnson St Coll, Johnson, VT; JR; BA; Bhvrl Sci Clb Treas 90-; Rgby Clb 88-; Vol Clarina Howard Nichols Ctr 90-; Psychlgy; Psychlgst.

**MC COY, THERESA M,** Auburn Univ At Auburn, Auburn, AL; SR; BSN; Sr Admsn Comm Ofcr 90-; Jr Cls VP 89-90; Campus Aflm Chi Alpha 90-; Sigma Theta Tau 90-; Chi Omega 87-; Kenneth Otis Physlgy Awrd; Auburn Assoc Nrsg Stu 90-; Nrsg; Crtcl Care Nrsg.

**MC COY, TIMOTHY S,** Univ Of Tn At Martin, Martin, TN; GD; Stdnt Govt Assn Dfndr 88; Poltcl Sci Club V P 90; Clg Democrats 86-90; Phi Kappa Phi 88-; Pi Sigma Alpha 89-; Phi Eta Sigma 86-; Kappa Alpha Order Schlrshp Chrmn 88; Rotary Fndtn Schlrshp 89; Poltcl Sci; Intl Politics.

**MC CRACKEN, KAREN L,** Indiana Univ Of Pa, Indiana, PA; JR; BS; Bio Clb; Stdnt Lit Corps; Kappa Delta Pi; Provost Schlr; Scndry Edn Bio; Teach.

**MC CRACKEN, LESLIE J,** Ringling School Of Art, Sarasota, FL; SR; BFA; Amer Soc Of Interior Designers 89-; Pr Lst 88-; Interior Design Merit Awd 89-90; BSW Univ Of W FL 81; Interior Design.

**MC CRACKEN, MICHAEL B,** Columbus Coll, Columbus, GA; SR; BS; SGA Rep Rep 90-; Crmnl Jstc Hon Scty 88-; Lamba Alph Epsln 88-; Arv Alv GA 85; Access 89; Deans List; Crmnl Jstc Stdnt Yr 90-; Pl Crmnl Jstc Natl Comp; Crmnl Jstc; Cnslr.**

**MC CRACKEN, W BRENT,** Indiana Univ Of Pa, Indiana, PA; JR; Actvts Brd 88-89; Ed Elem.

**MC CRACKIN, ANGELA M,** Univ Of Tn At Martin, Martin, TN; SO; Blck Stu Assn 89-; Alpha Kappa Alpha; Mu Epsilon Delta; Hppy Hs Dy Cr; Cane Creek Nrsng Hm; Recgntn GPA; Sci Phrmcy.

**MC CRACKIN, JAMES F,** Univ Of Sc At Columbia, Columbia, SC; GD; Flying Clb 86; Flght Instrc 88-89; Comm/Multi Engine/Inst/Flght Inst/Glider; Order Wig/Robe 90-; Phi Delta Phi 89-; Pro Bono 89; IMR Bsktbl/Rqtbl/Sftbl 88-; BA 86; JD; Law.

**MC CRANIE, WENDELL K,** Middle Ga Coll, Cochran, GA; JR; BS; Bio; Med.

**MC CRARY, ANITA B,** Univ Of Southern Ms, Hattiesburg, MS; SR; BCA; Psi Chi 90-; Psychology.

**MC CRARY, DAVID D,** Univ Of Fl, Gainesville, FL; JR; BA; Pre Lgl Soc; Phi Theta Kappa 88-90; Finance Intrn Martin Marietta Aerospc 89; AA 90; Finance; Invstmnt Bnkg.

**MC CRARY, DENISE M,** Middle Tn St Univ, Murfreesboro, TN; SR; BA; Gamma Beta Phi 89-; Kappa Delta Pi 90-; Elem Ed.

**MC CRAW, CLIFTON AMICK,** Univ Of Sc At Columbia, Columbia, SC; FR; BA; Amer Karate Clb Sec 90-; Tae Kwon Do Clb 90-; AIKIDO Clb 90-; Fllwshp Chrstn Athlts 90-; Crmnl Jstce; Law.

**MC CRAW, JENNIFER R,** Brewer St Jr Coll, Fayette, AL; SO; CMA; AS; Bus; Acctg/Corp Lawyer.

**MC CRAY, MAURICE S,** Fl A & M Univ, Tallahassee, FL; FR; BS; Pharm.

**MC CRAY, MELISSA J B,** Coll Of Charleston, Charleston, SC; SO; BA; Visual Arts Clb 90-; Studio Arts; Fine Arts.

**MC CRAY, RISPBA N,** Bennett Coll, Greensboro, NC; FR; BS; Intl Stdnts Assoc Pblc Rltns Offcr; Choir 90-; Biology Clb 90-; Mnrty Biomed Rsrch Smnr; NAACP 88-; Schlr/Deans List; All Star Tm; Biology; Medicine.

**MC CRAY, VICKY D,** Middle Tn St Univ, Murfreesboro, TN; SO; MBA; Gamma Beta Phi 90-; Alpha Kappa Psi; Bst Pldg Alph Akappa Psi 91; Acctg.

**MC CREARY, ARLINDA L,** Wilberforce Univ, Wilberforce, OH; FR; BA; Kappa Sweetheart Organ; Mktng; Wall Street Journals Mktng Dept.

**MC CREARY, TRACY D,** Ms Gulf Coast Comm Coll, Perkinston, MS; JR; BA; RA 89-90; Stdnt Cncl Exec Treas 89-90; Gospel Choir; Phi Theta Kappa 88-90; Acad Achvmnt Awd 90; Achvmnt Awd Engl 90; AA MS Gulfcoast Comm Coll 90; Jrnlsm News/Editorial; News Rptng.

**MC CREE, KATRINA P,** Johnson C Smith Univ, Charlotte, NC; SR; Bus Clb Pres 90-; Deans Lst; Vllybllf Sftbll 87-; BS; Bnkng; Mgmt.

**MC CRIMMON, MELISSA L,** Univ Of Sc At Columbia, Columbia, SC; FR; Alpha Lambda Delta; Phi Eta Sigma; Nrsng; RN.

**MC CROCKLIN, INES H,** George Mason Univ, Fairfax, VA; SR; BA; Ladies Aux Vtrns VFW 87-; Acct Spec Dept Pblc Wlfr 65-73; AA Nrthrn VA Comm Coll 80; Psychlgy-Art; Art Thrpy.

**MC CRORY, RICKY L,** William Carey Coll, Hattiesburg, MS; JR; BSN; Jr Cls Pres 90-; Amer Hrt Assoc Instr Trnr 89-; Pre Hosp Life Spprt Instr 87-; Schl Of Hlth Care Scns USAF 78; USAF 83; Nursing; EMS Educ.

**MC CRUM, ERIN MICHAEL,** Middle Tn St Univ, Murfreesboro, TN; SO; BA; Prsbyrn Stdnt Fllwshp Sec; Crss Cntry; Engl; Law.

**MC CUBBINS, KATHRYN B,** Spalding Univ, Louisville, KY; SR; Sub Tchr; Chruch Organist; BS; Elem Ed; Tchr.

**MC CUE, JACQUELINE G,** Fl International Univ, Miami, FL; SR; MSW; Natl Assoc Soc Wrkrs 90-; Phi Kappa Phi 89-; Deans Lst 89-; Intrnshp Chld Protection Tm; AA Miami Dade Comm Coll 88; BS FL Internation Univ 90; Soc Wrk.

**MC CULLAGH, EILEEN M,** Temple Univ, Philadelphia, PA; JR; BS; Amer Med Rec Assoc 90-; Hlth Rec Admin; Reg Rec Admin Dir.

**MC CULLAGH, NEIL E,** Radford Univ, Radford, VA; SR; BS; Pltcl Sci Soc 90; Radford Hon Soc 90-; Deans Lst; Pltcl Sci/Econ; Envrnmntl Law.

**MC CULLEN, JASON E,** Volunteer St Comm Coll, Gallatin, TN; SO; BS; Math; Engr.

**MC CULLISS, JENNIFER A,** Hillsborough Comm Coll, Tampa, FL; GD; AS; Rdtn Thrpy Clb 90-; Amer Cncr Soc Schlrshp; W FL Soc Rdtn Thrpy Tchnlgsts; Rdlgc Tchnlgst 89-; AS St Ptrsbrg Jr Coll 86-88; Rdtn Thrpy.

**MC CULLOUGH, AMANDA CRYSTAL,** Univ Of Sc At Spartanburg, Spartanburg, SC; SR; BS; Piedmnt Soc 89-; Gamma Psi Delta Sor Schlrshp Chrmn 89-; Fndrs Schlr 88-; Busn Admin; Finance.

**MC CULLOUGH, AMITY L,** Univ Of Sc At Spartanburg, Spartanburg, SC; FR; BA; Model Untd Ntns Prsnt Chrmn 90-; Fndrs Schlrshp; Pltcl Sci; Frgn Serv.

**MC CULLOUGH, ANISSA L,** Univ Of Sc At Columbia, Columbia, SC; SO; BA; NAACP; AAAS; Crmnl Jstc; Law.

**MC CULLOUGH, CHRISTOPHER T,** Middle Tn St Univ, Murfreesboro, TN; JR; BS; Mass Cmmnctns.

**MC CULLOUGH, DAVID A,** Wallace St Comm Coll At Selma, Selma, AL; FR; Eng.

**MC CULLOUGH, ERIKA L,** James Madison University, Harrisonburg, VA; SO; BA; Std Mnrty Otrch 89-90; Assc Dnc Ens 89-90; Cmtmpry Dnc Ens 90-; Alpha Kappa Alpha; Hnrs Schlrs Pgm 89-; Offc Mnrty Std Life Awd 89-90; Afrcn-Amer Imge Awd 90-; Clncl Psy.

**MC CULLOUGH, JULIE K,** Oh St Univ At Newark, Newark, OH; SO; MA; Ski Clb 89-90; Actvts Brd Co-Chrprsn 90-; Hnrs Clb 89-90; Alpha Lambda Delta/Phi Eta Sigma 89-90; 4-H 80-90; Phi Sigma Schlr 89-; Ambssdr 90-; AA; Clthng/Txtls: Desgn/Promotn.

**MC CULLOUGH, MEGAN,** Univ Of Sc At Columbia, Columbia, SC; SR; BS; Travelers Ins Co Schlrshp; J Key Powell Apprctn Awd; Mortor Bd VP Calendar Edtr 89-; Assc Hnr Stdnts 87-90; Kappa Kappa Gamma PR Chrmn 89-; Gamma Iota Sigma Tres 89-; Stdnt Alumni Assc 89-; Stdnt Fclty Rltns Chrmn 88-89; Gamma Beta Phi 88-; Business Adm; Insurance.

**MC CULLOUGH, PAM M,** Univ Of Al At Birmingham, Birmingham, AL; SR; BS; Kappa Delta Pi; Kappa Delta Epsilon; Gldn Key; Early Chldhd Educ; Tchr.

**MC CULLOUGH, SANDRA F,** Memphis St Univ, Memphis, TN; BA; BA; Alchl/Drgs; A/D Cnslr.

**MC CULLOUGH, STEVE,** Va Commonwealth Univ, Richmond, VA; SO; Nwspr Stf Wrtr 90; Frnch/Pol Sci; Tchng.

**MC CULLOUGH JR, THOMAS A,** Marywood Coll, Scranton, PA; SO; BS; Bio; Srgn.

**MC CULLOUGH, TRACY L,** Marywood Coll, Scranton, PA; SO; MS; Amrcn Dttc Assoc; Wght Cnsltnt Ntri Systm; Dtts; Cnslng.

**MC CULLOUGH, VANESSA,** Middle Tn St Univ, Murfreesboro, TN; SR; BA; Untd Greek Cncl; African Am Stdnt Assn; Zeta Phi Beta Pres 90-; Mrktng; Sales.

**MC CUMBER, NISSA R,** Univ Of Rochester, Rochester, NY; SR; BA; Sailing Clb 87; Spirit Org 88-89; Phi Sigma Sigma Rush Chmn 87-; Econ; Mgmnt.

**MC CUMBERS, DAVID G,** Univ Of Akron, Akron, OH; JR; BS; Bnd 88-; Kappa Kappa Psi VP 89-; Elem Ed/Art; Tchr.

**MC CUNE III, FRANK B,** Tougaloo Coll, Tougaloo, MS; JR; Acad Cmptr/Math 87-88; Bellcore Cmptr Pgmng Cntst; Cmptr Sci; Sys Analyst/Pgmr.

**MC CUNE, HEATHER C,** Va Commonwealth Univ, Richmond, VA; SO; BFA; Ramfrc 89-90; Hon Pgm 89-; Gldn Key Natl Hon Soc 90-; Pres Schlr-VCU Schlrshp 89-; Jackson Fund Intl Study Schlrshp; Art Hstry/Pntg/Prntmkng; PhD Art Hstry-Prof.

**MC CUNE, MARK S,** Univ Of Miami, Coral Gables, FL; SO; BS; Flm Assoc; AS Bnkr Hll Cmmnty Clg 90; Motion Pctres.

**MC CURDY, MOLLY A,** Univ Of Ga, Athens, GA; SR; BED; Chios Pldg Trnr 87-90; Cllgt Edctnl Srvc Corps 88; Sci Educ.

**MC CURDY JR, WILLIAM B,** S U N Y Coll Of Tech At Alfred, Alfred, NY; SO; BT; SME; Radio DJ 90-; IM 90-; AAS; Mech Eng; Eng Dsgn.

**MC CURLEY, JANETTE M,** Univ Of Akron, Akron, OH; JR; BS; Acctg Assn 90-; Fresh Frnds 88-89; Gldn Key 90-; Beta Alpha Psi; Alpha Delta Pi 87-88; Acctg.

**MC CURRY, CHARLES D,** Tn St Univ, Nashville, TN; SO; BA; ROTC Ast/Cmdr Clr Gd 90-; Elec Engr.

**MC CURRY, DENISE M,** Coll Of Charleston, Charleston, SC; SO; BS; Elem Educ; Elem Tchr.

**MC CURRY, PHILLIP K,** Northeast State Tech Comm Coll, Blountville, TN; SO; AAS; Inst Elec Engrs Inc 90-; Antioch Un Meth Chrch 68-; Stoney Crk Clggrs Applchn Trad Bg Cir 81-; Knxvl Intl Enrgy Expstn 82; Eli Witt Whlsl Inc 83-84; Allergan Phrmctls Inc 85-90; Comp Engr Tech; Comp Serv Tech.

**MC CURRY, SHERRI H,** Middle Tn St Univ, Murfreesboro, TN; SR; BS; SHEA Nwsltr Edtr Sec 88-; THEA 88-; AHEA 88-; Rita Davenport Schlrshp 90-; Tenn Rehab Schlrshp 90-; Fashion Merch; Mgmt/Buyer.

**MC CUSKER, HELEN S,** Oh Univ, Athens, OH; FR; BS; Society Women Engrs; Ohio Depart Transportation Internship; IM Volleyball; Engr; Civil Engr.

**MC CUTCHEN, VERONICA A,** Spartanburg Methodist Coll, Spartanburg, SC; FR; AA; Sga 90-; Phi Beta 90-; Phi Theta Kappa 90-; Pres Lst 90-; Chrldr 90-; Histry; Lawyr.

**MC CUTCHEON, BRANDY L,** Univ Of Sc At Columbia, Columbia, SC; SO; AA; Dean Lst 89-; Pres Lst/Hnr Rll 90; AA; Soc Sci; Educ.

**MC DADE, AIMEE K,** Middle Tn St Univ, Murfreesboro, TN; SR; BS; Chorus; Swing Choir; Dns Lst; Comm Plys; Best Actor; Dairy Sci Clb; Sftbl; Dyersburg St Comm Clg 87-89; Elem Ed; Tchr.

**MC DADE, CAROLYN,** Al St Univ, Montgomery, AL; FR; BED; Biology Educ; Tchr.

**MC DADE, JULIE A,** Union Univ, Jackson, TN; SR; BA; Linguae Mundi Sec 87-; Stdnt Activities Cncl 89-90; Bapt Stdnt Un 87-; Phi Sigma Iota 89-; Zeta Tau Alpha Schlstc Chmn 89-90; Honduras Bapt Med/Dntl Msn; Dept Human Serv 89; Spnsh; Soc Wrk Hispanics.

**MC DADE, MARY ASHLEY,** Ms St Univ, Miss State, MS; FR; BA; Rfrmd Univ Flwshp 90-; Stdnt Recrtmnt Organ 90-; Chi Omega Cmnty Srvc Comm 90-; Pres Schlr 90-; IMS 90-; Engl; Advrtsg.

**MC DANIEL, ANN O,** Tuskegee Univ, Tuskegee Inst, AL; JR; BS; Med Technlgy; Allied Hlth.

**MC DANIEL, CHARLOTTE LEE,** Univ Of Tn At Martin, Martin, TN; SR; BA; STEA 87-; OSA Chrprsn 87-; Dns Lst 88-; Elem Ed; Tchg.**

**MC DANIEL, DONNA J,** S U N Y Coll Of Tech At Alfred, Alfred, NY; GD; Hon Pgm 90; Sgm Tau Epsln 90; Hornell Ltl Leag BOD Chrmn 78-88; SKF Awrd Cmt Tres 87-88; ASSC 91; Sectrl Sci; Sec.

**MC DANIEL, HOLLY R,** Bowling Green St Univ, Bowling Green, OH; SO; BED; Marching Band 89-90; Athletic Band 90-; Help-A-Child; Hnrs Stdnt Assoc 89-; Phi Eta Sigma 90-; Math & Science; Education.**

**MC DANIEL, JAMES P,** Valdosta St Coll, Valdosta, GA; SO; BS; Natl Soc Prof Engrs 90-; Asc Coop Educ Std 90-; Pres Schlr Awd 89-90; Fdn Schlp 89-; Elec Engr.

**MC DANIEL, JENNIFER A,** Univ Of Sc At Spartanburg, Spartanburg, SC; JR; BS; Gamma Beta Phi 89-; Phi Theta Kappa 87-88; Sigma Delta Psi Treas 89-; Chldrns Hosp; Hbtt Hmnty 90; Fght Agnst Cncr Tdy 88-89; Cert Greenville Tech Col; Psychlgy.

**MC DANIEL, JESSIE R,** Univ Of Cincinnati-Clrmnt Coll, Batavia, OH; FR; BS; Phi Theta Kappa Secty 90-F Laubach Litry Tutor 90-; Certif Control Instit 88; Elec Engrg; Engrg.

**MC DANIEL, JEWELETTE G PETERSON,** Howard Univ, Washington, DC; GD; PHD; Peer Mntr Sprvsr 82-84; ASBC Orchstr Dir 89-; Chr 87-; Alpha Lambda Delta 82-; Soc Blck Phys Math Sci 83-; Fairfax Tchr Assn 88-90; Delta Sigma Theta Chrmn Msc 89-; Stu Yr; Chncllrs Awrd 83; Grad Tchng Awrd 86; Mntr Yr 83; Amer Bbl Soc Awrd 90; BS; Religion/Old Test; Prfssr.

**MC DANIEL, JOANN C,** Abraham Baldwin Agri Coll, Tifton, GA; FR; MFA; Arts Brd 90-; Drama 90; Deans Lst 90-; Art; Illust.

**MC DANIEL, LINC PARTON,** Univ Of Nc At Asheville, Asheville, NC; SR; MBA; Phi Theta Kappa 89; Cum Laude; UNCA Mngmnt Dept Dist; Mortimer Kahn Mgmnt Schlr 90-; Mgmnt Intrnshp With Med Pers Pool Of Asheville NC; AA Isothermal Cmnty Clg 89; BS; Bus Admin; Grad Schl.

**MC DANIEL, MARIA C,** Comm Coll Algny Co Algny Cmps, Pittsburgh, PA; FR; US Army Mltry Police Sldr Cycle 87-; Alld Hlth; Rsprtry Thrpy.

**MC DANIEL, MELANIE A,** Radford Univ, Radford, VA; JR; BS; Dance Theatre Stage Mgr 81-83; Natl Educ Assn 90-; Math Clb 90-; Legal Secy 80-85; Math; Math Tchr.

**MC DANIEL, MICHELE L,** Oh St Univ At Marion, Marion, OH; FR; PHD; Dns Stdnt Advsry Cncl 90-; Psych Clb 90-; Schdlng Comm; Grffn Hnr Soc 90-; Psych/Crimlngy; Psychlgst.

**MC DANIEL, MICHELLE LYNN,** Liberty Univ, Lynchburg, VA; SR; Nwspr Stf Wrtr 87-88; Coll Rpblcns 88-; Pre Law Clb 90-; Phi Alpha Theta 90-; Chi Alpha 90-; Chrstn Comm Serv Schlrshp 90-; Jrhi Yth Grp Thomas Rd Bapt Chrch 90-; GPA Schlrshp 89-90; Univ Asstnc Schlrshp 90-; Deans Lst 88-; Recog Exclnc 87-88; Hstry; Law.

**MC DANIEL, PESHEA ANNETTE,** Fl A & M Univ, Tallahassee, FL; SO; BA; Pre Law Clb 89-; Econ Clb; Chic Clb 89-; Phi Eta Sigma 90-; Dns Lst 89-; Busn Econ.

**MC DANIEL, ROBERT DEAN,** Univ Of Nc At Asheville, Asheville, NC; SR; MS; Assoc Of Comp Mach 90-; Phi Theta Kappa; AS Isothermal Cmnty Clg 89; BS; Comp Sci.

**MC DANIEL, SHEILAREE,** Morris Coll, Sumter, SC; JR; BS; Omega Psi Phi 87-; Bus Clb 89-90; Pres Lst 89-90; Dns Lst 90-; US Achvmnt Acad 90-; Bus Admin; Corp Mgmt.

**MC DANIEL, SHERRI L,** Owensboro Comm Coll, Owensboro, KY; FR; Namdra; Ausmetgy Lic Daviess Co Voc Sch 89; Radiogrphy; Radiogrphc Tech.

**MC DANIEL, SUSAN K,** Marshall University, Huntington, WV; JR; BED; Hall Advisory Cncl 88-89; Gamma Beta Phi 88-90; Phi Eta Sigma Sec 88-; Kappa Delta Pi; Pi Mu Epsilon; Paul Douglas Tchr Schlrshp 88-; Math Lang Arts; Math Tchr.

**MC DANIEL, SUSAN S,** Univ Of Southern Ms, Hattiesburg, MS; SO; BA; Gamma Beta Phi; Pres Lst 90; Comp Sci; Sftwr Dsgn.

**MC DANIEL, TRACEY P,** Johnson C Smith Univ, Charlotte, NC; JR; BA; Stdnt NC Assn Educators 90-; Harvey Gantt Cmpgn Wrkr 90; Deans Lst 90-; Navy Ofcrs Pgm Cand; Elem Edn; Tchr.

**MC DANIEL, VIRGINIA P,** Univ Of Sc At Columbia, Columbia, SC; JR; Best Buddies Sec 89-; Tchr.

**MC DANIELS, REBECCA K,** Defiance Coll, Defiance, OH; SR; BS; Assoc Stdnt Scl Wrkrs; Tau Mu 90-; Alpha Xi Delta 90-; Scl Wrk; Chld Wlfr Cs Wrkr.

**MC DAVID, CARY NICHOLAS,** Valdosta St Coll, Valdosta, GA; SR; BVE; USN Mchnst Mte 87; US Nvy Mchnst Mte 80; AS Ga Mltry Clg; Trde/Indstrl Ed; Nclr Pwr Trnr.

**MC DAVID, JACKIE J,** Bristol Univ, Bristol, TN; GD; MBA; MBA Schlrshp 89-90; Achvmnt Awd 89; Lsoc Serv 83-; Cert 75; BS 89; Bus Adm/Prsnl Hum Rsrc Mgmt; Prsnl Mgmt.

**MC DAVID, MARK S,** Va Polytechnic Inst & St Univ, Blacksburg, VA; FR; Rsdnce Hll Fed Hll Fclts; IM Sftbl; Comp Sci; Sftwre Eng.

**MC DERMET, DAVID A,** Catawba Valley Comm Coll, Hickory, NC; FR; Elec Engr Tech; Engr.

**MC DERMOTT, AMY L,** Univ Of Md Baltimore Prof Schl, Baltimore, MD; BSP; ASP; Rho Chi Schlstc Achv 90-; RN 87-; BSN RN Univ Lwll 83-87; Pharm.

**MC DERMOTT, BARBARA A,** Broward Comm Coll, Ft Lauderdale, FL; SO; BA; Phi Theta Kappa; Tchrs Asst; AA; Math/Spanish; Tch.

**MC DERMOTT, DEBORAH A,** Le Moyne Coll, Syracuse, NY; SR; BS; Blgy Clb Pres 90-; Glc Scty Yrbk Flk Grp; Echrstc Mnstr; Drm Cncl; Alpha Sigma Nu; Beta Beta Beta Pres 90-; Hmn Srvcs Assn; Prjcts In The Comm; Dept Hnrs; Magna Cum Laude; Sr Pure Sci Awrd; Blgy; Ph D.

**MC DERMOTT, KATHLEEN D,** Duquesne Univ, Pittsburgh, PA; SO; BA; Dbt/Frsncs Tm Treas 90-; Dir Ornttn Stf Co-Ldr; Hoby Almni Asc 87-; GSA 77-; Pres Awd Schlp 89-; Corp Comm; Law.

**MC DERMOTT, LISA M,** Elmira Coll, Elmira, NY; GD; MOA; Sch Picnic Harris Hill 90-; Hnr Rl 90-; St Josephs Hosp Intern 90-; Sftbl 90-; Med Ofc Asst; Med Asst/Phys Ther.

**MC DERMOTT, MICHAEL J,** Palm Beach Comm Coll, Lake Worth, FL; SO; AA; Phi Theta Kappa 89-; Stdnt Act Comm Schlrshp; Arch; Arch/Music/Law.**

**MC DERMOTT, MOLLY C,** Savannah Coll Of Art & Design, Savannah, GA; SR; BFA; Stdnt Prsrvtn Assn VP 90-; Hist Prsrvtn; Cmnty Dvlpmnt.

**MC DERMOTT, MONICA,** Villanova Univ, Villanova, PA; SO; Dem Sclsts Amer Cr 89-; Phi Kappa Phi; Pres Schlr 89-; Hist/Sclgy.

**MC DERMOTT, PATRICK M,** Memphis St Univ, Memphis, TN; SR; BS; Assoc Old Crows 85-; Boy Scouts Amer 72-; U S Navy Instr 84-; Elect Engr; U S Navy Ofcr.

**MC DERMOTT, TAMMIE J,** Castleton St Coll, Castleton, VT; JR; BS; All Amer Schlr; Elem Ed/Psychlgy; Tchr.

**MC DERMOTT, THOMAS L,** Germanna Comm Coll, Locust Grove, VA; SO; BS; Amer Crmnl Jstce Assn 89-; Jujitsu Fdrtn Asst Instrctr 88-; Shrfs Off Cadet 88-; Police Admin; Law Enfrcemnt.

**MC DEVITT, JOSEPH P,** Ms St Univ, Miss State, MS; SR; BS; Interfrat Cncl 88-90; Interfrat Jdcl Brd Rep 90-; Alpha Tau Omega VP 89-; Aerospace Eng.

**MC DEVITT, MOLLY D,** Chestnut Hill Coll, Philadelphia, PA; FR; BA; Cmps Mnstry; Std Pol Sci Asc Rep; Intdprtmntl Hnrs Pgm Rep; Hlpng Hmls Philly; Pol Sci/Phlsphy; Govt.

**MC DEW, SONJI F,** Saint Joseph Coll, West Hartford, CT; GD; Nrsng Club 88-90; Sisters Grp 86-90; Hartford Hospty Intern 87-90; Nrsng Assist 89-90; Hosp Mdl/Oncology Nurse 90-; BSN 90; Nursing.

**MC DILDA, MARTHA A,** Univ Of Va Clinch Valley Coll, Wise, VA; SR; BS; AAS VIR Hghlnds CC 88; Bus Admn/Accntng.

**MC DONALD, AMELIA E,** Univ Of Nc At Charlotte, Charlotte, NC; FR; BA; Soc Act Clb 90-; Bus Admin/Acctng; CPA.

**MC DONALD, ANDREA A,** Howard Univ, Washington, DC; JR; BS; Class 1992 VP 90-; Stdnt Natl Pharmaceutical Assoc Asst Sec; Golden Key 89-; Rho Chi Public Rltns Ofcr 90-; Kappa Psi; Deans Lst 88-; Recognition Awrd Rho Chi 90; Outstndng Achvmnt Awrd 89; Pharmacy; Drug Info Specialist.

**MC DONALD, ANNA H,** Daytona Beach Comm Coll, Daytona Beach, FL; FR; ADN; Grnpc Intl/Wrld Wldf Fnd; Envrnmntl Defns Fnd; Med Sec To RN; Cert 84; Nursing; Neonatal.

**MC DONALD, BONITA G,** Thomas Nelson Comm Coll, Hampton, VA; SO; AA; Dept Social Serv Vol 88-89; Liberal Arts; Teach/History.

**MC DONALD, CASSANDRA D,** California Univ Of Pa, California, PA; FR; BS; Blgy; Chrprctc.

**MC DONALD, CHRISTIAAN L,** Univ Of Al At Birmingham, Birmingham, AL; SR; BA; Better Earth Scty 90-; Gldn Key; Omicron Delta Epsilon; Ecnmcs; Rsrch Analysis.

**MC DONALD, CHRISTINE M,** Mount Saint Mary Coll, Newburgh, NY; SO; BA; Clg Dmcrts 89-; Gaelic Soc Sec 89-; CARE Stdnt Envrnmntl Grp 90-; Admssns Clb 90-; Mt St Mary Clg Merit Schlrshp 89-; Hist; Ed.

**MC DONALD, CHRISTY L,** Fl St Univ, Tallahassee, FL; JR; MA; Cncl For Excptnl Chldrn 90-; Golden Key 90-; Paul Douglas Schlrsph 88-; Deans List 89-; AA 89; Spec Edn; Teach.

**MC DONALD, CLIFTON M,** Millsaps Coll, Jackson, MS; FR; BBA; Clg Rpblcns; Kappa Alpha; Vrsty Soccer; Acctg; Law.

**MC DONALD, DANIEL C,** Ms St Univ, Miss State, MS; SR; BS; Choir; Nicholls St Engr Soc 88-89; LA Engr Soc 88-89; Tau Kappa Epsilon 87-; Outsdng Grad Sr Engr Tech 89; BS Nicholls St Univ 89; Elec Engr; Start Own Engr Firm.

**MC DONALD, DEBORAH D,** Lincoln Univ, Lincoln Univ, PA; SR; Accntng Clb 88; Bsnss Clb 88; NAACP Campus Chptr 89; Delta Sigma Theta Treas.

**MC DONALD, DEMETRA E,** Hampton Univ, Hampton, VA; SR; BA; Africa Stds Clstr; Sstrhd Coord 88-; SGA Attrny Gnrl 89-; Alpha Kappa Mu 89-; Deans Lst 90-; Pltcl Sci; Law Pltcl Scntst PHD.**

**MC DONALD, DENISE M,** Univ Of Rochester, Rochester, NY; SO; BA; Air Force ROTC 89-; D Lions Org 90-; Deans List 89-; Arnold Sir Soc Dpty Cmndr 90-; Selctd Resdnt Advsr Jr Yr; Cdt Of The Yr 90; Mac Guire AF Bs Run 1st Woman In 10k; Math; Tchng/AF.

**MC DONALD, DIANA G,** Univ Of Tn At Knoxville, Knoxville, TN; JR; BA; Accts Pybl; AS St Tech Inst At Knoxville 85; Accntng.

**MC DONALD, DONNA L,** Hampton Univ, Hampton, VA; FR; BSN; NROTC MPO; Prjct LEARN 90-; Stdnt Nrs Hlthcr Scrng; USN 87-90; USNR 90-; Mltry Nrs.

**MC DONALD, ELLEN,** Dowling Coll, Oakdale Li, NY; SR; BA; Phi Theta Kappa 89; Ins Clrk 73-86; AS SUNY 90; Elem Educ; Tchr.

**MC DONALD, HUGH W,** William Carey Coll, Hattiesburg, MS; SO; BSB; Pre Law Society Secty 90-; Phi Beta Lambda 90-; Accounting; Law.

**MC DONALD, JACQUELINE R,** Tn St Univ, Nashville, TN; JR; BS; Gospel Choir Secy 89-; T E Poag Plyrs Guild Secy 90-; Bapt Stdnt Union; Phi Beta Lambda 89-; Alpha Kappa Alpha 90-; Political Sci; Criminal Law.

**MC DONALD, JAMES F,** Alcorn St Univ, Lorman, MS; SR; MPA; Stdnt Govt Assoc Pres 89-90; Stdnt Sen VP 90-; Pol Sci Club Sen 90-; Alpha Kappa Mu Pres 90-; Hons Stdnt Org Pres 88-90; Southrn Regnl Hons Cncl VP 90-; Oasis Fox Masonic Ldg 75 Secy; Patricia Roberts Harris Publc Svc Fellowshp; Pol Sci; MA/LAW Sch.

**MC DONALD, JAMES W,** Univ Of Louisville, Louisville, KY; MBA; AIPE; Phi Eta Sigma 89-; Visit Nrsng Hm; Cooped Burroughs Wellcome Co; Chmcl Eng; Eng.

**MC DONALD, JENNIFER S,** Ms St Univ, Miss State, MS; JR; DVM; Rfrmc Univ Fllwshp 89-; Prsbytrn Coll Fllwshp 88-; Prsdnts Lst; Sci; Vet.

**MC DONALD, JESSICA D,** Ms St Univ, Miss State, MS; JR; BA; Campus Nwspr Staff; Yrbk Staff Section Edtr; Misscom; Gamma Beta Phi 90-; Phi Eta Sigma 90-; Vicksburg Theater Guild 90-; Univ Hnrs Coun 90-; Comm Mgt; Public Reltns.

**MC DONALD, JOSEPH D,** Univ Of The Dist Of Columbia, Washington, DC; GD; Epsilon Sigma; Natl Hon Soc; Grad Cum Laude 90; Staff Of Cmte On Judiciary U S House Of Reps 81-; U S Air Force 60-81; BBA 90; Bus Mngmnt.

**MC DONALD, LESLIE A,** Univ Of Nc At Greensboro, Greensboro, NC; JR; BA; Elem Educ; Tchng.

**MC DONALD, LISA K,** Indiana Univ Of Pa, Indiana, PA; SR; BED; PSEA 90-; NEA 90-; STRIDE Tutrg Pgm 88-89; Pre Tchng 89-90; Elem Ed; Edctr.

**MC DONALD, LULA A,** Asbury Theological Sem, Wilmore, KY; GD; MDIV; BA 86; Theology; Evangelist.

**MC DONALD, MARIE A,** Miami Jacobs Jr Coll Of Bus, Dayton, OH; ASSOC; Dayton Ostomy Pres; Sectrl/Info Procsng; Ofc Mgr.

**MC DONALD, MARY L,** Fl International Univ, Miami, FL; SR; BPA; Bg Brthrs/Bg Sistrs 86; AA Miami Dade Comm Coll 80; Pub Admin; Law/Govt.

**MC DONALD, MICHELE M,** Temple Univ, Philadelphia, PA; JR; BA; Psi Chi Sec 89-90; Alpha Lamda Delta; Gldn Ky; Crmnl Jst Soc 89-; Dean Lst 88-; Gldn Ky Awrd; Psychlgy.

**MC DONALD, MIRANDA D,** Tougaloo Coll, Tougaloo, MS; JR; BA/BS; Stdnt Support Svc 88-; Pre Hlth Club 89-; Hnrs Pre Med Pgm Baylor Med Schl; Psych/Bio; Med Schl.

**MC DONALD, PATRICK L,** Le Moyne Owen Coll, Memphis, TN; JR; BA; Phi Beta Lamda 86; Co-Op Stdnt IRS 85; Unresolved Accts Examiner IRS; Cert Qtrmstr Sch Ft Lee Va 81; AA Hinds Jr Comm Coll Raymond Ms 86; Acctng; CPA/ REVENUE Agent.

**MC DONALD, ROBERT L,** Selma Univ, Selma, AL; JR; BA; Natl Red Cross Life Guard 66-68; NAACP V P 88-; Religion/ Educ; Tch.

**MC DONALD, RODNEY J,** Wv Univ At Parkersburg, Parkersburg, WV; SO; BA; Boy Scouts Of Amer Eagle Scout Asst Sctmstr 80-; Cert Arch Moore Jr Voctnl Ctr 80-81; Soc Studies; Tchr.

**MC DONALD, ROSLYN L,** Norfolk St Univ, Norfolk, VA; JR; Student Gvt Assocf Yng Democrats VP 90-; Student Senate Secty 90-; Elk Gate Keeper 87-90; Vlybl Cptn 90; Political Sci/Pre Law; Law.

**MC DONALD, SCOTT C,** Spartanburg Methodist Coll, Spartanburg, SC; SO; BS; Newspr 90-; Phi Theta Kappa 90-; Alpha Mu Gamma 90-; Habitat Hmnty 90-; AS; Bio; Med Schl.

**MC DONALD, SHARON K,** Williamsburg Tech Coll, Kingstree, SC; SO; BA; Alchl Drg Abs Cncl Cmmnty Tsk Frc Chrprsn 90-; Phi Theta Kappa Pres 90-; AA; Psychlgy.

**MC DONALD, SHAWN E,** Old Dominion Univ, Norfolk, VA; JR; BS; Stdnt Senate Sntr; Mace/Crown Stdnt Nwspr Cmntry Ed; Acad Hon Assn 90-; Phi Kappa Phi; Pi Tau Sigma; Gold Key; ASME 90-; Dsgntd Natl Merit Schlr 89-; Left Flbck Div Champ Soccer Tm 90-; Mech Eng.

**MC DONALD, THOMAS A,** Medical Univ Of Sc, Charleston, SC; GD; DMD; ASDA Pres 90-; Phi Eta Sigma 83; Alpha Lambda Delta 83; Order Of Omega 89-; Psi Omega 89-; Phi Delta Theta VP 84-86; Cleveland Awd 89; Sneed Awd; BS Clemson Univ 86; Dental Medicine; Dentist.

**MC DONALD, THOMAS E,** Central Al Comm Coll, Alexander City, AL; FR; AA; Eng; Tch.

**MC DONALD JR, THOMAS J,** Ga Southern Univ, Statesboro, GA; FR; BSE; Distance Runner 86-; Scndry Ed/History; Teach.

**MC DONALD, VANESSA A,** Georgetown Univ, Washington, DC; SO; BS; Orgztn Intl Stdnts 89-90; AIBEC 89-90; Div Var Swmng 90-; Intl Afrs; Foreign Serv.

**MC DONALD, ZANDRA R,** Tougaloo Coll, Tougaloo, MS; JR; BA; Oprtn Shoestrng Tutrl Pgm 89-; Alpha Lambda Delta Pres 89-90; Pres Schlrshp 88-; Pres Schlr Lst 89-; Engl; Tchr/ Admnstrtr/Bus Ownr.

**MC DONNEHEAD, TOSHIKA C,** Fl A & M Univ, Tallahassee, FL; FR; BS; NASA Schlrs Assn 90-; Pres Schlrs Assn 90-; NASA Intern Kennedy Space Cntr; Chem Eng; Chem Biomed Eng.

**MC DONNELL, LORI A,** Elms Coll, Chicopee, MA; FR; BA; Grad Cmt; Pres Schlrshp; Hist; Prfsr.

**MC DONOUGH, JOHN B,** Thomas Nelson Comm Coll, Hampton, VA; GD; AAS; NASA/LARC Instr Rsrch 90; Elec Eng; BS Eng.

**MC DONOUGH, SEAN P,** Univ Of Fl, Gainesville, FL; SR; BS; Sigma Phi Epsilon Brotherhood Develpt Trainer 86-; Finance/ Acctng; Acctn Inverst Bnkng.

**MC DOUGALL, MIKKI P,** Central Fl Comm Coll, Ocala, FL; GD; ADN; Paramedic 88-; AS EMS 90; Nrsng; Trauma Nrs.

**MC DOWELL, COLLEEN J,** Fl St Univ, Tallahassee, FL; GD; BA; 1st Cls Orn Ldr 90; Lambda Chi Alpha 90; FEA 90; CEUSAC 90; Intrn Leila G Davis Elem Sch; AA 89; Elem Educ; Tchr.

**MC DOWELL JR, JAMES W,** Univ Of Cincinnati, Cincinnati, OH; FR; BA; Amer Mtrcyclst Assn 82-; Mech Eng.

**MC DOWELL, KARA E,** Richard Bland Coll, Petersburg, VA; SO; BA; Nwsppr Stff 89-90; Spnsh Clb 89-90; Phi Thetta Kappa 89-90; Dean Lst 89-90; Pres Lst 89; Cum Laude; AA; Ecnmcs.

**MC DOWELL, KATHERINE PENNY,** Oh Wesleyan Univ, Delaware, OH; JR; BA; Kappa Delta Pi; Mortar Bd Inc; Elem Edn; Tchr.

**MC DOWELL, KATHERINE R,** Spartanburg Methodist Coll, Spartanburg, SC; SO; Day Stdnts Assc 90-; Deans Lst 90-; AA.

**MC DOWELL, KIMBERLY D,** Fl A & M Univ, Tallahassee, FL; SO; BS; Army ROTC 89-; FFEA; White Gold Hnr Scty; Gamma Sigma Sigma Chaplain 90-; All Amer Schlr; Natl Cllgt Educ Awrd; AROTC Soph Superior Cadet Awrd; Rattlerette Bsktbl Mgr 89-90; Elem Educ; Teaching.

**MC DOWELL, SETH T,** Spartanburg Methodist Coll, Spartanburg, SC; FR; Psi Beta; Phi Theta Kappa 90-; Bsbl 90-; Sci; Med.

**MC DOWELL, TAMMY J,** Northern Ky Univ, Highland Hts, KY; JR; BA; Sigma Tau Delta Treas; Hon Prog 89-; English; Mktg.

**MC DUFFIE, KATHLEEN J,** Piedmont Coll, Demorest, GA; JR; BS; Torch Soc; Dean Schlr 88-90; Biol; Tchng.

**MC EACHERN, KARLA S,** Univ Of Nc At Greensboro, Greensboro, NC; GD; MED; Neo Black Soc 90-; Res Coll Orntn Staff; IM Prog; BS 90; Spec Edn-Cross-Categorical; Teach Disabled.

**MC EACHIN, CRYSTAL J,** Georgetown Univ, Washington, DC; SO; BSBA; NAACP Sec 90-; Busn Day Strng Comm; Stdnt Affrs Prog Asst; Delta Sigma Theta Tr; Acctg Intrn; Acctg/Mgmt.

**MC EACHRON, SUSAN M,** S U N Y Coll Of A & T Morrisvl, Morrisville, NY; FR; AS; Stdnt Govt Org 90-; Friars Drama Clb 90-; Newsmans 90-; Delta Psi Omega Sec 90-; Lib Arts; Sociology.

**MC ELHANON, NOREEN A,** Asbury Theological Sem, Wilmore, KY; GD; MA; Intl Soc Of Theta Phi 90; Alpha Delta Mu; Smr Inst Of Lingstcs 62-; ASW 90-; Wycliffe Bible Trnsltrs 62-; Lit/Commnty Dvlpmnt New Guinea 64-86; MSW Univ Of KY 90; Prsh Cnslng.

**MC ELHINNY, BRAD D,** Marshall University, Huntington, WV; FR; Stdnt Nwspr Athltc Crrspndnt; Soc Prfsnl Jrnlsts; Phi Eta Sigma; Rookie Yr Jrnlsm; Sports Wrtr Yr; Parkersburg Sentinel Intern; BA; Jrnlsm.

**MC ELHINNY, MARK E,** Westminster Coll, New Wilmingtn, PA; SO; BA; Hstry Clb; Sigma Nu 90-; William Botsford Schlrshp 90-; Dean Lst 89-; Bsktbl Crss Cntry Trck 89-; Hstry/Sec Educ; Law/Tchng.

**MC ELRATH, DERRICK S,** Central St Univ, Wilberforce, OH; FR; BA.

**MC ELRATH, TONYA L,** Univ Of Sc At Columbia, Columbia, SC; SR; BS; Early Chldhd Ed; Ed.

**MC ELROY, GINGER L,** Union Univ, Jackson, TN; FR; BA; Stdnt Fndtn; Un Univ Rep Spkr TN Bapt Cnvntn 90; Chi Omega Cmnty Serv Chmn; Engl; Scndry Edn.

**MC ELROY, JAMES MERLE,** Univ Of Nc At Asheville, Asheville, NC; GD; Hon Prog 88-89; Corp Trng 86-89; Sub Tchr 89; Tutor 89; Tch 66067; Un Cerebral Palsy 86-88; Kiwanis Cl 80-81; Mrktg Rep 67-76; AB Un/Ga 65; AA Campbell Colg 63; Edctn; Tch.

**MC ELROY, JENNIFER A,** Univ Of Nc At Greensboro, Greensboro, NC; SO; BA; Assn Ed Yng Chldrn 89-90; Stdnt NC Assn Edctrs 90-; Cmps Actvts Brd Film/Video Clb 89-; Schl Hmn Envrnmntl Sci Schlr 89-; Ed/Child Dvlpmnt; Tchng.

**MC ELROY, LYNN A,** Comm Coll Algny Co Algny Cmps, Pittsburgh, PA; SO; AAS; Stdnt Nrs Assn PA; Phi Theta Kappa; Nrsng Asst; Cert Cotech-Ptsbrgh Diocese 85; Nrsng.

**MC ELROY, NANCY M,** Immaculata Coll, Immaculata, PA; JR; Soph Cls Pres 89-90; Fresh Hall Rep 88-89; Campus Mnstry 88-90; Lambda Iota Tau Pldg Initiate Pres 89-; Delta Kappa Gamma Soc Awd 90-; UPS Schlrshp Awd 90-; English; Sec Educ.

**MC ELVEEN, CATHY L,** Ms St Univ, Miss State, MS; SR; BA; Blck Frrs Drma Cty Prop Hd 89-; Stdnt Hlth Advsry Com Chrmn 89-; Intrntl Stdnt Srvcs; Gamma Beta Phi 89-; Lambda Sigma Mmbrshp Com 90; Crdnl Ky 90-; Delta Gamma Art Com; Gamma Beta Phi 89-; Lambda Sigma Mmbrshp Com 90; Crdnl Ky 90-; Schlrshp 88-; Cmmnctns PR; Med.

**MC ELWAIN, MARY R,** Ramapo Coll Of Nj, Mahwah, NJ; SO; BA; Medcl Asstnt; Exec Secy; Cert Hohokus Sch 84-85; Litrtr.

**MC ELWAIN, NICOLE L,** Univ Of Ky, Lexington, KY; FR; BA; Alpha Lambda Delta 90-; Lambda Sigma; Pi Beta Phi 90-.

**MC ELYEA, BRIAN E,** Widener Univ, Chester, PA; SR; BS; Soc Adv Mgt; Delta Mu Delta; Omicron Delta Epsilon; Dean Lst; US Navy; Dir Self Hlp Prjts Navy Day Cr Cntr; AA Chaminade Univ 89; Dntl Asst US Navy 81; Hmn Rsrc Mgt; Hosp Admn.

**MC ENROE, DANNA M,** Brescia Coll, Owensboro, KY; JR; BA; KY Educ Assc Fr Stdnts 90-; Elem Educ/Engl; Tchr.

**MC ENTEE, THOMAS F,** Northern Ky Univ, Highland Hts, KY; JR; BA; Schlrshp Intlt Studies Summer Study Abroad Prog 90; German; Aviation Mgt.

**MC ENTYRE, JAMESIE H,** Birmingham Southern Coll, Birmingham, AL; JR; BA; Altrusa Clb Schlrshp; Phi Eta Sigma 90-; Alpha Lambda Delta 90-; Alpha Sigma Lambda 90-; Bus; Acctng.

**MC EVOY, DONALD A,** Life Coll, Marietta, GA; GD; DC; Cls Cncl Pres 90-; KC Frst Dgre 90-; BSA Eagle Sct 70-77; Amer Soc Rdlgc Tech 81-; Reg Rdlgc Tech Amer Rgstry 81-; Cert Bartone Schl Rdgrphy 81; Dctr Chrprctc.

**MC EVOY, KAREN A,** Kent St Univ Kent Cmps, Kent, OH; FR; BA; Krb Hl Hs Cncl Flr Rep 90-; Alpha Lambda Delta; Prsdnts Lst 90-; Psychlgy; Phd.

**MC EVOY, PAUL E,** Bristol Univ, Bristol, TN; SO; BA; Med Rtrd US Mrne Crps 70-86; US Post Srvc 87-; Bus Admn; US Pstl Srvc Mngmt.

**MC EVOY, SHARON A,** Teikyo Post Univ, Waterbury, CT; JR; BS; Assoc Gnrl Studies Mattatuck Cmmnty Clg; Fnce; Fncl Anlysr.

**MC EWEN, CHRIS J,** Univ Of Southern Ms, Hattiesburg, MS; FR; BS; Pride MS 90-; Symph 90-; Symph Bnd 90-; Phi Mu Alpha 90-; Music/Bus.

**MC FADDEN, JACQUELYN R,** Fisk Univ, Nashville, TN; SO; Hlth Careers Clb 89-; NAACP; Alpha Kappa Alpha; Biolgy/ Pre-Med; Med Dctr.

**MC FADDEN, JOSEPH P,** Bridgeport Engr Inst, Fairfield, CT; JR; BED; Tau Alpha Pi; Soc Plstcs Engrs; Engr Cnsltnt; CAE Plstcs; Assoc/Mech Engr Norwalk St Tech Clg 82; Mech Engr; Consltnt CAE.

**MC FADDEN, LISA A,** Bryant Stratton Bus Inst Roch, Rochester, NY; SO; AOD; Deans Lst 90-; Cmptrs; Prgrmng.

**MC FADDEN, MARK D,** Bapt Bible Coll & Seminary, Clarks Summit, PA; JR; BS; Married Stdnts Assoc Pres 90; Stock Brkr Robert Thomas Sec 87; Bible; Mssnry/Pstr.

**MC FADDEN, MAUREEN,** Glassboro St Coll, Glassboro, NJ; SR; BA; On Campus Job Personnel Ofc File Clerk & Typist 89-; Gamma Tau Sigma 90-; Eng Hnr Soc; Alpha Epsilon Phi Pres 90; Alpha Epsilon Phi Philanthropy Chiam Sheba; Deans List Member 89-; Tennis 87; Eng Secndry Ed; H S Eng Tchr.

**MC FADDEN, NANCY E,** Lenoir Rhyne Coll, Hickory, NC; SR; BA; Goldn Key 89-; Tchnlgy Trnsfr Soc 86-88; Chmbr Sngrs 87-90; Mstr Chorale 89; NASA Comp Sftwr Mgt Cntr 84-88; Engl; Grad Schl.

**MC FALL, CAROL RENEE,** Memphis St Univ, Memphis, TN; FR; Phi Eta Sigma 90-; Mgmnt Info Sys; Cmptrs.

**MC FALL, PATRICIA A,** Glassboro St Coll, Glassboro, NJ; JR; BA; SGA Sntr 88-89; Rsdnt Stdnt Assn-Dorm VP 88-89; Gamma Tau Sigma; Sigma Sigma Sigma Sec 88-; Wrstlng 88-89; Hstry; Tchng.

**MC FALL, SAMETRIA R,** Savannah St Coll, Savannah, GA; JR; BA; Yrbk Stf Edtr 90-; Debate Tm Sec 90-; Acdmc Cnsl Stdnt Rep 90-; Beta Beta Beta 89-; Beta Kappa Chi Asst Sec 89-; Delta Sigma Theta; Natl Hon Soc 89-; Biolgy/Engl; PhD Mcrobiolgy.**

**MC FALLS, BARBARA J,** Roane St Comm Coll, Harriman, TN; SO; BS; Deans Lst; PTO Sec 89-90; Prchsng Assc; AS; Educatin; Hmn Rsrcs.

**MC FARLAND, ANDREW B,** Univ Of Akron, Akron, OH; SO; BSEE; Campus Radio Sta 89-90; Phi Eta Sigma 90-; Alpha Lambda Delta 90-; Stdnt Asst Cmmnctns Dept 90-; Elec Engr.

**MC FARLAND, CECILIA E,** Sinclair Comm Coll, Dayton, OH; GD; BA; Dns Lst; Mt Olive Bapt Church Mass Choir 81-; Dayton Bd Ed Trng/Support Spec; AS 86; Mgmt; Mgmt/Cmptrs.

**MC FARLAND, DALTON E,** Univ Of Tn At Martin, Martin, TN; JR; BA; IEEE 90-; Elec Engr Tech; Engr.

**MC FARLAND, GLENDA F,** Daytona Beach Comm Coll, Daytona Beach, FL; FR; BA; Educ; Tchng.

**MC FARLAND, JAMES H,** Union Coll, Barbourville, KY; JR; BM; Choir Accmpst 88-; Iota Sigma Nu 89-; Chrch Music.

**MC FARLAND, JEANNIE MARIE,** Univ Of Nc At Charlotte, Charlotte, NC; JR; Brtndng; Psychlgy.

**MC FARLAND, KATHY R,** Univ Of Montevallo, Montevallo, AL; SR; BS; Speech Lang Hrng Assoc 87; Bapt Campus Mnstries 87; Deans Lst 88; Im 88; Speech Pthlgy.

**MC FARLAND, KELLY ANN,** Manhattanville Coll, Purchase, NY; SR; BA; Intl Clb Secr/V P 87-88; Core Crew/Tour Guide Co-Chr 88-; Model U N Clb Del 88-; Touchstone Wrtr 87-88; Manhattanville Ambsdrs 88-89; Judicial Bd 90-; Res Asst 89; Stdnt Advsr/Peer Advsr 88-89; Keio H S NY Tchg Asst; Embassy Japan Inter 90; Intl/Asian Studies; Govt.

**MC FARLAND, MARY K,** Bethany Coll, Bethany, WV; SO; BA; Chrstn Flwshp Co-Chr 90-; Nwspaper Nws Edtr; Soc Collgt Jrnlsts; Zeta Tau Alpha 90-; Res Asst 90-; Cmnctns; Phto Jrnlsm.

**MC FARLAND, SANDRA L,** Elmira Coll, Elmira, NY; SO; BA; Intl Clb; Dorm Cncl Rep; Math; Tchng.

**MC FARLIN, KATHRYN S,** Univ Of Montevallo, Montevallo, AL; JR; BS; Hnr Soc 88-89; Hnrs; Deans Lst 88-; Alpha Lambda Delta 88-; Elem Erly Chldhd Ed; Tchr.

**MC FATE, AUTUMN H,** Duquesne Univ, Pittsburgh, PA; SO; BS; Var Crw 89-; Camus Mnstry 89; IM Acvty 89-; ROTC 89-; Admsns Vol 89-; Lambda Sigma Prlmntrn 89-; Campus Mnstry; Fndrs Schlrshp; Arts/Sci Grnt; IM Tms; Bio; Med Sch.

**MC FEE, AMY L,** S U N Y Coll At Fredonia, Fredonia, NY; SO; BFA; Prfrmng Arts Co 89-; Aurora Plyrs Inc 90-; S Buffalo Theatre Co 90-; Alpha Psi Omega; Deans Lst 89-; Orchesis Dance Co 89-; Theatre Prfrmnc; Actress.

**MC FELEA, BEVERLY A,** Owensboro Comm Coll, Owensboro, KY; SO; ASSOC; Physical Sci.

**MC FELEA, COLEEN J,** Univ Of Louisville, Louisville, KY; SO; MENG; Stdnt Govt Rep 90-; Soc Of Women Engrs Chrprsn 90-; Amer Soc Of Mech Engrs; Phi Eta Sigma 90-; Golden Key; Pi Beta Phi Rush Chrmn 90-; Tchng Asst For Engr Graphics; Tau Beta Pi Frshmn Of Yr Alumni Schlrshp; IM Sports; Mech Engr.

**MC GARRIL, FREDERICK L,** Bergen Comm Coll, Paramus, NJ; GD; Phi Theta Kappa Pres 89-90; Tuchman Awd Mrt 89; Phi Theta Kappa Outstndng Srvc Awd 89-90; BCC Crim Jstc Awd Wnr; NJ Trfc Acdnt Rcnstrctnt Assoc; SGT Bergenfield Plc Dept 83-90.

**MC GARRY, ANDRYA M,** Embry Riddle Aeronautical Univ, Daytona Beach, FL; FR; BA; Yth All-City Tm Bowling Capt; Engr; Aerosp Engr.

**MC GARRY, TERENCE D,** Saint Thomas Univ, Miami, FL; FR; BA; Psych.

**MC GARVEY, MATTHEW P,** Le Moyne Coll, Syracuse, NY; FR; BA; Vrsty Golf Tm 90-; Bus Admin; Mktg.

**MC GARY, TERRANCE MARCEL,** Morehouse Coll, Atlanta, GA; JR; BA; Morehouse Acctg Assoc 90-; Morehouse Bus Assoc 88-; Morehouse Real Estate Club; Morehouse Clge Hnr Roll 89-; Cargill Schlrshp Recpnt; Fed Natl Mortgage Assoc Intrn; State Farm Ins Co Intr 90; Banking Finance Real Estate; Financial Conslt.

**MC GEE, AMANDA F,** Univ Of Sc At Aiken, Aiken, SC; SO; BA; Pre Law Clb Sec/Treas 90-; Amnsty Intl; Gamma Beta Phi Pres 90-; Pres Hon Roll 89-; Deans List 89-; Lgl Asst 89-; Pltcl Sci/Hist; Law.**

**MC GEE, ANDREA E,** Commonwealth Coll, Virginia Beach, VA; SR; AAS; Acctg Club; Alpha Beta Gamma; Pres Lst; Dns Lst; Acctg; Auditing/Tax Preparation.

**MC GEE, CYNTHIA H,** Hillsborough Comm Coll, Tampa, FL; SO; AS; Stdnt Nrs Org 90-; St Josephs Hosp-Hillsborough Cmnty Clg Nrsg Ed Challenge Grant Fund Schlrshp 90-; Nrsg.

**MC GEE, DEBORAH A,** Broome Comm Coll, Binghamton, NY; FR; BA; Newman Hse Cncl 90-; Lit/Creative Wrtng Law/Scty; Law.

**MC GEE, DEBRA A,** Williamsburg Tech Coll, Kingstree, SC; SO; BA; Phi Theta Kappa Sec; Chem.

**MC GEE, FRANCHESKA E,** Fl A & M Univ, Tallahassee, FL; FR; BA; SGA 90-; Math Chmstry; Elctrcl Engnrng.

**MC GEE, JAMES M,** Univ Of Southern Ms, Hattiesburg, MS; FR; BS; Bcchs 90; Stdnt Almn Assoc 90; Stdnt Egl Clb 90; Plymr Sci Clb 90; Bapt Stdnt Un 90-; Stdnts Agnst Rp; Alpha Lambda Delta Sec; Phi Eta Sigma; Gamma Beta Phi; Lambda Sigma; Alpha Epsilon Delta 90-; Lambda Sigma; IM Sprts 90; Plymr Sci.

**MC GEE, JASON D,** Valdosta St Coll, Valdosta, GA; FR; BS; Cmptr Sci; Cmptr Opr/Prog.

**MC GEE, JENNIFER L,** Colby Sawyer Coll, New London, NH; SO; BFA; Art Stdnts League V P 89-; Drama Club 89-; Key Assoc 90-; Stdnt Acdmc Cnslr 90-; Alpha Chi Pres 90-; Town Art Proj W/Tommy Depaola 90; Fine Arts; Prof/Maine Illustrator.

**MC GEE, JOSEPH P,** Glassboro St Coll, Glassboro, NJ; FR; BA; ROTC Guidon Bearer 90-; Hcky Capt 90-; Superior Cadet Awd ROTC; Smth Fndtn Awd ROTC; Psychlgy; Army/Aviation.

**MC GEE, KIMBERLY C,** Bethel Coll, Mckenzie, TN; SR; Stdnt Govt Assoc 88-90; Class Pres 89-90; Math Clb VP 88-; Gamma Beta Phi 89-; Alpha Phi Sigma Secy 89-; Stdnt Life Secy 90-; Hmcmng Comm 89-; Natrl Sci Scty 90-; Martha Stobbe Math Schlrshp 90-; Schlr 90-; Math; Medcl Physcs.

**MC GEE, MARILYN J,** Memphis St Univ, Memphis, TN; SR; BS; Assn On Yng Chldrn; Educator.

**MC GEE, MARY C,** Univ Of Southern Ms, Hattiesburg, MS; JR; BS; Baptst Stdnt Un 88; SUM Singers 88; Carillon Handbell Choir 89; Stdnt Alumni Assoc 90-; Alpha Lambda Delta 88-; Golden Key 88-; Gamma Beta 88-; Beta Gamma Sigma; Phi Chi Theta 90; Acctng; CPA.

**MC GEE, PAMELA S,** Wv Univ At Parkersburg, Parkersburg, WV; FR; Psy; Cnslng.

**MC GEE, RAQUEL J,** Alcorn St Univ, Lorman, MS; SO; Cmptr Sci; Cmptr Oper.

**MC GEE, TONI M,** Central Pa Bus School, Summerdale, PA; SR; AD; Acctg.

**MC GEE JR, WILLIAM B,** Hudson Valley Comm Coll, Troy, NY; FR; Cstmr Serv Rep Sprvsr Key Bnk Eastrn NY NA 86-; Pblc Hstry-Tchng.

**MC GEHEE, TRICIA K,** Middle Tn St Univ, Murfreesboro, TN; SO; Gamma Beta Phi.

**MC GEHEE, WILLIAM E,** Abraham Baldwin Agri Coll, Tifton, GA; SO; AA; AG Equip Tech Club Treas 90-; Stdnt Gov Trffc Crt Chef Just 90-; Whos Sho ABAC 89-90; AA Ag Bus; AA Lvstck Prd; Ag Mgmt.

**MC GHEE, ROBERT,** Savannah St Coll, Savannah, GA; SO; BS; IEEE Inst Elctrcl Elctrnc Engnrs Tres 90-; Blck Tn Union 86-; Engnrng.

**MC GHEE, STEVEN W,** Roane St Comm Coll, Harriman, TN; SO; BS; Bio/Chem; Nursing.

**MC GHEE, TAMI L,** Al A & M Univ, Normal, AL; SR; BS; Math Clb 88-; Assn Cmptng Mach 89-; Alpha Kappa Mu 89-; Cmptr Sci; Pgrmng.

**MC GHEE, VANESSA J,** Alcorn St Univ, Lorman, MS; JR; BA; MAESP Sec 90-; Yrbk Stf Layout 88-; Elem Educ; Tchr.

**MC GILL, CAROLINE E,** Valdosta St Coll, Valdosta, GA; FR; BED; Sprts Med; Tchr/Trnr.

**MC GILL, KATELLA Y,** Univ Of Sc At Columbia, Columbia, SC; JR; BA; Bus Drvr Org; FBLA Prlmntry 87-88; Sprntndnts Hon Rl; Pltcl Sci; Law.

**MC GILL, STEVEN T,** Cheyney Univ Of Pa, Cheyney, PA; JR; BA; Toastmasters Intrntl Ed VP 90-; Engl Clb; Aplastic Amer Fndtn Amer 90-; Trk/Fld Tm 89-; Engl; Tch.

**MC GILLIVRAY, ALISON M,** Fl St Univ, Tallahassee, FL; SR; BA; Acctg Soc Comm Chr 89-90; Clg Reps 86-87; Phi Eta Sigma 86-; Goldn Key V P 90-; Beta Alpha Psi 90-; Delta Zeta 87-; Librl Stds Hnrs Pgm 86-87; Acctg/Finance.

**MC GINLEY, ALICE R,** Daytona Beach Comm Coll, Daytona Beach, FL; FR; BS; Std Snt Asc 90-; DBCC Grns 90-; Peer Tutor 90-; Phi Theta Kappa 90-; Acad Schlr 90-; Pres Lst 90-; Engr.

**MC GINN, PAMELA E,** Univ Of South Al, Mobile, AL; JR; Math; Tchng.

**MC GINN, PATRICIA M,** Lesley Coll, Cambridge, MA; SR; BA; Rsdnts Lf Advsry Brd 90-; Kndrgrtn Cnfrnc Orgnztn 90-; Lsly Deans Lst 89-; Lsly Hnr Scty 89-; Dean Jr Coll Sccr/Sftbl 87-89; As Dean Jr Coll 89; Elem Edctn; Tchr.

**MC GINN-MOSS, JEANNETTE F,** Univ Of Charleston, Charleston, WV; SR; BA; UC/KP Production Three Penny Opera 87-88; Soloist Christmas Concert 87-; Nom Comm Mbr Conservatory Dean 89-90; Chorus Make-Up 87-88; Soloist 89-90; Dir Stage Mgr Props 89-90; Rint Ad Dir Millers Inc Lexington KY 78; Music/Volal Maj/Inst Min; Teach Writ Publish.**

**MC GINNIS, KATHLEEN B,** Thomas Nelson Comm Coll, Hampton, VA; GD; AAS; NASA Intern Chld Dvlp Cntr 89-; Erly Chldhd Dvlp.

**MC GINNIS, KRISTIN U,** Memphis St Univ, Memphis, TN; SR; BSN; Adult Stdt Assoc VP; NAACOG 89; RN Lbr/Dlvry; Chrg Nrs Surgies; OB ICU; RN 86-; RNC NCC 90; Nursing.

**MC GINNIS, MARIE K,** Kent St Univ Kent Cmps, Kent, OH; SR; BA; Kent Cncl Fmly Rltns VP 88-; Vol Hosp 90-; Stdnt Emplye Rgnl Cmps Kent St U 90-; Crown Ctr Intrn 90-; Natl Cncl Fmly Rltns 90; BA; Indvdl/Fmly Stds/Fmly Lf; MSW.

**MC GINNISS, CECILIA J,** Oh Wesleyan Univ, Delaware, OH; FR; BA; 4-H 90-; Nwmn Cntr VP 90-; Fresh Hnr Soc 90-; Ltr Chrch 90-; Tch Dance Jrvn Dtnt; CROP Wlk; Dean Lst; Jrnlsm; Law.

**MC GINNISS, KEVIN P,** Univ Of Sc At Columbia, Columbia, SC; SO; BA; Pres Hon Rl 90-; Cmmssn Scnd Ltnt SC Natl Grd Palmetto Mltry Acdmy; Acctg; CPA.

**MC GINTY, MATTHEW D,** Pittsburgh Tech Inst, Pittsburgh, PA; GD; Acad Achvmnt Ldrshp Awrd; Richard S Caliguiri Awrd; ASTD 90; Eng Math.

**MC GIRL, CAREY M,** Radford Univ, Radford, VA; JR; Amrcn Mrktng Assn 90-; Sigma Sigma Sigma Prsdnt 90-; Sigma Sigma Sigm Srvc Drctr 89-90; Sigma Sigma Simga; Mrktng Bsns; Mrktng Advrtsng.

**MC GLAMORY, ELEANOR F,** Central Fl Comm Coll, Ocala, FL; SO; Phi Theta Kappa 89-; Elem Ed; Tchr.

**MC GLANNAN, JULIA F,** Univ Of Miami, Coral Gables, FL; SR; BSN; Phi Kappa Phi 90-; Phi Theta Kappa 83-84; S FL Soc Of Hlthcare Risk Mgrs; ICU RN 84-; AS Miami Dad E Cmnty Clg 84; Cert Amercn Inst Of Medcl Law 90; Profsnl Nrsng; Clncl Spclst/Nrsng Admn.

**MC GLASSON JR, JACK E,** Middle Tn St Univ, Murfreesboro, TN; JR; BBA; Acctg; CPA.

**MC GLONE, EILEEN R,** Radford Univ, Radford, VA; JR; BA; Phi Sigma Sigma 90-; Pol Sci.

**MC GLONE, LORI A,** Alice Lloyd Coll, Pippa Passes, KY; SO; BA; Stdnt Govt Repr 89-; Actvts Brd 89-90; Deans List 89-90; Acad Deans List 90-; LMA 88-89; Radio Club 90-; Photographer 89-; Eagle Mascot 89-90; Soc Studies.

**MC GLOTHEN, DARRICK K,** Tuskegee Univ, Tuskegee Inst, AL; SO; BA; Boy Scouts Ldr; GM Schlrshp; Mchncl Engnrng Cmptr Sci; Company Engnr.

**MC GLOTHEN, SHELLEY L,** Marshall University, Huntington, WV; SR; BBA; Natl Mgmt Assn Pres 89-; Omicron Delta Kappa 90; Alpha Kappa Psi 89; Sigma Sigma Sigma Treas 88; Outstndg Mgmt Snr; Mgmt.

**MC GLOTHIN, MIQUELL L,** Univ Of Southern Ms, Hattiesburg, MS; SR; BS; Stdnt Judicial Brd; Mrchng Bnd; Chorus; Alpha Phi Alpha; Psychlgy; Clncl Psychlgst.

**MC GLOTHLIN, CHRISTOPHER L,** Radford Univ, Radford, VA; SR; BS; Plyrs Guild VP 88-; Pi Gamma Mu 90-; Alpha Lambda Delta 88-; Univ Publ Info Ofc Intern; Jrnlsm Pol Sci; Law.

**MC GLOTHLIN, JENNIFER R,** Univ Of Southern Ms, Hattiesburg, MS; SO; BA; Pre Law Soc; Intl Rltns Club; Gamma Beta Phi; Phi Delta Rho; Gamma Theta Upsilon; Kappa Delta Srgnt At Arms 88; DC Cngrssnl Intrnshp; IM Sftbl/Flag Ftbl; Intl Stds; Intl Law.

**MC GLOUGHLIN, KAREN E,** Saint Andrews Presbytrn Coll, Laurinburg, NC; SR; MS; Hlth Sci Clb 87-90; Hon Stdnt Assoc 87-; Hon Soc 90-; So Hons 88-89; Therptc Rec Intrnshp; Schlr Ath Awd; Dns Lst 88-; Vars Sftbl 89-; BA; Rec Admn/Thrptc Rec; Cert Therptc Rec Spec.

**MC GLYNN, COLLEEN R,** Life Coll, Marietta, GA; GD; DC; Interntl Chiropractrs Assoc; GA Cncl On Chiroprctc; Chiroprctc; Prvt Practc.

**MC GLYNN, SUSAN M,** Mount Aloysius Jr Coll, Cresson, PA; SO; ASSOC; Phi Theta Kappa 89-; Assoc Mount Aloysius Jr Clg; Legal Assistant.

**MC GOHAN, WAYNE M,** Vance Granville Comm Coll, Henderson, NC; SO; BED; Coll Actng Clb 89-; Enn Lns Clb Pres 87-; MADD Pres 90-; AAS Cayuga County Comm Coll Auburn NY 86; Psych; Cnslng.

**MC GOLDRICK, JENNIFER L,** Middle Tn St Univ, Murfreesboro, TN; FR; BA; Gamma Beta Phi 90-; Zeta Tau Alpha Dir Point Syst 90-; Advrtsng; Mktg.

**MC GONIGLE, RICHARD C,** Glassboro St Coll, Glassboro, NJ; SR; BA; Haddon Hgts HS Track Team Asst Coach 90-; NJ Soc Of Dispnsng Optcns 76-87; Fire Co 1 81-85; AAS Camden Cnty Clg 76; Secndry Ed/Hist; Tchr.

**MC GONNELL, SHARON P,** S U N Y Coll Of Tech At Frmgdl, Farmingdale, NY; SO; AS; Erly Chldhd Educ; Daycare.

**MC GORY, SHANNON M,** S U N Y Coll At Fredonia, Fredonia, NY; SO; BA; Spctrm Entrtnmnt Bd; Bus; Mktg.

**MC GOUGH, DEBORAH JONES,** Central Al Comm Coll, Alexander City, AL; FR; BA; ASEA-AL State Crrctnl Offcr 84-; Sgt Julia Tutwiler Prsn Wmn Wetumpka AL; Crmnl Juste.

**MC GOUGH, DEBRA C,** Western Piedmont Comm Coll, Morganton, NC; SO; AASC; Burke Co Extnsn Hmmkrs Quilters Guild 88-; NC Extnsn Homemkrs 88-; Phi Theta Kappa 90-; Wknd Mgr Options Inc 90-; Cont Ed Instrctn Sr Citzns 89-; Crmnl Jstc/Para Legal Technlgy.

**MC GOUGH, ROBERT P,** Univ Of Akron, Akron, OH; JR; BSEE; IEEE 90-; Tau Beta Pi; BSET 85; Elctrcl Engr.

**MC GOUGH, STEPHANIE A,** Radford Univ, Radford, VA; JR; BS; Cthlc Stdnt Assoc Ltrgy Co-Chrprsn 89; Stdnt Lfe Movie Cmmttee 89-90; Alpha Phi Omega VP Of Serv 89; Intrnshp At Grp Hm For Mntlly Retrded Adlts 90; Scl Wrk.

**MC GOUGH, TANYA R,** Univ Of Al At Birmingham, Birmingham, AL; JR; BA; Elem Ed; Tchr.

**MC GOVERN, BRENDA J,** Indiana Univ Of Pa, Indiana, PA; JR.

**MC GOVERN, BRIAN F,** City Univ Of Ny Baruch Coll, New York, NY; SO; BA; Acctng.

**MC GOVERN, ELIZABETH,** Univ Of Ky, Lexington, KY; SR; MA; Lit Mag Layout Edtr 88-89; Teach CCD Newman Cntr Cthlc Chrch 88-; Psi Chi; Kappa Kappa Gamma IM 87-; Soph Dlgt Ldrshp Conf 88; Sr Hnrs Thesis; Psych; Practice/Counseling.

**MC GOVERN IV, FRANK J,** Widener Univ, Chester, PA; SR; BS; Army ROTC Batt Comm 87-; Econ Cl 89-; Omicron Delta Epsilon Pres 89-; Pi Gamma Mu V P 89-; Phi Eta Sigma; Alpha Chi; Phi Kappa Phi; Middle Atlantic Cnfce All-Academic Tm 88-90; Outstndng Econ Stdnt; X Cntry Capt 87-; Econ/Mgmt; Law.

**MC GOVERN, THOMAS M,** Ny Univ, New York, NY; JR; BA; Data Arch; Orgztn Cmunctn; Info Sys.

**MC GOWAN, BARBARA A,** De Tech & Comm Coll At Dover, Dover, DE; GD; LPN; Nrsng Clb Asst Treas 90-; USAF Med Asst 89; Nrsng.

**MC GOWAN, BERNADETTE M,** Saint Francis Coll, Loretto, PA; SR; BS; RA 89-90; Stdnt Soc Physician Assists Treas 87; Physicians Assist; Emerg Dept/Surg Assist.

**MC GOWAN, BRIAN H,** George Mason Univ, Fairfax, VA; GD; AAHPERD 89-90; Stdnt Taught Parkview Hgh Sugarland Elmntry; BS GMU 90; Tchng; Phys Ed Hlth; Tchr.

**MC GOWAN, BRIAN S,** Indiana Univ Of Pa, Indiana, PA; JR; BA; Radio Brdcstr 90-; Alpha Phi Omega Prlmntrn 90; Cmnctns Media; Brdcstng/Prdctn.

**MC GOWAN, COLLEEN E,** Kings Coll, Wilkes-Barre, PA; FR; BS; Kings Sngrs 90; Crown Nwspr Stf 90; Wilkes Coll Wnd Ensmbl; Tutor Math/Physics; Pres Full Tuition Schlrshp; Wmns Tennis 90; Wyo Vly Oratorio Soc; Physics.

**MC GOWAN, DAVID A,** Savannah Coll Of Art & Design, Savannah, GA; JR; BFA; Grphx Clb 89-; Frncs Mclmn Schlrshp; AAS Grand Rapids Jr Clg 86-88; Grphc Dsgn/Ills; Advrtsng Crtv.

**MC GOWAN, GLORIA J,** West Liberty St Coll, West Liberty, WV; JR; BA; Wrtr Nwspr; Sigma Tau Delta; Chi Omega Corres 89-90; Engl; Jrnlsm.**

**MC GOWAN, SALESSIA D,** South Ga Coll, Douglas, GA; SO; ASCJ; Minority Odv Prog 89-; Stdnt Org/Black Unity Chpsn 89-; Stdnt Supp Svcs Tutor 89-; Stdnt Tutor/Math; Ntnl Collgte Hon/ Jr Colg 90; Outstndng Acad Awd; Tutor Church; Crmnl Jstce; Probtn Offcr/Parole Offcr.

**MC GOWAN, SHARON A,** Wilmington Coll, New Castle, DE; JR; Amer Hrt Assn CPR Instrctr 87-; DE Ar Natl Grd Capt Flght Nrse; 142 Ar Evctn Flght; Flght Instrctr 90-; Srvd Dsrt Shld Dsrt Strm 90-; RN 87-; AS St Peters School Of Nursing 82; Nrsng; Mstrs Nrse Anthtst.

**MC GOWAN, SHARON L,** Glassboro St Coll, Glassboro, NJ; SR; BA; Coll Bnd 87-88; Tlvsn Flm Assoc; WGLS Pblc Srvc DJ 90-; Sigma Sigma Sigma 87-; Intern Jns Intrcbl; Intern WFPG; Ftnss Arbcs Clb 88-89; BA 90; Cmmnctns Rd Tv Flm Tlvsn Rd.

**MC GOWEN, GRACE E,** Univ Of Montevallo, Montevallo, AL; FR; BA; Leadership Schlrshp 90-; Theatre Education; Teach/Act/ Mass Comm.

**MC GRAIL, KELLY B,** West Liberty St Coll, West Liberty, WV; JR; BA; Graphc Arts; Ph D.

**MC GRAIL, MADELINE L,** Univ Of Fl, Gainesville, FL; FL Plyrs 86-90; Alpha Psi Omega Pres 88-; Selby Found Schlrshp 90; Father Conne Daugherty Schlrshp 84-86; Dir Awd Manatee Comm Clg 86; Hippodrone State Theatre Yng Audiences 89; Actors Equity Assoc 89-; Theatre Perf; Acting Stage Mgng Theatre.

**MC GRANAHAN, LYLE L,** Univ Of Pittsburgh At Bradford, Bradford, PA; SO; BA; Math/Ec.

**MC GRATH, CHRIS M,** Schenectady County Comm Coll, Schenectady, NY; SR; BS; AAS; Chem; Orgnc La Rsrch.

**MC GRATH, KATHLEEN S,** Bethany Coll, Bethany, WV; JR; BA; Cir K Dist Sec 88-89; Coll Church Choir 90-; Coll Comm CCD Tchr 89-90; Gamma Sigma Kappa; Alpha Beta Gamma; Kappa Delta Pres 89-; Renner Schlrshp 88-; Elem Ed/Studio Art; Tchr.

**MC GRATH, SEAN P,** Georgian Court Coll, Lakewood, NJ; SR; BA; Hmnts.

**MC GRATH-BEDARD, PAULA M,** Newbury Coll, Brookline, MA; SO; AS; Drama Club Pres 89-; Areobic Club 89-; Bsktbl/ Ims/Crs Cntry 90-; Fashn Merchndsng Award; PALS 90-; Cnslng Ofc Peer Asst 89-; Crs Cntry Rnng 90-; Fashn Merchndsng; Tchng Deaf Stdnts.**

**MC GRAW, MATTHEW W,** Univ Of Md At Eastern Shore, Princess Anne, MD; JR; BED; Future Educrs Amer; Soc Sci; Tchng.

**MC GRAW, SHAUN L,** Southern Coll Of Tech, Marietta, GA; FR; BST; Bptst Stdnt Un 90-; Deans Lst 90; Love Inc Vol 90-; IM Ftbl/Sftbl 90-; Mech Eng Tech.

**MC GREGER, DANA K,** Itawamba Comm Coll, Fulton, MS; SO; Busn Tech; Comptrs.

**MC GREGOR, ANTONETTE A,** Fl Atlantic Univ, Boca Raton, FL; JR; BA; CLD; Afro-Amer Clb 90; Jr Clg HS 89-90; Pres Lst 89; Deans Lst 89; AA Brwrd Cmmnty Clg 90; Excptnl Stdnt Edctns Lrng Dsblties; MA.

**MC GREGOR, KATE M,** Eckerd Coll, St Petersburg, FL; SR; BA; Org Of Stdnts PR Adv Coord 87-89; Assoc Safer Envrnmnt Org Coord 90; Erth Soc 90; Stdy Of Intrntl Migrtn Econ Dev Wash DC Intrn 89; We Help St Petersbrg Free Clnc Intrn 90; Human Res Inst Intrn 90; Soc; Soc Actn Pol Wrk.

**MC GREGOR, KIMBERLIE R,** Ms St Univ, Miss State, MS; JR; BA; Art Clb 1st VP 88-90; Bapt Stdnt Un Cncl Comms Chrprsn 89-90; Bapt Stdnt Un Puppet/Drma Tm 89-90; Phi Theta Kappa 88-90; Gamma Beta Phi; NE MS Comm Clg 90; Art; Grphc Artst/Adv/Illust.

**MC GRELLIS, MICHAEL P,** Atlantic Comm Coll, Mays Landing, NJ; SO; BA; Ski Clb SGA 89-; Stu Govt Assoc Rep 89-; Sci Clb; AS; Chem; Rsrch.

**MC GREW, MARY K,** Commonwealth Coll, Virginia Beach, VA; GD; AAS; Comp Club Treas 90; Alpha Beta Gamma 90; Comp Sci; Prgmng.

**MC GREW, SUSAN M,** Kent St Univ Kent Cmps, Kent, OH; JR; BA; Gldn Ky; Sigma Tau Delta; Engl; Pblshng.

**MC GRIFF, ANTONIO L,** Methodist Coll, Fayetteville, NC; SO; BS; Cmnctns; Radio/TV Prgrmmng.

**MC GRIFF, BETSY ELLEN,** Miami Univ, Oxford, OH; FR; BS; Nwspr Stf 90-; 4-H 80-; Alpha Phi Omega 90-; IM Vlybl 90-; Mass Cmnctn; Prod/Pgmmng.

**MC GRIFF, DEBORAH L,** Valdosta St Coll, Valdosta, GA; JR; Phi Beta Lambda Abraham Baldwin Agric Clg; Sec 1st Un Meth Chrch 81-90; AS 80; Educ; Tchr.

**MC GRIFF, RUSSELL O,** Morehouse Coll, Atlanta, GA; FR; BS; Math Clb 90-; Space Endvr Clb 90-; Ronald E Mc Nair NASA Schlr 90-; Wm Penn Schlr 90-; Marshall Spc Flgt Cntr Intrnshp; Math/Engr; Professor/Engr.

**MC GRUDER, JONATHAN,** City Univ Of Ny Queensbrough, New York, NY; FR; AAS; Acctng.

**MC GUCKIN, DEBORA P,** Georgian Court Coll, Lakewood, NJ; SR; BA; Dns Schlr 90-; Spec Ed.

**MC GUIGAN, CHRISTINE ANN,** William Paterson Coll, Wayne, NJ; SR; BA; Prdced Spcl Series Reprt On Campus Plltn For Campus News Show Newslne 90; Active Membr Of NJ Animal Rghts Allnce 87; 1st Prze Wm P Clg Fmnst Essay Cntst; Engl Wrtng Mjr; Prof Wrtr.

**MC GUINESS, LISE M,** James Madison University, Harrisonburg, VA; SR; BS; NOW Treas 90; United Campuses To Prevent Nuc War; EARTH; Hons Schlr; Elem Engl Educ.

**MC GUINNESS, MARIANNE K,** Clarkson Univ, Potsdam, NY; FR; BA; Rugby Tm 90-; Soc Wmn Mngrs 90-; Finance Accntng; Fnncl Advsng CPA.

**MC GUINNESS, MAUREEN L,** Le Moyne Coll, Syracuse, NY; JR; BS; Human Resource Mgmt Clb Pres 88-; Indstrl Rltns Clb Sec Pblcty 88-; Ntnl Soc Hmn Rsrc Mgmnt; Indstrl Rltns Psychlgy; Scl Wrk.

**MC GUIRE, DORI L,** Daemen Coll, Amherst, NY; SR; Inter Grk Assoc Rec Sec 89-; Rsdnt Cncl 86-87; Kappa Delta Pi Treas 90-; Lambda Chi Iota Pres 89-; BA; Math; Tchng.

**MC GUIRE, ELIZABETH M,** Ny Univ, New York, NY; BA; Alpha Sigma Lambda; Deans List 90-; Cntng Ed Schlr 89-; Intrn Memrl Sloan Kettering Cancer Cntr; Jr League; Schl Prctcl Philosopy; 20 Yrs Wrkng Prfssnlly 79-90; Certfctn Katharine Gibbs 71; Psychlgy; Psychlgy.

**MC GUIRE, JULIE E,** Univ Of Al At Birmingham, Birmingham, AL; SR; Inthsp Eye Foundtn Hptl; Tn Tm; BS; Hlth Ed; Epidemiology.

**MC GUIRE, KIRSTY G,** George Mason Univ, Fairfax, VA; SO; Rsdnt Stdnts Assoc Chrmn Of Aux Serv 90; Cir-K 90; La Crosse Ims.

**MC GUIRE, MICHAEL T,** Old Dominion Univ, Norfolk, VA; SR; BSET; IEEE 88-; FCC Novice Class Radio License 89-; AAS VA Western Cmnty Clg 89; Elec Engr.

**MC GUIRE, MICHELE D,** Bowie St Univ, Bowie, MD; JR; BS; Educ Clb; PGCC Hnr Soc 89-90; Deans List 90-; Kappa Delta Pi 90-; Sigma Alpha E; Silon 81-83; Elem Educ; Teaching.

**MC GUIRE, MOLLY A,** Elmira Coll, Elmira, NY; JR; BS; Outing Clb 89-; Orchesis 88-89; Bus Clb Treas 90-; Phi Eta Sigma; Pupil Asst 89-90; Gold Key Ambssdr Awd; Wall Street Jrnl Bus Admnstrtn Awd; Deans List/Hon Schlr; Rsdnt Asst 89-90; Ad Hoc Com 89-90; Orientation Com 89-90; Exec Com 90; Bus Admnstrtn; Law.

**MC GUIRE, ROBERT W,** Atlanta Christian Coll, East Point, GA; SR; MBA; Hd Res 90-; Sr Superlatvs; Soccer Video Oper 90; Bsktbl Stats 90-; BS 78; AA; Bible/Bsn Adm; Tchr/Admnstr.

**MC GUIRE, SHERI R,** Longwood Coll, Farmville, VA; SR; BS; Phi Kappa Phi; Stdnt Rep Chrmn Fin/Ecnmcs Dept 90-; Wynne Schlrshp; Longwd Sml Bus Dvlpmnt Cntr Intrn; Full Time Stdnt Wife/Mthr; AAS Sthsd VA Comm Coll 89; Bus Admin; Fin.

**MC GUIRE, SHIRLEY S,** Univ Of Tn At Martin, Martin, TN; GD; BS; Bank Admnstrtn Inst Crtfd EDP Audtr 89; AS Dyersburg State Comm Clg 87; Mgt Info Sys.

**MC GUIRE, WENDY,** Brevard Coll, Brevard, NC; SO; BA; Cllgt Sngrs 89-; BPIU; Hon Rl 89-90; Deans Lst 89-90; AA; Early Chldhd Educ/Psychlgy; Day Cr/Psychtry.**

**MC GUIRT, MARY B,** Univ Of Nc At Greensboro, Greensboro, NC; SR; BS; AHEA 89-; Alpha Chi Omega Actvt Chrprsn 90-; United Way Intern 90; Hm Econ/Bus Cmmnty Serv; Spcl Prmtns/ Scl Plnn.

**MC GUNIGAL, ELIZABETH ANN,** Georgetown Univ, Washington, DC; FR; BS; GUSA Spirit Comm 90-; Intl Rltns Comm 90-; Army ROTC 90-; Intl Bus.

**MC HALE, ELIZABETH A,** Coll Misericordia, Dallas, PA; FR; Altrntv Lrnrs Prjct Notetkr 90-; Mdrgl Sngr 90-; IM Vlybl 90-; Chrldng 90-; Hlth Sci; Occptnl Thrpst.

**MC HALE, VIRGINIA M,** Commonwealth Coll, Virginia Beach, VA; SO; AAS; Tidewater Chapter Amer Iris Soc; St Gregorys Womens Club V Pres 90-; Vlntr With Little Theatre ; Sugar Plub Bakery; Bus Mgmnt.

**MC HAYLE, MARK M,** Cumberland County Coll, Vineland, NJ; FR; AA; Cadet Corp Crprl 85-87; Drama Clb 82-83; Engr; MBA.

**MC HENRY, AMY E,** Marshall University, Huntington, WV; FR; BA; Phi Eta Sigma 90-; Gamma Beta Phi; Sigma Sigma Sigma; Bus.

**MC HENRY, ANGELA D,** Alcorn St Univ, Lorman, MS; JR; BA; Nwsppr Edtr 89-; Engl Clb Sec 90-; Engl Educ; Tch Prfssnl Wrtng.

**MC HENRY, ELAINE M,** Hudson Valley Comm Coll, Troy, NY; JR; BS; AA 90; Elem Educ Engl; Educ.

**MC HENRY, JENNIFER A,** Westminster Coll, New Wilmingtn, PA; SR; Admssns Tm 88-89; Union Prgrmng Comm 87-89; Pnhllnc Grk Wk Comm Pres 90-; Pi Sigma Pi 89-; Tau Pi Phi 89-; Omicron Delta Kappa 90-; Mrtr Brd 90-; Sigma Kappa Schlrshp 88-; Adpt Grndprnt 89-90; Yth Dvlpmnt Ctr Vol 89-90; Bus Admin/Mrktg.

**MC HUGH, DAVID P,** Univ Of Vt & St Agri Coll, Burlington, VT; FR; BA; Econs/Pol Sci; Law.

**MC HUGH, MAUREEN A,** Comm Coll Algny Co Algny Cmps, Pittsburgh, PA; FR; BA; Law.

**MC ILWAIN, WANDA I,** Columbia Union Coll, Takoma Park, MD; SR; BS; Hlthcr Mngmnt; Mng Nrsng Hms.

**MC INERNEY JR, JOHN J,** Duquesne Univ, Pittsburgh, PA; FR; BA; Phi Eta Sigma 90-; Wrstlng 90-; Cmnctns; Publc Rltns.

**MC INNIS, DEBORAH DENISE,** Univ Of Southern Ms, Hattiesburg, MS; SR; BS; Prog Asst/Cnslng/Educ/Rsrcs For Stdnts; 101 87-88; Gamma Alpha Epsilon 89-; Phi Mu Schlrshp Ldg Trnr 88 -90; Stdnts Against Drnk Drvng 88-90; Alchl Aswrnss Tsk Frc 87-90; Stdnt Alumni Assoc 88-89; Prctm Cnslr; Cnslng Psych; Case Mngr.

**MC INNIS, JOHNNY R,** Fayetteville St Univ, Fayetteville, NC; JR; BA; Kappa Kappa Psi Sec Treas 89-; Stdnt Asst Bnd Dir 90-; Music Educ; Bnd Dir.

**MC INNIS, LISA J,** City Univ Of Ny Baruch Coll, New York, NY; JR; BBA; Inter-Var Chrstn Flwshp; Deans Lst 89; Acctng.

**MC INNIS III, WILLIAM L,** Ms St Univ, Miss State, MS; SR; MBA; Ntl Assoc Indstrl Tech 86-; Coll Rpblcns 89-; MBA Assoc; Phi Delta Theta Tres 90-; Prjct Brckfire 90; Meals On Whl 90; Adpt A Hwy; Co Op Educ Pro 88-89; Deans Lst 89; IM Ftbl/ Sftbl; BS; BBA; Mgmnt; Engr.

**MC INTIRE, SHERRI L,** Univ Of Akron, Akron, OH; JR; BA; Golden Key 90-; Kappa Delta Pi 90-; PADI Open Water SCUBA Divg; Asst Pee Wee Cheerldg Advsr Rittman 87-88; Secy Aetna Life Ins Co 82-85; Elem Edctn; Sci; Tchg.

**MC INTIRE, WILLIAM M,** Univ Of Southern Ms, Hattiesburg, MS; SO; BA; I M Ofcl Awd 89; Acctg; CPA.

**MC INTOSH, ADRIUNNE D,** Savannah St Coll, Savannah, GA; JR; BA; Cncrt Chr Mrchng Bnd 88-89; Chrldng Sqd Co-Cptn 89-; Dance Trp 90-; Delta Sigma Theta 90-; Bsns Mgmnt.

**MC INTOSH, CLARA,** Cumberland Coll, Williamsburg, KY; SR; BS; All Amer Schlr; J D Vllnghm Hnr Soc; Elem Ed; Tchng.

**MC INTOSH, DONNA J,** Edward Waters Coll, Jacksonville, FL; SR; BBA; Sut Govt Assn Sen 89-89; Kappa Diamond Treas 87-88; Natl Stu Bus Leag; Delta Sigma Theta VP 90-; Bus Admn; Mngmnt.

**MC INTOSH, IAN B D,** City Univ Of Ny City Coll, New York, NY; SR; BE; Caribbean Assoc Pub Rels; Tau Sigma Pr; SAE; PRES; Ath Hon Rl 88-90; Var Soccer 88-90; Mech Engr.

**MC INTOSH, J RANDALL,** Mayland Comm Coll, Spruce Pine, NC; FR; AS; Crim Just; Law Enfrcmnt/Pol.

**MC INTOSH, JEANNE R,** Univ Of Sc At Columbia, Columbia, SC; SR; BA; Art Studio; Artist.

**MC INTOSH, LORI A,** Thomas Nelson Comm Coll, Hampton, VA; FR; BA; Colony Civic Assoc; VA PTA; Army Aviatn Logstcs 81-; Spclst At Ft Eustis VA; Bus; Acctng.

**MC INTOSH, NANCY ELIZABETH,** Gallaudet Univ, Washington, DC; SR; BA; Reginald Lewis Schlrshp; Var Vlybl 85; Hist; Profr.

**MC INTOSH, SHERRY B,** Univ Of Sc At Columbia, Columbia, SC; SR; BS; USC Thtr 89-; Eeuc Mjrs Clb 89-90; Stdnt Educ Assn 88-89; Gamma Beta Phi 90-; Cncl Excptnl Chldrn 89-90; Gldn Mask Awd-Thtr 89-90; Vlybl-Richland Coll 87-88; AS Richland Comm Coll 88; Psychlgy; Psychlgy/Psychlgst.

**MC INTOSH, STACY L,** Univ Of Tn At Martin, Martin, TN; SO; Austin Peay Hall Assn 90-; Soc Hon Seminar Stdnts 90-; Hon Semnr 89; Ldrshp Res 89-90; Pi Sigma Epsilon 89-; Chi Omega Asst Pldge 89-; Acctg; CPA.

**MC INTOSH, WAYNE A,** Ny Univ, New York, NY; JR; BS; Fin/Econs; Bsns.

**MC INTOSH, YVONNE P,** Alcorn St Univ, Lorman, MS; JR; BA; Blgy Clb Tres 90-; Pre-Med Clb Sntr 90-; Alpha Kappa Alpha 90-; Blgy; Mdcl Tchnlgy.

**MC INTURFF, KEVIN J,** Southern Coll Of Tech, Marietta, GA; JR; CET; Envrnmntl Eng; Eng.

**MC INTURFF, NATALIE F,** East Tn St Univ, Johnson City, TN; SO; BBA; Alpha Lambda Delta 90-; Gamma Beta Phi; Acctg.

**MC INTYRE, ALICIA C,** Schenectady County Comm Coll, Schenectady, NY; SO; Deans List 89-; Intrnshp Walt Disney Wrld Clg Progrm Guest; Wrks At The Grand Floridian Hotel As Hosptlty Hosts; AS; Hotel/Rest Mgt; Gen Mgr Of Hotel.

**MC INTYRE, D MICHAEL,** Radford Univ, Radford, VA; FR; BA; Spanish Language; Tchng Univ Level.

**MC INTYRE, DANIEL B,** Wallace St Comm Coll At Selma, Selma, AL; FR; BS; Phi Theta Kappa Pres 90-; Sci.

**MC INTYRE, DAWN M,** S U N Y Coll At Fredonia, Fredonia, NY; SR; BED; Phi Theta Kappa; AA Jamestown Comm Coll 89; Elem Ed; Tchng.

**MC INTYRE, DEIRDRE E,** Oh St Univ At Newark, Newark, OH; SO; BA; Hstry.

**MC INTYRE, LATONIA R,** Al A & M Univ, Normal, AL; SO; BA; March Maroon/White Band Maroonette 89-; Tau Beta Sigma; Bus; Cmptr Op.

**MC INTYRE, RAYMOND J,** Bryant Stratton Bus Inst Roch, Rochester, NY; FR; Deans Lst; Acctng.

**MC INTYRE, RHONDA M,** Univ Of The Dist Of Columbia, Washington, DC; SR; BBA; Delta Mu Delta; Phi Sigma Pi Pres; C/P Tele Co Acad Schlrshp; Chevron Acad Schlrshp; Var Schlstc Achvmnt Awds; Brd Of Dir/Jewels Of Ann Prv Day Schl; Comp Info Syst Scinc; Mgmnt.

**MC INTYRE, SAMUEL S,** Longwood Coll, Farmville, VA; JR; Radio Sta Mgr 88-90; Psi Chi 90-; Tnns; Psychlgy; Rsrch.

**MC INTYRE, SETH D,** West Liberty St Coll, West Liberty, WV; JR; BS; Theta Xi Sgt Arms; Acad Schlrshp 88-; Bus Admin; Acctg.

**MC INTYRE, STEPHEN D,** Western Ky Univ, Bowling Green, KY; JR; BS; Phi Kappa Phi; Engrng.

**MC INTYRE, VALERIE LYNN,** S U N Y Coll At Fredonia, Fredonia, NY; JR; BS; Chautauqua Stdrs Tutoring Prog 89-; AA Jamestown Comm Clg 88-90; Elem Educ; Adminstrtr.

**MC INTYRE, WILLIAM R,** Owensboro Comm Coll, Owensboro, KY; SO; BA; Democrat Clb 90; Bapt Stdnt Un 90; Schl Nwspr Ed 90-; Envrnmntl Clb 89-; OCC Hon Pgm; OCC Judicial Bd Chrmn; Citizens Com Edn; Laubach Lit Cncl Instr 89-; US Navy; Carpentry; Electrician; Steelwrkr; Plmbr; Realtor Assoc; Bus/Cmnctns; Publ Rel Indstry Liason Cons.

**MC IVER, EDWARD L,** Oakwood Coll, Huntsville, AL; FR; BA; Dns Lst; Bsktbl; Engl/Bsn; Law.

**MC JILTON JR, ROBERT R,** Coppin St Coll, Baltimore, MD; SR; BS; AA 88; Spcl Ed; Tchg.

**MC KAHAN, ROBERT C,** Fl A & M Univ, Tallahassee, FL; SR; P T Clb 89-; Hon Soc 89-; Deans Lst 90-; APTA 90-; FPTA 90-; Physcl Thrpy; Physcl Thrpst.

**MC KASKLE, LISA F,** Ms St Univ, Miss State, MS; SR; BS; Voc Hm Ec Educ; Tchng.

**MC KAY, ADRIAN,** Alcorn St Univ, Lorman, MS; JR; Acctg; CPA.

**MC KAY, CONNIE F,** Middle Tn St Univ, Murfreesboro, TN; JR; BBA; Gamma Beta Phi 88-; Wrk Schlrshp; AAS Motlow State Cmnty Clg 90; Info Syst; Syst Analyst.

**MC KAY, GENOLA C,** Clark Atlanta Univ, Atlanta, GA; JR; BS; Hon Pgm 2nd VP 90-; Pre-Profl Hlth Soc VP 90-; Alpha Kappa Mu 90-; Beta Kappa Chi 90-; Delta Sigma Theta 90-; Pre-Hlth Soc VP 90-; Deans Lst 87-; Premed/Bio; Obstetrician/Gynecologist.

**MC KAY, GORDEN R J,** Univ Of Sc At Columbia, Columbia, SC; JR; BS; Young Replcns 89; IMA; Gamma Beta Phi; Finance; Law.

**MC KAY, KIMBERLY A,** Univ Of Ky, Lexington, KY; SR; BSN; Sigma Theta Tau; Gold Key; Treas Sr Cls Schlrshp Acad UK Hosp Treas 90-; IM Sftbl/Bsktbl/Flg Ftbl; Critical Care Nrsng.

**MC KAY, LA NELLE L,** Univ Of Med & Dentistry Of Nj, Newark, NJ; JR; BS; Lgue Wmn Vtrs Bd Dir 86-88; Biology Tchr 67-75; L D Spec Thrpst 82-89; BA Rice Univ 67; Phys Asst.

**MC KAY, LIA D,** Univ Of Sc At Columbia, Columbia, SC; JR; NRHH Pres 90-; Tau Beta Sigma 89-; March Band 89-90; Gamma Beta Phi 89-; Gold Key 90-; Sigma Iota Rho; Deans Lst 89-; Soviet Exchange; Intl Studies.

**MC KAY, LORI A,** Univ Of Nc At Charlotte, Charlotte, NC; FR; BA; Phi Eta Sigma 90-; Nrsng.

**MC KAY, PATRICK F,** Fayetteville St Univ, Fayetteville, NC; SO; BS; Psych 90; Psychology; Clincial/Ind Psychology.

**MC KAY, VEREATTA A,** Johnson C Smith Univ, Charlotte, NC; SO; Mrchng Bnd Capt 89-; Cnstttnl Cmmtt Chrprsn 90-; Alpha Kappa Alpha; BA; Bnkng/Fnnc.

**MC KEARIN, FRANCIS J,** Southern Vt Coll, Bennington, VT; JR; BSW; Stdnt Assoc VP 89-; Stdnt Assoc Acadmc Chrmn 90-; Yrbk Adv Chrmn 90-; Deans List 88-; Resdnt Asst Aldis Hall 89-90; Judcl Review Bd 89-90; Acadmc Stndng Comm 90-; Soc Wrk; Eductr.

**MC KEARNEY, JOHN L,** Niagara Univ, Niagara Univ, NY; SR; BA; Soccer; Cmmnctns; Sprts Indstry.

**MC KEE, DAVID R,** Bristol Univ, Bristol, TN; SR; BS; Grdtd Hgh Hnr VHCC 75; Wash Co Bs Clb 78-; Mntnc Sprvsr; AAS Va Hghlnds Cmnty Clge 75; Bsn Admin; Mgmt.

**MC KEE, DONYA C,** Univ Of South Al, Mobile, AL; JR; BED; Equestrian Clb; Jaguar Prod 89-; Conservancy Scty 90-; Omicron Delta Kappa; Alpha Gamma Delta Philantpy Chr 89-; Robert C Byrd Schlrshp 89-; Secondary Educ; Teacher Biol High School.

**MC KEE, JASON S,** Univ Of Tn At Knoxville, Knoxville, TN; JR; Bus Admin; CPA JD.

**MC KEE, LARRY MICHEAL,** Mayland Comm Coll, Spruce Pine, NC; SO; Stdnt Govt Repr; Phi Theta Kappa; Natl Assn Accts; AAS; Acctg.

**MC KEE, LORI A,** Volunteer St Comm Coll, Gallatin, TN; SO; ASSOC; Deans List 91; Med Rcds Tech; RN.

**MC KEE, MARYANN J,** Tallahassee Comm Coll, Tallahassee, FL; SO; AA; FL Future Educs Of Amer 90-; Phi Theta Kappa 89-; Deans Lst 89-; Vlybl 89-90; Lake Jackson Vol Fire Dept Treas 90-; Grad Lively Law Enforcmnt Trng Ctr 88; Cert Leon Co Sub Tchr; Elem Tchr.

**MC KEE, ROBYN L,** Oh Univ-Southern Cmps, Ironton, OH; FR; BA; Dns Lst; Soc Wrk; Drg Rehab.

**MC KEE, SHEILA S,** Univ Of South Al, Mobile, AL; SO; BA; Pi Kappa Alpha Frat; Alpha Gamma Delta Pub Chm 85-87; Mrchndsr & Former Mgr Of Eagles Eye Co Store; Elem Edn; Sch Teacher.

**MC KEE, SHELLEY L,** Memphis St Univ, Memphis, TN; SR; BPS; BREAK; Gamma Beta Phi; TN Prlgl Assoc; Prlgl Stds; Mgmt.

**MC KEE, STEPHEN T,** Pellissippi St Tech Comm Coll, Knoxville, TN; SO; MBA; Bus Mgmnt.

**MC KEE, TAINE E,** S U N Y Coll Of Tech At Alfred, Alfred, NY; FR; AS; Human Serv; Soc Wrk.

**MC KEE, THOMAS N,** Manhattan Coll, Bronx, NY; SR; Soc Of Automotv Engrs Chrmn 90-; ASME 89-; Deans List 88-; BSME; Mech Eng.

**MC KEEHAN, CASEY D,** Union Coll, Barbourville, KY; FR; Gamma Beta Phi; Deans List; Pres Laureate; Physcs; Cvl/Elect Eng.

**MC KEEL, CANDACE D,** Mount Aloysius Jr Coll, Cresson, PA; FR; Cardiovascular Techn.

**MC KEEVER, THOMAS J,** Dowling Coll, Oakdale Li, NY; SR; BBA; Mktg; Advrtsng/Mgmt.

**MC KEITHAN, ALBERTHA,** Saint Josephs Coll New York, Brooklyn, NY; BS; Med Tchnlgst 75; Hlth Admin.

**MC KELLAR, DIANNA L,** Christopher Newport Coll, Newport News, VA; SO; BA; Stdnt Ldrshp Inst 89-90; Amrcn Mrktng Assoc Pres 90-; Amrcn Mrktng Assoc Tres 91-; Mrktng; Advrtsng Cpywrtr.

**MC KELLAR, PRESTON L,** Christopher Newport Coll, Newport News, VA; SO; BS; IM Bsktbl; Biology; Education.

**MC KELVEY, BRIAN J,** Radford Univ, Radford, VA; SO; Math; Actuary.

**MC KELVEY, MAUREEN E,** Kent St Univ Kent Cmps, Kent, OH; SR; BA; Sigma Tau Delta; Goldn Key; Hnrs Clg Schlrshp Partl 88-; Pre Med/Engl; Med/Sci Wrtng.

**MC KELVEY, TERESA A,** Clayton St Coll, Morrow, GA; SR; BS; RN; AA 76; Nrsng.

**MC KENNA, BLAINE J,** Indiana Univ Of Pa, Indiana, PA; SO; BS; TV Sta; Empl M&m Mars; Communication Media; Brdcstng/Trng/Dev.

**MC KENNA, PATRICIA A,** Siena Coll, Loudonville, NY; SR; BA; Stdnt Sen Treas/Pblc Rltns 89-; Cmps Mnstry Mnstr Hsplty Vol Prgm 88-; Orien Comm; Ambsdrs Clb; Drmcncl Treas 87-; Pres Hnrs 87-; Dns List 87-; Cmps Mnstry; Intrnshp Marriott Food Svc Mgr 90-; Bsktbl/Vlybl IM Co-Cptn 87-89; Pltcl Sci; Law.

**MC KENNA, PATRICIA J,** Daemen Coll, Amherst, NY; SR; BS; Cmnty Srvc Daemen Clge; Ltrcy Vol 87-88; Cmpr Wst 87-; Eldr Hstl Arbcs 90; Lake Erie Inst Rhbltn; Rome Dvlpmntl Ctr 90; Physcl Thrpy; Rehab Thrpst.

**MC KENNA, PATRICK J,** Temple Univ, Philadelphia, PA; SO; BS; USAF Elect Tech; AAS Camden Co Coll 85; AAS Comm Coll AF 89; Elect Eng.

**MC KENNA, TIMOTHY J,** Univ Of Cincinnati, Cincinnati, OH; SR; BFA; Brdcstng Socty VP 88-; News Record Sprts Edtr 90-; Asst News Edtr 89-90; Socty Prof Jrnlsts 90-; Boy Scouts Of Amer Merit Bdg Cnslr 90; Brdcstng; Sales/Jrnlsm.

**MC KENNAN, DAVID J,** City Univ Of Ny City Coll, New York, NY; JR; BS; Sidney Millman Physics Schlrshp; Ward Mdl Hstry Dept 87; Stagehnd Mbr Of Thetrcl Protctv Union Loc 1 IATSE 82-; Physcs; Resrch.

**MC KENZIE, AMY D,** Lee Coll, Cleveland, TN; FR; Prsdntl Schlrshp Awd; Deans Lst Hnrs; Accntng.

**MC KENZIE, ANTOINETTE R,** Dutchess Comm Coll, Poughkeepsie, NY; SO; AA; Ntnl Mnrty Tlnt Rstr; Accnt Clr Dtchss Cnty; Lbrl Arts Hmnties; Psych.

**MC KENZIE, CARIE J,** Atlanta Christian Coll, East Point, GA; FR; Concert Choir 90; Music Edctr; Music Tchng/Prdcng.

**MC KENZIE, LORI A,** Univ Of Tn At Martin, Martin, TN; JR; BED; Alpha Tau Omega; Erly Chldhd Educ; Tch Kndrgrtn.

**MC KENZIE, MICHAEL J,** Va Commonwealth Univ, Richmond, VA; SR; BS; VCU Blck Stu Alnc; VCU Coll Bwl Tm Tres 90-; Rsdnc Hl Jdcl Brd 89-; VCU Coll Bwl Tm 89-; Gldn Key VP 89-90; Omicron Delta Kappa; Phi Sigma Bio; Prjct Umoja Frshmn Mntrshp Pro 90-; Nw Stu Orntn Vol; VCU Deans Lst 89; Bio; Orthpdc Srgn.

**MC KENZIE, ROBERT S,** Embry Riddle Aeronautical Univ, Daytona Beach, FL; SO; BA; Drama Clb Prsdnt 89; MENSA 85-; AOPA 90-; Deans Lst 90-; Hnr Roll 89; Aeronautical Sci; Prfsnl Pilot.

**MC KENZIE, SUZAN TABORY,** Livingston Univ, Livingston, AL; SR; BED; Stu Govt Sec 88-; Yrbk Clss Edtr 89-; Phi Mu Pres 88-; Emvoy 90-; Sis Yr; Elem Educ; Tchr.

**MC KENZIE, WILLIAM B,** Tn Wesleyan Coll, Athens, TN; SR; BA; Judcl Cncl Chrmn 89-; SGA 89-90; Alpha Chi 90-; TWC Ambsdrs 90-; Bsktbl 88-; Hstry; Law.

**MC KENZIE, YVETTE L,** City Univ Of Ny Baruch Coll, New York, NY; SR; BBA; INROADS Intrnshp Org 87-; W Indn Cltrl Clb 87-89; Crbbn Stdnt Assn 87-89; Acctg Soc 87; Goldn Key 90-; Beta Gamma Sigma 90-; Incntv Awrd 87-88; St Dvds Yth Grp Pres 87-88 Asst Dir 88-89; Deans Lst 88-89; Endwmnt Fnd Schlrshp 89; Bus/Acctg; Acctg/Audtng.**

**MC KEON, BERNADETTE M,** S U N Y Coll Of Tech At Frmgdl, Farmingdale, NY; JR; BA; Phi Theta Kappa Sec 90; Deans Lst 88-90; Pres Lst 89-90; AS 90; Psychlgy; Scl Wrkr.

**MC KEON, NANCY J,** Coll Of New Rochelle, New Rochelle, NY; SO; BA; Theatr Clb 89-; Cls Fndrsng Comm Chrprsn 89-90; Natl Coll Hnrs Cncl Conf Del 90-; Hnrs Brd 90-; Pol Sci; Law.

**MC KEOWN JR, ROBERT D,** De Tech & Comm Coll At Dover, Dover, DE; FR; BA; Self Employed Landlord/Gen Cntrctr 73-; Bus Admin; Law.

**MC KIBBEN, BOBBIE L,** Fl International Univ, Miami, FL; FR; Engl.

**MC KILLOP, MARY K,** Endicott Coll, Beverly, MA; SR; AS; Envrnmntl Clb Fitness Clb Aerobics Instrctr 90-; Fshn Dsgn Model 90-; Dns Lst 90-; Vic Micks Rstrnt Intern 90-; Scuba Cert 90-; Liberal Arts.

**MC KILLOP, SEAN J,** Univ Of Rochester, Rochester, NY; SR; BS; Newman Cmnty 87-; Wrstlng Club Pres 88-; Dorm Cncl Pres 87-90; Knghts Of Colombus 89-; Nvl Rsrv Ofcr Training Corps CC 87-; Mech Eng; Naval Svc/Engr.

**MC KINLEY, DEBRA A,** Univ Of South Al, Mobile, AL; JR; BA; Cooprtv Educ 89-; Acctg.

**MC KINLEY, EARL L,** Clark Atlanta Univ, Atlanta, GA; JR; BA; Professional Model; Coml Actor; Finance; Entertainment.

**MC KINLEY, ELNORE M,** Al A & M Univ, Normal, AL; JR; BS; Elem Schl Tchrs Clb 90-; Kappa Delta Pi 90-; AS Lewis Clark Comm Clge 89-90; Elem Ed; Tchr.

**MC KINLEY, KATRINA M,** Univ Of Montevallo, Montevallo, AL; FR; BSN; Rsdnc Hll Assoc 90-; Pr Rvw Brd 90-; Hghst Hnrs; Frshmn Clss Wnnr Prsdnts Awrd Excllnc Wrtng; Nrsng; RN.

**MC KINLEY, LAURA K,** Georgetown Coll, Georgetown, KY; JR; BMED; Chrl/Band Sctn Ldr 88-; Mrchng Bnd 88-; Hmcmng Show 89; Alpha Lambda Delta 89-; Delta Omcrn Sgt Arms; Alpha Chi Chr 90; Voc Rehab Cert Mrt 90; Msc Tutor 89-90; Most Outstdng Wmn Msc 89; Jay Parson Msc Schlp; Msc Educ; Tch.

**MC KINLEY, MARGARET E,** S U N Y Coll At Fredonia, Fredonia, NY; JR; BS; Tchr Ed Clb 90-; Rcqtbl Clb 90; Ttr 90; Kappa Delta Pi; Elem Educ; Tch.

**MC KINNEY, BEVERLY,** Southern Junior Coll, Birmingham, AL; SR; AAS; Peer Cnslr/Advsr; Intrnshp Eastern Mental Hlth Clinic; Asst To Assoc Dean; Mental Hlth Worker For St Of Ala 86-90; Substance Abuse Cnslr.

**MC KINNEY, COLLEEN M,** Emory & Henry Coll, Emory, VA; JR; BA; Stu VR Educ Assn Pres 88-; Math Assn 89-; Fllwshp Chrstn Athlts 90-; SS Tchr 89-; Chrch Orgnst 85-; K Mart Empl 89-; Emory & Henry Schlr 88-; Paul Douglas Tchr Schlrshp 89-; Math; Tchng.

**MC KINNEY, DAVID F,** Westminster Coll, New Wilmingtn, PA; JR; BA; Clg Radio Sprts Dir 89-90; Telecomm; Sprtscstng.

**MC KINNEY, DEBRA E,** Roane St Comm Coll, Harriman, TN; FR; BA; Dean Lst 90; Bus Admn; Accntng.

**MC KINNEY, DEBRA P,** Western Piedmont Comm Coll, Morganton, NC; SO; Marshall; Nrsng; RN.

**MC KINNEY, HAROLD L,** Duquesne Univ, Pittsburgh, PA; SO; BA; Northway Chrstn Comm Singles Grp Musician 90; Singles Conf Master Of Ceremony 90; Drama Tm Actor; Vietnam Vets Mem Schlrshp Fund 90-; Cranberry Comm Vlybl Trnmnt; U S Navy E-5 85-90; Cosmopolitan Lifestyles Hlth Spa Asst Mgr Physcl Cnsltnt 90; Pol Sci; Intl/Corp Atty.

**MC KINNEY JR, HOWARD G,** Middle Tn St Univ, Murfreesboro, TN; GD; BS; Scty Of Manuf Engs; Cert Manuf Tech; Manuf Eng Tech.

**MC KINNEY, JENNIFER L,** Middle Tn St Univ, Murfreesboro, TN; SR; BS; Gamma Beta Phi; Aerospc; Aerospc Frm.

**MC KINNEY, LACRECIA D,** Snead St Jr Coll, Boaz, AL; FR; BS; Sec Automobile Dlrshp; Engl.

**MC KINNEY, MELISSA C,** Western Piedmont Comm Coll, Morganton, NC; SO; ADN; Jr Choir Ldr 90-; Medcl/Bio; RN.

**MC KINNEY, PAMELA M,** Bloomfield Coll, Bloomfield, NJ; JR; Class Pr; Res Life Cmte Cnsl 90-; RA; Acad Hons; Deans Lst 89-; Acad Achvmnt 90-; Spanish Ling; Interpretor.**

**MC KINNEY, RONDA A,** Valdosta St Coll, Valdosta, GA; GD; BFA; Exec Cncl Schl FA; Thtr; Miss VSC 90; Alpha Lambda Delta; Sigma Alpha Chi; Alpha Chi; Phi Kappa Phi; Alpha Psi Omega; Omicron Delta Kappa; Pres Fresh Schlr; Alpha Lambda Delta Bk Awrd; Magna Cumme Laude; Thtr; Entrtmnt Law.

**MC KINNEY, SARAH L,** Lees Coll, Jackson, KY; SO; Cert Medctns Aide; Nrsng/Sci; Nrsng MA.

**MC KINNEY, SEAN P,** Fl St Univ, Tallahassee, FL; JR; BA; Musicae Antiquae; Music.

**MC KINNEY, STACIE C,** Mayland Comm Coll, Spruce Pine, NC; SR; AD; Outstndg Stdnt Awd Nrsng Edn Options Level I 90; Cert LPN 90; Nrsng.

**MC KINNEY, TAMMIE L,** Jackson St Univ, Jackson, MS; FR; Bibl Stdy Grp; Karate Clb; Alpha Lambda Delta.

**MC KINNEY, TEKITA M,** Univ Of Tn At Martin, Martin, TN; JR; BS; Bapt Stdnt Un Pres; Mnrty Stdnt Assn 88-; Deans Lst 90; Bio; Pediatrician.

**MC KINNEY, TINA S,** Univ Of Sc At Spartanburg, Spartanburg, SC; FR; ADN; Comm Yth Advsr Pres; Dir Comm Choir; Cmplt Nrsg Pro Obtn RN Lic; Nrsg; RN.

**MC KINNEY, TONY A,** Piedmont Coll, Demorest, GA; FR; BED; Svnth Day Sdvntst Chrch Deacon 90-; USAF 80-84; Arcrft Mechnc Lockhrd Corp 85-88; Early Chldhd Ed; Tch.

**MC KINNIS, KELLY A,** Milligan Coll, Milligan Clg, TN; JR; BS; Acad Deans Lst 88-90; Pres Schlrshp 88-; Schlrshps Bsktbl/ Sftbl/Vlybl 88-; Psychlgy; Phys Therapy.

**MC KINSTRAY, TERESA J,** Univ Of Sc At Columbia, Columbia, SC; FR; BS; Davis Besse Nclr Sta; Jrny Prsn-Instrmnt/ Cntrl Tchncn 81-89; Assoc Terra Tech Coll Fremont OH 85-; Dgnstc Sngrphy; Ultrsnd.

**MC KINSTRY, BARRY L,** Brewer St Jr Coll, Fayette, AL; FR; BA; VICA Sec 89-90; Hon Stdnt 89; Comp Sci; Comp.

**MC KINZIE, MONIQUE,** Shaw Univ, Raleigh, NC; SR; BA; Psychlgy Clb Pres 90-; Gspl Chr 88-89; Outstdng Hnr Psychlgy 90-; Psychlgy; Clin Psychlgst/Ph D.**

**MC KISSACK JR, DANIEL C,** Meridian Comm Coll, Meridian, MS; SO; BA; ASB Sntr 90-; Wall St Jrnl Clb; Clg Rpblcns; Chi Psi; Ec; Law.

**MC KISSACK, JEREMY D,** Middle Tn St Univ, Murfreesboro, TN; FR; BS; Marchng Bnd; Pres Hnr Soc; Outstndg Stdnt Schlrshp Cumberlnd Vly Schl Gospel Msc; Eng; Cmptr Tech.

**MC KISSICK, KELLY L,** Duquesne Univ, Pittsburgh, PA; FR; BSN; Drama Clb 90; Vol Tutor Soup Kitchen 90-; Nrsng; Psychtrc Nrs.

**MC KITRICK, KRISTIN L,** Anderson Coll, Anderson, SC; FR; Drama/Voice; Phi Theta Kappa; Acad Perf Frshmn Marshall; Science; Phys Therapy.

**MC KITRICK JR, ROBERT W,** Christopher Newport Coll, Newport News, VA; SR; BS; Private Pilot/Aircraft 85; Golf; Alpha Kappa Psi Alumni Dir 89; Prgrmng Awd; Nat Conf Undergrad Rsrch Physics Paper Publication; Prgmmr/Eng 83-; Cmptr Eng; Prgmng/Eng.

**MC KITRICK, VALERIE J,** Univ Of Akron, Akron, OH; JR; BA; St Martha Parent Grp V P 90-; Frnch Hnr Soc; Golden Key 90-; Alpha Sigma Lambda 90-; Intl Hnr Soc; French; Educ.

**MC KIVERGAN, BRIDGET T,** Univ Of Sc At Columbia, Columbia, SC; JR; BA; Gamma Beta Phi Cmmtt Chr 89-; Big Bro Sis 90-; IM Bsktbl Sftbl 88-; Engl/Anthrplgy; Prfssr.

**MC KNIGHT, ERIC,** Johnson C Smith Univ, Charlotte, NC; JR; BA; Union Pgm Bd Pres 90-; Delta Gent Org Treas 90-; Sftbl Mngr; WPEG Pwr 98 FM Radio Sta Intrn 90-; Cmnctns; Radio Ind.

**MC KNIGHT, GINA P,** Univ Of Md Balt Cnty Campus, Catonsville, MD; SO; BS; Bio; Med.**

**MC KNIGHT, JASON B,** Al A & M Univ, Normal, AL; SO; BS; Masnry 90-; Phi Beta Sigma 90-; Dns Lst 89-; Phi Beta Sigma 90-; Coop Nasa; Finc; Stock Brokr.

**MC KNIGHT, JOI M,** Bethune Cookman Coll, Daytona Beach, FL; JR; BA; Pres Schlrs Lst 88-89; Pres Schlrs Lst 90; Lakewood Jr Sprtns Ftbl Assn VP; Plng Pgrms; H R S Dist V St Of Fla Clrk Typst Spec 90-; Crim Just; Law.

**MC KNIGHT, JONATHAN C,** Univ Of Ky, Lexington, KY; SR; BA; Pltcl Sci Hons Clb 90-; Golden Key 90-; Coll Schlrs Amer 90-; Sigma Alpha Epsilon Comm Svc Hr 88-90; Pltcl Sci; Law.

**MC KNIGHT, LAURELEI,** Fl A & M Univ, Tallahassee, FL; SR; BS; Assctd Gnrl Cntrctrs Am 90-; Archtctrl/Cnstrctn Eng Tchnlgy; Mgt.

**MC KNIGHT, REGINA L,** Univ Of North Fl, Jacksonville, FL; JR; Employee Health Promo Subcommitte Mayo Clinic; Golden Key; Oltical Science; Law.

**MC KNIGHT, SHERRY L,** Mount Aloysius Jr Coll, Cresson, PA; FR; AS; Nrsng.

**MC KNIGHT, STACEY D,** Univ Of Md At Eastern Shore, Princess Anne, MD; SR; Alpha Angl Swthrt Crt 89-; Natl Stdnt Bus Lg 89-90; Phi Beta Lambda Sec 88-90; UMES Schlrshp 88; Acdmc Hnrs; BS.

**MC KNIGHT, TERESINA M,** Roane St Comm Coll, Harriman, TN; BSN; Crtfctn Brd Of Registry; Amer Soc Clinical Pthlgsts; St Marys Hosp/Phlebotomg Tech; ABS Cmptr Pgm/Acctg Draughons Jnr Clg 87; Nrsg; Critical Care.

**MC KONE, STACEY L,** Seton Hall Univ, South Orange, NJ; JR; BA; Elizabeth Ann Seton Ed Assoc Pres; Kappa Delta Pi; Alpha Gamma Delta Ritual Chair 90; Deans List; Psychology/ Elem Ed.

**MC KOWN, MATTHEW H,** Liberty Univ, Lynchburg, VA; SO; BA; Army ROTC 90-; Reserve Ofcr Achvmnt Awd 90-; Foreign Lang; Military.

**MC KOY, STACY L,** Bloomfield Coll, Bloomfield, NJ; JR; Afrcn Amer Asc Treas 90-; Zeta Phi Beta; Acctng.**

**MC LAIN, LAURA L,** Birmingham Southern Coll, Birmingham, AL; SO; BA; Bus Mktg; Sales/Accnt Exec.

**MC LAIN, LAURIE E,** Memphis St Univ, Memphis, TN; SO; BS; Hnrs Stdnt Assoc 89-; Gamma Beta Phi; Alpha Epsilon Delta; People Understanding Severely Handicapped 90-; Medcl Tchnlgy.

**MC LAIN, MARY R,** Chesterfield Marlboro Coll, Cheraw, SC; SO; AAS; Alpha Beta Delta 90-; Grad Marshall 90; Acctg.

**MC LAIN, POLLY R,** Chesterfield Marlboro Coll, Cheraw, SC; SO; ASSOC; Gen Bus.

**MC LAIN, RONALD C,** Fl Baptist Theological Coll, Graceville, FL; GD; MDIV; Magna Cum Laude 90; THI B Florida Bapt Thlgcl Clg 90; Thelogy; Bapt Chrch Pstr.

**MC LAMB, JANICE,** Morgan St Univ, Baltimore, MD; SR; BS; Cncrt Chr 88-; Kappa Delta Pi; Sigma Dove; US Army Rsrv 86-; Music Ed; Tchr.

**MC LAUCHLIN, ERIC E,** Salisbury St Univ, Salisbury, MD; JR; BA BA; French Club; French Soc; GA; Hon Prog; Deans Lst; Habitat Humnty; French/Pre Law; Law.

**MC LAUGHLIN, AMY V,** Al A & M Univ, Normal, AL; SR; BS; Early Chldhd/Elem Ed Clb Pres 88-; Kappa Delta Pi Treas 89-; Alpha Kappa Mu 89-; AB; Early Chldhd Ed; Tchr.

**MC LAUGHLIN, BRYAN F,** Nova Univ, Ft Lauderdale, FL; GD; MBA; Grp Ldr Sftware Eng 84-; BAS Fla Atlntc Univ 84; Bus/Cmptr Sci; Mgmnt Eng.

**MC LAUGHLIN, DAVID S,** East Stroudsburg Univ, E Stroudsburg, PA; SR; BS; Stdnt Nwsppr Cpy Ed 89-; WESSFM Stdnt Radio Prsnll 85-87; Scty Crtv Anchrnsm; Kdnkn Jjts Clb 85-87; Cum Laude Grad; BA ESU; BS ESU; Mgmt.

**MC LAUGHLIN, DEANA K,** Kent St Univ Kent Cmps, Kent, OH; SO; BS; SPN; Portage Faith Unit Meth Ch 87-; Nurs Asst 90-; Dipl Jr Acctg 85; Nurs; RN.

**MC LAUGHLIN, DEBORAH D,** Central Fl Comm Coll, Ocala, FL; SO; AA; Medical; Neonatal RN.

**MC LAUGHLIN, DIANE E,** Providence Coll, Providence, RI; JR; BA; Pastoral Cncl 88-89; Engl Clb 89-90; Phi Sigma Tau 90; Deans List 88; Liberal Arts Hnrs Prgrm 88; Engl; Clg Professor.

**MC LAUGHLIN, EILEEN URBANOWICZ,** Salisbury St Univ, Salisbury, MD; SR; MPS; Cycling Club 88-89; Intrml 88-90; Psi Chi 89-; Omicron Delta Kappa 90-; Deans List 90; Campus Life Awd 90; Wmns Club Soccer Cptn 88-90; BS 90; Public Admin; Persl Mangt.

**MC LAUGHLIN, ELLEN M,** Univ Of Sc At Spartanburg, Spartanburg, SC; JR; BA; Psych/Soc; Soc Work/Cnslng.

**MC LAUGHLIN, JAIME E,** Alcorn St Univ, Lorman, MS; JR; BS; Acctg Clb Pres; NAACP Sec 90-; Acctg; CPA/IRS Agnt.

**MC LAUGHLIN, NALANI-ALUA M,** Endicott Coll, Beverly, MA; SR; AS; Bus Clb/Clb Coutune 89-; Orient Ldr 90-; Theatre 90-; Phi Theta Kappa 90-; Bus Admin.

**MC LAUGHLIN, PATRICIA L,** Rivier Coll, Nashua, NH; SO; BA; Cmmtr Comm Pres 90-; Brd Appls 90-; Ornttn Comm 90-; Std Affrs Comm 90-; High Hnrs 89-; Dns Lst 89-; Prlgl Stds; Supreme Crt Judge.

**MC LAUGHLIN, PETER J,** Schenectady County Comm Coll, Schenectady, NY; FR; AAS; Gen Foreman Mntnc Al Tech Spclty Steel Corp 77-; Math/Sci; Engrng.

**MC LAUGHLIN, SARA L,** Otterbein Coll, Westerville, OH; JR; BA; Radio Bus Mgr 90-; TV Labeling Dir 89-90; College Bands 88-; Stdnt Sntr 90-; Res Hall Cncl 90-; Wmns Bsktbl Announcer 89-; Brdcstng/Bus; Accnt Exec.**

**MC LAUGHLIN, SHANNON L,** Western Piedmont Comm Coll, Morganton, NC; SO; AASC; Crmnl Jstc Clb 90-; Crmnl Jstc; Fed Law Enfrcmnt.

**MC LAUGHLIN, TIMOTHY A,** Catawba Valley Comm Coll, Hickory, NC; FR; Comrcl Art/Adv Dsgn; Adv/Photogrphy.

**MC LAUGHLIN, TRACY A,** Univ Of Ga, Athens, GA; JR; BS; Kappa Delta Epsilon Sec; Early Educ.

**MC LAUGHLIN, TRACY J,** Palm Beach Comm Coll, Lake Worth, FL; SO; BS; DPMA 90-; AA; Computer Infor Syst; Syst Analyst.**

**MC LAURIN, CAROLYN ELIZABETH,** Syracuse Univ, Syracuse, NY; SR; BSW; Undrgrad Stdnt Schl Wrk Org T 90-; Deans Lst 88-; Scl Wrk; Gov.

**MC LAURIN, SHEILA D,** Wilmington Coll, New Castle, DE; FR; BA; Svc Rep Damond State Tlphn; Acctg.

**MC LAURIN, SHONA D,** William Carey Coll, Hattiesburg, MS; SR; BSB; Phi Beta Lambd Prlmntrn 90-; Afro Amer Cltrl Scty 89-; Omcrn Dlt Kappa Sec 90-; Otstndng Bus Stdnt 90-; Wall St Jrnl Awrd 90-; Ldrshp Conf 90-; Crsdrs Capt 87-; Bus Mgmt; Tchng.

**MC LAURIN, TANYA T,** Johnson C Smith Univ, Charlotte, NC; SO; Lbry Clb Tres 90-; Psychlgy/Bio; Psychtry.

**MC LEAN, CAROLYN H,** Gaston Coll, Dallas, NC; SR; AAS; Beta Sigma Phi Pres 71-76; Charlotte City Cncl V P 76-77; Intrnshp WWMG 90 WSGE Clg Cblvsn; Presby Church Choir 88-; PTA 89-90; Bkkpr 69-79; Avon Sls Pres Clg 79-; Radio/TV Brdcstng.

**MC LEAN, DAVID M,** Union Univ, Jackson, TN; FR; BS; Pre Eng; Mech Eng.

**MC LEAN, DOREEN A,** Univ Of Miami, Coral Gables, FL; JR; Lrn To Rd Vols 89-; Mmi Dde Almni Assn; Stdnt Govt Sntr 90; Phi Kappa Phi; Phi Theta Kappa; AA Miami Dade Comm Coll 90; Educ And Pol Sci.

**MC LEAN, H KENNETH,** Pellissippi St Tech Comm Coll, Knoxville, TN; SO; AAS; Data Prcsng Mgmt Assn 90-; Phi Theta Kappa; Assn Engr Geologists 75-; BS East Carolina Univ 71; Cmptr Sci Tech; Cmptr Prgrmng.

**MC LEAN, JAMES N,** Coll Of Charleston, Charleston, SC; SR; BA 90; Bus/Fin.

**MC LEAN, JENNIFER L,** Bethany Coll, Bethany, WV; SO; BA; Bisons 89-; SBOG 89-; Frnch Clb 89-; Kappa Delta Hstrn 90-; Progmng Asst 90-; Rassias Asst Tchr 90-; Vars Swim Tm 89-; Frnch; Trnsltn.

**MC LEAN, MARIA L,** Newbury Coll, Brookline, MA; SR.

**MC LEAN, MATTHEW D,** Elmira Coll, Elmira, NY; FR; BA; Athletic Trainer 90-F Gold Key Ambsdr; Beta Beta Beta; Athletic Trainer Award; RA; Chem Award; Soccer/Wlybl; Sci; Envrnmntl Eng.

**MC LEAN, ROBERT S,** Univ Of Nc At Chapel Hill, Chapel Hill, NC; GD; JD; NC Law Review 89-90; Omicron Delta Epsilon 84-; Omicron Delta Kappa 85-; Phi Delta Phi; Simga Alpha Epsilon; Vars Trk 81-86; BA Davidson Coll 86; Law/Bus.

**MC LEAN, WILLIAM E R,** Saint Andrews Presbytrn Coll, Laurinburg, NC; FR; BA; Rgby Clb Sec 90-; Dbte Tm 90-; Acad Hnrs Schlrshp 90-; Natl Presb Schlr 90-.

**MC LEISH, STEPHANIE A,** Univ Of North Fl, Jacksonville, FL; SO; BA; Army Rsrvs E 4; Gldn Ky; Cert Nrsng Asst 89; Brgde Sldr Of Cycle 90; CNA Florida Comm Coll 89; Blgy; Med Dr.

**MC LELLAN, NELDA C,** Univ Of South Al, Mobile, AL; JR; BA; Phi Mu VP 87-; Lang Arts; Scndry Ed.

**MC LELLAND, DEBRA K,** Univ Of Nh Plymouth St Coll, Plymouth, NH; SR; BS; Kappa Delta Pi 90-; Crrclm Lab/Lbry Asst Fllwshp; Pres Lst 90-; Elem Educ/Ntrl Sci; Elem Educ Tchr.

**MC LEMORE, WANDA G,** Univ Of South Al, Mobile, AL; SO; BED; Phi Theta Kappa 89-; Socl Sci; Tchng.

**MC LENDON, KEITH O,** Fayetteville St Univ, Fayetteville, NC; SO; BA; Peer Asst 90-; Ldrs 90-; DECA; Engl Ed; Tchr.

**MC LENDON, SANDRA HARE,** Univ Of Sc At Sumter, Sumter, SC; JR; BA; Bus; Bus Mngmnt.

**MC LENDON, SYLVIA C,** Morris Brown Coll, Atlanta, GA; SO; BA; Gspl Chr Rec Sec 89-90; Gslph Chr 89-90; GA Assn Of Educ/NEA Rec Sec 89-; Hnr Rl 89-; Chrldr; Early Chldhd Eudc; Prmry Tchr.**

**MC LENDON, VICTOR K,** Univ Of Southern Ms, Hattiesburg, MS; SR; BS; Cmptr Sci; Sys Anlyst.

**MC LEOD, BANITA F,** Univ Of Nc At Greensboro, Greensboro, NC; FR; BS; Soc Wrk; Schl Soc Wrkr.

**MC LEOD, ELIZABETH R,** Univ Of Sc At Columbia, Columbia, SC; GD; BS; Eta Sigma Delta Treas 87-90; Deans List 87 90; Outstndng Clg Stdnts Am 89; Htl/Rstrnt/Trsm Admin; Mgt.

**MC LEOD JR, JOHN R,** Univ Of New Haven, West Haven, CT; JR; BS; Chem Clb Treas 89; Chem Eng Clb; Alpha Lambda Delta; Frshmn Chem Achievemnt Awd 87; AS Cmmnty Clg Of AF 89; Chem Eng; Grad Schl.

**MC LEOD, KATHRYN N,** Univ Of Sc At Columbia, Columbia, SC; FR; BA; Phi Eta Sigma; Hist; Tchng.

**MC LEOD, LOIS P,** Univ Of Sc At Columbia, Columbia, SC; SR; BA; Deans List/USC/SUMTER 90; Deans List Francis Marion Colg Florence S C 89; Furman H S Booster Cl; Sub Tchr Dist 2 Sumter S C; AA USC/SUMTER S C 87; Genl Edctn; Gdnce Coun.

**MC LEOD, MARLENE H,** Bloomfield Coll, Bloomfield, NJ; SO; BSN; Nrsng/Sociology/Nutrition Chem; Nurse.

**MC LEOD, MICHAEL A,** Fl St Univ, Tallahassee, FL; JR; BS; Eng Hnr Soc 90-; Phi Theta Kappa 88-89; AA 89; Gerald G Gould Sci Awd Grntd Emplymnt Nvl Cstl Sys Ctr 87-; Magna Cum Laude 89; Chem Eng; Eng.

**MC LEOD, MICHELLE A,** Fl International Univ, Miami, FL; SO; BA; Stdnt Govt Soc Comm Chrprsn 90-; Stdnt Govt Senate 89-90; Stdnts Advsry Brd 89-; Outstndng Fr Of The Yr 90; Finance; Law.

**MC LEOD, OSCAR B,** Alcorn St Univ, Lorman, MS; SR; BA; VITA 90; TMI Tele Mrktng Inc Tele Mrktr Rep 89-90; BA 89; Accntng; MBA CPA.

**MC LEOD, PHILLIP K,** Central Fl Comm Coll, Ocala, FL; SO; BA; Pi Kappa Alpha 86-87; Bus; CPA.

**MC LEOD, RUSSELL R,** Univ Of Sc At Sumter, Sumter, SC; FR; BA; Busn.

**MC LEOD, RUSSELL R,** Univ Of Sc At Columbia, Columbia, SC; FR; BA; Advrtsng Pblc Rltns; Jrnlsm.

**MC LEOD, SAMANTHA Y,** Fayetteville St Univ, Fayetteville, NC; JR; BA; E Gwynn Dancers Of NCA/T 85-; FSU Dncrs 90-91; FSU Drama Gld 90-91; Elem Educ; Teach/Grad Schl.

**MC LEOD, SCHANDRA G,** Bennett Coll, Greensboro, NC; JR; BA; Bio Med Rsrch Prog; Psychlgy Clb 88-; ARC; Zeta Phi Beta; Schlr Prog; Deans/Hon Lst; Psychlgy; Clngl Psychlgy.

**MC LEOD, SUSAN J,** Newbury Coll, Brookline, MA; SR; AS; Secy 87-; Bus Mngmnt; Customer Support Analyst.

**MC LEOD, SUZANNE W,** Portland School Of Art, Portland, ME; FR; BRA; Coord Audbn Soc Comm Grdn 87-; Audbn Soc Coor Of Vol; BA Univ Of PA 78; Painting.

**MC LEOD, VERONICA P,** Bloomfield Coll, Bloomfield, NJ; SO; BA; Exclnc Acctg; Assc Acctg Techncns 83-; MAAT Assc Acctg Techncns 85; AAS Union County Clg 90; Acctg; Bus.

**MC LEROY, D TODD,** Samford Univ, Birmingham, AL; GD; JD; AL Stdnt Br 90-; Chrstn Lgl Soc 89-; Cumberland Trl Brd; Law Rvw Assoc Ed 90-; Lgl Rsrch Wrtg Flw 90-; Phi Kappa Sigma Sec 87; Boy Scts Comm Chrmn 90-; Dstrct Exec Boy Scts Amer 88-89; BA Univ Alabama 88; Law.

**MC LEROY, MARGARET C,** Ms St Univ, Miss State, MS; SO; Pre-Vet Clb; Agri Econ Clb; Farmhouse Ltl Sis; Vet Med.

**MC LIN, MONICA E,** Univ Of Sc At Columbia, Columbia, SC; JR; BA; Stdnt Govt Advsry Brd 90-; Hmcmng Cmsn Qns Chrmn 90; Delta Gamma Vp 90-; Cmps Cltn Ltrcy 90-; Habitat Fr Humanity; Intl Edctnl Exchng 90; Deans Lst 90; Intl Studies; Law.

**MC LOCHLIN, SCOTT A,** Univ Of Louisville, Louisville, KY; SR; BS; Math Comp Sci; Eng.

**MC LOUGHLIN, REAGAN,** Villanova Univ, Villanova, PA; SO; BS; Bsktbl Clb 89-; Kappa Alpha Theta; Soup Ktchn 89-90; Spcl Olympcs 89-; Deans Lst 89-; Bio; Rsrch.

**MC LOUGHLIN, SUSAN C,** Le Moyne Coll, Syracuse, NY; JR; BS; Phi Theta Kappa 81-83; Delta Mu Delta; Cmptr Oprtr 89-; ASS Cayuga Cnty Comm Clg 83; Accntng; CPA.

**MC MAHAN, CHRISTINE D,** West Liberty St Coll, West Liberty, WV; FR; BA; 4-H 2nd Vp 80-; Untd Mthdst Yth Flwshp Pres 84-; Delta Pi; Bst 101 Orl Cmnctns Spkr; Bsns Admn Mth; Ststcl Anlyst.

**MC MAHAN, CHRISTOPHER S,** Ohio Valley Coll, Parkersburg, WV; SO; BA; IM Bsktbl Cptn 90-; Telecommunications; TV & Radio Announcer.

**MC MAHAN, KEITH H,** Memphis St Univ, Memphis, TN; SR; BET; AET St Tech Inst 89; Tdch; Eng.

**MC MAHAN, MARY MARCIA,** Wesleyan Coll, Macon, GA; JR; AB; Hnr Ct Jdcl Sec 88-; Washbrd Bnd Pres 88-; Frshmn Cls VP 89; Camp Fire Inc 88; Wottelo Medallion 88; Pierce Ldrshp Awd 88; Bd Of Dir 87-89; Intl Rel; Law.**

**MC MAHAN, MICHELLE E,** Univ Of Nc At Greensboro, Greensboro, NC; SO; BS; Mgmnt; Mrktg Dept.

**MC MAHON, ADDISON R,** Western Carolina Univ, Cullowhee, NC; SR; Deans Lst 89-90-; Study Abroad British; BS 90; Sociology; Bus.

**MC MAHON, ELEANOR M,** Hudson Valley Comm Coll, Troy, NY; SO; BA; Hist.

**MC MAHON, ERIN-KATHLEEN B,** Univ Of Rochester, Rochester, NY; SR; Cmtee Prfrmng Arts; Hartnett Gallery Cmtee 87-88; Alpha Psi Omega; Intrnshp Assn Blind; Hon Program 90; BA English; English; Prfrmng Arts/Crmnl Law.

**MC MAHON, JEREMY B,** Univ Of Ky, Lexington, KY; JR; BA; Mortar Bd; Pi Sigma Alpha; Gldn Ky; Sigma Nu Treas 89-90; Dns Lst 89-; Nominated Truman Schlrshp; Pol Sci; Law.

**MC MAHON, KATHLEEN M,** Longwood Coll, Farmville, VA; JR; BS; Rugby Clb VP 90; Psychlgy Clb; Hon Pgm 88-; Psi Chi 90-; Alpha Sigma Tau Pres; Peer Hlpr Org; Wrk Study; Psychlgy; Clncl Psychlgy.

**MC MAHON, KATHLEEN M,** Le Moyne Coll, Syracuse, NY; SR; BS; Acctng Soc Cmmctns Comm 90-; Delta Mu Delta 90-; Dns Lst 88-; Price Wtrhs Intshp 89-; Acctng.

**MC MAHON, MARYBETH K,** Marywood Coll, Scranton, PA; JR; BA; TOT; Engl/Secndry Ed; Tchr.

**MC MAHON, SHAWN C,** Siena Coll, Loudonville, NY; SR; BBA; NAA 87-; Fin Clb 88-; Siena Clg Acctg Clb 88-; Cmptrlrs Off 90-; Var Ftbl 87-88; Cert Real Est Aprsr; Natl Assn Real Est Aprsrs; NYS Life/Hlth Ins Lic; Acctg.

**MC MAHON, STACY J,** West Liberty St Coll, West Liberty, WV; JR; BS; Fashion Intern; Bus Admn; Fshn Mrktng.

**MC MAHON, SUSAN M,** Andrew Coll, Cuthbert, GA; SO; Head Start Vol 90-; Phi Delta 89-; Soccer 89-90; Psychlgy; Chld Psychlgst.

**MC MAHON JR, THOMAS W,** Daemen Coll, Amherst, NY; SO; BA; Flyng Clb 90; Schlr Ath Lst 87-88; Dns Lst 88-90; Phys Thrpy 87 90-; Chldrns Day Proj 90; Ftbl 87; CREW Capt 89-90; Phys Thrpy.

**MC MANUS, CHRISTINA J,** Cornell Univ Statutory College, Ithaca, NY; FR; BS; Eqstrn Tm 90-; Stdnts Hrsmns Assn 90-; Pre Vet Scty 90; Anml Sci; Vet Med.

**MC MANUS, DANIEL B,** Univ Of Ms Medical Center, Jackson, MS; GD; DMD; Stu Rsrch Grp 89-; Amer Stu Dntl Assoc 88-; Miss Dntl Rsrch 89-; Deans Lst 89-; BA 87; AA 84; Dntstry.

**MC MANUS, WENDY K,** Univ Of Sc At Columbia, Columbia, SC; SO; BA; SGA 89-; PAL 89-; Dns Lst 90-; IM Sftbl Vlybl Flg Ftbl 89-; B Ed; Bsn Mgmt; Grad Schl.

**MC MASTER, SCOTT A,** Duquesne Univ, Pittsburgh, PA; JR; BSBA; Res Hll Assn VP 90-; Intern Prudentia-Bache Scrts; Mrktng; Scrts Brkrng.

**MC MEANS, BRIAN L,** Memphis St Univ, Memphis, TN; JR; BBA; Mngd Specialty Clothing Stores; Mngmnt; Graduate Law School.

**MC MICHAEL, KIMBERLY DENISE,** Univ Of Southern Ms, Hattiesburg, MS; SO; BS; Almni Assc 90-; Rcrtn Mjrs Assc 90-; Hall Cncl 90-; Gamma Beta Phi; Deans List 90; IM Scr Sftbl 90-; Sprts Admn; Mgmt.

**MC MILLAN, CATHERINE E,** Univ Of Al At Birmingham, Birmingham, AL; SR; ASAHPERD VP 87-; P E Clb 87-; Asst Racquetbl Trnmnt Dir; Specl Olympics Vol 89-; Deans Lst 90; Pr Lst; Outstndng Undergrad Stdnt In Phys Educ 90-; Coop Wrk Pgm 88-; Tchng Asst; Phys Educ; Tch.

**MC MILLAN, DEBORAH E,** Univ Of Pittsburgh, Pittsburgh, PA; SO; BSE; Dept Defense Co-Op; Engrg Hnr Student; Sholokan Karate; Mechl Engrg; Engrg Test Pilot.

**MC MILLAN, KATHY L,** Univ Of Sc At Columbia, Columbia, SC; SR; MED; NAACP 86-90; Delta Sigma Theta 89-90; BAS; Cnslr Ed; Admin In Schl Syst.

**MC MILLAN, SHELLY CHRISTINE,** Gaston Coll, Dallas, NC; SO; BS; Pres List 90-; Sci; Nrsng.

**MC MILLAN, STEPHEN B,** Univ Of Fl, Gainesville, FL; JR; BA; Carribean Stdnts Assc 88-; Phi Eta Sgm 88-; Pres Mnrty Schlrs Scty 88-; Deans List; Presdntl Hon Roll 88; GMAC/AACSB Bus Inst At Un Of MI; IM Ftbl/Bsktbl 88-; Fin.

**MC MILLAN, SUSAN D,** Univ Of Nc At Greensboro, Greensboro, NC; SR; BS; Assn Educ Yng Chldrn VP 89-; Dns Lst 89-; Assoc Bus Mgmt Patrick Henry Comm Coll 82; Erly Chld/Elem Educ; Tch/Obtain Mstrs.**

**MC MILLEN, BONNIE L,** Indiana Univ Of Pa, Indiana, PA; SR; BS 90; Elem Educ.

**MC MILLER, FELICIA,** Univ Of Akron, Akron, OH; SO; BS; ACES 90; BES; SS Sec 85-; Chrch Choir Sec 86-89; Chrch Asst Yth Dir 87-89; Bsns Educ; Tchr.

**MC MILLER JR, LOVE V,** Al A & M Univ, Normal, AL; SO; BS; Drill Tm Exec Ofcr 89-; Hon Roll 89-; Schls Deans List 89-; Natl Hnry Soc Pershing Rifles Trng Ofcr 90-; Stdnt Drug Task Force 90-; Drill Tm Apprctn Cert 89-90; Chem Instrctr.

**MC MILLIN, ANN J,** Georgian Court Coll, Lakewood, NJ; SR; BS; Trnsfr Clb Treas 89-; Bus Clb 89-; Dns Schlr 89-; Intrcllgte Sftbl Wmns 89-; Acctng; CPA.

**MC MILLIN, JASON E,** Kent St Univ Kent Cmps, Kent, OH; JR; Acctng Assc; Alpha Lambda Delta 89-; Gldn Key; Beta Gamma Sigma; Acctng.

**MC MILLIN, KELLY D,** Va Commonwealth Univ, Richmond, VA; FR; BA; Hstry; Tchng.

**MC MILLON, BARRI V,** Fl A & M Univ, Tallahassee, FL; SR; MBA; Hlth Crt Mgt Clb Pres 90-; NAACP 89-90; Amer Coll Hlth Care Exec 90-; White/Gld Hnr Soc 89-; Cum Laude; Deans Lst; Univ Nght Exclnc; GSA Trp Ldr 90-; BA 90-; Hlth Care Mgt; Hosp Admin.

**MC MINN, GLYNNIS SCROGGINS,** Ms Univ For Women, Columbus, MS; SR; BSN; Stdnt Nrs Assc 89-; Stdnt Dir Cmt 89-; Sgm Theta Tau; Natl Stdnt Nrs Assc; Troubadour Soc Clb 87-88; Rotary Clb Schlrshp 89-; Sprt Nrsng Awrd; Nrsng; RN.

**MC MINN, LORRAINA L,** Saint Francis Coll, Loretto, PA; SO; BS; AS Altoona Sch Commerce 85; Elem Edn; Teach.

**MC MINN, MARTA E,** Ms St Univ, Miss State, MS; SO; S Miss Retrdtn Cntr 89-; Pltcl Sci/Cmmnctns; Law.

**MC MINN, MELINDA B,** S U N Y Coll At Fredonia, Fredonia, NY; SR; Wilderness Club 87-89; Beta Beta Beta Pres 88-; Intshp Chautauqua Cty Hlht Dept 90; Flwshp Jr Diabetes Foundation Research Syracuse Univ; Medl Techlgy; Med/Research.

**MC MINN, TARA P,** Univ Of Nc At Asheville, Asheville, NC; SO; Bsktbl Tm Capt 89-; Ed/Sociolgy; Tchng.

**MC MINN, VARSHA B,** Union Univ, Jackson, TN; SO; BSBA; Accntng; Accntng.

**MC MORRIS, JANICE L,** S U N Y Coll Of Tech At Delhi, Delhi, NY; SO; BS; Hotel Sales & Mktg Assoc 89-; Stdnts Against Driving Drunk Treas 89-; Student Senate Senator 89-; Campus Health Squad 90-; Holiday Inn Schlrshp 90; AAS 91f; Hotel/Resort Mgmnt; Catering Mgmnt.

**MC MORRIS, SABRINA R,** Alcorn St Univ, Lorman, MS; SO; BA; Hnr Rll 90-; Pre Nrsng; Nrs.

**MC MORROW, PATRICIA FLORENCE,** City Univ Of Ny La Guard Coll, Long Island Cty, NY; SO; AS; Dsbld Stdnts Org Pres Psych 88-; Phi Theta Kappa; Occuptnl Thrpy Club; Acadmc Exclnc Soc Sci Dept; Intrn Long Islnd Jewsh Psych Outptnt; Ctr For Rehab Neurolgcl Dsrdrs; Occuptnl Thrpy; Asstnt Thrpst.

**MC MULLEN, CARLA J,** Comm Coll Algny Co Algny Cmps, Pittsburgh, PA; FR; BA; Acctng.

**MC MULLEN, DORA K,** Memphis St Univ, Memphis, TN; JR; BA; Advrtsng 77-87; Mrktng; Advrtsng Sls.

**MC MULLEN, EDWARD M,** Hudson Valley Comm Coll, Troy, NY; FR; Cmmnty Theatre; Cnslr Wrkng Wth Dvlpmntly Disbld; Cmmnctns/Lit.

**MC MULLEN, ERIN M,** S U N Y Coll At Fredonia, Fredonia, NY; SR; BS; Circle K Clb 87-89; Chautauqua Day Cr Ctr Vol 88-89; Fredonia Hamburg Intern Pgm 90-; Elem Ed; Teacher.**

**MC MULLEN, KEITH C,** Univ Of Southern Ms, Hattiesburg, MS; SR; BS; Mech Eng Tech; Eng.

**MC MULLEN, TRACY L,** Univ Of Pittsburgh At Bradford, Bradford, PA; JR; BS; Bio Clb Pres 88-; Res Asst 89-; Tutor 90-; Alpha Lambda Delta; Beta Beta Beta Pres; Zeta Alpha Chi Crspndng Sec 89-; Alpha Phi Omega Pres 88-; Acad Exclnc Awd; J J Trow Undergrad Awd; Intercoll Sftbl 89-90; Bio; Med.

**MC MURPHY, CONNIE M,** Univ Of Montevallo, Montevallo, AL; JR; BS; Lambda Sigma Pi; Phi Mu Corr Sec; IMS; AA Central Alabama Comm Coll 90; Erly Chldhd Elem Educ; Tchng.

**MC MURPHY, MATTHEW A,** Villanova Univ, Villanova, PA; FR; IM Sccr/Sftbl/Flg Ftbl 90-; Lib Arts; Law/Pblc Srvnt.

**MC MURRAY, DEIRDRE E,** Erie Comm Coll, Buffalo, NY; FR; BA; Mgzn Edtr; Tutor Engl Skll Lab 90-; Cert NY St Piccolo Sch Hair Dsgn 90; Lib Art/Soc Sci; Soc Wrk.

**MC MURRAY, FONDA J,** Piedmont Tech Coll, Greenwood, SC; SR; Resp Thrpy.

**MC MURRAY, SHEILA M,** Fayetteville St Univ, Fayetteville, NC; JR; BA; Sclgy; Prbtn Offcr.

**MC MURRY, TERESA L,** Union Univ, Jackson, TN; SR; CERT; STEA 89-; Bsn Club 84; Phi Beta Lambda 81-82; Dns Lst 89; NEA 89-; BS 84; Math; Tchg.

**MC MURRY, WANDA B,** Univ Of Southern Ms, Hattiesburg, MS; FR; BS; Phi Beta Sigma; Alpha Lambda Delta; Elem Educ; Tchr.

**MC MURTRAY, SHEILA L,** Univ Of Southern Ms, Hattiesburg, MS; JR; BS; Gamma Beta Phi; Scl Rhbltn; Psycholgy Mntl Hlthl.

**MC MURTREY, RHONDA J,** Western Ky Univ, Bowling Green, KY; SR; BS; Ntnl Edc Assn Stdnt Cncl; Unv Mddl Schl Assoc; Cncl Excptnl Chldrn 90-; SNEA Schlrshp; Tchr Edctn Awd; AA Midway Cllg 87; Mddl Grds Edc; Spcl Ed & Math Tchr.

**MC MURTREY, ROBIN A,** Midway Coll, Midway, KY; SO; BA; Stu Gov Assoc Clbs Sntr 90-; KEASP Pres 89-; Phi Theta Kappa Tres 89-; BAACHAS Pres 89-90; Bapt Stu Union Sec 89-90; Deans Lst 89-; Vlybl/Bkstbl/Sftbl Tms 89-; Sci; Tchr.

**MC NAB, CRAIG A,** Hudson Valley Comm Coll, Troy, NY; SO; BA; Ski Clb 89-; Golf Clb 89-; AD 84; Telecmnctns Mgmt.

**MC NAB, LUANNE,** Union Univ, Jackson, TN; JR; BS; BSU 89-; Vision Clown Team 89-; ACT Acadmc Schlrshp 89-; Cld Psychlgst.

**MC NABB, GINA D,** Roane St Comm Coll, Harriman, TN; SO; IM Sprts; Nrsg.

**MC NABB, MARY K,** Middle Tn St Univ, Murfreesboro, TN; SO; BA; Bptst Stdnt Un 89-; IM Bsktbl Sftbl Tns Vllybl 89-; Grphc Dsgn; Art Drctr Chrstn Pblctn.

**MC NABB, SANDRA LEIGH,** Nova Univ, Ft Lauderdale, FL; GD; MBA; Serv Rep Southern Bell 90; BA Univ S Fla 81; Business.

**MC NABB, TRACY,** Memphis St Univ, Memphis, TN; SR; BS; Beta Beta Beta; Notary Public; Biology; Physical Therapy.

**MC NAIR, CHARLES J,** Fl A & M Univ, Tallahassee, FL; JR; BA; Bptst Cmps Mnstry Cmps Rltns; Cnsl Mbr 90-; Chld Cr Prvdr Bptst Chrch; AA Lake City Cmmnty Coll 90; Occptnl Thrpy; Alld Hlth Sci.

**MC NAIR, DEBRA A,** Kent St Univ Stark Cmps, North Canton, OH; SO; BS; Church Choir; PTA Clinton Elem VP 89-90; Pres Lst 90; NW Bd Of Educ/Cmptr Prctr; Elem Educ; Tchr.

**MC NAIR, LEAH D,** Memphis St Univ, Memphis, TN; SR; BS; Untd Meth Wmn; Mphs May Mphs Assoc Paralegals; Rice Rice Smith Bursi Veazey 87-; Paralegal Stud; Law.

**MC NAIR, MARY J,** Jackson St Univ, Jackson, MS; JR; BBA; Fnc Assoc 89-; Econ Clb 90-; Phi Kappa Phi 90-; Delta Mu Delta 90-; Alpha Kappa Mu 90-; Tutor 90-; Rsrch Asst 90; Bsn Admin; MA.

**MC NAIR III, MORRIS L,** Fl St Univ, Tallahassee, FL; SR; BS; Fncl Mngmnt Assoc Fnce Scty 89; Gold Key 90; Omicron Delta Epsilon 90; Phi Kappa Phi 90; Pi Kappa Phi 86-88; Ctr For Bnkng Fncl Inst Schlrshp 90; Gulf Pwr Fndtn Schlrshp 90; AA Gulf Coast Cmmnty Clg 89; Fnce; Bnkng.

**MC NAIR, REBECCA,** William Carey Coll, Hattiesburg, MS; JR; BSN; Bapt Stdnt Union 85-; Lambda Beta Rho Chpln 85-86; Belle Vista Adlt Cntr Dir 84-86; Sacred Hrt Hosp Vstn 84; Homes Of Grace Trtmnt Ctr Wmn Asst To Dir 89-; Chldrsn Chrch Tchr 90-; Nrsng; Nrs Prctntr.

**MC NALLY, ANDREW J,** Pa St Univ Delaware Cty Cmps, Media, PA; SO; BA; All Amer Shlr Cllgt Awrd; Fin; Anlyst.

**MC NALLY, DORNETTA E,** Al St Univ, Montgomery, AL; SO; ELEM; Stdnt Natl Educ Assoc Treas; Prog Career/Acad Enhncment 89-; Alpha Lambda Delta 89; Alpha Kappa Alpha 90-; Elem Educ; Tchr.

**MC NALLY, STEPHEN A,** Bloomfield Coll, Bloomfield, NJ; SO; BA; Musc Thtr/Arts Clb; Pre Law Clb; Tutor; Dcn Frst Pres Church Orng; Dns Lst Hgh Hnrs; Pltcl Sci.

**MC NAMARA, ERIN R,** Endicott Coll, Beverly, MA; FR; BA; Stdnt Govt Pres; Model U N Club Dlgt; Club Couture Sec; Phi Theta Kappa Treas; Intrnshp At 104.5 WVLO; Communications; Broadcast Journalism.

**MC NAMEE, JENNIFER S,** Birmingham Southern Coll, Birmingham, AL; SR; BFA; Quad Mag Layout Edtr 90-; Fr Peer Advsr 90-; Annual Stdnt Juried Art Show 87-; R J Macmahn Sr Art Awd; Alpha Lambda Delta 87-; Birmnghm Rec Coll 87-; Dana Stdnt Intrn Pgm; Graphc Artst 87-; Dns Lst Birm So Clg 87-; Gala Bk Desgn Lyout.

**MC NAMEE, NICOLE L,** Mount Saint Mary Coll, Newburgh, NY; FR; BA; Busn; Law.

**MC NARY, MARK E,** Belmont Coll, Nashville, TN; JR; BA; Chrstn Music Soc Tres 88-; Bapt Stu Union 88-; Music Bus; Album Prdcr.

**MC NARY, SANDRA M,** Hudson Valley Comm Coll, Troy, NY; SR; AAS; Hmn Srv Clb Treas 89; Hmn Srv Almn Comm Asst 89; Pres Lst 89-; Van Rensselaer Mnr Nrsg Hm Dtry 85-90; Eddy Mem Grtrc Ctr Pgm Asst 90-; Rn Own Nrsg Hm; Hmn Srv; Grntlgy.

**MC NEAL, ELAINE N,** Univ Of Akron, Akron, OH; SR; BS; ACES 90-; Alpha Lambda Delta 87-; Phi Eta Sigma 87-; Kappa Delta Pi 90-; Chi Omega Asst V P/Corr Secr 87-; Dns Lst 87 88 90-; Elem Ed; Tch/Libr Sci.

**MC NEAL, JETTIE D,** Central Fl Comm Coll, Ocala, FL; FR; AA; Law.

**MC NEAL, KENNETH A,** Ms St Univ, Miss State, MS; SO; BS; Phi Beta Lamda 89-; Yng Rpblcns 89-; Phi Eta Sigma 90-; Gamma Beta Phi 90-; Alpha Lamda Delta; Gamma Alpha Epsilon; Frmhs VP; Bus Info Sys; Anlyst.

**MC NEAL, MICHELYN RAE,** Valdosta St Coll, Valdosta, GA; JR; MBA; Dean Lst 89-; Dist Hnrs Grad Walter Reed Hosp 88; Phlbtmst Guthrie Hlth Cntr 88; Chmstry Lab Asst; Tutor 89-; US Army 86-88; Allrgy Immnlgy Spclst; Chmstry/Biol; MS Glbl Eclgy.

**MC NEAL, TAMMY E,** Comm Coll Algny Co Algny Cmps, Pittsburgh, PA; FR; Dsbld Amer Vets Aux 89-; Fmly Fndtns; US Census Bur Supv; Rsch Pharm.

**MC NEAR, KATHY L,** Muskingum Coll, New Concord, OH; FR; BA; Anl Stf 90-; Cntr Brd 90-; Theta Phi Alpha 90-; Elem Ed; Day Care Cntr.

**MC NEEL, SHANNON G,** Ms St Univ, Miss State, MS; SR; BS; Hons Soc Pres 87; Orientation Ldr Desk Sprvsr 90; Phi Eta Sigma 88; Phi Kappa Phi 90; Clg Wmn Am; Kappa Delta Pi 89; Ed; Tchng.

**MC NEELY, DEBORAH D,** Limestone Coll, Gaffney, SC; SR; BS; Empl Cncl NAVFAC 90-; Amer Soc Military Cmptrlrs Ed/Newsltr 90-; Tstmstrs Intl NAVFAC Eagles; Constr Contr Nvl Facilities Engr Cmd 81-; AS Indstrl Tech Trident Tech Clg 76; Bsn Mgmt/Psych; Contr Mgmt Cvl Svc.

**MC NEELY, LYNNE B,** Univ Of Rochester, Rochester, NY; SO; BA; Adopt A Grndprnt; Math; Acturl Sci.

**MC NEESE, JULIE A,** Lexington Comm Coll, Lexington, KY; FR; BA; Engr.

**MC NEESE, MARTHA ANN,** Mercer Univ Schl Of Pharm, Atlanta, GA; GD; PHARM; Amer Pharm Assn 87-; Acad Stdnt Pharm 87-; Cncl Stdnts 87-90; Rho Chi Hon 88-; Phi Kappa Phi; Alpah Lambda Delta 87-89; Kappa Epsilon Pres 89-90; Intra Frat Cncl Sec/Treas 89-90; Sigma Kappa Jr Dlgt 87-89; Pharm.

**MC NEIL, BARBARA D,** Univ Of South Al, Mobile, AL; SR; BS; BS AL A & M Univ 76; Erly Chldhd Ed Teaching Cert 90-; Bus Instr 89-90; Advsr Stdnts; Hoseparent Child Care Worker 88-90; Admstrtv Sec WA Univ St Louis MO; Grad C F Vigor H S Prichard AL; Erly Chldhd Ed.

**MC NEIL, BRUCE A,** Wv Northern Comm Coll, Wheeling, WV; FR; BA; NAVY P O; Nvl Rsrvs Cargo Hndlng P O; Bus Mgmt; Rstrnt.

**MC NEIL, CHARLENE S,** Fl St Univ, Tallahassee, FL; SR; Phi Theta Kappa 87-89; Phi Theta Kappa Natl Alumni Assoc 89-90; Phi Beta Kappa; AA Gulf Coast Cmnty Clg 89; Bio Sci; Fisheries Bio.

**MC NEIL, DAVID A,** Va St Univ, Petersburg, VA; JR; BS; Acctng Clb 87-; CPA Clb Pres; Union Actvts Brd Co Spnsr 89; Yng Peoples Imprvmnt Lgue VP 87; USDA Intrnhp Fnncl Acctng Asst 90-; Acctng; CPA.

**MC NEIL, FELICIA D,** Central St Univ, Wilberforce, OH; FR; Bio Pre Med; Obstetrcn.

**MC NEIL, JACKLYN SNOW,** Northern Ky Univ, Highland Hts, KY; GD; BSW; Soc Wrk Stdnt Org Sec 90-; Zeta Alpha Chi 89-; Tsk Frc Mnsg Expltd Chldrn 89-90; Hnr Roll 87-90; Dns Lst 87-90; Prctcns 89-; Cert Cndt Untd Meth Chrch 88-; NASW/NAACSW; Acctnt/Off Mgr 78-87; Soc Wrk; Pstrl Mnstry.

**MC NEIL, MARY L,** Univ Of Ga, Athens, GA; SR; BS; NSSLHA 90-; Golden Key 90-; Kappa Delta Pi 90-; Cmnctn Sci/Dsrdrs; Spch-Lang Path.

**MC NEIL, NICOLIE M,** Temple Univ, Philadelphia, PA; JR; BSE; IEEE Treas; Gold Key 89-; Intrnshp AT/T Bell Lab Allentown PA; Deans Lst 88-90; Elec Eng; Power Engr.

**MC NEIL, PAMELA R,** Memphis St Univ, Memphis, TN; FR; Paralegal Stud; Law.

**MC NEIL, STEPHANIE D,** Tougaloo Coll, Tougaloo, MS; SO; BA; Peer Helper 90-; Math Tutor 90-; Alpha Lamda Delta 89-; V Pres Scholar 89-; V Pres Hnr Slist 89-; Natl Clgte Minority Ldrshp Awd 90-; Economics/Bus Admnstrn; Law.

**MC NEIL, TONYA D,** Fayetteville St Univ, Fayetteville, NC; SR; BA; Bus Admin.

**MC NEIL, VERONICA,** City Univ Of Ny Baruch Coll, New York, NY; JR; BA; Afrcn Stdnts Assn Pub Rel 90-; Corp Cmmnctns; Pub Rel.

**MC NEILL, JENNIFER A,** Western Carolina Univ, Cullowhee, NC; JR; BS; Speech & Theatre Arts Dept Hnr Guild 90-; Alpha Espilon Rho; WWCU 291 Radio DS News Caster Campus Radio; WLOS-TV News Internship; AA Suny Orange Cnty Cmnty College 89; Radio & TV; Media Law.

**MC NEILL, KRISTI K,** Union Univ, Jackson, TN; SR; Accntng Clb Sec Tres 89-; Phi Theta Kappa 88-89; Arnld Spn Co CPA Intrnshp; Ntnl Assn Accntnts Awds; TN Soc CPA Schlrshp 90-; AS Jcksn St Cmmnty Clg 89; BSBA; Accntng.

**MC NEILL, PAMELA T,** Clark Atlanta Univ, Atlanta, GA; SR; BS; Math Clb 89-; Math.

**MC NEILL, VERONICA L,** Central St Univ, Wilberforce, OH; GD; BS; Offc Admin; Mgmt.

**MC NEILL, VICTORIA A,** Xavier Univ, Cincinnati, OH; FR; BA; Vrsty Swmmng Tm 90-; Spnsh Clb 90-; Biolgy Clb 90-; Univ Lctrs 90-; Biolgy.

**MC NELIS, ERIN K,** Coll Of Charleston, Charleston, SC; JR; BA; Alpha Phi Omega VP 89-; Omicron Delta Kappa; Math.

**MC NERNEY, JAMES D,** Oh Univ, Athens, OH; GD; DO; Undergrdt Amer Acdmy Ostpthy 89-; Fmly Prctc Clb 89-; Stdnt Ostpthc Med Assoc 89-; Soph Cls Pres 90-; Physcl Thrpst 75-89; BS PT W Va Univ 75; Ostpthc Med; Med Fmly Prctc.

**MC NETT, KRISTINA M,** Oh Univ, Athens, OH; FR; BS; Soc Physcs Stdnts 90-; Chem Clb 90-; Alpha Lambda Delta 90-; Worked For A Prof; Help Bld Elec Microscp 90-; Physcs; Res Physcs.

**MC NIEL, WILTINA F,** Sue Bennett Coll, London, KY; FR; BA; Edctn Clb 90-; Sigma Nu 90-; Elem Edctn; Tchr.

**MC NIESE, DEBRA R,** Univ Of Al At Birmingham, Birmingham, AL; AA; SPTO 90-; APTA 90-; Afflte Assmbly; Srvce Prjct 90-; BS 88; Phys Thrpy.

**MC NIFF, IAN S,** Central Fl Comm Coll, Ocala, FL; FR; AA; Med; Psychatry.

**MC NISH, TERESA D,** Benedict Coll, Columbia, SC; JR; Soc Physics Stdnts Pres 90-; Benedict Clg NAACP 90-; AASU 90-; All Amer Schlr 89-90; Deans Lst 89-; Xerox Eng Schlrshp 90-; Prfmng Arts 90-; Physics; Ind Eng.

**MC NUGE, AMANDA M,** Lesley Coll, Cambridge, MA; FR; BA; Lesley Scholar Award 90; Charles Oxnard Citizenship Award 90; Counseling Psychology; Law.

**MC NULTY, THOMAS P,** Southern Coll Of Tech, Marietta, GA; JR; BA; Mech Engr.

**MC NUTT, LISA G,** Middle Tn St Univ, Murfreesboro, TN; JR; BS; Kappa Delta Pi; Gamma Beta Phi; AS Columbia State Comm Coll 90; Elem Educ.

**MC PHAIL, JAMES RYAN,** East Carolina Univ, Greenville, NC; FR; BM; Mrchng Bnd; Cncrt Bnd; All Amer Schlrs; Music; Music Therpst/Tch.

**MC PHAIL, MONA L,** Univ Of Southern Ms, Hattiesburg, MS; JR; BS; Scuba Clb 89-; Alpha Epsilon Delta 89-; Psych.

**MC PHEE, KAREN M,** Saint Joseph Coll, West Hartford, CT; FR; BED; Chld Stdy Clb 90-; SADD 90-; Chld Stdy; Tchr.

**MC PHEE, PRESLEITH Y,** Nova Univ, Ft Lauderdale, FL; GD; MBA; Deans Lst 85-87; Pres Lst 87; Delta Sigma Pi 85; Alpha Kappa Alpha 85; Lvngstn Univ 88; Acad Achvmnt Bus Mgmnt 88; Most Outstanding Stdnt 85; HRS State Of Fla 89-; B Sc Bus Admin Livingston Univ 87; Bus Admin; Mgmnt Cnsltnt.

**MC PHERSON, CHESTER A,** City Univ Of Ny Baruch Coll, New York, NY; SR; BBA; Finance & Economic Soc Sec 90-; Golden Key 90; Diploma Clge Arts Science & Tchlgy 84; Business Ad; Finance; Law.

**MC PHERSON, DIANA L,** Cumberland County Coll, Vineland, NJ; FR; AS; Lgl Asst Clb 90-; EOF Hon Awd Pres Lst; Cert Acctg; Lwyr.

**MC PHERSON, EDGAR L,** Coll Of Charleston, Charleston, SC; SR; BS; Stdnt Govt Sr Clss Pres 90-; Coll Actvties Brd 87-88; Res Hall Judcl Brd 87-88; Sigma Alpha Phi Pres 89-; Pi Mu Epsilon Treas 88-; Phi Kappa Phi 89-; Alpha Epsilon Delta Pres 89-; Orgnc Chem Prz 90-; IM Sccr/Sftbl/Wtr Polo/Rqtbl 87-; Biolgy; Med.

**MC PHERSON, EDWARD L,** Wv Univ, Morgantown, WV; JR; BS; Gldn Key; Yau Beta Pi; Eta Kappa Nu; Assoc Engr Intrn Monongahela Power Co; Elec Engr; Prof Engr.

**MC PHERSON, GARY P,** Union Coll, Barbourville, KY; JR; BA; CRC Chemistry Awrd 88-89; Calculus Awrd 90-; Chemistry; Engrng Chemical.

**MC PHERSON, GARY W,** Northeast State Tech Comm Coll, Blountville, TN; SO; AS; Vctn Bible Schl; Wrte Artcles About Windows; Cmptr Eng; Tchncl Spprt For Microsft.

**MC PHERSON, JAMES B,** Univ Of Southern Ms, Hattiesburg, MS; FR; Ftbl Schlrshp 90-95; Bsns; Ftbl Cchng.

**MC PHERSON, JEREMY P,** Univ Of Sc At Columbia, Columbia, SC; FR; BA; Bus; Mgt.

**MC PHERSON, PAULA K,** Davis & Elkins Coll, Elkins, WV; SR; BA; Nwspr Copy Edtr 90; Order Diana Lil Strs Tau Kappa Epsilon Sec 85-88; Deans Lst 90; English Cmpostn; Wrtr/Edtr.

**MC PHERSON, ROBIN NICOLE,** Middle Tn St Univ, Murfreesboro, TN; JR; BS; Gamma Beta Phi 89-; Kappa Delta Pi 90-; Acdmc Wrk Schlrshp 88-; Elem Ed; Tchr.

**MC PHERSON, SHERI L,** Miami Jacobs Jr Coll Of Bus, Dayton, OH; SR; AS; Ofc Educ Assoc 85-86; Quality Circle 89-; Word Proc Secrtrl; Admin Asstnt.

**MC QUARTERS, MICHAEL A,** Central St Univ, Wilberforce, OH; SO; BS; Mnrty Sci Imprvmnt Pgm 89-; Pg Dvrsfd Vntrs 89-; Outstndng Chmstry Stdnt; Thurgood Marshall Schlr; Hnrs Pgm; Rsrch Asst; Wtr Rsrcs Mgmt; Envrnmntl Engrg.

**MC QUEEN, ARNITTA A,** Alcorn St Univ, Lorman, MS; SO; ROTC 1st Sgt 89-; Prcsn Drl Tm 1st Sgt 89-; Prshng Rflmn Trng Ofcr; Bio; Med.

**MC QUEEN, CINDY D,** Wilberforce Univ, Wilberforce, OH; FR; BS; Pre-Law Clb 90-; Poltcl Sci; Law.

**MC QUEEN, HENRI P,** Clark Atlanta Univ, Atlanta, GA; SO; BA; Mrchng Bnd 90; NAACP 89; Hons Prog 90-; Dns Lst 89-; Acad Schlrshp 89-; Cert Of Excl; Bsns Admn; Fin.**

**MC QUEEN, LARRY R,** Church Of God Sch Of Theology, Cleveland, TN; GD; MDIV; Grad Asstshp 89-; Tch Intshp 90-; BA Lee Clg 83; Thlgy; Tch.

**MC QUEEN, MARLON R,** Al St Univ, Montgomery, AL; FR; BED; Cmptr Info Syst; Prgrmmr.

**MC QUEEN, MICHAEL S,** Draughons Jr Coll Nashville, Nashville, TN; SO; BA; Acctg; CPA.

**MC QUEEN, SHANNON M,** Middle Tn St Univ, Murfreesboro, TN; JR; BS; Stdnt Ambsdr; Stdnt Hm Econ Assn; Kappa Delta Pi; Gamma Beta Phi; Tau Omicron; Chi Omega; Dns Lst; Early Chldhd Educ.

**MC QUEEN-GOSS, SHARON KAY,** Kent St Univ Stark Cmps, North Canton, OH; SR; Sigma Theta Tau 90-; Pres Lst 89-; Dns Lst; RN Akron City Hosp Neurosci Nrsg; BSN; AD; Nrsg/Appl Sci; Nrse Anesth.

**MC QUERREY, SANDRA L,** George Mason Univ, Fairfax, VA; SR; NCAA Vrsty Sccr; Erly Ed; Tchng.

**MC QUIGG, DAVID B,** Oh Wesleyan Univ, Delaware, OH; JR; BA; Hstry Brd 89; Phi Alpha Theta VP 90; Vrsty Ftbl 89; Hstry; Grad Schl.

**MC QUISTON, CATHIE J,** Westminster Coll, New Wilmingtn, PA; SO; BA; Lambda Sigma 90-; Kappa Delta; Intl Politics; Govt.

**MC QUOWN, CHERYL ANN,** Fl Southern Coll, Lakeland, FL; FR; MACC; Alpha Omicron Pi Socl Chrmn; Assn Wmn Stdnts Dorm Rep 90-; Intercoll Vlybl 90-; Acctng; Corp Law.

**MC RAE, ALEXIS N,** Lincoln Univ, Lincoln Univ, PA; FR; Lincoln U Gspl Ensmb Sprn 90-; Almn Mrt Schlrshp; Pres Schlrshp; Blgy/Psychlgy; Psychtry.

**MC RAE, COLLEEN G,** Huntingdon Coll, Montgomery, AL; FR; BED; Vlybl Tm 90-; Fllwshp Christian Athletes 90-; Phi Eta Sigma Secy 90-; Outstndng Frshmn Vlybl 90-; Vlybltm 90-; Sec Educ English; Professor.

**MC RAE, DENNIS C,** Fl St Univ, Tallahassee, FL; JR; BA; AA Genl Stud Brebard Comm Coll 89; Geography.

**MC RAE, KATHRYN M,** Va Commonwealth Univ, Richmond, VA; JR; BA; Actvts Pgmg Bd Fine Arts Chr 89-; Pntng/Prntmkng.

**MC RAE, KIMBERLY P,** Spartanburg Methodist Coll, Spartanburg, SC; FR; BA; Sex Aids Drgs Stdnt Adv Comm 90-; S Car Alatn Rep 87-88; Psi Beta 90-; Fst Pitch Sftbl 90-; Phy Educ/Math.

**MC RAE, ROBBIE L,** Univ Of Tn At Martin, Martin, TN; FR; BA; Hnrs Seminar Stdnts 90; Hnrs Schlrshp/Wrkshp; Acad Schlrshp; Agric/Animal Sci; Agri Bus.

**MC RAE, ROBERT L,** Hudson Valley Comm Coll, Troy, NY; JR; AAS; Pres List; Cert Mbr Rses 90-; Capt Dist Scty Hosp Eng 87-; Mgr Plnt Opertn; CM Rfrgrtn Svc Eng Scty 90; Plnt Utlts Tech Eng; Phys Plnt Eng.

**MC RAE, SALLY L,** Hillsborough Comm Coll, Tampa, FL; SO; BA; Phi Theta Kappa 90-; Hist; Doct Law.

**MC RARY, ANGELA D,** Lenoir Rhyne Coll, Hickory, NC; FR; BS; Psych Sclgy Clb 90-; Br Trckrs 90-; Prog Brd 90-; Psych Sclgy; Chld Pscyhlgst.

**MC RAVIN, GILLIAN A C,** Vance Granville Comm Coll, Henderson, NC; ADN; Cardlgy Tech/IV Thrpy Tech 87-; Nrsng.

**MC RAY, RHONDA M,** Campbellsville Coll, Campbellsvl, KY; BS; Phi Theta Cl 89-; Hmcmng Queen 89; Hon List 89; Deans List 90-; Marion Adjtmnt Cen Intnshp Case Wrkr/Distctn 90; AA St Catherin Colg 90; Psych; Scl Work.**

**MC REE, MARK CANIPE,** Catawba Valley Comm Coll, Hickory, NC; BS; Hstry Wstrn Cvlztn; Ed.

**MC REED, WENDY L,** Al St Univ, Montgomery, AL; SR; BS; Phi Eta Sigma; Alpha Kappa Mu; Ordr Estrn; Tns Tm Coachs Awd 89-90; SWAC Acdmc Awd; Cmptr Science; Cmptr Hrdwr Prgrmmng.

**MC REYNOLDS, ELIZABETH ANN,** Radford Univ, Radford, VA; JR; BA; Sr Cls Secr 90-; Ambsdrs Publ Chr 89-; Stdnt Awds Comm Chr 90-; Sigma Tau Delta; Engl; Tech Wrtng.

**MC REYNOLDS JR, JOHN T,** Ms St Univ, Miss State, MS; SR; BS; Alumni Dlgt 90-; Trffc Crt Chrprsn 90-; Phi Eta Sigma; Gamma Beta Phi; Beta Alpha Psi; Sigma Chi Treas 87-; IM Sports; Acctg.

**MC REYNOLDS, PHILLIP J,** Univ Of South Fl, Tampa, FL; SR; BM; Intl Assn Jazz Educ Pres 89-; Univ S FL Jazz Ensmbl 88-; Jazz Chmbr Ensmbl 87-; Themis 86-88; Gldn Ky 88-90; Piano Perf Schlrshp 86-88; Undergrad Jazz Schlrshp 89-; Alexandre Rudajer Composition Awd; Music Comp; Film Scrng/Music Media.

**MC REYNOLDS, SARA E,** Ms St Univ, Miss State, MS; JR; Stdnt Assoc Treas; Sen 90-; Beta Alpha Psi; Natl Assoc Accts; Kappa Delta Sec VP 90-; Campus Actvies Brd 90-; Ath Recrtr 89-90; Alumni Del; IM Flg Fbtl Bsktbl Sftbl 89-90; Acctg; CPA.

**MC ROBERTS, ROSE-MARIE A,** Kent St Univ Kent Cmps, Kent, OH; JR; Acctg; CPA.

**MC SHANE III, DANIEL E,** Univ Of Nc At Charlotte, Charlotte, NC; JR; BCA; Theatre; Actor.

**MC SHANE, JEANETTE L,** Molloy Coll, Rockville Ctr, NY; JR; BSN; Cmps Mnstrs Vp 88-; Glee Clb 89-; Gailc Scty 90-; Delta Epsilon Sigma; Sigma Theta Tau; Omicron Alpah Zeta; Nrsg.

**MC SHEPARD, ANGELA L,** Fisk Univ, Nashville, TN; JR; BA; Wesley Fndtn Orntatn; Positive Theory Semnr; Miss Fisk Univ; Lambda Iota Tau; Mrtr Bd; Tchr Educ Prog; English; Prfsr.

**MC SORLEY, ALICIA L,** Ramapo Coll Of Nj, Mahwah, NJ; SR; BA; Poltcl Intrnshp; Poltcl Sci.

**MC SORLEY, KATHRYN R,** Univ Of Sc At Columbia, Columbia, SC; JR; BS; Prnts Weekend Assn 90-; Car Pgm Un 89-90; Peer Conduct Brd Co Chr 89-; Alpha Phi Sigma 90-; Intrnshp Victms Witness Asst; Solctrs Offc; Crim Just; Inv Fed Bur Investgtn.

**MC STAY, ROBERT M,** Embry Riddle Aeronautical Univ, Daytona Beach, FL; JR; BS; Hon Rl 88-; Dns Lst 88-; IM Flg Fbtl 90-; Aerntcl Sci; Prof Pilot.**

**MC SWAIN, RONNIE D,** Meridian Comm Coll, Meridian, MS; SO; AA; Educ; Tchr.

**MC SWEENEY, DANNY K,** Marshall University, Huntington, WV; SR; BA; Intrnshp HCA Riverpark Hosp; Dist 1 Ltl League Bsbl WV 85-90; Boy Scouts Of Amer; CSX Transprtn 79-; Cnslng/Rehab; Pastrl/Christian Thrpy.

**MC TIGHE, JOHN J,** Hudson Valley Comm Coll, Troy, NY; SR; AOS; AOS; Elec Constrctn/Maint; Electrcn.

**MC TIGHE, MARY ANNE E,** Saint Vincents Coll & Seminary, Latrobe, PA; JR; BS; 4 H Pres 87-88; Stdnt Govt 87-89; Alpha Phi Omega 90-; Dns Lst; Vlybl 90-; Blgy; Med Schl/Pdtrcn.**

**MC TYRE, JOHN S,** Nova Univ, Ft Lauderdale, FL; MBA; Urban Lnd Inst; Rl Estat Aprsr; BBA FL Atlantic U 86; Rl Estate.

**MC VAY, JANET M,** Comm Coll Algny Co Algny Cmps, Pittsburgh, PA; FR; AS; Liberal Arts; Law Enfrcmnt.

**MC VAY, ROVERT L,** Memphis St Univ, Memphis, TN; SR; BFA; Fine Art.

**MC VAY, SHERRELL P,** Tn St Univ, Nashville, TN; SR; BS; Crim Just Org Pres 90-; NAACP Sgt Arms 89-90; Lambda Tau Epsilon V P 89-; Just Hnr Soc Prlmntrn 90-; Alpha Chi; Prince Hl Masonic Org Oak Grove Lodge 117; UPS 88-; Crim Just; Law Sch.

**MC VEY, CHARLES B,** Loyola Coll In Md, Baltimore, MD; FR; BS; Physcs Clb 90-; Math Clb 90-; Pres Schlrshp; Mrylnd Distgshd Schlr Schlrshp; MD Distgshd Schlr Tchr Schlrshp; Physcs/Cmptr Sci; Space Rsrch Dvlpmnt.

**MC VEY II, JON M,** Middle Tn St Univ, Murfreesboro, TN; JR; BS; Deans Pres Lst 90-; Aerospace; FFA.

**MC VICKER, BETTY C,** Muskingum Coll, New Concord, OH; SR; BA; Psi Beta Chrmn 88-89; Psi Chi; Phi Kappa Phi Recgn Schlstc Achvmnt 89; Mdtr Cambridge Mncpl Crt; Sthstrn Oh Symphnc Soc; Sclgy; Soc Wrk.

**MC WATERS, SHEILA O,** Coker Coll, Hartsville, SC; SR; CERT; BS 77; PE Hlth; Elem Ed.

**MC WEENEY, CHARLES J,** City Univ Of Ny Baruch Coll, New York, NY; SO; BBA; Acctng Socty; Baruch Schlrs 89-; Pres Full Schlrshp 89-; Acctng.

**MC WHIRTER, MICHAEL J,** Middle Tn St Univ, Murfreesboro, TN; FR; BS; Math.

**MC WHITE, MICHELE,** Valdosta St Coll, Valdosta, GA; SO; BA; Ftbl Rcttr 89-; Res Hll 89-90; Fresh Schlr 89; Deans Lst 89; Phi Beta Sigma Swthrt Sec 89-; Cmunctns; Bus/Pub Rltns.

**MC WHORTER, ANTOINETTE R,** Johnson C Smith Univ, Charlotte, NC; FR; BS; R W Sprtl Chr 90-; Omega Essnc Chpln; Psychlgy; Chld Psychlgst.

**MC WHORTER, DARREN E,** Union Coll, Barbourville, KY; JR; Bsbl/Ftbl NAIA All Dist All Conf; Hist; Phys Educ Tchr.

**MC WHORTER, GREGORY A,** Methodist Coll, Fayetteville, NC; SO; BA; Blgy Pre Med; Mdcl Fld.

**MC WHORTER, KEVIN L,** Univ Of Cincinnati, Cincinnati, OH; SR; BS; BASIS 85-; SNTA 90-; Phi Theta Kappa 85-86; Archtctrl Engr; MS.

**MC WHORTER, LYNDA J,** Schenectady County Comm Coll, Schenectady, NY; FR; AAS; Trvl/Trsm; Hotel Mgmt.

**MC WHORTER, MARLENE B,** Central Wesleyan Coll, Central, SC; SR; BS; Alpha Chi 90-; Phi Theta Kappa Pres 86-88; Outstndng Stdnt In Mgt 88; Cls Valedictorian; Loan Ofcr SC Natl Bank 77-86; Asst Registrar Central Wesleyan Clg 88-; AS Tri Cnty Tech Clg 88; Bus Admn; Ed Admnstrtr.

**MC WILLIAMS, BREGETTA T,** Jackson St Univ, Jackson, MS; FR; Alpha Lambda Delta.

**MC WILLIAMS III, GRADY,** Alcorn St Univ, Lorman, MS; SO; BA; Mrchng Bnd 89-90; Cncrt Bnd 89-90; Deans Lst 90-; USAA All Amer Schlrs 90-; Comp Sci; Prog.

**MC WILLIAMS, JACQUELYN M,** Univ Of Tn At Martin, Martin, TN; SO; BS; Blck Stdnt Assn Pub Rltn 90-; Blck Stdnt Assoc Choir Pub Rltn 89-; Alpha Kappa Alpha; Mnrty Schlrshp 90; BSA Ofcr Awd; Nurs.

**MC WILLIAMS, MARY D,** Univ Of North Fl, Jacksonville, FL; SO; BA; K-Mart Ofc Emplyee 85-; Acctng; CPA Or CMA.**

**MDIGOS-MULLI, SAMUEL,** Hudson Valley Comm Coll, Troy, NY; SO; AS; C Step; Afro Amer Stdnt Alnc; ASIS; Afrcn Stdnts Assc Cptl Dstrct; Scrty Adm; US St Dept Frgn Svc.

**MEACHAM, KIMBERLY K,** Univ Of Al At Huntsville, Huntsville, AL; SR; BSE; Amer Soc/Cvl Engrs; Soc/Wmn Engrs; Lambda Chi Alpha 77-79; Cvl Engr; Rsrch.

**MEACHAM, LISA M,** Union Univ, Jackson, TN; SO; BS; STEA 90-; Nacctg Clb 89-; Kappa Mu Epsilon; Interclgte Vybl Tm 89-; Math; Tchr.

**MEACHAM, SAMUEL ALEXANDER,** Middle Tn St Univ, Murfreesboro, TN; JR; BA; Rcrdng Indstry Mgmt; Rcrdng Artst.**

**MEACHON, SUSAN L,** Atlantic Comm Coll, Mays Landing, NJ; JR; BS; AS 90; Fnc; Fncl Anlyst.

**MEACHUM, BARBARA A,** Western Carolina Univ, Cullowhee, NC; SR; BA; Assisted Language Four 88-90; Sigma Chi Alpha Little Sis 88-90; French/Spanish; Frgn Cmnctns.

**MEAD, ALBA B,** Albertus Magnus Coll, New Haven, CT; SR; Kappa Gamma Pi 90-; Alpha Sigma Lambda 90-; Phi Theta Kappa 87-88; Psychology Awd High Achvment; Deans Lst 85-; Schl/Community Vol Work; Yale Univ Schl Of Med 68-71; AS S Cntrl Comm Clg 88; Psychology.

**MEAD, GENIENNE S,** Roane St Comm Coll, Harriman, TN; FR; BS; Natl Coll Eng Awrd; Crew; Sci.

**MEAD, MALCOLM G,** Univ Of Rochester, Rochester, NY; JR; BA; Stdnts Assn Chrncl Edtr In Chf 90-; Mag Fctn Wrtr 90-; Go Clb VP 89-90; Comm Intrracial Dialgue Pres 89-90; Stdnts Actv In Vol Envrnmnts Coord 90-; Comm Serv Awrd; Psychlgy.

**MEAD, STEPHANIE,** Comm Coll Algny Co Algny Cmps, Pittsburgh, PA; FR; BA; Sci; Vetrnarian.

**MEADE, KATHY L,** Oh Univ Belmont County, St Clairsvl, OH; FR; BA; Media Ctr Stdnt Wrkr; Telecmnctns; Media Prdctn Spec.

**MEADE, KATIE M,** Univ Of Va Clinch Valley Coll, Wise, VA; SO; BS; Finance; Acctg.

**MEADE, LEILA Y,** Marshall University, Huntington, WV; SO; BA; Intl Clb; Mrktng; Mrktng Exec.

**MEADE, LORI A,** Anne Arundel Comm Coll, Arnold, MD; FR; BA; Engl; Advrtsng/Educ.

**MEADE, MICHAEL S,** Carnegie Mellon Univ, Pittsburgh, PA; SO; BS; Natl Coll Bus Merit Awrd 90-; Bus Math; Fnnc.

**MEADE, MICHELE L,** Ga Southern Univ, Statesboro, GA; FR; BS; Baptist Stdnt Un Flwshp Drctr 90-; FCA; Deans Lst 90-; Math.

**MEADE, MICHELLE A,** Loyola Coll In Md, Baltimore, MD; JR; BA; Stdnt Hlth Advsry Com Treas 89-; April Fools; Evergreen Plyrs; Blood Dr Treas 89-; Classic Soc; Circle K; Psychlgy Clb; Psi Chi 89-; Eta Sigma Phi 89-; EMT Cranford 1st Aid Squad 86-; Sexual Assault Hotline Cnslr 89-90; Psychlgy; Ph D.

**MEADE, SHARON H,** Central Fl Comm Coll, Ocala, FL; SO; BS; Dsplcd Hmmkr Asc Rep 90-; AA 89; Crmnl Jstc; Lwyr.

**MEADE, VERONICA E,** Anne Arundel Comm Coll, Arnold, MD; SO; BARCH; Tlnt Rostr 90-; Achvmnt Awd 90-; Lgl Sec; Hon Grad Cert WA Sch Secys 78; Gen Stdies; Arch.

**MEADE, ZACHARY H,** Kent St Univ Kent Cmps, Kent, OH; FR; BA; Sigma Nu Fraternity 90-91; Bsns; Mrktng/Fin.

**MEADERS, DARCY M,** Univ Of Ga, Athens, GA; SR; BSED; SEEC 90-; AS Gainesville Clg 90; Spcl Ed; Tchng.

**MEADIOUS, CYNTHIA M,** Alcorn St Univ, Lorman, MS; SR; BA; Deans Lst; BA; Enlgh-Psych; Cnslr/Edctr.

**MEADOWS, CHRISTINE D,** Longwood Coll, Farmville, VA; SR; Phy Ed Majors Clb Treas 89-; Peer Helpers 89-; Longwodo Ambassadors 89; Delta Psi Kappa 89-; Order Of Omega 90-; Delta Zeta Pres 88-; Internship Fitness Sys; Assn Fitness In Bus; Intl Dance Exercise Assn; Phy Ed/Exercise Sci; Fitness Dir.

**MEADOWS, COREY,** Al St Univ, Montgomery, AL; SO; BS; M L K Jr Hl Drm Cncl Sec 90-; Greenwood Bptst Chrch Jrn Dcns 89-; Pres Schlrshp 89-; Elem Ed; Tchr/Prncpl.

**MEADOWS, DENISE M,** Schenectady County Comm Coll, Schenectady, NY; FR; AAS; Pres Lst 90; KY Drby Cncssn Mgr; Dsny Cll Prog; Untd Wy 85-; Mrch Of Dms 85-; K-Mrt Co 90; Htl Rest Mgmt; Bnqt Cnvntn Mgmt.

**MEADOWS, GARY R,** East Carolina Univ, Greenville, NC; GD; Jrs Awd Undrgrd Art Exhbtn 90 Grnvl Museum Proj 90; BFA 90; Art/Envrnmntl Dsgn; Arch.

**MEADOWS, KATHARINE U,** Gallaudet Univ, Washington, DC; GD; MA; Pres Schlr 90-; BA Bard Clg 85; Cnslng.

**MEADOWS, KEVIN M,** Roane St Comm Coll, Harriman, TN; SO; SGA Fee Bd 90-; Chrldr 90-; Gamma Beta Phi 90-; Bsn; Acctg.

**MEADOWS, LYNECIA A,** Alderson Broaddus Coll, Philippi, WV; FR; BA; Clge Cncrt Chr Sctn 90-; Yrbk Ed 90-; Bptst Cmps Mnstry 90-; Assoc Wm Stdnts Treas; WV St Wntr Spec Olympcs Vol; Hmcmng Crt; Sprng Crt; Dns Lst; Bsn Admin/Psychlgy; Htl Mgmt.

**MEADOWS, MISTY D,** Union Univ, Jackson, TN; FR; BS; Bapt Stdnt Un Puppet Mnstry 90-; Yrbk Stf 90; SPOTS Msn Tm; Dns Lst 90; Elem Educ; Tchng.

**MEADOWS, SHERRI L,** Univ Of Charleston, Charleston, WV; FR; BS; AARC 90-; Hlth Sci; Rsprty Thrpst.

**MEADOWS, SUSAN D,** Wv Univ At Parkersburg, Parkersburg, WV; SO; BA; Civitan Clb; Acctg; CPA.

**MEADS, CONNIE H,** Abraham Baldwin Agri Coll, Tifton, GA; FR; AS; Bus; Acctg.

**MEALEY, KIMBERLY S,** Marshall University, Huntington, WV; GD; MA; BS 89; Educ/Bio/Gen Sci; Tchng.

**MEALICK, RHONDA L,** Oh St Univ At Newark, Newark, OH; SR; BS; Phi Theta Kappa 87-88; Hon Soc; Htln Crs Vol 87-88; AA Del Mar Clg 88; Bsns; Fin/Acctg.

**MEALOR, STEPHANIE L,** Savannah Coll Of Art & Design, Savannah, GA; GD; Cum Laude; Illstrtn/BFA.

**MEANEY, GERALDINE G,** Mount Saint Mary Coll, Newburgh, NY; SR; Nrsng Stdnt Un Treas 90-; Sigma Theta Tau 90-; Alpha Chi 90-; Nrsng Faclty Awrd; BSN; Nrsng.

**MEANS, LEMUEL L,** Al A & M Univ, Normal, AL; SR; BS; IEEE 88-; Std Clstr Org 88-; Pres Schlrs Soc 88-; Natl Soc Blck Engrs 87-; Cert Bay Minette Area Voc Ctr 86-87; Elec Engr.

**MEANS, VERONICA SAMPSON,** Bryant Stratton Bus Inst Roch, Rochester, NY; FR; AS; Tchr Asst DC AC Elect Lab 90; Dean Lst 90; Co Ed Sftbll Asst Coach 90-; Elect; Eng.

**MEARNS, MELISSA M,** Methodist Coll, Fayetteville, NC; JR; BS; Acctng Club Sec 91; Phi Eta Sigma 90-; Alpha Chi; Chief Marshall; Marshall 90; Acctng; CPA.

**MEARNS, SUSAN E,** Univ Of Cincinnati-Clrmnt Coll, Batavia, OH; SO; Phi Theta Kappa 88-; Crrsn Tech Cinn Gas/Elec 83-; Elec Eng Tech; Eng.

**MEARS, MONIFA D,** Bloomfield Coll, Bloomfield, NJ; SO; BS; Sigma Swthrt 89; Bsns Admnstrtn.

**MEAU, AMELIA MAN CHU,** Univ Of Nh Plymouth St Coll, Plymouth, NH; JR; BSC; Hong Kong Mgstrcy Lay Sssr 80-89; Barbara Boyce Oakes Schlrshp; Rls Schls Cncl 77-89; Wan Chai Distrct Hdmstrs Cncl 85-89; Prncpl St Josephs Prmry Schl 77-89; Tchrs Certf Nrthct Clg Edctn Hong Kong 67; Tchrs Certf Japanese Flrl Arngmnt 89; Elem Edctn; Tchr.

**MEAUX, REBECCA H,** Univ Of Sc At Beaufort, Beaufort, SC; SO; BA; Early Childhood Ed; Tchr.

**MECCA, PAULETTE M,** D Youville Coll, Buffalo, NY; JR; BS; Elem And Spcl Educ; Tchr Admin.

**MECHALSKE, CASSANDRA H,** Bridgewater Coll, Bridgewater, VA; SO; BS; Brthrn Stdnt Fllwshp 89-; Dlln Hll Cncl Hll Rep 89-; Stdnt Atltc Trnr 89-; Lcrss Tm; Hlth Sci.

**MECHAS, ANTHONY M,** Davis & Elkins Coll, Elkins, WV; SO; BS; Delta Clb VP; ACM; Tau Kappa Epsilon; Bilogy/Math; Med.

**MECOMBER, VALOREE RACHELLE,** Univ Of Sc At Columbia, Columbia, SC; JR; BS; Gldn Key 90-; Sigma Pi Sigma 90-; Math Hnr Scty; Physcs; US Nvy.

**MECRAY, KURT L,** Pa St Univ Delaware Cty Cmps, Media, PA; JR; BA; Gen Arts/Sci; Bus Admin.

**MEDCROFT, CHAD E,** S U N Y Coll At Cortland, Cortland, NY; SO; BA; Ski Clb 90; Physcs Clb 90; Phi Eta Sigma Pres 90-; Hnrs Prog Fsclts Com 90-; Lynn Brown Gen Almni Schlrshp Awrd; H De Witt De Groat Pres Schlrshp; Dns Lst 90; Soph Awrd Fr Achvmnt In Math; IM Sccr Orgnzr 90-; Intrcllgte Trck And Fld 90; Math Mgmt Sci; Actrl Sci.**

**MEDDINGS, MARK A,** Glassboro St Coll, Glassboro, NJ; SR; BA; Math; Actuarial Prof.

**MEDEIROS, JOSEPH I,** Vance Granville Comm Coll, Henderson, NC; SR; Voc Clb Chr 90-; Indust Maint Awd; Cert Calcltng Indust Math; Indust Maint.

**MEDERO, HELEN MARIE,** Hillsborough Comm Coll, Tampa, FL; SO; BA; Phi Theta Kappa 90-; Math/Educ; Tchg.

**MEDEROS, EDILIO,** Miami Dade Comm Coll, Miami, FL; SO; BA; Fl Eng Scty 90; Ntnl Scty Of Prof Eng 90; AA; Civil Eng.

**MEDINA, BRIAN F,** Teikyo Post Univ, Waterbury, CT; SO; BA; Stdnt Ldr; Rsdnt Asst 90-; Mrktg.

**MEDINA, DARLENE T,** Fl Atlantic Univ, Boca Raton, FL; SR; BA; Mngmnt.

**MEDINA, EDDIEMARI DUCHENY,** Univ Of Pr At Mayaguez, Mayaguez, PR; JR; BS; Amer Inst Of Chem Engrs 90-; Natl Soc Prof Engrs 89-; Amer Soc Of Quality Control; Deans Lst 88-; Dept Of Engrng Hons Rl 88-; Engr.

**MEDINA, JAVIER,** Fl St Univ, Tallahassee, FL; SR; BA; Phi Eta Sigma 89-; Lib Stds Hnrs Prog 88-0; Dns Lst 88-90; Elec Engr; Engr Educ.**

**MEDINA, JUAN-CARLOS,** Univ Politecnica De Pr, Hato Rey, PR; SO; BSME; Mech Engr.

**MEDINA, LUIS F,** Newbury Coll, Brookline, MA; AS; Cntrl Aide Pblctns/Grphcs Mitre Corp; Comp Sci.

**MEDINA, LUZ C,** Bryant Stratton Bus Inst Roch, Rochester, NY; GD; ASSC; Wrd Prcssng.

**MEDINA, MANUEL E,** Fl International Univ, Miami, FL; JR; BA; Phi Theta Kappa; Gen Elec Mnrty Bsns Admn Schlrshp; AA Miami Dade Comm Clg 90; Bsns Admn; Acctg.

**MEDINA, MARTIN T,** Clarkson Univ, Potsdam, NY; JR; BS; US Fig Sktng Assoc 76-; Amer Speed Sktng Assoc 90-; Empire State Games 88-; Specl Olympics Vol 90-; Theta Chi Hse Mgr 89-; Deans Lst; JV Hockey 88; Mngmnt.

**MEDINA, NEYDA R,** Univ Of Pr Medical Sciences, San Juan, PR; SR; BS; Spch Therapy Grp Treas 90-; Orphans Hse Vol 87-89; Hon Grad Asstntshps 88-90; Spch Lang Therapy; MS Lang Pathology.

**MEDINA, NURIA,** Barry Univ, Miami, FL; JR; BA; Dnc Tm 90- Spnsh Clb 90-; Phi Alpha Delta Pbl Chrm 90-; Nwsppr Wrtr 90-; Pre Law/Phlsphy; Law.

**MEDINA, PATRICIA,** Gallaudet Univ, Washington, DC; SR; BA; Grmn Clb; Dnce Co; Tae Kwondo; Art Clb; Otstndng Artst; Bst In Art Shw; Dns Lst; Otstndng Spnsh; Delta Epsilon; Wbco Prntng Mdlnd TX 90; Dept Of Trans Wshngtn DC; Grphc Arts.

**MEDINA, PATRICIA C,** Saint Thomas Univ, Miami, FL; JR; BA; Crcl 5; Ttr ATM Rep 89-; AA 90; Elem Ed.

**MEDINA, RAFAEL A PEREZ,** Univ Of Pr At Rio Piedras, Rio Piedras, PR; SR; Scd Hnr Univ 86-; Scd Hnr Coll 85-86; Cncs Pltcs.

**MEDINA, ROXANNE,** Inter Amer Univ Pr Aquadilla, Aguadilla, PR; JR; BA; Arbcs Clb; Math/Hstry/Tprwrttng; Sec.

**MEDINA, SYLVIA,** Edison Comm Coll, Fort Myers, FL; JR; BABS; St Chrstphrs Hsptl Chldrn Sec 78-86; Spnsh Caucus Apprctn Stdnts Trdtnl; Admnstrtv Asst; Vsnry Sce Grntlgy; Optmtry.

**MEDINA, WEDNESDAY,** Teikyo Post Univ, Waterbury, CT; SO; BS; Res Assist 90; Minority Grant; Mgmnt; Hotel Mgmnt.

**MEDINA, YVETTE,** Newbury Coll, Brookline, MA; Tech Aide Mitre Corp; Bus Mgmt.

**MEDINA, ZENAIDES A,** City Univ Of Ny Coll Staten Is, Staten Island, NY; FR; Bsebl 88-90; Natl Hnr Rl 89-90; Salutatorian 89-90; Bsebl 90-; Acctg.

**MEDLEY, CAMILLE L,** Murray St Univ, Murray, KY; FR; BS; Deans Lst 90-; Mrchng Band 90-; Bus Admn; Mgmt.

**MEDLEY, CRYSTAL M,** Spartanburg Methodist Coll, Spartanburg, SC; FR; BA; Phi Theta Kappa; Bus Admin; Acctg.

**MEDLEY, JILL A,** Wv Northern Comm Coll, Wheeling, WV; FR; AAS; Phi Theta Kappa; Pres Lst 90-; Med Lab Tech.

**MEDLEY, MITZI J,** Tn Tech Univ, Cookeville, TN; SO; BS; Agrcltrl Eng Tech; Food Prod Prcssng.

**MEDLIN, DENISE J,** Union Univ School Of Nursing, Memphis, TN; JR; BSN; Stdnt Chrstn Assn 89-; Nrsng.

**MEDLOCK, CELESTE V M,** Cheyney Univ Of Pa, Cheyney, PA; JR; Hotel/Rest Inst Mgmt Secr 90-; Hnr Rl 89-; Omega Swthrt V P 89-; Hotel/Rest Inst Mgmt.

**MEDNIS, SARI L,** Cooper Union, New York, NY; JR; BEE; Brdg Clb 88-; Tau Beta Pi Pres; Eta Kappa Nu VP; Soc Wmn Engrs Pres 88-; Inst Elect/Elctrncs Engrs 90-; Fresh Chem Awd 89; IM Sftbl 89-; Elect Eng.

**MEDSKER, KIM J,** Miami Jacobs Jr Coll Of Bus, Dayton, OH; GD; Bus Admin Acctng; Mgmt.

**MEDVEDEV, MIKHAIL,** City Univ Of Ny City Coll, New York, NY; JR; BEE; Jwsh Cngrtn Agudath Achim 88-; Gldn Key 90-; Elctrcl Engnrng; Engnrng.

**MEDWYNTER, CLIVE G,** Nova Univ, Ft Lauderdale, FL; GD; MBA; Gld Undrgrad VP 83-84; UWI-GLD Undrgrad Intl Affrs Chrmn 82-83; Kiwanis Clb-N St Andrew Jamaica; Barbican Terr Ctzns Assn Exec; BSC Chem/Zlgy Univ W Indies 84; Dipl Mktg Jamaica Inst Mgmt 88; Mktg/Fin; Mgmt.

**MEDYNSKI, GREGORY F,** Saint John Fisher Coll, Rochester, NY; SO; BABS; Pol Sci; Eng/Law.

**MEE, CHRISTOPHER A,** Nyack Coll, Nyack, NY; SO; BA; Manhattan Gospel V P 89-; Jr Cls Rep; Christian Svc; Drama Ensmbl Chpln 89; Yth Mnstry/Bible; Mnstr.

**MEEDER, CURT N,** Cornell Univ Statutory College, Ithaca, NY; SR; BS; Pomology Clb 88-89; Gamma Sgm Dlt; Alpha Gamma Rho Stwrd 88-89; Tchng Asstnt; Intrnshp Farm Crdt WNY 90; Appl Econ/Bus Mgm; Law.

**MEEHAN, BARBARA J,** Teikyo Post Univ, Waterbury, CT; JR; BS; Amer Mrktng Assc 90-; Ski Clb Treas 88-89; BA; Mrktng.

**MEEHAN, CYNTHIA L,** Univ Of Cincinnati-Clrmnt Coll, Batavia, OH; SO; MBA; Civic Cntr Shltr Absd Wmn; Drug Rehab Cntr; Scl Serv Psychlgy; Hmn Serv; Psychlgy.

**MEEK, CHRISTINA MECHALE,** Middle Tn St Univ, Murfreesboro, TN; SR; BA; Alpha Kappa Phi 90-; Stdnt Programming 90; Gamma Beta Phi 90-; Mngmnt.

**MEEK, CLAY L,** Bethel Coll, Mckenzie, TN; SR; Math Clb 88-; Bus Clb SGA Rep 89-; Psyc Clb 90-; Gamma Beta Phi 89-; Sigma Phi Omega 90-; History; Law.

**MEEKER, GAIL M,** Coll Misericordia, Dallas, PA; FR; BA; Orient Com; Madrigal 90; Lit Clb 90-; Stdnt Hnr Assc 90-; Asst To Dr Regina Kelly RSM Eng Dept; Ast Sr Siena Finley Ethics Inst; English/Scndry Education.

**MEEKER, JAMI W,** Kent St Univ Kent Cmps, Kent, OH; GD; BABS; Kent St Unvrsty Hnrs Clg 87-; Gldn Key 90-; Grad Asst Romance Lang; Rssn Trnsltn; French Trnsltn; Rssn Frnch Ltrc.

**MEEKER, LARI M,** Salisbury St Univ, Salisbury, MD; SO; BA; RA 90-; Psych Clb 90-; Phi Eta Sigma; Psi Chi; Psych.

**MEEKER, LEE E,** Univ Of Sc At Columbia, Columbia, SC; SO; BA; SGA USC Sumter VP 90-; War Gamers At USC Sumter 89-; Deans List 89-; NBSC Lucile Mc Kiever Mem Schlrshp 90-; D L Scurry Fndtn Schlrshp 89-90; Comptr Sci; Progrmr/Sys Anlyst.

**MEEKER, LEE E,** Univ Of Sc At Sumter, Sumter, SC; SO; BA; Student Govt Assopc VP 90-; War Gamers 89-; Deans List 89-; NBSC Lucile Mckieven Mem Schlrshp 90-; D L Scurry Found Schlrshp 89-90; Computer Sci; Prog/System Analyst.

**MEEKINS, SALLY A,** Liberty Univ, Lynchburg, VA; SO; BS; Liberators Life 89-; Alpha Lambda Delta 89-; Liberty Stdnt Nrs Assoc Treas 90-; Youthquest 89-; Liberty Godparent Hm Hse Parent 90-; Urban Outreach 89-; Nrsg.**

**MEEKINS, WALTON D,** Saint Pauls Coll, Lawrenceville, VA; JR; BA; Stu Gov Rep 88-; NAACP 90-; Intr Frtrnl Cncl 90-; Alpha Kappa Mu; Alpha Phi Alpha VP 89-; Alpha Phi Alpha Sclrshp Awrd 89-; Mrs Whitehurst Schlrshp Awrd 90-; Glf 89-; Pol Sci; Law.

**MEEKS, ANTONIA J,** Anne Arundel Comm Coll, Arnold, MD; FR; BA; Mass Cmnctns; Brdcst Jrnlsm.

**MEEKS, LISA D,** Middle Tn St Univ, Murfreesboro, TN; JR; BS; Tchr Educ Pgm; Gamma Beta Phi 89-; AS Motlow State Cmnty Clg 90; Elem Tchr.

**MEEKS, MARK S,** Western Carolina Univ, Cullowhee, NC; JR; BS; SGA Attrny Gen; NC Stdnt Legislature Sec; IFC; Pi Gamma Mu; Ord Of Omega; Phi Alpha Delta V P; Sigma Phi Epsilon; SLED Intern; Rugby Clb; Pol Sci; Law.

**MEEKS, PATTY L,** Hocking Tech Coll, Nelsonville, OH; SO; Acctng Clb; Obleness Hosp Vol; Vol Of Yr Oblen 89; Dns Lst; Ldrshp Awd 90; Acctng; Tax Acctnt Law.**

**MEELER, JENNIFER A,** Longwood Coll, Farmville, VA; JR; BA; Nwsppr Stff 90; Lambda Iota Tau; Hnrs Prog 88-; Kappa Pi; Mary Clay Hiner Schlrshp; Dns Lst 88-; Engl; Edtng Jrnlsm.

**MEENACH, MICHELLE L,** Ashland Comm Coll, Ashland, KY; GD; AS; Data Info Systs.

**MEENAN, KATHERINE E,** Le Moyne Coll, Syracuse, NY; JR; BA; The Frhs Theatre; Envrnmtl Coalition; Brooklyn Dist Atty NYC; Engl; Tchg.

**MEERBOTT, COSETTE ANN,** Fl International Univ, Miami, FL; SR; BS; Future Ed Am 89-90; Ford Fndtn Intrnshp Pgm 90-; Chldhd Edn; Teach.

**MEESON, DANA E,** Union Univ, Jackson, TN; SR; BSBA; Mgmt/Mktg; Fin Anlyst.

**MEETZE, WILLIAM D,** Univ Of Sc At Columbia, Columbia, SC; SR; BS; BS Math 73; Cvl Eng.

**MEGGITT, BRIAN L,** Allegheny Coll, Meadville, PA; JR; BA; Stdnt Art Soc Co-Pres 89-; Alghny Commnty Exchng; Alden Schlr 90-; Studio Art/Hstry; Tchng.

**MEGGITT, TERESA F,** Anne Arundel Comm Coll, Arnold, MD; SO; BA; Hmn Srvcs Clb VP 85-86; Hmn Srvds Clb Pres 86-87; Phi Theta Kappa; AA Hmn Srvcs 87; Ed; Elem Erly Chldhd Tchng.

**MEGGS, MICHELLE R,** Johnson C Smith Univ, Charlotte, NC; SO; BA; FBLS VP 90; Poli Sci Clb; NBSA 89-90; Alpha Kappa Alpha Grmmts Epstls 90; Poli Sci; Corp Attrny.

**MEHAJ, MIZIJENE B,** City Univ Of Ny Baruch Coll, New York, NY; FR; BBA; Lahau/Hebrew Soc Treas 90; Bsn; Mgmt.

**MEHERKA, YALEW,** City Univ Of Ny Queensbrough, New York, NY; SO; BA; Pol Sci; Law.

**MEHLMAN, CHRISTOPHER T,** Wilmington Coll, Wilmington, OH; JR; BA; Natl Bnk Trust Intern; Pres Schlrshp 88-; Dean Lst 89-; Ftbl 88-; Fnnc Accntng; CPA.

**MEHNER, SYLVIA M,** Memphis St Univ, Memphis, TN; JR; BFA; Golden Key; Art-Grphc Dsgn; Grphc Dsgnr.

**MEHRAN, LALEH K,** Univ Of Fl, Gainesville, FL; SR; BFA; Art League 90-; Phi Kappa Tau 89-; Creative Phtgrphy; MFA.

**MEHRENS, JANE M,** Memphis St Univ, Memphis, TN; SR; BSN; Sigma Theta Tau; Pi Epsilon Iota; Flrn Nghtngl Hnr Awrd; RN TN Lcns; RN Stff Nrs; BS Mdcl Tchngy UTCHS; Nrsng.

**MEHROK, HARPAUL S,** Hahnemann Univ, Philadelphia, PA; SO; MD; Hatneman Homeless Clinic; Stdnt Affrs; Golden Key; BS UCLA 89; Med; Physician.

**MEHTA, AMISH A,** Temple Univ, Philadelphia, PA; JR; BSE; OAS Strng Comm 88-89; Alpha Lambda Delta 88-; Gldn Key; Eta Kappa Nu; IEEE; Elec Engr.**

**MEHTA, HEETA,** Beckley Coll, Beckley, WV; FR; BA.

**MEHTA, PAULA,** Univ Of Pittsburgh, Pittsburgh, PA; SO; BSE; Term Hnr Lst 90; Deans Hnr Lst; Elctrcl Eng; Eng.

**MEHTAJI, KAUSHAL D,** City Univ Of Ny Queensbrough, New York, NY; SO; AS; Math & Business Courses; Acctg.

**MEHU, FABRICIA,** Barry Univ, Miami, FL; JR; BA; Co-Anchor Stdnt Nws Pgm 88-90; Campus Stdnt Nwspr Assgnmnt Ed 88-90; Cmnctn; Advrtsng.

**MEI, HONG,** City Univ Of Ny La Guard Coll, Long Island Cty, NY; SO; Nrsg Clb; Med; Hlth Care Prfsns.

**MEIDES, HOLLY S,** S U N Y Coll At Postdam, Potsdam, NY; SR; BM; Band 88-90; Natl Assn Jazz Edn 88-90; Orchestra Violo 89-; Chorus 88; Opera Treas 87-90; Crane Stdnt Assn Treas 87-90; Music Edn Natl Conf 87-; Pres Schlr Motivat/Dsgntr 87-; All-Am Schlr 90-; Kappa Delta Pi 90-; Music; Tchr.**

**MEIER, ALISON,** Molloy Coll, Rockville Ctr, NY; JR; BSN; Nrsng Clb; Stdnt Rep Acad Brd Nrsng; Sigma Theta Tau; Epsilon Kappa Chptr 90-; Omicron Alpha Zeta 90-; Delta Epsilon Sigma 90-; Dns Lst 88-; Cert Red Crs 90; Nrsng.

**MEIER, CHRISTA M,** Hudson Valley Comm Coll, Troy, NY; FR; AS; Clg Cmnty Orchstr New Paltz 86-88; Hnry Scty Hnrs Comm 86-88; Physcn Asst.

**MEIER, CHRISTIAN E,** Glassboro St Coll, Glassboro, NJ; SR; BA; Stdnt Govt Assn Hstry Sntr 88-89; Cmps Radio Sta Comm Dept 88-89; Gamma Tau Sigma 90-; Phi Alpha Theta 90-; Sigma Beta Tau Secy 87-; Deans Lst 88-89; Stdnt Tchr; Assist Sftbl Coach; IM Sftbl 87-; Hist/Scndry Educ; Hist Tchr.

**MEIER, DAVID J,** Oh Wesleyan Univ, Delaware, OH; FR; BA; Stdnt Fdtn; Phi Eta Sigma; Chi Gamma Nu Prize; Chem; Med.

**MEIER, KAREN A,** City Univ Of Ny Queensbrough, New York, NY; AAS; Cert NY Sch Med Dntrl Asstnts 79; Nrsng.

**MEIER, KARYN E,** Temple Univ, Philadelphia, PA; SR; BSRPH; Am Soc Of Phrmcsts 89-; Am & Penn Soc Of Hosp Phrmcy 89-; Penn Phrmctcl Assoc 89-; Rho Chi 90-; Alpha Lambda Delta 87-89; Phrmcy Intern Lancaster Gen Hosp 90-; Citizens Schlrshp Fndtn Lancaster Co 87-; Chas Bonadio Lancaster Co Phrmctcl Schlrsp; Hosp Phrmcst.

**MEIER, MARK A,** Oh Wesleyan Univ, Delaware, OH; FR; BA; Wslyn Fndtn; Phi Eta Sigma; Chi Gamma Nu Chem Awd; Chem; Med.

**MEIERHANS, LAUREN R,** Univ Of Rochester, Rochester, NY; JR; BS; Eastman Sch Clarinet Lsns Orchstra 88-; Soc Of Women Engrs 88-90; Big Bro Big Sistr Vol 89-90; Deans List 88; Deans List 90; Phi Sigma Sigma Hd Of Judcl Bd 88-; Bausch/Lomb Merit Schlr 88-; Trck/Fld 88; Biomed Engrng; Medcn.

**MEIERHOEFER, KRISTIE R,** Columbus Coll Of Art & Design, Columbus, OH; FR; BA; SADD; AFS; Outstndg Stdnt Awd; Advrtsg Design; Cmrcl Art.

**MEIHOEFER, MARK R,** East Stroudsburg Univ, E Stroudsburg, PA; SR; BA; IM Scr Capt 87-90; IM Bsktbl Capt 88-; Econ Clb 87-; Dns Lst 87-; Vrsty Scr 87-89; Econ; Intrntl Bus.

**MEILE, TERESA M,** Lesley Coll, Cambridge, MA; FR; MBA; Poetry Clb Prsdnt 90-; Scl Sci Hmn Dev; Erly Chldhd Edctr.

**MEILHAMMER, DEBORAH S,** Salisbury St Univ, Salisbury, MD; SR; BS; SSU Dance Co 90-; Nalt Assoc Wmn Math 90-; Phi Eta Sigma 88-; D G Calcott Mem Schlrsp 90-; Math; M S.

**MEILI, KIMBERLY A,** Daemen Coll, Amherst, NY; FR; BS; Pshycl Thrpy.

**MEIMAN, MARGARET E,** Birmingham Southern Coll, Birmingham, AL; JR; BA; Alpha Lambda Delta; Sigma Tau Delta Sec; Deans Lst 88-; Schlrshp British Studies Oxford England; Engl; Law.

**MEINES, DARLA R,** Fl St Univ, Tallahassee, FL; FR; BM; Wesley U M Ch 90-; Choir 90-; Hnrs & Schlrs FSU 90-; Phi Eta Sigma 90-; Music; Music Thrpst.

**MEINZE, GILLIAN C,** Anne Arundel Comm Coll, Arnold, MD; FR; BA; Psychlgy.

**MEIR II, JOHN H,** Methodist Coll, Fayetteville, NC; FR; BS; USAF 86-; Comptr Sci; Progrmr/Anlys.

**MEISINGER, AMY A,** Villanova Univ, Villanova, PA; SO; BS; Spec Olympcs 89-; Kappa Delta Pi 90-; Big East Acad All-Amer 90-; Vars Sftbl; Math Ed; Tchr/Prfssr.

**MEISNER, JUDITH E,** Schenectady County Comm Coll, Schenectady, NY; FR; BSN; Fire Dept/Rescue Squad Lt 81-; EMS EMT Intrn 89-; RN St Clares Hosp 85-; Dip Ellis Hosp Schl Of Nrsng 72; Nursing; Hosp Admin.

**MEISSNER, KRISTEN L,** Bay Path Coll, Longmeadow, MA; GD; Tutorial Asst 89-; Maroon Ky 90-; Dns Lst 89-; Intr Dsgn Intrnshp BKM Dsgn; AS; Intr Dsgn; Dsgnr.

**MEISSNER, MELINDA L,** Fl Atlantic Univ, Boca Raton, FL; SR; BBA; Phi Theta Kappa; Beta Gamma Sigma; AA Palm Bch Comm Coll 89; Intl Bus; Bus/Mktg.

**MEISTER, ERIN S,** Anne Arundel Comm Coll, Arnold, MD; SO; BS; Erly Chldhd Ed; Ownr/Oper Day Care Ctr.

**MEISTER, MONICA A,** Univ Of Ky, Lexington, KY; FR; BA; Stdnt Dev Cncl; Kappa Alpha Theta 90-.

**MEIT, MORDECHAI,** Barry Univ, Miami, FL; JR; BA; Intl Studes; Frgn Affrns.

**MEITNER, STEVEN J,** Univ Of Rochester, Rochester, NY; SO; BS; Mini-Baja Eng Tm Dsgn Engr 90-; Univ Jazz Ensmbl 89-90; Argonne Natl Lab 88-89; RI St Dlgt Natl Yth Sci Camp 88-89; Mech Eng; Aerntcl Eng.

**MEIXELL, AMANDA S,** Franklin And Marshall Coll, Lancaster, PA; SR; Dance Clb 87-89; Spnsh Clb 87-89; Anthropology Clb 90-; Phi Beta Kappa; Pi Gamma Mu 90-; Sigma Delta Pi; BA Franklin Marshall Coll; Anthropology/Spnsh.

**MEIXELL, SUSAN A,** Portland School Of Art, Portland, ME; SO; BFA; Beatrice% Barrett Schlr; Fine Arts/Sculpture.

**MEJIA, DANY E,** Central Fl Comm Coll, Ocala, FL; FR; Hispanic Clb Assoc; Intl Clb; Intl Schlrshp; Machine Tool Tchnlgy; Engrng.

**MEJIA, MARIBEL,** City Univ Of Ny Hostos Coll, Bronx, NY; SR.

**MEJIA, MIGDALIA T,** Univ Of Pr Medical Sciences, San Juan, PR; GD; MS; NSSSLHA 90-; Psychlgy Treas 88-90; Chrcy Yth Pres 89-; Magna Cum Laude 90; BA Univ Of PR Rio Piedras 90; Speech/Lang Pthlgy.

**MEKUS, KEVIN P,** Univ Of Rochester, Rochester, NY; SR; BA; Linguistics; Law.

**MEKUS, NITA C,** Univ Of Ky, Lexington, KY; JR; BA; Scl Wrk; Achl Cnslr.

**MEKUS, SUSAN L,** Defiance Coll, Defiance, OH; FR; BED; Wrt Shrt Stry Chldrn; Hstry; Elem Ed.

**MELAMED, ALEJANDRO Y,** Yeshiva Univ, New York, NY; SR; BS; Accntng Scty 88; Sephardic Clb 88; Deans Lst 88; Joseph Herbst Awd; Accntng.

**MELAMED, DAVID NAVID,** City Univ Of Ny Queensbrough, New York, NY; FR; MAPHD; NY St EMT; Cert CPR/FRST Aid 90-; Biology; Doctor.

**MELAMED, NEDA N,** Yeshiva Univ, New York, NY; JR; BA; Sephardic Clb 89; Cltre Clb 90; Engl Lit; Law.

**MELANIE, CECILE A,** Fl International Univ, Miami, FL; JR; BA; Shape Assc Crdntr Asstnt; Hn Pgm Miami Dade Comm Clg 90; AS Degree Acctg Lycee Marie Curie France 87; AA Bus Admn Miami Dade Comm Clg 90; Tnns/Smwng Tm Frnc Tnns Refree/Plyr Swmng Un Cmptn 86-87; Mktg Intrntl Bus; Mstr Intrntl Bus.

**MELANSON, SCOTT A,** Western New England Coll, Springfield, MA; SR; Math Clb Treas 79-; Vrsty Bsktbl 90; BA.

**MELBA, ORTIZ ARCHILLA,** Caribbean Univ, Bayamon, PR; BA; Cltrl Ctr Carmen Rivera De Alvarado Vega Baja/Arts Culture Corp Manatuabon; Ind Oper; Mgmnt; Law.

**MELBOURNE, ERICA L,** Morris Brown Coll, Atlanta, GA; JR; BS; Dorm Cncl VP 88-89; Mock Trl 88-; All Amer Schlr; Cnslr For Yth 90; Tutor; Psychlgy; Tchng.

**MELCHER, MARGARET R,** Oh Univ-Southern Cmps, Ironton, OH; SO; BA; Office Mgt 85-88; Recrtl Therapy.

**MELCHIORRE, JOSEPH P,** Cumberland County Coll, Vineland, NJ; SO; EOF 87-; Mu Alpha Theta 88-; Deans Lst 87-; AA Pre Engrng; Math/Sci; Mech Engr.

**MELCHIORRE JR, LOUIS P,** Philadelphia Coll Pharm & Sci, Philadelphia, PA; SR; BS; Pre Med Scty Pres 89-; Amer Inst Of Blgcl Scis 87-; Phto Clb VP 89; Alpha Chi Treas; Alpha Lambda Delta 87-; IM Vlybl 90-; Blgy; Med.

**MELE, CHRISTOPHER,** Manhattan Coll, Bronx, NY; JR; BSCE; Amer Scty Civil Engineers Pres 89-; Concret Canoe Clb 89-; Chi Epsilo Edtr 90-; Engineering; Civil Engineer.

**MELE, HEATHER N,** Hamilton Coll, Clinton, NY; FR; Drama Clb 90-; Nwspr 90-; Natl Hon Scty 88-; Hon Pgm Clg 90-; Best Sprtng Actrs 90-; Engl Lit; Prfsr.

**MELE, KAREN E,** Franklin And Marshall Coll, Lancaster, PA; FR; BA; Porter Sci Soc 90-; Pre Healing Arts Clb 90-; St Joseph Hosp Vol 90-; Sci/Art Hstry; Med.

**MELE, MARGARET M,** Ny Univ, New York, NY; SR; BA; Alpha Sigma Lambda 90-; Anthrplgy; Ph D.

**MELE, PHILLIP A,** Davis & Elkins Coll, Elkins, WV; SR; BS; BS; Mktg; Bus.

**MELE, THOMAS L,** Nova Univ, Ft Lauderdale, FL; GD; Sthrn Schlrshp Fndtn Pres 80-82; Alpha Lambda Delta 78-79; Kiwanis Club; Advsry Engr IBM; Rl Est Lic 84; Dale Carnegie Grdte; BS Florida State Univ 83; MBA 90; Bsn/Mktg; Mgr.

**MELEAR, JENNI E,** Waycross Coll, Waycross, GA; SO; AA; Phi Theta Kappa Pres; Edn; Elem Edn.

**MELEI, STEVEN EDWARD,** Fl St Univ, Tallahassee, FL; SR; BA; Unico Natl Italian Amer Clb Sgt At Arms 86-89; Sons Of Italy Roma Lodge 88-; KC 89-; Pi Gamma Mu 90-; Phi Kappa Phi 90-; Tau Kappa Epsilon Temp Treas 90-; Italian Amer Clb 90-; Deans Lst; UNICO 90; Pol Sci/Intl Affairs; Law Schl.

**MELENDEZ LEON, MARIA V,** Univ Of Pr Cayey Univ Coll, Cayey, PR; JR; Read/Write/Study 87-; Hon Rl 89-; Tutor 89-; Acctng; Lawyer/CPA.

**MELENDEZ PAGAN, YANIRA,** Inter Amer Univ Pr San German, San German, PR; SR; Sci Clb 88-90; High Sch Hon Sq 88-; Sci Awrds 88-90; Schlrshp Awrds 88-; Chem Eng.

**MELENDEZ RIVERA, MARIA R,** Caribbean Univ, Bayamon, PR.

**MELENDEZ RODRIGUEZ, ILEANA,** Univ Politecnica De Pr, Hato Rey, PR; SO; BS; Brd Advsr AIESEC Bayamon Pres 89-90; AETI; ROTC; Ldrshp Smnr 88-; Chmbr/Cmmrc 89; Ecnmst Assoc 89; Engr; Civil.

**MELENDEZ, ISMAEL,** Univ Politecnica De Pr, Hato Rey, PR; FR; Engr.

**MELENDEZ, JONATHAN A,** Univ Of Pr At Rio Piedras, Rio Piedras, PR; SO; MD; The 100 Group; All Amer Schlr; Hnr Stdnt; Med/Surgery.

**MELENDEZ, LILIAN M,** Inter Amer Univ Pr Barranquita, Barranquitas, PR; SR; BA; Accntng; C P A.

**MELENDEZ, OLGA LUCIA,** Boston Univ, Boston, MA; JR; BS; Nwsppr Edtr 90-; Dean Hst 90-; Peer Cnslr 90-; Chorus 89-90; Trustee Schlr 88-; Natl Hspnc Schlr 89-; Physcl Thrpy; MS.

**MELENDEZ, OMAIRA,** Lincoln Univ, Lincoln Univ, PA; SO; BA; Laser Clb Chrprsn 89-; Chem Clb 89-; Alpha Chi; Mu Alpha Gamma; Alpha Kappa Alpha; Mst Otsdng Clcls Awd 89-90; Intrnshp NASA Cntr Space Propulsion 90; Engr Pennstate Univ; Univ Cmps Intrnshp Oak Rdge Assoc; Univ Natl Lab; Chemistry; Engr.

**MELENDEZ, RAPHAEL J,** City Univ Of Ny Baruch Coll, New York, NY; JR; BBA; Money/Fncl Invstmnts Assoc Secr 89-; Weightlifting/Exercise Prog 90-; Mgmt.

**MELENDEZ-CASTRO, VIVIAN D,** Bayamon Central Univ, Bayamon, PR; SO; Stdnt Support Serv 90-; WECN TV Tech 90-; US Army ROTC Cadet 90-; Engl; Telvsn Tech.

**MELFI, RENEE S,** Univ Of Rochester, Rochester, NY; SO; BA; Charles Drew Premed Soc 89-; Spnsh Interest Flr 90-; Varsity Soccer 89-90; Psychlgy; Physician.

**MELGAREJO, ORESTES G,** Fl International Univ, Miami, FL; SR; BS; IEEE; Natl Hispanic Schlrshp; GE Ocean/Radar Systems; Elect Eng; Prog Eng/Career Info.

**MELHADO, RIPTON A,** Morris Brown Coll, Atlanta, GA; JR; BS; Hon Cl; Hosptlty Mgmnt Asso V P 89-90; Am Inst; Gold Key Pres; Eta Sigma Delta; Intnshp Hyatt Regcy Atlanta 90-; Hotel Rstrnt/Tourism Admin; Hotel Mgr/Cnsltnt.

**MELIA, ANGELA M,** Germanna Comm Coll, Locust Grove, VA; SO; AAS; Thrptc Rdng Pgm Coord 84-89; 4-H Hrse Pgm Supt 88; Phi Theta Kappa; VA 4-H Cert Rcgtn/Ldrshp 88; Sci; Rdlgy.

**MELIA, DAWN M,** Seton Hall Univ, South Orange, NJ; JR; BSN; Nrsng; RN.

**MELIA, RHONDA G,** Commonwealth Coll, Virginia Beach, VA; SO; AAS; Acctg Clb Treas 90-; Acctg; CPA.

**MELIAN, JEANETTE C,** Fl International Univ, Miami, FL; SR; BS; FEA Sec 90-; Kappa Delta Pi 90-; AA Miami Dade Comm Coll 89; Elem Edn.

**MELICK, DAVID D,** Oh Univ, Athens, OH; FR; BA; Airway Sci; Pilot.

**MELILLO, SANDRA M,** Georgian Court Coll, Lakewood, NJ; GD; BA 90; Elem Educ/Psych; Tchg.

**MELINO, KRISTIN M,** Newbury Coll, Brookline, MA; SO; BA; Com Prprtn Sprng Fshn Show; Drssr Bob Mackie Fshn Show; Deans Lst 90-; Intrnshp Filenes Bsmnt-Newton MA Stck Assoc 90; Sftbl; Fshn Mrchndsng; Mrchndsng.

**MELINSKY JR, THOMAS R,** Oh Univ, Athens, OH; JR; BS; Alpine Clb 89-90; Ntl Soc Pro Eng; Golden Key 89-; Tau Beta Pi 90-; Eta Kppa Nu 90-; Outstndg Soph Rnnr Up EGE 89-90; Helen Hoover Schlrshp; IM Brmbl 87-89; Elec/Cmptr Eng.**

**MELISH, MARYANN M,** Central Fl Comm Coll, Ocala, FL; SO; AS; Reg Nrs.

**MELISKI, MARY C,** Hudson Valley Comm Coll, Troy, NY; FR; AS; GSA Chrmn 86-; Rlgn Instctr Tchr 89-; Share Dcsn Chldrn Schlp 89-; PTA Co-Pres 88-90; Evnt Coord 87-89; Early Chldhd; Tchr.

**MELLARD, ROBERT D,** Coll Of Charleston, Charleston, SC; JR; BA; Phi Kappa Phi; Phi Alpha Theta; Hist.

**MELLBERG, LAURA L,** Univ Of Rochester, Rochester, NY; SR; BS; Undrgrad Optcl Soc Amer VP 88-; Outsd Spkrs Com Bus Mngr 87-90; Rsdnt Advsr 89-; Tau Beta Pi 90-; Alpha Phi 90-; Optics Hon Pgm; Deans Lst; Optics; Eng.

**MELLEN, KATHERINE M,** Univ Of Nc At Asheville, Asheville, NC; JR; BA; Lit.

**MELLGREN, KIRSTEN S,** Clarkson Univ, Potsdam, NY; SR; BS; Pep Bnd 87-; Soc Acctnts Treas 87-; Phi Kappa Phi; Trustees Schlrshp 87-; Milton Carpenter Fndtn Schlrshp 87-; Acct/Fnc; Acctg CPA.

**MELLMAN, SAUL M,** Widener Univ, Chester, PA; SR; Amer Soc Cvl Engrs Treas 90-; Tau Beta Pi 89-; AS Eng DE Cnty Comm Coll 89; Cvl Eng; Eng Dsgn/Cnstr.

**MELLO, BROOKE,** Univ Of Ma At Amherst, Amherst, MA; FR; BS; Dunkin Donuts Corp Schlrshp 90-; Somerset Wmns Clb Schlrshp 90-; Science; Dental Schl.

**MELLO III, JOSEPH,** Univ Of Rochester, Rochester, NY; JR; BS; Crss Cntry Cpt 87-; Indr Trck/Outdr Trck 87-; ASME 90-; Mech Eng.

**MELLON, LAURA W,** Winthrop Coll, Rock Hill, SC; JR; BA; Notary Publ 83-83; Presbyterian Wmn 90-; AA Genl Ed Cleveland Comm Colg 81; AA EDP 82; Busn Admin; CPA.

**MELLON, ROBYN L,** Western Piedmont Comm Coll, Morganton, NC; FR; Paralgl Assn 90-; FDFR Incntve Prog Exec Comm; Option Inc Vol; Clfhvn Shltr; Crmnl Jstce; Soc Wrk.

**MELLOTT, KRISTY S,** George Mason Univ, Fairfax, VA; JR; BS; Alpha Chi; Deans Lst; Mkgt; Bus.

**MELNYK, DIANE E,** Mount Saint Mary Coll, Newburgh, NY; SO; BSN; Nrsng Stdnt Union; Nrsng; Nrs Prcttnr.

**MELO, FRANCISCA J,** Ny Univ, New York, NY; GD; Stu Ltrry Mag Edtr 86-88.

**MELO, KARLA C,** Fl International Univ, Miami, FL; FR; BA; Mrktng.

**MELO, MARGARET B,** Assumption Coll, Worcester, MA; JR; BA; Acctg/Cmptr Sci; CPA.**

**MELONE, ANGELIKA J S,** Hudson Valley Comm Coll, Troy, NY; SO; AAS; Taconic Vly Hist Soc Pres 87-88; Wmns Natl Farm Gdn Assn Taconic Vly Brnch Comm 87-; Catholic Med Msn Bd; Vol Svcs Honduras Mid 70s Dntl Asst,Haiti 78; Vol Baby Well Clnc Berlin N Y Renselear Cnty Hlth Dept 87-89; Dntl Asst 69-; Erly Chldhd Dvlpmnt; Erly Chldhd Tchr.

**MELONIO, LEIGH ANN,** Duquesne Univ, Pittsburgh, PA; SO; BS; Ski Clb 90-; Hmn Rsrc Mgmt Soc 90-; Phi Eta Sigma 90-; Bus.

**MELOON, ELIZABETH D,** Miami Chrisitian Coll, Miami, FL; JR; BS; SGA VP 90-; AWANA Youth Orgnztn Secy/Leader 88-; Vllybl 88-; Elmntry Ed; Professial Tchng.

**MELORE, JULIA A,** Lexington Comm Coll, Lexington, KY; FR; BA; Cmnctns; Teach.

**MELOVITZ, CHERYL A,** Univ Of Med & Dentistry Of Nj, Newark, NJ; SR; BS; Lambda Alpha Theta 88-; Amer PT Assc 89-; Welkind Rehab Hosp; Suburban PT; Physical Therapy.

**MELSHENKER, SCOTT A,** Savannah Coll Of Art & Design, Savannah, GA; SO; BFA; Grphc Dsgn.

**MELSON, MELISSA A,** Wilmington Coll, New Castle, DE; JR; BS; Dns Lst 89-; Alpha Eta Rho; Aviation Mgmt/Safety.

**MELSON, SHARON J,** Va Commonwealth Univ, Richmond, VA; JR; BS; Golden Key 90-; Psi Chi 90-; Alpha Sigma Alpha V P 89-; Psych; Acad Devel Dir.

**MELTON, BETTY M,** Christopher Newport Coll, Newport News, VA; JR; Elem Educ; Tchng.

**MELTON, CAPT GREGORY L,** Air Force Inst Of Tech, Wrt-Ptrsn Afb, OH; GD; MS; Sigma Iota Epsilon 90-; USAF 83-; BS West VA Univ 83; Engr Mgmt; USAF Engr.

**MELTON, CYNTHIA L,** Volunteer St Comm Coll, Gallatin, TN; SO; BA; Red Kap Industries Nashville TN Customer Serv Rep; Acctg; CPA.

**MELTON, DEBBIE L,** Chesterfield Marlboro Coll, Cheraw, SC; SO; AS; Comp Sci; Prgrmng.

**MELTON, DEREK S,** Gaston Coll, Dallas, NC; SO; BS; Cvl Engrg; Hwy Engr.

**MELTON, GABRIELE,** Fl St Univ, Tallahassee, FL; SO; BA; Phi Eta Sigma 90-; Deans Lst 90-; Acctg/Fnc.

**MELTON, JENNIFER A,** Wv Univ, Morgantown, WV; FR; BSN; Wesly Untd Meth Clg Chr; Hnrs Schlrs Pgm 90-; Alpha Phi Omega; Nrsng.

**MELTON, LANA N,** Memphis St Univ, Memphis, TN; SO; Stdnt Govt Assoc Sec Of State 90-; Res Hsng Assoc Chrmn Of Educ 90-; Rawls Hall Cncl 90-; Gamma Beta Phi; Pi Beta Phi; IM League Vlybl Tms 89-.

**MELTON, PAIGE C,** Univ Of Ga, Athens, GA; SR; Phi Beta Lambda Secy 89-90; Phi Beta Lambda VP 90-; Young Repblcns Rep; Big Sistr Prog; Im Tennis/Sftbl 89-; BSED; Bus Ed; Sales.

**MELTON, SHELBY D,** Spartanburg Methodist Coll, Spartanburg, SC; FR; BA; Phi Theta Kappa 90-.

**MELTON, SOPHIA L,** Sue Bennett Coll, London, KY; JR; BA; Nwspr Ed 86-87; Phi Beta Lamba 85-87; Soclgy/Psychlgy; Pre-Trial Svcs/Juvenile.

**MELTON, TRACY E,** Niagara Univ, Niagara Univ, NY; JR; BS; Math Clb 89; Kappa Mu Epsilon Treas 90-; Hon Soc 89-; Hockey 89-; Math/Econ; Econmst.

**MELTON-CRUZ, AMY L,** Bayamon Central Univ, Bayamon, PR; FR; BA; Pre Med; Medicine/Coroner.

**MELTSER, HENRY M,** Clark Univ, Worcester, MA; SR; Spkrs Frm 88-; Bio Clb 88-; Jwsh Stdnt Cltn 88-; Fiat Lux; Acad Hons 89-; Sigma Pi; Internshp UMASS 89; Org Chem Tchng Asst 89; Intrshp Worc Fnd Biol; Bio/Neurosci; Med.**

**MELVIN, BOBBY E,** Alcorn St Univ, Lorman, MS; SO; MBA; Inter Rsdntl Hall Cncl Bus Mgr 90-; Wesley Fndtn; Bus Admnstrtn; Pres Own Bus.

**MELVIN, CHRISTOPHER M,** Johnson C Smith Univ, Charlotte, NC; JR; BA; Carter Hl Actvts Brd Asst VP 90-; JCSU Yrbk Stf Wrtr/Ed Artst 89-; Phi Beta Sigma VP 90-; Hsng Athrts Smr Yth Pgm 90-; Asbury Prk Prs Intrn Lyt; JCSU Ftbl Tm Vrsty 89-; Cmnctns/Cmptr Sci; Grdt Schl.

**MELVIN, JOSEPH E,** Carnegie Mellon Univ, Pittsburgh, PA; GD; MS; Pres; Mrtr Brd Snr Hnr Scty 89-90; Scl Chrmn Crng Invlvmnt Assoc Scl Chr 89-90; Crng Mlln Bcyclng Clb Co Pres 89-90; Rgmccrdy Mmrl Schlrshp 89-90; Andrw Crng Scty Schlr 88-89; Rsrch Asst Dcsn Sci 89-90; BS 90; Ststcs.

**MELVIN, KELLEY R,** Memphis St Univ, Memphis, TN; JR; BFA; Chi Omega 81-82; Intr Dsgn.

**MELVIN, LINDA J,** Va Polytechnic Inst & St Univ, Blacksburg, VA; FR; BA; Frgn Svc/Intrntl Bus.

**MELVIN, MATT S,** Methodist Coll, Fayetteville, NC; JR; BS; Lambda Chi Alpha 89-; Meth Coll Chem Socty 89-; Stdnt Govt Assn Sntr; Amer Chem Socty; Crs Cntry/Trck/Fld 88-; Chmstry; Envrnmntl Cnsltnt.

**MELVIN, MELISSA D,** Ashland Comm Coll, Ashland, KY; SO; BA; Ch Pianist Danleyton Msnry Bapt Ch 89-; Acctng; CPA.

**MELVIN, VALERIE C,** Coppin St Coll, Baltimore, MD; SR; BS; Psych Clb 88-; Deans Lst; Dept Econ Emplyt Dev Claims Assoc 80; Psych.

**MENA, ALEIDA,** Antillian Adventist University, Mayaguez, PR; GD; BA; VP Stdnt Cnsl 90-; BA Andrews Univ 82; Hstry; Law.

**MENA, DAVID C,** The Johns Hopkins Univ, Baltimore, MD; FR; Optmst Clb Bsbll Coach; Chmstry; Medicine.

**MENAKER, HADAS L,** Univ Of Al At Birmingham, Birmingham, AL; SO; BA; Intrntnl Stdnt Assn Pblcty 90-; Intrntnl Bus; Pblc Rltns.

**MENAPACE, CHRISTINE M,** Glassboro St Coll, Glassboro, NJ; SR; BA; Venue Mag Assoc Edtr 88-; Ad Clb 89-; Advrtsng Dynmcs VP; Garden State Schlr; Advrtsng Dynmcs Tag Awd; Becker/Jani Inc Intrnshp; Cmnctns/Advrtsng; Cmnctns.

**MENAR, LORRAINE M,** Va Commonwealth Univ, Richmond, VA; JR; BFA; Otdr Advvntr Prgm Vol Trip Ldr 89-90; Cntmprry Crft Scty; Gldn Key 90-; Phi Eta Simga; Art Hstry; Art Admn.

**MENARCHICK, CATHERINE A,** S U N Y Coll Of Tech At Alfred, Alfred, NY; FR; ASSOC; Case Wrkr Fam Svcs Elmira NY; Soc Sci; Psych.

**MENARD, KAREN S,** Elms Coll, Chicopee, MA; JR; BA; Phi Theta Kappa 89; All Amer Schlr Clgt Awd; Convocation Awd 89; Mercy Hospital Nut Assist 89-; Elem Ed; Elem Schl Tchr.

**MENCARELLI, VICTOR A,** D Youville Coll, Buffalo, NY; SO; BS; Cmps Mnstry 89-; Beta Beta Beta 90; Ttr 89-; Pres Acad Schlrshp 89-; Blgy; Med.

**MENCHU, GLADYS EDILMA,** Central Fl Comm Coll, Ocala, FL; AS; Coop Assoc Of States For Schlrshp & Central Amer Schlrsp Prog 89-; Amer Soc For Quality Control; Phi Theta Kappa 90-; Deans List 90-; Qlty Control/Prodctn Mgmnt; Bus Admnstrtn.

**MENDEL, DANIELLE,** Glassboro St Coll, Glassboro, NJ; SR; BA; JR Achvmnt South Jersey V P 80-83; Cty Fdrl Svgs Bnk/Frst Fdlty Bnk 84-91; AA Gloucester Cnty Clg 86; Sclgy; Cnslng.

**MENDELS, KIM M,** S U N Y At Buffalo, Buffalo, NY; JR; BA; Jewsh Stdnt Union Cmpgn Treas; Sigma Delta Tau Treas 89-; Comm Actn Crps 90-; Dn Witter Reynolds/Intrn 90; Bus.

**MENDELSOHN, PAUL,** Univ Of Sc At Columbia, Columbia, SC; SO; BS; IEEE; U S Navy Pty Off 3rd Cls 82-85; S C Natl Grd Spec 86-; Hnr Mn Co 366 Nvy 83; Grdtd Tp 10% A Schl Nvy 83; IM Sftbl 90-; Engrg; Elec Engr.

**MENDELSON, MENUCHA D,** Yeshiva Univ, New York, NY; JR; BA; Intnshp Rusk Inst NYU Med Cen 90-; Intnshp Marsten Mandarajji Inc NYC Desgn 89; Spch Pathlgst.

**MENDEN, WILLIAM A,** City Univ Of Ny Baruch Coll, New York, NY; SR; BBA; Cmptr Clb 87-; Baruch Endwmnt Fnd Provosts Schlrshp 89; Mayors Schlrshp Fnd 89-90; Dns Hnr Lst 87-; MBA Systms Info; Cmptr Info Systms; Systms Anlyst.

**MENDES III, FORTUNATO J,** Va St Univ, Petersburg, VA; FR; BA; Histry Clb 90-; Pre Law Soc 90-; History; Envrnmntl Law.

**MENDES, KYLE R,** Fl International Univ, Miami, FL; SO; BA; Intl Stdnts Club; Fatima Coll Comp Club Trinidad; Trinidad Country Club; CXC/?GCE O Levels Fatima Coll Trinidad W I 87; GCE A Levels 89; Bus.

**MENDEZ RIVERA, BIBIANA,** Inter Amer Univ Pr Hato Rey, Hato Rey, PR; FR; BA; Blgy; Med Ob.

**MENDEZ, ALVARO F,** Univ Of Miami, Coral Gables, FL; SR; BSN; Fl Stdnt Nrs Assoc Dlgt 83-84; Amer Red Crs Vol 88-; Amer Hrt Assoc Instrctr/Trnr 86-; By Scts Amer Sct Mstr 84-86; Fl Scty Hlth Cr Ed Trnng 88-; S Fl Hosp Assoc Nrs Ed T Frc 90-; Nrsg; Hosp Admin.

**MENDEZ, CARLOS J,** Miami Dade Comm Coll South, Miami, FL; SO; BA; Miami Art Clb 88-; Comm Vol Pllwrkr 90-; Schlrshp Art 90-; Art Cert Robert Morgan Voc Tech Inst 88; Visual/Comm Art; Animation.

**MENDEZ, DENISE,** Miami Dade Comm Coll South, Miami, FL; SO; BA; Phi Theta Kapp Tres 90-; AA; Bus; Multntnl Bus.

**MENDEZ, FELIX RAMON,** Asbury Theological Sem, Wilmore, KY; SR; MDIV; Assn Smnrns Pres 86-87; Cir Evnglcl Wrtrs 87-88; Theta Phi; BA Tech Univ Santiago 87; BA Free Meth Smnry 86; Thlgy; Tchng.

**MENDEZ, ISABEL C,** S U N Y Coll Of Tech At Frmgdl, Farmingdale, NY; FR; Dntl Hygiene.

**MENDEZ, JOSE R,** Manhattan School Of Music, New York, NY; SR; BA; MBA Superior Cnsrvtry S Sebastian Spain 86; Piano.

**MENDEZ, LAWRENCE R,** Anne Arundel Comm Coll, Arnold, MD; SO; BA; MD Clssfd Employees Assoc; Am Crrctnl Assoc; Crrctnl Ofcr Srgnt State MD; Criminology; Crmnl Jstc Admnstrtn.

**MENDEZ, LOURDES,** City Univ Of Ny Baruch Coll, New York, NY; JR; Acctg Soc; Acctg; Law.

**MENDEZ, MARISOL,** Inter Amer Univ Pr San German, San German, PR; JR; Psych.

**MENDEZ, ROBERTO,** Georgetown Univ, Washington, DC; JR; BSBA; Latin Amer Student Assoc; Georgetown Invtmnt Alliance; Tennis; Busn/Finance/Intl Mgt.

**MENDEZ, SIMON J,** Colby Sawyer Coll, New London, NH; FR; BA; Phtgrphy; Bus/Photo.

**MENDEZ-RIVERA, CARMEN L,** Catholic Univ Of Pr, Ponce, PR; SO; Acctg; CPA.

**MENDIBURO, JOAQUIN P,** Nova Univ, Ft Lauderdale, FL; SR; MBA; Natl Sfty Cncl 89-; Amer Cmpnstn Asc 89-; Cuban Amer Natl Fndtn; BA FL St Univ 74; MA FL St Univ 75; Mrktng; Law.

**MENDIETA, PEDRO A,** Miami Dade Comm Coll South, Miami, FL; SO; BA; FL Engr Scty; Talent Roster 90; Engr; Mech Engr.

**MENDIOLA, JENNIFER R,** Hudson Valley Comm Coll, Troy, NY; SR; AAS; BA Emory & Henry Coll Emory Va 86; Mech Engr Tech; Mech Design.

**MENDOZA, BERNICE M,** Univ Of Pr Cayey Univ Coll, Cayey, PR; FR; Rec Assn Jard De Caguas P R 88-; Dns Lst 90-; Nat Sci; Phrmcy.

**MENDOZA, CARMEN F,** Radford Univ, Radford, VA; SO; BA; Photo Ed 89-; SCJ 90-; Catholic Stdnt Assoc 89-; Movie Comm 89-; Soccer IM Capt 90-; Jrnlsm/Spnsh; Law.

**MENDOZA, CYNTHIA I,** Central Fl Comm Coll, Ocala, FL; SO; Phi Theta Kappa Mrshl 90-; Almnmrcyclng Org 90-; Elem Ed; Evntlly Bcm Prncpl.

**MENDOZA, ELVA A,** Hudson County Comm Coll, Jersey City, NJ; GD; BS; Office Sys Tchnlgy Clb; Bus Admnstrtn.

**MENDOZA, ESTELA B,** Georgetown Univ, Washington, DC; FR; BSPS; Roundtbl Pol Cultr Mexclsn 90-; Orient Aide; AYUDA Vol 90-; Congrsmn Jim Bates Lyndon B Johnsn Intrn Leg Aide 89-90; Intl Affrs.

**MENDOZA, EVELYN,** Univ Politecnica De Pr, Hato Rey, PR; FR; Indl Engr.

**MENDOZA, JOSE A,** Univ Of Pr At Mayaguez, Mayaguez, PR; JR; BME; Hnr Stdnt 89-; Phi Sigma Alpha 90-; Math/Mech Engnrng.

**MENDOZA, KRISTINE,** City Univ Of Ny Kingsborough, Brooklyn, NY; SO; BA; AA; Psych.

**MENDOZA, MAYRA I,** Univ Politecnica De Pr, Hato Rey, PR; JR; Indstrl Eng.

**MENEDEZ, DANIEL,** Fl International Univ, Miami, FL; FR; Phi Lambda Beta.

**MENEELY, ELIZABETH A,** Ky Wesleyan Coll, Owensboro, KY; JR; BA; Chrldng 89-; Jdcl Cncl 90-; Kappa Delta Stndrds Brd; Pr Ttr 90-; Chrldng 89-; Nrsng.

**MENEFEE, KAREN D,** Georgetown Coll, Georgetown, KY; JR; BA; MAA; PBL; Alpha Lambda Delta; Envrnmntl Grp; Drm Cnslr Rsdnt Asst; Hnr Lst; Math; Intrnatl Law.

**MENEFEE, LARSHAUN E,** Al A & M Univ, Normal, AL; FR; BS; NAACP; Drg Tsk Frc; Apld Sci; Nrsng.

**MENEFEE, MARSHAUN L,** Al A & M Univ, Normal, AL; FR; NAACP; Drg Tsk Frc; Sttstcn Asst Trnr Grls Bsktbl; Apld Sci; Nrsng.

**MENENDEZ, KRISTINA M,** Fl International Univ, Miami, FL; SO; BA; Fclty Schlr Pgm 89-; Pol Sci; Law.

**MENENDEZ, RAMON J,** Fl International Univ, Miami, FL; SR; BA; Thespian Soc 86-; Phi Theta Kappa 88-; Psi Chi 90-; Phi Kappa Phi; Deans Lst 87-; ART Mus Intrn 90; Psych Acad Achvmnt Awrd; AA Miami Dade Cmnty Clg 88; Psych; Fine Arts/Tchr.

**MENENDEZ-CONDE, IDA,** Univ Of Miami, Coral Gables, FL; SR; BA; Phi Kapp Aphi 90; Golden Key 90; Hnr Stdnts Assoc; Prvsts Hnr Roll 90; Deans Lst; AA Miami Dade Cmmnty Clg 89; Pol Sci; Law.**

**MENGE, C J,** Univ Of Cincinnati, Cincinnati, OH; FR; BM; Hon Pgm 90-; Performance Percussion; Profl Percussionist.

**MENKHAUS, JILL K,** Northern Ky Univ, Highland Hts, KY; FR; BA; Natl Hnrs Scty 90; Rdlgy.

**MENNE, KRISTA S,** Northern Ky Univ, Highland Hts, KY; SR; BS; Human Serv; Mntl Hlth/Human Serv; Cnslng.

**MENNEFIELD, TARA T,** Talladega Coll, Talladega, AL; SO; BS; Blgy Clb Pres 90-; MARC; Beta Beta Beta; Dns Lst 89-; Sam Jackson Awd Schlstc Achvmnt 90; Blgy; Med/Physcn.

**MENON, MONISHA,** Bridgewater Coll, Bridgewater, VA; JR; BSC; Prog Cncl Pres 90-; Intnatl Clb 89; Dns Lst; Lambda Scty 90-; Phi Beta Lambda 90-; Bus And Econs; Mrktng Exec.

**MENSAH, PAMELA L,** Coll Of Charleston, Charleston, SC; SR; MBA; Urbn Stdies Clb Treas 90-; Outstndng Stdnt Awrd 90-; Co Clrk 81-87; Admin Asst/Acctnt 89-; Pub Admin; Hlth Care/Hmn Rsrces.

**MENSKY, LARISSA S,** Marywood Coll, Scranton, PA; SO; BS; Peer Tutoring 90; Deans Lst 89; Psych; Clinical Wrk.

**MENTGEN, PATRICIA J,** Memphis St Univ, Memphis, TN; SR; Grl Sct Ldr Trp Ldr 89-90; Parsh Cncl Pres 74-76; Ladies Cir Pres 71-74; Phi Theta Kappa 81-82; Extrdrnry Mnstr Of Euchrst 75-; Lay Mnstr Of Gods Word 79-; Ladies Of Chrty 70-81; Adv Catechist Cert 78; ASE Magna Cum Laude 82; Elem Educ; Relg Tchr.

**MENTH, ALLISON L,** George Mason Univ, Fairfax, VA; JR; BA; Deans Lst 89-; English; Edtng/Pblshng/Prof Wrtng/Tchng.**

**MENTZER, CASSANDRA S,** Oh St Univ At Marion, Marion, OH; FR; Deans List 90; Engr; Indstrl/Sys.

**MENTZER III, ROBERT L,** Kent St Univ Kent Cmps, Kent, OH; SO; BSMD; Hons Clg Kent State 90-; USAF Med Tech EMT.

**MENY, LISA M,** Bridgewater Coll, Bridgewater, VA; FR; BS; Ortrio Chr 90-; Pnn Plyrs Drma 90-; Dns Lst 90-; Psych; Gdnce Cnslr.

**MENZAK, ALEXANDRIA URSULA,** Beaver Coll, Glenside, PA; JR; BS; New Stdnt Orientation Ldr 90-; Soc Advcmnt Of Bus Admin 90-; Vars Tennis 89-; Zone Competition In Equestrian; Sftbl 88-; Equestrian Team 88-; Chem/Bus; Mgmnt.**

**MENZER, LAWRENCE WILLIAM,** Univ Of Ky, Lexington, KY; SR; BS Nrthrn KY Univ 89; Physics/Math/Elctrcl Engr; Engr.

**MERCADO DE JESUS, ANGEL J,** Univ Politecnica De Pr, Hato Rey, PR; FR; Math; Elec Engr.

**MERCADO DECLET, JANICE O,** Inter Amer Univ Pr Hato Rey, Hato Rey, PR; FR.

**MERCADO ESTRADA, JOSE E,** Inter Amer Univ Pr San German, San German, PR; SR; BBA; Bus Admn; Mrktng.

**MERCADO GARCIA, YADIRA,** Univ Politecnica De Pr, Hato Rey, PR; FR; Inst Ind Eng; Amer Bus Wmns Assn Schlrshp.

**MERCADO TORO, PABLO E,** Inter Amer Univ Pr San German, San German, PR; SR; BA; Psych Pub Rel Offcr 90-; Pres Chrch Sndy Schl Tchr; Phi Epsilon Chi 87-89; Psych; Ind/Clin Psych.

**MERCADO, ARNEL C,** City Univ Of Ny La Guard Coll, Long Island Cty, NY; SO; AA; Gldwtr Mem Hosp Data Prcssng Asst 90-; La Grdia Comm Coll Prgrmmr; Comp Sci.

**MERCADO, AWDELYN,** Univ Of Pr At Mayaguez, Mayaguez, PR; JR; Amer Chem Assn 90-; Hnr Stdnt 88-89; Phrmcy; Indus Phrmcy.**

**MERCADO, CLARIBEL M,** Univ Of Pr At Rio Piedras, Rio Piedras, PR; SR; AEPM VP 89-; ASDA; ADA; Golden Key VP 90-; Hon Tution 89-; Natural Scis Hon Grp 88-; SK/B Chem Intrnshp QA Anlyst 90; Athltc Tm 87-89; Natural Sci; Dentstry.

**MERCADO, DORIS E,** Inter Amer Univ Pr Hato Rey, Hato Rey, PR; FR; Seniors Yrs Sec 90; Intramer Acctng Assn; CPA.

**MERCADO, HILSA E,** Inter Amer Univ Pr San German, San German, PR; JR; Tutors Stdnt 87-; Noche De Lognos Uiv Interameni Cana 90; Yth Bus Offc 87; Tennis Cls Trny Wnr 90-.

**MERCADO, SUSAN L,** Va Commonwealth Univ, Richmond, VA; JR; Stdnt Govt; Greek Cncl; Phi Eta Sigma 88-; Phi Mu Secy Pldge Dir 90-; Deans Lst 88-; Schlrshp Awrd; Pldg Of Yr 90; Sccr Clb; IM Vlybl 88 90; Comml Illstrtn/Cmptr Graphics.

**MERCADO-CASTRO, NELSON A,** Univ Of Pr At Mayaguez, Mayaguez, PR; SO; DMD; ACE 89-; Chr 90-; Beta Beta Beta 90-; Biology; Dentistry.

**MERCADO-OTERO, SWANILDA,** Univ Of Pr At Mayaguez, Mayaguez, PR; SR; BBA; Natl Assoc Accntnts 90-; Band; Phi Kappa Phi 90-; Natl Hispanic Schlrshp Fund 90-; Dns Lst 90-; Info Syst.

**MERCED RAMOS, MAYRA,** Univ Of Pr Cayey Univ Coll, Cayey, PR; SO; Assn Rec La Loma Inc 89-; Pastoral Juvenil Grp 89-; Cuadro De Hon De La Rectora 90-; Liga Atletica Policiaca 89-90; Acctg.

**MERCED, MARIA M,** Miami Dade Comm Coll South, Miami, FL; SO; BA; Phi Theta Kappa; Old Cutler Wildlife Ctr Vol 90; Bsn Adm; Law.

**MERCED, MARIA V,** Univ Of Pr Medical Sciences, San Juan, PR; GD; MSA; Natl Stdnt Spch/Lang/Hrg Assoc 88-; Hnr Flrshp Univ PR Med Sci Campus 9-; BS Spch/Lang Ther 89; Audiolgy; Clncl/Habltv Audlgst.

**MERCED, VELMARIE,** Inter Amer Univ Pr Hato Rey, Hato Rey, PR; SR; BA; Hon Pgm; Bus Admin; Tchr.

**MERCED, VICTOR M,** Inter Amer Univ Pr Hato Rey, Hato Rey, PR; FR; Hnr Soc 90-; Neighborhood Sec Cncl 87-; Auto Show Assoc 87-; CPA.

**MERCER, ADRIENNE P,** Winthrop Coll, Rock Hill, SC; JR; BS; Hall Cncl 88-89; SNEA 90-; Deans Lst 90-; Elem Edn.

**MERCER, JENNIFER E,** Lexington Comm Coll, Lexington, KY; JR; MBA; Art/Pre-Med; Sports Med.

**MERCER, KELLIE,** Univ Of Al At Birmingham, Birmingham, AL; JR; BS; Gldn Key; Psychlgy; Psychthrpy.

**MERCER, KIMBERLY A,** Madisonville Comm Coll, Madisonville, KY; SO; Phi Theta Kappa 90-; Bus Mngmnt.

**MERCER, META H,** Univ Of Sc At Coastal Carolina, Conway, SC; JR; BED; Adlt/Chldrns Chr Dir Clarendon Bapt Chrch; Natl Fdrtn Msc Clbs Cnslr 86-; MENC Piano Tchr 85-; AFA Sthestrn Comm Clg 87; BA Meth Clg 90; Msc; Tchng.

**MERCER, TERRY B,** Christopher Newport Coll, Newport News, VA; JR; BA; Alpha Chi 90-; Phi Mu 90-; Hnrs Prog 88-; Chrldng Capt 90; Elem Educ.

**MERCHANT, JACQUELINE A,** Howard Univ, Washington, DC; SR; BSC; Acad Stdnts Phrmcy; Rho Chi Sec 90- Intrnshp Upjohn Pharmaceuticals; Phrmcy; Rsrch.

**MERCHANT, LISA,** Alcorn St Univ, Lorman, MS; SO; Pltcl Sci/Pre Law Clb Sec 90-; Soc Sci Clb 90-; Alpha Kappa Alpha 90-; Pres Lst; Deans Lst6.

**MERCHANT, LORI L,** Westminster Coll, New Wilmingtn, PA; SO; BS; Dance Thtr 89-; Lambda Sigma 90-; Upsilon Pi Epsilon Bk Awd 90-; Trustees Schlr 89-; Comp Sci/Math; Syst Analyst.

**MERCHANT, LYNN M,** Univ Of Nh Plymouth St Coll, Plymouth, NH; SR; Yrbk Assn Phtgrphy Edtr 90-.

**MERCIECA, PAULINE,** City Univ Of Ny Baruch Coll, New York, NY; SO; BBY; BBA; Comp Info Systms.

**MERCIER, JASON W,** Univ Of Southern Ms, Hattiesburg, MS; SO; BA; Business; Sales Mrktng Repr.

**MERCIER, JUDITH D,** Christopher Newport Coll, Newport News, VA; CERT; Nwspr 76-78; SGA Liason; Alpha Chi 79-80; Outreach Wrkr 90-; Just Say No 90-; Soc Wrk Serv/Prog Coord; Prog Dir; Grp Facilitator; BA U Of New Haven 80; Engl; MA Communications.

**MERCIER, NAOMI P,** Saint Elizabeth Hosp Sch Nurs, Utica, NY; SR; BSN; Amer Heart Assoc CPR Instrctr; Ntrtn Coor Head Strt; Nrsg; Nrsg Ped.

**MERCK, J PATRICK,** Tri County Tech Coll, Pendleton, SC; SO; BS; APS; Cert 90; Crmnl Juste; Law Enfrcmnt.

**MERCKLE, LISA A,** Indiana Univ Of Pa, Indiana, PA; SR; BS; PSEA 90-; Deans List 87-; Elem Ed; Tchng.

**MERCURI, JOANN,** S U N Y At Stony Brook, Stony Brook, NY; FR; BA; Pre Med Soc 90-; SADD 90-; Sigma Beta 90-; Deans Lst 90; Biology; Med.

**MEREDITH, CHARLOTTE R,** Univ Of Tn At Martin, Martin, TN; JR; BS; STEA Act Cord 90-; Mrtl Arts; Spec Ftns Clb; Elem Ed; Tchr.

**MEREDITH, DON E,** Tri County Tech Coll, Pendleton, SC; GD; AS 90; Mgmnt.

**MEREDITH, MARY JULIA,** Allegheny Coll, Meadville, PA; JR; BS; Circle K Sec 89-; Lambda Sigma 89-90; Alpha Phi Omega Pldg Pres; DUML; Sci; Envrnmntl Eng.

**MEREDITH, VICTORIA E,** Bethany Coll, Bethany, WV; JR; BA; Nwspr Cpy Edtr 89-90; Comm Theater 88-89; Lit Mag Stf/Contrbtr 90-; Lambda Lota Tau; Sigma Tau Epsilon 90-; Gamma Sigma Kappa; Oxford Semester 90; Cammie Pendleton Awd 89-; Flw; I M Ftbl 88; English; Wrtr/Pub/Tch.

**MERENA, ANN P,** Villanova Univ, Villanova, PA; JR; BA; Univ Chrstn Outrch 88-; Campus Mnstry 89-; Proj Sunshine 88-90; Theta Alpha Kappa; Religious Stds.

**MERGEL, CONNIE K,** Middle Tn St Univ, Murfreesboro, TN; JR; BS; Stdnt Hm Ecnmcs Assoc; Tn Hm Ecnmcs Assoc; Amrcn Dietetics Assoc; Ret Usaf Accntng 68-89; Assoc Science Comm Coll Of Usaf 85; Ntrtn/Fd Science; Rgstrd Dietetcian.

**MERGL, MICHELE L,** Suffolk Comm Coll Eastern Cmps, Riverhead, NY; SO; BA; Hosptlty Clb V P 89-; Stdnt Ldrshp Assoc; Cmptr Clb; Phi Theta Kappa; Pi Alpha Sigma; Dns Lst 89-; Alpha Beta Gamma; Fil Ballins/Goodfellow Schlrshp; Harvest Fest Schlrshp; AAS; Htl Adm-Finance; Cntrlr/Acctg.**

**MERHOFF, ELIZABETH G,** Univ Of Ky, Lexington, KY; FR; Clgns Acdmc Exclnc 90-; Pre Phrmcy Clb 90-; Ovrnght Tm Stdnt Rcrtmnt 90-; Phi Eta Sigma; Alpha Delta Pi 90-; Pres Schlr 90-; Cmnwlth Schlr 90-; Clge Arts/Sci Dns Lst 90-; IM Tns/Vlybl 90-; Phrmcy.

**MERICLE-CULVER, SUZANNE,** Medical Coll Of Ga, Augusta, GA; GD; DMD; Omicron Kappa Upsilon; Extrnshp-Augusta Crrctnl Med Inst 90; Sftbl Vlybl; BS Mcrblgy Univ GA 84-87; Dntstry.

**MERIDA, SONJA J,** Union Coll, Barbourville, KY; FR; BA; Bus Admn.

**MERIDTH, GENESE H,** Williamsburg Tech Coll, Kingstree, SC; FR; CERT; Tutor; Deans List; Med Ofc Clrcl Asst.

**MERIWETHER, CANDI R,** Howard Univ, Washington, DC; JR; BA; Sch Nwspr Copy Edtr 90-; Bapt Stdnt Un Sec 89-90; F Douglas Hon Soc 89-; Dom Res Asst 89-; Edtrl Intrn Amer Psychological Assn; Jrnlsm.**

**MERK, HOLLY J,** Holy Family Coll, Philadelphia, PA; JR; BA; Campus Mnstry 88-; Bus Soc 88-; Delta Epsilon Isgma VP; Natl Bus Hon Soc Treas; Acctg.**

**MERKERT, TRACY L,** S U N Y Coll Of Tech At Frmgdl, Farmingdale, NY; FR; Early Chldhd Ed; Chldhd Ed/Dev.

**MERKLE, MELISSA L,** Univ Of Sc At Columbia, Columbia, SC; JR; BA; Carolina Hsptlty; Clb Mngrs Assn America; HRT; Bsns.

**MERKLE, PAUL J,** Nazareth Coll Of Rochester, Rochester, NY; FR; Gheatre Leag 90-; Lit Magazine 90-; Nwspr 90; Theatre Arts; Prfsnl Theatre.

**MERKLE, TODD L,** Cornell Univ Statutory College, Ithaca, NY; JR; BS; Crnl Entrprnrs 90-; Ho Nun De Kah 90-; Rsrch Asst/Intrn Invstmnt Mgmt; IM Sftbl/Vlybl/Ice Hcky 87-; Ecnmcs; Brkrg Indstry.

**MERKLIN, DANIEL F,** Fl International Univ, Miami, FL; JR; BA; ACF 89-; Phi Kappa Phi; Bible Chrch Tchr Asst 87-; Grd Mgr Extrnshp 89; Brlr Chef Intrnshp; AS Culnry Inst Amer 90; Hosptlty Mgmt; Fd/Bvrg Mgmt.

**MERLE FELICIANO, LIND O,** Catholic Univ Of Pr, Ponce, PR; SR; JD; Amer Bar Assn Stdnt Div 88-; Revista De Derecho Puertorriguento Wrtr 89-; Delta Theta Phi Mstr Of Ritual 89-; Natl Guard Army 88-; B Co 1/296 Bn Infntry; Mos 11b Sabana Grande PR; BA Hnr Grad Cum Laude 86; Law.

**MERMER, CORY A,** Cooper Union, New York, NY; SR; BS; Amer Soc Cvl Eng 89-; Zeta Psi 89-; Baruch Schlr 86-87; Eng Sci Awrd Excllnc 89; AS Westchester Comm Coll 89; Cvl Eng.

**MERNIN, JAMES B,** Manhattan Coll, Bronx, NY; JR; BE; RA 89-; Encountr Retrt Ldr/Orgnzr 89-; RA Advsry Cncl 89-; Pen/Swrd; Am Socty/Mech Engr 90-; Plyrs Org Actr/Dncr 90-; Euchrstc Mnstr/Mnstr Of Word 89-; Mech Engrng.

**MEROLA, MICHAEL J,** Franklin And Marshall Coll, Lancaster, PA; SO; BA; Nwspr Asst Mgmnt Editor 89-; Tutor; Forensics 89-; Elderlink 89-; Cath Cmps Comm 89-; Spaulding Ldrshp Intrn 90-; Dana Schlr 90-; Govt Awd Clg Hnrs List 89-90; Govt/Economics; Law.

**MERONEY, VIRGINIA M,** Middle Tn St Univ, Murfreesboro, TN; SO; BBA; Campus Recrtn; Gamma Beta Phi; Acctg; CPA.

**MERRELL, JENNIFER A,** Oh Univ, Athens, OH; SR; BFA; Hist; Own Gallery.

**MERRELL, PAIGE,** Indiana Univ Of Pa, Indiana, PA; SR; BS; Paul Douglas Teacher Schlrshp 90-; Natl Mrt Schlrshp 85; Trstee Schlrshp Brigham Young Univ 85; Westinghouse Fam Schlrshp 85; AA Comm Coll Of Allegheny County Boyce Campus 88; Elem Educ; Educ Psych.

**MERRICK, JANET A,** Cornell Univ Statutory College, Ithaca, NY; SO; BS; 4-H Club Pres 90-; Agri Ambassador 90-; Alpha Zeta; Plant Sci; Research Scientist.

**MERRICK, TROY L,** Glassboro St Coll, Glassboro, NJ; FR; BA; Clg Pblctn 90; Wrstlng 90; Cmmnctns Advrtsng.

**MERRILL, ANGELA C,** Columbus St Comm Coll, Columbus, OH; FR; BED; Jobs Daughters Dist I Schlrshp; Cmptr Sci; Cmptr Prgrmr.

**MERRILL, LAURA M,** George Mason Univ, Fairfax, VA; JR; BS; Hlth; Physcl Thrpy.

**MERRILL, ROBERT C,** Univ Of Nc At Asheville, Asheville, NC; SO; BA; Univ Hnrs Stdnt Lst; Lit; Eductn.

**MERRIMAN, PAMELA G,** Lexington Comm Coll, Lexington, KY; FR; BA; Univeral Fasteners 89-; Advrtsng/Jrnlsm.

**MERRINGER, JAY M,** Oh St Univ At Newark, Newark, OH; FR; BS; Engr.

**MERRIS, LONA R,** Univ Of Sc At Coastal Carolina, Conway, SC; SO; BS; Psych Clb; Clncl Psych.

**MERRITT, ALISON D,** Univ Of Sc At Columbia, Columbia, SC; JR; BA; Tour Guide Assn 90; Intl Stds; Bsn.

**MERRITT, DEBRA S,** Hillsborough Comm Coll, Tampa, FL; SO; AA; Math Tutor 90-; Phi Theta Kappa V P 90-; Acad All-Florida Jr Clg Reg VIII 90-; NJCAA Acad All-Amer 90-; Outstndg Yng Wmn Amer Awd Jaycees; Sftbl Schlrshp 89-; Outstndg Math Stdnt 90-; Outstndg Acad Athl 90-; Lgl Asst/Paralgl 83-; Math.

**MERRITT, GLEN A,** Middle Ga Coll, Cochran, GA; SO; BA; Eng Clb; Rotarac Clb; Gamma Beta Phi; Co-Op Stdnt; Sci; Elctrcl Eng.

**MERRITT, PAUL D,** Va Highlands Comm Coll, Abingdon, VA; GD; AAS; Phi Theta Kappa; Cert; Cert; AAS; Bsn Mgmt.

**MERRITT, RENEE P,** Oh Wesleyan Univ, Delaware, OH; JR; BA; Modern Foreign Lang Bd Bd Mem 89-; Stdnt Fndtn; Intl Studies Bd Mem; Phi Sigma Iota 89-; Sigma Iota Rho VP 90-; Spnsh Econ; Peace Corps/Grad Sch.

**MERRITT, RICHARD L,** Marshall University, Huntington, WV; JR; BA; Dlbld Stdnts Org Pres 89-90; Deans Lst; Dstrct Fv Cnsmr Advsry Cmmtt; Acctg; Acctnt.

**MERRITT, TANYA ELESE,** Johnson C Smith Univ, Charlotte, NC; FR; BA; Hons Clg 90-; Clg Quiz Bowl 90-; Acadmc Schlrshp 90-; Engl/Comptr Sci; Techncl Wrtr.

**MERRITT, TANYA L,** Mount Olive Coll, Mount Olive, NC; SR; BS; Rec/Lsr Stdies Sec/Treas 90-; Mjrs Clb Pres; Rec/Lsr Stdes Mjrs Clb Nwsltr Edtr 90-; Spec Olympcs 90-; Aerobcs Instrctr 89-90; Ldrs Schlrshp; Hmcmng Crt 90-; Chrldr; Outstndng Achvmnt Awrd 90-; AA Wayne Comm Coll 89; Rec/Lsr Stdies; Therptc Rec.

**MERRONE, MARGUERITE M,** Elmira Coll, Elmira, NY; SO; BS; Commsn For The Blind 85-; Blind Assoc 85-; Tch 3rd Grdrs About Blindns; Humn Svcs; Soc Wrkr.

**MERRY, ELAINE K,** Fl Coll, Temple Terrace, FL; FR; BA; Phi Theta Kappa 90-; Phi Sigma Chi VP Elect 90-; Eng.

**MERSMAN, ELIZABETH N,** Univ Of Sc At Columbia, Columbia, SC; SO; BA; Epsilon Sigma Alpha Sec; Bus/Mktg; Exec.

**MERTENS, PATRICIA L,** Westminster Coll, New Wilmingtn, PA; SO; BA; Sdnt Wstmnstr Admiss Tm; Panhellenic Conf Sec 90-; Jur Phanhellenic Conf Sec 89-90; Phi Mu Pnhlc Rep 89-; VISA Tutor 89-90; Intrnshp Legal Aid Soc; Pol Sci; Law.

**MERWIN, KRISTE L,** Elmira Coll, Elmira, NY; SR; BS; Cmps Cntr Comm Prsdnt 89-90; Exectv Comm Orntatn Chrprsn 89-90; Edctn Clb 90; Deans Lst 89-90; JV Chrldng 89-90; Edctn; PHD.

**MESCHER, BRENDA M,** Ky Wesleyan Coll, Owensboro, KY; JR; ADRN; Stdnt Act Prgmg Brd 88-89; Sigma Nu Frat Little Sistr 89-; Kappa Delta Tr 90-; Dns Lst 88-; Nom Alpha Chi Natl Hnr Soc; Pres Athl Schlrshps 88-; Fstpitch Sftbl 88-; Nrsng.

**MESCHKE, MELISSA A,** Liberty Univ, Lynchburg, VA; SO; BS; Plyrs Clb 90-; Deans List 90-; Sport Mgt; Work Sport Org.

**MESERVE, RAYMOND S,** Fayetteville St Univ, Fayetteville, NC; SR; BS 90; Econs.

**MESHEL, MARCIA J,** City Univ Of Ny Grad School, New York, NY; SR; BA; Phi Theta Kappa 87; Abraham Multern Awd 87; Assist Ftbl Coach 86-90; Paraprof 84-; AA Kngsbrgh Comm Clg 87-; Speech/Educ; Tchr.

**MESHOTTO, KIMBERLY R,** Middle Tn St Univ, Murfreesboro, TN; SO; BBA; Bus.**

**MESITE JR, JOHN A,** Germanna Comm Coll, Locust Grove, VA; JR; ASSOC; Jaycee Dir Yr 87-88; Knight Mo 86; K C Dpty Grand Knight 88-89; Plnt Prtctn Offcr 90-; Cert Univ Ct 79; Plce Sci; Indust Secrty Mgmt.

**MESMER, ROSELLE D,** Hahnemann Univ, Philadelphia, PA; GD; MD; BA Cornell Univ 82.

**MESROBIAN, STEPHANIE M,** Villanova Univ, Villanova, PA; SO; BFA; Delta Delta Delta Mrshl; Art Hstry; Archlgy.

**MESSAM, PETERKAYE A,** Clark Atlanta Univ, Atlanta, GA; JR; BA; Bsn Assoc 89-; Acctg Clb 90-; Dance 90-; Hnr Stdnt; Hostss Annual Art Fstvl Hstss Head 87; Blck Stdnt Promise 90; Acad Excell; Precision Dance Tm 90-; Acctg/Finance; CPA/LAW Schl.

**MESSENGER, THOMAS J,** Springfield Tech Comm Coll, Springfield, MA; FR; BA; Music; Prod/Eng.

**MESSENKOPF, MICHAEL C,** Wagner Coll, Staten Island, NY; JR; BA; IM Ftbl Bsktbl Sftbl Hcky Vlybl Cptn 88-; Intra Frat Cncl VP 89-; Wrkd NYC Mrthn 90-; Schlr Athl 89-; Glf Tm Cptn 88-; Bus Adm/Econ.

**MESSENLEHNER, MARY L,** East Stroudsburg Univ, E Stroudsburg, PA; SR; BS; Cont Dancers Clb Pr 89-; Econs Clb 89-90; Pr Svc Awd; Mngmnt; Acctng.

**MESSER, GENA M,** Univ Of Cincinnati-Clrmnt Coll, Batavia, OH; FR; Tribunal 90-; Cmptr Tech; Sys Anlysis/Japnese Intrprtr.

**MESSER, RAYFORD D,** Western Piedmont Comm Coll, Morganton, NC; FR; BS; Math; Engrg.

**MESSER, RHONDA M,** Univ Of Nc At Chapel Hill, Chapel Hill, NC; JR; BSN; NCF 90-; ANS 90-; Awd Acad Excell 88-; Nrsg Extern Pgm Duke Univ Hosp; Nrsg.**

**MESSERIAN, GREGORY L,** Oh St Univ, Columbus, OH; SR; BA; Armenian Clb 87-; Phi Beta Kappa; Gldn Key 90-; Alpha Lamda Delta; Phi Eta Sigma 90-; Engl; Bus.

**MESSERSMITH, LAURA S,** Radford Univ, Radford, VA; JR; BA; SAM 90; Delta Zeta Banq Chr 89-; Bsn-Oper Mgmt; Bnkg Mgmt.

**MESSICK, SCOTT M,** Bowie St Univ, Bowie, MD; JR; BS; Pi Lambda Phi 90-; Vrsty Ftbl 88-; Crmnl Jstc; State/Fed Law Enfrcmt.**

**MESSICK, SUSAN M,** Wilmington Coll, New Castle, DE; SO; BS; Beebe Schl Nrsng Alumni Assn 90-; Beebe Med Cntr Nrs Advsry Com 90-; Stff Educ-Hosp Obstrcs Unit 90-; All Snts Epscpl Chrch-St Anns Chptr 87-; Clncl Nrs II 90-; Cert Inptnt Obstrc Nrsng 90; Bhvrl Sci; Nrsng.

**MESSIER, CLAIRE I,** Bentley Coll, Waltham, MA; JR; BS; Campus Activities Brd 89; Stdnt Admssn Corps 89; Cthlc Stdnt Org 90; Amnsty Intrntl 89-90; Hnrs Intrnshp Prog; Cmptr Info Syst; Instlltn Anlyst.**

**MESSINA, DIANE M,** Lesley Coll, Cambridge, MA; JR; BA; Erly Chldhd Educ; Tchr And Dy Cre Ownr Dir.

**MESSINA, LORI ANN,** Georgian Court Coll, Lakewood, NJ; GD; Yrbk Edit In Chf 90-; Amer Physcs Scty Pres 87-; Math Assn Of Amer 87-; Sigma Delta Pi 90-; Cmps Mnstry Rep 89; Echrstc Mnstr 88-; Dns Schlr 90; John N Shive Mem Schlrshp Physcs Awrd; BS 90; Physcs And Math; Tchng.

**MESSINA, TERESE A,** Mount Aloysius Jr Coll, Cresson, PA; FR; ADN; Phi Theta Kappa 90-; Nrsng; Ansthsia Nrsng.

**MESSING, DANIEL N,** Univ Of Tn At Knoxville, Knoxville, TN; SR; BS; Phi Eta Sigma 87-88; Phi Kappa Psi 90-; Beta Gamma Sigma 90-; Beta Alpha Psi 89-; Natl Alum Sclrshp 87-90; Jack Kiger Schlrshp 89-90; Schlrshp Head Mgr Tennis Tm 88-; Public Acctng.

**MESSINGER, DONNA MICHELLE,** Univ Of Nc At Charlotte, Charlotte, NC; SR; BA; Stdy Abrd In Italy 88; Spahish; Transltr.

**MESSMAN, JANE M,** Wilmington Coll, New Castle, DE; SO; LIBRL; Agnd Delaware Women; Jr Achvmnt Proj Bus Cnsltnt; AVP Oper 74-; FCC Natl Bnk; Human Rsrcs Mgmt BA.

**MESSMER, MICHELE C,** Ga St Univ, Atlanta, GA; SR; BS; SGAE 90-; Golden Key 88-; Phi Kappa Phi; Kappa Kappa Gamma Social Comm 84-; Deans List 88-; Deans Key; Early Childhood Awd; BA Boston Univ 88; Early Childhood Ed; Tch.

**MESTRE, ADELAIDA S,** Hillsborough Comm Coll, Tampa, FL; SO; BS; Phi Theta Kappa; Bus Sci; Phrmcy.

**METCALF, JAMA L,** Tn St Univ, Nashville, TN; JR; BS; Deans Lst 88-; Mgmt Asst Coop Sth Cntrl Bll; Comp Sci; Comp Prgrmmng.

**METCALF, SHEILA A,** Md Inst Coll Of Art, Baltimore, MD; SR; BFA; Sculpture; Educ.

**METCALF, SHIRVONNE L,** Comm Coll Algny Co Algny Cmps, Pittsburgh, PA; JR; AA; Home Sweet Home Hmls Advcy Pres 90-; Wmn Tkng Actn Effctvly 89-; Phi Theta Kappa 90-; NARAL 88-; Pittsburgh Now 89-; Vol Of Yr 89-; Anthrplgy; Curator.

**METCALF, TERI S,** Oh St Univ, Columbus, OH; SR; BS; Hons Peer Sprt Prog; Vol Dsablty Servs; Am Cncr Soc; OSU Hosps Emplyd Buckeye Gymnstcs; Stdnt Rsrch Asst; Alpha Lambda Delta; Phi Eta Sigma 88; Mortar Brd VP 90-; Alpha Epsilon Delta; Helix; Phi Kappa Phi; Zoolgy; Med Schl.

**METCALF, WILLIAM B,** Spartanburg Methodist Coll, Spartanburg, SC; SO; Day Stdnt Organization Assn Board 89; Deans List 90; Political Science; Lawyer/Dist Attny.

**METHENY, AMBER L,** Bapt Bible Coll & Seminary, Clarks Summit, PA; JR; BA; Stndt Gov Sec 90-; Dorm Ofcr Pres 88-90; Vars Vlybl/Bsktbl Co-Cpt 88-90; Hist; Ed.

**METHENY, MIDGE M,** Univ Of Nc At Greensboro, Greensboro, NC; SO; BS; Amer Scty Interior Designers 90-; BS 83; Interior Design.

**METHERELL, JAMES F,** Univ Of Sc At Columbia, Columbia, SC; FR; BS; Kappa Sigma Schlrshp Chrmn; Dns Lst 90-; Bio/Pre Med; Med/Orthpdcs.

**METHVIN, TIMOTHY S,** Embry Riddle Aeronautical Univ, Daytona Beach, FL; GD; BS; Nvl Aviation Clb 87-; Dns Lst 90-; AS; Assoc; Aero Stds/Aviatn Maint Tech; Mjr Airline.

**METLER, DAVID M,** Salisbury St Univ, Salisbury, MD; SR; BA; Tae Kwon Do Blue Belt 90-; Natl Acctg Assoc 90; VITA Fincl Mgmnt Sys; Co-Ed Sftbl; Acctg; Crmnl Invstgtns Auditor.

**METOYER, ANGELA L,** Oh Dominican Coll, Columbus, OH; SO; BA; United Negro Clg Fund Chrprsn 89-90; United Way Chrprsn 82-; Pblc Rltns; Pblc Rltns Trng.

**METOYER, TONI M,** Clark Atlanta Univ, Atlanta, GA; SO; BA; Bsn Admin; Mrktng.

**METRO, VALARIE M,** Comm Coll Algny Co Algny Cmps, Pittsburgh, PA; JR.

**METS, ANTHONY DUSTIN,** Oh Univ, Athens, OH; FR; BSC; Radio Asst Prdctn Dir 90-; Alpha Lambda Delta 90-; Brmbl 90-; Tlcmmnctns; Music Radio TV.

**METSGER, LORI J,** Westminster Coll, New Wilmingtn, PA; JR; BS; Cncrt Choir 90-; Show Choir; Lrng Cntr Teach Asst 89-; Math Clb 90-; Kappu Mu Epsilon Sec 89-; Mrtr Brd Sr Hnry; Omicron Delta Kappa Intn Chair 90-; Lambda Sigma Schlrshp Chair 89-90; Pi Sigma Pi; Alpha Phi Omega Pldg Cls VP; Math; Teach/Sec Schl.

**METTEN, RICHARD T,** Me Maritime Academy, Castine, ME; FR; AS; SNAME VP; Dean List 90-; Soccer 90-; Naval Archtcr; Engr.

**METZ, DANIELLE M,** Canisius Coll, Buffalo, NY; FR; BS; Phi Gamma Nu 90-; Accounting.

**METZ, JO E,** Ohio Valley Coll, Parkersburg, WV; FR; AA; Stdnt Govt VP Fresh 90-; Delta Scl Clb 90; Mssns Clb Com Chrprsn 90-; TIE 90-; Educ; Tchng.

**METZ, KENNETH W,** Clarkson Univ, Potsdam, NY; SO; BS; Ski Clb 90-; Slarkson Soc Actnts 90-; Delta Upsilon IFS Sports Rep 90-; Boy Scts Amer Eagle Sct 82-; Deans Lst 89-; Sccr 89-; Fin/Acctg; Bnkng/Fin.

**METZ, KIMBERLY M,** West Liberty St Coll, West Liberty, WV; JR; BS; Delta Mu Delta; All Amer Schlr Clgte Awd; Bus Admnstrn; Acctg.

**METZ, MICHAEL T,** Oberlin Coll, Oberlin, OH; FR; BA; Ofc Career/Dvlpmnt Intrn; Clg Conf Serv Asst; Ecnmcs/Govt; Mgmt Cnsltnt.

**METZ, VALERIE M,** Univ Of Cincinnati, Cincinnati, OH; JR; BFA; Mcmicken Hnrs Prog 90; Gldn Ky; Arthritis Fndtn Telethon; WSTR-TV Intern; IM Sftbl 89; Brdcstng; Jrnlsm.

**METZCAR, LORA T,** Wright St Univ Lake Cmps, Celina, OH; JR; BED; Math Cnvntn Tchr; Elem Ed Engl Cncntrtn; Elem Tchr.

**METZCAR, MELISSA S,** Fl St Univ, Tallahassee, FL; SR; BA; Zeta Tau Alpha 89-; Flying Hgh Crcs 89-; Cmnctns; Media Prdctn.

**METZER, RHONDA R,** Fl International Univ, Miami, FL; SR; BS; AA Santa Fe Comm Coll 88; Elem Educ; Socl Wrk.

**METZGAR, MATTHEW R,** Wv Univ, Morgantown, WV; FR; BS; Hon Prog 90-; Eng.

**METZGER, ANDREW T,** Oh Univ, Athens, OH; FR; BA; Karate Inst Of Amer Blue Blt; Cvl Engrng; Undrwtr Or Space Structrs.

**METZGER, BRADLEY J,** East Tn St Univ, Johnson City, TN; SR; BS; SME 85-; ASCET 90-; Epsilon Pi Tau 90-; Winds Surveying Co 90-; AS State Techl Inst Knoxville TN 85; Manuftng Engrg Techlgy.

**METZGER, CYNTHIA J,** Hudson Valley Comm Coll, Troy, NY; SO; BA; Alpha Phi Sigma; Phi Theta Kappa; Pres List 90-; Girl Sct Co-Ldr 90-; Sclgy/Scl Wk; Psychthrpy.

**METZGER, GREGORY S,** Bellarmine Coll, Louisville, KY; SR; BA; Pres Ldrshp Soc; Ecnmcs Clb 87-; Math Assn 87-; Pre Law Soc 87-; Drm Govt; Jrnlst Nwsppr 87-; Cardinal Hnrs Prog 87-; Acdmc All Conf; Crss Cntry Trck; IM Bsktbll Vllybl Capt 87-; Ecnmcs; Law.

**METZGER, JENNIFER L,** Univ Of Akron, Akron, OH; SO; BA; Hnr Stdnt 89; Phi Eta Sigma 89-90; IM Aerobics 89; Grphc Dsng.

**METZGER, LINDA K,** Emory Univ, Atlanta, GA; GD; MN; Stdnt Gvt Assn Grad Rep 89-90f Sigma Theta Tau; Wdrff Fllwshp 89-; Natl Clg Nrsng Awd 86-88; Amer Nrs Assoc; Stff Nrs Koscinsko Co Comm Hosp 88-90; BSN Goshen Clg Goshen IN 88; Fmly Nrs Prctnr; Prmry Hlth Care Prvdr.**

**METZGER, MARK J,** Fl St Univ, Tallahassee, FL; SR; BS; Goldn Key 90; Alpha Epsilon Delta; IM Sftbl/Bsktbl 89-; AA; Biolgy; Med.

**METZGER, SHELLY E,** Commonwealth Coll, Virginia Beach, VA; GD; AA; Fashion Clb VP 89-; Fashion Merch; Retail Mngmnt.

**METZGER, VINCENT PAUL,** Bowling Green St Univ, Bowling Green, OH; SR; BS; Vars Bsbl 87-; Acad All Mid Amer Conf 89; Epsilon Pi Tau; Genry Filters Inc Intern Rsrch/Dvlpr 89; City Eng Tech 90-; Arch/Envir Dsgn; Constr Mgr.

**METZGER, VIRGINIA ZEBLISKY,** Greenville Tech Coll, Greenville, SC; SO; Greenville Symph Principal Oboe 85-; BFA SUNY Purchase 79; MA CUNY Hunter 83; Comp Tech.

**METZLER, JOANNE E,** Kent St Univ Kent Cmps, Kent, OH; SO; BA; Stdnt Assn Gaming Enthsts 89-; Crmnl Jstc Hnr Socty; Intrnshp Lake Cnty Juv Ct Pnsvl OHIO; Green Dragon Kung Fu 89-90; Crmnl Jstc Stds; Crmnl Jstc/Corrections.

**METZLER, KAMILLA J,** Univ Of Sc At Columbia, Columbia, SC; FR; Mrchng Bnd 90; Jz Ensmbl; Symphny Orchstr; USC Hnrs Clge 90-; Frnch; Dplmtc Trnsltn.

**METZLER, LAWRENCE D,** Lancaster Bible Coll, Lancaster, PA; JR; BA; Clss Pres 88-; Chrch Assoc Pstr 89-; Res/Cmrcl Cnstrctn 78-; Bible; Pstrl Mnstry.

**METZLER, SANDRA JANE,** Edinboro Univ Of Pa, Edinboro, PA; SR; BED; Scndry Educ Assn VP 90; Cmmtr Assn VP 88-; Alpha Chi VP 89-; Kappa Delta Pi 89-; Pres Mdlln; EAPSU Otstndng Engl Mjr 90-; Pres Hnrs Stdy Abrd Schlrshp 90; Ttr Stdnt Ltrcy Corps 90; ODSS; PR Ttr Coor Fr Stdnts Lrngn Dsblts 90; Engl.

**METZMAN, MICHAEL S,** Univ Of Miami, Coral Gables, FL; GD; MD; Fl Kys Hlth Fr Chmn Lgstcs Com 88-; ASMA 87-; Alpha Omega Alpha; Alpha Tau Omega 84-; Cmls Hse Hlth Concrn 88-; Mgrnt Wrkrs Clncs 89-90; Intrnl Med Intern Univ Wa; IM Hcky 90-; BA 87; Med.

**MEYER, ANN RENEA,** Roanoke Coll, Salem, VA; FR; BS; Earthbound 90-; Comp Sci; Comp Prgrmng.

**MEYER, BOBBI J,** Ashland Comm Coll, Ashland, KY; FR; BA; Acad Excell Schlrshp Univ KY; Sci; Phys Ther.

**MEYER, BRIAN J,** Univ Of Cincinnati, Cincinnati, OH; FR; BM; OCMEA 90-; Jr Drum/Bgl Corps Drum Capt 88-; Jim Ott Schlrshp 90; Music Educ; Music Tchr/Bnd Dir.

**MEYER, CAROLYN S,** Fl St Univ, Tallahassee, FL; FR; BA; Ldy Sclphntrs; Pres Proj Cab Stdnt Govt 90; Lib Stud Hnrs Schlrs Pgrm 90-; Phi Heta Sigma 90-; Delta Gamma Pldg Cls Schlrshp Chrmn 90-; Hghst GPA Schlrshp Awd Delta Gamma Pld Cls 90-; Engl; Law/Educ.

**MEYER, CHARLES T,** Glassboro St Coll, Glassboro, NJ; SR; Law Jstce Clb 90; AAS Glcstr Cnty Clg 89; BA; Law/Jstce; Invstgtns.

**MEYER, DAWN C,** James Madison University, Harrisonburg, VA; SR; MED; Assn Educ Yng Chldrn VP 88-; Mrchng Royal Dukes Mrchng Bnd 87-; Gldn Key 89-; Mrtr Bd Sr 90-; Kappa Delta Pi 90-; Natl Assn Educ Yng Chldrns Cnfrnc 90; VA Assn Educ Yng Chldrns Cnfrnc 90-; BS; Early Chldhd Educ.

**MEYER, DEBORAH J,** Cincinnati Metropolitan Coll, Cincinnati, OH; JR; Medcl Asst Progrm Treas 90-; Nwspaper Stf Reprtr 90-; Fundrsr Chrprsn; Pres List; Perfct Attndnc Award; Intrnshp Univ Medcl Assoc ENT Spclsts; Sftbl 90-; ASMA; Medcl.

**MEYER, DEBORAH R,** Hillsborough Comm Coll, Tampa, FL; FR; AS; ASL 90-; Alpha Sigma Lambda; Phi Theta Kappa; Vol Chrch; Bld Dnr; Meyer Entrprs Sarasota Inc Sec Tres 90-; Intrrtr Deaf; Spec Educ Prog.

**MEYER, DEBRA J,** Wright St Univ Lake Cmps, Celina, OH; SO; BBA; FBLA 90-; Acctg; Finance.

**MEYER, DENNIS A,** Univ Of Louisville, Louisville, KY; JR; MENG; IEEE 90-; KY Bsktbl Offcls Asn 90-; Natl Clgt Engrs Awd; Elec Engr.**

**MEYER, GRETA A,** Johnson St Coll, Johnson, VT; FR; BA; Cert Office Mgmt; Bus Mgmt.

**MEYER, JESSICA LEE,** Oh Univ, Athens, OH; JR; BFA; Stdnt Snt Comm Dir 90; Scty Twrd Lrnng Enhncmnt Arts; Gldn Key; Alpha Lambda Delta 89univ Arbc Instrctr 88-90; Intern 90; Deans Schlrshp 90-; Deans Lst; Acdmc Achvmnt Aw; Art Hstry.

**MEYER, JOEL N,** Juniata Coll, Huntingdon, PA; JR; BA; Multcultrl Progmng Cmtee Co Chrmn 90; Human Concerns Cmtee Co Chrmn 89-90; Beta Beta Beta; Campus Mnstry Bd; Peace/Conflict Stdes; Soc Juste Rsrch/Lby.

**MEYER, JUNE R,** Georgetown Coll, Georgetown, KY; SR; BA; Bptststdnt Un 86-; Nespr Stf 87-88; Sigma Tau Delta Sec 88-; W B Jones Awd Bst Upprclsmn Prose 90-; Englsh; Wrtng Tchng.

**MEYER, KATRINA M,** Defiance Coll, Defiance, OH; SO; BA; Theta Xi Ltl Sis 90-; Chrldg 89-; Psych; Clncl Psych.**

**MEYER, KRISTINE M,** Defiance Coll, Defiance, OH; SO; BA; Elem Edn; Teach.

**MEYER, MICAH S,** Kent St Univ Kent Cmps, Kent, OH; FR; IM Sftbll 90; Pre Med.

**MEYER, MICHAEL S,** Univ Of Miami, Coral Gables, FL; SR; BS; Orient Coord 88-90; Hon Stdnt Assn 87-88; Phi Sigma Tau; Lambda Chi Alpha High Iota 87-; Peer Cnslr 89-90; Lambda Chi Alpah IM Tm; BS; Bio/Chem/Phlsphy; Med.

**MEYER, MICHELLE L,** Niagara Univ, Niagara Univ, NY; JR; BS; Intern Roswell Pk Mem Inst; Buffalo VAMC Valor Prog; Nursing/Psych.

**MEYER, NANCI J,** Middle Tn St Univ, Murfreesboro, TN; SR; BS; Delta Zeta 86-89; BS; Elem Educ; Teacher.

**MEYER, NATALIE K,** Birmingham Southern Coll, Birmingham, AL; JR; BA; Freshman Orient 89-90; Deans Advisory 90-; Student Judiciary 89-; Southern Chorale 88-89; Cocert Choir 89-; Attened Univ York England 91; Sigma Tau Delta 90-; Political Sci Hnry Treas 89-90; Alpha Lambda Delta; English/Policial Sci; Public Policy.

**MEYER, PATRICIA A,** Atlantic Comm Coll, Mays Landing, NJ; FR; BA; Engl; Spcl Ed Tchr.

**MEYER, PETER R,** Univ Of Nc At Asheville, Asheville, NC; FR; BS; Concert Band/Mrchng Bnd 88-89; VICA Pres 89-90; SADD 89-90; Deans/Chanc Lst 90; Phi Eta Sigma 90-; Comp Engr.

**MEYER, SANDRA A,** S U N Y Coll At Fredonia, Fredonia, NY; SO; BA; Igoe Hall Pres 89-90; Interdorm Cncl Rep 89-90; Grissom Hall V P 90-; Soph Cl Rep 90; Military Schlrs Awd Adcmc Exclnc & Extra Curricular Exclnc; Fredonia St Ldrshp Prog; IM Vlybl; Edn Club; Tutor Grd 10 Eng Stdnt; Amb Prog; Eng; Teach Jr Hi Sr Hi.

**MEYER, TRACI M,** Cornell Univ Statutory College, Ithaca, NY; JR; BS; Stu Advsr 90-; Phys Thrpy Vol 90-; Kappa Delta Crspndg Sec 89-; Red Crpt Soc 88-90; Crnl Trdtn Flw William Holt Awrd 89-; Deans Lst 88-; IM Swmg/Trck/Vlybl 89-; Bio; Med.

**MEYER, VIOLET U,** Univ Of Sc At Columbia, Columbia, SC; SR; BS; Res Hl Std Govt Sntr; Rsch Asst; Psy; Fmly Cnslr.

**MEYER JR, WAYNE M,** Comm Coll Algny Co Algny Cmps, Pittsburgh, PA; SO; BA; Moon Flyers Sec 91; Phi Theta Kapa; Meritorious Acdmc Achvmnt; Flght Tchnlgy; Eng/Flight Offc.

**MEYER, WILLIAM D,** Liberty Univ, Lynchburg, VA; JR; AA; Psi Chi; Psych; Scl Svc.

**MEYERER, MARK J,** Anne Arundel Comm Coll, Arnold, MD; FR; Mass Cmmcntns; Advrtsng.

**MEYERS, ALAN H,** Duquesne Univ, Pittsburgh, PA; SO; BA; Lambda Sigma 90-; Phi Eta Sigma 90-; Edctn; Tchng.

**MEYERS, ANDREW W,** Boston Coll, Chestnut Hill, MA; SO; BSN; Natl Stdnt Nrsng Assoc 89-; Deans Advsry Cncl; Rita P Kelleher Awd 90; Mary E Love Awd; EMT Husaan Serv Trng Inst 83; Nursing.

**MEYERS, APRIL R,** Univ Of Akron, Akron, OH; SO; Army ROTC Cadt Corp 89-; Res Hl Pgm Brd Educ Srvcs Comm 89-90; Gr Comm Stdnts 89-90; Phi Eta Sigma 90-; Unty Plyrs; Dghtrs Amer Rev Awd 90; Econ; Army Finc Offcr.

**MEYERS, BONNIE J,** Hilbert Coll, Hamburg, NY; SO; BA; AAS; Bus; Corp Law.

**MEYERS, CARRIE L,** Radford Univ, Radford, VA; SR; BBA; Acctng Socty 90-; VITA; Dns Lst 89-90; Acctng.

**MEYERS, COREY,** Life Coll, Marietta, GA; GD; Stdnt Gov Treas 87-90; Stdnt Alum Asso Frshmn; Entnmt Cmte Stdnt Chiro Org; Homecoming Cmte; Sid E W Ribley Schlrshp; IM Vlybl; Grad/Doctorate/Chiro 90; BA Psychlgy Rutgers Un 86; DC Chiro Life Chiro Colg 90; Chiro; Dr.

**MEYERS, DENISE,** S U N Y Coll Of Tech At Frmgdl, Farmingdale, NY; FR; AS; Mass Lector At St Annes R C Chrch 90-; AAS Suffolk Cnty Comm Coll 71-73; 2 Cert N Y S Dept Hlth 77-89; Nrsng; RN.

**MEYERS, ELLIOT M,** City Univ Of Ny La Guard Coll, Long Island Cty, NY; JR; BA; Phi Theta Kappa 90; Dns Lst 89-90; Cs Wrkr NYC HRA Casa 2 Hm Cr Srvc Pgm 90-; BA Queens Clge Cuny 77; BA Queens Clge Of Cuny 88; Cmptr Sci.

**MEYERS, GENE R,** Univ Of Akron, Akron, OH; JR; BS; Amer Soc Cvl Engrs 90-; Goldn Key 90-; Hon Schlrshp 88-; Deptmntl Schlrshp 90-; BP Amer Co-Op 90-; Cvl Engrng; Envrnmntl Engr.

**MEYERS, JACK H,** Univ Of Pittsburgh, Pittsburgh, PA; SO; BS; USN 83-89; Eng.

**MEYERS, JENNIFER G,** Garrett Comm Coll, Mchenry, MD; JR; AA; FFA Almn 90-; Natl Hnr Soc Pres 89-; Phi Theta Kappa 90-; Sec Sci.

**MEYERS, JENNIFER L,** Oh Wesleyan Univ, Delaware, OH; SR; BA; Cir K Intl Pres 88-; Habitat For Humanity 89-; Envrnmnt/Wldlf 89-90; Omicron Delta Epsilon 90-; Phi Beta Kappa; Phi Soc 89; Pi Beta Phi Corres Sec 88-; Comm Serv House; Stdnt Campaign Against Hunger 90; Econ Mgmnt; Auditing.

**MEYERS, KRISTINE M,** Seton Hall Univ, South Orange, NJ; JR; IM Ftbl; Elizabeth Ann Seton Offcr; Tchrs Natl Hon Soc; Kappa Delta Pi; Manfred Pakas Schlrshp; Ed/Cmnctns; Tchng.

**MEYERS, REBECCA L,** Saint Francis Coll, Loretto, PA; FR; BS; Stdnt Scty Of Physcn Assist 90; Hnrs Prog 90; Physcn Assist.

**MEYERS, SHANTI C,** Fl St Univ, Tallahassee, FL; JR; BA; Nwspr Nws Edtr 89-90; Phi Theta Kappa 89-90; AA Dean Jr Clg; Comms; Mrktng/Mrkt Res.

**MEYERSON, SARAH-KATE,** Univ Of Sc At Columbia, Columbia, SC; JR; BAIS; Rsdnce Hall Govt Pres 88-90; Deans Lst 90; Pres Lst 90; Outstndng Vol Of Mnth Awd 90; Erly Chldhd Ed; Tchr Spcl Ed.

**MEYERSON, SUSAN E,** George Mason Univ, Fairfax, VA; SR; BS; Amer Alliance Hlth 90; Alpha Chi; Golden Key 90; Kappa Delta Pi 90; Mst Outstndg Phys Educ Mjr; Phys Educ; Phys Educ Tchr/Coach.

**MEZINIS, PETER M,** Univ Of Miami, Coral Gables, FL; SR; BA; Sailing Clb; Psychology; Bus Grad Sch.

**MEZQUIDA, ARMANDO LUIS,** Saint Thomas Univ, Miami, FL; SO; BBA; Bus; Bus Admn.

**MIAH-LARGO, YUBEDA,** Fl International Univ, Miami, FL; SR; BS; FEA 89-; Logos Crdntr Kendau UMC 89-90; Montessori Tchrs Asst 89-90; Elem Ed; Spcl Ed.

**MIAL, LINDA L,** James Sprunt Comm Coll, Kenansville, NC; AS; Vst Asst Eldrly Nrsng Hm; Csmtlgy Compton Beauty Coll 81; Bio Eng Hst Antnmy Math Rdng; LPN.

**MIAN, A SABRINA,** Hillsborough Comm Coll, Tampa, FL; SO; BS; Frnch Clb 89-90; Blgy Bus Admn; MBA.

**MICALLEF, AMANDA C,** Middle Tn St Univ, Murfreesboro, TN; JR; Psychlgy; Psycho Thrpst.

**MICERI, DIANA,** Pa St Univ Delaware Cty Cmps, Media, PA; SO; BA; Prsdnt Frnch Clb Prsdnt; Phtgrphr Schl Nwspr 90-; Alpha Sigma Lambda Prsdnt; Arts Sciences; Photo Jrnlsm.

**MICH, CHRISTOPHER H,** Univ Of The Arts, Philadelphia, PA; FR; BFA; Film.

**MICHAEL, ANDREW S,** Marshall University, Huntington, WV; SR; MBA; Fncl Mgmnt Assoc; BBA; Bus Law; Corp Finance.

**MICHAEL, BRENT JAMES,** Emory Univ, Atlanta, GA; FR; Vrsty Swmmng 90-; Sigma Chi; Biolgy/Chem; Med.

**MICHAEL, DANYEL J,** Defiance Coll, Defiance, OH; JR; BA; Stdnt Scl Wrk Assn 89-; Tau Mu; Jr Yr Intrnshp At Dfnce Co Jvnle Prbtn Dept 90; Maumee Vly Gdnce Cntr Case Mgr; Scl Wrk; Cnslng Or Jvnle Prbtn.

**MICHAEL, DEBORAH K,** Memphis St Univ, Memphis, TN; SO; BA; Alpha Lambda Delta 67-68; Prtl Music Schlrshp 67-68; AMI; Cert Memphis Cty Schls 89; Psychlgy Music; Cnslnt Music Thrpy.

**MICHAEL, SUSAN L,** East Tn St Univ, Johnson City, TN; SR; BS; Phi Kappa Phi 90-; Dns Lst 76-90; Welcm Wagn Bristol Tn Va Hosp Chrmn; Prchsng Sec Trafc Coord 78-89; AAS Clevelnd St Comm Coll 81; Busn Educ; Tchng.**

**MICHAELES, CHRISTOPHER A,** Assumption Coll, Worcester, MA; SR; Rugby Cl 89-; Wachusett Mtn Ski Area Ski Instr 86-; Oprtn Frndshp Yth Exch Prog/Adul Member Advsr 80-; Delta Epsilon Sigma Pres 89-; Juvenile Diabetes Fllwshp 90-; Hon Convctn Awd/Excel/Biol/Chemsty 91; Biol; Chemsty; Med.**

**MICHAELIS, LAURA L,** William Carey Coll, Hattiesburg, MS; SO; BSN; Data Analyst/Mrktng Plnng Dept Tulane Med Cntr Hosp 84-; BS Tulane Univ 83f; Nursing.

**MICHAELIS, MELANIE A,** Teikyo Post Univ, Waterbury, CT; SO; BA; Drm Cncl Treas 89-90; Rsdnt Asst 90-; Sftbl 90-; Acctg.

**MICHAELIS, MICHELE,** Alfred Univ, Alfred, NY; SO; BS; Am Mktg Assn Newsltr Chrmn 89-; Natl Career Wmns Assn 90; Alpha Lambda Delta 89-; Highst Acdmc Indx In Clss 90-; Acctg.

**MICHAELS, ELISE M R,** Univ Of Rochester, Rochester, NY; SR; BS; AAS Hudson Vly Comm Coll 88; Optical Eng; Teach.

**MICHAELS, JAMIE R,** Indiana Univ Of Pa, Indiana, PA; SO; BED; Itza Pizza Empl Mnth; Elem Educ/Tchg.

**MICHAELS, ROBERT L,** Univ Of Rochester, Rochester, NY; SR; BS; Tau Beta Pi 90; Tau Alpha Pi 88; NY Air Ntnl Grd 85; AAS Hudson Vly Cmmnty Clg 88; AAS Cmmnty Clg Air Force 89; Optics; Electro Optical Eng.

**MICHAELS-GASPERSON, JACKIE,** Univ Of Nc At Asheville, Asheville, NC; SR; BA; Undrdg Prod Chrprsn 90-; Blue Banner Stf Wrtr 89; Sigma Delta Chi; Blue Rdg Bsn Jrnl Intrn 89; Amer Asc Univ Wmn Schlp; Mass Comm; Pblc Rltns.

**MICHAIL, NADIA,** Marywood Coll, Scranton, PA; FR; BS; Wnd Ensmble; Cmmnctn Dsordrs Clb; Envrnmntl Grp; Cmmnctn Disordrs; Speech Thrpy.

**MICHAILIDIS, EFFIE,** City Univ Of Ny Baruch Coll, New York, NY; JR; BBA; Gldn Ky Pres; Photo Clb Treas 89-90; Beta Gamma Sigma 89-; Acctg Soc 89-; Dns Lst 88-; Acctg; Hlth Reltd.

**MICHAL, DIXIE HUDNALL,** Emory & Henry Coll, Emory, VA; BA; Engl Litf Tchr.

**MICHALEC, CHERYL C,** Univ Of Nc At Greensboro, Greensboro, NC; SR; Marshall; Elem Educ.

**MICHALEC, MARK R,** Univ Of Nc At Charlotte, Charlotte, NC; SO; BS; Arts/Sci; Crmnl Jstc.

**MICHALEK, JOSEPH J,** Fl Atlantic Univ, Boca Raton, FL; SR; BA; Cltn Wldrnss Islands 88-; AA Palm Beach Comm Coll 89; Mrktng; Advrtsng.

**MICHALSKI, GARY J,** Comm Coll Algny Co Algny Cmps, Pittsburgh, PA; SO; BS; Sci; Engrng.

**MICHAUD, LISA A,** S U N Y Coll Of Tech At Alfred, Alfred, NY; SO; AA; Chrldr; Dns Lst; Liberal Arts/Humanities; Fshn Dsgn Mrchndsng.

**MICHEL, EDWARD,** City Univ Of Ny Baruch Coll, New York, NY; SR; Golden Key; Acctg; CPA.**

**MICHEL, JOSEPH S,** Oh St Univ At Newark, Newark, OH; FR; BSEE; Univ Chorus; U S Army 85-88; Elec Tchn 88-; Cert LCJVS Newark OH 85; Cert USAOMMCS Redstone Arsenal 86; Elec Engrng; Engrng.

**MICHEL, PATRICK R,** Bowling Green St Univ, Bowling Green, OH; BS; I M Sftbl 86-90; Visual Comm Tech; Prntr/Prod/Advtsng.

**MICHELIHI, ANN L,** Univ Of Rochester, Rochester, NY; SO; BA; Gamma Phi Beta Mthr Asst Rush 90-; Deans Lst; IM Flr Hcky/Inr Tube Wtr Polo 89-; Hlth; Admin.

**MICHELS, CATHY A,** Univ Of Ky, Lexington, KY; JR; BA; Kindercare Lrng Ctr Tchr 89-; Elem Edn/Math; Teach.

**MICHILLI, LUISA E,** Fayetteville St Univ, Fayetteville, NC; FR; Asn Stds Assn Caracas Ven Treas; Hon Soc 90-; Kyoto Acad D-Art Jpn Wtrclrst 80-81; Army Com Svc Cord 83-84; Chrbrgh Com Cncl Treas; Ft Bragg PTA Spc Actv Coord 89-90; Vlybl 89-90; Ft Brg Plyhse Cstm Coord 89-90; Ft Brg Prnt/Tchr Assn Cls Aid/Art 88-; Bus Adm; Archtc Dsgn.

**MICHINO, KAZUYO,** Colby Sawyer Coll, New London, NH; SO; BA; AA Showa Wmns Jr Clg Tokyo Japan 90; Intl Relations; Interpreter.

**MICHL, LINDA M,** Immaculata Coll, Immaculata, PA; SO; BS; Bio/Chem; Med Doc/Drmtlgst.

**MICHNOWICZ, MICHELLE L,** West Liberty St Coll, West Liberty, WV; FR; BS; Acctng; Law.

**MICIANO, EDOARDO S,** Church Of God Sch Of Theology, Cleveland, TN; FR; MDIV; Wrld Mssns Clb Tres; SGA Asn Smnry Chrstn Mnstrs VP 88-89; Yrbk Asian Smnry Chrstn Mnstrs Asst Edtr 86-87; Grd Hghst Hnrs Asn Smnry 90; Lovell Cary Awd Asn Smnry 90; Theology; Pstrl Mnstrs.

**MICKELL, CARMEN DEBORAH,** William Carey Coll, Hattiesburg, MS; SR; Natl Histrcl Scty Pres; Future Ldrs Amer; Acctng; CPA.

**MICKENS JR, JIMMY MAC,** Morehouse Coll, Atlanta, GA; JR; BA; Alpha Phi Omega 90; Schlr Athlete 88; Mthmtcs Awd; Russian Awd 88-; APO; Alpha Phi Omega 90-; Wansley Mvg Strg Co Crew Chf 90-; Ftbl 88-; Mgmt.

**MICKEY, AMY L,** Radford Univ, Radford, VA; SO; BA; Tchr Ed Prog; Elem Ed; Tchr.

**MICKLE, KATHERINE L,** Slippery Rock Univ, Slippery Rock, PA; JR; BFABA; Martha Gault Air Soc Secy 88-89; Sigma Delta Pi 90-; Martha Gault Art Schlrshp 90; Fine Arts/Span; Prof.

**MICKLE, STEPHANIE M,** Smith Coll, Northampton, MA; FR; BA; Spch/Debate Hse Repr Spch Capt 89-90; Vars Chrldr; FBLA 88-90; Frnch Hnr Soc 88-90; Svc Org Smith Tutor 90-; Amherst Clg Gospel Choir Bsn Mgr 90-; Precious Pearls Svc Clb 88-90; Selfo Run Publ Rels NY Intern; Engl; Jrnlsm/Publ.

**MICKLER JR, JOHNNY M,** Al A & M Univ, Normal, AL; SO; BS; Big Bro/Big Sis 89-90; Greenville Urban League Intrnshp 90-; Bsktbl League Hd Coach 89-; Pol Sci/Hist/Crmnl Jstc; Envrnmntl Law.

**MIDDLEBROOKS, LISA D,** John C Calhoun St Comm Coll, Decatur, AL; JR; AAS; Dns Lst 89-90; Pres Lst 90; Mst Otstndng Stdnt Elctrncs 90; Certif Electrncs Tech 90; Elctrncs Tech; BS Instrmntn.**

**MIDDLECOFF, MINDY E,** Univ Of Tn At Martin, Martin, TN; SR; BS; Fashn Merchndsng Assoc Pres 89-; Alpha Omicron Pi Asst Pldg Ed 87-; Retail Merch Intrnshp 90; Outstndng Mbr 90-; Deans List 87-; Home Ec/Fashn Merch; Retl Mgt/Law.

**MIDDLETON, ATESHIA S,** Univ Of Sc At Columbia, Columbia, SC; FR; MBA; Asc Afrcn Std 90-; Finance.

**MIDDLETON, ELAINE M,** Union Inst, Cincinnati, OH; GD; BA; Consort Belizean Dev Inc Asst VP; Mbr British Empire Awrd 76; Cert Tchrs Trng Clg 57; Cert Univ Clg Of Swansea 66; Socl Wrk.

**MIDDLETON, FELICIA S,** Johnson C Smith Univ, Charlotte, NC; SO; BA; Wmns Bsktbl/Track 90-; Math; Engrng.

**MIDDLETON, GAY L,** Benedict Coll, Columbia, SC; SR; BS; Alpha Chi; Rdrs Dgst 87-90; Bndct Col 87-; Bsns Admn; Gvt.

**MIDDLETON, JANET N,** Ms St Univ, Miss State, MS; FR; BABS; Anthrplgy Clb 90-; Gamma Beta Phi; Hnrs Prgm 90-; Univ Schlrshp; Cobb Inst Archlgy Rsrch Asstntshp; Anthrplgy/Geolgy; Marine Geolgy.

**MIDDLETON, JENNIFER A,** Bowie St Univ, Bowie, MD; FR; BA; Dns Lst 90-; Vars Vlybl 90-; Educ; Tchr.

**MIDDLETON, JUANICE G,** Fl A & M Univ, Tallahassee, FL; FR; Neumann Clb 90-; Mrchng 100 90-; Phi Eta Sigma 90-; Phi Eta Sigma 90; Sftbll 90-; IM Bsktbll 90-; Phrmcy; Ped Phrmcst.

**MIDDLETON, KIMBERLY A,** Livingston Univ, Livingston, AL; FR; BA; Phi Eta Sigma; Engl.

**MIDDLETON, KRISTIN L,** Univ Of Southern Ms, Hattiesburg, MS; SO; BS; Stdnt Almn Assc 89-; Phi Kappa Phi; Alpha Lmbd Dlt 90-; Gamma Beta Phi 90-; Kappa Dlt 89-; Elem Ed; Tch Mstrs.

**MIDDLETON, LORI C,** Middle Tn St Univ, Murfreesboro, TN; SR; BS; STEA 90-; Pi Mu Epsilon 90-; Zeta Tau Alpha 2nd VP 84-; BS GA Inst Tech 86; Math; Tchr.

**MIDDLETON, MARK L,** Me Maritime Academy, Castine, ME; FR; BS; Eng.

**MIDDLETON, TAMMY D,** Univ Of Southern Ms, Hattiesburg, MS; JR; BS; Univ Activities Council 89-; Speech Communication Assoc 90-; Payne Ctr Advsry Comm 89-; Sigma Phi Epsilon 90-; Deans List 89-90; Speech Communication; Communication Consultan.

**MIDDLETON, TRACEY G,** Memphis St Univ, Memphis, TN; JR; BA; Gamma Beta Phi 90-; Acctng; CPA.

**MIDDLETON, WILLIAM W,** Middle Tn St Univ, Murfreesboro, TN; JR; BA; Karate Ylw Blt 84; Chrch Invlvmnt Orch; Mass Cmnctns; Brdcst Prdctn.

**MIDGETTE, JACQUELINE H,** Fl St Univ, Tallahassee, FL; SR; BA; Dev Res Schl 90; Engl Educ.

**MIDGETTE-LUTHER, CAROL,** Fayetteville St Univ, Fayetteville, NC; SR; BS; Biolgy; PhD Biolgy.

**MIDGLEY, DIANA L,** Ringling School Of Art, Sarasota, FL; JR; BFA; Cnty Cmmssrn Spprt 90; Phi Theta Kappa 88-; Exhbtd Gllry Show; AA Edsn Comm Clg 87-89; Grphc Dsgn.**

**MIDKIFF, CYNTHIA D,** Fairmont St Coll, Fairmont, WV; FR; Im Sftbl; Eng; Eng Envrnmntl.

**MIDTSKOGEN, ERIK,** Temple Univ, Philadelphia, PA; JR; Haverford/Mrym Mawr Chmbr Sngrs 86-87; Journeyman Cabinetmaker 87-90; Archtctr; Engr.

**MIELE, DEBORA C,** Univ Of Al At Huntsville, Huntsville, AL; SR; BS; SWE 90-; IEEE; Tau Beta Pi 90-; Bng Eng 83-; BS 82; Elec Eng.

**MIELE, KAREN M,** Endicott Coll, Beverly, MA; FR; AS; SG 90; Cavendis Pointe Htl Intrnshp Desk Clerk 90; Bsn Admin; Clrcl/Bsn.

**MIELENZ, JENNIFER M,** Glassboro St Coll, Glassboro, NJ; FR; Stdnt Actvts Bd 90-; Deans List 90-; Cmmnctns; Brdcstng.

**MIERBETH, INGRID E,** Southern Coll Of Tech, Marietta, GA; JR; IET; ISA Pub/Soc Chrprsn; Gamma Phi Beta Fndrsr/Pnhllnc Pres 87-; Qulty Cntrl/Assrnce; Eng/Instrl.

**MIERES, JOSE E,** Inter Amer Univ Pr Hato Rey, Hato Rey, PR; SR; BA; Delta Tau Delta GA Tech 87; Greenpeace Action 89; Hnr Rl 90-; Engl Instr Madrid Spain 90; Bsn Adm; Phylosophy/Ed.

**MIERZWA, PATRICIA A,** Comm Coll Algny Co Algny Cmps, Pittsburgh, PA; SO; BA; Notary Pblc Alghny Cty PA 87-; PA Assc Notaries 87-; Amer Scty Notaries 87-; PNC Lsng Corp Pgh Pa Sr Sec 80-; Laurel Capital Corp Pittsburgh PA Ofc Mgr 86-; Engl; Clg Engl Tchr.

**MIESNER, TRENT C,** Univ Of Miami, Coral Gables, FL; JR; BS; Economics/Public Rltns; PHD/FINANCE.

**MIETZ, JANE A,** S U N Y Coll At Fredonia, Fredonia, NY; SO; BED; Natl Tchrs Clb 90-; Mdrn Brtsh Clb 90-; Engl; Ed Elem.

**MIGA, MIKE A,** S U N Y Coll Of Tech At Alfred, Alfred, NY; FR; BT; Deans Lst; Pres Hon Awrd; IM Sftbl/Bwlng/Ftbl; AAS; Dsgn/Drftng; Mech Eng.

**MIGHTY, CHRISTOPHER G,** City Univ Of Ny Baruch Coll, New York, NY; SR; BA; Gldn Key 89-; Acdmc Schlrshp 87-; Deans Lst 88-; Actrl Sci; Lf/Hlth Actry.

**MIGLIACCIO, MICHAEL,** Villanova Univ, Villanova, PA; SO; BA; Ecnmcs/Phlsphy; Law.

**MIGLINO, KELLY J,** Dowling Coll, Oakdale Li, NY; SR; Psi Chi 90-; Stdnt Tchr Of Pre K Speech Impaired 89; Stdnt Tchr Mdl Schl LD/ED 90; Stdnt Tchr 3/4 Grd LD/ED; Spec/Reg Educ.

**MIGLIORE, CARMEN,** Bloomfield Coll, Bloomfield, NJ; SR; BA; Bus Mgmt.

**MIGNOGNA, AMIE M,** Indiana Univ Of Pa, Indiana, PA; JR; BA; Dean Lst 88-90; Educ; Nrsry Schl.

**MIHAI, ADRIAN,** City Univ Of Ny La Guard Coll, Long Island Cty, NY; GD; BA; Deans Lst; Belle Zeller Schlrshp Awd 90; AS 90; TV; Flmmkng.

**MIHALEK, BALINDA R,** Tusculum Coll, Greeneville, TN; SO; BA; Res Advsr; Deans Lst; First Chrstn Church; Vlybl 89-90; Bus/Psych.

**MIHALIK, STACY L,** Va Polytechnic Inst & St Univ, Blacksburg, VA; SO; BA; Sccr 90-; Tae Kwn Do Clb 90-; Natl Wldlf Scty 90-; Alpha Zeta 90-; Wldlf Blgy.

**MIHOV, ILIYAN LJUBOMIROV,** Univ Of Sc At Columbia, Columbia, SC; JR; BS; Bus Econ; Econ Rsrch.

**MIKA, MOLLY B,** Coll Misericordia, Dallas, PA; SR; BS; Cmps Mnstry Exec Brd 89-; Peer Tutor; Stdnt Occptnl Thrpy Assoc Sec 90-; Cum Laude; Honors; Vac Bible Schl Coord; Occupational Thrpy.

**MIKALAJUNAS, SCOTT R,** Anne Arundel Comm Coll, Arnold, MD; SO; Seton Youth Grp Adlt Advsr 90-; Acctng; CPA.

**MIKE, LEIGH A,** Univ Of South Fl, Tampa, FL; FR; Univ Wide Hnrs Prgrm 90-; Bio; Med.

**MIKEL, ANGELIA L,** Jackson St Univ, Jackson, MS; JR; Les Exqust Ale Mode Bus Mgr 88-; Natl Stdnt Spch Lang Hrng Assn VP 88-; Spch Comm Organ 88-; Phi Kappa Phi 90-; Alpha Mu Gamma 89-; Alpha Chi 90-; Summer Rsrch Oppor Pgrm Nrthwstn 90-; Spch Dram Art; Spch Pathgst.

**MIKEL, RHONDA F,** Bethel Coll, Mckenzie, TN; SO; BS; Clss Pres; Gamma Beta Phi 90-; Soc Cllgt Jrnlsts 90-; Alpha Phi Sigma Sec/Treas 90-; Hon Roll 90-; Sec/Bkpng/Data Prcssng 85-; Clncl Psychlgy.

**MIKEO, BRENDA L,** Oh Univ, Athens, OH; FR; BFA; Theatre; Set Desgn.

**MIKLAS, DANUTE M,** Nova Univ, Ft Lauderdale, FL; GD; MBA; Cntmpraries Ft Ldrdl Museum Of Art; Prpsl Engr; BSED Univ DE 82.

**MIKLOVIC, PATRICIA L,** Columbus Coll Of Art & Design, Columbus, OH; SR; BFA; Illustrtn; Grtng Cards/Chldrns Bks.

**MIKO, AMY S,** Saint Francis Coll, Loretto, PA; SO; BA; Yrbk Stff 90-; Math Comps Clb 89-; IM Bsktbl Vlybl Sftbl 89-; Kappa Mu Epsilon; Math Comp Sci.

**MIKOLINSKI, NATASHA M,** Univ Of Ct, Storrs, CT; JR; BS; Stu Govt Area Cncl Liason 89-; Dorm Stu Govt Scl Chrprsn 89-90; IM Vlybl/Sccr Capt 89-90; Ntrtnl Sci; Dietician.

**MIKULLITZ, MARK A,** Western New England Coll, Springfield, MA; SO; Vrsty Lacrosse 89-; Engl; Law.

**MIKUSZEWSKI, VANESSA A,** Western New England Coll, Springfield, MA; SO; BA; Com Pgmg/Entrtnmnt 90-; Hall Assn 89-; Spec Olymp 90; Alpha Almbda Delta Pres 90-; Deans Lst 89-; Psychlgy.**

**MILAGROS, PALERMO,** Inter Amer Univ Pr San German, San German, PR; SR; BA; Beta Beta Beta 90-; Biology; Medicine.

**MILAM, CHERYL P,** Auburn Univ At Montgomery, Montgomery, AL; FR; BA; Mass Cmmnctn; Brdcstng.

**MILAN, JENNIFER L,** Univ Of Sc At Columbia, Columbia, SC; FR; BA; Phi Eta Sigma; Bus Admn.

**MILANA, FRANCESCO,** Alfred Univ, Alfred, NY; JR; Stdnt Actvts Brd Tres 90-; IEEE Tres; Tau Beta Pi Tres; Kappa Psi Upsln; Presdtl Schlrshp 88-.

**MILANAK, THOMAS M,** Comm Coll Algny Co Algny Cmps, Pittsburgh, PA; SO; AS; Advsry Brd 90; Envrnmntl Clb; Bus.

**MILANCZUK, JONATHAN,** Western New England Coll, Springfield, MA; JR; BA; MAA 88-; Peer Tutr 89; NCMA; REU; Tnns 88-; Math; Actrl Sci.

**MILANI, MARK T,** Univ Of Pittsburgh, Pittsburgh, PA; GD; BS; IIE Pre; Golden Key; Pi Kappa Alpha Hist 87-90; Tau Beta Pi; Alpha Pi Mu Corr Sec; Stdnt Govt Brd Athletic Comm 90-; Athletic Legsltv Subcomm; Placement Serv Comm; Ind Engr.

**MILARTA, SUSAN A,** Elmira Coll, Elmira, NY; SR; Nrsng Clb 89-; PAL 87-88; Dexchng Stdnt Hostess 90; Hon Schlr 89; NYSNA Dist 3 90-; Nrsng Crdntr Home Care Pgm Fmly Svc Chemung Co 89; Qlty Assrnc Cmt Mbr Fmly Svc 89-; RN Arnot Ogden Mem Hosp Sch Nrsng 89; Nrsng; Medcn/Grntlgy.

**MILASCHEWSKI, RICHARD W,** Central Fl Comm Coll, Ocala, FL; SO; BA; Phi Theta Kappa 90-; Deans Lst 89-; Tutoring Clg Pk Elem Schl 90; AA; Engl; Engl Educ.

**MILAZZO, ANDRAIA M,** Le Moyne Coll, Syracuse, NY; FR; BA BS; PIC 90-; Math.

**MILBERT, MICHAEL,** Fl International Univ, Miami, FL; BSE; IEEE V P 90-; TECHNISAL Comm 89; IEEE; Law Eng; Law.

**MILBURN, AIMEE S,** Smith Coll, Northampton, MA; JR; BA; 1st Grp Schlr 90-; Fclty Schlrshp Awrd Univ Of Colo Bldr 80-81; Fiske Schlrshp Awrd Univ Of Colo Bldr 79-80; Re Eval Co Cnslr; Wrtr Poetry/Essys/Shrt Stry/Cmpsr; Music; Wrtr.

**MILBURN, CRAIG T,** Tn Tech Univ, Cookeville, TN; JR; BS; Block/Bridle Club Pres; Delta Tau Alpha; W J Huddleston Agri Acadmc Award; Arnold W Hunter Anml Sci Award; TN Cncl Of Coop Schlrshp; Im Athletics; Anml Sci.

**MILBURN, DEBORA L,** Univ Of Miami, Coral Gables, FL; SR; BM; Phi Kappa Phi; Sigma Alpha Iota 90-; Kappa Alpha Theta 86-88; Karate Club 89-; AS Carnegie Mellon Univ 88; Music/Jazz Vocal/Studio Music; Perf/Tchng.

**MILBURN, MELVIN W,** Univ Of Louisville, Louisville, KY; SR; ME; ASCE 90; Golden Key 90; Civil Eng; Eng.

**MILBY, KRISTI D,** Christopher Newport Coll, Newport News, VA; JR; BA; Dixie Cnfrnce All Trnmnt Team 90-; Vrsty Sftbl 89-; Lsr Serv/Thrptc Rec; Cert Spclst.

**MILES YORK, REBECCA J,** Univ Of Tn At Martin, Martin, TN; SO.

**MILES, ALISHA E,** Syracuse Univ, Syracuse, NY; FR; BS; Campus Crsde Chrst Intl 90-; Inf Stdies; Conslt.

**MILES, AMANDA M,** Villanova Univ, Villanova, PA; SO; BA; Alpha Chi Omega Stdnt Actvts Chrprsn 90-; Prjct Sunshine Vol 90; Balloon Day Chrprsn; Engl.

**MILES, AMY M,** Univ Of Sc At Columbia, Columbia, SC; FR; BS; Pres Hnr Rl 90; Dns Lst 90; Phrmcy.

**MILES, ANJANEE D,** Va Commonwealth Univ, Richmond, VA; JR; Pre Lw Scty Sec Pres 89-; Fnncl Mgmt Assn Sec 90-; Stdnt Govt Sntr 90-; Afrcn Amer Schlrs Prog 90-; Ttr Mntr Prog 89-; Fll Schlrshp; Admin Of Jstce Pre Lw; Lw.

**MILES, DEIRDRE U,** Duquesne Univ, Pittsburgh, PA; SO; BA; Blk Stdnt Un 89-; Girl Scouts S Wstrn PA Asst Trp Ldrs 90-; DUV Duquesne Univ Vol Awd 90-; Inroads Phila Inc Intrn 89-; Cmunctns; Mgmt.

**MILES, DIANE J,** Bloomfield Coll, Bloomfield, NJ; FR; BA; CER Cmptr Process Inst 88; Cmptr Info Sys; Cmptr Sci.

**MILES, DINAH M,** Coker Coll, Hartsville, SC; FR; BA; Educ; Tch.

**MILES, ELIZABETH L,** Roane St Comm Coll, Harriman, TN; SO; ASSOC; Hlth Physcs Intrnshp Martin Marietta Smmr; Envrmntl Sci; Hlth Phys.

**MILES, GREGORY A,** Tn Temple Univ, Chattanooga, TN; SR; BRE; Pastrl Stes; Evangelist.

**MILES JR, JAMES E,** Comm Coll Algny Co Algny Cmps, Pittsburgh, PA; SO; BS; Blck Lge Afrcn-Amer Cltr 90-; Cntrl Govt Afrcn-Amer Std Uns 90-; Soc Crtv Mscns 90-; Grtr Pbg Std Chprt Natl Asc Blck Accntns 90-; Hmn Rsc Mgmt.

**MILES, JEREMY E,** Univ Of Sc At Columbia, Columbia, SC; SO; BA; Psychlgy.

**MILES, JERRY L,** Univ Of Md At Eastern Shore, Princess Anne, MD; JR; BED; Academic Honors; Art; Art Teacher.

**MILES, KAREN C,** Ashland Comm Coll, Ashland, KY; SO; BA; AA 90; Acctg.

**MILES, LISA M,** Univ Of Southern Ms, Hattiesburg, MS; SR; BS; Pres List 90; Social Sorvile Awd S Central Regl Medl Ctr 90; Nurse Yr 89; Adv Cardiac Life Support Inst 86-; Nursing.

**MILES, MARTHA L,** Northwest Al Comm Coll, Phil Campbell, AL; FR; Comp; Prog.

**MILES, MONICA E,** Univ Of Montevallo, Montevallo, AL; SR; MS; Natl Spch Lang/Hrng Assoc 88-; Spch/Hrng Assoc Of AL; Alpha Delta Pi Music Chrmn 87-; Delta Chi Ltl Sistr Secy 87-; BS; Undrgrad Ed Of The Hrng Imprd; Audiolgst.

**MILES, PENNY L,** Penn Coll Of Straight Chiro, Horsham, PA; GD; DC; Wrld Cngrss Chiropractic Stdnts; Chiropractic.

**MILES, ROBERT M,** Hampden Sydney Coll, Hmpden-Sydney, VA; FR; BA; Good Mn Good Ctzns 90-; Crss Cntry Vrsty Lttr 90-; Poli Sci/Hstry; Lwyr/Poltcn.

**MILES, SHELLY M,** Columbia Greene Comm Coll, Hudson, NY; FR; BA; Elem Edctn; Tchr.

**MILES, STEPHANIE A,** Watterson Coll, Louisville, KY; GD; DIPL; SGA Stuart Hall Treas 81-82; W Va Career Coll Spcl Hnr Grad; Watterson Coll Pres/Dns Lst Stdt; Intern OTT Ocmm Inc Adv Agy; Lungscty Vol; Hecks Ast Sls Prmtn/Adv Artist Wv; Diploma Clrk/Typist 84; Art; Comm Artist.

**MILES, TAMELA LA SHELLE,** Univ Of Al At Birmingham, Birmingham, AL; FR; BS; Afr Amrcn Med Clb 90-; Alpha Lambda Delta; Ambssdrs; Hnrs Prgm 90-; Prsdntl Schlrshp; Blgy Pre Med; Orthndntst.

**MILES, TRACI,** Radford Univ, Radford, VA; SR; Phi Sigma Sigma 89-; Dns Lst 89; Pub Rel Intrnshp; BS 91; Comm; Pub Rel/Reprtng.

**MILETIC, RENEE M,** Slippery Rock Univ, Slippery Rock, PA; SR; BS; Slppry Rock Dnc Theatre 87-; Spanish Clb Pres 91/87; HPERD 89; Sigma Tau Delta 90-; Sigma Delta Pi 88-; Kappa Delta Pi 90-; ACDFA 88-89; English/Spanish; Teacher.

**MILEY, DARYL F,** Central Al Comm Coll, Alexander City, AL; FR; Radio Annoucer; Radio Prgmr.

**MILEY, JIMMIE DEE,** Jackson St Univ, Jackson, MS; SR; BSED; SNEA 90-; Alpha Kappa Mu 90-; Phi Kappa Phi; Crystal Sprgs Jr Auxlry 86-; PTA St Brd 84-; Elem Educ.

**MILEY, SHERRY J,** Univ Of Southern Ms, Hattiesburg, MS; SR; B S Of Amer Ldr 90-; Phi Theta Kappa 88-; Golden Key 90-; Deans Lst; Pres Lst; Tee Ball Coach 88; AAS Degree In Cmrcl Design/Adv 79; Elem Tchr.

**MILEY, SUSANNAH M,** Clemson Univ, Clemson, SC; FR; BS; Flwshp Of Chrstn Athlts 90-; Reformed Univ Flwshp 90-; Res Hall Cncl 90-; Pblst 90-; Coll Big Sis 90-; Deans List; Bert & Johnnie Brantly Schlrly Achvmnt Awd 90-; Park Rcrtn & Trsm Mgmt; Resort Mgmt.

**MILFORD, FRANCIS T,** Southern Coll Of Tech, Marietta, GA; SR; BS; Pres Awd; AS Gainesville Clg 89; Indstrl Eng Tchnlgy; Tech Sales/Dstrbtn.

**MILFORD, SHIRLEY A,** Coppin St Coll, Baltimore, MD; SR; BS; AA Comm Coll Baltimore 87; Crmnl Jstc; Law.

**MILGRIM, ROBIN NICOLE,** Savannah Coll Of Art & Design, Savannah, GA; SO; Phtgrphy Clb; Art; Dsgn.

**MILHOAN, STEPHANIE M,** David Lipscomb Univ, Nashville, TN; FR; BS; Ftlghtrs; Fr Prsnlties; Tau Phi; Cwby Shw; WNH Coll Chrch Grp; Circle K; Deans Hon Schlrshp; Deans Lst; Hon Roll; Frtrnl Schlrshp; IM Vlybl/Bsktbl; Biochem/Biolgy; Med.

**MILHORN, BRANDON L,** East Tn St Univ, Johnson City, TN; FR; BS; Pre-Law Soc 90-; Cmte/1000 Schlrshp; Ftbl Place Kicker 90-; Fnce; Law.

**MILHORNE, BUFFY M,** Emory & Henry Coll, Emory, VA; JR; BA; Math Assn Amer 90-; Stdnt VA Educ Assn 90-; Phi Eta Sigma 88-; Gamma Beta Phi 89-90; Sigma Mu Schlrshp 90-; Pi Sigma Kappa Sec 90-; Alpha Phi Omega Sec 90-; J Brown Schlrshp 90-; Eastmn-Kdk Schlrshp 90-; Natl Cllgt Math Awds 90-; Math Edu; Scndry Schl Tchr.

**MILIAN FERNANDEZ, MAYRA N,** Univ Of Pr Cayey Univ Coll, Cayey, PR; SO; Engl/Spansh; Phrmcy.

**MILIC, MICHELLE M,** Duquesne Univ, Pittsburgh, PA; SO; BS; Pre Hlth Soc 89-; Delta Zeta Soc Chrmn 90-; Comm Vol Wrk Fndrsng MD Spch Hrng Imp 89-; Biol/Pre Med; Med.

**MILICI JR, SALVATORE,** Centenary Coll, Hackettstown, NJ; SR; BS; Phi Beta Lambda Prlmntrn 90-; Deans Trphy Trnmnt Capt Mktg Tm 90-; Alpha Chi 90-; Omega Rho Sec 90-; Big Bro/ Big Sis 90-; Cert Apprctn 90; Cett Merit Awd 90; Bus Admin; Law Schl.

**MILINER, MICHELLE P,** Andrew Coll, Cuthbert, GA; SO; Deans Lst; Spnsh; Edn.

**MILITELLO, ANTHONY J,** Univ Of New Haven, West Haven, CT; FR; BS; Fire Clb 90-; Vrsty Bsktbl Mngr 90-; Fire Prtctn Eng.

**MILITELLO, DAVID M,** Hudson Valley Comm Coll, Troy, NY; SO; Sclgy.

**MILKINS, BRUCE A,** Hudson Valley Comm Coll, Troy, NY; FR; Lab Tech Albany Intrntl; Owner Summit Slctng Co; U S Air Force Sec Pol Rsrvst; Mktng; Own Oper Bus In Fla.

**MILLARD, CASSANDRA A,** Univ Of Rochester, Rochester, NY; JR; BA; Soc Actvts Brd; Cmps Y 89-90; Deans List; Math; Bus Interntl.

**MILLARD, ELLEN A,** Newbury Coll, Brookline, MA; ADP; Estrn Star 89; ADB 89; Paralgl.

**MILLARD, JAY H,** Northern Ky Univ, Highland Hts, KY; SO; BA; Res Ofcrs Trng Corps 90-; Frat Order Of Police 84-; Alpha Phi Alpha Comm Rltns 83-; Ret Of Crs Assoc Ldrshp Medal; Mil Sci Acdmc Achvmnt Awd; Am Red Cross 84-; United Way 89-; Dir Of Guest Serv 89-; Pub Admn; Govt Serv/Law Sch.

**MILLARD, RICHARD,** Broward Comm Coll, Ft Lauderdale, FL; SO; MBA; Phi Theta Kappa 90-; Pres Lst 89-; U S Navy Vet 81-85; Good Conduct Mdl/Meritorious Unit Commendation U S Navy Sea Svc Rbn Ltr Comm 81-85; Math/Physics; Eng/Tchng.

**MILLAY, BRENT E,** Owensboro Comm Coll, Owensboro, KY; SO; ME; Engr.

**MILLBERG, MELISSA L,** Belmont Coll, Nashville, TN; SR; BS; Baptist Student Union; Stdnt Fndtn 89-90; Resident Asstnt 89-; BS; Elem Educ; Teaching.

**MILLEDGE, BEVERLY M,** Albany St Coll, Albany, GA; FR; Psychlgy.

**MILLENDER, CAROLYN,** Stillman Coll, Tuscaloosa, AL; JR; BS; Sclgy Clb; Stu Spprt; Miss Stillman Coll; Sclgy/Soc Wrk; Soc Wrkr Absd Chldrn.

**MILLENDER III, SHELLY,** Univ Of Al At Birmingham, Birmingham, AL; SR; BA; Spnsh Clb 89-; Pre-Law Soc VP 89-; Dmcrts 90-; Phlsphy Clb VP 90-; Debate Tm 89-; Kappa Alpha Psi Pres 90-; Achvr Year 90-; IM Ftbl/Bsktbl 89-; Engl; Law.

**MILLER, ADAM B,** Yeshiva Univ, New York, NY; JR; BA; Psy Chi 90-; Psy Club VP 90-; Philthpy Scty; Psy; Clinical Psy Pract/ Rabbinate.

**MILLER, ALISHA M,** Ky St Univ, Frankfort, KY; SO; BA; Yrbk Staff 89-; Engl Cl Sec 90; Phi Beta Lambda Recrdr; All Am Schol 90-; Deans List 89-91; Busn; Fince.**

**MILLER, ALISON L,** Univ Of Rochester, Rochester, NY; SO; BA; Glee Clb 89-; Acad Theatre Org 90; Adopt-A-Grandparent; Xerox Schlr 89-; Gum Clb 89; Engl; Ed.

**MILLER, AMANDA KAY,** Middle Tn St Univ, Murfreesboro, TN; JR; BA; Chi Omega Fnrsr Chrmn 89-90 Rush 90-; Elem Educ/Mktng; Phrmctcl Sls/Elem Tchr.

**MILLER, AMY R,** Coll Of Charleston, Charleston, SC; SR; Alpha Phi Omega Sec 87-; Intrnshp Dawn Center 90; IM 88; BS Clg Of Charleston; Psychology.

**MILLER, AMY S,** Bridgewater Coll, Bridgewater, VA; SR; BA; Day Stdnts Org Treas 89-90; Early Chldhd Educ; K-2 Tchr.

**MILLER, ANDREA M,** Univ Of Cincinnati, Cincinnati, OH; SR; BFA; Intl Tlvsn Assoc 89-; Schl Nwsppr Rep 90; Deans Lst 89-; Alpha Epsilon Rho Pblc Rltnskappa Alpha Theta 88-; Prctr Gmbl Prdctn Schlrshp; Intrnshp Gdng Lght 90; Brbr Prfft Cstng Intern Vdgrpher; Hcky Org Intern Pblc Rltns; Brdcstng.

**MILLER, ANDREA S,** Tomlinson Coll, Cleveland, TN; FR; ASSOC; Creatv Arts Minstry 90-; Spirtl Life Comm Asst Ldr 90-; Pres List 90-; Phi Theta Kappa Treas; Music Award; In-Touch Asst 90-; Music; Ed.

**MILLER, ANDREW W,** Indiana Univ Of Pa, Indiana, PA; SO; BS; IM Bsktbll 90-; Kappa Delta Pi 90-; Hnrs Cnvctn; Provosts Schlr; Biol; Educ.

**MILLER, ANGELA J,** Univ Of Nc At Charlotte, Charlotte, NC; JR; Fmly Wknd Plnng Cmmtt Pblcty Chrmn 88-90; Ldrshp Brd Sec 88-90; Etc Mgzn 90; Gldn Keyphi Sigma Alpha; Gamma Sigma Sigma Treas 87-90; Pltcl Sci; Law.

**MILLER, ANGELA JANE,** Union Coll, Barbourville, KY; SO; Vars Bsktbl/Sftbl 89-; Phy Ed/Hlth; Tch.

**MILLER, ANGELA R,** Mount Olive Coll, Mount Olive, NC; JR; BS; Clg Hnrs; Lab Prctr; Accntng; CPA.

**MILLER, ANN M,** Bridgewater Coll, Bridgewater, VA; SO; BS; Stdnt Cncl Religious Actvts 90-; Judicial Review Bd 90-; Concert Choir 90-; Lambda Soc 90-; Cross Country 89-90; Bio; Research/ Lab Wrk.

**MILLER, ANNA G,** Interdenominational Theo Ctr, Atlanta, GA; GD; MDIV; Gammon Stdnt Fllwshp Pres 90-; Gammon Stdnt Fllwshp Tres 89-90; Stdnt Chrstn Leg Exec Comm 90-; Deans Lst 90-; Melvia W Costen Msc Awd 88-; Ntnl Soc Scl Wrkrs 87; Zeta Phi Beta Dean Pldgs 69-70; Cub Scts Amrca Cub Mstr 80-88; Chrstn Edctn; Untd Mthdstmnstr.

**MILLER, APRIL J,** Marshall University, Huntington, WV; SR; Natl Mgmt Assoc Sec 90-; BBA 90; Mgmt.

**MILLER, ARNOLD R,** Brewer St Jr Coll, Fayette, AL; SO; BS; Phi Theta Kappa 89-; EMT 89; Sci; Med.

**MILLER, AUDREY M,** Clark Atlanta Univ, Atlanta, GA; SO; BA; Insprtnl Voices Of Faith 89-90; Dns Lst 90; Miss Merner Hall 89-90; 1st Attndt Ms Miss Morehouse Clg 90-; Marchng Pnthr Bnd 90-; Mass Media Arts; News Anchrwmn.

**MILLER, AUDRI J,** Johnson St Coll, Johnson, VT; SR; BS; Chessamore Hon Soc; Summa Cum Laude; Pro Vermont Citzns Cmtee 88; UVM Ext Hmkrs Clb 89-; Spec Educ Asst; AS Norwich Univ 86; Ele Educ; Educ.

**MILLER, BARBARA S,** Univ Of Cin R Walters Coll, Blue Ash, OH; SO; ASSOC; Stdnt Govt Sec/Treas 90-; Stdnt Serv Task Force Stdnt Rep 90-; Soroptomist TAP Awd 89-90; Clermonty Cnty Fmly Crisis Ctr Intern; Cert Wmns Studies 90-; Crisis Cnslng 90-; Med Office Tech; Hmn Serv.

**MILLER, BARRI LYNN,** Univ Of Med & Dentistry Of Nj, Newark, NJ; GD; Class Govt 88-90; Dvlpmntl Disabilites Coop 88-89; Educ Rvw Comm 89-90; BS Montclair State Clg 86; MPT Rutgers 90; PT.

**MILLER, BOBBIE R,** Endicott Coll, Beverly, MA; SO; AS; IBD 90-; Intr Dsgn Clb 90-; Arbcs 89; Phi Theta Kappa; Dns Lst 89-; Smth Offc Intshp 90; Intrs Intshp 90; Intr Dsgn.

**MILLER, BONITA JO,** Western Ky Univ, Bowling Green, KY; JR; BS; Prof Secs Intl Lincoln Trl Chptr Pres 89-90; Ltl Clifty Un Meth Chrch Sec Trstee Brd Of Dir; Assoc/Prof Sectyshp Elizabethtwn Comm Clg 76; Bsns; Ins Ind.

**MILLER, BONNIE L,** Kent St Univ Kent Cmps, Kent, OH; SR; BBA; Gldn Key 90-; Delta Nu Alpha 90; Bird Trckng Co 85-86; Frnch Trnsprt Inc 87-90; Trnsprtn/Lgstcs Mgmt.

**MILLER, BRENDA L,** Univ Of Nc At Greensboro, Greensboro, NC; SR; BS; Wmns Cnnctn VP; Clthng/Txtls Clb Pres 89-90; Kappa Omcrn Nu Pres; Fldcrst Fdn Schlp; Fldcrst Cannon Intshp; Ctzns Waste Rdctn/Rcyclng 89-; Wght Wtchrs Intl Lctr 80-82; Clthng/Txtls; Design.

**MILLER, BRIAN D,** Univ Of Nc At Chapel Hill, Chapel Hill, NC; FR; BA; Mrchg/Pep/Cncrt/Symphnc Bnd 90-; Clg Rpblcns 90-; Phi Mu Alpha Sec 90-; AM Guild Orgnsts 88-; AM Thtre Orgn Soc 90-; Hstrc Salisbury Assoc 89-; Robt C Byrd Hnr Schlr; Hstry; Law.

**MILLER, BRIAN G,** Oh St Univ, Columbus, OH; SR; BS; Ldr 21st Cntry Spkr Co/Chr 90-; Hon Peer Spnr Prog Asst Chr 88-89; Sphinx VP 90-; Hon Comm Assn VP 87-89; Bucket/Dpr Pres 89-90; Romophos VP 88-89; IM Sprts 87-; Buckeye Awd Stdnt Ldrshp/Svc 89; Glbl Affrs Conf Wnr 90; Univ Pres Acad Excel 90; Econ; Law.

**MILLER, BRIAN K,** Muskingum Coll, New Concord, OH; FR; Schlrshp Awd; IM Ftbl Bsktbl; Math.

**MILLER, BRIAN S,** Embry Riddle Aeronautical Univ, Daytona Beach, FL; SR; Prcsn Flght Demo Tm VP 90-; Amer Assoc Arprt Exec 90-; Deans Lst 89-; IM Bsktbl/Ftbl 89-90; Aerontcl Sci; Arln Pilot.

**MILLER, BRYAN J,** Providence Coll, Providence, RI; JR; IM Sccr Hcky 88-; Dean Lst 89-; Intern IDS Financial Serv; Fnnc; Fnncl Plnnr.

**MILLER, CARL E,** Univ Of Sc At Columbia, Columbia, SC; SO; BS; Cmps Crsd Chrst 89-; Math Clb 90-; Lower Div Otstndng Math Stdnt 89-; Math.

**MILLER, CAROL J,** Sue Bennett Coll, London, KY; FR; BA; Term Oper Appalchn Cmptr Svcs London Ky 40741 86-; Med; Nrsng.

**MILLER, CATHERINE A,** Peace Coll, Raleigh, NC; FR; AA; Peace Stdnt Recr Assc IM Asstnt 90-; Peace Stdnt Govt Assc 90-; Phi Theta Kappa 90-; Natl Assc Acctnts Tres Elect 90-; Marshall; Peace Clb Tns; Chem; Pharm.

**MILLER, CHANTEL E,** Miami Jacobs Jr Coll Of Bus, Dayton, OH; FR; Coll Sec Intl Tr; Stdnt Advsry Comm VP; Legal Offc Admin; Legal Sec.

**MILLER, CHARLES T,** Comm Coll Algny Co Algny Cmps, Pittsburgh, PA; GD; Chefs/Cooks Assoc 86-; Abel Org 86-.

**MILLER, CHERYL K,** Central Fl Comm Coll, Ocala, FL; FR; AA BS; Cert 90-; Fla Cert 88; Cmptrs; Engr.

**MILLER, CHRISTOPHER A,** Univ Of Akron, Akron, OH; SR; BSME; Amer Soc Mech Engrs Stdnt Chptr Univ Of Akron 88-; Tau Beta Pi Ctlgr 88-; Tau Beta Pi; Knights Of Columbus 86-; Full Fllwshp/Asstnshp Grad Stdy Univ/Akron; Biomed Engr Dept; Mech Engrf Biomed Engr.

**MILLER, CHRISTOPHER T,** Md Inst Coll Of Art, Baltimore, MD; SR; BFA; Tchrs Asst Drwng Cls 88-89; Exhbtd At The Rinehart Glry/Fox Bldg Baltimore MD; Mxd Med/Poetry Gen Fine Arts; Trvl/Tch MFA.

**MILLER, CHRISTY G,** Univ Of West Fl, Pensacola, FL; JR; BA; AA Pensacola Jr Clg 90; Erly Chldhd Elem Educ; Tchg.

**MILLER, CINDY C,** Mayland Comm Coll, Spruce Pine, NC; FR; AAS; Chrch Yth Grp; Dns Lst.

**MILLER, CINDY M,** Northern Ky Univ, Highland Hts, KY; SR; BS; AA 89; Human Srvcs/Mental Hlth; Child Cnslrd.

**MILLER, COLLEEN L,** Univ Of New Haven, West Haven, CT; JR; BS; Mgmt/Info Sys; Sys Anlyst.

**MILLER, COLLEEN S,** Atlantic Comm Coll, Mays Landing, NJ; JR; BS; Phi Deta Lambda Future Bus Ldrs Treas 88-90; Peer Mentor Prog 88-89; Economics State Of NJ 90; Cmnty Project Drunk Driving State NJ 89; Cmnty Project Homelessness State NJ 90; Acctng & Attend Stockton Clge; AAS 90; Health Admnstrn.

**MILLER, CONNIE WALTON,** Univ Of Al At Birmingham, Birmingham, AL; SR; MED; BFA Univ Montevallo 82; Kappa Pi 80; IM 78; Glenwood Mntl Hlth Svc Tchng Prnt 86-; AL Schl Fine Arts Art Tchr 90-; AL Schl Perf Arts Art Tchr 88-; Kings Rnch Shlby Co Tchr/Thrpst 85-88; DAY Pgm Shlby Co Tchr/Thrpst 87; Education; Art/Spcl Ed.

**MILLER, CONSTANCE S,** Wv Northern Comm Coll, Wheeling, WV; SO; BS; Phi Theta Kappa 89-; Cmnctns/Engl.

**MILLER, COREY D,** Univ Of Tn At Knoxville, Knoxville, TN; GD; DVM; PSU Pre-Vet Clb 87-90; PSU Block/Bridle Clb 88-89; SCAVMA UTCVM 90-; Phi Eta Sigma 90-; Gldn Key 87-; Stndrd Bearer Anml Biosci Mjr Grad Crmny; BS PA State Univ; Vet Med.

**MILLER, CORLA Y,** Southern Vt Coll, Bennington, VT; FR; BA; Crmnl Jstc Assn; Bus Clb; MISA; Sftbl; Crmnl Jstc; Law.

**MILLER, CRYSTAL D,** Univ Of Nc At Charlotte, Charlotte, NC; SR; BSW; Scl Wrk Clb 90-F Golden Key; Scl Wrk; Grad Schl.

**MILLER, CRYSTAL L,** Hudson Valley Comm Coll, Troy, NY; SO; AS; Phi Theta Kappa 90; Prsdnts Lst GPA; Bsns Admnstrtn; Mgmt.

**MILLER, CYNTHIA E,** Allegheny Coll, Meadville, PA; JR; BA; SAGE 88-90; Stdnt Govt Altrnt Hl Rep 88-89; Stdnt Orntn Advsr 90-; Lambda Sigma 89-90; Allghny Comm Exchng 88-90; Brooks Hl Cncl VP 88-89; Engl; Educ-Coll Lvl.

**MILLER, DANA K,** Radford Univ, Radford, VA; JR; BS; Sclgy Anthrplgy Clb 90-; Pi Gamma Mu; Sclgy.

**MILLER, DANIEL A,** S U N Y Coll Of A & T Morrisvl, Morrisville, NY; SO; BA; Stdnt Govt 89; Hall Cncl-Pub Rels 89-90; Hall Cncl VP 90-; Deans Lst 90-; Sociology; Psych.

**MILLER, DANIEL J,** Duquesne Univ, Pittsburgh, PA; JR; BA; Alpha Phi Omega VP 90-; AA Scott Comm Coll 89; Engl; Mgmnt MBA.

**MILLER, DANIEL J,** Univ Of Miami, Coral Gables, FL; SR; Arch.

**MILLER, DANIEL S,** Pellissippi St Tech Comm Coll, Knoxville, TN; SR; Knxvlle Gem And Mnrl Scty Lbrrn 86-; Clntn Cr Clb 87-; Phi Theta Kappa; Smky Mt Antque Engne And Trctr Assn 87-; Tau Alpha Pi; Vsn Vol 90-; Chem; Eng.

**MILLER, DANIELLE L,** Fl St Univ, Tallahassee, FL; JR; BA; Fin Soc; Amer Mktg Assoc; Pre-Law Soc; Little Sis; Sigma Alpha Epsilon; Bus Fin; Corp Law.

**MILLER, DARLEEN N,** Fl St Univ, Tallahassee, FL; FR; March Chiefs 90; Phi Eta Sigma; Music; Therapy.

**MILLER, DARREN E,** Western New England Coll, Springfield, MA; JR; BA; AS Lbrl Arts Springfield Tech Comm Clg 86-89; Mktg; Mktg Mgr.

**MILLER, DAVID A,** Univ Of Miami, Coral Gables, FL; SO; BS; Soccer Cl V P 90-; Alpha Lambda Delta 89-; Sigma Alpha Mu 89-90; IM Soccer Cl 89-; Biomed Engr.

**MILLER, DAVID L,** Meridian Comm Coll, Meridian, MS; FR; AS; VICA.

**MILLER, DAVID P,** Garrett Comm Coll, Mchenry, MD; FR; Pblshd Comm Coll Lit Jrnl; Mech Eng; Engr.

**MILLER, DAVID S,** Kent St Univ Kent Cmps, Kent, OH; FR; MBA; Wghtlftng Clb 90-; Alpha Lambda Delta; Bus.

**MILLER, DAVID T,** Univ Of Ky, Lexington, KY; SR; BABS; Phi Beta Kappa 90-; Omicron Delta Kappa 90-; Alpha Epsilon Delta 87; Alpha Tau Omega 87-; Tchr Asst Biol Dept; Oswald Rsrcrh Cmptn Winner 89; Chmsty/Biol; Med Sci.

**MILLER, DAVID W,** Univ Of Tn At Knoxville, Knoxville, TN; SR; BS; Res Hall Assn Eastern MI Univ Flr Gov 87-89; Beta Gamma Sigma; Gldn Ky; Econ; Bus.

**MILLER, DAWN B,** Va Commonwealth Univ, Richmond, VA; JR; RN 81-; ASN John Tyler Comm Clg 81; Nursing; Nursing BSN.

**MILLER, DAWN M,** Radford Univ, Radford, VA; FR; BA; Clgte Chrstn Lf Flw Up Coord 90-; Hnrs Stdnt Assoc 90-; Soc Wrk; Fmly/Mrg Cnslng.

**MILLER, DE INA D,** Thomas Nelson Comm Coll, Hampton, VA; SO; Stdnt Cncl Sec 90-; Upsilon Gamma Eta 90-; Cmps Otrch Opprtnty Lg; AA; Art.

**MILLER, DEBERAH A,** Univ Of Montevallo, Montevallo, AL; SR; AL Assn Yng Chldrn 90-; AL Cncl Scl Studies 90-; Stdnt AL Educ Assn 90-; Summ Cum Laude; Lambda Sigma Pi 90-; Pres Lst; Kappa Delta Pi 90-; Phi Kappa Phi 90-; Phi Theta Kappa 89-; AAYC Outstndng Achvmnt Awd 90-; Pres Ldrshp Schlrshp 89-; Early Chldhd/Elem Ed; Tch Grade Schl.

**MILLER, DEBORAH S,** Univ Of Ky, Lexington, KY; JR; BS; Goldn Key 90-; Psi Chi 90-; Phi Eta Sigma 90-; Acdmc Excllnce Schlrshp 90-; Psychlgy/Eng.

**MILLER, DEBRA L,** Indiana Univ Of Pa, Indiana, PA; FR; BED; Bnkng 78-81 85-86; Elem Educ.

**MILLER, DENISE N,** Univ Of Al At Birmingham, Birmingham, AL; SR; BA; Bapt Stdnt Un Sen 88-90; Govt Assoc; Stdnt Occup Thrpy Assoc Mbr Comm 90-; Phi Theta Kappa 88-; Assoc Cntrl AL Comm Clg 90; Occpu Thrpy; Rehab Med.

**MILLER, DESMOND R A,** Miami Dade Comm Coll North, Miami, FL; SR; Acctg.

**MILLER, DIANNE M,** Davis Coll, Toledo, OH; GD; AS; Data Prcssng.

**MILLER, DONALD Y,** Averett Coll, Danville, VA; SO; Bptst Stdnt Union Evnglsm 90-; Averett Plyrs 89-90; Sngrs Lbrn 90-.

**MILLER, DONNOUAM A,** Miami Dade Comm Coll, Miami, FL; SO; BA; Snppr Creek Hmownrs Assn Fnncl Advsr 90-; Accntng.

**MILLER, DOROTHY B,** Va Commonwealth Univ, Richmond, VA; BSN; Phi Kappa Phi 90-; AAS Felician Clg 74; Nrsng; Geropsychtry.

**MILLER, DOUGLAS J,** Le Moyne Coll, Syracuse, NY; JR; BS; Mktg Clb 90-; Alpha Sigma Nu; Edward M O'donnell Mdl Frshmn Bsn Adm; Vincent J Smith Mdl Soph Bsn Adm; IM Bsktbl 90-; Delta Mu Delta; Bsn Adm.

**MILLER, DOUGLAS R,** Univ Of Rochester, Rochester, NY; SO; BA; Vrsty Wrstlng 87-90; Elctd Mbr Stdnt/Fclty Appls Com 90-; Invstmnt Clb 90-; Elctd Sec 90; Wght Lftng Clb Soup Ktchn Vol 88; Deans List 90; Wrstling Vrsty Lafayette Clg; Ecnmcs; Finance/Bus/Bnkng.

**MILLER, ELIZABETH A,** Pa St Univ Main Cmps, University Pk, PA; JR; BED; Chrs 89-90; Educ Std Cncl; Alpha Lambda Delta 89-; Elem/Erly Chldhd Ed; Tchr.**

**MILLER, ELIZABETH K,** Salisbury St Univ, Salisbury, MD; JR; BA; IM 89-90; Spnsh Clb 89-; Phi Eta Sigma 90-; Phi Kappa Phi; Hnrs Prog 89-90; Acad Awd 89-90; Hnrs Prog Awd 90-; Engl/Spnsh; Intl Rel.

**MILLER, ELIZABETH T,** Coll Of Charleston, Charleston, SC; JR; BA; Nwsppr; Pltcl Sci Clb; Hstry Clb; Hstry Hnr Scty; Hstry Pltcl Sci; Frgn Corres.

**MILLER, ELLEN D,** Ga St Univ, Atlanta, GA; SR; CEC; PAGE; PTA; AA Dekalb Clg 80; Educ/Mntlly Rtrd; Teach.

**MILLER, ERIC A,** Oh Univ-Southern Cmps, Ironton, OH; SR; BBA; AAS Rio Grande Clg 82; Gen Bus; Finance/Bnkng/Invstmnts.

**MILLER, ERIC S,** Wv Univ, Morgantown, WV; JR; BA; Sigma Phi Epsilon 90-; Dry Ridge Fire Dept 89-; Pres Lst 90-; Deans Lst 89-; Schlrshp Harold Cathard Fund 90-; Mech Engr.

**MILLER, ERIC S,** Schenectady County Comm Coll, Schenectady, NY; SR; Pres Lst; AS; Food/Rstrnt Mgmt.

**MILLER, ERIC TODD,** Morehouse Coll, Atlanta, GA; JR; BA; Ed Clb; Morehouse Bus Assoc; NAACP Urbn Lg; Omega Psi Phi Cmmtt Chr 89-90; Ed; Ed Amdn.

**MILLER, ERICA K,** Univ Of South Fl, Tampa, FL; FR; BS; Themis Hnr Scty 90-; Blgy; Med Dctr.

**MILLER, ETHEL M,** Hillsborough Comm Coll, Tampa, FL; FR; Spcl Olympcs; Pizza Hot Rest Mgmt 87-; Cmptr Prog.

**MILLER, FRANKLIN K,** Wv Univ, Morgantown, WV; SR; BSME; ASME; SAE; Tau Beta Pi; Mech Engr; Engr.

**MILLER, GAYLE K,** Radford Univ, Radford, VA; SR; BBA; Intervrsty Christian Flwshp Sm Grp Ldr 89-; Intern Human Resources 89; AA Villa Julie Coll 89; Human Resource Mgmt; Coll Adm.

**MILLER, GEORGE E,** Univ Of North Fl, Jacksonville, FL; SR; BSC; Phi Kappa Phi; Gldn Ky; Blgy.

**MILLER, GERALD T,** S U N Y Coll At Fredonia, Fredonia, NY; JR; BS; Deans List 88-; AAS Erie Comm Coll S 90; Bus Admn; Fin Analyst.

**MILLER, GREGORY D,** Univ Of Sc At Aiken, Aiken, SC; JR; BS; Sci Clb 90; Bio; Med.

**MILLER, GWENDOLYN M,** Univ Of The Dist Of Columbia, Washington, DC; JR; BS; Presby Church Funds Comm Treas 81-; Deacon Bd Sec 77-80; NAACP 81-; NCBA; Ft Davis Civic Assn 63-; Retired Fed Employee 87-; AS 90; Econ; Bus Mgmt.

**MILLER, HASLYN A,** S U N Y Coll Of Tech At Frmgdl, Farmingdale, NY; FR; Arspc Tchnlgy.

**MILLER, HEATHER E,** Univ Of Montevallo, Montevallo, AL; FR; BFA; Internatl Art Frtrnty Treas; Art; Advrtsng.

**MILLER, HEATHER E,** Oh Wesleyan Univ, Delaware, OH; FR; Pres Clb 90-; Sg 90-; Phi Eta Sigma; Habitat Humnty 90-; Big Pal Ltl Pal Brd Mbr 90-; Proj Hope 90-; Env Stds/Elem Educ; Tch.

**MILLER, HERBERT A,** Northeast State Tech Comm Coll, Blountville, TN; SO; Stu Chptr IEEE 90-; Otstndg Stu Awrd 90-; Elctrnc Engr.

**MILLER, HOLLY K,** Indiana Univ Of Pa, Indiana, PA; SR; English Club Treas 87-88; Reserve Officer Training Corps Co Cmdr 89-90; Sigma Tau Delta; Sigma Delta Pi; Student Tchng; BS In Ed; English/Spanish; Tchng.

**MILLER, INGRID N,** Wagner Coll, Staten Island, NY; FR; Amnsty Intrnatl 90-; Rd Crss 90-; Pol Sci; Law.

**MILLER, IRENE A,** Oh St Univ At Newark, Newark, OH; SO; BS; Honor Society; Aviation.

**MILLER, JACQUIE M,** Middle Tn St Univ, Murfreesboro, TN; GD; BS; Sthstrn Arprt Mngrs Assoc.

**MILLER, JAMES A,** Univ Of South Fl, Tampa, FL; SR; BA; Natl Hnrs Soc 87-; Beta Club 87-; Art; Cmmrcl Artst.

**MILLER, JAMES B,** Tomlinson Coll, Cleveland, TN; FR; BA; Chrstn Stu; Pstr.

**MILLER, JAMES D,** Bowling Green St Univ At Huron, Huron, OH; SO; BA; Soc Mfg Engrs Treas 90-; Elctrncs Lab Asst 90-; Elctrncs; Engrg.

**MILLER, JAMES F,** Dowling Coll, Oakdale Li, NY; JR; BS; Crew Tm 88-; Cooper Ed Advisory Brd 90-; Conserv Awrns Comm; Intshp Port Authority NJ/NJ JFK Intnl Airport 90; Aeronautics/Mgt; Admin.

**MILLER JR, JAMES PERRY,** Gaston Coll, Dallas, NC; FR; BA; Pltcl Sci; Crmnl Law.

**MILLER, JANICE A,** Schenectady County Comm Coll, Schenectady, NY; SO; AAS; Deans Lst 89-90; Soroptimist Intl Schlrshp Awrd 90-; Acctng; CPA.

**MILLER, JEANINE M,** Univ Of Ky, Lexington, KY; JR; BA; SADD Pres 90-; Peer Edctr 90-; Stdnt Hlth Advsry Cncl 90-; Omicron Delta Kappa; Lances; Lambda Sigma; Alpha Gamma Delta Hse Chrmn 88-; Univ Hosp Emerg Dept 90; Kidney Fndtn Cntrl KY; Sunday Sch Tchr; Deans Lst 88-; Walt Disney Wrld Coll Pgm; Hlth Edn.

**MILLER, JEFF L,** Central St Univ, Wilberforce, OH; JR; BS; Pol Sci Assmbly Pres; Pol Sci; Law.

**MILLER, JEFFREY R,** Comm Coll Algny Co Algny Cmps, Pittsburgh, PA; SO; BA; U S Air Force Vets Assn 90-; Crim Just Clb Pr 90-; Powerlifting Tm; AAS Cmcnty Clg Allegheny Cnty; Admin Of Crim Just; Law.

**MILLER, JEFFREY S,** Columbia Union Coll, Takoma Park, MD; SR; BS; Hlth Fclts Assn MD; Admnstr Trng Spnsrd Mid Atlantic Advntst Hlth Servs; Dir Oprtns Shady Grove Advntst Nrsng/Rehab Ctr 88-; AA Montgomery Clg 81; Hlth Care Admnstrtn.

**MILLER, JENIFER D,** George Washington Univ, Washington, DC; FR; BA; Hillel 90-; Pol Sci; Envrmntl Law.

**MILLER, JENNIFER A,** Edinboro Univ Of Pa, Edinboro, PA; SO; BA; Hons Pgm 90-; Emplyd Bel-Aire Htl Erie PA 89-; Bus/Acctg; CPA.

**MILLER, JENNIFER L,** Eckerd Coll, St Petersburg, FL; SO; BA; ISA 90-; ELS Asst 90-; Wrk Study Fncl Aid Ofc 90-; Intl Studies; Intl Bus.

**MILLER, JENNIFER L,** Fl St Univ, Tallahassee, FL; JR; Flying High Circus 90-; AA 90; Eng Ed; High Schl Tchr.

**MILLER, JENNIFER S,** Cheyney Univ Of Pa, Cheyney, PA; SR; BED; Kappa Delta Pi VP 89-; Jack Jill Inc 88-; Big Bro Sis Brd 82-85; Cert FCC 72; Elem Educ; Tchr.

**MILLER, JENNIFER S,** Indiana Univ Of Pa, Indiana, PA; FR; BA; Kappa Delta Pi; Edctn; Elmntry Tchr.

**MILLER, JEWEL V,** Glassboro St Coll, Glassboro, NJ; SR; BA; Estrn Str; Mntr Tchncn 84-; Cetf Mddlsx Cnty Vctnl Schl 79; Sclgy; MSW Adlscnt Cnslr.

**MILLER, JOANNA,** Saint Thomas Univ, Miami, FL; SR; Prnt Tchr Assn Pres 85-87; Elem Ed; Tchng.

**MILLER, JOE R,** Ms St Univ, Miss State, MS; JR; BPA; Phi Kappa Phi 90-; Gamma Beta Phi 89-; Phi Eta Sigma 88-89; Alpha Lambda Delta 88-89; Hnrs Prog 88-; Beta Alpha Psi 90-; Presidents Schlr 89-90; Sr Acctng Schlrshp; Robert E Byrd Cngrssnl Schlrshp 88-89; Acctng.

**MILLER, JOHN C,** Middle Tn St Univ, Murfreesboro, TN; SR; BBA; Financial Mgmnt Treas; Deans Cir; Beta Alpha Psi; Beta Gamma Sigma; IM Sftbl; Finance; Mgmnt.

**MILLER, JOHN F,** Kent St Univ Stark Cmps, North Canton, OH; SO; BS; Pathway Vol 90-; U S Army 2 Yrs E-4 Spclst 87-89; Geo; Rsrch.

**MILLER, JOHN M,** Embry Riddle Aeronautical Univ, Daytona Beach, FL; SR; BS; Entrtnmnt/Stdnt Act 89-90; Hon Roll; Deans Lst 86-; Wlly Bl 90; Rcqtbl 88-; Cert Bill Law Avtn FAA 88-; Cert ERAU-FAA 89-; Avtn Maint Tech; Pilot.

**MILLER, JON PATRICK,** Univ Of Md At Eastern Shore, Princess Anne, MD; SO; BS; Acctng Clb 90-; VITA 90; Accounting; Cpa.

**MILLER, JOSEPH E,** Comm Coll Algny Co Algny Cmps, Pittsburgh, PA; SO; BA; Assoc/Acctg; Acctg; CPA.

**MILLER, JOSEPH R,** S U N Y Coll Of Tech At Alfred, Alfred, NY; FR; AAS; Yth Bsktbl 90-; Crtlnd Slw Ptch Sftbl; Bus Admin; Acctg.

**MILLER, JOY L,** Univ Of Akron, Akron, OH; SR; BED; Aces; Kappa Delta Pi; Gldn Key 90-; Phi Eta Sigma; Schlrshp Gnrl Die Cstrs; Elem Ed; MA Admin.

**MILLER, JULIE E,** Longwood Coll, Farmville, VA; JR; BS; Riding Tm 88-; Alpha Lambda Delta 88-; Phi Kappa Phi; Kappa Delta Pi; Edctn; Tchr.

**MILLER, JULIE L,** Medical Coll Of Ga, Augusta, GA; JR; GA Assc Nrsg Stdnts 90-; Wvmkrs 90-; Stdnt Nrs Apprntcshp Prog 90-.

**MILLER, JULIEANNE L,** Atlantic Comm Coll, Mays Landing, NJ; FR; Law.

**MILLER, KAREN M,** Bloomfield Coll, Bloomfield, NJ; JR; Alpha Chi 90-; Prjct Admin ITT Avncs Nutley NJ 84-; Acctng/CPA; Pblc Acctnt.

**MILLER, KARL B,** Western New England Coll, Springfield, MA; SR; BA; Tech Sprt Cnsltnt Mass Mutual Life Ins Co 79-; AS Holyoke Comm Coll 88; Bus; Mgmt.

**MILLER, KATHLEEN M,** Ny Univ, New York, NY; SO; BA; Psych.

**MILLER, KATHRYN R,** Hillsborough Comm Coll, Tampa, FL; SO; BA; Fl Inst Of CPA; Accntng Prncpls Perf Rcgnzd; Bsnss Admin; Mngmnt.

**MILLER, KEITH E,** Ms St Univ, Miss State, MS; SO; BE; Gamma Beta Phi 90-; Blgcl Eng.

**MILLER, KELLI N,** Kent St Univ Kent Cmps, Kent, OH; JR; BA; Gldn Key; Crmnl Jstc; Law Schl.

**MILLER, KELLY LYNN,** Wv Univ At Parkersburg, Parkersburg, WV; FR; BSW; Soc Work.

**MILLER, KENNETH N,** Middle Tn St Univ, Murfreesboro, TN; SR; BS; Delta Upsilon Univ FL VP 86-; Crmnl Justice Admin; Fed Law Enfrcmnt.

**MILLER, KIM A,** Univ Of Med & Dentistry Of Nj, Newark, NJ; SR; BS; APTA 89-; Lambda Alpha Sigma 89-; Rahway Hosp 90; Sbrbn Phys Therpy Cntr; Welkind Rehab Hosp; Phys Therpy.

**MILLER, KIMBERLY K,** Univ Of Sc At Columbia, Columbia, SC; SR; BS; Rho Chi VP 90-; Phi Beta Kappa 89-; Gldn Ky 89-; Kappa Epsilon Pres 89-; Phi Lambda Sigma Pres 90-; Acad Stdnts Phrmcy 89-; Mrtr Brd; Gamma Beta Phi 88-; Ntl Phrmctcl Cnsl Itrn-Smthkln; Phrmcy.

**MILLER, KRISTIE L,** Daytona Beach Comm Coll, Daytona Beach, FL; FR; Anthropology.

**MILLER, KRISTIN M,** Univ Of Akron, Akron, OH; SR; BSBA; Phi Eta Sigma 87-; Alpha Lambda Delta 87-; Gldn Key 89-; Delta Gamma Ast Rush Chrmn 88-; Pllsbry Schlrshp; Mrktng; MBA.

**MILLER, KRISTINE Y,** Wv Northern Comm Coll, Wheeling, WV; FR; MED; Engl Cmpstn Hon Cls 91; Engl/Lit/Elem Ed; Tchng.

**MILLER, KRISTY L,** Thomas Nelson Comm Coll, Hampton, VA; JR; PHD; Psych.

**MILLER, LABAN D,** Asbury Theological Sem, Wilmore, KY; GD; MDIV; Theta Phi 90-; Assoc Minister 85-88; BM Oh St Univ 81; MA Ohio St Univ 83; Theo; Religious Ldrshp.

**MILLER, LAURA B,** Longwood Coll, Farmville, VA; SO; BA; Intrvrsty Chrstn Fllwshp 89-; Wsley Fndtn Stdnt Fllwshp VP 89-; Orntatn Ldr 89-; Ambsdrs 89-; Fdrtn Stdnt Scl Wrkrs 89-; Camerata Sngrs 90-; Acdmc Achvmnt Schlrshp 89-; Deans Lst; Scl Wrk.

**MILLER, LAURA L,** Columbia Coll, Columbia, SC; FR; BS; Alpha Lmbda Delta 90-; Vrsty Volleyball 90-; Business.

**MILLER, LAURA M,** Northern Ky Univ, Highland Hts, KY; FR; BA; Hnrs Pgm 90-; Hnrs Clb 90-; Chldrns Hosp 85-; Pres Schlp 90-; Elem Ed; Tchr.

**MILLER, LAUREN L,** Univ Of Pittsburgh, Pittsburgh, PA; JR; BS; Engineers Wk Com 90-; Phi Eta Sigma 89; Merit Schlr/Schlrshp 88-; Hnrs Convocation Honoree 90-; NASA Lewis Research Ctr Intern; Mechanical Engineering.

**MILLER, LAURIE F,** Univ Of Montevallo, Montevallo, AL; SO; BS; Civitan Clb; Chi Omega Foods Chrmn; Home Econ/Dietetics; Nutritionist.

**MILLER, LEE FEE C,** Bristol Univ, Bristol, TN; GD; MBA; IIE VP 90-; SME; Prsnl/Sfty Spclst; BS ETSU 88; Prsnl/Hmn Rsrcs; Sfty Engr.

**MILLER, LINDA ELIZABETH,** Univ Of Cincinnati-Clrmnt Coll, Batavia, OH; SO; BA; Reunion Comm 86-; Secretarial 81-; Marketing; Communications.

**MILLER, LINDA S,** Springfield Tech Comm Coll, Springfield, MA; BA; Deans Admin Asst; Assoc Liberal Arts 91; Art Therapy.

**MILLER, LISA M,** Memphis St Univ, Memphis, TN; SR; BPS; Rcrtn Prks Scty 84-86; Univ Hnrs Prgm 83-84; Prvt Donor Schlrshp 83-87; Univ Coll Almn Schlrsp 90-; Crss Cntr Vol 90-; Rsdnt Cnslr Hosp 90-; Scl Wrk.

**MILLER, LORI W,** Indiana Univ Of Pa, Indiana, PA; JR; BED; Dns Lst 89-; Elem Ed; Tchg.

**MILLER, LYNN K,** East Carolina Univ, Greenville, NC; SR; BFA; Appln State Ski Clb 86-87; Pi Kappa Phi Ltl Sis 87-88; Ceramic Gld 90-; Art/Ceramics; Jewelry.

**MILLER, LYNNE M,** Univ Of Dayton, Dayton, OH; FR; IM Sftbll; IM Flg Ftbll 90-; BSKTBLL 90-; Elec Eng.

**MILLER, MACK A,** Ms St Univ, Miss State, MS; SR; BS; Stdnt Cncl Repr 89-90; Hnrs Cncl Repr 87-88; Inst Elctrcl Elctrncs Engrs 87-; Omicron Delta Kappa Secy Treas 90-; Mortar Brd Treas 90-; Phi Kappa Phi 89-; Phi Gamma Delta Correspndng Secy 89-; Hall Fame 90-; Blue Key; Hnrs Schlr; Elctrcl Engrng; Info Cnsltng.

**MILLER, MARCIA A,** Daytona Beach Comm Coll, Daytona Beach, FL; FR; AS; PTA 89-; Pres Lst 90; Acctng Tech; Pyrl A/P Supvr.

**MILLER, MARGARET S,** Birmingham Southern Coll, Birmingham, AL; SO; BA.

**MILLER, MARGOT J,** Va St Univ, Petersburg, VA; SR; BS; Alpha Kappa Mu; Wmns Aglow Flwshp Pres 85-; Acctg; Tchng.

**MILLER, MARILYNN ELAINE,** Univ Of West Fl, Pensacola, FL; SR; BS; Stdnt Hm Ec Assn Pres 90; Alpha Sigma Lambda 90; Delta Kappa Pi; Outstndng Stdnt Yr 90-; FL Hm Ec Assn; Hm Ec Ed; Tchr.

**MILLER, MARK W,** Middle Tn St Univ, Murfreesboro, TN; FR; BA; Dns Lst; Engl; Educ.

**MILLER, MARK W,** Hudson Valley Comm Coll, Troy, NY; SR; AOS; Elec Cnstrctn And Mntnce Clb 89-; Mntnce Mchnc AP Cntrl Schls 86-; AAS 75; Elec Cnstrctn And Mntnce; Indstrl Elec.

**MILLER, MAUDEEN A,** Wv Northern Comm Coll, Wheeling, WV; GD; BA; AS Acctng 90; BA Jesuit Coll; Hmn Rsrc Mgmt; Hlth Care.

**MILLER, MELANIE J,** Univ Of Md At Eastern Shore, Princess Anne, MD; SR; Yrbk; Stdnt Rehab Assn VP; Am Physcl Thrpy Assn.

**MILLER, MELISSA A,** Germanna Comm Coll, Locust Grove, VA; FR; BA; Stdnt Govt; Stdnt Nwsppr Stff Wrtr; Psych; Psychlgst.

**MILLER, MELISSA A,** Lindsey Wilson Coll, Columbia, KY; SR; MBA; Bapt Stdnt Un 88- Pres 90-; Stdnt Govt Assn Treas 89-; Phi Beta Lambda Treas 90-; BA 91; Bus Admn; Admn Non Profit.**

**MILLER, MELISSA A,** Villanova Univ, Villanova, PA; SR; BA; Phi Kappa Phi; Lbrl Arts; Bus MBA.

**MILLER, MELISSA A,** Mayland Comm Coll, Spruce Pine, NC; FR; AAS; Phi Theta Kappa; Crmnl Jstce Prtctve Serv Tchnlgy; Jvnle Ct.

**MILLER, MELISSA D,** Christian Brothers Univ, Memphis, TN; FR; Psychology/Biology; Occupational Therapy.

**MILLER, MELISSA G,** Fl St Univ, Tallahassee, FL; JR; BM; Natl Flute Assc 88-; FL Flute Assc 89-; Gldn Key 90-; Sigma Alpha Iota Sec 89-; FL Flute Assc Coll Cmptn; Schl Music Schlrshp 90; Deans Lst 89-; Music; Flute Per.

**MILLER, MELISSA J,** Longwood Coll, Farmville, VA; SR; Stdnt Educ Assc Pres 86-90; Ambssdr 86-90; Plyrs Pres 86-90; GEIST 90; Alpha Psi Omega Vp 86-; Sigma Alpha Iota 89-; VA Price Waller Schlrshp 89; B Ed 90; Elem Educ; Pre Schl Tchr.

**MILLER, MELISSA L,** Radford Univ, Radford, VA; JR; BS; Cath Student Assoc 88-; Delta Zeta Activ Chrmn 89-; Crim Justice; Juvenile Corrtl Facility.

**MILLER, MELLESSA M,** Memphis St Univ, Memphis, TN; JR; Espirt De Corps 90-; Amer Chem Socty 90-; Gamma Beta Phi 89-; Biology/Chmstry; Medicine.

**MILLER, MICHAEL D,** Univ Of Cincinnati, Cincinnati, OH; JR; BM; Symphny Bnd 88-; Phi Mu Alpha Tres 89-; Albert B Voorheis Mem Schlrshp 88-; Helga Daley Schlrshp; Music Oboe Prfrmnc; Prfsnl Mscn.

**MILLER, MICHAEL DAVID,** Marshall University, Huntington, WV; JR; Accntng Clb 90; Deans Lst; Ftbl 88; Accntng/Fnce; Law.

**MILLER, MICHAEL I,** Alcorn St Univ, Lorman, MS; FR; BS; Hnr Stdnt Orgnztn 90; Tennis Team 90; Special Olympics 88; Cmptr Scnce; Cmptr Eng.

**MILLER, MICHAEL P,** S U N Y Coll Of Tech At Alfred, Alfred, NY; FR; BS; IM Spts; Dns Lst; Elec Engr; Engr.

**MILLER, MICHELE R,** Glassboro St Coll, Glassboro, NJ; SR; BA; Stdnt Wrkr Asst Drctr 89-; Gamma Tau Sigma; Alpha Delta Epsilon Scl Chrmn 90-; Intrnshp Rancocas Vly Mmrl Hsptl Plbc Rltns Dpt; Cmmnctns; Pblc Rltns.

**MILLER, MICHELLE A,** Mount Aloysius Jr Coll, Cresson, PA; FR; Erly Chldh Edctn; Elem Tchr.

**MILLER, MICHELLE C,** Wittenberg Univ, Springfield, OH; FR; BS; Nwspr Prdctn Asst 90-; Alpha Lambda Delta; Alumni Schlrshp 90-; Bio; Envrnmntl Stds.

**MILLER, MICHELLE R,** Marshall University, Huntington, WV; FR; BBA; Inter Coll Vllybll Tm 90; Dean Lst; Vllybll 90-; Bus; Bus Exec.

**MILLER, NANCY K,** Catawba Valley Comm Coll, Hickory, NC; FR; AAS; Gamma Beta Phi 90-; Acctg/Bus Cmptr Prgrmmg.

**MILLER, NETTYEMARIE M,** Savannah St Coll, Savannah, GA; FR; BA; Mass Cmnctns Clb Pres 90-; Cls Pres; Nwspr Cntrbtg Edtr 90-; Alpha Aux VP 90-; Assoc Orgnl Man 90-; Sclgy.

**MILLER, NICHOLAS M,** Union Coll, Barbourville, KY; FR; BA; Stdnt Actvts Bd 90-; Stdnt Pblctn 90-; Union Schlr 90-; Faulkner Rushton Essay Awd; Varsity Bsbl 90-; Hist; CIA.

**MILLER, NICOLE M,** Northern Ky Univ, Highland Hts, KY; FR; XNRA; Nrsng; RN.

**MILLER, NITA P,** Middle Tn St Univ, Murfreesboro, TN; SO; BS; Brdcst/Jrnlsm; News/Feature Rptr.

**MILLER, PAMELA I,** James Madison University, Harrisonburg, VA; SO; BS; Cmps Crsd Chrst 89-; AEYC 89-; Pres Lst 89-90; Dns Lst 90-; Hnrs Prm 90-; Psych/Erly Chldhd Ed; Elem Schl Tchr.

**MILLER, PAMELA LYNNE,** Bridgewater Coll, Bridgewater, VA; SR; BS; Peace Forum Co Pres 89-90; Church Of Brthrn Peac Comm 88-; Intl Clb 88-; Commn Grnd Bd; Brethren Fllwshp 87-88; Stdnt Cnslr 90-; Soc Wrkr; Honduras Wrkcmp; IM Bsktbl/Sccr 87-88; Sociology; Soc Wrk/Cnslng.

**MILLER, PATRICIA A,** Saint Francis Coll, Loretto, PA; SR; BA; Psych Clb Sec 87-; Instmntl Enxmbl Pres 87-; Biology Clb 87-; Clg Hnrs Soc 90-; Hnrs Prog 87-; Dorothy Day Peace/Justice Ctr Vol 87-; Acad Schlrshp 87-; IM Sftbl/Sccr 88/90; Psych; Grad Schl.

**MILLER, PATRICIA H,** Springfield Tech Comm Coll, Springfield, MA; SR; AS; Hm/Schl Asso 87-; AS 75; Nrsng.

**MILLER, PAUL J,** Univ Of Med & Dentistry Of Nj, Newark, NJ; JR; BS; Deans Lst 89-90; Deans Lst CCM 81-89; Hgh Hnrs CCM 89; Rt Suprvsr 90; Invntry Supr; AA 89; Hlth Prfssns.

**MILLER, PENNY L,** Bapt Bible Coll & Seminary, Clarks Summit, PA; JR; BS; Alpha Gamma Epsilon; Missions.

**MILLER, PETER W,** Northeast State Tech Comm Coll, Blountville, TN; GD; AAS; Amer Dsgn Drftng Assn 89-; Drftng/Dsgn Tchncn.

**MILLER, RAYMOND M,** Univ Of Cincinnati, Cincinnati, OH; JR; BS; Constr Stdnt Assn V P 90; Assctd Gnrl Cntrctrs Pres 90; Prof Lnd Srvyrs OH Dlgte 87-88; AS Cincinnati Tech Clg 88; Cnstr Mgmt; Prjct Mgmt.

**MILLER, REBECCA LYNN,** Western Piedmont Comm Coll, Morganton, NC; SO; BS; Phi Theta Kappa 89-; Intrnshp Options Crisis Cnslng Victim Advocate; Achvmnt Awd Drug Alcohol Tech 89-; NC Regstrd Protctve Servcs Ind Sec Offcr 87-; AAS; Psychology; Mntl Hlth.

**MILLER, REBECCA S,** Univ Of Sc At Columbia, Columbia, SC; SO; BA; Mdl UN Sec 89-; Twrs Cncl Sec 90; Brny Govt Hl Repr 89-90; Tutor Iltrcy 90-; IM Scr 89; Internatl Stds; Govt Wrk.

**MILLER, RENAE R,** Indiana Univ Of Pa, Indiana, PA; JR; BS; RHA 88-; Natl Cmctns Coord 89-; Act Brd 89-; Phi Sigma Pi Natl 89-90; Theta Phi Alpha; Big Bros/Big Sis 89-; Campus G S 88-90; Deans Lst 89-; Rehab; Psych.

**MILLER, RICHARD D,** Marshall University, Huntington, WV; SR; Natl Mgmt Assoc 90-; BBA 90; Mgmt.

**MILLER, RICHARD F,** Temple Univ, Philadelphia, PA; SR; MD; Summa Cum Laude; Pres Schlr; Claude C/Mary Carson Bowman Awd High GPA Arts/Sci 90-; Dalhousie Univ Vars Vlybl; Mntl Hlth Tech 86-; BA; Psych; Med/Spclz Pedtrcs.

**MILLER, RICHARD T,** Atlantic Union Coll, S Lancaster, MA; GD; MA; Std Asc VP 89-90; Advntst Intclgt Asc Natl Dlgt 89-90; Cls PR Dir 88-89; Hvrd Natl Mdl UN Dlgt 90; Lncstrn Nwspr Rptr 88-90; Crew Clb Treas 88-89; Natl Hnr Soc 84-90; Phi Alpha Theta 90; Amer Red Crs 87-; Vol Peace; BA 90; Intl Rltns/Dplmcy; Law/Sttsmnshp.

**MILLER, ROBIN C,** Univ Of Nc At Greensboro, Greensboro, NC; SR; BS; Assn Edctn Yng Chldrn Prsdnt 86-; Intrcncl Advsry Comm Schl Hmn Envrnmntl Sci; Gldn Chain 88-; Kappa Omicron Nu 88-; Alpha Phi Omega 88-; Stdnt Exclnc Awd 90; Otstndng Snr Dpt Chld Dvlpmnt; Erly Chldhd Dvlpmnt; Tchr Chld Care Cntr.

**MILLER, RODNEY J,** Wv Northern Comm Coll, Wheeling, WV; FR; BA.

**MILLER JR, RONALD J,** Univ Of Ky, Lexington, KY; SO; Hold Patent Issued Last July/Invention Electronic Arch Ruler; Elctrcl Engr.

**MILLER JR, RONALD LEE,** Columbia Union Coll, Takoma Park, MD; SR; BA; Sls Mgr; AA York Clg 84; Busn Mgmt; Mktg Mgr.

**MILLER, S AYANNA,** Fl A & M Univ, Tallahassee, FL; FR; BS; Pre Physical Thrpy Clb; Frshmn Class Advsry Bd; Phi Eta Sigma; Deans Lst 90-; Leander L Boykin Awd; Sci; Phy Thrpy.

**MILLER, SANDRA A,** Davis Coll, Toledo, OH; AS; Admin Sec And Comps.

**MILLER, SARAH L,** Univ Of Nc At Asheville, Asheville, NC; SO; BA; Theatre Drama Dept 89-; Phi Eta Sigma 90-; Alpha Phi Omega Pblcty Ofcr 89-90; Outstndg Acad Achvmnt Drama Dept 89-90; Tutor Hill Street Mid Sch Lit Pgm 90-; Theater Arts; Edn K-12.

**MILLER, SCOTT,** S U N Y Coll Of Tech At Delhi, Delhi, NY; SR; AS.

**MILLER, SCOTT A,** Owensboro Comm Coll, Owensboro, KY; BS; Photogrphy Clb; IM 100 Mile Clb; BS Univ Louisville 83; Acctg.

**MILLER, SHANNON L,** Univ Of North Fl, Jacksonville, FL; JR; BA; Golden Key 90-; AA Fla Comm Clg Jcksnvl 90; Elem Educ; Teacher.

**MILLER, SHANNON Y,** Wv Univ At Parkersburg, Parkersburg, WV; FR; BA; Psych; Cnslg.

**MILLER, SHARI L,** Carnegie Mellon Univ, Pittsburgh, PA; SR; BA; BACCHUS 89-90; Res Asst/Res For Life Prog 88-90; Prog Asst Head R A 90-; Andrew Carnegie Slchlr Soc; Mortar Bd Sr Hnr Soc; Zets 87-; Womens Track Tm; Intern Della Femina Mcnanee WCRS Inc 89-90; Intern Negley Nrsng Rehap Ctr 90-; Prof Writing; Ph D Cnslng Psych.

**MILLER, SHARON G,** Alcorn St Univ, Lorman, MS; SR; BS; ROTC; Tnns; Prshng Rfls Sec 89-90; Distg Mltry Grad; Sec Sci; US Army Ofcr.

**MILLER, SHEILA ELIZABETH,** Miami Dade Comm Coll North, Miami, FL; GD; Acctg.

**MILLER, SHELLAYNE M,** Waycross Coll, Waycross, GA; SO; BS; Sigma Sci Club Secre/Treas 90-; Children Of Am Reval Scty Pres 70-; Daughters Of Am Rev 90-; AA Black Hawk Clg 88; Chemistry/Ed; High Schl Chemistry.

**MILLER, SHERRI C,** Bluefield Coll, Bluefield, VA; FR; Hist; Coll Prof.

**MILLER, SHERYL J,** Albertus Magnus Coll, New Haven, CT; FR; BA; Miss Jr Amer Clb 90; Explr Prog; Cmmnctns Or Sclgy; Wrtr Or Soc Wrk.

**MILLER, SHERYL LYNN,** Va Commonwealth Univ, Richmond, VA; SR; BFA; Natl Ed Assoc; VA Ed Assoc; Stdnt Ed Assoc VCU; Golden Key; Dns Lst 89-; Hnrs Pgm 89-; AA Bucks Co Comm Clge 89; Theatre Ed; Prof.**

**MILLER, SHERYL M,** Univ Of Miami, Coral Gables, FL; SR; BS; Cnmtc Arts Cmmssn Sec 89-90; Hmcmng Exec Cmmtt 89; Wmn Cmmnctns; Gldn Ky; Delta Gamma Coor Sec 90-; Dean Lst; Sally Jesse Rapheal Show Intern; Prvst Lst; Hnrs Prog 88-; Cmmnctns; Law.

**MILLER, SHON E,** West Liberty St Coll, West Liberty, WV; SO; BA; Tutr Cnslr; Sec Educ Soc Sci; Tch.

**MILLER, SNOW LYS,** Savannah Coll Of Art & Design, Savannah, GA; FR; JBFA; Butler Memorial Schlrshp 90-; Fiber Arts.

**MILLER, STACEY Y,** Meridian Comm Coll, Meridian, MS; SO; AA; Ambsdrs 89-; Nwspr Stf 90-; Pen Pals; Phi Theta Kappa 90-; H M Ivy Awrd; Pre Med; Pedtrn.

**MILLER, STACI A,** William Carey Coll, Hattiesburg, MS; SR; BSB; Chrldr; Omicron Delta Kappa; Gamma Chi; Deans Lst; Acctg; CPA.

**MILLER, STEPHEN L,** Hillsborough Comm Coll, Tampa, FL; FR; AA; Phi Theta Kappa; Electronic Tech Genl Cntrctr; Pre Eng; Elec Eng.

**MILLER, STEVE P,** Univ Of West Fl, Pensacola, FL; GD; BS; Assoc Gen Contr Stdnt Chap 90-; Campus Spnsrd I M Sprts 90; Res Const 81-86; AS Gulf Coast Comm Clg 87; Bldg Const; Engr.

**MILLER, SUNNI L,** Univ Of Sc At Columbia, Columbia, SC; FR; BA; Sci; Nrsng.

**MILLER, SUSAN,** Le Moyne Coll, Syracuse, NY; SO; BA; Pol Sci.

**MILLER, SUSAN E,** Wv Univ, Morgantown, WV; JR; BS; Ordr Grail 90-; Helvetia 89-90; ASP 90-; Gldn Key 90-; Phrmcy; Phrmcst.

**MILLER, SUSAN G,** Fl International Univ, Miami, FL; JR; BA; AA Miami Dade Comm Coll 90; Crmnl Just; Law Schl.

**MILLER, SUSAN R,** Fl St Univ, Tallahassee, FL; JR; BS; Bptst Stdnt Union Columbia Coll Pres 88-90; Alpha Lambda Delta Columbia Coll 89-90; Cncl Excptnl Chldrn Columbia Coll 88-90; FSU 90-; Trustees Schlrshp Columbia Coll; Bsktbl Columbia Coll 88-89; Spec Educ-Vsl Dsblts.

**MILLER, SUSANNE P,** Hillsborough Comm Coll, Tampa, FL; FR; AAS; Stdnt Nrs Org 90-; FISH Chrmn 70-79; Grl Sct Ldr 79-80; Boy Sct Den Mthr 76-78; CRA Dsgntn 79-88; SREA 80-88; NYS Rl Est Brkr 70-85; FHA VA Endrsd Mtg Undrwrtr 85-88; Fncl Anlyst 88-90; AAS Jefferson Cmnty Clg 66; Nrsg.

**MILLER, TABITHA L,** Bowling Green St Univ At Huron, Huron, OH; JR; BA; Deans Lst 89; James E Cole Mem Schlrshp; Rcyclng Schlrshp; Bsnss; Accntng.

**MILLER, TAMMY M,** Western Ky Univ, Bowling Green, KY; JR; BS; Gym Clb 88-89; Flag Ftbl 89-; SG 90-; Phi Eta Sigma 88-; Math; Scndry Educ.**

**MILLER, TARA E,** Spartanburg Methodist Coll, Spartanburg, SC; FR; BA; Phi Theta Kappa; Pres List 90-; Vlybl Sftbl Acdmc Schlrshps 90-; Bus.

**MILLER, TIMOTHY E,** Ms St Univ, Miss State, MS; FR; BS; ACS 90-; Chem; Rsrch.

**MILLER, TOMMY T,** Middle Tn St Univ, Murfreesboro, TN; SO; BA; D J/Sports Dir 84-; Hist; Tchr.

**MILLER, TONYA A,** Hampton Univ, Hampton, VA; JR; NAACP 88-; Un Bd 88-; Alpha Kappa Mu 90-; Psi Chi; Prd Sn; Psych; Instrl Org Psych.

**MILLER, TRAVIS L,** Fl St Univ, Tallahassee, FL; SR; BS; Hnrs/Schlrs Prog 87-; Genesis Ldrshp Grp 87; Grk Comm Ldrshp Conf 88; Mrtr Bd 90-; Phi Kappa Phi; Beta Gamma Sigma; Alpha Tau Omega Schlrshp Chrmn 88-; Outstdng Jr Male 90; Outstdng Acctng Schlr 90; Beta Kappa Alpha 89-; IM Ftbl/Bsktbl; Acctng/Finance; Law Schl.

**MILLER, VICKIE L,** Roane St Comm Coll, Harriman, TN; FR; BA; Cert; Science; Nursing-Surgical.

**MILLER, VIRGINIA R,** Coll Of Charleston, Charleston, SC; FR; Flwshp Chrstn Athls; Acctg; CPA.

**MILLER, VIRLANDA L,** Univ Of Nc At Charlotte, Charlotte, NC; JR; BA; Stdnt Md Asst Dvrsns Ed 88-; Blck Stdnt Un 89-; Univ Chrl; Smll Vcl Ensmbl; Thtr Wrk; Intern WFAEFM; Intern Spirt Square Cntr Arts; Engl; Pblc Rltns.

**MILLER, WENDY L,** Univ Of Miami, Coral Gables, FL; SR; BA; Frnch Clb; Pi Delta Phi; Miami Opera 90-; Urbn Lge 90-; Swtchbrd Miami 88-89; Natl Arbr Day Fdn 87-; Key Der Fdn 89-; NAFE 89-90; SFALL; Frnch/Spnsh; Lib Sci/Law.

**MILLER, WILLIAM BRETT,** Central Fl Comm Coll, Ocala, FL; SO; UAW Lcl 1821 85; Mrtn Mrtta 85; ASCET Tampa Tchnl Inst 84; Math; Accntnt Or Eng.

**MILLER, YVETTE A,** American Baptist Coll, Nashville, TN; FR; BA; Bapt Student Union; Busn Mgnt/Mktng.

**MILLER-PENSYL, ANNE R,** Oh St Univ, Columbus, OH; SR; BSLA; Am Soc Lndscp Architects 87-; Sigma Lambda Alpha 90-; Gold Key 89-; Eng Hon Stdnt 90-; Garden Clb Ohio Schlrshp Recpt 90-; Lndscp Architecture.

**MILLER-VANNEMAN, ANN L,** Atlantic Comm Coll, Mays Landing, NJ; SO; AS; Sci Club V P; Cmptr Sci; Engr.

**MILLERCHIP, CLAIRE,** Newbury Coll, Brookline, MA; SR; AA; AS; Htl Rstrnt Mgmt; Hsptlty.

**MILLETT, AMY L,** Clark Univ, Worcester, MA; SO; BA; Under Grad Fncl Aid Cmmtt 90-; Pr Ttrng 90-; Rsdnc Hll Strng Cmmtt 89-90; Econ; Bus.**

**MILLETT, DAVID A,** Oh Univ, Athens, OH; JR; BS; ASME 90-; Mrchng Bnd 89-; Trmbn Chr/Wnd Ensmbl 89-; Cmmnty Smmr Bnd 90; Co Op G E Aircraft Engns 90-; Mech Eng; Eng/Mngmnt.

**MILLETT, DENISE G,** Broward Comm Coll, Ft Lauderdale, FL; SR; BED; Marriott Sch Mgmnt; Mgmnt Soc Dir Day On The Job; Deans Lst 90; IM; Bus Mgmnt; Finance.

**MILLETTE, ALLISON M,** Norfolk St Univ, Norfolk, VA; SO; BS; Spartan Alpha Tau 90-; Vlybl Trck Fld Schlrshp 89-; Corrective Therapy; Physical Therapist.

**MILLEY, TAMMY M,** Univ Of Nh Plymouth St Coll, Plymouth, NH; GD; MED; Yrbk Photogphr; Res Hsng Assoc; Mntr Grp Sch Age Chldrn; Pres Lst 90-; BS Educ; Elem Educ; Tchr/Occup Thrpst.

**MILLICAN, JULIE A,** Snead St Jr Coll, Boaz, AL; FR; Phi Theta Kappa; Sclgy; Law.

**MILLIGAN, JAMES W,** East Stroudsburg Univ, E Stroudsburg, PA; SO; Bsbl 87-89; Law.

**MILLIGAN, JENNIFER L,** Univ Of Cincinnati, Cincinnati, OH; GD; BFA CCM 90; Musical Theatre; Prfrmr.

**MILLIGAN, KELLI A,** Northern Ky Univ, Highland Hts, KY; FR; BA; Campus Lit Mag Collage Ed Bd 90; St John Newman Ctr 90-; Engl; Jrnlsm.

**MILLIGAN, SASCHA B,** Memphis St Univ, Memphis, TN; FR; BA; Blck Assn; Activities Cncl; Army TROC Cadet 90-; Phi Eta Sigma Pres; Alpha Lambda Delta; Catholic Org 90-; Army Superior Cadet Awd 90-; Pol Sci/Intl Rel; Intl Publ Rel.

**MILLIGAN, SHANNON M,** Forsyth Tech Comm Coll, Winston-Salem, NC; FR; Kiwanis Schlrshp; Graphic Arts; Music Bus.

**MILLIGAN, STEPHEN M,** Univ Of Sc At Columbia, Columbia, SC; FR; BA; SAGE 90; Coll Rpblcns 90; Alpha Delta Lambda; Gamma Beta Phi; Scndry Educ; Tchr.

**MILLIKEN, CYNTHIA A,** Fl International Univ, Miami, FL; GD; BHSA; Hlth Serv Mgmnt; Cons Hlth Serv.

**MILLIMAN, HELAINE M,** Cleveland Inst Of Art, Cleveland, OH; FR; MFA; Illstrtn.

**MILLIN, NINO P,** Kent St Univ Stark Cmps, North Canton, OH; SR; Advrtsg/Mktg Intern 89; Art Hstry/Renaissance Florence Italy 90; BA Bsn Adm; Bsn; Intl Bsn/Law.

**MILLINER, ISABEL MARIA,** Univ Of Sc At Columbia, Columbia, SC; SR; BA; Intrnshp Fmly Scl Serv; Vol Woodland Pk Elem; Sclgy; Spnsh Ltrtr.

**MILLINGTON, LIESA P,** City Univ Of Ny City Coll, New York, NY; SO; BSN; CCAPP Org 89-; City Coll Schlr 89-; Sci; Nurse.

**MILLION, STEPHANIE B,** Lexington Comm Coll, Lexington, KY; FR; BA; Walk Hunger 89; Walk MS 90; Educ; Tchng.

**MILLIRON, SUSAN F,** Univ Of New England, Biddeford, ME; SR; BS; SOTA 89-; Lifestyles Alliance 88-; Non Trdtnl Stdnt Org 87-89; Alpha Chi; Vlybl/Sftbl League 78; Spec Educ Tchr; BS Mansfield Univ 77; Occup Thry: Clinician.

**MILLMAN, WENDY J,** Wilmington Coll, New Castle, DE; SO; BA; Rdng Elem Educ; Tchr.

**MILLOY, HEATHER L,** Bridgewater Coll, Bridgewater, VA; JR; BS; Stdnt Ed Assn 90-; IM Aerbcs 90-; Tutoring 90-; Elem Ed; Tchng.

**MILLOY, KEVIN L,** Alcorn St Univ, Lorman, MS; FR; BA; Indus Tech; Drftng/Grphc Dsgn.

**MILLS, ANGELINE L,** Northwest Al Comm Coll, Phil Campbell, AL; SO; Phi Thetta Kappa 90; Office Admin; Sec.

**MILLS, ANITA D,** Northwest Al Comm Coll, Phil Campbell, AL; FR; Phi Theta Kappa 90; Offc Sprvsn Mngmnt Lgl Option.

**MILLS, ANNA M,** Anne Arundel Comm Coll, Arnold, MD; FR; BS; Soc Work; Comm Work.

**MILLS, ANNE MARIE,** Univ Of Nc At Charlotte, Charlotte, NC; GD; MS; Crmnl Justice Assoc; Pre Law Soc Sec 89-; Etc Mag Assoc Edtr 89-; Phi Kappa Phi 90-; Alpha Phi Sigma V P 89-; MADD 89-; Southern Crmnl Justice Assoc 89-; Pre Law Stdnt Of Yr; Grad Asst Crmnl Justice Dept 90-; Pres Awd For Exclnc Wake Tech; Crmnl Justice; Ph D Crmnl Justice/Rsrch.

**MILLS, BARBARA P,** Bethune Cookman Coll, Daytona Beach, FL; SR; BA; Prsdnts Awrd; Deans Lst; Prfssnl Busnsswmn Lg; Accnt Exec 87-; Sclgy; Mdcl Schlgst.

**MILLS, BRETT A,** Brescia Coll, Owensboro, KY; SR; Clss VP 88-89; Stdnt Gov S 88-90; Jdcl Brd 89-90; Alpha Chi 89-; Glee Clb; All Amer Schlr; La Vega Clements Hist Awd; Hist; Diplmtc Corps.**

**MILLS, CONSTANCE R,** Wallace St Comm Coll At Selma, Selma, AL; SO; BA; SGA 87-; Civitan Intrnatl; Sprts Wrtr; Engl; Wrtr.

**MILLS, CRAIG A,** Cincinnati Bible Coll & Sem, Cincinnati, OH; GD; MA; Kappa Sigma VP 78-79; Intrclgt Knghts 80-82; Knghts Columbus 80-82; Kappa Sigma VP 78-79; BA/BS Arch/Eng 82-90; B Arch U Idaho 82; Mnstries; Prchng.**

**MILLS, CYNTHIA A,** Northern Ky Univ, Highland Hts, KY; JR; BA; May Festival Chorus 90-; Legal Secr Frost/Jacobs 89-; AA Tallahassee Cmnty Clg 86; Engl; Law.

**MILLS, DAVID C,** Duquesne Univ, Pittsburgh, PA; FR; BA; Pre Law Soc 90-; Union Prgrm Brd 90-; Orntatn Stf Co-Ldr; Frst Hnrs Deans Lst 90-; Ice Hocky 90; Ecnmcs Ltn; Law.

**MILLS JR, DAVID R,** Univ Of North Fl, Jacksonville, FL; JR; BBA; AA Fla Jr Clg 81; Corp Fin-Mktg; Slf Emplymnt.

**MILLS, DEL G,** Patrick Henry Comm Coll, Martinsville, VA; FR; AA; Bsbl Club 90-; Envrnmntl Concrns Soc 90-; Bsbl 90-; US Army Rsrvs 90-; Sci; Medcl.

**MILLS, DENA L,** William Carey Coll, Hattiesburg, MS; JR; BS; Club Med Secy 88-; Omicron Delta Kappa; Biol; Med Resrch.

**MILLS, ERIN M,** Univ Of Tn At Martin, Martin, TN; FR; BA; All Sing 90-; Alpha Omicron Pi Soph Chap Rel 90-; Intr Tennis; Vlybl; Sftbl 90-; Chemistry.

**MILLS, GINA A,** Union Coll, Barbourville, KY; FR; Deans Lst 90; Sci; Dentistry.

**MILLS, HEATHER L,** Memphis St Univ, Memphis, TN; JR; PHMD; Gamma Beta Phi 88-; Sigma Kapa Sorority Corres Sec 88-; Wmns Panhel Coum 3.0 Cl 88-; Microbiol; Phmcy.

**MILLS, JAMES E,** Medical Coll Of Ga, Augusta, GA; SR; BSN; Assn Nrsng Stdnts Tres 89-; Schl Cls Tres 89-; Amrcn Assn Crtcl Car Nrs; BBA Augusta Clg; Nrsng.

**MILLS, JANET H,** Asbury Theological Sem, Wilmore, KY; GD; MA; Chrstns Bblcl Eqlty Chptr Treas 90-; Rho Chi Hnr Pres 69-70; Alpha Lambda Delta; Kappa Epsilon Corr Sec Chptr 68-70; Res Hosp Phrmcy 70-71; BS N E La Univ 70; Amer Pharm Assn; Amer Soc Hosp Pharm; Ky Phar Assn; Stf Pharm; Christian Educ.

**MILLS, JASON J,** Me Maritime Academy, Castine, ME; SO; BA; Striker 90-; Yeoman 89-90; Deans Lst 89-; Cmndnts Lst 89-; Tae Kwon Do 90-; Marine Trnsprtn; Ship Dck Ofcr.

**MILLS, JEFFREY B,** Univ Of Southern Ms, Hattiesburg, MS; SO; BA; Mrchng Bnd 89-; Jz Bnd/Bsktbl Pep Bnd 90-; Sthrn Expsr 89-; Phi Kappa Tau 89-; Mktg.

**MILLS, JENNIFER L,** Univ Of Southern Ms, Hattiesburg, MS; SO; BA; Song/Dnc Trp 89-; Stdnt Alumni Assc 89-90; Phi Kappa Tau Ltl Sis 90-; IM 89-; Alpha Lambda Delta 90-; Lambda Sigma 90-; Gamma Beta Phi 90-; Gamma Beta Phi 90-; Acad Exc Schlrshp 89-; ACT Schlrshp 89-; Delta Delta Delta Pblc Rltns Chr 89-; Biolgy; Medicine.

**MILLS, JOHN M,** Univ Of Sc At Coastal Carolina, Conway, SC; SO; Psych Club; Bus; Mgmnt.

**MILLS, JOYCE H,** Al A & M Univ, Normal, AL; BA; Gamma Beta Phi; Exec Secy; Office Mgr; Bus Admin; Bus.

**MILLS, KATHY M,** James Sprunt Comm Coll, Kenansville, NC; FR; ASSOC; Nrsg Stdnts Natl Assn; Nrsg.

**MILLS, KENNETH R,** Ms St Univ, Miss State, MS; JR; ROTC 1st Serg 90-; Bus Mngmnt; Army Cmmssn.

**MILLS, LISA K,** Troy St Univ At Dothan, Dothan, AL; SR; BS; Data Proc Mgrs Assn; Gamma Beta Phi; Beta Sigma Phi Sec 89-; CIS Intrnshp; AS Wharton Cnty Jr Coll 81; Mngmnt Infor Sys; Cmptr Prgrmr/Analyst.

**MILLS, MARGARET K,** Concord Coll, Athens, WV; FR; BED; Sec Educ/Soc Stu.

**MILLS, MATTHEW T,** Liberty Univ, Lynchburg, VA; SR; BS; Yth Quest Mbr 88-; Strght St Yth Vol 90; Highest GPA Mjr Chrch Mnstries 90; Wrstlng Vrsty 87-; Chrch Mnstries; Semnry.

**MILLS, MICHAEL E,** Kent St Univ Kent Cmps, Kent, OH; JR; BS; Im Ftbl/Vlybl/Wlybl/Flr Hockey/Golf; Golden Key 90; Phi Epsilon Kappa Pres 90-; Phi Sigma Kappa Pres 89-90; Bro Of The Yr 90; Tim Tripp Mem Schlrshp Award 89-; Intrfratrnty Cncl Schlrshp Award 90; Phy Ed; Sport Psychlgy.

**MILLS, PAIGE W,** Piedmont Tech Coll, Greenwood, SC; FR; DIPL; Automated Ofc Tech; Clrcl.

**MILLS, PATRICIA L,** Univ Of Sc At Columbia, Columbia, SC; JR; BA; Gamma Beta Phi; Mrkng/Fin; Mgmr.

**MILLS, RHONDA K,** Univ Of Tn At Martin, Martin, TN; SR; BS; Ftbl Hstss; STEA; NEA; Spec Olymps; Deans Lst; Zeta Tau Alpha Rtul Chr 88-89; Kappa Alpha Lil Sis; BS; Ed Erly Chldhd Ed K-8; Tch.

**MILLS, SUSANNE D,** Univ Of Sc At Columbia, Columbia, SC; SO; BA; Natl Hon Soc 88-; Deans Lst 90-; French; PHD.

**MILLS, TAMMY G,** Union Coll, Barbourville, KY; JR; BS; Scl Sci Clb Sec 90-; Iota Sigma Nu; Gamma Reta Phi 90; Deans Lst 88-; Prsdntl Lrte 89sr Asstnt; Smpsn Pltcl Sci; Wrk Stdy Mrt Awrd; Psychlgy Sclgy Chld Psychlgy.

**MILLS, TAMMY R,** Beckley Coll, Beckley, WV; SO; Beta Sigma Phi; Paraoptometric Assist; Amer Optometric Assn; Assoc Vision Care; Psychology; Doctrine.

**MILLS, TARA A,** Winston Salem St Univ, Winston-Salem, NC; FR; BA; Hlth Careers Opport Pgm 90-; Atkins Hl Cncl Asst Secr 90-; Bio Clb 90-; Natl Inst Envir Hlth Sci Rsrch Triangle Pk Summer Intern; IM Bsktbl; Bio; Med Dr.

**MILLS, TRACY C,** Ms Univ For Women, Columbus, MS; JR; Phi Theta Kappa Pres 89-; Pres Lst 88-; Acctg; CPA.

**MILLS, VICKY L,** Miami Jacobs Jr Coll Of Bus, Dayton, OH; SO; ASB; Bus Admn.

**MILLSAP, MELANIE S,** Pellissippi St Tech Comm Coll, Knoxville, TN; FR; BA; Deans List; History; Edctn.

**MILLSAPS, CANDICE N,** Radford Univ, Radford, VA; SO; BS; Engl; Educ Tchng.

**MILLSAPS, SANDRA K,** Pellissippi St Tech Comm Coll, Knoxville, TN; FR; AAS; Prllgl Assoc 90-; Phi Theta Kappa; PTA Sec 88-90; Lbrry Rdng Prgm 86-; Chrch Yth Comm 86-; Lgl Asst Tchnlgy.

**MILLWARD, RODERICK A,** S U N Y Coll At Fredonia, Fredonia, NY; SR; Phi Theta Kappa; Ambassador Pgm; AA SS Jamestown Cmnty Clg 89; Hstry; Elem Ed.

**MILLWOOD, ANGELA L,** Univ Of Sc At Spartanburg, Spartanburg, SC; JR; BA; Stdnt Natl Educ Assoc 89-; Piedmont Soc 89-; Piedmont Schlr 88-; Deans List 88-; Chncllrs List; Elem Educ; Teach.

**MILNER, HEIDI R,** Ms St Univ, Miss State, MS; JR; BSU 90-; Presbytrn Chrstn Fllwshp 90-; Missionary 90; Spec Educ; Teach.

**MILNER, KELLY A,** Saint Leo Coll, Saint Leo, FL; JR; BA; SGA Cntr 89-90; Psychlgy Clb Pres 90-; Cncl Fr Excptnl Chldrn 90-; Delta Epsilon Sigma 90-; FL St Dnce Assc 83-; Orientn Ldr 89-; Outstandg Stdnt 90-; Outstndng Mrt/Prfrmnce 90-; Psychlgy/Dnce; Cnslng.**

**MILONOPOULOS, JULIE M,** Bunker Hill Comm Coll, Boston, MA; SO; Art Schl Certf.

**MILORO, MICHAEL J,** Univ Of Nh Plymouth St Coll, Plymouth, NH; SR; BA; RA 90; Peer Assist 89-90; Orient 89-90; SG 88-90; Newspapr 87-88; Fclty Stndng Cmmttee 87; Gvrnrs Sccss Grnt 88-89; Pres Lst; Elem Ed; Tchr.

**MILOSHEVSKI, MICHAEL,** Niagara Univ, Niagara Univ, NY; SO; BS; AIBS 89-; ACS 89-; Dorm Cncl 89-; Ski Clb 90-; Dns Lst; IM Sprts 89-; Bio/Pre-Med; Med/Pedtrcn/Dntst.

**MILOT, MARY ELLEN,** Teikyo Post Univ, Waterbury, CT; GD; Gen Studies.

**MILSON, BELVA E,** Univ Of The Dist Of Columbia, Washington, DC; SR; BBA; Carribbean Amer Intrcltrl Org Sec 87-89; Meth Wmn Treas 87-; Accts Rcvbl Spec; AAS 86; Acctg.

**MILSTEAD, CHRISTIE A,** Univ Of Md At Eastern Shore, Princess Anne, MD; JR; Newman Club Pres 89-; Drama Soc 90-; Hnrs Stdnt 89-91; Pom Pon Squad 89-90; Pharmacy.

**MILSTONE, JENYA,** Univ Of Rochester, Rochester, NY; SO; BA; Econs; Bus.

**MILTIADES, HELEN B,** Malone Coll, Canton, OH; JR; BA; Players Guild 88-90; Psych Club 88-; Cnslng Psych.**

**MIMMS, ROBIN S,** Kent St Univ Geauga Cmps, Burton Twp, OH; FR; Cmptr Sci.

**MIMNAUGH, EUGENE R,** Coker Coll, Hartsville, SC; JR; BS; US Amry 1st Serg 87-; Psychlgy; Law.

**MIMNAUGH, HEATHER Q,** Westminster Coll, New Wilmingtn, PA; JR; BA; Chem Clb 88-89; Psy Clb 88-89; J A Lrng Ctr 89; Adopt A Grndmthr Pgm 88; Mortar Bd; Pi Sigma Pi; Psi Chi; Phi Mu Hist 90-; Lambda Sigma 89-90; Otstndng Fresh Chem Awd 89; IM Vlybl-Sftbl 88-89; Psych; Cnslng.

**MIMS, ANDREA C,** Ms Univ For Women, Columbus, MS; JR; BA; Kappa Delta Epsilon; Mu Rho Sigma 90-; Elem Educ; Tchr.

**MIMS, BOBBI J,** Averett Coll, Danville, VA; FR; BS; Mbr Of Hmcmng Ct 90-; Phi Eta Sigma 90-; Phi Sigma Sigma 90-; Sports Med; Phys Ther.

**MIMS, JACQUELINE L,** Univ Of Md At Eastern Shore, Princess Anne, MD; JR; BS; Crmnl Jstce Soc VP 89-; NAACP 90-; Modeling 88-; Hon Cnvctn Splendid Achvmnt 89-; Zeta Phi Beta 90-; Vlybl Tm 88-90; Crmnl Jstce; Lawyer Juvenile Delinquents.

**MIMS, JENNIFER D,** Medical Univ Of Sc, Charleston, SC; SR; BSN; Stdnt Nurses Assoc 90-; Stdnt Govt Assoc 90-; Sigma Theta Tau; March Of Dimes Walk A Thon 90-; Spirit Nrsng Awrd; Deans Lst 89-90; AA 89; Nursing.

**MIMS, ROBIN S,** Univ Of Montevallo, Montevallo, AL; SR; BS; Educ; Tchg.

**MIMS, VIVIAN L,** Middle Tn St Univ, Murfreesboro, TN; JR; BSN; Hrsmns Assn Prgrm Dir 90-; Hrs Judging Tm 89-; TN Hrs Cncl 90-; TN Qrtr Hrs Assn 90-; TN Nrsng Assn; Staff Nrs RN 77-; AS UT Nashville 76; Nrsng/Hrs Sci; Prfsnl Hrs Judge.

**MIMS, WILLYE P,** Univ Of South Al, Mobile, AL; SR; BED; Kappa Delta Pi; BS Tuskegee Inst AL 76; Elem Ed; Pblc Schl Tchr.

**MINACH, SHELLY H,** Richard Bland Coll, Petersburg, VA; FR; AS; Rchrd Blnd Coll Fndtn 90-; Pres Hon Schlrshp.

**MINAMOTO, KAZUKO,** City Univ Of Ny La Guard Coll, Long Island Cty, NY; FR; AS; Intrnshps Asst TV Sta; Aerbics Wrkshp 90-; Plnnr Advrtsng Agncy 85-86; Mngr Cmmrcl Photo Studio 87-90; Bus Admin; Mktg.

**MINAR, MARYANN,** Glassboro St Coll, Glassboro, NJ; GD; BA; Stdnt Govt Sntr 86-90; Engl Club 86-87; Gamma Tau Sigma 90; Sigma Sigma Sigma Pres 88-90; Newman Ctr 88-90; Medallion Award 90; Engl; Scndry Educ.

**MINCAVAGE, KAREN M,** Univ Of Nc At Chapel Hill, Chapel Hill, NC; GD; JD; NC Jrnl Intl Law/Cmrcl Rgltn 90-; Stdnt Bar Fndtn 89-90; Golden Key Natl; Phi Alpha Delta 89-90; Grdte Assistantship Prof T Hazen 90-; Dns Lst 89; Nancy K Rhoden Schlrshp 90; Angell Schlr 89; William J Branstrom Fresh Prize 85; Law.

**MINCH, HEATHER K,** The Kings Coll, Briarclf Mnr, NY; JR; BS; Pol Awrns Cmte 90-; Stdt Govt Class Ofcr 90-; Deans Lst 88-90; Elem Tchr.**

**MINCHAK, STEPHEN J,** Glassboro St Coll, Glassboro, NJ; SR; MBA; Ecnmcs Clb Sec 89-90; Natl Hon Soc; Opened Own Bus 89; VP/TREAS Comp Pitsop; Fin; Anlyst.

**MINCY JR, EDWARD L,** Owensboro Comm Coll, Owensboro, KY; SO; MPA; Pres Awd 90-; Acctg; CPA.

**MINDEK, CATHY A,** Univ Of Ct, Storrs, CT; SO; BA; Assoc Stdnt Govt Pres 89-; Golden Key; Deans Lst 89-; Alumni Assn Awd; Mktg/Bus Law; Law.**

**MINDELL, DEBRA D,** Springfield Tech Comm Coll, Springfield, MA; JR; BA; Cert Med Asst Cert Phlbtmy Tech; Phlbtmst Prov 85-; AS 79 90; Mktg.

**MINDOCK, ERIC S,** Univ Of Fl, Gainesville, FL; SR; BS; Journal 89; Golden Key 90-; Anderson Schlr; Aerospace Engr.

**MINELGA, LEONIDA,** Daytona Beach Comm Coll, Daytona Beach, FL; FR; ADN; Nrsng; BSN.

**MINER, LEANNE R,** Kent St Univ Kent Cmps, Kent, OH; FR; BS; Med Tchnlgy; Med Lab Tchncn.

**MINER, MELISA M,** Garrett Comm Coll, Mchenry, MD; JR; Stdnt Govt 90; AA GCC 90; Psychlgy; Cnslng Psychlgst.

**MINES, ROXANNE E,** Va St Univ, Petersburg, VA; JR; NAACP 90; Big Bro Big Sis 89-; Stu Unn Actvty Brd 88-; Phi Beta Lambda 88-; Sftbl Tm 89-; Admn Sys Mgmnt; Entrprnr.

**MINEWEASER, JANE R,** Bowie St Univ, Bowie, MD; SO; BS; Educ Clb; Kappa Delta Pi; Grl Scts Cntrl Md Trp Ldr 85-; Comp Prgmr Fed Govt 65-77; Engl; Educ.

**MINGOLA, ANDREA,** City Univ Of Ny Coll Staten Is, Staten Island, NY; SO; BA; Nrsry Schl; Psychlgy; Chld Psychlgst.**

**MINGUEL, TINO F,** Fl A & M Univ, Tallahassee, FL; SR; BS; Crrbn Clb 87; Latin Clb; Curagao Lwn Tennis Clb; Archtctre Eng Tech; Dsgn Cnstrctn Fld.

**MINHAJ, MARYAM,** Univ Of Miami, Coral Gables, FL; SO; BS; Circle K; Hon Stdnt Assn; Indian Stdnts Assn; Smr Intrnshp Jackson Meml Hosp; City No Miami Yth Opprtnty Bd 90-; Bio; Med.

**MINIC, MICHAEL W,** Middle Tn St Univ, Murfreesboro, TN; SO; BS; Pi Mu Epsilon 90; Math Awd 89-90; Ntl Cllgte Math Awds 90; All Amer Schlr Cllgte Awd 90; Math; Statstcs.**

**MINICH, DAWN C,** Itawamba Comm Coll, Fulton, MS; JR; BS; Gamma Beta Phi; Smithville Bapt Ch; Elem Edn.

**MINICHELLO, STACIE L,** Kent St Univ Kent Cmps, Kent, OH; FR; BA; Fash Merchndsng; Whlsl Buyer.

**MINICK, JENNIFER A,** Univ Of Sc At Columbia, Columbia, SC; JR; BA; Psych; Clinical Psych.

**MINICK, LORI L,** Wv Univ, Morgantown, WV; FR; BA; Engr; Aerospace Engr.

**MINIUTTI, DAVID A,** Univ Of Nh Plymouth St Coll, Plymouth, NH; SR; BS; Skng/Scuba/Glf/Tnns 87-; Clg Wrkstdy Pgms 88-; Phi Kappa Phi; Snr/Day; St Louis Almni Schlp; Cid L Volandry Mem Schlp; IM Vlybl/Bkstbl/Tnns/Flr Hcry 87-; Bsn Admn; Intl Fnce/Law.

**MINK, ALBERT E,** Glassboro St Coll, Glassboro, NJ; JR; BED; Engl Hnr Scty; Engl; Scndry Engl Educ.

**MINK, JANICE G,** Saint Elizabeth Hosp Sch Nurs, Utica, NY; FR; AAS; Class Pres 90-; Girl Sct Of Amer Vol 89-; BA Angelo State Univ 77; Nursing; Psychiatric Nursing.

**MINK, NICOLE M,** Saint John Fisher Coll, Rochester, NY; JR; BS; Spnsh Clb Bdgt Mgr 89-; Acdmc Cncl 89-; Stdnt Senate 88-89; Frgn Lang Hon Soc VP 88-; Intrdscplnry/Mktg/Comm; Advtsng/Mktg.

**MINKS, HEATHER M,** Hillsborough Comm Coll, Tampa, FL; FR; BA; Adminstrtr Acctng Trng Sftwr Systems; Engrng.

**MINKS, KATHY M,** Fl International Univ, Miami, FL; SR; Ford Fdntn Otsdng Educ Majors 90-; Pi Kappa Phi 90-; AA Miami Dade Cmty Clg 86; Educ; Ele Educ Tchr.

**MINNEY, KIMBERLY M,** Wv Univ At Parkersburg, Parkersburg, WV; FR; BA; Brown Blt Tae Kwon Do; Rad Tech; Law.

**MINNICH, BARBARA L,** Duquesne Univ, Pittsburgh, PA; FR; BA; Psychlgy; Psychlgst.

**MINNICH, DAWN M,** Villanova Univ, Villanova, PA; JR; BA; Sclgy Clb 90-; Arbc Clb VP 90-; Vllnva Hngr Awrnss Wk Com Chrprsn 90; Sclgy Arbc Islmc Stds; Intrntl Affrs Mddle Es.

**MINNICK, JULIE S,** Memphis St Univ, Memphis, TN; SR; BS; Kappa Delta Pi 90-; AS NW MS Jr Clg 74; Rehab Ed.

**MINNICK, SHERRY L,** Radford Univ, Radford, VA; SR; Std Govt 89-90; SEA 89-90; BS; Erly/Mddl Chldhd Educ; Tchr.

**MINNICKS, TERRI E,** George Mason Univ, Fairfax, VA; FR; BS; Alpha Kappa Alpha Fin Sec; Deans Admsns Prog 90-; Acctg; CPA.

**MINNIG, JOHN W,** Columbia Union Coll, Takoma Park, MD; SR; BS; U S Army 71-; Hlth Care Admin; Hlth Care.

**MINNIS, DENISE M,** Notre Dame Coll, Cleveland, OH; SR; BA; Drama Soc Sec/Treas 87-; Coll Nwspr Edtr 87-90; Engl Soc 89-; Exclsr Awd; Marguerita C Banks Awd; Intrnshp Amer Cncr Soc; Cmnctns; Pblc Rltns.

**MINNIS, JESSICA L,** Liberty Univ, Lynchburg, VA; JR; Cltrl Awrns Comm 90; Clg Rpblcns 88-90; Pre Law 88-89; Alpha Lamba Delta 89; RA 90; Dns Lst 88; Gov; FBI/CIA.

**MINNITI, DANIELLE J,** Glassboro St Coll, Glassboro, NJ; SO; BA; Cmnctns.

**MINOR, ANNA R,** Ms St Univ, Miss State, MS; FR; BA; Lmbd Sgm; MSU Blldg Hsts; Cmps Actvts Brd; Alph Lmbd Dlt; Phi Eta Sgm; Gamma Beta Phi; Delta Delta Delta Asstnt Tres 90-; Cmps Clb Proj Dir 90-; Pres Schlr; Univ Hon Pgm 90-; Cmnctns; Law.

**MINOR, CARYL ANN,** Edinboro Univ Of Pa, Edinboro, PA; GD; MA; Nwspr Editr; Alpha Chi; Cmmtr Clb V P; Engl/Comp; Professor.

**MINOR, DEMETRIUS D,** City Univ Of Ny Baruch Coll, New York, NY; JR; BA; Intl Bnkng/La Bonque Francasie Du Commerce Exterieru 90; Mgmnt/Bus Admin; Intl Mrktng.

**MINOR IV, JAMES V,** Dowling Coll, Oakdale Li, NY; SR; BS; Crisis Intrvntn Htln Mngr 88-; Lions Den Stdnt Lng Mngr 89-; Aerontcs Clb 87; AVN OPS Spec US Army Aviation Cntr 90; Aerontcs/Mgmt.

**MINOR, JODY L,** Univ Of Tn At Chattanooga, Chattanooga, TN; SR; BSE; Amer Soc Mech Engr V Chrmn; Bapt Stdnt Union; Cooperative Ed Pgm; Phi Eta Sigma 86-; Alpha Lambda Delta 86-; US Achvmnt Acad Engr Awd 88-; IM Vlybl; Mech Engr; Engr.**

**MINOR, PATRICIA L,** Norfolk St Univ, Norfolk, VA; SO; BA; SG 89-90; Alpha Kappa Tau 90; Ins Clms Clrk 87-; Chld Care/Fmly Stdy; Day Care Admin/Tch.

**MINOR, SUSIE Y,** Fl A & M Univ, Tallahassee, FL; JR; BS; Pres Schlrsh Assn; Bptst Cmps Mnstry; Chem Clb; Phi Eta Sigma; Alpha Kappa Mu; White/Gld Key; Beta Kappa Chi; Non Verba Opera; Hon Premedcl Acdmy 90; Rsrch Careers Pgm; Chem; Med.

**MINORI, MICHAEL P,** City Univ Of Ny Queensbrough, New York, NY; FR; AS; Dsgn Drftng; Eng.

**MINOTT, BERNICE,** Saint Josephs Coll New York, Brooklyn, NY; SR; BS; New Lfstyl Flwshp; Bapt Chrch Pres World Wid Guild; Sndy Schl Tchr; Bedford Stuyvesant Chldhd Ctr Bd; Retired; Comm Hlth.

**MINOTT, MARK L,** Duquesne Univ, Pittsburgh, PA; FR; Blck Union 90-; Union Brd 90-; Bus Mgmt; Corp Law.

**MINOTTI, CLAUDIA A,** Elmira Coll, Elmira, NY; SR; BA; Tri Beta Pres 90-; Nwspaper Phto Edtr 88-90; Yrbk Phto Edtr 88-89; Hon Schlr 88-; Biolgy/Envrnmntl Sci/Educ; Sci/Tchng.

**MINSON, ARTHUR T,** Georgetown Univ, Washington, DC; JR; BSBA; Rsdnc Life Resid Asst 90-; Acctg Scty 88-; IM Bskbl Tm Capt 88-; Deans List 88-; Ernst/Young Summer Intern; A Andersen Intern; Coopers/Lybrand Intern; Equitable Int; Accounting/Finance; CPA.

**MINSON, HOLLY A,** Richard Bland Coll, Petersburg, VA; FR; BBA; Hotel Mgt.

**MINSTER, AVIVA S,** Yeshiva Univ, New York, NY; GD; AAS; Fine Arts Scty VP 88-90; Lit Arts Jrnl Asst Edtr Artst 88-90; Deans Lst 88-90; Creative Shwcse Mag Edtrl Staff Asst 90; Mlrm Mgr 88-90; Mlnrs Mrkt 88-89; Karate/Fncng 90; Cert 88; Fine Arts/Advrtsng Grphc Dsgn; Cmmrcl Dsgn.

**MINTER, CHERYL R,** Clark Atlanta Univ, Atlanta, GA; SR; Acctg Clb 90-; Natl Assn Blck Acctnts 90-; Acdmc All Amer Collgt Soc 88-; Acdmc Achvmnt 88; Prnce Hall Ordr Eastrn Strs Schlrshp 89; Outstndng Acdmc Achvmnt; BA; Acctg; CPA/LAW.

**MINTER, CRYSTAL A,** Middle Tn St Univ, Murfreesboro, TN; JR; BED; Alpha Omicron Pl Best Pldg 90-; Early Chldhd Educ; Tchng.

**MINTER, VISHAL S,** Oh Univ, Athens, OH; FR; Pi Kappa Alpha; Ohio Univ Ice Hockey Tm 90-; Elec Eng.

**MINTO, STEPHEN P,** Fl Atlantic Univ, Boca Raton, FL; JR; BA; Miami Dade Comm Coll Alumni Assn; AA Miami Dade Comm Coll 89; Acctng.

**MINTON, ALANA R,** Western Ky Univ, Bowling Green, KY; SR; Pi Delta Phi 89-90; Phi Kappa Phi 90-; Outstndng Sr German Awd 90-; Pres Schlr 90; BA 90; French/German; Seminary.

**MINTON, BARBARA J,** Asbury Theological Sem, Wilmore, KY; GD; MA; Chrstns Bblcl Eqlty 90-; Intrntnl Stdnt Fllwshp Hst Family 90-; Intrntnl Soc Of Theta Phi; T B Avery Mmrl Mrt Schlrshp 90-; Pansey Ethl Campbell Mmrl Schlrshp 90-; AA Lubbock Chrstn Clg 63; Cnslng; Pstr Tchr.

**MINTON, JEFFREY C,** East Carolina Univ, Greenville, NC; FR.

**MINTON, JILLANA N,** Clemson Univ, Clemson, SC; SR; BS; Goldn Key 89-; Phi Kappa Phi 90-; Sigma Theta Tau; Nrsng.

**MINTON, THOMAS D,** Asbury Theological Sem, Wilmore, KY; GD; MA; Chrstn Bib Equality Asbury Chptr VP 90-; OMS Intl Asbury Sem Flwshp Cab Chrmn 90-; Wrld Otrch Exec Comm 89-; Theta Phi 90-; ASM 89-; ACMC 85-; AIMS 88-; Srvng Stdnt Pstrls Msnry 61-89; Sba Abilene Chrstn Univ 66; Univ Zurch 66-67; World Msn Evangelism; Pstr/Tchr.

**MINTZ, BARA L,** Cornell Univ Statutory College, Ithaca, NY; JR; BA; Com Of Off Cmps Lvng; Pr Advsr 90-; Dns Lst 88-; Bus; Acctng.

**MIODRAG, JEFFREY L,** Westminster Coll, New Wilmingtn, PA; SO; Fresh Start 90-; Down Under Brtndr 90-; SWAT; Beta Beta Beta 90-; Phi Sigma Alpha Sec 89-; Deans List 89-90; Sigma Phi Epsilon 90-; Overlook 90-; Yth Dvlpmnt Ctr 90-; Bio; Neurologist.**

**MIOLI, RAE M,** Univ Of Sc At Columbia, Columbia, SC; FR; Wrld Tae Kwon Do Assoc 90; Pre-Med; MD Peds.

**MIRA, CYNTHIA G,** Central Fl Comm Coll, Ocala, FL; FR; AS; Busn Ofc Dept Store 90-; Ofc Tech; Busn Ofc.

**MIRABAL, ALEJANDRO J,** Fl International Univ, Miami, FL; JR; BS; AA Miami Dade Cmmnty Clg S Campus 90; Scl Studies; Ed.

**MIRABILE, DINA J,** Dowling Coll, Oakdale Li, NY; GD; Co-Orgnzr Of Campuses Without Drugs Nassau Cmnty Clg 89; Deans List Hons 90; AA Nassau Cmnty Clg 89; BA; Spcl Ed; Tchng.

**MIRABILLA, ALLYSON,** William Paterson Coll, Wayne, NJ; SO; BS; Ntrl Sci Clb 90-; Wyckoff Vol Amblnc Corp 90-; Deans Lst 90-; IM Sftbl; EMT Bergen Cty Emer Med Svc Trng Ctr 90; Blgcl Sci; Med Schl.

**MIRACLE, HAROLD WADE,** Univ Of Ky, Lexington, KY; SR; BA; SCEC Vp 89-; Deans Lst; Phi Delta Theta Pldg Trnr 87-89; Spcl Ed.

**MIRACLE, JOSEPH D,** Union Coll, Barbourville, KY; FR; BED; Ftbl 90-; Engl; Law.

**MIRACLE, KIMBERLY Y,** Roane St Comm Coll, Harriman, TN; SO; BA; Gamma Beta Phi; Psychlgy; Psychlgy/Law.

**MIRACLE, STACEY L,** Middle Tn St Univ, Murfreesboro, TN; SR; CERT; STEA; Deans List 90; So Cntrl Assc Young Children 85-; BS Univ Ky 80; Social Science/Elementary; Education.

**MIRACLE, TINA LEE,** Univ Of South Al, Mobile, AL; SO; BED; Spnsh Clb 89-; Alpha Lambda Delta 90; Czechoslvakian Sis Cty Prog Sec 90-; Spec Educ; Tch LD.

**MIRAGLIA JR, BENEDICT R,** S U N Y At Buffalo, Buffalo, NY; GD; DDS; BA Mnhtnvl Clg 89; Biology; Dentistry.

**MIRAGLIA, LISA M,** S U N Y Coll Of Tech At Frmgdl, Farmingdale, NY; SR; AS; Asst Dental Indus; Masters Dental Hygiene; Dental Hygiene; Reg Dental Hygnst.

**MIRANDA CORTES, CARMEN L,** Inter Amer Univ Pr Hato Rey, Hato Rey, PR; SR; BA; Bio Edn; Teach.**

**MIRANDA, DORYS D,** Univ Of Pr At Rio Piedras, Rio Piedras, PR; JR; Army ROTC Pgm Staff Sgt 88-; Army ROTC Schlrshp 88-92; ROTC Chnclr Trophy 89-; Chem; Med.

**MIRANDA, EVELYN,** Fl International Univ, Miami, FL; SR; BA; Kappa Delta Pi 90-; Kappa Delta Pi 90-; Werm/Treas 90-; Deans List 89-; Elmtry Int; NACOPRW 87; NAEA; DAEA; FAEA; WERM 90-; Mngmnts; AA MI Dade Cmm Clg 86; Art Ed; Art Tchr.

**MIRANDA, JEANEVETTE,** Univ Of Pr At Mayaguez, Mayaguez, PR; SO; BS; German Clb 90-; Church Yth Grp Mbr Of Directive 88-; NACME Schrlshp 90-; Chemical Engrng.

**MIRANDA, JUDYTH,** Inter Amer Univ Pr Hato Rey, Hato Rey, PR; JR; BA; Sci; Nrsg.

**MIRANDA, KATELYN,** City Univ Of Ny Baruch Coll, New York, NY; SO; BBA; Acctng; CPA.

**MIRANDA, MARILYN,** Inter Amer Univ Pr San German, San German, PR; FR; BA; Acctg.

**MIRANDA, MARK A,** Birmingham Southern Coll, Birmingham, AL; BS; Board Mbr Network Pblctn Judeo Chrisian Pblctn; Sls Mgr Partners Hlth Plan Of AL; Bus/Mgmnt.

**MIRANDA, MORAIS C,** Manhattan Coll, Bronx, NY; SO; BSEE; Min Stdnt Un; Ice Hcky; Gamma Alpha Sigma Fndg Bro; Intrnshp Lederle Lab; Elec Eng; Engrg.

**MIRANDA, RUSSEL A,** East Stroudsburg Univ, E Stroudsburg, PA; FR; BS; Chess Clb Treas 90-; ACM 90-; Comp Sci; Sftwr Eng.

**MIRANDA, VICKY LANDRON,** Caribbean Univ, Bayamon, PR; JR; BA; Maryknoll Fthrs/Bros; Mr Arnolds Excllnce Bty Cltre 88-89; Law.

**MIRANDA, WILLIAM E,** Inter Amer Univ Pr Hato Rey, Hato Rey, PR; SR; MBA; Nu Sigma Beta 89-; Fnnc.

**MIRANDA, YOLANDA,** Inter Amer Univ Pr San German, San German, PR; FR; BA; Sci; Scl.

**MIRANDA-SANTOS, YVONNE,** Inter Amer Univ Pr Hato Rey, Hato Rey, PR; SR; BA; Cmptrllr 86-; Acctg; CPA.

**MIRANTE, AUDRA M,** Clarkson Univ, Potsdam, NY; SO; BA; Clrksn Soc Acctnts; Soc Wom Mngrs; Pre Law Soc Tres 90-; Phi Sigma Sigma Jdcry Brd 90-; Intrn Prof Attry; Acctg/Pre Law; CPA.

**MIRAS ESTEVA, ROXANA,** Inter Amer Univ Pr Hato Rey, Hato Rey, PR; FR.

**MIRASDA, JAMES J,** Wv Univ, Morgantown, WV; SO; AS; Phi Kappa Phi; Elec/Comp Eng.

**MIRASOLA, NATALIE A,** Wv Univ, Morgantown, WV; FR; BS; Hon Pgm 90-; Civil Eng.

**MIRIDES, WENDY L,** West Liberty St Coll, West Liberty, WV; SR; BA; Elem Ed; Tchng.

**MIROLLI, KAREN T,** Va Commonwealth Univ, Richmond, VA; FR; BS; Phi Eta Sigma; Psychology; Photography.

**MIRTSCHEV, ANTON,** Columbia Greene Comm Coll, Hudson, NY; FR; BS; Acctng; Corp Law.

**MIRZA, IMRAN M,** City Univ Of Ny City Coll, New York, NY; SO; Indo-Pak Clb; Islamic Orgn; Pkstn Impct; Bdmntn; Elect Eng.

**MIRZA, KAMRAN M,** City Univ Of Ny City Coll, New York, NY; SO; EE; Muslim Club Indo Pak Clb 89-; Pakistani Im Pact 89-; Frgn Stdnt Schlrshp 89-; Science; Engnrng.

**MIRZA, MAVARA S,** Univ Of Miami, Coral Gables, FL; FR; BA; Circle K Intl 90-; Feeding/Impacting Hungry; Provosts Honor Roll 90-; J F Pearson Scholarship 90-; Hialeah Firefighters Schlrshp 90-; Acad Schlr 90-; Business; Accounting.

**MISDRAJI, ESTHER L,** Univ Of Miami, Coral Gables, FL; FR; MED; Alpha Lambda Delta; Music; Tchr.

**MISENER, ERIC A,** Univ Of Miami, Coral Gables, FL; SO; BA; Var Clb Bowl Treas 89-; Sng Hurrcns 89-90; J F Pearsan Schlrshp 89-91; U Miami Hon Prog 89-; J F Pearson Schlrshp 89-; I M Bkbl Sftbl 89-91; Hstry; Law.

**MISHKIN, MARGARET L,** Univ Of Miami, Coral Gables, FL; JR; BA; Pr Cnslng; Prsn Prog Cncl 90-; Cmps Sprts And Rcrtn 90; Klstr Crse Lmtd Intrnshp; Mgmt; Mrktng Pstn.

**MISHLER, SCOTT A,** Comm Coll Algny Co Algny Cmps, Pittsburgh, PA; SO; SNAP; Frat Assn Pro Prmdcs; Pro Prmdc 79-; Nrsng.

**MISIEWICZ, BARBARA J,** Central Fl Comm Coll, Ocala, FL; SO; ADN; Deans Lst; LPN Duluth Area Voc Tech Inst; LPN 81-; RN; BS.

**MISKA, JULIA I,** Cornell Univ Statutory College, Ithaca, NY; JR; BS; Pre-Vet Soc 89-; Orntn Cnslr; Alpha Phi; Anml Sci; Vet.

**MISKEY, DAWN M,** Alfred Univ, Alfred, NY; SR; BS; Amer Crmc Soc 88-; Soc Wmn Eng 88-F Tau Beta Pi VP 90-F Keramos VP 89-; Alpha Lambda Delta 87-88; Pres Schlrshp 87-; PPG Indust Schlrshp 88; Trnslco Div Ferro Corp Schlrshp 88f Equstrn Tm 88-; Vars Crss Cntry/Trk/Fld 87-88; Crmc Eng.

**MISKIMEN, SHEILA K,** Liberty Univ, Lynchburg, VA; SO; BS; Librty Assoc Chrstn Tchrs; Alpha Lambda Delta; Kappa Delta Pi; Elem Educ.

**MISLANOVICH, KAREN M,** Comm Coll Algny Co Algny Cmps, Pittsburgh, PA; SO; ASN; Phi Theta Kapa 89-; Nrsg Dept Hnr Awd; Med Asst 82-89; Nrsg; RN.

**MISNER, KENNETH R,** Newbury Coll, Brookline, MA; SO; AS; Hotel/Rstrnt Mngmnt.

**MISTER, KAREN L,** Salisbury St Univ, Salisbury, MD; SO; BA; Phi Eta Sigma 90-; Psy/Scl Wrk; Psy.

**MISUNAS, ANISSA L,** Providence Coll, Providence, RI; JR; BA; Educ Clb 90-; Comm Brd Sec 88-90; Chrch Choir 88-; Admn Ambsdr; Paul Douglas Tchrs Schlrshp 90-; Elem/Spec Educ; Tchr.

**MITCHAM, BRIAN J,** Southern Coll Of Tech, Marietta, GA; JR; BSEE; IEEE 89-; AIPE 89-; Tau Alpha Pi; Firefighter Vol 90-; Underwater Resc Spec 90-; GA Engr Fdtn Schlrshp 90; Elctrcl Engr; Engr.

**MITCHAM, CRYSTAL D,** Western Piedmont Comm Coll, Morganton, NC; FR; BA; Phi Theta Kappa; Math; Tchg.

**MITCHELL, ALLYSON C,** Jackson St Univ, Jackson, MS; FR; BA; Cmptr Sci/Engr.

**MITCHELL, ANGELA D,** Univ Of Montevallo, Montevallo, AL; SR; MA; Campus Outrch 89-; Bapt Campus Mnstrs 88-89; Campus Living Assoc 90-; Delta Gamma Pnhlnc Del 90; RUST Intl Corp Cmnctns Intern 90-; AS Northeast AL State Jr Clg 89; Engl; Law.

**MITCHELL, ANGELA L,** Radford Univ, Radford, VA; SR; BS; Intervrsty Chrstn Flwshp 90-; Interhsnp Prbtn Prl Agcy 90; Crim Jstc; Career Govt.

**MITCHELL, AUDRA IRENE,** Georgian Court Coll, Lakewood, NJ; SR; BS; SGA Cmmtr Rep 89-90; Bus Clb 90-; Delta Mu Delta; Dean Lst 89-90; Accntng; Accntnt.

**MITCHELL, BARBARA A,** Georgian Court Coll, Lakewood, NJ; SO; BABS; Math Assn Amer Stdnt Chptr Sec/Tr 90-; Acad Rep 89-; Schl Nwspapr; Sigma Phi Sigma 90-; Math/Physcs; Eng.

**MITCHELL, BAYYINAH M,** Strayer Coll, Washington, DC; FR; BA; Acctg; Bnkg.

**MITCHELL, BRIAN C,** Morehouse Coll, Atlanta, GA; SO; BA; Frshmn Cl Offcr Sec 89-90; Cl Offcr Sec 90-; STRIPES 89-; Hon Roll 89-; Deans List 89-; Mentoring Prog 89-; Ean; Mrktg; Adv/Mkt/Rsrch/Devl.

**MITCHELL, BRIAN W,** Univ Of Ga, Athens, GA; SR; BS; Baptst Un 88-; Big Bro 88-; Tutoring 90-; Golden Key 89-; Pharmcy Intrnshp 90; Pharmcy.

**MITCHELL, CAMILLIA R,** Univ Of Tn At Martin, Martin, TN; SO; BS; Clg Republicans 89; Phi Eta Sigma 90; Zeta Tau Alpha Asst Serv Chrprsn 90; Hnrs Seminar Schlrshp 89; Adopt/Schlr Schlrshp 89; Intrmural Sports 89; Mathematics; Bsn.

**MITCHELL, CARLA D,** Middle Tn St Univ, Murfreesboro, TN; JR; BBA; Business/Mrktng; Marketing.

**MITCHELL, CAROL A,** City Univ Of Ny Queensbrough, New York, NY; SO; AS; Science; Nurse.

**MITCHELL, CATHERINE A,** Middle Tn St Univ, Murfreesboro, TN; SR; BBA; Future Accntnts Assn 90-; Beta Alpha Psi 90-; AS Nashvl State Tech Inst 83; Acctg; CPA.

**MITCHELL, CATHY E,** Johnson C Smith Univ, Charlotte, NC; JR; BA; Artcls Pblshd Daily Post/Hampton Script Nwsprs Wrtr 90-; Stdnt Union Bd Actvty Orgnzr 90-; Cntrbtd Wrtngs Univ Mass Medial Jrnl 90-; Awrd Ldrshp Schlrshp Fresh Yr 88-90; Jrnslm Schlrshp Jr Yr Coll 90-; Jrnlsm-Print Media; Jrnlsm.

**MITCHELL, CHARLES R,** Southeastern Baptist Coll, Laurel, MS; JR; BA; Deans List 89-90; Natl Clgt Educ Awds 89-91; Pstr Bethel Bptst Chrch 90-; AA 90; Bible/Psych; Ministry/Cnslng.

**MITCHELL, CHARLES R,** Me Maritime Academy, Castine, ME; SO; BA; Ftbl 89-; Eng.

**MITCHELL, CHERA HOWARD,** Christopher Newport Coll, Newport News, VA; JR; BA; Intervarsity Chrtn Flwshp 89-; Bpt Student Union 90-; Rvrsd Rehbltn 89-90; Natl Level Assembly God Teen Talent Competion Vocal Ensemble 88; Biology; Phyl Therapy.

**MITCHELL, CRYSTAL A,** Longwood Coll, Farmville, VA; JR; BS; Soclgy Clb 89-; Anthrplgy Clb 89-; Psychlgy Clb 89-; Psi Chi 89-; Delta Zeta 89-; Hnrs Schlrshp 89-; Rdng Tm Capt 88-89; Psychlgy/Sclgy/Anthrplgy; Crmnlgy Doctorate.**

**MITCHELL, CYNTHIA A,** Univ Of Nc At Asheville, Asheville, NC; FR; Phi Eta Sigma; NC Tchng Fllws; Lit; Elem Tchr.

**MITCHELL, DAVID S,** Glassboro St Coll, Glassboro, NJ; JR; Psi Iota Pi VP 89; Stdnt Govt Psychlgy Sntr 90; Chrstn Flwshp 87-89; Psi Chi Pres; Gamma Tau Sigma; Newman Clb Serv Coordntr 89; Psychlgy; Cnclng.

**MITCHELL, DAVID SCOTT,** Univ Of Ky, Lexington, KY; SR; BS; Campus Crusade For Christ 90-; Baptist Stdnt Un 86-90; Schl Paper Wrtr 87-88; Tau Beta Pi 90-; Alpha Lambda Delta 86-87; Phi Beta Lambda 86-89; Pr Hs Assoc 87-89; Sci Awrd 86; IM Bsktbl/Ftbl/Spdbl/Vlybl 86-; Engr.

**MITCHELL, DAWN VICTORIA,** Wv Wesleyan Coll, Buckhannon, WV; FR; BA; SADD 90-; Intervrsty 90-; Zeta Tau Alpha; Cmp Fr 90-; Blgy; Vtrnry Med/DVM.

**MITCHELL, DONNA L,** Univ Of South Al, Mobile, AL; SR; BA; Cir K V P 89-90; Lit Cncl; Educ/Lang Arts; Tchng.

**MITCHELL, DONNA M,** Univ Of Sc At Columbia, Columbia, SC; SO; BA; Ed Clb Pres 87; SGA Sntr SAC Rep Acad SGA Rep 88; Phi Eta Sigma Pres 90; Kappa Delta Pi Pres 90; Sigma Tau Delta Sec/Treas 89; Omicron Delta Kappa 89; Affrs Lbry Advsry Cmps Serv Elctns; Chncllrs Lst 90; Mdnght Mdnss 89; Scndry Edc Engl; Tchr.**

**MITCHELL JR, EDDIE F,** Morehouse Coll, Atlanta, GA; SO; BA; Math Clb/Tm 87-89; Sci Clb 88-89; Drama Clb 88-89; Deca 88-89; Mu Alpha Theta 87-89; Crss Cntry 87-88; Wrstlng 87-89; Acctg; CPA.

**MITCHELL, ELIZABETH W,** Daytona Beach Comm Coll, Daytona Beach, FL; SO; MBA; Cmpssnt Frnds Nwsltr Edtr 90; Grl Scts Ldr 90-; Acctg; CPA.

**MITCHELL, EMERSON W,** Univ Of Rochester, Rochester, NY; SO; BA; Thurgood Marshall Pre Law Soc; D A Internshp; Owner/Oper Comm Photo Studio 85-90; Cr Ju Assoc Tmpkins Crtlnd Comm Clg 82; Pol Sci; Law.

**MITCHELL JR, ERSKIN,** Alcorn St Univ, Lorman, MS; SR; BS; ROTC Exec Ofcr 90; Univ Bnd 89-; AUSA 89-; Ind Tech Clb 89-; Kappa Alpha Psi 90-; Kappa Kappa Psi 89-; Adopt-A-Hwy 90-; Fed Aviatn Adm Trfc Cntrl Trne 90-; Dist Mil Cadet 89-90; Airborne Wngs 89; IM Ftbl Bskbl Capt 89-90; Elec Tech; Elec Engr.**

**MITCHELL, FAITH C,** City Univ Of Ny Queensbrough, New York, NY; GD; Cllgte Scrtries Intrntl VP; Day Stdnt Govt Sntr; 25 Plus Clb; Math Clb; Bsnss Depart Hnr Scty; Wrtrs Clb; Stdnt Fclty Dscplnry Cmmttee; DSG Sntr Of Yr 89; Ndlwrkrs Gld Of Amer NGA Inc; Queens Cnty Frm Museum; WP Cert; AAS; Bsnss Admin.

**MITCHELL, FAWN E,** Nyack Coll, Nyack, NY; FR; BA; Brass Choir 90-; Gospel Tm 90-; IM Tennis; Socl Sci; Secndry Ed.

**MITCHELL II, HAROLD M,** Univ Of Sc At Coastal Carolina, Conway, SC; SR; BSU Pres 88-89; Fllwshp Chrstn Athletes Treas 87-89; Biol V P 88-89; Omicron Delta Kappa 90-; Phi Sigma Tau; Deans Lst 87-90; Benediction 91 Grad; Vars Chrldr 89-90; Assist Coach Vars Chrldng 90-; Religion/Philosophy; Ministry.

**MITCHELL, HELEN CATHERINE,** Univ Of Pa, Philadelphia, PA; SR; Whrtn Evnng Schl Stdt Cncl Pres 89-; Sigma Kappa Phi 90-; Grad ABA Cum Laude Hnrs; Grad BBA Magna Cum Laude Hnrs; Chi Alpha Phi Awd; Clss 85 Awd Merit; Robt L Mac Donald Spec Achvmnt Awd; Deans List 88-; Management/ Marketing.

**MITCHELL, JAMES J,** Univ Of West Fl, Pensacola, FL; SR; MBA; AGC Treas 89-90; AIC Treas 89-90; Deans List 89-; Prod Support Sales Mgt; BS; Const; Engrg Mgt.

**MITCHELL, JEANNE M,** Univ Of Fl, Gainesville, FL; JR; BA; Fin Mgmt Assn 90-91; Kappa Delta 88-91; I M Sftbl 89-91; Bus Admn; Fin.

**MITCHELL, JEFFREY L,** Middle Tn St Univ, Murfreesboro, TN; SR; BS; STEA; Phi Kappa Phi; Hnr Rl/Dns Lst; Pol Sci; Higher Educ Admin.

**MITCHELL, JOHN W,** Union Coll, Barbourville, KY; SO; BA; Acad Tm 90-; Pep Bnd 90-; Theatre Tech 90-; Gamma Beta Phi; Alpha Kappa Psi 88-90; Pres Ldrshp Awd 90-; Bst Newcmr Theatre Tech Awd; Bst Cameo Actng Awd; Hstry/Pol Sci; Tch.

**MITCHELL, JOI A,** Tuskegee Univ, Tuskegee Inst, AL; SO; BS; MO Clb 89-; Crmsn Piprt Bnd 90-; Kappa Alpha Psi Swthrt Miss Kappa Alpha Psi 90-; Anml Sci; Vet Med.

**MITCHELL, KEVIN M,** Anderson Coll, Anderson, SC; FR; BA; Phi Theta Kappa 90-; Bsn; Mktg.

**MITCHELL, LA TRICE M,** Talladega Coll, Talladega, AL; SR; BA; Engl Majors Assn; Pre Alumni Cncl; Spnsh Clb; Alpha Chi; Engl.

**MITCHELL, LAURA L,** Oh St Univ At Marion, Marion, OH; SR; BA; OEA 90-; NEA 90-; Deans List 90; Elem Educ.

**MITCHELL, LEE ANN,** Univ Of Cincinnati-Clrmnt Coll, Batavia, OH; SO; Bsns Admn.

**MITCHELL, LINDA D,** Univ Of Akron, Akron, OH; SO; AS; Bus Prof Of Amer 90-; Deans Lst 89-; Business.**

**MITCHELL, LINNEY H,** Wv Univ At Parkersburg, Parkersburg, WV; FR; AAS; Emplyd Bennies Waffle Iron Wtrss 75-; Acctg.

**MITCHELL, LYNETTE M,** Marshall University, Huntington, WV; GD; MA; Grad Asst 89-; Active Duty Desert Storm Navy Res Charleston SC HM 2; LPN Bowling Green Sch Nrsng 74; BS Ed Ohio Univ 88; Cmnctn Arts; Media.

**MITCHELL, MACEO S,** Univ Of Sc At Columbia, Columbia, SC; FR; Bus Admn; Corp Law.

**MITCHELL JR, MARC C,** Livingston Univ, Livingston, AL; SR; BS; Lvngstn Univ Pro Bnd Dir 88-90; LU Jazz Bnd 88-90; Acctg Clb 88-90; VITA 88; Intrnshp Jcksn Acctg 90-; Rsdnt Asstnt 88-90; Acctg; CPA.

**MITCHELL, MARCUS A,** Fayetteville St Univ, Fayetteville, NC; FR; BA; 4 Club; US Naval Reserves 90-; US Navy Active 84-90; Criminal Justice; Law School.

**MITCHELL, MARCUS D,** Univ Of Tn At Martin, Martin, TN; JR; Alpha Phi Alpha Pres 89-90; BSA 90-; Alpha Epsilon Rho; IM Bsktbl; Cmnctns.

**MITCHELL, MARIA M,** Inter Amer Univ Pr Arecibo Un, Arecibo, PR; JR; Mu Alpha Phi.

**MITCHELL, MARIANNA T,** Univ Of Ky, Lexington, KY; SR; BA; Psychology; Sch Psych.

**MITCHELL, MARK T,** Univ Of Ky, Lexington, KY; JR; BS; Alpha Lambda Delta; Phi Eta Sigma; Golden Key; Pi Tau Simga; Tau Beta Pi; Stdnt Mbr Amer Soc Mech Eng/Soc Mfg Eng; Kappa Sigma; Outstdng Coll Stndts Amer; Deans Lst 87-; Schlrshps Acad Excell 87-88; Frat Ordr Frghtrs 89; Mech Eng.

**MITCHELL, MARK W,** Wv Northern Comm Coll, Wheeling, WV; FR; AAS; Phi Theta Kappa; Amer Culinary Fed; Ltl League Umpire 76-; Certif Columbia Sch Broadcasting 82; Culinary Arts; Chef/Restaurant Owner.

**MITCHELL, MARTIN E,** Nova Univ, Ft Lauderdale, FL; GD; MBA; Area Mgr Dayco Prod Inc; BBA Univ Toledo 81; Bsn.

**MITCHELL, MARVA G,** Benedict Coll, Columbia, SC; Benedict Stdnt Govt Assn Sr Sec 89-90; Natl Tchr Assn; Delta Sigma Theta; Manority Access Tchr Educ Trea 89-90; Alpha Chi; Alpha Kappa Mu; BED Ga St Univ 76; Natl Assn Advncmnt Colored People 89-; S Car Hlth Hmn Svc Fin Comm Pgrm Monitor; Early Chldhd/Elem Educ; Obtn Phd Educ.

**MITCHELL, MICHAEL C,** Cincinnati Bible Coll & Sem, Cincinnati, OH; GD; MA; Christian Campus Home Pres 89-90; Pres Scholar; Deans Lst; Honor Roll; Grad Teach Assist; BA SW MO State Univ 90; Religion Psychology; Teach.

**MITCHELL, MICHELE A,** Seton Hall Univ, South Orange, NJ; SO; BSN; Natl Stdnt Nrs Assn; Dns Lst 90; Unit Clrk Hackensack Med Ctr; Nrsng.

**MITCHELL, MICHELLE A,** East Central Comm Coll, Decatur, MS; SO; AS; SBA V-Pres 90-; Warior Corps Rcrtng; Ftbl/Bsktbl Hd Chrldr 90; Phi Theta Kappa; Mu Alpha Theta Vp 90-; Sigma Sigma Mu Tua Vp 90-; Phi Theta Kappa Adopt Hwy; Rndbll Rcrtrs; Coll Hall Fame; Miss ECCC; Hmcmng Queen; IM Sprts; Pre Med Microbio; Ansthslgy.

**MITCHELL, MICHELLE D,** Broward Comm Coll, Ft Lauderdale, FL; FR; AA; AASU 90-; Phi Theta Kappa; Pres Lst 90; Ed; Tch.

**MITCHELL, PAMALA M,** Pensacola Jr Coll, Pensacola, FL; SO; AA; Biochem; Med.

**MITCHELL, PEGGY S,** Newbury Coll, Brookline, MA; FR; BED; Intr Dsgn; Intr Dsgnr.

**MITCHELL, PHILLIP L,** Memphis St Univ, Memphis, TN; FR; BA; Busn.

**MITCHELL, RACHAEL A,** Goucher Coll, Towson, MD; SO; BA; Admns Exec Brd 89-; Cls Actvts Cmt Chrprsn 89-90; Brown Schlr 89; Deans Schlr 90-; Pol Sci; Law.

**MITCHELL, REBECCA A,** Fayetteville St Univ, Fayetteville, NC; SO; BED; Elem Ed; Elem Tchr.

**MITCHELL, RHONDA K,** Bridgewater Coll, Bridgewater, VA; SO; BA; IM Sports 90-; Lambda 90-; Pres Schlrshp; Bus Admin; Accounting.

**MITCHELL, RICHARD S,** Fl International Univ, Miami, FL; SR; BS; Scuba Clb Dive Mstr 90; ATRA; Therapeutic Rec Mgt.

**MITCHELL II, ROBERT B,** Ky Christian Coll, Grayson, KY; FR; BS; Fall Play; 90-; Madrigals; 90-; Concert Choir 90-; Acdmc Hnrs Schlrshp 90-; Bible Music; Mnstry.

**MITCHELL, ROBIN,** Univ Of Sc At Columbia, Columbia, SC; JR; BA; Psychlgy; Phd Clin Psychlgy.

**MITCHELL, ROBIN LYNN,** Harvard Univ, Cambridge, MA; FR; BA; NROTC Drill Tm 2nd In Cls 90-; Rep Clb 90-; Puerto Rican Assn 90-; IM Dorm Capt 90-; Biochem Sci; Doctr.

**MITCHELL, SANDY M,** Anderson Coll, Anderson, SC; SO; Acdmc Awrd 90-.

**MITCHELL, SCOTT D,** Univ Of Va, Charlottesville, VA; FR; BS; IM Tnns/Bwlng/Golf/Sftbl 90-; Acctng; Corp/Tax Law.

**MITCHELL, STACY,** Lane Coll, Jackson, TN; SO; BS; Stdnt Govt Assoc 89-; Bsn; CPA.

**MITCHELL, TAMIKA L,** Alcorn St Univ, Lorman, MS; FR; BS; Acctng; Corp Law.

**MITCHELL, TIMOTHY,** Al St Univ, Montgomery, AL; FR; BA; Arnold Air Soc ROTC Capt 90-; Mktg; Army Offcr.

**MITCHELL, TONYA R,** Livingston Univ, Livingston, AL; SO; Stdnt Support Serv 89-; Deans Lst; Pres Lst 90; Occuptnl Thrpy; Nurse.

**MITCHELL, TRACI B,** Univ Of Akron, Akron, OH; SR; BED; Deans Lst 87-; Edn; Elem Tchr.

**MITCHELL, TRACIE D,** Univ Of Nc At Charlotte, Charlotte, NC; FR; BA; Chrlt Interdscplnry Hon Prog; Poli Sci; Law.

**MITCHELL, TRINA L,** Tougaloo Coll, Tougaloo, MS; FR; BS; Pre Hlth Clb 90-; Stu Sprt Serv 90-; Bio; Physcn.

**MITCHELL, TYSON T,** Morehouse Coll, Atlanta, GA; SO; BA; Pre-Law Scty 90-; Swmg Instrctr 89-; Tutor Church; Intrnshp Fed Court Hse 90; Hnr Roll 89-; Nordstrom Schlrshp 90-; Swm Tm 89-; Hstry; Law.

**MITCHELL JR, URBAN GERALD,** Piedmont Tech Coll, Greenwood, SC; GD; AS; Phi Theta Kappa 89-; Psi Beta 89-; JP Strom Award/SC Crmnl Justc Acad; Crmnl Justc; Law Enfrcmnt.

**MITCHELL, WENDY J,** Atlantic Comm Coll, Mays Landing, NJ; GD; AAS; Culinary Arts,Catering.

**MITCHELL, WENDY Y,** Clark Atlanta Univ, Atlanta, GA; SR; BSW; UNCF Pre-Alumni Cncl 89-; Org Soc Change 89-90; Tour/ Recruitment Tm 88-89; Chld Welfare Traineeshp Awd 89-90; Dept Fmly Chldrn Serv Intrnshp 90-; NASW 89-; Soc Wrk; Grad Sch MSW.

**MITCHELL, WILLIAM ERIC,** Univ Of Sc At Columbia, Columbia, SC; JR; BS; Mthdst Yth Fllwshp Pres 86-87; Wtr Snw Ski; Fshng; Accntng; CPA.

**MITCHELL-PHILLIPS, KENNETH S,** Univ Of Md At Eastern Shore, Princess Anne, MD; SR; Pls Org 89-90; Drm Scty 89-90; Cmmnctn Clb Brd 89-90; Deans Lst 88-; Slf Enhncmnt Inc; Ppl Btfl Cnslr; Intern WESM Rdo 88-90; Schlr Athlt Yr 88-90; Otstndnt Achvmnt 89-90; Vrsty Bsktbll Capt 87-90; BA 90; Engl.

**MITCHEM, CHEREE A,** Univ Of Cincinnati, Cincinnati, OH; SR; BM; Music Perf/Viola; Orch Voc.

**MITCHNECK, IVY B,** Indiana Univ Of Pa, Indiana, PA; FR; BSED; Natl Std Spch Lang Hrng Asc 90-; Kappa Delta Pi; IM Bwlng; Spch Path/Adlgy.

**MITCHUM, JOSEPH A,** Embry Riddle Aeronautical Univ, Daytona Beach, FL; SR; Springstein Fan Club Pres 87; Naval Aviation; Sea Plane Adven Soc V P 89; IM; Aero Sci; Pilot.

**MITCHUM, RACHEL M,** Fisk Univ, Nashville, TN; SO; Delta Sigma Theta Treas; Vlybl/Bsktbl 89-; Psychlgy/Bus; Ind Psychlgst.

**MITHANI, SHAIL H,** Univ Of Rochester, Rochester, NY; JR; BA; Drm Cncl VP 89-90; Assoc Dvlpmnt Int India Pres 89-; Res Advsr 90-; Deans Lst 88-; Tiernan Dorm 90-; IM Fld Hcky 90-; Ecnmcs; Finance.

**MITHCELL, ANGELA C,** Ms St Univ, Miss State, MS; SR; BA; Spcttr Clb 87-89; Dela Dncr 87-88; Soc Adv Mgmt; Phi Theta Kappa 88-89; Phi Kappa Phi; Mu Kappa Tau 88-; Betta Gamma Sigma 89-; Gamma Betta Phi 89-; AA MS Delta Comm Clg 88; Mktg; Bsn.

**MITNICK, ANDREW K,** Franklin And Marshall Coll, Lancaster, PA; FR; Pi Lambda Phi; Ftbl; Govt; Law.

**MITRA, ANINDA S,** Bridgewater Coll, Bridgewater, VA; FR; Intrntl Clb 90-; Nwspr 90-; Intrntl Schlrhsp 90-; Ec/Bus Admn.

**MITRA, DANA L,** Brown Univ, Providence, RI; FR; BS; SOFA Outrch Coord 90-; Wmns Sccr Clb Tres 90-; Coalition For Peace In Mdl East; BOLT; WBRU FM Intern; CAP Advisor; Psychology.

**MITROPOULOS, JOHN,** Univ Of Sc At Columbia, Columbia, SC; GD; MSME; ASME 90-; Pi Tau Sigma 90-; Dns Lst 88-90; Grad Asstnshp Dept Eng; BSME 90; Mech Eng; Eng.

**MITTAS, THOMAS A,** Univ Of Akron, Akron, OH; SO; BS; Acctng.

**MITTEN, JEFFREY D,** Univ Of Akron, Akron, OH; SO; BSEE; Stewart L/Catherine E Dow Mem Schlp; NM St Dns Lst 90; Univ Akron Dns Lst 90-; Airman 1 Cls USAF 88-90; Cert Trng USAF 89; Elec Engr.

**MITTERANDO, DANIELLE,** Barry Univ, Miami, FL; SO; Stdnt Trng 89-90; NCAA Sftbl 89-90; Athletic Trng Sprts Med.

**MITUSINA, JULIE R,** Univ Of Hartford, West Hartford, CT; FR; BA; Acdmc Hnrs 90-; Deans Lst 90-; Bus; Finance Admin.

**MIU, LAWRENCE E,** Univ Of Akron, Akron, OH; SO; BS; Deans Lst 90; Clara Abbott Fndtn Schlrshp 89-; Elec Eng.

**MIX, JETAIME M,** Fl St Univ, Tallahassee, FL; FR; BMED; Mrchng Chfs 90-; Cncrt Bnd; IM Vlybl 90; Msc Educ; Bnd Dir.

**MIXON, MILDRED A,** Meridian Comm Coll, Meridian, MS; SO; ADN.

**MIXON, NICOLE,** Columbia Coll, Columbia, SC; FR; BA; Bapt Stdnt Un 90; Acctg.

**MIXON, OTIS S,** Fl St Univ, Tallahassee, FL; BA; Golden Key 90-; Outstndng Stdnt London Study Prog; Tanzey Schlrshp; Economics.

**MIXON, STEPHEN G,** Univ Of Southern Ms, Hattiesburg, MS; SO; BA; IM Bsktbll 90-; Nrsng.

**MIXTER, DAVID E,** Miami Dade Comm Coll, Miami, FL; SO; BA; Chrch Of Jesus Christ Of Latter Dy Sts; Phi Theta Kappa; Psych; Med.

**MIYAJIMA, HIROSHIGE,** Valdosta St Coll, Valdosta, GA; SO; BA; Bsn Mgmt; Mgmt.

**MIZAK, DIANE J,** Comm Coll Algny Co Algny Cmps, Pittsburgh, PA; SO; Boy Scts; Girl Scts; PTA; Exec Sec; Engl; Tchng.

**MIZE, JENNIFER L,** Western Ky Univ, Bowling Green, KY; JR; BA; Univ Cntr Brd Sp Evnts Chrprsn 89-; Panhlnc Pub Rltns Comm; Phi Kappa Phi; W Ky Univ Stdnt Rep 89-; Gldn Key Rcrdng Sec; Phi Eta Sigma 89-; Alpha Omicron Pi Pub Rltns 90-; Pres Schlr 89-; Jr Sor Woman 90-; Grk Hon Roll 89-; Corp Cmnctns; Bus Comm/Hmn Rsrcs.

**MIZELL, AMY T,** Clemson Univ, Clemson, SC; SO; BS; Central Spirit; SC Parks Recr Assoc; Rho Phi Lamda VP; Rape Crisis Cncl; Therapeutic Recreation.

**MIZELL, CHARLES E,** Ringling School Of Art, Sarasota, FL; SR; BFA; Greek Bible Study Co-Ldr 82-87; Pi Kappa Phi Chaplain 82-87; BBA Stetson Univ 87; Cmptr Design; Cmptr Animation.

**MIZELLE, STUART M,** East Carolina Univ, Greenville, NC; FR; BED; Intr Vrsty Chrstn Flwshp 90-; Hon Pgm 90-; Tchng Flws 90-; Music Educ; Educ.

**MIZERKIEWICZ, MICHELLE M,** S U N Y At Buffalo, Buffalo, NY; SO; BA; Alpha Sigma Lambda; Dns Lst MFC 86-; Empl W Seneca Dev Ctr; Hm Svcs Fld; Socl Sci/Psych; Cnslng.

**MIZOK, CAROLYN V,** Bethany Coll, Bethany, WV; SR; MBA; Gamma Sigma Kappa; Alpha Beta Gamma; Summa Cum Laude; Engl; Educ.

**MIZZELL, MICHELE N,** Univ Of Al At Birmingham, Birmingham, AL; AS; Phi Theta Kappa 90-; Deans Lst Cntrl Al Cmmnty Clg 90-; Prsdnts Lst 90-; AS Cntrl Al Cmmnty Clg; Certf; Physcl Thrpst Asstnt.

**MIZZELL, PAMELA LYNN,** Winthrop Coll, Rock Hill, SC; JR; BA; Campus Ministry Grps 88-; Res Stdnt Assn 89; Alpha Lambda Delta 89-90; Hon Soc 88-; Omicron Delta Kappa; Phi Kappa Phi; Stdnt Asst Kindergarten 89-; Visit Elderly; Winthrop Schlr 89-; Pr Lst 88-; Engl Bostic Rogers Schlrshp; Aerobics; Tchr.

**MIZZI, PIA S,** Dowling Coll, Oakdale Li, NY; GD; BA; Scl Sci; Admn/Pblc Serv.

**MJORNDAL, LENA C,** Univ Of Al At Birmingham, Birmingham, AL; FR; BA; Spnsh Clb Orgnzr; Stu Bettr Earth Nwslttr; Alchl Drg Awrnss Cmmtt; Alpha Lambda Delta; Pres Hnr Rl 90-; Crss Cntry Trck Schlrshp 90-; Sun Belt Hnr Rll; Crss Cntry Trck Tm; Engl; Sprts Med.

**MLECZKO, KEITH A,** Schenectady County Comm Coll, Schenectady, NY; FR; BA; Librl Arts; Psych.

**MLYNAREK, STEVEN P,** Univ Of South Fl, Tampa, FL; GD.

**MOATS, TAMMY L,** Univ Of Nc At Charlotte, Charlotte, NC; JR; BA; Interdisciplinary Hon Soc 88; Golden Key 90; Phi Alpha Theta 90; History.

**MOBERG, ERICA M,** Univ Of Sc At Columbia, Columbia, SC; JR; BA; Chrldr At Flnda Atlntc Univ 89; Psych; Rehab Chld Dev.

**MOBLEY, JANET L,** Univ Of Southern Ms, Hattiesburg, MS; SR; BS; Amer Advtsng Fed Treas 89-90; Pub Rltns Stdnt Soc Amer 88-90; Art Clb 86-88; Alpha Rho Tau Hinds Comm Coll 87-88; Pt Time Pub Prntng Svcs 88-90; BS 90; Phys Ftns Inst 89-90; AAS Hinds Comm Coll 88; Advtsng; Art Dir.

**MOBLEY, JENNIFER C,** Univ Of Sc At Columbia, Columbia, SC; FR; Schl Radio Station DJ; Litry Mag Stff; Carolina Pgm Union-Cntmpry Snds Com; Alpha Lambda Delta; Phi Eta Sigma; Stdnt Ethcl Treatmnt Anmls; Stdnts Alld Grnr Earth; Media Arts; Audio/Video Prdctn.

**MOBLEY, JENNIFER E,** Univ Of Southern Ms, Hattiesburg, MS; FR; BS; Dixie Darling 90-; Gamma Beta Phi 90-; Math; Engrng.

**MOBLEY, LISA A,** Univ Of Al At Birmingham, Birmingham, AL; SR; BED; Phi Eta Sgm 86-; Alpha Kappa Mu 89-; Gldn Key; Deans List Pres Hon 86-; Cert Hon/Schlrshp 87-89; Mdl Hghst GPA 89; Spec Art/Srvc Awrd 85 90; Elem Ed; Tchng.

**MOBLEY, LISA N,** Greenville Tech Coll, Greenville, SC; FR; PTA Allied Hlth; Phys Thrpy Asst.

**MOBLEY, PAXTON B,** Queens Coll, Charlotte, NC; JR; BA; Oasis; Art Clb; Kappa Epsilon Gamma VP; Pi Kappa Phi 89-90; Artst Of Yr Awd; Mint Museum Intrn; Art/Tennis Schlrshps; Varsty Tennis; Art Studio/Hstry; Artist.

**MOBLEY, TONJA M,** Fl St Univ, Tallahassee, FL; FR; BA; Seminole Ldrshp Fellows 90-; Hons Pgm 90-; Hons/Schlrs Pgm Writer 90-; Phi Eta Sigma 90-; Southern Schlrshp Fndtn Histrn 90-; FL Schlr 90-; Deans Lst; Acctng; Law.

**MOBLEY, VICKI M,** Averett Coll, Danville, VA; SR; BS; Alpha Chi; Garland Harriet Wyatt Schlrshp; Danville Bsns Prfsnl Wmns Clb Fin Chrmn; Rgstrd Nrs Spclty Crtcl Care; Dipl Mmrl Hsptl Schl Nrsng 85; Bsns Admnstrtn; Hsptl Admnstrtn.

**MOC, YULI B,** Fl International Univ, Miami, FL; SR; BA; AA Miami Dade Comm Coll 89; Educ; Elem Educ Tchr.

**MOCARILLA, MICHELLE SUZANNE,** Fl International Univ, Miami, FL; JR; BA; Wine Toasting Clb; Htl Fd Trvl Assc; AAS Schenectady Cty Comm Clg 90; Hosptlty Mgmt; Restrnt Mgmt.

**MOCHIZUK, TAKEYA,** Univ Of Tn At Martin, Martin, TN; SR.

**MOCK, ANITA D,** Livingston Univ, Livingston, AL; SR; Pi Kappa Phi Ltl Sis V P 88-90; B Ed; BS; Elem Ed; Tchr.

**MOCK, DIANA J,** Oh St Univ At Newark, Newark, OH; JR; BS; Erly/Mddl Chldhd Educ; Tchr.

**MOCK, LISA A,** Ms St Univ, Miss State, MS; FR; BS; Soc Wmn Eng 90-; Univ Hon Prg 90-; Hl Nwsltr 90-; Phi Eta Sigma; Alpha Lambda Delta; Gamma Beta Phi; Hon Res Hl 90-; Sci; Chem Eng.

**MOCK, MICHELE,** Mount Aloysius Jr Coll, Cresson, PA; SO; BA; Mdcn/Mdcl Tchnlgy; Mdcl Tchnlgst.

**MOCK, MICHELLE A,** Univ Of Akron, Akron, OH; JR; BA; Sclgy Clb 90; Soc Hmn Rsrc Mgmt; Gldn Key; Alpha Kappa Delta 90-; Sclgy; Hmn Rsrc Mgmt.**

**MOCK, RICHARD B,** Daytona Beach Comm Coll, Daytona Beach, FL; FR; BS; Air Cond; Eng.

**MOCK, WILLIAM L,** Lenoir Rhyne Coll, Hickory, NC; SR; BA; IM Sprts 87-; Theta Chi Asst Treas 89-; Pres Acad Schlrshp 87-; Pres Lst 90; Vars Sccr Co-Capt 87-; Bus Admin; Mfg Mgmt.

**MOCKBEE, PAMELA J,** Univ Of Akron, Akron, OH; JR; BFA; Repertory Dance Co Dancer 89-; Touring Ens Dancer 89-; Chrgrphrs Wrkshp Chrgrphr/Dancer 90-; Prfsnl Dancer.

**MOCKLER, HEATHER M,** Fl International Univ, Miami, FL; FR.

**MOCKLER, LINDA R,** Univ Of Nc At Asheville, Asheville, NC; SR; BA; Acctng Assoc 88-; Transylvania Trlblazers Wlkng/Rng Clb 89-; Spanish Clb 88-; Sigma Delta Pi Sec 89-; AAS Suffolk Cnty Comm Clg 77; BS 90; Spanish; Tax Acctg.**

**MODENBACH, CHRIS JOSEPH,** Kent St Univ Kent Cmps, Kent, OH; SR; BBA; Rbby Tm 89-; Alpha Chi Rho Schlrshp Repr 88-90; Cr Plng Plcmnt Ctr Extrn Pgm 90; BBA; Mktg/Trnsprtn Lgs Mgmt; Indstrl Rltns.

**MODERSKI, MARK M,** Univ Of New Haven, West Haven, CT; GD; BS; Fire Sci Clb 87-; Natl Fire Prctn Assn 89-; Yale Univ Fire Mrshl Off Intrn 89-90; Allingtown Fire Dist Live In Stdnt 90-; Unif New Haven Fire Prtctn Tech Stdnt Yr; AS Mech Engr; Fire Protection Engr; Engr.

**MODESITT, BRIAN J,** Franklin And Marshall Coll, Lancaster, PA; FR; BA; Econ Clb Treas; Charles A Dana Schlr; Pi Lambda Phi; Hnrs Lst 90-; Vrsty Ftbll; Bus Admn; Intl Fnc.

**MODESITT, PATRICK D,** Wv Univ At Parkersburg, Parkersburg, WV; FR; BA; Math; Mech Engrng.

**MODINE, THOMAS C,** Univ Of Nh Plymouth St Coll, Plymouth, NH; SR; BA; Snowbd Clb 89-; Philosophy; Tch/Grad Stdes.

**MODY, KASHMIRA N,** Southern Coll Of Tech, Marietta, GA; SR; BS; Act Bd Pres; Intrntl Organ Exhibit Chrprsn; IEEE; Tau Alpha Pi; Peer Facilitator 90-; Frshmn Experience Conf; Elec Eng Tech.

**MODZELEWSKI, LINDA A,** Glassboro St Coll, Glassboro, NJ; SR; BS; Pre Prof Soc Sec 89-; Bio Club 89-; Clg Bnd 86-89; Inter Vars Chrstn Fllwshp 86-88; Grdn State Schlr 86; Peter J Mcguire Schlrshp 88/89; Gnrl Assmbly Citation 88; Bio Sci; Vet Med.

**MOEBUS, JO VANCE,** Barry Univ, Miami, FL; SO; BSN; Alachua Cnty Schl Of Nrsng 65; U Of Fl Shnds Tchng Hosp 65; Pan Amer Wrld Arwys 67-74; Leg Aide State Of Fl Dstrct 85; Intr Dsgn 80-90; Vol Jackson Mem Hosp; USN Red Cross Cndy Strprs/Fndrsng; Drs Hosp Aux VP; Nrsng.

**MOELL, TODD E,** Columbus Coll Of Art & Design, Columbus, OH; SO.

**MOELLER, JADD DAVID,** Oh Univ, Athens, OH; JR; BS; Elec/Comp; Engr.

**MOELLER, KAREN M,** Radford Univ, Radford, VA; JR; BS; SEA/NEA; Kappa Delta Pi; Early Chldhd Ed; Montessori Tchr.

**MOELLER, LINDA L,** Barry Univ, Miami, FL; SR; BA; Delta Sigma Epsilon; Theta Alpha Kappa; Outstdng Grad; Dicese Of Se FL Socl Cncrns Chr 89-; Offc Bishop For Armd Frcs Liasion 89-; RN 71-; Ordained Deacon Epsicopal Chrch 88-; RN Flushing Hosp Schl Nrsng 71; Theology; Priesthood.

**MOEVES, PATRICK E,** Northern Ky Univ, Highland Hts, KY; SR; BA; Xi Omega Pres 90; Pol Sci Clb VP 90; Alpha Chi; Deans Lst 87; United Way; Pres Schlrshp; Cmmnwlth Schlrshp To Salmon P Chase; Pol Sci; Law Schl.**

**MOFFA, KELLY A,** Coll Of The Holy Cross, Worcester, MA; FR; BA; Sp Ktchn Vol; Bst Bdds Treas; Tr Gd 90-; Mntl Insttn Vol; Prpl Key; Econ; Corp Law.

**MOFFAT, BRIAN D,** Univ Of South Fl, Tampa, FL; GD; MSPH; Beta Beta Beta 87-89; USF Pub Hlth Trnshp 90-; Soc Envrnmntl Toxclgy/Chem 89; BS Univ Tampa 88; Envrnmntl Hlth; Aquatic Toxlgy.

**MOFFITT, LISA M,** Wv Northern Comm Coll, Wheeling, WV; SR; AAS; Phi Theta Kappa 87-; Amer Assoc Respiratory Care 90-; AAS Computers Inf Procsng 88; Cert Data Entry/Cmptr Oper 88; Respiratory Care; Resp Therapy.

**MOFFITT, LYNDA S,** Univ Of Al At Birmingham, Birmingham, AL; SR; BS; Pi Kappa Alpha 86-89; Phi Epsilon Kappa Auburn Univ 87-89; Pi Beta Phi Auburn Univ 85-89; BS Excercise Scnc Auburn Univ 89; Nursing.

**MOFFITT, SUSAN L,** Univ Of Rochester, Rochester, NY; JR; BA; Stdnt Assn Approp Comm Cntrlr 89-90; Univ Rel Comm Co Chair 90; Human Rel Adv Facltr 90-; Keidean; Delta Gamma 90-; YMCA Adopt A Grndprnt 88-; Literacy 88-90; Hugh Mcknz Mem Price 89; Stdnt Life Awd; Vntr Fellw Fndtn W Cult; Pol Sci; Public Pol/Law.

**MOFSKY, RUSSELL D,** Univ Of Miami, Coral Gables, FL; JR; BA; Soclgy.

**MOGAVERO, RICHARD,** Valley Forge Christian Coll, Phoenixville, PA; JR; BA; Teen Chllng Mnstry Tm Ldr 89-; Pstrl Internshp NE Urbn Chrch Pltng; Gspl Cmmnty Chrch Mnstr Music 77-82; Abndnt Life Chrstn Fllwhsp Dcn 82-86; Dcmnt Cntrl Clrk; Bblcl Stds; Pstrl Mnstry.

**MOGOLLON, RICARDO,** Univ Of Miami, Coral Gables, FL; SO; BS; Alpha Lambda Delta 90-; Jose Marti Schlrshp 90-; Narm Schlrshp 90-; Biology; Med.

**MOGUL, MARGUERITE M,** Hudson Valley Comm Coll, Troy, NY; FR; AS; Ladies Aux Jr V P 88-; Ind Stds; Law.

**MOHABIR, USHA,** City Univ Of Ny La Guard Coll, Long Island Cty, NY; BA; Acctng Clb Sec 90-; Intrnshps Law Firm Wall Street A/R Clrk 90; AAS Degree La Guardia Comm Coll; Acctng; CPA.

**MOHACSI, MICHELLE M,** Southern Ct St Univ, New Haven, CT; SR; Chrldr 88-89; Hall Cncl Sec 87; Florence Nightingale Hon Soc; Chrldr 88-89; BSN; Nrsng; RN.

**MOHAMAD, ROSZIATA,** Univ Of Miami, Coral Gables, FL; JR; BSC; Lbrrn Clb 90; Comp Clb 90; Bst Stdnt 90; Assc St Univ Of Buffalo 90; Comp Sci; Anlyss.

**MOHAMED, ALI,** City Univ Of Ny City Coll, New York, NY; SR; BA; Ghana Stdnts Assn VP 89-90; Afrcn Stdnts Assn Advsr Pres 90-; NY Rnbw Sccr Clb 88-; Gldn Key 90-; Wrld Assn Frmr UN Intrns/Fllws Inc 90-; BA Assoc Univ Du Benin Togo W Africa 86; Hstry; Law.

**MOHAMED, KASSIM,** City Univ Of Ny Queensbrough, New York, NY; SO; AAS; Tau Alpha Pi; Phi Theta Kappa; Driver Owner Operator; Mrchnt Seaman 73-83; Const Worker 84-88; 2nd Mate License Seamens Church Inst 84; Fire Fighting; Comp Tech; Engrng.

**MOHAMED, RADIKHA P,** City Univ Of Ny Queensbrough, New York, NY; SO; BS; Phi Theta Kappa; Biology; Rsrchr.

**MOHAMED, SALIMA,** Saint Petersburg Jr Coll, St Petersburg, FL; JR; BA; Phi Theta Kappa Hnrs Topic Chrprsn 90-; Tal Rstr Otstndng Minority Stdnts; Acctg; CPA.

**MOHAMEDKAMAL, SAMER S,** Shaw Univ, Raleigh, NC; SO; BA; Cmptr Eng.**

**MOHAMMED, ABDULMALIK A,** Columbia Union Coll, Takoma Park, MD; GD; BS; N VA Assn Rltrs 90-; VA Assn Rltrs 90-; Natl Assn Rltrs 90-; Mt Vernon Rlty Co Rltr 90-; Admin/Cmptrlr The Royal Embassy Of Saudi Embassy 87-; Bus Admin; MBA.

**MOHAMMED, ANDREW A,** Va Commonwealth Univ, Richmond, VA; FR; Clg Bowl 90-; Pre Med Clb 90-; Phi Eta Sigma 90-; Biology; Med.

**MOHAMMED, MOHAMMED YUSUF,** Howard Univ, Washington, DC; GD; MS; Amer Soc Cvl Engr Stdnt Mbr 90-; BS E Tenn State Univ 82; Engr.

**MOHAMMED, NIKKI N,** Fl St Univ, Tallahassee, FL; JR; Crrbn Clb Cltrl Exchng 90-; FSU Eng Hnr Scty; Akd Krt Shtln; Eng.

**MOHAMMED, SHALIZA,** Embry Riddle Aeronautical Univ, Daytona Beach, FL; SR; BA; Caribbean Assoc Pres 90-; Amer Assoc Airport Execs 90-; Phi Theta Kappa 89-90; AA Aviation Adm Miami Dade Cmnty Clg 89; PPL Briko Air Svcs 88; Mgmt/Opers/Pilot; Aviation.**

**MOHAMMED-ALI, KAMILA,** Univ Of Miami, Coral Gables, FL; JR; BA; Golden Key 90; Psi Chi; Psychlgy.

**MOHAN, SUE ANN,** Hudson Valley Comm Coll, Troy, NY; PSY; Tchr Asst; Psychlgy; Edn.

**MOHAR, TARA E,** Davis Coll, Toledo, OH; SO; Pres Lst; Mgmt Acctg Assoc; Acctg.

**MOHD ALI, ISMAIL,** Memphis St Univ, Memphis, TN; JR; BSME; Malaysn Assn VP 90-; AAD Mara Comm Clg Malaysia 90; Mech Eng.

**MOHD, KHAIRUL A,** Univ Of Rochester, Rochester, NY; GD; MSC; ASME 88-90; IM; Mchncl Engrg.

**MOHD-RAZALLI, AHMAD-ALBAKREE,** Univ Of Miami, Coral Gables, FL; JR; BS; Cmptr Sci.

**MOHL, RACHEL I,** Yeshiva Univ, New York, NY; SR; BA; Stdnt Nwspr Assc Edtr 88-; Israel Clb Chrprsn 90-; Yeshiva Sem Spvsr 90-; Proj Sages 88-89; Bnai Brith Hillel Jacy Intrn 90; Pol Sci/Judaic Stds; Law/Admin.

**MOHNEY, KERENSA M,** Longwood Coll, Farmville, VA; SO; BA; Coll Co Dncrs Wrdrb 90-; SGA Clss Sec 90-; Hall Cncl Treas 89-90; Elem Ed; Tchng.

**MOHON, BRIAN T,** Ms St Univ, Miss State, MS; FR; BA; Gamma Beta Phi; Phi Eta Sigma; Sigma Chi; Mrktng/Fnce.

**MOHR, CHRISTOPHER J,** Glassboro St Coll, Glassboro, NJ; SO; BA; Radio/TV/FILM; Audio Eng.

**MOHR, RICHARD L,** Kent St Univ Kent Cmps, Kent, OH; JR; BBA; Acctg Assoc 89-; Mrtr Brd; Hnrs Coll 88-; Beta Alpha Psi 89-; Delta Upsilon 89-; Acctg Intern; Acctg.

**MOHRMANN, SCOTT R,** Rensselaer Polytechnic Inst, Troy, NY; FR; BS; Jazz Ensmbl 90-; Pep Bnd 90-; Symph Band 90-; Tau Kappa Epsilon 90-; Chem Engr.

**MOHSENI, MAJID,** Southern Coll Of Tech, Marietta, GA; SR; Soccer Tm 89-.

**MOI, JUDY,** Barnard Coll, New York, NY; FR; Rcylng Clb; Gspl Choir; 1st Chinese Bapt Ch S Sch Prog Coor; Pell St Day Camp Prog Dir; Pltcl Sci-E Asian Stdes; Pub Interest Laa.

**MOINI, LISA A,** Berkerley Coll Of Business, W Patterson, NJ; SR; BA; Acctg; Bsns.**

**MOISE, MAY C,** Inter Amer Univ Pr San German, San German, PR; JR; Org Poly Ntra 90-; Comm Asntr Estdntls; Nrsng.

**MOJICA MORALES, ZOE M,** Inter Amer Univ Pr Hato Rey, Hato Rey, PR; GD; BBA Acctg.

**MOJICA-FLORES, ELIZABETH,** Univ Of Pr Medical Sciences, San Juan, PR; SO; MSN; Col Profl Enfermeria 85-; Hon Reg 90-; Pediatric Nurse Hosp El Maestro 85-86; ER/ICU Hosp Dr Federico Trilla 86-87; ER Trujillo Alto AFASS 87-; RN/BSN 84; Nrsng; Adminstr.

**MOKOS, DAVID J,** Oh Univ, Athens, OH; JR; BS; Flght Tm 90; Golden Key; Alpha Eta Rho 90; Acacia Intrntl VP 90; Cambier/Mc Clellan Schlrshp; Airway Sci; Prof Pilot.

**MOKRY, SHELLEY,** Coll Of Charleston, Charleston, SC; JR; BS; Math Clb 90; Math; Actrl Sci.

**MOLA, MADELINE S,** Saint Thomas Univ, Miami, FL; JR; BA; Elem Educ; Tchr.

**MOLALEGNE, DANIEL,** Bridgewater Coll, Bridgewater, VA; SR; BS; BCIC; Deans Lst; Schlrshp; Rcvd BS Degree; Biology; Med.

**MOLANO, LILIANA,** Nova Univ, Ft Lauderdale, FL; GD; MIBA; Accounting.

**MOLDOF, ALAN R,** Univ Of Miami, Coral Gables, FL; SR; BA; Chess Clb 90-; Chem Clb 87-88; Zeta Beta Tau 87-88; Pres Hon Roll 87-88; Grad W/Gen Hons; Hons Smr Rsrch Pgm 90-; Psych/Cmptr Sci.

**MOLENDA, SALLY M,** George Washington Univ, Washington, DC; FR; BA; Phi Eta Sigma; Pres Hnrs Schlrshp; Art Hstry; Corp Law.

**MOLES, ROBBIN A,** Roane St Comm Coll, Harriman, TN; FR; BA; SGA Sntr 90-; Oak Rdg Hsp Vol 90-; Sci; Phy Thrpy.

**MOLESWORTH, LAURA M,** Southern Coll Of Tech, Marietta, GA; JR; BA; Sigma Phi Epsilon 88-; Elec Eng.

**MOLETTIERI, BETH A,** Temple Univ, Philadelphia, PA; JR; Natl Scty Daughters Amer Rvltn 90; Technen Wrtr Intr Cnty Hosptlztn Plan Inc 86-; AGS Montgomery County Comm Clg 89; Engl; Tech Wrtng.

**MOLFETTA, FRANK S,** Carnegie Mellon Univ, Pittsburgh, PA; FR; BS; Deans Lst; Cvl Eng; Bus Mgmt.

**MOLIA, LEANNE M,** Coll Of Health Sci Stony Brook, Stony Brook, NY; GD; MD; Alpha Omega Alpha; Janet M Glasgow Mem Achvmnt Citation; Lenox Hl Hosp NYC Surg Intern; BS SUNY Stony Brook 87; Med.

**MOLINA PEREZ, MAYRA,** Inter Amer Univ Pr Aquadilla, Aguadilla, PR; JR; BA; Frgn Lang/Frnch.

**MOLINA ROQUE, LYNNETTE M,** Inter Amer Univ Pr Hato Rey, Hato Rey, PR; FR; Sec Svcs; Exec Sec.

**MOLINA VEGA, LUIS A,** Univ Politecnica De Pr, Hato Rey, PR; SR; BSEE; Dns Lst 88-89; Digital Design; Elctrcl Engr.

**MOLINA, MARITZA,** Univ Of Pr At Rio Piedras, Rio Piedras, PR; GD; MCR; Natl Rhbltn Assc; Asociacion De Estudiantes De Consejeria En Rehabilitacion; Tchr 75-79; Qlty Cntrl Inspctr Gen Elect Co 79-87; BA 75; Rhbltn Cnslng.

**MOLINA, MICHELLE,** Inter Amer Univ Pr San Juan, Hato Rey, PR; SO; Fontecha Mdlng Schl 84-88; Hgh Fshn Mdl; Karate 85-89; Hnr Rll 87-89; 4h Clb 83-86; Bsktbl Swmmng 85-89.**

**MOLINARO, LOU ANNE,** Wilmington Coll, New Castle, DE; FR; BA; Comm Arts.

**MOLINI SASTRE, LOURDES M,** Univ Of Pr At Rio Piedras, Rio Piedras, PR; SR; Karate Clb Brown Belt; Aerobics Clb; Natl Coll Architecture/Dsgn Awds.

**MOLITOR, RENEE M,** Univ Of Cin R Walters Coll, Blue Ash, OH; FR; BA; Deans Lst 89-; Thrftwy Cshr 87-; Bus; Acctg.

**MOLLENHAUER, PATRICIA A,** S U N Y Coll Of A & T Morrisvl, Morrisville, NY; SO; BA; AA; Engl; Elem Ed.

**MOLLENHOUR, MICHAEL S,** Univ Of North Fl, Jacksonville, FL; JR; BEET; Srvc Tchncn Mcrgrphc; AS Elctrncs Engnrng Tchnlgy 85; Elctrnc Engnr.

**MOLLER, VICTORIA A,** Fl International Univ, Miami, FL; JR; BA; Stdnt Asstnt Sch Pblc Afrs Deans Ofc 90-; AA Tallahasse Comm Clg 78; Spnsh; Tchng Mdrn Lang Tesol Pgm.

**MOLLEUR, CHRISTINE M,** Rivier Coll, Nashua, NH; FR; BA; Admssns Com; Stdnt Educ Assn Treas 90-; Educ; Tchng.

**MOLLICA, AMY M,** Indiana Univ Of Pa, Indiana, PA; SR; BA; Alpha Gamma Delta Rush Chr; Proj Stride Tutr; Stdnt Tchng Irelnd; Elem Educ; Tchr.

**MOLLOHAN, LINDA J,** Marshall University, Huntington, WV; SR; BA; Acctg Clb 90-; WV Soc CPA 90-; Westmorland Bapt Ch 80-; Vinson Bd Boosters 80-; Bus; Acctg.

**MOLLOY, MARILYN A,** Hilbert Coll, Hamburg, NY; SO; AA; Kairos Prsn Mnstry; Ntl Cursillo Mvmt/Wstrn NY Peace Ctr; Crmnl Jstc; Pnl Sys.

**MOLLOY, VELINE A,** Al St Univ, Montgomery, AL; SR; BA; Intl Stu Assn 89-; Phtgrphy Clb Sec 90; Intern WSVI; Brdcst Cmmnctns; Prdctn/Mngmnt.

**MOLNAR, DAWN I,** Niagara Univ, Niagara Univ, NY; SO; BS; Hon Pgm 89-; Deans Lst 89-; Alpha Kappa Psi; Bus Mgmt/Comp; MBA Becomea CEO.

**MOLNAR, HENRY A,** Univ Of Southern Ms, Hattiesburg, MS; SR; BSBA; Beta Gamma Sigma; Wl Mrt Intrnshp Prog Mgmt Spprt Tm 90-; Acctng.

**MOLNAR, MICHAEL J,** Duquesne Univ, Pittsburgh, PA; SO; MBA; Econ.

**MOLNAR, ZOLTAN,** Bridgeport Engr Inst, Fairfield, CT; JR; BSEE; AS Comm Coll Air Force 81-84; Elec Engr; MSEE.

**MOLYET, KEVIN E,** Univ Of Toledo, Toledo, OH; FR; BSME; By Scts Egle Sct Asst Sctmstr 89-; Ordr Of The Arrw Co Edit 90-; Phi Eta Sigma; Pres Lst; Dns Lst; Hnrs Stdnt; Mech Eng; Eng.

**MOMAN, RUTHIE I,** Tougaloo Coll, Tougaloo, MS; FR; Cncrt Choir 90-; Drill Tm VP 90-; Music.

**MONACO, ANN T,** Saint Johns Univ, Jamaica, NY; SR; Educ Clb 88-89; Itln Clb 88-89; Kappa Delta Pi 90-; Goldn Key 90-; Tutrng 86-88; Dns Lst 88-; Stdnt Tchng 91; Gold Awd Elem Jr High Educ; BS Educ; Educ/Sci; Tchg.

**MONACO, JENNIFER L,** Duquesne Univ, Pittsburgh, PA; JR; BSBA; Stdnt Acctg Assn; Beta Gamma Sigma Pres; Beta Alpha Phi; Acctg.

**MONACO, STEVEN J,** Carnegie Mellon Univ, Pittsburgh, PA; SR; BS; AICE 88-; Tau Beta Pi 90-; Lambda Sigma 88-89; Dns Lst 87-; UNIV Mrt Schlrshp 87-; Chem Eng; Engrg.**

**MONAGHAN, JESSIE F,** Univ Of Nc At Asheville, Asheville, NC; SO; BFA; Art Front Sec; Hnrs Prog Stdnt; Art; Teach.

**MONAGHAN, SEAN C,** Univ Of Sc At Columbia, Columbia, SC; SO; BA; Ldrshp Dev Prog; Gamma Beta Phi 90-; Piedmont Soc 90-; Chanclrs List 89-; Pres Hon Roll 89-; Jr Marshall; Pol Sci; Law.

**MONAHAN, PAMELA A,** Georgetown Univ, Washington, DC; JR; BA; Acctg Scty Pres 89-; Peer Edctr 89-; Tutr 89-; Price Waterhouse New York Intrn; Frst Hnrs; Acctg.

**MONAHAN, SUSAN A,** Mount Aloysius Jr Coll, Cresson, PA; SO; AS; All Cnty Crs 87-88; Mntbnk Plyrs Theater Co; Mnt Aloysious Chrs 90-; Phi Thet Kappa Sec 89-; St Frncs Xavier Yth Grp 84-90; Spcl Olympcs Chrprsn; Bshp Carroll Alumni Assn 88-; Ntnl Rght Life Afflt 87-90; Bsns; Hsptlty Mgmt.

**MONCADA, JOSE SANTOS,** Miami Dade Comm Coll, Miami, FL; SO; AA; Phi Theta Kappa Cmnty Serv Deleg 89-; Civil Eng; BA.

**MONCAYO, JOSEPH ARMANDO,** Becker Coll At Leicester, Leicester, MA; SO; BABED; Phi Theta Kappa VP 90-; Enrgy Cnsrvtn Cmmttee Stdnt Rep 90; Rsdnt Assist 90-; Phi Theta Kappa VP 90; Deans Lst Becker Clg 90f Var Bsebl 89; Red Cross Vol; USAF 85-89; Ca Dept Frstry/Fire Prot 89-90; Intrntl Rltns/Psych; Pblc Serv/Pri Prctce.

**MONCIL, BETTIE J,** Indiana Univ Of Pa, Indiana, PA; SR; BS; Tang So Do Korean Karate 87-88; Cncl Except Chldrn 89-; Univ Tutor 89-90; RHA Flr Rep 88-89; Kappa Beta Delta V P 90-; Spec Educ; Univ Instrctr.

**MONCRIEF, PHYLLIS I,** Alcorn St Univ, Lorman, MS; FR; BA; Hnrs Stdnt Org 90-; Pol Sci; Law.

**MONDA, MICHELLE LYNN,** Duquesne Univ, Pittsburgh, PA; SO; BA; Lambda Sigma 90-; RA 90-; Cmmnctns.

**MONDELL, LYNETTE,** Winthrop Coll, Rock Hill, SC; SR; Plmtto St Tchrs Assn VP 90-; Cncl Excptnl Chldrn 87-; Rfrmd Univ Flwshp 90-; Bg Brthr/Bg Sistr Prog 88-89; Asst Macfeat Kdg; BS; Spec Ed; Tch.

**MONDELLI, SHEILA K,** Lexington Comm Coll, Lexington, KY; FR; Cert Nrsng Asst; RN.

**MONDELLO, CHRISTINE,** Georgian Court Coll, Lakewood, NJ; SR; BS; AS Ocean Co Coll 88; Bus Admin; Corp/Acctg.

**MONELL CRUZ, JAVIER,** Inter Amer Univ Pr Hato Rey, Hato Rey, PR; SO; BA; Natl Hnr Soc; Bsktbl/Socr/Trck/Fld; Cmptr Prgrmng.

**MONEY, CONNIE S,** East Central Comm Coll, Decatur, MS; SO; AA; Mu Alpha Theta 89-; Phi Theta Kappa 90-; Phi Beta Lamda 90-; Bsktbl-Stdnt Asst 89-; Bedwell Ecnmcs Awd 90-; Schlstc Awd-Bsktbl 90-; Bsktbl 89-; Bnkng; Bus.

**MONEY, NISHA N,** Univ Of Miami, Coral Gables, FL; FR; BS; AF ROTC 90-; Indian Stdnt Assoc 90-; Pre Med Hnr Soc 90-; Alpha Lambda 90-; First Aid Squad 90-; Amer Leg Acad Excllnc Awd 90-; Provosts List 90-; Mstr Tutor; Tennis/Bsktbl/Tbltnns IM 90-; Comp Scnc/Pre Med; Medicine.

**MONEYPENNY, DONNA LEE,** Beckley Coll, Beckley, WV; JR; AS; Dns Lst 90-; Amer Pine Ldg Nrsng/Rehab Cntr 88-; Med/Sci; Rsprty Thrpy.

**MONFRADI, CHARLES M,** Bethany Coll, Bethany, WV; SR; MS; Gamma Sigma Kappa; Kappa Mu Epsilon; Soc Physics Stdnts; Kappa Alpha V P; IM Soccer/Bsktbl/Ftbl/Vlybl; Cmptr Sci.

**MONGAN, ELLEN M,** Villanova Univ, Villanova, PA; JR; BSBA; Vcl Ensmbl Dir 88-; Glee Clb Tr Dir 88-; Phi Kappa Phi 90-; Alpha Epsilon Delta; Phi Sigma; Kappa Alpha Theta 90-; Pres Schlrshp; Diamond St Schlrshp; Biol/Hnrs Lib Arts; Med.

**MONGE FERNANDEZ, SONIA,** Univ Of Pr Humacao Univ Coll, Humacao, PR; SR; BA; Stdnts Mgmt Assoc 89-; Hnr Stdnts; 2 Certif Achvmnt Acad Excell 90; Assoc 90; Mgmt; MA Hmn Res.

**MONGIELLO, STEPHEN,** S U N Y Coll Of Tech At Frmgdl, Farmingdale, NY; FR; Med; Physcl Thrpy.

**MONGULLA, MARC S,** Widener Univ, Chester, PA; JR; BA; Acctg Soc Pres 88-; Penn Inst CPA'S 88-; Ntnl Asso/Acctnts 88-; Alpha Sigma Phi 89-; Sartomer Schlrshp 90; Merit Schlrshp; La Crosse 88-; CPA.

**MONIE, ANN C,** Marywood Coll, Scranton, PA; JR; BS; Dns Lst 90; Cmptr Op/Off Wrk David Harris Sons Co; AA Penn St Univ 82; Elem Ed; Tchg.

**MONIE, MURELENE,** Univ Of Tn At Martin, Martin, TN; GD; Phi Beta Sigma 84-85; Soc Wrk Clb 87-88; Soc Wrk Intrnshp 87-88; Im Sftbl Tm; BA 90; Soc Wrk; Ombudsman Vol Coord.

**MONINGER, JEANNETTE R,** Bethany Coll, Bethany, WV; SR; BA; Pblc Rltns Clb Sec 90-; Gamma Sigma Kappa 90-; Sigma Delta Chi Sec/Treas 89-; Soc Cllgt Jrnlsts 90-; WWVA Radio Intrnshp/Linsly Schl 89-; Cmnctns Dept Sr Flwshp 90-; Acdmc Excllnc Awd Cmnctns; IM Ftbl; Cmnctns; Pblc Rltns.

**MONIRUZZAMAN, A B M,** S U N Y At Stony Brook, Stony Brook, NY; JR; BS; Bangladesh Clb SAC 90-; Phi Theta Kappa 90-; Elec Engr/Cmptr Sci; Bus.

**MONIZ, EARL J,** Fayetteville St Univ, Fayetteville, NC; FR; BED; Asst Drctr Chnclrs Schlrshp Pgm 90-; US Army 68-90; Elem Ed/Psych; Tchng.

**MONIZ, LISA A,** Suffolk Univ, Boston, MA; FR; BA; Trnsfr Stdnt Exchnge; Ornttn Ldr; Acctng; CPA.

**MONJU, J SHARON,** Univ Of Southern Ms, Hattiesburg, MS; JR; BS; Psy Chi 90-; Phi Beta Kappa 89-90; Gamma Beta Phi; Hon Clg 90-; AA Pearl River Cmuty Clg 90; Psychology; Soc Wrk.

**MONK, MARY F,** Rivier Coll, Nashua, NH; JR; BSW; Cmps Mnstry Core Grp 89-; Rsdnt Hll Cncl Flr Rep 90; Flk Grp Orgnst 89-; Prjct HUG Brd 90-; Scl Wrk.

**MONK, MARY R,** Univ Of Ms Main Cmps, University, MS; GD; PHD; Assc Grad Stdnt Bdy 89-; Hlth Cr Grad Stdnt Assn VP 89-; Rpho Chi 90-; Phi Kappa Phi 90-; Phi Delta Chi; Alpha Chi Omega; Outstdng Grad Stdnt Awd 89; Amer Socty Hosp Phrmcsts 87-; Alabama Socty Hosp Phrmcsts 87-; Hlth Care Admin; Acad/Rsrch/Phrmcy.

**MONK, VICTORIA A,** Furman Univ, Greenville, SC; FR; BA; Intvrsty Chrstn Fllwshp 90-; Sigma Nu Little Sisters 90-; Frshmn Advsr; Acdmc Schlshp 90-; Occptnl Thrpy.

**MONKELIS, CARRIE A,** Univ Of Pittsburgh, Pittsburgh, PA; SO; BA; Hand/Hand 89-; Lambda Sigma Soc 90-; Nrsg; RN.

**MONKS, JOSEPH C,** Slippery Rock Univ, Slippery Rock, PA; SR; BED; Intl Clb Pres; SRAPHERD Vp; Adptd Aqtrcs Prgm Crdntr; Delta Psi Kappa; Phi Epislon Kappa; Scl Olympcs Wrkshp Ldr Instrctr Skll Sts; Otstndng PE Mjr Yr; Acdmc Athltc Rcgntn; Deans Lst; Vrsty Crss Cntry; PSEA; NEA; Hlth Physcl Ed.

**MONLUX, ROXANNE M,** Springfield Tech Comm Coll, Springfield, MA; SO; RN; Hrtg Bptst Chrch; Sci; Nrsng.

**MONN, STACEY R,** Duquesne Univ, Pittsburgh, PA; FR; BA; Sclgy; Crmnl Jstc Fld.

**MONNIN, MARY JO,** Hilbert Coll, Hamburg, NY; SO; BED; Crmnl Just; Prbtn Offcr.

**MONNIN, TERESE L,** Oh St Univ, Columbus, OH; SR; BS; Golden Key 9o-; Phi Kappa Phi 90-; Phi Eta Sigma 87-; Alpha Lambda Delta 87-; Alpha Epsilon Delta 90-; Psi Chi 90-; Arts Sci Schlrshp 90-; Ohio Hse Repr Achvmnt Awd 90-; IM Arbcs 87-; Psychlgy; Med Schl.

**MONREAL, JANE L,** Univ Of Miami, Coral Gables, FL; JR; BBA; Hnrs Stdnts Assoc 89-; Golden Key 90-; NBC Corp Info Intern; Dns Lst 89-; Miss Asian-American Florida 89-90; Danceteam Capt 88-; Intl Finance/Mktg; Bsn Publctns.

**MONRO, GLENN A,** Lancaster Bible Coll, Lancaster, PA; SR; DR; Bsbl 90-; Dipl Prctcl Bible Trng Sch 90; Chrstn Educ Bible; Prfssr Tchr Pstr.

**MONROE, ANTIONETTE B,** Methodist Coll, Fayetteville, NC; JR; BA; Phi Theta Kappa 82-; NCSSA Pres 89-90; Cmbrlnd Co Dept Soc Svcs 90; AAS Halifax Cmnty Clg 80-82; Soc Work.

**MONROE, GINA M,** Univ Of Miami, Coral Gables, FL; SR; RN; BSN; Nrsng.

**MONROE, JENNIFER,** Wilberforce Univ, Wilberforce, OH; FR; BA; Voices Praise Gspl Choir 90-; Cmnctns/Jrnlsm; TV Brdcstng/Prdctn.

**MONROE, KEITH,** Vance Granville Comm Coll, Henderson, NC; NAACP.

**MONROE, KRISTA D,** Marshall University, Huntington, WV; JR; BBA; AMA 90-; Knn Yth Fllwshp VP 88-; Gamma Beta Phi Prsdnt 88-; Crdt Mrktng Assoc; Hntngtn Mll Mrchnts Assoc Intrn; Mrktng.

**MONROE, LA VERA R,** Peace Coll, Raleigh, NC; FR; BA; Stdnt Christian Assoc VP 90-; Chamber Singers 90-; Phi Theta Kappa 90-; Habitat Humanity; Cambridge Stdy Abroad Prog; IM Vlybl 90-; Elem Educ; Teacher.

**MONROE, MEREDITH LEE,** Univ Of Nc At Charlotte, Charlotte, NC; JR; BA; Phi Eta Sigma 88-; Golden Key; Deans List 87-; Chanclrs List 90; Philosophy; Envtl Wk/Visual Arts.

**MONROE, RUSS A,** Western New England Coll, Springfield, MA; SR; BSBA; Air Natl Guard Westfield MA Sgt; Intrnshp GA Cmnctns; Mktg/Advrtsng.

**MONROE-BERDAN, GRANT R,** Hudson Valley Comm Coll, Troy, NY; FR; AAS; Shpr; Mrtry Sci; Fnrl Serv.

**MONROIG-ARCE, MARILYN,** Inter Amer Univ Pr Arecibo Un, Arecibo, PR; FR; BA; Advntst Chrch Camuy P R Tchr; ASES SCRR Jr Clg 83.

**MONROY, MARTA R,** Miami Dade Comm Coll North, Miami, FL; SO; AA; AS CENEI Spain Cmptr Prog 81-84; Psychlgy.

**MONSEAU, ANISSA K,** West Liberty St Coll, West Liberty, WV; FR; BA; Wv Tns Fr Lf 88-; Wv Grls St Cnslr 89-; Deans Lst 90; Coll Sclr Athlt 90-; Vlybl; Dntl Hygn/Pre Dntstry; Dntstry Rsrch.

**MONSERRATE MORERA, MARISOL,** Univ Of Pr At Mayaguez, Mayaguez, PR; JR; BS; Amer Chem Soc 89-; Phi Kappa Phi; Arts/Sci Stdnt Hnr Rl 89-; Eastman Kodak Schlrshp; USAA Alla Mer Schlr; Chem; Pharmacy.

**MONSEUR, JANET L,** Oh Dominican Coll, Columbus, OH; JR; BA; Columbus Lit Cncl; Spnsh/Teach Eng.

**MONSOUR, MICHAEL M,** Le Moyne Coll, Syracuse, NY; SR; BA; Amnsty Intl VP; Stu Peace Pres; Hstry; Advrtsng/Pbl Rel; Fndtn Wrk.

**MONT BRUTON, JAIME J,** Inter Amer Univ Pr Arecibo Un, Arecibo, PR; JR; BA; Puerto Rico St Police 87-; Crmnl Jstc; Law.

**MONTAGLIONE, AARON D,** S U N Y Coll Of Tech At Alfred, Alfred, NY; FR; AAS; Alfred State Acctg Clb 90-; Indr/Otdr Trck Fld 90-; Bus Admn/Acctg.

**MONTAGUE, JAMES J,** Al A & M Univ, Normal, AL; JR; BS; Acctng Cl; Retail Asst Mgr 90-; Acctng.

**MONTAGUE, JANE M,** Belmont Coll, Nashville, TN; SR; BA; Religion.

**MONTAGUE, MONICA D,** Memphis St Univ, Memphis, TN; FR; BBA; Gama Beta Phi; Alpha Lambda Delta; Bus Acctg.

**MONTALBANO III, CARMINE,** Bloomfield Coll, Bloomfield, NJ; FR; BA; Crim Just; Law.

**MONTALBANO, KATHLEEN E,** Nova Univ, Ft Lauderdale, FL; GD; MBA; Hmn Res Soc V P; Hmn Res Assoc Brow Co; CPA Clb Ft Laud; Sigma Alpha Iota; Coral Ridge Presb Concert Choir; Sales Rep Commerce Clrg Hse Sales Rep Yr 90; BS Msc Ed Westchester Univ 76; Mgmt.

**MONTALDO, KAREN J,** Hillsborough Comm Coll, Tampa, FL; SO; AS; SNO 90-; Schlrshp St Jos Hosp; Legal Sec; Nurs Prog; RN.

**MONTALTO, BARBARA A,** Ramapo Coll Of Nj, Mahwah, NJ; JR; Deans List 89-; Art Thrpy.

**MONTALTO, JENNIFER HARGETT,** Univ Of Al At Birmingham, Birmingham, AL; GD; MA; Grad Stu Assoc 90-; Stu Btr Earth 90-; Amer Soc Trng/Dvlpmnt; Al Soc Hlth Care Educ Trng; Flwshp Prof Educ Serv Trng Dvlpmnt Dyson Inst; Athltc Schlrshp NWAL St Jr Coll 81-82; IM Bsktbl 83-; Sdwlk Safari Pro; Educ; Trng Dvlpmnt.

**MONTALVO CASTRO, IVELISSE,** Caribbean Univ, Bayamon, PR; SR; AAS; Secretarial Exec Sci.

**MONTALVO TOLEDO, HELVIA J,** Inter Amer Univ Pr San German, San German, PR; SR; BA; Cncrt Choir 86-; Music Band 88-90; UIA Inst Invstgtn 90-; Hnr Pgm Pres 86-; Hnr Pgm Nwspr Edtr 87-88; Anml Shltr PR 90-; Awrds Coop/Ldrshp 87-88; Hnr Cert 87-; Cert Crl Sngr Year/Story Cntst; Mayor/Psy/Msc; Indl Psy MBA.

**MONTALVO, ANGIE,** City Univ Of Ny Baruch Coll, New York, NY; JR; Hspnc Soc 90-; Bus Mgmt; Htl Mgmt.

**MONTALVO, BLANCA M,** Bayamon Tech Univ Coll, Bayamon, PR; SR; BBA; Hrnr Stdnt Assc 89-; Tennis 88-; Acctng; Cpa.

**MONTALVO, DEXIMARY,** Inter Amer Univ Pr San German, San German, PR; FR.

**MONTALVO, FARRAH,** Fl International Univ, Miami, FL; SO; BED.

**MONTALVO, MARIA D,** Atlantic Union Coll, S Lancaster, MA; SO; BA; CHISPA Sec 90-; Seventh Day Advntst Med Cadets Sub-Sec 89-90; Vlybl Tm 90-; Eng.**

**MONTALVO, MICHELE,** Inter Amer Univ Pr Hato Rey, Hato Rey, PR; FR; BS; Ntrl Sci; Med.

**MONTALVO-RODRIGUEZ, NYDIA,** Bayamon Central Univ, Bayamon, PR; SO; XA; Cmptr Sci Assoc 90; Cmptr Syst.

**MONTANA, MELISSA T,** Saint Johns Univ, Jamaica, NY; JR; BA; Sigma Chi Zeta VP 90-; Communication Arts; Public Reltns Pratr.**

**MONTANARO, RITA J,** Indiana Univ Of Pa, Indiana, PA; SO; BS; Provost Schlr 90-; Eng Ed; Tchg.

**MONTANEZ DEL VALLE, IAN J,** Inter Amer Univ Pr Hato Rey, Hato Rey, PR; SO; BA; Judo Fdrtn; Eng; Mech Eng.

**MONTANEZ, CHRISTINE H,** Inter Amer Univ Pr Hato Rey, Hato Rey, PR; SO; BA; Educ; Tchr.

**MONTANEZ, JACQUELINE,** Miami Dade Comm Coll, Miami, FL; GD; BA; Sec III Miami-Dade Comm Coll Wolfson Cmps 87-; Bus; Mgmt.

**MONTANEZ, RAMON E,** Univ Of Pr At Mayaguez, Mayaguez, PR; SO; BEEE; Univ Mrchng/Cncrt Bnd 1st Prcsn 89-; Spec Partcpatn/New Yrk Parad 86; Natl Hnr Soc Coll Brd Schlrshp 89; Engr Faclty Hnr Stdnt; NCMLA; EMPUT Ldr 89-; JAC Ldr 87; Gov Schlrshp 89; NACME Schlrshp 89-; Roberto Clemente Awrd 89; Engr/Sci; Elec Engr.

**MONTAREZ SUAREZ, JUDITH,** Inter Amer Univ Pr Guayama, Guayama, PR; FR; BBA; Secretary; Navy Rsrv; Acctg/ Auditor.

**MONTE, DENISE M,** Univ Of Tn At Martin, Martin, TN; SO; Pi Sigma Epsilon; Alpha Delta Pi Treasurer; Alumni Cncl; Honors Seminar Schlrshp 89-; Leaders In Residence 89-90; Ldrshp Schlrshp 89-90; Tennis 89-90; Marketing.

**MONTEITH, ANGELA M,** Western Carolina Univ, Cullowhee, NC; JR; BS; Bio Clb 88-; Pre-Med Clb 88-; IM Vlybl/Sftbl/ Bsktbl 90-; Delta Pi Pldg Mrshl; Std Advsr; Dns Lst 88-; Bio/ Pre-Optmtry; Optometry.**

**MONTELEONE, CHRISTINE M,** Saint Johns Univ, Jamaica, NY; SR; BS; Kappa Delta Pi 89-; Deans Lst 88-; Edctn Hstry; Tchng.

**MONTELEONE III, M MICHAEL,** Univ Of Miami, Coral Gables, FL; FR; BS; Scuba 90-; Alpha Lambda Delta 90-; Pres Hon Rl 90; Marine Sci/Bio; Med/Rschr/Tchng.

**MONTELEONE-BITONDO, LINDA E,** Temple Univ, Philadelphia, PA; JR; BA; APHA 90-; Actn Aids Vol; Itln Clb 87-89; Rho Chi Soc 90-; Deans Lst 87-; Alpha Epsilon Delta; Gamma Sigma Sigma 87-89; March Dimes Walk-A-Thon; BA-BLGY/CHEM La Salle Univ 85-89; Phrmcy Instnl; Hosp Phrmcy/Phrmcy Rsrch.

**MONTELL, ROBERT SCOTT,** Fordham Univ, Bronx, NY; JR; BA; RA 90-; MIS Clb; CEO Brkfst Clb; Peer Educ; Alcohol Awrns; Asst Rsrchr Mis Dept; Beta Gamma Sigma; Hnrs Seminar; Dns Lst; MIS Intrsnshp IT/T Stamford Ct Plt Prog; Natl Srvc League To Tch Cmptr Skls Coll Of Foreign Trade Budapest Hungary; Finance; Intl Bus.

**MONTELL, SARAH M,** Oh Dominican Coll, Columbus, OH; SO; BED; Hp Htln Vol 87-89; Insrnc Indstry Sls Srvc 70-90; BS 84; Elem Ed.

**MONTELLO, PATRICK J,** Hudson Valley Comm Coll, Troy, NY; SR; AS; HVAC.

**MONTENERO, SEAN S,** S U N Y Coll Of Tech At Frmgdl, Farmingdale, NY; SO; BA; Bus.

**MONTERO, PETER C,** Oh Wesleyan Univ, Delaware, OH; SR; OH Wesleyan Arnesen Inst Brd Co Chr 90-; Sgm Alph Epsln 87-; Habitat Humnities 89; Liebermar Senate Intrn 90; Intrnshp Sec State Masschsts Citizens Inf Svc 90; Vrsty Swmng 88-89; Real Est 89; Cert Lee Inst 89; Pol Sci/Engl; Govt/Law.

**MONTERREY RODRIQUEZ, JANIN,** Univ Of Pr Humacao Univ Coll, Humacao, PR; SO; BA; Amer Chem Scty 90-; MBRS 90-; Certif Schlrshp Hnrs Students 90-; Certif Acad Exce; Natl Sci Faculty; Pharmacy.**

**MONTES AVILES, ROBERTO L,** Univ Politecnica De Pr, Hato Rey, PR; JR; BSME; Soc Of Physics Stdnts Treas 88-89; Greek Cncl Co-Fndr Supreme Cncl 86-89; Phi Delta Gamma Sec 86-87; BS U Of PR Rio Piedras 89; Mech Engrng; HVAL Designer.**

**MONTES COLON, MONICA C,** Inter Amer Univ Pr Hato Rey, Hato Rey, PR; SR; BBABA; AMA 90-; Pol Sci Assc 90-; Hon Scty 90; Mktg/Mgmt; MBA.

**MONTES VIVAR, DORA M,** Inter Amer Univ Pr San German, San German, PR; GD; BSN; Hon Pgm 87-89; Assn Stdnts Enfermeria 88-; Assn Stdnts Physchlgy 88-.

**MONTES, DANIELLE K,** Fl International Univ, Miami, FL; JR; BA; Blk Stdnt Org; Haitian Stdnt Org 90; Sigma Tau Delta 90; Phi Lambda Pblctns Ed 90; Gldn Drum Schlrshp To Prsnt Univ 86; Fl Undrgrad Schlrs Grnt 86-88; Haitian Cmmnty Vol In Litrcy Wth Newly Arrved Immgrnts 86-87; Lgl Trnsltn 86-87; Engl/Mnr In Pblc Admin; Law/Sclgy.

**MONTES, EVELYN,** Inter Amer Univ Pr Guayama, Guayama, PR; SO; BA; Cert Cir 90-; Cuadro De Hnr 89-; Cmptr Sci; Anlyst Tchg.

**MONTESA, M GAIL,** Embry Riddle Aeronautical Univ, Daytona Beach, FL; SO; BS; Ninety Nines 90-; Bro Wind 90-; Swm Clb 80-; Aerntcl Sci; Mltry Pilot.

**MONTESINO, LEANDRO L,** Norfolk St Univ, Norfolk, VA; JR; BA; Co Cmmndr; (ROTC; Deans Lst 90-; Blue/Gld Soc Ftr Nvl Offcrs Srfc Wrfr Assn 90-; Citznshp Awd; Coach IM Sftbl Tm; Coord Adopt Schl Pgm; US Navy 81; Chf Petty Offcr; AA Campbell Univ 90; Pltcl Sci; US Nvl Offcr.

**MONTFORT, JACK M,** Southern Coll Of Tech, Marietta, GA; SR; EET; Bapt Stdnt Un; Tau Alpha Pi; Phi Theta Kappa 87-89; IEEE 90-; Cir K Treas; AS Andrew Clg 89; Electl; Engr Tech.

**MONTGOMERY, ALBERTNETTA R,** Univ Of South Al, Mobile, AL; SR; BS; SGA VP 87; Phi Beta Lambda Sec 87; SD Bshp St Sngrs Pres 87; Deans Lst 88 90-; Hon Roll 87-; SNEA; AATE; YWA Pres 89-90; US Senate Intrn 87; OCSA 87-89; AS 87; Elem Ed; Tchng.

**MONTGOMERY JR, ALVIN E,** Univ Of South Al, Mobile, AL; SR; BED; Ducks Unlmtd Gulf Coast Cnsrvn Assn; Wldlf Artst/Chrtr Fshng Capt 88-; BA 85; Ed Scl Sci/Engl.

**MONTGOMERY, ANITA D,** Tuskegee Univ, Tuskegee Inst, AL; SR; BA; Sigma Doves 89-; MS Clb 87-89; Lit Soc Treas 87-90; Lambda Iota Tau Sec 90-; Sigma Gamma Rho; Engl; Law/ Bus.

**MONTGOMERY, DAWN M,** Christopher Newport Coll, Newport News, VA; SR; BA; Music Clb 88-89; Art Clb 89-; Art.**

**MONTGOMERY, DEBORA D,** Coppin St Coll, Baltimore, MD; SR; BS; Delta Sigma Theta Treas 90-; Alpha Kappa Mu; Delta Sigma Theta Treas 89-; Spec Ed Priv Donor Schlrshp; Spec Ed; Tchg.

**MONTGOMERY, ERYN L,** Atlantic Union Coll, S Lancaster, MA; JR; BA; Schlrs Chpl 90-; Atlntc Union Cllgt Choir 89-; Hon Core 88-; Engl/Bus Admin.

**MONTGOMERY, FELISA C,** Bowling Green St Univ At Huron, Huron, OH; SO; AA; Cmptrs; Prgmng.

**MONTGOMERY, FRANCIS G,** Cooper Union, New York, NY; JR; BEE; Chess/Brdg 88-; Bwlng 89-; Tau Beta Pi V P; Eta Kappa Nu Pres; Deans Lst 89-; Elect Eng; Law.

**MONTGOMERY, FRANK L,** Birmingham Southern Coll, Birmingham, AL; SR; BA; Finance/Mrkting.

**MONTGOMERY, KATHY,** Duquesne Univ, Pittsburgh, PA; SR; BS; Comm Theatre 87-; Wddng Soloist 87-; Chrch Cantor 87-; Perf Trio 87-; Music; Educ.

**MONTGOMERY, LISA J,** Tn St Univ, Nashville, TN; SR; BS; Assoc For Yng Chldrn; Erly Chldhd Edn; Teach.

**MONTGOMERY, MARGARET BONITA,** Palm Beach Comm Coll, Lake Worth, FL; JR; BA; Phi Theta Kappa; Aerobics/Fitns Assoc Of Amer; Human Rsrcs; Human Rsrcs Mgt.**

**MONTGOMERY, MARGARET L,** Univ Of Southern Ms, Hattiesburg, MS; SO; Eagle Clb 89; Gamma Beta Phi 89; Accntng; CPA.

**MONTGOMERY, MONIQUE D,** Hillsborough Comm Coll, Tampa, FL; SO; BA; Plnt City Coord Stdnt Nwspr; Phi Theta Kappa; Beta Phi Gamma; Intrn TV Sta; Mass Communications.

**MONTGOMERY, ROBERT A,** Nova Univ, Ft Lauderdale, FL; GD; MBA; 100 Clb 89-90; Cruise Lines Mrkt Analyst 87-; BS Florida State Univ 86; Intl Bus; Exec Mgmt.

**MONTGOMERY, ROSALYN S,** Central St Univ, Wilberforce, OH; SO; BS; Soclgy Clb VP 90-; Clss Hnr Dns Lst 89-90; Clg Hnr 90-; Soc.

**MONTGOMERY, SUSAN J,** Oh Univ-Southern Cmps, Ironton, OH; JR; AA; Gldn Ky; Gamma Pi Delta 90-; Reg Higher Educ Schlrshp 90-; Secy 73-81; Exec Secy Cert Hntngton Jr Clg Of Bus 73; Elem Educ; BED.

**MONTGOMERY, SUSAN M,** Univ Of Cincinnati, Cincinnati, OH; FR; BA; Nrsng.

**MONTGOMERY, THERESA E,** Fl A & M Univ, Tallahassee, FL; FR; DVM; Anml Sci; Vet.

**MONTGOMERY III, THOMAS V,** Morehouse Coll, Atlanta, GA; FR; BA; Prspctv Stdt Seminar Grp Ldr; Morehouse Bsn Assoc 90-; Dorm Cncl/Stdt Sen Advsr 90-; Inroads/Atlanta Grnd Mtrpltn Pillsbury Co; Rsdnt Asst; IM Bsktbl 90-; Bsn Admin/ Mrktg; Bsn Sales/Mrktg.

**MONTGOMERY, TINA L,** Univ Of Nc At Charlotte, Charlotte, NC; JR; BA; Psychlgy; Substance Abuse Trtmnt.

**MONTIERO-PRIOLEAU, JEAN,** City Univ Of Ny City Coll, New York, NY; SO; BA; Alpha Sigma Lambda; Credit Union Spvr Comm; Nws Ltr Ed; Acctnt NY Pstl Data Ctr; Lbrl Arts; Bus Mgmt.

**MONTIGNY, JEFFREY L,** Worcester Poly Inst, Worcester, MA; FR; BS; Rugby Clb Treas 90-; Elec Eng.

**MONTILLA, MARIA ELENA,** Georgetown Univ, Washington, DC; SO; BA; PR Assoc 89-; Skilled Clergy Central Amer Schlrshp Pgm 90; Asst Prop Acctg Ofc; Acctg; CPA.

**MONTLE, KEITH R,** Hocking Tech Coll, Nelsonville, OH; SO; AAS; 4 H Advsr 89-; Sprtmns Scty 85-; Intern Lake Snowden 88-; Fsh Mgmt; Mngr.**

**MONTMINY, PAULA A,** Newbury Coll, Brookline, MA; SR; AAS; Phys Thrpy Asst Clb 89-; Dns Lst 89-90; Allied Hlth; Phys Thrpy Asst.

**MONTOR, JANET M,** Anne Arundel Comm Coll, Arnold, MD; SO; MBA; Dble Mjr Psych Scl Wrk; Cnslr.

**MONTOYA, MARIA DEL ROSARIO,** Fl Atlantic Univ, Boca Raton, FL; SR; BA; Vocbly Mastery Awd 89; Acad Actvt Awd 88; Striving Excell Awd; BA Food Engrg Uniersidad De Bogota Jorge Tadeo Lozanao 88; Mktng; MBA.

**MONTREUIL, FRANCE G,** Va Commonwealth Univ, Richmond, VA; JR; BS; Frshmn Ntnl Hnr Soc VP 88-; Physcl Thrpy Clb; Gldn Key; Vlntr Physcl Thrpy Dpt Vrs Hsptls; IM Vlybl Sftbl; Psychology; Physcl Thrpy.

**MONTY, KATHRYN M,** Schenectady County Comm Coll, Schenectady, NY; FR; AA; Tutorial Svc; SGA Return Adult Stdnt Achvmnt Schlrshp; Girl Boy/Pioneer Sctng Ldr 81-90; Sunday/Vctn Bible Schl Tchr 80-; Humanites; Elem Ed.

**MOO-YOUNG JR, HORACE K,** Morgan St Univ, Baltimore, MD; SR; BS; Crs Cntry/Trck/Fld Cptn 87-; NSBE 90-; ASCE; Alpha Kappa Mu; Alpha Lambda Delta 87-; NASA Morgan Pgm 87-88; NSWC Intrn 89; RPI Rsrch Intrn 90; Cvl Engrg; PH D Engrg.

**MOODIE, MARILYN J,** City Univ Of Ny Baruch Coll, New York, NY; SR; BBA; Fnce/Ecnmcs Clb 89; Gldn Key 89-; Phi Theta Kappa 87-88; Trnsfr Schlr 88-; Bsn Admn Schlp 88-; Colston Schlp Awd 88; AA Brnx Comm Clg 88; Fnce; Corp Law.

**MOODIE, WENDY A,** City Univ Of Ny Med Evers Coll, Brooklyn, NY; SO; BA; Bio; Pre-Med.

**MOODY, ANGELA L,** Clarkson Univ, Potsdam, NY; JR; BA; NSPA 89; NYSIA Tutor For Accntng I II NCCC 88-89; Phi Theta Kappa; Clksn Soc Of Accntnts; Pres Schlr 90; Deans Lst; Wayne Gregoire Mem Schlrshp 90; Ntl Soc Of Pblc Accntnts Schlrshp 90; AS N Cnty Cmmnty Clg 90; Accntng/Tech Cmmnctns Cncntrtn; CPA.

**MOODY, BONNIE C,** Anson Comm Coll, Ansonville, NC; JR; AS; Marshal; Human Svc Awrd; Sun Sch Tchr Sect Ushr Brd; Soc Svc.

**MOODY, CANDISE L,** Bethel Coll, Mckenzie, TN; SO; BS; Gamma Beta Phi 90-; Sclgy; Jvnl Law.

**MOODY, CASSANDRA G,** Radford Univ, Radford, VA; FR; BBA; Fin; Bus.

**MOODY, DANNY M,** Pellissippi St Tech Comm Coll, Knoxville, TN; JR; BS; Camp Radkio Univ AK Anchorage 89-90; Cmptr Sci; R/D Artjcl Intell.

**MOODY, IMANI D,** Morehouse Coll, Atlanta, GA; FR; Spnsh Clb 90-; Cncrt Bnd 90-; Econ/Spnsh; Bus/Law.

**MOODY JR, JAMES STEPHEN,** City Univ Of Ny Baruch Coll, New York, NY; SR; BBA; Fin/Econ Soc Sec 90-; Sigma Alpha Delta 90-; Golden Key 90-; Omicron Delta Epsilon; Pres Enterprise Zone Task Force 82; MD Park/Plnng Cmsn/Rsrch Analyst 83; Oakland Dvlpmnt Plnng Intern 80-81; Amer Plnng Assn 82-89; Amer Econ Assn 90-; Fin/Invstmnts; Law/Bsn.

**MOODY, JANICE M,** Univ Of Sc At Coastal Carolina, Conway, SC; BA; Phi Eta Sigma; Elem Educ; Teach.

**MOODY, JARED K,** Northeast State Tech Comm Coll, Blountville, TN; FR; AAS; Appl Sci; Elec Engr.

**MOODY JR, JOSEPH W,** Univ Of South Al, Mobile, AL; SO; BED; Scndry Edn/Soc Sci; High Sch Tchr/Prfsr.

**MOODY, LEASHIA L,** Walker Coll, Jasper, AL; SO; BA; W-Clb Clg Bowl; Jazz Bnd; Democrts; IM Vlybl; Psych; Cmnty Svc.

**MOODY, MARK K,** Univ Of Sc At Salkehatchie, Allendale, SC; SO; BED; Tau Kappa Epsilon; BED; Bsnss Admin; Bsnss Mngmnt.

**MOODY, MARY L,** Univ Of Sc At Columbia, Columbia, SC; JR; BSN; Gamma Beta Phi 90-; Delta Delta Delta 87-88; Nrsng.

**MOODY, PAULA S,** James Sprunt Comm Coll, Kenansville, NC; FR; AAS; Crmnl Jstc; Law Enfrcmnt.

**MOODY, SONIA R,** Meridian Comm Coll, Meridian, MS; JR; BS; Phi Theta Kappa Rprtr 89-; NARD ASP; Phi Theta Kappa Rprtr 89-; Gldn Key 90-; Phi Delta Chi Sec 90-; AA 90; Phrmcy; RPH.

**MOODY, TAMMY L,** Mount Olive Coll, Mount Olive, NC; JR; BS; Phi Beta Lambda 88-; Drm Cncl Pres 89-; Honors Prog 88-; Std Affrs Com 89-; Food Srvcs Com 90-; SGA 89-; Yrbk Stff 88-; Business Admin; Mngmnt.

**MOODY, TRICIA J,** Shaw Univ, Raleigh, NC; FR; BA; Dns Lst 90-; ROTC Mltry Dns Lst SGT 90-; Trck Fld 90-; Physcl Thrpy; Mltry Rsrvs PT.

**MOODY, VANESSA M,** Wilberforce Univ, Wilberforce, OH; SR; BA; New Phi Beta Pres 87-; Stdnt Govt Assoc 87-89; Sigma Omega Pres VP 88-; Delta Sigma Theta Sec 90-; Miss Wilberforce Pgnt 1st Rnnr Up 88-89; Indstl Psych; Corp Law.

**MOODY, W DERRICK,** Morehouse Coll, Atlanta, GA; SR; MD; Golden Key; Magna Cum Laude 90-; Hnr Rl 87-; Dns Lst 87-; Phi Beta Kappa; Beta Kappa Chi 90-; BS; Bio; Med.**

**MOOMAW, SCOTT A,** Bridgewater Coll, Bridgewater, VA; SO; BA; Math Clb Pres 90-; Physics Clb 89-; Assoc Cmptng Mach 90-; Lambda Soc 90-; Omicron Delta Kappa 89-; Acad Cmptr Ctr Asst 90-; Cmptr Sci/Math; Sftwre Engr.

**MOON, BRYAN S,** Air Force Inst Of Tech, Wrt-Ptrsn Afb, OH; GD; MS; Sigma Iota Epsilon; BSEE Univ Tex Austn 86; Contrctng Mgmt.

**MOON, H SUZANNE,** Kent St Univ Kent Cmps, Kent, OH; JR; BA; Korean Stdnt Assoc Chrprsn; Golden Key; Asian Assoc Of Cleveland Akron Treas 89; Birth Rght Holland Chptr VP 84-88; Pro-Lfe Holland Chptr Mi Acting Chrprsn 84-88; Psychlgy; Clncl Psychlgy.**

**MOON, HONEY M,** Central Fl Comm Coll, Ocala, FL; FR; AA; Bnd Coll Orchstr; Cmmnty Schlrs; Engl.

**MOON, MARK ANTHONY,** Nova Univ, Ft Lauderdale, FL; GD; MBA; Jaycees; Dir Oper 81; BA Deapul Univ 78; Intl Bsn; Bsn Mgmt.

**MOON, MELISSA M,** Univ Of Cincinnati, Cincinnati, OH; SR; BS; Res Advsr 88-90; Delta Sigma Beta Pldge Eductr 89-; Gene Carte Awd Crim Justice; Crim Justice; Masters Crmnl Jstce.

**MOON JR, RALPH L,** Union Inst, Cincinnati, OH; SR; BA; Gthc Ldg 122 Prnce Hl Free/Accptd Masons Wrshpfl Mstr 86-88; NAACP 75-; Hamilton Cnty Brd Elctns 80-; Trstee Brd New Prospect Bptst Sec 84; Proclmtn Offc Myr Key To City 90; Res Ohio Hse Reps 90; Ohio Snte Sntrl Citn 90; Bus Admin/Mrktg; Dctrl.

**MOON, ROBERT E,** Va Commonwealth Univ, Richmond, VA; JR; BS; Acctng/Law; Tax Atty.

**MOON, ROBERT L,** Salisbury St Univ, Salisbury, MD; GD; MA; VP Cmps/Comm Affrs 87-88; Rugby Tm Pres/Capt 88-90; Pltcl Sci Clb Pres 89-90; Pi Sigma Alpha; Rsrch Intrn-Dmcrtc Cngrssnl Cmpgn Comm Rsrch Intrn 89; Pltcl Sci; Law/Pltcs/Prfssr.

**MOON, SHIN-YOUNG,** Manhattan School Of Music, New York, NY; SO; BM; Presb Church Clg Grp 89-; Harbor Perf Arts Ctr; Sunny Msc Studio; Pianist 89-; Msc Piano; Pfrsr Perfmr.

**MOONA, SHERRIE Z,** Wagner Coll, Staten Island, NY; SR; BS; Alethea VP 89; Tri Beta 90; Im Vllybl 87; Bio; Med.

**MOONAN, JENNIFER C,** Boston Coll, Chestnut Hill, MA; JR; BSN; Mss Stdnt Nrs Assoc 88-; Schl Nrsng Sen Sec 88-89; Sigma Theta Tau; Smmr Pstn Dn Frbr Cncr Inst; Nrsng.

**MOONEY, ERICKA T,** Univ Of Va Clinch Valley Coll, Wise, VA; SO; BS; Deans Lst 90-; Soc Sci; Edn.

**MOONEY, GREGORY C,** Villanova Univ, Villanova, PA; SO; BA; Var Campus Minstry Act Lectr; Spgn Char Fundrsr Chrprsn; Omicron Delta Kappa; Stdnt Tutrng For Inner Cty Kids 89-; Spec Olymp Vol 89-; Stdnt Lector Habitat For Hum; IM Sprts 89; History.

**MOONEY, SARAH J,** Ms St Univ, Miss State, MS; JR; Bioengr Soc Pres 89-; Soc Wmn Engr Pblcty Chr 89-; Bapt Stu Union Srvdn Msn Comm 89-; Phi Eta Sigma Sec 90-; Alpha Lambda Delta 90-; Gamma Beta Phi 90-; White Rose Crt Sigmanu Ltl Sis 90-; Deans Schlr 89; Biolgcl Engr; Envrnmtl.

**MOONEYHAM, DEBRA A,** Snead St Jr Coll, Boaz, AL; FR; BA; Street Singrs 90-; Phi Theata Kappa; Acad Schlrshp; Street Sngrs Schlrshp; Comm; Advtsng/Pub Rltns.

**MOONEYHAN, DONNA J,** Lenoir Rhyne Coll, Hickory, NC; GD; Judcl Cncl 77-78; Sci Clb 75-78; Drama Clb 75-78; Alpha Chi; Physcs Awrd 76; Chrch Cncl Snday Schl Tchr; Chrch Aux Pres; Duke Pwr Co Chemst 79-85; BS Gardner-Webb Coll 78; Cert Lenoir Rynee Coll 90; Biolgy/Chem; Tch.

**MOORE, AARON J,** Me Maritime Academy, Castine, ME; FR; BS; Academy Band 90-; Fire Brigade 90-; Nautical Science; Shipping.

**MOORE, ABLE A,** Savannah St Coll, Savannah, GA; SO; BSW; Social Work.

**MOORE, ALLISON G,** Dyersburg St Comm Coll, Dyersburg, TN; SO; BA; Elem Ed; Tch.

**MOORE, ALMA L,** Jackson St Univ, Jackson, MS; SO; BED; Alpha Lambda Delta 89-; Pres Schlr 89-; Deans List Schlr 90-; Ed; Elem Ed.

**MOORE, ALTINA M,** Wilmington Coll, New Castle, DE; GD; BS; Phi Theta Kappa 81; Poultry Prcsng Equip; AAA 82; Bus Mgmt; Bus.

**MOORE, AMANDA L,** Queens Coll, Charlotte, NC; SO; BA; Cmnctns Club Secy/Treas 90-; Learning Soc Stdnt Chrprsn/Ticket Sls 90-; Clg Nwspaper Reprtr/Ads 90-; Alpha Delta Pi Corrspndg Secy 89-; Org Agnst Soc Injstc/Suffrng90-; Intrnshp Southeast Magzn Reprtr; Cmnctns/Engl; Publc Rltns.

**MOORE, AMY J,** Ms Univ For Women, Columbus, MS; JR; BS; Stdnt Msp Assn Of Edctrs 90-; Kappa Delta Epsilon; Lpn; Crtfct In Voc Tech Coll 85; Elem Edctn; Tchng.

**MOORE, ANDREA L,** Western Ky Univ, Bowling Green, KY; SR; MS; Cmps Crsd Chrst Stdy Ldr 89-; Cir K 86-88; Phi Kappa Phi 89-90; Natl Stu Spch Lng Hrng Assc 88-; Dean Schlr 86-; Magna Cum Laude; BS; Cmmnctns Dsrdrs; Spch Path.

**MOORE, ANGELA C,** Christopher Newport Coll, Newport News, VA; FR; BS; Bio; Doctor.

**MOORE, ANGELA D,** Univ Of Tn At Martin, Martin, TN; FR; BA; Psychlgy.

**MOORE, ANGELA L,** Thomas Nelson Comm Coll, Hampton, VA; SO; BS; Cmptr Info Syst; Pgmg.

**MOORE, ANGELA M,** West Liberty St Coll, West Liberty, WV; FR; Whlng Hosp Vol; Coll Srvce Tutor; Phys Thrpy.

**MOORE, AUDRA I,** Ms St Univ, Miss State, MS; JR; BA; Univ Hnrs Cncl Evltn Chr 89-; Russian Club Se C89-; Stdnt Adv Comm To Dean Arts/Sci; Phi Eta Sigma 89-; Gamma Beta Phi Soc Coord 90-; BARK 89-; Pres Schlr 89-; Phase I; Foreign Lang-Russian; Law.**

**MOORE, AUTUMN A,** Univ Of Nh Plymouth St Coll, Plymouth, NH; SO; Rugby.

**MOORE, BARRY R,** Fl St Univ, Tallahassee, FL; SR; BA; Retire USCG Lt Cmndr; Anthrplgy; Archlgy.

**MOORE, BENJAMIN G,** Coll Of Charleston, Charleston, SC; SR; BS; French 89-90; Ski Clb 87-88; Alpha Tau Omega Jdcl Brd 88; Acad Hnr Roll; Beta Xi Excllnce In Shclrshp; Ims Tennis/Soccer 87; Intrnshp Chrlstn Trdnt Chmbr Of Cmmrce 90; Bsnss/Frnch.

**MOORE, BETTY A,** Morehead St Univ, Morehead, KY; JR; BA; Spec Educ; Tchr.

**MOORE, BEVERLY A,** Roane St Comm Coll, Harriman, TN; SO; AAS; Medicine; Med Lab Tchnlgy.

**MOORE, BRADLEY T,** Oh Wesleyan Univ, Delaware, OH; FR; Phi Eta Sigma; Sigma Chi; Tns 90-; Hstry; Internatl Law.

**MOORE, CARLA L,** Middle Ga Coll, Cochran, GA; SO; BS; Gamma Beta Phi 89-; Deans List 89-; AS Busn Adm; Busn Admin; Acctng.

**MOORE, CARLA R,** Davis & Elkins Coll, Elkins, WV; JR; BA; Music Soc Pres 90-; Delta Comp Sci Treas 89-90; Stdnt Assmbly Rep 89-90; Hon Prog 88; Acdmc All Amer; Coll Trmptr 89-; Sngwrtr For Rcrdng Artsts 90-; Music Prfrmnce; Music.

**MOORE, CARMEN P,** Stillman Coll, Tuscaloosa, AL; FR; BA; Hstry Clb; Pre Law Soc VP; Gamma Iota Sigma; Alpha Phi Alpha Swthrt; NAACP; Dean Schlr; Dean Lst; Vllybl Tm; Hstry/Pre Law; Law.

**MOORE, CAROL SUZANNE,** Univ Of North Fl, Jacksonville, FL; SR; BSN; Amrcn Hrt Assn Mrktng 87; Blue Crs Blu Shld Sprvsr; ASN Floyd Jr Clg 80; Nrsng.

**MOORE, CAROLYN,** Fayetteville St Univ, Fayetteville, NC; JR; BS; Bio Clb; Bio Tutor; License Csmtlgy Walkers Beauty Ack 81; Dntl Asst Cert USA Army Ft Sam Huston 83; Bio; Med Schl.

**MOORE, CAROLYN R,** Patrick Henry Comm Coll, Martinsville, VA; SO; AAS; Bus Tech.

**MOORE, CECILIA A,** Univ Of Sc At Columbia, Columbia, SC; FR; BA; Rtrng Stdnts Assoc; Phi Eta Sigma 90-; Dns Lst/Chnclrs Lst 90-; Pi Kappa Delta/Pres Lst 90-; Elem Ed.

**MOORE, CHALISSA Y,** Fayetteville St Univ, Fayetteville, NC; FR; BS; Cls Ofcr Treas 90-; Res Ofcr Sec 90-; Univ Ambsdr 90-; LEAP Tutor 90-; Univ Human Rel Cncl; Biol; Phrmcy.

**MOORE, CHARLES C,** Ky St Univ, Frankfort, KY; SR; BA; Bkbl Captn 88-; Crmnl Juste/Mktg; Law Sch/Mktg.

**MOORE, CHRIS S,** Southeastern Comm Coll, Whiteville, NC; FR; Bsbll Tnns 90-.

**MOORE, CHRISTIE L,** Union Univ, Jackson, TN; FR; BS; Fllwshp Of Chrstn Athlts 90-; Chi Omega 90-; Vrsty Bsktbl 90-; Bus Educ.

**MOORE, CHRISTINA A,** Wv Northern Comm Coll, Wheeling, WV; FR.

**MOORE, CHRISTINA L,** Commonwealth Coll, Norfolk, VA; SO; AAS; Thspn Clb Tres; Nwspr; Alpha Beta Gamma; Alpha Tau; Prsdnts Lst; Deans Lst; Bsns Mgmnt; MBA.

**MOORE, CHRISTINA V,** Valdosta St Coll, Valdosta, GA; JR; BSN; GA Assoc Nrsng Stdnts Sec 90-; Tchr Sci 89; BSED 86; Nrsng.

**MOORE, CHRISTOPHER J,** Johnson C Smith Univ, Charlotte, NC; FR; Adv Brd 90-; IM Bsktbl 90-; Cmptr Sci; Sys Anlyst.

**MOORE, CHRISTY M,** Ms Univ For Women, Columbus, MS; SR; BS; Stdnt Govt Assn VP 89-; NAA VP 89-; Un Advsry Cabnt 89-; Phi Kappa Phi; Mortr Brd 90-; Amer Soc Womn Acctnts 90-; Univ Miss Grad Asstnshp; NAA Otstdng Acctg Stdnt; Otstdng Stdnt Acctg; Acctg; Mba.

**MOORE, CINDY W,** Middle Ga Coll, Cochran, GA; SO; BS; Tchrs Aid Brown 87; Mem Preschl/Pianist/Yth Chr/Dir/Bndy Schl Tchr 1st Assmbly God Wrightsvl 87-; Drvng Schl Bus 87-; Chem/Scndry Ed/Sci/Ed Mdle Grades; Tch Chem.

**MOORE, COLLEEN D,** Hudson Valley Comm Coll, Troy, NY; SR; AS; SCA Pres 90-; Pres Lst 90-; SCA Bk Tbl Bake Sl Food Dr Coord 90-; Yth Alive Yth Ldr 90; AIM Mssnry; Music Mnstry Vclst 88-; Hmn Serv.

**MOORE, CORA B,** Fayetteville St Univ, Fayetteville, NC; BS; NC Assoc Edtrs; Alumn Fayetteville Tchl Comm Clg; Lewis Chapel Missionory Bpt Chrch; Sunday Scl/Vaeahion Bible Schl Tchr; Sr Choir; Fmly Serv Vltr; Red Cross Vltr; Middle Edtn Mjr; AAS Fayetteville Tchl Comm Clg 80; Middle Edtn; Tch.

**MOORE, DANA E,** Hampton Univ, Hampton, VA; JR; BA; Natl Assoc Black Acctnts 90-; Alpha Kappa Mu 90-; Chrldng Capt 89-91; Acctng.

**MOORE, DARLENE K,** Va Commonwealth Univ, Richmond, VA; SR; BFA; Vol Work Grace House 90-; Art History Crafts.

**MOORE, DARRYL D,** Va St Univ, Petersburg, VA; FR; BA; Sci/Math; Mech Eng.

**MOORE, DAVID B,** Univ Of North Fl, Jacksonville, FL; SO; BA; Sigma Chi Schlrshp Chrmn 90-; Blgy; Med Dr.

**MOORE, DAVID B,** Roane St Comm Coll, Harriman, TN; SO; BS; SGA Fee Brd; Gamma Beta Phi; Raider Corps; Deans Lst; Outstndng Raider Corps; Bsbl; Bio.

**MOORE, DAVID C,** Southern Coll Of Tech, Marietta, GA; SO; BA; AIAS 90-; Co Ownr Rembrndt Entrprs 88-; Arch.

**MOORE, DAYTON I,** George Mason Univ, Fairfax, VA; GD; MA; Converse All-East Region 89; Bsbl Acad All-Amer 86; Bsbl Player 85-89; AA Garden City Cmnty 85-84; BS Phys Ed 88-90; Phys Educ; Coaching/Scouting.

**MOORE, DE ANNA R,** Cecils Coll, Asheville, NC; AAS; Paralegal; Law Criminal.

**MOORE, DEAN E,** Lenoir Rhyne Coll, Hickory, NC; JR; MBA; Bus Admin; Bus Mngr.

**MOORE, DEANNA,** Norfolk St Univ, Norfolk, VA; JR; BS; Mass Comm Std Asc 89-; Ldrshp Pgm 89-; Rdio Pgm Dir 90-; Alpha Kappa Mu 90-; Natl Clgt Comm Arts Awd; USAA All Amer Schlrs Awd; Mass Comm; Tlvsn Dir/Prdcng.

**MOORE, DEBBIE L,** Tn St Univ, Nashville, TN; SR; BS; NAACP Sec 88-90; SWE 88-; Natl Soc Blck Engrs 88-89; Alpha Kappa Mu Pres 88-; Tau Sigma Upsilon Treas; Detroit Edison Intrn 88-; Outstndng Sr Fclty Awrd; Elec Eng; Law.

**MOORE, DEMBRASKI M,** Stillman Coll, Tuscaloosa, AL; FR; BA; Prd Phi Prstg Tres; Dorm Actvs Comm 90-; Cordell Wynn Hnrs Pro; Gamma Iota Sigma; Bus Admin; Exec.

**MOORE, DIANA M,** Washington State Comm Coll, Marietta, OH; FR; AA; Acctg/Microcomputers; Microcomputer/Acctg.

**MOORE, DIHANNE A,** Univ Of Sc At Columbia, Columbia, SC; FR; Alpha Swthrt Clb; Mnrty Std Affrs/Acad Achvmnt Awd; Theatre; Acting/Directing.

**MOORE, DONNA H,** Western Piedmont Comm Coll, Morganton, NC; FR; Med Ast Clb 90-; Phi Theta Kappa Schlrshp 90; Med Asst.

**MOORE, DONNA L,** Univ Of Nc At Asheville, Asheville, NC; FR; BS; Biologist.

**MOORE, DONNA V,** Southwest Va Comm Coll, Richlands, VA; SO; AAS; Cmps Escrts 90-; Phi Theta Kappa Hstrn 90-; USA Tdy AACJC; Phi Theta Kappa Natl Schlrshp; Barry Goldwater Schlrshp Math Ntrl Scis; SVCC Mnrty Schlrshp; Tlnt Rstr Of Coll Brd Otstndng Stdts; Typst 89-; Educ Math And Bus; Tchng HS Or Coll.

**MOORE, DOREEN A,** City Univ Of Ny Queensbrough, New York, NY; SO; BA; Cmptr Clb 90-; Tutor; Stdnt Aide 90-; Alpha Beta Gamma 90-; Phi Theta Kappa; Bsn Dept High Avg Cmptrs; AAS; Bsn; Cmptr Pgmr/Syst Analyst.

**MOORE, EARL F,** Me Maritime Academy, Castine, ME; FR.

**MOORE, EDWARD A,** Davis Coll, Toledo, OH; FR; BA; Mngrl Acctg; CPA.

**MOORE, ELAINE S,** Univ Of Sc At Columbia, Columbia, SC; JR; BJAS; GAMMA 89-; LOCAL 89-; Delta Zeta Crtsy Chrmn 89-; Erly Chldhd Ed; Tchg.

**MOORE, ELIZABETH A,** Ms Univ For Women, Columbus, MS; SO; BS; Adptv Prnts Pgm 89-90; Math/Sci Clb 89-; Lntrn 90-; Torch; Deans Lst 89; Pres Lst 90-; Bus; Acctg.

**MOORE, ELIZABETH A,** Memphis St Univ, Memphis, TN; JR; BFA; Stdnt Nwspr Copy/Mngng Edtr 90-; Gldn Key 90-; Soc Pro Jrnlsts Sec 90-; Jrnlsm-News Edtrl; Jrnlst.

**MOORE, ELIZABETH LEE,** Middle Tn St Univ, Murfreesboro, TN; GD; ARMS 88-90; SEA 90; MTSU Equestrian Team 88-89; Inernship At Reptile Records 90; Equestrian 88-89; Recording Indstry Mgmnt; Mktg.

**MOORE, ELIZABETH M,** Univ Of Al At Birmingham, Birmingham, AL; SR; BS; Specl Educ Tchr.

**MOORE, ERICA P,** Converse Coll, Spartanburg, SC; SO; BS; Cnvrs Ldrs Prog 89-90; Stdnt Admssns Brd 90-; Yng Dmcrts 89-; Sec Fr Clss 89-90; Treas Jr Cls 90-; Crscnt Stdnt Govt Rep 90-; Deans Lst 89-; Cmptd Fr Converse Schlrs Prog 90-; Bus Admin/Mrktg; Mrktg Cnsltnt.**

**MOORE, ERIK A,** Ursinus Coll, Collegeville, PA; FR; BA; Nwspaper Cmptr Cnsltnt; Math/Econ.

**MOORE, GAYLA L,** Univ Of Southern Ms, Hattiesburg, MS; SO; Stdnt Almn Assoc; Gldn Grl Ftbl Rcrtr; Fshn Brd; Elem Ed.

**MOORE, GERALDINE M,** Radford Univ, Radford, VA; JR; BS; Bus Finance/Acctg; CPA.

**MOORE, GINA L,** Univ Of Nc At Charlotte, Charlotte, NC; FR; BS; Bapt Stdnt Union 90; Phi Eta Sigma 90; Physics; Engr.

**MOORE, GLENN CHRISTOPHER,** Siena Coll, Loudonville, NY; SR; BS; Comp Clb 87-; Sigma Pi Sigma 90-; Sigma Xi; Delta Epsilon Sigma; Gen Elec Res/Dev Intrn 90-; Rensselaer Polytech Inst; Track; Comp Sci; MS.

**MOORE, HARRY W,** Southern Coll Of Tech, Marietta, GA; GD; MS; Tau Alpha Pi 89-90; AT T Bell Lab Outstndng Achvmnt Awd 90; BSEET 90; Elctrcl Engrg.

**MOORE, HEATHER S,** Univ Of Ga, Athens, GA; SR; Kappa Delta Epsilon 89-; Adopt A Schl Comm 90-; Prtnrs Educ 90-; BSED In ECE; Early Chldhd Educ; Tchr.

**MOORE, HELEN M,** Univ Of Sc At Columbia, Columbia, SC; FR; BSN; Gamma Beta Phi 90-; Nursing; Midwifery.

**MOORE, HILLIARD L,** Fl A & M Univ, Tallahassee, FL; JR; Mdlng Trp 88-89; NAACP 88-; Urbn Leag 89-; Golden Key; Natl Mrt 86-; Phi Eta Sigma 88-; Kappa Alpha Psi Tr 90-; Eastmn Kodk Intrn; SBI Silvr Schlrshp; Eastmn Kodk Schlrshp; Busn Admin/Mktg; Mktg Mgr.

**MOORE, IRENE,** Al A & M Univ, Normal, AL; SR; BS; Ben Marcato Clb Sgt At Arms 89-; Lambda Sigma Pi Pres 88-90; Beta Beta Beta 88-90; Alpha Kappa Mu Rprtr 89-; Beta Kappa Chi 88-90; Martin Luther Kign Serv Clb 88; MARC Fllwshp 88-90; TRIO Desk Dir 87; MSRP Intrnshp UCLA 89; Zoology; Medicine.

**MOORE, JAMES M,** Ms St Univ, Miss State, MS; GD; Inter Frat Cncl Rep 87-88; Gamma Alpha Epsilon 87-90; Kappa Sigma Schlrshp Chrmn 85-90; BS 90.

**MOORE JR, JAMES R,** Old Dominion Univ, Norfolk, VA; JR; BS; IBEW Local 811; Cmnctns Elec Tech; AAS VA Wstrn Comm Coll 82; Elec/Electrnc Eng.

**MOORE, JANET K,** Oh Wesleyan Univ, Delaware, OH; JR; BA; Delta Zeta Almn Rltns 89-90; Sclgy/Anthrplgy; Bsn.

**MOORE, JEFFREY E,** Schenectady County Comm Coll, Schenectady, NY; FR; AOS; Asst Chef At Walt Disney World; Culinary Arts.

**MOORE, JENNIFER A,** Univ Of Miami, Coral Gables, FL; FR; BA; Alpha Lambda Delta; Intl Stds/Russian; Law Intl.

**MOORE, JENNIFER G,** Hillsborough Comm Coll, Tampa, FL; SO; AA; Phi Theta Kappa; Eng/Pblc Rltns; Law.

**MOORE, JEREMY D,** Univ Of Tn At Knoxville, Knoxville, TN; JR; BA; Phi Eta Sigma; Gamma Beta Phi; Gldn Key; IM Sccr Tnns; Bus Trnsprtn Lgstcs.

**MOORE, JERRY L,** Valdosta St Coll, Valdosta, GA; SO; BA; Computer Oper Leading Retailer; Math/Science; Mid Grades Ed.

**MOORE, JEWELL D,** Tri County Tech Coll, Pendleton, SC; FR; ADN; Stdnt Nurses Assn Pr 91-; Alpha Zeta Beta; Nursing.

**MOORE, JILL M,** Univ Of Nh Plymouth St Coll, Plymouth, NH; JR; BA; Amer Mktg Assoc Treas; Mktg; Advrtsg.

**MOORE, JOHN D,** Life Coll, Marietta, GA; GD; DC; Phi Kappa Phi 88; Otstndng Stdnt/Pol Sci Awrd Wnr 88; Un N FL; BA Un N Fl 88; Maga Cum Laude Pol Sci Un N FL 88; AA St Johns River Comm Clg 86; Chrprctc; Chrprctr.**

**MOORE, JOHN L,** Univ Of Montevallo, Montevallo, AL; SR; Alpha Kappa Appa Swthrt 78-88; Masonry 3rd & 7th Degree King 89; Wal-Mart Slpsrn 90; BS 90.

**MOORE, JOSEPH K,** North Greenville Coll, Tigerville, SC; SO; BA; Bptst Assc Yth Sndy Schl Dir 89-; AS No Greenville Coll; Cert EMT 78-; Outstndng Rescuer; Outstndng Ctzn 89; Lwr Piedmont Rescue Sqd Chpln 89-; Area Vol 85; Steering Com Teen Ctr; Church Rltd Vctn; Church Mnstry.

**MOORE, JULIE A,** S U N Y Coll At Postdam, Potsdam, NY; SR; MM; Opera Theatr 87-; MENC 87-; Pi Kappa Lambda 90-; Kappa Delta Pi 90-; Phi Kappa Phi; Sigma Alpha Iota VP 88-; Summa Cum Laude; Perfrmrs Cert; O D Goodrich Mem Awrd; BM Crane Schl Music/SUNY; Music; Voice Prfrmnce.

**MOORE, JULIE CATHARINE,** Richard Bland Coll, Petersburg, VA; JR; BA; Dns Lst 89-90; AS Richard Bland Clg; Engl; Law.

**MOORE, JULIE D,** Ms Gulf Coast Comm Coll, Perkinston, MS; SO; Nzrne Yth Intl Treas; Hnrs Prgm 89-; VP Lst 89-; AS; Acctg.

**MOORE, KATHERINE M,** Anne Arundel Comm Coll, Arnold, MD; SO; BS; Edctn; Tchng.

**MOORE, KATHLEEN M,** George Mason Univ, Fairfax, VA; JR; BA; Alpha Chi; Arbcs Instr 89-91; Acctg; Acctg Corprt Tax.

**MOORE, KATHY C,** Anson Comm Coll, Ansonville, NC; SO; AAS; Marshal; Annl Lrng Rsrc Ctr Media Ndlcrft Awd; Acctg.

**MOORE, KATINA A,** Bowie St Univ, Bowie, MD; FR; SGA VP 90; Engl/Sclgy; Law.

**MOORE, KATRINA L,** Memphis St Univ, Memphis, TN; JR; BBA; Mrchg Bnd 88-; Cncrt Bnd Pr Mntr Grp 88-; Ambsdr Brd 89-; Gamma Betaphi; Alpha Lambda Delta; Phi Eta Sigma 88-; Phi Kappa Phi; Gldn Key; Mrtr Brd 90-; Pi Sigma Epsilon VP Prsnl/Rcrtg 88-89; Finance; Fncl Anlys.

**MOORE, KAYLA M,** Marshall University, Huntington, WV; SR; BA; Amer Coll Hlth Cr Admin Chrmn 90-; Amer Coll Hlth Cr Exec; Delta Zeta Sorority Acdmc Chrprsn 89,Treas 90; Intrnshp Mdwbrk Acres Nrsng Ctr 90; Monica Ann Lucas Hlth Cr Mngmnt Schlrshp 90; Otstndng Coll Stdnts Amer 89; Hlth Care Mngmnt; Nrsng Hm Admin.

**MOORE, KELLIE J,** Johnson St Coll, Johnson, VT; SR; BA; Prsdnts Lst Intrnshp Stdnt Tchng; Spcztn Chldhd Edctn; Elem Edctn; Tchng.

**MOORE, KENNETH W,** Wilmington Coll, New Castle, DE; SR; BA; Hearn Schlrshp 76; Milford Hstrcl Soc Treas 83-; Actnt-Offc St Treas; AAS DE Tech/Comm Coll 77; Bsc/Stndrd Cert Amer Inst Bnkng 78; Acctg.

**MOORE, KIMBERLY A,** Vance Granville Comm Coll, Henderson, NC; FR; AAS; Ed Assoc Clb 90-; Early Chldhd; Occup Ther.

**MOORE, KRISTINA B,** Tn Wesleyan Coll, Athens, TN; SO; BED; SGA Sec 89-; Bapt Union 89-; Vrsty Bsktbl 89-; Hstry/Behav Sci; Guidance Cnslr.

**MOORE, LANITTA S,** Union Coll, Barbourville, KY; JR; NEASP; Sigma Nu Secy 89-90; Gold Medal 89-90; Hosp Vol; AA Sue Bennett 90; Elem Educ; Teacher.

**MOORE, LAQUITA M,** Univ Of Rochester, Rochester, NY; JR; BA; Spkr E Hgh Schl Annl Yth Mtvtn Day Rochester NY 89-90; Intrnshp/Pblc Dfndrs Offc Monroe Cty 89; Stdy Abrd Smstr Milan Italy; Pltcl Sci Mkt Frc Lctn Washington DC 88; Hstry; Prfssr Ancnt Cvlztn.

**MOORE, LATAUNYA D,** Jackson St Univ, Jackson, MS; JR; BS; Biolgy Clb 90-; Beta Beta Beta; Biolgy; Phys Therpy.

**MOORE, LATONYA,** Morris Coll, Sumter, SC; GD; MSW; Cnslr 88-90; Deans Lst 86-88/90-; Alpha Kappa Alpha Pres; H H Butler Awd 90; Social Wrkr.

**MOORE, LAURA MAE,** Roane St Comm Coll, Harriman, TN; SO; AAS; Med Lab; Tchnlgy Acad Awd 90; Med Lab Tchnlgy.

**MOORE, LEAH J,** Faulkner Univ, Montgomery, AL; FR; Hon Roll 90-; Medicine.

**MOORE JR, LEONARD DANIEL,** Spartanburg Methodist Coll, Spartanburg, SC; SO; BA; Psi Beta Kappa; Certif Spartanburg Techl Clg 86; Counseling Psychology.

**MOORE, LESLIE D,** Univ Of Ky, Lexington, KY; FR; BA; Soc Wmn Engrs 90; Estrn KY Hon Pgm; Lamda Sigma; Occptnl Thrpy.

**MOORE, LINDA B,** Medical Coll Of Ga, Augusta, GA; SR; BSN; Lamda Chi Nu Lander Coll; Sigma Theta Tau; ADN Lander Coll 84; Nrsng.

**MOORE, LINDA C,** Daytona Beach Comm Coll, Daytona Beach, FL; SO; BS; Otsdng Stdnt Educ 91; Excptnl Educ; Excptnl Ed Tchr.

**MOORE, LINDA D,** Ga St Univ, Atlanta, GA; SR; MBA; Phi Kappa Phi 90-; Kappa Delta Pi 89-; Gldn Key 89-; Dns Schlrshp Key 90; Mrtr Bd Awd Outstdng Schlrshp 90; Stdnt Qrtr Math 88; BED 90; Mdl Chldhd Ed; Tchr.

**MOORE, LINDA L,** Fl International Univ, Miami, FL; FR; BS; Ornttn Asst 90-; Hosp Vol 89-; Dns Lst 90-; Hnrs Pgm 90-; IM Vlybl 90-; Chem; Med.

**MOORE, LOUIS L,** Baldwin Wallace Coll, Berea, OH; SO; BA; Law Clb 90; Rep Clb 90; Inter Frat Cncl Permanet Rep 89-; Laurels Hnr Scty Sec 90-; Lambda Chi Alpha IFC Rep 89-; Summer Intrnshp 90-; Soccer 2 Yr Ltrmn 89-; Bsn/Pltcl Sci/Economics; Law.**

**MOORE, M ASHLEY,** Barry Univ, Miami, FL; SR; MA; Alpha Chi; Scl Act Dir Indpndt Rtrmnt Comm; BLS Barry U 90; Theo; Hlth Care Mnstry.

**MOORE, M GAYLE,** Gallaudet Univ, Washington, DC; SR; Never To Late Clb 89-90; Dns Advsry Brd 89-90; Phi Alpha Pi 89-; Dean Lst 89-; Pres Schlr 89-; Tx Bus Cncl 88-89; Psych/Engl; MA/CNSLNG.

**MOORE, MAE W,** Fayetteville St Univ, Fayetteville, NC; JR; BS; Young Amer Bowling Allnce VP 89-90; NCO Wives Clb 87-88; Parents/Tchr Stdnt Assn 90-91; Work Special Olympics 87-90; Red Cross Vol; Dental Asst; Sec; Cert Phillips Bus Clg 68; Cert 87; Drug/Alcohol Abuse Cnclr.

**MOORE, MARIUS A,** Morehouse Coll, Atlanta, GA; FR; BA; Bus; Acctg.

**MOORE, MARKILA K,** Univ Of Cincinnati-Clrmnt Coll, Batavia, OH; SO; MBA; Bus Mgmt.

**MOORE, MARTHA CHRISTINE,** Northwest Al Comm Coll, Phil Campbell, AL; GD; Msc; Art; LPN; RN.

**MOORE, MATTHEW M,** Univ Of Sc At Columbia, Columbia, SC; SO; MBS; Mech Engr; Dsgn Engr.

**MOORE, MAUREEN M,** Elmira Coll, Elmira, NY; JR; BS; SCOPE Leg Brd Rep 90-; ECOC Sec 90-; Orntn Ldr; Cmpgn Hmn Dvlpmnt WV 86-; HMS; Admin Scl Wrk.

**MOORE, MELANIE M,** Sue Bennett Coll, London, KY; FR; AAS; MA Cert; Spcl Ed Thrptc Rcrtn.

**MOORE, MELISSA K,** Univ Of North Fl, Jacksonville, FL; JR; BA; Fall Greek Rush 90; Phi Kappa Phi; Golden Key; Pol Sci; JD Ph D.

**MOORE, MELISSA R,** Marshall University, Huntington, WV; JR; BBA; IM Bsktbl/Soccr; Acctg; CPA.**

**MOORE, MELONY L,** Norfolk St Univ, Norfolk, VA; SR; BA; Alpha Kappa Mu 90-; Pi Sigma Alpha 87-; Poltcl Sci; Law Schl.

**MOORE, MICHAEL A,** Al A & M Univ, Normal, AL; SR; BA; Art Clb 90-; Kappa Delta Pi; Alpha Phi Alpha 90; Hon Roll 87-; Deans Lst 87-90; IM Athltcs 88-89; Grk Olympcs 90-; Commrcl Art; Illstrtn.

**MOORE, MICHAEL A,** Univ Of Al At Huntsville, Huntsville, AL; SO; EE; Sr Lead Elec Tech MSI Div Biontcs Corp 86-; Eng.

**MOORE, MICHAEL D,** Univ Of Al At Huntsville, Huntsville, AL; JR; BS; Pi Tau Sigma 90-; Amer Soc Of Mech Engrs 90-; Mech Engr; Design.

**MOORE, MICHELLE A,** Memphis St Univ, Memphis, TN; SR; BA; SGA Sec Pblc Rltns 88-89; Blck Stdnt Assoc Chr Mbrshp 89-90; Stdnt Actvty Cncl; Blck Hstry Mnth Cmte 88-89; Gamma Beta Phi 87-; Vol Yr Blck Stdnt Assoc 88-89; Psychlgy; Cnslng Psychlgy.

**MOORE, MICHELLE L,** Valdosta St Coll, Valdosta, GA; SO; BA; Erly Chldhd Ed; Teach.

**MOORE, MONICA Y,** Clark Atlanta Univ, Atlanta, GA; SO; BA; Bus Admn; Mrktng.

**MOORE, MYRIS D,** Al A & M Univ, Normal, AL; GD; BS; Soc Pres Schlrs 87-90; Delta Sigma Theta 90-; Dns Lst 87-90; Acad Schlrshp 88-90; Comp Sci.**

**MOORE, NICHELE A,** Tuskegee Univ, Tuskegee Inst, AL; SO; BA; Texas Clb VP 89-; IM Sftbl; Political Sci; Education.**

**MOORE, PAMELA A,** Wv Univ At Parkersburg, Parkersburg, WV; FR; BA; Spnsh; Scndry Educ.

**MOORE, PAMELA L,** Univ Of Pittsburgh, Pittsburgh, PA; FR; BA; Hnr Stu; Indstrl Eng.

**MOORE, PATRICE S,** Fl A & M Univ, Tallahassee, FL; FR; BED; Gspl Chr; Phi Eta Sigma; Acad Excllnce Awrd; Educ; Admin.

**MOORE, PATRICIA A,** Watterson Coll, Louisville, KY; SR; ASSOC; Wrd Prcssng; Wrd Prcssng Sec.

**MOORE, PATRICIA A,** Livingston Univ, Livingston, AL; FR; AS; Nrsng; RN.

**MOORE, PEGGY J,** Jersey City St Coll, Jersey City, NJ; SR; BSN; Sigma Theta Tau; Am Nurses Assn; Assn Of Nurses In Aids Care; Head Nurse Univ Hosp Newark N J; Nursing.

**MOORE, PRISCILLA M A,** S U N Y Coll At Fredonia, Fredonia, NY; FR; BS; Intrntl Cltrl Assn; Spnsh Clb 90-; Fstvl Chr 90-; Spch Pthlgy Adlgy; Tchr Of The Hrng Imprd.

**MOORE, RHONDA G,** Univ Of Nc At Greensboro, Greensboro, NC; JR; BSW; Univ Mrshlls Exec Com 90-; Alpha Delta Mu 90-; Pgm Dir-Mntl Hlth Assn Hgh Point NC 87-; BA-PSYCHLGY Univ NC Chapell Hill 89; Scl Wrk/Grntlgy; Grntlgst.

**MOORE JR, RICHARD FRANCES,** Hillsborough Comm Coll, Tampa, FL; FR; AA; HELP; Bsns; Law.

**MOORE, ROBERT D,** Univ Of Ky, Lexington, KY; FR; BS; Frshmn Cncl 90-; Bapt Stdnt Union V P 90-; Stdnts Affil Amer Chem Soc V P 90-; Stdnt Recruitmnt 90-; Karate Clb 90-; Chem Engr/Physics; Med.

**MOORE, ROBERT M,** Schenectady County Comm Coll, Schenectady, NY; JR; AAS; Mag Clb 90-; Acctg; Bus Admin.

**MOORE, ROBIN M,** Xavier Univ, Cincinnati, OH; FR; BS; Gold Star Dncrs 90-; Howard Hughes Biomed Schlr 90-; Biology/Pre Med; Physician.

**MOORE, ROCHELLE B,** Memphis St Univ, Memphis, TN; SR; BSN; Dip Methodist Hosp Schl Nrsng 86; Nrsng.

**MOORE, RONALD S,** Methodist Coll, Fayetteville, NC; SO; Adlt Chldrn Of Alchlcs; Elem Educ; Tchng.

**MOORE, SALIM,** Wilberforce Univ, Wilberforce, OH; SO; BS; Psychology; Indstrl Psychiatrist.**

**MOORE, SAMANTHA K,** Faulkner Univ, Montgomery, AL; SO; BS; Math Ed; Tch.

**MOORE, SCOTT E,** Oh Univ-Southern Cmps, Ironton, OH; JR; BA; Crmnl Juste; Law.

**MOORE, SHANNON V,** Clemson Univ, Clemson, SC; FR; BS; Cmptr Sci.

**MOORE, SHERRI D,** Northeast State Tech Comm Coll, Blountville, TN; SO; BED; Stdnt Ambssdrs; Chem Blgy Physcs Sclgy; Scndry Educ.

**MOORE, SHEVA V,** Univ Of The Dist Of Columbia, Washington, DC; SR; BA; Stdnt Mvmnt Kiamsha 90; Deans List 89-; Intrnd DC Cable/Potomac TV Cmnctns Inc; Natl Pblc Radio/Brdcst Fctry 87-90; Mass Cmnctns TV; Estblsh Prdctn Co.

**MOORE, SONJANITA LECHE,** Fl A & M Univ, Tallahassee, FL; FR; MBA; Dorm V P 90-; Mc Gunn Diamond Hall Nwsltr Rprtr 90-; Phi Eta Sigma; Deans Lst 90-; Bus; Mgmt Cnsltng.

**MOORE, SONYA G,** Tusculum Coll, Greeneville, TN; SR; Dns Lst 89-90; Alpha Delta Pi 82-; Natl Kidny Fndtn; Otstdng Psych Intrnshp 90; Case Wrkr 90-; Chld Abuse Prevtn Ctr; BA 90; Psych; Cnslng.

**MOORE, STACY L,** Tougaloo Coll, Tougaloo, MS; SO; BA; Engl Clb 89-; Engl; Lwyr.

**MOORE, STEPHANIE M,** Pellissippi St Tech Comm Coll, Knoxville, TN; SO; AS; Phi Theta Kappa; Bus; Bus Mgmt.

**MOORE, STEVEN S,** Hampton Univ, Hampton, VA; JR; BA; History Clb Treas 90; Hon Cncl; Alpha Kappa Mu; Phi Alpha Theta; Dans Fndtn Resrch; Tchng Apprentice; History; Pub Policy.

**MOORE, STEVEN T,** Bristol Univ, Bristol, TN; GD; Deans Lst 83; 1 Tnns Plyr Mllgn Coll 80-84; Tuppa Assn; Dcn Ust Chrstn Chrch 88-89; Mtrls Mgr/Sr Plnt Acctnt Erwin Utlties; MBA; BS Milligan Coll 84; Exec Mgmt; Hosp Admin.

**MOORE, SUKARI N,** Bryant Stratton Bus Inst Roch, Rochester, NY; SO; AS; Accntng.

**MOORE, TERESA L,** Fl A & M Univ, Tallahassee, FL; GD; PHARM; Alpha Kappa Mu 86-88; Delta Sigma Theta 87-; Sponsor Jr Sci Club 89-90; Co Sponsor Beta Club 88-89; Sci Tchr Physical Sci Biology Eart Sci 88-90; BS Albany State Clg 88; Biology; Pharmy; Hptl Pharmy.

**MOORE, TINA L,** Central Al Comm Coll, Alexander City, AL; FR; Computer Sci.

**MOORE, TRACEY L,** Middle Tn St Univ, Murfreesboro, TN; SR; BA; Ambsdr 89-; Psychlgy Clb 88-; Alpha 90-; Psi Chi; Alpha Delta Pi 87-; Pres Enrchmnt Schlrshp 88; Psychlgy; Gdnc Cnclr.

**MOORE, TRACY D,** Columbia Greene Comm Coll, Hudson, NY; FR; AS; Drama Club Secy 90-; Sigma Delta Mu 90-; Lang; UN Interpreter.

**MOORE, TREVAN C,** Al A & M Univ, Normal, AL; SO; BA; Choir; Pre Almn Assc; Kappa Delta Pi Hstrn; Psychlgy; Clncl Psychlgst.

**MOORE, TYSON D,** Va St Univ, Petersburg, VA; FR; BS; Outstndg Accmplshmnts Sclstc Achvmnt Awd; Bus Info Sys; Cmptr Prgrmr.

**MOORE, VALORIE F,** Liberty Univ, Lynchburg, VA; SO; BS; Dorm Sprtl Life Dir 89-90; Dorm Prayer Ldr 90-; Dns Lst 88-90; Engl Educ; H S Engl Tchr.

**MOORE, VERITA R,** Savannah St Coll, Savannah, GA; SR; BS; Crim Just; Law.

**MOORE, VICTORIA L,** Volunteer St Comm Coll, Gallatin, TN; SO; BS; Std Govt VP 90-; Nwspr Adv Mgr 90-; Outstdng Mnrty Std Awd 90-; Dist Std Ldrshp Awd 90-; Awd Exclnc 90-; Owner/Oper Vickis School Dance 82-84; AS; Comm/Pblc Rltns; Msc Industry.

**MOORE, VONDA P,** Itawamba Comm Coll, Fulton, MS; FR; BS; Bptst Stdnt Un 90-; Nwspapr Stff Rprtr 90-; Poltcl Sci Clb 90-; Phi Theta Kappa; Indnette Dncr 90; Pre-Med; Psychtry.

**MOORE, WENDI M,** Thomas Nelson Comm Coll, Hampton, VA; FR; BA; Art.

**MOORE, YAQUOI D,** City Univ Of Ny Baruch Coll, New York, NY; SO; BA; Jrnlsm.

**MOORE, YOLANDA,** Al A & M Univ, Normal, AL; SR; Kappa Delta Phi 87-90; Natl Assn Black Acctnts 88-90; Alpha Kappa Mu Sec; Pres Schlr Soc; Alpha Kappa Alpha Dn Pldgs Fincl Sec 89-90; Drug Tsk Awarns Force 89-90; Natl Assn Advcmnt Colored People 88-90; ALCPA Schlrshp; Acctg.

**MOORE, ZACHARY D,** Univ Of Sc At Columbia, Columbia, SC; SO; BA; Amnesty Intl Coord; Philosophic Soc Co Fndr 90-; Intl Stdnts Assoc; Models Of Mind Prog Of S C Coll On Human Rights Guest Lctr; Guest Lctr Grp Dynamics; Human Rights Study In Elem Sch Cnsltnt; Stdnt Amb Tver St Univ USSR 89; Intl Studies/Econ; Intl Bus.

**MOORE-HICKS, DIANA E,** Atlantic Comm Coll, Mays Landing, NJ; JR; BA; Minority Stdnt Un 88-89; Stdnt Govt Assn Sec 90; CARA 90-; AA 90; Psychology; Cnslng Domstc Violence Wmn.

**MOOREFIELD, ROBYN A,** Belmont Coll, Nashville, TN; GD; BBA; Natl Acctng Assn 90; Blmnt Bus Fnnce Assn 90; Blue Ky VP 90; Gamma Beta Phi VP 90; Fllwshp Chrstn Athlts 90; Bapt Stdnt Unn 90; Dns Lst 90; Tnns Tm 90; Fnnce; Fnnce Acctng.

**MOOREHEAD, KATHY M,** Meridian Comm Coll, Meridian, MS; FR; AA; Nrsng; RN.

**MOOREHOUSE, REBECCA LYNN,** Univ Of Cincinnati-Clrmnt Coll, Batavia, OH; FR; AS; The Quantum Chem Corp Schlrshp For Bus/Ofc Admn; Bus Admn; Ofc Admn.

**MOORER, SHELIA D,** Univ Of Sc At Columbia, Columbia, SC; SO; A Touch Of Faith Gspl Choir USC; Afro Americans 90-; Intern Orangeburg Hosp; Assist In Nrsgn Dept; Carolina Bsktbl Spirits 90-; Nrsg.

**MOORES, SARA J,** Univ Of Ky, Lexington, KY; FR; BS; Beta Clb Sec; Stdnt Cncl; Fllwshp Of Chrstn Athletes; Phi Eta Sigma; Gvrnrs Schlr Cndte; Hnr By Cngrssnl Yth Cncl; Optmst Clb Hnr; Chrldng Soccer; Acad Bstrs Hnr; Chem; Phrmcst.

**MOORHOUSE, JANET M,** Saint Josephs Coll, Windham, ME; SR; BS; Class Pres 89-; Superkids Pres 88-89; Currier Bus Soc Treas 90-; Livada Securities Intrnshp 89-90; IM 87-; Bus Admin; Sls/Mktng.

**MOORING, KEVIN L,** Barton Coll, Wilson, NC; FR; BS; Jazz Band 90-; Acctng; CPA.

**MOOS, HEIDI J,** Birmingham Southern Coll, Birmingham, AL; FR; Links-Up 90-; Southern Vltrs 90-; Adolscent Care Unit Intern; Psychology/English; Tch.

**MOOSA, SHAVZAB J,** Ny Institute Of Tech Ny City, New York, NY; SR; BTECH; Tau Alpha Pi 90-; Soccr Capt 88-89; Cmptr Tech; Eng.

**MOOSE, DONELL W,** Fayetteville St Univ, Fayetteville, NC; BA; Hstry; Educ.

**MOOT, GLORIA M,** Mount Aloysius Jr Coll, Cresson, PA; SO; AS; Stdnt Govt Treas 90-; PEAK-WMNS Advct Pgm Coll Spnsrd Spksprsn 89-; Intrnshp Natl Pk Serv Hstrcl Intrprtn; Deans Lst Natl Cllgt Stdnt Govt Awd 90-; Spec Olympc-Trck/Fld Meet 90-; BOD Cambria Cnty Spec Olympcs Pblc Rltns 84-; AS; Bus Ad Mgmt TT; Wrt/Bus Ethics.

**MOR, TAL,** Ramapo Coll Of Nj, Mahwah, NJ; SR; BS; Fnc/ Invstmnt Clb 90-; Delt Amu Delta; Englewood Cliffs Fire Dept 88-; Intern/Bckr Spielvogel Bates Media Rsrch; Marketing.**

**MOR, WEI L,** Univ Of South Al, Mobile, AL; SR; BS; Asean Stdnts Assoc Pres 90; Chinese New Year Celebration Coordinator 90-; Beta Gamma Sigma; Alpha Chi 90; Phi Kappa Phi 88-89; Beta Alpha Psi; VITA; Acctg/Finance; Internal Auditor.

**MORA, EDUARDO A,** Inter Amer Univ Pr San Juan, Hato Rey, PR; SO; MBA; Acctng Assoc; FBLA 86-89; Honors Prog; Business Admin; Acctng.

**MORABITO, CHRISTOPHER J,** Franklin And Marshall Coll, Lancaster, PA; SR; BA; Sch Nwspr Edtr Chf 87-; Wash Plygrnd Proj Chrprsn 90-; One On One Tutoring Pres; Phi Beta Kappa; Blck Pyramid; Phi Beta Kappa; Williamson Mdlst; Muhlenberg Goodwill Awd; B Albert Mem Awd; Rugby Cycling; Biology; MD Med.

**MORACEN KNIGHT, RUTH,** Univ Of Pr Cayey Univ Coll, Cayey, PR; SO; Hnr Rl 90-; Psychlgy/Mntl Hlth; Law.

**MORAITIS JR, GEORGE R,** United States Naval Academy, Annapolis, MD; JR; Naval Acad Foreign Affairs Conf V Chrmn Admin Comm 90-; Pol Sci Sec 90-; US State Dept Arms Cntrl Disarm Agency Intrnshp Wash DC Intern; Submarine Dolphins; Company Ftbl 89-; Pol Sci; Naval Ofcr Nuclear Submarines.**

**MORALES ARROYO, MARIA C,** Univ Politecnica De Pr, Hato Rey, PR; SO; BA; Indstrl Eng.

**MORALES COLON, JOSE A,** Inter Amer Univ Pr Guayama, Guayama, PR; JR; Club De Comercio Vocal De Contabilidad 90-.

**MORALES DIAZ, LOURDES ENID,** Univ Of Pr Medical Sciences, San Juan, PR; GD; MS; Usuanes Sat Resrch Asst 89; Hlth Educ Hon Schlrshp 88-89; NSSLAHA; USSLAHA; PRSLAHA; Speech; Lang Patho.

**MORALES RIVERA, CARMEN J,** Catholic Univ Of Pr, Ponce, PR; GD; BA; Assc Teacher DEP 87-; Hnr Lst 87-; Education; Elem Ed.

**MORALES RIVERA, SARAH,** Bayamon Tech Univ Coll, Bayamon, PR; GD; Cthlc Yng Univ Grp 89; Hnr Soc 85-89; BA; Acctng; Bus Admin.

**MORALES RODRIGUEZ, ARTURO,** Inter Amer Univ Pr San German, San German, PR; FR; MBA; Blgy Clb Pres 88; Comp Clb 89; Beca Maidenform 90-; Grad Hon 90; Achvmnt Awds George Bush Ronald Reagan 87-90; Bsbl 87-90; Fisicas/Math; Eng Aerontcl.

**MORALES RODRIGUEZ, FATIMA M,** Inter Amer Univ Pr San German, San German, PR; SR; BA; Cir Lit Jose Gautier Benitez Pres 90-; Assoc Hnr Pro 89-; Hnr Pro; Ntl Sci Fndtn Schlrshp; Spnsh Lit.

**MORALES SANTIAGO, JOANIE,** Inter Amer Univ Pr Hato Rey, Hato Rey, PR; SR; BA; Psychlgy Assn 90-; Karate Blue Blt 90-.

**MORALES SOSA, PATRICIO A,** Inter Amer Univ Pr San German, San German, PR; SR; BA; Cncrt Choir 87; Music; Tchr.

**MORALES, ALEXANDER,** Miami Dade Comm Coll, Miami, FL; SO; Wolfson Intl Jazz Sextet; Mscns Edctrs Natl Comm; Miami Dade Cmnty Clg Awd; Msc Ed; Elctrcl Engr.

**MORALES, ASTRID,** Univ Of Pr At Rio Piedras, Rio Piedras, PR; JR; Aspira Hlth Crrs Prog 89-; Drama Clb 90-; Hnr Stu Grp 90-; Gldn Ky; Yng Cathlc Ppl Grp 85-; Yng Yr Prz Exchng Clb 88; Med.

**MORALES, CARDONA JOSE IVAN,** Univ Politecnica De Pr, Hato Rey, PR; SO; BA; Yng Wrtrs Clb 86-88; Hgh Schl Theatr Co 88-89; Futr Bio Clb P R Univ Prog 87-88; Frst Pl Ltry Cntst 88; Eng.

**MORALES, GRICEL,** Univ Politecnica De Pr, Hato Rey, PR; SR; MIE; Inst Indstrl Engnrs 89-; San Pedro Apostol Prsh Msc Mnstry 87-; Cls Prsdnt; BIE Pltchnc Unv PR; Indstrl Engnrng; Engnrng.

**MORALES, ILIANA,** Miami Dade Comm Coll South, Miami, FL; SO; BA; AA; Busn; CPA.

**MORALES, KARLA MARIA,** Columbia Univ, New York, NY; FR; BA; Alianza Ltn Amer Chrprsn 90-; GED Tutrng Coord 90-; Vrsty Bsktbl Mgr 90-; Alpha Phi Treas 90-; Comm Impct Tutrng 90-; Biolgy; Pub Hlth Admin.

**MORALES, LUIS E,** Volunteer St Comm Coll, Gallatin, TN; SR; AD; Un Prmdcs Nshvl 86-; EMT 86; Parmdc Tech; EMS.

**MORALES, MARCIA,** S U N Y Coll Of Tech At Frmgdl, Farmingdale, NY; SO; AS; Acctg Scty VP 90-; Bus Admn.

**MORALES, MARIO J,** Miami Dade Comm Coll South, Miami, FL; SO; BA/MS; Outstndg Mnrty Stdnt 90-; AA; Crmnl Jstc; Law Enfrcmnt/Invstgtns.

**MORALES, MERCEDES,** Miami Dade Comm Coll North, Miami, FL; SO; Phi Rho Pi Spch Tm 90-; Tns Cnslng Tns 87-88; Coll Brd Tlnt Rstr Otstdng Mnrt Comm; AA; Engl; : Prfssnl Wrtng.

**MORALES, NANCY L,** Savannah Coll Of Art & Design, Savannah, GA; SR; BFA; Video Prdctn; TV.

**MORALES, NEVA,** Hamilton Coll, Clinton, NY; FR; BA; Blk/ Ltn Stdnt Union 90-; La Vangrda 90-; Wrtr Lit Mag; Engl; Med.

**MORALES, PATRICIA E,** Fl International Univ, Miami, FL; SO; MBA; Intl Thspn Soc 89-; Sth Miami Lang Arts Lrt 89; Bsn; Acctng.

**MORALES, REGINA M,** Barry Univ, Miami, FL; FR; Rspct Lf 90-; Hon Prog 90-; Campus Mnstry 90-; Psychlgy; PhD.

**MORALES, RICARDO,** Fl International Univ, Miami, FL; SO; BA; SGA Sntr 90-; Alpha Kappa Psi; Tau Kappa Epsilon Fndrsg Chr; Fclty Schlr 89-; Schlr 89-; IM Ftbl/Bsktbl 89-; Acctg; Law.

**MORALES JR, ROBERT D,** Mount Saint Mary Coll, Newburgh, NY; SR; BA; Acctg; Entrprnr.

**MORALES, YAMIRIS L,** Antillian Adventist University, Mayaguez, PR; SR; BA; Stu Govt VP 89-90; Educ Prof Clb 87-; Educ Prof Clb Vcl 87-88; Hnr Cnvctr 87-; Koinonia 87-90; Med Cdts Crop 87-88; Svn Dys Advntst Yth Soc 87-; Svn Dys Advntst Union Awrd/Pres Awrd 87-; Vlybl Coll Tm 87-90; Elem Educ; Psych.

**MORALES-GARCIA, ELBA J,** Univ Of Pr At Rio Piedras, Rio Piedras, PR; SO; BA; Amnesty Intrntl Prss Ofcr; Dstngshd Stdnt Awd 90-; Top 100 Bst Scrs Grp 89; Archtctr/Envrnmntl Dsgn; Urbn Dsgn.

**MORALES-VARGAS, JOSE R,** Univ Of Pr Humacao Univ Coll, Humacao, PR; SO; BA; Acdmc Hnrs Prog; Indstrl Chem; Sci Rsrch.

**MORAN, ALICE I,** Springfield Tech Comm Coll, Springfield, MA; GD; AS; Alpha Nu Omega; Crt Rprtng.

**MORAN, CHRISTY L,** Univ Of Al At Birmingham, Birmingham, AL; SR; BS; Stdnt Occptnl Therpy Assoc 89-; AL Occuptnl Thrpy Assoc 89-; Amercn Occuptnl Thrpy Assoc 89-; Phi Eta Epsilon 90-; Occuptnl Thrpy.

**MORAN, ELLEN M,** Villanova Univ, Villanova, PA; SR; BA; Stdnt Mscl Teatre Fndr/Chrprsn 90-; Wmns Glee Clb Tour Drctr 87-; Phi Beta Kappa 90-; Omicron Delta Kappa 90-; Phi Kappa Phi 90-; Phi Alpha Theta 90-; Cmps Mnstry Msc Crdntr 87-; Christopher Danson Medallion Top Hstry Grad; Honors/Histry; Unv Tchng/Rsrch British Hstry.

**MORAN, ERIC,** Schenectady County Comm Coll, Schenectady, NY; SO; AAS; Amer Soc Non-Destructive Tstg 90-; Mtrl Sci/ NDT Certif; Engr.

**MORAN, JOANNE E,** Springfield Tech Comm Coll, Springfield, MA; SR; Sci; Surgcl Tech.

**MORAN, LAUREN M,** D Youville Coll, Buffalo, NY; SO; BA; IM Vlybl 89-; Mngmnt; Marketing.

**MORAN, MARILYN,** Marymount Manhattan Coll, New York, NY; JR; BA; St Bartholomew Cmuty Clb; Tenants Assoc Pres 89-; Admn Asst; Bus Mgmt; Pub Rltns.

**MORAN, MICHAEL F,** Univ Of Sc At Columbia, Columbia, SC; FR; BA; NROTC Mdshpmn/Drill Tm/Pstl Tm; IM Ftbl/ Wlybl/Flr Hcky; Crmnl Jstc; Marine Crps Offcr.

**MORAN, MICHELLE L,** Boston Univ, Boston, MA; SR; BS; Stdnt Govt-Sgt Coll O T Rep 87-88; Occptnl Thrpy.

**MORAN JR, PATRICK J,** City Univ Of Ny Bronx Comm Col, Bronx, NY; SO; BAMBA; Acctg; CPA.

**MORAN, SEAN P,** Muskingum Coll, New Concord, OH; FR; BS; FCA 90-; Lambada Sigma VP; Beta Beta Beta Tri Beta 90-; Phi Kappa Tau 90-; Bsktbll; Blgy.

**MORAN, SHANNON N,** Longwood Coll, Farmville, VA; SO; BA; Coll Rd Dsc Jcky 89-90; Anthrplgy.

**MORAN, TRICIA J,** East Carolina Univ, Greenville, NC; SO; BA; Order Rainbow Girls; Pres Lst; Dns Lst; Hstry; Professor.**

**MORAN-REYNICS, MARY J,** Emory Univ, Atlanta, GA; GD; MN; Gamma Sigma Sigma 78-79; Lcrss 78-79; ANA; GNA 87-89; Asstn Unit Mgr; BSN Lebanon Valley Coll 82; Grntlgy; Clncl Nrs.

**MORAN-RUSSELL, ROSE M,** The Johns Hopkins Univ, Baltimore, MD; JR; BSN; Nrsg.

**MORANO, LAURA M,** Fl Atlantic Univ, Boca Raton, FL; JR; BS; Psi Chi 85-86; Cum Laude Grad 86; Comm Serv Vol England/Scotland 87-88; Tech Spprt Sftwr Dvlpmnt 90-; BA Drew Univ 86; Bus CIS; Syst Anlyst/Pgmr.

**MORANO, MICHAEL W,** City Univ Of Ny Grad School, New York, NY; SR; BS; Art Club/Rtrng Adults Grp/Eng Clb Tr 87-89; Nwspr Asst Edtr 88-; SG 87-89; Phi Theta Kappa; Gamma Gamma Gu; Fine Arts Awrd Gallery Awrd; Cert Of Merit; Masons; Amer Soc Of Notaries; Alfred A Varriales Healing Ministry; AS 89; Writing; Arts.

**MORATELLI, JACQUELINE S,** Cumberland County Coll, Vineland, NJ; SR; BA; Csmtlgy Vineland Acdmy Of Beauty Cult 83; Acctng; CPA.

**MORATH, TRACY D,** Saint John Fisher Coll, Rochester, NY; SR; BA; Nwspapr Nws Edtr 89; Fishr Jeffrsn Mntr Pgm 90; Pres Schlrshp; Grad MCC Hnrs 90; AS Monroe Comm Clg 90; Psych.

**MORATTO, LUANN,** Univ Of Sc At Columbia, Columbia, SC; FR; Blgy; Chrprctc.

**MORAVANSKY, JAMES J,** S U N Y Coll At Fredonia, Fredonia, NY; SR; BS; Fredonia Racquetbl Clb 89-90; Cmnctns/ Media; Engr.

**MORAVITZ, CARLA D,** Va Polytechnic Inst & St Univ, Blacksburg, VA; FR; BA; New River Vly Symphony Orch 90-; Math.

**MORAWIEC, MARGIE E,** Coll Of Charleston, Charleston, SC; SR; BA; Elem Ed; Tchng.

**MORDAS, GABRIELA E,** Univ Of Miami, Coral Gables, FL; JR; BS; Aikido Clb 90-; Org Tamsican Unity 90-; Hons Stdnt Assn 90-; Alpha Epsilon Delta 90-; Standford Schlrshp; AA Broward Comm Clg 90; Bio; Med.

**MORDCOVICH, XIOMARA,** Univ Of Miami, Coral Gables, FL; FR; BA; Intl/Cmprtv Stdes; Foreign Serv/Intl Law.

**MORDECAI, STACY E,** Jacksonville St Univ, Jacksonville, AL; JR; BS; JANS Pres; Sigma Theta Tau; Fac Schlr 88-; Nrsng; CRNA.

**MORDEN, TRISHA J,** Wright St Univ Lake Cmps, Celina, OH; SO; BED; Elem Educ.

**MORDER, VINCENT H,** Juniata Coll, Huntingdon, PA; SR; BS; Theatre; Math Soc; Crs Cntry Co Cptn 87-; Appld Math; Opertns Rsrchr.

**MORDES, JENNIFER,** Glassboro St Coll, Glassboro, NJ; JR; BA; Nwmn Clb 89-; Rght Lf Sec Treas 89-; Eng Hnr Soc 90-; Eng; Ph D/Clge Eng Prfsr.

**MOREAU JR, ABNER E,** S U N Y At Buffalo, Buffalo, NY; SR; BS; Rwng Tm Capt 89-; AMA; Fnncl Mgmt Assn; Gldn Ky; Assn Of Amer Advrstn Agncs Intrn; Bus Admin Fnnce Mrktng; Advrstn Invstng.

**MOREAU, TERRY L,** Western Carolina Univ, Cullowhee, NC; SO; BA; Reps 90-; Mrshll Clb 90-; US Army 89; Pol Sci; Law Law Enfrcmnt.

**MOREE, KATHERINE PATRICIA,** Univ Of Sc At Columbia, Columbia, SC; FR; Phi Eta Sigma 90-; Asst Den Ldr Boy Scts Amer 88-; Pres Mryvl Elem Schl PTO 87-88; VP Kensington Elem Schl PTO 89-90; Elem Ed; Tchng.

**MOREHAND, RENEE L,** Lincoln Univ, Lincoln Univ, PA; SR; BA; Chrstn Fllwshp Pres 89-90; Stu Govt Treas 89-90; Gspl Ensmbl Pres 90-; Coll Radio Sta DJ 90-; Natl Educ Awrd 90-; Inroads/Upstate NY Inc Intern 88-; Engl Educ; Tchr/Bnk Offcr.

**MOREHEAD, CHRISTIANA L,** Univ Of Southern Ms, Hattiesburg, MS; JR; BS; Hndbl Choir 89-; Bus.

**MOREHEAD, FLORIDA M,** Howard Univ, Washington, DC; GD; MDIV; Natl Assn Blck Seminarians Urban League 89-; Alpha Kappa Mu 70; Beta Kappa Chi; Alpha Kappa Alpha; Natl Coalition Blck Mtng Plnrs 88-; Ford Fndtn Flwshp; Magna Cum Laude Deans Awd; Preacher Tchr 82-; Assoc Mnstr Ebenezer AME Ch 87-; Religion; Exec/Mnstr.

**MOREHEAD, HAROLD V,** Wv Univ At Parkersburg, Parkersburg, WV; SR; 3 Rivers PC-SIG; Dns Lst; UCT; Cmptr Sci.

**MOREIRA, KATTIA M,** City Univ Of Ny Baruch Coll, New York, NY; SO; BBA; Latin American Yth Clb 90-; Cathlc Big Brthrs Big Sistrs Mntr; Inroads NYC Inc Chrprsn Scl Actvts Comm 89-; Mrktng.

**MOREIRA, MARIA E,** Saint Thomas Univ, Miami, FL; JR; BA; Elem Ed; Cont Elem Ed Stds.

**MOREJON, CARLOS E,** Miami Dade Comm Coll, Miami, FL; GD; AA 90; Business Adm; Cpa.

**MOREJON, MICHAEL J,** Fl International Univ, Miami, FL; SR; BS; SGA 90-; Intrgnztn Cmt 90-; Media Svc Cmt 90-; Phi Eta Sgm 88-; Phi Kappa Phi 90-; Alpha Epsilon Dlt Pres 87-; Dlt Chi Frat 89-; Otstndng Acad Achvmnt Fawrd 90; IM Flg Ftbl 89-90; Bio; Medcn.

**MOREL, JUDITH,** Univ Of Miami, Coral Gables, FL; JR; BA; Transfer Advsr Buddy Syst; Sigma Delta Tau 88-90; Dn Schl Cmnctns Hnr Lst; Provosts Hnr Rl; Engl/News Edtrl Jrnlsm; Law.

**MOREL, SYLVAIN M,** William Carey Coll, Hattiesburg, MS; SR; BS; Theatre Hstrn 90-; Alph Psi Omega; DVT Inst Univ Du Havre 89; Bus; Intrntl Mgmt.

**MORELAND, BENNIE L,** Alcorn St Univ, Lorman, MS; JR; BS; Bus Admin; Exec Mgr.

**MORELAND, CHERYL D,** Tougaloo Coll, Tougaloo, MS; SO; BA; Pre Hlth Clb 89-; Alpha Lamda Delta 90-; Psychology; Clin Psychlgst.

**MORELAND, DOUGLAS S,** Roane St Comm Coll, Harriman, TN; FR; AS; Epsilon Delta Phi 81-83; Rose City Vol 86-88; Amer Phys Therpy Assn 90-; BS Univ TX Tyler 87; AS TX St Tech Inst 83; Phys Therpy Asst.

**MORELAND, PHILLIP M,** Abraham Baldwin Agri Coll, Tifton, GA; SO; ASSOC; Assoc Sci; Forestry.

**MORELL, LE ALICE,** Savannah St Coll, Savannah, GA; SR; BA; Nwsppr Stff 90-; Pnhllnc Cncl 90-; Alpha Kappa Alpha Rprtr 90-; Hnr Rl; Dean Lst 88-; Intern WTOC News Sta; Mass Cmmnctns; Radio/TV Brdcstng.

**MORELLI, HEIDI A,** Jersey City St Coll, Jersey City, NJ; JR; BA; Psychlgy; Cnslng.

**MORELLI, TERESA M,** Comm Coll Algny Co Algny Cmps, Pittsburgh, PA; FR; BA; Occptnl Therapy.

**MORELLO, ANTONIO E,** Duquesne Univ, Pittsburgh, PA; SO; BA; IM Pep Bnd CYO Ply Drmmr; Sprts; Shk Scl Clb; CYO Ply Wrld Hngr Actr Drmmr; Prsdntl Schrlshp; Prsh Grnt Schlrshp; Bus Fnc.

**MORELLO, GINA L,** Univ Of Miami, Coral Gables, FL; JR; BBA; Delta Gamma Treas 89-; Mktg; Bus.

**MORELLO, LUCILLE R,** Bunker Hill Comm Coll, Boston, MA; FR; MBA; Nurs/Phys Thpry.

**MORELOCK, ALLEN L,** Northeast State Tech Comm Coll, Blountville, TN; SO; AAS; IEEE Chrmn 90-; Instrmnt Socty Of Amer; Outstdng Grad; Dns Lst; Elec; Engr.

**MORELOCK, LINDA A,** Univ Of Sc At Columbia, Columbia, SC; SR; BA; Gamma Beta Phi 87-; Tchrs Aide 79-; Psych; Fmly Cnslng.

**MORELOCK, TINA L,** Northeast State Tech Comm Coll, Blountville, TN; SO; AAS; Phi Theta Kappa 90-; Asst Mgr Opers Sears Roebuck Co; Mgmt Inf Sci; Comp Prog.

**MOREN, JENNIFER S,** Univ Of Cincinnati, Cincinnati, OH; SO; BED; IAJE 90-; OCMEA 90-; MENC 90-; Okinawan Karate 89-; Msc Ed-Clarinet; Tch.

**MORENINGS, VONDA S,** Va Highlands Comm Coll, Abingdon, VA; SO; Am Red Cross; Phi Theta Kappa; Alpha Gamma Rho; All-Am Schlr Coll Awd; Pres Hon Roll; Scholastic Awd 89-; Ofc Mgr; Facia Tek Corp; AAS Bus Adm; AAS Edn; Math; Profr.

**MORENO PEREZ, ODALIS I,** Univ Politecnica De Pr, Hato Rey, PR; SR; BSE; Inst Indstrl Engrs 90-; Engrg.

**MORENO, ALEXIS J,** Inter Amer Univ Pr Aquadilla, Aguadilla, PR; FR; Acctg.

**MORENO, CARLOS MIRAND,** Inter Amer Univ Pr Aquadilla, Aguadilla, PR; FR; Accntng.

**MORENO, MICHAEL C,** Univ Of Al At Birmingham, Birmingham, AL; SR; BS; Deans Lst 88-; Pres Hon Roll 90-; Spec Olympcs Vol 87-; Med; MD.

**MORENO, NICOLE,** Hillsborough Comm Coll, Tampa, FL; FR; Amer Sign Lang Clb 90-; Educ.

**MORENO, PAUL,** Western Ct St Univ, Danbury, CT; FR; BED; PAC Asst Chrmn 90-; Edn Clb 90-; Danbury West Ct St Univ Orch Violin 90-; Peace Activist Cmpgn Mgr 90-; Deans Lst 90-; Sftbl WCSU; Scndry Edn Earth Sci; Prfsr.

**MORENO-BERRIOS, SARA L,** Univ Politecnica De Pr, Hato Rey, PR; FR; Spnsh; Eng.

**MORESHEAD, KIM M,** Castleton St Coll, Castleton, VT; FR; BA; Brdg Clb 90-; Im Sprts 90-; Math/Scndry Ed; Tchng.

**MORETTI, DAVID,** City Univ Of Ny Queensbrough, New York, NY; FR; AAS; Comp Tech; Elec Engr.

**MORETZ, LAURA E,** Univ Of Nc At Charlotte, Charlotte, NC; FR; BA.

**MOREY, JILL A,** The Boston Conservatory, Boston, MA; SO; BFA; TA; Comm Thtre Intrn 87-; Mss Tntn Schlrshp; Dnce; Tch.

**MORFORD, JOAN M,** Milligan Coll, Milligan Clg, TN; GD; MENC 88-; Cncrt Choir 87-90; Chmbr Sngrs C Choir Asst Cndctr 87-90; Thtre Chrgrphr 86-90; Alpha Psi Omega 89-; Fine Arts Awd 87-88; Tchr Cert; BA 90; Music Ed/Voice/Thtre; Tch.

**MORGAN, ALEXANDRA CAROL,** Oh St Univ, Columbus, OH; JR; BSLA; Landscape Floriculture Frm Sec 88-; ASLA 88-; Engnrng Hnr Rl 90-; Hrtcltr TA 90-; Landscape Archtctr.

**MORGAN, ALLISON B,** Fl St Univ, Tallahassee, FL; JR; MS; Natl Stdnt Speech Lang Hearing Assoc Sec; Delta Zeta Sor Head Guard; Geriatric Intern At Barrington Terr Nursing Home 91; Communication Disorders; Speech Pathology.

**MORGAN, ALLISON N,** Alcorn St Univ, Lorman, MS; FR.

**MORGAN, AMECHA C,** Itawamba Comm Coll, Fulton, MS; FR; AAS; Pre Radiology Clb 90; Appled Hlth; Radiology.

**MORGAN, AMY E,** Marshall University, Huntington, WV; SO; Optmtry.

**MORGAN, ANDREA J,** Marywood Coll, Scranton, PA; SO; BS; Blgy Clb 89-; Delta Epsilon Sigma; Presdntl Schlrshp 89; Blgy; Med.

**MORGAN, ANTHONY E,** Univ Of Sc At Columbia, Columbia, SC; SR; BS; Prsdnt Advsr Slctn Comm 88; Rsdnt Advsr Dsk Oprtns Coordntr 88-90; Stdnt Ldrshp Cnfrnc 89-90; Peer Edctr Offc Alchl & Drgs89-90; Crlna Awrd 90; Lead Cnfrnc 90; Smr Hrid Prctcm 89; Vlntr Mcksck Museum 89; Htl Rstrnt/Trsm Admin; Prfsr.

**MORGAN, BARBEE A,** Ms St Univ, Miss State, MS; SO; BS; Ledrshp Class 89-90; Gamma Phi Beta 90; Alpha Lambda Delta; Chi Omega 89-; Natl Hungar Week 89-90; Vol Vanderbilt Hosp; Vol Southern Hills Hosp; IM Soccer 89-90; Biology; Physical Therapist.

**MORGAN, BILLIE S,** Itawamba Comm Coll, Fulton, MS; SO; BA; Amer Assn Medcl Assts Com Mbr 70-; MS Soc Medcl Assts Pres 70-; NE Chptr Medcl Assts Pres 70-; Ultrusa Clb Tupelo Sec 85-89; Acctg.

**MORGAN, BRENDA L,** Kent St Univ Kent Cmps, Kent, OH; SR; Gldn Key; Alpha Kappa Delta; Competition N Central Sociological Assoc; BA; Sociology; Law.

**MORGAN, BRENDA M,** Fl International Univ, Miami, FL; GD; MBA; Phi Theta Kappa 90-; Bible Tchr/Ch Chrst 74-; Tchr Twin Lakes Elem 90-; BS 90; AA Broward Comm Coll 86; Read Edn; Teach.

**MORGAN, BRIAN R,** Ms St Univ, Miss State, MS; SR; BA; Stdnt Publ Rels Org V P; Stdnt Assoc Comm 87-90; Campus Actvty Bd 90-; Asst Dir PR; Dns Schlr 87-89; Pres Schlr 89-; Sigma Phi Epsilon V P 87-; Circle K 90-; Clg Republ 90-; Asst Sports Info 89-; SEC Bsktbl Tourn Rep; Rubgy 89; Cmnctn-Publ Rels; Sports Info Dir.

**MORGAN, CHARISSE A,** Memphis St Univ, Memphis, TN; SR; BA; Clg Rep Clb 88; Deans List 90-; Hstry; Higher Ed.

**MORGAN, CHRISTOPHER W,** Commonwealth Coll, Virginia Beach, VA; SO; AAS; Stdnt Cnsl Rep Pres; Comp Clb; Acctg Clb; Comp Sci; Cnsltnt Sys Analyst.

**MORGAN, CINDY JO,** Newbury Coll, Brookline, MA; SR; BH; Makeup Artst Acct Coord; Esthetics Lic Cath Hinds Inst 84; Busn/Mktg.

**MORGAN, COLLEEN A,** Western New England Coll, Springfield, MA; SR; BA; Pre-Law Scty Tres 89-; Radio Dj 89-90; Peer-Advsng 89-90; Deans Lst 90-; Orchstra; Pr/Mkt Asst Sprngfrd Symphny Intrnshp; Englsh; Law.

**MORGAN, CYNTHIA L,** Longwood Coll, Farmville, VA; SO; BS; Jr Buddy Prog Cmtee 90; Clgte Natl Synchrnzd Swm Cmptn Ohio Sta U 90; P Morris Inc Schlrshp 90; Deans Lst; Synchrnzd Swim Clb 89; Spch Path/Audiology.

**MORGAN, DANA L,** Oh St Univ, Columbus, OH; SR; BM; OCMEA 89; ACDA Sec 90; Golden Key 90; Vocal Schlrshps 87; Arts/Sci Awd 90; Pres Acad Excellnce Rcgntn Awd 90; Music; Tchr.

**MORGAN, DANA M,** Fl St Univ, Tallahassee, FL; SO; BA; Lady Scalphunters Pub Rel Comm 90-; Delta Zeta Sor Actvts Chrmn 89-; United Way Communicatins Intern 91; AA 91; Communications; Broadcasting.

**MORGAN, DANIEL J,** Memphis St Univ, Memphis, TN; FR; BA; Spnsh/Frnch/Grmn; Law.

**MORGAN, DAVID L,** Univ Of Tn At Knoxville, Knoxville, TN; JR; BS; IIE; Alpha Pi Mu; Gamma Beta Phi 88-; IM Tnns/Bsktbl/Ftbl 88-; AS Roane State Comm Coll 90; AS Roane State Comm Coll 90; Eng/Sci/Math; Eng.

**MORGAN, DEBORAH A,** Germanna Comm Coll, Locust Grove, VA; FR; AAS; Cmptr Info Sys.

**MORGAN, DEXTER O,** Al A & M Univ, Normal, AL; SO; BS; Mktg.

**MORGAN, DONNA R,** Davis & Elkins Coll, Elkins, WV; SR; BA; SEA 90-F Alpha Delta Kappa 90-; Teacher/Voc Hm Ec 78-83/85-90; BS Berea Clg 78; MS Marshall Univ 83; Elem Educ; Teacher.

**MORGAN, ELAINE M,** Piedmont Tech Coll, Greenwood, SC; BA; Psi Beta 90; Dns Lst 89; Whitten Ctr Emplyee 90; Educ.

**MORGAN, FELICIA D,** Alcorn St Univ, Lorman, MS; JR; Engl/Poetry Club 90-; Dns Lst 90-; Engl; Underwriter/Tchr.

**MORGAN, GLENDA A,** Savannah St Coll, Savannah, GA; JR; BBA; Phi Eta Sigma 89-; Boy Scts Amer Den Ldr 86-87; Cathlc Dcse Svnnh Scl Brd Rep 90-; Our Ldy Lrds Cathlc Chch Prsh Cncl Vp 88-89; St Cnvntn Alt Dlg 89-90; Chatham Cnty Rep Prty Prcnctchrmn 89-90; Chrch Sec 80-; Acctng; CPA.

**MORGAN, GLENN C,** Widener Univ, Chester, PA; JR; BS; ASME 89-; Tau Beta Pi 90-; Mech Engrng.

**MORGAN, HELEN M,** Univ Of Ky, Lexington, KY; JR; BA; Phi Eta Sigma 89; Golden Key; Psi Chi 89; Clnc Assist Jesse G Harris Jr 90; Bluegrass United Ostomy Assoc Sec/Treas 87; Scrtry 7084; Psych; Clncl Psych.

**MORGAN, HYACINTH P,** Ny Univ, New York, NY; SR.

**MORGAN JR, JAMES D,** United States Naval Academy, Annapolis, MD; FR; BS; Chrchll Socty Treas 90-; Cthlc Mdshpmns Clb 90-; IMS 90-; Mdshpmn Serv Prgrm 90-; Co Plebe Of Mnth 90-; Poli Sci; Naval Flght Offcr.

**MORGAN, JEFFERY W,** Wv Univ At Parkersburg, Parkersburg, WV; SO; AS WVU-P; Sci; Phrmcst.

**MORGAN, JEFFREY D,** Univ Of Sc At Columbia, Columbia, SC; FR; BS; Garnet/Black Yrbk Photgrhs 90-; Phi Eta Sigma; Acceptance SC Hnrs Clg; Flag Ftbl/Bskbl/Sftbl 90-; Biology; Med.

**MORGAN, JOHNNA K,** Univ Of Tn At Martin, Martin, TN; FR; BS; Karate Clb; Pre Phy Thrpy Clb; Hnrs Seminar Schlrshp; Alpha Delta Pi Schlrshp Chrmn; Sci; Phy Thrpy.

**MORGAN, JULI G,** Andrew Coll, Cuthbert, GA; SO; SGA Sen Otstndng Sen Awd 90; Choraliers 89-; Phi Theta Kappa; Phi Delta Pres; Acdmc All Amer Sec Tm; Valedictorian Grad Cls.

**MORGAN, KIMBERLY A,** Fl St Univ, Tallahassee, FL; JR; BA; Ftr Ed Amer 89-; Phi Theta Kappa Hstrn 89-; Rdng Asst; Hnrbl Mntn Wrld Ptry Cntst; Edtrl Brd; AA Tallahassee Comm Clge 90; Eng Ed; Tchr.

**MORGAN, KIMBERLY D,** Ms St Univ, Miss State, MS; JR; BA; Phi Theta Kappa Rcrdg Sec 89-90; Gamma Beta Phi; Pres Lst Schlr 88-; AA 90; Sclgy; Teach.

**MORGAN, KINA L,** Fl A & M Univ, Tallahassee, FL; FR; BA; Inroads; Phi Eta Sigma; Sthwstrn Bell Telphn Intrnshp 90-; Acctg; CPA.

**MORGAN, LISA A,** Pellissippi St Tech Comm Coll, Knoxville, TN; SO; BS; Tau Alpha Pi; AS Roane St Comm Coll 87; Cvl Eng; Envrmntl Eng.

**MORGAN, LISA L,** Indiana Univ Of Pa, Indiana, PA; SR; BED; Forensics 89; Phi Sigma Pi 89-; RA 89-; Engl.

**MORGAN, LORRAINE,** Piedmont Tech Coll, Greenwood, SC; GD; LPN; LPN Stdnt Assn Treas 90-; Nursing.

**MORGAN, LOUELLA REBA,** Cumberland County Coll, Vineland, NJ; SO; Sclgy; Social Work.

**MORGAN, MALINDA L,** Univ Of Nc At Charlotte, Charlotte, NC; JR; Bapt Stdnt Un 87-; Res Stdnt Assn 87-; Hall Coun 87-; Gldn Ky; Res Advsr 88-; Otstndng Coll Stdnts Amer 89; Phi Alpha Theta 90-; Dns Lst Chnclrs Lst 88-; IM Coach 87-; Hist/Scndry Educ.**

**MORGAN, MARCUS TODD,** Middle Ga Coll, Cochran, GA; SO; Gamma Beta Phi 90-; Ag Engr.

**MORGAN, MARK D,** Univ Of Ky, Lexington, KY; FR; BS; Bapt Stdnt Union Frshmn Cncl Mbr 90-; Sgm Gamma Sgm Scty Govnrs Schlrs 90-; Otstndg Gen Chem Stdnt Awrd; Math; Clg Prfsr.

**MORGAN, MARY L,** Castleton St Coll, Castleton, VT; SO; BA; Hstry Clb 89-; Wmns Vrsty Clb 89-; USSA 84-; USSCA 89-; Dns Lst 90; Sem London Pgm; Rep US Sccr Trnmnt Russia; Schlrshp Steamfitters Lcl 501 89-; Wmns Sccr 89-90; Alpine Vrsty Ski Tm 89-; All Conf Sccr 89; History; Grad Schl Law.

**MORGAN, MERRIN J,** Univ Of Southern Ms, Hattiesburg, MS; FR; BA; Angl Flght; Stdnt Almn Assoc 90-; Bptst Stdnt Un 90-; Cmps Crsd Chrst 90-; Phi Eta Sigma; Alpha Lambda Delta; Pi Beta Phi 90-; SAAD 90-; Dmnd Drlngs 90-; Intl Rltns.

**MORGAN, MICHAEL J,** Saint Francis Coll, Loretto, PA; SO; BA; Vars Soccer 89-; Math 89-90; Deans Lst; Kappa Mu Epsilon; KC 89-; Pres Schlrshp 89-; Math; Eng.

**MORGAN, MICHELE R,** Marshall University, Huntington, WV; SO; BA; Gamma Beta Phi Rcrdng Sec 90-; Bus; Oper Mgmt.

**MORGAN, MICHELLE D,** Elmira Coll, Elmira, NY; SR; BA; Activ Bd Chrprsn 88-; Gold Key Ambassador Pres 87-; Orientation Chrprsn 88-; Kappa Delta Pi; Mcgraw Attainment Awd; Elem Educ/Engl Lit.

**MORGAN, NATHAN H,** Univ Of South Al, Mobile, AL; SO; BED; Yng Rpblcns Clb 90-; Scndry Educ; Tchr.

**MORGAN, NICOLAS E,** Univ Of Nc At Asheville, Asheville, NC; SO; BA; Drama; F P Hulme Plywrtng Awd 90-; T W Shrt Fctn Awd 90-; Engl/Lit; Crtv Wrtng.

**MORGAN, PAUL C E,** Germanna Comm Coll, Locust Grove, VA; FR; Poli Sci; Law.

**MORGAN, RANDALL J,** Tri County Tech Coll, Pendleton, SC; GD; AD; Mach Tool Tech; Tool/Die.

**MORGAN, ROBIN L,** Univ Of Sc At Aiken, Aiken, SC; SO; ADN; Dntl Asst; Assoc Peidmont Tech Coll 82-84; Nrsng; RN.

**MORGAN, ROGER T,** Atlantic Comm Coll, Mays Landing, NJ; SR; BA; Dns Lst 90; Prfct Attndnce Awrd; Otstndng Acad Achvmnt Awrd; Cert CA; AS; Clnry Arts; Exec Chf.

**MORGAN, RONI L,** Union Univ School Of Nursing, Memphis, TN; FR; BSN; Deans Lst 90-; Neontl Nrsng.

**MORGAN, SABRINA N,** Tuskegee Univ, Tuskegee Inst, AL; JR; BS; Biology Club; Alpha Kappa Mu; Hnr Roll 88-90; Dana Flwshp Awd 89-; Biology; MD/PH D.**

**MORGAN, SHAWN A,** Northeastern Christian Jr Coll, Villanova, PA; FR; BA; Gamma Delta Gamma; Vlybl/Sccr; Business Adm; Spcl Effects Tech.

**MORGAN, SONDRA R,** Norfolk St Univ, Norfolk, VA; JR; BS; Phi Theta Kappa Treas 87-; Cncrt Chr Treas 90-; Prnt Tchr Assoc Treas 84-; Phi Theta Kappa Treas 87-; Dstngshd Stdnt Awrd 86-89; Msc Edctrs Natl Cnfrnc 89-; Nnsmnd Rvr Bapt Chfrch Chrch Orgnst 74-; AA 89; Music Ed.

**MORGAN, STEPHANIE M,** Hudson Valley Comm Coll, Troy, NY; SR; Pres List 89-90; Deans List 89; State Senate Certif Merit 90; AAS; Criminal Justice; Continue Clg.**

**MORGAN, STEVEN D,** Duquesne Univ, Pittsburgh, PA; SO; BS; Acctng Assn 90-; Phi Eta Sigma 89-; Delta Sigma Pi Treas 89-; Teledyne Borwn Eneg Merit Schlr; Acctng; CPA.

**MORGAN, STEVEN M,** Northeastern Christian Jr Coll, Villanova, PA; SO; AS/BS; KOCS 90-; Gamms Delta Gamma 90-; NJCAA Academic All Amer 90-; Scr 89-; Yth Mnstr Falls Church Vir; Acctg; CPA.

**MORGAN, SUZANNE RENAE,** Univ Of Akron, Akron, OH; FR; BSN; Cmps Focus Mnstrs 90-; Nrsng.

**MORGAN, THAYRA J,** Fl International Univ, Miami, FL; SO; BA; FL Pblc Intrst Rsrch Grp Core Mmbr Cmpgn 90-; Kiwanis Clb Hndcpd Park Orgnzr Vol; Habitat Hmnty Miami Prjct; Dsgn Archtctr; Arctctr.

**MORGAN, THOMAS C,** Owensboro Comm Coll, Owensboro, KY; SO; BA; DPMA 89-90; Cmptr Sci; Eng.

**MORGAN, TISHA M,** Livingston Univ, Livingston, AL; SR; BA; Alpha Chi; Cardinal Key; Societos Excell De Mercatus Lit V P 90-; Bus; Cmptr Sci.

**MORGAN, TROY C,** Auburn Univ At Montgomery, Montgomery, AL; SO; BS; Almn Assoc 89-; Yrbk Grk Ed 89-90; Coop Ed Pgm 89-90; Phi Eta Sigma 89; Omicron Delta Kappa; Schlr; Pi Kappa Phi VP 88-; Hst Grp 89-; Cir K Internatl Treas 89-90; IM Tm 88-; Mech Engrg.**

**MORGISON, TCHULA L,** Va Polytechnic Inst & St Univ, Blacksburg, VA; FR; BS; Amer Soc Mcrobiolgy; Hon Porg 90-; C Mccormick Schlrshp 90-; VA Tech Almni Schlrshp 90-; Biolgy; Clncl Mcrobiolgst.

**MORGRAGE, SANDRA L,** Colby Sawyer Coll, New London, NH; SO; BA; Key Assoc; Stdnt Athletic Trnr; Var Bkbl; Sprts Med; Athletic Trng.

**MORHARDT, KEMP A,** Univ Of Nc At Charlotte, Charlotte, NC; JR; BA; Rugby Clb 85-86; Venture 90-; Grad High Hons HSTC Deans List 88-90; AS Hartford State Tech Clg 90; Archtctr; Archtct/Entrprnr.

**MORIARTY, DAWN M,** Holy Family Coll, Philadelphia, PA; FR; BSN; Nrsng.

**MORIARTY, HOLLY M,** Southern Vt Coll, Bennington, VT; JR; SA Sec 90-; Var Bsktbl MPV/CAPT 88-; Bus Mgt; Rsrt.

**MORIARTY, JODI A,** Springfield Tech Comm Coll, Springfield, MA; SR; Alpha Nu Omega 90-; Telecmnctns; Film.

**MORIARTY, SHAWN T,** Springfield Tech Comm Coll, Springfield, MA; SR; Alpha Nu Omega 90-; Telecmnctns; Film.

**MORILLO, JUAN P,** Univ Of Miami, Coral Gables, FL; SR; BA; Peer Cnslr/Tutr 90-; Frnch Clb VP 90-; Frnch Natl Hon Soc; Chldrns Hm Soc Vol; Phlsphcl Natl Hon Soc; Hstry/Phlsphy/Frnch/Psychlgy; Law.

**MORILLO, MARITZA ALTAGRACIA,** Inter Amer Univ Pr Guayama, Guayama, PR; FR; BA; Hnr Stu 90-; Wrkd Sec Engr Const Co; Bus Admin/Acctg.

**MORIN, BETHANY L,** Univ Of Sc At Columbia, Columbia, SC; JR; BA; Ntnl Stdnt Exchng 88-89; Erly Chldhd Edctn.

**MORIN, JAMES M,** Western New England Coll, Springfield, MA; SR; BS; Fin Mgt Assoc 89-; Mgt Assoc 89-; Im Hockey Cptn 87-90; Fin; Law.

**MORIN, JENNIFER R,** Cornell Univ Statutory College, Ithaca, NY; SO; BS; Crnll Pre Vet Scty 89-; Crnll Coll 4 H 89-90; Crnll Rnd Up Clb 89-90; Under Grad Tchng Asst; Pre Vet Med; Vet.

**MORIN, KARA A,** Smith Coll, Northampton, MA; JR; BA; Debate Tm 88-89; Theatre Comm Stdnt Fac Liasn 89-90; SOS 88-; Theater; Wrtng.

**MORIN, MARY T,** Wagner Coll, Staten Island, NY; FR; BA; Psych.

**MORIN, PATRICIA A,** Central Me Medical Center, Lewiston, ME; FR; AS; Natl Hnr Soc 80; Alpha Delta Pi 85-86; Mntfr Med Ctr Cancer Rsch Asst 86; BS Univ ME 86; Nrsng.

**MORIN, RITA L,** Fl International Univ, Miami, FL; SR; BA; Kappa Delta Pi; Comm Clg Mnrty Trnsfr Schlrshp; Deans List 90-; Golden Dzzlrs Dnc Sqd; AA Miami Dade Comm Clg 89; Elem Educ; Teacher.

**MORIN, SHARON K,** Hillsborough Comm Coll, Tampa, FL; FR; BA; Phi Theta Kappa 90; Fmly Serv Hickam AFB Pres 77-80; Accntng Awd 90; Accntng; CPA.

**MORIN, TRACY E,** Saint Josephs Coll, Windham, ME; SO; BS; Sprkds Dlb Undrprvlgd Chldrn Treas 89-; IM Vlybl/Flr Hcky/Sftbl; Bus Admin/Acctg; CPA.**

**MORISANI, SILVIA J,** Univ Of South Al, Mobile, AL; JR; Un Prog Bd 88-90; Alpha Lambda Delta 88-; Phi Eta Sigma 88-; Kappa Delta Pi; Phi Kappa Phi; ARC Blood Donor 87-; IM Sftbl 88-; Elem Ed; Tchr.

**MORISON, SAMUEL T,** Univ Of Nc At Chapel Hill, Chapel Hill, NC; GD; JD; Fdrlst Scty Fr Law/Pblc Plcy Vp 90-; Lgl Educ Asst Prog Tchg Asst 89-; Claude Lambe Flwshp Awd 88-89; William Joyner Awd; Windchase Hmownrs Assc Pres 89-; Valerie Hubbard Memrl Fndtn Dir; BIS George Mason Univ Fairfax VA 87; Law.

**MORISSEAU, JON M,** Fl St Univ, Tallahassee, FL; JR; BA; Pi Delta Phi; Englsh Frnch; Tchr.

**MORISSETTE, REBECCA L,** George Mason Univ, Fairfax, VA; JR; Hlf Sky Wms Clb Embry Riddle Aero Univ 88-89; IM Tbl Tns ERAU 88; Princess Ann Ruritan Clb Schlrshp 87; Virginia Drewry Mem Schlrshp 87; Slctd Prtcpt Spch Nght 88; Vrsty Wms Glf Tm Embry Riddle Aero Univ 88-89; Mktg; Avtn/Sprtg Gds Mktg.

**MORITA, CHIE C,** Radford Univ, Radford, VA; SR; BS; Psychology Clb 90-; Intrntnl Clb 88-; Soc Hmn Rsrc Mgmt Tres 89-; Psi Chi 90-; Deans Schlr Awd; Otstndng Stdnt Awd 89-90; IM 88-89; Wrkd Citibank Tokyo Br 87-88; Psychlgy; Hmn Rsrc Mgmt.

**MORITA, RIKA,** Brevard Coll, Brevard, NC; SO; AA; Phi Theta Kappa 90-; Intrntl Stds.

**MORLEY, MARK A,** Miami Dade Comm Coll South, Miami, FL; SO; BS; Untd Blck Stu Tres 89-; Otstndg Comm Coll Mnrty Stu 89-90; Im Ftbl/Sftbl/Baktbl 89-; Elec Engr.

**MORMAN, LINDA W,** Howard Univ, Washington, DC; GD; MSW; BA Univ DC 89; Soc Wrk; Mntl Hlth.

**MORMAN JR, MICHAEL W,** Birmingham Southern Coll, Birmingham, AL; SO; AS; Alpha Lambda Delta 90; Phi Eta Sigma 90; Sccr 89-.

**MOROCH, KAREN A,** Mount Saint Mary Coll, Newburgh, NY; JR; BA; Math; Tch.

**MORONEY-FRATIANNI, MARGARET K,** Saint Josephs Coll New York, Brooklyn, NY; SR; BS; Comm Demo Clb; Chrprsn Cncl Nrse Prctnrs 84-; NY Nrs Assoc MMC; Cert Cnslng; Hlth Care Adm.**

**MOROZ, LINDA,** Thomas Nelson Comm Coll, Hampton, VA; FR; BS; Red Crs Instr 88-; Marine Tech Soc; Sea Scouts Asst 90-; U S Navy Rsrvs; M M Diving Pres 86-; AS Clg Ocerng 90; Engr Ocean Engr.

**MORPHIS, MARSHA J,** Union Univ, Jackson, TN; GD; Stdnt Ed Assoc 90-; TN Ed Assoc 90-; Natl Ed Assoc 90-; Girl Scout Ldr 89-; Empl Alamo Pre-Sch; BS 89; Elem Ed; Tchr.

**MORREALE, JOSEPHINE F,** Niagara Univ, Niagara Univ, NY; SO; BS; AIBS 90; ACS 90; NUCAP 89; Deans Lst 80; Rugby 90; Im Bsktbl Capt 89; Bio/Pre Med; Med.

**MORRELL, BARBARA A,** Georgian Court Coll, Lakewood, NJ; JR; BA; AA Brookdale Comm Coll 90; Engl; Elem Educ.

**MORRELL, BYRON D,** Tomlinson Coll, Cleveland, TN; JR; BA; Various Areas Of Ministry 84-90; AS Music 83; Ministry.

**MORRELL, LEEAN W,** Memphis St Univ, Memphis, TN; JR; BA; Sftbl Fld Hcky 86-89; Fshn Brd Model 90; Drm Cncl 88-89; Gamma Beta Phi 81; Alpha Chi Omega 88; Nutrtn Physlgy; Whlstc Dnstry.

**MORRELL, VANESSA C,** King Coll, Bristol, TN; FR; BA; Nwspaper Stf 90-; Choir 90-; Behvrl Sci; Tchr.

**MORRET, DENISE L,** Temple Univ, Philadelphia, PA; SR; BS; Amer Phrmctcl Assoc 88-; Rho Chi Treas 89-; Lambda Kappa Sigma Sec 88-; Phrmcy.

**MORRICE, PETER D,** Villanova Univ, Villanova, PA; JR; BA; Cmncmnt Spch Com; Run Hunger, Feed Chldrn Spnsr; Deans Lst 88-; Right Guard Big East Acad All-Star Tm Golf 90-; Schlrshp Vrsty Golf 89-; Ltrd Vrsty Golf 88-; Engl; Law.

**MORRILL, FREDERICK S,** Clarkson Univ, Potsdam, NY; SR; BS; Society Of Acct Sec 89; Phi Theta Kappa 88; Phi Kappi Phi; St Lawrence County Democratic Committee 78-90; Town Hermon Board Assess Review 80-90; AS Sumy Canton 89; Acct; Assoc Cost Analyst.

**MORRILL, MARY E,** Utica Coll Of Syracuse Univ, Utica, NY; FR; BS; Occup Ther Soc 90-; Yrbk Fr Photog 90-; Vol United Cerebal Palsy 90-; Novacare Inc Intern Occup Ther Asst 90-; IM Vlybl/Bsktbl 90-; Occup Ther.

**MORRIS, ADAM M,** Manhattan Coll, Bronx, NY; FR; BA; Lit Mag Cmptr Cnsltnt 90-; Jazz Ensmbl; Itln Clb; De La Salle 90-; Pres Schlrshp; Engl; Professr.

**MORRIS, ALISSA S,** Walker Coll, Jasper, AL; FR; BS; Pi Beta Phi 90-; Nrsg; Neo Natal Nrs.

**MORRIS, AMY D,** Univ Of Tn At Martin, Martin, TN; SR; MA; Hstry Clb 89-; Span Clb; Phi Kappa Phi; Pi Sigma Alpha; Phi Alpha Theta 90-; Zeta Tau Alpha Judcl 89-; Tn Hstrl Cmns Awd; Hstry Awd; Chi Omega Awd; BA; European Hstry; Ph D.

**MORRIS, AMY L,** Univ Of Sc At Columbia, Columbia, SC; SO; BS; Angel Flght 89-90; Chemistry; Pharmacy.

**MORRIS, AMY LYNN,** Univ Of Sc At Coastal Carolina, Conway, SC; SO; Psychology Clb 90-; Bsns Clb 90-; Theta Sigma Chpln 89-; Bsns Mgmt.

**MORRIS, ANGELA,** Va Union Univ, Richmond, VA; SR; BS; Cmmnty Schlrs; Alpha Kappa Alpha VP 89-90; Erly Mdl Edctn; Tchng.

**MORRIS, ANNE F,** Felician Coll, Lodi, NJ; SR; Asprng Wrtrs 88-; Art Clb Sec 87-; Schlstc Schlrshp; Eng/Art; Pblshng.

**MORRIS, BENNIE R,** Ky St Univ, Frankfort, KY; FR; BS; Fisheries Mgmt.

**MORRIS, BILLIE J,** Univ Of Louisville, Louisville, KY; JR; BS; Cntr Acdmc Achvmt 89-; Geology Clb 90-; Phi Eta Sigma 88-; Cntr Acdmc Achvmt Schlrshp 89-; Dns Lst 88-; IM Vlybl Cptn 89-; Phy Ed/Math; Tchg/Coaching.**

**MORRIS, BRENTON KIRK,** Univ Of Montevallo, Montevallo, AL; FR; BS; Flwshp Chrstn Ath Pres 90; Ftbl Acad Awd 87-90; Ntl Hon Soc 89-90; Mu Alpha Theta 89-90; GA Pcfc Schlrshp; Montevallo Ldrshp Schlrshp; Ftbl/Bsbl; Scl Sci; Law.

**MORRIS, BRIAN MICHAEL,** Livingston Univ, Livingston, AL; FR; BA; Theatre; US Army Rsvs; Trustee Schlp; Hstry; Law Schl.

**MORRIS, CHARLES J,** Univ Of Med & Dentistry Of Nj, Newark, NJ; GD; MPT; Amer Phys Thrpy Assoc 90-; BS Temple Univ 81; Phys Thrpy.

**MORRIS, CHERYL L,** Medaille Coll, Buffalo, NY; FR; BED; TEACH; PTO; Med Sec; Soc Sci; Spcl Ed.

**MORRIS, CHRISTINA L,** Salisbury St Univ, Salisbury, MD; SR; BS; Elem Ed; Tch.

**MORRIS, CHRISTINE D,** Marshall University, Huntington, WV; FR; BA; Bapt Cmps Mnstry 90-; Phi Eta Sigma; Gamma Beta Phi; Spnsh/Frnch Educ; Educ Scndry Stdnts.

**MORRIS, CYNTHIA D,** Morris Brown Coll, Atlanta, GA; SR; BS; Phi Eta Sigma; Pi Mu Epsilon; Prsdntl Schlr; Smmr Undergrad Rsrch Asstnts; SURP U OK/U CA San Diego; URPC; Chem; Rsrch.

**MORRIS, CYNTHIA L,** Western Ky Univ, Bowling Green, KY; SO; Math.

**MORRIS, DARREN T,** Coll Of Charleston, Charleston, SC; JR; BS; Alpha Epsilon Delta 89-; Alpha Chi Sigma; Biochem; MD.

**MORRIS, DE LINDA V,** Al A & M Univ, Normal, AL; JR; BA; Art Clb 90-; Kappa Delta Pi 90-; Art Educ; Tchng Art.

**MORRIS, DEBORAH A,** Teikyo Post Univ, Waterbury, CT; SO; BA; Phi Theta Kappa; Untd Church Of Christ Vistn Comm 90-; Supprtr Of The Cathlc Wrkr Mvmnt 89-; Mgt Postns Fred Harvey Co/Grnd Cnyn Natl Pk Concsnr; Soclgy/Pol Sci; Law.

**MORRIS, DEBORAH J,** Ny Univ, New York, NY; SR; MA; Continuing Edn Schlr 89-; Personnel Admnstr 84-; Sociology; Law.

**MORRIS, DIALLO K,** Hampton Univ, Hampton, VA; SO; BA; Undrwtr Explrs 89-; Acdmc Schlrshp Hmptn Emnt Schlr 90-; Deans Lst 89-; Pltcl Sci; Law.

**MORRIS, EDDIE L,** Ms St Univ, Miss State, MS; SR; BA; Phi Beta Lambda Bus Club Intr Sports 87-89; Beta Gamma Phi 90-; Phi Kappa Phi 90-; Deans & Pres List 87-; Acdmc Schlrshp 90-; Gen Bus; Bus/Mrktng.

**MORRIS, GAY S,** Bennett Coll, Greensboro, NC; FR; PHD; Vlybl Bsktbl Co Cptn 90-; Acadmc Affrs Frshmn Rep 90-; Trck; Hnr Stdnt 90-; Prsdntl Schlr 90-; Deans Lst 90-; Fsk Prmdcl Intrnshp Prgrm; Bsktbl Vllybl Trck 90-; Biology Prmdcl; Grad Schl.

**MORRIS, GLORIA S,** Chattanooga St Tech Comm Coll, Chattanooga, TN; SO; AD; Natl Stdnt Nrs Assc 90-; Chrch Pianist 87-; Chi Omega Mthrs Clb UTC 90-; Bkkpr 84-; Nrsng; RN.

**MORRIS, HENRY,** Holyoke Comm Coll, Holyoke, MA; SO; MA; Afro Am Clb 89-; Lrng Asst Ctr Tutor 90-; Phi Theta Kappa 90-; Natl Jr Clg Athltc Assn Acdmc All Am 90-; Nmntd USA Today/NJCAA Acdmc All Am Tm; Alexander Crummell Summer Hmnts Inst; Vrsty Bsktbl Co-Capt 89-; AA; Hist; Law/Tchng.

**MORRIS, JEAN,** Owensboro Jr Coll Of Bus, Owensboro, KY; GD; CERT; Central City Bsn/Profsnl Wmn Pres 86-88; Muhlenberg Co Dem Wmns Clb; Bookkeeper; Law; Paralegal.

**MORRIS, JEFFERY A,** Lexington Comm Coll, Lexington, KY; SO; BHS; Stephen A Thomas Schlrshp Award 90-; Deans List 90; Physcl Thrpy.

**MORRIS, JEFFREY A,** Yeshiva Univ, New York, NY; SR; BA; Intrn Local Cngrsmn; I M Bkbl League Capt 90-; Trck Tm; Hstroy; Law.

**MORRIS, JERI L,** Marshall University, Huntington, WV; FR; BA; Phi Mu Schlrshp Chrmn 90-; Finance; Stockbroker.

**MORRIS, JOELL H,** Western Carolina Univ, Cullowhee, NC; SR; BSW; Natl Assoc Soc Wrks; Soc Wrk Clb 90-; Stdnt Mrshls Clb; Pi Gamma Mu; Phi Alpha; Clge Schlrs Amer; All Amer Schlr; Soc Wrk; Schl Soc Wrkr.

**MORRIS, JOHN M,** Univ Of Sc At Columbia, Columbia, SC; JR; BA; Gamma Beta Phi 88-90; Pi Kappa Phi; AA Anderson Coll 90; Bus; Mktg.

**MORRIS, KEITH D,** Univ Of Tn At Martin, Martin, TN; SR; Work Partime Pizza Hut 89-; Alpha Phi Sec 89-; E TN St Univ Prep Mst Impvd Stdnt 90; Premed Renfrcmnt Envrnmnt Prog; Biology; Dentistry.

**MORRIS, KELLY M,** Univ Of Med & Dentistry Of Nj, Newark, NJ; GD.

**MORRIS, KLEVIN P,** Embry Riddle Aeronautical Univ, Daytona Beach, FL; FR; BS; Mrtl Arts Clb 90-; Drvr Chrch Vn 90-; Wrk Hlfx Mdcl Cntr 90-; Hnrs Roll; Deans Lst; Advnc Plcmnt Spnsh & Grmn 90-; Yoshukai Karatee 90-; Arntcl Sci; Pilot.

**MORRIS, LARRY E,** Central Al Comm Coll, Alexander City, AL; FR; BA; Phi Theta Kappa; Eng.

**MORRIS, LESLIE JANINE,** Clark Atlanta Univ, Atlanta, GA; SR; MD; NAACP 87-; Yng Dem 88-90; Insprtnl Vcs Fth Chr 88-; Kappa Mu 89-; Alpha Kappa Mu 90-Vol Grady Mem Hosp 90-; Deas Lst 87-; Magna Cum Laude Grad; BS Blgy; Med; Mdcl Schl.

**MORRIS III, MANUEL K,** Morehouse Coll, Atlanta, GA; JR; BS; Morehouse Clg Research Inst 90-; Morehouse Mathletes Clb 88-; Natl Scty Blck Engrs 88-89; Morehouse Clg Hnrs Prog 88-; Boys Clb Amer Vol 90-; Frederick Douglas Tutorial Prog Vol 90-; GTE UNCF Smmr Sci Prog 89-90; Math; Clg Professor.**

**MORRIS, MARIAN,** James Madison University, Harrisonburg, VA; GD; BS; Stu Educ Media Assoc 86-90; Hmn Rsrcs Mgmt Assoc 89-90; JMU Wmns/Univ Chorus 88-90; Stu Alumni Assoc Sec 87; Stu Ambsdrs Sec/Tres 87-90; Pres Lst 89-90; Intrnshp Offc Admin 88; Intrnshp Ofc Sys Mgmt Prsnl Dept Rcknghm Mem Hosp 90; Offc Admin.

**MORRIS, MARLA M,** Valdosta St Coll, Valdosta, GA; SO; BA; Alpha Lambda Delta 89-; Kappa Delta Guard 90-; Chldrns Hosp Richmond VA; Natl Comm Prevent Chld Abuse; Blazers Batgirl 89-; Pre-Phrmcy; Phrmcy.

**MORRIS, MARY S,** Univ Of Cin R Walters Coll, Blue Ash, OH; SO; BA; Engl/Frnch; Educator/Wrtr.

**MORRIS, MELANIE A,** Indiana Univ Of Pa, Indiana, PA; JR; BA; PHEAA; Gymnstc; Mccullough Elem Aide; Spcl Olympcs; Elem Educ.

**MORRIS, MICHAEL G,** Univ Of Nc At Asheville, Asheville, NC; JR; BA; Biolgy Clb; Deans/Chnclrs Lst 89-; Bsktbl 74-78; NC Elctrcl Cntrctrs Lcnse 86-; Bsbl/Bsktbl Coach; Biolgy; Tchng.**

**MORRIS, MIN X,** City Univ Of Ny Baruch Coll, New York, NY; SR; BBA; Frgn Trd Eco Clb Shanghai Inst Frgn Trd China VP 85-87; Golden Key; Cert Shanghai Inst Frgn Trd China 87; Acctg; Intntl Mktg Offcr.

**MORRIS JR, PATRICK J,** Gettysburg Coll, Gettysburg, PA; FR; Stdnt Govt Treas 90-; Phi Kappa Psi; V Ftbl; V Trck And Fld 90-; Hlth Phys Educ; Phys Thrpst.

**MORRIS, REBA DE ANN,** Middle Ga Coll, Cochran, GA; FR; AS; Nrsng; RN.

**MORRIS JR, RICHARD M,** Liberty Univ, Lynchburg, VA; SR; Debate Team 89-90; Clge Republicans Recdng Sec 88-90; Stndt Senate 90; Phi Alpha Theta 90-; Alpha Lambda Delta 89-90; Intrnshp Senate Repblcn Policy Comm; Oxford Study Prog 90; BS; Govmnt; Law.

**MORRIS, ROBERT B,** Univ Of Tn At Knoxville, Knoxville, TN; FR; BA; Reese Hall Rest Assoc 90-; Raquetball Club 90-; Alpha Lambda Delta Treas 90-; Bus Admnstrn-Finance; Post Grad MBA & JD.

**MORRIS, ROGER P,** Memphis St Univ, Memphis, TN; JR; BA; Md-South Mdl Un Natns; Hstry/Poltcl Sci; Law.

**MORRIS, SCARLET L,** Faulkner St Jr Coll, Bay Minette, AL; SO; MBA; Pow Wow Ldrshp Scty Pres 89-; Singers; Phi Theta Kappa; James B Allen Awrd; Pow Wow Ldrshp Awrd; Best Actress 90-; Faulkner Singer Awrd 90; Stdnt Hosts Stdnt Coordinator; ASS Science; English; Teacher.

**MORRIS, SCOTT,** Morris Brown Coll, Atlanta, GA; SO; BS; Natl Soc Blck Eng Pub Comm; Morris Brown Coll Eng Clb Cnsttn Comm; Nw Blck Voices; Hnrs Pgrm; Big Bro YMCA; Hnr Rl; Dual Degree Hnr Rl; Math/Physics; Eng.

**MORRIS, SHIRLETTE R,** Albany St Coll, Albany, GA; SR; BA; Intercoll Studies Inst Inc Campus Rep 90-; Dougherty Cnty Sch Vol Strng Com Sec; Sch Vol Sys 89-; Smr Schlrs Pgm Columbia Univ; Smr Intern Schlrshp Awd; Am Bus Wmns Assn Pres 89-; Floral Dsgnr; Teach; Spcl Edn; Teach.

**MORRIS, SUSAN L,** Glassboro St Coll, Glassboro, NJ; SR; BA; Psi Chi; Prov Hse Intern; Psychlgy; Cnslng Psych.**

**MORRIS, TERRI L,** Middle Tn St Univ, Murfreesboro, TN; SR; BS; News Anchor/Rep 89-90; Hnr Stdnt Assn 87-88; Rho Lambda 90-; Phi Kappa Phi; Tau Omicron 89; Gamma Beta Phi 88-; Soc Prof Jrnlsts 89-; Speech Cmnctn Assn 90-; Alpha Delta Pi Exec V P 87-; Intrnshp Talk Shw WTVF Nshvlle; Brdcst Jrnlsm/Speech; TV Brdcstng.

**MORRIS, TIMOTHY S,** Univ Of Sc At Columbia, Columbia, SC; FR; BS; Eng; Elect Eng.

**MORRIS, TISHA L,** Western Ky Univ, Bowling Green, KY; SO; BS; Pre Law Clb 89-; SGA 89-; Phi Eta Sigma 89-90; Alpha Gamma Delta Rsh Chrmn 89-; Clg Hghts Fndtn Schlrshp 90; Pres Schlr 89-; Im Flg Ftbl; Vlybl; Tenns; Socr 89-; Gov/Busn; Law.

**MORRIS JR, TOMMY L,** Coker Coll, Hartsville, SC; JR; BS; Hist Ed; Tchng.

**MORRIS, TRINA Y,** Univ Of Southern Ms, Hattiesburg, MS; SR; BS; Paralegal Soc; Afro-Am Stdnt Org; Alpha Lambda Delta; Alpha Kappa Alpha Anti-Grammateus; Intrnshp US Dept Of Jstce Montgomery AL; Paralegal; Law.

**MORRIS, VICKI A,** City Univ Of Ny Baruch Coll, New York, NY; JR; BBA; Chrstn Mssn USA Yth Dept Tr 89-; Chrstn Mssn USA Sndy Schl Sec 90-; Acctg.

**MORRIS-MASON, KATHERINE,** Atlantic Comm Coll, Mays Landing, NJ; JR; BA; Sales Mgr; Law; Law Schl.

**MORRIS-PLESS, CATHERINE M,** Univ Of Ga, Athens, GA; SR; BS; SG 87-88; SHEA Sec 87-88; Cthlc Assn VP 87-88; Lambda Sigma Sec 88-89; Phi Upsilon Omicron Initiatn Chrmn 90-; Foods/Ntrtn Assn Nutr Wk Chrprsn 90-; Deans Aide 90-; Fmly Cnsmr Sci; Dietcn.

**MORRIS-YOUNG, SEAN L,** Middle Tn St Univ, Murfreesboro, TN; SO; BA; Grmn Clb VP 89-90; Rsdnt Asst 90-; Gamma Beta Phi 90-; Engl; Scndry Ed.

**MORRISEY, DWIGHT L,** Fayetteville St Univ, Fayetteville, NC; SR; BS; Crmnl Jstce Clb 89-; Kappa Delta Pi 90-; Alpha Kappa Mu; Athletic Ofcls Assn 82-; Brothers Christ 76-78; Warsaw Elem Advsry Cncl 86-; Cumberaldn Cnty Dispute Mediation; Cmnty Serv Intern; Hsng Assn 81-88; Crmnl Jstce; MS Teach.

**MORRISEY, TERESA M,** S U N Y Coll Of A & T Morrisvl, Morrisville, NY; FR; Mddle Sts Com 90-; Stdnt Srvcs Com Fctly Congrss 90-; Offce Asst Prof J Schlausne; Scl Sci; Law.

**MORRISON, CAROL A,** Tallahassee Comm Coll, Tallahassee, FL; SO; BFA; Phi Theta Kappa 84-87; Pres Lst Daytona Bch Comm Coll 85-86; Deans Lst St Petersbur Jr Coll 88-89; Deans Lst 90; Phtgrphy; Instrctr.

**MORRISON, CHERYL H,** Univ Of Sc At Columbia, Columbia, SC; JR; BA; Gamma Beta Phi 89-; Gldn Ky 90-; History; Applied History Advncd Degree.

**MORRISON, DARLENE M,** Newbury Coll, Brookline, MA; SR; AAS; Deans Lst 89-; System One Corp Intrnshp; Merit Schlrshp 89-; Travel/Tourism Mgmnt/Bus Admin; Corp Travel.

**MORRISON, DENNIS RAY,** Howard Univ, Washington, DC; JR; Japan Karate Assn; Intl Karate Fed; Red Cross; Swmmng; CAIUB Clg Art Sci/Tech; Architect.

**MORRISON, ELLEN L,** Broward Comm Coll, Ft Lauderdale, FL; SO; BS; Broward Cnty Dietetic Assn 89-; Amer Dietetic Assn 89-; AVP Amer 1st S/L Assn 83-87; AVP Cmnwlth Svngs/Loan Assn 87-89; AS; Ntrtn; Dietician.

**MORRISON, EMILY M,** Univ Of Nh Plymouth St Coll, Plymouth, NH; SO; BS; Chorale 89-90; Voice Pfmrmnce Schlrshp 89-90; Bus; Mngmnt.

**MORRISON, ESTHER K,** O'more School Of Design, Franklin, TN; FR; BA; BS John Brown Univ 88; Fshn Dsgn; Mrchndsng.

**MORRISON, JANICE M,** S U N Y At Buffalo, Buffalo, NY; SO; BA; Bus.

**MORRISON, JENNIFER L,** Univ Of Sc At Columbia, Columbia, SC; FR; BA; Nwspr Carnegie Mellon Univ Pitts 89-90; Engl; Art Consult.

**MORRISON, JULIA L,** Middle Tn St Univ, Murfreesboro, TN; SO; BA; Hypers Clb; Fllwshp Chrstn Athlts; Gamma Beta Phi; Bsktbl Schlrshp; Phys Thrpy; Sprts Thrpsts.

**MORRISON, JULIE A,** Wv Univ At Parkersburg, Parkersburg, WV; SR; AS; Stdnt Govt Sec 90-; Bd Of Advsrs 90-; Dsplnry Hrng Bd 90-; Phi Theta Kappa 88-; Physiology; Phys Thrpy.

**MORRISON, KATHY D,** Central Fl Comm Coll, Ocala, FL; FR; AS; Dntl Hygn; Dntl Hgnst.

**MORRISON, KELLI JO,** West Liberty St Coll, West Liberty, WV; SO; AB; Mltcltrl Ed Comm 90-; Tutrng Serv 90-; Rsdnt Asst 90-; W Liberty St Clg Hnrs Pgm 90-; Elem Ed; Tchg.

**MORRISON, KRISTI M,** Cornell Univ Statutory College, Ithaca, NY; FR; BA; Wmns La Crosse 90-; Cornell Tradition Flw 90-; Wmns La Crosse 90-; Statistics/Biometry; Med/Rsrch.

**MORRISON, LEE A,** Univ Of Al At Birmingham, Birmingham, AL; FR; Blazer Bnd 90; Psychlgy; Art Thrpy.

**MORRISON, LESLIE C,** Abraham Baldwin Agri Coll, Tifton, GA; SO; Ga Assoc Nursing Stdnts Sec 89-; Phi Theta Kappa 89-; Ladies Aux VFW 88-; Dorming Nrsng Schlrshp 90-; ASN; Nrsng.

**MORRISON, MARYBETH,** Wagner Coll, Staten Island, NY; JR; BS; Stdnt Act Brd 88-; Schl Nwpr 89-; Schl Fnd Rsng Functns 88-; Omicron Delta Kappa 89-; Alethea 89-; Tri Beta 89-; Vol St Vincnts Med Ctr 88-90; Intrnshp Phy Thrpy Prac 90-; Var Sftbl Tm 88-; Chrldng Tm/Trck Tm; Bio; Phy Thrpy.

**MORRISON, MEGHAN A,** Christopher Newport Coll, Newport News, VA; JR; BA; Dns Lst; Kinder Care Lrng Cntr Tchr 88-; Early Chldhd Ed; Corp Trainer.

**MORRISON, PATRICIA A,** Wv Univ At Parkersburg, Parkersburg, WV; JR; BA; Asst 4h Ldr Chrch Mmbr Asst Ldr 89-; Elem Edctn; Elem Tchr.

**MORRISON, PRECIOUS D,** Morgan St Univ, Baltimore, MD; JR; BS; Alpha Kappa Mu; Beta Kappa Chi; Alpha Nu Omega Pres 88-; Currclm Brd Hon Schlrshp 88-; Biolgy/Pre-Profsnl Chem; Med.

**MORRISON, RODNEY,** Univ Of Rochester, Rochester, NY; SR; BA; Thurgood Marshall Pre Law Scty Bus Mgr 90-; Dorm Cncl 88-; Black Stdnts Un 88; Big Brthr/Big Str Pgm 90-; Vol Svc Awd; Intern Merrill Lynch Asst Brkr; Ralston Purina Intern Dstrt Sls Rep 90; Intrctv Prtnrs Mrktng Asst; Var Bsktbl 88-90; Hist; Bus.

**MORRISON, SUZANNE E,** Fl International Univ, Miami, FL; FR; B SC; W Indian Stdnt Assn Sec; Sec Dpl Alpha Bus Clb 90; Advtsng/Pub Rltns; Exec.

**MORRISS, CHRISTINE L,** Birmingham Southern Coll, Birmingham, AL; FR; Cnsrvncy Clb 90; Chi Omega Pldg Class Spirit Chrmn 90; Erly Chldhd Ed; Ed.

**MORRISSETTE, MARIA C,** Rivier Coll, Nashua, NH; SO; Bsktbl 89-; Hmnty Comm 90-; Math.**

**MORRISSEY, MARILYN M,** Tn St Univ, Nashville, TN; JR; BA; Allnc Frncs 89-; Eta Sigma 89-; Rape/Sxl Abuse Ctr Vol; Pblc Rltns Hosp; Frnch; Law Schl.

**MORROW, BECKY L,** Duquesne Univ, Pittsburgh, PA; FR; BS; Concert Choir 90-; Opera & Brodway Workshops 90-; Church Folk Choir 90-; Phi Eta Sigma 90-; Founders Award 90-; Biology.

**MORROW, CECELIA A,** Univ Of Al At Birmingham, Birmingham, AL; SR; BS; Hmcmng Comm 88; Delta Sigma Theta Srgnt At Arms 88-; Jffrsn Cnty Dept Hlth Intrnshp Educ; Pres Hnrs; Health Educ; Tch.

**MORROW, JEFFREY O,** Univ Of Ky, Lexington, KY; JR; BA; Mens Bkbl Mgr 88-; History; Tch/Coach.

**MORROW, KAREN D,** Univ Of Tn At Knoxville, Knoxville, TN; JR; BS; Mktg.

**MORROW, LOU-ANN,** Clarkson Univ, Potsdam, NY; SR; A; Pres Lst 89; Dns Lst 89-90; Wmn Ldrs Acad Smnr Schlp; AAS Cntn Clg Tech 87; Indl Mgmt.

**MORROW, SHARON,** De Tech & Comm Coll At Dover, Dover, DE; GD; AAS; Stdnt Sprt Orgnztn 89; Hmn Svc Orgnztn 89-; Phi Theta Kappa; Human Svc; Sbstnc Abuse Cnslng.

**MORROW, THERESA A,** Judson Coll, Marion, AL; SR; BS; Interior Desgn Intnshp Barberry Sq Dec Cen; Interior Desgn.

**MORROW, VICTORIA ELIZABETH,** Fl International Univ, Miami, FL; SR; BS; Stf Wrtr 90-; Std Nwspr Edtr Chief 89-90; Std Ornt Mag Ed Chief 90; Phi Theta Kappa 88-; Soc Prof Jrnlsts Pres; Grad Hghst Hnrs; Pres Lst 90; Dns Lst 90-; PTK Outst Prov Mbr 88; PTK Sev Awd 88; Std Life Awd 90; AA 90; Jrnlsm; Edtr/Pblshr.

**MORROW, WILLIAM B,** Embry Riddle Aeronautical Univ, Daytona Beach, FL; JR; BA; Am Assn Airprt Exec 89-; Vrsty Bsktbl 89-90; Aerntcl Sci; Airln Plt.

**MORSCH, EUGENE P,** S U N Y Coll Of Tech At Alfred, Alfred, NY; FR; Acctg Clb 90-; Acctg.

**MORSE, CARLIN P,** Al A & M Univ, Normal, AL; SO; Thespial Soc 90; Lwendolyn Brooks Poetry Contest; Hnr Rl Deans List 90-; Bus; Law.

**MORSE, FORTIS D,** Va Commonwealth Univ, Richmond, VA; FR; BA; Phi Eta Sigma; Provost Schlr; Hon Pgm; Pre-Law Soc; Pol Sci; Law.

**MORSE, MICHAEL A,** Middle Tn St Univ, Murfreesboro, TN; SO; BS; Assc Recrdng Mngmnt Std 89-; RIM Wrtrs 90-; Audio Engnrng Scty 89-; Hbtt Humnty; Std Envrnmntl Actn 90-; Recrdng Indstry Mngmnt; Audio Engnrng/Prdctn.

**MORSE, MIRIAM A,** Allegheny Coll, Meadville, PA; SR; BA; Soc Advncmnt Gndr Eqlty 90; Psi Chi Sec 89-; Alpha Chi Omega Clgte Rsh Infor Chrprsn 88; Fmly Plnng Svcs Intrnshp 90; Sesqui Cntnl Schlrshp 87-; Alden Schlr 89-90; Engl/Psych; Law.

**MORSE, TERESA E,** Univ Of Nc At Greensboro, Greensboro, NC; JR; BS; Kappa Omcrn Nu; Gamma Sigma Sigma Natl Serv Sor VP 87-; NC Tchng Flws Schlr 88-; Almni Schlr 88-; Hmn Env Schlr 88-; Home Ec Ed; Tchr.

**MORSE, VICTORIA A,** S U N Y Coll At Buffalo, Buffalo, NY; SO; BA; Hnrs Prog 89-; Regents Schlrshp 89-; Hnrs Prog Schlrshp 89-; Psychology; Neuropsychology.**

**MORT, HELEN M,** Indiana Univ Of Pa, Indiana, PA; JR; Sigma Tau Delta 90-; Engl Ed; Tchr H S.

**MORTIMER, GREG W,** Life Coll, Marietta, GA; SR; DC; Dean Lst; Rugby Ftbl Clb 87-; Chrprctc; Dr.

**MORTIMER, KARL B,** S U N Y Coll Of Tech At Alfred, Alfred, NY; SO; BS; Eng Sci Clb 89-; Dorm Cncl 90; Chem Eng.

**MORTIMER, PAULA M,** Life Coll, Marietta, GA; GD; DC; BS Muhlenberg Coll 86; Chrprctc.

**MORTON, ADRIANNE N,** D Youville Coll, Buffalo, NY; SR; BA; Blck Stu Union 89-; Stu Assoc Sntr 90-; Scl Wrk Clb 89-90; J C Penney Mgt Intrn 90; Sclgy; Prsnl Admin.

**MORTON, APRIL M,** Pellissippi St Tech Comm Coll, Knoxville, TN; SO; BS; Phi Theta Kappa 90-; Whos Who Amng Stdngs Amer Jr Coll 91; Bus Mgmt.**

**MORTON, CARISSA G,** Univ Of Southern Ms, Hattiesburg, MS; SR; BS; Stdnt Nurses Assoc S MS 90-; Stndt Alumni Assoc .0-; Gamma Alpha Epsilon Sec 89-; Pi Tau Chi 89-; Chi Omega Rush Chrmn 89-; Rotoract 89-90; Nursing; Intensive Care.

**MORTON JR, GEORGE E,** Atlantic Comm Coll, Mays Landing, NJ; SO; BA; Hstry/Govt Clb; Pre Law.

**MORTON, JONATHAN LEE,** Birmingham Southern Coll, Birmingham, AL; FR; BS; Alpha Lambda Delta 90-; Poltcl Sci; Law.

**MORTON, JULIE E,** Longwood Coll, Farmville, VA; JR; BS; Phy Educ Majrs Clb; IM Sprts; Delta Psi Kappa Pldg Eductr 90-; Sigma Kappa Schlrshp Chrmn 90-; Phy Educ; Tchng.**

**MORTON, KIMBERLY R,** Comm Coll Algny Co Algny Cmps, Pittsburgh, PA; FR; Law.

**MORTON, LASONGIA M,** Ms St Univ, Miss State, MS; SO; BS; SG Pll Com; Hlth Advsry Com; Ambssdrs Pr Asst; Gamma Beta Phi; Pre Med Blgy; Med.

**MORTON, LESLIE A,** Middle Tn St Univ, Murfreesboro, TN; FR; BA; Presbyterian Stdnt Fllwshp; Fllwshp Of Christian Athletes; HPERS Clb; Gamme Beta Phi; IM Sftbl; Physical Educ; Teacher.

**MORTON, NEAL F,** Univ Of Tn At Knoxville, Knoxville, TN; JR; BBA; Jrpblcns; Alpha Kappa Psi; Wllm Bls Fndtn Schlrshp; Fnc.

**MORTON, SHELLY B,** Marshall University, Huntington, WV; SR; BA; Kappa Delta Pi; Elem Ed; Tchg.

**MORTON, TERESA A K,** Southern Vt Coll, Bennington, VT; FR; BA; Amer Legn Aux 87-; Bsns; Comms/Adv.

**MORVAN, LAURENCE EDWARD,** Bunker Hill Comm Coll, Boston, MA; FR; BA; Psych; Rehab Cnslg.

**MORVILLE, KENNETH,** Ny Univ, New York, NY; SO; AAS; Deans Lst 90-; DPMA 89-; Dept Mgr Phtfnshng Indust 81-; Cert Long Island U 88; Bus; Cmptr Prgrmr BA NYU Schl Bus.

**MORWAY, DEBRA S,** Manhattanville Coll, Purchase, NY; JR; BA; Hnrs Schlr; O'gorman Prize Fichon Wrihing 90-; Exective VP Laby Syst VT 87-; CLV Amer Clg 81; AS Norwalk Commty Clg 90; History; Law.

**MOSCA, MARIA H,** Glassboro St Coll, Glassboro, NJ; GD; BA; Pol Sci Clb Sec 89-90; RA 87-; Dns Lst; Natl Panhellenic Pres 88-90; Alpha Epsilon Phi 87-90; Callaghan/Thompson Attys At Law Intrnshp 90; Pol Sci/Sec Educ; Pol Career/Pub Offc.

**MOSCARDELLI, GEORGIA A,** Ga St Univ, Atlanta, GA; JR; BSED; Gamma Beta Phi 89; Golden Key 90-; Middle Sch Sci; Edn/Teach.**

**MOSCARITOLO, STEVEN J,** Merrimack Coll, North Andover, MA; FR; BA; Cmmtr Clb 90-; Frontiers 90-; Acctng; Bus.

**MOSCOSO, CLAUDIA P,** Oh Wesleyan Univ, Delaware, OH; SO; Stdnt Fndtn 90-; Wmn Crs Cltrl Undrstdng 90; Tutor Mdrn Foreign Lang Dept 90-; Phi Socty; Newman Comm 89-90; Intl Bus/Jrnlsm.

**MOSELEY, DONALD,** Norfolk St Univ, Norfolk, VA; GD; Cmps Psychlgy Clb VP 88-89; Cmps Yng Dmcrts 89-90; Psi Omega Phi 89-90; Amrcn Psychlgcl Assn 89-; BA Nrflk Unv 90; Psychlgy; Thelgy MA MD.

**MOSELEY, DOROTHY M,** Fl St Univ, Tallahassee, FL; JR; BS; Genisus Ldrahp Clb 88-89; Hnrs/Schrs 88-89; Bapt Campus Mnstry Coor Of Evnglsm 89-; Psychlgy; Socl Wrk/Marriage Family Thrpy.

**MOSELEY, JAMES H,** Middle Tn St Univ, Murfreesboro, TN; FR; BBA; Acctg.

**MOSELEY, KATHY S,** Middle Ga Coll, Cochran, GA; SO; BED; Pres SELL; Mdle Grds Educ; Tchng.

**MOSELEY, PAMELA,** Catawba Valley Comm Coll, Hickory, NC; FR; BA; Gamma Beta Phi 90-; US Navy Rsvs Crpsmn 89-; Hlth Unit Coord; Cert John Robert Powers Schl Fshn Careers 86; Psy; Med/Phscn.

**MOSELEY, REX W,** Univ Of Sc At Columbia, Columbia, SC; SR; BA; SG 90; AA 89; Psych Sclgy; Scl Wrk.

**MOSELEY, ROBERT D,** Central Al Comm Coll, Alexander City, AL; FR; AS AA; Mthmtcs & Physcs; Engnrng.

**MOSELEY, SALLY E,** East Carolina Univ, Greenville, NC; SR; BM; Music Tchrs Natl Assoc 90-; Grnvl Piano Tchrs Assoc 90-; Pi Kappa Lambda 89-; Phi Eta Sigma 88-; Omicron Delta Kappa 90-; ECU Univ Awd; Schl/Music Otsdng Sr; Wnner ECU Yng Artst Comptn 90; Music/Piano; Arts Admin/Teach.

**MOSELEY, WILLIAM BRETT,** Univ Of Sc At Columbia, Columbia, SC; SO; BAS; Fencing Club Pres 90-; Assn Hnrs Stdnts 89-; Gamma Beta Phi 89-; Engl/Psych; Tch/Write.

**MOSELEY, WILLIAM J,** Lexington Comm Coll, Lexington, KY; FR; BS; Cmptr Sci; Cmptr Pgmng.

**MOSELY, HELENA J,** Cheyney Univ Of Pa, Cheyney, PA; GD; MS; BS Ed 90; Elem Ed Cert NJ PA Ntl Merit Deans Lst Stdnt 89-90; Deans Hon Rll 88-90; Cum GPA 3.86 Kappa Delta Phi Ntl Ed Hon Soc 89-; Chr Hood St Prnt Advsry Cncl 88-89; Quinton Twnshp Brd Ed/Erth/Life Sci Tchr 90-; Laurls Montessori Day Care 86-87; Crrclmn Dev/Envrnmntl Sci.

**MOSER, ANNE C,** Columbus Coll Of Art & Design, Columbus, OH; JR; BFA; IDSA 89-; Indstrl Dsgn; Retail Envrmntl Dsgn.

**MOSER, BRADLEY B,** Hillsborough Comm Coll, Tampa, FL; SO; Stdnt Govt 90-; Phi Theta Kappa; Bio; Dntstry.

**MOSER, CHRISTINA M,** Bowling Green St Univ, Bowling Green, OH; SO; BA; Vsl Cmnctns Tech Orgnztn Sec 89-; Phi Eta Sgm 89-; St Thomas Moore 89-; Co Op Upjohn Co; Deans List 90; Vsl Cmnctn Technlgy; Vsl Cmnctns.

**MOSER JR, DAVID B,** Southern Coll Of Tech, Marietta, GA; SR; BSMET; ASME 89-; SME 90-; Mfg Engr.

**MOSER, MICHAEL R,** Oh Wesleyan Univ, Delaware, OH; SR; Hll Govt Pres 90; Phi Beta Kappa; Phi Alpha Theta Sec 89-; Mrtr Brd 90-; Crcle K 88; Govrs Hnrs Prog Intrnshp 90; A Russoff Otstndng Hstrcl Rsrch Ppr Awrd; Vrsty Bsktbl Vrsty Trck 87-; Hstry; Law.

**MOSER, NORA E,** Columbia Union Coll, Takoma Park, MD; SR; BS; Med Advsry Comm Rep 90-; Pre-Med Soc; Deans Lst 87-; Soup Kitchen; Acad Schlrshp; Vlybl; Resprtry Care; Med.

**MOSER, SHEILA A,** Bridgewater Coll, Bridgewater, VA; SR; Fllw Chrsstn Athltc Clb; Intrnshp Wdrw Wlsn Rhb Cntr; Bsktbll Sftbll Tms Capt; BS; Psychlgy.

**MOSES, ARI H,** Ramapo Coll Of Nj, Mahwah, NJ; SR; Fin Invstmnt Assn Pres 89-; Delta Mu Delta; BS; AAS Rcklnd Comm Coll 89; Bus; Fin.

**MOSES, COREY L,** Ms St Univ, Miss State, MS; SR; BS; Ambssdrs Famous Maroon Bnd Sec/Ambsdrs 89-; Intrschl Cncl 87-; Fash Focus 89-90; Phi Kappa Phi 90-; Phi Eta Sigma 88-; Gamma Beta Phi 88-; Kappa Omicron Nu Exec Brd 90-; Cmps Crsd Christ Srvnt Tm 88-; Clg Cncl 88-.

**MOSES, KESHA D,** Columbia Union Coll, Takoma Park, MD; JR; AA; Theta Alpha Beta Sec 90-; Loaves/Fishes 90-; Teach A Kid 90-; Bus; Law.

**MOSES, LILLY F,** Columbia Union Coll, Takoma Park, MD; GD; BS; Emrgncy Nrs Assn 84-; Emrgncy Med Serv 88-; S Asia Advntst Assn 74-; Basic Lf Support Cert 74-; CPR Instrctr Cert; Hlth Care Admin; Clncl Sprvsr.

**MOSES, SAMUEL C,** Univ Of Sc At Columbia, Columbia, SC; FR; BA; State Senate Clerk 90-; Honors College; IM Bsktbl 90-; Internatl Sutdies German; Internatl Corp Atry.

**MOSHER, JACK T,** Allegheny Coll, Meadville, PA; SR; BS; Orientation Advsr 90-; Alden Schlr 90; Athl Hnr Rl 90; Bsebl Capt 87-; Psych; Neurosci.

**MOSHER, PATRICIA J,** Univ Of Ct, Storrs, CT; JR; S; Block/Bridle Cl Marshal 90-; Dairy Cl 90-; Golden Key 90-; Alpha Zeta 90-; Phi Theta Kappa 85-86; Sigma V P 90-; Alumni Schol Awd; Anml Sci; Vet Med.

**MOSHER, REBECCA A,** S U N Y Coll Of Tech At Alfred, Alfred, NY; SR; Drama Club 89-; Dorm Cncl; Delta Psi Omega 90-; Res Asst; IM Sftbl 90-; Elem Edn; Teach.

**MOSHIRFAR, ALI,** Univ Of Md At College Park, College Park, MD; FR; BA; Alph Lmbd Dlt 90-; Acad Hon 90-; Frfghtr/EMT 90-; Hlndl Vol Fr Dept; Medcn Bus Mgmt.

**MOSHTAGHI, MAHSA,** Univ Of Al At Birmingham, Birmingham, AL; FR; BS; Stdnt Govt Chrprsn Intl Comm; Intl Stdnt Assoc VP Chrprsn Cultrl Comm; Ambsdr; Lectr Series Comm; Chldrns Hosp Vol; Chldrns Hosp Vol Serv Awd; Intl Stdnt Assoc Dedctd Hrd Wrk Awd; Ldrshp Awd; Biol; Med.

**MOSIELLO, MICHAEL L,** Fordham Univ, Bronx, NY; JR; BA; Bsns.

**MOSIER, NANCY L,** Marshall University, Huntington, WV; JR; BA; AM Clg Hlth Care Exec 90-; Phi Eta Sigma 89-; Alpha Kappa Psi; Frshmn Rsdnt Schlr Awrd 89; Hlth Care Mngmnt Intrnshp; Hosp Admin.

**MOSKEL, PAULA J,** Indiana Univ Of Pa, Indiana, PA; GD; BED; IM Vlybl 90; BED IN Univ PA 90; Elem Ed; Masters.

**MOSKO, SAUNDRA A,** Marshall University, Huntington, WV; JR; BA; Stu Govt Assn Offc Mngr 89-90; Stu Actvts Hmcmng Co Chrm 90; Gamma Beta Phi 89; Sigma Sigma Sigma Pers 89-; Intern Mcdowell Co Natl Bnk 91; IM Vllybl 90-; Fnnc; Bnkng.

**MOSKOWITZ, ERIC I,** Univ Of Rochester, Rochester, NY; JR; BA; Camp Times Sprts Ed 88-; Intrnshp London Slctrs/Bnstrs 89; Inst Eurpn Stds; Pltcl Sci.

**MOSKOWITZ, LOIS LEAH A,** Va Commonwealth Univ, Richmond, VA; SR; BA; Pres PTA Rudlin Torah Acdmy 85-86; Dressmaker 88-89; BS Georgia Sothern Univ 76; Elem Ed; Tch.

**MOSLEY, CAROL F,** Miami Dade Comm Coll, Miami, FL; SO; AA; Phi Theta Kappa 90-; Lgl Sec; Sociolgy; Law/Educ.

**MOSLEY, ELIZABETH A,** Univ Of Sc At Columbia, Columbia, SC; JR; BSN; Nrsg; MSN.

**MOSLEY, ERNEST A,** Jackson St Univ, Jackson, MS; FR; Alpha Lambda Delta 90-; Prsdnts Lst 90-; Deans Lst 90-; Physcl Thrpy.

**MOSLEY, IRIS R,** Al A & M Univ, Normal, AL; SO; BSN; SHARP Prog 89; Nursing; RN.

**MOSLEY, KEVIN,** Univ Of Akron, Akron, OH; SO; Rsdnc Hl Prgrmg Brd Mjr Evnts Comm 90-; Rsdnc Hl Prgrmg Brd Major Pblcty Comm 90-; IM Ftbl/Sftbl/Baktbl & Vlybl 89-; Bus; Mrktg.

**MOSLEY, LORENZA D,** Al A & M Univ, Normal, AL; SO; BS; US Army Rsrvs Spc E4 88-; Bus; Mrktng/Mngmnt/Advrtsng.

**MOSLEY, REGINALD V,** Alcorn St Univ, Lorman, MS; SO; BS; FFA Alcrn 90-; Mnrts Agri Ntrl Rsrcs Rltd Sci 90-; Mrchg/Cncrt Bnd 89-; Alpha Tau Alpha VP 90-; Agri Ed; Tchr.

**MOSLEY, RHONDA L,** Univ Of Miami, Coral Gables, FL; SR; BBA; Fnce Clb 89-; Hrrcn Hny Clb 89; Phi Kappa Phi 90-; Gldn Key 90-; Beta Gamma Sigma; Alpha Epsln Phi 89-; Pres Lst; Prvst Hnr Rl; Dns Lst; Bowman Ashe Schlp; AA Broward Comm Clg 89; Fnce; Bsn.

**MOSLEY, SHARON W,** Valdosta St Coll, Valdosta, GA; SO; BSED; Seaboard Const Co Accts Pay Clerk 73-82; Gold Kist Feed Mill Payroll Ins Clerk 82-84; East Coweta High Schl Attendance Sec 85-88; Early Chldhd Ed; Tchng.

**MOSLEY, TAMMY R,** Univ Of Southern Ms, Hattiesburg, MS; JR; BS; Stdnt Alumni Assn 89-; Stdnt Eagle Clb 90-; Res Asst 90-; Polymer Sci/Math; Engr.**

**MOSLEY, WILLIE M,** Hillsborough Comm Coll, Tampa, FL; FR; AA; SGA V P 90-; Better Stdnts United 90-; Phi Theta Kappa Corres Sec; Serv Awd 90-; Rcgntn Awd 90-; Acctng-Bus Admn; Law-Judgeship-Psych.

**MOSMEN, KEVIN J,** Hudson Valley Comm Coll, Troy, NY; JR; BA; Jdcl Review Brd Membr 88-90; Alcohol Review Brd Elcted Membr 88-90; Phi Theta Kappa; Pi Kappa Alpha C Chrmn 88; Psychlgy; Dntstry.

**MOSORJAK, SUZANNE J,** Indiana Univ Of Pa, Indiana, PA; SR; MED; Stdnt Lit Corps 90-; Sgn Lng Clb 89-90; Grdt Asstshp; B Ed; Ed Excptnl; Tchg.

**MOSS, ADANUS S,** Norfolk St Univ, Norfolk, VA; FR; BA; Choir 90; NABA 90; NAACP 90-; Spartan Alpha Tau; Acctg.

**MOSS, ALISON C,** Elmira Coll, Elmira, NY; JR; BABS; Orientn Ldr 89-; Actvts Bd Lctr/Chrmn 89; Theatr Mgr 88-; Phi Eta Sigma 90; Kappa Delta Pi; Hnrs Schlr; LISP; Medlln/Schlrshp Awd 90; Deans Lst 89-; Theatr/Spch/Hearg; Prfrmng.**

**MOSS, BRENDA H,** Limestone Coll, Gaffney, SC; GD; MED; Alpha Chi 89-; Kappa Delta Epsilon 89-; S C Gov Schlrshp; Paul Douglas Awd 90; Magna Cum Laude 90; Elem Ed 90-; Cmptr Pgrmr 70-90; AS Spartanburg Tech Clge 70; BA Limestone Clge 90; Elem Ed.

**MOSS, CHARISSE R,** Lexington Comm Coll, Lexington, KY; SR; Am Dntl Hygnst Assn 89-; Ownr Dance Studio 87-; Charisse Schl Dance; Mbr KY Army Natl Grd; Dntl Hygiene.

**MOSS, DANA R,** Univ Of Ky, Lexington, KY; GD; BA; KCSS NEA 90-; Alpha Gamma Rho Aux; Deans Lst 85-; Elem Ed; Tch.**

**MOSS, DOROTHY L,** Pellissippi St Tech Comm Coll, Knoxville, TN; SO; AAS; Prod Tchncn; Offc Syst Tchnlgy; Exec Sec.

**MOSS, ERIN J,** Wv Univ, Morgantown, WV; FR; BA; Air Force ROTC 90-; ROTC Schlrshp; Nrsng; Med.

**MOSS, ERNESTINE D,** Livingston Univ, Livingston, AL; SR; BA; Intl Stdnts Assn 90-; Acctg Clb 90-; Delta Sigma Theta Sec 89-; Acctg.

**MOSS JR, JERRY N,** Univ Of Southern Ms, Hattiesburg, MS; SR; CCT; PE Knsthrpy.**

**MOSS, KENNETH H,** Middle Tn St Univ, Murfreesboro, TN; SR; BS; BA Univ Calif Los Angeles 66; Intrdsplnry Stds/Elem Educ; Tchr.

**MOSS, LA TICCA W,** Fl A & M Univ, Tallahassee, FL; FR; BA; Epcrn Mdlng Sqd; Gspl Choir; Pres Schlr; All-Amer Awd; Elect Eng Tchnlgy; Eng.

**MOSS, MARY C,** Mary Holmes Coll, West Point, MS; SO; AD; Bsn Adm.

**MOSS, MELISSA N,** Pellissippi St Tech Comm Coll, Knoxville, TN; SO; AAS; Paralegal Assn 89-; Phi Theta Kappa 89-; Faculty Cncl Schlrshp 90-; Licensed Cosmetologist 84-; Legal Asst Tech; Paralegal.

**MOSS, RACQUEL M,** Hampton Univ, Hampton, VA; FR; BA; SC Pre Alumni Assc 90-; Army ROTC 90-; Hampton Commty Orchstr 90-; Citation Superior Cadet Dcrtn Awrd 90-; Army ROTC Ldrshp Awrd 90-; Army ROTC Schlstc Achvmnt Awrd 90-; Bsn; Acctng.

**MOSS, RODNEY D,** Alcorn St Univ, Lorman, MS; SO; BA; Alpha Phi Omega; Phi Beta Sigma VP 90-F; Acctg; CPA.

**MOSS, SHARAI B,** Johnson C Smith Univ, Charlotte, NC; SO; BA; Acctg; CPA.

**MOSS, TRACEY A,** Southern Coll Of Tech, Marietta, GA; JR; BA; Amer Inst Archtctrl Stdnts 90-; BSU 88-; Coop Stdnt L Hurd Engrs Inc 88-90; IM Flg Ftbl/Sftbl; Archtctrl Eng Tech.

**MOSS, TRACY L,** Al St Univ, Montgomery, AL; FR; Ftbl; Dean Lst 90-; Art; Archtctr.

**MOSS, WALTER S,** Ms St Univ, Miss State, MS; FR; BS; Phi Eta Sigma 90-; Lambda Chi Alpha Rsk Mgr 90-; Mss St Schlrshp Rcgntn; Econs; Law.

**MOSSALLAM, USAMAH,** City Univ Of Ny City Coll, New York, NY; SR; BS; Stdnt Gov Clss Rep 90-; Stdnt Acad Prgrss Comm Clss Rep 89-; Amnsty Intrntl Treas 87-89; Biomed Stds; Med.

**MOSSER, HEATHER J,** Kent St Univ Kent Cmps, Kent, OH; SR; BA; Delta Sigma Pi 89-; Bus Mgmt; Law.

**MOSSER, JENNIFER E,** Wv Univ, Morgantown, WV; FR; RHA 90-; Hevetia Honorary 90-; Hnrs Prog 90-; Pres Schlrshp 90-; Chem Eng.

**MOST, JAMES D,** Atlantic Comm Coll, Mays Landing, NJ; SO; BA; History; Teacher.

**MOSTAFAVI, ARMAGHAN AMY,** Boston Univ, Boston, MA; GD; MD; Phi Beta Kappa; Alpha Omega Alpha; Golden Key; All Amer Coll Soc; NIH Surg Oncology 90; BA 83; MD; Biol; Med.

**MOSTAR, LINDA A,** Kent St Univ Kent Cmps, Kent, OH; GD; Pres List 90; Deans List 87-90; Intrnshp Summit Co Chldrn Svc Brd 90; BA; Indvdl/Fmly Stds; Emplyd Jvnl Crt Geauga Cty.

**MOSTEL, CLAIRE R,** Fl International Univ, Miami, FL; GD; MPA; Pblc Admin Soc VP 88-; Inter-Org Com Sec 90-; Amer Soc Pblc Admin 90-; Natl Yng Pro Forum; AA Miami Dade Comm Coll 84; BPA 90; Pblc Admin.

**MOSTELLER III, DOUGLAS E,** Anderson Coll, Anderson, SC; JR; BS; Dns Lst 90; BA; Busn/Mktg.

**MOTAI, TAKEHIRO,** Comm Coll Algny Co Algny Cmps, Pittsburgh, PA; FR; Bus Mgmt.

**MOTEKI, WINONA F,** City Univ Of Ny Baruch Coll, New York, NY; SR; BSED; Tchrs Tomorrow; Phi Theta Kappa 87-; Goldn Key; AAS Kingsbrgh Comm Clg 88f; Spec Educ; Tchr/Dir.

**MOTES, PAMELA T,** Ga St Univ, Atlanta, GA; SR; BA; Gldn Key; Kappa Delta Phi; Assoc Clayton State Coll 89; Early Chldhd Educ; Tchr.

**MOTESHARREI, BITA,** Univ Of Miami, Coral Gables, FL; FR; BS; Wrkng Rsrch Grp Chem; Bio; Med.

**MOTICHKA, JANEL S,** Marywood Coll, Scranton, PA; SR; BFA; SG Pres Stdnt Mntr 87-89; Art Clb 87-90; Artsts Fr Arts Sake; Zeta Omicron Vp 90-; Clgte Vol 87-89; Hghlghts Fr Chldrn 89; Michael Sporn Amntn Inc; Tchr Chce Exhbts 88-90; Illstrtn; Dsgn.

**MOTLEY III, ALBERT E,** Old Dominion Univ, Norfolk, VA; SR; BA; Stdnt Eng Cncl 89; IEEE 89; Eng Crr Dy Com 90; Schlrshp Com 86; Eta Kappa Nu 90; Alpha Chi 90; Omicron Delta Kappa 90; Phi Theta Kappa 86; Dgtl Equip Comp Usrs 83-; Assn Of Comp Mchns 88-; Stdnt Srvce Awrd 90; AS Thomas Nelson Comm Coll 86; Elec And Comp Eng; Eng.

**MOTLEY, ANTHONY J,** Howard Univ, Washington, DC; GD; MDIV; DC Bible Inst 87-; Biblcl Inst For Soc Chng 89-; Frnds Of The Wash Hghlnds Libry Pres 85-; Gerald Durley Award; Assoc For The Study Of Afro-Amrecn Life/Hist 87-; Natl Assoc Of Blck Seminarns; Relign; Pastor.

**MOTLEY, BYRON M,** Middle Tn St Univ, Murfreesboro, TN; JR; BS; FOP Lodge; Tenn Sec Sch Athletic Assn 86; Ftbl Ofcl; M L King Schlrshp Fndtn Bd; Police Bnvlnt Assn 89; Masons 87; Police Patrol Sgt 78-89; Crmnl Juste Admn; Prfsr.

**MOTLEY, NATHANIEL,** Norfolk St Univ, Norfolk, VA; SR; BS; NABA 87-; Big Bro/Big Sis Pgm 88-; Acctg Tutor 89-; Alpha Kappa Mu 90-; Beta Gamma Sigma Pres 90-; Kappa Alpha Psi Treas 90-; IM Bsktbl 87-; Acctg; Pblc Acctg.

**MOTLEY, RHONDA J,** Radford Univ, Radford, VA; SO; BA; Univ Hnrs Prog; Elem/Spec Educ; Tchr.

**MOTON, CASEY J,** United States Naval Academy, Annapolis, MD; SR; Astrnmy Clb Sec 87-; Srfr Wrfr Clb 88-; Tau Beta Pi 89-; Sigma Xi 90-; Phi Kappa Phi 89-; Soc Nvl Archtcts/Mrn Engrs 88-; Amer Soc Nvl Engrs 90-; Trident Schlr 90-; Sec Navy Dist Grad; BS; EIT St MD; Nvl Archtctr; Nvl Serv.

**MOTT, LEAH R,** Univ Of South Al, Mobile, AL; SO; BED; Stdt Cncl Excptnl Chldrn 90-; Spec Ed.

**MOTT, NORMA J,** Gaston Coll, Dallas, NC; FR; ASN; Beta Clb; Sgt NC Air Natl Guard Aeromed Evacuation Tech 88-; Air Force 86-88; Nrsng; RN.

**MOTTA, KERYL,** Univ Of Pr At Rio Piedras, Rio Piedras, PR; FR; BA; Ch Yth Grp; Lib Blind Univ Vol 90-; Chem; Ph D.

**MOTTER, JIMMY E,** Tn Temple Univ, Chattanooga, TN; SO; BA; Pi Kappa Delta 90-; Missions; Fultime Chrstn Wrkr.

**MOTTERN, DONNIE A,** Northeast State Tech Comm Coll, Blountville, TN; FR; BA; Elec; Tech.

**MOTZNIK, STACEY ANN,** Immaculata Coll, Immaculata, PA; JR; Chorale VP 88; SAM Pres 89; Hnr Scty Sec 90; Bsnss; Ecnmcs/Admin.

**MOUA, NA LEE MISTIE,** Winthrop Coll, Rock Hill, SC; FR; BED; Intl Clb; Baptist Student Union 90-; Amer Scty Interior Dsgn 90-; Big Brother Big Sister Prog 90-; Guidance Intl Kids Field Day 90; Elem Educ.

**MOUGHAL, SARWAT TASNEEM,** City Univ Of Ny Brooklyn Coll, Brooklyn, NY; FR; Biolgy; Phrmcst.

**MOULDER, VICKI M,** Univ Of West Fl, Pensacola, FL; GD; MED; AA Art Pensacola Jr Clg 87; BA Art Hist Univ Of FL Gnsvlle 90; Educ Ldrshp; Museum.

**MOULTON, BROOKE R,** Andrew Coll, Cuthbert, GA; FR; Phi Theta Kappa 90-; Phi Theta Kappa 90-; Bio-Pre Med; Physician.

**MOULTON, REGINA M,** Volunteer St Comm Coll, Gallatin, TN; FR; BS; Elem Educ; Tech.

**MOULTRIE JR, HERMAN L,** Cheyney Univ Of Pa, Cheyney, PA; SR; BS; Elctrnc Clb Treas 89-; Video Prod Clb Treas 89-; Alpha Phi Sigma 90-; Phi Beta Sigma Pres 89-; U S Achvmnt Acdmy 86; Wrstlnb Tm/All Amer Capt 86-; NCAA Div II Acdmc All Amer Tm Wrstlng; BS; Elctrncs/Drwng/Dsgn; Elect Eng.

**MOULTRIE, MONICA R,** Al St Univ, Montgomery, AL; SR; BA; Stdnt Govt Class Rprsntve 87-88; Stdnt Orient Ldr 88-89; Hnr Roll 90; Intrnshp Dept Of Pblc Sfty; Offce Admin.

**MOULTRIE, NATHANIEL A,** Fl A & M Univ, Tallahassee, FL; FR; Mrchng 100; Symph Band.

**MOULTRY, DEANNA L,** Clark Atlanta Univ, Atlanta, GA; SO; BA; Acctg Clb; Spanish Clb; Hnrs Prog; Acct Intrn Ct St Treas 90; Acctg.

**MOUNT, JERI L,** Schenectady County Comm Coll, Schenectady, NY; SR; Dns Lst 87; Pres Lst 87-; Tough Trvlr Ltd 82-; AS; Math/Sci; R D Lab Tech.**

**MOUNTAIN, DEBORAH E,** Va Highlands Comm Coll, Abingdon, VA; FR; Nursing Clb 90-; Presidential Honro Roll/ Deans List; RN.

**MOUNTFORD, MEAGHAN E,** Georgetown Univ, Washington, DC; FR; Cmnty Serv Vlntr 90-; Ski Club 90-.

**MOUNTS, SARAH A,** Castleton St Coll, Castleton, VT; SO; BS; Chrstn Flwshp Clb Stdnt Cdr 90-; Calvery Bible Chrch; Cmptr Inf Systms; Cmptr Systm Anlys.

**MOUNTS-TACKETT, RITA K,** Marshall University, Huntington, WV; SR; BBA; Stdnt Spprt Serv 87-; Natl Mgmnt Assoc Sec 89-; Wal Mart Stores Inc Merch Clrk; Bus Mgmnt; Retail.

**MOURAD, DAVID LAWRENCE,** Univ Of New Haven, West Haven, CT; SO; BSEE; IEEE Vice Chrmn 90-; Radio DJ 89-; SPAJ Oversr 87-; Alpha Lambda Delta; Elec Engr; Audio.

**MOURADIAN, VIRGINIA,** George Mason Univ, Fairfax, VA; SR; BSED; Spnsh Clb 89; Ltl Str Sigma Alpha Mu 86; SS Tchr Soorp Khatch Chrc; MCI Mc Lean VA Co Op Stdnt Tech Intrnshp; Erly Ed; Tch/Grdt Schl.

**MOURATOFF, JOHN G,** Hahnemann Univ, Philadelphia, PA; GD; MD; AMSA 89-; ASAPP 89-; SOBR Pr 90-; Chi Phi 86-88; MDA Sup Coord 87-88; SPCA Adopt Cnslr 88-89; IM Vlybl/ Sftbl/Rqtbl 90-91; BA Univ Cal Berkely 88; Med.

**MOUSAW, DEBRA L,** Clarkson Univ, Potsdam, NY; SR; BS; AAS Canton Clg Technology 89; Mgmt; Hmn Rsrc Mgmt.

**MOUTON, PORTIA Y,** Al St Univ, Montgomery, AL; SO; Bsktbl Tm 89-90; IM Bsktbl Tm; Comp Sci; Analyst.

**MOUTSIAKIS, DEMETRIUS LEONIDAS,** Coll Of Health Sci Stony Brook, Stony Brook, NY; GD; MD; Leningrad St Brk Med Schl Exc 89-; BA SUNY At Stony Brook 89; Med; Physicn.

**MOUZANNAR, NABIL R,** Univ Of New Haven, West Haven, CT; SO; BS; ISA Treas 90-; Cmptr Sci; Eng.

**MOUZON, CHRISHAUN T,** Univ Of Sc At Columbia, Columbia, SC; FR; Pltcl Sci; Corp Lawyer.

**MOVASSAGHI, PATRICIA E,** Hillsborough Comm Coll, Tampa, FL; FR; BFA; Advrtsng Accntnt Exctv 82-; Art.

**MOWEN, ANTHONY RAYMOND,** Wilmington Coll, New Castle, DE; SR; SGA VP 89-90; Nwspr Edtr 90; Delta Epsilon Rho 89; Dr Hilda A Davis Schlrshp 87.

**MOWER, JOANNA E,** North Greenville Coll, Tigerville, SC; FR; AS; Bptst Std Un 90-; Flwshp Chrstn Atlts VP; Govt Sec; Hnrs Smnr; Singing Grp 90-; Pres Schlp 90-; Elem Ed; Tchng.

**MOWERY, BARRY S,** Wv Univ, Morgantown, WV; JR; BCE; Cvl Engr.

**MOWERY, DEBORA D,** Commonwealth Coll, Virginia Beach, VA; AA; AA Ntl Univ 87; Med Ofc Mgmt; Bus Admin.

**MOWERY, KRISTINE M,** William Paterson Coll, Wayne, NJ; SO; BA; Actvts Pgmg Bd Vice-Chr Entrtnmnt 90-; Alpha Phi Omega Treas 90-; Tnns Tm 89-90; Intl Mgmt.**

**MOWERY, MICHAEL T,** Northern Ky Univ, Highland Hts, KY; SO; BFA; AS Antonelli Inst Of Art/Photo 88; Grphc Dsgn; Dsgnr.

**MOWERY, TINA M,** Wv Univ At Parkersburg, Parkersburg, WV; FR; BA; Math.

**MOWREY, BONNIE S,** Univ Of Tn At Martin, Martin, TN; SO; BS; RLDS Church Pres 87; Rainbow Sound Chorus Pres 87-89; Yth Cnslr 85; Home Ec-Dietetics; Own Cnsltg Firm.**

**MOWREY, KELLY L,** Indiana Univ Of Pa, Indiana, PA; SR; BED; ACEL 90-; Alpha Phi Omega 88-; Dns Lst 89-; Elem Educ; Tch.

**MOWRY, DENISE J,** Felician Coll, Lodi, NJ; SO; BA; Drama Clb; Questing/Aspiring Authors; PR Felicianews; Drozd/Skawinski Schlrshp; Art; Cmrcl Art/Phtgrphy.**

**MOX, TAMMY S,** Defiance Coll, Defiance, OH; SR; BA; Amer Mktg Assoc; Tau Pi Phi Secr 90-; Alpha Xi Delta Pldg Cls Pres 90-; Herbet Willet Schlrshp/Intern; Mktg/Mgmt; Cmptr Sci.**

**MOXON, SERENA E,** Colby Sawyer Coll, New London, NH; FR; Equestrian Tm 90; Psych; Clncl Psych.

**MOY, HOK F,** Norfolk St Univ, Norfolk, VA; SO; Chns Cmmnty Assoc 80-; Hrbrfst Sb Cmmtt Chr Pckng Trnsprtn 90; Certy 79; Acctg.

**MOY, JAN ERIK,** Manhattan Coll, Bronx, NY; SO; BS; Amer Inst Chem Engrs; AS Rockland Comm Clg 90; Chem Engr.

**MOY, TENLEY,** Union Coll, Barbourville, KY; JR; BA; Acdmc Tm; Alpha Kappa Psi By Laws Chp 89-; Bus Admn/Econ/BA Spanish; Bus.

**MOYA, SYLVIA C,** Radford Univ, Radford, VA; JR; BA; Sigma Sigma Sigma; Brdcstrs Gld Clb; Vlntr Oprtr; Phi Kappa Phi; Sigma Sigma Sigma; Deans Lst; Intrnshp Futura Advrtsng VA Bch; Cmmnctns; Advrtsng.

**MOYAD, MARK A,** Univ Of South Fl, Tampa, FL; GD; MPH; Kappa Chi Pres 87-88; Vrsty Bsktbl 83-86; Dean Lst 89-; Untd Way Shltr Assn Hmlss; Save Chldrn 86-; Asst Envrmntl; Occptnl Hlth; BA Col Wooster 88; Infcts Diseases; Med.

**MOYD, PAIGE M,** Univ Of Ga, Athens, GA; SR; BED; DECA Sec 90-; AMS 87-88; PR Intern Dalton Publ Sch 87-88; Stdnt Teach Northwest High Sch Dalton GA 90; Cert Gemology Dalton Coll Dalton GA 88; Mktg Edn; Tchr.

**MOYE, DEBRA D,** Comm Coll Algny Co Algny Cmps, Pittsburgh, PA; SO; BLAC Club 90-; Orntn Ldr 90-; Natl Orntn Dir Assn/Trng; Deans List 90-; ASS; Acctng Spclst.

**MOYE, LUANNE B,** Commonwealth Coll, Virginia Beach, VA; SR; AAS; Ofc Adm Clb VP 90-; Coll Sec Intl VP 90-; Alpha Beta Gamma; Legal Ofc Admin.

**MOYER, ELIZABETH ANN,** Commonwealth Coll, Virginia Beach, VA; SO; MBA; Commonwlth Law Scty Historian; Fraternal Order Police 8 80-; Amer Hrt Fnd Drive 85-; Navy Lgl Serv Office NLSO Intshp; State Certif Police Officer 87-88; Crim Justice Credits TCC/OLD Dominion Univ Norfolk VA 80-88; Paralegal/Criminal Just; Law.

**MOYER, GWEN E,** Oh St Univ At Newark, Newark, OH; SO; BED; Phi Eta Sigma; Alpha Kappa Lambda; Elem Educ; Tchg.

**MOYER, JENNIFER A,** Liberty Univ, Lynchburg, VA; SR; BS; Nrsng Clb 90-; Spnsh Hrnr Scty 89-90; Godparent Hm Unwed Mthrs Hse Prnt 87-89; Spnsh Hnrs Awd 89; Comm Hlthintern Med Tech 89-; Nsg/Comm Hlth; Med Surg Nsg.

**MOYER, JESSICA A,** Kutztown University Of Penna, Kutztown, PA; FR; BS; Crmnl Jstce Clb 90; Univ Orchstra 90; Crmnl Jstce; Prle Offcr.

**MOYER, JULIE A,** Kent St Univ Kent Cmps, Kent, OH; FR; MBA; Hon Clg 90-; Alph Lmbd Dlt; Bus Mgmt/Mktg; Own Co.

**MOYER, KIMBERLY A,** Univ Of Akron, Akron, OH; SR; BA; Dnc Lnc Capt 89-90; Elem Educ; Lwyr.

**MOYER, LORI ANN,** Gallaudet Univ, Washington, DC; SR; BS; Acctg; CPA.**

**MOYER, LORI BETH,** S U N Y Coll At Fredonia, Fredonia, NY; JR; BS; Fredonia Symphnc Winds 90; Music Thrpy.

**MOYER, MOLLY B,** Univ Of Cincinnati, Cincinnati, OH; SO; BA; Nrsng; RN.

**MOYER, SHARON A,** Mansfield Univ, Mansfield, PA; FR; Vlybl 90-; Acctng.

**MOYER, STEPHANIE D,** George Mason Univ, Fairfax, VA; JR; BS; Early Chldhd Ed; Tchr.

**MOYERS, BRADLEY J,** Bridgewater Coll, Bridgewater, VA; JR; BA; Residence Hall Cncl 90-; Student Senate 90-; Stdnt Govt President Elect; Lambda Scty 90-; Alpha Chi 90-; Vrsty Golf Tm 88-; History Political Sci; Teaching.

**MOYERS, GREGORY W,** Bridgewater Coll, Bridgewater, VA; SR; BS; Lmbda Scty 88-; Alpha Chi 89-; Wllm L Brwn Blgy Schlrshp; Hnr Schlrshp 87-; US Frst Srvc Intrnshp; Intrmrl Tnns 87-88; Blgy.

**MOYERS, JULIE A,** Columbia Union Coll, Takoma Park, MD; SO; BA; Yrbk Asstnt Editor 90-; Phi Eta Sigma VP 90-; English Communications.

**MOYKA, ANA S,** Rensselaer Polytechnic Inst, Troy, NY; FR; BS; Latin Stdnt Assoc 90-; Soc Hispanic Prof Engrs 90-; Fencing Clb 90-; Indstrl Engr; Engr.

**MOZEE, LINDA B,** Fayetteville St Univ, Fayetteville, NC; JR; BS; St Thomas AME Zion Chrch Asst Pstr 87-; Yth Ldr 85-; Elem Ed; Tchr.

**MOZEE, THOMACINA F,** Alcorn St Univ, Lorman, MS; FR; Cncrt Chr; Msc Educ; Msc Instrctr.

**MOZEE, TIMOTHY B,** Fl A & M Univ, Tallahassee, FL; FR; MBA; Cmptr Inf Systm Clb 90; Trck/Fld 90; Cmptr Inf Systm/ Math Sci; Inf Systms.

**MOZINGO, JASON W,** West Liberty St Coll, West Liberty, WV; FR; BA; Crmnl Jstc; Law Enfrcmnt.

**MOZNY, CHRISTINE M,** City Univ Of Ny Brooklyn Coll, Brooklyn, NY; SO; BA; Newman Cthlc Clb 89-; Judaic Stds Clb 90-; Deans Lst 90-; Med.**

**MPINGA, PETER,** Allen Univ, Columbia, SC; FR; BA; Spch Tm 90-; Dns Lst 90-; Work Aid 90-; Video Flmng 88-90; Chrch Chr 90-; Cert Uganda Posts Telecomm Corp 87; Acctg.

**MRAMOR, VERONICA J,** Univ Of Akron, Akron, OH; SR; BS; Cncl Educ Stdnts 90-; Golden Key 90-; Kappa Delta Pi 90-; YMCA St Sach 90-; Elem Educ; Tchr.**

**MRAVICH, BARBARA M,** Ms St Univ, Miss State, MS; SR; BS; Phi Alpha Theta; Pi Delta Phi; Pi Sigma Epsilon; French/ Mrktng; Intrntl Mrktng.

**MROWCA, GARY A,** Kent St Univ Kent Cmps, Kent, OH; FR; BA; Film/Video; Film Editing/Sound/Directing.

**MRSH, WAYNE B,** Anson Comm Coll, Ansonville, NC; SR; AAS; Phi Beta Lambda 90-; Cmptrs; Prgrmmr.

**MT PLEASANT, KRISTI L,** D Youville Coll, Buffalo, NY; SO; BS; Cmps Mnstry 89-90; Biol; Vet Med.

**MUCHLER, JULIE A,** Tn Tech Univ, Cookeville, TN; SR; BA; Dns Lst 86-; AS Schl Crft Clg 88; Hortcltr; Landscp/Nrsry Mgmt.

**MUCKLE, ALLEN A,** Comm Coll Algny Co Algny Cmps, Pittsburgh, PA; SO; BS; Percussion Team Local Church 87-; Prof Sales Cnsltnt 87-; Human Rsrcs Mgmtn; Sales Cnsltnt.

**MUCKLE, SANDRA B,** Savannah St Coll, Savannah, GA; JR; BA; Scl Wrkrs Tmrrw 89-; Scl Wrk/Psychlgy; Clncl Scl Wrkr.

**MUCKLOW, MARC M,** Barry Univ, Miami, FL; SR; BS; Econ Clb 87-88; ACM Cmptr Clb 88-90; Pres Lst 89-; Dns Lst 89-; Cmptr Sci; Data Proc Mgr.

**MUDD, BRYANT S,** Brevard Coll, Brevard, NC; FR; AA; Envrnmntl Awrns Grp 90-; Phi Theta Kappa; Biol/Env Sci; Envrmntlst.

**MUDD, JACQUELINE M,** Univ Of Louisville, Louisville, KY; JR; BS; Res Stu Assoc Hl Rep 89-90; Pr Admsns Cnslr 88-90; Phi Eta Sigma 89-; Tau Beta Pi 90-; Cooprtv Intrnshp Burroughs Wlcm Co 90-; IM Trck 90; Mech Engr.

**MUDD, JENNIFER K,** Brescia Coll, Owensboro, KY; SR; BS; SNEA Hstrn 87; SCEC 87-89; SGA 87-88; Alpha Chi Treas 88-; Wendel Foster Center Vol 86-90; Acdmnc Exclnc Awrds 88; Acdmc Deans List 87-90; Alpha Chi 90; Spcl Ed/Elmntry Ed; Tch.

**MUDENGE, THANDO D,** Teikyo Post Univ, Waterbury, CT; JR; BA; Intl Clb Pres 90-; Stdy Japan Prog; Mrktg; Intl Bus.

**MUDRYK, WILLIAM P,** Comm Coll Algny Co Algny Cmps, Pittsburgh, PA; SO; BA; Assoc Penn Tchncl Inst 79; Cmptr Sci Infrmtn Bsns; Law.

**MUECK, ANDREW G,** S U N Y Coll Of Tech At Frmgdl, Farmingdale, NY; SO; ASSC; Phlsphy Clb 90; Lbrl Arts; Eng.

**MUEHLBAUER, DARLENE D,** Niagara Univ, Niagara Univ, NY; FR; BA; Pltcl Sci; Govt.

**MUELLER II, ALFRED G,** Wilkes Univ, Wilkes-Barre, PA; SO; BA; Debate Union Pres 90-; Law Asso Pres 90-; Pol Sci Intnl Studies Cl V P 89-90; Pi Kappa Delta Pres; Proj Mgr Historical Atlas; Legstve Intern Rep P Mundy 89-; Debate/Forensics Awds 89-; ASA 89-; OAH 90-; Cmmctns/History/Philopshy; Politics.**

**MUELLER, DOLORES A,** Centenary Coll, Hackettstown, NJ; SR; BA; Educ Clb 87-; Right Ot Life 87-; Nwsppr 89-90; Alpha Chi 90-; US Natl Coll Awrd 89-; Big Bro Sis 88-90; Pres Schlrshp 87-; Assc Sprvsn Crrclm Dev; Assc Kndrgrtn Tchrs; Engl/Educ; Elem Educ.

**MUELLER, ERIC M,** Fl St Univ, Tallahassee, FL; SR; MBA; MBA Assc; Fncl Mgmt Assc 90-; Gldn Key; Sigma Alpha Epsilon 89; IM; BS; Finance; Bus.

**MUELLER, GUSTAVE F,** Univ Of Fl, Gainesville, FL; SR; BA; Amer Mktg Assn 90-; Omicron Delta Epsilon 89-; Econ; Mba Jd.

**MUELLER, MELISSA A,** Central Fl Comm Coll, Ocala, FL; SO; AA; MASH 89-90; Phi Theta Kappa; Comm Schlrsh Hon Pgm 89-; Intrn St Attrnys Offc 90; IM Sports Capt; Bus/Acctg; Law.

**MUELLER, MICHELLE E,** Western Ky Univ, Bowling Green, KY; JR; BA; Library Media Edn; Publ/Art Library.

**MUELLER, REBECCA A,** Univ Of Ms Medical Center, Jackson, MS; SR; BSN; MS Assn Stdnt Nrs St Sec 89-90 Chptr Pres 90-; Sigma Theta Tau; MASN Hall Fm 90; Y Bertolet-Pressgrv Schlrshp 90; H Hess Schlrshp 90-; Qulty Cntrl Micrbiolgst 68-78; Rsrch Assoc Univ MS Med Ctr 79-89; BS Memphs St Univ 68; Nrsng.

**MUELLER, ROSEMARIE,** Manhattan Coll, Bronx, NY; SR; BE; Amer Soc Cvl Engrs 88-; NY Water Pollution Control Assoc Stdnt Ch Pres 90-; Soc Wmn Engrs Secr 88-; Epsilon Sigma Pi 90-; Tau Beta Pi 89-; Chi Epsilon 89-; St La Salle 87-; Manhattan Clg Jazz Ensmbl 89-; Stearns/Wheeler Envir Engr Schlrshp; Engr.

**MUELLER, TROY J,** Fl International Univ, Miami, FL; SR; Am Dietetic Assn; AS Broward Comm Coll 86.

**MUERMANN, ROY,** Univ Of Rochester, Rochester, NY; SO; BS; Colg Repbl 89-90; Amnesty 89-; IM Vlybl 90-; Elec Engrng; Engrng.

**MUGG, CATHY L,** George Mason Univ, Fairfax, VA; JR; BS; Acctg Clb; Beta Alpha Psi; Acctg; CPA Law.

**MUGHAL, SHAZIA P,** Edison Comm Coll, Fort Myers, FL; SO; AABA; Chmstry; Pre-Med Fmly Dr.

**MUGUERCIA JR, RAMON,** Inter Amer Univ Pr Aquadilla, Aguadilla, PR; BA; PR Army Ntnl Grd Btln Lgl NCO 90-; Lgl Spclts US Army Civ Eqp Para Lgl 87-90; Pltcl Sci; Law.

**MUHAMMAD, ABDULLAH R,** Comm Coll Algny Co Algny Cmps, Pittsburgh, PA; AFO Amer CCAC Algny Cmps 90; History Certif; Teachers Educ.

**MUHAMMAD, AYESHA X,** Al A & M Univ, Normal, AL; SO; BS; Mdcl Tchnlgy Med.

**MUHAMMAD, NAOMI R,** Al A & M Univ, Normal, AL; SO; BA; Amer Hm Econ Assn 89-; Trendsetters Fshn Clb VP 89-; Alpha Zeta; Hnr Rl 89-; Dns Lst 89-; Fshn Mrchndsng; Fshn Cnsltnt.

**MUHAMMAD, SIA SAFIYAH,** Al A & M Univ, Normal, AL; JR; BA; AHEA Sec/V P; NAACP Treas Sec; Alpha Zeta V P; Kappa Omnicron Du; Post Scndry Schlrshp; Fashion Mrchndsng/ Family Studies; Teach.

**MUIR, GARY S,** S U N Y Coll Of Tech At Frmgdl, Farmingdale, NY; FR; AAS; Dns Lst 90-; Auto Eng; Bus.

**MUIR, MICHAEL J,** Mount Saint Mary Coll, Newburgh, NY; SO; BS; AAS Orange Cty Cmnty Clg 90; Bsn Adm.

**MUIR, MICHELLE A,** Fl St Univ, Tallahassee, FL; JR; BA; Golden Key 90-; Chem Sci; Chem Fld.

**MUJICA, SAMUEL,** Univ Of Pr At Rio Piedras, Rio Piedras, PR; GD; MA; Grad Assoc 89-90f Pltcl Sci Assoc 87-88; Professor Asstnt 89-; Judo Vrsty Capt 86-90; BA 89; Sociology.

**MUKASA, STEPHEN N,** White Pines Coll, Chester, NH; SR; AA; Phi Theta Kappa; Alpha Zeta Zeta Secr 90-; Alpha Zeta Zeta Peer Tutor Pgm Cnsltnt 90-; ED Inst Tchr Ed Kyambogo Uganda 86-88; Lib Arts; Law/Tchr.

**MUKASE, YVONNE B,** Central St Univ, Wilberforce, OH; BSC; SGA 90; ISA; Red Cross 83; Bus Admu; CIS/ACCT.

**MUKUWA, RICHARD M,** Fl A & M Univ, Tallahassee, FL; SR; BS; Pltcl Scnc; Lbr Rltns.

**MULANAX, TINA L,** Cedarville Coll, Cedarville, OH; FR; BA; IM Vlybl/Sftbl 90-; Bus Gomm Tech; Secretary.

**MULARZ, MARY,** Atlantic Comm Coll, Mays Landing, NJ; SO; BA; Bsktbl Co-Capt 89-90; Holy Trinity Greek Folk Dancing Lead Dancer 89-; Sndy Sch Tchr 87-; Dvlpmntl Engl Tutor 90; Deans Lst 89-; General Studies; Elem Edn.

**MULAY, DENENE R,** Univ Of Cincinnati, Cincinnati, OH; FR; BFA; Conservatorys 90-; Mainstage Prod; Musical Theatre.

**MULCAHEY, MELINDA A,** Allegheny Coll, Meadville, PA; JR; BA; Panhllnc Assn Rsh Cnslr 90-; Kappa Alpha Theta Chrprsn; Aldn Schlr 89-90; Stdnt Orientatn Advsr 90-; IM Vlybl 88-89; Engl; Pub Rltns/Advtsng.

**MULCAHEY, TAMARA M,** Univ Of Nc At Greensboro, Greensboro, NC; FR; BS; Fmly Development; Cnslg.

**MULDROW, JENNIFER,** Morgan St Univ, Baltimore, MD; FR; BS; YWCA; Kappa Tau 90-; INROAS; Sywca; Undrwrtr Intrnshp; Hons Prog; Bsns; Ins.

**MULE, COLETTE A,** Fordham Univ, Bronx, NY; SR; BS; Mrktng Scty 90-; Cmmtng Stdnts Assoc 88-; Internshp Sprts Chnnl 90; Mrktng.

**MULFORD, DEBRA S,** Salisbury St Univ, Salisbury, MD; JR; BS; Chi Alpha Treas 90-; Cmps Crsd Christ 89-; Yng Adlt Grp Co-Ldr 90-; PGHMC Vol 90-; Deans Lst 90-; Miss Missionette Potomac Dist Assmbly God 89; Rsprtry Thrpy; Neontl/Pdtrc Care.

**MULFORD, VICTORIA L,** Glassboro St Coll, Glassboro, NJ; SO; Bio Clb Pres 90-; Peer Tutor; Chrmns Awrd 90-; Peter J Mcguire AFL-CIO Schlrshp; Educ Opprtnty Fnd Pro Cert Achvmnt 90-; Asstn NJ Dept Envrnmtl Prtctn Div Fish/Game/ Wldlf 90-; Bio Sci; Marine Bio Rsrch.

**MULHERIN, HOLLY G,** Union Univ, Jackson, TN; SO; BA; Bapt Stdnt Unn 89-; Sigma Alpha Iota Prog Chr 90-; Sigma Tau Delta; Zeta Tau Alpha; Dns Lst; Schlrs Of Excllnce Schlrshp Awrd; Kathryn Sullivan Bowld Orgn Schlrshp Awrd; Engl Ppe Organ; Coll Prfssr Wrtr.

**MULHOLLAND, DANIEL J,** City Univ Of Ny Baruch Coll, New York, NY; SR; BBA; Accntng Soc 89-; Trvl Clb 87-89; Baruch Schlrshp 87-89; Accntng; Accntng Finance.

**MULHOLLEM, LISA A,** Univ Of Nc At Chapel Hill, Chapel Hill, NC; SO; BS; March Band Flag Corps 90-; Phi Eta Sigma 90-; Intrnshp Analytical Chem Merck/Co Inc Rahway NJ 90-; Chem; Genetic/Molecular Bio Rsrch.**

**MULKEY, LORA L,** Oh Univ-Southern Cmps, Ironton, OH; SO; MBA; Alpha Beta; Mgmt & Law; Bus Mgmt.

**MULL, CHRISTI D,** Meredith Coll, Raleigh, NC; FR; BA; Meredith Christian Assc 90-; Alpha Lombda Delta 90-; Engl; Tchr.

**MULL, DANIEL R,** Oh Univ, Athens, OH; JR; Alpine Club; Triathlon Club Secy; Water Ski Club; AS Larcin Cnty Cmnty Clg 89; AS Jordon Clg 84; Engrng; Renwbl Energs/Enrgy Consrvtn.

**MULL, HEATHER M,** Allegheny Coll, Meadville, PA; SR; BA; Coll Radio Music Dir 87-; SAGE; ASAD; Alden Schlr 88-; Womens Soccer Most Val Rookie 87-88; Eng/Minor In French; Arts Mgmt.

**MULL, KIMBERLY L,** Old Dominion Univ, Norfolk, VA; SR; BS; Vctnl Indust Club Sec 87-89; Electrncs Clb Pres 87-89; Phi Theta Kappa 87-; Resue Sqd Vol Chpln 86-; AAS Southside Va Comm Clg 89; Elect Engr Tech; Engr.

**MULL, SHARI B,** Mount Aloysius Jr Coll, Cresson, PA; SO; AS; Chrldng Squad 89-90; Intrnshp Packwood House Musem Lewisburg PA 89-90; AS Mt Aloysius Jr Clg Cresson PA; Travel/ Tourism.

**MULL, WILLIAM E,** West Liberty St Coll, West Liberty, WV; SR; BS; Gamma Sigma Tau V P 87-90; Hmlss Vol 89-90; Nwspr Photo Intrn 90-; Weirton Wmns Clb Schlrshp 86-87; Graphic Dsgn; Advtsng/Photo.

**MULLA-FEROZE, JOHANN D,** Franklin And Marshall Coll, Lancaster, PA; FR; BA; Intl Clb 90-; Cricket Clb 90-; Dns Lst; Hnrs Lst; Chem.

**MULLALY, MICHAEL E,** Univ Of Akron, Akron, OH; GD; MS; Amer Prod Invntry Cntrl Soc Pres 90; Dns Stdnt Avsry Coun; Intntl Bus Clb; Dns Lst 89-90; IM Ftbl,Bsktbl,Vlybl,Rqtbl 85-90; BS; Mngmnt Infor Sys.

**MULLARKEY, D SEAN,** Salisbury St Univ, Salisbury, MD; SO; BS; Phi Eta Sigma 90; Army Achvmnt Mdl Natl Gd; Blgy; Marine Blgy.

**MULLARKEY, DORIS A,** Ny Univ, New York, NY; GD; MS; Deans Lst 88-90; GJC Deans Lst 76-78; Fndrs Schlr; GJC Vldctrn 78; AS 78; BA; Fncl Mgmt.

**MULLARKEY, J SCOTT,** S U N Y Coll Of Tech At Delhi, Delhi, NY; SR; Amrcn Dsgn Drftng Assn; Phi Theta Kappa; AOS; Cmptr Drftng; Indstrl Engnr.

**MULLEN, BARBARA A,** Villanova Univ, Villanova, PA; FR; BSN; Undergradutae Nrsng Senate Frshmn Rep 90-; Stdnt Nrsng Assc PE 90-; Stdnts Agnst Drnk Drvng 90-; Campus Mnstry Blln Day Cmmt Chr; Spcl Olyms Fstvl 90; Sigma Theta Tau Cmmtmnt Nrsng Awrd; Deans List; Johnson/Johnson Nrsng Schshp; IM 90; Nrsng; Ped Onclgy.

**MULLEN, CARY S,** Wv Univ At Parkersburg, Parkersburg, WV; FR; BA; IM Bsktbl/Vlybl 90-; Bus; Self Employment.

**MULLEN, CRAIG P,** Western New England Coll, Springfield, MA; SO; BS; Alpha Lambda Delta 89-; Mech Engr/Math; Process Control.

**MULLEN, DAVID P,** Western New England Coll, Springfield, MA; FR; BA; American Soc Of Mech Engr; Lcnsd MA Constr Supv Unrstrctd; Engr/Mech.

**MULLEN, JACQUELINE P,** Wv Univ At Parkersburg, Parkersburg, WV; GD; Bus Admin; Acctg.

**MULLEN, KELLIE A,** Southern Vt Coll, Bennington, VT; JR; BS; High Sch Intern 90-; Sr Hsg Complex Intern 90-; Scl Wrk.

**MULLEN, MELANIE D,** Univ Of Southern Ms, Hattiesburg, MS; SO; Rotoract; Phi Mu; Pi Kappa Alpha Ltl Sistr 89; Chld Lf Speclst; Cnslr.

**MULLEN, RICK D,** Wv Univ At Parkersburg, Parkersburg, WV; FR; BA; CJO EARS Rep 90; Intrnshp Wd Co Prsctrs Offce; IM Bsktbl And Tble Tnns 90; Crmnl Jstce; Tax Law Enfrcmnt.

**MULLEN, VICTORIA M,** Clemson Univ, Clemson, SC; SR; BS; Ssc Park/Rec Assn 87-; Delta Gamma 87-89; IM Tennis 87-; Park/Rec/Trsm Mgmt.

**MULLENIX, PRISCILLA M,** Wv Univ At Parkersburg, Parkersburg, WV; FR; AAS; Untd Mthdst Wmn Chpsn Mbrshp 90-; Untd Mthdst Chrch Pstr/Prsh Comm 89-; H/R Block Offc Mgr 89-; Bus Admin.

**MULLER IV, AUGUST,** Liberty Univ, Lynchburg, VA; SR; BS; Stdnt Govt Senator 89-; Cycling Team Treas 89-; Bus Admin/ Finance; Aerospace/Defense.

**MULLER, BRADLEY J,** Univ Of Sc At Columbia, Columbia, SC; JR; BA; Rgby Clb VP 89-; Dns Lst 89-90; Radio Sta Intrn 90; Brdcst Jrlsm; TV Sprts Prod/Anncnt.

**MULLER, CATHERINE L,** Hudson Valley Comm Coll, Troy, NY; SO; BA; Psych.

**MULLER, DONNA LYNNE,** City Univ Of Ny Baruch Coll, New York, NY; GD.

**MULLER, ELIZABETH A,** Univ Of Miami, Coral Gables, FL; SO; BA; Phi Eta Sigma 89-; Alpha Lambda Delta 89-; Dns Lst 89-; Provosts Hnr Rl 89-; Art.

**MULLER, GLENN D,** West Chester Univ, West Chester, PA; GD; MA; Wnd Ensmbl Symphnc Bnd Brs Chr 86-90; Jazz Ensmbl Trmpt Ensmbl Mrchng Bd 86-90; Cncrt Chr Frshmn Chrs Insrptn Brs 86-90; Kappa Kappa Psi Prlmntrn 87-88; Comm Msc Schl Instrctr 87-90; Dir Chrl Act Hgh Schl 90-; BS 90; Msc Educ; Tchr Admin.

**MULLER, TIMOTHY P,** Villanova Univ, Villanova, PA; SR; BA; New Stdnt Orntn Pgm Cnslr 90; PA Spcl Olympics Com 88-; Don Guanella Sch Rtrd Boys 87-90; Mother Teresas Soup Kitchen 90-; St Edmonds Hm 87-; Deans Lst 88/90-; Jake Nevin Spirit Awd; Athletic Schlrshp 90-; Econ; Invstmnt Bnkg.

**MULLICAN, DEREK D,** Middle Tn St Univ, Murfreesboro, TN; SO; BS; Clg Rpblcns; Wrk Stdy Schlp; Paul Douglas Tch Schlp; TN Tchr Schlp; Sci; Tch.

**MULLIGAN, BRIAN M,** Webb Inst Of Naval Archt, Glen Cove, NY; FR; BS; Stdnt Crt 90-; Athltc Awrd 90-; Ultmt Frsbee/Bsktbl 90-; Nvl Archtctr/Marine Eng.

**MULLIGAN, JOHN THOMAS,** Villanova Univ, Villanova, PA; SO; BA; Big Bro Sis 90-; Cmps Mnstry Hsptlty Mnstr 90-; Ornttn Cnslr; Phi Gamma Delta Sec; Peer Ttr Wrtng Cntr; Engl.

**MULLIGAN, KRISTIE D,** Univ Of Sc At Spartanburg, Spartanburg, SC; SR; BA; Sclgy Clb Secr 90-; Gamma Beta Phi 87-; Sclgy; Hosp Scl Wrk.

**MULLIKIN, PHYLLIS M,** Dyersburg St Comm Coll, Dyersburg, TN; SO; ASSCS; Frst Untd Meth Chrch Preschl Dir 87-90; Elem Educ.

**MULLIN, MARCUS P,** Wv Northern Comm Coll, Wheeling, WV; FR; BS; GUTS; Foreign Lang Hnry 90-; Natl Hnr Scty; Ftbl Wrstlng Capt; Chem Engr.

**MULLIN, WENDY R,** Univ Of Sc At Sumter, Sumter, SC; JR; BA; Prvntn Tm 89-; Explrs Law Enfrcmnt; Educ Clb 90-; S Sch Tchr 89-; Deans Hon 90; Cert Dstngshd Schlrshp 88-; AS 90; Ele Educ; Tch.

**MULLINAX, AMANDA E,** Univ Of Sc At Columbia, Columbia, SC; FR; BA; Bptst Stdnt Un Comm 90-; Jrnlsm; Frgn Mssnry.

**MULLINGS, MELINDA J,** Savannah St Coll, Savannah, GA; SR; BS; Campus All-Star Challenge Quiz Bowl Schlrs Stdnt Coach 90-; Dns Lst 89-; Hnr Rl 89-; Campus All Star Schlrs; Concert Choir Schlrshp 90; Bsn Mgmt.

**MULLINGS, VICTOR G,** Fl International Univ, Miami, FL; SR; BS; Adlt Lit Pgm; Brnt Bnk South FL; AA Miami Dade Comm Clg 90; Fnce; MBA Banking.

**MULLINS, AMY L,** Univ Of Nc At Greensboro, Greensboro, NC; SR; BS; Ambssdr 90-; Mrshl 89-; Intrnshp Foust Elem Schl; Deans Lst 89-; Elem Educ; Tchr.

**MULLINS, B IRENE,** Univ Of Va Clinch Valley Coll, Wise, VA; JR; BA; UM Wmn Dist VP; Schl Vol Prog; VA Comm Coll Assn; SW VA Comm Coll Fscl Asst 86-; AAS S W VA Comm Coll 75; Elem Educ; Tch.

**MULLINS, BETTY E,** Bennett Coll, Greensboro, NC; SO; BA; NAACP Pres 90-; UNCF Pre Alumiea 90-; Campus Scouts Actng Pres 89-; Schlr 90-; Inroads; Acctng; Corp Lawyer.

**MULLINS, CERIANNE L,** Smith Coll, Northampton, MA; JR; BA; Smith Debate Soc 89-90; Deans Lst 88-89; 1st Grp Schlr 89-90; Eatng Dsordrs Tsk Frc 89-90; Sen Bingaman Wash DC Intrn 90; Hist.

**MULLINS, DIANNA L,** Va Commonwealth Univ, Richmond, VA; SR; MED; Golden Key; Psych/Elem Educ; Tch.

**MULLINS, JERRY C,** Univ Of Al At Huntsville, Huntsville, AL; FR; BA; Alpha Lambda Delta; Mech Engrng.

**MULLINS, JOHNNY DARREN,** Univ Of Tn At Knoxville, Knoxville, TN; FR; MBA; Alpha Lambda Delta 90-; Bus; Law.

**MULLINS, MARY H,** Va Highlands Comm Coll, Abingdon, VA; SO; AAS; Phi Theta Kappa 90-; Retail J C Penney Co/Parks Belk 70-; AA Hiwassee Clg 67; Mgt; Sls/Mktg.

**MULLINS, MYLA D,** Middle Tn St Univ, Murfreesboro, TN; FR; BS; Nursing; MS Pedtrc Nrsng Prctnr.

**MULLINS, REBECCA A,** Lees Coll, Jackson, KY; JR; BA; Phi Kappa Phi Morehead St Univ; Kappa Delta Pi Morehead St Univ; Phi Theta Kappa 85-86; Rgnts Schlrshp Morehead St Univ 90-; Pres Schlrshp Morehead St Univ 85-86; Griffith Schlrshp 90; Bsn Ed; Tchg Sec Stdnts.

**MULLINS, RHONDA M,** Webber Coll, Babson Park, FL; JR; BA; Stdnt Govt Assoc 89-90; Castle Of King Spnsh Spkng Chldrns Puppet Mnstry 88-90; Chldrns Mssn Trp El Salvdr 90; Int Yth Cnclr Dsny Cruise Lns; Chrldr SE Clg Lakelnd FL 88-89; Intl Trvl/Toursm.

**MULLINS, ROBERT S,** Univ Of Al At Huntsville, Huntsville, AL; FR; MSE; US Marine Corps Rsrv PFC; Twin Dragon Scty; Mech Eng; Robotic Eng.

**MULLINS, STUART R,** Univ Of Va Clinch Valley Coll, Wise, VA; SR; Psychlgy Clb Pres 88-; Envrnmntl Cncrns Org 90-; Darden Socty; Dns Lst; Awd Outstdng Achvmnt Socl/Behav Sci; BS Clinic Vly Coll/Univ Of VA; Pyschlgy/Socioloby; Cnslng.

**MULLINS, SUZANNE R,** Univ Of Va Clinch Valley Coll, Wise, VA; SO; BA; Deans Lst; Acctg; CPA.

**MULLINS, WENDY,** Univ Of Cincinnati, Cincinnati, OH; JR; BA; Itln Clb Ofcr 88-90; Ski Clb 89-90; Kappa Omicron Nu 90-; Dns Lst 88-; Eta Sigma Gamma; Gldn Key; Chrst Hosp Diet Cntrl Clrk 90-; Lng Lab Clrk Cmps 89-; Arbc Instrctr 90-; Trmnstcs 88-90; AFS 86-90; Ntrtnl Sci/Dtcs; Ntrtnl Edctr.

**MULLINS, WILLIAM A,** Memphis St Univ, Memphis, TN; SR; BFA; CMSA 89-90; Ancnt Ordr Samurai 90-; NARAS Stdnt Music Awd 90; NARAS 90-; Commrcl Musci/Rcrdng Eng; Rcrd Prdctn.

**MULLIS, JAMES C,** Valdosta St Coll, Valdosta, GA; SR; BED; USAF Tsgt 83-; Occup Sfty Hlth Tech 84-; AAS Munitns Mgmt/ Sfty Tech Comm Clg Air Frc 90-; Trade/Indstl Educ; Sfty Mgmt Engr.

**MULLIS, JAMES M,** Middle Ga Coll, Cochran, GA; FR; BPHAR; Gamma Beta Phi 90; Chemistry; Pharmacy.

**MULLIS JR, JIMMY E,** Middle Ga Coll, Cochran, GA; SO; Sftbl/Bsktbl 89-; Cert 88-89; Hstry; H S Tchr.

**MULLIS, JULIE R,** Middle Ga Coll, Cochran, GA; FR; Hm Ec Clb 90-; GHEA 90-; AHEA 90-; Hm Ec Awd; Hm Ec; Chld/Fmly Dvlpmnt.

**MULLIS, STEPHANIE A,** Univ Of Nc At Charlotte, Charlotte, NC; SO; BSBA; Mngmnt Info Systems; Computer Syst Oper.

**MULLOY, JOSEPH B,** Middle Tn St Univ, Murfreesboro, TN; SR; FCA 86; Pi Kappa Alpha Sgt At Arms 87; Big Bro Of Amer 87; Bsebl 86; BS; Crmnl Jstce Admin; Law.

**MULLOY, STEPHANIE G,** Union Univ School Of Nursing, Memphis, TN; FR; BED; Nrsng.

**MULLRAY, WILLIAM T,** Merrimack Coll, North Andover, MA; SR; Stdnt Hl Rep 88-89; Beta Sigma Epsilon Sec 89-90; Pegasus House Cnslr; IM 87-; Sociology; Real Estate.

**MULTALA, HENRY V M,** Univ Of Rochester, Rochester, NY; SR; BS; Naval ROTC 86-; Actv Duty Miltry US Navy 82-86; Mech Eng; Navl Offcr/Eng.

**MULVANY, CRISTINE J,** Univ Of North Fl, Jacksonville, FL; SR; BA; Gldn Key 90-; IATA; Mjr Arln Chgo; Whlsl Trvl Ornt Vir; Trvl Agnt Tr Co; Assoc 83; Acctg; CPA.

**MULVEY, ANNE L,** Marymount Manhattan Coll, New York, NY; SO; BA; St Joseph Sch Parents Assn Pres 90-; Psych; Teach.

**MULVEY, JAMES E,** S U N Y Coll Of Tech At Frmgdl, Farmingdale, NY; GD; BA; Crmnl Just.

**MULWEE, MELISSA LYNNE,** Univ Of Sc At Columbia, Columbia, SC; FR; Zeta Tau Alpha Asst Pldg Trnr.

**MULYCA, JONAS J,** Schenectady County Comm Coll, Schenectady, NY; FR; AAS; Mtrl Sci; Eng.

**MULZAC, DIANNA M,** Howard Univ, Washington, DC; JR; BSP; Mrchng Bnd 87-88; Tae Kwondo Clb 89-90; Kappa Psi Pldg Mstr 90-; NY St Phrmcy Intrng Prmt 90-; Coll Phrmcy Trustee Schlrshp 89-90; Phrmctcl Frat Schlrshp Hon; Phrmcy.

**MUMPER, RICHARD T,** Temple Univ, Philadelphia, PA; JR; BS; ASME 90-; Bsktbl; IM Sftbl; IM Ftbl; Mchncl Engnrng; Engnrng Mgmt.

**MUMPOWER, ALICE A,** Radford Univ, Radford, VA; SO; BA; Stdnt Actvty Bdgt Com 89-90; Trfc Bd; Campus Beautification 90-; Stdnt Ldrshp Conf Dnc Coord 89-90; Intrnl Gov Rep Stdnt Ldrshp Conf 90-; Interdisciplinary Studies; Teacher.

**MUMPOWER, AMY N,** Patrick Henry Comm Coll, Martinsville, VA; FR; ASN; Nursing; Rn.

**MUNCHBACH, CANDICE E,** Schenectady County Comm Coll, Schenectady, NY; FR; AAS; Greater Galway Comm Serv Assov Pres 89; V P 90-; Math Tutor; Music Dir Barkersville Ch 89-; Music Dir Wood Winds Singing Grp 84-; Word Prcsng; Sec.

**MUNCHMEYER, LORI M,** Univ Of Ky, Lexington, KY; SO; BS; Act Brd 90-; Campus Crusade 90-; Alpha Hon 90-; Alpha Delta Pi Schlrsh Brd 89-; Orient Ldr; SG Ldrshp Conf 90; Nursing.

**MUNCY, PAMELA A,** Marshall University, Huntington, WV; FR; BED; Bsn; Tchng.

**MUNDAHL, MERRILEE M,** Eckerd Coll, St Petersburg, FL; SO; BS; Chr Grps Madricals Sensations 89-90; Dorm Pres 90-; Academic Afrs Comm 90-; Habitat Humanity 90; Cnslr Chrch Rtrts 90; CASPHE Schlr Wk Proj Prof 90; Psychology; Grad Schl Cognitive Psychlgy.

**MUNDO, MONICA A,** Westminster Coll, New Wilmingtn, PA; SO; BS BA; Stdnt Govt Pblcty 90-; Hse Cncl Com Mmbr 93-; Frsh Strt 90-; Lambda Sigma 90-; Kappa Mu Epsilon; Pi Delta Phi; Alpha Gamma Delta Asst Treas 90-; Chrldr 90-; Kappa Mu Epsilon Bk Awrd 90-; Elizabeth Nixon Mem Schlrshp; Wstmnstr Coll Hnrs Schlr; Math Frnch.

**MUNDY III, GEORGE L,** Va St Univ, Petersburg, VA; FR; BA; Coop Ed Sec 90-; Vet State Treas 90-; Elect Tech; Avtn.

**MUNDY, MEREDITH C,** Smith Coll, Northampton, MA; FR; Chr Omega 90-; Deans Lst; Frst Grp Schlr; Engl; Edtng Wrtng.

**MUNFORD, JOCELYN D,** Fl A & M Univ, Tallahassee, FL; FR; PHARM; Choir 90; Phi Eta Sigma 90-; Pharm Sci.

**MUNGAI, DANIEL M,** Univ Of Southern Ms, Hattiesburg, MS; SO; BA; Vlbl IM; Table Tennis; Vlybl; Jrnalism Pol Sci.

**MUNGO, WILTON L,** Anderson Coll, Anderson, SC; SO; BA; Clg Choir Pres 89-; Gamma Beta Phi V P 90-; Denmark Soc; Cmpus Mnstres Otrch Dir; Chrstn Rltd Vocatn 89; AA; Cmunctn.

**MUNI, JENNIFER L,** Univ Of Central Fl, Orlando, FL; SO; BA; Frnds Expctnt Mthrs Pres-Fndr 90-; Stdnt Actvts Bd Asst Dir 90-; Intrcllg Un Allc; Phi Theta Kappa 90-; Stdnt Spprt Svc Tutr 90-; Pregn Crs Cntr 90-; 10 Pct Schlrshp; Fla Undgrd Schlr; AA DBCC; Soc Psychlgy.

**MUNIZ IRIZARRY, KIRIAM JAVIER,** Univ Politecnica De Pr, Hato Rey, PR; FR; Sci/Math; Engr.

**MUNIZ, ADELAIDA M,** Univ Of Miami, Coral Gables, FL; SR; BA; Hnrs Stu Assoc; Solon Soc Sec; Miami Dade Comm Coll; Phi Theta Kappa Comm Serv Dir; 89 Mst Otstndg Exec Brd Comm Serv Dir; Dir Awrd Phi Theta Kappa; Miami Chldrns Hosp 89 Adlt Vol Awrd; Fclty Awrd 88-89; Stnfrd King Acdmc Schlrshp; Pol Sci; Law.

**MUNIZ, ALICIA,** Fl International Univ, Miami, FL; SR; BA; Future Edctrs Of Am 90-; Campus Mnstry 90-; Delta Phi Omega 88-90; AA Miami Dade Comm Coll 90; AS 90; Elem Edn.

**MUNIZ, OMARIS M,** Univ Of Rochester, Rochester, NY; SO; YMCA Vol 90-; Bio; Phrmcy.

**MUNIZ-VALLADARES, HARRY,** Inter Amer Univ Pr San Juan, Hato Rey, PR; GD; Ntl Law Stu Assoc Tres 88-; Pol Sci Assoc 85-88; Cum Laude; Awrd Gvn By Inst Dvlpmnt Law; JD; BA 88; Pol Sci; Law.

**MUNK KEGELER, BONITA L,** Miami Dade Comm Coll, Miami, FL; SO; AA; Phi Theta Kappa; ANSI 80; Atomic Enrgy Clearance; Beta Sigma Phi Pres 72-76; Beta Sigma Phi Pres 72-77; US Gov Cert Scntst; Trng Crdntr; Nclr Plnt Tech; Med Claims Exmnr; Waste Mngmnt; LPN; Tchrs Aide; LPN Ambrdg Schl Prctl Nrsng 66; Cmptrs; Electcl Engrng.

**MUNKELWITZ, ROBERT A,** Coll Of Health Sci Stony Brook, Stony Brook, NY; GD; MD; Amer Med Assoc 89-; Alpha Omega Alpha 90-; Phi Beta Kappa; Phi Kappa Phi; BS The Univ Of RI 83-87; Medicine.

**MUNN, CASEY S,** Univ Of Sc At Columbia, Columbia, SC; FR; BS; Assoc Hon Stdnts 90-; Nwspr Copy Ed; Gamma Beta Phi 90-; Phi Eta Sigma 90-; Alpha Lambda Delta 90-; Page SC State Hs Hs Of Rep; Bus Admin; Law.

**MUNNERLYN, GINGER R,** Univ Of Sc At Columbia, Columbia, SC; JR; BFA; Pen/Ink Pblshd Sumter Sandhill USC 89; Awd Blue Crs/Blue Shld Purch Awd 91; Taught Thomas Sumter Acad Fld/Art 83-90; Assoc Degree Arts; AA USC Sumter 90; Art Ed.

**MUNNINGS, MONIQUE M,** City Univ Of Ny City Coll, New York, NY; JR; BA; Seck Mntr Entrng Fresh; Chrldng Sqd; Clncl Psychlgy.

**MUNNS, MELINDA R,** Longwood Coll, Farmville, VA; SR; BS; Amnsty Intl 88-89; Octoberfst Klwns 90-; Kappa Delta Pi Pgm Dir 88-; Phi Kappa Phi 90-; BS; Elem Educ; Tchg.

**MUNOZ RUIZ, BELKIS,** Univ Of Pr Medical Sciences, San Juan, PR; FR; Spnsh; Cmnctns.

**MUNOZ, ALEX,** Bowling Green St Univ, Bowling Green, OH; SO; BS; Cnstrctn Mgmt Assoc; Delta Tau Delta; Cnstrctn Mgmt/Tecit; Field Engr.

**MUNOZ, ASTRO,** Univ Of Pr At Rio Piedras, Rio Piedras, PR; SR; Asoc Ex Alumnos Proyecto CAUSA VP 89-90; Gldn Key; Deans Hnr Lst; Ntrl Sci; Hsptl Admnstrtn.

**MUNOZ, IRLIM,** Inter Amer Univ Pr San German, San German, PR; SO; BBA; Natl Hnr Scty 89-90; Accounting; Cpa.

**MUNOZ, JORGE H,** Fl International Univ, Miami, FL; FR; BA; Hstry; Educ.

**MUNOZ, SANDRA E,** City Univ Of Ny La Guard Coll, Long Island Cty, NY; SO; AAS; Phi Theta Kappa; Math/Engl; Cmptr Pgmg.

**MUNRO, ERIKA D,** Hampton Univ, Hampton, VA; SO; BA; Stdnt Govt Assn Comm Chr 89-; Stdnt Ldrshp Pgm 90-; Exec Cncl 89-; Emnnt Pres Hnrs Schlr 89-; Intrnshp Burgr King Corp 89-90; Mass Comm; Law.

**MUNRO, JOYCE E,** Castleton St Coll, Castleton, VT; SO; BS; Pres List; Tutor; Corp Comm; Human Resources Mgmt.

**MUNRO, KIMBERLY J,** Salisbury St Univ, Salisbury, MD; GD; Resident Asstnt 90; Lambda Iota Tau; BA 90; English; Student Affairs.

**MUNROE, KAREN C,** City Univ Of Ny Queensbrough, New York, NY; SO; Wrd Prcssng.

**MUNSEY, LINDA G,** Averett Coll, Danville, VA; FR; BS; Soph Pres; Res Assist; SOAR Ldr; Vllybl/Chrldng; Cosmetologists License 89-90; Clinical Psychologist.

**MUNSEY, MELODY F,** Radford Univ, Radford, VA; SO; BS; Std Govt Asc Vol Srv Coor 90-; Jdcl Brd Advct 90-; Ambssdr 90-; Alpha Lambda Delta 90-; Hosp Vol 89-; Sntr Leigh Hosp Vol 86-; Outstdng Std Awd 90-; Lib Stds; Hosp Admn.

**MUNSON, BRIAN M,** Teikyo Post Univ, Waterbury, CT; SR; BS; Jr/Sr Cls Pres 89-90; Manchester Cmuty Clg Stdnt Sntr 88-89; Amer Mktg Assn; Food Cmtee Chrmn 89-; Stdnt Amsdr 90; Alumni Assn Cls Agnt; Hm Cmng King 90-; I M Ftbl Vybl 89-90; AS Manchester Cmuty Clg 89; Mktg; Intl Mktg.

**MUNSON, KRISTI L,** Salisbury St Univ, Salisbury, MD; JR; BS; Stdnt Ntl Ed Assn 89-; Kappa Delta Pi; Elem Ed; Tchr.

**MUQTASID, ADRIENNE FELYCE,** Hampton Univ, Hampton, VA; SO; BS; VOT 87-88; FBLA 87-88; Spnsh Clb 87; Phi Theta Kappa 89; Chem Eng; Eng.

**MURACA JR, VICTOR,** Carnegie Mellon Univ, Pittsburgh, PA; JR; BS; Mrchng Bnd 88-90; Outstndg Coll Stdnts Amer 89-; Theta Xi 89-; Ntl Coll Bus Merit Awds; IM Sccr/Hocky 89-; Indust Mgmt; Bus/Med.

**MURAK, KIMBERLY A,** S U N Y Coll At Buffalo, Buffalo, NY; FR; BFA; Earth Alliance Buffalo St Clgs 90-; Set Constr Stdnt Plys Upton Theatre 90-; Prof Wedding Photogrphr 86-; Visions Unltd Prof Wddng/Prtrt/Mdl Phtgrphr Owner 89-; Fine Art.

**MURAKAMI, YUMIKO,** Endicott Coll, Beverly, MA; FR; AA; Chldrns Museum Boston Intrnshp; Mngmnt; Bsn.

**MURAKHVER, NATALYA,** Ny Univ, New York, NY; SO; BA; Pre-Law Soc 90-; Newspr Rep 89-90; Engl; Writing; Law.

**MURAWSKI, MARK D,** Univ Of Pittsburgh, Pittsburgh, PA; FR; BS; Phi Eta Sigma 90-; Elect Eng.

**MURBERG, ELIANN,** City Univ Of Ny Baruch Coll, New York, NY; JR; BBA; Golden Key 90-; Deans Lst 89-; Endowmnt Fund Provosts Schlrshp 89-; Acctng; CPA.**

**MURCHIE, CAROLYN,** Providence Coll, Providence, RI; JR; BS; Coll Radio Offc Mgr 88-; Hd Of Fndrsng; Finance; Bnkng.

**MURCIA, ALGIS,** Southern Coll Of Tech, Marietta, GA; SO; Natl Soc Pro Engrs; GA Soc Pro Engrs; Soc Manuf Engrs; Eng.

**MURDOCH, KATHERINE H,** Birmingham Southern Coll, Birmingham, AL; JR; BA; Hmn Res Mgt.

**MURDOCK, DONAVIN D,** Univ Of South Al, Mobile, AL; SR; BED; Dns Lst; Sci.

**MURDOCK, KAREN M,** Lesley Coll, Cambridge, MA; JR; BED; Lesley Coll Trans Schlrshp 90-; AA Bunker Hill Comm Coll 89; Elem Edn; Teach.

**MURDOCK, MELISSA A,** Alcorn St Univ, Lorman, MS; SO; BA; Chf Staff SGA; Indl Tchnlgy Soc Sec; Hon Soc 89-; NAACP Hstrn 90-; 1st Runner Up Ms Black/Gold 90-; Co-Op Eng Tchncn Aide USDA Soil Cnsrvtn Servs; Sci; Eng.

**MURDOCK, SHERITA R,** Jackson St Univ, Jackson, MS; SO; BED; Alpha Lambda Delta; Elem Ed; Educatr.

**MURER, SASHA E,** Univ Of Miami, Coral Gables, FL; SO; BS; Microbio Clb 90; Vllybl Clb 89-90; Hnr Stdnt Assoc 89-90; Alpha Epsilon Delta 90; 1st Aid Sq 90f Alph Epsilon Delta 90; Prvsts Hnr Roll 90; Var Trk 89; Henry King Standard Acad Schlrshp Half Tuition U Of M 89; Math/Bio; Med.

**MURFIN, MELISSA A,** Bethany Coll, Bethany, WV; SO; BABA; Sigma Tau Epsilon Sec/Tr 90-; Alpha Psi Omega; Alpha Xi Delta 90-; Math/Acctg.

**MURICEAK, DENISE R,** Franklin And Marshall Coll, Lancaster, PA; FR; Ornttn Advsr Incmng Fresh/Wmn; Clg Wrk Study Pgm; Chi Omega; Step Pgm Asst; Geo/Govt; Env Stds.

**MURICEAK, EDWARD J,** Saint Francis Coll, Loretto, PA; JR; BA; PNA Schlrshp; Lynnanne Wingard Awd; IM Bsktbl/Sftbl Capt 89-; Acctg.

**MURICEAK, JEFFREY A,** Juniata Coll, Huntingdon, PA; SR; BA; Class Pres 90; Judicial Board/Chairperson 89; Clg Honor Society 89; Political Science Intership; History; Law.

**MURKIS, PAUL A,** City Univ Of Ny Baruch Coll, New York, NY; SO; BBA; Law Scty Sec 89-90; Hlll Clb Sec 89-; Alpha Phi Delta 90-; Cntr Rtrn 89-; Stdnt Rsrch Asst 90; Intrnshp Oppnhmr Qlfr 90; Brn USSR; Rckw Awrd Hnr 89-90; Fnc.

**MURLING, JACKI L,** Bridgewater Coll, Bridgewater, VA; JR; BA; Stdnt Senate Senator 88-; Band Pres 88-; Alpha Psi Omega 90-; Music; Coll Teach.

**MURNAHAN, JAMES R,** Oh Univ-Southern Cmps, Ironton, OH; SR; BHS; Non Trdtnl Org Sec 90-; Deans Lst 89-; Hnrbl Dschrg Nvy E5; Prsnnlmn 2nd XO Ymn; Nvy Achvmnt Mdl; Egls Frst Batp Chrch; Hdsn Med Cntr; Sp 92 BHS Hlth Hmn Srv Admn; Hlth Hmn Srvcs.

**MURPH, CAROL A,** Savannah St Coll, Savannah, GA; JR; BA; Acctng; CPA.

**MURPHY, ALISON M,** Converse Coll, Spartanburg, SC; FR; BA; Synchrnzd Swm Tm 90-; Cncpt Ltry-Art Mag Stff 90-; Stdnt Admssns Bd 90-; Alpha Lambda Delta VP 90-; Art Hstry/Sclgy/Latin.

**MURPHY, ANNE M,** Columbia Greene Comm Coll, Hudson, NY; SO; BA; Indiv Stdes; Crmnl Invstgtn.

**MURPHY, ANTHONY JEROME,** Saint Josephs Coll New York, Brooklyn, NY; GD; BSC; New York Nrs Assn; Knghts Col St Francis Assissi; Psychtrc Nrs 23 Yrs; Hlth Admin 3 Yrs; Reg Nrs San Fern Gen Hosp 68; Hlth Admin; Hlth Care.

**MURPHY, BONNETTA D,** Central St Univ, Wilberforce, OH; SR; BS; Nation Assn Blck Bus Prof Wmns Clb Inc 88-; Mktng Clb 89-; Dns Lst 87-; Acad Schlrshp 87-; Mktng/Mngmnt.

**MURPHY, BRIDGET,** Villanova Univ, Villanova, PA; FR; IM Scr Capt; Villanovan Stf Rptr; Stdnt Govt Comm Ofcr; Liberal Arts; Law/Journalis.

**MURPHY, CARLINE,** City Univ Of Ny Baruch Coll, New York, NY; JR; BBA; Rigerball Athltc Assc Brklyn Clg Treas 86; Dun/Bradstrt 84-87; Allnc Cptl 87-89; Chmcl Bnk Pres 89; Statistics; Graduate Degree Ecnmcs.

**MURPHY, CATHERINE J,** Fl A & M Univ, Tallahassee, FL; SR; MBA; Goldn Key 89-; Cancer Soc 88-; Madsn Boostr Clb 87-; MADD 87-; BA FAMU 90; N FL Jr Coll Almni 89-; Elem Ed.

**MURPHY, CECILE M,** Cornell Univ Statutory College, Ithaca, NY; JR; BS; Stu Adv 89-; Dean Lst; Ag Econ Intern; Agri Ecnmcs; Gvt/Law.

**MURPHY, CHARLOTTE W,** Univ Of Al At Birmingham, Birmingham, AL; JR; BA; Dns Schlrshp Awd 90; ASD Wallace State Cmnty Clg 89; Acctg; CPA.

**MURPHY, CHRISTOPHER J,** Molloy Coll, Rockville Ctr, NY; JR; BS; Acad Brd Chrprsn; Sci Clb Pr 90-; Math Clb Sec 89-90; Gaelic Soc 90-; Mu Sigma Mu 90-; Chi Beta Phi 90-; Math/Sci; Med Schl.

**MURPHY, CHRISTOPHER W,** Oh Univ, Athens, OH; FR; BA; Engr.

**MURPHY, CLAUDIA J,** Anne Arundel Comm Coll, Arnold, MD; SO; Spec Ed; Tchg.

**MURPHY, CONSTANCE D,** Atlantic Comm Coll, Mays Landing, NJ; SO; AAS; Goshen Vol Fire Co Wmns Aux 89-; Restaurant Mgmt; Acctf; CPA.

**MURPHY, CRYSTAL N,** Newbury Coll, Brookline, MA; FR; BA; Accnt Crdntr Surgi Care Inc; Mgmt; Intl Business.

**MURPHY, DANA S,** Union Univ, Jackson, TN; SO; BA; Rutldg Hstry Clb 90-; Bapt Un 89-; Hnr Assn 89-; Elem Educ; Tch.

**MURPHY, DAVID C,** S U N Y Coll Of Tech At Alfred, Alfred, NY; SR; BD; Psi Beta; Deans Lst 89-; Cert Acdmc Dstnctn; Hmn Serv; Psychlgst.

**MURPHY, DEANNIA J,** Roane St Comm Coll, Harriman, TN; FR; Raider Corps; Hstry; Professor.

**MURPHY, DERRON B,** Univ Of Montevallo, Montevallo, AL; SO; BA; Black Male Coalition; Chapel Hill Harvester Church; Deans List; Bsktbl Capt; Brdcst Eng.

**MURPHY, DORIS J,** Univ Of New Haven, West Haven, CT; SR; BA; Iterary Mag; Crmnl Jstc Clb; Alpha Lmbd Dlt 89-; Natl Kaplan Mem Schlrshp 89-90; Wiggins/Dana Schlrhsp 89; Deans List 87-; Engl Lit/Crmnl Jstc; Tchng.

**MURPHY, ERIN K,** Indiana Univ Of Pa, Indiana, PA; JR; BS; Englsh Clb 89-90; Pr Mntr Prgrm 90-; Sigma Tau Delta Tres 90-; Mcfrlnd Schlrshp 90-; Prvst Schlr 90-; Adlt Ltrcy Ttr 89-; Englsh/Spnsh Scndry Edctn; Tchng.

**MURPHY, ETHEL I,** Wilmington Coll, New Castle, DE; GD; BS; Delta Epsilon Rho 90; Pres Citation-Salem Comm Coll 88; Deans Lst 88-; USPS Spec Achmvmnt Awd 89; PTA; Grl Scts; Wmns Sftbl Leag; Jvnl Cnfrnc Comm; Sprntndnt Pstl Oprtns-USPS; AS Salem Comm Coll 88; Acctg; CPA.

**MURPHY, FRANK J,** Fl A & M Univ, Tallahassee, FL; SR; BA; Amer Inst Arch Stdnts; AA Broward Cmunty Clg 88; Arch.

**MURPHY, GRETA L,** Va Commonwealth Univ, Richmond, VA; SR; BA; Phi Eta Sigma; Phi Kappa Phi; Gldn Key; Art Hstry.

**MURPHY, HANNESSON I,** Fl International Univ, Miami, FL; FR; BS; Archtctr.

**MURPHY, HEATHER M,** Hillsborough Comm Coll, Tampa, FL; SO; BA; HELP 90-; BCM Bptst Cmps Mnstrs 89-; Insight 89-; Phi Theta Kappa 90-; Asstnt Drctr Ruth Eckerd Hall Prdctn 89; Intenshp Jones Intercable 90-; Mass Cmmnctns; Tlvsn Flm Prdctn.

**MURPHY, IVA B,** Volunteer St Comm Coll, Gallatin, TN; FR; AAS; Acctng; CPA.

**MURPHY, JAMES E,** Oh Univ, Athens, OH; SO; BFA; E Green Cncl VP 89-; Studio Art; Artist.

**MURPHY, JEAN M,** Notre Dame Coll, Cleveland, OH; GD; CERT; Postulant/Sister Of Notre Dame Who Run Notre Dame Clg 90; Rcrtnl Thrpst 4 Yrs; BA Cntrl Michigan Univ 86; Theology/Engl; Tchng.

**MURPHY, JENNIFER E,** Georgian Court Coll, Lakewood, NJ; SR; BA; Clionaes Soc Pres 88-; Phi Alpha Theta Secy 90-; Intnshp Ocean County History Soc; Deans Schol 90-; History; Colg Prof.

**MURPHY, JENNIFER H,** Univ Of Sc At Columbia, Columbia, SC; SR; BA; PAJI GA State Pres 87-90; BAHAI Clb SC Sec 90-; Radio 90-; Hon Schl GA State 87-90; SAGE 90-; Amnesty SC GA 87-; Hbtat Hmnty 88-90; Intrntl Stds; Ed.

**MURPHY, JOHN CHARLES,** Villanova Univ, Villanova, PA; JR; BA; RA 90-92; Hse Cncl Pres 89-90; Ecnmcs Soc 89-; Omicron Delta Epsilon; Omicron Delta Kappa 90-; Phi Kappa Phi; Deans List 89-; Economics; Bus.

**MURPHY, JOHN D,** Anne Arundel Comm Coll, Arnold, MD; FR; BS; Deans Lst; Cmptr Sci.

**MURPHY, JOHN J,** Colgate Univ, Hamilton, NY; FR; Delta Kappa Epsilon; Vrsty Bsbl; Ecnmcs/Rssn.

**MURPHY, JOHN M,** Roanoke Bible Coll, Elizabeth Cy, NC; JR; BA; Jr Class VP 90; Schlrshp From Roanoke Bible Clg, Rotary Club Schlrshp; Bsktbl Sftbl Tennis; Ministry.

**MURPHY, JULIE A,** Allegheny Coll, Meadville, PA; SR; BA; Vrsty Sccr 87-90; Tutr 90-; Alden Schlr 89-; Alpha Chi Omega 88-; Intrnshp Fdrtd Invstrs Pittsburgh 90; Econ.

**MURPHY, KAITLIN M,** Villanova Univ, Villanova, PA; FR; BA; Univ Yrbk Uncerclassmen Editor; Deans List; Project Sunshine Tutoring; Homeless Comm Soup Kitchen; SWAOO; Deans List.

**MURPHY, KARLA E,** Va St Univ, Petersburg, VA; SR; BS; Data Proc Mgmt Assn Pr 90-; Pan Hellnc Cncl 90-; Stdnt Busn Adv Comm 90-; Delta Sigma Theta 90-; Busn Inf Syst; Cmptr Sci.

**MURPHY, KATHERINE A,** Bellarmine Coll, Louisville, KY; JR; Beta Psi VP 88-; Chrl Dpt Sec 88-; Delta Epsln Sigma; Psi Chi Pres 90-; Rsch Asst Psy 90-; Psy; Grad Schl Psyd.

**MURPHY, KRISHNA ALBERT,** Univ Of Miami, Coral Gables, FL; JR; BBA; VITA; Beta Alpha Psi; SEEP; Vet US Army/Rsvs 82-90; AA Miami-Dade Comm Clg 90; Acctng; Intl Bsn/Fnce.

**MURPHY, KRISTIN L,** Western New England Coll, Springfield, MA; SO; BS; Soc/Wmn Engr Treas 89-; Chrldng Cl Pres 89-; SG 89-90; Peer Adv; Ambass; Pa Dept/Trans Intnshp 90-; Mechncl Engrng.

**MURPHY, LAURA M,** Glassboro St Coll, Glassboro, NJ; FR; BA; Radio Stn; FCC Lcnse; Wrk Prmtns; Scndry Ed/Math; Math Tchng.

**MURPHY, LAURIEANN,** City Univ Of Ny Baruch Coll, New York, NY; SR; BBA; AS; Queensborough Cmmty Clg 89; Hmn Resource Mngmnt; Mngmnt Hmn Resource Dept.

**MURPHY, LEANNE M,** Le Moyne Coll, Syracuse, NY; SR; BA; Lit Mag Co Edtr; Englsh/Mrktng Clb 90; Open Hse Vol 88; Intrnshp Coolican-Le Mon Adv Agncy; Intrnshp Prdgy Bus Serv 90; English/Communications; Adv.

**MURPHY, LEIGH A,** Univ Of Scranton, Scranton, PA; JR; Acctg Soc Treas; Natl Hon Soc Bus Admin 90-; Wmns Bus Hon Soc 90-; Pres Schlrshp; Horizons 88-; IM Bsktbl 90-; Acctg; Actnt.

**MURPHY, LISA A,** Coll Misericordia, Dallas, PA; FR; BA; Bndfrnt/Drll Sqd 87-89; Theatr Prdctn/Actng 87-90; Yrbk Stf 87-89; Ntl Hnr Scty Treas 88-90; Tchng Asst Discrete Math Wth Isetl; Pres Schlrshp 90-; Bshps Awd Fr Rlgs Educ/Yth Mnstry 90; Hstry; Govt Wrk/Tchng.

**MURPHY, LISA S,** Univ Of Sc At Columbia, Columbia, SC; FR; Band; Interdisciplinary Studies; Linguistics.

**MURPHY, M KAY,** Univ Of Miami, Coral Gables, FL; FR; Amnsty Intrntl Freedom Wrtr 88-; Natl Hon Soc 89-; Hons Stdnt Assoc 90-; IN Univ Hons Prog In Frgn Lang 89; Provsts Hon Roll 90; Motion Pictrs/Engl; Film Mkr.

**MURPHY, MARGARET,** City Univ Of Ny Queensbrough, New York, NY; FR; AAS; Nursing; Rn.

**MURPHY, MARILYN S,** Miami Jacobs Jr Coll Of Bus, Dayton, OH; FR; AA; Trvl/Trsm.

**MURPHY, MARLO M,** Le Moyne Coll, Syracuse, NY; SR; BA; Scrtc Clb St Francis Coll 87-88; Stu Art Shw 90; Deans Lst Sprng 88-; Asst Ads Crdntr At Manlius Pblshg Intrn; Grad Magna Cum Laude; X Cntry Trck St Francis Coll 87-88; Enlg.**

**MURPHY, MARTHA E,** Univ Of South Al, Mobile, AL; JR; BS; SGA; Jaguar Prdctns 89-; Chi Omega 89-; Educ; Tchng/Cnslng.

**MURPHY, MATTHEW J,** Juniata Coll, Huntingdon, PA; SO; BS; Scalpel/Probe; Beta Beta Beta; Frshmn Chem Awd; IM Vlybl/Soccer; Bio; Med.

**MURPHY, MAURA A,** Daemen Coll, Amherst, NY; JR; BS; Phys Ther.

**MURPHY, MELISSA K,** Radford Univ, Radford, VA; SR; BMT; Natl Assoc Music Thrpy 89-; VA Assoc For Music Thrpy 89-; Music Thrpy Clb 87-; Bapt Stdnt Un 87-; Bapt Festvl Sngrs European Choir Tour 88; Chrtr Westbrk Psych Hosp Music Thrpy Intrn; Aganst All Odds Clbhse Clncl Stdnt 90; Music Thrpy.

**MURPHY, MICHAEL E,** Univ Of Sc At Columbia, Columbia, SC; FR; BS; Lambda Chi Alpha Rush Chr 90-; Math; Mltry.

**MURPHY, MICHELLE L,** Broward Comm Coll, Ft Lauderdale, FL; SO; AA; Phi Theta Kappa; Erly Admssns 89-90; Psychlgy; Educ.

**MURPHY, NICOLE N,** Fl International Univ, Miami, FL; FR; BS; Math; Actuarial Sci.

**MURPHY, PATRICIA E,** City Univ Of Ny Baruch Coll, New York, NY; JR; BBA; Sigma Alpha Delta; Acct Assist; Acctg.

**MURPHY, PATRICIA J,** Bloomfield Coll, Bloomfield, NJ; SR; BA; Bdwsr Blls 88-90; Hgh Hnr 90; Deans Lst; Deans Lst Jr Cllg; All Amrcn Sftbll Tm 88-90; Jr Cllg All Amrcn Sftbll Tm 87; Crmnl Jstc Pstl Inspctr.

**MURPHY, PAUL D,** Washington State Comm Coll, Marietta, OH; GD; ASC; Pres Lst 90; Deans Lst 90; Rmdlng; Elec Eng.

**MURPHY, PAULA A,** Lasell Coll, Newton, MA; SO; AA; Intnl Cl Pres; Jap Sis Prog; Deans List; Libl Arts; Cmmctns; Acting.

**MURPHY, PENNY L,** Oh St Univ At Marion, Marion, OH; FR; BS; Stdnt Alumni Cncl Treas; Griffen Soc; Econ/Bsnss Soc; Phi Eta Sigma; Alpha Lambda Delta; Stdnt Alumni Cncl Treas; Deans Lst 90; Rasor Mth Test; Psych; Psych Prof.

**MURPHY, PETER-CHRISTOPHER,** Cornell Univ Statutory College, Ithaca, NY; FR; BS; Cornell Civil Lib Un 90-; Bus Mgmnt; Intl Bus/Diplomacy.

**MURPHY JR, RONALD L,** Comm Coll Algny Co Algny Cmps, Pittsburgh, PA; FR; Engl; Tch Shakespearan Lit/Wrtr.

**MURPHY, ROSALYN D,** Clark Atlanta Univ, Atlanta, GA; FR; BA; NAACP 90-; Bstrs Clb 90-; Frnscs Achvmnt 90-; Mass Cmmnctns/Pbl Rel.

**MURPHY, SEAN M,** Savannah Coll Of Art & Design, Savannah, GA; SO; BFA; Illstrtn; Grphc Dsgn.

**MURPHY, SHAUNA L,** Newbury Coll, Brookline, MA; FR; BA; Fshn Mrchndsng; Rtl Mrchndsng.

**MURPHY, SIOBHAN E,** James Madison University, Harrisonburg, VA; SR; Univ Prog Bd 88-; Cncl Excptnl Chldrn 88-; Stdnt Cncrns Comm Sec 90; Kappa Delta Pi 90-; Golden Key 90-; Spec Olympics 87-89; Schlr Athlete 89; Pres Lst 89-; Outstndng Stdnt Lrng Dis; Intercoll Swmmng 87-89; Spec Ed/LD; Masters Spec Ed.

**MURPHY, STACEY L,** George Mason Univ, Fairfax, VA; SR; BSED; Early Childhood Education; Teacher.

**MURPHY, STEPHEN M,** Univ Of Southern Ms, Hattiesburg, MS; SR; BS; Std Jdcl Cncl 90-; Math; Statistics.

**MURPHY, SUZANNE E,** Marywood Coll, Scranton, PA; SR; SGA VP 89-; Res Advsr 89-; Cls Actvts/Offcr VP 87-; Sigma Pi Epsilon Delta 89-; Kappa Delta Pi 89-; Kappa Gamma Pi 90-; Cllgt Vol 88-; Cmps Mnstry Com Chrprsn 87-; Cncl Excptnl Chldrn 87-; St Catherine Mdl Ldrshp/Serv 90; BS; Elem/Spec Ed; Educ/Mnstry.

**MURPHY, SUZZETTE T,** Ohio Valley Coll, Parkersburg, WV; FR; AA; Ambsdr 90-; Missns Clb 90-; Tghr Eternity Clb 90-; Alpha Delta Chi Wmn 90-; Mus/Ele Educ; Prod Engr/Tch.

**MURPHY, THADDEUS S,** Univ Of Sc At Columbia, Columbia, SC; SR; BA; AFACT Pres 87-; Rsme Bldrs Flms Wrtr/Pblshr 90-; Hnr Rl 87-; Engl; Edtr/Wrtr.

**MURPHY, THOMAS D,** Oh Univ-Southern Cmps, Ironton, OH; SO; BS; Math/Chem Tutor Tutorng Prog 90; Prctr For Ohio Tests Of Schlstc Achvmnt; Deans Lst 90; Karate 89; Chem/Math.

**MURPHY, TIMOTHY A,** Le Moyne Coll, Syracuse, NY; SO; BA; Le Moyne Coll Dns Lst; Vrsty Crss Cntry Tm 89-; Bus Mgmt.

**MURPHY, TORRII ALONZA,** Nc Agri & Tech St Univ, Greensboro, NC; FR; BA; Natl Soc Blck Engrs 90-; INROADS 89-; IBM Supplemntl Cust Engr Intern 90-; Elctrcl Engr; Cmptr Engr.

**MURPHY, XAVIER A D,** Miami Dade Comm Coll North, Miami, FL; GD; BA; Jamaican Stdnts Assoc Pres 88; Stdnt Govt Offcr 88-89; Stdngs Expo Assn Pres 89; Stdnt Actvts Awd Cntrbutn Stdnt Actvts Prog 89; Bus/Mktg; Pub Rltns Mktg.

**MURRAL, DEBRA J,** Kent St Univ Kent Cmps, Kent, OH; SR; BS; Wght Clb 88-; Golden Key 90; Outstndg Coll Stdnts Amer 89; OH Estrn Stars 87-; Tchng Asst; Pres Lst 89; Deans Lst 88-90; Bio; Entmlgy.

**MURRAN, ANN R,** Univ Of Fl, Gainesville, FL; SR; BFA; Docent Univ Gallery 87-88; Art Hstry Assn 90-; Amer Ins Foreign Study 90; Golden Key; Exhbtd Juried Stdns Show; Paintng; Art.

**MURRAY, AMELIA G,** Univ Of Sc At Columbia, Columbia, SC; SO; BS; Stdnt Nrs Assn; Phi Eta Sigma; Delta Gamma; Nrsng.

**MURRAY, AMY J,** Atlantic Union Coll, S Lancaster, MA; FR; BS; Amnesty Intl 90-; Frshmn Schlrshp; Biology/Pre Med; Medicine.

**MURRAY, BRYAN L,** Alcorn St Univ, Lorman, MS; FR; BA; Mrch Bnd 90-; Pol Sci; Lwyr/CIA.

**MURRAY, CAROL L,** Hampton Univ, Hampton, VA; SR; Spch Cmunctns Clb 90-; Per Cnslrs 89-90; Hampton Univ Choir 89-90; U S Achvmnt Acad; Pres Eminent Schlr Awd 87-88; BA 91; Mass Cmunctn/Brdcstng.**

**MURRAY, CLAUDIA M,** Univ Of Montevallo, Montevallo, AL; JR; BS; Rsdnts Asst; Wesley Fllwshp 90-; Sigma Alpha Pi; AL Speech Hrng Assn 90-; Ntnl Stdnts Speech Hrng Lang Assn 90-; Zeta Tau Alpha Srvc Phlnthrpy Chrprsn 88-; Circle K 88-; News Intrn WHMA Radio 89; Speech Lang Pthlgy Intrnshp; Speech Lang Pathlgy.

**MURRAY, DAVID C,** Franklin And Marshall Coll, Lancaster, PA; SR; BA; Stdnt Congress VP Sec 90-; Govt Clb VP 89-; Tour Guide 90-; Phi Alpha Theta; Pi Gamma Mu; Phi Beta Kappa; Boy Scouts Am Asst Scoutmastr 87-; Hackman Schlr 88; Dona Schlr 88-; Moffet Schlr 87-; Intl Rel; Public Policy.

**MURRAY, DIANE,** Duquesne Univ, Pittsburgh, PA; GD; MA; Psi Chi; Cinn Psych Assoc Awd 90; Cinn Bsns Prof Wmns Clb Schlrshp 88-90; Asst Duquesnes Mstrs Prog Psych 90-; BS Xavier Univ Cinn OH 90; Psych; Clncl Psych.

**MURRAY, DONNA A,** Ny Univ, New York, NY; JR; BA; Sch Contn Educ Stdnt Cncl 90-; Dns Lst 89-; Contn Educ Schlrshp 88-; Shimkin Schlrshp 88-89; Mgr Human Res 79-; AAS; Org Comms; Comms.

**MURRAY, ERIN,** Immaculata Coll, Immaculata, PA; JR; BA; Life Acdnt/Hlth Ins Agnt 88-; Engl/Bus Mgmt/Edn; Scndry Edn.**

**MURRAY, GREGORY R,** Allegheny Coll, Meadville, PA; SR; BS; IM Sprts; Stdnt Orient Advsr; Beta Beta Beta; Lambda Sigma; Theta Chi Sec 90-; Allegheny Schlrshp; Alden Schlr; Bio; Med.

**MURRAY, JAMI C,** Saint John Fisher Coll, Rochester, NY; SR; BA; Soc Clb Pr 87-; Drama Clb 89-90; Alumn Assn Sec 90; Pi Gamma Mu 89-; St John Fishr Jeffrsn Prtnrshp Tutrng 90-; Hllside Chldrns Hm Vol 90; Acad Adm Schrlshp 87-; Soclgy; Socl Work.

**MURRAY, JASON B,** Oh Wesleyan Univ, Delaware, OH; JR; BA; Dublin Mrtl Arts Ctr Red Belt; Phi Eta Sigma 89; Phi 90; Mortar Brd; Order Of Omega 90; Sigma Phi Epsilon VP 90; Outstndng Greek Pldg 89; Clifford B Scott Mem Awd 90; Vars Ftbl 88-89; Pltcs/Gov; Law.

**MURRAY, JENNIFER L,** Le Moyne Coll, Syracuse, NY; SO; BS; Intrntl Hse; Admsns Tr Guide; Lctr Cmps Masses; Psychlgy Spec Ed; Tchr.

**MURRAY, JOAN A,** Centenary Coll, Hackettstown, NJ; SR; BA; Alpha Chi; H G Dubois Awrd; AA Co Coll Morris 88; Engl; Tchng/Wrtng.

**MURRAY, JOHN M,** Elizabethtown Coll, Elizabethtown, PA; FR; BA; SAM 90-; Mktng/Advtng Club; Alpha Lambda Delta 90-; Busn Admin; Finance/Mgt/Computer.

**MURRAY, JOSEPH J,** William Paterson Coll, Wayne, NJ; JR; BA; Cty Clg Morris Deans List 88; Deans List 90; AS Cty Clg Morris 90; Math.

**MURRAY, JOYCE A,** Western Piedmont Comm Coll, Morganton, NC; SO; BA; Phi Theta Kappa 90-; Coop Ed Tchr Asst 90; S S Tchr 89-; Ch-Comm Prof Strytlr 89-; BA Pillsbury Bapt Bible Coll 77; Speech/Comm; Teach.

**MURRAY, JOYCE A,** Univ Of Charleston, Charleston, WV; SO; ADN; Nrsng; Cont Ed.

**MURRAY, KATHLEEN A,** Germanna Comm Coll, Locust Grove, VA; SO; BLS; Acctg Clrk; Sec; Hstry/Soc Stdies; Tchr.

**MURRAY, KEASIA D,** Fl A & M Univ, Tallahassee, FL; FR; BS; Std Govt Asc 90-; Miss Fresh 90-; Natl Soc Blck Engrs 90-; Soc Wmn Engrs 90-; Phi Eta Sigma 90-; Pres Schlrs Asc 90-; Hnywl Inc 90-; Cvl Engr; City Plng/Urbn Dvlpmnt.

**MURRAY, KELLY C,** Ashland Comm Coll, Ashland, KY; SO; BA; Ofc Admin; Med Sec.

**MURRAY, KIERAN N,** Merrimack Coll, North Andover, MA; SO; BA; Orien Com 90-; Ski Clb 89-; Nu Phi Kappa 90-; Dns Lst 89-90; Mns Crs Cntry Tm 89-; Poli Sci; Law.

**MURRAY, LAURA A,** Mount Aloysius Jr Coll, Cresson, PA; FR; Phi Theta Kappa; Occptnl Thrpy; Cert Occptnl Thrpy Assn.

**MURRAY, LORI J,** Memphis St Univ, Memphis, TN; JR; BA; Acad Toss Up Tm V P 89-; French Clb 89-; Philosophy Clb 89-; Red Crs; Philosophy/Hstry; Prfsr.

**MURRAY, LORRAINE E,** Middle Tn St Univ, Murfreesboro, TN; SR; DVM; Cmptr Clb 87-88; Hon Soc 90-; Delta Tau Alpha 90-; Block/Bridle Awd 90; AS Frank Phillips Clg 89; Animal Sci; Vet Med.

**MURRAY, MARGARET M,** Univ Of Southern Ms, Hattiesburg, MS; SR; BS; Psi Chi 90-; Gamma Beta Phi 90-; Sexual Assault Crisis Cen 90-; Psychlgy.

**MURRAY, MARY P,** Duquesne Univ, Pittsburgh, PA; JR; BS JD; SHARP 88-89; Frnscs 88-89; Bsn/Law.

**MURRAY, MELVIA M,** Coppin St Coll, Baltimore, MD; JR; BS; SIFE Treas 90-; Big Brother/Big Sis 90-; Kilimingaro Invstmnt Clb Treas; Mgmt Sci; Law.**

**MURRAY, MICHELLE A,** Castleton St Coll, Castleton, VT; SO; Comm Lbry; Elem Tutor; Kids Meeting Kids Russia Exch Coord; Bnk Proof Clrk; Elem Lbry Aide; Elem Educ/Rdng; Tch.

**MURRAY, MICHELLE Y,** Howard Univ, Washington, DC; SR; BA; Film Prod.

**MURRAY, MYRON D,** Fl A & M Univ, Tallahassee, FL; SO; BS; NAACP 89; Phi Eta Sigma 90-; Econ.

**MURRAY, NANCY ELIZABETH,** Le Moyne Coll, Syracuse, NY; JR; BA; Humn Serv Assoc VP Pres 90-; Soc Clb Pub Rel Ofcr 90-; Chldrns Aids Ntwrk Exec Ofcr 90-; Intrnshp Auburn Mem Hosp; Soc/Biol; Hlth Care Admn.

**MURRAY, NANCY L,** Mercyhurst Coll, Erie, PA; GD; AIDS Cncl Erie Co Bd Of Dirs Sec; Am Red Cross HV/AIDS Instr; Cnslr/AIDS Spclst; BA Gannon Univ 79; Adm Jste; Crrctns.

**MURRAY, NICHOLE S,** George Mason Univ, Fairfax, VA; JR; BS; SEA 89-; NEA VEA 89-; Gldn Key; VA Acad Schlrshp 88-; Deans Lst 90-; Early Educ; Tchr.**

**MURRAY, ROSE A,** Savannah St Coll, Savannah, GA; SO; BBA; Phi Delta Chi/Chi Delta Phi 76-77; Cub Scts Asst Cub Mstr 88-; Busn Admin; Acctg.

**MURRAY, TANYA L,** Benedict Coll, Columbia, SC; JR; BA; Intl Stdnts Assoc Bus Mgr 90-; Drg Fr Achvrs Bus Mgr 87-88; Natl Stdnts Bus Lg; Alpha Chi; Alpha; Kappa Mu; Dnc Ompny; Vllybll Tm; Bus Admn.

**MURRAY, THURSTON P,** Coll Of Charleston, Charleston, SC; SO; BA; Hstry; Law.

**MURRAY, TIMOTHY E,** Fl St Univ, Tallahassee, FL; SR; BA; Pi Gamma Mu; Deans Lst 90; IMS Ftbl Bsktbl 89-; Intl Affairs; Law.

**MURRAY, TRACIE L,** Johnson C Smith Univ, Charlotte, NC; SO; BA; Soph Clss VP 90-; Alpha Lambda Delta 89-; Dns Lst 90; Pres Lst 90; Cmmnctns; PR Agncy.**

**MURRAY, UWADA M,** City Univ Of Ny City Coll, New York, NY; SR; BS; Amer Medl Student Assoc 87-; Third World Orgtn Day Student Govt 89-; Amer Acad Fmly Phys 90-; Golden Key VP 89-; Deans List 89; Sophie Davis Hurricane Hugo Relief Fund Coordtr 89; Role Model/Inshp Prog 89; Biomedical Ed; Med MD.

**MURRAY, VREGE A,** Univ Of Southern Me, Portland, ME; FR; BA; Bsn; Bsn Admin.

**MURRAY, WILLIAM ROBERT,** Coll Of Charleston, Charleston, SC; SO; BA; Hnrs Engl.

**MURRAY JR, WILLIAM S,** Fl St Univ, Tallahassee, FL; JR; BA; AA 90; Engl; Tchr.

**MURRELL, HOLLY P,** Coll Of Charleston, Charleston, SC; JR; BS; Stdnt Govt Sr Cls Pr; Alpha Lambda Delta 88-89; Phi Kappa Phi; Omicron Delta Kappa 90-; Alpha Epsilon Delta V P 89-; Fr Acad Hnr Awd Col Clg 88-89; Bio; Md.**

**MURRELL, JENNIFER L,** Marshall University, Huntington, WV; SR; BED; MENC 87; Delta Omicron Treas 90; Delta Omicron Pres Awd; Tchng Music.

**MURRELL, SHERRY HONEYCUTT,** Faulkner Univ, Montgomery, AL; SR; BA; SAEA 89-; Phi Lambda VP 89-90; Univ Math Awd 89-90; Pres Schlp 87-; Math; Tchr.

**MURRELL, STEVEN W,** Univ Of Tn At Martin, Martin, TN; JR; BS; Stdnt Tnnss Ed Assoc; Kappa Omicron Pres 73; Bnd Bstrs Pres 90-; Mnstr Chch Chrst 78; AA 73; Scndry Ed Math.

**MURRISH, MELINDA L,** Fl Atlantic Univ, Boca Raton, FL; SR; BBA; Comp Info Systms; Comp Tech Wrtr.

**MURRY, DEBRA YVETTE,** Lane Coll, Jackson, TN; SR; Soph Clss Pres/Cmnctns Clb/Stdnt Chrstn Org 88-89; Hon Roll Frsh Yr; Nwspr Clb; Yrbk Staff 87-; Phtgrphy Clb 88-; Intrnshp Kix-96 90-; Chrldr Capt 87-88; Cmnctns.

**MURSCH, SANDRA E,** Univ Of Nc At Charlotte, Charlotte, NC; JR; BA; Relgs Studies; Tchng.

**MURTHA JR, JAMES,** Glassboro St Coll, Glassboro, NJ; JR; BA; IM Vlybl 89-; GSC Vlybl Clb VP 90-; Deans Lst; WRNJ Radio Intrnshp; Advtsng/Cmnctns.

**MURUGI, GATHONI,** Immaculata Coll, Immaculata, PA; FR; BA; Stndt Govt VP 86-; Athltcs Clb Vc Capt 80-89; Lang Clb 90-; Immaculata Coll Nrh Sctytn Vc Clb 85-90; Sci Cngrss Awrd 87-88; Swm Tm Pres 80-89; Bus Admn; Law.

**MUSA, ASHRAF F,** Univ Of Louisville, Louisville, KY; JR; BS; IEEE; Elctrcl Eng.

**MUSANTE, JULIE ANN,** Carnegie Mellon Univ, Pittsburgh, PA; SO; BA; Ind Mgmt; Actnt.

**MUSCATO, STEPHEN J,** Univ Of Rochester, Rochester, NY; JR; BS; IEEE 89-; Tau Beta Pi 90-; Wrstlng Clb 89-; Tau Beta Pi 90-; Delco Prdcts Div GM Eng 90-; Accptnce U Of R EE Grdte Prog; Elec Eng.

**MUSCELLA, JOSEPH M,** Widener Univ, Chester, PA; SR; BS; Tau Beta Pi; Alpha Chi; IEEE; AS Delaware Cnty Comm Colg 90; Elec Engrng; MBA Mas/Envmntl Engr.

**MUSE, ALEXIS M,** Va St Univ, Petersburg, VA; FR; BA; Hnr Rl 90-; Deans List 90-; History; Law.

**MUSE, KAREN D,** Commonwealth Coll, Virginia Beach, VA; SR; Acctng Clb 89-; Bus Mgmt Clb 89-; Pres Lst 89-; Phi Beta Lambda 89-; Alpha Beta Gamba 89-; AAS 90-; Acctng/Bus Mgmt.**

**MUSGRAVE, JAN A,** Va Commonwealth Univ, Richmond, VA; JR; BSW; Alcohol/Drug Peer Eductrs 90-; Natl Assn Soc Wrkrs 89-; Golden Key 90; Soc Wrk.

**MUSGROVE, DENISE C,** Middle Tn St Univ, Murfreesboro, TN; SR; BA; Gamma Beta Phi; Phi Alpha Theta 90; Pi Gamma Mu 90; AACN; RN Critical Care Certified 87; History.

**MUSGROVE, LISA R,** Univ Of Md At Eastern Shore, Princess Anne, MD; SO; BS; Pom Pom Sqd Co Capt 89-; Hmn Eclgy Clb Pres; Kappa Omicron Nu 90-; Fshn Mrchndsng; Advrtsng/Coordntng.

**MUSGROVE, MARY D,** Univ Of Southern Ms, Hattiesburg, MS; SR; BS; Psi Chi; Psychology; Law.

**MUSHARRAF, BILAL,** Univ Of Miami, Coral Gables, FL; FR; BS; Tns 90-; Usr Asstnt Scrty Mngr 90-; Instrctnl Sprt Fctly Cmptr Cntr; Alpha Lambda Delta; Hnrs Prgrm; Intrnshp Dpt Cnsrvtn Energy; Elctrcl Engnrng Math; Engnrng.

**MUSIC, BRIAN K,** Marshall University, Huntington, WV; JR; BBA; Deans Lst 89-; Mel Triola Schlrshp; Logan H S Parent Advsry Schlrshp 90; A E Booth Mem Schlrshp; Marshall Univ Tuition Waivers 90-; W P Black Schlrshp; Century III Schlrshp; Fin; Bnkg; Invstmnt Bnkg.

**MUSIC, DENISE L,** Oh Dominican Coll, Columbus, OH; SO; BA; Ohio Assn Schl Bus Offcls Pres 80-; Ohio Govt Fin Offrc Assn 89-; Fiscal Offcr Met Educ Cncl 83-; Bus Admn Accntng; Pblc Fin.

**MUSICK, KENNETH R,** Patrick Henry Comm Coll, Martinsville, VA; FR; Cert; Indus Eldng.

**MUSICK, TRACI L,** Marshall University, Huntington, WV; JR; BA; Phi Eta Sigma 89; Sigma Tau Delta; Lang Arts; HS Engl Tchr.

**MUSIK, JEFFREY S,** Averett Coll, Danville, VA; SO; BS; Act Brd 89-; Stdnt Fndtn; Bapt Stdnt Un 89-; Alpha Chi 90-; Phi Eta Sigma 89-90; IM 89-; Acctg.

**MUSKAT, JAMIE L,** S U N Y Coll At Fredonia, Fredonia, NY; JR; BS; Deans Lst 89-90; Kappa Delta Pi; Soph Acad Achvmnt Educ Awd 90; Erly Chldhd Educ; Tchng.

**MUSKAT, MICHAEL,** Emory Univ, Atlanta, GA; JR; BA; Non-Profit Karate Org Fndr-Instr 89-; Bsn/Anthrplgy; Bsn.

**MUSOLINO, ANTOINETTE,** City Univ Of Ny Baruch Coll, New York, NY; JR; Teachers Of Tomorrow 90-; Big Bros/Big Sis 88-90; Spec Edn; Teacher.

**MUSSELMAN, ROBIN A,** George Mason Univ, Fairfax, VA; SR; BS; SEA 89-; VEA 89-; NEA 89-; Golden Key 89-; Alpha Chi 90-; Erly Chldhd Educ; Tchr.

**MUSSELWHITE, TINA E,** Abraham Baldwin Agri Coll, Tifton, GA; FR; BA; Phi Theta Kappa 90-; Alpha Beta Gamma 90-; Bus Admin; Real Est/Bus Mgmnt.

**MUSSER, MARILEE A,** Fl St Univ, Tallahassee, FL; JR; BA; Delta Tau Delta Ltl Sis 90-; Deans Lst 88-; IM Athltc Trnr 89-; AA 90; Cmnctns; Rec Thrpy.

**MUSSULMAN, LAURA M,** Univ Of Nc At Greensboro, Greensboro, NC; JR; BS; Exrcs/Sprt Sci Dept Bd 90-; Susan Stout Schlrshp; Vrsty Sccr 88-; Exrcs/Sprt Sci Blgy; Rsrchr Coach.

**MUSTAFIC, NEZIR,** Fordham Univ, Bronx, NY; SR; BS; Fordhm Univ Fed Cred Un VP Fin 90-; Fordham Univ Fin Soc Treas 89; Dns Lst 89-; Prudntl Secrties Intrnshp 89-; Fin; Law.

**MUSTARD, JULIANA J,** Wagner Coll, Staten Island, NY; SO; BA; Theatre 89; Opera Workshp 90; Capri Film Scty/Mntgmry AL 89; Theatre; Actor.

**MUSTELIER, CARLOS E,** Fl International Univ, Miami, FL; SO; BBA; Mgmt Info Syst/Acctg; Law.

**MUSTELIER, TERESA,** Univ Of South Fl, Tampa, FL; GD; MPH; Assc FL Old Girls Scl Chrprsn 89-; Tampa Aids Ntwrk Vol 89-; Share Tampa Bay; Natl Assc Accrdttn Phys Asst 82-; FL Acdmy Phys Asst 80-; AM Acdmy Phys Asst 89-; BS Univ FL 82; BA 80; Pblc Hlth; Occptnl Med.

**MUSTO, JEAN E,** Georgian Court Coll, Lakewood, NJ; SO; BA; Wrtr Nwspr; Stdnt Govt Cmps Mnstry Chrprsn; Sigma Tau Delta; Deans Schlr 90; English/Rlgus Stdes; Fam Law.

**MUSTO, JENNIFER E,** Springfield Tech Comm Coll, Springfield, MA; JR; BS; Lil Miss Sftbl Coach; AS 90; Indstrl Tech Graphic Arts; Mgmnt/Teach.

**MUTASA, BATSIRAI M,** Bennett Coll, Greensboro, NC; SO; BA; Interntl Stdnt Org V Pres 90-; Bennett Tennis Team; Union Gospel Choir 90-; Fermi Natl Accelerator Lab Intern 89-; Exchange Prog With Union Clge 90-; Physics & Business; Biomedical Engrng.

**MUTER, LAURA A,** Bethany Coll, Bethany, WV; SO; BS; SPS Sec 90-; Chrstn Flwshp Clb 89-; Stu Brd Govr Rep 90-; Soc Coll Jrnlsts; Kappa Mu Epsilon; Paper Crws Rprtr 90-; Intrn Crnl Univ; Physics; Astrophyscs.

**MUTEWERA, PERI,** Lincoln Univ, Lincoln Univ, PA; SO; BS; Bio Clb; Secr Intl Clb; Tennis; RA; Bio/Chem; Med Dr.

**MUTH, CHARLES A,** Capitol Coll, Laurel, MD; SR; BS; Inst Elec/Electrnc Eng 88-; MD Beta Chptr Alpha Chi 90-; Tau Alpah Pi VP; Elctrnc Eng Tech.

**MUTH, MARY-ANN,** Eckerd Coll, St Petersburg, FL; SO; BA; Nwspaper Edtr 89-; Radio DJ 89-; Media Comm/Pet Cncl 90-; Omicron Delta Kappa; Campus Mnstry 89-90; Boyd Hill Nature Pk Intrn 90-; Envrnmntl Stdies; Wldlf Mgmt.

**MUTHARD, SHERI L,** Central Pa Bus School, Summerdale, PA; SR; ASB; Acctng.

**MUTISO, ANDREW M,** Ky St Univ, Frankfort, KY; JR; BSC; Westley Fndtn 90-; Camp All Star Capt 90-; Deans Lst 90-; Pres Schlrshp 90-; Cmptr Sci/Math; Cmptr Eng/Sci.

**MUTO, DENA J,** Mount Aloysius Jr Coll, Cresson, PA; FR; BA; Chrldr; Theater; Elem Educ.

**MUTSCHLER, MELINDA J,** Livingston Univ, Livingston, AL; SR; BED; Mrchng/Cncrt Bnd Sctn Ldr 87-; IM Sprts 87-; Spec Ed/Lrng Dsbld; Tch.

**MUTTO, JULIE,** Seton Hall Univ, South Orange, NJ; JR; MIS Scty 90-; Lgn Mary Pres 89-; Prsh Cncl 90-; Beta Gamma Sgm; Dean List 89; HK Home Ec Assc 87-88; Tchr Engl Home Ec Rlgs Stds 88-89; BSMIS; Mgmt Inf Systm; Cmptr Cnsltnt.**

**MUTUA, EDWIN M,** Brevard Coll, Brevard, NC; FR; AA; Phi Theta Kappa VP; Prjct Insde/Out; Bus Mgmt; Hotel Mgmt.

**MUTUBERRIA, RICARDO,** Muskingum Coll, New Concord, OH; JR; BS; Beta Beta Beta 90-; Sigma Xi 90-; Vars Sccr 90-; Bio; Rsrch/Dvlpmtn Appld Bio.

**MUTZFELD, CHRISTE L,** Daytona Beach Comm Coll, Daytona Beach, FL; SO; Sigma Phi Delta Aux 90-; Pltcl Sci; Law.

**MUXO, SUE W,** Fl International Univ, Miami, FL; JR; BA; Yth Karate; S S Tchr; Bilingual Prschl; Cancer Soc; Rotary; Hnr Soc; AA Miami Dade Comm Coll 90; Soc Wrk; Prv Prctc.

**MUZIK, CECILIA B,** Univ Of South Al, Mobile, AL; JR; BA; Deans List 88-; Elem Ed.

**MWAMBA, JAY C K,** City Univ Of Ny City Coll, New York, NY; SR; BA; Jrnlsm 82; Currently Wrtng Papers NY/LONDON/LUSAKA/ZAMBIA; AA Evelyn Hone Clg 81; Engl; Jrnlsm.

**MWAMBA, NOEL M,** City Univ Of Ny Baruch Coll, New York, NY; SO; BBA; Afrcn Stdnts Assoc 89-; Soccer 89-; Cert Natl Inst Pub Admin 86-88; Finance.

**MWAMBA, ROBERT,** City Univ Of Ny Baruch Coll, New York, NY; SO; BBA; Jazz Bnd 90-; Bnd 90-F Deans List; Tutor 90-; Soccer 89-; Acctng.

**MYER, DINA F,** Ms Univ For Women, Columbus, MS; JR; BA; Lntrn Scty 87-90; Kappa Delta Epsilon; Dns Lst 88-; Elem Ed; Tch.

**MYER, GISELE B,** City Univ Of Ny Baruch Coll, New York, NY; SR; BBA; AA Suffolk Cty Comm Clg 83; Oper Mgmt; Mfg.

**MYER, STACY L,** Fl Atlantic Univ, Boca Raton, FL; JR; Hillel Pres; Sntr Stdnt Govt; Amer Mrktng Assoc 88-89; Phi Eta Sigma; Delta Sigma Pi Sec Chncllr 90-; Alpha Epsilon Phi 89-; Alpha Phi Epsilon Rho 90-; AA Univ Of FL 90; Acctg; CPA.

**MYERS, AMBER L,** Fl International Univ, Miami, FL; SR; PSYD; Soclgy/Anthplgy Soc 90-; Phi Lambda 90-; Psi Chi 90-; Phi Kappa Phi; Assoc Behvr Anlsys; Amer Psych Assoc 90-; AA Miami Dade Comm Clg 90; BA; Clncl Psych.

**MYERS, AMY E,** Univ Of Sc At Columbia, Columbia, SC; SR; BA; SGA 89-90; Hnrs Awds Commssn Co-Chr 89-90; Almni Assc 89-; Mrtr Brd Pres 90-; Omicron Delta Kappa 90-; Ordr Omega 90-; Recyclng 90-; Hnrs Assc 88-; Acdmc Plng 88-; Delta Delta Delta Treas 87-; Schl Vol 90-; Dns Lst 87-; Hnrs 87-; S Swanger Awd; BA; Psychlgy; Mgmt.

**MYERS, BENNETT H,** Cornell Univ Statutory College, Ithaca, NY; FR; BS; Lmbd Chi Alph Stwrd; Rgby 90; Bio.

**MYERS, CHAD C,** Southern Coll Of Tech, Marietta, GA; FR; BA; Applied Computer Sci; Programming.

**MYERS, CHRISTINE H,** Johnson St Coll, Johnson, VT; SR; BA; Behavioral Sci Clb Co Pres; Grad Summa Cum Laude; Recpnt Behavioral Sci Dept Awrd; Mensa Intl 86-; Vly Plyrs Theater 83-; Psychology.

**MYERS JR, DANNY J,** Univ Of Charleston, Charleston, WV; JR; BA; Athltc Dept Assist 89-; Alpha Lambda Delta 89-; Pi Gamma Mu 90; Cmptr Info Sys.

**MYERS, DAVID K,** Pellissippi St Tech Comm Coll, Knoxville, TN; SO; BA; Phi Theta Kappa 90-; Bus/Pblc Admin.

**MYERS, DEBORA S,** Univ Of Ky, Lexington, KY; SR; BA; Russian Clb Soc Dir 89; SAB Cinema Cmmttee 89; Hall Govt Sec 89; Phi Beta Kappa; Phi Eta Sigma 87-88; RA Grnt; Russian; Russian Lit Prof.

**MYERS, DONNA MARIE,** S U N Y Coll Of Tech At Frmgdl, Farmingdale, NY; JR; BS; Theatre Apprctn Clb Sec 89; NY Pub Int Rsrch Grp 90; Dns Lst 87-90; Yth Cnslr; Cntrl Aftr Schl Prog; Nutritional Sci.

**MYERS, EDDIE L,** Bishop St Comm Coll, Mobile, AL; SO; BA; Phi Theta Kappa 90-; BSCC Fine Arts Wk Poetry Cntst 90; Short Story Cntst 90; Engl; Author/Edctr.

**MYERS, ELIZABETH,** Univ Of Sc At Columbia, Columbia, SC; SO; BA; Psychlgy.

**MYERS, ELIZABETH K,** Oh Wesleyan Univ, Delaware, OH; FR; BA; Frnds Of Beta Theta Pi Exec Comm 90-; Dns Lst 90-; Secndry Ed/Hstry; Hstry Tchr.

**MYERS, ERIN N,** Oh Univ, Athens, OH; FR; BSCE; Ecology Club; IM Tennis; Chem/Envrnmntl; Engr.

**MYERS, EVE L,** Emory Univ, Atlanta, GA; GD; MN; Sigma Theta Tau 84-; Schlrshp; Amer Nrs Assn 84-; NAPNAP 90-; BSN Duke Univ 84; Chld Hlth Nrsng.

**MYERS, FRANK A,** Trenton St Coll, Trenton, NJ; SR; BSN; Prfssnl Nrsng Orgnztn Of Stdnts Pres 90-; Sigma Theta Tau; Phi Epsilon Kappa VP; IM Sftbl Shrt Stp; Nrsng; Prfssr Ph D Educ Nrsng.**

**MYERS, HAROLD T,** Wagner Coll, Staten Island, NY; SO; BS; Rsdnc Hall Cncl Tres 88-90; Dhist Pol Sci Clb 90-; Guitar Lute Ensmbl 88-; Omcrn Dlt Kappa 90-; Dlt Dlt 90-; Tau Kappa Epsln VP 90-; Acad Schlrshp 88-; IM Sprts 88-; Bus Admn; Bus.

**MYERS, HEATHER L,** Coker Coll, Hartsville, SC; JR; BA; Sprt Com; Tutor; Stdnt Invlvmnt Com; Pi Gamma Theta Sec 90-; IM; Engl Educ/Frnch; Tch.

**MYERS, JEAN C,** Ky St Univ, Frankfort, KY; GD; BA Alice Lloyd Jr Coll 69; Erly Elem Ed; Tchr.

**MYERS, JENNIFER E,** Univ Of Nc At Charlotte, Charlotte, NC; JR; BA; Tchng Fellws Schlr; Alpha Delta Pi Pr 88-; Stdy Abrd London Eng 90; IM; Middle Grds Educ; Tchg.

**MYERS, JOHN D,** Andrew Coll, Cuthbert, GA; FR; Stdnt Govt Sen 90-; Phi Theta Kappa 90-; Omega Tau Lambda 90-; Intrmrls 90-; Sci.

**MYERS, KATHERINE M,** Univ Of Montevallo, Montevallo, AL; JR; BS; Phi Mu 89-90; Spch Pthlgy.

**MYERS, KEVIN D,** Wright St Univ Lake Cmps, Celina, OH; SO; BA; Deans Lst 89; Elctrncs; Eng.

**MYERS, KEVIN E,** Schenectady County Comm Coll, Schenectady, NY; FR; Vica 88-90; Golf; Clnry Arts.

**MYERS, KIM E,** Villanova Univ, Villanova, PA; SO; BS; Spcl Olympcs Fl Fstvl Chr; 24 Hr Dnc Mrthn Evnt Chr; Rsdnt Stu Assoc Dor VP 90-; Prjct Snshn Tutor 89-; SADD Pro Chr 90-; Safe Rides 90-; Bus; Chld Psychlgy Fld.

**MYERS, KIM M,** Saint Francis Coll, Loretto, PA; FR; BS; Physicians Assist Frshmn Rep 90-; Hstrns Of Rnd Tbl 90-; Socratic Clb 90; Med; Physician Assist.

**MYERS, KIMBERLY D,** Radford Univ, Radford, VA; FR; House Cncl Flr Rep; Alpha Lambda Delta; Nom Otstndng Stdnt Awd 90-; IM Tennis 90; Elem Edn; Teach.

**MYERS, LAURIE L,** Indiana Univ Of Pa, Indiana, PA; JR; BS ED; Sgn Lngge Clb 90-; Sgn In Prfrmnce Co Prfrmnce Coor 90-; Tme Ot Chrstn Fllwshp 88-; Phi Eta Sigma 88-; Prvsts Schlr; Ed Of The Hrng Imprd; Tchr.

**MYERS, LISA A,** Stockton St Coll, Pomona, NJ; JR; BJ; EARTH 89-90; Psych Clb; Alpha Epsilon Delta; Psi Chi; Gldn Key; Thrptc Rdng; BJ J Madison Univ 90; Physcl Thrpy.

**MYERS, LISA L,** Va Commonwealth Univ, Richmond, VA; SR; BA; Stdnt Dsgn Show; Cmmnctn Arts/Dsgn; Illustrator.

**MYERS, LORA A,** Univ Of Sc At Columbia, Columbia, SC; SR; BSN; Sigma Theta Tau 90-; All Metro Conf Plyr 90-; Tm Capt 90-; Best Offns Awd 90-; Coachs Awd 89-90; Deans Lst 87-; Full Schlrshp Vlybl Ath Capt 87-; Nrsng; Onclgy Nrsng/Masters.

**MYERS, LORI E,** Tn Temple Univ, Chattanooga, TN; FR; BS; Annl Stff Asst Ed 90-; Chr 90-; Comp; Prgrmmr.

**MYERS, MARK E,** Wv Univ, Morgantown, WV; JR; BA; Gldn Key 90-; Eta Kappa Nu 90-; Asstnt Engnrng Consol Coa Co; Elctrcl Engnrng.

**MYERS, MARY C,** Villanova Univ, Villanova, PA; SR; BS; Kappa Delta Pi 90-; Crew 87-89; Engl; MA.

**MYERS, MICHAEL A,** Marshall University, Huntington, WV; SR; BBA; Bptst Chmps Mnstrs Steerg 87-; Bus Info Syst; Mgmt.

**MYERS, NANCY H,** Fl International Univ, Miami, FL; JR; BA; Deans List Santa Fe Cmnty Clbe 90; Marketing.

**MYERS JR, PATRICK C,** Wv Univ, Morgantown, WV; FR; BS; Mntnr Cncl; Mntnr Wk Strng Comm; Sigma Phi Epsln Rep 90-; IMS; Chem Engr.

**MYERS, PENNY A,** Oh St Univ At Newark, Newark, OH; FR; Campus Stdnt Senate Com Chair 90-; Campus Psychlgy Clb 90-; Hon Soc 90-; Alpha Lambda Delto 90-; Phi Eta Sigma 90-; Jaycees Proj Chrmn 89-; Teach Asst; Notary Publ 89-; New River Personnel Assn 87; Nws Crspndnt Newark Adv; Orgztnl Psychlgy; Human Resources.

**MYERS, RAY P,** Kent St Univ Geauga Cmps, Burton Twp, OH; SO; BS; Pharmacy.

**MYERS, STACI J,** Volunteer St Comm Coll, Gallatin, TN; FR; BA; Excercize Sci.

**MYERS, STEPHANIE P,** Norfolk St Univ, Norfolk, VA; SR; Med Rcrd Admin Clb 88; BS; Med Rcrd Admin.

**MYERS, STEPHEN C,** Oh Univ-Southern Cmps, Ironton, OH; SR; BGS; Aa 89; Bhvrl Sci Comm.

**MYERS, SUSAN BLAIR,** Va Commonwealth Univ, Richmond, VA; SO; BFA; Arts/Jewlry.

**MYERS, TERESA M,** Northern Ky Univ, Highland Hts, KY; SR; BS; Communications Ohio Natl Life Ins Co 77-86; Acctng; CPA.

**MYERS, TERI R,** Neumann Coll, Aston, PA; SO; BA; Profsnl Educ Soc Treas 90-; VIVA Vol Ass Stdnts 90; Yrbk Stf 90; Spec Educ Hrng Imprd; Eductr.

**MYERS, VIRGINIA L,** Miami Jacobs Jr Coll Of Bus, Dayton, OH; FR; AB; Am Lgn Aux Post 675 Dayton OH; Sec/Word Prcsr; Info Sys Mgt; Comp Sys.

**MYERS, VONDA K,** Ashland Comm Coll, Ashland, KY; SO; MBA; Ashland Adlt Lrng Ctr Vol; Psych; Child Psychologist.

**MYINT, MAUNG W,** City Univ Of Ny La Guard Coll, Long Island Cty, NY; SR; MS; Cmptr Clb 89-90; IEEE 89-; Burmese Bdhst Assoc 88-; Intrnshp IBM T J Watson Rsrch Ctr N Y Cmptr Oprtr 89-90; BS Univ Mandalay Burma 85; Cmptr Sci; Systm Anlyst.

**MYLES, MITICHUELL J,** Morehouse Coll, Atlanta, GA; SO; BA; Mrhse Bus Assn 90; Mdl Hmcmng Fshn Shw 90; Mr LA Of LA Clb 90; Hnr Rll 89-; Cnslr Fr Upwrd Bnd Sthrn Univ; Cnslr Fr Bys St 90; Mrktng; Entrprnrshp.

**MYLES, VICTORIA E,** Marywood Coll, Scranton, PA; JR; BFA; Amrcn Scty Intr Dsgnrs 89-; Intr Dsgn Cncl; Deans Lst 90-; Cathers Assoc Inc; Chrldng Capt 90-; Intr Dsgn.**

**MYLIN, LELAND H,** City Univ Of Ny City Coll, New York, NY; JR; BE; Intr Varsty Christn Fellowshp; Natl Engr Hon Soc 90-; Golden Key 90-; Alpha Sigma Lambda 88; Frshmn Hon Soc 86; Deans List Cty Clg Sch Of Gen Stds 87-90; Fellowshp Chapel Brethren In Christ Ch Bd Mbr; Electrncs Techncn 77-; AT 76; Elec Engr.

**MYNATT, KIMBERLY S,** Fl A & M Univ, Tallahassee, FL; FR; BA; Cmptr Infor Sys Clb; Phi Eta Sigma; Arts Sci; Cmptr Infor Sys.

**MYNATT, KRISTOPHER L,** Roane St Comm Coll, Harriman, TN; FR; BS; Criminal Justice; Law.

**MYNATT, SHELLEY V,** Pellissippi St Tech Comm Coll, Knoxville, TN; FR; BS; Central Point Bapt Chrch Chr 88-; Cntrl Point Bapt Chrch Sftbl Tm 90-; Bapt Young Wmn 89-; Dns Lst 90-; Pre Med; Nrsng.

**MYRACLE, ANGELA G,** Memphis St Univ, Memphis, TN; SO; MBA; Pnhlnc Cncl Schlrshp Chr 90-; Gamma Beta Phi; Delta Gamma; Acctng; CPA.

**MYRIAM, CRESPO,** Univ Of Pr At Rio Piedras, Rio Piedras, PR; GD; BA; Us Aikido Fed 90-; Intnl Aikido Fed 90-; Gldn Key 90-; Mcroblgy Asstshp 89-; Biology; Medicine.

**MYRICK, CAROLYN S,** Univ Of Southern Ms, Hattiesburg, MS; JR; BED; Cncl Fr Excptnl Chldrn 90-; Kappa Delta Phi; Spcl Educ; Tchg.

**MYRICK, CHARLOTTE L,** Vance Granville Comm Coll, Henderson, NC; FR; AAS; Acctng; CPA.

**MYRICK, RODNEY J,** Univ Of Tn At Martin, Martin, TN; SR; BS; Sigma Pi Frst Cnslr 88-; Adopt A Schlr; Sghlrshp Prog Sigma Pi Intl Educ Fnd; Intl Schlrshp; Biology; Envrnmntl Sci.

**MYRICK, TERESA D,** Univ Of Southern Ms, Hattiesburg, MS; GD; MBED; NEA 90-; DECA Almna 90-; BED 90; Mktg Ed; Mktg Instrctr.

**MYRICK, TINA N,** Central St Univ, Wilberforce, OH; SO; BA; Roses Plyrs Pres 90-; NABJ 90-; PDV 89-; Deans Lst 90-; Chrldr 90-; Cmnctns; Radio/TV Brdcst.

**MYRICK-PENDARVIS, EMILY ELIZABE,** Univ Of Sc At Columbia, Columbia, SC; SO; BA; CA Cares Commt Chrpsn 90-; CA KIDS Mbrshp Chrmn; Sorority Council Cabnt Head; Nurturing Ctr 90-; Ronald Mc Donald House; Alpha Delta Pi Corrpdng Secty 90; English; Ed.

**MYRICK-PENDARVIS, STEPHANIE S,** Univ Of Sc At Columbia, Columbia, SC; SR; Stdnt Alumni Assn Sec/Treas 89-; Cmps Jdcl Brd 90-; Stdnt Govt 88-90; Assist Stdnt Advcte 88-90; Phi Beta Kappa 89-; Golden Key 89-; Mortar Brd 90-; Mortar Brd 90-; Omicron Delta Kappa 90-; Alpha Delta Pi Pres 87-; Phlsphy/Engl; Law.

**MYRIN, ALARIK F,** Cornell Univ Statutory College, Ithaca, NY; SR; Cvl Air Ptrl Arspc Educ Offcr 89-; Karate 84-; BS; Agrcltrl Ecnmcsf Cttl Rnchr.

**MYRTO, KIMBERLY A,** Niagara Univ, Niagara Univ, NY; SR; BBA; Natl Assn Actnts 89-; Acct Soc Treas 87-; VITA 89-; Alpha Kappa Psi VP 88-; Acctg; Actnt Taxes.

**MYSLIWCZYK, RICHARD J,** Univ Of Pittsburgh, Pittsburgh, PA; SO; Amer Inst Chem Engrs 90-; Clairton Sprtsmn Clb 87-; Univ Schlr 89; Wayne Rawley Schlr 89-; Chem Engr.

**MZWAKHE MSIMANGA, FRANS,** Teikyo Post Univ, Waterbury, CT; JR; BS; S African Clb Tr 88-; Intl Org Exec Mbr 88-; Ldrshp Pgm Asst Dir; Soweta Yth Svcs S Africa Pr 85-88; RA 90-; Shukokai Martial Arts Asst Inst 81-88; AS Teikyo Post Univ 90; Mktg; Mktg Prof.

# N

**NAAMAN, MARWAN G,** Univ Of Miami, Coral Gables, FL; JR; Pre Lgl Scty; Pi Dlt Phi; Dpsi Chi; Sgm Tau Dlt; Alph Sgm Phi Cmnctns Chrmn 89-90; Hosp Vol 88-89; Deans List; Prousts Hon Roll; Engl/Psychlgy; Law/Jrnlsm.

**NABERS, MARION K,** Commonwealth Coll, Virginia Beach, VA; FR; Tstmstrs 90-; Comp Clb 90-; Lillian Vernon 90-; Comp Sci.

**NABESHIMA, KAORU,** Oh Wesleyan Univ, Delaware, OH; FR; BA; Cmps Prog Brd; Hrzn Intl Tres; Far East Stu Pres; Phi Eta Sigma; Ecnmcs.

**NABORS, ALEXANDER J,** Univ Of Al At Birmingham, Birmingham, AL; SO; Fire Dept Vol; EMT; Med RN Medic; Flight Nurse/Medic.

**NABORS, GWENDOLYN A,** Univ Of Nc At Charlotte, Charlotte, NC; JR; BA; Stf Wrtr Asst Featrs Edtr For Etc Mag 90-; Alpha Delta Pi 89-; Otrch 90-; Stf Wrtr Daily Independent Nwspr 90-; Engl/Comms/Frgn Lang; Intl Consult.

**NABUTETE, MARJORIE F,** Bergen Comm Coll, Paramus, NJ; SO; BS; BCC Alumuni; Org Mgmt.

**NACE, RODERICK F,** Ms St Univ, Miss State, MS; FR; BS; Scty Ptrlm Eng; Gamma Beta Phi; AMOCO Prdtcn Co; Ptrlm Eng.

**NACHAZEL, DAVID C,** Univ Of Ky, Lexington, KY; JR; BA; Poli Sci; Ph D/Tch.

**NACHMAN, ELIZABETH S,** Christopher Newport Coll, Newport News, VA; SO; BA; Sigma Tau Delta; Englsh.**

**NACHTIGAL, ALINA,** Univ Of Sc At Columbia, Columbia, SC; SR; Assn Hnr Stdnts 87-90; Phi Beta Kappa 90-; Beta Gamma Sigma 90-; Goldn Key 89-90; Delta Gamma; Coop Educ Merrill Lynch 89-90; Otstdng Clg Stdnts Amer 89-90; Pres Lst 87-90; BA; Mgmt Inf Syst; Syst Anlyst.

**NADEAU, LISA D,** Providence Coll, Providence, RI; SR; BS; Pstrl Cncl Soc Action Com 90-; Double Helix 87-88; Res Bd 87; Pre-Med Hon Soc Pres 89-; Early Identification Brown Med Sch 88-; Rsrch Asstntshp 90-; Bio; Med.

**NADER, FRANCES M,** Univ Of Ga, Athens, GA; SR; BSED; PAGE; Delta Zeta 87; Cm Univ Big Str 90-; I M Vybl Sftbl 87-; Early Chldhd Educ; Tch.

**NADORFF, PAMELA J,** Spalding Univ, Louisville, KY; JR; BS; KY Educ Assn 90-; Delta Epsilon Sigma 90-; Pi Lambda Theta 90-; AA Jefferson Comm Coll 90; Erly Chldhd Educ; Tchng.

**NAFF, ROBYN R,** Univ Of Al At Birmingham, Birmingham, AL; SR; BS; Occptnl Thrpy.

**NAGEL, BRADLEY R,** Defiance Coll, Defiance, OH; SR; BA; Tau Pi Phi 90; Cmpbll Soup Co 85; AAB NW Tchncl Clg 89; Accntng/Fnce; Bnkng.

**NAGEL, DEVIN K,** D Youville Coll, Buffalo, NY; SO; BS; Sngrs 89-; Dns Lst; Pyscl Thrpy.

**NAGEL, JEFFREY D,** S U N Y At Buffalo, Buffalo, NY; JR; BAMBA; Schussmeisters Ski Clb Inc Pub Dir Vice Chrmn 90-; Ski Tm 90-; Golden Key; Greece Rotary Intl; BAMBA 90-; Intrclgte Ski Racing; Mgmt; Mktg.

**NAGEL, JENNIFER J,** Villanova Univ, Villanova, PA; JR; BS; Spec Olympics 90; Proj Sunshine 90-; Habitat For Humanity 90-; Phi Kappa Phi; Pi Mu Epsilon; Math; Statistics.

**NAGEL, MEREDITH C,** Fl St Univ, Tallahassee, FL; SR; BA; Psychlgy; Law.

**NAGLE JR, DAVID W,** Univ Of Louisville, Louisville, KY; FR; ME; Cnmtc Arts Comm 90-; Newman Comm; Aikido Clb 90-; Phi Eta Sigma 90-; Deans List 90-; IMS 90-; Mech Engr; Rsrch.

**NAGLE, JENNIFER L,** Duquesne Univ, Pittsburgh, PA; SO; Orientn Co-Ldr 89-; Alpha Gamma Delta Actvts 90-; Sigma Nu Ltl Sistr 89-; Resdnt Asst; Ed/Hist; Tchng.

**NAGLE, KELLY ANN G,** Siena Coll, Loudonville, NY; SR; BA; Admssns Tour Guide 87-88; Hall Govt Pres 88; Yrbk Acad Ed; Mnstr Of The Altar; Frshmn Orient Ldr 88-89; Intrntl Studies Clb; Wntr Wkend Cmmttee 89; Alpha Kappa Alpha; Vol At Nrsng Hm 87; JCA Admssns Offce Intrn; Womens La Crosse 88; Engl; Lwyr.

**NAGUCKI, ROBERT E,** Univ Of Toledo, Toledo, OH; GD; JD; Knyn Coll Ftbl Capt All Amer Mst Val Plyr 89; Beta Thet Api Knyn Coll Treas; BA Econs Kenyon Coll 90; Law.

**NAGY, CHRISTINE J,** Univ Of Charleston, Charleston, WV; JR; BA; Stdnt Govt Assc Jr Cls Pres 88-; Stdnt Actvts Brd 89-; BACCHUS Pres 89-; Psi Chi Vp 89-; Alpha Lambda Delta 88-; Pi Gamma Mu Sec/Treas 89-; Orntn Tm Coordntr; Liston Awd Fr Dist; Vrsty Bsskbl Tm Cpt 88-; Psychlgy; Fmly Thrpy.

**NAGY, DANIEL A,** Kent St Univ Kent Cmps, Kent, OH; SO; MBA; Hs Cncl Res Hall Tr 90-; Acctg Assn; Hs Cncl Res Hl Flr Rep 90; Im Bsktbl Capt 89-; Acctg.

**NAGY, HAROLD,** Mount Olive Coll, Mount Olive, NC; GD; Bus Mngmnt; Indstrl Mngmnt.

**NAGY, JENNIFER A,** Fl Atlantic Univ, Boca Raton, FL; SO; BS; Mrktng/Interior Dsgn; Advertising.

**NAGY, KAREN S,** Kent St Univ Kent Cmps, Kent, OH; FR; BA; Hs Cncl Flr Repr 90-; Arbcs Clb 90-; Alpha Lambda Delta 90-; Alpha Xi Delta 90-; Dns Lst 90-; Bsn; Acctng.

**NAGY, LYDA KATHERINE,** Univ Of Southern Ms, Hattiesburg, MS; JR; Gldn Ky 90-; Gamma Beta Phi; Ins Wmn Of Hattiesbrg Pres 79-85; Hattiesbrg Ins Wmn Of Yr 82-83; Ins Adjstrs 79-90; BS; Elem Educ; Tchr.

**NAGY, TRACY C,** Comm Coll Algny Co Algny Cmps, Pittsburgh, PA; FR; Phi Theta Kappa; Word Proc Oper/Secr; Nrsg; Anesthetist.

**NAH, JANICE U,** George Mason Univ, Fairfax, VA; JR; BS; Korean Chrstn Fllwshp 90-; Accntng Clb; Gldn Key Ntnl; Bsns; Accntng.

**NAHABEDIAN, DONNA L,** Univ Of Tn At Martin, Martin, TN; JR; BS; Phi Chi Theta 90-; Deans Lst 90; Legal Secy 85-88; Cert Retter Bus Clg 85; Mngmnt.

**NAHHAS, RAMZI W,** Oh St Univ, Columbus, OH; SR; BS; New Life Bible Stds 88-; Math Asc Amer 89-90; Phi Kappa Phi; Pi Mu Epsln; Ultmt Frsbee Clb 89; Math.

**NAHMIAS, MORDECHAI MOTTY,** Univ Of New Haven, West Haven, CT; JR; ISA; Clnry Clb; Htl Rstrnt Mgmt.

**NAIK, RAKSHA R,** Univ Of Med & Dentistry Of Nj, Newark, NJ; GD; CERT; BS India 80; Lbrtry Science; Med Tech.

**NAIL, DEBRA L,** Eckerd Coll, St Petersburg, FL; JR; BS; Dorm Pres 89-; Blgy Clb Evnts Chrprsn 88-; Earth Soc Cmps Eclgy 90-; Ford Apprntc Schlrshp Pgm 90-; Wrtng Excllncy Awd; Vrsty Tnns 88-; Marine Sci-Blgy; Ntrl Rsrc Mgmt.

**NAIL, EILEEN A,** Memphis Academy Of The Arts, Memphis, TN; SO; BFA; Art.

**NAILS, STEPHANIE R,** Lincoln Memorial Univ, Harrogate, TN; JR; BSBA; Stu Govt Assn Attrny Gen 88-; Stu Nws Rprt Tm 88-90; Pres Ambssdrs Cncl 88-89; Kappa Pi Omega 89-; TN Leg Intern; Intern WREG 3 Nws; Nws Anchr Rpprt 89-; Vrsty Tnns 88-89; Vrsty Chrldr Bsktbl 88-89; Brdcst Cmmncnts/Engl; Law.**

**NAIM, YOUSSEF M,** Temple Univ, Philadelphia, PA; GD; MS; Gold Key 87-90; Pres Schlr 90; 1st Hon Awd 90; Teach Asstntshp 90-; BS 90; Mech Eng.

**NAIMEY, DARLEEN ANN,** Western New England Coll, Springfield, MA; SR; BA; Psi Chi; Crisis Serv; Psychology; Grad Sch/Neuroscience.

**NAING, ANDREW,** Cornell Univ Statutory College, Ithaca, NY; JR; BA; Cornell Univ EMS 88-89; Cornell Chinese Bible Stdy Games Coordntr 89-; Cornell Chinese Bible Stdy Choir 89-; Golden Key 90-; Deans List 6 Semstrs 88-; Biochem Tchng Asst; PEW Fndtn Summer Rsrch Prog; Im Vlybl 90; Biolgcl Scis; Medcl Sch.

**NAING, GRACE,** Cornell Univ Statutory College, Ithaca, NY; SO; BS; Peer Counseling 89-90; Rsrch Asst; Blgcl Sci; Medicine.

**NAIR, CHARLOTT,** Roane St Comm Coll, Harriman, TN; FR.

**NAIR, SUSAN C,** Kent St Univ Kent Cmps, Kent, OH; FR; BA; Bus; Mrktg.

**NAISANG, JUDITH L,** East Carolina Univ, Greenville, NC; SR; Music Ed Natl Cnvntn 86-87; Amer Chrl Drctrs Assc Pres-Sec 85-; Hspc 89-; Msc Thrpy Clb Stdnts Sec-Treas 86-90; Sigma Alpha Fota Msc Drctr 86-; BMED 90; Musc; Perfmnc Voice.

**NAITO, MEGUMI,** Ny Univ, New York, NY; SR; BA; Alpha Sigma Lambda 90-; Psych.

**NAJAFZADEH, HALEH,** Hudson Valley Comm Coll, Troy, NY; FR; Cert Labor Dept Iran 87; Bio; Phrmcy.

**NAJDA, CHRISTOPHER R,** Allegheny Coll, Meadville, PA; SR; BS; Econs Clb 89; Alden Schlr 89-90; IM Golf 87-; Econs; Mktg.

**NAKAGAMI, KYOKO,** Univ Of Nc At Charlotte, Charlotte, NC; JR; BCA; Arts; Artst/Grphc Dsgnr.

**NAKAHARA, MARI,** Miami Dade Comm Coll, Miami, FL; SO; Outstndng Intl Stdnt 88-89.**

**NAKAMURA, KAZUYO,** Univ Of New Haven, West Haven, CT; JR; BS; Phi Eta Sigma 88-89; Alph Lambda Delta; Deans List 88-; Mrktng.

**NAKANO, HIROE,** Duquesne Univ, Pittsburgh, PA; Obirin Step ESS Japan 89-90; Julia Tennis Tm Meiji Univ In Japan 89-90; Intl Bus.

**NAKANO, MISAKI,** Oh Dominican Coll, Columbus, OH; FR; Art.

**NAKANO, YOSHIKO,** Ky Mountain Bible Coll, Vancleve, KY; SO; BA; Yrbk 89-; Yth Tmprnc Cncl 90-; Sngng Grp 90-; Chr 89-; Chrch Pnst S S Tchr 90-; Rlgn Music; Chrstn Wrkr Tchr.

**NAKATSU, YUKO,** Andrew Coll, Cuthbert, GA; FR; AA; E/W Fndtn 90-; Deans Lst 90; Bdmntn Trnmnt.

**NAKHOUL, NABIL,** Merrimack Coll, North Andover, MA; SR; BA; Assoc North Shore Cmnty Clg 88; Mktg.

**NAKONECHNY, WALTER S,** Univ Of Ct, Storrs, CT; JR; BS; Gldn Key; East Of The Rvr Bsbl Tour Trnmnt Asst Coach 90; Hartford Twilight League Bsbl 90-; NJCAA All Starm Tm 89; Annual Avery Point Awd; Outstdng Schlstc/Ldrshp Cert; UCONN Avery Pt Bsbl 88-90; UCONN Bsbl Tm Vrsty 90-; Nat Rsrcs/Biology; Prof/Rsrch.

**NALBACH, CHARLES D,** Kent St Univ Kent Cmps, Kent, OH; SR; BBA; Co-Op Intern TRW 90; ROTC 89-; AAS Cmnty Clg Of The Air Force 87; Cmptr Sci; Air Force Cmsnd Officer.

**NALBONE, LESLIE J,** Allegheny Coll, Meadville, PA; JR; BS; Chrldng Capt 89-; Orchesis; Alden Schlr; Alpha Chi Omega; Economics.

**NALBONE, SHERRY,** Northeast State Tech Comm Coll, Blountville, TN; GD; Am Design & Drftng Assn Treas 90-; Phi Theta Kappa V P 90-; Tx Bd Of Rltrs 87-; AAS; Drftng Design Tech.

**NALEPINSKI, KATHLEEN M,** Commonwealth Coll, Virginia Beach, VA; FR; EDA; Pres List 90-; Acctng/Sec Skills; Banking.

**NALEWAJEK, JOEL,** Univ Of Nh Plymouth St Coll, Plymouth, NH; JR; BS; MENC Sec/Treas 88-; Symphnc Bnd 88-; Jazz Ensmbl 88-; Chmbr Wnds 88-; Chorale 88-; Music Educ.

**NALLEY, LENORA H,** Saint Catharine Coll, St Catharine, KY; FR; New Bus Ownr Tanning Unlimited Bardstown KY; Bus.

**NALLS, IDA D,** Central St Univ, Wilberforce, OH; JR; BSE; Stdnt Cncl Excptnl Chldrn P 90-; Camp Fire Cncl Instr 88-90; Ntl Hon Soc Edctr; Sigma Gamma Rho P 78-79; Camp Fire Cncl Dayton 87-89; Dayton Schl Comm Vlntr 87-; Cert Ntl Inst Tech 83; Spec Ed; Prvd Erly Inrntn Svcs Chldrn.

**NALLS, SABRINA ELEASE,** Ms St Univ, Miss State, MS; JR; BA; Mktg.

**NAM, JOO H,** Ramapo Coll Of Nj, Mahwah, NJ; SO; BS; Intl Stdnts Org; Acctg.

**NAMBIAR, PRITA C,** Fl International Univ, Miami, FL; JR; BBA; BA Hnrs Univ Delhi New Delhi India 89; Mgmt Inf Sys.

**NAMIAS, KIMBERLY D,** Dowling Coll, Oakdale Li, NY; SR; BSPLS; Kappa Delta Pi Chmn; Elem Edn; Tchr.

**NANCE, ANDREA F,** Marshall University, Huntington, WV; SO; BBA; Spch Tm 88-90; Mktg; Advtsng.

**NANCE, ANGELA R,** Saint Catharine Coll, St Catharine, KY; SO; Phi Theta Kappa 90-; Yth Choir Dir Accmpnst Yth Grp Coord; Bus; Acctg.

**NANCE, CRAIG E,** Fl St Univ, Tallahassee, FL; SR; BS; IEEE 89-; EARS Cofndr E Wk Rep 90-; N E Fla Astrnml Soc Bd Dir 87-; Eng Honr Soc 90-; AA Fla Comm Jacksnvl 88; Elec Eng; Electromgntc.

**NANCE, DAVID K,** Univ Of Al At Birmingham, Birmingham, AL; EMT P; Emer Med Tech; Fire Fghtr.

**NANCE, DENISE L,** Oh Univ-Southern Cmps, Ironton, OH; FR; BS; Dns Lst; IM; Hrng/Speech; Spch Pthlgst.

**NANCE, JANICE E,** Univ Of The Dist Of Columbia, Washington, DC; JR; BA; Yng Adlts Actv Mmbr 88-; Delta Sigma Theta Sec 88-90; Otstndng Grd 90-; Financial Adtr Offc DC Adtr DC Gvrnmnt 89-; BA Unv Maryland 82; Accngnt.

**NANCE, MAGGIE C,** Univ Of Nc At Greensboro, Greensboro, NC; SR; BS; SCNAE 89-90; Eta Phi Beta Sorority Sec 87-; NC Hdstrt Assn Mem Dev Cntr High Point NC Sec 89-; NAACP 89-; Plng To Entr Grad Schl Fall 91; Elem Educ.

**NANCE, RACHEL B,** Winthrop Coll, Rock Hill, SC; JR; BME; Music Educ Natl Conf 88-; Rock Hill Chmbr Orch 90; Winthrop Symphnc Bnd 88-; Delta Omicron VP 89-; Kappa Delta Pi; Chi Omega Sec 89-; Wesley Fndtn 89-; Intl YMCA Coll Ambsdr To Israel Winthrop Panhellenic Wmn Of Yr; Music Educ; Admin.

**NANGLE, JENNIFER E,** Providence Coll, Providence, RI; FR; BA; Ski Clb 90-; Pol Sci; Law.

**NANGLE, KEVIN M,** Temple Univ, Philadelphia, PA; FR; BS; Temple Un Diamond Mrchng Bnd 88-90; Temple Univ Clgt Bnd 89-90; Elec Eng Technlgy; Audio Eng.

**NANNEY, PHILIP W,** Univ Of Tn At Martin, Martin, TN; SR; BS; Tri-Beta 89-; Phi Eta Sigma 89-; Ordr Omega 89-; Phi Kappa Phi 90-; Kappa Alpha Pres 90-; Univ Schlr 88-; Biolgy; Med.

**NANNI, MARY BETH,** Indiana Univ Of Pa, Indiana, PA; SR; BS; Elem Edctn; Tchr.

**NANNI, TRACI L,** Bloomfield Coll, Bloomfield, NJ; JR; BS; Alpha Chi; Dns Lst 90; Dns Lst Hi Hons 90; IM Ftbl Capt 86-88; Psych/Biol; Med Sch/Physcn.

**NANTON, MARK R,** Howard Univ, Washington, DC; JR; BA; AIAS 90-; AFS Intercltrl Pgms Cnslr 89-90; Tomln Voss Arch 86-87; Govt St Vincnt Mnstry Wks Eng Div 87-90; Dipl Humber Clg 86; Arch.

**NAPIER, ANGELA J,** Middle Tn St Univ, Murfreesboro, TN; SO; BED; Bptst Stu Un 90-; Fllwshp Chrstn Athlts 90-; Elem Educ.

**NAPIER II, BENNETT E,** Univ Of Nc At Charlotte, Charlotte, NC; SR; Amer Pol Sci Assn 89-; Southern Pol Sci Assn 89-; Natl Eagle Sct Assn 87-; Coll Schlrs Amer 90-; Prog Asst Pres Clssrn 90; Cngrssnl Intern Howard Coble 90f; BA; Pol Sci/Sclgy; Law/PHD Govt.

**NAPIER, CHRISTI L,** Univ Of Charleston, Charleston, WV; FR; BSN; Nrsng; Nrse Ansthtst.

**NAPIER, JAMES ALLEN,** Pittsburgh Tech Inst, Pittsburgh, PA; FR; AST; Cmptr Draft; Cmptr Sys Mgr.

**NAPIER, JULENA D,** Ashland Comm Coll, Ashland, KY; SO; BSC; Home Econ; Clncl Dietetcian.

**NAPIER, MIRANDA G,** Ashland Comm Coll, Ashland, KY; SO; Elem Ed-Tchr.

**NAPIER, STANLEY,** Lexington Comm Coll, Lexington, KY; JR; BA; Archtctrl Tchnlgy; Bldg Cds Enfrcmnt.

**NAPIORSKI, CATHY A,** Univ Of Med & Dentistry Of Nj, Newark, NJ; GD; Orientation Asstnt 89; Ski Club 87; Cert Of Acadmc Exclnc 90; Amercn Soc For Medcl Technlgy 89-; Medcl Technlgst 90; MT Amercn Soc Of Clincl Pathlgsts 90; CLS Natl Cert Agncy For Medcl Alb Prsnl 90.

**NAPLES, ANNA HART,** Mount Olive Coll, Mount Olive, NC; SR; BS; Natl Bus Wmn Amer; Actnt CPA Firm; Acctg; CPA.

**NAPLES, DAVID A,** Germanna Comm Coll, Locust Grove, VA; FR; PH D; Govt V P 90-; Nwspr Asst Edtr/Wrtr/Bus Mgr/Typstr 90; Physics/Astronomyf Sci Rsrch/Tch.

**NAPOLES, LUIS,** Fl International Univ, Miami, FL; SR; BHSA; Comm Coll Trnsfr Schlrshp Recpnt; AA Miami Dade Comm Coll 87; Hlth Svs Admin; Pbl Hlth Edctr.

**NAPOLES, ZENAIDA,** Miami Dade Comm Coll South, Miami, FL; SO; RPH; U S Army Rsrv Prvt Frst Cls 87-; Miami Dade Comm Clg Trnsfr Schlrshp 88-89; Deans List 88; AA; Pharm; Dr.

**NAPOLI, DENISE A,** Georgian Court Coll, Lakewood, NJ; FR; BA; Psychlgy Club 90-; Psychlgy/Elem Educ; Chld Psychlgst.

**NAPOLI, STEPHANIE A,** Western New England Coll, Springfield, MA; SO; BS; Hlpng Hnds Soc 90-; Stdnt Tchng Asst; Fin Mgmt Clb; Fin; Fin Mgmt.

**NAPOLI, SUSAN S,** S U N Y Coll Of Tech At Frmgdl, Farmingdale, NY; LPN 76; Nrsng.

**NAPPER, PAUL D,** The Kings Coll, Briarclf Mnr, NY; FR; BS; IM Bsktbl/Ftbl 90-; Pres Schlp; Acct; CPA.

**NAPULI, CHONA O,** Univ Of Fl, Gainesville, FL; GD; PHARM; Acad Stdnt Pharmcy 87-; Clg Phrmcy Stdnt Gov Clb 89-90; Natrl Sci Cncl 86-87; Kappa Epsilon Stdnt Cncl Rep 87-; AA Univ So Fla 87; Sundown Vitmns Schlrshp Awrd 88; Intrnshp Walgreens Phrmcy 90; Clin Pharm Res.

**NAQUI, IMRAN H,** D Youville Coll, Buffalo, NY; JR; BA; Stdnt Govt Sen 88-; Delta Kappa 88-; DYCNAA 90-; Dns Lst 88-; Acctntng.

**NARAGON, MOLLY L,** Tn Temple Univ, Chattanooga, TN; FR; Athletic Dir Flr 90; Stdnt Msns Fwlshp 90; Vybl 90; Math; Sec Educ.

**NARANG, JOHN M,** Univ Of Sc At Columbia, Columbia, SC; FR; BA; Alpha Tau Omega Bro 90-; Carolina Chldrns Home Visits 90-; Top Rep Trophy; Vector Mktg Firm; Golf 86-90; IM 90-; Bus Admin; Law.

**NARASIMHAN, AJIT,** Oh Wesleyan Univ, Delaware, OH; JR; BA; WCSA Stdnt Govt Geographic Repr 89-90; Hall Gvrng Prgrmmg Brd Supv; Academic Affairs Comm 90-; AD HOC; Fclty Schlr; Omicron Delta Kappa; Mortar Brd; Pi Mu Epsilon; Omicron Delta Epsilon; Deans Lst; IM Tnns Rcktbl; Acctng Math Econ Mngmnt; Finance Acctng.

**NARAYANAPPA, ARUNDATHI P,** Univ Of Ky, Lexington, KY; JR; BS; Clgns For Acadmc Exelnc 88-; Actvts Bd 88-; Phi Eta Sigma 90-; Lances 90-; Mortar Bd VP; Alpha Epsilon Delta 90-; Delta Delta Delta Treas 88-; Pres Schlrshp 88; Bio; Medcn.

**NARCISO, MORALES MONTALVO,** Univ Politecnica De Pr, Hato Rey, PR; FR; BA; Catholic Church Chorus 87-88; Hnr Lst Polytechnic Univ P R 90-; BA; Eng; Electric.

**NARDELLI, BRENDA M,** Univ Of Med & Dentistry Of Nj, Newark, NJ; SR; Lambda Alpha Sigma 89; Cert Acad Dstnctn 87-; BS Kean Clg 87-; Cert Physcl Thrpy 89-; Physcl Thrpy.

**NARDI, MARIA I,** Univ Of Miami, Coral Gables, FL; SR; BA; Archtctr; MA Lndscp Archtctr.

**NARDONE, CYNTHIA L,** Marywood Coll, Scranton, PA; SR; BFA; ASID Sec 87-; Interior Dsgn; Dsgnr.

**NARDONE, VINCENT J,** Duquesne Univ, Pittsburgh, PA; JR; BA; Pre-Law Soc 90-; Mktg Frat; Alpha Tau Omega 88-; Ftbl; Mktg; Law.

**NAREMORE, TINA M,** Livingston Univ, Livingston, AL; SR; BA; Envoys 90-; Clg Nwspr Edtr 88-90; Univ Press Asst Dir 90-; Omicron Delta Kappa Pres; Sigma Tau Delta V P 88-; Alpha Chi 90-; Alpha Sigma Tau Pres 88; Summer Orntatn Ldrl; Jrnlsm Awd; Intrnshp Western Star Nwspr 89; GPA Yr; I M; English; Jrnlsm.

**NARENTHIRAN, NADESAN,** Ms St Univ, Miss State, MS; SO; BS; Gamma Beta Phi; Prsdnts Schlr; Dept Schlrshp; Elec Eng.

**NARESE, NICOLE,** Saint Peters Coll, Jersey City, NJ; FR; BA; Schl Nwspr Writer; Soup Kitchen 90-; Kappa Alpha Alpha 90-; Pol Sci/Engl; Public Rel/Law.

**NARIANI, MAHESH G,** City Univ Of Ny La Guard Coll, Long Island City, NY; SR; AAS; Deans List; Intrn Gen Elec; Acctng; CPA.

**NAROTHAM, ANUPAMA,** Columbus Coll Of Art & Design, Columbus, OH; JR; BFA; Repr Body Clg/Fine Arts India 89-90; Pres List 90-; Prctcl Trng 88-89; Diploma 88-89; Int Dsn; Art Therapy.

**NARTEY, DESMOND A,** City Univ Of Ny City Coll, New York, NY; JR; BAMA; Ghandaian Stdnts Assn Pblc Rltns Offcr; Econ; Law/Finance.

**NARTKER, SUE A,** Defiance Coll, Defiance, OH; SR; BS; AS Cmptr Sci Northwest Tech Clge 86; Bsn Admin.

**NARVAEZ, CARMEN L,** Univ Of Pr At Mayaguez, Mayaguez, PR; SO; Natl Hon Soc Treas 88-89; Math; Indstrl Engr.**

**NARY, SEAN J,** Castleton St Coll, Castleton, VT; SR; BA; Karate Clb 89-; Crim Just Clb Sec 89-; Chorale Grp Strng Ensmbl 89-; IM Sftbl 89; Intrnshp Woodside Juvnl Corctn 90-; Crim Just/Psychlgy; Juv Just.

**NASCIMENTO, ADRIANA F,** S U N Y At Buffalo, Buffalo, NY; JR; BSEE; IEEE; Soc Wmn Eng; Eta Kappa Nu Rec Sec; Tau Beta Pi Coor Sec; Gldn Ky; Motorola Inc Intern; Cmputel Comp S Amer Inter 88; Elect Eng; Mngmnt.

**NASH, BRENDA R,** Univ Of Al At Birmingham, Birmingham, AL; SR; Natl Hnr Soc 87-; Kappa Delta Pi 89-; Phi Theta Kappa 87-; Outstndng Undrgrdte Elem Ed 90-; AS Snead St Jr Clge 89; BS; Ed.

**NASH, CHRISTIE L,** Germanna Comm Coll, Locust Grove, VA; GD; Spanish Clb Pblcty/Sec 88-90; Mu Phi Epsilon Tres 86-90; Kappa Delta Pie 89-90; Mary Washington Coll Comm Orch 85-; BA Mary Washington Coll 90; Music/Business; Secretary/Music Teacher.

**NASH, CHRISTIE M,** Univ Of Tn At Martin, Martin, TN; SO; BS; Bptst Stu Unn 89-; Phi Eta Sigma; Mu Epsilon Delta 90-; Hnrs Smnr Schlrshp 89-; Dean Lst 89; Biol; Med.

**NASH, DAVID E,** Barry Univ, Miami, FL; GD; MSOB; Fndr/Exec Natl Assn Shftwrk Help; Masters; Cnsltnt Chrnblgcl Applctns; ASCE Marion Tech Coll 80; ASIE 81; Orgnztnl Bhvr; Ind Cnsltnt.

**NASH, GLENN I,** East Tn St Univ, Johnson City, TN; SR; BS; Scabbard/Blace 89-90; Amtr Radio Clb 90; Epsilon Pi Tau 89-90; Elctrncs Eng Tchnlgy; Tchng.

**NASH, GOLDIE A,** Cuyahoga Comm Coll, Cleveland, OH; SR; BA; Phi Theta Kappa; Tlnt Rstr Crtfct Achvmnt; Crtfct Prfcncy; Bsns; Admnstrtn.

**NASH, GWENDOLEN D,** Southern Coll Of Tech, Marietta, GA; SO; BS; Hl Govt 89-90; Cmptr Sci.

**NASH, JENNIFER A,** Duke Univ, Durham, NC; FR; BA; Chpl Choir 90-; Delta Gamma; Pblc Plcy; Law.

**NASH, JUDY D,** Univ Of Sc At Columbia, Columbia, SC; GD; BA; Key Acct Mgr 83-; AS Midlands Tech Coll 83; Intrdscplnry Stdies/Bus.

**NASH, MICHELLE DIANE,** Longwood Coll, Farmville, VA; JR; BS; Camerata Sngrs Lncr Edtn Show Chr Sec 89-; Cncrt Chr; Eqstrn Tm 89-; IM Dsprts Pgm Stdnt Accmpnst 89-; Phi Kappa Phi 89-; Pi Mu Epsln 89-; Geist Honry Elizabeth Burger Johnson Awrd Schlrshp; IMS Riding Tm 90; Math Cncntrtn Comp Sci; Actuary.

**NASH, MILTON H,** Univ Of Al At Birmingham, Birmingham, AL; FR; S; Alpha Lambda Delta; Math/Lngstcs.

**NASH, NATHANIEL R,** Brevard Coll, Brevard, NC; FR; BA; Jzz Ensmble 90-; Gtr Ensmble; Phi Theta Kappa; Msc Prfrmnce; Clsscl Gtrst.

**NASH, SARAH C,** Hampton Univ, Hampton, VA; FR; BA; Hmptn Univ Chr 90-; Hmptn Univ Gspl Chr 90-; Hnr Stdnt In Hnrs Dorm 90-; Math.

**NASH, SHERRIE M,** Wilmington Coll, New Castle, DE; SO; BS; Acctg; CPA.

**NASH, TOYIA G,** Clark Atlanta Univ, Atlanta, GA; SR; BA; PRSSA Treas 90-; Nwspr Contr Wrtr 90; NCBC 90; Rchstr Assoc Blck Comm 90-; Assoc Arts Monroe Comm Clg 89; Publ Rels; Corp Comms.**

**NASH, TROY L,** Wilmington Coll, New Castle, DE; JR; BS; US Ar Frc; Acctg; Law Schl.

**NASON, KEITH,** Nc Agri & Tech St Univ, Greensboro, NC; JR; BA; Alpha Phi Alpha; Acctg.**

**NASSER, JANICE,** Fl International Univ, Miami, FL; SR; BA; Phi Kappa Phi; Elem Ed; Tchng.

**NASSIF, GEORGIA R,** Univ Of Nc At Charlotte, Charlotte, NC; JR; BS; East Carolina Stdnt Un Com Spcl Evnts 88-89; Scott Hall Cncl Suite Rep 89-90; Pres Cncl 90; Gamma Beta Phi 88-89; Orientation Cnslr SOAR; Res Advsr Sanford Hall; Hon Roll 88-89; Deans Lst 90; Pol Sci; Bus Mgmnt.

**NAST, DAVID B,** Villanova Univ, Villanova, PA; SO; BA; Image Bible Study Fndg Mbr; New Directions Msc Grp/Bnd Ld Sngr/Guitrst Fndg Mbr 86-; Gen Arts; Law/Msc-Cmpsr/Sngr/Sngwrtr.

**NASWORTHY, ELAINE L,** Hillsborough Comm Coll, Tampa, FL; SO; AA; Sunday Schl Tchr; Tchr Bell Shoals Baptist Acad; Elem Tchr.

**NATAL, CELSO L,** Univ Politecnica De Pr, Hato Rey, PR; FR; BS; Engr/Elctrcl.

**NATAL, JESSICA GONZALEZ,** City Univ Of Ny Bronx Comm Col, Bronx, NY; SO; BA; NYS Soc CPA Awrd; Dean Lst 89-; Accntng; CPA.

**NATALE, NICHOLAS A,** North Greenville Coll, Tigerville, SC; SO; BA; BSU 89-; FCA 89-; Stdnt Life Comm 90-; Religion; Air Force Chaplin.

**NATALI, SUSAN M,** Villanova Univ, Villanova, PA; SR; BS; Vllnvns Peace; Deans Lst 90-; Blgy; Cnsrvtn/Sustnbl Dvlpmnt.

**NATALIE, JOHN S,** Schenectady County Comm Coll, Schenectady, NY; FR; AS; Math/Sci/Librl Arts; Tchng/Engr.

**NATALINI, MICHELE MARIE,** City Univ Of Ny Baruch Coll, New York, NY; SR; BBA; Mgt.**

**NATARAJAN, S,** Gallaudet Univ, Washington, DC; SO; BS; Duke Undrgrdte Fllwshp NC NSF/ERC; Indian Overseas Bnk Asst Offcr 76-88; Eng Tchnlgy.

**NATARELLI, BETH E,** Seton Hall Univ, South Orange, NJ; SR; BED; Ski Club Sec 89; Kappa Delta Pi 89-; Unvrsty Grnt 89-90; Good Stdnt Schlrshp 88; Magna Cum Laude; Elem Edctn Englsh; Tchr.

**NATER NATER, MARGARITA C,** Inter Amer Univ Pr Hato Rey, Hato Rey, PR; FR; Cert De Grad De Acdmc De Guitarra 89; Ana B Del Valle Grdt Cert Guitar Acdmy Ana B Del Valle; Hnr Pgm 90-; Bsn Admin; Mrchnds.

**NATH, KRISTY M,** Univ Of Cincinnati-Clrmnt Coll, Batavia, OH; FR; BA; Bus; Mgmt.

**NATHAN, CHITRA,** Allegheny Coll, Meadville, PA; JR; BS; Envrnmntl Awrns 88; Intl Clb Pub Rltns Rep 90-; Alden Schlr 90; Hosp Vol 88-; Allegheny Sesquicentennial Humntrn Schlrshp 88-; Biology; Med.

**NATHAN, COURTNEY,** Univ Of Ky, Lexington, KY; JR; BA; Psi Chi; AIDS Vol Lexington; Phi Eta Sigma 89-; Psi Chi 90-; Kappa Kappa Gamma 88-; Frshmn Eng Cmp Awd 88-89; IMS 88-; Psychlgy; Soc Wrk/Law.

**NATHAN, JANET S,** Colby Sawyer Coll, New London, NH; SR; BS; Stdnt Alumni Assn Treas 88-; Choices; Early Chldhd Clb VP 90-; Yrbk 90; Key Assn 88-; Stdnt Acad Cnslr 90; Stdnt Tchng; Chld Stdy; Tchng.

**NATHAN, TIMOTHY E,** Al A & M Univ, Normal, AL; SO; BED; Art Clb Treas 90-; Gospel Choir Chpln 90-; Kappa Delta Pi; Art Edn; Tchr.

**NATION, ADAM P,** Duquesne Univ, Pittsburgh, PA; GD; PHD; Phlsphy Clb VP 89-; Tchg Asst Logic 90; Tchg Asst Aesthetics Crng Mln Univ Pgh Pa; BA 87; Phlsphy; Tchg.

**NATION, HEATHER L M,** Fl International Univ, Miami, FL; SR; Barry Univ Cmptr Clb Sec 87-88; DPMA 90-; Natl Assn Fml Exec 89-; Pres Lst 87-88; Dean Lst 88-; BBA; Mngmnt Infrmtn Sys.

**NATIONS, DONNA J,** Ms St Univ, Miss State, MS; SR; BA; Sigma Alpha Epsilon V P 87-; Deans Schol 88-; Pres Schol 90-; Mu Kappa Tau; Phi Eta Sigma 90-; Chi Omega Actv Chmn 90; Very Specl Arts/Ms; Sls Rep Intern/Amagi-Nations Inc 90; Mrktg; Advtsg.

**NATIONS, JANET M,** Truett Mc Connell Coll, Cleveland, GA; FR; Phi Thetta Kappa 90-; Bsn; Acctng.

**NATIVIDAD, BRIDGET M,** Hillsborough Comm Coll, Tampa, FL; SO; Bus; CPA.

**NATIVIO-BOTTOMLY, RENEE,** Central Fl Comm Coll, Ocala, FL; FR; Campus Dplmt; Phi Theta Kappa; Phi Beta Lambda VP; Bus/Acctg; Bus Ownr.

**NATOLE, VICKY L,** Oh Univ-Southern Cmps, Ironton, OH; SR; BED; Phi Kappa Phi; Gamma Pi Delta 90-; Jr League 85-89; Deans List 90-; Deans List St Univ Of NY Oneonta 84; Paramount Arts Womens Assoc; KY Highland Museum Soc Ladies Of The Mnr 90-; AAS Univ Of KY 79; Elem Ed; Tchng.

**NATTILINE DUNSTAN, CHERYL-ANN,** Barry Univ, Miami, FL; FR; BS; Jamaicn Assn Tr 90-; Camps Mnstry Lectr 90-; Chrstn Mnstry; Beta Beta Beta Fr Yr 90-; Bio; Dentistry.

**NAUGHTON, JENNIFER A,** James Madison University, Harrisonburg, VA; BS; Cleveland Hll Intr Hll Cncl VP 89-; Psychlgy Dept Stdt Advsry Comm 89-; DJ WXJM Stdt Run Radio Stat 89-; Editing Stf Chrysalis Art/Literary Mag 89-; Psych Clb 89-; Univ Prog Brd Flm Crw 89-; Psi Chi 89-; Deans/Pres List; Psychology/English Minor.

**NAUGLE, AMY M,** Radford Univ, Radford, VA; SO; BS; Jrnlsm; Nwspaper Jrnlst.

**NAULT, CHRISTINE M,** Saint Josephs Coll, Windham, ME; JR; BS; Stdnt Govt Exec Bd 90-; Interhall Cncl Dir 90-; Hall Cncl Pres 89-; Folk Grp Pres 88-89; Stdnt Alumni Assn Pres 88-; Collegiate Awd 88-; All Amer Schlrd 88-89; Elem Educ; Tchr.

**NAUMAN, ERIC A,** Univ Of De, Newark, DE; FR; ME; Hmlss Shltr 90-; Frshmn Schlrhsp Eng Almn Assoc; Mech Eng; Eng.

**NAUMANN, MICHELE A,** Anne Arundel Comm Coll, Arnold, MD; SO; BA; Vol Marley Elem Schl 89-90; AA; Gnrl Studies.

**NAVARRE, LENELL Q,** Jackson St Univ, Jackson, MS; FR; BA; Ftbl 90-91; Mathmtcs; Acctg.

**NAVARRO COLON, ZORILUZ,** Inter Amer Univ Pr Hato Rey, Hato Rey, PR; SO; Church Activities Young Catholic Group; San Juan Bautista Awd 89; Interamerican Univ Of PR Hnr Soc 90-; Commonity Group Q Womon Prinz; Commerce; Manager.

**NAVARRO ROMERO, MARIBEL,** Univ Of Pr At Rio Piedras, Rio Piedras, PR; SR; BBA; Amer Mktg Assn; Golden Key; Natl Collegiate Of Bus; USAA All Amer Schlrs; Bus Admin; Quantitative Mthds.

**NAVARRO, GLADYS C,** Georgetown Univ, Washington, DC; FR; BS; Puerto Rican Clb 90-; Lctr Fnd; Frst Hnrs Deans Lst 90-; Bsns Admnstrtn.

**NAVARRO, HECTOR O,** Univ Politecnica De Pr, Hato Rey, PR; FR; Natl Jr Hon Soc 86-88; Pres Acdmc Ftnss Awd 87.

**NAVARRO, JENNIFER L,** Bunker Hill Comm Coll, Boston, MA; FR.

**NAVARRO, JOSE E,** Miami Dade Comm Coll, Miami, FL; SO; BA; Gen Mgr Chf 83-; Econ; Bus.

**NAVARRO, ROEHL B,** Fl International Univ, Miami, FL; JR; BA; Stdnt Govt; Sigma Pai Epsilon Asst Comptrllr 90-; Rcqtbll; Wghtlftng; Acctg.

**NAVARRO, VIVIANA L,** Fl International Univ, Miami, FL; JR; AA; AA Miami Dade Comm Coll S 90; Educ; Elem Tchr.

**NAVARRO, YAYLEENE CALZADA,** Univ Of P R Bayamon Tech Univ, Bayamon, PR; FR; Poetry Awd; Education.

**NAVAS-AUGER, AILEEN M,** Inter Amer Univ Pr San Juan, Hato Rey, PR; SO; JURIS; Natl Assoc Law Stdnts Treas 89-; Amrcn Br Ass Mmbr 89-; Asstnt Lw Dvsn Inst 91; Rsrch Wrkr TV Prgm 90; BA 84-88; Smnr 87; Crmnl Cnsttntl Law.

**NAVIA, PEDRO A,** Antillian Adventist University, Mayaguez, PR; GD; Pblc Rltnshp SGA 88-90; Yearbook 89-90; Offical Mag 87-90; Wrkng Brdcst Radio Sta 88-90; Advsng About Drugs/Tobacco/Alcohol SEHS 88-90; Wrkng Tchr Assist 88-90; BA 90; Theology/Spanish; Tchr.

**NAVIA-FRIPP, KIM D,** Savannah Coll Of Art & Design, Savannah, GA; SR; BFA; Nghbrhd Assoc 88; Intern WSAVTV 90; Cmr Asst 89; Vldctrn; Vol Fld Prdctn 87-88; Cbl Advrtsr Prdctn Edtng; Pht Rtl; Cert Phtgrphy 80; Vd Prdctn; Prdctn Pst Prdctn Dcmntry.

**NAVIN, EMILY J,** Le Moyne Coll, Syracuse, NY; JR; BA; Stu Govt 87; Sclgy Clb 90-; Dean Lst 89-; Wood Co Sr Cntr 87; Vera House; Well Actvts Hndcppd Tnagrs; Sclgy; Soc Wrk/Rsrch.

**NAVIN, TERENCE F,** Villanova Univ, Villanova, PA; FR; BS; Blck Cltrl Soc 90-; Univ Hon Prog 90-; Alpha Phi Alpha Crspndg Sec; Cndt Day Repr/Spkr; Dns Lst 90-; VU Blck Cltrl Soc Fr Awd 90-; Bio/Pre-Med; Med.

**NAWROCKI, ROBERT M,** Atlantic Comm Coll, Mays Landing, NJ; SO; Criminal Justice; Police Off/Prosecutor.

**NAWROCKI, SHERRIE A,** Atlantic Comm Coll, Mays Landing, NJ; FR; Ed; Tch.

**NAYAK, KRISHNA S,** Fl St Univ, Tallahassee, FL; SO; Chess Clb Tm; Assn Comptng Mach Tm; Math Assn Amer; Phi Eta Sigma 90-.

**NAYAK, LAXMEESH D,** Yale Univ, New Haven, CT; FR; BA; A Capella Singing Grp Tour Mgr 90-; Psychology; Medicine.

**NAYLOR, MICHELE L,** Methodist Coll, Fayetteville, NC; SR; BS; Stdnt Act Cncl 90-; Spcl Olympics 89-; Soc Wrk Intrnshp Chldrns Treatmnt Ctr; Soccer Tm 87-; Soc Wrk/Sociology; Cnslr.

**NAYLOR, NAN W,** Union Univ, Jackson, TN; FR; BA; Elem Edn; Teach.

**NAYLOR, VICTORIA L,** Blue Mountain Coll, Blue Mountain, MS; SO; BA; Athltc Cncl VP; Alpha Psi Omega Drama Soc VP; Modenian Soc Pres; Modenian Scl Clb 90-; Blue Mt Coll Tns Tm No1 Plyr 89-; Engl Prof; Engl; Prof.

**NAZAR, KATHLEEN J,** Life Coll, Marietta, GA; GD; DC; Sacro Ocptl Clb 90-; Actvtr Clb; Orthospihology Clb; Phi Beta Kappa 84-; Cmptr Prgrmng; A T & T Cmunctns 85-89; BS 85; Chiropractic.

**NAZARENO, ANN,** Strayer Coll, Washington, DC; SO; BS; Acctng Clb; Pres Lst 89-; Acad Schlrshp 90-; Acctng; CPA.

**NAZARENO, DARREN R,** Old Dominion Univ, Norfolk, VA; SR; BS; Phi Kappa Phi 90-; Gldn Key; Tau Beta Pi; Cmptr Engr.

**NAZARIO CUEVAS, YANIRA,** Inter Amer Univ Pr San German, San German, PR; SR; BS; Cum Laude; Bio; Microbio.

**NAZARIO DETRES, DARIO,** Inter Amer Univ Pr San German, San German, PR; FR; Erly Admsn Pgm 90; Un Frst Yr Hon 90-; Tchr Piano Lessons 88; Un Frst Yr Hon 90-; Scntfc Fair Frst Prz 87-88; Vlybl Tm 90-; Acctg; Law.

**NAZARIO LEBRON, CARMEN IRIS,** Caribbean Univ, Bayamon, PR; MBA; BA; Cmrcl Ed; Law.

**NAZARIO, FRANCES M,** Inter Amer Univ Pr San German, San German, PR; SR; Soridad Eta Gamma Delta.

**NAZARIO, LUIS A,** Inter Amer Univ Pr San German, San German, PR; GD; BS; IEEE 89-90; Elect Eng.

**NAZARIO, MAY-LING DEL C,** Inter Amer Univ Pr San German, San German, PR; JR; BS; Tnns Vrsty 88-; Blgy; Dr Sprts Med.

**NAZZARO, LUISA A,** Va Commonwealth Univ, Richmond, VA; JR; BFA; Golden Key 90; Graphic Dsgn.

**NDERITU, FLORENCE A W,** Immaculata Coll, Immaculata, PA; FR; BA; Econ/Bsns Admnstrtn; Tchng.

**NDIAYE, OULIMATA L,** Georgetown Univ, Washington, DC; JR; BSBA; Alesel Assc Int 89; Frnch Bcclrt Inst 88; Intrntnl Mngmnt; Htl Mngmnt.

**NDOYE, MAKHTAR,** Ny Univ, New York, NY; FR; AASB; NASA Treas 90-; Ins Brkr Certfd NYAIP Pres; Bkkg NYU 90; BPC L T M Delafosse Sengal 78; Acctg; CPA/CPCU/LLD/ECNMST.

**NE SMITH, KIMBERLY A,** Univ Of Al At Birmingham, Birmingham, AL; SO; AAS; Std Govt Asc Sntr/Rep 90-; Med Rcrd Std Clb Rep 90-; Phi Theta Kappa 90-; Dns Lst 90-; Pres Lst; Acad Schlp 90; Med Rcrds Mgmt.

**NEAL, ANGELA M,** Union Univ, Jackson, TN; FR; BS; Bptst Stdnt Un 90-; Kappa Delta Scl Chrmn; Sci; Phrmcy.

**NEAL, ANTHONY,** Alcorn St Univ, Lorman, MS; SR; BA; Pol Sci Clb Pres 88-90; Hon Orgnztn 90-; Soc Sci Scty 89-90; Phi Beta Lmbd Bus Mgr 87-90; Pol Sci; Pblc Afrs.

**NEAL, BUFFIE FORTNER,** Univ Of Southern Ms, Hattiesburg, MS; JR; BA; Phi Kappa Phi; Englsh; Edctn Cnsnlg.

**NEAL, CHERIE K,** Univ Of Southern Ms, Hattiesburg, MS; SR; BS; Signing Eagles 89-; CAID VP 89-; Fllwshp Christian Athletes FCA 87-89; Golden Key 90-; Gamma Beta Phi 89-; MVP Sftbl; Most Versatile 88; Ldng Hitter 88; All Region 88; All State 89; Tm Dedication 89; Vrsty Sftbl 87-89; AA 89; Deaf Educ; Teach Elem Deaf.

**NEAL, CHRISTOPHER P,** Middle Tn St Univ, Murfreesboro, TN; JR; BS; RIM Writers 89-; ARMS 90-; Recording Ind Mgmt; Sound Engineering.

**NEAL, FELICIA R,** Jackson St Univ, Jackson, MS; SO; BS; WEB Dubois Hnrs Coll; Acctg.

**NEAL, FRED A,** Southeastern Baptist Coll, Laurel, MS; SR; BS; SGA Treas 90-; Mnstrl Allnc VP 90-; Hosp Chpln Vol 90-; Corr Chpln Vol 89-; Ctznshp Awd 89-90; Bptst Chrsh Msc Mnstry 89-; AA 90; Pstrl Trng; Cnslng.

**NEAL, GARY K,** Roane St Comm Coll, Harriman, TN; SO.

**NEAL, JAMES D,** Atlantic Union Coll, S Lancaster, MA; SO; BS; Class President 90-; Newspaper Staff Writer 90-; Honors Cove Hnrs Comm Rep 90-; Local Newspaper Intern 89-; Biochemistry; Medicine.

**NEAL, JUDY S,** City Univ Of Ny Baruch Coll, New York, NY; SR; BBA; Comp Qnttv Mthds Scty 88-; Beta Gamma Sigma; Gldn Key 89; Comp Info Systms.

**NEAL, KEVIN T,** Vance Granville Comm Coll, Henderson, NC; FR; AS; Hstry Clb 90-; Scntst 90-; Ntl Grd Assn 90-; NC Ntl Grd Corp 90-; US Army 87-90; Plymr; Mtrl Sci.

**NEAL, KEYA D,** Spelman Coll, Atlanta, GA; FR; BA; Dns Lst 90-; NASA Summer Sci Engr Prog 90; Most Outstdg Stdt Awd Stats 90; Analysis; Mnrty Aprntcshp Fed Govt; Cmptr Sci; Syst Analysis.

**NEAL, KIMBERLY D,** Va Commonwealth Univ, Richmond, VA; SR; BS; Acctng Soc 90-; Beta Gamma Sigma 90-; Phi Kappa Phi; Phi Eta Sigma 87-; Golden Key 90; Acctng.

**NEAL, KRISTIE L,** Middle Tn St Univ, Murfreesboro, TN; FR; BA; Gamma Beta Phi; Bsn; Mrktng.

**NEAL, LINDA A,** Norfolk St Univ, Norfolk, VA; JR; BA; Alpha Phi Alpha Parlmntrn 88-90; Clin Psych.

**NEAL, LORAINE C,** Barry Univ, Miami, FL; GD; MBA; Employee Of Mnth Awd Southeast Bank 86; Outstndng Sdtnt Achvmnt Awd 88; Intl Schlrshp FIU; BA Barry Univ 90; AA Miami Dade Comm Clg 88; Bus/Bus Educ; Bus Info.

**NEAL, LU ANN D,** Middle Tn St Univ, Murfreesboro, TN; JR; BA; Golden Key 89-; Phi Alpha Theta Sec/Tres; History/Wmns Studies; Ms.

**NEAL, MICHAEL L,** Univ Of Akron, Akron, OH; JR; BED; Stdnt Cncl For Excptnl Chldrn; Golden Kety; Kappa Delta Pi; Spec Edn.

**NEAL, REVA D,** Central Fl Comm Coll, Ocala, FL; GD; BA; Phi Thetta Kappa; AA; Nrsng.

**NEAL, SHANIKA L,** Memphis St Univ, Memphis, TN; FR; BBA; Peer Mentor Pgrm 90-; Phi Eta Sigma; Otstndng Minority Merit Schrshp 90-; Acctng; Acctnt.

**NEAL, SHEILA R,** Radford Univ, Radford, VA; JR; BA; SEA 90-; Erly Educ; Tch K-3.

**NEAL, SHEILA R,** Univ Of Cincinnati-Clrmnt Coll, Batavia, OH; FR; BA; Bus-Acctg; CPA.

**NEAL, WENDY M,** Tn Temple Univ, Chattanooga, TN; SR; BS; Chr Sec; Piantist Fall Prdctn; Zeta Nu Rho Tres 90-; Msc/Math; Tchng.

**NEALE, CHANCE H,** City Univ Of Ny City Coll, New York, NY; SR; PHD; Rsrch Schlrs Asst 88-90; Mt Sinai Mdcl Cntr; Biology Hnrs Orgnztn 88-; BS; Mlclr Blgy Rsrch Med.

**NEALE, SCOTT C,** Univ Of Sc At Columbia, Columbia, SC; JR; BA; Natl Stdnt Exc Prog 90-; Phi Kappa Phi 88; Dns Lst; Psych; Law.

**NEALON, MARK J,** Univ Of Akron, Akron, OH; SO; BA; Busn; Busn Mgmnt.

**NEALON, TARA J,** Syracuse Univ, Syracuse, NY; FR; BA; Univ Union TV Msc News Dir/Promos Dir 90-; Univ Union Concert Bnd; Radio DJ; Dns Lst 90-; Pi Beta Phi 90-; Brdcst Jrnlsm/Pol Sci/Frnch/Msc; Brdcst Jrnls.

**NEALY, CAMILLE Y,** Clark Atlanta Univ, Atlanta, GA; SR; Stdnt Ga Asso/Ed PR; Early Chldhd Ed.

**NEALY, LISA N,** Jackson St Univ, Jackson, MS; JR; Pre Law Club 90-; Student Staying Straight 87-88; Bpt Student Union 88-89; Pi Sigma Alpha Pres; Dir Boy L Brown Chr 87-91; 1st Union Bpt Church; AA Meridian Commty Clg 90; Political Sci; Pre Law.

**NEAPOLITANO, DARRYL J,** Hudson Valley Comm Coll, Troy, NY; SO; BS; Wste Mgmnt; Envrmntl Eng.

**NEARY, MARGARET M,** Spalding Univ, Louisville, KY; SR; Adlt Stdnt Org Scrty 90; Delta Epsilon Sigma; WRKA Cmmnctn Intrnshp 90; Coed Vllybl 90; BA; Cmmnctn; Mngmnt/Sales.

**NEARY, PATRICK J,** Erie Comm Coll South Cmps, Orchard Park, NY; SR; BS; Phi Theta Kappa 90-; BSEET 87-89; BS CRT; Eng Tech; Elec/Cmptr Eng.

**NEAT, JAMES W,** Univ Of North Fl, Jacksonville, FL; SR; BA; Alpha Sigma Pi 90; IMA; U S Navy 81-87; AA Fl Comm Coll Jacksonville 89; Acctng; Mgmt Acctng Or Internal Auditing.

**NEAT, KRISTINA A,** Anne Arundel Comm Coll, Arnold, MD; FR; BA; Un Cmps Min Treas 90-; Crcl Frnqs; Intl Ord Jobs Dghtrs Hon Qn; Ms Md Jobs Dau 90-; Intl Stds; Fgn Srv.

**NEATE, LAURA M,** Anne Arundel Comm Coll, Arnold, MD; FR; BA; Bsnss; Law.

**NEATHERY, S DIANE,** Univ Of Ga, Athens, GA; JR; BSED; Goldenkey 90-; Kappa Delta Pi 90; Rgnts Schlr; Schlrshp; Ga Dept Correctns Sec; Early Chldhd Educ; Tch.

**NEBBIA, ERIC J,** Univ Of Scranton, Scranton, PA; SO; BA; Knghts Clmbs 89-; Yng Rpblcns Treas 89-; IM Bsktbl 89-; Deans Lst 89-; Hon Soc 90-; Bsktbl 89-; Bus.

**NEBESH, ADRIANNA L,** Columbus Coll Of Art & Design, Columbus, OH; SR; BA; Ukrainian Girl Scts Head Cnslr; Stdnt Cncl; Commercial Arts Pgm; Painting/Art Therapy; Art Therapist/Psych.

**NEBOT-MARIN, CARLOS ALBERTO,** Miami Dade Comm Coll, Miami, FL; SO; BA; Msc; Snd Eng.

**NECE, SUZANNE E,** Va Commonwealth Univ, Richmond, VA; JR; BFA; James Madison Univ Contmpry 88-89; Dance Ens Assoc Dance Ens V A Comm Univ; Deans Lst 88-90; Reg Natl Levels Amer Clg Dance Festivl 89-90; Dance; Performng Arts.

**NEDD, NICOLE M,** Univ Of Fl, Gainesville, FL; JR; BSN; Phi Theta Kappa 89-90; Deans List 88-; LPN 88-; Brevard Comm Clg 90; Nursing.

**NEDD, RUPERT A,** Morris Brown Coll, Atlanta, GA; JR; BED; Cmptr Sci Clb Edtr Chief 89-; Morris Brown Coll Hnrs Clb 89-; Ambsdr Coll Grad Clb 90-; Apex Museum Vol Grp 89-90; Frdrckjrdn Acdmc Schlrhsp 89-; Judge Coco Cola Anl Art Expstn 90-; African Amer Pnrmc Exprnc Museum 89-90; Art Educ; Graphcs.

**NEDOMA, TIMOTHY K,** Univ Of Sc At Aiken, Aiken, SC; JR; BS; Bsbl Team; Comp Sci; Syst Anlyst.

**NEED, SARAH J,** Anne Arundel Comm Coll, Arnold, MD; FR; BA; Intrntl Thspn Soc; Emerg Med Tech MEIMSS; Phlbtny Soc; Lang; Mstrs Lngustcs/Intrprtr.

**NEEDHAM, ADAM M,** Univ Of Tn At Chattanooga, Chattanooga, TN; FR; Natl Soc Of Pro Engrs 90-; Amer Soc Of Civil Engrs 90-; US Acad Achvmnt Awd 90-; Elec Engr.

**NEEDHAM, JACKIE C,** Northeast State Tech Comm Coll, Blountville, TN; SO; AS; Amer Dsgn Drftng Assn 89-; Drftng Asst TN Eastmn Co 90-; Drftng Dsgn Tchnlgy; Dsgn Engr.

**NEEDHAM, MARY A,** Elizabeth City St Univ, Elizabeth City, NC; FR; RN BS; Nurs.

**NEEDHAM, REGAN A,** Central Fl Comm Coll, Ocala, FL; SO; BA; Cmps Dplmt 90-; Miss CFCC Pageant Prtcptn Wnnngs; Cmmnctns Pblc Rltns; Stdnt Actvts Drctr.

**NEEDLER, DIANE L,** Kent St Univ Kent Cmps, Kent, OH; SO; BA; Acctng; CPA.

**NEEL, JOHN F,** Anderson Coll, Anderson, SC; FR; AA; Clg Nwspr Spts Edtr 90; Hnrs Prog 90; Phi Theta Kappa 90; Deans List 90; Journalism/Commun; Nwspr Writer.

**NEEL, LAURA S,** Va Commonwealth Univ, Richmond, VA; JR; BSN; Nursing Clb Sec/Tr 89-90; Nurses Assn Class Rep 90-; Golden Key; CAIS 90-; VIEW 90; Hosp Nursing Externshp; Nursing.

**NEEL, MARY E,** Mount Olive Coll, Mount Olive, NC; JR; BS; Hndrsn Sci Clb Pres 88-; Sci Fair Jdg 90-; Math Fair Jdg; Hnrs Pgm 88-; Hnry Mrshl 89-; Fresh Sci Awd 89; CRC Prs Fresh Chem Awd 90; Asst Math Lab Dir; Bio; Gntc Cnslr.

**NEEL, SARA J,** Univ Of Pittsburgh At Bradford, Bradford, PA; SO; BA; Amer Stds Club 90; Amer Stds; Tchr.

**NEELEY JR, FRANK,** Patrick Henry Comm Coll, Martinsville, VA; BA; Lib Arts; Comm Artist.

**NEELEY, SUSAN N,** Fl St Univ, Tallahassee, FL; SO; BS; Pre Law Soc 90-; Hon/Schlrs 89-; Chi Omega; AA FL St 90; Cmnctns; Law.

**NEELLEY, JUDITH A,** Central Al Comm Coll, Alexander City, AL; FR.

**NEELY, COLLEEN M,** Saint Francis Coll, Loretto, PA; SO; BA; French/Engl Clbs 90-; Resp Life Clb Treas/Sec 90-; Singers/Staff Wrtr For Paper 90-; Hons Pgm 89-; Sigma Tau Delta; Vlybl 89-90; Engl; Pub Rels.

**NEELY, EDWARD M,** Washington & Jefferson Coll, Washington, PA; FR; Delta Tau Delta; Wrstlng 90; Chem; Med.

**NEELY, RICHARD S,** Winthrop Coll, Rock Hill, SC; SO; BA; Pi Kappa Alpha Corr Sec 90-; Pres Lst; Hstry/Pltcl Sci; Lcl/State Gov.

**NEELY III, WILLIAM T,** Univ Of Ms Medical Center, Jackson, MS; GD; Amer Dental Assoc 87-; Acad Gen Dentstry 89-; Phi Kappa Phi; Deans Hon Lst 88-; Omicron Kappa Upsiler; Chi Chi Chi; Sisters Robyns Charity Dental Clinic; Thomas P Himan Schlar 90; Wm S Kramer Awd Exclnce 90; BS 87; DMD 91; Dentistry; USAF.

**NEERGAARD, LINDA F,** Univ Of Southern Ms, Hattiesburg, MS; SR; BA; Musc Indstry Clb Pres 87-90; Musc Hnry Scty 87-; Musc Schlrshp; Schlstc Excllnc Schlrshp; Musc; Grad Schl/Physcs.

**NEFF, BRIAN JOHN,** New Comm Coll Of Baltimore, Baltimore, MD; SO; BA; Raymond T Bender Awd; Egl Sct; Emplyd Rcrtn/Prks Baltimore Co Md; Bsn Mgmt.

**NEFF, DENISE L,** Richard Bland Coll, Petersburg, VA; SO; Phi Theta Kappa VP 90-; AS; Bus; Acctg.

**NEFF, GREGORY A,** Univ Of Cincinnati, Cincinnati, OH; SR; BA; Assoc Community Coll Air Force 84; Elec Eng.**

**NEFF, MICHELE A,** Juniata Coll, Huntingdon, PA; SO; BA; Band Front Clrguard 90-; Aerobics Clb 89-; Beta Beta Beta Biological Hon Soc; Biochem/Pre Med; Med.

**NEFF, STEPHEN D,** Va Polytechnic Inst & St Univ, Blacksburg, VA; FR; BA; Bus; Mgmt.

**NEFF, WILLIAM S,** Memphis St Univ, Memphis, TN; BS; Hons Forum; Physics.

**NEGRI, LYNN E,** Univ Of Sc At Columbia, Columbia, SC; JR; BA; Disk Jockey 89-; Hnr Soc; Tau Beta Sigma Hstrn 88-; Alpha Phi Omega Prsdnt Admnstrtv VP 90-; Fencing; Grphc Dsgn.

**NEGRON DAVILA, FLOR,** Inter Amer Univ Pr Hato Rey, Hato Rey, PR; SR; BS; Biologcl Sci Assn Attndg Sympsm 86-; Ethcl Soctl Issues Biotech; Summr Jobs Dept Navy Def 89-90; Beta Beta Beta 86-; Chptr; Bio; Med Career; Biomed Sci.

**NEGRON GARCIA, MARIA I,** Inter Amer Univ Pr San Juan, Hato Rey, PR; JR; JD; Pol Sci Assn 80-83; Model UN 82; Stdy Of Presidency Symposium 82; Oxford Univ 86; P R Cmnty Dept 87; Cum Laude 83; Magna Cum Laude 88; Grad Hist Stdnts Assn Sec 85; Resrchr Ctr Of Hist Invest 87-88; BA Univ Of P R 83; M A Univ Of P R 88; Hist; Pol Sci/Law.

**NEGRON GONZAEZ, ELISA,** Univ Metropolitano, Rio Piedras, PR; SR; BED; Excell Acad PR Jr Coll 85-86; Univ Metropolitan 90-; Artes Del Lang Escuela Elem; BED PR Jr Coll 86; Soc Wrk/Comm Dvlpmnt; Elem Edn.

**NEGRON GONZALEZ, ENID,** Univ Of Pr Cayey Univ Coll, Cayey, PR; SR; BS; Math Clb 90-; Math Dept Stdnt Rep 89-90; Alpha Lambda Delta 87-89; Hons Lst 89-; Math.

**NEGRON MATOS, LILLIAN,** Univ Del Turabo, Gurabo, PR; SR; Grup Hnr De Quimica Tecnicode Labo Ratorio De Investigocion 89-; Pell Grant; Chmstry.

**NEGRON ZAPATA, ELIZABETH,** Inter Amer Univ Pr San German, San German, PR; FR.

**NEGRON, ALBA ROSA,** Barry Univ, Miami, FL; SO; BS; Acctng.

**NEGRON, BRENDA L,** Univ Of Pr At Mayaguez, Mayaguez, PR; SO; Fin; Law.

**NEGRON, FRANCES N,** Univ Of Pr At Mayaguez, Mayaguez, PR; SO; BED; AEMC 89-90; Chem Engrg.

**NEGRON, JANICE,** Inter Amer Univ Pr San German, San German, PR; FR; Eta Gamma Delta; Comp.

**NEGRON, LUIS O,** Univ Of Pr Medical Sciences, San Juan, PR; GD; CERT; BS Colegio Universitario De Cayey 90; Microbiology; Tecnologo Medico.

**NEGRON, MIGUEL A,** Inter Amer Univ Pr Aquadilla, Aguadilla, PR; SO; BS; Biology; Medicine.

**NEGRON JR, RICHARD,** Bayamon Tech Univ Coll, Bayamon, PR; JR; BA; Hnr Stdnts Assn 89-; Almni Mrt Schlrhsp 89-; AA Bayamon Tech Univ Coll Univ Of PR 90; Elec Tech; Eng Elec Tech.

**NEGRON-APONTE, JOSE A,** Univ Of Pr At Rio Piedras, Rio Piedras, PR; SO; HS 90; Sci.

**NEGRON-GONZALEZ, MARIE DEL C,** Bayamon Central Univ, Bayamon, PR; FR; Chrch Aux Treas 89; Cath Yth Ldr 90.

**NEHER, LINDA S,** Va Commonwealth Univ, Richmond, VA; JR; BS; Stdnt Govt Assoc Sntr 90-; Panhellenic Assco Sec 90-; Hum Rels Cmte Chr 90-; Omicron Delta Kappa Pr 89-; Psi Chi VP 90-; Golden Key Treas; Phi Mu Sdnd Chr 89-; Sco Schlrshp; Most Outstndng Greek Soph 90-; Psych.

**NEHMAD, LEON A,** S U N Y Coll Of Optometry, New York, NY; SR; OD; VOSH 87-90; Beta Sigma Kappa 87-; MSW Jr Coll Schl Soc Wrk 84; BARUTGERS Coll 79; Optometry.

**NEIDIG, DANIEL ANDREW,** Bob Jones Univ, Greenville, SC; SO; Opera; Beta Gamma Delta; Bus; Engr.**

**NEIER, TAMMY E,** Christian Brothers Univ, Memphis, TN; JR; BS; Ntnl Soc Prfsnl Engnrs 90-; Amrcn Inst Chmcl Engnrs Prsdnt 87-; Prctr Gmbl Intrnshp 90; Deans Lst 90-; Chmcl Engnrng.

**NEIGER HOLLANDER, MARCIA,** City Univ Of Ny Queensbrough, New York, NY; SO; AS; Phi Theta Kappa; Lic Massage Ther 88; Lib Arts/Sci; Phys Ther.

**NEIGHBORGALL, ELIZABETH A,** Univ Of Nc At Greensboro, Greensboro, NC; SR; BS; SNCAE Treas 90-; Zeta Tau Alpha 86-; Dns Lst 89-; GPA Awd 90; Educ/Cnsl Ctr Tutor; Elem Ed; Tch Spec Ed MS.**

**NEIL, JILL ADAMS,** Univ Of Tn At Martin, Martin, TN; SR; Wkly Cnty Prk Cncl Wmn; STEA; BS Elem Ed; Elem Ed; Tchng.

**NEIL, LANCE D,** City Univ Of Ny City Coll, New York, NY; JR; BME; ASME Stdt Mbr 90-; SAE Stdt Mbr; AIAA Stdt Mbr; Pi Tau Sigma Pres; Dns Lst 88-; Aerospace; Mech Engr.

**NEIL, REBECCA S,** Anne Arundel Comm Coll, Arnold, MD; FR; Gen Educ.

**NEILL, MARK D,** Univ Of Sc At Columbia, Columbia, SC; FR; BA; Bus; Law.

**NEILL, TERRY A,** Birmingham Southern Coll, Birmingham, AL; SO; BA; Psi Chi; Sigma Alpha Epsilon 90-; Vrsty Tennis 90-; Psychlgy; Rdlgy.

**NEILSON, TAMMY M,** Judson Coll, Marion, AL; SR; BA; Stdnt Govt Assoc Rpes 89-; SIFE 90-; Strategic Plng Comm 90-; Circle K 88-89; Bus Mgmnt; Mgmnt & Info Systms.

**NEIMAN, JOY D,** Univ Of Sc At Coastal Carolina, Conway, SC; FR; BS; Chnclrs Hnr Rl; Marine Sci; Rsrchr Bio Oceangrphy.

**NEIMAN, PIPER M,** Univ Of Sc At Columbia, Columbia, SC; FR; BA; Engl; Educ.

**NEIRA, DIANA P,** Tusculum Coll, Greeneville, TN; FR; BA; Stdnt Ambssdr; Theatre; Chld Abuse Prvntn Ctr 90; Deans Lst 90; Soccer 90; Bsnss; Advrtsng Exctve.

**NEIRA, LUIS E,** Tusculum Coll, Greeneville, TN; SO; MBA; Res Advsr 90-; Var Soccer Tm; MVP; Fresh Hon; Soccer; Cmptr Sci; Cmptr Anlyst.**

**NEIRO, MICHAELA Z,** Univ Of Rochester, Rochester, NY; SR; BA; Alpine Ski Tm Trnr 87-; Art Cncl Co-Pres 89-; Outng Clb 89-; IM Soccr/Hockey 89-; Dcrtv Arts Intrnshp 89; Art Hstry; Intl Art.

**NEISSER, DONNA L,** Wv Univ At Parkersburg, Parkersburg, WV; FR; BA; Phi Theta Kappa; Educ; Tchg.

**NEITZEL, THERESA L,** Central Fl Comm Coll, Ocala, FL; SO; BA; Dns Lst; FL Undrgrad Schlr; AA; Org Comms; Bsns Admn/Law.

**NEJEDLY, BRIAN A,** Savannah Coll Of Art & Design, Savannah, GA; SO; BFA; Grphc Dsgn; Advrtsng Dsgn.

**NEKOOASL, JANET B,** Univ Of Nc At Charlotte, Charlotte, NC; SR; BA; History; Tchr.

**NELL, ANGELA L,** Saint Thomas Univ, Miami, FL; SO; BS; Eng; Ind Engr.

**NELLI, WILLIAM R,** Univ Of Ky, Lexington, KY; SR; BA; Bands 87-90; Cncl Econ Priorities 90-; Phi Beta Kappa; Sigma Delta Pi 90-; Kappa Kappa Psi 88-89; Dns Lst 90-; Pres Hnrs Awd 87; Linguistics/Spanish.

**NELLY, PEREZ V,** Univ Of Pr Cayey Univ Coll, Cayey, PR; SO; BA; Natl Sci; Phrmcst.

**NELSON III, ALFRED F,** Fl St Univ, Tallahassee, FL; JR; BM; Newman Clb 86-87; Music Ensmbl 90-; Folk Mass Ensmbl 90-; Music Cmpstn; Film Scoring/Coll Profr.

**NELSON, ALYSSA Y,** Univ Of Sc At Columbia, Columbia, SC; SO; BA; Cmptr Sci; Sys Anlyss.**

**NELSON, AMANDA R,** Appalachian St Univ, Boone, NC; FR; BA; News Edtr; Gamma Beta Phi; Intrnshp At The Caldwell News In Hudson NC; Engl; Journlsm.

**NELSON, ANDREW R,** Tn Temple Univ, Chattanooga, TN; SR; BA; Wrd Lf Clbs 89-90; Stdnt Msn Flwshp 89-90; Pryr Grp Ldr 90-; Alpha Epsilon Theta; Pi Kappa Delta; Smr Intern Clry Bptst Chch 90; Summa Cum Laude; Bsktbl; Sftbl 89-; Cerf Wrd Lf Bl Inst/Msn/Yth Mnstrs 86-88; Bible; Msns Ovrseas.

**NELSON, ANN FRANCES,** Saint Josephs Coll New York, Brooklyn, NY; GD; BS; Cntrbtng Ed Mgmt Crr 86; Amrcn Cncr Scty Drctr 88-; NYC Rd Rnnrs Clb 81-; AAS; Cmmnty Hlth Frnsc Psychlgy.

**NELSON, ANNOLYN M,** City Univ Of Ny La Guard Coll, Long Island Cty, NY; JR; Otstndng Acad Achvmnt Awrd 89; Dstngshd Acad Prfrmnc Talent Rstr; Nrs Aide Cert; Cert Med Aid Trng Sch Inc 87; Nrsng LPN; RN.

**NELSON, AUDREY E,** City Univ Of Ny Queensbrough, New York, NY; JR; AS; 25 Plus Clb 89-; ICF 89-; Jmca Ctr; Daycare Vol 89-; Stndrd Frst Aid; Hnr Lst 90; Magna Exmplry Hnr Dgr 90; Cert Achvmnt; Sgnfcnt Serv Awd; Nrsng.

**NELSON, BARBARA I,** Christopher Newport Coll, Newport News, VA; SO; BA; Served 4 Yrs USAF 85-89; English; Tchng.

**NELSON, BRIGITTE R,** Univ Of Md At Eastern Shore, Princess Anne, MD; SR; BA; Music Ed Natl Conf Pres 88-; Concert Choir 87-90; Alpha Kappa Mu 88-; Dinner Theatre/ Drama Soc Stdnt Music Dir 87-90; Fine Arts Citation/Awd UMES 88; Music Ed/Math; Tch MS Guid Cnslg.

**NELSON, C ADRIENNE,** Saint Thomas Univ, Miami, FL; JR; Pre Med Clb; Bio; Vet Med.

**NELSON, CHRISTINE F,** Marywood Coll, Scranton, PA; FR; BS; Ski Clb 90-; Tchrs Tmrw 90-; Cmps Chr/Wnd Ensmbl 90-; Flk Grp Cmps Mnstry 90-; Elem Ed/Frnch K 12 Ed; Tchg.

**NELSON, CHRISTOPHER TODD,** Paducah Comm Coll, Paducah, KY; SO; BA; Bapt Stu Union 89-; Phi Theta Kappa 90-; Co Val Grad Cls; Recip Comm Coll Trnsfr Cmnwlth Schlrs Schlrshp Univ Ky; AA; Spnsh; Tchg.**

**NELSON, CLAIRE D,** Schenectady County Comm Coll, Schenectady, NY; JR; AOS; Intrnshp Qlty Food Mgmt Schlrshp; Clnry Arts.

**NELSON, COLETTE G,** Univ Of South Al, Mobile, AL; JR; BED; Elem Edctr.

**NELSON, DANELLE J,** Hampton Univ, Hampton, VA; JR; BA; Stdnt Govt Mntrshp Pgm 90-; Otstdng Mnrty Schlrshp Awd 88-89; AA Grnd Rpds Jr Clg 90; Comm Disrdrs; Spch Pathlgst.

**NELSON, DAVID E,** Comm Coll Algny Co Algny Cmps, Pittsburgh, PA; SO; BA; Phi Theta Kappa 90-; Mktg; Bus.

**NELSON, DAVID F,** Univ Of Al At Huntsville, Huntsville, AL; SR; SCI Systems 13000 87; Industrial Engr; Mnfctrng Engr.

**NELSON, DELONDIA M,** Al St Univ, Montgomery, AL; FR; BA; Dns Lst 90-; Frgn Lng Stdy; Internatl Law.

**NELSON, DIEDRE S,** Vanderbilt Univ, Nashville, TN; FR; BS; Cncrt Choir 90-; Alpha Lambda Delta 90-; Eta Sigma Phi 90-; Math; Medicine.

**NELSON, ERIK C,** Univ Of North Fl, Jacksonville, FL; JR; BA; Golden Key; Dns Lst 90-; Msc; Msc-Perf/Tchg.

**NELSON, GREGG D,** Cheyney Univ Of Pa, Cheyney, PA; FR; MD; Q Roni VP; La Orgnl Mdlng Fshn Gld Mdl 90-; Radio Sta Stf; Bio; OB/GYN.

**NELSON, IDRISSA ATO,** Morehouse Coll, Atlanta, GA; SO; BA; Bnkng/Fin; Stockbrocker.

**NELSON, JACK D,** Saint Thomas Univ, Miami, FL; JR; BA; AA Miami Dade Comm Clg 87-90; Sprts Admin; GM Prof Sprts Tm.

**NELSON, JAMES A,** Piedmont Comm Coll, Roxboro, NC; FR; AAS; Sht Mtl Wrkr 73-89; AAS Danville Comm Coll 73; Cmptrs; Prgrmmng Data Cmmnctns.

**NELSON, JAMES C,** Daytona Beach Comm Coll, Daytona Beach, FL; SO; BA; Chemistry; Research.

**NELSON, JANE ARTHUR,** Gaston Coll, Dallas, NC; FR; ASN; Cls Co-Pres 90-; BA Cedarville Coll 78; Nrsng; RN.

**NELSON, JOANNE,** Univ Of The Dist Of Columbia, Washington, DC; SR; BA; Oprtng Acctnt 87-; AAS 84; Acctng.

**NELSON, JOY L,** Univ Of Nc At Greensboro, Greensboro, NC; SO; BED; Intern Morhead Elem; Elem Educ; Tchng.

**NELSON, KAREN E,** Univ Of Akron, Akron, OH; SR; BS; Acctng Assoc 90-; Beta Alpha Psi 90-; Beta Gamma Sigma; Golden Key 90; Delta Sigma Pi 89-; Log Audit Agent 88-89; Mortgage Loan Processor 85-88; Acctng; Industrial Acctng.

**NELSON, KATHERINE J,** Hilbert Coll, Hamburg, NY; FR; Psychlgy.

**NELSON, KATHRYN M,** Fl International Univ, Miami, FL; SR; BA; FEA 89-; Kappa Delta Pi 89-; Dns Lst 89-; AA Brward Comm Clg 89; Elem Educ; Tch.

**NELSON, KATHY L,** Snead St Jr Coll, Boaz, AL; SO; Phi Theta Kappa 90-; Radiology; Cert Rdlgst.

**NELSON, KEITH LAWRENCE,** S U N Y Coll At Fredonia, Fredonia, NY; JR; BS; WNYF TV Prog Host On Amer; Dns Lst; Jamestown Comm Coll; Bd Of Trustees Stdnt Trst; Mdl States Assn; Evltn Tm; Jamestown Comm Coll 90; NFL Buffalo Bills Org 90; Pur Rel Intrn 90; IM Sftbl/Ftbl/Bsktbl 88-; AS Jamestown Comm Coll 90; Bus Admin/Mktg; Indstry.

**NELSON, KELVIN W,** Morehouse Coll, Atlanta, GA; SR; BA; Morehouse Sls/Mktg Inst 90; Morehouse Bus Assn 90-; Morehouse Realestate Clb 90; Acad Hon Roll 90; Chrmn At/T Qrtr Rcgntn Event 90; Mgr Asst AT/T 90-; Mktg; Cons.

**NELSON, KENNETH R,** Univ Of South Al, Mobile, AL; SR; BS; Chi Alpha Chrstn Fllwshp USA Chptr Rsdnt Mgr 90; Coop Educ Prog Coop Eng 90; IM Sprts Sftbl And Flg Ftbl 89-; Systms Cnsltnt; Bus Mgmt; Oprtns And Systms Mgmt.

**NELSON, KENNETH R,** Memphis St Univ, Memphis, TN; SO; BSME; Peer Mentor Prog 89; Phi Eta Sigma 90-; Alpha Lambda Delta 90-; Deans List 89-; Honors Certificate; Engineering; Biomedical Engineering.

**NELSON, KIMBERLY G,** Univ Of Southern Ms, Hattiesburg, MS; SR; BS; Phi Theta Kappa 89-; AA Copiah Lincoln Comm Clg 87-89; Elem Educ; Tchr.

**NELSON, KIMBERLY W,** Longwood Coll, Farmville, VA; SR; BS; APE Clb Sec 87-; IM Sprvsr 90-; Geist Kids Games 90; Dlt Psi Kappa Tres 89-; Alph Dlt Pi 89-90; Olive T Iler Awrd; Geist Schlrshp; Fld Hcky 87-89; Hlth/Phys Educ; Teach.

**NELSON, KRISTIAN E,** Fl St Univ, Tallahassee, FL; JR; BA; Stdnt Alumni Fndtn; GAMMA; Gldn Key; Sigma Nu Frat Schlrshp Chrmn 90-; Schlrshp Key Rcpnt Sigma Nu 89-; Finance Mltntnl Bsns; Bsns Admnstrtn.

**NELSON, LEONESE,** Tuskegee Univ, Tuskegee Inst, AL; SO; BS; Pre-Law Scty 90; Hnr Roll 90; Pltcl Sci; Lawyer.

**NELSON, LINDA J,** Univ Of North Fl, Jacksonville, FL; JR; BA; Wmns Cncl 89-90; Jacksonville Bd Of Rltrs 84-; Fla Assn Realtors 84-; Realtor Assoc Watson Rlty 84-; AA Fla Comm Coll 82; Psychlgy; Indus Org Psychlgy.

**NELSON, LISA A,** Univ Of Al At Birmingham, Birmingham, AL; SR; BSN; AACN; Prcptrshp Bptst Mntclr Hosp; RN UAB Hosp Cardio Vas ICU ACLS Cert; ADN Jefferson St Jr Clg 85; Nrsng.

**NELSON, LORETTA S,** Saint Joseph Coll, West Hartford, CT; FR; BS; Intrcltrl Clb 90-; Amnsty Intl 90-; Mrch Hmlss People; Dns Lst; Hons Sympsm; Tnns Bdmntn; Econs/Fin; Stck Brkr.

**NELSON, LOWELL A,** Air Force Inst Of Tech, Wrt-Ptrsn Afb, OH; GD; MS; Sigma Iota Epsln 90-; Soc Amer Mltry Engrs 88-; USAF Capt; BE Duke Univ 87-; Engr Mgmt.

**NELSON, MARISHA K,** Univ Of West Fl, Pensacola, FL; SR; Alpha Beta Gamma Treas 87-88; AA Pensacola Jr Coll 88; Elem Edn; Tchr.

**NELSON, MELISSA D,** Univ Of Tn At Martin, Martin, TN; FR; Vngrd Thtr 90-; PEP 90-; Deans Lst 90-; Alpha Omicron Pi Scl Fvrs 90-; Fine Arts/Thtr; Actress.

**NELSON, PATRICIA A,** Univ Of Southern Ms, Hattiesburg, MS; SR; BS; Angel Flight Ofcr 90-; MS St Bd Nrsng 86-; RN 86-; ASN MS Gulf Cst Comm Coll 86; Pre Prof Psych.

**NELSON, PATTY S,** Southern W V Comm Coll, Logan, WV; FR; BA; Elem Edctn; Tchr.

**NELSON, REE A,** Faulkner Univ, Montgomery, AL; FR; BS; Nwspr Rprtr; Bus; Mrktng.

**NELSON, SAMARTIAN M,** Faulkner St Jr Coll, Bay Minette, AL; SO; BA; Phi Theta Kappa; Assoc Degree Busn Admin; Busn; Bnkng/Finance.

**NELSON, SCOTT L,** Muskingum Coll, New Concord, OH; JR; BA; First Tm Acad Ohio; Athletic Conftn Bskbl 90-; Varsity Bsktbl 88-; Busn; Busn Mgt.**

**NELSON, SEAN A,** Univ Of North Fl, Jacksonville, FL; JR; BBA; Fnc Invstmnt Scty Pres; Stdnt Govt Assoc Sen Pres Pro Tmpr; Bus Assoc Cncl Chrprsn; Phi Theta Kappa Almn 90-; Gldn Key; Delta Sigma Pi Chncllr; Distilled Spirits Wholesalers FL Schlrshp 90-; Financial Exec Inst Jackvll Schlrshp; Fnc; Fnc Bnkng.

**NELSON JR, THOMAS BOYE,** Strayer Coll, Washington, DC; SO; BSC; Deans Pres List 90; Ecnmcs; Ecnmst/Financer/Banker.

**NELSON, TINA M,** Univ Of Sc At Spartanburg, Spartanburg, SC; SO; BS; Bio; Med Hlthfld.

**NELSON, TRACY D,** Norfolk St Univ, Norfolk, VA; SR; BSW; Socl Wrk Clb Hmcmng Comm 88-; Lake House Girls Grp Hm Cnslr; Hnr Rl 88-90; Dns Lst 90-; IM Bsktbl Coach; Socl Wrk; Law JD MSW.

**NELSON, WILLIAM J,** Univ Of Southern Ms, Hattiesburg, MS; SR; BA; Young Democrats Prlmntrn 90-; ROTC 90-; ROTC Drill Team; Natl Hnr Soc 86-; Phi Theta Kappa 89-; Phi Alpha Thetar; Miss State Clg Spkng Chmpnshp 2nd Plc 89; JR Clg Prgmng Cntst 1st Pl 89; Mississippi Yth Cngrs Snte Mnrty Ldr 88; Poltcl Sci/Pre Law/Econ; Law.

**NELTNER, LOUISE A,** Univ Of Cincinnati, Cincinnati, OH; JR; Kappa Delta Pi.

**NEMBHARD, NICOLE C,** City Univ Of Ny Baruch Coll, New York, NY; JR; BBA; SGA VP 89-90; Fnnc; MBA Intl Bus.**

**NEMET, DEBORAH A,** Saint Josephs Coll, Windham, ME; SR; BA; Delta Epsilon Sigma; All Amer Clgte Schlr Award; Bio; Rsrch/Chem.

**NEMETH, JAMES R,** Univ Of Akron, Akron, OH; JR; BA; Ntnl Acct Assc 90; Acct Assoc 90; Beta Alpha Psi VP Finance 90; Acct; CPA.

**NEMETH, VINCENT G,** Univ Of Akron, Akron, OH; SR; BA; Ntnl Strenth/Conditioning; Assc AM Alliance; Hlth Phys Ed Rcrtn/Dance; Physcl Ed; Tchr.

**NEMETZ, BARBARA J,** Christian Brothers Univ, Memphis, TN; SR; BA; Wmns Assoc Motivate Spirit 87-; Little Sister Tau Kappa Epsilon 87-; Intrnshp Biostatistics St Jude Childrens Resrch Hosp 90; Psychology.

**NEMODA, CHRISTINE M,** Lasell Coll, Newton, MA; SO; AA; Open Studies.

**NEMTSEV, IRINA,** Fl International Univ, Miami, FL; SO; BS; Sclgy Anthrplgy; Law.

**NEOPHYTOU, NEOPHYTOS A,** City Univ Of Ny Baruch Coll, New York, NY; GD; MBA; Stdnt Cncl Advsr 90-; Golden Key Natl 89-; Grad Asstnshp Stdnt Lfe Clg Ins 90-; BA 90; Actuarial Sci; Actuarial.

**NEPTUNE RIVERA, VIVIAN I,** Univ Of Pr At Rio Piedras, Rio Piedras, PR; JR; BS; Ecnmcs Stdnts Assn 90-; Gldn Key; Hnr Stdnts Clb; Hghst Index Entr Score Scl Sciences Fclty 88; Econ Social Sciences; Law.

**NEPTUNE, JOY R,** Milligan Coll, Milligan Clg, TN; FR; BS; Ggrphy Achvmnt Awd; Psy; Chrstn Cnslng.

**NERIS, ESTHER M,** Univ Of Pr Medical Sciences, San Juan, PR; GD; MSPH; Clg Phrmctcs PR 86-; Grad Rsrch Assoc Grad Stdnts Phrmctcs; Amer Assoc Phrmctcl Sci 89; BS Ph Univ PR 85; Phrmctcs.

**NERO, LEONARD V,** Fordham Univ, Bronx, NY; FR; BSMBA; Pre-Law Soc 90-; Acctg Soc 90-; Comp Asst 90-; Sftbl 85-; Piano 85-; Beta Alpha Psi 90-; Big Brthrs 90-; Law Clrk Intrnshp; IM Sprts 90-; Pub Acctg; Law.

**NERSWICK, THOMAS A,** Univ Of Cincinnati, Cincinnati, OH; SR; BSN; STAFF; Nrsng; Nrs.

**NESBIT, APRIL A,** Western Ky Univ, Bowling Green, KY; SR; Phi Eta Sigma 89-; Sigma Delta Pi VP 90-; Phi Kappa Phi 90-; Gldn Key 90-; Pi Sigma Alpha; Intrnshp Cmmnwlth Attrnys Ofc 90; BA; Govt; Law.

**NESBITT, JAYNE H,** Coker Coll, Hartsville, SC; FR; BA; Educ; Tchr.

**NESBITT, RHONDA F,** Univ Of Sc At Columbia, Columbia, SC; FR; BS; Deans Lst 89-90; Assoc Sumter Area Tech Clg 86; Crmnl Just; Law Enfrcmnt.

**NESI JR, ALBERT,** Dowling Coll, Oakdale Li, NY; SR; Yr Bk Phtgrphr 90-; Prntmkng Tchr Asstnt; Visual Arts; Tchr.

**NESMITH, HARRIETTE ANTRONETTE,** Univ Of Sc At Coastal Carolina, Conway, SC; SO; BA; Data Prcssng Mgmt Assn Pres 86-88; Phi Theta Kappa 87-; Natl Beta Clb 78-81; MB Fdrl Cr Un Comp Oprtr 87-89; AS H Grgtwn Tech 88; Comp Sci.

**NESMITH, MARILYN S,** Indiana Univ Of Pa, Indiana, PA; SO; BED; Elem Ed; Tchr.

**NESMITH, VERLENE H,** Williamsburg Tech Coll, Kingstree, SC; SO; Deans Lst; Mthdst Mary Kay Cnsltnt; Pres Of Chldrn Chorus; Gnrl Clg Stdy; Tchr.

**NESNAS, ISSA A,** Manhattan Coll, Bronx, NY; SR; BSEE; Elec Clb Pr 88-; Intl Stdnt Assoc Pr 88-; Crew Tm 88; Tau Beta Pi 90-; Epsilon Sigma Pi; Eta Kappa Nu 90-; Pen/Sword 90-; Pr Schlr 80-; Grad Medals; Our Lady Of Lourdes In FL; Elec Engr.

**NESPOR, JULIE A,** Faulkner St Jr Coll, Bay Minette, AL; SO; AAS; Office Admin; Mgmt.

**NESTER, MICHAEL B,** Univ Of Nc At Charlotte, Charlotte, NC; JR; BA; Mdl UN Pres 89-; SGA Leg 90-; Yr Video Edtr 89-90; Sigma Phi Epsilon Chpln 89-; Prlgl Intern 90-; Ntry Pblc; COOP Dir; Poli Sci Hstry; Law.

**NESTER, MICHELLE L,** Univ Of Akron, Akron, OH; JR; BA; ACES 89-; Elem Educ.

**NESTOR, JOYCE M,** Davis & Elkins Coll, Elkins, WV; SR; BS; Jnngs Rndlph Ldrshp Pgm 88-; Alpha Chi Pres 90-; Beta Alpha Beta Hstrn 90-; M M Osullivan Awd; Wall St Jrnl Awd; Crs Cntry 88-89; AS 89; Bsn; Mgmt/Sales.

**NESTOR, LINDA B,** Vance Granville Comm Coll, Henderson, NC; SO; BED; Phi Theta Kappa; Empl Roses Stores Inc Mgr IS Adm; Comp Sci; MBA.

**NESTOR, MARY J,** Columbia Union Coll, Takoma Park, MD; SR; BSBA; Sprvsr Cbra Retree 86-; Bnfts Admin Marriott Corp; AA Montgomery Coll Rockvl MD 85; Bus.

**NESTOR, NESTOR B,** Lycoming Coll, Williamsport, PA; JR; BS; Beta Beta Beta 88-; Deans Lst 89-; Theta Chi Acad Brthr 90-; Bio/Chem; Med/Srgry.**

**NESTOR, ROCKY E,** Davis & Elkins Coll, Elkins, WV; JR; BA; Ntl Educ Assoc Photo Hstrn; Educ.

**NESTORE, JANINE M,** Glassboro St Coll, Glassboro, NJ; JR; BA; Cmmnctns.

**NETT, CAROLINE O,** Univ Of Sc At Columbia, Columbia, SC; SR; BS; Gldn Ky 90-; Beta Gamma Sigma 90-; Phi Eta Sigma 88-; Mktng/Bus; Mktng.

**NETTLEFORD, PAUL A,** Columbia Union Coll, Takoma Park, MD; JR; BS; Stdnt Assn Sntr 89-; Pre Law Clb Tres 88-; Soph Cls Tres 89-90; Trck Fld Cptn90-; BS; Bsns; Law.

**NETTLES, ALAN H,** Univ Of Miami, Coral Gables, FL; SO; BS; Nwscstr 89-; Cameraman 90-; Alpha Lambda Delta 89-; Phi Eta Sigma 89-; Alpha Phi Alpha 89-; Deans Lst 89-; Prsdnts Hnr Rl 89; Prvst Hnr Roll 89-; Admnstrtv Asst 89-; Mtn Pctrs Englsh Lit; Mtn Pctr Prdctn.

**NETTLES, WILLIAM K,** Al St Univ, Montgomery, AL; JR; BS; Stdnt Govt Assoc Chrmn Constitution 90-; Nwspr Bus Mgr 90-; AA Jefferson Davis Jr Clg 84; Lang Arts; Tch.

**NETTLETON, LAURA L,** Elms Coll, Chicopee, MA; JR; BA; Stdnt Ambss; Toys Lcl Chldrn; USAA All Amer Schlr; Res Advsr; Pres Ldrshp Awd; Deans Lst; Ed; Tchng.

**NETTLETON, MARIA A,** Columbia Greene Comm Coll, Hudson, NY; SO; BA; AIB 90-; Bsn Adm; Hmn Res Mgmt.

**NETUS, LINDA,** Ny Univ, New York, NY; FR; MBA; Jrnlsm.

**NEU, SCOTT R,** Middle Tn St Univ, Murfreesboro, TN; FR; BS; Computer Sci; Programming.

**NEU, TODD W,** Univ Of Ky, Lexington, KY; JR; BA; Clncl Psychgy.

**NEUBACHER, JILL E,** Univ Of Sc At Columbia, Columbia, SC; SO; BMUED; Bands 89-; Gamma Beta Phi; Pi Kappa Lambda; Delta Omicron Crm Pblcty Committee 90-; Drum Major; Music Educ; Band Dir.

**NEUBECK, TAMATHA J,** Oh Univ-Southern Cmps, Ironton, OH; SR; BA; Mrchng Bnd 87-89; Chorus 87; Chrch Choir 86-90; Nrsng Homes/Hosp Phys Therpy Vol; Deans Lst 89-; Sociolgy; Tchng.

**NEUBECKER, CHRISTOPHER A,** Alfred Univ, Alfred, NY; JR; SGA; AMA; NYS Rgnts Schlp 88-; Dns Lst; Vars Tnns 90-; Bsn Admn; Intl Bsn.

**NEUGER, JENNIFER M,** Bay Path Coll, Longmeadow, MA; FR; AS; Intr Dsgn.

**NEUKIRCH, ANNETTE M,** Univ Of North Fl, Jacksonville, FL; JR; BA; AA Fla Comm Clg 89; A T & T Comm 69-; Lit; Tch.

**NEUMANN, ROLF,** Savannah Coll Of Art & Design, Savannah, GA; BA; Jesse Corrine Ward Flemming Schlrshp; Deans List 88-90; Graphic Design; Designer.

**NEUMANN, TINA M,** Gallaudet Univ, Washington, DC; SR; BA; Lambda Scty 90-; Wmns Grp Co Mdrtr 90-; Kappa Delta Pi 90-; Phi Alpha Pi 90-; Pres Schlr 90-; Eng Lit; Grad Schl/ Linguistics.

**NEUMEISTER, LORI A,** Univ Of Akron, Akron, OH; FR; BA; Hnr Clb; Phn Thn 90-; Phi Eta Sigma 90-; Amrcn Chmcl Scty 90-; Intern Rsrch Dvlpmnt; 2M Vllybll 90-; Chmcl Eng.

**NEUNER, DANIEL J,** Holyoke Comm Coll, Holyoke, MA; FR; BA; Ed; Tchng.

**NEUSE, RAYMOND E,** Memphis Academy Of The Arts, Memphis, TN; SO; BFA; Entrd Art Art US Exhbtn Shwn Grmny Won Merit Awd Hawkins Mem Awd; Vlybl/Tnnlbl; Fine Art; Pro Artst.

**NEUSTADTER, DAVID M,** Yeshiva Univ, New York, NY; GD; PHD; Ralph Behrends Physics Soc Pres 89-90; Hamevasser Ed Bd 89-90; Max Stern Schlrshp 86-90; Prfr Lowan Meml Awd Excell Physics 90; Deans Lst 86-90; Biomed Eng.

**NEVALA, HOPE A,** Columbia Union Coll, Takoma Park, MD; FR; BS; Perf Wrkshp 90; Phi Eta Sigma 90; Amtrak 20th Annvrsry 1000 Schlrshp Wnnr; Biochem; Med Neonatlgy.

**NEVARES, MERCEDES M,** Univ Of Central Fl, Orlando, FL; FR; BA; Inter Hall Cncl Sec 90-; Hispanic Am Stdnt Assn 90-; Lambda Chi Alpha Lil Sis 90-; UCF Hon Pgm 90-; Cmptr Sci.

**NEVAREZ, FELIX J,** Univ Politecnica De Pr, Hato Rey, PR; JR; BS; Soc Physics Stu Pres 89; BS 89; Engr; Elec.

**NEVEL, MICHAEL A,** Bloomsburg Univ Of Pa, Bloomsburg, PA; SR; BS; Acctg Clb 87-; Cmtrs Assn 87-; Delta Mu Delta 89-; Phi Beta Lambda 90-; Prfsnl Intrnshp Bloomsburg Hosp Staff Accnt 90; Acctg; Staff Accnt Hlth Care Ind.**

**NEVELLS, FRED E,** Casco Bay Coll, Portland, ME; FR; Acctng/Cmptr Applctns; Acctnt.

**NEVILLE, CHRISTIE M,** Western New England Coll, Springfield, MA; SR; BA; Deans List 90-; AA Greenfield Comm Clg 89; Engl.

**NEVILLE, DIANE S,** Clayton St Coll, Morrow, GA; GD; Stdnt Govt Tech Rep 89-90; Amer Tech Educ Assn Pres 89-90; AAS 90; Drftng/Dsng Tech.

**NEVILLE, KRISTINA,** Schenectady County Comm Coll, Schenectady, NY; SR; AAS; Stdnt Govt Scrtry 90; Jrsprdnce Clb 90; Tutor 90; Phi Theta Kappa 84; Phi Kappa Phi 87; Golden Key 87; BFA U Of Ill At Chgo 88; AA Hrpr Clg 84; Prlgl; Law.

**NEVILLE III, R LESTER,** Medical Univ Of Sc, Charleston, SC; GD; DMD; Amer Stdnt Dntl Assn Clss Rep; Acad Chrmn Clss Rep; Gross Antmy Tchng Asst; IM Ftbl/Vlybl 90; Phrmcutcl Sls Rep 89-90; BS Wofford Coll 87; Dntl Med; Orl Srgry.

**NEVIN, KRISTINA M,** Univ Of Rochester, Rochester, NY; JR; BA; Kappa Delta Scl Chr 89-; Deans Lst 89-; Blgy.

**NEVIN, NICHOLAS D,** Broward Comm Coll, Ft Lauderdale, FL; SO; AA; Nrsng.

**NEVIUS, JAMES C,** Ny Univ, New York, NY; SO; BA; Literary Mag; NYC Jr Chmbr Of Cmmrce 89; Graphic Dsgnr For Ntnl Arts Clb 89; Engl; Tchng.

**NEW, RACHEL GARRETT,** Ms St Univ, Miss State, MS; JR; BS; MS Assc Chldrn Under Six 89-; Rpblcns 88-; Bapt Stdnt Union Priorty Grp 89-; Gamma Beta Phi 89-; Phi Kappa Phi; Order Of The Owl 89-; Kappa Delta Phi 90-; Order Of Omega; Chi Omega Crspndng Sec 90- Asst Recrd Sec 89-90; Pres List Schlr 89-; Elem Ed; Tchr.

**NEWBERN, CAROLINE B,** Toccoa Falls Coll, Toccoa Falls, GA; SR; BED; Prfssnl Assn GA Educrs; Choir 81-83; Trng Mssns Choir Pianst 82-83; Magna Cum Laude B Ed; Choir Dir 87-89; Fant Hall Drm Cncl 82-83; AA 88; Elem Ed; Tchng.

**NEWBERRY JR, CURTIS R,** Miles Coll, Birmingham, AL; SR; BA; Miles Clg Gspl Chr Treas 87-; Mssnry Evnglst Cmps Outrch Birmingham Al Srvnt 89-; Cmmnctns/Jrnlsm; Intrntl Mssns/Affrs.

**NEWBERRY, TANYA L,** Northern Ky Univ, Highland Hts, KY; FR; BA; Delta Zeta; Wmns Crisis Ctr; Dnc Hrt; Ntl Acteen Cnvtn Rep; Innr Cty Vac Bible Schl Wrkr; Talnt Shw Wrkr Florence Y All Festvl; Golden; Nrsng; RN.

**NEWBILL, GAIL L,** Tougaloo Coll, Tougaloo, MS; SO; BA; Soph Class Treas; Wakadzi Jr Class Pres Elect; Stdnt Fclty Discpln Comm; Yrbk Staff; Alpha Kappa Alpha; V Pres Schlr; Business; Bus Admnstrn.

**NEWBILL, ROBERT B,** Birmingham Southern Coll, Birmingham, AL; SR; BS; Lit Mag Prose Ed 88-; Alpha Lambda Delta; Phi Eta Sigma; Alpha Epsilon Delta; Phi Beta Kappa; Alpha Phi Omega 88-89; Teach Asst Econ; Outstndg Sr Econ Major; Econ; Grad Sch MBA.

**NEWBOLD, JOHN W,** Norfolk St Univ, Norfolk, VA; FR; BA; Asc Gen Cntrctr Amer 90-; Bldn Cnstrctn; Cntrctr.

**NEWBROUGH, MARCIA A,** Wv Northern Comm Coll, Wheeling, WV; FR; AA; Sec Assn 90-; Stdnt Mnth; Asst Rehab Serv Coord; Sec Sci; Exec Sec.

**NEWBROUGH, SHAWN R,** Wv Univ At Parkersburg, Parkersburg, WV; FR; Amer Wldg Scty; Phi Theta Kappa; Deans Lst; Wldg Mgmt Tech.

**NEWBRY, EVERETT G,** Univ Of Rochester, Rochester, NY; SO; BS; Marine Option NROTC; Dns Lst; Elec Engr.

**NEWBY, CHRISTOPHER P,** Al A & M Univ, Normal, AL; SO; BA; Computer Sci.

**NEWBY, KIMBERLY A,** Neumann Coll, Aston, PA; SR; BA; Pro Educ Soc 87-; Psychlgy Clb 87-; Cmps Mnstry 87-; BA; Elem/ Early Chldhd Educ.**

**NEWBY, SHARON L,** Alcorn St Univ, Lorman, MS; SO; BS; Gospel Chr 89-; Pre Med Clb Treas 90-; Biology Clb 90-; Biology; Pediatrician.

**NEWCOMB, ADAM J,** Oh Univ, Athens, OH; SO; BFA; South Green Radio Treas 89-; Clq Mdlng 89-; Acting.

**NEWCOMB, ROGER L,** Roane St Comm Coll, Harriman, TN; SO; BS; Elem Ed; Tchg.

**NEWCOMB, ROY S,** Hillsborough Comm Coll, Tampa, FL; FR; BA; Priv Invstgtr 90-; Pol Sci; Law Enfrcmnt.

**NEWCOMB, SHARON M,** Longwood Coll, Farmville, VA; SR; BS; Natl Hon Soc 86; Phi Theta Kappa Treas 87-89; AAS Southside VA Comm Clg 89; Bsns Admn; Mgmt Inf Sys.

**NEWCOMB, WILLIAM L,** Tn Temple Univ, Chattanooga, TN; FR; BA; Clss Chpln 90-; Campus Quest 90-; Ensmbl 90-; Sccr Mngr 90-; Rlgn; Mnstry.

**NEWCOMBE, RICHARD E,** Ny Inst Tech Old Westbury, Old Westbury, NY; JR; BA; Asst Yth Mnstr 89-; Sacristan Holy Name Mary Ch 84-; Deans Lst 88-; Bus Mktg; Food Chains Mktg.**

**NEWELL, ANDRE E,** Alcorn St Univ, Lorman, MS; FR; BME; MENC; Mrchng Bnd; Wind Ensmbl; Jazz Bnd; Msc Edctn; Instrctr.

**NEWELL, BARBARA L,** Univ Of Miami, Coral Gables, FL; FR; BBA; Hnrs Assoc 90-; Alpha Lambda Delta; Delta Sigma Pi; Cmptr Info Syst; Cmptr Pgmr/Mgmt.

**NEWELL, CRYSTAL L,** Coll Misericordia, Dallas, PA; FR; BS; Thomas A Marvel Schlrshp; All Amer Schlr; Bsn Merit Awards; Acad Schlrshp; Erly Chldhd Elem; Spec Educ.

**NEWELL, GAIL A,** Glassboro St Coll, Glassboro, NJ; JR; BA; Vail Communications/Security Owner; Hist/Educ.

**NEWELL, LINDA,** Alcorn St Univ, Lorman, MS; SR; Cmptr Sci Clb Asst Sec; Intrfaith Gosp Chr; Yrbk Stf; Dean List Stdnt; BS; Un Schlrshp Acadmc; Cmptr Sci Apld Math; Cmptr Pgmr.

**NEWELL, PATRICIA J,** Univ Of North Fl, Jacksonville, FL; SR; BSH; Golden Key 89-; Amer Occuptnl Therapy Assoc 79-; 1st Coast Esprit De Corps; Baptist Med Ctr Jcksnvl Wolfson Chldrns Hosp 80-; AS Quinsigamond Cmnty Clge 79; Health Science; Occupational Therapy.

**NEWELL, PETER T,** Univ Of Miami, Coral Gables, FL; JR; BBA; Tae Kwon Do Clb 89-; Res Coll Prog Cncl 90; Golf Clb 90-; Gldn Key 90-; Hon Stdnts Assn 89-; Personnel Clb 90-; Mktg Clb 90-; Provosts Lst 89-; Var Trck Tm 89-90; Var X-Co Tm 89; Mgmt/Mktg; Bus.

**NEWELL, TONY L,** Oh Univ, Athens, OH; SR; BFA; Dns Lst 90-; Gldn Ky; Phtgrphy/Vsual Comm.

**NEWHALL-GEORGE, N SUSAN,** Lasell Coll, Newton, MA; FR; BA; High Hnrs 90-; Hd Tchr Daycare Ctr 88-90; HTECE Middlesex Comm Clg 90; Phy Thrpst.

**NEWINGHAM, AMY J,** Mount Aloysius Jr Coll, Cresson, PA; FR; Assn Surgcl Techgst; Surgcl Techngy.

**NEWINS, LEE A,** Suffolk Comm Coll Eastern Cmps, Riverhead, NY; JR; AAS; Acctng.

**NEWKIRK, ANGELA N,** Alcorn St Univ, Lorman, MS; JR; Mrch Bnd; Inst Mgmt; Rest Mgmt.

**NEWKIRK, DESEREE,** Saint Josephs Coll New York, Brooklyn, NY; GD; BSN; Chi Eta Phi 87-; AS NYC Tech Clg 87; Nrsng; MA.

**NEWKIRK, FRANCES S,** Hillsborough Comm Coll, Tampa, FL; SO; BED; Acdmc All FL 90-; All Natl Athltc Assn Rgn VIII; Tnns Tm HCC Capt.

**NEWKIRK, NORMAN K,** Univ Of Miami, Coral Gables, FL; FR; BS; Cane Computer Organ 90-; Alpha Lambda Delta 90-; Math; Engineering.

**NEWKIRK, SHEILA,** Fayetteville St Univ, Fayetteville, NC; SR; BA; Sclgy Clb 87-; Jynr Hll Bsktbl Tm; BA; Sclgy; Instrctr.

**NEWLAND, MICHELLE G,** Fl St Univ, Tallahassee, FL; JR; Fsu Cuong Nhu Karate Clb 88-; Music Educ.

**NEWLON, TAMMY L,** Ms St Univ, Miss State, MS; FR; Vars Lttrmns Clb; Flwshp Chrstn Athlts; Lambda Sigma; Reformed Univ Flwshp; Gamma Beta Phi; Alpha Lambda Delta; Phi Eta Sigma; Pres Schlr; Vars Bsktbl Tm; Physcl Thrpy.

**NEWMAN, ANDREW SCOTT,** Cornell Univ Statutory College, Ithaca, NY; SR; DVM; Wind Ensmbl 87-; EARS 88-89; Gamma Sigma Delta; Lab Rsrch Asst 90; Stockroom Asst 90-; BS; Bio; Vet Med.

**NEWMAN, BARBARA G,** Georgian Court Coll, Lakewood, NJ; SR; BA; Deans Lst 89-; Hmnts/Cmprhnsv Sci Blgy; Tchr.

**NEWMAN, BRONJELYN P,** Alcorn St Univ, Lorman, MS; FR; Chem Clb; Pre Med Clb; Pre Med Chem; Med Sch.

**NEWMAN, CHRISTOPHER T,** Ms St Univ, Miss State, MS; SO; BS; Bapt Stdnt Union; Phi Eta Sigma; Gamma Beta Phi; Deans Lst; Forestry; Forest Mngmnt.

**NEWMAN, CYNTHIA L,** Union Univ, Jackson, TN; JR; BA; Elem Ed; Teach.

**NEWMAN, CYNTHIA L,** Marshall University, Huntington, WV; SO; BA; Rehab; Gndc Cnslr.

**NEWMAN, DOROTHY F,** Dyersburg St Comm Coll, Dyersburg, TN; FR; Phi Theta Kappa; Nrsng.

**NEWMAN, DUANE E,** Southern Coll Of Tech, Marietta, GA; JR; BSIET; Natl Soc Prof Engrs V P 89-; GA Soc Prof Engrs; Bapt Stdnt Union 88-90; Habitat Humanity 90-; Augusta Boys Clb; Reid-Rowell Pharmceuticals Intern; Milliken Abbeville Plant Co-Op 90-; Milliken Spartanburg Plant Co-Op 89-90; Indstrl Engr; Engr.

**NEWMAN, HAROLD R,** Va Commonwealth Univ, Richmond, VA; JR; BA; Wrkd Rtl Bkstrs Vd; Comprtv Lit.

**NEWMAN, KATHRYN R,** Long Island Univ C W Post Cntr, Greenvale, NY; SR; BFA; Art League Pres 89-; Undrgrte Assist/ Sclptr Dept 90-91; Prntmkng Wrkshp 89-90; Art Dept Award Excel Sculpture 90-91; Fine Arts.

**NEWMAN, KELCEY L,** Norfolk St Univ, Norfolk, VA; JR; BA; Art Gld 90-; Lttn Pblctns Clrk Intrn; Grphc Dsgn; Advrtsng.

**NEWMAN, KELLY J,** Ga St Univ, Atlanta, GA; JR; BES; Kappa Delta Pi; Pres Plq; Erly Chldhd Educ; Tchr K-4.

**NEWMAN, KIMBERLY B,** Ms St Univ, Miss State, MS; SR; BA; Bptst Stu Unn 87-89; Univ Fshn Brd 87-; Phi Mu 87-; Univ Alchl Awrnss Wk Comm 89-; Chldrn Mir Ntwrk Tlthn; Mdl Act Phi Mu 90-; 3rd Alt Miss MI St Univ 89; Mrktng/Mngnt.

**NEWMAN, KRISTIN E,** Juniata Coll, Huntingdon, PA; JR; BS; Psychology Clb 90-; RHA 88-89; Lit Mag Art Ed 88-90; Varsity Swmng 88-89; Psychlgy.

**NEWMAN, MARTHA A,** Univ Of Tn At Knoxville, Knoxville, TN; JR; BA; Bnk Admn Inst; Intl Audtr/Comp Ofcr/AVP 1st Natl Bk; Acctg/Audtng; Audtng.

**NEWMAN, MELISSA S,** Webber Coll, Babson Park, FL; SR; BA; AA Polk Comm Coll 89; Mktg; Corp Law.

**NEWMAN, MICHAEL E,** Ms St Univ, Miss State, MS; GD; PHD; Grad Stdnt Assoc Pres 90; Clg Of Ed Dctrl Stdnts Assoc Pres 89-90; Phi Kappa Phi; Gamma Sigma Delta; Phi Kappa Phi; Omicron Tau Theta; Alpha Gamma Rho; Grad Rsrch Assist Ms State 89-90; Grad Rsrch Assist Ohio State 85-86; BS; MS; Ag/ Extnsn Ed; Univ Prfssr.

**NEWMAN, MICHELE L,** Mount Saint Mary Coll, Newburgh, NY; SR; BA; Cthlc Yth Org Yng Adlt Advsr 87-89; Flk Grp 87-; Dtchs Cmnty Clg Dns Lst 87-89; Alpha Chi; Natl Rght Lf Cmte 90-; Ytn Mnstry Awd 87; Aquinas Schlr; AA Dutchess Cmnty Clge 89; Hstry/Elem Ed; Tchg.**

**NEWMAN, MICHELLE M,** Wv Univ At Parkersburg, Parkersburg, WV; AAS; Accg.

**NEWMAN, PAUL A,** Bloomfield Coll, Bloomfield, NJ; JR; BA; Economics Club 84-85; Black Action Soc 83-87; Alpha Chi 90-; Soccer Tri Cap 83-84; Insurance Fraud Investigator 89-; Economics; Law School.

**NEWMAN, PHYLIS DIANN,** Univ Of Tn At Knoxville, Knoxville, TN; JR; BS; Gldn Ky 88-; Ft Sanders/Sevier Med Ctr Pyrl Spec Proj 76-; Acctg/Bus.

**NEWMAN, ROBERT J,** Hellenic Coll/Holy Cross, Brookline, MA; GD; MDIV; Orthodox Chrstn Fllwshp 90-; Phi Beta Kappa 77-; Am Philological 74-; Asst Prof/Classics 84-90; BA MA Catholic Un/Am 77; PH D Johns Hopkins Un 84; Theology; Orthodox Ch Priesthd.

**NEWMAN, ROCHELLE S,** Yeshiva Univ, New York, NY; SR; BA; Jnt Bus Soc VP 89-90; Jnt Bus Soc-Chrprsn Annl Awds Dnnr 89-90; Deans Lst 88-; Com Lbry Rltns Chrprsn 89-90; Undrgrad Nwspr Sr Rprtr 88-; Soph Cls Stdnt Cncl Pres 88-89; Stern Coll Drmtcs Soc Pblcty Coord 87-88; Mktg/Cmnctns Engl Lit.

**NEWMAN, ROGER,** Fayetteville St Univ, Fayetteville, NC; SR; BA; Pol Sci Clb 89-90; Alpha Kappa Mu 89-90; Pol Sci Awd 89; Chnclrs Lst 89-90; AAS Fytvl Tech Comm Clg 88; Pol Sci; Law.**

**NEWMAN, SCOTT D,** Univ Of Ma At Amherst, Amherst, MA; FR; BS; IM Bsktbll; Hnrs Prgm 90-; Bus; Mrktng Mgmt.

**NEWMONES, GEOGEANNA,** Atlantic Comm Coll, Mays Landing, NJ; SO; BA; Nrsng; Nrsng Admin.

**NEWNAM, LUCY D,** Fl St Univ, Tallahassee, FL; SR; BS; Tdys Ntrtn Clb 89-90; Mrchng Chfs U Mrchng Bnd 87-89; Phi Kappa Phi 90-; Kappa Omicron Nu 90-; Golden Key 89-; Lbrl Stds Hons Cmptn 90; Ntrtn; Dtetc Intrnshp/Mstrs Degree.

**NEWPHER, STACEY L,** Birmingham Southern Coll, Birmingham, AL; FR; BS; Conservancy 90-; Phi Eta Sigma 90-; Alpha Lambda Delta 90-; Chi Omega 90-; Alphi Phi Omega 90-; Biology; Medicine.

**NEWPORT, KEVIN L,** Liberty Univ, Lynchburg, VA; FR; BS; Acctng.

**NEWSHAM, CAROLYN J,** Winthrop Coll, Rock Hill, SC; JR; BA; Stdnt Govt Assoc Senator 90-; Dinkins Stdnt Union V P; Panhellinic Assoc 90-; Sigma Sigma Sigma Parlmntrn 90-; Mass Communicaitons; TV Broadcasting.

**NEWSLOW, PAULA L,** Southern Vt Coll, Bennington, VT; SO; BSN; AD Berkshire Cmnty Clg 85; Nrsg; Nrsg Mgmt/Tchg.

**NEWSOM HARPER, LORI A,** Western Ky Univ, Bowling Green, KY; SR; BS; Phi Eta Sigma 88; Phi Kappa Phi; Presidents Lst 89-; IM 88; Educ; Teach.

**NEWSOME, DEBORAH K,** Ashland Comm Coll, Ashland, KY; FR; ASSOC; Schlrshp Franciscan Sisters Poor 90-; Our Lady Bellefonte Hosp; Allied Hlth Nrsng.

**NEWSOME, GLORIA R,** Norfolk St Univ, Norfolk, VA; SO; BA; Assoc Mnstr First Bapt Ch Evnglstc Dir 88-; Ombudsman Bus Off; Depaul Med Ctr To Promote & Iknsure Customer Serv Rltnshps; CES/BED Va Un Sch Of Theo Ext Prog 84; Soc/Rel; Fulltime Asst Pastor.

**NEWSOME, KAREN K,** Medical Univ Of Sc, Charleston, SC; SR; BSN; Sigma Theta Tau; VALOR Stdnt VA Med Cntr 90; Offcrs Wvs Clb 82-; Combat Support Grp Wvs Clb 82-; EMT Cty Coll Chicago 86; Nrsng; Fed Prog.

**NEWSOME, MARY R,** Kent St Univ Stark Cmps, North Canton, OH; SR; BA; Ltry Mag Asst Edtr 88-; Psychlgy Clb; Psi Chi; Sigma Tau Delta 90-; Engl Awd; Pres Lst 87-; Univ Schlrshps 89-; AA 89; Psychlgy/Engl; Clncl Psychlgy.**

**NEWSON, CASSANDRA D,** Univ Of Southern Ms, Hattiesburg, MS; SR; BS; Med Tech.

**NEWSON, LISA L,** Fl A & M Univ, Tallahassee, FL; FR; Phi Eta Sigma; Housing Dept Awrd; Phrmcy Achvmnt Awrd; Indstrl Phrmcy.

**NEWSON, MARIAH M,** Shepherd Coll, Shepherdstown, WV; FR; ADN; SNA; Catherine C Fix Essay Cntst Schlp 90-; Nrsng; Midwifery.

**NEWSTAD, WILLIAM J,** Saint Johns Univ, Jamaica, NY; FR; BA; Dance Marathon 90; Alpha Phi Delta Cmnty Serv Chr 90; Dns Lst 90-; Competitive Schlrshpf Cthlc Hgh Schl Schlrshp St Johns Univ; Pltcl Sci; Law.**

**NEWTON, CARLETTA S,** Owensboro Comm Coll, Owensboro, KY; FR; AS; Dns Lst 90-; Pr Pblshd Ocrncs Chsng Lftm Mt; Nrsg; RN.

**NEWTON, KATHLEEN ANN,** Bethany Coll, Bethany, WV; JR; BA; Cir K 88-; French Club 88-; Pol Affairs Club Pres; Amnesty Intl 90-; Gamma Sigma Kappa; Pi Gamma Mu; Pol Sci Intl Cnsltnt Pol.

**NEWTON, KELLY R,** D Youville Coll, Buffalo, NY; JR; BA; AOS Bryant/Stratton 86; Mktg Mgmt; Corp Amer.

**NEWTON, NELLIE H,** Vance Granville Comm Coll, Henderson, NC; SO; AAS; Phi Theta; Depart Awd; Data Processing Tech 77-; Business/Computer.

**NEWTON, NIKKI R,** Western Piedmont Comm Coll, Morganton, NC; FR; Mdcl Asst Clb 90-; Mdcl Asstng.

**NEWTON, NORMAN,** Albany St Coll, Albany, GA; GD; BA; Scl Sci Clb 89-; Mrchn Gbnd 88-89; Psychlgy; Cnslng Crrctns.

**NEWTON, PENNIE-JEAN,** Castle Jr Coll, Windaham, NH; FR; Frshmn VP 90-; Scl Actvs 90-; Bus Admin; Mrktg.

**NEWTON JR, ROBERT L,** Hampton Univ, Hampton, VA; FR; PSYD; Psy; Fmly Therapist.

**NEWTON, ROGER W,** Univ Of Ky, Lexington, KY; SR; Assn Hlth/Phys Ed/Rcrtn/Dnc 88-; NEA Ed Assn 90-; Phy Ed Mjrs Clb 87-; Rick Pitino Wildcat Bsktbl Camp Coachng Staff 90-; Randy Ayers OH St 89-; Wade Houstons TN Bsktbl Schl Coachng Staff 89-; Phy Ed; MS Ed Sprts Mgmt Baylor U.

**NEWTON, SABINA O,** Hampton Univ, Hampton, VA; SR; Stdnt Educ Assn 89-; Cncl For Exceptnl Chldrn 90-; Kappa Delta Phi 89-; BS; ASSOC Thomas Nelson Cmnty Clg 86-87; Specl Educ.**

**NEWTON, STEVEN B,** Savannah Coll Of Art & Design, Savannah, GA; SR; BA; Res Asst 87-88f Video Wrkstdy Prog 89-; Art Work 87-; Soccer Tm 88-89; Video/Graphic Dsgn; Adv/Teach/Artist.

**NEWTON, TRACY L,** Univ Of Tn At Martin, Martin, TN; JR; BA; Alpha Delta Pi 90-; Sigma Tau Delta; Alpha Delta Pi VP 88-; Eng; Law.

**NEWTON, VIRGINIA D,** Wallace St Comm Coll At Selma, Selma, AL; SO; A; Sci; Bus.

**NEWTON, WINNIE E,** Univ Of Nc At Charlotte, Charlotte, NC; SR; BCA; Golden Key; Phi Eta Sigma 86-; Chnclrs List 87-90; Deans List 86-; Visual Art; Artst.**

**NEWYEAR, KARL D,** Univ Of Miami, Coral Gables, FL; SR; BS; Hnrs Stdnts Assn 87-88; Phi Beta Kappa; Phi Kappa Phi 90-; Golden Key 90-; Fllwshp UM RSMAS 89-90; Stdnt Yr 90-; Trck Crs Cntry 87-; Marine Sci Physcs; Ocnrgrphc Rsrch.**

**NEY, MARTIN F,** Atlantic Comm Coll, Mays Landing, NJ; SO; BA; AA; Hstry; Educ.

**NEYER, PATRICIA A,** Univ Of Cincinnati, Cincinnati, OH; JR; BED; Girl Scouts Troop Leader; Elem Ed Math; Teach.

**NEYLAND, LA SHUND S,** Univ Of Cincinnati, Cincinnati, OH; FR; Interior Arch; Entrprnr/Intrr Dsgn.

**NEZBETH, ERIN A,** West Liberty St Coll, West Liberty, WV; SO; BED; Physcl Ed/Health; Tchng/Coaching.

**NG, AH CHUAN,** Univ Of South Al, Mobile, AL; SR; BS; ACM; DPMA; Alpha Chi; Mngmnt Infrm Sys; Mngmnt.

**NG, ANGELA,** Univ Of Fl, Gainesville, FL; Phi Kappa Phi 90-; Grphcs Intrn 90; Deans List 90; BD 90; Grphcs Dsgn.

**NG, ANNETTE S,** City Univ Of Ny Baruch Coll, New York, NY; JR; Hong Kong Clb 87-88; Acctg.

**NG, CHI WING,** City Univ Of Ny La Guard Coll, Long Island Cty, NY; JR; BS; Asian Clb 88-; Hong Kong Clb 88-; Phi Theta Kappa 90; Pharmacist.

**NG, CHING-WANG,** Univ Of South Al, Mobile, AL; SR; BS; Asn Stdnt Assn Com 90; Beta Gamma Sigma; Asst Adtr; Dplma Ungku Omar Polytechnic Malaysia 86; Acctng.

**NG, HUEY LIN,** Oh Wesleyan Univ, Delaware, OH; FR; BA; Horzns Intl; Wmn For Crss-Cltrl Undrstndng Treas; Phi Eta Sigma; Stdnt Asst Wmns Stdies Dept; Awrd F Leas Prz For Mathmtcs; ATCL Trnity Coll Of Music Englnd 89; Intl Bus/Acctg; Intl Bus Mgmt.

**NG, KWAI-FONG RAINA,** Muskingum Coll, New Concord, OH; SO; BED; Intl Stdnts Org Sec/Treas 90-; Lambda Sigma 90-; Sigma Alpha Iota Sgt-Arms; Phi Eta Beta 90-; First Yr Awrd 90-; Deans Lst 89-; Specl Child Care Wrkr 85-89; Child Care Cert Lee Wai Lee Tec Inst 85; Music Educ; Tchr.

**NG, LAI KUEN,** Univ Of South Al, Mobile, AL; JR; BSC; Prmry Schl Tchr; Diploma Of Chinese Lang And Lit Hong Kong Shue Yan Coll 87; Acctng.

**NG, PAULINE Y,** S U N Y Coll Of Tech At Frmgdl, Farmingdale, NY; JR; BA; Intl Bus.

**NG, RIGOBERTO,** Fl International Univ, Miami, FL; JR; BS; Amer Dietetic Assn 90-; Fla Dietetic Assn Stdnt Dietetic Assn 90-; Dietetics/Nutrition; Med.

**NG, SANDRA,** Hillsborough Comm Coll, Tampa, FL; FR; Law.

**NG, SIU H,** Univ Of The Dist Of Columbia, Washington, DC; JR; BBA; Amer Acct Assn; Acctg Clb; High Hon 90-; Deans Lst 89-; Bus Admin Acctg.

**NG, SU-PENG,** Winthrop Coll, Rock Hill, SC; FR; BA; Alpha Lambda Delta; Vars Tennis.

**NG, SUTMAN,** Bunker Hill Comm Coll, Boston, MA; FR.

**NG, SZE CHUNG,** City Univ Of Ny La Guard Coll, Long Island Cty, NY; SO; AS; Phi Theta Kappa; Deans Lst 90-; Computer Sci; Programmer.

**NG, SZE-HUNG,** City Univ Of Ny City Coll, New York, NY; GD; ME; Untd Chinese Stdnt Assoc VP 87-88; Tau Beta Pi Treas 88-89; Golden Key; BE 90; Comptr Sci; Engrng.

**NG, WAI MING,** Univ Of Tn At Knoxville, Knoxville, TN; JR; BA; Hong Kong Assoc Pres 90-; Lingnan Clg Mgmt Assoc Intl Admn 88-89; Gldn Ky 90-; Yuen-Leung Mo-Tak Schlrshp 89-; Mgmt; Bsns.

**NG, YIM LING,** City Univ Of Ny La Guard Coll, Long Island Cty, NY; GD; AAS; Acctg.

**NGAN, CHING-YUK P,** Univ Of Rochester, Rochester, NY; FR; BS; Campus Chrstn Fllwshp 90-; Chnese Stdnt Assoc 90-; Genesee Schlrshp; Provdnce Schlrshp; Psyscs; Acad Res.

**NGARE, BEN NJOROGE,** Tomlinson Coll, Cleveland, TN; FR; BS; Deans Lst; Ntrl Sci; Comp Eng.

**NGO, HY L,** Univ Of The Dist Of Columbia, Washington, DC; SO; AA; Tau Alha Pi 89; Electronic; Eng Tchnlgy.

**NGO, VAN T,** Univ Of Fl, Gainesville, FL; PHARM; Vietnamese Org; Amer Soc Hosp Pharm; Rho Pi Phi; Pharm.

**NGOUYASSA, ERIC N,** Central St Univ, Wilberforce, OH; JR; BS; Hnr Pgm; Cmptr Sci; Engr.

**NGUMBA, RAHAB W,** Fl International Univ, Miami, FL; SR; BS; Kenya Profnl Bus Wmns Assn; YWCA; Sarova Hotels Kenya Asst Mgr Intrn 87; Kenya Assn Htlkprs Ctrs; Lctrer Frnt Ofc Mngmnt Kenya Utalii Coll 87-90; AAS Kenya Utalii Coll 87; Cert Assn Sls Mktng Exec 86; Hsptlty Mngmnt; Hotelier.

**NGUYEN PONG, ANH-THO T,** City Univ Of Ny City Coll, New York, NY; SR; BSEE; IEEE Pres 89-90; Hnr Soc Pres 87-88; Tau Beta Phi; NFS Rsch Exp; John Von Neuman Natl Flwshp; Super Cmptr Ctr; Elec Engr.

**NGUYEN, ANH T,** City Univ Of Ny Baruch Coll, New York, NY; GD; Stdnt Govt V P 88-89; Golden Key 88-90; Helpline 87-89; NY Telephone Schlrshp 87-90; Provosts Schlrshp 87-90; Becker Fmly Schlrshp 88-90; Engl.

**NGUYEN, ANN,** Va Commonwealth Univ, Richmond, VA; SR; Pre-Dental Clb; Phi Eta Sigma; Phi Sigma; Outstndg Bio Stdnt Bk Awd 89-90; BS; Bio; Dntstry.

**NGUYEN, CHIEU ANH,** Va Commonwealth Univ, Richmond, VA; JR; BFA; Juried Exhbtn; Honord Awrd Wnnr 89; Intrn At Mktg Gen/Alxndria; Grphc Dsgn; Commncatns Art/Dsgn.

**NGUYEN, CHUONG H,** Eckerd Coll, St Petersburg, FL; SO; BS; Finance Comm; Mgmt Super METP Mpls; Bus Mgmt.

**NGUYEN, DANH T,** Temple Univ, Philadelphia, PA; JR; BS; Vietnamese Stu Assn 88-89; Dean Lst CC Of Phil 88-89; Dean Lst 90-; Elect Eng; Eng.

**NGUYEN, DIEM-SUONG T,** Franklin And Marshall Coll, Lancaster, PA; JR; BA; Amer Chem Scty Stdnt Afflte Treas; Bdgt Priorities Cmmttee Stdnt Cngrss 90; Yr Bk Bsnss Edtr 89-90; Phi Beta Kappa 90; Dana Schlr; Spldng Ldrshp Fllw 89-90; Rsrch Asst Hckmn/Hughes Fllw Rsrch Ast 89; Hmltn Bnk Wrk/Stdy Intrnshp 89-90; Chem/Bsnss/Ecnmcs; Law.

**NGUYEN, DO V,** Piedmont Tech Coll, Greenwood, SC; JR; BS; AD 81; Elec Eng Tech; Eng.

**NGUYEN, DUONG,** Temple Univ, Philadelphia, PA; SR; BS; Rho Chi 89-; ASHP 90-; BS Saigon Univ Sch Phrmcy 69; Prrmcy; Phrmcy/Res.

**NGUYEN, DZUNG B,** Univ Of Miami, Coral Gables, FL; FR; BA; Vtnms Asc 90-; Hosp Vol; Engr Sci.

**NGUYEN, HA Y,** Memphis St Univ, Memphis, TN; JR; BS; SWE; Tau Beta Pi; Dns Lst; Elec Eng.

**NGUYEN, HAN D,** Norwalk St Tech Coll, Norwalk, CT; SR; AS; Tau Alpha Pi VP 90-; Phi Theta Kappa VP 90-; Elec Engr; Engrng.

**NGUYEN, HANH P,** Univ Of Cincinnati, Cincinnati, OH; FR; Chem Eng.

**NGUYEN, HENRY HUNG-DINH,** Manhattan Coll, Bronx, NY; JR; Elec Engr/Applied Math.

**NGUYEN, HIEN N,** Univ Of South Al, Mobile, AL; FR; BS; Vietnamse Assoc 90-; Phi Eta Sigma; Alpha Lambda Delta; Bsns.

**NGUYEN, HIEU K,** Bunker Hill Comm Coll, Boston, MA; FR; Engl; Cmptr Tech.

**NGUYEN, HUNG V,** Univ Of Rochester, Rochester, NY; JR; BS; Vietnamese Stdnts Assn Monroe Comm Clg VP 87-88; Vietnamese Comm Rochester 87-89; Vietnamese Cthlc Org Choir 86-; Assoc Monroe Comm Clg 89; Microbio/Immunlgy; Med Schl MD.

**NGUYEN, HUY V,** Middle Ga Coll, Cochran, GA; SO; BA; Math/Sci; Eng.

**NGUYEN, HUYENLINH TRUC,** George Mason Univ, Fairfax, VA; FR; Business; Accounting.

**NGUYEN, JAY PHUONG L,** Ny Univ, New York, NY; FR; BA; Fin Bus; Fin Anlyst.

**NGUYEN, KIM-THANH T,** Howard Univ, Washington, DC; SR; BS; Rho Chi 90; Phrmcy.

**NGUYEN, LINH T,** Christian Brothers Univ, Memphis, TN; FR; BA; Interculture Club 90-; Chem; Medcn.

**NGUYEN, LYNH THI,** Univ Of Sc At Columbia, Columbia, SC; FR; BS; Gamma Beta Phi; Chmstry-Mathematics; Eng.

**NGUYEN, MINHCUONG C,** Univ Of Louisville, Louisville, KY; JR; BED; Elec; Engr.

**NGUYEN, MINHTAM C,** Univ Of Louisville, Louisville, KY; GD; Tau Beta Pi 89-90; Ntl Awrd Wnr 90-; Gldn Key 90-; Schlstc Achvmnt Deans Lst 85-86; BED; Elec; Engr.**

**NGUYEN, MONG-HOAI T,** Univ Of Rochester, Rochester, NY; SO; BA; Cmpn Rfg Yth 89-90; Frnds Vol 90-; Tutorng Clara Barton Schl; Janet Griswold Schlrshp 89-; Psychlgy; Ed.

**NGUYEN, MYHANH T,** City Univ Of Ny La Guard Coll, Long Island Cty, NY; SR; Acctng.

**NGUYEN, NGOC VAN T,** Boston Univ, Boston, MA; FR; BS; Vietnamese Assn Asst To Treas 90-; IM Vlybl 90-; Biology; Phys Thrpst.

**NGUYEN, NGOC-DIEP T,** Bunker Hill Comm Coll, Boston, MA.

**NGUYEN, NHU Q,** Univ Of Nc At Charlotte, Charlotte, NC; JR; Sga Co Dir Multi Cultr; Phi Eta Sigma; Pi Sigma Alpha Pr; Goldn Key; Amnsty; Dns Lst 89-; Pols/Econ; Law Schl.

**NGUYEN, RICHARD,** S U N Y At Buffalo, Buffalo, NY; SO; BS; Vietnamese Assoc V P 90-; Phi Eta Sigma 90-; IEEE; Elctrcl/Cmptr Engr; Elctrcl Engr.

**NGUYEN, ROBERT HUNG,** Middle Ga Coll, Cochran, GA; SO; BS; Phi Theta Kappa; Biol; Med.

**NGUYEN, SON K,** Va Commonwealth Univ, Richmond, VA; SO; BA; Accntng.

**NGUYEN, TAM T,** Jersey City St Coll, Jersey City, NJ; SO; BS; Chem.

**NGUYEN, TAN M,** Hillsborough Comm Coll, Tampa, FL; SO; BA; Acctng; Bus.

**NGUYEN, TEO H,** Univ Of Sc At Columbia, Columbia, SC; SR; Acctng; CPA.

**NGUYEN, THAI,** Manhattanville Coll, Purchase, NY; JR; Ciba-Geigy Intshp; Chem/Biochem; Env.

**NGUYEN, THANH T,** Va Commonwealth Univ, Richmond, VA; FR; BS; Phi Eta Sgm 90-; Bio; Med Dr.

**NGUYEN, THUY T,** S U N Y Coll Of Tech At Frmgdl, Farmingdale, NY; SO; BA; Asian Clb Pres/Scrtry 90; Accntng Scty Treas 89-90; AAS; Hlth Admin; Law Schl.

**NGUYEN, THY L A,** Va Commonwealth Univ, Richmond, VA; JR; Intrntnl Orgnztn 87-88; Mu Alpha Theta 87-88; Fr Hnr Scty 88-89; Comp Sci; Prgrmmr.

**NGUYEN, TOUYEN H,** Fl International Univ, Miami, FL; SO; BA; Intl Stu Clb 89-; Phi Eta Sigma 90-; Educ; Edctr.

**NGUYEN, TRUCMAI C,** Univ Of Louisville, Louisville, KY; JR; BED; Elec Engr.

**NGUYENDON, TAMMY H,** Univ Of Ky, Lexington, KY; GD; Kappa Alpha Theta 87-90.

**NGUYENDUC, MONICA D T,** Birmingham Southern Coll, Birmingham, AL; JR; BA; Pre Law Scty Intr Crdntr; Triangle Clb 88-89; Phi Alpha Theta; Phi Eta Sigma; Alpha Lambda Delta; Links/Up Prgrm Cnslr 88-89; Pre Law Clrkshp 89-90; History; Law Schl.

**NIBOH, MARTIN MBANGTANG,** Kent St Univ Kent Cmps, Kent, OH; GD; PHD; Taught Physcs Mthmtcs Vice Prncpl High Schl 87-90; BS Univ Yaounde 87; Physcs; Univ Tchng Reserch.

**NICE, JENNIFER L,** Marywood Coll, Scranton, PA; SO; Adpt/Grndprnt Campus Mnstry 89-90; Adpt/8th Grdr 90-; Fshn Clb 89-; Kappa Omicron Nu; Deans Lst 89-; Bus Admin/Mktg; Mktg/Intl Bus.

**NICE, NATALIE A,** Tallahassee Comm Coll, Tallahassee, FL; SO; BS; Sun Sch Tchr; AA 90; Pol Sci/Math; Law.

**NICE, TARA L,** Milligan Coll, Milligan Clg, TN; SR; BA; SGA Soc Affrs 89-; Delta Kappa Cls Rep; Relgs Affrs; Dns Lst; Fndrs Dghtr Swthrt Cand; Busn Admin/Econ/Comm; Publc Reltns.

**NICELY, TIMOTHY A,** Bridgewater Coll, Bridgewater, VA; SR; BS; Vars Bsebl Capt 87-; Magna Cum Laude Grad; Pol Sci; Adm/Mgmt.

**NICELY, WARREN L,** Bowling Green St Univ, Bowling Green, OH; JR; BS; Mnfctrng Tech; Eng.

**NICHOLAS, FRANK A,** Bridgeport Engr Inst, Fairfield, CT; SR; BS; Tau Alpha Pi Sec 84-85; Eng Asst 85-; Sikorsky Aircrft Main St Stratfrd; AS Norwlk St Tech Clg 85; Mech Eng.

**NICHOLAS, TERESA L,** Univ Of Southern Ms, Hattiesburg, MS; FR.

**NICHOLAS-YAGHOUB, ARIS,** Univ Of Ct, Storrs, CT; SO; BS; Bio; Premed.

**NICHOLLS, BETH A,** George Mason Univ, Fairfax, VA; SO; Cir K 90-; Busn; Acctg.

**NICHOLLS, DAWN M,** Seton Hall Univ, South Orange, NJ; SR; BSN; Stdnt Nrs Assc 89-; Nrs Pinning Ceremony Co Chrmn 90-; Sgm Theta Tau 90-; Nrsng; Med/Surg Nrsng.

**NICHOLLS, JODY L,** Univ Of Rochester, Rochester, NY; SR; BA; Glee Club 87-; Dorm Council 87-89; Independent Study 90; Sr Thesis; Geology; Envrmntl Communications.

**NICHOLS, ALISON,** Gaston Coll, Dallas, NC; FR; AAS; Mech Drftg/Dsgn Tech; Mech Engr.

**NICHOLS, ALLISON E,** Middle Tn St Univ, Murfreesboro, TN; JR; BS; HSA 89-; TRPA 90-; HPERS 90-; Tau Omicron Sec 90-; Gamma Beta Phi 90-; Phi Kappa Phi; Natl Wmns Hist Month Chr; Jr Honors Awd 89-90; Reynolds Schlrshp; Recreation; Church Recreation.

**NICHOLS, ANN B,** Coker Coll, Hartsville, SC; SR; BED; Ntl Cncl Math Tchrs; Assc Sprvsn/Crrclm Dvlpmnt 90-; Deans Lst 90-; Cncl Fr Excptnl Chldrn; EH Autstc Asst 87-; BS Psychlgy Francis Marion Clg 78; Spcl Educ; Tchr.

**NICHOLS, ANNETTE C,** Wv Univ, Morgantown, WV; SR; Jr Cl Treas 89-90.

**NICHOLS, CAROLYN,** Methodist Coll, Fayetteville, NC; SR; Beta Beta Beta; Phi Sigma Iota; Alpha Chi; BS Methodist College; Blgy; Ph D In Blgy.

**NICHOLS, CONNIE F,** Middle Tn St Univ, Murfreesboro, TN; SO; BBA; Bsns; Ofc Mngmnt.

**NICHOLS, DEBORA L,** Memphis St Univ, Memphis, TN; JR; BPS; Gamma Beta Phi 89; Glden Key 90; Phi Kappa Phi; Deans List 88; AM Psych Scty 89; Human Services; Cnslng/Psychlgy.

**NICHOLS, DENAY C,** Univ Of Tn At Martin, Martin, TN; JR; BS; STEA 88-; Spec Ed; Tch.

**NICHOLS, JOY W,** Piedmont Coll, Demorest, GA; JR; BA; Torch; Erly Chldhd Ed; Tchng.**

**NICHOLS III, JULIAN E,** Central Al Comm Coll, Alexander City, AL; SO; AA; Psychlgy.

**NICHOLS, KATRINA M,** Alcorn St Univ, Lorman, MS; SO; BA; Bwlng Tm 90-; Fashn Merch Econ; Dsgng/Retl.

**NICHOLS, KENNY A,** Univ Of Nc At Asheville, Asheville, NC; FR; Christian Action Flwshpf Rifle Tm; Stdnts For Amer VP 90; Phi Eta Sigma; Fairmont Proj Zeta Alpha; Bowery Mission; Upper Rm Midnigh Run Mssn Grp; Sccr; Math Educ; Teacher.

**NICHOLS, KIMAKA,** Winthrop Coll, Rock Hill, SC; FR; BA; PACE; Pol Sci; Law.

**NICHOLS, LAURA A,** Salisbury St Univ, Salisbury, MD; GD; Psychology; Law Schl.

**NICHOLS, LINDA S,** Liberty Univ, Lynchburg, VA; SR; BS; Lib Mktg Assn 90; Soc Humn Res Mgmt 90; Alpha Lambda Delta 87-90; Cir K Sec 89-90; Intrnshp Mgmt Trnee J C Penny 89-90; Busn; Mgmt/Mktg.

**NICHOLS, LYNDA D,** Memphis St Univ, Memphis, TN; SO; BA; Phi Eta Sigma 90; Alpha Lambda Delta 90; Sbsdm Memphis Oral Schl/Deaf 86-; Exec Sec/Sec/Admin/Bkkpr/Lffc Mngr; TN Rl Est Lic TN Rl Est Cmmssn Nshvl 85-; Art; Teach Univ Level.

**NICHOLS, MARK D,** Daemen Coll, Amherst, NY; JR.

**NICHOLS, MARY-SUE O,** Daytona Beach Comm Coll, Daytona Beach, FL; SO; AA; Phnx Envrmntl Clb 89-; Stdt Actvts Brd Rep 88-; 1st Annual Vol Fstvl Fndr 90; Intercollegiate Un Allncs Rep 90-; Phi Theta Kappa Pres 88-; Halifax Med Ctr 88-; Untd Wy Stdt Rep 88-; Hbitat Hmnty 88-; Yth Mtvtr Pblc Schl 90-; Chem/Wrtng Awd 90-; Pre Medicine; Biochemist.

**NICHOLS, MELISSA M,** Northern Ky Univ, Highland Hts, KY; JR; BA; Lckng Rvr Rvw Asst Ed 90-; Pr Tutor 90-; Lst Cs Rvw Stf Wrtr 90-; Eng; Lit/Crtv Wrtng Prfsr.

**NICHOLS, PAULETTE,** Northwest Al Comm Coll, Phil Campbell, AL; SO; Phi Theta Kappa.

**NICHOLS, REBECCA A,** Univ Of Tn At Martin, Martin, TN; FR; Bptst Stdnt Union Nesltr Edtr 90-; Elem Edctn; Tchng.

**NICHOLS, RHONDA D,** Univ Of Sc At Columbia, Columbia, SC; JR; BA; Engl; Sec Educ/Engl.

**NICHOLS, SHARON F,** Livingston Univ, Livingston, AL; SR; BS; Sprngfld Meth Prot Chrch; Sec/Bnk Cstmr Asst; Patrick Henry State Jr Coll 78; Math; Tchr.

**NICHOLS, SHARON L,** Bob Jones Univ, Greenville, SC; SR; BS; Nu Alpha Phi 88-; Pre-Med.**

**NICHOLS, TIFFANY A,** Belmont Abbey Coll, Belmont, NC; SR; BA; Clg Union Bd 88-90; Yrbk Stf 89; Natl Assn Accntnts 90-; Commuter Cncl 88-90; Pi Gamma Mu Secy 90-; Delta Epsilon Sigma 90-; Lambda Xi Sorority Pres 88-; Super Senior Awd; Natl Assn Accntnts Schlrshp 90-; Martin-Irene Kehoe Schlrshp 90-; Acctng; CPA.**

**NICHOLS, TRACY A,** Univ Of Md Baltimore Prof Schl, Baltimore, MD; SR; BS; Qst Care Comm VP 90-91; Stdnt Amrcn Dntl Hygiene Assn 89-; Deans Lst 89-; Stdnt Amrcn Dntl Hygn Scl Comm Chrmn 90-; Orthdntc Clrkshp 90; Dntl Hygiene; Prvt Prctc Dntl Hygiene.

**NICHOLS, VALERIE L,** Univ Of Pittsburgh At Bradford, Bradford, PA; FR; BA; Hmn Rels; Tchg/Cnslr.

**NICHOLS-HOLDEN, KATHERINE E,** Univ Of Cincinnati-Clrmnt Coll, Batavia, OH; SO; AS; BA; Crmnl Jstc; Police Offcr.

**NICHOLSON, AMY E,** Memphis St Univ, Memphis, TN; SO; BSED; Tiger Tamers 89-; Delta Gamma Anchora Pr 89-; Deans List; Special Education; Teaching.

**NICHOLSON, AMY S,** Medical Coll Of Ga, Augusta, GA; SR; BSN; GANS 89-90; Nrsng Asst St Josephs Hosp 90-; North GA Nrsng Career Fair Chrmn 90; Outstndng Clg Stdnts Am 88; Deans List 89-90; IM Sftbl 88-89; Nrsng; Trnsplnt Crdntr.

**NICHOLSON JR, BOBBY G,** Middle Tn St Univ, Murfreesboro, TN; SR; BBA; Stdnts For Envrnmntl Actn Treas 90-; Phi Sigma Epsilon 82-83; Bus Admin.

**NICHOLSON, CANDACE A,** Univ Of Nc At Asheville, Asheville, NC; JR; BS; Phi Eta Sigma 88-; Mgmt.

**NICHOLSON, DAVID A,** Truett Mc Connell Coll, Cleveland, GA; SO; BS; Bptst Mnstr; Gspl Sngr; Spcl Olympcs; Tchrs Aid Spcl Edctn 88-; Spcl Edctn N GA Clg; Tchr.

**NICHOLSON, GRADINE S,** Inter Amer Univ Pr Hato Rey, Hato Rey, PR; FR; BA; Red Cross Pres; Yng People Church Grp VP; Engl/Span; Comm.

**NICHOLSON, HEATHER R,** Univ Of Southern Ms, Hattiesburg, MS; SO; BA; Crusade Chrst 90-; Alumni Assn 90-; Bapt Stdnt Un 90; Dns Lst 90; Foreign Lang; Intrptr/Trnsltr.

**NICHOLSON, JARRETT L,** Tn Tech Univ, Cookeville, TN; SO; BS; Flwshp Chrstn Athlts 90-; Intl Agri Clb 90-; Agri.

**NICHOLSON, JENNIFER MELISSA E,** Univ Of Sc At Columbia, Columbia, SC; SR; BA; Educ Majors Clb 87-; S Carolina Educ Assn 90-; Natl Educ Assn 90-; Spec Olympics VOC 89-90; Educ Mjrs Schlrshp 90-; Elem Educ; Tchng.

**NICHOLSON, JENNIFER T,** Univ Of Tn At Martin, Martin, TN; SR; BA; Stdnt Afflts Amer Chem Soc 87-; Alpha Phi Omega Tres 89-; Eng Soc 8.-; Sigma Tau Delta 89-; Mu Epsilon Delta Pldg Trnr 87-91; Kappa Alpha 90-; Hnrs Smnr Schlrshp 87-88; Deans List; English/Biology; Med Rsrch/Educ Psych.

**NICHOLSON, JOSEPH H,** Alfred Univ, Alfred, NY; JR; BS; IEEE VP 89-; Trck Tm; Elec Engr.

**NICHOLSON, SAMANTHA C,** William Carey Coll, Hattiesburg, MS; JR; BS; Elem Ed; Tchg.

**NICHOLSON, STEPHANIE L,** Glassboro St Coll, Glassboro, NJ; JR; BA; Math; Clg Prof.

**NICHOLSON, WILLIAM J,** Franklin And Marshall Coll, Lancaster, PA; FR; Pre-Healing Arts Clb; Hnrs Lst; Dns Lst.

**NICINSKI, TIMOTHY R,** William Paterson Coll, Wayne, NJ; SO; USMC Reserves Lance Cpl; Oper Desert Storm/Shield; Hstry; Sec Sch Tchr.

**NICKEL, CARL A,** Comm Coll Algny Co Algny Cmps, Pittsburgh, PA; SO; MS; Deans Lst 90-; Spcl Olympcs Sprts Coord Athltcs Coach 88-; Rhbltn Inst Pttsbrgh Physcl Thrpy Vol 90; Chld Aid Hm Inc Pstn Site Mngr Mntly Hndcppd Adlts 90-; AS; Physcl Thrpy.

**NICKELSEN, ERIC S,** Birmingham Southern Coll, Birmingham, AL; FR; BA; Habitat Hmnty 90-; Triangle Clb; Alpha Lambda Delta 90-; Phi Eta Sigma 90-; Theta Chi Asst Tres 90-; Bsns; Bnkng.

**NICKELSON, KAY J,** Christopher Newport Coll, Newport News, VA; SR; BA; Educ Erly Chldhd.

**NICKERSON, BETHANIE HOLLY,** Univ Of Tn At Martin, Martin, TN; FR; BA; Clgte 4 H; Univ Schlr Fresh Rep 90-; Kappa Alpha Southern Belle; Chem Soc Sec; Wildlife Soc Sec; Proj Recycle Pub Chrmn 90-; Acad All Amer Schlr 90-; Mrchng/Cncrt Band; 4 H Natl Wildlife Proj Awd 90-; Envrnmntl Mgmt; Envrnmntl Rsrsh/Law.

**NICKERSON, JILL K,** Univ Of Ky, Lexington, KY; JR; Epsilon Delta 90-; Pi Beta Phi 90-; Epsilon Delta 90-; Epsilon Delta 90-; IM Chrmn 90-; Soc/Bhvrl Sci; Elem Educ Tchr.

**NICKERSON, KURT H,** Univ Of Rochester, Rochester, NY; SR; BS; Am Soc Mech Engrs 88-; Tau Beta Pi 90-; Alpha Delta Phi 88-; Mech Eng.

**NICKERSON, LISA ANN,** Newbury Coll, Brookline, MA; SO; AS; Stdnt Cncl Cls Rep 89; Boston Co 90-; Bus Mgmnt; Mgmnt.

**NICKERSON, MELISSA ELAINE,** Liberty Univ, Lynchburg, VA; SO; BS; Cncrt Chr Chpln 90-; Sprtl Lf Prog Dir 90-; Radio Anncr 89-; Alpha Lambda Delta Edtr 90-; Telecmnctns; Radio Brdcstng.

**NICKLAS, DEBORAH A,** Allegheny Coll, Meadville, PA; JR; BA; Allies Mbr 90-; Allegheny Comm Exch Coord 88-89; Kappa Alpha Theta 90-; Am Heart Assoc Instr 90-; Emerg Med Tech P A Cert 88-; Med/Rescue Tm 87-; Alden Schlr 89-90; Stdnt Athletic Trainer 88-; EMT Cert 88; CPR Instr Cert 90; Pre-Med/Math; Medicine.

**NICKLE, MELODY J,** Wilmington Coll, New Castle, DE; SR; BS; AS Wstrn OK State Coll 87; Bus Mgmnt.**

**NICKLIN, DEBRA M,** Garrett Comm Coll, Mchenry, MD; SO; BA; Raiders Lost Arts Secy 89-90; Phi Theta Kappa 90-; AA; Elem Mddl Educ; Teacher.

**NICKLIN, SHAWN D,** Garrett Comm Coll, Mchenry, MD; SO; EDUC; Raiders Art Clb Pres 89-90; Phi Theta Kappa V P 90-; Hs Of Hope Bkbl Game; Grad GCC High Hon; AA 91; Coach/Tch.

**NICKLIS, KIMBERLEY L,** George Mason Univ, Fairfax, VA; SR; BS ED; Golden Key 90-; Kappa Delta Pi 90; Phys Educ/Tchr Cert; Adptve Phys Educ.

**NICKLOW, PAULA M,** Liberty Univ, Lynchburg, VA; GD; Kappa Delta Pi 88-; Hons Pgm 87-89; Alpha Lamda Delta 86-90; Engl Hon Soc 88-90; Res Asst Schlrshp 88-90; Chncllr Schlrshp 86-87; GPA Schlrshp 88-90; Hons Schlrshp 87-88; IM Vlybl 87-90; BS; Engl; Tch.

**NICKOLAI, NICOLE K,** S U N Y Coll Of A & T Morrisvl, Morrisville, NY; SO; BA; Engl; Sec Educ.

**NICKS, JULIE D,** Univ Of Montevallo, Montevallo, AL; JR; BA; SAEA Pres 89-; Alpha Lambda Delta 89-; Kappa Delta Pi VP; Omicron Delta Kappa; Elem/Early Chldhd Educ; Tch.

**NICOL, DEBRA D,** Ga St Univ, Atlanta, GA; SR; BSED; Tchng Asst Fulton Cty Bd Of Ed 87-; Math; Tchr.

**NICOL, MARIANNE R,** Lesley Coll, Cambridge, MA; SR; BA; AS N Essex Comm Coll 89; Early Chldhd Educ; Tchr/Art Thrpst.

**NICOLADU, STELLA T,** Univ Of Md At Eastern Shore, Princess Anne, MD; SR; BA; Dns Lst; Hstry; Clg Tchr/Hstry.

**NICOLAOU, DANAE A,** Duquesne Univ, Pittsburgh, PA; JR; BA; Intrntnl Stnt Orgnztn Pres 90; Phi Eta Sigma; Lamda Sigma; Intrnshp Shrsn Lhmn Brothers; Bsn Finance; Finance.

**NICOLAY, KATHLEEN H,** Univ Of Md Baltimore Prof Schl, Baltimore, MD; JR; BS; Cls Tres 90-; Phi Kappa Phi; Dentl Hygn.

**NICOLETTA, ROBERT J,** Univ Of Rochester, Rochester, NY; JR; Activities Cncl; Amesty Intl 88-90; Dorm Cncl; Scty Undergrad Biology Stdnts; Alpha Lambda Delta 87-; Phi Eta Sigma; Dean Lst; Big Bros Big Sisters Prog; Orthopedic Intrnshps Strong Meml Hosp 88-90; Vrsty Ftbl 87-; Biology; Medicine.

**NICOLINI, MARK J,** Suffolk Comm Coll Selden Cmps, Selden, NY; FR; BA; Cmptr Sci; Cmptr Pgm.**

**NICOLL, WILLIAM ALEXANDER,** Western New England Coll, Springfield, MA; SO; BS; Peer Tutor 90-; Dns Lst; Vars Soccer 89-; Elctrcl Engr.

**NICOLUSSI, CHRISTOPHER L,** Allegheny Coll, Meadville, PA; SR; BA; Interfrat Cncl Pres 90; Stdnt Govt Sen 90-; Pub Events Comm 90-; Order Of Omega 90-; Alden Schlr 90; Delt Tau Delta Corres Sec; Comm On Racial Issues 90-; Stdnt Orntn Adv 90-; Annual Giving Office Intern 90; Carson Grp Inc Intern 90; Comm Arts; Pub Rltns.

**NICOME, PATRICIA,** City Univ Of Ny City Coll, New York, NY; SO; ICF Sec 89-90; Hosp Chld Psychtry Intern 89-; Dns Lst 90-; Blgy; Med.

**NICOTRA, BEVERLY A,** Saint Francis Coll, Loretto, PA; JR; BA; Cinema Shwcs Chrprsn 88-; Jrn Cls Ofcr Sec 90-; Chrs 89-; Cmps Mnstry 90-; Big Sister Pgm 88-; Soc/Crim Jstc; Law.

**NICOTRA, CHRISTA D,** Duquesne Univ, Pittsburgh, PA; JR; BA; Orntn Entrnmnt 89-; Sign Waves Cmtr Cncl Pro Chr 88-89; Cncl Excptnl Chldrn 89-; Mrtr Brd; Kappa Delta Epsilon 90-; DUV; Freewhlrs 89-; Educ; Tchg.

**NICOTRA, CHRISTOPHER M,** S U N Y At Buffalo, Buffalo, NY; SR; BS; IEEE 90-91; Ny Army National Guard 90-; U S Army 88-90; Arvin Arvin Calspan Intrn; Cmptr Engr; Engr MS.

**NIDA, LESA L,** Marshall University, Huntington, WV; SR; BA; Band Flg Corp Capt 86-; Spnsh/Math; Tchr.

**NIDAY, MELINDA W,** Winthrop Coll, Rock Hill, SC; GD; MBA; AMA V P 90; Econ Club Pres 90; Alpha Kappa Psi/ Alumni Sec 90; Grdte Assistantship; BS Winthrop Clg; Bsn Admin; Mktg.

**NIDIFFER, KATHI A,** George Mason Univ, Fairfax, VA; SR; BED; IMBSKTBL 88-; IM Vlybl 89; IM Sftbl 89-90; Athltc Acad Hon Rl 89-; Dns Lst; Sccr Cpt 87-; Physcl Educ/Hlth; Tchng.

**NIDO, RAFAEL J,** Emory Univ, Atlanta, GA; SR; BBA; Emry Mktg Assn 87-; Intl Assn 87-; Latn Amer Intrst Org 90-; US Achvmnt Acdmy All Amer Schlr; GA Bus Pln Competitn; IM Sprts Co-Capt 87-; 5th Annl Intl Bus Pln Competitn; Bus/Mktg; MBA.

**NIEDZWIECKI, ELIZABETH A,** Ny Univ, New York, NY; SO; BA; J Walter Thompson 88-; Socl Sci; Envrnmntl Law.

**NIEHAUS, JOANNA M,** Univ Of Cincinnati, Cincinnati, OH; JR; BSN; Stdnt Nurses Assn; 500 Hr Vol Awd; Bs Nrsng; Oncology Nurse Clinical Spclst.

**NIEHUS, JAMES P,** Radford Univ, Radford, VA; SO; BED; Vars Lcrs Tm 89-; Hstry; Tch/Coaching.

**NIEKREWICZ, DEBRA K,** Felician Coll, Lodi, NJ; SR; Edn Clb 86-87/90-; Edn/Soc Bhvrl Sci; Teach.

**NIELSEN, CONNIE L,** George Mason Univ, Fairfax, VA; GD; MSW; Soc Wrk Stdnt Assn Treas 89-90; Golden Key 89-90; NASW; Thrpst Mntl Hlth Fld; BSW George Mason Univ 90; Soc Wrk; Mntl Hlth Thrpst.

**NIELSEN, JEFFREY A,** Albertus Magnus Coll, New Haven, CT; FR; BA; IM Sftbl 90-; Dns Lst 90; Bsktbl Crss Cntry Tms 90-; Math.

**NIELSEN, KELLY R,** Fl St Univ, Tallahassee, FL; SR; BA; Lambda Pi Eta; Advrtsng Intrnshp Jack Eckerd Corp; Advrtsng Cmmnctn.

**NIEMAN, JAMES,** Univ Of Nc At Charlotte, Charlotte, NC; JR; BA; Pre-Law Soc 89-; Crmnl Jstce Assn; Rugby Clb 89-; Pi Sigma Alpha; Tau Kappa Epsilon; Intrnshp DA Off 90; UNCC Rugby Clb; Poltcl Sci; Law.

**NIEMANN, PATRICIA L,** Saint Francis Coll, Loretto, PA; SO; BS; Physcns Asst Soc 90-; Hnrs Prgrm 89-; Vlntr Dorothy Day Cntr Cmps 90-; Hnrs Prgrm 89-; Phi Delta Kappa; CV Starr Schlrshp 90-; Physcns Asst.

**NIEMEL, KAREN S,** Univ Of Rochester, Rochester, NY; SO; BA; Un Symp Orch 89-; USO Orch Bd Co-Chpsn 89-; Tae Kwon Do 90-; Pol Sci; Law.

**NIERMEYER, ERIC P,** Saint John Fisher Coll, Rochester, NY; JR; BS; Acctg Clb 89-; IM Bsktbl 90-; IM Sftb 89-; Soc CPA Cndidts 90-; Tchrs Asst 90-; Tutr 89-; Vars Tnns 90-; Pblc Acctg.

**NIETO, JOSEPH I,** Norfolk St Univ, Norfolk, VA; JR; BS; Phi Theta Kappa VP 89-; SME Secty; Air Natl Guard Civil Engrs Assn; Mech Eng Tch; AAS Comm Clg Air Force; Indtl Mgt; Mfg Mgt.

**NIEVES CARABALLO, GLADYS N,** Catholic Univ Of Pr, Ponce, PR; SR; Clb De Avnzda Arstca 90; Actvdds Expscns De Pntras; Assn De Ftrs Prfsnl De La Educ; Lista De Honor Del Decano 89-; Arts.

**NIEVES CRUZ, RAMON F,** Inter Amer Univ Pr Barranquita, Barranquitas, PR; SO; Ass Estudiantil Ciencia 90; Voluntarios En Accion; Otorgacion De Cert De Aprovecha 89; Miento Por La Univ 90-.

**NIEVES QUINONES, DANIEL A,** Univ Central Del Caribe, Cayey, PR; SO; MD; Svnth-Day Advntst Med Cadet Corp 85-88; Pthfndrs Clb Cnslr 82-85; US Pub Hlth Serv COSTEP; Mcgrw Hill Awrd Med Stdnts 90; Bsktbl Sftbl; BS Univ Of P R 89; Med; Intrnl Med.

**NIEVES, DAYANA,** Univ Of Pr Medical Sciences, San Juan, PR; GD; BA; Juvenile Coop Of Comerio Org 89-; Cath Yth Proj Coord 90-; Cultural/Sociol Stdy Dominican Republic 90-; Magna Cum Laude Dental Assist; Acad Achvmnt Cert 90-; Ldrshp/Acad Achvmnt; Admin.

**NIEVES JR, JESUS MANUEL,** Manchester Comm Coll, Manchester, CT; SO; BA; Mahatuk Cmnty Clg Pres List 89; Acctng; CPA.

**NIEVES, JOSE S,** Univ Of Pr At Rio Piedras, Rio Piedras, PR; SO; BA; Mnrty Rsrch Cntr Exclinc; Cntr Enrgy/Envrnmntl Rsrch; Axlry Rsrchng Scntsts/Dept Of Natrl Rsrcs 90-; Hnr Stds Prog 90-; Rsrch MARC; Biology; Neurobiological Scncs.

**NIEVES, KAREN,** Daytona Beach Comm Coll, Daytona Beach, FL; SO; BA; Acctg; CPA.

**NIEVES, LUCIA,** Univ Of Pr Humacao Univ Coll, Humacao, PR; SR; BBA; Assc Univ Stu Gerencia 90; Hnr Stu Assc Pres 89-; Stu Rep Title Iii Hnr Prog 89-90; Catechist 90; Mngmnt; Indus Psychlgcl.

**NIEVES, YOLANDA,** Univ Of Pr At Rio Piedras, Rio Piedras, PR; JR; Hnr Roll 89-; Communications; Advrtsng.

**NIEVES-DE JESUS, CARLOS E,** Univ Of Pr At Mayaguez, Mayaguez, PR; SR; BA; Amer Soc Qulty Cntrl; Phi Kappa Phi; Alpha Pi Mu; NSF Incntv Exclince Schlrshp; Indstrl; Eng.

**NIEVES-MINDEZ, DEBORAH E,** Univ Of Pr Humacao Univ Coll, Humacao, PR; SO; BA; Assn Biology Stdnts 89-90; Hnr Acad Prog HUC; Microbiology; Molecular/Cellular Biology.

**NIEVES-PADILLA, MADELINE,** City Univ Of Ny City Coll, New York, NY; GD; BA; NYPIRG; Fld Plcmnt Acad Adusing Off; Alumni Assn Peer Acad Advsrs; Cmuty Hlth Educ; Pharm.

**NIEVES-ROSA, ANA,** Univ Of Pr At Rio Piedras, Rio Piedras, PR; JR; Inter Amer Soc Psych; Soc Cmnty Rsrch/Action; Div 27 Amer Psych Assn; Golden Key; Dns Lst 90-; Hispanic Marc Trng Biopsychosocial Rsrch 90; Pres Cathl Org 89-; Rsrch Assist 90; Vlybl; MARC Pgm; Psych.

**NIEWIEROWSKI, BRADLEY J,** Kent St Univ Kent Cmps, Kent, OH; JR; BS; Golden Key Natl; Ex Sci; Grad Schl.

**NIGAGLIONI, ANNIA,** Fl International Univ, Miami, FL; SO; Cmptr Sci; Cmptr Pgrmg.

**NIGHTINGALE, JOHN C,** Christopher Newport Coll, Newport News, VA; SR; BSBA; FMC Corp Mrn/Rl Div 79-86; Mgr Mrn Cnstrctn 79-86; Prod/Mtrl Cntrl Mgr 86-; Fin; Pblc Acctg.

**NIGRO, DANA M,** Cornell Univ Statutory College, Ithaca, NY; SO; BS; Magazine Prdctn Mngr 90-; Eqstrn Tm 89-; Ho Nun De Kah; Cmmnctnf Jrnlsm Pblshng.

**NIJHOF, MARGREET G,** Bunker Hill Comm Coll, Boston, MA; SO; BA; Dptmnt Awd Spcl Achvmnt Comm; Acdmc Exclnc Awd Lbrl Arts; Grad Hghst Hnrs; Intrntnl Ecnmcs; Intrntnl Law.

**NIKLAS, CHRISTIAN E,** Kent St Univ Kent Cmps, Kent, OH; SO.

**NIKODEM, BARBARA L,** Bowling Green St Univ, Bowling Green, OH; FR; Theatre Prdctn 90-; Orchstr 90-; Chr 90; Hon Stdnt Assc 90; Phi Eta Sgm.

**NIKSTAITIS, DAWN R,** Fayetteville St Univ, Fayetteville, NC; FR; BA; Acctg; CPA.

**NILES, ADRIAN L,** City Univ Of Ny Baruch Coll, New York, NY; JR; BBA; Gldn Ky; Acctg; Acctg/Cmptr Info Sys.

**NILES, ELIZABETH C,** Fl St Univ, Tallahassee, FL; JR; BA; Alumni Fndtn 90-; Stdnt Govt 89-90; Cmpus Sing 90-; Chi Omega Alumni-Advsr Chrprsn; Chi Omega Head Stndrds Bd 90-; Comm; Mgmt.

**NILES, LYNN E,** Ma Inst Of Tech, Cambridge, MA; JR; BS; March Band Pres 88-; Musical Theater Guild Mem Lrg 88-; Soc Wmn Engrs 88-; Sigma Kappa Rec Sec 88-; Louis Stahl Schlr Chem 89-; Envrnmntl Chem.**

**NILL, ROBERT W,** Coll Misericordia, Dallas, PA; JR; BA; AS Comm Clg Luzerne Cty 90; Hstry; Professor.

**NILLES, DONALD A,** Univ Of Sc At Coastal Carolina, Conway, SC; JR; BS; Num/Bytes 90-; Dns Lst 89-; Comp Sci; Syst Anlyst.

**NILO, TINA G,** Oh St Univ At Marion, Marion, OH; SR; BS; Hmn Rsrce Assn 90; Soc Hmn Rsrce Mgmt 90; Dns Lst; Hmn Rsrce Assn Svc Award; Summer Intrnshp Soundsation Inc 91; Bsn; HRM.

**NILSEN, LAUREN J,** Duquesne Univ, Pittsburgh, PA; FR; BA; Most Imprvd Player Awd; Phi Eta Sigma; Lambda Sigma; Duquesne Exmplry Acad Effrt Awd; Vlybl; Nrsng; RN.

**NILSSON, PER J,** Univ Of Southern Ms, Hattiesburg, MS; SR; BA; Omicron Delta Epsilon VP; Gldn Key 90-; Gamma Beta Phi 90-; Delta Phi Eta Sigma 90-; WSM Wl St Jrnl Awd; Econ; Finc.

**NIMMONS, DANIELLE L,** S U N Y Coll Of Tech At Frmgdl, Farmingdale, NY; JR; Sec Erly Chldhd Clb 90; Dns Lst 88-90; Chrldr; AS 90; Erly Chldhd Educ; Pub Schl Tchr.

**NIMOX, TERRENCE M,** Tougaloo Coll, Tougaloo, MS; JR; BA; SGA Ofc Mgr 90-; Nwspr Phtgrphr 88-; Peer Hlprs Pgm Acad Afrs Ofc Cnslr 90-; Meta Phi Sgm Engl Clb; Minds Prdctv Stdnts VP 89-; Radio Intrn DJ 90-; Engl/Jrnlsm; Pblc Rltns/ Advrtsng/Law.

**NINNESS, RICHARD J,** Univ Of Sc At Columbia, Columbia, SC; JR; BA; Hstry; Tchng.

**NIRMALANI, SANGEETA,** George Mason Univ, Fairfax, VA; SO; BS; Assoc Of Indian Stdnts 89-; Internatl Stdnts Assoc 89-; Acctng Club 89-; Deans List 89-; Hon Roll 90-; Acctng; CPA.

**NISCHAN, MELISSA L,** Franklin And Marshall Coll, Lancaster, PA; SO; BA; Astrnmy Clb; Physics Clb; Dance Clb; Physics; Rsrch.

**NISHIYAMA, TAKASHI,** Univ Of Southern Ms, Hattiesburg, MS; JR; BA; Bapt Union 88-; Dewey R/Wilma Sanderson Schlrshp Fnd 89-90; Intl Stds.

**NISSLE, SUSAN M,** Cornell Univ Statutory College, Ithaca, NY; FR; BS; Chrs Cncrt Mgr; PB Jm Thtr T Grp; Deans Lst; Mdrn Dnc; Blgcl Sci; Rsrch Nrblgy.

**NIST, LORRIE A,** Duquesne Univ, Pittsburgh, PA; JR; BA; Stdnt Acctg Assoc 90-; Beta Alpha Phi 90-; Acctg Bus.

**NISWANDER, DONNA K,** Univ Of Montevallo, Montevallo, AL; FR; BA; Bsn.

**NISWONGER, CHAD D,** Wilmington Coll, Wilmington, OH; FR; BA; Drama Clb; Bsktbl; Bsn Admn; Mgmt.

**NITCHMAN, ROBERT A,** Schenectady County Comm Coll, Schenectady, NY; FR; AAS; Music Certif 90; Music Perf; Ed.

**NITSUN, FIONA J,** Yeshiva Univ, New York, NY; GD; MS; Spch Path Clb Treas 88-90; Yrbk Bus Ed 90; Deans Lst 86-90; JPSY Advsr 89-90; AA 90; BA Cum Laude 90; Cmnctn Diordrs; Spch Ther.

**NITTOLO, SHERI LEIGH,** Middle Tn St Univ, Murfreesboro, TN; JR; BS; Child Cr Ctr Asst Tchr 90-; Math/Art.

**NITZSCHKE, JOHN D,** Roane St Comm Coll, Harriman, TN; SO; MBA; Sunbright Boys Clb 88-; Deans Lst 90-; Booster Clb 89-; Ldrshp Pgm 87; St Trnmnt Bsbll 89; Electrical Eng.**

**NIV, LAVI,** Duquesne Univ, Pittsburgh, PA; JR; BA; Bsn; Intl Bsn/Mktg.

**NIVENS, ANGELA,** Savannah Coll Of Art & Design, Savannah, GA; JR; BFA; Frlncng Cmmssn Wrk Spclzng Fntsy Sci Fictn 87-; Art Hstry.

**NIVENS, CATHERINE E,** Univ Of Sc At Spartanburg, Spartanburg, SC; JR; BA; Clemson Univ Chorus 88-90; Clemson Plyrs 90; Clemson Univ Spirit Clb 89-90; Gamma Sigma Sigma 90; Early Chldhd Ed; Elem Tchr.

**NIX, CRAIG L,** Univ Of Sc At Columbia, Columbia, SC; SO; MBA; Gamma Beta Phi; Golden Key Ntnl; Acctng.**

**NIX, JOE K,** Univ Of Nc At Asheville, Asheville, NC; JR; BA; CERT Natl Inst Autmtv Serv Exclnce 89; Math; Tch.

**NIX, PATRICIA D,** Truett Mc Connell Coll, Cleveland, GA; FR; BED; Emplyd Milliken Avalon; Sci; Physcl Thrpy.

**NIX, RALESHIA L,** Univ Of Montevallo, Montevallo, AL; FR; BA; Std Govt Asc; Cvtn Clb Treas; Chem Clb; Bio Clb; IM Sftbl Ptchr; Bio; Med.

**NIX, REBECCA D,** Univ Of Montevallo, Montevallo, AL; JR; BS; Dean Lst Jeff St Jr Coll 90-; Dean Lst Univ Montevallo 90-; Elem Educ/Erly Chldhd; Tchr.

**NIX, VIRGINIA P,** Valdosta St Coll, Valdosta, GA; FR; BA; Chi Omega Sor 90-; SGA 90-; Campus Act Brd 90-; Bus Admin/ Spanish.

**NIXON, ALISA L,** Al A & M Univ, Normal, AL; FR; BS; Made Deans Lst Hnr Roll AAMU 90-; Cmptr Sci; Cmptr Prgrmmr Systm Analysts.

**NIXON, DENISE R,** Univ Of Sc At Columbia, Columbia, SC; FR; Sclgy; Scl Wrk.

**NIXON, GWENDOLYN G,** Va Commonwealth Univ, Richmond, VA; SR; VA Natl Grd E4 Spclst 84-90.

**NIXON, JULIA B,** Anderson Coll, Anderson, SC; FR; MBA; Phi Theta Kappa 90; Psych/Sclgy; Scl Wrk/Tchng.

**NIXON, ROBIN M,** Univ Of Md At Eastern Shore, Princess Anne, MD; JR; BSMS; Assoc Commuting Mchnry Sec; AA Hagerstown Jr Coll 86; Comp Sci; Comp Sys Anlst/Sftwr Design.

**NIXON, SHAWN J,** Savannah St Coll, Savannah, GA; SR; BA; Cert Savanah Vo-Tech Schl 85; Bus/Mgmt; Mgmt Cnsltnt Firm.

**NIZAM, JANET K,** Emory Univ, Atlanta, GA; SR; BSN; Class Offcr Secy 89-90; Sigma Theta Tau 90-; Task Force/Homeless Vol 90; Grad/Hon; Nrs Extern/Emroy Hosp 89-90; Ntl Stdnt Nrs Asso; Working Emory Hosp; BA Grinnell Colg 85; Nrsg; Nrs.

**NIZIOL, CHRISTOPHER J,** Univ Of Pittsburgh, Pittsburgh, PA; SR; BA; Soc For Creative Anachronisms; Karate Clb; Info Sci; Comp Graphics.

**NIZZA, VINCENT A,** Saint Josephs Coll New York, Brooklyn, NY; SR; BS; Law.

**NIZZICO, DANA N,** Fordham Univ, Bronx, NY; JR; BS; Vol Income Tax Asstnce Pgm; Deans Lst Fordham 88-; All-Am Schlr 90-; Alpha Beta Psi; Beta Gamma Sigma; Pub Acctg; CPA.

**NJIE, AWA E,** Allen Univ, Columbia, SC; GD; Business Club; Ainternatl Stdnt Sec 90-; Zeta Phi Beta; Phi Beta Lambda; Pan Hellenic Cncl; BA; Bus Admnstrtn.

**NJOROGE, CATHERINE W,** Coppin St Coll, Baltimore, MD; FR; BS; Intl Stu Assoc Org Comm; Pres Awrd Scheme Tm Ldr 87; Cmptr Sci; Prog.

**NKOSI, MANDLA M,** Univ Of The Dist Of Columbia, Washington, DC; SO; BA; Assn Acctg Tchncns 88-89; Phi Sigma Pi 89-90; Swmmng 89-; Acctg; CPA.

**NNADI, MICHAEL C,** Howard Univ, Washington, DC; SR; PHARM; SNPHA 87; SCODAE; ASP; Beta Sigma Rho Chi Pharm Pres 90; Hnr Soc; Golden Key 89-; Intl Stdnt Union Advsr Pres; Pharm.

**NNOLIM, ONWUNEME O,** Univ Of Rochester, Rochester, NY; JR; Chem Res 90-; IM Soccr; Chem Eng.

**NOAH, JENNIFER R,** The Johns Hopkins Univ, Baltimore, MD; FR; BA; Psych.

**NOAR, JILL R,** Life Coll, Marietta, GA; FR; DC; Chrprctc Class At Lfe Intrntl Chrprctic Assoc Pres; Bsnss/Prof Women Org 89; Intrntl TV Asoc 87; Video Prdcr In Entrtnmnt/Corp Areas 82; BS Syracuse Univ 82; Telecomm Mgmt/Mrktng; Dr.

**NOBILE, JUDITH A,** Erie Comm Coll, Buffalo, NY; SR; AAS; Ftr Scrtrs America 90-; Phi Theta Kappa 90-; Offc Tchn Wrd Prcsng; Wrd Prcsng Scl Wrk.

**NOBLE, BRIDGET M,** Univ Of South Al, Mobile, AL; JR; BA; SGA 88-90; Kappa Delta Sec 90-; Erly Chldhd Ed; Teacher.

**NOBLE, DARLENE Y,** Colby Sawyer Coll, New London, NH; JR; Erly Chldhd Clb Sec 88-91; Key 90-; Alpha Chi 88-; BA; Chld Stdy.

**NOBLE, ELIZABETH B,** Ky Wesleyan Coll, Owensboro, KY; GD; MA; BA 90; Psych.

**NOBLE, INELL M,** Jackson St Univ, Jackson, MS; SR; Alpha Lambda Delta 90; Edctn; Tchr.

**NOBLE, JAMILLE V,** Lincoln Univ, Lincoln Univ, PA; SO; BA; Chinese Club 89-; Educ Club 89-; Stdnt Govt 90; Blck Conf On Hghr Educ Schlrshp; Elem Educ; Tch.

**NOBLE, JEANNIE A,** Miami Univ, Oxford, OH; JR; BS; Alpha Lambda Delta; Phi Eta Sigma; Bus Finance.**

**NOBLE, LAURA T,** Univ Of Southern Ms, Hattiesburg, MS; JR; Spch Pthlgy Adlgy; Spch Pthlgst.

**NOBLE, MEKO A,** Fl A & M Univ, Tallahassee, FL; FR; BS; Couture Mdlng Inc 90-; Phi Eta Sigma; Dean Lst 90-; Hnr Rll 90-; Brdcst Jrnlsm; TV Anchrwmn.

**NOBLE, NANCY D,** S U N Y Coll At Fredonia, Fredonia, NY; SO; BA; Acctg Soc 90-; Dns Lst 89-; TOPS Mkt Schlrshp; Schlr Awd; All-Amer Schlr; Acctg.

**NOBLE, RICHARD,** Jackson St Univ, Jackson, MS; SO; BS; Alpha Lambda Delta; Math; Actry.

**NOBLE, ROGER K,** Eckerd Coll, St Petersburg, FL; FR; BA; EC TV Sta Anchor 90-; Radio Sta DJ 90-; Cmps Tour Guide 90-; Campus Perspective Stdnt Host 90-; Res Advsr 90-; Intl Bsn; Bsn Admin.

**NOBLE, SUZANNE L,** Gallaudet Univ, Washington, DC; GD; PHD; So Snd RHICE Pres 89-; Phi Betta Cappa; Deaf Ed; BS Penn State Univ 81; Deaf Ed; Admin.

**NOBLE, TAMMY R,** Savannah St Coll, Savannah, GA; SR; BS; Crmnl Justice Clb Sec 89-; SG Elctn Comm; Actvts Apprprtns Brd; Savannah Police Dpt Intrn; US Marine Crps Rsrvs; Crmn Jstc; US Marine Corps.

**NOBLES, CHERYL L,** Livingston Univ, Livingston, AL; SR; BS; Deans Lst 89-90; Pres Lst; Elem Ed.

**NOBLES, JOHN STACY,** Valdosta St Coll, Valdosta, GA; SR; BBA; Var Ftbl 88-89; Fnce; Bnkng.

**NOBLES, SHEILA D,** Oh Univ-Southern Cmps, Ironton, OH; FR; BA; Ohio Assc Garden Clbs Inc Sec 90-; Bus Mgmt; Acct Exctv.

**NOBLES, SHELLI R,** Methodist Coll, Fayetteville, NC; SO; BS; Clncl Psych.

**NOBLES, TONI R,** Beaufort County Comm Coll, Washington, NC; SO; AAS; Gamma Beta Phi 90-; Acctng/Bsn Admin; Acctng.**

**NOBLETT, VICTORIA HARRISON,** Crichton Coll, Memphis, TN; SR; BED; Deans Lst 89-90; Church/Comm Affairs; Elem Educ; Educ/England.

**NOBLIN, ELEANOR,** Freed-Hardeman Univ, Henderson, TN; SO; BS BA; Schl Yrbk Editor 89-; Schl Paper 89; Comm Mjrs/Mnrs Assc 89-; Phi Kappa Alpha 89-; Scndry Ed/Gen Comm; English/Speech Tchr.**

**NOBLIN, TAMMY R,** Richard Bland Coll, Petersburg, VA; FR; AS; Delta Tau Chi 90-; Deans List 90-; Chrldr 90-; Phys Edn.

**NOBREGA, WILLIAM K,** Providence Coll, Providence, RI; JR; BA; Stdnt Ambssdr 90-; Msc Com Frst Bapt Chrch RI 90-; Brd Of Dcns Frst Bapt Chrch 90-; Nrth Str Rcrds Intrnshp 90; Hmnts And Msc; Hmn Rsrcs And Or Msc Cmpstn.

**NOCE, KIMBERLY J,** Pellissippi St Tech Comm Coll, Knoxville, TN; SO; AS; Accntng; Trvl Trsm.

**NOCENTINO, STEFANIE,** Drexel Univ, Philadelphia, PA; FR; BS; Phi Eta Sigma 90-; Bsn Adm; CPA.

**NOCERA, KRISTI,** Glassboro St Coll, Glassboro, NJ; SR; BA; IGC Rep 88-89; Alpha Epsilon Phi Inc Asst Rush Chr 89; Dns Lst 89-90; Alumi Assn Awd; Awd Cumberland Cnty Mntl Hlth Assn 87; IM Vlybl; Psychology; Personnel Admin.

**NODA, HIROSHI ALEX,** Univ Of Southern Ms, Hattiesburg, MS; SR; BA; Gamma Beta Phi 90-; Gldn Ky 90-; Engl; Tchng.

**NODURFT, MICKI L,** Univ Of Southern Ms, Hattiesburg, MS; SR; Almni Asc 90; Gamma Beta Phi; Psy; Scl Wrk.

**NOE, DAVID M,** East Tn St Univ, Johnson City, TN; FR; BS; Engr Dsgn Graphics; Dsgn.

**NOE, DONALD F,** Univ Of Sc At Columbia, Columbia, SC; FR; BED; FCA 90-; ARETE 90-; Crmnl Justc; Law.

**NOE, JEROD C W,** Univ Of Nc At Asheville, Asheville, NC; JR; BS; Ambassador Hd; SGA Assoc Justice 90-; Outdoor Clb; Phi Theta Kappa Hstrn 88-89; Mgmnt; Hlth Care Admin.

**NOE, JOHN J,** Comm Coll Algny Co Algny Cmps, Pittsburgh, PA; FR; BA; Art Assoc 90-; Advsr Pgh Job Corps Stu Arts/Crfts; Grphc Cmnctn.

**NOEL, KAREN S,** Wv Univ At Parkersburg, Parkersburg, WV; JR; BED; PTA Pres 86-87; Black Diamond Girl Scout Ldr 85-89; Phi Theta Kappa 90-; Art Dir Pappas Brothers Fahlgren/Ferris Ad Agency Free Lnc Dsgn; Grphc Dsgn Art Inst Of Pttsbrg 73; Math; Tchr.

**NOEL, MARCIA L,** Va St Univ, Petersburg, VA; JR; BS; Drftng Tech Clb 90-; Big Bro/Sis 90-; Htl/Rest Mgt Clb 88-90; Ds Lst 88-; Acad Awd Pin 89-; Indl Tech Awd; Drftng Tech; Archtctr.

**NOEL, MICHAEL E,** East Tn St Univ, Johnson City, TN; JR; BS; Alpha Lambda Delta 89-90; Gamma Beta Phi 90-; Bus Educ; Tchng.

**NOEL, SUSAN L,** Saint Catharine Coll, St Catharine, KY; SO; BA; Jrnlsm Clb 90-; Stdnt Sen Jdcry Brd 90-; Phi Theta Kappa Treas 90-; CPMA Axllry Ldr; AA; Scndry Ed; Tchr.

**NOFFSINGER, NATALIE LURA,** Middle Tn St Univ, Murfreesboro, TN; SO; Gamma Beta Phi; Kappa Delta Pi 90-; Chi Omega 89-90; Elem Edctn; Tchr.

**NOFTSIER, JILL A,** The Kings Coll, Briarclf Mnr, NY; SR; RA 89-; Bsktbl Stats 87-; Tble Frncs 87-89; Std Tchr 90-; Frnch; Law.

**NOGALSKI II, GILBERT L,** Fl Atlantic Univ, Boca Raton, FL; SR; BS; Intl Bus Clb; Phi Theta Kappa; AA Brevard Community Coll 90; Jintl Bus; Intl Bus Mgmt.

**NOGUERAS MARTINEZ, RICARDO,** Inter Amer Univ Pr Hato Rey, Hato Rey, PR; FR; BS; Aeronautical Sciences; Aviation.

**NOH, JAE J,** Cornell Univ, Ithaca, NY; FR.

**NOHARA, MICHIKO,** Brevard Coll, Brevard, NC; FR; PTK 90-; Athlete Highest Schlstc Average 90-; Brevard Clg Frshmn Schlr Awrd 90-; Tnns 90-; Communication; Broadcaster.

**NOLAN, AMY F,** Hillsborough Comm Coll, Tampa, FL; FR; Bsktbl; USAF; Biol.

**NOLAN, EDWARD T,** Univ Of Fl, Gainesville, FL; JR; BA; AA Manatee Comm Clg 90; Bsns; Mgmt.

**NOLAN, ELLEN T,** Univ Of Ky, Lexington, KY; SR; Crrclm Comm/Phsphy Dept 89-90; Arts/Sci Phlspy Dept Rvw Comm 89-90; Phi Beta Kappa 90-; Matchette Fdn Awd Otsdng/Phlsphy Undrgrad 90.

**NOLAN, ERIN E,** Villanova Univ, Villanova, PA; SR; BA; Pre-Law Scty 89; Im Sftbl; Rush Cnslr 90; Deans Lst 89; Delta Delta Delta 87; Spcl Olympcs 88; Grk Wk 87; Engl/Hstry Mnr; Law.

**NOLAN, JANELLE K,** Northern Ky Univ, Highland Hts, KY; FR; BED; Tutoring 89-; Exclnc Award; Mdl Grd Ed; Tchng.

**NOLAN, JENNIFER A,** Westminster Choir Coll, Princeton, NJ; JR; BA; MENC; Sigma Alpha Iota; Alpha Omicron Pi; Cvnt Presb Chrch Awd; Aden G Lewis Schlrshp; Prnctn Chrch Of Christ; Music Educ.

**NOLAN, KATHY M,** Wesley Coll, Florence, MS; FR; BED; Stdnt Cncl Repr 90-; Choir 90-; Ensemble 90-; Missionary Prayer Band 90-; Yrbk Staff 90-; Drama 90-; Libr Staff 90-; Religion; Missions.

**NOLAN, KENNETH B,** Commonwealth Coll, Virginia Beach, VA; JR; Phi Beta Lambda Treas 90-; Pres Lst 90; Excel Attdnce Awards 90; Assoc Degree Bsn Mgmt; Assoc Degree Acctg; Bsn; Acctg/Bsn Mgmt.

**NOLAN, LORA A,** Chesterfield Marlboro Coll, Cheraw, SC; FR; BA; Alph Beta Dlt; Vctry Chrstn Ctr Tchr 87-; Dean Of Stdnt Chstrfld Mrlbr Tech Clg Sec; Engl; Educ.

**NOLAN, MARY J,** Univ Of Pittsburgh, Pittsburgh, PA; JR; BA; Aids Org 87-; Soc Work.

**NOLAN, MICHAEL T,** Villanova Univ, Villanova, PA; JR; BA; Coll Rpblcns 88-90; Phi Kappa Phi 90-; Pi Sigma Alpha Treas 90-; Prjct Sunshine Tutrng Undrprvlgd Chldrn 89-90; Smmr Intrnshp Monmouth Cnty Prsctrs Offc; Deans Lst 88-; Pltcl Sci; Crmnl Law.

**NOLAN JR, RONALD DEAN,** Radford Univ, Radford, VA; SR; BBA; AMA 88-; Tau Kappa Epsilon Soc Chrmn 87-; IM Sftbl/Ftbl 87-; Mrktng.

**NOLAN, SHANNON C,** S U N Y Coll At Geneseo, Geneseo, NY; FR; BS; Equestrian Clb 90-; Bio; Pharm.

**NOLAN, STEPHANIE FRANCES,** Va Commonwealth Univ, Richmond, VA; SR; MSW; Alchl Drg Ed 90; Univ Sbstnc Abs Cmmtt 90-; Alchl Bvrg Cntrl Strng Cmmt; Alchl Awrnss Cmmtt 89-90; Phi Mu Pr Edctr Sbstnc Abs 88-; Fldwrk Internshp; BS; Psychlgy; Sbstnc Abs Cnslr.

**NOLAND, CARLETTA M,** Tougaloo Coll, Tougaloo, MS; SR; Stdnt Govt Sr VP 89-90; Educ Clb VP 89-90; Stdnt Natl Educ Assn 87-; Alpha Kappa Alpha 89-; Natl Assn For Advncmnt Of Colored People 86-; Stdnt Tchr Sem 90-; Cheerleader 86-87; BA; Elem Tchr.

**NOLAND, PATRICIA E,** Medical Coll Of Ga, Augusta, GA; SR; DMD; Amer Stdnt Dntl Assn 88-; Amer Soc Clncl Pthlgsts 76-; Omicron Kappa Upsilon; Smmrvl Nghbrhd Assn Treas 84-86; BS Med Tech 76; Dntstry; Dntst.

**NOLAND, WENDY K,** Univ Of Akron, Akron, OH; JR; BED; IM Vlybl 90; Elem Ed; Tchr.

**NOLD, KELLY L,** Maria Coll, Albany, NY; FR; AAS; Erly Chldhd Educ; Elem Educ.

**NOLDER, STACIA T,** Univ Of Pittsburgh At Bradford, Bradford, PA; SO; ASN; SNO; Hnrs; Deans Lst 90-; Nrsng; Rn.

**NOLEN, KRISTINA J,** Univ Of Al At Birmingham, Birmingham, AL; JR; BA; Educ; Tchng.

**NOLEN, REGINA A,** Univ Of Al At Birmingham, Birmingham, AL; JR; BS; Gldn Ky 90-; Elem Educ; Tchr.

**NOLEN, SHANNON E,** Allegheny Coll, Meadville, PA; SO; BA; Alpah Phi Omega 90-; First Runner Up Comp Exam 89; Alden Schlr 80-; Srf Hnry Sco/Natl Hnrs Soc 88-89; Engl.

**NOLES, KRISTIE M,** Univ Of Tn At Martin, Martin, TN; FR; BS; Mrchng Bnd 90-; Elem Ed.

**NOLES, NATALIE M,** Truett Mc Connell Coll, Cleveland, GA; JR; BA; Bptst Un VP 89-; Stdnt Assn 89-90; Gamma Beta Phi 90-; Englsh Edctn; Tchng Edctn.

**NOLES, TINA L,** Univ Of Al At Birmingham, Birmingham, AL; JR; Stdnt Ocptnl Thrpy Assoc; Phi Theta Epsilon; Dns Mrt Schlrshp; Sci; Ocptnl Thrpy.

**NOLL, JEANNINE A,** Comm Coll Algny Co Algny Cmps, Pittsburgh, PA; SO; BA; Lib Arts/Sci; Law.

**NOLTE, MARY ANN,** Wv Northern Comm Coll, Wheeling, WV; FR; ASSOC; Stdnt Nurs Assn; Dns Lst Acad Schlrshp 90-; Nrsng Asst Whlng Hosp Whg W V 88-; CERT Marshll Co Adlt Educ 85; Hlth/Nrsng.

**NOMI, AKI,** Converse Coll, Spartanburg, SC; SO; BFA; ASID; Engl Tchr In Japan 86-87; AAS Cazenovia Clg 84; Int Dsgn.

**NONAMAKER, PAULETTE D,** George Mason Univ, Fairfax, VA; SR; BSED; Stu Vr Educ Assn Pres 89-; Gldn Ky 90-; Kappa Delta Pi 89-; Erly Educ; Elem Tchng.

**NOONEY JR, JAMES F,** Univ Of Sc At Columbia, Columbia, SC; FR; Wtrski Clb 90-; Tennsi Tm Mngr 90-; Gamma Beta Phi 90-; Alpha Lambda Delta 90-; Phi Eta Sigma 90-; Pi Kappa Alpha Hs Mngr 90-; Pres Hnr Rl 90-; Deans List 90-; Pltcl Scnc/Bus; Law.

**NORBECK, KIMBERLY I,** Pembroke St Univ, Pembroke, NC; FR; BA; Ambass 90-; Marshall 90-; Theta Kappa 90-; Chnclr Schlr; Vars Chrldng; Telecmnctns; Brdcst Rprtr.

**NORBURY, NICKY E,** Univ Of Sc At Columbia, Columbia, SC; SO; BS; Phi Eta Sigma 90-; Delta Gamma 90-; Carolina Cares 90-; Presidents Hnr Rl 90-; IM Sccr 90; Biology; Dr Optometry.

**NORBUT, CHRISTINE M,** Stockton St Coll, Pomona, NJ; SR; MSW; Intern Div Yuth/Fmly Serv 90-; Deans List 89-; Intern Mntl Hlth Assoc 90; Intern Atlantic Mental Hleth Alcohol/Drug Univ 89; NCAA Chrldng 87-90; NASW; CCD Tchr St Clements Church 90-; Jr High Chrldng Coach 90-; BSW; Social Work; Social Wrk Admintr.

**NORBUTT, KEITH A,** Duquesne Univ, Pittsburgh, PA; FR; BM; Music; Flutist.

**NORBY, LISA A,** Alfred Univ, Alfred, NY; SO; BS; Stdnt Alumni Assoc Treas; Campus Guide 90-; Orientation Guide; Alpha Lambda Delta; Phi Sigma Iota; Sigma Delta Pi; Pres Schlrshp 89-; Dns Lst 89-; Bsn Adm; Bsn.

**NORBY, MICHELE L,** Alfred Univ, Alfred, NY; SO; BS; Stdnt Alumni Assoc Secr; Campus Guide 90-; Orientation Guide; Alpha Lambda Delta; Phi Sigma Iota; Sigma Delta Pi; Pres Schlrshp 89-; Dns Lst 89-; Bsn Adm; Bsn.

**NORCLIFFE, SYLVIA R,** Atlantic Union Coll, S Lancaster, MA; JR; BA; Orchestra 87-89; Bsktbl Clb 90-; Vrsty Vlybl Tm 89-; Engl; Psychlgy/Psychoanalyst.

**NORCROSS, MARY ANNE,** Coll Of Charleston, Charleston, SC; SR; Ed Forum; Deans Lst 90-; Fcltys Lst 90-; Hghly Dstngsh Hnr 90-; BA; Elem Ed; Tchng.

**NORDAN, ERIC C,** William Carey Coll, Hattiesburg, MS; SO; Univ AL Ofcls Assoc; Vars Soccer 89-; Jrnlsm; Free-Lance Wrtr.

**NORDBERG, CARRIE LYNN,** Atlantic Comm Coll, Mays Landing, NJ; SO; AA; EMT New Jersey State Dept Hlth 89; Liberal Arts/Cmptr Art Cncntrtn; Intr Dsgnr.

**NORDBY, KARENA S,** Radford Univ, Radford, VA; SO; BA; Fashion Dsgn.

**NORDIN, GAMAL ADLAN,** Univ Of Miami, Coral Gables, FL; JR; BA; Malaysian Martial Art Org Comm 88-90; Malaysian Stdnt Assoc 90-; AA State Univ NY Buffalo 90; Acctg.

**NORDLAND, HEATHER L,** S U N Y Coll Of Tech At Alfred, Alfred, NY; SR; Radio D J 90-; SICA 90-; Hall Doorguard 90-; Psi Beta V P 90-; Hon Convctn; Deans Lst; AS; Psychology/Child Care Educ.

**NORDMANN, LAWRENCE W,** Univ Of North Fl, Jacksonville, FL; JR; BBA; Finance/Invstmnts Soc Natl Invstmnt Challenge Chrmn 90-; UNF Deans Lst 90-; AA Sante Fe Cmnty Coll Gainsville FL 89; Finance; Cmrcl Lending Banking.

**NOREN, DAWN P,** Univ Of Md At College Park, College Park, MD; FR; BA; Wtr Pl Clb; Hll Govt VP 90-; Phi Eta Sigma; Alpha Lambda Delta; GPA Awrd; Deans Lst 90; Mrn Blgy.

**NOREN, SHAWN R,** Univ Of Md At College Park, College Park, MD; FR; BA; Watr Polo Clb; Res Hll Govt Treas 90-; Phi Eta Sigma; Alpha Lambda Delta; All As Awrd 90-; 101% Givr For Watr Polo; Dns Lst 90; Marine Bio.

**NORFLEET, DAVID S,** Western Ky Univ, Bowling Green, KY; SO; MBA; I M Sprts; Pres Lst; Hstry; Tch.

**NORFLEET, EBEN C,** Univ Of Rochester, Rochester, NY; JR; BA; Coll Rpblcns Chrmn 88-89; Soc Act Bd Co-Chair 89-90; Fac Cncl Rep 89-90; Outstndg Coll Stdnts Am 89-; Res Advsr 90-; Comm Serv Awd 89-90; Ldrshp Awd 89-; Intern Oswego Cnty Dist Attys Ofc; Pol Sci; Law.

**NORIEGA, VAUGHN CADIAN,** City Univ Of Ny Queensbrough, New York, NY; FR; AASET; Chi Alpha Chrstn Flwshp Pres 90-; Elctrncs; Engr.

**NORIEGA, VERA L,** Columbia Univ, New York, NY; FR; BA; News Dept Radio Nwsrdr 90-; Cmnty Impact 90-; Advocacy Hmls 90-; One To One Tutor 90-; Classics/Hist; Profr.

**NORIEGA-PAGAN, CAROL I,** City Univ Of Ny La Guard Coll, Long Island Cty, NY; SO; B ED; Sinai Chrstn Chrch Sndy Schl Tchr Yth Crdntr 87-; Chrstn Mnstry Ny Thlgcl Smnry 90; Blngl Edctn; Bchlr/Mstr Spcl Edctn.

**NORKET, LOIS B,** Univ Of Sc At Coastal Carolina, Conway, SC; JR; BS; Psychlgy Clb 89-; Psi Chi 90-; Pres Hnr Roll 90-; Spec Olympcs; Instnl Rsrc Coastal Carolina Clge; Psychlgy; Hmn Rsrc Mgmt.

**NORKUS, DENISE M,** East Stroudsburg Univ, E Stroudsburg, PA; SR; MBA; Psych Assoc Secr 90-; Psi Chi Secr 90-; Chldrn/Yth Svcs; BS Psych; Psych; Ph D Clncl Psych.

**NORKUS, EDWARD C,** Glassboro St Coll, Glassboro, NJ; JR; BA; Cmmnctns; Wrkng Cmr.

**NORMAN, CAROLYN J,** Seton Hall Univ, South Orange, NJ; FR; BS; Nrs Assn 90-; Sci; Nrsng.

**NORMAN, JOSEPH E,** Univ Of Nc At Asheville, Asheville, NC; SO; BS; Fllwshp Chrstn Athlts 89-; IM 89-; Math/Cmptr Scnc; Actuary/Statistician.

**NORMAN, LORI L,** Univ Of West Fl, Pensacola, FL; JR; BA; Aerobic Instr Bapt Ch; Off Mgr; AS Jr Clg 86; Bus Tchr Educ; Bus Tchr.

**NORMAN, MARK A,** De Vry Inst Of Tech, Columbus, OH; SO; BA; Peer Advsr 90-; Natl Hnr Scty 89-; Computer Info; Programming.

**NORMAN, RACHEL E A,** Prince Georges Comm Coll, Largo, MD; FR; Sci; Occptnl Thrpy.

**NORMAN, RUTH H,** Va St Univ, Petersburg, VA; FR; BA; Stu Ntl Tech Assc Tres 90-; Inrds Tlnt Pool 90-; Deans Lst 90-; Bus Acctg.

**NORMAN, TERRI E,** Western Carolina Univ, Cullowhee, NC; SR; BFA; Art Students Lge 89-F Mktng/Mgt Club 86-87; Panhellenic Cou Activ Chprsn 89-90; Sorority. Rush Clr 90-; Phtghyg Club Treas 90-; Delta Zeta Sorority Wy/Means Chr 86-; Outstndng Sr Delta Zeta Sor 90-; Golden Grest 92-; Natl Alhl Awns Conv Dlgt 88-89; Fine Arts Phtghy; Arts Admin.

**NORMANDEAU, SHEILA M,** Univ Of South Al, Mobile, AL; SR; BED; Symphnc Bnd 90-; NAUI 88-; USCG Petty Ofcr Frst Cls 85-; Radioman Navy; Spec Ed; MED.

**NORMOYLE, LAURIE A,** Ramapo Coll Of Nj, Mahwah, NJ; SR; BS; Bus Admn Acctg; CPA.**

**NOROIAN, ALISON K,** Newbury Coll, Brookline, MA; GD; ASSOC; Drama Club VP 89-; Sgn Lang Clss; Deans List; Cum Laude; Intrnshp At Chintz-N-Prints; Interior Dsgn; Arch.

**NORRIS, ALMA C,** Stillman Coll, Tuscaloosa, AL; SR; BS; Sci Clb Pres 90-; Gamma Iota Sigma; Alpha Kappa Mu; Alpha Kappa Alpha Pres 90; Purdue Univ Res Intrn 89; Univ TX Res Intrn 90; Biol/Chem; Phrmcy.

**NORRIS, AMY C,** Livingston Univ, Livingston, AL; JR; BA; AS Wallace Comm Clg Selma 90; Acctg.

**NORRIS, AMY L,** Longwood Coll, Farmville, VA; SR; MS; Pom Pom Squad Dnce Tm 88-90; Psychlgy Clb 88-89; Alpha Psi Omega Sec 89; Alpha Sigma Tau 90; Cncl For Exptnl Chldrn 88-89; BS; Psychlgy/Spcl Ed; Tchng/Cnslng The Autistic.

**NORRIS, BRIAN R,** Southern Coll Of Tech, Marietta, GA; SR; BSEET; IEEE 88-; AET Clayton State Clg 87; Elec Engr.

**NORRIS, CHERYL DENISE,** Marshall University, Huntington, WV; GD; MA; BACCHUS PR 89-90; Stdnt Rep Pres Task Cmte 89-; Gamma Beta Phi 88-; Psi Chi 90-; Alpha Chi Omega V P 88; Cabell County Child Prot Tm Workshp Ldr 89; MD Asso; Deans List 87-90; Stdnt Asst; Grad Asst Stdnt Hlth Prog 88-90; Coun/ Rehab; Stdnt Prsnnl Hi Ed.

**NORRIS, CHERYL M,** Univ Of Tn At Chattanooga, Chattanooga, TN; JR; BS; Coop Eddtn 88-; Chmcn Engnrng Soc 87-; Co-Op Dupont 88-; Chmcl Engnrng; Engnrng.

**NORRIS, COREY L,** Morris Brown Coll, Atlanta, GA; JR; BA; Vrsty Ftbl Tm 88-; Bus; Mgmt.

**NORRIS, DAVID D,** Kent St Univ Kent Cmps, Kent, OH; SO; MBA; Hon Prg 89; Edinbr Univ; Art Hstry; Tchng.

**NORRIS, JEFFREY L,** Oh Wesleyan Univ, Delaware, OH; FR; BA; Zoolgy Semnr Grp 90-; Zoolgy Bd 90-; Flwshp Of Chrstn Athlts 90-; Phi Eta Sigma 90-; Sigma Chi Tribune 90-; Marston Wells Schlrshp 90-; Pre Profsnl Zoolgy; Profsnl Rsrch Secndry Ed.

**NORRIS, JENNIFER L,** Oh St Univ At Marion, Marion, OH; SR; BS BA; Human Resource Assoc 90; Clg Business Deans List; Human Resource Mngmt.

**NORRIS, KAREN M,** Mayland Comm Coll, Spruce Pine, NC; FR.

**NORRIS, KASSANDRA JO,** Univ Of Southern Ms, Hattiesburg, MS; JR; BS; Ermnl Jstc; Law Schl.

**NORRIS JR, KIETH E,** Chattanooga St Tech Comm Coll, Chattanooga, TN; SO; AAS; Hon Stdnt; US Army Rsrve Capt; BA Brgham Yng Univ 79; Hzrds Matrls Tech.

**NORRIS, KIMBERLY,** Tuskegee Univ, Tuskegee Inst, AL; SO; BS; Stdnt Gov Assn Pblc Rltns Comm 89-90; Mrchng Crmsn Pipr Brd 90-; Alld Hlt-Occ Ther.

**NORRIS, KIMBERLY L,** Troy St Univ At Troy, Troy, AL; FR; BED; Cllgt Singers 90-; History/English; Education/Acting.

**NORRIS, LISA M,** Cheyney Univ Of Pa, Cheyney, PA; JR; Who's Who Among African Amer Wmn In Blck Colleges & Univ; Dietcs; Ntrntn.

**NORRIS, MARY A,** Univ Of Ky, Lexington, KY; JR; BSW; Big Bro/Sis Bluegrs 89-; Soc Wrk.

**NORRIS, NANCY D,** Patrick Henry Comm Coll, Martinsville, VA; FR; Erly Edn Major; Elem Tchr.

**NORRIS, NATALIE R,** Edward Waters Coll, Jacksonville, FL; SR; BBA; Stdnt Supprt Spclst For The Alachua Multi Cnty Migrnt Ed Progrm 82-; Bus; Mgt/Migrnt Ed.

**NORRIS, NATHAN J,** Univ Of Pittsburgh, Pittsburgh, PA; SO; BSE; Soc Auto Eng 90-; Eng Trainee LTV Steel Co 90-; Univ Schlr/Eng Hnrs Schlrshp 89-; Mech Eng.

**NORRIS, NICOLE,** Tuskegee Univ, Tuskegee Inst, AL; SR; BS; SNEA 89-; Phi Delta Kappa; Alpha Omega 87-; Eastern Star 90-; Honor Roll 90-; Deans Lst; Elem Educ.

**NORRIS II, RICHARD A,** Memphis St Univ, Memphis, TN; SO; BS; Kappa Alpha 89-; Engr.

**NORRIS, ROGER C,** Birmingham Southern Coll, Birmingham, AL; FR; BA; Circle K 90-; Phi Eta Sigma; Alpha Lambda Delta; Sigma Nu 90-; Bus/Acctng.

**NORRIS, RUTHANNA C,** Indiana Univ Of Pa, Indiana, PA; JR; BS; Phi Sigma Pi Fndng Fthr 88-; Deans Lst 89-; Prvst Schlr 89-; PA State Edctn Assn Stdnt Mmbr 90-; Scndry Edctn Math; Clg Math Prfsr.

**NORRIS, TERRI L,** Marshall University, Huntington, WV; JR; BS; Dietetic Advsry Bd 90-; Amer Dietetic Assn 90; Kappa Omicron Nu 90; Dietetics.

**NORRIS, TRISHEENA L,** Spartanburg Methodist Coll, Spartanburg, SC; FR; Bus.

**NORRIS, VALDA T,** Norfolk St Univ, Norfolk, VA; SR; BS; Univ Gospel Chr Sec 88-89 87-89; Fin/Bnkng Clb 90; Hon Stdnt; Bus Fin; Real Est Brkr/Dvlpr/Dsgnr.

**NORRMAN, KELLY A,** Newbury Coll, Brookline, MA; FR; AS; Physcl Thrpy Clb 90; Deans Lst 90-; Physcl Thrpy Asst Stdnt Intern; Physcl Thrpy.

**NORSEN, MICHELE R,** Canisius Coll, Buffalo, NY; FR; BA; Ltl Theatre 90-; Suny Brckport Model European Cmuty; Intl Rltns; Foreign Serv.

**NORSKOG, JEFFREY J,** Georgetown Univ, Washington, DC; SR; BA; Student Judicial Commt 88-89; Pres Schlrshp 87-89; Amer Advtng Fedtn Exec Dir 90-; Amer Mktng Assoc 88-; Johnson N Johnson Indonesia Assist Gen Mgr 88; Johnson N Johnson Japan 90; Mktng Intl Busther.

**NORSWORTHY, TAMMY M,** Ms St Univ, Miss State, MS; SR; BFA; Comm Hlp Hndcp Stdnts Comp 90; !hmcmng Comm 89-90; Electns Comm 88-90; Kappa Pi 89-; Delta Delta Delta Asst Rsh Chrmn 87-; Grphc Dsgn Intrnshp 90; Grphc Dsgn.

**NORTH, ELIZABETH A,** Beckley Coll, Beckley, WV; FR; Sci; Envrmntl/Nrsg.

**NORTH, MARK E,** Univ Of Hartford, West Hartford, CT; JR; BA; Vrsty Lacrosse 88; Cmmnctns; Advrtsng.

**NORTH, MARY L,** Hillsborough Comm Coll, Tampa, FL; FR; BA; Phi Theta Kappa; Nursing.

**NORTH, MELISSA J,** Juniata Coll, Huntingdon, PA; JR; BS; Jun Clg Adm Assn 90-; Psych Clb Tr 89-; Jun Clg Hnr Soc; Sftbl 89-; Psych; Psychgst.

**NORTH, ROBIN L,** Clarkson Univ, Potsdam, NY; SO; BS; Panhellenic Cncl Sec/Treas 91; Phi Mu Pub Rel 91; Pres List 89; Deans List 90; Var Soccer Lacrosse; Indstrl Mgmnt.

**NORTH, SUSAN K,** Kent St Univ Kent Cmps, Kent, OH; JR; BBA; Wmns Ntwrk Pres; Accss Std Asc Treas 89-90; Acctng Clb 89-90; Beta Alpha Psi; IRS 90; Pres Lst; Dns Lst 89-90; Natl Asc Lgl Asst; Lgl Asst Adv Comm; Free Lance Prlgl; Cert Lgl Asst Summa Cum Laude Thomas Nelson Comm Clg 78; Acctng; CPA.

**NORTH, TRACEY M,** Univ Of South Al, Mobile, AL; JR; BED; Med Culture Soc; Alpha Chi; Sec Educ/Soc Sci; Tch.

**NORTHCOTT, BETH R,** Union Univ, Jackson, TN; FR; Chi Omega 90-.

**NORTHCUTT, LARRY B,** Univ Of Tn At Martin, Martin, TN; SR; BS; Philosophy Clb; Park/Rec Adventure Clb 89-; Geo Clb 89-; Phi Kappa Tau 82-; Geography; City Plng.

**NORTHENER, MELINDA A,** Western Ky Univ, Bowling Green, KY; JR; BS; Phi Eta Sigma; Beta Beta Beta; Alpha Epsilon Delta; Alpha Delta Pi Hstrn 89-90; Biology.**

**NORTHINGTON, JANEL A,** Central St Univ, Wilberforce, OH; FR; BS; Econs Clb Sec 90-; Stdnt Comms Brd Co Chrmn 90-; Vllybl Tm; Pol Sci; Crmnl Law.

**NORTHROP, CHRISTY,** Auburn Univ At Auburn, Auburn, AL; FR; BED; Chrch Chr; Phi Eta Sigma; Alpha Lambda Delta; Frm Hs/Ltl Str; Math; Ed.

**NORTHROP, MARY ALLYSON,** Emory Univ, Atlanta, GA; FR; Res Hall Assc Pblc Rltns 90-; Dooleys Wk Pgm Chr; Kappa Alpha Theta.

**NORTON, BRYAN S,** Northern Ky Univ, Highland Hts, KY; JR.

**NORTON, CAROLINE R,** Spartanburg Methodist Coll, Spartanburg, SC; FR; BA; Day Stdnt Assn 90-; Crmnl Jstc Clb 90-; Phi Theta Kappa 90-; Soclgy; Law Enfrcmnt/FBI/DEA.

**NORTON, CHRISTIAN M,** Old Dominion Univ, Norfolk, VA; SR; BS; Chi Omega Care Series Chrprsn 88-89; Intrn Designs Levi Strauss Co 90; Mktg Educ/Fsn Merch; Dsply.

**NORTON, DENISE L,** Glassboro St Coll, Glassboro, NJ; SR; BS; Blgy; Tchr.

**NORTON JR, GUY A,** Savannah Coll Of Art & Design, Savannah, GA; SR; BA; Phtgrphy; Educ.

**NORTON, JEFFREY R,** Wagner Coll, Staten Island, NY; JR; BS; Outstndg Perf Scl Fldwrk Head Start 90-; Bayley Seton Cont Trtmnt Pgm Mntly Ill; Vars Ftbl 88-; Track/Field Vars MVP 88-; Sclgy/Fmly Studies; Scl Wrk-Admin.

**NORTON, KAREN A,** Hilbert Coll, Hamburg, NY; SO; Assoc; Law.

**NORTON, KEVIN S,** Southern Coll Of Tech, Marietta, GA; JR; BA; Intrfrat Cncl VP; Grk Plnng Com Chrmn; Orntn Ldr 89-; Pi Kappa Phi VP; Cvl Eng Tchnlgy; Eng.**

**NORTON, KIMBERLY D,** Univ Of Southern Ms, Hattiesburg, MS; JR; SAVE; Hlcrst Hl Cncl Pres 90; Psi Chi; Hnrs Clge; Pres Lst; AA Hinds Cmnty Clge 89; Clin Psychlgy.

**NORTON, LESLIE A,** Univ Of Ky, Lexington, KY; JR; BA; Phi Eta Sigma; Hstry; Law.

**NORTON, PAULA,** Fl Atlantic Univ, Boca Raton, FL; SR; BS; Amer Mktg Assn ICC Rep 90-; Mst Otsdng New Mbr 90-; Mktg; Mktg Rsrch/Grad Sch.

**NORTON, RICHARD B,** Glassboro St Coll, Glassboro, NJ; FR; Chem.

**NORTON, RICHARD P,** Univ Of Hartford, West Hartford, CT; SR; BS; IEEE; Tau Alpha Pi; Alpha Chi: ASEET Hartford State Tech Coll 89; Elec Eng Tech.**

**NORTON, SCOTT L,** Hiwassee Coll, Madisonville, TN; FR; BA; Eng Clb 90-; Phi Theta Kappa 90-; Bsbl 90-; Civil/Elect Eng.

**NORTON, TIMOTHY M,** Southern Coll Of Tech, Marietta, GA; SR; BSEET; Pres Cert Acad Excell; AS AET 89; Elec; Eng.

**NORTON-COKE, ETHLYN M MC K,** Nova Univ, Ft Lauderdale, FL; GD; Kiwanis Clb New Kingston Jamaica W I 89-; Jamaican Bar Assn Cntng Educ Com 74-; Hosp Bd Univ Hosp W Indies/Nuttall Memrl Hosp; Jamaica Soc Prvntn Crlty Anmls Bd; St Andrew Old Grls Assn VP 90-; Attrny Law 74-; Assoc Tutor; Norman Manley Law Schl; Bus Admin; Tchng Bus Univ Lvl.

**NORVELL, ELLEN H,** Clayton St Coll, Morrow, GA; SO; BS; Prestl Schrls 77-78; Army Intern 85-87; Army Mgt Analyst 85-88; Pjt Mgr 88-89; Busn Admin; Optns Mgt.

**NORWOOD, CANDRA M,** Tougaloo Coll, Tougaloo, MS; FR; BA; Pre Hlth Clb 90-; Biol; Obstetrics/Gynecology.

**NORWOOD, DORIS A,** Univ Of Nc At Charlotte, Charlotte, NC; SO; BA; Psi Chi 91-; Psychology; Cnslng Pblc Schls.

**NORWOOD, LAURA E,** Bridgewater Coll, Bridgewater, VA; FR; BS; ICP Exeuc Tm 90-; Stdnt Cnslrs 90-; Deans Lst 90-; Physcs/Math; Tch.

**NORWOOD, MARSHALL A,** Morehouse Coll, Atlanta, GA; JR; BA; Bus Assn; Glee Clb; SGA; Yrbk Stff; Hmcmng Comm; Golden Key; Deans Lst; Hon Rll; Mntrng Pgm; Tutrl; Feed Hngry; Blood Drvs; KPMG Pet Marwik Intrn; AICPA Schlr; Monsanto Schlr; Cargill Schlr; IM; NTL Assn Blck Acctnts; Acctg.

**NORWOOD, REBECCA L,** Castleton St Coll, Castleton, VT; SO; BA; Intl Clb Pres; Phi Eta Sigma 90-; Sigma Delta Pi; Tutoring 90-; Emplymnt Foreign Lang Lab 90-; Spnsh; Intl Bus.

**NORWOOD, SHARLETTE,** Tougaloo Coll, Tougaloo, MS; JR; Pre-Hlth Clb 88-; Soc Hmn Res Clb Sec 90-; Pre-Alumi Clb 88-89; Alpha Kappa Alpha; Ntl Cncr Soc 88-; Asstnt PR 88-89; Asstnt Coll Devpmnt 88-89; Body Condtng; Aerobics/Rnng 88-89; Soc/Bio; Ped MD.

**NORWOOD, SHEILA D,** Nc Agri & Tech St Univ, Greensboro, NC; JR; BS; Gspl Choir 82-84; Acdmc Achvmt Awd 89-90; Alpha Phi Omega 83-84; Child Dvlpmt; Day Care Cntr.**

**NORWOOD, STEPHANIE D,** Alcorn St Univ, Lorman, MS; SR; DECA 86-87; Hm Ec Clb 87-89; MS Hm Ec 88-89; Pres Lst 86; Deans Lst 86-87; Hnr Grad 87; AAAS Hinds Jr Coll 87; BS; Fshn Mrchndsg; Mrktg.

**NORWOOD, VERONICA M,** Al St Univ, Montgomery, AL; SO; BA; SOS Intake Offcr 90; SAM 89; Invstmnt Clb 90; Finance; Invstmnt Brkr Corp Lawyer.

**NOTA, ALYSSA A,** Fl St Univ, Tallahassee, FL; JR; BA; Hons Pgm Nwsltr Asst Edtr 90-; Florence Italy Study Pgm Cnslr 90-; Tutor 90-; Hons Pgm 88-; Thomas J Martino Schlrshp For Italian Studies 90-; IM Sftbl Capt 88-90; Italian/Wrtng.

**NOTARBERARDINO, JOSEPH G,** Bowling Green St Univ, Bowling Green, OH; SO; BS; Stdnt Cnstrctn Mngmnt Assn; Dns Lst 90; Cnstrctn Mngmnt; Eng/Proj Mngmnt.

**NOTARIANNI, LENORA M,** Neumann Coll, Aston, PA; JR; BD; AD DCCC 90; Educ; Early Chldhd Ed.

**NOTHNAGEL, PAMELA S,** Univ Of North Fl, Jacksonville, FL; JR; BA; Mu Phi Epsilon Rcrdng Sec; Sec Chmpn Intl 79-84; Blue Crs Blue Shld Sec 78-79; AA Lon Morris Jr Clge 74; Msc; Chrl Cndctr/Tch Prvtly.

**NOTO, JOSEPH,** Univ Of Nc At Asheville, Asheville, NC; SR; BS; Envrnmntl Stds; Eclgst.

**NOTTINGHAM, BRIAN D,** Kent St Univ Kent Cmps, Kent, OH; SR; BS; Phys Fitness Spec; Cardiovsclr Rehab.

**NOTTINGHAM, PATRICK A,** Bryant Stratton Bus Inst Roch, Rochester, NY; GD; Elec Clb.

**NOTTO, CANDACE T,** Christian Brothers Univ, Memphis, TN; FR; CORE; Chorale; Tau Kappa Epsilon Aux; Math; Tch.

**NOVAK, ANDREA M,** Marywood Coll, Scranton, PA; SO; BS; Commuter Club; Speech/Hearing Club; Cmnctn Disorders; Speech Lang Pthlgst.

**NOVAK, JAMES E,** Cornell Univ Statutory College, Ithaca, NY; FR; BS; Lunatic Writing Stf Sls Stf; Stdnt Asmbly Cand Cmpgn Mgmnt Poster Cmpgn Pet Advoc; A Capella 90; Deans Lst 90-; Regents Schlrshp 90-; Dr George Hess Prof Biochem Rsrch Asst; Biochem; Medicine.

**NOVAK, KEITH G,** Kent St Univ Kent Cmps, Kent, OH; SR; BSMD; Wghtlftng Clb; Homeless Shltr; Harry Truman Schlrshp Semi Fin; IM Vlybl Sftbl 89-; Intgrtd Lf Sci; Med.

**NOVAK, MATTHEW,** Duquesne Univ, Pittsburgh, PA; FR; BS; Lambda Sigma Parlmntrn; Physcs; Physcst/Grad Sch.

**NOVAK, NICOLE,** Duquesne Univ, Pittsburgh, PA; FR; BED; Lambda Sigma; Kappa Delta Epsilon; Elem Ed; Tchng/Grad Sch.

**NOVAK, ROBERT A,** Piedmont Bible Coll, Winston-Salem, NC; SR; THB; Stdnt Cncl Rep 87-89; Sr Class VP 90; Prchrs Fllwshp Pres 90; T P Sanders 88; Deans Lst 88-90; Alumni Achievemnt Awd 90; Assist Pstr 89f Yth Pstr 89; Brlngtn Bible Inst 80-81; Theology; Pstr.

**NOVAK, TERESA A,** Marywood Coll, Scranton, PA; JR; BS; Commuter Club; Delta Epsilon Sigma; Kappa Delta Pi Treas; Elem Educ; Tch.

**NOVAKOSKI, SHARON A,** Indiana Univ Of Pa, Indiana, PA; JR; BA; Pa State Ed Assoc; Assoc For Chldhd Ed Intrntl; Erly Chldhd Ed; Tchng.

**NOVAKOVICH, JULIE A,** Indiana Univ Of Pa, Indiana, PA; JR; BED; Penn St Educ Assn; Assn Chldhd Educ Intl; Penn Sci Tchrs Assn; Elem Educ; Tchng.

**NOVEAN, SARAH A,** Univ Of Cincinnati, Cincinnati, OH; SO; BSN; Nrsg; Ped Nrsg.

**NOVELL, JENNIFER A,** Univ Of Rochester, Rochester, NY; SO; BA; Meridian Soc; Stdnt Intrvwrs; Delta Gamma VP Rsh; Intrn W/Crmnl Just Dept; Pltcl Sci/Ethcs; Law.

**NOVELLI, PATRICIA A,** Merrimack Coll, North Andover, MA; SO; BS; Cmmtr Cncl Sec 89-; Benzene Ring 90-; Biology Clb; Deans List 89-; Stdnt Ldrshp Recgntn Awd; Chem/Bio; Medicine.

**NOVELLI JR, RICHARD JOHN,** Western New England Coll, Springfield, MA; JR; BA; Res Hl Assoc 90-; Crmnl Jstc; DEA/FBI.

**NOVICK, ELIZABETH,** Fl International Univ, Miami, FL; JR; BA; Mktg/Intl Bsn; Intl Bsn.

**NOVICK, NANCY L,** Schenectady County Comm Coll, Schenectady, NY; FR; AAS; Drama Clb 90; Msc; Msc Cmpstn.

**NOVOA-COLBERG, KEVIN,** Inter Amer Univ Pr Hato Rey, Hato Rey, PR; SR; BA; Hnr Rl 88-; Mktg; Law.

**NOVOBILSKI, PATRICIA M,** Marywood Coll, Scranton, PA; JR; BS; Choir 88-; Wnd Ensmbl Orchstra 88-90; Flt Ensmbl 88-90; Biolgy Clb VP 88-; Chem Clb 88-; Connaught Labs Intrnshp; Biolgy/Chem; Med.

**NOVOTNY, KEVIN A,** Kent St Univ Kent Cmps, Kent, OH; JR; BBA; Gldn Key; Mrktng Bus Mgmt; Grad Schl.

**NOWACEK, DOUGLAS P,** Oh Wesleyan Univ, Delaware, OH; SR; BA; Stdnt Govt VP 90-; Stdnt Fndtn Adm Asst 88-; Res Asst 89-90; Phi Beta Kappa; Omicron Alta Kappa 90-; Mortar Bd 90-; Order Of Omega Pres 89-; Sigma Chi Sec 88-; Intrnshp Duke Marine Lab 90-; Columbus Zoo Aprntcshp 90-; IM 87-91; Zoology; Marine Sci.

**NOWAK, KATHLEEN N,** S U N Y Coll At Fredonia, Fredonia, NY; JR; BS; Spectrum Entrnmnt Bd VP 90-; Superdance Dance Marathon Benefit MDA Finance; Math; Teach.

**NOWAK, RAYMOND R,** Greenville Tech Coll, Greenville, SC; SO; AA; Scctng; Bus Admn.

**NOWAKOWSKI, GREGORY A,** Niagara Univ, Niagara Univ, NY; JR; BA; Tutor; Cmnty Brkfsts-Grand Isl 87-; Intern Airborne Exp; Intrn Natl Fuel-Gas; Niagara Univ Opport Pgm Highest Acad Average 88-; IN Sftbl/Bsktbl/Wght Lftng 88-; Bus Mngmnt.

**NOWELL, LAURIE A,** Meridian Comm Coll, Meridian, MS; JR; BPA; Phi Theta Kappa Brd Mbr 88-90; Batgirl 89-90; Assoc Of Arts 90; Acctng; CPA.

**NOWLIN, KATHERINE A,** Kent St Univ Kent Cmps, Kent, OH; SO; BA; Stdnt Educ Assn 89-90; Spnsh; Educ.

**NOWLIN, SHAWN,** Hudson Valley Comm Coll, Troy, NY; SO; BA; C-Stp Prog; Mnrty Mntrng Clb: Afro-Amer Stdnt Alliance Treas; Sherfs Schlrshp 90; Outstndng Acdmc Achvmnt; DA Asst Crt Clrk; AAS; Crmnl Jstce; Crmnl Lwyr.

**NOWLIN-NISSEN, STACEY G,** Univ Of Southern Ms, Hattiesburg, MS; FR; Phi Etta Sigma; Wrk Mntly Rtrd Chldrn/Adlts; Spec Ed; Df Educ.

**NOWZAMANI, NARMIN,** Univ Of Miami, Coral Gables, FL; FR; BBA; Cmmtrs Clb Orgnztn 90-; Intrntl Fnnce And Mrktng; Law.

**NOYES, BRIAN P,** Embry Riddle Aeronautical Univ, Daytona Beach, FL; JR; BS; Dvng Eagls Scuba Clb VP 88-; Yoshukai Karate Clb 88-; Amer Assn Arprt Exec 90-; Windsrfng Sailng Clb; Omicron Delta Kappa 90-; Boy Scts Amer Eagle Sct 90-; Ordr Arrow Ordl 90-; Intrn Amer Airlns Arprt Svcs Per; Aerntcl Sci; Pilot-Mgr.

**NOYES, HEATHER A,** Berry Coll, Rome, GA; FR; Bsn; CEO.

**NOYES, HELEN F,** Univ Of Sc At Columbia, Columbia, SC; SO; BED; S Strand La Sertoma Clb Treas 89-; Phi Theta Kappa 88-89; Stff Actnt; AD Horry-Georgetown Tech Coll 89; Elem Ed; Tchr.

**NOYES, JEFFREY W,** Temple Univ, Philadelphia, PA; SO; BS; Actf Dty USCG; 1st Clss Elec Tech; Elec Eng.

**NOYES, KELLY J,** Merrimack Coll, North Andover, MA; JR; BS; Acctng.

**NOZAR, MINA,** Old Dominion Univ, Norfolk, VA; JR; BS; Tau Beta Pi 88-; Sigma Pi Sigma; IEEE Secr 87-; SPS V P 87-; CEBAF Intern; Physics; Physics Ph D.

**NOZELL, SUSAN E,** Lexington Comm Coll, Lexington, KY; JR; MBA; Math Clb 87-88; Spirit Clb 87-88; Yrbook Clb 87-88; Stdnt Gvrnmnt 86-88; Sr Exctv Cmmt 87-88; Ski Clb 86-88; Crop Walk 84; Cmmty Serv Undprvldgd Fmls 84; Asst Bookeeper Darryls 1891 88-; Employee Mont Oct 89 Dec 89-90; Acctng; CPA.

**NSOULI, NADIM M,** Georgetown Univ, Washington, DC; SR; BS; Beta Gamma Sigma; Deans List; Fin/Interntl Mgt; Law.**

**NTEZINDE, SIMON M,** Commonwealth Coll, Virginia Beach, VA; SO; BSCET; Aviation Storekeeper U S Navy 86-; AAS-ET; Elec; Engr Tech.

**NTUBA, WILFRED M,** Coppin St Coll, Baltimore, MD; SO; BSC; Intl Assoc 89-; Mgmt Sci Scty 89-; NABA; SIFE; Cert 89; Mgmt Sci.

**NUCKOLS, ALYSON D,** Radford Univ, Radford, VA; FR; BS; Frst Bapt Chrch Choir 90-; Bapt Stdnt Union 90-; Mxd Ensmbl 90; Bio/Pre Med; Med.

**NUEL, CRAIG E,** Cornell Univ Statutory College, Ithaca, NY; SO; BS; Orntn Comm; Sailing; Ski Clb 88-90; Phi Beta Sigma; Intrn Deloitte/Touche Acctg Tax Stf 90; Deans Lst 88-; Ag Ecnmcs; Law.

**NUGENT, GREGORY M,** S U N Y Coll Of Tech At Alfred, Alfred, NY; SR; AAS; Envrnmntl Sci.

**NUGENT, HEIDI M,** George Mason Univ, Fairfax, VA; JR; BBA; Decision Sci VP 90-; Laptop Users Grp; Gldn Ky 89-; Beta Gamma Sigma; Coop Educ Mitre Corp 90-; Schlrshp Anderson Consulting 91; Bus; Cmptr Infrmtn Sys.

**NUGENT, SUE A,** Coll Of Charleston, Charleston, SC; JR; Hnrs Prog; Early Childhood Devptmt; Tchng.

**NUJOMA, YVONNE N,** Beaver Coll, Glenside, PA; JR; BS; Amer Chem Soc Sec; Coll Hnr Pgm; Chem.**

**NULL, DONNA E,** Neumann Coll, Aston, PA; SO; BSN; Dns Lst 90; BS Phila Coll Phrmcy Sci 86; Nrsng.

**NULTY, JACQUELINE A,** City Univ Of Ny Baruch Coll, New York, NY; Stdy Abrd Org; Baruch Schlr; Beta Gamma Sigma; Gldn Key Ntl; Schlrshp Stdy Abrd Mdlsx Plytchnc Lndn England; BBA 90; Mrktg Mgt.

**NUNES, ANDREA H,** Md Inst Coll Of Art, Baltimore, MD; SR; Natl Soc Art/Ltrs Cmptn Photography; Maryland Inst Trvlng Flwshp Photography Turkey; Intrnshp Johns Hopkins Univ Med Photography; BFA Cum Laude; Photography; Artist.

**NUNES, HEIDI L,** Central Fl Comm Coll, Ocala, FL; FR; MBA; Cmnty Schlrs 90-; Bsns; Crprt Lwyr.

**NUNES, IRENE,** S U N Y Coll Of Optometry, New York, NY; GD; PH D; Am Optmtrc Assoc; N Y St Optmtrc Assoc 88-; Minority Flwshp 88-90; MS 90; OD 90; Molecular Cell Bio.

**NUNEZ REYES, CARMEN N,** Univ Of Pr Medical Sciences, San Juan, PR; GD; MS; Ntl Stu Spch/Lang/Hearng Assoc 90-; Sec Cls; Mstr Spch Lang Pthlgy 89-; Cum Laude Ba Spch Thrpy; Assoc Degree 87; BA 89.

**NUNEZ, CHRISTIAN J,** Manhattan Coll, Bronx, NY; SO; BME; Deans Lst; Mech Eng.

**NUNEZ JR, GERMAN R,** Fl International Univ, Miami, FL; FR; BSME; Inst Indstrl Engnrs 90-; Engnrng; Mchncl.

**NUNEZ, JOSE L,** City Univ Of Ny La Guard Coll, Long Island Cty, NY; GD; BT; La Guardia Cmptr Clb 89-90; Phi Theta Kappa; IEEE 90; Intrnshp At IBM 90; Intrnshp IBM La Guardia Cmmnty Clg 89-90; Electro Mchncl Eng Tchnlgy; Eng Tchnlgy.

**NUNEZ, MATTHEW GARCIA,** Univ Of Ky, Lexington, KY; FR; BS; Phi Eta Sigma; Beta Theta Pi Exec Cncl; Pre-Med.

**NUNEZ, RODOLFO P,** Barry Univ, Miami, FL; JR; BS; Rspct Life Org Treas 90-; Cir K Intl Serv Org 90-; Crmnl Jstc; Educ.

**NUNEZ, VIVIAN,** Fl International Univ, Miami, FL; JR; BA; MI Dade Chrldrs Co Capt 88-90; Gldn Dzzlrs 90-; Phi Theta Kappa 89-; Acctg Assoc; AA 90; Acctg; CPA.

**NUNLEY, JEANETTA,** Al St Univ, Montgomery, AL; SR; BS; Stdnt-Alumni Rels Comm 88-90; Kappa Delta Pi Nu 90-; Alpha Kappa Mu; Elem Ed; Tch.

**NUNLEY, NORMA JANAY,** Union Univ, Jackson, TN; FR; BME; Bptst Stdnt Union; Prclmtn; Zeta Tau Alpha; Intrn Mnstr W Palm Bch FL; IM Sftbl/Bsktbl; Music Educ/Yth Mnstry; Mnstr.

**NUNN, BONNIE M,** Franklin And Marshall Coll, Lancaster, PA; FR; BA; Sight/Sound 90-; Ice Hockey Clubs Mgr 90-; Math/French.

**NUNNALLY, GRAHAM R,** Longwood Coll, Farmville, VA; SR; BA; Phi Theta Kappa SVEC 87-88; Cum Laude 88-90; AA/S Southside Va Comm Coll 88; Hstry/Socl Sci; Tch H S.

**NUNNALLY, MONTREL Y,** Johnson C Smith Univ, Charlotte, NC; SO; NABA 90-; Hon Coll 89-; SGA 89-; Bus Mgmt/Acctg; Mngr/CPA.

**NUNNARI, NANCY G,** Niagara Univ, Niagara Univ, NY; SR; BBA; Acctg Soc Niagara Univ; Natl Assoc Acctnts; VITA CTE; AAS Niagara Co Cmnty Clg 83; Acctg; CPA.

**NUNNERY, PATRICIA A,** Alcorn St Univ, Lorman, MS; SR; BS; SNEA Treas 89-90; NAACP; Natl Cllgt Awd 90-; Elem Ed; Tchng.

**NUNNERY, SHELLEY R,** Oh Univ-Southern Cmps, Ironton, OH; FR; BA; Sclgy; Hmn Svcs.

**NUNZIATO, KATHLEEN M,** Hudson Valley Comm Coll, Troy, NY; SO; BA; Spec Ed Tchr Assist; Psych; Tchng.

**NUON, SANITH C,** Univ Of Cincinnati-Clrmnt Coll, Batavia, OH; FR; BED; Cambodian Assoc Grtr Cnti Exec Dir; Kiwanis; Rotary Clb; Cinti Pblc Schl; Red Crs; Slvtn Army; St John Soc Serv; Free Store; Trvlrs Aid Inst; Spec Hnr Awd 84; Gen Hosp; Chldrn Hosp; Bsn/Acctg.

**NUOVO, KRISTA J,** S U N Y Coll Of Tech At Frmgdl, Farmingdale, NY; GD; AAS; Horticulture Club 90; Ornamental Horticulture; Horticulture Mgmt.

**NURNBERGER, DONALD A,** Hillsborough Comm Coll, Tampa, FL; FR; BA; Bsnss.

**NUSBAUM, LISA C,** Md Coll Of Art & Design, Silver Spring, MD; SO; AAF; Art; Graphic Designer.

**NUSRALA, AMY L,** Georgetown Univ, Washington, DC; JR; BS; Acctg.

**NUSZ, TONI L,** Univ Of Sc At Spartanburg, Spartanburg, SC; SR; Acctg Club Pres 89; Advsry Cncl 90; Omicron Delta Kappa 89; Gamma Beta Phi 88; Piedmont Soc 88; Gamma Psi Delta V P 87-; Marshall 90; Acctg; CPA.

**NUTLER, SUSAN K,** Endicott Coll, Beverly, MA; SO; BA; Stdnt Govtmnt Assoc Pres 90-; Envrnmntl Ldrshp Club 90-; Edtr Poeby Mag; Jrnlst Nwspr 89-; Phi Theta Kappa 90-; Intrnshp Interntl Museum Phtgrhy 89-90; Intrnshp At Monroe Cahly Leg Ofc 90-; AS; English.

**NUTTER, CYNTHIA M,** Northeast State Tech Comm Coll, Blountville, TN; SO; AS; Bsn Mgmt Tech; Mgmt.

**NUTTER, JEFFREY A,** Oh St Univ At Marion, Marion, OH; SR; BSBA; Ass Arts 90; Acctg; CPA Firm.

**NUTTING, REBECCA L,** Endicott Coll, Beverly, MA; FR; AA; Bus Clb 90; Deans List 90; Liberal Arts/Psychology; Child Psychologist.

**NUZZI, JOSEPH F,** Villanova Univ, Villanova, PA; SO; BA; Itln Clb Pres 89-; Hmls Comm Vol 89-; Phi Kappa Phi; Deans Lst; Phlsphy.

**NUZZO, PATRICIA M,** Univ Of Pittsburgh At Bradford, Bradford, PA; JR; BS; Stdnt Govt 89-; Geology Club Sec 90; Alpha Lambda Delta; Bus Mgmt; MA Interior Dsgn.

**NUZZOLO, LISA M,** Boston Coll, Chestnut Hill, MA; SR; BS; NSNA 88-; Mendels Clb Annual Biomedical Ethics Conf; Independence Study-Post Anesth Care Unit/ Surg ICU; Neurosurgery Intrn 90-; Nursing; Cardiac-Med Unit.

**NWACHUKU, ADINDU O,** Manchester Comm Coll, Manchester, CT; SR; BA; Econ; Law.

**NWOKEAFOR, COSMAS U,** Howard Univ, Washington, DC; GD; PH D; Dept SG; Gen Sec 90-; IGBO Cath Assn Amer Choir Mstr 86-; K Of C Knight 86-; Orlu Peoples Assn In Americas Gen Sec 88-90; Grad TA 90-; Radio Intern News 85-86; PBS TV News 88-89; BA 86; MA 90; Mass Comm; Tchng/Cnsltng Job.

**NWOSU, CORDELIA N,** Cheyney Univ Of Pa, Cheyney, PA; SR; BS; Accounting.

**NYARKO, YAW O,** Central St Univ, Wilberforce, OH; FR; BA; Internatl Stdnts Org; Flwshp Chrstn Stdnts; Engrg.

**NYCUM, DONNA R,** Kent St Univ Geauga Cmps, Burton Twp, OH; JR; BA; Cncrt Bnd 89-; Symphny Bnd; Grl Scouts Ldr 88-90; Natl Assn Educ Yng Chldrn 86-; Tri-Co Assn Ed Yng Chldrn 86-; Early Chldhd Educr 86-; AAS Cuyahoga Comm Coll 86; Educ.

**NYUNT, DARRYL T,** City Univ Of Ny Baruch Coll, New York, NY; JR; BS; Chinese Cult Clb Pr 89-90; Var Tennis 89-90; Asian Assoc 90-; Baruch Schlr; Deans Lst; Alex Brown/Sons Intrn; Acctng/Fin; Intl Bus.

# O

**O BANION, JOY L,** Ashland Comm Coll, Ashland, KY; SO; BA; Honorable Odr Ky Colonels Col 77-; Girl Scout Ldr 90-; Office Intern; Notary Public 88-; Telecommunications Admin Clerk 81-; Elementary Education.

**O BANNON, LAWANDA J,** Univ Of Al At Birmingham, Birmingham, AL; SR; Natl Sci/Math SGA 85-86; Nclr Med Allied Hlth SGA 89-90; Mnrty Schlrshp 89-90; BS; Cert; Nclr Med Tchnlgy; Law.

**O BEIRNE, HUGH S,** Merrimack Coll, North Andover, MA; SO; BA; Philosophy/Hist; Teach/Rsrch.

**O BERRY, DAVID T,** Univ Of Sc At Columbia, Columbia, SC; SO; BA; Amnsty; Yng Coll Rpblcns; Gamma Beta Phi 90-; Gldn Key 90-; Ruth C Patrick Blgcl Rsrch Pgm 89; Hstry Pre-Law; Law Crprt.

**O BOYLE, BRETT M,** Berry Coll, Rome, GA; FR; BA; Hm Ec Assn Tchr 90-; Cath Stdnts Assn 90-; Emergng Ldrs 90-; Dnc Tm 90-; Int Dsgn/Frnch.

**O BOYLE, GREGORY P,** Bapt Bible Coll & Seminary, Clarks Summit, PA; SR; BA; Pstrl Intrst Flwshp Pres 90-; RA 88-; Camp Cnslr 87-90; Wrstlng 87-89; Mnstry; MA.

**O BRIEN, AIMEE L,** Endicott Coll, Beverly, MA; FR; BA; Club Coutier Fshn Show; Radio/TV Cmmnctns; Brdcstng.

**O BRIEN, AMY C,** Notre Dame Coll, Manchester, NH; JR; BA; Res Lf Stff RA 89-; Stu Snt Offc Cncl 89-; Clss VP 89-; Alpha Chi 90-; Dean Lst; NH Humanities Cncl Intern; Engl/Psychlgy; Clncl Psychlgy.**

**O BRIEN, AMY P,** Allegheny Coll, Meadville, PA; JR; BA; Gymnastics Club 89-90; Lambda Sikgma 89-90; Animal Shelter Vol Work 90-; Comm Arts; Entertainment Ind-Film Comedy.

**O BRIEN, CATHERINE E,** Wilmington Coll, New Castle, DE; SR; BA; Crmnl Jstc Law Enfrcmnt.

**O BRIEN, CATHY A,** Seton Hall Univ, South Orange, NJ; JR; BS; Acctng Clb 90-; Fox Gearty Std Rep; Beta Gamma Sigma; Beta Alpha Psi Pres 90-; Seton Hl Dist Acad Schlr 90-; Acctng Intrn; Stf Acctnt Meeker Sharkey Fncl Grp 88-; Pblc Acctng.

**O BRIEN, CHRISTINE A,** Boston Univ, Boston, MA; SR; BS; Phys Ther Clb T 90-; Nrntmy Tutr Acad Stdnt Advsry Pgm 89-; Res Asst 89-; Phys Ther; MA Med Sci.

**O BRIEN, COLLEEN B,** Niagara Univ, Niagara Univ, NY; JR; BS; Intrnshp Cath Charities; Socl Wrk.

**O BRIEN, COLLEEN I,** Old Dominion Univ, Norfolk, VA; SR; BED; Pi Beta Phi VP; Adopt A Hwy 90-; Mrktng; Adv.

**O BRIEN, DEBORAH L,** Alfred Univ, Alfred, NY; JR; BS; Natl Assoc Actnts 90-; Delta Mu Delta VP Elect; Alpha Iota Delta; AAS Alfred State Univ NY Agri/Tech Coll 82; Bus; Acctg.

**O BRIEN, DENNIS J,** Univ Of Ky, Lexington, KY; SR; Fnnc; Fnncl Plnnr.

**O BRIEN, EILEEN T,** Va Commonwealth Univ, Richmond, VA; FR; BS; Hnrs Prog; Psych/Soc; Counselor.

**O BRIEN, HAROLD D,** Spalding Univ, Louisville, KY; SO; BSN; Cl Rep 90-; Acad Hon 89-; Sons/Dau/Erin 88-; KC 3rd Deg 86-88; MTG/COMM Bnkg 7yrs; USNASAS Nuc Reactor Oper; BSBA Un/Louisville 83; Nrsg; Psych Nrs.

**O BRIEN, JANET L,** Comm Coll Algny Co Algny Cmps, Pittsburgh, PA; SO; BS; Bsn; Admn.

**O BRIEN, JOHN A,** Me Maritime Academy, Castine, ME; FR; BS; Stdnt Life Exec Treas; Engrng; Maritime.

**O BRIEN, JOHN C,** Jersey City St Coll, Jersey City, NJ; JR; BA; Math Clb Pres 88-; Math/Sec Edn; High Sch Math Tchr.

**O BRIEN, JOHN F,** Georgetown Univ, Washington, DC; SO.

**O BRIEN, JUSTIN,** Inter Amer Univ Pr San German, San German, PR; FR; BBA; Blngl Eng/Spnsh Org 90-; Mrktng; Bus.

**O BRIEN, KAREN M,** Univ Of Cincinnati, Cincinnati, OH; SR; BFA; Co Drctd One For The Rd Amnesty Intrntnl; Intrnshp Videowrks Blue Ash OH 90; Asstnt WGUC 90-; Certf Cntacts Euroval Tours France 88; AA 88; Brdcstng Elctrnc Media; Drctng Wrtng.

**O BRIEN, KELLY L,** Le Moyne Coll, Syracuse, NY; SR; Newspr Asst News Edtr 88-; Folkgroup Violinist 87-89; Poltcl Sci Acdmy 87-90; Hnrs Prog 88-; Deans List 87-; Cropwalk 88; NY Atrny Gen Consumer Rep Intern; IM Vlybl 88-89; BA; Poltcl Sci English; Law.

**O BRIEN, KIMBERLY A,** Comm Coll Algny Co Algny Cmps, Pittsburgh, PA; JR; AS; Elem Ed.

**O BRIEN, MARC M,** Eckerd Coll, St Petersburg, FL; SO; BUS; Deans Lst 89-; Nrthwstrn Mtl Lf Ins Cmpny Intern; Mgmt.

**O BRIEN, MARIE,** Univ Of South Al, Mobile, AL; JR; BS; Dns Lst 89; Pres Lst 89-; Intl Bus; Fncl Cnsltnt.

**O BRIEN, MATTHEW S,** Univ Of Sc At Columbia, Columbia, SC; SO; BS; Econ; Forcstng.

**O BRIEN, MICHAEL E,** Georgetown Univ, Washington, DC; SO; BSBA; Congressional Intern Honorable Geo J Hochbrueckner 90; Accounting.

**O BRIEN, MICHELLE A,** S U N Y Coll Of Tech At Alfred, Alfred, NY; FR; AS; Bus Mktg Clb; Alfrd Assoc Wmn Schlrshp; Bus; Corp Exec.

**O BRIEN, PATRICK T,** Univ Of South Al, Mobile, AL; FR; BED; Cthlc Yth Orgn Ftbl Coach 90; Phi Kappa Sigma VP 90-; Red Crss 90; IM Ftbl Vllyb Sftbl Wtr Polo 90-; Bus Mngt; Mrktng.

**O BRIEN, PAULINA M,** Coll Of The Holy Cross, Worcester, MA; FR; BA; Mrchng Band 90-; Wmns Vrsty Swim Tm 90-; Classics; Medicine/Law.

**O BRIEN, PHYLLIS D,** George Mason Univ, Fairfax, VA; SR; BIS; Amrcn Rd Crss Instrctr 90-; Alxndr Cmmnty Shltr Intern; Whtmn Wlkr Clnc Vol; Aids Ed.

**O BRIEN, SUZANNE,** Georgetown Univ, Washington, DC; SR; BSN; Sigma Theta Tau 89, Nrsng, Peds Nrsng.

**O BRIEN, TARA J,** Eckerd Coll, St Petersburg, FL; JR; BS; Theatr Clb 90-; IM Sprts Clb 88-; Coll Hon 88-; Vol Tutr 88-; Food Drv 88-; G Matter Acctg Awrd 89; Clrwtr Cntrl Cthlc Schlrshp 88-; Vrsty Vlybl Capt 88-; Mgmt; Acctnt.

**O BRYAN, ERIN C,** Univ Of South Al, Mobile, AL; JR; BS; Res Lf Cncl 89-; Bapt Cmps Mnstries 89-; AL Rec Prks Assoc 90-; Therptc Rec; Rec Thrpy.

**O BRYAN, KATHY L,** Owensboro Comm Coll, Owensboro, KY; SO; BA; Natl Edctn Assoc 90-; KY Edctn Assoc 90-; Phi Theta Kappa; Math; Tchng.

**O BRYAN, PAUL A,** Univ Of Louisville, Louisville, KY; GD; MENG; Weight Clb 89-; Tau Beta Pi 90-; Gold Key 90-; BS 90; Elec Eng.

**O CALLAGHAN, JENNIFER L,** Manhattan Coll, Bronx, NY; SO; BS; SWE 90-; New York Water Pollution Cntrl Assn; Water Pollution Cntrl Federation; Intrnshp AT/T 90-; Cvl Engr; Envrnmntl Lawyer.

**O CALLAGHAN, NIKKI M,** Niagara County Comm Coll, Sanborn, NY; FR; BA; Lib Arts; Stable/Farm Mgmnt.

**O CLAIR, MICHAEL J,** Hudson Valley Comm Coll, Troy, NY; Paramedic Intern Leonard Hosp 90-; St Peters Hosp 90-; Prof Firefghtr; Advncd Cardiac Lf Sprt; Pre Hosp Trauma Lf Sprt; Pre Hosp Pdtrc Care; Paramedicine; Firefghtr/Paramedic.

**O CLAIRE, JOSEPH R,** Fl Baptist Theological Coll, Graceville, FL; GD; MDIV; Thlgy Clb 87-88; Cum Laude 90-; Thlgy; Tchr.

**O CONNELL, ALICE J,** Catholic Univ Of America, Washington, DC; FR; BA; Phi Eta Sigma 90-; Kappa Tau Gamma Rsh Co-Chrmn 90-; Dns Lst 90-; Pol Sci.

**O CONNELL, ANN E,** Daytona Beach Comm Coll, Daytona Beach, FL; SO; BA; Tchl Supsr; Phi Theta Kappa; Art; Professional Artist.

**O CONNELL, ERINBETH J,** Coll Of Charleston, Charleston, SC; SO; BS; Frnch Clb 89-90; Trguide 89-90; Yrbk Stf 89-90; Hnrs Pro 89-; Hnr Pro Stu Assoc Treas 89-; Phi Mu; Deans Lst 89-; Sthrn Rgnl Hnrs Cnvtn; Bus Admin.

**O CONNELL, KAREN J,** Duke Univ, Durham, NC; FR; BA; Dk Eqstrn Tm 90-; Intern Coop Dvlpmnt Fndtn; Pre Med Grmn; Med.

**O CONNELL, PATRICK H,** Widener Univ, Chester, PA; SR; MBA; Chester Eastside Ministry Rec Prog Cordntr 88-; Univ Ambsdr 89-; Judicial Brd 89-90; Omicron Delta Epsilon 89-; Phi Delta Theta Rush Chrmn 89-; Rotarcet Club V P 90-; Vlntr Of The Year 88-89; Phi Delta Theta Edctnl Schlrshp 90-; BA.**

**O CONNOR, CAROL M,** Indiana Univ Of Pa, Indiana, PA; SR; New Stdnt Asst 87-89; Swim Tm Mngr 86-87; Deans Lst 89-; Phi Mu 87-; Stdnt Art Exhbt 86; BS Educ.

**O CONNOR, CATHERINE P,** Manhattan Coll, Bronx, NY; FR; BA; Parish Lector 89-; Deans Lst 90-; Computer Sci; Syst Analyst/Prgmr.

**O CONNOR, CHRISTINE E,** George Mason Univ, Fairfax, VA; SR; BS; Gldn Ky; Alpha Chi; Gldn Ky; Alphi Chi; Acctng; CPA.

**O CONNOR, COURTNEY E,** Lesley Coll, Cambridge, MA; SO; BED; Class Offcr Pres 89-; Stdnt Life Condct Brd Chrprsn 89-; Eductnl Pgm Comm 90-; Lesley Schlrshp 89-; Middle Schl Math/Sci Schlrshp 90-; Phy Sci; Tchr.

**O CONNOR, ELIZABETH A,** Georgian Court Coll, Lakewood, NJ; JR; BA; Mchlnglst Art Clb Pres 90-; Stdnt Serv Tutor 90-; Opt AR Amer Optmtrc Assn 86; Art/Elem Ed; Tchng.

**O CONNOR, ELIZABETH L,** Univ Of South Al, Mobile, AL; JR; Elem Educ.

**O CONNOR, JACQUELINE M,** S U N Y At Binghamton, Binghamton, NY; SO; BS; Acctg Mgmt Orgztn 89-; O'connor Hall Exe Bd Soc V P 90-; Bus; Acctg.**

**O CONNOR, KATHERINE P,** Univ Of Sc At Columbia, Columbia, SC; SO; BA; Gamma Beta Phi; English; Law.

**O CONNOR, KATHLEEN M,** Western New England Coll, Springfield, MA; SR; BA; WNEK-FM Prog Dir 89-; Pre-Law Soc 89-; Intrnshp In Psych 90-; Sccr/Karate 87-88; AA 89; Psych; Human Serv/Law.**

**O CONNOR, KRISTIN B,** Radford Univ, Radford, VA; JR; BS; Radford Univ Hon Prog 90-; Pi Gamma Mu; Radford Univ Vybl Tm 88-; Pltcl Sci; Envrnmtl Plcy/Plng.

**O CONNOR, LINDA BERKHOUDT,** S U N Y At Buffalo, Buffalo, NY; GD; Alpha Sigma Lambda; Sarah Helen Kish Awrd; Free Lance Wrtr; BA 90; AS 87; Engl Cmmnctns; Jrnlsm.

**O CONNOR, MARGARET M,** Iona College, New Rochelle, NY; SO; BA; Spec Olympics Sec 89-; Bowling Clb Treas 89-; Frshmn Orien Grp Sprvsr 90; CCD Tchr 86-; Full Acad Schlrshp 89-; Dns Lst 89-; IM Sftbl 89-; Psychlgy; Educ.**

**O CONNOR JR, MELVIN J,** Univ Of South Al, Mobile, AL; JR; BED; History; Edctn.

**O CONNOR, PATRICIA DARLINE,** Univ Of Nh Plymouth St Coll, Plymouth, NH; SR; BA; Status Wmn Cmsn Task Frc; Domestic Violnc/Sexual Asslt Tsk Frc; Paralegal; Pltcl Sci; Law.

**O CONNOR, RHONDA P,** Univ Of Tn At Martin, Martin, TN; FR; BS; Asst Mgr At Long John Silvers 86-90; Nursing.

**O CONNOR, RUAIRE J,** Duquesne Univ, Pittsburgh, PA; GD; MA; Holy Ghost Fthr CSSP; Prst/Mssnry Kenya E Africa Rctr 71-90; Dip Philsphy Hly Ghst Clg; Dip In Thlgy Dublin Ireland; Frmtve Sprtlty/Mnstry; Sprtlty Frmtn.

**O CONNOR, SEAN P,** Iona College, New Rochelle, NY; SR; BS; Stdnt Gov 90-; Bwlng Clb Pres 87-; Domp Clb VP 88-; Delta Epsilon Sigma 90-; Upsilon Pi Epsilon; Cornelian Hnr Scty; Tutor 87-; Acad Schlrshp 87-; Outstndng Sci Stndt Awd; Math/Comp Sci Awds; Math/Comp Sci; Pgrmr/Professor.**

**O CONNOR, SHELLEY ELIZABETH,** Providence Coll, Providence, RI; SR; Yrbk Edtr 90-; Psi Chi 90-; Vol Providence 87-89; Vol RI Coll Litrcy Prog 88-89; Pstrl Cncl 87-; Dorcas Pl Litrcy Cntr Asst Coor 90-; IM Frsbe 87-; BA; Psych.

**O CONNOR, SUZANNE,** Univ Of The Dist Of Columbia, Washington, DC; SR; BA; Bus Finance Assn 89-; Mrktng Clb; Deans List 88-; Highest Hons; Outstndng Jr 90; Asst Chief Fincl Offcr Jellinek/Schwartz/Connolly/Freshman 88; Finance.

**O CULL, JEANNIE R,** Wilmington Coll, Wilmington, OH; FR; Psychlgy; Clncl Psychlgst.

**O DANIEL, CHRIS L,** Kent St Univ Kent Cmps, Kent, OH; FR; BS; Math; Cmptr Sci.

**O DAY, JESSE S,** S U N Y Coll Of A & T Morrisvl, Morrisville, NY; FR; BS; Hmn Sci; Coun/Byc Frame Bldr Dsgnr.

**O DEA, EILEEN E,** Hudson Valley Comm Coll, Troy, NY; SR; Credentialed Alcohalism Counsellor.

**O DEA, JENNIFER L,** Coker Coll, Hartsville, SC; BA; Stdnt Athltc Trnr Sftbl Trnr 90-; Phys Educ Mjrs Clb VP 90-; Wmns Sccr 88-; Pol Sci And Phys Educ; Athltc Trnr Certfd.

**O DELL, DONNA M,** King Coll, Bristol, TN; JR; Biol Awd 90; Biol; Marine Biol.

**O DELL III, JAMES E,** Nc St Univ At Raleigh, Raleigh, NC; FR; BA; IM Scr; Elctrcl Engrg/Bsn.

**O DELL, JOHN S,** Univ Of Al At Birmingham, Birmingham, AL; SR; BA; Gldn Key 89-; Otstndg Stu Gadsden St Comm Coll 88-89; Mtrls Engr.

**O DELL SR, MICHAEL P,** Bryant Stratton Bus Inst Roch, Rochester, NY; SR; AAS; Elec; Comp Repr.**

**O DELL, SHERRY C,** George Mason Univ, Fairfax, VA; SR; BED; Tae Kwon Do Club; Kappa Delta Pi; Golden Key; AED Northrn Va Cmnty Clg 89; Physcl Ed; Physcl Therapst.

**O DONALD III, ARTHUR J,** Holyoke Comm Coll, Holyoke, MA; SO; BA; Green Key Tres 90-; Vol Kates Ktchn 90-; AA; Pol Sci; Intl Law.

**O DONALD, LISA E,** Villanova Univ, Villanova, PA; JR; BA; Villanova Un 88-89; Philosophy Hon Soc; Delta Delta Delta Exe Pres 88-; Proj Sunshine; I M Vybl Ftbl Sftbl; Philosophy.

**O DONNELL, AMELIA C,** Longwood Coll, Farmville, VA; GD; BS; Thrputc Rcrtn Org 87-90; Syncrnzd Swmng Pres 86-90; Prince Edw Cty Vol Rsce Squd; Spec Olympcs Chrprsn 87-90; Intrn Land Bwtwn Lks 90; Intrn Dominon Psy Hosp; BS 90; Rcrtn Thrpst Geratrics.

**O DONNELL, DAVID R,** Hudson Valley Comm Coll, Troy, NY; SR; AA; Rdlgy Tchnlgy Clb Treas 85-86; Pres Lst 90; Amer Rgstry Rdlgc Tchnlgst 86-; Stf Rdlgc Tchnlgst St Marys Hosp Troy NM 86-; AAS Hudson Vly Comm Clge 86; Lib Arts; Ed/Hstry.

**O DONNELL, JOHN M,** Univ Of Pittsburgh, Pittsburgh, PA; GD; MSN; Amer Assn Nunse Ansthtsts 89-; Crtcl Cr Nrsng Assn 88-; Grad Stdnt Nrsng Assn; Sigma Theta Tau 90-; US Army Rsrv Nrs Corp 1st Lieut; BSN Carlow Coll 83; Anesthesia Nrsng.

**O DONNELL, KAREN E,** Springfield Tech Comm Coll, Springfield, MA; GD; Empl Remdr Publ Inc E Longmdw MA 87-; AS 90; Busn Admin; Mktg.

**O DONNELL, KAREN M,** Duquesne Univ, Pittsburgh, PA; JR; BA; Dqsn Dk Ed Chf 88-; Cmmtr Asst 89-; Spnsh Ttr 89-90; Orttn Stff 89; Phi Kappa Phi; Deans Lst; Natl Coll Cmmnctns Arts Awrd; Capone Schlrshp 90; Schlrs Awrd; Intern Family Srvcs Western PA; Cmmnctns; Jrnlsm.

**O DONNELL, KAREN M,** Rivier Coll, Nashua, NH; SO; BS; Prlgl Soc Pres; Mdl UN Del 89-90; RAID-DAY; Dean Lst 89-90; Arbcs; Wght Trnng; Bld Drv; Law; Prlgl.

**O DONNELL, KELLIE A,** Indiana Univ Of Pa, Indiana, PA; SR; BS; PSEA 90-; Res Hall Assoc 88-89; Wmns Ldrshp Caucus 88-89; Provost Schlr 88-; Sigma Delta Pi 88-; Amer Assn Tchrs Span/Portugse 88; Res Asst 88-90; Study Abrd Spain 90; Soph Ldrshp Awd; Wmns Advsry Cncl; Span; Tch.

**O DONNELL, KELLY A,** Univ Of Akron, Akron, OH; SO; BSN; Coll Nrsng Club 90-; Deans List 89-; Nursing.

**O DONNELL, KEVIN,** William Paterson Coll, Wayne, NJ; FR; BA; Hstry; Frgn Serv.

**O DONNELL, MARY E,** Univ Of Ct, Storrs, CT; SO; BS; Blck/Brdl Clb 89-; Pre Vet Clb 89-; SENAA Mrshl 90-; Anml Sci; Vet Med.**

**O DONNELL, SHERYL L,** D Youville Coll, Buffalo, NY; JR; BSN; Stdnt Fllwshp; DAWO; SNA; Soc Wrk Club; Cmtrs Club; Natl Hnr Soc 67; Alpha Chi 71; Delta Psi Omega 70; AIDS Cmnty Svc Wstrn New York Hotline Vol 89-; NY State Hlth Svc Corps Schlrshp 90-; Distr 1 NYSNA Wstrn Area; UCC; Nrsg; Chrstn Mnstry.

**O DONOGHUE, DIANA L,** Providence Coll, Providence, RI; SR; Nwspr Orgztn 87-88; AISEC 87-88; Big Bro/Big Sis Exe Bd Ofcr 87-; Dance Tm 88-; Figure Sktng Clb Pres 88-; BA; Ele/Spec Educ; Tch/Law.

**O DONOGHUE, PETER J,** Old Dominion Univ, Norfolk, VA; SR; BSME; Pi Tau Sigma 90-; Tau Beta Pi 90-; Vrsty Swm 87-90; Grdt Schl/Nasa Rsrchr.

**O DONOGHUE, RUTH N,** Brescia Coll, Owensboro, KY; SR; BS; Alpha Chi 90-; All Amrcn Schlr Cllg Awd; Pblc Spkng 87; Assn Handicapped Drctrs 89-; Democrat Exctv Comm 87-; Edctn Scl Stds; HS Tchr.

**O FARRELL, JENNIFER D,** Marywood Coll, Scranton, PA; SO; BA; Cls Ofcr Vol Chrmn 90-; Orntn 90-; Vols In Actn Publ Chrmn 90-; Campus Mnstry; Mu Alpha Gamma; Ireland Exchg Schlrshp; Elem French Tchr; Frnch; Tchr.

**O FARRELL, MEL FRANCIS,** Univ Of Pa, Philadelphia, PA; JR; BSC; Economics; Strategic Mngmnt.

**O GARRO, PAULA C,** Fl International Univ, Miami, FL; SO; BSBA; West Indian Stdnt Assn 89-; Pre-Med Soc 90-; Intl Stdnt Assn 90-; Phi Lamda Beta; Comp Imm Asstshp 90-; Bio/Chem; Med.

**O GUIN, MICHAEL K,** Volunteer St Comm Coll, Gallatin, TN; GD; AS; Med Recs Tech; Med Recs Dir.

**O GUINN, KELLEY M,** Central Fl Comm Coll, Ocala, FL; FR.

**O GWIN, GARY L,** Univ Of Al At Birmingham, Birmingham, AL; SR; BS; HEPE Majors Clb 89-; AAHPERD 89-; ASAHPERD 89-; Ala Spec Olymp 89; Ala Army Natl Grd 89-; SMI Steel Inc Birmhm Al 84-; AS Wallace St Comm Clg 82; Histry Physcl Educ; Tchr.

**O HAIR, EDWARD B,** Hillsborough Comm Coll, Tampa, FL; FR; AA; Jhoon Rhee Tae Kwon Do 90-; Jstc Admin; Fed Law Enfrcmnt.

**O HALLARON, THOMAS P,** Va Commonwealth Univ, Richmond, VA; SR; MBA; Jennings Soc; Omicron Delta Epsilon; Dir Rtl Oprtns/Mrktng 84-; BS; Bus.

**O HALLORAN, THOMAS J,** Me Maritime Academy, Castine, ME; FR; Band/Fire Brigade/EMT/SCUBA; Dns Lst; Marine Trnsprtn/Nvgtn; Deck Officer/Paramedic.

**O HARA, HEATHER M,** Cornell Univ Statutory College, Ithaca, NY; JR; BA; CUDS 89-; Cal Poly Dairy Exhng 90; Equestrian Tm 88-90; Alpha Phi Unity Officer; Cargill Nutreria Feeds Intshp; Animal Sci; Livestock Nutrition.

**O HARA, KATHLEEN M,** West Chester Univ, West Chester, PA; SR; BS; Athltc Trnrs Clb 88-; Microbiomedics Schlrshp; Athltc Trng; Phy Thrpy.

**O HARA, MICHELE A,** Le Moyne Coll, Syracuse, NY; JR; Alpha Sigma Nu 90-91; English/Span.**

**O HARA, SEAN T,** S U N Y At Buffalo, Buffalo, NY; GD; BSMBA; Upstate Milk Coop Inc; Athletic Dept Tutor 90-; Sccr 88-89; Acctng.

**O HARE, MAURA E,** Villanova Univ, Villanova, PA; SO; BA; Rprtr Asst Edtr/Ftrs Edtr Stdnt Nwspr 90-; Hs Cncl Scl Awrnss Offcr 90-; Omicron Delta Kappa; Villanova Com Phldlph Hmlss; Habitat Hmnty Cmps Chptr Chrprsn; Lctr Euchrstc Mnstr; Stdnt Mnstr Trng; IM Ftbl 89-; Engl; Tchng.

**O KEEFE, CAROL L,** Mount Saint Mary Coll, Newburgh, NY; FR; BA; Finance Brd; Hnrs Alliance; Big Bro Big Sis 89-; Pres Schlrshp 90-; Math; Elem Educ.

**O KEEFFE, CELINE,** City Univ Of Ny La Guard Coll, Long Island Cty, NY; GD; AAS; Nrsng Clb 90; Soc Sci Hon 89; Frmr Elem Schl Tchr; BED St Patrcks Coll 81; Cert Montessori Schl 86; Nrsng; MS.

**O KELLEY, HOLLE L,** Converse Coll, Spartanburg, SC; SO; BFA; Stdnt Activ Comm Soph Rep 90-; Stdnt Admssns Bd 90-; Keybrd Comm 90-; Deans Lst 90-; Crs Cntry; Int Dsgn; Architecture.

**O LEARY, CHRISTINE M,** Duquesne Univ, Pittsburgh, PA; JR; BS; PA Phrmctcl Assn Chrprsn 90-; Ski Clb 90; Alpha Gamma Delta 89-; Rho Chi Cert Of Rcgntn; Dns Lst; Phrmcy.

**O LEARY, MARY E,** Broward Comm Coll, Ft Lauderdale, FL; FR; AS; Med Rcrd Assoc; Amer Med Rcrd Assoc; Med Rcrds Tech; Med Office Mgr.

**O LEARY, PATRICIA A,** Mount Aloysius Jr Coll, Cresson, PA; SO; Medical Assistant Club VP 90-; AS Mount Aloysius Jr Clge; Medical Assistant.

**O MALLEY, EDWARD THOMAS,** Anne Arundel Comm Coll, Arnold, MD; SO; BA; Dstngshd Hon Grad 88; Good Cndct Medal 89; US Army Infntry 87-89; Engl; Wrtr/Tchr.

**O MALLEY, PATRICK F,** Providence Coll, Providence, RI; SO; BA; AIESEC Dir PR 89-; Spanish Club Treas 89-; Intrn Lt Govnr 89-; Hist/Mdrn Lang; Intrntl Bus Law.

**O MALLEY, SUSAN M,** Univ Of Nc At Charlotte, Charlotte, NC; GD; PHD; Pre Law Scty 87; Rsdnc Lf Ste Rep 86-90; Stdnt Govt Assoc ; Phi Kappa Phi 89-90; Phi Eta Sigma 86-90; Alpha Phi Sigma 89-90; Cum Laude Grad 86-90; Deans Lst; Chnclrrs Lst; Custmr Srvc Rep Insrnc Frm; BA 90; Crmnl Jstc.

**O MARA, ELLA K,** George Mason Univ, Fairfax, VA; SR; BS; Alpha Phi 87-; Elem Educf Tchr.

**O MARA, PATRICK J,** Manhattan Coll, Bronx, NY; FR; BS; Deans Lst 90-; IM Bsktbl 90-; Eng; Cvl Eng.

**O MARA, SHANNON M,** Univ Of Rochester, Rochester, NY; SO; BA; Vrsty Sccr 89-; Dlion Orgnztn 90-; Deans List 89-; Sgm Dlt Tau Tres 90-; Almn Schlr 89-; Actrl Stds Schlrshp; Ec; Actry.

**O MARA, TODD M,** D Youville Coll, Buffalo, NY; GD; MSPT; Stdnt Physcl Thrpy Assoc 88-; Amer Clg Of Hlth Care Exec; Buffalo Back Neck PT Schlrshp; Intrnshp Lakeside Meml Hosp 89-90; Intern Mt Sinai Medl Ctr 90; Intern Miami Chldrns Hosp 90; Physical Therapy.

**O NEAL, BARBARA DIANNE,** Ms St Univ, Miss State, MS; SR; BS; Phi Theta Kappa 65-69; Band Dance Team 68-71; CASA; Imp Lrng Cntr Uppr Elem; Judge Regnl Sci Eng Fair; PTA Chrprsn Career Day; Deans Lst Schlr 65-90; Pres Lst; NAEYC IRA MPE MACUS/SACUS NEA/MAE 90-; AA Music Perkinston Clg 71; Elem Educ; Tchr.

**O NEAL, BILLY R,** Kent St Univ Kent Cmps, Kent, OH; JR; BBA; Golden Key 90-; Beta Gamma Sigma 90-; Arthur Andersen Tax/Audit Intrn 90-; Sherri Jo Luft Mem Awrd 89-; Acctng/ Comp Sci; Database Admin.

**O NEAL, BONNIE J,** Wv Northern Comm Coll, Wheeling, WV; SO; BA; Marshall Cnty Sheriffs Dept Intern; Criminal Justice; Fedl Law Enfrcmnt.

**O NEAL, CAROLEE,** Univ Of Ky, Lexington, KY; FR; BA; Trimble Co Silver Stirrups 4-H Horse Clb Pres 88-; Mt Hermon Bapt Church; Phi Eta Sigma 90-; Elem Ed; Elem Sch Tchr.

**O NEAL, CLIFFORD,** Monroe Comm Coll, Rochester, NY; SO; AS; Cmptr Sci; Cmptr Math.

**O NEAL, LISA R,** Ashland Comm Coll, Ashland, KY; JR; BA; AS; Acctng.

**O NEAL, LOIS M,** Salisbury St Univ, Salisbury, MD; SO; BS; Phi Beta Lambda Sec 90-; Fin Mgmt Assn 90-; Phi Eta Sigma 89-; Bsn Admin; Fin/Econ.**

**O NEAL, LORA L,** Univ Of Cincinnati-Clrmnt Coll, Batavia, OH; FR.

**O NEAL, LORRY SUNSHINE,** Univ Of Nc At Wilmington, Wilmington, NC; FR; BA; Stdnt Gov Pres 90-; Clg Repb 90; Sigma Sigma Sigma Fndng Sr 90-; Attnd Natl Conf Stdnt Govt Assoc TX A/M; Spec Sec VP Quayles Visit Wilmngtn; Crmnl Jstce; Law DA.

**O NEAL, SEAN E,** Central Fl Comm Coll, Ocala, FL; SO; MA; AA; Arch.

**O NEAL, SUSAN P,** Volunteer St Comm Coll, Gallatin, TN; FR; AS; Acctg Clb 90-; Bus Mgt.

**O NEIL, BONNIE SUE,** Comm Coll Algny Co Algny Cmps, Pittsburgh, PA; SO; AS; Lfgrd/Cert Swmng Instrctr; Phi Theta Kappa; Sftbl; Phys Ed; Coach/Tch Athltcs.

**O NEIL, DEANNA L,** Jefferson Comm Coll, Watertown, NY; FR; Pres Lst; Phtgrphy; Wldlife Phtgrphy.

**O NEIL, ELLEN M,** George Mason Univ, Fairfax, VA; SR; Beta Gamma Sigma; Gldn Ky; Alpha Chi; BS; Bus Mgmt.

**O NEIL, MAUREEN L,** Univ Of Ct, Storrs, CT; FR; BA; Business.

**O NEIL, PATRICIA A,** Western New England Coll, Springfield, MA; JR; BSEE; Sigma Beta Tau; Sigma Beta Tau Merit Schlrshp; Elect Eng Dept Awrd; Elect Eng.

**O NEIL, ROBERT J,** Univ Of Akron, Akron, OH; SR; BFA; Stdnt Schlrshp Art; Phtgrphy; U Lvl Tchng.

**O NEILL, CAROLE E,** Mount Saint Mary Coll, Newburgh, NY; SR; Hon Alliance 88-90; Alpha Chi 89-90; Aquinas Schlr 90; Deans Lst 86-; Engl; Educ/Elem Tchr.

**O NEILL JR, EFRAIN,** Univ Of Pr At Mayaguez, Mayaguez, PR; SO; BA; Mthdst Chrch Yng Adlt Scty 86-; IEEE; NACME 90; Eng.

**O NEILL, JENNIFER L,** Comm Coll Algny Co Algny Cmps, Pittsburgh, PA; SO; BED; Spec Olympics; Vars Tennis 90-; Scdry Engl Ed; Teach.

**O NEILL, JENNIFER T,** Cornell Univ Statutory College, Ithaca, NY; JR; BA; Rd Crpt Soc Exec Brd 89-; Trdtn Flwshp 89-; Scl Comm Rsdnc Hl 89-90; Ambsdrs; Rsrch Ntrtn Dept; Lacrosse IM Rwg 89-; Bio; Orthopdcs.

**O NEILL, JOSE E CABAN,** Inter Amer Univ Pr Hato Rey, Hato Rey, PR; BA; Bus Admn/Ecnmc; Law.

**O NEILL, KAREN B,** Radford Univ, Radford, VA; JR; BS; Hse Cncl Pres 89-; Inter Res Hse Cncl Sec; Hse Cncl Flr Rep; Early/ Mdl Educ; Grad Sch/Admn Educ.

**O NEILL, KATHLEEN,** Glassboro St Coll, Glassboro, NJ; SR; BA; Venue Mag Mgng Dir 89-90; Bureau Of Stdnt Pblctns Prers 89-90; Glassboro Impvsvn Grp Wrtr/Prfrmr 89-90; Pub Rel Jrnl Stdnt Intrn; Cmmnctns/Lib Arts; Mag Jrnlsm.

**O NEILL, KELLY M,** Bryant Stratton Bus Inst Roch, Rochester, NY; SR; AS; Lawyers Asst; Prlgl Career.

**O NEILL, MICHAEL C,** Niagara Univ, Niagara Univ, NY; SR; BS; Alpha Hi Sigma; Criminology Crmnl Justice; Law & Govt.

**O PRANDY, SUSAN M,** Longwood Coll, Farmville, VA; FR; BA; IM Flag Ftbl 90; IM Co-Ed Sftbl 90; Fresh Hall Of Fame 90; Alpha Lambda Delta Pres; Poltcl Sci; Law.

**O QUINN, VICKIE M,** Univ Of Va Clinch Valley Coll, Wise, VA; JR; BA; AS SW VA Comm Coll Summa Cum Laude 88; Hstry/Psyc; Tch/Cnslng.

**O REILLY, ANGELA D,** Casco Bay Coll, Portland, ME; FR; AS; Bus Mngt/Paralegl Cert; Paralegal.

**O REILLY, CHRISTOPHER H,** Andrew Coll, Cuthbert, GA; SO; AA; Grk Cncl; Admssn Tm Chrmn; Phi Theta Kappa; Phi Kappa Pres; Athltc Schlrshp; Vrsty Bsbl; Intl Bus; Intl Sls.

**O REILLY, CLAIRE P,** Seton Hall Univ, South Orange, NJ; SO; BA; Kappa Delta Pi; Stdnt Tchr 90-; Elem Educ/Engl; Elem Tchr.

**O REILLY, ERIN K,** S U N Y Coll At Fredonia, Fredonia, NY; SO; BS; Dorm Cncl Sec 89; Orchesis 89-; Deans Lst 89-; Clscl Ballet Awd; U S Fish Wild Lfe Serv Fld Tech; Zoology Lab Tchng Asst; Rcmbnt Gene Tech; Rsrch/Astronaut Corps.

**O REILLY, PETER T,** Coll Of Insurance, New York, NY; JR; BS; Stdnt Cncl Tr 88-; Bowlng Co Capt 88-90; Actrl Sci; Actry/ Entreprnr.

**O REILLY, SHAWN M,** George Mason Univ, Fairfax, VA; JR; BS; US Mrn Crps CPS 82-88; Physcl Ed.

**O RIELLY, MICHAEL P,** Univ Of Rochester, Rochester, NY; SO; BA; Pltcl Sci; Law/Govt.

**O ROURKE, COLLEEN M,** Boston Univ, Boston, MA; SR; BS; Sargent Clg Stdnt Govt Rep 89-; Spnl Crd Unt Intrnshp 90; P T Asscts PC Orthpdc Prvt Prctc Intrnshp 90-; Fransican Chldrns Hsp Intrnshp; Aerobc Instrctr 88-; IM Sftbl; IDEA Cert Ntl Fndtn 88-; Cert Aerobc Instrctr; Phy Thrpy; Med.

**O ROURKE, ERIN M,** Oh Coll Of Podiatric Med, Cleveland, OH; GD; DPM; Amer Clg Ft Srgns 89-; Amer Assc Fr Wmn Podtrsts 88-90; Podtrc Poli Actn Comm 88-; Pi Delta 90-; Alpha Gamma Kappa 90-; Clevelnd Free Med Clnc 89-; Clvlnd Clnc PVD Rotn Slctee; Deans Lst 88-; BS Siena Hts Clg 88; Podtrc Med.

**O SCULLIVAN, KERRY,** S U N Y Coll At Fredonia, Fredonia, NY; JR; BS; BA SUNY Oneonta 77; Erth Sci 2 Ed; MA Sci Ed.

**O SHAUGHNESSY, BRENDA J,** Univ Of Montevallo, Montevallo, AL; SO; BS; Psychlgy Clb Sec Treas; Alpha Lambda Delta 90-; Psi Chi Sec; Rsng Schlr Awrd; Pres Lst 89-; Dean Lst 89-; Hghst Hnrs 90-; Ldrshp Schlrshp 89-; Psychlgy; Clncl Chld Psychlgst.**

**O SHEA, HARMONY D,** Central Me Medical Center, Lewiston, ME; SR; ASN; Hlth Care Ctr Vol; Sci; Nursing.

**O SHEA, JOHN C,** S U N Y Coll Of Tech At Frmgdl, Farmingdale, NY; FR; AAS; Karate Clb 84-87; Knights Columbus 85-; Niagara United Way Intern; Sheahan/Conniff Advrtsg Agcy Acct Exec Intern 87-89; Sheahan Publ Co Asst-To-Ed Intern 87-89; BA Niagara Univ 87; Mortuary Sci; Funeral Dir.

**O SHEA, JOHN G,** Christopher Newport Coll, Newport News, VA; JR; BA; Amnesty Intl Coord 87-; Psych Clb 87-88; Psi Chi; Psych; Ph D.

**O SHEA, LISA A,** Albertus Magnus Coll, New Haven, CT; FR; BA; Var Bsktbl/Sftbl:; Psych; Engl.

**O SHELL, ROBIN L,** Roane St Comm Coll, Harriman, TN; FR; Frlnc Comp Grphcs Bus 90-; Gamma Beta Phi; Comp Grphcs; Eng Grphcs.

**O SHENSKA, BRIAN J,** Anne Arundel Comm Coll, Arnold, MD; FR; AA; Cmmnctn Arts Tchnogy; Tlvsn Engnr.

**O SULLIVAN, JEANMARIE,** Wv Univ At Parkersburg, Parkersburg, WV; FR; BA; YWCA Day Care Com; Sftwre Sls; Exec Sec Washington School For Secretary 82; Nrsng.

**O TOOLE, JOSEPHINE J,** Univ Of Cincinnati-Clrmnt Coll, Batavia, OH; SO; BA; Education Club; Education English; Teaching.

**O TOOLE, KATHLEEN L,** Allegheny Coll, Meadville, PA; FR; BA; Nwspaper 90-; Im Suprvsr 90-; Hall Cncl Rep 90-; Lambda Sigma 90-; Im Bsktbl; Math/Comp Sci; Actuarial Math.

**O TOOLE, STEVEN,** Univ Of Rochester, Rochester, NY; SR; BS; IEEE 87-; Elec Eng; Eng.

**O-SAKA, LINDA B,** Univ Of Toledo, Toledo, OH; SO; BA; Outstdng Mnrty Stdnt Achvmnt Awd; Case Mgr IDECMHC Tol Oh; AA; Socl Wrk.

**OAKES, CHRISTINE C,** Univ Of Pittsburgh, Pittsburgh, PA; JR; BSIS; Info Sci.

**OAKES, DEBORAH L,** Southern Vt Coll, Bennington, VT; JR; BSW; Hghst Rnkng Fr 89; Assc Dgree Slttrn Of Clss 90; Hghst GPA Dgree Prog Hmn Srvce 89-; AS 90; Scl Wrk Psychlgy; Cnslng Adlscnts Fmls.

**OAKES, DONNA E,** Clayton St Coll, Morrow, GA; JR; AAS 88-90; Sci; Med Tech.

**OAKES, MICHAEL J,** Immaculata Coll, Immaculata, PA; SO; Pre Med; Medcn.

**OAKES, RICHARD B,** Univ Of Louisville, Louisville, KY; SO; MS; Hi Eta Sigma 90-; Srvc Mgr Tchncn 81-88; AAS 81; Elec Eng.

**OAKES, SAMRA G,** Univ Of Nc At Greensboro, Greensboro, NC; SR; BS; NC Tchng Fllws 87; UNC Greensboro Chem Lab Assist 88; Deans Lst; Mddl Schl Ed.

**OAKES, SCOTT A,** Elmira Coll, Elmira, NY; SO; BA; Chrstn Flwshp Grp Co-Ldr 89-; Martial Arts Clb 89-; Legislative Bd; Beta Beta Beta 90-; Phi Eta Sigma 90-; Borden Prize 90; Phi Beta Kappa Prize; Biochem; Pre-Med.

**OAKLEY, BECKI M,** Lee Coll, Cleveland, TN; FR; BA; Yrbk Stff/Phtgrphr 90-; Drama Clb 90-; Asst Dir Fall Drama Prdctn 90-; Crmnl Psych.

**OAKLEY, JONNIE C,** Thomas Nelson Comm Coll, Hampton, VA; GD; AAS; Bus Mngmnt; Mrktng.

**OAKLEY, SHELIA D,** Univ Of Tn At Martin, Martin, TN; SO; BA; Phi Chi Theta 90-; Acctng.

**OATHOUT, THOMAS E,** Hudson Valley Comm Coll, Troy, NY; SR; ECM Clb; Emrald Ath Clb; Gunther Schlrshp; Intern Asst Elec Est; AOS; Elec Cnstrctn Mn Tenure; Electrcn.

**OATIS, SHARON Y,** Jackson St Univ, Jackson, MS; JR; BBA; Acctng Socty 89-; Alpha Lambda Delta 89-; Hnrs Coll 88-; IRS Intrnshp; Acctng.

**OATLEY, JEFFREY A,** Univ Of Al At Huntsville, Huntsville, AL; JR; BS; ASME; Mech Eng; Rsrch.

**OATS, LA TONYA T,** Central Fl Comm Coll, Ocala, FL; SO; AA; Phi Theta Kappa 90-; Psych; Clin Psychtry.

**OBEAHON, ALEXANDER COLERIDGE,** Coppin St Coll, Baltimore, MD; JR; Std Govt Sntr 90-; Pi Gamma Mu; Pol Sci; Law.

**OBEDIAN, ROBERT,** Va Commonwealth Univ, Richmond, VA; FR; BS; Phi Aeta Sigma; Blgy; Med.

**OBEN, KAREN E,** Georgetown Univ, Washington, DC; JR; BSN; Emerg Resp Med Serv EMT CPR Instr 89-; PR Stdnt Assoc 88-; Nrsng; Dr.

**OBENSHAIN, MARGARET ELAINE,** Univ Of Sc At Coastal Carolina, Conway, SC; SO; Phi Eta Sigma Sec Treas 90-; Bio Tutor Schl Spnsrd 90-; Skills Lab; Dist Mngr Retail Chain; Bio/ Psy; Pre/Med.

**OBERG DOITTEAU, HAKAN R,** Inter Amer Univ Pr San German, San German, PR; FR; Swdsh AI Scty 89-; B Ed Stockholm Univ 90; Comp Sci.

**OBERG, THERESA H,** Univ Of Sc At Coastal Carolina, Conway, SC; JR; BA; Coach Elem Chrldrs 90-; AD Bus Mgmt Eastern Maine Tech 87; Elem Edn; Edctr.

**OBERHOLTZER-MEZA, E KATRINA,** Barry Univ, Miami, FL; SR; BA; Assc Stu Coll Notre Dame Treas 83-84; Assc Stu U AZ 84-85; Dean Lst 88-89; Alpha Delta Pi 86; Alpha Chi Omega Rsh Chrmn 85-86; Cir K 84; Intern Ser Lautenburg; Intern Jacqueline Speier 89; Vllybll 83-89; Vol Natl Parkinson Assn 90; BA N D; Pol Sci; Pblc Rltns.

**OBERLE, MONICA L,** Fl St Univ, Tallahassee, FL; SO; MBA; Phi Eta Sigma; Bus; CPA/CORP Law.

**OBERLIES, JOHN M,** Central Fl Comm Coll, Ocala, FL; JR; BS; Phi Theta Kappa; Pres List 89-90; Deans Lst 90; AS Broward Comm Clg 78; AA 90; Srvyng/Mppng; Hydro Srvyng.

**OBERMAN, WINDY M,** Radford Univ, Radford, VA; SR; Phys Educ Mjr Clb 89-; Stu Trnr 90-; Mst Imprv Stu Trnr 90-; Physcl Thrpy Intern; Stu Trnr Gymnstc Tm 90-; BS; Phys Educ; Sprts Med/Exrcs Physlgy.

**OBERMARK, JEROME L,** Christian Brothers Univ, Memphis, TN; FR; BS; Fncng Clb 90-; Chess/Gaming Clb 90-; Phlsphrs Forum; Elec Engr.

**OBERMILLER, KRAIG E,** Univ Of Pittsburgh At Bradford, Bradford, PA; FR; MS; Cmptr Sci Clb 90-; Cmptr/Chmcl Eng; Rsrch.

**OBERWAGER, BRADFORD S,** Georgetown Univ, Washington, DC; JR; Jr Class Cmte; Lacrosse 89-; Fin; Entrepeneur.

**OBESO, VIVIAN T,** Fl International Univ, Miami, FL; FR; Bio; Med.

**OBI, BETTY J,** Univ Of North Fl, Jacksonville, FL; JR; BA; Gldn Ky 90-; Phi Kappa Phi; Mu Phi Epsilon Treas 89-90; Music Dir/Orgnst 90-; Music.

**OBINGER, DANIEL M,** Bapt Bible Coll & Seminary, Clarks Summit, PA; SR; Hall Tr 88-90; Alpha Gamma Epsilon; Var Soccer 87-89; BS; Pastoral Care; Minister.

**OBLAD, CHRISTOPHER J,** David Lipscomb Univ, Nashville, TN; FR; BS; Fr Prsnlts Drama Sngrma; Envir Clb Sprtl Life Com; Sci; Med.

**OBREGON, DALIA O,** Va Highlands Comm Coll, Abingdon, VA; SO; BA; Phi Theta Kappa; Ofc Svcs Suprvsr At Local Hlth Dept; Cert Drftng ICS Scranton PA; Lang; Tch Spanish.

**OBREGON JR, JOSEPH E,** Abraham Baldwin Agri Coll, Tifton, GA; FR; AS; Frstry/Wldlfe Clb; J Baldwin Davis Schlrshp; Wldlfe Tchnlgy; Wldlfe Tchncn.

**OCANA-CASTILLO, ROSE M,** Caribbean Center For Adv Stds, San Juan, PR; GD; PH D; SHRM Fin Dir 89-; Soc Indus Orgztnl Psychlgy; Amer Psychlgcl Assn; Better Wrld Mvmnt; Magna Cum Laude 89; BA 89; MS; Spychlgy; Indust Orgztnl Psychlgy.

**OCANTO, MARIA G,** Miami Dade Comm Coll, Miami, FL; FR; AA; New Wrld Dnc Ensmbl 90-; Danc; Choreogrphr.

**OCASIO, ELVYN D,** Inter Amer Univ Pr San German, San German, PR; FR; BA; Math; Indstrl Engrg.

**OCASIO, MARTIN,** Caribbean Univ, Bayamon, PR; JR; BA; Human Serv Assoc Educ Dept 89; Soc Wrkrs Clg 89; Magna Cum Laude 85-86; Eplpsy Assoc Of PR; AS 85; Soc Serv; Soc Wrkr.

**OCASIO, MIRIAM,** Medaille Coll, Buffalo, NY; SR; BS; Jacquelyn M Downey Schlrshp 90-; Bank Secy 89-; Hmn Resource Dvlpmnt; Trning/Dvlpmnt.

**OCCHIALINI, THOMAS O,** Univ Of New Haven, West Haven, CT; JR; BA; Phi Theta Kappa 90-; AS Mohegan Cmnty Clg 90; Law Enfrcmnt; Law.

**OCHOA, JUAN C,** Suffolk Comm Coll Selden Cmps, Selden, NY; SO; BS; Phi Theta Kappa; Elctrcl Engnrng.

**OCKER, REBEKAH E,** Shippensburg Univ, Shippensburg, PA; FR; BSED; Mrchng Bnd 90-; Hnrs Prog 90-; Big Sis 90-; GPA Awrd 90-; Trm Paper Pblshd 90; Elem Educ; Tch.

**ODAI, MICHAEL D,** Univ Of Rochester, Rochester, NY; SO; BS; Theta Chi Sec; Golf Tm 89-; Econ Pltcl Sci.

**ODEMS, SONIA Y,** Jackson St Univ, Jackson, MS; FR; Jackson St Univ Symphonic Bnd; Alpha Lambda Delta Bus Mngr; Natl Collgt Nat Sci Awrd; Herin/Hess Schlrshp Rec 90; Cmptr Sci; Drafting.

**ODEN, DAWN,** Northwest Al Comm Coll, Phil Campbell, AL; FR; Sco Clb 90-; Clg Bowl Tm 90-; Phi Theta Kappa; Pre Elem Educ; Erly Chldhd Educ.

**ODEN, MARK A,** Rust Coll, Holly Springs, MS; JR; BA; Fshn Clb 89-; NAACP 89-; Ln H Mccrd Intern 90; Mass Cmmnctns Awrd 90-; Mass Cmmnctns.

**ODEN, MARSHA N,** Univ Of Montevallo, Montevallo, AL; SO; BS; Civitan Intl; 4h Cnty Pres; Alpha Lambda Delta 89; 4 H Pres Awd 90-; Kappa Mu Epsilon Bk Awd; E G Cochrane Vldctrn Schlrshp; Natl 4h Clthng Schlrshp; Math.

**ODENDAHL, LAURA J,** Goucher Coll, Towson, MD; SO; BA; Womns Issues Grp 90-; Stdnt Govt Rep 90-; Sga Soc Comm 90-; Hnr Pgm 89-; Stdy Skls Cons Acad Ctr Excell 90-; Hstry; Law/Hstry Stds.

**ODERMATT, SANDRA G,** Hillsborough Comm Coll, Tampa, FL; SO; BA; SNO 89-; Phi Theta Kappa 90-; Lic Clncl Lab Tech; Med; Nrsng.**

**ODOM, BILLY G,** Spartanburg Methodist Coll, Spartanburg, SC; FR; Crmnl Jstc Clb 90-; Scuba Dvng Clb 90-; IM Sprts Sftbl/Bsktbl/Vlybl 90-; Crmnl Jstc; Law.

**ODOM, DAVID I,** Norfolk St Univ, Norfolk, VA; FR; BA; Naval ROTC 90-; Spartan Alpha Tau 90-; Adopt A Schl 90-; IM Vlybl 90-; Hghst GPA Cmptr Sci Dept 90-; Cmptr Sci; Nvl Ofcr/Cmptr Eng.

**ODOM, FRANKIE B,** Coker Coll, Hartsville, SC; FR; BA; Hist Clb; Behavior/Sci Clb; T/T Jewelry Sls; Hist Soc; Tchr.

**ODOM, JAMES K,** Gallaudet Univ, Washington, DC; JR; BA; Hon Stdnt; Advtsg Art.

**ODOM, KELLY S,** Univ Of Southern Ms, Hattiesburg, MS; SR; BS; Phi Kappa Phi; Gold Key; Chi Omega Alum; Spch Cmnctn; Mgmnt.

**ODOM, KIMBERLY G,** Middle Ga Coll, Cochran, GA; FR; BED; Edctn; Erly Chldhd Tchr.

**ODOM, LA RHONDA,** Alcorn St Univ, Lorman, MS; SR; BA; Sclgy Scl Wrk Clb Pres 90-; Cls Secy 90-; Scl Sci Scty Prlmntrn 90-; Alpha Kappa Mu 88-; Alpha Mu Gamma Pres 90-; Univ Hnr Scty; Wmn Church Of God 90-; Chrch Of God Yth Flwshp MISS VP 90-; Sclgy Scl Wrk.

**ODOM, LYN E,** Radford Univ, Radford, VA; SR; Delta Zeta Srty SGA Senate VP 88-; MSAC Cncl Pahellenic Cncl Extn Crd 89-90; Greek Week Sec 90; Rho Lamanda 89-; Kappa Omicron Nu; Delta Zeta VP 88-; Quest Asst Orntn 89; Quest Admin Asst 90; Intrnshp Rnbw Riders 90-; Srty IM 89-.

**ODOM JR, MICHAEL G,** Greenville Tech Coll, Greenville, SC; SR; BA; Electrnc Engrng Tchnlgy.

**ODOM, PATRICK L,** Fl St Univ, Tallahassee, FL; JR; BA; Phi Theta Kappa Cmnctn Secr 89-90; FL Acad Undergrad Schlr 88-; AA Tallahassee Cmnty Clg 90; Cmnctn/Advrtsg; Urban-Reg Plnr.

**ODOM, PEGGY R,** Pensacola Jr Coll, Pensacola, FL; SO; Phi Theta Kappa 90-; First Bapt Yng Adult Choir; Usher Bd; Yng Wmn Aux; Psychology; Dr Of Psychology.

**ODOM, REGINA D,** Ky Wesleyan Coll, Owensboro, KY; GD; BA; Alpha Epsilon Rho Sec 89-90; Black Stdnt Union Sec 87; Deans List 89-90; Order Oak/Ivy 89; PR Intrn KY Wesleyan Clg 90; PR Intrn Owensboro-Daviess Cty Hosp 89; IM Bsktbl 88-89; BA KY Wesleyan Clg 90; Mass Cmnctns.

**ODOM, SHANAH D,** Livingston Univ, Livingston, AL; SO; BA; IMS 90-; Phys Educ/Hstry; Tchng.

**ODOM, SHARON R,** Roane St Comm Coll, Harriman, TN; FR; BA; Gamma Beta Phi 90-; TN St Bd Of Regents 90-; Business; Acctng/Finance.

**ODOM, SHEILA DARLENE MOFFETT,** Northeast State Tech Comm Coll, Blountville, TN; GD; Cls Ofcr Milligan Clg Secy 73-74; Phi Eta Tau 73-74; Moffetts Siding Inc VP 81-88; AAS; Ofc Systems Technology; Certfd Public Secy.

**ODOM, VALERIE A,** Univ Of South Al, Mobile, AL; FR; BA; Blck Stdnt Union 90-; Yth Outrch Mnstrs 90-; Future Bus Ldrs Of Amer Sec 87-90; Abeneefoo Kuo; Beta 88-90; Teen Pub Srvc Org 88-90; Acctng; CMA.

**ODOR, D LAWRENCE,** Savannah Coll Of Art & Design, Savannah, GA; FR; BARCH; Archtctr.

**ODUBENG, MICHAEL GAUTA,** Al A & M Univ, Normal, AL; SR; BS; Mktng Clb 88-; Intl Stdnt Assoc 88-; African Stdnt Assoc 89-; PTA; Gaborone Soccer Clb Mngr 87-88; Div Mngr/Whlsl/Distn Boswana Coop Union; Mrktng; Mngr.

**ODUM, IRENE R,** Midlands Tech Coll, Columbia, SC; SR; ADN; La Leche League SC Treas 88-; La Leche League Central Columbia Lstd Ldr 87-; Part Time Stdnt Hnr Rl 88-; Grace Chapel Church Hostess 89-; Bapt Med Ctr Columbia Nrs Tech 90-; Nrsg; RN.

**ODVARKA, ZDENEK,** Bunker Hill Comm Coll, Boston, MA; SR; Masaryk Clb Boston 89-; Ping-Pong; Soccer; Czechoslovak Cmnty; Intl Bsn; Bsn.

**ODVINA, RODNEY M,** Univ Of North Fl, Jacksonville, FL; FR; BS; Info Sci; Cmptr/Bus.

**ODZGA, JOHN,** Duquesne Univ, Pittsburgh, PA; SR; BSBA; Dns Lst; Cmptv/Minnie Hyman Schlp; Fnce; Prchsng/Qlty Cntrl.

**OEFFINGER, DONNA J,** Univ Of Ky, Lexington, KY; SR; BS; K-Clb Rep 90-; Stdnt Athlt Advsry Cncl 90-; All Sthestrn Conf Acdmc Awrd 88-90; Vrsty Gymnstcs 87-; Phys Ed/Exrcs Sci; Biomechncs.

**OEHLER, EMILY E,** Mary Baldwin Coll, Staunton, VA; SO; Hnr Cncl 90-; Stdnt Hndbk/Stdnt Gvmt Hndbk Editor In Chief; Comm Dvlpmnt Tm 90-; Alph Lambda Delta 90-; Big Str 90-; Peer Advsr 90-; Tutor Msc/Psych 90-; Comm/Media Wrtng; PR/MAGZN Editor.

**OEHMIG, ANNALIZA G,** Coll Of Charleston, Charleston, SC; JR; BS; Coll Rpblcns 88-89; Hnrs Coll 88-; Hnrs Prgm Stu Assn 88-; Omicron Delta Kappa 90-; Omicron Delta Epsilon; Alpha Delta Pi Pldg Pnhllnc 88-; Intern Cngrssm B Derrick; Hghst Big Sis Lttl Sis GPA 89; Ecnmcs/Math; Intl Bus.

**OEI, MELINA E,** Birmingham Southern Coll, Birmingham, AL; SO; BS; Amnsty Intl 89-; Cnsrvncy 89-; Mc Coy Tutrg 89; Alpha Epsilon Delta; Fncng 89-; Alpha Phi Omega Rcrdng Sec 90-; Peer Advsr 90; Guy B Snavely Awd 89-; Blgy; Med.

**OELBERG, GARY A,** James Madison University, Harrisonburg, VA; JR; BS; Drctr Wrkshp Prfrmncs Stage Mngr 88-89; Pyschlgy Clb 90-; Otng Clb; Psi Chi; Gldn Key 90-; Cntr Srvc Lrnng 90; Sftbl IM Sccr IM 88-; Psychology.

**OELRICH, BRIGITTE L,** Central Fl Comm Coll, Ocala, FL; SO; BA; Newpr 89; Theatre Arts 89-; Bus; Mgmt.

**OELTGEN, RYAN C,** Univ Of Ky, Lexington, KY; FR; BS; Chemistry; Engrng.

**OERTLING, MELINDA M,** Univ Of Southern Ms, Hattiesburg, MS; SR; BS; Hon 90; Amer Libry Assc 90-; MAE/NEA MS 90-; LA Libry Assc; Assc Gulf Park Clg 69; Library Sci; Media Specist.

**OESTERLE, DARCY J,** Southern Vt Coll, Bennington, VT; SO; BA; Com Affrmtv Actn Sxl Hrrssmnt Hmphbia Bd Stdnt Rep 90-; Com Dvlpmnt Chld Cr Cntr Stdnt Rep 89-; Tutrl Cntr Sr Tutor 89-; Hghst Rnkng 1st/2nd Yr Stdnt 90-; Hghst Rnkng Chld Dev Mjr; Chld Dvlpmnt; Chld Psychlgy/Scl Rsrch.

**OFFERDAHL, AMY L,** Univ Of Nc At Greensboro, Greensboro, NC; SR; BFA; John Casablancas Choreographer 89-90; Greensboro Prime Movers Dance Choregraped; Track Field 86-87; Performing Arts Dance.

**OFFHAUS, BRIAN J,** S U N Y Coll At Fredonia, Fredonia, NY; JR; BS; Physics Clb Pres 90-; Soc Physics Stu 90-; Mech Eng.

**OFFORD, ROSE M,** Central St Univ, Wilberforce, OH; FR; MBA; Chorus; Band; Music.

**OFFUTT, JESSICA L,** Md Coll Of Art & Design, Silver Spring, MD; FR; BA; Vsl Cmnctn; Advrtsg.

**OFMAN, PYOTR U,** Univ Of The Dist Of Columbia, Washington, DC; JR; BS; M S Moscow Polytechn Inst Moscow Ussr 88; Cmptr Sci; Bio; Med.

**OFRAT, ERAN,** Rutgers St Univ At Newark, Newark, NJ; JR; BA; Israeli Scouts Grp Ldr 89; Deans Lst; Acctg; Pblc.**

**OGAWA, MOANA M,** Oh St Univ At Newark, Newark, OH; SO; BS; Dow Chem Co Co-Op; Bus Admin; Acctg.

**OGAYONNE, RIGOBERT P,** Central St Univ, Wilberforce, OH; FR; Gold Hnr 90-; Fin/Mgmnt.

**OGDEN, CHERYL A,** George Mason Univ, Fairfax, VA; SR; BS; Gld Ky 89-; Alpha Chi; Bus Mngmnt; Corp Law.

**OGENESKI, STEPHANIE A,** Univ Of Sc At Columbia, Columbia, SC; SO; BA; SC Craft Assn; Kappa Alpha Theta Frat Asst Schlrshp; Univ SC Deans Lst 90-; Kappa Alpha Theta Acdmc Excllnc Awd 90; Univ SC IM Pgm 89-90; Art Studio/Engl Lit; Phtgrphy.

**OGG, ROBIN S,** Castleton St Coll, Castleton, VT; JR; BA; Pltcl Discsn Grp 90-; Chittenden Cmuty Assoc Pres 87-; Educ/Psychology; Tch/Gudnce.

**OGI, RANDALL J,** Cornell Univ Statutory College, Ithaca, NY; SO; BS; Zeta Psi Frtrnty Treas 90-; Vrsty Trck 89-; Mgmt Mrktng; Bus.

**OGILVIE, KATHY A,** Howard Univ, Washington, DC; GD; JD; Rsrch Asst Prof Rogers 89-; Intrn Jdg Burnett Supr Ct; Asst VP Rpblc Bnk Dlls 77-87; BA Univ Of Hrtfrd 74; MBA Atlntc Univ 77; Law.

**OGINO, RYOKO,** Hilbert Coll, Hamburg, NY; FR; AA; Vlybl 90; Hmn Srvcs; Instrctr.

**OGLE, JODY J,** Oh St Univ At Newark, Newark, OH; FR; BA; Alpha Lambda Delta Phi Eta Sigma 90; Bsnss; Accntng.

**OGLE, KARLA D,** Middle Tn St Univ, Murfreesboro, TN; FR; Poli Sci; Law.

**OGLE, RODNEY A,** Columbus Coll Of Art & Design, Columbus, OH; JR; BFA; Fine Arts.

**OGLES, JACK D,** Univ Of Al At Birmingham, Birmingham, AL; SR; BA; Tau Beta Pi; Pi Tau Sigma; ASME; ASHRAE; Mech Engr.

**OGLESBY, ALAN K,** Liberty Univ, Lynchburg, VA; JR; BS; Hlth Dmnsn Clb 90; SGA Sntr; Haiti Hlth Tm Intrnshp; Comm Hlth; Pblc.

**OGLESBY, DAVID A,** Pensacola Jr Coll, Pensacola, FL; SO; MBA; Phi Theta Kappa; Phi Theta Chi; Asst Stdnt Cch Vrsty Ftbll; Engl; Ed.

**OGLESBY, GARY D,** Univ Of Al At Birmingham, Birmingham, AL; SR; BS; Mchncl Eng.

**OGLESBY, GREGORY L,** Beckley Coll, Beckley, WV; SO; AS; Comp Tech.

**OGLESBY, MATTHEW T,** Fl Coll, Temple Terrace, FL; FR; Phi Beta Lamda VP 90-; Omega Chi Sec; Accntng.

**OGLESBY, RHONDA M,** Blue Mountain Coll, Blue Mountain, MS; SR; BS; Bapt Stdnt Union Worshop Chrmn 89-90; Stdnt Govt Assoc Pres 90-; Stdnt Govt Assoc Rep 88-89; Modenian Scl Soc 87-; Elem Ed; Tch.

**OGLESBY, ROBERT J,** Memphis St Univ, Memphis, TN; JR; BS; Sigma Chi Frtrnty VP 88-; Arnold Air Scty 88-90; Elctrncs Tech; Engnrng.

**OGLESBY, STELLA C,** Greenville Tech Coll, Greenville, SC; SR; BSN; IMAGE Pgm 88-; Admssns Com Rep 88-; Schlrshp Grenvll Memrl Hosp; ANA 88-; ADN; Nrsng; Nrs Ansthst.

**OGONOWSKI, SEAN C,** S U N Y Coll Of A & T Morrisvl, Morrisville, NY; FR; BA; Dean Lst; Sci; Physcl Thrpst.

**OGORZALY, MATTHEW M,** Cleveland St Univ, Cleveland, OH; JR; BA; )ieee 90-; Electronics; Electrical Eng.**

**OGUERI, UDO PEACE,** Daytona Beach Comm Coll, Daytona Beach, FL; FR; Phi Theta Kappa; Physics; Medicine.

**OGUNYOMADE, TOLULOPE,** Bowie St Univ, Bowie, MD; SO; BSC; Intl Stdnt Assn 89-; Math Tutoring Club 90-; Bowie Hnrs Pgm 90-; Soccer Club 90-; Math; Engr.

**OGURCHAK, ELIZABETH A,** Saint Francis Coll, Loretto, PA; FR; BS; Le Cir Frncs 90-; Std Soc Physcns Asst 90-; Physcns Asst/Mgmt; Bsn Admn.

**OH, CHARLES J,** Univ Of Miami, Coral Gables, FL; SO; BA; Korean Stdnts Assn; Res Hall Prog Cncl; Hon Stdnt Assn; Alpha Lambda Delta; Provost Hon Rl; Biology; Med.

**OH, JUNG S,** Hillsborough Comm Coll, Tampa, FL; FR; Comptr/Acctng; Bus.

**OHASHI, KAYO,** Indiana Univ Of Pa, Indiana, PA; FR; BS; Spec Educ.

**OHLER, SHERI A,** Westmoreland County Comm Coll, Youngwood, PA; FR; Nursing.

**OHLIGER, EILEEN SUZANNE,** Georgian Court Coll, Lakewood, NJ; GD; Cncl Excptnl Chldrn 89-; NJ Cncl Lrng Dsblties 89-; Georgian Ct Spec Svcs Note Tkr Hard Hrng 89-90; Deans Lst 88-90; Georgian Ct-Spec Ed Awd Hon Mntn; Ed Opp Fnd Pgm-Georgian Ct Awd Acad Excell 88-90; Spec Ed; Tchng.

**OHLIN, PATRICK K,** Carnegie Mellon Univ, Pittsburgh, PA; JR; BA; Nwsppr Ed; WRCT Sprtsln Sprtscstr 90-; Rsdnc Lf Stff Hd Rsdnt 89-; Natl Rsdnc Hll Hnrry; Earle Swank Schlrs; Deans Lst 89; Earl Swank Schlrshp 89; IM Ftbll Bsktbll Vllybll; Engl; Pblc Rltns.**

**OHMER, CHERYL L,** Daemen Coll, Amherst, NY; SO; BS; Spcl Olympics 90-; Cmnty Serv Clb 90-; Phys Therapy.

**OHMS, MARSHAE L,** Oh Univ, Athens, OH; SO; BED; Alpha Lambda Delta 90-; Psh Chi; Psychlgy/Art Thrpy; Cert Art Thrpst.

**OHREL JR, RONALD L,** Univ Of Sc At Coastal Carolina, Conway, SC; JR; BS; RA 90-; Hnrs Cncl Chrprsn 88-; Omnicron Delta Kappa 90-; Chmstry Stdnt Of Yr 88-89; Hurricane Hugo Rsrch Asst 90; Hnrs Prog Asst; Vrsty Crs Cntry 88-; Marine Sci; Envrnmntl Policy/Law.

**OHSON, ASPAN S,** Cornell Univ Statutory College, Ithaca, NY; SO; BS; Habitat For Hmnty 89; Indian Stdnt Assoc; Syosset Cmmnty Hosp 90; Cross Cntry Rnng Vrsty 89-90; Bio; Med.

**OHTSUKA, YUKA,** Endicott Coll, Beverly, MA; SO; Phi Theta Kappa; Lib Arts/Soc Sci.

**OIRICK, JEFFREY T,** Univ Of Miami, Coral Gables, FL; JR; BA; Res Asst 90-; Master Tutor 90-; Miami Hurrican Clmnst 89-90; Psi Chi Psychology V P 90-; Standford Schlrshp 88-; Psychology; Clncl Psychlgy.

**OJALA, ILKKA J,** Univ Of Miami, Coral Gables, FL; SR; BBA; Mngrl Finc Org 90-; Scndnvn Stdnt Org; Gldn Ky 90-; Pres Hnr Rll; Prvsts Hnr Rll 90; Dns Lst 88-90; Finc; Real Est/Finc.

**OJEDA, GENEVIEVE K,** Hillsborough Comm Coll, Tampa, FL; SO; BA.

**OJIIWAWH, ERIIDINA L,** Clark Atlanta Univ, Atlanta, GA; FR; BS; Allied Hlth Soc Secr 90-; Ohio Clb 90-; Hnr Rl 90-; Dns Lst 90-; Vars Track 90-; IM Bsktbl 90-; Phys Ther.

**OKELLO, DAVID O,** Morehouse Coll, Atlanta, GA; SR; B Sc; Bio Chem; Med.

**OKERE, CLEOPHAS N,** Rust Coll, Holly Springs, MS; SR; Pres Internatl Stdnt Assn Pres 89-90; Alpha Kappa Mu; Tutr/Specl Serv Prgrm; BS Bus/Comp Sci; Comp Engrng.

**OKHRAVI, SIMINDOKHT J,** Strayer Coll, Washington, DC; JR; BS; BSCS Streyer Clg; Cmptr Sci; Ph D Cmptr Info Sys.

**OKINE, ANTOINETTE,** City Univ Of Ny Bronx Comm Col, Bronx, NY; SO; Chem Clb 89-; Phi Theta Kappa 90-; AAS; Phrmcy.

**OKRAH, DORA,** Memphis St Univ, Memphis, TN; SR; BA; Gldn Ky 88-; Memphis Shelby Co Med Aux 76-; Prncpls Adv Cncl Double Tree Elem 86-89; Tax Clrk IRS Ahana W Africa 73-74; A Asc St Tech Inst Memphis 83-87; Acctg; CPA.

**OKRASINSKI, SCOTT M,** Univ Of Sc At Columbia, Columbia, SC; JR; BS; Stdnt Orntn Ldr 90; Rsdnt Advsr 90; RHA Sntr Chrmn Of RHA Nwslttr 89; Gldn Ky 90-; Alpha Phi Sigma 90-; Natl Rsdnce Hll Hnrry Fndng Mmbr 89-; Crmnl Jstce; Instgtr.

**OKUNOLA, LOLA O,** City Univ Of Ny Bronx Comm Col, Bronx, NY; SR; Fusionst Clb Pres 89-; Tutorng Serv Math Chem Phy 89-; Lib Art/Biol; Med.

**OKUYAMA, KAZUKO,** Elms Coll, Chicopee, MA; JR; BA; Intl Clb 90-; Assoc Seibo Jr Coll Japan 90; Hstry/Sclgy; Intl Tour Gd.

**OLAND, EMILY A,** Western Md Coll, Westminster, MD; FR; PHD; Cmps Radio DJ Nws Dir 90-; Stdnt Envrnmntl Actn Coaltn 90-; Chrstn Fllwshp Grp 90-; Hnrs Prog Repr 90-; Circle K 90-; Sbacchus 90-; Fall Orntn Ldr; Stdnt Repr Hnrs Prog 90-; Vlybl/Bsktbl 90-; Eng/Hist; Professor.

**OLAWSKI, SUZANNE,** East Stroudsburg Univ, E Stroudsburg, PA; SR; BA; Engl Clb 89-; Asst Edtr Cllpe 90-; Krstn Leone Awd; Engl/Wrtng; Govt/Pblshng.

**OLAYA, NAYIBE,** City Univ Of Ny La Guard Coll, Long Island Cty, NY; GD; Deans Lst 89-; AA; Occupational Therapy.

**OLD III, EPHRIAM M,** Univ Of Tn At Martin, Martin, TN; JR; BA; Finance; Stck Anlysis.

**OLDAKER, JEFFREY S,** Wv Univ, Morgantown, WV; SO; BS/EE; Elctrcl/Cmptr Engr; Engr.

**OLDFIELD, KELLY J,** Kent St Univ Kent Cmps, Kent, OH; JR; BA; Gldn Key 90-; Dns Lst 89-90; Pres Lst; Fnce; Hghr Educ Admn.

**OLDHAM, AMY,** Univ Of Tn At Martin, Martin, TN; SO; BS; CC Stdnt Cntr 89-90; Phi Eta Sigma; Sigma Pi Pres; Cir K V P 90; Cir K Pres 90; Biol; Med Schl/Pathology.

**OLDHAM, CLAYTON M,** Nova Univ, Ft Lauderdale, FL; GD; MBA; BA Cntrl Wash Univ 87; AA Yakima Vly Cmnty Clg 85; Bsn Admin; Mgmt/Prof Rcrtmnt.

**OLDHAM, KATHY A,** Middle Tn St Univ, Murfreesboro, TN; JR; BBA; Alpha Omicron Pi VP 90-; Acctg; CPA.

**OLDS, TAWANA T,** Va Union Univ, Richmond, VA; SO; BA; Stdnts For Soc Justice 89-90; Comm Schlrs 89-; Natl Hnr Soc 89-; Psychology; Law.

**OLEARCEK, PATRICK F,** Western New England Coll, Springfield, MA; SO; Pre Law Soc 89-; Govt Soc 89-; Lamda Delta 89-; Peer Tutr 89-; Fr Bsbl Plyr Adv 90-; Concsn Wrkr; Dns Lst 89-; Hnr Soc 89-; Var Bsbl 89-; IM Ftbl/Bsktbl 90-; Govt/Pre Law; Law Corp.

**OLEARCHYK, CHRISTINA N,** Drexel Univ, Philadelphia, PA; FR; BVA; Karate Clb 90-; Ukrnan Dnc Ensmbl Phila 87; Ukrnan Yth Ass SUMA; Karate Tm 90-; Intrntl Area Stds; Dplmtc Srvc.

**OLEJARZ, LYNN D,** Springfield Tech Comm Coll, Springfield, MA; SR; AS; Coop Educ 90-; Alpha Nu Omega 90-; Cmptr Info Sys; Cmptr Prgmmr.

**OLEKSZYK, JEFFREY T,** Bowling Green St Univ, Bowling Green, OH; JR; BS; Flyng Tm 90-; Ordr Omega Sec/Treas 90-; Alpha Lambda Delta 89-; Hnr Std Assc 89-90; Alpha Eta Rho 89-; Epsilon Pi Tau 90-; Phi Kappa Psi Pldg Ed 89-; IM Sccr/Vllybll/Sftbl 89-; Aerotech; Airline Pilot.

**OLENCHAK, REBECCA L,** Univ Of Sc At Columbia, Columbia, SC; JR; BA; Sigma Tau Delta Sec Treas 89; Gamma Beta Phi 90-; Chncllrs Lst 88; Dns Lst 90-; Pblshd Phtgrphr Wrtr Pt In Cpy Rck Scne IRH And Am Ptry Anthlgy 79-; Engl; Prcssr Of Engl Lit Fctn Ptry Wrtr.

**OLENICK, JOHN M,** Univ Of Nc At Charlotte, Charlotte, NC; JR; BA; Delta Sigma Phi Almn Chr 88-; IM Sccr; IM Bsktbll; BDMTTN 88-; Engl; Ed.

**OLESIEWICZ, TIMOTHY W,** Fl International Univ, Miami, FL; SR; BS; ASME 90-; Media Sys Inc Co-Ownr 89-90; AA Univ FL 87; Mech Eng.

**OLESKIEWICZ, MARK L,** Kent St Univ Kent Cmps, Kent, OH; SO; BA; Grn Drgn Kung Fu Clb 89-90; Acct Assn 90; Deans Lst 90-; Pres Lst 90-; Acctg; Bus.

**OLEWNICKI, JOSEPH S,** Cooper Union, New York, NY; SR; BE; ASME; Mechanical Engrng.**

**OLFERS, ROBERT C,** Anne Arundel Comm Coll, Arnold, MD; FR; AA; Arch Tech.

**OLIGA, TERENCE C,** Livingston Univ, Livingston, AL; SO; BS; Engl; Prfsr.

**OLIPHANT, IRENE E,** De Tech & Comm Coll At Dover, Dover, DE; FR; AOS; Acctg; Sec.

**OLIVA, ANA M,** Fl International Univ, Miami, FL; FR; BA; Psych; Cnslng.

**OLIVA, MARTHA I,** Nova Univ, Ft Lauderdale, FL; GD; MBA; Sftwr Engr 80-; BS 86f; Cmptr Sci/Bus; Sftwr Engr.

**OLIVA, ROBERT D,** City Univ Of Ny Baruch Coll, New York, NY; JR; BBA; Phlsphy VP 89-90; Mgmt; Entrpnr/Wrtr.

**OLIVARES, MARCEL U,** Abraham Baldwin Agri Coll, Tifton, GA; JR; BA; Tnns; BA; Bus; Mngmt.

**OLIVE, MELISSA K,** Chattanooga St Tech Comm Coll, Chattanooga, TN; SO; BS; Phi Theta Kappa 90-; Bus Admin; Mktg.

**OLIVE, PAUL ANTHONY,** Savannah Coll Of Art & Design, Savannah, GA; SO; BFA; Graphix Grp Treas 90-; Juris Corp Intrnshp Grphc Dsgnr 90; Scad Sccr 89-90; IM Bsktbl 89-90; Grphc Dsgn/Cmnctns.

**OLIVEIRA, DEBORA S,** Nova Univ, Ft Lauderdale, FL; GD; Fl Occptnl Ther Asso; Tallahassee Occptnl Ther Forum Co Chmn 89-; Stdnt Advsy Coun Chair-Elect.

**OLIVENCIA PETITON, CARMEN I,** Catholic Univ Of Pr, Ponce, PR; GD; Stdnt Psych Assn 87-; Luis T Nadal Thtrcl Wrkshp 89-; Lit Comp 89; Deans Hon Roll 88-; Ptrnl Rspnsblties Orgnzr 89; Drama Schlrshp 90-; BA 90; Sci; Indust Psych.

**OLIVENCIA, EIRA J,** Inter Amer Univ Pr San German, San German, PR; SR; MBA; Assc Ex Alumnos Fund Jose Orgy Gasset; Ntnl Assc Acctnts Treas 89-; Beca Harris 87-; BBA; Acctng; CPA.

**OLIVER, AIXABEL F,** Univ Of Pr Medical Sciences, San Juan, PR; JR; BS; Yrbk Sec 89-; Ldrshp Wrkshp; Rsrch Prof ; Rho Chi 89-; Deans Awd 89; Rectors Awd; Acad Stdnts/Pharmcy; Assoc Stdnts Pharmacy; Assoc Stdnt Pharmacy; Assoc Stdnt Councellors; Leo Club Pres 85-90; Hlth Clinic Vol 89; Cancer Cos 89; Pharmacy.

**OLIVER, ANITA L,** Wilberforce Univ, Wilberforce, OH; FR; BA; Natl Stdnt Bus League 90; John F Morning Mem Bus Aw%d 90; Acctng.

**OLIVER, CANDACE C,** Univ Of Ga, Athens, GA; SR; BA; Magna Cum Laude Assoc Dgr Spanish Educ 90; AA Truett Mcconnell Coll 90; Tch Spanish.

**OLIVER, CHERIE Y,** Univ Of Ky, Lexington, KY; SR; BA; SAVE; PETA; BAWL; Deans Lst 88-; Vol Estrn State Mntl Hosp Vol Envrnmntl Proj 88-; Clncl Psychlgy; Forensic.

**OLIVER, DEBORAH M,** Comm Coll Algny Co Algny Cmps, Pittsburgh, PA; SO; AS; CCAC Med Rcds Assoc Sec/Treas 89-; Phi Theta Kappa 90-; Full Hnr Schlrshp 89-; Comm Coll Of Allegheny Co Deans List 89-91; Awarded Chm Pass Pt Auth Transit 89; Liaison Block Parent Prog 87-88; Med Rec Tech.

**OLIVER, DEBORAH S,** Andrew Coll, Cuthbert, GA; SO; AA; Stdnt Govt Assoc VP 90-; Ltry Mag Art Ed 89-90; Hmcmng Ctr; Phi Theta Kappa 89-; Phi Delta VP 90-; Andrew Ambssdr Stdnt Tr Gd; Pres List 89-; Most Otsdng Greek; English; Brdcst News.

**OLIVER JR, DONALD G,** Dyersburg St Comm Coll, Dyersburg, TN; FR; BA; Const Prof 80-; Arch.

**OLIVER, JAMES E,** Univ Of Al At Birmingham, Birmingham, AL; SO; BS; College Youth Group At Church 89-; Alumni Achvmnt Awd Schlrshp 89; Cooperative Ed Emplymnt Northern Telecom; Elec Engrng.**

**OLIVER JR, JAMES O,** Univ Of Sc At Columbia, Columbia, SC; SR; BSED; Kappa Delta Pi 90-; SEA 89-90; Deans Lst 88-; Prsdnts Lst Chnclrs Lst 90-; Intrnshp Smtr H S 90-; IM Bsktbl 88-; Deacon Crswll Bptst Chrch; Prsdnt Chldrns Bootery Inc 82-; BSED Coastal Carolina Clg USC; AS USC Sumter 82; Math Edctn; Mddl H S Tchr.

**OLIVER, KYLE M,** Univ Of Fl, Gainesville, FL; SR; BSBA; FMA 90-; Vrsty Scr 86-87; Sigma Alpha Epsilon 87-; Pres Rcgntn Awd 87; Acctg Intrn 89; IM Scr Sftbl Ftbl 87-90; Fin; Bus.

**OLIVER, LINDA S,** Memphis St Univ, Memphis, TN; BSN; Gamma Beta Phi; Nrsg.

**OLIVER, LISA A,** Westminster Coll, New Wilmingtn, PA; SR; BA; Argo Yrbk Edtr Chf 89-; W Hl Wnd Engl Alumn Nwsltr Edtr Chf 90-; Hlcad Nwspr Chr 87-; Soc Coll Jrnlsts; Omicron Delta Kappa; Sigma Kappa Publ Rel Chr; Publ Intrnshp; Im Sftbl; BA; Engl/Elem Educ; Adv/Tchr.

**OLIVER, LISA D,** Bethel Coll, Mckenzie, TN; SR; BA; Stdnt Govt Assoc 90-; Cmnty Chrs 90; Wmns Issues Orgnztn 90; Lambda Sigma Chpln 90-; Diakonoi Pres 90-; Chrstn Issues Orgnztn 90-; Intrnshp Chldrns Drctr 90; Amrcn Bible Scty Awrd 90-; As Vlntr St Comm Coll 89; Rlgn; Chrch Mnstry.

**OLIVER, LYNDA A,** Ramapo Coll Of Nj, Mahwah, NJ; SR; BS; Finance/Investment Assn 90-; Delta Mu Delta; Intl Bus Machines Admin Spplmntl 87-89; Bus; Finance.

**OLIVER, MARY L,** Owensboro Jr Coll Of Bus, Owensboro, KY; FR; AD; SGA V P Elect; Pres List 90-; Street Relief Prog; Green River Comp Care; Comp Sci; Computerized Office Prof.

**OLIVER, MATTHEW C,** Oh Univ, Athens, OH; SR; BFA; Ultimate Frsbee Clb Capt 87-; Visual Comm.

**OLIVER, MICHELLE R,** Savannah St Coll, Savannah, GA; JR; BS; IEEE 90; Math Sci BS Armstrng State Clg 88; Electrncs Eng Tchnlgy; Eng.

**OLIVER, REBECCA L,** Middle Tn St Univ, Murfreesboro, TN; SR; BS; Stdnt Cncl Excptnl Chldrn 88-; Stdnt TN Edn Assn 89-; Gamma Beta Phi Chair 89-; Kappa Delta Pi 88-; Stdnt Ambassador Exec Com 89-; Deans Lst 88-F; Spcl Edn; Tchr.

**OLIVER JR, ROBERT B,** Univ Of Al At Birmingham, Birmingham, AL; SR; BS; Registered Respiratory Therapist; AAS 82; Resprtry Thrpy Cert 82; Allied Health Admin; MSHHA MBA.

**OLIVER, RONALD A,** Va Polytechnic Inst & St Univ, Blacksburg, VA; SO; BS; Co Op Wrkng IBM; Pres Lst; Elect Engr.**

**OLIVER, SHAWYNNE M,** Savannah St Coll, Savannah, GA; SR; BS; ASCE 89-; Wrkd Dept Trnsprtn Cvl Engr Trn 90; AS Tampa Tech Inst 86; Cvl Engrg Tech; PE Cvl Engrg.

**OLIVER, TERAMIA L,** Clark Atlanta Univ, Atlanta, GA; JR; BA; Alpha Kappa Alpha VP 89-; Fshn Mrchndsg Clb 89-90; Atlanta Metro Big Sis 89-; Kappa Delta Episolon 89-; Prjct Outrch Tutrl Oglethorape Tutrl Pgm 90-; Crestview Nrsng Hm/Bttrd Chldrns 90-; Coca-Cola Comm Serv Awd Honoree; Early Chldhd Educ; Edctr/Admnstrtr.

**OLIVER, TRACEY A,** Roane St Comm Coll, Harriman, TN; JR; MBA; SGA Prlmntrn 88-89; Clg Rpblcns Pres 90; Lifeguard 87-; Miss Broane State Comm Clg 88-89; Miss TN Schlsrhp Pageant 89; Sftbl; Natl Collegiate Math Awd 88-89; Econ.**

**OLIVER, YVETTE T,** Tn St Univ, Nashville, TN; SO; BS; Bnd Majorette; Alpha Kappa Alpha; Peer Cnslr; Gspl Chr; Tri St Univ Hnrs Pgm; Engl; Tchr.

**OLIVERA, CHARLES H,** Ponce School Of Medicine, Ponce, PR; JR; MD; Acad Sntr 90; Amer Med Assn 89-; Amer Med Stdnt Assn 88-; Alpha Omega Alpha; Free Mason 90-; Appleton Lange Book Award 88-89; Mcgraw Hill Book Award 88-89; Dns Lst 88-89; BS Univ Puerto Rico 85; Medicine.

**OLIVERAS, DAN-EL VIERA,** Univ Of Pr At Rio Piedras, Rio Piedras, PR; SO; BA; AIAS 89-; Natl Hnr Soc 86-89; NCADA; Acdmc Awrd 89-; Ambiental Dsgn; Arch.**

**OLIVERO, HERMINIO,** Univ Of Pr At Rio Piedras, Rio Piedras, PR; SR.

**OLIVERO, LUIS A,** Hillsborough Comm Coll, Tampa, FL; SO; BA; Club I Benco Espanol 85-; Talent Roster 90-; Cmctns; Radio/TV.

**OLIVEROS, YESENIA,** Saint Thomas Univ, Miami, FL; FR; BA; Crmnl Jstce; Cstms Invstgtr.

**OLIVETO, AARON P,** Valdosta St Coll, Valdosta, GA; SR; BA; Pi Gamma Mu 90-; Phi Alpha Delta; Political Sci Pre Law; Corporate Law.

**OLIVETT, REBECCA A,** Niagara Univ, Niagara Univ, NY; SR; BA; Karate Clb 88-89; Niagara Univ Com Actn Prog 89-90; Dns Lst VP 89-90; Sigma Tau Delta VP 89-; Engl; Elem Educ.

**OLIVIER JR, LEON L,** Ga St Univ, Atlanta, GA; SR; BSE; Kappa Delta Pi; Dns Schlrshp Key; Initial Tchr Preparation Awd; AA Oxford Coll Emory Uni 80; Chmstry; Tchr.

**OLIVIER, PASCALE,** City Univ Of Ny La Guard Coll, Long Island Cty, NY; SR; AAS; Physical Therapy Clb Pres 89-; Physical Therapy.

**OLIVIERI, MICHELLE A,** Ny Univ, New York, NY; FR; BA; Inter Srrty Cncl 90-; Newman Clb 90-; Delta Phi Epsilon Scl Cmm Chrprsn 90-; Hstry; Law Govt.

**OLIVO-FONTANEZ, ALEJANDRO,** Inter Amer Univ Pr Hato Rey, Hato Rey, PR; FR; BA; Air Frc ROTC 90; Drama Clb Lght Sprvsr 84-90; Hon Soc 90; Sccr Trnmnts Chmps 84-90; Airway Elctrnc Syst; Aviation Elctrnc.

**OLLIC, CYNTHIA R,** Univ Of Cin R Walters Coll, Blue Ash, OH; SO; ASN; Nrsng.

**OLLINGER, JESSICA L,** Indiana Univ Of Pa, Indiana, PA; SR; Big Bro/Big Str 88-; PSEA 90; NEA 90; Kappa Delta Pi; Alpha Gamma Delta Pres; Delta Kappa Gamma Educ Sor Schlrshp 90; Otsdng Stdnt Tchr Awd; BS Ele Educ; Ele Educ.

**OLLIS, CINDY Y,** Western Piedmont Comm Coll, Morganton, NC; SR; AASD; Bsn Admin; Sprvsn.

**OLMEZER, LUCY,** Broward Comm Coll, Ft Lauderdale, FL; SO; BS; Presdnts Lst 90; Sec Myr Cty Cmmssn 90-; Pltcl Sci.

**OLMO, IVONNE M,** Univ Of Pr At Rio Piedras, Rio Piedras, PR; SR; MBA; Hnr Stdnts 87-; Summa Cum Laude; Dns Awrd; Hnr Rgstrtn 87-; BED 89; Pol Scis; Law.

**OLMSTEAD, BRYAN K,** Meridian Comm Coll, Meridian, MS; SO; BS; Phi Theta Kapa 90-; Brv Hrt; Gym/Taiwan; Sml Trdng Co; Elec Engr; In/Exprt Comp Dsgn.

**OLOHAN, DANIEL P,** Providence Coll, Providence, RI; JR; BA; Spnsh Clb 90-; Phi Sigma Tau 90-; Sccr/Bsktbl 90-; IM Sftbl; Lbrl Arts; Law.

**OLORTEGUI, MONICA R,** Anne Arundel Comm Coll, Arnold, MD; SO; AA; Intrl Assn Sec 89-; Phi Theta Kappa; Finance.

**OLSAVICKY, KIMBERLY A,** Christopher Newport Coll, Newport News, VA; GD; Cmps Activ Bd Trvl Comm 87-88; Lit Mag Assoc Edtr 89-90; Alpha Chi 88-90; Mcmurran Schlr Hnrs Prog 88-90; Sigma Tau Delta Pres 87-90; Stdnts Of VA Educ Assn 89-90; Tchng Intrnshp 90; BA 90; Engl; Tchng.

**OLSCHEWSKI, MICHAEL R,** Bryant Stratton Bus Inst Roch, Rochester, NY; GD; AOS 88-90; Elctrncs; Eng.

**OLSEN, ALBERT H,** Univ Of Pittsburgh, Pittsburgh, PA; FR; BS; Mech Eng.

**OLSEN, CLIFFORD S,** S U N Y Coll Of Tech At Frmgdl, Farmingdale, NY; FR; Frmngdl Art Asc 90; Uppr Tm Tbrncl Chrch 90-; Frlnc Art Wrk; Sbarro Inc 89-90; Oystr Ay Nssn; Adv Art/Dsgn.

**OLSEN, DONA K,** Faulkner Univ, Montgomery, AL; SO; AA; Phi Lambda; SGA Exec Cncl; CWIA; Deans Lst; Soc Sci; Soc Wrkr/Cnslr.

**OLSEN, DORENA L,** Clarkson Univ, Potsdam, NY; SR; BS; Society Of Accountants Pres 90-; Phi Theta Kappa Pres 90-; AAS Canton Clg Technology 89; Acctng; CPA.

**OLSEN, GREGORY J,** Hudson Valley Comm Coll, Troy, NY; SR; AAS; Pres Lst 89-; St Catherines Ctr Chldrn 89-; R/E May Sch Intern 89-; Scl Wrk; MA.

**OLSEN JR, H EARNEST,** Central Fl Comm Coll, Ocala, FL; SO; BS; Math/Sci Hon Clb Fld Trp Coord 90-; Phi Theta Kappa 89-; Ml Chrldr 89-90; AA Cntrl Fla Comm Coll; Mrn Bio; Fshrs Mgmt.

**OLSEN, HEATHER ANN,** Midway Coll, Midway, KY; SO; AA; Chrch Sngls Grp 89-; Phi Theta Kappa 89-; Erly Chldhd Ed; Preschl Tch.

**OLSEN, JENNIFER A,** Wagner Coll, Staten Island, NY; FR; BS; Acctng; CPA.

**OLSEN, LAURA LEE,** Fl St Univ, Tallahassee, FL; SR; BS; Intl Affrs Soc Mbr Offc 89; Clg Rep Del 87-90; Phi Alpha Theta 90-; Gold Key 90-; Sigma Chi 87-89; Zeta Tau Alpha V Pres 89-90; Cap City Jaycees 89-90; Big Sis Riley Elem 88-89; Gamma Mbrshp 90-; Intrn U S Sentr Bob Graham 90; Histry Pol Sci; Attrny.

**OLSEN, LISA M,** Saint Josephs Coll, Windham, ME; SR; BS; Womens Varsty Bsktbl Co Capt 87-; Womens Varsty Sftbl 89-90; Elem Ed Club 87-; Dist 5 Sftbl All Star 90; MVP Dist 5 Bsktbl 90; Partcpnt In Natl Bsktbl Tourn 87-; Intrnshp Kindrgrdn A 90; Stdnt Tchng 3rd Grd A 90-; Im Sftbl/Bsktbl Co Cpt 87-; Elem Ed; Tchng.

**OLSEN, MATTHEW P,** S U N Y At Buffalo, Buffalo, NY; FR; MBA; Psychlgy.

**OLSOMMER, SHANNON M,** East Stroudsburg Univ, E Stroudsburg, PA; FR; BS; Trck Fld Tm 90-; Hnrs Prgrm 90-; Won $500 Hnrs Schlrshp; PA Cnfrnc Schlr; Athlt Crtf; Attnded Ntnl Hnrs Cnvtn; Psychology; Psychlgst.

**OLSON, BETH J,** Univ Of Toledo, Toledo, OH; GD; Envrnmntl Law Soc Co Chrprsn 90-; Burton Maddock Academic Schlrshp 89-; Regulatory Affrs Spec Envrnmntla Svcs; BS Western Mich Univ 83; Chmstry/Biomedical Science; Law.

**OLSON, BRIAN D,** Memphis St Univ, Memphis, TN; FR; Stdnt Activities Cncl Chmn 90-; Midwest Model UN Delg; Hon Stdnt Assn 90-; Tutorcore 90-.

**OLSON, ERIK A,** Univ Of Ky, Lexington, KY; FR; BA; Pol Sci/ Engl; Law.

**OLSON, GAYLE L,** Atlantic Comm Coll, Mays Landing, NJ; SO; BS; Phi Beta Lambda NJ State Pres 89-90; Phi Beta Lambda Pres 87-; Phi Beta Lambda NJ State Ldrshp Confrnc 89-; Regstrd Radiolgst Technlgst 85-; Cert Burdette Tomlin Mem Hosp Sch Of Radiolgc Technlgy 85; Hlth Care Admn.

**OLSON, MICHELLE C,** Thomas Nelson Comm Coll, Hampton, VA; SO; BA; Deans Lst 89-; Intern Pht Rflctns 90-; Jrd Exhbtn; AA; Phtgrphy.

**OLSON, PAUL M,** Georgetown Univ, Washington, DC; FR; Delta Sigma Pi Co-Chm Soc Comm; Georgetown Univ Swim Tm 90-; Acctng; Fin & Law.

**OLSON, PRESTON R,** Piedmont Tech Coll, Greenwood, SC; AA; 2 Yrs Tchncl Studies In Suand Eng; Elctrnc Eng; Eng.

**OLSON, SUSAN C,** Brevard Coll, Brevard, NC; FR; BS; Phi Theta Kappa; Envrnmntl Sci; Envrnmntl Law.

**OLSON, WENDY J C,** Averett Coll, Danville, VA; FR; MBA; Deans Lst 90; Engl Lit.

**OLSZEWSKI, THERESA M,** Univ Of Rochester, Rochester, NY; JR; BA; Univ Symphny 88-90; O Lions Scl Chr; Undrgrdt Psy Cncl 89-; Alpha Psi Snshne Chr 90-; Rsdntl Advsr 90-; Psychlgy; Indstrl Psychlgst.

**OLUGBODI, LYDIA O,** Gallaudet Univ, Washington, DC; JR; BS; Ngr Natl Assoc Df Sec 90-; Hnr Stdnts Org; Accnts Clrk 89-; Dplm 81-84; Acctg.

**OLWINE, ELIZABETH A,** Univ Of Md At Eastern Shore, Princess Anne, MD; JR; BA; Eta Sigma Delta 90; Eta Sigma Delta 89; Delta Delta Delta 87-; Motel Mgmr Intrn; Tennis 89; Hotel/Rstrnt Mgmt; Sls Dept Hotel/Chain.

**OMAN, TARA M,** Univ Of Tn At Martin, Martin, TN; FR; DPH; Zeta Tau Alpha 90; Pharmacy.

**OMAYRA, MEDINA DEL C,** Univ Of Pr At Rio Piedras, Rio Piedras, PR; SR; Amrcn Inst Archtctr Stdnts; Archtctr.

**OMENE, CORAL O,** City Univ Of Ny City Coll, New York, NY; SO; BS; Caduceus Scty; Vol Svc St Lukes Roosevelt Hosp NY; Bio; Medcn.

**OMO-OSAGIE, SOLOMON I,** Coppin St Coll, Baltimore, MD; SO; BA; Stdnt Senate Pres 90-; Intl Stdnts Assn VP 90-; Afr-Am Soc; Stdnt In Poltcs; Stdnt Hon Assn 90-; Nwspaper Featrs Edtr; Pst-Baccalreat Achvmnt Prog; Tutor 89-; Deans Lst Awrd 90-; Outstndng Stdnt Awrd 89-90; Goldn/Slvr Poet Awrd 90; Tennis Tm; Soc Sci/Poltcl Sci; Law.

**ONATIVIA, JOSE E,** Catholic Univ Of Pr, Ponce, PR; GD; USA Retiree; Engl; Tchr.

**ONDERKO, CHRISTINE E,** Mount Aloysius Jr Coll, Cresson, PA; SO; AA; Childrens Advocacy Assc Rep 90-91; Phi Theta Kappa 89-90; Big Brother/Big Sister 89-90; Early Childhood Ed; Teaching.

**ONDREJACK, LEE A,** Juniata Coll, Huntingdon, PA; JR; BS; Barristers Clb 90-; Legal Intern; Vlybl 88-90; Pol Sci/Hstry; Lawyer.

**ONDRICK, SUSAN A,** Newbury Coll, Brookline, MA; FR; AS; Paralgl Assn; Paralgl Stdies; Lgl Asst.

**ONEY JR, ROGER L,** Kent St Univ Kent Cmps, Kent, OH; SR; BA; Psychology Philosophy.

**ONG, DARYL GIM LOO,** Columbus Coll Of Art & Design, Columbus, OH; JR; BA; Singapore Armd Frcs Lt 87-89; Dns Lst 89090; Indstrl Dsgn Schlrshp 90-; Cert Singapore Polytechnic 87; Indstrl Dsgn.

**ONG, JONATHAN A,** Embry Riddle Aeronautical Univ, Daytona Beach, FL; JR; BS; Aero Engr.

**ONG, JULIAN,** City Univ Of Ny Baruch Coll, New York, NY; SR; Beta Gamma Sigma 90; BBA; Intrntnl Mrktng; Intrntnl Bsns Int Affrs.

**ONG, MEI-SUEN ELLEN,** Southern Coll Of Tech, Marietta, GA; SR; BAEET; IEEE 89-; Tau Alpha 90-; Pres Cert Of Acad Excllnce 89; Elec Eng Tech; Systm Eng.

**ONO, MIDORI,** Truett Mc Connell Coll, Cleveland, GA; SO; Tnns 90; Bus.

**ONO, NORIKO,** Univ Of South Al, Mobile, AL; SR; BS; Acctng Club Treas 90-; Beta Alpha Psi Rprtng Sec 90-; Deans List & Pres List 88-; Diploma Orlando Coll 88; Acctng; CPA.**

**ONO, SACHIKO,** Univ Of Tn At Martin, Martin, TN; SR; BS; Phi Kappa Phi; AA Toita Wmns Clg 80; Geo/Trvl/Trsm.

**ONODIPE, OLUSEUN A,** Univ Of Pittsburgh, Pittsburgh, PA; SO; BS; Elec Engr; Cmptr.

**ONORATO, DAWN C,** Clarkson Univ, Potsdam, NY; SR; BS; Amer Mktg Assoc 90; Soccer Capt 87-; Mktg/Mgmt; Mktg Rep.

**ONTL, RICHARD C,** Memphis St Univ, Memphis, TN; SR; BSET; Holiday Inn Schlrshp St Tchncl Inst; Grad St Tch Hnrs; Ntwrk Engnr Crtf Ntwrkng Data Cmmnctns; Hitech Data Cmmnctns Inc 87-; ASET St Tchncl Inst Mmphs 87; Electncs Engnrng; Engnrng.

**ONUFREY, NICOLE S,** Oh Wesleyan Univ, Delaware, OH; SO; BA; Delta Delta Delta Pldg Scl Trident Hstrn 89-; Cmnty Svc Comm 90-; Jrnlsm; Publ Rels.

**ONUOHA, AUGUSTINA A,** Al A & M Univ, Normal, AL; SO; BS; Miss ISA African Stdnt Assn; Hon Rl; Deans Lst; Zoology; Med.

**ONWUGBOLU, ESTHER N,** Jackson St Univ, Jackson, MS; SR; BS; Biol Clb; Alpha Lamda Delta; Beta Kappa Chi; Dean Lst; Biol/Pre Med; Med.

**ONYEAKA, CATHY I,** Al A & M Univ, Normal, AL; SR; BS; Finance; Bsn.

**ONYEAKA, SAMUEL O,** Univ Of Al At Huntsville, Huntsville, AL; SR; BS; Amer Soc Civil Engr 89-; Soccer Club; Civil Engr; Engr.

**ONYEUKA, ANGELA A,** Cheyney Univ Of Pa, Cheyney, PA; SR; Int Std Assc Tres 87-89; Nvosi Std Un VP 83-85; Dns Lst; Bsktbl 90; TCII Lasbrey Tchrs Clg 82; WASC WAYEC 76; BSC Dietcs/HRIM; Cnslt.

**OOI, TAT S,** City Univ Of Ny Baruch Coll, New York, NY; SR; BBA; Untd Malaysn Stdnts Assn Pr 90; Finc/Econ Soc Mbr 89-; Goldn Key 90; Dns Lst 90; Devel Bk Singapore N Y Intrn 90; Intl Stdnts Schlrshp 89-; Finc/Inv; Inv Bnkg.

**OOKUBO, RIE,** Bay Path Coll, Longmeadow, MA; FR; AA; Gldn Z Clb 90-; Sec 83-90; Hmn Serv; Psychtrst.

**OON, SIN YING,** Univ Of Ky, Lexington, KY; JR; BS; Malaysian Stdnt Org Sec 90-; Math.

**OOTEN, JOSEPH F,** Roane St Comm Coll, Harriman, TN; SO; AS; Bsbl Tm; Police Sci; Lawyer.

**OPEL, MATTHEW R,** Cornell Univ Statutory College, Ithaca, NY; SO; BS; Japanimation Soc 90-; Teatown Lk Rsrvtn Intern 90; Biol/Botany; Rsrch.

**OPGENORTH, SCOTT ALLAN,** Univ Of Sc At Columbia, Columbia, SC; JR; Mat/Sci; Medcl.

**OPHER, ALBERT W,** Hampton Univ, Hampton, VA; FR; BA; Stdnt Gvrnmnt Assn Rep 90-; Frshmn Exctv Cncl 90-; SEMS Schlrshp Rcpnt 90-; Rsrch OH St Unv; Math.

**OPIE, PAUL J,** Indiana Univ Of Pa, Indiana, PA; SO; BA; Provost Schlr; Math Educ; Tchr.

**OPIELA, SCOTT K,** Clarkson Univ, Potsdam, NY; JR; BS; AMA Treas 90-; Class Pres 88-89; Clarkson Hall Assoc Dorm Rep 89-90; Dorm Cncl Flr Rep 88-89; Stdnt Orient Svc 90-; Host A Prospective Frshmn Pgm 88-89; Sigma Chi 90; Nwsltr 90-; Clarksons Trustees Schlrhsp 89-; Clarkson Hon Schlrshp 89-; Mktg; Mngmnt.

**OPIPERY, PAULETTE A,** Univ Of Cincinnati, Cincinnati, OH; SO; BA; St George Newman Cntr; Alpha Lambda Delta; Sigma Alpha Iota Corr Sec 90-; Flute Prfrmnc; Mscl Prfrmnc/Educ.

**OPON, JULIE M,** Elms Coll, Chicopee, MA; JR; BA; Col Art Shows; Etching Dsgn Awd; Art Educ; Advrtsng/Tchng.

**OPPENHEIMER, MICHAEL W,** Univ Of Akron, Akron, OH; SO; BEE; Univ Akron Hnrs Pgm 89-; Alpha Lambda Delta 90-; Phi Eta Sigma 90-; Acad Schlp Univ Akron; Dns Lst; Vars Bsbl 90-; Elec Engr; Dntstry.

**OPPERMAN, TAMMY C,** Lake Erie Coll, Painesville, OH; FR; BS; Intrclgte Riding Clb Treas 90-; Cmpus Bible Flwshp 90; Equestrian.

**OPPERMAN, WILLIAM J X,** Comm Coll Algny Co Algny Cmps, Pittsburgh, PA; FR; BA; Art Ed; Tch.

**OPPOLD JR, THOMAS M,** Univ Of Sc At Columbia, Columbia, SC; JR; BA; Chi Psi Pres 90; Rsdnce Hall Govt Treas 88-89; Judical Brd; Gamma Beta Phi 89-; Order Of Omega Treas 90-; Cmnty Svc Chrn Chi Psi 89-90; Derrick Schlrshp; Thomas B Pierce Mem Schlrshp; IM Bsktbl/Sftbl/Vlybl/Floor Hcky/Ftbl; Bsn Mgmt/Mgmt Sci; Bsn.

**OPRE, BARBARA M,** Rivier Coll, Nashua, NH; SR; BED; Elem/Spcl Edn.

**OPUDA, ANNE C,** Univ Of Fl, Gainesville, FL; SR; BSM; FL Nrs Assn 77-; Sigma Theta Tau; VA Schlr Hlth Pro Schlrshp Pgm 90-; Fawcett Schlr; Civitan Rgnl Bld Cntr; Dept Vet Affrs Medcl Cntr 82-; Nrsng; Grntlgcl Nrsng.

**OQUENDO, AIDA M,** Univ Of Pr At Rio Piedras, Rio Piedras, PR; SR; BA; SG VP 90-; Envntmtl Dsgn; MBA Archtcre.

**OQUENDO, CARMEN W,** Univ Of Pr Humacao Univ Coll, Humacao, PR; SO; Acctg; Law.

**ORABONI, NADINE M,** Ramapo Coll Of Nj, Mahwah, NJ; JR; Rsdnt Stdnt Assn Mbr 89-; Dns Advsry Bd Mbr 89-90; Pre Law Socty Mbr 89-; Oxford Hnrs Prog Mbr 88-; Dns Lst 88-; Phi Alpha Delta Mbr 90-; Intrnshp Ocean Cnty Prob/Prsctrs Offc 89-; Pre Law; Law.

**ORAMA, ALYCE M,** Endicott Coll, Beverly, MA; SO; AS; Tutor 90-; Bus Clb 90-; Psychology Clb; Phi Theta Kappa 89-; Intrnshp 90-; Pres Awd; Fshn Mrchndsng; Buyer.

**ORAMA, LIONEL R,** Univ Politecnica De Pr, Hato Rey, PR; JR; BA; IEEE; ROTC 1st Lt 87-88; Phi Eta Mu Inctn Comm 89; ROTC Awd 87; IM 86; Electrl; Engr.

**ORAVECZ, LISA M,** Notre Dame Coll, Cleveland, OH; SO; BS; Nu Delta Mu Sec 90-; Pall Mall Engl Clb 89-; Coll Nwspr Ed 89-90; Vars Bsktbl 89-; Vars Sftbl; Math/Mech Eng.

**ORDERS II, JAMES MICHAEL,** Anne Arundel Comm Coll, Arnold, MD; FR; MBA; Econ/Finc; Brokgr/Bnkg.

**ORDONEZ, IVAN F,** City Univ Of Ny City Coll, New York, NY; SO; MBA; Seek 90-; Deans Lst 90-; Urbn Archtct.

**ORDONEZ, JUANA PATRICIA,** Miami Dade Comm Coll, Miami, FL; SO; BA; Phi Theta Kappa; Talent Rstr Otstndng Mnty Com Coll Grad; Acdmc Ascvmnt Awrd 89; Hispanic Schlrshp Awrd; AA; Math; Prfssr.

**ORDWAY, DAWN M,** Defiance Coll, Defiance, OH; SO; BS; Restoration Ecology Soc Treas 90-; Ohio Pgm Intensive Engl Cnvrstn Partner 89; Odyssey Mind Coach; Engl; Teach.

**ORDWING, ANDREA L,** Fl International Univ, Miami, FL; SR; BS; FL Rstrnt Assn Schlrshp 90; Ft Laudrdl Chart Hs Intrn; Hsptlty Mgmt.

**OREBAUGH, ANGELA R,** Bridgewater Coll, Bridgewater, VA; SO; BA.

**OREHGO-RODRIGUEZ, NESTOR,** Univ Politecnica De Pr, Hato Rey, PR; JR; BSIE; I E Toc Univ Of Puerto Rico 90; Sci; Engrng.

**ORELLANO COLON, ELSA M,** Univ Of Pr Medical Sciences, San Juan, PR; SO; BS; Sci; Occ Ther.

**ORFANAKOS, KATHERINE S,** Cornell Univ Statutory College, Ithaca, NY; SO; BS; Yrbk Ed Of U Sctn 90; Mscl Theater Grp 89-90; Ho-Nun-Do-Kah; Alpha Omicron Pi; Orient Cnslr 90; Tchng Assist Introd To Cmmnctn; Im Vllybl 90; Tri-Cnty Cornell Alumni Schlrshp 89; Cmmnctn; Pbl Rltns.

**ORGAIN, GAVIN L,** Univ Of Tn At Knoxville, Knoxville, TN; JR; BA; Phi Eta Sigma 90-; Alpha Tau Omega 88-; Alpha Tau Omega 90; Deans List 88-; Acctg Bus Law; Professor.

**ORGERON III, HORACE J,** Hillsborough Comm Coll, Tampa, FL; SO; AA; Optcnry Asst 89-; Rcqutbll Trnmnt; Psychlgy.

**ORIE, STACI L,** Allegheny Coll, Meadville, PA; SO; BA; La Crosse Clb 89-; Hapitat Hmnty 89-; Orntatn Advsr; Lambda Sigma Hstrn 90-; Alpha Delta Pi 90-; Meadville Cncl Arts 90-; Alden Schlr 89-; I M Vybl 89-; Art Hstry; Law/Arts Admn.

**ORION, RHEA A,** Norfolk St Univ, Norfolk, VA; SO; BS; Interior Dsgn Stdnt Org Tidewater Comnty Clg 89-90; Tidewater Ballet Sch Stdnt/Perfrmr 86-; Bernina Club Of Sthestrn US 87-; Hm Sewing Bus Lions Windws Wardrbs Crfts Interiors; Cert Tidewtr Cmnty Clg 90; Soc Sci/Hm Ec; Coop Extnsn Svc/Cnslr.

**ORIZONDO, IVETTE M,** Fl International Univ, Miami, FL; SR; BS; Future Ed Am 89-90; Campus Radio Sta DJ 89-; Grk Cncl VP 90-; Panhellenic Cncl Voting Deleg 90-; Phi Kappa Phi; Order Omega; Phi Sigma Sigma Exec Bd 90-; Delta Kappa Schlrshp Awd 90-; Elem Edn/Early Chldhd; Plans/Admin.

**ORKWIS, DOUGLAS R,** Dowling Coll, Oakdale Li, NY; FR; BA; Prsdntl Hnrs Clb 90-; Mdcl; Ntrnst Dtcn.

**ORLANDO, GONZALEZ ZAYAS,** Catholic Univ Of Pr, Ponce, PR; GD; BSSE; MBSE.

**ORLANDONI, ENRICO F,** William Paterson Coll, Wayne, NJ; SR; BS; Res Lf Res Asst 88-; Bacchus Fndng Mbr Pres 89-90; Gln Soc; Ntl Sci Clb; IM Sprts; Beta Beta Beta; Res Asst Yr Awd 89; Bio; Med Schl.

**ORLIAN, ETAN,** Yeshiva Univ, New York, NY; GD; MA; Phlthrpy Sco 90-; ACM Prgrmng Cmptn Tm 89-90; Cmptr Sci.

**ORLICK, PAMELA A,** East Stroudsburg Univ, E Stroudsburg, PA; SO; BA; Mthr/Hmkr; Pltcl Sci; FBI.

**ORLOFF, WARREN D,** Oh St Univ, Columbus, OH; SR; BS; Sundial Stdnt Humr Mag Ethcs Chr 88-89; Bllrm Dnc Assn 89-; Bicyclng Clb 88-90; Dns Lst 87-; Vlntr Ushr 88-; Excllnc/Schlrshp Awrd 90-; IM Hcky; Bio; Ed.

**ORLOWSKI, JULIANNE S,** Villanova Univ, Villanova, PA; SO; BS; Blue Key 90-; Campus Mnstry; Alpha Epsilon Delta; Phi Sigma; Alpha Phi 90-; Spec Olympics Comm Mbr 89-; Bio; Med.

**ORLOWSKY JR, EDWARD L,** George Mason Univ, Fairfax, VA; SR; BS; Bus Mngmt.

**ORLOWSKY, JENNIFER L,** Delaware Valley Coll, Doylestown, PA; FR; Chrle 90-; Envir Awrnss Clb Pres 90-; Apry Scty; Otdrs Clb 90-; Pres Dplmt 90-; Crss Cntry 90-; Anml Sci Pre Vet; Vet.

**ORMANDY, LESLIE J,** City Univ Of Ny City Coll, New York, NY; GD; Gold Key 89; BFA City Coll 90; BA City Coll 90; Engl; Masters Lib Sci.

**ORME, CHERI L,** Univ Of Ky, Lexington, KY; SR; BS; Coll Prog Fclty Brd 90-; Pi Mu Epsilon; Epsilon Delta 89-; Omicron Delta Kappa; Lances And Links 89-; Gldn Ky 89-; Alpha Lambda Delta; Lambda Sigma; Phi Eta Sigma; Alpha Lambda Delta Rcrdng Secr 87-; Sllvn Awrd; Pnce Awrd; KEA Dlgte NEA RA; Math Educ Scndry; Tch Hgh Schl Math.

**ORMSBY, DAWN M,** Western New England Coll, Springfield, MA; SR; BSBA; Pre-Law Soc 87-91; Radio 87; Peer Adv 88-90; Tutor 88-90; Bowling Clb 89-91; SG 91; Deans Lst 87-; Sec Of States Ofc Intrn; Bus; Law.

**ORMSBY, HEATHER E,** De Tech & Comm Coll At Dover, Dover, DE; FR; AAS; Crmnl Jstce Orgnztn; Crmnl Jstce; Prbtn Or Prle Ofcr.

**ORMSBY, MICHELLE L,** Western New England Coll, Springfield, MA; SO; BA; Pre Law Soc 90-; Bowling Clb 90-; Peer Tutor 90-; Helpins Hand Soc 90-; Deans Lst 90-; Field Hcky 90; Engl; Law.

**ORNDORF JR, THOMAS P,** Nova Univ, Ft Lauderdale, FL; GD; MBA; NAA V P 78; US Coast Guard Lt Cmndr 75-; Occidental Chem Corp Cntrlr 87-89; BS Pembroke State Univ 75; Fin; Bsn Analyst.

**ORNDORFF, SUSANNE M,** Pa St Univ Main Cmps, University Pk, PA; SO; BA; ACF 90; Phi Eta Sigma 89; Phi Kappa Phi 90; Intrnshp; Jrnlsm; Pblc Rltns.**

**ORNDORFF, TIFFANY L,** Glassboro St Coll, Glassboro, NJ; SR; BS; Alpha Delta Epsilon Hstrn 88-; Bio; Med.

**ORNER, LISA E,** Pa St Univ Mont Alto Cmps, Mont Alto, PA; FR; AS; Business Adm.

**ORNER, RACHEL E,** Univ Of Sc At Columbia, Columbia, SC; FR; MBA; Hillel VP 90-; Alpha Lambda Delta 90-; Bsns; Mrktng.

**ORNER, TODD M,** Schenectady County Comm Coll, Schenectady, NY; SO; BS; Comp Sci; Sftwr Engr.

**OROBITG, MARIELSA,** Inter Amer Univ Pr Hato Rey, Hato Rey, PR; JR; MBA; Acctg; CPA.

**OROLOGIO, TANA L,** Schenectady County Comm Coll, Schenectady, NY; FR; AAS; Travel/Tourism; Hotel Mgmnt.

**OROPALLO, BARBARA A,** Hudson Valley Comm Coll, Troy, NY; SO; BA; Bsn Admn.

**OROZCO, MERCEDES,** City Univ Of Ny City Coll, New York, NY; SR; BS; Alpha Sigma Lambda; AAS Borough Manhattan Cmty Clg 89; Early Chldhd Educ; Child Psychology.

**ORR, BRIAN S,** Univ Of Va Clinch Valley Coll, Wise, VA; SR; BS; Assn Cmptng Mchnry 90-; Cmptr Info Systs.

**ORR, CHRISTINE M,** Villanova Univ, Villanova, PA; SR; BA; Pr Cnslng Cr Cntr Stdnt Coord 88-90; Hse Cncl VP 87-88; Amnsty Internatl 87-88; Order Omega 90-; Eng Hnr Soc 90-; Hstry Hnr Soc 90-; Kappa Kappa Gamma 1st VP 90-; Eng.

**ORR, DEREK W,** Univ Of Cin R Walters Coll, Blue Ash, OH; FR; BA; Acctg; Busn.

**ORR, DONNA D,** Univ Of Sc At Columbia, Columbia, SC; FR; BA; Chrch Pianst 86-; OH Brss/H Hubble Schlrshp 90-; Deans Lst 90-; Acctg/Comp Sci; CPA.

**ORR, KAREN E,** Salisbury St Univ, Salisbury, MD; SR; BA; MENC Pres 90; Outdoor Clb 87; Phi Kappa Phi 90; Pres Schlr 87; Im 87; Music; Music Thrpy.

**ORR, MARK D,** Birmingham Southern Coll, Birmingham, AL; JR; BA; Sigma Tau Delta 90-; Alpha Kappa Delta; Tutr; Radio Nws Intrn; IM Sprts 88-; Engl/Sclgy; Brdcst Jrnlsm.

**ORR, PENNY L,** Appalachian Bible Coll, Bradley, WV; SO; BS; Bible Clb Ldr 89-90; SBC 90; Bblc Cnslng; Cnslng.

**ORR, REBECCA J,** Wv Northern Comm Coll, Wheeling, WV; SO; BBA; Stdnt Govt Rcrdng Sec 89-90; Communications.

**ORR, RICHARD WILLIAM,** Wv Univ, Morgantown, WV; JR; BSIE; Rcqtbl Clb Pres 88-; Inst Indl Engrs 89-; AT/T Bell Labs Intshp; Indl Engr.

**ORR, SHANNON E,** Univ Of Tn At Martin, Martin, TN; JR; BED; STEA 90-; Chi Omega Pnhllnc Offcr; IM Actvts; Elem Educ; Spch Pthlgy And Adlgy.

**ORR, TAMI L,** De Tech & Comm Coll At Dover, Dover, DE; GD; BED; Hmn Serv Org 89-; Intrnshp Lake Forest North Elem Schl; AA DE Tech/Comm Clg; Elem Ed; Tchng.

**ORR, TIFFANY D,** Univ Of Ky, Lexington, KY; FR; BS; Coll Acad Excel; Res Hall Gov; Alpha Lambda Delta; Phi Eta Sigma; Emrgng Ldr Inst; Math; Tchr.

**ORR, TINA L,** S U N Y Coll At Fredonia, Fredonia, NY; JR; BS; BCIC 90-; Newman Cntr Religious Ed Tchr 90-; Psychology; MSW.

**ORR, TODD C,** Syracuse Univ, Syracuse, NY; SR; BARCH; Outing Club Photo Club Architecture Stdnt Orginization 87-; Inter Russel Gibson Von Drolen Arch Farmington CT Modee Bldger 87; Intern Sargent & Merrman Arch Asst Designer 88-90; Architecture.

**ORRANGE, JOHN J,** Univ Of New Haven, West Haven, CT; JR; BS; Alpha Lambda Delta; Comp Science; Sftwr Engnrng.

**ORRELL, STACY SPENCER,** Univ Of Nc At Charlotte, Charlotte, NC; JR; Psychlgy Clb; Outstdng Coll Stdnts Of Amer 87-; Gldn Key 88-; Psi Chi 90-; Pi Sigma Epsilon 90-; Psychlgy.

**ORRICK, PATZE M,** Belmont Coll, Nashville, TN; FR; BM; Chrstn Music Scty 90; Opera Scanes Assist Cstme Coord; Slctd Womens Choir Slst; Ftred Mikado Opera Scene Slst; Cmmrcl Music; Sngr/Sngwrtr Rcrdng Artst.

**ORRICO, ANDREA L,** City Univ Of Ny Baruch Coll, New York, NY; JR; BSED; Sec Clb Pres 89; Kingsborough Comm Coll Off Admin Advsry Cncl 89; Phi Theta Kappa 89-; Phi Beta Lambda 89-; AAS Kingsborough Comm Coll 89; Bus; Tchr.

**ORRICO JR, DONALD A,** Old Dominion Univ, Norfolk, VA; SR; BA; IEEE 90-; Tau Beta Pi 90; Gldn Key 90; Phi Theta Kappa 89; Tau Kappa Epsilon 87-; Eta Kappa Nu 90; FAA Awrd 90; AS 89; Elec Eng.

**ORRIN, CHEVARA L,** Memphis St Univ, Memphis, TN; SR; SGA Senator 86-87; BSA 86-; Blck Allnc Scl Eqty Base 90-; Silver Star News Cmmnty Serv Awrd 89; Natl Cvl Rights Museum Sympsm Plng Comm; Highland Hundred Clb James Mc Clelland Schlrshp 87; First Tenn Bnk Intrnshp.

**ORSAG, SUSAN S,** Gallaudet Univ, Washington, DC; JR; BA; Chrldng Squad 88-90; Mstr Tutor In Spanish 89; Sec Ed Math; Tchr.

**ORSINI, ANGELA L,** Lesley Coll, Cambridge, MA; JR; BS; Class Pres 88-; Dns Lst 88-; LING 88-; SOAR Sec 88-89; Cath Comm Pres 90-; Cnslng; Clin Psych.

**ORSINI, ANTONIETTA,** Long Island Univ Brooklyn Cntr, Brooklyn, NY; JR; BS; Acctng Scty VP 90-; Vol Incme Tx Asst Prog 90-; Cmps Rep Fr Chykn CPA Rvw 90-; Acctng; CPA.**

**ORSINI, KRISTIN D,** Lesley Coll, Cambridge, MA; SO; Stdnt Govt Assn Sec 90-; Cath Comm VP 90-; Walk For Hunger 90; AIDS Actn Comm Dncng Time 90; BA Univ So Cal; Theatre-Busn; Entrtnmnt.

**ORSOLICS, ERIC J,** Indiana Univ Of Pa, Indiana, PA; SO; BA; Cmmnctns Media.

**ORTA, MARIA M,** D Youville Coll, Buffalo, NY; GD; BA; Teachers Aide 76 Herman Padillo; Sec Bilingual Adv Bd; B Ed; Bilngl Elem & Spanish; Teach.

**ORTALDO, MONICA L,** Univ Of Sc At Columbia, Columbia, SC; JR; BA; Cmps Cltn Ltrcy 90; Gamma Beta Phi 89-; Deans Lst 88-; Cncl Chld Abs 88-90; Kappa Kappa Gamma Asst Treas 88; Elem Ed; MA Spch Pthlgy.

**ORTEGA COTTE, IVAN OSVALDO,** Univ Politecnica De Pr, Hato Rey, PR; FR; BSA.

**ORTEGA VELEZ, MILAGROS LUZ,** Univ Politecnica De Pr, Hato Rey, PR; FR; In Tthr; Bsktbl; Eng.

**ORTEGA, LEE CORBIN,** Newbury Coll, Brookline, MA; FR; HMFH Architects Inc Cambridge Office Assist; Secty; Certif Univ Granada Spain 90; Interior Design.

**ORTEGA, MARGARITA,** Georgetown Univ, Washington, DC; SO; BA; Georgetowns Mntr Pgm 90; Christian Life Comm 87-90; First Hon 89-90; Deans Lst 89-; Christian Life Comm 87-90; Vol Home Abused Chldrn 89; Mktg; Advrtsng.

**ORTEGA, MARIA,** Inter Amer Univ Pr San German, San German, PR; GD; ACS 89-; Chmstry.

**ORTEGA, MARIBEL,** Newbury Coll, Brookline, MA; SR; AAS; Fashn Dsgn Club Fashn Show 89-; AAS; Fash Dsgn/Art; Fash Dsgnr.

**ORTEGA, RICARDO J,** Fl International Univ, Miami, FL; SR; BA; Alpha Lambda Delta; Chi Phi; Mod Architecture History.

**ORTEGA-RAMIREZ, WENDOLLY,** Univ Of Pr At Mayaguez, Mayaguez, PR; SO; BA; Drll Tm; AFROTC Admn Offcer 90-; CESA 89-90; Eng Hnr Rll 89-; Comp; Comp Eng.

**ORTIZ COLLADO, CARLOS E,** Inter Amer Univ Pr Hato Rey, Hato Rey, PR; GD; BA; Natl Assoc Acctns 89-; Hnr Scty 90-; Finance; Law.**

**ORTIZ COLON, MARICARMEN,** Univ Of Pr At Rio Piedras, Rio Piedras, PR; JR; BA; Acctg Assoc 89-; Gldn Key; Hosp Vol 87-88; Acctg; CPA.

**ORTIZ COSME, MILDRED J,** Inter Amer Univ Pr Hato Rey, Hato Rey, PR; FR; Sci; Med Tech.

**ORTIZ FRANCESCHI, LUIS E,** Univ Of Pr At Mayaguez, Mayaguez, PR; SO; Comp Sci.

**ORTIZ JUSTINIANO, MILDRED,** Inter Amer Univ Pr San German, San German, PR; FR; Sec Sci; Baccalaureate.

**ORTIZ MALDONADO, ZULMA I,** Inter Amer Univ Pr Fajardo, Fajardo, PR; FR; BA; Math; Comp Pgmr.

**ORTIZ RIVERA, EILEEN,** Inter Amer Univ Pr San German, San German, PR; FR; BBA; Acctg.

**ORTIZ RODRIGUEZ, EFRAIN,** Inter Amer Univ Pr Hato Rey, Hato Rey, PR; SO; BA; Asstnt Admsn Offc 89-; Deans Lst 89-; Hnr Rl 90-; Airways Sci; Air Traffic Cntrl.

**ORTIZ ROSARIO, EDGARDO,** Univ Politecnica De Pr, Hato Rey, PR; FR; Elctrncs; Eng.

**ORTIZ SILVA, LISANDRA,** Inter Amer Univ Pr Hato Rey, Hato Rey, PR; FR; BA; Bsns Mgmnt.

**ORTIZ TORO, MELVIN D,** Inter Amer Univ Pr San German, San German, PR; JR; BA; Comp; Prgrmmr.

**ORTIZ, ANNIE E,** Univ Of Pr Medical Sciences, San Juan, PR; GD; Prof Clg Nrsg 87-; RN; BA Univ PR Med Sci Campus 86; BA Sci Nrsg; MA Nrsg Adm.

**ORTIZ, CARLOS E,** Inter Amer Univ Pr San Juan, Hato Rey, PR; GD; BA; NAA 90-; Hnr Scty 90-; Finance; Law.**

**ORTIZ, CARMEN M,** City Univ Of Ny Baruch Coll, New York, NY; JR; BBA; AAS NY City Tchncl Clg 83; Ofc Admnstrtn Tchnlgy.

**ORTIZ, CAROLINA M,** S U N Y Coll Of Tech At Frmgdl, Farmingdale, NY; JR; BA; AA 90; Psychlgy.

**ORTIZ, CIRA D,** Hudson County Comm Coll, Jersey City, NJ; JR; Hlth/Hmn Serv Assist Adult Yuth Grp West NY Treasf; Oustdng Achiev Awd 89-90; Deans List 89-90; St Joseph's H Schl Click Pres 90-F; Tchr Assist N Bergein Hd Start; Early Childhood Psy; Tchr Child Care.**

**ORTIZ, EFRAIN,** Reading Area Comm Coll, Reading, PA; SR; BA; Church God Minister 82-; Pastor Flwshp Pres; BA Theology PR 80; B Ed PR State Police 70; Psych-Religion; Cnslr.

**ORTIZ JR, EFRAIN,** Inter Amer Univ Pr San Juan, Hato Rey, PR; SO; BA; Lit Esy Cntst Frnch Rvltn 90; Hnr Rl 90-; Arwys Sci Mgmt; Ar Trfc Cntrlr.**

**ORTIZ, ELSIE M,** Univ Of Pr At Rio Piedras, Rio Piedras, PR; JR; BS; Amrcn Chmcl Sct; Pre Med Stdnts Assoc; Hnr Rll; Chmstry; Med.

**ORTIZ, GRISEL,** Univ Of Pr Cayey Univ Coll, Cayey, PR; JR; BS; Med Sci Enclsr Smnry 90-; Chmstry Grp 90; Asst Vol Menoritas Hosp 90-; Hnr Stdnt 90-; Smr Rsrchr Tufts Med Schl Imnlgy Rsrchr; Gen Sci Pgm; Med Cr.

**ORTIZ, HENRY,** Univ Of New Haven, West Haven, CT; JR; Un Latin Stdnt Assc Sec 90; Eta Sgm Dlt 90-; CLAS 89-; Robert Bryd Schlrshp 88; Deans List 89; Htl/Rstrnt Admn; Htl Admn.

**ORTIZ, JAVIER R,** Inter Amer Univ Pr Hato Rey, Hato Rey, PR; FR; PHD; Tllr Tho Inter Metro 90-; Assn Ex Almns CROEM 89-; Phi Epsilon Chi 90-; Psychlgy.

**ORTIZ, JEANNETTE,** Inter Amer Univ Pr Hato Rey, Hato Rey, PR; SR; BA; Bus Admnstrtn/Mrktng; MBA.

**ORTIZ, JOEL,** Boston Univ, Boston, MA; SO; Deans Lst 88-; Bsns Admnstrtn.**

**ORTIZ, JOSE L,** Atlantic Comm Coll, Mays Landing, NJ; GD; AS; Marine Corps Reserve 85-89; Cmptr Infor Sys; Prgmg.

**ORTIZ, JOVITA,** Boricua Coll, New York, NY; SR; BS; Cert Am Lung Assn; Borinquen Plaza Sr Ctzn Ctr Vol; AA 90; Cert SCS Bus/Tech Inst Brooklyn NY 85; Hmn Serv.

**ORTIZ, JULIETTE G,** Fl International Univ, Miami, FL; JR; BS; Pi Theta Epsilon; Deans Lst 89-90; AA Miami Dade Comm Coll 86; Occptnl Therapist.

**ORTIZ, LOREEN M,** Atlantic Comm Coll, Mays Landing, NJ; SO; Prlgl; Law.

**ORTIZ, LUIS F,** Univ Of Pr Medical Sciences, San Juan, PR; GD; Clg Prof Entfermeria 84-; Clg Prof De La Enfermerie PR Tenny Olivo 84-; BSN U Inter-AM 84; Nrsng.

**ORTIZ, MAGDALISSE MONTENEGRO,** Catholic Univ Of Pr, Ponce, PR; JR; Vsl Arts; Educ.

**ORTIZ, MARCO A,** Univ Of Sc At Columbia, Columbia, SC; FR; BS; Gamma Beta Phi 90-; Cmptr Sci.

**ORTIZ, MARIEN,** Schenectady County Comm Coll, Schenectady, NY; FR; Fund Raisers; Hvn Schidy Schidy Orch Symphny; M,Gr Wmns Shoe Accssry Store; Bus.

**ORTIZ, MARILIZ,** Univ Of Pr At Rio Piedras, Rio Piedras, PR; JR; BS; Amer Chem Soc 89-; Golden Key 90-; USAA 90; Delta Phi Etha Treas 90-; Natural Sci Faculty 88-89; Hon Rl 89-90; Chem.**

**ORTIZ, MIGUEL R,** Univ Of Pr At Mayaguez, Mayaguez, PR; SO; BA; Poltcl Sci; Law.

**ORTIZ, MYRIAM A,** Ponce School Of Medicine, Ponce, PR; GD; MD; Stdnt Cncl Rep 90-; Amer Med Assc 88-; Damer Med Stdnt Assc 88-; BA Un PR 88; Medcn; Dr Medcn.**

**ORTIZ, NITZA IVETTE,** S U N Y Coll At Fredonia, Fredonia, NY; JR; BA; Span Clb 90-; Silver Cert 90; Deans Lst 90-; Span/Soc Wrk.

**ORTIZ, OMAIRA,** Bayamon Central Univ, Bayamon, PR; JR.

**ORTIZ, ONEIDA,** Univ Of Pr At Rio Piedras, Rio Piedras, PR; SO; Acad All Amer 90-; Natl Bus Hnr Soc 90-; Math; Acctng.

**ORTIZ, REISAMARI,** Univ Of Pr At Rio Piedras, Rio Piedras, PR; FR; Govt Offcr 90; Lbrry Clb 88; Sci Awrds 90; Chrch Cmps Fr Chldrn 88; Natl Hspnc Schlr Awrd Prog 90; Scl Scis; Psych.

**ORTIZ, ROBINSON I,** City Univ Of Ny City Coll, New York, NY; JR; Elem Educ; Tchr.

**ORTIZ, RUTH MARIE D,** Dickinson Coll, Carlisle, PA; FR; SGA 90-; Actvts Brd 90-; Scty Of Law And Jstce 90-; Alpha Phi Omega 90-; Pol Sci; Law.

**ORTIZ, SEAN P,** Savannah Coll Of Art & Design, Savannah, GA; FR; BA; Portfolio Schlrshp 90-; Grphc Dsgn; Advrtsng.

**ORTIZ, TERESA,** Evangelical Seminary Of P R, Hato Rey, PR; SO; MASTE; Circulo De Dietetica 77-78; Hon Stdnt Home Econ 75-78; Hon Stdnt Univ PR 74-78; Dietetic Intrnshps Vet Adm Hosp San Juan PR Dietetic Intern 78-79; Fund Theological Edn Inc Schlrshp; NCMLA Winner; Col Nutricionistas Dietistas 79-; Theological Studies; Pastor.

**ORTIZ, VANESSA,** Univ Of Pr Medical Sciences, San Juan, PR; GD; Amer Soc Clinical Pathologists 89-; Amer Soc For Microbiology; 7th Stdnt Forum For Scientific Research 90-; BS 88; Microbiology; Medicine.

**ORTIZ, WANDA I,** Dowling Coll, Oakdale Li, NY; GD; BA; Arep Stdnt Review Bd 90-; Translator & Interpreter For Dr Camilo Jose Cela Sumpo 91; Srum At Dowling Clg Nobel Prize Lit 89; Deans List 87-; Selected By Pres Of Coll To Rprsnt Stdnt Body Sat Mediterranean XIII Conf Spain; Sci; Law Integrated To Med Prof.

**ORTIZ, YVETTE M,** Columbia Union Coll, Takoma Park, MD; SR; AA/BA; Stdnt Gov Senator 90-; Pro Musica Pastor 90-; Theta Alpha Beta 87-89; Offc Admin; Music Prfmnce.

**ORTIZ-FOSTER, ARGELIS V,** Christopher Newport Coll, Newport News, VA; SR; BA; Intl Stdnt Assn VP 90; Spnsh Clb Liasn 90; Natl Blck Chld Dvlpmnt 89-90; AS Univ Panama 73; Spnsh; Tchng.

**ORTIZ-ORTIZ, MARIA E,** Univ Of Pr Humacao Univ Coll, Humacao, PR; JR; BA; Engl Stu Assoc Tres 88-89; Hnr Pro 90; Hnr Enrlmnt 89-; Acdmc Exclnc Certf; Hnr Enrlmnt 89-; Acdmc Exclncert; Engl; Phd.

**ORTIZ-ORTIZ, SONIA M,** Bayamon Central Univ, Bayamon, PR; FR; MBA; LPN Tomas O Ongay Bayamon 74; RN.

**ORTIZ-ROSA, LUIS,** Univ Of Pr Medical Sciences, San Juan, PR; GD; CERT; Magna Cum Laude BA 77; Ruerto Rico Psychlgst Assn; BA Univ PR 77; MA 83; Clncl Psyclgst; Grntlgy; Clncl Psychlgst.

**ORTNER, TAMMY L,** Columbus Coll Of Art & Design, Columbus, OH; SO; BA; Assoc 89; Cmmrcl Art; Illstrtn.

**ORTOLEVA, DEBORA M,** Univ Of Miami, Coral Gables, FL; SR; BBA; Intl Bsn Assoc 90-; Golden Key 90-; Beta Gamma Sigma; Dns Lst 88-; Provost Lst 88-; Sportsfest Co-Capt 90; Intl Finance/Mktg; Invstmnt Bnkg.**

**ORTON, JOLEIGH D,** Univ Of Sc At Coastal Carolina, Conway, SC; JR; BED; Educ Clb 89-90; Math Clb 90-; Math; Engr.

**ORTT, KATHRYN H,** Kent St Univ Kent Cmps, Kent, OH; SR; BBA; Delta Sigma Pi; Mgt/Mktng; Research.

**ORWAT, LYNETTE M,** Daemen Coll, Amherst, NY; SR; BS; Educ Clb V Pres 89-90; Educ Clb 88-89; Kids Day Vol 89-90; EPIC Vol 88; Elem Educ; Tchr.

**OSA-YANDE, TANALA B,** Morris Brown Coll, Atlanta, GA; JR; BA; Foreign Lang Clb VP 88-; Hnrs Clb Pres; Gldn Key; Phi Sigma Iota VP 90-; Socty 100 Blck Yth; Pres Schlrshp 88-; Carnegie Mellon Smr Pub P.cy Inst; Frnch/Intl Stds; Intrprtr.

**OSAGHAE, ANTHONY O,** Central St Univ, Wilberforce, OH; SO; BS; Acctng Club 90-; Hon Soc; MEHA; Deans List; Acctng; CPA.

**OSAKWE, LUCY V,** Howard Univ, Washington, DC; GD; JD; Blck Stdnt Law Soc; Intrntnl Law Soc; Rsrch Asst 90-; Amrcn Jrsprdnc Awd 90-; Deans Recntn Awd 90-; Intrntnl Law Admnstrtv Law 90-; BA BBA MBA Andrews Unv MI 83-88; Law.

**OSAMOR, EVA J,** Saint Thomas Univ, Miami, FL; SR; BA; Pltcl Actn Clb Sec 90-; Seagull 90-; Delta Phi Epsilon 90-; Msntry Wrd Lctr; Pltcl Sci; Law.

**OSAWA, AKEMI,** Elmira Coll, Elmira, NY; JR; BS; Intl Clb 88-; Internshp Japanese Co 90-; Econ.

**OSBORN, H LOUISE,** Columbia Greene Comm Coll, Hudson, NY; FR; AS; Nurs; RN.

**OSBORN, SANDRA K,** Memphis St Univ, Memphis, TN; JR; BBA; Baptist Stdnt Un Exec Cncl; Laubach Literacy Action Tutor; MIS; Consulting Tchncl Wrtng.

**OSBORNE, AMY E,** Ashland Comm Coll, Ashland, KY; FR; BS; Engr/Math; Civil.

**OSBORNE JR, CHARLES E,** Univ Of Akron, Akron, OH; SR; BS; Fncl Mgmt Assn Hrn Scty 90-; Gldn Key; Beta Gamma Sigma; Fnc.

**OSBORNE, CHRISTINE E,** Erie Comm Coll, Buffalo, NY; SO; AAS; Paralegal Clb 89-; Natl Hnr Soc; Phi Theta Kappa; Relgs Vol; Law Firm Intrnshp; Paralegal; Law.

**OSBORNE, DANA L,** Bellarmine Coll, Louisville, KY; JR; BA; Dorm Govt 88-89; Mock Trl Tm 89-90; Acctg Assn 90-; Deltqa Epsilon Sigma; Vol In Serv In Our Neighbrhd 88-89; Pres Schlrs 89-; Pres Schlrshp/Bellarmine 88-; Asst To Jeanne Baird-Shofner CPA; IM Vlybl; Acctg; CPA.

**OSBORNE, DONNA R,** Patrick Henry Comm Coll, Martinsville, VA; FR; Dean Lst 90-; Miss Patrick Co 90; Arbcs Ftnss Prog; Biol/Pre Med; Pdtrcs.

**OSBORNE, DORINDA A,** Saint Catharine Coll, St Catharine, KY; FR; Phi Theta Kappa; Math.

**OSBORNE, GRETA L,** Bridgewater Coll, Bridgewater, VA; JR; BA; Lambda Soc 89-; Alpha Chi 90-; Hstry.

**OSBORNE, IDA F,** Commonwealth Coll, Virginia Beach, VA; FR; BA; Busn Cl Pres 90; Stdnt Gov Dir 90; Ntnl Org/Wmn 90-; Phi Beta Lambda; Busn; Fince.

**OSBORNE, J A TERRY,** Va Commonwealth Univ, Richmond, VA; FR; BS; ROTC 90-; Phi Eta Sigma 90; Lambda Alpha Epsilon; VA Dfns Frc Mltry Police Stf Sgt 85-90; Amer Red Crs Instrctr 88-90; W End Vol Rescue Sqd Emer Med Tech 79-81; Cmmdntn Mdl VA Dept Mil Affrs 89; Admin Of Jstc; Law.

**OSBORNE, J ALLEN,** Belmont Coll, Nashville, TN; SR; BBA; Belmont Bus/Finance Assoc 90-; AMA 90-; Pinnacle Schlstc 90-; Blue Key 90-; Gamma Beta Phi 90-; Finance; Corp Fincl Mgmnt.

**OSBORNE, JAMES M,** Piedmont Tech Coll, Greenwood, SC; FR; Natl Hon Soc Pres 90-.

**OSBORNE, JOELLE E,** Marywood Coll, Scranton, PA; JR; BA; Chnnl 20 Nws Cmps Anchr 87-; WVMN 91.5 Radio Cmps DJ 88-; Chnnl 22 Intrnsp Various; Radio TV; Scriptwrtng.

**OSBORNE, KEVIN R,** West Liberty St Coll, West Liberty, WV; JR; BS; Delta Mu Delta; AAB Jefferson Tech Clg 88; Bus; Entrepreneur.

**OSBORNE, KIMBERLY D,** Univ Of Sc At Columbia, Columbia, SC; SR; BS; Phi Beta Kappa; Psi Chi 88-; Gldn Key 89-; Gamma Beta Phi 89-; Pres Lst 90-; Dns Lst 88-89; Schlrshp; Psychlgy; Ph D Psych.

**OSBORNE, LINDA C,** Radford Univ, Radford, VA; SO; MUBM; Pbtst Stu Unn 90-; Chmbr Orch; Sigma Alpha Iota 90-; Douglas May Mem Schlrshp; New River Vlly Sym Orch; Music; Tchng/Prfrmng.

**OSBORNE, LORI A,** Radford Univ, Radford, VA; JR; BS; Natl Stdnt Speech/Hearing Assoc 90-; Amer Spch/Hrng Assoc 90-; Goolsby Schlrshp; Cmctn Sci/Disorders; Speech Pathology.

**OSBORNE, MECHELLE L,** Patrick Henry Comm Coll, Martinsville, VA; FR; Comp Art Art Tchr Comp Anlysts.

**OSBORNE, NANCY E,** Middle Tn St Univ, Murfreesboro, TN; JR; BA; Cmptr Info Systms; Systms Anlyst.

**OSBORNE, SHAWN V,** Wallace St Comm Coll At Selma, Selma, AL; SO; Bus; Bnkng Admin/Govt Job.

**OSBORNE, SHIRLEY W,** Truett Mc Connell Coll, Cleveland, GA; JR; BA; Spec Ed/Psychlgy; Educ/Cnslng.

**OSBORNE, THEODORE C,** Bridgeport Engr Inst, Fairfield, CT; SR; BS; ASME 89-; AS Nrwlk St Tech Coll 84; Mech Eng.

**OSBORNE, TRACI LOUISE,** Spalding Univ, Louisville, KY; SR; BA; SGA 89-; Stdnt Actv Bd 89-; IM 89-; Busn Admin; Law.

**OSBORNE, WENDY W,** Pellissippi St Tech Comm Coll, Knoxville, TN; FR; BA; Hnr Role 90-; Bsns; CPA.

**OSBORNE, YOLUNDA F,** Alcorn St Univ, Lorman, MS; JR; Cmptr Sci/Math Clb; Most Dedicated Mem ASU Gospel Choir; Best Fndrsr ASU Gospel Choir; Cmptr Sci.

**OSBORNE-RYE, KENNETH A,** Morehouse Coll, Atlanta, GA; SO; BA; Natl Assn Of Blck Jrnlsts 88-; Atlnta Assn Of Blck Jrnlsts 88-; Mss Cmmnctns Clb 88-; Chcgo Assn Of Blck Jrnlsts; Sprts Intrn Cble Nws Ntwrk Atlnta; Sprts Intrn Atlnta 90; Mss Cmmnctns; Brdcst Mgmt Law.

**OSBY, CYNTHIA M,** Ms St Univ, Miss State, MS; SR; BBA; SAM 90; Blck Stdnt Cncl 89; Chrch Chr; Otstndng Coll Stdnts Of Amer 88-; Dns Schlr 90; SAM Tp 10 Nw Mmbr; Gen Bus Admin; Mrktng Bus Law Fnnce.

**OSCAR, CORLISS N G,** City Univ Of Ny Baruch Coll, New York, NY; SR; BBA; Soc Hmn Rsrc Mgmt VP 89-; Deans Lst 87-90; Mgmt; Hmn Rsrc Mgmt.

**OSEGUEDA, MAURICIO E,** Fl International Univ, Miami, FL; SR; BA; Pol Sci.**

**OSEI-TUTU, DOLOROSA,** Georgian Court Coll, Lakewood, NJ; SO; BS; Intl Clb Pres 89-; Cncl Exceptional Chldrn 89-; Business Clb 90-; Sigma Phi Sigma 90-; Pi Delta Phi 90-; Eucharistic Minister 89-; Vol Campus Ministry 89-; Business Admin; Corporate Law.

**OSGOOD, BRYAN A,** Me Maritime Academy, Castine, ME; SO; BS; Engineering.

**OSGOOD, CHRISTINA L,** Johnson St Coll, Johnson, VT; JR; Chesamore Hnrs Scty 89-; JSC Dist Serv Awd Winner 90-; Wrtng Dept Dist Serv Awd Winner 90-; BFA; Tchng.

**OSIAN, NELLIE W,** Univ Of Nc At Charlotte, Charlotte, NC; FR; BA; IM Vlybl/Bsktbl/Sftbl/Ftbl/Tennis; Phi Theta Sigma; Crmnl Justc; Law.

**OSINSKI, JEFFREY M,** Comm Coll Algny Co Algny Cmps, Pittsburgh, PA; SO; BA; Priv Pilot; Instr/Shodan Pennsylvania Karate; Acad Dormont PA; Altar Boy St Mary Magdalene Parish Homestead PA; Aeronavtics; Pilot.

**OSLE, HARRY C,** Nova Univ, Ft Lauderdale, FL; JR; MBA; Tstmstrs Intl 89-; Am Mgt Assn 89-; Deans List 84-85; FL Power/Light Co 85-; BBA 85; Bus; Hmn Rsrcs.

**OSMAN, MOINUL IM,** Northern Ky Univ, Highland Hts, KY; SR; Eng.

**OSMUNDSVAAG, BRITA,** Eckerd Coll, St Petersburg, FL; JR; BA; SAM 89-; Intnl Stdts Assoc 88-; Intl Hnr Scty Econ 90-; SAISA Wmns Coord Chr; Ford Scholar 90-; Sailing Capt 90-; Economics.

**OSORIO, HAYDEE S,** Univ Of Pr At Rio Piedras, Rio Piedras, PR; JR; BBA; Hnr Stdnts Pgm 89-; NCBM Awd 89-; All-Amer Awd 89-; Bsn Adm; Cmptr Info Syst.**

**OST, DEBORAH J,** Liberty Bible Coll, Pensacola, FL; SO; BA; Vlybl Coach 85-87; AA Acctng F P Ferrari Valladolid Spain 89; AA Bible 89; Missions.

**OST, JANA M,** Univ Of Al At Birmingham, Birmingham, AL; SR; Dorm Cncl Rep 86-87; Natl Cncl Tchrs Math; Nom Mortrs Brd Auburn Univ 89; Nom Natl Yth Ldrshp Cncl Wash D C 89; Pres Hnrs; Habitat For Humnty 91; Intrnshp Pelhm High Schl 91; Rec Alabama Comm Highr Educ Schlrshp 90-; BS; Math; Educ.

**OSTA, HEIDI MICHEL,** Tri County Tech Coll, Pendleton, SC; FR; BS; Cert Of Achvmnt Rly 90; Comp.

**OSTEEN, MARIE A,** Southeastern Coll Of Hlth Sci, N Miami Beach, FL; JR; BA; Phrmcy Schl; AA/HGH Hon Broward Comm Coll 89; Phrmcy.

**OSTER, TERRI E,** Univ Of South Fl, Tampa, FL; JR; BA; Stdnt Govt Supreme Ct Chf Jstce 89-; USF Ambassador 90-; Pres Clb 90-; Omicron Delta Kappa; Alpha Phi Sigma; Pi Gamma Nu; Delta Delta Delta; Gold Key; Sr Cls Com; Woman Of 90 Nwspr; Hon Stdnt; IM; Crmnlgy; Law.**

**OSTERBERGER, GLEN A,** Savannah Coll Of Art & Design, Savannah, GA; SR; BFA; Soc Of Illustrators 87-88; Illustration.

**OSTERGARD, KERRY M,** Indiana Univ Of Pa, Indiana, PA; SR; BS; Assoc Chldhd Ed Intrn 89-; PSEA 90-; Phi Sigma Pi 89-; Big Bro/Big Str 89-; Proj Stride 90-; Ele Educ; Tch.

**OSTERHAUS, TIMOTHY D,** King Coll, Bristol, TN; SO; BA; Stdnt Govt Assoc Parlmntrn 90-; Judcl Cncl 90-; Const Rev Comm 90-; Tchng Asst 90-; Vars Soccr 89-; Clncl Psych.

**OSTERHOUT, SHELLY A,** Nova Univ, Ft Lauderdale, FL; GD; MBA; Amer Bus Wmns Assn; Oprtns Cntrl Spclst 90-; BBA Nrthwd Inst 88; Mktg/Mgmt; Mgmt.

**OSTERMEIER, AUDRA A,** Villanova Univ, Villanova, PA; JR; BA; Villanovans For Jewish Awrns 88-; Villanova Env Grp 89-; Villanova Astro Soc 88-; Hist Hon Soc; Alpha Omicron Pi 90-; Hist; Tchr.

**OSTRANDER, PATRICIA A,** Marywood Coll, Scranton, PA; FR; BA; Elem Edctn; Tchr.

**OSTRANDER, ROBYN L,** Smith Coll, Northampton, MA; SO; BA; Outng Clb Eqpmnt Offcr 89-; Advsng Asst/Acdmc Rep 90-; Circus Clb 90-; Frst Grp Schlrs 89-; Serv Orgs 90-; Cncr Spprt Grp 90-; Deans Lst 89-; A E Hamm Awd 89-90; IM Indr Sccr 90-; Psychlgy/Neurosci; PHD/RSRCH.

**OSTRISHKO, ANATOLY,** Wilmington Coll, New Castle, DE; SR; BA; Wlmngtn Plce Dept Mdl Of Hnr; Crtcl Incdnt Strss Dbrfng Tm; Crmnl Jstce.

**OSTROM, DAWN M,** Boston Univ, Boston, MA; FR; BA; Stdnt Radio Nwscstr 90-; Ski Tm Sec 90-; Pltcl Sci/Brdcst Jrnlsm; Intl News Crrspndnt.

**OSTROM, JILL M,** Univ Of Miami, Coral Gables, FL; SR; BA; Hnrs Stdnt 87-; Lttl Sstr Sigma Alpha Mu Pres 88-90; Phi Kappa Phi 90; Gldn Key 90; Deans Lst; Prs Hnr Rll; Prvsts Hrn Rll; IM; Crmnl Jstc.

**OSTROOT, MARK C,** Savannah Coll Of Art & Design, Savannah, GA; FR; BFA; Photo Grp 90-; Bsebl 90-; Photography; Photojrnlsm.

**OSTROWSKI, JENNIFER A,** S U N Y Coll Of A & T Morrisvl, Morrisville, NY; SR; BA; Consrvtn Clb 89-; Chem Clb 89-90; Phi Theta Kappa 90-; NATURAL Rsrcs GPA Awd 89; Phi Theta Kappa Serv Clb 90-; Deans Pres Lsts 89-; Individual Stdes; Forrest Biologist.

**OSUMI, ANDRE N,** Univ Of Sc At Columbia, Columbia, SC; FR; Math Cmptr Sci; Tchr.

**OSVALD, SANTIAGO,** Univ Politecnica De Pr, Hato Rey, PR; JR; BA; Lion Clb Treas 87-90; Phi Delta Gamma 88-; Indl Eng.

**OSWALD, AMY D,** Univ Of Sc At Columbia, Columbia, SC; SR; BA; Dns Lst 88-; Pres Lst 90; Gldn Ky 90-; Phi Beta Kappa; Erly Chldhd Educ; Tchr.

**OSWALT, ALISA G,** Memphis St Univ, Memphis, TN; SO; BA; Hnrs Stdnt Assc Pres 90-; Frnds Untn Jpns Int Pres Fndr 90-; Stdnt Govt Assc Sec 90-; Rpblcns Sec 90-; Res Hll Assc; Alpha Lambda Delta; Gamma Beta Phi; Phi Eta Sigma; Mrch Dms Tm Capt 90-; Natl Cllgt Stu Govt Awrd 90; Delgt Awrd 90; Dean Lst 90; Mrktng; Intl Bus.

**OSWALT, TAMARA L,** Univ Of Ga, Athens, GA; SR; BSED; Bapt Stdnt Union 87-; SCEC; Dns Lst; Mntl Retardtn; Tch.

**OTALORA, JULIAN,** City Univ Of Ny Queensbrough, New York, NY; SO; BS; IEEE; Tau Alpha Pi; Deans List 90-; AAS; Electrical Engineering; Engineer.

**OTANO, SUZANA E,** Fl International Univ, Miami, FL; JR; BS; Soc Wmn Engrs; Alpha Omega Chi 89-; Schlrshp Amer Soc Plmbng Engrs; Mech Engr.

**OTCHET, FELICIA B,** Smith Coll, Northampton, MA; SR; Head Rsdnt 90-; Srvc Org At Smith Hse Rep 87-90; Gldy Key 88-; Sigma Xi 90-; Cum Laude; Psychlgy.

**OTE, YOSHINO,** Elmira Coll, Elmira, NY; SO; BS; Intl Clb 89-; Psychlgy.

**OTERO CARABALLO, GRISEL,** Univ Politecnica De Pr, Hato Rey, PR; Hghst Hnr Math Precalculus/Calculus/Englsh 90-91; Library Comm Prgrm Vlntr 90-; Chrty Spnsrshp Prgrm Sec 90-; Math Sci; Industrl Engnr.

**OTERO, LYDIA E,** Bayamon Central Univ, Bayamon, PR; SO; PR Army Ntl Grd Sgt 80-; Mgmt; Mgr.

**OTERO, MICHELLE,** Fl St Univ, Tallahassee, FL; JR; B ED; Neuman Club Catholic Campus Mnstry 88-; ALPHA Retreat Co Dir 88-89; Genesis Frshmn Ldrshp Soc 88; Phi Eta Sigma 89-; Golden Key 90-; FEA 90-; St Thomas More Choir Cathedral 90-; Elem Edn; Teach.

**OTERO, SANDRA S,** City Univ Of Ny La Guard Coll, Long Island Cty, NY; SR; AAS; Stdnt Rep Lag Co-Prep 88-; Phi Theta Kappa 90; Dns Lst 89-; Kings Hrbr Care Cntr; Mt Vernon Hosp; Untd Crbral Plsy Phy Thrpy Aide 82-; Sci; Psy Thrpy.

**OTHERSEN, MARGARET B,** Emory Univ, Atlanta, GA; SR; BSN; Hon Cncl Chmn 89-; Univ Senate Hlth Serv Stdnt Sub Com; Sigma Theta Tau 90-; Kappa Kappa Gamma Hse Chmn 87-90; Vrsty Vlybl 87-89; Nrsng.

**OTIENO, ROSE AKINYI,** Rust Coll, Holly Springs, MS; SO; Compuer Sci Clb; Intl Stdnts Assoc.

**OTIS, SHARON L,** Broward Comm Coll, Ft Lauderdale, FL; SR; AA; Pres Lst; Deans Lst; Grad High Hnrs; Business; Accounting/Cpa.**

**OTIS, VICTORIA L,** Newbury Coll, Brookline, MA; FR; AD; Stdnt Govt 90-; Thm Dnrs 90-; Htl Rstrnt Mgmt.

**OTS, JAN C,** Univ Of Al At Birmingham, Birmingham, AL; SR; BA; Gldn Ky 90-; All Amer Schlr 89; Snblt Hnr Rll 88-; Tnns 87-; Fnncl Mgmt; Scrty Anlyst.

**OTT, CASEY K,** Touro Coll, New York, NY; SR; Stdnt Govt Pres 90-; Pres Athltc Clb 89-90; Alpha Chi 90-; Deans Lst 88-; BS; Biolgy; MD.**

**OTT, JANET M,** Middle Tn St Univ, Murfreesboro, TN; SR; STEA 90-; Kappa Delta Pi; Elem Educ; Tchng.

**OTT, JENNIFIER MICHELLE,** Univ Of Sc At Columbia, Columbia, SC; FR; MBS; Univ Band; Chem; Phrmcy.

**OTT, JODI B,** Va Commonwealth Univ, Richmond, VA; SR; BSN; Stdnt Nurs Assoc 90-; Hnr Cncl Repr 89-; Deans List 90; Accptd Med Clg Of VA Hosp Intrnshp Med Resp Intnsv Care Unit; BA Biology Univ Of Tex 81-87; Nursing; Critical Care.

**OTT, LYNETTE J,** East Stroudsburg Univ, E Stroudsburg, PA; JR; BA; Omicron Delta Epsilon; Cb Sct Pck 105 Dn Ldr 88; Trp 105 Adlt Com Treas 85-; Econs.

**OTT, ROBERT A,** Bowie St Univ, Bowie, MD; Rocky Gorge Rgby Clb 89-; Salisbury St Univ Almn Clb 86-; Deans Lst 90; ROTC Schlrshp 1lt 84-86; Salisbury St Univ Rgby Clb Vp 82-86; Colesville Mns Clb 89-; BS Salisbury St Univ 86; Geo/Educ; DEA.

**OTT, STACY L,** Coll Of Charleston, Charleston, SC; SO; BA; Im Gymnstcs; Wtrskng Clb; Clmsn Jwsh Stdnt; Union Hillel Scrtry 89; Hnrs Prog; St Francis Hosp Vol 88-89; Intrnshp Rsrch Inc 89; Gymncstcs Sprvsr 90; BA; Engl; Bsnss/Cmmnctns.

**OTT, WARREN H,** Livingston Univ, Livingston, AL; FR; BS; Comp Sci; Comp Prgrmr.

**OTTAWAY, GAIL L,** Univ Of Cincinnati, Cincinnati, OH; SR; BSN; Nrsng.

**OTTEN, LAUREN M,** Univ Of Cincinnati, Cincinnati, OH; SO; BSN; Nrsg.

**OTTERNESS, TERESA M,** Christopher Newport Coll, Newport News, VA; SR; BA; Stdnt VA Educ Assoc 90-; Alpha Chi 90-; Peninsla Litrcy Cncl 89; Rotary Club Schrlshp 90-; Athlt Of The Wk 90; Varsity Vlybl 90; Mdl Lvl Educ Math; Tchr.

**OTTEY, KRISTA L,** Longwood Coll, Farmville, VA; JR; BS; Stdnt Union 89-; Earth Clb 90-; Psi Chi 90-; Deans Lst 90; Psychlgy.

**OTTEY, SANDRA A,** City Univ Of Ny Med Evers Coll, Brooklyn, NY; SR; BS; Cert Exclnc Acad Achvmnt 90; Deans List 88-90; Asstnt Acctnt Consolidated Edison Co NY Deprctn Statistcs Sectn 89-; Fin; Finc Anlyst/Cnsltnt.

**OTTINGER, MICHELLE Y,** Univ Of Sc At Columbia, Columbia, SC; JR; BA; Career Advsry Bd 89-90; Gamma Beta Phi; Alpha Phi Omega 86-90; Zeta Tau Alpha Pres 87-90; Alpha Phi Omega 86-90; Deans Lst 90; Stdnt Athltc Trnr 89-90; BS-BLGY Wofford Coll 90; Phrmcy.

**OTTMAN, CHRISTOPHER W,** Castleton St Coll, Castleton, VT; SO; BS; Glgcl Soc 90-; WIUV 89-90; Elect Tech 81-85; Prototype Tech 85-89; AAS Spartan Schl Aeronautics 80; Corp Cmmnctns; Doc Film Dir.

**OTTO JR, CHARLES F,** Univ Of Miami, Coral Gables, FL; JR; BA; Pre Lgl Scty 90-; Hnrs Stdnts Assoc 88-; Math.

**OTTO, JOHN D,** Mayland Comm Coll, Spruce Pine, NC; MBA; Cert 90; Eng/ Under Wtr Wldng.

**OTTS, MELISSA S,** Clarkson Univ, Potsdam, NY; JR; BS; Stdnt Orntatn Srvcs 88-; Soc Accntns 90-; Alpha Kappa Psi 90-; Stdnt Admsns Rep 90-; Phalanx Awd; Trst Schlrshp 88-; Hnry Schlrshp 88-; Accntng Finance.

**OTWELL, CHRISTINA A,** Salisbury St Univ, Salisbury, MD; SR; BS; Am Mktg Assoc 90-; Phi Beta Lambda 88-90; Bus Intrnshp 90; IM Vlybl 89; Bus Admin/Mktg.

**OTWELL, SHANA M,** Truett Mc Connell Coll, Cleveland, GA; SO; Basketball Scholarship 89-; Physical Therapy.

**OU-TIM, CHRISTOPHER J,** Birmingham Southern Coll, Birmingham, AL; JR; BA; Socco Clb V P 88-; Amnesty Intl 88; Pre Law Sec 90-; Chi Sigma Chi Rush Chrmn 89-90; Hstry/Pltcl Scif Law.

**OUDEKERK, DEBORAH J,** George Mason Univ, Fairfax, VA; SR; BA; Stu Tchg; BSED; Erly Chldhd Educ; Tchg.

**OUELLETTE, ADAM J,** Davis & Elkins Coll, Elkins, WV; SO; BA; Jennings Randolph Ldrshp Prog 89-; Vrsty Bsktbl 89-; Mngmnt/Mrktng; Law.

**OUELLETTE, DENISE M,** Western New England Coll, Springfield, MA; FR; BS; SWE 90-; Alpha Lambda Delta Sec 91-; Bioengrng.

**OUELLETTE, LYNEE,** Fl St Univ, Tallahassee, FL; JR; BS; St Judicial Brd Just 88-89; Stdnt Govt Rep 88-89; Goldn Key 90-; Sailng Clb 88-89; AA 90; Erly Chldhd Educ; Grad Schl/Tch.

**OUELLETTE, MATT J,** Merrimack Coll, North Andover, MA; FR; BA; Nu Phi Kappa; Elctcl Engrng; Engrng.

**OUELLETTE, MICHAEL C,** Teikyo Post Univ, Waterbury, CT; JR; BS; Deans List; Acctng; CPA.

**OUKA, PETER M,** Rust Coll, Holly Springs, MS; FR; BA; Stdnts Fr Entrprs VP; Intl Stdnts Assoc VP 90-; Prsdnts Lst 90-; Math Arntcl Eng.

**OUKROP, BENNY B,** Univ Of Louisville, Louisville, KY; SO; MES; Surveying 86-; Mech Engr.

**OURS, MELISSA R,** Davis & Elkins Coll, Elkins, WV; JR; BS; Stdnt Ed Assc 89-; Stdnt Advsry Cncl Retention; Hnrs Prgrm 90-; Elmntry Ed; Elmntry Tchr.

**OUSLEY, PAMI F,** Auburn Univ At Montgomery, Montgomery, AL; SO; BA; Phi Eta Sigma 89-; Elem Ed; Tchg.**

**OUTEN, NANCY M,** Univ Of Sc At Columbia, Columbia, SC; JR; BED; Gamma Beta Phi 90-; Goldn Key 90-; BA USC Lancaster 90; Psychlgy; Early Chldhd Ed.

**OUTERBRIDGE, VERSIE A,** Owensboro Comm Coll, Owensboro, KY; FR; BA; Nrsng Or Indstrl Mgmt; Nrsng Or Mgmt.

**OUTIN, MICHAELLE J,** Univ Of North Fl, Jacksonville, FL; SR; BA; Phi Theta Kappa Sec 87-; Natl Cllgte Mnrty Ldrshp Awrd; US Achvmnt Acad Awrd; AA St Johns River Comm Coll 88; Elem Educ; Tchng.

**OUTING, TAMMIE J,** Albany St Coll, Albany, GA; SR; BS; Bnd 87-89f Crmnl Jstc Clb 90-; Stdnt Govt 86-87; Chrch Wom Sec 90-; Yth Serv Pres 86-88; Dghty Cnty Jvnl Crt/Intrn Prob Offcr; Crmnl Jstc; Invstgtn/Law Enfrcmnt.

**OUTING, WANDA T,** Howard Univ, Washington, DC; SO; BA; Archit Intern Develop Corp Col Hts; Indstrl Eng Intern Ortho Pharm Corp 89-; Architecture.

**OUTLAND-GENELLE, WANDA E,** Catawba Valley Comm Coll, Hickory, NC; FR; Cmmty Clg Schlrshp; Cochrane Furniture Persl Dept; Computer Prog.

**OUTLAW, DEV,** Univ Of Pa, Philadelphia, PA; JR; BBA; Wharton Schl Deans Lst 90; Amer Mgmt Assn 90-; Fclty Mgr Advncd Envrnmntl Tech Corp 81-; Emerg Rspns/Fire Fghtng Burlington Cnty Fire Schl 88-89; Bus Admin/Mgmt; Envrnmntl Sci.

**OUTLAW, EDWARD M,** Central St Univ, Wilberforce, OH; SO; BS; Biolgcl Soc Pre Prof Hlth Soc 90-; Biology/Pre Med; Orthopedic Surg.

**OUWENGA, JULIE A,** The Kings Coll, Briarclf Mnr, NY; FR; BS; Tourney Vlybl; Bio.

**OUYANG, LEYIN,** Glassboro St Coll, Glassboro, NJ; SR; Pres List Del Co Comm Coll 86-88; Cert 90; Law.**

**OVERBECK, STEPHANIE A,** Univ Of Al At Birmingham, Birmingham, AL; SO; Psychlgy; Fmly Thrpy.

**OVERBEE, TAMELA L,** Lexington Comm Coll, Lexington, KY; FR.

**OVERBEEKE, MARIE M,** Springfield Tech Comm Coll, Springfield, MA; FR; AS; CDA Springfield Tech Comm Coll 90; Dntl Hygiene.

**OVERBERGER, BETH M,** Indiana Univ Of Pa, Indiana, PA; JR; BA; Delta Gamma VP; Elem Ed; Tchr.

**OVERBEY, JACQUELINE L,** Univ Of Tn At Martin, Martin, TN; SR; MED; Stu Govt Assoc 87-88; Stu Tenn Educ Assoc 88-; Ftbl Hsts 88-; Chi Omega Sng/Sprt Chrmn 88-; Delta Kappa Gamma Intl Schlrshp 89; Miss Tenn Schlrshp 88; Spcl Olympcs 88-; BED; Elem Ed.

**OVERBEY, MELANIE R,** Univ Of West Fl, Pensacola, FL; JR; BA; Pensacola Jr Clg 89-90; Comm Tech 84-89; AA Pensacola Jr Clg 89-90; Educ; K-6 Tchr.

**OVERBY, ARNOLD D,** Va Commonwealth Univ, Richmond, VA; SO; BA; Phlsphy/Rlgn; Prfsr.

**OVERBY, GINA L,** Va Commonwealth Univ, Richmond, VA; SO; BA; Phi Eta Sigma 90-; Bus; Mgmt/Admin.

**OVERBY, JASON S,** Univ Of Tn At Martin, Martin, TN; JR; BS; ACS 88-; Clg Rpglcns Pblcty Chrmn 88-; Phi Eta Sigma Prsdnt 90-; Phi Kappa Phi; Mu Epsilon Delta Pldg Mstr 88-; Phi Eta Sigma TA 90-; Chemistry Pltcl Sci; Prfsr.

**OVERGAARD, NANCY K,** Gordon Conwell Theol Sem, S Hamilton, MA; GD; MDIV; Cum Laude 88; For Rel Intrn U S Sen 88; State Dept Embsy Intrn 89; Alan Emory Schlrshp Awd 90; Pol Conv 86-87; Elder Pres Chrch; MA Tufts Univ 90; BA Univ Minn 88; Theo.

**OVERHOLT, MICHAEL L,** Oh St Univ, Columbus, OH; JR; BS; Phi Eta Sigma 88-; Alpha Lambda Delta 88-; Phrmcy Intrnshp 90; Bsktbl 88-89; Phrmcy.**

**OVERHOLTZER, KAREN L,** Franklin And Marshall Coll, Lancaster, PA; FR; BA; Rugby Club 90-; Bio/Chem; Marine Bio.

**OVERLAY, CHARLES J,** Bethel Coll, Mckenzie, TN; FR; BS; Busn Club; Psychology; Counselor.

**OVERMAN, CAROL L,** East Carolina Univ, Greenville, NC; SR; BFA; Indust Arts Clb Sec 89; Hse Cncl Mem 90-; Intrvrsty Chrstn Flwshp 90-; Phi Kappa Phi; Intrvrsty Sprts 87-88; Txtl Dsgn; Art Ed.

**OVERMIER, BECKY LYNN,** Bowling Green St Univ, Bowling Green, OH; FR; BA; Am Inst Archit Stdnts; Phi Eta Sigma; Archit/Envrnmntl Dsgn.

**OVERTON, CHERYL A,** Longwood Coll, Farmville, VA; JR; BA; Drl Tm; Show Choir; Pi Delta Phi Pres; Book Awd 90-; Mdrn Lang/Frnch.

**OVERTON, JEAN K,** Vance Granville Comm Coll, Henderson, NC; FR; AAS; Phi Theta Kappa; N Granville Jaycees Sec 85-86; Dns Lst; Spoke Of The Year Awd N Granvl Jaycees 86; Outstdng Yng Wmn Of Amer 87; Flat Rock United Meth Chrch; NFIB; US Chmbr Of Comm; Intl Inst Mncpl Clrks; Bus Admin.

**OVERTON, MARTI L,** Roane St Comm Coll, Harriman, TN; SO; BS; Elem Ed.

**OVERTON, REHAN D,** Bennett Coll, Greensboro, NC; JR; BA; WICI Mbr 90-; Nwspr Asst Ed Rptr 89-; Judcry Comm 90-; Hnr Soc Rptr 90-; Symph Orch Pub Rel Intrn 90-; TV Promtn Intrn 90-; Comm; Pub Rel.

**OVERTON, SUSAN FAITH,** Columbia Greene Comm Coll, Hudson, NY; FR; BA; Phi Theta Kappa; Sigma Delta Mu; Elem Educ/Lang; Tchng.

**OVERTON, THOMAS R,** Cornell Univ Statutory College, Ithaca, NY; SR; MS; Dairy Hend Mgmnt Flwshp 89-; Acad Integrity Bd 90; Sprt Teach Com 90; Deans Lst; Alpha Gamma Rho VP 88-; Army ROTC Schlrshp 88-; Cmsnd 2nd Lt US Army; Univ IL Rsrch Asstntshp; Teach Asst; BS; Anml Sci; Profr Ruminant Nutrition.

**OVERTON, TWYANDA C,** Springfield Tech Comm Coll, Springfield, MA; SO; BA; Key Clb 87-88; AWARE 87-88; Trck/Fld 86-88; CVS Phrmcy Tech 90-; Phrmcy.

**OVIASOGIE, ALPHONSUS O,** Daemen Coll, Amherst, NY; JR; BA; Hsng Cmt Rsdnt; Asstnt; Pi Gamma Mu 90-; Rosicrucian Order AMORC 6th Degree 88-; Crisis Svcs Phone Cnslr 90-; Rcgntn Awrd; Deans List 90-; Bsktbl 88-; Psychlgy; Clncl Psychlgy.

**OVIASOGIE, DORCAS ESE,** Jackson St Univ, Jackson, MS; GD; MBA; Fin Assc Hstrn 89-; Afrc Dstdnt Assc 88-; Deans List Schlr 88-; BS; Fin; Rltr.

**OWEN, AMANDA V,** Union Inst, Cincinnati, OH; SR; BA; Philadelphia Astrlgcl Soc Pres 87-90; Scl Wrkr Astrlgr; Psychology.

**OWEN, BRADLEY,** Atlantic Union Coll, S Lancaster, MA; SR; MS; Amer Allnc For Hlth Physc 88-; Educ Rec/Dance; PE Clb Pres 89-90; Natl Awd US Achvmnt Acad 89-90; Bsktbl Trnr 90-; BS PE; AS Ftns Mgmt; Hlth Fitness.

**OWEN, DINAH BARKOWSKY,** Univ Of Sc At Aiken, Aiken, SC; FR; ADN; Outstndg Schlstc Achvmnt Awd; Pres Hnr Rl 90; Nrsg Tech; Nrsg.

**OWEN, DONNA M,** Tri County Tech Coll, Pendleton, SC; SO; AS; Phi Theta Kappa 90-; Qlty Technen 73-; Textile Mgmt; Qlty Assur Engr.

**OWEN, ERIC S,** Asbury Theological Sem, Wilmore, KY; GD; MA; Theta Phi 89-; Amer Acdmy Physcns Assts 81-; Physcns Asst 81-83 85-87; BS Chem GA Inst Technlgy 78; BS Physcn Asst Med Coll Of GA 80; Wrld Mssns/Evnglsm; Mssnry.

**OWEN, JAMES C,** Univ Of Miami, Coral Gables, FL; FR; BA; Sngrs 90-; H K Stanford Schlrshp; Music Schlrshp; Studio Music/Jazz Vocal; Music Prfrmnc/Rcrdng.

**OWEN, JAMES M,** Univ Of Nc At Asheville, Asheville, NC; SR; BS; Amer Mtrlgcl Soc 87-; Untd Mthdst Clb Pres 87-89; Hbt Hmnty 89-; Mtrlgy Intrn 89-90; Natl Clmtc Data Ctr Met Intrn 89-91; Mtrlgy Lab Asst 89-90; Wthr Frcstng; T V Wthr Frcstng.

**OWEN, JEFFERY C,** Wv Northern Comm Coll, Wheeling, WV; FR; AD; Stdnt Cncl Rep Next Semester; Phi Theta Kappa; Prsdnt Lst; Hnrs Clg Comp II; Lcl 438 Indstrl Pntrs Union 87; Nrsng; RN.

**OWEN, JIM D,** Ms St Univ, Miss State, MS; JR; BS; Gamma Beta Phi 88-89; Beta Beta Beta 90-; Phi Delta Theta Schlrshp Chrmn 89-; Rsrch Asst 90-; Microbiolgy; Grad Schl/PhD.

**OWEN JR, JOHN W,** Belmont Coll, Nashville, TN; JR; BA; Gamma Beta Phi Pres 88-; CMS VP 88-89; Yth Mnstry Itrn Blmnt Chrch Bthl Chpl 90; IM Prgmg; Religion; Mnstry.

**OWEN, KENT H,** Northern Ky Univ, Highland Hts, KY; SO; BA; Dns Lst 89-; Acctg; CPA.

**OWEN, LAURA M,** Vance Granville Comm Coll, Henderson, NC; FR; AAS; Photon Clb Rdlgy Clb 90-; NC Soc Rdlgc Tchnlgy 90-; Phi Theta Kappa 90-; Red Cls Spcl Olympcs 89; Deans Lst 90-; AA Peace Clg Raleigh 89; Rdlgc Tchnlgy; Nclr Med.

**OWEN, MARY L,** Queens Coll, Charlotte, NC; JR; BA; Clge Un Brd Dir Pres; Clge Un Brd Dir Rlgs Lf Chr 90-; Admsns Core 89-; Mrtrbrd; Stdy Tr Great Britian; Internshp Orthopaedic Hosp Charlotte 90; Bsn Admin.

**OWEN, RANDALL SCOTT,** Emory Univ, Atlanta, GA; SR; BBA; Beta Gamma Sigma; Acad All Am; Ntl Bus Hon Soc; Bus.

**OWEN, REGINA L,** Univ Of Sc At Columbia, Columbia, SC; SR; BS; Crlna Hosp Soc Sec 89-; Clb Mgr Assc Am 89-; Dns Lst 90-; Htl/Rstrnt/Trsm Adm; Sls Fd Svc Co.

**OWEN, ROBERT H,** Univ Of Nc At Charlotte, Charlotte, NC; SO; BA; H S Beta Club Vp 89; Kappa Sigma; IM Bsktbl Ftbl Vlybl Water Polo Sftbl 89-; English; Law.

**OWEN, TERRY L,** Univ Of Akron, Akron, OH; SO; BA; Amer Soc Mech Engrs 89-; Stdnt Auto Engr 90-; Ganyard Schlrshp 89; Optmst Clb Schlrshjp; Engr Schlrshp; Mech Engr; Engr Med.

**OWEN JR, THOMAS G,** Univ Of Md At College Park, College Park, MD; FR; Trrpn Gaming Clb 90-; Alpha Lambda Delta; Cmptr Sci.

**OWEN-PEER, WILLIAM D,** Hudson Valley Comm Coll, Troy, NY; FR; MBA; Physic; Eng.

**OWENBY, TONIA A,** Limestone Coll, Gaffney, SC; JR; BS; Acctg Asst TW Servs Inc Spartanbrg SC; AA Acctg Spartanbrg Tech Clg 88; Bsns.

**OWENS, ANGELA D,** Lincoln Univ, Lincoln Univ, PA; SR; Sch Newspaper Copy Ed 88-89; Gospel Ensmbl 88-89; Res Advsr 89-91; All Amer Schlr; NAACP 87-; Intern John Hopkins Hosp 88-89; BS; Sclgy Hmn Svcs; Psych Scl Wrkr.**

**OWENS, ANGIE,** Southwest Va Comm Coll, Richlands, VA; FR; MBA; Phi Theta Kappa; Educ; Elem Educ.

**OWENS, ANN M,** Wv Univ At Parkersburg, Parkersburg, WV; FR; Educ; Teaching.

**OWENS, CARLISA S,** Memphis St Univ, Memphis, TN; SO; BA; Res Hall Cncl Sec 89-; Inroads 89-; Intrnshp Bapt S S Bd 89-; Bus; Acctng.

**OWENS, CYNDI L,** Oh Univ-Southern Cmps, Ironton, OH; SR; Hnds Of Praise 88-90; Dvtnl Grps 88-90; Elem Ed; Tch.

**OWENS, DANA L,** Liberty Univ, Lynchburg, VA; JR; BS; Lib Assn Chrstn Tchrs 89; Ythquest 88-89; Elem Edn; Non Teach Role Chldrn.

**OWENS, DANA R,** Univ Of Al At Birmingham, Birmingham, AL; SR; MBA; Kappa Kappa Gamma; Pres Hnr 91; BS/CERT Auburn Univ 91; Elem Ed; Tchr/Dodds W Germany.

**OWENS, DEBRA A,** City Univ Of Ny Med Evers Coll, Brooklyn, NY; JR; BS; Stdnt Govt Treas; Soc Advncmnt Mgt VP 90-; MEC Peer Advsng Advsr; Pblc Acctg.

**OWENS, DOLORES L,** Glassboro St Coll, Glassboro, NJ; SR; BA; Paralegal; AAS 88; Commctns; Law Schl.

**OWENS, DONNA JEAN,** Wilmington Coll, New Castle, DE; SR; Deans List 90-.

**OWENS III, EDDIE L,** Daytona Beach Comm Coll, Daytona Beach, FL; FR; AA; Art; Cmptr Grphc Arts.

**OWENS, ELIZABETH G,** Ms St Univ, Miss State, MS; FR; Angel Flight 90-; Bulldog Hostess Recruit Tm 90-; Phi Eta Sigma 90-; Hns Pgm 90-; Delta Delta Delta Corr Secr 90-; Compass Clb 90-.

**OWENS, ERIC W,** Univ Of Md At College Park, College Park, MD; FR; BA; Cmmnctns; Advrtsng Mrktng.

**OWENS JR, G STANLEY,** Univ Of North Fl, Jacksonville, FL; JR; BED; Gldn Key 89-; Kappa Delta Pi; Scty Auto Eng 78-; 4 H Ldr: Advsry Brd Crhmn 81-; Advsry Brd FL Cmmty Coll 76-81; Dstrc Srvc Mgr Trnng Mgr Auto Mfg 71-; AA FL Junior Coll 81; Vctnl Ed; Auto Indsltrl Voc Ed.

**OWENS, JASON,** Johnson C Smith Univ, Charlotte, NC; SO; BA; Phi Beta Sigma Secr; WBTV Chnl 3 Intern; Cmnctns; News Anchor.

**OWENS, JENNIFER A,** Union Coll, Barbourville, KY; FR; BED; Ed; Tchr.

**OWENS, KAREN M,** Saint Francis Coll, Loretto, PA; SR; BS; Educ Clb 89-; Hnr Soc; Amer Legion Ladies Aux 89-; Elem Educ; Tchr.

**OWENS, KATINA D,** Univ Of Southern Ms, Hattiesburg, MS; FR; BA; Afro/Am Stdnt Org 90-; Gamma Beta Phi; Cmptr Sci; Data Proc.

**OWENS, KELLY A,** Salisbury St Univ, Salisbury, MD; SR; BS; Ntl Assn Acctnts 87-; Delta Mu Delta; Perdue Farms Inc Credit Anlyst 90-; Acctg; FDIC Bnk Exmnr.

**OWENS, LA RHONDA R,** Tougaloo Coll, Tougaloo, MS; JR; BA; English Club Alpha Challenbe Tm 90-; Army Reserve Officers Trng Corp; VP Scholor 88-; IM Bskbl Tm 89-; English Liter; Lawyer Of US Army.**

**OWENS, MARK A,** Coll Of Charleston, Charleston, SC; JR; BA; Accntg Assc; Accntg.

**OWENS, MARK T,** Emory & Henry Coll, Emory, VA; SR; Sigma Mu 90-; Snavely Schlrshp; Clinard Schlrshp; Emory Schlrshp; Lucille Webb Schlrshp; AAS Wytheville Cmnty Clg 89; Engl Lit; Clg Tchr.

**OWENS, MICHELLE S,** Tn Tech Univ, Cookeville, TN; FR; BS; Int Vars Chrstn Flwshp Co-Ldr; Std Ornttn Ldr; Std Admssns Rep; Cir K Intl; St/Rgnl Hnrs Conf; Dns Lst 90-; Acctng.

**OWENS, NICOLE M,** Univ Of Fl, Gainesville, FL; SR; BS; Soc Hmn Rsrce Mgmt VP; Classcl Hon 89-90; Wlt Dsny Wrld Coll Prog 90; AA 89; Mgmt; Bus Admin/Hmn Rsrces.

**OWENS, NICOLE O,** City Univ Of Ny City Coll, New York, NY; GD; BA; Psychlgy; Child Psychlgst.

**OWENS, PAMELA,** Fort Valley St Coll, Fort Valley, GA; FR; BS; Agric Econ Clb; Agric Econ; Exten Agnt.

**OWENS, RACHEL L,** Hudson Valley Comm Coll, Troy, NY; SO; AA; Psych.

**OWENS, REBECCA A,** Christian Brothers Univ, Memphis, TN; JR; BA; Wmns Assn Motivate Sprt VP 90-; Soc Cllgt Jrnlsts; Tau Kappa Epsilon Ltl Sis; NY Times Intrnshp; Amer Heart Assn Intrn; Cmnctn Arts; Pblc Rltns.

**OWENS, REBECCA S,** Lexington Comm Coll, Lexington, KY; FR; AS; Dental/Med; Dental Hygne.

**OWENS JR, ROBERT C,** Mercer Univ Schl Of Pharm, Atlanta, GA; FR; PHD; Amer Soc Hosp Pharmcsts 90-; Acad Stdnts Phrmcy 90-; Kappa Psi; Pi Kappa Phi Soc Chrmn 86-; Phrmcy; Clin Phrmcy.

**OWENS, SHONDA D,** Al A & M Univ, Normal, AL; SO; BS; SGA 90-; Bsn; Fnce.

**OWENS, SUSANNA S,** Va Commonwealth Univ, Richmond, VA; SR; BS; Psi Chi 90; Golden Key 90; Stdnt Afflte Amer Psych Assoc; Psych; MS.

**OWENS, TAMMY R,** Rust Coll, Holly Springs, MS; JR; Socl Wrk Clb 89-; Alpha Kappa Mu; Hnr Trck Std; Dns Lst 89-; Delta Sigma Theta; Tennis 90-; Scl Wrk; Cnslr.

**OWENS, WENDELL R,** Mayland Comm Coll, Spruce Pine, NC; FR; BA; Indstrl Art; Eng.

**OWENS JR, WILLIAM C,** Birmingham Southern Coll, Birmingham, AL; JR; BA; Phi Eta Sigma 89; Alpha Lambda Delta 89; Mathematics; Actuary.

**OWENSBY, AMY JEREE,** Lenoir Rhyne Coll, Hickory, NC; SR; BA; Psych Scl Clb 89-90; Engl Clb 89-90; Mu Sigma Epsilon 90; Sr Hnr Thesis 90; Psych Intrnshp Ten Broeck Hosp 90; Psychlgy; MA Clncl Psychlgy.

**OWENSBY, JONIA V,** Wilberforce Univ, Wilberforce, OH; SR; BS; Ntl Soc Blk Eng 88-90; Alpha Kappa Alpha Prlmntrn 90-; Rsrch; Math/Comp Sci; Syst Eng.

**OWENSBY, KATRINA ANNETTE,** Clark Atlanta Univ, Atlanta, GA; SO; MBA; Fnnce Clb; Univ Hnrs Prog 89-; Otrch Prog 90; E L Simon Schlrshp 90; Univ Schlrshp; Lions Clb Schlrshp; Atlnta Mtrpltn Schlrshp 90-; Acctng; CPA.

**OWNBEY, CAROL J,** Piedmont Tech Coll, Greenwood, SC; GD; RRT; Tutr 88-90; S Schl Clss Pres 88-90; NYTHS 89-90; Ldr Shp Retrt 89; CRTT 90; Amer Assn Resp Care 89-; Resp Therpy Tech 90-.

**OWNBY, BENJAMIN S,** Pellissippi St Tech Comm Coll, Knoxville, TN; SO; BS; Phi Theta Kappa 89-; Math/Sci; Mech Eng.**

**OWNBY, LISA L,** George Mason Univ, Fairfax, VA; SR; BS; Gldn Key; Alpha Chi; Intrn Wdbrdg Nrsg Cntr 89-90; Intrn Intl Assoc Dvlpmntl Dsblty Cncls 90-; AS 89; Scl Wrk.

**OWOSO, TAIWO F,** Tuskegee Univ, Tuskegee Inst, AL; SR; BED; Extnsn Tchncl Ectn.

**OWSLEY, LAURA L,** Georgetown Coll, Georgetown, KY; JR; BS; Govt Assoc Parlmntrn 89-90; Eta Delta Phi 90-; Alpha Lambda Delta 88-; Phi Beta Lambda Parlmntrn 90-; Intrnshp Georgetwn Bnk Trst Co Loan Dept Int 90; Intrnshp E-Town UK Sml Bsns Dev Ctr; Anncr Vllybl 90-; Anncr Bsktbl 89-; Marktng/Fin; Bnkng/Mgmt.

**OXENDINE, JENNIFER L,** Neumann Coll, Aston, PA; JR; BA; Psychlgy Clb 90-; Nwspr; Prisn Flwshp Mnstrs 89-; Deans Lst 89-; Coop Edn Adult Care; Aston Jaycees Comm/Sch Invlvmnt Personal Integrity 88; Psychlgy; Soc Wrk.

**OXFORD, ANGELA K,** Brevard Coll, Brevard, NC; SO; BS; Spnsh Clb 90-; Athltc Trnr Bsktbl Tm 89-; Sprts Med; Athltc Trng.

**OXFORD, IKE T,** Savannah Coll Of Art & Design, Savannah, GA; FR; BFA; First Bapt Chrch Yth Grp 90-; Dns Lst 90-; Illustration.

**OXLEY, GEORGE R,** Norfolk St Univ, Norfolk, VA; SR; BS; Alpha Kappa Mu; U S Navy 97-88; AA Univ Central Fla 78; Biology; Sec Educ.

**OXNARD, BARBARA A,** Kent St Univ Kent Cmps, Kent, OH; SR; Stdnt Med Assoc 88-; Biology Clb 89-90; Gldn Key; Biology; Med.

**OYEDIRAN, OYENIYI A,** Wilberforce Univ, Wilberforce, OH; SO; BA; Blk Ed Entrprs VP; Cmptr Info Sys.

**OYELARAN, ADEDOYIN A,** Morehouse Coll, Atlanta, GA; FR; BS; Chess Clb 90-; NSBE 90-; INROADS 89-; Kodak Schlrshp Awrdee Schlr; GM Schlrshp; Inrds Schlr 89-; Spr Comp Rltd Rsrch 90; IBM Intrn; Asst Pstn; Physcs Elec Eng Math; Eng Comp Dsgng.

**OYER, JENNIFER M,** S U N Y Coll At Geneseo, Geneseo, NY; FR; BA; Wnd Ensmbl 90-; Deans Lst 90-; Engl/Frnch; Tchng.

**OYSTER, MICHAEL D,** Univ Of Akron, Akron, OH; SO; BS; Mrchng Bnd; Amrcn Soc Mchncl Engnrs; Mchncl Engnrng.

**OZ, SHLOMIT J,** Univ Of Miami, Coral Gables, FL; SR; MBA; Org Jewsh Stdnts Scl Chr 88-; Mahoney Pgm Cncl Scl Chr 88-; Phi Sigma Tau 89-; Master Tutor 89-; Bowman-Ashe Schlrshp 88-; Stanford Schlrshp 88-; Regents Schlrshp 87-; Aerobics Instr 88-; BA; Hist; Law.

**OZDAMAR, AYSE C,** Southeastern Coll Of Hlth Sci, N Miami Beach, FL; GD; BS; Kappa Epsilon Soc Chrmn 89-; BS Hucettepe Univ Turkey 78; Phar; Pharm D.

**OZMENT, SONYA A,** Univ Of Nc At Greensboro, Greensboro, NC; JR; BA; Elem Ed/Hstry; Tchg.

**OZUZU, ONYEKWERE P,** Fl St Univ, Tallahassee, FL; JR; BA; Orchesis Modern Dnc Co; Eigh Days Of Dance; Hnrs English Dept; Golden Key; English/Economics; PHD English/Clg Prof.

# P

**P POOL, JASON R,** Western Ky Univ, Bowling Green, KY; SO; BA; Blck And Brdle Clb Almni Sec 89-; Ag Educ Clb Rprtr 89-; Natl Voc Ag Tchrs Assn 89-; Ag Dept Otstndng Soph; Lil Nrth Amer Sprtsmnshp Awrd; Lil Nrth Amer Hrdsmn Awrd; Anml Sci Ag Educ; Tchng Rsrch.**

**PAAR, NADINE,** Glassboro St Coll, Glassboro, NJ; FR; BA; Glsboro Chrstn Flwshp; AROH Fndtn Chrmn; YDI; Grdn St Dist Schlr; Psych; Adlscnt.

**PABIS, DENNIS J,** Philadelphia Coll Pharm & Sci, Philadelphia, PA; SR; BS; Acdmy Stdnts Pharmacy 87-; Interfraternity Cncl Repr 88-; Phi Delta Chi Alumni Liaison 87-; Drug Abuse Educ Comm 88-89; Deans Lst 90-; CVS Schlrshp 90; Rifle 86-87; Pharmacy.

**PABLO, RIVERA VALE,** Inter Amer Univ Pr Aquadilla, Aguadilla, PR; SO; BA; Biol/Pre Med; Med.

**PABON, AIDA I,** Univ Of P R Bayamon Tech Univ, Bayamon, PR; FR; Grl Scts 90-; Natl Hspnc Schlr Awds Pgm Smfnlst 90; Indstrl Engrg; Engr/Law.

**PABON, JAMES OWEN,** Suffolk Comm Coll Selden Cmps, Selden, NY; SO; BFA; Pi Alpha Sigma 89-; Otsdng Mnrty Clg Stdnt; AA; Photo; Photo Jrnlst/Photogrphr.

**PACCHINO, CARMINE E,** Oh Dominican Coll, Columbus, OH; SR; BA; Coll Choir Pres 87-; Radio St Gen Mgr 88-; Kappa Gamma Pi; Delta Epsilon Sigma; Music Ldrshp Awrd 88-90; Chld Wrtng Awrd 90; CLIO Awrd Excl Hstry; OH Ctzn Actn; Hstry; Law.

**PACE HOWARD, SHERRIE LYNN,** Univ Of Nc At Greensboro, Greensboro, NC; SR; BSHES; Prnt-Tchr Assoc 87-; Gamma Sigma Sigma; Turrentine Schlrshp Awd; Asst Youth Bsbl Coach 90-; Sls Asst Regent Lghtg Corp 88-; Hmn/Envrnmnt Sci-Psy.

**PACE, BRANDON L,** Christopher Newport Coll, Newport News, VA; SO; Biology; Pharm.

**PACE, CHRISTOPHER S,** Univ Of Southern Ms, Hattiesburg, MS; FR; BA; Student Eagle Club; HSA Hnr Students Assoc; Speech Commtns; Law.

**PACE, CRAIG C,** Winthrop Coll, Rock Hill, SC; SO; Econ Clb 90-; Alpha Kappa Psi; Econ; Govt Self Employeed.

**PACE, KELLY R,** Va Commonwealth Univ, Richmond, VA; JR; BAMBA; Stdnt Educ Assc 89-; Golden Key 90-; Philip Morris Schlrshp 90-; Engl/Educ; Elem Tchr.

**PACE, LIANA T,** Coker Coll, Hartsville, SC; SO; BA; Stdnt Govt VP 89-90; Singers 90; Christians Helping Others 89-90; Commissioners 90-; Top 10 Class 90-; Math; Professor.

**PACE, MELANIE D,** Western Piedmont Comm Coll, Morganton, NC; FR; Int Desgn Clb; Int Desgn; Desgnr.

**PACE, NATALIE D,** Clayton St Coll, Morrow, GA; JR; BA; Pol Sci; Law.

**PACE, PAMELA J,** Univ Of South Fl, Tampa, FL; GD; MSN; Stdnt Nurses Assoc Treas 89-90; AACN 89-; CCRN 89; AS Edison Comm Coll 87; BSN 90; Nrsng; Edn.

**PACE, PATRICIA E,** Judson Coll, Marion, AL; SR; Stdnt Govt Assoc VP 88-90; Clss Rep 89-; Jdsn Schlrs Pres 88-; Deans Lst; Pres Lst; Eta Epsilon Gamma 89-; APA Afltn 90-; Crcl K Pres 89-; Ambssdrs 89-; Yng Rep 89; Intern Sxl Abs Drg Alchl Abs Fm Cn; Magna Cun Ladue 90-; Tnns Vllybll Bsktbll Capt; Psychlgy; Clncl Psychlgy.**

**PACE, PATSY J,** Roane St Comm Coll, Harriman, TN; FR; BA; Psychology Crmnl Jstc; Law.

**PACELLA, TERESA C,** Comm Coll Algny Co Algny Cmps, Pittsburgh, PA; SO; BS; Activ Comm V Chrprsn 89-; Phi Theta Kappa; Hosp Neurosurgery Adm Sec 88-; Psychology; Psychotherapy.

**PACEWIC, GREGORY A,** Greenville Tech Coll, Greenville, SC; GD; Wade Hampton Taylors Jcs 90-; Pi Lambda Phi 77-; CADD; Eng.

**PACHANO, PEDRO R,** Tallahassee Comm Coll, Tallahassee, FL; SO; BA; Nwspr Feature Edtr 90-; English/Journlm; Writer.

**PACHECO, CIRA M,** Montclair St Coll, Upr Montclair, NJ; FR; BA; Bio; Med.

**PACHECO, FRANCES,** Univ Of Pr At Rio Piedras, Rio Piedras, PR; JR; BS; Gldn Ky; Architecture.**

**PACHECO, IVONNA J,** Caribbean Center For Adv Stds, San Juan, PR; GD; PHD; Human Rsrcs Mgmnt Soc Pres 90- V P 89-90; Ind/Org Psychology Prog 88-; Magna Cum Laude U Of PR 86; Quality Clg Philip Crosby Ad Assn; Psychologist License 90; Banco Sanlander Puerto Rico Quality Serv Officer 90-; Ind/Org Psychology.

**PACHECO, JOSUE,** Univ Of Pr Medical Sciences, San Juan, PR; GD; Assoc De Jovenes Embajadores De Cristo Nivea Oliveras 75-; Assoc De Ninos Joyas De Cristo Rafael Frientes 89-; USAA All-AM Schlrs; Ntl Clgt Nrsng Schlrs; US Achv Acdmy; Clg Prof De La Enfermeria De J Olivo 88-; Nrsn Adm.

**PACHECO, RAMONA,** Catholic Univ Of Pr, Ponce, PR; BBA; BPW Treas 89-; Liga Atltca Pol Srgnto 87-; Cdro De Hrn Del Clgio De Cmrcio UCPR 90; Contbldd.

**PACHECO, REBECCA E,** Va Commonwealth Univ, Richmond, VA; JR; BS; Stdnt Alumni Ambsdrs 90-; Res Hall Judcl Bd Sec 90-; VA Stdnt Edn Assoc 89-; Gold Key 90-; Psi Chi 89-; VA Tchr Schlrshp/Loan 90-; Psychlgy Rsrch Intrnshp 90-; Psychlgy/Early Edn; Teach.

**PACHECO-LABOY, CYNTHIA N,** Catholic Univ Of Pr, Ponce, PR; JR; BA; Scrtrl; Exec Sec.

**PACHECO-ROMAN, SONIA,** Inter Amer Univ Pr San Juan, Hato Rey, PR; GD; JD; Col Trabajadores Soc; Exec Dir Juvenile Ct 87-; BA Univ PR 68; MSW Univ PR 76; Law.

**PACHON, HELENA,** Cornell Univ Statutory College, Ithaca, NY; SO; BS; Natl Schlr; Alpha Phi Hse Clrk 90-; Biology; Medicine.

**PACHTER, JEAN M,** S U N Y Coll Of Tech At Frmgdl, Farmingdale, NY; SO; Alpha Beta Gamma; Pres List 89; Deans List 90; AS; Bus Admin; Mgmnt.

**PACHUCKI, ANNE C,** Schenectady County Comm Coll, Schenectady, NY; SO; BA; Psychology/English; Teacher.

**PACHUTA, LISA M,** Beckley Coll, Beckley, WV; FR; Rsjprtry Thrpy.

**PACIONI, JOHN A,** Ramapo Coll Of Nj, Mahwah, NJ; JR; BS; Poli Sci Clb PR 89-90; USAF ROTC Flght Sgt 86-87; Delta Mu Delta; Deans Lst 89-; Intern SONY Corp Am Inv Acctnt; Bus Adm/Acctg; CPA Lcl/St Pltcs; Tchr.

**PACK, BENJAMIN C,** Univ Of Ky, Lexington, KY; SR; BS; Hnrs Prog; Commonwlth Schlrshp; Byrd Schlrshp; Henry Mason Lites Engrg Schlrshp; Mech Engrg; Law.

**PACK, DONNA S,** Beckley Coll, Beckley, WV; FR; Wmn Of Moose Chrprsn 81-; Leg Sec.

**PACK, JOE M,** Bridgewater Coll, Bridgewater, VA; FR; Bsktbl; Bio/Pre-Med; Dr.

**PACK, KELLI E,** Clark Atlanta Univ, Atlanta, GA; FR; BS; Natl Soc Blck Eng Jr Pblcty Chr 90-; Biol Clb 90-; Hnrs Prog 90-; Inrds NE Ohio 89-; E Ohio Gas Inter 90-; Dean Lst 90-; Biol/Eng; Biomed Eng.

**PACK, PAULINE A,** Univ Of Pittsburgh, Pittsburgh, PA; FR; BSN; Nrsng.

**PACKARD, MELISSA A,** Elmira Coll, Elmira, NY; JR; BA; Ski Club 89-; YWCA Latchkey Pgm Intrnship 90-; Ice Skating; Elem Educ; Tchng Elem Sch.

**PACKETT, RUSSELL W,** Univ Of Ma At Amherst, Amherst, MA; JR; BS; Bg Brthr/Bg Sistr 83-90; Stdnt/Faclty Rep; MRPA 89-; NRPA 89-; AS Grnfld Comm Coll 90; Rec Rsrces Mgmt; Rec Admin.

**PACKMAN, ANDREA R,** Univ Of Miami, Coral Gables, FL; JR; Pblc Rltns Stnd Scty Amer PR Dir 89-; Frnch Clb 89-; Pres Co 90-; Deans List; Provost Hon Roll 90-; Pi Dlt Phi 90-; Orientation Advsr 90; Aerobic 89-; Summer Intrshp Gymns Clb 90-; BS 92; Pblci Rltns Frnch/Mkgt; Bus Law.

**PACKMAN, DAVID,** Atlantic Comm Coll, Mays Landing, NJ; SO; BA; Pol Scnc Clb Sec 88f Perf Arts Clb 90; Clb Actvty Trnmnt Day Coord 90; Pol Scnc/Sec Ed; Teach.

**PACKWOOD, THERESA G,** Georgetown Univ, Washington, DC; SO; BS; Nursing.

**PACOLAY, LAURA JEAN,** Comm Coll Algny Co Algny Cmps, Pittsburgh, PA; SO; BA; Ntrnt Fd Mngmnt Clb Sec 90-; Clncl Dietetics Ntrtn; Dietitian.

**PADAMADAN, SARRY M,** Univ Of Akron, Akron, OH; GD; MA; Pi Sigma Epsilon 90-; Myers Ind Intern 90-; Adv; Writing.

**PADGETT, CYNTHIA K,** S E Coll Of Assemblies Of God, Lakeland, FL; SO; BA; Cllg Chr Msc Lbrn 89-90; Tchr Pal 89-90; Nrsng Hm Otrch Mnstry Ldr 90-; Elem Edctn; Msnry Chldrn Pblc Schl Tchr.**

**PADGETT, DAVID L,** Truett Mc Connell Coll, Cleveland, GA; JR; Bus Oprtns; Cmptr Applctns.

**PADGETT JR, EDWARD E,** Univ Of Sc At Columbia, Columbia, SC; FR; Shng Stars CCH Kids 90-; Elec Engr.

**PADGETT, FREDA A,** Gaston Coll, Dallas, NC; SO; Chem; Phrmcy.

**PADGETT, JANELLE L,** Central Fl Comm Coll, Ocala, FL; FR; BA; Co-Op I 90-; Bus Admin; Str Mgr.

**PADGETT, JOHN I,** Fl Atlantic Univ, Boca Raton, FL; SR; BS; Phi Theta Kappa 90-; Phi Kappa Phi 90-; Beta Gamma Sigma 90-; Willard J Sullivan Schlrshp; A A Ind Rvrs Comm Coll 88; Finance; Ins Sales.

**PADGETT, KAILLE M,** Saint Andrews Presbytrn Coll, Laurinburg, NC; SO; Dorm Cncl Ste Ldr.

**PADGETT, KELLY L,** Bellarmine Coll, Louisville, KY; JR; BA; Natl Ed Assoc Bellarmine Chptr Pres 90-; Crdnl Sctn Hnr Clqm 88-; Delta Epsilon Sigma 89-; Bellarmine Fncl Aid Ofc 88-; Eng; Tchg/Wrtng.

**PADGETT, MELINDA L,** Ga St Univ, Atlanta, GA; JR; BED; Math; Tchg.

**PADGETT, TINA C,** Livingston Univ, Livingston, AL; FR; Phi Eta Sigma.

**PADGETT, TRACY ANNE,** Univ Of Sc At Columbia, Columbia, SC; SO.

**PADGETT, WALTER J,** Oh St Univ At Newark, Newark, OH; SO; BA; Stdnt Senate Pres 90-; Hons Soc 90-; Cty Teen Inst Adult Fcltr 89-; Golf Tm 90; Engl/Phlsphy; Jrnlsm.

**PADILLA ORTIZ, CLARISA,** Catholic Univ Of Pr, Ponce, PR; JR; BED; Mc Nair Pgm 90-; Alcance Pionero 90-; Deans List 89-90.

**PADILLA RAMOS, JUAN A,** Univ Of Pr Humacao Univ Coll, Humacao, PR; JR; BBA; Acctng; CPA.

**PADILLA, ALFONSO,** Fl International Univ, Miami, FL; FR; BA; Intrntl Stdnt Clb 90; Vlg Cncl 90; Fclty Schlr 90; Hnrs Prog 90; Im Flag Ftbl 90; Eng; Indstrl Eng.

**PADILLA, JEAN-PIERRE T,** City Univ Of Ny Baruch Coll, New York, NY; SO; BBA; Filipino Amer Clb VP 90-; Untd Filipino Yth Cncl Vice Chrmn Pol Affrs; Acctg.

**PADILLA, JENNIFER R,** Fayetteville St Univ, Fayetteville, NC; SR; BA; Soclgy Club 89-; Alpha Kappa Delta; Grad Sr Soclgy Mjr W/Hghst Cumltv GPA; Asst Mgr; BA; Soclgy.

**PADILLA, LYMARIES,** Univ Of Pr At Rio Piedras, Rio Piedras, PR; JR; BA; Ldrshp Schl Caguas PR 88; Jvnl Pstrl Caguas PR Orgnztn 88-; Hnr Pgm 89-; MARC Pgm Bpsychscl Trng Rsrch 89-; Amer Psychlgcl Assoc 89-; Interamer Soc Psychlgy 89-; Psychlgcl Stdnts Assoc 90-; MARC Pgm 89; Hnr Pgm 89; Psychlgy; Clncl Psy.

**PADILLA, MARIEL,** Bayamon Tech Univ Coll, Bayamon, PR; JR; BSIE; Stdnt Cncl/Crrclm Comm Cnlsr 89-90; Hon Certs/Hon Pgms 88-; Tenns Tm IM Tennis 90-; AA Sci; Eng; Indust Eng.

**PADILLA, MILDRED IVETTE,** Inter Amer Univ Pr San German, San German, PR; SR; BA; Sociedad De Pre-Medica-Caduceus Tres 90-; Sociedad De Histeria Natural-Poly-Natura; Sorroridad Nu Delta Sigma; BA; Biology; Physician.

**PADILLA, PETER LLOYD,** Embry Riddle Aeronautical Univ, Daytona Beach, FL; SO; BA; Wrstlng Clb 90-; Aeronautical Sci; Pilot.

**PADILLA, ROSEMARY,** City Univ Of Ny City Coll, New York, NY; GD; Alpha Sigma Lambda; Tchr At Nuestros Ninos Dy Cr Ctr Bklyn; BS; Erly Chldhd Educ; Tchr.

**PADILLA, SUYAPA M,** Central Fl Comm Coll, Ocala, FL; SO; Clb Intl CASS Prog 89-; Presntn Typical Dances From CA 89-; Phi Theta Kappa 90-; Blessed Trinity Church 89; Diploma Recognition; Deans List 90; Pres List 90.

**PADIOS, BONNIE G,** Memphis St Univ, Memphis, TN; JR; BED; AFAA; Arbcs/Ftnss Instr Hlthy Adlst/Rehab Lcl Psych Hosp; Tch Adlscnts W/Bhvrl Prblms; Phys Ed; Cnslng/Instr Ftnss.

**PADOVANI OLIVER, FABIOLA B,** Univ Of Pr At Mayaguez, Mayaguez, PR; JR; BSA; Alpha Zeta; Beta Beta Beta; Vtwrd Bnd Smmr Elry Enrllmnt Prgm 88; Anml Sci.

**PADOVANI, FABIOLA B,** Univ Of Pr At Mayaguez, Mayaguez, PR; SO.

**PADOVANI, JULIO C,** Inter Amer Univ Pr San German, San German, PR; FR; BS; Nu Sigma Beta; Aerospcl; Eng.

**PADRON, BELKIS,** Palm Beach Comm Coll, Lake Worth, FL; SO; BA; Educ; Elem Educ Teach.

**PADRON, OTTO M,** Univ Of Miami, Coral Gables, FL; SR; BS; ROTC Cmdr 90-; Gldn Key 90-; Scbbd Blde Sgt 89-; AA Miami Dade Comm Clg 88-89; Brdcstg/Ec; Media Law.

**PADRON, RUBEN J,** Fl International Univ, Miami, FL; FR; BA; Theater Clb Dsgnr; Schlr 90-; Pltcl Scn/Theater; Law.

**PADRON, SONIA V,** Univ Of Miami, Coral Gables, FL; JR; BA; FL Intl Bllt Co 88-; Miami Intl Ballet; Bowman Ashe Schlp 89-; Dns Lst 89-; Psy; Chld Psy.

**PADUA, JOSEPH M,** Rensselaer Polytechnic Inst, Troy, NY; GD; MBA; Stdnt Orientation Co Chair 88-; Pep Band Co Mgr 88-; Parents Weeked Staff Co Chair 89-90; Mgmnt Of Technology; Mgmnt.

**PADULA, JO ANNE M,** Lasell Coll, Newton, MA; JR; BA; Rsdnt Asstnt Stdnt Govt 90-; Lip Sync Nght 90-; Tour Guide 88-; Hgh Hon 89-90; Hon Stdnt Tchng Chld Dvlpment 89-90; Deans List 90-91; Sftbl; AS 90; Erly Chldhd Educ; Tchng.**

**PADULA, KATHLEEN,** Middlesex County Coll, Edison, NJ; SR; AAS; Clge Asmbly 90-; Stdnt Amer Dntl Hygn Assoc Hstrn 90-; Dvsnl Cncl 89-90; Dns Lst 88-; Dntl Asst 79-96; CT St Ins Agts Exm 88; Cert Berekely Bsn Schl 86-87; Sci; Dntl Hygn.

**PADULA, SUSAN A,** Siena Coll, Loudonville, NY; SR; BS; Cmptr Clb 87-; Karate Clb 88-89; Alpha Kappa Alpha; Delta Epsilon Sigma; Music Mnstgry 87-; Bowl For Kids Sake 87-; GE Rsrch Intrn 90-; Fed Watervliet Arsenal Flwshp 87-90; Cmptr Sci; Prgrmr.

**PAEZ, ANNA M,** Brevard Coll, Brevard, NC; FR; AABA; SGA VP Judicial Brd; Blck People Unity; Phi Theta Kappa Pres; Prjt Inside Out 90-; Cross Cntry/Sccr/Trck 90-; Pltcl Science; Intrntnl Law.

**PAEZ, CARLOS M,** Univ Politecnica De Pr, Hato Rey, PR; SO; BS; ICE 90-; Cvl Eng; Arch M S.

**PAEZ, JUAN D,** City Univ Of Ny City Coll, New York, NY; SO; BE; Ecudrn Clb 90-; SHPE 90-; Laesa; Golden Key 90-; Math Tutrng 90-; Best Fnl Math 202 90; NY Law Schl Word Prcssr Oper 89; Cvl Eng.

**PAGAN CRESPI, ROBERTO IVAN,** Inter Amer Univ Pr San German, San German, PR; SO; Hon Prog.

**PAGAN FERRER, ROSANNA,** Univ Of Pr At Rio Piedras, Rio Piedras, PR; SO; BA; Acctg; CPA/ACCTG Mstry.

**PAGAN GONZALEZ, RAMON ANTONIO,** Catholic Univ Of Pr, Ponce, PR; GD.

**PAGAN HERNANDEZ, HILDA Y,** Univ Politecnica De Pr, Hato Rey, PR; FR; Close-Up Fndtn 89-90; Upwrd Bnd Pgm 88-90; Math; Eng.

**PAGAN MARTI, CARMEN M,** Univ Of Pr Cayey Univ Coll, Cayey, PR; JR; BA; Espanish; Ed.

**PAGAN MENDOZA, JUAN A,** Univ Politecnica De Pr, Hato Rey, PR; GD; Spnsh/Math; Mech Engr.

**PAGAN VEGA, ELIZABETH,** Inter Amer Univ Pr Aquadilla, Aguadilla, PR; GD; BA; Sec Ed Scl Studies; MBA.

**PAGAN, ANGEL R,** Inter Amer Univ Pr Hato Rey, Hato Rey, PR; JR; BA; Science; Engnrng.

**PAGAN, ARTURO,** Univ Of Rochester, Rochester, NY; SO; BA; Spanish Int Flr 89-; Inter Frat Cncl; Tau Kappa Epsilon; Pol Sci; Intl Affrs.

**PAGAN, EDWARD M,** Boricua Coll, New York, NY; SR; BS; Stdnt Gvmt Pres 87-88; Bus Clb Pres 88-; Roberto Clemente Acad Awd 88; Math Tutor 87-; Hstry Tutor 87-; Acctng Tutor 89-; AS 89; Business Adm; Acctnt.

**PAGAN, GILBERTO,** Ny Univ, New York, NY; SO; BS; Elmhrst Gen Hosp Comm Bd 90-; St Claires Hosp 89-; Beth Isreal Hosp 90-; Stdnt Cncl Sntr; Aids Intrnshp Beth Isreal Hosp 88; Rsrch Assoc; AAS Hlth Admin; Hlth Care Admin; Theological.

**PAGAN, MAYRA,** Univ Of Pr Cayey Univ Coll, Cayey, PR; SO; BA; Chem; Med.

**PAGAN, VANNESSA,** Univ Of Pr At Mayaguez, Mayaguez, PR; SO; Cath Apstlshp Grp; Chorus; Beta Beta Beta Bio Soc 90-; All Amer Schlr Coll Awrd 90; Ntl Coll Ntrl Sci Awrd; Univ Hnr Rl 90; Pre Med.

**PAGAN, VELLISSE M,** Fl St Univ, Tallahassee, FL; SR; BS; Psi Chi Treas 90-; Ph D Clncl Psychlgy.

**PAGAN-CANCEL, MICHELLE M,** Univ Of Pr At Mayaguez, Mayaguez, PR; SR; BS; AICHE 89-; Tau Beta Pi 90-; Chml Engrg Hnr Student 88-; USAA All Amer Schlrs 90-; Chem Engrg; Engrg.

**PAGANO, DONNA MARIE,** Wagner Coll, Staten Island, NY; SR; BA; Snug Harbor Gllry Instlr Intern; Visual Arts; Gallery Work.

**PAGANO, LEONARD J,** City Univ Of Ny La Guard Coll, Long Island Cty, NY; SO; AAS; Acctng.

**PAGANS, BETTY M,** Patrick Henry Comm Coll, Martinsville, VA; AAS; DPMA 90-; Phi Theta Kappa 90-; AAS 90; Microcmptrs; Cmptr Prgrmr.

**PAGE SR, ADRIAN COOPER,** Coppin St Coll, Baltimore, MD; JR; BA; Aa Essex Comm Coll 89-90; Business; Tchng.

**PAGE, ALMA L,** Phillips Jr Coll Spartanburg, Spartanburg, SC; SO; AASD; Med Admin Asst; AASD; Med Admin.

**PAGE, ANN J,** East Stroudsburg Univ, E Stroudsburg, PA; SR; BA; Spch Cmnctns Org Treas 90-; Sigma Tau Delta; Stdnt Secy In Ofc Of The Pres 87-; Pres Award Of Merit; Spch Cmnctns.

**PAGE, BARBARA A,** Univ Of Sc At Columbia, Columbia, SC; SO; Psych.

**PAGE, CATHY HOOPER,** Gaston Coll, Dallas, NC; SO; AAS; Comp Sci Clb 90-; Real Est Ofc Mgr 86-90; Bus Comp Pgmr.

**PAGE, CRYSTAL L,** Lincoln Univ, Lincoln Univ, PA; JR; Chrldng Sec 90-; Stdnt Ntwrk 91-; Big Str/Big Bro 90-; Yng Popls Div Mt Zion Fenwick Ch; Cmrnl Juste; Corrctn Ofcr Jvnls/ Lawyer.

**PAGE, CYNTHIA D,** Middle Tn St Univ, Murfreesboro, TN; FR; BA.

**PAGE, ERIC JOHN,** Schenectady County Comm Coll, Schenectady, NY; FR; Math/Sci; Cvl/Mech Eng.

**PAGE, ERIC ROBERT,** Ms St Univ, Miss State, MS; SR; Rugby Ftbl Club Cptn 86-; SCAPE 90-; Graphic Dsgn; Tch/ MFA.

**PAGE, KERRI L,** Univ Of Al At Birmingham, Birmingham, AL; FR; BS; Hons Schlrshp 90-; Rtry Clb Schlrshp 90-; Alpha Kappa Alpha/Alpha Phi Alpha Schlrshp 90-; Crmnl Just/Spnsh; Law.

**PAGE, LAUREL J,** Univ Of Nc At Charlotte, Charlotte, NC; JR; BA; Psych; PHD.

**PAGE, MARY A,** Univ Of New England, Biddeford, ME; JR; BS; Phys Thrpy Clb 90-; Rrl Hlth Prjct 90; Phys Thrpy; Hm Hlth Care.

**PAGE, MICHAEL A,** Univ Of Tn At Martin, Martin, TN; GD; MS; 3 Time Billiards Chmpn/Rep 87-; Geography; Envrnmtlst.

**PAGE, NICOLA M,** Univ Of Sc At Columbia, Columbia, SC; SR; BA; Radio Stat 87-88; Gamma Beta Phi 88-; Phi Beta Kappa 90-; Spnsh; Educ.

**PAGE, NICOLE L,** Clark Atlanta Univ, Atlanta, GA; SR; BA; Psych Clb 87-; Ronald E Mc Nair Pgm 90-; Amer Schlr Achvmnt Awd 90-; Subst Use Prev Ed Resrce Asst Eval 90-; Ronald E Mc Nair Post Baccalurate Asst 90; Psych; Clncl Psych.**

**PAGE, PATRICIA A,** Oh Dominican Coll, Columbus, OH; FR; Outrch Pgm St Johns Episcopal; Emplyd Care After Sch; Tchr Elem Grade.

**PAGE, PATTY L,** North Ga Coll, Dahlonega, GA; SO; BA; Phi Eta Sigma VP 89-90; Phi Kappa Phi 90-; Phi Mu 90-; N GA Clg Acad Schlrshp Recipt 89-; LBMA Craig Meml Schlrshp Recipt 89-90; Cherokee Co Serv League Schlrshp Recipt 90-; Physical Therapy.

**PAGE, ROCHELLE L,** Bunker Hill Comm Coll, Boston, MA; GD; BS; Innr City Grls Grp Hm; Intshp Cable Sta; Schlp Suffolk Univ; AS; Comm; Anchor.

**PAGE, STACEY L,** Middle Tn St Univ, Murfreesboro, TN; SR; BS; Stdnt Amb Chp 88-; Gamma Beta Phi Pub Serv 88-; Beta Beta Beta 87-; Phi Mu Delta 90-; Kevin Driver Mem Schlrshp 90; Wiser Pre Med Prof Schlrshp 91; Bio; Phys Thrpy.

**PAGE, TAMMY L,** Fl Atlantic Univ, Boca Raton, FL; GD; MBA; Beta Alpha Psi Chrmn Fndrsng 90-; Beta Gamma Sigma 90-; Asstshp Exec BBA Prog; Horses/Hndccpd Fndrsng Comm 88; Empl By Deloitte/Touche; BBA 90; Cert State Of Fla 88; Bus; Acctng.

**PAGE, THERESA M,** Univ Of Sc At Columbia, Columbia, SC; SR; BSN; Stdnt Nrsg Assoc V P/Secr 89-; Nrsg; RN.

**PAGE, TINA M,** Valdosta St Coll, Valdosta, GA; SR; BS; Alpha Chi; AA Waycross Clge 89; Mid Chldhd Ed; Teaching 7th Grd.

**PAGE, TROY L,** West Liberty St Coll, West Liberty, WV; SO; AB; Pgmng Bd 90-; Ski Clb 89-90; Kappa Delta Rho Pres 89-; Tnns Tm 89-; Bus Educ; Tchng.

**PAGE, VIVIAN E,** Va Commonwealth Univ, Richmond, VA; SO; BA; Stdnt Almn Ambsdrs 90-; Vcu Dnc Tm 90-; Phi Eta Sigma 90-; Vcu Hnrs Prgrm; Untd Wy Vlntr; Deans Schlrshp; Pltcl Sci Intrnshp Gen Asmbly Of Va; Englsh; Law.

**PAGE, YVETTE D,** Univ Of Sc At Columbia, Columbia, SC; FR; BA; Red Cross Vol; Deans Lst 90-; Bio; Med.

**PAGEL, ANGELA D,** Univ Of Cin R Walters Coll, Blue Ash, OH; SO; AS.

**PAGENDARM, EDWARD M,** Wv Univ, Morgantown, WV; SR; BS; Amer Inst Chem Engrs 88-; Hnrs Prog 87-; Phi Kappa Phi 90; Golden Key 88; Tau Beta Pi 89; Omega Chi Epsilon 90; Chimes 89-90; Helvetia 88-89; Chf Engr Dsgn 90-; Achvmnt Schlrshp 88-; Scty Amer Mltry Engrs Schlrshp 89; IMS; Chem Engrng.

**PAGLIARULO, ROBERT PAUL,** Newbury Coll, Brookline, MA; FR; CERT; Clss Repr; BFA Boston Univ Schl/Fine Arts 86; Culinary Arts; Pastry Chef.

**PAGLIUCA, DOMINCO A,** Univ Of Miami, Coral Gables, FL; JR; BM; Symphny Orchstra Prncpl Chr 89-; Miami Symphny Orchstra Prncpl Chr 90-; Orchstra Snfnca Venezuela Prncpl Chr 87-; Symphnc-Wind Orchstra Soloist 90-; Miami Bch Comm Sypmhny Orchstra Prncpl Chr; Cncrto Cmptn 89; Instrmntl Music Prfrmnc.

**PAGNIANO, THOMAS A,** Oh Univ, Athens, OH; SR; BFA; Natl Head Injury Fndtn Ohio Chapt VP 89; Gold Key; Am Art Therapy Assn; Rec Therapist 57-62/80-83; Rehab Cnslr 62-64; Arts/Crafts Dir US Air Force 68-74; Self Employed Potter 83-; Art Therapy/Psychlgy; Univ Instr.

**PAGNOTTA, MICHELE A,** Dowling Coll, Oakdale Li, NY; SR; BA; Babylon Chorale Hstrn Bx Ofc 88-; S Bay Chamber Singers 88-; Future Music Edctrs 89-; AS Suffolk Cnty Cmnty Clge 89; Music; Music Education.

**PAGUIA, SAMSON T,** Comm Coll Algny Co Algny Cmps, Pittsburgh, PA; FR; Scl Wrk Clb; Phi Theta Kappa; Alpha Mu Tau; Glry Rbts Lit Awd 88; Frnk Gspro Awd 86; Dem Prty Allghny Cty 65-; Amer Isrl Ms Asc; Med Tech; AA Prtrvl Clg 59; Sci/Math.

**PAHL, MARCY L,** Western New England Coll, Springfield, MA; SO; BA; Res Hall Assn Treas; Hlpng Hnds Soc; Bus Mngmntr Mktg; Htl Mgr.

**PAHMAN, DAVID A,** Faulkner Univ, Montgomery, AL; SO; BA; Natl Lads To Ldrs Spkng Tm 89-; Preachers Clb 90-; SAEA Pres 90-; Kappa Sigma Phi Sec 89-; Hnry Citizen Huntington Tenn; Math Educ; Tchr.

**PAHOSKI, LYNNE F,** Marywood Coll, Scranton, PA; SR; BS; Spch/Hrng Clb Pres 88-91; Natl Stdnt Spch Lang Hrng Assn Pres 88-; Delta Epsilon Sigma 90-; Amer Cncr Soc Vol 90-; Intrnshp Allntwn Hosp/Leigh Vlly Hosp Cntr; Spch Pthlgy; Grad Schl.

**PAIANO, CHRIS D,** Pellissippi St Tech Comm Coll, Knoxville, TN; SO; BA; Comp Sci; Comp Pgmng.

**PAIGE, CAROLYN D,** Wallace St Comm Coll At Selma, Selma, AL; SO; BA; Engl; Elem Ed.

**PAIGE, CHRISTINE HUNT,** Alcorn St Univ, Lorman, MS; SO; Ele Educ.

**PAIGE, DARCY M,** Castleton St Coll, Castleton, VT; JR; BA; Stg Lft Pres; Phi Eta Sigma; Alpha Psi Omega; Thtr Arts; Cstm Fshn Dsgn.

**PAIGE, LANA LEE,** Lesley Coll, Cambridge, MA; SR; BA; Soph Cls Brd Stdnt Actvts Cncl 89-; Sr Cls Brd VP; Rsdnc Life Comm Sec 88-; LINC Pblcty; Elem Edctn Spcl Edctn; Tchng.

**PAIGE, MARK A,** Stonehill Coll, North Easton, MA; JR; BA; DJ Radio 88-; Cmnctn Org 88-; Cmnctns.**

**PAIGE, MELISSA H,** Casco Bay Coll, Portland, ME; FR; BA; Bus Admn; Mgr.

**PAIGE, MONICA A,** Fl A & M Univ, Tallahassee, FL; FR; BS; Phi Eta Sigma 90-; Psych; Psychlgst.

**PAILES, EDWARD W,** Nova Univ, Ft Lauderdale, FL; GD; Broward County Yng Rep 86-; Tstmstrs 86-; Ins/Clms Sprvsr; BA Monmouth Coll Il 84; MBA; Bus; Ins Mgmt.

**PAINE, DAVID O,** Air Force Inst Of Tech, Wrt-Ptrsn Afb, OH; GD; MS; BSEE OK St Unv 82; Engnrng Mgmnt.

**PAINE, IRENE M,** Rivier Coll, Nashua, NH; SR; BA; Campus Mnstry Cnsl; Delta Epsilon Sigma; Hghst Hnrs 90-; Vldctrn Cls 90-; Mdtn Assoc Nashua Mdtn; Psych; Law Sch.

**PAINE, JANET L,** Johnson St Coll, Johnson, VT; SO; BA; Chambermaid Factory Wrkr Offc Clrk 77-; Bus Mgmnt; Accntnt.

**PAINE, JOHN J,** Merrimack Coll, North Andover, MA; SO; Sociolgy.

**PAINTER, DAVID H,** Univ Of Sc At Columbia, Columbia, SC; FR; BA; Fr Rep SGA Fr Rep 90-; Stdnt Govt Assn Pres; Gmck Ambssdr 90-; DA Coll Intrn 90-; Stdnt Ornttn Ldr; IMS 90-; Bus Admin; Lwyr.

**PAINTER, DONALD M,** Univ Of Nc At Asheville, Asheville, NC; JR; BA; SAM; Mgmnt; Law.

**PAINTER, GABRIELA E,** S U N Y Coll At Fredonia, Fredonia, NY; JR; BED; Phi Theta Kappa JCC 89-; Kappa Delta Pi; Roger Seager Schlrshp JCC 90-; 1st Plc Literary Comp JCC 90; Quaolity Markets 71-81; AA Socl Sci Jamestown Comm Coll 90; Elem Educ/Socl Stds; Tchr.

**PAINTER, JAMES V,** S U N Y At Buffalo, Buffalo, NY; SR; BS; Univ Bflo Acctg Assn 89-; NAA 89-; Gldn Ky 90-; Beta Alpha Psi 89-; Mgmt Acctg Intrnshp; NCAA Div II Ftbl 87-89; Bus Adm; Law Schl.

**PAINTER, JEANNETTE L,** Fl St Univ, Tallahassee, FL; SR; BSN; Natl Stdnt Nrs Assoc; AA 90; Nrsg; Ob/Gyn Nrsg.

**PAINTER, MELISSA A,** Blue Mountain Coll, Blue Mountain, MS; SR; BS; Bapt Stdnt Union 87; Koinania 89-90; Ms Assoc Of Edctrs Stdnt Prog 90; Modenian Scl Scty 87; Elem Ed; Tchr.

**PAINTER, NOVA J,** Averett Coll, Danville, VA; SR; BS; NARP Frst VP 90; NAA; Mangr Prpty Taxes Norfolk Southern Corp Emplyd 25 Yrs; AAS; Virginia Western Cmmnty Clg 87; Hmn Resource Dvlpmnt.

**PAINTER, ROBIN L,** Northern Ky Univ, Highland Hts, KY; JR; BA; Un Meth Wesley Fndtn Pres 89-; Elem/Spec Ed; Teach.

**PAINTER, TRACY A,** Immaculata Coll, Immaculata, PA; SO; BA; Soc Advncmnt Mgmt Sec 89-; Schl Nwspr Assoc Edtr 90-; Stdt Assoc SAIC Rep 90-; Cmps Mnstry 89-; Bus Admin/Econ; Bus Field.

**PAINTON, CHRISTINA ELIZABETH,** Endicott Coll, Beverly, MA; SO; ASS; Student Govt Senator, Co Chair Student Gvt Finance Somm Co Chair; Student Orient Ldr Ldr Hlpng Nwsstudent; Phi Theta Kappa Mbr; Deans List; Intshp TV Stations Rptr Prod Lanchor; Commts/Radio RV; Brdct Journlm.

**PAIR, VANESSA P,** Richard Bland Coll, Petersburg, VA; SO; MBA; Hlth Sci; Phy Thrpst.

**PAIT BOBBEY, HEATHER S,** Liberty Univ, Lynchburg, VA; SR; Prayer Ldr; Liberty Assoc Chrstn Tchr Sec Rep 90-; Kappa Delta Pi 89-; Sigma Tau Delta 90-; Chancellors Schlrshp; BS; Engl Ed; Ed.

**PAK, SANG-CHUNG,** Old Dominion Univ, Norfolk, VA; SR; AMA 87-88; KSA Treas; Mktg Ed; Hmn Rsrc.

**PAKES, LAURI M,** Washington State Comm Coll, Marietta, OH; FR; AA; Micro Cmptr Applctns Tchnlgy.

**PAKULSKI, SCOTT J,** Univ Of Toledo, Toledo, OH; FR; MBA; Brdcstg 90-; Rpblcns 90-; Pi Kappa Phi Cmps/Cmnty Invlv Chrmn 90-; Intl Mktg/Frnch; Intl Bsn/Ed.

**PALACHI, HILEL ILAN,** Fl International Univ, Miami, FL; SR; BS; Grd Hnrs; Crtf Edctnl Inst AH MA 88; AA Miami Dade Com Clg 90; Hsptlty Mngmnt; Fd Srvc Mgmnt.

**PALACINO, CHRISTINE,** City Univ Of Ny Queensbrough, New York, NY; SO; BA; AA; Erl Chldhd Ed; Tchr.

**PALACIO, JAYLIN D,** Methodist Coll, Fayetteville, NC; JR; BA; Hon Soc 88-90; Engl; Tchr.

**PALACIO, MARLENE,** City Univ Of Ny La Guard Coll, Long Island Cty, NY; JR; BA; Trvl/Tourism; Mktg.

**PALACIOS FRAU, ALEIDA M,** Inter Amer Univ Pr Hato Rey, Hato Rey, PR; SR; Acctg Assn 86; Mktg Assn 86; Intramrcn Hon Soc 86; Deans Lst 86-; Acctg/Math; Mgr Acctnt.**

**PALACIOS VAZQUEZ, SYLVIA,** Inter Amer Univ Pr Hato Rey, Hato Rey, PR; SR.

**PALACIOS, LUZ M,** City Univ Of Ny La Guard Coll, Long Island Cty, NY; SO; Alpha Theta Kappa 90-; Dns Lst 89-.

**PALAGONIA, KATHERINE M,** Georgian Court Coll, Lakewood, NJ; SR; BA; Dir Rllng Hls Jr Tenn Trvl Pgm 88-; AS Ocean Cnty Coll 89; Sclgy; Elem Schl Tchr.

**PALASINSKI, JENNIFER D,** Villanova Univ, Villanova, PA; SO; BS; Musical Theatre 90-; Spcl Olympcs Vol 90-; Hall Cncl Secy/Treas 89-90; Stdnt Un 89-90; Alpha Phi Chpln 90-; Blue Key 90-; Fin; Bus.**

**PALATAS, DIAN B,** Miami Jacobs Jr Coll Of Bus, Dayton, OH; FR; AS; Colg Sec Intl Rec Sec 90-; Outstndg Stdnt Sprg Qtr; Pres Lst Dir Lst; Schlrshp CSI; Inf Proc; Law Office.

**PALAU, JENNIFER M,** S U N Y Coll At Fredonia, Fredonia, NY; JR; BS; Psychlgy; Cnslng.

**PALAURO, TONJA IELENE,** Va Commonwealth Univ, Richmond, VA; SO; BS; Phi Eta Sigma 90-; Sccr Clb Tm; Blgy; Med.

**PALAZZO, ANTHONY J,** Univ Of Southern Ms, Hattiesburg, MS; SR; BSBA; Assoc Stdnt Body Treas 89-; Clg Republicans Pres 88-; Amer Mktng Assn V P 88-90; Golden Key; Omicron Delta Kappa; Lambda Sigma; Beta Alpha Psi V P 89-; Kappa Sigma Treas 87-; Rotaract Serv Org Treas 88-90; Outstanding Acctng Major; Acctng; CPA.

**PALAZZO, HELEN E,** Ms St Univ, Miss State, MS; FR; Intl Vlybl; Alpha Lambda Delta; Gamma Beta Phi; Kappa Delta; Biological Sci; Marine Biology.

**PALCHUK, MATVEY,** Franklin And Marshall Coll, Lancaster, PA; FR; BA; Hillel; Rssn Clb; Biol; Med.

**PALEXAS, ZACHARIAS GEORGIOU,** Georgetown Univ, Washington, DC; Coord Comm Karpasia Rep US 90-; Accntng Soc Pres 90-; Hellenic Clb Prsdnt 90-; Beta Gamma Sigma 90-; Omicron Delta Epsilon 90-; Washington DC Alumni Assn Cyprus Co Fndr 89; AIESEC 88-; Cmps Rep Epp Adtrs 90-; Bsns; MBA.

**PALEY, ELLA,** Bunker Hill Comm Coll, Boston, MA; FR; MBA; Intl Clb; Engl; Med.

**PALIVODA, SHERI L,** Comm Coll Algny Co Algny Cmps, Pittsburgh, PA; JR; BA; Scl Wrk Clb Sec 89; Social Wrk/Ed; Education.

**PALKOVIC, VIRGINIA E,** Schenectady County Comm Coll, Schenectady, NY; SO; AS; Anlytcl Stds Grp; Phi Theta Kappa; Rttrdm Boys/Girls Clb; Brd Dir Oasis Daycare Ctr; Bsn Admn/Math; Scndry Schl Math Tchr.

**PALLADINO, JO ANNA L,** Emory Univ, Atlanta, GA; JR; BBA; Phi Theta Kappa 88-; Beta Alpha Psi 90-; Deans Lst 87-; Cert Achvmnt Future Ldrs 90; Past Dir FL Legal Assts Inc 87-88; Bus Educ Adv Cmte 87-89; Cert Legal Asst; Acctng; CPA.

**PALLADINO, LEO,** City Univ Of Ny Baruch Coll, New York, NY; JR; BA; Pol Sci; Teach.

**PALLATTO, VALARIE A,** Indiana Univ Of Pa, Indiana, PA; SR; Assoc US Army 87-; Rsrv Offcr Trng Corps 87-; PA Cncl Tchrs Math 90-; Dist Mltry Grad 90; Dist Wmn Ldrshp Recog 90; Dghtrs/Fndrs Amer Rev Awrd 90; BS 90; PA 90; Math; Oprtnl Rsrch.

**PALMATEER, JASON B,** Eckerd Coll, St Petersburg, FL; JR; BA; Org Stdnts/Stdnt Govt Finance Dir 89-; Mdl UN Pres 89-; Nwspaper Edtr In Chf 88-90; Omicron Delta Kappa 90-; Omicron Delta Epsilon; Ford Fndtn Schlr 90-; Pres Schlrshp Slctn Comm 88-; Econ; Profssr.

**PALMATIER, ANDREW D,** Univ Of Al At Birmingham, Birmingham, AL; JR; BA; Psychlgy Clb; Gen Studies Undecided Peer Cnslr 90-; Psychlgy; Cnslg

**PALMER, AMANDA R,** Christian Brothers Univ, Memphis, TN; SR; BS; Tau Kappa Epsilon Ltl Sis 88-; Assn Mtvt Schl Spirit 87-; Intrnshp ATS-TLPHN/DATA Serv; Mktg; Bus.

**PALMER, AMY L,** Muskingum Coll, New Concord, OH; FR; BA; Cncrt Choir 90; Chmbr Sngrs 90; Lambda Sigma; Sigma Alpha Iota; FAD Clb; 1st Yr Schlrshp Awd.

**PALMER, ANNE C,** Samford Univ, Birmingham, AL; GD; JD; Delta Kappa Gamma; Assoc Supervision Curriculum Dvlpmnt; Internship Federal Judge 11 Cir; Rotary Intl Grantee; Secndry Univ Tchr 78-; MA French 86; MA English 82; BA 77; Public Serv Educ Law.

**PALMER, AUDRA A,** Newbury Coll, Brookline, MA; SR; APICS; Invntry Analyst.

**PALMER, BRENDA L,** Averett Coll, Danville, VA; JR; BS; BSU Campus Life 88; Phi Eta Sigma 88-89; Sigma Lampda Epsilon Pres 89-; Alpha Chi 90-; Deans Lst 88-90; Pres Lst; Educ; Tch.

**PALMER, BRIAN S,** S U N Y Coll Of A & T Morrisvl, Morrisville, NY; SO; AAS; Phi Theta Kappa 90-; Microcmptr Tech; Cmptr Eng.**

**PALMER, BRUCE W,** Oh Univ, Athens, OH; SR; BFA; Stdnt Nwspr Stff Phtgrphr; William Randolph Hearst Phtjrnlsm Cmptn 90-; Winter Intrnshp Yngstwn Vndctr 90; Smmr Intrnshp Troy Daily News; Natl News Phtgrphrs Assn; Vsl Cmnctn; News Phtgrphr.

**PALMER III, CARL,** Alcorn St Univ, Lorman, MS; SO; BS; Mississippi American Lgn Boys State Snr Cnty Adv 89-; New Vision Gospel Choir Pblc Spkr 89-; Co-Op Stdnt Grnd Gulf Nclr Intrn Chmst; Alcorn St Univ Dns Lst Stdnt 89-; Pre Med/Chem; Doctor Pediatrician.

**PALMER, CHERITH A,** Bapt Bible Coll & Seminary, Clarks Summit, PA; SO; BA; Nrsng Hm Vol 89; Mssns; Mssnry Nrse.

**PALMER, DAMON C,** Comm Coll Algny Co Algny Cmps, Pittsburgh, PA; FR; BS; Cmptr Sci; Cmptr Sys Anlyst.

**PALMER, ESTER S,** Hudson Valley Comm Coll, Troy, NY; GD; MBA; BA Russell Sage Coll 83; Bus Acctng; Law And Or Fnnce Acctng.

**PALMER, JERRY T,** Christopher Newport Coll, Newport News, VA; SR; DPMA 90-; AABA San Diego Coll SD CA 77; Cert VA Hsng Auth 89; BSIS Cert Christopher Newport Coll; Infos Sci; MIS Elec/Comm Indust.

**PALMER, JONATHAN M,** Univ Of Nc At Asheville, Asheville, NC; SR; BA; Math Assn Of Amer 90-; Prof Military Educ Cert; NCO Cert 82; USAF 79-83 Sgt Weapons/Ammun Inspctr 81-83; Math; Educ.

**PALMER, JULIE W,** Union Univ, Jackson, TN; SO; BA; Flwshp Christian Ath V Pres; Sigma Tau Delta; Chi Omega Lodge Mngr 90-; Babtist Stdnt Union Spots Tm; English; Law.

**PALMER, KAREN A,** City Univ Of Ny City Coll, New York, NY; SO; BA; Wrld Pltcs Org Tres; Intl Org Ntwrk; Lambda Alpha Mu 90-; Political Sci; Law.

**PALMER, LAUREN A,** Wv Univ, Morgantown, WV; SO; BS; Morgntwn Ronald Mcdonald House Vol 90-; Soc Wrk.

**PALMER, LINDA E,** Univ Of Cin R Walters Coll, Blue Ash, OH; SO; BA; Tri-Cnty React Treas 78-80; Warren Cnty Kennel Clb VP 75-81; Super Food Serv Inc Grocery Whlslr/Serv 79-90; Mktg/Cmrcl Art; Mktg.**

**PALMER, MICHAEL A,** Univ Of Med & Dentistry Of Nj, Newark, NJ; GD; All Atlantic Coast Capt 86; Conf Track 88; BS 88; Phys Thrpy.

**PALMER, MICHAEL C,** Milligan Coll, Milligan Clg, TN; SO; BS; Vars Bsktbl 89-; Bsn Admin/Econ; Entrepreneur/Ecnmst.

**PALMER, MURIEL J,** Central St Univ, Wilberforce, OH; FR; BS; Bio Soc 90-; Pre Hlth Club 90-; ROTC 90-; Beta Beta Beta 90-; Acdmc Achvmnt 90-; Acdmc Achvmnt 90-; Res Officers Assn Awd 90-; Bio/Chem Pre-Med.

**PALMER, NANCY R,** Alcorn St Univ, Lorman, MS; SR; BS; Bio 89-; Senate SGA 89-; Prayer Bnd 89-; Chem 89-; Wesley Fdtn 89-; Pre-Med 89-; Alpha Kappa Mu 89-; Beta Kappa Chi 90-; Awd Excell 90-; Chem Awd 89-90; Pres Lst 87-; IM Bsktbl/Sftbl 87-; Chem/Pre-Med; Physician.

**PALMER, PAUL M,** Johnson St Coll, Johnson, VT; FR; BS; Math; Tch.

**PALMER, ROBIN L,** Clayton St Coll, Morrow, GA; SO; BBA; Assoc Arts Diplomaf IM Vlybl; AA 90; Bus; Own Bus.

**PALMER, RYAN S,** Saint Josephs Coll, Windham, ME; SR; BS; Class VP 89-90; Clg Theatre Guild Pres 87-; Yrbk Commt 90-; IM Sftbl Soccer Vlybl Aerobics 88-; Elem Ed; Tchr.

**PALMER, SANDRA J,** Saint Pauls Coll, Lawrenceville, VA; SR; MS; Math Club Treas 89-90; Sci Club Treas 89-90; Pep Bnd 87-88; Wdwnd Chmbr Ensmbl 87-88; Alpha Kappa Mu Pres 90-; Magna Cum Laude; Alden Schlr; BS; Microbiolgy; Medcn.

**PALMER, TIMOTHY A,** Univ Of Pittsburgh, Pittsburgh, PA; JR; BENG; Bnd 88-; Mu Kappa Upsilon Sec 89-; Iota Beta Kappa Mmbr 89-; Pi Tau Sigma 90-; Tau Beta Pi 90-; Spcl Hnrs 8-; Chncllrs Nmn Schlrshp 88-; Fssndn Trtt Schlrshp 88-; Univ Schlr 90-; Cpt Endwd Schlrshp; Mchncl Eng.

**PALMER-SMITH, VICTORIA C,** Oh Wesleyan Univ, Delaware, OH; JR; BA; Chem Club; Chem Stdnt Fclty Brd; Chem Club Chrmn Actvts 88-; Wmn In Sci 89; Stdnt Fndtn 90; Chi Gamma Nu; Phi Society; Phi Eta Sigma; Mortar Board; Crestview Mntrng Pgm 89; Habitat Hmnty 90; Mortar Board Sec 90-; Chem/Zoology; Med.

**PALMERI, LINDA,** Univ Of Rochester, Rochester, NY; SR; BA; SG Chrprsn 90-; Italian Club Co Pres 87-88; Deans List 87-; Omicron Delta Epison; Partnrs In Rdng; Advest Inc Intrnshp; Im Soccer; Econ; Bus.

**PALMERTREE, MELANIE R,** Ms St Univ, Miss State, MS; SO; BA; Gamma Beta Phi 90-; Alpha Lambda Delta 90-; IM Sprts 90-; Arts; Med Tchnlgy.

**PALMIERI, FRANCINE G,** Mount Saint Mary Coll, Newburgh, NY; JR; BA; Deans Lst 90; AS Dutchess Comm Coll 90; Bus Mgmt; Finance.

**PALMIERI, LORI B,** Saint Vincents Coll & Seminary, Latrobe, PA; SR; BS; Natl Assc Of Accts Treas 87-; Bus Frm 90; Clss Cncl Ornttn Com 89; Intrnshp Sthwst Natl Bnk Tx Prprtn Asst 90; Wstnghse Elec Corp Acctng Asst 90; Acctng; Stff Acct.

**PALMIOTTO, GRACE,** Fl International Univ, Miami, FL; FR; Hsptlty; Hsptlty Mngmnt.

**PALMISIANO, JEAN L,** Univ Of Pittsburgh, Pittsburgh, PA; SR; BSW; Legstve Asst; Social Work.

**PALMQUIST, MITCHELL E,** Univ Of North Fl, Jacksonville, FL; SR; BBA; Amer Soc Mltry Cmptllrs 88-; Acctng; Bdgt Anlyst.

**PALMUCCI, CHRISTINE M,** Seton Hall Univ, South Orange, NJ; SO; BA; Nrsng Asst Intrn; Nrsng.

**PALOMBARO, KERSTIN M,** Saint Josephs Univ, Philadelphia, PA; FR; BA; Spnsh Tutor 90-; Hon Pgm 90-; Vrsty Crew 90-; Psychlgy; Physcl Thrpy.

**PALOVICH, MICHAEL R,** Allegheny Coll, Meadville, PA; SR; BA; Chemii Clb; Phi Kappa Psi; Chem; Ph D.

**PALSSON, MAGNUS,** Fl International Univ, Miami, FL; JR; BA; Mgr 80-90; Stu Prof Mtrcltn Exam Trnsfr Stu 77; Mrktg; Intl Bus.

**PALUCH, ROCCO A,** West Liberty St Coll, West Liberty, WV; SR; BS; Psy Clb 90-; Exprmntl Psy.

**PALUMBO, CHRISTOPHER J,** Fl Atlantic Univ, Boca Raton, FL; SR; BA; Alpha Tau Omega Scl Dir 87-90; Intrnshp IBM Intl Assgnmnts; Pre Professional Acctnt; Intl Bus; Intl Consultant.

**PALUMBO, JOHN R,** S U N Y Coll Of Tech At Alfred, Alfred, NY; FR; AOS; Sigma Tau Epsilon; Construction Maint Elctrcn.

**PALUMBO, LYNN,** Glassboro St Coll, Glassboro, NJ; SR; BA; Ad Clb 90-; Yrbk Lyt Ed 90; Delta Seta 1st VP 90; Intern Jamieson Advrtsng; Delta Zeta Awrd Acdmc Achvmnt 90; Deans Lst; Cmmnctns; Advrtsng.

**PALUSCI, JOUMANA M,** Duquesne Univ, Pittsburgh, PA; SO; Dns Lst 89-90; Intl Bus.

**PALUSZKIEWICZ, RICHARD J,** S U N Y Coll Of Tech At Frmgdl, Farmingdale, NY; FR; BET; Elect Engrng.

**PALUZZI, THOMAS M,** Merrimack Coll, North Andover, MA; SR; BS; Co-Op Ed 86; Deans Lst 89; Cmptr Sci; Sftwre Eng.

**PAMBIANCO, AMY B,** Marywood Coll, Scranton, PA; SR; BA; Hlth Serv Admin Clb Pres 89; Pi Gamma Mu; CPACA Visiting Nrse 90; Hlth Serv Admin; Hlth Care.

**PAMIC, EDDIE,** Ny Institute Of Tech Ny City, New York, NY; GD; BA; Co-Op Symbl Technlgs; Deans Lst 88-; Eng Tech.

**PAMON JR, STEPHEN R,** Morehouse Coll, Atlanta, GA; GD; Stdt Govt; Gldn Key 90-91; NAACD 87-91; HS Kenwood Acdmy 87; Banking/Finance; Invstmt Banking.

**PAN, JIN-PING,** Lake City Comm Coll, Lake City, FL; SO; Rcgnzd Dstngshd Acdmc Prfrmnc Tlnt Rstr; Excllnc Peer Tutrg Awd; AA; Comp Eng.

**PAN, KONG-FAN,** Oh Univ, Athens, OH; SR; Chnse Stdnt Assn 87-; Natl Soc Prfssnl Engrs 90-; IEEE 90-; Intl Stdnt Un 89-; Elec/Comp Eng.

**PAN, YOUNG-HUI,** Ms St Univ, Miss State, MS; SR; BBA; Chinese Stdnt Assn 90-; Malaysia Stdnt Assn 88-; Pres Schlr 89; Dean Schlr 90-; Mgmt Info Sys; Bus Mgr.

**PANAGIOTIS, HELEN E,** Bristol Univ, Bristol, TN; GD; Natl Mgmt Assoc; Manuf Prt Sply Buyr 79-; AA Cuyahg Comm Clg 74; BA Cal St Univ 78; MBA 90; Busn Admin/Hum Res; Purchsng.

**PANAGIOTOPOULOS, CONSTANTINA,** Montgomery Coll At Rockville, Rockville, MD; FR; AA; Pep Clb 90; Chrch Fstvl 90-; Sndy Schl Tchr 90-; Snr Grk Orthdx Yng Adlt Lge 90-; Maids Athena 90-; Ecnmcs Undstdng Cert 90; Omega Ins Agcy Intshp 90; Bsn Law; Corp Lawyer.

**PANAGOPOULOS, JUNE M,** Bunker Hill Comm Coll, Boston, MA; FR; AA; Linden Tenants Org Pres 89-90; Hdstrt Prschl Chrprsn 87-88; Ins Co Acctg Sprvsr/Cllctn Coord 73-82; Liberal Arts.

**PANARIELLO, ANGELA G,** S U N Y Coll Of Tech At Frmgdl, Farmingdale, NY; FR; AS; Bsn Admin.

**PANAS, EDWARD A,** Liberty Univ, Lynchburg, VA; SR; BS; Rape Comm 89-90; Acad Comm 88-89; RA 89; Thlgcl Stds/Chrch Hstry Award 89-90; Natl Stdnt Ldrshp Forum 90; IM Bsktbl 87-90; Pstrl Mnstrs; Pstr.

**PANAS, STEPHANIE L,** Duquesne Univ, Pittsburgh, PA; SO; BS; Campus Ministry; Alpha Gamma Delta; Var Swim Tm; Mktg.

**PANASETHANED, SUPANEE,** Univ Of Md At Eastern Shore, Princess Anne, MD; JR; BA; Bus Admnstrtn; Acctng.

**PANASUCK, SUZANNE J,** Marywood Coll, Scranton, PA; FR; BS; Opera IV 87-; Coll Vol 90-; NE Penn Lgl Asst Assn 87-; Psychlgy; Tchr.

**PANAYIOTOU, NICOLETTE M,** Tn Temple Univ, Chattanooga, TN; FR; BS; Stdnt Govt Sec Of Soph Clss; Vrsty Chldr 90-; Elem Educ; Tchr.

**PANCAKE, CINDY A,** Marshall University, Huntington, WV; SR; BBA; Natl Mgmt Assoc 90-; Alpha Kappa Psi Chr Res Comm 90-; Mgmt.

**PANCARI, JULIANN V,** Univ Of Pittsburgh, Pittsburgh, PA; SR; BSN; Dir S Fayette Sch Board Pres 87-; NCCDN Prog Coord Hickory Ridge; Adolescent Treatmnt Chem Depndny 87; Dip St Josephs Hosp Ch Nurs; # Rn Cac Natl CertfRN C Ana Psychiatric Mntl Hlth 87; CAC PCACB Cert Addictions Cnslr 89; Nurs; Grad Prog Hlth.

**PANCZAK, CHRISTINA M,** Saint Francis Coll, Loretto, PA; JR; BED; The Educ Clb 88-; Commtr Schlrshp 88-; Acdmc Schlrshp 88-; Elem Ed; Tchng.

**PANDEYA, VANDANA,** King Coll, Bristol, TN; SR; BA; Stdnts Free Entrprs Chr 90-; Camp Life Comm 89-90; Orient Comm Co-Chr 89-; Hlth Sci Clb 88-90; Pre Pro Soc 87-88; Alpha Delta Pi Pldg 87-88; Bsktbl Admin Asst Coachs Asst 90-; All Amer Schlr Coll Awd 90-; Econ/Bus Admin; Mktg/Pblc Rltns.

**PANDORA, TARA B,** Univ Of Nh Plymouth St Coll, Plymouth, NH; JR; BA; Pace 89-90; Kappa Delta Pi Treas 90; Phi Kappa Phi; Pres Schlr 88-; Swim Team 88-89; Math/Elem Educ; Educ.

**PANDROCK, RENEE L,** Slippery Rock Univ, Slippery Rock, PA; FR; Dnc Thtr 90-; SRAHPERD 90-; Dnc/Phy Ed; Tchng Scndry Schls.

**PANE, BETSY K,** Marywood Coll, Scranton, PA; SO; BS; Phi Beta Lambda 90-; Dance Educ Of Amer; Stdng Room Only; Acctng; Law.

**PANEK, ROBERT C,** Rochester Inst Of Tech, Rochester, NY; SO; MS; Engr Hse 89-; Xerox Co Op; Comp Engr; Engr.**

**PANELLA, MICHELE,** Castleton St Coll, Castleton, VT; JR; BSBUS; Chrldng Cptn 88-; ACE Sec 90-; Hall Cncl Prsdnt 90-; Earth Day Comm; RA Intrvwr; Acdmc Deans Lst 90; ASOAD; Mgmt; Mngr.

**PANEPENTO, PETER V,** Le Moyne Coll, Syracuse, NY; SO; Stu Nwsppr Mngr Edtr 90-; Stu Sen Cmmtt 90; Clss Rep 90-; Coll Intgrl Hnrs Prog 89-; IM 89-; Engl/Cmmnctns; Prfssr/Jrnlst.

**PANEPUCCI, DANA M,** Kent St Univ Kent Cmps, Kent, OH; SR; BA; All Campus Progrmng Bd Sec 88-89; Kent State Hon Assoc Sec 87-88; Alpha Lambda Delta; Golden Key; Phi Beta Kappa; Phi Alpha Delta Pre Law Clb; Ohio Govt Hon Int; Crmnl Juste; Pub Admnstrtns.

**PANFIL, KATHERINE,** Kent St Univ Kent Cmps, Kent, OH; FR; BA; AIESEC Intl 90-; PNA Flk Dncr 87-90; Polsh Natl Allianc Cncl 90-; Acad Hnr Rl; Dns Lst; Intl Rel; Dipl Wk/Poltcs.

**PANFILE, PAULA M,** S U N Y Coll Of Tech At Alfred, Alfred, NY; SO; BS; AS; Sociology.

**PANG, FIONA SUK HAN,** Northern Ky Univ, Highland Hts, KY; SR; BS; Alpha Chi Soc 90-; Acctg.

**PANG, TAK-YU,** City Univ Of Ny City Coll, New York, NY; SO; BA; Cmptr Sci.

**PANGBURN, TAMI C,** Chattahoochee Vly St Comm Coll, Phenix City, AL; SO; BS; Gamma Beta Phi; Engr; Comptr Sci.**

**PANIGUTTI, CARA A,** Coll Of Charleston, Charleston, SC; SO; BS; Coll Chrlstn Swm Tm 89-; Kappa Alpha Theta 90-; Intrmrls 90-; Mrn Blgy.**

**PANIKAR, JOHN MATHEW,** Univ Of Rochester, Rochester, NY; SR; BS; St Thomas Episcopal Church 89-; Sigma Phi Epsilon Schlrshp Chrmn 87-; Natl Starch/Chem Intern 90; Rugby 90; Mgmt Certif; Chem Engr.

**PANKO, LAURA J,** Cornell Univ Statutory College, Ithaca, NY; SR; PHD; Jordani Nat Hist Club Pres 88-; Wait Terr Coop Hse Mgr 88-; CU Sci Fiction Assoc 90; Ho-Nun-De-Kah At Cornell U 89-; Gamma Sigma Delta 90-; Phi Kappa Phi 90-; Merrill Prsndtl Schlr 91; Smithsonian Zoology Intern 88; Biology; Research/Teaching.

**PANKOW, SARAH L,** Cornell Univ Statutory College, Ithaca, NY; JR; BS; Yrbk Edtr 90-; Cmpfr Boys/Grls; Gldn Key 90-; Alpha Phi Edctr; IM Ice Hcky/Ftbl/Sftbl; Educ; Engl.

**PANNELL, DAVID J,** Alcorn St Univ, Lorman, MS; SR; BA; Stdnt Senate Prlmntrn 90-; Econ Treas 90-; Panhellenic Cncl Sec 89-90; Omega Psi Phi 89-; Econ; Corp Law.

**PANNELL, DONNA D,** Univ Of Al At Birmingham, Birmingham, AL; SO; BA; Spctr Edtr 90-; Std Amb Asc 90-; Clmbs Miss Hosp 90-; Lntrn 90-; Outstdng Serv Awd; Lckhrt Scl Clb 89-; Bsn/Prof Wmns Clb 90-; Camp Rising Sun Cnslr 90-; MS St Snte Page; Gold Star Awd; Pblc Rltns Acctng.**

**PANNELL, LESLIE S,** Abraham Baldwin Agri Coll, Tifton, GA; SO; BS; Student Govt Assoc 90-; Pre Vet Club Pres 89-; Soph Class Pres 90-; Phi Theta Kappa Nwsltr Edtr; Mu Alpha Theta; 4-H Club; Animal Sci; Vety Med.

**PANNELL, MELANIE E,** Univ Of Ga, Athens, GA; JR; BSED; Math Educ Stu Assoc; Ga Cncl Tchrs Math 90-; Prof Assoc Ga Educ; Mdl Sch Math; Educ.

**PANNO, TINA M,** Univ Of Cincinnati, Cincinnati, OH; SO; Stdnt Govt Escort Serv 89-90; Hlth Fairs 90-; Advsr 4h Jr Fair Bd Clermont Co Oh 90-; IM Vlybl 89-90; Nursing; Neonatal RN.

**PANNU, JASDEEP S,** Univ Of Sc At Columbia, Columbia, SC; JR; BA; Inter-Frat Cncl 90-; GAMMA Pres; Golden Key; Gamma Beta Phi; Psi Chi; Pi Kappa Phi; Olympic Karate Champion; IM Bsktbl/Flr Hockey; Psych; Med.

**PANNUCCI, JAMES A,** Univ Of Ct, Storrs, CT; JR; BS; Tae Kwon Do Clb; Alpha Zeta; Pathobiology; Disease Rsrch.

**PANNULLO, DAREN M,** Glassboro St Coll, Glassboro, NJ; FR; BA; Cpmtr Sci; Sys Analyst.

**PANTALIONE, CHRISTINA E,** Cumberland County Coll, Vineland, NJ; SO; MBA; History; Educ.**

**PANTALONE, BRETT A,** Univ Of Akron, Akron, OH; JR; BS; Eng.

**PANTANO, JENNIFER A,** Le Moyne Coll, Syracuse, NY; JR; BA; Engl Clb 90; Cmmnctns Intrnshp 90; Var Vllybl 88-90; Engl; Cmmnctns.

**PANTOJA, ENRIQUE A,** S U N Y At Buffalo, Buffalo, NY; GD; MUP; Fulbrght Schlrshp 88-90; Intrnshp OAS 90; Rsrch Asst/Tchng Asst 90-; BA/ARCH Univ Del Valle Cali Colombia 83; Arch/Urban Plnng; Urban Dsgn/Comm Dvlpmnt.

**PANYALEUTH, PHOTHONG THONG,** Bloomfield Coll, Bloomfield, NJ; FR; Dns Lst 90; Hnr Rl; BA; Acctg.

**PANZA, ANTHONY R,** Univ Of Pittsburgh, Pittsburgh, PA; SO; Coaching Summer Bsbl; Pi Kappa Alpha VP; Hon Rl; IM Bsktbl 90; Mech Eng.

**PANZARINO, JOANNE E,** Elmira Coll, Elmira, NY; SR; MS; Corning Tchrs Assoc; AS Corning Cmnty Clg 83; BA SUNY 85; Elem Tchr; Engl.

**PAOLI, GIOVANNI A,** Univ Of New Haven, West Haven, CT; SR; BA; Latin Assn Pres 88-90; Comm Racial Dvrsfctn Stdnt Rep 90-; Dns Lst 90; Delta Sigma Alpha Pldg Edctr 90-; Delta Sigma Alpha 89-; Music/Sound Rcrdng; MA Educ.

**PAOLINI, DENISE M,** Temple Univ, Philadelphia, PA; SR; BS; Ctr Early Chldhd Serv 89-90; Intern Lwr Bucks Hosp Cardiac Rehab; W W Smith Charitable Trust Schlrshp 90-; Deans Lst 89-; Am Heart Assn 89-; Am Coll Sports Med 89-; Fitness Cons 89-; Med Sec 80-88; Cert Digital Tech RETS 82; Phys Edn/Exercise Sci; Instrctn/Physiology.

**PAOLINI, LAURA A,** Barry Univ, Miami, FL; SR; BA; Ambassadors Clb 90-; Hosp Vol 90; Outstanding Grad Liberal Studies 90-; Crisis Ctr Intern 88; Lib Studies/Psychology; Mntl Hlth Cnslng.

**PAOLUCCI, LISA M,** Kent St Univ Kent Cmps, Kent, OH; SR; BBA; AMA 89-90; IM Co-R Ec Vlybl 89; Alpha Lambda Delta 88; Golden Key 90; Summit Mrktng Serv Inc Inter 90; Pillsbury Schlrshp Mrktng 90; Victor P Gravereau Mrktng Hnry Schlrshp Awd; Tennis 88-89; Mrktng/Bus Mgmt; Sales Rep.

**PAONE, CRISTINA M,** Le Moyne Coll, Syracuse, NY; JR; BA; Ski Clb Sec 89-; Pol Sci Acad 88-; Dorm Cncl Pres 90; Tour Gde 89-; Echrstc Mnstr 90-; Lcrsse Tm 90; Pol Sci Hstry; Law.

**PAONE, TONJA M,** Elms Coll, Chicopee, MA; JR; Stdnt Scl Wrk Org Co-Chr 89-; Deans Lst 88-; Ldrshp Awd 90-; Scl Wrk.**

**PAPA, DAVID M,** Providence Coll, Providence, RI; SR; BS; Prvdnc Acctng Clb 88-; Tau Pi Phi; Spec Olymc Vol 87-; IM 87-; Acctng; CPA.

**PAPA, REBECCA S,** Univ Of Sc At Columbia, Columbia, SC; JR; BS; Scuba Clb Sec 90-; Marine Sci; Mar Eclgst.

**PAPA, SUSANNE F,** Univ Of Southern Ms, Hattiesburg, MS; SR; BS; AA Hinds Comm Clg 88; Hotel Restrnt Mngmt.

**PAPADATOS, CLEVOULOS D,** S U N Y Coll Of Tech At Frmgdl, Farmingdale, NY; SO; BA; AAS; Intl Bus.

**PAPADOPOULOU, CORINNA J,** Univ Of Miami, Coral Gables, FL; JR; BA; 1st Cls Dipl St Godrics Coll London England 86; Fine Arts/Pntng/Phtgrphy; Advrtsng.

**PAPADOPULOS, MIGUEL F,** Ms St Univ, Miss State, MS; SR; BBA; Internatl Stdnt Assoc 90-; Latin Stdnt Assoc 90-; Gamma Beta Phi; Dns Lst 90; Pres Schlr 90; Bsn; Mgmt.

**PAPANIKOLAOU, ARISTOTLE,** Hellenic Coll/Holy Cross, Brookline, MA; SR; MDIV; NCCJ 89-; Phi Beta Kappa 88-; BA Fordham U Bronx NY 88; Theo; Ph D Stds U Chgo Dvnty Schl.

**PAPARATTO, LAURA M,** Bloomfield Coll, Bloomfield, NJ; SR; BA; Alpha Chi 90-; Bloomfield Symph/Orchestra 73-; Inductee Bloomfield Msc Hall Fame; Prfsnl Mscn; Rctlst/Ensemble Plyr; Dir Christ Church Sndy Schl/Vestry Mbr; Fine/Prfrmng Arts.

**PAPARO, ARI,** Georgetown Univ, Washington, DC; JR; BA; Environmental Scty; Fine Arts Painting; Bus Admin.

**PAPAS, ELAINE D,** Barry Univ, Miami, FL; GD; MPSY; Delta Epsilon Sigma; Phi Theta Kappa 86-87; Asstshp Dr Frederica Muller 89-; Intrnshp Under Dr Frederica Muller 90-; Mais Blas Schlrshp 85-87; Deans List 90-; Museum/Art Docent Trng Prog 89; Various Fnd Rsng Chldrn 84-89; Ind/Soc Psych; Gdnc Prvntv/Lrng Bhvrs.

**PAPAS, WASSILLI,** Georgetown Univ, Washington, DC; SO; BS; Bsn Adm; Invstmnt Bnkg.

**PAPATRYPHON, ELEFTHERIOS,** City Univ Of Ny Baruch Coll, New York, NY; SR; BBA; Grk Clb 88-; Deans Lst 88-; Frgn Stdnt Schlrshp 89-; Finance.

**PAPAY, JULIE I,** Ms St Univ, Miss State, MS; GD; BS 90; Blgy.

**PAPAY, MICHELLE S,** Univ Of Sc At Aiken, Aiken, SC; FR; Spec Painting Bdrm/Bath Banksin Museum.

**PAPE, DAWN R,** S U N Y At Stony Brook, Stony Brook, NY; FR; Anthrplgy.

**PAPE JR, EUGENE H,** Western Carolina Univ, Cullowhee, NC; JR; BA; Suncoast Sierra Clb Cnsvrtn Chr 88-89; Natl Rsrc Mgmt; Frstry.

**PAPERMASTER, ELLEN SUE,** Lesley Coll, Cambridge, MA; SO; BA; Lit/Ele Educ; Ele Ed Tchr.

**PAPINEAU, TONYA M,** Johnson St Coll, Johnson, VT; FR; BS; Biology; Tch.

**PAPOUTSAKIS, CHRISOULA,** City Univ Of Ny Baruch Coll, New York, NY; SO; Law Soc 90-; Acctg Soc 90-; Deans Lst; AHEPA Grk 88-; Acctg; Law.

**PAPP, DAVID R,** Thomas Nelson Comm Coll, Hampton, VA; SO; BA; Bsns.

**PAPPAS, JOHN-PAUL,** Pa St Univ Delaware Cty Cmps, Media, PA; FR; BA; Business.

**PAPPAS, VANESSA M,** Univ Of Nc At Charlotte, Charlotte, NC; JR; BCA; NAEA Pres Elect 91-92; NEA Pblctn 90-; National Golden Key 90-91; Vol Intrn Enrchment Prog Newell Elem; LPN Fayette County Vo Tech; Visual Arts.

**PAPPO, BARUCH,** Fl International Univ, Miami, FL; GD; MA; Beta Gamma Sigma 90-; Phi Kappa Phi 90; Dns Lst; BBA Fl Intnl Univ 90; AS Cntl Htl Trng Sch 85; Acctng.

**PAPURA, DAVID P,** Univ Of Scranton, Scranton, PA; SR; BS; Cmptr Sci Bsnss Clb 89-90; Omicron Delta Epsilon 2 VP 89-90; Delta Mu Delta 89-90; United Way 89; Sheriffs Dept Rsrve Spec Deputy Sheriff 89; Deans Lst 89-90; Natl Cllgte Bsnss Merit Awd; AS Pa State Univ 88; Mngmnt; Mngmnt Cmptr Info Systms.**

**PAQUETTE, JENNIFER L,** Endicott Coll, Beverly, MA; SR; ASSOC; Phi Theta Kappa 90; Internshps 89-90; Interior Decrtng; Dsngr.

**PAQUETTE, MARC J,** Univ Of Nh Plymouth St Coll, Plymouth, NH; SR; BFA; ALSO Pres 90-; Pres List 90; Artist/Graphic Design 81-89; Prntmakng & Drwng Art.

**PAQUETTE, SUSAN B,** Castleton St Coll, Castleton, VT; SR; BS; Tennis Tm 87-89; Res Hall Stf 88-; Food Cmtee 88; Otng Clb 87-; Stdnts Art Lgue 87-88; Stdnt Educ Assn; Tennis Tm 87-89; Educ; Tch.

**PARA, RAYMOND A,** Univ Of Akron, Akron, OH; SR; BSBA; FMA 90-; AOPA 84-; Golden Key 88-; Alpha Sigma Lambda 89-; Phi Theta Kappa 90-; Tri Cty EAP VP/BRD Dir 88-; Jrnymn Elctrcn Goodyear Tire/Rubber; AAB Comp Prgrmng Tech 90; Finance; Law.

**PARACHINI, SUSAN J,** City Univ Of Ny Baruch Coll, New York, NY; SR; BA; Gldn Key; Awrd Hghts GPA 83; Comp Prgrmmr 78-87; AAS 83; Cert Comp Prgrmmng 78; Spnsh.

**PARADIES, JENNIFER,** Newbury Coll, Brookline, MA; FR; BA; Fasion Merchndsng; Fshn Rtl/Byng.

**PARADIS, ADRIENNE E,** Columbia Union Coll, Takoma Park, MD; GD; BS; Assn Of Fed Hlth Org Sect 87-; Natl Assn Of Govt Employees 78-; AA Montgomery Clg 76; Bus Admin; Hlth Care.

**PARADIS, LINDA A,** Newbury Coll, Brookline, MA; ASSOC; Acctng; CPA.

**PARADISE, MELANIE M,** Univ Of Ga, Athens, GA; SR; BSHE; Phi Upsilon Omicron 88-90; Fshn Mrchndsng.

**PARADISE, MICHELLE A,** Hillsborough Comm Coll, Tampa, FL; SO; Phi Theta Kappa; Acctng/Bsn; CPA.

**PARADISO, MARIA C,** Cornell Univ Statutory College, Ithaca, NY; SO; BS; Big Sis/Big Bro; Alpha Epsilon Phi 90-; Ntl Schlr 89-; Sccr Tm; Bus; Law.

**PARADOWSKI, MARK R,** S U N Y At Buffalo, Buffalo, NY; SR; BS; Fncl Mgmt Assoc Treas 89-; Data Proc Mgmt Assoc 90-; Beta Gamma Sigma 90-; Sch Mgmt Annual Rep Fncl Dir 90-; Fncl Mgmt Assoc Natl Hnr Soc 89-; Marine Midland Bank Inc Intern; Prudentials Future Ldrs Conf 90; Finance/Mgmt Info Syst.

**PARADY, KELLY J,** Concord Coll, Athens, WV; GD; MFA; Owner/Bus 85-; Indpndnt Artis/Bus Woman/Teacher 85-; BFA Poartland Sch Of Art Portland Me 85; Fine Arts; Work Sm Bus/Teach.

**PARAGI, JOYCE A,** Comm Coll Algny Co Algny Cmps, Pittsburgh, PA; SO; BSN; Vol Amer Dbts Assn; Trvl Agnt; Rtrn To Schl Nrsng; Cert Sawyer Schl 85; Nrsng; BSN Ansthsia.

**PARAKILAS, CHRISTINA E,** Western New England Coll, Springfield, MA; JR; MBA; Attic Players 87-88; Mgmnt Asso 90-; Alpha Kappa Psi; Chrldg 87-88; Mrktg; Advtsg.

**PARANAL, ROWENA R,** Univ Of Sc At Columbia, Columbia, SC; FR; BA; Asian-Am Assoc 90-; Clb Asia 90-; Alpha Phi Omega; Tau Beta Sigma PR Chrprsn 90-; Bsn; Acctg.

**PARANGELO, VICTOR T,** Univ Of Rochester, Rochester, NY; SR; BS; ASME 89; Mens Vrsty Trck/Fld 87; Mchncl Engr; Engr.

**PARASMO, SERGIO,** A D Little Mgmt Educ Inst, Cambridge, MA; GD; MSM; BA 87; Bus Admin.

**PARAVATI JR, JOSEPH S,** Manhattan Coll, Bronx, NY; SR; BSME; ASME; SAE; Pi Tau Sigma VP 90; Epsilon Sigma Pi; Tau Beta Pi; Mchncl Eng.

**PARCHER, JUDITH A,** Fl International Univ, Miami, FL; SR; BS; Future Edctrs Amer 90-; Phi Kappa Phi; Grad Hnrs; Girl Scts USA Ldr 86-89; PTA Sec 85-86; Miami Spgs Jr Wmns Clb Pres 84-85; Elem Educ; Tchng.

**PARCHMENT, DIONNIE M,** Miami Dade Comm Coll South, Miami, FL; JR; CERT; Stdnt Govt Assoc Corr Secr 88-89; Phi Theta Kappa; Future Ed Amer 89-; Mnrty Stdnts Schlrshp 89-90; AA 89; Early Chldhd Ed/Elem Ed; Tchr.

**PARDEE, SUSAN C,** Teikyo Post Univ, Waterbury, CT; SO; BA; Amer Mktng Assc; Drama Clb; Exec Asst; Mktng; Advtsng.

**PARDO VARGAS, DIANNA L,** Inter Amer Univ Pr San German, San German, PR; JR; Accmplshmn Nght Stdnt 90-; Spnsh/Engl; Elem Tchr.

**PARDO, MAYTE,** Fl International Univ, Miami, FL; SR; BA; Future Educ Amer 90-; Kappa Delta Pi 90-; AA Miami Dade Comm Coll 89; Elem Educ; Tchg.

**PARDOE, ROBERT E,** Widener Univ, Chester, PA; JR; BS; Busn Admin; Acctg.

**PARDUA, CHRIS R,** Hiwassee Coll, Madisonville, TN; SO; AA; Drama Clb 90-; Phi Theta Kappa 90-; Mass Cmctns; Brdcstng.

**PARDUE, AMY A,** Univ Of Nc At Greensboro, Greensboro, NC; SO; BA; Elem Ed; Tchng.

**PARDUE, CLINT,** Univ Of Al At Birmingham, Birmingham, AL; SR; Interfraternity Cncl Prsdnt 89-90; Air Force ROTE 90-; Tau Kappa Epsilon VP 89-90; Arnold Air Soc Dpty Cmmndr; Prsdntl Hnrs; Hstry.

**PARDUE, KAREN H,** Univ Of Sc At Lancaster, Lancaster, SC; JR; Adlts In Ed 89-; ARETE Hnr Scty 90-; Half Tuition Spcl Awd 90-; Immanuel Bptst Chrch Chldrns Chr 86-; A Min Sthrn Baptist Thlgcl Smnry 85; Erly Chldhd Ed; Teacher.

**PARE, LOIS A,** Holyoke Comm Coll, Holyoke, MA; FR; AA; Spch Awd; Care Prvdr Spec Needs Indvduls 79-; English; Wrtr.

**PARE, MELISSA A,** Providence Coll, Providence, RI; SO; BA; IM Sftbl Clb 89-90; Erly Educ; Tchr.

**PAREDES VELEZ, SARA A,** Inter Amer Univ Pr Aquadilla, Aguadilla, PR; SR; MBA; New Stdnts Recruitmnt Comm 88-89; Future Tchrs Assoc 88-89; Stdnts Cncl Treas 90-; Dns Lst 87-; Hnr Soc 87-; Stdnt Orientation Assoc 87-; Medal Ldrshp; Certif Campaign Against Drugs/Alcohol Abuse; BA Ed Sec Spnsh; MA Cnslg/Orientation.

**PAREDES, MIKE C,** Embry Riddle Aeronautical Univ, Daytona Beach, FL; JR; BS; Amer Asso Airport Execs Daytona Bch 90-; Scuba Clb 90; Intrnshp Phoenix E Avtn Flght Dsptchr 90-; SCUBA 90; Cert Eagle Avtn 90; Arntcs/Flght; Pro Pilot.

**PAREKH, BOBBY H,** Comm Coll Algny Co Algny Cmps, Pittsburgh, PA; FR; BA; Cert Inst Cert Cmptr Prof 89; Chem Engr.

**PAREL, AMETHEL A,** Western Ky Univ, Bowling Green, KY; SO; Phtgrphr WKU Pblctns; Natl Assoc Blck Jrnlsts VP 90-; Phi Eta Sigma 90; Pht Intrn Nws Sntnl; Clge Hgts Fndtn Schlrshp 90; WKU Kodak Schlrshp Phtjrnlsm; Phtjrnlsm; Flk Stds/Grphc Arts.

**PARENT, JAMES W B,** Winthrop Coll, Rock Hill, SC; SR; BS; Resid Students Assoc 86-; SC Army National Guard E-4 88-; Deans List 90; Delta Psi Kappa 90-; Pi Kappa Alpha Big Brother Cord 87-; Berau Fist Bapt Chrch Cmp; Critical Issves Symposin 102 Student Dir; Amer Red Cross Instr 90-; Phys Ed; Tchr Certif.

**PARENT, KIM C,** Univ Of Ct, Storrs, CT; BS; Nat Res; Envir.

**PARENT, TAMARA A,** Comm Coll Of Philadelphia, Philadelphia, PA; FR; AGS; Gen Stds Math; Tchr.

**PARENT, VALORIE R,** Newbury Coll, Brookline, MA; FR; BA; Bsn.

**PARENTE, PETER A,** Brevard Coll, Brevard, NC; FR; BA; Chrldng Stnt Sqd Tornados 90-; Auditorium Co-Ord Dunham Hall Cltrl Actvty Cntr 90-; Wright Lftng 90-; Music; Prfrmnc.

**PARES AGOSTO, GILMARTIN,** Inter Amer Univ Pr Hato Rey, Hato Rey, PR; SR; BS; Phd Biology.

**PARES COTTO, WILKIA W,** Univ Of Pr Cayey Univ Coll, Cayey, PR; JR; BA; Cuadro De Hon De La Rctra CUS 88-; Estdnts Dstcds Del Prgm De Srvcs Espcls 88-; Mtrcla De Hon 88-; Psych/Mntl Hlth; Pblc Rltns.

**PARGITER, LUKE R,** East Tn St Univ, Johnson City, TN; SR; BS; Upsilon Pi Epsilon Treas; Comp Sci; Sys Analysis.

**PARHAM, ANGELA J,** Vance Granville Comm Coll, Henderson, NC; SO; BS; Ambsdrs Org Pres 90-; Phi Theta Kappa 90-; Trnsfr Schlr 88-; Deans Lst 88-; AA; AS; Elctrncs Engr; Air Trfc Cntrl.

**PARHAM, JERRY W,** Liberty Univ, Lynchburg, VA; SR; MA; Natl Guard Assoc US 80-; Miss Army Natl Grd Trng Offcr 80-; BGS; BS; Counseling; Personnel Mngmnt.

**PARHAM, ROVANDA L,** Commonwealth Coll, Norfolk, VA; FR; MA; Attndn Awrd; Dean Lst Awrd; Lit; RN.

**PARHAM, RUSSELL S,** Piedmont Tech Coll, Greenwood, SC; FR; AAS; Power Refrig Capsugel 90-; AAS 85-88; Htng Vntltn Air Condtng; Engrng.

**PARHAM, WANDA L,** Memphis St Univ, Memphis, TN; SR; BS; Blck Stdnt Assoc 87-; Gamma Beta Phi 90-; Blck Schlr Unlmtd 90-; U S Army Rsrvs; ROTC State Univ; OR Tech 88; Chem; Optometrist.

**PARHETTA, MARY T,** Comm Coll Algny Co Algny Cmps, Pittsburgh, PA; FR; AS; Chfs/Cooks Asc Pgh; Amel Bmbrlt Epcrn Lge; BS Duquesne Unv 85; Clnry Arts; Chef.

**PARIGIAN, BONNIE LYNN,** Radford Univ, Radford, VA; SR; BS; Crim Just Clb 89-; Zeta Tau Alpha 89-90; Dns Lst; Crim Just; U S Marshall.

**PARIKH, MANISH K,** City Univ Of Ny City Coll, New York, NY; SR; BS; Dbte Tm 90-; Cdgss Scty Pre Med Clb Treas; Gldn Ky; Pre Med Vol 90-; CRS Rsrch Prog; Psych Pre Med; Med Schl.

**PARINI, DARILYN M,** S U N Y Coll Of Tech At Frmgdl, Farmingdale, NY; SO; BA; Early Chldhd Ed.

**PARIS, ALFONSO C,** Wv Univ, Morgantown, WV; JR; MBA; Tau Beta Pi; Golden Key; Sigma Gamma Tau; Aero Engr.

**PARIS, ANDREW L,** Cincinnati Bible Coll & Sem, Cincinnati, OH; GD; Alpha Delta Tau 70-; Greek Awd 70, New/Old Testament Awds 70; Assoc Porf Theol 85-90; Of New Tstmnt/Dctrn 75-85; ABMAM Div; Theology/Religion.

**PARIS, ANN MARIE C,** Marywood Coll, Scranton, PA; FR; BSN; Nrsng.

**PARIS, DWIGHT J,** Univ Of Md Univ Coll, College Park, MD; FR; BA; Hmcmg Comm 90; Alpha Lambda Delta; Alpha Epsilon Rho 90-; IM Crss Cntry 90; Radio/Film/T V; Brdcstng.

**PARIS, JAMES T,** Hellenic Coll/Holy Cross, Brookline, MA; GD; MDIV; Stdnt Gvnmt VP 90; Deans List; Brnch Retail Oprtns Bank Of AM 86-88; Acct Wells Fargo 88-90; BS BA CA State Unvrsty Haywrd 85; Theology; Priest.

**PARISE, DONNA M,** Fl International Univ, Miami, FL; JR; BA; FEA Pres 89-; SG Chair-Scribe 89-; Kappa Delta Pi 90-; Day Care Vol 90-; Florida Ldr Mag Awd; AA Hnrs Broward Comm Coll 89; Educ; Elementary School Teacher.

**PARISH, AYANNA T,** Columbia Univ, New York, NY; FR; BA; Carman Dorm V P 90-; Dorm Cncl 90-; Prod Theatre; John Jay Schlr 90-; English/Philosophy; Law.

**PARISH, JANE C,** Tallahassee Comm Coll, Tallahassee, FL; SO.

**PARISH, TERI K,** Univ Of North Fl, Jacksonville, FL; FR; BA; Lit; Coll Prfssr.

**PARISI, IRENE M,** Wagner Coll, Staten Island, NY; SR; MBA; Blgy; Tchng.

**PARIZI, GHAZALEH,** Bunker Hill Comm Coll, Boston, MA; FR; Lbrl Arts; Pharmacy.

**PARK, ANNETTE M,** Unity Coll, Unity, ME; FR; BA; Nwmns Clb; Hlth Cncl; Radio Clb; Cross Cntry; BA Soc Sci; Env Policy.

**PARK, BERNARD J,** Cornell Univ Statutory College, Ithaca, NY; SO; BA; Radio Sta 90-; Burke Rehab Ctr Intrn 90-; Comms; Wrtr.**

**PARK, EMMA J,** Oh St Univ At Marion, Marion, OH; SO; BA; OCCL Pres 85-86; United Meth Wmn Pres 83-84; Martha Horne Cir Pres 87-88; Psychlgy Clb 90-; Griffin Socty 90-; Chrprsn Amer Cncr Sec La Rue Area Chrprsn 87-88; Recog Tchrs Elgin W Schl 86; Chrprsn Amer Cncr Socty Area Chrprsn 87-88; Elem Educ.

**PARK, EUN C,** Anne Arundel Comm Coll, Arnold, MD; FR; BA; Intrntl Stdnts Assn 90-; Phi Theta Kappa; Eng.

**PARK, EUNSOOK,** Univ Of Akron, Akron, OH; SR; BFA; Graphic Design.

**PARK, FELICITY A,** Anne Arundel Comm Coll, Arnold, MD; FR; ASN; Am Sing Lang Clb; Schl Vol; Orgnztnl Com Annapolis City Plygrnd; Office Mgt/Band Mgr/Phtjrnlst/Instrctd Sr Ctzns Arts Crafts Prog; Nrsng.

**PARK, JI-AH,** Eckerd Coll, St Petersburg, FL; JR; Fine Art.

**PARK, JIN-YONG,** Temple Univ, Philadelphia, PA; SO; BED; Physics; Engr.

**PARK, JOANNE H,** Case Western Reserve Univ, Cleveland, OH; FR; BA; Alpha Chi Sigma 90-; Biochem; Rsrch.

**PARK, JOHN C,** Univ Of Ky, Lexington, KY; FR; DVM; FFA KY St Rprtr 90-; Pre Vet Clb 90-; Pre Vet Med; Vtrnrn.

**PARK, JOHNNY L,** Middle Tn St Univ, Murfreesboro, TN; FR; BFA; BA W KY Univ 87; Grphc Dsgn.

**PARK, KIM M,** Kent St Univ Geauga Cmps, Burton Twp, OH; GD; BS; Selected For Voc Edn Srch Comm Spg 85; Superior Schlrshp Awd; Grad Cum Laude; Oh Bus Tchrs Assoc; Taught Adult Sec Trng 87-89; Elem Edn.

**PARK, MARIA C,** Dartmouth Coll, Hanover, NH; FR; BA; Big Bro/Sis 90-; Elec Nwspr Wrtr 90-; Hstry; Med.

**PARK, MI HYUN,** Columbia Union Coll, Takoma Park, MD; SO; MBA; Coll Korean Assns; Comp Grphc Art; Grphc Dsgnr.

**PARK, MICHELE M,** Hudson Valley Comm Coll, Troy, NY; GD; MBA; BA SUNY Nw Pltz 89; Bsns Admnstrtn.

**PARK, SANG-OK,** Univ Of Rochester, Rochester, NY; SR; BA; Physcl Thrpy Strong Mem Hosp 90-; BA; Biol.

**PARK, SEUNG HO,** Salisbury St Univ, Salisbury, MD; SO; BA; Bsn; Acctg/Fin.

**PARK, SO YOUNG,** City Univ Of Ny Baruch Coll, New York, NY; SO; BBA; Acctg.

**PARKER, ALICIA L,** Southeastern Baptist Coll, Laurel, MS; FR; BA; Assn Sec Treas Bapt 90-; SG Sec; S Central Reg Med Ctr Vol 90-; Music; Piano Tch.

**PARKER, ALLISON M,** Univ Of Sc At Columbia, Columbia, SC; FR; DVM; Blgy Clb 90-; Theta Sigma 90; Intern; Blgy Pre Vet.

**PARKER, ANDREA DAWN,** Univ Of Ms Main Cmps, University, MS; FR; Phi Beta Lambda 90-; Bnd 90-; Assc Stdnt Body; Prog Brd 90-; IM Ftbl 90; Acctng.

**PARKER, ANNIE LEE R,** Southern Junior Coll, Birmingham, AL; JR; Cosmtlgy.

**PARKER, APRIL M,** Harcum Jr Coll, Bryn Mawr, PA; FR; AS; Ebony Soc Clb; Partcpn Awd Ebony Soc Clb; Bsns Admn; Bkkpr/Acctg.

**PARKER, BERNADETTE,** Elmira Coll, Elmira, NY; JR; BA; Art Ed; Ther.

**PARKER, BERNICE C,** Stillman Coll, Tuscaloosa, AL; BA; Gamma Iota Sigma; Alpha Kappa Mu; Zeta Phi Beta Anti Basil 90-; Ford Schlr 89-; Cordell Wynn Hnrs 87-; Dns Schlr 88; Engl; Tchr.

**PARKER, BEVERLY COX,** Roane St Comm Coll, Harriman, TN; SO; BA; Gamma Beta Phi 81-82; Alpha Delta Pi 81-; Deans Lst 90-; AS Roane St Comm Coll; Acctg.

**PARKER, BRYAN A,** Univ Of Nc At Asheville, Asheville, NC; JR; BS; Soc Hnr Soc; Theta Chi Pres; Deans List; Hnr Roll; IM Ftbl Bsktbl 88-; Soc/Criminal Justice.

**PARKER JR, CECIL LAMAR,** Univ Of North Fl, Jacksonville, FL; JR; BS; Acctg Awd 87-88; AS LF Comm Clg/Jcksnvle 88; Acctg.

**PARKER, CHAD E,** Catawba Valley Comm Coll, Hickory, NC; SO; AASC; Bus Admin; Cmmnctns.

**PARKER, CHRISTINE B,** Valdosta St Coll, Valdosta, GA; FR; Pre-Phrmcy Chem.

**PARKER, DANIEL EDWARD,** Middle Tn St Univ, Murfreesboro, TN; SR; BS; Recycle Rutherford 90-; TN State Univ Swm 84-86; Blck Capt City Curbside Recycling Prog 90-; Mass Comm; Brdcst Sls/Mgmnt.

**PARKER, DEREK E,** Southern Coll Of Tech, Marietta, GA; JR; BSMET; BSU; Mech Engr; Engr.

**PARKER, DUSTY A,** Memphis St Univ, Memphis, TN; FR; BS; Hl Cncl Pres 90-; Engl Clb Treas 90-; Peer Mntr Prog 90-; Alpha Lambda Delta Hstrn; Gamma Beta Phi; Phi Eta Sigma; Hon Stdnt Assoc 90-; Mech Engr.

**PARKER, ELLEN L,** Andover Coll, Portland, ME; GD; Excell Shrthnd; Excell Typng 90-; Assoc Sec Sci; Legal Sec.

**PARKER, GARY L,** Ky Wesleyan Coll, Owensboro, KY; JR; BME; Stdnt Govt Assoc 89-; Music Educ Natl Conf Pres 89-; Singers 88-; James Graham Brown Soc 88-; Alpha Chi; Sigma Phi Epsilon Pres 89-; Wrtng Awrd 90; United Meth Ministers Schlrshp 88-; Music; Choral Dir.

**PARKER, GINA L,** Univ Of Montevallo, Montevallo, AL; SR; BA; Sigma Tau Delta Treas 89-; Alpha Lambda Delta 87-; Kappa Delta Pi 89-; Lambda Sigma Pi 90-; Eva O Golson Schlrshp 90-; Schlrshp 90-; Hnrs Chrldr Co-Capt 89-; Engl; Ed.

**PARKER, HEATHER,** Gallaudet Univ, Washington, DC; SR; BS; Phi Alpha Pi 89-; Pres Schlr 90-; Home Ec/Chld Dvlpmnt; Hmn Serv.

**PARKER, IRIS B,** Fl St Univ, Tallahassee, FL; SO; BA; WEB Dubois Soc; Engl/Bus; Lawyer.

**PARKER, JAMES D,** Vance Granville Comm Coll, Henderson, NC; FR; BA; Phi Theta Kappa; Dept Schlrshp 90-; Pht Jrnlsm; Newsppr Rep Phtgrphr.

**PARKER, JANINE R,** Central St Univ, Wilberforce, OH; SR; BA; Comp Sci/Math Clb 89-; Hon Stdnt 89-; Unisys Intrnshp 90; Unisys Schlrshp 90-; BA; Comp Sci; Syst Anlyst.

**PARKER, JEFFERY B,** Pellissippi St Tech Comm Coll, Knoxville, TN; SO; AS; Acad Work Study; Dsng Drftsmn DMC Bach Eng Seco 84-86; Cmptr Integrated Dsgn; Cad Sys Mgr.

**PARKER, JERRIE L,** Central Al Comm Coll, Alexander City, AL; SO; Sthrn Union St Jr Coll Chrldr 89; Ed; Erly Chldhd/Elem Tchr.

**PARKER, JODY A,** Springfield Tech Comm Coll, Springfield, MA; FR; Mass Ntl Grd; Sec Yr US Army 89; Adm Spclst US Army; Comp Oper; Ct Rptng.

**PARKER, JON C,** Ga Southern Univ, Statesboro, GA; JR; BA; Phi Theta Kappa; Acctg; Cpa.**

**PARKER, JULIE B,** S U N Y Coll At Fredonia, Fredonia, NY; JR; BA/BC; Music Therapy Clb 88-; Opera Thtr 88-; Orchesis Dance Grp 90-; Pi Kappa Lambda; Music; Vocal Perf.**

**PARKER, KAREN R,** Western Piedmont Comm Coll, Morganton, NC; SO; BA; AA; Bsn Admnstrtn.**

**PARKER, KARLA M,** Portland School Of Art, Portland, ME; JR; BFA; Pres List 90-; Studio Sprvsr 90-; Ringling Schl Art/Dsgn 88-; Fine Arts/Prntmkng; Grad Schl/Prntr.

**PARKER, KEVIN C,** Wallace St Comm Coll At Selma, Selma, AL; SO; BA; Prof Bowling Assoc; Smithsonian Assoc; Al State Trooper Booster; Crmnl Justice; Pre Law Paralegal.

**PARKER, KIMBERLY L,** Univ Of Sc At Columbia, Columbia, SC; FR; Drm Bible Stdy 90-; Educ.

**PARKER, KRISTY M,** Brewer St Jr Coll, Fayette, AL; SO; SGA 89-; Paula Thompson Meml Schlrshp; Hodges Schlrshp; Hnrs Schlrshp/Sr Natl Hnr Scity Schlrshp; IM 90; Chemisty; Med Schl.

**PARKER, LARA J,** James Madison University, Harrisonburg, VA; JR; BS; Natl Assn Educ Yng Chldrn 88-; Stdnt Cncrns Comm Cls Rep; Gldn Key 90-; Kappa Delta Pi Pres 89-; Kappa Delta Pi; Alpha Phi 90-; Cntr Srvc Lrng 89-; Ride For Hndcppd 89-; Future Tchr Awd Schlrshp 88; Dns Lst 88-; Pres Lst 89-; Early Chldhd Educ; Tchng/Admin.

**PARKER, LISA M,** Castleton St Coll, Castleton, VT; FR; BS; Bus; Acctg.

**PARKER, LISA MARIE,** Fl Atlantic Univ, Boca Raton, FL; SR; BA; Amer Mktg Assn 89-; Phi Theta Kappa Schlrshp 87-; Hnr Rl Palm Bch Comm Coll; Hnr Rl Fla Atlantic Univ; Mktg; Bus.**

**PARKER, MARCIA A,** Snead St Jr Coll, Boaz, AL; SO; Human Resources Field Adolescents; Behavoiral Sci; Social Wk.

**PARKER, MARGARET E,** Saint Andrews Presbytrn Coll, Laurinburg, NC; SR; BA; NCAE Pres 88; Gospel Choir 89; Alpha Chi 89; Hnr Soc 89; Christian Serv Org 87; Sr Ed Awd 90; Delta Kappa Gamma Rcrtmnt Grnt 90; Paul Douglas Tchng Schlrshp 89; Elem Ed; Tchr.

**PARKER, MARIAN L,** Portland School Of Art, Portland, ME; SO; BA; Stdnts Peace; Edctr Rec Spclst 86-; B Ed U MA 80-85; Cermacs; Artist/Tchr.

**PARKER, MARK S,** Middle Tn St Univ, Murfreesboro, TN; FR; BA; Air Force ROTC 90-; Arnold Air Soc 90-; Cadet Of Yr; IM Bsktbl; Aerospace Eng.

**PARKER, MARY M,** Middle Tn St Univ, Murfreesboro, TN; JR; BS; Campus T V Sta Nws Dir 89-; Channel 12 Promo Mgr 89-; SGA Sen 88-89; Gamma Beta Phi 89-; Tau Omicron 90-; Rho Lambda 90-; Soc Prof Jrnlst 89-; Alpha Delta Pi Chrmn 88-; Intrnshp WSMV Chnl 14 Nshvl Tn; MTSU Ldrshp Perf Sch; Radio/TV Brdcst Jrnlsm; TV Nws Rptr/Anchor.

**PARKER, MELODI J,** Duquesne Univ, Pittsburgh, PA; GD; Psi Chi Ntl Hnr Soc Psych 90-; BA 90; MA; Psych; Hmn Serv.

**PARKER, MINNIE I,** Rust Coll, Holly Springs, MS; FR; BS; Acapello Choir; Tennis; Chem; Phrmcy.

**PARKER, PAMELA N,** Alcorn St Univ, Lorman, MS; SO; BA; Bapt Stdnt Union 90-; Pryr Bnd; Trk; Acctg; CPA.

**PARKER, PATRICIA A,** Ms Univ For Women, Columbus, MS; SR; BS; Jones Hall Cncl Wing Rep 90-; Home Econ Hostess Squad Pres 90-; Bapt Stdnt Un 90-; Mortar Bd 90-; Phi Upsilon Omicron Sec/Treas 90-; Phi Theta Kappa VP 88-89; Mamselle Soc Clb 90-; MS Home Econ Assn; Outstndg Stdnt Yr; Dept Stdnt Yr; Clothing/Textiles Merch; Dept Store Buyer.**

**PARKER, PAUL E,** Commonwealth Coll, Virginia Beach, VA; SO; AAS; Commonwlth Clg Acctg Clb Pres 90-; Alpha Beta Gamma V P 90-; Pres Lst 90-; Acctg; Fncl Cnsltg.

**PARKER, REBECCA L,** Christian Brothers Univ, Memphis, TN; SR; BS; Am Mktg Assn VP 90-; Grad Cum Laude; Mktg.

**PARKER, REESE W,** Wilmington Coll, New Castle, DE; SR; BA; Prnts Anonymous 88-; 803 House Georgetown DE Intrnshp 89; Lions Clb 90-; Elctrcn 88-; Bhvrl Sci.

**PARKER, RENNA D,** Johnson C Smith Univ, Charlotte, NC; JR; BA; Sociology/Scl Wrk Clb; Yrbk Staff; RW Spiritual Choir; RA; Alpha Kappa Alpha Ivy Leaf Rprtr 90-; Sociology; Grad Schl.

**PARKER, ROBERT S,** Middle Tn St Univ, Murfreesboro, TN; SO; BA; Englsh; Tchng.

**PARKER, SAMANTHA J,** Endicott Coll, Beverly, MA; JR; J Lewis-London Englnd Sls Assoc 89; Mikeys Sprtng Goods Byr 88; Rtlng/Fash Merch.

**PARKER, SAMUEL T,** Univ Of Md At Eastern Shore, Princess Anne, MD; FR; B; Agric.

**PARKER, SANDRA J,** Univ Of Sc At Columbia, Columbia, SC; SR; Psychlgy Clb 85-87; Educ Clb 89; Kappa Delta Pi 89-; Rsrch Ppr Carolina Psyc Conf; Empl J C Penney 87-; BS 87; Psych Educ; Tchng.**

**PARKER, SHUNDA L,** Va St Univ, Petersburg, VA; JR; AS; Big Bro/Strs 90; N J Pre Alumni 90; Soc Wrk Clb Prlmntrn 90-; Urban Plnrs Chpln; NAACP; Urban Lgue 90-91; Sociology; Ph D Soc/Rsrch.

**PARKER, STEPHANIE E,** Morgan St Univ, Baltimore, MD; JR; BS; Telecomm Socty Camera Dir 90; 4 Yr Acad Schlrshp 88-; Awd Of Merit Acad Excel 89; Telecomm; Brdcst Prod.

**PARKER, SUSAN G,** Univ Of Sc At Columbia, Columbia, SC; SR; BA; Education.

**PARKER, SUZANNE H,** Univ Of Sc At Columbia, Columbia, SC; SO; BA; SC Philharmonic Chorus 90-; Assn Hnrs Stdnt; Gamma Beta Phi; Sec 85-; Intl; Law.

**PARKER, THOMAS C,** Norfolk St Univ, Norfolk, VA; SO; BA; Ftbl 89-; Phy Educ.

**PARKER, VICTOR S,** Union Univ, Jackson, TN; SR; BA; Mnstrl Assn 87-; Jdcl Brd 87; Prfssrs Aid 89-; Sigma Alpha Epsilon 87-; Mdl Excllnc Bblcl Grk Lang; Rlgn/Grk; Mnstr.

**PARKER, VIRGINIA F,** Middle Tn St Univ, Murfreesboro, TN; SR; BBA; FMA 90-; Bus Awd; Pres Enrchmnt Schlrshp 90-; Kodak Intrn 89-; Bus Fin; Bus Plng MBA.

**PARKER, VIRGINIA H,** Univ Of North Fl, Jacksonville, FL; SR; BA; Alpha Sigma Phi 90-; GSA 87-; Acctng; CPA.

**PARKER, WENDY K,** Chesterfield Marlboro Coll, Cheraw, SC; FR; BS; Phi Delta Kappa VP; Psychlgy; Cnslr.

**PARKER, WILLIAM A,** Talladega Coll, Talladega, AL; FR; BA; Crimson Ambassador 90-; Campus All Star Challenge Tm; Dns Lst 90-; Bsn Adm; MBA Bsn.

**PARKES, JAY T,** Indiana Univ Of Pa, Indiana, PA; JR; BED; Unvrsty Chrl 88-90; Stdnt Ldrshp Dvlpmnt Comm 90-; Sigma Tau Delta 90-; Kappa Delta Pi; Alpha Phi Omega Chptr Prsdnt 88-; Dstngshd Achvr Schlr 88-; Prvst Schlr 89-; Scndry Englsh Edctn; Bed.

**PARKES, JODY L,** Bridgewater Coll, Bridgewater, VA; FR; Ortr Chr 90-; Bsn; CPA.

**PARKES, TONYA KAYE,** Ms St Univ, Miss State, MS; SO; BA; Spanish Club 90; Sociology Corrections; Law.

**PARKHILL, AMY E,** Va Commonwealth Univ, Richmond, VA; JR; MFA; Amrcn Soc Interior Dsgn 90-; Gldn Key; Interior Dsgn.

**PARKHILL, GREGORY J,** Oh St Univ, Columbus, OH; SR; BS; Brd Gvrnrs 90-; Eta Sigma Gamma Sec 89-; Batelle Memrl Rsrch Inst Intrn 90; Ashland Chem Co Med Affrs Intrn 90-; Unv Hnrs Grad; Comnty Hlth; Hlth Promo/Hlth Prdct Salesmrktg.

**PARKHURST, CINDY L,** Northeastern Christian Jr Coll, Villanova, PA; FR; BA; Acctg.

**PARKHURST, KELLY M,** Univ Of Tn At Martin, Martin, TN; SR; BS; Lutheran Flwshp 89-90; Gamma Beta Phi 87-89; Pi Sigma Alpha 90; Phi Alpha Delta 90; Zeta Tau Alpha 89-90; Governors Cmndtn Awd 90; Govt Intern; AS Motlow State Comm Coll 89; Publ Admin; Law.

**PARKHURST, SHAWN L,** Johnson St Coll, Johnson, VT; SO; BA; Vol Srv Lngng 90-; Red Crss Bld Dr Coor 90; Chesamore Hnr Soc 90-; Tutor 89-; Ornttn Wrkr 90; Fclty Stff Schlrshp 90; Vrsty Bsbl 89; Elem Educ Spc Ed; Elem Tchr Prncpl.

**PARKINSON, BARBARA A,** Kent St Univ Kent Cmps, Kent, OH; SR; MA; Alpha Delta Pi 85-87; Wmns Ntwrk 85; Danceline 85; Amer Psy Soc; AS Univ Akron 87; Comm Cnslng; Psy.

**PARKINSON, BRIAN S,** City Univ Of Ny Brooklyn Coll, Brooklyn, NY; FR; BA; Engl; Tchr.

**PARKMAN, CINDY M,** Fl Atlantic Univ, Boca Raton, FL; JR; BA; Stdnt Actvts Comm/PBCC; Phi Theta Kappa/Fau/PBCC; Phi Kappa Phi; Delta Sigma Pi; IM Sftbl/PBCC; AA Plm Bch Comm Coll 90; Bus; Acctg.

**PARKMAN, ERICA L,** Tougaloo Coll, Tougaloo, MS; FR; NAACP; Miss Blck/Gold Pgnt; Biology/Pre Med; Medicine.

**PARKMAN, JAMES N,** Middle Ga Coll, Cochran, GA; SO; AS; Psychlgy/Bsn; Cnslng.

**PARKMAN, JANE M,** Clayton St Coll, Morrow, GA; SR; BSN; AHA; BLS Instr/Trnr; PALS Instr; ICEA; NAACOG; NACES; Ed Coord; RN GA Bapt Hosp Sch Nrsg 75; CPCE NACES 88; Nrsg.

**PARKMAN, STEPHANIE S,** Univ Of Sc At Columbia, Columbia, SC; SO; BS; NARD Stdnt; Mrchng Bnd Squad Ldr 89-; Bsktbl Pep Bnd 90-; FCA 89-; BSU 89-; SC Hnrs Clg 89-; Assn Hnr Stdnt 89-; Phi Eta Sigma 89-; Alpha Lambda Delta 89-; Gamma Beta Phi VP 89-; Pharmacy Intrn; Prsdnt Lst 90-; Deans Lst 89-; Pharmacy.

**PARKS, BARRY E,** Western Carolina Univ, Cullowhee, NC; SO; BS; Sylva Chrch Christ Yth Grp 89-; Flwshp Chrstn Athlts 90-; Alpha Lambda Delta 89-; Athltcs Dir Acad Achv Awd 89-; Vrsty Chrlding Co Cpt 89-; Bio; Vet Med.

**PARKS, BERLIE E,** Mountain Empire Comm Coll, Big Stone Gap, VA; SO; BSA; Tn Eastmn Co Trnee; Drftng/Dsgn; Drftg.

**PARKS, BETHANY ANN,** Mount Saint Mary Coll, Newburgh, NY; GD; Nwspr Sec 90-; Asst Layout Edtr 90-; Nwsltr Sec 90-; Tri Beta 88-; Math/English; Actuarial Sci.

**PARKS, CHAD W,** Fl International Univ, Miami, FL; SO; BS; Gvrng Cncl V P; Stdnt Srvcs Cmmtee SGA V Chr; Mnr Intrnatl Rltns; Hsptlty Mgmt; Trvl Trsm.

**PARKS, CHRISTIAN HUNTER,** Fl Atlantic Univ, Boca Raton, FL; JR; BBA; Fnc; Lwyr.

**PARKS, CHRISTOPHER A,** Middle Tn St Univ, Murfreesboro, TN; SR; Sigma Chi Pres 87-; Entreprenuers Assc 89-; St Thomas Hosp Intern 89-; BS; Wellness/Fitness-Mrktng; Import/Export Bus.

**PARKS, COLLEEN M,** East Carolina Univ, Greenville, NC; SO; BFA; Art Grphc Dsgn.

**PARKS, DONNA L,** Wilberforce Univ, Wilberforce, OH; JR; BA; Cntrl State Univ Spec Hlth Prjcts 4th Pl Wnnr CSU AIDS Pstr Cntst 90-; Cmmrcl Art; Advrtsng Agncy.

**PARKS, GLENDA L,** Christian Brothers Univ, Memphis, TN; FR; BA; Acctg/Info Syst; Acctg/Telecmnctns.

**PARKS JR, JAMES D,** Univ Of Tn At Knoxville, Knoxville, TN; SR; BS; Soc Nuclear Med 86-; Beta Gamma Sigma; J H Williamson Awd Schlrshp 90; Soc Nuclear Med 86-; AS Walter State Comm Clg 85-; Cert U Tenn 86; Bus Mgmt; Hosp Admn.**

**PARKS JR, JOHN W,** Savannah St Coll, Savannah, GA; JR; BA; Hall Assc VP 90-; Drmtry Cmt 90-; Ftbl/Trck 88-; Acctg; Bus.

**PARKS, KAREN M,** Coll Of New Rochelle, New Rochelle, NY; SO; BA; Theatre Grp Pr 89-; The Wash Ctr; Hons Pgm 89-; State Sntr Suzi Oppenheimer Intrn 90; AFS Schlrshp; Hons Schlrshp; Cmctn Arts; Actress.

**PARKS, MARK S,** Univ Of Cincinnati-Clrmnt Coll, Batavia, OH; SO; BSEE; Elec Eng.

**PARKS, NICOLE D,** Fayetteville St Univ, Fayetteville, NC; SO; BS; Bio/Premed; Pedatrcs.

**PARKS, PORTIA L,** Norfolk St Univ, Norfolk, VA; SR; BS; Math/Cmptr Sci Clb Pres; Alpha Kappa Mu 88-; Spartan Alpha Tau 87-88; NASA Langley 89; NASA Goddard 90; GPA Awd; Math; MS.

**PARKS, ROCHELLE EVE,** Central St Univ, Wilberforce, OH; FR; BA; Hnrs Dorm Queen 90-; Busn; Cpa.

**PARKS, STUART A,** Va Highlands Comm Coll, Abingdon, VA; SO; BA; Deans Lst 90; Pres Lst 90; AAS; Elec Eng.

**PARKS, SUSAN E,** Univ Of Nc At Greensboro, Greensboro, NC; SR; BS; Amer Soc Int Dsgnrs Stdnt Chptr 90-; Hnrs Studio Participant Dept Hsg/Int Dsgn 89-; Univ Marshall 88-90; Outstndg Sr Dept Hsg/Int Dsgn; Lyndon Bray Co Intern 89; Brayton Intl Intern; Graphic Dsgnr 74-; Envir Dsgn; Museum/Exhib Dsgn.

**PARKS, SUSAN G,** George Mason Univ, Fairfax, VA; SR; BS; AS Charles Co Cmnty Clge 81; Erly Ed; Tchr.

**PARKS, TIMMEKO D,** Ga St Univ, Atlanta, GA; GD; NAUW; GCSS 90-; BED 90; Middle Chldhd Educ; Admin.

**PARLANTI, JOSEPHINE,** Wagner Coll, Staten Island, NY; FR; MBA; Intl Mktg.

**PARLAPIANO, MARIA I,** Atlantic Comm Coll, Mays Landing, NJ; GD; AAS; Aerobics/Dance/Gymnstcs; Chrldng; ACC 90; Court Stngrphr.

**PARLATO, MICHELLE L,** S U N Y Coll At Brockport, Brockport, NY; FR; BA; Nrsg.

**PARLER, PENNY I,** Univ Of Sc At Columbia, Columbia, SC; FR; BS; Bsn; Mgmt.

**PARLIKAR, DAKSHESH D,** Temple Univ, Philadelphia, PA; SO; BA; IEEF; Alpha Lambda Delta 90-; Digital Signal; Elect Eng.

**PARLIMENT, TAMMY J,** Stockton St Coll, Pomona, NJ; FR; Crss Cntry 90-; Schlr Mntr Prog 90-; Pres Schlr 90-; Dns Lst 90-; Crss Cntry 90; Math; Actuary.

**PARLOW, GINA L,** Union Univ, Jackson, TN; SO; BM; Music; Tch.

**PARLSEY, ROBIN L,** Middle Tn St Univ, Murfreesboro, TN; FR; Deans Lst; Gamma Beta Phi; Delta Zeta Sor Treas 90; 4 Yr Acad Wrk Schlrshp 90; Wrk For Dean Haskew Clg Of Bsnss; Mngmnt W/BA Finance Mnr; Bsnss Mngmnt.

**PARMAN, TRACY L,** Fl International Univ, Miami, FL; SO; MBA; Accntng; Bsns Mgmnt.

**PARMEGIANI, ANTHONY C,** Saint Johns Univ, Jamaica, NY; FR; MBA; Stdnt Govt 90-; Psych.

**PARMELEE, HEIDI A,** S U N Y Coll Of Tech At Delhi, Delhi, NY; SO; DVM; NYSAVT 89-; AALAS 90-; Vet Med; Bovine Vet.

**PARMENTER, DONITA S,** Univ Of Miami, Coral Gables, FL; JR; BBA; Hnrs Prgm 90-; Cert Rsprtry Thrpy Tchncn 85; Rsprtry Thrpst 84-89; AAS 85; Bus.

**PARNABY, JEFFREY A,** Univ Of Miami, Coral Gables, FL; SR; BBA; Orntatn Asst 88-89; Ltcl Sci Stdnt Assn 89-; Coconut Grove Social Clb 88-; Hon Stdnts Assn 87-; Lambda Chi Alpha 87-89; Amer Cvl Libtes Un Intrn; Univ Miami Athletic Dept Intrn 87-; Pres Hon Rl 88-; Pltcs; Law.

**PARNELL, CHARLES GILBERT,** Univ Of Tn At Martin, Martin, TN.

**PARNELL, KEITH M,** Memphis St Univ, Memphis, TN; SO; BA; SGA Prss Sec 89-; Phi Eta Sigma 90-; Fr Essy Wrtrs Cmpttn 90-; Hnrs Cert; Jrnlsm; Brdcst Mngmnt.

**PARNELL, KENYA V,** Univ Of Sc At Columbia, Columbia, SC; SO; BA; Hall Govt Rep; Early Chldhd Edn; Teach.

**PARNELL, KIMBERLY A,** Walker Coll, Jasper, AL; SO; RN; Bptst Cmps Mnstrs 90-; Jzz Ensmbl 90-; Coll Chr 90-; Cmpss Clb 90-; Sci; Nrsng.**

**PARNELL, LINDA D,** Va Commonwealth Univ, Richmond, VA; SR; BS; Phi Kappa Phi; Vlr Prgrm Mcguire VA Mdcl Cntr 90; Nrsng.

**PARNELL, REGINA G,** Northern Ky Univ, Highland Hts, KY; FR; BA; Educ; Engl/Math Tchr.

**PARNELL, TAMMY G,** Volunteer St Comm Coll, Gallatin, TN; SO; BA; Math; Tchng.

**PARNELL, TRACI D,** Birmingham Southern Coll, Birmingham, AL; FR; BA BE; Art Stdnts League 90-; Chrmn Of Greek Wk 90-; Comm Outrch; Fndrsng; Spring Frml Comm Co Chr; Dns Lst; Pi Beta Pi 90-; Art/Hnrs Schlrshps 90-; Pi Beta Phi Hse Mgr; Engl/Art; Wrtr.

**PARNESE, TED V,** Wagner Coll, Staten Island, NY; FR; BS; Ftbl; Acctg; Acctnt/Law.

**PARNITZKE, ERIC G,** Northern Ky Univ, Highland Hts, KY; JR; BS; Finance.

**PARONG, FIL A,** Old Dominion Univ, Norfolk, VA; JR; BS; Golden Key; NASA 89-; Engr; Elctrcl Engr.

**PARONISH, NICHOLAS M,** Mount Aloysius Jr Coll, Cresson, PA; FR; AS; Nrsng; Nrs Ansthtst.

**PAROUS, AURISTELA BATISTA,** Comm Coll Algny Co Algny Cmps, Pittsburgh, PA; SO; Engl Cmmnctns/Jrnlsm.

**PARR, MISTY L,** Fl International Univ, Miami, FL; JR; BS; Vars Clb 90-; Schlr Athlete 90-; Vars Soccer 90-; AA Anne Arundel Comm Clg 90; Scndry Educ/Biol; Tch.

**PARR, THOMAS G,** Life Coll, Marietta, GA; GD; DC; Gnstd Clb 90; Actvtr Clb 90; Amer Gld Of Orgnst 79; Fllwshp Cath Mscns 89; Intrntl Chrprctc Assoc 90; Amer Scty Of Clncl Pthlgst 87; Chrch Music Dir/Orgnst 79; Med Tchnlgst 87; BSMT Ga State U 87; Chrprctc; Dr Of Chrprctc.

**PARRA, CARLOS,** Passaic County Comm Coll, Paterson, NJ; SO; Subst Tchr Passaic Brd Educ ; Army Natl Grd; Bus Admn; Ec.

**PARRA, RACHEL M,** Univ Of Nc At Greensboro, Greensboro, NC; SO; BA; Elmntry Edctn; Spnch Edctn.

**PARRA, RENE X,** Ma Inst Of Tech, Cambridge, MA; FR; BS; SHPE 90-; Mtrls Sci Rsrch; Intern Hewlett Parckard; Elec Eng; Rsrch Artfcl Intllgnc.

**PARREIRA, ANABELA S,** Ct Coll, New London, CT; FR; BA; Bio Med Rsrch Grp; Asst Masters Candidate Caffeine/Stress Rsrch; Psych.

**PARRENT, ELIZABETH A,** Me Maritime Academy, Castine, ME; JR; BS; BA Colby Coll 83; Nautcl Sci.

**PARRETT, JANET F,** Meridian Comm Coll, Meridian, MS; SO; BS; Ms State U Meridian; Elem Ed; Tchng.

**PARRETT, KIMBERLY G,** Univ Of Ky, Lexington, KY; JR; BED; Dns Lst 88-; K-4 Elem Ed; Tchng.

**PARRINO, CAROLINE M,** James Madison University, Harrisonburg, VA; JR; BS; Univ Prog Brd 89-91; Univ Chorus 90-91; Cmps Cadet 90-91; Alpha Phi 90-91; Train A Champ Vol 90-91; Pyshc; PHD Cnslng Psych.

**PARRIS, BRIAN W,** Univ Of Sc At Columbia, Columbia, SC; FR; BS; AS EET Spartanburg Tech Coll 90; Elec Eng.

**PARRIS, JAMASON R,** Walker Coll, Jasper, AL; FR; BS; Chrch Yth Grp; Dns Lst; Math; Scndry Educ Math Tchr.

**PARRIS, PAMELA C,** Phillips Jr Coll Spartanburg, Spartanburg, SC; GD; AD; Dns Lst 90-; Pres Lst; Sec Sci; Lgl Exec Sec.

**PARRIS, SHARON V,** City Univ Of Ny Baruch Coll, New York, NY; SR; BA; Art Soc 88-; Bus Clb VP 87-88; Psi Chi 89-; Gold Key 90-; Trnsfr Schlrshp 88-; Sybil C Simon Art Admn Intrnshp Art/Bus Cncl 90; Baruch Almni Assn Schlrshp 90-; Prnt Tchr Vol Dist 26 88-; Trvl Coord 88-90; Art Agent 87-88; Clncl Psychlgst.

**PARRIS, SUSAN M,** Univ Of Sc At Spartanburg, Spartanburg, SC; FR; BS; Math; Eng.

**PARRISH, ALLISON A,** Ms St Univ, Miss State, MS; SO; BS; Chi Omega Asst Corr Secr 89-90; Very Spec Arts Vol 90-; MADD 90; IMS 89-90; Elem Ed; Tch.

**PARRISH, AMELIA W,** Univ Of Nc At Charlotte, Charlotte, NC; JR; BA; Media Srvcs Intrn 90-; Tutor 88-90; Engl; Brdcstng.

**PARRISH, CHRISTINE T,** Univ Of Akron, Akron, OH; SR; BA; ACES; NCTE; Assoc Cuyahoga Comm Coll 89; Comm Comprehensive/Educ; Tchng.

**PARRISH, CHRISTOPHER R,** Univ Of North Fl, Jacksonville, FL; BA; Histiory.

**PARRISH, DAVID R,** Ms St Univ, Miss State, MS; SO; BA; Co-Op Stdnt; Indstrl Engr; Engr/Mgmt.

**PARRISH, DONNA L,** Univ Of Ga, Athens, GA; GD; MED; Delt Epsln Ch Deca State Rep 88-89; 88 Stdnt Of Yr; ASSC Gainesville Clg 88; BSED 90; Mktg Educ.

**PARRISH, GENEVA L,** Marshall University, Huntington, WV; JR; BA; Stdn Torgnztn Almn Rltns Mmbr 90-; Deans Lst 89-; Ornttn Stdn Tasst; Stdnt Affrs Wrk Stdy 88-; Intrnshp Nw Stdnt Ornttn; L; Cnslng Rhblttn.**

**PARRISH, GEOFFREY ALLEN,** Southern Coll Of Tech, Marietta, GA; SR; BSIET; Hewlett-Packard Intrnshp; Inst Indus Engr 90; Amer Soc Quality Cntrl 90; Indus Engr.

**PARRISH, JEANA R,** Univ Of Miami, Coral Gables, FL; JR; BS; Scuba Clb; Dwntwn Tampa Bus/Prof Wmn Assn 88-89; JR Achvmnt Advsr 86-87; Citizen Southern Natl Bnk 85-88; AA Hillsborough Comm Coll 90; Accntng; CPA/FNNCL Plnnr.

**PARRISH, KATHLEEN M,** Tn Temple Univ, Chattanooga, TN; JR; BA; Word Life Clb 89-90; Practicum I Ii 90-; Psych; Cnslg.

**PARRISH, KIMBERLY B,** Univ Of Sc At Sumter, Sumter, SC; JR; BA; Rape Crisis Adv YWCA; Dom Shltr Vol; AA; Psych; Clin Psych/Thrpy.

**PARRISH, LEAH A,** Wv Univ At Parkersburg, Parkersburg, WV; FR; AA; Nrsng; RN.

**PARRISH, LISA M,** Univ Of Ms Medical Center, Jackson, MS; JR; BSN; Natl Stdnt Nrs Assn 90-; Miss Stdnt Nrs Assn; Gamma Beta Phi 84-; Phi Mu 83-; Sigma Alpha Epsilon Ltl Sis 83-; Stdnt Nrs Extrnshp Univ Med Ctr; BS Miss State Univ 88; Nrsng; RN.

**PARRISH, MICHELLE E,** Manhattanville Coll, Purchase, NY; JR; BA; Stdnt Prog Brd Soc Co Chrmn 90-; Publ Chrmn; Intrnshp Rye Hstrcl Soc; Art Hstry.

**PARRISH, TERESA A BOND,** Ky St Univ, Frankfort, KY; SO; BA; Grls Actn Ldr 87-; BYW 90-; PTO Prsdnt 86-; Erly Elem Edctnf Tchr.

**PARRISH, VALERY J,** Itawamba Comm Coll, Fulton, MS; SO; BA; Elem Educ; Tchr.

**PARROTT, GLENISE B,** Gaston Coll, Dallas, NC; GD; AA; Psychology; Soc Wrkr.

**PARROTT, MICHAEL S,** Univ Of Sc At Columbia, Columbia, SC; SO; BA; Naviagtors; BSU; Cmptr Sci; Analyst.

**PARROTT, SCOTT D,** Tn Tech Univ, Cookeville, TN; SR; BS; Agrbsnn Clb Pres 87-; Rgby Clb 89-; Delta Tau Alpha VP 89-; Omicron Delta Epsilon 89phi Kappa Phi 90-; Acdmc Schlrshp 89-; Agrcltr Awrd 89-; Vrsty Ftbll 87-88; Agrbsnss Econ.

**PARROTT, THERESA L,** Nova Univ, Ft Lauderdale, FL; GD; MBA; Phi Kappa Phi; Hnrs Proj; Magna Cum Laude Grad; Tstmstrs Intl 90-; Natl Assn Female Execs 90-; Sr Sls Mgr; BA U Of NC 84; Mktng; Sls/Mktg Mgmnt.

**PARROTT, VIRGINIA W,** Vance Granville Comm Coll, Henderson, NC; SO; AAS; Phi Theta Kappa; Bsn Cmptr Pgm.

**PARSCHAUER, ROBERT J,** Tn Temple Univ, Chattanooga, TN; JR; BA; Sngng Ensmbl Sng Ldr 90-; Sccr 90-; Bible Dipl Word Lf Bible Inst 89; Mssn/Yth Dipl Word Lf Sch Yth Mnstrs/Mssns 90; Pulpit; Cmnctns; Mssnry.

**PARSH, ANN MARIE,** Bethany Coll, Bethany, WV; SR; BA; Pblc Rltns Clb Pres 90-; Yrbk 89-90; Nwspr Sbscrptn Mgr 89-90; Soc Cllgt Jrnlsts; Gamma Rho Omicron 89-; Kappa Delta VP 89-90; Fine Art Cntr ; Pr Intrn; Btncl Grdn PR Intrn 90; Communications; Pblc Rltns.

**PARSON, ANGELA C,** Univ Of Sc At Columbia, Columbia, SC; FR; BA; Math; Acctnt.

**PARSON, MINNETTE J,** Rust Coll, Holly Springs, MS; SO; NAACP 90-; Asstn Press Sec Stdnt Govt Assn; Hon Track Orga 89; Sigma Tau Delta Sec; Bearcat Chrldr Squad 90-; English.

**PARSON, PAMELA S,** Hampton Univ, Hampton, VA; SR; BS; Pr Cnslrs 89-90; SVEA 88-; Kappa Delta Pi 90-; Hnr Cncl Awrd Otstndng Achvmnt; Mddl Sci.

**PARSON, SHANE C,** Va Polytechnic Inst & St Univ, Blacksburg, VA; SO; BS; Am Soc Agri Engrs 90-; Ernestine Mattews Schlrshp; George C Vaughn Schlrshp; Agri Eng.**

**PARSON, TRACEY E,** Univ Of Sc At Columbia, Columbia, SC; SR; BA; USC Ad Clb 89-; Alpha Lambda Delta 87-; Phi Eta Sigma 87-; Sirrine Schlr 87-; Deans Lst 87-; Intrnshp Henderson Advrtsng 90; Jrnlsm; Assist Editor.

**PARSONS, ANTHONY D,** Marshall University, Huntington, WV; FR; BBA; Busn/Fince.

**PARSONS, BRENDA L,** Indiana Univ Of Pa, Indiana, PA; SR; BI ED; Rsdnce Lfe Rsdnt Asst 89-; Erly Chldhd Educ; Tchng.

**PARSONS, EMILY MARIE,** James Madison University, Harrisonburg, VA; FR; BS; Sigma Pi Ltl Sis; Living Sci Clb; Delta Gamma Sr B-Days; Walter Reed Army Med Ctr Intern; Nrsg; Ped Nrs.

**PARSONS, JANET,** Tn St Univ, Nashville, TN; JR; BA; Nashville Artists Gld Perm Gllry 89-; Alpha Mu Gamma 90-; Gldn Key 89-; WPLN Radio Patron Gala Chrmn; Med Asst/Lcnsd Xray Tech; Prof Art Career Reg Exhbts; Intrdscplnry French/Art; Prof Lecture Coll.

**PARSONS, JULIA A,** Livingston Univ, Livingston, AL; FR; ASN; Nrsng.

**PARSONS, LISA A,** Univ Of Sc At Columbia, Columbia, SC; FR; BA; Fine Arts/Music.

**PARSONS, MELODY J,** Tn Temple Univ, Chattanooga, TN; FR; BA; Sngng Mn Tmpl Pianst; Univ Choir 90-; Theta Mu Rho; Acad Schlrshp; IM Bsktvl/Vlybl 90-; Musc Educ; Tchg.

**PARSONS, PATTI L,** Greenville Tech Coll, Greenville, SC; SO; ASB; Deans Lst 89-; Sftbl/Vlybl 90-; CLC Univ Spain 87; Bus Mgmt/Mktg; Intl Bus.

**PARSONS, REBEKAH J,** Gettysburg Coll, Gettysburg, PA; FR; BA; Envrnmntl Clb 90-; Martial Arts 90-; Stdnt Actvies 90-; Recog For Recvng A Perfct Score On Biol Fnl; Biol.

**PARSONS, SANDRA M,** Univ Of Al At Birmingham, Birmingham, AL; SR; BS; Amer Soc EEC Tchnlgsts 80-; Al Soc EEG Tchnlgsts 80-; Sr EEG Tech UAB Hosp; Assoc Appld Sci Alexander City St Jr Clge 77; Alld Hlth Admin; Hlth Admin Mgmt.

**PARSONS, SHARON J,** Villanova Univ, Villanova, PA; JR; BS; Acctng Scty; Pr Cnslr; Phi Kappa Phi 89-; Omicron Delta Kappa 90-; Gamma Phi 89-; Beta Gamma Sigma; Alpha Phi Prmtns 89-; Prjct Snshne; Smkss Agncy Intrnshp; Natl Assn Of Blck Acct Schlrshp; IM Bsktbl; Acctng; CPA.**

**PARSONS, T SCOTT,** Kent St Univ Kent Cmps, Kent, OH; JR; BA; Engl; Grad Schl.

**PARSONS, VIRGINIA PIAZZA,** Fl A & M Univ, Tallahassee, FL; JR; BS; SOTA VP; Mortar Bd Troy St Univ 89; Phi Kappa Phi Troy St Univ 89; Omicron Delta Kappa Troy St Univ 89; Phi Mu Troy St Univ Pnhllnc Pres 89; Amer Occup Thrpy Assoc; BS Magna Cum Laude Troy St Univ 89; Occup Thrpy.

**PARSONS, WENDIE F,** Bowling Green St Univ, Bowling Green, OH; JR; BS; Stdnt Advsry Brd Schlrshp 88-89; U Schlrshp 88-89; Deans Lst 88-90; Social Sci Clb Schlrshp 89-90; Ohio Acad Schlrshp; Psych; Cnslng/Clncl Psych.**

**PARTEE, PATRICIA G,** Memphis St Univ, Memphis, TN; FR; BBA; Blck Schlrs Unlmtd; Acad Schlrshp Recptnt; Bsns; Mgmt.

**PARTHUM, KIMBERLY A,** Merrimack Coll, North Andover, MA; SR; Benzene Ring Scty Sec 88-; Amer Chem Scty 87-; Phi Lambda Upsilon; Grad Cum Laude; BS; Chemistry.

**PARTIN, JAN L,** Valdosta St Coll, Valdosta, GA; JR; BS; Cum Laude; Phi Theta Kappa; Nursing.

**PARTIN, RHETTA E,** Tri County Tech Coll, Pendleton, SC; SO; BA; English; Tch.

**PARTIN, SHIRLEY S,** Chattanooga St Tech Comm Coll, Chattanooga, TN; SO; AD; Phi Theta Kappa 90-; Nrsng Hnrs 89-; Calvry Bapt Chrch Sec 85-; Nrsng.

**PARTLO, CHRISTIE I,** Oh St Univ At Newark, Newark, OH; JR; BS; Broad Street Church Head/Nrsry 89-; Waldons/Daltons Buok Clubs 80-; Cntmpry Karate Studio 89-; Newark Hnrs Soc 89-; Dns Lst 89-90; Fmly Cnslng Svcs 89-; Newark Hlth Care Fclty 89-90; Newark Hnrs Soc 89-; Psychology.

**PARTLOW, CHRISTOPHER L,** Castleton St Coll, Castleton, VT; JR; BA; Crmnl Jstc Clb 88-; Tnns Trnmnt 88-; AS Castleton St Coll; Bus Admn; FBI Agnt.

**PARTLOW, KELLI S,** Wv Univ, Morgantown, WV; SR; BS; Alpha Lamdba Delta 87; Phi Sigma 87; Pharmacy.

**PARTLOW, KEVIN E,** Itawamba Comm Coll, Fulton, MS; FR; BS; Phi Theta Kappa; GPA Awd 90-; Elec Eng; MBA.

**PARTLOW, TAMMY C,** Saint Josephs Coll Suffik Cmps, Patchogue, NY; SR; BS; Bsns Clb 87-; Sigma Iota Chi 89-; Dns Lst 87-; Delta Epsilon Sigma 89; Delta Mu Delta; Summa Cum Laude; Intl Ord Of Rainbow Grls; Bsns Admn.**

**PARTON, CINDY G,** Middle Tn St Univ, Murfreesboro, TN; GD; Res Hall Cncl VP 90-; Pi Sigma Epsilon 89-90.

**PARTON, RHONDA,** Savannah Coll Of Art & Design, Savannah, GA; Vlybl.

**PARTRICK, DELIA M,** East Carolina Univ, Greenville, NC; SR; BA; Art History.

**PARTRIDGE PHILIPPS, ROBIN KAYE,** Owensboro Jr Coll Of Bus, Owensboro, KY; GD; AD; Stdnt Bvrnmnt Chrmn; Prsdnts Lst Prfct Attndnc; Mdcl Oc Asst; Science.

**PARTRIDGE, ADAM L,** John C Calhoun St Comm Coll, Decatur, AL; FR; BA; Computer Engineering.

**PARTRIDGE, WILLIAM P,** Christian Brothers Univ, Memphis, TN; JR; BS; Cordntr Chemical Testing Procter & Gamble 78-; Bus Mgmnt; Telecommunications.

**PARUTA, JACK L,** S U N Y At Buffalo, Buffalo, NY; GD; MARCH; Amer Inst Arch Stdnts; Res Hall Counc; Grad Stdnt Assn; Phi Kappa Theta; IM Sftbl; New York St Rgnts Schlrshp; BPS 90; Arch.

**PARVIN, SHAWN M,** Cumberland County Coll, Vineland, NJ; SO; BYE 87-; Phi Theta Kappa Pres 90-; Deans List 89-90; N J Dist Schlr 89-; AA; Math/Sci; Dental Hygiene.

**PASCAL, JULIE A,** Duquesne Univ, Pittsburgh, PA; SO; BBA; Phi Eta Sigma 89-; Delta Sigma Pi 90-; SHARP Vol 89-90; Dns Lst 89-; Crew 89-; Mktg.

**PASCAL, STACY J,** Univ Of Hartford, West Hartford, CT; SO; BA; Student Dudicial Brd Brd; AA Univ Hartford 91; Psy; Forensir Psylt.

**PASCAL, VALENTINE G,** Al A & M Univ, Normal, AL; JR; BS; Caribbean Stu Assoc Chpln 89; Bapt Stu Union 90; Mrktg Clb; Agribus; Mrktg Cnsltnt.

**PASCARELLA, JULIE L,** Univ Of Pittsburgh At Bradford, Bradford, PA; SO; BS; Alpha Lambda Delta 89-; Bsktbl 89-; Bus; Mrktng.

**PASCHAL, DARLENE,** Al St Univ, Montgomery, AL; JR; Elem Ed/Hlth Sci Ed; Tchr MA Ph D Ed.

**PASCHAL, MELANIE J,** Univ Of Nc At Greensboro, Greensboro, NC; FR; BS; Dance Education; Teach.

**PASCHALL, KATHY LYNN,** Middle Tn St Univ, Murfreesboro, TN; SR; BA; Fla Clg Forensics Un 87-89; Drama Clb 88; MTSU Frnsc Un 89-; ARETE; Omega Chi; G E Warner Awd 89; Otsdng Cmptr Awd 89; AA Fla Clg 89; Spch/Cmunctn; Clg Educ.

**PASCHALL, MELISSA A,** Middle Tn St Univ, Murfreesboro, TN; SO; Gamma Beta Phi.

**PASCHALL, WILLIAM M,** Boston Univ, Boston, MA; FR; BA; Chess Club Mstr Chess Plyr; Ecnmcs; Pltcl Sci.

**PASCHER, MOSHE C,** Cooper Union, New York, NY; SR; IM Sftbl 87-88; BS; Math/Engr; Actry.

**PASCO, ANNA L,** Peace Coll, Raleigh, NC; SO; BA; Schlrs 89-90; Deans Lst 90; Deans Lst Dstnctn; AA; Hstry.

**PASCUAL, PAUL J,** City Univ Of Ny Bronx Comm Col, Bronx, NY; SR; BS; Fshn Clb VP 88-89; Fncng Clb Pres 89-90; Physcs Clb VP 90-; Mnrty Hon 89-; Pgm Star; Fncng Tm; Mech Eng; Aerdnmcs Air Frc.

**PASCUAL-VELEZ, MIGUEL A,** Inter Amer Univ Pr San Juan, Hato Rey, PR; GD; JD; Boy Scout Cncl Dir 90-; La Villa De Torrimar Res Assoc Repr 89-90; First Boston Corp V P-Trading 80-; BS Univ Penn 76; Law.

**PASCUCCI, MICHELLE A,** Hudson Valley Comm Coll, Troy, NY; SO; BS; Accntng; CPA.

**PASHEL, ROBERTA W,** Comm Coll Algny Co Algny Cmps, Pittsburgh, PA; MBA; Natl Exec Hskprs Assn; Cert 85; Bus Mgt/Admnstrtn; Hosp Admnstrtn.

**PASHLEY, GEOFFREY K,** Le Moyne Coll, Syracuse, NY; FR; BS; Integral Hnrs Prog 90-; Psychology; Law.

**PASHO, MARIA,** S U N Y Coll At Fredonia, Fredonia, NY; SR; BS; Radio Station News Rprtr Edtr 89-90; Dorm Cncl Soc Chr 89; Deans List 87-90; WA Smstr Prog Nwslnk News Bureau TV News Rprtr Intern; IM Vlybl 89; AAS Onondaga Comm Clg 89; Cmnctn/Media; Brdcst Jrnlsm.**

**PASHOUKOS, CHRISTOPHER M,** S U N Y Coll At Postdam, Potsdam, NY; Stdy Abrd UK 89; Pi Kappa Lambda; Prssr Schlr 89-90; Pres Schlr 86-90; Envrnmntlst/Mscn.

**PASLEY, PAMELA R,** Univ Of Cincinnati, Cincinnati, OH; SR; BS; Band 87-89; Flag Corps Cptn 87-89; Kappa Delta Ki; Elem Ed; Tchng.

**PASQUALE, CESARE,** Manhattan Coll, Bronx, NY; FR; BS; Amer Soc Mech Engrs 90-; Soc Auto Engrs 90-; Engr.

**PASQUALE, EDWARD A,** Comm Coll Algny Co Algny Cmps, Pittsburgh, PA; FR; Deans Lst; Bus Mgmnt; Topline Mgmnt.

**PASQUALE, RUSSELL G,** Fordham Univ, Bronx, NY; SR; Dean Lst 89-; IRS Vol VITA Prog.

**PASQUARELLA, ARTHUR M,** Schenectady County Comm Coll, Schenectady, NY; FR; BA; Clnry Arts Clb; Dean Acdmc Affrs; Asst Chef; Wghtlftng; Sccr; Own Bus; Engl; Mgmt.

**PASQUARETTE, SUSAN L,** Clarion Univ Of Pa, Clarion, PA; SO; ASN; Nrsng Club 90-; Phi Theta Kappa; R N.**

**PASS, STEVEN E,** Univ Of Ky, Lexington, KY; JR; BS; Internatl Frat Concl Chptr Rep 90; Sigma Alpha Mu 88-; Pharmacy.

**PASSAFIUME, LAURIE A,** Univ Of Tn At Chattanooga, Chattanooga, TN; SO; BS; Ntnl Cllgt Engnrng Awd; Coop Stdnt S Cntrl Bell Mgmt 90-; Rowing Tm 89-; Mchncl Engnrng; Aerospace Indstry.

**PASSALACQUA, JILL E,** Pellissippi St Tech Comm Coll, Knoxville, TN; FR; BED; Recreation; Educ.**

**PASSALAQUA, KIM,** S U N Y Coll Of Tech At Frmgdl, Farmingdale, NY; SO; AA; Sccr 89-90; Lbrl Arts; Physcl Thrpy.

**PASSANANTE, JOSIANNE,** William Paterson Coll, Wayne, NJ; GD; MED; Phi Beta Kappa; NJ Assoc Lrng Consltnts; Cncl Lrng Disablts; Amer Assoc Tchrs Frnch Treas 90-; NY State Assoc Foreign Lang Tchrs; Amer Assoc Tchrs Spnsh/Portuguese; New Rochelle H S Tchr; Frnch Clb Advsr; Spec Ed-Lrng Disblts; Tchg/Clnc LD Chldrn.

**PASSERELLO, NICOLE,** Widener Univ, Chester, PA; JR; BS; SAM 90-; Fld Hckry Capt 87-88; Bus Mgmt; Mktg.

**PASSIEU, SUSAN R,** Waycross Coll, Waycross, GA; SO; MBA; Phi Theta Kappa; Sci/Math; Educ.

**PASSINO, JANET A,** Nova Univ, Ft Lauderdale, FL; GD; MBA; BS Physcl Thrpy Fl Intrntl U 79; Bsnss; Admin.

**PASSMAN, FRANCES C,** Ms Gulf Coast Comm Coll, Perkinston, MS; FR; V Pres Lst 90-; Paralgl Tech; Paralegal.

**PASSONS, RUTH A,** Roane St Comm Coll, Harriman, TN; JR; BS; Stdnt Govt Assoc 89-90; Phi Kappa Phi; Kappa Delta Pi; STEA; Practicum 90; AS 90; Sec Educ English History; Educator.

**PASSWATER, STEPHEN E,** Wilmington Coll, New Castle, DE; SR; BS; Phi Theta Kappa Publ Rel 86-87; Grad DTCC High Hnrs 87; Phi Theta Kappas; Assc Acctnt; AA Del Tech Comm Clg 87; Acctg; Corp Acctg.

**PASTAKIA, NEPA,** S U N Y Coll Of Optometry, New York, NY; GD; OD; Natl Optometric Stdnt Assn 89-; Amer Optometric Stdnt Assn 89-; Beta Sigma Kappa 90-; Grad Adelphi Univ Magna Cum Laude BS Biology 90; BS Adelphi Univ 90; Optometry.

**PASTERICK, KELLY M,** Duquesne Univ, Pittsburgh, PA; JR; BA; Orntn Stf 89; Stdnt Acctg Assc 89-; Deans List; Dlt Zeta Tres 90-; Zeta Beta Tau; Intrnshp Eqtbl Gas Co 90-; Acctg Schlrshp 90-; Acctg; CPA.

**PASTERNAK, CHARLES J,** Indiana Univ Of Pa, Indiana, PA; SO; BED; Kappa Delta Pi; Soc Sci Hist; Edn.

**PASTERNAK, DAVID J,** Duquesne Univ, Pittsburgh, PA; JR; BS; Nwsppr Prod Asst 90-; Penn St Nwsppr Edtr Chf 88-90; PSM SG 88-90; Almn Soc 90-; Mngmnt.

**PASTEUR, REGINALD L,** Va St Univ, Petersburg, VA; JR; BS; Agri Sci Org 88-; Mrchng Trojan Explsn 89-; Pep Bnd 89-; Kappa Alpha Psi; Co-Op/Intrnshp CIBA-GEIGY Corp Agri Div 90; Anml Sci; Wrk Dept Agri.

**PASTO, LESLIE A,** Hillsborough Comm Coll, Tampa, FL; FR; AA; Sci; Engr/Aerospace.

**PASTOR, DENNIS W,** S U N Y Coll Of Tech At Alfred, Alfred, NY; SR; AS; Stdnt Senate; Peer Tutr; Trgde; IM Sprts; Sigma Tau Epsilon; Drftng/Cad Achvmnt Awrd; Drftng/Cad.

**PASTOR, IRMINA BOSCH,** Saint Thomas Univ, Miami, FL; SR; BA; Untd Teach Of Dade; ESOL Teach 90-; Cert Educ Dept Of FL 88; Teach Sec/Spanish; MBA.

**PASTORA, MAURICIO J,** Miami Dade Comm Coll South, Miami, FL; JR; BA; French Clb; French Alliance Of Miami; French Hnr Soc; Kappa Psi; Internship Dade Cnty Spanish Court Interpreter; AA 90; Dipl Southeastern Acad Travel Career Trn 86; French/Span Trnsltn; Interpretation.

**PASTORELL, SCOTT A,** Alfred Univ, Alfred, NY; SR; Radio Stn 88-89; Tlthn 88-89; Im Sprts 87; Klan Alpine Treas 88-90; Wegmans Food Mkt Schlrshp 87; BS; Bsnss Admin; Music Bsnss.**

**PASTORIUS, JUDITH,** Comm Coll Algny Co Algny Cmps, Pittsburgh, PA; FR; AS; Acct; CPA.

**PASTORIUS, SUSAN,** Comm Coll Algny Co Algny Cmps, Pittsburgh, PA; FR; ASSOC; Business; Bus Executive.

**PASTRICK, CHRISTOPHER L,** Allegheny Coll, Meadville, PA; SR; BA; The Camps Nwspr Arts Leisur Edtr 89-; WARC EM D J Brd Mbr 87-90; SET 87-90; Aldn Schlr 89-90; Apprentc Of Yr Awd 89; Hollrn Awd 87; Comm Arts; Jrnlsm.

**PATANE, BRYAN M,** S U N Y Coll Of Tech At Delhi, Delhi, NY; FR; AOS; Phi Theta Kappa 90-; Plumbing/Htng/Pipe Fitting/A/C/Refriftn.

**PATANELLA, DANIEL F,** City Univ Of Ny Lehman Coll, Bronx, NY; JR; BA; Schlrs Prgm 88-; Rd Sttn Dsc Jcky 88-89; Gldn Key 90-; Psi Chi; Deans Lst Prsdntl Schrl 90; Lhmn Mrt Schlrshp 88-; Psychlgy.

**PATCH, JONATHAN F,** Univ Of Southern Ms, Hattiesburg, MS; JR; Phi Kappa Phi 90-; Gamma Alpha Epsilon 89-90; IM; Zoology; Medicine.

**PATCHELL, EMILY R,** Univ Of Nc At Wilmington, Wilmington, NC; FR; BA; Educ Engl; Tchr.

**PATCYK, ARLENE L,** Indiana Univ Of Pa, Indiana, PA; SR; Pi Gamma Mu 90-; Grdtd Cum Laude; Smthsn Assoc; PA Cncl Scl Stds Natl Cncl Slc Stds; BA Ed IN Univ PA; Scl Sci Hstry Cncntrtn; Tchng.

**PATE, BONITA S,** Ky Wesleyan Coll, Owensboro, KY; SR; BA; Alpha Chi 89-; Keasp 90-; Lbry Intrnshp 87-; BA; Library Sci/Engl; Clg Prfsr.

**PATE, BRYAN TODD,** Memphis St Univ, Memphis, TN; SR; MA; Peer Mntr Undrgrads 87-; Stdnt Aide Wrkr 87-; Outstndng Coll Stdnts Amer 89-90; Goldn Key 89-90; Chi Beta Phi 90-; St Brd Rgnts Schlrshp 87-; BA; Merit Acdmc Schlrshp 87; Psychlgy.**

**PATE, CARA R,** Chesterfield Marlboro Coll, Cheraw, SC; FR; BED; Nrsng.

**PATE, JANET C,** Wallace St Comm Coll At Selma, Selma, AL; SO; BS; Elec Engr.

**PATE, KAREN J,** Mobile Coll, Mobile, AL; SR; BS; Cmptr Sci Clb Trea 89-; Alpha Chi; Coop; Cmptr Sci/Accntng; Adtr.

**PATE, MICHAELA A,** Radford Univ, Radford, VA; SR; BSN; Sigma Theta Tau Intrntnl; LPN; Manhatten Vctnl Tchnl Schl 79; Nrsng.

**PATEL, ALPESH J,** Univ Of Sc At Columbia, Columbia, SC; SR; BA; FMA Financial Mgmnt Assoc; Gama Iota Sigma; Deans List 88-; Pres List 90; Deans Schlrshp 90; CPUC Schlrshp; Finance & Insurance; Business.

**PATEL, ALPESH K,** Salisbury St Univ, Salisbury, MD; SO; BS; Chem.**

**PATEL, ARUNKUMAR S,** Rutgers St Un At New Brunswick, New Brunswick, NJ; FR; BS; AIR 90-; Nardipur Swm Nryn Sewa Tmpl; Engr.

**PATEL, BHAKTI V,** Univ Of Tn At Martin, Martin, TN; SO; BS; Mu Epsln Delta; Bio; Doctor.

**PATEL, BINTA K,** Fl A & M Univ, Tallahassee, FL; SR; BS; Intra Sprts 86-8; Indian Clb Assoc 86-88; Amer Pharm Assoc 89-; Stdnt Natl Pharm Assoc 89-; Deans Lst 89-; Hnr Roll 86-88; AA Univ Of Fla 89; Pharmcy; Mstrs Hosp Admin.

**PATEL, DAKSHESH S,** Boston Univ, Boston, MA; GD; MD; MA Med Soc 89-; AMA; Alpah Omega Alpha V P 90; Golden Key 86; Ralph Taylor/Case Schlrshps 88; Valedictorian 88; BA Boston Univ 88; Biol; Physician.

**PATEL, DASHANT K,** Southern Coll Of Tech, Marietta, GA; SR; BS; Tau Alpha Pi; Chrmn Ind Comm Assn Chrmn 86-88; Elec Eng Tech.

**PATEL, DAXSHA,** Univ Of Tn At Martin, Martin, TN; JR; BS; ACM 90; Econs Clb 90; Dns Lst 90-; Comp Sci; Systms Anlyss Prgrmmng.

**PATEL, DHARMESH RAMESH,** Univ Of Sc At Columbia, Columbia, SC; FR; Math/Sci Club; Computer Sci/Masters; Computer Related.

**PATEL, DIPA N,** Elms Coll, Chicopee, MA; SO; BA; Std Govt Asc Sec 90-; Pax Christi 90-; Dns Lst 90-; Amer Stds/Hstry; Pol/ Law/Govt.

**PATEL, GEMINI S,** Va Commonwealth Univ, Richmond, VA; SO; BS; Acctng.

**PATEL, GITA BIPIN,** Univ Of Sc At Columbia, Columbia, SC; FR; BA USC Aiken 92; Math Ed; Tchng.

**PATEL, GITESH C,** Univ Of Miami, Coral Gables, FL; FR; BS; Excel Prog 90-; Res Clg Sprtsfst; Alpha Lambda Delta; Pres Hon Rl; CSR I M; Biology; Med.

**PATEL, HIREN K,** Univ Of Al At Birmingham, Birmingham, AL; SR; Phi Sigma Tres; Alpha Epsilon Delta VP/TRES; Omicron Delta Kapp; BA; Med.

**PATEL, JABEEN,** George Mason Univ, Fairfax, VA; SR; Sec Indian/Pakistani Stdnts Assn; Yth/Sports Coord.

**PATEL, JATIN K,** Vance Granville Comm Coll, Henderson, NC; SO; AAS; Electronics; Tech.

**PATEL, JAYANT R,** Univ Of Nc At Charlotte, Charlotte, NC; SR; BS; APA 90-; SGE 90-; GTU 90-; Geog/Earth Sci; Plnr/ Constlt.

**PATEL, KALPANA M,** Middlesex County Coll, Edison, NJ; FR; MLT; Natl Schlrshp India 75-80; Bed; Med; BS Math; Medcl Field; Medcl Tchnlgst.

**PATEL, KAUMUDI,** Abraham Baldwin Agri Coll, Tifton, GA; JR.

**PATEL, LINA I,** Middlesex County Coll, Edison, NJ; SR; MLT; Pres MLT Club 90-; All Coll Awd; BS Microbiology Bhavans Coll India 88; Sci.

**PATEL, MAYANK R,** Univ Of Sc At Columbia, Columbia, SC; FR; BS; Sci Clb 90-; Gamma Beta Phi; Alumni Ambssdr; Chmstry; Med Dr.

**PATEL, MEERA R,** Niagara Univ, Niagara Univ, NY; FR; Engr.

**PATEL, NAMRATA A,** Glassboro St Coll, Glassboro, NJ; SO; BA; Am Advtsng Fed 90-; Nwspr Asst Ad Mgr 90-; Stdnt Govt Assn Sen 90-; Boost Alchl Concsns Cnrng Hlth Univ Stdnts 90-; Advtsng/Cmmnctns.

**PATEL, NAVIN K,** Univ Of Pittsburgh, Pittsburgh, PA; SR; BS; AAS Delaware Tech/Comm Clg 87; Mech Eng.

**PATEL, NAYAN S,** Southern Coll Of Tech, Marietta, GA; SR; AIAS 89-90; Tau Alpha Pi.

**PATEL, NEETA A,** S U N Y At Buffalo, Buffalo, NY; SR; Indian Stdnt Assn Sec 89-90; Acctg Assn 89-90; BS SUNY; Acctg; CPA MBA Fnce.

**PATEL, NIRAV C,** Univ Of Sc At Columbia, Columbia, SC; FR; BSC; Internatl Stdnt Assoc; Flyng Clb; Indian Stdnt Org; Phi Eta Sigma; Asian Amer Assoc; Chmstry/Blgy; Pharmacy.

**PATEL, PARUL A,** Memphis St Univ, Memphis, TN; SO; BA; Intrntnl Rltns; Dplmcy.

**PATEL, PRAHLAD R,** Univ Of Sc At Columbia, Columbia, SC; SO; BA; Bio Clb 90-; Gamma Beta Phi 89-90; Pres Lst 89-; USC-AIKEN Prtnrshp Schlrshp 90-; Wstnghse Sci/Educ Schlrshp; Bio; Prctc Med.

**PATEL, PRITI V,** Hillsborough Comm Coll, Tampa, FL; SO; Math; Eng.

**PATEL, RAHUL,** Univ Of Fl, Gainesville, FL; FR; BA; Ldrchp Asst Dir; Ldrshp; Stdnt Govt Crse Gde Cbnt; Hnrs Prog; Engl; Med.

**PATEL, RAJEN P,** Univ Of Rochester, Rochester, NY; SO; BA; Vars Tennis 89-; Med Emerg Resp Tm 89-; Bio; Med.

**PATEL, RAJENDRA R,** Univ Of Med & Dentistry Of Nj, Newark, NJ; SR; CERT; MS Univ Bomberg India 82; Toxicology.

**PATEL, RAJUL A,** The Johns Hopkins Univ, Baltimore, MD; FR; Hopkins Indian Assc 90-; Tutorial Pgm 90-; Mntr/Mntc Pgm 90-; Chem Psychlgy; Medcn.

**PATEL, SANJAY A,** Univ Of Rochester, Rochester, NY; JR; BSBA; Neurosci/Psychlgy; Med.

**PATEL, SHARMISHTHA R,** Ms St Univ, Miss State, MS; FR; India Assoc Of MS; Gamma Beta Phi; Deans List; Sci; Medcl.

**PATEL, SHREETI,** City Univ Of Ny City Coll, New York, NY; JR; BSMD; Amrcn Mdcl Stdnt Assn Treas 88-; Biomed Asian Hlth Coalition VP 88-; Epicurean Scty Pres 90-; IM Vllybll 89-; Blgy; Medicine.

**PATEL, SHREYA MANUBHAI,** Pa St Univ Main Cmps, University Pk, PA; FR; BA; Ebrly Coll Sci Peer Advsng Pgm; Alpha Epsilon Delta; Pres Frsh Awd 90-; Hons Ebrly Coll Sci 90-; Pre-Med; Med.

**PATEL, TARLA C,** Fl Atlantic Univ, Boca Raton, FL; SR; Beta Alpha Psi Rcrdng Secy 90-; Phi Kappa Phi 89-; Deans Lst 81-83; Acctng Mgr Visage Inc Frmnghm Mass 84-88; ASBA 86; Acctng.

**PATEL, TEJAL S,** Bloomfield Coll, Bloomfield, NJ; SO; Blmfld Clg Stdnt Almni Assoc 90-; Yrbk Stf 90-; Intl Clb 90-; MCOSS Nrsng Serv Hm Hlth Aide; Hon Awd Cert 90; Calculus/Biol/ Psych; Nrsng/Gnclgy.

**PATEL, VIPUL D,** City Univ Of Ny La Guard Coll, Long Island Cty, NY; SO; PT Asst.

**PATEL, VIPUL K,** City Univ Of Ny City Coll, New York, NY; JR; BE; Indo Pak Soc 87-; Eta Kappa Nu VP; IEEE 90-; Elec Engr; Comp Sci.

**PATEL, VIREN C,** Southern Coll Of Tech, Marietta, GA; GD; MS; ACM 87-88; Tau Alpha Pi 89; BS Sthrn Coll Tchnlgy 90; Artfcl Intllgnc.

**PATERNOSTER, JANET L,** De Tech & Comm Coll At Dover, Dover, DE; FR; AN; AA Comm Coll Air Force 86; Nrsng.

**PATERRA, JUDITH B,** Radford Univ, Radford, VA; JR; BSN; Pta Gilbert Linkous Elem 89-; Sigma Theta Tau; Montgomery Reg Hosp Extrnshp; Schrlshp; BA Bio Stn Hl Coll 75; Nrsng; ICU.

**PATERSON, SHARYN M,** Georgian Court Coll, Lakewood, NJ; SR; BA; St Pauls Bell Choir 87-88; EOF Acdmc Achvmnt Awrds 89-; St Acdmc Achvmnt Awrd; Georgn Ct Coll Deans Schlr Awrd 90; AA Ocean Co Coll 89; Elem Ed/Psychlgy; Tchr/Cnslr.

**PATINELLA, LILIA,** Wagner Coll, Staten Island, NY; SO; PHD; Psych Club 89-; Deans Lst Awds 89-; Psych.

**PATINO, JOSEPH,** Nova Univ, Ft Lauderdale, FL; GD; Phi Theta Kappa; Fla Engr Soc; IEEE; I M Bkbl; Motorola Inc 83-; BSEE U Of Fla 81; MBA 90-; Bus Admn/Engr; Engr Mgmt.

**PATITUCCI, TINA E,** Allegheny Coll, Meadville, PA; JR; BS; Dance Ens; Beta Beta Beta 3rd V P 90-; Kappa Kappa Gamma Rec Sec 89-; ALLIES; Alden Schlr 89-90; Summer Flwshp Cellular Bio; Teaching Asst Human Bio 90; Bio; Med Sch.

**PATNAIK, MISHA M,** Va Commonwealth Univ, Richmond, VA; JR; MD; Rhoads/Johnson Assn 89-; Gold Key 89-; Phi Sigma 90-; Hon Stdnt 88-; Hon Dorm RA 89-; Jane Jones Thornton Awd 89-90; Provost Pres Hon Schlrshp 88-; Stdnt Ldrshp/Serv Awd 90; BS VA Cmnwlth Univ; Med; Physician.

**PATNAIK, SUMEETA,** Beckley Coll, Beckley, WV; FR; BA; French Clb Offr 87-88; Hnrs Mbr 90-; Nwspr Wrtr 90-; Ntnl Hnr Scty Mbr 87-88; Scty Dstngshd AM HS Stdnts 87-88; Special Olympcs Plcst 89-; Englemphs Wrtng; Wrtr Edtr.

**PATNAIK, SUMEETA,** Beckley Coll, Beckley, WV; FR; BA; Hons Clg; Spcl Olympcs Bd 89-; Engl; Wrtr/Edtr.

**PATNODE, KIMBERLY L,** Schenectady County Comm Coll, Schenectady, NY; FR; AAS Hotel Rest Mngmnt; Bnqt Hl Mngmnt.

**PATOKI, CHRISTIN M,** Duquesne Univ, Pittsburgh, PA; SO; BS; Phi Chi Theta 90-; Acctng; CPA.

**PATREGANI, MICHAEL R,** Hudson Valley Comm Coll, Troy, NY; FR; Elctrcl Cnstrctn Maint; Elctrcn.

**PATRIARCA, DANIELA,** Georgian Court Coll, Lakewood, NJ; FR; BA; Math Assc Amer 90-; Cmmtr Clb; Georgian Ct Acad Schlrshp 90-; Garden St Schlrshp 90-; Math.

**PATRICIOS, ARLANA K,** Univ Of Miami, Coral Gables, FL; SR; BARCH; Phi Kappa Phi; Gold Key; Tau Sigma Delta; Architecture.

**PATRICK, AUDREY S,** Bristol Univ, Bristol, TN; JR; BS; Brnch Mgr 82; Bsnss Admin/Accntng; Mngmnt.

**PATRICK, BRYAN W,** Fl Coll, Temple Terrace, FL; SO; MS; Swrs Clb 89-; Bnd 89-; Yrbk Phtgrphr 90-; Chorus 90; Phi Theta Kappa 90-; Arete 90-; Kappa Omicron 89; Mr Fl Coll Crt; Mr Royal Palm; IM Sftbl 90; AA; Educ; Prch.

**PATRICK, CHUCKIE,** Alcorn St Univ, Lorman, MS; SR; BS; Cmptr Sci Clb; Kappa Alpha Psi; Bsbl Tm; Bus; Mltry Ofcr.

**PATRICK, CINDY R,** Ms Univ For Women, Columbus, MS; SR; Bench/Gavel Paralgl Assn 88-; EM Yrbk E MS Comm Coll 85-87; Diamond Batgrl Sqd E MS Comm Coll 85-87; Nu Epsilon Delta; W Law Cmptr Lgl Rsrch Cert 90; Phi Beta Lambda 85; Silhouette Socl Clb 87; Paralegal Stds; Law Schl.

**PATRICK, FRANCES,** Rhodes Coll, Memphis, TN; FR; Chrldr 90-; Delta Delta Delta; Bsn Admn/Ecnmcs/Grmn.

**PATRICK, JANET A,** Commonwealth Coll, Virginia Beach, VA; SO; AS; Acctng; Bsn.

**PATRICK, LISA,** Morris Brown Coll, Atlanta, GA; SO; BA; Untd Negro Coll Schlr 89-; Fndtn Schlrshps; Crdnl Strtch Coll Bsktbl Tm Mbr 88-89; Crmnl Jstc; Law.

**PATRICK, LISA D,** Roane St Comm Coll, Harriman, TN; SO; BA; Gamma Beta Phi V P 88-90; Phi Beta Lambda 88-89; Grad Summa Cum Laude; Rcpnt Of Pres & St Bd Of Regents Schlrshp; Assoc Bus Adm 90; Acctng; CPA.

**PATRICK, LISA M,** William Paterson Coll, Wayne, NJ; SR; BA; Elem Educ Soc 87-F Kappa Delta Pi 90-; Alpha Kappa Delta 90-; Tchrs Aid Tutor; Elem Educ/Sociology; Tchr.

**PATRICK, MELISSA P,** Univ Of Sc At Columbia, Columbia, SC; FR; MBA; Intl Clb Hstss 90-; Gamma Beta Phi 90-; IM Sftbl 90-; Intl Bus/Frgn Lang.

**PATRICK, MELVIN D,** Lexington Comm Coll, Lexington, KY; SO; EET; KY Amateur Archaeology Scty 75-; KY Woodworkers Assoc 82-; Engrng Electrcl.

**PATRICK, MICHAEL E,** Wv Univ, Morgantown, WV; SR; BA; Helvetia 88-89; Chimes 89-90; Sigma Gamma Tau Pres 89-; Tau Beta Pi 90-; Kappa Alpha Order Treas 88-; Aerospace Eng.

**PATRICK, NANCY L,** Longwood Coll, Farmville, VA; JR; BS; Stu Educ Assn 88-; Alpha Lambda Delta 89; Kappa Delta Pi 90-; Dean Lst 89-; Phi Kappa Phi 91; All Amer Schlrs; Elem Educ; Tchr.

**PATRICK, PAMELA M,** Marywood Coll, Scranton, PA; FR; BA; Elem Educ; Tchng.

**PATRICK, PAUL E,** Univ Of South Al, Mobile, AL; SR; BS; SHAPE Clb Pres 90-; AAHPERO 89-; USGF 89-; Otsdng Sr P E 90-; Deans Lst 90; Pres Lst 90; Chrldr 87-89; Educ; Tch.

**PATRICK, RICHARD L,** Beckley Coll, Beckley, WV; United Mine Workers AM VP 87-90; Legal Asst WV 87-90; Coal Miner Prlgl 87-; Prlgl Stds AA; Prlgl.

**PATRIKIOS, ANGELIQUE,** Memphis St Univ, Memphis, TN; JR; BA; Gamma Beta Phi 90-; Alpha Chi Omega Prsnl Dvlpmnt Chrmn 88-; Stamo Llato Schrlshp 88; Early Schrls Schrlshp 88; Deans List 89-; English; Law.

**PATRIKUS, PAUL J,** Pellissippi St Tech Comm Coll, Knoxville, TN; JR; BS; FFA 81-84; 4h 78-81; U S Army Infnty S F Sgt 83-; AS Pell State Com Clg 90; CJA; Law.

**PATSIS, THOMAS G,** Bridgeport Engr Inst, Fairfield, CT; SR; BSEE; Deans Lst 86-90; ASEE Norwalk St Tech Clg 82; Electrncs; Eng.

**PATTEN, PATRICIA G,** Northern Ky Univ, Highland Hts, KY; SR; BA; MOE PTO Treas 90-; SDRC Financl Plnr 86-90; Finance; Corp Finance.

**PATTEN, SUSAN,** Ursinus Coll, Collegeville, PA; SR; BS; Lab Asst 87-89; Pre Mdcl Scty 86-89; Brdwo Chmcl Scty Nwslttr Comm 86-89; Physcs Prctblgy Clb 86-89; Arbcs Instrctr 86-89; Arbcs Mrthn 86-89; Rd Gld Dy Hst 86-88; BS 90; Blgy.

**PATTERSON, ALAN D,** Tri County Tech Coll, Pendleton, SC; FR; Humanities; Law Enfrcmnt Ofcr.

**PATTERSON, ASHLEY N,** Univ Of Sc At Spartanburg, Spartanburg, SC; SO; BS; Gamma Beta Phi Crspndc Sec 90-; Peer Edctrs 89-; Piedmont Scty 89-; Physical Therapy.

**PATTERSON, BETH A,** Univ Of Miami, Coral Gables, FL; FR; BA; S G Acad Affrs Comm 90; Alpha Lambda Delta; Delta Sigma Pi Cls Pr; Kappa Kappa Gamma Pan Rep 90-; Acctg; Tax Atty.

**PATTERSON III, CHARLES O,** Watterson Coll, Louisville, KY; FR; ASSOC; DPMA Prsdnt; Prsdnts Lst 90-; Cmptr Sci; Prgrmr.

**PATTERSON, CHRISTAL A,** Al St Univ, Montgomery, AL; SO; Elem Educ.

**PATTERSON, CHRISTY A,** Roane St Comm Coll, Harriman, TN; SO; BS; Elem Ed.

**PATTERSON, CINDY J,** Univ Of Tn At Martin, Martin, TN; JR; BS; Outstndng Jr Stdnt 90-; Natl Clgte Nrsg Awd 90-; BS 83; Nrsg.

**PATTERSON, CORNELIA A,** Northern Ky Univ, Highland Hts, KY; SR; BA; ICF Mtg Coord 90; Gldn Ky 88-; Theatre; Stg/ Radio/Law.

**PATTERSON, CYNTHIA M,** Univ Of Nc At Charlotte, Charlotte, NC; SO; BA; Psych; Child Thrpst.

**PATTERSON, DANA AMANI,** Clark Atlanta Univ, Atlanta, GA; SO; Stdnt Govt Sec/Rep; Stdnt GA Assn Edctrs Com Chrprsn 90-; Hon Pgm Miss Hon Pgm 90-; Sprt Batra Clb Bus Mngr 90-; Kappa Delta Epsilon; Acdmc Schlrshp; Early Chld Educ; Tchng.

**PATTERSON, DANA E,** Lexington Comm Coll, Lexington, KY; FR; BA; Chld Psy.

**PATTERSON, DANA L,** Northwest Al Comm Coll, Phil Campbell, AL; SO; BA; Phi Theta Kappa 89-; Stdnt Govt Assn Sen 90-; Pblctns Edtr 90-; Phi Theta Kappa 89-; Deans Or Pres List 89-; Highest Acdmc Awd; Bsktbl Vlybl Sftbl Capt 89-; AS Lib Arts; Hlth; Nrsng Thrpst.**

**PATTERSON, DARVIN OKERA,** Morehouse Coll, Atlanta, GA; SO; Endeavor Space Clb 90-; Ronald E Mc Nair NASA Schlrs Pgm 89-; Dns Lst; Hnr Rl; NASA Intern Lewis Rsrch Ctr 89-; Engr.**

**PATTERSON, DAWN M,** Oh St Univ At Marion, Marion, OH; FR; BA; Acctg; CPA.

**PATTERSON, GINA L,** Oh Dominican Coll, Columbus, OH; SO; BA; Cmps Mnstry VP 90-; Cir K Sec 90; Battdle Schlrshp; Psych.

**PATTERSON, IMMAURI M,** Morehouse Coll, Atlanta, GA; JR; BA; Hlth Careers Scty Chr Hmcng 89-; Busn Assoc 89-; Organ Africaan Amer Consic 89-; Hnr Rl 90-; Deans List 90-; D C Metropolitan Club 88-; Optng Serv Assist Yth 88-; Mayor Barrys Yth Ldrshp Inst 88-89; Hnr Rl 90-; Deans List 90-; Hltcr Intern; Admin/Mgt; Public Hlth/Hptl Admin.

**PATTERSON, IRETTE Y,** Fl A & M Univ, Tallahassee, FL; FR; Biology Pre Med Scty 90-; Phi Eta Sigma 90-; Outstndng Biology Student 90-; Biology; Research Biologist.

**PATTERSON, JODY M,** Ashland Comm Coll, Ashland, KY; SO; AS; Re-Entry Pgm; Acctg.

**PATTERSON, JOHN A,** Univ Of Nc At Charlotte, Charlotte, NC; SO; BA; Intrvrsty Chrstn Flwshp 89-; Spnsh Clb; Spanish; Tchr.

**PATTERSON, JON RANDALL,** Ms Coll, Clinton, MS; GD; JD; C Clark Am Inn Ct 90-; Phi Delta Phi 89-; Acad Schlrshp 89-; Law Rvw Artcl Edtr 89-; Am Jrsprdnc Awd 90; Dns Lst 89-; Am Bar Assn 89-; Army Ofcr 79-84; BA Citadel 79; Law; Ltgtn Prctc.

**PATTERSON, JOYCE A,** Hillsborough Comm Coll, Tampa, FL; SO; AA; Phi Theta Kappa; Blck Awareness Clb Pres 89-; PTA; Co-Owner Metal Fabr Co; Scl/Behav Sci; Rahab/Guid Cnslr.

**PATTERSON, JULIE A,** Comm Coll Algny Co Algny Cmps, Pittsburgh, PA; SO; BA; Info Sci; MIS.

**PATTERSON, KAREN W,** Salisbury St Univ, Salisbury, MD; SO; BS; SADD 89-90; Math Assc Amer 89-; Amer Math Scty; Geogrphy Scty; Phi Eta Sigma 90-; Henson Schl Sci Schlrshp 89-; Univ Pres Schlrshp 89-; Delegate Dixon Schlrshp 89-; Math/Geography; Geodetics/Cartography.

**PATTERSON, KEVIN DWAYNE,** Tougaloo Coll, Tougaloo, MS; SR; BA; History Club 87-; Student Const Revision Comm 88; Student Tutor 88; Pan African Ed Ntwk 88-89; Pre Schl 87; Top Hist Awd 88-; Exchange Student Brown Unv; CBS Schlr 88-89; BA Toygaloo Clg Tougloo Ms; History; Law.

**PATTERSON, LARRY R,** Univ Of Tn At Knoxville, Knoxville, TN; JR; BA; Acctg.

**PATTERSON, LEIGH A,** Mobile Coll, Mobile, AL; GD; BA; Modern Lang Clb; Save A Life Vol; Alpha Chi; Sigma Tau Delta VP; Engl/Sociology; Tchng.

**PATTERSON, LORI B,** Indiana Univ Of Pa, Indiana, PA; JR; BED; Tns Tm Co-Cpt 88-; Phi Mu 89-; Elem Educ; Tchr.

**PATTERSON, MONICA R,** Lincoln Univ, Lincoln Univ, PA; SR; Sclgy Clb 90; Alpha Chi 90-; Alpha Kappa Alpha 90-; Cum Laude; Sclgy Scl Wrk; Scl Wrk Educ.

**PATTERSON, NATHAN W,** Birmingham Southern Coll, Birmingham, AL; JR; BA; Rgby Clb; Beta Beta Beta; Alpha Epsilon Delta 90-; Kappa Mu Epsilon 90-; Phi Eta Sigma 89-; Theta Chi Frtnry Scl Chrmn 89-; Chmstry; Mdcl Schl.

**PATTERSON, PHYLLIS,** Al St Univ, Montgomery, AL; SO; BS; Phi Eta Sigma 90-; Bus Comp Info Systms; Systms Anlyst.

**PATTERSON, RHONDA M,** Hampton Univ, Hampton, VA; FR; BA; Univ Choir 90-; New Jersey Pre-Alumni 90-; Continental Insurance Intern 90-; Adolescent Psychlgst.

**PATTERSON, RICHELLE A,** Morgan St Univ, Baltimore, MD; JR; BS; Std Govt 90-; Peer Cnslr 89-; Alpha Lambda Delta Snr Advsr 90-; Phi Eta Sigma 90-; Pi Gamma Mu; Kappa Delta Pi Sec 90-; Curr Bsd Schlp 88-; Sntrl Schlp; Harry S Truman Schlp 90; Elem Ed; Ed.

**PATTERSON, SCOTT E,** Liberty Univ, Lynchburg, VA; SR; BS; Hnrs Pgm 88-; Govt; Law.

**PATTERSON, SUSAN MARGARET,** Lesley Coll, Cambridge, MA; JR; BS; Emerald Key Ambsdr 90-; Deans Lst 89-; LINC 90-; Erly Chldhd Ed/Mdrt Spcl Needs; Spcl Ed Tchr.

**PATTERSON, TODD H,** Widener Univ, Chester, PA; SR; Acctg Soc 87-90; CPA Intrn 90-; Squash Capt 87-; Acctg.

**PATTERSON, TRACY A,** Medical Univ Of Sc, Charleston, SC; JR; BSN; Jr Cls Rep To Clg Nrsng Stdnt Govt 90-; Fellwshp St Francs Hosp; Nrsng; Gerntlgy Nrsng.

**PATTERSON, VICTORIA L,** Vance Granville Comm Coll, Henderson, NC; SO; AA; Phi Theta Kappa Scl Coor 90-; Pres Trnsfr Schlr; Oxfrd Wmns Clb VP 86-; Oxfrd Bus And Prfssnl Wmn 90-; Chem; Chem Eng.

**PATTERSON, VINCENT T,** Faulkner St Jr Coll, Bay Minette, AL; JR; BA; Phi Theta Kappa 90-; Pblc Rltns Stdnt Scty 90-; Intern Rd 90; Pblc Rltns Scty 90-; Exctv Offcr A Cmpny Army Natl Grd; Natl Grd Assoc US 86-; Natl Grd Assoc 86-; AA 90; Pblc Rltns; Crprt Law.

**PATTIE, CHRISTIE L,** Villanova Univ, Villanova, PA; SR; PHYD; ACE Program 87-89; Psi Chi 90-; Phi Kappa Hi 90-; DCCC Alumni Schlrshp 88; Presidnets Hnr List 7-89; Deans List 89-; BA; Psychology; Clinical Psychology.

**PATTISHALL, AMY J,** Univ Of Nc At Charlotte, Charlotte, NC; FR; BSN; Nurs.

**PATTISON, KARA K,** Springfield Tech Comm Coll, Springfield, MA; FR; AS; Accntng.

**PATTON, ADDIE RENEE,** Western Piedmont Comm Coll, Morganton, NC; SO; BA; Phi Theta Kappa 90-; English; Teach.

**PATTON, ANGELA,** Alcorn St Univ, Lorman, MS; FR.

**PATTON, BEVERLY L,** Valdosta St Coll, Valdosta, GA; JR; BSN; GANS Hstrn 90-; NCNA; AAUW Schlrshp 90-; Nrsng; Nrse Ansthtst MSN.

**PATTON, BRADLEY G,** Kings Coll, Wilkes-Barre, PA; SR; BA; Comm Clb 87-88; Nwspr Rprtr 87-88; Theta Alpha Kappa 90-; Deans Lst 87-; Communications; Jrnlsm/Brdcst.**

**PATTON, CHRISTI C,** Memphis St Univ, Memphis, TN; FR; BSN; Scrtry 80-90; Nrsng.

**PATTON, EDITH W,** Univ Of Tn At Knoxville, Knoxville, TN; SR; BS; Phi Kappa Phi; Beta Gamma Sigma; Accntng.

**PATTON JR, GEORGE W,** Western Piedmont Comm Coll, Morganton, NC; FR; MBA; Nwspr Cl Treas; SG; Mgmnt; Indus Mgmnt.

**PATTON, HAROLD G,** Fl A & M Univ, Tallahassee, FL; SO; BSN; Stdnt Nurses Assoc Pres 90-; Campus Ministry Co Chairman 89-; Natl Stdnt Nurses Assoc; Phi Eta Sigma Chaplain 89-; Nursing; Profssnl Nurse.

**PATTON, JAN M,** Ms St Univ, Miss State, MS; SO; BS; Phi Eta Sigma 89-; SWE Pres 89-; Comm Mnrty Wmn Rcrtmnt; Cvl Engr.**

**PATTON, JAN-EDWARD,** Duquesne Univ, Pittsburgh, PA; SR; BS; Stu Acctg Assoc 89-; Beta Alpha Phi 90-; Intrnd Alpern Rosenthal/Co CPA Pgh Pa; Tx Dept; AFTRA 89-; Radio Ancr Crntly Radio Pgh; Acctg; CPA.

**PATTON, KENYA L,** Draughons Jr Coll Nashville, Nashville, TN; GD; ASSOC; DPMA Vp; Incrprtd Bus Tn Vcs Amrc 90-; Comp Sci.

**PATTON, LORI A,** Ms St Univ, Miss State, MS; SR; Soc Hmn Rsrc Mgt 89; Soc Advncmnt Mgt 89; Mu Kappa Tau 90; Phi Theta Kappa 86; Delta Sigma Pi Pres 88-; Pres Schlr 89; Deans Schlr 88-90; BBA 90; Mrktng/Mgt; Hmn Rsrc Mgt.

**PATTON, ROBERT ALEX,** Roane St Comm Coll, Harriman, TN; SO; AS; Stdnt Envrnmntl Hlth Assoc; Deans Lst; Knights Pythias Vice Chnclr 89-; Independent Scientific Investigation Bio; Indstrl Hygiene; Environmental Hlth.

**PATTON, SEAN A,** Fl A & M Univ, Tallahassee, FL; SO; BS; Mrchng Band/Symphnc Band 89-; Jazz Ensmbl; Prayer Group; Hnr Roll 89-; Deans List 90; Music Ed; Edctn/Prfrmnc.

**PATTON, SUSAN T,** Radford Univ, Radford, VA; SR; BS; Stdnt Educ Assn 89-; Assn Educ Of Yng Chldrn; Kappa Delta Pi 90-; AAS Educ New River Comm Coll 89; AAS Sec Sci Wytheville Comm Coll 86; Early/Mdl Educ; Tchr.

**PATTS, MERSINE,** Hellenic Coll/Holy Cross, Brookline, MA; SR; BA; Grad Comm Chr 90-; Dscplnry Brd 89-90; Accrdtn Slf Stdy Comm 89-90; Stdnt Gov Jr Clss Rep 89-90; Deans List 89-; Maids Athena Pres 86-87; Yng Adlt Leag Grk Orthdx Chrch 87-; Lbrl Arts; Law/Intrntl Affrs.

**PATTY, MICHAEL S,** Roane St Comm Coll, Harriman, TN; SO; BS; Envir Hlth; Indstrl Hygiene.

**PATZ, M JOYCE,** Duquesne Univ, Pittsburgh, PA; SR; BED; Demo Comm Wmn Etna Pa; Zng Hrg Brd Sec; Ltrgcl Mnstr; Phi Theta Kappa; Alumnae Assoc; Ltrgcl Comm All Sts Chrch; Exec/Lgl Sec; AED 89; Sci Educ; Tchr.

**PAUGH, MIA A,** Ramapo Coll Of Nj, Mahwah, NJ; SR; BS; Rsdnt Stdnt Assc VP 90; Mbr Advsry Board Dean Stdnts 89-90; Reading Tutor Division Basic Studies 89-90; Finance Invstmnt Clb 89-90; Mrktng Clb 89; Ntnl Residence Hall; IBM 90; Bsn Admin/Mngmnt; Bsn.

**PAUL, ADAM C,** James Madison University, Harrisonburg, VA; FR; Kappa Delta Rho Frtrnty Cncl; IM Sccr; Pltcl Sci Econ; Law Schl.

**PAUL, ANGELA L,** Christopher Newport Coll, Newport News, VA; SR; Deans List 89-; Grad Cum Laude; Elem Sch Tchr; BA CNC; Elem Educ; Tchr.

**PAUL, CATHERINE E,** Boston Coll, Chestnut Hill, MA; FR; BA; Campus Right To Life 90-; Vrsty Sftbl 90-; Nursing.

**PAUL, CHRISTINE G,** Livingston Univ, Livingston, AL; SR; BA; Cardinal Key 90-; Alpha Chi 90-; Spec Ed; Tchr.

**PAUL, CHRISTINE L,** Central Pa Bus School, Summerdale, PA; SR; ASB; Data Prcssng Mgmt Assn Chr 90-; Vlybl 90-; Stdnt Govt Achvmnt Awrd 90-; Deans Lst 90-; Comp Info Syst; Anlyst/Prog.

**PAUL, CYNTHIA L,** Wv Northern Comm Coll, Wheeling, WV; SR; AAS; Phi Theta Kappa 89-; Teller Med Pk Fed Credit Un 90-; Cert 90; Bus; Banking.

**PAUL, FRANCOIS,** Bunker Hill Comm Coll, Boston, MA; FR; Bsktbl/Vlybl; Partners In Hlth; Honrs From The Pres Of Partnrs In Hlth For Wrk Done In My Cmnty; Hlp People To Undrstnd How Protct Thmslvs Agnst Aids; Engl; Acctng.

**PAUL, GATHUNGU N,** Howard Univ, Washington, DC; GD; M; ASCE 87-; Tau Beta Pi 89; Schl Eng Deans Lst 88-89; BSCE 89; Cvl Eng; Rsrch.

**PAUL, JENNIFER C,** Dowling Coll, Oakdale Li, NY; FR; BA; Stdnt Govt; Dorm Cncl VP; Orchestra 90-; Blood Drive Asst Coord; Stdnts Assn Serv Awd; Math/Bio; Scndry Edn.

**PAUL, KAREN E,** Long Island Coll Hosp Of Nrsng, Brooklyn, NY; FR; AD; Office Mgr 87-90; BS SUNY 90f; Nrsng.

**PAUL, MICHAEL A,** Georgetown Univ, Washington, DC; SO; BA; Brown T V Prdcr; Ftbl Bsbl 89-; Eng; Film Production.

**PAUL, NATASHIA R,** Va Union Univ, Richmond, VA; SO; Miss Frsmn 89-90; Pearl Omega Psi Phi VP 89-90; Natl Schlrs Com 90-; Cmnctn/Radio/TV/FILM; Film Dir.

**PAUL, RUTH L,** George Mason Univ, Fairfax, VA; SR; BSED; SEA George Mason Chptr 88-; Wmns Damer ORT VP 70-; Kappa Dlt Pi 90-; Alph Chi 90-; Deans List Nrthrn VA Comm Clg; Wmn Clb Schlrshp; Synagogue Sisterhd; Annadale Bus/Prfsnl Wmn Schlrshp; Educ Grant; AS Nrthrn VA Comm Clg 88; Erly Chldhd Ed; Tch.

**PAUL, SANDRA M,** Univ Of Hartford, West Hartford, CT; SO; BA; Alpha Eisilon Phi 89-; Psychlgy.

**PAUL, TAMMY L,** Daytona Beach Comm Coll, Daytona Beach, FL; FR; AS; Pres Lst 90; Grphc Dsgn.

**PAUL, VERONICA C,** Springfield Tech Comm Coll, Springfield, MA; SO; BFA; Fine Arts; Art.

**PAULEY IV, DON R,** Marshall University, Huntington, WV; SR; BA; WV Soc Of CPAS 90-; Acctg; CPA/PROFESSIONAL Accountant.

**PAULEY, SCOTT F,** Wv Northern Comm Coll, Wheeling, WV; SO; BA; Bus Admin.

**PAULEY, VICTORIA L,** Marshall University, Huntington, WV; FR; BBA; Dns Lst Schl Of Bus; Employed By Putnam Co Schl Systs; Bus; Mgmt.

**PAULHAMUS-NOLEN, ROBIN L,** Asbury Theological Sem, Wilmore, KY; GD; MA; Christns Biblcl Equalty 89-; Theta Phi 90-; Evang Soc Act 90; Cris Cnslr; Youth Advoc 84-87; BA Ind Univ Of Pa; World Msn/Evangelism; Mnstry; Cnslng.

**PAULING, BRIAN L,** Hampton Univ, Hampton, VA; JR; BS; Gspl Chr Prlmntrn 90; Mrchng And Cncrt Bnd Sctn Ldr 88-; Rsdnt Asst Asst Drm Dir 89-; Alpha Kappa Mu 90-; Phi Beta Sigma VP 90-; Acctng Intrn 90-; Fll Schlrshp 90-; All CIAA 90-; Acctng; CPA.

**PAULING, SHERRY B,** Embry Riddle Aeronautical Univ, Daytona Beach, FL; JR; BS; Fut Prof Wmn Aviation 88-; Wndsrfg Clb 90; Sigma Chi 90-; Intl Ordr Rnbw Grls Wrthy Advsr 82-90; Aerontcl Sci; Prof Pilot.

**PAULINHO, JOYCE M A,** Newbury Coll, Brookline, MA; SO; AS; Cls Rep 90-; Deans Lst 90-; Catechist 90-; Bus; Fshn Merch.**

**PAULINO MARTINEZ, RAMON A,** Bayamon Central Univ, Bayamon, PR; FR; BA; Cmptr Sci.

**PAULINO, JOANNE G,** Univ Of Akron, Akron, OH; JR; Coop Ed Wth G E Cptl; Edith Mae E Schlrshp; Accntg; Law.

**PAULK, LAURIE E,** Memphis St Univ, Memphis, TN; FR; BS; Stdnt Ambsdr Brd; Stdnt Actvts Cncl; Phi Eta Sigma; Pi Beta Phi 90-; Cecil C Humphries Pres Schlrshp; Math Sci Schlrshp; Math; Hghr Lvl Math Tchr.

**PAULK, MIRANDA L,** Valdosta St Coll, Valdosta, GA; SO; BA; Alpha Lambda Delta 89-90; Kappa Delta 89-; Ttr Ltrcy Prgm 90-; Psychlgy Spcl Edctn; Psychlgst.

**PAULO, JOSEPH T,** Liberty Univ, Lynchburg, VA; SR; BS; Alpha Lambda Delta 88-; Rsdnt Asst Full Schlrshp 89-90; Math; Tchg.

**PAULSEN, FAYME G,** Endicott Coll, Beverly, MA; SO; ASSOC; Res Asst 90-; Peer Tutr 90-; Intrnshp 89-90; Intrnshp Jrdn Mrsh 90-; Fld Hcky 90-; Retlng.

**PAULSON, JESICA A,** Univ Of South Al, Mobile, AL; JR; BA; Jgr Prdctns; Sec Ed.

**PAULSON, KATHERINE D,** Univ Of South Al, Mobile, AL; SO; BA; Equestrian Clb 90-; Soc Sci/Educ; Tch.

**PAULSON, KRISTEN,** Georgetown Univ, Washington, DC; JR; BA; Clg Repbl 88-; Nw Stdnt Orntn Stff 89-90; Dns Lst 89-; Stdnts Georgetwn Inc Gen Mgr Vital Vittles Str; Fin/Intl Mgmt; Rl Est Brkr.

**PAULSON, PAMELA S,** Univ Of South Al, Mobile, AL; JR; BA; AS Wallace Coll Of Dothan 89; Educ; Tchr.

**PAULUS, CYNTHIA A,** Elmira Coll, Elmira, NY; SO; BS; Lge Intrn Spch Pthlgsts 89-; Orntn Comm 90-; Outng Clb 90-; Phi Eta Sigma Sec 90-; Spch/Hrng; Spc Pthlgst.

**PAUYO, MARIE-FRANCOISE,** Bunker Hill Comm Coll, Boston, MA; FR; MBA; Ch Act Resota Lady Pity Cambridge MA Asst Mgr 89-; AS Inaghei Haiti 85; Engr Elect.

**PAUZA, MICHAEL,** Embry Riddle Aeronautical Univ, Daytona Beach, FL; SR; BS; Dns Hnr Lst 89-; United Airlies Flgt Offcr Intrnshp; United Airlines San Fran Intl Airport 79-; AS Dual Mjrs Coll San Mateo 79-81; Aeronautical Sci; Airline Pilot.**

**PAV, MICHELLE L,** Duquesne Univ, Pittsburgh, PA; JR; BS; Lambda Kappa Sigma; Phi Delta Chi Little Sis; Deans List; Aerobics Instr; Phrmcy.

**PAVEY, STEPHEN C,** Asbury Theological Sem, Wilmore, KY; GD; M DIV; Quartet 89-90; Rlgus Life Dir 88-89; Alpha Kappa Epsilon 89-90; AGORA 87-88; Orange Beret 87-89; Wilson King Awd 90-; BA Greenville Clg 90; Relgn; Prfsr.

**PAVLATOS, JENNIFER C,** Immaculata Coll, Immaculata, PA; JR; BA; Nwsppr Edtr 89-; Immts Pr Cncl Co Chrmn 90-; Nrsng Hm Vol; Sclgy; Pblc Rltns.

**PAVLIC, PAULA S,** West Liberty St Coll, West Liberty, WV; JR; BA; Engl.

**PAVLICK, ANDREA,** Allegheny Coll, Meadville, PA; SO; BS; Plyshp Thtre Crpntr 89-; Lambda Sigma 90-; Hbtt Fr Hmnty 91; Aldn Schlr 90; Allghny Fncng Clb 89-; Chem; Envrnmntl Sci.

**PAVLICS, MARY L,** Georgian Court Coll, Lakewood, NJ; JR; BS; St Lanslaus Parish Coun Rep Large; Natl Assn Female Exec; Delta Mu Delta Sec 90-; Bus Admin/Acctng.

**PAVLOCK, MARY E,** Hillsborough Comm Coll, Tampa, FL; FR; MD; Phi Theta Kappa; Med; Frnsc Psychtry/Rsrch.

**PAVLOVSKY, KELLY S,** Salisbury St Univ, Salisbury, MD; SR; MBA; Lambda Iota Tau; Deans Lst 89-; Cum Laude Hnrs; BA; Engl.

**PAVONE, JODIE A,** Central Fl Comm Coll, Ocala, FL; SO; Chld Care; Day Care/Tchr.

**PAWELSKI, BRIAN M,** City Univ Of Ny Baruch Coll, New York, NY; SR; BA; Foreign Trade Soc 90-; Golden Key 90-; AAS 89; Intl Mktg; Exprtng.

**PAWLEY, JASON R,** United States Naval Academy, Annapolis, MD; SO; BS; Naval Acad Mens Glee Clb 89-; Masqueraders Roles Mystery Plays 89-; Westside Story 90-; Catholic Choir 89-; Pol Sci; Naval Aviator.**

**PAWLEY, JONATHAN C,** S U N Y At Buffalo, Buffalo, NY; SR; BA; AIAS 89-; UB Planning Dsgn Assc 89-; Gldn Key 90; Intrnshp Je Role Assc 88-; Basebll/Soccer/Hcky 86-90; AAS Suny Alfred Tech 86; Archtcr/Planning; Mstrs Cty Plnng.

**PAWLICZAK, LAWRANCE J,** Manhattan Coll, Bronx, NY; SR; BS; SAE 89-; Tau Beta Pi 88-; Pi Tau Sigma 89-; Epsilon Sigma Pi 90-; Pres Schlrshp 87-; 2M Ftbl Bsktbl Sftbl Vlybl 87-; Mech Eng; MBE.

**PAWLIKOWSKI, SCOTT M,** Univ Of Akron, Akron, OH; FR; BS; Lacorsse Clb; ASME; Phi Eta Sigma; Alpha Lambda Delta; IM Sprts Capt; Mech Eng.

**PAWLOWSKI JR, JAMES R,** S U N Y Coll At Fredonia, Fredonia, NY; JR; BA; Theatre 88-; Natl Guard 88-; Hist; U S Army.**

**PAWNELL, YVETTE P,** Ky St Univ, Frankfort, KY; FR; BS; Busn Admin; Intrnl Audtr.

**PAXTON, JOSEPH D,** Univ Of Al At Huntsville, Huntsville, AL; SO; Cnslr Eng Smr Res Pgm; Mech Eng.

**PAXTON, ROBERT G,** Tn Tech Univ, Cookeville, TN; SR; BS; Agri Bus Clb Sec 87-; Agri Cncl 90-; Delta Tau Alpha 90-; Agri Bus Econ; Mgmnt Agri Firm.

**PAYACK, LAURA C,** Castleton St Coll, Castleton, VT; JR; BA; Dorm Cncl Interdorm Rep 88-89; Phi Eta Sigma 88-; Psych; Med.

**PAYEUR, MELISSA A,** Middle Tn St Univ, Murfreesboro, TN; SO; Elem Edn; Tchr.

**PAYLOR, KARLA M,** Howard Univ, Washington, DC; SR; BSP; Stdnt Natl Pharmctcl Assoc VP 89-; Stdnt Assmbly Rep; Natl Soc Of Blck Engrs 87-88; Golden Key 88-; Rho Chi 90-; Youth On The Rise Tutor 89-; YMCA Big Sis 90-; Dupont Medcl Prodcts Div Intrn 90; Patricia Roberts Harris Publc Affrs Intrn; Pharmcy.

**PAYN, ROBERT M,** Univ Of Southern Ms, Hattiesburg, MS; JR; BA; Student Alumni Assoc 89-; Interfty Council Public Relat Officer 90-; Phi Eta Sigma 88-; Gamma Beta Phi 89-; Delta Tau Delta VP 88-; Selected Exchange Univ Wales UK; English.

**PAYNE, CAROL A,** Comm Coll Algny Co Algny Cmps, Pittsburgh, PA; SO; AA; BLAC 90-; Girl Scout Troop Ldr; Phi Theta Kappa; Kappa Swthrt Pres Line 88 87-88; African Amer Stdnt Schlstc Awd; History; Professor.

**PAYNE, CHANTA S,** Jackson St Univ, Jackson, MS; FR.

**PAYNE, DAIVD A,** Univ Of Pittsburgh, Pittsburgh, PA; FR; BS; Phi Eta Sigma; Eng; Materials Sci Eng.

**PAYNE, DEBORA G,** Middle Tn St Univ, Murfreesboro, TN; SR; BFA; Gamma Beta Phi 87-; Tau Omicron 88-; Graphic Dsgn; Comm Artist.

**PAYNE, DEBRA K,** Univ Of Charleston, Charleston, WV; SR; AD; AD Crmnl Justice WV St Coll 77; Nursing.

**PAYNE, DEITRA C,** Univ Of The Dist Of Columbia, Washington, DC; SR; BA; Acad Achvmnt Awd 89-90; Real Estate Cert EWW Real Estate Academy 90; Cmptr Prog Cert ICS Schl Cmptr Trng 87; Acctng; Real Estate Law.

**PAYNE, GEORGE L,** Asbury Theological Sem, Wilmore, KY; GD; M DIV; Intl Stdnts Clb Chpln 87-; Otrch Mnstres Tm Ldr 87-; World Otrch Flwshp Tm Ldr 87-; Deans Lst 88 89; BA Messiah Clg 89; Theology/Bibcl Stdes; Mnstry/Tchng.

**PAYNE, GERALD L,** Al St Univ, Montgomery, AL; SO; BED; AL St Univ Mrchng Bnd Tuba Sec Ldr 90-; Equip Mgr 89-; Kappa Kappa Psi; Msc Educ; Bnd Dir Coll.

**PAYNE, HOWARD H,** Tougaloo Coll, Tougaloo, MS; SO; BA; Pre-Alumni Club Pres 90-; Stdnt Ldrs Org Peer Hlprs 90-; Stdnt Supprt Svcs Club 89-; Boy Scouts Of Amer Scout Mstr; Upwrd Bound Prog Tutor Of Yr 90; Upward Bound Prog Tutor Of Yr; Econ; Law.

**PAYNE, JENNIFER L,** Ms St Univ, Miss State, MS; JR; Yavapai Coll Hmcmng Maid 87; Hmcmng Queen 88; Bible Sch Tchr Nettleton U M Ch; Buckeye Comm Ch 86-87; Pres List; Elem Edn.

**PAYNE, JOANNE R,** Al St Univ, Montgomery, AL; JR; Gldn Ammbsdr 90-; Biomed Sci Clb 89-; Gift Life Fndtn; Alpha Kappa Mu; Alpha Kappa Alpha 90-; Acdmc Schlrshp 88-; Dns Lst 88-; MARC 89-; AS Solano Comm Cllg 90; Chem; Med.

**PAYNE, JUDITH M,** Owensboro Comm Coll, Owensboro, KY; SO; BED; Anthrplgy Club 89-90; Ky Tchrs Assn 89-; KHEAA 89-; Deans List 90-; Eng/Math; Edn 5-8 Grades.

**PAYNE, JULIE E,** Bethany Coll, Bethany, WV; FR; BS; Drama; Nwspaper Photo Edtr; Soc Of Profsnl Jrnlsts; Dixcples Of Christ Church; Actvts Cncl; Yrbk Photogrphr; Cmnctns; Profsnl Photogrphy.

**PAYNE, KATHY R,** Savannah St Coll, Savannah, GA; SR; BS; Model Arab Leag Tm 90; AS Cntrl Carolina Comm Coll 89; Acctg.

**PAYNE, KELLY J,** Unity Coll, Unity, ME; FR; BA; Vlybl 90-; Soc Sci; Pk Mgt.

**PAYNE, KIMBERLY D,** Jackson St Univ, Jackson, MS; JR; BBA; Alpha Lambda Delta 89-; Delta Mu Delta Histrn 90-; Delta Sigma Theta Secy; Acadmc Schlrshp 88-; Pres List Schlr 88-; Deans List Schlr 89-90; Fin; Mgt.

**PAYNE JR, LARRY D,** Longwood Coll, Farmville, VA; FR; BS; Alpha Lambda Delta; Sys Engr.

**PAYNE, LEE ANN,** Oh Univ-Southern Cmps, Ironton, OH; FR; BA; Excllnc Schlrshp 90-; Elem Educ.

**PAYNE, LISA A,** Brescia Coll, Owensboro, KY; SO; BA; Stdnt Govt Pres; Yrbk Co Edtr; Theatre Troupe 89-; Alpha Chi 90-; Deans List 89-; Acdmc Exclnc Awd 90-; Soc Stds; Law.

**PAYNE, LORELEI A,** Oh Univ-Southern Cmps, Ironton, OH; JR; BA; OUSC Ironton Jdcry Brd 89-; Stdnt Gov Cmnctns Dir 88-; Camp Nwslttr Ed 88-; Phi Kappa Phi 90; Gamma Pi Deltqa 89; Alpha Lambda Delta 89; Wmn Wllnss Pres 89; COGSWA 87; Vlntr Mnr Cr Nrsng Ctr Westerville OH 84-88; Psych/Sclgy; Grtrics Cnslr.**

**PAYNE, M JILL,** Brescia Coll, Owensboro, KY; FR; BA; In Town Rep Frshmn; Cls 90-; Senate Seat 90-; Deans Lst 90-; Acad Exellence 90-; Math.

**PAYNE, MELISSA A,** Niagara Univ, Niagara Univ, NY; SR; BSN; Swm Tm Mgr 87-; Stdnt Govt Cls Rep 89-90; Chpl Erchrstc Msntr 87-; Dlt Phi Eplsn 87-88; Comm Actn Pgm 87-89; Roswell Park Inst Intrnshp 90-; Asstntshp Tchr Asstnt 90-; Slf Brst Exam Amer Cncr Scty Instrctr 90; Nrsng Bio.

**PAYNE, MELISSA M,** Winthrop Coll, Rock Hill, SC; SO; BA; Cmptr Sci; Syst Pgm.

**PAYNE, MICHAEL S,** Western Ky Univ, Bowling Green, KY; JR; BA; Phi Kappa Phi; Hnr Roll; Math/Chmstry; Physcn.

**PAYNE, MICHELLE R,** Oh Univ, Athens, OH; JR; BFA; Cmps Crsd Chrst; IM Sprts; Deans List; Photo Ills; Fshn Phtgrphy.

**PAYNE, MORGANNA C,** Albertus Magnus Coll, New Haven, CT; SR; BA; Act 2 Theatre 87-; Originals Co-Fndr 87-; Di Jon Productions Co-Fndr/V P; Dns Lst 89-; Intern Browning-Ferris Ind 90; Indstrl/Org Psych; Ther Theatre Chldrn.

**PAYNE, NORALYN R,** Morgan St Univ, Baltimore, MD; SR; BS; Chrldrs; Psychlgy Clb; Pi Gamma Mu; Psi Chi 89; Alpha Kappa Alpha Prlmntrn 89-; SMRI Univ DE 90; Rsrch Asstshp-Bhvrl Phrmclgy Rsrch Frances Cott Key Med Ctr 90-; Psychlgy; Scl Psychlgy Rsrch.

**PAYNE, PATRICIA LOUISE,** Christopher Newport Coll, Newport News, VA; SO; BA; Soc Wrk Club; Zeta Phi Beta; Soc Wrk; Soc Wrkr.

**PAYNE JR, PHILIP W,** Fl St Univ, Tallahassee, FL; SR; MS; Amer Soc Cvl Eng Pres 88-; FAMU Stdnt Exec Cncl 90-; FAMU Career Plcmnt Stdnt Advsry Cncl 90-; Tau Beta Pi 89-; Pi Eta Sigma 87-; Golden Key 87-; Schlrshp 86-90; FSU Lbrl Stds Hons/Schlrs Pgm 87; Deans Lst 86-; Cvl Eng U CA Berkeley; Const Eng/Mgmt.

**PAYNE, R STEVEN,** Ga Southern Univ, Statesboro, GA; JR; BS; Blgy; Rsrch Mllclr Genetics.**

**PAYNE, RAYMOND V,** Asbury Theological Sem, Wilmore, KY; GD; MDIV; Theta Phi; BS Oh Unvrsty 73; Theology; Parish Mnstry.

**PAYNE II, ROBERT G,** Univ Of Fl, Gainesville, FL; SR; BA; Amer Clsscl Leag 90-; Phi Kappa Phi 90-; Eta Sigma Phi 90-; Stdnt Tchng P K Yonge HS Gainesville FL 90-; Paul Douglas Schlrshp Tchrs 90-; Eta Sigma Phi Schlrshp 90-; Clsscs; Scndry Ed.**

**PAYNE, RONALD D,** Northeast State Tech Comm Coll, Blountville, TN; SO; AAS; Comp & Engrng.

**PAYNE, SANDRA,** Univ Of Tn At Martin, Martin, TN; SO; BAS; Mu Epsilon Delta 90-; Delta Sigma Theta; Biol; Med.

**PAYNE, SARA E,** Univ Of Al At Birmingham, Birmingham, AL; JR; BS; Coll Rep Club Spring Hill Coll V P 88; Stdnt Adv Bd Soph Rep 88; Acctng Stdnt Adv-Spprt Grp 90; Current Events Comm 88; Phlsphy Club 88; Beta Gamma Sigma; Phi Kappa Phi; Golden Key Prog Chm; Betas Alpha Psi V P; Acctng; CPA & Big Six Acctng.

**PAYNE, SEAN C,** Birmingham Southern Coll, Birmingham, AL; SO; BA; Phi Eta Sigma 89; Bank And Intrchnge 89-; Fnnce; Fnncl Cnsltnt.

**PAYNE, SHELLEY R,** Western Ky Univ, Bowling Green, KY; JR; BSN; Assoc Stdnt Govt; Dorm Flr Rep; KY Assn Nrsng Stdnts; Phi Kappa Phi; Pres Schlr 88-, IM Sftbl Flag Ftbl Vlybl 88-; Nrsng.

**PAYNE, SHERRY L,** Univ Of Louisville, Louisville, KY; GD; MENG; Natl Soc Of Profsnl Engrs 88-; IEEE 90-; Assoc For Comptng Machnry 90-; Vlybl 86-90; BES 90; Eng/Math/Comptr Sci; Engrng.

**PAYNE, TINA C,** Midway Coll, Midway, KY; SO; AD; Law; Paralegal.

**PAYNE-DUBLIN, PHYLLIS BARBARA,** Saint Josephs Coll New York, Brooklyn, NY; GD; St Vincent/Grenadines Ex-Nrs Assn; Dir Nrs.

**PAYNTER, BRIDGET J,** Memphis St Univ, Memphis, TN; FR; BBA; Stdnt Ambsdr Bd; Wmns Panhellenic Cncl; Alpha Lamda Delta; Hnrs Stdnt Assc; Delta Gamma 90-; Gamma Beta Phi; Economics; Law.

**PAYNTER, PATRICIA A,** Concord Coll, Athens, WV; SR; BS; BS; Multi-Subject; Tchng.

**PAYSON, ANDRIANNE S,** City Univ Of Ny Med Evers Coll, Brooklyn, NY; SO; BS; Nwspr Assoc Edtr 90-; Natl Assn For Black Acctnts; Crwn Hts Yth Cllctv G S Trp Ldr; Belle Zeller Schlrshp; Dr Mattie Cook Mem Schlrshp Awd; Constans Culver Awd; Acctng/Math; CPA/AUDITOR.

**PAYSON, JEREMY P,** Western New England Coll, Springfield, MA; FR; BA; Alpha Lambda Delta 90-; Dns Lst 90; Acctng.

**PAYTON, DERRICK ARSHELL,** Morehouse Coll, Atlanta, GA; FR; BA; Chess Tm 90-; Martin Marietta Manned Space Sys Intern 89-; Swim 90-; Math; Eng.

**PAYTON, HEATHER H,** Ky Wesleyan Coll, Owensboro, KY; SR; BMUSE; SGA Pres 87-; Yrbk Edtr 87-89; Music Educ Ntl Cnfrnc VP 88-; Alpha Chi 89-; James Graham Brown Schlr 87-; Sigma Kappa VP 87-; Compass Clb 87-88; Oak/Ivy Hnr Soc 90; Mitchell Kybrd Muisc Awrd 89; Muisc Educ; Stu Prsnl.

**PAYTON, KIMBERLEE S,** Univ Of Montevallo, Montevallo, AL; SR; BA; Elem Mddl Schl Educ; Math Tchr.

**PAYTON, SHANNON C,** Ms St Univ, Miss State, MS; SO; BS; Alpha Lambda Delta 90-; Phi Eta Sigma 90-; Math/Sci; Bio Engr.

**PAYTON, TANJA L,** Wilmington Coll, New Castle, DE; JR; BS; Delaware Qrtr Hrs Assn Mmbr 89-; Estrn Shr Wstrn Hrs Shw Assn Pntkpr 89-90; Obtng Bchlrs Degree Ftthr Myslf St Frm Ins; Assoc Delaware Tchncl Comm Clg 86; Bsns; Insrnc.

**PAYTON, WENDY L,** Bapt Bible Coll & Seminary, Clarks Summit, PA; FR; BED; Yth Grp Ldr; Deans Lst; Hstry Educ; Hgh Schl Tchr.

**PAZDERAK, MATTHEW B,** Kent St Univ Kent Cmps, Kent, OH; SO; BA.

**PAZIENZA, STACIE A,** Chatfield Coll, Saint Martin, OH; JR; BA; Vol Spcl Olympics 85-90; Vol Stdnt Tchr; Elem Edn; Tchr.

**PAZOGA, VICTORIA A,** Univ Of Sc At Coastal Carolina, Conway, SC; SR; BA; Ntl Coll Cmptn 90; Cox Cbl Myrtle Bch SC 90; Mrktg; Rsrch.

**PAZOS, JOHN C,** Univ Of Southern Ms, Hattiesburg, MS; SO; BS; Stdnt Alum Assn Stdnt Rep 89-; Mbr Exec Brd; Assc Stdnt Bdy Sen Hattiesbrg Hall 90; Dns Lst 90; Alpha Tau Omega Wrthy Sentnl 90; Crim Just; Investgtn.

**PEACHEY, CYNTHIA A,** West Chester Univ, West Chester, PA; SO; BS; Camp Crsd Christ Ldrshp 90-; Sigma Alpha Iota 90-; Clss 37 W Chester U Schlrshp 89-90; W Chester Alumni Assn Schlrshp 90-; Ephrata Amer Bus Wmn Assn Schlrshp 89-; Opera Delaware 90; Music Ed; Tch/Prfrm.

**PEACHEY, KENT D,** Juniata Coll, Huntingdon, PA; SR; BS; Dir Church Boys Clb 88-90; Head Usher Church 90-; 4-H Dairy Clb 78-83; Deans List 84-86 90-; AA Lbrl Arts Hesston Clg 86; Acctg.

**PEACOCK, CECELIA JEFFORDS,** Univ Of North Fl, Jacksonville, FL; SR; BSN; Stff Nrse At Univ Med Cntr In Cardio Vsclr Intnsve Care Unit; ADN Joliet Jr Coll Joliet IL 74; Nrsng.

**PEACOCK, CHRISTOPHER M,** Middle Ga Coll, Cochran, GA; FR; BA; Tenns; Gamma Beta Phi; Dorm Cncl; Math; Eng.

**PEACOCK JR, CLAYTON E,** Univ Of Southern Ms, Hattiesburg, MS; JR; BS; Un Brd 90-; Bapt Un 89-; Hnrs Assn VP 89-; Cmptr Sci.

**PEACOCK JR, JAMES W,** Univ Of Nc At Charlotte, Charlotte, NC; SO; BS; Allied Hlth Clb 89-; Int Var Chrstn Flwshp 89-; Dns Lst 90-; Intrnshp St Gov; Blgy; Med Sci.

**PEACOCK, KIMBERLY J,** Glassboro St Coll, Glassboro, NJ; FR; BA; Hnrs Concntrtn; Poetry Comp Hnrbl Mntn; Jrnlsm; Edtg.

**PEADEN, LINDA L,** Univ Of West Fl, Pensacola, FL; SR; BS; Phi Beta Lambda; Alpha Sigma Lambda 90-; AAS NE AL State Jr 74; Bus Educ Tchr.

**PEAK, DERON G,** Liberty Univ, Lynchburg, VA; SR; BS; Music Mnstry Clb 90-; Yth Quest 90-; Chmbr Sngrs 90-; Music Educ; Tchr.

**PEAK, ERIC A,** Marshall University, Huntington, WV; JR; BBA; Intrfrat Delgt; Natl Ord Of Omega; Pi Kappa Phi Sec 89-; Bsns; Mrktng.

**PEAK, KARA E,** Middle Tn St Univ, Murfreesboro, TN; SR; BS; Hm Ecnmcs Assn 89-; Orntatn Asstnt Tm Cptn 88-; Chi Omega Tres 87-; Intrnshp Oprylnd Htl Nshvl TN 90; Fshn Mrchndsng; Rtl Mgmnt.

**PEAKE, ERVILA A,** Schenectady County Comm Coll, Schenectady, NY; FR; AAS; Phi Theta Kappa 90-; Exec Brd Pivt Indstry Cncl Clirpro Comm 88-90; Law.

**PEAKE, J TRAVIS,** Univ Of Sc At Columbia, Columbia, SC; JR; BS; LDS Stdnt Asso V P 90-; BSA Scoutmaster; Ntnl Hon Mechncl Engrng Soc; Pi Tau Sigma; Phi Eta Sigma 86-; Mechncl Engrng; Engrng.

**PEAKE JR, JAMES T,** Univ Of Sc At Columbia, Columbia, SC; JR; BA; Deans Lst; Elect Eng; Elctrncs.

**PEAL, TERESA L,** Univ Of Charleston, Charleston, WV; FR; BS; Marmet Pub Lbry Bd 89-; Educ; Tchr.

**PEALE, MICHAEL R,** Memphis St Univ, Memphis, TN; JR; BA; Gamma Beta Phi 89-; Ntl Intrcoll Rodeo Assn; Bus Mgmt; Corp Lvl Mgmt.

**PEAPER, JEFFREY W,** James Madison University, Harrisonburg, VA; SR; MA; Psychlgy Clb 89-; Ordr Of Omega 90-; Goldn Key 90-; Psi Chi 90-; Deans Lst 89; Sigma Nu VP/RSH Chrmn 88-; Spec Olympcs Coach 88-; Pres Lst 89-; Outstndng Undrgrad 90; IM Sftbl/Bsktbl 88-; Psychlgy; Indstrl/Org Psychlgy.

**PEARCE, BARBARA M,** Albertus Magnus Coll, New Haven, CT; SR; BA; Tau Pi Phi 90-; Alpha Sigma Lambda; SNET Co Comptrllrs 85-; AA; Busn/Econ; Acctng.

**PEARCE, GARY L,** Ashland Comm Coll, Ashland, KY; FR; Art.

**PEARCE, MELODIE R,** Univ Of Sc At Columbia, Columbia, SC; FR; BA; Yrbk Ads Edtr 90-; Stdnt Govt Assoc Senator 90-; Gamma Beta Phi 90-; Presidental Hnr Rl 90-; Education; Elem Tchr.

**PEARCE, RONALD K,** Tallahassee Comm Coll, Tallahassee, FL; SO; Santander Homeowners & Crime Watch Assoc Officer 88-; Paper Ind 79-86; USAF; USAF Resesrves; Bus; Acctng/Tax Law.

**PEARCE, SCARLET P,** Livingston Univ, Livingston, AL; SR; BS; Bus Admin.

**PEARCE, SHERYL A,** Univ Of Ct, Storrs, CT; JR; BA; Gldn Ky 90-; Manchester Elderly Outreach Intern; Alumni Schlrshp; Hmn Dvlpmnt Fmly Rsrcs; Soc Wrkr.**

**PEARCE, WILLIAM S,** Univ Of Al At Huntsville, Huntsville, AL; JR; BSE; US Army 80-88; AAS Calhoun Comm Coll 88; Elect Eng; Dsgn/Mgmt.

**PEAREN, NICOLE B,** Philadelphia Coll Pharm & Sci, Philadelphia, PA; JR; BS; ASP V P 90-; IPSF Stdnt Exch Officer 90-; Peer Cnslr/Stdnt Dvlpmnt Cntr 90-; Rho Chi; Rho Pi Phi 89-; Alpha Delta Theta 88-; Hstrn 90-91; Vol Tutor Team Ldr 88-; Pharm.

**PEARL, DENNIS J M,** Owensboro Comm Coll, Owensboro, KY; FR; ASSOC; Nursing; Work Emergency Rm.

**PEARLINGI, PATRICIA M,** Va Commonwealth Univ, Richmond, VA; SR; Stdnt Edn Assn 89-90; Edn.

**PEARLMAN, DAVID W,** Western New England Coll, Springfield, MA; SO; BSBA; Com Prgmg Entrtnmnt Subcom Hd 90-; Stdnt Snt 90-; Alpha Lambda Delta Sec 90-; Stdnt Tchng Asst 90-; Acctg; Bus Admin.

**PEARLMAN, ELIZABETH H,** City Univ Of Ny Baruch Coll, New York, NY; GD; BBA; Advtsng Clb 89-90; Intrn Cntr Comm 89; Intrn Jacksina Co 89-90; AA Tallahassee Comm Coll 87; Mktng; Advrtsng.

**PEARLSON, JENNIFER B,** Boston Univ, Boston, MA; GD; BS; Pi Theta Epsilon Pres 90-; Gldn Key Natl Hnr Scty; Alpha Delta Pi Pldg Clss V P 88; Mortar Bd Soph Cls Awd; Occup Ther.

**PEARMAN, ELBA I,** Fl International Univ, Miami, FL; JR; BA; Std Diet Asc 90-; Amer Diet Asc 90-; Diet/Nttrtn; Reg Diet.

**PEARROW, ZENDA K,** Union Univ, Jackson, TN; SR; BS; Baptist Yng Wmn 87-; Baptist Stdnt Union 87-; STEA 90-; Elem Educ; Tchr.

**PEARSALL, DAVID L,** City Univ Of Ny La Guard Coll, Long Island Cty, NY; SO; AAS; Phi Theta Kappa; Qlty Cntrl Sprvsr 90-; Bsns Mgmnt; Qlty Cntrl Mgmnt.

**PEARSON, ALAN S,** Univ Of Ky, Lexington, KY; FR; BS; Radio 90-; LD Aide; ACM; Cmptr Sci; Prgrmmng.

**PEARSON, AMY E,** Daytona Beach Comm Coll, Daytona Beach, FL; SO; AS; Photo Soc 89-; Prof Photo; Comm/Adv.

**PEARSON, ANDRE J,** Univ Of Md At Eastern Shore, Princess Anne, MD; JR; BA; Sclgy; Cnslrng.

**PEARSON, ANGELA M,** Columbia Greene Comm Coll, Hudson, NY; SO; Taconic Farms Anml Crtkr 88-; Chrch Actvts 81-; Intern; Vllybl; Sci; Chrpctcs.

**PEARSON, CHARLES T,** Greenville Tech Coll, Greenville, SC; SR; AD; AD 2 Clb 90; Phi Theta Kappa 90; Ntl Cllgte Bus Mrt Awrd 90; All Amer Schlr 90; Dns Lst 90; Leslie Advrtsng Intrnshp 90; PR Frm; Mrktng; Advrtsng PR.

**PEARSON, ENID P,** Fayetteville St Univ, Fayetteville, NC; GD; Stdnt Orntatn Ldr 89-; Kappa Delta Pi Scl Comm 89-; Sigma Gamma Rho 90-; Otstndng Stdnt; Hghst Rnkng Sr 90; Intrnshp Cngrsmn Charlie Rose Offc; Bs 90; Tchng.

**PEARSON, JAMIE L,** Univ Of Ga, Athens, GA; SR; MSW; Scl Wrk Clb 89-; NASW 89-; Stdnts Envrnmntl Awrnss 89; Gldn Key 89-; Phi Kappa Phi; Alpha Delta Pi Pldg Trnr 88-; Psychtrc Hosp Intrn 90; State Hosp Intrn; BSW; Scl Wrk; PHD.

**PEARSON, JANA L,** Medical Coll Of Ga, Augusta, GA; SR; BSN; Sigma Theta Tau; Nrsg.

**PEARSON, LECIA B,** Fayetteville St Univ, Fayetteville, NC; NAE; Zeta Phi Beta 90; Chancellors Lst 90; BS 90; Early Chldhd Ed; Tchr.

**PEARSON, LEE ANN,** Univ Of Sc At Columbia, Columbia, SC; JR; BA; Bus Admn; Rl Est Apprsng.

**PEARSON, LISA M,** Dyersburg St Comm Coll, Dyersburg, TN; SO; AS; Phi Theta Kappa 90-; Sci; Elem Ed.

**PEARSON, MARTHA JENAE,** Ms St Univ, Miss State, MS; SO; BA; Campus Actv Bd 89-; BSU 89-; Gamma Beta Phi 90; IM 90-; Occptnl Ther; Clin Ther.

**PEARSON, MELISSA L,** Central Al Comm Coll, Alexander City, AL; SO; AA; Ssga Senator 90-; Phi Theta Kappa 89-; Yth Grp Lvng Word Chrch Pres 86-; Sylacauga Beautification Cncl 90-; Tlnt Schlrshp Miss Ala Pgnt; 2 Yr Univ Of Ala Hnrs Schlrshp; Bsbl Plate Mate 90-; Biology; BA/MEDICAL.**

**PEARSON, MICHELLE R,** Longwood Coll, Farmville, VA; SR; Stu Educ Assoc 89-; BS; Elem Ed; Tchr.

**PEARSON, NANCY L,** Univ Of Al At Birmingham, Birmingham, AL; JR; BS; Little Sister/Alpha Tau Omega 87-88; Acad Schlrshp; Pres/Deans List; Nursing; Neonatology.

**PEARSON, RICHARD E,** Lincoln Univ, Lincoln Univ, PA; SR; BS; Psychlgy Club 88-; Psi Chi; Minrty Biomed Rsrch Schlrshp Progrm 90; Psychlgy; Clincl.

**PEARSON, SARA J,** Benedict Coll, Columbia, SC; SR; Library Clb Treas; Natl Cncl Negro Wmn; Alpha Kappa Alpha; Stdnt Tchr 90; BS; SC Stdnt Ed Assc; Natl Ed Assc; Scnd Attndnt Hmcmng Queen 90; Elem Ed.

**PEARSON, SHERRY L,** Memphis St Univ, Memphis, TN; SR; BA; Stdnt Act Cncl Fash Brd VP 90-; Alpha Delta Pi; Intrn TV Sta; Mktg; Pblc Rltns.

**PEARSON, SHERRY P,** Abraham Baldwin Agri Coll, Tifton, GA; SO; Prfssnl Mom 69-87; Nrsng Edctr( Rgstrd Nrs.

**PEARSON, TINA F,** Bennett Coll, Greensboro, NC; SO; BA; Campus Grl Scouts Rcrdng Sec 90-; NAACP 89-; Bus/Acctg Clb 90-; Deans Lst; Bus Admin; Ins Undrwrtr.

**PEARSON, TINA S,** Univ Of Ga, Athens, GA; SR; BED; NSSLHA 89-; Gldn Ky 90-; Phi Kappa Phi; Cmmncn Scis And Dsrdrs; Spch Pthlgst.

**PEARSON, TRACY MICHELLE,** Univ Of Nc At Charlotte, Charlotte, NC; FR; BA; Phi Eta Sigma 90-; Im Sftbl 90-; Bus Admn; Adv.

**PEARSON, VICTORIA J,** Univ Of Sc At Columbia, Columbia, SC; SO; BA; Jap Study Cl 90-; Gamma Beta Phi 89-; Alpha Lambda Delta 89-; BCNB Schlrshp Intnshp 89-; Astronomy Lab Instr/Asst 90-; Fnce; Bnkg.

**PEART, KELLEY M,** Univ Of Sc At Columbia, Columbia, SC; FR; PHD; Hnrs Coll 90-; Physcs/Math; Nuclr Physcs.

**PEASE, LAURA C,** Elms Coll, Chicopee, MA; SR; BSN; Stdnt Nrs Assoc Treas 89-; Choir 88-90; Sigma Theta Tau; Kappa Gamma Pi; Shea Awrd; Nrsing.

**PEATROSS, VONDA K,** Longwood Coll, Farmville, VA; SR; Stdnt Educ Assn 87-; Baptist Stdnt Union 87-89; Hall Cncl Rep 90; Elem Educ; Tchr.

**PEAVY, RUTH B,** Univ Of South Al, Mobile, AL; JR; BA; Art Patrons League; Early Chldhd Ed; Tch.

**PECHMAN, HELEN R,** Yeshiva Univ, New York, NY; GD; JD; Stdnt Senate 89-90; Pre-Law Soc Pres 89-90; Yrbk Ed 89-90; Samuel Belkin Acad Schlr 86-90; BA 90; Psych; Law.

**PECHMAN, STACY L,** Ramapo Coll Of Nj, Mahwah, NJ; GD; AS; Italian Clb 90; Delta Mu Delta; Alpha Beta Gamma 89; Phi Sigma Omicron 89; AAS Rockland Comm Clg 89; Cmptr Info Sys; Dsgn Cmptr Sys.

**PECHT, MELANIE C,** Va Commonwealth Univ, Richmond, VA; FR; BS; Phi Eta Sigma; Psychology; Counselor/Case Worker.

**PECHULIS, MARK J,** Western New England Coll, Springfield, MA; JR; MS; Wghtlftng Clb 87-89; Judo Clb 87-88; Sigma Beta Tau; Pi Kappa Alpha 88-89; IM Ic Hcy; Mchncl Eng; Eng.

**PECK, ANDREW C,** Villanova Univ, Villanova, PA; JR; BA; Pres Residence Hall Part Dorm Cncl Pres 88-89; Active Part Pres Plnng Cmmt 88-89; Phi Kappa Phi; Psi Chi; Part EVE Clntr Serv 88-89; Stdnt/Tchr Liasion 90-; Intrmural Sftbll/Bsktbll Capt 88-89; Psychlgy; Doctorate Social Psychlgy.

**PECK, CHRISTOPHER L,** Coll Of Charleston, Charleston, SC; GD; JD; Bard Soc P 88-90; Yng Rpblcns 90; Sierra Clb 88-; Spec Olymps 80-; USN Elctrncs Wrfr 83-87; L-Tec Dsgn Asst 87-88; UPS Spec Air Drvr 89-; BA Coll Charleston 90; Envrnmntl Law; Law.

**PECK, JILL L,** Beckley Coll, Beckley, WV; FR; BS; Deans Lst; Marlinton Presbyn Chrch; AS Clercl Fairmont St Coll 87; Nrsng.

**PECK, LISA RENEE,** Marshall University, Huntington, WV; JR; BA; Gamma Beta Phi 89-; Ronald Mcdonald Hse; Deans Lst 88-; Acctg; CPA.

**PECK, RICHARD E,** Bridgeport Engr Inst, Fairfield, CT; SO; BS; Stdnt Snt Pres 90-; Cmnctns Fclty Tchncn 86-; Elect Eng; Eng.

**PECK, TERRI L,** D Youville Coll, Buffalo, NY; SO; BSMS; Ithc Clg SAB Flm Cmt 83-87; Eaber Union Rcrtmn Chrprsn 86-87; Rgnts Sclrshp; Cmt Amer Mktg Assc 85-86; Vol Buffalo Gen Hosp Occptnl Thrpy Dept; BS 87; Bus Mgmt; Cuyahoya Svngs/ Loan Intrnl Auda 88-89; Dlwr Nual Co Sales Tax Anlyst 89-90; Occptnl Thrpy; Phys Disablilites.

**PECK, TRACY L,** Springfield Tech Comm Coll, Springfield, MA; JR; AS; Chrch Yth Grp Advsr 90; SS Tchr 88-89; Bsnss Med; Med Admin.

**PECKINPAUGH, CARRIE J,** Cumberland Coll, Williamsburg, KY; FR; MBA; Bkbl 90-; Biology; Pharm.

**PECORA, JOHN V,** Le Moyne Coll, Syracuse, NY; JR; BA; Bus Clb; Engl Clb; Dean Lst 89-; IM 89-; Acctg; CPA.

**PECORA, PATRICIA G,** Wv Univ, Morgantown, WV; SR; BS; ASP; Gldn Ky; Pres Awd Exclnc; Phllps Schlr; Pharm D.

**PECORA, PHILIP L,** Univ Of Rochester, Rochester, NY; JR; BA; Pre-Law Soc 88-89; Oracle Soc Ithaca Coll 88-89; Deans Lst IC 88-89; Deans Lst 89-90; YMCA Yth Pgm 89; Dist Attys Intern; Lacrosse 88-89; Econ; Law.

**PECORARO, BRENDA,** City Univ Of Ny Queensbrough, New York, NY; SO; AAS; Phi Theta Kappa; Nrsg; MSN Nrsg.

**PEDDICORD, CLAUDE M,** Anne Arundel Comm Coll, Arnold, MD; SO; AA; Emplee Full Time; Gen Stdes; Defense Dept Emplee.

**PEDERSEN, RIKKE K,** Univ Of Al At Birmingham, Birmingham, AL; SR; Allnc Frncs 88-; Phi Kappa Phi 89; Gldn Key 89; Omicron Delta Kappa 90; Beta Gamma Sigma; Omicron Delta Epsilon; Dns Lst 88; Pres Hnrs 89-; Wall St Jrnl Stdnt Achvmnt Awd; UAB Acdmc Excell Awd; Finance/Ecnmcs; Fncl/ Bsn Mgmt.

**PEDERSON, LOIS E,** Queens Coll, Charlotte, NC; JR; BA; New Dmnsns Flwshp; New Dmnsns Schlrshp; Prsbytrnwmns Schlrshp; Olde Prvdnce Grdn Clb Sec 80-; Crml Prsbytrn Wmn Hstrn 80-; Bnk Tlr/Nrsry Schl Tchr; Elem Ed; Tchr.

**PEDIGO, CHANDRA S,** Western Ky Univ, Bowling Green, KY; FR; BS; Bus; Acctng.

**PEDIGO, KATHRYN M,** Western Ky Univ, Bowling Green, KY; JR; BA; Gldn Key 90; AA 88; Math/CS; Edctn.

**PEDIGO, MARK A,** Middle Tn St Univ, Murfreesboro, TN; SR; Scty Brdct Students 89-; Scty Profl Jourlts 89-; WTVF Channel 5 Talk Town 90; Prodr Air Personality Cable 33 Murfreesboro 88-90; BS Mass Com 90; AS Criminial Justice 90; Brdct Jourlm; Brdctng.

**PEDONE, LORI P,** Schenectady County Comm Coll, Schenectady, NY; JR; Trvl/Trsm.

**PEDRAZA SANTIAGO, I ELSIE,** Inter Amer Univ Pr Hato Rey, Hato Rey, PR; FR; Hm Ec Clb 89-; Lions Clb Aux Awd 88; Math; Bsns Admn.

**PEDRAZA, MILDRED E,** Inter Amer Univ Pr Guayama, Guayama, PR; FR; Prlnzco Llst De Estnts Dstcn 90-; Spnsh; Cmmrcl Admn.

**PEDRO, CARLOS D,** Western New England Coll, Springfield, MA; JR; BS; Jnr Achvmnt Assmbly/Sls 85; AS Sprngfld Tech Comm Clg 90; Cmptr Info Sys; Cmptr Prgmmr.

**PEDROGO NUNEZ, AIDA MIRIAM,** Inter Amer Univ Pr Guayama, Guayama, PR; SR; BA; Blgy Med Tech.

**PEDROSA, SHEILA D,** Hillsborough Comm Coll, Tampa, FL; SO; ADN; Phi Theta Kappa; AACN; BNA 90; LVN Cisco Jr Clg 77; Nrsg.

**PEEBLES, GAYLIN L,** Ky St Univ, Frankfort, KY; SR; BA; Clge Rcrtr Univ 87; Hrmb Org Srgt Arms 86-87; Alpha Phi Alpha Actng VP 87-89; Alpha Phi Alpha Sec 88-90; Fund Rsng Can Fd Drv 87-88; Bld Drv; Adpt Chld/Bg Bro Pgm Asst Dir 87; Coop Aprctn Awd Rcrds Mgr 90; Dns Lst 89-90; Bsn Admin/Mgmt; Admin/Mgmt.

**PEED, TROY G,** Univ Of South Al, Mobile, AL; JR; BS; Cndmnm Brd VP 90-; Indstrl Eng Dsgnr 86-; AS Faulkner St Jr Coll; Accntng; Tx Accntnt/CPA.

**PEEK, MICHAEL S,** Bowie St Univ, Bowie, MD; SR; BS; Deltma Mu Delta; AA Univ MD Germny 87; Bus Mgmt; Intl Bus.

**PEEKER, VICTORIA,** Emory Univ, Atlanta, GA; FR; BA; Sor/ Frat Pldg Bd 90-; Kappa Kappa Gamma 90-; Intl Bus; Intl CPA.

**PEEL, CAROLYN A,** Va Commonwealth Univ, Richmond, VA; MD; Big Sis 89-90; Phi Omega VP 87-88; BS Coll Of William/ Mary 88; Medicine.

**PEEL JR, GALEN E,** Liberty Univ, Lynchburg, VA; JR; BS; Engl.

**PEELE, JAMES E,** Broward Comm Coll, Ft Lauderdale, FL; FR; AA; Pro Muscn; Music Educ; Music Cmpstn.

**PEELE, MARILYNN P,** Williamsburg Tech Coll, Kingstree, SC; JR; BA; 4-H Clb Pres 87-89; Alpha Kappa Alpha Tres 84-85; Cosmetology/Business Adm; Cosmetologist.

**PEELER, JAYNE S,** Lenoir Rhyne Coll, Hickory, NC; SR; AB; Plymkrs 89-; Crnvl Lit Mgzn 90-; Ltrry Scty; Mu Sigma Epsilon 90; Clvry Lthrn Chrch; AA 88; Engl.

**PEELMAN, GEORGIA S,** Univ Of Nc At Greensboro, Greensboro, NC; SR; BS; Natl Assn Educ Yng Chldrn 89-; Univ Mrshls 90-; Sec/Sev Companies; Schl Bd Mbr; Happy Days Nrsry Schl; 4h Advsr; Rlgs Educ; Elem Educ.

**PEEPLES, DWIGHT A,** Southern Coll Of Tech, Marietta, GA; SR; BS; Big Brother/Big Sister 88-90; Natl Soc Blck Eng 89-90; Cnstrctn Specif Ins 87-90; Construction; Proj Mgmnt.

**PEER, KATHLEEN,** Wagner Coll, Staten Island, NY; JR; BA; Psychlgy.

**PEER, SUSAN R,** Western New England Coll, Springfield, MA; JR; BA; Mrktng Assn 90-; Delta Mu Delta Sec; Alpha Kappa Psi 90-; Fld Hcky All Star 88; Mrktng.

**PEERCY, ANGELA M,** Univ Of Tn At Martin, Martin, TN; FR; BSN; Ldrds Res 90-; Hnrs Smnr 90-; Arts/Scncs; Nursing.

**PEERCY, LATRICIA K,** Brescia Coll, Owensboro, KY; GD; SGA Rep; Pep Clb Sec; NEASP; BA 90; Engl; Tchng.

**PEERY, STARLA G,** Univ Of Tn At Martin, Martin, TN; FR; BS; Mu Epsilon Delta 90-; Blgy; Med.

**PEET, JOHN E,** Carnegie Mellon Univ, Pittsburgh, PA; SR; BS; Advsry Cncl 89-; Deans Lst 89-; Beta Gamma Gisma; NCBMA; Indstrl Mgmt.

**PEET, JULIE A,** Marywood Coll, Scranton, PA; FR; BED; Elem Early Chldhd Educ; Teacher.

**PEEYACHAIPRAPA, CHANPEN,** Univ Of Cincinnati, Cincinnati, OH; JR; BFA; Cert UCLA Extnsn 90; BA Chulalongkorn Univ 88; Thtr Dsgn Prdctn; Makeup Artist.

**PEGG, KEITH J,** Kent St Univ Stark Cmps, North Canton, OH; SO; BA; Ftbl; Pre Med; Sports Med.

**PEGRAM, CYNTHIA D,** Univ Of Nc At Charlotte, Charlotte, NC; FR; BA; Phi Eta Sigma 90-; Math; Tchng.

**PEGRAM, JENNIFER S,** Univ Of Sc At Columbia, Columbia, SC; SO; BA; Stdnt Govt SGA Sec/Treas; Bst All Arnd Stdnt 90-; Union Math Awrd 90-; AS Union; Acctg; CPA.

**PEGUES, CONRAD R,** Memphis St Univ, Memphis, TN; SR; BA; Engl; Start Grad Sch/Eng.

**PEH, HUIE LING,** Univ Of Southern Ms, Hattiesburg, MS; SO; BA; Gamma Beta Phi; GCE A Level Anderson Jr Clg Singapore 89; Radio/TV/FILM; Film Prodctn.

**PEHANICH, DIANE P,** Marywood Coll, Scranton, PA; SR; MBA; Tutor 90; Delta Epsilon Sigma; BS; Accounting.

**PEIFER, MICHELLE J,** Lancaster Bible Coll, Lancaster, PA; SR; BS; Vlybl; Bible; Educ.

**PEIFFER, WENDY J,** East Stroudsburg Univ, E Stroudsburg, PA; FR; BS; Univ Prog Cncl Pub 90-; Psychlgy Assoc 90-; Honrs Prog/Schlrshp 90-; Psychlgy.

**PEINHARDT, CLINT W,** Birmingham Southern Coll, Birmingham, AL; SO; BA; SGA 89-; Concrt Choir 90-; Hltp Singrs 90-; Alpha Lambda Delta 89-; Phi Eta Sigma 89-; Hon Prog 89-; UMC N Al Confrnce On Yth Mnstry Chr 89-; Scnd Yr Rsn Stdnt 90-; Fr Ldrshp Smnr Sec 89-90; Deans Lst 89-90; IM Scr Bsktbl 90; Intl Stdies; Coll Tchng/Admin.

**PEIRIS, BIMAL V,** Oh Wesleyan Univ, Delaware, OH; FR; BA; Cmps Prog Brd; Hl Govt Treas; Phi Eta Sigma; Bnkg/Acctg; Dvlpmntl Econ.

**PEIRIS, LASANTHA A,** Bridgewater Coll, Bridgewater, VA; SO; BS; Ingl Clb 89-; Physics Clb VP 89-; Ski/Outing Clb 89-90; Deans Lst 89-; Crp Wlk; Radio Station 90-; Coll Dshrm 89-; Lab Asstnt Gen Physics; Rsrch Prjct With Prof; Physics; Cvl Engr.**

**PEIRSON, EDWARD K,** Indiana Univ Of Pa, Indiana, PA; JR; BS; Cmnctns Media; Naval Aviation.

**PEIXINHO, SCOTT A,** Providence Coll, Providence, RI; JR; BS; Mngmnt.**

**PEKAREK, PAMELA J,** Southern Coll Of Tech, Marietta, GA; FR; Stdnt Govt Dana Lib Arts Clg 83-84; Dns Lst Dana Lib Arts Clg 82-84; Dns Lst; Rgnts Schlrshp 82-84; Acad Schlrshp 84-86; MT ASCP 86-; BA Univ NE Med Ctr 86; Engr.

**PEKARIK, THOMAS J,** Anderson Coll, Anderson, SC; SO; Ntl Oldsmobile Ownrs Assn 89-; Auto Detail 90-; Mktg.

**PEKARSKY, AMY M,** Coll Of Charleston, Charleston, SC; FR; Hnrs Pgm; Biology; Med Dr.

**PELACHICK, KEITH J,** Widener Univ, Chester, PA; SO; BSEE; Elect Eng; Eng.

**PELCYGER, LISA R,** City Univ Of Ny Brooklyn Coll, Brooklyn, NY; FR; BA; Cncl Unty; Mlt Cltrl Actn Comm; Psychlgy; Fmly Cnslng.

**PELCZAR, GARY E,** Univ Of Miami, Coral Gables, FL; JR; Alumni Mentor Pgm 90-; Hon Stdnt Assoc 88; Hon Stdnt Pgm 88-; Intrnshp Harris Corp Melbourne FL 90-; Bsebl 88; Sys Analysis.

**PELEK, KATHERINE M,** Eckerd Coll, St Petersburg, FL; SR; BA; Amer Mgmt Assn; Stdnt Ambssdr 88-89; Phi Theta Kappa Treas 88-89; Alpha Mu Gamma 88-89; Hon/Ldrshp Schlrshp 89-; Alumni Schlrshp 90-; Outstndng Ldrshp/Serv Awd 89; AA St Petersburg Jr Coll 89; Mgmt; CPA.

**PELGER, JUDITH M,** Univ Of Al At Huntsville, Huntsville, AL; SO; MA; Soc Wmn Engr 89-; Math Club 89-90; Chem Club 89-90; Alpha Lambda Delta 89; Dns Lst 89; All Amer Schlr Clgte Award; Chem Engr; Engr.

**PELHAM, TRACEY L,** Saint Pauls Coll, Lawrenceville, VA; FR; BA; Bus.

**PELICK, JOHN D,** Marywood Coll, Scranton, PA; JR; BS; Nrsng Clb 90-; Deans List 86-87; Deans List; Prior Second Class Petty Offc Hosp Corpsmn US Navy 82-88; BS Southern IL Univ 88; Nrse Prctnr/Hlth Care Admin.

**PELINE, YVETTE MARIE,** Newbury Coll, Brookline, MA; SR; AA; Fd Show; Dns Lst; Cul Extrnshp; Culnry Arts; Chef.

**PELL, LISA A,** Miami Dade Comm Coll South, Miami, FL; SO; AS; FL Eng Soc 88-89; Outstndng Acdmcachvmnt Awrd 90; Deans Lst; Vlybl; Eng/Comp.

**PELLA, LORI L,** Indiana Univ Of Pa, Indiana, PA; JR; ACEI Actvts Comm 90; Alpha Sigma Alpha Schlrshp Chrmn 89-; Spec Olympics; Elem Ed.

**PELLARD, BRIDGET L,** Springfield Tech Comm Coll, Springfield, MA; GD; Bio Clb Tutor 89-90; Spfld Tech Comm Clg 89-90; Mcknght Nghbrhd Cncl 89-; Sci; Engr.

**PELLEGRINELLI, LARA V,** Univ Of Rochester, Rochester, NY; SO; BA; Glee Clb Pblcty Offcr 90; Trnsfr Assist Prog 90; Grdn State Schlr; Clmbn Assoc Schlrshp; Ramapo Clg Oxfrd Hnrs Prog; Chubb/Sons Inc Schlrshp; Mildred Burton Fllwshp For Smmr Stdy Abrd; Music.

**PELLEGRINO, ALISON A,** S U N Y Coll Of Tech At Frmgdl, Farmingdale, NY; SO; Ele Educ.

**PELLEGRINO, AUDREY JEAN,** Univ Of Nh Plymouth St Coll, Plymouth, NH; SR; Boy Scts Amer Sec 90-; Phi Kappa Phi 90-; Nrs Tchr; BSED; Elem Ed.

**PELLEGRINO, ELIZABETH M,** S U N Y Coll Of Tech At Frmgdl, Farmingdale, NY; SO; AA; Lib Arts.

**PELLEGRINO, VICKY M,** Seton Hall Univ, South Orange, NJ; SO; BSN; Stdnt Nrs Assoc; Alpha Phi Phlnthrpy Asst; Deans Lst; Intern Med Cntr Nrsng Asst; 2M Flg Fotbll; Nrsng.

**PELLEGRONI, MICHELLE L,** S U N Y Coll Of Tech At Frmgdl, Farmingdale, NY; FR; AS; Bus Admin.

**PELLETIER, BRENDA J,** Andover Coll, Portland, ME; SR.

**PELLETIER, LISA A,** Providence Coll, Providence, RI; SO; BA; Junior Ring Comm 90-; Big Sis In Big Brthrs/Big Sis Org 89-; Vol Tutor Prov Elem Schl 89-; Dns Lst 89-; Applied/Selected Attend Univ Of Glasgow; Spec Elem Educ; Tchr/Adminstrtr.

**PELLETIER, SHEILA J,** Schenectady County Comm Coll, Schenectady, NY; SR; AAS; SGA Treas 89-; Stu Actvts Brd Pres 89-; Jr Achvmnt Advsr 89-; Dean Lst 90; SGA Merit Awrd 90-; Elston Schlrshp 90; Bus Admn; Bus Mngmnt.

**PELLETIER, TRICIA M,** Mount Saint Mary Coll, Newburgh, NY; SO; Stdnt Govt Fin Brd Asst Vp Fin 90-; BACCHUS 90-; Orntntn Ldr 90-; Deans List 90; Math Cmptr Sci.

**PELLICANO, THERESA,** S U N Y Coll Of Tech At Frmgdl, Farmingdale, NY; FR; AAS; Tau Kappa Epsln 86-87; Spec Plympcs 87; BA St Unv NY Stnybrk 90; Dntl Hygn.

**PELLICONE, MARIA A,** Georgian Court Coll, Lakewood, NJ; FR; BA; Deans Lst; Indstrl Psy.

**PELLITTERI, DANIELLE M,** S U N Y Coll Of Tech At Frmgdl, Farmingdale, NY; FR; BED; Elem Ed; Tchr.

**PELLMAN, ALLAN,** Fl International Univ, Miami, FL; SR; HILLEL Fndtn 87-; Indstl Engr Soc 90-; Dns Lst; Engr Vol Cedars Med Ctr 90; Engr Vol Hialeah Hosp; Bst Indstl Engr Sr Proj.

**PELLON, VINCENT F,** Central Fl Comm Coll, Ocala, FL; FR; AS; Elks Ldg; Crppl Chldrn Fla; Rdlgy; Nrsng; Crdc Care; Rdlgs Hlth Nrsng; Nrsng.

**PELLOT, MARIA DE LOS ANGELES,** Fl International Univ, Miami, FL; JR; Natl Hnr Soc 88-89; Pell Grant 89-90; Barry Adrian Dominican Grnt 89-90; Dns Lst 89-90.

**PELLOT, MIGUEL H,** Univ Of Pr At Mayaguez, Mayaguez, PR; SO; BS; Hnr Scts Cvl Engnr Fclty 90-; Civil Engineering.

**PELMON, JOSEPHINE C,** Comm Coll Algny Co Algny Cmps, Pittsburgh, PA; FR; BED; Tchng.

**PELPHREY, MARY MARGARET,** Oh St Univ At Marion, Marion, OH; JR; BA; AA Sci Ohio State Marion Branch 90; Edn; Masters.

**PELSKI, JILL M,** Bay Path Coll, Longmeadow, MA; FR; AS; Acctg.

**PELTIER, MARLENE B,** Univ Of Sc At Columbia, Columbia, SC; FR; BA; Sn Admn; Law.

**PELTON, JONATHAN R,** S U N Y Coll Of Tech At Alfred, Alfred, NY; SO; BA; Wrstlng 89-; Rugby; Psi Delta Omega 89-; AS Lib Arts/Sci Math Sci; Hlth Sci; Scndry Edn.

**PELUSO, LISA C,** Duquesne Univ, Pittsburgh, PA; JR; BA; Stdnt Acctg Assoc 90-; Italian Clb Sec 90-; Phi Eta Sigma 88-89; Lambda Sigma 89-90; Beta Gamma Sigma 90-; Beta Alpha Phi 90-; Pi Sigma Epsilon VP Finance 90-; GNC Co Accnts Payable Div 89-90; Tax Xpress 89-; Acctg; Lawyer.

**PELUSO-RICCARDI, STEPHANIE A,** City Univ Of Ny Baruch Coll, New York, NY; SR; BBA; Mktg Mgmt.

**PELZ, BONNIE L,** S U N Y Coll At Fredonia, Fredonia, NY; SO; BS; Erly Chldhd Tchr 87; AAS Erie Comm Coll South 84; Elem Educ; Tchr.

**PEMBAMOTO, KANIMU MARK,** Coppin St Coll, Baltimore, MD; SR; BS; AA Comm Coll Baltimore 89; Mgmt Sci/Acctg.

**PEMBER, SUSAN D,** Univ Of Cin R Walters Coll, Blue Ash, OH; BA; Acctng.

**PEMBERTON, ALI-SHA,** Bergen Comm Coll, Paramus, NJ; SO; BSW; SGA Sen 90; RAH Sec 90; Alpha Epsilon Phi 90; Walt Dsny Wrld Clg Prog; AA 90; Soc Wrk; Clncl Soc Wrk.

**PEMBERTON, DONNA M,** Va Commonwealth Univ, Richmond, VA; SR; BFA; Chancel Choir Pianist 90-; Taberncl Untd Methdst Church Pianist 87-; Phi Kappa Phi; Cmnctn Art/Dsgn; Graphc Dsgnr.

**PEMBERTON JR, ROY A,** Hampton Univ, Hampton, VA; SO; BS; Virgn Islnds Pre Alum Pres; Marine Sci; Cons Envrnmntl Prot.

**PEMBERTON, VERONICA H,** Fl A & M Univ, Tallahassee, FL; SO; Cncrt Chr; NABJ; Phi Eta Sigma; Rd Intern; Brdcst Jrnlst; Nws Anchr.**

**PEMBERTON, VICTORIA,** Univ Of The Virgin Islands, St Thomas, VI; JR; BED; Pres Clb; Cmmtrs Clb Soc Com 89-; Tchng Assn 89-; Crls Brgd Ldr Asst 78-80; 4-H Clb Sec 79-81; Pres Awd Acad Excl; Var Tns 90-; Cert Univ WI 84; Elem Educ/Bus Mgmt; Tchr/Bus.

**PENA CONCEPCION, JEANNETTE,** Inter Amer Univ Pr Guayama, Guayama, PR; FR; Admn Cmrcl.

**PENA DE LA VEGA, LOURDES S,** Univ Of Pr At Rio Piedras, Rio Piedras, PR; SO; BA; Pre Med Sci Assn 89-90; Academic Awds 89-; Chmstry; Med.

**PENA, JOSE R,** Evangelical Seminary Of P R, Hato Rey, PR; GD; MDIV; BS Biology Univ Of PR 75; Theology; Ministry.

**PENA-FELIZ, BANI,** Univ Of Pr Humacao Univ Coll, Humacao, PR; SR; BA; Univ Assoc Acctg Stu VP 89-90; Univ Assoc Acct Stu Pres 90-; Univ Assoc Stu Acdmc Tlnt Mbr 88-; Acdmc Tlnt Awrd 89-90; Who Who Amng Stu Awrd 89-; Acctg; CPA.

**PENALVA, LUIZ A,** D Youville Coll, Buffalo, NY; SR; SOTA 89-; Untd Crbrl Palsy Assn Actvts Prog Aide 90-; Occptnl Thrpy; Mntl Hlth.

**PENALVER, ANA M,** Barry Univ, Miami, FL; SR; BMED; Barry Educ Assoc 89-; French Clb 87-89; Barrytones 88-90; Deans Lst 87-; Presidents Lst 90-; Stdnt Tchr Miami Cnty Day Schl Music Tchr 90-; Music Educ.

**PENCE, ROBERTA,** Va Commonwealth Univ, Richmond, VA; JR; BPE; Pre Phys Thrpy Club 88-89; New Stdnt Orient Ldr 89; Vol Wrk Mtrpltn Hosp 89; RCU Sprts Med Ctr 90; Phys Educ; Phys Thrpst.

**PENCEK, CAROL J,** Marywood Coll, Scranton, PA; SR; BA; Delta Epsilon Sigma 90-; Theta Alpha Kappa; Lds Aux; PTA; Abngtn Hts Bnd Bstrs; Trnty Luth Chrch; GS; Cb Sct Mthr; Abngtn Sprts Bstr; Treas Jr Wmns Clb; Exec Sec; Mky Rdio Dvsn Of ITT; Asst Nrsry Schl Tchr; AS Lackawanna Jr College 63; Sclgy; Pstrl Care.

**PENCEK, MARK D,** Kent St Univ Kent Cmps, Kent, OH; JR; Mrtr Brd 90; Vrsty Bsbl 88; IM Sftbl Bsktbl 88-; Cmptr Sci; Cmptr Indstry/Bus.

**PENDARVIS, CANDACE M,** Coll Of Charleston, Charleston, SC; JR; BS; Psych Clb 90-; Psi Chi 90-; Psych; Soc Wrk.

**PENDARVIS, WALKER THOMAS,** Univ Of Sc At Columbia, Columbia, SC; FR; BS; Alpha Tau Omega 90-; Acad Achvmnt 90-; Bus; Dentistry.

**PENDER, GEORGE V,** Ny Univ, New York, NY; SR; BA; Intl Studies.

**PENDERGAST, SCOTT D,** Boston Univ, Boston, MA; GD; MA Med Scty Med Serv Cmmtt 89-; Amer Med Std Assoc 87-; Amer Med Assoc 89-; Alpha Omeag Alpha 90-; BA MD Case Western Reserve Univ 86; Med; Ophthlmlgy.

**PENDERGRAFT, DONNA M,** Comm Coll Algny Co Algny Cmps, Pittsburgh, PA; FR; BA; Engl; Nrsg.

**PENDERGRASS, KELLI R,** Jackson St Comm Coll, Jackson, TN; FR; Ofc Adm.

**PENDERGRASS, SANDRA H,** Al A & M Univ, Normal, AL; SR; Kappa Delta Pi; Schlr Of Yr 90-; Pres Cup; Boy Scouts Of Amer; AS Calhoun Comm Coll 88.

**PENDERGRASS, VALERIE L,** Snead St Jr Coll, Boaz, AL; FR; BA; Elem Ed.

**PENDLEY, AMY R,** Owensboro Comm Coll, Owensboro, KY; FR; English; Writer.

**PENDRY, JENNIFER L,** Marshall University, Huntington, WV; FR; BA; SOAR; Phi Eta Sigma; Gamma Beta Phi; John Marshall Schlr 90-; Acctg.

**PENDYGRAFT, TRACY D,** Georgetown Coll, Georgetown, KY; SR; MBA; Stdnt Sprm Crt Jstce 89-; Spch Tm Pres 87-; Mskrftrs Drama Clb Pres 87-; Pi Kappa Delta Pres 87-; Phlsphcl Soc; Sigma Kappa Actvties Cmn 88-; Grad Cum Laude; Pi Kappa Delta Cmnctn Awrd; IM Sftbl Rferee 90-; BA; Cmnctn Arts/Phlsphy; Prfssr Arts.

**PENFOLD, DELPHINE C,** Merrimack Coll, North Andover, MA; JR; BS; Scrtry; Accntng; Accntnt.

**PENG, ERIC W,** Princeton Univ, Princeton, NJ; FR; BA; Triangle Clb 90-; Orchestra 90-; Sngrs 90-.

**PENGELLY, H MEGAN,** Univ Of Nc At Charlotte, Charlotte, NC; SO; BA; Emrgng Ldrs Almni Ambssdr 89-; Soph Clss Cncl 90-; Rsdnce Hlls Adpt A Dlgte 90; Mntrshp Emrgng Ldrs 90-; Pltcl Sci Hstry; Pltcs.

**PENICK, BETTY L,** Univ Of Al At Birmingham, Birmingham, AL; JR; BS.

**PENLAND, BETTY R,** Va Highlands Comm Coll, Abingdon, VA; SO; AA&S; Mnstr Un Chrstn Chrch/Mnstrl Assn Cvlnd Tn 82-; Psychlgst.

**PENLAND, JENNIFER A,** Univ Of Tn At Knoxville, Knoxville, TN; SO; BS; Yrbk Wrtr Vol 90-; Mstrs Hnds Pupt Tm 89-; Exec Undrgrdts 89-; Almn Schlrshp 89-; TN Acdmc Schlr 89-; Pblc Admin; Law.

**PENN, ARTHUR W,** Western Ky Univ, Bowling Green, KY; SR; BA; Bapt Stdnt Un Choir 89-; Chrstn Stdnt Flwshp 89-; Phi Kappa Phi 90-; Phi Alpha Theta 90-; Gold Key 90-; Awd Excell 88-; A M Stickles Awd 90-; A M Stickles Schlrshp; Hist/Spnsh; Foreign Policy/Serv.

**PENN, EDWARD,** Cheyney Univ Of Pa, Cheyney, PA; SO; Indtl Arts; Audio Engrg.

**PENN, JOHN W,** Howard Univ, Washington, DC; BA; VI Clb 88-; AIAS 88-; Asstntshp 89; Var Vlybl Univ VI 86-88; CXC Crbn Exmntn Cncl 82; GCE; Archit/Cnstrctn Mgmt; Dvlpr.

**PENN, LORI,** Oh Univ, Athens, OH; SO; BMUS; Alpha Lmbd Dlt 89-; Sch Msc Tlnt Schlrshp 90; Deans Schlrshp; Soph Hghst GPA Awrd; Msc; Educ.

**PENN JR, MICHAEL LAWRENCE,** Morehouse Coll, Atlanta, GA; FR; BS; Hlth Crrs Soc Edtr 90-; Real Est Clb 90-; Hnrs Prog Clb 90-; Mntrng Prog 90-; Biol; Med.

**PENN, RICHELYN E,** East Stroudsburg Univ, E Stroudsburg, PA; JR; BA; Black Stdnt Assoc 90-; 1st Runner Up Howard Univ Miss Phila Pageant 87-88; Pol Sci; Law.

**PENN JR, THOMAS E,** Univ Of Nc At Charlotte, Charlotte, NC; SR; Psych Clb 89-; Transition Opptuntes Prog; Otsdng Clg Stdnts Of America; BA; Psych; Pub Rltns.

**PENNELL, KIMBERLY M,** Seton Hall Univ, South Orange, NJ; SO; BA; Stdnt Sen 89-; Stdnt Ambssdr 89-; Delta Phi Epsilon Co Chr 89-; Ldrshp Awd; Engl.

**PENNELL, LAWRENCE J,** Bloomfield Coll, Bloomfield, NJ; SR; BS; Alpha Chi; Socty Lgstcs Engrs Schlrshp Awd; APICS; AS Middlesex Cnty Coll 81; Bus Mgmt.

**PENNEY, DERRICK S,** Fl St Univ, Tallahassee, FL; GD; JD; IM Sftbl 89-90; BS Univ Toronto 87; BA Univ NC 90; Law.

**PENNIE, LORI A,** Newbury Coll, Brookline, MA; JR; AS; Phys Thrpy Clb 89-; Amer Phys Thrpy Assn 90-; Phi Theta Kappa; Phys Thrpy; Phys Thrpst Asst.**

**PENNINGTON, KRISTA R,** Univ Of Cincinnati-Clrmnt Coll, Batavia, OH; FR; BA; Bsnss; Accntng.

**PENNINGTON, MARY J,** Itawamba Comm Coll, Fulton, MS; SO; BS; Choir 88-90; Bnd 88; BSU 88-; Phi Theta Kappa; Cmmnctns; Speech Pthlgy.

**PENNINGTON, SHAWN M,** Beckley Coll, Beckley, WV; FR; ASN; Nrsng.

**PENNISI, LINDA A,** Centenary Coll, Hackettstown, NJ; SO; BA; Fashn Grp Mbrshp Chr Pr 89-; Phi Beta Lambda 90-; Sigma Epsilon Phi; Mentrshp Schlrshp 89-; Fashn Grp Phila Eductnl Schlrshp; Fashn Merch; Visual Merchdsr.

**PENNIX, JOEY L,** Cheyney Univ Of Pa, Cheyney, PA; SO; BA; Math Comp Sci Clb; Comp Sci Math.

**PENNOCK, SCOTT M,** Kent St Univ Kent Cmps, Kent, OH; JR; BA; Radio Sta Asst Msc Dir 90-; Jrnlsm; Photo Jrnlst.

**PENNY JR, JOSEPH MARSHALL,** Nc Agri & Tech St Univ, Greensboro, NC; JR; BS; Natl Sci Awd; Amer Chem Soc 90-; Chem; Biochem.

**PENNYPACKER, JENNIFER L,** Marywood Coll, Scranton, PA; FR; BS; Psych Clb 90-; Psych.

**PENROD, JANET B,** Owensboro Comm Coll, Owensboro, KY; FR; BA; Natl Educ Assn PR 90-; KY Educ Assn 90-; Educ.

**PENROSE, MATTHEW A,** Saint Francis Coll, Loretto, PA; FR; BS; Biol Clb 90-; Ftbl Indr Trck Otdr Trck 90-; Biol; Med.

**PENSABENE, MICHAEL J,** Ny Univ, New York, NY; JR; BA; Dns Lst 89-90; Awd For Excel 90; Position Sr Bus Analyst Shearson Lehman Brothers; AAS Finance NYU 90; Lic Series 7/63 NY State Brokers Lic Cert 90; Econ; Brkrg Analyst.

**PENSUVAN, PATRICIA JOAN,** Univ Of Sc At Columbia, Columbia, SC; SO; BS; Psychlgy; Medicine.

**PENTECOST JR, GERALD GASTON,** Univ Of Al At Birmingham, Birmingham, AL; JR; BA; Gldn Key; Phi Theta Kappa 90; Beta Alpha Psi; Hnrs Schlrshp 90; IM Ftbl Bsktbl 90-; AS Gdsdn St Cmmnty Clg 90; Accntng; Pblc Accntng.

**PENTOLINO, SAMUEL G,** Univ Of Rochester, Rochester, NY; SO; BS; Optics; Engrng.

**PENTON, HJORDIS V,** Univ Of Cincinnati, Cincinnati, OH; JR; BS; AIAS 87-88; Lutheran Campus Mnstry Msn Com Ldr 87-89; Math; Profl Educator.

**PENTON, MISTI L,** Univ Of Montevallo, Montevallo, AL; SR; BS; Hnrs Prog 88-; Phi Mu Schlrshp Asst 88-; Chrldr 88-89; BS; Educ; Tchng.

**PENTON, PAMELA D,** Livingston Univ, Livingston, AL; BS; Stdnt Govt Assoc Sen; Alpha Simga Ta; Chi Delphia Pldg Cncl Pres 88-; IM All Str Tm; Elem Ed; Tchng.

**PENTON, ROXANNE,** Ms St Univ, Miss State, MS; FR; Bark Clg Rpblcns 90-; Gamma Beta Phi; Alpha Lambda Delta; Kappa Delta Actvts Chrmn 90-; Indl Eng; Corp Law.

**PENUEL, ANGELA A,** Huntingdon Coll, Montgomery, AL; FR; BA; Chi Omega Natl Pnhllnc Del 90-; Bus Admn; Fnc.

**PENUEL, CHRISTOPHER M,** Wilmington Coll, New Castle, DE; SO; BA; BED DE Tech/Cmnty Clg 90; Bus; Ins Agnt.

**PEOPLES, GEORGEANN J,** Univ Of South Al, Mobile, AL; JR; BS; Phi Theta Kappa 88-89; Bus Mgmt; ACCTNG.

**PEPE, DEANNA A,** Glassboro St Coll, Glassboro, NJ; JR; BS; AA 90; Bio; Dntl Sch.

**PEPE, MARK E,** S U N Y Coll Of Tech At Frmgdl, Farmingdale, NY; SO; BS; Math Hnr Soc 88-; Deans Lst; Physis; Mdcl Schl.

**PEPE, MATHEW E,** Oh Dominican Coll, Columbus, OH; SR; BA; Alpha Sigma Lambda 84; Mu Kappa Tau 83; Tele Pioneer Amer 89-; AT/T Sys Cnsltnt 88-; Gen Stds.

**PEPE, RAYMOND P,** S U N Y Coll Of Tech At Frmgdl, Farmingdale, NY; JR; BA; SME 89-; IM Vlybl Sftbl 88-; AAS Suny At Farmingdale 90; Mech/ Mfg Eng Tech; Eng.

**PEPER, CATHERINE A,** Univ Of North Fl, Jacksonville, FL; JR; BA; First Cst Hlth Care Execs; Dir Blue Cross Blue Shld; AA FL Comm Coll 89; Cmmnctns; Mgm.

**PEPIN, MARY A,** Memphis St Univ, Memphis, TN; SO; BFA; Art Hstry; Lbry Sci.**

**PEPMILLER, STEVEN W,** Fl St Univ, Tallahassee, FL; GD; BA; Intl Bus Soc 90-; Frnch Hon Soc 88-; W King Schlrshp 89-90; IM Tns Fnlst 90; AA Gulf Cst Comm Coll 88; Fin; Intl Fin.

**PEPPER, CHRIS J,** Methodist Coll, Fayetteville, NC; SO; BA; Glf Tm 89-90; Bus; Asstnt Glf Prfssr.

**PEPPER, PENNY C,** Ms St Univ, Miss State, MS; JR; Phi Theta Kappa Holmes Cmmnty Coll 88-90; Gamma Beta Phi 90-; IM Sftbll Ftbll 88-90; AA 90; Math; Eng.

**PEPPER, SHARI L,** Univ Of Miami, Coral Gables, FL; SR; BA; Chrldng Ftbl/Bsktbl 87-88; Pgm Cncl Assn Chr 90-; Hons Stdnts Assn 87-; Manor Dscplnry Pnl 90-; Alpha Lambda Delta 87-; Phi Eta Sigma 87-; Golden Key 89-; Lamba Chi Alpha 88-; Fndy-Lead Act Spec Olymp 88-89; Spnsh/Bus Mnr; Law.

**PEPPER, THOMAS E,** East Tn St Univ, Johnson City, TN; JR; BS; Epsln Pi Tau; SME 90-; Retired Navy Air Trfc Cntrlr 67-87; AA Pensacola Jr Clg 78; Eng Technlgy; Mfg.

**PEPPIN, CHRISTIAN C,** Hudson Valley Comm Coll, Troy, NY; SR; Lang Audio Vsl Drctr Hdsn Vly Comm Clg 70-; Hstry.

**PERA, JOSE,** Fl International Univ, Miami, FL; FR; DOCTR; Math; Cmptr Engnrng.

**PERAGINE, JOHN N,** Fl St Univ, Tallahassee, FL; JR; BA; GO Clb Assn Yhns Mstr And Tchr 90-; Alpha Mu Alpha Treas 90-; Tlphne Cnclng 89-; SYSOPS Cnsltnt 90-; Tp Mscn In Lttle Thtr 85-; Msc And Msc Educ.**

**PERAGINE, MARIA,** City Univ Of Ny Baruch Coll, New York, NY; SR; BBA; Amer Mktg Assn; Deans Lst 90; Mktg; Bus.

**PERALES, JOSE R,** Univ Of Pr At Rio Piedras, Rio Piedras, PR; SR; BA; BA Pol Sci 88-; Mnrty Accss Pgm 90; Wdrw Wlsn Natl Flwshp Fdn 90; Dist Std 90; Hnr Stds Pgm 89-; Contornos Mag Edtg Comm 89-; SOLAR 89-90; Pol Sci Std Asc 88-; Ltn Amer Stds Asc 90-; Crbbn Stds Asc 89-; Amer Pol Sci Asc 89-; Pol Sci; Pblc/Intl Affrs.**

**PERATT, PHYLLIS D,** Maysville Comm Coll, Maysville, KY; GD; ADN; Natl Coll Nrsng Awds Wnr; Nrsng.

**PERAZA, JAVIER,** Saint Thomas Univ, Miami, FL; SR; BA; Scndry Educ/Hstry; Ph D Hstry.

**PERCOCO, JOSEPH,** Wagner Coll, Staten Island, NY; SR; BA; Fr Cls Offcr V P 87-88; Pol Sci Clb 88-90; Offc Stn Isl Borgh Pr Intrn 89; N Y St Sen Admin Asst 90; Offc Gov N Y Adv Asst 90; Var Ftbl 87-88; Pol Sci; Law.

**PERCY, KENDRA A,** Marymount Manhattan Coll, New York, NY; SR; MBA; Stdnt Newspaper; Gallery Talent Coord; Dns Lst 89-90; Art Hstry Awd; BA; Art Hstry; Art Ther.

**PERDIGAO, CHRISTOPHER A,** Merrimack Coll, North Andover, MA; SR; BS; Drama Soc 88-; Altrntv Voice Mag Art Dir 90-; Nwspr Art Dir 89-; Mrmck Rvw Ilstr 89; Pro Brd 87-88; Wrtg Cntr Peer Tutor 89-; Deans Lst; Appnt Marshall Grad Cls; Mrktg; Ad Cmnctns.

**PERDOMO, NESTOR A,** Univ Of Sc At Sumter, Sumter, SC; FR; BA; ISO 90-; SGA 90-; SOL; Cmuty Dev Prog Honduras Coord 88-; CASS Schlrshp; Bkbl Soccr Tns Rckbl; Small Bus Mgmt; Bus.

**PERDUE, CHARLES D,** Marshall University, Huntington, WV; SR; BBA; Amer Mktg Asc 90-; Big Bro/Sis 89-; Jnr Achvmnt Ohio Vly Cnsltnt; Fed Exprs 82-; Mktg/Fnce; Intl Bsn.

**PERDUE, JAQULINE E,** Thomas Nelson Comm Coll, Hampton, VA; SO; Nwspr 78; Cert 80; Assoc 90-; Bus; Mrktg.

**PERDUE, LORETTA L,** S U N Y Coll Of Tech At Frmgdl, Farmingdale, NY; BA; Engl; Tchng.

**PERDUE, MICHAEL V,** Ferrum Coll, Ferrum, VA; SO; Actvts Committee 89-; Cmptr Clb Prsdnt 90-; Tbl Tns Clb 87-; Cvl Air Ptrl C/LTC Cdt Cmmndr 83-; Bsns Mgmt Cmptr Sci Music.**

**PERDUE, MILLIE M,** Greenville Tech Coll, Greenville, SC; ASSOC; BFA-ART Valdosta St 79; Engrng Graphics.

**PERDUE, PATRICK R,** Nc Agri & Tech St Univ, Greensboro, NC; SO; BED; Special Ed; Phys Therapy.

**PERDUE, TIFFANY M,** Patrick Henry Comm Coll, Martinsville, VA; FR; ASSOC; Nrsng.

**PEREA, JOSEPH R,** Univ Of Cincinnati, Cincinnati, OH; SO; BM; Amateur Radio Clb 90-; St Georges Food Pntry 89-90; Msc Soc Nrthrn KY; Deans List 89-; Intrnshp Drum Band; Msc; Prcssn Prfrmnc.

**PEREIRA, DAVID D MOLINARI,** Univ Politecnica De Pr, Hato Rey, PR; SO; NEB; Nu Sigma Beta Iniciation Cmtee.

**PEREIRA, JOHN S,** Univ Of Sc At Columbia, Columbia, SC; FR; BS; IEEE 90-; Nazareth Pub Spkrs Acad Bombay 88-; Catholic Stdnts Org; BSC Physics Univ Of Bombay 90; Comp Engr.

**PERELES CASTRO, HECTOR A,** Univ Of Pr At Mayaguez, Mayaguez, PR; JR; BSEE; IEEE 90-; Coll Athl Stdnts Assn Swmng Rep 90-; Cls Treas; Tau Beta Pi; Hnr Stdnt Rgstrgn Schlrshp 88-; Hnr Stdns Lst 88-; Vrsty Swmng Tm Capt 88-; Elec Engr.

**PERELLO, MAYTE D,** Univ Of Pr At Rio Piedras, Rio Piedras, PR; FR; Cert Awd 90; Business Adm; Acctng.

**PERENICH, CHRISTINE M,** Saint Andrews Presbytrn Coll, Laurinburg, NC; SO; BA; Hnrs Clb 89-; Bsns Clb 90-; Deans Lst 90-; Scts Fr Yth 90-; Bsns; Acctng.

**PEREWICZ, DYAN L,** Colby Sawyer Coll, New London, NH; FR; BS; Vars Bsktbl; IM Vlybl Capt; Sprts Med; Ath Trnr.

**PEREYO, NEVILLE G,** Ponce School Of Medicine, Ponce, PR; SR; MD; Admissions Comm 88-; Faculty Evaluation Comm 90-; Alpha Omega Alpha 90-; Mc Graw Hill Bk Awd 88; Appleton/Lange Bk Awd 89-; Pharmacology Awd 88; Bsktbl/Tennis/Bsebl 87-; Catholic Univ Puerto Rico 87; Med; Dermatology.

**PEREYRA, RODRIGO,** Christian Brothers Univ, Memphis, TN; JR; Vrsty Sccr Capt 90-; Spnsh Clb; Prfsnl Memphis Rogues SISL; Pi Kappa Phi; Dean List; Eng Dsgn Contest; Athltc Schlrshp; Mgmt/Mktg.

**PEREZ ALBERTORIO, VANESSA,** Univ Of Pr Medical Sciences, San Juan, PR; JR; BA; Oquimpiadas 1st Offc 90; Hnrs Soc 88-90; Sci; Phrmcy Stu.

**PEREZ AVILES, RESTITUTO,** Inter Amer Univ Pr Aquadilla, Aguadilla, PR; JR; BA; US Army Res Instr 89-; Credit/Loan Comm Coop 89-90; Recruiting Cmdr US Army 78-89; Paramed EMT UPR 88-89; AA 90; Acctg; MBA.

**PEREZ CASTILLO, ESTHER M,** Univ Of Pr At Mayaguez, Mayaguez, PR; JR; BS; AICHE 87-; ASQC; Chem Engrg Hnr Soc 87-; Dns Lst 89-90; Pres Awd 86; Chem Engrg.**

**PEREZ COLON, EDDIE,** Inter Amer Univ Pr Hato Rey, Hato Rey, PR; GD; BS; Coop Prgm Ar Trffc Cntrl 88-; Three Ar Trffc Cntrl Intern FAA; One Intern PR Govt; Arwy Sci Mgmt.

**PEREZ GARCIA, VILMA MARIA,** Inter Amer Univ Pr Hato Rey, Hato Rey, PR; JR; BS; Stdnt Chmsty Asso 90-; Org/1st Chmsty Olympiad; Chmsty/Math; Ph D/Chmsty.

**PEREZ HERNANDEZ, ORLANDO,** Univ Of Pr Humacao Univ Coll, Humacao, PR; SO; BA; Judo Clb 87-88; Math; Eng.

**PEREZ LOPEZ, ALEXANDRA R,** Inter Amer Univ Pr Hato Rey, Hato Rey, PR; SO; Math; Acctg.

**PEREZ MORALES, FRANCISCO,** Inter Amer Univ Pr Hato Rey, Hato Rey, PR; FR.

**PEREZ ORTIZ, MARIA P,** Inter Amer Univ Pr San German, San German, PR; FR; BA; Cthlc Yngstrs Actn; Nrs Asst Grdt 90; Mdl Cprtn Schl Lbry Lbry Asst 87; Plc Athltc Lg 87-89; Cert Northeast Tech Clge 90; Bsn Admin/Cmptr Systms; Bnk Mgr.

**PEREZ ORTIZ, RICARDO,** Inter Amer Univ Pr Hato Rey, Hato Rey, PR; GD; Engl.

**PEREZ RAMOS, ELISAMUEL,** Inter Amer Univ Pr Hato Rey, Hato Rey, PR; JR; BA; Bsns Admn; Acctg.

**PEREZ RIVERA, CARMEN M,** Univ Of Pr Humacao Univ Coll, Humacao, PR; SO; BA; Hnr Acad Prog U Of PR; Languages; Humanities.

**PEREZ RODRIIGUEZ, CARMEN,** Inter Amer Univ Pr Hato Rey, Hato Rey, PR; JR; Social 90-; Clb De Futuros Vabajatores Scls; Hon Roll 90-; Law.

**PEREZ VALENTIN, OSVALDO,** Inter Amer Univ Pr Aquadilla, Aguadilla, PR; SR; BA; Sci; Med Technlgy.

**PEREZ VAZQUEZ, SARA N,** Inter Amer Univ Pr Hato Rey, Hato Rey, PR; SO; MBA; Cuadro De Hnr 90-; Assoc De Psicologia; BA; Psychlgy; Psychlgy Indstry.

**PEREZ, ALBA I,** Univ Of Pr Medical Sciences, San Juan, PR; GD; Stdnt Clb Nrsg CUH 87; Plt Cnslng Cmte Cntn Ed CUH 88-; Prfsnl Nrsg Clge PR 87-; Amer Red Crs PR; Magna Cum Laude 87; Cert Mrts Dctn Dvlpmnt Prfsnl Nrsg 90; Nrsg Ed/Dir Asst Nrsg 87-; Nrsg; MA/NRSG Ed/Admin.

**PEREZ, ALEJANDRO E,** Fl International Univ, Miami, FL; FR; BA; FBLA Pres 89-90; Natl Key Clb 87-90; Sci Hon Soc 87-90; Math Hon Soc Prlmntrn 88-90; Pres Fitness Awd 89-90; Bus Appl Awd 89-90; Finance; Real Estate Banking Inds.

**PEREZ, ALEJANDRO M,** Fl International Univ, Miami, FL; JR; Accntng; CPA.

**PEREZ, ALFREDO J,** Saint Thomas Univ, Miami, FL; JR; BA; Vol Emer Disaster Tm 83-84; Miami Dade Bsbl Tm 82-83; Sls Cnsltnt 85-; AA 83; Bus Admin; Law Degree.

**PEREZ, ANA M,** Univ Of Rochester, Rochester, NY; SO; Soc Of Hispanic Profsnl Engrs VP; Intrnshp Lab Of Laser Energtcs 90-; Eastman Kodak Lab Asstnt 90-; Mech Engr.

**PEREZ, ANTHONY J,** Southern Coll Of Tech, Marietta, GA; JR; BS; GA Fed Clg Rpblcns 88-90; Cir K V P 89-; Clg Nwspr; Clg Radio Sta; Phi Theta Kappa 88-89; Elect Eng Tech; Eng.

**PEREZ, ARIS M,** Inter Amer Univ Pr Aquadilla, Aguadilla, PR; SR; Chrch; Edctn; Tchr.

**PEREZ, BARBARA M,** Manhattanville Coll, Purchase, NY; SO; Dns Lst Manhattnvl Clg 90; Asstntshp Engl Lang Inst Manhtnvl Sec Wrk; Fld Hcky 90; Econs; Bsns.

**PEREZ, BELEN,** Fl Atlantic Univ, Boca Raton, FL; JR; BA; Acctng Stdnts Assn; Deans/Pres Lsts 89-; Acctng; CPA.

**PEREZ, CHRISTINA,** Fl International Univ, Miami, FL; FR; BSN; Deans List 90-; Nursing.

**PEREZ, CHRISTOPHER J,** Salem-Teikyo Univ, Salem, WV; JR; BS; IFC; Gamma Beta Phi 89-; Sigma Pi T 90-; Sccr/Tnns Capt 90-; Sprts Mgmt; Tm Mgr.

**PEREZ, CRISTINA S,** Univ Of Hartford, West Hartford, CT; JR; BA; AA Univ Of Hartford 90; Cmmnctns; Advrtsng.

**PEREZ, DAMARYS,** Miami Dade Comm Coll South, Miami, FL; JR; BA; Blgy; Dttcs And Ntrtn.

**PEREZ, DANELLE M,** Univ Of Southern Ms, Hattiesburg, MS; SR; BS; Pnhlnc Cncl Prsdnt 89-; Omicron Delta Kappa Sec; Gldn Key; Ordr Omega Sec; Lambda Sigma; Alpha Delta Lambda; Phi Eta Sigma; Phi Delta Rho; Gamma Beta Phi; Beta Alpha Psi Sec; Kappa Delta Prsdnt 90-; USM Hall Of Fame Pnhlnc Cncl Prsdnt; Accntng; CPA.

**PEREZ, DIANNE,** Miami Dade Comm Coll South, Miami, FL; GD; BA; Deans List 88-90; Talent Rooster Outstndng Minority Comm Clgs Grad Distigd Acad Perfor 2 Yrs Clg; Ed; Tchng.

**PEREZ, DONNA LEE,** Fl International Univ, Miami, FL; JR; BS; Stdnt Advsry Comm; Intl Stdnts Clb; STA Summer Pgm Univ CT Med Ctr 88; IM Vlybl 90-; Nrsg/Engl; Nrsg Abroad/Literature.

**PEREZ, DOREEN A,** Univ Of North Fl, Jacksonville, FL; SR; BSN; Sigma Theta Tau 90-; Phi Kappa Phi; Amer Heart Assoc Instrctr Trnr; Amer Red Crs Instrctr; RN Spclst U N FL; AS U St NY 86; Nrsg.

**PEREZ, FRANCIS CUADRADO,** Univ Of Pr At Rio Piedras, Rio Piedras, PR; SR; BA; Goldn Key 90-; Psychlgy; Clncl Psychlgy.

**PEREZ, FRANCISCO J,** Univ Politecnica De Pr, Hato Rey, PR; FR; BA; Mech Engrng.

**PEREZ, GRISELDA C,** Fl International Univ, Miami, FL; GD; BA; Miami Dadd Comm Clg Stdnt Govt Senate Secy 86-87; FJCSGA 86-87; Phi Kappa Phi 90-; AA Miami Dade Comm Clg 87; Elem Educ; Tchng.

**PEREZ, IRIS D,** Tn Temple Univ, Chattanooga, TN; JR; BA; Intl Stdnts Fllwshp Sec Asst 90-; Zeta Tau Ro 90-; Art Educ.

**PEREZ, JEAN,** Fl International Univ, Miami, FL; JR; BA; AA Miami Dade Comm Clg 90; Psych; Cnslng Psych.

**PEREZ, JERRY F,** Fayetteville St Univ, Fayetteville, NC; FR; BA; Art Clb VP 90-; Hmcmng Offcl Art Dir 90-; Beauty Pgnt Offcl Art Dir 90-; Hnrs Prog 90-; Chnclrs Schlrs 90-; Dns Lst 90-; K Of C 3rd Deg 89-; Rgt To Lf Org Sprtr 89-; Cmptr Rsrch Artfcl Intlgnc 90-; Cmptr Rsrch Chip Rsrch; Cmptr Engr/Math; Cmptr Rsrchr/Scientist.

**PEREZ, JUAN F,** Fl International Univ, Miami, FL; FR; MBA; Bus Mgmt.

**PEREZ, JUANA M,** Miami Dade Comm Coll, Miami, FL; FR; AS; Nrsng; RN Prsfct.

**PEREZ, LIDA R,** Fl International Univ, Miami, FL; SO; BA; Fl Pub Interest Envrnmntl Soc; Ch Choir 90-; Elem Edn; Teach.

**PEREZ, LIZA A,** Univ Of Miami, Coral Gables, FL; SR; BS; Rsdnt Asst 90-; Pres 100 88-; Microbiology Clb 88-; Mortar Bd/ Gldn Key 89-; Alpha Epsilon Delta 88-; Beta Beta Beta 88-; Kappa Kappa Gamma 88-; Hnrs 351 Rsrch Schlrshp 90-; Micriobiology; Medicine.

**PEREZ, LUIS A,** Embry Riddle Aeronautical Univ, Daytona Beach, FL; JR; BS; Gliding Clb 86-87; U S Hang Gliding Assn 86-; Draggin Flyers Hand Gldng Assn 90-; Amer Airlines Intrnshp; Aero Studies/Mgmnt; Airline Industry.

**PEREZ, MARIA ELENA,** Inter Amer Univ Pr Hato Rey, Hato Rey, PR; FR; BBA; Mktg; Bus.

**PEREZ, MARIA I,** Caribbean Univ, Bayamon, PR; JR.

**PEREZ, MARIE I,** Inter Amer Univ Pr Hato Rey, Hato Rey, PR; JR; BA; Amer Mrktng Assc; Mrktng.

**PEREZ, MARILIZ,** Univ Of Pr At Mayaguez, Mayaguez, PR; SO; BBA; Acctg.

**PEREZ, MARTA M,** Univ Of Pr At Rio Piedras, Rio Piedras, PR; SR; BA; Fine Arts Assn Pres 87-; PR Art Exhibit 87-; US Art Exhibit 87-; Hnr Prog 87-; Act Up 90-; Girl Scout Ldr 87-89; Arlington Arts Cntr Intern 89-; Pres Schlrshp 89; Wash D C Semester Prog 89; Prntmkng/Visual Arts; MA.

**PEREZ, MICHELLE M,** Univ Of Rochester, Rochester, NY; JR; BS; Mnrty Stu Ambsdr 88-89; Spnsh/Latin Stu Assoc 88-89; Deans Lst 90; Microbio; Phrmcy.

**PEREZ, NOEMI,** Fl International Univ, Miami, FL; SR; BS; Kappa Dlt Pi FEA 90-; Kappa Dlt Pi 90-; Educ; Tchr.

**PEREZ, PAULA D,** Miami Jacobs Jr Coll Of Bus, Dayton, OH; FR; Mdcl Asstg/Appld Sci; Mdcl Asstng.

**PEREZ, PETER L,** Ny Univ, New York, NY; SR; BA; Jrnlsm-Lit Criticsm; Jrnlst Criticsm.

**PEREZ, RAMON L,** Inter Amer Univ Pr Hato Rey, Hato Rey, PR; JR; BS; Sigma Chi 89-90; AMR 90-; Biol; Dntl Med.

**PEREZ, REBECCA,** City Univ Of Ny City Coll, New York, NY; GD; BS; Bs Ed; Erly Chldhd Ed; Tchng.

**PEREZ, ROXY,** Univ Of Miami, Coral Gables, FL; SO; BA; Psi Chi; TABS; Psychlgy; Clncl Psychlgst.

**PEREZ, SARA A,** Univ Of Fl, Gainesville, FL; SR; BHSOT; Am Occptnl Thry Assoc 89-; Fl Occptnl Thrpy Assoc 90-; Stdnt Assoc Thrpy Assoc 89-; Pres Hnr Roll 89-90; Level II Intrnsp Phys Dysfunction V A Med Ctr Gainesville Fl; Level II Intrnshp Physosocial Dysfunction Vista Pavilion Gainesville Fl; AA 88; Ped Occptnl Thrpy.

**PEREZ, SILVIA M,** Fl International Univ, Miami, FL; SR; Dns Lst; Global Awareness Pgm 89-; MDA Cnclr; Respect Life Dir 86-; Yth Grps Pres 84-; Tchr Intern; Don Juan Awd Cmnty Svc 89; Respect Life Awd 90; AA Miami Dade Cmnty Clg 89; BS FIU; Scl Studies Ed; Tch.

**PEREZ, STEVEN M,** Hillsborough Comm Coll, Tampa, FL; BA; Yth Ldr Bibl Schl Instr Tchr 88-; Mnstry Cand PTA 90-; Ownr Strt Snd Inc 80-86; Dir Tech Svcs Ctc Gte 86-87; Bibl/Theolgy; Pres Mnstr.

**PEREZ, VICTOR,** Miami Dade Comm Coll, Miami, FL; SO; Phi Theta Kappa 89; Awrd Exc Phlsphy; Under Hnrs Schlrshp 89-; Dean Lst 89-.

**PEREZ, WANDA,** Cumberland County Coll, Vineland, NJ; FR; Bus; Scrtrl.

**PEREZ, WILLIAM D,** Univ Politecnica De Pr, Hato Rey, PR; FR; MBA; Eng.

**PEREZ, YOLANDA M,** Univ Of Pr At Rio Piedras, Rio Piedras, PR; JR; APRU 90-; Gldn Key; Cmnctn Advtg.

**PEREZ, YUANET,** Univ Of Miami, Coral Gables, FL; JR; BS; ASCE Secy; FL Eng Soc; NSPE; Chi Epsilon Treas; Tau Beta Pi; Pres Hon Roll; Univ Deans List; Vicil Engr.

**PEREZ-BEAUCHAMP, ROBERTO O,** Univ Of Pr At Rio Piedras, Rio Piedras, PR; SO; BED; Stdnt Cncl Nwsppr Edit In Chf 88; Art Clb Treas 87; Dns Lst 90-; Magna Cum Laude 88; Acad Coor Prjct Scss Univ Or PR 90-; BA 88; Archtctre.

**PEREZ-CRUZ, AWILDA,** Univ Del Turabo, Gurabo, PR; GD; BA; Hstry.

**PEREZ-ESPINAR, ANTONIO,** Hudson County Comm Coll, Jersey City, NJ; JR; BS; Comp Sci; Telecommnctns.**

**PEREZ-LLANA, MERCEDES,** Catholic Univ Of Pr, Ponce, PR; JR; BBA; Acctg Stdt Assoc 90-; Dns Lst 89-; Astra Clb 86-; Acctg; CPA.

**PEREZ-LOPEZ, R,** Univ Of Pr At Rio Piedras, Rio Piedras, PR; SO; Hnrs Pro; Psych Stu Assoc; Asstntshp Rsrch Cmptv Anxty; Rsrch Exprnc Undrgrad Suny Stry Bk Part; MARC Pro Biopsych Rsrch Mbr; Psych.

**PEREZ-MORALES, JOSE L,** Univ Of Pr At Mayaguez, Mayaguez, PR; JR; BS; ASME 89-; NSPE 90-; NSS 90-; Tau Beta Pi 90-; NACME Schlrshp 88-; Mechanical Engrng.

**PEREZ-ORTIZ, MELANIE A,** Univ Of Pr At Rio Piedras, Rio Piedras, PR; GD; BA; Prog Of Hnr Studies Dir Of Extrcrrclr Activities; Grad Wth Hnrs 90; Cert Fndtn Ortega Y Gasset 89; Spnsh; PHD Phlsphy Hspnc Studies.

**PEREZ-RIVERA, EIDAN MARIA,** Tuskegee Univ, Tuskegee Inst, AL; GD; DVM; Aesclpn Hstrn 87-88; SCAUMA 89-; Newman Clb 88-; Deans Lst 89-90; Cum Laude Biolgy 86; BS Univ PR 86; Sml Anml Prvt Prctce.**

**PEREZ-RODRIGUEZ, ANER E,** Univ Of Pr At Mayaguez, Mayaguez, PR; JR; BS; Amiga Usr Grp 90-; Intrn Bellcove; Engr.

**PERFETTI, VINCENT,** Manhattan Coll, Bronx, NY; JR; BEE; Elect Clb 89; IEEE 90; Eta Kappa Nu 90-; Bsbl 89; Elect Eng; Med.

**PERIASWAMY, RAMALIGGAM,** Livingston Univ, Livingston, AL; SR; BS; Acct Clb 89-; Intl Std Asc; Sci Univ Mlys Bst Serv Awd 88; Acct; CPA.**

**PERICO, ANTHONY,** Central Fl Comm Coll, Ocala, FL; FR; AA; Silver Garland Awd Nominee For Jrnlsm 90; Grader For Eng Class Taught By Cen Fl Comm Coll Pres W Campion; Eng Tchr.

**PERIN, JOSHUA B,** Franklin And Marshall Coll, Lancaster, PA; FR; BA; Goethean Literary Scty; Nwspr 90-; Frnch Clb 90-; Crs Cntry Vrsty 90; Vrsty Indr/Otdr Trck 90-.

**PERINGER, JASON D,** Univ Of New Haven, West Haven, CT; SR; BS; Alpha Lambda Delta 90-; Pres Schlrshp 87-; Crmnl Jstc; Fed Law Enfrcmnt.

**PERIS, JENNIFER L,** Syracuse Univ, Syracuse, NY; SO; BARCH; Phi Kappa Phi; Dns Lst; Arch.

**PERITORE, DEBORAH-LYNN,** Dowling Coll, Oakdale Li, NY; SR; BBA; Cnsrvtn Awrns Comm 90-; Academic Hnr Schlrshp 89-; Dns Lst 90-; AAS Suffolk Conty; Comm Coll 87-89; Bus; Admin/Mngmnt.

**PERKINS MD, DIANNE A,** Boston Univ, Boston, MA; GD; MD; Primary Care Soc 87-89; Amer Med Stdnt Assoc 88-; Med Soc 89; Alpha Omega Alpha; BS 87; Medicine; Pediatrics.

**PERKINS, AVIS K,** Mercer Univ Schl Of Pharm, Atlanta, GA; JR; PHARM; Acad Of Stdnts Pharm Vice Chrmn 90-; Amer Soc Of Hosp Pharm 90-; Alpha Chi 82; Golden Key 82; Phi Delta Chi Rush Coord; Merit Schlrshp 90-; Pr Upper Level Schlrshp SW TX State Univ 83; Med Tech; BS SW TX Univ 84; Pharmacy.

**PERKINS, CHARISSA D,** Methodist Coll, Fayetteville, NC; SO; Acctg.

**PERKINS JR, CHARLES A,** Ms St Univ, Miss State, MS; SR; MBA; Natl Cattlemens Assn; AA Hinds Jr Coll 77; Agri Bus; Consltng/Mgmnt.

**PERKINS, CHERYL E,** Univ Of Nc At Greensboro, Greensboro, NC; SR; MBA; SGA VP 77-78; Schl Vlntr; Stdnt Intrn Peller Elem Greensboro NC Grds 1-2 90; Stdnt Tchr C W Mc Crary Elem Schl Asheboro NC Grd K 90; Preschl Tchr Ags 4-5 78-80; Tchrs Asst 1st Grd 78-80; Mem Assn Chldhd Ed Intrntl; Intrm Pstn; BS 90; Ed; Tchr K-6.

**PERKINS, CHRISTOPHER E,** Tn St Univ, Nashville, TN; JR; BSEE; NSBE 89-; IEEE 89-; Delco Elctrncs Intern; Elctrcl Engr.

**PERKINS, DANA L,** Radford Univ, Radford, VA; FR; BA; Alpha Lmbd Dlt; Phi Sgm Pi; Mgr Bsktbl 90-; Bio.

**PERKINS, DAVID S,** Methodist Coll, Fayetteville, NC; SR; BS; Alpha Chi 90; Bsnss Fnce; Invstmnt Serv Fnce.

**PERKINS, DAWN MARIE,** Methodist Coll, Fayetteville, NC; SR; BS; Grad Mrshl 89-90; Ntl Assoc Of Accntnts; Alpha Chi 90, Clrk Awd In Accntng; Pres Lst Deans Lst 87; Crlna Tlephne Tlgrph Schlrshp; Accntng; CPA.

**PERKINS, GWENDOLYN P,** Univ Of South Al, Mobile, AL; JR; BS; Phi Kappa Phi; Alpha Chi; Beta Alpha Psi; Bsn/Acctg; CPA.

**PERKINS, IRENE E,** Western New England Coll, Springfield, MA; SR; BSBA; Mktg Assn Treas 89-; Rsdnt Hall Assn Pres 87-88; Delta Mu Delta 90-; Alpha Kappa Psi 87-; Intrnshp H P Hood Inc 89-90; Vrsty Fld Hcky 87-; Mktg.

**PERKINS, JENNIFER L,** Snead St Jr Coll, Boaz, AL; FR; BA; Art; Phtgrphy.

**PERKINS, JILL R,** Liberty Univ, Lynchburg, VA; GD; BA; Coll Rpblcns; Ythqst Clb; Lght Clb; Lbrtrs For Lf; Bptst Stdnt Un; Sigma Tau Delta; Lbrty Gdprnt Home Htln Vol; Engl Dirctd Rsrch 90; Engl; Ed/Law.

**PERKINS, JOE WAYNE,** Memphis St Univ, Memphis, TN; SR; BA; Golden Key 90; Alpha Kappa Delta 90; Chi Beta Phi 90; Phi Kappa Phi 91-; Addington Awd; Tch Clg Level; Pschlgy; Grdt Schl/Tchg.**

**PERKINS, KAREN L,** Memphis St Univ, Memphis, TN; MA; BA Union Univ 90; Art Hist; Museum Wrk.

**PERKINS, KASSANDRA F,** Wesley Coll, Florence, MS; SO; Beacon Co Editor 90-; Choir Pres 90-; Player 90; Soph Sec/Treas 90; Alpha Chi Omega 89-; Pres Lst 90; Dns Lst 89-90; Cheerleader 90; AS; Law.

**PERKINS, KEVIN B,** Radford Univ, Radford, VA; SR; BA; Bus Admin.

**PERKINS, LA KESHYA N,** Al A & M Univ, Normal, AL; SR; Extra Touch Tutorial Prog 89-90; Ntl Ed Hnr Scty; NAACP 88-90; Ntl Stdnt Speech Lang Hrng Assoc VP 88; Al State Assistntshp 90; Speech Pthlgy; Speech Thrpst.**

**PERKINS, LARRY TODD,** Lexington Comm Coll, Lexington, KY; SR; AIAS Treas Elect; Arch Tech; Cvl Engr.

**PERKINS, MATTHEW S,** Western Piedmont Comm Coll, Morganton, NC; FR; Paralgl Assn Pres; SGA Sntr; Paralgl; Law.

**PERKINS, MELISSA L,** Univ Of Al At Birmingham, Birmingham, AL; JR; BED; Jfrsn St Almni Assn 90-; Pres Hon Roll; AS Jfrsn St Comm Coll 90; Early Chldhd Ed; Tchr.

**PERKINS, MICHELE,** Temple Univ, Philadelphia, PA; JR; BS; Envir Engr Assoc 90-; Golden Key 89-; Phi Eta Sigma 88-89; Anna M Vincent Schlrshp; Pres Frshmn Schlrshp; Achvmnt Awds; Envir Engr; MS.

**PERKINS, RAQUEL C,** Jackson St Univ, Jackson, MS; FR; WEB Du Bois Hons Clg 90-; Alpha Lambda Delta 90-; Pr Lst 90-; Mktg; Pharmaceutical Sls.

**PERKINS, REBECCA R,** Univ Of Ky, Lexington, KY; FR; BA; Biology Clb; Phi Eta Sigma; Psychology.

**PERKINS, RENEE,** Univ Of Ga, Athens, GA; SR; BSED; CCF; Golden Key; Kappa Delta Pi; Art Tchr.

**PERKINS, ROBERT T,** Univ Of Cincinnati, Cincinnati, OH; SR; BFA; AERHO Tr 89-90; Dns Lst 88-90; 3 Mnth Intrnshp Prgmmg 90; Brdcstng/Comm; Entertnmnt/Music/Tele.

**PERKINS, SARAH A,** James Madison University, Harrisonburg, VA; SO; BA; Amnsty Intntl 89-; Alpha Chi Rho Aux; Psych; Clncl Chld Psych.

**PERKINS, SHARON D,** Rust Coll, Holly Springs, MS; SO; BA; NAACP 89-90; Pom-Pom Squad 90; Pre-Law Clb 90-91; Crmsn Schlrs 89-; Alpha Kappa Mu; Morris Marion Schlrshp 90; Hon Trk Acad Schlrshp 89-; Pres Lst 89-; Pltcl Sci; Law.

**PERKINS, STEVEN W,** Casco Bay Coll, Portland, ME; FR; Bg Brthr; Bg Brthr Yr 85; Prlgl Ins.

**PERKINS, TARA L,** Univ Of Ky, Lexington, KY; FR; MBA; Educ/Spec Educ; Tchr.

**PERKINS, WILLIAM R,** Daytona Beach Comm Coll, Daytona Beach, FL; FR; BS; Software Engr 84-; Engrng.

**PERKINSON, CHRISTINA E,** Chowan Coll, Murfreesboro, NC; FR; BA; Aces; Marshall; Art Gallery Picture Pblshd Magazine; Comml Art.

**PERKINSON, DOROTHY H,** Vance Granville Comm Coll, Henderson, NC; SR; AAS; Stdnt Govt Rep 90-; Essay Cntst 90-; Asst Actvties Dir Nrsng Hm; Therptc Rec; Actvty Dir/Soc Dir.

**PERKINSON, FREDA GALE HIGHT,** Vance Granville Comm Coll, Henderson, NC; SR; Totor 78-790; AAS 80; AAS 80; Acctg/ Bus Adm/Cptr Prog; Accnt/Mgmt Ceer.

**PERKO, AMY J,** Wv Northern Comm Coll, Wheeling, WV; FR; Hlth Sci; Nrsng.

**PERKO, JOSEPH A,** Univ Of Akron, Akron, OH; SR; BS; Gldn Ky 87-; Otstndng Coll Stu Amer 87-; Beta Gamma Sigma 90-; Magna Cum Laude; IM Bstkbl 89-; Bus Admn/Mrktng; Actrl Sci.

**PERKOWSKI, LEON J,** Cornell Univ Statutory College, Ithaca, NY; SO; BS; Gl Clb Pres 89-; AF ROTC 89-; Natl Schlrs 89-; Mtrlgy; Air Force Offcr.

**PERKOWSKI, PETER E,** Univ Of Rochester, Rochester, NY; JR; BA; Glee Clb Prsdnt 88-; Gay Lesbian Bisexual Frnds Assn Drctr 90-; Nwmn Comm 88-; Vrsty Trck Fld 88-; Math; Edctn.

**PERKS, REBECCA,** Pa St Univ Wilkes Barre Cmps, Lehman, PA; FR; BS; Stdnt Govt; Sch Paper Ed 90-; Campus Actvts Bd 90; Circle K 90; Math Ed; Sec Ed Math.

**PERLMAN, TRACY A,** Hofstra Univ, Hempstead, NY, JR, BA; Dncwrks Sec 90-; Kckln Capt; Deans Lst 89-90; Fndr Phi Mu Hstrn; Cmmnctns Elec Jrnlsm.**

**PERLOFF, DAVID E,** Univ Of Miami, Coral Gables, FL; GD; MD; Outstndg Yng Men Am Assoc Awd 88f Am Med Stdnt Assn 87-; Am Med Assn 87-; Alpha Lambda Delta 84; Phi Kappa Phi 86-87; Alpha Omega Alpha; Phi Lambda Upsilon Awd 85; James Mcknight Awd 86-87; Dept Biochem Awd 86-87; Internal Med; Cardiology.

**PERMAN, AMY J,** Kent St Univ Kent Cmps, Kent, OH; FR; Var Trck Acad Capt 90-; Ele Educ.

**PERMENTER, DEBBIE L,** Univ Of Nc At Wilmington, Wilmington, NC; FR; BA; Cape Fear Dycr Asc Org 90-; Dns Lst 90-; New Hnvr Reg Med Ctr Vol 90-; Chldrns Chrch Vol 90-; Wntr Prk Prschl Crgvr 90-; Amer Bsn Wmns Asc Schlp 90-; Prsbytrn Wmn Schlp 90-; Elem Ed; Tchr.

**PERNA, DAVID M,** Le Moyne Coll, Syracuse, NY; SO; MBA; Clg Radio Station 89-; Hcky 89-; Pol Sci; Law.

**PERNA, KEVIN A,** Wilmington Coll, New Castle, DE; SR; BS; Amer Legion 84-; DE State Police Intern 90-; Athl Bsebl Schlrshp 89-; Bsebl Capt 87-; BS; Crmnl Jstc; DE State Police.

**PERNELL, CINDY L,** Vance Granville Comm Coll, Henderson, NC; FR; AAS; Phi Theta Kappa; Elec Eng; Elec Techncn.

**PERNG, IRENE,** S U N Y At Buffalo, Buffalo, NY; SO; BA; Ski Clb 89-; Wmn Mgmt; IM Vllybll; IM Sftbll 89-; Acctg; CPA.

**PERNG-FUSSELL, HWEY-FEN,** Tallahassee Comm Coll, Tallahassee, FL; FR; AA; Mgr Of A Lgge Schl In Twn 89; Hstry Wstrn Cvlztn; Educ.

**PERODIN, ABNER J,** Saint Thomas Univ, Miami, FL; FR; BED; Haitian Task Force Treas 87-; Intrnshp Miami Edison Sr High 89-; Public Asst Supervisor 87-; AA Miami Dade Cmty Clg 88-; Social Sciences; Teaching.

**PEROTTI, JEAN A,** Marywood Coll, Scranton, PA; SR; Kappa Delta Pi 90-; Val Lackawanna Jr Coll 88; Assoc Lckwn Jr Coll 88; Elem Educ; Tchng.**

**PEROZICH, JOHN P,** Lebanon Valley Coll, Annville, PA; JR; BS; Blgy Clb 89-; Swmng Clb 88-89; Wlns Wk Cmte 90; Beta Beta Beta 90-; Dns Lst 88-; Pres Ldrshp Schlrshp; Achvmnt Awd Chmstry; Blgcl Schlrshp Awd; Vrsty Ftbl 88-90; Blgy; Gntcs Prof.**

**PERPETUA, CAROLYN M,** Duquesne Univ, Pittsburgh, PA; SO; BA; Latin Cmmnctns.

**PERRAULT, ALEXANDER D,** Savannah Coll Of Art & Design, Savannah, GA; FR; BFA; Soc Of Illustrtrs 90-; Librn At Telfair 90-; Deans List; Illustrtn; Art.

**PERRI, GIOVANNA,** Teikyo Post Univ, Waterbury, CT; SO; BA; Taught Religion 89-90; Tutor 90-; Acctng Bus; CPA.

**PERRI, STEPHEN J,** Clarkson Univ, Potsdam, NY; JR; BS; Stu Govt Wstchstr Comm Coll VP 89-90; Nwspr Bus Mgr WCC Bus Mgr 89-90; Alpha Beta Gamma Ntl Bus HS Ntl Pres 90-; Alpha Beta Gamma VP 89-90; Pres Lst WCC 89-90; Deans Lst 89-90; Sml Bus Ownr 87-90; AS 90; Finance; Stckbrkr.

**PERRICELLI, ANN MICHELLE,** Univ Of Rochester, Rochester, NY; JR; BS; Optcl Scty Amer 85-; Optcl Eng.

**PERRICELLI, KIMBERLY A,** Endicott Coll, Beverly, MA; FR; BS; Envrnmntl Ldrshp Clb 90-; Shpmts; Phi Theta Kappa; Hons Prog; Up Wth People 89-90; Intrnshp MA Aubudon Soc; Biol; Med.

**PERRICONE, CARRIE L,** Univ Of Miami, Coral Gables, FL; JR; BS; Dnce Corp 89; NIV Clbe Sta Rprtr Anchr 89-; NIV Rdo Sta Nwscstr 89; Miami Hrld Wrtr 89-; Alpha Epsilon Rho Pres 89-; Hnrs Prog 88-; Vol Rdng Ttr YMCA; Smmr Intrnshps WPTV Wst Plm Bch; Schlrshp NATAS; Schlrshp UM Schl Cmmnctns; Brdcst Jrnlsm; TV Rprtng And Anchrng.

**PERRICONE, MARY,** S U N Y Coll Of Tech At Frmgdl, Farmingdale, NY; JR; Winthrop Rsrch Intern; Deans Lst 90; Vet Sci Tech; Lab Tech.

**PERRIE, CYNTHIA K,** Univ Of Akron, Akron, OH; SR; BS; Brd Of Rltrs; Smythe Crmr Co 90-; Frstne Tre & Rbbr Co 89; Mrktng.

**PERRIGAN, LOIS J,** Va Highlands Comm Coll, Abingdon, VA; FR; AAS; Chrstn Clb Rprtr 90-; Alpha Gamma Rho/Phi Theta Kappa Sec 90-; Substnc Abuse 90-; Intrnshp Brstl Retg Mntl Hlth Cnslng Ctr 90-; Tutor/Chrch Yth Ldr 89-; Wash Cnty Lttl League Hosp Hostess 68-89; Psych; Soc Serv.

**PERRINE, JAMES B,** Univ Of Al At Birmingham, Birmingham, AL; SR; BS; Gldn Key; Phi Kappa Phi; 88-89 Otstndng Frshmn Chm Stdnt; 90- Otstndng Chem Stdnt; IM Bsktbl Sftbl 88-; Chmstry; Law.

**PERRINO, JANET M,** Le Moyne Coll, Syracuse, NY; SR; BA; Bio Clb 88-; Eucharist Mnstr 87-; Beta Beta Beta 89-; Alpha Sigma Nu 89-; Prjcts Comm Tutor 90-; Syracuse Univ Mrchng Band 88-; Bio; Phrmcst.

**PERRO, DAWN MARIE,** Dowling Coll, Oakdale Li, NY; JR; BA; Alpha Chi 90-; Spec Educ; Spec Educ/Psychology.

**PERRON, DEANA MICHELINE,** Univ Of New England, Biddeford, ME; JR; BA; AOTA 90-; MEOTA 90-; MUNESOTA 90-; IM Bsktbl Vllybl; Occptnl Thrpy; Pdtrc Rehab.

**PERRON, NICOLE S,** Endicott Coll, Beverly, MA; SR; AS; Lrng/Understndng New Challenges 89-; Dorm Treas 90-; Club Couture 90; Deans Lst 90-; Intrnshp Sportswear Designs 90; Intrnshp Susan Bristol Traditional Designs; Apparel Design.

**PERRONE, CYNTHIA,** Wagner Coll, Staten Island, NY; JR; BA; Ltry Mag; Sgm Tau Dlt; Engl; Law.

**PERROTTO, KAREN L,** Edinboro Univ Of Pa, Edinboro, PA; JR; BMA; Mrchng Bnd 89-; Prcssn Ensmbl 90-; Cert Lfgrd YMCA 90; PAS; Kappa Delta Pi; Alpha Phi Omega Sec 90-; Pres Stdy Abrd Schlrshp Italy 90; Fresh Hnrs Schlrshp 89-90; IM Vllybl Bwlng 90-; Math; Tchr Coll Univ.

**PERROTTO, MICHELLE C,** Ri Coll, Providence, RI; FR; BED; Coffee Shop Emplee 90-; Psychology; Tch.

**PERRY, ALEXANDER S,** Nc Central Univ, Durham, NC; GD; JD; AM Bar Assc; BLSA 90-; NALBEEMS 89; Deans List 90; Delta Theta Phi; IM 90; Altrntvs Mddl Schl Prgm; Pwr Lght Co Law Clrk Intrn; NC Bar Assc Mnrty Smmr Crk; Dept Crrctns Vol 89; AME Zion Chrch; BS NC A T State Univ 89; Law.

**PERRY, ANNA D,** Univ Of Cin R Walters Coll, Blue Ash, OH; AD; LPNAO; NAPNES; WARF Analy Comm; Nrsng.

**PERRY, BRENT L,** Univ Of Tn At Martin, Martin, TN; SR; BS; Crmnl Jstce Soc 89-90; Deans Lst 88-90; Crmnl Jstce; Law.**

**PERRY, CELENDA H,** Valdosta St Coll, Valdosta, GA; SR; BA; Ga Water/Polutn Cntrl Assn; Camden Cty Humne Soc; Hospice S E Ga; Coastal Ga Wtlnds Tsk Frce; Natl Bus Eductrs Assn; Plnr 85-; AA Ga Military Clag 90; Pub Admn; Law.

**PERRY, CHRISTIE S,** Savannah St Coll, Savannah, GA; JR; BS; Newtonian Soc Cmptr Sci Clb 90-; Beta Kappa Chi; Alpha Kappa Alpha; State Farm Ins Co Intrn; Cmptr Sci Tech; Sys Anlys.

**PERRY, CHRISTINE E,** Mount Saint Mary Coll, Newburgh, NY; SR; BS; Hnrs Allnc Sec 89-90; Soup Kitchn 89; Alpha Chi 88-; Ralph Schlr 88-89; Aqnas Schlr 89-; Math.

**PERRY, CYNTHIA M,** Bunker Hill Comm Coll, Boston, MA; FR; AS; Bsn Adm.

**PERRY, DANNETTA A,** Atlantic Comm Coll, Mays Landing, NJ; FR; BA; Bus Admin; Acctnt.

**PERRY, DIANE M,** Univ Of South Al, Mobile, AL; SO; Athltc Trnrs Clb 90-; Intrnshp Athltc Trng 90-; Crs Cntry/Trck Tm 90-; Sprts Sci; Athltc Trng.

**PERRY, DOROTHY P,** Bryant Stratton Bus Inst Roch, Rochester, NY; GD; AS; Acctg; CPA.

**PERRY, G ALLEN,** Univ Of Ky, Lexington, KY; SR; BA; Phi Alpha Theta; Hstry; Pblc Srvc.

**PERRY, KAREN B,** Longwood Coll, Farmville, VA; FR; MOLAS; Modern Lang Clb 90-; SEA 90-; F Wygal Schlrshp Awd; Stdnt Invlmnt Ldrshp Awd; Cert Recgntn High Schlstc Achvmnt Hon Soc Phi Kappa Phi; Lacrosse Trng; Span/French; Intrprtg/Educ.

**PERRY, LORI J,** Fl International Univ, Miami, FL; GD; Dean Lst 86-90; Stu Tchng Intern 90; Prog Ltrcy 88-90; Sub Tchr 90-; AA Miami Dade Comm Coll 87; BA Fla Intl Univ 90; Engl; Tchng.

**PERRY, MARK W,** Marshall University, Huntington, WV; SR; BBA; Amer Mktg Assoc 90-; US Army Corp Engrs Intern 90-; BBA; Mktg/Mgmt; Sales.

**PERRY, MIA S,** Newbury Coll, Brookline, MA; FR; BSD; Fresh Start Pgm 87-90; Future Bus Ldrs Of Amer 90; 8th Annual Ldr Dev Inst Gov 89-90; Fash Mrchndsng.

**PERRY, MICHELLE L,** Le Moyne Coll, Syracuse, NY; JR; BS; Mktg Clb Mbrshp Cmtee; Bus Clb; Bus.

**PERRY, PAULETTE J,** City Univ Of Ny Med Evers Coll, Brooklyn, NY; SR; BA; Elem Ed.

**PERRY, REBECCA L,** Longwood Coll, Farmville, VA; JR; BA; Lngwd Ambsdrs 90-; Lngwd A/S Hon Prog 88-; Peer Adv 89-90; Alpha Lambda Delta 89-; Zeta Tau Alpha 2nd VP 89-; Red Crs Bld Dnr 88-; Adpt Grndprnt 89-; Lngwd Schlr 88-; Arts/Sci Hon Prg Schlrshp 88-; Soc; Jstce/Sclgy.

**PERRY, RHONDA M,** Anderson Coll, Anderson, SC; SO; BED; Spnsh Clb 90-; Hnrs Prgm 90; Phi Theta Kappa VP 90-; Erly Chldhd Ed; Tchng.

**PERRY, ROBERT R,** Ms St Univ, Miss State, MS; JR; BA; Phi Kappa Phi 89-; Gamma Beta Phi 89-; Mechncl Engrng; Plant.

**PERRY, S LEE,** Ms St Univ, Miss State, MS; SO; Pnhlnc Dlgt 90-; Grk Wk Comm Rep 90-; Jr Pnhlnc Pres 90; Lambda Sigma 90-; Gamma Beta Phi 90-; Deans Lst Schlr; Kappa Delta Cncl Mbrs Dlgt 89-; Kappa Alpha Ltl Sis 90-; Old South Queen; Alumni Dlgt; Phys Thrpy.

**PERRY, SARI R,** Northern Ky Univ, Highland Hts, KY; SR; BA; Psych Clb; Psi Chi; Alpha Chi; Phi Beta Kappa; Psych; Clincl Psych.

**PERRY, SHALAUNDA M,** Central St Univ, Wilberforce, OH; FR; BA; Acctg; CPA.

**PERRY, SHAUN N,** Al St Univ, Montgomery, AL; SR; DOMA 90-; Cltrl Org; Prof Intrnshp Campus Police; Hmcmng Game Usher 89; Crmnl Jstc; Fed Agnt DEA.

**PERRY, SHENITA Y,** Al St Univ, Montgomery, AL; SO; BA; Mrchng Symph/Pep Band Sctn Ldr 90-; Tau Beta Sigma Hist 90-; Music; Rcrd Prdcng/Performane.

**PERRY, STACEY M,** Chattanooga St Tech Comm Coll, Chattanooga, TN; SO; AS; Chattanodga Soc Rad Tech; Chattanooga State Rad Soc VP; Rad Tech Merit Awrd; Rdlgc Tech; Med Sch.

**PERRY, STEPHANIE R,** Wv Univ At Parkersburg, Parkersburg, WV; SO.

**PERRY JR, THEODIS L,** Univ Of Nc At Charlotte, Charlotte, NC; SO; BA; SAFE 89; NAACP V P 89; Black Union 90; Phi Eta Sigma 90; Kappa Alpha Psi; Arch Dsgn.

**PERRY, TONI E,** Hudson Valley Comm Coll, Troy, NY; JR; AS; Emrgng Bttrfly Yng Wdwd Sprt Grp Treas 90-; Begnng Exprnc Sec 90-; Humn Srvcs.

**PERRY, TRACI L,** East Carolina Univ, Greenville, NC; FR; BED; Phi Eta Sigma; Elem Educ; Small Bus.

**PERRY, TWYLA D,** Univ Of Al, Tuscaloosa, AL; FR; BED; AL Frnscs Cncl 90-; Wmns Hnr Pgm Tres 90-; Phi Eta Sigma Tres 90-; Alpha Lambda Delta 90-; Lambda Sigma; Elks Natl Fndtn Most Vlbl Stdnt Runner Up 90-; IM 90-; Math; Teaching.

**PERRY, VALERY L,** Univ Of Rochester, Rochester, NY; JR; BA; Stdnts Assoc Apprprtns Cmmttee Cntrllr 88; Mrdn Scty Stdnt Admssns Vol 90; Clg Rpblcns Pres 88-90; Phi Beta Kappa; Ordr Of Omega Greek; Alpha Phi Frt Ed 90; U Stdnt Lfe Awd; Marmon Potter Memorial Schlrshp; Sylvia Griffith Schlrshp; Russian/Pol Sci; Intrntl Rltns.

**PERRY, VERTONYA J,** Johnson C Smith Univ, Charlotte, NC; SR; BA; Engl Clb VP 88-; Pol Sci Clb 78-89; Alpha Kappa Mu Pres 89-; Alpha Chi Sec 89-; Sigma Tau Delta; Alpha Kappa Alpha Asst Sec 89-; Southern Educ Fndtn Schlr 89; Vanderhorst Meml Chrch Yng Adlt Coun 90-; S Carolina Elec Gas Co Intrn 90; Engl; Fld Educ.

**PERRY, WENDY R,** Inter Amer Univ Pr Hato Rey, Hato Rey, PR; SR; BA; Pltcl Sci Assoc Treas 89-; Dns Lst; Pltcl Sci; Law.

**PERRY, WESLEY L,** Ms St Univ, Miss State, MS; JR; BS; Wsly Fndtn 89-; Frshmn Acdmc Schlrshp 88-90; IM Sprts Tm Capt Rep 88-; Blgcl Eng; Dsgn Eng.

**PERRY, WILLIAM G,** Alfred Univ, Alfred, NY; SR; BS; Alph Phi Omg Tres 90-; Radio Fin Dir 89-90; Tau Beta Pi Pres 90-; Keramos; Hot Dog Day Cmt Anl All Day Fndrsr Fin Dir 88-89; Alpha Lmbd Dlt; Mark S Miller Mem Schlrshp; Smr Job Expermental Stn Dupot; Ceramic Eng; Ph D Material Sci.

**PERRY III, WILLIAM W,** Ms St Univ, Miss State, MS; JR; BS; Gamma Beta Phi 90-; Mech Eng.

**PERRYMAN, AMY LYNN,** Univ Of Nc At Greensboro, Greensboro, NC; SO; BED; Intrnshp 90-; Elem Educ; Tchr.

**PERRYMAN, JANNA C,** Univ Of West Fl, Pensacola, FL; JR; Stdnt Cncl Exceptnl Chldn 90-; AA Pensacola Jr Clg 90; Spec Educ; Teaching.

**PERRYMAN, OCTAVIA K,** Memphis St Univ, Memphis, TN; FR; BS; Peer Mntr Pgm 90-; Amer Chem Soc Stdnt Affil Tr 91-92; Alpha Lambda Delta; Gamma Beta Phi; Chem; Resrch.

**PERSAD, IVANOV K,** Fl International Univ, Miami, FL; JR; BA; Phi Eta Sigma 90-; Fclty Schlr 89-; Bio/Chem/Elctrncs; Eng/ Med Lab Sci.

**PERSAD, SABBITHRY,** Univ Of Md At Eastern Shore, Princess Anne, MD; JR; BA; Pre-Law Soc; Carbbn Clb; NAACP; Tnns Tm; Hons Prog; Natl Grd Res; Soclgy; Law.

**PERSAD, STEVE S,** Univ Of Al At Birmingham, Birmingham, AL; SO; ASSOC; Bio Med Tech Sci; Elec Eng.

**PERSAUD JR, GUNANAND,** Fairleigh Dickinson Hackensack, Hackensack, NJ; FR; BS; Pre Prof Clb 90-; Deans Lst 90-; Biol; Med.

**PERSAUD, JANET,** Bloomfield Coll, Bloomfield, NJ; JR; BA; Psychlgy; Optmtry.

**PERSAUD, KHEMRAJ,** Mount Olive Coll, Mount Olive, NC; GD; MSA; US Air Force Med 76-90; Lab Spclst; Assoc Cmnty Clg Air Force 89; Bsn Admin.

**PERSAUD SR, NARAYAN D,** Catawba Valley Comm Coll, Hickory, NC; FR; AAS; Arch; Engr.

**PERSAUD, OARMILLA P,** City Univ Of Ny La Guard Coll, Long Island Cty, NY; SR; AAS; Bus Mgmt; Invstmnts/Fin Wrld.

**PERSELLIN, THEREASA L,** Univ Of North Fl, Jacksonville, FL; JR; BA; Gldn Key 90-; Sexual Asslt Ctr Intshp; State Attys Offc Intshp; Crmnl Jstc; Law.

**PERSON, SHERYL E,** Columbia Union Coll, Takoma Park, MD; SR; BS; Phi Theta Cappa; LDS Tchr Lbrn 79-; Lbry Aide 90; Accnt Mgr Nwspr; Acctng; CPA MA.

**PERSON, THERESA M,** Al St Univ, Montgomery, AL; FR; BA; Bsns; Mgmnt.

**PERSONTE, JOSEPH M,** S U N Y Coll At Fredonia, Fredonia, NY; JR; BA; Rsdnt Assist Advsry Brd VP 90; Orient Ldr Orient Ldr 90; Rsdnt Assist VP 89; Cmmnty Actvties Rsdnt Assist 89; Hmbrg Stdnt Tchng Prog; Im Ftbl Sftbl Bsktbl 88; Elem Ed; Tchr.

**PERSSON, CAROL J,** Daytona Beach Comm Coll, Daytona Beach, FL; SO; BS; Offc Mgr 89; AA; Bsns Admnstrtn; Intrntnl Bsns.

**PERSTROPE JR, GENE F,** Crichton Coll, Memphis, TN; SR; BS; Phi Theta Kappa 88; Pstrl Intrnshp First Bptst Frbnks Ak 90; Pstrl Intrnshp First Bptst Arnold Mo 89; Dept Awd Chrch Mnstrs 90-; AA Jefferson Cllg 88; Church Ministries.**

**PERSUITTE, CHRISTINE R,** Indiana Univ Of Pa, Indiana, PA; SR; BS; PSEA NEA 90-; Theta Phi Alpha 88-; Elem Educ.

**PERTL, FRANZ ANDREAS JOHANNES,** Wv Univ, Morgantown, WV; SO; BA; Internatl Stdnt 89-; Elctrcl/Cmptr Engrg; Engr.

**PERULLO, BETH A,** Becker Coll At Leicester, Leicester, MA; SO; AS; Early Chldhd Educ.

**PERZ, LISBEL,** Fl International Univ, Miami, FL; SR; Intrnshp Douglas Elem 90-; Intrnshp Sweetwater Elem; AA Miami Dade Comm Clg 89; Elem Ed.

**PERZANOSKI, KAREN E,** Savannah Coll Of Art & Design, Savannah, GA; FR; MBA; Dorm Cncl; Ttr 90-; Illstrtn; Advrtsng.

**PESANTES, EILEEN R,** Univ Of Pr At Mayaguez, Mayaguez, PR; SO; BA; Cvl Eng.

**PESCATORE, MAURA J,** Providence Coll, Providence, RI; SR; Accntng Assn Exec VP 90-; Rsdnc Brd 87-89; Stdnt Cngrs Tchr Evltn Comm 89-; Tau Phi Pi; BS; Accntng.

**PESHO, RENEE K,** Univ Of Akron, Akron, OH; JR; BA; Deans List 89; Bsn; Ed Secondary.

**PESI, CHRISTINE M,** Indiana Univ Of Pa, Indiana, PA; SR; BED; PSEA-STDNT Tchr Union 88-; Elem Ed; Tchng.

**PESTANA, JULIA ESTHER,** Fl International Univ, Miami, FL; SR; BA; Phi Kappa Phi 90-; AA 88; AS 88; Elem Ed.

**PESTANO, NIGEL A,** Coll Of Aeronautics, Flushing, NY; FR; BET; Chess; Pres Lst; Vlybl/Sccr; Avionics; Aernautcl Engr.

**PESUIT, MARGARET M,** Manhattanville Coll, Purchase, NY; SO; BA; Hstry; Prfssr.

**PETE, DANIEL J,** S U N Y Coll At Fredonia, Fredonia, NY; SR; BA; LVA; Anmsty Intl; Phi Alpha Theta; Kappa Delta Pi; Hon Grad; Hstry; Tchng.

**PETEL, NATHAN A,** Fl International Univ, Miami, FL; SO; BS; Hotel/Food/Tourism Assn 90-; IM Bsktbl Capt 90-; Hosp Mgmnt.

**PETERKIN, PAUL M,** Bridgeport Engr Inst, Fairfield, CT; SR; BE; Brdgprt Eng Inst Schlrshp Grnt Sec Sem 90-; Instrmnt Soc Amer 88-; Qlty Assr Insptr Drssr Ind Newtwn Ct 88-; Dipl Clg Arts Sci Tech 87; Elec Eng.

**PETERMAN, DEBORAH R,** Univ Of Central Fl, Orlando, FL; FR; BS; Hsptlty Mgmnt.

**PETERMAN, ISTVAN,** City Univ Of Ny City Coll, New York, NY; JR; BS; Evening Stdnt Govt Sen; CCNY Vars Swim; Cmptr Sci Pgm; Syst Dev.

**PETERMAN, JAIYME J,** Marshall University, Huntington, WV; JR; BA; Elem Educ Math; Tch.

**PETERMAN, MELISSA K,** Cumberland Coll, Williamsburg, KY; JR; BS; Psych Clb 88-; Love In Actn 87-; Chldrns Mnstry 87; Acdmc Schlrshp 87-; Hnr Crt; Psych; Cnslg.

**PETERMANN, MICHAEL A,** Ny Inst Tech Old Westbury, Old Westbury, NY; SR; Amer Inst Of Arch Stdnts 89-90; Nu Ypsilon Tau 89-; Exhib Cmte 90-; AIA Schlstc Schlrshp Awd 89; Pr Svc Awd 90; NYIT Gold Medal Achvmnt Arch; AAS Orange Cnty Cmnty Clg 86; Arch.**

**PETERS, ALEXANDRA C,** Marymount Manhattan Coll, New York, NY; SR; BA; Intrnshp At CBS Nws Spcl Evnts Dsk Asst 88; Phllps Actnrs PR Dept Asst Mgr; Abitur Nicolaus Cusanus Gymnasium Bonn Germany 86; Cmmnctn Arts; PR.

**PETERS, BARBARA M,** Univ Of Al At Birmingham, Birmingham, AL; SR; BA; Elem Educ; Tchr.

**PETERS, DOUGLAS E,** Nc Agri & Tech St Univ, Greensboro, NC; JR; BS; NSBE 88-89; Tau Beta Pi 90-; Eta Kappa Nu 90-; CORBEST Schlrshp; Internshp Corning Inc Corning N Y; Elect Engrng.

**PETERS, ELAINE J,** Alcorn St Univ, Lorman, MS; JR; BS; Mrchng Bnd 88-; Natl Hon Org 88-90; Acdmc Schlrshp 88-; Deans Lst 88-; Bus Admin; Financl Anlyst.

**PETERS, JEFFREY S,** George Mason Univ, Fairfax, VA; JR; BS; Stdnt Laptop Cmptr Users Grp Pres; US Air Force Achvmnt Mdl 87,Commndtn Mdl 88; Fin Sys Analyst White Hs 88-; Decision Sci; Mngmnt Info Sys/Exprt Sys.

**PETERS, JOAN M,** Coll Of New Rochelle, New Rochelle, NY; SR; BSN; Nwsltr 89; Sigma Theta Tau; Acadmc Hon 89-90; Hope Comm Prog 87-90; Mls On Whls 87-88; Tchr 70-77; BA 70; MS 75; Nrsng; Stf Nrs.

**PETERS, LISA K,** Fl International Univ, Miami, FL; JR; BA; Hotel Rsrvtns Mgr Summit Hotel Dallas 80-; Sheraton Riverhouse Omni Intl Miami Fl 90; AS Richland Jr Coll 83; Bus; Mgmt Info Sys.

**PETERS, MICHAEL S,** Daytona Beach Comm Coll, Daytona Beach, FL; JR; BSBA; Phi Theta Kappa 89-; Prsdnts Lst DBCC 89-; Earn MBA Rtrn Career Prdctn Oprtns Mgmt; AA 90; Mgmt; Prdctn Oprtns Mgmnt.

**PETERS, MICHAEL W,** Union Coll, Barbourville, KY; SR; BS; Phi Theta Kappa 88-90; E KY Essay Awd; Earl Wallace Excell Ed Awd 89; AA Sue Bennett Clg 90; Bio; Sec Ed.

**PETERS, MICHELE M,** Univ Of Scranton, Scranton, PA; SR; Psych Club 87-89; Soc Acctg Stdnt 88; Delta Mu Delta 90; Omega Beta Sigma 90; Bsn Schlr 88-89; BS; Acctg.**

**PETERS, MICHELLE K,** Mary Baldwin Coll, Staunton, VA; SO; BS; Stdnt Senate 90; Co-Chr Acad Affrs Cmmttee; Extracrrclr Cmmttee 90f; Alpha Lambda Delta Sec/Treas 90; Pres Sco 90; Frnch/Ed; Tchr.

**PETERS, NICOLE M,** Niagara Univ, Niagara Univ, NY; JR; BA; Accntng Soc 89-; Ntnl Assn Accntnts 89-; Delta Epsilon Sigma; Vlntr Incm Tax Asstnc Prgrm 89-; Awd 90; Accntng; CPA.

**PETERS, RENEE M,** Univ Of Md At Eastern Shore, Princess Anne, MD; JR; BA; Pom Pom Sqd 90-; Alpha Phi Alpha 89-; Cndy Strpr Martin Army Hsptl 87-88; Intrnshp Greenebaum & Rose Assctes Leasing & Real Est; Bus Adminstrtn; Real Estate.

**PETERS, ROBERT T,** Cornell Univ Statutory College, Ithaca, NY; SO; BS; Tae Kwon Do Clb 90-; Cooprtv Eng Prog G E Crprte Rsrch/Dev Bio Sci Lab; Lghtwght Crw Tm 89-90; Bio Eng; Rsrch/Eng.

**PETERS, ROBIN M,** Hudson Valley Comm Coll, Troy, NY; SO; BA; Pres Lst; Prud Bache Sec 86-90; Mktg; Busn Mgmt.

**PETERS, SCOTT D,** William Paterson Coll, Wayne, NJ; SR; BA; WRRC-FM Rider Clg Gnrl Mgr 86-89; Army ROTC 86-88; Avion Newspapr Staff Wrtr 85-86; Phi Alpha Theta; Hillel Rider Clg Exec Brd 87-88; Deans Lst 86-90; Hstry; Rsrch Or Tchng On Clg Lvl.

**PETERS, SHERRIE L,** Univ Of Montevallo, Montevallo, AL; FR; Stdnt Advsry Cncl Freshmen Repr 90-; Alpha Lambda Delta 90-.

**PETERSEN, ANDREW J,** Nova Univ, Ft Lauderdale, FL; GD; MBA; Thtr Clb 87-; Phltns Accmpnst 83-85; Trp Cmmtt By Scts Amrc Cmmtt Chrmn 89-91; Tchncl Comm Sftwr Eng 90-; Stfwr Eng 81; BS 81; Bus Admn.

**PETERSEN, ANNE M,** Christopher Newport Coll, Newport News, VA; GD; CERT; Stdnt VA Educ Assn 90-; BA Blgcl Sci Univ Nrthn CO 88; Tchng.

**PETERSEN, CHRISTY L,** William Paterson Coll, Wayne, NJ; JR; BA; Specl Educ Club 90-; Catholic Campus Ministry; Specl Ed CCD Tchr 90-; Assumption Grammar Schl Girls Vrsty Hd Coach 90-; Pi Lambda Theta 90-; Kappa Delta Pi 90-; CYO Bkstbl Coach 90-; CCD Tchr Specl Educ 90-; Deans Lst 89-; Spec Educ; Teacher.

**PETERSEN, JAN C,** Georgetown Univ, Washington, DC; SR; BSBA; Mktg Soc Pr 89-; Busn Schl Asst 88-90; Tutr 87-88; Im Golf; Socr; Sftbl 87-; Mktg; Busn.

**PETERSEN, KATHY J,** Michael J Owens Tech Coll, Toledo, OH; FR; AD; Deans Lst 90-; Bus; Admin Sec.

**PETERSEN, KRISTIN K,** Bapt Bible Coll & Seminary, Clarks Summit, PA; SO; AA; Sec Intrst Fllwshp Pres 89-; SG 90-; Hll Jdcl Brd 90-; Mrt Lst 89; Deans Lst 90-; Trng Music Grp 89-; Chrldng 89-; Scrtrl.

**PETERSEN, RUTH A,** Univ Of Nc At Greensboro, Greensboro, NC; SR; BM; Clgt Msc Edctrs Natl Conf Dir 87-; Cncrt Bnd 87-; Trmbn Ens 87-; Gldn Chn; Alpha Lambda Delta 88-; Unv Mrshl 89-; Mu Phi Epsln Pres 88-; P Dlgs Tchr Schlp 88-; Msc Educ; Tchr.

**PETERSEN, THOMAS J,** Univ Of Ky, Lexington, KY; JR; B; Ky Assn Of Stdnts Of Phrmcy 90-; Chem Clb 87-88; The Fun Clb 87-; Bsl Cole Bio Awrd; Alpha Epsilon Delta 87-88; Beta Beta Beta 87-88; Dns Lst 87-; Sigma Alpha Epsilon; Fellwshp Emory Univ Dept Of Biochem 88-89; Glen Dooley Chem Awrd 87-88; BS Ky U 88; Pharmacy.

**PETERSON, ANGELIQUE D,** Georgian Court Coll, Lakewood, NJ; JR; BA; G C C Sdnt Chptr Math Assn Amer Pres 90-; Pi Mu Epsilon 90-; Paul Douglas Schlr 89-; Jr Wmns Clb Freehold Pres 87-89; Manalapan Rec Chrldng Coach 87-89; Manalapan L L Sftbl Bd Dir Comm 89-; Sr Stephanie Sloyan Math Awd 89; Math/Educ; Tchng.

**PETERSON, BECKY L,** Goldey Beacom Coll, Wilmington, DE; FR; Natl Assoc Asstnts 90-.

**PETERSON, CHARLES L,** Univ Of North Fl, Jacksonville, FL; JR; BA; AA Gulf Coast Comm Coll Panama City Fla 76; Trans/Lgstcs.

**PETERSON, CHRISTOPHER JOHN,** Richard Bland Coll, Petersburg, VA; SO; BA; Spnsh Clb 89-; Soccer Clb 89-; Phi Theta Kappa; Bus Adm; Accntnt.

**PETERSON, CHRISTOPHER M,** Univ Of Ga, Athens, GA; GD; BS; APLA Gpla 90-; AED Pre Mdcl Hnr Scty; Kappa Psi Corres Sec 90-; Phrmcy Intern 90-; Chmstry Lab Asst 89-90; Chmstry Ttr 89-90; IM Sprts 88-; BA 90; Med.

**PETERSON, DANIELLE K,** Univ Of Cincinnati, Cincinnati, OH; SO; BA; Alpha Beta Chi; Assn Fitness Bus; ETA Sigma Gamma Mbr 90-; Dns Lst 90-; Awd Ath Schlrshp 89-; Co-Capt Univ Cin Vlybl; Univ Cinc Intrcoll Vlybl 89-; Cardiovascular Ftns; Ftns Coord/Rehab.

**PETERSON, DEAN T,** Brevard Coll, Brevard, NC; JR; BA; COA Mbr; Phi Theta Kappa; Magna Cum Laude Grdtd; AA; Engl; Law.

**PETERSON, GARY D,** Belmont Coll, Nashville, TN; BA; Psychology.

**PETERSON, GERALD P,** Fayetteville St Univ, Fayetteville, NC; SR; Stdnt Acctng Assc 88-90; Natl Stdnt Bus Lge Treas 89-90; Deans Lst 86-90; New Bethel Afrcn Meth Epscpl Zion Chrch Usher Bd 86-90; Acdmc Schlrshp 86-90; Dist Svc Awd Intern Small Bus/Tech Dvlpmnt Ctr 90; BS 90; Bus Adm.

**PETERSON, GERARDINE T,** De Tech & Comm Coll At Dover, Dover, DE; SO; AAS; Gen Mgr/Jos R Peterson Co Inc; Aerntcl Sci.

**PETERSON, JANNA K,** Coll Of Charleston, Charleston, SC; JR; BA; Choir 88-; Madrigal Singers 88-; Intern Ashley Hall Girls Sch; Music; Masters Music Edn.

**PETERSON, JOHN GREGORY,** Embry Riddle Aeronautical Univ, Daytona Beach, FL; SO; BA; Fld Rep Pwrhse Fclty 86-90; Aerntcl Sci; Airline Plt.

**PETERSON, JULIE L,** Longwood Coll, Farmville, VA; FR; Modern Lang/Spnsh; Govt Intprtr.

**PETERSON, KATHY L,** Salisbury St Univ, Salisbury, MD; SO; BA; Newman Catholic Club Pres 89-91; Perdue Schlrs Assoc Rep 89-; Phi Eta Sigma 90-; Deans List 89-; Firefighter Level Vlntr Fire Co 89-; Handicapped Facilities; Perdue Bus Schlrshp 89-; Purchasing Mgmnt Assoc Awd; Hnrs Prog Awd 89-; IM Sports; Business Admin Leisure Studies.

**PETERSON, KEITH A,** Univ Of Nc At Charlotte, Charlotte, NC; SO; BA; Music.

**PETERSON, KEITH ROLAND,** Kent St Univ Kent Cmps, Kent, OH; SR; BA; Parks Karate Clg Ravenna Instrctr 83-; Golden Key; IM Tae Kwon Do Clb Mgr/Instrctr 87-; Anthrplgy/Archlgy; Prfssr.

**PETERSON, KEVIN D,** Univ Of Louisville, Louisville, KY; FR; MCHE; Phi Kappa Tau Fnd Rsng Chrmn Assoc Clss; Comm Serv Proj Affiliated Soc Fraternity; IM Sprts Bsktbl/Tck/Free Thrw Shootout; Chem Eng.

**PETERSON, KEVIN M,** Atlantic Comm Coll, Mays Landing, NJ; SO; BA; Minority Student Un Pres 90-; Stdnt Govt Assoc MSU Rep 89-90; Phi Theta Kappa 90-; Pleasantvl Police Athletic League Dir 90-; Kudos Scl Clb Advsr 88-; Pleasantville Police Dept Offcr 87-; AS; Criminal Justice; Police Admin.

**PETERSON, KEVIN W,** Va St Univ, Petersburg, VA; FR; BA; Bsbl; Elctrncs; Engnrng.

**PETERSON, LINDA ANN,** Vance Granville Comm Coll, Henderson, NC; SO; ADN; Phi Theta Kappa 90-; Kairos Fndtn Lcnsd Mntr; Oncolgy Intrnshp; Vlybl 90; Pres Merit Schlrshp 90-; NC Fndtn Nrsng Schlrshp 90-; Hstiocytsis Assn Amer 87-; Oncolgy; Nrsng.

**PETERSON, MICHELLE N,** City Univ Of Ny La Guard Coll, Long Island Cty, NY; AAS; Rcgntn Clg Brd Schlp Serv; Bkkpr Chld Care Agcy 89-; Acctng.

**PETERSON, ROBERT M,** Central St Univ, Wilberforce, OH; JR; BA; VP Dorm Cncl 88; Water Res Mgmt; Urbn Plng.

**PETERSON, SCOTT J,** Fl International Univ, Miami, FL; JR; BSCE; AA Broward Comm Coll 84; AS Comm Coll Air Force 88; Eng.

**PETERSON, SCOTT J,** S U N Y Coll Of Tech At Delhi, Delhi, NY; FR; AOS; Hlth Squad 90-; Dns Lst 90-; Carpentry.

**PETERSON, SHANDRIKA O,** Barry Univ, Miami, FL; SR; BA; Intl Stdnt Org 89-; Dance Tm Cptn 89-; Entmnt Bsktbl Season 89-; Math; Law.

**PETERSON, STEPHEN G,** Univ Of Nc At Charlotte, Charlotte, NC; JR; BA; Krte Clb Pres 90-; Hlshsr Hll Cncl 89; Phi Eta Sigma 89; Gldn Ky; Otstndng Coll Stdnts Of Amer 89; Psych; Rl Est.

**PETERSON, TREVOR P,** Univ Of Tn At Knoxville, Knoxville, TN; FR; BA; Carrick Hall Res Assoc 90-; Alpha Lambda Delta; Phi Eta Sigma; Fin; Invstmnt Banking.

**PETIT, BARBARA E,** Univ Of Cincinnati-Clrmnt Coll, Batavia, OH; SO; BA; Ed Engl; Elem Tchr.

**PETITO, PATRICIA A,** Saint Johns Univ, Jamaica, NY; SR; BED; CAUSE 88-; Spch Clb 89-; Grad Schlrshp; Gold Mdl Spec Ed; Deans Awd; Educ/N-6/Spec Ed; Tchng.

**PETKA, JAMES C,** Wilmington Coll, New Castle, DE; JR; BS; Bsn Mgmt; Sales Rep Mgmt.

**PETKANAS, JOHN D,** Ny Univ, New York, NY; GD; DDS; Emerg Rm Orderly Astoria Genl Hosp Aide 85-89; Kastorian Yth Cultural Soc Bd Dir; Dntl Materials Rsrch 88-; Trustee Schlr 84-87; Deans Lst 88-89; Xi Psi Phi 88-90; BA 88; Bio; Dntstry.**

**PETNICK, KELLY L,** Atlantic Comm Coll, Mays Landing, NJ; FR; Certif Natl Rest Assoc; Certif Amer Hotel/Motel Assoc 90; Hosptlty Mgmt; Hotel/Rest Mgmt.

**PETOFF, SCOTT D,** Univ Of Rochester, Rochester, NY; SO; BA; Stdnt Assn; Wlsn Cmmns Prog Brd Chrprsn 89-; Intr Clss Lvng Cntr Hll Mmbr 90-; Dns Lst; Stdnt Lfe Awrd; Psych; Advrtsng.

**PETRACCO, LAWRENCE,** Bloomfield Coll, Bloomfield, NJ; FR; Carpenter; Pre-Chiro; Chiropractor.

**PETRACCORO, MARIA T,** Manhattanville Coll, Purchase, NY; SR; BA; Econs/Mgmt Clb 90-; Oxford Un Soc 89; Stdy Abroad Oxfrd Venice 89-90; Dns Lst 89-; Lacrsse Clb 88; BA; Econs; Fin.

**PETRAK, TERI A,** Bapt Bible Coll & Seminary, Clarks Summit, PA; SR; BA; Clss Offcr ASC Rep 89-90; Assc Stdnt Cncl 89-90; Dns Lst 87-88; Mert Lst 88-90; Alpha Gamma Epsilon 89-; Concrt Chr 87-; Gospl Muscl Tm 88-90; Res Asst Dorm 89-90; Elem Educ; Tchg.

**PETRAZZI, ANTOINETTE R,** Duquesne Univ, Pittsburgh, PA; GD; MA; St Vincent Psychlgy Clb Co Pres 86-87; Grad Cum Laude St Vincent Coll 87; Asst W/Spec Olympics 86-; Rcvd St Vincent Ldrshp Schlrshp 83-87; Grad 1st Co Ed Grad Cls Of St Vincent Coll 87; Powder Puff Ftbl 85-87; Psychlgy; Pursue Ph D.

**PETREE, DEBBIE H,** Roane St Comm Coll, Harriman, TN; SO; AAS; Active Little League Ftbl Prog Wrkng 5-8 Yr Old Chrldrs Hd Chch 87-; Tchng Office Skills; Bus Admin/Acctg; Bus Mgmt/Industry.

**PETRETSCHEK-SHELTON, ROSWITHA M,** Va Commonwealth Univ, Richmond, VA; SR; BA; J Sargent Reynolds Stdnt Govt Assoc Actng Pres 86-87; SACS Sdty Cmmtt Mem 87-88; VCU Hnrs Prgm 89; Gldn Key; Alpha Gamma Omicron Pres 89-90; Ttr 87-89; Rep 90; Yng Vrgns Sctn Rchmnd Nws Ldr Nws Ldr Cmps Corres 88; Prsdntl Schlrshp Awrd 89; Jrnlsm; Nws Ed.

**PETREYCIK, JANE M,** Mount Saint Mary Coll, Newburgh, NY; SR; BA; Schl Nwspr Entrtnmnt Edtr 89-; Theatre Grp 87-; Alpha Chi 89-; Dns Lst 87-; Aquinas Schlr; Comm Media; Tlvsn/Film.

**PETRI, KIMBERLY L,** Allegheny Coll, Meadville, PA; JR; BS; Alden Schlr 88-90; Math.

**PETRICK, PAUL J,** Kent St Univ Kent Cmps, Kent, OH; FR; BA; Bowling 90-; Fnce; Invstmnt Bkg.

**PETRILLI, NICOLINA,** Comm Coll Algny Co Algny Cmps, Pittsburgh, PA; FR; RN; Nrsng.

**PETRILLO, ELLEN M,** Saint Johns Univ, Jamaica, NY; FR; BA; Comptr Psy Ntwrkng; Psychlgy; Law.

**PETRILLO, ROSE D,** Indiana Univ Of Pa, Indiana, PA; JR; BSED; House Of Yahweh F G Church Bible Tchr 80-; Engl Educ.

**PETRIN, JAMIE S,** Fl St Univ, Tallahassee, FL; SR; BS; Blrm Dnc Clb; Intrnshp Tallahassee Chmbr Commrc 90; Tchng Asst Cmnctn Clsses 90-; Bus Cmnctn; Hmn Rsrcs.

**PETRIN, MAURICE M,** Bryant Stratton Bus Inst Roch, Rochester, NY; AOS; Elec Tech Clb Pres 90-; Elec Tech.

**PETRIN, MICHELE M,** Bryant Stratton Bus Inst Roch, Rochester, NY; FR; AOS; Medcl Club Treas 90-; Amercn Assn Of Medcl Assts 90-; R T French Co 73-75; Neisner Bros Dept Store Ofc 75-77; Lincoln 1st Bnk Inc Comptr Ctr 77-82; Trvl Agnt 82-90; Medcl Asstng.

**PETRIN, SUSAN M,** Newbury Coll, Brookline, MA; SR; ASSOC; MADD 89-; Bostons Rock Agnst Drgs 90-; Para Legal Assn; Paralegal; Law.

**PETRINI, MARCIA E,** Univ Of Rochester, Rochester, NY; SO; BS; Campus YMCA Pgm Coord 90-; Nrsng.

**PETRO, ANTHONY M,** S U N Y At Buffalo, Buffalo, NY; SO; BS MA; Wnd Ensmble 89; Cgntve Sci Clb; Phi Eta Sigma 90; Eta Kappa Nu; Kodak Schlr 90-; UB Cntr Fr Cgntve Sci Fllwshp; UB Pres Hnrs Schlr 89-; Elec Eng Phlsphy; Cgntve Sci Comp Rsrch.

**PETRONIO, TRACY L,** Le Moyne Coll, Syracuse, NY; SO; BA; Acctg Scty 90-; Hll Rep 90-; Deans Lst 90-; Arbcs Instrctr 90-; Acctg.

**PETROSKY, BRENDA A,** Pa St Univ Beaver Cmps, Monaca, PA; FR; BA; Psychlgy; Psychlgst.

**PETROSKY, WILLIAM T,** Ga Inst Of Tech At Atlanta, Atlanta, GA; SO; BSEE; IEEE Tres 90-; Swim Clb 90; Schlumberger Co-Op Org Pres; Phi Eta Sigma 90; Phi Kappa Theta; Co-Op Schlumberger Ind 90-; Elec Engineering.**

**PETROU, TREVOR S,** Slippery Rock Univ, Slippery Rock, PA; SO; BA; Army Natl Guard 89-; Track/Field 90; Physical Educ; Physical Therapy.

**PETROVIC, MARC T,** Cleveland Inst Of Art, Cleveland, OH; SR; First Agnes Gund Mem Schlrshp; BFA; Art Glass.

**PETROVIC, STANKO,** Edinboro Univ Of Pa, Edinboro, PA; SO; BA; Intl Stu Assn 89-; Frshmn Hnrs Soc 90-; Ecnmcs; Grad Schl.

**PETROVSKY, JULIE A,** Indiana Univ Of Pa, Indiana, PA; SO; BA; Elem Educ; Tchr.

**PETROZZA, CARMELA,** Bloomfield Coll, Bloomfield, NJ; FR; Acctng; CPA; Law.

**PETRUCCI, LOUIS C,** Univ Of New Haven, West Haven, CT; SR; BS; Stdnt Govt 88-; Alpha Lambda Delta 88-; Delta Chi Pres 90-; Man Of Yr Campus Ldrshp 89-90; Music/Sound Rcrdng.

**PETRUSH, CHRISTINE E,** Kent St Univ Kent Cmps, Kent, OH; JR; BFA; Interior Design.

**PETRUSKY, JOLENE A,** Duquesne Univ, Pittsburgh, PA; FR; BA; Pittsburgh Yth Symph 90-; MENC 90-; Dir Cir; Mu Phi Epsilon; Pres Schlrshp 90-; Music Schlrshp 90-; Music Educ.

**PETRUSKY, JOSEPH J,** Comm Coll Algny Co Algny Cmps, Pittsburgh, PA; JR; BA; Bus Fin; Crprt Fin.

**PETRUZZI JR, PETER T,** Birmingham Southern Coll, Birmingham, AL; SO; BA; Soccer Clb 89-90; Alpha Epsilon Delta 90-; Alpha Lambda Delta 90-; Kappa Mu Epsilon 90-; Phi Eta Sigma 90-; Sigma Nu Treas 90-; Habitat Humanity; Urban Mnstrs Tutor 89-; Soph Pre-Med Intern; Math; Med.

**PETRY, FREDERICK Z,** Univ Of Pittsburgh At Bradford, Bradford, PA; FR; BA; Stdnt Gov Assoc VP; Judicl Brd 90-; RA; Alpha Lambda Delta Pres; Dns Lst 90-; Hstry/Pol Sci; Law.

**PETRY, NINA S,** Wv Northern Comm Coll, Wheeling, WV; SO; BA; Phi Theta Kappa 89-; Communicatins Studies Psychology.

**PETSCHONEK, CAROL E,** Univ Of North Fl, Jacksonville, FL; JR; BA; MO Reg Medcl Asstnt Assoc Treas 83-85; Advsry Comm Mdcl Ofc Asstnts 84-85; Stndt Mbr St Louis Comnty Clge Comm For Re Accredidation 86; Grad Amer Youth Fndtn Ldrshp Conf 78-80; AA St Louis Cmnty Clge 87; Spcl Ed; Teaching Lrng Disabled Stdnts.

**PETTELLA, ANGELA L,** Univ Of North Fl, Jacksonville, FL; SR; BA; Sierra Clb; Phi Kappa Phi; Cmnctns Intrnshp; AS FL Cmnty Clg 81; AA FL Cmnty Clg 88; Cmnctns.

**PETTESCH, JAMES F,** Seton Hall Univ, South Orange, NJ; SO; BS; Acctg.**

**PETTESCH, KAREN M,** Seton Hall Univ, South Orange, NJ; JR; BA; Engl.**

**PETTIE, CHARON A,** Ms Gulf Coast Comm Coll, Perkinston, MS; SO; BS; Rflctn Rcrtr; VP Lst; Sci; Med Nrs.

**PETTIFORD, DELORES HAWKINS,** Vance Granville Comm Coll, Henderson, NC; SO; A; Educ Clb; Payne Schlrshp; Intrnshp Dabney Schl.

**PETTIGREW, CARLA M,** Nc St Univ At Raleigh, Raleigh, NC; FR; BA; Schl Yrbk 90-; Chld Phych.

**PETTIGREW, DONNA L,** Memphis St Univ, Memphis, TN; SO; BA; Prdcr Hst 7SU Pblc Affrs Shw; Jrnlsm; TV Nws Prsnlty.

**PETTIGREW, JOHN R,** Fl International Univ, Miami, FL; FR; BS; Engnrng.

**PETTIGREW, TONYA E,** Ga Coll, Milledgeville, GA; FR; BS; NOVA Ldr; Hnrs Prog 90-; Blgy; Med.

**PETTINI, LORI A,** Wv Northern Comm Coll, Wheeling, WV; SO; BA; Human Serv; Scl Wrk Retarded Chldrn.

**PETTIS, AARON F,** D Youville Coll, Buffalo, NY; FR; Lambda Sigma; Bsktbl 90-.

**PETTIS, CHARISSE D,** Wilberforce Univ, Wilberforce, OH; JR; 4.00 Average 90-; AS Sinclair Comm Coll 89; Bus Mgmt.**

**PETTIS, JAN R,** Central St Univ, Wilberforce, OH; SR; BED; Alpha Kappa Mu; Delta Sigma Theta 70-; Yng Wmns Chrstn Coun 80-; OSEA 90-; Elem Educ.

**PETTIT, JEREMY M,** Ga Inst Of Tech At Atlanta, Atlanta, GA; FR; Civil Eng Co-Op; Civil Eng.

**PETTIT, MARK L,** Ga St Univ, Atlanta, GA; SO; BS; Therapeutic Recr.

**PETTIT, MICHELLE S,** Univ Of Miami, Coral Gables, FL; SR; BA; Sailing Club 87-88; Scuba Club 88-89; Earth Alert 90-; Golden Key 88-; Phi Kappa Phi; Wild Life Rhbltn Ctr Vol 90; Bowman Ashe B Schlrshp 87; IM Sports Vlybl/Sftbl 87-88; Marine Affairs; Envir Sci.

**PETTIT, PAULA K,** Ms St Univ, Miss State, MS; SO; BA; Gamma Beta Phi 90-; Phi Eta Sigma 90-; Peggy Howerton Schlp; Elem Ed; Tchr.

**PETTIWAY, TARINA S,** Fl A & M Univ, Tallahassee, FL; JR; BS; Comp Info Syst Clb VP 90-; Elctrl Cmmssn 89-; NAACP 89-; Urbn Leag 89-; Eastmn Kodal Schlr; Nght Excllnc Schlr 89; Intrnshp Eastman Kodak 90; Amoco; Miss CIS 89-90; Comp/Info Syst.

**PETTKO, THEODORE M,** Saint Vincents Coll & Seminary, Latrobe, PA; SO; BA; Cmpus Mntry; Orntatn 90; Cls Treas; NAA Treas; Vol Income Tax Asst VITA 90-; I M Bkbl Ftbl 89-90; Acctg; Law/Corp Tax.

**PETTRY, CYNTHIA J,** Univ Of Charleston, Charleston, WV; SR; BSN; Cptl Assoc Nrsg Stu 88-; Nrsg Cap/Pin Comm 89-; Nrsg Hnr Soc; Univ Schlrshp 87-; Deans Lst 88-; Nrsg.

**PETTUS, LUCINDA L,** Howard Univ, Washington, DC; JR; BA; Campus Crusade For Christ 88-; Res Hall Choir Pres 89-; Kappa Delta Pi; Big Bro Big Sis 90-; Sachs Foundation Schlrshp 88-; Trustee Schlrshp 90-; Elem Ed; Teaching.

**PETTUS, RICHARD C,** Manhattan Coll, Bronx, NY; SR; BSME; Amer Nuclear Soc 88-; Amer Soc Mech Engrs 88-; Garlic Soc 86-; Pi Tau Sigma 88-; Presidntl Schlrshp 86-; I M Bkbl Ftbl 86-; Mech Engr.

**PETTUS, RICHARD S,** Univ Of Sc At Columbia, Columbia, SC; FR; BA; Art; Graphc Dsgnr.

**PETTWAY, EARTHA M,** Stillman Coll, Tuscaloosa, AL; SR.

**PETTY, CHRISTY M,** Northern Ky Univ, Highland Hts, KY; FR; BA; Bsn; Mktg Anlyst.

**PETTY, MICHAEL D,** Old Dominion Univ, Norfolk, VA; SO; BS; Crrntly Attndng ODU Schlrshp Empl Vir Intl Ter Inc; Eng; Cvl Eng.

**PETTY, STEPHANIE R,** Univ Of Sc At Spartanburg, Spartanburg, SC; FR; BA; Elem Ed; Tchr.

**PETURSSON, GRACIELA,** City Univ Of Ny Grad School, New York, NY; GD; BA; Over 25 Clb 87-89; Stdnt Assn 88; Alumni Merit Schlrshp 89; Golden Key 90; Deans Hnr Lst 87-; Nrsng Stdnts Psychology Tutor 88-; Daytop Vlg Substance Abusing Teens 90-; Gracie Square Hosp Substance Abusers; Psychology; Soc Wrk.

**PEURA, JAMI B,** Strayer Coll, Washington, DC; GD; Alpha Chi 90-; A Nova 89; Acctg; CPA.

**PEYKO, MARC A,** Bloomfield Coll, Bloomfield, NJ; SR; BS; Sci Clb Treas 90-; Chmstry Dept Ttr 90-; Hcknsck Mdcl Cntr Vol 90-; Cmmtt Vol 90-; Chmcl Rbbr Co Frshmn Achvmnt Awrd 90; Bsbll 87-89; Blgy.

**PEYREBRUNE, JOHN C,** Le Moyne Coll, Syracuse, NY; JR; Proj Comm Vol 90-; H S Tutor Liberty Partnership Prog 90-; Varsity Bsktbl Ltrmn 88-90; Pol Sci.

**PEYTON, GERALD F,** Alcorn St Univ, Lorman, MS; SO; BA; Acctng; CPA.

**PEYTON, LISA M,** Hampton Univ, Hampton, VA; FR; BA; Edctnl Tlnt Srch; Tutor; Deans Lst 90; Cnslng/Edctnl Psychlgy.

**PEZAEZ, JULIO C,** City Univ Of Ny City Coll, New York, NY; SR; BFA; Paintng/Prnt Making; Fine Artist.

**PFAFF, LAWRENCE J,** Northern Ky Univ, Highland Hts, KY; SR; BS; Scty Mfg Eng Pres 90-; Advncd Elcntrncs Lab Asst 90-; Grvs Schlrshp 90-; Elctrnc Eng Tchnlgy.

**PFAHLER, ELIZABETH K,** Fl St Univ, Tallahassee, FL; SO; BS; Wsly Fndtn Fl St Univ Pro Cncl; Phi Eta Sigma 90; Bio; Vet Sci.

**PFALLER, MICHELLE L,** Christian Brothers Univ, Memphis, TN; SO; BA; Namaste Pres 90-; Pryr/Bible Stdy Grp; IM Sprts 89-; Hon Prog 89-; Stdnt Ambsdr; Peer Cnslr; Chrldr 89-; Elem Ed.

**PFALZGRAF, SALLY A,** Wv Northern Comm Coll, Wheeling, WV; FR; AAS; Acad Schlrshp; Emerg Med Tech Vol 89; EMT/A Bethal Graysville E/Sqad 89; Nrsg.

**PFANSTIEL, ROXANE K,** Northern Ky Univ, Highland Hts, KY; SR; Art Club 90; Dns Lst 90; Artist; Dsgnr/Seamstress 88-; Fine Arts/Thtr; Fshn/Cstme Dsgnr.

**PFEFERSTEIN, MICHAEL,** Columbia Union Coll, Takoma Park, MD; JR; BS; Natl Assn Real Estate Appraisers 90-; Fld Serv Mgr CPT Corp 83-87; Cert TESST Scl Of Elect 78-78; Bus Admin; Finance.

**PFEFFER, KRISTI L,** Savannah Coll Of Art & Design, Savannah, GA; JR; Jwlry Clb; Dns Lst; Grphc Dsgn Pntng; Dsgn Frm.

**PFEFFER, KRISTIN,** S U N Y Coll Of Tech At Frmgdl, Farmingdale, NY; SO; AAS; Dept Liberal Arts & Sciences 90-; Pres List 89-; Academic Excellence Awd; Liberal Arts; Psychology.

**PFEIFER-SKELLY, MARYANN,** Wv Univ At Parkersburg, Parkersburg, WV; JR; BS; Crmnl Justice Org Sec 88-; Deans List 90; Hons List 89-; Sr Ctzn Ctr Vol 88; Intrnshp Parkersburg Rgnl Jvnl Dtntn Ctr; Intrnshp Wood Cty Magistrate Ct; Church Orgnst; AAS WV Univ Parkersburg WV 90; Crmnl Justice Tchnlgy.

**PFEIFF, HEATHER M,** Radford Univ, Radford, VA; SO; BA; Sigma Sigma Sigma; Crmnl Jstc; Law.

**PFEIFFER, DAYNA L,** Westminster Coll, New Wilmingtn, PA; JR; BA; Orientation Stf 89; SWATW 90-; Greek Week Staff 89-; Kappa Delta 89-; VISA 88-; Admssns/Financial Aid Comm 90-; Sociology; Prsnl/Hmn Rsrcs Cnsltnt.

**PFEIFFER, FRITZ W,** Univ Of Rochester, Rochester, NY; SR; BA; NROTC 87-; Phi Beta Kappa; Top Grad; Stdnt Lf Awrd; Pol Sci; Lt USMC.

**PFEIFFER, SHANNON M,** East Stroudsburg Univ, E Stroudsburg, PA; JR; BS; Amrcn Qrtr Hrs Assoc 78-; Kystn Qrtr Hrs Assoc 88-; Blgy Scndry Ed; Prfssr.

**PFENDER, SHARON L,** Anderson Coll, Anderson, SC; FR; BFA; Art; Prfssr.

**PFENNINGER, ALICIA A,** Centenary Coll, Hackettstown, NJ; SR; Phi Beta Lambda 90; Peer Advisor 89; Alphi Chi 90; Alphi Sigma Lambda; AAA Raritan Vly Cmnty Clge 88; BS 90; AS 90.**

**PFENNINGER, TOBI A,** Univ Of Nh Plymouth St Coll, Plymouth, NH; SO; BS; Jzz Ensmbl 89-; Symph Bnd 89-; Scuba Clb 90-; Asst Tchr German 90-; Spnsh/Grmn Educ; Tchr.

**PFEUFER, ANGELA T,** Bloomfield Coll, Bloomfield, NJ; JR; BS; NJAS 90-; Alpha Chi; Pre-Chrprctc Sci; Chrprctr DC.

**PFISTER, FRANK C,** Schenectady County Comm Coll, Schenectady, NY; FR; BA; Culnary Arts; Head Chef.

**PFISTER, JAN M,** Coll Of Charleston, Charleston, SC; SO; BS; Alpha Epsilon Delta; Delta Delta Delta 89-; Deans Lst; Hon Lst; Biolgy; Med.

**PFISTER, JENNIFER L,** Radford Univ, Radford, VA; SO; BS; Res Asst 90-; Gaelic Asst/Ed 90-; Cath Stdnt Assn Flwshp Co-Chr 89-; IM Sccr; Mktg; Advrtsng/Pblc Rltns.

**PFISTERER, RACHEL L,** Villanova Univ, Villanova, PA; FR; Prgmmng Cncl 90; SADD 90-; Pi Delta Phi; Dean Lst 90-; Engl; Law.

**PFOUTS, DANA L,** Winthrop Coll, Rock Hill, SC; SR; MED; Cncl Excptnl Chldrn Scrpbk Chr 89-; Wffrd Hll Cncl 86-87; Prsdnts Lst 90-; Chi Omega Pldg Trnr 88-; Pptr 90; Stdnt Tchr 90-; BS; Elem Gdnc.

**PFUETZE, RACHAEL K,** Savannah Coll Of Art & Design, Savannah, GA; SR; BFA; Soc Illustrtrs 89-; Illustration; Art Educ/Med Illstrn.

**PFUND, JOLINDA K,** Defiance Coll, Defiance, OH; FR; MSW; Stdnt Social Wrk Assoc 90-; Defiance Clg Chamber Singers 90-; Stdnt Asstnt 90-; Library Asstnt 90-; Social Work.

**PFUNTER, JEANINE M,** Niagara Univ, Niagara Univ, NY; SO; BA; Kids Adjstg Through Sprt; Pltcl Sci/Nrsg; Pblc Plcy/Pblc Hlth.

**PHAM, CHINH N,** Catholic Univ Of America, Washington, DC; SR; BA; Schl Phlsphy Rep 90-; Phi Sigma Tau; Phlsphy.

**PHAM, DAO H,** Auburn Univ At Auburn, Auburn, AL; FR; Rnng/Tnns/Wght Lftng 90-; Alpha Lambda Delta 90-; Phi Eta Sigma 90-; Hnr Intl Std 90-; Dorm Desk Asst 90-; Tnns 90-; Chem Engr/Pre-Med; Med/Engr.

**PHAM, DAVID C,** Howard Univ, Washington, DC; SR; BS; Cls Pres 90-; Rho Chi; Pharm.

**PHAM, HANG T,** Temple Univ, Philadelphia, PA; SO; BS; Vietnamese Stdnt Assn Clb 89-; EESA 89-90; BCM Schlrshp 89-; Phrmcy.

**PHAM, KHANH T,** Bunker Hill Comm Coll, Boston, MA; English/Sec Lang ESL; Tech.

**PHAM, MAIHANH H,** Georgetown Univ, Washington, DC; SO; BA; Vietnamese Stdnts Assn VP 89-; D C Schl Proj 90-; Intrnshp Nike Intl; Finance/Intl Bus.

**PHAM, SON HOANG,** Bunker Hill Comm Coll, Boston, MA; SO; Electrncs Tech 87-89; Cmptr Pgmng; Dsgn Systm.

**PHAM, TOAN VAN,** Bunker Hill Comm Coll, Boston, MA; Hs Bldng; Archtctr; Engl.

**PHAN, ANH H,** Univ Of Sc At Columbia, Columbia, SC; JR; BS; Carolina Schlr Organ 88-; Alpha Laud Delta Soc 88-; Vietnamese Act Grp 88-; Pres Hnr Rl 89-90; Biology; Hlth Prof.**

**PHAN, KHANH THI HONG,** Univ Of Louisville, Louisville, KY; SR; BS; Soc Wmn Engrs; Inst Indstl Engrs; Vietnmse Stdnts Assoc Edtr Chf 86-87; Natl Wldlf Soc 89-; Amer Orchid Soc 90-; Natl Geogphc Soc 89-; Au-Co Sch Vol Tchr 86-87; Nrth Mkt Plnng Coaltn Comm Org 87; AS Fllrtn Clg 82-85; Indstl Engr; Engr.

**PHAN, LAN T,** Old Dominion Univ, Norfolk, VA; SR; BSEE; Vietnamese Assn 88-; Elec Engr.

**PHAN, PHUC T,** Davidson Coll, Davidson, NC; FR; BS; Cls Cncl 90-; IVCF 90-; Sigma Phi Epsilon 90-; City Govt Charlotte Intrnshp; IM Tennis/Vlybl/Indoor Soccer 90-; Math; Med.

**PHAN, QUANG T,** Univ Of Sc At Columbia, Columbia, SC; SO; BS; Deans Lst 89-90; Mech Eng.

**PHARES, DONA L,** Christopher Newport Coll, Newport News, VA; JR; BS; Advsry Brd Legl Stds; Dns Hnr Lst 90-; Intrnshp Riechie Berrane Law Frm; AA Olympic Clg 87-89; Govt; Law.

**PHARO, JENNIFER A,** Univ Of Cin R Walters Coll, Blue Ash, OH; FR; Dntl; Dntl Hygnst.

**PHARR, KELLY A,** Clayton St Coll, Morrow, GA; SO; BBA; AAS 90; Cmptr Infrmtn Systms; Cmptr Prgrmr/Systms Anl.

**PHARR, SARAH R,** Mercer Univ, Macon, GA; FR; Bptst Stdnt Un 90-; Nwsppr 90; Chi Omega Almn Rltns Chrprsn; Bus Law.

**PHELAN, CATHY M,** Glassboro St Coll, Glassboro, NJ; JR; BA; Chrldng 88-; Deans Lst 90; Phi Sigma Sigma 89-; Math; Actry.

**PHELAN, CHARLES,** Springfield Tech Comm Coll, Springfield, MA; SO; BA; Bsn/Acctg; CPA.

**PHELAN, KATHLEEN M,** Univ Of Md Baltimore Prof Schl, Baltimore, MD; JR; BS; Chrstn Phrmcsts Flwshp Intl 90-; Phi Beta Kappa 81; Sigma Phi 80; UW Schl Prhmcy Alumni Assn Schrshp 90-; Coll Park Coop Nrsry Schl Pres 86-87; Elem Schl/Comm Vol 81-89; BS Univ Maryland Coll Park 80; Phrmcst.

**PHELAN, MARY LEE,** Ms St Univ, Miss State, MS; SR; BBA; Alumni Assoc Advsry Cncl Secr; Pres Schlr; Gamma Beta Phi 90-; Fncl Mgmt Assoc V P 90-; FMA Carl Jones Schlrshp; US Army Res 1st Lt 85-; Signal Regmntl Assoc 89-; Rental Mgr/Cmptr Adm 87-89; BS 90; Finance; Law.

**PHELAN, TIMOTHY A,** Savannah Coll Of Art & Design, Savannah, GA; JR; MFA; Schlstc Art Awds Schlrshp; Phtgrphy; Fine Art Phtgrphy.

**PHELPS, GLORIA M,** Valdosta St Coll, Valdosta, GA; SO; Sigma Alpha Chi; Pres Fresh Schlr 90-; Psy.

**PHELPS, JAMES M,** Ms Gulf Coast Comm Coll, Perkinston, MS; FR; BS; Phi Theta Kappa; Med.

**PHELPS, JEFFRY D,** Castleton St Coll, Castleton, VT; FR; BA; Radio Brdcstng Advrtsng; Educ/Psyc; Spec Educ.

**PHELPS, JENNIFER L,** Baldwin Wallace Coll, Berea, OH; FR; BM; Opera Prod; Orch Wind Ensmbl 90-; Campus Crsde Christ 90-; Alpha Lambda 90-; Mu Phi Epsilon; Mus-Piano; Piano Prfrmnc Thrpy.

**PHELPS, JULIE L,** Univ Of Cincinnati, Cincinnati, OH; FR; BFA; Stdnt Govt Persnnl Comm 90-; Clg Cons Music Tribnl Mbr 90-; Brdcstng Soc 90-; Alpha Lambda Delta Sec 90-; Dns Lst 90-; Brdcstng; Socl Wrk.

**PHELPS, KATHY C,** Greenville Tech Coll, Greenville, SC; AS; Forest Acres Elem Sch PTA 84-; Grd Mthr 85 87 90; Vol Awd; Sec Recpt 81-; Ofc Sys Tech; Exec Sec.

**PHELPS, LINDA J,** Central Fl Comm Coll, Ocala, FL; FR; AASBA; Psi Beta; Phi Theta Kappa Treas; Crmnl Justice Deptmntl Schlrshp 90; Crmnl Justice; Field Work With Juveniles.

**PHELPS, LINDA R,** Valdosta St Coll, Valdosta, GA; SO; BED; Sigma Alpha Chi; Awarded Paul Douglas Tchrs Schlrshp; Mdl Chldhd Sci/Math; Tch.

**PHELPS, MICHELE J,** Western New England Coll, Springfield, MA; JR; BA; Alpha Lambda Delta 89-; Psi Chi; Psychlgy.

**PHELPS, PATRICK H,** Le Moyne Coll, Syracuse, NY; SO; MBA; Mdrn Lang Allnc Pres 90-; Spnsh; Intl Rltns.

**PHELPS, REGINA A,** Univ Of Sc At Columbia, Columbia, SC; FR; FCA; Schlrshp.

**PHELPS, REVA B,** Owensboro Comm Coll, Owensboro, KY; FR; AAS; Pres Awd Outstndg Acad Achvmnt 90-; Secr/Ofc Mgr; Acctg.

**PHELPS, ROSE V,** Fayetteville St Univ, Fayetteville, NC; JR; BS; Physcl Thrpst Asst Stdnt Actvbts Clb VP 85-87; NC Physcl Thrpy Assoc PTA Cmm Chr; AAS 87; Blgy.

**PHELPS, TONYA J,** Eastern Ky Univ, Richmond, KY; FR; BS; Early Elem Ed; Tchg.

**PHELPS, TRICIA R,** Christian Brothers Univ, Memphis, TN; SO; BA; IM Dir 90-; Bsktbl 89-; Schlr Athlete Awd 90-; Bus; Mktng Cnsltnt.

**PHELPS, WILLIAM D,** Schenectady County Comm Coll, Schenectady, NY; FR; Stdnt Gov Com; Deans Lst 90-; Wrk Walt Disney Wrld; Hotel Tech; Self Emp/Food Indstry.

**PHENES, DANIELLE R,** S U N Y Coll Of Tech At Alfred, Alfred, NY; FR; AA; Bnd 90-; Lib Arts Humanities; Art Thrpy.

**PHIFER, JAMES K,** Ms St Univ, Miss State, MS; SO; BS; Eng Clb 87-89; ACT Schlrshp 87; Acctg.

**PHIFER, REBECCA A,** Hampton Univ, Hampton, VA; SR; BA; Alpha Kappa Mu 88-; Kappa Tau Alpha 89-; Natl Assn Blck Jrnlsts 89-; Mass Media; Advrtsng Sls.

**PHILBIN, SANDRA L,** Asnuntuck Comm Coll, Enfield, CT; SO; Phi Theta Kappa 87-; NAFE; Sprvsr; Cert 87; Bsn; Cntrct Law/Fnce.

**PHILBRICK, FAUSTENA L,** Longwood Coll, Farmville, VA; SR; BS; Vars Bsktbl 88-; Phys Educ Mjrs Club V P 88-; IM Supv 89-90; USAA Acad All Amer; Delta Psi Kappa V P 89-; Pres 91-; US Natl Guard 88-89; Dns Lst 88/90; Intrshp Xerox; Athl Hnr Roll 88/89; Vars Bsktbl 88-; Phys Educ; Hlth/Exercise Sci.

**PHILEMON, DANNY R,** Central Fl Comm Coll, Ocala, FL; Intrntl Assc Firefghtrs Lcl 3362 80-91; Prfssnl Firefghtrs FL 80-90; Orange Pk Assc Firefghtrs 80-90; Clay Cnty Prfssnl Firefghtrs; Intrntl Assc Arson Invstgtrs 90; Ntl Fire Prtctn Assc; FL St Firemns Assc; Fire Sci.

**PHILEMONT, GUITHO GUS,** S U N Y Coll Of A & T Morrisvl, Morrisville, NY; SO; ASUBA 89-; Deans Lst; Human Serv Intrnshp; Bkbl Capt 89-.

**PHILIPPE, EMILY J,** Fayetteville St Univ, Fayetteville, NC; SO; BS; US Army 86-88; Med; Nrsng.

**PHILIPPE, SHEILA,** Univ Of Med & Dentistry Of Nj, Newark, NJ; SR; BS; West Indies Clb 86-89; Zeta Delta Pi Fndng Sister 86-89; Haitian Assoc 86-89; Zeta Delta Pi Fndng Sister 86-89; Med Tech.

**PHILIPPI, BRUCE M,** Univ Of Al At Birmingham, Birmingham, AL; SR; BS; IEEE 90; ACM 89-; Tau Beta Pi 90; Eta Kappa Nu; BS 89; Elec Eng.

**PHILIPPOU, PHILIPPOS C,** City Univ Of Ny Baruch Coll, New York, NY; SR; BA; Pncyprian Assoc Amer 86-; Acctg Soc 86-; Acctg.

**PHILIPS, BRIAN J,** Allegheny Coll, Meadville, PA; JR; BS; Alden Schlr 90-; Beta Beta Beta; Biology; Mdcl Schl MD.

**PHILIPS, MARGARET A,** Univ Of North Fl, Jacksonville, FL; FR; BA; Zeta Tau Alpha 90-; Fla Undergrad Schlrshp; Criminal Justice/Political Sci; Law.

**PHILLEY, CHRISTOPHER R,** Ms St Univ, Miss State, MS; JR; BPA; Schl Accntncy Prsdnt; Intrschl Cncl; Kappa Sigmma Ktchn Mngr 89-; Untd Way; Arthur Andersen Ldrshp Cnfrnc; Accntng.

**PHILLINGANE, DONNA G,** Va Commonwealth Univ, Richmond, VA; SR; CERT; Golden Key; NBEA Awd Merit; AS Richard Bland Clg 84; Bus Ed; Tch.

**PHILLIP, ETHEL Y,** Howard Univ, Washington, DC; GD; Hlth Prfssnl Clb Pblc Rel 89-90; Intrnshp/Awd D C Superior Ct Prbtn Offcr 87; Intrnshp Dept Commerce 89-; BS Columbia Union Clg 89; Scl Wrk.

**PHILLIPPE, KIMBERLY D,** Germanna Comm Coll, Locust Grove, VA; SO; ASSOC; Gen Studies; Sociology.

**PHILLIPPE, MELODYE D,** George Mason Univ, Fairfax, VA; JR; BS; Decsn Sci/Mis Clb VP 90-; Golden Key; STARS; Decision Sci/Mis Dept Intrnshp Prog 90-; Andersen Cnsultine Schlrshp; Decision Sci/MIS; Cnsulting.

**PHILLIPPI, AMY J,** Seton Hill Coll, Greensburg, PA; JR; BA; Interclrl Stdnt Org 90-; Dns Lst 88-90; Fmly Stds/Soc Wrk; Soc Wrkr.**

**PHILLIPPI, MELISSA A,** Faulkner St Jr Coll, Bay Minette, AL; SO; BA; Spec Ed; Tchr.

**PHILLIPS BROWN, BETH L,** Immaculata Coll, Immaculata, PA; SR; BA; Planning Cmte 90-; Stdnt Life/Devl 89; Immaculata 90-; Delta Epsilon Sigma; Kappa Gamma Pi; Lambda Iota Tau; NWAF Exch Schol 89-90; Bd/Ntnl Welsh-Am Foun; Poet/Resd Tyler Arboretum 89-; English.

**PHILLIPS JR, ALWYN A,** City Univ Of Ny Med Evers Coll, Brooklyn, NY; FR; AAS; Medgar Evers Yth Intrnshp Prog 88-89; Cmptr Splctns; Prgrmr.

**PHILLIPS, ANDREW B,** Univ Of Tn At Chattanooga, Chattanooga, TN; FR; BS; Jazz Bnd Pianist 90-; Phi Eta Sigma; Elctrcl Engr; Engr.

**PHILLIPS, ANTHONY S,** Univ Of Sc At Spartanburg, Spartanburg, SC; SO; BS; Pep Band 89-; Lambda Chi Alpha Eductn Ofcr 89-90; Sirrine Schlr 89-; Byrnes Schlr Founded By James F Byrnes 89-; Psychology; Law Enfrcmnt.

**PHILLIPS, ARTHUR B,** Talladega Coll, Talladega, AL; JR; BA; U S Army Resf Math Club; Alpha Chi; Beta Kappa Chi; Phys/Math; Engrg.

**PHILLIPS, BENJAMIN F,** Boston Univ, Boston, MA; FR; BS; Nwspr Clmnst 90-; Trustee Schlr 90-; Jrnlsm.

**PHILLIPS, BEVERLY C,** Bishop St Comm Coll, Mobile, AL; FR; Phi Thetta Kappa 90-; Nrsg.

**PHILLIPS, BONNIE P,** Univ Of Nc At Asheville, Asheville, NC; SR; BA; Stdnt Paper The Blue Bnr Sprts Edtr 90-; Sprts Intrn 90; Sprtswrtng Awd Blue Banner; AA Fla Comm Coll Jcksnvl 89; Mass Comm; Sprtscstng.

**PHILLIPS, BRENT W,** Clarkson Univ, Potsdam, NY; SR; BS; APICS 90; Sgm Gamma 87-89; AA Canton CTC 89; Mgmt; Bus.

**PHILLIPS, CARRI A,** California Univ Of Pa, California, PA; FR; AA; Bus Mgmt; Ofc Mgr.

**PHILLIPS, CELIA L,** Milligan Coll, Milligan Clg, TN; SO; Vlybl; Biology; Physical Therapy.

**PHILLIPS, CHANDRA L,** Duquesne Univ, Pittsburgh, PA; SO; Bsktbl 89-; Hmn Rsrc Mgmt/Intl Bsn.

**PHILLIPS, CHARLES H,** Livingston Univ, Livingston, AL; SO; Sci; Engr.

**PHILLIPS, CHRISTIE L,** Castleton St Coll, Castleton, VT; SO; BA; Math/Scndry Edn; Teach.

**PHILLIPS, CHRISTOPHER J,** Va Commonwealth Univ, Richmond, VA; SR; BS; Fnncl Mgmnt Assn; Extern Lawyers Title Ins Corp; Fnnc; Fnncl Mgmnt.

**PHILLIPS, CONNIE F,** Roane St Comm Coll, Harriman, TN; SO; AAS; Amer Med Rec Asc; Med Rec Tech.

**PHILLIPS, CONSTANCE M,** Univ Of Nc At Chapel Hill, Chapel Hill, NC; FR; BA; Hnrs Stdnt Assc 89-90; Chorales 89-90; Physical Therapy Intern 89-; Psychology; Occptnl Therapy.**

**PHILLIPS JR, DAVID E,** Univ Of Southern Ms, Hattiesburg, MS; SO; Polymer Sci Clb 89-; Dns Lst 89-; Polymr Sci; Res/Dev.

**PHILLIPS, DAVID J,** S U N Y At Buffalo, Buffalo, NY; JR; BS; Deans Lst 89; AAS 90; Mgt; Acctg.

**PHILLIPS, DEBRA L,** George Mason Univ, Fairfax, VA; SR; BS; Rcqtbl Clb 87-88; Gamma Phi Beta Hstrn 90; Intrnshp At Alxndra Hosp; Hlth; Physcl Thrpy.

**PHILLIPS, DENISE C,** Pa St Univ Delaware Cty Cmps, Media, PA; FR; BA; Elem Educ; Elem Ed Tchr.

**PHILLIPS, DION A,** Saint Thomas Univ, Miami, FL; JR; BA; S FL Netball Assc VP 90; Dsunshine Royals Netball Clb Pres 89-90; Pol Sci/Engl; Law.

**PHILLIPS, DONNA S,** Univ Of Al At Birmingham, Birmingham, AL; JR; BS; Phi Theta Kappa 88-; Cmtlgst 80-85; Accnts Rcvbl Clrk 85-87; AS Shelton St Comm Col; Rdlgc Sci; Rdtn Thrpst.

**PHILLIPS, DORA ELIZABETH,** Ms St Univ, Miss State, MS; JR; BED; Gamma Beta Phi; Pres Schlr; BPA Univ MI; Foreign Lang; Tchng H Schl/Clg.

**PHILLIPS, DOUGLAS A,** Central St Univ, Wilberforce, OH; JR; ASMT/OSMT 88-; MLT Apollo Clg Tucson AZ 89; Nursing; Dr.

**PHILLIPS, E NADINE,** Univ Of Southern Ms, Hattiesburg, MS; SO; BS; Sociology; Peace Corp.

**PHILLIPS, HEATHER L,** Beckley Coll, Beckley, WV; FR; Prlgl Stds.

**PHILLIPS, HOLLIS,** Univ Of Rochester, Rochester, NY; SR; SFIC Pres; Akido Clb Bsn Mngr 90.

**PHILLIPS, JACQUELYN Y,** Averett Coll, Danville, VA; SR; BS; Math; Clge Prfsr.

**PHILLIPS JR, JAMES G,** Bunker Hill Comm Coll, Boston, MA; SO; AD; Negro Psych Tech Sch Valedctrn; Cmndg Ofcrs Merit Awd Schlstc Excell 80; High Hnrs Hosp Corpsman Sch 79; In-Patient Psych Unit USN Vet Cnslr; Nrsg; Psych Clncl Nrs Speclst MSN.

**PHILLIPS, JASON L,** Central St Univ, Wilberforce, OH; FR; BA; De Jallu Mdlng Clb Rep 90-; Univ Dns Lst 90-; Cmmtr Schlrshp 90-; Cntrl St Univ; IM Bsktbl Co Capt 90-; Bio/Chem; Eng/Bio Res.

**PHILLIPS, JENNIFER R,** Columbus Coll Of Art & Design, Columbus, OH; JR; BFA; Illustratn; Illustrte Chldrns Books.

**PHILLIPS, JIMMY SCOTT,** Ms Univ For Women, Columbus, MS; JR; BS; Natl Assn Acctnts; Acctg Honrary; Bus Week; Mgmt Info Syst Mgr; Acctg; Finance.

**PHILLIPS III, JOHN H,** Univ Of Nc At Charlotte, Charlotte, NC; FR; BA; Hnrs Clg; Tchng Fllws Schlrshp; Math; Teaching.

**PHILLIPS, JULIA C,** Ky St Univ, Frankfort, KY; SO; BS; Pre Hlth Clb 89-; Acdmc Achvmnt; Jr Mrshl Grad Crmny; Biol; Med.

**PHILLIPS, JULIE A,** Valdosta St Coll, Valdosta, GA; SR; BA; YABA V P 78-90; Affil APA; Alpha Lambda Delta 89-; Sigma Alpha Chi 90-; Pi Gamma Mu; Alpha Chi; PYOC V P 82-90; Frshmn Schlr 89-90; Psych/Mdl Chldhd Ed; Elem Sch Cnslr.

**PHILLIPS, KAREN L,** Georgetown Univ, Washington, DC; SR; BSBA; Cmpus Nwsppr Bus Mgt 89-90; Georgetown Univ Invstmnt Alliance Sec 89-90; Mktg Socty 87-; Stdnt Assst Georgetown Bus Schl 89-90; Alpha Mu Alpha; Intrnd Sev Pol Cand 87-88; Intrnd Earle Palmer Brown Advrtsng Agency Bethesda MD; Doubla Mjr Mktg/Intl Mgmt; Retail Exec Buyer.

**PHILLIPS, KAREN R,** Oh St Univ At Newark, Newark, OH; JR; Grl Sct Trpldr Vol; Elem Ed/Sci; Tchr.

**PHILLIPS, KAREN S,** Davis & Elkins Coll, Elkins, WV; JR; BS; Phi Beta Lambda 90-; Beta Alpha Beta; Jennings Randolph Ldrs Pgm; Dns Lst 88-; Mgmt/Acctg AA.

**PHILLIPS, KARYN A,** Wilberforce Univ, Wilberforce, OH; FR; BA; Bus Mgmt.

**PHILLIPS, KELLY D,** Univ Of Ga, Athens, GA; SR; Math Ed Stdnt Assn; Natl Cncl Tchrs Of Math; GA Cncl Tchrs Of Math; Goldn Key; Kappa Delta Pi; Grad Cum Laude; BSED 91; Math Ed.**

**PHILLIPS, KEVIN A,** Morehouse Coll, Atlanta, GA; JR; BA; Morehouse Bus Assn 88-; Spnsh Clb 88-; Hon Roll Stdnt 88-; Deans Lst 89-; Ftbl/Bsebl Tm 88-; Bus Finance; Fncl Cons/Profl Ftbl Plyr.

**PHILLIPS, KRISTEN,** Univ Of Southern Ms, Hattiesburg, MS; SO; Alumni Assn VP 90-; Lambda Sigma; Chi Omega Sec 89-; Grk Lf Bk Edtr; IM Bwlng Sftbl; Lbrl Arts.

**PHILLIPS, LAURIE K,** Defiance Coll, Defiance, OH; SR; BS; Gamma Omega Kappa Sorority Prlmntrn 89-90; Acctg/Finance Clb 88-; Mrktng Clb Sec 88-90; Tau Pi Phi 90-; Sun Mgt Serv Co-Op 90-; Acctg/Mgt; Acctg/Audtng.

**PHILLIPS, LEE ANN,** Indiana Univ Of Pa, Indiana, PA; SR; BED; Std Adv Cncl; PSEA; Kappa Delta Pi 89-90; Alpha Gamma Delta Schlp 89-; Prvst Schlr 89-; Elem Ed; Tch Elem Stds.

**PHILLIPS, LESLIE MEREDITH,** Ny Univ, New York, NY; SR; BA; Mgzn Mngng Ed 88-91; Deans Lst 87-90; Schl Cntng Ed Schlr; Alpha Lambda Sigma; SCE Dgr Stds Stdnt Cncl 87-; Engl.

**PHILLIPS, LINDA L,** Chattanooga St Tech Comm Coll, Chattanooga, TN; GD; AAS; Sighn Chr 2nd Time Around Clg Bound 89-; Phi Theta Kapa 90-; Psi Beta; Track/Trail Support Agency; Ntl Assoc Deaf CCTRID 90-.

**PHILLIPS, MARGARET C,** Erie Comm Coll, Buffalo, NY; FR; AAS; Para Legal Clb; Para Legal; Law.

**PHILLIPS, MARGARET J,** Central St Univ, Wilberforce, OH; SR; BS; Wild Hrs/Burro Adptn Pgm Intrnshp 90; Fin Mgmt.

**PHILLIPS, MARGIE D,** Troy St Univ At Dothan, Dothan, AL; SR; BS; Elmntry Ed; Edctn.

**PHILLIPS, MARY L,** Univ Of Tn At Martin, Martin, TN; JR; PH D; Undergrad Alumni Cncl Sec Treas 89-; Phi Eta Sigma; Order Omega; Amer Chem Soc 90-; Alpha Omicron Pi Pres 90-; Univ Serv Awd; Pre Pharm; Pharm Sch.

**PHILLIPS, MATTHEW J,** Castleton St Coll, Castleton, VT; SO; BS; Schlrs Nwspr 90-; IM 89-; Commtns; Journalism.

**PHILLIPS, MICHELLE D,** Va St Univ, Petersburg, VA; FR; BA; Big Bros/Big Sis; Mltcltrl Affairs Cncl; Hnrs Clg; Bus Admin; Bus Owner.

**PHILLIPS, NICKIE D,** Volunteer St Comm Coll, Gallatin, TN; SO; BS; Hon Rl; Deans Lst; Crmnl Juste.

**PHILLIPS, PAMELA R,** Methodist Coll, Fayetteville, NC; JR; BA; Stf Wrtr Nwspr; Gamma Beta Phi 88-89; Sigma Sigma Sigma Pnhlnc 88-90; Comm/Mass Media.

**PHILLIPS, PHYLLIS H,** Central Al Comm Coll, Alexander City, AL; SO; BS; Phi Theta Kappa 90-; Elem Edn; Teach.

**PHILLIPS, RACHEL L,** Va Commonwealth Univ, Richmond, VA; JR; BFA; Trnsdentl Mdttn Clb 90-; Phi Kappa Phi 90-; Hnrs Prog 89-; Music Schlrshp 87-; Phi Kappa Phi Schl Arts Schlrshp 90; Sclptr; MFA.

**PHILLIPS, REBECCA D,** Middle Tn St Univ, Murfreesboro, TN; SR; BS; SHES 89-; Smth Mmrl Schlrshp 90-; Edctn Awrd; Erly Chldhd Ed.

**PHILLIPS, REBECCA K,** Ky Christian Coll, Grayson, KY; SO; BS; Womens Bsktbl 90-; Mens Bsktbl Statstcn 90-; Bus Admn; Law.

**PHILLIPS, REECIA S,** James Sprunt Comm Coll, Kenansville, NC; SO; BA; Amer Svgs Bank Custmr Serv Rep; Assoc 83; Crmnlgy; Histry; Elem Educ.

**PHILLIPS, RITA GRIGGS,** Univ Of Sc At Coastal Carolina, Conway, SC; SO; AS; Nursing.

**PHILLIPS, RONALD G,** Univ Of Tn At Martin, Martin, TN; JR; BA; Ed; Tchr.

**PHILLIPS II, RONALD W,** Western Carolina Univ, Cullowhee, NC; FR; BS; Delta Chi Fndng Fthr Almn Sec; Frshmn Math Awd Hnrbl Mntn 90-; Frshmn Bus Mjrs Hgst GPA 90; Math; Teaching.

**PHILLIPS, SABINE L,** Northern Va Comm Coll, Annandale, VA; FR; BA; Agrctrl Econ; Law.

**PHILLIPS, SAMUEL H,** Indiana Univ Of Pa, Indiana, PA; SR; MED; Dns Lst; Most Vlbl Emplyee Holiday Inn IN; Grad Cum Laude; BED IN Unv PA; Hstry/Pol Educ; Tchng.

**PHILLIPS, SANDRA R,** Mayland Comm Coll, Spruce Pine, NC; JR; BA; Intrnshp Riversd Elem Schl Sprc Pine N C; Educ; Tchg.

**PHILLIPS, SCOTT A,** Piedmont Tech Coll, Greenwood, SC; FR; AS; Hlth Sci; Radiologist Tech.

**PHILLIPS, SHERRI R,** Univ Of Montevallo, Montevallo, AL; FR; BA; Univ Of Montevallo Wind Ensmbl 90-; Alpha Lambda Delta; Engl; Jrnlsm.

**PHILLIPS, TAMI ANTOINETTE,** Fl A & M Univ, Tallahassee, FL; JR; BA; Golden Hgt Church Of Christ Youth Grp 79-; Pol Sci Club 88-; AROTC Plt Sgt 90-; The Hachett 90-; US Achvmnt Acad; All Amercn 90-; White/Gold 90-; Spcl Olympcs 90-; AROTC Schlrshp 90-; Delta Sigma Theta Schlrshp Award 88-89; Pol Sci; Intrntl/Corp Law.

**PHILLIPS, TAMMI E,** Univ Of Nh Plymouth St Coll, Plymouth, NH; JR; BA; Chrldng Ftbl 89-; Aerobcs Instr; Psych.

**PHILLIPS, TAMMY R,** Appalachian St Univ, Boone, NC; FR; BSBA; Phi Eta Sigma; Alpha Phi; Bus; Fnc.

**PHILLIPS, TERRI J,** Longwood Coll, Farmville, VA; FR; BS; Alpha Lambda Delta 90-; Dntl Asst Dr J Keller Vernon DDS; Dntl Hygnst.

**PHILLIPS, TERRY M,** Snead St Jr Coll, Boaz, AL; FR; AA; Bsn; Acctng.

**PHILLIPS, TIM L,** Roane St Comm Coll, Harriman, TN; SO; BED; Lit Prjct; Sec Ed/Hstry; Tchng/Rsch Lbrn.

**PHILLIPS, TINA L,** Univ Of New England, Biddeford, ME; SO; BS; Non-Trdtnl Stdnt Org Sec 89-; Lfstyls Allnc Org Treas 89-; Hspc Vol-Brnswck 85-90; Mrrymtng AIDS Educ Pgm 86-88; Phy Thrpy-Tchng/Prctc.

**PHILLIPS, TOMMY M,** Clayton St Coll, Morrow, GA; SO; BA; Envrnmntl Awrns Club Exec Asst 90-; Lyceum Comm 89-90; Creative Arts Festival 89; Deans List; IM Sftbl 88; Bus Admn; Mgmt.

**PHILLIPS, TOMMY W,** Tn Temple Univ, Chattanooga, TN; SR; BS; RA; Phi Beta Delta Snr Advsr; Ftbl/Bsktbl/Sftbl; Pstrl/Chrstn Ed; Pstr/Educ Admin.

**PHILLIPS, TONYA L,** Beckley Coll, Beckley, WV; FR; MBA; FHA 89-90; Pep Clb 87-90; March Dimes Fnd Rsr 87-; Four Sml Acdmc Schlrshps; Dance Sqd 87-89; Spch Pathology Audiology; Clncl Spech Pthlgy.

**PHILLIPS, TRACI B,** Piedmont Coll, Demorest, GA; FR; BA; BSU 90-; IM Spts; Dns Schlr Lst 90; Dns Lst; Educ; Tchr/Coach.

**PHILLIPS, TRACY L,** Nova Univ, Ft Lauderdale, FL; GD; MBA; AATCC Pres 82-88; Phi Lambda Upsilon 86-; Phi Psi Textile V P 83-; ATOE Awd 87; AATCC Schlrshp 82-86; Soc Plast Eng 86-; Appl Eng PMS Cons Corp Tech Ctr 88-; BS Aubrn Univ 86; Text Chem; Eng/Plastcs Ind.

**PHILLIPS, TRICIA R,** Fisk Univ, Nashville, TN; SO; BS; Stdnt Ct Psdng Offcr 88-89; Mock Trial State/Local Judge 89; Bus Prof Prlmntrn 88-89; Deans Lst 89-; Delta Sigma; Nasa Database Assist 89-90; Tenneco Oil Cntrct Assist 88-89; Assist Legal Secy 88; Stdnt Spprt Serv 90-; Pol Sci/Pblc Admin; Corp Law.

**PHILLIPS, TWYLA J,** Roane St Comm Coll, Harriman, TN; SO; AS; Nrsng; BS Nrsng.

**PHILLIPS, ZELPHIA T,** City Univ Of Ny Baruch Coll, New York, NY; JR; BA; Wmn Color Netwrk; Photog/Wrtr Ticker Baruch Nwspr; Deans Lst; Seek Acad Achvmnt; Jrnlsm.

**PHILLIPS-GOLDER, RENEE,** Memphis St Univ, Memphis, TN; FR; BFA; Grphc Dsgn; Advrtsng Dsgnr.

**PHILMORE, SAMARAH L,** Fl A & M Univ, Tallahassee, FL; SR; BS; FLSIATE 88-; Mdlng Trp 87-88; Alpha Kappa Alpha 89-; Gldn Sable 87; Hnr Rl 88-; Dean Lst 89-; Elem Educ; Tchr.

**PHILPOTT, LAUREL B,** Birmingham Southern Coll, Birmingham, AL; SR; Kappa Delta 91; Intshp Physical Therepy Rehab Assoc 90; NAIA All Amer 89; NAIA All Amer 88-91; Varsity Tennis 88-91; Psychology; Dentisry.

**PHILYAW, KITTY A,** Tri County Tech Coll, Pendleton, SC; FR; AIT; Deans Lst 90; Elctrncs/Elctrcty; Elctrnc Tchncn.

**PHINAZEE, LINDA J,** Saint Josephs Coll New York, Brooklyn, NY; GD; MSN; Assoc Operating Room Nurses; Amer Nurses Assoc; Hnr Rl; Regents Schlrshp 72; Registered Prof Nurses; AAS 78; Nursing; Professor.

**PHINNEY, JENNIFER L,** Andover Coll, Portland, ME; SR; Stdnt Mod 90; Typng Shrt Hnd Awds.

**PHINNEY, LOUIS S,** Utica Coll Of Syracuse Univ, Utica, NY; JR; BS; CCAF 89; Cmptr Sci; Prgmr.

**PHINNEY, MICHAEL W,** Niagara Univ, Niagara Univ, NY; SO.

**PHIPPS, ADAM P,** Bunker Hill Comm Coll, Boston, MA; SO; ADN; Nursing; BSN.

**PHIPPS, DAVID L,** Radford Univ, Radford, VA; SR; BS; Phi Kappa Phi; Pi Gamma Mu 90-; Scl Sci.

**PHIPPS, HAROLD W,** Western Ky Univ, Bowling Green, KY; SR; BS; Phi Beta Lambda State Treas 90-; Beta Gamma Sigma VP 89-90; Omicron Delta Kappa; Pi Kappa Phi; Beta Alpha Psi; Phi Beta Lambda Accntng II Ntnl Evnt; Accntng; Copr Accntng.

**PHIPPS, JAMES M,** Univ Of Sc At Columbia, Columbia, SC; SR; BMA; Cmps Crusade Christ 87-; Scuba Clb 89; Media Arts; Snd Eng.

**PHIPPS, JERROLD DION,** Al A & M Univ, Normal, AL; SO; Physics.

**PHIPPS, LINDA O,** Univ Of Sc At Columbia, Columbia, SC; JR; BA; Elem Ed; Tchng.

**PHISTER, DAVID T,** Univ Of Akron, Akron, OH; SO; BA; Phi Eta Sigma 90-; Alpha Lambda Delta 90-; Dns Lst; Math/Electrncs; Elec Engr.

**PHLIPOT, SHARON M,** Univ Of Tn At Martin, Martin, TN; SR; BA; Cmps Engl Socty 88-; IM Sprts Vlybl/Bsktbl Chmpns 88-; Edtrl Assg Lcl Mag 90-; Phi Kappa Phi; Sigma Tau Delta 90-; Engl; Pblshng.

**PHLIPOT, TAMARA S,** Defiance Coll, Defiance, OH; JR; BS; Intr Srrty Cncl Sec; Phi Alpha Theta; Beta Sigma 90-; Ed Tchng.

**PHONG, LANH QUOC,** Bunker Hill Comm Coll, Boston, MA.

**PHRANER, WENDY A,** Clarkson Univ, Potsdam, NY; SO; Amer Mrktng Assn 90-; Stdnt Ornttn Srvce; Delta Zeta 90-; Mrktng And Mgmt; Mrktng Sales.

**PI COLLAZO, LIZ ANETTE,** Inter Amer Univ Pr San German, San German, PR; SR; BBA; Hstry; Acctng.

**PIACENTINI, LAURIE A,** Providence Coll, Providence, RI; SR; Magna Cum Laude; Hghst Acdmc; Rcrd; BA; Egnglsh.**

**PIACENTINI, LISA A,** Providence Coll, Providence, RI; JR; BA; Pastrl Cncl 90-; Psi Chi Pres 90-; Tchrs Asstnt 90-; Deans List 88-; Psychlgy.

**PIANIN, MARK D,** Cumberland County Coll, Vineland, NJ; FR; AA; Bsn Admin.

**PIANO, CHRISTIANE M,** Immaculata Coll, Immaculata, PA; FR; Schl Nwspr 90-; Outng Clb 90-; Intrntl Law/Bus.

**PIANTANIDA, DEBRA L,** Schenectady County Comm Coll, Schenectady, NY; SO; Drama Clb; Crmnl Juste Clb Sec 90; Sftbl; Crmnl Juste; Law.

**PIASECKY, DYANN M,** Indiana Univ Of Pa, Indiana, PA; JR; BED; Cir K Intrntl State Exec Ofcr 90-; Assn Chldhd Ed Intrntnl Clb Pres 90-; Ed; Erly Chldhd.

**PIATOS, NIKI,** City Univ Of Ny Baruch Coll, New York, NY; GD; Advrtsng Clb Tres 89-; Deans List 89-; Advrtsng.

**PIAZZA, JENNIFER R,** Glassboro St Coll, Glassboro, NJ; JR; BA; Gamma Tau Sigma Pres; Sigma Delta Upsilon Pres 88-; Engl; Tch.

**PIAZZA, MICHAEL J,** S U N Y Coll Of Tech At Alfred, Alfred, NY; SR; BE; IM Soccer Capt; Arch Engr; Engr.

**PIAZZA, PHILIP G,** Univ Of Rochester, Rochester, NY; SO; BA; Ftbl 89-; IM Bsktbl 89-; Campus Times Sports Rep 90-; Delta Kappa Epsilon Rsh Chrmn 90-; Engl; Jrnlsm/Advrtsg/TV.

**PICA, KELLY A,** Rivier Coll, Nashua, NH; SO; Lbrl Stdies; Ed.

**PICA, ROSEMARI,** Univ Of South Al, Mobile, AL; FR; BS; Phi Chi Theta; League Wmn Vtrs; Bay Area Conf Wmn; Amer Cancer Soc Cmm Rsrc Mnl; Intl Stu/Asian/Bus; Intl Corp Law.

**PICANO, JASON L,** Old Dominion Univ, Norfolk, VA; JR; BS; Karate Instr 90-; Acad Hnrs Pgm 88-89; Dns Lst 90-; Cvl Engr.

**PICARD, KAREN A,** S U N Y Coll At Fredonia, Fredonia, NY; JR; BS; Chamber Singers 89-; Clg Ambassadors; Pi Kapp Lambda; Hillman Schlrshp 90-; Carlyon Mem Schlrshp; Art/Music.

**PICARD, KATERI S,** Middle Tn St Univ, Murfreesboro, TN; JR; MSW; Scl Wrk; Pblc Hlth Admn.

**PICARD, KERRI LYNN,** Marist Coll, Poughkeepsie, NY; SR; BA; Garlic Scty; Tour Guide Vol; Deans List Frst Hon; IM Sprts; D; Psychlgy; Soc Wrk.

**PICARELLI, SHARON E,** Wilmington Coll, New Castle, DE; GD; BA; Judg Battle R Robns Fmly Ct; AS D E Tech Comm Clg 89; Behavrl Sci; Humn Res Mgt.

**PICARO, LUCIA,** Bloomfield Coll, Bloomfield, NJ; SR; BS; Sec Almn Assc 89-90; Sec Sci Clb 90-; Eye Dry Tech 84-; Pre Med Biol; Dr/Tchr.

**PICCALO, GINA LOUISE,** Univ Of Nc At Charlotte, Charlotte, NC; SR; BA; Magazine Edtr 88-; Nespr Sr Stf Wrtr 88-; Amrcn Cllgt Pblctn Cnvtn 88; Deans Lst 89; Hall Govt 88; Wlcome Week 88; City Magazine Intrn Rprtr 89; Radio Inten Prdctn Asst 90; TV Intern Nes Assistant 91; IM Flag Ftbl Sftbl 88; Englsh; Brdcst Jrnlsm.

**PICCININI, MIRIAM C,** Univ Of New Haven, West Haven, CT; SR; BS; Htl Rstrnt Scty Sec; Eta Sigma Delta; Htl Rstrnt Mgmt; Htl Mgmt.

**PICCININNI, CHRIS F,** S U N Y Coll Of Tech At Frmgdl, Farmingdale, NY; JR; BA; IM Sftbl; Vol Wrk St Anthnys Chrch; AA; Lbrl Arts; Tch.

**PICCIRELLI, LINDA ANN,** S U N Y Coll Of Tech At Frmgdl, Farmingdale, NY; FR; BA; Liberal Arts; Law.

**PICCIRILLO, ANGELO A,** Adelphi Univ, Garden City, NY; JR; BA; Hstry Soc; MD Dnce Marathn Chrmn; Cathcst; IM Hcky Sftbl; Hstry; Law.**

**PICCOLI, PETER D,** S U N Y Coll Of Tech At Delhi, Delhi, NY; FR; Auto Mech; Auto Tech.

**PICCOLINO, JOHN A,** Marywood Coll, Scranton, PA; SR; BS; Comp Info Sys; Prgrmr/Analyst.

**PICHIARELLO, MARY BETH D,** Univ Of Scranton, Scranton, PA; SR; BS; Acctg Soc; Amnsty Intl; Bus Clb; VITA; Delta Mu Delta 90-; Omega Beta Sigma; PICPA Schlrshp 90; KPMG Peat Marwick Intrnshp; Acctg.

**PICHULO, ANASTASIA S,** Albertus Magnus Coll, New Haven, CT; JR; BA; Amnsty Intl Pres 88-; Orientatn Stff 89-; Arts Clb; Intrn Art Gllry 90; Intrn St Dept; Humnties/Poltcl Sci; Frgn Serv.

**PICK, KATHERINE E,** Liberty Univ, Lynchburg, VA; FR; BS; Actd Prod The Lost Key One Act Play 90-; Alpha Lambda Delta; Grls IM Sftbl Mgr 90-; Psych.

**PICK, TRACY MARTIN,** Nova Univ, Ft Lauderdale, FL; GD; MBA; Sve The Mntee Fndtn 85-; BS BA Florida Southern Coll 89; Bus Mgmt; Intrnatl Bus Rltns.

**PICKARD, REBECCA J,** Lesley Coll, Cambridge, MA; JR; BS; Chld Cr Serv Hd 89-; Undrgrad Schlrshp; Vrsty Sftbl Capt 89-; Early Chldhd Educ; Tch.

**PICKARD, TERRY L,** Univ Of Southern Ms, Hattiesburg, MS; SR; BS; Gldn Key; Oil Fld Lease Oprtr 84-88; Electrncs; Eng Tech.

**PICKENS, JOHN C,** Univ Of Ga, Athens, GA; JR; BA; Lndscp Archtr; Envrnmntl Dsgn.

**PICKERING, MARGOT E,** Salisbury St Univ, Salisbury, MD; JR; BA; Sphns Theatre Org; Comm; Tlvsn Prod/Dir.

**PICKERING, SEAN P,** City Univ Of Ny Baruch Coll, New York, NY; GD; BA; Biomed Soc Treas 88-90; Gldn Ky; Bellvue Prvt Ttr; Pres Awd Achvmnt Ntrl Sci; BA 91; Bio; MD.

**PICKERING, WENDOLYN M,** Univ Of De, Newark, DE; SR; BA; Vrsty Swim/Dvng Tm 87-89; Nwspr Stff; Intrnshp Du Pont De Nemours 90; H S Sports Strngr 89-90; Scripps-Howard Schlrshp Rcpnt 90-; Swmmng/Dvng Tm; Engl Jrnlsm; Wrtr.

**PICKETT, CATHERINE L,** Fl St Univ, Tallahassee, FL; JR; BA; Golden Key 90-; Delta Zeta Public Reltns Chrmn 88-; Intshp Data Express; Communication Busn.

**PICKETT, CONNIE LEIGH,** Univ Of Sc At Columbia, Columbia, SC; JR; Bptst Stdnt Un Cncl 89-; Alpha Lambda Delta Cncl 89-; Gamma Beta Phi; Biolgy; Med Sci.

**PICKETT, DAVID B,** Union Univ, Jackson, TN; SO; BA; Impct Drm Tm 89-; Un Univ Plyrs; Deans Lst 89-; Rsdnt Asst 89-; Tlvsn Rd Intern; Cmmnctn.

**PICKETT, DUANE A,** Univ Of Southern Ms, Hattiesburg, MS; FR; Music/Jazz.

**PICKETT, JEANINE M,** Univ Of Md Baltimore Prof Schl, Baltimore, MD; SR; BS; Stdnt Amer Dntl Hygiene Assn 89-; Phi Kappa Phi; Dns Lst Catonsvl Comm Coll 86-89; Dns Lst 89-; Maryland State Delegate Schlrshp Awd 90-; Reg Dntl Asst 82-; Dental Hygiene; Reg Dntl Hygieniest.

**PICKETT, NICOLE M,** Al A & M Univ, Normal, AL; JR; BS; Ford Fndtn Schlrs 89-; Kappa Delta Pi 90-; Acad Schlrshp 89-; Spch Pathology.

**PICKETT, PAUL A,** Ms St Univ, Miss State, MS; SR; BBA; Campus Crusade For Christ Servant Tm 88-; Army ROTC Bulldog Battery; Bible Study Ldr; Phi Kappa Phi; Beta Gamma Sigma; Gamma Beta Phi; BBA 90; Mrktng; Bus Mgmt Sales.

**PICKETT, REBECCA A,** Fl International Univ, Miami, FL; FR; PHD; Psychlgy; Psychthrpy.

**PICKETT, SUZETTE D,** Tn Wesleyan Coll, Athens, TN; JR; BS; Elem Educ; Schl Tchr.

**PICKLE, LESLIE N,** Itawamba Comm Coll, Fulton, MS; SO; MBA; Mdlg Squad 90-; Indianette 89-90; Elem Ed.

**PICKLE, MARY E,** Itawamba Comm Coll, Fulton, MS; SO; Bnd; Indntt Capt; Sprng Dnc Ln Co Capt; AA; Educ Elem.

**PICKLESIMER, ROBERT A,** East Tn St Univ, Johnson City, TN; SO; BS; Upward Band Tutor; Spcl Svcs Inside Track Tutor; Cmptr Sci; Cmptr Prog.

**PICKWORTH, AMY J,** Oh Wesleyan Univ, Delaware, OH; SR; BA; Stdnts Against Apartheid 88-90; Phi Beta Kappa; Phi Society 89; Phi Eta Sigma 88; Art Editor/Lit Magzn 90-; Intern/Dlg Arts In The Mdwst 90-; Hnrs Stdnt 87-; Fine Arts.

**PICO, DAVID H,** Life Coll, Marietta, GA; GD; DC; Upper Crvcl Clb; SOT Clb; Thomson Clb; Chrprctc Dr Chrprctc.

**PICON, LISA,** Dowling Coll, Oakdale Li, NY; SR; BA; Educ Clb 89; Dowling Dance Ensmbl 90-; Anyseed; Kappa Delta Pi; Steffi Nossen Dance Schlrshp 90; Dowling Kickline Coach 90-; Spec/Elem Educ; Speech Pathologist.

**PIECUCH, JANE H,** Western New England Coll, Springfield, MA; SR; BSBA; Mgmt Club; Yrbk Comm; Snr Comm; Admin Assist Med Ctr; Mgmt.

**PIEDRAHITA, JAIRO,** Nova Univ, Ft Lauderdale, FL; GD; MBA; Deans List 90-; CYF/KIDS Crusaders; Mrktng V P; BA Ind Engrng U De Am Bogota 80; BA Econ Sci U Tadeo Lozano Bogota Columbia S A 84; Econ; Engrng.

**PIEGER, GERARD E,** Albertus Magnus Coll, New Haven, CT; SO; AA; Fncl Svc Rep Mech/Frmrs FSB 89-; Bus-Mgmt; Ptlcl.

**PIEKARSKI, JENNIFER A,** Fairfield Univ, Fairfield, CT; FR; BA; Class Senate 90-; Paul Douglas Teach Schlrshp; Am Studies; Scndry Edn.

**PIEKARSKI, TIMOTHY,** Univ Of Nc At Charlotte, Charlotte, NC; FR; BS; NTSO; IEEE; US Nvl Rsrve Ptty Offcr 90-; Nvy Actv Dty 81-90; Elec Tech; AS Univ St NY 89; Elec Eng.

**PIENN, ROCHELLE THEO,** Univ Of Miami, Coral Gables, FL; GD; BS; Cmps Cmmtr Org Hstrn 87-88; Lit Mag Co Editor 90; Hnrs Prog 87-90; Bowman Asche Schlrshp 87-90; BS 90; Engl/Comm; Grad Schl.

**PIEPER, LEE ANNE,** Univ Of Sc At Columbia, Columbia, SC; FR; Dns Lst; Gamma Beta Phi; Schlr Athlte Awrd; Vrsty Vlybl 90-; Pscyhlgy; Cnslr.

**PIERBERG, SUZANNE M,** Univ Of Nc At Asheville, Asheville, NC; SR; Mssng Lnks Blgy Clb 88-; Hon Schlrs 89-; Memrl Mission Hosp Dept Rdlgy; BA; Blgy; Rdtn Thrpy Tchnlgy.**

**PIERCE, BARBARA E,** Univ Of Nc At Greensboro, Greensboro, NC; SR; BS; Stdnt Art Alliance 88-; Clthg/Textile Clb 89-; Stdnt Govt Repr 87-88; Kappa Omicron Nu 89-; Marithe/Francois Girbaud Intern; Am Bsn Wmns Asc Schlrshps 88-; Rockingham Cty Fine Arts Fest 3rd Pl 90; AS Arts Rockingham Cmnty Clg 89; Clthg/Text; Apparel Dsgn.

**PIERCE, BARNEY W,** Wallace St Comm Coll At Selma, Selma, AL; FR; BA; Pres List; Chldrn Mrcl Ntwrk Tlthn; Acad Achvmnt Awd; Math; Aerospace Engr.

**PIERCE, CECELIA W,** Vance Granville Comm Coll, Henderson, NC; SR; AAS; SGA Scl Chrprsn 90-; Ambsdr Sec/Treas 90-; Phi Theta Kappa Treas; Acctng; CPA.

**PIERCE, CHRISTINE C,** Hudson Valley Comm Coll, Troy, NY; FR; EOA; Word Prcsng/Cmptr Sci; Mgmt.

**PIERCE, DEBORAH A,** Univ Of Sc At Columbia, Columbia, SC; FR; BA; Educ.

**PIERCE, DEBORAH R,** Springfield Tech Comm Coll, Springfield, MA; GD; CERT; Alpha Nu Omega; Trng Wrkshps Comp Asstd Trnscrptn Stngrphc Notes 90; Natl Crt Rprtrs Assn 89-; MA Shrthnd Rprtrs Assn 89-; AS 90; Crt Stngrphy/Clrcl Spprt Crt Rprtrs 82-; Wstrn MA Dairy Goat Brdrs Assn Pres 85-; Crt Rprtng/Lngstcs.

**PIERCE, DIANA S,** Univ Of Nc At Greensboro, Greensboro, NC; GD; Univ Marshall 87-90; Alison Schlrshp; Univ Stores Schlrshp 90; Deans Lst 86-90; BS Elem Edn K-6 Cert 90; K-8 Educ Ohio/WV; Elem Edn/Math; MA.

**PIERCE, ELIZABETH G,** Univ Of Sc At Aiken, Aiken, SC; SR; BS; Grmn Clb Pres; Frgn Lng Plcmnt Tst Prctr 88-; Frgn Lng Plcmnt Tst Smr Sprvsr 90-; Frshmn Scs Wk 90-; Lit Mgzn Cntrptng Phtgrphr 90-; Yrbk Cntrbtng Phtgphr 90-; Grmn Lng Tr 89-90; Bsn Admin/Psychlgy; Law Schl.

**PIERCE, HOPE M,** Salem Comm Coll, Penns Grove, NJ; SO; BA; AA; Law Jstc; Law.**

**PIERCE, JAMES C,** Glassboro St Coll, Glassboro, NJ; JR; BA; Sclgy Clb Treas; Alpha Phi Delta Pldge Mstr; Ftbl; Sclgy Scndry Educ.

**PIERCE, JOY D,** James Sprunt Comm Coll, Kenansville, NC; FR; Sftbl; Hist/Phy Ed.

**PIERCE, JUDITH L,** Columbia Union Coll, Takoma Park, MD; SR; BSN; Deans Lst Loma Linda 77-80; Deans Lst 82-83; AS Shepherd Clg Wv 85-; BS 80; Nurs; RN.

**PIERCE, JULIE A,** Fl International Univ, Miami, FL; SR; BSW; Phi Kappa Phi; Certificate Awrd Otstndng Udrgrdt Schlr; Intrnshp Imperial Pnt Med Cntr Psych Unit 90; Intrnshp JASP Prgrm Juvenile Criminal Offenders 90; Social Work.

**PIERCE, KIMBERLY L,** Valdosta St Coll, Valdosta, GA; SO; BED; Band Marching & Concert General Assistant 89-; Choir Chamber Singers 89-; Baptist Stdnt Union Sec 89-; Music; Teaching.

**PIERCE, KIMBERLY S,** Lexington Comm Coll, Lexington, KY; SO; Army Comm Svcs Fmly Sprt Grp 89-; Grad Hgh Dstnctn; Wrkng Cntrl Bapt Asst Nrs Wmns Care Plaza; ADN; Nrsng.

**PIERCE, KRISTY L,** Wv Univ, Morgantown, WV; JR; BS; Chimes 90-; Gldn Key 90-; Sphinx; Delta Gamma 88-; Schlrs Pgm 88-; Health Sci; Physical Therapy.**

**PIERCE, LAWRENCE H,** Volunteer St Comm Coll, Gallatin, TN; GD; ASSOC; Stdnt Msnry Srvc S Pacific 87-88; Clin Intrnshps Vndrblt Unit Med Cntr In Fld Of Phys Comprhnsv Med Rehab Cntr; Natl Hlth Care Inc; Phys Thrpy.

**PIERCE, LU ANN,** Univ Of Sc At Columbia, Columbia, SC; JR; BA; Sc Assn Of Homes For Chldren Chrprsn Pgm Dir; Asst Natl Trnng Com; Dir Of Indpndnt Living/Carolina Childrns Home 86-; Interdisc Studies.

**PIERCE, LYNDA M,** Lima Tech Coll, Lima, OH; SO; Hnrs; Deans Lst; AS; Erly Chldhd Dev; Tch.**

**PIERCE, M ROCHELL,** Brescia Coll, Owensboro, KY; JR; BA; Ichbd Scty Pres 88-; Amnsty Intl 8-; Stdnt Govt Rep 88-; Engl.

**PIERCE, M THERESE,** Gallaudet Univ, Washington, DC; GD; PH D; Kappa Delta Pi Pres 90-; Co Ldr Cnslng Grp Hlf Wy Comm Hse 88; Ttr Hgh Schl Grads 87; B App Sci Curtin Univ Of Tech W Australia 81; Dip Ed Monash Univ Victoria Australia; GDSE Victoria Coll Australia 83; MA 89; Grp Fclttr Fr Grad Stdnts 90-; Pres Awrd; Spcl Educ Admin; Spcl Educ Admin And Cnslng.

**PIERCE, MARY W,** Elms Coll, Chicopee, MA; JR; BA; Clg Nwspr Asst Edtr 90-; E Longmeadow Comm Theatre 90-; Theatre Co 88-; Ldrshp Awd 90-; Nation Endowment Humanities Schrlshp 90; Diocesine Schlrshp 88-; English; Teaching.

**PIERCE, MEMORIE R,** Fl St Univ, Tallahassee, FL; SR; BS; Deans Lst 89-; Intrnshp Fla State London Prog; Educ; Tchng.

**PIERCE, PAULA A,** Univ Of South Al, Mobile, AL; SR; BS; Elem Ed; Tchng.

**PIERCE, ROBERT J,** Wv Univ, Morgantown, WV; FR; BA; 4H Pres 81-; Hnr Sprgm 90-; Comp Elec Eng.

**PIERCE, SHANNON D,** Rutgers St Un At New Brunswick, New Brunswick, NJ; SO; BM; Mrchng Bnd/Pep Bnd Rcrtng Ofcr 89-; Jazz Ensmbl 90-; Wnd Ensmbl 89-; Mu Upsln Alph Asstnt VP 89-; Msc Edctn; Tchng.**

**PIERCE, SHARON G,** Daytona Beach Comm Coll, Daytona Beach, FL; FR; AS; Mktg Mgt; Byr.

**PIERCE, STACEY E,** Longwood Coll, Farmville, VA; JR; BS; Psychology Clb 90-; Hall Cncl 90-; Panhellenic Cncl Pres 89-90; Psi Chi 90-; Zeta Tau Alpha; Res Assist; Psychology; Ind Psychology.

**PIERCE, TAMMY V,** Eckerd Coll, St Petersburg, FL; SR; BA; Vol Pinellas Co Schl Systm 89-90; Intrnshp High Schl Tchr 90-; Hstry; Sec Schl Socl Stds Tchr.

**PIERCE, TERRI L,** Univ Of Sc At Columbia, Columbia, SC; SR; BS; Jyccs VP 90-; Omicron Delta Kappa 90; Mrktng Rsrch Asst 90-; Bus Admn; Mrktng.

**PIERCY, MICAH A,** Saint Andrews Presbytrn Coll, Laurinburg, NC; SR; BA; Math Computer Sci Clb Pres Cofounder 89-; Bridge Clb Pres 89-; Gospel Choir 87-90; Hnr Scty 89-; Hnrs Stdnt Assoc 87-; Elymosynary Posse 88-; Kum Laude; Intrnshp Lcl Area Ntwrk Instlltn 90-; IM Ftbl Bsktbl Vlybl Tm Capt 87-; Math/Computer Sci; Consulting.

**PIERCY, TERESSIA L,** Western Piedmont Comm Coll, Morganton, NC; FR; BA; Phi Theta Kappa; Nurs/Sci; Nurs/O B Ped.

**PIERMAN, PATRICIA M,** Glassboro St Coll, Glassboro, NJ; FR; Elem Ed/Psych.

**PIERMATTEO, VICTORIA I,** Temple Univ, Philadelphia, PA; GD; MBA; Amblr Press 90-; Res Hl Snte 89-; Hnrs Pgm 87-90; Asstshp Temple Hosp 90-; IM Vlybl 87-; BBA 90; Fnce; Mgmt.

**PIEROTTI, CRAIG A,** Univ Of Pittsburgh At Bradford, Bradford, PA; SO; BS; Applied Math; Actrl Sci.

**PIERRE LOUIS JR, EDNER,** City Univ Of Ny Med Evers Coll, Brooklyn, NY; JR; BBA; Haitian Stdnts Assc 90-; Assc Stdy Afrnc Amer Life/Hist; Sls Mgr Beverage Corp NY; Bus Admn; Mktg Natrl Bvrgs.

**PIERRE, GILBERT E,** City Univ Of Ny Baruch Coll, New York, NY; GD; BBA; Computer Clb 87-; Haitian Clb 87-; Clg Acdmc Awrd Excllnc 89-; Oper Mngmnt; Cmptr Info Syst.

**PIERRE, KENNETH L,** Felician Coll, Lodi, NJ; SO; BA; Ntl Cath Ed Assn; Yth Outrch Mnstry VP 80-85; HS Tchr; Dip Spnsh Inst Lang Trinidad W Indies 85; Dip Theory Music Ryl Schls Music London England 86; Dip Ed Cambridge England 78; Elem Ed/Engl; Tchg.

**PIERRE, KEVIN,** American Baptist Coll, Nashville, TN; SO; BA; NAACP; Baptst Stdnt Un 90-; Amer Bptst Theolgcl Smnrys Yrbk Stf Photo Edtr 90-; Nshvle Rscue Mssn Tmwrk Cnslr/Prchr 90-; Biblcl Theolgcl Stdies; Sociolgy.**

**PIERRE, MAYOBANEX,** Bunker Hill Comm Coll, Boston, MA; SO; Intl Stdnt Clb 90-; Electronics; Engineering.

**PIERRE, MICHELE T,** Marywood Coll, Scranton, PA; SR; BM; MENC Pres 86-; PCMEA Sec 86-; St Cecelia Music Soc V P 86-; Kappa Gamma Pi; Music Educ; Tch.

**PIERRE, SANDRA MARIE,** City Univ Of Ny City Coll, New York, NY; SR; BA; Dn Ldr By Scts Clb; Erly Chldhd Ed; Dir Day Care Pgm.

**PIERRE-CANEL, MARIE J,** Bunker Hill Comm Coll, Boston, MA; SO.

**PIERRE-LOUIS, LUCILE,** City Univ Of Ny Baruch Coll, New York, NY; JR; BBA; Haitian Cltrl Soc Sec 89-90; Accntng; CPA.

**PIERRE-LOUIS-PINNOCK, MAGGY M,** City Univ Of Ny City Coll, New York, NY; SR; BSN; Nrsng Stdnt Orgnztn Cls Rep 89-; Ntnl Key Hnr Soc; Sigma Theta Tau; Manhattan Vet Admnstrtn Vltr Prgrm Stdnt Extrn 90-; Nrsng.

**PIERRO JR, LEONARD,** Univ Of Med & Dentistry Of Nj, Newark, NJ; SR; PBM; Delta Phi Comm Serv Rep 86; BA 88; Phys Thrpy.

**PIERRO, MICHELE R,** Savannah Coll Of Art & Design, Savannah, GA; SR; BFA; AIGA N Y Chptr 88-89; AIGA Atlanta Chptr; Deans Lst 89; M E Effing Schlrshp 89-; Magna Cum Laude; Grphic Dsgn; Art Dir.

**PIERRO, RENEE,** S U N Y Coll Of Tech At Frmgdl, Farmingdale, NY; SO; ASA; Law/Crmnl Jstce.

**PIERRON, NICK E,** Wright St Univ Lake Cmps, Celina, OH; JR; BSE; Tutor 89-; Elec Engrg; Engrg.

**PIERSON, DEBRA M,** Defiance Coll, Defiance, OH; SR; BS; Acad Awd; Grad Magna Cum Laude; Central Fndry Div GMC; Psych.

**PIERSON, KARLA J,** Kent St Univ Stark Cmps, North Canton, OH; FR; BA; Deans Lst; Bus; Financing/Mtkg.

**PIERSON, LEIGH A,** Univ Of Montevallo, Montevallo, AL; SO; BFA; Art Clb; Deans List; Hons Awd; Art.

**PIESCOR, ANN RENEE,** Georgian Court Coll, Lakewood, NJ; SR; Soc Actvts Comm 87-90; De La Salle Clb 87-; Big Str/Ltll Str 89-; Stdnt Ambssdr 87-; Vlybl Clb 90-; Crss Cntry Tm Co Capt 87-90; BA; Elem Educ/Soc; Teacher.

**PIESKI, JOHN H,** Georgetown Univ, Washington, DC; FR; BS; Delta Sigma Pi; Finf Invstmnt Bkng.

**PIETERS, DANIEL A,** S U N Y Coll Of Tech At Alfred, Alfred, NY; SO; AAS; Archtctrl Clb 88-; Deans List 88-90; Archtctr; Rgstrd Archtct.

**PIETLOCK, SHARON M,** Wilmington Coll, New Castle, DE; GD; Amer Hosp Rad Admin 88-; ARRT 68-; Mgr Christiana Hosp Day Opers; AS Del Tech Cmnty Clg 85; BS 90; Soc Sci.

**PIETROPAOLO, ROSE,** Villanova Univ, Villanova, PA; JR; BA; Stdnt Theatre 90-; Spnsh Clb 88-89; Chi Alpha Pres Elect; Balloon Day 88-; Spcl Olympics 88-; WPVI TV Chnl 6 Intern; IMS 90-; Cmnctn; Brdcstng.

**PIETROPAOLO, VINCENZO,** Kent St Univ Kent Cmps, Kent, OH; SR; BBA; Interfrat Cncl Treas 90-; Finance Assn; Deans Lst 88-; Delta Tau Delta 89-; Grk Acad Hon 89; Delta Tau Delta Rush Chrmn Asst Treas 89-; MD Assn; IM Ftbl/Sftbl/Rcqtbl 87-; Mgmnt; Corp Finance/Bnkng.

**PIETRUSINSKI, CAROLYN A,** Duquesne Univ, Pittsburgh, PA; SO; BA; Pharmacy.

**PIETRUSZKIEWICZ, ALAN J,** Va Commonwealth Univ, Richmond, VA; FR; MPT; Phi Eta Sigma; Kappa Delta Rho; X-Cntry/Trck Fld Vrsty Ltr 90-; Pre Physcl Thrpy.

**PIFER, RICHARD G,** Temple Univ, Philadelphia, PA; JR; BSEE; IEEE 89-; Army ROTC Exec Ofcr 89-; Eta Kappa Nu; Elctrnc Tchncn 85-89; ASEE Rets Elctrncs Schls 85; Elec Eng.

**PIGATT, TERRIN D,** Univ Of Nc At Charlotte, Charlotte, NC; JR; BA; Blck Std Un 89-; Natl Asc Adv Clrd People 89-; Engl/Jrnlsm.

**PIGFORD, GERALD B,** Middlesex County Coll, Edison, NJ; SR; Student Assoc Radiography 89-; Phi Theta Kappa 90-; Radiography; Medical Doctor.

**PIGG, TERI S,** Middle Tn St Univ, Murfreesboro, TN; GD; BS; Sigma Delta Sigma 87-; Kappa Delta Pi 89-; Rho Lambda; Zeta Tau Alpha Svc Chrmn 89-; Psychlgy; Gdnc Cnslr.

**PIGGOTT, PHILIP G,** Samford Univ, Birmingham, AL; GD; JD; Hnr Crt Jstc; Amer Jrnl Trl Advcy Assoc Ed; BA Rhoden Clge 85; Law.

**PIGMAN, ANIK E,** S U N Y Coll At Fredonia, Fredonia, NY; JR; BA BS; ACA Sec 90-; Frnch Clb VP 90-; Alpha Mu Gamma VP 90-; Pi Delta Phi; Cmmnctns Media/Frnch; Pub Rel.

**PIGMAN, KIMBERLY M,** Capital Univ, Columbus, OH; FR; BSN; Stdnt Ambssdr 90; Nrsng.

**PIGNATO, JEFFREY LAWRENCE,** Fl St Univ, Tallahassee, FL; SO; BS; Phi Eta Sigma 89-90; Hnrs/Schlrs Soc 89-; Acctng.

**PIKE, ANGELA T,** Western Ky Univ, Bowling Green, KY; SR; Nwmn Clb Pres 86-88; Assn Undrgrad Gntcsts 90-; Phi Kappa Phi 90-; Phi Theta Kappa 86-; Gldn Key 89-; Outstndng Blgy Stdnt Yr 90-; BS; Btncl Soc Amer Yng Btnst Rcgntn Awd 90-; AS Elizabthtwn Comm Coll 87; Rcmbnt Gntcs/Chmstry; Lab Tech.

**PIKE, BRENDA J,** Univ Of Nc At Asheville, Asheville, NC; SR; BA; Alpha Kappa Delta; Dns Lst 87-; Vrsty Sccr 88; Sclgy; MA.

**PIKE, CINDY C,** Univ Of Cincinnati, Cincinnati, OH; SR; BM; Ohio Coll Music Edctrs Assn Co Edtr 86-; Alpha Lambda Delta; Music Educ; Tchr.

**PIKE, KIMBERLY M,** Siena Coll, Loudonville, NY; SR; BA; Kickline Tm 90-; Yrbk 89-90; Sibling Wkend Cmtee; Delta Epsilon Sigma 90-; Human Rsrce Intrn 90-; Alpha Kappa Alpha 90-; Alpha Mu Gamma; Kickline 90-; English; Tch Hum Rsrcs.

**PIKE, MARILIYN A,** Univ Of Ky, Lexington, KY; SO; SW; KY Cncl Chld Abuse; Photo Studio 85-; Soc Work; Clinical.

**PIKE JR, WILLIAM D,** Dyersburg St Comm Coll, Dyersburg, TN; SO; BED; Acctg/Econ Tutr 90-; Natrl Sci; Tchr.

**PIKER, CHRISTOPHER W,** Univ Of Southern Ms, Hattiesburg, MS; SO; Scty Physics Stdnts Sec/Treas 90-; Outstdng Fresh Physics Stdnt 89-; Physics; Prof.

**PIKULA, NANCY A,** D Youville Coll, Buffalo, NY; SR; BS; Amer Occup Thrpy Assoc 88-/Schlrshp; Occup Thrpy.

**PILATE, MARCENIA S,** Jackson St Univ, Jackson, MS; SO; BED; Wsly Fndtn; Chem Soc; NSBE; Web Debois Hnr Soc; Alpha Lambda Delta; Cmps Crusade; Biomed Rsrch Prog; Chem; Environ Eng.

**PILCHER, DEBRA F,** Commonwealth Coll, Norfolk, VA; FR; MA; Amercn Medcl Assoc 90; Medcl Asst.

**PILESKI, GAIL A,** Mount Aloysius Jr Coll, Cresson, PA; FR; ASSOC; Hosp Nrs Extrn; Nrsng.

**PILEWSKI, JENNIFER M,** Slippery Rock Univ, Slippery Rock, PA; FR; BSED; Phi Eta Sigma; Lambda Sigma Sec; IM Bsktbl Capt; Math; Tchng.

**PILEWSKI, ROBERT J,** Methodist Coll, Fayetteville, NC; JR; BS; Resdnt Advsr; Lambda Chi Alpha Treas 89-; Stdnt Govt Hall Of Fame; Sykes Cap Athltc Award 90; NCAA Div III Golf Champ Mdlst; Varsty Mens Golf Team; Bus Admn.

**PILGRIM, AMY M,** Ga St Univ, Atlanta, GA; SR; BA; Kappa Delta Pi 90-; Cert Med Offc Asst Claytn St Clg Morrow Ga; Erly Chldhd Educ; Tchr.

**PILGRIM, ANDERSON M,** City Univ Of Ny Baruch Coll, New York, NY; GD; BBA; AMA 89-; Beta Gamm Sigma 90-; Baruch Schlr 88-90; AAS Borough Of Manhattan Cc 88; Mkrt; Retl Mngmnt.

**PILGRIM, LISA G,** Univ Of Tn At Martin, Martin, TN; SR; BS; Nrsng.

**PILGRIM, MARLON D,** Morehouse Coll, Atlanta, GA; FR; BSC; Internatl Stdnt Org 90-; Exclnc Math Awds 90-; Acctng.

**PILGRIM, STEVEN S,** S U N Y Coll Of Tech At Alfred, Alfred, NY; FR; AOS; Sigma Tau Epsilon 90-; Hvy Equip Trk/Dsl; Entrprnr.

**PILIERO, KIMBERLY A,** Georgetown Univ, Washington, DC; JR; BSBA; Sch Bsns Admn SBA Stdnt Nwsltr Edtr 89-; Bsns Day Steerng Comm Brochre Comm 89-; SBA Mentr Prog Alumni 90-; SBA Stdnt Adv; SBA Dns Lst 88-90; Our Lady Mercy Cath Chr Rdr 89-; SBA Ldrshp Retrt 90-; SBA Fac Cand Intrvws; Mgmt; Law.

**PILKINGTON, WENDY E,** Spartanburg Methodist Coll, Spartanburg, SC; SO; AA; Crmnl Juste Clb 89-; Crmnl Juste; Law.

**PILLAI, DYLAN R,** Cornell Univ Statutory College, Ithaca, NY; FR; BS; Bio; Publ Hlth.

**PILLERI, THOMAS M,** Boston Coll, Chestnut Hill, MA; SR; BS; Entrprnr Soc 89-; Acctg Acad 89-; Golden Key 89-; Beta Gamma Sigma 90-; IM Bsktbl 90-; Acctg; CPA.**

**PILLING, HEATHER M,** West Liberty St Coll, West Liberty, WV; FR; BA; Educ; Tchr.

**PILLOW, ERIC A,** Memphis St Univ, Memphis, TN; JR; BA; Campus Crus/Christ; Gold Key; Gamma Beta Pi; Commctns; Ministry.

**PILLOW, KIMBERLY G,** Univ Of Sc At Columbia, Columbia, SC; JR; BS; Women In Business 88-90; Host Carolina Bus Dialogue; Phi Eta Sigma 89-; Gamma Beta Phi 89-; Gamma Beta Phi Hnr Soc 89-; USC Deans List 88-; USC Presidents List; Davis-Garvin Agency Schlrshp; Finance Insurance.

**PILLOW, TINA R,** Jackson St Univ, Jackson, MS; FR; BA; Alpha Lambda Delta 90-; Deans Lst 90-; Finance; Corp Law.

**PILNY, ANTHONY A,** Central Fl Comm Coll, Ocala, FL; FR; AA; Phi Theta Kappa 90-; Sci; Vet Med.

**PILOT, PETER J,** Univ Of Fl, Gainesville, FL; JR; BA; Art Hstry Assn 90-; Natl Trst Hstrc Presrvtn 88-; Amer Flm Inst 89-; Psychtrc Cnslr; Dir Comm Crisis Cntr; Edtr Socl Srvc Nwsltr; Edtr Lit Mag; Art Hstry; Law/Arts Museum Stds/Tchg.

**PILZ-DAY, JOAN,** Saint Joseph Coll, West Hartford, CT; JR; BA; Psych Clb Sec; Phi Theta Kappa 89-; Religious Educ Instr 89-; Assoc 89; Lgl Sec; Psych; Cnslg.

**PIMENTEL, FLERIDA M,** City Univ Of Ny Hostos Coll, Bronx, NY; SR; Coll Boards Coll Schlrshp; Socl Wrkr.

**PIMENTEL, LOIDA V,** Bunker Hill Comm Coll, Boston, MA; FR; Clb 20-30 87-88; Ping Pong/Tns 90; Cert 88; Engl; Flght Attdnt.

**PIMPERL, E TREMAINE,** Mobile Coll, Mobile, AL; JR; BS; AS Faulkner State Jr Coll 90; Math; Tchr.

**PIMPINELLI, MICHELE L,** Atlantic Comm Coll, Mays Landing, NJ; SO; Bwlng 88-90; Chld Cr Dvlpmnt/Scndry Educ; Tchng.

**PINARD, JULIE A,** Elms Coll, Chicopee, MA; JR; BA; Judicial Brd 88-; Field Hockey 90-; Wuti Gallery Enfield CT Ast Dir 90-; Field Hockey 90-; Art Education.

**PINCH III, ROY E,** Fl St Univ, Tallahassee, FL; SR; BA; USA Karate Blckblt 86-; Aikikai 90-; Rssn Clb/Rssn Tbl 90; Phi Eta Sigma 88-; Gldn Ky 90-; Psi Chi; Psychlgy.

**PINCHES, WILLIAM L,** Bates Coll, Lewiston, ME; SO; BA; Chapel Brd Secty 90-; Students Admissions Tour Guide 89-90; Vltr Coord Officer 90-; Hunger Clean Up Prjt Commt Co Ldr 90-; Crop Walk Commt Co-Ldr 90; Deans List 89-; Dana Schlr 90-; Religion; Ministry/Ed.**

**PINCKNEY, MICHELE F,** Johnson C Smith Univ, Charlotte, NC; JR; Soc For Opport In Sci 89-; Alpha Chi 90-; Beta Kappa Chi 90-; Alpha Kappa Mu 90-; MBRS 90-; MARC; Bio; Env Hlth Sci.

**PINDELL III, ALLEN H,** Anne Arundel Comm Coll, Arnold, MD; SO; BA; Drama Clb 89-; Crtv Wrtng Org VP; Engl; Playwriting.

**PINDELL, JENNIFER LYNN,** Ky Christian Coll, Grayson, KY; SR; Bsbl/Vlybl/Aerobics Instrctr 90-; Erly Ed; Tchng.

**PINDER, JOHN JOSEPH,** City Univ Of Ny Queensbrough, New York, NY; FR; BS; Audio Engr.

**PINEDA, ALBINO ARIEL,** Univ Politecnica De Pr, Hato Rey, PR; SO; Deans Lst 89-90; Math; Civil Eng.

**PINEIRO SANTIAGO, LUIS A,** Univ Of Pr At Mayaguez, Mayaguez, PR; SO; BSME; Eng; Mech Eng.

**PINELLI, CYNTHIA A,** Elon Coll, Elon, NC; JR; BA; Student Adm Commt Tour Guide 89-; Athletic Recruite Adm Tour Guide 89-; Athletic Dept Tutor; Lambda Pi Eta VP; Alpha Epsilon Rho Secty 90-; Deans Commdtn Deans List 89-; Corp Commtns; Corp Reltns Law Field.**

**PINER, KENNETH E,** Columbia Union Coll, Takoma Park, MD; JR; BS; Jrnlsm.

**PINERO, ANTONIO,** Univ Of Pr At Rio Piedras, Rio Piedras, PR; SR; BS; AEPM; Micro Biol Stdnt Assn; Reg Hnr List; Deans Lst; Golden Key 89-; Natural Sci; Med Doctor.

**PINERO, MARISEL,** Miami Dade Comm Coll North, Miami, FL; SO; AA; Phi Theta Kappa 89; AA; Acctg; CPA.

**PING, DOUGLAS E,** S U N Y At Buffalo, Buffalo, NY; SR; BS; Gold Key 90-; Sarah Helen Kish Meml Fndtn Schlrshp 88; VP Johnson Park Entertainmnt Inc 89-; AAS 89; Bus Admin; Law.

**PINGELSKI, CAROLINE M,** Hudson Valley Comm Coll, Troy, NY; SR; AAS; Internshp NY State Asmbly Sec; Bsn; Admin/Mgr.

**PINGITORE, ANDREW F,** S U N Y Coll At Fredonia, Fredonia, NY; SR; BED; Pi Mu Epsilon; Edn Hon Soc; Wnr Nysmatic Excell Awd Math Schlrshp 88; AS Jamestown Comm Coll 88; Math; Sec Edn.

**PINHEIRO, ANGELA M,** Univ Of Ga, Athens, GA; SR; BSED; Deans Lst 90-; Engl; Tch.

**PINHO, ANABELA A,** Saint Joseph Coll, West Hartford, CT; FR; BS; Acctg Scty 90; Bus Scty 90; VA Med Ctr; Hon Symposium; Acctg/Ec; Bus.

**PINILLA, FREDY,** Atlantic Union Coll, S Lancaster, MA; JR; BA; Chispa Vp 88-89; Cmps Mnstry Stdnt Assoc Codrctr 90-; Sa Sntr 90-; Theta Alpha Kappa 90-; Cmmnty Cntr 90-; Theolgy/Scl Wrk; Pastor.

**PINILLOS, JOSE F,** City Univ Of Ny City Coll, New York, NY; JR; BA; Spanish Lit; Mba Bus Adm.

**PINION, PEGGY S,** Alice Lloyd Coll, Pippa Passes, KY; SR; BA; Phi Beta Lambda Hstrn 89-; SIFE 89-90; Alpha Chi 90-; St Conf/Natl Conf Bsn Law 90; St Conf Acctng; Fred J Becker Awd 90; Outstdng Snr Awd; Acctng; CPA.

**PINKARD, PHAIDRA H,** Univ Of South Al, Mobile, AL; SR; BS; BSU 89-; SCEC 90-F SGA 89-90; Hon Soc 89-; Order Of Omega; Delta Sigma Theta Pres 90-; Deans List 89-90; Ed; Tchr.

**PINKERMAN, GINA K,** Coll Of Charleston, Charleston, SC; SO; BA; Concert Choir Centre Stage 89-90; Flwshp Chrstn Athls; Phi Mu 90-; Carolina De Fabritils Schlrshp 90-; Frnch.

**PINKHAM, CARL A,** Liberty Univ, Lynchburg, VA; JR; BS; Crss Cltrl Mnstrs; Mssnry.

**PINKHAM, DOREEN,** Newbury Coll, Brookline, MA; FR; Asst Mgr Pier 1 Imports Woburn MA; Hotel/Rstrnt Mngt.

**PINKHASOV, DOLLILA,** Miami Dade Comm Coll, Miami, FL; SO; BA; Business; Finance.

**PINKSTON, JEWELSTINE,** Savannah St Coll, Savannah, GA; JR; ASME Sec 89-; Mech Eng Tchnlgy; Machine Dsgnr.

**PINNEY, GLEN W,** Springfield Tech Comm Coll, Springfield, MA; SR; AS; Mchncl Tchnlgy CAD Cam; CAD Dsgn.

**PINNICK, THAYLENE D,** Va Commonwealth Univ, Richmond, VA; JR; BFA; Act Arts Comm 89-; Crtv Arts Mnstries; Guild Tmlnsn Coll Dir 89-90; Golden Key; Ntl Hon Soc 89-; Hons Pgm; Phi Theta Kappa 89-90; Maymont Fndtn Intrn Asst Ed Prgrmr; AA Tomlinson Coll 90; Art Hist/Museum Currclm; Ed Prgrmng.

**PINNICKS, LORI A,** Muskingum Coll, New Concord, OH; SR; BA; Chrldng 87-90; Choir 87-90; Phi Theta Beta 89-; Sr Hnry 89-; Delta Gamma Theta Alum Sec 88-; Edn; Teach.

**PINO, ANTHONY,** Schenectady County Comm Coll, Schenectady, NY; SR; AAS; Engrng.

**PINO, MARIA DEL CARMEN,** Inter Amer Univ Pr Hato Rey, Hato Rey, PR; Mrtg Bnk Cash Cntrl/Teller Cstmr Serv Intrntnl Prvt Bnkng 85; Acctncy; CPA.

**PINSON, PAMELA C,** Middle Tn St Univ, Murfreesboro, TN; JR; BA; Future Acctnts Assn VP 90-; Stdnt Orntn Ldr 89-90; Rho Lambda; Beta Alpha Psi; Tau Omicron; Beta Gamma Sigma; Kappa Delta Pres; Wrk Schlrshp 88-; Accntng; Private Accntng.

**PINSON, PAUL L,** Lexington Comm Coll, Lexington, KY; SO; Data Cmnctns.

**PINTABONA, ROBERT J,** Jersey City St Coll, Jersey City, NJ; SR; BA; Engl; Jrnlsm.**

**PINTADO, ANITA M,** Barry Univ, Miami, FL; SR; BA; Hstry Asc Sec 88-89; Hnr Std Asc 90-; Pi Gamma Mu VP 90-; Phi Alpha Theta Pres 89-; Hstry; Ed.

**PINTAGRO, MICHAEL R,** Univ Of Rochester, Rochester, NY; SO; PH D; Deans List 89-; Hse Mrcy Intrn 90; Hist; Rsrch Wrtng Tchng.

**PINTAL, ANNMARIE,** Rivier Coll, Nashua, NH; SR; BS; Howard F Greene Mem Schlp NEAGSC 90; Acctng/Cmptr Sci.

**PINTO, ALEXANDRA T,** Inter Amer Univ Pr San German, San German, PR; SO; BBA; Accntng; Archtctr.

**PINTO, MARJORIE H,** Univ Of Md At Eastern Shore, Princess Anne, MD; SO; BS; Phys Thrpy.

**PINTO, NINA G,** Carnegie Mellon Univ, Pittsburgh, PA; SR; BS; VP Action Comm 90-; Orientation Cnslr 88-; Senate Affrs Comm 88-89; Envrnmntl Action Comm 89-90; Deans Lst 90; Intrnshp Proctor Gamble 90; Intrnshp Software Engrng Inst 89; Aerobics Instructor 89-; Info Systems; Analyst.

**PINTOR, JERI B,** Shawnee St Univ, Portsmouth, OH; JR; BA; Rght Life Org 90-; AS Ashland Comm Coll 89; Envrnmntl Sci; EPA.

**PIONTKOWSKI, PATRICIA K,** West Chester Univ, West Chester, PA; SR; BMUS; Music Ed Natl Cnfrnce 88-89; Wind Ensmbl 87-; Cncrt Choir 89-; PA Intrcoll Bnd; Pblshd Artcl In Todays Msc Ed; Deans Lst 89-90; Music Ed.

**PIOTROWSKI, MICHAEL J,** Univ Of Rochester, Rochester, NY; SO; BS; Act Brd 90-; Crew 90-; Mech Eng.

**PIPER, CARLENE R,** Bapt Bible Coll & Seminary, Clarks Summit, PA; SO; BS; Stdnt Mssns Fllwshp; Mgr Jhnstwn Str; AA 85; Mssns.

**PIPER, LORRIE L,** Endicott Coll, Beverly, MA; JR; BS; Stdnt Ambsdr; Deans List; Advertising Intrnshp; AS 90; Visual Communications; Advertising.

**PIPER, TONY L,** Middle Ga Coll, Cochran, GA; SO; AS; Deans List; Physical Therapy.

**PIPERSBURGH, OLIVIA H,** Saint Josephs Coll New York, Brooklyn, NY; SR; BS; Bkkpr Agncy Fr Chld Dev 85-; Tchr In Cntrl Amer; Acctng Clrk; Dns Advsry Cncl 89-; Tchrs Cert Board Of Educ Belize CA 58; Mgmt Cert 90; Hmn Rsrcs Mgmt.

**PIPES, MICHAEL J,** Univ Of Al At Huntsville, Huntsville, AL; GD; MS; IEEE; BSE; Elec Engr.

**PIPILES, KAREN E,** Niagara Univ, Niagara Univ, NY; JR; BA; Phi Theta Kappa 90-; Delta Epsilon Sigma; AAS Niagara Cty Comm Coll 90; Acctng.

**PIPITONE, CRISTINA M,** Fl Atlantic Univ, Boca Raton, FL; SR; BBA; AA Cmmnty Coll 84; Crprt Mgmt; Govt.

**PIPKIN, SINA I,** Univ Of Nc At Greensboro, Greensboro, NC; SO; Stdnt NC Assoc Of Educ 89-; Assoc Educ Yng Chldrn Stdnt Mbr 89-; Univ Mrshls 90-; Alpha Lambda Delta 90-; Omicron Nu Fres Awd 90; Josephine Kramer Soph Awd; Phi Beta Kappa Soph Bk Awd; Chld Dev K-6 Certif; Teach Preschl/Elem Schl.

**PIPPEN, CRAIG J,** Univ Of Ky, Lexington, KY; JR; HPR Hlth Physcl Rcrtn VP; Christ Kng Bsktbl Coach Hd Coach; Edctn Hlth PE; Tchr Coach.

**PIPPIN, JAMES A,** Tallahassee Comm Coll, Tallahassee, FL; FR; AA; Criminology; Law Enfrcmnt/Invstgtn.

**PIRET, BRIAN T,** East Stroudsburg Univ, E Stroudsburg, PA; JR; BA; IM Flg Ftbl Bsktbl Sftbl 88-; Ec/Mgmt; Fin.

**PIREZ, CRISTINA M,** Fl International Univ, Miami, FL; FR; BA; Pre Med Soc 90-; Bio; Med.

**PIRILLA, KIMBERLY L,** Methodist Coll, Fayetteville, NC; GD; MBA; Psych Clb Pres 89-90; Sclgy/Scl Wrk Clb 89-90; Psi Chi 90-; Sigma Omega Chi 90-; Guardian Ad Litem Vol 90-; YMCA Inst 90-; BS 90; Psychology; Industrial/Orgnztnl Psych.

**PIRKLE, KEVIN M,** Southern Coll Of Tech, Marietta, GA; JR; MBA; Elect Eng Tech; Eng Tech.

**PIRMOHAMED, ROSEMIN A,** Mercer Univ Schl Of Pharm, Atlanta, GA; SO; Gpha 88-90; Ptnt Edctn Comm Phrmcst; Phrmckntc Srvc Due; Rho Chi 90-; Phi Kappa Phi 88-; Srvc At Mosq 88-; Poison Prvntn Week Comm; Deans Lst 90; Acdmc Schlrshp 88; Clncl Phrmcst.**

**PIROUMOFF, ANN A,** Oh Wesleyan Univ, Delaware, OH; JR; BA; Econ Bd; Sfty Bd; Ortntn Asst; Phi Sigma Iota; Delta Delta Delta Treas 88-; Smng Tm 88-90; Acctg.

**PIRZADA, NUSRAT M,** City Univ Of Ny Queensbrough, New York, NY; SO; Frnch Clb Pres; Muslim Clb; Certif Sch Diagnostic Ultra Snd 89-90; Physlgy/Chem; Biochem.

**PISANA, GINA M,** Seton Hall Univ, South Orange, NJ; SO; BED; Archeolgy Clb 90-; Spec Olympcs Comm; Kappa Delta Pi 90-; Deans Lst 89-; Dvlpmntl Dsordrs; Spec Ed Tchr.

**PISANI, CHERYL D,** Endicott Coll, Beverly, MA; SR; AS; Int Dec/Mrchndsng.

**PISANI, GREG A,** Cecils Coll, Asheville, NC; SR; AAS; Law/Paralegal.

**PISANO, MELAINEY J,** Schenectady County Comm Coll, Schenectady, NY; SO; AS; Walt Disney World Clg Prog; Invitational Culinary Quadrathlon 90; Hotel/Rest Mgmnt; BA.

**PISAPIA, JOSEPH J,** Salisbury St Univ, Salisbury, MD; SR; BA; Sprts Clb Cncl 90-; Athlt Advsry Com 90-; Res Hl Assn 87-; Phi Eta Sigma 87-; Phi Alpha Theta 90-; Pi Gamma Mu 90-; Omicron Delta Kappa 90-; Yng Rpblcns Clb 87-90; Rsdnt Asst 89-; Mst Imprvd Swmmr 88; Mst Vlbl Swmmr 90-; Hstry/Scndry Educ; Grad Schl-NC St Univ.

**PISARIS, JOHN B,** Oh Northern Univ, Ada, OH; GD; Dns Lst; USAA All Amer Schlr; BLS Hillsdale Coll 88; Juris Doctor.

**PISHIONERI, GINA M,** Mt Saint Marys Coll & Seminary, Emmitsburg, MD; SR; BS; Commuter Clb 89-; Geo H Miles 89-; Hon Stdnts Assoc Co Chrprsn 87-89; Delta Mu Delta 90-; Dns Lst 87-; AA Frederick Comm Clg 89; Acctg.

**PISKAC, LAURA E,** Univ Of Akron, Akron, OH; JR; Lbrian Asst Akrun Summit Cnty Pblc Lbry 77-90; Elem Ed; Tchr.

**PISKOVICS, CHRISTINE J,** Glassboro St Coll, Glassboro, NJ; SO; BA; Laser Inst Amer 84-86; Laser Techn 86-90; AAS Camden Cnty Clg 86; Psychology; Drug Alcohol Abuse Cnslr.

**PISTACCHIO, UGO SALVATORE,** Strayer Coll, Washington, DC; SO; Acctg Clb 90-; Comp Info Clb 90-; Tea Kwon Do Karate Clb Blk Blt Instrctr 88-89; JROTC 2nd LT 86-90; BA; Comp Sci; Comp Anly/Bsn Adm.

**PISULA, JAMES N,** Georgetown Univ, Washington, DC; FR; Prog Brd; 2nd Hons 90; 1st Hons; CREW Tm.

**PITA-LOOR, KAREN J,** Barry Univ, Miami, FL; FR; BA; Phi Alpha Delta 90-; Psychlgy/Thtr; Law.

**PITCHER, JEFFREY C,** Temple Univ, Philadelphia, PA; JR; BS; Natl Assn Rtl Drggst; PA Phrmctcl Assn; Kappa Psi 90-; Phar; Rtl Phrmcst.

**PITCHER, MARIA O,** Al A & M Univ, Normal, AL; SR; BS; Cncl Except Chldrn 90-; Acad Hnrs 86-; Kappa Delta Pi; Spec Ed; Tch.

**PITCHER-WESTBROOKS, JANICE MAY,** Univ Of Tn At Martin, Martin, TN; SR; BA; STEA 90-; AA Jackson Comm Clg 70; Elem Ed; Tchng.

**PITCHFORD, CHERYL LA NAY,** Central Al Comm Coll, Alexander City, AL; SO; BS; Stu Gov Assoc Sec 90-; Chem; Phrmcy.

**PITCOCK, EDNA C,** Wv Northern Comm Coll, Wheeling, WV; BS; Hmer Laughlin China Co Newell W Va; Nrsng; BSN.

**PITEL, SCOTT R,** Embry Riddle Aeronautical Univ, Daytona Beach, FL; JR; BS; AAAE 90-; Mgmt Clb 90-; Assoc Degree Bus Admin; Bus Mgmt.

**PITLUCK, SUSAN O,** Neumann Coll, Aston, PA; SR; BA; Charlotte Newcombe Schlrshp 90-; Deans Hnr Lst 90; Congregation Oheo Shalom; BA; Erly Chldhd; Teach.

**PITMAN, SANDRA L B,** Medical Coll Of Ga, Augusta, GA; SR; BSN; Sigma Theta Tau; AA FL St Univ 88; Nrsng; Nrsng NICU.

**PITONYAK, EDDIE T,** Troy St Univ At Dothan, Dothan, AL; SR; BS; Gamma Beta Phi; Phi Theta Kappa 89-; Otsdng Achvmnt 89; Untd Assoc Mfg Repr 89-; Knights Of Columbus; Terr Mngr/Vicon Inc Memphis TN 84-; AS Wallace Comm Clg 89; Bus Mgmnt.

**PITSENBARGER, LISA M,** Bridgewater Coll, Bridgewater, VA; FR; BS; Hlth Sci; Occptnl Therpy.

**PITT, ALISON C,** Univ Of Ma At Amherst, Amherst, MA; FR; BS; Mrchng Bnd 90-; RA; Blgy; Rsrch.

**PITT, CATHERINE C,** Univ Of Miami, Coral Gables, FL; JR; BS; Pres 100 Orientation Asst 90-; Mstr Tutor Prog; Stdnt Govt Undrsecty 88-89; Phi Beta Kappa 90-; Phi Kappa Phi 90-; Psi Chi 89-; Alpha Lambda Delta 89-; Sigma Alpha Epsilon Delta; Pi Kappa Alpha Ltl Sis 88-89; Gldn Key 90-; Psychlgy; Physician.

**PITTARI JR, DOMINICK A,** Univ Of Southern Ms, Hattiesburg, MS; JR; Amer Mktng Assoc 90-; Gamma Beta Phi 89-.

**PITTELLI, RANDAL L,** Univ Of Rochester, Rochester, NY; JR; BA/BS; Tchng Asst EE 111 Elec Circts Rectatn Cls 89-90; Math/Elec Eng/Pre Med; Pblc Hlth Med.

**PITTER, ANDREW DAVID,** City Univ Of Ny Queensbrough, New York, NY; SR; AAS; Radio Clb; Tau Alpha Pi Pres; Merit Cert Coll Arts Sci Tech 89; Comp Tech; Eng.

**PITTMAN, AUBREY G,** Univ Of West Fl, Pensacola, FL; JR; BA; AA Pensacola Jr Clg 90; Social Work.

**PITTMAN, CHERICA CHARMAINE,** Southeastern Comm Coll, Whiteville, NC; SO; BA; Talent Roster Cert 90-; AA; Mrktng.

**PITTMAN, COLDEN DELORES,** Bristol Univ, Bristol, TN; SR; BA; Blacks Gvt Ntl Bd Dir 88-; NAACP Knxvl Chptr Exec Bd Mbr; Ntl Pltcl Cngrs Black Wmn Knox Pres 87-; Optimist Clb E Knxvl; Regnl Dir; Business Admin/Paraleagalism; Management.

**PITTMAN, JAYNE M,** Univ Of Nc At Charlotte, Charlotte, NC; FR; BA; Psych Clb; Holshser Hl Cncl; Creatv Arts Leag 90; Univ Hons; GTE Schlrshp 90-; Res Adv; Psych; Clncl Thrpy.

**PITTMAN, JENNIFER A,** Univ Of Ga, Athens, GA; SR; Georgia Girl 89-90; Panhellenic Sec 87-88; Rsdnt Assist 88; Golden Key 90; Outstndng Clg Stdnt Amer 90; Kappa Delta Epsilon; Kappa Delta; N Ga Clg Tour Guide; Tutorial Pgm; Ldrshp Schlrshp 86-88; Paul Douglas Tchng Schlrshp 88-; Educ/Erly Chldhd; Tchng.

**PITTMAN, JOETTA L,** Univ Of Ga, Athens, GA; SR; BSCFC; Hall Govt Pres 90; WCU Bnd 88-90; Alpha Zeta Scrbe 90; Golden Key 90; Phi Upsilon Omicron Pres 90; Stdnt Hm Ec Assoc 90; Deans Lst; Alpha Chi Omega Cmmnctns Chrmn 88-90; Chld Dvlpmnt Erly Chldhd Ed; Day Care.

**PITTMAN, KELLY E,** Fl St Univ, Tallahassee, FL; JR; BA; Gldn Key 90-; Intrnd Kathy Hanson Cmnctns Spclst Educ Cmmssnr Betty Castor; Univ Gold Tm 88-; Cmnctns/Pblc Rltns; Pblc Rltns.

**PITTMAN, KIMBERLY W,** Fl A & M Univ, Tallahassee, FL; FR; BS; Ladies Aux Knghts Of Peter Claver 89-; Elec Engr.

**PITTMAN, LATONYA Y,** Alcorn St Univ, Lorman, MS; FR; BS; Hons Clb 90-; Bus; Acctg.

**PITTMAN, NATASCHA K,** Alcorn St Univ, Lorman, MS; FR; Natl Hnr Soc Secr; Acad Schlrshp; Elem Ed.

**PITTMAN, ROGERS S,** Fl A & M Univ, Tallahassee, FL; FR; FAMU Symph Bnd 90-; Phi Eta Sigma; Leander L Boykin Schrlshp; Hsng Recog; Cmptr Inf Syst; Prgrmmg.

**PITTNER, DAVID A,** Univ Of Miami, Coral Gables, FL; SO; BA; Clg Bwl Miami Vrsty Tm 89-; IM Coordntr 90-; Pearson Schlrshp 89-; Hstry; Law.

**PITTS, AMBER E,** Atlantic Comm Coll, Mays Landing, NJ; Bus; Acctg/CPA.

**PITTS, BIANCA M,** Cleveland St Univ, Cleveland, OH; FR; BA; English; Law.

**PITTS, C ADELE,** Birmingham Southern Coll, Birmingham, AL; SR; BS; Student Govt Assoc Adult Studies Rep 89-90; Adult Studies Adv Commt Mtr 89; Adult Studies Adv Council Recr 90-; Alpha Sigma Lamdba 90-; Mortar Brd 90-; Alpha Kappa Psi 90-; Amnesty Intl 89-; Mktng/Mgt; Consultant.

**PITTS III, DAVID M,** Morehouse Coll, Atlanta, GA; FR; N Car Clb Dentstry Clb; Mentrng Pgm; Schlrshp Rec; Bio; Dentstry.

**PITTS, DENISE L,** Winthrop Coll, Rock Hill, SC; SR; BS; SNEA 90-; Orntn Asst 90; Rsdnt Asst 90-; PACE 88-; Deans Lst 90-; Delta Sigma Theta Prlmntrn 90-; Rdng Tutor-Richmond Drive Elem 90; Tchng Aide 88; Ft Mill Prmry 90-; Vrsty Chrldng 87-89; Elem Ed; Tchng.

**PITTS, ELLEN S,** Univ Of Sc At Columbia, Columbia, SC; JR; BA; Amer Mktg Assn 90-; Bsn Admin; Fin/Mgmt.

**PITTS, JAMES M,** Wv Univ At Parkersburg, Parkersburg, WV; AS; Epwrth Un Meth Chrch Admn Brd Pres/Prop Comm; Ltl Leag Coach; Welder Applacn Pwr Co Mtnr Pwr Plnt 80-; Cert Ben Frnkln Vo Tech Ctr 78; Wldng Mgmt; QC Spec.

**PITTS, JOHN A,** Univ Of Ky, Lexington, KY; SO; BA; Tau Kappa Epsilon 85-86; Engl/Hstry; Tch Coll/Publish Essays.

**PITTS, LINDA JOAN,** Middle Tn St Univ, Murfreesboro, TN; SO; BSN; Phi Theta Kappa 79-80; Nrsng; Nrsng Anthslgy.

**PITTS, MELINDA S,** Middle Ga Coll, Cochran, GA; JR; BA; Acctng; CPA.

**PITTS, NATALEE P,** West Liberty St Coll, West Liberty, WV; FR; Biology; Medl Tchnlgy.

**PITTS, REVA LYNETTE,** Central St Univ, Wilberforce, OH; JR; BS; Jr Achvmnt Advsr 89-90; Frst Natl Bnk Corp Ln Div 83-; Bus Admin/Finance; Corp Attrny.

**PITTS, STEPHEN MITCHELL,** Fl A & M Univ, Tallahassee, FL; JR; BED; Grnsboro Un Meth Chrch; AA Tallahassee Comm Clg 90; Elem Educ; Tchr.

**PITTS, TARA L,** Clark Atlanta Univ, Atlanta, GA; SR; BED; Stdnt GA Assn Eductrs Asst Sec 88-; Kappa Delta Epsilon 90-; Deans Lst 88-; Educ; Tchng.**

**PITTS, VALERIE V,** Al St Univ, Montgomery, AL; SO; Elem Ed; Prncpl.

**PITTSON, ANNEMARIE S,** Central Fl Comm Coll, Ocala, FL; FR; BA; Hnrbl Dschrg US Navy 82-88; Pgmr 89-; Cert BE/E US Navy 83; Cert Cmnctns US Navy 83; Bus Admin; Bus.

**PITZER, DANIEL P,** City Univ Of Ny Baruch Coll, New York, NY; SR; Psychlgy Soc Pres 90-; Gldn Key 90-; Psi Chi 90-; Incntv Awd 87-88; Provst Awd 89-90; Psychlgy.

**PITZER, MICHELE L,** Kent St Univ Kent Cmps, Kent, OH; SR; BA; Fin Assoc Pres; Rho Epsilon; Ski Club; Golden Key; Fincl Mgt Assoc; Fin/Real Est.

**PIVAWER, JOLIENNE,** City Univ Of Ny Baruch Coll, New York, NY; SR; BBA; Ttr 87-88; Nwsppr Ed Chf 90-; Deans Slt 88-; Gldn Key 89-; Beta Gamm A Sigma 90-; Jls Rsnthl Mmrl Schlrshp 88; Brch Schlr 87-; Acctncy.

**PIVEC, CLARE M,** Coll Of Notre Dame Of Md, Baltimore, MD; SO; BA; Stdnt Tm Admsns Rep 89; Clg Radio Sta D J 90; Wmn Cmunctns Inc 90; Cmunctn Arts; Advtsng/Pub Rltns.**

**PIVIK, GEORGE A,** Duquesne Univ, Pittsburgh, PA; SO; BA; Wrld Affr Cncl Pgh; Intl Affr Cncl 90-; Army ROTC Cdt 89-; Lambda Sigma Pres 90-; Alpha Phi Omega; Amer Univ Intern Leg Deloitte & Taude; Hstry/Pol Sci; Law.

**PIXLEY, MARK C,** Univ Of Akron, Akron, OH; GD; BSME; ASME; Sigma Pi Sigma 89-; BS Kent State Univ 89; Mech Engr.

**PIZARRO, JOSE C,** Univ Of Pr At Rio Piedras, Rio Piedras, PR; SR; Gldn Key 90-; BA Pltcl Sci; Pltcl Sci; Law.

**PIZEM, RICHARD D,** Bowling Green St Univ, Bowling Green, OH; SR; BS; SCMA VP 90-; NAHB 90-; OH Cntrctrs 90-; Epsln Pi Tau; Natl Hnrs Asc; Epsln Pi Tau; Kulhman Schlp; Cnstrctn Mgmt Mgr.

**PIZIO, MARRA,** Glassboro St Coll, Glassboro, NJ; SR; MA; Phi Alpha Theta; BA 90; Hist; PhD Publc Hist.

**PIZZA, THERESA L,** Univ Of Md At Eastern Shore, Princess Anne, MD; JR; BA; Intl Food Svc Exec Assn 90-; Eto Rho Mu Hsptlty Club 90; Htl Rstrnt Mgmt; Exec Chef.

**PIZZANO, KRISTINA M,** Univ Of Ga, Athens, GA; JR; BA; PRSSA; Cert Aerobics Instrctr 88-; Golden Key 90-; Pi Beta Phi Im Chrmn 89-90; Deans List 88-; Jrnlsm; Publc Rltns.

**PIZZINO, PHYLLIS E,** Beckley Coll, Beckley, WV; JR; BS; Scndry Edctn Scl Stds; Tchr.

**PIZZY, CARLA L,** Broward Comm Coll, Ft Lauderdale, FL; JR; BA; Assoc Chldhd Edctn Intrtn 90-; As Brwrd Comm Coll 90; Erly Chldhd Edctn; Tch.

**PLACEK, BRADY J,** Nova Univ, Ft Lauderdale, FL; GD; MBA; DPMA Dir 87-88; Sr Systs Engr GTE Data Srvcs 80-; Bus; Quality Assurance.

**PLACER, ROBERT E,** Reformed Episcopal Seminary, Philadelphia, PA; JR; MDIV; Stdnt Govt Treas 90-; Bishop Higgin Mem Prize In Liturgics 90-; Pastrl Minstry; Church Plntng Minstry.

**PLACIDE, KAREN F,** City Univ Of Ny Baruch Coll, New York, NY; JR; BBA; Natl Assoc Blck Accts 91; Beta Alpha Psi 91; CXC Holy Fth Convent Trinidad 87; Acctg.

**PLACIDE, PATRICK,** Ky St Univ, Frankfort, KY; SO; BA; Phi Beta Lambda; Bus Admin; Entrepreneur.

**PLADEL, KEITH J,** Hudson Valley Comm Coll, Troy, NY; FR; AAS; Deans List 84-; Pres List 90-; Track/Field 84-85; AAS Hudson Vly Commty Clg 84-86; Resp Therapy.

**PLANAS, EDWIN J,** Inter Amer Univ Pr Hato Rey, Hato Rey, PR; FR; Clb Sodiet 87; Clb Dcrtn Clss Actvts 88-90.

**PLANELL, JONAS J,** Tn Temple Univ, Chattanooga, TN; SO; BA; Bus Clb 90-; BA PR Bapt Coll 86; Acctg; CPA.

**PLANEY, PATTY M,** Miami Jacobs Jr Coll Of Bus, Dayton, OH; SO; Drctrs Lst; Acctng; CPA.

**PLANK, CARRIE A,** East Carolina Univ, Greenville, NC; FR; BFA; Art; Med Illstrtn.

**PLANKERS, JAMES M,** Univ Of Tn At Knoxville, Knoxville, TN; FR; BA; Rssn Clb 90-.

**PLANTE, BRIAN C,** Hudson Valley Comm Coll, Troy, NY; SO; BA; Germn Clb 90-; Lacrosse 90-; AA; Cmnctns; Brdcst Jrnlsm.

**PLANTE, JENNIFER L,** Univ Of Rochester, Rochester, NY; JR; BA; Prtnrs In Rdg 89-90; Cmps YMCA; Amnsty Intrntl; Phi Sigma Sigma Insgn Chr 89-; Psychlgy Intrnshp 89-; Hlth/Scty Intrnshp; Psychlgy.

**PLASENCIA, AMELIA,** Fl International Univ, Miami, FL; JR; BS; AIAS Brd 89-; Phi Kappa Phi; Fclty Schlr 88-; Arctctrl Tchnlgy; Arctctr.

**PLASENCIA, MIREYA,** Fl Atlantic Univ, Boca Raton, FL; FR; BS; Phi Eta Sigma 90-; Bus; CPA.

**PLASSIO, JAMIE LEE,** Univ Of Pittsburgh At Greenbrg, Greensburg, PA; FR; Mgmt; Acctnt.

**PLASTER, DAVID L,** Univ Of Akron, Akron, OH; JR; BA; Pi Sigma Epsilon 89-; Mrktng; Sls Advrtsng.

**PLASTER, WANDA C,** Patrick Henry Comm Coll, Martinsville, VA; SO; BA; Ldr GEMS; Sndy Sch Tchr; Vol Fire Dept Lady Aux; Tchrs Asst; AAS; Educ; Tchr.

**PLASTINO, KRISTEN A,** Philadelphia Coll Pharm & Sci, Philadelphia, PA; JR; BS; Stdt Ttrl Serv Vol Liason 87-; Dorm Cncl 87-; Acdmy Stdts Phrmcy 87-; Rho Chi; Alpha Delta Theta Serg/Arms 88-; SHAPE 90-; Se Pa Scty Hosp Phrmcsts Schlrshp 90-; Deans List 87-; Vrsty Vlybl Capt 87-; Pharmacy; Doctor Of Pharmacy.

**PLATANIA, JOSEPH C,** Memphis St Univ, Memphis, TN; SR.

**PLATER, MARGO L,** Hampton Univ, Hampton, VA; SO; Univ Chr Treas 89-; Cncrt Chr 89-; NAACP 90-.

**PLATERO, TELMA C,** Central Fl Comm Coll, Ocala, FL; SO; Phi Theta Kappa; Amer Soc Q C; Schlrshp 89-.

**PLATKIN, STEVEN A,** City Univ Of Ny Baruch Coll, New York, NY; SR; Alpha Phi Delta VP 89-90; BBA Baruch Clg; Bsnss Mgt; Mngmnt/Entrprnr.

**PLATT, CELIA R,** Fl St Univ, Tallahassee, FL; JR; BA; Acctng Soc 90-; Synch Swim Tm 90-; Bus; Acctng.

**PLATT, SANDRA L,** Livingston Univ, Livingston, AL; JR; BS; IM Sports 88-90; Tau Kappa Epsilon Aux 88-90; Biolgy; Phrmcy.

**PLATT JR, WILLIAM H,** Univ Of Sc At Aiken, Aiken, SC; FR; BS; Bsn/Fnc.

**PLATZ, SARAH L,** Univ Of Toledo, Toledo, OH; GD; JD; Jdcl Bd Sr Cmte 79-81; Alpha Lambda Dleta 77-81; Phi Eta Sigma 77-81; Gamma Sigma Pi 79-81; Phi Mu 79-81; Genl Mills Schlrshp; Med Technlsgt 83-; Law.

**PLAVCHAN, JOAN,** Daytona Beach Comm Coll, Daytona Beach, FL; FR; VIPS; PTA Secy; CCD Coor; Tchrs Asst; Sub Tchr; Elem Ed; Tchr.

**PLAYER, LAUREN E,** Radford Univ, Radford, VA; SO; BA; Prsbytrn 89-; Gymnstcs 89-; Hstry; Educ/Law.

**PLAYTON, CHRISTINA L,** Univ Of Miami, Coral Gables, FL; JR; BA; BACCHUS 90-; BACCHUS Pres; Rho Lambda; Sigma Delta Tau VP 90-; CRS Vlybl 89-90; Cmnctns/Eng; Lawyer.

**PLAZA MALDONADO, LISSETTE,** Catholic Univ Of Pr, Ponce, PR; GD; BED; Cum Laude; Bellas Artes; MA Educ.

**PLAZA TOLEDO, OMARIS,** Catholic Univ Of Pr, Ponce, PR; JR; BA; Busns Admnstrtn; Mngmnt.

**PLEBANIAK, ANITA B,** Fl International Univ, Miami, FL; SO; BS; Lds Hrt; Biology; Med Drmtlgy Grtrc.

**PLEDGER, RONALD K,** Truett Mc Connell Coll, Cleveland, GA; SO; BA; Baptist Stdnt Union 89-; Majesty 90-; Music.

**PLEIS, CYNTHIA E,** Cumberland County Coll, Vineland, NJ; SO; AAS; Phi Theta Kappa 90-; Nursing; Rn.

**PLEKKENPOL, JACQUELINE M,** Ny Univ, New York, NY; SO; BA; Psi Chi 89-; Legal Secty 85-; Industrial/Org Psy.

**PLEMMONS, SEAN F,** Memphis St Univ, Memphis, TN; JR; BA; Film Prod; Dir/Prod/Wrtng.

**PLESKA, SHAWN C,** Duquesne Univ, Pittsburgh, PA; FR; BS; Res Hall Assoc 90-; Bus; Acctg.

**PLESNER, CARL E,** Fl St Univ, Tallahassee, FL; SR; BA; AA Glf Cst Comm Coll 89-; Accntng.

**PLETCHER, DAWN D,** Duquesne Univ, Pittsburgh, PA; SR; BA; Crss Cntry Trck And Fld 88-; NARD Clb 89-; ASP Clb 89-; Rho Chi; Intrnshp Smrst Drg 89-; Phrmcy.

**PLETCHER, ERIC D,** Duquesne Univ, Pittsburgh, PA; FR; BA; Union Pgm Bd; Cmps Mnstry; MENC; Music; Educ/Cmpstn.

**PLETCHER, ROBERT J,** Muskingum Coll, New Concord, OH; SR; Yrbk Sprts Edtr 88-89; Nwspr Stff Wrtr 89-; Phi Sigma Iota Treas 89-; Sigma Tau Delta; Omicron Delta Kappa; BA; Grmn Engl; Tchng.

**PLETT, THERESA CHERYL,** Union Univ, Jackson, TN; FR; BS; Vision Clown Team 90-; BSU 90-; Revival Teams 90-; Vol Wrk Hosp 90-; Bio; Pediatrician.

**PLICHTA, ANJANETTE L,** Coll Of William & Mary, Williamsburg, VA; FR; BA; Fld Hcky Clb Sec 90-; Pre-Law Clb 90-; Phi Eta Sigma Sec; Alpha Lambda Delta; Delta Gamma Mchdse Chrmn 90-; Pub Polcy/Engl; Law.

**PLINTA, LYNN M,** Comm Coll Algny Co Algny Cmps, Pittsburgh, PA; AD; Diploma Connelley Voc Trade Schl 87-88; Nursing.

**PLISKANER, ANNE,** Comm Coll Algny Co Algny Cmps, Pittsburgh, PA; SO; BA; Psychlgy; Counselor.

**PLISNER, SYLVIA K,** City Univ Of Ny John Jay Coll, New York, NY; JR; BS; Law.**

**PLITMAN, LAURA,** City Univ Of Ny Baruch Coll, New York, NY; SO; BBA; Jwsh Soc/Hillel 90-; Real Est Kingsbrgh Comm Coll 90; Fin/Invstmnts.

**PLOCK, KATHERINE M,** Univ Of Nh Plymouth St Coll, Plymouth, NH; SO; BA; Erly Chldhd Clb Pres; Elem/Erly Chldhd Ed; Tchr.

**PLOETZ, NICOLA S,** Birmingham Southern Coll, Birmingham, AL; SO; BA; Global Studies Assoc 91; Intl Student Assoc 91; Bskbl 91; Abitur Franz-Stock-Gymnasium Germany 90; Intl Studies; Engrg.

**PLOSS JR, EUGENE G,** S U N Y Coll At Fredonia, Fredonia, NY; JR; BFA; Rl Plyrs Gld 90-; Assoc Jmstwn Com Coll 89; Art; Ilstrtn.

**PLOTKIN, MARTIN L,** Va Commonwealth Univ, Richmond, VA; SR; MA; Roadrnnr Clb; Grnpc; Deans Lst; BA 86; BS 90; Engl-Educ; Tch.

**PLOTNIK, MICHAEL F,** City Univ Of Ny Baruch Coll, New York, NY; JR; Russn Clb VP; Acctg Soc; Mngmnt Soc.

**PLOURDE, EMELIE M,** Smith Coll, Northampton, MA; GD; Frnch Clb 87-90; Hs Pres VP Treas 88-90; SC Frst Grp Schlrs 90; Holyoke Comm Clge Srv Awd 85; Holyoke Comm Clg Stdnt Snt Awd Outstndg Chrctr/Intv/Ldrshp 85; Amer Stds; Ins Fld.

**PLUCKTER, TAMMY L,** Univ Of Sc At Columbia, Columbia, SC; SR; BS; Sorority Cncl Treas 89-90; Tae Kwon-Do Club VP 88-; Body Bldg Club 88-; Golden Key; Kappa Alpha Theta; Intrnshp With The Equitalbe Life Assurance Soc 90-; Fin/Mgt Info Sys; Invstmnt Bnkng.

**PLUMB, BRIAN M,** Univ Of Akron, Akron, OH; SO; BA; IM Vlybl; Elec Engr.

**PLUMMER, JILL E,** Anne Arundel Comm Coll, Arnold, MD; SO; BS; Sign Lngge Clb 90-; St Albns Chrch Sftbl Lgue 89-; AA Anne Arundel Comm Coll; Educ; Deaf Edctr.

**PLUMMER, SONIA MARIE,** City Univ Of Ny Med Evers Coll, Brooklyn, NY; SR; BS; Untd Chrstn Fllwshp Tres 89-; Elem Edctn; Tchr.

**PLUNK, JERRY D,** Memphis St Univ, Memphis, TN; SO; BFA; Fdrl Exprss Info Coord 89-; OCSA 89; Art/Grphc Dsgn; CAD/COMP Grphcs.

**PLUNKETT, DANA C,** Bloomfield Coll, Bloomfield, NJ; JR; Bsktbl 90-; AD Lackawanna Jr Coll 90; Bus Admn Mang.

**PLUNKETT, KAREN E,** Hudson Valley Comm Coll, Troy, NY; SO; AAS; Phi Theta Kappa 90-; Tutrng 89-; Pres Lst 89-; Librl Arts; Frnch/Sec Educ.

**PLUNKETT, MARGARET P,** Methodist Coll, Fayetteville, NC; SR; BA; Tapestry Art Edtr 89-; Fine Art Schlrshp 89-; Fayetteville Art Guild 89-; Fine Art; Artist Museum Vol.

**PLYBON, NANCY A,** Averett Coll, Danville, VA; SR; BS; Grc Crnshw Awrd; Deans Lst; AAS 89; Acctg.

**PLYLER, ANDREAS P,** Western Carolina Univ, Cullowhee, NC; SR; MPA; Spnsh Clb Sec 89-; Stdnt Gov Sen Pro Tempore 90-; Alpha Lanbda Delta 87-; Delta Sigma Phi Socl Chrmn 88-; Orientation Ldr; Washington Seminar Grad; BA; Public Affrs; US Govt.

**PLYLER, JULIE A,** Coker Coll, Hartsville, SC; JR; BA; Christmas In April; Sigma Tau Delta; Coll Commrs 89; Stu Elec May Ct; Top Ten; Var Bsktbl M Imprvd 89; Crew Team 90; Coaches Awd; Eng Educ; Tchng Sec Level.

**PLYMALE, JOSEPH A,** Oh St Univ At Marion, Marion, OH; SR; BS; Alumni Cncl 89-; Campus Committee 90-; Show Choir 90; Honor Scty 90-; Ambassadors 89-; Financial Aid Student Internship 90-; Elem Educ; Teach.

**PLYSER, GRACE A,** Fl International Univ, Miami, FL; SR; MS; FEA 90-; Deans Lst 90-; Ele Educ.

**POATES, VERA E,** Univ Of South Al, Mobile, AL; JR; BS; Mbl Jycs Brd Dir 87-; Mbl Azl Trl Fstvl VP Brd Dir 87-; Natl Bus Cnsrvtn Assoc 90-; Sec Offc Mgr 79-; Lsr Srvcs; Rcrtn Mgmt.

**POCAI, LINAE M,** Ky Mountain Bible Coll, Vancleve, KY; SO; Drm 89-90; Scl Cmmtt 90-; Clss VP 90-; Ed; Tchng.

**POCCIA, FRANK,** Pace Univ At White Plains, White Plains, NY; FR; BS; Bsn Mgmt.

**POCHAS, ERIC M,** Marywood Coll, Scranton, PA; FR; BA; Amrcn Advrtsng Fdrtn 90-; Pblc Rltns Stdnt Soc America 90-; Stdnt Nwspr 90-; Pblc Rltns Advrtsng; Corp Pblc Rltns.

**POCHINSKY, ANN M,** Saint Vincents Coll & Seminary, Latrobe, PA; JR; BA; Psychology Clb 88-; Adult Literacy Prgrm 90-; Career Dvlpmnt Cls 89; Acdmc Schlrshp 88-; Prtl Hsptlztn Cswrk Asst 89-90; Rsrch Asst Stdnt Tutor Englsh Prfsr 89-90; Psychology; Clinical Psychology.

**POCHIRO, ANTHONY M,** Youngstown St Univ, Youngstown, OH; JR; BE; Amer Chem Soc 90-; Intrfrat Cncl Treas 89-; Stdnt Govt Acdmc Snt 90-; Phi Kappa Tau Treas 89-; Cntrns Fresh Hon Soc 89-90; AMER Nclr Soc Srgnt Arms 90-; IM Bsktbl Ftbl Bsbl Sccr Vlybl 89-; Amer Inst Chem Engrs 90-; Chem Eng; MBA.

**POCKL, JOHN J,** Comm Coll Algny Co Algny Cmps, Pittsburgh, PA; SO; BA; Nwspr Clmnst; Amrcn Soc Bkry Engnrs Mmbr 90-; Amrcn Inst Bnkng Alumni Mmbr 89-; Crtf Amrcn Inst Bnkng 89; Crtf Amrcn Inst Bnkng 89; Bsns.

**POCRATSKY, MICHAEL W,** Defiance Coll, Defiance, OH; SO; AA; Crmnl Jstc Hnr Scty 90; USAA All Amer Schlr 90; Cngrssnl Yth Ldrshp Cncl 90; Hnrs Lst 89-90; Crmnl Jstce; Probtn Wrk.**

**POCZATEK, ROBERT B,** Birmingham Southern Coll, Birmingham, AL; JR; BA; Music Com Rep 90-; Soc Composers Treas 90-; Alpha Epsilon Delta; EMT I Hlth Profsns UAB 90; Music; MD.

**PODEST, PETER,** Me Maritime Academy, Castine, ME; JR; BS; Drl Tm Hon Grd 88-90; Yeoman 88-90; Alpha Phi Omega Soc Cncl 89-; Pres Commndtn Awd 90; Fr Cruise Awd 88; Commndnts Lst 88-89; Nautcl Sci; Maritime Fld.

**PODGAYETSKY, GRIGORY Y,** Bunker Hill Comm Coll, Boston, MA; FR; Engl; Acctg.

**PODGORSKI, MARJORIE J,** Univ Of Pittsburgh, Pittsburgh, PA; JR; BA; AS Alllegheny Cmnty Clg 73; Legal Studies/Sociolgy; Svc Flds.

**PODKOWKA, LISA A,** Western New England Coll, Springfield, MA; SO; BS; Stu Sen Rep; Psychlgy; Chld Psychlgst.**

**PODRON, ALEXIS,** Miami Dade Comm Coll South, Miami, FL; JR; PHD; Cert Crisis Intrvntnist AAS 90-; Boy Scts Amer Ptrl Ldr 85-90; Dice Master 90-; Shape; Greenpeace/W W F 89-; Tnns Tm 88; BA FL Intrntl Univ; Clcnl Psych.

**PODURI, ANNAPURNA,** Radcliffe Coll, Cambridge, MA; FR; BA; Mdl United Ntns Scrty Cncl VP 90; Mag Staff; Phillips Brooks Hse Pbl Serv Org 90; Cmbrdge HS Vol Tutor; Strng Mem Hosp Chldrns Rsrch Ctr Shapiro Schlrshp; Bio Neurosci; Med.

**POE, LAURA E,** Longwood Coll, Farmville, VA; JR; BS; Bapt Un Bible Stdy Co Ldr 90-; Union Bd Sec; Kappa Delta Pi; Alpha Phi Omega Cls Sec; AS Tidewater Comm Coll 87; Elem Educ; Tch.

**POE, THOMAS A,** Ky St Univ, Frankfort, KY; FR.

**POFOK, CASSANDRA M,** Univ Of New Haven, West Haven, CT; SO; BA; Art; Grphc Dsgn.

**POGGEMILLER, EUGENIA E,** Liberty Univ, Lynchburg, VA; FR; BA; Chi Alpha 90-; Alpha Lambda Delta 90-; Sigma Tau Delta Poetry Awd; Modern Lang/Linguistics; Diplomatic Intrptr.

**POGGEMILLER, EVANGELINE E,** Liberty Univ, Lynchburg, VA; SR; BS; Adv Clb 90-; Alpha Lambda Delta 87-; Zeta Chi; Oxford Stdy Pgm 90; Graphc Art/Educ; Art.

**POGOZELSKI, ANN M,** Univ Of Akron, Akron, OH; SO.

**POGUE, DAVID D,** Central St Univ, Wilberforce, OH; FR; BA; Msc Educ; Msc Tchr.

**POHLE, LEAH R,** Univ Of Tn At Knoxville, Knoxville, TN; FR; BA; Phi Eta Sigma; Alpha Lamda Delta; Zeta Tau Alpha 90-; Bsn; Fnce.

**POINDEXTER, ANNE R,** Anderson Coll, Anderson, SC; SO; BA; IM 89-; Hons Pgm 89-; Gamma Beta Phi 89-90; 2 Tm All Amer Vlybl 89-90; 2 Tm Reg X Plyr Yr 89-F Vlybl; Bio; Chiro.

**POINDEXTER, MONTEZ B,** Austin Peay St Univ, Clarksville, TN; SO; BS; Philosophy Clb; Psychlgy Clb; Sigma Gamma Rho; Ch Musician; Med Tech; Natl Yng Ldrs Cnvntl Schlr; AAS; Clncl Microbio; Bacteriologist.**

**POINT, ERICKA H,** Saint Andrews Presbytrn Coll, Laurinburg, NC; SO; BA; Athltc Trnr 90-; Hnrs 90-; Vlybl/Bsktbl Tms 90-; NATA; Sprts Med/Athltc Trng.

**POINTER, JAMIE L,** Univ Of Sc At Columbia, Columbia, SC; SR; Phlhrmnc Chorus 87-88; Cncrt Choir 88-90; Deans Lst; BA; Elem Ed.

**POIRIER, KATHLEEN M,** Columbus Coll Of Art & Design, Columbus, OH; FR; BA; Illstrtn; Fr Lance Illstrtn.

**POIRIER, SUZANNE M,** Newbury Coll, Brookline, MA; FR; AS; Bus Mngmt; Bus.

**POISSON, CHRISTINE E,** Endicott Coll, Beverly, MA; SO; AS; Fitness Cl Ldr 90-; Busn Cl 90-; Ofc/Atty Genl Paralgl Intrn 90; Law Ofc/Richards/Gaoury/Mac Allister Paralgl Intrn; Deans List 90; Paralgl.

**POIST, MICHAEL G,** Columbia Union Coll, Takoma Park, MD; JR; BS; Stu Assn Soc VP 89-; Cmmnctns; Tch Grphc Art/Brdcst Media/Cllgt.

**POKALSKY, ROBERT M,** Le Moyne Coll, Syracuse, NY; JR; BA; Ornttn Comm 90; Pol Sci Acad 89-90; Nwsprs Rptr/Asst Ed 89-; Hnrs Pgm 89-; Alpha Sigma Nu; Brkfst Truck Prjct Coord 88-; IM Bsktbl; Pol Sci.

**POKORNY, JEFF J,** Kent St Univ Kent Cmps, Kent, OH; JR; BS; Hosp ER Nrsng Asst 90-; Deans Lst 90-; Hbtt Hmnty 90-; Hnrs Schlrshp 90-; Med.

**POLA, MARTALINA,** Oh Univ, Athens, OH; SR; BBA; Indonesian Stdnt Org 88-; Finance Clb 90-; Finance/Genl Bus.**

**POLAND, JULIA D,** Va Commonwealth Univ, Richmond, VA; SR; BSN; Natl Stdnt Nrs Assoc 89-; Phi Eta Sigma 88-; Sigma Theta Tau.

**POLAND, LISA R,** Saint Andrews Presbytrn Coll, Laurinburg, NC; SO; BA; Mdl Untd Ntns Pblcty 90; Ecctn 89-; Rdng Cncl 9-; Sphmr Hnrs; Stdnt Athlt 90; Eqstrn Tm 9-; Elem Ed.

**POLAND, MICHELLE R,** Roane St Comm Coll, Harriman, TN; FR; MBA; Math; Tch.

**POLANSKY, PAULA S,** Bunker Hill Comm Coll, Boston, MA; FR; BS; Creative Wrtr Rdng Fishing Wlkng; Vol Sci Museum; Aids Quilt; NCIA; Awd Merit; Hon Mntn; World Poetry 88; Vol Income Tx Asst 90; Cert DDES Opr IRS 71; Acctg; CPA.

**POLCYN, DONNA M,** Hilbert Coll, Hamburg, NY; SO; BA; Amer Pltry Asc 90-; Learn/Play Day Care Intshp; Rfges Fndng Jobs/Hm/Clthng Vol 88-; Sclgy/Scl Work; Cnslr.

**POLEN, DAVID A,** Univ Of Sc At Columbia, Columbia, SC; FR; BA; Bus; Mktng Prod.

**POLEN-DORN, LINDA F,** Nova Univ, Ft Lauderdale, FL; GD; MBA; Intl Assn Bus Comm; Pblc Rltns Soc; V Pres Cmmnctns Mgr Glndl Fed Bnk; BA Univ Miami 67; Bus.

**POLETTI, LAWRENCE F,** Va Commonwealth Univ, Richmond, VA; GD; MD; Amrcn Mdcl Assn 89-; Amrcn Mdcl Stdnt Assn 89-; VA Mdcl Soc 89-; Pi Lambda Phi Tres 81-85; A D Williams Smmr Rsrch Fllwshp 90; Lt Navy Indvdl Ready Rsrv; Nclr Engnr Nvl Nclr Prplsn Prgrm; Medicine.

**POLIAK, JOHN P,** Univ Of Akron, Akron, OH; FR; BS; Hnrs Club 90-; Phi Eta Sigma 90-; Stdnt Summer Intern; Chem Engrng.

**POLICASTRO, JULIE A,** Elmira Coll, Elmira, NY; SO; BSN; Intrntnl Clb 89-; Nrsng Clb 89-; Red Crs Vlntr; IM Vlybl 90; Nrsng; RN.

**POLICASTRO, LORRAINE A,** Univ Of Sc At Columbia, Columbia, SC; SO; BAIS; Soccer Club 89-90; Elem Educ; Tchng.

**POLIDOR, AMBERLY C,** Northeastern Christian Jr Coll, Villanova, PA; SO; BA; AA 90; Jrnlsm.

**POLIDORO, JENNIFER A,** Marywood Coll, Scranton, PA; SO; BA; Orntn Comm Moderator/Stdnts Svcs 90-; Fshn Cl 90-; Helping Stdnts Secy 90-; Parent Wk End 89-90; Kappa Omicron Nu 90-; Blood Drive 89-90; Fund Raiser Proj 89-; Big Sis/Frshmn 90-; Kappa Omicron Nu 90-; Deans List 90; Fshn Ret.

**POLING, LINDA F,** Univ Of Cincinnati-Clrmnt Coll, Batavia, OH; FR; ADS; PTO Stu Aid Chrprsn 87-89; Bptst Chrch Brd Chrst Ed 90-; Gir Scts Co Ldr 84-; Nrsng.

**POLINSKI, KEVIN L,** Wv Northern Comm Coll, Wheeling, WV; SO; Phi Theta Kappa 90-; ASE Cert Master Auto Tchn 85-; AAS 92; AAS 92; Acctg/Bus Mgmnt.

**POLINSKI, RICHARD E,** Nyack Coll, Nyack, NY; JR; BA; Yrbk Edtr 88-89; Drama Ensmbl 89-; Alpha Chi Pres 90-; Bible Dept Asst; Orngtwn Police Aux; Theolgy; Coll/Univ Prof.

**POLITE, SANDRA J,** Saint Johns Univ, Jamaica, NY; SR; BS; CBC 88-89; AS 90; Bsn; Mgmt.

**POLIZOS, KATHERINE M,** Anne Arundel Comm Coll, Arnold, MD; FR; BA; Art Educ; Scndry Tchr.

**POLIZOS, THANOS M,** Old Dominion Univ, Norfolk, VA; SR; BS; Scty Mfg Eng Pres 90-; Natl Scty Prfssnl Eng VP; Scty Auto Eng 90-; Schlrshp Ahepa Org 88; Schlrshp Daughters Penelope Scty 88; Rwng Clb 89; Dvng Tm 90; Mech Eng.

**POLIZZOTTO, DANA M,** Georgian Court Coll, Lakewood, NJ; SR; BA; Sigma Tau Delta 90-; Deans List 90; AA Ocean Cty Coll 88; Eng; Book Pblshng.

**POLK, DAVID C,** Univ Of Southern Ms, Hattiesburg, MS; FR; BS; Phi Eta Sigma; Natl Reg Emer Med Tchncn 84-; Nrsng.

**POLK, KAWANIS FELICIA,** Rust Coll, Holly Springs, MS; FR; A Cappella Choir 90-; Hlth Career Opportnty Prog 90-; Jrnlsm Club; Chem; Pharmcst.

**POLK, LAURA E,** Capital Univ, Columbus, OH; SO; BSN; Dns Lst; Nrsng.

**POLK, LAURA E,** Univ Of Tn At Martin, Martin, TN; FR; BSBA; Univ Schlrs Org 90-; Mrchg Symph Bnd 90-; Bapt Stdnt Un Worship Chr 90-; Andy Holt Alum Schlrshp 90-; Dns Lst 90-; Math/Music; Educ.

**POLK, STACIE R,** Univ Of Sc At Columbia, Columbia, SC; FR; BA; Alpha Lamda Delta 90-; Eng; Comp Eng.

**POLK, TAMMY M,** Tuskegee Univ, Tuskegee Inst, AL; JR; BS; Delta Sigma Theta; BS Jackson State U 90; Occupatnl Thrpy.

**POLKA, LYNN M,** Cornell Univ Statutory College, Ithaca, NY; FR; BS; Deeans Lst; Mcrblgy; Physcns Asst.

**POLLACK, BRIAN R,** Manhattan Coll, Bronx, NY; FR; BE; BSA Eagle Sct; Mech Engrng.

**POLLAK, DENA REBEKAH,** Georgian Court Coll, Lakewood, NJ; FR; BA; Stdnt Govt Acdmc Rep 90-; Mth Assoc Ame Clge Chptr 90-; Concert Band 90-; Soccer 90-; Math; Secondary Ed Tchr Of Math.

**POLLARD, CHRISTINE L,** Fl St Univ, Tallahassee, FL; JR; BM; Alpha Mu Alpha 89-; Sigma Alpha Iota Pres; Schl Of Music Brd Adv 90-; Deans Lst 90; Sigma Alpha Iota Sword Of Hon; Music Therapy.

**POLLARD, DAWNE K,** Fl A & M Univ, Tallahassee, FL; SO; MBA; Pres Schlrs Asc 89-; Gspl Choir 89-; Art Exclnc Awd 90-; Blck Hstry Ortrcl Cntst; Gold Awd 89-; Bsn Admn; Mktg/Adv.

**POLLARD, EDWARD G,** Comm Coll Algny Co Algny Cmps, Pittsburgh, PA; FR.

**POLLARD IV, ERIC W,** Univ Of Rochester, Rochester, NY; JR; BA; Scl Actvts Brd 89-; Hm Cmng Coor 88-; LBJ Cngrssnl Intrshp Awrd Cngrssmn B Lwry; Vrsty Lcrsse 88-; Pol Sci; Govt Admin.

**POLLARD, KEVIN L,** Saint Pauls Coll, Lawrenceville, VA; SR; BA; Phi Beta Lambda 87-90; NAACP 87-90; Yrbk Edtr 88-90; Govt Soil Survey Off Intrn; Pltcl Sci; Law.

**POLLARD, LEIGH ANNE,** Samford Univ, Birmingham, AL; GD; JD; Client Cnslng Competn; TN Stdnt Bar Assn 90-; R B Donworth Fr Competn; Deans Lst 90; BA Carson-Newmn Coll 90; Law.

**POLLARD, MARIE,** Fl International Univ, Miami, FL; FR; BA; Intl Stdnts Clb Plbcty; Elec Eng.

**POLLARD, NANCY A,** Coll Of Charleston, Charleston, SC; SO; BS; Stdnt Alumni Assn 90-; LEADS 89-; Hnrs Pgrm Stdnt Assn 89-; Frederick J Collins Schlrshp 89-; Biology; Envrnmntl Sci.

**POLLARD, ROBIN L,** Chattahoochee Vly St Comm Coll, Phenix City, AL; FR; AA; Lbrl Arts.

**POLLARD, SUSAN S,** Va Commonwealth Univ, Richmond, VA; SR; BS; Urban Studies Stdnt Assoc Pres 90-; Phi Eta Sigma 87-; Intrnshp City Mgrs Office Richmond Va; Lurban Studies; Grad Sch Law Or M S.

**POLLEY, LESA L,** Memphis St Univ, Memphis, TN; SO; Hnrs Prog 88-; Sigma Phi Epsilon Lttl Sis 89-; Psychlgy.

**POLLICOVE, KERRI B,** Cornell Univ Statutory College, Ithaca, NY; JR; BS; Biol Stu Advsr 90-; Chi Omega Chrprsn 90-; Intern Cornell Biol Field Sta; Biol/Eclgy; Grad Schl.

**POLLINGER, KEVIN R,** Clarkson Univ, Potsdam, NY; FR; Stdnt Nwsppr The Integrator Nws Edit 90-; Amer Inst Of Chem Engs 90-; Dns Lst 90-; Chem Eng; Eng.

**POLLOCK, AMY D,** Oh St Univ At Marion, Marion, OH; JR; BA; Psych Soc; Psychlgsts.

**POLLOCK, CAROLE SUMNER,** Blue Mountain Coll, Blue Mountain, MS; JR; BS; Engl Clb Pres; Phi Theta Kappa; Co Dir Youth Activities; Euclatubba Bapt Bhurch Co Dir; Saltillo Drama Costume Dsgn Vol; Tchr Assist; AA North East Comm Clg 90; Engl; Tchng.

**POLLOCK, DAVID S,** Univ Of Md Baltimore Prof Schl, Baltimore, MD; GD; MSW; Phi Kappa Phi 90-; Greater Wash Soc Clncl Soc Wkr 91; Common Bndry 90; BA U M D Clg Pk 70; Clncl Soc Wrk; Psycho Thrpy.

**POLLOCK, GARY M,** S U N Y Coll Of Tech At Alfred, Alfred, NY; SR; Sftbl Ice Hockey; AAS; Math Physcl Science; Engnrng.

**POLLOCK, JUDSON B,** Univ Of Cincinnati, Cincinnati, OH; SR; BM; Intl Assoc Jazz Edtrs 89-; Jazz Studio Music.

**POLLOCK, KERRI L,** Middle Tn St Univ, Murfreesboro, TN; SO; BED; Gamma Beta Phi Sec 89; Tau Omicron; Kappa Delta Pi; Ntl Cllgte Ed Awd; Elem Ed; Prmry Grade Edctr.**

**POLLOCK, TRACI Y,** Fl A & M Univ, Tallahassee, FL; FR; BA; Stdnt Gvrn Assn Sntr 90-; Phi Eta Sigma 90-; Jrnlsm-Pblc Rltns; Corp Natl Liaison.

**POLNARYOVA, ALLA,** Newbury Coll, Brookline, MA; FR; Envrnmntl Protctn Org Kharkov USSR 86-88; Kharkov Water Rsrcs 82-88; Ophthalmic Dspnsng; Optcn Bus.

**POLNASZEK, SUE E,** Smith Coll, Northampton, MA; FR; BA; Head New Stdnts Sessions Hse; Stdnt Escort Serv 90-; Serv Orgztn 90-; I M Vybl 90-.

**POLO, ISABEL,** Southeastern Coll Of Hlth Sci, N Miami Beach, FL; SR; PHARM; Amrcn Phrmctcl Assoc 87-; Sth Flrd Scty Hosp Phrmcsts 87-; Rho Chi; Wllcm Schlrshp; Phrmctcls Awrd 90; Phrmcy.

**POLOKA, STEPHEN A,** Jersey City St Coll, Jersey City, NJ; SR; BS; NW St Assn Of Chfs Of Plce; Intrntl Assn Of Chfs Of Plce 90-; Intrntl Assn Of Chfs; Mddlsx Cnty Assn Of Chfs; NJ Nrctcs Offcrs Assn Brd Of Dirs; Chf Of Plce NJ; Ptrlmn 65; Sgt; Lt; Capt; Dpty Chf; Crmnl Jstce; Law Enfrcmnt.

**POLSON, JOHN S,** Univ Of Ky, Lexington, KY; JR; BA; Ky Edn Assoc Stdnt Prog; Phi Eta Sigma; Pi Sigma Alpha; Lances; Big Bro Big Sis; Deans List; Acdmc Exclnc Schlrshp 90-; Carl D Perkins Mem Schlrshp KEC; Hist/Pol Sci; Teach.

**POLTIE, KELLY A,** Daemen Coll, Amherst, NY; JR; BA; Stdnt Physcl Thrpy Assoc Sec 90-; Dns Lst 89-; IM Sftbl Vllybl Bsktbl 90-; Sci; Physcl Thrpy.

**POLTROK, GINA M,** Univ Of De, Newark, DE; FR; Prcsn Dnc Tm 90-.

**POMARES, VIVIAN,** Fl International Univ, Miami, FL; SR; BA; Amer Inst Architecture Stdnts Brd Mbr 87-; Pereira Martinez Intrnshp Dsgnr; De Soto And Associates Intrnshp Dsgnr 89-; Architecture.

**POMBO, MARK A,** Lancaster Bible Coll, Lancaster, PA; SR; MA; BA Spokane Bible Clg 87; Cnslng Educ.

**POMERANTZ, LINDA R,** Carnegie Mellon Univ, Pittsburgh, PA; SR; BS; Chi Omega Secy 88-; NCR Corp Intnshp 91; Cognitive Psych/Vsl Cmmctns; Hmn Intfce Dsgnr.

**POMERANZ, LISA E,** Univ Of Rochester, Rochester, NY; SR; BA; D'lion Peer Coun Org 88-89; Sigma Delta Tau Ritlst 88-; IM Flr Hockey 90; Psychlgy; Hlth Care.

**POMERLEAU, TAMMY M,** Newbury Coll, Brookline, MA; FR; BA; Fshn Mrchndsng.

**POMEROY, DAWN M,** Kent St Univ Kent Cmps, Kent, OH; JR; BA; Natl Hnr Soc 87-88; Schlrshp Clb 86-88; Dir Dance Rctl 90; Drll Tm Lt 85-88; Dance; Prfrmnc.

**POMEROY, SEAN F,** Radford Univ, Radford, VA; JR; BA; Psychlgy Clb Pres; Geography Clb; Psychlgy/Geography; Ph D Indstrl Psychlgy.

**POMPANO, TERESA M,** Albertus Magnus Coll, New Haven, CT; SR; BA; Lit Mag 90-; SG 87-88; Coll Exec Bd 89-; Advrtsng Mgr Nwsppr 90-; Engl Clb 88-; Chrch Cncl; Jr High Alumni Comm Blood Donor; Stf Wrtr Intrn; Engl; Bnk Prsnl.

**POMPEI, MONIQUE D,** Manor Jr Coll, Jenkintown, PA; SO; AS; Stdnt Snt VP 89-90; Cvl Air Ptrl Cdt Lieut 83-; Yrbk Stff Edtr 89-; Alpha Beta Gamma VP 90-; Extrnshp Prlgl; Wawriw Acdmc Schlrshp 89-; Cvl Air Ptrl Flght Schlrshp 88; Vlybl Intrcllgt Capt 89-; Law Prlgl; Law.

**POMPEL, LAURA M,** Smith Coll, Northampton, MA; FR; BSBA; LBA 90-; Col Choir 90-; Dean Lst 1st Grp; Crew 90-; Wmn Stu/Pre Med; Dr Sprts Med.

**POMPILIO, TRUDY A,** Manor Jr Coll, Jenkintown, PA; SR; AA; Hnr Rl Summa Cum Laude 90; Dns Lst; Comm Coll Cnstrm Bucks/Montgomery Allied Hlth 85; Mntrng Acutely Ill Cert Of Achvmnt; La Salle Schlrshp 71; Infnt/Chld Svr Crs Nazareth Cert 86; Multimedia Frst Aid Cert 86; Lib Arts; Tchng Chldrn/Wrtng.

**POMPONIO, BERNADETTE A,** Eckerd Coll, St Petersburg, FL; SO; Swm Clb 89-90; Intl Bus Clb 90-; Flt Ensbl 90-; Swm Clb 89-90; Frnch/Rssn; Intl Bus.

**PONAK, WENDY M,** Univ Of Nc At Charlotte, Charlotte, NC; SO; BA; Psychlgy; Clin Wrk/Rsrch.

**PONCE DE LEON-GONZALEZ, LEYDA,** Univ Of Pr At Mayaguez, Mayaguez, PR; SR; BS; Anml Sci Stdnts Assoc 90; Future Agronomst Of PR 90; Alpha Zeta 89-; Anml Sci; Agronomst.

**PONCE, JAMES E,** Univ Of Sc At Sumter, Sumter, SC; FR; BA; Media Arts.

**PONCE, RAMON,** Broward Comm Coll, Ft Lauderdale, FL; SO; BS; Florida Eng Society 89; Catholic Clb Trea 90; Pres List 89; Mathematics Awrd 89; Tuition Schlrshp Awrd 90; Intrntnl Assc Mchnsts 80; Toys For Tots Vlntr 90; Aviation Mntnce Tchncn 80-89; AS 89; Eng; Elctcl Eng.

**PONCE-DE-LEON, LEILA I,** Univ Of Pr At Mayaguez, Mayaguez, PR; SO; BA; Natl Clg Minority Ldrshp Awrds; Ind Engr.

**PONCHOT, KELLY E,** Western Ky Univ, Bowling Green, KY; JR; BS; Wstrn Plyrs 88-; Hnr Scty; CP Mcnally Undrgrd Schl Chem 90-; Regents Schlrshp 88-; Chem.

**POND, LORI A,** Wv Northern Comm Coll, Wheeling, WV; SO; ASSOC; Phi Theta Kappa; Phi Theta Kappa; Nrsng.

**PONDEK, THERESA A,** Anne Arundel Comm Coll, Arnold, MD; SO; AA; Phi Theta Kappa; Psychlgy; Thrpst.

**PONDER, AMY E,** Univ Of Southern Ms, Hattiesburg, MS; SR; BS; Almni Assn 88-89; USM Clb 87; Gamma Beta Phi 90-; Gamma Alpha Epsilon 88-; Psi Chi 90-; Alpha Delta Pi Soc/ Schlrshp Chrmn 87-; IM Bwlng 89; Psychlgy; Cnslng.

**PONDER, AMY E,** Valdosta St Coll, Valdosta, GA; SO; BA; Mddl Chldhd Ed Cnslng Gdnc; Tchr Schl Cnslr.

**PONDER, CHANDRA A,** Morris Brown Coll, Atlanta, GA; GD; BS; Assn Educ Pres 89-; Hnrs Clb Co Chrprsn 90-; Pi Lambda Theta; Zeta Phi Beta; Atlanta Inst Real Est 85; Early Chldhd Educ; Tchr.

**PONDER, MONA C,** Middle Tn St Univ, Murfreesboro, TN; JR; BA; Math; Teach.

**PONDER, TRAVIS O,** Chattahoochee Vly St Comm Coll, Phenix City, AL; SR; MBA; BS Troy St Univ; Cert Lasalle Ext Univ 70; Cmptr Sci/Bus Admn; Mngmt Inds.

**PONDOFF, KIMBERLY A,** Fl St Univ, Tallahassee, FL; GD; JD; Omicron Delta Epsilon 90-; Pi Gamma Mu 90-; Goldn Key 90-; Sigma Sigma Sigma Ethcs Chrmn 88-90; Hsng Schlrshp S Schlrshp Fndtn 89; BA 90; Intl Law.

**PONG, CHEE LONG,** City Univ Of Ny Queensbrough, New York, NY; SO; BA; Acctg.

**PONGER, ROBERT L,** City Univ Of Ny Baruch Coll, New York, NY; JR; BBA; Acctng Scty 90-; Pres Schlr; Provost Schlr; Basebll; Acct; Lawyer.

**PONRAJ, MERLIN D,** Columbia Union Coll, Takoma Park, MD; GD; BS; BS; Bus.

**PONTANI, DE ANNA M,** Indiana Univ Of Pa, Indiana, PA; SR; BS; PSEA 90-; Jr Wmns Cvc Clb 89-; Elem Ed; Tchr.

**PONTANILLA, JOEY P,** Radford Univ, Radford, VA; SR; BBA; Rdfrd Univ Asian Assoc 90; Rdfrd Univ Otdrs Clb 90; Phi Beta Lambda 89-90; Kappa Delta Rho Pldg Cls Pres; Admin Sys; Cmptr Mgmt Info Sys.

**PONTE, SUSAN ELAINE,** Univ Of South Fl, Tampa, FL; JR; BA; Network Peace/Justice 90-; FPIRG 90-; Amnesty Intl; Arts/ Sci Hnr Soc; Golden Key; Hnrs Cnvctn 89-; Natl Merit Schlr; Wmns Stds/Anthrplgy; Academia/Tchng/Rsrch.

**PONTIUS, AMANDA M,** Kent St Univ Kent Cmps, Kent, OH; FR; Bus; Bus Mngt.

**PONTZER, ALICIA M,** Univ Of Pittsburgh, Pittsburgh, PA; JR; BS; Outdr Clb; Pitt Ski Clb; Phi Eta Sigma; Inst Ind Engrs; Soc Wmn Engrs Treas 90-; Deans Lst; Intrnshp ICI Amer 89-90; Co-Op GE Aircraft Engines Co-Op Chrprsn; Ind Eng; MA.

**PONZIO, RICHARD J,** Columbia Univ, New York, NY; FR; BA; Wrld Fdrlsts Hpkns Pres; Wtnss Theatr; Model UN Treas; Army ROTC Cadet Corprl; Sigma Phi Epsilon; Grp For Dvc Prgrss Tutr; Amer Cntr Intl Ldrshp Rsrch Asst; IM Lacrsse/ Soccr; Intl Rltns; Intl Law.

**POOL, TINA A,** Hillsborough Comm Coll, Tampa, FL; FR; AA; Hstry; Tchr.

**POOLE, ANGIE J,** Spartanburg Methodist Coll, Spartanburg, SC; FR; Hmcmng Ct 90-; Yrbk 90-; Phi Theta Kappa 90-; Deans Lst 90-; Sftbl 90-; Educ/Bus.

**POOLE, CINDY S,** Radford Univ, Radford, VA; FR; Rdfrd Univ Hnrs Prog 90-.

**POOLE, CYNTHIA DENISE,** Univ Of Nc At Greensboro, Greensboro, NC; BS; Educ K-6 Teacher; Geography Spanish.

**POOLE, JENNIFER L,** Rivier Coll, Nashua, NH; FR; ADN; Protestant Campus Mnstry Co-Ord 90-; Proj Hug 90-; Open Hse Comm 90-; Natl Stdnt Nrs Assoc 90-; Hnr Schlrshp 90-; DAR Awd 90-; Dan Moffet Schlrshp 90-; Nrsg; Med Msnry.

**POOLE, KIMBERLY J,** Univ Of Md At Eastern Shore, Princess Anne, MD; JR; BA; Rehab Club; Certif Aced Achiev 90-; Mental Ill Rehab 89-; Rehab Serv; Aids Rehab.

**POOLE, LISA L,** Endicott Coll, Beverly, MA; JR; BS; AS 88; Visual Comm; Photographer/Wrtr.

**POOLE, LORETTA A,** Alcorn St Univ, Lorman, MS; SO; BA; Snds Of Dynamite; Cmptr Scnc.

**POOLE, MARCUS T,** Ms St Univ, Miss State, MS; JR; BA; Graphic Dsgn.

**POOLE, MICHELLE,** Jacksonville Univ, Jacksonville, FL; FR; BA; Honr Assn 90-; Alpha Kappa Psi; Phi Sigma Iota 90-; Cath Stdnt Org 90-; Finc; Bnkg.

**POOLE, NANCY L,** Owensboro Jr Coll Of Bus, Owensboro, KY; FR; AS; Stdnt Govt Treas; Stdnt Tutor; Goodwill Ambsdr; Pres List 90-; St Relief For Homeless Through Stdnt Govt; Muscular Dystrophy Assoc Stdnt Govt; Bluff City Liquors Sales Clerk; Med Ofc Asstnt; Medical.

**POOLE, STEPHANIE M,** Va Commonwealth Univ, Richmond, VA; FR; BS; Commonwealth Times Rprtr 90-; Phi Eta Sigma 90-; Mass Cmnctns; Brdcst Jrnlsm.

**POOLE, THOMAS L,** Shaw Univ, Raleigh, NC; JR; BA; Peer Tutoring Coord; Tutoring 87; AS Lenior Cmmnty Clg; Math Scl; Tchng.

**POOLE, VICKIE N,** Univ Of South Al, Mobile, AL; SR; BS; AA Patrick Henry Jr Coll 88; Hist; Ed.

**POOLER, JASON C,** Univ Of Tn At Knoxville, Knoxville, TN; FR; MBA; Bus; Mktng.

**POON, DAVID,** Newbury Coll, Brookline, MA; FR; AAS; Intr Dsgn; Archtctre.

**POON, HARRY H,** City Univ Of Ny La Guard Coll, Long Island Cty, NY; SO; AA; Phi Theta Kappa 90-; Lib Arts/Sci; Cmptr Sci.

**POON, VIVIAN,** Cooper Union, New York, NY; JR; SWE IEEE Schl Athletic Assoc 88; Untd Ntns Badminton Clb; United Stdnts Assoc; Smith Badminton Clb VP 90; Amer Red Cross Instr 89; Raymond E Kirk Awd Chem 88-89; Deans Lst At Plytchnc U 88-90; SWE Awd 90; Con Edison 89; AT&T Bell Labs; Elctrcl Eng; Elctrcl Eng.

**POON, YUK-SHAN,** City Univ Of Ny Baruch Coll, New York, NY; SR; BBA; Amer Mktng Assn 90-; Gldn Ky 90-; Beta Gamma Sigma 90-; Mktng Mngmnt; Mktng/Advtsng.

**POORE, BRAD D,** Fl St Univ, Tallahassee, FL; FR; BA; Music.

**POORE, TAMMY R,** Salisbury St Univ, Salisbury, MD; SO; BA; Univ Nwsppr Stfwrtr; Panhellenic Assn Pres; Phi Eta Sigma 90-; Phi Mu Socl Srvc Chrprsn 89-; Cmmnctns; TV/RADIO.

**POP, ERIC W,** Fl International Univ, Miami, FL; SO; BS; Cmptr Sci.

**POPADYCH, HEATHER L,** Oh Univ, Athens, OH; JR; BFA; STYLE; OCPA; Rho Lambda; Alpha Xi Delta Hs Pres 90-; Intrnshp Art Schl; Fn Arts/Stdio Arts; Cmrcl Arts.

**POPE, ANGELA E,** Winthrop Coll, Rock Hill, SC; JR; BS; CEC 90-; CEC Puppet Grp 90-; SC CEC Pan 90-; Kappa Delta Pi; Spcl Edctn; Tchng Spcl Edctn.

**POPE, ARLENE L,** Norfolk St Univ, Norfolk, VA; JR; BA; Alpha Kappa Mu 90-; Bus Mngmnt.

**POPE, BARRY W,** Meridian Comm Coll, Meridian, MS; SO; AA; Phi Beta Lambda Proj Coord 90-; Dns Lst 90-; Schlrshp Acad Achvmnt 90; State Competition; Cmptr Tech; Pgmr/Syst Analyst.

**POPE, CAZZIE R,** Univ Of Sc At Columbia, Columbia, SC; SR; Kappa Delta Pi; Zeta Phi Omega Pldg Cnclr; Erly Chldhd Ed.

**POPE, DOROTHY B,** Montgomery Comm Coll, Troy, NC; GD; BA; SG 88-89; Marshl 89; N C Soc Svcs Assn; Income Maint Casewrkr; Human Srvcs.

**POPE, JOY A,** Clemson Univ, Clemson, SC; FR; BS; Flwshp Chrstn Athlts 90-; Nrsng.

**POPE, JUDY S,** Lenoir Rhyne Coll, Hickory, NC; GD; NCAE; BA; Elem Ed.

**POPE, LYDIA E,** Wv Univ, Morgantown, WV; SO; BSC; Cvl Eng.

**POPE, NATHAN D,** Samford Univ, Birmingham, AL; GD; JD; Envrnmntl Laws Soc 90-; Ala Stdnt Bar Assoc 90-; AL Cntr Legal/Civic Educ 90-; Cumberland Schl Law Deans List 90-; Cumberland Law Review 90-; BS Univ Of S AL 90; BA Univ Of S AL 90; Law.

**POPE, OHRIDIA A,** Emory Univ, Atlanta, GA; JR; BS; Sigma Teta Thau; Sci; Nrsng.

**POPE, PATTY L,** Pfeiffer Coll, Misenheimer, NC; FR; DVM; Blgy; Vet Med.

**POPE, ROBIN RENAE,** Univ Of The Dist Of Columbia, Washington, DC; SR; BBA; Delta Sigma Theta 81-; Dns Lst 89; Fclttr Fr Mns Dmstc Vlnce Grp 88; PTA 90-; Bus Mgmt; Prsnnl Mgmt.

**POPE, THOMAS C,** Va Commonwealth Univ, Richmond, VA; JR; Amer Chem Soc 90-; Gldn Key 90-; Chem; Medcl.

**POPE, WILLIAM B,** Univ Of Ky, Lexington, KY; GD; MED; BA Tulane Univ 74; Educ; Scndry Educ.

**POPEK, MICHELLE V,** Broward Comm Coll, Ft Lauderdale, FL; JR; BA; AA; Cmnctns; Brdcstng.

**POPELESKI, TIFFINIE M,** Fl St Univ, Tallahassee, FL; SR; Stdnt Govt Assn VP 88-89; FL Pblc Rltns Stdnt Assn VP 90-; Wmn Cmnctns 90-; Lambda Phi Eta 90-; Phi Theta Kappa 88-89; Sigma Sigma Sigma 89-90; Walt Disney World Coll Pgm 90; Pres/Deans Lst 87-; Schlrshps 87-; BS; Pblc Rltns; Law.

**POPELLA, DENNIS M,** Piedmont Tech Coll, Greenwood, SC; SR; Std Govt Assc; Phi Theta Kappa 90-; Tau Kappa Epsilon 88-; IM; AA; Eng Grphcs Tech.

**POPENDIEKER, KEITH A,** Univ Of Pittsburgh At Bradford, Bradford, PA; SR; BSCS; Cmptr Sci Clb; Sigma Lambda Chi Rush Chrmn 89-; Thrift Drug Co Intrn 89-90; I M Bkbl Ftbl Hcky 88-.

**POPHAM, CHERI L,** Muskingum Coll, New Concord, OH; JR; BS; Rsrch Assist 89; Psi Chi Pres 89; Omicron Delta Kappa 89; Psi Chi Prsntn Of Papr; Ntl Sci Week Pstr Prsntn; Im 88-89; Psych; Schl Psychlgy.

**POPIOLEK, DAWN M,** Central Ct St Univ, New Britain, CT; SR; BS; United Way Vltr 89-90; Delta Mu Delta; Office Syst Mgt Awd; Office Syst Mgt; Sect/Mgt.**

**POPISH, TIMOTHY G,** Mount Aloysius Jr Coll, Cresson, PA; FR; Legal.

**POPLAR, PAMELA R,** Tougaloo Coll, Tougaloo, MS; SO; BS; Econ/Bus Admin.

**POPLI, RAAJ K,** Va Commonwealth Univ, Richmond, VA; FR; BSC; IM Bsktbl/Sftbl 90-; Biology; Medicine.

**POPOCHOCK, LYNN M,** Allegheny Coll, Meadville, PA; JR; BS; Theatre 90; Psi Chi Sec 90-; Kappa Kappa Gamma Sng Chrmn 90-; Marie/Eugene Cease Schlrshp; Alden Schlrshp 90-; Psych/Biol; Child Psych.

**POPOLO, GLEN J,** Bloomfield Coll, Bloomfield, NJ; SR; BS; APICS 87-89; NAA 91; Brd Dir S Hntrdm Lttle League 88; Umpire In Chief SHLL 88; Invntry Cntrlr; BA William Paterson Clg 80-84; Acctg; Invtry Cst Acct/Auditing.

**POPOVITCH, SUSAN M,** Seton Hall Univ, South Orange, NJ; JR; BSN; Phi Delta Pi 89-; Nrsng/RN.

**POPP, JANIS E,** Univ Of Cin R Walters Coll, Blue Ash, OH; SO; AAS; Specialink Vol 90-; Libr Sci; Librarian.

**POPP, KAREN A,** Salisbury St Univ, Salisbury, MD; JR; BS; IABC 89-; Black/Norris Acctg Svc Intrnshp; IM Vlybl/Tnns/Sftbl/Wlybl 88-; Acctg; CPA.

**POPP, KRISTIN L,** Univ Of Fl, Gainesville, FL; SR; BS; Delta Delta Delta Tres 88-89; Dean Lst 90-; Bus Fnnc; Bnkng.

**POPP, SUZANNE E,** Savannah Coll Of Art & Design, Savannah, GA; JR; BFA; Illustration; Freelance.

**POPPE JR, JOHN D,** Wagner Coll, Staten Island, NY; JR; BS; Proj Hospitality; Omicron Delta Kappa; Delta Mu Delta; Bank Mktng Dept 89-; Deans Lst 88-; IM Hcky/Bsktbl/Sftbl; Econ/Bus Admin; Mkt Frcstng/Opportunties.

**POPPELL, CLARESSA P,** Fl International Univ, Miami, FL; SR; BS; AA Miami Dade Comm Clg 73; Sci Educ; Tch Bio.

**PORCARO, IRENE J,** Columbia Greene Comm Coll, Hudson, NY; FR; BA; PADI; Art Office Sply Store; Ele Educ; Tch Handcpd Ele.

**PORCHER, LISA YVETTE,** Norfolk St Univ, Norfolk, VA; GD; Pblc Rltns Stdt Scty Amer Sec/Treas 90; Hmptn Rds Black Media Prfssnls Mntrshp 90; Ntl Assoc Advncmnt Colored People Dept Socl Serv Youth Cncl Pres Exec Brd; Ruder Finn Exec Training Prog Exec Trne; Virg Bus Intern 90; Journalism Minor/Public Relations.

**PORCO, JOHN J,** Univ Of Pittsburgh, Pittsburgh, PA; SR; BA; Beta Gamma Sigma; Sigma Pi Sigma; Univ Schlr 90-; Golden Key 89; Peat Marwick Schlrshp 89; Physics/Astronomy/Bsn; Bsn/Law.**

**PORELLE, SUSAN M,** Merrimack Coll, North Andover, MA; SR; BA; Ski Clb 88-89; Math Clb VP 90-; Dns Lst 87-; Pres Schlr 90-; Math; Sec Ed.

**PORFIDIO, JOSEPH A,** Church Of God Sch Of Theology, Cleveland, TN; SR; MDIV; Stdnt Govt Pres 90-; BS MKT Ferris St Univ 90; Theology; Mssnry/Pstr/Teacher.

**PORNPRINYA, JARATPONG ANDY,** Univ Of Miami, Coral Gables, FL; SR; BA; Vrsty Bwlng Capt 87-; Treas Of The Grmn Clb 90; VP Of Amer Asn Stdnt Assn 90; Bowman Ashe Acad Schlrshp 87-; Bwlng Capt 87-; Fnnce; Mutintl Frm Mgmt.

**PORPORA, GINA M,** Widener Univ, Chester, PA; SO; BA; Acctg Soc 90-; Modern Lang Soc 89-; Phi Eta Sigma; Widener Univ Hon Pgm 90; Sch Mgmnt Hon Pgm; Acctg; CPA.

**PORRAS, ADRIAN,** Brevard Coll, Brevard, NC; FR; AA; Chrstn Stdnt Flwshp 90-; Proj Inside/Out 90; Theology; Tch/Prsthd.

**PORRAS, JESUS,** Saint Thomas Univ, Miami, FL; SR; BBA; Dns Lst 90; Acctg.

**PORRATA VEGA, CARLOS A,** Inter Amer Univ Pr Guayama, Guayama, PR; JR; BBA; Univ Cmrcl Clb Tres 90; Hnr Stdnt 90-; Hnr Ert 90; Bsktbl/Vlybl 90-; Acctng/Cpa.

**PORRATA, MANUEL F,** Inter Amer Univ Pr San Juan, Hato Rey, PR; JD; Phi Alpha Delta 89-; Hnr Schlp 90-; Amer Bnkrs Asc 90-; Amer Bar Asc 90-; Crdt Offcr Comm Lndng 89-; BSBA Univ Dayton 87; Law.

**PORRECA, CARLO,** Rutgers St Univ At Camden, Camden, NJ; BS; NAA 90; Acctg; CPA Law.

**PORTAL, ROLANDO E,** Miami Dade Comm Coll, Miami, FL; SO; BA; AA 90; Hstry; Tchng.

**PORTALE, CYNTHIA A,** Columbia Union Coll, Takoma Park, MD; JR; BS; AA Montgomery Clg Rockville MD 90; Bus Admn; Cnsltng Bus.

**PORTE, ALICE R,** Univ Of Cincinnati, Cincinnati, OH; JR; BFA; Chmbr Sngrs/Motet Chrl Ens; Horton Mdron Dnc; Clg Consv Msc Perf; Dee Wacksman Schlp Awd; Mscl Theater; Entrtnmnt.

**PORTELLA JR, CHARLES F,** Bishop St Comm Coll, Mobile, AL; SO; Babl; Math/Physics; Engr.

**PORTER LAMBERT, TOMMYE M,** William Carey Coll, Hattiesburg, MS; JR; BSN; Yth Crdntr Church Crdntr 90-; Church Choir 90-; AA City U Bellevue WA 90; Nrsg; Nrs Anesthelist.

**PORTER, AMY B,** Bryant Stratton Bus Inst Syrac, Syracuse, NY; FR; AS; Deans Lst 90; Exe Sec; Profsnl Exec Sec.

**PORTER, ANITRA K,** Ky St Univ, Frankfort, KY; JR; BA; Gspl Ens 89-; Cncrt Chr 90; Alpha Kappa Mu; Inrds Intern Shell Pipeline Corp 90; Math; Scndry Cert.

**PORTER, BARBARA ANN,** Wv Univ, Morgantown, WV; SR; BS; Natl Stdnt Nrs Assoc 90-; Sigma Theta Tau; Alpha Omicron Pi Pldg Phlnthrpst 89-; Nrsg.

**PORTER, D ANDREA N,** Clark Atlanta Univ, Atlanta, GA; JR; IVOF Gospl Chr 88-89; Alpha Phi Alpha 89-; Busn Admin; Entreprnr.

**PORTER, DEBORAH A,** Comm Coll Algny Co Algny Cmps, Pittsburgh, PA; SR; ASN; Phi Theta Kappa Sec 90-; Nursing.

**PORTER, DORIS C,** Northwest Al Comm Coll, Phil Campbell, AL; Phi Theta Kappa 90; New Bethelhmem Bptst Chrch; LPN 90-.**

**PORTER, EVA S,** Alcorn St Univ, Lorman, MS; SO; AD; Nursing.

**PORTER JR, GEORGE A,** Univ Of Md Baltimore Prof Schl, Baltimore, MD; GD; MDPHD; Rugby Ftbl Clb 89-; Med Physiology; Med DR Rsrch.

**PORTER, GLORIA L,** Al St Univ, Montgomery, AL; JR; Stdnt Ori Asst Rep VP 90-; Pi Mu Epselon 90-; Phi Eta Sigma Sec 90-; Pres Schlrshp 88-; Math; Air Force Offcr.

**PORTER III, HAYDEN S,** Univ Of Sc At Columbia, Columbia, SC; SR; Soc Advcmnt Of New Music & Letters; Music Dept Stdnt Cncl; Phi Kappa Lambda.

**PORTER, JACKIE W,** Gaston Coll, Dallas, NC; ADN; RN; Sci; RN.

**PORTER, JARED K,** Univ Of Southern Ms, Hattiesburg, MS; JR; Bptst Stdnt Un Exec Cncl 88-90; Phi Theta Kappa 88-90; Lttr J Awrd 89-90; IM BsktblIM Sftbl Ftbll 88-90; AA Jones Cnty Jr Coll 90; Blby; Mdcl Dctr.

**PORTER, JOZELDA S,** Lane Coll, Jackson, TN; SR; MBA; Schlrly Affrs 89-; Tnage Cnslnc Cntr Vol 90-; Grl Sct Trp Ldr 87-; Rtl Store Mgr 82-89; Soclgy/Hstry; Edctnl Cnslr.

**PORTER, KATHERINE A,** Interdenominational Theo Ctr, Atlanta, GA; GD; MDIV; Mason Flwshp VP 90-; Gospel Chr Ld Vocalist 90-; Drama Pres 89-; UNCF 90-; Ministy Intern 90-; Mason Schlrshp Pioneer Awd 88-; BA Univ N Col 83; Ministry; Clg Chlpn Christian Ed Dir.

**PORTER, KATHLEEN R,** Ky Mountain Bible Coll, Vancleve, KY; JR; BA; Chorus & Choir 88-; Class Officer Sec 88-; Chrstn Serv 89-; Intrnshp Ch Music Dir; Rel/Sacred Music; Ch Music/Youth Ministries.

**PORTER, KELLY L,** Univ Of Nc At Charlotte, Charlotte, NC; SO; BA; Welcome Week 90; Alpha Delta Pi; Adopt-A-Hwy Clean-Up 90-; Feed The Homeless 90-; Psychology Child; Erly Chldhd Counselor.

**PORTER, KELLY M,** Indiana Univ Of Pa, Indiana, PA; SO; BS; Bio/Pre Vet; Vet Sci.

**PORTER, KIMBERLY N,** Univ Of Nc At Chapel Hill, Chapel Hill, NC; FR; BS; Phi Eta Sigma; IM Bsktbll 90-; Bus Admn; Law.

**PORTER III, L WILLIAM,** Fl St Univ, Tallahassee, FL; SR; BS BA; Hnrs Prog; Fla Acad Schlrshp; AA; Pol Sci/Spnsh; Law Schl.

**PORTER II, LARRY W,** Union Coll, Barbourville, KY; SR; BS; Stdnt Govt 90-; Hse Cncl V P 90-; Fllwshp Chrstn Athl 89-; Gamma Beta Phi 90-; Iota Sigma Nu 89; Soph Acctg Award 88-89; Jr Award Hghst Schlstc Avcr 89-90; Snr Award Shwng Mst Prof Achvmnt 90-; Ftbl 87-89; Acctg/Bsn; CPA.

**PORTER JR, LEON M,** Wilmington Coll, New Castle, DE; JR; BS; Phi Alpha Theta 88-89; Alpha Eta Rho 90-; Aviation Mgt; Air Traffic Contrl/Pilot.

**PORTER, LESLIE,** Union Inst, Cincinnati, OH; SR; BA; Natl Tumor Registrars Assoc Midwest Dir; OH Tumor Registrars Assoc Pres 86-87; SW OH Tumor Registrars Assoc Pres 83-84; Natl Assoc Hlth Svcs Execs; Amer Med Red Assoc; Cancer Data Dir 84-; AAS Cincinnati Tech Clg 84; Hlth Svcs Adm.

**PORTER, LESLIE J,** Ms St Univ, Miss State, MS; SR; Coll Rep 89-90; Socty Advncmnt Mgmt 89-; Pres Schlr 90.

**PORTER, LOLA M,** Lees Coll, Jackson, KY; SO; MLS; Engl.

**PORTER, MARK D,** Kent St Univ Kent Cmps, Kent, OH; JR; BA; Fin Assc Pblc Rltns 90-; Gold Key; Delta Sigma Pi; Mrktng/Bus Mngmt.

**PORTER, MARY E,** Univ Of Nc At Greensboro, Greensboro, NC; FR; BS; Alpha Lambda Delta; Teach Flws 90-; Edn K-6; Teach.

**PORTER, MIA R,** Al A & M Univ, Normal, AL; FR; BED; Math Tutor; Math; Tchr.

**PORTER, MICHELE S,** Defiance Coll, Defiance, OH; SR; BA; Hstry; Elem Educ.

**PORTER, PEGGY JO,** Univ Of Va Clinch Valley Coll, Wise, VA; SR; BA; Pstr The Ark Faith; SS Tchr; Headstart; AS SW Comm Coll 90; Elem Educ; Tchr.

**PORTER, RANDI K,** Muskingum Coll, New Concord, OH; SR; BA; Theatre Productions 87; Phi Sigma Iota 88-90; FAO Scl Clb V P 88-90; BA 90; Spnsh; Tch.

**PORTER, TAMMY A,** Ma Inst Of Tech, Cambridge, MA; FR; BS; Park St Church Seekers 90-; IM Ftbl Bsktbl Vlybl Sftbl 90-; Biology; Marine Biology.

**PORTER, TIMOTHY O,** Fordham Univ, Bronx, NY; JR; Summit Cncl World Peace Intern; Acctg; Law.

**PORTER, WARREN D,** Northern Ky Univ, Highland Hts, KY; JR; BS; Intshp Unv Cnccti Ctr Cltrl Rsc Mgmt 87-88; Grd Stds Grnt Anthrplgy UC 87-88; Hstrc/Prehstrc Arch/Hstrc Antqs Apprs 86-90; BA Univ Cinn 85; Bio/Scndry Ed; Bio/Edctr.

**PORTERFIELD, DEBRA M,** Marshall University, Huntington, WV; JR; Mrchng Bnd 89-90; Phi Eta Sigma 90-; Phi Alpha Theta; Undrwd Smth Tchr Schlrshp 89-; Soc Stdies Educ; Tch.

**PORTERFIELD, KIMBERLY L,** Univ Of Ga, Athens, GA; SR; BSED; Erly Chldhd Educ; Tchr.

**PORTH, DENISE G,** Western New England Coll, Springfield, MA; JR; BA; Vars Sftbl 88-; All-Distr 89-90; All-Amer All-Stars; High Batting Avg 89-90; Most RBI 89-; Sftbl; Psych.

**PORTIS, DEBORAH M,** Fl St Univ, Tallahassee, FL; JR; BS; Hall Cncl Sec 90-; FL Pr Assn 90-; Concert Bnd 90; Phi Kappa Phi; Hnrs/Schlrs Assn 89-; Natl Rsdnce Hall Hnry 90-; Dudd & Sons Intern; AA 90; Cmnctn; Pblc Rltns.

**PORTKA, DEBORAH A,** S U N Y Coll Of Tech At Alfred, Alfred, NY; FR; BA; Lbrl Arts/Hmnties.

**PORTMANN, NICKLAUS F,** Southern Coll Of Tech, Marietta, GA; GD; BSEET; IEEE Fndr Edgr 87-; AIM Inst Undrprvlgd Yth Math/Sci Instr 90-; Deans Lst 90-; Pres Cert Acdmc Exclnc 90; Elec Engr Tech; Indstrl Cntrl Engr.

**PORTNOY, MICHAEL ELLIOTT,** Univ Of Miami, Coral Gables, FL; SR; MA; Radio D J Exec Bd Nws Dir 89-90; Mnrty Theatre Ensmbl 90-; Natl Press Phot Assn; Phi Alpha Delta Sec 88-; Eaton Dorm Cncl 90; Shepley Hse Cncl 87-88; Grad Asstshp English; Res Asst Altrntе; BA; English; Grad School.

**PORTS, NICOLE M,** Savannah Coll Of Art & Design, Savannah, GA; FR; MFA; Pntg; Ilstrtr Thtr Dsgn.

**PORTWOOD, KRISTINE D,** Brescia Coll, Owensboro, KY; JR; BS; Phi Beta Lambda; All Amer Schlr Awd; Deans Lst; Acad Awd; IM Bsktbl; Acctng; CPA.

**POSADA, BALDEMAR,** Bunker Hill Comm Coll, Boston, MA; Cmbrdg Chrch Nzrn Mmbr 88-; Fremnt Templ Bptst Chrch Spnsh Ldr 84-88; Spnsh Chrch Plntr Spnsrd; Cambridge Pstr Ldr Chrch Nzrn 88-91; Prfsnl Cls I Drvr 83-; Theology; Evnglst.

**POSEY, BRIAN L,** Wilmington Coll, New Castle, DE; SR; BS; Delta Epsilon Rho 90-; Deans List 89-; Business Mgmt; Marketing.

**POSEY, JAMES PEPPER,** Univ Of Southern Ms, Hattiesburg, MS; JR; BS; Cochng Adm Educ.

**POSEY, MONICA D,** Snead St Jr Coll, Boaz, AL; FR; AAP; Phi Theta Kappa; Data Proc; Cmptr Sci.

**POSEY, WILLIAM J,** Univ Of Akron, Akron, OH; SR; BS; Hll Govt Flr Rep 89-90; IM Athltcs 87-; Dns Lst; Natl Assn Of Acctnts; Air Force ROTC 87-88; IM Athltcs 87-; Acctg; Pblc Acctg.

**POSEY, WYLA M,** Middle Tn St Univ, Murfreesboro, TN; FR; BA; Acctng; Law.

**POSNER, AVRAM E,** Yeshiva Univ, New York, NY; SR; BA; T V Cmntr Wrtr Nwspr; Phlnthrpy Soc; Res Asst; Econ; Law.

**POSNER, DANIEL E,** Yeshiva Univ, New York, NY; GD; JBC Exec Brd Treas 90; Fr Clss Pres 88; Stdnt Strggle Fr Svt Jwry VP 90; Hbrw Lt Hnrs Scty; Bnei Akva; Ivn Tllm; Ychd ; Bs Ezra Sprvsr 89-; Hbrw Lit Awrd 90-; BA; Econs; Strtgy Cnsltng.

**POSNER, JONATHAN SCOTT,** Hofstra Univ, Hempstead, NY; FR; BA; Delta Sigma Phi Fndng Fthr 90-; Accounting; Law.

**POSNER, MARY ELLEN,** Memphis St Univ, Memphis, TN; JR; PRSSA VP; Canterbury Episcopal Yth Org Chpln Asst; Dns Lst; Kappa Delta; Habitat For Humanity; Intrnshp Intl Paper.

**POSS, ALISSA M,** Middle Tn St Univ, Murfreesboro, TN; SR; BS; Orntn Advsr 90; Pnhlnc Cncl 88-; Pnchlnc Cncl Treas 90-; Alpha Omicron Pi 87-; Alpha Omicron Pi Treas 90-; Eta Zeta Swthrt; Pltcl Sci.

**POSS, GREGORY D,** Middle Tn St Univ, Murfreesboro, TN; SR; BS; Mass Cmnctns.

**POSS, JONATHAN C,** Ga St Univ, Atlanta, GA; FR; BA; Alpha Lambda Delta 90-; Deans Lst 90-; Hon Day 90-; Hist/Sociology; Univ Hist Profr.

**POSS-KENNEDY, LAURA A,** Savannah Coll Of Art & Design, Savannah, GA; JR; BFA; Amer Scty Of Intr Dsgn Treas 90; Stdnt Prsrvtn Assoc; Bapt Stdnt Union; Ga Trust For Historic Prsrvtn Schlrshp; Amer Bsnss Womens Assoc 90; Bwlng Tm 90; Interior Dsgn/Hstrc Prsrvtn; Prsrvtnst.

**POSSON, CHRISTINE J,** Casco Bay Coll, Portland, ME; FR; Stdnt Sen Pol Rec Comm; Phi Beta Lambda Treas; Phi Beta Lambda VP; Dns Lst; Trvl/Toursm Mgmt; Trvl Conslt/Agnt.

**POST, DELORA J,** Savannah St Coll, Savannah, GA; SR; BA; Recipient Of Ntl Merit Schlrshp 83-86; Deans Lst 83-89; Rcpnt Of Frank Davis Schlrshp 90; Real Estate Loan Prcssr 90; Info Syst; Cmptr Sci.

**POST, JACQUELYN A,** Wright St Univ Lake Cmps, Celina, OH; SO; BS; Math.

**POST, MELANY D,** Wv Univ At Parkersburg, Parkersburg, WV; FR; BA; Pscyh; Indstrl Psych Cndct Wrkshps.

**POST, NICOLE,** James Madison University, Harrisonburg, VA; JR; BS; Grace Campus Mnstrs 89-; Intrhl Cncl Pblcty Chrprsn 90-; Mdl Sch Educ; Tchng.

**POSTELL, JAMIE A,** Oh St Univ At Marion, Marion, OH; FR; BA; Ecnmcs/Bus Stdnt Soc; Alpha Lambda Delta; Phi Eta Sigma; Bus; Finance/Law.

**POSTELL, JOHNNIE,** Tuskegee Univ, Tuskegee Inst, AL; SO; Cmps Digest Stff Rprtr 90-; Larabee Schlrshp 89-; Hnr Rll 89-; Dns Lst 89-; Hstry/Poli Sci; Law.

**POSTLE, JOHN M,** Wv Northern Comm Coll, Wheeling, WV; JR; AAS; Yth Serv Sys Inc 88-; Stdnt Mnth; Cmnty Serv Awd; Heat/Air Cond/Refrig; Bus Owner.

**POSTLES, TAMERA M,** Wilmington Coll, New Castle, DE; JR; BA; Phi Theta Kappa; Alpha Epsilon Epsilon 87-88; DE Tech/Comm Coll; Outstndg Stdnt Curriculum DTCC 88; Deans Lst Wilmington Coll 89; DE Tech; Ednl Lab Spclst 88-; Genl Mgr Southern Campus In-Hse Radio Station; Cmnctn Arts; Jrnlsm/Ednl Field/Free-Lance.

**POSTON, KRISTA M,** Univ Of Ky, Lexington, KY; JR; PHARM; Res Hall Assn Rep 88-89; Alpha Lambda Delta 88-; Arts & Sci Deans List 88-; Phrmcy Intern; Phrmcy.

**POTANOVIC, THOMAS J,** Hudson Valley Comm Coll, Troy, NY; SR; AAS; Rdlgc Tchnlgy; Rdlgc Tchnlgst.

**POTEET, JAMES S,** Union Univ School Of Nursing, Memphis, TN; FR; MS; Nrsng; Cert RN Ansthst.

**POTEET, PATTI L,** Columbus Coll, Columbus, GA; SR; BS; Alpha Phi Sigma V P; Am Crmnl Justice Assoc Lambda Alpha Epsilon 90-; Crmnl Justice; Law Enfrcmnt.

**POTERO, EDWARD K,** Temple Univ, Philadelphia, PA; SO; MBA; Exrcs Physlgy.

**POTKOVIC, TROY M,** Stetson Univ, Deland, FL; JR; BS; Rngr Chlnge 88-90; Phi Eta Sigma 89-; Psi Chi 90-; Sigma Phi Epsilon 88-; US Army Arbrn Schl 89; Air Asslt Schl 90; Supr Cadet Awd 89-; Psych; US Army Ofcr.**

**POTOMA, SCOTT J,** Salisbury St Univ, Salisbury, MD; SR; Res Hall Cncl 88-; Phi Alpha Theta 90-; Pi Gamma Mu 90-; Omicron Delta Kappa 90-; Sigma Alpha Epsilon Pres 88-; Res Asst Hsng Dept 88-; Vrsty Track & Fld Tm Capt 87-; BA; Hist; Law Tulane Law Sch.

**POTRAFKE, KARYN F,** Univ Of Cincinnati-Clrmnt Coll, Batavia, OH; SO; B ED; Deans List 89-; B Ed; Human Soc Serv; Psych.

**POTRATZ, MARY E,** S U N Y Coll At Fredonia, Fredonia, NY; JR; BED; Kappa Delta Pi; Natl Cncr Crds Chrmn 90; Hrt Fdn 88-90; Easter Sls 89-90; Lgl Sec 81-84; Scl Stds; Elem Ed Tchr.

**POTT, JASON A,** Broward Comm Coll, Ft Lauderdale, FL; SO; BA; Phi Theta Kappa 90-; Chem; Med.

**POTTER, DEBRA A,** Norfolk St Univ, Norfolk, VA; JR; AAS; Summa Cum Laude 88-; Cedar Rd Academy Tchr 88-; Tidewater Comm Clg; Edctn; BA.

**POTTER, ELIZABETH E,** Converse Coll, Spartanburg, SC; FR; BA; Alpha Lambda Delta; Stcnt Vol Svcs 90-; Chem/Bio.

**POTTER, ELIZABETH R,** Snead St Jr Coll, Boaz, AL; SO; Varsity Sftbl All Rgnl 89-; Hmcmng Ct; Phi Theta Kappa Sec 89-; Pres Lst 89-; Schlr Athlete Awd; Varsity Sftbl Pitcher All Rgnl 89-; Nrsng; Anesthetist.

**POTTER, HOPE VICTORIA,** Salisbury St Univ, Salisbury, MD; JR; BA; Rsprtry Thrpy Assn V P 90; Rsprtry Thrpy; Hlth Care.

**POTTER, JEFFREY L,** Hudson Valley Comm Coll, Troy, NY; SR; AAS; Assoc Gen Cntrctrs Stdnt Chptr 90-; Trckstp Mgr; Cert 90; Cert 90; Cnstrctn Tchnlgy.

**POTTER, KELLEY L,** Glassboro St Coll, Glassboro, NJ; SR; BA; Glee Clb York Clg Of PA 87-88; Sigma Delta Rho York Clg Of PA 88-; Artcl Publ In Protection Officer Mag 88; Crmnl Jstc; Fed Govt Wrk.

**POTTER, KENNETH D,** Middle Tn St Univ, Murfreesboro, TN; JR; BSN; Nrsng.

**POTTER, KIMBERLY D,** Alice Lloyd Coll, Pippa Passes, KY; GD; Kappa Delta Epsilon 88-; BA; Educ.

**POTTER, LISA M,** Univ Of Cin R Walters Coll, Blue Ash, OH; FR.

**POTTER, LISA M,** Anne Arundel Comm Coll, Arnold, MD; SO; Amer Sign Lang Clb; Omicrontheta; Dev Psychlgy; Chld Psychlgst.

**POTTER, MARY LOU E,** Albertus Magnus Coll, New Haven, CT; SR; BA; Judcl Cmte; Alpha Sigma Lambda; AA Albertus Magnus Colg 90; Engl: MA.

**POTTER, MICHELLE R,** Fl St Univ, Tallahassee, FL; JR; BA; Golden Key 90-; Statistics/Math; Actuary.

**POTTER, RICHARD A,** Ramapo Coll Of Nj, Mahwah, NJ; SR; BA; Lit Clb VP 88-; Sigma Tau Delta; Lit/Ed; Ed.

**POTTER, RITA L,** Merrimack Coll, North Andover, MA; SO; BS; Benzene Ring Chem Cl 90-; Yrbk Staff 89-90; Pharmctcl Chem.

**POTTER JR, ROBERT C,** Bridgeport Engr Inst, Fairfield, CT; FR; BSEE; Eng Clb Pres 90-; Audiophile Soc 90-; Amer Pwdr Mtllrgy Inst; Qlty Tchncn; Elctrncs/Radio Cmcntns; Eng Dsgn/Prtypng.

**POTTKOTTER, TINA M,** Wright St Univ Lake Cmps, Celina, OH; FR; BA; Educ; Elem Educ.

**POTTRATZ, ANITA R,** Savannah Coll Of Art & Design, Savannah, GA; JR; BFA; Baptist Stdnt Un V P 90-; Bwlng/Tnns 89-; Graphic Dsgn; Advrtsng.

**POTTS, AMY L,** Memphis St Univ, Memphis, TN; JR; BED; Kappa Alpha Theta; Jr Chbr Comm 90-; Elem Ed; Tchr.

**POTTS, GREGORY L,** S U N Y Coll At Fredonia, Fredonia, NY; SR; Nstl/Crntn Co.

**POTTS, HOLLY J,** D Youville Coll, Buffalo, NY; SO; BSN; Lambda Sigma 90-; Lambda Sigma Chr Cake Sls 90-; IM Vllybl 90; Science; Nrsng.

**POTTS, JULIE K,** Univ Of Nc At Greensboro, Greensboro, NC; JR; BS; Wsly/Lthrn Hse Untd Meth/Lthrn Cmps Mnstry Cncl 89-; Chld Dvlpmnt; Educ.

**POTTS, KHRISTIN J,** Univ Of Nc At Greensboro, Greensboro, NC; SO; BS; Chld Dvlpmnt; Child Abuse Cnslr.

**POTTS, MEREDITH L,** Ringling School Of Art, Sarasota, FL; JR; BFA; BA Auburn Univ 88; Ills; Cmnctns.

**POTTS, MICHELLE A,** Defiance Coll, Defiance, OH; SO; BA; Cmnctns Clb Pblc Rltns VP 90-; Frnscs Tm 89-; Clg Yrbk Edtr 89-; Pi Kappa Dlt 89-; Natl Frnscs Assc Cmptr 90; Cmnctns Arts; Clg Prfsr.

**POTTS, NICHOLE D,** Al St Univ, Montgomery, AL; SO; BA; Dinkins Stdnt Union; Ebonite Assn; Gospel Chr; Sclgy; Entrprnr.

**POTTS, REGINA D,** Daytona Beach Comm Coll, Daytona Beach, FL; SO; Prs Lst; Math/Sci; Rehbltve Thrpy.

**POTTS JR, TERRY L,** Columbia Union Coll, Takoma Park, MD; SR; BS; Cum Laude; Austo Sls Rep Licns; AS Panama Canal Clg Republic De Panama 88; Orgnztnl Mgt.

**POTWIN, LISA M,** Slippery Rock Univ, Slippery Rock, PA; JR; BA; CV Soccer Assoc Bd Secy 89-90; Phi Theta Kappa 88; Adlt Litry Progrm Tutor 89-; Laubach Litrcy Intrntl 89-; BC 3 Day Care Ctr Bd 87-89; Hlth/Phy Ed; Tchng.

**POU, JAVIER A,** Bridgewater Coll, Bridgewater, VA; FR; Pre Med Scty 90-; Ski And Otdr Clb 90-; Blgy; Med.

**POUCH, MELISSA M,** Duquesne Univ, Pittsburgh, PA; SO; BA; Cmmtr Asstnt 90; Phi Eta Sigma 90; Phi Chi Theta; Bsns; Accntng MIS.

**POUGET, LAWRENCE A,** Va Commonwealth Univ, Richmond, VA; JR; BS; Stdnt Govt Assn Sub-Com Chrprsn 90-; Urban Studies Stdnt Assn VP 90-; Acdmc Intgrty Appls Bd Rep 90-; Phi Sigma Kappa Pblc Rltns Dir 90-; Cmps Scrty 89-90; Cthlc Cmps Mnstries 90-; Grace Street Task Frc Rep 90-; Navy Achvmnt Mdl 86; Urban Studies/Pblc Admin; Law.

**POUGH, GWENDOLYN D,** William Paterson Coll, Wayne, NJ; JR; BA; Black Stdnt Assoc Pres 90-; Sis For Awrns Black Ldrshp & Eqlty 88-; Orntn Ldr 90-; Delta Sigma Theta Dean Of Pldgs 90-; Dean Of Stdnts Awd For Campus Serv Soph 90; Highest GPA Soph Black Stdnt Assoc 90; Eng; Pblshd Writer.

**POUKISH, JUDY R,** Asbury Theological Sem, Wilmore, KY; GD; MDIV; Intrvrsy Chrstn Fllwshp Yuba Clg Ldr 78-79; Nwspr Asst Ed 78-79; Stdnt Cncl Wom IM Dir 82-83; UC Davis Pblcty Offc Intrnshp Wrtr 79-80; IM Dir 82-83; Japan/Amer Soc Of KY; Calif Assoc Tchng Englsh 88-89; Biblical Studies; Christian Missions.

**POULIN, DAVID W,** Holyoke Comm Coll, Holyoke, MA; SO; BA; Green Key 90-; Alpha Xi Omege 90-; Natl Mtpl Sclrss Scty; AS; Acctg; CPA.

**POULIOT, GEORGE A,** Saint Vincents Coll & Seminary, Latrobe, PA; JR; BA; Physcs Clb 88-; Rspct Fr Lfe Clb 88-; CRC Prss Fr Chem Achvmnt Awd 88-89; Summer Inst Fr Atmsphrc Sci 90; NOAA; Math/Cmptr Sci; Sci.

**POULIOT, JOAN F,** Fl A & M Univ, Tallahassee, FL; JR; BS; Cls Sec 90-; Wntr Prk Mem Hsptl Physcl Thrpy Dept 87; Crw Tm 85-86; BS Univ Cntrl Fl 88; Physcl Thrpy.

**POULIOT, MATTHEW,** Me Maritime Academy, Castine, ME; JR; BS; Indctntn Stf Bravo Co Cmmndr; Intrnshp Brd Oil Tnkr Cdt 90; Lfbtsmn Crtf US Cst Grd 90; Ntcl Sci; Dck Offcr Mrchnt Marine.

**POULOS, JAMES,** Johnson St Coll, Johnson, VT; SR; BA; Chesamore; Pres List; All Am Schlr Clgt Awd; Psychlgy.

**POUNCEY II, WILLIAM J,** Nc Agri & Tech St Univ, Greensboro, NC; SR; BS; Kappa Alpha Psi Pres; Elect Eng; Elect Eng.

**POUND, DARCIE L,** Univ Of Akron, Akron, OH; JR; BA; Univ Mrchng Band Feature Twrlr 88-; Madison Mrchrs Asst Dir 90-; IM Ftbl 88; Phy Ed.

**POUND, SANDRA J,** Itawamba Comm Coll, Fulton, MS; SO; BA; Comp Sci Clb 90-; Natl Hnr Scty; Cmptrs; Info Systems.

**POUND, TOYA D,** Coll Of Charleston, Charleston, SC; SR; BA; Ldrshp Educ 89-; Alumni Assn 89-; Omicron Delta Kappa 90-; Alpha Hnr 89-; Alpha Delta Pi 88-; Hghly Dstngshd Hnrs Lst 89-; Blgy; Med.

**POUNDS, MICHAEL A,** Univ Of Tn At Martin, Martin, TN; JR; BS ED; Stdnt Tn Educ Assn 90-; US St Achvmnt Acad All-Am Schlr 90-; Spcl Olympcs 90-; Scndry Educ/Eng; Tchr.**

**POUPORE, DARREN L,** Univ Of Nc At Asheville, Asheville, NC; SR; BA; Stdnt Govt Assn Senatr 88-; Phi Alpha Theta 90-; Pi Sigma Alpha 90-; Hstry.

**POURNARAS, VASILIKI C,** Univ Of Sc At Columbia, Columbia, SC; JR; Educ Clb 90-; Kappa Delta Pi 90-; Outstndg Stdnt Awd Elem Educ; Intrnshp Tchg Thrd Grd Clss Myrtle Bch Elem; Elem Educ.

**POURROSTAMIAN, MAHNAZ,** Yeshiva Univ, New York, NY; JR; Bio/Pre-Hlth; Dentistry.

**POUTENIS, MARK V,** Wagner Coll, Staten Island, NY; FR; BA; Radio Prog Dir 90-; Theater/Art; Illstrtn.

**POVLICK, DEBRA K,** Schenectady County Comm Coll, Schenectady, NY; SO; AS; Prgrmr Anlyst Ny St Tchrs Rtrmnt Sys 89-; Comp Sci; Engrng.

**POWE, CHARMELL F,** Univ Of Al, Tuscaloosa, AL; FR.

**POWE, TAHELIA C,** Alcorn St Univ, Lorman, MS; SR; Krte Clb Treas 89; Stdnt Govt Assn Stdnt Sntr 89-; Pn Hllnc Cncl 89-; Alpha Kappa Mu 89-; Beta Kappa Chi Prlmntrn 90-; Beta Beta Beta Pres 88-; Alpha Kappa Alpha Phlctr 89-; Natl Cllgte Educ Awrd 90; Pn Hllnc Cncl ASU; BS; Blgy Pre Med.

**POWELL, ANDREA D,** James Madison University, Harrisonburg, VA; SO; BA; Amnsty Intrntl 89-; Phi Sigma Iota 90-; Study Schlrshp; Psychlgy/Frnch; Chld Psychlgst.

**POWELL, BARBARA A,** Hudson Valley Comm Coll, Troy, NY; FR; AAS; Pres Lst 90-; Med; Resp Therpy.

**POWELL, BRANDON C,** Univ Of Ky, Lexington, KY; JR; BA; Amer Inst Archtctr Stdnts 90-; Phi Delta Theta Eastern KY Univ 88-89; John L Cutler Awd 90; Bk Awd 1st Yr Dsgn Excllnc Archtctr; Archtctr; Prctc/Tch.

**POWELL, BRENDA WHITE,** Va Commonwealth Univ, Richmond, VA; SR; BS; Stdnt Nrs Of Th Yr 70; Pres Sr Cls 70; Jnstn-Wls Almn Assoc Chr Dir Chrch Orgnst; Amrcn Hrt Assoc; Rn Jnstn-Wls Hsptl Scl Of Nrsng 71; Nrsng; Grtrc Nrs Prctnr.

**POWELL, BRIAN M,** West Liberty St Coll, West Liberty, WV; GD; IM 86-90; Reg Ldrshp Awrd 84-85; Ftbl/Bsbl 84-85; BS 90; Chem/Bio; Lab Tech.

**POWELL, CAROLYN H,** Thomas Nelson Comm Coll, Hampton, VA; FR.

**POWELL, CATHY L,** Newbury Coll, Brookline, MA; SR; AS; Fshn Shw Exprnc 89-; Phi Theta Kappa; Intrnshp E Drumm Dsgns; AS Wlmsprt Area Comm Coll 79; Fshn Dsgn; Dsgnr/Ptrnmkr/Own Bus.

**POWELL, CHRISTINE E,** Univ Of Akron, Akron, OH; JR; BA; Gldn Ky; Kappa Delta Pi; Elem Educ/Hstry.

**POWELL, CHRISTINE Y,** Anne Arundel Comm Coll, Arnold, MD; JR; BA; Phi Theta Kappa; AA Anne Arundel Comm Clg 90; Acctg; CPA.

**POWELL, CHRISTOPHER A,** Nova Univ, Ft Lauderdale, FL; GD; MBA; Univ Intl Stdnts Assn 89-; Plantation Eagles Soccer Clb Capt 89-; Los Perfectos Soccer Clb Jamaica WI 87-88; All-Dist Soccer Tm NAIA 89; All So Soccer Tm NAIA 89; All Area Soccer Tm NAIA 89; U Soccer Capt 88-89; BSC; Bus Admin; Human Resource Mgmnt.

**POWELL, CHRISTOPHER J,** Univ Of Cin R Walters Coll, Blue Ash, OH; FR; BA; Phi Theta Kappa; Engl/Jpnese; Tchng.

**POWELL, DARNISHA N,** Stillman Coll, Tuscaloosa, AL; FR; Hstry Clb 90-; Stdnt Gvmt 90; Ford Schlrs 90-; Cordell Wynn Hnr Scty.

**POWELL, DAVID FREDERICK,** Niagara Univ, Niagara Univ, NY; SR; BS; AIBS Treas 90-; Scabbard/Blade Actng Cpt 90; Pi Sigma Alpha 89-; Coll Arts/Sci Hnrs; Bio/Pol Sci; Env Law.

**POWELL, DAWN M,** Univ Of Tn At Martin, Martin, TN; SR; BS; Soc Wrk Clb Sec; Sigma Kappa Sec 87-88; Hnrs Smnr Schlrshp; Soc Wrk; Scl Wrk Adlt Clnts.

**POWELL, DELON R,** Morehouse Coll, Atlanta, GA; FR; BA; Hnrs Pgm; Army ROTC; MS Clb; Nrthwstrn Mtl Life Intshp; IM Bsktbl/Ftbl; Ecnmcs/Math; Intl Corp Tax Law.

**POWELL, DOUGLAS N,** S U N Y At Buffalo, Buffalo, NY; SO; BS; Amnesty Intl USA City Msn Soc Buffalo 89-; Water Pollution Cntrl Fed 90-; Vet USAF 80-; Bio; Envrnmntl Serv.

**POWELL, ERIC M,** Hudson Valley Comm Coll, Troy, NY; FR; BA; Phi Theta Kappa; Phi Theta Kappa; Pres Lst; Eng.

**POWELL, EVRIL H,** Al St Univ, Montgomery, AL; SR; Intrntl Stdnts 87-; Alpha Kappa Mu Sec 90-; Cnty Dist Atty Chld Spprt Intrn 90; BS; Hmn Srvcs Cncntrtn Jvnle Jstce; Prbtn Offcr.

**POWELL, FELISSA A,** Al A & M Univ, Normal, AL; SO; Cheerleading 89-90; Psychology; Clinical Psychology.

**POWELL, FRANCINE P,** Saint Thomas Univ, Miami, FL; JR; Natl Lbrry Ptry 89-; SADD 89-; All Fr On Assoc 90-; Rbrt Mccb Trnsfr Schlrshp 88-; AA 90; Elem Ed.**

**POWELL, GEORGE R,** Old Dominion Univ, Norfolk, VA; JR; BS; Brd Of Dcns; Oklnd Chr Of Chrstn Chrch; Nwprt Nws; Shpbldng; Mgmt; Mech Eng.

**POWELL, GERALDINE S A,** Coppin St Coll, Baltimore, MD; JR; BA; GSA Cntrl Mrylnd Trp Ldr 86-; Trp Ldr Daisy Grl Scts; Tchr Asst/Cnslr 81-; AA 84-87; Cert 78-81; Elem Ed.

**POWELL, HOPE M,** Univ Of West Fl, Pensacola, FL; SR; BA; AA Okaloosa Walton Jr Clg 89; Early Chldhd/Elem Ed; Ed.

**POWELL, HUGH E,** Central St Univ, Wilberforce, OH; FR.

**POWELL JR, JAMES J,** East Tn St Univ, Johnson City, TN; FR; BA; Bus Mgmt; Cnstctn Cmpny.

**POWELL II, JAMES R,** Marshall University, Huntington, WV; FR; BA; Alpha Sigma Phi; Acctg; CPA.

**POWELL, JEANNIE A,** Marshall University, Huntington, WV; SR; BA; Grls Scts; Kappa Gammi Phi 90-; Kappa Omicron Phi; Womans Clb; Merchndsng; Clthng Buyer.

**POWELL, JOHN M,** Univ Of South Al, Mobile, AL; SO; BA; Amer Hrt Assn Com 90-; Amer Lung Assn 89-; VP Gen Mgr New Dmnsns Ftnss Cntr Inc 83-; Bus Mgmt; Intrprnr.

**POWELL, JOSEPH C,** Fl A & M Univ, Tallahassee, FL; SR; BA; Surf Clb; BA FL State; Engl; Jrnlsm.

**POWELL, JUDITH F,** Vance Granville Comm Coll, Henderson, NC; AS; Phi Theta Kappa 90-; Max Factr Schlrshp Endwmnt Schlrshp; AAS 90-; Sci Cmptr Prgmg.

**POWELL, JULIE A,** Union Univ, Jackson, TN; JR; BS; Bsktbl Mgr; Phy Ed/Hlth; Athletic Trnr.

**POWELL, KAREN L,** Comm Coll Algny Co Algny Cmps, Pittsburgh, PA; Mscl Thtr Grp; USAF; Blgy; Physcl Thrpy.

**POWELL, KIMBERLY A,** Salem-Teikyo Univ, Salem, WV; JR; BS; Deans Lst 88-; Gamma Beta Phi 89-; All Amrcn Schlr 89-; Otstndng Coll Stdnts Amrc 89-US Achvmnt Acdmy 89-; Natl Coll Bujs Mrt Awrd 89-; Acctg.

**POWELL, LAURA N,** Bellarmine Coll, Louisville, KY; GD; BA; Delta Epsilon Sigma 89-; Womens Club Schlrshp 86-87; BA 90; Bus Admin.

**POWELL, MARK A,** Columbia Greene Comm Coll, Hudson, NY; SR.

**POWELL, MARLA HOPE,** Middle Ga Coll, Cochran, GA; FR; Bsn Admin; Acctng.

**POWELL, MARY C,** Univ Of Va, Charlottesville, VA; FR; Chi Omega 90-; Biol; Med.

**POWELL, MELANIE M,** Stillman Coll, Tuscaloosa, AL; JR; Class Pres; Yrbk Staff; Gamma Lota Sigma; Cordell Wynn Hnrs Prog; Alpha Kappa Alpha; Cmptr Sci/Math.

**POWELL, MELISSA C,** Radford Univ, Radford, VA; JR; Tau Kappa Epsilon 90; Limited Inc 86-; Bus Mktg; Mktg Cnslnt.

**POWELL, NIGEL R,** Lincoln Univ, Lincoln Univ, PA; JR; BA; Natl Blacks In Crmnl Justice Assoc; Lincoln Univ Deans List 90-; Most Dependable Rendall Hall 88-89; Crmnl Justice; Law.

**POWELL, PATRICIA E,** Western Piedmont Comm Coll, Morganton, NC; SO; ASN; Nrsng; Hosp RN.

**POWELL JR, RAY D,** Fl A & M Univ, Tallahassee, FL; JR; BSEE; Dorkus Drake Chrstn Party; USN Rank E-6; AS FL Jnr Clg 89; Elec Engr; USN Engr Offcr.

**POWELL, RHONDA K,** Univ Of Sc At Columbia, Columbia, SC; JR; BED; Pres Hon Lst 89-90; Deans Lst 89-90; S S Bible Sch Tchr 80; Ele Sch Vol 85-89; AA Cerro Coso Cmty Clg 88; Ele Educ; Tch.

**POWELL, RHONDA K,** Univ Of Sc At Sumter, Sumter, SC; JR; BED; Deans List 89-90; Pres Hnr List 89-90; Sunday Schl/ Bible Schl Tchr 80-; AA Cerro Coso Comm Clg 88; Elem Ed; Tchng.

**POWELL, RICHARD M,** Birmingham Southern Coll, Birmingham, AL; SO; BS; Gtr; Chss; Alpha Tau Omega; Acctg.

**POWELL, ROBIN DIANE,** Univ Of Sc At Columbia, Columbia, SC; SO; BS; Occupational Thrpy.

**POWELL, SHALISA D,** Fl A & M Univ, Tallahassee, FL; FR; BA; Gaspel Choir 90-; Concert Choir 90-; Phi Eta Sigma 90-; Elite Tour Guide 90-; Busn Admin; Mktng.

**POWELL, SHARMAN L,** Va St Univ, Petersburg, VA; SO; BBA; Outstndng Schlrshp In Acad; Deans Lst; Bsnss Info Syst; Corp Lwyr.

**POWELL, SHARON D,** Univ Of Sc At Columbia, Columbia, SC; SR; BS; Assn Hon Stdnts Rep 87-; Peer Cndct Dscplnry Bd 89-90; Ordr Omega 90; Gamma Iota Sigma 89-; Delta Zeta Sec V P 88-; Carolina Camp Cnslr 90; Mgmt/Bus Admn.

**POWELL, SHELIA L,** Alcorn St Univ, Lorman, MS; JR; BSN; Sigma Star Sweetheart Club Chpln 88-90; NAACP 89-90; Inter Rsdnce Hall Cncl Sec 89-90; Beta Beta Beta 89-; US Pblc Hlth Svc 89/90; Costep Nrse; Outstndg Fmle On Drill Team Staff Sgnt 87-90; Nrsg.

**POWELL, STACEY M,** Longwood Coll, Farmville, VA; JR; BS; Stdnt Educ Assn 90-; AAS Sthsd VA Comm Coll 90; Elem Ed; Tchng.

**POWELL, STEVEN J,** Comm Coll Algny Co Algny Cmps, Pittsburgh, PA; FR; AA; Avtrs Clb Pres 90-; Flgt Tchnlgoy; Arntcl Sci.

**POWELL, SUZANNE M,** Oh Coll Of Podiatric Med, Cleveland, OH; GD; DPM; Amer Clg Ft Srgns Clb 90-; Alpha Gamma Kappa 90-; Mrt Schlrshp 90-; TA 89; BS St John Fisher Clg 89; Podtrc Med.

**POWELL, TAMARA M,** Tri County Tech Coll, Pendleton, SC; SO; BA; Assoc Prof; AA; Sociology; Cnslng/Juv Victims Of Crime.

**POWELL, WANDA D,** Gaston Coll, Dallas, NC; FR; BA; Bptst Chrch; Prjct Mngmnt Assc 87-88; Cert Kings Coll 87; Educ; Tch.

**POWELL, WAYNE,** City Univ Of Ny Med Evers Coll, Brooklyn, NY; FR; BA; Acctg.

**POWELSON, JARED T,** Univ Of Tn At Martin, Martin, TN; JR; BS; Resident Hall Assc Sec/Treas 88-89; Society Hnrs Seminar Stdnts 90; IFC Sec 89-90; Order Of Omega 90; Sigma Alpha Epsilon VP 89-90; Cert Merit; Biology; Optometry.

**POWER, BERTINA MARIAN,** Hampton Univ, Hampton, VA; FR; BA; Wmns Senate 90-; Frshmn Cls Bd 90-; Ill Alumni 90-; High Hnr Rl 90-; Howard Hughes Med Inst Sci Enrchmnt Prog 90; Trck/Long Jmp 90-; Acctng; CPA.

**POWER, JAMES R,** Valdosta St Coll, Valdosta, GA; SR; BA; Pi Gamma Mu; Hstry; Clg Prfsr.

**POWER, MENTORIA A,** Fl A & M Univ, Tallahassee, FL; SO; BS; Bio Nvl Rsrch Pgm; Deans Lst; Bio; Peds.

**POWERS, ALANA S,** Fayetteville St Univ, Fayetteville, NC; SR; BA; Pltcl Sci Clb Pres 89-; Alpha Kappa Mu; Chnclrs List 89-90; Pltcl Sci Dept Hon Awd 89-; US Army Rsrvs Staff Sgt 89-; US Army 81-89; AAS Cntrl TX Clg 86-88; Pltcl Sci; Law.

**POWERS, CAROL J,** Univ Of Sc At Aiken, Aiken, SC; SO; AD; Nrsng; Alcohol Drug Rehab.

**POWERS, CHRISTOPHER G,** Univ Of Sc At Aiken, Aiken, SC; JR; BA; SGA Snte Elctns Comm Chr 89-90; SGA Sec/Treas; Yng Dems Vp 88-; Tchg/Excllnc Comm 90-; LIFE Sec/Treas 89-; Cmps Crsde Fr Christ 88-; Aiken Cnty Dem Prty Thrd Cnty Co Chr 89-; Greenpeace 89-; Deans Lst; Poli Sci; Law.

**POWERS, CHRISTOPHER M,** Wagner Coll, Staten Island, NY; JR; BS; Delta Mu Delta; Douglas Gee Morton Mem Awd; Bsn Admn; Dns Lst 89-; Ecnmcs.

**POWERS, DENISE M,** Converse Coll, Spartanburg, SC; JR; BED; Cncl Excptnl Chldrn Secr/Treas 89-; Stdnt Govt Assoc 90-; Alpha Lambda Delta 88-90; Comprhnsv Spec Ed; Tchg.**

**POWERS, DON E,** Kent St Univ Geauga Cmps, Burton Twp, OH; SO; BA; Comp Sci; Acctg; Dsgnr/Mgmt.

**POWERS JR, EVERETT K,** Capitol Coll, Laurel, MD; SR; BS; Alpha Chi 90-; Tau Alpha Pi; AA Prince Georges Cmnty Clg 89; Elec Engr Tech.

**POWERS, FAITH A,** Dickinson Coll, Carlisle, PA; SO; BA; Spnsh Clb Treas 89-; Dickinson Sml Bsn Alnc Sec 89-90; Alpha Lambda Delta 90-; Delta Delta Delta Asst Pldg Trnr 89-; Dns Lst 90-; IM Tns 90-; Spnsh/E Asian Stds; Intrprtr.**

**POWERS, FELICIA D,** Univ Of Tn At Martin, Martin, TN; JR; Stdnt TN Ed Assn; Erly Chldhd Ed; Tchr.

**POWERS, GAIL M,** Vance Granville Comm Coll, Henderson, NC; SO; AA; Hstry Clb Pres 89; Stdnt Govt Soc Com 90; Drama Actng Grp Stge Mgr 89; Top Schlr Clg Transfr 89; Sci Demo Tm Sr Scientst 89; H S Coach Track 89; 4th July Cmtee Chrprsn 90; Bio Chem Lab Asst 90; Physical Thrpy; P T Sprts Med.

**POWERS, GAYLE B,** Univ Of Sc At Columbia, Columbia, SC; SR.

**POWERS, JEANNINE F,** Mount Aloysius Jr Coll, Cresson, PA; FR; BA; Genl Stud; Nrsng.

**POWERS, JEREMY A,** Allegheny Coll, Meadville, PA; SR; Chemii Clb 87-; Camps Nwspr 87-88; Allegh Comm Exch Dir 87-; Stdnt Ldrshp Svc Comm 90-; Comm Vol 90-; Aldn Schlr 88-; IM Vlybl B Ball Ftbl Sftbl; Camps Cons Next Inc 90-; Chem; Tchng/ Ind.

**POWERS, KIMBERLY D,** Radford Univ, Radford, VA; JR; BS; Stdnt Ed Asso 90-; Kappa Delta Pi 90-; Deans List; Early/Middle Ed; Tch.

**POWERS, MARGARET M,** Univ Of Akron, Akron, OH; JR; BA; Akron Cncl Educ Stdnt 90-; Fmly Svc Summit Cty Vol Yr 90-; Engl Lang Inst 89; Kappa Dlta Pi 90-; Gldn Key 90-; Rho Lmbd 90-; Alpha Gamma Dlt Pnhlnc Dlgt 90-; Acad Schlrshp 89-; Co Operative Educ Boys/Girls Clgs 90; Scndry Educ; Tchng Univ Level.

**POWERS, MARK A,** Owensboro Comm Coll, Owensboro, KY; SO; Fnce; Law.

**POWERS, MARTHA N,** Univ Of Miami, Coral Gables, FL; JR; BA; UMFA 88-; Film Festival Awrds; Little Sister Sigma Chi 88-; Motion Pictures/Theatre; Prdcng Talent Agnt.**

**POWERS, MELISSA A,** S U N Y Coll Of Tech At Frmgdl, Farmingdale, NY; FR; MBA; Ed.

**POWERS, MELISSA B,** Roane St Comm Coll, Harriman, TN; JR; BS; AS 90; Educ; Tchr/Cnslr.

**POWERS, MELISSA G,** Owensboro Comm Coll, Owensboro, KY; FR; BA; Chmstry; Phrmcst.

**POWERS, PATRICIA E,** Nazareth Coll Of Rochester, Rochester, NY; FR; BA; Lit Mag 90f Radio Statn 90; Frnch Art; Intrntl Advrtsng Dsgn.

**POWERS II, ROBERT P,** Fordham Univ, Bronx, NY; SO; BA; Goelic Soc 90-; Accntng; CPA.

**POWERS, SABRINA J,** Northeast State Tech Comm Coll, Blountville, TN; SO; AAS; Phi Theta Kappa 90-; Wrk Schlrshp 89-90; Outstndng Stdnt Mjr; Grdtd Hnrs; Ofc Systms Tech; Bsn.

**POWERS, SAMANTHA L,** Univ Of Ky, Lexington, KY; SR; BSN; ADN Paducah Comm Coll 89; Clinical Nurse Spclst CCU.

**POWERS, SCOTT W,** Rochester Inst Of Tech, Rochester, NY; SO; AAS; Str Trk Clb Capt; Acctg Lab Tr; Citicorp Citibank Schlrsp; Lillian M Cowin Schlrsp; Security Bank Trust Intern Accts Pybl 90; 1st Amrc Bank Intern Smmr Inter; Acctg; Bus Bnkng.**

**POWERS, SHARON RENEE,** Western Ky Univ, Bowling Green, KY; JR; BA; Stdnt Repr 88-90; Phi Eta Sigma 88-; Univ Brdcstg Assoc 90-; Brdcstg; TV Prod/Dir.

**POWERS, STACEY R,** East Central Comm Coll, Decatur, MS; SO; BA; Mu Alpha Thea 89-; Phi Beta Lambda 90; Fshn Sqd 89-; Phi Theta Kappa 90-; AA; Bus Admn.

**POWERS, STEPHANIE M,** Glassboro St Coll, Glassboro, NJ; JR; BA; AA Cumbrlnd Cnty Coll 90; Spnsh; Intrprtr.

**POWERS, STEPHEN T,** Abraham Baldwin Agri Coll, Tifton, GA; SO; BSFR; Frst Rsrcs; Wldlf Blgst.

**POWERS, TRACEY L,** Memphis St Univ, Memphis, TN; FR; BBA; Acctg; CPA.

**POWERS III, WILLIAM,** Univ Of North Fl, Jacksonville, FL; SO; BA; Mktg; Bsn Exec.

**POWERY, LINDA M,** Univ Of Miami, Coral Gables, FL; SR; BA; Econ/Fin.

**POWLEDGE, PATRICK W,** Bayamon Central Univ, Bayamon, PR; SO; BBA; Stdnts Assn Busn Admin VP 90-; Inst Comm Drg Alchl Free Cmps 90-; Cat Rev Comm 90-; Inst Libry Stndg Comm 90-; Inst Comm Sel Otstdng Prof 90-; Acctg; Prof Acctg.

**POWLETT, STEPHEN L,** Ms St Univ, Miss State, MS; SR; BA; Sigma Alpha Epsilon 87-90; Deans Schlr 90; IM Ftbl Sftbl 87-90; Mktg; Sls.

**POWLUS, JODI L,** Wilkes Univ, Wilkes-Barre, PA; FR; BS; Math Cmptr Sci Clb 90-; Schlrs 90-; Biochem; Ob/Gyn.

**POYNER, JONATHAN M,** Roanoke Bible Coll, Elizabeth Cy, NC; JR; BA; Kempsville Church Of Christ Yth Minister; Intrnshp To Jamaica 90; Bsktbl Tm 89-90; Christian Ministries; Missionary.

**POYNER, M JOANN,** Univ Of Tn At Martin, Martin, TN; SR; BSW; Oldr Stdnt Assoc Pres 87-88; Soc Wrk Clb Cmte Chrprsn 89-90; Natl Assoc Scl Wrkrs 90-; Natl Assoc Chrstn Scl Wrkrs 90-; Soc Wrk; Soc Srvc.

**POYNOR, KAREN E,** Nyack Coll, Nyack, NY; JR; BA; Innr Cty Yth Outrch New York City 89-; Asst Psychlgy Dpt; Deans Lst 89-; Grls Sccr Clb 90; Spychlgy; Childrns Thrpy/Cnslng.

**POYSER, KAREN M T,** Nova Univ, Ft Lauderdale, FL; FR; BA; Blck Stdnt Assoc Crspndng Sec 90-; Internatl Stdnt Assoc 90-; Vlybl; Bsn Admin; Corp Law.

**POYTHRESS, ANTOINE F,** Ky Wesleyan Coll, Owensboro, KY; JR; BA; Order Oak/Ivy; Ftbl Tm Cptn 88-; Acctng.

**POZAR, AMY M,** Indiana Univ Of Pa, Indiana, PA; FR; B ED; Sgn Lng Clb 90-; Alc Pl Hs Vintr 90-; IM Grls Bsktbl 90-.

**POZEN, BARBARA R,** Univ Of Ga, Athens, GA; JR; BED; Stdnt Cncl Excptnl Chldrn Treas Elect; Educ; Spec Educ Tchr.

**POZNIAK, LAURIE E,** Univ Of Md At College Park, College Park, MD; FR.

**POZON, ANGELICA Z,** Univ Of Rochester, Rochester, NY; JR; BA; Undergraduate Mngmnt Scty; AEISEC; Alpha Lambda Delta; Omicron Delta Epsilon; Banque Nationale De Paris Internship; Rugby Tm Mgr 89-; Economics; Intl Finance.

**POZUN, LAURA M,** Kent St Univ Kent Cmps, Kent, OH; SR; BED; Amrcn Chrl Drctrs Assn 90-; OH Msc Edctrs Assn 90-; NN Chorale 88-90; Gldn Key 90-; Alpha Lambda Delta 88-; Delta Omicron Chpln 89-; NW Hnrs Schlrshp 87-90; Schl Msc Schlrshp Voice; Msc Edctn; BED Chrl Msc Edctr.

**POZZUTO, ANGELO A,** City Univ Of Ny Baruch Coll, New York, NY; SO; BBA; Mrktng.

**POZZUTO, BRIDGETTE D,** Oh Wesleyan Univ, Delaware, OH; SR; BA; Westezun Stdnt Fndtn 88-; Campus Pgrms Bd 89-90; Engl Stdnt Bd 90-; Chi Eta Sigma Phi Soc 88-89; Omicron Delta Kappa 90; Sigma Tau Delta 89; Psi Chi 90; Pres Schlrshp 87-; Grad Phi Beta Kappa; Engl; Law.

**PRADHAN, NEETA,** George Mason Univ, Fairfax, VA; JR; BA; Acctg; Banking.

**PRADO, JESSICA V,** Fl International Univ, Miami, FL; FR; Phi Mu; Bsn; Law.

**PRADO-SEVILLA, IRIS VANESSA,** Bayamon Central Univ, Bayamon, PR; SR; Assc Future Scl Wrkr; Edctnl Alliance Nicolas Sevilla Sec 87-90; Youngs Hope Seed Clb Sec 87-88; Marie Legion Young VP 88-90; Marie Legion Adults Sec 88-90; History/Social Work; Social Wrk/Law.

**PRAGER, ERIC H,** Slippery Rock Univ, Slippery Rock, PA; SO; BA; HPERD Clb 90-; Athltc Trng Clb 89-90; Lambda Sigma 90-; Delta Psi Kappa; Wrstlng Tm 89-90; Sport Mgt/Lftm Ftns; Cnsltnt/Clb Owner.

**PRAGER, SHARON L,** Newbury Coll, Brookline, MA; FR; BA; Jwsh Big Bro Big Sis 90-; Jwsh Phlnthrps 89-; Law.

**PRAKASH, GAUTAM B,** Univ Of Rochester, Rochester, NY; SR; BS; Cinema Grp Thea Mgr 89-; Bridge Cl Publ Dir 89-; Study Abroad Oxford Un England; Biochem; Academia.

**PRAKOBCHATI, SUCHATE,** Manhattan Coll, Bronx, NY; JR; BS; IEEE 89-; Eta Kappa Nu 90-; Tau Beta Pi 90-; Acadmc Support Svc Tutor/Comptr Cnsltnt 89-; Elec Eng.

**PRALL, DEAN V,** Kent St Univ Kent Cmps, Kent, OH; SR; BA; Gldn Ky; US Army 84-88; Fnnc; Govt Fnnc Fld.

**PRANCL, CHRISTOPHER L,** Rollins Coll, Winter Park, FL; FR; BA; Biology.

**PRANTKE, SHARON E,** Erie Comm Coll, Buffalo, NY; JR; AAS; Chld Care; Erly Chldhd Educ.

**PRASADA-RAO JR, THOMAS W,** Columbia Union Coll, Takoma Park, MD; BS; Org Mgt; Public Hlth.

**PRASHAD, ROMONA,** Ny Univ, New York, NY; FR; BA; Engl; Ed.

**PRATER, MECHELLE L,** Oh Univ Chillicothe Branch, Chillicothe, OH; SO; BS; Home Ecnmcs; Fashion Mrchndsg.**

**PRATHER, DENNA R,** Northern Ky Univ, Highland Hts, KY; SR; BA; Mktg.

**PRATT, AARON H,** Rensselaer Polytechnic Inst, Troy, NY; SR; Chrmn Jud Bd Chr 89-; Amer Soc Of Mech Engr Pr 90; Pr Cmsn Acad Integ 90; Deans Lst Of Dist Stdnts 86-; Phi Gamma Delta 86-; Awd Recog For Rips Asme; BS Rensselaer Polytech Inst; Mech Engr; Mfg Mgmt.

**PRATT, CONNIE W,** Western Piedmont Comm Coll, Morganton, NC; FR; AAS; Phi Theta Kappa 90-; Thrptc Rcrtn.

**PRATT, CYNTHIA D,** Middle Tn St Univ, Murfreesboro, TN; SR; BED; STEA 90-; Elem Educ; Tch.

**PRATT, DAWN C,** Fisk Univ, Nashville, TN; SO; BA; Fisk Clb VP 90-; Intrnshp Stfr Htl; Intrnshp Hskns Vnc/Co; Pblc Accntng.

**PRATT, DONA CHIMENE,** Bennett Coll, Greensboro, NC; SR; BA; Psychlgy Clb; Marshall Bd Clb; Deans Lst 90-; Intrnshp Watsons Grp Home ICF 90-; Psychlgy.

**PRATT, DOUGLAS G,** Middle Tn St Univ, Murfreesboro, TN; SR; BS; Behvrl Sci Clb; Fmly Stds Stdnt Yr; Behvrl Sci; Psych/Cnslr/Tchr.

**PRATT, ELIZABETH J,** Radford Univ, Radford, VA; JR; BA; Amer Horse Shw Assn 87-; U S Drssg Fed 87-; Bus Mngmnt.

**PRATT, ELIZABETH S,** Franklin And Marshall Coll, Lancaster, PA; JR; BA; Sigma Pi Sigma 90-; John Kershner Schlr Physcs 90-; Hons Lst 89-; Phycs; Res.

**PRATT, JANET L,** Newbury Coll, Brookline, MA; GD; BA; Resp Therapy Clb Sec 89-; Cystic Fib Walk-A-Thon 89-; Comm Vol Rt Camp Chstnt 89-; Phi Theta Kappa; Lambda Beta; Inter Sputum Bowl Compt Wnr 89-; Magna Cum Laude; Aerobics; Thrpst Mass Genl Hosp; AS; "CRTT Natl Brd Resp Care; Rep Therapst.

**PRATT, JEFFREY S,** Western New England Coll, Springfield, MA; JR; BS; DPMA 90-; Tchng Prog 90-; Deans List 90-; AS Greenfield Comm Clg Greenfield 90; Comp Info Sys; Bus/Comp Sys.

**PRATT, KENNETH J,** Old Dominion Univ, Norfolk, VA; JR; PHD; Cmptr Sci.

**PRATT, KJERSTI L,** Univ Of Sc At Coastal Carolina, Conway, SC; SO; BS; Hnrs Pgm 89; Phi Eta Sigma 89; Sftbl 89; Scndry Educ/Engl; Tch.

**PRATT, LAURA B,** Roane St Comm Coll, Harriman, TN; GD.

**PRATT, LAURA CAROL,** Tougaloo Coll, Tougaloo, MS; SO; BS; Spanish Clb 89-; Pre Health Clb 89-; Alpha Lambda Delta; Presidents Lst 90; Biology; Medicine Pediatrics.

**PRATT, LOUIS L,** Broome Comm Coll, Binghamton, NY; SO; BS; Phi Theta Kappa 90-; Acad All Regn III; RITS Otstndng Transfr Schlrshp; Frank G Paul Schlrshp; Vars Bsbl; AS; Elec Engr.**

**PRATT, SUSAN J,** Springfield Tech Comm Coll, Springfield, MA; SR; AS; Bus Clb VP 90-; Alpha Nu Omega; Amer Mktg Assn; AS 89; Grphc Arts/Mktg; Exec Pos.

**PRATT, SUSAN L,** Wilmington Coll, New Castle, DE; SO; BS; Trst Oper Sprvsr Bank Of Delaware; Bnkng/Fin; Bnkng.

**PRATT, TAWANDA M,** Alcorn St Univ, Lorman, MS; JR; BS; Hon Stdnt Org; Alpha Kappa Mu; Acctg; CPA.

**PRAVER, FRANCES,** Long Island Univ C W Post Cntr, Greenvale, NY; SR; Psych Clb; Psy Chi; Hon Pgm; BA Summa Cum Laude; Psychlsy Art Thrpy; Clncl Pgm.

**PRAZNIK, SANDRA R,** Kent St Univ Stark Cmps, North Canton, OH; FR; PHD; Psychlgy; Cnslng.

**PREACHER, BELINDA L,** Nc Agri & Tech St Univ, Greensboro, NC; FR; BA; Hometown Clb VP; Cls Fndrsr; INROADS; Bristol Myers Squibb Intern; Indstrl Eng.

**PREECE, RAYMOND L,** Marshall University, Huntington, WV; JR; BA; Chrch God Bible Grp Intr 88-90; Baptist Stdnt Un 88; Switzer Chrch Of God 87-; Acctng; CPA.

**PREGGER, BECKY C,** Castleton St Coll, Castleton, VT; SO; BA; Marine Blgy.

**PREISCHE, JODY R,** Salisbury St Univ, Salisbury, MD; FR; Sprts Med Clb 90-; Physcl Ed Scty 90-; Athltc Trnr 90-; MAHPGRD 90-; Physcl Ed; Athltc Trnr.

**PREMA, PAUL D,** City Univ Of Ny Queensbrough, New York, NY; AAS; Phi Theta Kappa; Elec Engr.

**PREMO, DAWN B,** Springfield Tech Comm Coll, Springfield, MA; GD; BA; Alpha Nu Omega 90; Sr Yr HS STCC For Clg Credit 88; Liberal Arts.

**PRENDERGAST, ANNE,** Seton Hall Univ, South Orange, NJ; JR; BS; Stdnt Ambsdr Soc; Fresh Stdes Dept Per Advsr; Kappa Delta Pi; Campus Mnstry Vol; Ele Educ/Psychology; Tch.

**PRENDERGAST, CHRISTOPHER S,** City Univ Of Ny Baruch Coll, New York, NY; JR; BBA; Evngn Accntg Scty; Sigma Alpha 90-; Mlbnk Twd Hdly And Mc Cly 89-; AAS Kingsborough Comm Coll 89; Acctng; Law.

**PRENDERGAST, KATHLEEN A,** Cornell Univ Statutory College, Ithaca, NY; SO; BA; Ambassadors Recorder Strng Comm 89-; Sage Chapel Choir 89-90; Orntn Cnslr; Suprvsry Orntn Cnslr 90-; Advisor; Deans Lst 90-; Tradition Fllwshp 89-; Biology; Medicine.

**PRENTICE, DAMON S,** Memphis St Univ, Memphis, TN; SR; BSET; ASCE State Tech Inst Memphis 89; Engineering Technology; Engineering.

**PRENTICE, MICHAEL J,** Clarkson Univ, Potsdam, NY; JR; BS; Amer Mktg Assn Exec VP 90-; Clrksn Mini-Indy 90-; Clrksn Automtv Assn 88-90; Mngmnt Info Syst/Mktg; Cnsltng.

**PRENTISS, JOHN D,** Univ Of Southern Ms, Hattiesburg, MS; SO; BSBA; Activities Cncl 90; Hnrs Stdnt Assoc 89; Accntng; CPA.

**PRESCHER, CRAIG R,** Ms St Univ, Miss State, MS; JR; PGM Clb 88-90; Band 88-90; Cmps Crusd 88-90; Dns Schlr; Phi Eta Sigma; IM Bsktbl; Bus; Pro Glf Mngr.

**PRESCOD, ANDRU J A,** Morehouse Coll, Atlanta, GA; FR; BS; Natl Soc Blck Engr; Intl Stdnt Orgztn; Clg Hon Prog; Otsdng Stdnt Atlanta U 90; Ctr Dual Dgre Engr Prog; Physics/Engr; Aeronautical Engr.

**PRESCOTT, DONNA G,** Univ Of Sc At Columbia, Columbia, SC; SO; BA; Citizens/Southern Natl Bank Adm Asst 88-89; Elem Ed.

**PRESCOTT, MICHELLE L,** Allegheny Coll, Meadville, PA; JR; BS; Cltrl Escape Soc Sec 88-89; Nwspr Phtgrphr 89-; Psi Chi; Alpha Gamma Delta Treas 90-; Chldrns Home Incrn 90; Alden Schlr 89-90; Bsktbl Statistician 90-; Psychology.

**PRESCOTT, RUSSELL D,** Univ Of Sc At Columbia, Columbia, SC; FR; BCHME; Outstndng Physics Stdnt 90-; AEET Aiken Tech Coll 90; Chem; Chem Engr Spclzng Envrnmntl Cntrl.

**PRESCOTT, STEPHEN M,** Mount Olive Coll, Mount Olive, NC; JR; BS; Mt Olive Clg Sngrs Danc Capt 89-; Hnrs Schlr 88-; Busn Mgmt.

**PRESCOTT, W WALKER,** Savannah St Coll, Savannah, GA; SR; BA; Tybee Islnd Jycs; IM Ftbl/Bsbl/Bsktbl; Systm Oprtr Savannah Fds Indstrs; Cmptr Info Systms; Prgmr.

**PRESH, LEE A,** Western New England Coll, Springfield, MA; SR; Dean List 89-; BSBA; Human Rsrc Mgmt; Dir.

**PRESLEY, PAULA R,** Univ Of Nc At Greensboro, Greensboro, NC; JR; BS; ASID 88-90; Alpha Lamda Delta 89-; Dean Lst 88-; Erly Childhd Educ.

**PRESLEY, TRENT J,** Union Univ, Jackson, TN; SR; BS; Stdnt Fndtns P 88-; Sen 87-; Stdnt Pblc Rltns Soc VP 89-; Admssns Intrnshp 90-; Mr Union 90-; Mgmt/Mktg.

**PRESLEY, WANDA ALLEN,** Tn St Univ, Nashville, TN; JR; BS; Sociology Clb 90-; Goodlark Educ Fndtn Schlr 90-; Mt Lebanon United Meth Chrch Chrprsn PPR Comm 90-; CPS Prof Sec Intl 86; Sociology; Hlth/Comm Srvc.

**PRESNELL, DAVID W,** Univ Of Nc At Asheville, Asheville, NC; SR; BS; Amer Meteorological Soc 87-88; Natl Forecast Contest; IM Ftbl/Bsktbl; Cert Exec Cntrl Lang; Atmospheric Sci; Meteorologist.

**PRESSIMONE, DARIO A,** City Univ Of Ny Baruch Coll, New York, NY; GD; BBA; Itln Scty 86-90; CIAO Pres 88-89; Axlry Brd 89-90; Stdnt Achvmnt Awrd 87-88; Deans Lst 86-87; IM Hcky 87-90; Mrktng.

**PRESSIMONE, DOREEN,** William Paterson Coll, Wayne, NJ; SR; Early Childhd Org Pres 87; Kappa Delta Pi Pres 90-; Pi Lambda Theta 88-; Alpha Kappa Delta 90-; Deans Lst; NAEYC; SNJEA; BA; Soc/Kindergrtn Tchr.

**PRESSLEY, CARL C,** City Univ Of Ny Baruch Coll, New York, NY; SR; BBS; Mrktng Mgmnt.

**PRESSLEY, JANNIE J,** Comm Coll Algny Co South Cmps, West Mifflin, PA; GD; BS; Stdt Intern 89-90; Hmn Resource Mgmt Ind Corp; AS 90; Human Resource Mgmt; Executive.

**PRESSLEY, LA KISHA T,** Nc Agri & Tech St Univ, Greensboro, NC; SO; BS; Mrchg Bnd 89-; Symph Bnd 89-; Mu Phi Epsilon 90-; A J Fletcher Msc Schlrshp 89-; Msc Ed; Msc Ther.

**PRESSLEY, TINA MARIA,** Radford Univ, Radford, VA; JR; BS; English Club V Pres; IM Soccer Sftbl 90; English; H S Teacher.

**PRESSMAN, CHRISTIAN M,** Univ Of Miami, Coral Gables, FL; SO; BA; Stdnt Lit Corps 90; SCALE Peer Cnslr 90; Zeta Beta Tau Pledge Pres; Hist/Edn; Law.

**PRESSNELL, MICHAEL R,** Univ Of Al At Huntsville, Huntsville, AL; SR; BSE; Co-Op Pgm Wrk Phs III Syst 90-; Hon Forum Calhoun Comm Coll 87-89; Doers Clb Calhoun Comm Coll Sec 88-89; Bsbl-Calhoun Comm Jr Coll 88-89; Elect Eng.

**PRESSON, BLAIR A,** Union Univ, Jackson, TN; SR; BSBA; Accntng Clb Treas 90-; Hstry Clb VP 90-; Alpha Chi 90-; Phi Theta Kappa 88-89; Faclty Awrd JSCC 89; Hmnts Awrd JSCC 89; IM Vllybl 89; AA Jackson St CC 89; Accntng; Accntng Law.

**PRESTAMO-TORRES, NYDIA AMANDA,** Univ Of Pr At Rio Piedras, Rio Piedras, PR; SR; Amer Inst/Archtctr Stdnts 87-.

**PRESTIEN, LAURA A,** Univ Of Akron, Akron, OH; SR; BA; Pre Law Club 90; Golden Key 89-; Acadmc Schlrshp 87-; Deans List 87-; Bus Mgt; Law.

**PRESTON, ANTHONY E,** Norfolk St Univ, Norfolk, VA; SR; BS; Mass Comm Stdnt Assoc 89-; Cmps All Star Chllng Acad Tm; Natl Assoc Blk Jrnlsm 90; Alpha Kappa Mu; Spartan Alpha Tau; Brdcst; Mass Comm Acad Awd; Wnsb Trlblzr Yr Awd; Mass Comm; Brdcst Mgmnt.

**PRESTON, EDWIN H,** Morehouse Coll, Atlanta, GA; FR; BS; Blgy; Med.

**PRESTON III, GEORGE E,** Bishop St Comm Coll, Mobile, AL; SO; BS; Deans Lst; AA 90; Sclgy.

**PRESTON, JAMES L,** Fl St Univ, Tallahassee, FL; JR; Todays Ntrtn Clb 90-; Gulf Wnds Trck Clb 90-; FPIRG 89-; AA FSU 90; Nrsng.

**PRESTON, KENNETH G,** Univ Of Nh Plymouth St Coll, Plymouth, NH; SO; BS; Assoc Non Trad Stdnts; Presidents Lst 89-; Achvmnt Schlrshp 90-; Geography; Hydrology Research.

**PRESTON, PATRICIA A,** Concord Coll, Athens, WV; GD; BA; Cnty Rdng Cncl 89; Crdnl Key 90; Kappa Delta Pi 89; All-Amer Schlr Cllgte Awd; Grad Cum Laude; BA Sci; Multi-Sbjcts; Edctn.

**PRESTON, TRACY L,** Kent St Univ Kent Cmps, Kent, OH; SO; BA; Hse Cncl KIC-RED 90; Alpha Lambda Delta 89-; Delta Sigma Pi 90-; Acctng.

**PRESTON, VICKI J,** West Liberty St Coll, West Liberty, WV; JR; BS; Stdnt Amer Dntl Hygnsts Assn Pres; Lght Hill Blb Stdy 90-; Chi Beta Phi; BS Fairmnt St Coll 89; Dntl Hygn; Dntl Hygnst.

**PRESTOPINO, PATRICIA A,** Univ Of Nc At Charlotte, Charlotte, NC; SR; BCA; NAEA Tr 87-; Phi Kappa Phi 90-; Visual Arts.

**PRESTRIDGE, KAREN E,** Univ Of Southern Ms, Hattiesburg, MS; JR; BA; Mgng Edtr Sch Paper 90-; S E Jrnlsm Conf Pres; Coalition Stdnt Invlmnt V P 90-; Soc Prfsnl Jrnlst Sec; Gamma Beta Phi 89; Hathesburg Amer Copy Edtng Intern; Jrnlsm; Nwspr Rprtr/Copy Edtr.

**PRESTWOOD, ANGELA S,** Univ Of Southern Ms, Hattiesburg, MS; JR; BS; Assoc Stdnt Govt Senator 89; Traffic Appeals Comm Secy 89; Orientation Ldr 89; Phi Theta Kappa 88-; Gamma Beta Phi; Comm Serv Pblc Rltns Comm 89; Persuasive Speech Contest Finalist 89; AA Hinds Comm Clg 90; Oceanography; Rsrch.

**PRETE, JEAN M,** S U N Y Coll Of Tech At Alfred, Alfred, NY; SR; AAS; Lib Arts Crmnl Jstce; Law.

**PRETTY, CHRISTINA M,** Newbury Coll, Brookline, MA; SO; BA; Cls Rep; Nwspr Crcltn Dist Mgr; Eng/Mktg.

**PRETTYPAUL, DONALD L,** City Univ Of Ny City Coll, New York, NY; SO; BS; MBRS Student; Chem & Physics; Research.

**PREVATT JR, JAMES NORMAN,** Fayetteville St Univ, Fayetteville, NC; SO; BS; Comp Sci; BS Engrng.

**PREVOST, CURTIS A,** Al A & M Univ, Normal, AL; JR; BS; Caribbean Stdnts Assoc Treas 89-; Engr Natl Hnr Soc Treas 90-; NAACP; Acad Asst Cen Math Spec; All-Amer Schlr; Acad Hnr Rl; Dns Lst; Elctrcl Engr Tech; Entreprenuer.

**PREVOT, LYNN M,** Duquesne Univ, Pittsburgh, PA; FR; Kappa Delta; UMCA Of Allegheny Co Vol 90; Milliones Middle Sch Tutor; Elem Edn; Coll Prof.

**PREW, LOIS A,** Western New England Coll, Springfield, MA; SO; BA; Committee Progrmmng And Entertainment 90-; Deans Lst 89-; Psychology; Clinical Psychologist.

**PREWITT, LINDA K,** Western Piedmont Comm Coll, Morganton, NC; GD; AAS; Interior Dsgn Club Secy 90-; A B Hon Roll 90-; Interior Dsgn.

**PREYEAR, CAROLYN L,** Al A & M Univ, Normal, AL; FR; BS; Dns Lst 90-; Med; Phys Thrpy.

**PREYER, LESLIE A,** Castleton St Coll, Castleton, VT; JR; BA; Outing Clb 88-89; Acdmc Excllnc Awd 90; Vol Dismas Hs; Asst Store Mngr 90-; AA 88; Psychlgy; Frnsc Psychlgy.

**PREYER, TYRONE P,** Atlantic Comm Coll, Mays Landing, NJ; FR; AA; Comp Clb VP 90-; Peer Mentor 90-; Deans Lst 90; Natl Frght Inc Spvrsr 89-90; Bsktbl Asst Coach; ; Little League Bsbl Head Coach; Diesel Mech 85-90; Cert Atlantic Cnty Voc Tech Schol 84; Cert OH Diesel Tech Inst 85; Tchr.

**PREZIOSO, MARLA S,** Kent St Univ Kent Cmps, Kent, OH; GD; Acctng Assoc 89-90; AIESEC 87-88; Golden Key 90-; Beta Alpha Psi 89-; Stdnt Vol Awd 90; Conviser Miller CPA Review Awd 89; 4 Yr Italian Schlrshp 86-90; Youngstown St Univ Acdmc Schlrshp 86; BBA 90; Acctng.

**PREZZANO, DENISE ANN,** S U N Y Coll Of Tech At Frmgdl, Farmingdale, NY; SO; AS; Chrldng Coach 89-90; Tch Rlgn Clss 88-; Phi Theta Kappa 90-; Deans Lst 89-90; Pres Lst 90-; NAEYC 89-; Fthr P Carey Schlrshp 89-90; Early Chldhd Grnt 89-; Day Care Cntr Tchr; Prvt Tutr; Early Chldhd Ed/Spch Pathlgy/Autiolgy.

**PRIAR, SUZETTE R,** Owensboro Comm Coll, Owensboro, KY; FR; BA; Nrsng; RN.

**PRIBELL, KEVIN J,** Samford Univ, Birmingham, AL; GD; JD; Am Jrsprdnc Book Awd; BSBA Univ FL 87; Real Est/Urban Analysis; Law.

**PRIBETIC, LILLIAN E,** City Univ Of Ny La Guard Coll, Long Island Cty, NY; GD; Sls Rep 81-; Elec Spply Hse; Bus.

**PRIBISCO, TRACEY L,** Univ Of Miami, Coral Gables, FL; JR; BBA; Program Cncl; Gen Hnrs Pgm Hnrs Clb; Delta Gamma V P Rush-Asst; FL Undergrad Schlrshp; J F Pearson Schlrshp; Finance; Bsn Mgmt/Professor.

**PRICE, AARON C,** Thomas Nelson Comm Coll, Hampton, VA; SO; BA; Acctg; CPA.

**PRICE, ANGEL L,** Ms Univ For Women, Columbus, MS; JR; Lockhrt Scl Clb P 88-; Masker Scl Clb P 90-; Stdnt Alumnae Assn 89-; Stndt Gov Assn Ed Sen 89-90; Hottentots 90-; Mortar Brd; Torch 90-; Kappa Delta Epsilon VP 90-; Union Advsry Cbnt 89-; Elem Ed; Tchng.

**PRICE, CHERYL L,** George Mason Univ, Fairfax, VA; JR; Stdnt Ed Assn 89-; Kappa Delta Pi 90-; Alpha Chi; Golden Key; Zeta Tau Alpha Alumnae Rltns 90-; Hist; Tchng.

**PRICE, CHRISTOPHER A,** Tuskegee Univ, Tuskegee Inst, AL; SO; NSBF 90-; CA Club; Silver Trvl Ldg #10 Sr Wrdn 89-; Intern Dept Wtr/Pwr 90-; Mech Eng.

**PRICE, DAWN R,** Le Moyne Coll, Syracuse, NY; GD; Chmbr Cmrc; Ads Dir 86-; BPS 81; Crmnl Jstc; Spcl Ed Tchr.

**PRICE, FREEDA L,** Tri County Tech Coll, Pendleton, SC; SR; ASSOC; Sec Sci; Sec.

**PRICE, GABRIELLE M,** Fl St Univ, Tallahassee, FL; JR; BS; Phi Theta Kappa Exec Bd 89-90; Garnet Key; Magna Cum Laude Grad; Deans Lst; AA Gulf Coast Comm Clg 90; Elem Educ; Educator.

**PRICE, GLYNN E,** Central Al Comm Coll, Alexander City, AL; FR; BA; Psych/Hist; Tchr.

**PRICE, GRETCHEN A,** Coll Of Charleston, Charleston, SC; SO; BA; Chrstn Chpl Assem Of God Sndy Schl Tchr/Fllwshp Banquet Coord/Worship/Sng Ldr89-90; Elem Educ; Tchng.

**PRICE, JAMES A,** East Stroudsburg Univ, E Stroudsburg, PA; SR; BA; Biol Treas 87-89; Wrk Stdy Prog 87-; Ftbl 87; Envir Studies; Water Quality/Analysis.

**PRICE, JASON J,** Coll Of Charleston, Charleston, SC; FR; BA; IM Ath 90-; Hon Coll 90-; Psych.

**PRICE, JEFFREY R,** Slippery Rock Univ, Slippery Rock, PA; SO; Clncn Prcptul Mtr Dvlpmnt Pgm; Pres Lst; Deans Lst; IM 90-; Bio/Pre-Med; Dr.

**PRICE II, JOHNNY T,** Germanna Comm Coll, Locust Grove, VA; FR; BA; Phys Ed/Sprts Med.

**PRICE, KAREN M,** Mobile Coll, Mobile, AL; SR; BS; SLATE Sec 88-90; Psi Chi VP 87-90; Alpha Chi 90-; Kappa Delta Epsilon 89-90; ATE; Deans Lst 87-89; Presdnts Lst 89-; Erly Chldhd Elem Ed; Tchr.

**PRICE, KATHY D,** Central Al Comm Coll, Alexander City, AL; FR; BA; Goree Wellness Ctr 90; Pub Rltns/Speech; Pub Rltns/T V.

**PRICE, KELLIE W,** East Tn St Univ, Johnson City, TN; FR; BS; Infrmtn Sci; Comp Prog.

**PRICE, KIM H,** Al St Univ, Montgomery, AL; SR; BA; Focal Inc 90-; FHA 87; Alpha Kappa Alpha 89-; Educ; Tch.

**PRICE, KIMBERLY M,** Marshall University, Huntington, WV; FR.

**PRICE, KRISTEL A,** Unity Coll, Unity, ME; SO; BS; Wldlf Clb; Wldlf.

**PRICE, LA TONYA D,** Fisk Univ, Nashville, TN; SR; Choir Sec 87-; Psi Chi 90-; Alpha Kappa Alpha 90-; BA; Psych; Indstrl Psych.**

**PRICE, LORI T,** Cecils Coll, Asheville, NC; SO; AAS; Paralegal Prog.

**PRICE, MAREA A,** Clayton St Coll, Morrow, GA; FR; AD; Hlth Sci; Nrsng.

**PRICE, MAYLON D,** Glassboro St Coll, Glassboro, NJ; JR; BA; Cinema Wrkshp 89-; Vet U S Coast Guard 80-84; AA 88; Comm; Grad Sch/Tch.

**PRICE, MICHAEL A,** Univ Of Nc At Charlotte, Charlotte, NC; SO; BS; Boston Arch Ctr 89-90; Dns Lst; Chnclrs Lst 90-; Arch; Arch/Prfsr Dsgn.

**PRICE, MICHAEL B,** Univ Of Al At Birmingham, Birmingham, AL; FR; MBA; Alpha Lambda Delta; Bus; Accntng/Bus.

**PRICE, MICHAEL E,** Univ Of Montevallo, Montevallo, AL; SO; BA; SGA 90-; Chi Omega Chpln Assn Rush Chrmn 89-; Bptst Cmps Mnstrs Cmps Otrch; Alpha Lambda Delta VP 89-90; Prsdnts Lst 89-; Dean Fine Arts Schlrshp 89-; Cmmnctn Arts Advsry Brd 90-; Mass Cmmnctns Hstry; Tchng.

**PRICE, RHONDA R,** Old Dominion Univ, Norfolk, VA; GD; SDBC 86-87; Alcohol Awareness 87-88; Tour Gd 87-90; Alpha Kappa Alpha 87-90; Boys Clb Vol 89-90; J C Penny Intern 89; BS 90; Mktng Educ; Adult Trng.

**PRICE, ROBERT B,** Tn Temple Univ, Chattanooga, TN; SR; BS; Choirs; Knox Soc Athl Dir; Dns Lst 88-90; Chpl Pgm 86-90; Bst Def Bsktbl 88-90; Sprtl Ldr Awd 87-90; Bsktbl 86-90; Psych; Mnstr/Soc Svc.

**PRICE, ROBERT H,** West Liberty St Coll, West Liberty, WV; JR; BA; Schlr Athl; Golf 89-; Grphc Dsgn.

**PRICE, RONNIE L,** Beckley Coll, Beckley, WV; SO; BA; Art; Tchr.

**PRICE, RUBY K,** Univ Of Sc At Coastal Carolina, Conway, SC; SO; BS; Phys Ed Mjrs Clb; IM Sftbl; Cstl Statcn Mens Bsktbl; Phi Eta Sigma; Hons Pgm; Crss Cntry Tm All Conf 89; Phys Ed; Tchng/Phys Ther.

**PRICE, RUBY K,** Univ Of Sc At Columbia, Columbia, SC; SO; BA; Pi Epsilon Mu 89-; Phi Eta Sigma 89-; Hnrs Prgrm; Crs Cntry NCAA 89-; Physcl Edctn.

**PRICE, RUTH E,** Comm Coll Algny Co Algny Cmps, Pittsburgh, PA; FR; AS; Alld Hlth; Med Rcrds Tech.

**PRICE, SARA E,** Univ Of Sc At Columbia, Columbia, SC; SO; BA; Walt Disney World Coll Pgm; Journalism; Public Relations/Advrtsng.

**PRICE, SARAH L,** Middle Tn St Univ, Murfreesboro, TN; SR; BS; SHEA 87-; Omicron Nu 88-; Kappa Delta Pi 89-; Tau Omicron 90-; Erly Chldhd Ed.

**PRICE, SONYA J,** Middle Tn St Univ, Murfreesboro, TN; SR; BS; Assoc Stdnt Body Sntr 87-; Stdnt Orien Asst Cnslr 90; Pre Law Socty; Rho Lambda; Rho Chi Cnslr; Chi Omega Prsnl/Socl 87-; Priv Intrnshp W/M Lee Smith Pub/Prntr 97th Gen Assmbly TN; Pol Sci; Law.

**PRICE, STEFFANI M,** Liberty Univ, Lynchburg, VA; SO; RN; Lbrty Assoc Chrstn Tchrs 89-90; Nrsng.

**PRICE, STEPHANIE K,** Piedmont Tech Coll, Greenwood, SC; FR; Secr; Secr Med.

**PRICE, STEVEN W,** Univ Of Montevallo, Montevallo, AL; FR; Alph Lmbd Dlt; Pr Rvw Brd; Pres Awrd Exclnc Wrtng; Hon Cert; Math; Educ.

**PRICE, TAMARA D,** Univ Of Nc At Charlotte, Charlotte, NC; GD; BA; NC Press Assoc 83-88; NC Wmns Press Assoc 83-88; Soc Prof Jrnlst Hstrn 82-84; Lincln Co Hospce Brd Dir 86; Nwspr Rep Lncln Tms Nws 83-88; BA 83; Engl; Tchr.

**PRICE, THELMA J,** Univ Of Sc At Sumter, Sumter, SC; SR; BA; Order Eastrn Star; Am Lgn Aux; VFW Aux; Soclgy/Psychlgy.

**PRICE, TRACY A,** Atlantic Comm Coll, Mays Landing, NJ; SO; AAS; Phi Beta Lambda 90; Bus Sec.

**PRICE, TRACY A,** Univ Of Akron, Akron, OH; JR; BA; Gldn Ky; Phi Etta Sigma 88-; Alpha Lambda Delta/Sigma Delta Pi 88-; Engl/Span; Scndry Educ.

**PRICE, TRACY Y,** Queens Coll, Charlotte, NC; SR; BA; SGA Pres 90-; Hrvrd Mdl UN 89; Yrbk 90; Mrtr Brd VP 90-; Ordr Of Omega VP 90-; Vlkyrie 89; Phi Alpha Theta 88-; Chi Omega VP 90; Afro Amer Cltrl Cntr Intrn 89; Sprt Sqre Cntr Fr Arts Intrn; Hstry And Art Hstry; Tch MA.

**PRICE, WENDY R,** Univ Of Sc At Columbia, Columbia, SC; SR; BS; Campus Crusade For Christ 90-; Omicron Delta Kappa 90-; Pi Epsilon Mu 89-; SCAHPERD 89-; Educ Schlrshp 90-; Athletic Achvmnt Awrd 88; Sftbl Tm 88-90; AA Spartanburg Meth Clg 88; Physical Educ; Sports Medicine.

**PRICE, ZOANA O,** Clark Atlanta Univ, Atlanta, GA; FR; BA; Step Tm 90-; Hnrs Prog 90-; Dorm Cncl Treas 90-; Prsdntl Acad Exclince Awrd 90-; Dns Lst 90-; Cert Of Exclince In Math 90-; Dance 90-; Mass Cmmnctns; TV Flm Prdcr Dir And Dnce.

**PRICE-GAINEY, MEIKE A,** Univ Of Tn At Martin, Martin, TN; SO; BS; Pre-Physcl Thrpy Clb 89-90; Nrsng; RN.

**PRICHARD, LEIGH ANN,** Memphis St Univ, Memphis, TN; SR; BPS; Gamma Beta Phi 89-; Lakeside Hosp Intern; Memphis Recovery Ctrs Intern 90-; Edward Hamilton Schlrshp 90; Firefighters Schlrshp 87; Alcohol/Drug Abuse Svcs; Scl Wrk/Hmn Rels.

**PRIDDLE, KRISTINA M,** Schenectady County Comm Coll, Schenectady, NY; FR; AS; Hmn Svc Clb 90-; Hmn Svc; Soc Wrk.

**PRIDDY, GARY W,** Ms St Univ, Miss State, MS; GD; MBA; MBA Assoc 90-; Rho Epsilon Pr 88-89; Rho Epsilon VP 89-90; Gamma Iota Sigma Tr 89-90; Ldrshp Real Est Awrd 88-89; BBA MS State Univ 90; Fin/Mngmnt.

**PRIDE, TERRY A,** Livingstone Coll, Salisbury, NC; JR; BA; Pres Schlr; Omega Psi Phi KRS; Wrstlng Tm Capt 90-.

**PRIDEMORE, EDYTHE A,** Alice Lloyd Coll, Pippa Passes, KY; SO; BA; Otstndng Frshmn Achvmnt 89-90; Csy IGA Schlrshp Cmmtmnt Applcha 90-; Alyc Llyd Coll Fctn Awrd 90-; Engl.

**PRIEST, AARON H,** Middle Tn St Univ, Murfreesboro, TN; SR; BBA; Beta Gamma Sigma 90-; Phi Beta Lambda VP 90-; AS Columbia St Comm Coll 89; Bus Fnc; Fncl Mgmt.

**PRIEST, DOUGLAS L,** Central Fl Comm Coll, Ocala, FL; SO; BS; Phi Theta Kappa 75; Mrhd Eng Awrd 75; USAF Lgstcs Cmmnd Cvl Eng Awrd 80; Mrtrs Srvce Mdl 81; USAF Cmmndtn Mdl 79; USAF Gd Cndct Mdl 79; Chldrns Chrch Dir; Prnt Tchr Advsry Brd 88; US Pstl Srvce 82-; BS Southern IL Univ 78; AS 75; Bldng Cnstrctn At Univ Of FL; Bldng Cntrctr.

**PRIEST JR, JAMES A,** Coppin St Coll, Baltimore, MD; SR; BS; Psychlgy Clb 89-; Psychlgy; Cnsl.

**PRIEST, MARY E,** Memphis St Univ, Memphis, TN; SO; BA; Stdnt Act Cncl 89-90; Engl/Dept Hnrs; Tch Lit Sec Educ.

**PRIESTLEY, JOHN S,** Cumberland County Coll, Vineland, NJ; FR; BA; Internatl Mgmt Cncl Pres Mktg Dept 90-; Pres Lst 90-; Mktg; Mktg Mngr.

**PRIETO, ELIZABETH M,** Georgetown Univ, Washington, DC; SR; Coalition Advncmnt Hspnc Amer 89; DC Schls Prjct Tutor 89-90; BS; Acctg; Pblc Acctg/Arthur Andersen.

**PRIETO, HELEN G,** Nova Univ, Ft Lauderdale, FL; GD; MBA; Ldrshp Miami Alumni Mbrshp Dir 82-83; Coalition Of Hispanic Amer Women Dir 86-90; S Bell Tel/Tel Co Oper Mgr 62-; BS Barry Univ Miami Shrs FL 83; Bus.

**PRIETO, MIGUEL A,** Catholic Univ Of Pr, Ponce, PR; SR; BA; Phi Eta Mu Tres 90-; Acctg Stdnt Assc 90-; Fin Assc 89-; Acctg/Fin; MBA Intrntl Bus.

**PRIEUR, WENDY N,** S U N Y Coll At Fredonia, Fredonia, NY; JR; BA; SADD 88-89; Psy Clb 88-90; Phi Theta Kappa 88-90; Seager Schlp Rcpnt 90-; AA Jamestown Comm Clg 90; Psy; Prfssr.

**PRIHODA, KIMBERLY A,** Marywood Coll, Scranton, PA; SR; BS; Cncl Excptnl Chldrn Pres 89-90; Tchrs Of Tomorrow V P 89-90; Vol In Action; Alpha Mu Gamma; Delta Epsilon Sigma V P 90-; Sigma Pi Epsilon Delta V P 90-; Kappa Gamma Pi; Kappa Delta Pi; Spec Educ/Elem Ed; Tchr.

**PRIM, DEBRA L,** Washington State Comm Coll, Marietta, OH; FR; BED; Vol Fr Marietta Cty Schls 90-; Math; Educ.

**PRIMAVERA, DONNA M,** Va Intermont Coll, Bristol, VA; FR; BS; Bapt Stdnt Union 90-; Natl Hnr Soc 90-; Psych.

**PRIMMER, DEBRA LEE,** Kent St Univ Kent Cmps, Kent, OH; SO; BA; Busn/Acctng; CPA.

**PRINCE, ADRIENNE D,** Morris Brown Coll, Atlanta, GA; SO; YPD Ldr; Hon Cert.

**PRINCE, ARTIE LAMONT,** Tn St Univ, Nashville, TN; SR; NAACP 90-; Pol Sci Clb 90-; Ambsdr 86-90; NSBE 86-90; Intrn Congrss Bob Clements Ofc PR 90-; BS; Arts/Sci; Pol Sci.

**PRINCE, CHERYL J,** Yeshiva Univ, New York, NY; SO; BA; Psychlgy/Crtve Wrtng; Clncl Psych Or Jrnlsm.

**PRINCE, CHRISTOPHER D,** Univ Of Cincinnati, Cincinnati, OH; JR; PHD; SG 88-; Soc Amateur Jrnlsts Prince Prod 89-; Brandenburg Fndtn 89-90; Ae Rho 89-; TV Intern 90-; Scripps Howard Schlrshp; Indstrl Prod Bus 88-; Video Film Prod 88-; Film Dir.

**PRINCE, CYNTHIA A,** Beckley Coll, Beckley, WV; SO; BA; Elem Ed.

**PRINCE, DIA D,** Ky St Univ, Frankfort, KY; SO; BS; Future Doctors Of Amer 90-; Intern UC Hosp/Clin Rsrch; Biology; Med Rsrch.

**PRINCE, LINDA A,** Univ Of Sc At Spartanburg, Spartanburg, SC; SR; ADN; Gamma Beta Phi 90-; Pres List 90-; Deans List 89-90; Nrsng.

**PRINCE, MARK DWANE,** Univ Of Ky, Lexington, KY; JR; BS; SMART 89-; HCOP 90; Hrt Assoc Inst 90-; Alpha Epsilon Delta; Clg Schlrs; Dns Lst; Med Ctr Vol 89-; UK Acad Schlrshp; Biol; Med.

**PRINCE, MARYANN,** Bunker Hill Comm Coll, Boston, MA; SO; BA; Exec Sec; Bus Admin; Acctng.

**PRINCE, NATASHA A,** Alcorn St Univ, Lorman, MS; FR; MBA; Cmptr Sci; Data Proc.

**PRINCE, SUZANNE L,** Southern Coll Of Tech, Marietta, GA; SR; BS; IEEE 89-; Elecs Clb Pres 87; Tau Alpha Pi 88; AAS Stanly Comm Coll 87; Elec Eng Tech; Eng.

**PRINCE, TERRA L,** Central Al Comm Coll, Alexander City, AL; FR; Phi Theta Kappa.

**PRINCE, THOMAS J,** Neumann Coll, Aston, PA; SO; BS; Psychology Clb 89-; Very Important Vol For Admssns 90-; Alpha Phi Delta Pldgmstr 89-; IMS 89-; Industrial Psychology.

**PRINCE, TONY D,** Univ Of Sc At Columbia, Columbia, SC; FR; BS; TARS Cnty Chrmn 90; Beta Clb 89; Phi Eta Sigma; Lfegrd 87-; SC By St 89; Comp Sci; Sftware Dev.

**PRINCE, TROY S,** Case Western Reserve Univ, Cleveland, OH; FR; BS; Prgrmng Brd Entrtnmnt Comm; Delta Upsilon; Pres Schlr 90-; Mech Eng.

**PRINCE, VICTORIA J,** Talladega Coll, Talladega, AL; FR; BA; Cmptr Sci; Cmptr Analyst/Tech.

**PRINDIBLE, JAYNE L,** Fl Atlantic Univ, Boca Raton, FL; SR; BA; Beta Alpha Psi; DPMA Pres 85-86; Paint Your Heart; AA Jefferson Tech Coll 86; Acctng/Finance; Forecasting.

**PRINTZ, SCOTT A,** Towson St Univ, Baltimore, MD; FR; BA; Math.

**PRIORE, CHRISTINE L,** Marshall University, Huntington, WV; SO; BA; Bsn Mgmt.

**PRISCIANDARO, ANN M,** Saint Thomas Univ, Miami, FL; SO; BS; PAC 89-; Sundy Sch Tchr; Deans List 89-90; Pol Sci; Law.

**PRISCIANTELLI, DONNA A,** Fl Atlantic Univ, Boca Raton, FL; GD; BBA; Citicorp Employee Clb Pres 87-89; Phi Beta Lambda; Citicorp Prchsng Mngr Sthamer Div 84-90; Fin; Fin Plnnr.

**PRITCHARD, BARBARA A,** Mayland Comm Coll, Spruce Pine, NC; FR; AAS; Erly Chldhd Tchr.

**PRITCHARD, CAROL A,** Hudson Valley Comm Coll, Troy, NY; FR; ASSOC; Mortuary Sci Clb Treas; Vermnt Fnrl Dir Assoc 88; Ntl Fnrl Dir Assoc Hospice 87; Fnrl Hm Pres 87; BA Indiana U Of Pa 69; Mortuary Sci; Fnrl Dir Emblmr.

**PRITCHARD, DAVID K,** Middle Ga Coll, Cochran, GA; FR; Eng Clb 90-; Gamma Beta Phi 90-; Eng.

**PRITCHARD II, DENNIS DAVID,** Itawamba Comm Coll, Fulton, MS; SO; BS; Frstry Clb VP 89-; Ag Clb 89-90; Soc Mnfctrng Eng 88-89; Phi Theta Kappa Pres 89-; Frstry Hnr Stu Yr; AAS; Frrstry/Wldlf; Educ Cnsltng.

**PRITCHARD, ELIZA C,** Univ Of New England, Biddeford, ME; SO; BA; Ecnmcs Tutor; Engl.

**PRITCHARD, PARMELY J,** Savannah Coll Of Art & Design, Savannah, GA; SR; Drama Clb 87-88; SCAD Schlrshp 87-; Deans Lst 87-; Grad Magna Cum Laude; Sccr 87-89; BFA; Painting.

**PRITCHARD, PATRICIA A,** Western Piedmont Comm Coll, Morganton, NC; SO; Hortcltr Tech; Landscp Desgnr.

**PRITCHARD, REBECCA I,** George Mason Univ, Fairfax, VA; JR; BSW; Soc Wrk.

**PRITCHARD, TARA M,** Glassboro St Coll, Glassboro, NJ; FR; BA; Cmnctns; Flm Indstry.

**PRITCHETT, CLYVIVE L,** Livingston Univ, Livingston, AL; SO; MBA; Stdnt Spprt 90-; Stdnt Yr 89-90; Elem Educ.

**PRITCHETT, JENNIFER L,** Southern Coll Of Tech, Marietta, GA; SR; BA; Inst Industrl Eng 88-; Indus Eng; Mgmt.

**PRITCHETT, JERRI A,** Gaston Coll, Dallas, NC; FR; AS; Gamma Beta Phi; Acctg; Actnt.

**PRITCHETT, JOHN F,** Eastern Christian College, Bel Air, MD; FR; BA; Deans Lst; Cnslr M/R Fld; Biblcl Stds.

**PRITCHETT, STEPHANIE A,** Cumberland County Coll, Vineland, NJ; SO; BA; Cert Assoc Erly Chldhd Educ; Erly Childhd Educ/Math; Busn.

**PRITT, ROBERT W,** Kent St Univ Kent Cmps, Kent, OH; FR; BA; Alpha Lambda Delta 90-; Army 89; Acctng.

**PRITZ, ALLISON L,** Coll Of Charleston, Charleston, SC; SO; Zeta Tau Alpha Scl Wl Serv 90-; Bio; Pdtrcn.

**PROBST, CHRISTINE MARIE,** Dowling Coll, Oakdale Li, NY; SR; BA; Acad Schlp 87-; Dns Lst 90-; Elem Ed; Tch.

**PROBST, KATHLEEN A,** Cumberland County Coll, Vineland, NJ; FR; Nrsng.

**PROCACCINO, GREGORY J,** Northern Ky Univ, Highland Hts, KY; JR.

**PROCKO, GEORGE S,** Saint Vincents Coll & Seminary, Latrobe, PA; SO; BA; Deans Lst 89-; All Amrcn Schlr Coll Awrd; Engl.

**PROCOPIO, MICHAEL D,** East Stroudsburg Univ, E Stroudsburg, PA; SR; BS; Assc Cmptng Mach VP 87-; Res Hl Cncl VP 87-; Univ Prgmng Cncl Cncrt Comm 88-90; ESU Hnrs Comm Schlrshp 87-; Dns Lst 88-; RA 89-; One To One Vol 89-90; Cmps Tour Gde 89; Univ Prgmng Cncl Flm Comm 89-; IM Sftbl 90-; Trck/Field 87-89; Comp Sci; Sftwr Engnrng.

**PROCTOR, BETTY A,** Chattanooga St Tech Comm Coll, Chattanooga, TN; SO; AS; Editor/Chief 90; Art Clb; Stdnt Gov Assc Exec Comm Mbr; Phi Theta Kappa Sec; Phi Theta Kappa Alpha Beta Mu Chapter Reporter 90; Deans List 90; 2nd Pl/Fall Advrtsng Arts Juried Show 90; SHHH 90; Girl Scts Dir 79; Untd Chrch 90; Advertising Art; Grphc Desng/Art.

**PROCTOR, DIANNE G,** Clayton St Coll, Morrow, GA; JR; BED; AA; Scndry Soc Stud; Tchng.

**PROCTOR, JASON M,** Univ Of North Fl, Jacksonville, FL; SO; BS; Assn Fr Cmptng Mchnry VP 90-; DPMA; Hnrs Cncl Stdnt Rep 90-; ACM SE Rgnl Prgrmmng Cntst Capt Elct 90-; Comp Sci; Univ Tchr.

**PROCTOR, LISA A,** Memphis St Univ, Memphis, TN; JR; BA; Golden Key 90; Phi Kappa Phi; Engl; Law.

**PROCTOR, STEPHEN P,** Univ Of Sc At Coastal Carolina, Conway, SC; SR; BA; Fine Arts Educ.

**PROCTOR, SUNDI L,** Broward Comm Coll, Ft Lauderdale, FL; SO; AA; Crmnl Jstc; Lw Enfrcmnt.**

**PROFANT, MICHELE A,** Northern Ky Univ, Highland Hts, KY; JR; BA; Alpha Chi 90-; Engl; Scndry Educ.

**PROFFITT, KIMBERLY A,** Union Coll, Barbourville, KY; SO; BA; CAB VP 90-; FCA 89-90; Cmt Spec Olympcs Swmng Div 89-; Swmng; Coachs All Amer 90-; Spec Olympics Athltc Rep 90-; Engl; Scndry Ed.

**PROFFITT, ROBYN L,** Univ Of Ky, Lexington, KY; FR; Sigma Kappa 90; Bio; Med.

**PROFFITT, STEPHANIE L,** Alice Lloyd Coll, Pippa Passes, KY; SR; BA; Kappa Delta Epsilon 90-; Erly Chldhd Ed; Tchng.

**PROFFITT, TERESA R,** East Tn St Univ, Johnson City, TN; SO; BBA; Acctg Soc; IM 89-; Alpha Lambda Delta 90-; Gamma Beta Phi; Acctg.

**PROFFITT, TIFFANY M,** Va Commonwealth Univ, Richmond, VA; FR; BSW; BSW Assoc 90-; Hnrs Prog 90-; Phi Eta Sigma; Soc Work: Soc Worker For Protective Servcs.

**PROFITT, SHELLY A,** Northern Ky Univ, Highland Hts, KY; SO; BA; Elem Ed.

**PROGER, WILLIAM B,** Villanova Univ, Villanova, PA; FR; BA; Stdnts Against Driving Drunk Sec/Treas; Univ Chrstn Otrch 90-; Handicapped Prog 90-; Geography; Cartography.

**PROKSA, ALYSSA E,** Savannah Coll Of Art & Design, Savannah, GA; JR; BA; Graphic Design Grp 90-; Crew Tm 88; Grphc Dsgn/Illustr.

**PROKUSKI, CARA A,** Savannah Coll Of Art & Design, Savannah, GA; FR; BARCH; Arch/Hist Pres; Arch.

**PRONI, FREDERICK P,** Utica Coll Of Syracuse Univ, Utica, NY; SO; BS; Amer Chem Soc 89-; Mid-York Beekprs Assoc; St Thomas Ushers Clb 87-; Mens Clb 88-; St Thomas Golf League; Griffiss AFB Rome Lab-Lab Mgr; Griffiss AFB Rome Air Dev Ctr Trainee 88-90; Chem; Chemist/Chem Engr.**

**PRONKO, JAMES M,** Unity Coll, Unity, ME; SO; BA; SADD Pgm; Outdoor Ext Svc; Restaurant Mgmt 85; AS Paul Smith Clg 85; Outdoor Recr; Wldrness Med.

**PROPP, ALISON L,** Savannah Coll Of Art & Design, Savannah, GA; FR; BA; BACCHUS; ASID; ISID; JAM Ldr; Intr Dsgn.

**PROPRI, COLETTE M,** Kent St Univ Kent Cmps, Kent, OH; SO; BA; Itln Clb Pres 90-; Undrgrdt Stdnt Senate 89-90; Alpha Lambda Delta; Pres Lst; Itln/Pltcl Sci; Trnsltng.

**PROPST, DARRELL W,** Univ Of Nc At Greensboro, Greensboro, NC; FR; BA; Cncrt Band 90-; Rsdntl Clg 90-; Alpha Lambda Delta 90-; NC Tchng Flw 90-; Catherine Smith Reynolds Schlr 90-; Deans List 90-; Engl Ed/Msc; Tchr.

**PROROCK, DENISE M,** Neumann Coll, Aston, PA; SO; BA; Hnrs Pgrm 89-; Psy Clb 89-90; VIVA; Scrd Hrt Med Cntr Aux 84-; St John Neumann Frncscn Schlrshp 89-; Comm Arts; Mktng/P R Dir.

**PROSEUS, TIMOTHY E,** Univ Of Nc At Wilmington, Wilmington, NC; FR; BS; Biology Clb 90-; Phi Eta Sigma; Marine Biology.

**PROSKE, NICOLE A,** Duquesne Univ, Pittsburgh, PA; SR; MBA; IM Ftbl Bsbl Vlybl 87-; SHARP Rcrtng Vol 90; Lambda Sigma; Omicron Delta Kappa 90; Rho Chi; Lambda Sigma; Omicron Delta Kappa 90; Univ Schlr Phrmcy Intrnshp 87-; Dqsne Dvng Tm Lttrmn 88; Phrmcy.

**PROSPERI, ANNE H,** Saint Vincents Coll & Seminary, Latrobe, PA; JR; BS; Biology/Chmstry Clb 88-; Pyhscs Clb/Envrnmntl Awrns Clb 90-; Yrbk Clb 89-; Cmps Mnstry 90-91; Intrnshp Pittsburgh Enrgy Tech Cntr 90; Crs Cntry 88-; IM Vlybl 89-; Biology; Med.

**PROSPERIE, DESIREE A,** Fl St Univ, Tallahassee, FL; SR; BSEE; SWE; Golden Key 90-; Engrg Hnr Scty; Go-Op Student 90-; Elec Engrg; Engrg.

**PROSPERINO, SERGIO,** Pace Univ At Pleasantville, Pleasantville, NY; FR; BBA; Soccr; Busn; Acctg.

**PROST, CHRISTINE C,** Villanova Univ, Villanova, PA; SR; LAW; Blue Key Offcr 89-; Hmls Comm 89-; Spnsh Clb 87-; Delta Gamma Sprt Ldr 88-; Dns Lst 87-; BA; Arts; Law.

**PROTASS, MITCHELL O,** S U N Y At Buffalo, Buffalo, NY; SR; BS; Gldn Ky 90-; Bus Mngmnt.

**PROTONO, DARIA A,** Georgian Court Coll, Lakewood, NJ; SR; BA; AA Ocean Co Clge 88; Psychlgy; Cnslr/Soc Srvc.

**PROTOS, POLLY C,** Cornell Univ Statutory College, Ithaca, NY; FR; BS; Stdnt Ambsdr; Evntng Clb; Deans List; Intrnshp/Asstntshp Equine Rsrch 90-; Anml Sci; Veterinarian.

**PROUDLER, LAURA R,** Newbury Coll, Brookline, MA; SR; BE; Assoc; Lgl; Law.

**PROVALL, WILLIAM ANTOINE,** Univ Of Tn At Knoxville, Knoxville, TN; FR; BA; Exec Undrgrad Pgm 90-; Inroads Inc 90-; Phi Eta Sigma; Intrnshp Mgmt Trainee Kroger Co; Bus Acctg.

**PROVANCE, ELIZABETH E,** Wv Northern Comm Coll, Wheeling, WV; JR; ADSN; Natl Stdnt Nrsng Assn Rprtr; Phi Theta Kappa Campus Rep; Prfssnl Nrsng Asst; Pres Lst 90; Acdmc Schlrshp 90-; Fstr Prnt Prog 84-; RN.

**PROVEDO, LINDA,** Fl International Univ, Miami, FL; SR; BED; Future Edctrs Am; Deans List 90-; Elem Ed.

**PROVENCHER, DIANNE L,** Castleton St Coll, Castleton, VT; SR; BS; Stdnt Ed Assn 90-; Kappa Delta Pi 90-; Elem Ed.

**PROVENZA, MICHAEL K,** Univ Of Toledo, Toledo, OH; GD; JD; Im Stfbl 87-; Itln Law Assn; Delta Theta Phi 89-; W Publshng Co Awd 90; Dns Lst 90; Cum Laude 89; BA Ohio St Univ 89; Law/Pol Sci.

**PROVENZANO III, MICHAEL J,** Merrimack Coll, North Andover, MA; JR; BSA; Nu Phi Kappa Pldg Master 88-; Ski Clb Pres 88-; Law Soc 90-; Rsdnt Asst 89-90; Co-Op Pgm 88-; Nu Phi Kappa Pldg Mstr 88-; Vrsty Tnns/Trck Capt 88-; Acctg; Law Schl/CPA.

**PROVOST, GAYLA JEAN,** Middle Tn St Univ, Murfreesboro, TN; JR; BS; AS Motlow Clg 89; LS Cert Phillips Clg 80; Acctg; CPA.

**PROVOST, TRACEY A,** Lasell Coll, Newton, MA; SO; BA; Intrnatl Clb Pres 90; Hmn Srvce Clb Pres 89-; Hnrs Engl; Intrn Comm Cntr Schl 90-; Pres Schlrshp; Otstndng Stdnt Awrd; Sftbl Bsktbl Tms 89-; Hjn Srvcs; Psychlgst.

**PRUDEN, DIANNA,** Univ Of Fl, Gainesville, FL; JR; BS; Mrchng Band 88-; Hlth Rel Prof Clg Cncl Class Rep 90-; Golden Key 90-; Alpha Lambda Delta 88-; IM Soccer Tm Co-Capt 88-90; AA 89; Med Tchnlgy.

**PRUDEN, RONDA S,** Defiance Coll, Defiance, OH; FR; BA; Cmpus Actvtsnbd Intrvar; Deans Lst; English; Ele Educ.

**PRUDEN, VIVIAN A,** Defiance Coll, Defiance, OH; JR; BA; Deans Lst; March Dimes Clntn; Cancer/Heart Fund; Coach Sftbl Tm; Hstry; Educ/Archaeology.

**PRUDENT, PIERRE,** City Univ Of Ny Med Evers Coll, Brooklyn, NY; JR; MBA; Math; Ed.

**PRUDY, BRIAN E,** Old Dominion Univ, Norfolk, VA; SR; BS; Vol Spec Engr Fndr/Pres 90-; AAS N VA Cmnty Clg 89; Elctrcl Engr Tech; Engr.

**PRUE, LINDA M,** Southern Vt Coll, Bennington, VT; FR; BA; Accntng.

**PRUETT, DANIEL W,** Southern Coll Of Tech, Marietta, GA; SR; BSEET; S Tech Natl Alumni Assoc 90-; Dns Lst 85-86/90-; Bsebl Gordon Jr Clg 82-84; Bsebl 84-85; FMA; IEEE 90-; T Drill Sr Proj Engr FMS 90-; Dsgn Engr FMS 86-90; AA Gordon Jr Clg 84; BSMET 86; Elctrcl Engr.

**PRUETT, ELISA A,** Univ Of North Fl, Jacksonville, FL; FR; BM; UNF Jazz Ensmbl Bass; Msc-Jazz; Prfsnl Mscn/Tchr.

**PRUETT, KENNETH S,** Southern Coll Of Tech, Marietta, GA; SR; BA; AS Gainesville Clg 89; Cmptr Scnc; Prgrmmr.

**PRUETTE, SHANNA D,** Gaston Coll, Dallas, NC; SO; BA; Gamma Beta Phi 90-; Math; Ed.

**PRUITT, BRETT DOROTHY,** Morris Brown Coll, Atlanta, GA; SO; Vol Tutor For Elem Chld.

**PRUITT, DARLENE,** Bunker Hill Comm Coll, Boston, MA; SR; BA; Crmnl Law; Attrny.

**PRUITT, EVELYN Y,** Meridian Comm Coll, Meridian, MS; SO; BA; Dex-DECA Dist Ed Clb Of Amerca 90-; Phi Beta Lambda Treas 89-90; Actvty Brd 89-90; AA Mktg Meridian Comm Coll; Bus Admin; Bus Rep.

**PRUITT II, JAMES H,** King Coll, Bristol, TN; JR; BA; Cmps Lf Comm Chrmn; Dogwood Comm 90-; Ambsdr Co-Cptn 90-; New Stdnt Orient Comm; Hstry/Pltcl Sci; Prof.

**PRUITT JR, JOHN A,** Fl St Univ, Tallahassee, FL; SR; BA; Hons/Schlrs Cncl Nwsltr Ed 90-; Lit Mag Assoc Ed Layout/Dsgn 90-; Genesis-Fresh Ldrshp Trng 88-; Lmabda Iota Tau; Hons Mjr Pgm; Intrnshp FL Dept Ed Asst Ed Wkly Nwsltrs Midweek/Mndy Rprt Asst Ed 90-; Engl Lit; Tch.

**PRUITT, KATHY O,** Chattahoochee Vly St Comm Coll, Phenix City, AL; SO; BSED; Vol United Way 90; Educ; Rhbltn Spc Educ.

**PRUITT, LINDA D,** Meridian Comm Coll, Meridian, MS; SO; ADN; Stdnt Nrs Pgm 90-; Phlbtmy Cert 86; Medcl-Nrsng.

**PRUITT, MERI H,** Univ Of Sc At Columbia, Columbia, SC; SO; BA; Phi Eta Sigma; Zeta Tau Alpha Pub Rel 90-; Dns Lst 90-; Pres Lst; Best Pledge 90; Early Chldhd Educ; Tchr.

**PRUITT, NANCY L,** Univ Of Ga, Athens, GA; SR; BSHE; Alpha Omicion Pi Crspndng Sec 87-88/Bnqt Hd 90-/Cntrbtr Natl Rsh Kt 90-; Tutor U Athltc Dept; Cnsmr Econ; Assoc Mgmt.

**PRUITT, SANDRA G,** Ms Gulf Coast Comm Coll, Perkinston, MS; FR; BS; Hnrs Pgm 90-; Perkette Dnce Tm 90-; Bsn.

**PRUITT, STEVEN D,** Milligan Coll, Milligan Clg, TN; JR; BS; Bays Mountains Amateur Astronomers 90-; Grace Flwshp Youth Staff 89-; Limestone United Meth Administrative Board 89-; Psychology; Christian Ministry/Physics.

**PRUITT, VICKI D,** Union Univ, Jackson, TN; SR; BA; Educ; Elem Tchr.

**PRUNEAU, JOANNE B,** Univ Of Fl, Gainesville, FL; SR; BFA; Potters Gld Sec 90-; Phi Theta Kappa Co-Chr 88-89; Exec Asst 80-88; Ins Clrk 76-79; AA Daytona Bch Comm Coll 89; Art Educ; Tch/MED.

**PRUNER, LISA B,** Daytona Beach Comm Coll, Daytona Beach, FL; FR; ADN; EMT Flagler Hosp 88-; EMT-A St Augustine Tech Cntr 88; Nrsng; RN.

**PRUNTY, SANDRA K,** Marshall University, Huntington, WV; GD; MSN; Amer Nrs Asc; WV Nrs Asc; WV Nrs Asc Adv Prctc Grp; Amer Acad Nrs Prctnrs; Omicron Delta Kappa 81-; Sigma Theta Tau; Sigma Sigma Sigma 80-; Asst Nrsng 90-; Bptst Chrch 88-; RN 80-; Stf Nrs; LPN Pgm Tch; Home Hlth Asmts; ASN 80; BSN 83; Fmly Nrs Prctnr; Edctr.

**PRUSH, YVONNE,** Daytona Beach Comm Coll, Daytona Beach, FL; FR; AS; SOS Clb 90-; Act Corp CM Asst 90-; Aids In Srvce Trng; Osteen Otstndng Prnt 89-; Hmn Srvcs; Mntl Hlth Fld.

**PRUSIK, RENEE S,** Rutgers St Un At New Brunswick, New Brunswick, NJ; FR; Math Sci Orgztn 90-; Envrntl Wrk Stdy 90-; Bio Chem; Rsrch.

**PRUSKI, THOMAS A,** Niagara Univ, Niagara Univ, NY; FR; BS; Pol Sci Frm St Vincent De Paul Soc 90-; NSNA; Comm Actn Pgm 90-; IM Bsktbl/Vlybl/Sftbl Sftbl Cptn 90-; Nrsg; RN.

**PRUTER, GLENN D,** Middle Tn St Univ, Murfreesboro, TN; SR; MA; Activities Brd 87-; SHRM 90-; Natl Cncl Pblc Hstry; Pi Gamma Mu 89-; Psi Chi; Sigma Chi Rush Chrmn 89-; Elizabeth Buford Shepherd Schlrshp 86-90; BS; Indstrl Psychlgy; Human Resources.**

**PRUTZMAN, JANET L,** Boston Coll, Chestnut Hill, MA; SR; BS; Stylus Poetry Pblctn 90-; Sch Of Nrsng Sen Sec 87-89; Res Hall Cncl Pub Coord 90-; Sigma Theta Tau Intern; Nursing.

**PRY, MARGARET ANN,** Marywood Coll, Scranton, PA; SR; Pa Stdnt Nrs Assc 88-; Nrsng Clb Tres 88-; Deans List 88-; Natl Deans List; Amer Heart Assc MD Assc MS Assc Vol 85-; Lackawanna Med Scty Schlrshp 89-; Nrsng; MSN Nrs Prctnr Wmns Hlth.

**PRYCE, ALTHIA L,** Tuskegee Univ, Tuskegee Inst, AL; SO; BA; Alpha; Psych; Chld Psych.

**PRYCE, KAREN L,** Mount Aloysius Jr Coll, Cresson, PA; SO; AS; O T Clb 89-; Affltns Phy Psych Dysfnctn; Occup Thrpy Asst.

**PRYOR, AMY L,** Oh St Univ, Columbus, OH; SR; All Amer 88-; Natl Collgt Champion 88; Olympc Trls Comp 88; US Natl Chmpnshp 88-; St OH Hs Of Reprcgntn Athltc Exclince 90-; Bg Ten Cnvrnce Medal Hon 88-; Golden Key 89-; Phi Kappa Phi 90-; Acdmc All Amer; Deans Lst; Exclnce Schlrshp Awrd; Engl; Law Schl.

**PRYOR, MARSHA R,** Fl A & M Univ, Tallahassee, FL; SR; BS; Preprfssnl Mnrty Scty 90; Gldn Ky 89-; Dns Lst 90; Hnr Stdnt Awrd 89; Hnr Stdnt Awrd 90; AA Univ Of South Florida 89; Phrmcy.

**PRYOR, STEFANIE E,** Boston Univ, Boston, MA; FR; BA; SG Clss Treas 90-; Admssns Lnch Ovrnght Acdmc Hst Schl Mgmt Pr Advsr 90-; Hll Cncl 90; Trst Schlr Strng Cmmtt 90-; AIESEC Almn Dir 90-; Admssns Intrvwr; Intl Bus; Intl Trd.

**PRYSLAK, JACQUELINE A,** Elmira Coll, Elmira, NY; GD; MS; Alpha Sigma Lambda; Bruce Beaty Meml Prze 90; Rd Crss Bld Donr; AAS Corning Comm Clg 82; BS 90; Erly Chldhd Educ; Educ.

**PRYTHERCH, TAMERA D,** Kent St Univ Kent Cmps, Kent, OH; FR; BA; Interhall Cncl 90; Varsity Gymnastics 90; Phys Edn; Phys Therapy.

**PRZYBELSKI, THOMAS R,** Univ Of Sc At Columbia, Columbia, SC; SO; BS; Ski Clb; Amer Hnr Soc; Inst Elec Eng Fndrsng Mngr; Hnrs Coll 89-; Pres Lst; Elec/Cmptr Eng; Eng.

**PRZYBELSKI, TOM R,** Univ Of Sc At Columbia, Columbia, SC; SO; BS; Ski Clb; IEEF; Amer Hnr Soc 89-; NCR Intrnshp; Elect Eng.

**PRZYBYSZEWSKI, BETH A,** Niagara Univ, Niagara Univ, NY; SR; Clb Intrntl Treas 88-90; Delta Epsilon Sigma 89-; Phi Sigma Iota 90-; Phi Alpha Theta; Intrntl Studiess/Spnsh; Frgn Serv.

**PRZYCHODNIECZ, BRYAN,** Fl St Univ, Tallahassee, FL; FR; BME; Clgt Msc Edctrs Natl Conf 90-; Phi Eta Sigma; Phi Mu Alpha; FL Acad Schlrs 90-; Acad Schlp/Msc Schlp 90-; Hnrs Pgm 90-; Msc Educ.

**PRZYTULA II, LEON J,** Marist Coll, Poughkeepsie, NY; SO; BA; Msc; Prdcr.**

**PSZCZOLKOWSKI, DEBRA K,** Muskingum Coll, New Concord, OH; JR; BA; Centrbrd 88-89; Vol Coord 88-; Bacchus 89-; IM 88-90; Elem Educ; Tch.

**PTASICK, THERESA A,** Salisbury St Univ, Salisbury, MD; JR; BA; Medl Careers Club; Peninsula Gen Hospt; Bethany Luthran Church; Biology; Phsy Therapist.

**PUCCIA, PAMELA A,** Bunker Hill Comm Coll, Boston, MA; FR; ASSOC; Lbrl Arts.

**PUCH, DIANE,** Mount Aloysius Jr Coll, Cresson, PA; FR; AS; Crdvsclr Tchnlgy.

**PUCHALSKI, JONATHAN T,** Denison Univ, Granville, OH; FR; BA; Mens Bbl Stdy 90; Coll Lf 90; Admssns Offc Hst Ambssdr Stdnt Pnl 90; Sphmr Hnr Scty; Denison Cmmnty Assoc 90; Hty Yth Adlt Stff Advsr; Prtnrs Prvntn Prgm; Denison May Trm; OH St Univ Rsrch Asst; Fclty Achvmnt Schlr Hnrs Prgm; Chmstry; Med.

**PUCILLO, MICHELLE L,** Merrimack Coll, North Andover, MA; SR; BA; Orientation Comm Coord 88-90; Comm Coun 87-90; MORE Rtrd Prgrm Tm Ldr 88-; Men Of Mnth Schlrshp 90-; Ldrshp Hnr 89-90; Bus Mngmnt/Biology; Hlth Care/Med/Biotechnogy.

**PUCKETT, DALE C,** Middle Ga Coll, Cochran, GA; FR; AS; Gamma Beta Phi; Bus Admn.

**PUCKETT, DEBRA C,** Univ Of Ga, Athens, GA; FR; Cmmnvrsty; Alpha Lambda Delta; Hnrs Day; Educ Hnrs Bnqt; Scl Sci Educ; Tch.

**PUCKETT, ELLEN B,** Oh St Univ, Columbus, OH; SR; BLA; Co Op Stdnt By Dsgn Chgo 90-; Lndscp Archtctr.

**PUCKETT, GERALD C,** Fayetteville St Univ, Fayetteville, NC; SO; BA; Fayetteville St U Drm Gld; Alpha Psi Omega Plyrs Drm Gld; 1st Pl Infrmtv Schlrshp Pblc Spkng Cntst; Fayetteville St U Ftbl Tm 89-; Spch; Spch Pthlgy.

**PUCKETT, MELISSA M,** Roanoke Bible Coll, Elizabeth Cy, NC; SO; BA; Soph Cls Pres 90-; Tennis Club Pres 90-; Co Yrbk Staff Photogrphr 90-; Im Vlybl Cptn 90-; Christn Ed/Cnclng.

**PUCKETT, TECIA L,** Belmont Coll, Nashville, TN; SO; BABBA; Stdnt Fndtn Svp 90-; Rsdnc Hl Cncl Pres 90-; Bapt Stdnt Union Cmmnctns Dir 90-; Gamma Beta Phi; Soph Cls Favorite; IM Bsktbl; Engl/Bus Admin; Law/Professor.**

**PUEBLA, MARGARET G,** Fl International Univ, Miami, FL; SR; BA; AA Miami Dade Comm Clg 88; Elem Ed; Schl Admn.

**PUEHLER, LORI S,** Univ Of North Fl, Jacksonville, FL; SO; BA; Hnrs Cncl Rep; Hnrs Pgm 90-; Pres Schlrshp 90-; Dns Lst 90-; Vlybl Mng Stat; Lit/Bio.

**PUENT, MEYON E,** Longwood Coll, Farmville, VA; SO; BA; IM 90-; Alpha Gamma Delta 90-; Fld Hcky; Psychology/Spec Educ; Spec Educ Instrtr.

**PUENTE, RICARDO H,** Fl International Univ, Miami, FL; JR; BBA; Fncl Mgmt Assn; Dns Lst; Natl Dns Lst; AA Bus Miami Dade Comm Coll 90; Finance/Intl Bus; Corp Lawyer.

**PUERTA RENDON, ANA MARIA,** Inter Amer Univ Pr Hato Rey, Hato Rey, PR; JR; BA; Natl Hnr Soc Puerto Rico 86-88; Beta Beta Beta 90-; Biomed Sci; Optmtry.

**PUERTO, LUZ E,** Methodist Coll, Fayetteville, NC; JR; BA; Spanish; Tchng.

**PUFFENBARGER, MICHAEL B,** Radford Univ, Radford, VA; SR; BS; Brdcstrs Gld Pub Affrs Chrmn 88-; TV Nws Exec Prod 90-; WVRU Brd Oprtr 89-; Hon Prog 89-; Alpha Epsilon Rho Pub Affrs Chrmn 90-; Deans Lst 89-; IM Sftbl 88-; Intrnshp NASA; Cert Univ NC 88; Cmnctns/Radio/TV; TV/VIDEO Prodcr.

**PUGA, FERNANDO GABRIEL,** Inter Amer Univ Pr Hato Rey, Hato Rey, PR; FR; BA; Mdl UN 89; Comp Clb 90; Sci Clb 90; Gd Shprd Cath Yth Grp 88; Swmmng Vlybl Sccr Tns; Sn Igncio Engl Yth Grp 90; Sn Lcs Yth Grp Treas 90; FL St Spnsh Confrnce Otstndng; Bus; Bus Mgmt.

**PUGH MACK, N BETH,** Ky Christian Coll, Grayson, KY; SR; PH D; Psi Sigma Chi VP 90; Pr Er 90; Nrsng Hm Scl Wrk Intrn; Hlpng Fllwshp Awrd 90; Dns Lst; Amer Psychlgcl Assn 90; Chrstn Assn Psychlgcl Stds 90; AA 89; BS 90; Phsyclgy; Prvte Prctce.

**PUGH, ANDREW M,** Va Commonwealth Univ, Richmond, VA; FR; Phi Eta Sigma; Bus; Acctng.

**PUGH, CHARLES R,** Piedmont Bible Coll, Winston-Salem, NC; JR; THB; Missions Flwshp 89-; Conquerors In Missions Group Asstnt Ldr 87-; Awana Clubs Internatl Club Dir 87-; Deans List 87-; Var Church Activities 87-; Alumni Canvessing Team Grp Ldr 89; Schl Social Comm 88-; Dorm Res Asstnt 89-90; Tgheology; Church/Ministry.

**PUGH, DALE G,** Univ Of Al At Birmingham, Birmingham, AL; SR; BED; Phys Ed Clb 90-; Golden Key 90-; Pres Lst 90-; Dns Lst 90-; Spec Olympics; Yth Minister 1st Bapt Irondale 89; Recr Asst Mc Elwain Bapt 82-90; Undrgrd Stdnt Yr Phy Ed; Repr Dn Stdnt Affrs 90-; AS Sci Jefferson St Cmnty Clg 89; Phys Ed/Bio; Coachg/Tchg.

**PUGH, DANA M,** Mount Aloysius Jr Coll, Cresson, PA; FR; BA; Lic Csmtlgst Admiral Peary AUTS 85; Bus/Accntng.

**PUGH, JENNIFER A,** Wv Inst Of Tech, Montgomery, WV; SR; Amer Inst Chem Engrs 88-; Circle K 86-88; Natl Enrgy Dsgn Comp 90; Coop Educ 88-; Chem Eng.

**PUGH, JILL A,** Davis Coll, Toledo, OH; SR; AAB; Stu Actvts Brd; Davis Dsgn Grp; Pres Lst 90-; Intrr Dsgn.

**PUGH, KEITH W,** Savannah Coll Of Art & Design, Savannah, GA; SR; BFA; Grphc Dsgn; Advtsng.

**PUGH, KIMBERLY RENEE,** Norfolk St Univ, Norfolk, VA; SO; BS; AROTC 90-; AROTC Color Guard 90-; Spartan Alpha Tau; Amer Red Cross Vol 88-89; Alpha Kappa Alpha Schlrshp 89; Military Order World Wars Awd; Nrsg; Med Surg Nrs.

**PUGH, LORA M,** Kent St Univ Stark Cmps, North Canton, OH; JR; BA; Jaycees VP; Tenants Assoc Lndwd Apt Pres 90-; Sdn Infnt Dth Syndrm E Oh Bred 76-80; Vctm Asst Strk Cnty 90-; Vctm Advct Strk Cnty Prsctr 85-; Crmnl Jstc; Law.

**PUGH, MARILYN R,** Radford Univ, Radford, VA; SR; Radford Chmbr Orch; Prog Stdnt Allnce; Alpha Lambda Delta; BS; Engl.

**PUGH, MELINDA D,** Ohio Valley Coll, Parkersburg, WV; FR; AA; Sigma Epsilon Chi 90-; Cmmnctns.

**PUGH, RANDY L,** Northeast State Tech Comm Coll, Blountville, TN; JR; AAS; Fin; Mngmnt.

**PUGH, REBECCA A,** Beckley Coll, Beckley, WV; SO; BA; 4-H Sec 88-; AQHA 87-; WVQHA 89-; RCHA 87-; Blgy.

**PUGH, SENETRA C,** Fisk Univ, Nashville, TN; SR; BA; Psychlgy Clb 87; Tnnssee Clb 87; Engl/Math; Bus.

**PUGH, SHERRARD L,** Longwood Coll, Farmville, VA; JR; BA; Psych Clb 90; Natl Hnr Soc Psych; AAS Rappahannock Cmnty Clg 90; Psych; Cnslg.

**PUGH, SHERRI M,** Al A & M Univ, Normal, AL; SR; BS; AAMV Treas 90-; Amer Mktg Assn 90-; Alpha Kappa Mu Natl Asst Sec 89-; Delta Mu Delta Treas 89-; Tutor 90-; USDA Forest Svc Coop Educ Stdnt 90-; Superior Acad Achvmnt Awd Mktg Dept 90; Mktg.

**PUGH, SHERRY A,** Radford Univ, Radford, VA; JR; BA; Poli Sci Clb 90-; Kappa Mu Epsilon; Phi Kappa Phi; Poli Sci; Law.

**PUGH, TRACI L,** Univ Of Akron, Akron, OH; JR; BA; Ski Clb 88-89; Edctn; Elem Tchng.

**PUGLIELLI, EDWARD,** Bunker Hill Comm Coll, Boston, MA; FR; Bus; Bus Mngmnt.

**PUGLIESE, EUGENE RICHARD,** Southern Coll Of Tech, Marietta, GA; JR; AET; Air Force Res TSGT 80-; Akin & Flanders Inc Asst Proj Mgr 89-; Arch.

**PUHARIC, ERIN M,** Glassboro St Coll, Glassboro, NJ; SR; PRSSA Praction Pres; Delta Zeta Acdmcs/Pblcty Chrprsn; Chldrns Hosp Philadelphia Intrnshp Plbctns Asst; BA; Cmnctns/Pblc Rltns.

**PUIG MEDINA, MARINES,** Univ Of Pr At Mayaguez, Mayaguez, PR; SR; BS; IEEE 88-; Sprcmptr Pgm Undrgrdt Rsrch Cornell Univ 90-; Tau Beta Pi 90-; Engrg Hnr Stdnt 88-; Elctrcl Engrg; PHD Elctrcl Engrg.

**PUIG, NEYDA M,** Fl International Univ, Miami, FL; JR; MBA; Future Educ Amer 89-; Elem Educ; Teacher.

**PUJOUE, KATHERINE A,** Al St Univ, Montgomery, AL; SO; BA; Natl Hnr Soc 90-; Yng Peo Actn Chrst Sec 89-; Acad Schlrshp 89; Elem Educ; Tchr.

**PULA TAVERAS, PEDRO A,** Univ Politecnica De Pr, Hato Rey, PR; SR; BA; BED Tchnlgcl Inst PR 83-85; Elec Eng.

**PULASKI, DONNA J,** Saint Elizabeth Hosp Sch Nurs, Utica, NY; SR; BSNMS; Clss Sec; Dean Lst 89-; Suny Hlth Sci Cntr Univ Hosp; Nrsng Sci.

**PULASKI, LAURA E,** Coll Of Charleston, Charleston, SC; FR; BS; Alpha Delta Pi; Catherine Correlli Schlrshp; Bsn Adm; Law.

**PULCINI, MASSIMO,** Univ Of Miami, Coral Gables, FL; SR; Mktng Clb 90-; Amer Mktng Assn 89-; Dns Lst; Intrn Amer Express; Mktng; MBA Fin.

**PULICE, FRANK,** Manhattan School Of Music, New York, NY; FR; BM; Clscl Vlc Music; Opera.

**PULLAM LEROY, SUSAN J,** Western Ky Univ, Bowling Green, KY; SR; BS; Deans Lst 88; Prsdnts Schlr 89-; Elem Edctn; Edctn.

**PULLANO, PATRICK,** Univ Of Rochester, Rochester, NY; JR; BA; Mock Trial Org Sec 89-; Pre Law Org 89-90; Pltcl Sci; Law.

**PULLEN, GINNENE NATHERA,** Fl A & M Univ, Tallahassee, FL; SO; BA; NAACP; Pres Schlrs Clbs; Hnr Soc; Spec Pres Schlrshp; Gannett Schlrshp; Dns Lst; Jrnlsm; Publ Rels.

**PULLEN, MARK A,** Middle Tn St Univ, Murfreesboro, TN; JR; BS; Assoc Computing Machinery Pres 90-; Gamma Beta Phi 90; Outstndng Jr Computer Sci; Computer Sci Alumni Awrd; Amer History Awrd 90; Computer Sci; Computer Programmer Analyst.

**PULLEY, CAMILLE A,** Va St Univ, Petersburg, VA; FR; Engl Educ.

**PULLEY, CINDY K,** Radford Univ, Radford, VA; JR; BA; Std Govt Asc VP 90-; Ornttn Asst 90-; Jdcl Brd Advct 89-; Alpha Lambda Delta 88-89; Phi Sigma Sigma Rep 90-; Pol Sci; Law.

**PULLIAM, ANNA LEIGH GUIN,** Univ Of Ms Medical Center, Jackson, MS; SR; Nurses Assn 88-; Class VP 90-; Phi Kappa Phi 90-; Sigma Theta Tau 90-; Alpha Delta Pi 87-88; Deans List Schlr 88-89; IM Ftbl 90-; BSN.

**PULLIAM, JOHN W,** Univ Of Louisville, Louisville, KY; JR; MENG; Peer Admssns Cnslr 88-; Comp Lab Asst 88-; Res Hl Scrty 90-; Phi Eta Sigma 89-; Tau Beta Pi 90-; Gldn Key 90-; Phi Kappa Phi; Govrnrs Schlr 88-; Tau Beta Pi Outstndng Fresh/Soph 88-90; Mech Eng.

**PULLIAM, LEAH M,** Morris Brown Coll, Atlanta, GA; SO; BS; Psychology Clb 90-; Calif Clb 89-; Alpha Kappa Alpha 90-; MARC Adamha Marc Intern; MBRS Awrd 89-; Psychology; Research Psychologist.

**PULLIAM III, MALLA L,** Alcorn St Univ, Lorman, MS; FR; Math; Elem Ed.

**PULLIAM, RUTH L,** Bloomfield Coll, Bloomfield, NJ; SO; Nwspr Stffwrtr 90-; Peer Cnslrs Assn; Music Thtr Arts Clb 90-; Psychlgy; Psychlgst Chld.

**PULLIN, KENNETH B,** Hillsborough Comm Coll, Tampa, FL; FR; MD; Sccr Tm; Mdcl Dctr.

**PULLIN, PATRICK B,** Morehouse Coll, Atlanta, GA; FR; BS; Bio; Med.

**PULLMAN, JANICE L,** Northern Ky Univ, Highland Hts, KY; JR; BS; Marshal; Wmns Cntr Asst 90-; Biology; Mdcl Tchnlgy Rsrch.

**PULLY, BENJAMIN F,** Va Commonwealth Univ, Richmond, VA; JR; BS; Math Clb Co Presdnt 90-; Math Assoc Amrc; Gldn Key; Delta Upsilon Co Scl Chrmn 88-; Deans Lst 90; Ftbll Vrsty Bsbll 87-89; Ststcs Math Sci.

**PULVER, SYLVIA DIANNE,** Univ Of Southern Ms, Hattiesburg, MS; SR; BMED; Tau Beta Sigma VP 87-88; Mu Phi Epsilon; Music Ed; Tchng.

**PUNJ, GUARAV,** Duquesne Univ, Pittsburgh, PA; JR; BS; Fin Mgt Assoc Publc Reltns 90-; Intrntl Stdnts Org 88-; Duke Of Edinburghs Gold Award 88; Lloydinsulations Inda VPT Ltd Intrnshp 90; Metacon Sys Co Intrnshp; Fin; Bus Mgt.

**PUNTUS, NOAH J,** Georgetown Univ, Washington, DC; SR; BA; Frshmn Orient 88-89; Bicentennial Comm 88-89; Alpha Kappa Delta 90-; Beta Gamma Sigma 90-; Acctng Soc 88-; Price Waterhouse Audit Intrnshp Prog 90; Louis Shayemde Abizaid Schlrshp 90-; Stdnt Ldrshp Conf 90; IM Sprts 87-; Acctng/Sociology.

**PUPPOLO, MARIA T,** Elms Coll, Chicopee, MA; SO; BA; Intl Clb Treas 90-; Amrcn Chmcl Scty VP 90; Orntn Advsr 90-; Vol Byst Mdcl Cntr 90-; Asst Tchr Prsh 90-; Blgy.

**PURBA, HUDSON,** Radford Univ, Radford, VA; SR; BS; Indonesian Stdnt Assoc Pres 89-90; Internatl Clb 89-; Asian Assoc Pblcty Ofcr 89-90; Kappa Mu Epsilon; Math; Engrg.

**PURCEL, LORI L,** Northern Ky Univ, Highland Hts, KY; SO; BA; Psychlgy; Cnslr.

**PURCELL, HANNAH M,** Fl International Univ, Miami, FL; SR; BS; Girl Scouts Am Co-Ldr/Asst Ldr 87-; Future Ed Am 90-; Intl Read Assn 90-; Sec/Ofc Mgr Publ Sch 80-89; AA Miami Dade Com Coll 83; Elem Edn.

**PURCELL, MICHAEL J,** Eckerd Coll, St Petersburg, FL; SR; BA; Search/Resuce Wtch Ldr Coxswain EMT 87-; Radio Station DJ 87; Bike Club 88; Waterfront Student Asst 88-; Pineallas Co Sheriffs Office Intern 90; Sociology; Law Enforcement.

**PURCELL, MICHELLE C,** Univ Of Sc At Columbia, Columbia, SC; SR; BS; Delta Zeta 88; BS; Blgy; Med Schl.

**PURCELL, PAIGE E,** Fl St Univ, Tallahassee, FL; FR; MBA; Marching Chiefs 90-; IM Sftbl 90-; Hnr Prgm 90-; Psych.

**PURDHAM, PENNY L,** Tomlinson Coll, Cleveland, TN; SO; Sldrs Undr Const Chldrns Mnstry Sec 89-; CAM 89-; Stu Govt Grls Drm Rep 89-90; Chrldr 90-; AS; Elem Ed; Tchr.

**PURDHAM, ROY TODD,** Univ Of Sc At Columbia, Columbia, SC; SR; MS; Asst Coach 90-; Bsebl Tm 87-89; BS 90; Phys Ed/Sports Admin; Coach.

**PURDIE, BARBARA J,** Fayetteville St Univ, Fayetteville, NC; SR; Phi Beta Lambda 90-; Stdnts Free Enterprise 90-91; Acctg Assn 90-; Fayetteville Finance Dept Intern; State NC Schlrshp 90-; BS; Acctg; CPA/MBA.

**PURDUE, PAUL R,** Univ Of Ky, Lexington, KY; SR; Bapt Stdnt Un 88; Bapt Smmr Mssnry Cncl Worshp Cordntr 86-87; Phi Beta Kappa 90-; Psy Chi 90; Gldn Key 90-; Chrch Yth Mnstr; BA 90.

**PURDUM, KIMBERLY G,** Univ Of Md Baltimore Prof Schl, Baltimore, MD; JR; BS; Stdnt Dntl Hygn Assn 90-; Dntl Asst 77-85; Dntl Lab Tech 79-; AA Montgmry Jr Coll 76; Dntl Hygn.

**PURDY, ADRIENNE C,** Kent St Univ Trumbull Cmps, Warren, OH; SO; BA; IM Softball; Deans/Pres Lst; Nrsng/Chem/Biol.

**PURDY, DEBBY E,** Pellissippi St Tech Comm Coll, Knoxville, TN; FR; AAS; Pellissippi Prlgl Assoc 90; Assoc Of Rcrds Mngrs & Admnstrtrs; Rcrds Mngr Law Frm Baker,Worthngton,Crossley,Stansberry & Woolf; Lgl Asst Tchnlgy; Law.

**PURDY, MICHELLE L,** Ms St Univ, Miss State, MS; FR; BPA; Hon Prog 90-; Acctg; CPA.

**PURDY, SABRINA L,** Anne Arundel Comm Coll, Arnold, MD; FR; BS; Cmptr Sci; Prgrmr.

**PURDY, SAMANTHA L,** Bethany Coll, Bethany, WV; JR; BA; Renner Union Pgmng Brd 90-; Art Clb 89-90; Kappa Dlt VP Mbrshp 90-; Deans List 90-; Kalon Leadership Schlrshp 88-; Intrds Art Hist; Educ Cnsltng Rsrch.

**PURDY, VIOLET ROLEN,** Roane St Comm Coll, Harriman, TN; SO; Cert Income Tx Preparer; Maryville Coll 85; Bus Admin; Acctng.

**PURDY, WALTER E,** George Mason Univ, Fairfax, VA; SR; BIS; Plc Assoc Pres 88-; White Hs Stf 90-; IM Bsktbl 88; Sthrn Pol Sci Assoc 90-; Cntr Study Pres 90-; Law.

**PURDY, WILLIAM C,** Glassboro St Coll, Glassboro, NJ; JR; BA; Delta Sigma Phi Asst Soc Chr 87-88; Proj Lit; Ntl Soc Arts/Ltrs 1st Prz Lit 89; Engl; Tech Wrtng.

**PURGASON, LORI D,** Tusculum Coll, Greeneville, TN; SR; Choir Sec/Treas 87-88; Alpha Chi VP 89-; Acdmc Excllnce Awrd 87-88; BA; Elem Ed.

**PURIFOY, OMEKIA D,** Al St Univ, Montgomery, AL; FR; Crmnl Jstce; Law.

**PURKS, CHRISTIE,** Univ Of Ga, Athens, GA; FR; ABJ; GA Recrtmnt Tm 90-; Pandora Stf; All Campus Hmecmg Comm 90; Pnhlnc Cncl; Pi Beta Phi Pldg Cls Pres 90; GA Girl Ofcl Ftbl Hostess; Jrnlsm.

**PURNELL, CRYSTAL R,** Va St Univ, Petersburg, VA; SR; BS; New Gen Cmps Ministries 90-; Truman Schlr Clb 89-; Data Prcssng Mgtm Assoc 88; Alpha Kappa Mu; Alpha Mu Gama 88-; Bus Inform Systems; Computer Programmer.

**PURNELL, RUBY S,** Roane St Comm Coll, Harriman, TN; SO; AA; Rdlgc Schlstc Awd; Highest GPA; Radiologic Tech.

**PURNELL, STEPHANIE R,** Lincoln Univ, Lincoln Univ, PA; SO; BS; Fornsc Soc VP 90-; Stdnts In Free Entrps Chf Exec Ofcr 90-; Bsns Admn; Publ Rels.

**PURSER, LINDA S,** Memphis St Univ, Memphis, TN; SO; BA; Clinical Psychlgst.

**PURSLEY, SEAN F,** Hudson Valley Comm Coll, Troy, NY; SR; AOS; Pres Lst; Atbdy Rpr; Auto Fld.

**PURVES, DENNIS P,** Seton Hall Univ, South Orange, NJ; SO; MA; English.**

**PURVIS, RANI D,** Newbury Coll, Brookline, MA; SR; AS; Dns Lst; Alpha Beta Gamma; Mktg.

**PURVIS, SUSAN A,** Univ Of Miami, Coral Gables, FL; SR; BHS; Carondelet Hist Soc St Louis MO Treas 88-89; Stfng Clrk 89-; Media Buyer 86-89; AA St Louis Comm Coll Meramec 81; Hlth Sci; Cytotechnologist.

**PURYEAR, JOANNE S,** Birmingham Southern Coll, Birmingham, AL; JR; BA; NAA Adult Studies Rep; AS Mrktng Jefferson State 86; AS Acctg Jefferson State 90; Acctg.

**PURYEAR JR, SAMUEL GIBSON,** Tn St Univ, Nashville, TN; JR; BA; Gold Key 90-; Alpha Phi Alpha 90-; Intshp Golf Digest Mag; Natl Minorty Schlrshp 88-; Sports Writing Awd 90-; Golf Tm Cptn 90-; Media Comm/Spch; Nws Caster/Sptwrtr/PR.

**PURYEAR, TAMMY C,** Vance Granville Comm Coll, Henderson, NC; SO; AAS; Beta Phi Upsilon Secy 90-; Admin Ofc Technology; Secretary.

**PUSCAS, LIANA,** Univ Of Miami, Coral Gables, FL; FR; BS; Coll Of Arts And Scis Stdnt Cncl Crrspndng Sec 90-; Alpha Lamda Delta 90-; Bapt Cmps Mnstry St And Cmps Exec Cncl; Pres Hnr Rll 90-; Dns Lst 90-; IM Vlybl And Sftbl; Blgy; Med Dr.

**PUSCH, GABRIELA S,** Kent St Univ Kent Cmps, Kent, OH; JR; BA; Amer Crmnl Jstc Assc; Dns Lst; Pres Lst; Gldn Key; Lamba Alpha Epsilon; Crmnl Jstc/Bus; Law Crcts.

**PUSCHMANN, SHANNAN K,** Fl St Univ, Tallahassee, FL; JR; BS; SID; IBD; Int Concept 4 Intrs; Du Pont Dsgn Of Times Comp; IBD Day 6 Dsgn Comp; AA 90; Int Dsgn; Dsgn/Spce Plnng.

**PUSEY, DANIEL L,** Bapt Bible Coll & Seminary, Clarks Summit, PA; SO; MDIV; Pstrl Intrst Flwshp Treas; Crs Cntry/Trck 89-; Pstrl.

**PUSEY, JENNIFER E,** Salisbury St Univ, Salisbury, MD; GD; MED; Sdtnt Natl Educ Assn 88-; Kappa Delta Pi Pres 89-; Phi Kappa Phi 89-; Campus Tour Gd 87-; Salisbury State Univ Deans Lst 88-90; BS 90; Erly Chldhd Educ; Tchr.**

**PUSPOKI III, LOUIS J,** De Tech & Comm Coll At Dover, Dover, DE; SO; ADN; Nurs Clb Treas 90-; Clg Deans Lst 89-; Nurs; Emrgncy Rm Nurs.

**PUSTULKA, PAUL J,** Alfred Univ, Alfred, NY; JR; BS; Amer Crmc Soc Stdnt Brnch Tread 88-; Ntl Inst Crmc Eng 88-; IM Sprts Capt 88-; Keramos 90-; Crmc Eng.

**PUTNAM, CINDY L,** Hudson Valley Comm Coll, Troy, NY; FR; BA; Lit Vol Amer; Tutrng 89-; Unit Sprvsr NYS Tchrs Rtrmnt Syst 79-; Psychlgy.

**PUTNAM, CRISTI G,** Belmont Abbey Coll, Belmont, NC; FR; BA; Anne Horne Little Acdmc Schlrshp Rcpnt 90-; Erly Chldhd Ed; Elem Schl Tchr.

**PUTNAM JR, PAUL DAVID,** North Greenville Coll, Tigerville, SC; FR; MBA; Frbl; Bus; Bldg Cntrctr.

**PUTNAM, TRACEE L,** Western Carolina Univ, Cullowhee, NC; FR; BS; Westrn Gld 90-; Pre Med Clb 90-; Hnrs Pgm Pre Univ Hnrs Pgm 90-; Alpha Lambda Delta; Wstrn Car Univ Dns Lst 90; Fr Math Awd; Stdnt Marshll; Bio; Med.

**PUTT, MICHAEL P,** Memphis St Univ, Memphis, TN; JR; BS; AS 86; AS 87; Fire Science; Fire Serv.

**PUTZ, SONGCHA K,** Strayer Coll, Washington, DC; SR; BS; Amer Red Crs Vol 87-; Schlrshp U S Army Ofcrs Wives Clb 89; U S Army Ofcrs Wives Clb Actvtes Chrprsn 88-89; AS Bus Admn 84; Bus Admn; Chf Exec Ofcr.

**PUTZBACH, JENNIFER R,** S U N Y Coll At Fredonia, Fredonia, NY; JR; BS; Audio Engrng Scty Treas 88-; Tonmeister Assoc Treas 88-; Hnrs Prog 88-; Sci/Math/Music; Sound Recording Tchnlgy.

**PYBURN, MAUREEN D,** Middle Tn St Univ, Murfreesboro, TN; SO; BSN; Delta Zeta Alumnae; BS 85; Nrsg.

**PYE, JASON T,** Spartanburg Methodist Coll, Spartanburg, SC; FR.

**PYLE, JILL M,** Clarion Univ Of Pa, Clarion, PA; FR; BSN; Nrsg Clb 90-; Oil Cty Area Hlth Cntr Aux Schlrshp 90-; Stu Wrk Stdy 90; Alumni Phn Athn Nrsg Pro; Nrsg; Crdlgy Dept.

**PYLE, SCOTT R,** Indiana Univ Of Pa, Indiana, PA; SO; BS; Wghtltng/Eycling/Fantasy Gaming; BS English; Tchng Pgh Public Schlrs.

**PYLES, TERRY L,** Wv Univ At Parkersburg, Parkersburg, WV; SO; BS; Phi Theta Kappa 90-; US Army/Army Natl Grd; Sci; Elec Eng.

**PYLES, TRACEY D,** Piedmont Comm Coll, Roxboro, NC; FR; AAS; Stdnt Govt Assn; Admin Offc Tchnlgy; Admin Sec.

**PYO, JIAE,** Memphis St Univ, Memphis, TN; FR; MUSIC; Piano.

**PYOTT, WENDY L,** Muskingum Coll, New Concord, OH; SR; Phi Kappa Tau Ltl Sis 87-; Cntrbd 87-; Tour Gd 90-; Habitat Hmnty Coord 90-; BA; Elem Ed; Tchng.

**PYRCZAK, RICHARD M,** Oh St Univ, Columbus, OH; SR; BA; AIESEC Dir 88-90; Frnch Clb V P 88-90; Span/Portuguese Clb Sec 89-90; Romophos Activ Dir 88-89; Bucket/Dipper 89-90; Gldn Key 88-; Refugee Serv YMCA 90; Dept Intl Studies Schlrshp 89; Rotary Schlr; Frnch/Spnsh.

**PYRON, JULIA M,** East Carolina Univ, Greenville, NC; SR; BS; ST Wooten Const Co Inc 85-; AS Rockingham Comm Coll 84; Indust/Tech Cnstrcnt Mang; Cnstrctn.

**PYROS, VARVARA A,** Allegheny Coll, Meadville, PA; SO; BA; Chrstn Otrch Chpl Chr Allghny Lders Lsns Ed Spprt; Chpl Decn Prr Alchl Edctr; Rd Nwscstr Intrn; Lambda Sigma 90-; Hbtt Hmnty 89-; Sp Ktchn 89-90; Aldn Schlr; Stdnt Srvc Ldrshp Comm 89-90; Chmstry Tchng Asst Tt; Vrsty Bsktbll Chrldng; Math.

**PYSK, MARY BETH,** Comm Coll Algny Co Algny Cmps, Pittsburgh, PA; FR; BA; IFMA 90-; GPAUG 87-; Cadvance Usrs Grp Pres 89-90; Dean Lst 90-; La Roche Coll Adjunct Fclty; Cmptr Fclts Cnsltnt; AS Pittsburgh Tech Inst 83; Bus; MIS.

# Q

**QAOUD, MOHAMMED K,** Northern Ky Univ, Highland Hts, KY; SR; BS; Intl Stdnt Un Acdmc Chrmn 90-; Physics; Engrng.

**QIAN, KAIFENG,** Univ Of Md Baltimore Prof Schl, Baltimore, MD; GD; PHD; Metro Acupuncture Assn 88-; Chinese Med Assn 85-; Grad Rsrch Assist 87-; Grad Merit Fllwshp 88-; Radiologist 84-87; MD Shanghai Clg Trad Chinese Med 79-84; Molecular Endro; Sci Rsrch/Med.

**QUACKENBUSH JR, MICHAEL P,** Univ Of Fl, Gainesville, FL; JR; MACC; Goldn Key 90-; Alpha Lamda Delta 89-; IM Socr/Bsktbl/Ftbl/Vlybl 88-; AA 90; Acctg.

**QUALLS, ERROL C,** Alcorn St Univ, Lorman, MS; FR; BA; Hnr Scty Orgn 90-; Math; Cmptr Prgrmmr.

**QUALLS, JEREMY S,** Memphis St Univ, Memphis, TN; SO; BS; Actvts Cncl 89-90; Phi Eta Sigma 90-; Beta Beta Beta 89-; Hnrs Assoc 89-90; RA; Physcs; Med.

**QUALLS, JOHNNY W,** Northeast State Tech Comm Coll, Blountville, TN; SO; AAS; Mgmnt Inf Sciences; Programmer Analyst.

**QUALLS, LISA A,** Alcorn St Univ, Lorman, MS; SR; Bus Admin; Finance.

**QUALLS, PAMELA L,** Columbus Coll Of Art & Design, Columbus, OH; SO; BA; Blck Stdnt Un 89-; Stndt Cncl 89-90; Iota Phi Theta; Clr Whls Instrctr 90; Art Wrk; Advrtsng Dsgn.**

**QUAM, ERIC S,** Liberty Univ, Lynchburg, VA; SR; BA; Sigma Phi Delta Sec/Treas 87-89; Cir K Clb; Vars Intclgt Bsktbl 87-90; Bsn Mgmt; Entprnr.

**QUAN, LUPITA T,** Fl International Univ, Miami, FL; SR; BA; Phi Kappa Phi; Omicron Delta Epsilon 90-; Phi Lambda 90-; Econ; Busn.

**QUANDT, BELINDA F,** East Tn St Univ, Johnson City, TN; FR; BBA; United Way Recycler Musalar Dist Chrmn 90; RHA 90-; Hmcng Partcipant 90-; Alpha Lmdb Delta; Regents Schlrshp Prog 90-; Acctng; Corporate Law.

**QUARLES, AYANNA Y,** Al A & M Univ, Normal, AL; FR; Acctg.

**QUARLES, GLENDA J,** Valdosta St Coll, Valdosta, GA; SO; BS; Chi Omega 90; Sprts Med; Athltc Trnr.

**QUARLES, IVEY L,** Univ Of The Dist Of Columbia, Washington, DC; SR; BA; UDC Prcrmnt Clb 90-; AAS 88; Prcrmnt/Pblc Cntrcng Law.

**QUARLES, SUSAN B,** Univ Of Sc At Columbia, Columbia, SC; SR; Soc Med Lab Tech Pres 85-87; Natl Assoc Female Exec; Soc Med Lab Tech 87; Natl Clgt Med Prof Awd 87; Amer Soc Med Tech 85-90; Amer Soc Clncl Path 87-; Med Tech; BAIS 90; AHS Trident Tech Clg 87; Med Tech.

**QUARLES-NUR, VALEYN R,** Univ Of The Dist Of Columbia, Washington, DC; SR; BA; Acctng Tech US Dept Of Justice 84-; AAS 87; Cert 87; Business Mgmt; Sm Business Owner.

**QUARTARONE, JOSEPH R,** Merrimack Coll, North Andover, MA; FR; Crss Cntry 90; Nu Phi Kappa; DPMA Schlrshp; Crss Cntry 90; Bus Admin; Mgmt Or Acctng.

**QUARTERMAN, TAMMY L,** Savannah St Coll, Savannah, GA; JR; BA; ASME Edtr Treas Rcrt Ofcr 89-; Mech Engr Tech; Engr Tech.

**QUARTERMAN, TRICIA CLARK,** Mercer Univ Schl Of Pharm, Atlanta, GA; FR; PHARM; ASP V Chr Spec Citizens Comm 90-; ACS 88-; Newspaper 87-90; Bapt Stdnt Union 87-; Big Bro/Big Sis 88-90; United Way Vol 87-88; Savannah Pharm Assoc Dean Smith Schlrshp 90-; Outstndg Yng Wmn Amer Awd 90-; Phrmcy.

**QUASHIE, KEVIN E,** Fl International Univ, Miami, FL; SR; MA MS; Stdnt Actvts; Outstndng Sr; Grd Schl Schlrshp; Edctn; Stdnt Affrs.

**QUASHNOCK, DAWN D,** Indiana Univ Of Pa, Indiana, PA; JR.

**QUASNEY JR, ROBERT S,** Anne Arundel Comm Coll, Arnold, MD; FR; AA; Embedded Syst Prgrmng 90; Robotics 90; UNIX Assc 90; Deans Lst 89-90; Computer Sci; Prgrmng.**

**QUAST, NANCY J,** Widener Univ, Chester, PA; JR; BS; Data Proc Mngmnt Assn Pres 90-; Pioneer Yrbk Sr Sect Edtr 89-; Stdnt Jud Bd Jdg 89-; Chster Eastside Mnstrs Stdnt Vol Tutor Asst Coor 89-; Rotaract Clb Intrnl 89-; Dns Lst 90-; Bus Mngmnt/MIS; Infor Sys.

**QUATTLEBAUM, AMBER D,** Auburn Univ At Auburn, Auburn, AL; SR; BSN; Angel Flght 89-; Assn Nrsng Stdnts 89-; Bptst Cmps Min 87-88; Phi Eta Sigma 88-; Alpha Almbda Delta 88-; Sigma Theta Tau 90-; Outsdng Stdnt Nrsng; Deans Lst; Nrsng.

**QUATTLEBAUM, CAROLINE B,** Univ Of Ga, Athens, GA; SR; BSED; Clg Rpblcn 88-89; Chi Omega Pres 87-; Erly Chldhd Educ; Tchr.

**QUATTLEBAUM JR, CYRUS J,** Piedmont Tech Coll, Greenwood, SC; SR; AS; Engr.

**QUEEN, CHRISTINE D,** Washington State Comm Coll, Marietta, OH; FR; AAB; Accntng; CPA.

**QUEEN, DEBBIE E,** Univ Of Nc At Chapel Hill, Chapel Hill, NC; GD; JD; Wmn Law 88-; Amer Jurisprudence Awd Trsts Est 90; BA Univ N Car Charlotte 88; Law.

**QUEEN, KIMBERLY N,** Univ Of Nc At Asheville, Asheville, NC; FR; BA; Ambassador 90-; Phi Eta Sigma; Hnr Scty; Busn.

**QUEEN, LINDA S,** Oh Univ-Southern Cmps, Ironton, OH; SR; BA; WOW 89-F Deans List; Gamma Pi Delta 90-; Santa Fe Lodgers Assoc 81-85; AS Huntington Clg Busn 77; Busn; Busn Admin.

**QUEENER, LEISHA D,** Roane St Comm Coll, Harriman, TN; SO; AD; Extern UT Hosp; Nrsng.

**QUEENER, PATRICIA GRACE,** Roane St Comm Coll, Harriman, TN; FR; BED; Gamma Beta Phi Socty; Educ; Tchr.

**QUEIRUGA, ANA Y,** Bloomfield Coll, Bloomfield, NJ; FR; BS; Hosp Vol 89-; Adcma Schlrshp 90-; High Hnrs Acdmc Exclnc Asan 90; Otstndng Frshmn Awd 90-; Nursing.

**QUENON, GREGORY E,** Lexington Comm Coll, Lexington, KY; FR; MBA; MBA; Hstry; Tchr/Prof.

**QUERESHY, FAISAL A,** S U N Y At Buffalo, Buffalo, NY; GD; DDS; Pakistani Ontario Yth Cltrl Forum Exec 88-90; Delta Sigma Delta 90-; Red Cross 87-88; Entrnc Schlrshp 87; Ontario Schlr Awd 87; BS Univ Toronto 90; Hmn Blgy BS; Dntstry.

**QUESADA MEDINA, MARIFE,** Inter Amer Univ Pr Arecibo Un, Arecibo, PR; FR; Home Ec Assn 85-89; P E Clb 86-87; Math Clb 85-86; Club FLCA Pres; Futuros Lideres Del Comercio De America Pres 87-; Amer Cancer Soc 87; Pres Acad Fitness Awd 90; High Hnrs 90; Phi Sigma Omicron 87; Criminal Justice.

**QUESENBERRY, ANGELA M,** Radford Univ, Radford, VA; SR; Phy Ed Mjrs Clb 87-; Coached Girls Bsktbl 89-90; Coached Vlybl; Sftbl Tm 90; BS; Phy Ed/Hlth; Tchng/Coaching.

**QUESENBERRY, CAROL A,** Beckley Coll, Beckley, WV; BSN; Nrsng.

**QUESENBERRY, LORA LYNN,** Radford Univ, Radford, VA; SR; BS; Tri M 89-; Stdnt Ed Assoc 89-; Math; Tchg.**

**QUESTEL, ALLISON P,** City Univ Of Ny Baruch Coll, New York, NY; SO; BBA; Bnk Cntrl Spec Dean Witter Reynolds 89; Acctg; Law.

**QUETTAN, SAUREL,** Nova Univ, Ft Lauderdale, FL; GD; MBA; Tst Mstrs Intrnatl Pres 89-; Hllywd Chrch Of Rlgs Sci Pres 89-; Sthrn Bll Eng 85-; Div Chmpn Tstmstrs Int Spch Cntst 90; FL Bst Of The Bst Spkr Sthrn Bll; BSEE Univ Of FL 85; MBA; Orgnztnl Bhvr; Mgmt Cnsltng.

**QUEVEDO, DIANA I,** City Univ Of Ny Kingsborough, Brooklyn, NY; SO; BA; Peer Advsr 89-; AA Kingsborough Comm Coll; Chld Psychlgy.

**QUEZADA, ANGELA M,** Georgian Court Coll, Lakewood, NJ; FR; De La Salle Educ Clb 90-; Spec Ed/Elem Ed; Tchr.

**QUI, THUY T,** Memphis St Univ, Memphis, TN; SO; BA; Sci; Nrsng.

**QUICK, DORIS A,** Coker Coll, Hartsville, SC; SR; BA; Coll Schlstc Awd 87-90; Deans Lst 87-90; Stdnt Rep Ed Tchr 90; Srch Comm; Prnt Rep Chstrfld Chrw 90-; Co Schl Imprvmnt Comm Elem 90-; AAS Richmond Tech Coll 77; AAS 84; Elem Ed; Tchng.**

**QUICK, MICHELLE S,** Daytona Beach Comm Coll, Daytona Beach, FL; SO; AA; Restaurant Manager; Education; Law School.

**QUICK, SARAH L,** Univ Of Sc At Columbia, Columbia, SC; SO; BA; Symphny Orch 89-; SCC Hon Clg 89-; SAGE 89; Amanesty Intl 89; Anthropology.

**QUICK, SHERYL D,** Methodist Coll, Fayetteville, NC; JR; BA; Art Clb 90-; Fayettevl Art Cnsl Annl Art Cntst 1st Pl; Art Gld Annl Art Cntst 2nd Pl; Fine Arts; Prfssnl Artst/Psychlgy.

**QUICK, VAN R,** S U N Y Coll Of Tech At Delhi, Delhi, NY; SO; BBA; Delhi Bus Assoc 90-; NJCAA Bsbl Sr All Star; NJCAA Bsbl; AAS; Acctg; Law Enfrcmnt.

**QUIGLEY, BARBARA M,** Univ Of Nc At Greensboro, Greensboro, NC; SO; BS; IM Sports; Gamma Sigma Sigma Alumnae Liason 90-; Hstry/Pltcl Sci; Govt.

**QUIGLEY, CARLA J,** West Liberty St Coll, West Liberty, WV; SO; BA; Hnrs Prog; Math Tutor 89-; Underwood Smith Tchrs Schlrshp 89-90; Elem Edn/Math Minor; Teach.

**QUIGLEY, KRISTINE M,** S U N Y Coll Of Tech At Frmgdl, Farmingdale, NY; SO; AS; Legal Ofc Mngmnt Clb VP 88-89; Deans Lst 87-90; Legal Secy Intern 88-; AAS SUNY Farmingdale 90; Criminal Justice; Law.

**QUIGLEY, SUZANNE L,** Villanova Univ, Villanova, PA; SO; BA; Spec Olympcs Cnslr 89-; Proj Sunshine Tutor 89-90; M L K Clbrtn Stdnt Fcltr; Alph Phi 90-; Natl Right To Life Soc Cntrbtr 87-; Villanovans For Life 89-; IM Bsktbl Capt 89-; Pol Sci/ Womens Studies; Law/Pub Serv.

**QUIJANO VEGA, OMAYRA M,** Inter Amer Univ Pr Hato Rey, Hato Rey, PR; SO; Biomed; Med.

**QUILDON, MICHAEL K,** Morehouse Coll, Atlanta, GA; FR; BS; Hnrs Pgm Clb 90-; Math Clb 90-; Cmptr Sci Clb 90-; Morehouse Clge Hnrs Pgm 90-; Natl Soc Blck Engrs 90-; Morehouse Clge Mntrng Pgm 90-; Hnr Rl 90-; Acdmc Schlrshp 90-; Frshmn Stp Tm 90-; Math; Univ Prfsr.

**QUILES RAMOS, ROSA J,** Inter Amer Univ Pr Aquadilla, Aguadilla, PR; FR; Offic Cont Francisco Mendoza School 90; History; Busn Admin.

**QUILES, ANNETTE MARTINEZ,** Caribbean Univ, Bayamon, PR; SR; Deans Lst 90; Assc Scrtrl Sci 82-; Assc Clg Rgnl Arcbo 82; Scrtrl Sci; Cmptr Sci.

**QUILES, LISA,** Univ Of Miami, Coral Gables, FL; FR; BM; Msc; Tchr.

**QUILES, TANIA E,** Inter Amer Univ Pr Hato Rey, Hato Rey, PR; FR; BA; Young Christian Assoc Treas 89-; Bio; Med Tech.

**QUILLEN, PATRICIA E,** Bluefield Coll, Bluefield, VA; JR; BS; Stdnt Govt Assn Sec V P 90-; Yrbk Staff 89-; Phi Mu Delta Little Sis 88-; Res Asst 90-; Edn Practicums 90; Chrldr 88-89; Psych/ Eng.

**QUILLER, LA RONNA A,** Univ Of Sc At Columbia, Columbia, SC; JR; BA; Assn Afro Amer Stdnts 88-; Natl Assn Advncmnt Color People 89-; Delta Sigma Theta Crspndng Sec 90-; Mnrty Hnr Stdnt 88-; Dns Lst 89-; Wstnghse Savannah Rvr Co PR Intrnshp; Media Arts; Corporate Media.

**QUINLAN, CAROLYN M,** Univ Of Southern Ms, Hattiesburg, MS; SO; BA; Stdnt Alumni Assn 90-; Coll Rpblcns 89-; Pnhlnc Rsh Cnslr; Psi Chi; Gamma Alpha Epsilon VP Elect; Alpha Lambda Delta/Phi Eta Sigma 89-90; Chi Omega Hmcmng/Sprt Chr 90-; Gamma Beta Phi; Acdmc Exclnc Awd; IM Sftbl Flg Ftbl; Psychlgy; Clncl Psychlgy.

**QUINLAN, HILARY A,** Memphis St Univ, Memphis, TN; JR; Stdnt Sen 89-90; Hmcmng Comm 89-90; Actvty Cnsl 89-90; Deans List 90-; Chi Omega Prayer & Sharer Ldr 89-90; Super D Phrmcst-Tech 87-; Bellvue Bapt Schlrshp 88-90; Parmacist.

**QUINLAN, KELLY B,** Univ Of Ct, Storrs, CT; FR; BA; Anml Sci; Vetrnrn.

**QUINLEY, DANIEL BLAINE,** Memphis St Univ, Memphis, TN; SR; Delta Nu Alpha.

**QUINN, DAVID T,** Hudson Valley Comm Coll, Troy, NY; SR; BA; Bus; Acctng.

**QUINN, ERIK-JON,** Univ Of New Haven, West Haven, CT; FR; BARCH; Archtctr.

**QUINN, ERIN E,** Fordham Univ, Bronx, NY; SR; Clgt Sci/Tech Pgm 90-; Beta Alpha Psi 89-; Beta Gamma Sigma 90-; Acctng Soc 89-; Gold Awd; Hugh J O'reilly Cath Acctnt Awd; Dns Lst/Hnr Rl 87-; Intshp US Cncl Intl Bsn 88-89; Asst Audtr Arthur Andersen 89-; BS; Acctng; CPA.**

**QUINN, ERIN G,** Glassboro St Coll, Glassboro, NJ; SR; BA; Radio T V Assn; Hm Shpng Ntwrk Intrn; Mag Show Tech Dir; Music Prog Tech; Cmunctns; T V Production.

**QUINN, FREDERICK DOUGLAS,** Tougaloo Coll, Tougaloo, MS; FR; BS; Pre Almn Clb 90-; Pre Hlth Clb 90-; Art Clb 90-; Dillard Univ Howard Hughes Flwshp Smmr 90; Meridian Almn Schlrshp 90-; Inst Schlrshp 90-; Intrmdt Bwlg Tm 90-; Bio/ Pre-Med; Physcn.

**QUINN, JEANNE M,** S U N Y At Buffalo, Buffalo, NY; JR; BS; Beta Alpha Psi; Acctg Assoc Prsntly Nom Pres 90-; Schussmeisters Ski Clb 89-; Gold Key 90-; Beta Alpha Psi; Jr Achvmnt Com; Deans Lst 89-90; Acctg.

**QUINN, JENNIFER L,** Lenoir Rhyne Coll, Hickory, NC; SR; BA; Yng Democrats 88; Amnesty Intl 88-89; Mu Sigma Epsilon 90-; Omicron Delta Epsilon Pres 90-; Sigma Kappa Corrspndg Sec 89-; Lineberger Schlr 87-; French Drill Instr 89; Deans/Pres Lsts 87; Econ/French; Fin Analyst.

**QUINN, JOAN E,** City Univ Of Ny Baruch Coll, New York, NY; SR; BBA; Golden Key 90-; Ntry Pblc 80-; Clrk 78-88; Acctg; Estblsh Acctg Prctc.

**QUINN, JOHN THOMAS,** Univ Of Pa, Philadelphia, PA; JR; BBA; Real Est Clb 89-; Fin Clb 89-; Bus Admin; Cnsltng.

**QUINN, KEELY M,** Va Commonwealth Univ, Richmond, VA; GD; BS; Gldn Key 90; Phi Kappa Phi 90-; Psi Chi Pres 90-; Magna Cum Laude 90-; VCU Srv Awd 90-; Res Intrnshp Psychphrmclgy 89-; Hon Psychlgy 90-; Psychlgy; Schl Psychlgst.

**QUINN, KIMBERLY D,** Univ Of Sc At Coastal Carolina, Conway, SC; FR; Soc Undersea World; Coastal Carolina Hnrs Prog; Phi Eta Sigma; USC Hnrs Schlrshp; Marine Scinc; Chem Oceanography.

**QUINN II, LUTHER J,** Eckerd Coll, St Petersburg, FL; SR; DVM; Bio Club V P 90-; AS Panama Canal Coll 89; Vet Med; Rsrch.

**QUINN, PATRICIA E,** Central Fl Comm Coll, Ocala, FL; SO; AA; Phi Theta Kappa Pres; Para Legal Assn Pres 90; PTK Advsrs Recog Awd 90; Tla Dvlpmntl Schlrshp; Southern Crim Just Assn 90-; Crim Just/Psych Legal Asst; Law.

**QUINN, ROBERT T,** Georgetown Univ, Washington, DC; FR; Bus.

**QUINN, ROBIN L,** Gaston Coll, Dallas, NC; SO; AAS; Comp Sci Clb Treas 90-; Comp Prog.

**QUINN, SHERRY P,** Oh Univ-Southern Cmps, Ironton, OH; FR; BA; Psych.

**QUINN, TIMOTHY S,** Siena Coll, Loudonville, NY; SR; Internshp 90-; IM Ftbl Bsktbl Sftbl 87-; BBA; Acctg.

**QUINN, VIRGINIA CAROL,** Univ Of Cincinnati, Cincinnati, OH; SO; BSN; Univ Stdnt Nrs Assoc VP; Natl Stdnt Nrs Assoc 90-; Amer Red Cross Instr; Cert Paramedic Colombus Tech 89; Nursing; Rsrch/Gntcs.

**QUINN, WILLIAM T,** Nova Univ, Ft Lauderdale, FL; GD; MBA; Assoc Cmptg Mach 85-86; Phi Kappa Phi 86; Phi Beta Lambda V P 79-80; Grad W/Hnrs FL Atlantic Univ 86; Grad W/ Hnrs Broward Cmnty Clg 83; A T T Accnt Exec 90-; BAS FL Atlantic Univ 86; AA Broward Cmnty Clg 83; Bsn Adm/Intl Bsn; Bsn Mgmt.

**QUINN, WINIFRED M,** Comm Coll Algny Co Algny Cmps, Pittsburgh, PA; SO; VFW Leetsdl PA 89-; Amer Lgn 89-; Kngs Fmly Rest; Hlth Cr Admn; Hosp Admn.

**QUINONES ALICEA, LOUISE MARIE,** Inter Amer Univ Pr Hato Rey, Hato Rey, PR; SR; BA; Theater 90-; Summer Missionary; Preschl Pedagogy; Tch.

**QUINONES AQUINO, JACQUELINE,** Inter Amer Univ Pr Hato Rey, Hato Rey, PR; FR; BA; Cls Treas 88-89; Lit Mgz Ed 88-89; Stdnt Cncl Repr 88-89; Blgy; Crdvsclr Srgn.

**QUINONES BELAZQUEZ, JAVIER E,** Inter Amer Univ Pr Aquadilla, Aguadilla, PR; JR; BA; Data Entry/Acctg/Bkkpg 87-; Acctg; CPA.

**QUINONES NEGRON, JOSE L,** Univ Politecnica De Pr, Hato Rey, PR; FR; Eng.

**QUINONES, ALINA J,** Inter Amer Univ Pr San German, San German, PR; SR; BA; Psychlgy Assn 87-; Beca Harris Clb 87-; Psychlgy Assn 87-; Rsrch Hist Ctr San German 89-; Harris Awd 87-; Excell Acad Awd 87-; Psychlgy/Valedictorian; Sabana Eneas Grp; Psychlgy; Doctorate.

**QUINONES, ANTONIO,** Univ Of Pr Medical Sciences, San Juan, PR; GD; MS; Clss Pres 88-89; Assn Ctzn Untd Hlth Envrmnt 90-; Toxic Sub Dis Reg Intern; BS Univ PR 88; Sci; Rsrch.

**QUINONES, CARMEN L,** City Univ Of Ny La Guard Coll, Long Island Cty, NY; SR; AAS; Phi Theta Kappa; Sec Sci; Psych.

**QUINONES, DESIREE M,** Catholic Univ Of Pr, Ponce, PR; JR; BS; Pre-Med Clb 90-; Hons Pgm 89-; Bio; Med.

**QUINONES, JOHN R,** George Mason Univ, Fairfax, VA; SO; BS; French Club Treas 89-; Tau Kappa Epsilon 90-; Pre Busn; Law.

**QUINONES, LUIS A,** Univ Politecnica De Pr, Hato Rey, PR; SO; BEE; Elctrncs; Eng.

**QUINONES, LYMARI,** Inter Amer Univ Pr Hato Rey, Hato Rey, PR; FR.

**QUINONES, MARA I,** Univ Of Pr At Rio Piedras, Rio Piedras, PR; GD; MBA; Italian Cir 85-87; Frnch Cir 86-87; Internatl Amnsty 90-; Pblc Admin Soc 90-; Orphn Hm 87-89; Patricia Robert Harris Flwshp 90-; Vol Trnsltr St Dept 89-; Prmtn Repr Trsm Co 87-; BA 87; Pblc Admin; Law/Internatl Rltns.

**QUINONES, MARCOS A,** Inter Amer Univ Pr Hato Rey, Hato Rey, PR; SR; BS; AAS Univ Of MD 89; Comp Sci; Phd.

**QUINONES, REINALDO PACHECO,** Caribbean Univ, Bayamon, PR; JR; Stdnt Cncl 90-; Bus Admn Clb 90-; Admn; Mgmt.

**QUINONES-DIAZ, MAGDALEN C,** Univ Of Pr At Mayaguez, Mayaguez, PR; JR; BA; Leo Clb; Rotaract Clb; Hnr Rl 89; Bsn Admn/Acctng; CPA.**

**QUINONEZ, MARGARITA,** Fl International Univ, Miami, FL; SR; BS; U S Jaycess 90-; Phi Theta Kappa 86-; Adele Smith Achvmnt Awd; Twns Schlrshp Awd 90; Apparel Mngmnt; Fshn Dsgn.

**QUINTANA, JOANNA,** Saint Thomas Univ, Miami, FL; JR; BA; AA Miami Dade Comm Clg N 90; Educ; Elem Educ.

**QUINTANA, MARY E,** Fl International Univ, Miami, FL; FR; BA; Elem Educ; Tchr/Principal.

**QUINTAS, JOHN CHARLES,** Hahnemann Univ, Philadelphia, PA; JR; MD.

**QUINTAVELLA, SCOTT J,** Bloomfield Coll, Bloomfield, NJ; GD; Stdnt Nwspr Stf Wrtr 89-90; Sigma Phi Epsilon 89-; Intrnshp T V 89-90; Shadow Traffic Ntwrk Assnshp 90; Prfsnl Tutor; BA 90; English/Cmunctns; Brdcst Mgmt.

**QUINTELA, MERCY G,** Fl International Univ, Miami, FL; JR; BS; Chi Alpha Theta Pres 90-; Scl/Cltrl Comm SGA Asst Chrmn 90-; Acctg; Law.

**QUINTER, STEPHANIE A,** S U N Y Coll Of Tech At Alfred, Alfred, NY; FR; AAS; Sci.

**QUINTERO, ELIZABETH R,** Miami Dade Comm Coll South, Miami, FL; SR; BA; Real Est Tax Rep 81-; Ed.

**QUINTERO, LUIS E,** Bayamon Central Univ, Bayamon, PR; SR; BA; Bus Admn Assn; Peroetuo Socorro Chrch 88; Bus Admn.

**QUINTERO, MARIA LUGO,** Univ Of Pr At Rio Piedras, Rio Piedras, PR; SR; BA; AIAS 89-90; Golden Key 88-; Schlstc All Am Awd 88-; Chrstn Yth Soc 84; Highest Grade Avg Dsgn Class 86; Highest Grad Avg Cmps 86; Rector Awd 86; Interior Dsgn Cert Colegio Rgnl Carolina Cmps 86; Mstr Archtctr.

**QUINTI LIANI, ANTHONY C,** Fl International Univ, Miami, FL; JR; BA; Phi Theta Kappa Chrmn Tutrg Comm 88-89; Acdmc Awrd; Sftbl Tm 88-89; AA 90; Scl Stdy Educ.

**QUINTIN, EMILIA P,** Commonwealth Coll, Virginia Beach, VA; BS; Acctg Clb Sec V P 90-; City Assn Sec 89-; Red Crs Clrk; CCD Asst Tchr; Offcrs Wives Clb 89-90; Magna Cum Laude 89; AA Commonwealth Clg 89-; Acctg; MS.

**QUINTON, LORI MAJORS,** Auburn Univ At Auburn, Auburn, AL; GD; MED; Pi Lambda Theta 90-; Phi Kappa Phi 90-; AA Southern Union St Jr Clg 88; BED 90; Elem Educ; Schl Admin.

**QUIRK, KERI,** Wagner Coll, Staten Island, NY; FR; Nrsg; RN.

**QUIRK, STEPHANIE B,** Elms Coll, Chicopee, MA; GD; MAT; BS Syracuse Univ 89; Elem Ed.

**QUIROGA, DAVID,** Embry Riddle Aeronautical Univ, Daytona Beach, FL; SO; BS; Avtn Maint Tech Avncs; Mech Avncs Tech.

**QUISENBERRY, ANNETTE,** Radford Univ, Radford, VA; JR; BS; Foods/Ntrn Clb 90; Va Dietetic Assn; Amer Dietetic Assn; Kappa Omicron Nu; Fds/Ntrtn; Dietetics.

**QUISENBERRY II, RANDALL J,** Ky St Univ, Frankfort, KY; JR; BS; Phi Beta Lambda; Mech Eng.

**QUIST, MARNI L,** Ky Wesleyan Coll, Owensboro, KY; SO; DVM; Sigma Kappa Phlntrpy Chrm 89; Pre Prfsnl Soc Pub Rltns Chrm 90-; Parnassus Soc 89-90; Brown Schlr 89-; Sigma Kappa Phlntrpa Chrmn 89-; Sigma Kappa Schlrshp Awd 90; Brown Schlrshp 89-; Deans Lst 89-; Biology; Vet Med.

**QUITO, ANA Y,** City Univ Of Ny Kingsborough, Brooklyn, NY; SO; BBA; Kingsborough CC Chrstn Clb; Phi Theta Kappa; AAS; Pblc Acctg.

**QURESHI, FARAZ,** Fl International Univ, Miami, FL; FR; BA; Sigma Phi Epsilon Fndrsng Chr 90-; Deans List; IMS; Math; Eng.

**QURESHI, MOHAMMAD M,** Univ Of Rochester, Rochester, NY; SO; BS; Drm Cncl Sec 90-; Mag Assc Ed 90-; Intrntl Univ Ambssdr 90-; Econ; Bus/Fin.

**QURESHI, SEEMA N,** Va Commonwealth Univ, Richmond, VA; FR; BS; Lddrs Scsss; Pkstn Stdnts Assoc; Hnrs Prgm; Blgy; Med.

# R

**RA, YONGSUN,** Univ Of Rochester, Rochester, NY; SO; Neuroscience/Psychlgy; Med Sch.

**RAAB, JOHN B,** Atlantic Comm Coll, Mays Landing, NJ; SO; Dental Lab Tech; Mktg.

**RAAB, JOHN G,** S U N Y Coll Of Tech At Frmgdl, Farmingdale, NY; SO; BA; Flyng Clb 89-90; Alpha Eta Rho Tr 90-; Aerospc Tech; Prof Pilt.

**RABANAL, NATOSHA L,** Wv Univ, Morgantown, WV; SO; Natl Stdnt Nurs Assn 90; Deans Lst.

**RABE, CLIFFORD L,** Northern Ky Univ, Highland Hts, KY; FR; MBA; Englsh; Tchng.

**RABEENANDAN, VIMLA,** City Univ Of Ny City Coll, New York, NY; GD; NY Soc Physician Asst Mmbr 88-; Amrcn Acad Physcian Asstnts; High Achvmnt Awd PA Prgrm 90; Intrnshps Maj Med 89-90; Physician Ssst Crtfd; BSC City Cllg 90; PA Ccny Hrlm DSP PA PROG 90; Science; Medicine.

**RABER, CHRISTOPHER D,** Wilmington Coll, Wilmington, OH; SO; BS; Acrvts Prgmng Bd Movies Chr 90-; Res Hall Assn V P 90-; Hnry Degrees Comm 90-; Tau Kappa Beta Alum Coord 90-; Ldr Schlrshp 89-; Hnr Schlrshp 89-; Sports Med; Phys Thrpy.

**RABER, JENNIFER L,** Wv Univ At Parkersburg, Parkersburg, WV; JR; BBA; PTA Pres; FBLA; Delta Zeta Almna; AAS 89; Acctg.

**RABI, CHRISTINE,** Miami Dade Comm Coll, Miami, FL; JR; BA; Presch Tchr/Afternoon Care Dir Plymouth Pres 87-; AA 87; AS 90; Edn; Elem PE Tchr.

**RABI, MASOODA,** Tn St Univ, Nashville, TN; FR; EE; Star Fillet; Phi Theta Kappa 88; Tau Alpha Pi Secy 89-; AAS Nashville State Technol Inst 90; Sci/Electrncs; Engr.

**RABIA, DANIEL,** City Univ Of Ny Baruch Coll, New York, NY; JR; BBA; Israeli Def Frcs Lt 84-88; Ofcr Chrg Oprtns Mltry Police Corps; Fin.

**RABINOVICH, IRINA,** City Univ Of Ny Baruch Coll, New York, NY; JR; BBA; Acctng Scty; Beta Gamma Sigma; Acctng; CPA MBA Txtn.

**RABINOVITCH, ERICA L,** Lesley Coll, Cambridge, MA; SO; BA; Hillel Brd Treas 90; Hnr Roll 89; Frshmn Yr Stdnt Tchng 89; Soph Stdnt Tchng 90; Mddle Schl Ed/Humnties; Ed.

**RABON, KIMBERLY A,** Univ Of Sc At Columbia, Columbia, SC; FR; BM; Marching Bnd 90; Concert Bnd; Music Educ; Teach Perform.

**RABUS, ALAN L,** Asnuntuck Comm Coll, Enfield, CT; SO; AS; Comp Pgmr 90-; BS Univ CT 81; Comp/Info Syst; Comp Pgmg/Syst Anlys.

**RABUSSEAU, THEODORE J,** Strayer Coll, Washington, DC; GD; MIS; Alpha Chi 90-; Sr Trng Anlyst Cae Lnk Corp 87-; Inf Tech; Eng.

**RACE, JUDITH D,** Adelphi Univ, Garden City, NY; SR; BA; Summa Cum Laude; Hadassah 85-; Coalition Advncmnt Jewish Educ 88-; Art Dir Clb Long Island 90-; Vlg Art Clb Rockville Centre 88-; Art Design; Artist/Graphic Arts.

**RACENIS, LARISA R,** Dowling Coll, Oakdale Li, NY; SR; Green Key 86-88; Alpha Beta Gamma 86-88; AAS Suny Farmingdale 88; Cmptr Inf Syst/D P.

**RACER-HANEY, LINDA S,** Marshall University, Huntington, WV; SR; BBA; Fin; Fin Mgmt/Invstmnts.

**RACETTE, JENNIFER R,** Ky St Univ, Frankfort, KY; SR; Otstndng Sr Awrd; Chld Dev; Scl Wrk Spcl Educ.

**RACH, FRANCIS ED,** Comm Coll Algny Co Algny Cmps, Pittsburgh, PA; SR; Loyl Ordr Of Moose /Belle Vernon Pa Prelate 80-81; AARC 90; Staff Resprtry Thrpst; AS; Resprtry Thrpy.

**RACHE, THOMAS,** Middle Tn St Univ, Murfreesboro, TN; SR; BS; Phlsphy.

**RACHKO, CYNTHIA,** Marywood Coll, Scranton, PA; SO; BA; Dietetics Clb 90-; Pa Stu Dietetic Assoc; Deans Lst; Chrch Serv 87-; Dietetics.

**RACHKO, MARY E,** Georgian Court Coll, Lakewood, NJ; SO; Girl Scout Ldr 86-88; Relgus Educ Tch 86-90; Paraprfsnl Tchr Ade 86; Humanities; Ele Sch Tchr.

**RACIC, MARY A,** Duquesne Univ, Pittsburgh, PA; SR; BS; Intrntnl Bsns Assn Rcrdng Sec 90-; Duquesne Orntatn Stf 90-; Tau Delta Tau Rcrdng Sec 89-90; Bst Actrs 88-89; Bst Fml Vclst 90; MD Dance Marathon 88; Intrntnl Bsns; Mgmnt.

**RACINE, KATHLEEN L,** Castleton St Coll, Castleton, VT; JR; BA; Vrsty Clb 88-; Athltc Awrds Comm 90-; Res Asst 89-90; Deans Lst 90-; Vrsty Soccr 88-; IM Sftbl/Bsktbl/Indr Soccr 88-; Elem Ed; Tch.

**RACINE, TODD M,** Castleton St Coll, Castleton, VT; SR; BA; Dean Lst 89-90; Natl Bus Educ Assn Awrd Mrt; IM 88-; Bsbll 88-; Sccr 88; Bus Educ; Tchr Coach.

**RACINES, AILIEN MARIA,** Miami Dade Comm Coll, Miami, FL; JR; BA; PRSSA; Tlnt Rstr Outstndng Mnrty Comm Coll Grad; Miami Bk Fair Intl Asst Chrprsn 89; Paella 88-90; Help Rvsn Oakland Pk FL Wlcm Hndbk; AA 90; Cmnctns; Pblc Rltns/Psychlgy.

**RACITI, ROSARIA LINDA,** Univ Of Scranton, Scranton, PA; SR; BS; Hlth Admn Club Fndr 90-; Humn Resrce Assoc 89-; Fall Revw Chorus 88-; Telespond Sr Svc 87-; Taylor Nrsng Ctr Admn Intrn 90-; Moses Taylor Hosp Cmnctns Intrn 89-90; Stdnt Assoc Of Amercn Clg Hlth Care Exec 90-; Hlth Admn; Nrsng Hm Admnstrtr.

**RACKI, ELAINE K,** Boston Univ, Boston, MA; SR; BS; APTA 86-89; Phys Thrpst Asstnt Peds Spcl Needs Chldrn 86-89; AS 86; Phys Thrpy.

**RAD, SHALAH B,** Howard Univ, Washington, DC; GD; MSW; Soc Sci Awds; Hosp Wrk Intrn 90-; Grad Assist 90-; BA U Of HI 87; AA U Of HI 89; Soc Wrk; Clncl Thrpy.

**RADANOF, DAVID M,** Univ Of Akron, Akron, OH; SR; BS; Dns Lst; IMS Ftbl Sftbl Bsktbl; Indstrl Mgmt Prchsng; Cnsdrng Law.

**RADANOVICH, MICHAEL A,** Univ Of Akron, Akron, OH; SR; BSEE; Elctrcl Eng.

**RADCLIFF, JENNIFER ELLEN,** Duquesne Univ, Pittsburgh, PA; SR; BA; AMA; TV Shw Assoc Prod; Deans Lst 88-; Phi Sigma Epsilon; Crngie Sci Cntr Intrn; Spkrs Bureau The Crngie Coord 90-; Sls/Mktg.

**RADCLIFFE, DAVID B,** Duquesne Univ, Pittsburgh, PA; FR; BA; Dns Lst; Crim Just; Law Enfrcmnt.

**RADCLIFFE, SHARON L,** Salisbury St Univ, Salisbury, MD; SR; BASW; Soc Wrk Hon Soc; Intrnshp Chld Prtctv Serv Seaford DE 90-; Soc Wrk; Chld Prtctv Serv.

**RADDALGODA, LALITH S,** Anne Arundel Comm Coll, Arnold, MD; FR; AA; Intrntnl Stdnts Clb 90-; Bsn Cmpt Info Systms; Systms Anlyst.

**RADE, ALLISON LYNN,** Le Moyne Coll, Syracuse, NY; SO; BS; Acct Soc 89-; CAN Pblcty 90-; People Action 90-; Le Moyne Sprng/Wntr Olympcs Capt/Pblcty 90; Peopel Actn Tutor Chldrn 90-; Intrnshp Brstl-Myers Squibb 90-; Deans Lst 90; IM Vlybl/Sccr 89-; Acctg; CPA.

**RADE, JUDITH A,** Endicott Coll, Beverly, MA; FR; Shipmts Club 90-; Librl Arts.

**RADECKI, SANDRA C,** Le Moyne Coll, Syracuse, NY; SO; BS; Acctng Scty 89-; Cmmtr Affrs Com 90; Bus Clb 90; Vrsty Sftbl; Acctng; CPA.

**RADELL, ELAINE J,** Indiana Univ Of Pa, Indiana, PA; SR; BS; PSEA 90-; Alpha Phi Omega 88-; Elem Educ; Teacher.

**RADEMACHER, LISSA F,** D Youville Coll, Buffalo, NY; SO; BSN; Nrsg.

**RADEMAKER, RICHARD L,** Univ Of Cin R Walters Coll, Blue Ash, OH; SO; BA; Beta Theta Pi 87-; Engl; Wrtng.

**RADEN, ROBERT W,** Yeshiva Univ, New York, NY; SR; BA; Bio Clb 87-F Chem Clb 87-F Hebrew Hon Soc 89-F Sigma Delta Rho Pre-Med Soc 88-; Tillen Spec Svcs Eldrly; Samuel Belkin Schlr 88-; Bio; Med Dr.

**RADER, BEVERLY A,** Wv Univ At Parkersburg, Parkersburg, WV; SO.

**RADER, JOSEPHINE E,** Hillsborough Comm Coll, Tampa, FL; FR; AA; Sulphur Sprgs Action League Exec Bd 88-90; Save Our Earth Sec/Treas 87-90; Medicine; Schl Of Phrmcy.

**RADER, KARIN A,** Middle Tn St Univ, Murfreesboro, TN; SR; Pre-Vet Soc 90-; Gamma Beta Phi 90-; Kappa Gamma Pi 89-; BA St Marys Clg 90; Pre-Vet Sci; Vet.

**RADER, LYNN D,** Radford Univ, Radford, VA; SO; BGS; Bus; Bus Mgmt.

**RADER, MICHAEL D,** Oh Univ, Athens, OH; JR; BSME; Amer Nclr Soc 89-90; SME; Gldn Key; Achvmnt Acdmy; US Nclr Rgltry Cmmssn Intern 89-90; IM Ftbl Sftbl; Mech Eng.

**RADER, PATRICK N,** Fl International Univ, Miami, FL; JR; BA; Pre Med Soc; Otstndg Acdmc Achvmnt Awrd 88; AA 86; Mgt Info Systms; Med.

**RADER, TERESA M,** Wv Inst Of Tech, Montgomery, WV; FR; BA; Wmn Tech Schlrshp 90-; Cvl Survyr.

**RADESI JR, FELIX J,** Univ Of Rochester, Rochester, NY; Optical Soc 88-90; U Of Rochesters Optical Soc Educ Comm 89-90; Deans Lst 88-90; IM Hcky/Bsktbl/Ftbl 86-90; BS 90; Optics; Eng.

**RADETICH, IVAN,** William Paterson Coll, Wayne, NJ; JR; BA; Humanities Clb; Phi Alpha Theta Treas 90-; Deans List 89-; Hist; Bus.**

**RADFORD, CYNTHIA L,** Radford Univ, Radford, VA; SR; BS; P E Mjrs Clb Treas 88-; Aerobcs Clb 89-; VAPHERD; Bg Bros/Bg Strs 90-; Deans Lst; Asst Vlybl Coach; Vlybl Tm Mgr/Scrkpr; BS; Helth/P E; Educ.

**RADFORD, KAREN M,** Univ Of Sc At Spartanburg, Spartanburg, SC; JR; BA; SNA VP; Mary Black Hosp Schlrshp 88-; Nrsng; Nurse Ansthst.

**RADFORD, KEVIN T,** Savannah Coll Of Art & Design, Savannah, GA; SR; BFA; Photog.

**RADFORD, MYRA E,** Memphis St Univ, Memphis, TN; SR; BA; Vol St Peter Mnr; Fin; Rsk Mngmnt Cnsltnt.

**RADINSKY, MOCHE D,** Yeshiva Univ, New York, NY; SR; BA; Math Clb 88-89; Actry Soc VP 90-; Belkin Schlr 88-; Deans Lst 88-; Math/Physcs; Actrl Sci.

**RADITZ, JOSHUA A,** Coll Of William & Mary, Williamsburg, VA; FR; Hillel; Tns Clb; Cir K; Sqsh.

**RADKA, ALEX J,** Univ Of Southern Ms, Hattiesburg, MS; FR; BS; Phi Eta Sigma 90-; Lamda Sigma 90-; Gamma Beta Phi 90-; Alpha Tan Omega Pres 90-; Deans List 90-; Polymer Science; Polymer Chemistry.**

**RADLE, CATHRYN L,** Cleveland Inst Of Art, Cleveland, OH; FR; BFA; Schl Schrlshp; IM Soccer 90-; Drawing; Art Educ/Artist.

**RADLEY, THERESE M,** George Mason Univ, Fairfax, VA; SO; BA; Stdnt Coalition Agnst Racism 89; Stdnts Envrnmntl Action 90; Circle K 90; Habitat For Hmnty; Appalachian Sprg; Fldwrk/Fairfax Co Dept Hsng/Comm Dev 90; Amer Stds; Socl Chng.

**RADNEY, ANGIE L,** Clayton St Coll, Morrow, GA; SO; BBA; Acctg Clb; Deans List; Bnk Emp Asst Sprvsr Acctg Dept; Acctg; CPA.

**RADOMSKI, KIMBERLY A,** S U N Y Coll At Fredonia, Fredonia, NY; JR; BA; Bsn Clb VP 90-; Bsn Admin/Finance.

**RADOMSKI, WILLIAM C,** Nova Univ, Ft Lauderdale, FL; GD; MBA; BS Admin Westfield State Coll 87; Bus; Fin.

**RADOSTA, LORI L,** Daytona Beach Comm Coll, Daytona Beach, FL; FR; Phtgrphy.

**RADTKE, MICHAEL J,** S U N Y At Buffalo, Buffalo, NY; GD; M; Asstnshp Adaptv Envrnmnt Lab 90-; Prof Phtgrphr 84-87; Freelnc Phtgrphr 87-; BS Rochester Inst Of Tech 83; Arch.

**RADZEWICZ, SANDRA M,** Schenectady County Comm Coll, Schenectady, NY; FR; AS; Bus Admnstrtn.

**RADZWILL, DEBORAH L,** Fl Atlantic Univ, Boca Raton, FL; JR; BA; Phi Theta Kappa 89; Deans Lst Fau; Prsdnts Lst BCC 89; Deans Lst 88-89; Math Tutor 89-90; AA Broward Comm Clg 89; Bsns; Legal.

**RAEBIGER, ANTONIA C,** Rutgers St Un At New Brunswick, New Brunswick, NJ; FR; BA; Video Yrbk Pres; Prog Cncl Flm Cmmttee Vice Chr; Clg Newspapr; Phi Sigma Pi; Gnrl Hnrs Prog; Merit Schlrshp; Engl/Art; Film.

**RAEBURN JR, CRAIG N,** Western New England Coll, Springfield, MA; SR; BSBA; Cupola Staff Yrbk Co Edtr; COPE 87-88; RHA 87-88; Finance.

**RAEDER, BONITA M,** Columbia Greene Comm Coll, Hudson, NY; SO; ASSOC; Bus; Mgmt.

**RAEDY, ROSEMARIE,** Clemson Univ, Clemson, SC; SO; BSN; Med Asst; Nrsng; RN.

**RAEHMANN, JENNIFER C,** Hudson Valley Comm Coll, Troy, NY; SO; Phi Theta Kappa; Pres List 90-; Lgl Secy 86-; Katharine Gibbs Schl 86; Psychlgy.

**RAESHAUN, IRIS,** Wesley Coll, Florence, MS; SO; BA; Chcgo Intrfth Cncl; 4 Yrs Gnntt Co Inc To Earn Cmmnctns Dgree; Cmmnctns; Bcme Jrnlst And Mag Pblshr.

**RAEUBER, CAROL R,** Tri County Tech Coll, Pendleton, SC; SO; AA; Bs Univ Of S FL 81; Computer.

**RAFALSKI, STEPHEN P,** Utica Coll Of Syracuse Univ, Utica, NY; FR; Hnr Sprgm; Blgy; Mdcl Physcn.

**RAFF, DANIEL D,** Wilmington Coll, New Castle, DE; JR; BA; Acctg; Scrts Brkr.

**RAFFA, ROSARIO MARK,** Embry Riddle Aeronautical Univ, Daytona Beach, FL; JR; BS; Stdnt Gvmt Middlesex Comm Coll Stdnt Sntr 87-88; Windsrfng Clb 88-89; Drama Clb Entrtnmnt Comm 89-90; Lambda Chi Alpha Rsk Mgr 89-; Deans Lst; Hnrs; Indr Soccr Middlesex Com Coll 86-88; Cert Embry Riddle Aero Univ 89; Aero Sci; Airline Pilot.

**RAFFALDT, BRENDA C,** Univ Of Sc At Columbia, Columbia, SC; JR; BA; AA 90; Psych; Educ.

**RAFFERTY, CAROLE J,** William Paterson Coll, Wayne, NJ; SR; BA; Schl Nwsppr Stff Wrtr 90; Blmngdle Crnt Bnd VP 84-; Sbrbn Trnds Corr Flm Rvws 90; BA 82; Engl; Msc Hstry.

**RAFFERTY, JOHN Y,** Comm Coll Algny Co Algny Cmps, Pittsburgh, PA; SO; Chem; Chrprctc.

**RAFFERTY, LESLIE M,** Univ Of Ky, Lexington, KY; JR; PHARM; Acad Of Stdnt Pharmst 88-; Alpha Lambda Delta 86-87; Lambda Sigma Treas 86-87; Lances Jr Mens Hon 87-88; Natl Key 90-; Lambda Kappa Sigma Sec 88-; Deans Lst 85-; Pharm Intrn 88-; Pharmacist.

**RAFFERTY, NANCY L,** Univ Of Cincinnati, Cincinnati, OH; JR; BSN; Coll Nrsng Tribunal Class Rep 90-; Nrsng Asst Jewish Hosp 89-; Nrsng; Anesthesia.

**RAFFERTY, PATRICK A,** Christian Brothers Univ, Memphis, TN; SR; BA; Kngts Clmbs 87-; Spnsh Clb 87-89; IM Drm Rep/Tm Cptn 87-90; Echrstc Mnstr; Cannon Staff/Rptr 87-90; Scty Cllgt Jrnlsts 88-; Deans Lst 88-; Magna Cum Laude; Outstdng Clg Stdnt Amer 87-; Pblc Intern Mntl Hlth Assc 90-; Schicks Super Hoop 90; Comm Arts; Advrtsng.

**RAFFERTY, RICK A,** Temple Univ, Philadelphia, PA; JR; BARCH; Phi Sgm Pi Hstrn Elect; Archtctr.

**RAFFIANI, CASSANDRA L,** Columbia Greene Comm Coll, Hudson, NY; FR; Mgr Restaurant 87-90; Sales Reptvt 86-87; Busn.

**RAFIQUI, AISHA,** Allegheny Coll, Meadville, PA; SR; BA; Math Club; Stdnt Fclty Libr Comm; Intl Club; VISA; Stdnt Orient Advsr; BA; Econ; PHD.

**RAFTER, JOHN D,** Oberlin Coll, Oberlin, OH; FR; Intrnshp Wth K Sbrmn U Of Il At Chgo Dept Of Gntcs 90; Oberlin Swmmng Tm 90; Biochem.

**RAFTICE, MICHAEL P,** Univ Of Fl, Gainesville, FL; SR; BA; Gainesville Chamber Orch Bass Sect 89-; Mark Spee Jazz Quintet Bassist; Richard Dickson Dinner Theater Bassist; Madison Street Sch Ocala Fl Music Intern; Bronson Middle H Sch Bronson Fl Music Intern; Music Ed; Tchng.

**RAGANO, CHRIS E,** Tallahassee Comm Coll, Tallahassee, FL; JR; BS; Dive Clb 90-; AA FL State Univ 90-; Ecnmcs; Law.

**RAGAULT, GUY G,** Merrimack Coll, North Andover, MA; SO; BSC; Class Pr 88; Yrbk Cnsl 88; Prom Cnsl 88; Hockey East All Acad Tm 90; Quebecs Midget AAA Hockey Lg 89; Var Hockey 89-; Elec Engr.

**RAGGHIANTI, JEFFREY W,** Limestone Coll, Gaffney, SC; JR; US Navy Offcr; Accntng; Naval Offcr.

**RAGGS, KATRINA M,** Alcorn St Univ, Lorman, MS; JR; BA; Cmnctns Club; Yrbk Stf; Deans List; Natl Hon Soc; Collgt All Amercn; Ladies Auxlry For Vetrns Of Frgn Wars; Cmnctns/Publc Rltns; Publc Rltns Rep.

**RAGIAB, ALI T,** Al A & M Univ, Normal, AL; JR; BS; MSA 90-; ISNA 88-; MAYA 89-; Electrncs; Engr.

**RAGLAND, KEVIN D,** Middle Tn St Univ, Murfreesboro, TN; FR; BS; SGA Frshmn Sntr 90-; Agrcltr Cncl Rep 90-; Agrcltr; Tchr Gen Unvrsty.

**RAGOLIA JR, SALVATORE,** City Univ Of Ny Baruch Coll, New York, NY; SR; BA; Deans Lst 90-; Bmtrc Ntern; Clncl Psychlgy.

**RAGONE, ARTHUR P,** Manhattan Coll, Bronx, NY; SR; ASCE; Chi Epsilon; BE CE.

**RAGOOBARSINGH, NYLA R,** Morgan St Univ, Baltimore, MD; SO; BSC; ACS Mbr 89-; Promethean Kappa Tau 89-; Phi Eta Sigma 89-; Alpha Lambda Delta 89-; Chem; PHD Toxicology.

**RAGOONANAN, NATHASHA A,** Miami Dade Comm Coll North, Miami, FL; SO; BA; Tlnt Stdo 90-; Rprtry Dnc Thtr 89-; Chrgrphr/Dncr; Phi Theta Kappa 89-; Glbl Cprtn Fr Bttr Wrld UN; AA 89; Crtfct Fr Otstndng Acdmc Achvmnt; Bsnss; Fnnc.

**RAGSDALE, PAMELA A,** Univ Of Southern Ms, Hattiesburg, MS; JR; BS; Yrbk; Zeta Phi Beta 90-; Order Of Omega; Mol Biology; Rsrch.

**RAHAL, FADI E,** Hudson Valley Comm Coll, Troy, NY; SR; BA; Intrntnl Clb Prsdnt 89-; Engnrng Assn VP; Phi Theta Kappa Tres; Tutor; GPA Plaque; Engnrng Science; Mechanical Engnr.

**RAHAMAN, SHARON,** Saint Thomas Univ, Miami, FL; FR; BA; Math; Tchng.

**RAHAMUT-ALI, CAMILLE L,** Saint Thomas Univ, Miami, FL; SO; Intl Stdnt Orgztn; Pre Med Clb PRO; Cir K Intl; Tennis Tmf; Biology; Optometrist/Optician.**

**RAHAMUT-ALI JR, CLIVE LAUREL,** Saint Thomas Univ, Miami, FL; JR; BA; Intrntl Stdnt Org Treas 90-; Pre Med 90-; Sccr Clb 90-; Deans Lst 89-90; Bio; Vet Med.

**RAHGOZAR, MOHAMAD,** Bunker Hill Comm Coll, Boston, MA; FR; Intl Org 90; Iranian Educ Assoc 89; Med Asst Army Mash Unit Iran/Iraq Ward 85-87; Blue Ribbon Awrd 87; Med Rdlgy; Bio Med Engr.

**RAHMAN, AFM S,** City Univ Of Ny La Guard Coll, Long Island Cty, NY; SO; AAS; B Com Dhaka Univ Bangladesh 80; Nrsng; RN.

**RAHMAN, SEEMA,** S U N Y Coll At Fredonia, Fredonia, NY; SR; MBA; Dorm Cncl Pres 87-89; Intl Cltrl Asc Treas 87-88; Jdcl Brd Chrp 89-; Res Asst VP 88-; Tutor Lrng Ctr 89-90; Grls Otrch Awd Rcrtr 87; BS Comm; Law.

**RAHMAN, SHARIF M,** Oh Wesleyan Univ, Delaware, OH; SO; Scty Physcs Stdnts 89-; Assoc Comp Mchnry 90-; Univ Flm Srs 89-; Sigma Pi Sigma; Pi Mu Epsilon; Phi Eta Sigma 90; Flrnc Ls Award 89-; Physcs.

**RAHMING, JASON D,** Morehouse Coll, Atlanta, GA; SO; BSC; Intl Stdnt Org 89-; Asst; Trck Tm 90; Comp Sci; Anlyst.

**RAHN, PATSY A,** Atlantic Comm Coll, Mays Landing, NJ; SO; BA; Frshmn Clb Sec 89-90; SGA Rep 89-90; Psych.

**RAHR JR, CARL H,** S U N Y Coll Of Tech At Alfred, Alfred, NY; SR; BS; Outstndg Grad 90-; AAS; Cmptr Sci.

**RAI, SANJIV,** Old Dominion Univ, Norfolk, VA; SR; BSEET; Dns Lst; Vehicle Electr Singapore Armed Forces 87-89; Tech Dipl NGEE Ann Polytech 84-87; Elctrcl Engr Tech; Mgmt.

**RAICHE, LISA M,** Western New England Coll, Springfield, MA; SO; BA; Comm Prgmng/Entrtnmnt Treas 89-; Alpha Lambda Delta 89-; Ambssdr; Bsn; Accntg.

**RAIF, LISA A,** Ms Gulf Coast Comm Coll, Perkinston, MS; FR; BFA; Hons Pgm 90-; Bnd 90; Studio Art.

**RAIFORD, ALJUAN J,** Morehouse Coll, Atlanta, GA; JR; BA; Orgnztn Afrcn Amrcn Cnscns 88-; Kemet Frtnrty 90-; Mass Cmmnctns; Film Mkng.

**RAIFORD, GRACE ELIZABETH,** Peace Coll, Raleigh, NC; FR; AA; Drama Clb 90-; Delta Sigma Mu; Liberal Arts; Broadcst Jrnlsm.

**RAIFORD JR, JAMES B,** Univ Of Al At Birmingham, Birmingham, AL; SO; SOTA 89-90; Hlth Rel Prof Assoc 89-90; Pres Lst 89-90; O T Cert 90; AS John Calhoun Comm Clg 90; AAS John Calhoun Comm Clg 89; Occup Thrpy Asst.**

**RAIFORD, LISA R,** Univ Of Sc At Aiken, Aiken, SC; FR; BSN; Afro Amer Students Alliance; Wmns Missionary Cir VP; Nursing; RN.

**RAILEY, FRANCES R,** Central Al Comm Coll, Alexander City, AL; JR; BA; Phi Theta Kappa; AS 90; Hstry; Hstrcl Rcrds For St.

**RAILEY, RENE H,** Nc Agri & Tech St Univ, Greensboro, NC; SR; BSE; Tau Beta Pi; G E Mbl Cmmnctns Coop; Snyder Schlrshp; AAS Forsyth Comm Clg 88; Elctrcl Engnrng; Engnrng.

**RAILEY, SHERRY L,** Western Carolina Univ, Cullowhee, NC; FR; BED; Wstrn Gld 90-; Last Minute Prod 90-; Std Cncl Excptnl Chldrn 90-; Alpha Lambda Delta 90-; Spec Ed; Tchng.

**RAIMO, DAVID V,** Hudson Valley Comm Coll, Troy, NY; JR; BA; OCS USMC 90; AA 90; Cert OCS USMC 90; Sociology; USMC Aviator.

**RAIMUNDO, TRIO MARTINEZ,** Univ Politecnica De Pr, Hato Rey, PR; BS; Eng; Mech Eng.**

**RAIN, MELISSA M,** Endicott Coll, Beverly, MA; FR; AD; Ski Clb 90-; Cmrcl Art; Artst.

**RAINBOLT, DAWN E,** Spalding Univ, Louisville, KY; SO; BSN; Deans List 89-; Army Reservist Retired Pv-2 87-; Cert Ivy Tech 88; Nursing; ER Nurse/Practitioner.

**RAINE, MEREDITH E,** Wv Univ, Morgantown, WV; FR; Smmr Intrnshp Estrn Amer Enrgy Corp Chrlstn WV 25304; Jrnlsm; Wrter/Editor.

**RAINER, ANGELIA J,** Itawamba Comm Coll, Fulton, MS; FR; CRTT; Respiratory Thrpy.

**RAINES, CYNTHIA M,** Dyersburg St Comm Coll, Dyersburg, TN; JR; BED; Phi Theta Kappa 90-; Luth Womens Mssnry League VP 87-; Deans List 90-; DSCC Hmcmng Fres Maid 77; BS Erly Chldhd Educ/Psych BS; Teach/Cnslng.

**RAINES, DANNY L,** Kent St Univ Stark Cmps, North Canton, OH; SO; BA; Cov Singls Felwshp Pr 87-90; Hon Disch U S Army 83-86; Empl Prices Cont 86-; Indstrl Mgmt.

**RAINES, DEBORAH L,** Memphis St Univ, Memphis, TN; SR; BED; Stdnt Cncl Excptnl Chldrn 90-; Srch Chrstn Matrty Codir 87-88; Goldn Key 90-; St Ann Yng Adlts 89; Lamda Chi Alpha Crscnt 90; Spec Olympcs/Ftnss Clb; Cert Bsktbl Coach 90-; Deans Lst 89-; Spec Ed.

**RAINES, JOAN M,** Middle Tn St Univ, Murfreesboro, TN; SR; BS; Math Org 89-; Tau Omicron Treas 89-; Phi Theta Kappa Treas 87-89; Gamma Beta Phi 90; Pi Mu Epsilon 90-; Kathryn Chamber Hay Awrd; Natl Clg Math Awrd 90-; Math.

**RAINES, LATONIA R,** Spelman Coll, Atlanta, GA; SO; BS; Chemistry Club V Pres; Michigan Club; Alpha Lamda Delta; Natl Soc Black Engineers; Intern Dow Chem Co; Maxwell House Scholar 89-; Outstanding Award 90; Biochemistry/Chem Engrng.**

**RAINES, LORRIE A,** Univ Of Sc At Spartanburg, Spartanburg, SC; FR; BA; Psych Clb; Chrldr; Cmptr Clb; Psychology; Psycho Analyst.

**RAINES, NANCY M,** Univ Of Sc At Columbia, Columbia, SC; FR; Bus Mgmt.

**RAINES, ROSHAN P,** Univ Of Al At Huntsville, Huntsville, AL; JR; BS; Natl Soc Blck Engrs Secr 88-; Chrstn Stdnt Org 90-; Blsk Stdnt Assoc 90-; Minority Engr Schlrshp Pgm 88-90; SMART Pgm Univ CO Boulder; Martin Luther King Jr Essay Contest; Mech Engr; Engr Consultant.

**RAINES, SUSAN E,** Western Carolina Univ, Cullowhee, NC; JR; BSW; Debate Tm Pres/Capt 89-90; Scl Wrk Clb 89-90; Scl Wrk; Chld Wlfare/Prison Reform/Gerentlgy.**

**RAINES-ROBINSON, ROSARIO,** Savannah St Coll, Savannah, GA; JR; BA; Newtonian Soc; Comp Sci Clb; Blck Chrstn Flwshp; Math; Law.

**RAINEY, JEANNETTE R,** Christopher Newport Coll, Newport News, VA; JR; BS; Lw Clb 90-; Msc Clb 89; Govt Admin; Law.

**RAINEY, JOHN DWIGHT,** Univ Of Sc At Spartanburg, Spartanburg, SC; SR; BS; Comp Club 90-; Gamma Beta Phi 0-; Piedmont Soc 90-; Deans List 89-; Comp Sci.

**RAINEY, LISA D,** Queens Coll, Charlotte, NC; SO; Soph Sec/Treas 90-; Stdnts For Blck Awrnss Sec 90-; Stdnt Admiss Core 90-; Dana Schlr 90-; Oustndng Minority Schlr 89-; Alpha Kappa; Org Against Soc Injustices/Suffering; Elem Educ; Tchng.

**RAINEY, MARY E,** Coll Of Charleston, Charleston, SC; SO; BA; Hstry Clb 89-; Pltcl Science Clb 89-; Intrntl Studies Clb 90-; Wesley Fndtn 90-; Pltcl Science/Hstry; Intelligence Serv.**

**RAINEY, MICHAEL O,** Central Fl Comm Coll, Ocala, FL; FR; Math; Engrng.

**RAINEY, PERRY C,** City Univ Of Ny Baruch Coll, New York, NY; GD; BA; Omega Psi Phi V Basileus 90-; NAACP Yth Cncl 88-90; Baruch Clg Schlrhsp 86-90; NY State Rgnts Schlrshp 86-90; Omega Psi Phi Frat Schlrshp 90; Actrl Sci; Actrl Cnsltnt.

**RAINEY, SHARON D,** Al St Univ, Montgomery, AL; SO; BA; Cmptr Infrmtn Systm; Prgrmmr.

**RAINEY, WILLIAM D,** Univ Of Tn At Martin, Martin, TN; FR; BS; Bnd Schlrshp; Mrchng Bnd/Symp Bnd; Acctng; CPA.

**RAINGE, STELLA LOUISE,** Bryant Stratton Bus Inst Roch, Rochester, NY; AOS; Bus Mgmt Clb V P 90-; Bus Mgmt Clb Pres 90-; Spec Olympc Hndcpd Vol 90; Mem Chldrn Fund Vol 90; Cert Deans Lst 90; Bus Mgmt.

**RAINS, KIMBERLY R,** Univ Of Tn At Martin, Martin, TN; SO; BED; Sigma Tau Delta 90; All Amercn Schlr; Swim Team 90; Engl; Tchr.

**RAINSBURG, MONICA M,** Univ Of South Fl, Tampa, FL; FR; Sigma Phi Epsilon Ltl Sis 90-; Pell Grants.

**RAINWATER JR, DAVID BRUCE,** Ms St Univ, Miss State, MS; JR; BA; Prfssnl Glf Mgmt Clb Pres 89-; Prfssnl Glf Mgmt Mrktng; Glf Prfssnl.

**RAISHE, JENNA S,** Fl St Univ, Tallahassee, FL; FR; BA; Alpha Retreat; Phi Eta Sigma 90-; Florida Acad Schlr 90-; Psychlgy; Clin Psychlgst.

**RAITZ, KRISTIN MARIE,** Bowling Green St Univ, Bowling Green, OH; JR; BA; Visual Cmnctn Tech Org Sec 90-; TVAS Land Between The Lakes Photo; Cedar Point Amusement Park Photo 90; Visual Cmnctn Tech; Photo.

**RAJ, VIMALA,** City Univ Of Ny Queensbrough, New York, NY; SR; BA; IN Rlwys Aus Pres 69; Tchr 72-83; Bnk 84-89; BA Ut Unv India 69; Accntng; Cpa.

**RAJA, JAMIL M,** Strayer Coll, Washington, DC; SO; BSCS; DPMA; Alpha Chi; BA/EC Univ Of Karachi 86; DPCS Strayer Coll; Computers/Econ; Mgmt Info Syst.

**RAJACIC, JEANE,** Wagner Coll, Staten Island, NY; SO; BS; APA; Psy Clb; Asst State Isl Univ Hosp; Dns Lst 89-; IM Sftbl; Frsnc Psy.

**RAJACK, CAROLINE J,** Fl International Univ, Miami, FL; FR; BS; Intrntl Clb 90; Physcl Thrpy.

**RAJAGOPALAN, POORNA,** Gallaudet Univ, Washington, DC; SO; Stdnt Bdy Govt Asst Dir Of Soc Affr 89; Plys Trng Grp 90; Trck Tm Mgr 90; Ntl Collegiate Mnrty Ldrshp Awd; Intrntl Stdnt Advsry Brd; Trck Tm 90; Best Spprtng Actress Awd 90; Ed/Theater Arts; Ed Admin.

**RAJAH, COLIN,** Duquesne Univ, Pittsburgh, PA; JR; BA; Cmpus Mnstry Sacristan 89-; Intl Stdnts Orgztn 89-; Vol 90-; Allegheny Cty Jail 89-; Deans Lst Hon 89-90; Soc/Pltcl Sci; Admn.

**RAJAN, RALLIS M,** Columbia Union Coll, Takoma Park, MD; FR; BA; Phi Eta Sigma 90-; Vstng Nrsng Hms 90-; Rsng Fnds 90; Amer Lng Assn Schlrshp 90; MD St Schlrshp 90; Rsprtry Thrpy Pre Med; MD.

**RAJAR, HARRY,** Coll Of Aeronautics, Flushing, NY; SO; AAS; Magna Cum Laude 91; Pres Lst 89-90; Dns Lst 90; AOS; Avtn Maint; Maint Tech.

**RAJNIK, SUSAN,** Mt Saint Marys Coll & Seminary, Emmitsburg, MD; FR; BA; Phi Beta Delta; Pep Bnd; Grg Hnry Mls Hnr Scty; Hnrs Prgm; CRC Achvmnt Awrd; Bio Chmstry.

**RAJOO, SHARI K,** Univ Of Southern Ms, Hattiesburg, MS; JR; BS; Alpha Epsilon Delta; Acad Exec Awd 89-; Fred J Walker Schlrshp; Nicrobiology/Biology; Med.

**RAKER, DAVID A,** Fl International Univ, Miami, FL; GD; MS; FL Pblc Intrst Rsrch Grove 87-89; Amnsty 90-; Kappa Alpha 86-; Tchr Wrld Hist 90-; BS Union Clg 82-86; Educ/Scndry Soc Stds; Tchr/Crclm Dvlpr.

**RAKES, BERNARD R,** Averett Coll, Danville, VA; GD; BS; Envrnmntl Eng 90-; AAS; Hmn Rsrcs Mgmt; Mgmt.

**RAKES, GREGORY D,** Patrick Henry Comm Coll, Martinsville, VA; FR; BA; SGA Sen 90-; ECCO Co Fndr Chrmn 90-; Otstndng Frshmn Sen 90-; USAA Stdnt Govt Awrd800 Rsrch Grnt VA Campus Outreach Opportunity League; Pltcl Sci Blgy; Envrnmntl Law.

**RAKESTRAW, JANET L,** Univ Of Ga, Athens, GA; JR; BED; Kappa Delta Pi; AA Gordon Coll 90; Ed; Tch.

**RAKESTRAW, TINA R,** Blue Mountain Coll, Blue Mountain, MS; SO; BS; Cmmtr Clb 90-; MAESP 90-; Modenian Soc 90-; Sec NY Life Ins Notary Publ State MS 89-90; Elem Edn; Teach.

**RAKITA, STEVEN S,** Univ Of South Fl, Tampa, FL; FR; BS; Sigma Tau Gamma; Bio; Med.

**RALEIGH, EDWARD L,** Univ Of Sc At Columbia, Columbia, SC; FR; BA; Model UN Com Chair 90-; Emerging Ldr Pgm; Chem; Intl Envrmntl Affairs.

**RALEIGH, KELLY J,** Kent St Univ Kent Cmps, Kent, OH; SO; BS; Biolgy/Chmstry; Med Tchnlgy.

**RALEY, MARLA A,** Univ Of South Al, Mobile, AL; JR; BS; Newman Clb Sec 89-90; Share Tm 89-; SHRM 90-; Phi Eta Sigma 89-; Phi Chi Theta VP/TREAS 89-; Natl Deans Lst 89-90; Deans Hon Lst 90; Pres Schlrs; Bus; Personnel/Indstrl Rel.

**RALEY JR, ROBERT C,** Pellissippi St Tech Comm Coll, Knoxville, TN; FR; BS; Sci Clb 87-88; Spnsh Clb 87-88; Cvl Eng.

**RALL, LAURA D,** Oh St Univ At Marion, Marion, OH; JR; BA; Dntl Asst; Elem Educ; Educ/Tchr.

**RALPH, THERESA A,** Owensboro Jr Coll Of Bus, Owensboro, KY; SO; AS; Pres Lst 90-; Bsns; Acctg.

**RALPH, WENDY R,** Hilbert Coll, Hamburg, NY; SO; Phi Beta Lambda Hstrn 90-; Paralegal Clb 90-; Hnrs Lst 90-; W NY Paralegal Assoc; Attny Gen Intern; Law; Paralegal.

**RALSTON, MARC A,** S U N Y Coll Of Tech At Alfred, Alfred, NY; FR; AS; Natl Voc Tech Hon Soc 90-; Deans Lst 90-; Sigma Tau Epsilon 90-; V Lockwood Mem Schlrshp Awd 90-; AS Comm Clg Finger Lakes 88; Drftng/CAD.

**RALSTON, MICHELLE ELIZABETH,** Univ Of Sc At Columbia, Columbia, SC; SO; BFA; Schlrshp Vlybll; Art; Tch.**

**RAMACH, JENNIFER B,** Univ Of Miami, Coral Gables, FL; FR; BS; Amnesty Intl 90-; Habitat For Humanity 90-; Earth Alert 90-; Alpha Lambda Delta; Deans List 90; Jrnlsm.

**RAMADAN, BASMA F,** Wagner Coll, Staten Island, NY; JR; BA; Psych Clb VP 89-; Psych/Ed Dept Stdnt Asst 89-; Mag Cvr Dsgnr 89-; Psi Chi Ntl VP 89-; Omicron Delta Kappa; Althea; Deans Lst 88-90; Psych Mjr Lit Mnr.

**RAMAGE, ANDREA S,** Univ Of Ky, Lexington, KY; SR; BA; Bptst Stdnt Un Exctv Cncl Smmr Mssns Chmn 89-90; Bptst Stdnt Un Grtr Cncl 87-89; Alpha Lambda Delta Sec 88-89; Epsilon Delta 89-; Phi Alpha Theta 90-; Vldctrn Schlrshp 87-88; Deans Lst 87-; Scl Stds Edctn; Clg Hstry Prfsr.

**RAMAKRISHNAN, MEENAKSHI,** Yale Univ, New Haven, CT; FR; BA; Instrmntl Cnnctn 90-; Yale New Haven Hosp Vol 90-; Biology.

**RAMAL, CYNTHIA L,** Barry Univ, Miami, FL; JR; BS; Econ Clb VP 89-; Assn Coll Entrprnrs; Delta Mu Delta Pres 90-; Goldn Z 90-; Deans Lst/Pres Lst 88-; Outstndng Jr; Bus; Mgmt.

**RAMANI, JAYSHREE D,** Lesley Coll, Cambridge, MA; FR; BS; LIIF 90-F Emerald Key 90-; AHANA 90-; Scl Sci/Elem Ed.

**RAMANJULU, JOSHI M,** Villanova Univ, Villanova, PA; SR; PHD; Amer Inst Of Chemists 90-; BS; Chemistry; Rsrch.

**RAMATOWSKI, PATRICIA L,** Univ Of Ga, Athens, GA; SR; BSED; Encore 88; Dns Lst 90-; Alpha Chi Omega Soc Chr 89; Stdnt Tchr Intern; Erly Chldhd Educ; Tchr.

**RAMBLER, CHRISTIAN A,** Kent St Univ Kent Cmps, Kent, OH; SO; Rgby Clb Pres 90-; Bus.

**RAMBO, JANIE R,** Univ Of Nc At Greensboro, Greensboro, NC; SR; BSN; Nrs Chrstn Flwshp 90-; Unv Mrshls 89-; Sigma Theta Tau; BS Med Unv SC 80; BA Elon Clg 81; Nrs; Med/Srgcl Nrs.

**RAMBO, JOHN C,** East Tn St Univ, Johnson City, TN; SR; BS; Stdnt Govt Stdnt Jdg 89-; Clg Rpblcns Chrmn 88-; Phi Kappa Phi; Omcrn Dlt Kappa 90-; Ec/Pol Sci; Law.

**RAMCHANDANI, NARESH K,** Fl International Univ, Miami, FL; FR; BA; Amer Mrktg Assoc 90-; Educ; Elem Ed.

**RAMES, CLIFFORD N,** Univ Of Nh Plymouth St Coll, Plymouth, NH; SR; BA; Intl Assoc Pres 89-; Radio DJ 88; Newspaper Photo Ed 88-89; Tutor; Clarice Parker Mem Bk Awd; IM Soccer 90-; AAS Brookdale Cmnty Clg 85; Engl/Wrtg; Author.

**RAMEY, DONALD G,** Univ Of Va Clinch Valley Coll, Wise, VA; SR; BS; Im MVP 90-; AS Lees Mc Rae Clg 89; BS; Psychlgy/Soclgy; US Army.

**RAMEY, MICHAEL T,** Va Commonwealth Univ, Richmond, VA; SO; BA; Inter Vrsty Chrstn Flwshp Bible Stdy Ldr 90-; Colonial Hts Bapt Chrch Sanc Orchstra 88-; Msc Educ; Mnstr.

**RAMEY, SUSAN A,** Ashland Comm Coll, Ashland, KY; SO; Elem Ed; Tchng.

**RAMEY, WILLIAM T,** Bristol Univ, Bristol, TN; MBA; Licensed Prfsnl Engr; Commonwealth Of VA; Dist Constrn Engr VA Dept Transp; BSCE WV Univ 64; Mgmnt; Engrng.

**RAMEZANIAN, MITRA,** Youngstown St Univ, Youngstown, OH; SO; BSIE; Amer Inst Ind Eng 90; Ind Eng.

**RAMHOFF, LORRAINE A,** Bethany Coll, Bethany, WV; SO; BS; Am Chem Soc 90-; Beta Beta Beta; Varsity Vlybl 90; Chem.

**RAMIREZ LUGO, ANGEL L,** Univ Of Pr At Mayaguez, Mayaguez, PR; JR; BA; Stdnt Cncl/Fclty Arts/Sci 89-; AEPSIC 88-; EPSOA 90-; Psychology; Phd/Scl Psych.**

**RAMIREZ MIRANDA, EDUARDO A,** Univ Politecnica De Pr, Hato Rey, PR; SR; Inst Of Indstrl Eng; Eng Sci; Indstrl Eng.

**RAMIREZ VILELA, JOSE E,** Bayamon Central Univ, Bayamon, PR; SR; BA; Nghbrhd Scrty Clb Plc 90-; Mmbr Hmnts Scty 87-; Lns Clb 86-; Mmbr Pntfcl Mssns 88-; Ftbll Assoc 89-; BED Phlsphy 86; Phlsphy.

**RAMIREZ, ALEJANDRA J,** Univ Of Miami, Coral Gables, FL; SO; MBA; LASA 89-; CCO 89-; Hnr Std 89-; H King Stanford Schlrshp Awd 89-; Finc/Bus Admnstrtn.

**RAMIREZ, ANA M,** Univ Of Sc At Columbia, Columbia, SC; JR; MBA; Am Mrktng Assn 89-90; Natl Stdnt Exch 89-90; BA Univ Of Puerto Rico; Bus Admn-Mrktng; Law.

**RAMIREZ, BRENDA L,** Univ Of Pr At Rio Piedras, Rio Piedras, PR; SR; BBA; Acctg Stdnts Assn Stf Mbr 90-; Golden Key 89-; All Amer Schlr Awd 89-90; Acctg; Juris Doctor.

**RAMIREZ, ELENA M,** Fl International Univ, Miami, FL; JR; BA; AA Miami Dade Comm Coll 90; Spec Educ/Mntl Rtrdtn.

**RAMIREZ, FRANCISCO V,** Tallahassee Comm Coll, Tallahassee, FL; SO; AA; Phi Theta Kappa V P; Wel Bck Leg Spec Fntcn Coord; Pre Med.

**RAMIREZ, HIRAM A,** Univ Of Pr At Rio Piedras, Rio Piedras, PR; JR; BA; Golden Key; 2nd Prze 23rd Engl Litrcy Cntst 89; Fllw Mnrty Smmr Rsrch Prog; Pol Sci; Law.

**RAMIREZ, JESUS GREGORIO TORRES,** Inter Amer Univ Pr Hato Rey, Hato Rey, PR; SO; BA; Hrt Assoc 88; Msclr Dstrphy 89; Suma Cum Laude; Assoc Dgr; Vrs Hnrs Prfssnl Cvl Lbr; TV Prdcr Tlvsn Std Schl RCA 83; Mrktng; Law.

**RAMIREZ, JOANN C,** Nova Univ, Ft Lauderdale, FL; GD; MBA; Bsn.

**RAMIREZ, JOSE R,** Inter Amer Univ Pr Hato Rey, Hato Rey, PR; SO; Biology; Vet.

**RAMIREZ, MARITZA,** Univ Of Pr At Mayaguez, Mayaguez, PR; JR; MS; Comp Eng Stdnts Assn VP 90-; Mrchng Bnd 88; Tau Beta Phi 90-; Schl Of Eng Hrn Chrt; IEEE 90-; ACM 90-; Comp Eng; Eng.

**RAMIREZ, MICHELLE K,** S U N Y Coll Of Tech At Frmgdl, Farmingdale, NY; GD; AAS; Dntl Hygn.

**RAMIREZ, ROLANDO A,** Bloomfield Coll, Bloomfield, NJ; FR.

**RAMIREZ, RONNY O,** Miami Dade Comm Coll South, Miami, FL; SO; RPH; SICA; Eckerd Drugs 88-; Pharm Tech Intern; AA Pharmacy; Chem Biology; Pharmacy.

**RAMIREZ, TERESA C,** Inter Amer Univ Pr Hato Rey, Hato Rey, PR; Prnctn Univ Glee Clb Pblcty Mngr 87-90; Accion Prtrrqna Amigos VP 86-90; IMHOTEP Mnrty Pre-Med Soc 87-89; Gspl Choir 87; Gamma Kappa Alpha; Prnctn Medcl Cntr 88-90; Stdnt Vol Cncl 86-87; Assn Jovenes Torrimar Chrch Grp; Lang Frnch/Itln; Med.

**RAMIREZ, WANDA J,** Inter Amer Univ Pr San German, San German, PR; SR; BA; Stdnt Assn Spec Educ V P 90; Bilingual English Span Orgztn Sec 89; Dep Awd Acad Exclnc Ldrshp Coop; Spec Educ; Tchr.**

**RAMIREZ-GARNICA, GABRIELA,** Fl International Univ, Miami, FL; GD; MPH; Pub He Stdnt Almni Assc; Amer Pub Hlth Assoc; Fla Pub Hlth Assoc; French Clb Nwstr Edtr; Mex Cntrl Amer Clb V P; Latin Amer Clb Pres; BA French 88; BS Lbrl Arts 88; Trnsltn Cert 87; Pub Hlth Epidemiology.

**RAMIREZ-RIVERA, ELIZABETH,** Inter Amer Univ Pr Hato Rey, Hato Rey, PR; SR; BA; Certif Aux Nrsg Southern Prfsnl/Tech Clg Inc Yauco PR 80; Mgmt.

**RAMIREZ-RODRIGUEZ, ARLENE I,** Univ Of Pr At Mayaguez, Mayaguez, PR; JR; BA; Beta Beta Beta 89-; Hnr Rll 89; Dns Lst 90; Marine Blgy.**

**RAMIS, LUISA M,** Saint Thomas Univ, Miami, FL; SR; BA; Ph D Havanna Univ Cuba 59; Spanish; Education.

**RAMJISINGH, SASE R,** City Univ Of Ny City Coll, New York, NY; JR; BA; Guyanese Clb 88; Eta Kappa Nu; Electrical Eng.

**RAMJOHN, STEPHANIE I,** Wilberforce Univ, Wilberforce, OH; FR; BA; Choir 90-; Gospel Choir 90-; Ambsdr 90-; Deans Lst 90-; Wrk Stdy Awd 90-; Pol Sci; Law.

**RAMLOW, SUSAN P,** Univ Of Sc At Columbia, Columbia, SC; SO; Entrtnmnt Editor Nwspr; Gamma Beta Phi 90-; AA; Bus Admin; Acctnt.

**RAMMEL, RICHARD D,** Univ Of New England, Biddeford, ME; SR; BS; Phys Thrpy Clb Pres 89-; Otstng Stu 90-; Bsktbl Coach 89-; Amer Phys Thrpy Assn 89-; Phys Thrpy Aide; BS Auburn Univ 84; Phys Thrpy.

**RAMMINGER, NATASCHA M,** De St Coll, Dover, DE; SO; BA; DE Regnl Ballet Co 79-; Ed; Early Chldhd Ed.**

**RAMNARAYAN, ANITA,** City Univ Of Ny Queensbrough, New York, NY; SO; AA; Alfa Beta Gamma 90-; Acctg; Acctnt.

**RAMOS BONILLA, LUIS A,** Univ Of Pr At Mayaguez, Mayaguez, PR; SO; BED; Sci; Math; Eng.

**RAMOS CASANOVA, AIXA,** Inter Amer Univ Pr Fajardo, Fajardo, PR; FR; BA; Hnr Roll Prgrm 90-; Sec Mssnry Dptmnt Chrch; Elem; Tchng.**

**RAMOS CUBERO, WANDA,** Univ Of Pr At Rio Piedras, Rio Piedras, PR; JR; Golden Key; Educ; Bio.

**RAMOS LOPEZ, MARIA DE L,** Inter Amer Univ Pr Aquadilla, Aguadilla, PR; JR; BA; Ftr Ldrs Bsns America 86-89; Scrtrl Sci.

**RAMOS MARZAN, NORA I,** Bayamon Central Univ, Bayamon, PR; SR; Mkgt; Cmmnctns.

**RAMOS MEDINA, IDSA,** Univ Of Pr At Rio Piedras, Rio Piedras, PR; JR; BA; Acctg Stdnts Assn P R Chptr 90-; Gldn Key 90-; All Amer Schlr Coll Awd 90-; Acctg.

**RAMOS MENDEZ, NEREIDA,** Inter Amer Univ Pr Aquadilla, Aguadilla, PR; SR; BA; Univ Assn Sec Sci Stu 88-; Yng Ppl Chrst Pres 87-90; Mncplty Asst 87-; Sec Sci; Bus Educ/MS.

**RAMOS MORALES, RAFAEL,** Inter Amer Univ Pr Aquadilla, Aguadilla, PR; SR; BS; By Scts Amrc Sctmstr 87-88; AUSA 88-89; Comp Prgrmmng.

**RAMOS NEGRON, RAFAEL LUIS,** Inter Amer Univ Pr San German, San German, PR; FR; MBA; Psych Assoc; Phi Eta Mu; Leo Clb; Acacia Frat Grd Ldg 88; Bsbl; Bus Admin.

**RAMOS ORTIZ, LUIS R,** Inter Amer Univ Pr Hato Rey, Hato Rey, PR; FR; BSCHE; Sci; Chem Eng.

**RAMOS RODRIGUEZ, JOHANNA,** Inter Amer Univ Pr San German, San German, PR; FR; BA; 1st Natl Conf Governor Young People; Cert Inst De Banca 90; Mktg; Publ Rel.

**RAMOS, CARLOS I,** Inter Amer Univ Pr Hato Rey, Hato Rey, PR; FR; Boy Scouts Amer Eagle Scout 89; Eagle Scout Awd 89; Swiming Tm 88-; Scif Aernctl Engr.

**RAMOS, CRISTINA J,** City Univ Of Ny Lehman Coll, Bronx, NY; SR; BA; Stdnt Elctns Cmpgng 87; Lhmn Thtr Clb 87-; Nwyrk Jgglr Clb 88-; Lhmn Schlrs Prgm 87-; Deans Lst; Prsdntl Schlr 90; Gldn Key 90; Strlght Fndtn Vol 86-88; Exxn Smmr Jbs Grn Tvsns Srvcs Blnd 90; Psychlgy.

**RAMOS, DAPHNE,** Univ Of Pr Cayey Univ Coll, Cayey, PR; JR; BA; Techno-Chem; Oquimpiadas; Chem Comp; Deans Lst 89; Chemsty; Med Ped.

**RAMOS, FRANCISCO J,** Miami Dade Comm Coll, Miami, FL; BED; S Fl Dry Indstrs Assoc; Indpndnt Ordr Odd Flws; Outstndng Acdmc Achvmnt; Bch In Blgy; Basic Crs Spclty Sci Havana Univ 73; Advncd Crs Blgcl Sci Ed Havana U 79; Blgy; MD Blgy.

**RAMOS, GLORIA B,** Fl International Univ, Miami, FL; SR; BS; Soc Phys Stdnts 90-; Argonne Natl Lab Summer Stdnt Rsrch Prog; Physics; Phys Engr.**

**RAMOS, HECTOR R,** Inter Amer Univ Pr San Juan, Hato Rey, PR; SO; BA; Amrcn Hnr Scty 90-; Eng; Arspc Eng.**

**RAMOS, JIMMARIE,** Univ Of Pr At Mayaguez, Mayaguez, PR; JR; Biology Stdnts Assoc Sec 90-; Beta Beta Beta Brd/Dir 89-; Cllbrtr/Rsrch Brkhvn Natl Lab Long Isl NY; Vlybl IM 89; Dentistry.

**RAMOS, JOLLYVETTE,** Cumberland County Coll, Vineland, NJ; FR; BED; Psychology; Guid Cnslnr.

**RAMOS, JOSE GABRIEL,** Saint Thomas Univ, Miami, FL; FR; Save Pine; Sccr 90-.

**RAMOS, JUAN D,** Ma Inst Of Tech, Cambridge, MA; SO; BS; APR Athl Chrmn 89-; JV Vlybl Cpt/Tm MVP 90-; Arch/Cvl Eng; Dsgn/Bld Tech.**

**RAMOS, KAREN L,** Inter Amer Univ Pr Hato Rey, Hato Rey, PR; JR; Bio Assn 90; Beta-Beta-Beta; 1st Pl In Chem Olympics; Bio; Med/Pharm.

**RAMOS, LATRICE A,** Commonwealth Coll, Virginia Beach, VA; SR; Acctng Clb Sec 89; Water Aquatist Soc 90; Alpha Beta Gamma 90; Pres Lst 89; Cert Rcgtn Jvnl Crt Serv Unv; AS; Acctng; Self Emplymnt.

**RAMOS, LETICIA,** Univ Of Rochester, Rochester, NY; JR; BA; SALAS 88-90; Undrgrd Ecnmc Cncl 89-90; Spcl Intrst Grps 88-; Eccmnc/Stttcs; Intl Bus.

**RAMOS, LUCIA I,** Univ Of Miami, Coral Gables, FL; SR; BS; Lbrry Stff Assn 90; Phi Theta Kappa 87-; Phi Kappa Phi 90-; Pi Mu Epsilon 90-; Chldrns Hm Scty Of FL Vol 90; Prvsts Hnr Rll 90-; Hnrs Math Awrd 89; AA Miami Dade Comm Coll 89; EKG Tech Miami Rsprtry Thrpy Inst 84; Math; Med Schl.

**RAMOS, LUIS R,** Inter Amer Univ Pr Aquadilla, Aguadilla, PR; JR; BA; Knight Of Columbus; Psychlgy; PHD.

**RAMOS, MARIA A,** Univ Of Pr At Rio Piedras, Rio Piedras, PR; SO; BED; Blgy; Med.

**RAMOS, MARIA DEL P,** Inter Amer Univ Pr San German, San German, PR; GD; Lista De Hnr Del Decano 87-90; Futuros Lideres De Comercio Amer Pres 87; Lista De Hnr Del Decano Univ Catoliea 87-89; Elem Ed; Maetria En.

**RAMOS, MARIA M,** Bloomfield Coll, Bloomfield, NJ; SR; BSN; Alpha Phi Seton Hl Univ Fndg Mbr 88; Nrsng.

**RAMOS, MARTA,** Inter Amer Univ Pr San Juan, Hato Rey, PR; GD; JD; Asst VP; BA; Bsn Admn; Law.

**RAMOS, MICHAEL JAMES,** Miami Dade Comm Coll, Miami, FL; JR; BS; Phi Theta Kappa 90-; Deans Lst 89-; Acdmc Awrd 89; Ahd Schlrshp 90; AA 89; Crmnl Jstc Admn.

**RAMOS, ORLANDO,** Bayamon Tech Univ Coll, Bayamon, PR; GD; BBA; Hnrs Assembly 87-90; Tutor 87-; Hnrs Certif 87-90; Acad Schlrshp 87-90; BBA 86-90; Acctg.

**RAMOS, PEDRO I,** Inter Amer Univ Pr Arecibo Un, Arecibo, PR; JR; BA; Clg Hnr Prog; Hnr Stndt; Army Achvmnt Mdl 88; Army Cmmdtn Mdl 89; BED Acad Hlth Sci 85; PE.

**RAMOS, RAFAEL,** Inter Amer Univ Pr Hato Rey, Hato Rey, PR; FR; Mrktng; Bus Admnstrtn.

**RAMOS, REBECA E,** Univ Of Pr At Rio Piedras, Rio Piedras, PR; SR; BS; Assn Premed Stu 89-90; Natl Hnr Soc 85-87; Natl Stu Exchng Prog 88-89; Vllybl Clb 88-89; Biol; PHD Cellular Mlclr Biol.

**RAMOS, VANESSA,** Univ Of Pr Medical Sciences, San Juan, PR; JR; BS; SGA Cls Treas 90-; Amercn Pharmctcl Assoc 89-; Rho Chy 90-; Cathlc Dghtrs Of Amer 86-; Pharmcy; Pharm D.

**RAMOS, VENUS F,** Univ Of Miami, Coral Gables, FL; FR; BS; Amnesty Intrntl Urgent Action Coord 90-; Biology Clb Stfr 90-; Pizzazz Dance Clb; Alpha Lambda Delta; Kappa Kappa Gamma Jr Pnhlnc Rep 90-; Biology; Pediatrics.

**RAMOS-FERNANDEZ, MARISOL,** Univ Of Pr At Rio Piedras, Rio Piedras, PR; JR; BA; Golden Key; Matricula De Hnr 90-; History; Law.

**RAMOS-MERCADO, FABIOLA B,** Univ Of Pr At Rio Piedras, Rio Piedras, PR; JR; Yng Luthrn League Sec/Treas 90-; Hon List 89-; Biol; Med.

**RAMP, RENEE L,** Oh Coll Of Podiatric Med, Cleveland, OH; GD; DPM; Amer Coll Foot Surgeons 90-; Ohio Podtrc Med Stdnts Assn Dir Of Cmmnctns 88-89; Alpha Gamma Kappa 87-; Amer Bus Wmns Assn 87-; BSN Thiel Coll 85; Podiatric Med.

**RAMPEY, DEBRA E,** Coll Of Charleston, Charleston, SC; SR; BS; Sclgy.

**RAMSARAN, DHANRAJ,** City Univ Of Ny Baruch Coll, New York, NY; SO; BBA; Acctng/Law; Corp Law.

**RAMSAY, ROBERT J,** Univ Of Miami, Coral Gables, FL; SO; BA; Miami Cmmtmnt Stdnt Plnng/Inst Rsrch/Test Cntr 90-; Alpha Lambda Delta; Empl Of Yr Clg Wrk Stdy Stdnts 90-; Acctg.

**RAMSBY, SHANNON G,** Va Commonwealth Univ, Richmond, VA; SR; BA; Recycling Co-Op 90-; Golden Key; Top 1 Percent Award; History; Poltcl Sci.

**RAMSDALE, JERRY E,** Univ Of Southern Ms, Hattiesburg, MS; JR; BSBA; Beta Gamma Sigma; Hnrs Clg; Acctg.

**RAMSDALE, RUTH ANNE ARLINE,** Univ Of Sc At Columbia, Columbia, SC; JR; BA; Amow Outstndg Tchr Award Comm Stdnt Chr 89-; V P/Treas 89-90; Model Untd Ntns Club Pres 90-; Stdnts For A Better Cenolina 89-90; Wmns Stdnts Assn 89-90; Mortar Brd; Omicron Delta Kappa 90-; Alpha Delta Pi 89-90; Intl Stds; Pediatric Oncology.

**RAMSDELL, KAREN E,** Middle Tn St Univ, Murfreesboro, TN; JR; BA; Soc Wrk Soc 90-; Delta Zeta 88-; Actvies Chrmn 89-90; Pep Chrmn 88-89; Rush Prty Chrmn 90-; Judcry Brd Sr Rep; Soc Wrk/Spec Ed.

**RAMSDELL, KENNETH A,** Univ Of South Al, Mobile, AL; GD; MED; Tchr Enrchmnt Pgm Gftd Stdnts; US Coast Guard Aviation 71; BS Embry Riddle Aero Univ; Educ.

**RAMSDEN JR, JOHN W,** Al A & M Univ, Normal, AL; BS; Cert Photogrammetric Engr 84-; Am Soc Photogrammetry/Remote Sensing 82-; BS Univ N AL 74; Elec/Cmptr Eng.

**RAMSEY, AGNES S,** Fl Atlantic Univ, Boca Raton, FL; SR; Amer Soc Mech Engrs Sec 90-; Soc Wmn Engrs 89-; Soc Auto Engrs; ASME Stdnt Sect Awd; Pres Hons Lst; Schlstc Schlrshp 87; Medcr Blng Spec Good Smrtn Hosp 87-90; BSME; AS Palm Bch Comm Clg 88; Mech Engr.

**RAMSEY, CHIQUITA M,** Al A & M Univ, Normal, AL; JR; BS; Pres Schlr 89-; Phi Beta Lambda 90-; Awd Mgmt; Dns Lst/Hnr Rl 88-; Chrldr 89-90; Bus Mgmt.

**RAMSEY, CHRISTINE A,** Oh Dominican Coll, Columbus, OH; SR; BA; Delta Epsilon Sigma; Outstndg Sr Acctng Mjr Awd ODC; Tax Acctng Intnshp Beall/Rose CPAS; Bd Mbr/Mtl Hlth Assn Franklin Cty; Harp/Voclst Celtic Mus Grp 87-; Emp State Ohio Rehab Ser Comm Fin Div 88-; Accounting; CPA Cert/MA Tax/Fin Plnng.

**RAMSEY, ELIZABETH G,** Savannah Coll Of Art & Design, Savannah, GA; GD; MFA; Intern Ptr Brwrs Assocts Dsgn Asst 88-90-; Intern Hltn Hd Intrs; 2SID; BA 83; Intr Dsgn.

**RAMSEY, GEORGETTA L,** Marshall University, Huntington, WV; JR; BBA; Fnce/Bsn Law.

**RAMSEY, JULIANNE PATRICIA,** Middle Tn St Univ, Murfreesboro, TN; SR; PHD; Assc Non Trdntnl Stdnts 89-; Hnr Stdnts Assc 90-; Sigma Tau Delta 89-; Gamma Beta Phi 89-; Phi Theta Kappa 89-; Hnrs Motlow State Cmmt Clg; Deans List; AA Summa Cum Laude; Hnrs Mdl TE State Univ; AA Motlow State Cmmty Clg 89; BA; Engl; Acdmcs.

**RAMSEY, KATHERINE L,** Salisbury St Univ, Salisbury, MD; JR; BA; Deans Lst 90; Hstry/Scndry Educ; Tchng.

**RAMSEY, KIMBERLY D,** Indiana Univ Of Pa, Indiana, PA; SR; BED; PSEA 90-; PSTA 90-; Prjct STRIDE 90; Elem Ed; Tchng.

**RAMSEY, KIMBERLY L,** Radford Univ, Radford, VA; FR; BS; Alpha Lambda Delta; Zeta Tau Alpha Pldg Class Social Chrmn; INTR Bsktbl/Sftbl; Thrptc Rec.

**RAMSEY, LAURA A,** Fl A & M Univ, Tallahassee, FL; JR; BA; Vlybl 87-89; Bsktbl 88-90; Sftbl 90-; IM Vly Dir 90; AA Polk Comm Coll 89; Phys Edn; Teach/Coach.

**RAMSEY, LESLIE S,** Western Piedmont Comm Coll, Morganton, NC; FR; BA; Sci; Ed.

**RAMSEY, LISA K,** Univ Of Tn At Martin, Martin, TN; SO; BA; Soc Hnrs Seminar Stdnts 90-; Phi Chi Theta; Alpha Delta Pi; Acctg.

**RAMSEY, MARIAN A,** Northwest Al Comm Coll, Phil Campbell, AL; FR; AS; Baptist Bible Study Cl 89-; Nightingale Awd; Perf Atten Awd; Acad Achvmnt Awd; Prac Nurse; CE; Sci; Nrsg.

**RAMSEY, MARY A,** Rutgers St Univ At Camden, Camden, NJ; GD; BS 90; Accounting.

**RAMSEY, MELANIE D,** Univ Of Al At Huntsville, Huntsville, AL; FR; BS; Hnr Schlrshp; Mech Engrng.

**RAMSEY, MELISSA A,** Converse Coll, Spartanburg, SC; JR; BA; Stdnt Admssns Brd 88-; Cnvrs Wllnss Assoc 89-; Stdnt Govt Treas 90; Alpha Lambda Delta 89-90; Mrtr Brd Almn Affrs Chrprsn; Crscnt 89-90; Trstt Hrn Shclrscnvrs Kybrd; Engl.

**RAMSEY, MELISSA K,** Central Fl Comm Coll, Ocala, FL; SO; BSN; FSNA 88-; NSNA 88-; Amblnc Srvc EMT 81-; Nrsng.

**RAMSEY, MICHAEL W,** Winthrop Coll, Rock Hill, SC; SO; BME; Music Ed; Chrl Drctr.

**RAMSEY, NANCY D,** Northern Ky Univ, Highland Hts, KY; SR; Conner Hgh Sch Athltc Boosters 90-; Pltcl Sci Clb 90-; Pinnacle VP; Pl Sigma Alpha 90-; Law-Chase Coll Law NKU.

**RAMSEY, REBECCA W,** John Wesley Coll, High Point, NC; SO; BA; Biblcl Theolg; Tchr.

**RAMSEY JR, ROBERT C,** Emory & Henry Coll, Emory, VA; SO; BA; Math Assoc Amer 90-; Stdnt VA Educ Assoc 90-; Natl Clgt Math Awds 90-; All Amer Schlr 90-; Math; Tchr.

**RAMSEY, ROBIN M,** Univ Of Nc At Asheville, Asheville, NC; FR; Chancellors List Outstanding Stdnts; Deans List; Pol Sci/History; Teaching.

**RAMSEY, STELLANIA L,** Walters St Comm Coll, Morristown, TN; FR; BA; Sec Tchr.

**RAMSEY-CALDWELL, SHEILA F,** Howard Univ, Washington, DC; GD; MSW; Fellowship Club Yth Dir 84-87; Pi Sigma Delta; Wash Urban League 90; Iona Hse Snr Svcs 90; NASW 90; BS Univ Maryland 88; AA Cmnty Clg Air Force 87; Social Work.

**RAMSEYER, ROBERT B,** Oh Wesleyan Univ, Delaware, OH; FR; BA; Stu Cntr Entrtnmt Comm 90-; Phi Eta Sigma 90-; Sigma Chi 90-; Alumni Rltns Chrmn; Adpt Hwy 90-91; IM Bsktbl/Sftbl 90-; Var Glf 90-; Ecnmcs Mgmt; Bus.

**RAMSHORN, SALLY-ANN T,** Coll Of Charleston, Charleston, SC; JR; BA; AA Nassau Comm Clg 90; Scl Sci/Educ.

**RAMSUMAIR, SAMUEL P,** City Univ Of Ny City Coll, New York, NY; GD; MBA; Econ Soc V P Tutoring 88-89; Tae Kown Do Oh Do Kwan 85-88; Gldn Ky 89; Econ; Acctng/Bus.

**RAMUSEVIC, FETIJE,** City Univ Of Ny Baruch Coll, New York, NY; SR; BBA; Busn Mktg Soc; Gldn Key; Dns 87-90; Mktg Mgmt.

**RANAGLIA, GIA M,** La Salle Univ, Philadelphia, PA; FR; Young Adult Musins Sacred Heart Church Church Reboardist Ld Soloist/Hrmzr 89-; Commit Hmls 90-; Adult Children Alcoholics 90-; Math/Italian; Law.

**RANAL-GUERRA, MARGARITA C,** Univ Of Pr At Rio Piedras, Rio Piedras, PR; GD; PHD; Prnts/Tchrs Assc Cristo Rey Pres 90; Acad; BA Mgn Cum Laude 70; BA 70; MA 75; Intramer Psychlgy Assc Natl Educ Assc; Puerto Rico Psychlgy Assc; Puertorican Unv Prfsr Assc; Psychlgy; Clg Tchng/Cnsltnt.

**RANALLI, KARLA S,** Kent St Univ Stark Cmps, North Canton, OH; SO; BS; Spanish Club Pres 90-; Stdnt Govt Bd Of Elctns Mbr; Spanish Dept Awd; Phys Thrpy.

**RAND, LISA M,** George Mason Univ, Fairfax, VA; SO; BA; Res Asst 90-; Natl Res Hall Hon Assn; Tutor Refugees Through United Way 90-; Psy/Edu; Tch.

**RAND, RENATA,** Saint Johns Univ, Jamaica, NY; JR; BS; Swim 90-; Army ROTC 89-; Cmptr Sci; Math.**

**RANDAL, JOEL P,** Comm Coll Algny Co Algny Cmps, Pittsburgh, PA; FR; BA; Hlth Scncs; Rdlgst.

**RANDALL, CYNTHIA B,** S U N Y Coll Of Tech At Alfred, Alfred, NY; FR; Wellsville Actvts Cncl Stdnt Spcl Evnts Chrprsn; Sigma Tau Epislon; Electrncs; Techncn.

**RANDALL, JAN E,** Clarkson Univ, Potsdam, NY; JR; BS; Amer Mrktng Assn 90-; Yrbk Clb Asst Edtr 89-90; Fnnc/Ecnmcs; Invstmnt Bnkng.

**RANDALL, JEFFREY J,** Teikyo Post Univ, Waterbury, CT; SR; MSOB; Intl Stdnts Assoc 87-; Bsktbll Tm 87-; Afr Amrcn Assoc Pres 90-; BS; Acctg; CPA.

**RANDALL, JILL,** Albertus Magnus Coll, New Haven, CT; JR; BA; Cls Pres; Cls Treas 90-; Exec Bd Mbr 90-; Fd Bd Consltnts 90-; Dns Lst 88-; Hosp Vol; Math; Med.

**RANDALL, LESLIE A,** Union Coll, Barbourville, KY; FR; BA; FCA 90; Bsktbl; Engl/Phy Ed; Ed.

**RANDALL, LIA L,** Claflin Coll, Orangeburg, SC; FR; Hnrs Prog; Ctznshp Awd; Hnr Rl; Claflin Coll Schlrshp; Sociolty; Socl Wrk Law.

**RANDALL, LYNDA H,** Northern Ky Univ, Highland Hts, KY; FR; BA; KHEAA Tchr Schlrshp 90-; Honors List; Northery Knty; Bptst Chrch Lksd Pk; Elem Educ/English; Elem Teacher.

**RANDALL, MARCIA K,** Dowling Coll, Oakdale Li, NY; SR; BA; Fdrtn Nrs/Hlth Pro; Ctzns Cmpgn Envrnmnt; Friends Smithtown Lbry; Scl Sci; Educ.

**RANDALL, MARK A,** Bob Jones Univ, Greenville, SC; FR; BS; Sigma Alpha Chi 90-; Hstry; Ed.

**RANDALL, MARYROSE T,** Winthrop Coll, Rock Hill, SC; JR; BED; Cncl Excpt Chldrn 90-; Girl Scts Ldr 86-; Kappa Delta Pi; Amer Red Crss Instr 84-; Sub Tchr 88-; Wtrfrnt Spec 88-; AA Univ S FLA 73; Cert York Tech Inst 89; Spec Educ EMR LD EH; Tchr.

**RANDALL, MATTHEW M,** Univ Of Cin R Walters Coll, Blue Ash, OH; SO; BA; Finance; Bus.

**RANDALL, SALLIE J,** Univ Of Southern Ms, Hattiesburg, MS; JR; BA; Golden Key 90-; Most Outstndng Frshmn Thea Dept 88-89; Svce Awd Schlrshp 90-; Deans List 89-; Thea.

**RANDALL, SHARON A,** Univ Of Akron, Akron, OH; SR; BS; Amrcn Soc Mchncl Engnrs VP 89-; Soc Atmtv Engnrs Sec 89-; Alpha Lambda Delta 86-; Chi Omega Actvts Chrmn 88-; Mchncl Engnrng.

**RANDALL, VALERIE D,** Fayetteville St Univ, Fayetteville, NC; JR; BS; Chnclrs Lst; Black Employmnt Pgm Cmte; Greater Fayetteville Dental Hygiene Soc; Reg Dental Hyg 80-; AAS FTCC Fayetteville NC 80; Psych.

**RANDAZZO, JOHN F,** Univ Of Ky, Lexington, KY; JR; BSW; Deans Lst 90; Coc Wrk; Pub Welfare Plcy.

**RANDAZZO, KIRK A,** Univ Of Sc At Columbia, Columbia, SC; FR; BMUS; March/Jazz/Concert/ PEP Bands; Bsktbl; Schl/Music Stdnt Coun; Kappa Kappa Psi; IMS Vlybl; Music Edctn; Band Instr/Composer.

**RANDAZZO, LOUISE JANE,** Ny Chiropractic Coll, Glen Head, NY; GD; DC; Schlp 90-; Cert Prfcny 90; RA 83-87; BS Mnchstr Unv 83; Chrprctc.

**RANDAZZO, RENEE E,** Coll Misericordia, Dallas, PA; SR; BA; Educ Clb VP 90; Elem Educ; Tchr.

**RANDLE, KATHERINE M,** Itawamba Comm Coll, Fulton, MS; FR; AS; Health/Science; Rn.

**RANDLE, KEVIN D,** Wilmington Coll, New Castle, DE; BS; US Ar Frce 85-; AA Community College Of The Air Force 90; Bus Mgmt.

**RANDO, CHRISTOPHER J,** Alfred Univ, Alfred, NY; JR; BA; Radio Disc Jockey 89-; RSVP Prgrm 88-; Cllg Bowl 88-; Alpha Lambda Delta 88-; Tau Beta Pi 90-; Keramos Sec 90-; Alpha Chi Rho Sec 89-; IM 88-; Crmc Engnrng.

**RANDOLPH, BRIAN S,** Univ Of Ky, Lexington, KY; SR; BS; Chi Epsilon 90-; Sigma Alpha Epsilon 88-; Cvl Eng; Engrg.

**RANDOLPH, CAROLYN S,** Memphis St Univ, Memphis, TN; FR; BA; Japanese Clb Pres; Phi Eta Sigma; Alpha Lambda Delta; Intl Relations; Govt Work UN.

**RANDOLPH, CHERYL A,** Al A & M Univ, Normal, AL; JR; Choir 88-; Ford Schlr 89-; Alpha Kappa Alpha 90-; Elem Educ; Tchr.

**RANDOLPH, CHRISTOPHER L,** Thomas Nelson Comm Coll, Hampton, VA; SO; AAS; Stdnt Ltrry Artstc Jrnl Artst 90-; Cmmrcl Art.

**RANDOLPH, CONSUELA D,** Johnson C Smith Univ, Charlotte, NC; SO; Soph Cls Pres 90-; NAACP; Vrsty Chrldr 89-90; FCA; Psych Clb 90-; Deans Lst; Kappa Diamond Aux 90-; Project Vote; MAP; Fine Arts Com; Blck Hstry Mo Com; Outstndng Svc Awd 90-; Stdnt Orient Ldr; Cross Country; Communications; Pblc Relations.

**RANDOLPH, DORIS D,** City Univ Of Ny City Coll, New York, NY; SO; BA; Alpha Sigma Lambda; Dns Lst 90; Church Gethsemane Elder 88-; CAFJ Advsry Bd 88-; AOS Interboro Inst NYC 77; Sclgy; Scl Rsrch Sci.

**RANDOLPH, GINGER R,** Univ Of Nc At Charlotte, Charlotte, NC; SR; Bapt Stdnt Union 88-89; Golden Key; Delta Zeta Stndrds Board Chrmn 87-; Peace Acad Schlrshp; AA Peace Clg 87; Engl; Tchr.

**RANDOLPH, HOWARD G,** Hillsborough Comm Coll, Tampa, FL; SO; BS; Phi Theta Kappa 90-; Eastside Bapt Chrch Dover Chrch Trng Dir 89-; Fndtns Schlrshp Wnr 90; Dns Comm Coll Schlrshp; Awd Acad Excel Engl 88-89; AA; Aerospace Engr; Flight Strctrs.

**RANDOLPH, JASON D,** Wv Univ, Morgantown, WV; FR; BS; Hmn Rsrcs 90-; Dean Lst 90-; Crwmn 90-; Aero Eng; USAF Plt/Astrntcl Eng.

**RANDOLPH, KIMBERLY A,** Limestone Coll, Gaffney, SC; SR; BA; Bptst Yng Wmn; Chrch Chr; Gamma Beta Phi; AS Cleveland Comm Coll 88; Elem Ed; Mba Library Sci.

**RANDOLPH, LINDSAY DYANNE,** Univ Of Sc At Columbia, Columbia, SC; SR; Carolina Prog Union 87-88; Golden Key 89-; Psi Chi Sec 87-; Phi Beta Kappa 90-; Gamma Beta Phi 88-; Undergrad Intrnshp Wm S Hall Psych Inst Forensic Unit 89-90; Psych; Grad Sch Clinical Psych PHD.

**RANDOLPH, STEPHANIE S,** Univ Of Ga, Athens, GA; FR; BA; Colonial Comm Serv 90-; Seagram Schlrshp; Bus; Acctg.

**RANDOLPH, VICKIE T,** Univ Of Ga, Athens, GA; SR; BED; Erly Chldhd Edctn; Tchng.

**RANELLONE, ELIZABETH M,** Long Island Univ C W Post Cntr, Greenvale, NY; SR; BA; Undgrad Asstshp Frgn Lang Dpt; Clg Frnch Awd 90-; Dns Lst 89-; Engl/Frnch; Tchr.

**RANGASWAMY, CHANDHIRAN,** Univ Of Louisville, Louisville, KY; FR; BS; Soc Porter Schlrs 90-; Phi Eta Sigma 90-; Govrnrs Schlrs Awd 90-; Woodford Porter Awd 90-; Chem Eng; Med.

**RANGEL, CARLOS A,** Univ Politecnica De Pr, Hato Rey, PR; SO; L D Sports 87-89; Little Leagues 87-89; Neighborhood Security Cncl 90-; Bsktbl/Vlybl 87-; Engr; Indstrl Engr.

**RANII, LOUIS C,** Comm Coll Algny Co Algny Cmps, Pittsburgh, PA; SO; AAS; Art Clb; Assertvist Clb 89; Wmns Clb Sanitation 87-88; Assertiveness Trng Plaque 90; Grphc Dsgnr; CCAC; Phlsphy/Psychlgy; Art Dir.

**RANII, WILLIAM G,** Comm Coll Algny Co Algny Cmps, Pittsburgh, PA; JR; Physics Clb Pres; Chem Clb VP 90-; Chpstck Vol 89-; Dntl Offc Dntl Lab Tech; Denist Pre Prof; BA; Scinc; Dentist.

**RANKIN, CATHERINE A,** Atlantic Comm Coll, Mays Landing, NJ; SO; BA; Sprvsr; Bus/Hmn Res; Mgmt.

**RANKIN, DUANE M,** Marshall University, Huntington, WV; FR; BA; Jrnlsm; Sports Castor/Jrnslst.

**RANKIN, KINDRA A,** East Tn St Univ, Johnson City, TN; SO; Campus Crusade; Fllwshp Christian Atheletics; Hall Cncl; Gamma Beta Phi; ETSU Vol; Vlybl; Business; Bus Mngmnt.

**RANKIN, TAMMY J,** Mount Aloysius Jr Coll, Cresson, PA; JR; BA; Phi Theta Kappa Sec 89-90; Gamma Sigma Sigma; AS 90; Crmnlgy; Juv Prob/Parole.**

**RANKIN, TAMMY L,** Tougaloo Coll, Tougaloo, MS; SR; BS; Educ Clb 88-; Elem Educ; Tchrs.

**RANKIN, TINA L,** Radford Univ, Radford, VA; SR; SEA 89-; Kappa Delta Pi Gst Spkr Com Chrmn 90-; BS; Educ; Tchng.

**RANKINS, JAMES L,** Central St Univ, Wilberforce, OH; JR; BA; Lions Clb Dir; Psi Chi Treas 90-; Kent State Univ Intrn; Clin Psychlgst.

**RANKINS, MICHAEL A,** Al St Univ, Montgomery, AL; SR; Msnc Ldg 90; Bio Medical Sci Clb 88-; Kappa Alpha Psi 89-; Guide Rght Comm; Bsbl Tm Cptn 89-.

**RANSOM, CAROL J,** Springfield Tech Comm Coll, Springfield, MA; SR; BA; Alpha Nu Omega 90-; AA; Bio/Educ; Tch.

**RANSOM, GENE M,** Anne Arundel Comm Coll, Arnold, MD; SO; BS; Intern To St Sen James Simpson; IM Soccer; AA; Econ; Bankruptcy Law.

**RANSOM, JENNIFER A,** Univ Of Ky, Lexington, KY; SO; Campus Crusade For Chrst 90; Stdnts Agnst Drvng Drnk 89-90; Ims Srty 89; Phi Beta Phi Dlgte 89; Clg Schlrs Of Amer; Mst Outstndng Pldge Of Pi Beta Phi 90; Hghst Grde Pnt Ave Of Pi Beta Phi Pldge Class 90; Scndry Ed/Hstry; Tchr.

**RANSOM, JOHN F,** Providence Coll, Providence, RI; JR; BA; Pi Mu Epsion; Math; Insurance.

**RANSOM, KELLY L,** Cornell Univ Statutory College, Ithaca, NY; JR; BS; Central NY IFT 890-; Food Science Club 91-; Work Study Jobs 88-; Alpha Chi Omega Pldge Sec 89-; Nabisco Biscuit Co Resch & Dvlpmnt Assoc; Food Science; Product Development.

**RANSOM, ROBIN B,** Va St Univ, Petersburg, VA; JR; BA; Bus Admin Clb Treas 89-; NAACP Sec; BSAD Sec; Big Sis 90; Cnvlsnt Home Vol; Pres Pin Awd 90; Dns Lst 89-90; Bus Admin.

**RANSOM, SANDRA C,** Hillsborough Comm Coll, Tampa, FL; FR; BSC; Acctgs Analyst; Globus Gateway; Cosmos Tourama; Bus Admn/Nurs; Human Rsrc Dev.

**RANSOME JR, JAMES E,** Norfolk St Univ, Norfolk, VA; SO; BA; Hist Clb 90-; Hist/Pre Law; Tchng.

**RANTA, MARGARET E,** Bristol Univ, Bristol, TN; SR; BA; Acctng; Contrlr/Tchr.

**RANZIE, FRANCES,** S U N Y Coll Of Tech At Frmgdl, Farmingdale, NY; FR; AS; Bsnss; Accntng.

**RAO, DANILO,** Northwest Al Comm Coll, Phil Campbell, AL; SO; Phi Theta Kappa 90-; AAS 89; AS 90; Mchncl; Engrg.

**RAO, FRANK N,** City Univ Of Ny Baruch Coll, New York, NY; SO; BBA; Fin/Econ Soc Pres 89-; Deans Lst 90; Fin; Invstmnt Bnkg.

**RAO, GEETHA,** Univ Of Pittsburgh, Pittsburgh, PA; FR; BA; Amnsty Intl Coord 90-; Intl Stds; Foreign Serv.

**RAO, RAJEEV K,** Univ Of Miami, Coral Gables, FL; SO; BS; Indian Stdnts Assn; Psychlgy; Med.

**RAO-KATHI, PRASANTH BURRI,** Georgetown Univ, Washington, DC; FR; BSBA; Ambsdrl Admsns Pgm Reg Coord 90-; Model UN Clb Mex Crisis Stf 90-; Engl Tutor; Finance; Law.

**RAPACHIETTA, CAROL J,** Saint John Fisher Coll, Rochester, NY; SR; BS; Acctng Clb; Phi Theta Kappa 89; Fncl Exec Inst Awd; Duplessis Wolfe Schlrshp 90; Pres Schlrshp 90-; A C Rochester; AS Monroe Comm Coll 90; Acctng; Fncl Analysist.

**RAPAGLIA, NICOLE C,** Wagner Coll, Staten Island, NY; JR; BS; Physician Assist.

**RAPAPORT, AIMEE J,** Univ Of Miami, Coral Gables, FL; SR; Rprtr Nwspr 88-; Hnr Cncl 89-; Nwspr Intrn 88-; Sec Stdnt Govt 89-90; Hnr Stdnt Assn; Henry King Stanford Schlrshp; Acdmc Schlrs Schlrshp; Phi Alpha Delta; Alpha Epsilon Pi; Org Of Jewish Stdnts 88-; Sportsfest Canoeist; BS With Hnrs; Eng/News Edtrl Jrnlsm; Law.

**RAPAPORT, DEBORAH,** Lesley Coll, Cambridge, MA; SO; BA; Hillel Pblcty Dir Otrch Dresp 89-; Psychlgy.

**RAPE, STEPHEN CHRISTOPHER,** Univ Of Fl, Gainesville, FL; SR; BS; Kapa Psi 89-; Kappa Sigma 85-88; Pharmacy Intrnshp 89-90; AA 87; BS; Pharmacy; Pharmacist.

**RAPER, LEIGH C,** Univ Of Miami, Coral Gables, FL; SR; JD; Hnrs Stdnt Assoc 88-; Pre Legal Soc 88-90; Amnesty Intl 89-; Sigma Tau Delta 90-; Phi Eta Sigma 89-; English/Pltcs & Pblc Affrs; Law.

**RAPER, LORI L,** Northwest Al Comm Coll, Phil Campbell, AL; SO; AS; Schl Nwsppr 90; Socty Tech/Sci Finance Dir 90-; Dns Lst 89-90; Sci; Phys Thrpy.**

**RAPER, SANDRA L,** Walker Coll, Jasper, AL; SO; ADN; Student Nurses Assoc 90-; Pres List; Deans List; Amer Red Cross 83; 1st Freewill Bapt Church; LPN Walker State Tech Clg 88; Sci; Nrsng.

**RAPHAEL, TODD E,** Oh Wesleyan Univ, Delaware, OH; SO; BA; SGA 89-90; Hillel Treas 89-; Phi Eta Sigma 89-90; Phi 90-; Pol/Govt Dept Intrn 89-; Var Indr/Outdr Trck 89-; Politics.

**RAPP, JAMES L,** Salisbury St Univ, Salisbury, MD; SR; BS; Eco-Concerns 90-; Earth Day Cmte Co Chrprsn 90; Salisbury Zoo Vol 88-; Belize Zoo Vol Central Amer 88; Cross Cntry Var 87; Bio; Zoo Dir.

**RAPP, LAURA N,** Fl International Univ, Miami, FL; SR; BS; Interum Gvrng Cncl Scrty; Stdnt Govrnmnt Assoc Hosp Sntr 90; Stdnt Serv Cmmttee Chprsn 89-90; Intrntl Food Serv Exec Assoc 89-90; Hotel Rstrnt Clnry Scty SBCC VP 88-89; CC Santa Barbara Cty Clg 89; Hosp Mngmnt; Hotel Mngmnt.

**RAPP, LISA J,** Catholic Univ Of America, Washington, DC; JR; BA; Clg Young Repubs 88; CUA/CAN Vol Pgm 89-90; Elem Tchr; Phys Ther.

**RAPP, SHERRY A,** Bapt Bible Coll & Seminary, Clarks Summit, PA; SO; BS; Cert Lancaster Bible Clg 75; Elem Educ; Teach.

**RAPP, TAMMY FRAZER,** Le Moyne Coll, Syracuse, NY; JR; BS; Corp Acctng 85-; AA Columbia Clg 90; Acctng; Publc Acctng.

**RAPPL, CLAUDIA J,** Savannah Coll Of Art & Design, Savannah, GA; JR; BA; Interntnl Stdnts Orgnztn 89; Savannah Symphy Training Orchstr Asst Concertmaster 90; Illstrn; Psychlgy.

**RAPPOLD, JAMES A,** Carnegie Mellon Univ, Pittsburgh, PA; SO; BS; AIESEC 90-; Invstrs Grp 89-90; Assn Indstrl Mgmnt Econ 90-; Lambda Sigma Pres 90-; Math; Manuf.**

**RAPPU, LENA E,** Univ Of Southern Ms, Hattiesburg, MS; SO; BA; Intl Bus.

**RAPUZZI, MARIA A,** Saint Josephs Coll New York, Brooklyn, NY; GD; BS; Deans List 79-80; Explors Clb Fin Aid Cnslr 90-; Acad Achvmnt NYC Tech Clg; Gst Rltns Meth Hosp 89-90; AAS NYC Tech Clg 80; Hlth Care Mgmnt; Admin/Hlth Care Fclty.

**RARDON, MICHELLE D,** Oh St Univ At Newark, Newark, OH; FR; BA; Stdnt Sent Sec 90-; Vlybl 90-; Bus Admin.

**RARDON, SHIRLEY J,** Oh St Univ At Newark, Newark, OH; SO; BED; VIPS Publ Rel; Ongoing Stdnts Pgm Asst; Theatre Arts Publ Rel; Hon; Utica Emergency Squad Sec; ECHO; VISTA Publ Rel; Outstndg Stdnt Ldrshp Awd 90; Soroptimist Midwest Region Awd 90; Cmndtn Ohio Hse Rep 90; A Emt A Utica Squad 84; Med Cmnctns; Hosp Admin.

**RASBERRY, NANCY B,** Univ Of Montevallo, Montevallo, AL; SR; BS; GPA Hon Stdnt; Delta Kappa Pi; Elem/MS Lang Arts; Tchr.

**RASBERRY, SANDRA A,** Wallace St Comm Coll At Selma, Selma, AL; SO; BAS; Academic Achvmnt Awd 90-; Pres Lst 89-; Dns Lst 89-; Al Rl Est Lic 87-; Microfilm Clrk Clms Clrk 80-83; AAS; Bus Sci; Actnt/Envrnmntl.

**RASCHE, LAWRENCE,** Northern Ky Univ, Highland Hts, KY; SR; BA; Amer Scty Clinical Pathologists Registrant 79-; BA Thomas More Cllg 70; Geography.

**RASH, CRYSTAL D,** Spartanburg Methodist Coll, Spartanburg, SC; JR; BA; Natl Assn Accntnts 90; AA 90; Acctng; Accntnt.

**RASH, GREGORY S,** Univ Of Miami, Coral Gables, FL; FR; MBA; UM Minor Dscplnry Hear Panel; Army ROTC 90-; Alpha Lambda Delta; Lambda Chi Alpha 90-; Intl Finance/Mktg; Invstmnt Bnkg.

**RASH, JENNY M,** Gallaudet Univ, Washington, DC; JR; Stdnt Body Gov Asst Dir Pblc Rltns 89-90; Phi Kappa Zeta 90-.

**RASH, LEA J,** Saint Andrews Presbytrn Coll, Laurinburg, NC; SO; BS; Clg Chrstn Un 90-; Riding Cncl Sec 90-; Soph Hon; Cmuty Serv Scotland Co Humne Soc; Interclgte Horse Show Assn 89-; Equine Stdes/Visual Arts; Comp Graphics.

**RASHEED, CHRISTOPHER H,** Ky St Univ, Frankfort, KY; BA; Mrchng Band 87-; Engl/Crmnl Justice; Law.

**RASHEED, MICHELLE CHRISTIAN,** Mary Baldwin Coll, Staunton, VA; SR; BA; Cmmtr Stdnt Assn 89-; Sigma Tau Delta; Pres Lst; Dns Lst 90; Tchg Asst 90; Engl; Tchg.

**RASHEED, SHA KA A,** Morehouse Coll, Atlanta, GA; SO; BA; Bsn Assoc 89-; Pre-Alumni Assoc Secr 90-; SGA 89-; Stars Mentoring Pgm 89-; Fed Natl Mortgage Assoc Fannie Mae Intern; Keyes Realty Co Intern 89; Metropolitan Dade Cty Audit/Mgmt Intern 90; IM Ftbl 90-; Urban Studies; Rl Est/Law.

**RASHLEY, BRADFORD C,** Univ Of Sc At Columbia, Columbia, SC; SO; BM; Phlhrmnc Chrs 90-; Msc Thry Cmpstn; Msc.

**RASIAH, PRASANNA W,** Wesleyan Univ, Middletown, CT; FR; Wslyn Argus Co Nwspr Phtgrphr 90-; WA/ASU; Ultmt Frsbe.

**RASKIN, ROY,** Syracuse Univ, Syracuse, NY; FR; Israel Chrmn 90-; Arch Dsgn; Arch.

**RASMUS, JOHN D,** Embry Riddle Aeronautical Univ, Daytona Beach, FL; JR; BS; FAPA 88-90; Comm Pilot; Deans Lst 90; IM Flg Ftbl 89-90; Aero Sci; Pilot.

**RASMUSSEN, ANGELA D,** Salisbury St Univ, Salisbury, MD; SO; BA; Busn Admin/Mgmt; Mktg.

**RASMUSSEN, ANNE BRITH,** Life Coll, Marietta, GA; JR; Mohon Palpahon Cert 90; Gonstead 89-.

**RASMUSSEN, BONNIE B,** Norfolk St Univ, Norfolk, VA; SR; BED; SVEA 90-; Alpha Kappa Mu; Edn; Teach.

**RASMUSSEN, DONNA J,** Dowling Coll, Oakdale Li, NY; SR; BBA; Stdnt Bus Assn Sec 90-; Intl Clb; Natl Hon Soc Bus Admin 90-; AS SUNY Farmingdale Clg Tchnlgy 89; Mrktng; Mrkt Rsrch.

**RASMUSSEN, GLENN S,** S U N Y Coll Of Tech At Delhi, Delhi, NY; SO; BA; Am Inst Architecture Stdnts 90-; AAS; Architecture.

**RASMUSSEN, KRIS R,** S U N Y Coll Of Tech At Delhi, Delhi, NY; FR; BA; Elec Constrctn/Maint; Elec Engr.

**RASMUSSEN, NIEL C,** Birmingham Southern Coll, Birmingham, AL; SR; MD; Pres Stdnt Serv Org 89-; Stdnt Alumni Assn 89-; Alpha Epsilon Delta VP 90-; Kappa Mu Epsilon 90-; Sigma Nu Pldg Cls Pres 88-; Gnrl Chmstry Lab Asst 89-; IM Ftbl Bsktbl Sftbl 88-; BS; Math; Med.

**RASMUSSEN, ROBIN H,** Memphis St Univ, Memphis, TN; GD; Memphs Prlgl Assn; BA Memphis Unv 90; Law.

**RASSER, CHRISTINE,** Dowling Coll, Oakdale Li, NY; GD; BA; Alpha Chi 90-; Kappa Delta Pi; Paw Douglas Tchr Schlrshp; Charlotte Raebeck Schlrshp; Tchr Spl Ed Terryville Lrng Ctr Pt Jefferson NY; Special Ed; Tchng.

**RAST, KIMBERLY A,** Coll Of Charleston, Charleston, SC; JR; BS; Bapt Stdnt Union 87-89; Exec Comm Stdnt Recruitmnt 88-89; Omicron Delta Kappa; Alpha Phi Omega V P 87-89; High Distinguished Hnrs Lst 90-; Marshall; Spec Ed; Tch.

**RAST, KIMBERLY G,** Davis & Elkins Coll, Elkins, WV; SR; BS; Stu Educ Assc 88-; Zeta Tau Alpha Tres 88-; Elem Educ; Prof.

**RAST, LISA A,** Univ Of Sc At Columbia, Columbia, SC; SR; BA 90; Retailng; Byr.

**RASTEGAR, RAHA,** Radford Univ, Radford, VA; SO; BS; Psychology.

**RASTETTER, DANIELLE N,** Hiram Coll, Hiram, OH; FR; BA; Sprngfst Comm; IM Vlybll 90; Biology; Vet.

**RASUL, AMJAD SHAWQI,** Youngstown St Univ, Youngstown, OH; SO; BA; Gnrl Un PlstN Stdnts Sec 89-; Yngstwn St Fndtn 90-; Deans Lst 89-90; Amrcn Inst Chmcl Eng 90-; Amrcn Chmcl Scty 90-; Brd Intl Stdnts Scl Cmmnty Crdntr 89-Yngstwn St Fndtn Schlrshp 90-; Arb Stdnt Ad Intl Schlrshp Excllnt Achvmnt 90-; Chmcl Eng.

**RATAJCZAK, TRACIE A,** Muskingum Coll, New Concord, OH; FR; BA; Sprtswrtr Nwspr 90-; Fres Clss Offcr Sec 90-; Fllwshp Chrstn Athlts 90-; Delta Gamma Theta; Deans List/Msknm Clg 90; 1st Pl Mskngm Clg Speech Comp 90; Var Vlybl 90; Elem Educ; Teach.

**RATCLIFF, GLENN C,** Univ Of Nc At Asheville, Asheville, NC; SO; BS; ACS 90-; Chem.

**RATCLIFF, KELLY A,** Long Island Univ C W Post Cntr, Greenvale, NY; SR; BFA; Post Thtr Stdnt Assn Sec 88-89; Phi Eta; Hnrs Pgm CW Post; PTC Bnfctrs Award 90-; Diet Of The Arts Award 88-89; Acad Perf Award 87-; Thtr Schlrshp 87-; Tae Kwon Do; Thtr; Plywrtng/Drctng.

**RATCLIFF, KIMMBERLY E,** Oh St Univ, Columbus, OH; SR; Frnch Clb 89-; Stu Choice 89-; Grad Summa Cum Laude Hnrs Dist; BA; Frnchf Tchng Coll Lvl.

**RATCLIFFE, JOHN ALLEN,** Salisbury St Univ, Salisbury, MD; SO; BA; Phlsphy/Bus/Admin.

**RATH, MARY J,** S U N Y At Buffalo, Buffalo, NY; SR; BS; Women In Mngmnt Secy 89-; Scty Human Resource Mngmnt 90-; Undergrad Psychology Assoc 89-; Golden Key; Stdnt Asstnt Ofc Acdmc Advsng; Bus Admin/Human Resources; Educ Psychlgcl.

**RATH, MICHELLE L,** Saint John Fisher Coll, Rochester, NY; SR; BS; Deans Lst 89-90; AS Monroe Comm Clg 86; Acctng.

**RATHBONE, DEBORAH L,** S U N Y Coll Of Tech At Delhi, Delhi, NY; SO; BA; Phi Theta Kappa; Hnrs Grad; AAS Bus Admn; Bus; Undrwrtng/Brkrng.

**RATHER, ELIZABETH A,** George Mason Univ, Fairfax, VA; SO; BA; Deans Lst 90-; Accntng; CPA.

**RATHMELL, KIMBERLY M,** Bapt Bible Coll & Seminary, Clarks Summit, PA; FR.

**RATHSWOHL, LUKAS K,** Manhattan Coll, Bronx, NY; JR; BSEE; Elec Clb 89-; IEEE 90-; Eta Kappa Nu Brdg Corrspndt; Tau Beta Pi Treas; Tau Kappa Epsilon Treas 90-; Deans Lst; Elec Eng.

**RATHWAY, LARISSA J,** Slippery Rock Univ, Slippery Rock, PA; JR; Delta Psi Kappa 90-; Phi Epsilon Kappa 89-; Hlth/Phy Ed; Tch.

**RATKOVICH, THOMAS J,** Ms Valley St Univ, Itta Bena, MS; SR; MS; Beta Kappa Chi 90-; Pres Schlr; Ntnl Achvmnt Acdmy Hghst Math GPA; Tchng Asstshp Univ So Ms; BS; Math; Instrctr.

**RATLIFF, BECKY J,** Christopher Newport Coll, Newport News, VA; JR; BSDA; Hnrs Prog 88-89; Alpha Chi; Deans List 88-; Bus Mgmnt.

**RATLIFF, CAROL A,** Univ Of Tn At Martin, Martin, TN; SO; BS; Hnrs Seminary Socty 89-; Mu Epsilon Delta 90-; Alpha Omicron Pi Cls VP 90-; Pre Med Biology; Anesthesiologist.

**RATLIFF, CHRIS A,** Univ Of Ky, Lexington, KY; SR; BSME; Hghlnds Reg Ches Scty 87-88; Tours Com GE 89; Deans Lst 86-; 4 Ptnt Dsclsr GE Co Op 89-90; AS Prestonsburg Comm Coll 88; AS 87; Mech Engineering.

**RATLIFF, JEAN E,** Winthrop Coll, Rock Hill, SC; SO; BED; Wesley Newman Westminster 89-; Wesley Fndtn Bd; Red Cross/ Kiwanis Club Learn To Swim Progrm Instrctr 90-; Schlr 89-90; Im Sftbl 89-90; Elem Ed; Tchr.

**RATLIFF, KENNETH D,** Marshall University, Huntington, WV; GD; MAT; MAA; Grdt Asstnt 90-; BS 89; Math.

**RATLIFF, KIMBERLY J,** Methodist Coll, Fayetteville, NC; JR; BA; Hist/Pol Sci Club VP 89-; Stdnt Govt Assoc Sen 90; Stdnt Govt Assoc Pres; Phi Sigma Iota 90-; Washington Ctr Intrnshp 90; Yolanda L Cowley Award Spanich 90-; Pol Sci/Spanish; Fedrl Govt.**

**RATLIFF, RACHEL E,** Smith Coll, Northampton, MA; GD; Plstne Sldrty Com 90; Arbc Clb 90; Fve Coll Mddle Estrn Stds Grnt 90; Pol Sci; Intrnatl Rltns.

**RATNER, STACY J,** Brandeis Univ, Waltham, MA; FR; BA; Crtv Fntsy; Corp Lit.

**RATTERMAN, JANICE C,** Univ Of Cincinnati, Cincinnati, OH; SO; BMUS; Mc Micken Hon Soc 90-; Music Hist.

**RATTNER, MARK L,** S U N Y Coll Of Tech At Frmgdl, Farmingdale, NY; FR; AS; Business; Acctg.

**RATZ JR, JOHN J,** Niagara Univ, Niagara Univ, NY; FR; BA; Natl Warplane Museum 88-; Bus Mgmt.

**RATZEL, MARNI H,** Univ Of New Haven, West Haven, CT; SR; BA; Phi Sigma Pres 90-; Habitat Hmnty New Have Vol; Pre Arch/Sclgy; Urban Plng/Dsgn.

**RAU, VEENA,** Univ Of Pa, Philadelphia, PA; FR; BSE; Penn Dnc 90-; South Asia Socty 90-; Socty Wmn Engrs; Bioengr Socty 90-; Alpha Phi; Bioengr; Bus.

**RAUDENBUSH, VICKI A,** Broward Comm Coll, Ft Lauderdale, FL; FR; BA; Phi Theta Kappa 90-; Bus; Acctg.

**RAUHE, GINGER M,** Kent St Univ Kent Cmps, Kent, OH; SR; BA; Coun/Fam Rltns 88-; County Dept/Hmn Svcs Intnshp; IM Vlybl 90; Indiv Fam Studies; Socl Wrkr.

**RAULERSON, TRACI F,** Saint Leo Coll, Saint Leo, FL; JR; Psychlgy Clb Sec 88-; Emrgng Ldrs Pgm 90; Delta Epsilon Sigma Sec 90-; Theta Phi Alpha Pres 89-; Clge Ambsdrs; Sigma Phi Epsilon Swthrt; Orntn Ldr 90-; Psychlgy; Prsnl Psychlgy.**

**RAULLI, DEBORAH A,** Fitchburg St Coll, Fitchburg, MA; FR; BA; Dance Club 90-; Hstry; Ed.

**RAULS, VALERIE D,** Alcorn St Univ, Lorman, MS; SO; BS; Dns Lst 89-; Vac Bible Sch Vol 89; Lfgrd Undrprvlgd 89-90; Erly Chldhd Educ; Educ.

**RAUM, FRANK K,** Neumann Coll, Aston, PA; SR; BA; Diane Hisler Mem Schlrshp 90; Pol Sci; Govt Srvc.

**RAUSCH, JEFFREY C,** Alfred Univ, Alfred, NY; JR; BD; Am Mktg Assoc VP Advrtsng 89-; Fncl Mgmnt Assoc Dir Mktg; Delta Mu Delta; Mgmnt Hon Soc VP; JV/VARSITY Ftbl 89-; Bus/ Admin/Mktg; Advrtsng/Promo.

**RAUSCH, MICHAEL W,** Duquesne Univ, Pittsburgh, PA; SR; BS; APHA 89-; ASP 89-; PPA 89-; PSHP 90-; WPSHP 90-; Dean Lst 90-; Intern Forbes Cntr Gerontolgy 88-; Cmpttv Schlrshp 90-; Phrmcy.

**RAUSCH, ROBERT A,** Le Moyne Coll, Syracuse, NY; SR; Pol Sci Academy Treas 87-; Pre Law Soc 89-; Dolphin Stdnt Nwspr News Staff 89-; WLMU Coll Radio Disk Jockedy 89-90; Deans List 88-; IM Bsktbl Vlybl Sftbl Tm Capt 87-; BA; Pol Sci; Albany Law Sch.

**RAUTON, DENISE M,** Univ Of Sc At Aiken, Aiken, SC; SR; BA; Gamma Beta Phi 87-88; Edctn Majors Clb 87-; Advsry Cncl Schl Edctn 90-; Gamma Beta Phi 87-88; Prsdnts Lst 90-; Deans Lst 87-90; Ntnl Edctn Assn 90-; Schl Imprvmnt Cncl Sec VP 87-88; AS Augusta Tchncl Clg 75; Elem Edctn; Edctn Tchng.

**RAUTON, KELLI K,** Univ Of Sc At Columbia, Columbia, SC; SR; BS; Amer Mktg Hon; Top Mktg Grad Stdnt; Bus Admin/Mktg; Rsrch.

**RAVAL, ASEEM H,** Univ Of Sc At Columbia, Columbia, SC; FR; BS; Alpha Phi Omega 90-; IM Bsktbl 90; Physcs; Med.

**RAVAL, PANKAJ M,** Embry Riddle Aeronautical Univ, Daytona Beach, FL; SR; BS; Indo Amer Stdnts Assc Vp 90-; Mngmt Clb 88-; Assc Amer Arprt Exec 88-; Omicron Delta Kappa 90-; Eastern Airlines Inc Intrn 90-; Indo Amer Stdnts Assc Spcl Awd 90-; Ldrshp Awd Stdnt Actvts; Sr Cls Cncl Comm Chrmn; Aviatn Mngmt; MBA Bus.

**RAVALLI, JENNIFER K,** Hudson Valley Comm Coll, Troy, NY; SO; BS; AAS Erly Chldhd Educ; Educ; Tchng.

**RAVELING, SUZANNE M,** Univ Of Fl, Gainesville, FL; JR; BA; Art Dir Fine Line Grphcs 82-90; Fine Art/Pntng.

**RAVEN, MICHELE L,** Glassboro St Coll, Glassboro, NJ; SR; BS; Wmn Cmmnctns Inc Treas; TV Intrn 90; Cblvsn Vol 90; Cmmnctns; TV Prdctn.

**RAVENHORST, WILBUR H,** Fl St Univ, Tallahassee, FL; FR; BCE; Christian Flwshp Fund Raising Cord 90-; Peer Mentor Prog; Phi Eta Sigma; Hnr Schlrs Prog 90-; IM 90; Civil Engrg.

**RAVENHORST, WILBUR H,** Fl St Univ, Tallahassee, FL; FR; BS; Intr Vrsty Spec Evnts Coord 90-; Phi Eta Sigma 90-; IM Vlybl/Bsktbl/Sftbl 90-; Cvl Engrng.

**RAVI, CARMELA V,** Ny Univ, New York, NY; FR; Exec Secy Flat USA Inc 84-; Intl Econ/Pltcl Sci; Intl Law.

**RAWICZ-TWAROG, CHRISTINE,** City Univ Of Ny Baruch Coll, New York, NY; SR; BA; Gldn Key; Finance.

**RAWLINS, PAULA D,** Bethune Cookman Coll, Daytona Beach, FL; JR; BSN; Intl Rlths Clb Prlmntrn 87-; Stdnt Cnslr 89-; Delta Sigma Theta Hist 90-; Nrsng.**

**RAWLS, ANGELIQUE,** Jackson St Univ, Jackson, MS; SO; BA; Les Wxquisite A La Mode 89-; Mu Alpha Theta; Mktng; Intl Mktg/Rsrch.

**RAWLS, JON A,** Central Al Comm Coll, Alexander City, AL; SO; AS; Narcotics Anonymous Draper Chapter 89-; DAVIC Asst Sec 90; Draper Chpl Chr 89-; Dean Lst 89-; Pres Lst 89-; Bus Ofc/Mgmt; CPA.

**RAWLS, PENNY E,** Univ Of Sc At Aiken, Aiken, SC; JR; BS; Gamma Beta Phi 88-; Bus Admin Mrktng; Mrktng Rsrch.

**RAWLS, RHONDA L,** Univ Of Southern Ms, Hattiesburg, MS; GD; BS; Soc Nrsng Prfssnls 90-; Sigma Theta Tau 90-; Emrgncy Nrs Assn 87-; RN 81-; AD Lvngstn Univ Schl Nrsng 81; ACLS 83 86 90; BTLS Instrctr Candidate 85; Bsc Cardc Lf Supprt Instrctr 90; Neonatl Resusctatn Cls; Nrsng.

**RAWSON, MARY L,** Fl St Univ, Tallahassee, FL; SR; BS; Smnl Ambsdr Rectmnt Ofcr 89-; Lambda Pi Eta 90-; Intern-Tallahassee Magz 90; Dns Lst/Coll Comm 90-; IM Sftbl 87-91; Commnctn; Sprts Adm.

**RAWSON, MARY Q,** Christopher Newport Coll, Newport News, VA; SR; BA; SG R 87-88; Lt Mag 88-; Sigma Tau Delta 89-; PA Radio Blnd Rdr Vol 89-; Engl Lit/Wrtng.

**RAWSON, SHEILA R,** Livingston Univ, Livingston, AL; JR; BED; Phi Theta Kappa Treas 78-80; Art Clb Treas 79-80; Stdnt Govt Assn Rep 79-80; Bapt Stdnt Un 79-80; Jones Cty Jr Clg Hall Fame 80; Sci Awd 90; AA 80; AA 90; Sci Cmprhnsve; Sec Educ/Sci.

**RAY, ALEXANDRA,** Samford Univ, Birmingham, AL; GD; JD; Wmn Law Scty VP 90-; Law.

**RAY, AMANDA L,** Univ Of Al At Birmingham, Birmingham, AL; SR; BS; Elem Educ; Tchr.

**RAY, AMY L,** Memphis St Univ, Memphis, TN; JR; Dance Sqd 89-90; Sccr; Chrldng Coach Shelby Yth Sprts 88; Mid-South Fair Yth Tltn Show 82-87; Erly Chldhd Educ.

**RAY, ARIANNE D,** Univ Of Sc At Columbia, Columbia, SC; FR; BA; Phi Eta Sigma 90-; Gamma Beta Phi 90-; Alpha Lambda Delta 90-; ROTC 90-; Nrsg; Med.

**RAY, CARRIANN,** S U N Y Coll Of A & T Morrisvl, Morrisville, NY; GD; Hnr Grad 89-; Tour Gd Smstr Hnr 89-; Tchr Asst 90-; AS; Elem Educ; Tchr/Cnslr.

**RAY, CARRIE A,** Indiana Univ Of Pa, Indiana, PA; JR; BED; Indiana U Of Pa Mrchng Bnd Drill Instr 89; Elem Ed; Tchr.

**RAY, CATHY J,** Anne Arundel Comm Coll, Arnold, MD; FR; AA; Bsn Asst/Med Offc Mgr; Nrs.

**RAY, CATINA A,** Livingstone Coll, Salisbury, NC; FR; BS; Bus.

**RAY, CHRISTIE J,** Saint Vincents Coll & Seminary, Latrobe, PA; SO; BS; Biology; Medicine.

**RAY, DAIRIA L,** Lincoln Univ, Lincoln Univ, PA; FR; BA; Mltnts Chrst 90-; Gspl Ensmbl 90; Hnrs Prgm 90-; Psychlgy.

**RAY, DANIEL E,** Univ Of Southern Ms, Hattiesburg, MS; SR; MS; Alpha Tau Omega Sprts Dir 81-; Assoctd Gen Cntrctr; Home Bldrs Assn; AA Jones Co Jr Coll 85; Cnstrctn Eng; Prfssnl Eng/Law.

**RAY, DEWEY W,** Christopher Newport Coll, Newport News, VA; SO; BS; Bsebl; Med.

**RAY, ELIZABETH A,** Roane St Comm Coll, Harriman, TN; SO; AS; Natl Envrnmntl Hlth Clb 90-; SGA Judcl Brd Membr 89-90; Soc Sci.

**RAY, ELMER P,** Univ Of Tn At Martin, Martin, TN; FR; BA; Alpha Phi Omega 90-; Pre-Law Clb 90-; Poltcl Sci; Law.

**RAY, GWEN E,** Univ Of Southern Ms, Hattiesburg, MS; SR; MS; Mrchng Bnd Flag Corps 84-86; Trailblazers 85-86; Engl Clb; Art Clb; Pres Cncl Pres 84-86; One Clb Sec 86-88; Kappa Mu Epsilon 90-; Phi Theta Kappa 85-; Alpha Omega 84-; Bapt Stdnt Union 84-86; Hall Fame 86; Math Cmptr Sci; Rsrch.

**RAY, JACQUELINE M,** Le Moyne Owen Coll, Memphis, TN; SO; BS; Pre Hlth Prof Soc 89-; Nwsppr Typst 90-; SGA; Dubois Schlrs Prog 90-; Dean Lst 89-; Biol; Med.

**RAY, JANICE A,** Al A & M Univ, Normal, AL; SR; Bsn Admn; Lgstcs.

**RAY, JEFFREY W,** Fayetteville St Univ, Fayetteville, NC; SO; BS; 4.0 Soc; Sci Clb; Chem; Biochem Res.

**RAY, JO ANNE W,** Mayland Comm Coll, Spruce Pine, NC; JR; AAS; MCC Schlrshp 90; Peer Advsry 90-; Instr Amer Thread Co; Gen Ofc; Secr.

**RAY, KENDALL B,** Allen Univ, Columbia, SC; JR; BA; Dean Hon Lst 89; Kappa Alpha Psi V Pdmrch 90-; Bsbl Capt 89-; Bio; Lab Tech.**

**RAY, KIMBERLY L,** Vanderbilt Univ, Nashville, TN; SR; MSN; SNA 87-; NSNA 87-90; TNA 90-; Alpha Chi 90-; Nrsng Hnrs Scty; Heart Awareness Month Coord; Deans List 87-; Cum Laude 89-; Hnrs Stdnt 88-; ASN 89; BSN; Fmly Nrs Prctnr; Provide Fmly Prmry Care.**

**RAY, LYNN S,** Oh St Univ, Columbus, OH; SO; BA; Operators/Engrs Vallon 88-; Natl Lime/Stone Co 88-; Larchf Landscare Arch.

**RAY, MADELYN MARIE,** Germanna Comm Coll, Locust Grove, VA; SO; AAS; Alpha Beta Gamma 90; Dns Lst 90; Bsn Mgmt; CS.

**RAY, MARY E,** Northern Ky Univ, Highland Hts, KY; SR; BA; Phi Alpha Theta Sec/Treas 89-; Kappa Delta Pi 90-; Alpha Chi 90-; SNEA 90-; Red Cross Adv Vol 85-; Dns Lst 87-88; Hon Lst 89-; Educ Dept Sftbl Vlybl Tms 90; AA Hpknsvl Comm Coll 88; Soc Stds/Sec Educ; Law.

**RAY, MELISSA A,** Alcorn St Univ, Lorman, MS; SO; BS; Chem Pre Pharm; Pharm.

**RAY, MICHELLE L,** Central Al Comm Coll, Alexander City, AL; SO; Acctng; CPA.

**RAY, MONICA T,** Fayetteville St Univ, Fayetteville, NC; FR; MBA; Vars Bsktbl 90-; Bus; Law.

**RAY, RACHEL L,** Spartanburg Methodist Coll, Spartanburg, SC; SO; BA; Psi Beta 90-; Sccr Capt 89-; Sftbl Capt 90-; AA; Spec Ed; Spec Ed Tchr.

**RAY, REGINA G,** Univ Of Va Clinch Valley Coll, Wise, VA; SO; BA; IM Ftbl 90; Hstry; Ed.

**RAY, SHANOVA L,** Union Univ, Jackson, TN; SR; BA; Bapt Stdnt Union Cncl 89-90; Bapt Yng Wmn Mission Study 87-89/Pres 89-90; Porter Cable Intern; Religion/Cmnctns Arts; S Bapt Foreign Msnry.

**RAY, SHARON DENICE,** Union Univ School Of Nursing, Memphis, TN; JR.

**RAY, SHEILA D,** City Univ Of Ny Baruch Coll, New York, NY; SO; BA; Math; Acctg.

**RAY, TIMOTHY A,** Univ Of Sc At Aiken, Aiken, SC; JR; BA; German Clb 90-; USC Aiken Ranger Clb Treas 90-; USC Aiken Army ROTC 90-; Gamma Beta Phi; Psych.

**RAYBON, CATHERINE D,** Univ Of Nc At Greensboro, Greensboro, NC; SO; BS; Actvts Brd 90; Nwsppr Sprts Wrtr 89; Lsr Stds Assoc; Prks Rcrtn Vol ; Hlthsth Rehb Cntr; Lsr Stds.

**RAYBORN, JO BETH L,** Northern Ky Univ, Highland Hts, KY; JR; BS; Blgcl Soc 90-; Deans Lst; Blgy; Rsrch.

**RAYBOURN, JOHN D,** Univ Of Southern Ms, Hattiesburg, MS; SO; BA; Hstry; Tchg.

**RAYBUCK, KERRY L,** Indiana Univ Of Pa, Indiana, PA; JR; BA; Sigma Delta Pi; Spnsh; Educ.

**RAYBURN, DONNA M,** Univ Of Montevallo, Montevallo, AL; SR; BS; NSSHLA 87-90; Alpha Lambda Delta 87-; Kappa Delta Pi Treas 89-; Lambda Sigma Pi 90-; Sigma Alpha Pi 90-; Sr Elite Cmnctn Dsrdrs 90-; Alpha Lambda Delta Schlrshp; Robert E Wolfe Awd; Ed Hrng Imprd; Audlgy/MS.

**RAYBURN, NANCY R,** Blue Mountain Coll, Blue Mountain, MS; JR; BS; Hmmkr 18 Yrs; Elem Ed; Tch.

**RAYFIELD JR, SIDNEY B,** Catawba Valley Comm Coll, Hickory, NC; FR; NC Landscape Cntrctrs Assn Awrd; Hrtcltr; Lndscp Dsgn.

**RAYFORD, CELESE R,** Spelman Coll, Atlanta, GA; FR; Hon Rl 90-; Chld Dvlpmnt; Ownr Day Cr Cntr.

**RAYFORD, EBONIE Z,** Ky St Univ, Frankfort, KY; SO; Stdnt Ambsdr; Ldrshp Tm 88-89; Future Bus Ldrs Amer Treas 87-89; Ldrshp Awd 89; Erly Elem Educ; Tchr/Peace Corps.

**RAYFORD, SHIRLEY A,** American Baptist Coll, Nashville, TN; SO; BA; Theology; Evnglz.

**RAYLE, B PAIGE,** West Liberty St Coll, West Liberty, WV; SR; Kappa Delta Pi 89; Phi Theta Kappa 87; Sigma Tau Delta; Pres Lst; Dns Lst; US All-Amer Schlr; BA Summa Cum Laude; Engl/Lang Arts; Tchng.

**RAYLINSKY, WENDY A,** Hudson Valley Comm Coll, Troy, NY; SO; BAD; Tutor Acctng 89; Defen Driving Course Natl Sfty Council Assist Tchng 90; Deans List 90; Pres List 89-90; AS; Acctng; CPA.

**RAYMAT, MAYRA M,** Fl International Univ, Miami, FL; SR; BS; Intrnshp Shenandoah And Henry M Flagler Elem Schls 90; Stdnt Tchng At AL Lewis Elem; Elem Educ; Tchr.**

**RAYMIS, TODD S,** Univ Of Miami, Coral Gables, FL; JR; MS; Pre-Phys Therapy Clb; AS Data Proc Lehigh Cnty Comm Coll Schnecksville PA 83; Phys Therapy.

**RAYMOND, AARON J,** Schenectady County Comm Coll, Schenectady, NY; FR; AOS; Culinary Arts; O/O Rstrnt.

**RAYMOND, BRION S,** Univ Of Rochester, Rochester, NY; JR; BS; Crew Tm 88-; Optical Soc 90-; Dns Lst; Psi Upsilon Steward 89-; Cmnty Contributor; Optical Engr; Engr.

**RAYMOND, JAMES T,** Univ Of Ct, Storrs, CT; SR; BS; Amer Hpkd Pres 87-; Karate Clb 90; Pre Vet Clb Sec 87-90; Phi Kappa Phi 90-; Mrtr Brd 90-; Gldn Key 90-; Pthblgy; Vet Med.

**RAYMOND, KIM M,** Tallahassee Comm Coll, Tallahassee, FL; SR; AS; GA Assn Phys Ed/Rec/Dnce 88-89; Stdnt Asst Vlybl Coach 88-89; Vlybl Schlrshp 83-87; BSED W GA Coll 89; Resp Therpy; Hlth Cr Facilty.

**RAYMOND, RONALD A,** Pellissippi St Tech Comm Coll, Knoxville, TN; SO; AAS; Phi Theta Kappa 89-; Tau Alpha Pi 90-; Full Tuition Acad Schlrshp 90; Lab Assist/Infor Sys Tech 90-; Grdtd Summa Cum Laude; Knoxville Jaycees Pres 77-88; Tennessee Jaycees Rgl Dir 77-88; Cmptr Intgrtd Drftng/Dsgn; Engr.

**RAYMORE, NATALIE H,** Barry Univ, Miami, FL; GD; MED; Sci Lb Asst Indn Rvr Comm Coll 88-; Phlsphy; Educ.

**RAYNOCK, DOUGLAS C,** East Stroudsburg Univ, E Stroudsburg, PA; SR; BA; Psych Assoc Pres 88-; Htln 90; Psi Chi 89-; Crbn Monroe Pk Drug/Alcohol Cmsn Intrn; Otstndg Sr; Psych; Cnslg.

**RAYNOR, HAROLD B,** Univ Of Sc At Columbia, Columbia, SC; JR; BS; Math Cmptr Sci Clb Tres 88-; Coop Savannah Rvr Eclgy Lab 90-; Math Cmptr Sci; Prgrmr Cmptr Tchncn.

**RAYO, JUDITH C,** Miami Dade Comm Coll, Miami, FL; SO; Cert Hon Tlnt Rstr; Intr Dsgn Archtctr.

**RAYON, ANJELA N,** Wilberforce Univ, Wilberforce, OH; SR; Univ Gspl Chr VP 89-; Natl Stu Bus Leag Sec 89-; Ill Pre Almn Tres 90-; Dean Lst 90-; Blck Wmn Hstry Cmmtt 89-; Bus Mngmnt; CEO.

**RAZ, DALIT,** Univ Of New Haven, West Haven, CT; SR; BA; Prctcl Eng Tel-Aviv U 88; Elctrcl Eng.

**RAZA, AYSHA,** Fl St Univ, Tallahassee, FL; JR; BS; Stu Govt Assoc Vice Chrmn 88-90; Intl Stu Assoc 89-90; Phi Theta Kappa VP 88-; Pre Med Soc 90-; AA 90; Bio; Med.

**RAZAK, GHULAM M,** Oh Wesleyan Univ, Delaware, OH; SO; BA; Cncl On Stdnt Affrs SGA Rep; Res Asst; Tr Gd Admssns Office; Phi Eta Sigma; Econ/Acctg; Invstmnt Bnkng.

**RAZI, AFSHIN,** Yeshiva Univ, New York, NY; SO; BA; Blgy; Medicine.

**RAZZANO, ERNEST J,** Wilmington Coll, New Castle, DE; SR; BS; Paralyzed Vetrns Assoc 89-; Red Cross CPR Instr 90-; USAF Master Sgt 76-; AA Rollins Clg 86; AA Commty Clg Air Force; Criminal Justice; USAF Real Estate Invtr.

**RAZZANO, VANESSA A,** Univ Of Nc At Asheville, Asheville, NC; FR; BA; Greenpeace; Nature Cnsrvncy; Pet Savers; Frshmn Wrtng Cntst 3rd Pl; Biltmore Forest Cntry Clb Pblc Rltns; Psy; Adlcnt Cnclng.

**REA, ANNETTE,** Northwest Al Comm Coll, Phil Campbell, AL; GD; AAS; Phi Theta Kappa 89-; Off Supvr/Mgmt.**

**REA JR, DONALD P,** Schenectady County Comm Coll, Schenectady, NY; SO; BS; Bicycling/Jogging/Btng/Stk Investg/Trpcl Fish/Trgt Shtng/ Fshng; Spndg Time With Wife To Be; Pres Lst; AOS Serv Tech; AAS Bus Admin; Ecnmcs; Mgmnt.

**READ, MICHAEL L,** Tusculum Coll, Greeneville, TN; FR; Fr Clss VP 90-; Dns Lst; Ambssdr 90-; 2nd Clss Fr; Scl Stds; Frgn Srvce.

**READING-MURPHY, KYLIE L,** Georgian Court Coll, Lakewood, NJ; SR; BS; Phi Theta Kappa Ocean Cnty Clg 85-86; Acad Tutor 85-86; Deans Schlr 89-90; Full Time Sec 86-; AS Bus Admin 89; Acctng; CPA.

**REAGAN, BONITA J,** Univ Of New England, Biddeford, ME; SO; BS; Alpha Lmbd Dlt 79-87; Unesota 90-; Winn Parish EMT Assc 86-88; Athltc Scrngs 89; Wrk Stdy Physcl Thrpy Pinecrest State Schl 82; Sr Olympics Scrng 88-89; EMT A 86-88; Ocptnl Thrpy/Phys Thrpy Techcn 79-; EMT A Natl Rgstry Emer Med Techcn 86; Ocptnl Thrpy; Certf Hand Thrpst.

**REAGAN, BRIDGET A,** Daemen Coll, Amherst, NY; FR; BS; Biol; Phy Thrpy.

**REAGAN, ERIN C,** Atlantic Comm Coll, Mays Landing, NJ; SO; BA; Elem Edn; Tchr.

**REAGAN, JENNIFER LEE,** Radford Univ, Radford, VA; SR; BSN; Nrsng Class VP 89-90; Chrstn Flwshp Sm Grp Crdntr 89-90; Sigma Theta Tau 90-; Phi Kappa Phi 90-; Alpha Lambda Delta Sec 88-89; Radford Univ Fndtn Schlrshp 87-; Nrsng.

**REAL, LILLIANA M,** Univ Of Miami, Coral Gables, FL; SR; BA; Biscayne Bay Yng Rpblcns Soc Dir 89-90; Coconut Grv Jaycees 88-; Hugh Obrian Youth Fndtn Cnslr 90-; FL Fedrtn Of Yng Rpblcns Pub Rltns Dir 88-89; Bush/Quayle 88 Campgn Vol 88; State Rep Bruce Hoffman Vol 88; Jrnlsm/Pol Sci; Law Sch.

**REALE, MARGUERITE GIALLOMBARDO,** Georgian Court Coll, Lakewood, NJ; SR; Spec Educ; Handcppd Tchr.

**REAM, BRENTON J,** Coll Of William & Mary, Williamsburg, VA; FR; BS; Intervar Christian Flwshp 90-; Chem.

**REAM, SUNNY,** Pratt Inst, Brooklyn, NY; FR; BFA; Charles Pratt Schlrshp Wnnr 90-; Fll Ttn Rm And Brd Allwance Fr Bks And Sppls; Fne Art; Cstme Dsgn.

**REAMS, GILBERT W,** Germanna Comm Coll, Locust Grove, VA; FR; BA; Mrg CVS Peoples Drug 90-; Accountng; Economics.

**REANEY, WILLIAM S,** Middle Tn St Univ, Murfreesboro, TN; GD; CERT; HPERS Clb Pres 89-90; STEA; Table Tennis; US Army; Restaurant Mgmt; BS MTSU 83; Elem Ed; Phys Ed/Elem Tchr.

**REARDON, KERRIE A,** Comm Coll Algny Co Algny Cmps, Pittsburgh, PA; FR; White Wtr Rftng Gde; Phys Thrpy.

**REARDON, REBECCA D,** Va Commonwealth Univ, Richmond, VA; JR; BS; Gldn Key 90-; Phi Eta Sigma 89-; Betta Gamma Sigma; S Richmond Rtry Clb Schlrshp; Bus Admin/Mgmt; Invstmnt Anlyst.

**REARIC, MELINDA S,** Kent St Univ Kent Cmps, Kent, OH; SR; Am Mktg Assc 89-; Alpha Lmbd Dlt 87-88; Superior Sclrshp Awrd; BBA; Bus; Mktg.

**REARICK, HOPE K,** Livingston Univ, Livingston, AL; FR; BED; Univ Sngrs Choir; Phi Mu; IM Spts Sftbl Vllybl Tnns; Biol; Med Sch/Ophthlmgst.

**REARICK, LISA A,** D Youville Coll, Buffalo, NY; JR; BSMS; Amer Occptl Thrpy Assoc 90-; Lambda Sigma 89-90; Hon Lambda Sigma 90-; Hons Convctn 88-; Dns Lst 88-; Occptnl Thrpy.

**REAVES, DANIELLE M,** Univ Of Al At Birmingham, Birmingham, AL; JR; BA; Vlybl; Bus; Finance.

**REAVES, JENNIFER C,** Longwood Coll, Farmville, VA; JR; BA; Earth Clb Sec 90-; Hall Cncl Rep 90-; Soc/Anthrop 89-; Alpha Lambda Delta 90; Phi Kappa Phi; Alpha Kappa Delta; Sociology.

**REAVES, WADE A,** Old Dominion Univ, Norfolk, VA; SR; BS; USCF Lteam Junque Bicycle Racing Tm; Am Soc Civil Engrs 90-; Chi Epsilon 90-; Civil Eng.

**REAVIS, JAMES A,** Univ Of Miami, Coral Gables, FL; JR; BA; Lacrosse Clb 88-; After School House Vol; Clncl Psych.

**REAVIS, TALEASHA A,** Hampton Univ, Hampton, VA; FR; BA; Psychlgy.

**REAY, JENNIFER L,** Castleton St Coll, Castleton, VT; FR; BA; Envrnmntl Grp 90-; Elem Ed.

**REBECCA, MARIE,** Ny Univ, New York, NY; FR; BA; Free Entrprs Clb Ofcr 85-86; Phys Thrpy Clb 85-86; USGF Coach 81-; Rgnts Schlrshp Recp 85; Cystic Fibrosis Fndtn Wl St Rep 90-; Gldl Sr Asst Pro Vol 84-85; PGI Athltc Instr Phys/Mntly Hndcpd Chldrn 85-86; Acctg; Bus.

**REBOLLIDA, YOLANDA M,** Miami Dade Comm Coll, Miami, FL; SR; AA; Dns Lst 89-90; Hnrs Day 90; AS Ofc Syst Tech; Bsn; Acctg.**

**RECCHIA, JOYCE M,** Teikyo Post Univ, Waterbury, CT; SR; BS; Rose Traurig Schlrs Sec 90-; Stdnt Orien Prog 90; Alpha Chi 90-; Rowland For Governor Cmpgn 90; State Of CT Legis Intrnshp Prog 90-; Awd Excel Hstry/Pol Sci 90-; State Of CT Cntrl Hsng Comm 90-; Lic Real Est Brkr 89-; Pol Sci; Govt.

**RECEK, CAROLE A,** Fl St Univ, Tallahassee, FL; JR; BSW; SGA 87-/Sec 89; Phi Theta Kappa 87-88; Amer Bus Wmns Assn 89-; AA 84-89; CES 90; Natl Assn/Socl Wrkrs; Tallhsse Coiltn On Hmlss; Assn For Rtrded Citzns; Dns Lst; Oak Coiltn On Hmlss VP 90; Asst Displcd Hmmaker Prgm Oak/Wltn Comm 84-89; Socl Wrk; Socl Wrk MSW/PSYCH.

**RECEVEUR, ALBERT ALEC,** Columbia Union Coll, Takoma Park, MD; SR; BA; Alpha Chi 86-; Phi Eta Sigma 83; Org Mgmt.

**RECEVEUR, SUZANNE J,** Columbia Union Coll, Takoma Park, MD; SR; BA; Org Mgmt.

**RECEVEUR, TERRANCE JEFFREY,** Memphis St Univ, Memphis, TN; MBA; Amercn Assoc For Lab Anml Sci Pres-Elect 85-; Anml Rsrc Ctr St Jude Chldrns Rsrch Hosp Mgr 90-; BS Purdue Univ 85; Fin; Tchng.

**RECH, SHARON A,** Pa St Univ Ogontz Cmps, Abington, PA; FR; BA; Educ.

**RECHENBERG, CHRISTINE A,** Northern Ky Univ, Highland Hts, KY; FR; BA; Psychlgy; Clncl Psychlgy.

**RECHTMAN, AMALIA,** Ny Univ, New York, NY; FR; BA; Investment Banks; Business; Banker.

**RECIO, BLANCA I,** Barry Univ, Miami, FL; FR; BS; Hnrs Pgm; Mktg; Corp Law.

**RECIO, GISELLE,** Antillian Adventist University, Mayaguez, PR; SR; BA; Music Clb Pres 90-; Mayro Guide Clb Cnslr 88-89; Music Educ; Educ.

**RECK, LINDA B,** Immaculata Coll, Immaculata, PA; JR; BA; Pool Mgr/Swm Instr/Lionville YMCA; Sclgy; Tchr.

**RECKNER, JILL E,** Anne Arundel Comm Coll, Arnold, MD; BS; Adult Day Care Ctr Vol; AA 90; Psychology.

**RECTOR, MICHELLE L,** Western Piedmont Comm Coll, Morganton, NC; SO; AABAM; Early Chldhd Ed K-6; Tchr.

**RECTOR, PATRICIA R,** William Paterson Coll, Wayne, NJ; SR; BS; Alumni Schlrshp; NJASFAA Schlrshp; Envrnmntl Sci.

**REDA, CHRISTINE,** Coll Of New Rochelle, New Rochelle, NY; JR; BSN; Natl Stdnt Nurses Assn; Sigma Theta Tau; Nursing.

**REDCROSS, KENNETH E,** Va Commonwealth Univ, Richmond, VA; FR; BA; Phar Clb 90-; George W Clarke Schlrshp 90; IM 90-; Bio; Med.

**REDD, AMY E,** Samford Univ, Birmingham, AL; FR; BA; Chorale; Bells Buchanan 90-; Bapt Stdnt Un 90-; Step Sing; Cls Hon Hon Day Cnvctn; Psychlgy.

**REDD, DANA L,** Rutgers St Univ At Camden, Camden, NJ; JR; Mgmt-Acctg; Mgmt/Fin Occptn.

**REDD, HARRY H,** Morehouse Coll, Atlanta, GA; JR; BA; PA Clb 88-90; Hlth Careers Soc Hmcmng Com 88-89; Morehouse Bus Assn 89-; Jr Achvmnt-Bus Basics 90-; Intrnshp W/Continental Bnk Ft Washington PA 89-; Coll Acdmc Schlrshp; IM Bsktbl; Bnkng/Fin; Hosp Admin/Corp Fin.

**REDD, KATHRYN M,** Univ Of Sc At Columbia, Columbia, SC; FR; BS; Bptst Std Un 90-; Bio.

**REDD, KELLIE M,** Stetson Univ, Deland, FL; FR; BA; Fllwshp Chrstn Aths 90-; NOW 90-; Kappa Alpha Theta; Aerbcs 90-; Geogrphy; Zoogrphy.

**REDD, LORETTA,** Christian Brothers Univ, Memphis, TN; FR; Nom For Frshmn Class VP; Willing Wrkrs Help People In Cmmnty; Membr Of Wrd Rcrdng Artsts; O'landa Drpr/Assoc; Accntng; Tax Accntng.

**REDDEN, NATHAN A,** Univ Of Louisville, Louisville, KY; SO; B ENG; Prgrsve Stdnts Lgue Chrmn Cvl Rgts 88-89; Cmptr Sci Engr.

**REDDEN, STEPHENIE D,** Bethany Coll, Bethany, WV; SO; BA; Bethany Clg Theatre 90-; Instrmntl Engmbl 89-90; SIFE; Amnesty Intl 89-; Renner Stdnt Un Prgrmng Bd 90-; Deans Lst 90-; Fclty Awd Schlrshp 89-90; Acctg Intrn MAF Serv; Chrldr 89-90; Acctg/Theatre; Acting.

**REDDIC, JOHN E,** Univ Of Sc At Columbia, Columbia, SC; SO; Delta Upsilon Hse Mgr 90; Chem Physcs; Tchng.

**REDDICK, ELLEN E,** Univ Of Sc At Columbia, Columbia, SC; SR; BS; Cath Stdnt Org 88-; Omega Chi Epsilon 90-; Golden Key 90-; Gamma Beta Phi Proj Coord 88-; AALCHE 89-; Resrch Asst 89-; Chem Engr.

**REDDICK, LINDA L,** Columbia Union Coll, Takoma Park, MD; SR; Alpha Chi; Amer Reg Rdlgc Tech; Mrlynd Reg Rdlgc Tech; Chf Tech/Hlth Tech MRI; BS; Magna Cum Laude Hlth Care Admin.

**REDDIN, ANTHONY J,** S U N Y At Buffalo, Buffalo, NY; JR; BA; Acctng Assoc 90-; Beta Alpha Psi 90-; Deans List; Im Ftbl; Acctng; CPA.

**REDDING, KENNETH L,** Hillsborough Comm Coll, Tampa, FL; JD; Law.

**REDDISH, CARLA G,** Temple Univ, Philadelphia, PA; SR; BSN; Stdnt Nrs Assc 89-90; Nrsng Schl Cls VP 89-90; Nrsng.

**REDDITT, CLINTON B,** Alcorn St Univ, Lorman, MS; SR; BS; SIFE; Alpha Kappa Mu; Phi Beta Lambda; NAACP; Deans Lst; Bus Admin; Mgmt.**

**REDDOCH, REGINA E,** William Carey Coll, Hattiesburg, MS; SR; BS; Stdnt Tchr Of The Yr William Carey Clg Maintnd 3.9 GPA 90-; 1st Responder Hebron Vol Fire Dept; Elem Ed.

**REDDOCK, TROLICE L W,** Saint Pauls Coll, Lawrenceville, VA; FR; BA; Bus Admn/Educ; Tch.

**REDDY, GAYATRI,** Univ Of Sc At Columbia, Columbia, SC; SR; BA; Intl Stdnts Assn; Early Chldhd Ed.

**REDDY, VENKATA NB,** Memphis St Univ, Memphis, TN; SR; BS; Intl Stdnt Assn 90-; Indn Stdnt Assn 90-; Comp Sci Rmt Site Oper 90-; Mis Trans India Shpg Pvt Ltd 85-90; As Inst Of Eng India 85; Math Sci; Comp Sci/Mgmt.

**REDFERN, JENNIFER L,** Hilbert Coll, Hamburg, NY; FR; AAS; Math; Acctng.

**REDING, LAURA J,** Oh Univ, Athens, OH; SR; BA; 1st Tm Acad All-Mac Mid Amer Conf; Womens Bsktbl Tm Capt 87-; Graph Design; Studio Design.

**REDINGTON, AMY E,** Marywood Coll, Scranton, PA; SO; BA; Nwspaper Stf 90-; Drama Clb 90-; Vol In Actn 90-; Orientatn Comm 90-; Engl/Sco Sci; Law.

**REDINGTON, REGINA L,** Glassboro St Coll, Glassboro, NJ; JR; BA; Free Lanc Cpywrtg Prnt Elec Media 90-; Comm; Advtsng.

**REDMAN III, GEORGE W,** Univ Of Sc At Columbia, Columbia, SC; SO; BS; Wrstlng Clb 90-; Tae Kwon Do Clb 90-; Dns Lst SD Schl Mines/Tech 89-90; Chem; Med.

**REDMAN, WILLIAM M,** Univ Of Miami, Coral Gables, FL; SO; BM; Msc Engnrng Tchnlgy; Prdcr Cmpsr Engnr Prfrmr.

**REDMON, GLENDA B,** Mayland Comm Coll, Spruce Pine, NC; SO; BA; Bus Mnstry/Yth Choir New Manna Bapt Ch; Property Mgr Resort; Nrsng RN.

**REDMON, KIMBERLY BETH,** Fl A & M Univ, Tallahassee, FL; JR; BA; Engl Lit Guild PR Chrprsn 90-; Lambda Iota Tau; Dns Lst; Hnr Rl; Engl; Law.

**REDMON, PATTY A,** Middle Tn St Univ, Murfreesboro, TN; JR; Stdnt Tchr Educ Assn 90-; Stdnt Cncl Excptnl Chldrn 88-; Omega Phi Alpha Almn Sec 88-89; Co-Ed Sftbl Wmns Sftbl Flg Ftbl 88-; Spec Ed; Tchr.

**REDMON, RODNEY G,** Georgetown Coll, Georgetown, KY; GD; BA; Rlgn; Pstrl Care.

**REDMON, SELENA E,** Samford Univ, Birmingham, AL; FR; BA; Univ Radio Sta News Rprtr; Bsbl Offc Sec; IM Bsktbl/Sftbl.

**REDMON, SHERRI S,** Union Inst, Cincinnati, OH; SR; BA; Vol Mntl Hlth Assn; Vol Prbtn Offcr Btlr Cnty; Nite Club Ownr/Mgr; Crisis Cnslng Univ Cinnti 90-; Wmns Stds Cert Univ Cinnti; Scl Work; Crmnl Jstc.

**REDMON, TAMMY R,** Tn Tech Univ, Cookeville, TN; JR; BS; Intervars Christian Flwshp 90-; Math; Tchr.

**REDMOND, DANIEL P,** Hilbert Coll, Hamburg, NY; SO; BS; US Cstms Explorer Pst Rules Chrprsn 90; Govt Serv; Law Enfrcemnt.

**REDMOND, DAVID M,** Univ Of Akron, Akron, OH; JR; BS; Am Inst Aeronautics Astronautics VP; Dns Lst; ASME; Engr Mech; Aerospace Engr.

**REDMOND, DOUGLAS W,** Univ Of Sc At Columbia, Columbia, SC; SR; BS; Stdnt Gov Legl Res Comm Chrmn 90-; Fincl Mgmt Assn; Dns Hnr Lst 90; IM Ftbl/Bsktbl/Hcky/Wrstlng 87-; Busn Finc/Econ; Bnk Mgmt Consltng.

**REDMOND JR, EDWIN C,** Univ Of Cincinnati-Clrmnt Coll, Batavia, OH; SO; ASSOC; Commrcl Art.

**REDMOND, IDELLA L,** Tougaloo Coll, Tougaloo, MS; SR; BA; Sclgy Clb 87-; Hnr Rll; Lxngtn Mnr Nrsng Hme Intrnshp Actvts Dir Asst; Sclgy; Attnd Grad Schl.

**REDMOND, JAYNE M,** Miami Chrisitian Coll, Miami, FL; SR; BS; Grdn Ad Ltm 88-; Psychlgy/Cnslng.

**REDMOND, KATHLEEN,** Glassboro St Coll, Glassboro, NJ; SR; BA; Phi Alpha Theta 89; AA Glouceller Co Clg 72; Hstry; Tchr.

**REDMOND, RHONDA J,** Utica Coll Of Syracuse Univ, Utica, NY; GD; Alpha Omicron; Psi Chi 90-; Hnrs List 89-; Psi Beta 88; Pres List Mohawk Vly Coll; Smohawk Vly Psych Ctr 89; Ctr Against Sexual Assault 85; Parents Anonymous 87-88; Spec Olympcs 83; Psych.**

**REDMOND, RODNEY W,** Rust Coll, Holly Springs, MS; SR; BA; SGA Pres 88-; Bd Of Trustees Rep 89-; Rpes Ldrs Forum 89-; Sigma Tau Delta 89-; Alpha Kappa Mu Chpln 90-; Crimson Schlrs Chpln 90-; Phi Beta Sigma Pres 90-; Engl Educ; Professor/Educator.

**REDMOND, SHEILA A,** Va St Univ, Petersburg, VA; SR; BS; Phi Beta Lambda Secr; SCLS; FBLA Secr; Dns Lst; Adm; Syst Analyst.

**REDNER, DEBRA E,** Ramapo Coll Of Nj, Mahwah, NJ; SR; BS; Acctng Clb; NAA; Delta Mu Delta; Deans Lst 88-; Acctng Acad Exc; SAB Awd; Cum Laude; Business Adm; Acctng.**

**REDRICK, P LAMONT,** Morehouse Coll, Atlanta, GA; SO; BS; Atlanta U Ctr Chmstry Clb 90-; Natl Soc Blck Engrs 89-; Morehouse Clge Dns Lst 89-; Morehouse Clge Hnr Rl 89-; Chrstn Yth Flwshp 88-89; Morton Thiokol Corp Intrn; Digital Equip Corp Schlrshp; Dupont Corp Schlrshp; Chmstry; Chem Engrg.

**REEB, DORRAINE L,** Davis & Elkins Coll, Elkins, WV; SR; BS; Stdnt Educ Assoc 88-; Jennings Randolph Ldrshp Prog 89-; Hnrs Prog 88-; Hnrs Assoc Secy 88-; Alpha Chi; Acdmc Achvmnt Awrd Educ Dept 90-; USAA All Amer Schlr; AA Catonsville Comm Clg 88; Elem Educ; Teach.

**REECE, DEBORAH N,** Gaston Coll, Dallas, NC; FR; BS; Cvl Clb 90-; Art 89-90; Bnd 89-90; Gamma Beta Phi; Cvl/Envrnmntl; Engrg.

**REECE, KIMBERLY I,** Emory & Henry Coll, Emory, VA; FR; BS; Tnns; Acctg/Math; CPA.

**REECE, PATRICIA T,** Western Piedmont Comm Coll, Morganton, NC; SO; AASC; Phi Theta Kappa 89-90; Crtfd Arbcs Instrctr; Crtf 90; Accntng; Bsns Admnstrtn.

**REECE, PHYLLIS R,** Alcorn St Univ, Lorman, MS; SO; BS; ASU Tech Clb 89-; Alpha Kappa Mu; ASU Dean List Schlr 89-; Ntnl Cllgt Eng Awrs 90-; Cntrct/Sales; Cevron 89-90; Band 89-; Industrial Tech; Mnfctrng.

**REECE, RHONDA G,** Univ Of Akron, Akron, OH; SO; BA; Natl Spch Lang Hrng Assc 90-; Natl Stdnt Spch Lang Hrng Assc 90-; Deans Lst 90; Comm Dsrdrs; Spch Lang Path.

**REECE, STACEY R,** Milligan Coll, Milligan Clg, TN; JR; MA; Bsktbl 90-; Sftbl 90-; Engl; Tchng/Coaching.

**REECE-LE FEVERS, JANN,** Western Piedmont Comm Coll, Morganton, NC; Drexel Booster Club; Henry River Environmental Organization; Horticulture Tech; Horticulture Technology.

**REED ANDERSON, GAIL E,** William Carey Coll, Hattiesburg, MS; JR; BSN; Stdnt Nrs Assn 90-; Eastrn Star 60-; Nrs Tech Biloxi Rgnl Med Cntr 89-; Nrsng; Pediatrc Nrs.

**REED, AMY D,** Endicott Coll, Beverly, MA; SO; AS; Hse Cncl P 90-; Deans Lst 89-90; K-Mart Intern 90; Casa De Moda Intern; Rtlng; Mktg.

**REED, ANGELIA M,** Tougaloo Coll, Tougaloo, MS; JR; BS; Pre-Health Club 89-90; Alpha Lambda Delta Sec 88-89; Delta Sigma Theta 90-; Chemistry; Medical School.

**REED, BRENDA L,** Livingston Univ, Livingston, AL; FR; BS; Prgms Brd; Math/Sci Soc; Math Assn Amer; Phi Eta Sigma; Phi Mu; Stdnt Sprt Clb Sec; Deans Lst; IM Sftbl; Chem; Pharm.

**REED, CARRIE L,** Wv Univ At Parkersburg, Parkersburg, WV; GD; Phi Theta Kappa 90; Lgl Asst WV; Actrs Gld Prksbrg Dir 90-; Rpblcn Wmns Serv Lge.

**REED, CHERYL E,** Univ Of Tn At Martin, Martin, TN; SO; Blck Stdnt Assn; Med Nrs.

**REED, CHRISTOPHER P,** Syracuse Univ, Syracuse, NY; SR; Archtctr Stdnt Org 86-; Peer Advsr 89; Stdnts Agnst Styrfm 86-; Accptd Study Abd Florence Italy 89-90; B Arch; Archtctr.

**REED, CINDY A,** Middle Tn St Univ, Murfreesboro, TN; SR; BSW; Scl Wrk Stdnts Frm Pres 90-; Deans Lst 90-; Intern Plnn Prnthd Assoc; Scl Wrk.

**REED JR, CLIFFORD,** Bethune Cookman Coll, Daytona Beach, FL; SR; BA; Bsktbl Tm 89-; US Army 89; Sldr Month 89; Good Condct Medal 89; MVP Bsktbl Tm; Schlstc Achvmnt Awd; Peoples Choice Std Athltc Yr; Physcl Educ; Tch.

**REED, COURTNEY J,** Daemen Coll, Amherst, NY; JR; BA; Nwspr Jrnlst 88-89; Ltry Rvw Wrtr 89-; Dns Lst 90-; Engl; Freelance Wrtr.

**REED JR, CRAIG A,** Anne Arundel Comm Coll, Arnold, MD; FR; AA; Comp Info Sys.

**REED, DARRELL L,** Univ Of Ky, Lexington, KY; SR; BA; Golden Key 90-; Phi Theta Kappa 87-; Mu Alpha Theta 87-; Intern Gen Elec 90; Deans List 87-; IM Ftbl/Bsktbl/Vlybl 88-; Elec Engr.

**REED, DAWN M,** Coppin St Coll, Baltimore, MD; SO; BS; Mc Nair Pgm; Chi Sgm Chi; Comm Svc Lbrty Med Ctr; Math; Mech Eng.

**REED, DE ANNA P,** Middle Tn St Univ, Murfreesboro, TN; SR; BED; Elem Edctn.

**REED, DIANNA L,** Glassboro St Coll, Glassboro, NJ; SR; Crmnl Just Soc 90; In-Svcs Cts 90; BA Glassboro St Coll; Law-Just.

**REED, DOROTHA G,** Bethel Coll, Mckenzie, TN; SR; BS; Gama Beta Phi 88-; Theta Psi 89-; Bob Hope Hon Schlrshp 87-; Busn.

**REED, DOUGLAS D,** Univ Of Al At Huntsville, Huntsville, AL; GD; BSE; IEEE 90-; Flwshp Chrstn Stdnts Offcr 89-90; Eta Kappa Nu 89-90; Tau Beta Pi 90; Elec Engr.

**REED, ELIZABETH ANN,** Ms St Univ, Miss State, MS; FR; BARCH; Unv Hnrs Prgrm 90-; Michael C Johnston Mmrl Awd; BA Intln Stds Unv Padova 89; Arch.

**REED, GARY K,** Clayton St Coll, Morrow, GA; JR; BS; Chem Eng.

**REED, GERRY D,** Salisbury St Univ, Salisbury, MD; SO; BA; Bapt Stdnt Mnstrs 89-90; Hon Pgm 89-; Schlstc Hon Soc; Phi Eta Sigma; Foreign Lang Lab Asst 90-; Aerobic Classes 89-; Psychlgy; Cnslng.

**REED, JACQUE A,** Univ Of Cincinnati, Cincinnati, OH; SR; BA; Golden Key; Chldrns Hosp Vol; Hons Schlrshp 90-; Indpndnt Cntrctr; Scndry Ed/Engl; Tchng MA.

**REED JR, JAMES B,** Roane St Comm Coll, Harriman, TN; SO; BBA; Jdcry Brd Chrprsn 89; Snte 90; Annl Staff 89; Awds Comm 89-90; Bplctns Comm 90-91; Plnng Comm 90; Bapt Stdnt Union 89; Stdnt Bdy Pres 90; Clg Rpblcns Chrprsn 90; TISL Comm Sec 90; TN Stdnt Pres Cnsl 90; Bsnss; Bsnss/Law.**

**REED, JAMES KEVIN,** Clemson Univ, Clemson, SC; FR; BS; Cvl Eng.

**REED, JAYSYN P,** Springfield Tech Comm Coll, Springfield, MA; SR; AS; Grphc Arts Clb 90-; Alpha Nu Omega 90-; Std Actvts Chldrns Prtys 90-; Std Tutor 90-; Grphc Arts Tech; Adv/Dsgn.

**REED, JILL A,** S U N Y Coll Of Tech At Delhi, Delhi, NY; SO; Assoc Trvl Exec Pres 90-; Stdnt Govt Sec 90-; Chrldng Ch 90-; AAS Trvl Trsh Mgmt; AAS Bus Admn 88; Trvl Trsm Mgmt.

**REED, JOHN K E,** Clark Atlanta Univ, Atlanta, GA; JR; BA; English/Bus Data Entry; Tch/Bus Progmr.

**REED, JOHN W,** Southern Coll Of Tech, Marietta, GA; SO; BS; Radio DJ 90; Crim Just: U S Marshall.

**REED, JULIE A,** Spartanburg Methodist Coll, Spartanburg, SC; FR; Soccer; Acctntng.

**REED, KAREN E,** Ms St Univ, Miss State, MS; JR; BA; Soc Advcmnt Mgmt 90-; Bus Adm; Bus.

**REED, KATHRYN E,** Miami Jacobs Jr Coll Of Bus, Dayton, OH; SO; Acctg.

**REED, KERRY L,** Wv Univ, Morgantown, WV; JR; BS; Aero Eng.

**REED, KIMBERLY A,** Le Moyne Coll, Syracuse, NY; FR; BA; Pltcl Sci.

**REED, LANE B,** Ms St Univ, Miss State, MS; SR; BA; Clg Rep State V P 88-; Stdnt Assn Comm 82; Stnns Schlrs Forum 89-; Phi Kappa Phi 90-; Mortr Brd; Omicron Delta Kappa Pr 90-; Gamma Beta Phi St Pr 89-; Pi Sigma Alpha 90-; Amer Pol Sci Assn 89-; Statesmn Pr 90-; Bapt Stdnt Un 88-; Pr Schlr Cert 89-; Pol Sci; Law.

**REED, LORRI M,** Middle Tn St Univ, Murfreesboro, TN; JR; BSN; Nrsng; Nrs Prctnr.

**REED, MARILYN W,** Alcorn St Univ, Lorman, MS; GD; MS; Englsh Clb 88-89; Alpha Swthrt Orgnztn 88-89; Ordr Estrn Str 87-; Alpha Kappa Mu; Alpha Mu Gamma Prsdnt 87-88; Alpha Kappa Alpha Sor; Intrnshp TV 89; USDA Intrn 90; BA 90; Englsh Edctn; Tchr.

**REED, MARSHA K,** Northeast State Tech Comm Coll, Blountville, TN; FR; BA; Jhnsn Cty Jr Mndy Clb 86-89; Engl.

**REED, MARY L,** Mount Aloysius Jr Coll, Cresson, PA; FR; BSN; Phi Theta Kappa; Waitress 87-90; Nrsng; Psychiatric Nrs.

**REED, MELANIE A,** Castleton St Coll, Castleton, VT; FR; AS; IM Sftbl/Horseshoes 90-; Crmnl Jstce; Law.

**REED, MELISA A,** Marshall University, Huntington, WV; GD; MA; Stdnt Cncl For Exceptnl Chldrn Pres 83-86; Huntington Area Soc For Autistic Chldrn/Adlts; ; Wv Soc For Autistic Chldrn; Educ Specist; BA 86; Behavior Disorders.

**REED, MICHAEL S,** Univ Of Richmond, Richmond, VA; FR; BA; Hist Club Treas 90-; Bapt Stdnt Un 90-; Phi Kappa Sigma Pres Pldg Cl 90-; Hist/Am Studies; Law.

**REED, MICHELLE D,** Va Commonwealth Univ, Richmond, VA; SO; BA; Pre Phrmcy Clb 89-; Phrmcy.

**REED, MICHELLE R,** Univ Of Ky, Lexington, KY; SO; BA; Phi Eta Sigma 90-; Elec Engrng.

**REED, MILISSA E,** Univ Of Nc At Asheville, Asheville, NC; JR; BA; Econ Clb 90-; Cncrt Bnd 80-; Hon Stdnt/Indpndnt Schlr 80-; Hon Stdnt 90-; S W Bufton Mem Grnt 90-; D Reiner Poltcl Econ Awrd 90-; Pres Schlr 79-80; MENSA 89; Sprtswr Syst/Procdrs Mgr 89; Buyers Rep 90; Econ/Poltcl Sci/Poltcl Econ; Law.

**REED, PAMELA L,** S U N Y Coll Of A & T Morrisvl, Morrisville, NY; SR; BA; AS; Cmptr Sci; Pgmmng.**

**REED, PHILIP A,** Old Dominion Univ, Norfolk, VA; JR; BED; ODU TECA V P 90-; TECA Edtr; ITEA; VTEA; TSA; Surf Clb; Iota Lambda Sigma; Tech Educ.

**REED, REBECCA,** West Chester Univ, West Chester, PA; SR; BS; Chmbr Choir 89-; Stdnt Teach 90-; Music; Edn.

**REED, SALLY L,** Univ Of Sc At Columbia, Columbia, SC; JR; BA; Edn Clb VP 88-; Edn; Teach.

**REED, SANDRA R,** Coll Of Charleston, Charleston, SC; JR; BS; Tour Guides 90-; Pi Mu Epsilon; Math; Tchng.

**REED, SHENISE R,** Stillman Coll, Tuscaloosa, AL; FR; Gamma Iota Sigma; Blue White Swthrt; All Amer Schlr; Dns Schlr; Dns Lst.

**REED, SUSAN J,** Fayetteville St Univ, Fayetteville, NC; FR; BS; Spec Educ; Tchng.

**REED, TALLY L,** Univ Of West Fl, Pensacola, FL; SR; MA; Educ Assn Treas 89-90; Hon Rl 88-; BA; Educ; Tch.

**REED, TODD L,** Univ Of Tn At Martin, Martin, TN; JR; BS; Bapt Student Union 90-; Phi Theta Kappa 89-90; Gamma Beta Phi VP 89-90; Martin Meth Clg Acad Shlrshp 88-90; Bsbl 88-90; AA Martin Meth Clg 90; Agriculture; Soil/Water Conservation.

**REED, WILEY ZANE,** Univ Of Sc At Columbia, Columbia, SC; SR; BS; ASME; Phi Beta Theta 82-84; Fluor-Daniel Eng Schlr 89-; Lebby-Ellis Eng Schlr 89-; Fluor-Daniel Eng Intern 90; AS Orangeburg-Calhoun Tech Coll 84; Mech Eng.

**REED, YOLANDA N,** Fl A & M Univ, Tallahassee, FL; SO; BS; Riology Premed Socty; Most Outstdng Biology Stdnt 89-90; Mahlon C Rhaney Awd 90-; Med.

**REEDER, ANNETTE M,** Juniata Coll, Huntingdon, PA; SO; BS; Mrchng Bnd Mjrtte 90; Jz Bnd Pianst; IM Vlybl 89-; Phi Chi Theta; Acctg Txtbk Awrd; Bus/Frnch; Intl Bus.

**REEDER, DARLENE K,** Cumberland County Coll, Vineland, NJ; FR; BA; Bsn Admn/Acctng; CPA.

**REEDER, JENNIFER A,** Christopher Newport Coll, Newport News, VA; FR; Hnrs Pgrm 90-; Hnrs Coun 90-; Franklin O Blechman Schlrshp 90-; Bus.

**REEDY, AMY LEIGH,** Emory & Henry Coll, Emory, VA; FR; BA; Emry And Hnry Schlr 90-; Psych; Scl Wrk.

**REEL JR, DAVID A,** Fl Coll, Temple Terrace, FL; FR; Crest 90-; Phi Theta Kappa; Phi Sigma Chi 90; Biology Dept Awd; Deans Lst; Pre Med; Med.

**REENTS, MARK J,** Embry Riddle Aeronautical Univ, Daytona Beach, FL; SR; BS; Precision Flight Team 90-; Army Aviat Assc; Future Aviat Prffnls Amer; Pilot US Army Attack Helicopters; Aviation Mgmt; Pilot/Mngr Mjr Airline.

**REEP, MARK A,** Gaston Coll, Dallas, NC; SO; BA; Math; Cmptr Sci.

**REEP, PHILLIP D,** Univ Of Nc At Asheville, Asheville, NC; FR; BS; Dns Lst; Chnclrs Lst; Chrch Cong Sng Ldr/Dir Of Outrch Prog; Elec/Cmptr Engr.

**REES, ANNETTE M,** Kent St Univ Kent Cmps, Kent, OH; JR; BA; Golden Key; Lambda Alpha Epsilon 90-; Sheri Jo Luft Mem Awd 90; Psych/Crmnl Just; Chld Psych.

**REESE, CHRISTIE A,** Indiana Univ Of Pa, Indiana, PA; JR; BA; Rehab Clb 89-; Sign Lang 89-90; Alpha Gamma Delta 88-89; Lrng Ctr Peer Advsr 90-; Voc Rehab Cnslr.

**REESE, DONNA M,** Schenectady County Comm Coll, Schenectady, NY; JR; AAS; Ladies BPO Elks Schenectady/Cobleskill NY; Clms Exmnr Prdntl Ins Albany 88-; Bus; Acctg.

**REESE, DONNIETA M,** Ky St Univ, Frankfort, KY; SO; Natl Cncl Ngro Wmn; Intrnshp W/Wstnghs Matrls Co; Vlybl 89-; Acctg; CPA.

**REESE, ERIC W,** Univ Of Miami, Coral Gables, FL; SR; BA; Lambda Chi Alpha; Hstry; Law.

**REESE, JOHN T,** Samford Univ, Birmingham, AL; GD; JD; BS Univ Of TN 89; Law.

**REESE, KATHLEEN PATRICIA,** Univ Of Ky, Lexington, KY; JR; BSW; Practicum Primitive Camp Emtnly/Bhvrlly Dstrbd Chldrn Asst Prog Dir; Soc Work.

**REESE, LEE D,** Southern Coll Of Tech, Marietta, GA; SR; Natl Soc Prof Engrs 88-; AS Gainesvl Clg 88; Mech Engr Tech; Engr.

**REESE, LESONJO Q,** Alcorn St Univ, Lorman, MS; FR; Hlthf Med Tech.

**REESE, MARQUITA CELESTE,** Wilberforce Univ, Wilberforce, OH; FR; BA; Phi Beta Sigma Spokes Person; Drama Clb; Clinical Psychlgy; Pre Law.

**REESE, MARYANN,** Hudson Valley Comm Coll, Troy, NY; SR; BA; Phi Theta Kappa 90; Peer Tutor 90; Engl/Sec Ed; Engl Prof.

**REESE, MICHAEL D,** Daemen Coll, Amherst, NY; SO; Booga Booga Beta; Psyc Thrpy.

**REESE, RACHEL E,** Univ Of Nc At Asheville, Asheville, NC; SO; BS; AAS Sandhills Comm Coll 79; Envrnmntl Sci-Geo; Envrnmntl Geo.

**REESE, ROBIN N,** Clark Atlanta Univ, Atlanta, GA; JR; BA; Beta Gamma Sigma; Hon Rl 88-89; Natl Cllgt Bus Merit Awd 90; Bus Admin; Mgmt.**

**REESE, SALENA A,** Univ Of Sc At Aiken, Aiken, SC; FR; MBA; Bsns; Acctg/Audtr.

**REESE, SHANE C,** Coll Of Charleston, Charleston, SC; FR; BA; Engl; Ed.

**REESE-YOUNG, REGINA L,** Lane Coll, Jackson, TN; SR; BS; SGA Pres 90; Cncrt Choir Chpln 89-90; St Paul CME Chrch Jcksn Tn Ast Pstr 89; Clvry CME Chrch Pasadena Ca Asst Pstr 87-89; Pres Awd For Outstndng Ldrshp Awd 90; SGA Awd For Devoted Ldrshp Awd 90; SGA Awd For Outstndng Acad Achievemnt 90; Bsnss Ed; Mnstry.

**REESOR, ELAINE C,** Univ Of Louisville, Louisville, KY; JR; BS; South Central Bell Tele Oper 79-; Comp Sci.

**REEVE, JONATHAN T,** Univ Of Ky, Lexington, KY; FR; BA; Vars Debate Tm 90-; Phi Eta Sigma 90-; Alpha Lambda Delta 90-; Lab Ldr; Debate Inst; Engl/Art Hstry; Tchr.

**REEVE III, WILLIAM H,** Nova Univ, Ft Lauderdale, FL; GD; MBA; Scty Rl Est Apprsrs Prs 86-87; Chrmn Ed Comm 84-89; Chrmn Admssns Comm 82-84; Treas 82-83; Sec 83-84; Amrcn Instt Rl Est Apprsrs 88-; Apprsl Inst 90-; Rgstrd Rel Est Brkr; Tchng Bnkng Fnc Rl Est; Apprsr 76; USMC 62-66; Real Est.**

**REEVES, CASSANDRA D,** Memphis St Univ, Memphis, TN; SR; BM; Blck Schlrs Unlmtd; MENC; Pr Mntr Prog; Gamma Beta Phi; Sigma Alpha Iota Treas; Msc Educ; Tchr.

**REEVES, CHARLES D,** Tn Temple Univ, Chattanooga, TN; Alpha Epsln Theta; Cert TN Dpt Educ; Math; Admn.

**REEVES, DONNA E,** Univ Of Nc At Charlotte, Charlotte, NC; SO; BA; A Luta Con 90-; Blck Stu Unn 90-; Dsbld Stu Serv 89-; Hstry; Educ Univ/Law.

**REEVES, ELIZABETH C,** Univ Of West Fl, Pensacola, FL; JR; BA; Socratic Soc; Relig Studies; Mssn Flds/Furthering Ed.

**REEVES, HEATHER D,** Univ Of Southern Ms, Hattiesburg, MS; JR; BS; U Activities Cncl Membr Of Yr 88f Stndt Eagle Clb; Alcohol Awareness Task Frce 90; Res Assist 90; Ancient Egypt Class Wrtng Coach 90; Yr Abroad Studies In Wales; Engl; Ed.

**REEVES, KELLY CHRISTINE,** Univ Of Sc At Columbia, Columbia, SC; JR; BA; Psi Chi 89-; Yng Rpblcns 90-; Tri Delta Ref Chrmn 90; Actvs; Deans Lst 89-90; Day Care 90-; Awrd Acdmc Exclnc; Bus Admin; Corp Law.

**REEVES, KENNETH G,** Broward Comm Coll, Ft Lauderdale, FL; SO; AA; Ntl Eng Soc 88-90; Read Campgn 90-; Soc Photogrphc Art 88-89; Phi Theta Kappa 90-; Broward Read Camp; Pres Lst; Rinker Schlrshp 90-; Coll Assoc Schlshp 90-; Cmptr Oper 77-; Cmptr Eng.

**REEVES, KIMBERLY J,** Medical Coll Of Ga, Augusta, GA; JR; BSN; Coll Rpblcns Grks Agnst Mis Mgmt Alchl; Alpha Lambda Delta; Delta Zeta; Natl Nrsng Stdnt Schlr Awrd; Nrsng.

**REEVES, LORRAINE MARY,** Glassboro St Coll, Glassboro, NJ; SR; BA; Stdnt Govt Sen/Rec Sec 88-89; Phi Alpha Theta VP 90-; Pres Lst/Dns Lst 88-90; Marius Lvngstn Hstry Awrd; W D Grls Sccr Coach 79-80; CCD Tchr 78-87; Sub Tchr; AA Gloucstr Co Coll 89; Hstry; Tchr.

**REEVES, LUCIAN E,** Middle Tn St Univ, Murfreesboro, TN; SO; Kappa Delta Phi; Gamma Beta Pi; Intl Rltns; Law.

**REEVES, MARCUS C,** Alcorn St Univ, Lorman, MS; JR; BS; Phi Theta Kappa 89-90; Alpha Kappa Mu; Bsktbl 88-90; AA Coahoma Comm Clg 90; Biol; Med.

**REEVES, MARY MANNON,** Middle Tn St Univ, Murfreesboro, TN; SR; BA; Currents Lit Mag Rhodes Coll Edtr 84-85; Natl Hnr Socty 80-81; Engl Hnr Socty 90; Southwstrn Schlr; Natl Hnr Socty Letter Of Cmdntn; Trinity Luth Chrch Tullahoma; Prog Asst 88-; Engl; Tch/Write.

**REEVES, SANDRA D,** Memphis St Univ, Memphis, TN; FR; BS; Alpha Chi Omega 90-; Sci; Nrsng.

**REEVEY, EDWARD A,** Univ Of Sc At Columbia, Columbia, SC; FR; BA; Glf Tm 90-; Outstndg Schlstc Achvmnt 90-; Acctg; Golf.

**REF, HOVAV,** City Univ Of Ny Baruch Coll, New York, NY; SR; BBA; Clge Frgn Trd Soc 89-; Beta Gamma Sigma; Gldn Key; Dns Lst 89-; Endwmnt Fnd Provosts Schlrshp 90; Internatl Mktg.

**REGAN, AMY E,** Bristol Univ, Bristol, TN; SR; BA; Acctg.

**REGAN, ELLEN P,** Syracuse Univ, Syracuse, NY; FR; BS; Nrsng.

**REGAN, JENNIFER A,** Miami Univ, Oxford, OH; FR; BA; Phi Eta Sigma; Alpha Sigma Alpha 90-; Deans Lst 90-; Pres Lst; Culler Awd; Aeronautics/Math; Engineering.

**REGAN, JENNIFER C,** Univ Of Southern Ms, Hattiesburg, MS; SO; BS; Gamma Beta Phi 90-; Phi Eta Sgm 89-90-; Beta Beta Beta Frshmn Bio Awrd 90; Bio; Resrch/Dvlpmnt.

**REGAN, MATTHEW M,** Duquesne Univ, Pittsburgh, PA; FR; BMUS; Natl Mrt Schlrshp; Schlrshp Schl Music; Music Prfrmnc.

**REGENT, RHONDA S,** Nova Univ, Ft Lauderdale, FL; GD; MBA; Pnhllnc Cncl 86-88; Stdnt Educ Lflng Ftnss Co-Prdcr 88-89; Grk Wk Asst Dir Slctns 87; Omicron Delta Kappa 87-89; Alpha Lamda Delta 86-89; Pi Rho Sigma 88-89; Delta Phi Epsilon 85-89; Grad Cum Laude; Gator Gals 86-87; Mktg; Mktg/Cmnctns.

**REGENTIN, JOHN E,** Radford Univ, Radford, VA; JR; Tour Guide 90-; Stdnt Govt Multi Cultral Affrs Cordntr 90-; Resident Asstnt 89-; Quest Assistant Frshm Orientation 90; Phi Beta Sigma Vic Pres 89-; Rectration; Thereputic Rec.

**REGER, JUDY G,** Middle Tn St Univ, Murfreesboro, TN; SR; BSW; Soc Wrk Forum VP 88-; Gamma Beta Phi 87-89; Phi Kappa Phi 90-; Alpha Delta Mu VP 89-; Joe Ramsey Leatherman Awd 89-90; Clayton L James Awd 90-; Soc Wrk/Psychlgy; Cnslng.

**REGINELLI, DAVID R,** Utica Coll Of Syracuse Univ, Utica, NY; GD; MBA; BS 90; Fince; Corp Fince.

**REGIS, ELLEN M,** Albertus Magnus Coll, New Haven, CT; SR; BA; Act II Theatre Albertus Magnus Campus Musl Dir 89; Frdns Kings Clg London 90-; English Club 88-; Intshp Tyler Cooper/Alcon PC New Haven; English/French; Law.

**REGISTER, DIANNA L,** Univ Of West Fl, Pensacola, FL; SR; BS; US Nvl Reserve Cmnctns Elctrcn 90-; US Navy Flight Simulator Tech 81-85; Co-Op Stdnt Telecmnctns Spec Nvl Cmptr/Telecmnctns Sta Naval Air Sta Pensacola 88-; AS Pensacola Jr Clg 89; Elctrcl Engr Tech; Cmptr/Telecmnctns.

**REGISTER, ERIC L,** Morehouse Coll, Atlanta, GA; SO; BA; Pre Law Soc V P 89-; Hon Prog Clb Com Chrmn 89-; Pltcl Sci Clb 89-; Clg Hon Prog; Uhlmann Fndtn Schlr 90; Pltcl Sci; Law.

**REGISTER, GREGORY D,** Fl A & M Univ, Tallahassee, FL; JR; BA; Architecture.

**REGO RIOS, HILDA L,** Univ Of Pr At Mayaguez, Mayaguez, PR; SO; BS; Hnr Roll; NCMLA; Chmstry; Chem Engnrng.

**REGUEIRO, MONICA,** Miami Dade Comm Coll, Miami, FL; FR; AA; Law.

**REHAN, FARRUKH,** Univ Of South Al, Mobile, AL; FR; BBA; Deep South Model United Nations; Phi Kappa Phi; Business; Marketing Firm.

**REHAR, SUSAN M,** Indiana Univ Of Pa, Indiana, PA; SR; Frnch Clb ACEI PSEA NEA; Dns Lst; BS Educ 90; Elem Educ; Tchng.

**REHBERG, DELBERT JOHN,** Columbia Greene Comm Coll, Hudson, NY; SO; BS; Clb Ftbl; Pres Schlr 90-; As; Crmnl Jstce; Law Enfrcmnt Arsn Invest.

**REHDER, MELISSA D,** Fl St Univ, Tallahassee, FL; SR; BA; Phi Beta Kappa; Golden Key; Phi Kappa Phi; Biology; Horticulture.

**REHM, PATRICK G,** Univ Of South Al, Mobile, AL; SO; BA; Glf; Bsn/Eng; Cmnctn Sprts.

**REIBER, GINA M,** Columbus Coll Of Art & Design, Columbus, OH; FR; BFA; Ilstrtn; Free Lnc Artst.

**REICH, KAREN E,** Yeshiva Univ, New York, NY; SR; BS; Acctng Soc Peer Tutor 88-; Acctng.

**REICHARD, PATRICIA G,** Fl International Univ, Miami, FL; SR; BS; Future Educators Of Am 87-88; Phi Kappa Phi; Natl Assoc Ednl Young Chldrn 90-; Assoc Supvrsn Curriculum Dvlpmnt 90-; AA Miami Dade Comm Coll 88; Elem Edn; Teach.

**REICHENBACH, ROBERT,** Embry Riddle Aeronautical Univ, Daytona Beach, FL; FR; BS; Bowling League 90; Dns Lst 90; Priv Pilot Lic; Aerunautical Sci; Comm Airline Pilot.

**REICHENBERGER, CHARLES S W,** Nova Univ, Ft Lauderdale, FL; GD; Intrntl Stdnt Organ 84-86; Nwspr Bus Mgr 85-87; Fin Mngmnt Assn Natl Hnr Soc 90; BS 87; MBA 90; Bus Fin.

**REICHERT, JAMES M,** Wagner Coll, Staten Island, NY; FR; BS; Alld Hlth Clb; Sci; Phys Asst.

**REICHERT, KEVIN E,** Abraham Baldwin Agri Coll, Tifton, GA; FR; AS; Bnd Prcssnst 90-; Mu Alpha Theta 90-; Bptst Stdnt Ynion 90-; Phi Theta Kappa 90-; Suprr Hon Stdnt; Hon Stdnt; Pres Lst Deans Lst 90-; Mech Drftng Dplm Moultrie Area Tech Inst 89; Math; Eng.

**REICHERT, TRACEY C,** Le Moyne Coll, Syracuse, NY; SO; BS; Intrgrl Hnrs Prog 89-; Psych; Cnslr.

**REICHGUT, STEVAN G,** S U N Y At Buffalo, Buffalo, NY; JR; BA; Delta Sigma Pi; Bus Admn; Intl Trd/MBA.

**REICHNER, STEPHANIE S,** Bloomsburg Univ Of Pa, Bloomsburg, PA; FR; BS; Studio Bnd Alto Sax III Libr/Equip Mgr; Early Chldhd/Elem Ed; Ed.

**REICIS, SANDRA S,** S U N Y At Buffalo, Buffalo, NY; GD; MA; Amer Inst Archtctr Stdns; Fine Arts Acad; Spidola; TWIGS Pres 89-; BA York Univ Toronto CN 77; Architecture.

**REID, AMY L,** Duquesne Univ, Pittsburgh, PA; SR; Natl Clgte Cmunctn Arts Awd; Pittsburgh Blind Assn Intrn 90; Pub Rltns; Cmunctns.

**REID, ANDREW K,** Ny Univ, New York, NY; SO; BA; Alpha Sigma Lambda; Deans List 90-; Prog Dir YMCA Of Greater NY; Boys Club Of NY Vlntr; Program Dir; AA 90; Cum Laude; Education; Youth Services.

**REID, APRIL A,** Univ Of Nc At Charlotte, Charlotte, NC; JR; BA; Gldn Key; Sanford V Davenport Schlr; AA Surry Cmmnt Coll 90; Hstry Engl; Tchng.

**REID, ASEEM B,** Atlantic Comm Coll, Mays Landing, NJ; SO; MBA; Prosecuting Atty.

**REID, CHARMAINE A,** City Univ Of Ny Bronx Comm Col, Bronx, NY; SR; AS; Stdnt Govt VP 89-90; Interorgnztnl Cncl Pres 89-90; MBRS 90-; Phi Theta Kappa 90-; Dstngshd Serv Awd 90; Deans Lst 88-; Bio; Med.

**REID, CHRISTOPHER BRIAN,** Western Carolina Univ, Cullowhee, NC; FR.

**REID, CHRISTOPHER M,** Fl International Univ, Miami, FL; SR; BS; Cthlc Yth Org Advsr VP 87; Hly Fmly Cthlc Chrch 84-; Euchrstc Mnstr; Mstr Crmns Lctr 85-; Alchlc Bev/Tobacco Intrn; Crmnl Jstc; Law Enfrcmnt.

**REID, DEAN C,** Va Commonwealth Univ, Richmond, VA; JR; BA; History/Education; Teaching.

**REID, DEXTER A,** Morris Brown Coll, Atlanta, GA; JR; BS; Mrchng Bnd 90-; Symphnc Bnd 90-; Cmptr Clb 90-; Pep Bnd 90-; Cncrt Bnd; Prvst Lst 89-90; Phi Mu Alpha Sec 90-; Intshp Hghs Arcrft Co; Cmptr Sci; Sys Anlysts.

**REID, DIANE M,** Saint Andrews Presbytrn Coll, Laurinburg, NC; SR; Chorale/Chmbr Sngrs VP 87-; Stdnt Gov VP Res Hall VP 89-; St Andrews Highland Plyrs 89-90; St Andrews Hon Soc 90-; Pi Gamma Mu 90-; Coll Chrstn Union Pltcl Comm Chr 89-90; Eco-Action 90-; Deans Lst 87-; Pltcs/Rlgn; Tch Pltcs/Law/Theo Coll Lvl.

**REID, DONNA K,** Wv Inst Of Tech, Montgomery, WV; SO; BS; Hall Cncl Drm Cncl 89-90; Chrstn Stdnt Union 89; Cmptr Sci; Cmptr Anlyst/Prog.**

**REID, HEATHER L,** Hillsborough Comm Coll, Tampa, FL; SO; AA; Phi Theta Kappa VP 90-; Phi Theta Kappa Srvc Awd 90-; Media Prfrmnc; Cmmntns BA.

**REID, JANET G,** Univ Of The Dist Of Columbia, Washington, DC; SO; BA; Admin Asst Fed Resrv Brd; Bus Mngmnt.

**REID, JEFFREY D,** Univ Of Sc At Columbia, Columbia, SC; SO; BA; Mrktng Assoc; Lamda Pi Lamda 89-; Prsdnts Ldrshp Scty 89-; Frshmn Hnr Rll 89; Deans Lst 90-; Pi Kappa Phi Push Chrmn 89-; Snt Pg 90-; Mrktng.

**REID, JOHN W,** Univ Of Fl, Gainesville, FL; SR; BS; Financial Mgmt Assoc 90-; Phi Kappa Phi 90-; Beta Gamma Sigma 90-; Omicron Delta Epsilon 90-; Finance; Law.

**REID, KAREN L,** Coll Of Charleston, Charleston, SC; SR; BS; Tstmstrs 87-; Omicron Delta Kappa 90-; Zeta Tau Alpha 87-; Bus Admin.

**REID, MICHELLE ANTOINETTE,** Manhattan Coll, Bronx, NY; FR; BSENG; ACAC 90; Eng.

**REID, NOREEN B,** Commonwealth Coll, Virginia Beach, VA; Ofc Admn Clb; Dns Lst 90; Pres Lst 90-; St Marys Acad Vol 90-; AS; Med Offc Prod/Trmnlgy; Med Offc Mgmt.

**REID, STEPHANIE N,** Univ Of Al, Tuscaloosa, AL; FR; Delta Zeta; Bus; Acctg.

**REID, STEVEN H,** Fl International Univ, Miami, FL; JR; BA; SGA 90-; Otstndng Schlr 90-; Pblc Admn; MA PA.

**REID, TINA J,** Univ Of North Fl, Jacksonville, FL; SR; BA; Brd Dir Clay Cnty Cmbr Cmmrc 90-; Bsn Cncl Pres 90; Grn Cove Sprgs Bsn Cncl VP; Beta Gamma Sigma 90-; Asst Mgr Barnett Bank 90-; Acctng; CPA.

**REID, WAYNE P,** Duquesne Univ, Pittsburgh, PA; JR; BA; Dir Ornttn Stf Co-Ldr 89-; Sngrs 89-90; Phi Eta Sigma 88-89; Lambda Sigma 89-90; Mrtr Brd 90-; Phi Kappa Phi 90-; Pi Sigma Alpha 89-; Pol Sci Intshp 90; IM Athlcts 88-; Pol Sci/Bsn; Law Schl.

**REIDELBERGER, DARLENE KAY,** Watterson Coll, Louisville, KY; SR; BA; Mu Phi Epsilon VP 89; Paralegal Assoc; Minor Music ED Southern Ill Univ 86-89; AS John A Logan Clg 84-86; Paralegal; Law Schl.

**REIDELL, JENNIFER,** Univ Of Miami, Coral Gables, FL; SR; BA; RA 88-; Conf Asst 89; Phi Beta Kappa 90-; Phi Kappa Phi 90-; Psi Chi 89-; Dns Lst 87-; Prvst Hnr Rl 89-; Pres Hnr Rl Psy 88-; Psy/Educ; Grad Stdy Psy.

**REIDHEAD, PARIS W,** Cornell Univ Statutory College, Ithaca, NY; SO; BS; Sage Chpl Chr 90; Outdr Educ Instctr; Res Hall Govt Rep 89-90; Trdtn Flwshp 89-; Agri Ecnmcs; Bsn/Ecnmcs.

**REIER, STACY A,** Wright St Univ Lake Cmps, Celina, OH; FR; Stdnt Snt 90; Vol Hosp 89-; Occptnl Thrpy.

**REIFF, CHRISTINE M,** Oh Wesleyan Univ, Delaware, OH; SR; BA; Sentral OH Symphny Orchstra 87-; SPS Secy 87-; WIS 89-; Phi Eta Sigma 87-88; Phi Soc 88-89; Sigma Pi Simga 88-; Roger D Rusk Award 90-; Cosen Grant Intrnshp 89-90; Physcs; MA.

**REIFF, RONNA L,** Comm Coll Algny Co Algny Cmps, Pittsburgh, PA; FR; BSN; Deans Lst; Harmarville Rehab Ctr; Cellular One 86-; Cert ICM Sch Of Business; Cert ICM Sch Bus 84; Nurs-Sci; Nurs Anesthetist.

**REIFSNYDER, ROBERT EMMETT,** Oh Univ-Southern Cmps, Ironton, OH; JR; BNE; ASTM; SSPC; NACE; Qlty Engr; Lead Auditor; Nuclear Lvl Iii Inspctr; Sci; Engr.

**REIGEL, SUSAN L,** Fl St Univ, Tallahassee, FL; SO; BA; Phi Heta Sigma; AA Fsu; Math/Psych.

**REIL, G LYNN,** Radford Univ, Radford, VA; JR; BBA; Cardinal Key 89-90; Bus; Paralegal.

**REIL, REBECCA E,** Radford Univ, Radford, VA; FR; BS; Art Educ; Tchr.

**REILLEY, ROBERT T,** Franklin And Marshall Coll, Lancaster, PA; FR; BS; Clg Rpblcns 90-; BACCHUS Club 90-; Bus Club 90-; Deans List 90-; Clg Hons List; Im Ftbl/Bsktbl 90-; Bus; Corp.

**REILLY, ALICE T,** Columbia Greene Comm Coll, Hudson, NY; SO; BA; Dmcrtc Clb; AS; Bus Admn; Mngmnt Trsn.

**REILLY, ANDREW T,** Univ Of Sc At Columbia, Columbia, SC; SO; BS; Disc Jcky 89; Ski Tm Colgate Univ 88-89; Mntnrng/Whtwtr Clb; Clgt Ftbl 86-88; Marine Sci/Cstl Mgt; Cnsltnt/Envrnmntl Law.

**REILLY, DAVID J,** Anne Arundel Comm Coll, Arnold, MD; FR; AA; Bsn; Mktg.

**REILLY, DOREEN K,** City Univ Of Ny Hunter Coll, New York, NY; GD; MS; Ntnl Stdnt VP 90-; Spch Lang Hrng; Assn Hntr Clg Chptr; Vlntr Rsk Ints 90-; Chlngr Fllwshp 90-; BA SUNY Binghmtn 90; Spch Pthlgy.

**REILLY, DOUG,** Springfield Tech Comm Coll, Springfield, MA; SO; BS; Elctrncs Tech.

**REILLY, MICHAEL G,** County Coll Of Morris, Randolph, NJ; FR; Bus Admin; Bus Owner.

**REILLY, SALENA M,** Mount Saint Mary Coll, Newburgh, NY; SR; BS; Flk Grp 89-90; St Columba Flk Grp 87-; Coll Sngrs 89; Alpha Chi 88-; Hon Soc 88-; Dns Lst 88-; Alpha Chi 88-; E Fshkl Librn 90; Newbrgh Comm Schl Imprvmnt Cntr Intern 90-; Psychlgy; Schl/Comm Psychlgst.

**REILLY, SHANNON M,** Univ Of Sc At Columbia, Columbia, SC; SO; BA; Assn Hnrs Stdnts 89-; Yrbk Stfr Sctn Edtr 89-; Gamma Beta Phi 89-; Kappa Kappa Gamma Crrspndng 89- Sec; Jrnlsm; Pblc Rltns.

**REILLY, TERRY W,** Temple Univ, Philadelphia, PA; JR; BS; Penns Pharmctcl Assn 89-; Amer Pharmctcl Assn 89-; Phi Delta Chi 89-; Phrmcy.

**REIMER, TROY G,** Bridgewater Coll, Bridgewater, VA; SO; BA; Golf 89-; Bsns Admnstrtn.

**REIMOLD, REID ELIZABETH,** Syracuse Univ, Syracuse, NY; SR; BA; Scl Wrk Org 89-; Big Sis Pro 88-; SADD 88-; Gldn Key 89-; Ntl Assoc Scl Wrkrs 88-; Ntl Org Wmn 88-; Lnd A Hnd 88-90; Barnabas Otrch Pro 88-90; Cnslr/Shltr Mgr Hmls Shltr Intrnshp 88-90; Scl Wrk.

**REIN, JESSICA K,** Marymount Manhattan Coll, New York, NY; SO; BFA; Theatre; Theatre; Actng/Dir/Chrgrphy.

**REINER, KEVIN C,** Columbia Union Coll, Takoma Park, MD; FR; BS; Drm Clb 90-; Phi Eta Sigma.

**REINER, STEVEN C,** Allegheny Coll, Meadville, PA; JR; BA; Alden Schlr 88-90; Physics; Engr.

**REINERS, TANJA,** Univ Of Nc At Charlotte, Charlotte, NC; JR; BA; AIAS 89-; Gldn Key 90-; Natl Coll Archtctr Dsgn Awrd Wnnr 90-; Archtctr; Rgstrd Archtct.

**REINERTSEN, ELSABETH,** Liberty Univ, Lynchburg, VA; JR; BS; Ythqst Clb Pblcty Offcr 89-90; Chrstn Srv Intrn 90; Elem Ed.

**REINERTSON, M YVONNE,** Daytona Beach Comm Coll, Daytona Beach, FL; FR; MBA; Ecnmcs; Bus.

**REINHARDT, AMY L,** Univ Of Ga, Athens, GA; SO; BED; Alpha Delta Pi 89-; Communication Sci Disorders; Spch Pathology.

**REINHARDT, INGRID,** D Youville Coll, Buffalo, NY; SR; MS; SPTA Sec 90-; Tutor 89-90; Senior Hon Soc 90-; Zeta Tau Alpha 88-; PT Clncl Intrnshp 90-; Excell Phys Therapy Awd; Phys Therapy.

**REINHARDT, JENNIFER L,** Glassboro St Coll, Glassboro, NJ; FR; BA; NJPIRG 90-; Voice Choice Green Amnesty 90-; Peace Orgnztns Peta Amnsty Intrntnl Deans Lst 90-; Rsdnt Asstnt; IM Aerobics 90-; Englsh; Tchr.

**REINHARDT, JULIE A,** Northern Ky Univ, Highland Hts, KY; JR; BA; Cmps Rep VP 90; Pol Sci Clb; Alpha Chi; Xi Omega; Pol Sci; Law.

**REINHARDT, ROCK D,** Pittsburgh Tech Inst, Pittsburgh, PA; SR; Comp-Aided Drftng.

**REINHART, KRISTEN S,** Westminster Coll, New Wilmingtn, PA; SO; BS; Dance Theatre 89-; Liturgical Dance 89-; Lit Mag 89-90; Kappa Mu Epsilon; Sigma Pi Sigma; Alpha Phi Omega VP Flwshp 90-; Trustees Schlrshp 89-; Deans List 89-; Physics; Eng.

**REINIG, DONNA R,** Union Inst, Cincinnati, OH; SR; BA; Outstndg Stdnt Recog Kirkwood Cmnty Clg 80; Telephone Pioneers; Alumni Bd Kirkwood Cmnty Clg 82-83; AT/T 80-; Dipl Kirkwood Cmnty Clg 80; Hmn Res Mgmt; Cnsltnt.

**REINIKE JR, VERNON R,** Ms St Univ, Miss State, MS; JR; BS; AA MS Gulf Coast Cmnty Clg 90; Petro Engr.

**REINKE, LYNN F,** Univ Of Pittsburgh, Pittsburgh, PA; GD; MSN; Grad Stdnt Org 89-90; Res Nrsng Soc 90-; Sigma Theta Tau; PA Threic Soc 90-; Lung Assn Cnltnt/Spkr 90-; Rsrch Instr U Pittsburgh Plmnry Clncl Nrs Spec; MSN 90; Nsng; Rsrchr.

**REINOSO, WASHINGTON A,** City Univ Of Ny La Guard Coll, Long Island Cty, NY; SR; AAS; Intrnshp Laguardia Comm Coll; AAS 88; Cmptr Tech; Eng.

**REINSEL, DARLA L,** Edinboro Univ Of Pa, Edinboro, PA; SO; BA; Psychlgy Clb 89-90; Phi Eta Sigma 89-; Hnrs Prgrm 90-; Psychlgy; Clncl.

**REIS, CYNTHIA L,** Duquesne Univ, Pittsburgh, PA; JR; BS; Beta Alpha Phi 90-; Delta Sigma Pi 89-; Intrnshp USX Corp 89-; MIS; Bus.

**REIS, VARONICA B,** Valdosta St Coll, Valdosta, GA; JR; BED; Page; Jr Wmns Clb Educ Co Chrmn; Intl Reading Assoc; AA 87; Erly Chldhd Educ.

**REISER, JENNIFER A,** Univ Of Pittsburgh, Pittsburgh, PA; JR; BS; Tau Beta Pi Crspndng Sec 90-; Omega Chi Epsilon; Gldn Key; Provost Schlrshp; Paul F Fulton Schlrshp; Lord Corp Schlrshp; Chem Engr.

**REISER, PATRICIA A,** Glassboro St Coll, Glassboro, NJ; SR; BA; Amer Aerobic Assn 89-; Intl Sprts Med Assn; Alpha Epsilon Phi; Sigma Sigma 86-87; IM 89-; Psychlgy; Drug/Alcohol Abuse Cnslng.

**REISERT, LORRAINE M,** Le Moyne Coll, Syracuse, NY; JR; BS; Bus Clb 88-; Mrktng Clb 90-; Deans List 89-; Delta Mu Delta 90-; CAN 9--; Con Edison Smmr Intrnshp; Jesuit Schlrshp 88-; Reilly Schlrshp 88-; IM Vlybl 89-; Bus/Info Syst; Analyst.

**REISINGER, BETH A,** Radford Univ, Radford, VA; FR; Mrktng Analyst.

**REISINGER, JASON M,** Univ Of Pittsburgh, Pittsburgh, PA; SR; BS; Intramural Basketball; Mathematics/Scie; Mechanical Engineering.

**REISINGER, KIMBERLY S,** Salisbury St Univ, Salisbury, MD; SR; BSW; Socl Wrk Clb Sec 89-; Dance Co 87-; Pi Gamma Mu 90-; Phi Kappa Phi; Phi Alpha Phi Chi Eta; Socl Wrk; Socl Svcs W/Chldrn.

**REISMAN, VALERIE A,** S U N Y Coll Of Tech At Alfred, Alfred, NY; SR; AAS; Cellular Biotech Clb Sec 89-; Sigma Tau Epsilon 89-; Phi Theta Kappa 90-; Sci.

**REISNER, MICHEAL B,** Christian Brothers Univ, Memphis, TN; JR; BA; Phi Alpha Theta 90-; Hstry; Atty.

**REIST, JESSICA A,** Glassboro St Coll, Glassboro, NJ; SO; BA; PRSSA 90-; Cmmnctns; Pblc Rltns.

**REITER, ELIZABETH R,** Kent St Univ Kent Cmps, Kent, OH; JR; BS; Dance Mrthn; New Stdnt Orient Ldr; Pre Law Scty; Yng Rpblcns; Alpha Lambda Delta; Pres Lst; Lamplight Awd; Delta Gamma; St Rep Intern 90-; Rsrch Grant; Asst Prof; Schl Spnsrd Aerobic Inst; Pltcl Sci/Business; Law.

**REITLER, JENNIFER L,** Univ Of Sc At Columbia, Columbia, SC; JR; FMA; Gamma Beta Phi 89-; Golden Key 89-; Delta Sigma Pi 90-; Finance; Bnkg.

**REITMAN, ELIZABETH,** Univ Of Cincinnati, Cincinnati, OH; SR; BSN; Univ Cinn Std Nrs Asc Pres 88-; OH Std Nrs Asc VP 88-; Natl Std Nrs Asc 88-; Sigma Theta Tau; VALOR Std Vets Affrs Med Ctr 90-; Amer Irish Clb Pres 84-; Ladies Ancnt Ordr Hbrmns 89-; BA Ed Univ KY 82; Emrgcy Nrsng.

**REITZ, ANNE M,** Elmira Coll, Elmira, NY; JR; BS; Elem Educ.

**REKART, CANDYCE E,** Caribbean Center For Adv Stds, San Juan, PR; GD; MA; Am Assn Cnslng/Dvlpmnt 89-90; Tchr 70-89; MA NY Univ 80; BA Loyola Univ 70; Clncl Psychlgy; Mntl Hlth.

**REKER, MICHELLE R,** Northern Ky Univ, Highland Hts, KY; SO; BA; Queen City Clb 87-; Lawyer.

**REKOWSKI, THOMAS J,** Comm Coll Algny Co Algny Cmps, Pittsburgh, PA; FR; BS; Untd Stlwrkrs Union Lcl 14034 Dstrct 20; Cplng Syst Inc; Math/Sci; Educ.

**RELIFORD, HELEN J,** Ashland Comm Coll, Ashland, KY; FR; AS; Earn Assoc Degree BA; Nrsng; Psych.

**RELLICK, JENNIFER M,** Saint Andrews Presbytrn Coll, Laurinburg, NC; JR; BA; Stdnt Govrnmnt Assoc Dorm VP 89-90; Envrnmntl Chr Cmmttee 90; Stdnt Lfe Cmmttee 90; Alpha Chi 90; Pi Gamma Mu; Hnr Scty; Tchng Prctcm Assistntshp 90; Phlsphy Pol Sci; Law.

**RELYEA, CHRISTOPHER K,** Schenectady County Comm Coll, Schenectady, NY; SR; Acctg; CPA.

**REMALEY, CONNIE L,** Univ Of Al At Birmingham, Birmingham, AL; SR; BS; Med Rcrd Clb 89-; Med Rcrd Admin.

**REMBERT, LAURIE K,** Coker Coll, Hartsville, SC; SR; BA; Outstndg Educ Stdnt 89-90; Suzanne G Linville Schlr 87-; Deans Lst 87-; Natl Clgte Educ Awd 90-; Clss Top Ten 89-90; Elem Educ; Tch.

**REMBOWSKI, AVERY K,** Smith Coll, Northampton, MA; FR; BA; Svc Org Vol Pine Rest Nrsg Hme 90-; First Grp Schlr 90-; Hstry.

**REMEDIOS, MARLEN M,** Univ Of Miami, Coral Gables, FL; SR; BA; Fed Cuban Stdnts; Cand Cmtr Org; Sigma Phi Epsilon Lil Sis 87-89; Msns Unides De Buena Vlntr; Bus Fnc/Mktg; MBA.

**REMEL, KATHRINE DIAHN,** Univ Of Southern Ms, Hattiesburg, MS; SO; BS; Bnd; Arnld Air Soc ROTC; Nrsng; Air Frc Ofcr.

**REMER, RONALD E,** Fl St Univ, Tallahassee, FL; SO; BA; Crmnlgy; US Sec Serv.

**REMEUR, SARA J,** Memphis St Univ, Memphis, TN; JR; BA; Peer Mntr Pgm 88-89; Grk Pblc Rltns Bd 90-; Natl Downs Syndrm Sympsm; Ordr Omega 90-; Alpha Gamma Delta Pres; Spec Olympcs 88-; Jvnl Dbts 88-; Alpha Gamma Delta Grk Wk Chrmn VP 89-; Sor IMS 88-; Advrtsng Jrnlsm Spnsh; Advrtsng.

**REMILLARD, CYNTHIA S,** Georgetown Univ, Washington, DC; FR; BSN; IM Vlybl 90-; Nursing; RN/MIDWIFE.

**REMILLARD, KRISTINE M,** Univ Of Ma At Amherst, Amherst, MA; JR; BS; Cmnctn Dsrdrs Clb Cls Repr 89-; Golden Key; Rsrch Asst; Cmnctn Dsrdrs; Adlgy.**

**REMINGTON, LAURA J,** Immaculata Coll, Immaculata, PA; JR; BA; Hstry Pltcs Clb 90; SADD; Intrntnl Rltns Soc; Alpha Alpha Rho 91; Intrnshp San Diego D A Offc Vctm Wtns Asst Prgrm 89-; Hstry Pltcs; Law Crmnl Jstc Systm.

**REMINGTON, SHARON K,** Univ Of Akron, Akron, OH; SR; BS; Loan Ofcr 87-90; Elem Ed.

**REMINGTON, SHARON L,** Castleton St Coll, Castleton, VT; SO; Hll Cncl Sec 90; Crtve Dscvry; Elem Educ Fne Arts; Tch.

**REMO, JAMES-EDWARD C,** Univ Of Cincinnati, Cincinnati, OH; JR; BA; Mech Eng Tech; Dsgn Eng.

**REMOLDE, JAMES A,** Anne Arundel Comm Coll, Arnold, MD; FR; AA; Lab Technology.

**REMPFER, SHERRI CELEST,** Cumberland County Coll, Vineland, NJ; SO; BA; Bus Clb; Phi Theta Kappa 90-; Bus Admn; Bus.

**REMSEN, GLENN C,** Citadel Military Coll Of Sc, Charleston, SC; FR; BA; Cordell Army Rngr Co 90-; St Albans Episcopal Choir 90-; Gold Stars 90-; Deans Lst 90-; Pol Sci; Army Ofcr.

**REMY, DONALD M,** Howard Univ, Washington, DC; GD; JD; Howard Law Jrnl Exec Articles Edtr 90-; Kappa Alpha Psi; Am Jurisprudence Awd 88-; Am Bar Assn; Natl Bar Assn; Asst Gen Cnsl Dept Of Army; BA La St Univ 88; Law; Judiciary.

**REMY, STEVEN,** Westminster Coll, New Wilmingtn, PA; SO; BA; Visa Svc Tm Chr 90-; Phi Sigma Tau 89-; Alpha Phi Omega 90-; Eliz Nixon Mem Schlrshp; Engl/Phlsphy; Tch.

**RENARD, KENNETH D,** Univ Of Pittsburgh, Pittsburgh, PA; SO; BS; Coop Ed Pgm; Phi Eta Sigma 90-; Elec Eng.

**RENAUD, STACI K,** Univ Of Pittsburgh At Bradford, Bradford, PA; FR; Bus/Acctg; CPA.

**RENAULT, MARIA D,** Western New England Coll, Springfield, MA; SO; BA; Big Sis Untd Way 89-; Scl Wrk; Prbtn Ofcr.

**RENDER, JOHN W,** Univ Of Sc At Columbia, Columbia, SC; SR; Mrchn Bnd 88; AMA 90; BS; Mrktng; Mrktng Hsptlty.

**RENDER, SUSAN R,** Univ Of Sc At Columbia, Columbia, SC; FR; BA; Dorm Govt 90-; Assct Hon Clg Stdnt 90-; Mountaineering Clb 90-; Gamma Beta Phi 90-; Alpha Dlt Lmbd 90-; Carolina Cares 90-; Carolina Kids Tres 90-; Fmly Abuse Agncy Vol; Pres List 90; Deans List; Intrntl Stds; Soviet/US Rltns.

**RENEHAN, GAIL E,** Providence Coll, Providence, RI; SR; BS; Envrnmntl Clb 90-; Friar Fntc 88; Biol Clb 88-90; Dean Lst 88-; Alpha Epsilon Delta 88-; Cncl Excptnl Chldrn Treas 90-; Magna Cum Laude; Rgby 89-; Biol; Vet.

**RENFROE, DWAYNE K,** Univ Of Al At Huntsville, Huntsville, AL; FR; BSE; Cncrt Chr; Bapt Cmps Mnstrs; Alpha Lambda Delta; Alpha Tau Omega; Hnr Schlr; Indstrl And Systms Eng; Cnsltng.

**RENFROW, KIRSTEN A,** Univ Of Sc At Columbia, Columbia, SC; FR; BA.

**RENFROW JR, LEONARD C,** Owensboro Comm Coll, Owensboro, KY; SO; AA; Dns Lst 90-; Law Enfrcmnt; Plc Ofcr.

**RENGARAJAN, BADRINATH,** Harvard Univ, Cambridge, MA; SO; BA; Model Congr Spkr Hse 89-; S Asian Assoc; Masters Swim; US Nvl Acad Foreign Affrs Conf 90; Woods Hole Oceangrphc Inst Marine Pol Intern 90; Bio; Med/Sci Rsrch.**

**RENGER, JANE K,** Radford Univ, Radford, VA; SO; BA; Psych; Sch.**

**RENGERS, STEPHEN E,** Westminster Coll, New Wilmingtn, PA; SO; BA; Intnl Cultures Clb 89-; Fresh Schlrs 89-90; Asst Tchr German 90-; Econ; Intnl Bus.

**RENGLE, KIMBERLY A,** Castleton St Coll, Castleton, VT; FR; BA; Castltn Env Grp; Castltn Plyrs Theatr Grp; Sprtn News Corr Stdnt Nwspr; STEP Lrng Ctr Tutr; Comm; Mag Jrnlsm.

**RENNALLS, GRACE L,** Saint Thomas Univ, Miami, FL; JR; BA; Cir K Clb Asst Sec; Tutoring Ele Sch; AA Miami Dade Commclg 84-86; Trvl/Tursm Mgmt.

**RENNER, AMY L,** Goucher Coll, Towson, MD; SR; BA; Psych Clb Sec; Chmbr Ensmb Towson St Unv Cello Chr Cellist; Chrst Fllwshp Org; Phi Beta Kappa; Dns Schlr; J Van Meter Almn Fllwshp; Annl Dnc Cncrt Bllt/Mdrn; Psych/Dnc Thrpy; MSOT/OCCPTNL Thrpst.

**RENNER, CRYSTAL L,** Coll Of New Rochelle, New Rochelle, NY; JR; BA; Yrbk Cpy Edit 90-; Cmps Nwsppr 90; Sbcom Cmps Actvts 90; Hnrs Prog Brd Rep 88-; NCHC Com 90-; Prog Nwslttr 90; Fr Ornttn Com Chrmn 90; Natl Orgnztn Fr Wmn 88-; Pres Schlrshp 88-; Hnrs Lst 88-; Engl Commncins Arts; Jrnlsm.

**RENNER, JENNIFER D,** Saint Francis Coll, Loretto, PA; SR; BS; Acctng; CPA.

**RENNER, ROBERT A,** Charles County Comm Coll, La Plata, MD; FR; BA; SGA Tres; Stdnt Newspaper Asst Edtr/Photo Edtr 90-; Stdnt Actvts Com 90-; Acctng; Cpa.

**RENNICK-BALL, JOYCE M,** Univ Of Akron, Akron, OH; SR; BS; Golden Key 90; Beta Gamma Sigma; Sigma Iota Epsilon; Indstrl Mngmnt; Info Syst.

**RENNINGER, LESLEY T,** Long Island Univ Brooklyn Cntr, Brooklyn, NY; SO; BA; Sftbl 89-; Psychology; Cnslr.**

**RENOT, SUSAN V,** Ms Gulf Coast Comm Coll, Perkinston, MS; SO; ASSOC; Mcrcmptr Spclst.

**RENOT, VIVIANE DAFTARI,** Univ Of Ky, Lexington, KY; JR; BA; GSA Asst Ldr 87-88; Pi Delta Phi 89-; Golden Key Ntnl Hnr Scty 89-; Acdmc Excllnce Schlrshp 90-; Coll Edctn Schlrshp; KY State Tchr Schlrshp; Elmntry Frnch Tchr 74-76; Clnry Cert FORCOTEL 85; Scndry Frnch Ed; Tchng.

**RENSHAW, MELISSA H,** Blue Mountain Coll, Blue Mountain, MS; SR; BS; Univ Hnrs Pro 87-90; Campus Actv Brd 88-90; Right To Life 89-90; Phi Kappa Phi; Gamma Beta Phi; Phi Eta Sigma; Alpha Lambda Delta; Crdnl Key; Ordr Omega; Gamma Alpha Epsilon 88-90; Omicron Delta Kappa 89-90; Delta Delta Delta Pldg Trnr; Math; Tchg.

**RENTAS VARGAS, JESUS M,** Univ Of Pr Cayey Univ Coll, Cayey, PR; JR; BBA; CADE 90-; NASHA 89-90; Cuadro De Hon 88-; Gerencia; Law.

**RENTOS, MICHAEL D,** Northern Ky Univ, Highland Hts, KY; SR; ASBS; YAL Secy 88-89; Jr Cncl Wrld Affrs 84; Art Clb 84; Hnr Scty 84; Hmn Serv/Mntl Hlth; Cnslng/Hlpng People.

**RENTZ, JAMIE N,** Medical Univ Of Sc, Charleston, SC; SR; Alpha Omega Alpha 89-90 Sigma Nu Clemson Univ 84-87; Superhealth 2000 88-89; Interfaith Crisis Mnstry Clinic 89-90; BS Zoology 87; MD; Apprentice Dr Chas M Webb Pathologist Spartanburg Regnl Med Ctr 86; IMS 83-87; Medicine MD.

**REOTT, SUZANNE M,** Univ Of North Fl, Jacksonville, FL; FR; BS; Navy Offcrs Wvs Clb/Parent Teacher Assoc/Navy Relief Soc; Trust Co Bk/Atlanta Bnk Oper; Bus; Bnkng/Fin.

**REPACI, VINCENT A,** Providence Coll, Providence, RI; JR; BA; IM Ath Bureau 88-; Career Plcmnt Prog Intrnshp Prog 90-; Dns Lst 89-; Intrnshp Kidder Peabody Inc 90-; IM Aths 88-; Mrktg/Bsns.

**REPHAN, DINA,** Yeshiva Univ, New York, NY; GD; MED; Bsktbl Tm 86-87; Phy Educ; Hlth Clb Mgmt.

**REPIEDAD, AGUINALDO L,** Central Fl Comm Coll, Ocala, FL; SO; AA; Bus; Acctg.

**REPKO, JOHN S,** Mount Aloysius Jr Coll, Cresson, PA; GD; AS; Skng Emplymnt Soc Serv Org; Genl Studies/Psychlgy Bckgrnd; Soc Serv Wrkr.**

**REPKO, MATTHEW C,** Univ Of Akron, Akron, OH; SR; BS; IEEE; Golden Key; Eta Kappa Nu; Milton L Kult Awd; Pres Schlrshp 85-; Firestone Schlrshp 85-; Elec Eng.

**REPKO, ROBERT T,** Coll Misericordia, Dallas, PA; JR; BA; Stdnt Govt Jdcl Coordntr; Hons Assoc Rep; Intrclgt Ldrshp Wilkes Barre; Alpha Delta Kappa Pres; Orientn Cnslr; Ambsdrs; Tutor; Presdntl Schlrshp; All Amercn Schlr; Natl Merit Award; Im Vlybl; Hist; Profsr.

**REPKO III, WILLIAM E,** Central Fl Comm Coll, Ocala, FL; FR; Physics; Engr.

**REPLOGLE, PAMELA S,** Saint Francis Coll, Loretto, PA; SO; BSN; Stdnt Nurses Org 89-; Meml Hosp Bedford Cnty Schlrshp; Deans Lst 89-90; St Pauls UCC Preschl Sndy Schl Tchr; Dntl Asst; Cert Altoona Area Voc Tech Schl 86; Nrsng; RN.

**REPLOGLE, SHAWN M,** Bridgewater Coll, Bridgewater, VA; JR; BS; Hnr Cncl Invstgtr 90-; Drm 88-; Internatl Clb 88-90; Lambda Soc Stdnt Repr 89-; Alpha Chi 90-; Interdstrct Yth Cbnt Crspndg Sec 90-; Brthrn Flwshp 88-; Scr Clb Co Cptn 89-; Pltcl Sci; Pblc Admin.

**REPSYS, ANDREA M,** Elms Coll, Chicopee, MA; SR; BA; Chmstry Clb 88-; Yrbk; Accreditation Comm Pblcty/Pub Rel Grp 90-; Biology; Med Rsrch.

**RESCH, JENNIFER D,** Middle Tn St Univ, Murfreesboro, TN; FR; BA; Skydvng Assn Sec; Biolgy Clb; Chem Clb; Delta Zeta; Sigma Phi Epsilon; Sftbl/Soccr; Biolgy; Pre-Med.

**RESICK, CHRISTIAN J,** Saint Francis Coll, Loretto, PA; JR; BS; Radio DJ 89-90; Delta Sigma Phi Pres 89-; Mercy Hosp Admn Intrn; Ftbl 88; Trck 89; Mgmt; Org Psych.

**RESIG, ANDREA J,** Pellissippi St Tech Comm Coll, Knoxville, TN; SO; DVM; Pre Vet Club Univ Tenn; PC Spclst 90-; ASB Sthrn Clg 84; Vet Med; Doctorate.

**RESNICK, GWEN L,** American Univ, Washington, DC; FR; BS; Bsns Clb Asst To Pres 90-; Orntn Asst; Phi Mu Asst Treas 90-; Bsns/Jstce; Acctg.

**RESNICK, JODIE A,** Atlantic Comm Coll, Mays Landing, NJ; SO; AA; Phi Theta Kappa 90-; Educ; Tchng.

**RESNICK, MARCIA B,** Univ Of Nc At Chapel Hill, Chapel Hill, NC; GD; JD; Hldrnss Moot Ct Bnch; Clnt Cnslng Tm; Crvn Entrtnmnt Com Hd 89-; NC Jrnl Intl Law 90-; Ortn Cnslr 89-90; Prspctv Stdnt Assn 88-90; Amer Bar Assn-Stdnt Div 88-; UNC Phtgrphy Clb 88-90; Omicron Delta Epsilon; Undrgrad-Bus Mgmt; Law.

**RESPASS, CHRISTOPHER J,** Morehouse Coll, Atlanta, GA; SO; BA; Bus Assn 90-; Pre-Law Soc 90-; Atlanta Univ Carolina Clb Pr; Golden Key; Summer Intrn GTE Hdqtrs; Hon Roll 89-; Deans Lst; Bnking/Fin; Law/Bus.

**RESPESS, REBECCA A,** Liberty Univ, Lynchburg, VA; JR; BS; Taekwondo Clb Sec/Tres 90; Alpha Lmbd Dlt 89-; Psychlgy; Cnslr.

**RESSEL, YVONNE D,** Memphis St Univ, Memphis, TN; SR; BA; Psych.

**RESTER, LESLEE J,** Univ Of Al At Birmingham, Birmingham, AL; JR; BA; Phlsphy Clb 90-; Pres Hnrs; Eng/Phlsphy; Pblshng/Edtng.

**RESTIERI, GINA C,** Georgetown Univ, Washington, DC; SO; BSN; NSO 90; NSNA 89-90; Alpha Phi Omega Pblcty Cochr Serv Crdntr 89-; Nrsg.

**RESTO REYES, JOSE M,** Univ Politecnica De Pr, Hato Rey, PR; FR.

**RESTO, CARMEN H,** Inter Amer Univ Pr Hato Rey, Hato Rey, PR; SR; BA; Spnsh Clb 88-90; Hon Soc 88-; Spnsh; Nwspr Clnst.

**RESTO, GELSYS M,** Barry Univ, Miami, FL; SO; Barry Univ Ambsdrs 89-90; Beta Beta Beta 89-90; Psychlgy.

**RESTREPO, ADRIANA,** Fl International Univ, Miami, FL; SR; FL Ftre Edctr Of Amer 90-; Dns Lst 89-; AA Miami Dade Comm Coll 89; BA Elem Educ; Tchr.

**RESTREPO, CLAUDIA E,** Univ Of Miami, Coral Gables, FL; JR; BFA; Advsry Cncl Pres 88-; Trnsfr Advsr 90-; Cane Cmutr Orgztn 90-; Phi Theta Kappa Pres; Omicron Fla Alumni Assn 90-; Wmn Cmunctns Inc V P; Wmn Grphcs Prntg Indus 89; Multi Ethic Tsk Frc 88-89; Cath Cmpus Mnstry 89; Hon Mntn 90-; AA 89: AS 90; Graphc Dsgn/Ullustr.

**RETAN, MARK B,** Niagara Univ, Niagara Univ, NY; SR; BA; Psychlgy Clb 90-; Hdstrt Pgm 89-90; Psi Chi 90-; BA; Psychlgy; Chld Psychlgst.

**RETANO, JONATHAN,** Glassboro St Coll, Glassboro, NJ; FR; MBA; Stdnt Govt Treas 90-; Stdnt Financl Cntrl Brd 90-; Econ/Advtsng Clb 90-; Res Stdnt Assn 90-; Hon Clb 90-; Sigma Beta Tau Asst Pldgmstr; Dean Lst 90-; Sigma Beta Tau; Grdn St Schlrshp 90-; IM Ftbl/Hockey/Soccr/Sftbl/Bsktbl; Econ; Us Treasry/Fdrl Rsrv.

**RETELL, KEVIN R,** Hudson Valley Comm Coll, Troy, NY; SR; Crmnl Juste; Law Enfrcmnt.

**RETHWILM, CRAIG R,** Univ Of Tn At Chattanooga, Chattanooga, TN; SR; BS; Amer Socty Mech Engrs 90-91; Amer Socty Cvl Engrs 91-; Phi Theta Kappa 88-; Mu Alpha Theta 88-; IM Vlybl 90-; Mech/Cvl Engr.

**RETMAN, DEBORAH J,** Miami Jacobs Jr Coll Of Bus, Dayton, OH; SO; CSI Pres; Outstndg Stdnt Awd; Info Syst Proc; Secr/Supv Mgmt.

**RETTEW, PAULA S,** Elms Coll, Chicopee, MA; JR; BA; Lgl Sec 85-88; AS Holyoke Comm Clg 85; Prlgl; Law.

**RETTIG, LINDA F,** Univ Of Med & Dentistry Of Nj, Newark, NJ; GD; MS; Golden Key 87-; Phi Kappa Phi 86-; Outstndng Stdnt Yr 87; Magna Cum Laude 88; BS Univ Maryland 88; Physcl Thrpy.

**RETTIG, SUSAN B,** Kent St Univ Kent Cmps, Kent, OH; SO; BS; Vollybl Clb 89-; Alpha Lambda Delta 90-; Ind Chem.

**RETZNER, MARY V,** Immaculata Coll, Immaculata, PA; JR; BA; Psych Clb Sec 90-; Psi Chi Sec 90-; Psych; Indstrlst Psych.

**REUS, JUAN L,** Fl International Univ, Miami, FL; SR; Intl Clb SW Univ Sec 87-88; Tennis/Sccr Tm 87-88; Ecnmcs; Pblc Plcy.

**REUSCH, SHARMON D,** Northern Ky Univ, Highland Hts, KY; JR; BA; Wmns Stdies Wrtng Cntst; PTA Cltrl Arts; Wmns Magckl Art Coaltn; Grphc Artst 80-86; Cert Gable Advrtsng Art Schl 79; Art/Secndry Educ; Art Tchr.

**REUSCHER, TRACEY L,** D Youville Coll, Buffalo, NY; SR; MSBS; Occupational Therapy.

**REUSS, VICKI A,** Univ Of Cincinnati-Clrmnt Coll, Batavia, OH; SO; AD; Natl Acad Hnr Scty; Records/Infor Mgt; Busn Records Mgt.

**REUTER, BRONWYN J,** Academy Of The New Church, Bryn Athyn, PA; JR; BA; Peer Advsry Cncl Strng Cmmt 89-90; Stdnt Union Games Cmmt 90; Scty Hmn Resouce Mngmnt 90; Tau Phi Delta Scty Co Chrmn Special Evnts 90; Theta Alpha Awrd 90; IM 90; AA Acdmy New Chrch Clg 90; Psychlgy; Human Resource Mngmnt.

**REUTHER, DANA E,** Saint Vincents Coll & Seminary, Latrobe, PA; JR; BA; St Vncnt Review Bsn Mngr 90; In Touch Clb Pblcty Drctr 89; Choir Drctr 90; Grass Roots; Orntn Cmmt; Psychlgy Clb; Ltrcy Outreach Prgrm; Rsdnt Asst 90; Psychlgy; Cnslng.

**REUTTER, RICHARD ALEXANDER,** Princeton Univ, Princeton, NJ; FR; Yo-Yo Clb First VP 90-; Coll Bowl 90-; Sim Games Un 90-; IM Cptn 90-; Mathematics.

**REVAH, ALBERT,** Georgetown Univ, Washington, DC; FR; BSBA; Hlnc Clb 90-; Bsktbl IM 90-; Bsn.

**REVEL, MARK C,** Campbell Univ, Buies Creek, NC; FR; BS; Bsn Adm; Mgmt.

**REVELL, ARETHLIA B,** Norfolk St Univ, Norfolk, VA; SR; BS; Std VA Educ Asc VP 89-90; Minie Ludford Awd 90; YMCA Tdwtr Prk Tutor Pgm Coord 88-90; Cloth Tech AS 83; Erly Chldhd Educ; Tch.

**REVELL, EDWIN,** Univ Of Al At Birmingham, Birmingham, AL; SO; BA; Natl Scty Black Engrs 89-; Amer Scty Cvl Engrs 90-; Hnrs Prog 89-; Admin Intern; Cvl Engrng.

**REVELS, ALICE D,** Tri County Tech Coll, Pendleton, SC; SO; BA; Real Estate Clsng Sec 83-89; Psychlgy; Child Psychlgy.

**REVELS, TINA I,** Univ Of Nc At Charlotte, Charlotte, NC; SR; BA; Natl Frshmn Hon Soc 86-87; Spirit Square Educ Dept Under April Carder 90; Cum Laude; Sftbl Tm Stats 87; Vis Arts Educ; Tchr.

**REVER, ROBYN K,** Ms St Univ, Miss State, MS; FR; BA; Rfmd Univ Flwshp 90-; Cncrt Choir 90-; Delta Chi Frat Swthrt 90-; Deans Schlr; Sclgy; Chrstn Cnslg.

**REVILLA, TANIA MARIE,** Fl International Univ, Miami, FL; SR; BA; Fut Eductrs Amer 89-; Biscyne Bay Yng Rep Soc Dir 89-; Rep Tr 90-; Kappa Delta Phi 90-; Recog Peer Adv 90-; AA Miami Dade Comm Clg 89; Educ; Tchg.

**REVIS, JENNIFER B,** Brevard Coll, Brevard, NC; SO; BA; Work Stdy Fincl Office 89-; Frgn Lng Club 89-90; Phi Theta Kappa Crspndg Sec 90-; Am Cancer Scty 89-; AA; Radio Tv Mtn Picts.

**REVIS, MICHAEL G,** Old Dominion Univ, Norfolk, VA; SR; BS; Am Soc Civil Engrs 90-; Tau Beta Pi; Chi Epsilon; Civil Eng/Geotech/Structrl; Eng Firm/Cons.

**REVOREDO, ROSA M,** Fl International Univ, Miami, FL; FR; BA; Hnrs Pgm 90-; Fclty Schlr 90-; Sci; Chem Engr.

**REVUELTA, JANICE,** Fl International Univ, Miami, FL; SR; BS; Stdnt Govt Elctns Comm 90-; DPMA 90-; Omicron Delta Kappa Treas 90-; Delta Phi Epsilon Pres 87-; Deans List 90-; Intern Ryder Sys Inc; Mgmt Inf Sys.

**REVUELTA, KAREN,** Fl International Univ, Miami, FL; SR; BS; Future Ed Am VP 90-; Kappa Delta Pi; Omicron Delta Kappa VP Proj; Phi Kappa Phi; Delta Phi Epsilon Spcl Evnts Alumni Rel 89-; Schlr 88-; Fac Schlr 88-; Elem Edn; Tchr.

**REWIS, SHANE H,** Abraham Baldwin Agri Coll, Tifton, GA; FR; BS; Bptst Stdnt Un; John H Dorminey Schlrshp 90; IM Ftbll; Vet Med.

**REWITZER, DAVID A,** Tn St Univ, Nashville, TN; SO; BS; Chess Clb Pres 90-; Physcs Clb Pres-Elct; Tutr Prog 90-; Goldn Key 90-; Math/Physcs Tutr 90-; Cert Nashvle Tech 89; Elec Eng.

**REXER III, WILLIAM F,** Broome Comm Coll, Binghamton, NY; SR; BS; AMO 89-; Pres Lst 87; Deans Lst 88; AS 89; Mgmt Mrktng.**

**REY, NINA BAELLO,** Caribbean Univ, Bayamon, PR; SO; BA; Hnr Lst 90-; Kappa Delta Phi 90-; Poetry Award 90; Cert; Elem Educ English.**

**REYES AGOSTO, PEDRO N,** Univ Of Pr Humacao Univ Coll, Humacao, PR; GD; BA; BED 90-; Law.

**REYES CALDERON, MARIRENE,** Inter Amer Univ Pr Hato Rey, Hato Rey, PR; SR; BA; Magna Cum Laude; Hnr Rll 88-; Myr Mdl Awrd 86-; Tchng Intrnshp; Spcl Educ Spch And Hrng Imprmnts; Spch And Ln.

**REYES DE JESUS, JAVIER A,** Univ Of Pr At Rio Piedras, Rio Piedras, PR; MPA; Assn Stdnts Grad Schl Pub Admin 90-; Judge Sci Comp 90-; Asst Prof 90-; DPMA 89-; BBA 86.

**REYES DIAZ, SANDRA A,** Inter Amer Univ Pr Hato Rey, Hato Rey, PR; FR; Cl Treas 88-; Spanish Hnr Soc 89-90; Grl Scts Coun Co Ldr 87-; Chess Chmpnshp 2nd Plc; Acctg; Bus Admin.

**REYES MAISONET, LEILA,** Univ Politecnica De Pr, Hato Rey, PR; SO; Engl; Eng.

**REYES, ALEXANDER,** Broward Comm Coll, Ft Lauderdale, FL; JR; BA; Crim Jstc; Law.

**REYES, ALEXANDRIA,** William Paterson Coll, Wayne, NJ; SR; Spnsh Clb 90-; Hstry Clb 86-88; Kappa Delta Pi 89-; Phi Alpha Theta 90-; Otstng Sr Awrd; Academic Superiority; The Livio Stecchine Awrd; BA WPC; Hstry/Spanish; Tch.

**REYES, AMADO A,** Saint Thomas Univ, Miami, FL; SR; BA; Coll Schlrshp; Serv Cert Achvmnt Awrd; Mens Tennis Tm; AA 90; Psych; Marriage/Fmly Thrpy.**

**REYES, ANTONIO C,** Univ Of Med & Dentistry Of Nj, Newark, NJ; FR; Amrcn Assn Rsprtry Cr 90-; Intgrtd Inst Elctrcl Engnr 82-; BS Hapua Inst Tchnlgy Phlpns 80; Rsprtry Thrpy Tchncn; Biomdcl Engnrng.

**REYES, BOBBIE L,** Fl St Univ, Tallahassee, FL; SR; BA; Ldrshp Effect/Dev Pgm 89; Phi Beta Kappa; Phi Theta Kappa 88-89; Phi Theta Kappa 89-; Golden Key 90-; Maude Smith Awrd 89; Cir Of Excel 89; AA Meridian Cmnty Clg 89; Engl/Bus; Law.

**REYES, BONNIBELLE,** Univ Of Sc At Columbia, Columbia, SC; FR; BS; Phrmcy; Phrmcst.

**REYES, CARLOS AVILES,** Inter Amer Univ Pr San Juan, Hato Rey, PR; SR; BA; 4 H Clb Psych Stdnts Assn 87-; Bible Stdy Grp; Rmdl Assn; Pre Law Assn; Hnr Stdnts Assn 90-; Hnr Prog 90-; Yng Chrstns Assn 87-; Rlgn Prfssr 87-; Dn Lst; Hnr Sq; Bsktbl 87-; Cert UPR 88; BA; Psych.

**REYES JR, EFRAIN,** Univ Politecnica De Pr, Hato Rey, PR; SO; BA; Bsebl 90-; Orntn Other Stdnts; Hon Stdnt 90-; Cert Cmptr Gallery Cmptr/Dsgn 88-89; Math; Eng/Surveying.

**REYES, GEORGE,** Harvard Univ, Cambridge, MA; FR; Envtlt Action Commt; Perspective Libl Monthly Cart 90-; Al Viento Hnrd Spanish Literary Mag Artist; Drama 90-; Peer Reltns Grp Counlr; Student Per Counseling Grp; Univ Lthrn Hmls Shltr; History/Sci; Law.

**REYES, HENRY,** Univ Of Ct, Storrs, CT; SO; BA; CAP Part 89; Smr Precoll Pro; Career Bgngs Pro Alumnus 88-; Alpha Gamma Phi 90-; Alpha Nu Chptr; Ag Frat; Alpha Gamma Rho 90-; Trnty Coll Smr Rsrch Intrn Psychlgcl Assmnt Prtcpnt 90; Anml Sci; Vet.

**REYES, IGNACIO J,** Fl A & M Univ, Tallahassee, FL; JR; BARCH; Amer Inst Archtctrl Stu 87-; Hstrcl Soc Palm Beach Co; Gldn Ky 89-; Palm Beach Co Plnng Intern; AA Broward Comm Coll 89; Archtctr; MS Urbn Plnng.

**REYES, IVELISSE,** Ny Univ, New York, NY; SR; BA; ACE Awrds Pr 84-; Friends Of ACE; Alpha Sigma Lambda; Soc Sci/Intl Stds; Cmctn Media.

**REYES, IVETTE,** Univ Of Sc At Columbia, Columbia, SC; JR; BA; Natl Stdnt Exhnge 90; Bus Acctg Fin.

**REYES, JAIME A,** Univ Of Pr At Rio Piedras, Rio Piedras, PR; SO; Karate; Cdr Hnr Decano; Sci; Dr Med.

**REYES, JAMES,** Catholic Univ Of Pr, Ponce, PR; GD; MA; Bsktbl; JD Univ Catilica; MA Univ 87; Law.

**REYES, LEXY S,** Inter Amer Univ Pr Hato Rey, Hato Rey, PR; JR; Yaucano Clb 89-90; Spnsr Wrld Vsn 90-; Cath Mssn 90-; Spec Hon 88; Mdl Hist 89; Spnsh; Prof.

**REYES, MARIA D,** Caribbean Univ, Bayamon, PR; JR; BBA; Acctng; CPA.

**REYES, MELISSA M,** Va Commonwealth Univ, Richmond, VA; SR; BED; Cncl Except Chldrn; Alpha Sigma Alpha Panhellenic Rep 85-89; Spec Educ; Tch Mntl Rtrd Stdnts.

**REYES, NAYRA L,** City Univ Of Ny Baruch Coll, New York, NY; JR; BBA; Endwmnt Fnd Prvsts Schlrshp; Deans Lst; Acdmc All Amer Schl Prog 86; Feit Smnr/The Bible Wstrn Cltr; Comp Info Syst.

**REYES, REINALDO,** Univ Central Del Caribe, Cayey, PR; JR; MBA; Clss Pres; Nu Sigma Beta; Tutor; 1st Rnkng Stu; Awrd Hghtst Stu; Intrnl Med.

**REYES, ROSALIE L,** Univ Of Southern Ms, Hattiesburg, MS; FR; BSN; Pulley Hall Cncl Pres 90-; Hnrs Stdnt Assn Hmcmng Chr 90; Alumni Assn 90; Intl Rltns Clb 90; Lambda Sigma; Gamma Beta Phi; Nrsng.

**REYES-MEDINA, SELENA,** Evangelical Semimary Of P R, Hato Rey, PR; MDIV; Concert Bnd 85-89; Acctg Assn 86-89; Cum Laude 89; BBA Univ PR 89; Acctg/Mgmnt; Mnstr.

**REYLE, SERENA M,** Wilmington Coll, New Castle, DE; GD; BSN; Evangelical Presby Ch Of Newark Yth Ldr 88-; Hosp/Sch Pediatricians Ofc RN 84-; ASN Grace Coll 84; Nrsng.

**REYMAN, CAROL A,** Univ Of Cincinnati-Clrmnt Coll, Batavia, OH; SO; AA; Amer Legion Post 484; Clinical Med Tech/Biological Research Tech; MT Eastern Schl Physicians Aids Inc 63; Business Admin; Human Resources.

**REYMANN, MARY M,** Kent St Univ Kent Cmps, Kent, OH; SR; BBA; Flying Clb 89-; CYO Co-Ed Sftbl 86-; CYO Co-Ed Vlybl 89; Stonehedge Pl Vlybl; Beta Gamma Sigma 90-; Bus Mgt; Flight Ofcr.

**REYNOLDS, ANDREW M,** Univ Of New Haven, West Haven, CT; JR; BA; Rcrdng Eng Soc 88-89; Music/Snd Rcrdng.

**REYNOLDS, ANESSA LYNN,** Univ Of Southern Ms, Hattiesburg, MS; SR; BA; Amercn Mktg Assn Soc Comm VP Of Fndrsng; Assoc Jones Cnty Jr Clg 89; Mktg; Law.

**REYNOLDS, BRADLEY G,** Walker Coll, Jasper, AL; SO; BA; Phi Theta Kappa 90-; Var Bsktbl 89-; AS Walker Jr Coll; Biology; Medical Dr.

**REYNOLDS, DANIEL P,** Southern Coll Of Tech, Marietta, GA; JR; BS; IEEE; Tau Alpha Pi; Prs Hon Rl 86-87; Svc Tech Black/Decker; Cert Spartan Schl Of Aero 81; Elec Engr.

**REYNOLDS, DAVID J,** Saint Vincents Coll & Seminary, Latrobe, PA; SR; BA; Bus Forum 89-; Vol Inc Tax Asst 90-; Cmps Mnstry 89-90; Alpha Sigma Lambda; Intrnshp USX Corp 90-; Bus Dept Fin Awd; Career/Bus SW Natl Bk 86-90; Finance; Economics MBA.

**REYNOLDS, DONALD J,** Wv Univ, Morgantown, WV; SR; BSEE; IEEE; Taekwon Do Club; Intern Natl Radio Astrony Obsel; Westmoreland Sprague Schlrshp; C/P Telphone Schlrshp Pres List; Elec Engrg; Engeg.

**REYNOLDS, DONNA M,** Univ Of South Al, Mobile, AL; FR; BS; Phi Eta Sigma; Church; Little League; Boy Scouts; Elem Ed; Teacher.

**REYNOLDS, EUGENIA DENISE,** Univ Of Al At Birmingham, Birmingham, AL; FR; BA; Dnc/Engl; Tch.

**REYNOLDS, JEFFREY S,** Life Coll, Marietta, GA; JR; DC; Gnstd Clb; Mtn Plptn Clb; Chrprctc Rsrch Vol; Chrprctc.

**REYNOLDS, JENNIFER L,** Northern Ky Univ, Highland Hts, KY; JR; BS; Stdnt Spprt Srvcs Tutr 90-; Lrning Asstnc Cntr Tutr 90; Info Syst; Info Syst/Finc.

**REYNOLDS, JULIE A,** Middle Tn St Univ, Murfreesboro, TN; SR; BS; Stdnt Tchr Educ Assn; Stdnt Home Ec Assn; Early Chldhd Educ; Tchr.

**REYNOLDS, KATHY S,** Pellissippi St Tech Comm Coll, Knoxville, TN; SO; BA; Nrsg.

**REYNOLDS, KELLY D,** Univ Of Ky, Lexington, KY; SR; BS; Alpha Epsilon Delta 89-; Biology/Pre Med; Medicine.

**REYNOLDS, KELVIN M,** Draughons Jr Coll Nashville, Nashville, TN; GD; DPMA Treas 90-; AS; Cmptr Sci.

**REYNOLDS, KIMBERLY,** Kent St Univ Kent Cmps, Kent, OH; SO; Scuba/Sftbl; Vol Robinson Mem Hosp 90-; Biol/Pre Phy Thrpy; Phy Thrpy.

**REYNOLDS, LINDA L,** Cumberland Coll, Williamsburg, KY; SR; BS; Dntl Hygiene U Of Lsvle 78; Elem Ed; Tchr/Cnslr.

**REYNOLDS, LYNN,** Univ Of Al At Birmingham, Birmingham, AL; JR; BA; USGA Lgsltr 89-; Ad Hoc Cmt Non Trdtnl Stdtn Chrmn 90-; Srvc Cmt 90-; Pgm Cmt 89-90; Ad Hoc Cmt S Afrc 90; Omcrn Dlt Kappa Mbrshp Chr; Gldn Key 90; Deans List; Brd Stdnt Pblctns 90-; Natl Assc Legal Asstnts; AALA 90- Pres; Pol Sci; Law.

**REYNOLDS, MARCIA E A,** Bloomfield Coll, Bloomfield, NJ; SO; US Embssy Kgn Jmc 84-87; Srvc Rep 87-; Comp Prgrmmng.

**REYNOLDS, MARIANNE,** Univ Of Nc At Asheville, Asheville, NC; JR; BA; Psi Chi VP 90-; Rsrch Grnt 90-; Rsrch Asstnt; Psych.

**REYNOLDS, MARY A,** Univ Of Southern Ms, Hattiesburg, MS; JR; BS; Alumni Assn 90-; Jdcl Brd; Eagle Cnnctn; Alpha Lambda Delta; Phi Eta Sigma; Gamma Beta Phi; Phi Beta Lambda; Phi Chi Theta; Angel Flight Cmptrlr 89-90; Pacers; Bpts Union; Awrds Day Prgrm; Schlrshp Banquet; AASO Rcgntn; Bnkng Finance; Bsns.

**REYNOLDS, MARY A,** Univ Of Cincinnati, Cincinnati, OH; JR; Beta Chi Pres 79-81; Alumni Schlrshp 90-; Payroll Benefits Admin 84-88; AD 81; Elem Educ/Hist; Tchng.

**REYNOLDS, MARY S,** Tn St Univ, Nashville, TN; SR; BA; Lbrl Arts; Actng.

**REYNOLDS, MARY S,** Beckley Coll, Beckley, WV; FR; Assoc Resprtry Cr; Resprtry Thrpst.

**REYNOLDS, MICHELLE L,** Defiance Coll, Defiance, OH; FR; BA; Gamma Omega Kappa; Pres Schlrshp; Cmnctns.

**REYNOLDS, PATRICIA A,** Patrick Henry Comm Coll, Martinsville, VA; SO; MBA; Va Msm Ntrl Hstry Lab Asst Vol; Spch Cmnctns; Spch Pthlgy.

**REYNOLDS, PATRICIA LYNN,** Roane St Comm Coll, Harriman, TN; SO; BS; DAR 89-; BS Tn Tech Univ; Elem Educ; Teach.

**REYNOLDS, RANDAL A,** Fl International Univ, Miami, FL; SR; BA; Amer Mrktng Assc Vp Prmtns 90-; Tau Epsilon Phi V-Chnclr 89-; Bus Mrktng/Mgmt.

**REYNOLDS, ROBIN M,** Averett Coll, Danville, VA; FR; Phi Sigma Sigma Treas; Acctg; CPA.

**REYNOLDS, SCOTT L,** Tn St Univ, Nashville, TN; SO; BA; Lit Gld 90-; Engl.

**REYNOLDS, SHARON D,** Norfolk St Univ, Norfolk, VA; FR; BS; Stdnt Assn 90-; Gspl Choir 90-; Spartan Alpha Tau; Chem; Rsrch.

**REYNOLDS, SHERRIE L,** Univ Of Nc At Greensboro, Greensboro, NC; JR; BS; Elem Edctn; Tchr.

**REYNOLDS, STACY A,** Liberty Univ, Lynchburg, VA; SR; Intrnshp Babcock/Wilcox; Grad Magna Cum Laude; Data Cntrl Tech Babcock/Wilcox; Bus Admin; Acctg.

**REYNOLDS, SUSAN W,** Northern Ky Univ, Highland Hts, KY; BA; Maplewood Gld 90-; BS Eastern KY Univ 84; Elem Ed; Tchr.

**REYNOLDS, TARA M,** Providence Coll, Providence, RI; SR; Pltcl Sci Clb Prs 88-90; Vrsty Sftbl 87-88; Yng Rpblcns 87-; Pi Sigma Alpha 91; Pltcl Sci Hnrs Prgrm 87-; New England Sclgy Cnfrnc Awd Wnnr; Pblc Admnstrtn Certf; IM Bsktbl 87-91.

**REYNOLDS JR, THOMAS K,** Univ Of Ky, Lexington, KY; SO; BS; Math; Sci Electrcl Eng.

**REYNOLDS, TRENEICE L,** Al A & M Univ, Normal, AL; SO; BA; Palmer Hl VP 90-; Edtr A & M Nwsppr 90-; Mrktng/Bus.

**REYNOLDS, YVONNE E,** Fl International Univ, Miami, FL; SR; BPA; West Indian Stdnt Assn; Grl Scts Asst Trp Ldr 90-; AA Broward Comm Coll 89; Pub Admin; Pursue Masters Same Fld.

**REYNOSO, THERESA B,** Jersey City St Coll, Jersey City, NJ; SR; BSN; Sigma Theta Tau; Hnrbl Mntn Fclty Rcgn; Sprng Hlth Fair; Prof RN; AAS Bergen Comm Col 82; Nrsng.

**REZAZADEH, HASSAN,** Erie Comm Coll, Buffalo, NY; SO; BA; Bahai Faith Prtcptn 87-; Eng Sci.

**REZVANI, GOLNAZ,** Middlesex County Coll, Edison, NJ; SO; EOF Actvts; Bio; Med.

**RHEA, ELIZABETH HOPE,** Roane St Comm Coll, Harriman, TN; FR; ASN; Nursing.

**RHEE, JOHN S,** Coll Of Health Sci Stony Brook, Stony Brook, NY; GD; MD; Med/Hmnts Mag Edtr 89-; Cancer Inst Onclgy Fllwshp 90; Med Schl Admissions Comm 90; BA Dartmouth Clg 89; Med; Physician.

**RHEE, PATRICIA,** S U N Y At Albany, Albany, NY; FR; Korean Clb; Chinese Clb; Math; Prfssr.

**RHEE, WILLIAM,** Yale Univ, New Haven, CT; FR; BA; US Grnt Fndtn Tchr 90-; CSA Asst Sctmstr; Red Cross 90-; Yale Pol Mo Assoc Edtr Art Dir 90-; Lbrl Prty; Yale Pol Union Whip 90-; Army ROTC Cadet PFC 90-; DC Pblc Dfndr Serv Invstgtr Intrnshp; Hstry; Law.

**RHEW, TINA L,** Univ Of Nc At Greensboro, Greensboro, NC; SR; Educ; Tchr.

**RHINEHART, SCOTT C,** Emmanuel Coll Schl Chrstn Min, Franklin Sprg, GA; FR; BA.

**RHINES, CANDACE H,** Cumberland Coll, Williamsburg, KY; FR; Mnstrl Assn 90-; Soclgy Socl Wrk Clb 90-; Appalachian Mnstrs Mtn Outrch Chpln; Love In Action Tm Ldr; Spec Chldrn Asst Stdnt Crdntr; Smr Msnry Yth Tchr; Rlgn/Psychlgy; Msnry/Set Up Shtlrs.

**RHINES, GWENDOLYN L,** Memphis St Univ, Memphis, TN; SR.

**RHINESMITH, KIM M,** Merrimack Coll, North Andover, MA; SR; BA; Psych Clb; Prog Brd Treas 88; Fd Comm; Psi Chi; Merrimactian 88; Stdy Abroad Granada Spain 90; Psych.

**RHOADES, CHRISTY L,** Liberty Univ, Lynchburg, VA; JR; BA; SCORE; Alpha Lambda Delta 88-; Kappa Delta Phi 89-; Chrldng 88-; Elem Educ; Tchr.

**RHOADES, DAVID F,** Pa St Univ Delaware Cty Cmps, Media, PA; FR; BS; Campus Nwspr Prdctn Edtr 90-; SADD V Pres 90-; Camera Club 90-; Tutoring 90-; The Keystone Soc; Pres Frshmn Awd; Academic Excellence Awd; Deans List; Aerospace Engrng; Engrng.

**RHOADES, DUANE B,** Indiana Univ Of Pa, Indiana, PA; SO; BS; Mrchng Band 90; Chrstn Show Chr 89-; Comm Media; Photographer.

**RHOADES, LAURA E,** Univ Of Al At Birmingham, Birmingham, AL; JR; BA; Phi Theta Kappa 89-90; Stdnt Occptnl Thrpy Assc 90-; Phi Theta Kappa 89-90; SOTA 90-; AS Snead St Jr Coll 90; Occptnl Therapy.

**RHOADES, LORI A,** Thomas Nelson Comm Coll, Hampton, VA; FR; BA; Hmns Srvcs; Cnslr.

**RHOADHOUSE, PAMELA A,** S U N Y Coll At Fredonia, Fredonia, NY; JR; BS; MAA 90-; Math Club 89-; All-College Band 88-; Pi Mu Epsilon; VAX Lab Asstntshp 89; Learning Center Tutor 89; AAUIW Award 90; Computer Science Math; Programming Software.

**RHOADHOUSE, SUSAN M,** S U N Y Coll At Fredonia, Fredonia, NY; JR; BM; MENC 88-; Asta Pres 89-; Kappa Delti Pi; Pi Kappa Lambda; Msc Educ; Tchng.

**RHOADS, ALAN C,** Univ Of Akron, Akron, OH; SR; Gldn Key; Leone/Franklyn Dickinson Endwmnt; Clvrlf Sr H Trch Asst Coach; Clvrlf Sr H Ftbl Asst Coach; Cmpnt Anlys Tchncn-Milk Mktg Inc Strngsvl OH 81-87; Scndry Educ-Cmprhnsr Bus/Phy Ed/Tch/Coach.

**RHOADS, CHRIS E,** Univ Of Ky, Lexington, KY; SO; BA; Phi Eta Sigma; Elec Eng; Eng.

**RHOADS JR, DONALD E,** Univ Of Sc At Columbia, Columbia, SC; FR; BA; Cmptr Clb 87-90; Sci Clb 87-90; Mu Alpha Theta 87-90; Beta Clb 88-90; Ntl Hnr Scty 88-90; Gamma Beta Phi; Deans Lst 90-; Bio; Med.

**RHOADS, GERALD W,** Christopher Newport Coll, Newport News, VA; SR; BSGA; Cmpltd Intrnshp Tres Suffolk VA; Admn Asstnt Rndtr Const Co Suffolk VA; Pol Sci; Prsnl/Pblc Mgmt.

**RHODE, ABBEY J,** Teikyo Post Univ, Waterbury, CT; FR; BS; Outstndng Ldrshp Awd; Bus; Fin.

**RHODES, BENAE L,** Univ Of Nc At Charlotte, Charlotte, NC; JR; BA; Sclgy/Wmns Studies.

**RHODES, CHARISE R,** Fl A & M Univ, Tallahassee, FL; SO; BS; Math Clb Tr 89-90; Pres Schlrs Assn 89-; Tau Beta Sigma Tr 90-; Life Gets Better Schlr 89-; Dns Hnr Rl 89-90; Actrl Sci; Actry.

**RHODES, DANIELLE L,** Clark Atlanta Univ, Atlanta, GA; SR; Politicial Science Club Treas; Honor Roll 88; Deans List 90; Hosp Volntr 90; Legislative Aide; BA Clark Atlanta Univ; Political Sci Public Policy; Grad School.

**RHODES, DEBORAH L,** Univ Of Md Baltimore Prof Schl, Baltimore, MD; JR; BS; Deans Lst 90; Amer Phrmctcl Assc 90-; Acdmy Stdnts Phrmcy 90-; Rad Hnrs 88; Edward J Stegman Awd 89; Rsrch Lab Mgr/Rsrch Tech 85-; Comm Emmnl Utd Meth Chrch 88; BS Penn St Univ 84; MAS MGMT John Hopkins Univ 88; Pharmacy.

**RHODES, GAVIN T,** Ms St Univ, Miss State, MS; JR; BA; Amer Soc Lndscp Archtcts 90-; Gamma Beta Phi 90-; AAS 87-89; Ag; Lndscp Archtct.

**RHODES JR, JAMES E,** Bridgewater Coll, Bridgewater, VA; FR; BS; Nwspr 90-; Radio 90-; Debate 90-; Drama 90-; Biol.

**RHODES, JANIS A,** Merrimack Coll, North Andover, MA; SR; BA; Litry Mag 90-; Contemporary Affairs Scty 87-89; Mod UN Delegate 88; Presdy Study Con 88; Certif Trvl Consult 87; Awd Winning Barizon Model 85-87; YWCA Tchr/Afterschl Prog 89-90; AA History Northern Essex Co Clg 88; History/Internat Rela; Religion Law.

**RHODES, JENNY L,** Wake Forest Univ, Winston-Salem, NC; FR; MA; Bostwick House Cncl Secy 90-; Harbinger Corps 90-; Resdnt Stdnt Assoc Delgt 90-; Delta Delta Delta 90-; Im Sftbl; Math/Cmptr Sci.

**RHODES, KATHARINE A,** Memphis St Univ, Memphis, TN; SR; BA; Classcl Piano 87-; Fam Trbl Cntr; Isac E Brown Mem Music Schlrshp 88; Psychlgy.

**RHODES, KATHRYN S,** Bridgewater Coll, Bridgewater, VA; SO; Cncrt Chr 89-; Chrl 90-; Altrnatvs For Abusd Adlts/Untd Way Chldrns Coord 90-; Big Bro/Big Sis/Untd Way 90-; Soclgy; Cnslr.

**RHODES, LORI L,** Indiana Univ Of Pa, Indiana, PA; JR; BED; Concert Dance Co 88-; Kappa Delta Pi 90-; Phi Sigma Pi 89-; JUP Stdnt Literacy Corps 90; Lutheran Campus Cntr Secy Of Directing 88-; Provost Schlr 90-; Elem Educ; Teaching.

**RHODES, LOU ANN,** Kent St Univ Kent Cmps, Kent, OH; SR; BA; Prctcm-Lorain Cnty Bd MR/DD; Deans Lst 90-; Indvdl/Fmly Studies/Grntlgy; Scl Serv/Hmn Ser.**

**RHODES, MARCIA J,** Beckley Coll, Beckley, WV; FR; AD; Law; Prlgl.

**RHODES, MARILYN A,** Tn St Univ, Nashville, TN; JR; BA; Bio Clb 89-; Beta Kappa Chi 90-; Golden Key 90-; Delta Sigma Theta 89-; Bio; Med.

**RHODES, MICHELLE A,** Radford Univ, Radford, VA; FR; BS; Crmnl Juste Clb 90-; Phi Sigma Pi; Crmnl Juste; Law-Jvnl Dlnqncy.

**RHODES, PATRICK B,** Middle Ga Coll, Cochran, GA; JR; Eng Clb 88-; Gamma Beta Phi 88; Hon Day Awd Deans Lst 88-; Civil Eng.

**RHODES, PAULA C,** Life Coll, Marietta, GA; GD; Gnstd Clb; Mtn Plpttn Clb; Sccr; GA Hroptlgcl Scty; ACA; ICA; Prdct Mgr; BA Rutgers St Univ 84; DC Life Chiropractic Coll; Physlgy; Chrrprctc.

**RHODES, ROBBIE ALYSON,** Univ Of Nc At Greensboro, Greensboro, NC; JR; BS; Univ Ambssdrs 90-; Clthng Txtls Clb 90-; Dnc Cmpny 88-; Univ Mrshls 89-; Alpha Lambda Delta 89-; Kappa Omicron Nu; Rsdntl Coll Cncrns Otrch Cmmtts 89-90; Rsdntl Coll Almn; Orttn Ldr Rsdntl Coll 90; Intern Chralotte Apparl Mart; Clthng Txtls; Fshn Mrchndsng Mrktng.**

**RHODES, ROBERT B,** Western Carolina Univ, Cullowhee, NC; SO; BA; Pre-Lthl Pro Org Pres; Wstrn Gld Pres; Chcllrs Ambssdr; Woodfin Fire Dept/EMS Sfty Offcr 86-; Wstrn NC Athltc Offcl Assn; Chem Pre-Med; Medcl Dctr.

**RHODES, RUTH E,** Edinboro Univ Of Pa, Edinboro, PA; JR; BA; Crw Tm VP; Stdnt Govt 88-90; Cmmnty Plyrs 88-; Deans Lst 88-; Engl.

**RHODES, TINA M,** Edinboro Univ Of Pa, Edinboro, PA; JR; BA; Ski Clb 88-89; Alpha Chi 90-; Alpha Phi Sigma Pres 90-; Pres Hon Schlrshp 88-89; Hon Stdy Abrd Schlrshp 90; Intrnshp W/L Ambrose; IM Vlybl/Soccr 90-; Crmnl Jstce; Law.

**RHODUS, SAMUEL L,** Univ Of Ky, Lexington, KY; FR; BS; Mrchng Bnd 90; Bsktbl Pep Bnd 90-; Prcsn Soc 90-; Math/Sci; Elctrcl Engrg.

**RHONE, GUY C,** Univ Of West Fl, Pensacola, FL; SR; MEA; Kappa Delta Pi 90-; Phi Beta Lambda Pres 89-90; BS; MPA Golden Gate Univ 76; Educ; Tchr.

**RHONE, JACQUELINE M,** Stillman Coll, Tuscaloosa, AL; SO; BA; Chnclrt Scl Clb; Delta Sigma Theta; Cmptr Sci; Systms Anlyst.

**RHONEY, CLINT R,** Univ Of Nc At Greensboro, Greensboro, NC; SR; BS; Bapt Stdnt Union Rec Chrprsn 88-89; Alpha Lambda Delta 87; IM Chmpn 87-; Leisure Srvcs.

**RHONEY, DENISE H,** Univ Of Ky, Lexington, KY; GD; PHARM; Amer Soc Hosp Phrmcsts Ky Soc Hosp Phrmcsts 89-; Res Hall Govt Pr 87-89; Amer Phrmctcl Assn 87-; Rho Chi VP 88-; Lambda Kappa Sigma 87-; Excell Clin Comm; IM Ftbl 86-88; BS 90; Phrmcy; Clin Phrmcy.

**RHONEY, TIMMY L,** Catawba Valley Comm Coll, Hickory, NC; SO; AAS; Gamma Beta Phi 89-90; Certif Auto Mechanics 86; Indstrl Engrng.

**RHUDY, BRENDA J,** Northwest Al Comm Coll, Phil Campbell, AL; FR.

**RHYMER, DENISE P,** Fl A & M Univ, Tallahassee, FL; JR.**

**RHYMES, LAURA A,** Va Commonwealth Univ, Richmond, VA; SR; BA; Nwspr Wrtr/Photo 86-88; Yrbk Photo Edtr 86-88; Keyettes 86-87; Lyndon Johnson Congrsnl Intrn 90; La Crosse 87-88; Pol Sci; Law.

**RHYNES, PEGGY G,** Chesterfield Marlboro Coll, Cheraw, SC; GD; BA; Otstndng Achvmnt Assc Bsn Acctng Prgrm 90; Assc Bsn Acctng Prgrm; Bsn Mngmnt; Bsn Mgmnt.

**RHYS, VANESSA AUDI,** Ny Univ, New York, NY; SR; BA; Hsg Coop Sec 9-; NAFE 89-; Alpha Sigma Lambda; Dept Cmmrc Int ; AA Macomb Clg 85; Ecnmcs; Intl Bsn Plnng.

**RIAL, JEFFREY R,** Univ Of Tn At Martin, Martin, TN; FR; BS; Mngmnt; Business Mngmnt.

**RIALS, KELLIE L,** Univ Of Southern Ms, Hattiesburg, MS; SR; BS; Paralegal Soc 89-; Pre Law Soc 90-; Kappa Delta; Paralegal Stds.

**RIBAUDO, PHYLLIS D,** City Univ Of Ny Baruch Coll, New York, NY; GD; BSED; Thtr Actors Inst; Sec Tchr; BSED.

**RIBAUDO, REBECCA T,** Bloomfield Coll, Bloomfield, NJ; FR; BA; Bus; Admin.

**RIBAVARO, RUTHANN,** Widener Univ, Chester, PA; JR; Lcrsse 89-; Bus Mgmt; Hmn Rsrcs.

**RIBEIRO, LINDA A,** Teikyo Post Univ, Waterbury, CT; JR; BSGS; Stdnt Govt Assn Pres 89-90; Rose Taurig Schlrs 89-90; Cmnctns.

**RIBO, MICHAEL E,** Kent St Univ Kent Cmps, Kent, OH; SR; BM; Oh Coll Music Edctrs Assoc V P 88-; Pi Kappa Lambda Natl Music Hnr Soc 90-; Golden Key 90-; Kappa Kappa Psi 88-; Roy D Metcalf Otstndng Bandsman Awd 90; Edward L Masters Otstndng Band Frshmn Awd 88; Sheri J Luft Mem Awd Acdmc Achvmnt 89-; Music Edn; Public Sch Teaching.

**RICARD, HEATHER M,** Univ Of Sc At Columbia, Columbia, SC; FR; BVA; LOCAL 90-; Alpha Lambda Delta; Jrnlsm/Bus.

**RICARDO, MARIA D,** Inter Amer Univ Pr Hato Rey, Hato Rey, PR; JR; BA; Hstry Lit Stdnts Assn Sub Sec 89-; Hstry; Phd Hstry.

**RICCI, ANTHONY R,** Bloomfield Coll, Bloomfield, NJ; SO; BA; Dns Lst 89-; Pre Med; Med Dr.

**RICCI, ZINA J,** City Univ Of Ny City Coll, New York, NY; GD; BSMD; Italian Club CCNY 88-90; Deans Lst 87-; Pre Med/Bio Med; Med Schl.

**RICCIARDI, PAULA A,** Schenectady County Comm Coll, Schenectady, NY; FR; AAS; Amer Assoc Medical Assistants; Bus Admnstrn.

**RICCIO, REBECCA A,** Radford Univ, Radford, VA; SR; BA; Ski Clb; Alpha Sigma Alpha.

**RICE, AMY L,** Oh Univ, Athens, OH; SR; BMUS; Msc Stdnt Advsry Cncl 89-; Natl Assoc Msc Thrpy Inc 89-90; Ohio Assoc Msc Thrpy 89-90; Phi Eta Sigma 88; Alpha Lambda Delta 88; Pi Kappa Lambda 90; Mac S Bethel Schlrshp 89-; Dns Schlrshp 88-89; Msc; Msc Thrpy.

**RICE, BROOKE E,** Univ Of Nh Plymouth St Coll, Plymouth, NH; SO; BS; Psychlgy 90-; Erly Chldhd Clb Sec Elect; Deans Lst 89-90; Pres Lst; Elem Ed; Tchr.

**RICE, CHAD E,** Thomas Nelson Comm Coll, Hampton, VA; GD; AS; Mech Tech.

**RICE JR, CLYDE L,** Univ Of Nc At Greensboro, Greensboro, NC; JR; BS; Bapt Stdnt Un Tms Coord 89; Alpha Lambda Delta Ind Comm Mbr 89-90; NC Teach Fellows Schlrshp 88-; Intrnshp Guilford Primry Schl 90; Intrnshp Hmptn Elem; Elem Educ; Teacher.

**RICE, CONSERVERINA Y,** Univ Of Sc At Columbia, Columbia, SC; FR; BA; Carolina Classics; NAACP; Educ; Tchr.

**RICE, CYNTHIA D,** Al A & M Univ, Normal, AL; SO; BA; Bus; Bus Admin.

**RICE, DAVID M,** Northern Ky Univ, Highland Hts, KY; SR; BSW; Socl Wrk Clb; Pi Kappa Alpha Alum Comm Serv 89-; Brigadon Ctr Vol Drk Hosp Vol; Lakeside Nrsng Hm Shrt Long Term Res Spec; Arobic Danc; Socl Wrk/Humn Serv; Minstry/Semnry.

**RICE, DAVID P,** Atlantic Comm Coll, Mays Landing, NJ; FR; Culinary Chef; Rstrnts.

**RICE, DEBORAH F,** Davis & Elkins Coll, Elkins, WV; SO; BS; Hnrs Assoc 89-90; Biolgy Clb 90-; Bio Envir Sci Achvmnt Awd; USAA All Amer Sclr; Biology; Tchr.**

**RICE, GRANT J,** Marshall University, Huntington, WV; FR; BA; Nwslttr Asst Edtr 90-; Ltrgcl Actvts Com Nwmn Assn Chrmn 90-; Nwmn Asscn Chr 90-; M Nwmn Clb 90-; PROWL 90-; Rsdnc Hall Assn 90-; Soc Yeager Schlrs 90-; IM Vlybl 90-; Fin/Spnsh; Bus.

**RICE, JANA L,** Univ Of Tn At Martin, Martin, TN; SR; BS; Alumni Cncl 89-; Ordr Omega 90-; Phi Eta Sigma 88-; Phi Kappa Phi; All Amer Schlrs; Pi Sigma Epsilon VP Mktg 89-; Chi Omega Schlrshp Del 87-; Intrnshp CBK Ltd 90; Mrktg; Indstrl Sales.

**RICE, JENNIFER C,** Va Commonwealth Univ, Richmond, VA; SO; BS; Clin Psych.**

**RICE, JO B,** Lesley Coll, Cambridge, MA; JR; BS; Commuter Clb 88-; Acad Achvmnt 90-; Elem Ed; Tchr.

**RICE, JO-ELLE M,** Indiana Univ Of Pa, Indiana, PA; SO; BA; Hstry Clb; Spcl Olympics Hlpr; Provost Schlr; Kappa Delta Pi; Brthrn Youth Grp; Drm Vlybl; Hstry; Tchg.

**RICE, JODI L,** Coll Of Saint Rose, Albany, NY; FR; BA; Hist/Pol Sci; Law.

**RICE, JOHN F,** Univ Of Nc At Asheville, Asheville, NC; SO; MD; Hnrs Prog 90-; SG Crt Justice 90-; Phi Eta Sigma; Chancellors/Deans Lsts; IM 90-; U S Navy 84-89; Biol; Physician.

**RICE, KATHRYN P,** Davis & Elkins Coll, Elkins, WV; FR; AS; Stdnt Nrs Assn 90-; D/E Hnrs Schlrshp; Nrsg.

**RICE, KEISHA L,** Hampton Univ, Hampton, VA; FR; BA; Alumni Assn 90-; Accntng; Corp Law.

**RICE, KIMBERLY A,** Cumberland Coll, Williamsburg, KY; SR; BED; Campus Mnstrs 87-90; Show Choir 87-; Chorale Sec 87-90; Saxton Bapt Ch 89-; Deans Lst 86-; Math/Music.

**RICE, KIMBERLY S,** Davis & Elkins Coll, Elkins, WV; SO; BS; Elem Ed.

**RICE, KRISTI M,** Oh St Univ At Newark, Newark, OH; SR; BED; AA; Elem Edn; Teach.

**RICE, LAURANNA LOUISE,** Univ Of Southern Ms, Hattiesburg, MS; JR; BA; Stdnt Spch/Hrng Assn; Assoc Arts Hinds Comm Coll 90; Spch/Lang Pthlgy; Spch Thrpy.

**RICE, LINDA M,** East Stroudsburg Univ, E Stroudsburg, PA; FR; BS; Ins Sales 84-; Mgmt; State Farm Ins Agcy.

**RICE, LORI A,** Siena Coll, Loudonville, NY; SR; BA; Coll Pblctn Copy Edtr 88-89; Alpha Mu Gamma 89-; English.

**RICE, MARI L,** Savannah St Coll, Savannah, GA; SO; BS; Sclgy Clb Ms Sociology 90-; Newspaper Wrtr; Peer Cnslr; Flg Corp; Sclgy; Professor.

**RICE, MARTHA E,** Christian Brothers Univ, Memphis, TN; SO; BA; Chrstn Edctn Comm Cordova Prsbytrn Chrch; Kentwood Est Nghbrhd Assn Tres 89-; Hillhaven Corp Sr Accntnt 79-87; Acctng.

**RICE, MARY V,** Defiance Coll, Defiance, OH; SO; BED; NW OH Dive Clb Pres 87; Engl.

**RICE, MEGAN R,** Lesley Coll, Cambridge, MA; JR; BS; Deans Lst 90-; Mid Sch Math/Cmptr Sci; Tchr.

**RICE, MELISSA A,** Bethany Coll, Bethany, WV; JR; BA; Alpha Beta Gamma; Gamma Sigma Kappa; Heritg Hs Co Ed Ind Hsng Unit Pr; Phi Alpha Theta; Elem Educ; Spec Educ.

**RICE, MELISSA A,** Stillman Coll, Tuscaloosa, AL; SR; BS; Gamma Iota Sigma 87-88; Cmptr Sci; Data Processing.

**RICE, MICHAEL E,** Univ Of Md Baltimore Prof Schl, Baltimore, MD; JR; BSMT; Amercn Soc For Medcl Technlgy; Medcl Technlgy; Medcn.

**RICE, MICHAEL K,** Univ Of Montevallo, Montevallo, AL; SR; MA; SGA Sentr 90; Phi Theta Kappa Pres 87-; Phi Alpha Theta Pres 88-; Kappa Delta Pi 90-; Alpha Tau Omega Hstrn 88-; Yng Rpblcns 88; BA 90; Coll Dplmts Pres 87-88; IM Ftbl/Bsktbl/Vlybl/Sftbl 86-; AA Wallace Coll 88; Soc Sci; Ed.

**RICE, NANCY H,** Life Coll, Marietta, GA; GD; DC; Gonstead Study Clb; Motion Palpation Clb; Point Zero Philosophy Clb; BA Univ NC 86; Chiropractic Doctor.

**RICE, PATI A,** Middle Tn St Univ, Murfreesboro, TN; JR; BA; Girl Scouts; Shoneys Inc Menu/Cost Analysis 85-; Grphc Cmmnctns; Grphc Dsgn.

**RICE, RAE ANNE,** Southern Vt Coll, Bennington, VT; SO; BS; Acctg.

**RICE, REGINA C,** Roane St Comm Coll, Harriman, TN; SO; AS; IM Bsktbl Vlybl 89-90; Nursing; RN.

**RICE, ROBIN ERIC,** Univ Of Louisville, Louisville, KY; SR; MCHE; Tau Beta Pi; Golden Key; Tau Beta Pi; Chem Engrng.**

**RICE, RONNIE D,** Ms St Univ, Miss State, MS; JR; BA; Miss Comm 89-; Arbour Acres Socl Prog Dir 90-; Phi Kappa Phi; Omicron Delta Kappa; Gamma Beta Phi Asst Dir 89-; Phi Eta Sigma 89; Pres Schlr 89-; TV Intrnshp 90; Vlybl Anncr 90; Corp Cmmnctns.

**RICE, RUSSELL C,** Birmingham Southern Coll, Birmingham, AL; SO; Amnsty Intrntnl 89-; Quad Mag Stf 90-; Sthrn Acdmc Revw Asst Edtr 90-; Phi Eta Sigma; Alpha Lambda Delta; Chi Sigma Chi Pblc Rltns Chrmn 89-; Mrktng Englsh; Advrtsng Media.

**RICE, SHARON L,** Hudson Valley Comm Coll, Troy, NY; SR.

**RICE, SHERRY L,** Middle Tn St Univ, Murfreesboro, TN; SO; BS; Early Childhood Edctn; Tchr.

**RICE, SONYA M,** Al A & M Univ, Normal, AL; JR; BA; Amer Soc Cvl Eng VP 90; St Hwy Dept; Cvl Eng.

**RICE, STAYCIE WORLEY,** Anderson Coll, Anderson, SC; SO; BS; Gamma Beta Phi; Glenn Huey Award; AA; Secndry Ed Math; Tchng.

**RICE, THOMAS H,** Columbia Union Coll, Takoma Park, MD; SR.

**RICE, TIFFANY A,** Murray St Univ, Murray, KY; FR; BS; Theta Chi Delta Hstrn 90-; Pres Schlr 90-; Educ; Tchr.

**RICE, TIMOTHY S,** Valley Forge Christian Coll, Phoenixville, PA; SR; BS; Barth Schlrshp; Pstrl Studies/Theology; Ministerial.

**RICE, TINA R,** Middle Tn St Univ, Murfreesboro, TN; SO; BSN; Nrsng; RN.

**RICE, V DIANNE,** Garrett Comm Coll, Mchenry, MD; SO; BS; Phi Theta Kappa; Elem Ed; Tchr.

**RICE-IQBAL, MELONY G,** Midway Coll, Midway, KY; JR; BA; Amer Bus Wmns Assn Sec 90-; Intntl Clb Sec Treas 89-; Phi Theta Kappa Rptr Pres 89-; Xi Gamma Chptr Phi Theta Kappa Pres/Rep 90-; Phi Theta Kappa; Intrntl Clb Sec Tr 89-; Habitat Humanity; Dns Lst 88-90; Span Awd 88-89; Presdntl Schlrshp 88-90; AA; Bus Admin; Intrntl Mktng.

**RICH, ALISON B,** Nova Univ, Ft Lauderdale, FL; MBA; BS State Univ Of NY At Binghmtn Schl Of Mgmt.

**RICH, BRYAN M,** Liberty Univ, Lynchburg, VA; JR; BS; Dns Lst 90; Acad Schlrshp 90-; Busn/Finc; Fincl Mgmt.

**RICH, CAROL M,** Owensboro Jr Coll Of Bus, Owensboro, KY; SR; Magna Cum Laude; Missions Comm Calvary Temple Asmbly Chrmn 90-; Ladies Auxiliary Vly Inst Of Psychiatry 89-90; BA Siena Hts Clge 68; Diploma Bus Ofc Prfsnl; Computerized Office Professional.

**RICH, DANA D,** Fl St Univ, Tallahassee, FL; JR; BA; Gldn Key 90-; Psi Chi 90-; Engl; Law.

**RICH, JEFFREY M,** Anne Arundel Comm Coll, Arnold, MD, SO; AA; Cmnctn Arts Prctcm; Video Prdctn Intrnshp; Cmnctn Arts; Video Prdctn.

**RICH, KATRENNA S,** Fayetteville St Univ, Fayetteville, NC; SO; BS; Sndy Schl Tchr; Choir; Pblc Schl Sys Vol; Educ/Math; Tchr.

**RICH, KRISTIN E,** Merrimack Coll, North Andover, MA; SR; BA; Commuter Coun Chrprsn 89-90; APICS 90-; Bus Admin; Ins Prop Casualty Claims.

**RICH, STEVEN L,** Memphis St Univ, Memphis, TN; SR; BA; Golden Key 88-; Dns Lst 87-90; Paul H Sisco Awd Geography; Geography; Cartography.

**RICHARD, DAVID W,** Univ Of Southern Ms, Hattiesburg, MS; SR; Kappa Omicron Nu 90-; Act Acad Achvmnt Schlrshp 87-89; Statler Hosp Schlrshp 89-90; Outstanding Jr Schlrshp 90-; Hotel/Rest Mgmnt.

**RICHARD, EILEEN G,** Bridgeport Engr Inst, Fairfield, CT; SR; BSEE; Dns Lst 83-; Vllybl 82-83 86-90; IEEE 86-; Elect Engr; Citizens Utlties Co Stamford CT 81-; ASEE 89; Elec Engr.

**RICHARD, ELIZABETH,** City Univ Of Ny City Coll, New York, NY; SR; BA; Gldn Key Schlrshp 90-; Kelly Prize; Assn Gheatre Hghr Edctn; Ntnl Stdnt Speech Lang Hrng Assn 90-; Certf Ntnl Shakespeare Cnsrvtry 84; Speech Lang Pathology; Voice Speech Spclst.

**RICHARD, FREDRICK,** Clark Atlanta Univ, Atlanta, GA; JR; BA; Var Bsktbl Capt 89; Hlth P E Clb Pres; Hlth P E; Sprts Adminstrtr Tchr.

**RICHARD, GWENDOLYN D,** Jackson St Univ, Jackson, MS; SO; BS; NABJ; NAACP 90-; WJSU Announcers Club SGA Repres Miss WTSU; Alpha Lambda Delta Asst Secy 90-; Mbr Jackson States Hnrs Clg 89-; Edtr Variety Section Blue/White Flash; Music Announcer WJSU Campus Radio Station 90; Mass Communication; Criminal Justice System.

**RICHARD, MALCOLM RAY,** Alcorn St Univ, Lorman, MS; FR; BA; Hon Stdnt Org; Chrldng Squad; Engl/Cmnctns; Law.

**RICHARD, REGINA KATHERINE,** Univ Of Al At Birmingham, Birmingham, AL; SO; AA; Std Physcl Thrpy Asc Rep 90; Amer Physcl Thrpy Asc; Dns Lst; Physcl Thrpy Asst; Educ.

**RICHARD, SHERYL L,** Bapt Bible Coll & Seminary, Clarks Summit, PA; SO; AA; Dns Lst; Bible; TESL.

**RICHARD, THEFARRO V,** Howard Univ, Washington, DC; FR; BS; NSBE 90-; Dormty Pres 90-F Harriet Tubman Qmadrangle Pageant 90; Prefreshman Prog Incmng Engrg Students 90-F Varsity Vlybl 90-; Chemical Engrg; Med.

**RICHARDE, CATHERINE,** Univ Of Southern Ms, Hattiesburg, MS; SR; BA; Wesley Fndtn Cncl Mbr 88-89; Womens Soccer Club 87-89; Res Asst 90-; Phi Chi 90-; Phi Kappa Phi 89-; Alpha Lambda Delta 87-; Omicron Delta Kappa 90-; Gamma Beta Phi; Golden Key 89-; $5000 Un Schlst Schlrshp: $1600 Hnrs Col Schlrshp 87-; Prs Dns Lists; Psych; Hist Edn.

**RICHARDELLA, SUSAN L,** Saint Francis Coll, Loretto, PA; SR; CERT; YMCA Instr; Mbr Of ASCD; Presch & Prog Dir 81-90; BA Psych Penn St Univ 79; Elem Edn; Teach.

**RICHARDS, ADAM N,** Univ Of Al At Birmingham, Birmingham, AL; SR; Art Gld Pres 90-; Hulsey Hnry Schlp; Pres Hnrs; BA; Art/Grphc Dsgn.

**RICHARDS, AVIS A,** Fl A & M Univ, Tallahassee, FL; FR; BS; Thrd Flr Dmnd Hll Pres 90-; Phi Eta Sigma 90-; Cert Schlrshp 90-; Deans Lst 90; Math Ed.

**RICHARDS, BETTY J,** Univ Of Rochester, Rochester, NY; JR; Sbs Blgy Clb 90-; D Lns Clb 90; Rsrch Wth Blgy Prfssrs 90-; MD Wlk A Thns 90-; Charles Mem Fllwshp 90; Nom Fr Rlstn Prna Schlrshp 90-; Crss Cntry 90; Indr And Otdr Trck 90; Mlclr Gntcs; Rsrch Prfssr In Mlclr Blgy.

**RICHARDS, BRIDGETTE L,** Pa St Univ Main Cmps, University Pk, PA; FR; BA; Linguistics; Professor.

**RICHARDS, BROWYN P,** Univ Of The Dist Of Columbia, Washington, DC; FR; BA; Hon Prog 90-; Mtgmry Hspc Soc 90-; USN Hstlgy Tech Ldg Ptty Offc 89-; EMT Ntl/Lcl Cert; Med.

**RICHARDS, C VANN,** Univ Of Sc At Columbia, Columbia, SC; SR; Phi Theta Kappa 80-81; Data Serv Schlrshp NE MS Jr Clg 80; Prog/Anlyst 91; AAS NE MS Jr Clg 81; BS Univ SC Aiken 90.

**RICHARDS, CHRISTY R,** Volunteer St Comm Coll, Gallatin, TN; SO; AAS; Sci; Nrsg.

**RICHARDS, CRYSTAL L,** Nova Univ, Ft Lauderdale, FL; GD; MSHSA; Sigma Theta Tau 85-; Natl Std Nrs Asc Schlp 85; Clg Nrs Hnrs Pgm 85-86; Univ FL Clnc Admstrn Intshp; Med-Surg Nrs 86-88; Utlztn Rvw/Qlty Assrnc Nrs 88-; BSN Univ FL 86; Hlth Serv Admn; Hlthcr Admnstrtr.

**RICHARDS, DWIGHT H,** City Univ Of Ny City Coll, New York, NY; JR; BE; Goldn Key 90-; Tau Beta Pi; Eta Kappa Nu; Tutr 90-; Cert Coll Arts/Sci/Tech 85-88; Elec Eng.

**RICHARDS, EUNICE,** S U N Y Coll Of A & T Morrisvl, Morrisville, NY; SO; Afrcn Stdnt Union Blck Allnc; Jdcl Brd; Sch Sfty Brd; Latino Amer Stdnt Org; Deans Lst; Taft Huntly Schlrshp; Fclty Stdnt Assn Schlrshp; Tlnt Rstr Schlrshp; Res Asst.

**RICHARDS, GEORGE C,** Barry Univ, Miami, FL; GD; Phi Theta Kappa 86-88; AA Miami Dade North 88; BS Barry Unvrsty 90; Psychlgy; Psychlgy/Law.

**RICHARDS, JEFFREY R,** Western New England Coll, Springfield, MA; SO; BS; WNEC Jr High Prgrm; Deans Advsry Comm 89; Indstrl Engr; Engr.

**RICHARDS, JOHN P,** S U N Y Coll Of Tech At Delhi, Delhi, NY; SR; BA; Amer Inst Of Archtcts 90-; AAS 90-; Archtctre; Archtct.

**RICHARDS, JUDIMARIE,** Elmira Coll, Elmira, NY; SO; BA; Stu Cltn Peer Educ Pblcty Chrmn 90-; Pupil Asst Lrnng Vol 89-; Clss Trea 89-90; RA 90-; Phi Eta Sigma 90-; Acdmc Prfrmnc Schlr 89-; Empire St Chllngr Awrd; Paul Douglas Awrd Wnnr; IM Bdmntn 90-; Frnch Educ; Tch.

**RICHARDS, JUDY A,** Borough Of Manhattan Comm Coll, New York, NY; SR; BA; Caribbean Clb 87-; Chrstn Flwshp 88; Natl Talent Rstr; Aarion/Janifer Schlrshp; Certif Excell Awd ECE Dept BMCC; Henry I Siegel Co Asst Cmnctns Mgr 87-; Penticostal Gospel Tabernacle Christ Yth Grp Pres 87-; AAS; Edctnl Cnslg.

**RICHARDS, KAREN F,** Univ Of Sc At Columbia, Columbia, SC; SO; BS; Orient; Kings Jwlrs Bkkpr 90-; Crmnl Just/Sclgy; Law.

**RICHARDS, KIMBERLY M,** Gulf Coast Comm Coll, Panama City, FL; FR; AA; Spnsh; Spnsh Tchr.

**RICHARDS, LEONA D,** Tougaloo Coll, Tougaloo, MS; SO; BA; Pre-Alumni Cncl 90-; Eboni Danz VP 89-; Stdnt Spprt Serv/Upwrd Bnd Tutor 90-; Natl Cncl Negro Wmn 87-; Debs/Beaus Cls Fndng Sis Asst/Coord; Chrldr Capt 89-90; Pblc Hlth; Clncl Psychlgst/Epdmlgst.**

**RICHARDS, LEONARD J,** Tn St Univ, Nashville, TN; JR; BSEE; Forest Pk Handbl Clb; Chess; Biking; AA Forest Pk Cmnty Clg 90; Elec Engr; Patent Law.

**RICHARDS, MICHAEL J,** Western New England Coll, Springfield, MA; FR; BS; Work Stdy 90-; Natl Alpha Lambda Delta 90-; Tnns Tm 90-; Math; Acctnt.

**RICHARDS, MICHELLE K,** Alcorn St Univ, Lorman, MS; SO; BA; Pol Sci Clb 90-; Hons Stdnts Org 90-; Pol Sci; Law.

**RICHARDS, REBECCA L,** Holyoke Comm Coll, Holyoke, MA; FR; AS; Vet/Anml Sci.

**RICHARDS, REUBEN RAYMOND,** James Madison University, Harrisonburg, VA; SR; BS; Cmtr Stdnt Cncl VP 90-; Psi Chi; Drctd Rsrch Prjct 90-; Prkng Advsry Comm 90-; Indstrl Psychlgy.

**RICHARDS, SEAN A,** Univ Of Miami, Coral Gables, FL; SO; BM; Audio Engr Socty Treas 89-; IM Soccer 89-; IM Soccer; Phi Eta Sigma; Joan Handleman Sadoff Schlrshp; FLA Undergrad Schlrshp; Henry King Stanford Schlrshp; Music Engr Tech; Audio/Music/Engr.

**RICHARDS, SUSAN B,** Coll Of Charleston, Charleston, SC; GD; MBA; Natl Assn Exec Females; Dept Of Trfc/Transp Transit Info Spclst; BS 90; AA Univ Md 87; Bus Admin.

**RICHARDS, TERRY L,** Franklin And Marshall Coll, Lancaster, PA; SR; Pi Gamma Mu; Golden Key 89; Wall Street Journal Bsn Adm Prize; Magna Cum Laude; Honeywell Inc Export Coord; Continental Ins; Bsn Adm-Mgmt; Ins.

**RICHARDS, TODD S,** Fl St Univ, Tallahassee, FL; FR; PHD; Rsdnc Hl Govt Rep 90-; Phi Eta Sigma; Meteorlogy.

**RICHARDS, TRACI L,** Fl A & M Univ, Tallahassee, FL; JR; Hatchett Prelaw Clb 90-; Stdnt Govt Assoc Jr Senator 90-; Golden Key; Summer Research Opportunity Prog; Political Sci; Law.

**RICHARDS, VIRGINIA R,** Univ Of Ga, Athens, GA; SR; BSED; Phi Theta Kappa 88-90; Kappa Delta Pi 91; Kappa Delta Epsilm 90; Golden Key 90; Delta Epsilon Chi Treas 90-; Serv Awd 89-90; AS Dalton Clg 90; Mktg Educ; Educ.

**RICHARDS, WENDY D,** Univ Of Al At Huntsville, Huntsville, AL; JR; BS; ASME V Chr 90-; Alpha Lambda Delta 88-89; Tau Beta Phi 89-; Phi Tau Sigma 89-; Phi Kappa Phi; Tau Beta Phi 89-; Phi Tau Sigma 89-; NASA Co-Op 90-; Mech Engr Schlrshp 89-; Engr; Mech Engr.

**RICHARDS, WENDY G,** Livingston Univ, Livingston, AL; SR; Oaapn 90-; ANA; AL State Def Force 90-; Mnstr Music 90-; Sndy Sch Tchr 90-; Annie Louise Pruitt Schlrshp 90; Acad Achvmnt Awd Nrsng; ASN; Rn.**

**RICHARDS, WILLIAM B,** Duquesne Univ, Pittsburgh, PA; FR; MBA; Sharp 90-; Stdtn Orientation 90-; Phi Eta Sigma 90-; Allstate Financial 90-; Bus; Financial Plng.

**RICHARDSON SOTO, PATRICIA L,** Univ Of Pr Cayey Univ Coll, Cayey, PR; FR; BS; Deans Lst; Chem Cir 90-; Sftbl/Trck/Fld Vars 87-90; Chem; Med.

**RICHARDSON, ADRIENNE V,** Univ Of Sc At Columbia, Columbia, SC; SO; BS; Chi Omega; Math; Physician.

**RICHARDSON, ALETA L,** City Univ Of Ny Queensbrough, New York, NY; SO; BA; Phi Theta Kappa 90-; Freehold Ladies Auxilary Brd Dir 89-90; Acctg.

**RICHARDSON, AMANDA L,** Western Ky Univ, Bowling Green, KY; JR; BS; Phi Eta Sigma 90; Phi Kappa Phi; Pres Schlr 90-; Awd Excel Schlrshp 89-; Natl Collgt Ed Awd; Elem Ed; Tchr.

**RICHARDSON, AMY S,** Cornell Univ Statutory College, Ithaca, NY; JR; BS; Gldn Key 90-; Advsr 90; Kossoff Awrd Prnsl Entrprs Pro; Merch Kraft USA; Deans Lst 89-; Var Crs Cntry/Trck 89-; Bus Mgt; Food Indstry Bus.

**RICHARDSON, ANDREW,** Alcorn St Univ, Lorman, MS; JR; BS; Indstl Tech Clb 89-; Trck 87-89; Elec/Comp Tech; Engr.

**RICHARDSON, BARBARA A,** Fl A & M Univ, Tallahassee, FL; SO; BS; Plymkrs Guild; Cncrt Chr 89-; Ec Dclb 90-; Hon Roll 89-; SBI Bronze Awrd 89-90; Pres Schlrs 89-; Bus Admn; Logistics.**

**RICHARDSON, BARBARA C,** Coppin St Coll, Baltimore, MD; JR; BA; Hnrs Assoc 88-; Newspaper Ed 90-; Hnrs Pgm; Chi Sigma Chi 89-; Sigma Tau Delta; Mc Nair Schlr 84-; Rsrch Asst Intern; Newspaper Rep Intern 90-; Clg PR Intern 90-; Engl; Jrnlsm.

**RICHARDSON, CHARLES H,** Univ Of Sc At Columbia, Columbia, SC; JR; Chi Psi 88-.

**RICHARDSON, CHARLES K,** Univ Of Al At Birmingham, Birmingham, AL; SO; Sch Hlth Rltd Prfsns SGA 90-; BMET VP 90-; SGA Vly Coll 89-90; Intrnshp Univ Hosp Oprtg Rm; Prtcptd Ofctd IM Sprts 90-; AAS; Cert; Med; Dr.

**RICHARDSON, CHRISTOPHER A,** Ms St Univ, Miss State, MS; SR; BBA; Econ Clb 89; Band 87-90; Fincl Mgmt Assn; Amer Econ Assn Summr Mnrty Pgm Temple Univ 90; Econ; Finc.

**RICHARDSON, CRYSTAL,** Marshall University, Huntington, WV; SR; BBA; Acctg Clb 88-; W Va Soc CPA'S 89-; U S Army Corp Eng 87-; Acctg; CPA.

**RICHARDSON, DA META J,** Tougaloo Coll, Tougaloo, MS; FR; World Hstry Club 90; Pre Hlth Club 90; Alpha Lambda Delta; Outstndng Achvmnt Mission Invlmnt; Bio; X-Ray Tech.

**RICHARDSON, DANA F,** City Univ Of Ny Baruch Coll, New York, NY; JR; BA; Chrldng; Modeling; Dance; Computer Sci; Comp Analyst.

**RICHARDSON, DANA VINCENT,** Univ Of Sc At Spartanburg, Spartanburg, SC; SO; BA; Erly Chldhd Edn; Teach.

**RICHARDSON, DENA N,** Radford Univ, Radford, VA; JR; BBA; Alph Lambda Delta 89-; Delta Um Delta Pres; Acctg; CPA.

**RICHARDSON, DENISE N T,** Midlands Tech Coll, Columbia, SC; FR; Dip H S; Pharm Tech; Phys Thrpst.

**RICHARDSON, DENISE R,** Ky St Univ, Frankfort, KY; FR; BME; Cncrt Chr; Gspl Ensmbl; KY Hll Clb VP 90-; Sftbll 90-; Music Ed; Tch Music.

**RICHARDSON, DESDEMONA D,** Fisk Univ, Nashville, TN; SR; BS; Cmptr Sci Clb Pr 90-; Eductnl Tutr Pgms 89-90; Carolina Clb 87-; Beta Kappa Chi; Gld Key Mortr Brd; Alpha Kappa Alpha Parlmntrn; Exxn Co USA Intrnshp 90-; Cmptr Sci; Anlyst.

**RICHARDSON, DIANNE P,** Limestone Coll, Gaffney, SC; SR; BA; IAPES; Budget/Policy Analyst SC Emplymnt Sec 73-; AS Univ SC 73; Mgmnt.

**RICHARDSON, DOLORES J,** Tallahassee Comm Coll, Tallahassee, FL; SO; BA; Phi Theta Kappa 90-; Army Spcl Act Awd 87-88; Natl Contract Mgmnt Assn 83-85; Cntractng Ofcr/Spclst 80-89; Bus Mgmnt; Personnel.

**RICHARDSON, DOUGLAS B,** Memphis St Univ, Memphis, TN; FR; BFA; Aperature Flm Soc 90-; Lambda Pi Eta 90-; Phi Eta Sigma 90-; Film; Dir Commcl Flms.

**RICHARDSON, DULCIE RENEE,** Univ Of Fl, Gainesville, FL; SR; BHS; Stdnt Dietetic Assoc Treas 89; Fla Dietetic Assoc 89; Amer Dietetic Assoc 89; Alpha Lambda Delta 88; Golden Key 89; Phi Kappa Phi 90; Pres Awd For Outstndng Achievemnt; Outstndng Stdnt Awd For Clncl Cmmnty Dietetics; Clncl/Cmmnty Dietetics; Mstr Of Pbl Hlth.

**RICHARDSON, DWAYNE A,** Fl A & M Univ, Tallahassee, FL; GD; BS; Engr Clb V P 90-; Cmptr Sci Assoc 88; Blck Stdnts Union 88; Dns Lst 89-; Phi Theta Kappa 88; Federal Aviation Engr Asst; Southern Bell Tech 89-90; SONY Test Engr 90; AA Miami-Dade Cmnty Clg 87/90; Elctrncs; Engr.**

**RICHARDSON, EILEEN M,** Providence Coll, Providence, RI; SR; BS; Deans Lst 89-; ACT Schlrshp 87-; Cum Laude; Biology; Medicine.

**RICHARDSON, ERIC A,** Bethune Cookman Coll, Daytona Beach, FL; JR; BS; Cncrt Chrl 88-90; Jr Cls Exec Brd Dir P R 90-; Alpha Chi; Alpha Mu Gamma 90-; Psi Chi Sec 90-; Fl Ftr Ed Amer Prlmntrn 89-; Ed Prfsnl Smnr Brn Bwl 88-; Pthfndrs Amer 88-; Sthrn Fndtn Smr Schlrs Pgm; Psychlgy; Schl Psychlgst.

**RICHARDSON, ERIC S,** Al St Univ, Montgomery, AL; SR; BA; Phi Mu Alpha Sinfonia 89-; Presser Schlrshp Awrd 90-; Ntl Mnrty Educ Awrd 90-; Music.

**RICHARDSON, GABRIELLE R,** Roane St Comm Coll, Harriman, TN; SO; AAS; Hlth Sci; Nrsng.

**RICHARDSON JR, HOMER ALLEN,** Norfolk St Univ, Norfolk, VA; JR; BS; Pre-Med Scty 89-; Alpha Kappa Mu; Vis Cst Grd 85-89; Blgy/Pre-Med; Medicine.

**RICHARDSON, JACINTA R,** Hampton Univ, Hampton, VA; SR; BS; Natl Assn Blck Acctnts 87-; Stdnts Free Entrprs 89-90; Pre Alum Clb 87-; Alpha Kappa Mu 89-; Vol Inc Tax Asst 89-90; Deptmntl Awd 90-; Acctg.

**RICHARDSON, JACQUELINE M,** Alcorn St Univ, Lorman, MS; SO; BS; Bus Admin; Finance.

**RICHARDSON, JENNI A,** Univ Of Cincinnati, Cincinnati, OH; SR; BA; Educ; Tchr.

**RICHARDSON, JENNIFER M,** City Univ Of Ny Baruch Coll, New York, NY; SR; BA; Caribbean Stdnts Assn Sec 88-89; Frshman Orientation Ldr 88-90; Assist Fixed Assets Clg Mgr 90-; Communications; Pblc Rltns.

**RICHARDSON, JOANNA,** Old Dominion Univ, Norfolk, VA; JR; Alph Phi Omega 90-; Mktg Educ; Retail.

**RICHARDSON, JOHN CHRISTOPHER,** Coll Of Charleston, Charleston, SC; FR; BA; Busn; Law Schl/MIB/MBA.

**RICHARDSON, JOSEPH TULLOSS,** John C Calhoun St Comm Coll, Decatur, AL; SO; BS; Tech Stdnts Assn Pr 90-; Educ Soc 90-; Chamber Of Cmmrce Cmnty Invlvmnt Awd 90; F O Smith Awd 90; AAS; Mach Tool Tech; Mech Engr.**

**RICHARDSON, KELLY L,** Winthrop Coll, Rock Hill, SC; SO; BA; Comp Sci Lab Inst 90; Critical Issues Symp Stdnt Dir 90; Baptist Stdnt Union 90-; Alpha Lambda Delta 90; Deans Lst 89-90; Pr Lst; Engl; Educ.

**RICHARDSON JR, LACY R,** Univ Of Sc At Coastal Carolina, Conway, SC; BFA; Hnrs 81; Art Instctr 88-; Cert Pntng/Sclptr Ringling Schl Art/Dsgn 81; Art/Ed; Tchr/Art.

**RICHARDSON, LAURIE A,** Queens Coll, Charlotte, NC; SR; BA; Un Bd Dir Sec 88-; Justinian Scty 87-90; Cltrl Evnts Chrmn 88-90; Mrtr Bd 90-; Ordr Omega Pres 90-; Ordr Alpha 89-; Delta Omicron 90-; Alpha Delta Pi Treas 87-; Pres Schlr 87-; Chem Lab Asstshp 88-; Law Intern 90; Pltcl Sci; Law.

**RICHARDSON, LLOYD T,** Truett Mc Connell Coll, Cleveland, GA; SO; BA; Bsns; Entrprnrshp/Ftnss Fld.

**RICHARDSON, MARK H,** Vance Granville Comm Coll, Henderson, NC; SO; Eng Asst Harriet/Henderson Yarns Inc 87-; Bus Cmptr Pgmng.

**RICHARDSON, MATTHEW M,** Univ Of Tn At Knoxville, Knoxville, TN; FR; MBA; SGA; Undrgrd Acdmc Cncl; Exec Undrgrd Bus Prog 90-; Alpha Epsilon Delta 90-; Pi Kappa Alpha; Accntng; Med.

**RICHARDSON, MAURICE,** Jackson St Univ, Jackson, MS; FR; BA; Engl; Scndry Ed.

**RICHARDSON, MELISSA A,** Spartanburg Methodist Coll, Spartanburg, SC; SO; BED; Clge Chrstn Mvmnt Sec 90-; Bptst Stdnt Un 90-; Stdnt Sprt Srvc 89-; Ilsns Lit Mgz Ed; Yrbk Sprts Phtgrphr 90-; Hbt Hmnty Vol; A J R Helmus Ptry Awd 1st; Tns Cptn 89-; Spec Ed; Tchr.

**RICHARDSON, MICHAEL LEE,** Memphis St Univ, Memphis, TN; SO; BA; Bys Clb Cmp Cnslr; Psychlgy Sclgy; Clncl Indstrl Psychlgy.

**RICHARDSON, MISTY L,** Univ Of Montevallo, Montevallo, AL; GD; Bptst Cmps Mnstrs 88-90; Assoc Hmn Sev 89-90; BS 90; Sclgy; Soc Serv.

**RICHARDSON, NIKITA R,** Stillman Coll, Tuscaloosa, AL; FR; BA; Alpha Phi Alpha Aux; Gamma Iota Sigma; Stillman Schlr 90; Deans Lst 90; Sociology; Child Psych.

**RICHARDSON, PAUL D,** Air Force Inst Of Tech, Wrt-Ptrsn Afb, OH; GD; MSC; Sigma Iota Epsilon; Engr Ofcr Royal Australian Air Force; Be Swinburne Inst Tech 78; Info Res Mgmt.

**RICHARDSON, PAUL M,** Univ Of Sc At Columbia, Columbia, SC; JR; Coll Pharm Stdnt Gov VP 90-; Phi Beta Kappa; Golden Key 88-; Gamma Beta Phi 88-; Kappa Psi Treas 89-; S C Sen Page 90; Pharm Intrn 90-; Pharm.

**RICHARDSON, PAUL W,** Savannah Coll Of Art & Design, Savannah, GA; JR; BA; Photogrp SCAD 90-; Photo; Prntr/Phr.

**RICHARDSON, ROBBIE B,** Northwest Al Comm Coll, Phil Campbell, AL; SO; BA; Stdnt Govt Assoc Pres 88-90; Publc Rltns/Mktg Comm 89-90; Stdnt Afrs Comm 89-90; Discplnry Comm 89-90; Athlts/Stdnts Actvts Comm 89-90; Bus/Acctng/Fin; CPA Profsr.

**RICHARDSON, ROBERT DENNIS,** Fl A & M Univ, Tallahassee, FL; SR; PH D; ACM; IEEE; Sigma Alpha Epsilon Rgnl Offcr; Grad Summa Cum Laude; Deans Lst 89-90; Adlt Ldr Boy Scts Amer Asst Dist Cmmssn; Sr Syst Archtct; BS CIS; Comp/Info Syst; Sftwr Eng Dstrbtd Syst.

**RICHARDSON, SHANNON E,** Middle Tn St Univ, Murfreesboro, TN; SO; Spcl Ed.

**RICHARDSON, SHARLYN,** Bloomfield Coll, Bloomfield, NJ; SO; Deans Lst 89-90; Psychology; Psychologist.

**RICHARDSON, SHEILA M,** Meridian Comm Coll, Meridian, MS; SO; BS; Coll Act Bd 88-; CAB Hlth Wlns Pblcty Chr Prsn 89-; CAB Exec Bd Co Chrprsn 89-; Ambassador 88-; Literacy Tutor 89-; Elem Educ; Tchr.

**RICHARDSON, TAUNYA MONIQUE,** Univ Of The Dist Of Columbia, Washington, DC; SR; BBA; Hmcmng Cmt 88; Phi Smg Pi 89-; Data Prcsng Mgmt Assc Sec 87-; Dlt Mu Dlt; Alpha Kappa Alpha VP 88-; SOME 89-90; Fedrtd Kings Daughter Sr Ctzn Home 79-; Christmas April 89-; AA Benjamin Franklin Univ Acctg 83-85; Cmptr Inf Systms Sci; Pgrmr.

**RICHARDSON, TRACY E,** Villanova Univ, Villanova, PA; JR; BA; Prjct Sunshine 88-90; Spec Olymp 88; Kappa Alpha Theta; Deans Lst 88-90; Pltcl Sci; Law.

**RICHARDSON, VALERIE D,** Univ Of South Al, Mobile, AL; SR; BS; Dns Lst; Pres Lst; Stdnt Tchng; Bsktbl 89-; AS Jfrsn Dvs St Jr Coll 89; Elem Educ; Tchr.

**RICHARDSON, VALERIE S,** Coker Coll, Hartsville, SC; SO; BS; Natl Hlth Care Rcrtrs Assn 89; S C Area Hlth Care Rcrts Assn 89; Nurs Rcrtmnt Specist 89; AS 80; Mgmt; Human Rsrcs/Personnel.

**RICHARDSON, VENENCIA A,** Saint Josephs Coll New York, Brooklyn, NY; GD; MA; BS H Admn 90; Hsptl Adm.

**RICHARDSON, WILLIAM E,** Coker Coll, Hartsville, SC; JR; BS; SC Army Natl Guard; Cvl Svc Empl; Bsn Adm; Mgmt.

**RICHART, MICHELE D,** Coll Misericordia, Dallas, PA; SR; BS; Campus Mnstry Adpt Grndprnt 87-90; CMSOTA Co Chr Sr Brqt 87-90; Tutor 88-90; Deans Lst 90; St Hosp Intrnshp; Rhb Hosp; Occptnl Thrpy.

**RICHBOURG, BRENDA L,** Univ Of West Fl, Pensacola, FL; SR; BA; Alpha Sigma Lambda; AA Okaloosa Walton Cmnty Clg 89; Educ/Erly Chldhd; Tch.

**RICHBOURG, PAULA MARGARET,** Coll Of Charleston, Charleston, SC; SR; BS; Coll Rpblcns Vc Chrmn 90-; Fin Clb 90-; Omicron Delta Kappa 90-; Outstndng Stdnt Awd Sch Bus; Natl Cllgt Bus Merit Awd; Hghly Dstngshd Fac Hon Lst; IM Vlybl Bsktbl Wtrpolo Capt 88-; Bus; Mktg.

**RICHBURG, JOSEPH D,** Emory Univ, Atlanta, GA; FR; BA; Blck Stdnt Alliance 90-; Bible Study 90-; IM Bsktbl 90-; Deans Lst 90-; Pol Sci; Law.

**RICHBURG, VICTORIA R,** Univ Of Cin R Walters Coll, Blue Ash, OH; GD; MD; Minrty Premed Allnc VP 87-88; Spnsh Clb Treas 88; Sigma Delta Pi 88; Min Acad Schlrshp 85-89; Alpha Kappa Alpha Rec Sec 88; Lgthse Runaway Shltr Vol 88; Deaconess Hosp 86-88; Alaskian Nrsng Hm 87-88; Intra Soccer 85-86; Blgy Spansh; Medcl.

**RICHEME, MAURICE F,** Teikyo Post Univ, Waterbury, CT; SR; BA; Intl Stdnt Clb Treas 88-90; Amer Mktg Assn; Sccr Vrsty All New England; All Distrct All Star Nominee 90; Mktg/Mgmt; Pltcl Sci/Fin.

**RICHER, CHRISTINE E,** Defiance Coll, Defiance, OH; FR; BS; Nrsg.

**RICHERT, CANDACE S,** Eastern Coll, Saint Davids, PA; JR; BA; Hbtat Fr Hmnty 88-; Bible Stdy Grp 90-; Clwng Mnstry 89-; W W Smith Schlrshp 89-; Psychlgy Hnr Scty; Nrsg Hm Vol 90; Feedg Hmlss 89-90; Stdnt Chpln 88-90; EDT 90; Grw Grp Ldr 90; Flwshp Chrstn Athl Ldr 88-90; Psychlgy.**

**RICHERT, GABRIEL S,** Oh Wesleyan Univ, Delaware, OH; FR; MD; Horizons Intl 90-; Phi Eta Sigma; Tennis 90-; Med; Doctor.

**RICHESON, JUANITA H M,** Univ Of Fl, Gainesville, FL; GD; BAA; Golden Key 90-; Ldrshp Schlrshp Franklin Univ; BS Bus Admnstrn 92; 20 Yrs Retail Mgmnt Exp; Trade Book Manager FL Book Store 86-88; Field Sales Rep The Pressworks Corp First Impressions Inc 84-86; Hearing Rptr 84; Business; Art Production/Mgmnt.

**RICHEY, JASON L,** Allegheny Coll, Meadville, PA; SO; BA; Alcohol Cnslr; RA; Judicial Hnr Comm; Academy For Acad/Athl; Phi Gamma Delta; Acad All Amer Wrstlng; Alden Schlr; Wrstlng; Pol Sci/Econ; MBA.

**RICHEY, KEITH A,** Ms St Univ, Miss State, MS; SR; BA; Bptst Stdnt Un; Mthdst Stdnt Cntr; Miscm; Phi Theta Kappa; Phi Kappa Phi; Acdmc Schlrshp; Cmmnctns.

**RICHEY, LEE M,** Winthrop Coll, Rock Hill, SC; SR; BS; Lee Whicker Hl Cncl VP; Pblctns Drm Lf Edtr 87-88; Pblc Sfty Adv Cmmtt 90-; RA 89-; Stu Hlth Advsry Cmmtt 89-; Intern 90-; Bus Educ; Tchr.

**RICHEY, MARCIA D,** Wv Univ, Morgantown, WV; SR; BS; Amercn Inst Of Chem Engrs; Phi Kappa Phi; Omega Chi Epsilon Secy 90-; Tau Beta Pi; Golden Key; Alpha Phi Omega; AICHE Profsnl Promise Award: 3m Schlrshp; Awarded Du Pont PhD Flwshp; Monsanto Schlrshp; Outstndng Sr Amercn Chemsts Fndtn; Chem Engr.

**RICHEY, SONYA A,** Clark Atlanta Univ, Atlanta, GA; SR; BS; Stdnt Recruit Tm 87-89; Natl Soc Of Black Engrs 87-; Beta Kappa Chi; Alpha Kappa Mu; Pi Mu Epsilon; Delta Sigma Theta 88-; Outstndng Stdnt Awd; Natl Schlr; Hon Rl 87-; Math/Mech Engr.

**RICHEY, VIVIAN M,** Itawamba Comm Coll, Fulton, MS; JR; BA; Laser Club; Soc Mfg Engrs; Phi Theta Kappa; All Am Schlr; Pres List; Deans List; Grad Spec Hnrs 86; AAS Itawamba Comm Coll 86; Elem Edn.

**RICHMOND, ANGELA V,** Marshall University, Huntington, WV; SR; BA; Frshmn Stdnt Govt Cncl Mbr 87; Mrchng Spclsts Inc 86-; Jr Achvmnt Bus Cnsltnt 90-; Deans List 90-; Bus Mgmt; Mgr.

**RICHMOND, DAVID S,** City Univ Of Ny Baruch Coll, New York, NY; SR; BBA; Dip Agri Sc Guyana Schl Agriculture 80; Accty; Insur.

**RICHMOND, JACKIE A,** Univ Of Southern Ms, Hattiesburg, MS; FR; Jrnlsm; Editorial.

**RICHMOND, ROBYN A,** Univ Of Akron, Akron, OH; SR; BS; Mgmt; Ins Ind.

**RICHMOND, RONALD E,** Wv Northern Comm Coll, Wheeling, WV; SO; AA; Hbltn Spclst Nrthrn Pnhndl Bhvr Hlth Cntr 85-; Hmn Srvcs; Rsrch Psychlgy.

**RICHMOND, VALERIE A,** Clark Atlanta Univ, Atlanta, GA; SR; MSW; Org Socl Chng 88-; Chld Wlfr Trnshp Awd; Socl Wrk; Attnd Grad Schl.

**RICHTER, KATHLEEN A,** Univ Of South Al, Mobile, AL; JR; SGA 88-89; Varsity Golf 88-90; Phi Eta Sigma; Alpha Lambda Delta; Chi Alpha 89-90; Pres Lst; IM Sftbl 90; Mktg.

**RICHTER, MARY C,** Univ Of Cin R Walters Coll, Blue Ash, OH; FR; BA; Chesters Pizzeria Inc Admin Asst 89-; Bus; Teach.

**RICHTER, PHILIP,** Yeshiva Univ, New York, NY; SR; BA; Coll Dmcrts 88-; Jnt Bus Soc 88-; Comp Sci Soc 88-; Chess Clb 88-; Pre-Law Soc 88-; Ecnmcs Soc 88-; Hbrw Hon Soc 89-; Untd Jwsh Appl 90; Prjct Achi 87-88; Dean Witter Rynlds Intern 90-; Shearson Lehman Hutton Intern 89-90; Ecnmcs; Law.

**RICK, KAREN A,** S U N Y Coll Of Tech At Canton, Canton, NY; SO; BA; Phi Theta Kappa Schlrshp Cmte 90-; Client Bd/N Cnty Lgl Svcs St Lawrence Cnty; Psychlgy; Coun.

**RICKABAUGH, ROBERT M,** Salisbury St Univ, Salisbury, MD; JR; BA; Acctg/Finance.

**RICKARD, KATRINA L,** Univ Of Tn At Martin, Martin, TN; JR; BA; Pep Bnds 88-; Piano Ensembl 89-; Sigma Alpha Iota 90-; Phi Mu Alpha Swthrt 88-; Zeta Tau Alpha 88-; Msc.

**RICKARDS, DAVID A,** Univ Of North Fl, Jacksonville, FL; JR; BMUS; Intervar Chrstn Flwshp 88-90; Ivy Refrmtn Lgue Lit Clb V P; AA Edison Cmuty Clg 90-; English/Jazz; Music.

**RICKARDS, LEXIE L,** Univ Of North Fl, Jacksonville, FL; JR; BA; ICF 88-90; Lit Clb Secr; AA Edison Cmnty Clg 90; Art Hstry; Hmemkg.

**RICKELS, LISA A,** Univ Of Al At Birmingham, Birmingham, AL; SR; BA; Soc Of Prof Jrnlsts Sec 91-; Kaleidoscope Stdnt Nwspr Sr Staff Writer 91-; Sigma Delta Chi Elect; Mills Schlrshp 91-; Jrnlsm Major/Bus Minor; Novelist.

**RICKENBACKER, SALLEY A,** Univ Of Sc At Columbia, Columbia, SC; SR; BA; Carolina Cares 89-90; Carolina Prog Union 89-90; Cath Stdnt Org 88-89; Gamma Theta Upsilon VP 89-; Geography; Grad Schl.

**RICKENBAKER, MELISSA E,** Limestone Coll, Gaffney, SC; FR; BS; Sccr/Sftbl Trnr 90-; Phys Ed/Athltc Trng.

**RICKER, LISA D,** Salisbury St Univ, Salisbury, MD; SO; BS; Med Careers Soc Sec 90-; Phi Eta Sigma; Biology; Dr Of Med.

**RICKER, TRACY L,** Fl St Univ, Tallahassee, FL; FR; BA; Phi Eta Sigma; Pol Sci; Law.

**RICKER, VANESSA J,** Tusculum Coll, Greeneville, TN; SR; BS; Dorm Rep; Ambsdr Clb: Hm Vol; Sftbl Capt; Vybl; Bkbl; Phys Educ/Spec Educ; L D.

**RICKERT, LISA J,** Liberty Univ, Lynchburg, VA; SR; Kappa Delta Pi; Dns Lst 87-90; BS 90-; Elem Educ.

**RICKETT, LUCINDA F,** Georgetown Univ, Washington, DC; FR; BA; Bus; Mrktng.

**RICKETTS, RICHARD D,** Oh St Univ, Columbus, OH; SR; BS; Geology Clb Sec 90-; Golden Key 90-; SGE Chapt Natl Earth Sci Hon Soc 90-; Mrtr Bd Pres 90-; Geology/Pltcl Sci; Grad Sch.

**RICKETTS, SUZANNE M,** Bethany Coll, Bethany, WV; FR; BA; Soc Prof Jrnlsts; Alpha Xi Delta; Comms; Publ Rels/Adv.

**RICKLES, ANGELA,** Brewer St Jr Coll, Fayette, AL; SO; BS; Cncrt Bnd 89-; Brewer Sngrs 90-; Dept Mgr 87-; Music; Educ.

**RICKSGERS, THOMAS H,** Kent St Univ Kent Cmps, Kent, OH; JR; BM; Muisc.

**RICO, MARTHA L,** City Univ Of Ny City Coll, New York, NY; JR; BA; Sftbl Tm St Thomas Univ 86-87; Exbtn Arch Dsgn 87; Stdnt Natl Arch Assoc Pres Cult Actvies 85-87; BA Arch Dsgn Sch Arts Bogota Colombia 80; Arch.

**RICONDO, PEDRO,** Fl St Univ, Tallahassee, FL; SR; BS; Tau Beta Pi; AA Miami Dade Cmnty Clg 88; Engrng; Civil Engrng.

**RICOTTA, PATRICK J,** Oh Coll Of Podiatric Med, Cleveland, OH; GD; DPM; Amer Clg Ft Surgeons 90-; Deans List 89-; Alpha Gamma Kappa 90-; BS St Bon Aventure Univ 89; Podiatric Medicine; Foot Dr/Surgeon.

**RICOTTONE, LEANNE L,** S U N Y At Buffalo, Buffalo, NY; JR; BA; Phi Eta Sigma 88-; Bus/Acctng; CPA/GRAD Sch.

**RIDDELL, DAWN,** Columbia Greene Comm Coll, Hudson, NY; SO; AOS; Columbia Green C C State Grant; Architictural Design; Cmptr Aided Drafting.

**RIDDELL, RICHARD B,** Univ Of Ky, Lexington, KY; FR; BA; Stdnt Athletic Clb 90-; Res Hall Govt 90-; Phi Eta Sigma 90-; Lambda Chi Alpha 90-; Univ KY Safe Six Lifestyles Ldrs Theatre Trp 90-; Engl/Theatre; Wrtng/Film/Theatre.

**RIDDICK, MELISSA,** Lincoln Univ, Lincoln Univ, PA; FR; BA; Psychgy Clb; Japanese Clb; Chld Psychlgst.

**RIDDICK, SIMONE,** Bloomfield Coll, Bloomfield, NJ; SR; Mddl Sts Tsk Frc Crrclm 90-; Res Life Cncl 90-; Coll Nwsppr; Intern TV 90; Dean Lst 89-; Engl Cmmnctns; Pblc Rel Brdcstng.

**RIDDLE, BEVERLY L,** Wv Univ At Parkersburg, Parkersburg, WV; FR; Crmnl Jstce Orgnztn 90-; 4 H Ldrs Assn Sec 84-; Law.

**RIDDLE, CHRISTY L,** Delta St Univ, Cleveland, MS; FR; BA; Wal-Mart Fndtn Schlrshp; Acad Schlrshp; Computer Info Syst Frshmn Schlrshp; Computer Info Syst; Syst Analyst.

**RIDDLE, EVELYN DUVALL,** Univ Of Nc At Charlotte, Charlotte, NC; SR; BS; Criminal Justice; Teach.

**RIDDLE JR, JACK M,** Greenville Tech Coll, Greenville, SC; SO; BS; Stdnt Govt; Alumni Assn; Greenville Tecs Dns Lst; HVAC Greenville Tech Coll; Cert Greenville Tech Coll 90; Indus Mech/Electrncs; Indus Mntnc/Dsgn.

**RIDDLE, JENNIFER A,** Indiana Univ Of Pa, Indiana, PA; SO; SADD 90; Deans Lst 90-; I M Vybl 90; Ele Educ; Tch.

**RIDDLE, KEVIN R,** Spartanburg Methodist Coll, Spartanburg, SC; FR; BA; Law.

**RIDDLE, KRISTIE L,** Radford Univ, Radford, VA; JR; BS; Stdnt Ed Assoc 90-; Amnesty Intrntl 90-; Pi Gamma Mu 90-; Phi Kappa Phi 90-; Alpha Lambda Delta 88-; Deans List 88-; Natl Clgt Soc Scis Award; Hons Prog 88-; Soc Sci; Law Sch.

**RIDDLE, NICOLE A,** Univ Of Sc At Columbia, Columbia, SC; FR; BS; Stdnt Govt 90-; Gamma Beta Phi 90-; Biolgy; Pre-Med.

**RIDDLE, PAMELA J,** Fayetteville St Univ, Fayetteville, NC; SR; Hstry Clb VP 90; Kappa Delta Pi 88; Outstndng Hstry Achievemnt Awd 90; Deans Lst 88; BS; Hstry Ed; Tchr.

**RIDDLE JR, SAMUEL T,** Marshall University, Huntington, WV; SO; BA; Bus Mngt; Own Music Str.

**RIDEMAN, RONALD L,** Nova Univ, Ft Lauderdale, FL; GD; MBA; Phi Delta Chi 79-; BS Mercer Univ 78.

**RIDEN, EDIE R,** Middle Tn St Univ, Murfreesboro, TN; JR; BS; Chem; Phys.

**RIDENBAUGH, CYNTHIA K,** Bowie St Univ, Bowie, MD; JR; BS; Kappa Delta Pi; AA 89; Elem Ed; Tchr.

**RIDENHOUR, DAVID E,** Southern Coll Of Tech, Marietta, GA; SR; BS; Crdt Un Chf Fncl Offcr 86-8 9; SG 86-87; ACM; Tau Alpha Pi; Msnc Ldg; Vllybll Clb; Appld Comp Sci.

**RIDENHOUR, JAMIESON M,** Coker Coll, Hartsville, SC; SR; BA; Plyrs 88-; Stndrds Comm 90; RA 88-; Alpha Psi Omega Pres 90-; Drama; Muscl Perf.

**RIDENOUR, BILLIE J,** Western Ky Univ, Bowling Green, KY; SO; MS; Lib Ntnl Prty; Phi Eta Sigma; Spch/Cmnctn Dsrdrs; Tchng.

**RIDENOUR, MICHELE R,** Oh St Univ At Newark, Newark, OH; FR; BA; Psych; Cnslng.

**RIDEOUT, KRISTIN M,** James Madison University, Harrisonburg, VA; JR; NEAYC; Kappa Delta Pi; Erly Chldhd Educ; Tchng.

**RIDER, ANDREW S,** Western New England Coll, Springfield, MA; FR; BA; Photo Clb 90-; Lacrosse 90; Govt; Law.

**RIDER, ANDREW W,** Fl St Univ, Tallahassee, FL; SR; BS; Rugby Clb VP 86-; Am Soc Civil Engrs 89-; IM Ftbl/Sftbl 90; Engr In Trng Cert FL 90; Civil Eng.

**RIDER, KATHLEEN,** City Univ Of Ny Grad School, New York, NY; SR; BA; Magna Cum Laude Hnrs Grad 90; N Y St Assn Vet Tech Pres 84-85; Metro N Y Brnch Amer Assn Lab Animal Sci Educ Comm Chrprsn; Vet Tech; AAS St Univ N Y Delhi 78; N Y St Educ Dept 81; Comm/Mngmnt; Pursue Grad Stud Animal Sci.

**RIDER, KATHLEEN A,** Central Pa Bus School, Summerdale, PA; SR; Phi Beta Lambda; Acctg.

**RIDGEWAY, LAQUITHA R,** Livingston Univ, Livingston, AL; FR; LU Almn Schlsrhp 90-; Frst AL Schlrshp; Prsdnts Lst 90-.

**RIDGEWAY, MARK A,** Oh Univ-Southern Cmps, Ironton, OH; SR; BSED; Scl Stds.

**RIDGEWAY, RUTH L,** Univ Of Sc At Columbia, Columbia, SC; FR; BA; Senate Page; Res Hall Govt Pres 90-; Baptist Stdnt Union 90-; Pol Sci; Law/Politics.

**RIDGEWAY, SANDRA T,** Birmingham Southern Coll, Birmingham, AL; FR; BA; Mentor Pgm-Adlt Studies; Alpha Lambda Delta; Phi Eta Sigma; Engl.

**RIDGLEY, DOUGLAS M,** Wilmington Coll, New Castle, DE; GD; Prfsnl Karate Leag Blck Blt 80-; Smma Cum Laude Grad; AA Gen Stds 88; USAF Enlstd Radio Rprmn 74-; AS Electrnc Tech 89; Bus Mgmt.

**RIDGWAY, JAMES W,** Univ Of Southern Ms, Hattiesburg, MS; SR; BS; Assn Cmptng Mchnry; Grmn Club Crspndng Sec 90-; Kappa Alpha Pldg Class Pres 86-87; Cmptr Sci; Software Engr.

**RIDGWAY, JENNIFER L,** Ga St Univ, Atlanta, GA; FR; BA; Consrvncy; Hmcmng Comm; Phi Eta Sigma; Alpha Lambda Delta; Alpha Xi Delta; Acctng; CPA.

**RIDGWAY, JESSICA M,** Bridgewater Coll, Bridgewater, VA; FR; BA; Nwspr Rprtr 90-; Yrbk Stf 90-; Brthrn Stdnt Fllwshp 90-; Engl/Spec Ed; Tchr/Jrnlst.

**RIDING, JANINE L,** Univ Of Sc At Columbia, Columbia, SC; SO; MA; Journlsm; Editr.

**RIDLEY, M CAROL,** Bethel Coll, Mckenzie, TN; SO; BS; STEA Sec 89-; Gamma Beta Phi 90-; Tnns Tm 89-; Elem Educ; Tchr.

**RIDLEY, MONA C,** Bethel Coll, Mckenzie, TN; SO; BS; STEA Sec; Gamma Beta Phi; Tns Tm; Elem Educ; Elem Schl Tchr.

**RIDLEY, PAMELA J,** Middle Tn St Univ, Murfreesboro, TN; SR; Amer Psych Nrss Assn Chrtr Mmbr; Amer Nrss Assn Cert Psych And Mntl Hlth RN 88; ADN Motlow St Comm Coll 84; BSN; Nrsng; MSN.

**RIDLEY, WINIFRED L,** Va St Univ, Petersburg, VA; JR; BA; Txtl Apprl Merch/Mgmt Sec; Trjns Rctng Univ Std 90; Gspl Chr 90; Frst Bptst Chrch; Bsn/Home Ec; Fshn Mrchndsng.

**RIDLOFF, JASON B,** Univ Of Pa, Philadelphia, PA; SO; BS; Penn Invstmnt Allnc; Mgt Clb 89-; Finance Clb 89-; Zeta Beta Tau 90-; Dai-Ichi Kangyo Bk Ltd Copr Finance Dept/Ln Admin; Deans 89-90; Bus; Finance.**

**RIEBE, THERESA E,** Lehigh Univ, Bethlehem, PA; FR; BS; LUV 90-; Adopt A Grndprnt 90-; Food Phone 90-; Biology; Medical Rsrch.

**RIEBOCK, MISTI A,** Univ Of Southern Ms, Hattiesburg, MS; SO; BED; Coaching/Sprts Admin; Math Tchr.

**RIECK, THOMAS A,** George Mason Univ, Fairfax, VA; SR; BS; Decision Scis Club; Beta Gamma Sigma 90-; Alpha Chi 88-; Golden Key 88-; Mgt Info Sys.

**RIEDEL, BARBARA E,** Kent St Univ Geauga Cmps, Burton Twp, OH; JR; BED; Cncl Excptnl Chldrn 86-; Lake Cty Soc Crpld Chldrn/Adults 84-89; AAS Lakeland Comm Coll Magna Cum Laude 87; Orthopedically/Multiple Hndcpd Ed; Teach.

**RIEDEL, PHYLLIS R,** Kent St Univ Kent Cmps, Kent, OH; SR; BA; Amer Plng Assc 90-; Gamma Theta Upsilon 90-; James R Beck Awd 90; Ballet Tchr 87-89; Intern Akron Metro Area Trns90; Intern Portage Cty Rgnl Plng Com; Sec 84-85; Prof Ballet Dncr; Akron Art Museum; Progress Thru Preservation; Medina Cty Hist Scty; Geography; Urban Planning/Dvlpmnt.

**RIEDEL, STEVEN M,** Me Maritime Academy, Castine, ME; SO; BS; NROTC Pltn Ldr 89-; Rgmnt Mdshpmn Striker 89-; Lacrosse Club 89-; Propeller Club 90-; Legore Schlrshp 89-; NROTC Schlrshp 89-; Deans List 89-; Commandants List 89-; Marine Systms Engnrng; Marine Engnrng.

**RIEDER, JILL LYNETTE,** Sue Bennett Coll, London, KY; FR; BA; Flwshp Cntmpry Collegians; Inn Rserv Mgr 88-90; Cmptr Sci; Cmptr Analyst.

**RIEDLEY, LISA M,** Univ Of Louisville, Louisville, KY; SR; BSI; AF ROTC Eastern KY Univ 87-88; Arnold Air Soc 88; Marching Band; Computer Programming.

**RIEFF, JOEL E,** Univ Of Rochester, Rochester, NY; JR; BA; Stdnt Asso Senate Towers Senator 89-90; Stdnt Asso Apprtns Cmte Cntrllr 89-90; Chi Phi Histrn Rush Athl 89-; D'lion Org ; Ra Helper 89-90; UR Cinema Grp; UIR Mag Ed/Chf; Deans List 89-; Boar's Head Dinner Host 89; Rugby Tm 90-; Euro History/ Pol Sci; Busn/Politics/Law.

**RIEGER, TONYA F,** Miami Jacobs Jr Coll Of Bus, Dayton, OH; SO; Hgr Acctg; CPA.

**RIEGGER, PATRICK M,** Suffolk Comm Coll Eastern Cmps, Riverhead, NY; SO; AA; Pi Alpha Sigma 89-91; Euchrstic Mnstr 91; Crss Cntry Tm Capt 90-91; Hotl Mgmt.**

**RIEGNER, DANIEL J,** Kent St Univ Kent Cmps, Kent, OH; SR; Kent Wgt Clb Pres 87-; I M Cmpus Rcrtn Assoc V P 90-; Orntatn Instr 90-; Sprts Clb Cncl Rep 90-; Fin/Real Est; Cnslnt.

**RIEGO DE DIOS, RICARDO L,** Univ Of Sc At Columbia, Columbia, SC; JR; BS; Hll Govt 90-; Rsdnce Hll Assn Sntr 90-; Phi Beta Kappa; Gldn Ky 90-; Natl Rsdnce Hll Hnrry Rha Lsn; Gamma Beta Phi 90; Alpha Lambda Delta 88-; Pres Lst 89; Dns Lst 90; Blgy; Med.

**RIEHL, ADAM J,** Oh Univ, Athens, OH; SO; BA; Pres List 89-90; Dept Transp; Assist Const Engr Intern; Engrg; Structural Const Engrg.

**RIEHM, APRIL,** Daytona Beach Comm Coll, Daytona Beach, FL; FR; AS; Pres List; Photography.

**RIEKER, JAMI M,** Midway Coll, Midway, KY; SO; BS; Horse Patrl 89-; Phi Theta Kappa 90-; Rsrch Alltech Biotech Cntr; Intrcllgt Rdng Team 89-; AS; Lbrl Arts; Equine Rsrch.

**RIEL, ERIN L,** Brevard Coll, Brevard, NC; SO; MBA; Spnsh Clb; Ttrd Engl; Coll Sngrs Mem; Lf Cltr Prfmr Attndr Scl Brd Stdn Govt Assoc; Hnr Rll; Fd Srvc Cmmtt; Srvyr Rcl Prjdcs Cmps; IM Sprts Rep; AA:; Psychlgy.

**RIELEY, DINA J,** Radford Univ, Radford, VA; JR; BS; Stdnt Edctn Assn 89-; Early Ed; Tchr.

**RIELS, KELLI J,** Univ Of Southern Ms, Hattiesburg, MS; SO; BS; Stdnt Alumni Assns Chrmn; Diamond Darling Bat Grl; Archtctrl Eng/Tech; Archtctr.

**RIEMERSMA, KURT R,** Savannah Coll Of Art & Design, Savannah, GA; SR; BFA; Tnns Tm 89-; Rsng Star Prgm Crdntr; Outstndg Sr Awd; Outstndg Soph Awd 89; Tnns 89-; Grphc Desgn/Illstrtn; Advrtsng Agncy.

**RIENDEAU, PATRICK DANIEL,** Radford Univ, Radford, VA; JR; BA; Pltcl Sci/Phlsphy.

**RIEPL, MAUREEN L,** Fayetteville St Univ, Fayetteville, NC; SO; BS; Chancellors Lst 89-; Fmly/Soldier Spt Grp 7th Spcl Forces Grp Maint Sect 90-; 2nd Bat D Co Sctn Coord; Greenpeace; Natl Geographic Soc; Ft Bragg Flying Clb 89-; Civil Eng/Constr.

**RIERA AYALA, GUILLERMO M,** Univ Of Pr At Mayaguez, Mayaguez, PR; SO; BSEE; Ntnl Hnrs Soc 89-90; Ntnl Actn Cncl Mnrtts 89-90; Engnrng NACME Schlrshp 90-; Elctrcl Engnrng.

**RIES, MELISSA J,** Ky Christian Coll, Grayson, KY; SR; BSW; Psi Sigma Chi Pres 90-; Pr Ears Stu Crdntr 89-; Hnds Praise Asst Dir 88-89; Intrn Safe Hrbr 89-; NCCAA Div Ii All Reg Tm 88-90; Var Vlybl Capt 87-90; Var Bsktbl Capt 87-; Scl Wrk.

**RIESE, KIMMI K,** Univ Of Akron, Akron, OH; JR; BA; Golden Key; Readers Digest Fndtn Schlrshp 90-; Schlrshp Deans Schlr Pgm; Elem Ed; Tchng.

**RIESS, ALISON PATRICIA,** Oh Univ, Athens, OH; SR; STA 88-89; PRSSA 88-90; Advtng Club 88-90; UAL 88-90; Alpha Xi Delta; Baxter Trvl Hlthcre Corp 87-90; BFA; Studio Arts; Artist/ Model.

**RIFAI, MAHMOUD M,** Comm Coll Algny Co Algny Cmps, Pittsburgh, PA; SO; Phrmcy.

**RIFFEY, LINDA C,** Roane St Comm Coll, Harriman, TN; SO; AS; Yrbook 75-76; Omicron Nu 77-78; Social Science; Chld Family Cnslng.

**RIFKIN, JULIE B,** Yeshiva Univ, New York, NY; JR; BS; Acctng Scty Pres/Tres 89-; Fine Arts Scty 89-; Deans Lst 88-; Hebrew Hnr Scty 89-90; Intern Deloitte/Touche 90-; Acctng; Cpa.

**RIGATTI, AMY L,** Univ Of Rochester, Rochester, NY; GD; Optical Soc Of Amer; Lab Engr 90-; BS Univ Of Rochester 90; Engr.

**RIGDON, KELSI,** Ms St Univ, Miss State, MS; JR; MBA; Gamma Beta Phi 90-; Mrktng; Bus.

**RIGDON, TAMMIE C,** East Central Comm Coll, Decatur, MS; SO; BS; Warrior Corp 90-; ECCC Bsktbl 90-; Sigma Sigma Mu Tau 90-; Phi Theta Kappa 90-; Bsktbl Best Defensive Player 90-; Nrsg.

**RIGG, BRYAN M,** Yale Univ, New Haven, CT; FR.

**RIGG, KATHLEEN S,** Norfolk St Univ, Norfolk, VA; SO; BA; Wk Recovering Addicts 85-; Legal Asst 81-; English; Law.

**RIGG, SARAH A,** Milligan Coll, Milligan Clg, TN; FR; BA; Clg Nwspr 90-; Borderview Chrstn Ch 90-; English; Wrtng Fctn.

**RIGG, TODD M,** Hudson Valley Comm Coll, Troy, NY; SO; AS; Crdt Invstgtr/Analyst 86; Math/Sci; Astronomy.

**RIGGAN, JENA R,** Vance Granville Comm Coll, Henderson, NC; FR; AAS; Phi Theta Kappa 89-90; Owens Ill Acad Achvmnt Schlrshp 90-; Endowment Schlrshp; Early Chldhd Assoc; Day Care Owner/Dir.

**RIGGINS, KEITH E,** Al A & M Univ, Normal, AL; GD; MS; Huntsville Prsnl Cmptr User Grp Pres 90-; AL Lib Auto Ntwrk; BS Univ AL 82; AS Alexander City State Jr Coll 79; Cmptr/Info Sci.

**RIGGINS, LANA A,** Fisk Univ, Nashville, TN; JR; BA; Stagecrafters 88-90; Psych Clb 90-; Univ Choir 88-90; Psi Chi; Mortar Bd; Concrnd Stdnts Fisk Univ V P 89-; Dns Lst 88-; Psych; Corp Lawyer.**

**RIGGINS, MARCUS D,** Tri County Tech Coll, Pendleton, SC; FR; BSEE; Elctrncs Tech Untd States Air Force 86-90; Sci; Elctrcl Engr.

**RIGGINS, PAMELA J,** Valdosta St Coll, Valdosta, GA; SO; BA; Concert Choir; Chamber Singers; Soc Internatl Stdnts; Alpha Lambda Delta; Sigma Alpha Chi; Frshmn Scholar; Economics.

**RIGGINS, TRACY L,** Pellissippi St Tech Comm Coll, Knoxville, TN; SO; BBA; Stdnt Ambssdr 90-; Phi Theta Kappa 90-; Acad Schlrshp 88-; Days Inns Schlrshp 89-90; Natl Deans Lst 89-90; Bus; Acctng.

**RIGGINS, WILLIAM F,** Kent St Univ Geauga Cmps, Burton Twp, OH; SO; BA; St Helens Choir 74-; Chagrin Vly Choral Un 89-; Choral Arts Perf Soc 89-; Serv Tech Amerigas A P Propane 70-; Bus Admn.

**RIGGLE, CHARLOTTE N,** Va Highlands Comm Coll, Abingdon, VA; SO; Phi Theta Kappa; Engl; Tchr.

**RIGGS ANDERSON, HOLLY MARIE,** Univ Of Sc At Columbia, Columbia, SC; JR; BS; PEO Sisterhood Chpln 70-; Sumter Clarendon Lee Med Aux 90-; YWCA Wom/Achvmnt 89; Chrstn Wmns Cl Durham N C Chmn 81-84; Dntl Asst; Mgr/ Consul/Med/Dntl Offc 69-90; Cert RDA St Mn Dntl Asst Prog 73; Busn Admin; Mgmnt.

**RIGGS, ALLEN J,** Univ Of Tn At Martin, Martin, TN; JR; BS; Undergrad Alumni Cncl 89-; Frshmn Orien 89-; Phi Eta Sigma Sec 88-; Order Of Omega 90-; Pi Kappa Alpha Pres 88-; Intrnshp W/Wilson Sprtng Goods 89; Econ/Finance; Cmmdts Broker.

**RIGGS, JENNIFER A,** Univ Of Al At Huntsville, Huntsville, AL; JR; BS; Chmstry Clb Hstrn 90; Math Clb 89; Grmn Clb 89-90; Alpha Lambda Delta Scrtry 88; Omicron Delta Kappa VP; Cir K Intrntl; Nasa Spce Grnt Undrgrad Fllwshp; Amer Inst Of Chmst Awd; Rsdnt Assist 90; Rsrch Assist 90; Chmstry; Physical Organic Chmstry.**

**RIGGS, KENNETH J,** Univ Of Sc At Sumter, Sumter, SC; JR; BS; Asst Br Mgr Am Gen In Sumter S C; AAS U Of Md/Comm Coll Of A F 88; Bus/Fin; Bankikng Officer/Financial Plnr.

**RIGGS, L MELISSA,** Tomlinson Coll, Cleveland, TN; FR; BS; Phi Theta Kappa 90-; Pres Lst 90-; Ntrl Sci; Tchng.

**RIGGS, MICHAEL S,** Bethel Coll, Mckenzie, TN; JR; BA; Lttl League Ch 87-90; Edctn Hstry Hlth; Scndry Edctn Tchr.

**RIGGS, PATSY J,** Christopher Newport Coll, Newport News, VA; SR; BS; Alpha Kappa Psi 90-; Newport News Shipbldg Drydock Co Intern 90; NCOA 89-; Bus Admin Mgmnt.

**RIGHTER, JAMES A,** Memphis St Univ, Memphis, TN; FR; BS; Nvl ROTC 90; Memphis State Rgby Clb 90; Semper Fidelis Scty 90; Alph Lmbd Dlt; Phi Eta Sgm; Apptmnt USN Acad; Mech Eng; Nvl Ofcr/Pilot.

**RIGHTLEY, CORNELIUS J,** Univ Of Scranton, Scranton, PA; JR; BS; Crs Cntry Var Capt 88-; Trck Clb Pres 89-; Fin Clb Pres 89-; Bus Clb 89-; Omicron Delta Epsilon; Delta Mu Delta; Clg Vol 90-; Hand In Hand Prog; Sch Mgmt Stdnt Advsry Comm 90-; Crs Cntry Var Capt 88-; Econ/Fin; Intl Corp Fin.

**RIGHTMEYER, JULIE R,** Longwood Coll, Farmville, VA; SO; BS; Ambassador; Peer Hlpr; :Cec Publcty 90-; Sigma Kappa Fndrsng Chrmn 89-; Psych/Specl Educ; Tchr.

**RIGHTMIRE, APRIL L,** High Point Coll, High Point, NC; JR; BS; Sr Cls VP 91-; Wmns Vars Tnns 88-90; Alpha Chi 90-; Delta Mu Delta SGA Rep 90-; Phi Sigma Iota 90-; Phi Mu Sor Pres 88-; Jerry Lewis Telethn Vol 91; Handicp Chldrn Vol 89-91; Sto Ag W Germany Intrnshp 90; Intl Bsns.**

**RIGLER, SUSAN E,** Univ Of Cincinnati, Cincinnati, OH; SR; BFA; Alpha Epsilon Rho 87-88; Cmunctns; Brdcstng.

**RIGNEY, PATRICIA L,** William Carey Coll, Hattiesburg, MS; SR; BFA; Art Clb Cncl Pres Chair 89-; BSU; Gallery Asst 89-; Art; Teach.

**RIGSBEE, JACKIE A,** Longwood Coll, Farmville, VA; SO; BS; Psychology; Phys Therapy.

**RIGSBY, ADRIEN D,** Univ Of Southern Ms, Hattiesburg, MS; JR; BS; Amer Soc Intr Dsgnrs 89-; Stdnt Hm Econs Assoc 90-; Stdnt Alumni Assoc 90-; Int Dsgn.

**RIGSBY, MARTHA C,** Univ Of Al At Birmingham, Birmingham, AL; JR; BA; Ftr Tchrs Clb; Spec Ed.

**RIGSBY, WILLIAM D,** Oh Univ-Southern Cmps, Ironton, OH; SR; BBA; Gen Bus; Bus Mgmt.

**RIHA, BRENT C,** Univ Of Miami, Coral Gables, FL; SO; BA; Bus; Mrktng.

**RIHA, JERRY A,** Univ Of Cincinnati, Cincinnati, OH; FR; BA; Comp Clb VP 90-; Mntnrng Clb 90-; IEEE; Hon Stdnt Assn 90-; Tau Alpha Pi; Elec Eng Technlgy; Elec/Comp Syst.

**RIHANI, RUDY Z,** Old Dominion Univ, Norfolk, VA; FR; Math/Cmptr Sci; Elec Engr.

**RIHM, ANGELA JO,** Memphis St Univ, Memphis, TN; JR; BSED; World Plc/Fire Games; Educ; Tchng.

**RIHM, LUCINDA J,** Saint Joseph Coll, West Hartford, CT; SR; BS; Liturgical Choir Treas 87-90; Coll Tour Guide 87-90; Res Asst 88-90; Cum Laude; CT Tchr Cert; Elem Edn; Teach.

**RILEY, BRIAN P,** Villanova Univ, Villanova, PA; SO; BA; Rsdnt Stdnt Assn 89-; Prjct Sunshine 90-; Theatre 90-; Deans List 89-; Engl; Law/Tchng.

**RILEY, CASSIE L,** Univ Of Tn At Martin, Martin, TN; FR; BS; The Soc For Hnrs Sem Stdnts; Leaders In Res; Mu Epsilon Delta; Vlntr Hospital; Deans List; Biology; Physician.

**RILEY, CATHERINE A,** Saint John Fisher Coll, Rochester, NY; SR; BA; Sociology Clb VP 89-; Pi Gamma Mu 90-; Asst Coord Fshr/Jfrsn Prtnrshp 90-; Constantino Schlr 89-; Sociology; Cnslng.

**RILEY, CHRISTINA L,** Univ Of Southern Ms, Hattiesburg, MS; SR; BM; CLCC Mrchg/Concert/Jazz Bnds 87-89; Sojourners; Choir 87-89; USM Chorale 89-; Convenant 90-; Carillon 90-; Oratorio Chorus 90; Gamma Beta Phi 89-; Kappa Phi; Golden Key 89-; Pi Kappa Lambda 90-; Sunny Jean Jones Msc Schlrshp 89; Msc-Piano Perf.**

**RILEY, DEBRA A,** S U N Y Coll Of Tech At Alfred, Alfred, NY; FR; AS; Wllsvle Vlntr Amblnc Crp; Scio Fire Dprtmnt Co 1; NYS Rgnt Schlrshp; GPN; Blmnt Vctnl Schl 90; Nrsng; Prmdc Flght Nurs.

**RILEY, DINEE M,** Hampton Univ, Hampton, VA; SR; BA; AIBS 90-; Bio Tutor 90-; Stdnt Vol Hampton Genl 90-; Beta Kappa Chi 89-; Alpha Kappa Mu 89-; Dept Awd Outstndg Achvmnt; Miss Gertrude Lee Awd; Bio/Pre-Med; Medicine.

**RILEY, DONNA D,** Univ Of Tn At Martin, Martin, TN; JR; BSBA; Intnshp/1 Vol Bank; All Am Schol Collgte Awd; Work/1st Vol Bank Union City Tn; Acctng; CPA.

**RILEY, GINA Y,** Univ Of North Fl, Jacksonville, FL; SR; BA; Phi Kappa Phi 90-; Golden Key 90-; Psych; Crim Just.**

**RILEY, JANET B,** Oh Univ-Southern Cmps, Ironton, OH; SR; BSED; Gldn Ky; Dns Lst; Gamma Pi Delta; Clifford E Jean Peters Allen Schlrshp; Trumbo Fam Schlrshp; Elem Educ; Prmry Tchr.

**RILEY, JENNIFER M,** Ms St Univ, Miss State, MS; JR; BS; Stdnt Adv Cncl Dn Arts/Sci 90-; Gamma Beta Phi 89-; Frgn Lang; Intl Bsns.

**RILEY JR, JOHN H,** Le Moyne Coll, Syracuse, NY; JR; BA; Pol Sci Acam VP 88-; Natrl Mdl Untd Natns 88-90; Intrnl Bltns Clb 88-; Alpha Sgm Nu; Tutor Jamesville Prsn 90-; IM Bsktbl Capt 88-; Pol Sci/Bio; Medcn.

**RILEY, JOSEPH R,** Georgetown Univ, Washington, DC; JR; BS; Dorm Cncl Rep 88-89; Hand-In-Hand 89-90; IMS 88-; Acctng.

**RILEY, KARA M,** Geneva Coll, Beaver Falls, PA; FR; BSN; Sen Fml Rep 90-; Varsity Tennis 90-; Nrsng; MSN Profsr.

**RILEY, KERRA V,** Univ Of South Al, Mobile, AL; JR; BED; Alpha Lambda Delta 89-; Lang Arts; Sec Educ.

**RILEY, KRISTA L,** Methodist Coll, Fayetteville, NC; SR; BS; Acctng Club Secy 90-; Peer Advsr 88-; Marshall For Grad 88-90; Phi Eta Sigma 90-; Alpha Chi 90-; Phi Sigma Iota 90-; Natl Assoc Of Acctnts 90-; Acctng.

**RILEY, LA TANJA N,** Christopher Newport Coll, Newport News, VA; FR; BA; Yth Grp 90-; Engl/Scndry Educ; Tchr.

**RILEY, MARYANNE N,** Hudson Valley Comm Coll, Troy, NY; FR; AAS; Early Chldhd Clb 90-; Sndy Schl Tchr 87-; Early Chdhd Dvlpmnt; Educ/Day Care Oper.

**RILEY, MELINDA HELEN,** Academy Of The New Church, Bryn Athyn, PA; JR; BS; Hall Govt 88-89; Peer Advsry Cmt 89-; RA 89-; Lacrosse 89-90; Jazz Dnc 89-90; AA 90; Education.

**RILEY, MEMRIE E,** Ms St Univ, Miss State, MS; SR; BA; Alumni Delgts; Phi Gamma Delta Ltl Sis Pres 90-; Stdnt Assn Comm; Omicron Delta Kappa; Gamma Beta Phi; Phi Eta Sigma; Delta Gamma Frat Treas 90-; Stdnt Spprt Srvcs; Un Way Vol; IMS; Math.

**RILEY, MICHAEL W,** Wv Univ, Morgantown, WV; SO; BS; AM Institute Chmcl Engrs 90-; Alpha Phi Omega 90-; Bowling 90-; Chml Engrng; Engrng.

**RILEY, NANCY A,** Clark State Comm Coll, Springfield, OH; SO; BED; Phi Theta Kappa 89; Vol Spec Olympcs 89-; Math/ Spec Educ; Tch.

**RILEY, PATRICIA M,** Fl International Univ, Miami, FL; JR; BA; Stdnt Govt Assoc 90-; Brd Govnr Comm; Anml Protctn Assoc 89-; Realtr Assoc Sls Assoc 90-; Re Assoc Dept Prof Regltns 90; Bsns Admn; Inf Sys/Res Mgmt.

**RILEY, REGINA L,** Middle Tn St Univ, Murfreesboro, TN; SR; BS; STEA 90-; Deans List 90-; Kappa Delta Pi; Gamma Beta Phi; AS Columbia St Comm Clg 89; Elem Educ; Teacher.

**RILEY, RHONDA K,** Marshall University, Huntington, WV; JR; BBA; Alpha Kappa Psi Sec 90-; Mgmnt.

**RILEY, SHANNON E,** Trenton St Coll, Trenton, NJ; FR; BA; Nwmn Clb 90-; Theta Phi Alpha VP Clss 90-; Psych/Erly Chldhd Ed; Nrsry Schl.

**RILEY, TAMMY,** Univ Of Southern Ms, Hattiesburg, MS; JR; BA; Afro Amer Stdnt Orgnztn Acad Awrd 89-; Deans List 90-; Elem Educ; Scsfl Tchr.

**RILEY, TIFFANY J,** Univ Of Tn At Martin, Martin, TN; FR; BA; Stdnt Affiliates Of Am Chem Soc 90-; Alpha Omicron Pi 90-; Hon Roll 90-; Chem/Bio; Med Doctor.

**RILEY, TIMOTHY H,** Fl International Univ, Miami, FL; JR; BS; Frmr Pgmr 89-; AS Troy State Un 84; Cmptr Sci; Sftwr Eng.

**RILEY, TRACY L,** Voorhees Coll, Denmark, SC; SO; Acctng; CPA.

**RILLO, SUSAN L,** Fl St Univ, Tallahassee, FL; BED; Early Chldhd Educ; Educ.

**RIMBEY, JANET L,** Westminster Coll, New Wilmingtn, PA; JR; BA; Lambda Sigma 89-90; Mortar Bd; Kappa Delta Pi; Kappa Delta Secr 89-; Dns Lst 89; Elem Ed; Tch.

**RIMICK, KATHY L,** Teikyo Post Univ, Waterbury, CT; JR; Bus; Mgmt.

**RIMLI, MICHAEL R,** Drew Univ, Madison, NJ; FR; BS; Schl Nwsppr Advrtsng Mgr 90-; Arl Hspnc Scty 90-; Abcs Mth Lg 90-; Bcchs Alchl Grp; Ttr Comp Sci Math Spnsh 90-; IM Tnns; VLLYBLL 90-; Comp Sci Spnsh Lang; Comp Sci.

**RIMMEL, BRAD A,** Kent St Univ Kent Cmps, Kent, OH; JR; BA; Amer Inst Arch Stdnts 89-90; Natl Golden Key 90-; Pol Sci/ Intl Rel; Law.

**RINALDI, ANN MARIE C,** Cornell Univ Statutory College, Ithaca, NY; JR; BS; Low-Rise Res Govt Fac 88-89; Alpha Epsilon Delta 89-; Tch Asstshp Comms 89-90; Tch Asstshp Biochem 90-; Biol Sci; Ped Med.

**RINALDI, ELZA M,** Univ Of Miami, Coral Gables, FL; SR; MARCH; Indonesian Stdnt Assn; Golden Key 90-; Amer Inst Of Arch Stdnts 90-; Deans Lst 89; Arch.

**RINALDO, MARY B,** Daemen Coll, Amherst, NY; SR; BS; Informer Co Edtr 90-; SPTA 89-; Res Cncl 90; Cmnty Serv Advsry Brd Stdnt At Lg 90; Admsn & Fincl Aid Comm Rep 88-90; Special Olympics 90-; SABAH 83-; Affiliations WYN PT LLUMC BGMC School 84; Coops St Jos Prost By Nelson; Physical Therapy.

**RINCON, GABRIEL A,** Fl International Univ, Miami, FL; JR; BS EE; Alpha Omega Chi; Phi Kappa Phi; Eta Kappa Nu Sec; Inst Elec/Elctrncs Engrs; Fl Undergradschlrs Fnd 89-; Fclty Schlrshp 89-; IM Bsktbl 90-; Elec Engr.

**RINCON, JOANNE,** Univ Of Miami, Coral Gables, FL; FR; BA; Chrstn Flwshp Cordntr; Alpha Lambda Delta; Deans List Roundtable Comm 90-; Miami Commitment Program; English.

**RINDONE, JENINNE,** Dowling Coll, Oakdale Li, NY; SO; BED; Elem Educ.

**RINDONE, REBECCA R,** S U N Y Coll Of Tech At Alfred, Alfred, NY; SR; AAS; Florcltur Merch; Mgmr Flwr Shop.

**RINE, KIMBERLY ANNE,** Memphis St Univ, Memphis, TN; JR; BA; Engl/Cmnctns; Corp Bsn.

**RINEHART, CHRISTOPHER A,** Wittenberg Univ, Springfield, OH; FR; BA; Pre Law Assn 90; SG 90; Salt Hse 90; Phi Eta Sigma 90; Univ Schlr 90; RA 90; Pol Sci Bus Admin; Corp Law.

**RINEHART, PHILIP CHURCHILL,** Old Dominion Univ, Norfolk, VA; SR; BS; Assoc Gen Contr Pres 90-; Constr Specfctns Inst 90-; Sigma Phi Epsilon 78-81; Masonic Ldg 87-; BA Univ Del 81; Cvl Engr Tech; Engr/Grad Sch.

**RINEHART, THERESA R,** Columbia Union Coll, Takoma Park, MD; SR; BS; SG 90-; Vienna Stars Pathfndr Clb Cnslr 87- Alpha Chi 1; Bus Admin; Gerontolgoy.

**RINES, BARBARA A,** Andover Coll, Portland, ME; SR; AAS; VITA; Acctng.

**RINES, CHRISTINE M,** Bay Path Coll, Longmeadow, MA; SR; AS; Law/Legal Asst; Law.

**RING, CYNTHIA J,** Fl Atlantic Univ, Boca Raton, FL; SR; BA; Bus/Fin; Bnkng/Invstmnts.

**RING, YVETTE D,** Guilford Tech Comm Coll, Jamestown, NC; FR; AD; Med; Med Asstng.

**RINGER, DARLENE B,** Miami Jacobs Jr Coll Of Bus, Dayton, OH; SO; Greeters Comm Pres; Wom Clb VP; Roth Hnrs Soc; NJROTC Hnr Soc; SE Acad 83; Faith Temple PCDG; Apstlcs Untd Christ; Travel/Tourism.

**RINGLER, BARON J,** Davis & Elkins Coll, Elkins, WV; JR; BA; Wldrnss Coop VP 90-; WCDE Coll Radio 90-; Dead Mjrs Scty Wrtrs Clb 90-; AA Butler Cnty Commnty Coll; Engl; Tchr.

**RINI, SYLVIA M,** Univ Of Miami, Coral Gables, FL; JR; BS; Stdnt Govt Athltc Affrs Offcr 90-; Strm Frnt 90-; Orttn Ldr Prgm 88; Eastern Airlines Bus Internshp 90; Louis Wolfson Ii Media Hstry Cntr Internshp; Ftbll Prty Gvwy Plnng Cmmtt 90; Mtn Pctrs Hstry; Tchng.

**RINKER, LISA K,** Univ Of Md At Eastern Shore, Princess Anne, MD; SR; Natl Rhbltn Assn 89-; BA 90; Rhbltn Serv; Rhbltn Spclty.

**RIO, JESSICA E,** Allegheny Coll, Meadville, PA; SR; BS; Stdnt Jdcl Brd 90-; Admssns Fnncl Aid Com 90-; Nwsppr 90-; Lambda Sigma 89; Jr Prze Envrnmntl Stds Dept 90; IM 90; Envrnmntl Stds.

**RIOPELLE, JASON E,** Univ Of Sc At Columbia, Columbia, SC; FR; Symphnc Bnd; Wnd Ensmbl; Alpha Lambda Delta; Gen Acdmc Schlrshp; Music Schlrshp; SC Hon Coll.

**RIORDAN, ELIZABETH A,** Immaculata Coll, Immaculata, PA; SO; BA; Stdnt Govt Cmtr Rep 90-; Envrnmntl Clb Co Fndr 90-; Nwspr Stf Wrtr 90-; Engl; Wrtr.

**RIOS RODRIGUEZ, WILLIAM,** Univ Politecnica De Pr, Hato Rey, PR; Engr.

**RIOS SOTO, GADIEL I,** Univ Of Pr At Mayaguez, Mayaguez, PR; GD; BS; Chrst Emsdrs Yth Assc Tres 90-; Hon Brd Eng 87-; Tau Beta Pi 89-; Phi Kappa Phi 89-; P R Mfg Assc Schlrshp 86-; Mech Eng; Cnsltng.

**RIOS VALLE, OMAYRA,** Inter Amer Univ Pr Arecibo Un, Arecibo, PR; SO; BA; Pertenezco Al Programa De Hnr De La Univ; Oficinista Sec Espanol Escuela Superior De Camercio Abelardo Martinez Otero 89; Admin Comercial; Leyes.

**RIOS, CARLOS E,** Pellissippi St Tech Comm Coll, Knoxville, TN; SO; BS; Intl Clb; Elec Eng.

**RIOS, EMILY,** City Univ Of Ny Baruch Coll, New York, NY; JR; BBA; Civil Serv Emp For CUNY; Mrktng; Cnsmr Bhvr.

**RIOS, JORGE L,** Inter Amer Univ Pr Hato Rey, Hato Rey, PR; JR; BA; Prvt Pilots Lic; Arcrft Sys; Air Trnsprt Pilot.

**RIOS, JUAN A,** Univ Of Pr At Rio Piedras, Rio Piedras, PR; SR; BS; Chem Stdnt Assn 88-89; Micro Bio Stdnt Assn 90-; Pre Med Stdnt Assn 88-; Dns Hnr Roll 89; Bio; Med.

**RIOS, LILLIAN,** Bloomfield Coll, Bloomfield, NJ; SR; BA; Lib Stdnt Asst; Monclr Chld Dev Ctr Soc Wkr Tchr Asst; Columbus Hosp Csewrkr Asst 90-; Soclgy/Med Soc Wrk; Soc Wrk/Spec Aid Tchr.

**RIOS, LORI A,** Inter Amer Univ Pr Hato Rey, Hato Rey, PR; FR; Bio Clb 90-; SPELL 90-; Mnrty Bio Rsrchr 90-; Rsrch Stdnts Proj; NIH-MBRS Pgm; Bio; Med.

**RIOS, MARIA DEL PILAR VAZQUEZ,** Inter Amer Univ Pr Hato Rey, Hato Rey, PR; SR; AIESEC 87-89.

**RIOS, MELVA N,** Univ Of Pr At Rio Piedras, Rio Piedras, PR; JR; BS; Amer Chem Scty 90-; Wrld Vsn Spnsr 89; Natl Geogrphc Scty 90; Deans Hon List 90-; Estmn Kodak Schlrshp; Chem; Txclgst.

**RIOS, VIVIAN A,** Univ Of Pr At Rio Piedras, Rio Piedras, PR; GD; MRC; Biblcl Stdnts Un Sec 85-89; Psychlgy Stdnts Acdmc Orientatn 88-89; Psychlgy Stdnts Assn 88-89; Hon Roll Schlrshp 90-; MS Soc PR Chapt 88-90; BA Univ PR 89; Rehab Cnslng; Psychlgy.

**RIOS-LYLE, LEANDRO V,** Inter Amer Univ Pr Hato Rey, Hato Rey, PR; FR; MBA; U S Customs Explorers 87; Hnr Stdnts Roll Carvin Sch 90; Hnr Soc 87; Air Force ROTC Cadet 90-; Bsktbl Swimming 87-89; Comp Sci; Engr.

**RIPA, MARK C,** Embry Riddle Aeronautical Univ, Daytona Beach, FL; SR; BS; Aerospc Soc; Amer Assn Airprt Execs; Aircrft Ownrs/Pilots Assn 87-; Cert Flght Instr/Multi-Engine Instr 88-; AS 90; Arntcl Sci; Airline Pilot.

**RIPATO, CAROLYN S,** Maysville Comm Coll, Maysville, KY; FR; AS; Nrsg; RN.

**RIPELLINO, ROME A,** Kent St Univ Kent Cmps, Kent, OH; SO; BA; Wmns Ntwrk 90-; Alpha Xi Delta Tres 89-; Bus Mgt.

**RIPERI JR, JOSEPH C,** Oh Coll Of Podiatric Med, Cleveland, OH; SR; DPM; Sprts Medcn Clb 89-; Alpha Gamma Kappa 89-; Surgcl Rsdncy St Louis MO; BS John Carroll Univ 87; Bio; Dr Podiatric Medcn.

**RIPLEY, DARCY A,** Johnson St Coll, Johnson, VT; SO; BED; Elem Edctn; Tchng.

**RIPLEY, TRISHA L,** Univ Of West Fl, Pensacola, FL; SR; BA; AA Okaloosa Waltom Cmnty Clg 89; Early Chldhd/Elem Ed; Primry Age Tchr.

**RIPOLI, ERIC A,** City Univ Of Ny Baruch Coll, New York, NY; JR; BBA; Dns Lst 89-; Acctg.

**RIPPE, ANN E,** Saint John Fisher Coll, Rochester, NY; JR; BS; Chem Clb Treas 88-; Chem.

**RIPPEE, TRACY D,** Memphis St Univ, Memphis, TN; SO; BA; Acctg; CPA.

**RIPPLE, AMMON S,** Saint Francis Coll, Loretto, PA; SO; BA; Cmps Mnstry Retreat Comm Chrmn 89-; SAO Cinema Shwcs 89-; New Theatre Bd Comm 90-; Hnrs Pgrm; Secular Franciscan Order 89-; Knights Of Columbus; Engl.

**RISCH, ANDREW M,** Savannah Coll Of Art & Design, Savannah, GA; SO; BACH; Archtctre.

**RISCHAR, BRENDA J,** Valdosta St Coll, Valdosta, GA; SO; BA; Blgy; Cmmnty Hlth Nttrtn.

**RISCHITELLI JR, ROBERT J,** Kent St Univ Kent Cmps, Kent, OH; JR; Umprs Assn; Amtr Hcky Assn US Rfree 89-; Gld Key Soc; Bsbl 88-89; Pltcl Sci-Pre Law; Law-Cnstttnl Law Prfssr.

**RISELING, MICAELA A,** Memphis Academy Of The Arts, Memphis, TN; JR; BFA; Bingham Kurts Art Gallery Inernship; Painting; Design.

**RISERVATO, PAMELA J,** Clarkson Univ, Potsdam, NY; SO; BA; Outting Clb Peer Facltr; RA Lifegrd; Tutor; Pres Schlr; Womens La Crosse; Bus Mngmnt; Elem Educ.

**RISHTON, VIVIAN D,** East Tn St Univ, Johnson City, TN; SO; BS; Manpwr Tmpry Agncy 87; Kelly Girl Temp Emplymnt 90; Tchngy; Eng.

**RISING, CORINNE E,** Oh Univ, Athens, OH; FR; BA; Phi Mu Rcrdng Secy 90-; Airway Sci; Corp/Comm Pilot.

**RISING, KATHLEEN A,** Smith Coll, Northampton, MA; SR; BA; Chamber Orch 87; Phi Beta Kappa 90; Bio Chem Grant 90; Dns Lst 87-90; Arthur Ellis Hamm Mem Prize/Acad Excel 87-88; Bio Chem.

**RISKA, MICHAEL D,** Duquesne Univ, Pittsburgh, PA; FR; BS; Phi Eta Sigma; Acctg.

**RISKO, JENNIFER L,** Longwood Coll, Farmville, VA; FR; BSBA; Bus Adm; Acctg.

**RISLEY, LYNN PLUMPTON,** Ms Coll, Clinton, MS; GD; JD; Law Revw Editr 90-; Natl Moot Ct Team 89-90; Wmns Stdnt Bar 89-90; Phi Delta Phi 89-; Inns Of Court 90-; AA Leees Mcrae Clg 83; BBA Millsaps Clg 87; Law.

**RISLEY, WENDY JILL,** Mayland Comm Coll, Spruce Pine, NC; FR; FBLA 80-83; Dean Lists 90-; Cnty Ofc Clrk 90-; Gen Ofc; Bus Ownr.

**RISSER, CONSTANCE A,** Nova Univ, Ft Lauderdale, FL; GD; MBA; Hnrs For Undergrad Degree 82; BS FSU; Spring Support Grp 89-; Stock Broker; MBA; Bus.

**RISSMILLER, LISA L,** S U N Y Coll Of Tech At Frmgdl, Farmingdale, NY; JR; BS; Erly Chldhd Rsrcs Clb 88-90; AS SUNY Coll Tech Farmindale 90; Elem Ed/Sci; Tch.

**RISSMILLER, RICHARD W,** Villanova Univ, Villanova, PA; FR; BS; Rsrch Fllw; Chmstry; Med.

**RISTER, JEROME E,** Univ Of Louisville, Louisville, KY; SO; MENG; Amer Inst Chem Engr 90-; ASSOC; Chem Engr.

**RITA, ROSA M,** Fordham Univ, Bronx, NY; SR; BS; Mktng Scty 90-; Commty Serv Prog 88; Beta Gamma Sigma; Hnrs Prog 90-; Financial Wmns Assoc Intern 90; Finance; Bnkng/Law.

**RITCH, GEORGANNA L,** Univ Of Montevallo, Montevallo, AL; SR; BS; Lambda Sigma Pi; Kappa Delta Pi; Bill E Fancher Awd; Schlrshp Achvmt; Frances O Cannon Awd; AS Alexander Cty Jr Clg 82; Elem Ed; Tch.

**RITCHEY, DEBORAH A,** Saint Francis Coll, Loretto, PA; SO; BS; Up With Downs Fndr 87-; SATS Sltn ACOA Fcltr 88-; Peak Prog 89-; Hndcp Aid 85-86; Ntrtn Cert Cambria Cty Extnsn Ofc 83; Tchrs Aid Cert Johnstown Vo-Tech 85; Soc Wrk; Cnslng.

**RITCHEY, EMILY M,** Kent St Univ Kent Cmps, Kent, OH; FR; MBA; Stopher Hall Wing Rep 90; Alpha Lamda Delta 91-; Resid Staff Assist; Busn; Human Res.

**RITCHEY, GINGER L,** Indiana Univ Of Pa, Indiana, PA; JR; BED; Elem Ed; Tchg.

**RITCHIE, ANNETTE M,** Wv Univ At Parkersburg, Parkersburg, WV; FR; Phi Theta Kappa; Acctg.

**RITCHIE, CHRISTI M,** Univ Of Nc At Charlotte, Charlotte, NC; FR; Phi Eta Sigma; Math Ed.

**RITCHIE, JARRYL B,** Ms St Univ, Miss State, MS; SR; BA; German Clb 90-; USCF 87-; Ms Cyclng Assn 87-; Phi Alpha Theta 88-; Acad Schlrshp 87-88; Dean Schlr 89-90; Pres Schlr 89-90; History; Coll Prof.

**RITCHIE, MARY C,** Wv Northern Comm Coll, Wheeling, WV; SO; BA; Stdnts Fr Entrprs 89-; Prsdnts Lst; Bus.

**RITCHIE, PAMELA F,** Watterson Coll, Louisville, KY; Boy Scouts Amer Vol.

**RITROSKY, MICHAEL L,** Hudson Valley Comm Coll, Troy, NY; FR; Auto Tech Srvcs; Auto Eng.

**RITSON, CARRIE S,** Portland School Of Art, Portland, ME; SR; BFA; Intrnshp/William Wegman-Phtgrhr Intrn 90-; Phtgrphy.

**RITTER, ANN MARIE N,** S U N Y Coll Of A & T Morrisvl, Morrisville, NY; SO; BA; SADD; AS Clg Agri/Tech; Engl; Wrtr/Prfssr.

**RITTER II, DAVID T,** Univ Of Nc At Greensboro, Greensboro, NC; SR; BS; Marshals; US Air Force Hon Dschrg 84-88; Elem Ed K-6; Clssrm Tchr.

**RITTER, KATHLEEN MARIE,** Ramapo Coll Of Nj, Mahwah, NJ; SR; BA; Phi Alpha Theta 90; Hstry/Pltcl Sci; Scndry Scl Studies Tchr.

**RITTER, LINDA E,** Indiana Univ Of Pa, Indiana, PA; FR; BA; Elem Educ; Tchng.

**RITTER, TAMMY L,** Indiana Univ Of Pa, Indiana, PA; SR; BSED; Phi Sigma Pi; Gamma Sigma Sigma Pres 90; IM; Scl Studies; Edctn/History; Tch.

**RITTER, TYRONE M,** Cheyney Univ Of Pa, Cheyney, PA; SR; BA; Engl/Theatr Arts/Cmnctns Clb VP 90-; Cheyney Yrbk Stf 90-; Debate Team 90-; Natl Cnvntn Afrcn/Amercn Stdnt Hghr Educ 89-90; Intrnshp NYNEX Cmnctns Exec Asst 89-90; AA Hudson Vly Comm Coll 88; Cmnctns Arts; Educ.

**RITTER, W JANE,** Bowie St Univ, Bowie, MD; JR; BS; Senate Pres Intrnshp; Prk/Rec Advsry Brd Comm Chr 81-; Symphnc Assn Pres 74-81; USS Swim Offcl 78-89; Euchrstc Mnstr Hly Spirit Cthlc Chrch 84-; Paralgl/Offce Mgr Law Offces 70-; Poltcl Sci; Law.

**RITTER, WENDY A,** Palm Beach Comm Coll, Lake Worth, FL; SO; BS; Phi Theta Kappa 89-; Pres Schlrshp 89-; AA; Physics.**

**RITTNER, JOHN D,** Allegheny Coll, Meadville, PA; SR; BS; Phi Beta Kappa 90-; Phi Kappa Psi 88-; Circle K V P 87-90; Cornell Natl Rsrch Pgm 90; Cross Cntry Co Capt 87-90; Physics; Mtrls Sci.

**RITZ, RONALD R,** Univ Of Akron, Akron, OH; SR; BS; Vol All Am Soap Box Derby Top Side Oprtns 82-90; Jazz Combo 90-; Sigma Nu Goals Chrmn 87-; Co-Op Dow Chem Co 89-; Mech Eng; Prdctn Eng/Entrprnr.

**RITZMAN, THOMAS F,** Univ Of Akron, Akron, OH; JR; BS; IEEE; Golden Key 90-; Macedoniasn Businessmens Club Schlrshp 90-; Elect Engrng.

**RIVARD, BRIGITTE K,** Western New England Coll, Springfield, MA; SR; BSIE; Soc Wmn Engrs Pres 89-; Inst Indl Engrs 89-; Amer Prod/Inv Cntrl 89-; Sigma Beta Tau; AA LA Mnchstr Comm Clg 89; Indl Engr.

**RIVAS, ENOC F,** Central Fl Comm Coll, Ocala, FL; FR; Indstrl; Eng.

**RIVAS, EVELYN J,** Inter Amer Univ Pr Guayama, Guayama, PR; GD; Clb De Cmrc Sec; BA.

**RIVAS, ROBINSON M,** City Univ Of Ny City Coll, New York, NY; JR; BE; Amercn Inst Of Chem Engr Publc Rltns 90; Secy 90; LAESA-SHPE Publc Rltns; Tau Beta Pi; Golden Key 90; Soc Of Profsnl Hispnc Engrs 90; Delancy 7th Day Advntst Ch Sub Dirctn Y Outh 89; Proctr/Gmbl Min Schlrshp Award 90; Chem Eng.

**RIVCHUN, SUZANNE M,** Life Coll, Marietta, GA; SR; DR; Thompson Clb 87-; Motion Palpation Clb 87-; Kappa Delta Pi 76; Alpha Delta Upsilon Sority 89-; Excellance Awd Number Chrpractic Adjst Bynd Requmnt; Chiropator Cline Awd Excellance; BS St Univ Coll Buffalo 76; Chiropractic.

**RIVENBURG, TIMOTHY J,** Columbia Greene Comm Coll, Hudson, NY; FR; AA; Crim Just; Law Enfrcmnt Ofcl.

**RIVENSON, JOYCE A,** City Univ Of Ny La Guard Coll, Long Island Cty, NY; AS; Hosp Phys Rehab Vol 90-; Aid/Hlth Care Symposium; Phi Theta Kappa 86-; Mu Sigma Alpha MIFS 87-88; Cert Mc Allister Inst/Funeral Svc 88; Phys Ther Asst.

**RIVERA ACOSTA, LEYLA,** Inter Amer Univ Pr Hato Rey, Hato Rey, PR; FR; Scdd De Jns Y Snrts Embjdrs De Crsto Ry 85-; Dcno De Estdnts VIIPR 90-; Mdla Alto Hnr Ingls; Mdlla Alto Hnr Espnl; Cert De Mrto Ingls; Psclgia.

**RIVERA ALVAREZ, BRENDA,** Univ Politecnica De Pr, Hato Rey, PR; FR; AJEC 89; Ftre Ldrs Bus Acctng 89; Cvl Eng; GA Escuela Superior Pedro Falu 90; Crso Gen Esc Sup; Math; Eng.

**RIVERA ALVAREZ, DILLIAN M,** Inter Amer Univ Pr Hato Rey, Hato Rey, PR; SR; BA; Amer Mktng Assn 90-; Hnr Prog 89-; Deans Lst 88-; Bus Admin; MBA/ACCTG Law.

**RIVERA BONET, SHEILA L,** Univ Of Pr At Mayaguez, Mayaguez, PR; SR; MBA; JR Achvmnt Advsr 90-; NAA 89-; Dt Prcssng Mgmt Assoc 90-; Phi Kappa Phi 90-; BSBA; Bus Admn.

**RIVERA CARDONA, ROBERT,** Inter Amer Univ Pr Arecibo Un, Arecibo, PR; SR; BA; Natl Fire Protection Assoc Rep 90-; Anti Fire Control Tchncl Advsr Sls Rep 89-; Teller Loan Clerk 84-89; Magna Cum Laude; Certif 88; Bus Admin; Sales Mrktng.

**RIVERA CARRASQUILLO, YILDA B,** Univ Of Pr At Mayaguez, Mayaguez, PR; SO; Adv Orchstra Prog Yng Muscns 87-89; Bell Choir 89-90; Eng Hnr Brd 90-; Chrstn Smmr Cmp 88-89; Cvl Eng; Envrnmntl Eng.

**RIVERA CORREA, JOSE A,** Univ Politecnica De Pr, Hato Rey, PR; FR; MBA; Engr.

**RIVERA CRUZ, ASTRID,** Inter Amer Univ Pr Hato Rey, Hato Rey, PR; SO; BA; Church Youth Grp; Monumiento Cursullo De Cristiandad 90-; Deans Lst 89-; Psychology.

**RIVERA CRUZ, TERESA,** Inter Amer Univ Pr Hato Rey, Hato Rey, PR; SR; BA; Cmptr Sci; Lic Pilot.

**RIVERA DE JESUS, MAYDA I,** Catholic Univ Of Pr, Ponce, PR; JR; BBA; AESEC; Genercia; MBA.

**RIVERA DEL TORO, DANIEL A,** Univ Of Pr Ponce Tech Univ Col, Ponce, PR; JR; BA; Acctng Stdnt Assn 89-; Tlnt Rstr; Bus Admin; Acctng.

**RIVERA FIGUEROA, FELIPE M,** Univ Politecnica De Pr, Hato Rey, PR; SO; BA; Bsktbl Bsebl; BED Mtrpltn Inst Of Sci/ Tech 89; Elctrncs; Elctrcl Eng.

**RIVERA GONZALEZ, BERENICE O,** Univ Of Pr At Rio Piedras, Rio Piedras, PR; SO; Msc Studies Cnsrvtry Msc PR 87-; Phlrmnc Choir San Juan; Fclty Ntrl Sci Deans List 90-.

**RIVERA GUADALUPE, SOCORRO,** Bayamon Central Univ, Bayamon, PR; GD; BA; Ldr Cmmty; Soc Wrk.

**RIVERA ISAAC, EMILY,** Univ Politecnica De Pr, Hato Rey, PR; JR; MBA; Engineering/Law.**

**RIVERA LEON, MIGUEL A,** Catholic Univ Of Pr, Ponce, PR; GD; BSSE; CVL Def Comm SUC; Phy Ed; MA Ed.

**RIVERA LLORENS, CARLOS M,** Inter Amer Univ Pr Hato Rey, Hato Rey, PR; JR; BA; Assoc Estdnts De Cntbld 90-; Natl Assoc Accntns 90-; Hnr Rl 90-; Mktg.**

**RIVERA MALAVE, LAURA,** Inter Amer Univ Pr Hato Rey, Hato Rey, PR; SO; Phsclgy Orgnztns 90-.

**RIVERA MEDINA, AMARILIZ,** Univ Of Pr At Mayaguez, Mayaguez, PR; SO; BA; Assn Clg Evngl Sec 90-; Biol; PHD Mcrblgy.

**RIVERA MEDINA, WILLIAM G,** Inter Amer Univ Pr Hato Rey, Hato Rey, PR; SR; BA; Arntcs IAU Assoc 90-; Dns Lst 88-; Hnr Roll 88-; Red Crs Vol 87-; Rotary Internatl 87-; Reg/St Sci Prjcts Wnr 87-88; Arwy Sci; Arwy Sci Mgmt.

**RIVERA MENDEZ, MELVIN J,** Univ Of Pr At Mayaguez, Mayaguez, PR; SO; MBA; Bus Admn; Hnr Stdnt; Phi Eta Mu; Bus Admn.

**RIVERA MIRANDA, CARLOS J,** Inter Amer Univ Pr Arecibo Un, Arecibo, PR; JR; BA; Phrmcy Clb 87-88; Biolgy; Microbiolgy.

**RIVERA MORALES, IVONNE YANIRA,** Inter Amer Univ Pr San German, San German, PR; FR; Assn Ex Stdnt Upwrd Bnd 90-.

**RIVERA PADILLA, BELMARI,** Inter Amer Univ Pr San German, San German, PR; SO; BA; Evnglcl Assoc 89-; Hnrs Pro 89-; Tutor 90-; Cert Acdmc Exclnc 90; Ntl Asstntshp 90; Sec Sci.

**RIVERA PEREZ, EDITH J,** Inter Amer Univ Pr Hato Rey, Hato Rey, PR; FR; MBA; Honor Roll Interamer Univ; Psychology.

**RIVERA PEREZ, JOSE LUIS,** Univ Politecnica De Pr, Hato Rey, PR; FR; BA; Cvl Eng.

**RIVERA PIZARRO, DORILIE,** Inter Amer Univ Pr Hato Rey, Hato Rey, PR; FR; MBA; Villa Capri Tns Clb 90-; PRTA 88-; Sociology; Law Schl.

**RIVERA QUINONES, CARMEN M,** Inter Amer Univ Pr San German, San German, PR; SR; BA; Bus Admi(; Mgmt.

**RIVERA REYES, RICHARD,** Univ Politecnica De Pr, Hato Rey, PR; JR; BIE; Iglesia Fuente Salv Misnr Inc Mbr 90; Agrpcn Jehova Rafah VP 91; Soc Jovns Mbr 90; Drama Mbr 91; Indstl Mgmt; Engr/Bsns Admn.**

**RIVERA RIVERA, BRENDA L,** Univ Of Pr Cayey Univ Coll, Cayey, PR; SO; Math/Hmnts; Acct.

**RIVERA RIVERA, CARMEN M,** Inter Amer Univ Pr Barranquita, Barranquitas, PR; SR; BA; Llemental Educ.

**RIVERA RIVERA, MARILEEN,** Inter Amer Univ Pr Hato Rey, Hato Rey, PR; FR; BA; Science; Airway Mngrshp.

**RIVERA RODRIGUEZ, GENOVEVA,** Inter Amer Univ Pr San German, San German, PR; SR; BA; Hon Pgm; Jrnlst.**

**RIVERA RODRIGUEZ, JOSE A,** Univ Politecnica De Pr, Hato Rey, PR; SO; BS; Boy Scouts Amer Sctmstr 85-87; Knights Of Columbus 74-; Yng Rpblcns State Co-Chr; Eagle Scout 73; Vigil Hnr 83; Pres Constr Firm 89; Civil Engr.

**RIVERA RODRIGUEZ, MARALEXI,** Univ Of Pr At Mayaguez, Mayaguez, PR; JR; Premed Cir 90-; Beta Beta Beta Sec 90-; Arts/Sci Fclty Hnr Dplm 88-90; Blgy; Med.

**RIVERA ROMAN, EDWARD,** Univ Politecnica De Pr, Hato Rey, PR; FR; Movimiento Juan XXIII; Engr.

**RIVERA RUIZ JR, JOSE N,** Inter Amer Univ Pr San German, San German, PR; SO; BS; Bibl Chrch Yth Dir 90-; Rsrch Inst/ Tlntd Stdnts; Pro Bsktbl Stats Keepr 89-; Bio; Osthpthc Med.

**RIVERA SANCHEZ, DOLORES,** Caribbean Univ, Bayamon, PR; GD.

**RIVERA SANCHEZ, LETICIA,** Inter Amer Univ Pr Hato Rey, Hato Rey, PR; GD; OFA P R Yth Off Govt Rep 89; Hon Prog Univ Assc P R Rep IAU 88; Stdnts Orgztn 89-; Hon Prog Stdnt Assn V P Pres 88-91; 4.0 Grde Rtng Adults 90; Assoc Degree; BBA Mgmt; Bus Admn; CPA.

**RIVERA SANTIAGO, MARIA M,** Univ Politecnica De Pr, Hato Rey, PR; FR.

**RIVERA, ABIMAEL E LAFUENTE,** Univ Politecnica De Pr, Hato Rey, PR; SO; Phi Eta Mu 90-; Engrng.

**RIVERA, AGNES V,** Inter Amer Univ Pr Hato Rey, Hato Rey, PR; SR; BBA; Model UN Rider Coll 87; Amer Mktg Assn 90-; Intl Stdnts Clb 87-89; Hon Stdnts Assn; Delta Phi Epsilon; Rep Ofc Of Govrnr For Juv Affrs; Panhellenic Cncl Chrprsn 89; Spelling Bee Champ 90; Mktg; Law.

**RIVERA, AIDA B,** Univ Of Pr At Rio Piedras, Rio Piedras, PR; SR; Stdnt Cncl Rep 89-; Anthrplgy Stdnts Assoc 88-; Gldn Ky 88-; Magna Cum Laude; Asst Curator Archlgy UPR Msueum 89-; BA; Anthplgy; Museum Stdies.**

**RIVERA, ALMA I,** Cumberland County Coll, Vineland, NJ; BA; Talent Roster Otsdng Mnrtes; AA 91; Sociology; Soc Wrkr.

**RIVERA, ARTEMIO,** Inter Amer Univ Pr San Juan, Hato Rey, PR; GD; JD; Amer Bar Assn 90-; Summa Cum Laude 90; Natl Tire Dealers/Retreaders Assn 90-; Pr Pro/Goma Inc 90-; BSIF Purdue Univ 87; MBA Inter Amer Univ 90; Law; Bus.

**RIVERA, CAMILLE,** Inter Amer Univ Pr Guayama, Guayama, PR; FR; AD; Rep Clb Pres 90-; Sci; Nrsng.

**RIVERA, CARMEN I,** Inter Amer Univ Pr Guayama, Guayama, PR; FR; Engl; Tchr.

**RIVERA, CARMEN J,** Univ Of Pr Cayey Univ Coll, Cayey, PR; JR; Cdro De Hon De La Rectra Del Colgo Univ De Cayey 89-; Psychlgy; Indstrl Psychlgy.

**RIVERA, CARMEN L,** Inter Amer Univ Pr Guayama, Guayama, PR; FR; Clb Cazadores Unidos Los Magnificos Inc Treas; Inst Banca Comp Prgmg Cert 90; BA Comp.

**RIVERA, CARMEN M,** Univ Of Pr At Rio Piedras, Rio Piedras, PR; JR; BA; Golden Key; Muncpl Schlrshp 88-; Hon Tuition 89-; Hispanic Stdes; Tch.

**RIVERA, CHRISTINA M,** Fl International Univ, Miami, FL; SO; BA; English Educ; Teacher.

**RIVERA, CLARIBEL,** Univ Of Pr At Rio Piedras, Rio Piedras, PR; SR; BA; Hon Achvmnt Awd 90; Mdrn Lang; Trnsltr.

**RIVERA, DAISY R BONILLA,** Caribbean Univ, Bayamon, PR; SR; BED; Ed Svcs Pgm Engl Tutor 83-86; Catholic Movement Pres 85; Kappa Delta Pi; Medal Outstndng Stdnt Lions Clb; Certif Airlines Bayamon Tech/Comm Inst 87; Ad Comp Sci UPR Bayamon 84; Engl; Tchr.**

**RIVERA, DANIEL,** Coll Of New Rochelle, New Rochelle, NY; SR; MDIV; BA; Theology-Philsophy; Mnstry Pedagogy.

**RIVERA, DIANA M,** Antillian Adventist University, Mayaguez, PR; GD; BSN; BSN Antillian Advntst Univ; Nrsng.

**RIVERA, ELAINE M,** Univ Of Pr At Rio Piedras, Rio Piedras, PR; FR; Sci; Pdtrcn.

**RIVERA, GENARO L,** Inter Amer Univ Pr Hato Rey, Hato Rey, PR; GD; BA; Stdnt Hist/Lit Assoc; Knght Of The Altar; Music Minstry; Cancer Cmpgn Andres Grillasca Hosp; Spanish; Educ.

**RIVERA, GUILLERMO A,** Univ Of Pr At Rio Piedras, Rio Piedras, PR; SR; BA; Hnrs Pgm 88-; MICEFA Tchg Asstshp Spnsh; Cmprtv Lit/Frnch; Frnch Prfsr/Intrprtr.

**RIVERA, HECTOR C,** Bayamon Tech Univ Coll, Bayamon, PR; GD; Elec Techlgy Student Assoc 87-90; Edtl Serv Dept Tutor 89-90; Deans List 86-89; Elec Techlgy; Elec Engrg.

**RIVERA, INA C,** Christopher Newport Coll, Newport News, VA; JR; BA; Stdnt Govt 89-89; Theatrcl Prodctns 88-89; Spnsh Clb 88-89; Munich Camps Tele 87-89; Cath Yng Adlts 90; Litrgy Word Chldrn 90; Chrldng 88-89; AA Univ MD 89; Busn Admin; Mktg.

**RIVERA, IRMA L,** Univ Of Pr Medical Sciences, San Juan, PR; GD; MBA; BA 89; Math; Demography.

**RIVERA, IVETTE R,** Long Island Univ C W Post Cntr, Greenvale, NY; JR; BFA; Prod Asst CNBC Station 90; Radio Anncr WNJ Station 90; Radio Anncr B91 Station Coll 89; AAS Brdcstng Kingsborough Comm Coll 89; Cert Brdcstng Cntr Media Art 90; Brdcstng; TV Anncr/Rprtr.**

**RIVERA, IVIA G,** Inter Amer Univ Pr Hato Rey, Hato Rey, PR; FR; BA; Bapt Un 87-; Justas Colgate 88; Tchr 88-; Bus Admin.

**RIVERA, JOSE F,** Inter Amer Univ Pr Hato Rey, Hato Rey, PR; SR; BA; 4-H Pres 87-89; Concert Corps Inter-Metro 90-; Assoc Psychlgy Stdnts 89-90; Msnry Saint Spirit 87-89; Youngs Against Aids 87-89; Outstndg Stdnt UCB Medal 88; Homage To Stdnt Plaque 88; Poet Plaque 89; Talent Show Plaque 90; Psychlgy; Masters.

**RIVERA, JUANA M,** Bayamon Central Univ, Bayamon, PR; JR; Gen Sci.

**RIVERA, JULIE,** Inter Amer Univ Pr Aquadilla, Aguadilla, PR; SO; ASSOC; Accntng; CPA.

**RIVERA, LILLIAM E,** Catholic Univ Of Pr, Ponce, PR; SR; BA; Elem Schl First Cords.

**RIVERA, LYNNETTE,** Univ Of Pr Humacao Univ Coll, Humacao, PR; SO; Assn De Estudianted En Ciencias Sociales Pres 90-; Assn Universitaria JOYTO Sec 89-; Stdnt Cncl Nom 90; Hnr Prog; Socl Sci; Law.

**RIVERA, MARIA LUISA,** Inter Amer Univ Pr Aquadilla, Aguadilla, PR; FR.

**RIVERA, MARIA R MELENDEZ,** Caribbean Univ, Bayamon, PR; SO.

**RIVERA, MARIADELI,** Univ Of Pr At Rio Piedras, Rio Piedras, PR; SR; BA; Gldn Ky 90-; Natl Hispanic Schlr Awds 87-88; Hnr Stdnt 89-90; Biol; Med.**

**RIVERA, MICHELLE A,** Univ Of Sc At Columbia, Columbia, SC; FR; Bdy Bldg Clb 90-; Dns Lst 90-; Orgnz Multp Sclrs Wlk SC; Phrmcy.

**RIVERA, MILDRED,** Inter Amer Univ Pr Hato Rey, Hato Rey, PR; SR; BA; Assoc Accntnts 89-; Assoc Geographics In Action 90-; Acctng.

**RIVERA, MILITZA,** Univ Of Pr Humacao Univ Coll, Humacao, PR; SO; BA; Univ Assoc Acctg Stdnts 90-; Bapt Yth Flwshp 89-; Bapt Study Grp 89-; Pres Awd; All Amer Schlrs; Acctg; Law.

**RIVERA, NELSON,** City Univ Of Ny Baruch Coll, New York, NY; JR; BBA; Baruch Schlrshp Pro 88-; Rgnts Schlrshp 88-; Dean Lst 90; Acctg; CPA.

**RIVERA, RAUL,** Univ Politecnica De Pr, Hato Rey, PR; Assoc Degree Elctrnc; BA 85; Cmptrs; Engr.

**RIVERA, RICHARD VELAZQUEZ,** Univ Politecnica De Pr, Hato Rey, PR; FR; Mech Eng.

**RIVERA, RIVERA JACQUELINE,** Catholic Univ Of Pr, Ponce, PR; JR; Newspaper Pres 88-89; Red Cross Secr 87-88; Spanish; Sec Ed.

**RIVERA, SUSANA T,** Fl International Univ, Miami, FL; SR; BA; Kappa Delta Pi V P 90-; Elem Educ; Tchr.

**RIVERA, SYLVIA A,** Bunker Hill Comm Coll, Boston, MA; SR; AS; Comp Prog/Micro Appl Tech.

**RIVERA, WILLIAM,** Brown Univ, Providence, RI; SR; BA; ACLU Pres 87-; Radio Disc Jkcy Adm/Dir 87-; Third Wrld Cntr Spprt Staff 87-89; Amnsty Intrnl 87-89; Critical Review Writer/ Edtr 87-89; Radio Advtmn Acct Exc 89-; Grassroots Cood 89-; Fulbrght Schrshp Exchng; Deans List 87-; Hnrs Crppntr Awrd; Pblc Plcy AM Inst; Law.**

**RIVERA, WILMA E,** Inter Amer Univ Pr Barranquita, Barranquitas, PR; SR; BA; Ccontabilidad; Maestria.

**RIVERA, WILMA I,** Univ Of Pr Medical Sciences, San Juan, PR; GD; CERT; BA Univ PR Cayey Cmps 87; Grntlgy; Psychlgy.

**RIVERA, ZACARIAS,** City Univ Of Ny City Coll, New York, NY; SR; Gldn Ky; Phi Theta Kappa; Lbrl Arts Awrd 87; AA Kingsborough Comm Coll 87; Engl; Tchng.

**RIVERA, ZAIDA E,** Univ Of Pr Medical Sciences, San Juan, PR; GD; MS; NSSLHA 87-; BA 90; Spch Therapy; Spch Lang Pathology MS.

**RIVERA-CASTILLO, ENID,** Univ Of Pr Medical Sciences, San Juan, PR; GD; MS; Air Force ROTC Eagle Angel Glight Cmptrlr 84-88; Natl Stdnt Spch Lang Hrng Assn; BA 88; Spch Lang Pathology.

**RIVERA-COLLAZO, CARMEN IRIS,** Caribbean Univ, Bayamon, PR; SO; Scl Wrk.

**RIVERA-MERCADO, ROSA M M,** Univ Of Pr Cayey Univ Coll, Cayey, PR; SR; Hnr Stdnt 90-F.

**RIVERA-NIEVES, JOSE J,** Univ Of Pr At Mayaguez, Mayaguez, PR; GD; BSEE; IEEE Stdnt Chap; Hon Rl; Hon Schlrshp; Elect Engr.

**RIVERA-RIVERA, DIANA G,** Univ Of Pr At Rio Piedras, Rio Piedras, PR; SR; Stdnt Cncl Schl Of Archtctr Rep Dsgn Bd; AIAS 87-88.

**RIVERA-SEPULVEDA, JOSE A,** Bayamon Central Univ, Bayamon, PR; SR; BED; AETE Pres 89-; FTA Chrprsn 89-; COOP Dstrct Pres 84; PR Natl Grd Stff Sgt 79-; AS 88-; Engl; Educ.

**RIVERA-SOTO, RICARDO,** Univ Of Pr At Mayaguez, Mayaguez, PR; JR; BBA; Hnr Rl 89-; Deans Lst 89-; Acctng; Law.**

**RIVERO, FERNANDO J,** Fl St Univ, Tallahassee, FL; SR; SGA Sntr 90-; United Latin Soc Hmcng Coord 90-; Phi Theta Kappa Cmuty Serv Chrmn; Phi Theta Kappa 88-90; Fla Pub Intrst Rsrch Grp; Natl Hispanic Schlr 90-; Phi Theta Kappa; Karen Simmons Schlr 90-; BA; English; Intl Law.

**RIVERON, JULIE,** Fl International Univ, Miami, FL; SR; BS; Kappa Delta Pi 90-; Phi Kappa Phi 90-; FEA 90-; Youth Ctr Archdiocese Of Miami 87-90; Elem Educ.

**RIVERS JR, CHARLES C,** S U N Y Coll Of A & T Morrisvl, Morrisville, NY; FR; ASN; Colgate Inn Hamltn NY; Nrsng; LPN/RN.

**RIVERS, GABRIELLE L,** Livingston Univ, Livingston, AL; FR; BA; Phi Mu 90-; Engl; Educ.

**RIVERS, H KEVIN,** Ms St Univ, Miss State, MS; SR; BS; ASME 87-; SAE 87-; Aiaa 87-; Phi Kappa Phi 89-; Tau Beta Pi 89-; Pi Tau Sigma 89-; Bell Undergrad Asstshp Colman Dxeesign Awd; NASA Langley Rsrch Ctr Rsrch Engr; Mech Engr; Rsrch Aero Dynamic & Astro Dynamic.

**RIVERS, NANCY L,** Castleton St Coll, Castleton, VT; JR; BA; Poster Prsntn Psychological Research Conf Univ Winnipeg; Research Asstnt Psych Dept; Parent Teacher Orgnztn 89-; Partnrshp Computer Graphics Bus; Psychology.

**RIVERS, PRINCE R,** Morehouse Coll, Atlanta, GA; SO; BA; Yth NAACP; Clss VP 90-; GA Clb; Lab Asst 90-; Rsrch Asst 90-; ADAHHA MARC Fllw; Psychlgy; Educ.

**RIVERS, STARELLA D,** Ms St Univ, Miss State, MS; JR; BPA; Natl Soc Blck Engrs VP Pblcty 89-90; Acctg; CPA.

**RIVES, ERIC M,** Univ Of Al At Huntsville, Huntsville, AL; SO; BS; Math Clb Sec 90-; Alpha Lamda Delta 89-; Engrg.

**RIVEST, MICHELLE Y,** Niagara Univ, Niagara Univ, NY; JR; BA; Secrty Cncl; Psi Sigma Iota; Res Asst; Chrldr; Frnch; Gov Wrk.

**RIVIELLO, CYNTHIA R,** Widener Univ, Chester, PA; SR; BS; Soc Advncmnt Mgmt SAM; Wrk Study Prog; Co Op Prog; Phi Eta Sigma Pres 89; Alpha Chi; Phi Kappa Phi; Fin Exec Inst Schlrshp Awd 89-90; Medallion Awd 90-; Bus.

**RIVIERE, ROLAND,** Coppin St Coll, Baltimore, MD; JR; Crmnl Jstc Club 88-; Bsbl Cptn 88-; Crmnl Jstc; Law.

**RIVIEZZO, KRISTIN M,** Boston Coll, Chestnut Hill, MA; SO; BS; Glgy Clb 89; Envrnmntl Actn Ctr 89-90; Glgy; Envrnmntl Eng/Cnsltng.**

**RIVKIN, RENA M,** Yeshiva Univ, New York, NY; GD; MS; Stdnt Cncl Judaic Stds Sec 89-90; Fine Arts Soc 88-90; Blood Drv Coord 88-89; Pre Hlth Hnr Soc Mbr Sec 86-90; Cum Laude 90; Deans List 86-90; Natl Conf Synogogue Yth Advsr 86-90; Chai Lifeline 89-; Lincoln Sq Synogogue 88-; Biolog; Y Physc Therapy.

**RIVLIN, DAN G,** Fl International Univ, Miami, FL; SR; BS; Kenes Convntns Empl Of Year Chf Tech 89; Hosp Mgmt; Conv Plnnr.

**RIVLIN, JENNIFER NINA,** Coll Of Charleston, Charleston, SC; JR; Untd Way Cris Hotln; Vol; Psych; Ind Psych.

**RIZK, CHRISTINE M,** Georgian Court Coll, Lakewood, NJ; JR; BS; Yrbk; Court Singers; Amnesty Intl; Deans Lst; Acctg.

**RIZVI, SYED SHAUKAT ABBAS,** City Univ Of Ny Med Evers Coll, Brooklyn, NY; SO; BS; Asian Stdnt Clb 89-; Mntr Pgm Hmnts Dept 89-90; Dns Lst 90-; Ntrl Sci Dept Awd 90-; Cmptr Sci; Engrg.

**RIZZA, ROBERTA A,** Albertus Magnus Coll, New Haven, CT; SR; BA; Campus Paper 89; Editor 90; Literary Magazine 88; Staff 90; Intern Reporter Wallingford Post 90; Eng/Communications; Writing.

**RIZZARDI, ANITA PAIGE,** Lexington Comm Coll, Lexington, KY; SO; BA; Nrsng.

**RIZZARDI, LISA A,** Central Pa Bus School, Summerdale, PA; SR.

**RIZZI, GREGORY M,** Western Piedmont Comm Coll, Morganton, NC; SO; AAS; US Army 85-89; Mech Dsgn; Mech Eng.

**RIZZO, ADAM,** Bridgeport Engr Inst, Fairfield, CT; FR; BSEE; BS Univ Conn 87; Electrcl Engrng.

**RIZZO, BRENDA A,** Univ Of Sc At Columbia, Columbia, SC; JR; BS; Beta Gamma Sigma 90; AS Cntrl TX Coll 87; Bus Admin/Finance.

**RIZZO, CHRISTINE M,** Cornell Univ Statutory College, Ithaca, NY; JR; BS; Crnl Cthlc Comm Prsh Cncl Vice Chrmn 89-; Risley Res Clg Comm 90-; Ho Nun De Kah; CALS Rep 90; Std Tchr Rep ATANY; Educ; Tch.

**RIZZO, CLAIRE C,** Comm Coll Algny Co Algny Cmps, Pittsburgh, PA; SO; Elem Educ; Tchr.

**RIZZO, DAVID R,** Saint Vincents Coll & Seminary, Latrobe, PA; FR; BS; Life Club 90-; Camps Mnstry Sprts Frndshp 90-; Dns Lst 90-; CRC Chem Awd 90-; Bio; Med Doctr/Chrprctc.

**RIZZO, ELIZABETH M,** Fl Atlantic Univ, Boca Raton, FL; FR; BS; Phi Eta Sigma Treas; Pres List; Acctg.

**RIZZO, EUGENE A,** Niagara Univ, Niagara Univ, NY; FR; BA; Hstry; Sec Ed.

**RIZZO, JOSEPH J,** Widener Univ, Chester, PA; SR; BA; Econ Clb 89-; Natl Scl Sci Hnr Soc; Rsrch Asst Univ PA; Econ.

**RIZZO, JOSEPHINE,** City Univ Of Ny Baruch Coll, New York, NY; JR; BBA; Dns Lst; Mktg.

**RO, RAYMOND I,** Wv Univ, Morgantown, WV; JR; BSEE; IM Ftbl 88-90; Cmptr Eng.

**ROACH, BROOKS A,** Western Ky Univ, Bowling Green, KY; JR; AB; Phi Kappa Phi; Phi Eta Sigma; Math; Educ.

**ROACH, DARREN S,** Univ Of Miami, Coral Gables, FL; SR; BBA; Air Force ROTC Fnc Offcr 87-; Rathsklr Advsry Bd Cmptr Chmn 89-; Beta Gamma Sigma 90-; Phi Kappa Phi 90-; Gldn Key 90-; Lambda Chi Alpha Socl Chm 88-; Amer Lgn Schlstc Slvr Mdl; Amer Lgn Schlstc Brnz Mdl; Cmptr Info Systs; Air Force Offcr.

**ROACH, HEIDI M,** Fl International Univ, Miami, FL; FR; Hon Pgm 90-.

**ROACH, JEAN T,** Ky St Univ, Frankfort, KY; SO; BA; Mdlng; Nrsng; Anesthesiology.

**ROACH, KERRY J,** Villanova Univ, Villanova, PA; FR; BA; Blue/White Clb 90-; Pi Beta Phi 90-; Cmnctns; Jrnlsm/Brdcstng.

**ROACH, KRISTIN L,** Univ Of Rochester, Rochester, NY; FR; BA; Intvars Chrstn Flwshp 90-; Sigma Alpha Iota Treas 90-; Exclnc Accmpnyg; Kochanski Mdl; Piano Perf; Tch/Orchestra.

**ROACH, LISA MARIA,** Norfolk St Univ, Norfolk, VA; FR; BA; Member Spartan Alpha Tau Hnr Scty; Vllybll; GCE Olevel St Jsphs Cnvnt Trnd West Indies 89; Finance; Financial Cnsltnt.

**ROACH, ROBERT J,** Embry Riddle Aeronautical Univ, Daytona Beach, FL; SR; BA; Mngmnt Clb 90-; Phi Beta Lambda; FAA Cmmrcl Pilot Cert 90; Phi Beta Lambda St Cmpttn Bus Plcy; Arntcl Stu; Avtn Law.

**ROACH, SUSAN D,** Atlantic Comm Coll, Mays Landing, NJ; FR; BA; Newspr Bsn/Mgr 89-90; Cmnctns; Radio/Tv/Film.

**ROACHE, DENISE M,** Saint Thomas Univ, Miami, FL; SR; BA; Intl Stdnts Org; Minority Stdnt Union; Acctg Club; Tele Mrktr Admsns Dept Supv; Cert ST Louis Delia Scndry Schl 87; Bsn Mgmt.

**ROADCAP, PATRICIA M,** James Madison University, Harrisonburg, VA; JR; Ambsdrs 89-90; Phi Theta Kappa Sec 89-90; Sprt Stf Schlrshp 89-90; AAS Blue Ridge Comm Clg 90; Early Chldhd Edctn: Tchr.

**ROADMAN, CHARLES W,** Ms St Univ, Miss State, MS; JR; BS; Mktg/Prof Golf Mgmnt.

**ROADMAN, SAMUEL E,** Univ Of Pittsburgh, Pittsburgh, PA; JR; AICHE; Tau Beta Pi; Omega Chi; Co-Op Pgm Arco Chem; Chem Eng; Eng Rsrch.

**ROAMER, SUSAN I,** Rensselaer Polytechnic Inst, Troy, NY; FR; BS; G M Wk Plng Cmte 90-; Ski Clb 90-; Sftbl 90-; Engrg.

**ROAN, KATHLEEN M,** Univ Of Southern Ms, Hattiesburg, MS; FR; Gamma Beta Phi; Alpha Lambda Sigma; Phi Eta; Anthrplgst.

**ROANE, JULIA L,** Truett Mc Connell Coll, Cleveland, GA; FR; Deans Lst; Pres Clb; Wmsn Fire Aux; Fund Raising Comm Chrmn; Liberty Mutual Ins 89-; Bus/Acctng; Acctng.

**ROARK, JOHNIE S,** Fayetteville St Univ, Fayetteville, NC; SR; BS; Air Frc ROTC Cmdr Col 90-; Arnold Air Soc; Bsns; Air Frc Ofcr.

**ROARK, LORI A,** Hudson Valley Comm Coll, Troy, NY; GD; AAS; Human Serv Clb 90-; Pres Lst 90; Prctcn Viking Child Care Ctr Tchrs Aide 90; The Ark Prcticum II Tchrs Aie 91; Human Serv; Ele Educ Tchr.

**ROARK, SANDRA R,** Fl International Univ, Miami, FL; SR; BA; Dns Lst; Natl Hnr Scty; Elem Intrnshp 90-; Erly Chldhd Intrn; Elem Educ; Elem Erly Chldhd Tchr.

**ROATEN, JEFFREY B,** Memphis St Univ, Memphis, TN; SO; BS; Anthrplgy/Chem; Hrt Srgn/Meso-Amer Archlgst.

**ROBAINA, TERESA I,** Fl International Univ, Miami, FL; JR; BA; AA 90; Elem Ed; Tchg.

**ROBARDS, JANET L,** Eckerd Coll, St Petersburg, FL; SR; BA; Cls Cncl Pres 90-; Spch Dbte Tm Pres 87-88; SG Chrprsn 87-; Sigma Xi; Omicron Delta Kappa; Phi Rho Pi Pres 87-88; Sch Dist Vol; Ambsdr 88-; Assoc Edtr Rsrch Annual 90; I M Sprts 90-; LWV 88-; AA 89; Human/Machine Sys; Law.

**ROBARGE, KAREN L,** Univ Of Nc At Greensboro, Greensboro, NC; SR; BS; Exrcs/Sport Sci Assn 89-; Deans Lst 88-; AAHPERD 89-; Co-Mngr Fmly Ftnss Cntr 87-90; Exrcs/Sport Sci; Tch.

**ROBATOR JR, JAMES W,** Holyoke Comm Coll, Holyoke, MA; FR; AA; Constr Trades; Sci, Med.

**ROBAYO, JOSE M,** Miami Dade Comm Coll North, Miami, FL; SR; Talent Roster Certif Achvmnt; Gymnastics; AA Arch.

**ROBB, ALFREDA DENISE,** Alcorn St Univ, Lorman, MS; SR; BS; MS Edctn 87-88; Psychlgy 87-88; MS Gammette 88-89; Gammette Clb Prs 87-89; Wsly Fndtn 86-87; Kappa Alpha Psi Swthrt 87-; Stdnt Ntl Ed Assn Sec 87-88; Deans Lst 89-; Acdmc Exclnc 89-; Sigma Gamma Rho 89-; Dr Ralph Lwry Sr Hgh; Elem Edctn; Tchr.**

**ROBB, LARRY PAUL,** Indiana Univ Of Pa, Indiana, PA; SR; BSED; NCTM 90-; PCTM 90-; MCWP 90-; Ftbl 85-88; BS Clarion Univ PA 88; Math.

**ROBB, LAURA A,** Univ Of Cincinnati, Cincinnati, OH; JR; BFA; Univ Cntr Bd Dir Of Pblcty 90-; PAC Dir Multicltrl 90-; SOAR 89-; Mc Micken Hnrs Prog 89-; Fredrick Ziv Awd Intrn; Galvin Siegel/Kemper Advrtsng Intrn; Elec Media; Mktg/Advrtsng.

**ROBB, LORI A,** Kent St Univ Kent Cmps, Kent, OH; SR; BA; Stdnt Rprdctv Choice Co Chrprsn 89-; Undergrad Stdnt Senate Allctns Com 89; Psy Chi 88-; Golden Key; Support Htln 87-88; Dr Elizabeth Mullins Schlrshp; Psychlgy; PHD Indl Psychlgy.

**ROBB, MICHELLE L,** Liberty Univ, Lynchburg, VA; FR; BS; Fnnc.

**ROBB, REBECCA J,** Western New England Coll, Springfield, MA; FR; BA; Peer Alcohol Rsrce Tm 90-; Soc Wrk; Soc Wrkr.

**ROBB, ROSEMARY,** Saint Vincents Coll & Seminary, Latrobe, PA; JR; BA; Psychlgy Clb Asst Sec 89-90; Ltry Mag Stf Lay-Out Edtr 90-; Deans Lst Stdnt; Alpha Phi Omega 89-90; Priorty Cr Intrn Latrobe Area Hosp 90; Stdnt Asst Assoc Acdmc Dean 90-; Psychlgy; Thrpy Cnslng Chld Cr.

**ROBB, SHANNON M,** O'more School Of Design, Franklin, TN; FR; BA; Omore Fshn Mrchndsng Assn 90-; Fshn Mrchndsng/Dsgn; Retail Bus Owner.

**ROBB, WENDY A,** Radford Univ, Radford, VA; FR; BS; Stdnt Govt IRHC Flr Rep 90-; Busn.

**ROBBINS, CHRIS P,** Liberty Univ, Lynchburg, VA; SR; BA; Lttrmn Bsbll Vrsty 87-.

**ROBBINS, DENNIS B,** Tn Tech Univ, Cookeville, TN; JR; Stdnt Govt Assc Assc Chf Jstc 89-; Bapt Stdnt Union Comm Msns Dir 88-; Cmps Demcrts Pres 89-; Phi Kappa Phi 90-; Alpha Lmbd Dlt 88-; Fincl Mgmt Hon Scty 90; IM Bsktbl Vlybl Sftbl 88-; Fin; La/Chrstn Ethics.

**ROBBINS, JO ANN,** Sue Bennett Coll, London, KY; GD; Phi Beta Lambda Hstrn 89-; Goldn Key; Deans Lst Hnr Rll 88-; Acdmc Hnrs 88-; AA; Bsns Mgmt Admnstrtn.

**ROBBINS, JULIA E,** Univ Of Ky, Lexington, KY; SR; Mdle Schl Assn 89-; KY Mdle Schl Assn; Natl Mdle Schl Assn; KY Cncl Soc Stds 90-; Stdnt Actvty Bds Spec Actvty Comm 86-87; Clg Educ Advsry Cncl 90-91; Dns Lst 88-; Chi Omega Rush Chrmn 86-90; Prsntr/Spkr Mdle Schl Conf; Dance Cats 88-90; Mdle Schl Educ; Tchr.

**ROBBINS, KATHY A,** Fayetteville St Univ, Fayetteville, NC; FR; BA; Biolgy,Med/Marine Biolgy.

**ROBBINS, KEITH A,** Portland School Of Art, Portland, ME; FR; BFA; Vissually Enlghtnd Footbggrs; Prntmkng/Sclptur/Artist.

**ROBBINS, KELCY J,** Sue Bennett Coll, London, KY; SO; BA; Natl Ed Assoc Stdnt Prog V P 89-; Dest Grad Tutor 89-; Wells Scholar 89-; U S Achvmnt Acdmy All Amer Schlr; Sigma Nu Sec/Treas; Elem Ed K-4; Elem Schl Tchr.

**ROBBINS, KELLY G,** Univ Of New England, Biddeford, ME; SR; BS; UNESOTA Occup Thrpy Assn 89-; Active Mem Sr Cls 89-; Dns Lst; Head Rsdnt Rsdnc Hl 89-; RA 88-89; Schl Stdnt Swtchbd Crdntr 90-; Vrsty Sftbl 88-; Occup Thrpy.

**ROBBINS, KELLY-JO,** Daemen Coll, Amherst, NY; SO; BFA; Psi Xi Omicron Pres 90-; Spc Olympc Vol 89-90; Grphc Dsgn; Dsgn/Art.

**ROBBINS, MARK A,** Univ Central Del Caribe, Cayey, PR; SO; MD; Flwshp Chrstn Athlts; Funds; Spkr Altrntv Schl; Terry Guinn Awd; Acad All Conf; BS Zoology Ark St Univ 87; Medical.

**ROBBINS, MICHELE L,** Alfred Univ, Alfred, NY; JR; BA; Deans List; Busn Admin; Mgmnt.

**ROBBINS, PATRICIA L,** Endicott Coll, Beverly, MA; FR; BA; Clb Couture 90-; Fitness Clb Ldr 90-; Shipmates Clb 90-; Honors Pgrm; Tutor; First Yr Intrn; Fshn Mrchndsng; Entrepreneurship.

**ROBBINS, RICHARD C,** Memphis St Univ, Memphis, TN; SR; BA; Glf Tm 87-88f; Phlsphy; Peace Corp Law.

**ROBBINS II, RICHARD E,** Univ Of Sc At Columbia, Columbia, SC; JR; BS; Phi Beta Lamda 89-; Sigma Phi Epsilon Rsh Chrmn 88-; Ttr 90; Dns Lst 90; Spnsrd Natl MS Wlk; Atlnta Apprl Mrt Intrnshp; Mrchndsng Prmtn; Fshn Mrchndsng.

**ROBBINS, SUE P,** Nc Central Univ, Durham, NC; GD; JD; Eclectic; Hnrs Lst 90-91; Page Brd; Hopeln Crisis Intvntn Brd; Leg Asst 90; BA NYU; Law.

**ROBBINS, SUSAN J,** Stetson Univ, Deland, FL; FR; BS; BCM 90-; Aletheia Chrs; Blgy; Medicine/Pediatrics.

**ROBBINS, SUZANNE J,** Liberty Univ, Lynchburg, VA; BS; Reading Cncl 90; Curriculum Dev Assn 90; Chrstn Tchrs Assn 90; Elem Educ.

**ROBBINS, TONYA R,** Phillips Jr Coll Charlotte, Charlotte, NC; GD; Deans Lst; Pres Lst; Acctg.

**ROBBINS, WANDA D,** Al St Univ, Montgomery, AL; SO; BS; Intrdscplnry Hnrs Pro 89-; Sigma Gamma Rho; Hnr Rl 89-; Finance; Prtnrshp Loan Co.

**ROBBINS, WILLIAM S,** Univ Of Montevallo, Montevallo, AL; JR; BS; Hstry; Mssnry.

**ROBER, TERESA R,** S U N Y Coll Of Tech At Frmgdl, Farmingdale, NY; SO; AS; Bus Admin.

**ROBERSON, CHRISTINA M,** Univ Of Nc At Greensboro, Greensboro, NC; FR; BS; Hon Pgm; Nmntd All Amer Clgt Awrd; Educ; Mnr Engl Tchr.

**ROBERSON, DENNIS S,** Vance Granville Comm Coll, Henderson, NC; Stdnt Mnth 90; Dns Lst; Wrkng Txtls; Indstrl Elctrncs; Elctrnc Engrg Pgm.

**ROBERSON, JAMES H,** Middle Tn St Univ, Murfreesboro, TN; SR; BS; Tri Beta Pr; Bio; Grad Stdy/Resrch.

**ROBERSON, JOHN S,** Radford Univ, Radford, VA; SO; BA; Acctg; CPA.

**ROBERSON, JONNE C,** Clayton St Coll, Morrow, GA; SO; BA; Charter Mbr Apics Stdnt Dvsn Prgrm Cmmtt 90; Stdnt Tutor Hlpng; AA; Cmptr Infrmtn Systms; Cnsltng.

**ROBERSON, KIMBERLY S,** Nc Agri & Tech St Univ, Greensboro, NC; FR; BS; Womens Cncl 90-; Alpha Lambda Delta 90-; NC Tchng Flws Prog 90-; Acadmc Hon Stdnt 90-; Elem Ed; Tchr.

**ROBERSON, LINDA CAROL,** Thomas Nelson Comm Coll, Hampton, VA; GD.

**ROBERSON, LISA A,** Georgian Court Coll, Lakewood, NJ; SR; Michlnglst Clb Art Clb VP 90; Art Ed.

**ROBERSON, MARVIN C,** Univ Of Al At Birmingham, Birmingham, AL; GD; BS; IM Bsktbll Ftbll Capt 88-; Rdlgy; Med Schl.

**ROBERSON, STEPHANIE E,** Univ Of Tn At Martin, Martin, TN; SO; BS; Sigma Alpha Epsilon Ltl Str; Natl Hon Soc; Natl Beta Clb; Cmunctns.

**ROBERSON, SUSAN C,** George Mason Univ, Fairfax, VA; SR; BA; SEA 89-; Early Chldhd Educ; Tch.

**ROBERSON, TRAVELON E,** Bloomfield Coll, Bloomfield, NJ; SR; BS; Alpha Kappa Psi Treas 89-90; Fin; Invstmnt Bnkr.

**ROBERSON JR, WILLIAM H,** Lincoln Univ, Lincoln Univ, PA; JR; BA; Bus Club; Acctng Club; Deans List; Acctng/Math; Entreprenuer.

**ROBERTA, ROSEMARIE,** Univ Of Al At Birmingham, Birmingham, AL; SR; BS; Amer Mrktng Assoc 90-; Bus; Marketing.

**ROBERTI, ANTHONY J,** Univ Of Nc At Asheville, Asheville, NC; SO; BS; Weizenblat Endwmnt 90-; Math; Academia.

**ROBERTS, ANDREW T,** Embry Riddle Aeronautical Univ, Daytona Beach, FL; JR; BS; Screaming Eagles Mdl Arplne Clb 89-90; Tau Alpha Pi; I M Soccer 90; Aircraft Engr Tech; Aeronutcl Engr.

**ROBERTS, ANGELA C,** Univ Of Tn At Martin, Martin, TN; JR; BED; Coll Rep VP 89-; Stdnt Govt Assoc 90-; Natl Stdnt Spch Lng Hrng Assoc VP 89-90; Chi Omega Commnty Srvc Chr 90-; Stdnt Org Df Awrnss 88-89; Spcl Olympcs Cch 87-90; Spch Hrng Srvcs.

**ROBERTS, ANGELA K,** Union Coll, Barbourville, KY; FR; Acctg/Bus Admin; Bus.

**ROBERTS, BARBARA J,** Toccoa Falls Coll, Toccoa Falls, GA; SR; BS; Delta Epsilon Chi 90; ETTA Evnglcl Tchr Trng Assoc 90; Wrld Mssns; Mssnry.

**ROBERTS, BECKY L,** Univ Of Southern Ms, Hattiesburg, MS; JR; BS; Am Adv Fed VP; Jrnslm; Advtsng.

**ROBERTS, BELINDA L,** Christian Brothers Univ, Memphis, TN; JR; OD; Pre/Optmtry; Optmtry.

**ROBERTS, BONITA L,** Christopher Newport Coll, Newport News, VA; JR; BS; Pub Admn; Govt/Non Profit Orgztn.

**ROBERTS, BRENDA L,** Clemson Univ, Clemson, SC; SR; BSN; Slng Golf 90-; Vol Hosp Wrk Physcl Thrpy 89-90; Blue Key Ldrshp Awd; Herbert N Shearin Awd; Delta Sigma Mu 88-; Natl Stdnt Nrs Assn 89-; Chi Omega 88-; Nrsng Extrnshp Condel Hosp 90-; Nrsng; RN/HOSP Crtcl Care.

**ROBERTS, BRENT D,** Univ Of Tn At Chattanooga, Chattanooga, TN; FR; BSE; Bptst Stdnt Un 90-; Mech Engrng.

**ROBERTS, CANDICE M,** Richard Bland Coll, Petersburg, VA; SO; BS; Rotaract 90-; AS; Bio; Phrmcy.

**ROBERTS, CAPRICE L,** Rhodes Coll, Memphis, TN; FR; JD; Stdnt Assmbly 90-; Stdnt Life Comm 90-; Delta Delta Delta 90-; Ntl Inter Coll Mock Trl Champ 90-; Grk Day Champ 90-; Pltcl Sci/Intrntl Stds; Law.

**ROBERTS, CHERYL C,** Colby Sawyer Coll, New London, NH; SO; BS; Stndt Acad Cnslr; Ski Vol; Sftbl Vol; Chld Study; Teach.

**ROBERTS, CHRISTOPHER C,** Univ Of Southern Ms, Hattiesburg, MS; JR; BS; Grmn Clb 90-; Soc Polymer Sci 88-; Fncg Clb 90-; Plymr Sci; Rsrch Dvlpmnt.

**ROBERTS, CONNIE J,** Savannah St Coll, Savannah, GA; SO; BS; Award Mst Outstndng Yng Wmn Amer 88; AME Mnstr Wives/Widows Alliance Pres 86-; Cmnty Chldcre Food Spplmnt Inc Pres 87-; Owner/Dir Daycare 85-; Chld Dev I Cstl Ga Ctr Cntng Educ 83; Chld Dev 22 Cstl Ga Ctr Cntng Educ 86; Bsn Mgmt.

**ROBERTS, DALE S,** Columbia Union Coll, Takoma Park, MD; SR; BSBA; By Scts Of Amer 82; Pres Awd Fairchld Spce Co 89; 5 Yr Serv Awd Fairchld Spc Co 89; NASA Spec Serv Rec Awd Hubble Spc Telscpe Repair Mssn 90; HI Trck Tm 72-74; Supr Oper 84-; AAET Un Electr Inst 80; Tech Mgmt.

**ROBERTS, DALLAS R,** Abraham Baldwin Agri Coll, Tifton, GA; FR; BS; BSU Cmmtt 90-; Phi Theta Kappa 90-; Dns Lst 90-; Hnr Std 90-; Bio; Marine Bio Resrch.

**ROBERTS, DEANNA M,** Itawamba Comm Coll, Fulton, MS; FR; Cmptr Clb; Phi Theta Kappa Pres; Bus; Cmptr/Mgmt Inf Systms.

**ROBERTS, DERRICK L,** Northeast Ms Cc, Booneville, MS; FR; BSU; Soc Sci Educ.

**ROBERTS, DIANE F,** Bunker Hill Comm Coll, Boston, MA; SO; RN; Tutorng Lit 90-; Dorchestr Comm Actn Cncl 73-74; MA Fair Shre Exec Cncl Mbr 75-79; Fair Shr VP 75-81; Fstr Mthr 85-86; Asst Ofc Mgr 78-85; Nrsng/Soc/Educ; Ped Nrs.

**ROBERTS, DIANNE C,** Univ Of Tn At Knoxville, Knoxville, TN; SO; BS; Amer Mktg Asc; Exec Undgrad Pgm 90-; Phi Eta Sigma 90-; Alpha Lambda Delta 90-; Delta Nu Alpha 91-; Amer Bsn Wmns Asn 91-; Lgstcs/Trnsprtn.

**ROBERTS IV, EDWIN,** Commonwealth Coll, Virginia Beach, VA; SO; AA; USMC E3 83-85; Chrysler Mtrs Srv Trng Tech 89-; ASE Cert Automtv Mech 87-; ASE Ntl Inst Fr Automtv Serv Exclnc 87; Electrncs Tech; Electrncs Eng.

**ROBERTS, ERIC W,** Univ Of Miami, Coral Gables, FL; SO; BHS; Sigma Alpha Epsilon; Physcl Thrpy.

**ROBERTS, ERROL F,** City Univ Of Ny La Guard Coll, Long Island Cty, NY; SR; AAS; Computer Sci Clb 90-; Carribbean Clb; Phi Theta Kappa Stdnt Actvts Rep; Learning Proj Tutor; Computer Sci.

**ROBERTS III, FRANK H,** Marshall University, Huntington, WV; SO; BA; Gamma Beta Phi 90-; Phi Eta Sigma 90-; Scl Stds; Tchng.

**ROBERTS III, HARDY L,** Univ Of Fl, Gainesville, FL; JR; BS; Amer Judicature Soc; R James & Assoc Auditor Intrn; 1st Fla Bk Intrn 90-; AA 90; Fin; Law.

**ROBERTS, HARRIETT E,** Central Carolina Comm Coll, Sanford, NC; FR; Nursing; Ob Rn.

**ROBERTS, HOLLY E,** Queens Coll, Charlotte, NC; JR; BA; Pr Advsr Advsry Comm 89-90; Oasis Exec Comm 89-; Religious Life Comm 88-; Beta Beta Beta 89-; Mrtr Brd; Psych; Cnslg.

**ROBERTS, JAMIE M,** Birmingham Southern Coll, Birmingham, AL; FR; BA; Stdnt Judiciary; SGA Com 90-; Nws Stf Wrtr 90-; Hon Pgm 90-; Alpha Lambda Delta; Phi Eta Sigma; Alpha Chi Omega 90-; Habitat Hmnty 90-; IM Bsktbl/Vlybl; Engl; Jrnlsm/Cmnctns.

**ROBERTS, JENNIFER A,** Memphis St Univ, Memphis, TN; JR; BPS; Stdnt Assoc Amer Clge Hlth Cr Exe; Admin Intrn Rgnl Med Ctr Memphis Lucy Shaw CEO Pres; Crtfd Med Lab Tchn Amer Soc Clncl Pthlgy; AS Jackson St Cmnty Clge 85; Hlth Cr Admin; Hosp Admin.

**ROBERTS, JENNIFER K,** Va St Univ, Petersburg, VA; SR; BS; Natl Cncl Of Soc Studies 90-; Stdnt Educ Assoc 90-; Alpha Kappa Mu 89-; Kappa Delta Pi Treas 90-; ASS Richard Bland Clg 82; Elem Educ; Eductnl Instrctr.

**ROBERTS, JO ANNA L,** Mount Saint Mary Coll, Newburgh, NY; SO; BS; Hnrs Alliance 90-; Biol Div Rep 90-; Tri Beta 90-; Biol; Vet.

**ROBERTS, JOHN C,** Coker Coll, Hartsville, SC; JR; BA; SGA 88-90; Library Comm 88-90; Drama Clb 88-90; ACS 90-; Chrch Chr 88-; Biology Clb Pres 88-; Academic Schlrshp; ACS; Chmstry Awd; Sci Awd; Chmstry; Med.

**ROBERTS, JOHN M,** Univ Of Fl, Gainesville, FL; JR; BA; Cmps Crsd/Christ 88-; Undrgrd Ecnmc Soc; IM Ftbl 88-90; Golden Key 90-; Intrnshp Walt Disney World Clg Prog; Mgmnt; Hotel.

**ROBERTS, JOHNSIE B,** Univ Of Cin R Walters Coll, Blue Ash, OH; JR; AAS Deg; Soc Sci; Elem Ed.

**ROBERTS, JOYCE ANNE,** Radford Univ, Radford, VA; SR; BS; Stdnt Ed Assoc 90-; Hs Cncl VP 88-90; Early Mdl Ed; Elem Tchr.

**ROBERTS, KAREN,** Mount Saint Mary Coll, Newburgh, NY; SR; MBA; Coll Nwsppr Ast Bus Edtr 90-; Heop Nwsltr Edtr N Chf 90-; Bsns Assoc 87-; Hnrs Alnc 90-; Ambsdr 89-90; Dept Insttnl Rsrch Intrn; Acdmc Exclnc; Cmps Ldrshp; Bsns Admnstrtn; Mrktng; Instnl Rsrch.

**ROBERTS, KATHERINE E,** Villanova Univ, Villanova, PA; SO; BA; SCAAR Co-Coord 90-; Yr Dvrsty Strng Com Mntr 90-; Phlsphy Clb Co-Coord; Pom Pom Sqd 89-90; Alpha Phi 90-; Hon Phlsphy; Prfssr.

**ROBERTS, KATHLEEN A,** D Youville Coll, Buffalo, NY; JR; BS/MS; Rsdnt Asst 90-; Delta Zeta 1st VP 86-; BA UNH 88; Occptnl Thrpy.

**ROBERTS, KENDRA L,** Alfred Univ, Alfred, NY; JR; BS; The Plyrs Of Allgny Cnty VP 82; Bsnss Admin; Hlth Fld.

**ROBERTS, KENNETH D,** Univ Of Southern Ms, Hattiesburg, MS; JR; BSBA; Phi Theta Kappa 90-; Tutor PIE; U S Mrchnt Marines Capt 84-; Emplyd NOARL Stennis Spc Ctr Pres Sty Schl Pgm; Aad Pearl River Cmnty Clge 90; Ecnmcs; Internatl Bsn.

**ROBERTS, KENNETH W,** Oh Univ, Athens, OH; FR; BA; 3 AD Anmtn Aprctn Athns Dlwre; Pre Art; Phtgrphy.

**ROBERTS, KERRY L,** Duquesne Univ, Pittsburgh, PA; JR; MBA; Alpha Tau Omega Crnvl Chrmn 88-; Delta Sigma Pi VP 89-; Beta Alpha Phi 90-; Acctg/Law.

**ROBERTS, KIMBERLY M,** Union Univ, Jackson, TN; SR; Bstbl/Tns Lingue Mundi; Alpha Chi; Kappa Mu Epsilon; Alchl Drg Prvntn Comm; NAIA Acdmc All Amer; BS; Math; Tchg.

**ROBERTS, KRISTEN N,** Univ Of Tn At Martin, Martin, TN; SR; BFA; New Pacer Singers 88-90; Univ Singers 88-90; Choral Soc 88-90; Vanguard Theater; Sigma Alpha Iota Rec Sec 88-90; Alpha Delta Pi Hist 88-90; Miss Madison Cnty; Non-Finalist Talent Awd Miss TN Pageant; Theater; Performance.

**ROBERTS, LANA R,** Wright St Univ Lake Cmps, Celina, OH; SO; BA; Ltn Clb; Chrldng 83-86; Schlrshp Awrd St Mrys Jnt Twnshp Dist Mem Hosp 90-; Nrs; Nrs Ansthtst.

**ROBERTS, LINDA D J,** Georgetown Coll, Georgetown, KY; SR; Stdnt Court Review Justice 89-; Yng Rpblcns 1st Vice Chrmn 89-90; WRVG FM Station Mgr 90-; Kappa Delta Stndrds Bd 88-; WLRS FM Intrnshp 90; BA; Cmnctn Arts; Advrtsng.

**ROBERTS, LORRIE A,** Univ Of Cincinnati, Cincinnati, OH; FR; BA; Dietetics; Reg Dietitian.

**ROBERTS, LUCINDA R,** Midway Coll, Midway, KY; SO; BA; Stdnt Govt Assc Pres; Intrntl Clb Sec 90-; Phi Theta Kappa Rgnl Sec; Amer Bus Womens Assc 90-; Summa Cum Laude; Deans List Schlr; AA; Equine Ofc Admn Mjr Fld Awrd; Intrntl Comnctns; Intrntl Law.

**ROBERTS, LYDA A,** Clayton St Coll, Morrow, GA; SR; AAS; GA Schl Brtndng 86; Mech Drftng Tchnlgy.

**ROBERTS, MARCIE D,** Miami Jacobs Jr Coll Of Bus, Dayton, OH; GD; Profl Therapeutic Serv Ofc Mgr.

**ROBERTS, MARK M,** Hillsborough Comm Coll, Tampa, FL; FR; BA; Phi Theta Kappa 90-; Cmptr Eng.

**ROBERTS, MELANIE D,** Ga St Univ, Atlanta, GA; SR; BS; GSU Conservncy Cncl Excptnl Chldrn 90; Bptst Stdnt Union; 20/20 Vision; Nicholas Castri-Cone Awrd; Deans Schlrshp Key; Pres Plaque; Paul Douglas Tchr Schrsp; Clairmont Hills Bptst Chrch Schlrshp; Ballet; Ed Mentally Retarded; Tchng.

**ROBERTS, MELANIE M,** Va St Univ, Petersburg, VA; SR; BS; Mrchng Bnd Pres 89-; Acctng Clb 90; Dns Lst 88-; Outstdng Bus Achvmnt Awd 89-; Acctng; CPA.

**ROBERTS, MELISA L,** Univ Of Montevallo, Montevallo, AL; JR; BS; Baptist Student Union 88-89; Kappa Omicron Nu; Home Econ; Child Care.

**ROBERTS, MELISSA A,** Pellissippi St Tech Comm Coll, Knoxville, TN; FR; MBA; Psychlgy/Lbrl Arts.

**ROBERTS, MELISSA JOYCE,** Emory & Henry Coll, Emory, VA; SO; Kappa Phi Alpha; Mss Cmmnctns.

**ROBERTS, NICOLE L,** Va St Univ, Petersburg, VA; SO; BS; Bsn Info Systms; Cmptr Pgmr/Anlyst.

**ROBERTS, NICOLE Y,** Saint Pauls Coll, Lawrenceville, VA; SR; BS; Gospel Choir 89-90; ROTC Lt 87-90; Enrlmnt Mgt Soc 88-89; Sigma Gamma Rho 89-; IFC Chapln 89-; VITA 90-; Acctnt Intrnshp 90; Amercn Legion Bronz Medal 87-88; Bus Admn/Acctng; CPA Taxtn MS.

**ROBERTS, PATRICIA A,** Oh Univ-Southern Cmps, Ironton, OH; SR; BS; Elem Ed; Tchng.

**ROBERTS, PAUL LAWRENCE,** Norfolk St Univ, Norfolk, VA; SR; Alpha Kappa Mu 90-; Pres Hnrs/Deans Lst/Hnr Rl 84-; AAS Tidewater Comm Clg 88; BS; Acctng; CPA.**

**ROBERTS, POLLY J,** Memphis St Univ, Memphis, TN; SO; BA; Jr League Memphis 76-; Tres 76-; Craddock/Roberts Partner 89-; Sr VP Leader Srvcs Inc 80-89; Communication; Ins Consultant.

**ROBERTS, REBA A,** Memphis St Univ, Memphis, TN; SO; BS; Hnrs Prog 89-; Gamma Beta Phi 90-; Alpha Epsilon Delta; Pre Med Blgy; Med.

**ROBERTS, RENITA L,** Central Fl Comm Coll, Ocala, FL; SO; AA 90; Law.

**ROBERTS, ROSALIE N,** Univ Of Miami, Coral Gables, FL; SO; BA; ICF 89-; Gspl Choir 90-; Hnrs Pro; Engl; Law.

**ROBERTS, ROSILAND S,** Saint Pauls Coll, Lawrenceville, VA; SR; BA; Grl Sct Ldr; Elem Tchr; Assoc; Elem Educ; Tchr.

**ROBERTS, SHARAN E,** Univ Of Al At Birmingham, Birmingham, AL; SR; BSN; Nrsng Assn UAB Schl Of Nrsng Lvl Rep 90-; Phi Theta Kappa 87-88; AA Jefferson State Jr Coll 88; Nrsng.

**ROBERTS, SHARON L,** Univ Of Nc At Charlotte, Charlotte, NC; JR; BS; Crim Jstc.

**ROBERTS, SHARON L,** Northern Ky Univ, Highland Hts, KY; SR; BED; Grad Top Cls; Am Registry Radiologic Tech; Radiologic Tech Cmptd Axial Tech; AS Radiology Lexington Cmnty Coll 87; Elem Edn/Chem; Teach.

**ROBERTS, SHIRLEEN C,** Colby Sawyer Coll, New London, NH; FR; BA; Alumni Assoc 90-; Habitat Humanity 90-; Science; Medicine.

**ROBERTS, SONJA H,** Ga Southern Univ, Statesboro, GA; JR; BA; Gamma Beta Phi; Beta Alpha Psi; Dns Lst 88-; AS BA 90; Acctg; Acct.

**ROBERTS, STEPHEN E,** Faulkner St Jr Coll, Bay Minette, AL; JR; BE; Phi Theta Kappa 90-; Elect Eng; Cmptr Sftwr Dsgn.**

**ROBERTS, STEPHEN J,** Univ Of Miami, Coral Gables, FL; SO; BA; Bus Mgmt.

**ROBERTS, STEVEN L,** Wv Univ At Parkersburg, Parkersburg, WV; FR; AAS; 4h Cmpng 69-73; Un Meth Yth 70-77; Glfng Trvlng; Hon Rl 86-87; Mtns St Clg Dip; Jr Acctg Mgmt; Bureau Of Ccensus Enmrtr; AAS Mtn St Clg 87; Bsns Admn; Mgmt.

**ROBERTS, SUSAN R,** Univ Of Southern Ms, Hattiesburg, MS; SR; BS; Phi Theta Kappa 89; Kappa Delta Pi 90-; AA Copiah-Lincoln Comm College 89; Elem Educ; Tchr.

**ROBERTS, SUSAN W,** Valdosta St Coll, Valdosta, GA; FR; BM; GMEA Piana Awd 90; Music Prfrmnce; Prfssr.

**ROBERTS, TAMARA L,** Univ Of West Fl, Pensacola, FL; JR; BA; PJC Acad Hnrs 88-90f AA Pensacola Jr Clg 90; Educ; Elem Educ.

**ROBERTS, TAMMY M,** West Liberty St Coll, West Liberty, WV; SR; Foreign Stdnt Clb 89-; Certif Dntl Asst Career Canada Clg 86; A Sc; Dntl Hyg.

**ROBERTS, TARA L,** Univ Of Tn At Knoxville, Knoxville, TN; GD; DVM; Avian Exotics Clb; Phi Eta Sigma 87-; Phi Beta Kappa 90-; BS 90; Vet Med.

**ROBERTS, TASHA A,** Tougaloo Coll, Tougaloo, MS; JR; BA; Stu Govt Assoc 90-; VP Cls 90-; Pre Heath Clb 89-; Gspl Choir Pan Afrcn Clb 88-; Deans Lst 89-; Delta Sigma Theta; Life Coll Marietta Georgia Intrn; Drl Tm 90-; Clncl Psych.

**ROBERTS, THOMAS G,** Ny Univ, New York, NY; FR; AAS; Hsop Audiences Inc 87-; GMHC 87-; Hlth/Hmn Serv; Psychlgy.

**ROBERTS, TIMOTHY G,** Univ Of Sc At Columbia, Columbia, SC; JR; BS; Econ/Finance; Entrepreneur.

**ROBERTS, TODD S,** Barry Univ, Miami, FL; JR; BA; ROTC Capt 90-; Phi Alpha Theta; AS Comm Clg Of Air Frc 89; Hstry; USAF Ofcr.

**ROBERTS, TONIA L,** Univ Of Ky, Lexington, KY; JR; BS; Phi Beta Lambda 89-90; Phi Eta Sigma 89; Secondary Sci Edn; High Sch Sci Tchr.

**ROBERTS, TYRANE L,** Clark Atlanta Univ, Atlanta, GA; SR; BA; Acctng Clb Treas 90-; Ntl Assoc Black Acctnts; Alpha Kappa Mu; Beta Gamma Sigma; Business/Accounting.

**ROBERTS, URSULA D,** Johnson C Smith Univ, Charlotte, NC; SO; BA; Choir; Bellmont Boys/Girls Club Vol; Psychlgy; Clin Psychlgst.

**ROBERTS, VICKI L**, Chatfield Coll, Saint Martin, OH; SO; Earth Day Cmmt; Buckeye Trls Girl Scout Assc Group Ldr 87-90; Deans List 89-; Freelance Artst 89-; Cert Art Instrctn Schl 90; Creative Arts; Commerical Artst.

**ROBERTS, VICTORIA L**, Owensboro Comm Coll, Owensboro, KY; SO; Bus; Mgt.

**ROBERTS, WALTER E**, Univ Of Sc At Columbia, Columbia, SC; FR; BA; English; Writer.

**ROBERTS, WILLIAM C**, Univ Of Tn At Knoxville, Knoxville, TN; GD; DVM; Frst Yr Vet Med Clss Pres 90-; TN Army Natl Grd 1st Lt 86-; Gamma Beta Phi 86-; Phi Eta Sigma 86-; Gamma Sigma Delta 89-; Alpha Zeta 89-; Almni Natl Mrt Schlrshp 85; Bonham Fndtn And Ag Fclty Almni Schlrshp 86; Merek Awrd From Coll Of Vet Med; BS; Vet Med.

**ROBERTS, WILLIAM T**, Univ Of Rochester, Rochester, NY; JR; BS; Rgby Clb 89-; Optcl Scty Of Amer 88-; Nwsppr Phtgrphr 90; By Scts 79-; Alpne Ski Tm 88-; Optcl Eng.

**ROBERTSON, AILEEN J**, Univ Of Sc At Columbia, Columbia, SC; JR; BA; Psi Chi 90-; Deans Lst Univ 87-90; Wmns Glf Team 87-; Psychlgy; Sprts Psychlgy.**

**ROBERTSON, ALETA B**, Salem Coll, Winston-Salem, NC; JR; BA; Salem Coll Dmcrts 90-; Incunabula 90-; Lbry Comm 89-90; Circle K 89-; Fremdendieren 89-90; Archlgcl Lab Intrnshp; Sclgy; Biblical Archlgst.**

**ROBERTSON, ANGELA N**, Univ Of Southern Ms, Hattiesburg, MS; SR; BA; Elem Educ.

**ROBERTSON, BRYAN C**, Univ Of Akron, Akron, OH; JR; BS; AAB; Busn Mgr; Cmptr Prgmg/Busn.

**ROBERTSON, CHARLES B**, King Coll, Bristol, TN; SO; BA; SGA Pres 90-; Theater 89-; Choir 89-; King Schlr 89-; Acctng; Law.

**ROBERTSON, CHRISTINE E**, Indiana Univ Of Pa, Indiana, PA; SR; Open Door Ind Cnty Vol/Fcltr 89-; Kappa Delta Pi 90-; Pi Gamma Mu 89-; Deans List 88-; Provost Schlr 88-89; Summa Cum Laude; AA Univ Of S FL 88; BS; Sec Soc Scnc Educ; Teach Jr/Sr HS.

**ROBERTSON, CHRISTOPHER R**, Central Fl Comm Coll, Ocala, FL; SO; BA; Eng/Bus; Career Nvl Ofcr.

**ROBERTSON, CLINTON D**, Univ Of Tn At Chattanooga, Chattanooga, TN; SO; BA; Amer Soc Cvl Engrs; Art Sci Hstry Archlgy; Archtctr.

**ROBERTSON, CRAIG FRANCIS**, Niagara Univ, Niagara Univ, NY; JR; BS; Poltcl Sci Forum 89-; Hstry Forum 90-; Vars Soccer/Club Bsbl 88-; Poltcl Sci; Law.

**ROBERTSON, DALE M**, De Tech & Comm Coll At Dover, Dover, DE; FR; BS; Nursing.

**ROBERTSON, DANNY J**, Saint Vincents Coll & Seminary, Latrobe, PA; SR; BS; NAA 89-; Alpha Sigma Lambda; Ntnl Asso/Acctnts; Awd/Excel; Awd Excel Outstndng Achvmnt; Ntnl Asso/Acctnts; Asso Penn St 77; Acctng; MBA.

**ROBERTSON, DEBORAH A**, Univ Of Nc At Charlotte, Charlotte, NC; JR; BA; Grmn.

**ROBERTSON, DREAMA A**, Univ Of Nc At Asheville, Asheville, NC; SO; BA; SNEA 89-; Hl St Ltrcy Prjct Lit Tutr 90-; NC Tchng Flws Prog 89-; Biolgy; Teaching.

**ROBERTSON, GINA L**, Middle Tn St Univ, Murfreesboro, TN; JR; BBA; Math Org Stdnt 88-89; Natl Soc Publ Acctnts 90-; Pi Sigma Epsilon VP Mktg Fin 89-; Young Am Bowling Alliance Bd Dir 88-; Coachs Awd 88-89; Bill Zelna Dye Schlrshp; Gold Medallion Schlrshp Undrclsmn Awd Merit Pi Sigma Epsilon Mktg Frat; Acctg; CPA.

**ROBERTSON, JAMES D**, Niagara Univ, Niagara Univ, NY; JR; BA; Math Clb; Kappa Mu Epsilon; Delta Epsilon Sigma; Vrsty Bsbl Tm; Math; Engrng Cvl.

**ROBERTSON, JEANETTE S**, John Wesley Coll, High Point, NC; FR; BA; Gvrnrs Offce Cert Of Apprctn For Vol Wrk 89; ASK Prison Mnstry Dir 88; Crossroads Prison Mnstry Brd Membr; Scrtry 87; Cert Liberty U 88; Bible Thlgy; Chldrns Mnstry/Cnslng.

**ROBERTSON, JERMAINE A**, Old Dominion Univ, Norfolk, VA; SO; BS; ASME 89-; ASHRACE 90-; VA Pwr Intrn 90-; Urban Lg Schlrshp 89; Mail Hndlrs Schlrshp 89; VA Pwr Schlrshp 90; ASRACE 90; Mech Engr.

**ROBERTSON, JOYCE M**, Lane Coll, Jackson, TN; SR; BS; Bio Clb 87; Beta Kappa Chi Treas 89-90; Zeta Phi Beta 87; Bstkbl Tm 87-88; BS 90; Bio; Mdcl Tchnlgst.

**ROBERTSON, KENDRA A**, Univ Of Sc At Lancaster, Lancaster, SC; FR; Bsn Admin; ACCTG.

**ROBERTSON, KEVIN CHRISTOPHER**, Columbia Union Coll, Takoma Park, MD; FR; BA; Phi Eta Sigma; Crss Cntry Tm 90-; Chem; Arch.

**ROBERTSON, KIMBERLY M**, Fayetteville St Univ, Fayetteville, NC; JR; Dnc Tchr; Elem Ed; Tch 1st Grd.

**ROBERTSON, LARUA S**, Christopher Newport Coll, Newport News, VA; JR; BS; Beta Sigma Phi Pres 84-85; AAS Paul D Camp Cmnty 88; Physical Ed; Teacher.

**ROBERTSON, LEA P**, Ky St Univ, Frankfort, KY; SO; Stdnt Sntr Govt 90-; Ms Mcculium Hall 89-90; Pres Schlrshp 89-; Bio Art; Fshn Dsgn City Plng.

**ROBERTSON, LESLIE F**, Univ Of Ms Main Cmps, University, MS; SR; BA; Coll Rpblcns 88-90; Gldn Key 89-; Gamma Beta Phi Invtns Chr 88-; Alpha Epsilon Delta 89-90; Kappa Delta Activ Chr 87-; Kappa Sigma Little Sis 88-; Chancellors Hnr Roll 88-; Deans Hnr Roll 87-; Accounting.

**ROBERTSON, LISA ANN**, Oh St Univ, Columbus, OH; SR; BA; Environ Action Treas 89-90; Stdnts For Choice 89-90; Stonewall Union 88-; Phi Kappa Phi; Golden Key; Phi Beta Kappa; Phi Beta Delta; Wmn Against Rape 89-; Excellence In Schlrshp Awd 90-; Engl/Wmns Studies; Engl MA.

**ROBERTSON, LORI A**, Duquesne Univ, Pittsburgh, PA; SO; BA; Stdnt Nwsppr 90-; Phi Eta Sigma Pres 90-; Awrd Fndrs Schlrshp 89-; Intgrtd Hnrs Prgm; Commnctn.

**ROBERTSON, MALCOLM E**, Tougaloo Coll, Tougaloo, MS; SR; BA; Assoc Dgr 89; Psychlgy.

**ROBERTSON, MEREDITH C**, Memphis St Univ, Memphis, TN; JR; BA; Gamma Beta Phi; Alpha Delta Pi 88-; Psychlgy; Spch Pthlgy.

**ROBERTSON, MIRENDA V**, Al A & M Univ, Normal, AL; FR; BS; Dns Lst 90; Pol Sci; Law.

**ROBERTSON, PANDORA**, Univ Of Akron, Akron, OH; SR; BS; Beta Gamma Sigma; Prof Ballet Dancer 83-90; Pt Dance Faculty 89-; Mktg.

**ROBERTSON, PHYLLIS A**, Univ Of Al At Birmingham, Birmingham, AL; JR; BED; AS Wallace State Coll Hanceville AL 86; Elem Educ; Tchr.

**ROBERTSON, SHARON A**, Miami Jacobs Jr Coll Of Bus, Dayton, OH; JR; BA; Accntng; Med Admn.

**ROBERTSON, STEPHANIE J**, Memphis St Univ, Memphis, TN; JR; BED; Kappa Delta Pi 90-; Jr Acad Achvmnt Awd; Elem Educ; Tchg/Admin.

**ROBERTSON, SUSANNA L**, Coker Coll, Hartsville, SC; SR; BA; SGA Sntr 89-90; Union Cmtr Chrprsn 90-; Otstndng Stdnt Div Ntrl Physcl Sci Math 89-90; Top Ten Stdnts 87-; Ntnl Cncl Tchrs Math 88-90; Math; Epdmlgy.**

**ROBERTSON, SUZETTE D**, Winthrop Coll, Rock Hill, SC; FR; BS; Bptst Stdnt Un 90-; Alpha Lambda Delta 90-; Pres Host 90-; Elem Ed; Tchng.

**ROBERTSON, TOMMIE L**, Union Inst, Cincinnati, OH; SR; BS; Alliance Blck Telecomm Employees Chptr Contact 89-; AT/T Analyst 72-; Info Systs Mgmt; Socl Wrk.

**ROBERTSON, TUNYA T**, Tuskegee Univ, Tuskegee Inst, AL; JR; BA; Bus Admn; Offcr USAF.

**ROBERTSON JR, WAYNE M**, Liberty Univ, Lynchburg, VA; SO; BS; Chrstn Tchrs Assc Pres 89-90; Alpha Lambda Delta 90-; Ftbll 90-; Engl; Tch.

**ROBESON, MARK E**, Old Dominion Univ, Norfolk, VA; GD; MS; Tau Beta Pi VP 88-; Pi Tau Sigma 88-; Alpha Chi 89-; Cooper Dominion Schlrshp 90; Fclty Awrd 90; BS 90; Eng.

**ROBEY, MELANIE D**, Univ Of Tn At Martin, Martin, TN; FR; BA; Alpha Delta Pi; USAA All Amer Schlr; Soc Wrk.

**ROBICH, MARILYN M**, Kent St Univ Trumbull Cmps, Warren, OH; JR; BBA; Ed Twrds Chng Sec/Treas 90-; Stdnt Sen Sen 90-; Pres Lst 89; Deans Lst 89-90; Lcnsd Real Estate Agnt 88-90; Lcnsd Actnr 84-90; AA; Acctg/Cmptr Sci; Acctnt/Cmptr Pgrmr.

**ROBICHAUD, MICHELLE M**, S U N Y Coll At Fredonia, Fredonia, NY; SR; MS; Psyhlgy Club 87-89; Alpha Delta Kappa; BA; BA; Psychology; Schl Psychologist.

**ROBICHEAUX, CHRISTINA M**, George Mason Univ, Fairfax, VA; SR; BS; Stu Educ Assoc 90-; Virginia Educ Assoc; Ntl Educ Assoc; Erly Chldhd Educ; Tchg.

**ROBILLARD, DENISE A**, Newbury Coll, Brookline, MA; FR; Travel/Tursm Mgmt; Trvl Agnt.

**ROBINETTE, MELINDA F**, Univ Of West Fl, Pensacola, FL; JR; BS; Phi Theta Kappa 88-89; AA Tidewater Cmnty Clg 89; Elctrcl Engr Tech; Appl Engr.

**ROBINETTE, MELISSA A**, Univ Of Ky, Lexington, KY; JR; BA; Bptst Std Un 90-; Athltcs Cncl 89-; Gldn Key 90-; RA 89-; Asst Hl Dir; MCAT/DAT Prep Pgm 90; Hlth Admn; Optmtry.

**ROBINETTE, ROBIN S**, Hillsborough Comm Coll, Tampa, FL; SO; AA; Edn/Humanities; Edn.

**ROBINETTE, SHELLEY J**, Middle Tn St Univ, Murfreesboro, TN; JR; BA; Clgt Secretaries Intrntl; Gamma Beta Phi 89-; Sgm Iota Epsln; Mgmt/Psychlgy Mnr; Prsnl/Hmn Rsrcs Mgmt.

**ROBINETTE, TAMMY SUTHERLAND**, Univ Of Va Clinch Valley Coll, Wise, VA; JR; BA; IM Bsktbll 90-; Psychlgy.

**ROBINS, AMANDA G**, Univ Of Tn At Martin, Martin, TN; FR; PHD; Amer Chem Soc 90-; Hon Smnr Soc 90-; Phrmcy.

**ROBINSON, ALBERTINA**, Tougaloo Coll, Tougaloo, MS; FR; BA; Ecnmcs.

**ROBINSON, AMANDA H**, Denmark Tech Coll, Denmark, SC; JR; ASA; Esquire Sweethrts Frat; ECI Co-Op Wstnghse Svnnh Rvr Ste; ASA; Electronics Eng Tech; Eng.

**ROBINSON, ANDRADE N**, Coppin St Coll, Baltimore, MD; SO; BA; Coll Athltcs; Advsry Brd; Stdnt Snte; Coll Hnrs Treas Elct Prog; Hosp Vol; Trck Tm 90-; Comp Sci; Comp Eng Arntcs.

**ROBINSON, ANDREA**, City Univ Of Ny Baruch Coll, New York, NY; GD; BBA; Mgmt; Law.

**ROBINSON, ANDREW C**, Md Inst Coll Of Art, Baltimore, MD; SR; Stdnt Actn Cmtee Stdnt Govt Co Fndr 88; Exchange Prog; BFA; Ceramic Sculpture; Fine Arts.

**ROBINSON, ANGELA D**, Gaston Coll, Dallas, NC; JR; BA; Acctg; Real Est Dev.

**ROBINSON, ANGELA L**, Central St Univ, Wilberforce, OH; JR; BS; Stdnt Govt Assn Rec Sec 89-; Cmptr/Math Clb Sec 89-; Alpha Kappa Alpha; Im Sftbl Co Capt; Cpa.

**ROBINSON, ANGELA Y**, Al St Univ, Montgomery, AL; JR; Psychlgy; Police Psychlgst Jvnls.

**ROBINSON, ANN H**, Teikyo Post Univ, Waterbury, CT; GD; MLS; Rose Traurig Schlrs Publcty Chmn 87-; Phi Theta Kappa; Alpha Chi; Valedictorian Post Coll 90; Engl Awd Post Coll 89; Estrn Comm Coll Soc Sci Awd 86; Arts/Humanities Awd Maltatuck Comm Coll 86; Cnvlscnt Hosp Vol; Misc Comm Ch Act; Lib Studies/Humanities; Writer/Engl Tchr.

**ROBINSON, ANTOINETTE**, Al St Univ, Montgomery, AL; SO; Peer Alliance Career Cnslng Awrnss V P 90-; Mrchng Bnd Prctr 89-; Whitney Yng Soc Wrk Club Pblc Rltn 90-; Alpha Sweetheart Club V P Pblc Rltn 89-90; Ldrshp Schlrshp 89-90; Univ Lady Hornet Bsktbl Mgr 89-90; Social Work; Social Worker.

**ROBINSON, AVA NELL**, Ms Univ For Women, Columbus, MS; SO; BS; Nu Epsilon Delta 90-; NAFE 89-; Lgl Sec Offce Mgr 72-; Prlgl; Law.

**ROBINSON, BARBARA A**, Meridian Comm Coll, Meridian, MS; GD; Nrsng.

**ROBINSON, BEATRICE O**, Commonwealth Coll, Norfolk, VA; FR; AAS; Cmptr Clb Sec; Alpha Betta Gamma; Hon/Pres Lst; English; Cmptr Progrmr.

**ROBINSON, BECKY S**, Univ Of Al At Birmingham, Birmingham, AL; JR; BSN; AD Sci 90; Nrsng; Mstrs In Nrsng.

**ROBINSON, BOYD A**, Oh Coll Of Podiatric Med, Cleveland, OH; SO; DPM; PPAC; AGK Treas; Dns Lst 90; OCPM Acdmc Schlrshp 90; BS Mt Union Clge 89; Podiatric Med; Pdtry.

**ROBINSON, BRENT D**, Fl International Univ, Miami, FL; SO; BS; IM Soccer 90-; Cmptr Sci; Cmptr Pgmg.

**ROBINSON, BRIAN E**, Radford Univ, Radford, VA; SO; BS; Govt Assoc Treas 90-; VP Res Hall 89-90; Bus; Finance.

**ROBINSON, CALVIN O**, Fl A & M Univ, Tallahassee, FL; SR; BS; Kemetic Math Soc 1st V P 90-; Stdnt Tchr James A Shanks H S; Math; Ed.

**ROBINSON, CAROL A**, Central St Univ, Wilberforce, OH; FR; Chorus 90-; Mus Educ; Tch.

**ROBINSON, CHRISTOPHER L**, Broward Comm Coll, Ft Lauderdale, FL; SO; BA; Hons Inst 90-; Phi Theta Kappa; Pres List 90-; Merit Schlrshp 90-; Pre Med.**

**ROBINSON, CYNTHIA L**, Univ Of Sc At Aiken, Aiken, SC; FR; BS; Nrsng/Bus Mgmt; Nrsng/Hosp Admin.

**ROBINSON, CYNTHIA M**, Univ Of The Dist Of Columbia, Washington, DC; SR; BBA; Busn Finc Assn Pr 88-; Univ Stdnt Adv Cncl 88-90; Delta Mu Delta Mbr 90-; Urbn Leag 88-; Smithsn Assoc 88-; Frnd Natl Zoo 89-; Pepco Schlrshp 89-90; Ambssdr Mexico 89; Tuitn Fees Schlrshp 89-90; Busn/Econ/Finc; Postsecndry Educ.

**ROBINSON, DANIEL**, Bridgeport Engr Inst, Fairfield, CT; JR; BSEE; Nrwlk St Tech Coll 87-; Almni Assn; ASEM Nrwlk St Tech Coll 87; Elect Eng; Eng/Rbtcs/Bus.

**ROBINSON, DAPHANE M**, Univ Of Al At Birmingham, Birmingham, AL; FR; Dpt Rdtn/Onclgy Intshp; Mnrty Pres Schlp 90-; Bio; Gntcs.

**ROBINSON, DARLENE Y**, Univ Of Md At Eastern Shore, Princess Anne, MD; JR; BS; Yrbk Stf Phtgrphr 88-89; Pre Prfsnl Soc 88-90; Amrcn Physcl Thrpy Soc 90-; Hnrs Prgrm 88-; Rcgnzd Hnrs Cnvntn 88-; Naacp 88-; Physcl Thrpy; Physcl Thrpst.

**ROBINSON, DEBRA A**, Central St Univ, Wilberforce, OH; SR; BS; OSEA 89-; NCTE; AAS Medcl/Dntl Tech Inst 87-88; Elem Ed; MS Tch.

**ROBINSON, DERRICK E**, Morehouse Coll, Atlanta, GA; SO; BA; Pol Sci Soc 90-; Proj Success Prog Tutor 90-; Pol Sci; Law/Educ/Politics.

**ROBINSON, DEXTER J**, Tougaloo Coll, Tougaloo, MS; SR; MBA; Std Govt Asc VP 90-; Gspl Choir Treas 89-; Spprt Serv Pres 88-; Alpha Lambda Delta 88-89; Alpha Kappa Mu 90-; Alpha Phi Alpha; Untd Way Amer 87-88; NAACP 89-; Hrtfrd Ins Grp Intshp 90; BA; Bsn Admn/Acctnt.

**ROBINSON, DIANA L**, Wv Northern Comm Coll, Wheeling, WV; SO; RN; Nrsg Pgm Repr 89; Phi Theta Kappa; Acad Schlrshp 90-; Natl Stdnt Nrs Assoc 90-; Nrsg; Ped Nrsg.**

**ROBINSON, DONNA LEE**, Southern Coll Of Tech, Marietta, GA; SR; B; ASCE; Pnllnc P 88-; Alpha Delta Pi Chpln 88-; Cvl Eng.

**ROBINSON, DOUGLAS A**, S U N Y Coll Of Tech At Frmgdl, Farmingdale, NY; FR; AD; Vars Lacrosse; Lib Arts; Educ/Psychology.

**ROBINSON, DOYLE W**, Livingston Univ, Livingston, AL; JR; BS; Lynnville Meth Church 87-; Elem Ed/Sci Studies; Tch.

**ROBINSON, DWIGHT**, Univ Of Nh Plymouth St Coll, Plymouth, NH; SO; BS; Eta Sgm Gamma; Phi Mu Dlt 89-; Paul E Arold Mem Schlrshp; Brennan Hart Mem Schlrshp; P E Exrcs Sci.

**ROBINSON, E RAYNETTE**, Columbia Union Coll, Takoma Park, MD; BS; Business Adm; Mgmt Trng FDIC.

**ROBINSON, EDWARD J**, Harding Grad School Of Relig, Memphis, TN; GD; PHD; G P Bowser Mnstrl Awd 87; Hon Grad SW Chrstn Clg 88; Dns Lst; AA BA SW Chrstn Clg 88; MAR Hardng Univ Grad Sch Rel; Amer Chrch Hstry; Tchr.

**ROBINSON, ELEANOR J,** Cumberland County Coll, Vineland, NJ; FR; Choir Dir Heisterville UM Ch 75-85/89-; Admin Bd Heisterville UM Ch; Claims Corr Durand Intl; Liberal Arts; Edn.

**ROBINSON, ELLIOTT S,** Norfolk St Univ, Norfolk, VA; GD; Spartan Alpha Tau 88-90; Kappa Alpha Psi 90-; Cert Sup Achvmnt 90; Cert Accmplshmnt 90; IM Bsktbl 87-88; AS 89; BS 90.

**ROBINSON, ERIC B,** Christian Brothers Univ, Memphis, TN; SR; BS; BBA Millsaps Coll 89; Telecmnctns.

**ROBINSON, GINA M,** Memphis St Univ, Memphis, TN; SR; BFA; Peer Mntr Prog 87-88; Hon Prog 87-90; Goldn Key 90-; Pi Kappa Alpha Ltl Sistr 87-89; Art Hstry; Law.

**ROBINSON, GINA M,** Wilberforce Univ, Wilberforce, OH; SR; Std Govt Asc Sec 90-; Sigma Omega 90-; Alpha Kappa Mu 89-; Alpha Kappa Alpha; BS; Bio/Pre-Med.

**ROBINSON, GLENDA S,** Chesterfield Marlboro Coll, Cheraw, SC; ASSOC; Business.

**ROBINSON, GREG S,** Univ Of Nc At Asheville, Asheville, NC; FR; BA; Chemistry.

**ROBINSON, GREGORY D,** Al St Univ, Montgomery, AL; FR; BA; Acctng; Bus.

**ROBINSON, GREGORY K,** Liberty Univ, Lynchburg, VA; JR; BS; Acctng.

**ROBINSON, HELJA I,** Univ Of Ms Main Cmps, University, MS; GD; PH D; European Stdnt Assoc 90; Phi Delta Kappa 89; Kappa Delta Pi 90; Phi Kappa Phi; Grad Instrshp 89; Grad Sch Achvmnt Awd; Lamar Grad Schlrshp; Ele Educ; Prfsr.

**ROBINSON, JAN,** East Central Comm Coll, Decatur, MS; SO; AA; Elem Edn.

**ROBINSON, JANE E,** Norfolk St Univ, Norfolk, VA; FR; BED; Interdisciplinary Studies; Teach.

**ROBINSON, JEAN M,** East Carolina Univ, Greenville, NC; SR; BM; Am Choral Dir Assoc Pres 90-; Music Edctrs Natl Conf; Hon Choir 89; Music; Edn.

**ROBINSON, JEFFREY A,** Univ Of Akron, Akron, OH; JR; BS; Res Hl Prog Brd Asst 89-; Stdnt Govt Treas 90-; Acctg Assc 90-; Res Asst 91-; Alpha Lambda Delta 89-; Phi Eta Sigma 89-; Golden Key 90-; Beta Alpha Psi 90-; Beta Gamma Sigma; Deans Lst 88-; Hnrs Prog 88-; Ntl Res Hl Hnry 91-; Acctg; CPA.

**ROBINSON, JENNIER D,** Univ Of Charleston, Charleston, WV; JR; BA; Amer Scty Interior Desgrs 88-; BA Interior Design AS Busn Admin; Interior.

**ROBINSON, JENNIFER S,** West Chester Univ, West Chester, PA; SO; BS; Athletic Trng Club 89-; RHA Hall Treas; Hnrs Student Assoc 89-; Prestl Schlrshp 89-; Deans List 90-; Athletic Trng.

**ROBINSON JR, JERRY D,** Liberty Univ, Lynchburg, VA; JR; BS; Acad Cncl Exclnc 88-89; Old Dmn Ob Core Tutor 89-; Bsn; Mgmt Info Sys.

**ROBINSON, JUDITH H,** Univ Of Rochester, Rochester, NY; SR; BA; Rel & Classics Stdnt Cncl V P 90-; Deans List; Rel; Law.**

**ROBINSON, KAREN B,** Middle Tn St Univ, Murfreesboro, TN; FR; Assn Prsbytrn Chrch Edctrs 90-; Psychlgy; Dir Of Chrstn Educ.

**ROBINSON, KAREN K,** Middle Ga Coll, Cochran, GA; FR; AA; VA Vol Awd 87; Word Proc Hnr Grad Heart GA Tech 87; Ed-Early/Mdl/Spec; Tchg.

**ROBINSON, KELLIE A,** Ky St Univ, Frankfort, KY; SR; AS; Chrch Chr 87-; Boyscout Trp 281 85-; Dns Lst Ky State 89-; Academic Awd Nrsng; Nrsng; Stf Nurse.**

**ROBINSON, L C,** Alcorn St Univ, Lorman, MS; FR; Baptist Stdnt Un Chpln; Prayer Band; Math Club; Math.

**ROBINSON, LANCE E,** Savannah Coll Of Art & Design, Savannah, GA; SR; BFA; Chess Clb VP; Ultimate Frisbee Clb; BGS; Video; Field Prod.

**ROBINSON, LAURA K,** Mayland Comm Coll, Spruce Pine, NC; FR; AGE; Phi Theta Kappa 90-; Deans Lst 90-; Sci/Blgy; Envrnmntl Sci/Blgst.

**ROBINSON SR, LEWIS C,** Roane St Comm Coll, Harriman, TN; SO; AS; Stdnt Natl Envrnmnt Hlth Clb Pres 90-; Physcs Stdnt Of Yr 90-; Envrnmntl Wst Mgmt/Ind Hygne.

**ROBINSON, LINDA R,** Dyersburg St Comm Coll, Dyersburg, TN; SO; AS; Business Ofc Systems Assoc Pres 90-; Ambassador 90-; Phi Theta Kappa Secy 90-; Outstndng Grad; Ldrshp Awrd; Amer Bus Wmns Assoc; AS; Business; Paralegal.

**ROBINSON, LISA C,** Samford Univ, Birmingham, AL; GD; JD; Hon Ct 89-90; AL Stdnt Bar 88-; Envrnmntl Law Scty 90-; Phi Alph Dlt 88-; Women In Law 88-; Deans List; BSA Converse Clg BA 88; Law.

**ROBINSON, LISA R,** Sinclair Comm Coll, Dayton, OH; JR; BA; United Yth Grp Home Inc Brd Pres 88-; Fstr Prntng Ntwrk; Sinclair Comm Clg; Talent Rstr Cert Achvmnt; Man Cosmetology Dayton Acad Hair Dsgn 84; Asstd Chemst Dave Seagraves Fantastic Hair Prodcts 84-87; Chem/Math; Chem Csmtcs.

**ROBINSON, LORI A,** Univ Of Sc At Lancaster, Lancaster, SC; FR; BA; ARETE; Busn Admn; Prsnnl Mgmnt.

**ROBINSON, MARCIE H,** O'more School Of Design, Franklin, TN; SO; BA; ASID 89-; Hnr Rl 89-; Dns Lst 89-; Prsvtn Intrs Intshp; Dsgn; Arch.

**ROBINSON, MARION E,** Johnson C Smith Univ, Charlotte, NC; FR; BA; X-Cntry 90-; Indr/Outdr Trck 90-; Math; Elec Engr.

**ROBINSON, MARY JEAN,** Al A & M Univ, Normal, AL; SO; BS; Chrch Chr; High Bstrs Clb; Offc Systmes Mngmnt; Cert TN Valley Coll 83; Cert TN Vlly Coll 83; Cert Madison Co Tech 72; Office Systms Mngmnt; Offc Mgr.

**ROBINSON, MATTHEW T,** Central St Univ, Wilberforce, OH; JR; BA; Jr Cls Pres Stud Gov 90-; AA Louis Tech 89-; Accntng/ Pre Law; Law Schl.

**ROBINSON, MAXWELL T,** Morris Brown Coll, Atlanta, GA; JR; BA; Prlgl Clb 90-; Natl Cllgt Comp Sci Awd; IM Bsktbl Chmpn Capt; Prlgl Studies; Law.

**ROBINSON, MELONE A,** City Univ Of Ny Med Evers Coll, Brooklyn, NY; SR; BA; Chrstn Flwshp Secr 87-88; Peer Cnslr 88; Elem Ed; Tchr.

**ROBINSON, MELVIN DARRELL,** Mayland Comm Coll, Spruce Pine, NC; SR; Grocery Mgr 84-85; AS MD Comm Clg 90; Bsn Admn.

**ROBINSON, MICAKL,** Central St Univ, Wilberforce, OH; SO; BA; Cmptr Infor Sys; Prgmmr.

**ROBINSON, MICHAEL D,** Cumberland County Coll, Vineland, NJ; SO.

**ROBINSON, MICHAEL J,** Univ Of Southern Ms, Hattiesburg, MS; FR; BS; German Clb 90-; Gamma Beta Phi; Math; NASA.

**ROBINSON, MICHAEL W,** Central Al Comm Coll, Alexander City, AL; SO; BA; Soc Sci Awd 90-; USMC; Police Ofcr; Deputy Cnty Sheriffs Ofc; Jstce/Publ Safety Jurisprudence; Law.

**ROBINSON, MICHELLE D,** Alcorn St Univ, Lorman, MS; FR; BS; Biology Club 90-; Honors Biology Club 90-91; Hnrs Soc Organization 90-; Biology; Medicine.

**ROBINSON, MICHELLE M,** City Univ Of Ny City Coll, New York, NY; JR; BA; Am Museum Ntrl Hstry 85-86; Rego Pk Nrsng Hm Vol 85; Queens Btncl Grdn 85-86; Sec Sci Hnr Soc Pres 87-88; Dns Lst 87-; General Mtrs Schlrshp 89-90; Ciby Clg Tennis Tourn; AAS/CERTIF Queensborough Cmnty Clg 89-; Hstry; Law/Ed.

**ROBINSON, MICHELLE R,** Ms Coll, Clinton, MS; FR; BSBA; Nenamoosha Soc Tribe 90-; Bptst Stdnt Union; Alpha Lambda Delta; Deans List 90-; Bus; Fshn Mrchndsng.

**ROBINSON, MYRA C,** Ms St Univ, Miss State, MS; FR; BFA; IM Tennis Capt; AIAS 90; Kappa Pi; Fine Art/Graphic Design Awd; Art/Graphic Design.

**ROBINSON, NANCY M,** Daytona Beach Comm Coll, Daytona Beach, FL; FR; AS; Photo Soc 90-; Gallery Of Fine Arts 90-; Photo Career Aspirations; Photography; Jrnlsm.

**ROBINSON, NANCY M,** Piedmont Bible Coll, Winston-Salem, NC; FR; BA; Deans List; ACT Score Schlrshp 90; Elem Edn; Teach.

**ROBINSON, NIKKI H,** Hampton Univ, Hampton, VA; JR; BA; Natl Assc Blck Jrnlsts Miss NABJ 90-; Stdnt Ldrshp Pgm 90-; Dlt Sgm Theta Jrnlst 90-; Spec Tutor Pre Clg Pgm 90; Intrnshp Dept Soc Svc; White House Advncd Tm Stf Asstnt; Mass Media; Entrtnmnt Law.**

**ROBINSON, PAMALA S,** Oh St Univ At Marion, Marion, OH; JR; BS; Psych Clb 88-90; Ed Soc V P 88-; Griffen Soc; Ridgemont Music Boosters Pres 80-; Mt Victory Un Meth Church Yth Advsr 81-; Elem Ed; Tchr.

**ROBINSON, PAMELA J,** West Liberty St Coll, West Liberty, WV; SO; BED; Dean Lst 89; Mthdst Chrch; Rdlgy Sec 76-88; Data Prcssng Clrk 88-89; Elem Educ/Gen Sci; Tch.

**ROBINSON, PETER C,** The Kings Coll, Briarclf Mnr, NY; SR; BA; Deans Lst 90; Briarcliff Manor Vol Fire Dept 90-; Soccer 87; Bio; Med.

**ROBINSON, RAPHEL R,** Central Fl Comm Coll, Ocala, FL; SO; BA; Afro-Amer Stdnt Union 90-; AA; Econs.

**ROBINSON, RHONDA L,** Univ Of Sc At Columbia, Columbia, SC; JR; BA; NAACP; Assn Of Afrcn Am Stdnts; Golden Key; Intrdscplnry Studies; Erly Chldhd Edctr/Admn.

**ROBINSON, RHONDA Y,** Al St Univ, Montgomery, AL; FR; BS; Nwspr Edtr 90-; Std Govt Snt Sec 90-; Std Govt Exec Sec; Lawyer.

**ROBINSON, RITA RAE,** Oh St Univ At Marion, Marion, OH; SR; BA; Envir Stdnts Assoc 88-; Distr Sci Fair Jdg Envir Sci 89; AA; Elem Ed; Tchr.

**ROBINSON, ROBBIN M,** Middle Tn St Univ, Murfreesboro, TN; SO; BS; Gamma Beta Phi; Sci; Agribus.

**ROBINSON, ROBERT M,** Kent St Univ Kent Cmps, Kent, OH; SO; BA; IM 89-; Pltcl Sci.

**ROBINSON, ROBYN M,** Fl A & M Univ, Tallahassee, FL; SR; BS; Educ Ldrs Assn 89-90; Pershing Kisses Secy 88-89; Pres Schlrs 88-89; Pblc Schls Intern 90; AA Seminole Comm Clg 87; Elem Educ; Rdng.

**ROBINSON, RON B,** Univ Of Sc At Columbia, Columbia, SC; FR; BA; Mech Eng.

**ROBINSON III, SAM A,** Tuskegee Univ, Tuskegee Inst, AL; SR; BS; Amer Inst Of Chem Engr; Soc Of Amer Mltry Engr; Natl Soc For Blck Engr; Chem Engr-Omega Chi Epsilon-VP 90-; Pi Mu Epsilon; Beta Kappa Chi; Outstndng Yng Men Of Amer; Distngsh Mltry Stdnt; Chevron Schlr; Chem Engr.

**ROBINSON, SANDRA M,** Ny Univ, New York, NY; SO; BA; Assoc Rtrng Stdnts 89-; Dip Coll Arts Sci Tech Kingston JA WI 86; Intl Bus.

**ROBINSON, SANYA B,** Howard Univ, Washington, DC; FR; BS; Phys Thrpy.

**ROBINSON, SCOTT R,** Univ Of Pittsburgh, Pittsburgh, PA; JR; BS; Inst Indstrl Engr; Alpha Pi Mu VP 90-; Tau Beta Pi; Gldn Key; Alghny Gen Hosp; Indstrl Engr.

**ROBINSON, SHANA L,** Univ Of Sc At Columbia, Columbia, SC; FR; MBA; SC Dept Of Labor Adm Spprt Spec; Psychtry/ Guidance Cnslng; Cnsl HS Stdnts.

**ROBINSON, SHANGO I,** S U N Y Coll Of Tech At Alfred, Alfred, NY; SR; BS; AAS; Mech Engr Tech; Automotive.

**ROBINSON, SHANNON K,** Wv Northern Comm Coll, Wheeling, WV; SO; Nrsng.

**ROBINSON, SHANNON R,** Ky St Univ, Frankfort, KY; FR; Stdnt Govt Assoc Sen 90-; Amrcn Rd Crss 87-89.

**ROBINSON, SONYA LYNNE,** Univ Of Charleston, Charleston, WV; JR; BA; Std Educ Asc 89-; Paul Douglas Tchr Schlp; Pres Schlp 88-; Elem Ed; Tchr.

**ROBINSON, STACY E,** Troy St Univ At Dothan, Dothan, AL; SR; U S Coast Grd Res E-5 88-; Port Securityman; Police Dept Intrn; BS; Crim Just; Law Enfrcmnt.

**ROBINSON, STEVEN M,** Davis & Elkins Coll, Elkins, WV; SO; Hnrs Soc; Deans Lst; Sccr; Engnrng Biology; Med Engnrng.

**ROBINSON, TAMMY J,** Auburn Univ At Auburn, Auburn, AL; JR; BS; Crusade Christ 88-; UPC Pblcty Com 88; Pool Lfgrd/Mgr; Kappa Omicron Nu Treas; Apparel Dsgn.

**ROBINSON, TANEA K,** Lincoln Univ, Lincoln Univ, PA; SO; Russian Club Sec; Thurgood Marshall Law Soc; SGA & Stdnt Council; Hnrs Soc; Intern MD Dept Of Health & Mental Hygience Contracts & Compliance Unit; Intern Theiblot Ryan Martin Ferguson 89-90; Englsh; Law.

**ROBINSON, TARA A,** Cornell Univ Statutory College, Ithaca, NY; SR; BS; Mrchng Bnd Asst Rnk Ldr 89-; Pep Bnd Cndctr 89-; Rd Crpt Hstng Scty 88-89; PEW Fndtn Under Grad Rsrch Fllwhsp 89-90; Deans Lst 90-; Coed IM Bwlng 89-90; Blgy; Blgy Rsrch.

**ROBINSON, TAWANA M,** Univ Of Md At Eastern Shore, Princess Anne, MD; SR; BA; Cmps Pal Orgztn VP 87-89; Nwspr Edtr 89-90; Stdnt Gvrnmnt Assn Mmbr 89-; Delta Sigma Theta Sor Inc Sgt Arms 88-; Adopt A Hwy 89-; Wediko Chldrns Srvcs Intrnshp Thrptc Cnslr 90; Seton Cntr Intrnshp Thrptc Cnslr 90-; Sociology; Clinical Psychology.

**ROBINSON, TERESA P,** Univ Of Sc At Columbia, Columbia, SC; SR; BS; Psy Clb 90-; Psy; Hlth Fld.

**ROBINSON, TERESITA M,** Univ Of Southern Ms, Hattiesburg, MS; JR; Act Cncl Advrtsng Comm 88-89; Afro Amer Stdnt Org 88-89; Golden Girls; Fash Merch/Mktg; Image Cnsltnt/ Byr.

**ROBINSON JR, TERRY E,** Wv Univ At Parkersburg, Parkersburg, WV; FR.

**ROBINSON, THEA M,** Va Commonwealth Univ, Richmond, VA; JR; BS; Pre Physical Therapy Clb Treas 88-; Stdnt Athletic Trainer 90-; IMS Vlybl Sftbl Flag FB Capt 88-; Physical Hlth Educ; Athletic Trng.

**ROBINSON, TODD A,** Anne Arundel Comm Coll, Arnold, MD; SO; BS; Bsns/Publ Admn; Mgmt.

**ROBINSON, TODD T,** Va St Univ, Petersburg, VA; JR; BA; Stdnt Advsry Cncl 90-; Bg Brthr Bg Sstr Org 90-; NJ Pre Almn 88-; Phi Beta Lambda Pres 89-; Bus; Wrd Prcssng Info Systms.

**ROBINSON, TOM E,** S U N Y Coll At Oneonta, Oneonta, NY; FR; BS; IM Sftbl; Bsn Ecnmcs; Acctng/Finance.

**ROBINSON, TRACEY M,** Fayetteville St Univ, Fayetteville, NC; SR; BED; Alpha Kappa Sor Tr 88-90; Yng Dems 86-90; Res Hall Res Asst 87-88; Chancllrs Lst 88-90; Stdnt Acad Adv Brd 86-88; Alpha Kappa Alpha 88-; Stdnt Tchg 90; NEA Natl Educ Assn 87-90; Bnd Anncr Chrldr Mgr 87-88; Elem Educ; Tch.

**ROBINSON, TROPHIA D,** Alcorn St Univ, Lorman, MS; SO; Hnr Soc 89-; Biol Educ/ Instrctr.

**ROBINSON, VERNISHIA C,** Tuskegee Univ, Tuskegee Inst, AL; SO; BS; Biol Chmstry Clb 90-; Gspl Chr 90-; Drma Clb 89-90; Howard Hughts Med Inst Schlrshp; Howard Univ Grad Schl Intern 90; Biol; Med.

**ROBINSON, VICKI R,** Univ Of Southern Ms, Hattiesburg, MS; JR; Theapeutic Recreation.

**ROBINSON, VIRGINIA L,** Livingston Univ, Livingston, AL; JR; BS; Cardinal Key Sec; Lynville Meth Church 87-; AAS E MS Cmnty Clg 90; Engl Ed; Tchg.

**ROBINSON, VIVIAN L,** Benedict Coll, Columbia, SC; SR; Crmnl Jstc Clb 89; NAACP 88; Army ROTC Bst Sqd 89; Dept Yth Serv Intrnshp 90; Crmnl Jstc.

**ROBINSON, WANDA D,** Jackson St Univ, Jackson, MS; SO; BS; Natl Assoc Advncmnt Clrd Pl 89-; Alpha Lambda Delta 89-; Pi Lambda Theta; Ed; Tchr.

**ROBINSON, WHITLEY H,** Univ Of Miami, Coral Gables, FL; SR; BARCH; Amer Inst Arch Stdnts 90-; Amer Soc Interiro Dsgn Stdnts 88-89; Phi Kappa Phi; Fairchild Trpcl Grdn 83; Lcnsd Interior Dsgnr 89-; BS FL State U 89; Arch/Int Dsgn.

**ROBINSON, WILMA J,** Meridian Comm Coll, Meridian, MS; GD; BA; PBL 89-90; Deans Lst 89-90.

**ROBINSON, YOLANDA L,** Coppin St Coll, Baltimore, MD; JR; BA; Crmnl Justice Club 88-; Intern M D Div Of Parole & Prbtn; Crmnl Justice/Psych; Crmnlgst.

**ROBINSON, ZELPHIA V,** Alcorn St Univ, Lorman, MS; SR; SNEA 89-; Elem Educ.

**ROBINSON-GATO, SUSAN L,** Bergen Comm Coll, Paramus, NJ; GD; AAS; Natl Org Wmn 68-; Parent/Tchr Guid Cncl 90-; Day Care Comm Englewood Hosp 90-; Phi Theta Kappa; Horticulture Clb 90-; Mission Dev Comm Good Shepherd Churdh 89-; VFW Ladies Aux; Girl Scouts Cookie Mgr; High Schlstc Avg Awd; Ornmntl Hortcltr Awd; Sci; Nrsg/Hortcltr/Politics.

**ROBISCH, RICK T,** Univ Of Cincinnati, Cincinnati, OH; JR; BA; Welsh Schlrshp; Whiting Schlrshp; Educ/Socl Stds; Tchr/Politician.

**ROBISON, DEAN E,** United States Naval Academy, Annapolis, MD; SR; Brigade Offcr 5 Strps; Semper Fi 88-; Tau Beta Pi 89-; Spcl Olympc 87-; Lghtwght Crew 87-88; BS; Sys Eng; USMC Offcr.

**ROBISON, DIANNE L,** Allegheny Coll, Meadville, PA; JR; BA; SAS 89-; ANTS 89-; Alden Schlr 89-90; SHAL 82-; Art & Womens Studies.

**ROBISON, JENNIFER G,** S U N Y Coll At Fredonia, Fredonia, NY; JR; BMED; Music Educrs Natl Cnfrnce 88-; Piano Clb Sec 89-; Amer Chrl Dir Assn Pres 90-; Hon Smnr 88-90; Pi Kappa Lambda; M/A Davis Acmpnst Schlrshp 89-90; Fredonia Acdmc Schlrshp 89-90; Rgnts Schlrshp 88-; Music Educ Schlrshp 88; Music Educ.

**ROBISON, JENNIFER H,** Univ Of Sc At Columbia, Columbia, SC; SO; Kappa Delta Sec 89-90; Phys Thrpst.

**ROBISON, MITZI V,** Memphis St Univ, Memphis, TN; SR; BPS; Phi Gamma Nu M2-73; Amer Scty Of Cncl Pthlgsts 77; W Tenn Scty For Med Tchnlgsts 86; Hardin Cnty Hosp Savannah Tn; AS Copiah-Lincoln Jr Clg Wesson Ms 77; Hlth Care Admin.

**ROBISON, REED R,** Western Carolina Univ, Cullowhee, NC; SO; BS; Stdnt Marshalls; Alpha Lambda Delta 90-; Soph Computer Science Awd; Computer Science.

**ROBISON, SHERRY E,** Univ Of Sc At Spartanburg, Spartanburg, SC; SO; BS; Bsktbl Chrldr 89-90; Bus Admin; Acctg.

**ROBITTAILE, LUCIE,** Fl International Univ, Miami, FL; SR; BA; Pi Theta Epsilon 90-; BA Physcl Edctn 84; Hlth; Occptnl Thrpy.

**ROBKE, GINNY L,** Northern Ky Univ, Highland Hts, KY; SR; La Link Treas 89; Sigma Tau Delta; Alpha Chi; Kappa Delta Pi; Wrtng Ctr Engl Tutor 90; Stdnt Support Servs Spnsh Tutor 88-; Frgn Lang Cert Merit 90; Frgn Lang Spcl Achvmnt Awd; Alumni Fmly Schlrshp; Engl/Scndry Ed; Tchr Engl/Spnsh.

**ROBLEDO, JESUS H,** Inter Amer Univ Pr Hato Rey, Hato Rey, PR; SR; BA; DPMA; Sr Progrmr Anlyst; Bus Admn; MBA.

**ROBLES RAYA, BRENDA M,** Inter Amer Univ Pr Hato Rey, Hato Rey, PR; FR; Soc Sci; Soc Wrkr/Law.

**ROBLES RIVERA, DORY JEAN,** Inter Amer Univ Pr San Juan, Hato Rey, PR; GD; Puerto Rico Bar Assn 90; Pol Sci Assn Jr Rep 85-87; Genl Bar Exam 89-90; Notary Publ Exam Stdnt Schlrshp 83; Smng Tm Sports Schlrshp 84-87; LLM LLB.

**ROBLES RIVERA, MADELINE,** Inter Amer Univ Pr Guayama, Guayama, PR; SR; BACH; Nurses Prof Clg; Nurses Laboral Union; Comrcl Amer Lique Fed 79-81; Lion Frat Clb 87-89; Religios Orientation At Catholic Church; Guayama Area Hosp Fld Day 86-; Class Pres; Assoc Degree Nursing 83; Dact Ofcr 81; Nursing.

**ROBLES JR, DAVID A,** Western New England Coll, Springfield, MA; SO; BA; Mrktng Assn Tres; Alpha Lambda Delta 90-; Lambda Delta 89-90; Karate 89-90; Finance; Law Schl.

**ROBLES, HILDA E,** Evangelical Semimary Of P R, Hato Rey, PR; GD; MDIV; BS Gnrl Prgrm Unvrsty PR 87; Theology; Mnstry.

**ROBLES, JOHN A,** Univ Politecnica De Pr, Hato Rey, PR; FR; Beta Theta Phi 87; Computers Mechanics; Engineering.

**ROBRECHT, MARY E,** Salisbury St Univ, Salisbury, MD; JR; BA; Psi Chi 91-; Sec; Psychology; Cnslr.

**ROBRECHT, THERESA C,** Salisbury St Univ, Salisbury, MD; SR; BS; IM Sports; Phi Eta Sigma 87-; Delta Mu Delta; Intrnshp Law Office; Bus Admin; Law.

**ROBSON, CHAD E,** Nc St Univ At Raleigh, Raleigh, NC; FR; BS; Ftbl; Bio Chem.

**ROBSON, JAMIE L,** Univ Of Al At Birmingham, Birmingham, AL; JR; BS; Soc Wmn Engr; Amer Soc Mech Engr; Amer Soc Prof Engrs; Tau Beta Pi; Gldn Key; Habitats Hmnty; Mech Engr Fml Stu Yr 90-; Mech Engr.

**ROBUSTO, GERALD R,** Kent St Univ Geauga Cmps, Burton Twp, OH; Fin Exec Inst 76-; Beta Gamma Sigma; Grtr Clvldn Grwth Assoc 85-89; BSC Ohio Univ 62; MBA 63; Finance; Cnsltng/Tchng/Bus.

**ROBY, DEBORAH J,** Univ Of Ky, Lexington, KY; SO; BA; Crs Cntry/Trch Mgr 89-90; Natl Guard 90-; Agri; Landscape Architecture.

**ROBY, HEATHER R,** Owensboro Comm Coll, Owensboro, KY; FR; AD; Nrsng.

**ROBY, ROBERT J,** Oh Univ, Athens, OH; SO; BSME; Mrchng Bnd/Vrsty Bnd 89-; Gldn Key 90-; Tau Beta Pi 90-; Alpha Lambda Delta 89-; Theta Tau Crspndng Sec 90-; Trsts Schlrshp 89-90; Dns Schlrshp 90-; IM Ftbl; Mech Engrg; Law Schl/Ptnt Law.

**ROCA, AMPARO,** Miami Dade Comm Coll South, Miami, FL; JR; BA; Psy Chi; Vol Chldrns Hm Soc; Certf Adhvmnt Coll Brds Clg Schlrshp Srvc Tlnt Rstr; AA 90; Psychology; Erly Chldhd Psychology.

**ROCCAPRIORE, MARIE C,** Albertus Magnus Coll, New Haven, CT; SO; BA; Italian Clb Treas 89-; Sftbl 89-; Bus; Law.

**ROCCO, DEAN A,** Kent St Univ Kent Cmps, Kent, OH; JR; BA; Stdnt Data Proc Assoc 90-; Natl Hnr Soc 90-; Phi Kappa Tau 87-88; Deans List 87-91; Pres List 90-; Kent St Ex Trnshp 90-; Cmptr Sci; Law Schl.

**ROCH, DENISE L,** Dowling Coll, Oakdale Li, NY; SR; BA; Bible Enrchmnt Clb Pres 89-90; Elem Educ.

**ROCHA, ANDREW G,** Univ Of Rochester, Rochester, NY; SR; BSME; Pep Bnd Pres 87-; Chmbr Sngrs Tour Mgr 87-; ICF 89-; Tau Beta Pi 89-; Phi Beta Kappa; Amer Soc Mech Eng Treas 88-91; Soc Hispanic Prof Eng 88-91; Mobil Schlr 89-91; Bausch/Laumb Schlr 87-; Mech Eng; Aero Eng.

**ROCHAT, LAURELLA C,** Pellissippi St Tech Comm Coll, Knoxville, TN; FR; AAS; Phi Theta Kappa; Bus; Logistics/Transp.

**ROCHE, ANTHONY T,** Adelphi Univ, Garden City, NY; JR; BS; AA SUNY Frmngdl 90; Elem Ed; Elem Tchr.

**ROCHE, DANIEL E,** Oh Dominican Coll, Columbus, OH; SO; BA; Clge Cncl Repr Lrg 90-; Pre Law Scty; Air Frc Achvmnt Mdl; U S Air Force Vet; Ohio Air Natl Grd 86-89/89-; Eng; Grdt Schl Pltcl Sci.

**ROCHESTER, JODI L,** Tri County Tech Coll, Pendleton, SC; FR; AB; Govt 90; Alpha Beta Zeta 90-; Sec Sci.

**ROCHESTER, JULIAN A,** Spartanburg Methodist Coll, Spartanburg, SC; FR; AS; Coll Chrstn Mvmnt VP 90-; Bapt Stdnt Union 90-; Cmptrs; Systs Analyst.

**ROCHFORD, SHARON M,** City Univ Of Ny Queensbrough, New York, NY; SO; AAS; Foreign Stdnt Assoc Rep; Cmptr Pgm Clb 90-; 25 Plus Clb; Alpha Beta Gamma; Phi Theta Gamma V P; Cmptr Pgm; Cmptr Syst Analyst/Pgmr.

**ROCHON, PAULA CHRISTINE,** Marywood Coll, Scranton, PA; SO; BA; Schl Nwspr Ftr Wrtr 90-; &RSSA 90-; AAF 90-; Deans Lst 1st Hon 90-; Pro Prctcm Halcyon Assoc; Pblc Rltns Pblc Affrs Mktg Grphc Dsgn PR Intrn; Archtctrl Hrtg Assn PR Intrn; Ski Clb PA State 90-; Cllgrphrs Gld NE PA 90-; PR/ADVRTSNG; Pblc Rltns/Jrnlsm.

**ROCHON, SHELLY L,** Northeastern Christian Jr Coll, Villanova, PA; SO; Alph Chi Omega Pres 89-; RA; Pres List; Deans List; Sccr Kpr 90; Sec Exprnc 85-89; Psychlgy; Chld Psychlgy Ph D.**

**ROCK, CHRISTINA M,** Coll Of Charleston, Charleston, SC; SR; BS; Student Gvt 85-86; Biology Club Pres 84-87; Clg Activities Brd 84-87; Psi Chi 90-; Alpha Phi Omega VP 84-; Peer Mentor Assoc Treas 85-87; Intshp Social Reltns 87-88; Alpha Phi Omega Sectional Distghd Serv Key; Psychology/Biology; Indstl Psy.

**ROCK, DARLENE K,** Fl A & M Univ, Tallahassee, FL; FR; MBA; Prsdntl Schlrs Assn Mmbr 90-; Schl Bsns Indstry Srvc Inc Elite Tr Gd 90-; Schl Bsns Indstry Hmn Rsrcs Inc Asst Trnr 90-; Phi Eta Sigma 90-; Prsdntl Schlr Assn 90-; Otstndng Srvc Awd SBI Srvcs Inc 90-; Deans Lst 90-; Bsns Admnstrtn; Corp Bsns.

**ROCK, DOUGLAS J,** Schenectady County Comm Coll, Schenectady, NY; FR; BA; Drama Clb Schl Nwspr Rprtr 90-; Pro Sngr Wrtr Music; Rcrdng Artst Real Estate Agnt Crpntr Busnssmn; NYS Rltrs Licnc 87; Engl Hstry Scl Sci; Cmnctns.

**ROCK, JAMIE A,** Daytona Beach Comm Coll, Daytona Beach, Fl; SR; BA; Mtn Pctr Tech; Film Prod.

**ROCK, MATTHEW THOMAS,** Hudson Valley Comm Coll, Troy, NY; FR; BA; Pres Lst 90; Waiter; Wrehse Man; Math; Law JD.

**ROCKEL, DONNA M,** Liberty Univ, Lynchburg, VA; SO; BS; Yth Quest Clb 89-90; Psych Clb 90-; Psi Chi; Prvntn Ctr Child Abuse 90-; Psych; Psychotherapist.

**ROCKETT, JOHNNIE M,** Alcorn St Univ, Lorman, MS; JR; Alpha Kappa Mu Hon Stdnts Org 90-; Engl/Cmnctns.

**ROCKETT, KAREN S,** Western Piedmont Comm Coll, Morganton, NC; SO; Paralegal.

**ROCKHILL, SALLY A,** Kent St Univ Kent Cmps, Kent, OH; SR; BA; Psi Chi; Abuse Shltr Vol 91; Vol Awd Plnnd Prnthd 89-90; Psychlgy; Cnslng/Hmn Srvcs.

**ROCKMAN, LINDA D,** S U N Y Coll At Fredonia, Fredonia, NY; SO; BED; Delta Phi Epsilon Pldg Mom; Elem Ed; Tchr.

**ROCKMAN, SUSAN K,** Univ Of Cincinnati, Cincinnati, OH; JR; BSN; IM Rep 90-; Alpha Beta Chi 90-; Kappa Kappa Gamma Hse Chrmn 88-; Chrldngn 3rd Natl; Nrsng; MS/MED Schl.

**ROCKMORE, ELIZABETH J,** Univ Of Ga, Athens, GA; SR; BS; Deans List 89-90; Interior Design Intrnshp The Plan Room; Clge Of Fmly & Cnsmr Sci; Interior Design.

**ROCKOFF, FRANCYN,** Yeshiva Univ, New York, NY; GD; MA; Spch Lang Path/Adlgy Clb Pres 89-90; Ntl Stdnt Spch Lang/Hrng Assn 89-90; Deans Lst 88-90; Rusk Inst Intrnshp 89; Svc Spch Dept Awd 90; BA 90; Spch Lang Path.

**ROCKWELL, CHRISTINA L,** Univ Of Tn At Martin, Martin, TN; SO; BS; Jrnlsm.

**ROCKWELL, DAVID M,** Western New England Coll, Springfield, MA; SR; BSME; Amer Soc Mech Eng Tr 89-; Dns Adv Comm 89-; Sigma Beta Tau 90-; Intl Gas Turbine Inst Schlrshp 90-; Alum Schlrshp 90-; Dns Lst 90-; AS Mohawk Vly Comm Clg 89; Mech Eng.

**ROCKWELL, HOLLY JUNE,** Bunker Hill Comm Coll, Boston, MA; SO; AS; The 3rd Rail Paste Up/Lay Out 89-; Cls Rep Rdgrphy Prog Stdnts 90-; Alpha Kappa Mu; Hnrs Prog 90-; Stdnt Success Proj Tutor Engl; Vol 1990 US Census On Cmps 90; Vol Engl Tutor Adlt Lrng Cntr 89-90; EMT 80; Rdgrpy; Ultrasound/Mgntc Rsnc Imgng.

**ROCKWELL, KEVIN J,** Pa St Univ Delaware Cty Cmps, Media, PA; SO; BA; Stdnt Actvts Cncl 90; Nwspr Staff Rprtr 90-; Peer Tutoring Math Tutor 90-; Bus Admnstrtn; Law.

**ROCKWELL, MICHELLE D,** Univ Of Tn At Martin, Martin, TN; SO; BS; Vetrnrn.

**ROCKWELL, MOLLY L,** Ms St Univ, Miss State, MS; JR; BED; Mdrgl Sngrs 90-; MS Magic 89-; Choir 88-; PALS; Elem Ed; Music Therpy.

**RODA, ANA I,** Endicott Coll, Beverly, MA; FR; BA; Intl Clb 90-; Peer Tutrng; Stdnt Orientn Ldr; Phi Theta Kappa; Engl Hon Prog; Intrnshp W/Tmlss Intrior; Intrior Dsgn.

**RODA, CHERYL J,** Columbia Union Coll, Takoma Park, MD; SR; BA; Stdnt Assoc Pres 89-90; Adventist Intercoll Assoc Pres 90-; Campus Mnstrs Dir 90-; Alpha Chi 90-; Pro Musica 88-; Bio Lab Tchr 90-; Med.

**RODA, DOMINICK,** Clarkson Univ, Potsdam, NY; SO; BA; Econ; Law.

**RODAK, JOY L,** Nova Univ, Ft Lauderdale, FL; GD; MBA; Rtry Intl; Fund Raising Cmts Broward Co Alzheimers Assoc; Graduated Hnrs Summa Cum Laude 89; Amer Hosp Assc Scty Hlth Cr; Plng/Mrktng; Svrl Chmbrs Cmmrc; Mgr; Physcian; Sprt Ser; Hlth Cr Mrktng; BS 89; Bus; Hosp Marketing/Development.

**RODDEN, JULIE M,** Winthrop Coll, Rock Hill, SC; SR; BS; Phi Gamma Nu VP 88-89; Kappa Alpha 88; Fndrs Schlrshp 87-89; Bus Admn; Hmn Rsrcs Mngmnt.

**RODDEY, TERRY MC GUIRE,** Winthrop Coll, Rock Hill, SC; JR; Kappa Delta Pi 91; Elem Educ; Tchg.

**RODDY, TERRI L,** Ga St Univ, Atlanta, GA; GD; Grad Magna Cum Laude 90; Initial Tchr Prep Awd 89-90; Dns Schlrshp Key 89-90; Cmptr/Acctng Rel Fnctns Sev Employers 80-90; BSED 90; Math; Scndry Lvl Tchr.

**RODE, LAURA I,** Defiance Coll, Defiance, OH; SR; BA; Acctg Clb 87; Accntnt 88-90; AAD Intl Bus Coll Ft Wayne IN 86-87; Bus Mgt/Acctg.**

**RODE, LAURA I,** Defiance Coll, Defiance, OH; SR; BA; Tau Pi Phi; Bus/Acctg/Mgmnt; Bus Exec.

**RODEBAUGH, WILLIAM A,** Bapt Bible Coll & Seminary, Clarks Summit, PA; GD; MBA; Symphnc Band 1st Chr 88-89; Symphnc Band; Pep Band; Youth Pastr 89-90; Tchr Grace Baptst Church 87-89; Temple Baptst Churc Tchr 90-; Geo W Lawlor Greek Award 88-89; Hghst Grd Point Avrg In Greek; BA Cedrvl Clg 89; Bible; Minstry/Pastrt.

**RODERICK, STACEY A,** Norfolk St Univ, Norfolk, VA; JR; BS; NAACP 88; Alpha Swthrt Crt Sec 89 Pres 90; Poltcl Sci; Law.

**RODES, WILMA,** Beckley Coll, Beckley, WV; SO; PTA 75-87; Natl Prk Tsk Frce Mbr 88-89; Hrdrssr 71-; Rl Est Sls 89-; Soc Wrk/Sec Educ.

**RODGERS, BETH A,** Univ Of Tn At Martin, Martin, TN; JR; BA; Sigma Tau Delta 90-; Englsh; Tchng.

**RODGERS, CAROL A,** Christopher Newport Coll, Newport News, VA; SO; BA; Econ; UN IMF/FRGN Serv.

**RODGERS, CHARLES A,** Univ Of Miami, Coral Gables, FL; SO; Sigma Alpha Epsilon.

**RODGERS, DEBORAH J,** Indiana Univ Of Pa, Indiana, PA; SR; Alpha Xi Delta Treas 86-90.

**RODGERS, DENINA C,** Univ Of Southern Ms, Hattiesburg, MS; FR; BM; Stdnt Eagle Club; Music Indus Stdnts Assn; Music Indus; Perf/Prdcng.

**RODGERS, JAMES A,** Univ Of Sc At Columbia, Columbia, SC; FR; BA; Navy ROTC 90-; Blue/Gold 90-; Drill Tm 90-; Reserv Ofcr Assoc Awd; Intl Studies; Nvl Ofcr.

**RODGERS, JOHN B,** Univ Of Med & Dentistry Of Nj, Newark, NJ; GD; TRIO; AARC; Zeta Beta Tau-Glassboro St Coll; Purtn Bennett Stdnt Excell Awd; UMDNJ Awd Cncl Excell; Rsprtry Care; Eng/Tch.

**RODGERS, LESLIE J,** Rivier Coll, Nashua, NH; JR; BA; Berlin Clge Sftbl State Chmps 80; Kitchen Mgr 87-90; Fish Mrkt; Clnry Arts 81-; AS NH Tech Inst Berlin 81; Elem Ed Spec; Tch.

**RODGERS, LYNDON F,** Fl A & M Univ, Tallahassee, FL; SR; BS; Pltcl Scie Clb VP 89-; Hatchett Pre Law Clb 88-; SGA Sen 87-; Phi Theta Kappa 84-; Alpha Kappa Mlt 88-; All Amer Schrs 90-; Stdt Actvts Cmt 87-; Cmty Clg Schrlshp 88; AA Plm Bch Cmty Clb 88; Political Scie; Law Schl/Wrk IRS.**

**RODGERS, STACY L,** Glassboro St Coll, Glassboro, NJ; JR; BA; Kappa Delta Pi; Sigma Sigma Sigma Exc Brd Ed Dir; 2 Articles Published In Book Wright Like This; Elem Ed/Communictions; Education.

**RODGERS, TASHA MICHELLE,** Va St Univ, Petersburg, VA; SO; BS; Acctg Clb VP 89-; Trck Tm 90; Natl Assoc Blk Acctnts 89-; Spec Serv Awd Pres Asst 89-90; Ldrshp Awd VP 90-; Acctg; CPA.

**RODICIO, SERGIO,** Fl International Univ, Miami, FL; JR; BA; AA Miami Dade Comm Clg S Campus 90; Acctg.

**RODIL, CARLA M,** Georgetown Univ, Washington, DC; JR; BA; Intl Rltns Clb 90-91; Bus Admin; Intl Fncr.

**RODIO, GINA M,** Atlantic Comm Coll, Mays Landing, NJ; SO; AS; Spec Educ; Educ.

**RODMAN, CINDY B,** Rutgers St Univ At Camden, Camden, NJ; SR; BS; Dns Lst 90-; Bsn Mgmt.

**RODMAN, SHANNON G,** Ms St Univ, Miss State, MS; FR; Hll Cncl Bptst Stdnt Un; Alpha Lambda Delta; Gamma Beta Phi; Phi Eta Sigma; Zeta Tau Alpha Music Chrmn 90-; Grk Cncl Chrst; IMS; Acctg; Tax Law.

**RODOCKER, MELISSA G,** Radford Univ, Radford, VA; FR; Bus Fin; Law.

**RODRIGO, DANIEL,** Castleton St Coll, Castleton, VT; SR; BA; Stage Left Thtre Grp Co-Fndr Co-Fcltatr 89-; Alpha Psi Omega Co-Fndr Bus Mgr 90-; Acas Achiev Awd 89; Pres Schlrshp 89; Thtre 88-; BA; Thtre/Actr.

**RODRIGUEZ AYALA, ANA BEATRIZ,** Univ Politecnica De Pr, Hato Rey, PR; FR; Soc De Jovns; Igls Dispbs De Crsto Srra Baymn; Cvl Engnrng.

**RODRIGUEZ BAEZ, YVONNE,** Inter Amer Univ Pr San German, San German, PR; SR; BA; Beta Beta Beta; Bio/Med Tchnlgy.

**RODRIGUEZ BORGES, DAMARIS,** Univ Of Pr Cayey Univ Coll, Cayey, PR; SO; Cuadro De Honor De La Rectora 90-.

**RODRIGUEZ CABALLERO, CARMEN I,** Univ Politecnica De Pr, Hato Rey, PR; JR; BA; Alpha Kappa Omicron Mayaguez Campus 88; Apolo Angel Lght Mayaguez Camps Lt 88; Microbio Sci Fair 87; Ind Eng.

**RODRIGUEZ CARMONA, OSCAR,** Univ Politecnica De Pr, Hato Rey, PR; FR; Eng.

**RODRIGUEZ CARRASQUILLO, ALICIA,** Univ Del Turabo, Gurabo, PR; SR; BA; Damas Perpetuo Socorro 75-; Mgt BA Sec; Mgt; MBA Mrktng.

**RODRIGUEZ COLON, MARICARMEN,** Inter Amer Univ Pr Hato Rey, Hato Rey, PR; FR; Acctng; CPA.

**RODRIGUEZ DIAZ, MILAGROS,** Inter Amer Univ Pr San Juan, Hato Rey, PR; JR; Sume Cum Laude; BA.

**RODRIGUEZ IRIZARRY, RAQUEL,** Inter Amer Univ Pr Aquadilla, Aguadilla, PR; FR; Girl Scouts Amer Cadet 87-89; Spec Ed; Tchr.

**RODRIGUEZ JIMENEZ, KAREN J,** Inter Amer Univ Pr San German, San German, PR; JR; BBA; Hnrs Pgm 88-; Mvmnt Jn 89-; SADD 89-; Beca El Quijote; Cmptr Systms Info; Engrg.

**RODRIGUEZ LAZU, ISMAEL,** Bayamon Tech Univ Coll, Bayamon, PR; SR; MBA; Hnr Soc 86-90; Dean Hnr Awd; CPA.

**RODRIGUEZ LOPEZ, NITZA E,** Univ Of Pr At Rio Piedras, Rio Piedras, PR; SR; MBA; Sociedad De Jouenes Universitarios De La Iglesia Presbiteriana Unida De Bayamon 89-; Peograma De Estudeos De Honor De La Universidad De Puerto Rico 88-91; Soc Sci; MBA Soc Worker/Law.

**RODRIGUEZ MATOS, MARIA DEL C,** Bayamon Central Univ, Bayamon, PR; SR; MBA; Psychlgy Stdnts Assoc; Arprt Cmptr Panamerican Schl Trvl NY Cty 83; Indstrl Psychlgst; Prsnl Admin.

**RODRIGUEZ OCASIO, RUBEN,** Inter Amer Univ Pr Hato Rey, Hato Rey, PR; FR; Oficina Gob Asuntos Juventud; Categvista Iglesia Catolica 90-; Eagle Scout 90; Natl Eagle Assn 90-; Order Of The Arrow 88-.

**RODRIGUEZ PEREZ, FRANCISCO J,** Univ Politecnica De Pr, Hato Rey, PR; JR; Engr.

**RODRIGUEZ PEREZ, JANNETTE,** Univ Of Pr Cayey Univ Coll, Cayey, PR; JR; Hnr Std; Spnsh/Std Behav; PHD Sp Ed.

**RODRIGUEZ PEREZ, NANCY,** Univ Of Pr Medical Sciences, San Juan, PR; FR; MSN; CPPR; BSN 86; Nrsg Admin; Sprvsr.

**RODRIGUEZ RAMOS, HERMES,** Univ Politecnica De Pr, Hato Rey, PR; FR.

**RODRIGUEZ RIOS, OLGA I,** Inter Amer Univ Pr Barranquita, Barranquitas, PR; FR; BA; Hon Cert 89-; Admin Comrcl.

**RODRIGUEZ ROBLES, YOLANDA,** Univ Of Pr At Mayaguez, Mayaguez, PR; JR; Elec Engrg.

**RODRIGUEZ RODRIGUEZ, PEDRO J,** Inter Amer Univ Pr San German, San German, PR; FR; Boy Scts Amer 88; Intl Sci/Eng Fair Fnlst 89; US Army Mdlln Sco/Eng Fairs 88; US Navy Sci Awds 89; US Marines Crps Sci Awds 89; Eng; Cvl Eng.

**RODRIGUEZ ROSA, GLADYS A,** Inter Amer Univ Pr Arecibo Un, Arecibo, PR; SR; BA; Assoc Crmnl Jstce Pres 88-; Hon Prog Intramrcn Univ Mbr 90; Awd Nght Of Entramercn; Crmnl Jstce; Law.

**RODRIGUEZ ROSADO, MABEL,** Univ Of Pr At Mayaguez, Mayaguez, PR; SR; BIE; NSPE 90-; Tau Beta Pi Ctlgr; Inds Eng.

**RODRIGUEZ VAZQUEZ, JUAN F,** Inter Amer Univ Pr Hato Rey, Hato Rey, PR; GD; BA; Tennis; Sci; Bus Admin.

**RODRIGUEZ, AIDA L,** Univ Of Pr Humacao Univ Coll, Humacao, PR; JR; BA; Chem.

**RODRIGUEZ, ALBA N,** Bayamon Central Univ, Bayamon, PR; BA; Soc Wrk.

**RODRIGUEZ, ALBERT I,** Univ Of Miami, Coral Gables, FL; SO; BA; Wrked In Various Archtcts Offcs 87-; Architct.

**RODRIGUEZ, ALEJANDRO A,** Broward Comm Coll, Ft Lauderdale, FL; FR; Phi Theta Kappa; Math; Elec Engr.

**RODRIGUEZ, ALEJANDRO M,** Fl International Univ, Miami, FL; SO; BA; Acad Schlrs Prog Schlrshp; Fclty Schlrs Awd; Cmptr Eng.

**RODRIGUEZ, ALINA B,** Fl International Univ, Miami, FL; GD; MFA; Flrda Art Edctn Assoc 90-; Phi Theta Kappa 86; Artfcts Grp Exhbtn 84-89; Msrt Glry Trbt To Wrhl; Mdwln Elmntry Intrn 90; Art Ed Assoc Ntnl Cngrs 90-; Fn Arts Edctn; Prfsr.

**RODRIGUEZ, AMARDO JOSEPH,** Univ Of The Dist Of Columbia, Washington, DC; GD; Caribbean Stdnts Assoc; BA 90; Mass Media; Academia.

**RODRIGUEZ, ANA M,** Univ Of Miami, Coral Gables, FL; JR; BS; Latin Amer Stu Assoc 89-90; Assoc Cmptr Mchnry 90-; Pro Cncl 89-90; Peer Cnslr 90-; Cmptr Sci; Prog.

**RODRIGUEZ, ANELYS,** Endicott Coll, Beverly, MA; JR; BS; Shipmates Clb 88-; RA 89-; Radio Intrnshp 88-89; TV Intrnshp 89-90; AS 90; Communications; News Anchor.

**RODRIGUEZ, ANGELA M,** Barry Univ, Miami, FL; SO; BA; D Phi E 89-; Biomed Sci; Cyrotechnology.**

**RODRIGUEZ, ANNA L,** Univ Of Miami, Coral Gables, FL; FR; BA; Key Clb Pres 88-90; Cir K Intl Dist Edtr Fl; Nlt Frnscs League Debate Tm HS Var Capt 89-90; Hnr Stu Assoc 90-; Ntl Hnr Soc VP 89-90; Sci Hnr Soc Hstrn 89-90; Sthrn Bell Comm Serv Awrd 89; Pol; Law.

**RODRIGUEZ, ANTONIO L,** Catholic Univ Of Pr, Ponce, PR; SR; Acctg Stdnts Assoc; Natl Bus Hon Soc; Natl Coll Bus Merit Awds; Acctg.

**RODRIGUEZ, ANYELINE VARONA,** Antillian Adventist University, Mayaguez, PR; JR; BA; Campus Mnstrs Pres 87-88; Elem Ed/Hist/Music Ed.

**RODRIGUEZ, ARELYS E,** Univ Of Miami, Coral Gables, FL; FR; Frnch Clb; Coral Gables Yth Ctr Vol; St Brendas Catholic Church Vol; Vlybl; Soccer; Tennis; Pol Sci; Law.

**RODRIGUEZ, AXEL L,** Bayamon Central Univ, Bayamon, PR; FR; Power Lifting 90-; Pstrl Universitaria 90-.

**RODRIGUEZ, BARBARA,** Miami Dade Comm Coll North, Miami, FL; SO; AA; Collector; Philsphy; Law.

**RODRIGUEZ, BEATRIZ RODRIGUEZ,** Caribbean Univ, Bayamon, PR; SR; BA; Pre Med Clb 87-88; AS CUTB Univ PR 88; Ntrl Sci; Vet.

**RODRIGUEZ, CARLOS,** Univ Of Pr At Rio Piedras, Rio Piedras, PR; JR; BA; Hnr Stu; Fllwshp Chinese Natl Taiwan Normal Univ 90-; For Lang; MA Trnlstn.

**RODRIGUEZ, CARMEN H,** Univ Of Pr At Rio Piedras, Rio Piedras, PR; GD; B Arch 90; Arch.

**RODRIGUEZ, CARMEN IVELISSE,** City Univ Of Ny City Coll, New York, NY; JR; BED; Golden Key 90; Ele/Bilngual Educ; Educ Tchr.

**RODRIGUEZ, CAROLYN M,** Fayetteville St Univ, Fayetteville, NC; SO; BS; Phi Sigma Iota 83-; BA Blmsbrg Univ Of Penn 83; Comp Sci; Comp Prgrmmng.

**RODRIGUEZ, CYNTHIA D,** Univ Of Miami, Coral Gables, FL; SR; BSN; Stdnt Nurses Assn Pres 89-; Air Force Reserve Officer Trng Corps 88-; Omicron Delta Kappa; Sigma Theta Tau; Phi Kappa Phi; IM Soccer; Outstanding Nrsng Stdnt Awd; Nrsng; Air Force.

**RODRIGUEZ, DAN F,** Univ Of Pr At Mayaguez, Mayaguez, PR; JR; IEEE 89-; Sci; Elec Engr.

**RODRIGUEZ, DANIEL,** Cumberland County Coll, Vineland, NJ; FR; BED; Clg Music Clb Founder; Latin American Clb 90; Yth Fedrtn SDA Cnslr 89-; Mailman 88-89; Music/Aviation; Recording Studio/Teach Avtn.

**RODRIGUEZ, DAVID,** Univ Of Miami, Coral Gables, FL; SO; BS; Orntntn Asst; Trnsfr Advsr Buddy; Scuba Clb; Marine Sci Hon Scty; Marine Sci/Bio; Marine Biolgst.

**RODRIGUEZ, DAVID,** Inter Amer Univ Pr San Juan, Hato Rey, PR; GD; Law Review Assoc Dir 90-; Professor Assistantship 89-90; Co Prod Talk Show 90-; BA Political Sci 87.

**RODRIGUEZ, DELMALIZ NEGRON,** Catholic Univ Of Pr, Ponce, PR; SR; BA; Hstry Clb 88-89; Dean Lst 88-; Hstry; Archlgy.**

**RODRIGUEZ, DEYRA MARIE,** Univ Of Pr At Rio Piedras, Rio Piedras, PR; JR; BS; APM 88-; Amer Chem Scty 90-; Golden Key; Candy Stripe Hpst Auxilio Mutuo 86-88; Deans List 89-; Pred Flwshp Minorities Ford Found 90-; Biology; Med.

**RODRIGUEZ, DORIS I,** Inter Amer Univ Pr Hato Rey, Hato Rey, PR; FR; Accnt; Finance Mngmnt.

**RODRIGUEZ, EDDIE J,** Strayer Coll, Washington, DC; SO; BA; Girl Scout Cncl Natl Cptl Svc Unit Mgr 90; Air Force Mbr; Cmptr Infor Sys; Sys Analysis.

**RODRIGUEZ, ERIC S,** Bowling Green St Univ, Bowling Green, OH; SO; Stdnt Cnstrctn Mngmnt Assoc 90-; Ntnl Assoc Hme Bldrs 90-; Co-Op Cottys Cnstrctn Asst Gnrl Cntrctr 90; Co-Op ODOT Dist 7 Prjct Inspctr; Cnstrctn Mngmnt; Cntrctr.

**RODRIGUEZ, ESTHER LIDIA,** Rutgers St Un At New Brunswick, New Brunswick, NJ; SR; BA; Psych; Mrrg/Fmly Ther.**

**RODRIGUEZ, G PATRICIA,** Ny Univ, New York, NY; SO; BS; Math; Engr.

**RODRIGUEZ, GEORGE E,** Univ Of Miami, Coral Gables, FL; SO; Slng Clb 90-; Univ Schlr 89-90; IM Bsktbl 90-; Ecnmcs.

**RODRIGUEZ, GILDA J,** Miami Dade Comm Coll, Miami, FL; SO; BA; Math Tchr In Cuba 79; Came To USA; Math Tchr Since 82 City Of Miami; & Yrs U Of Havana Pedagocic In Physics & Astrnmy 78; Math; Acctng.

**RODRIGUEZ, GRISSELL,** Univ Of Pr At Rio Piedras, Rio Piedras, PR; SR; Law.

**RODRIGUEZ, HERIBERTO,** Univ Politecnica De Pr, Hato Rey, PR; SO; U S Navy Petty Ofcr; Elect Eng.

**RODRIGUEZ, ILEANA M,** Univ Of Pr At Rio Piedras, Rio Piedras, PR; JR; Lector Chrch 86-; Hon Stds Pgm 89-; Cert Acad Exclnc; Hist; Law.

**RODRIGUEZ, INGRID G,** Univ Of Pr Cayey Univ Coll, Cayey, PR; FR; BS; Clb Leo 85-88; Sci; Phrmcy.

**RODRIGUEZ, IVAN,** Saint Thomas Univ, Miami, FL; JR; BA; St Thomas Schlry Achvmnt 90; Mngr BTM Trnng; Rlgs Stds; Theology.

**RODRIGUEZ, IVAN,** Inter Amer Univ Pr Hato Rey, Hato Rey, PR; SR; BBA; Ajedrez Fed 80-; Ajedrezcentro De Caguas 79-; Amer Inst Of Bnkng High Dist Plaque 90; Bsktbl 82; Bnkng; Cert 89/90/; Bus Admin; Law.

**RODRIGUEZ, IVETTE M,** Fl International Univ, Miami, FL; JR; BA; AA 89; Mngmnt; Hsptlty.

**RODRIGUEZ, IVETTE M,** Univ Of Pr Medical Sciences, San Juan, PR; FR; MHS; Sociedad Estdnts Microbiology Indstrl 89-90; Sociedad Mcrblgy 90-; BA UPR Recinto Univ Mayaguez 90; Salud Ambiental.

**RODRIGUEZ, JENNIFER D,** Univ Of Sc At Columbia, Columbia, SC; SO; Gamma Beta Phi 90-; Biology; Medicine.

**RODRIGUEZ, JOEL O,** Univ Politecnica De Pr, Hato Rey, PR; FR; BA; Spanish; Engrng.

**RODRIGUEZ, JORGE L,** Fl International Univ, Miami, FL; SR; BS; Languedoc Rousillon Wine Fstvl 90; Natl Feed Hungry Campaign 90; Deans Lst 89-90; Am Hotel/Motel Schlrshp; Sigma Alpha Mu 87-89; VMS Realty Partners Intrnshp 88; Hospitality Mgmnt.**

**RODRIGUEZ, JOSE A,** Caribbean Univ, Bayamon, PR; JR; BS; APICS 87-; SPC MRPII Proj Tm; Sprvsr Dupont Med Prods; BS Chem Univ Of PR 80; MBA Inter Amer Univ 87; Engr; Grad Work.

**RODRIGUEZ, JOSE A,** Southeastern Coll Of Hlth Sci, N Miami Beach, FL; SR; BS; AA Broward Commnty Clg 88; Pharmacy; Medicine.

**RODRIGUEZ, JOSE A,** Nova Univ, Ft Lauderdale, FL; GD; MBA; S FL Assn Law Lbrn 86-; Sls Rep Lwyrs Coop Pblshng 83-; BA Univ Interamericana 83; Bus Admin; Mktg/Sls Mgmt.

**RODRIGUEZ, JULIA E,** Nova Univ, Ft Lauderdale, FL; GD; MS; Pharmacist Assn Puerto Rico; Pharmacist; BS Univ PR 80; Hlth Serv Admin.

**RODRIGUEZ, KAREN L,** Al A & M Univ, Normal, AL; JR; BS; Am Hom Ec Assn; Kappa Omicron Nu VP 90-; Exquisite Catering Ownr 84-90; Home Ec Ed; Tchr.

**RODRIGUEZ, LIZA I,** Univ Of Pr At Rio Piedras, Rio Piedras, PR; GD; Hnr Prog; Magna Cum Laude 90; Mdrn Lnnge And Lit; Oprtns Agnt Amer Arlns 90-; BA 90.

**RODRIGUEZ, LIZETTE,** City Univ Of Ny Baruch Coll, New York, NY; JR; BA; Cust Serv Rep; Elem Ed; Educ.

**RODRIGUEZ, LYVIA N,** Univ Of Pr At Rio Piedras, Rio Piedras, PR; SR; BA; Am Inst Arch Stdnts 90-; Envrnmntl Dsgn; Architecture.

**RODRIGUEZ, MAGDALINE F,** Fl International Univ, Miami, FL; SR; MS; Stu Dietetic Assoc 89-; AED 86; BS; Dietectics.

**RODRIGUEZ, MARIA ELENA,** Bergen Comm Coll, Paramus, NJ; SO; Blgy; Dntstry.

**RODRIGUEZ, MARIA MICHELLE,** Inter Amer Univ Pr Hato Rey, Hato Rey, PR; FR; Profl Modeling Fontechan Academy 87; Close Up Washington 88; Pres Acad Fitness Awds Secty 89-90; Reconocimienta San Juan Bautista 89-90.

**RODRIGUEZ, MARIA YAQUELIN,** Miami Dade Comm Coll, Miami, FL; SR; BA; Phi Theta Kappa Sec 88-; AA 89; Education; Teaching.

**RODRIGUEZ, MARLENE,** Univ Of Miami, Coral Gables, FL; FR; BA; Cable TV Sta 90-; Radio Sta 90; Cane Commuter Org 90-; Hnr Assoc 90-; Natl Forensic League 90-; Political Awareness 90; Gov Intern-Cmnty Rels; Stanford Schlrshp Awd 90-; FL Undergrad Schlrshp 90-; Brdcst Jrnlsm/Theatre Arts; Cmnctn Law.

**RODRIGUEZ, MARLYNA,** Univ Of Pr At Rio Piedras, Rio Piedras, PR; SR; BED; Spec Ed.

**RODRIGUEZ, MARTA A,** Fl International Univ, Miami, FL; FR; BA; Sci; Drmtlgy.

**RODRIGUEZ, MERCEDES ONELIA,** Fl International Univ, Miami, FL; SR; BED; LDS Ch Primary Tchr; PURG Sprtr; Phi Kappa Phi; FACE; TCHR Intrn; After Sch Prog Dir 83-; Educ; Tch MBA.

**RODRIGUEZ, MIGUEL F,** Univ Politecnica De Pr, Hato Rey, PR; FR; Math; Elec Engr.

**RODRIGUEZ, MILDRED,** Univ Of Pr At Rio Piedras, Rio Piedras, PR; SR; BS; Dns Lst 88-; Gldn Ky 90-; All Amer Schlr 90-; Rehab Grp Chldrns Hosp 89; MARC Jpgrm Rsrch Grnt 90-; Dns Lst 88-; Hnr Matriculation 88-; Biology; Med/Pedtrcn.

**RODRIGUEZ, MILDRED,** Univ Of Pr Medical Sciences, San Juan, PR; JR; BA; Cls Svp 90-; All Amer Schlr Coll Awd 90-; Phys Thrpy.

**RODRIGUEZ, NATHALIE ANNE MARIE,** Univ Of Sc At Columbia, Columbia, SC; JR; BA; Tennis Schlrshp 89-; Finance/ Mgmt; Mgmt.

**RODRIGUEZ, NOEL,** Univ Of Pr At Rio Piedras, Rio Piedras, PR; JR; BS; APHA-ASP 90-; SG Treas 90-; Stdnts Affairs Comm 90-; Golden Key 89-; Leo Clb 88-; Natural Sci Dns Hnr Lst 88-; IM Bsktbl 90-; Phrmcy.

**RODRIGUEZ, PEDRO,** Schenectady County Comm Coll, Schenectady, NY; AAS; Acctg; Public Acctg.

**RODRIGUEZ, PROVIDENCIA,** Univ Of Pr At Mayaguez, Mayaguez, PR; SR; BSEE; IEEE 89-; Tau Beta Pi 89-; Stdnts Cncl 90-; Hnr Registration 88-; Elctrcl Engr.

**RODRIGUEZ, RAQUEL E,** Teikyo Post Univ, Waterbury, CT; SO; BA; Excell Cnvctn Comm Awd Teikyo Post U; Fash Merch; Rtl Byng.

**RODRIGUEZ, REGINA A,** Miami Dade Comm Coll South, Miami, FL; SO; BA; Psychgly.

**RODRIGUEZ, REGINO R,** Miami Dade Comm Coll North, Miami, FL; SO; BA; Phi Theta Kappa; Math/Physics; Elec Eng.

**RODRIGUEZ, RODOLFO,** Fl International Univ, Miami, FL; JR; BA; AA Miami Dade Community Clg 89; Elem Edctn; Prncpl Tchr.

**RODRIGUEZ, ROMUALDO,** Inter Amer Univ Pr Hato Rey, Hato Rey, PR; SR; BBA; Amer Mktg Assn Exec VP 89-; Mktg; Law.

**RODRIGUEZ, ROSA E,** Univ Of Pr Cayey Univ Coll, Cayey, PR; JR; BED; Fclty Hon Roll 89-; Vol Wrk Ctr Exptnl Chldrn Cayey P R; Engl; Tchr Exptnl Chldrn.

**RODRIGUEZ, SANDRA E,** Univ Of Pr At Rio Piedras, Rio Piedras, PR; JR; BS; Amer Chem Soc Chem Dept 90-; UNICA Mdlng Agcy 90-; Dns Lst 90-; MARC 90-; Chem.

**RODRIGUEZ, SANTIAGO,** Antillian Adventist University, Mayaguez, PR; SR; MA; Mnstrl Clb Trnsltr 88-; Assoc Youth Ldr 88-; Pthfndrs/Mstr Guides Org 88-; Summa Cum Laude 88-; Sftbl Team; Assoc Pstr Miami Sprngs SDA 90; Prt Time Musician/X Ray Tech/Ultrasound Tech/Pastor 86-; BA 90; AS 84; Theology; Church Pastor/Univ Professor.

**RODRIGUEZ, SARAI,** Inter Amer Univ Pr Hato Rey, Hato Rey, PR; FR.

**RODRIGUEZ, SONIA E,** Inter Amer Univ Pr Guayama, Guayama, PR; FR; ASC; Sec.

**RODRIGUEZ, VIC C,** S U N Y Coll Of Tech At Frmgdl, Farmingdale, NY; SO; BA; Tllr Bowery Svngs Bnk; Bus Admin; CPA.

**RODRIGUEZ, VICTORIA E,** Georgetown Univ, Washington, DC; FR; BA; Deans List 90-; Delta Simga Pi; Bread For The World 90-; Bus Admn; Bus Exec.

**RODRIGUEZ, VILMA ENID MATIAS,** Inter Amer Univ Pr Aquadilla, Aguadilla, PR; FR; Cmmnctns; Trsm.

**RODRIGUEZ, VIVIAN M,** Univ Of Miami, Coral Gables, FL; SR; Fnce Clb; Untd Mssns Gdwl 88-; Aspira 89-; Beta Gamma Sigma 90-; Magna Cum Laude; Cert Acad Exclnc; Fnce Acad Schlp 90; BBA 90; Fnce; Crmnl Law.

**RODRIGUEZ, WANDA D,** Inter Amer Univ Pr Arecibo Un, Arecibo, PR; Tchng Bible/Being Counselor; Social Wk/Ed; Prof Counselor.

**RODRIGUEZ, YDALMI,** Univ Of Pr At Mayaguez, Mayaguez, PR; SO; BSIE; Inst Ind Eng 90-; Natl Soc Prof Eng 90-; Amer Soc Qlty Cntrl 90-; Assn De Padres De Ninos Irupedidos Colabrath 89-; Natl Hisp Schlrshp Fndtn 88-; Dns Lst 88-90; Sci; Eng.

**RODRIGUEZ, ZOE M,** Univ Politecnica De Pr, Hato Rey, PR; SR; BS; AFA 82-84; AAS Ntnl Prjct Offcr 83-85; IIE 89-; Air Force ROTC Sqad Ldr 80-82; Army ROTC Rcrtng Offcr 87-88; Army ROTC Smltns Mmbrshp Prgrm Cadet 87-88; Mu Alpha Phi 87-; Green Vlg Rsdnts Assn Vcl 90-; Vly Bl Tm Offcr Bsc Crw Cls 90; Indstrl Engnrng; Sty Mstr Degree Bsns Admn.

**RODRIGUEZ-ARROYO, ADAN,** Univ Of Pr At Mayaguez, Mayaguez, PR; SR; IEEE 90-; UPR Ponce Reg Coll Mayaguez Cmps Dean Lst 86-; Tau Beta Pi 90-; Ortr Ponce Reg Coll Deal Lst 86; Cert NASA Wallops Flth Fclty 90; Elec Eng; Cmmnctns.

**RODRIGUEZ-BURGOS, WANDA J,** Catholic Univ Of Pr, Ponce, PR; JR; BBA; Civil Defense 89; Deans Lst 89-90; Bus Admin; Bus Cmptrs.

**RODRIGUEZ-CAYRO, NARCISO ALEJAN,** Nova Univ, Ft Lauderdale, FL; GD; MBAJD; BA Ind Univ Of Pa 88; Bus; Law.

**RODRIGUEZ-DIAZ, SANDRA M,** Univ Of Miami, Coral Gables, FL; JR; BA; Intsnv Engl Trnng 87; Smmr Hstry Prgm 85; Gldn Key 89-90; Beta Gamma Sigma; Deans Lst 87-88; Beta Gamma Sigma; Hnr Rll; Pltcs Sci.

**RODRIGUEZ-DURAN, DAVID,** Catholic Univ Of Pr, Ponce, PR; SO; Jr Comm Asst 89; Legn Marie 88; Pres Clsrm 90; Bsktbl Trnmnts; Sci; Med.

**RODRIGUEZ-GRANADOS, ERNESTO,** Univ Central Del Caribe, Cayey, PR; JR; MD; Med 92 Cls Drctv 88-90; Gnl Stdnts Cncl 89-90; AMA; AMER Med Stdnts Assc; PR Med Assc; Phi Delta Gamma; BS Univ PR 87; Medicine; Ob/Gyn.

**RODRIGUEZ-LAMPON, CARLOS R,** Inter Amer Univ Pr Barranquitas, Barranquitas, PR; SR; BA; Hist & Lit Stdnts Assoc 90-; Hnr Soc 90-; ADREDE Inc Chp 88-; Hist.

**RODRIGUEZ-MARTIN, ARTURO,** Univ Of Pr At Mayaguez, Mayaguez, PR; SO; BS; Italian Cir V P 90-; Research Asst Zoology Spec Pgm Dr Sonia Borges; Univ Perugia Italy 90; Univ CO Research Schlrshp SMART Pgm; Certif USAF Sheppard AFB TX 85; Pre-Med Sci; Med.

**RODRIGUEZ-MULET, HECTOR M,** Inter Amer Univ Pr San German, San German, PR; FR; MBA; Bsn Adm; MA Acctg.

**RODRIGUEZ-PARAJA, M CRISTINA,** Strayer Coll, Washington, DC; JR; BA; Cert 90; Econ/Infrmtn Sys; Interntl Econ Cnslt.

**RODRIGUEZ-PEREZ, JUANA,** Univ Of Pr Medical Sciences, San Juan, PR; GD; Cncl Higher Ed Advsry Bd 90; Prof Nrs Assoc PR 66; PR Hrt Assoc Instr 82; US Army Res Ltc/Chf Nrs; RNA Univ Hosp Sch Anesthesia 72-74; Care Adults-Citizens/ Anesthesia.

**RODRIGUEZ-RAMOS, INGRID,** Caribbean Center For Adv Stds, San Juan, PR; GD; Chrs 84-; Asc Banday Orq PR 85-; Rndl Clg RUM Pres; Std Psy Asc 87-88; Crbn Ctr Adv Stds Psy Asc Org; Dist MA Std 90; BA UPR 88; MA 90; Psy; Rsch.

**RODTS, SHANNON M,** Fl St Univ, Tallahassee, FL; FR; PHD; Phi Eta Sigma 90-; Pi Beta Phi; Psychology; Child Psychology.

**ROE, CHERYL L,** Coll Misericordia, Dallas, PA; JR; BA; Acctg Clb; Exec Bd Campus Mnstry; Adopt-A-Grandparent Pgm; Acctg; CPA.

**ROE, GARY D,** Portland School Of Art, Portland, ME; FR; BFA; Graphc Dsgn.

**ROE, KAREN L,** Christian Brothers Univ, Memphis, TN; SR; Soc Chartered Property/Casualty Underwrtrs 87-; Crump E/S Memphis V P; BS; Econ/Fiance.

**ROE, LEIGH ANN,** Univ Of Sc At Columbia, Columbia, SC; FR; BA; Carolina Pro Union 90-; Bus Admin.

**ROE, MARGARET A,** Elmira Coll, Elmira, NY; JR; BS; Crnng Pntd Pst PTA Cncl VP 87-89; By Sct Com Chrprsn 86-90; Erwn Vlly Prschl Tchr; AAS 73; Elem Ed.

**ROEDER, LAUREN C,** George Mason Univ, Fairfax, VA; SR; BS; Gmu Coll Repblcns 87-; Gmu Acctng Clb 89-90; Beta Alpha Psi Pres 90-; Chi Omega Vp 88-; Arthr Andrsn Schlrshp 90-; Accntng; Cpa.

**ROEHNER, RODNEY,** Villanova Univ, Villanova, PA; FR; BA; Delta Tau Delta Pledge Pres; Liberal Arts/Sci; Ethics.

**ROEPER, ANDREW P,** Rivier Coll, Nashua, NH; JR; BSCS; Eng Pos 78-84; Prod Mgr 84-90; AAS Elec Tech Orange Cnty Comm Clg Middltn N Y 78; Cmptr Sci; Softwr Eng.

**ROEPER, KARL F,** Indiana Univ Of Pa, Indiana, PA; SR; BS; Live Studio Prod/Rprtd/Prdc News Ftrs/Wrt Nws Cpy Dly; Kappa Delta Rho VP 80-83; KDKA-TV; USMC Sgt 82-90; Cmnctns Media; TV Prod.

**ROESCH, SUSAN M,** Capital Univ, Columbus, OH; FR; Stdnt Ambass; Zeta Pi Lambda; Natl Coll Nrsng Awd; Dns Lst.

**ROESE, BARBARA A,** Suffolk Comm Coll Eastern Cmps, Riverhead, NY; SO; BA; Dns Lst 88-; Alpha Beta Gamma; Pi Alpha Sigma; Bus Admi(; Exec.

**ROESSEL III, FRED P,** Radford Univ, Radford, VA; SR; Phlsphy Clb Pres 90; Pysch Clb 90; BS 90; Psyc/Phlsphy; Cvl Svc.

**ROESSLER, JOYCE A,** Portland School Of Art, Portland, ME; SO; BFA; Pieces Art Perm Collctn Prtlnd Mus Art; Pntng; Prof Artist.

**ROETHLER, KATHY E,** Wright St Univ, Dayton, OH; FR; BSE; Acad Invol Com 90-; SWE 90-, Univ Hnrs Prog; IM Sccr 90; Eng; Biomed Eng.

**ROETHLISBERGER, TAMMY E,** Radford Univ, Radford, VA; SR; BA; Hnrs Prog 87-; Early Educ; Tchr.

**ROFEIM, OMID,** City Univ Of Ny Queensbrough, New York, NY; JR; BS; Frnch Clb 89; Dns Lst 88-90; AS; Bio; Dntstry.

**ROGAN, THOMAS B,** S U N Y Coll Of Tech At Frmgdl, Farmingdale, NY; FR; AA; Librl Arts/Sci.

**ROGERS, ALAINE M,** Lincoln Univ, Lincoln Univ, PA; SR; BS; Stu Ldr Ntwrk Pres; Soc Physcs Stu Trea; Stu Prog Brd 89-90; RA 89-; Beta Kappa Chi 90-; Delta Sigma Theta Sec 89-; Nal Cncl Negro Wmn 90-; INROADS 88-; Oadk Ridge Assc Univ Fllwshp; Lincoln Fndrs Schlrshp; Fllwshp; Physic/Sec Educ; Law/ Educ.

**ROGERS, ANGELA K,** Memphis St Univ, Memphis, TN; SO; Bsnss/Cmmnctn; Fnce Or Real Estate.

**ROGERS, ANGELA R,** Savannah St Coll, Savannah, GA; SR; BA; Mrchg Bnd 87-89; Acctg Clb 87-89; Gamma Beta Phi 87-89; Alpha Gamma Delta 87-89; Dns Lst; Rl Est Lgl Asst 90-; Acctg; CPA.

**ROGERS, AUTUMN R,** Coll Of Charleston, Charleston, SC; SO; BED; Bptst Stdnt Un Prgrms Chrprsn 89-; Edctn; Tchr Yth Mnstr.

**ROGERS, BRETT R,** Newbury Coll, Brookline, MA; SO; BE; AA; Bus.

**ROGERS, BRIAN S,** Western Piedmont Comm Coll, Morganton, NC; GD; AAS; Indstrl Eng; Eng.

**ROGERS, CARL M,** Anderson Coll, Anderson, SC; SO; Vrsty Wrstlng; Industrial Eng.

**ROGERS, CATHERINE J,** Gordon Conwell Theol Sem, S Hamilton, MA; GD; MDIV; BA Gordon Clg 90.

**ROGERS, CHERIE L,** Univ Of Sc At Columbia, Columbia, SC; SR; Stdnt Govt/Stdnt Afrs Cmt 89; USC NAACP Sec 88-90; Assc Afro Amer Stdnt 88-90; Gldn Key 89; Omcrn Dlt Kappa 89; Dlt Sgm Theta 2nd VP 88; Sickle Cell Assc 88-; Proj Rapp Ii Hendley Homes 90; Frshmn Mntr Pgm 89-90; USC Co Op Pgm 90-; BA; Pol Sci; Law Sch.

**ROGERS, CHRISTA R,** Clark Atlanta Univ, Atlanta, GA; JR; BA; Deans Lst 90-; Bus Admin; Mktg.

**ROGERS, DE ANNA L,** Univ Of Tn At Martin, Martin, TN; SO; MBS; Occptnl Thrpy Clb Fndr; Mu Epsilon Delta Pldge Treas; Psych Occptnl Thrpy; Occptnl Thrpy.

**ROGERS II, DONALD F,** Univ Of Tn At Martin, Martin, TN; SO; BS; RA; Mu Epsilon Delta Ofcr 90-; Pre-Dntl; Dentst.

**ROGERS JR, EDWARD J,** Va Commonwealth Univ, Richmond, VA; FR; BA; Phi Eta Sigma; Sheltering Arms Hosp Vol 90-; Chippenham Hosp Vol; Wldr; Pre OT Prog; Occptnl Thrpst.

**ROGERS, EVANS M,** Tuskegee Univ, Tuskegee Inst, AL; SR; BS; Intl Assoc; Carribn Assn Med Tech; Amer Soc Med Tech; AS Clg Arts Sci Tech Jamaica Wi 86; Med Tech; Hlth Svcs Mgmt.

**ROGERS, FADRA B,** Central Al Comm Coll, Alexander City, AL; SO; BA; Phi Theta Kappa 89-; Magna Cum Laude; Ed; Elem Ed.

**ROGERS, FRANCES M,** West Chester Univ, West Chester, PA; SR; Hnrs Cncl Stdnt Repr 88-89; Newman Catholic Ctr Vol 87-; Wmns Bsktbl Tm 87-; Hnrs Pgm 87-; Highest GPA Athl PSAC Conf; Carol Eckman Mem Awd 90; Bsktbl 87-.

**ROGERS, GARY L,** Oh St Univ, Columbus, OH; SR; BS; Spch Tm 87-90; Phi Beta Kappa; Phi Kappa Phi; Phi Alpha Theta 90-; Alpha Lambda Delta 87-; Phi Eta Sigma 87-; Gldn Key Rcrdg Sec 89-; Arts Sci Awd 90-; Sydney Fisher Prz 89-90; REU Rsrch Intrnshp Mich St 90; Physics/Hstry; Law.

**ROGERS, HEATHER L,** Indiana Univ Of Pa, Indiana, PA; JR; BA; Anthropology Clb Sec 89-; Anthropology Intrnshp Chevy Chase Comm Ctr; Anthropology; Scl Sci Educ.**

**ROGERS, JACK A,** Johnson St Coll, Johnson, VT; JR; BED; AA Comm Colg Vermont 90; Art; Tchh.

**ROGERS JR, JAMES ALLEN,** Ga St Univ, Atlanta, GA; SR; BS ED; GA Assn Of Edctrs Com Chr 90-; Natl Educ Assn 90-; Gldn Ky; Kappa Delta Pi; Natl Sci Tchrs Assn 90-; Natl Assn Tchrs Of Math 90-; GA Cncl Fr Scl Stds 90-; Natl Cncl Of Tchrs Of Engl 90-; GSU Awrd; PTA 90-; AA De Kalb Comm Coll 77; Mddle Grds Educ Sci And Scl Stds; Tchr.

**ROGERS, JAN E,** Univ Of Sc At Columbia, Columbia, SC; JR; BS; Parents Wknd Strng Cmtee; Club Mgrs Assn Amer Pres 90; Catering Cnvtns/Cruises 90; Kappa Delta Alumnae Rltns Chrmn 88-; Gamecocks Agnst Msmgmt Misuse Alcohol 90; C Trident Chmbr Cmrce Intrnshp 90; Clb Mgrs Amer Schlrshp; Motel Assn Schlrshp; Cnvtn/Tursm Mgmt; Hosptly Prgrmng/Mgmt.

**ROGERS, JEAN M,** Univ Of Cincinnati-Clrmnt Coll, Batavia, OH; SO; BA; Mgr Rstrnt 84-; Bus/Ofc Mgmt; Acctng Asst.

**ROGERS, JEREMY W,** Middle Ga Coll, Cochran, GA; SO; BS; Acctg; Bus Law.

**ROGERS, JESSICA,** Univ Of Nh Plymouth St Coll, Plymouth, NH; JR; BA; Philosphy Tutor 90-; Woms Vllybl Clb 89-; Philosphy; Prof/Law.

**ROGERS, JOHN A,** Lexington Comm Coll, Lexington, KY; FR; Bus; Acctg.

**ROGERS, JULIE L,** Tusculum Coll, Greeneville, TN; SR; BA; Yrbk 87-88; Cl Officer V P 88-; Alpha Chi 89-; Psych; Ind/ Orgnztnl Psych.

**ROGERS, JULIE R,** Christopher Newport Coll, Newport News, VA; JR; BSA; Stdnt Orntn Ldr; Army-Ft Eustic Sldr Mnth 88; Acctg; CPA.

**ROGERS, KAREN L,** Chesterfield Marlboro Coll, Cheraw, SC; SO; AA; Alpha Beta Delta 90-; High GPA; Psy.

**ROGERS, KATHERINE T,** Univ Of Rochester, Rochester, NY; SO; BA; Grk Wk Strng Cmt Phlntrpy Co Chr; Ethnc Rcl Dvsty Comm Bd; Cir K 90-; Gamma Phi Beta Pldg Dir 90-; Pol Sci Hist.

**ROGERS, KERRYE J,** Memphis St Univ, Memphis, TN; SR; BBA; Gamma Beta Phi 89-90; Mktg.

**ROGERS, KEVIN B,** Middle Ga Coll, Cochran, GA; SO; BA; Pianst Chrch 84-; Bio; Med/Denstry.

**ROGERS, KIMBERLY ANN,** Middle Tn St Univ, Murfreesboro, TN; SR; BS; STEA 90-; Elem Educ; Tchg.

**ROGERS, KIMBERLY S,** Univ Of Sc At Columbia, Columbia, SC; FR; Psychlgy; Psychtrst.

**ROGERS, KRISTEN LYNN,** Anderson Coll, Anderson, SC; FR; BA; Phi Theta Kappa 90-; Gamma Beta Phi 90-; Mrshl; NJCAA Bsktbl Acdmc Awrd 90-; Science; Physcl Thrpst.

**ROGERS, LA JUANA,** Clark Atlanta Univ, Atlanta, GA; SR; BA; Mktg Clb 89-; Miss Soph Morehouse Coll; Miss Pfeiffer Hall; Rcrtng Offc; Dns Lst 89-; No Hope To Dope 90; S C Johnson/ Wax 90; Sci Trek/Sci Tech Museum 90; Bus Admin/Mktg; Area Sls Mgr.

**ROGERS, LATONIA S,** Lincoln Univ, Lincoln Univ, PA; SR; Psychlgy Clb 86-90; Blgy Clb 87-; Trck 88-89; Crss Cntry 88-90; Psychlg.

**ROGERS, LEON,** Fl A & M Univ, Tallahassee, FL; JR; BS; SACD 89-; Opera Hon Soc; White/Gold; Phi Beta Sigma Treas 90-; Math Sci; Statscn.**

**ROGERS, LINDA J,** Univ Of Akron, Akron, OH; GD; Mu Kappa Tau VP 89-90; Alpha Lambda Delta 87-90; Phi Eta Sigma 87-90; Pi Sigma Epsln VP 87-90; Delta Gamma Actv/Hstrn 86-90; Aid/Blind 86-90; Red Crs 86-90; Co Op Gnrl Elec Mbl Comm; Univ Akrns A-Key Awd.

**ROGERS, LISA N,** Norfolk St Univ, Norfolk, VA; SO; BS; Dozoretz Ntl Inst Fr Mnrts Appl Sci Stdnt Assc 89-; Spartan Alpha Tau 90-; DNIMAS Schlr 89-; Bnd 90-; Cmptr Sci; Cmptr Eng.

**ROGERS, MARK G,** Pellissippi St Tech Comm Coll, Knoxville, TN; SO; BSMSW; Phi Theta Kappa 90-; AA; Soc Work/Psych Soc; Caseworker.

**ROGERS, MELANIE L,** Oh Univ, Athens, OH; FR; Ntl Soc Blck Eng 90-; Soc Wmn Eng; IM Sftbl; OURS; Intrnshp B F Goodrch Chem 90-; Deans Lst 90-; Sadie T M Alexander Schlrshp; Chem Eng.

**ROGERS, MELINDA,** William Carey Coll, Hattiesburg, MS; SR; BS; Stdnt Govrnt Assc Ed Rep 90; Stdnt Ntnl Ed Assc Pres 90; Bptst Stdnt Union Mbr Clbs Activities 90; Carpenters Wood 90; Clg Chorale Mbr 89; Stdnt Fndtn Committee 90; Ed Ldrshp Adwrd 90; Assc Jones Cnty Jr Clg 80; Elmntry Ed; Tchng.

**ROGERS, MELISSA,** Methodist Coll, Fayetteville, NC; JR; BS; Stdnt Govt Assoc 90; Fr Shmn Hnr Soc 88-90; Deans List 88-90; Newswriter Nwspr Campus Tour Guide For Incoming Recruits 90; Dorm Comm Treas 90; Publ Artwork Tapestries Mag 89; Publ Articles Small Talk Nwspr 90; Art; Advtsng.

**ROGERS, MELISSA A,** Bunker Hill Comm Coll, Boston, MA; SO.

**ROGERS, MICHELE L,** Northern Ky Univ, Highland Hts, KY; SR; MBA; Psychlgy Clb 89-; Psi Chi 89-; Alpha Chi 89-; Deans Lst 89; Hon Lst 88 90-; Trneeshp Grad Schl; BA; Psychlgst Clncl.

**ROGERS, NANCY C,** Saint Catharine Coll, St Catharine, KY; FR; BA; Phi Theta Kappa Pres Elect; Phi Theta Kappa State Pres; Honors Institute; PTO Pres 89-; Educ Math; Tchr.

**ROGERS, NEIL D,** Univ Of Sc At Aiken, Aiken, SC; SR; BA; Sports Med Stf 90-; Pres Hnr Rl 90-; Dns Lst 89-; Vars Bsktbl Asst Coach 87-; Phys Ed; Tchg/Coachg.

**ROGERS, PAMELA E,** Va Commonwealth Univ, Richmond, VA; SR; BFA; Natl Art Ed Assoc 90-; VCU Art Ed Scty 89-; Gldn Key; Phi Eta Sigma 89-; Deans Lst; Art Ed.

**ROGERS, RAYMOND A,** Savannah St Coll, Savannah, GA; SR; BS; Nvl ROTC Cmndr 88-; Stdnt Govt Chf Jstc 89-90; Beta Kappa Chi Pres 90-; Alpha Kappa Mu 90-; Cmptr Sci; US Nvl Avtn.

**ROGERS, RITA-MARIE,** Southern Ct St Univ, New Haven, CT; SR; NSNA 90-.

**ROGERS, ROBERT T,** Kenyon Coll, Gambier, OH; FR; BA; Envrnmntl Cmmttee 90; Head Start Vol 90; Engl.

**ROGERS, ROY S,** Central St Univ, Wilberforce, OH; SR; Poltcl Sci Clb Hstrn 90-; Trstee Awrd; Kappa Alpha Psi Hstrn 90-; BA; Poltcl Sci; Law.

**ROGERS, SANDRA L,** Alcorn St Univ, Lorman, MS; JR; BS; Khm Clb Treas 90-; Hnrs Stdnt Orgnztn; Alpha Kappa Mu; Chem; Rsrch.

**ROGERS, SHARON A,** Univ Of Sc At Sumter, Sumter, SC; BA; Psychlgy; Socia Work MSW.

**ROGERS, SHELIA A,** Alcorn St Univ, Lorman, MS; JR; BS; Khem Clb Sec 90-; Alpha Kappa Mu 90-; Hon Orgztn 88-; Clgte Hon Cncl 89-90; Pres Schlr; Clgte Mississippi; Chem; Pharm.

**ROGERS, STEPHAN L,** Savannah Coll Of Art & Design, Savannah, GA; SO; Soccr 89-; Arch/Photogrphy.

**ROGERS, STEPHANIE M,** Talladega Coll, Talladega, AL; FR; Socl Wrk Clb 90-; Comp Sci.

**ROGERS, TAMMY R,** Liberty Univ, Lynchburg, VA; SO; BS; Ythqst Clb 89-; Lght Clb 90-; Dns Lst 89-; IM Vlybl/Sftbl/Bstkbl Capt 89-90; Bsn/Cmptr Sci; Mgmt Info Sys.

**ROGERS, TINA L,** Western Piedmont Comm Coll, Morganton, NC; SO; AA; Mass Comm/Jrnlsm; Jrnlst/Rprtng.

**ROGERS, TONY M,** Livingston Univ, Livingston, AL; JR; BS; Math; Tchng.

**ROGERS, TRICIA D,** Central Fl Comm Coll, Ocala, FL; FR; MBA; Celebrtn Singrs St Pauls Untd Meth Chrch 89-; Phi Theta Kappa 90-; Comm Schlrs 90-; Intrn Phy Thrpy 90-; Intrn Phy Thrpy Ctr; Phy Thrpy; Phy Thrpst/Athl Trnr.

**ROGERS, WENDY S,** Newbury Coll, Brookline, MA; FR; Fashion Dsgn; Business.

**ROGERS, WILLIAM M,** Nova Univ, Ft Lauderdale, FL; GD; Scty Rl Est Apprsrs Dir; SRA; Apprsl Mgr/Rsdntl Glendale Fdrl Bnk Ft Laud FL 81-; MBA; Rl Est Dvlpmnt/Mgmnt.

**ROGERS, WILLIAM T,** Broward Comm Coll, Ft Lauderdale, FL; SO; AS; Brwrd Cty Fire-Rescur Frfghtr EMT 86-; Fire Sci; Career Lddr Fire Serv.

**ROGERS-DEAS, YOLANDA F,** Hillsborough Comm Coll, Tampa, FL; FR; AS; Radiolgy Tchnlgy; Med.

**ROGERSON, TERESA A,** West Liberty St Coll, West Liberty, WV; SR; MENC 88-; ACDA 88-; John Philip Sousa Awd; Arion Awd; USMC Musicianshp Awd; Private Piano Instr; Organist; Piano Accmpnst 78-; BA West Lib State Coll; Music Edn; Teach.

**ROGGE, JENNIFER A,** Colby Sawyer Coll, New London, NH; JR; BA; Key Assoc 89-; Campus Actvtes Bd Treas 90-; Res Coord 90-; Res Hall Pres 90; Cmunctn; Pub Rltns.

**ROGILLIO, SCOTT E,** Ms Coll, Clinton, MS; GD; JD; Law Stu Bar Assn Tres 90-; Hst Cmmtt 89-; Ornttn Tm 90-; Dean Lst 90; Miss Bar Fndtn Schlrshp; IM Bsktbl Flg Fltbl; Untd Wy 88; Jr Achvmnt 87; Mrktng Rep 87-88; BBA Miss St Univ 87; Law.

**ROGINSKI, PATRICIA T,** Kings Coll, Wilkes-Barre, PA; FR; BA; Elem Educ; Tch.

**ROHAL, KRISTINA M,** Bethany Coll, Bethany, WV; SO; BS; Amer Chem Soc Treas 89-; Soc Physics Stdnts 90-; Alpha Xi Delta 90-; Rsrch James Madison Univ; Chem Eng.

**ROHAN, CATHERINE M,** S U N Y Coll Of Tech At Alfred, Alfred, NY; FR; AS; Soc/Behavrl Sci Clb 90-; Boy Scouts Of Amer Den Ldr 88-; Campfire Boys/Girls Ldr 85-; Sub Tchr Aide 87-; Psych; Spcl Educ Tchr.

**ROHENA HANCE, HECTOR,** Univ Politecnica De Pr, Hato Rey, PR; FR; Mech Eng Stdnt Assoc; Raw Mlk Indstry Sprvsr 86-; Sci Tech; Eng.

**ROHER, DIANNE L,** S U N Y Coll Of A & T Morrisvl, Morrisville, NY; FR; BA; Cnslng Yngr Stdnts; Soc Sci; Cncl Soc Wrk.

**ROHR, CAROL A,** Univ Of Akron, Akron, OH; JR; BS; Gldn Ky 90-; Beta Gamma Sigma 90-; Deans Awd Outstndng Achvmnt 89; Bus/Acctng; Accntnt.

**ROHR, KATHLEEN A,** Kent St Univ Kent Cmps, Kent, OH; SO; Nrsng.

**ROHR, MICHAEL L,** Fayetteville St Univ, Fayetteville, NC; SO; BSEE; Natl Hstrc RR Soc 89-90; Black/Decker 88-89; U S Navy 84-87; Nec 7988 U S Army 85; Math; Eng.

**ROHRBACHER, ERIC G,** Asnuntuck Comm Coll, Enfield, CT; SO; AS; Phi Theta Kappa 88-; Hamilton Stndrd Oper Mgt Dev Progrm; Hamilton Stndrd Pres Award 89; Hamilton Stndra Mgt Club; MFG Engr 87-; Bus Mgt; Engr Mgt.

**ROHRBAUGH, TIMOTHY R,** Widener Univ, Chester, PA; SO; BA; Phi Eta Sigma; Alpha Tau Omega; Bus; Mktg.

**ROHRER, DION P,** Fl St Univ, Tallahassee, FL; SR; BA; Sigma Alpha Epsilon Pldg Trnr 87-; BA; Bsn/Mktg.

**ROHRER, ZOE M,** Brescia Coll, Owensboro, KY; FR; BA; Art.

**ROIG, ANNA PATRICIA,** Fl International Univ, Miami, FL; SR; BED; AA Miami Dade Comm Clg 89; AS; Elem Educ; Kndergrtn Tchr/Own Day Care.

**ROJAS ANDRACA, MAXIMO A,** Univ Politecnica De Pr, Hato Rey, PR; FR; BA; Hato Rey P R Hosp Er Vol 81-86; Dntl Tech Awd 87; Elec Tech 81-83; Dntl Tech 83-87; Cert Elec Clg 83; Cert York Dntl Schl 85; Mech Eng.

**ROJAS, CARLOS O,** Fl A & M Univ, Tallahassee, FL; SR; Surf Tm And Clb 87; AIA 90-; RTKL Intrnshp 90; Hnr Rll 88-; AA Univ Of FL; Archtctre; Prof.

**ROJAS, JAIME,** Cooper Union, New York, NY; JR; BE; Scty Hispanic Prof Engnrs Pres 90-; Amer Scty Mech Engnrs 90-; Gldn Key 89-; Cooper Un Schl Engnrng Full Schlrshp 89-; Mech Engnrng.

**ROJAS, JIMMY,** S U N Y Coll Of Tech At Frmgdl, Farmingdale, NY; GD.

**ROJAS, NANETT A,** Fl International Univ, Miami, FL; SO; BA; Std Pgm Comm 89-; Phi Lambda; Peer Advsr 90-; Engl; Wrtr.

**ROJAS-CARMELINO, ROBERTO,** Fl International Univ, Miami, FL; SR; BS; Alpha Omega Chi; Phi Kappa Phi; Mech Eng.

**ROJEWSKI, BONNIE A,** Georgian Court Coll, Lakewood, NJ; FR; PHD; Psychlgy Clb 90-; Pi Delta Phi; Dean Schlr 90-; Psychlgy/Frnch; Cnslng.

**ROKICKI, PAMELA D,** City Univ Of Ny Baruch Coll, New York, NY; SO; BA; Provost Schlrshp; Pres Schlrshp; Bus Cmnctns; Pblc Rltns.

**ROKOFF, GREGORY W,** Kent St Univ Kent Cmps, Kent, OH; SO; Mrchng Bnd; Hse Cncl VP 89-90; Knt Inrhl Cncl; Alpha Lambda Delta 89; Red Crs Bld Mbl Coord; Dns Lst 89-; Outstdng Svc Stdnt Actvts; Outstdng Prog Res Svcs; Bus; Mgmt.

**ROKOSZ, SUSAN M,** Elms Coll, Chicopee, MA; JR; BED; Jdcl Brd 90-; Future Tchrs Assn VP 88-89; Elem Ed/Spnsh; Tch.

**ROLAND, GRETCHEN P,** Cumberland Coll, Williamsburg, KY; FR.

**ROLAND, JENNIFER D,** Saint Vincents Coll & Seminary, Latrobe, PA; SO; BS; Psych Clb In Touch-Wrld/Soc Awareness 89; Rspct For Lfe Clb 89; Im Ftbl/Sftbl 89; Campus Mnstry Choir Spec Chldrn 89-91; Deans Lst 89; Psychlgy; Rsrch/Cnslng.**

**ROLAND, LYNN MARIE,** Erie Comm Coll South Cmps, Orchard Park, NY; JR; BA; PTA 90-; SS Tchr 89-90; Intern People Inc; Asst Wrtrs Guild; AA Bryant Stratton Bus Inst 81; Engl; Jrnlsmn/Pblc Cmmnctns.

**ROLAND, MELISSA A,** Univ Of Ga, Athens, GA; SR; Educ/Erly Chldh; Tch.

**ROLAND, PHILLIP W,** Ms St Univ, Miss State, MS; JR; Est Cntrl Cmmnty Coll Bnd Mrchng Cncrt; Phi Theta Kappa 87-89; AS 89; SS 89; Wldlf Blgy; Wldlf Blgst.

**ROLAND JR, ROBERT L,** Va Commonwealth Univ, Richmond, VA; SR; BS; Kappa Delta Rho; Bus Admin/Mgmt.

**ROLAND, TEANDREA NICOLE,** Al A & M Univ, Normal, AL; SO; BA; BA; Cmptr Sci; Engr.

**ROLDAN CORTES, GLADYS E,** Inter Amer Univ Pr Arecibo Un, Arecibo, PR; JR; BA; Engl; Tchng.

**ROLEWSKI, SHERI R,** Comm Coll Algny Co Algny Cmps, Pittsburgh, PA; SO; BA; Business; Mgmt/Mrktng.

**ROLEY, JASON D,** Faulkner St Jr Coll, Bay Minette, AL; SO; BS; Pow Wow Ldrshp Soc; Eng; Mat Eng.

**ROLFE, KATHERINE A,** Castleton St Coll, Castleton, VT; JR; BS; Castltn St Coll Phy Ed Dept 90; Top Ten Stdnt; Wmns Sccr 88; Wmns Sftbl 90; Phy Ed Tchng; Hlth.

**ROLL, MARY V,** Dowling Coll, Oakdale Li, NY; GD; BA; CSEA Svp 87-89; APL/CIO AFSME Lcl 1000 Unit 8772; Xi Alpha Chi Kappa Dlta Pi 90-; NY Alpha Rho Chptr Of Alpha Chi Mbr 90-; Dns Lst/Dowling 89-; Rcpnt Of Kenneth Stellenwerf Mem Endowed Schlrshp 90-; Girl Sct Ldr 86-88; Educ/Spec Educ; Tchr.

**ROLLAND, SANDRA C,** Endicott Coll, Beverly, MA; SO; AS; Phi Theta Kappa; Ski Clb; Jz/Mdrn Dnce; Deans Lst; Intr Dsgn; Archtctrl Rndrer.

**ROLLE, ADRIAN L,** Morehouse Coll, Atlanta, GA; JR; BSC; Coll Hlth Crrs Scty 88; Bg Brthrs Bg Sstr Prgm 89-90; Smmr Rsrch Emory Univ; Blgy; Obsttrcn Gynclgst.

**ROLLE, NATASHA MICHELLE,** Fl International Univ, Miami, FL; SR; BA; W Indn Stdnts Assn; Phi Kappa Phi; AA Coll Bahamas 87; Pub Admin.

**ROLLE, SPENCER H,** Toccoa Falls Coll, Toccoa Falls, GA; GD; Yth Rcgntn Cert Of Hon 90; B Carter Mem Awrd Prmsng Tchr 90; AS Coll Bahamas 81; Elem Schl Tchr.

**ROLLER, PENNY P,** Coker Coll, Hartsville, SC; SO; BA; CARE Hmlss Shltr Bd Advsrs 90-; Hrt Hrt Fmly Rcrtn Cntr 90-; Cmmnctns.

**ROLLIN, JAMES A,** Kent St Univ Kent Cmps, Kent, OH; SO; BA; Alpha Tau Omega Jdcl Revw Mbr; Bus; Fin.

**ROLLING, MARJORIE D,** Niagara Univ, Niagara Univ, NY; JR; BA; AA Niagara Cnty Comm Clg 89; Elem Educ/Soc Stds; Tchr.

**ROLLING, RONALD,** Morgan St Univ, Baltimore, MD; JR; BA; Cncrt Bnd 88-; Jazz Bnd 88-; Pep Bnd 88-; Mrchng Bnd 8-; Kappa Kappa Psi Prsdnt 89-; Msc Edctn; Msc Thrpy Edctn.

**ROLLINS, CAROL J,** Univ Of Cincinnati, Cincinnati, OH; SR; BS; OCAS Stdnt Tribnl VP 89; IEEE Sec 89; Soc Of Women Eng Pres 88; Tau Alpha Pi 88; Electrical Eng Tech; Cmptr Eng.

**ROLLINS, KERI L,** Univ Of Sc At Columbia, Columbia, SC; FR; BA; Stu Govt Rsdnc Hl VP 90-; Gamma Beta Phi; Symphnc Bnd; Rsdnt Advsr Rsdnc Hl; Music Ed; Dir.

**ROLLINS, RACHELLE R,** Northern Ky Univ, Highland Hts, KY; SO; BA; Bptst Stdnt Un Co Chrprsn Cmnctns 90-; Mntl Hlth/Hmn Srv; Hmn Srv.

**ROLLO III, FREDERICK F,** Neumann Coll, Aston, PA; FR; BS; Newspaper Stf Wrtr 90-; VIVA 90-; Hnrs Prog 90-; Tutoring Serv 90-; Acctng.

**ROLLO, THERESA A,** New Comm Coll Of Baltimore, Baltimore, MD; SR; AA; Fast Food Mgmt; Nrsng; RN.

**ROLNICK, PAUL,** Yeshiva Univ, New York, NY; JR; BS; Joint Bus Soc Sec 89; Acctng Soc 88-; Sr Yrbk Bus Edtr; Cong Shomrei Torah 87-; Mens Clb Cong Shomrei Torah 87-; Acctng.

**ROLON, WINA I,** Univ Of Pr Medical Sciences, San Juan, PR; GD; BA; Magna Cum Laude 90; BA Sci Univ Interamericina Bayamon 83-88; EMT Prmed 89-90; Bio; Med.

**ROLOSON-SCHWAB, KAREN E,** Marywood Coll, Scranton, PA; SO; BS; Coun Excptnl Chldrn 90-; Sigma Pi Epsilon Delta; Spec Educ; Tchr.

**ROMAGUERA, DENISE M,** Univ Of Miami, Coral Gables, FL; JR; BS; Chmbr Sngrs 89-; Intrnshp Chnl 23 90-; Intrnshp Unvsn Nws Dept Asgnmnt Ed; Brdcstng/Psychlgy; TV Prdcr.

**ROMAIN, DONNA R,** City Univ Of Ny Med Evers Coll, Brooklyn, NY; JR; BS; Soc Adv Mgmt 90-; AS Bus Admn 90; Bsn Admn/Finance; Law.

**ROMAN DAVILA, LUIS D,** Inter Amer Univ Pr Hato Rey, Hato Rey, PR; FR; BA; Hnr Prog Vcl Rep 90-; Sci And Tech; Arospce Eng.

**ROMAN PINEIRO, DIANA,** Inter Amer Univ Pr Aquadilla, Aguadilla, PR; SO; Admnstrtv Asst.

**ROMAN SANTIAGO, JOHANNA,** Inter Amer Univ Pr Hato Rey, Hato Rey, PR; SO; BA; Scrtrl Sci.

**ROMAN, ALBERTO,** Saint Thomas Univ, Miami, FL; JR; BA; AA Miami Dade Comm Clg 90; Soc Studies/Hist Geography; Sec Educ.

**ROMAN, DEAN J,** Savannah Coll Of Art & Design, Savannah, GA; GD; MFA; Zeta Beta Tau Hstrn 86-88; Asst Prof Studio Pntng 90-; BA Univ Of S Fla 88; Sclptr; Tchr/Wrtr.

**ROMAN, JACQUELINE,** Inter Amer Univ Pr Guayama, Guayama, PR; FR; BBA; Bus; Acct.

**ROMAN, JOSSIE I,** Inter Amer Univ Pr San Juan, Hato Rey, PR; Latin Clb; Cncl Yth Orgnztns Pres 90-; Mdl Untd Natns; Hon Pgm 90-; Otstndng Yth Puerto Rico 90; Intrntl Rltns; Law Mstr Degree Jstc.**

**ROMAN, JUDIBELLE,** Univ Of Pr Humacao Univ Coll, Humacao, PR; SR; BS; Amrcn Chmcl Scty 90-; Univ Hnr Lst 88-90; NSF Reu 90 Smmr Fllwship 90; Mnrty Bmdcl Rsrch Spprt 88-90; Mnrty Accss Rsrch Crrs 90-; Chmstry.

**ROMAN, LUCINDA,** Caribbean Univ, Bayamon, PR; SO; BA; Bus Admin Mgmnt.

**ROMAN, MARITZA,** Univ Of The Virgin Islands, St Thomas, VI; SR; BSN; Stdnt Nrs Assn VP 89-90; Bapt Stdnt Union 87-; Cath Clb 88-89; Pres Clb; Proj Access Intrnshp Univ Az Nrsng Res 90; Nrsng.

**ROMAN, NICULAE,** Bridgeport Engr Inst, Fairfield, CT; SR; BSEE; ASEE 89; Eng.

**ROMAN JR, ROMAN,** Miami Dade Comm Coll, Miami, FL; JR; BA; Bsnss Mngmnt.

**ROMAN, STEPHEN S,** Univ Of New Haven, West Haven, CT; SR; BS; Bus Admn.

**ROMAN-TIRADO, MARILYN,** Mount Saint Mary Coll, Newburgh, NY; SR; BA; Co-Op Ed; Alpha Chi; Human Servcs/Hispanic Studies.

**ROMANGO, JAMES D,** Columbus Coll Of Art & Design, Columbus, OH; SO; BA; USN Elctrcn Mtr Rwnd Oprtr EM 2 84-88; Art Illstrtn.

**ROMANISHAN, CONSTANCE M,** Chattahoochee Vly St Comm Coll, Phenix City, AL; SO; Artst; AA; Art.

**ROMANO, CARL S,** Embry Riddle Aeronautical Univ, Daytona Beach, FL; SR; BS; Senate Clb Str 89-; Law Club 90-; Engl Hnr Scty 90-; Red Cross 82-; Civil Air Ptrl 78-82; Deans Lst; Tennis IM 89-; USAF Rsrvs Staff Sgt 87-; US Army 83-86; Prof Aeronatics; Law.

**ROMANO, JOHN V,** Univ Of Pittsburgh, Pittsburgh, PA; FR; Clssc Car Clb; Stck Brkr.

**ROMANO, KRISTIN A,** Villanova Univ, Villanova, PA; JR; BA; VEG Co Pres 88-; Amnsty Intl 88-; Comm Phil Hmls 88-; Habitat Hmnty 89; TA Crtgrphy 90; Geogrphy; Envrnmntl Cnsltg.

**ROMANO, LISA,** Teikyo Post Univ, Waterbury, CT; JR; BA; Deans Lst 90; AS Becker Jr Coll 90; Bus Mgmt; Trvl Agncy.

**ROMANO, LYNNETTE D,** Le Moyne Coll, Syracuse, NY; JR; BA; The Curriculum Hnr Awd 89; Citizens Schlrshp Fdn Awd 89-; Assoc Deg Onondaga Cmnty Clge Syracuse NY 89; Psychology/Spcl Ed; Spcl Ed Tchr.

**ROMANOWICZ, LESLIE,** S U N Y At Buffalo, Buffalo, NY; FR; MBA; Crew Team; Ski Clb; Bsns; Envrnmntl Stds.

**ROMANS, DERE G,** Middle Tn St Univ, Murfreesboro, TN; SO; BA; Business; Acctng.**

**ROMANS, H JORDAN,** Univ Of Al At Huntsville, Huntsville, AL; SO; BS; Phi Theta Kappa 90-; Pres Lst; Dns Lst; AS Rets Elctrncs Instit 85; Elctrcl Engr; Engr.

**ROMANS, JENNIFER P,** Univ Of Sc At Columbia, Columbia, SC; SO; BA; Gamma Beta Phi; Phi Mu Treas 89-; Chrldr; Elem Ed; Tchr.

**ROMANSKY, LINDA S,** Comm Coll Algny Co Algny Cmps, Pittsburgh, PA; SO; AS; Tri State Radiation Oncology Soc; Phi Theta Kappa; Science; Radiation Therapy Technologist.

**ROME, KIMBERLY J,** Marywood Coll, Scranton, PA; FR; BA; Karate Clb Org 90-; Bsns/Econs.

**ROMEO, SEAN J,** Miami Dade Comm Coll, Miami, FL; SO; MBA; Phi Theta Kappa 90; Outstndng Acad Achvmnt Awd; Hnr Stdnt Bsnss Depart; Ntl Cllgte Bsnss Merit Awd; AA; Fnce; Urban Redvlpr.

**ROMER, RHONDA K,** Hudson Valley Comm Coll, Troy, NY; FR; BA; Sftbl; Pres Lst 90; Dietary Aide Rosewood Gdns; Bsn Adm; Finance.

**ROMERO ZAMBRANA, ELISAMUEL,** Univ Politecnica De Pr, Hato Rey, PR; FR; Mth Sci.

**ROMERO, ALICIA E,** Barry Univ, Miami, FL; JR; BA; Yng Democrt Clb Sec 89-; Circle K 89-90; Rspct Lf 89-; Hon Stdnt Assn Rep 89-90; Phi Alpha Theta 90-; Pres Schlrshp 89-; Hstry; Govt.

**ROMERO, CHA LOE A,** Wilberforce Univ, Wilberforce, OH; FR; BA; Kappa Sweetheart Of Kappa Ct; Psychlgy; Clncl Psychlgst.

**ROMERO, DOUGLAS J,** Univ Of Pr At Mayaguez, Mayaguez, PR; SO; BA; Model Untd Ntns Pres 86-89; Stdnt Cncl 87-89; Beta Beta Beta 90-; Cir Pre Mdcs 90-; Untd States Natl Stdnt Cncl Awd 88-89; Schlstc All Am Mbrshp 88-89; Natl Ldrshp/Serv Awd 88-89; Pre Med Studies.

**ROMERO, ELOISA V,** George Mason Univ, Fairfax, VA; JR; BA; Cmps Biblestdy 89; Yth Advsry Cncl Sec 88-; Educ; Elem Educ Schl Tchr.

**ROMERO, JEANNIE P,** Univ Of North Fl, Jacksonville, FL; FR; BA; SGA Sen 90-; Stdnt Prgrmmng Brd Chrprsn Flms Cmmtt 90-; Rcrtnl Sprts Clb 90-; Cmmnctns; Pblc Rltns Spclst.

**ROMERO, JOSE A,** Univ Politecnica De Pr, Hato Rey, PR; JR; Work P R Sewer Auth Engrng Aid 91; ADT Propg Ldrshp Grp With Chldrn 89; Hnrbl Mntn CBC 89; Hnrbl Mntn Bayamon Univ P R 90; Rcqtbl; BA; Hydrlc Sys; Engrng.

**ROMERO, LILLIE A,** Univ Of Tn At Martin, Martin, TN; SO; BS; Mu Epsln Dlt 90-; Alpha Phi Omg 89-90; Cytotechnlgy; Cytotechnlgst.

**ROMERO, ROMULO H,** Fl International Univ, Miami, FL; SR; BS; Amer Chem Scty Pres 90-; Phi Kappa Phi; Fclty Schlrs 87-; Marc Schlrshp; Amer Lgn Schl Awd 87; Chem; Rsrch/Grdte Schl.

**ROMERO-PINEIRO, ANTONIO G,** Inter Amer Univ Pr Hato Rey, Hato Rey, PR; FR; BA; Ass Sct Mstr Boys Scts America 88-; US Army Rsrv 89-; Pltcs; Law.

**ROMESBERG, JILL A,** Indiana Univ Of Pa, Indiana, PA; SR; BED; IM Vlybl 88-90; Eqstrn Tm 89-90; Outstndng Stdnt Tchr Awd 90-; Erly Chldhd Ed.

**ROMETO, NICOLE M,** Temple Univ, Philadelphia, PA; JR; ACSM.

**ROMIG, JAMES M,** Temple Univ, Philadelphia, PA; SR; BS; Envir Eng Stdnts Assn 89-; Envir Eng Tech; Eng.

**ROMINE, ALLISON M,** Univ Of Montevallo, Montevallo, AL; SO; BS; RHA Historian 89-; RA 90-; Alpha Lambda Delta 89-; Presidents Lst 89-90; Deans Lst 89-90; Vldctrn Schrlshp 89-; Gold Vlybl Tm; Elem Early Chldhd Ed; Teaching.

**ROMINE, SHEILA A,** Univ Of West Fl, Pensacola, FL; JR; BA; AS; Erly Chldhd/Elem Ed.

**ROMP, CYNTHIA B,** Kent St Univ Kent Cmps, Kent, OH; SO; BS; Gymnstcs Clb 90-; Pres Lst 90; Hon Schlrshp 90-; Exclnce Schlrshp 90-; IM Sftbl 90-; Vrsty Gymnstcs 90-; Lf Sci; Med.

**RONAGHAN, GERALD J,** Univ Of Hartford, West Hartford, CT; JR; BA; Stdnt Nwspr 88-89; Stdnt Radio Sta 88-90; AA 90; Engl; Educ.

**RONAN, JANICE L,** Mount Aloysius Jr Coll, Cresson, PA; GD; Nrsn Gorg 89-; Emplyd Tlmtry Unit.

**RONCA, EILEEN M,** Villanova Univ, Villanova, PA; JR; BA; Newspaper Stf Rep 90-; Proj Sunshine 88-89; Pi Delta Phi 90-; Pi Beta Phi Arrow Corr 90-; Dns Lst 88-; Coxswain Crew Tm 89; Engl/Frnch.

**RONCA, KRISTINE ANNE,** Univ Of Hartford, West Hartford, CT; SO; BFA; Painting/Art Hstry.

**RONCONI, NICHOLAS,** Broward Comm Coll, Ft Lauderdale, FL; FR; NY Commodities Exchange; Engl; Law.

**RONDINELLI, ANTHONY,** Springfield Tech Comm Coll, Springfield, MA; SO; BA; Deans List; Bus Adnstrn; Marketing Advertising.

**RONEN, TAL,** Univ Of Miami, Coral Gables, FL; FR; MD; Alpha Lambda Delta; Sigma Phi Epsilon Hse Chrmn; Deans Lst 90-; IM Bsktbl; Bio; Med Doc.

**RONEY, AMY E,** Bethel Coll, Mckenzie, TN; FR; BS; Chrstn Issues Org 90-; STEA 90-; Writing Cons/Tutor 90-; Chrldr 90-; Elem Edn; Teach.

**RONEY, EDITH ANN,** Clayton St Coll, Morrow, GA; JR; BA; Psych; Clin Psych.

**RONEY, JOHN P,** S U N Y Coll At Fredonia, Fredonia, NY; JR; BS; Physics Clb Treas 90-; Sigma Pi Sigma 90-; Pi Mu Epsilon 90-; Rensselaer Eng/Sci Awd For Excel 90-; Deans Lst 89-; J V Soccer 89-; Aero Eng.

**RONEY, SCOTT M,** Pa St Univ Delaware Cty Cmps, Media, PA; SO; BA; Outstndng Acdmc Achvmnt Awrd; Mktg; Adv/Phrmctcl.

**RONEY, STEPHEN C,** Merrimack Coll, North Andover, MA; JR; BS; ACM 90-; Cmptr Sci; Cmptrs.

**RONG, YI-BIN,** Marywood Coll, Scranton, PA; FR; BS; Multcltrl Clb 90-; Deans Lst 90; First Hnr; Assoc 87-89; Cmptr Info Sys; Mngrl Position.

**RONK, CAROL E,** Hahnemann Univ, Philadelphia, PA; MD; Med/Lit; Princeton Clb Of Phila; Habitat Humanity; Peer Advsr; St George Soc Flwshp 89; BA Princeton Univ 84; Med; Physician.

**RONNING, JESSICA L,** Piedmont Bible Coll, Winston-Salem, NC; JR; BS; Soph Class Sec/Treas 89; Jr Class Sec Treas 90; RA 90; Beta Sigma Phi VP 89 90; All Amer Schlr; Var Bsktbl 89-90; Elem Ed; Tchr.**

**ROOD, SHEILA A,** Bryant Stratton Bus Inst Roch, Rochester, NY; GD; Mdcl Clb 90-91; Stdnt Cncl Mdcl Rep 90; Emplyd Mrtg Srvcng Swtch Mdcl Asstng; AOS; Mdcl Asstng; Mdcl Asstnt.

**ROODE, DONNA C,** Dowling Coll, Oakdale Li, NY; SO; BA; Nwsppr 89; Intl Exchng Clb 89; Vsl Art; Educ.

**ROOK, BRIAN T,** Alfred Univ, Alfred, NY; SO; BA; AMA Pres 89-; SG Fnc Cmmtt; Intr Grk Cncl; Alph Alambda Delta; Kappa Psi Upsilon Se; Fnc.

**ROOKER, MARGIE ELAINE,** Univ Of Sc At Aiken, Aiken, SC; JR; BA; Edctn Mjrs Clb 90-; Gamma Beta Phi; Spcl Olympcs Vlntr; AS Mnt Olive Clg 90; Edtn; Tchr.

**ROOKS, AMY T,** Norfolk St Univ, Norfolk, VA; FR; BS; Sprtn Alpha Tau; Cnsmr Svcs/Fmly Stds; Fshn Dsgn.

**ROONEY, CATHLEEN A,** Saint Johns Coll At Annopolis, Annapolis, MD; FR; King Williams Plyrs 90-; Lit Soc 90-F Rowing Club Crew Team 90-; Librl Arts.

**ROONEY, CHARITY A,** Emory & Henry Coll, Emory, VA; SO; BA; Vrsty Wmns Bsktbl 89-; Vrsty Wmns Crs Cntry 89-; Phi Sigma Iota 90-; Alpha Beta Chi 90-; Most Vlbl Rnr Crs Cntry 89-; Hstry/Clscl Stds.

**ROONEY, JAY D,** Allegheny Coll, Meadville, PA; SO; BA; Yng Reps 89-; SG 90-; Aldn Schlr 89-90; Im Sprts 89-; Econ.

**ROONEY, JEFFREY J,** S U N Y At Buffalo, Buffalo, NY; SR; BA; Dsgn Assn Treas 90-; UB Seido Karate Clb 87-; UB Ski Clb; Outstdng Acad Achvmnt 91; Dsgn; Grphc/Prdct Dsgnr.

**ROONEY, MARGARET P,** Univ Of Cincinnati, Cincinnati, OH; JR; BA; SCEC 88-89; Kappa Delta Pi 90-; Spec Ed; Wrk Absd/Nglctd Chldrn.

**ROONEY, RAE M,** Oh St Univ At Newark, Newark, OH; JR; Engl; Educ.

**ROONEY, WALTER G,** Coll Of Charleston, Charleston, SC; JR; BA; LEADS 89-90; Actvts Brd 89-; Rugby Tm 89-; Sailng Tm 89-; Tutor 89-; Alpha Chi Sigma 89-; Alpha Epsilon Delta 89-; E Emerson Towell Chem Prize; Philosphy; Med Schl.

**ROOP, BARBARA G,** Emory & Henry Coll, Emory, VA; JR; BA; Stdnt VA Ed Assn Pres; Sigma Mu; Henry Clay Graybl Schlrshp; Creed Fultn Schlrshp; AS Ed VA Highlnds Comm Coll 90; Intrdscplnry Engl; Ed.

**ROOP, JANET L,** Bristol Univ, Bristol, TN; JR; BA; Dean Lst 87-; Rtl Mngmnt 88-; Dept Mgr; Bus Admn/Accntng; Accntnt Adtr.

**ROOS, MICHELLE L,** Ms St Univ, Miss State, MS; FR; BA; Hightower Hall Cncl Pres 90-; Bulldog Hsts; Gamma Beta Phi; Alpha Lambda Delta; Zeta Tau Alpha 90-; Pres Schlr 90; Hnr Pldg Zeta Tau Alpha 90; Business Adm; Intl Bus/Mrktng.

**ROOT, CHAD M,** Oh St Univ, Columbus, OH; SO; BS; AM Inst Archtctrl Stdnts 90-; Phi Eta Sigma 90-; IM Rcqtbl 89-90; Archtct.

**ROOT, KEVIN A,** Gaston Coll, Dallas, NC; SO; BS; Knights Of Columbus Fincl Sec 88-; AAS; Bus Mgt; Admnstrtr.

**ROOTES, DAVID,** Univ Of Akron, Akron, OH; JR; BS; Phi Eta Sigma 89-; Tau Beta Pi; Eta Kappa Nu; Pi Mu Epsilon; Elec Eng.

**ROPER, HOLLIS E,** Univ Of Sc At Columbia, Columbia, SC; SR; BS; Habitat/Humanity; Piedmont Soc 89-; Gamma Beta Phi 90-; Upstate Schlrshp 89- ; BS Greenville Tech Colg 90; Busn Admin; Bnkg; FDIC.

**ROPER, KERRY L,** Middle Tn St Univ, Murfreesboro, TN; JR; Acad Schlrshp 4 Yrs MBU; 2yr Schlrshp Motlow St Comm Clg; Assoc Sci Motlow State Commty Clg 90; Elem Ed; Tchng.

**ROPER, ROGER J,** Spartanburg Methodist Coll, Spartanburg, SC; SO; BS; Head Athlc Trnr 89-; Bio/Sclgy; Doctor Sports Med.

**ROPER, SCOTT C,** Clark Univ, Worcester, MA; SR; BA; Geography Stdnt Org Pres 88-; Film Scty 88-90; Phi Beta Kappa 90-; Magma Cum Laude; Ellen Churchill Semple Awd; Paul P Vouras Scl Sci Awd; Assc Amer Geogrphrs Schlrshp; Gamma Theta Upsilon; IM Sftbl/Vlybl/Sccr/Cptn; Geography; Educator/Researcher.**

**ROPER, SUSANNE,** Univ Of Nc At Asheville, Asheville, NC; SO; BA; Mass Cmmnctn; Prnt Media Pblc Rltns.

**ROQUE FALCON, BRIAN A,** Bayamon Central Univ, Bayamon, PR; FR; BA; Stdnt Assc Ed Tchnlgy Pblc Relations Offc; Ed Tchnlgy; Motion Picture Prod.

**ROQUE, MERCEDES JIMENEZ,** Miami Dade Comm Coll, Miami, FL; SO; BA; Lgl Asst Blackwell/Walker PA Miami 89-; Lgl Asst/Arts/Sci; Bchlrs Degree Arts/Sci.

**ROQUE, VIVIAN M,** Miami Dade Comm Coll, Miami, FL; SO; BA; Mtrpls Stf Wrtr; Otstndng Acdmc Achvmnt Awd 90-; Pltcl Sci; Jrnlsm.

**ROQUE-GAFFNEY, ELIZABETH,** Univ Of Med & Dentistry Of Nj, Newark, NJ; CERT; Mid Atlantic Soc Of Toxicology; Bio Tchr Bergen Cath H S 84-90; BS Scndry Sci Edn Oneonta St Coll 82; MA Bio Montclair St Coll 89; Bio/Toxicology; Phrmctcl Rsrch Lab.

**ROQUE-NIEVES, PEDRO JOSE,** Bayamon Central Univ, Bayamon, PR; GD; BA; Peers Cnslr 85-87; Catechisis 87-; Trck Fld 90; CPR San Pablo Hosp/Civil Dfns 86-; Air Transprtn Univ Of Puerto Rico 86; Eductnl Technlgy; TV Prodcr/Tchr/Photogrphr.

**ROQUES, ANNIE,** Fl International Univ, Miami, FL; SR; BBA; Dns Lst 90-; Mktg; MBA Mktg JD Law Sch.

**ROQUES, JOSE FINA V,** Bunker Hill Comm Coll, Boston, MA.

**ROQUES, MERRI-LYNN LOIS,** Gordon Coll, Wenham, MA; FR; BA; Brkfst Clb 90-; A J Gordon Schlrshp 90-; Bsktbll Mgr; Tnns Sftbll 90-; Engl.

**RORIE, IVEY,** Univ Of Sc At Spartanburg, Spartanburg, SC; SR; BA; Stu Govt Pres 88-; Soc Fr Thnkrs Pres 88-90; Mntnrg Clb VP 87-; Pi Sigma Alpha Pres 90-; Odk Omicron Delta Kappa Pres 90-; Rsrch Asst Bill Rghts Stdy; Carolina Pdmnt Schlr; Pol Sci; Law.

**RORISON, DAVID W,** Comm Coll Algny Co Algny Cmps, Pittsburgh, PA; FR; BA; Acctg; CPA.

**ROSA JIMENEZ, MARIBEL,** Inter Amer Univ Pr Hato Rey, Hato Rey, PR; SO; Cuadro De Honor; Chem Pharm.

**ROSA REYES, VICTOR MANUEL,** Inter Amer Univ Pr Hato Rey, Hato Rey, PR; SR; BA; Bands De Concr; Cuadro Hon; Beta Beta Beta 89-; Pres Fitns Awd; Pub Paper Resrch Asst; Biology; Pub Hlth.

**ROSA, ANGELICA Y,** City Univ Of Ny Baruch Coll, New York, NY; GD; Ofc Adm Tech Clb 89-90; BBA 90; Ofc Tech/Adm; Hlth Cr Mgmt/Adm.

**ROSA, BRYAN P,** Southern Vt Coll, Bennington, VT; FR; Bus Clb 90-; Bus Mgmnt; Psych.

**ROSA, CUEVAS CESAR,** Inter Amer Univ Pr San Juan, Hato Rey, PR; SR; BA; Acctg; MBA.**

**ROSA, FRANCISCO J,** Univ Politecnica De Pr, Hato Rey, PR; FR; BA; Clb Santurce Trck Fld 87-89; Stdnts Athl Assn 87-90; Little Leag Bsbl Coach 87-; Trck/Fld Rookie Yr 89-90; Civl Eng.

**ROSA, HECTOR WM COLON,** Univ Of Pr Cayey Univ Coll, Cayey, PR; JR; PH D; Math Cir 89-; CAUSA Assn 90-; MSIP Prog 89; Rctr Benitezs Hnr Bd 88-; Hnr Stdnts Socty Spec Srvcs Prog 89-; Mbrs Prog Schlrshp Berkeley Lab 89-; Rctrs Hnr Bd 90; Appl Math; Rsrchr/Prfsr.

**ROSA, JEANETTE M,** Lesley Coll, Cambridge, MA; JR; BA; LINC Treas 89-; Human Serv Intern 89; Elder Serv Intern 89-90; Short Stop Intern; Human Serv/Cnslng Psychlgy; Scl Wrk.

**ROSA, JOSE D,** City Univ Of Ny City Coll, New York, NY; SO; Aspira Hispnc Clb 90; Cadcs Soc; Dns Lst 90-; Bio; Med.

**ROSA, RITA Y,** City Univ Of Ny City Coll, New York, NY; JR; BS; Vlybll Team Borough Manhattan CC 85-87; AA Borough Manhattan CC 85-87; Elmntry/Bilingual Ed; Tchng.

**ROSADO COLON, MARINELBA,** Univ Of Pr At Mayaguez, Mayaguez, PR; JR; Inst Indstrl Engrs; Engrg.

**ROSADO GONZALEZ, CARMEN YERITZA,** Univ Of Pr Medical Sciences, San Juan, PR; SR; Amrcn Phrmctl Assc 89-; Rho Chi 90-; Phrmctcl Scncs.

**ROSADO SANTIAGO, LUIS E,** Caribbean Univ, Bayamon, PR; SR; Info Systems; Mis.

**ROSADO, ANTONIO,** Inter Amer Univ Pr Aquadilla, Aguadilla, PR; SR; Seventh Day Adv Ch; ADRA; LPN; LPN Ponce Tech Sch 81; Hstry; Tchr.

**ROSADO, JULISSA M,** City Univ Of Ny Baruch Coll, New York, NY; SO; BBA; Hspnc Soc 90; Acctg; CPA.

**ROSAGE, JENNIFER LEE,** Indiana Univ Of Pa, Indiana, PA; SR; BS; Res Hall Assoc Advsr 87; Ntl Womens Ldrshp Awd; Ntl Rsdnce Hall Hnr 88; Prog Of Yr 87; Im Vllybl Womens/Co-Ed Bsktbl 86-90; PSEA Ntl Ed Assoc 90; Bio Ed/Psyclgy/Sexlty Ed.

**ROSAGE, LISA A,** Indiana Univ Of Pa, Indiana, PA; SR; BED; Sign Lang Clb 87-89; Cntmpry Chr 89-; Dns Lst; Tchng Jr High Engl Rdng 90; PSEA NEA; ARA Svcs Stdnt Mng 88-; Hrg Imp Elem Educ; Tchr Deaf.

**ROSALES, OSCAR W,** Fl A & M Univ, Tallahassee, FL; JR; BS; AID Schlrshp 86-87; Georgetown Univ Schlrshp 90-; AAS Kirkwood Cmnty Clg 88; Ag Bus; Intl Mktg.

**ROSAMOND, GEOFFREY N,** Villanova Univ, Villanova, PA; JR; BA; Pre Law Soc 90; SADD; Spcl Olympics 90; Phi Kappa Phi; Omicron Delta Kappa Sec; Pi Sigma Alpha; Delta Tau Delta Fndrsng Chmn 88-; IM Bsktbl/Sftbl 88-; Pol Sci; Law.

**ROSARIO HERNANDEZ, FRANCES J,** Inter Amer Univ Pr Hato Rey, Hato Rey, PR; JR.

**ROSARIO MATOS, JOSE E,** Inter Amer Univ Pr Hato Rey, Hato Rey, PR; JR; BA; Sci; Airway Sci Mgmnt.

**ROSARIO MORALES, ENEIDA,** Univ Of Pr At Mayaguez, Mayaguez, PR; SO; BS; Pre Med Assn Stf 90-; Beta Beta Beta Sec,Yrbk Edtr; Med Asst; Dns Hnr Rl 90-; Biology; Med.**

**ROSARIO RIVERA, MARISOL,** Inter Amer Univ Pr Hato Rey, Hato Rey, PR; JR; BA; Yng People Of PPD 87-; Tchrs Ed Prog 89-; Photo Clb 89; Red Cross 90; Alphabetization Prog 88; Cthlc Church Instrctr 89-90; Alphabetization Cert 88; Fidelity Medal 88; Cert Of Merit 88; Elem Educ; Law.

**ROSARIO RIVERA, SONIA M,** Univ Of Pr Humacao Univ Coll, Humacao, PR; SO; BA; Hnr Acad Prog 90-; Cthlc Yth Grp 90-; Elem Educ.

**ROSARIO, ANGELO L,** S U N Y Coll At Fredonia, Fredonia, NY; SR; BA; Omicron Delta Epsilon; Wall St Jrnl Awrd; Schlrshp Fund Awrd 89-; Deans Lst 88-; US Marines 83-87; Economics; Public Policy.

**ROSARIO, CAROLINE,** Bayamon Central Univ, Bayamon, PR; GD; BED; Math Tutor 88; Dnatl Hon Scty 85-87; Stdnt Cncl 85-87; Summa Cun Laude; BED; Elem Ed; Aiming Mstrs Degree Educ.

**ROSARIO, DARLENE ROSE,** Felician Coll, Lodi, NJ; SO; BA; Psych Clb 89-; Peer Asst Pgm 90-; Dns Lst 89-; Tutrng 90-; Drozd Schlrshp 89-; Dns Lst 89-; Bill Brdly Awd 88-89; Psych; Clin Psychlgst.

**ROSARIO, LISSETTE,** Inter Amer Univ Pr Hato Rey, Hato Rey, PR; SO; Cmptr Prgrmr Cert; Magna Cum Laude 89; Natural Sci; Cmptr Sci.

**ROSARIO, MICHAELANGELO,** Inter Amer Univ Pr Hato Rey, Hato Rey, PR; SR; BA; Hspnc Org Univ Brdgport 87-88; Hnr Stdnt Assn 90-; Soclgy; Law.

**ROSARIO, MICHELLE A,** Felician Coll, Lodi, NJ; FR; MBA; Psych Clb; Peer Supporter; Zata Alpha Zata; Psych.

**ROSARIO, MIGUEL A,** Fl International Univ, Miami, FL; SO; BA; Sci; Cmptr Eng.

**ROSARIO-DIAZ, EMUEL,** Univ Of Pr At Mayaguez, Mayaguez, PR; SO; BA; Dfndrs Yng Chrstn Assc 90-; Boy Scts Amer 87-89; Cmptrs; Eng.

**ROSAS, ANGEL L,** Univ Of Pr At Mayaguez, Mayaguez, PR; JR; BS; ACS 89-; All Amer Awd 89-; Med/Orgnc Chem.**

**ROSAS, PAMELA S,** Union Univ, Jackson, TN; SR; BS; STEA; Alpha Chi; Elem Educ; Teaching.

**ROSATO JR, JOSEPH A,** Univ Of Rochester, Rochester, NY; SO; BS; IEEE Micromse Comp 90; NROTC Unit 89; Ntl Grnt; Mchncl Eng; Avtr Nvl.

**ROSBOROUGH, HEATHER L,** Unity Coll, Unity, ME; JR; BA; SADD 90-; Envir Ed; Elem Ed.

**ROSCOE, MICHAEL A,** Wilmington Coll, New Castle, DE; JR; BA; Dover AFB 1st Serg Cncl Sec 90-; Air Force Assn 87-; USAF 75; 1st Serg 88-; Hmn Rsrc Mgmt; MS Cnslng.

**ROSE, ADRIENNE M,** Fl International Univ, Miami, FL; JR; BSW; AA Miami Dade Cmmnty Clg 90; Soc Wrk.

**ROSE, AMY R,** Univ Of Al At Birmingham, Birmingham, AL; JR; BA; Gldn Key; Deans Lst 89-; Prsdntl Hnrs Lst 90-; Erly Chldhd Ed; Tchng.

**ROSE, ANN M,** Univ Of Ms Medical Center, Jackson, MS; JR; BSN; MS Assoc Stdnt Nrs 90-; Wesley Fdtn Bapt Stdnt Union 88-89; Chi Omega 88-89; Med Chrstn Stdnts Chrstn Nrs 90-; Flwshp Chrstn Athl 88-89; Wesley Fdtn 88-89; Honduras Med Mission 87-; DCP MS Bapt Med Ctr; Flg Ftbl 88-; IM Bsktbl 88-89; Nrsg.

**ROSE, ANTHONY,** Indiana Univ Of Pa, Indiana, PA; SO; BA; SADD 90-; Deans Lst 89-90; Deans Lst 90-; Hnrs Cnvctn Dnnr; Deans Lst 89-; IM Vllybll Sftbll Capt 90-; Elem Ed.

**ROSE, AUDREY J,** Youngstown St Univ, Youngstown, OH; SR; BS; Gldn Key; Hnrs Cnvctn 87; Fndtn Schlrshp 85; NAEYC; Child Day Care Hm; AS 88; Erly Chldhd Spc Ed; Tchr.

**ROSE, BARNEY M,** Adelphi Univ, Garden City, NY; SO; BBA; Actvts Brd 90-; Hillel Sngng Cuitar/Kybrds/Drums/Phlsphy/Poetry/Rdng/Bdy Bldg 89-; Radio Sta Nwsmn/Dir/Prod 89-90; Trustees Schlr 89-; Deans List 89-; Bus Mgmnt/Fin Cncntrtn; Businessman.**

**ROSE, BONNIE S,** Middle Tn St Univ, Murfreesboro, TN; SR; BS; Gamma Beta Phi 90-; Kappa Delta Pi 90-; Natl Coll Educ Awd; Margaret Boutwell Early Chldhd Educ Schlrshp 90; Albert L/Ethel Carver Smith Mem Schrshp 90; AS Motlow State Comm Coll 79; Early Chldhd Educ; Prof Educ Primary Lvl.

**ROSE, CHERIE L,** Kent St Univ Geauga Cmps, Burton Twp, OH; FR; BA; Bus; Fin.

**ROSE, CYNTHIA M,** Saint Thomas Univ, Miami, FL; SR; BA; Acctg Clb Sec 89-90; Intrntl Stdnt Org 88-90; Fnc; Law Intrntl.

**ROSE, DANA,** Cumberland Coll, Williamsburg, KY; FR; BA; Bapt Stdnt Union; Flwshp Chrstn Athlts; IM Vlybl; Chem; Phrmcy.

**ROSE, DAVID C,** Univ Of Southern Ms, Hattiesburg, MS; SR; BS; Hattiesburg Jaycees 90-; Golden Key 90-; Arnold Air Soc 89-; AAS Cmmnty Cllg Air Force 83 89; Engnrng.

**ROSE, DAVID E,** Coppin St Coll, Baltimore, MD; JR; BA; Concerned Veterans 90-; Epilepsy Assoc Chm 88-; Jaycees Treas 88-90; U S Navy Vet Bten 76-82; Cert NEC Corres 86; Man Sci; Bus/Acctng.

**ROSE, DEBBIE G,** Middle Tn St Univ, Murfreesboro, TN; JR; Stdnt Envrnmntl Actn 90-; Hnr Stdnt Assn 90-; Sigma Tau Delta 90-; Gamma Beta Phi 82-; AS Columbia State Cmmnty Clg 82; Englsh; MSLS Wrk Clg Library.

**ROSE, DONNA,** Cumberland Coll, Williamsburg, KY; FR; BA; Bapt Stdnt Un; Flwshp Chrstn Athletes; IM Vlybl; Sci Chem; Med Profsn.

**ROSE, EDWARD K,** Columbia Greene Comm Coll, Hudson, NY; GD; BA; US Army Spc 4 86-89; Natl Grd Spc 4 89-; AA; Hstry/Pol Sci; Tchng Sec Educ.

**ROSE, JAMES D,** Ashland Comm Coll, Ashland, KY; SO; MBA; Phi Beta Lambda; SG 90-; Hon Stdnt Of The Yr 89-90; Phi Beta Lambda Pres 89-; Tutor 89-90; Drug Info Unit 90-; Appeals Ct 90-; Tennis 90-; Acctng; Law/CPA.

**ROSE, JAMES R,** Kent St Univ Geauga Cmps, Burton Twp, OH; SO; BA; Architecture; Architect.

**ROSE, JEAN M,** Univ Of Ms Medical Center, Jackson, MS; SR; Nrsng Cls Tres 89-90; Nrsng Cls Tres 90-; Nrsng Stdnt Body Sec 90-; Assn Stdnt Nrs 89-90; Ntnl Stdnt Nrs Assn 89-90; Wshngtn Wmns Luncheon Schlrshp 90; IM Ftbl; BS Sclgy Mlsps Cllg 88; BS Nrsng.

**ROSE, JERRY W,** East Tn St Univ, Johnson City, TN; SR; BSMNT; Soc Mnfctrng Engnrs 90-; Engnrng Lab Tech Asst; Engnrng Asst; AS Tri Cty St Tch 85; Mnfctrng Engnrng Tchnlgy; Engnrng Bsns Indstr.

**ROSE, JOSEPH A,** Univ Of New England, Biddeford, ME; SO; BS; SG; Phys Thrpy.

**ROSE, JOSEPH JOSHUA,** Yeshiva Univ, New York, NY; JR; BA; Hstry Soc 87-; Pre-Law Soc 87-; Beta Schl Jwsh Music 87-; Deans Lst 89-90; Phlnthrpy Soc 88-90; Law.

**ROSE JR, LEONARD A,** Univ Of Al At Birmingham, Birmingham, AL; SO; BSN; EMT Basic 90; EMT Interm; Nrsng.

**ROSE, LESLYN M,** City Univ Of Ny Baruch Coll, New York, NY; JR; BBA; Goldn Key 90-; Chrch Nzrn Yth Wrkr/Tutr 89-; Comp Info Syst; Syst Anlyst.

**ROSE, LINDA M,** Univ Of Montevallo, Montevallo, AL; SO; BA; Grmn Clb 90-; Deans Lst; Tutor Btny Stu Sprt Serv; Stu Sprt Serv; Psych; Corp Law.

**ROSE, LORRE G,** Ms Univ For Women, Columbus, MS; JR; BS; SMEA 90-; Kappa Delta Epsilon 90-; ARRT 82-; X-RAY Tech 82-; Cert Jones Cnty Cmnty Hosp Schl Rdlgy 82; Elem Educ.

**ROSE, MARY ELLEN,** Indiana Univ Of Pa, Indiana, PA; FR; Clarien Univ Hnrs Pgrm; BED; Spch Path/Aud; Spch Path.

**ROSE, MARY F,** Slippery Rock Univ, Slippery Rock, PA; FR.

**ROSE, MAUREEN,** S U N Y Coll Of Tech At Frmgdl, Farmingdale, NY; GD; AS; Deans Lst 90; Michael T Flemming Hon Awd; Acctg Dept 86-; Bus Admin; Mgmnt.

**ROSE, MICHAEL A,** Lexington Comm Coll, Lexington, KY; FR; BA; Crmnl Justc Club; Crctns/Jvle Svcs; Crctns Cnslr.

**ROSE, MICHELLE K,** Northern Ky Univ, Highland Hts, KY; FR; Dean Lst 90-; Hnrs Lst; Psych; Fmly Law/Fmly Cnslng.

**ROSE, MORGAN T,** Oh Univ, Athens, OH; FR; BA; Karate Clb; Art Ed; H S Tchr.

**ROSE, RHONDA M,** Univ Of Ky, Lexington, KY; SR; BA; Social Work.

**ROSE, ROGER E,** Tallahassee Comm Coll, Tallahassee, FL; SO; BA; Cmps Nwspr Entrtnmnt Edtr; Phi Theta Kappa Pub Rel/Hist; Phi Theta Kappa; Schlrshp Serv To The Talon; Elec Eng/Film; Eng Univsrl MGM Orlando.

**ROSE, SANDRA C,** Ga St Univ, Atlanta, GA; JR; BED; Rtl Sls; Sls Mgr; Asst Byr; Erly Chldhd Ed; Tchr.

**ROSE, SANDRENE A,** Bloomfield Coll, Bloomfield, NJ; FR; BA; Alpha Omega Epison/Iota Phi Theta Swthrt; Medcl Sclgst.

**ROSE, SHARON K,** Juniata Coll, Huntingdon, PA; SR; BS; Deputation Club 87-; Multicultural Comm; Psych Club 88-; Coll Hnr Soc; Univ Of Leeds Eng 89-90; Bio Psych; Clinical Psych.

**ROSE, STACY J,** Pellissippi St Tech Comm Coll, Knoxville, TN; GD; Wrk Study Schlrshp; Grad Cum Laude Hnrs; Philips Consumer Elec; Finance.

**ROSE, STEPHANIE L,** Christopher Newport Coll, Newport News, VA; SO; BS; Bio.

**ROSE, SUE ANN,** Kent St Univ Geauga Cmps, Burton Twp, OH; SO; Apple Scntfc 90-; Comp Tech.

**ROSE, SUSAN L,** Univ Of Ky, Lexington, KY; FR; Pharm.

**ROSE JR, THOMAS A,** Univ Of Sc At Columbia, Columbia, SC; SO; BS; Art Grphc Dsgn; Advrtsng.

**ROSE, TRACY L,** Va Commonwealth Univ, Richmond, VA; SO; BA; Gldn Ky; SASAC Rep 90-; Intrnshp Crtve Mtlwrks 90-; Helene Safire 90; Crfts; Artst.

**ROSEBERRY, MARK O,** Memphis St Univ, Memphis, TN; GD; MBA; Sons Of Liberty Club Sec 77-78; Dns Lst 90; Union Univ Schlrshp 77; Head Coach; Fndr NWA Fitness Ctr; ESE Nrthwst Airlines 79; Speech Pathology.

**ROSEBERRY, TREVOR D,** Fl A & M Univ, Tallahassee, FL; JR; BS; Alcohol/Drg Awrnss Prog 88-; NAACP 88-; Bg Brthrs/Bg Sistrs 89-; Gold/White; All Amer Schlr; Omega Psi Phi 90-; Hon Roll 88-; Deans Lst 88-; IM Ftbl 90-; Omega Psi Phi Chptr Schlr 88-; Zion Hl Bptst Schlrshp Awrd 90; Bus Econmcs.

**ROSEBORO, SUSAN D,** Central St Univ, Wilberforce, OH; SR; BME; Central State Univ Chorus 85-; Mrchng Bnd Treas 89-90; Concert Bnd Treas 89-90; Tau Beta Sigma; Stdnt Govt Assn Sec 89-90; Music Educ/Voice.

**ROSEBOROUGH, TIFFANY A,** Norfolk St Univ, Norfolk, VA; SO; Mass Cmmnctns Stdnt Assoc Pblc Rltns Prsn; Deans Lst; WNVZ Radio Promtns Dept.

**ROSEBROUGH, CATHERINE M,** Univ Of Akron, Akron, OH; FR; BA; Univ Prog Brd 90-; Res Hall Govt 90-; Educ Info Comm Brd Of Dir 90-; Phi Eta Sigma; Natl Hon Soc 90; US Achvmnt Acdmy 87-90; Alpha Lambda Delta; Sr Grl Scout Amer; Val Marion Hrdng Hgh Schl 90; Pres Schlr; Exchng Clbs Yth Of The Yr 90; Spec Educ; Dvlpmntly/Orthpdcly Hndcpd.

**ROSEHART, STEPHANIE A,** Univ Of Southern Ms, Hattiesburg, MS; FR; BS; USM Stdnt Sports Med Assn; SAA; Gamma Beta Phi; Pi Beta Phi 90-; Stdnt Athletic Trnr; Athletic Trnr/Edn; Profl Trnr/Pro Sports.

**ROSELL, KIM M,** Central Fl Comm Coll, Ocala, FL; FR; AA; Bio; Ethlgy.

**ROSELL, SONJA J,** Newbury Coll, Brookline, MA; FR; ASSOC; Bsns Mgmt; Humn Res Mgr.

**ROSELLI, ANTHONY T,** S U N Y Coll Of Tech At Alfred, Alfred, NY; JR; BS; Rsdnc Cncl Pres 88-89; AAS 90; Mgmt; Bus.

**ROSELLI, LAURIE A,** James Madison University, Harrisonburg, VA; SR; BS; IM Sftbl/Bsktbl 87-; Pi Kappa Phi Aux 89-; Pres List 90; Var Field Hockey 87-; Early Chldhd Ed; Tch.

**ROSEMAN, ANGELA D,** Univ Of Miami, Coral Gables, FL; SR; BS; Carni Gras Exec Comm Exec Chrprsn 89-; Frst Aid Sqd Chf Oper 87-; Bnd 87-90; Phi Kappa Phi 90-; Golden Key 89-; Mortar Brd Sec 90-; Pi Mu Epsilon Sec Treas 89-; Alpha Lambda Delta 87-88; Phi Eta Sigma 87-88; Amer Red Cross 89-; Math; Actuary.

**ROSEMAN, DELILAH G,** Talladega Coll, Talladega, AL; FR; Dance Tm 90-; Bus/Acctg Clb 90-; Inroads 90-; Intrnshp Mark Twain Bnk Ladue Teller; Finance; Loan Officer.

**ROSEMAN, EDWARD F,** Cornell Univ Statutory College, Ithaca, NY; JR; BS; Cobleskill Fisheries/Wldlf Club Pres 88-89; Amercn Fisheries Soc 90-; Phi Theta Kappa 88-89; Biolgcl Fld Sta On Oneida Lk Intrnshp; Firemns Assn Schlrshp 90; Dorwin Hamm Mem Schlrshp 89; 4-H Instrctr; AAS; Natrl Rsrcs; Fisheries Bio.

**ROSEMAN, MICHELE D,** Queens Coll, Charlotte, NC; SR; BA; Stdnts For Black Awrness 88-; Sec Sr Class 90-; Alpha Kappa Alpha 90-; Hsng Auth Stdnt Of Yr 89-90; Bus Admin; Law Schl.**

**ROSEMOND, HEATHER M,** Mary Baldwin Coll, Staunton, VA; SR; Cir K Scl Com 89; Pr Advsr Coll Lfe 90; Pres Of Drm Pres 90-; Alpha Lambda Delta; Mary Baldwin Hnr Schlr Scty; Tchrs Asst 90-; Pr Advsr 90; BED; BA; Sclgy Elem Educ; Tch Elem Educ.

**ROSEMOND, YVONNE T,** Greenville Tech Coll, Greenville, SC; Gen Offce Dplma; Cert Wrd Prfct; Cert Clrk Typst.

**ROSEN, ALIZA N,** Fl International Univ, Miami, FL; SR; BA; Psi Chi VP 89-; Phi Kappa Phi; Outstndng Acad Achiev Awd 90; Rsrch Asst Psych 89-; Deans Lst 88-90; Psych; Clncl Psych-Dr.

**ROSEN, ALIZA Y,** Univ Of Rochester, Rochester, NY; SR; BA; Phi Sigma Sigma Pdg Cls Pres 88-; Sch Nwspr Rprtr 87-88; Phi Beta Kappa; Advntg Fresh Orntatn Cmtee Stdnt Advsr Pnl Spkr 88-; Adopt Grndprnt Vol 87-88; Amer/Cndns Israel Vol 89-90; H C Goldsmith Schlrshp 89-; Tch Asst Psy 90; FAIR; Psychology; Jrnlsm/Brdcst.

**ROSEN, DAVID A,** Cornell Univ Statutory College, Ithaca, NY; FR; BS; Mrchng Bnd 90-; Symphnc Bnd 90-; Pep Bnd 90-; Chmbr Wnds 90-; Biology; Marine Biology.

**ROSEN, ERICA L,** Cedar Crest Coll, Allentown, PA; JR; BA; Amnsty Intl Pres 87-; Jdcl Bd Rep 88-; Preterite Ltry Soc Sec/Treas 89-; Espejo Yrbk Advrtsng Edtr 89-90; Alpha Kappa Delta; Asstg Our Comm-Serv 90; Scl Wrk/Sclgy; Cnslng/Wrtng.

**ROSEN, KEVIN D,** Univ Of Fl, Gainesville, FL; JR; BSBA; Financial Mgmnt Assn; Stdnt Govt Finance Assist; Phi Kappa Psi V P 88-; FL Undrgrd Schlr 88-; AA 90; Finance; Law.

**ROSEN, LOTTA E,** Broward Comm Coll, Ft Lauderdale, FL; SO; AA; Intrntnl Bsn; Bsn.

**ROSEN, ROSA INES,** City Univ Of Ny City Coll, New York, NY; JR; BA; Law And Govt Scty 88; SG; Urbn Lgl Stds; Dns Lst; Hspnc Aid Scty 84-; GM Schlrshp; Sim Vlybl 88; Hspnc Aid Scty 84-; AAS Gregg Dominican Institute 73; Urban Lgl Stds; Law.

**ROSENBALM JR, LARRY F,** Roane St Comm Coll, Harriman, TN; SO; MBA; Hardees Mgr 87-; Aerospace Eng.

**ROSENBERG, ERIC I,** Univ Of South Fl, Tampa, FL; GD; MSPH; Pub Hlth Stdnt Assn 90-; Madison Hse Med Serv Prog Dir 85-87; Asstnshp 90-; U S Pub Hlth Trneshp Schlrshp; BA Univ Va 87; Epidemiology/Biostatistics; Med.

**ROSENBERG, ERIC T,** Univ Of Cincinnati, Cincinnati, OH; SO; BM; Jazz Combo 89-; IAJE 89-90; Sci Fiction Clb; Alpha Lambda Delta 89-; Mc Micken Arts/Sci Hon Pgm 89-; Phi Mu Alpha Treas 90-; Univ Cincinnati Piano Cmptn; Wnr State U Of NY Piano Cmptn 88; Consrvtry Music Schlrshp; Piano/Jazz Piano Performance; Pianist/Cmpsr.

**ROSENBERG, JOHN P,** Georgetown Univ, Washington, DC; JR; BA; Asst Assoc Prdcr; Asst Prdctn Coor 90; Fnnce; Mtn Pctre Prdctn.

**ROSENBERG, SUZANNE,** Georgetown Univ, Washington, DC; SO; BA; Radio DJ 89-; Blck Mvmnts Dnce Theatr 90-; Envrnmntl Clb 89-; Psi Chi 90-; DC Schl Kids Tutr 89-; Deans Lst 89-; Hghst Hon 89-90; Bus Admin/Mktg; Law/Advtsng.

**ROSENBERG, TAMI J,** Kent St Univ Kent Cmps, Kent, OH; FR; BED; Clg Life 90-; US Vlybl Assoc 90-; Engl; Sec Ed.

**ROSENBERGER, BRIAN E,** Univ Of Al At Huntsville, Huntsville, AL; JR; BS; Mechl Engrg; Engrg.

**ROSENBERRY, CHRISTOPHER S,** Juniata Coll, Huntingdon, PA; JR; BS; Tri Beta 90-; Fsh Commssn Intrnshp; CRC Fr Chem Awrd 90; Ftbl Ltrmn 90; Vrsty Ftbl; Biolgy; PhD.

**ROSENBLATT, HOWARD S,** Cooper Union, New York, NY; SR; M ENG; Eta Kappa Nu; Bwlng; B Eng; Elect Eng.

**ROSENBLATT, MARK I,** Univ Of Miami, Coral Gables, FL; JR; BS; Vrsty Debate Tm 89-; Phi Eta Sgm 89-90; Phi Kappa Phi 90-; Pres Hon Roll 89-90; Asstnt Un MI Radio Phrmclgy Lab 90; Henry King Stanford Schlrshp 89-; Bio; Medcn.

**ROSENBLOOM, LAWRENCE A,** Univ Of Rochester, Rochester, NY; SR; BA; Univ Rochester Mock Trial Org Co Fndr 87; Young Democrats 87; Cmps Radio Sprts Announcer 89; Dns Lst; Univ Rochester Wash Cngrssnl Dnstr 90; IM Bsktbl/Sftbl/Ftbl; Poltcl Sci/Amer Hstry; Law.

**ROSENBLUM, BENJAMIN G,** Coll Of Insurance, New York, NY; FR; BS; Actuarial Sci.

**ROSENDE, STACY M,** Hillsborough Comm Coll, Tampa, FL; SO; ASSC; Juried Stdnt Art Show; Pblshd HCC Galleria Mag; Awrded Tlnt Bsd Schlrshp; Visual Arts; Visual Art Educ.

**ROSENECKER, LORA ANNE,** Wv Univ, Morgantown, WV; JR; BS; Wnd Ensmbl 88-90; Crnrstn Flwshp VP 88-; Mrgntwn Comm Bnd; Goldn Key; Acdmy Stdnts Phrmcy 90-; Gen Hosp Vol 88; Phrmcy Intrnshp 90-; WVU Music Schlrshp Awrd 88-90; Phrmcy.

**ROSENFELD, AMY R,** Endicott Coll, Beverly, MA; SO; AS; Erly Chld Educ/Psych; Tchr.

**ROSENHAUS, JASON C,** Univ Of Miami, Coral Gables, FL; SR; BA; Tae Kwon Do 2nd Degree Blck Blt 83-; Deep Water Lfgrd Cert 87-; Gold Key 90-; Beta Gamma Sigma 90-; Phi Kappa Phi 90-; Reg Athlete Agent; Acctg Excell Awd 89-90; Acad Excell Awd; Robert Baileys Cntrct Negotiator; Acctg; Sports Agent.

**ROSENHOLM, CARL A,** Univ Of Nh Plymouth St Coll, Plymouth, NH; SR; BS; Clg Rpblcns 87-88; Disk Jcky Radio Sta 85-86; Clmnst Newspr 87-88; Dns Lst; Pres Lst; Bsn Admin; MBA.

**ROSENKRANZ, THOMAS,** Bridgeport Engr Inst, Fairfield, CT; GD; BSEE; Elec Engr 88-; Ptnt Mtr Cntrls 88; AS 86; AAS 81; Elec Engr.

**ROSENSTARK, DAVID M,** Yeshiva Univ, New York, NY; SR; Wkly Schl Pblctn Editor In Chf 89-; Deans Lst; Cmptr Oper; Samuel Belkin Schlr Acad Achvmnt; Swim; Cmptr Sci; Cmptr Prgmng.

**ROSENSTEEL, TRACY V,** Indiana Univ Of Pa, Indiana, PA; JR; BSED; Panhellenic Exec Bd Sec 90-; Natl Stdnts Spch Lang Hear Assoc Treas 89-; Actvtes Bd 88-89; Phi Sigma Pi 89; Alpha Gamma Delta 89; Visit Aged 89-90; Vol Amer R C Blood Dr 90; Alpha Gamma Delta 89-; I Ms 89; Spch Path/Audiology; Spch Pathology M A.

**ROSENSTROCK, JEFFREY S,** Cornell Univ Statutory College, Ithaca, NY; JR; BS; Cornell Univ Orntn Cnslr/Stdnt Advsr 89-; Cornell Ambassador 88-; Gold Key 89-; Ho Nun De Kah VP 90-; Robert Purcell Un Cncl Co-Chair 88-; Teach Asst Intermediate Microeconomics Teach Asst; Athletes Schlstc Tutor 90-; Bus Mgmnt/Mktg; Law.

**ROSENTHAL, ANDREA P,** Bowie St Univ, Bowie, MD; SR; BED; Engl Clb 89-; Sigma Tau Delta VP 90-; Kappa Delta Pi 90-; Engl; Educ.

**ROSENTHAL, GEOFFREY L,** Univ Of Md Baltimore Prof Schl, Baltimore, MD; GD; MDPHD; Phi Kappa Phi; Amer Fed Clncl Rsrch Med Stdnt Awd; MD PLD Prog Tuition Awd; Amer Fed Clncl Rsrch Med Stdnt Awd; Short Tm Rsrch Trng Flwshp 89-; Soc Epidemiologic Rsrch; Amer Ststcl Assn 90; Study Dsgn; BA; MS; Epidemiology; Acad Med.

**ROSENTHAL, JODY A,** Fl International Univ, Miami, FL; SR; BS; Le Amis Du Vin 90; Hotel Food/Travel Assoc; Phi Kappa Phi; Phi Lambda Beta; Hospitality Management; Law.

**ROSENTHAL, RICHARD R,** Samford Univ, Birmingham, AL; GD; JD; Trl Advcy Brd; Mt Crt; Amer Jr Trl Advcy Stdnt Mtrls Ed; Sigma Phi Epsilon; Big Bros Amer; Ltr Rcgntn Montgomery AL; Fncl Anlyst Ryder Systms Inc; BA Fla Interntl Univ 85; Law.

**ROSHAL, ANNA,** Univ Of Rochester, Rochester, NY; SO; BS; Neurosci; Med.

**ROSIER, MEREDITH L,** Univ Of Sc At Columbia, Columbia, SC; SR; BA; Gamma Beta Phi 88-; Art Allince 88-; Intrnshp U SC Art Gallry Gallry Asst 88-; Recpnt VA Kaplan Awd P/Excell Expsng Wrtng 89; Crss-Cntry 89-; Studio Art; Grad Sch Ph D Pntng.

**ROSIGNOLI, DAVID A,** Rensselaer Polytechnic Inst, Troy, NY; FR; BS; Elect Clb Pres 90; RPI Ambulance Attndnt 90; Elect Engr; Engr.

**ROSINSKI, SHERYL A,** Western New England Coll, Springfield, MA; JR; BA; Quantttv Mthds; Actry.

**ROSINSKI, THOMAS W,** Hilbert Coll, Hamburg, NY; FR; Chess Clb; Lbrl Arts.

**ROSKOS JR, ROBERT E,** Univ Of Rochester, Rochester, NY; GD; Amtr Radio Clb 90; IEEEI 89-; Sigma Phi Epsilon 87-; BS 90; Elect Eng; Eng Bus.

**ROSMAN, DEANNA LYN,** Univ Of Miami, Coral Gables, FL; SR; Mrktng Clb 88-; Alpha Kappa Psi 88-; Sigma Delta Tau 88-; BA Univ Miami; Bus Admn/Mrktng.

**ROSNER, GITTY N,** Yeshiva Univ, New York, NY; JR; BA; Fshn Mrchndsng; Buyer.

**ROSOWSKI, DONALD,** D Youville Coll, Buffalo, NY; JR; BS; Hath Dist Bsbl Coach; Un Steward; AAS Erig Comm Coll 76; Spec Educ; Tchr Spec Educ.

**ROSPOND, LIA A,** Seton Hall Univ, South Orange, NJ; SR; BSN; Stdnt Nrs Assn 90-; Dns Lst 90-; Vol Hillside Hlth Fair 89-; Allergy Cnsltnts Med Aid 88-; Vol Spec Olympics; Nrsng; Pediatrics.

**ROSS, ADDIE G,** Norfolk St Univ, Norfolk, VA; JR; BA; Summer Schlrshp Virginia Cncl Hghr Educ; Engl; Tch.

**ROSS, ALVATINA G,** Tuskegee Univ, Tuskegee Inst, AL; SO; BA; Medicine; Nursing Intensive Care.

**ROSS, AMANDA K,** Bluefield St Coll, Bluefield, WV; FR; BS; Phi Eta Simga; Outstndng Frshmn Eng Tech 90-; Deans Lst 90-; Computer Sci; Programmer.

**ROSS, AMY J,** Allegheny Coll, Meadville, PA; JR; BA; ANTS Pres 89-; ACA Schlrshp 87-88; Walsh Schlrshp 88-89; Dist Alden Schlr 89-; Preschool TA 87-89; English; Elem Tchr.

**ROSS, AMY J,** Duquesne Univ, Pittsburgh, PA; FR; BSBA; Bus; Corp Acctg.

**ROSS, BRIAN A,** United States Naval Academy, Annapolis, MD; FR; Cath Midshipmens Clb 90-; Vrsty Rifle Tm 90-; History; UR Marine Corps Ofcr.

**ROSS, BRIAN K,** Fl A & M Univ, Tallahassee, FL; SO; BS; Res Ofcrs Trng Corps; Campus All-Star Challenge Tm Capt; Intrnshp Dist Attys Ofc Cndtd Govt 90; Pol Sci; Law.

**ROSS, BRIAN K,** Western New England Coll, Springfield, MA; SR; BSBA; IM Hcky/Sftbl/Ftbl 87-; Deans Lst 89-90; Intrnshp MA State Plc 90; NRA Mem YMCA; Mgmt; Law Enfrcmnt Ofcr.

**ROSS, CATHERINE S,** Univ Of Rochester, Rochester, NY; SO; BA; Undrgrad Hist Cncl 89; Peer Cnslng Phnelne 90f TMCA 89; Alpha Phi Schlrshp Chrprsn; History.

**ROSS JR, CHARLES A,** Fl St Univ, Tallahassee, FL; JR; BA; Flying High Circus 88-; Golden Key 89-; Bio/Psych; Marine Bio.

**ROSS, DANA M,** Allegheny Coll, Meadville, PA; SR; BS; Allghny Psych Assn VP 87-; Psych Dept Brd Stu Rep 89-; Stu Jdcl Brd 89-; Lambda Sigma Fndrsng 88-89; Psi Chi Fndrsng 89-; Kappa Lalph Theta 88-; Alden Schlr; Intern Hosp Prog 90-; Orchesis 87-; Psych; Occptnl Thrpy.

**ROSS, DAVID A,** Coll Of Charleston, Charleston, SC; SO; PHD; Bio Club 90-; Phi Kappa Phi; Marine Bio; Rsrch.

**ROSS, DAVID L,** Central St Univ, Wilberforce, OH; SO; BS; Biolgcl Soc Clss Rep 89-; Pre-Hlth Clb 89-; Blck Mn On The Move VP 90-; Beta Kappa Chi 90-; Beta Beta Beta 90-; Biolgy; Med Schl/MD/PHD.

**ROSS, DAVID W,** Univ Of Pittsburgh, Pittsburgh, PA; SR; BS; ASCE VP 89-; Chi Epsilon 90-; Gldn Ky 89-; Delta Tau Delta Dir Acad Affrs 87-; Kershner Awd 89; Cvl Engr; Engr.

**ROSS, DENIA J,** Alcorn St Univ, Lorman, MS; FR; Deans List; Pol Sci; Lawyer.

**ROSS, DENISE M,** Oh St Univ At Newark, Newark, OH; SO; BS; Phi Sigma; Elem Educ; Tchng.

**ROSS, DONALD,** Fayetteville St Univ, Fayetteville, NC; SO; BA; Fayetteville Cumberland Adv Cncl For People With Disabilities Empl Comm; Fayetteville Area Bd Of Rltrs Sls Person 87-89; Soc; Cnslr.

**ROSS, GERALD E,** George Mason Univ, Fairfax, VA; SR; BS; Acctng Hnr Scty 90-; Summa Cum Laude 89; Hnrs Tuition Schlrshp 87-88; Certif Hnr Outstndng Perfmnc; IM Flg Ftbl 87-89; AS Bus Admin 89; Acctng.**

**ROSS, GERRIT D,** Morehouse Coll, Atlanta, GA; JR; BA; IN Clb 90-; Mrhse Bus Assn 90-; Fnnce; Fnncl Anlyst.**

**ROSS, GLADYS L,** Fayetteville St Univ, Fayetteville, NC; JR; BA; Dept Corrections Mccain Corr Hosp Corr Ofcr 85-; Elem Edn; Teach.

**ROSS, GWENDOLYN J,** Univ Of Tn At Martin, Martin, TN; FR; BSN; Nrsng; RN.

**ROSS, JAMES P,** Manhattan Coll, Bronx, NY; JR; BS; Lambda Chi Alpha Ice Hcky 89-90; Natl Hon Soc 87; Natl Spnsh Hon Soc 87; Lambda Chi Alpha 89-91; Mgr Cty Islnd Ltl Leag; Engr.

**ROSS, JANET L,** Univ Of Sc At Columbia, Columbia, SC; SO; Gamma Beta Phi; Middleburg Phrmcy Intern 90-; Phrmcy.

**ROSS, JENNIFER M,** Oh Univ, Athens, OH; FR; BA; Sci; Elec Engr.

**ROSS, JENNIFER M,** Northern Ky Univ, Highland Hts, KY; JR; Vrsty Socer Wright State Univ; Jr Marshal; Grphc Dsgn; Advtsng.

**ROSS, JOYCE Y,** Salisbury St Univ, Salisbury, MD; JR; BS; Pi Gamma Mu; Ecnmcs; Bus/Ecnmcs.

**ROSS, KERRY W,** Union Univ, Jackson, TN; SO; BS; Sigma Zeta 90-; Sigma Alpha Epsilon Coorspndt 90-; Chem Lab Asstshp 89-; Chem; Med.

**ROSS, KIMBERLY M,** Univ Of Sc At Columbia, Columbia, SC; SO; Gamma Beta Phi 90-; Beta Gamma Sigma; Pres Schlrshp 89-; Bus Prtnrshp Fndtn Schlrshp; Deans Lst 89-90; Pres Lst 90-; Bus; Mktg.

**ROSS, LA TOYA N,** Tougaloo Coll, Tougaloo, MS; JR; CBS Scholar; Bio; Med/Peds.

**ROSS, LAURA L,** Ms St Univ, Miss State, MS; FR; BED; Phi Eta Sigma; Gamma Beta Phi; Alpha Lambda Delta; Elem Ed; Edctr.

**ROSS, MARIA ANTOINETTE,** Columbia Union Coll, Takoma Park, MD; JR; BA; Bsn Adm.

**ROSS, MITCHELL J,** Yale Univ, New Haven, CT; SO; Marching Band Soc Shrprsn 89-; Rifle Club 89-90; Bridge Club 90; Hosp Er Vol 90; Yale Alumni Assn Intern; Chem; Med.**

**ROSS, NICOLLA R,** Oh St Univ, Columbus, OH; SR; BA; Stdnt Cncl 87-89; African Amer Media Assoc Scl Chr 89-90; Rsrch Opport Pgm 89-90; Mortar Bd 90-; Hnrs Soc 87-; Minority Schlrs 87-; African Amer Schlr Awd 90; Outstndg Clg Stdnts Amer Flwshps 88; Cmnctns; Sls Promo/Spec Events.

**ROSS, PAUL W,** Wilmington Coll, Wilmington, OH; SO; BS; Dns Lst Southern St Cmnty Clg 89-90; Dns Lst 90-; Sci Achvmnt Awd; Sci; Med.

**ROSS, REBECCA L,** S U N Y Coll At Fredonia, Fredonia, NY; JR; BS; PTA Sec 89-; Grl Scts Asst Trp Ldr Nghbrhd Sec 90-; Hstry; Tchng.

**ROSS, ROBERT J,** Norfolk St Univ, Norfolk, VA; FR; BA; Ftbl 90-; Bus; Cmptr Prgrmr.

**ROSS, ROBIN L,** Glassboro St Coll, Glassboro, NJ; SO; PRSSA; IM Vlybl 89-90; Cmmnctns; Pblc Rltns.

**ROSS, SHARI N,** Columbia Greene Comm Coll, Hudson, NY; FR; BA; Crmnl Jstc; Law.

**ROSS, SHERRY D,** Univ Of Sc At Columbia, Columbia, SC; FR; BS; Delta Gamma Pledge Secr; Dns Lst 90; Psych; Psychother.

**ROSS, STEVE A,** Christopher Newport Coll, Newport News, VA; JR; BA; AS TNCC 90; Pltcl Sci; Pltcs Gvrnmnt.

**ROSS, TAB S,** Univ Of Tn At Martin, Martin, TN; SO; BA; Undgrad Almni Cncl 90-; Dns Lst 90-; Alpha Tau Omega Hstrn 90-; Ldrshp Conf 90-; Bsn Admn Mgmt.

**ROSS, THERESA,** Al A & M Univ, Normal, AL; FR; MANRRS V P 90-; Circle K Treas 90-; Dns Lst 90-; Hnr Rl 90-; Soil Conserv Intern; Agri Awd; MANRRS Natl Essay Awd; Agri Econ; Rsrchr.

**ROSS, THERESA A,** Univ Of Cin R Walters Coll, Blue Ash, OH; SO; AS; Cmptr Sci Tech; Cmptr Prgmng.

**ROSS, THERESA K,** Prince Georges Comm Coll, Largo, MD; FR; RC Wtr Sfty/CPR Inst; Sftbl 90-; Phys Ed; Gymnastics Coach.

**ROSS, TRAVIS F,** Univ Of Sc At Columbia, Columbia, SC; FR; MBA; Tennis; Spec Olympics; IM Soccer Captf; Intl Studies.

**ROSS, TZIVIA,** City Univ Of Ny Baruch Coll, New York, NY; SR; BA; Baruch Schlr 89-; Soc Srvc Intrn; Dns Lst 89-90; Bnos Chang Tchrs Semnry Jerusalem; Cert; Sociology; Soc Wrk.

**ROSS, VICKY L,** Oh St Univ At Marion, Marion, OH; SO; BA; Soc Wrk.

**ROSS-WADE, KIM,** City Univ Of Ny Baruch Coll, New York, NY; JR; BBA; Acctg; CPA.

**ROSSEL, CHERYL S,** West Liberty St Coll, West Liberty, WV; SR; BA; Multicultural Comm Pres 89-90; Internatl Org 89-90; Elem Ed; Teacher.

**ROSSELAND, NICOLE J,** Savannah Coll Of Art & Design, Savannah, GA; JR; BFA; Illustration/Pntng; Prof Illustrator/Prof.

**ROSSETTI, KRISTINE L,** Univ Of Akron, Akron, OH; JR; BS; ACES 90-; Golden Key; Kappa Delta Pi; Alpha Lambda Delta 89-; Phi Eta Sigma 89-; Gen Acad Schlrshp 89-; Deans Lst 88-; Elem Ed.

**ROSSI JR, FRANK JOSEPH,** Bloomfield Coll, Bloomfield, NJ; FR; BS; Chrprctc Clb 90-; IM Bsktbll 90-; Sci.

**ROSSI, JAMES J,** S U N Y Coll Of Tech At Frmgdl, Farmingdale, NY; SO; MBA; Acctg Scty 90-; Acctg; CPA.

**ROSSI, KRISTINE M,** Longwood Coll, Farmville, VA; SR; MS; Ldrshp Comm 89-90; VA Psychological Assoc 89-90; Pyschology Clb 87-88; Psi Chi 90-; Alpha Sigma Tau VP 89-90; Internship Psychological Cnsltnts Inc; Top Tau Awrd 88-; Silent Leader Awrd 89-; Psychology; Indstrl Psychlgst.

**ROSSI JR, MICHAEL J,** Ms St Univ, Miss State, MS; SO; BA; Frnch Clb; Alpha Lambda Delta; Phi Eta Sigma; Kappa Alpha Order; IM Sftbll; Hstry; Law.

**ROSSI, MICHELE A,** Teikyo Post Univ, Waterbury, CT; JR; BA; Bus; Acctng.

**ROSSI, RICHARD J,** Kent St Univ Kent Cmps, Kent, OH; FR; BA; Yng Rpblcns 90-; Alpha Lambda Delta 90-; IM Ftbl/Sccr 90-; Pol Sci.

**ROSSI, STEVEN K,** Manhattan Coll, Bronx, NY; FR; BS; Crew 90-; Engr.

**ROSSINI, DAN J,** Bridgeport Engr Inst, Fairfield, CT; SR; BS; Natl Assoc Of Left Handed Golfers 89-; AS ME Norwalk St Tech Coll 84; Mech Engr.

**ROSSITER, RENEE B,** Elms Coll, Chicopee, MA; SR; BA; Cls Ofcr Treas 89-90; Soph Show Chorgrphr 88; Dns Lst 87-90; Stdnt Tchr 90; Drama Dept Bulltn Brd Dsgnr 89; Hons Convctn Cover Dsgnr; Art Educ; HS Art Tchr.

**ROSSON, GINO S,** Kent St Univ Kent Cmps, Kent, OH; JR; BA; Accntng Assn VP 89-; Beta Alpha Psi 89-; Intrnshp Ernst & Young Pblc Accntng Adtr; Rlnc Elctrc Intrnl Adtr; Accntng.

**ROSSON, JAMIE A,** Middle Tn St Univ, Murfreesboro, TN; JR; BS; Deans List; AS Columbia St Comm Clg 90; Elem Educ; Teach.

**ROSTAMIZADEH, MARYAM,** Fl St Univ, Tallahassee, FL; SR; BS; A M Erdman Schlrshp 90-; AAS Tallahassee Comm Clg 88; Nutrtn/Food Sci; Food Sci Tech.

**ROSTCHILD, MARY L,** Concordia Coll, Selma, AL; JR.

**ROSZKO, DIANE B,** Rutgers St Univ At Camden, Camden, NJ; SR; Athnm 90-; Lab Tech 79; Ownd Oprtd Swng Mchne Bus 87; CLA Medical College Of PA 74; Acctng; Fnnce.

**ROTH, ALLISON M,** Millersville Univ Of Pa, Millersville, PA; SO; BA; Karate Clb 90-; Indstry/Tech Assn 90-; PSEA 90-; Indstrl Tech Edn.**

**ROTH, ANNE F,** William Paterson Coll, Wayne, NJ; JR; BA; Spec Educ Clb 89-; Kappa Delta Pi Sec 90-; Cncl Excptnl Chldrn 89-; PTA-TEANECK Schls 80-; Bogota Swm Clb Trustee 85-; Admin Asst 81-89; Spec Ed/Cnslng; Tch Spec Ed Grad Schl.

**ROTH, DAVID JAMES,** Univ Of Ky, Lexington, KY; JR; BS; KASP; KSHP; NARD; Kappa Psi Phlnthrpc Chr; Acad Excell Schlrshp; BA Bellarmine Clg 84; Bio; Phrmcy.

**ROTH, DAVID P,** Kent St Univ Kent Cmps, Kent, OH; JR; BM; Rcqtbl Clb 90-; Kent Music Educ Clb V P 89-; Golden Key; Kappa Kappa Psi Natl Hon Band Frat Pres 88-; Delta Imicron 88-89g; Sec Music Educ; H S Band Dir.

**ROTH, EDIT,** Ny Univ, New York, NY; SO; BA; Prs Ears Advsr 90-; The Frm Wrtr 90-; Jwsh Cltrl Fndtn 90; Chem Hnr Scty 90-; Dns Ldrshp Cir 90-; All Univ Orntn Ldr; Trstee Schlrshp Schlr 89-; Collins Schlrshp Schlr; Biochem; Med.**

**ROTH, ERIC H,** The Boston Conservatory, Boston, MA; SR; BM; Phi Kappa Lambda; Asst Music Div Chrprsn; BA SUNY Binghamton 79; Music Perf Cello; Tchng.

**ROTH, JANINE E,** Univ Of Akron, Akron, OH; JR; BA-MA; Hon Clb 88-; Cmps Crsd 90-; HSSLHA; Grt Cmmssn Stdnts; OSU Grnt-Rsrch; Hon Pgm 88-; Gldn Key 90-; Ohio Spch/Lang/Hrng Assn; Vol Physcl Thrpy Grp; Vol Amer Hrt Assn; Hon Schlrshp; Deans Lst 88-; Cmnctv Dsrdrs; Adlgy.

**ROTH, JASON M,** Allegheny Coll, Meadville, PA; SR; BS; Psychlgy Clb 88-; Itln Clb 87-88; Psi Chi 90-; Theta Chi Schlrshp Chrmn 89-; Alden Schlr 89-; Lacrosse Clb 88-; Psychlgy; Psychlgy Proffsr.

**ROTH, KIMBERLY C,** Converse Coll, Spartanburg, SC; FR; BA; Stdnt Govt; Stdnt Chrstn Assoc; Spanish Club; Stdnt Admsn Brd; Deans List; Pre-Law; Law.

**ROTH, MICHAEL J,** Univ Of Ct, Storrs, CT; SO; BA; Fncl Invstmnt Clb 89; Ecnmc Debate Tm; Tutor Hstry Math Sci Physics Chmstry 89; Deans Lst 89; Chess Clb 89; 3rd In 1991 CT Inter-Cllgte Ecnmc Debate; Hstry; Corp Law.**

**ROTH, RACHEL D,** Ursinus Coll, Collegeville, PA; FR; MBA; 4-H Horse Clb Pres 89-; Horse Bowl Tm Capt 90-; Bsn.

**ROTH, ROB E,** Pa St Univ Main Cmps, University Pk, PA; FR; BA; IM Ftbl/Vlybl 90-; Bsn; Econ.

**ROTHAN, ANN LEE,** Columbus Coll Of Art & Design, Columbus, OH; SR; BFA; DSI Alter Med Ctr Dir 75-77; YES Sympsm Wmn Over 40 Dir 87-88; Art Therapy; Fine Art; Fine Art; Art Therapy.

**ROTHE, SUSAN K,** Univ Of Tn At Knoxville, Knoxville, TN; FR; Campus Crsde Chrst; Alpha Lambda Delta; Phi Eta Sigma Sec; Delta Delta Delta Pldg Clss Chpln 90-; Habitat For Hmnty; UT Crew; Bus; Acctg.

**ROTHENBERGER, JUDY,** Bloomfield Coll, Bloomfield, NJ; SO; BS; Bio; Doc.

**ROTHENBERGER, KELLY A,** Bethany Coll, Bethany, WV; SR; Nwspr Clmnst The Tower 89; Yrbk Stf 87-88; Tri Beta Bio Hnry Soc Pres 89-90; Res Asstnt 89-; Yng Schlrs Pro Hd Res 90; BS; Bio; Nutrition.**

**ROTHERMEL, STACY L,** Savannah Coll Of Art & Design, Savannah, GA; SR; BSA; Graphic Design.

**ROTHFEDER, ANDREW E,** Emory Univ, Atlanta, GA; SR; BBA; Beta Gamma Sigma; Bus; Rl Estte.

**ROTHHAAR, MELINDA S,** Oh Wesleyan Univ, Delaware, OH; JR; BA; Wesleyan Stdnt Fndtn Tour Guide 88-; Orntn Asstnt 89-; Pres Club 88-90; Phi Eta Sgm Sec 88-89; Phi Scty 89-90; Omcrn Dlt Epsln VP 90-; IM Vlybl 90; WCSA Acad/Ldrshp Awrd; Deans List 88-; Sgm Chi Ltl Sis 88-90; Economics; Law.

**ROTHMAN, NICOLE IVETTE G,** Cecils Coll, Asheville, NC; AA; Spnsh Hnr Scty 85-86; Paralgl; Law.

**ROTHROCK, DONNA L,** Va Commonwealth Univ, Richmond, VA; JR; BS; Biology 100 Clb 89-90; Gldn Key 91; Bsns Admnstrtn; MBA Tchng Unvrsty Lvl.

**ROTHROCK, EDWARD K,** Pa St Univ Main Cmps, University Pk, PA; FR; BS; Boy Scouts Amer Asst Scout Mstr 90-; Eagle Scout Boy Scouts Amer; Sec Ed/Scl Studies; Tchr.

**ROTHROCK, PATRICIA L,** Lenoir Rhyne Coll, Hickory, NC; JR; BA; DPMA Pres 86-87; APICS Assoc Mbr 86; Phi Thetta Kappa Assoc 90; AAS Wstrn Piedmont Comm Coll 90; Cert Wstrn Piedmont Comm Coll 90; Bus Admin/Cmptr Prgrmng; Bus.

**ROTHROCK, TAMMY R,** Bapt Bible Coll & Seminary, Clarks Summit, PA; FR; BS; His Hddn Hnds Puppt Tm; Elem Educ; Elem Schl Tchr.

**ROTHSTEIN, MICHELE D,** Lehigh Univ, Bethlehem, PA; JR; BA; Stdnt Actvts Cncl Flm Chr 88-; Rsdnce Hll Cncl 90; Wmn Invlvd In Stdnt Educ Big Sis; Sigma Tau Delta 90-; Tch Fr Amer Dy Tchr 89; Stdnt Hstss 89; Henry C Pfaff Schlrshp; Robert Littner Schlrshp 90-; IM 89; Engl And Govt; Law.**

**ROTRUCK, JOHN R,** Univ Of Miami, Coral Gables, FL; SO; BS; Stdnt Cncl Secy 90-; Tbl Tennis Club 90-F Hons Stdnts Assoc 90-; Alpha Lambda Delta 90-; Beta Beta Beta 90-; Bio; Medcl Doctr.

**ROTSTEIN, JONATHAN ISAAC,** Univ Of Toledo, Toledo, OH; GD; JD; Stdnt Bar Assn 90-; Governing Bd 90-; Deans Lst 90-; Stdnt Am Bar Assn; Stdnt Ohio Bar Assn; BA Univ Of FL 82; Law.

**ROTTENBERG, JASON L,** Georgetown Univ, Washington, DC; JR; BSBA; Triathlon Fed USA 90-; German Clb 90-; Invstmnt Alliance 88-; Delta Phi Epsilon 89-; Harif/Arogeti/Wynn PC Intern; Crew Tm 88; Ftbl 89-90; Intl Mgmt/Acctg.

**ROTTER, JONATHAN C,** Coll Of Charleston, Charleston, SC; JR; Inter Frat Cncl Schlrshp Chr 90- SC State Coord; Kappa Alpha Order Corr Sec; Prsntr/State Ldrshp Conf/SE Inter Frat Cncl Conf; Poli Sci; Law.

**ROTTER, NATHAN A,** Memphis St Univ, Memphis, TN; JR; BSET; Memphis P C Users Grp; Comp Oper 90-; Comp Syst.

**ROTTMANN, HANS E,** S U N Y At Buffalo, Buffalo, NY; SR; BS; VITA 88; Hon Pgm 86-89; Beta Alpha Psi 89-; Phi Eta Sigma 87-; Deans Lst 86-90; IM Sftbl/Ftbl/Soccer 86-; Acctg/MIS; CPA.

**ROTUNNO, DONALD T,** Cooper Union, New York, NY; SR; BE; AICHE Pres 87-; Stdnt Cncl 89-; Athltc Assn 90-; ACS Treas 87-; Zeta Psi Pres 87-; Habitat Hmnty 88-; 4 Yr Tuitn Schlrshp; Bsktbl Sftbl Vlybl 87-; Chem Eng; Prcss Engr.

**ROTZKO, VICKI LYNN,** Univ Of Pa, Philadelphia, PA; GD; Sigma Kappa Phi 90-; Cls 1972 Awd 90; Wharton Evening Schl Alumni Assc Awd 90; DP Project Mgr; BBA 90; AS Burlington Comm Coll 86; Acctng/Mgmt.

**ROUDA, KIM S,** D Youville Coll, Buffalo, NY; JR; BA; SOTA 88-89; Res Cncl S 88-90; Lambda Sigma 89-90; Occ Ther.

**ROUDEBUSH JR, RONALD E,** Tomlinson Coll, Cleveland, TN; FR; BA; Phi Theta Kappa 90-; Sci; Medicine.

**ROUELLE, MARTIN D,** Rensselaer Polytechnic Inst, Troy, NY; FR; Ski Clb; Sigma Chi; Deans Lst; IM Sccr/Hcky/Lacrosse; AIAA; Engineering.

**ROUGHGARDEN, SHARON L,** William Paterson Coll, Wayne, NJ; JR; Specl Educ Clb At William Paterson 90-; CEC 90-; Young Adult Grp 89-; Reformed Church; Fidelians Camp For Exceptnl 89-90; Garden State Schlrshp 89-; Govrnrs Tchng Schlrshp 89-; Specl Ed Tchr.

**ROUGIA, MICHAEL J,** Hudson Valley Comm Coll, Troy, NY; SR; AOS; Elec Constr/Maint; Indstrl Electrcn.

**ROULLARD, PATRICIA D,** Univ Of Nc At Asheville, Asheville, NC; JR; BA; Cb Scts Cb Mstr 89-; Accts Rcvbls Coord Hot Springs Hlth Pgm 81-90; Hstry; Tch.

**ROUMAIN, DANIEL B,** Vanderbilt Univ, Nashville, TN; SO; BM; Blair Schl Music Stdnt Cncl V P 90-; Stdnt Prjcts Fnd Comm Chr 90-; Blck Stdnt Alliance Arts Comm Pres 90-; Phlhrmnc Orch Florida Intern 90; Benjamin E Mays Acad Award; Sue Brewer/Sngwrtr Award 90; Cmpstn/Theory; Violin Perf.

**ROUNDING, ROSLYN F,** Central Fl Comm Coll, Ocala, FL; SO; BA; Phi Teta Kappa 90-; AA; Pub Rltns; Poltcs.

**ROUNDTREE, CHERELIA D,** Fort Valley St Coll, Fort Valley, GA; SO; BA; Coop Dvlpmntl Engry Prgm 89-; Jdcry Cmmtt 89-; SGA; Mss Sphmr 90-; Prtr Schlr 89-; Bank Pierro Rutland Schlr 89-; Intern Dept Enrgy NV Oprtns 90-; Pltcl Sci Chsmtry: Envrnmtl Law.

**ROUNDTREE, TRACIE L,** Hillsborough Comm Coll, Tampa, FL; SO; BS; Tampa Bay Bucnrs Chrldr; Phi Theta Kappa Pres; Sci; Phys Thrpy.

**ROUNSAVALL, CHRIS M,** Daytona Beach Comm Coll, Daytona Beach, FL; SO; AA; Math Awd; Cmptr Sci.

**ROUNTREE, NATASHA M,** Wilberforce Univ, Wilberforce, OH; SR; BS; Wmn Holding Interest/Prfssnlm Chpln 89-90; Oh Pre Alum; Ntnl Stdnt Busn League; Ntnl Stdnt Busn League; Sigma Omega; Alpha Kappa Alpha Treas 90-; J F Morning Schlrshp 87-89; Rust Pres Hon 89-90; Busn Mgmnt; Hmn Rsce Mgmnt.

**ROUNTREE, ZELOMA C,** Vance Granville Comm Coll, Henderson, NC; GD; Stdnt Govt Assn Wmns Cncl Sec 65; Drma Clb 65; Glee Clb 73; Delta Psi Omega 65; Voc Stdnt Awrd 86; Chrch Mnstr Of Msc Orgnst Pnst 70-; Admin Prncpl N Hndrsn Schl; BCA Univ Of North Carolina 73; MA Pensacola Christian Coll 90; Msc; Tch.

**ROUPP, LORI A,** West Chester Univ, West Chester, PA; JR; BS; Cls Hrmny Jazz Shw Choir Dir Chrgrphr 88-; Cncrt Chr 90-; Music Edctrs Ntl Conf 89-; Hons Stdnt Assn 89-; Res Hall Assn Hall Rep 88-89; Fred Warings US Chrus 87-; Wilkinson Music Ther Schlrshp 90; Dnc Prdctn Wrkshp 89-; Music Ed Voice Mjr; Tchng.

**ROUSCULP, ANDREA G,** Anne Arundel Comm Coll, Arnold, MD; SO; BA; Elem Educ; Tchg.

**ROUSE, ERIC C,** Univ Of Rochester, Rochester, NY; JR; Poli Sci; Govt.

**ROUSE, KELLY E,** William Carey Coll, Hattiesburg, MS; SR; BS; Sci Soc VP 87-; Stdnt Govt Jstc Chf Jstc 88-90; Psychlgy Club 88-89; Omicron Delta Kappa 88-; Alpha Chi Pres 89-; U Of S AL Stdnt Fellow Rsrch 90; Presdntl Schlrshp 87-; Magna Cum Laude; BS; Bio; Tchng.

**ROUSE, MELISSA P,** Ms Gulf Coast Jr Coll Jeffersn, Gulfport, MS; FR; BA; Std Govt Sec 90-; Pol Sci; Intl Law.

**ROUSE, REBECCA H,** Central Fl Comm Coll, Ocala, FL; SO; BS; Hstlgst; Elem Ed; Spec Ed.

**ROUSE, SCOTT L,** Univ Of Southern Ms, Hattiesburg, MS; FR; BS; Hon Stdnt Assc VP 90-; Nwspr Asst Nws Edtr 90-; Presdntl Schlr 90-; IM Athltcs 90-; Jrnlsm.

**ROUTH, CARMEN R,** Univ Of New Haven, West Haven, CT; SO; BA; Communications; Mass Media.

**ROUTH, REGINA F,** Truett Mc Connell Coll, Cleveland, GA; FR; BA; Pres Clb; Hero Elbert Cnty; Cstmr Serv Rep 1st Natl Bank Elberton; Bus; Bnkng Offcr.

**ROUTH, TRUDY A,** Blue Mountain Coll, Blue Mountain, MS; FR; BA; BSU Fres Cncl 90-; Modenian Soc Soc 90-; Fres Cls VP 90-; Religion; Church Voc.

**ROUZER, EVONNE N,** East Stroudsburg Univ, E Stroudsburg, PA; SR; BS; Cum Laude Grad; Bus Mgmt; Govt Serv.

**ROVET, RICHARD J,** Univ Of Sc At Columbia, Columbia, SC; SO; BA; Sgt USAF 85-; Plyr Coach Brtsh Hcky Assc 87-90; Bio/Psychlgy; Ocptnl Thrpst.

**ROVETTO, LUCY R,** Jersey City St Coll, Jersey City, NJ; SR; BFA; Art Editor Schl Nwspr; Art Assn 87-; V P Photo Assn; Hnrs Prog 87; Intern Jersey City Museum 89; Artwork 89-; Stdnt Photo Show Awd; Fine Arts; Prntmkr/Phtgrphr.

**ROVIRA, JOSE B,** Fl International Univ, Miami, FL; JR; BS; FL Eng Soc 88-90; Crmnl Juste Hon Soc; Alpha Phi Sigma; FLA Army Natl Gd 86-; Hghst Hon 90; AA Miami-Dad Comm Coll 90; Crmnl Juste; Law.

**ROVITO, KRISTEN M,** Indiana Univ Of Pa, Indiana, PA; JR; BS; Concert Dance Co 89-; Scndry Scl Studies Ed; Sclgy Tchr.

**ROW, DEANNE M,** Savannah Coll Of Art & Design, Savannah, GA; FR; BFA; Rsdnts Cncl VP 90-; Intrntnl Stdnts Assc 90-; Int Stdnts Orntn Prgrm Fndr; Painting; Illustration.

**ROWAN, JAMES C,** Morehouse Coll, Atlanta, GA; FR; BA; TN Clb; Bnkng/Finance/Engl; Law.

**ROWAN, ROSLYN,** Marywood Coll, Scranton, PA; SO; BA; Spch/Hrg Clb 90-; Cmnctn Dsordrs; Spch Pthlgst.

**ROWDEN, MICHELLE E,** Memphis St Univ, Memphis, TN; SR; BPS; Gamma Beta Phi 89-; Paralegal Intern Pblc Dfndrs Ofc; Law.

**ROWE, ANGELA E,** S U N Y Coll Of Tech At Delhi, Delhi, NY; SO; BSN; Stdnt Govt Exec Sec 90; Wmn Of Cln 90; Blck Stdnt Union 90-; Beta Blckrs Nrsng Orgn; Rsdnt Asst 89-; AAS SUNY Delhi; Nrsng; Cert Emer Nrse.

**ROWE, ARTHUR T,** Univ Of Sc At Columbia, Columbia, SC; SR; BA; Naval ROTC USC 89-; Navy Enlisted Comm Prog USC 8-; Deans Lst 90; Pres Lst 89-; US Navy 81-; AA St Leo Clg 88; Mgmnt/Mgmnt Sci; U S Naval Officer.

**ROWE, ASTON K,** Nova Univ, Ft Lauderdale, FL; GD; MBA; Caribbean Stdnts Assn Cltrl Dir 88; W Indies Stdnts Assn Cncl Rep 89; BBA Fla Intl Univ 90; Mktg; Mgmt.

**ROWE, GERALD L,** Oh Univ-Southern Cmps, Ironton, OH; SO; YMCA; US Peace Corps Thlnd Vlntr 88-90; Geology; Rtnrng US Peace Corps.

**ROWE, JACQUELYN M,** Cornell Univ Statutory College, Ithaca, NY; SO; BS; Mrchng Bnd 89-; Pep Bnd 89-; Ski Clb 90-; Nat Rsrcs; Mgmt.

**ROWE, JOSEPH E,** S U N Y Coll Of Tech At Alfred, Alfred, NY; FR; AS; Elec Eng; Eng.

**ROWE, JULIE D,** Wilmington Coll, Wilmington, OH; FR; CBS; Frshmn Hmecmg Ct Attendant; Repr Xavier Clg Expo; Miss Black Cincinnati Pageant 90; Cin Career Conf Telephone Tech 1st Pl 90; MBA Psych BA Theatre.

**ROWE, KIRSTIN T,** Mary Baldwin Coll, Staunton, VA; SR; BA; Yrbk Fnncl Mgr 90; Big Sis Prog 90; Dev Com Fr Pnhll Cntr Sr Rep 90-; Crstr Bnk Scrts And Trst Dept Systms Cnvrsn Mgr 90; Mildred E Taylor Schlrshp Math; Wll St Smnr In NY Cty; Asstnshp Math Dept At MBC 88-; Math And Econs; Fnncl Anlyst.

**ROWE, LENFORD A,** De St Coll, Dover, DE; JR; BS BA; CASC Acad Quiz Bowl Tm Capt 89-; Jr Cls Pres 90-; Radio Sta Oprtns Mgr 89-; Alpha Chi 90-; Alpha Phi Alpha 90-91; W Wilson Flw Princeton U 90-; Law Firm Intrn; English; Econ; Law.**

**ROWE, LYNDA J,** Fl A & M Univ, Tallahassee, FL; SO; PHD; Natl Jr Hnr Soc 84-85; Natl Hnr Soc 87-89; FL Acdmc Schlr 89-; Pres Schlr 89-; Excllnc Achvmnt Schlr 89-; Phrmcy/Math; Indstrl Phrmcy.

**ROWE, MELANIE LEIGH,** Ga Southwestern Coll, Americus, GA; SO; BBA; Mktg Clb; Gamma Beta Phi; Alpha Lambda Delta; Pi Kappa Phi Swthrt; Vol Hndcpd Chldrn; Deans Lst; Mktg; Sls Rep.**

**ROWE, MICHAEL M,** Duquesne Univ, Pittsburgh, PA; SO; BS; Phrmcy.

**ROWE, OLIVIA M,** Bennett Coll, Greensboro, NC; JR; BA; Wmn Cmnctns Chrwn Pblcty; NAACP; Staff Reprtr 90-; Bennett Banner Awd; Intrnshp Greensboro News/Record 90-; Intrdscplnry Stds Awd 90-; Tutr/Mntr Ntl Blck Chld Dvlpmnt Inst 90-; Mayors Cncl Prsns W/Dsblties; Intrdscplnry Stds; Pblc Rltns.

**ROWE, SHAWN D,** Thomas Nelson Comm Coll, Hampton, VA; SO; BA; Sci; Elect Engr.

**ROWE, TOBY-LEE M,** Philadelphia Coll Of Bible, Langhorne, PA; FR; BA; Chorale 90-; Newspr 90-; Dns Lst 90-; Tchr Educ 90-; Pres Schlrshp; Music Schlrshp; Music Awd; Music Educ; Bible; Tchr Perfrmnc.

**ROWE, VEDA L,** Western Piedmont Comm Coll, Morganton, NC; JR; BA; Amer Nurses Assn 88-; Emerg Nurses Assn 90-; RN 78-; ADN 78; Nursing.

**ROWELL, ALLISON J,** Ms St Univ, Miss State, MS; JR; BA; Revielle Staff Co-Ed 88-; BARK; Athl Advsy Cmte 90-; Stdnt Asso 90-; Phi Kappa Phi; Gamma Beta Phi 88-; Phi Eta Sigma 88; IM; AA N E Ms Comm Colg 90; Secndry Edctn; Tch.

**ROWELL, DANA STEELE,** Auburn Univ At Auburn, Auburn, AL; GD; MED; Stdnt AL Ed Assoc 89-90; Phi Kappa Phi 89-90; Kappa Delta Pi 89-90; Sigma Kappa 88-90; Deans Hon Roll; BED 90; Erly Chldhd; 1st Grd Tchr.

**ROWELL, DEBORAH D,** Antonelli Inst Of Art & Photo, Cincinnati, OH; SO; AS; Alpha Beta Kappa 90-; Photgrphy.

**ROWELL, GRAHAM T,** Atlanta Christian Coll, East Point, GA; GD; Southwest Chrstn Church Intern 88-; Assoc Church Christ; Minister; BA; Chrstn.

**ROWELL, KARIN E,** Chesterfield Marlboro Coll, Cheraw, SC; FR; BA; Acctg Bus.

**ROWELL, RICHARD W,** Univ Of Sc At Columbia, Columbia, SC; JR; BA; Newspr 88-; Judicial Brd 89-; Hmecmng Comm Treas 88-90; Gamma Beta Phi 89-; Golden Key 89-; Mortar Bd Treas; Kappa Sigma Phlnthrpy Chr 90-; Jesse A Rutlege Schlrshp 90-; Elizabeth Junker Schlrshp 88-; Schlrs Schlrshp 88-; Jrnlsm; Advrtsng.

**ROWELL, TERI C,** Memphis St Univ, Memphis, TN; FR; BA; Hm Bldrs Assn Memphis; Yng Rlty Grp; Lgl Asst; Bsn; Law.

**ROWLAND, ALLEN T,** Valdosta St Coll, Valdosta, GA; JR; BSN; Nurs; Nurs Anesthetist.

**ROWLAND, HARMONY-FAYE,** Strayer Coll, Washington, DC; SR; BS; Alpha Chi 90; Cntrl Intllgn Agncy 83-90; Anlytc Sciences Corp TASC Reston VA 90; AA Allentown Bsn Schl Allentown PA 82; Cmptr Info Systms; Systms Anlys.

**ROWLAND, LISA A,** Univ Of Tn At Martin, Martin, TN; JR; BA; Chrch Chrst Std Ctr 88-; Dns Lst; Erly Chldhd Educ; Tchr.

**ROWLAND, RANDALL S,** Brewer St Jr Coll, Fayette, AL; SO; BA; Im Ftbl/Bsktbl 89-; Hist; Educ.

**ROWLAND, ROCKY A,** Univ Of Cincinnati-Clrmnt Coll, Batavia, OH; SO; AS; Deans List 90; H S Ser Prac 90-; Civil War Reinactor; S M Paper; Vol Nrsng Home 89-; Cub Scout Den Ldr/S Sch Chrch Wrkr 87-90; H/S Serv; Case Wrkr/Human Serv.

**ROWLAND, SUSAN E,** Univ Of Southern Ms, Hattiesburg, MS; SO; BS; Stdnt Alumni Assn 90-; Alpha Lambda Delta; Phi Eta Sigma; Lambda Sigma; Gamma Beta Phi; Chi Omega Frtrnty V P 90; Micro Bio/Chem; Sci.

**ROWLEY, BELINDA L,** Clarkson Univ, Potsdam, NY; JR; BS; Acctg Clb 90; Ntl Assc Acctnts 90; Deans Lst 89-90; Vrsty Sccr 88-90; Acctg/Mgmt Info Sys; CPA.

**ROWLEY, DORIS E,** Univ Of Sc At Coastal Carolina, Conway, SC; SR; AS; Daughters Amer Rvltn; High Hnrs; Natl Nurses Assoc; LPN Conway Schl Prctcl Nrsng 85; Nursing; MSN.

**ROWLEY, JENNY R,** Duquesne Univ, Pittsburgh, PA; SO; BA; Lambda Sigma Hstrn 90-; Lambda Kappa Sigma 90-; Phrmcy; Hosp.**

**ROXBURY, LINDA F,** Commonwealth Coll, Virginia Beach, VA; SO; AAS; Trvl Clb 90-; Phi Beta Lambda; Deans Lst 90; Pres Lst; Bus Adm Trvl; Flght Attndnt.

**ROY, ANJANA,** City Univ Of Ny Kingsborough, Brooklyn, NY; SR; Pthlgy Asst; Dwnst Med Cntr; MA Banasthali Vidyapith India 75; M PHIL U Delhi India 81; Nrsng.

**ROY, DENISE EDNA,** Fl St Univ, Tallahassee, FL; SR; BS; NAEYC; Intrn Gilchrst Elem 90-; Erly Chldhd Ed; Tchr.

**ROY, JENNIFER R,** Marshall University, Huntington, WV; FR; BA; Chrldr 90-; Dns Lst 90-; Acct.

**ROY, LAURA R,** Allegheny Coll, Meadville, PA; SR; BA; Psych Clb 89-; RA 89-; Allegheny Chrstn Outrch 89-; Psi Chi Pres 89-; Alpha Delta Pi 88-; Allegheny Comm Exchng 88-90; Psychlgy; Hlth Admin.**

**ROY, PAMALA M,** Fort Valley St Coll, Fort Valley, GA; SR; BA; Alpha Kappa Mu; Fd And Ntrtn; Hlth Admin.

**ROY, SIMONE,** Inter Amer Univ Pr San German, San German, PR; SO; BA; Intl Clb 89-90; Phi Beta Chi VP 90-; Grls Serv Clb 88-89; Outstdng Ldrshp 88-89; Engl; Elem Ed.

**ROY, SUSAN E,** Univ Of Rochester, Rochester, NY; SO; BS; Intrvrsty Chrstn Flwshp Sml Grp Ldr 89-; Res Hl Dorm Cncl Rep 90-; Soc Undrgrad Blgy Stdnts 89-90; Sailg Clb 89-90; Deans Lst 89-; Envrnmntl Sci.

**ROYAL, CHRISTOPHER B,** Univ Of Montevallo, Montevallo, AL; SR; BS; Montevallo Mstr 88-89; Phi Alpha Theta 89-; Omicron Delta Kappa Pres 89-; Kappa Delta Pi 90-; Delta Chi Pres 88-; IM Ftbl/Bsktbl/Sftbl 87-; Soc Sci; Tchr.

**ROYAL, COENA LA VETTE,** Tuskegee Univ, Tuskegee Inst, AL; JR; BS; Pltcl Sci Clb Rep 88; Pre Law Scty 89-; SGA Stdnt Sen Rep 89-90; Alpha Kappa Alpha Srrty Inc Mmbr Lrg 90; Cndy Strp Vol 87-88; Macon Cnty Cmmnty Actn Cntr Vol 90; Pltcl Sci; Corp Law.**

**ROYAL, JENNIFER G,** Medical Coll Of Ga, Augusta, GA; SR; BSN; Sigma Theta Tau Inc; Nrsng.

**ROYCROFT, CHERYL A,** Daemen Coll, Amherst, NY; JR; BS; Ed Policy Comm 90; Business Club 90; Delta Mu Delta; Kappa Delta Pi; NY Christmas Tree Growers Assoc 90; Familys Interested In Adoption 90; AOS; Bryant/Stratton Bsn Inst 86; Business/Ed; Teacher.

**ROYE, KENNETH M,** Al St Univ, Montgomery, AL; FR; BS; Trck Tm 90-; Biology; Doctor.

**ROYE, TERRI S,** Al St Univ, Montgomery, AL; JR; BA; Alpha Kappa Alpha; Pan Hllnc Cncl AKA Rep; Erly Chldhd Educ.

**ROYER-BERGEN, SABRINA K,** Univ Of Ga, Athens, GA; SR; UGAYC Treas 89-90; GORP; Communiv; Golden Key 90-; Ed.

**ROYSTER, DEMETRIA L,** Vance Granville Comm Coll, Henderson, NC; SO; AAS; Educ Clb 89-; Dns Lst 89-; Educ Intrnshp; Educ; Tchr.

**ROYSTER, DENISE L,** Al St Univ, Montgomery, AL; JR; NSE 90-; Fnnce; Fnncl Cnsltnt.

**ROYSTER, LAURA A,** Longwood Coll, Farmville, VA; JR; BS; Longwood Ambsdrs Pblcty Comm 89-; Kappa Delta Pi; Phi Kappa Phi; Elem Educ/Engl, Tchr.

**ROZEBOOM JR, VICTOR E,** Middle Ga Coll, Cochran, GA; JR; BE; Choras 90-; Drama Theatre 90-; Phi Kappa Sigma 87-; GA Power Co-Op 86-90; Elctrcl Engr; Engr.

**ROZENSHTEYN, GARY,** City Univ Of Ny Baruch Coll, New York, NY; JR; BA; Beta Gamma Sigma; Baruch Schlrshp; Dns Lst; Gldn Key 90; Accntg.

**ROZENSON, DAVID E,** Yeshiva Univ, New York, NY; SO; BA; Pluilan Thrpy Soc Drctr 89-; Camp Gan Israel Wrcstr MAS Drctr 87-; Otrch Prgrm Svt Jews Chrmn 89-; Assn Svt Jews Drctr 89-; Prsdntl Rcgntn Srvcs Immgrnts Rcgntn Scl Srvcs 88-89; Pltcl Sci Hstry; Law.**

**ROZENVELD, JAN,** Fl International Univ, Miami, FL; GD; MS; Stdnt Govt Chrmn PR 87-88; Primus Inter Pares 86-; MHS Mddlbr Htlschl Grnngn 89; BA FL Intl Univ 90; Hsptlty Mgmt; Htl Mgmt.

**ROZEWICZ, MARILYN L,** Erie Comm Coll, Buffalo, NY; FR; BA; Mntl Hlth; Cnslg-Alcohol.

**ROZEWSKI, TRICIA A,** Oh Wesleyan Univ, Delaware, OH; SO; BA; Wmn Vrsty Crs Cntry 90-; Wmnvrsty Indr/Otdr Track 90-; FCA 90-; Indr NCAC Chmpnshps 90; Edctn/Sprts Med.

**ROZMAN, DONALD N,** Comm Coll Algny Co Algny Cmps, Pittsburgh, PA; SO; Lab Tech 88-; Chmsty; Chmcl Engrng.

**ROZZELLE, DONICE L,** Central St Univ, Wilberforce, OH; SR; BS; Alpha Kappa Alpha Treas 90-; Intrnshp Dupont Co Inc 90-; Am Chmcl Soc Anlytcl Chmstry Awd 90-; Chmstry Schlrshp Bill Cosby 87-; Westinghouse Mtrls Schlrshp 89-90; Bk Spply Schlrshp Drifters 87-; Chmstry; Cosmtc Chmstry.

**ROZZELLE, SERGIO A,** Lincoln Univ, Lincoln Univ, PA; SR; Chrprsn Fndrsng Entrmnt Yrbk Chrprsn 89-90; Sntr SGA Jr Cls Hstrn Sntr 87-90; Bus Pol Sci Clb; Pre Law Soc; Theatre Grp; S Robinson Schlrshp Awd 90-; S W Nghbrhd Schlrshp; M Miner Schlrshp 88-; Lincoln Univ Hlth/Welfare Cmtee 88-89; Pltcl Sci; Law/Pltcs.

**ROZZI JR, ANDREW,** Duquesne Univ, Pittsburgh, PA; FR; BS; Work Stdy Prog 90-; Bus; Mgmt Acctng.

**RUA, SUSAN A,** Comm Coll Algny Co Algny Cmps, Pittsburgh, PA; RN.

**RUAN, SHULAN,** City Univ Of Ny Baruch Coll, New York, NY; JR; BA; Actrl Sci Soc; Seek Schlp Awd 88-; Endwmnt Fnd Prvsts Schlp; Actrl Sci.

**RUANE, JOHN G,** Embry Riddle Aeronautical Univ, Daytona Beach, FL; FR; BA; Sns Amer Lgn Sec 87-; Hnr Grdt US Nvy Armn Aprntcshp Schl 1st Cls 100 88; U S Nvy Rsrvs Pty Ofcr 3rd Cls; Actv Dty U S Nvy/Occup Pln Capt/Avtn Elctrcn 88-90; Arntcl Sci; Cmrcl Plt/Astrnt.

**RUBADEAU, ROBERT E,** Univ Of Rochester, Rochester, NY; JR; BA; Undrgrd Engl Cncl 89-; Pre Law Assn 89-; Engl/Psychlgy; Law Schl.

**RUBENSTEIN, LEANNE,** Univ Of Ga, Athens, GA; JR; BED; Bnai Brith Hillel 90-; Cncl For Exceptnl Chldrn 89-; Communiversity 90-; Spcl Ed; Tchng.

**RUBENSTEIN, LISA R,** Univ Of Ga, Athens, GA; FR; IM Sprts Sccr Vllyvll 90-; Delta Phi Epsilon 90-; Spcl Olympics; Ed; Tchng.

**RUBENSTEIN, RANDEE M,** Univ Of Rochester, Rochester, NY; SO; BA; Jdscl Cncl Jstc 89-; Kappa Dlt Tres 90-; Dist Atty Intrn; Fld Hckty; Psychlgy; Law.

**RUBENSTIEN, MICHAEL-ANNE,** Univ Of Miami, Coral Gables, FL; SO; Pres 100 90-; Prog Cncl 90-; Hnrs Stdnt Assoc 89-; Marine Affrs/Anthrplgy; Envrnmntl Educ.

**RUBERRY, KAREN A,** Goucher Coll, Towson, MD; JR; BA; Vsl Arts Org 90-; Intrn MD St Arts Cncl 90-; By Scts Amer Fndrsng Chr 89-; Shrn Ltl Flwr Hm Schl Assc Pblcty Chr; Educ Asst Walters Art Glry 88-90; Art; Musm/Educ.

**RUBIN, ALAN L,** Allegheny Coll, Meadville, PA; SR; Vrsty Tnns 87-88; Rsdnt Advsr Allegheny Rsdnc Life 89-; Intr Frtrnty Cncl Trs 89-; Ordr Omega 89-; Phi Gamma Delta Chptr Cnslr 87-; Intrnshp Lgl Rsrch Pineot Pineot Pratt Atrns Law 89-90; Alden Schlr 88-; Psychology; Law Bsns.

**RUBIN, DAVID,** City Univ Of Ny Baruch Coll, New York, NY; SR; BBA; Golden Key 90-; Beta Gamma Sigma; Cmptr Info Syst.

**RUBIN, JAN G,** Fl International Univ, Miami, FL; SR; BA; Hsptlty Clb 90-; Sprts Soc 81-; FL Prk/Rcrtn Assn 90-; RCRA; Mgmt Intrnshp; Coll Vlybl Offcl; ASA Sftbl Umpire; Cert PADI Scuba Dvr Instrctr; AA Miami-Dade Comm Coll 81; Rcrtn Mgmt; Dir Rcrtn Actvties.

**RUBIN, JODI B,** Va Commonwealth Univ, Richmond, VA; SO; BS; Ocptnl Thrpy Clb 89-91; Jr Vrsty Chrldr 89-; Vrsty Chrldr 90-; Phi Eta Sgm; Ocptnl Thrpy.

**RUBIN, KENNETH A,** George Mason Univ, Fairfax, VA; SO; BA; SADD Pres 85-88; Bus Comp.

**RUBIN, RICK D,** Univ Of Miami, Coral Gables, FL; SR; Hons Stdnt Assoc 87-; Disc Jcky 89-; Golf Club 87-; Phi Kappa Phi; Golden Key; Econ.

**RUBIN, ROSELYN,** Coll Of Insurance, New York, NY; JR; BS; Deans Lst; Act Sci; Acctg.

**RUBIN, SUSAN R,** Lesley Coll, Cambridge, MA; JR; Chamber Singers Vocal Jazz 88-; Marching Bnd Stdnt Cncl 88-; Chorale; Childrens Hospt Vol; Sing Along Singers; Bowman Schl Kndrgrtn Intrn 89; Cmnty Theater; Bicent Bnd 88-; Human Svcs; Art/Psych.

**RUBINO, NANCY M,** Duquesne Univ, Pittsburgh, PA; SO; BS; Rsdnt Asstnt 90-; Deans Lst 89-; Kappa Psi 89-; Intrnshp Olsons Phrmcy; Phrmcy; Phrmcst.

**RUBINO, RENEE A,** East Stroudsburg Univ, E Stroudsburg, PA; SR; BA; Stdnt Senate Chair Acad Affairs 89-; Omicron Delta Kappa; Hist; Pol Sci; Hist/Pol Sci; Law Sch.

**RUBINSTEIN, REENA D,** Univ Of Sc At Columbia, Columbia, SC; SO; Psych Club Repr; RA; Hillel; Zeta Beta Tau Aux; IM Tennis; Engl/Psych; Prof.

**RUBIO, ALEX,** Fl International Univ, Miami, FL; FR; B ACC; Deans Lst 90-; I M Ftbl 90; Acctg; Law.

**RUBIO, JORGE E,** Fl International Univ, Miami, FL; SR; BED; Fut Educ Amer; Coll Demo; FIV Chptr Cuban Amer Stu; Vol Wrk Prjct LEAD; Cmnd Coop Tchr/Scl Stdy Dept Hd Stu Intrn; Scl Stdy; Tchg.

**RUBIO, NANCY V,** Bunker Hill Comm Coll, Boston, MA; FR; BA; Cmptrs; Systms Anlyst.

**RUBY, JENIFER J,** Gettysburg Coll, Gettysburg, PA; FR; BA; Cbnt 90-; Rcgntn Lst 90-; Engl; Law.

**RUBY, ROBERT H,** Ms St Univ, Miss State, MS; JR; BA; Stndt Corr Assoc 89-; Filwhsp Chrstn Athlts 89-90; Refrm Univ Fllwshp 89-; Elder Statesman Hnry 90-; Kappa Sigma VP 88; Roadrunner Stdnt Rcrtr Alumni Delg; Soc; Law.

**RUCCI, SERGIO,** Univ Of Rochester, Rochester, NY; SR; Amer Soc Mech Engrs 88-; Sigma Phi Epsilon Fnd Rsg Chrmn 88-89; IM Soccer 87-; Mech Engr.

**RUCH, JOHN B,** Oh Wesleyan Univ, Delaware, OH; SO; BA; East Asian Studies Clb Treas; Bacchus Formula Host 90-; Student Radio Dir 89-; Community Serv Roundtable 89-; English.

**RUCK, CAROL W,** Middle Tn St Univ, Murfreesboro, TN; SR; THEA 89-; HEA 89-; HYPER 89-; Wllnss/Ftnss; Physcl Thrpy.

**RUCKEL, DIANNE D,** Seton Hall Univ, South Orange, NJ; SR; BSE; Educ Clb 90-; Kappi Delta Phi 90-; Spec Olympcs 89; Stdnt Tchng 89; Soccer Track 87-89; Ele Spec Educ; Tch.

**RUCKER, ANGELA,** Le Moyne Owen Coll, Memphis, TN; SO; BA; Peer Cnslr 90-; Class Ass Sec 90-; Pres Schlr 89-; Math; Engrng.**

**RUCKER, DREAMA D,** Ashland Comm Coll, Ashland, KY; FR; Baptst Stdnt Union 90-; Dns Lst 90-; Sci; Med Lab Tech.

**RUCKER III, IKE,** Selma Univ, Selma, AL; FR; BA; Rlgn.

**RUCKER, JENNIFER C,** Univ Of Rochester, Rochester, NY; SO; BA; Otsd Spkrs Comm Publ Rels 89-; Lit Jrnl 89-; Gamma Phi Beta Asst Schlrshp Chrmn 90-; Engl/Hstry; Educ.

**RUCKER, JENNIFER S,** Union Univ, Jackson, TN; SO; BA; Hstry Clb Treas 90-; Baptist Stdnt Union 89-; Zeta Tau Alpha 89-; Hstry; Law.

**RUCKER, PATRICIA A,** Oh Univ-Southern Cmps, Ironton, OH; SO; BA; Coach Mdgt Lge Chrldrs VP; Chesapeake PTA VP; Deans Lst 90; Elem Ed/Engl Lit.

**RUCKER, PHILIP S,** S U N Y Coll Of Tech At Delhi, Delhi, NY; SR; BA; Indr Trck/Fld 89-90; Spec Olympcs Vol; Trck/Fls 89-90; AAS; Bsn.

**RUCKER, SHERRICE L,** Bennett Coll, Greensboro, NC; FR; BS; Acctng; CPA.

**RUCKMAN, LINDA P,** Western Piedmont Comm Coll, Morganton, NC; JR; RN; Cub Sct Mstr 90-; Sndy Schl Tchr 89-90; Nrsng.

**RUDASILL, RICHARD S,** Itawamba Comm Coll, Fulton, MS; SO; BS; Acad Schlrshp; Cmptr Sci/Math.

**RUDD, REBECCA L,** Univ Of Ky, Lexington, KY; SR; BA; Rssn Clb Rep 88-; Pol Camp Rep 90; Pre-Law Soc 90-; Pi Sigma Alpha 89-; Scts Pro Lgls 90-; Delta Gamma; KY Gnrl Assmbly Intrshp 90; Hnrs Dist; Pol Sci/Rssn Stds; Law.

**RUDDELL, DOUGLAS L,** Christopher Newport Coll, Newport News, VA; JR; BA; Gov Policy Ofc Intern; Bk Store Mgr; Asst Mgr Auto Parts Store; Pol Sci; City Policy Analyst.

**RUDDER, GAIL J,** Long Island Coll Hosp Of Nrsng, Brooklyn, NY; FR; AS; Manfacturers Hanover Trust Co Spvsr 87-; AOS Taylor Bus Inst 86; Hlth Sci; Nursing.

**RUDGE, RANDY R,** Mount Aloysius Jr Coll, Cresson, PA; SO; Phi Theta Kappa 90-; Shtz Inc; Assoc; Prlgl; Bus.

**RUDGE JR, THOMAS L,** Univ Of Akron, Akron, OH; GD; PHD; Bike Clb Treas 88-90; Bulger Hall Gov Flr Rep 86-90; Hons Clb 86-90; Alpha Lambda Delta 88-90; Phi Eta Simga 88-90; BS Ntrl Sci 90; Mlclr Gntcs Rsrch.

**RUDGUNAS, JESSE M,** Embry Riddle Aeronautical Univ, Daytona Beach, FL; FR; BS; Lackawanna Bicycle Clb Rcng Tm 88-; US Cycling Fdrtn Ctgry 3 Rcr 89-; Aerntcl Sci; Prfsnl Airline Pilot.

**RUDIN, KERRI A,** Radford Univ, Radford, VA; SO; BS; Speech Path/Audio.

**RUDISILL, DAWN J,** Lenoir Rhyne Coll, Hickory, NC; JR; BA; Alpha Lambda Delta; Mu Sigma Epsilon; Deans Lst; Pres Lst; Elem Ed; Tch.

**RUDMAN, MICHELE L,** Univ Of Miami, Coral Gables, FL; SR; BS; Wmns Intl Znst Org Vchrmn; Gldn Key; Krt Clb; Jrnlsm.

**RUDNEY, PAULETTE R,** Daemen Coll, Amherst, NY; SO; BA; Wtrss; Phys Thrpy Aide; Hstry Govt; Lwyr.

**RUDNICKI, AMY M,** D Youville Coll, Buffalo, NY; FR; BSN; Artsts/Wrtrs Asn 90-; SNA 90-; Cmps Mnstry 90-; Pres Hnrs Schlp 90-; Nrsng; Pediatric/Natal.

**RUDNIK, DOUGLAS O,** Saint Francis Coll, Loretto, PA; SR; BS; Deans Lst; Treas 3 Brethren Chrch; Health Mngmt.**

**RUDOLF, KATHRYN A,** Fl St Univ, Tallahassee, FL; JR; BA; Chi Omega Chrmn 88-90; Std Govt Rep 89-90; Pol Sci.

**RUDOLPH, HELGA,** Univ Of Sc At Coastal Carolina, Conway, SC; FR; Pre Schl Tchr Dsbld Chldrn; Fraunenfachschule Lubeck Germany 66; Ed; Elem Schl Tchr.

**RUDOLPH, JOACHIM C,** Univ Of Sc At Columbia, Columbia, SC; SO; BS; Sailing Clb Pres 90-; Gamma Beta Phi; Bus; Fncl Mgmt.

**RUDOLPH, MEDRIDGET S,** Talladega Coll, Talladega, AL; BA; Chrstn Assn Pres 83; Tour Choir; Alpha Kappa Alpha; MARC Schlr 85-86; Deans Lst 90-; Hon Stdnt; Prmry Sndy Schl Tchr; Sr Choir; Comm Chorus; Biolgy; Allied Hlth.

**RUDOLPH, TARA A,** Suny Health Sciences-Buffalo, Buffalo, NY; FR; BA; Alpha Beta Gamma Zeta Chptr 90-; Phi Theta Kappa Mu Omega Chptr 90-; Bus; Bus Law Admin.

**RUDOLPH, TERRANCE O,** Al A & M Univ, Normal, AL; FR; Football.

**RUDOLPH, TIMOTHY B,** Al A & M Univ, Normal, AL; FR.

**RUDOLPH-THOMPSON, MARILYN J,** Bowie St Univ, Bowie, MD; SR; BS; Edctn Clb Pres 90-; Ftr Tchrs Treas 90-; Schlstc Awrds Ed Clb 90-; Schlstc Awrd Alpha Kappa Alpha 90-; Tchrs Assoc 89-; Natl Edctn Assoc 89-; Elctn Jdg; Mn Cnfrnc FTM Prsntr; AA 90; Elem Ed.

**RUDY, GEORGE,** Miami Dade Comm Coll South, Miami, FL; JR; BA; AA; Eng.

**RUDY, STACEY R,** Northampton County Area Coll, Bethlehem, PA; FR; AAS; Stdnt Assn Dntl Hygientists 90-; Phi Theta Kappa; Dental Hygiene.

**RUDZINSKI, J SCOTT,** Edinboro Univ Of Pa, Edinboro, PA; JR; BFA; Pntng/Crfts; MFA/ART Hstry.

**RUED CONLEY, SUSANNE,** Lesley Coll, Cambridge, MA; JR; BA; Elem Ed; Tchr.

**RUEF, CAROLYN E,** Atlantic Comm Coll, Mays Landing, NJ; BSN; Dns Lst; Phi Theta Kappa 90; Schlrshp Sth Jrsy Nrsng Assn 89; Schlrshp Vstng Nrss Assn 90; RN Cape May County Vo-Tec 90; Cert Cape May County Vo-Tec 78; Nrsng; Nrsng Onclgy Cert Spclst.

**RUEGG, MARK A,** Univ Of Akron, Akron, OH; SR; BFA; Good Yr Theater 85; Dance; Ballet Dncr.

**RUEHL, PAMELA S,** Northern Ky Univ, Highland Hts, KY; SR; BA; Acctg; MBA.

**RUEHL, PHILLIP J,** Oh Univ, Athens, OH; FR; BA; Engr/ Math; Elec.

**RUEHLE, DIRCK R,** Winthrop Coll, Rock Hill, SC; JR; BS; AS York Tech Clg Rock Hill SC 89; AS York Tech Clg Rock Hill SC 89; Bsns; Fin.

**RUEHLE, JANET G,** Va Commonwealth Univ, Richmond, VA; JR; BS; Stdnt VA Ed Assoc; Psychlgy Spcl Ed; Tchr.

**RUEHLE, MELANIE L,** West Liberty St Coll, West Liberty, WV; JR; AS; SADHA 89-; Chi Beta Phi 89-; Dntl Hygn; BS.

**RUF, ANITA A,** Kent St Univ Geauga Cmps, Burton Twp, OH; SO; BA; Tutrng; Deans Lst; Hstry/Scndry Ed; Admin Ed.

**RUF, MERLE A,** Cumberland County Coll, Vineland, NJ; JR; RN AS; Nrsng Club Pres Elct; Nrsng Class Pres; Beta Sigma Phi 70-80; Wmns Club Vineland Rcrdng Sec 70-80; AA Mrktng Rider Coll 67; Nursing.

**RUFENER, LYNDA S,** Univ Of Akron, Akron, OH; JR; BBA; Womens Network 87-88; Mrktng; MBA/ENVRNMNTL Law.

**RUFF, AMY N,** Allegheny Coll, Meadville, PA; JR; BA; Judo Clb Stdnt Gov Rep 88-89; Chrldr 89; Cmmnty Exchng 89-; Alden Schlr; Kappa Alpha Theta 89-; Mdcl Intrnshp; Latin; Med Physcn.

**RUFF, KEVIN R,** Univ Of Sc At Spartanburg, Spartanburg, SC; JR; BA; Gamma Beta Phi; Acctng; CPA.

**RUFF, MICHAEL J,** Univ Of Nc At Charlotte, Charlotte, NC; JR; BA; Kappa Alpha Order Athl Chrmn 90-; Atlantic States Diving Meet Bronze Mdl; Diving Record 90; Swim Tm Capt 89-90; Diving 1 88-; Crim Just; Air Force/Law/Navigatn-Pilot.

**RUFF, VALERIA C,** Johnson C Smith Univ, Charlotte, NC; JR; BA; Stdnt Assoc Of Educ 89-; Pi Delta Tau 90-; Elem Educ; MA.

**RUFFIN, JEFFREY D,** Ms St Univ, Miss State, MS; SR; BS; Reflector Sportswriter 88-; Mbr Reformed Univ Flwshp 90-; IM Bsktbl Sftbl Ftbl Tennis Golf 87-; Deans Schlr 87-88; Mu Kappa Tau 90-; Pub Rltns Comm; Winner Of Midnight At Mccarthy Bsktbl Competition; Mrktng.

**RUFFIN, LEERNEST M,** Al St Univ, Montgomery, AL; JR; BS; Tutor For Ala Urban League For Advncemnt Of Ed 90; Arnold Air Soc; Acad Schlrshp 90; Hnr Stdnt Clg Of Arts/Sci; AAS Lawson State Cmmnty Clg 89; AA Tarrant Cnty Jr Clg 89; Cmptr Sci; Cmptr Eng.

**RUFFIN, SHARON Y,** Norfolk St Univ, Norfolk, VA; JR; BED; Bus Educ; Tchr.

**RUFFNER, ROMI R,** Saint Vincents Coll & Seminary, Latrobe, PA; FR; BA; Chem Club; Chemistry; Analytical Chemist.

**RUFFNER, VALARIE J,** Mount Aloysius Jr Coll, Cresson, PA; FR; BA; O T Club; Phi Theta Kapa Prsdnt; PTA Prsdnt 86-87; AA Harcum Jr Cllg 75; Hlth Srvcs; Occtptnl Thrpy.

**RUFUS, FREEMAN,** Morehouse Coll, Atlanta, GA; JR; BS; Chess 88-; IL State Clb Treas 89-90; Ntnl Hnr Scty Treas 88-89; AT & T Hnr Awd 88-; Math; Engnrng.

**RUGENSTEIN, MARY LEE A,** Univ Of Miami, Coral Gables, FL; Wmn Cmnctn 90-; Publ Rels Soc 90-; Libr Arts Cncl Pres 83-90; Jaycees Just Say No Pgm Natl Awd 86; US Jaycees Proj Coord 86 88; Drug/Alcohol Awareness Task Force Pres 86-88; Dept Agri 82-90; Publ Rels/Pol Sci; Govt Publ Affairs.

**RUGGERI, GINA M,** Univ Of Ct, Storrs, CT; SO; BS; Stdnt Union Brd Of Govrnrs 90; Stdnts Thnkng Ahead Rflctng Sprt 89-90; Hsky Ambssdrs; Golden Key; Soph Chem Intrnshp 90; Chemistry; Engr.**

**RUGGIERO, CHRISTINE R,** Liberty Univ, Lynchburg, VA; SO; BS; Clg Repblns 89-; Big Sister 90-; Elem Ed; Tchng.

**RUGGIERO, CINDI ANN,** Bloomfield Coll, Bloomfield, NJ; SR; BA; Sigma Phi Delta VP 88-; Hoffmann-La Roche Intrn 90-; Chld Psychlgy.

**RUGGIERO, DONNA MARIE,** Cedar Crest Coll, Allentown, PA; SO; MBA; Cncrt Chr VP 89-; Cdr Crest Chrstn Flwshp 89-90; Theatre Prdctns 89-; Alpha Psi Omega Prse; Clg Ambsdr 90; Deans List 89-; Elem Educ/Psychlgy; Elem Schl Tchr/Actrs.

**RUHE, KAREN L,** Radford Univ, Radford, VA; SR; BBA; Chrldg Capt 87-89; Ru Snw Ski Clb 90-; Cls Ofcrs Cncl Soph Scrt 88-89; Pi Omega Pi Pres 90-; Phi Beta Lambda VP 90-; Otstndg Stu Admin Systms 90-; Chrldg Capt 87-89; Bus; Educ.

**RUHNAU, ROLAND B W,** Juniata Coll, Huntingdon, PA; SR; BS; Biol.

**RUIZ GOMEZ, WILLIAM,** Univ Politecnica De Pr, Hato Rey, PR; FR; Karate Blue Belt; Math; Elect Engr.

**RUIZ MELENDEZ, PEDRO E,** Inter Amer Univ Pr San Juan, Hato Rey, PR; GD; JD; Amer Bar Assn 87-; Natl Assn Law Stdnts 87-; Alumni Assn Law Stdnts 90-; Hon Rl; Legal Rsrch Asstshp 88-89; Law Review 88-90; Bkbl 88-90; BBA Univ Puerto Rico 86; Law; Lawyer.

**RUIZ RIVERA, BETSY Y,** Inter Amer Univ Pr San German, San German, PR; FR; Sccss Nght Excllnt Stdnts 90-; Hon Stdnts 90-; Bio; Med Tech.

**RUIZ RODRIGUEZ, JULIO DANIEL,** Univ Politecnica De Pr, Hato Rey, PR; FR; Recre Spts Club; Students Council; Bsbl/ Swmng/Tns; Indtl Engr.

**RUIZ TOMASSINI, MARITZA,** Inter Amer Univ Pr Aquadilla, Aguadilla, PR; GD; BA; Cmptr Prgmmr Cncl 90-; Hnr Std 90-; Cmptr Sci; Cmptr Prgmmr.

**RUIZ, JOHN L,** Inter Amer Univ Pr Hato Rey, Hato Rey, PR; FR; Math; CPA.

**RUIZ, JOY,** Univ Of Pr At Rio Piedras, Rio Piedras, PR; SR; Amer Inst Archtctr Stdnts Sec 88-90; Stdnt Cncl Treas 90-; Archtctr.

**RUIZ, LUIS F,** Univ Of Miami, Coral Gables, FL; JR; BM; Kairos-Prison Mnstrs 88-; Fmr Sprvsr Rgstrn 86-90; AA Miami-Dade Comm Coll 89; Music Ind; Rcrdng Ind.

**RUIZ, MARIA B,** Inter Amer Univ Pr San German, San German, PR; FR.

**RUIZ, MARISOL,** Bloomfield Coll, Bloomfield, NJ; SO; Stdnt Govt; Ldrshp Prog; Bloomfield Clg Deans Lst 90; Delta Phi Chi Pres; Acad Hnrs 90; Sftbl; Bio/Pre Chrprctc; Chrprtc Dr.

**RUIZ, MERVIN,** Univ Of Pr At Mayaguez, Mayaguez, PR; JR; MBA; Soc Stu Unn Pres 90-; CISA Rsrch Asst; Thrd Prz Lit Fable Cntst 90; Pol Sci; Jrnlsm.

**RUIZ, NEREIDA,** Catholic Univ Of Pr, Ponce, PR; SR; BBA; ALESEC 88; Acctg Stdt Assn; Puerto Ricotesol; Acctg/English; Law.

**RUIZ, RICHARD,** City Univ Of Ny City Coll, New York, NY; SR; BA; Cvl Air Ptrl Manhattan Grp Asst Trnr 88-90; Psychlgy; Clncl Psychlgst.

**RUIZ-AGUIRRE, IRLANDA,** Univ Of Pr Humacao Univ Coll, Humacao, PR; SO; SSSA Stdnts Repr 90; Editor Impacto 90; Joy To Univ Assn 89-90; Hnr Pgm Stdnt Repr 90; Poetry Cntst Award 89-90; Art; Law.

**RUIZ-TORRES, JEANNETTE,** Univ Of Pr At Rio Piedras, Rio Piedras, PR; GD; MLS; SG VP 89-; Research Asstnt 90-; Bed 88; Librarian.

**RUKES, JACQUELYN A,** Middle Tn St Univ, Murfreesboro, TN; SR; BA; Kappa Delta Pi 88-; Elem Educ; Tchr.

**RULAND, CAROL A,** Long Island Coll Hosp Of Nrsng, Brooklyn, NY; SR; AAS; Paul Doyle Awd 90; Switzer Fdtn Schlrshp 89; Nrsg.

**RULAND, GARY E,** George Mason Univ, Fairfax, VA; JR; BS; Sprts Med Physcl Edctn; Med.

**RULEY, REBECCA K,** Watterson Coll, Louisville, KY; SO; AD; Bus Admin; Business Owner.

**RUMANCIK, WILLIAM P,** Wv Univ, Morgantown, WV; SO; MBA; IEEE; Cmptr Soc; Helevetia 89-90; Chimes VP; Pi Mu Epsilon; Cmptr/Elec Eng; Rsrch/Dvlpmnt.

**RUMBERGER, JOANN M,** Mount Aloysius Jr Coll, Cresson, PA; FR; AS; Sci; Med Lab Tech.

**RUMFELT, BRENDA E,** Western Piedmont Comm Coll, Morganton, NC; SO; Nursing Clb; Phi Theta Kappa; Amer Student Nurses Assoc; Science; Nursing.

**RUMLEY, LISA A,** Middle Tn St Univ, Murfreesboro, TN; SO; BA; Gamma Beta Phi 89-; Natl Hon Roll 90-; Psychlgy; Psychiatric Soc Wrkr.**

**RUMMEL, CAROL A,** Wv Univ At Parkersburg, Parkersburg, WV; SO; AS; Hosp Mdcl Trnscrptnst 67-; Psychlgy.

**RUMMEL, MARGARET E,** Bloomfield Coll, Bloomfield, NJ; SR; BSC; Alpha Phi 87-; Hgh Hon-Sclgy Awd 86; Natl Pres Amvets 81-82; Natl Trng/Coord; Lab Tchncn/Prsnnl Asst; BA 86; Prsnnl Mgmt.

**RUMRILL, MARTIN R,** Me Maritime Academy, Castine, ME; SR; ME; NROTC; TSB; US Coast Grd Eng Lic; Mrn Eng; U S Navy.

**RUNEY, KAREN M,** Coll Of Charleston, Charleston, SC; SO; BA; Blgy Clb 90-; Intl Clb 89-90; Frnch Clb 90-; Alpha Epsilon Delta 90-; Chrldng 89-; Blgy.

**RUNFOLA, RANDALL P J,** S U N Y Coll At Fredonia, Fredonia, NY; JR; BA; Pol Sci Clb 87-89; City Of Jamestown NY Intrn 88; City Of Jamestown Mayro Intrn 89; City Of Jamestown Dept Of Dev Intrn 90-; AA Jamestown Cmnty Clg 89; Pol Sci; Law.

**RUNGE, ANITA J,** Univ Of Southern Ms, Hattiesburg, MS; SO; Hall Govt Rep 89-90; Gamma Beta Phi 90-; Archtctrl Eng; Archtctr.

**RUNGE, JOHN P,** Fl Atlantic Univ, Boca Raton, FL; SR; BS; Pres Lst 90; Mrktg; Entrprnrshp.

**RUNGE-HIX, DEBORAH K,** Univ Of Al At Birmingham, Birmingham, AL; SR; AS; Beta Alpha Psi; Golden Key; Phi Kappa Phi; Am Soc Clncl Pathlgst; Med Tech Lab Mngr; Bkkpr; Sales; Accntng.

**RUNGTA, SANJAY,** Western New England Coll, Springfield, MA; SR; BSEE; Intl Stdnt Assn 88-; Alpha Lambda Delta 90-; Sigma Beta Tau 89-; Peer Tutor 89-; Tchng Asst Mech Eng Dept 89-; Elec Eng.

**RUNKLE, SARA J,** Fl St Univ, Tallahassee, FL; FR; Student Alumni Fndtn; Phi Eta Sigma; Kappa Delta Asst Secy 90-; Business; Acctng.

**RUNNELS, COURTNEY A,** Ms St Univ, Miss State, MS; FR; BA; Delta Gamma 90-; Alpha Tau Omega Ltl Sis 90-; Pres Lst 90; Bsn; Mktg.

**RUNNELS, MELISSA A,** Ms St Univ, Miss State, MS; FR; BS; Pre Vet Clb 90-; Act Schlrshp 90-; Pr Lst 90-; Bio/Sci; Phys Ther.

**RUNNELS, MICHAEL S,** Fl St Univ, Tallahassee, FL; FR; BA; Phi Etha Sigma 90-; Lambda Chi Alpha Chrmn; Dns Lst; Phi Etha Sigma; Chem; Dntl Schl.

**RUNYON JR, JAMES MICHAEL,** Cecils Coll, Asheville, NC; FR; AA; CCAP; Vet Frgn Wars US 90-; US Navy :Uss Nimitz 86-90; Prlgl; Law.

**RUOTOLO, RACHEL A,** Duke Univ, Durham, NC; FR; Clscl Ballet Pgm 90-; Project Bld 90; Cancer Sprt Pgm Vol; Biology; Medicine.

**RUPARD, JENNIFER L,** Salisbury St Univ, Salisbury, MD; JR; BS; Jr Achvmnt 89-90; Kappa Delta Pi Chrmn; Elem Ed; Tchg.

**RUPE, JOE M,** Emory & Henry Coll, Emory, VA; JR; BS; Pre Hlth Prfssns Clb :Vp Pres 90-; Beta Beta Beta VP 90; Blue Key; Blgy Chmstry.

**RUPERT, JOY L,** Indiana Univ Of Pa, Indiana, PA; BA; Biology; Sec Educ.

**RUPERT, MARY MADELINE,** Indiana Univ Of Pa, Indiana, PA; SO; BED; PARALEGAL 88; Cert 88; Excptnl Stdnt; Tch.

**RUPERT, SUZANNE L,** Oh Univ, Athens, OH; SR; BA; Prog Cncl 89; Radio DJ 88; Alpha Lambda Delta 88; Phi Kappa Phi 89; French Art Clny 88; Mc Guffey Schlrshp 88; Deans Lst Schlrshp 89; Ohio Vlly Bnk Schlrshp 88; Visual Cmmnctns; Freelnce Phtgrphr.

**RUPERT, SYLVIA A,** Bristol Univ, Bristol, TN; GD; Blck Wmns Prfssnl Ntwrk 89-; E TN Dev Cncl Advsr 89-; Mnrty Entrprse Dev Pblc Pvte; Sctr Plnng Com; DJ Wrd Ensmble Drma Ok Rdge Plyhse; Univ Of TN Drma Dept; NAACP; Socioecon Progs Spclst; MBA.

**RUPLE, MICHELLE R,** Coll Of Charleston, Charleston, SC; SO; BS; Bio Clb 89-; Alpha Epsilon Delta 90-; Chi Omega 89-; Bio; Med Pediatrics.

**RUPP, ANGELA K,** Univ Of West Fl, Pensacola, FL; JR; BA; Std Acctng Soc; Phi Eta Sigma 89-; Alpha Sigma Lambda; Outstdng Std Lwr Div 89-90; Pres Lst 88-; AA 90; Acctng; CPA.**

**RUPP, STACY D,** Univ Of Pittsburgh, Pittsburgh, PA; JR; BSN; Natl Std Nrs Asc 89-; Sigma Theta Tau 90-; Chldrns Hosp Pttsbrgh Extnshp; Nrsng.

**RUPPE, SUSAN A,** West Chester Univ, West Chester, PA; FR; BB; Stdnt Govt Rsdnce Hll Assn 90-; IM Vlybl Sftbl; Mrktng.

**RUPPEL, KIM B,** Kent St Univ Kent Cmps, Kent, OH; SO; BM; Marching Bnd; Symphony Bnd; Univ Bnd; Tau Beta Sigma; Music Ed; Teach.

**RUPPERT, MARYA,** S U N Y Coll Of Tech At Frmgdl, Farmingdale, NY; FR; AD; SNA Pres; Nrsg; Nrs Prctnr.

**RUSCHE, RANDALL J,** Tallahassee Comm Coll, Tallahassee, FL; SO; BA; Sigma Pi Intl Beta Class Pres 90; Clin Psychlgy.

**RUSCITTI, TERESA M,** Wagner Coll, Staten Island, NY; FR; BA; Sngfst; Hmcmg; Hnrs Pro; Alpha Sigma Omega; Elem Ed; Tch.

**RUSCITTO, DIANE M,** Coll Of Charleston, Charleston, SC; SR; BS; Biology Club 89-; Phi Theta Kappa 81-83; Omicron Delta Kappa 89-; Burkart Academic Schrshp 90-; Vlntr Roger Hop 90-; AAS SUNY At Canton 83; Biology; Physcl Therapy.

**RUSE, DEBORAH L,** Hillsborough Comm Coll, Tampa, FL; FR; BA; Faith Bapt Ch S Sch Tchr 86-; Ele Educ; Tch K-3 Grades.

**RUSE, GLENN R,** Comm Coll Algny Co Algny Cmps, Pittsburgh, PA; FR; AS; Alum Brick/Glass Wrkrs Intl Financial Secy 89-; Nrsng; Hosp Exec.

**RUSH, BARBARA L,** Univ Of Montevallo, Montevallo, AL; SR; BS; Kappa Delta Pi 90-; Lambdo Sigma Pi 90-; Phi Kappa Phi 90-; Elem Educ; Tchr.

**RUSH, MATTHEW J,** Allegheny Coll, Meadville, PA; JR; BA; Chrs 89-; Stdnt Exprmntl Thtr 89-; Tsk Frce Spprt Of Hmsxl Bscl Pple Co Chrprsn 90-; Aldn Schlr 90-; Engl; Engl Prfssr.

**RUSH, ROXANE N,** Lenoir Rhyne Coll, Hickory, NC; JR; AB; Bapt Union Sec 87-; Spnsh Clb 87-; Phi Beta Lmbd 90-; Sgm Kappa Soc Chrmn 89-; Mktg Awrd; Vrsty Sccr 89; IM 90-; Intrntl Bus; Mktg/Acctg.

**RUSHER, SHARON D,** Brescia Coll, Owensboro, KY; SR; BS; Natl Spch Lang/Hear Assn VP 90; Cmnctn Sci/Disorders; MS.

**RUSHIN, JAMILYN M,** Univ Of Akron, Akron, OH; GD; BS; Law Library Fl Time Stdnt; Golden Key; Phi Eta Sigma; Alpha Lambda Delta; Mu Kappa Tau; Pi Sigma Epsilon; Mktg; Sales.

**RUSHING, BONNIE E,** Ms St Univ, Miss State, MS; SR; AATSP; AATSP Of MS; Spanish Hon Soc Sec/Treas; Spanish Clb Sec/Treas; Italian Clb; Pre-Law Soc; Hist Hon Soc; Choir; Hist Hon Soc Advsry Com/Sec/Treas 90; Deans Stdnt Rep Lang Dept; Phi Mu Sor; Phi Mu Sor; Vol Court House Vol Cnty Hosp; Foreign Lang/Romance Lang; Romance Lang Prof.

**RUSHING, DANIEL HARRY,** Univ Of South Fl, Tampa, FL; FR; BA; Futore Busn Ldrs Amer Treas 88-90; Marching Band 87-90; Spanish Natl Hnr Scty 89-90; Acctng Econ.

**RUSHING, EILEEN F,** Univ Of Ky, Lexington, KY; SO; BA; Scl Wrk; Chld Gdnc Spec.

**RUSHING, HEATHER R,** Meridian Comm Coll, Meridian, MS; SO; AA BS; Clogging Tm 85-90; Debte/Frnscs Clb; Natl Rural Elec Yth Tour Rep 88; Batgirl 90-; Crmnl Jstc/Pre Law; Law.

**RUSHING, TANYA R,** Univ Of Tn At Martin, Martin, TN; SO; BS; Spanish Clb; Math Clb; Hons Seminar; Phi Eta Sigma; Deans Lst 89-; Comp Sci.

**RUSHING, TRENA L,** Lee Coll, Cleveland, TN; JR; BS; Pscy Clb; Alpha Chi; Epsilon Lambda Phi; Psch; Educ.**

**RUSHTON, ANGELA C,** Queens Coll, Charlotte, NC; SO; NC Stdnt Legs Delgtn Chr; Jdcl Bd Dorm Rep 90-91; Mdl UN 90-; Flwshp Of Chrstn Athlts 90-; Janusian Soc 90-; Order Of Omega; Phi Mu Panhlnc Secy; Dana Schlr; Belk Schlr; Soccer MVP; Varsty Womens Soccer Cptn.

**RUSHTON, MIKI L,** Crichton Coll, Memphis, TN; SO; BS; Stdt Gvt 89-; Drama Clb; Annual Stff Co Edtr; Honor Roll 89-; Stdt Servs Asst; Psychology; Counselor.

**RUSHTON, PAMELA S,** Winthrop Coll, Rock Hill, SC; FR; BA; Engl Clb; Bg Bro Bg Sis Prog 90-; Chrldng 90-; Engl; Scndry Educ.

**RUSHTON, STEPHEN T,** Univ Of Sc At Aiken, Aiken, SC; FR; BS; Chmstry; Med.

**RUSIN, LEAH M,** Daemen Coll, Amherst, NY; SR; BA; Grntlgy Clb Pres 88-89; Hmn Serv Clb Sec 89-90; Scl Sci Asc 90-; Pi Gamma Mu; Natl Asc Scl Wrkrs 90-; Lord/Life Adlt Day Care Intrn 89; Dr Wnstn Schlp Arts 89; Chktwg Snr Ctr Intrn 90; Cntlcn Ctr Lrng Intrn 90-; Dns Lst 89-; Spec Olymp; AAS 89; Scl Wrk; MA Doctorate.

**RUSMAN, JARED M,** Georgetown Univ, Washington, DC; SR; Pre Law Soc; Clg Rep; Beta Gamma Sigma 90-; Fincl Mgmt Assn; Res Asst; Acad Frst Hnr; Summa Cum Laude; BSBA; Finc/Intl Mgmt; Law.

**RUSNAK, BARBARA A,** Richard Bland Coll, Petersburg, VA; SO; BS; Art.

**RUSNAK, MARK A,** Clarkson Univ, Potsdam, NY; SO; BS; Rsdnt Advsr 90-; IM Sprts Cptn 89-; Mgmnt Infrmtn Systm.

**RUSS, DAWN M,** Southern Vt Coll, Bennington, VT; JR; BA; Animal Rights Forum 89-; Deans Lst 89-90; Acctng.**

**RUSS, HOWARD B,** Fl St Univ, Tallahassee, FL; SR; BS; Amercn Mktg Assoc 90-; Im Bsktbl/Sftbl 88-90; Bus; Mktg/Sports.

**RUSS, JONATHAN D,** Emory & Henry Coll, Emory, VA; SR; Intrnshp Dana Corp 90; Bsbl 86-87; BA 90; Mathmtcs; Educ.

**RUSS, JUANITA F,** Thomas Nelson Comm Coll, Hampton, VA; SO; AAS; Office Sys Tchnlgy; Exec Sec.

**RUSS, MARY-MARGARET,** Richard Bland Coll, Petersburg, VA; FR; AA; Engl; Pblc Rltns BA.

**RUSS, TRINA D,** Princeton Univ, Princeton, NJ; FR; BSE; Gospel Choir Sec; Imani Ensmb; Natl Soc Blk Engrs; David Sarnoff Rsrch Cntr Intrn; MEP Schlrshp; Elec Engr.

**RUSSEL, DEBBIE C,** Goldey Beacom Coll, Wilmington, DE; FR; BA; Girl Scouts; Bus; Acctg.

**RUSSEL-AGOSTO, JACQUELINE,** Univ Politecnica De Pr, Hato Rey, PR; FR; Math; Cvl Engr.

**RUSSELL, ALLISON A,** City Univ Of Ny Med Evers Coll, Brooklyn, NY; SO; BS; Psychlgy.

**RUSSELL JR, ANDREW DAVIS,** Columbia Union Coll, Takoma Park, MD; SR; BS; AA Prince Georges Cmnty Clg 79; Psych-Mgmt; Grad Sch.

**RUSSELL, ANGELES L,** Meridian Comm Coll, Meridian, MS; FR; BA; Sndy Sch Tchr; Bathsheba; Srvd Mgr Diesel Trmnl; Radiology; Tchr.

**RUSSELL, BARRI L,** Univ Of Southern Ms, Hattiesburg, MS; JR; BSBA; Rnld Mcdnld Hs 88-90; Alpha Delta Pi Hstrn 89-90; Finance.

**RUSSELL, BETH M,** Western Ky Univ, Bowling Green, KY; JR; BS; Cncrt Bnd 89-; Phi Eta Sigma 89-; Beta Alpha Psi 90-; Pres Schlr 89-90; Acctng; CPA.

**RUSSELL, CHAD S,** Northeastern Univ, Boston, MA; FR; Hnr Pgm; Bsn; Finance/Intl Bsn.

**RUSSELL, CHARLES A,** Savannah Coll Of Art & Design, Savannah, GA; BA; Pntng Clb 90; Exprssnst Cf 89-90; Vllybll 89; Lit.

**RUSSELL, CHRISTINE H,** Schenectady County Comm Coll, Schenectady, NY; SO; BS; Phi Theta Kappa; Pres List; AS; Physcs; Tchng Rsrch Physcs.

**RUSSELL, CONSTANCE M,** Methodist Coll, Fayetteville, NC; JR; BS; AAS Fayetteville Technical Comm Coll 87; Blgy.

**RUSSELL, DANIEL P,** Roane St Comm Coll, Harriman, TN; FR; AA; SG; Psychlgy; Clncl Psychlgst.

**RUSSELL, DANNIELLE L,** Paine Coll, Augusta, GA; SR; BS; Bio Clb Cmte 89-; Alpha Kappa Mu 89-; Alpha Kappa Alpha 90-; Educ MASTER Inst; Ctr For Disease Cntrl Intrn; Bio; Forensic Sci.

**RUSSELL, DARLENE E,** Fayetteville St Univ, Fayetteville, NC; SO; BED; Vet US Army Ret SSG 84-90; Hstry; Tchng.

**RUSSELL, DARRYL E,** S U N Y Coll Of A & T Morrisvl, Morrisville, NY; FR; AS; Deans List 90-; Christian Hrld Children 90-; City Ministries Schlrshp Fund; Elec Engrg Techlgy.

**RUSSELL, DAVID C,** Union Coll, Barbourville, KY; FR; BS; Vrsty Ftbl 90-; Chmstry.

**RUSSELL, DAWN A,** Middle Tn St Univ, Murfreesboro, TN; SR; BS; Univ Ctrl Ark Concert Choir 80-81; Oratorio Soc 80-81; Alpha Psi Omega 80-82; V P 81-82; Best Actress 82; Dir Of Prchsng 88-90; Speech/Theatre; Teach.

**RUSSELL, DENA L,** Univ Of Sc At Columbia, Columbia, SC; SO; BS; Alpha Mu Gamma; Psi Chi; Phi Eta Sigma 90-; Psychology.

**RUSSELL, DOLAN L,** Savannah St Coll, Savannah, GA; SR; BSC; Clb Royal Banamian Pr 88-90; IEEE Pr 89-90; Natl Clg Engr Awrd 90-; Elects; Engr.

**RUSSELL, EILEEN,** Hudson Valley Comm Coll, Troy, NY; FR; Cmptr Sci; Pgrmr/Anlyst.

**RUSSELL, EVA C,** Memphis St Univ, Memphis, TN; JR; BBA; Acctnt Mgr 88-; Acctng; CPA.

**RUSSELL, EVELYN H,** Vance Granville Comm Coll, Henderson, NC; AAS; Edn Clb 90-; Deans Lst 90-; Dept Schlrshp 89-; AAS Schlrshp; Museum Arts Raleigh NC; Dip; Edn; Tchr Asst.

**RUSSELL JR, GARY,** Fl Memorial Coll, Miami, FL; SR; BS; Acctng Clb Pres VP 90-; FJC SGA Assn Exec Offcr 87; Prlmntrn; Brn Bwl Tm Capt; Alpha Kappa Mu 90-; Cum Laude; Beta Phi Psi Sec Dn Of Pldgs 90-; Dbbs Hss Mgmt Intrn; AA Miami Dadge Wolfson Cmps 87; BS; Ctbnk Intrn 90-; Bus Admin Mgmt; Law.

**RUSSELL, JAMES M,** Savannah St Coll, Savannah, GA; SR; BA; Bus Mngmt; Mngmt.

**RUSSELL, JEANNE R,** Oh St Univ At Newark, Newark, OH; SR; BED; Phi Sigma 89-; Paper Publ Sch Lit Mag 89; Outreach Chrstn Pre-Sch Bd 89-; AA; Elem Ed; Tchg.

**RUSSELL, JENNIFER R,** Allegheny Coll, Meadville, PA; JR; BA; Yth Soccer Assn Rfree 87-; Lambda Sigma 89-; Kappa Alpha Theta 90-; Aldn Schlr 88-; Cathlc Daughtrs Amer 86-; Vrsty Soccer Capt 88-; Biolgy; Phrmclgy.

**RUSSELL, JOHNNIE-MAE,** City Univ Of Ny City Coll, New York, NY; GD; BSED; Gldn Key 87-; Dns Lst 89-90; Bapt Chrch Sec 86-88; Blck Entrprs Mag 81-84; Blue Crs/Blue Shld 85-86; AAS Bronx Comm Coll 77; Elem Educ; Rdng Spclst.

**RUSSELL, JULIE L,** Middle Tn St Univ, Murfreesboro, TN; JR; BS; Gamma Beta Phi Nmntng Comm 89-; Kappa Delta Pi 89-; Cavalry Bnkng FSL 82-86; Frst Cty Bnk 87-89; Elem Edctn; Tchng.

**RUSSELL, KAREN R,** Interdenominational Theo Ctr, Atlanta, GA; GD; M DIV; Blk Wmn Chrch Soc Sec 90-; Deans Lst; Kappa Swthrt; Assoc Clncl Pstrl Edctn Inc 90-; Ga Adctn Cnslrs Assoc 90-; Mi Assoc Chldrns Alncs 88-90; Say No T Drgs Stdnt Awrd; Fmls Agnst Drgs; Lcnsd Soc Wrkr; Sbstnc Abs Thrpst Fmls & Adlscnts; Bs Estrn Mi Univ; Pstrl Cnslng; Clncl Pstrl Edctn.

**RUSSELL, KAREN R,** Coppin St Coll, Baltimore, MD; SO; BSC; Sci Clb 89-; Zeta Phi Beta 89-; Bsktbl Cnfrnc Chmps 89-; Blgy; Pedtrcn.

**RUSSELL, KEITH L,** Commonwealth Coll, Virginia Beach, VA; FR; AAS; Cmptr Clb 90-; SGA 90-; Alpha Betta Gamma; Phi Beta Sigma 76; Wedgewood Vol Cmmt Treas 90-; Cmpt Science; Systms Anlyst/Prgrmr.

**RUSSELL, KIMBERLEY F,** Coll Of William & Mary, Williamsburg, VA; JR; BS; Hlth Car Assn 90-; Phi Theta Kappa; Rita Welsh Adlt Skls Ctr Tutr 90-; Pres Lst 89-90; All Amer Schlrs Coll Acad 90; AS R Bland Clg 90; Bio; Optmtry.**

**RUSSELL, KIRK S,** City Univ Of Ny La Guard Coll, Long Island Cty, NY; GD; BA; King Wallenberg Cnsmr Law Club; Phi Theta Kappa; Sclgy Award; AS; Mrkt/Mgt.

**RUSSELL, MACRESIA L,** Al A & M Univ, Normal, AL; FR; Cmptr Sci; Cmptr Syst Anlyst.

**RUSSELL, MARY H,** Western Ky Univ, Bowling Green, KY; JR; BA; FCA 87-90; Golden Key 89; Pi Mu Epsilon 89; Psi Chi; Math; Actrl.**

**RUSSELL, MELISSA Y,** Liberty Univ, Lynchburg, VA; FR; BED; Marching Band 90; Alpha Lambda Delta; Education; Elem Tchr.

**RUSSELL, MICHELLE A,** Elmira Coll, Elmira, NY; SR; Stdnt Ambass Tour Guide 87-90; Orient Ldr 88-90; Exec Comm Orient Prnts Wknd Chr 89-90; Beta Beta Beta 87-88; BA; Math; Scndry Ed Tchr.

**RUSSELL, PAUL L,** Marshall University, Huntington, WV; FR; BED; Vrs Clrcl Sprvsry Pstns 83-90; Cmptr Sci; Systms Analysis Prgrmmng.

**RUSSELL, RAYLENE,** Comm Coll Algny Co Algny Cmps, Pittsburgh, PA; SO; ASSOC; Sclgy Clb; SNAP; Hlth Sci; Nursing.

**RUSSELL, REBECCA A,** Walker Coll, Jasper, AL; FR; Pres List; Busn; Acctng.

**RUSSELL, REBECCA L,** Fulton Montgomery Comm Coll, Johnstown, NY; FR; AOS; Sky-Life Flying Camp Priv Pilot 90-; Cvl Air Patrol; Aviation; Prfsnl Pilot.

**RUSSELL, RHONDA,** Merrimack Coll, North Andover, MA; SR; BA; Alpha Mu Alpha; Dns Lst 87-; Mktg.

**RUSSELL, RICHARD R,** Memphis St Univ, Memphis, TN; FR; BA; Hnr Stdnt Assn Tr; Sga Sentr; Stdnt Ambsdr Brd; Phi Eta Sigma; Alpha Tau Omega; Engl Clb; Pr Mentr Pgm 90; Highst Pldg GPA; Dns Lst; Engl; Env Law.

**RUSSELL, ROBERT T,** Jersey City St Coll, Jersey City, NJ; JR; BA; Coll Choir 88; Karate Clb 88-89; Intrnshp Prod Asst; Asst Mgr Media Arts Dept 90-; Media Arts; Music Prod.

**RUSSELL, SCOTT,** Slippery Rock Univ, Slippery Rock, PA; SO; BS; Barbell Clb 90-; Phi Epsilon Kappa; IM Ftbl Vlybl Sftbl 89-; Phys Educ; Phys Educ Tchr.

**RUSSELL, SHENA R,** Al A & M Univ, Normal, AL; SO; Soc Work Clb Pres; Hntsvl Hosp; Oper Santa Clause; Soc Work.

**RUSSELL, SHERRI R,** Comm Coll Algny Co Algny Cmps, Pittsburgh, PA; SO; BA; English Comm; Pub Brdcstng.

**RUSSELL, TERESA A,** Faulkner St Jr Coll, Bay Minette, AL; JR; BS; Early Chldhd Ed; Ed.

**RUSSELL, TERESA T,** Central Fl Comm Coll, Ocala, FL; SO; AA; Phi Theta Kappa 90-; Yth Orgnztn Of 1st Bapt Invrnss FL; Engl; Elem Educ.

**RUSSELL, VELASQUE G,** Fl A & M Univ, Tallahassee, FL; JR; BS; White/Gld; Bsbl Hghst GPA; Offc Admin/Bus; Ins Agncy.

**RUSSELL, WILMA V,** Coll Of New Rochelle, New Rochelle, NY; SR; MDVI; Clss Pres Treas 90-; Natl Cthlc Assoc Chrprsn 70-81; Cncrt Slst 55-; Cdng Clrk 54-60; Jnr Fr Adjstr 63-69; Orgnst; Chr Dir; Piano Vc Ch 69-; :Ba Psych; Rlgs Stds Cnsllng; Pstr Cmps Cnsllr.

**RUSSO, ALISON A,** William Paterson Coll, Wayne, NJ; GD; Ele Educ Clb 87-; Early Chldhd Educ Clb 88-90; Alpha Kappa Delta 90-; Deans Lst 87-90; Stdnt Tch 90; Practicum II 89-; BA 90; Early Chldhd Educ; Tch.

**RUSSO, ANNA NICOLE,** Birmingham Southern Coll, Birmingham, AL; JR; BA; Alpha Lambda Delta 88-89; Phi Eta Sigma 88-89; Alpha Kappa Psi Pres 90-; Zeta Tau Alpha 1st V P 88-; Southern Vol Svcs 88-89; Admin Intern 90; Bsn Jrnl Intern; Chattanooga Marriott Intern 90; IM Ftbl/Sftbl 88-; Bsn Adm; Mktg/Mgmt.

**RUSSO, CHRISTINA M,** Saint Johns Univ, Jamaica, NY; SR; MS; Kappa Delta Pi Gen Mem 89-; Silver Medal Spec Ed SJU; Deans Lst 87-; BSED; Elem Ed/Spec Ed; Elem/Spec Ed Tchr.

**RUSSO, DENISE R,** Univ Of Fl, Gainesville, FL; SR; BA; Bnds Pres 88-89; Fine Arts Cncl Treas 88; Celebration 1991 Dir/ Musical Affairs; Omicron Delta Kappa Solicitations Dir 90; Mortar Bd; Tau Beta Sigma VP 89-; MENC Pres 89; Sigma Alpha Iota Cls Pres 88; Pres Ldrshp 90-; Frnds Of Music Schlr; Music Educ/Bus; Music Rcrdng Indstry.

**RUSSO, ELENA,** City Univ Of Ny Baruch Coll, New York, NY; SO; BBA; Schlrshp; Acctng; CPA.

**RUSSO, JENNEFER A,** Cornell Univ, Ithaca, NY; FR; BS; SAFER Peers; Aerobics Instrctr; Concert Commsn; IDEA Fndtn Certn; Bio/Soc; Law/Jrnlsm.

**RUSSO, JOAN K,** De Tech & Comm Coll At Dover, Dover, DE; GD; Cmptr; Systm Analysis Cmptr Prgrmmng.

**RUSSO, KENNETH M,** S U N Y Coll Of Tech At Frmgdl, Farmingdale, NY; FR; Acctg Soc; Tns Tm Var; Bus Adm; Mgr.

**RUSSO, LAURIE A,** Mount Saint Mary Coll, Newburgh, NY; JR; Flk Grp; Bcchs; Anlyts Stds Tm Sec; Rsdnt Lvng Cncl Chrprsn; Vllc Scty Treas; Scrd Hrt Yth Grp; Cmps Mnstry88-; Vssr Bro Hops 90-; Psychlgy.

**RUSSO, LORI J,** Duquesne Univ, Pittsburgh, PA; SO; BED; MENC; PMEA; Msc Ed; Tchr.

**RUSSO, LUCILLE G,** Seton Hall Univ, South Orange, NJ; JR; E A Seton Ed Assn 89-90; Phi Alpah Theta; Kappa Delta Pi 90-; Helen/Ruth Warren Schlrshp 90-; Scndry Ed/Hist.

**RUSSO, MARIE Q,** Va St Univ, Petersburg, VA; SR; BS; Pi Omega Pi 90-; Kappa Delta Pi 90-; Alpha Kappa Mu; Bsns Ed; Tchng.

**RUSSO, MELISSA A,** Wagner Coll, Staten Island, NY; SR; BS; Kappa Delti Pi; Phi Eta Sigma 89; Coll Tutoring Serv 90-; Edn; Teach Elem Edn.

**RUSSO, RICK J,** Wagner Coll, Staten Island, NY; GD; AM Mngmnt Assc 90-; Delta Mu Delta 87-; High Scholastic Achmnt; Tutor 87-; Deans List 87-; Magna Cum Laude 87-90; Summa Cum Laude 90-; BA Wanger Clg 90; MBA Wagner Clg; Ecnmcs Mngmnt.**

**RUSSO, STACEY J,** Manhattanville Coll, Purchase, NY; SO; BFA; Chrs 89-; Art; Advrtsng Dsgn.

**RUSSO, SUSIE M,** Newbury Coll, Brookline, MA; FR; BA; Fshn Dsgn Clb Expressions; Peer Actvty Ldr; Certif Merit; Fshn Dsgn-Merch.

**RUSSOM, TRACY L,** Univ Of Al At Birmingham, Birmingham, AL; SR; BS; Alpha Gamma Delta 83-84; Crmnl Juste; Law.

**RUSSWURM, LINDA,** S U N Y Coll Of Tech At Frmgdl, Farmingdale, NY; GD; BA; Amer Yth Hostels; Bsns; Mgmt.

**RUST, KEVIN J,** Univ Of Ky, Lexington, KY; SR; BS; Amer Soc Of Civil Engrs 89-; Deans Lst 90-; KY Transp Cab Schlrshp 90-; Engr.

**RUST, REBECCA,** Indiana Univ Of Pa, Indiana, PA; SO; BS; Kappa Delta Pi 91; Speech Pathlgy/Audiology; Speech Pathlgy.

**RUTAN, KIMBERLY J,** Coll Of Charleston, Charleston, SC; FR; BS; Bio; Med.

**RUTENBAR, MARY E,** Indiana Univ Of Pa, Indiana, PA; JR; Radio Station DJ 88; Delta Zeta Hstrn 90; Asstnshp Phtgrphr; Commnctns Media; Phtgrphy Prof.

**RUTH, CRYSTAL L,** Shippensburg Univ, Shippensburg, PA; FR; Geoenvir Stds.

**RUTH, DAVID M,** United States Naval Academy, Annapolis, MD; SR; MA; Phi Kappa Phi 90-; Sec Navy Dstngshd Grad; Prf H R Robrts Awd Exclnc Math; Ntnl Sci Fndtn Hnrbl Mntn; Lghtwght Crew 88-90; Math; Nclr Pwr Submarine Srvc USN.

**RUTH, JEANNE E,** Wilmington Coll, New Castle, DE; SR; BA; Delta Epsilon Rho; Prfsnl Sectres Intl Corr Sec 89; Natl Assn Legal Sec Bar Liasn; Legal Sec/Exec Asst; Beauty Sys Cnslnt; Bus Mgmt/Mis; MIS Mgmt.

**RUTH, REBECCA L,** Kent St Univ Kent Cmps, Kent, OH; SR; BA; Kent Cncl Fam Rltns Treas 88-; Pres Lst 90-; Dns Lst 90-; Indvldl/Fam Stds; Drg Cnslng/Drg Educ.

**RUTH, TINA M,** Westminster Coll, New Wilmingtn, PA; SR; BA; SGA Exec 88-90; Cmps Prog Comm 88-90; Dance Theatre 87-; Pi Sigma Pi 90-; Omicron Delta Kappa 90-; Tau Pi Phi 89-; Lambda Sigma Secy 88-89; Amer Express Mktng Schlrshp; Bus Mgmnt; Stdnt Prsnnl Serv.

**RUTHENBECK, KRISTA M,** Univ Of Sc At Columbia, Columbia, SC; FR; Prsdnts Hnr Roll; Elctrcl Engnrng.

**RUTHERFORD, DEVON C,** Miami Dade Comm Coll North, Miami, FL; GD; AA; Christian Clb 89-90; Utd Way Scty 90-; Soccer Tm 89-90; Business; Administration.

**RUTHERFORD, ELISE M,** Anne Arundel Comm Coll, Arnold, MD; FR; BA; Phi Theta Kappa; Deans Lst 90-; Elem Educ.

**RUTHERFORD, NICOLLE R,** Univ Of Sc At Columbia, Columbia, SC; SO; BS; Blgy Clb VP 90-; Phi Eta Sigma 90-; Alpha Mu Gamma Sec; Hon Pgm Rcrtmnt Offcr; Marine Sci/ Blgy.

**RUTHERFORD, NICOLLE R,** Univ Of Sc At Coastal Carolina, Conway, SC; SO; BS; Blgy Clb VP 90-; Phi Eta Sigma 90-; Alpha Mu Gamma Sec; Hon Pgm Rcrtmnt Offcr; Marine Sci/Blgy.

**RUTHERFORD, REBECCA A,** Spartanburg Methodist Coll, Spartanburg, SC; FR; BA; Scndry Educ; HS Tchr.

**RUTHERFORD, RUTH A,** Univ Of Cincinnati-Clrmnt Coll, Batavia, OH; FR; BED.

**RUTHERS, CHRISTY J,** Marshall University, Huntington, WV; SR; Nwmn Asc Sec/Treas 89-; Magna Cum Laude; BA Ed; Engl Lit/Math; Educ.

**RUTLAND, SHELLEY,** Ms St Univ, Miss State, MS; JR; BS; Kappa Delta Pi; Hi-Stepper; Elem Ed; Tch.

**RUTLEDGE, ALEXANDRA L,** Cornell Univ Statutory College, Ithaca, NY; JR; BS; Hsng Coop Treas Elect; Alpha Phi Omega V P Serv 90-; Biology; Grad Sch.

**RUTLEDGE, ANGELA K,** Radford Univ, Radford, VA; SR; BS; P E Clb 89-; Var Vybl 87-; Hped; Tch Coach.

**RUTLEDGE, BENJAMIN T,** Univ Of Cincinnati-Clrmnt Coll, Batavia, OH; MDA; AS Cincinnati Bible Coll 79; BM 80; Music.

**RUTLEDGE, JOCELYN YVETTE,** Al St Univ, Montgomery, AL; SO; Phi Eta Sigma 90-; Math/English; Law.

**RUTLEDGE JR, JOSEPH L,** Miles Coll, Birmingham, AL; SR; BA; SGA VP 89; Hmnts Clb Pres; Mem Miles Gntlmn Clb Govr 90-; Kappa Alpha Psi Plmch 89; Intern Birminghman News Stff Wrtr 87-88; Dean Lst; Engl/Cmmnctns; Wrtr/Instr.

**RUTLEDGE, MARTHA E,** Erie Comm Coll, Buffalo, NY; SO; AAS; Paralegal Assoc Pres 90-; Outstndng Mbr ECC Paralegal Assn Pres 90-; Owner Rutledge Photography Profssnl 86-90; Paralegal Studies.

**RUTLEDGE, MICHELLE QUILLEN,** East Tn St Univ, Johnson City, TN; SO; BS; Assn Stdnt Nrs; Alpha Lambda Delta 88-89; Nrsng.

**RUTLEDGE, SALLY E,** Radford Univ, Radford, VA; FR; BMT; Msc; Thrpst.

**RUTNER, HEATHER W,** Yeshiva Univ, New York, NY; GD; MBA; Psychlgy Clb/Fn Arts Soc/Frnch Clb 88-; Drctry Ed 87-; Yrbk Sr Coord 89-90; Hst Cmte 87-; Syng Yth Coord 88-89; Fine Arts Intrn 89-90; Soc Sci Awd 89-90; Vlybl; AA Yeshiva Univ; Indstrl/Orgnztnl Psychlgy; Rcrtng Dir/Hmn Rsr.

**RUTTER, SCOTT A,** Memphis St Univ, Memphis, TN; JR; BS; Sprng Musical Dnce Ld 86; Summer Musical Supt Rl 86; Alpha Lambda Delat 82-83; Make A Wish Fndtn Vol; Natl Merit Schlrshp Finlst 82; Hons Crs Wrk Chem/Lab/Frnch Univ Cinn 83-85; Var Supv Rls Cust Serv 87-90; Anthrpogy; Ph D Med Anthplgy.

**RUTTER, WENDY J,** Oh Univ, Athens, OH; JR; BFA; Sngrs 88-89; Wmns Glee Clb 90-; Msc Ed; Msc Tchr/Elem.

**RUTTY, SOPHIA A,** Cheyney Univ Of Pa, Cheyney, PA; SO; Psychlgy Pre Law Major; Entrtnmnt Law.

**RUTZ, ADAM K,** Univ Of New Haven, West Haven, CT; SR; BS; Helen Anne Hall Cncl Pres 89-; Clb Mgrs Assn V P 89-; Res Assist 90-; Alpha Lambda Delta 90-; Eta Sigma Delta V P 90-; Alpah Beta Gamma 87-88; Vol Homeless Shltr 89-; Amer Red Cross 88; Senior Book Awd; Senior Acad Awd; Hotel/Rest Admin; Entrepeneur.

**RYALS, CHRISTY R,** Truett Mc Connell Coll, Cleveland, GA; FR; Concert Choir 90-.

**RYALS, DEBORAH M,** Daytona Beach Comm Coll, Daytona Beach, FL; FR; AA; Phi Theta Kappa Rec Sec; Pres Lst 90-; Pell Grnt 90-; Educ; BA Math Tchr.

**RYALS, WENDY D,** Univ Of Fl, Gainesville, FL; SR; BS; Grmn Clb 87; Stdnt Diettc Assn Sec 89-; Amer Diettc Assn 89-; Pres Lst.

**RYAN, ANNE L,** Coll Misericordia, Dallas, PA; SR; BS; Educ Clb Cllg Misericordia 90; Delta Epsilon Sigma; Acad Schlrshp Part 90-; Deans List 89-; AA Pa State Univ 88; Elem Educ; Teaching.

**RYAN, ARLENE M,** Merrimack Coll, North Andover, MA; JR; English Clb VP 90-; Orientation Comm 90; Wrtng Ctr Peer Tutor 89-; Big Brother Big Sister; Private Tutor Foreign Children 89-; Prepracticum Tchr Asstnt 90-; English Educ; Law.

**RYAN, BETH ANNE,** Comm Coll Algny Co Algny Cmps, Pittsburgh, PA; FR; BA; Law.

**RYAN, BRIDGET A,** Univ Of Cincinnati, Cincinnati, OH; SO; BFA; Deans Lst 89-; Bllt Frnch.

**RYAN, DANIEL S,** Middle Tn St Univ, Murfreesboro, TN; JR; BA; Gamma Beta Phi 89-; Intrnshp Dstrct Attrny; Crmnl Jstce Admin; Law.

**RYAN, DENNIS J,** Merrimack Coll, North Andover, MA; JR; BA; Math Rsrc Ctr Tutor 88-; Congrsnl Intrn Rep Chrtr Alkns D Ma 90; Vrsty Bsktbl 87-; Harry S Truman Schlrshp 88; NE All Acad Tm 87-89; Ec; Pblc Fin.

**RYAN, ELIZABETH A,** Hudson Valley Comm Coll, Troy, NY; SO; AAS; Phi Theta Kappa 90-; Mktg; Mktg/Mgmt.

**RYAN, ELIZABETH GAYLE,** Univ Of Ky, Lexington, KY; JR; BA; Kappa Alpha Theta Rush Rcmmndtn Chrmn 88/86; Intrnshp 88-90; Pblc Radio; IM 86-89; Communication; Fsh Mrktng.

**RYAN, J BARRY,** Univ Of Rochester, Rochester, NY; SR; BS; NROTC Univ Rochester Co Cmdr 87-; St John Fisher Clg Campus Mnstry Co Coord 87-89; St John Fisher Clg RA 88-; Phi Beta Kappa; Tau Beta Pi; BA St John Fisher Clg 90; Mech Engr; US Navy Nuclr Pwr.

**RYAN, JANET MARIE,** Ga St Univ, Atlanta, GA; JR; BS ED; Bus Ed; Tchr/Scndry Schl.

**RYAN, JENNIE L,** East Stroudsburg Univ, E Stroudsburg, PA; SO; BA; E Stroudsburg Univ Hnrs Prog Secty; Deans List 89-; Hnrs Prog Schlrshp; IM Sftbl/Vlybl 89; Busn Mgt; Accountant.

**RYAN, KAY S,** Univ Of Al At Birmingham, Birmingham, AL; SR; BA; Pres List 90-; AA Jefferson St Jr Coll; Education/Comp Social Studies; Teach.

**RYAN, KEVIN J,** Springfield Tech Comm Coll, Springfield, MA; JR; BS; Pioneer Vly Stamp Clb 75-82; Lope De Vega 80-81; HBO Inc Pgrmmr Anlyst 85-88; Cert Bsn Ed Institute 84; Cmptr Science; Software Engrng.

**RYAN, LEANNE M,** Northern Ky Univ, Highland Hts, KY; SR; BA; KY Cncl Tchrs Math 90-; Cncl Tchrs Math 90-; Dns Lst 88-; Drill Tm 87-90; IM Vlybl 87-90; Elem Ed/Mdl Grd Ed/Engl/ Math; Tchr.

**RYAN, LISA A,** Pa St Univ Delaware Cty Cmps, Media, PA; SO; BA; Comm Svcs; Deans Lst; Sftbl; Bus; Mktg.

**RYAN, MARGARET A,** Va Commonwealth Univ, Richmond, VA; SO; BA; Pre Occptnl Thrpy Clb Co Pres 90; Phi Eta Sgm 90-; Deans Schlrshp 89; Bus.

**RYAN, MARY A,** Marymount Manhattan Coll, New York, NY; JR; BS; Admn Acctg Asst Pfizer Inc; Exec Sec Dip Mildred Elley Sch Albany NY; Acctg/Bsns Mgmt; Fin.

**RYAN, MELISSA A,** Le Moyne Coll, Syracuse, NY; SO; BS; Acctg Soc 90-; Bowling 90-; Vol Firefighter 90-; Bristol-Myers Squibb Acctg Intern; Acctg; Law.

**RYAN, PATRICIA L,** S U N Y Coll At Fredonia, Fredonia, NY; SR; Bus Clb Admin Asst 89-; Acctg Soc Nwlttr Asst Ed 89-; Phi Theta Kappa 86-87; Deans List Tompkins Cortland CC 86-87; Onondaga Comm Clg Deans List 87-89; Suny At Fredonia Deans List 87-; Suny At Fredonia Alumni Schlrshp 89-90; BS; BS 89; Acctg.

**RYAN, PATRICK C,** Coll Of Charleston, Charleston, SC; JR; BS; Phi Kappa Phi; Premed Hnr Soc 90-; Rest Mngmnt; Biol; Med.

**RYAN, ROBIN WILLIAM,** S U N Y Coll Of Envr Sci & For, Syracuse, NY; JR; BS; Forest Engrng Clb 90-; Alpha Xi Sigma 90-; Presidents Hnr Lst 90; AAS Natural Resources Cnsrvtn 89; Water Resource Engrng.

**RYAN, STACEY E,** City Univ Of Ny Baruch Coll, New York, NY; JR; BBA; Natl Assn Blck Acctnts VP; Gldn Key; Beta Gamma Sigma; Mitchel Titus Awd Excel; NABA NY Chptr Schlrshp; NABA Gratitude Awd; Acctng; CPA.

**RYAN, TRACEY L,** Indiana Univ Of Pa, Indiana, PA; JR; BA; Comm Media; Phtgrphy/Grphcs.

**RYANS, ESTHER G,** Al A & M Univ, Normal, AL; JR; BA; Psychlgy Clb 89-; NAACP 88-; Delta Sigma Theta Parlimentarian 90-; Dns Lst 88-90; Clinical Psychologist.

**RYBAK, KEVIN R,** Niagara Univ, Niagara Univ, NY; SR; BA; Psychology Clb VP 88-; Stdnt Advsry Comm 89-; Fd Comm; Delta Epsilon 89-; Psi Chi 89-; Wrkng Psychlgst Curraine Scizzrrd G J Main Elem Schl; Psychology; Schl Psychlgst.

**RYBARCZYK, MARIA A,** Univ Of Pittsburgh At Bradford, Bradford, PA; FR; BA; Act Cncl Co-Pres 90-; Stdnt Govt Assn Sec 90-; Union Pgmng Bd; NACA Showcase Select Com; Publ Rel; Dir Stdnt Act.

**RYBICKI, JEAN M,** Fl International Univ, Miami, FL; SR; BS; Phi Theta Kappa 86-88; Elem Ed; Elem Tchng.

**RYCE, ANGELA M,** Duquesne Univ, Pittsburgh, PA; SO; BA; Dns Lst 89-; Vlybl 89-90; Math; Scndry Educ.

**RYCHLICKI, JENNIFER M,** Allegheny Coll, Meadville, PA; SO; BA; SAGE Flm Series Chr 90-; Amnsty Intl 89-90; Alpha Gamma Delta Corres Sec; Alden Schlr 90-; IM Vlybl 90; Engl/ Rlgs Stdies; Tch.

**RYCRAW, RAMSEY G,** Georgetown Univ, Washington, DC; SO; BS; Invstmnt Alliance 90-; Asst Career Edctr; Dns Lst 90; IM Bsktbl 89-90; Finance; Bnkg.

**RYCZEK, PETER F,** William Paterson Coll, Wayne, NJ; JR; BS; Comp Sci.

**RYDELL, JODY A,** Duquesne Univ, Pittsburgh, PA; SO; BA; Bus Admn; Acctg.

**RYDER, KATHY J,** Newbury Coll, Brookline, MA; FR; ASSOC; Fashion Design; Consultant/Costume Desiging.

**RYGALSKI, SHANNON L,** Methodist Coll, Fayetteville, NC; FR; BS; Monarch Playmakers; U S Army 83-87; Socl Wrk; Prof Cnslr.

**RYLKE, PATRICE L,** Saint Francis Coll, Loretto, PA; JR; BS; Invstmnt Clb VP 90-; Stdnt Govt 90-; Scrtc Clb 90-; Deans Lst 88-; IM Bsktbl; AS Mt Aloysius Jr Coll 90; Bus Admin/Mgmt; Fin/Bnkng.**

**RYMER, DAVID A,** Life Coll, Marietta, GA; GD; DC; Stdnt Soc Orthspinology Sec 89-; Gonstead Stdy Clb 89-90; Upper Cerv Spec Clb 89-90; Chi Rho Prof Hnorary Frat Sec 90-; Rymer Chrpractc Offc Dr Al Rymer 87-90; Southern Chrprctc Clnc Dr Joel Joyce; Mc Alpine Orthspinology Schlrshp; Chrpractc; Phsycn.

**RYMER, GREGORY A,** Wv Univ At Parkersburg, Parkersburg, WV; JR; BA; Bshps Clrk Lcl LDS Chrch Clrk 86-; Gnlgst Lcl LDS Chrch 85-; Hll Cmrh Pgnt Amrcs; Lrgst Otdr Drm; Schl Imprvmnt Cncl 90-; LDS Stk Sngl Adlt Chrmn 88-; 550 Hr Pn Vol Wrk Lcl Hosp 82-83; Wd Cnty Fdrtn Tchrs Sec 90-; Wd Cnty Hd Trm Assoc; Ed Spcl Ed; Tchng Admn.

**RYMER, SUSAN J,** Univ Of Akron, Akron, OH; SR; BS; Campus Focus Pres 88-90; IM Vlybl 89; Elem Edn; Teach.

**RYMER, TODD M,** Fl International Univ, Miami, FL; GD; MS; Anarciet; Chef Ectrsm Mgmt; BA; Hsptlty Mgmnt; Ectrsm.

**RYNASKO, CARLA G,** Schenectady County Comm Coll, Schenectady, NY; SO; AS; Phi Theta Kappa; Bus; Bus Admin.

**RYNDAK, KARIN L,** Columbia Greene Comm Coll, Hudson, NY; FR; AS; Stu Chrstn Fllwshp; Med Cntr Career Fld Stu; Amer Sccr Ambssdr 88; Sr Grl Athl Awrd; Gail M Gabriele Athltc Schlrshp Awrd; Vrsty Sccr MVP 87-; Vrsty Bsktbl Sftbl; Physcl Thrpy/Sci; Sprts Thrpy.

**RYON, DAVID B,** Central St Univ, Wilberforce, OH; FR; BS; Rsrv Offcr Trn Corp 90-; Food Serv Comm; Army Comndtn Medal 90; Good Cndct Medal 90; ROTC Sftbl Team; US Army Mltry Intlgnce Asst 88-90; US Army 88-90; Poltcl Sci; Tchng.

**RYON, JULIE M,** Fl St Univ, Tallahassee, FL; SR; BA; Phi Theta Kappa 90-; AA Lake City Comm Coll; Engl Educ; H S Tchr.

**RYOO, SHANNON H,** City Univ Of Ny Baruch Coll, New York, NY; JR; BBA; Golden Key Natl 90-; Acctg.

**RYS, STANLEY J,** Springfield Tech Comm Coll, Springfield, MA; FR; AS; CAD CAM Mechncl Tchnlgy; Dsgn Engrng.

**RYSINGER, LISA A,** Glassboro St Coll, Glassboro, NJ; SO; BA; Pblc Rltns Stdnt Scty Of Amer PR Actn Assn; Grdn St Schlrshp; Almni Schlrshp; Pblc Rltns.

**RYTER, PATRICIA A,** Kent St Univ Stark Cmps, North Canton, OH; JR; BED; Elem Educ.

**RZEWNICKI, PETER,** Springfield Tech Comm Coll, Springfield, MA; SR; AS; Mrktng; Publ Rels/Mrkt R D.

**RZEZNIKIEWICZ, ANDREW R,** Unity Coll, Unity, ME; FR; BA; Cnsrvtn Law Clb 90-; Natl Audubon Soc 89-; Ntr Cnsrvncy; Envrmntl Sci; Cnsrvtn Law Enfrcmnt.

**RZEZNIKIEWICZ, NANCY E,** Western New England Coll, Springfield, MA; SO; BA; Mktng Assoc VP 89-; Alpha Lambda Delta 89-; Alpha Kappa Psi 90-; Chrlng 89-90; Mktng; Law.

# S

**SAAB, ALEXANDRA M,** Georgetown Univ, Washington, DC; JR; BA; Frnch Cir; Spnsh Clb 88-90; Mdl UN Chrpsn 89-90; Dns Lst 90; GU Hosp Vol 88-90; Intrnshp Bk/Frnc; Mktg Intrnshp Frnc; Intl Dipl Univ Lyon III Frnc; Intl Bus/Econ; Wld Bk IMF.

**SAAD, TONY A,** Marshall University, Huntington, WV; SO; Acctg Clb 90-; Deans List; BA; Acctg; CPA.

**SAADOULI, NASREDDINE,** Univ Of Tn At Knoxville, Knoxville, TN; FR; BA; TSS 90-; Busn Mgt.

**SAALFELD, DANIEL A,** Univ Of Nc At Charlotte, Charlotte, NC; JR; BA; Golden Key; Phi Alpha Theta; Phi Eta Sigma 89-; Cecil Prince Schlrshp 89; Engl/Hstry; Write.

**SAAM, ELLEN J,** Le Moyne Coll, Syracuse, NY; SO; BA; Five House Theater Stage Mgr 89-; Math Club 89-; Comp Sci Club 89-; People In Action Grade Sch Tutor 89-90; Goldwater Natl Schlrshp Nom; Deans List 89-; Comp Sci/Math; Comp Prgmng/ Cnsltng.

**SAARI, PAULA J,** Framingham St Coll, Framingham, MA; FR; BA; Stdnt Unions Actvts Brd; Psych; Child.

**SAARI, THOR,** Univ Of Sc At Columbia, Columbia, SC; SR; BSC; Amnsty Intl Anti-Death Pnlty Co-Ordntr 88-; Deans Hon List 88-; South Carolinians Agnst War In Middle East 90-; Columbia Film Soc Brd Dir 88-; Reykjavik Union Seamen Trustee 84-; Fed Icelandic Stdnts Abrd Trustee 88-; Mrktng; Ecnmcs.

**SAATHOFF, JOHN D,** Univ Of Md At Eastern Shore, Princess Anne, MD; SR; BS; Collgt FFA Pres 87-; Phi Kappa Phi 90-; UMES Ag Stdnt Yr 88-90; Delmarva Corn/Soybn Tech Conf Schlrshp; All Amer Schlrs 90-; Ag.

**SABAHAT, KEN,** City Univ Of Ny City Coll, New York, NY; GD; MBA; Econ Soc Pres 89-90; Day Stdnt Govt Sen 88-89; Inf Syst Mgr Bnk Sadrt N Y 85-; Intl Finc; Intl Busn.

**SABATER, CHRISTINA M,** Yale Univ, New Haven, CT; FR; BA; Amnsty Intl 90-; Cmmnty Serv Hispanics 90-; Big Sis Hspnc Stu 90-; IM Ping Pong 90; Ecnmcs; Bus.

**SABATER, SHAWN J,** Morehouse Coll, Atlanta, GA; JR; BA; Male Mntrng Prgrm Exectv Brd 89-; Hstry Mjrs Clb VP 90-; Phi Alpha Theta 90-; Gldn Key 90-; Anti-Apartheid Comm Atlanta 88-90; Hmls Vlntr Tsk Frc 90-; Frd Fndtn Mrhs Schlrs Prgrm 89-90; Dana Tchr Apprtceshp Prgrm 90-; Hstry; Entrprnr.

**SABBAGH, MOHSEN P,** Univ Of Nc At Charlotte, Charlotte, NC; SR; BS; Allied Hlth Clb; Tri Beta; Gldn Key; Hosp Vol; Biology; Physician.

**SABEL, BRENT G,** Belmont Coll, Nashville, TN; JR; BBA; Fin; Corp Law.

**SABELLA, TERRI-MARIE E,** The Boston Conservatory, Boston, MA; SR; Stdnt Gvmt Pres 89-; Stdnt Rep 87-89; Peer Sprt Aide 89-90; Res Drctr 90-; BFA; Musical Theatre/Acting/Speech.

**SABGA, CAROLLYNN K,** Saint Thomas Univ, Miami, FL; SR; BA; CARIBSA; Deans Lst; Lcnsd Intr Dsgnr; Prctcng Intr Dsgnr; AA Intl Fine Arts Coll 85-87; Fin; MBA.

**SABHARWAL, YASHVINDER S,** Univ Of Rochester, Rochester, NY; JR; BS; ADITI VP 89-90; Tau Beta Pi Pr 90-; Phi Beta Kappa; Summer Intrnshp At Hughes Danbury Optical Syst; Optics; Engr.

**SABIA, BETTINA M,** Le Moyne Coll, Syracuse, NY; FR; Psych Clb 90-; IM Sccr; Blgy; Med Schl Fr Psychtry.

**SABILLON, EDUARDO A,** Miami Dade Comm Coll, Miami, FL; JR; BA; Peo Ctdrl Yth Grp; JESUS Drm Clb; Vol Wmns Crs Preg Ctr; Cnslr Intrmrcn Chrstn Sch; Sunday Sch Tchr Peo Ctdrl; Outstdng Awd Acad; Tlnt Rstr Cert; Grad Hon; Coll Bd Tlnt Rstr; Outstndg Coll Grad; Clncl Psychlgy.

**SABINE, JOHN A,** Westminster Choir Coll, Princeton, NJ; SR; BM; Chrstn Fllwshp VP 89; Chr 87-; Pi Kappa Lambda; Amer Gld Of Orgnsts; Hymn Scty; Amer Gld Of Engl Hndbll Rngrs 90-; Cncrt Hndbll Chr 90; Chrch Msc; Msc Mnstry Grad Stdy.

**SABINE, NAROPA,** Memphis Academy Of The Arts, Memphis, TN; SO; BA; Art Painting/Sculpture.

**SABO, CHRISTOPHER E,** Marshall University, Huntington, WV; JR; BA; FMA VP; SGA; Alpha Kappa Psi Pres 90-; Natl Collgt Bus Merit Awrd; Finance; Sprts Cntrct Ngotiatns.

**SABO, EDWARD P,** Clarkson Univ, Potsdam, NY; JR; Hcky Schlrshp; Mrktng.

**SABO, TAMMY J,** Oh Univ-Southern Cmps, Ironton, OH; FR; Attnded Profsnl Secy Dinner; Bus; Exec Secy.

**SABOL, SHERYL A,** Kent St Univ Kent Cmps, Kent, OH; SO; BSN; SPN Fndrsng Chr On Exec Brd 90; ONSA Nom/Elctns Cmmttee Chr 90; NSNA 90; Bcclrte Crrclm Comm Soph Rep 90; Golden Key; Nrsng.

**SABOURY, DAWN M,** Salisbury St Univ, Salisbury, MD; GD; Alpha Omega Secy 87-88; PE Cl 87-90; Deans List 88-90; Salvation Army Vol 90; YMCA Vol 89; Jump Rope/Heart Chmn 90; PE Stdnt Tchr; Vara Soccer 88-89; IM 86-90; MAHPRED 89-; Phys Ed.

**SABREE, RACHEL,** Claflin Coll, Orangeburg, SC; SR; Student NEA.

**SABY, ANTHONY W,** Temple Univ, Philadelphia, PA; SR; BS AR; Golden Key 89-; Intl Hrtge Soc 88-89; Arch Stdnts Wrk Exhbtn; AS Lehigh Cty Cmuty Clg 88; Arch; URBN Plng.

**SACCO, SHARON N,** Indiana Univ Of Pa, Indiana, PA; SR; BA; Math Ed.

**SACCO, STEPHEN P,** Providence Coll, Providence, RI; SO; BA; Debate Tm 90-; Chorus 90-; IM Soccer 90-; Modern Lang/ Humanities; Law.

**SACCO, TODD A,** Allegheny Coll, Meadville, PA; SR; BA; Judicial Bd 89-; Jazz Lab 87-; Judo Clb 88-90; Phi Sigma Iota; Amnesty Intl 87-; Allegheny Sesquicentennial Schlrshp 87-; Frank J Haskell Mem Schlrshp 90-; Alden Schlr 88-; Vrsty Trck 89-90; Intl Stds; Law.

**SACHS, DANA J,** Albertus Magnus Coll, New Haven, CT; JR; BA; Hmnts Trng Grp Dir 90; Artspace Inc Brd Of Dir 90; Fndr/ Artistic Dir 78-; Hmnts; Thtr Dir/Plywrght.

**SACIA, CHRISTINE M,** Le Moyne Coll, Syracuse, NY; SO; BA; Intl Hse 90-; Acctng; CPA.

**SACK, DAVID J,** Yeshiva Univ, New York, NY; JR; BA; Pol Sci Soc 89-; Econ Soc 89-; Stdnt Radio Sta Tlk Shw Hst 90-; Trck 90-; Econ.

**SACKNOVITZ, ILANA M,** Yeshiva Univ, New York, NY; SR; BA; Yauneh Olami Brd 89-; Hamevaser Stdnt Jrnl Assc Brd 89-; Proj Sages 89-; Am Istrl Chmbr Cmrc Intrn 89-90; Wjalfederation Ovrseas Afrs Div; DBA; Jewish Stds/Hstry; Urban Plng.

**SACRA, AMY M,** Longwood Coll, Farmville, VA; SO; BS; Psi Chi; Tnns Tm 89; Psychlgy.

**SADAT-AKHAVI, MAHMOUD,** Northern Ky Univ, Highland Hts, KY; JR; BS; Dental Tech; Chemistry; Engr.

**SADEGHI, ABBAS ALI,** Miami Dade Comm Coll, Miami, FL; SO; Mercy Hosp Miami Vol 90-; Crmc/Mrbl Tl Cntr Tps Instltn Frntr Prdctn; Pharm; Phrmcst.

**SADEN, LU ANN G,** S U N Y Coll At Fredonia, Fredonia, NY; JR; BS; SPIE Treas 89-; Fredonia Food Co-Op Treas 88-; Chem.

**SADIQ, YUSUF A,** Fayetteville St Univ, Fayetteville, NC; SO; BS; Muslim Cmmnty Imam/Ldr 88-90; Psy.

**SADLER MOORE, DEBORAH L,** Oh Univ-Southern Cmps, Ironton, OH; SO; BED; Women Of Wellness 89-; Gamma Pi Delta 90-; Alpha Lambda Delta 89-90; EMT Green Twnshp 81-89; Storms Cr Missionary Baptist; Elem Tchr.

**SADLER, BARRY C,** Vance Granville Comm Coll, Henderson, NC; FR; ASD; Stdnt Month 90; Elect Dprtmnt; Elctncs; Eng.

**SADLER, JAMIE E,** Oh Univ-Southern Cmps, Ironton, OH; SR; BA; Camps Wmns Org Brd Dir 88-90; SG 89-90; Phi Kappa Phi 88; Gldn Key 89; Alpha Lambda Delta 87-88; 4 H Clb Adv 88-; Twrd Pcfl Wrld Sem 88; Med Transcptnst 90; Psych/Engl; Phd Engl/Educ Fld.

**SADLER, MARY A,** William Carey Coll, Hattiesburg, MS; JR; BS; Afro Amer Cltrl Soc Pres 88-F Stdnt Gov Assn Psych Rep 90-; Phi Beta Lambda 90-; Alpha Chi 90-; Omicron Delta Kappa 90-; Chld Psychlgst.

**SADLER, REBECCA L,** Newbury Coll, Brookline, MA; FR; Bus.

**SADLER, RONNIE D,** Memphis St Univ, Memphis, TN; JR; BA; Phi Theta Kappa 88-; Deans List 87-89; Automotive Tchnglty & Mgmnt; BPS; Criminology; Law Politics Vriting.

**SADLER, SCOTT M,** Memphis St Univ, Memphis, TN; JR; BS; Stdnt Actvts Cncl 88; Memphs Mrchng Cncrt Jzz Bnds 89-90; Gldn Key 90-; Phi Sigma Kappa Sntnl 88-; Blgy; Med.

**SADLON, AMY M,** Schenectady County Comm Coll, Schenectady, NY; SO; AAS; Walt Disney Intern 90; Hotel Restaurant Mgmnt.**

**SADOCK, DR JENNIFER B,** Life Coll, Marietta, GA; GD; DC; Motion Plptn Clb Sgt Arms 88-90; Pedtrc Assc 89-; Almn Assc 89-; Dlt Sgm Chi 87-; Phtgrphc Edtr Life Frc 88-; BS Syracuse Univ 86; Chiropractic.

**SADOWSKI, DAVID C,** D Youville Coll, Buffalo, NY; JR; MS; Vol Fr Dept Rsc Sqd EMT Lvl I; Schlr Athltc Yr 90-; Dyouville Clge Rgn III Bsktbl Tm; Ocptnl Thrpy.

**SADOWSKI, DENISE L,** West Liberty St Coll, West Liberty, WV; JR; BED; Stdnt Cncl Excptnl Chldrn; Clge Hnrs Pgm 89-90; GA Haught Cochran Mem Schlrshp; Elem Ed; Tchr.

**SADOWSKI, LORRIE A,** Duquesne Univ, Pittsburgh, PA; SO; BMED; Mu Phi Epsilon Almn Sec 90-; Music Ed Prfrmnc.

**SADOWSKI, THEODORE J,** Kent St Univ Kent Cmps, Kent, OH; SO; BA; Phi Epsilon Kappa; Exercise Phys; Cardiac Rehab.

**SAEED, SHAHROKH,** S U N Y Coll Of Tech At Frmgdl, Farmingdale, NY; FR; AAS; Flying; Deans Lst; Cert 90; Aerospace; Engrng.

**SAEGER, SALLY A,** Oh St Univ, Columbus, OH; SR; BA; French Clb 86-; Pi Beta Phi Chrmn 90; Arts/Scnc Awd 90; OSU Wom Lacrosse Club; French; Intl Bus.

**SAETHER, DEBRA L,** Dowling Coll, Oakdale Li, NY; SR; BA; Alpha Chi; Comm Block Capt For Scotts Beach ; Pvt Bch Clb; AA Suffolk Cnty Comm Clg 88; BA; Spanish/Sec Educ; Teach HS/TUTOR.

**SAFAR, PAUL V,** Univ Of Cincinnati, Cincinnati, OH; SR; BM; Envir Grp 90; Sigma Alpha Iota Compos Prize 90; Compos/ Theory; Mscl Endeavors.

**SAFEEK, ABRAHAM,** Tn St Univ, Nashville, TN; JR; BS; Blgy Clb 88-; Alpha Lambda Delta 87-; Amer Rd Crss 87-; Blgy Pre Med; Dr Of Med.**

**SAFFER, MARY ELLEN,** Bellarmine Coll, Louisville, KY; JR; BA; Pol Sci Clb V P 89-; Pre Law Soc 90-; Spouse Abuse Ctr Intrnshp 91-; Pol Sci/Soc; Law Schl.

**SAFKO JR, JOHN L,** Univ Of Sc At Columbia, Columbia, SC; SR; BA; Psi Chi Social Chrmn 88-; Golden Key 89-; Gamma Beta Phi 89-; Psychology; Music/Psych.

**SAFRIT, JULIE A,** Univ Of Sc At Columbia, Columbia, SC; JR; BS; Phi Beta Kappa; Gamma Beta Phi 88-; Beta Gamma Sigma; Kappa Alpha Theta Srty Cncl Delg; Bsns Admn Acctng; CPA.

**SAFTNER, S CLAYTON,** Allegheny Coll, Meadville, PA; JR; BA; 2FC VP 90-; Trgd 89-; Lambda Simga Treas 89-90; Delta Tau Delta R Chr 90-; Alden Schlr 88-; Econ; Bus.

**SAGAN, JENNIFER J,** The Boston Conservatory, Boston, MA; SO; BFA; Dance Edctrs Of Am 87-89; Prof Dance Tchrs Assoc 87-89; Prof Theatre Experience 90; Dance; Prof Dance Teacher.

**SAGANES, RENE L,** Commonwealth Coll, Virginia Beach, VA; SO; AA; Med Clb; Pres Lst; Dns Lst; Alpha Beta Gamma; PTA; AAB Lorain Cnty Comm Clg 87; Med.

**SAGAR, LORI S,** Muskingum Coll, New Concord, OH; JR; BA; Bacchus Orgnztn 89-; Lmbd Sgm 88-89; Phi Theta Beta; Prsdntl Schlrshp 88-; Deans List 88-; Msc Dept Piano Tchr Comm Div 88-; Elem Ed/LD; Tchng LD Stdnts/Elem Ed.

**SAGE, BRADFORD L,** Fl Atlantic Univ, Boca Raton, FL; JR; BA; Phi Kappa Phi; Prof Golfers Assoc/Amer 81-; Golf Prof; BS Nova Univ 85; Acctg.

**SAGENDORPH, JIM,** Hudson Valley Comm Coll, Troy, NY; SO; Pres Lst 89-; Bsn Admin; Ed/Mgmt.

**SAGESER, SANDY,** Ky St Univ, Frankfort, KY; FR.

**SAGRAVES, LINDA K,** Lexington Comm Coll, Lexington, KY; SO; BA; Bapt Stdnt Unn 89-; Acctng; CPA.**

**SAGSVEEN, RITA A,** S U N Y Coll Of Tech At Frmgdl, Farmingdale, NY; GD; AS; Sci; Nrsg.

**SAI, DAVID,** Ny Univ, New York, NY; FR; BS; Asst Portfolio Maint Sec 89-; Finance; Fixed Income Analyst.

**SAIA, ANTHONY J,** Bunker Hill Comm Coll, Boston, MA; FR; AS; Grphc Dsgn.

**SAIA, TARA LYNN,** Ms St Univ, Miss State, MS; JR; BA; Pnhllnc Cncl Rep 89; Psych Clb Pres 90; Gamma Beta Phi 89; Phi Eta Sigma 89; Hnrs Prog 88-; Alpha Gamma Delta 88-; Sthestrn LA St Mntl Hosp 89-; IM Vllybl Capt; Psych; Clncl Psychlgst PHD.

**SAID, RICHARD,** S U N Y Coll Of Tech At Frmgdl, Farmingdale, NY; SO; BA; Bus Admin; Film Prod.

**SAIER, BRIAN D,** Western New England Coll, Springfield, MA; SO; BS; ACM Pres 90-; MAA Pres 90-; Bwlng Clb 89-; Tchng Asst 90-; Comp Sci Math; Sftwr Eng.

**SAIGEON, KERI A,** Memphis St Univ, Memphis, TN; FR; Phi Eta Sigma; Alpha Lambda Delta; Gamma Beta Phi.

**SAILER, CARL V,** Seton Hall Univ, South Orange, NJ; SR; BS; Stdnts Free Enterprise Pres 89-; Wrtr Sch Newsper Sprtswrtr 88-; Founder/Editor Sch Newsletter Mng Ed 88-90; Perrier Grp Intern Sls Rep 90; Thomas S Boron Inc Intern Telemark Rep 87-90; IM Bsebl Capt 87-; Mktg/Jrnlsm; Bsn.

**SAILS, HARLOW B,** Coppin St Coll, Baltimore, MD; SR; BS; Psychlgy Clb Pres 90-; Stu Govt Clss Pres 87; Psychlgy/Clncl Serv; Mntl Hlth Serv.

**SAIN, MARGIE I,** Bethel Coll, Mckenzie, TN; JR; BA; Judicial Bd 90-; STEA 88-; Gamma Beta Phi Prlmntrn 89-; Iota Alpha Omega VP 88-; Bob Hope Hon Schlrshp 88-; Wms Bstkbl 90-; Edn; Teach.

**SAINE, AMANDA M,** Caldwell Comm Coll & Tech Inst, Lenoir, NC; FR; CCC & TI Occptnl Thrpy Clb 90-; Phi Theta Kappa 90-; Psychology Biology; Occptnl Thrpy.

**SAINI, TINA K,** Univ Of Pa, Philadelphia, PA; JR; BA; Pre Hlth Soc V P Pblcty 88-; Biomed Rsrch Soc Exec Bd 88-; Biological Basxis Of Bhvr Soc 89-; Econ Soc 89-; Soc Plannikng & Events Comm 88-; Orntn Comm Hd Adv 89-; Peer Adv 90-; Res Hall Govt Comm Chm Flr Rep 88-; Econ/Biological Basis Of Bhvr; Med.**

**SAINI, VANITA,** City Univ Of Ny City Coll, New York, NY; SO; BS; Soc Wmn Engrs 90; Dns Lst 89-; Cvl Engr; Engr.

**SAINT JUSTE, ARLANDE,** City Univ Of Ny City Coll, New York, NY; GD; MA Pub Admn.

**SAINT-AIME, PASCALE,** Coll Of Insurance, New York, NY; JR; BS; Rsdnt Lfe Offce Cnfrnce Asst; Brklyn Coll Wmns Cntr 89; Gamma Iota Sigma Sec; Citibank Schlrshp Brklyn Coll 89-; Actrl Scis; Fnnce Ins.

**SAINZ, GEMA M,** Nova Univ, Ft Lauderdale, FL; GD; MBA; Comp Prgrmr/Analyst; BA FL Intl Univ 84; Bus Admnstrtn; Comp Fld.

**SAITO, HIROSHI,** Univ Of South Al, Mobile, AL; SR; BS; Maruzen Showa Unyu Co Ltd; BS Takai Univ Japan 85; Mktg/Intl Bus; Mgmt.

**SAITOWITZ, HADLEY N,** New England Coll Of Optometry, Boston, MA; SR; OD; Rep So Africa Wrld Mallabiah Gms 89; Intern Bstn VA Hosp 90; AOA 90-; Intern Brghtn Marine Hosp 90; Hnrs; So African Optmtrc Assc 87-; So African Med/Dntl Cncl 87-; Dip Optom FOA Technikon Witwatersrand 86; Optometry.

**SAJA, RAYMOND F,** Atlantic Comm Coll, Mays Landing, NJ; SO; AAS; Clnry Arts.

**SAJNER, TARA M,** Oh Univ, Athens, OH; SO; BED; Alpha Lambda Delta 89-; Phi Mu Song Chrmn 90-; Elem Ed; Tchr.

**SAK, GILBERT,** Manhattan School Of Music, New York, NY; GD; BM; Deans Lst 90; All Amer Schlr Clgte Awd; Violin Prfrmnc; Chmbr Mus/Orch Playr/Tch.

**SAKAYA, HELIO S,** Nova Univ, Ft Lauderdale, FL; GD; MBA; Brzln-Amer Chmbr Of Cmmrc 89-; Gen Mngr ENA Tech Inc 89-; PG Getulio Vargas Bus Schol 77; BE Aeronautics Inst Of Tech 73; Bus; Gen Mgnt.

**SAKELLARAKOS, DINA N,** Radford Univ, Radford, VA; SO; BA; Crmnl Jstc Clb; Greek Orthdx Yth Assoc; Cnslr; Psychlgy; Cnslg/Drug Rehab.

**SAKKAB, DALIA H,** Le Moyne Coll, Syracuse, NY; SR; PH D; Cmprhnsv Anlytcl Grp Elctrn Mcrscpy Intrn; Brstl Myers Squibb Co Intrn; Chem; Rsrch Prfsr Indstry.

**SAKKALLOU, ELENI I,** City Univ Of Ny Baruch Coll, New York, NY; GD; MBA; Accntng Soc; Greek Cypriot Stdnt Assn; Community Tax Aid; BBA 90; Cmptr Infrmtn Systm; Accntncy.

**SAKON, BRENDA ALLEN,** Livingston Univ, Livingston, AL; SR; BS; Alpha Delta Pi Sorority Stnd/Pldg Board 86; Cmps Inter 87-89; Omega Phi Alpha 88-89; Stdnt Peer Tutor/Stdnt Spprt Svc 90-; Cmptr Sci Tutor Schlrshp 90-; L M Fitten/Mark Florersch Schlrshps 86-88; Acctg; CPA.

**SAKOWICZ, CHRISTINE A,** Radford Univ, Radford, VA; SO; BS; Rsdnce Hall Athl Coord 89-90; IM Flag Ftbl 89; Psych.

**SAKS, JEFFREY N,** Yeshiva Univ, New York, NY; SR; NJ Conf Yth Dir Com Asst 87-; JP Dunner Pol Sci Soc Treas 90-; Ben Zakkai Hon Soc 87-; Belkin Schlr; BA; Pol Sci; Jewish Educ.

**SAKSA, SHIRLEY G,** Oh St Univ At Marion, Marion, OH; SO; BA; Psych Club 90-; Stdnt To Stdnt Mentor Prog 90-; APA 90-; House Mgr For Homeward Bound T Rnstnl Home For Mentally Disabled; Child Psychlgst.

**SAKURAGAWA, TOKIKO,** Lasell Coll, Newton, MA; SO; AA; Internatl Clb 89-; Opn Stds; Advrtsng.

**SAKURAI, KUNIHIKO,** S U N Y Coll Of A & T Morrisvl, Morrisville, NY; SR; AD; Jazz Bnd 90-; Indvdl Stdies.

**SAL, NATALIE J,** Wv Univ, Morgantown, WV; SR; JD; IIE Nwsltr Comm Chrprsn 87-; WVU Mrchng Bnd Rnk Ldr 86-; Alpha Pi Mu Pres 89-; Stdnt Marshl; Outstdng Sr Awd IE Dept; Outstdng Jr Awd IIE 90; Wstrmrlnd Sprague/Kirkland Engr Schlrshps 90-; BSIE; Law.

**SALAAM, AL-NISA,** Benedict Coll, Columbia, SC; JR; BA; Stdnt Govt 89-90; NAACP 89-; SEA Of S C; Dns Lst Awd 88-89; Eunice Ponder Schlrshp 88-89; Alpha Kappa Alpha Schlrshp 89-; Erly Chldhd Educ.

**SALABARRIA PENA, YAMIR,** Univ Of Pr Medical Sciences, San Juan, PR; GD; PH D; Assc Hlth Ed PR 86-; Comm Afrs Cmt Med Sc Cmps 88-89; BS 88; MPHE; Stdnt Cncl Sch Pblc Hlth Tres 88-90; Harvard Hlth Prfsnl Pgm Intrnshp 87; Awrd Schlrshp Cncl Hghr Ed PR 88-90; Awrd Natl Hspnc Schlrshp Fund 88-90; Bhvrl Sci/Hlth Ed; Ph D.

**SALAC, TERRI E,** Faulkner St Jr Coll, Bay Minette, AL; SO; BS; Phi Theta Kappa 90-; AS; Bus Admn Mngmnt; Mngmnt.**

**SALADIN, CINDY M,** Univ Of Med & Dentistry Of Nj, Newark, NJ; SR; BS; Biological Soc Mbr 90-; Beta Beta Beta Mbr 90-; Maplewd Frst Aid Sqd Mbr 90-; Intrnshp Inst For Sci; Intrnshp Met Path Lab Inc; Dns Lst 83-; Midlantc Soc Toxlcgy Mbr 90-; Natl Geog Mbr; U S Army Act 84-88; AA Univ MD 87-; Clin Lab Sci; For Toxclgy.

**SALAHUDDIN, ALI A,** Franklin And Marshall Coll, Lancaster, PA; SO; BA; Intrntl Club Mbr 89-; Hons List 90-; Deans List 89-90; Michael Albert Lewis Mem Physcs Prize Recpnt 89-90; John Hackman Schlr 90-; Cricket Club; Math; Rsrch.

**SALAM, BASILIO,** Central Fl Comm Coll, Ocala, FL; GD; AS; Stdnt Govt Assoc 89-; Cedar Grp Assoc Post Chrmn 85-86; Mopan Mayon Cult Grp 80-86; CASS/CASP Schlrshp Pgm 89-; Ldrshp Ctr Of Amer Schlrshp; Beliz Govt Schlrshp 85-89; Soccer Tm 84-86; Dip Punta Gorda 89; Cert Ldrshp Ctr Of Amers; Quality Contrl/Prod Mgmnt.

**SALAMY, KAREN A,** Univ Of Sc At Columbia, Columbia, SC; SO; BA; Slng Clb 90; Gamma Beta Phi 89-; Phi Eta Sigma 89-; Alpha Lambda Delta 89-; IM Sftbl/Vlybl; Marine Sci; Rsrch.

**SALARY JR, LEROY,** Fisk Univ, Nashville, TN; SO; MBA; Cmptr Sci Clb; MBM Chorus Dir 89-; Alpha Phi Alpha Pres; FASE; Eng/Cmptr Sci; Eng.

**SALATINI, FARZANEH,** Central Fl Comm Coll, Ocala, FL; SO; AA; Tutor Scty 90-; Lbrn Asst; Dns Lst 90-; Comm Actvts; Tnns; Pngpng; Bwlg; Swmng; HSD 83; Phrmcy; Cont Hghr Ed.

**SALAZAR JR, ALFREDO,** Miami Dade Comm Coll North, Miami, FL; SO; BA; Intrnshp Jewsh Fed TV; AA; Cmnctns; Brdcstng.

**SALAZAR, CYNTHIA L,** Univ Of North Fl, Jacksonville, FL; JR; BA; Stdnt Wlns Assessmnt Tm 90-; Intrnshp Forrest Sr Hgh Phys Ed 90; Intrnshp Mandarin Sr Hgh Phys Ed 90; Vol Asst Bsktbl Coach Grls Vrsty 90-; Ftns Instrctr/Prnsl Trnr/Triathlete 87-; Scndry Phys Ed; Hgh Sch Coachng.

**SALAZAR, J OCTAVIO,** Nova Univ, Ft Lauderdale, FL; GD; MBA; Florida Med Assn; Amer Psych Assn; Amer Acad Child/Adlscnt Psychtry; Ocala Chmbr Cmrce 89-; Psych Clncl Assist Prof 90-; Marion Cnty Med Soc 89-; Child/Adlscnt/Adult Psych 89-; MD Univ Valle Cali-Colombia 72.

**SALAZAR, MARIA E,** City Univ Of Ny City Coll, New York, NY; JR; BA; YMCA Phtgrphy Vdo Clb; Cmmnctns/Film/Vdo.

**SALAZAR, MARIA R,** City Univ Of Ny La Guard Coll, Long Island Cty, NY; GD; BA; NEST; Dns Lst La Guardia Cmnty Clg; Latin American Comm; Fllwshp Ctr 3rd Wrld Orgnzng; Mnrty Actvst Apprntcshp Pgm; AA La Guardia Cmnty Clg 90.

**SALAZAR, SYLVIA,** Fl International Univ, Miami, FL; SR; BS; Ftr Edctrs Amer 89-90; AA Miami Dade Comm Coll 89; Spec Ed; Tchr Emtnlly Hndcppd.

**SALCEDO, ALMA NORMA,** Bergen Comm Coll, Paramus, NJ; SO; AA; Educ; Tchr.

**SALCI, JENNIFER J,** Univ Of Sc At Columbia, Columbia, SC; FR; BA; Std Alld Grnr Earth 90; Comm; Brdcstng.

**SALCINES, DANIA,** Miami Dade Comm Coll South, Miami, FL; JR; BA; AA; Engl; Elem Ed.

**SALDANA, JAVIER A,** Methodist Coll, Fayetteville, NC; SO; Amer Bsbl Congress; US Army Yth Actvts; Letter Of Apprctn Kitzingen Yth Actvts; Business.

**SALEEM, FAZANA S,** Bryn Mawr Coll, Bryn Mawr, PA; FR; BABSC; Intl Stdnts Assn Sec 90-; Islamic Cultural Assn 90-; Math/Econ/French; Bus/Law.

**SALEH, AWATIF,** Felician Coll, Lodi, NJ; BA; Deans Lst 89-; AAS; Bio.

**SALEHI, MASOUD,** Southern Coll Of Tech, Marietta, GA; SR; Elctrcl Engr.

**SALEM, JIHAD M,** Univ Of Akron, Akron, OH; SO; BA; Ei Biereh Clb 89-; Palestine Clb 89-; Dns Lst 89-; Eng; Elec Eng.

**SALERA, CHRISTINA L,** Va Commonwealth Univ, Richmond, VA; SO; BA; Alpha Omicron Pi PR 89-; Emerg Shltr Wmn Chldrn; Soc Wrk.

**SALERNI, CHRISTINE M,** Saint Joseph Coll, West Hartford, CT; SR; BS; Chem Clb Pres 87-; Amer Chem Scty 87-; Intern Walsworth Atheneum Hartford CT 90; CRC Press Fresh Chem Awd 88; Amer Inst Chem Awd; Chmstry/Fine Arts; Frnscs Cnsrvtn/Rstrtn.

**SALERNO, CONCETTA M,** Marywood Coll, Scranton, PA; SR; MBA; Rtl Fshn Cbl 88-; Kappa Omicron Nu; Intrnshp The Bon Ton 90; Intrnshp Scrntn Chmbr Cmrc; Mrktg.

**SALERNO, JANELLE S,** Pellissippi St Tech Comm Coll, Knoxville, TN; SO; AS; Phi Theta Kappa Pr 89-; Blue Grass PTA Vol 88-; Pellissippi Sts Cler/Support Staff Cncl 89-; Pellissippi St Tech Cmnty Clg 89-; Nursing.

**SALES, SUSAN A,** Univ Of Nc At Asheville, Asheville, NC; SR; BS; Asheville Buncombe Cmnty Chrstn Mnstry; Amer Int CPA Achvmnt Lvl II Exam; Acctg; CPA.

**SALGADO, CARLOS J,** Univ Politecnica De Pr, Hato Rey, PR; FR; Eng.

**SALGADO, CLAUDIA P,** Fl International Univ, Miami, FL; JR; BA; Occptnl Thrpy Clb 90-; Bapt Campus Mnstry Pblc Rltns 88-; FIU Deans Lst; Bapt Campus Mnstry 88-; Occptnl Thrpy.

**SALGUEIRO, MARY OTERO,** Saint Thomas Univ, Miami, FL; JR; BA; Sthrn Bell Tlphn Co Pioneers 90-; Assoc Antiguas Alumnas Havana Clb 75-; Grad Dale Carnegie 90; BSA Troop 205 Chrmn Prtns Comm 81-87; Rl Est Asso Gldn Line Prpty Inc 90-; Mbr Hialeah Miami Lakes Brd Rltrs 90-; Mrktg; Bus Mgt.

**SALICHS-VERA, FLORENCE J,** Inter Amer Univ Pr Hato Rey, Hato Rey, PR; GD; MED; Bio; Med Tech.

**SALINAS RAMIREZ, FRANCISCO J,** Univ Politecnica De Pr, Hato Rey, PR; FR.

**SALINAS, KATHIE B,** Va Commonwealth Univ, Richmond, VA; JR; BS; Acctg; Hair Salon Owner.

**SALINAS, ROSA D,** Saint Lawrence Univ, Canton, NY; FR; MBA; Ahora Clb 90-; Blck Stu Union 90-; Chrldrg Tm 90-; Spcl Olympcs Ftns Arbcs 90-; Ecnmcs; Corp Law.

**SALINAS, YVONE,** Ringling School Of Art, Sarasota, FL; SR; BFA; Swedish Clb Sarasota 88-; Cnty Med Auxillary 88-; Ship Radio Op 83-87; Cet Aland Maritime Coll 83; Fine Arts/Illus; Tchr.

**SALINE, LAURA C,** Manhattanville Coll, Purchase, NY; SO; BA; The Cmmtr Cncl 89-; Cmmtr Nwslttr Asst Edtr 89-; Vrsty Vllybl 89-; Engl; Tchng.

**SALING, RHONDA B,** Oh St Univ At Newark, Newark, OH; SR; Phi Sigma 88-; AA; BS Ed; Elem Ed; Tchng.

**SALINSKY, HEATHER L,** Indiana Univ Of Pa, Indiana, PA; SR; BED; PSEA 89-; Stdnts Of Crtve Arts Chrgrphr 88; Rsdnt Hll Assn Brd 90; Ordr Of Omega 89-; Kappa Delta Pi 89; Phi Mu Exec Offcr 89-; Cir K Sec 89; Otstndng Pldge 89; Otstndng Sis 89; IM Vlybl; Prfssnl Stds Of Educ; Tchng Elem.

**SALISBURY, BRAD D,** Duquesne Univ, Pittsburgh, PA; FR.

**SALK, JILL L,** Lesley Coll, Cambridge, MA; FR; BA; Educ Advsng Comm 90-; Soc Sci; Elem Tchr.

**SALL, JAMES A,** West Liberty St Coll, West Liberty, WV; JR; BS; Crmnl Jstc; Fdlr Law Enfrcmnt.

**SALLEE, KRISTIN M,** Middle Tn St Univ, Murfreesboro, TN; SO; BA; Gamma Beta Phi 89-; Alpha Delta P Asst Treas 90-; Wrk Schlrshp 89-; Acctng.

**SALLER, TIMOTHY R,** Fl International Univ, Miami, FL; SR; BA; IM Flg Ftbl/Bsktbl/Sftbl Capt 88-; B Ed; Mgmnt.

**SALLEY, ANN B,** Univ Of Sc At Columbia, Columbia, SC; JR; BA; Delta Zeta Natl Soc 90-; Hon Clb 88-; Assoc Hon Stdnts 88-; Ele Educ; Tch.

**SALLEY, LAGUAMNA M,** Norfolk St Univ, Norfolk, VA; FR; BS; Norfolk Naval Shipyard Auditing Clrk 89-; Cmptr Sci; Prog Analyst.

**SALLIS, YOLANDA,** Johnson C Smith Univ, Charlotte, NC; JR; PHD; SOS Club 90; - Beaufort Elem Progrm; Tuesday Club 90; Duke Univ Marine Lab Flwshp; UNCF Schlrshp; J C Smith Schlrshp 90-; Bio; Scintst.

**SALLIS, YVONNE L,** Va St Univ, Petersburg, VA; JR; Bsnss Admin 89; Big Bro/Sis 90; Bus Admin; Lwyr.

**SALLOT, JEFFREY P,** Capital Univ, Columbus, OH; SO; BSN; Nurs Curr Cmtee Stdnt Rep; Deans Lst; I M Athletics; United Way; Hosp Emplee; Emergcy Rm Reg Clrk; Nurs; Med.

**SALM, JENNIFER M,** Cornell Univ Statutory College, Ithaca, NY; FR; BS; Bio; Med Rsrch/Doctor.

**SALMON, CYNTHIA H,** Fl International Univ, Miami, FL; SR; BED; Phi Kappa Phi; US Cst Guard Petty Offcr 74-78; Comp Prog Anlyst 80-86; BA Phlsphy Ca St Univ 74; BA Psychlgy Ca St Univ 79; Elem Ed; Tchng.

**SALMON, GAIL A,** Georgian Court Coll, Lakewood, NJ; SR; Phi Theta Kappa 87; Sigma Delta Mu 85; Tchrs Aide/Sub Tchr/Tchr 80-90; BA; AA Ocean Cty Clg; Hmnts; Elem Ed.

**SALMON, GINA K,** Univ Of Tn At Martin, Martin, TN; SR; Peer Enblng 89-; Alumni Cncl 90-; Alpha Tau Omega Aux 90-; Ordr Omega Sec/Treas 89-; Pi Sigma Epsilon PR 88-; Alpha Omicron Pi Chpln 87-; Sor Offcr Awd 88-; Univ Serv Awd; Ldrs Rsdnc Schlrshp 87-88; Ecnmcs/Fin; Fin.

**SALO, TIMO H,** Tomlinson Coll, Cleveland, TN; SO; MAS; Intrntnl Stdnts Assc 90; Industrial Elec 89; Mnstry.

**SALOIO, KENNETH P,** Western New England Coll, Springfield, MA; JR; BA; Asst Jr High Eng Pgm 90-; Indus Eng.

**SALOM, VERONICA M,** Fl International Univ, Miami, FL; SR; BS; Polc Intern; Crmnl Justc; Law Enfrcmnt.

**SALOMON, RAFAEL C,** Univ Of Rochester, Rochester, NY; SO; BA; Hist.

**SALOOM, CHARLENE R,** Univ Of Miami, Coral Gables, FL; SR; BS; Hons Stdnts Assoc; Bio; Med.

**SALSBERY, KIMBERLY S,** Northern Ky Univ, Highland Hts, KY; SR; Rdlgc Tchnlgy Clb; Nrthrn KE State Rdlgc Tchnlgst 90; Deans List 89; Assc Dgr; Rdlgc Tchnlgy; Radiologic Tchnlgst.

**SALSER, JANICE MARIE,** Birmingham Southern Coll, Birmingham, AL; SO; BS; Intntl Stdnt Assoc Asst Sec 88-90; Alpha Phi Omega 87-89; Pres 87; Phi Eta Sigma 88; Beta Beta Beta VP 89; Alpha Epsilon Delta 88; Blgy; Medicine.

**SALTER, ERICA L,** Bennett Coll, Greensboro, NC; SR; BAIS; Stdnt Union Brd Prsdnt 90-; Bnnr Edtr 90-; Sec Sr Cls Sec 90-; Alpha Kappa Alpha; All Amrcn Schlr; Ntnl Cllgt Stdnt Gvt Allgt Awd; Intrnd Greensboro News Rcrd 88-; Bsktbl Sftbl 88-90; Cmmnctns Medif Jrnlst.

**SALTER, JENNIFER J,** Ms St Univ, Miss State, MS; JR; BA; Coll Rpblcns 89-90; Fnncl Mngmnt Assn 89-90; Alpha Gamma Delta 89-; Bus; Bus Admn.

**SALTER, RANDOLPH H,** Univ Of Nc At Charlotte, Charlotte, NC; SR; BS; Canterbury Clb Pres 87-; Heliconia Soc Intl 90-; NC Piedmont Orchid Soc 88-; Tri-Beta Bio Hist; IM Sftbl 90-; Botany; Rsrch/Dvlpmnt.

**SALTER, SUZIE C,** Univ Of Pittsburgh At Bradford, Bradford, PA; FR; Alpha Lambda Delta; Occup Thrpy.

**SALTERS, ROBIN D,** Univ Of New Haven, West Haven, CT; SR; BA; Alpha Lambda Delta; Vrsty Vlybl Co Cptn 87-; AA Lake Michigan College 89; Sociology.

**SALTMARSH, TAMEE L,** Catonsville Comm Coll, Catonsville, MD; FR; Stdnt Govt Org 88-; Shw Chr; Ensmbl; Dnc Clb Pres; All St Bnd; All Cntry Chr 88-89; NHS 89-90; Prfct Attndnc 89-90; 2nd Plc Wnnr Spch Cntst 89; Whos Who Among Am High Schl Stdnts Schlrshp 90-; Tr Gd; Music Cert; Hnrs Mert Cert; Bus Mgmt; Mdlng Spcl Ed Cnslr.

**SALTS, TRACEY L,** Univ Of Cincinnati, Cincinnati, OH; JR; Alpha Lambda Delta 88-; Kappa Delta Pi Cmnty Svc Comm 89-; Richard Hagedorn Youngblood Schlrshp 90-; Elem Ed; Tchg.

**SALTSMAN, ROSS L,** Kent St Univ Kent Cmps, Kent, OH; SO; Physical Therapist Vol; IM Vlybl; Mortor Brd; Scholar Athlete Banquet; Vrsty Track Field.

**SALTZ, MICHAEL E,** Va Commonwealth Univ, Richmond, VA; JR; BS; Rugby Clb 90-; Deans List 89-; FBI Hnrs Intrnshp Prgrm; Div I Collegiate Bsbl 88-89; Bus Admin; Fdrl Law Enfrcmnt.

**SALTZBERG, CHERYL A,** Univ Of Ma At Amherst, Amherst, MA; SO; Leisure Studies/Resources Soc 89-; Leisure Studies/ Resources; Cmcl Rec.

**SALTZMAN, JAMES M,** Glassboro St Coll, Glassboro, NJ; JR; BA; Advrtsg Clb 90-; Mktg Clb 90-; Cinema Wrkshp 87-88; Zeta Beta Tau Parlmntrn 85-; Glassboro Today Stf 86-88; IM Ftbl/ Hockey/Sftbl 85-; Cmnctns-Advrtsg.

**SALTZMAN, JENNY L,** Ms St Univ, Miss State, MS; SO; BA; Hnrs Cncl Traffic Ct Appls Sec 89; Diamond Girl; Jr Panhellenic; Gamma Beta Phi; Chi Omega; Psychlgy.

**SALTZMAN, TARA L,** Fl International Univ, Miami, FL; SR; Anmsty 87-; Grnpc 85-; Phi Lambda; Vol Jackson Memrl Hosp 90-; Red Crss Bld Don Gallon Dnr Clb 88-; BA; Scl Studies Educ; Tch Mddl Schl/Sr H.

**SALTZSTEIN, SARA LORIN,** United States Naval Academy, Annapolis, MD; SR; MD; Hnr Comm 87-; Airborne Trng Unit 89-; Brigade Staff 90-, Phi Kappa Phi 89-; Wom Prof Assoc 87-; All Amer 88-89; All Conf 88-; Varsity Swmmng 87-; BS; Oceanography; Navy Physician.

**SALUME, BEATRIZ,** Univ Of Miami, Coral Gables, FL; JR; BBS; Tennis Tm 88-89; VITA; Beta Alpha Psi 90; Golden Key 90; Deans Lst 88-; Acctg; Taxation.

**SALUS, LORI A,** Marywood Coll, Scranton, PA; JR; BS; Ski Clb Pres 88-90; Rsdnt Cmmtt 87; Ski Clb Trp Crdntr Pres 88-90; Htl Rstrnt Clb Scl Crdntr 90; BA 90; Htl Rstrnt Mgmt; Edctnl Hlth Cr Fd Srvc.

**SALUS, TODD MARTIN,** Anne Arundel Comm Coll, Arnold, MD; SO; AA; Phi Theta Kappa 90-; Bus Admin.

**SALVA FIGUEROA, LUIS RAUL,** Inter Amer Univ Pr Hato Rey, Hato Rey, PR; JR; BA; NAA 90-; Acctng Assn 89-; Deans Lst 90-; Hon Rl 89-; IM Tennis Gold Met 90; Acctng; CPA.

**SALVA, CATHERINE E,** Univ Of Pr At Rio Piedras, Rio Piedras, PR; GD; MBA; Exclnc Medal; Assoc Bibliotecarios Juridicos; Assoc De Bibliolecarios; Crclm Tech Dept Educ 79-85; BA 76; MBA 85; Lbry Sci; Acdmc.

**SALVA, ERIC W,** Edinboro Univ Of Pa, Edinboro, PA; SO; BS; Edinboro Univ Of Pa Hnrs Prog 90-; Envrmntl Sci Earth Sci.

**SALVA, IVETTE SANTIAGO,** Caribbean Univ, Bayamon, PR; SR.

**SALVA, KIMBERLY,** S U N Y Coll Of Tech At Frmgdl, Farmingdale, NY; SO; BA; Lbrl Arts/Sci Acdmc Exclnc Awd 90-; Deans Lst 90-; Lbrl Arts; Cmnctv Dsrdrs.

**SALVADOR, WENIMAR D,** Univ Of Sc At Columbia, Columbia, SC; FR; BS; Phi Eta Sigma; Pharmacy; Medicine.

**SALVATORE, DINA A,** Duquesne Univ, Pittsburgh, PA; SR; BSBA; AMA Soc Chrmn 89-90; Dance Tm 87-89; Mrtr Bd 90-; Themis 89-90; Beta Alpha Phi 89-; Zeta Tau Alpha 89-; Painewebber Intrn 90; Derby Days 88-; Winter Olympics 88-; Finance; Financial Analyst.

**SALVATORE, JEAN C,** Bloomfield Coll, Bloomfield, NJ; JR; BA; Nwsppr; Frlnc Wrtr 90-; Natl Hnr Soc; Engl; Law Schl.

**SALVATORE, WILLIAM V,** Ny Chiropractic Coll, Glen Head, NY; GD; Amer Chrprctc Assn; Phi Chi Omega; Deans Lst 88-90; NYCC-SLTTRN 90-; Core Sci Awd; Acdmc Excllnc Awd; ACA Acdmc Schlrshp 85-86; Rsrch Asstshp-Cytgntcs/Gynclgc Onclgy; Stony Brook Rugby Clb 86-87; Chrprctc Nrlgy; Dctr Chrprctc Nrlgy.

**SALVI, ALEJANDRO,** Miami Dade Comm Coll South, Miami, FL; SO; BS; So Cross Astronomy Clb; Bapt Hosp Auxlry; Outsdng Acad Achvmnt Awd 90; Clg Tlnt Rstr; Biochem/Humanities; Emerg Physcn.

**SALVUCCI, ROBERT M,** Univ Of Akron, Akron, OH; SR; BS; Fin Mgmt Assoc Pres 89-; Stdnt Adv Cncl Rep; Gallucci Hall Fl Rep 89; Natl Hnr Soc; Golden Key; IM 88-89; Fin; Bus.

**SALWAN, RITA M,** Notre Dame Coll, Cleveland, OH; JR; BS; Nutrition Assn V P 90-; Amer Dietetic Assn 90-; Cleveland Dietetic Assn 90-; U S Achvmnt Acad 90-; Natl Collegiate Nat Sci Awd 90-; Deans Lst 89-; Home Ec Assn Schlrshp; Dietetics/ Nutrition; Reg Dietitian.

**SALYER, ANDREA D,** Alice Lloyd Coll, Pippa Passes, KY; SO; BA; Memorial Schlrshp 89-; Kndgrn Educ/Hmnts/Arts; Tch Elem Schl.

**SALYER, MELISSA J,** Univ Of Tn At Knoxville, Knoxville, TN; FR; BA; Acctng; Acct.

**SALYERS, O ROBERTA,** Univ Of Va Clinch Valley Coll, Wise, VA; SO; BS; Judd Lws Soc 90-; Darden Soc 90-; Dns Lst 89-; Std Mrshl; Peer Advsr; Hst Chnclr; Clncl Psy.

**SAM, VALERIE D,** Al St Univ, Montgomery, AL; SO; CASET Pgm; Dorm Treas 89-90; Pr Schlr; Deans Lst; 1st Runnerup Miss Frshmn 89-90; Engr.

**SAMAHA, MAYSSAM,** Teikyo Post Univ, Waterbury, CT; SO; BS; Intl Clb Sec/Treas 90-; Intr Dsgn.

**SAMAN, TANIA A,** Univ Of Nc At Charlotte, Charlotte, NC; FR; BA; Arts/Sci.

**SAMARASINGHE, DEEPTHI J,** Eckerd Coll, St Petersburg, FL; SO; BS; Crckt Clb; Cmptr Sci; Instrct.

**SAMAROO, HOAMESHWAR,** City Univ Of Ny City Coll, New York, NY; JR; BA; Pltcl Sci; Law.

**SAMAROO, MARLYN S D,** City Univ Of Ny La Guard Coll, Long Island Cty, NY; SO; BA; Phi Theta Kappa; Cmptr Oper Intern; Spec Intern Consolidated Edison; Spec Intern Chemical Bank; AAS; Cmptr Sci; Cmptr Analyst.

**SAMI, SAMINA,** Villanova Univ, Villanova, PA; SO; BA; So Asian Cultural Soc PR Ofcr 90-; Lit Mag 89-; Envrnmntl Clb 90-; Vol Tutor Phila Lit Ctr 90-; Engl; Jrnlsm.

**SAMI, SHABANA,** Pellissippi St Tech Comm Coll, Knoxville, TN; FR; BS; Intl Clb 89-; Muslim Comm 90-; Bsns Mgmt.

**SAMICK, JENNIFER A,** Indiana Univ Of Pa, Indiana, PA; SR; BED; ACEI 90-; Erly Chldhd Ed; Tchr.

**SAMLOW, NADINE M,** Comm Coll Algny Co Algny Cmps, Pittsburgh, PA; FR; BSN; Bio/Behav Sci; RN.

**SAMMONS, KRISTEN V,** Bristol Univ, Bristol, TN; GD; MBA; Phi Kappa Phi 84-; Kappa Mu Epsilon 84-; Upsilon Pi Epsilon 84-; Natl Mgmt Assn 90-; Systs/Cmptng Analyst 86-; BS East TN State Univ 86; Cmptr Sci/Exec Mgmt; Cmptr Bus Mgmt.

**SAMMONS, SHAUN W,** Middle Tn St Univ, Murfreesboro, TN; FR; BA; Univ Theatre Actor; Aerospace; Prof Pilot.

**SAMMONS, TANIA L,** Wallace St Comm Coll At Selma, Selma, AL; FR.

**SAMMS, DONOVAN A,** Nova Univ, Ft Lauderdale, FL; GD; MBA; Sccr 76-79; BSC Mgmt Stds; Bus Admn.

**SAMOL, DEBORAH T,** Fl International Univ, Miami, FL; JR; Phi Lambda Beta 89-; Bsn Adm; CEO.

**SAMPLE II, BYRON,** Rensselaer Polytechnic Inst, Troy, NY; FR; BA; Sci; Eng.

**SAMPLE JR, EDDIE BOOKER,** Central St Univ, Wilberforce, OH; SR; BS; Opprtnty For Psych Stdnt Invlvemnt VP 89-90; Psi Chi 90; Undrgrad Rsrch Assist 90; Psychlgy; Grad Schl.

**SAMPLES, KIMBERLY M,** Univ Of North Fl, Jacksonville, FL; JR; BSN; Phi Kappa Phi 90-; Nrsng.

**SAMPLES, ORETA M,** Fort Valley St Coll, Fort Valley, GA; SO; AAS; Vet Sci Clb Sec 90-; USDA Schlrshp 90; Hls Pt Fd Schlrshp; Med Exmnr/Nrs 83-; Cert Crandall Jr Coll 83; Vet Tech.

**SAMPLES, SABINA S,** Abraham Baldwin Agri Coll, Tifton, GA; JR; BSED; Phi Theta Kappa Soc 89-; Child Day Care; Early Chldhd Educ; Tch.

**SAMPSON, AMY E,** Ms St Univ, Miss State, MS; FR; MBA; Lambda Sigma Soc RUF 90-; Intr Resdnc Hall Cnsl; IRHC Hall Govts Comm Hl Rep 90-; Gamma Beta Phi 90-; Chi Omega 90-; Lambda Sigma; Chi Omega Pldg Cls VP 90-; Accptd In Hons Prog 90-; MS State Univ Aerobics Club; Bnkng/Fin; Bus.

**SAMPSON, CARMEN L,** S U N Y Coll Of Tech At Alfred, Alfred, NY; SR; BED; Hnrs Prog 90-; Hnrs Prog Comm 90-; Phi Theta Kappa; Physical Ed; Teacher/Coach.

**SAMPSON, DEBORA L,** Memphis St Univ, Memphis, TN; JR; BA; PSI 90-; AAS 79; Cert 89; Psych; Chld.

**SAMPSON, DEBORAH L,** Marshall University, Huntington, WV; SR; BA; Hall Advsry Cncl; Pnhllnc Cncl Sec 90f Kappa Delta Pi; Order Omega VP 90-; Gamma Beta Phi 89-90; Beta Hphi Phi Mu Prvsnl Mbr Dir 89-90; Otstndg Cll Stdnts Amr; Elem Ed.

**SAMPSON, JERMAINE L,** Converse Coll, Spartanburg, SC; FR; Stdnt Admssns Brd; Stdnt Govt Assoc; SVS Pre Law Scty; SC Stdtn Lgsltr Hrn Brd Rep; Alpha Lambda Delta; Crscnt; Deans Lst; Bsktbll Sttcn; Engl.

**SAMPSON, KAREN LENEE,** Al A & M Univ, Normal, AL; GD; BS; Stdnt Natl Educ Assn 89-; Al Educ Assn 89-; Natl Cncl Tchrs Of Engl 90-; Alpha Kappa Mu 89-; Sigma Tau Delta 89-; Zeta Phi Beta 87-; Educ/Engl Poltcl Sci; Law.

**SAMPSON, KELLI M,** Memphis St Univ, Memphis, TN; SO; Tiger Paws 90-.

**SAMPSON, MICHELLE K,** Daytona Beach Comm Coll, Daytona Beach, FL; SO; BS; Dns Lst 88-; Pres Lst 88-; Blgy Stdnt Of Yr; AA Daytona Beach Comm Coll 90; Phrmcy.**

**SAMPSON, RICHARD J,** Middle Tn St Univ, Murfreesboro, TN; SR; BS; Maths Tchrs Assoc 89-; Kappa Delta Pi 90-; Enlisted Assoc Tenn Army Natl Grd 86-; Elem Educ; Teach.

**SAMPSON, THERESA E,** Springfield Tech Comm Coll, Springfield, MA; JR; BA; Stdnt Govt; Hmels Shltr Vol; Police Assn Schlrshp Grad W/Hon 90; Tennis Univ Lowell 90; Crmnl Jstce/Engl; Law.

**SAMS, CASSANDRA M,** Albany St Coll, Albany, GA; JR; Allied Hlth Clb 90-; Phi Beta Lambda 90-; Gospel Choir 90-; Alpha Eta; Allied Hlth Acad Schlrshp 90-; Allied Hlth; Hlth Care Admin.

**SAMS, ELIZABETH A,** Wv Univ At Parkersburg, Parkersburg, WV; FR; BA; Wood Co Hrng Imprd Pres 88-90; Bus; Mrktng.

**SAMS, GREGORY B,** Morehouse Coll, Atlanta, GA; SO; MBA 89-; Morehouse Glee Clb Tenor 89-90; IL Clb AUC 89-; Hon Roll 90-; Deans Lst 90-; Inroad Chgo Inc 89-; Zurich Am Ins Co Intern Tax Analyst 90-; Northern Trust Bank Co-Op Intern Process Gnrlst 88-89; Acctg; CPA Lawyer.**

**SAMSELL, MARY-ELIZABETH A,** Va Commonwealth Univ, Richmond, VA; SO; BA; Englsh.

**SAMSON, BRENT A,** Comm Coll Algny Co Algny Cmps, Pittsburgh, PA; JR; MBA; Physcl Thrpy.

**SAMSON, DANIEL C,** Hillsborough Comm Coll, Tampa, FL; JR; BS; Stdnt Govt Sgt At Arms 89-90; Mech Eng.

**SAMSON-RODRIGUEZ, SHERILYN M,** Commonwealth Coll, Virginia Beach, VA; SO; AS; Elctrncs Clb Pres 90-; NESDA 90-; Tstmstrs 90-; Beta Chi/Alpha Beta Gamma 90-; Cox Cable Intrnshp 90-; Adopt A Beach 91; Msclr Dystrphy Assoc 86-91; Elctrncs/Cmptr Scnc 90-92; Engr.

**SAMU, TAYIB I,** Central St Univ, Wilberforce, OH; FR; Muslim Stdnt Assoc Treas; Mfg Engr.

**SAMUEL, ANTHONY J,** Fl A & M Univ, Tallahassee, FL; JR; BS; IEEE V Chrmn 90-; Phi Eta Sigma; Elctrnc Engr Tech; Engr.

**SAMUEL, MODESTINE J,** Coker Coll, Hartsville, SC; GD; BA; Natl Educ Assn 80-; SC Educ Assn 80-; Sec Florence Schl Dist 1 83-90; Elem Educ; Tchr.

**SAMUEL, SOPHIA,** Morgan St Univ, Baltimore, MD; SR; BS; Soc Advncmnt Mgmt; Alpha Kappa Mu; Alpha Lambda Delta; Phi Eta Sigma; Mgmt; Bsn.

**SAMUELS, DEBORAH,** Converse Coll, Spartanburg, SC; FR; BED; Chrstn Assoc 90-; Alpha Lambda Delta 90-; Vol Serv 90-; Religion; Ele Spec Educ.

**SAMUELS, JENNIFER L,** Univ Of Sc At Columbia, Columbia, SC; FR; BS; Sclgy/Anthrplgy Clb 90-; Sclgy; Prof.

**SAMUELS, NICOLE S,** Fl A & M Univ, Tallahassee, FL; FR; Phi Eta Sigma; Elec Eng.

**SAMUELS, STANLEY E,** Norfolk St Univ, Norfolk, VA; JR; BS; Acctng; Publc Acctng.

**SAMUELS, TERRANCE E,** Columbia Union Coll, Takoma Park, MD; GD; MED; AA Prince Georges Comm Clg 73; Stdnt Admin; High Rnkng Schl Admin.

**SAMUELSON, GARY M,** Oh Northern Univ, Ada, OH; GD; JD; Federalist Soc; Chrstn Legal Soc; Comm Chrs; Cncrnd Wmn Amer; BA Harding Univ 76; Law/Constitutional.

**SAN JORGE, PATRICIA A,** Fl International Univ, Miami, FL; FR; Hons Prog.

**SAN MIGUEL JR, ANGEL A,** Inter Amer Univ Pr San German, San German, PR; SR; BBA; Phi Eta Mu-Beta; Jr Chmbr Intl; Profssnl Ins Agnts Of PR; Mktg; Mstr Degree.

**SAN SEVERINO, ANITA R,** Bunker Hill Comm Coll, Boston, MA; SO; AS; Mahoney Wrght Insrnc Agncy Inc Intrnshp Lgl Asst; Lgl Admnstrtn; Law.

**SANAN, ABHAY,** Boston Univ, Boston, MA; GD; PHD; Mdl United Ntns India Clb 85-87; Amer Med Stdnt Assoc 87; Golden Key 90; Alpha Omega Alpha Pres 89; Mc Graw-Hill Awd 89; CIBA-GEIGY Awd; BA; MD; Hewlett-Packard Awd; Med; Nrlgcl Srgry.

**SANBORN, DIANNE G,** Merrimack Coll, North Andover, MA; GD; Pres Schlr 90-; Summa Cum Laude; BS; Fin; Fund Acctg.**

**SANBORN, ELIZABETH M,** Hillsborough Comm Coll, Tampa, FL; SO; BA; Erly Chldhd Edctn; Kndrgrtn Tchr.

**SANBORN, KATHARINE J,** Atlantic Comm Coll, Mays Landing, NJ; FR; AA; Educ; Spec Ed Tchr.

**SANBORN, KEITH R,** S U N Y Coll At Fredonia, Fredonia, NY; SR; BS; Governor Cuomos Athl Agnst Alcohol/Drgs; Omicron Delta Epsilon; SUNYAC Acad Player Of Yr For Soccer; All New York State Soccer; Vrsty Soccer Capt 87-; Cmptr Sci; Prgrmg/Mgmt.

**SANBORN, KIMBERLY A,** Neumann Coll, Aston, PA; JR; BA; Grad Hnrs 90; AAS 90; Erly Chldhd Educ; Tchg.

**SANCHEZ ZEA, DHARMA S,** Univ Of Pr Medical Sciences, San Juan, PR; GD; Asstn Pfsr 90-; Cum Laude 85; BA 85; MS; Psychlgy/Cmmnctns Dsrdrs; Speech/Lang Path.

**SANCHEZ, ARNALDO,** Miami Dade Comm Coll South, Miami, FL; SO; SAFE 90-; Phi Theta Kappa 89-; Emmanule Snty Hr 87-89; Acad Awd 89; Awrd Brd Trustees 90; Awd Ntl Hispnc Fndntn; Talent Rstr Outstndng Mnrty Stdnts 90; AA; Bio-Chem/Mlclr Bio; Med Dr.

**SANCHEZ, BRENDA L,** Antillian Adventist University, Mayaguez, PR; FR; Secretarial.

**SANCHEZ, CRAIG A,** Suffolk Comm Coll Selden Cmps, Selden, NY; SO; BS; AAS; Engl/Mrktng; Pblc Rltns.

**SANCHEZ, DAVID,** Univ Of Pr Medical Sciences, San Juan, PR; GD; MPHB; UPR 90; BA; MPHB; Biostatistics.

**SANCHEZ, DIANA MARIA,** Univ Of Miami, Coral Gables, FL; JR; BA; Immaculate Cath Chrch Yth Grp 88-; Bowman Ashe Schlrshp 89-90; Music Schlrshp 88-; Music; Teaching.

**SANCHEZ, ELDALIZ,** Inter Amer Univ Pr Guayama, Guayama, PR; FR; Hnr Cert; Sci; Nrsg.

**SANCHEZ, ELIA,** Newbury Coll, Brookline, MA; FR; BA; Admn Asst Pioneer Grp 89-; Bsn Mgmt.

**SANCHEZ, ELISA A,** Univ Of Southern Ms, Hattiesburg, MS; SO; BA; Pnamer Stdnt Assn Treas 89-; Intl Rltns Clb VP Pub Rltns 89-; Amer Mktg Assn 90-; Bus; Mktg Mgmt.**

**SANCHEZ, ERNESTO,** Inter Amer Univ Pr Guayama, Guayama, PR; SO; Meth Yth Soc 90-; Hnr Lst 90-; Civil Defense; Communications.

**SANCHEZ, GIOVANNY F,** City Univ Of Ny City Coll, New York, NY; JR; BA; Stdnt Govt Sen 90-; Aspira Hispanic Clb Publ Rels 89-; Intl Org Ntwrk VP 90-; Hons Prog 89-; Chrch Yth Soc Pres 88-90; Econs Soc; Hubert Humphrey Publ Pol 90; Intrnshp Natl Puerto Rican Coaltn Wash DC; Natl Hispanc Schlrshp Fnd; Pol Sci/Publ Pol; Law.

**SANCHEZ, GRISEL,** Fl International Univ, Miami, FL; SR; BED; Fclty Schlrs Schlrshp Pgm 88-; Spnsh; Educ.

**SANCHEZ, HELGA M,** Univ Politecnica De Pr, Hato Rey, PR; FR; BA; Mech Eng.

**SANCHEZ, JEAN NOEL R,** City Univ Of Ny Baruch Coll, New York, NY; JR; BBA; Comptr Club; Golden Key; Comptr Info Sys.

**SANCHEZ, JEANETTE M,** Fl International Univ, Miami, FL; FR; MBA; Un Cerebal Palsy Fndrsr 88-; Deans Lst 90-; Intl Rltns.

**SANCHEZ, JULIE A,** Univ Of Sc At Coastal Carolina, Conway, SC; SO; BA; Dns Lst; Psy; Doctor PHD.

**SANCHEZ, LESLIE ANN,** Amherst Coll, Amherst, MA; SO; Wmn In Sci; Sntr Dorm; Howard Hughes Grnt; Vrsty Sqsh Cptn; Psychology; Pre Med.**

**SANCHEZ, MANUEL,** Fl International Univ, Miami, FL; FR; BA; FBLA 88-89; Bwlng; Hstry Edc; Tchr.

**SANCHEZ, MARCELA M,** Univ Of Cincinnati-Clrmnt Coll, Batavia, OH; SO; BA; Bus; MBA.

**SANCHEZ, MARLON MIKHAIL,** Morehouse Coll, Atlanta, GA; FR; BA; Morehouse Coll Glee Club 90-; Morehouse Bus Assn 90-; Spelman Coll Drama Club 90-; Bus Admn Mrktng; Securities Broker.

**SANCHEZ, MARY E,** William Paterson Coll, Wayne, NJ; SO; BA; Spec Educ Clb Chrprsn; Spec Educ.

**SANCHEZ, MAYRA C,** Miami Dade Comm Coll, Miami, FL; SO; AA; Psi Beta; Soc Psych Comm/Jr Coll; Psych.

**SANCHEZ, OLGA M,** Univ Of Pr Medical Sciences, San Juan, PR; SO; Amer Stdnt Dental Assoc 89-90; Stdnt Govt Cls Sec 89-90; Investigation & Teacher Sstnt Surgical Sciences Dept 90-; Deans List Mbr 89-90; Omicron Kappa Upsilon Awd Of Achvmnt 90-91; BA Univ Of Puerto Rico 91; Biology; Pedodontics.

**SANCHEZ, ORLANDO,** Inter Amer Univ Pr Hato Rey, Hato Rey, PR; SO; Comp; Comp Prgrmmng.

**SANCHEZ, PEDRO L,** Inter Amer Univ Pr San German, San German, PR; SR; BA; COPANI; Hnr Std; Phi Zeta Chi 90; Army ROTC 2lt; USA Natl Grd; La Solucion Orchstr 86-; Mc Donald All Amer Band; Sftbl Phi Zeta Chi; Ba; Music; Med.

**SANCHEZ, RITA M GONZALEZ,** Univ Of Pr Humacao Univ Coll, Humacao, PR; SR; BA; ACS Stdnt Chptr UPR Humacao 90-; Ind Chem; Ph D.

**SANCHEZ, ROBERT B,** Univ Of Sc At Columbia, Columbia, SC; FR; BS; IM Sccr/Swmng 90-; Engineering.

**SANCHEZ, ROSEMARY,** Fl International Univ, Miami, FL; GD; Phi Lambda 90; Deans Lst 88-90; Natl Home Frtrnty 90; Hnr Lst 88-90; Natl Hnr Soc 84-87; Phi Lambda Pi; Hnrs Grad 90; Carlson Hipp Radisson Normandie 89; Copr Mgmt Trng Prog; Amer Hotel/Motel Assn; BSHM FIU 90; Hosp Mgmt; Bus/Law.

**SANCHEZ, ROXANNA N,** Coastal Carolina Comm Coll, Jacksonville, NC; SO; BS; Phi Theta Kappa; AA/PRE-BUS; Acctg; CPA.

**SANCHEZ, TERESA,** Ny Univ, New York, NY; FR; BA; NY St Lib Prty Chrprsn 88-90; Bsn/Ecnmcs; Admn.

**SANCHEZ, WILLIAM R,** Inter Amer Univ Pr San German, San German, PR; JR; Police Org Corp 87-; Pol Dept San German PR Homicide Div 87-; Cmptr Pgm.

**SANCHEZ-PICO, GUILLERMO,** Saint Andrews Presbytrn Coll, Laurinburg, NC; JR; BA; Chess Clb Prsdnt 88-; Wrld Cltr Soc Prsdnt 88-; Bsns Clb VP 88-; Amnesty Intrntnl 90-; Chldrn Intrntnl Spnsr 89-; Intrnshp Sprit De Corp New Orleans 90; Intrnshp Peace Corps Costa Rica; Bsns Ecnmcsf Intrntnl Bsns.

**SANCHEZ-WALKER, YANIRA,** Bayamon Central Univ, Bayamon, PR; FR; BA; Deans Lst 89-90; Catholic Ch Religious Instr Coord; Young Grp Instr; Spnsh.

**SAND, PAULA R,** Univ Of Cincinnati, Cincinnati, OH; SO; BSN; Nrsng.

**SANDBERG, JOHN C,** Columbia Greene Comm Coll, Hudson, NY; Math/Science; Pharmacy.

**SANDBROOK, DOUGLAS D,** Hudson Valley Comm Coll, Troy, NY; SO; CERT; Prmdc.

**SANDEL, ANABEL,** Elms Coll, Chicopee, MA; SO; BA; Campus Ministry 90-; Pay Christi 90-; Affirmative Action Committee; Intl Studies; Architecture.

**SANDELIN, LEVI D,** Tn Temple Univ, Chattanooga, TN; SO; BA; Security Cncl Repr 90-; Pi Kappa Delta Actvts Dir 90-; IM Flg Ftbl 90; IM Bsktbl Asst Coach 90-; Msc; Law.

**SANDER, DOUGLAS W,** Union Univ, Jackson, TN; SR; BS; Psy Club 90-; Bpt Student Union BSU 88-90; Outdrs Club 90-F Cir K Club 89-90; Psy; Clinical Psylgt.

**SANDER, EUSTACIA M,** Castleton St Coll, Castleton, VT; SR; BA; Kappa Delta Pi 90-; Engl And Scndry Educ; Hgh Schl Engl Tchr.

**SANDERS, AMY C,** Wilmington Coll, New Castle, DE; SO; BED; Mthdst Church Christian Ed Ldr 90-; Caregiver Support Grp 90-; Day Care Owner 89-; AAS Del Tech Com Clge 90; Elem Sci Mth; Elem Sec Ed Tchr.

**SANDERS, AMY MICHELLE,** Ms St Univ, Miss State, MS; SR; BS; MSU Fashion Brd VP 88-; Stff Wrtr Clg Nwspr; Presidents Schlr 90; Deans Schlr 90-; Pi Kappa Alpha Little Sister 90-; Miss Assoc Educators; Elem Educ; Teach.

**SANDERS, BRENDOLYN D,** Univ Of Tn At Martin, Martin, TN; SO; BS; Blck Stdnt Assn 89-; Blck Stdnt Assn Gspl Choir 89-; Phi Eta Sigma; Delta Sigma Theta; Phi Kappa Phi; Delta Sigma Theta Higheste Acad Achvmnt; U Of TN Cert Of Merit; Psychology; Ind/Org Pscyhologist.

**SANDERS, CARLA L,** Middle Tn St Univ, Murfreesboro, TN; SO; Chem Clb 90-; Phi Mu Delta; Blgy Pre Med; Med.

**SANDERS, CAROLE L,** East Tn St Univ, Johnson City, TN; SO; BS; Eng Technlgy; Indstrl Eng.

**SANDERS, CARRIE ANN L,** Univ Of Sc At Columbia, Columbia, SC; SO; Thtr Plyrs; Plygrnd Plyhse; Robert E Benjamin Schlrshp; Thtr/Indstrl Psychlgy; Tchr.

**SANDERS, CATHERINE P,** Radford Univ, Radford, VA; FR; Alpha Lambda Delta; Bsns.

**SANDERS, CHAD N,** Mercer Univ, Macon, GA; FR; Alpha Tau Omega 90-; Mbr Emrld Cmmty Chrch Seattle 89-90; Track Team State Chmps 89-90; Arospace Engnrng; Engrng.

**SANDERS, CHANITA N,** Al A & M Univ, Normal, AL; FR; Hnr Rll; Bus; Bus Admn.

**SANDERS, CONNIE JARA H,** Meridian Comm Coll, Meridian, MS; SR; BS; Stdnt Nrs Assn 87-89; Orgnztn Assc Nrs 87-89; Frst Bptst Chrch Of Lake Sndy Schl Tchr 88-; Acadmc Schlrshp 90-; Emily Louise Mcdonald Schlrshp 88-89; Bst Cls 89; Elizabeth C Harkins Undrgrd Awd; Nrsng; Edctn Adlt Hlth.

**SANDERS, CYNTHIA JOY,** Ga St Univ, Atlanta, GA; GD; MED; Ntl Ed Assn 89-; Golden Key 89-; Phi Kappa Phi 89-; Unicef Vlntr Wrk 88-90; Grad Magna Cum Laude; Pres Awd; B Ed 90; Erly Chlhd Ed; 2nd Grade Tchr Cobb Cnty.

**SANDERS, DANDERIA A,** Jackson St Univ, Jackson, MS; FR; BS; Alpha Lambda Delta 90-; Chemistry; Dr Anesthesiology.

**SANDERS, DAVID J,** Chattahoochee Vly St Comm Coll, Phenix City, AL; FR; AS; Criminal Justice; Law Enfor Officer.

**SANDERS, DAVID L,** Tn Temple Univ, Chattanooga, TN; SR; BA; Alpha Epsilon Theta; Zeta Chi Delta; MD.

**SANDERS, DELCY S,** Alcorn St Univ, Lorman, MS; JR; BS; DC Comm; Senate; Pan-Hellenic Cncl; Dns Lst 88-89; Zeta Phi Beta V P 89; IM Bsktbl; Pol Sci; Corp Law.

**SANDERS, DEMETHA M,** Alcorn St Univ, Lorman, MS; SO; BA; Psych Club 90-; All Amer Schlr 90-; Indus Psych.

**SANDERS, DEVIN D,** Kenyon Coll, Gambier, OH; FR; BA; Carolina Ohio Sci/Engr Ntwrk 90-; Stdnt Alumni Assn 90-; Vrsty Ftbl 90-; Biology/Chmstry; Medicine.

**SANDERS, DONA M,** Marshall University, Huntington, WV; SO; BA; CA Assoc Rltrs 84-87; Untd Wy 82-84; Cmptr Sci; Cmptr Pgrmr.

**SANDERS, EDWIN C,** Morehouse Coll, Atlanta, GA; SR; Glee Clb Pres 90-; S Reg Hnrs Cncl V P 89-90; Stdnt Govt Sen 90-; Phi Beta Kappa 90-; Pi Mu Epsilon 90-; Omicron Delta Epsilon 90-; Phi Mu Alpha Sinfonia V P-FEO 90-; Sigma Tau Delta 89-; BUILD Pgm Fndr/Instr; Asstntshp Fed Res Bd Wash DC; Econ; Prfsr.

**SANDERS, GLADYS E,** Univ Of Sc At Columbia, Columbia, SC; SR; Aiken Sci Clb 87-90; Omicron Delta Kappa 89-; Gamma Beta Phi 86-; USCA Sr Schlr Schlrshp 89-90; BS Unv SC 90; Biology Scndry Edctn; Tchr.**

**SANDERS, GORDON PAUL,** Central Al Comm Coll, Alexander City, AL; SO; BA; Phi Theta Kappa; Sec Ed/Blgy/Psyclgy; High Schl Tchr.

**SANDERS, GREGORY O,** Univ Of Ct, Storrs, CT; SR; BS; American Fisheries Soc; AA Grossmont Clge 85; Natural Resource Mgmt & Engrng; Fishery Bio.

**SANDERS JR, JAMES L,** Univ Of Sc At Lancaster, Lancaster, SC; SO; Deans List; Arete; Stdnt Govt Assc; Yrbk Edtr; Hist; Tchr.

**SANDERS, JAMES T,** Alcorn St Univ, Lorman, MS; SO; BA; ROTC Tech Clb; Alph Phi Omega VP 90; Im Bsktbl Bsebl 89; Tchnlgy; Tchncl Ed.

**SANDERS, JEANNETTE,** Mattatuck Comm Coll, Waterbury, CT; GD; Cert Meriden-Wallingford Hsp; Mattatuck Cmnty Clg 90; Nrsg; RN.

**SANDERS, JENNIFER L,** Clark Atlanta Univ, Atlanta, GA; SO; BA; Stdnt Grg Assoc Edctrs 90-; Insprtnl Vcs Fth Chr 89-90; Upwrd Bnd Cnslr; Erly Chldhd Ed.

**SANDERS, JUDITH SUSAN,** Central Al Comm Coll, Alexander City, AL; FR; MBA; Ambsdr; Phi Theta Kappa Dir; CACC Fvrt; Math; Tch.

**SANDERS, JULIE D,** Middle Tn St Univ, Murfreesboro, TN; JR; BS; Intrn Bracey Campbell Pub Rels/Adv 90; Mass Cmctns; Pub Rels.

**SANDERS, JULIE M,** East Tn St Univ, Johnson City, TN; JR; BS; Constrctn Mgmnt Assn; Epsilon Pi Tau; Epsilon Pi Tau; Constrctn; Architecture.

**SANDERS, KATHERINE E,** Catawba Valley Comm Coll, Hickory, NC; FR; AIM Art Clb; Gamma Beta Phi; Comml Art; Computer Graphic Design.

**SANDERS, KAZ G,** Morehouse Coll, Atlanta, GA; SO; BS; Endvr Space Clb Svp 90-; AMOCO Schlr Clb 90-; Ronald E Mc Nair Schlr 90-; NASA Intrnshp 90-; Bsktbl; Math; Engr.

**SANDERS, KEEVIN C,** Al St Univ, Montgomery, AL; SO; Music; Music Ed.

**SANDERS, KENNETH H,** Middle Ga Coll, Cochran, GA; FR; BA; IM Bsktbl; Math; Engr Tech.

**SANDERS, KERRY M,** Univ Of North Fl, Jacksonville, FL; JR; BS; Gldn Key; Otstndng Achvment Blgcl Sci 88-90; AA FL Cmmnty Coll 90; Blgy; Envrnmntl Eng.

**SANDERS, KIMBERLY M,** Middle Tn St Univ, Murfreesboro, TN; FR; BED; BSU 90-; FCA 90-; Gamma Beta Phi; IM Sports 90-; Interdiscply Studies; Tchr.

**SANDERS, KYNA T,** Lane Coll, Jackson, TN; SR; BS; Mrchng Band 90-; Chrldr; Layout Edtr Yrbk 90; Alpha Kappa Alpha; BS 87-; Bus Admn; Mktg/Sls.

**SANDERS, LARA K,** Radford Univ, Radford, VA; SO; BA; Spnsh Natl Hnr Soc 89; Jr Avt 89; Sclgy.

**SANDERS, LARRY J,** Alcorn St Univ, Lorman, MS; SO; BA; Hon Stdnt Assn; Soc Sci; Law.

**SANDERS, LAURA J,** Schenectady County Comm Coll, Schenectady, NY; SR; BA; Assoc SCCC; Pol Sci; Law.

**SANDERS, LEE ANN H,** Univ Of Southern Ms, Hattiesburg, MS; SR; BSW; Soc Work Clb 90-; Soc Work.

**SANDERS, LEE C,** Rochester Inst Of Tech, Rochester, NY; FR; BS; Singers; Imaging Sci; Digital Data Comprssn.

**SANDERS, MARGARET C,** Allen Univ, Columbia, SC; JR; BA; Library Club 88-89; Member NAACP 88-89; Bsktbl Trnr 88-89; Trck Fld Events 88-89; Elem Edctn Psychology; Clncl Psychlgst.

**SANDERS, MARIE E,** Bellarmine Coll, Louisville, KY; JR; BA; NEASP Pub Rel 90-; Delta Epsilon Sigma 90-; Elem Educ; Tchr.

**SANDERS, MARY ELIZABETH,** Univ Of Nc At Chapel Hill, Chapel Hill, NC; GD; JD; Law Review; BA Davidson Clg 87; Law.

**SANDERS, MERCEDES J,** Tougaloo Coll, Tougaloo, MS; JR; BS; SGA 88-89; Pre Eng/Phy Sci Clb Pres 89-90; Math/Cmptr Sci Clb 88-; Alpha Lambda Delta 88-89; Spprt Srvcs Rep 88-; Ldr 89-90; Peer Hlpr 89-90; Math/Physcs; Aerospc Eng.

**SANDERS, MICHAEL P,** Embry Riddle Aeronautical Univ, Daytona Beach, FL; FR; BA; Nav Aviation Clb 90-; CARAL 90; Interm Sports 90-; Aeronavtical Sci; Aviation.

**SANDERS, NICK A,** Northern Ky Univ, Highland Hts, KY; JR; BA; Cmnctns; Perform/Record Music.

**SANDERS, PAMEKA T,** Alcorn St Univ, Lorman, MS; FR; BS; SADD Stdnt Cncl Pres 89-90; FBLA; Stdnt Cncl/4 H Clb; Natl Hnr Soc; Key Clb Intl 87-90; Hall Fo Fame Inductee 90; Chrlder 87; Med Tech.

**SANDERS, PAMELA J,** Univ Of Sc At Sumter, Sumter, SC; JR; BS; Desk Clrk 89-; Univ Maryland 88; Accntng; CPA.

**SANDERS, PAMELA J,** Univ Of Sc At Columbia, Columbia, SC; JR; BS; Desk Clrk 89-; CPA; Acctg; Fin.

**SANDERS, ROBIN J,** Livingston Univ, Livingston, AL; JR; BS; Debating Club; Phi Theta Kappa; AS Faulkner St College 88-90; Elem Ed; Teacher.

**SANDERS, RUBY L,** Southern Junior Coll, Birmingham, AL; FR; Cmptr Science; Cmptr Inf Systems.

**SANDERS, S DARRYL,** Brewer St Jr Coll, Fayette, AL; SO; MBA; Phi Theta Kappa; Cotler Inc; Hist; Prfsr.

**SANDERS, SANDRA C,** Univ Of Al At Birmingham, Birmingham, AL; SO; AAS; Stdnt Phys Thrpy Org 90-; Acad Schlrshp Schl Of Hlth Related Profs 90-; Pres Lst 90-; AL Chptr Amer Phy Thrpy Assn; Phy Thrpy.

**SANDERS, STEPHANIE A,** Memphis St Univ, Memphis, TN; SO; BBA; BACCHUS 90; Beta Gamma Sigma; Delta Gamma 90-; Acctg.

**SANDERS, TAMMY L,** Johnson C Smith Univ, Charlotte, NC; FR; BA; Cmmnctns; Pblc Rltns.

**SANDERS, TANYA M,** Middle Ga Coll, Cochran, GA; FR; Bptst Stdnt Union 90-; Spch Pthlgy.

**SANDERS, TIMOTHY A,** Franklin And Marshall Coll, Lancaster, PA; FR; BA; Res Hall Assoc 90-91; J Marshall Schlr; Hackman Schlr; Vybl; Biopsychology; Med.

**SANDERS, VICKI L,** Jackson St Univ, Jackson, MS; FR; Pre Law/Engl; Lwyr.

**SANDERS-KLAHR, DEBORAH E,** Yeshiva Univ, New York, NY; GD; JD; Pltlcl Sci Soc 85-89; Drm Soc 85-89; Fn Arts Soc 85-89; Dns Hnr Rl 85-89; Torah U Mada Flwshp 88-89; Belkin Schlrshp 85-89; Awd Exclnc Pltcl Sci 88-89; BA 89; AA 89; Pltcl Sci/Fine Arts; Law.

**SANDERSON, CHARISA R,** Volunteer St Comm Coll, Gallatin, TN; SO; AS; Nrsng; Psychiatric Nrsng.

**SANDERSON, JAMES L,** East Tn St Univ, Johnson City, TN; GD; MD; Amer Med Assn 90-; Amer Acdmy/Famly Physcns 90-; BS King Coll 90; Med; Surgry.

**SANDERSON, LISA M,** Saint Josephs Coll, Windham, ME; FR; BS; Elem Edn Club Frshmn Rep 90-; Superkids; Elem Edn Teacher.

**SANDERSON, MANDALYN S,** Savannah Coll Of Art & Design, Savannah, GA; SO; BFA; Grphx Grp Sec 90-; Art Grphc Dsgn.

**SANDERSON, RUSSELL J,** Fl St Univ, Tallahassee, FL; SR; FL Pblc Intrst Rsrch Grp 89-90; Deans Lst 89-90; BS 90; Blgy; Med.

**SANDFORD, DAVID A,** East Carolina Univ, Greenville, NC; JR; BFA; AIAS; IM Bsktbl/Rqtbl 88-89; Envir Mntl Dsgn; Arch.

**SANDIFER, ALISA R,** East Central Comm Coll, Decatur, MS; SO; BS; Sigma Sigma Mu Ta Sci Clb 89-; Med Sci Awrd; AD; Nrsg.

**SANDIFER, GERALDINE W,** Roane St Comm Coll, Harriman, TN; SO; AA; Sec; Bus Mgmt; Bus.

**SANDIFER, PRISCILLA R,** Alcorn St Univ, Lorman, MS; SO; BS; Sci Blgy; Med Tech.

**SANDLES, JOAN E,** Nova Univ, Ft Lauderdale, FL; GD; MA; Loricco Williams Wndr Croslnd 85-; BS Miami Univ 85; Acctg.

**SANDLIN, ROBIN A,** Fl Coll, Temple Terrace, FL; SO; AA; Phi Theta Kappa Sec 90-; ARETE 89-; Yng Wmns Trnng Orgnztn Treas 90; Phi Theta Kappa Sec 90-; ARETE 89-; Elem Educ; Tchng.

**SANDONATO, ANTHONY G,** Saint John Fisher Coll, Rochester, NY; SR; BS; Clg Rpblcns Treas 88-89; Acctg Clb 90-; Rochester Taekwondo Clb VP 87-89; Delta Epsilon Sigma 90-; Schlstc Hon Soc; Xerox Clg Exprmntl Lrng Intrnshp; Outstndng Clg Stdnts Am Awd 89; Deans List 87-90; Acctg; Law.**

**SANDOR, GEORGE J,** Norwalk St Tech Coll, Norwalk, CT; SR; AS; Data Processing.

**SANDOR, PAULA,** Widener Univ, Chester, PA; SR; BA; Ntnl/Ord Omega; Phi Sigma Sigma Pres 90-; Chester Eastside Minis 88-; Var Chrldg 87-; Acctng.

**SANDORFY, MICHAEL E,** City Univ Of Ny Baruch Coll, New York, NY; SR; BBA; Jewish Soc Baruch Clg VP 90-; Fin Soc Brklyn Col 87-89; Golden Key 90-; Deans Lst 88-90; Finance.

**SANDOVAL, CHRISTOPHER J,** Villanova Univ, Villanova, PA; JR; BA; Radio Dir 88-89; Engl Lit; Brdcstng.

**SANDS, CHRISTOPHER D,** Bloomfield Coll, Bloomfield, NJ; CERT; Army Natl Grd Capt 87-; Opers Supv Lechters Inc 90-; BA Jersey Cty St Clg 84; Matls Mgmt.

**SANDS, CHRISTOPHER W,** Univ Of Ga, Athens, GA; SR; BLA; GSLA 87-; ASLA 87-; Sigma Lambda Alpha 89; Acacia Intl Sic Chrmn 86-88; Toro Irrgtn Schlrshp 88; C Adamson Schlrshp 90; Club Soccer 86-87; Landscape Arch; Envrnmntl Dsgn MLA.

**SANDS, IRENE G,** Bloomfield Coll, Bloomfield, NJ; SR; BA; Engl Hndbll Org 90-; Chrs 88-89; Psi Chi Pres 87; Alph Asigma Lambda 89-; Srvc Awrd 90; Ltrcy Awrd Prjct Rd 89; Hmnrts Hnrs Prgm 88; Hmnts Intern Prgm ; Ltrcy Prgm 88; Hnrs 87; Hgh Hnrs 90; Deans Lst; Engl.

**SANDS, JAMES M,** Univ Of Nc At Greensboro, Greensboro, NC; FR; BS; Alpha Lambda Delta 90-; Mddl Grds Educ; Tchr.

**SANDSTROM, KERSTIN B,** Academy Of The New Church, Bryn Athyn, PA; SO; MBA; PAC Orntn Pgm Ldr 90; Alpha Kappa Mu 88-89; Deans Lst 89-; Comm Svc 90; Vlybl Co Capt 89-90; Lacrss 90-; Bio/Eclgy; Envrnmntl Eng.

**SANDVIG, MARIE C,** Univ Of Pittsburgh, Pittsburgh, PA; GD; MSN; Grad Stdnt Nrsng Orgnztn 88-90; Sigma Theta Tau 86-89; Sigma Theta Tau 89-; Tchng Asst Univ Pittsburgh 89-90; West Penn Schl Nrsng Fclty; BSN Laroche Clg Pgh PA 82; Nrng; Nrsng Ed.

**SANDVOSS, INGA E,** S U N Y Coll At Fredonia, Fredonia, NY; SR; BA; Nwspr Cntrbtr 88-; Alpha Mu Gamma 89-; Summa Cum Laude; Engl; Wrtg Jrnlsm.

**SANFELIZ, ANA E,** Bayamon Central Univ, Bayamon, PR; FR; BA; Educ Tech.

**SANFORD, DEBORAH J,** Central Al Comm Coll, Alexander City, AL; FR; AS; Baptist Ch; Hospe; Supv Mrkt Planning Russell Corp; Genl Busn.

**SANFORD, ERIC S,** Cumberland Coll, Williamsburg, KY; SO; BS; Math Clb 90; High Hnr 89; US Achvmnt Acad; Im Bsktbl 89-90; Cmptr Info Sys/Math; Prog Opr.

**SANFORD, JOY L,** Daytona Beach Comm Coll, Daytona Beach, FL; FR; AA; Daytona Playhouse 90-; Phi Theta Kappa; Hospice Of Volusia Flagler Co; Aviation Psych.

**SANFORD, KAREN A,** Univ Of Al At Birmingham, Birmingham, AL; SR; BS; Amer Med Rcrd Assn 89-; AL Med Rcrd Assn 89-; Stdnt Med Rcrd Assn 89-; Intrnshp Med Recs/Centinela Hosp Med Ctr; BA Miss State Univ 86; AS Calhoun Cmnty Clg 89; Med Rcrd Amin; MRA/DIR.

**SANFORD, P DENISE,** William Carey Coll, Hattiesburg, MS; SR; BS; Coll Chr 86-; Hndbell Chr 86-87; Omicron Delta Kappa Sec 89-90; Delta Omicron Pres 89-; Elem Educ.

**SANFORD, TRICIA E,** Defiance Coll, Defiance, OH; FR; Frnscs Tm; Coll Play; Phi Kappa Delta; Engl Ed; Tch.

**SANFORD, VANESSA L,** Fl A & M Univ, Tallahassee, FL; JR; BS; Cert Empire Tech Sch 86; Dip Mech Inst 84; Arch/Constr Engr Tech; Constr Mgmt/Engr.

**SANFORD, WANDA J,** Brewer St Jr Coll, Fayette, AL; SO; AS; Phi Theta Kappa; Sci; Nrsng.

**SANFREY, STEVEN L,** Kent St Univ Kent Cmps, Kent, OH; SR; BS; Geological Scty Treas 89-; Sigma Gamma Epsilon 90-; Natl Sci Stdnt Awrd; ABA 89; Geology.

**SANG, SHIWEI,** City Univ Of Ny City Coll, New York, NY; SR; Han Wave Stdnt Assoc Sec 88-; Tau Beta Pi 90-; BE; Elec Engr.

**SANGEMINO, NICOLE,** Siena Coll, Loudonville, NY; SR; BS; Ambsdrs Clb Tr Gd 87-89; Thtr 87-89; Alpha Kappa Alpha; Delta Sigma Pi Sr VP 88-; Pres Schlr Lst/Acdmc Hnrs Lst 87-; Chrldng 87-89; Fnce; Fncl FDIC.

**SANGER, KAREN E,** Daytona Beach Comm Coll, Daytona Beach, FL; SO; BA; Cmmnctns Stds/Engl.

**SANGINITI, J GARTH,** Kent St Univ Kent Cmps, Kent, OH; SR; BBA; Intrfrat Cncl VP Schlrshp Educ 89-90; Ordr Omega 89-; Gldn Key 90-; Delta Tau Delta Dir Acdmc Afrs 89-90; Hghst Pldg 88; Super Schlrshp; Grad Cum Laude; Bus Financ; Law Sch.

**SANGSTER, WAYNE E,** Abraham Baldwin Agri Coll, Tifton, GA; SO; BA; Agric Equip Tech Clb 88-; Sunblt Expo Schlrshp 89-90; Jessie/Dolly Chambles Schlrshp 90; Agric Mech Tech; Frmr.

**SANGUEDOLCE, SUSAN,** Fl International Univ, Miami, FL; SR; BS; Amrcn Occptnl Thrpy Assn 89-; FL Occptnl Thrpy Assn 89-; Occptnl Thrpy Clb 91; Pi Theta Epsilon 90-; Unv FL Deans Lst 88-89; Deans 89-; AA Unv FL 89; Occptnl Thrpy; Occptnl Thrpst.

**SANKIES, DAVID G,** Suffolk Comm Coll Western Cmps, Brentwood, NY; SR; BBA; Afrcn Ppls Assoc Pres 90-; Stdnt Sen 90-; Alpha Beta Gamma; AAS; Bus; Arln Mgmt.

**SANKOWSKI, ALEX J,** Univ Of Sc At Columbia, Columbia, SC; SO; BA; Deans Lst USC Aiken 90; Deans Lst USC Salk; Vrsty Bsbl 90-; AS USC Salk; Bus Adm/Finance; Law/Finance.

**SANO, LAURA K,** Saint Bonaventure Univ, St Bonventure, NY; SO; BED; Bg Bro/Bg Sis 89-; Wms Cncl 89-90; Stdnt Ambsdr; Elem Ed; Tchg Rmdl Rdng.**

**SANON, REGINALD,** Fl International Univ, Miami, FL; FR; MBA; FAF/AOP Schlrshp 90; Chem; Med.

**SANOQUET, LINDA L,** Univ Of Pr At Rio Piedras, Rio Piedras, PR; JR; BA; Engl Mjrs Assn 90-; Lector For Blind 89-; Engl.**

**SANROW, CAROLUS W,** Oh Univ, Athens, OH; SR; BS; Inst Indust Eng VP 90-; Ntl Soc Pro Eng Pgm Dir 90-; Indonesian Stdnt Assn; Alpha Pi Mu; Tau Beta Pi; Phi Kappa Phi; Indust/Sys Eng Bus.

**SANS, STEPHANIE C,** Saint Joseph Coll, West Hartford, CT; JR; BA; Spec Ed/Elem Ed.

**SANSALONE, ROSEMARIA PIA,** Saint Josephs Coll Suffflk Cmps, Patchogue, NY; SO; BA; Tnns Tm Rec Clb 89-; Deans Lst 90-; Prsh Otrch 89-; Tennis Tm 89-; Thrptc Rcrtn; Thrpst.**

**SANSANELLI, JOSEPHINE A,** S U N Y Coll Of Tech At Frmgdl, Farmingdale, NY; FR; BA; Phy Ed.

**SANSANOWICZ, LEONARD H,** City Univ Of Ny City Coll, New York, NY; SO; BFA; Stdnts For Israel Pres 90-; New Arts Grp 90-; Actng; Entrtainmnt.

**SANSOM, CATHERINE E,** Marshall University, Huntington, WV; JR; BA; Natl Art Educ Assn; Art Educ; Tchng.

**SANSONE, ELIZA R,** Univ Of Med & Dentistry Of Nj, Newark, NJ; GD; MPT; Outdrs Clb 83-84; Tae Kwon Do Clb 85-86; Bg Sistrs 84-85; Cmps Crsde 83-85; IM Sprts 83-90; Hsp Vol 85-86; Deans Lst 89-; Robert Wood Johnson Univ Affltd Schlrshp Prog 90-91; BA Rutgers Univ 87; Phy Thrpy.

**SANSONE, JAMIE L,** Oh St Univ At Marion, Marion, OH; SO; Fshn Merchandiser.

**SANTA MARIA, RAFAEL P,** Fl Memorial Coll, Miami, FL; JR; MBA; Pres Congressional Task Force 81-; Ellis Island Centnnial Commission 84; Busn/Econ Awd 90-; LO Clg Varsity Bskbl 70-71; Hnrbl Discharge USAF 68; Finacl/Ins Cons 82-; Busn Mgt; Law.

**SANTA, JESUS J,** Univ Of Pr At Rio Piedras, Rio Piedras, PR; JR; BA; Pre-Med Stdnts Assn 90-; Hon Stdnt 89-; Pre-Med; Med.

**SANTA-CRUZ, GUILLERMO M,** Fl St Univ, Tallahassee, FL; SR; BA; 1800 Seconds TV Prog Cmps TV Prdcr 90-; Lambda Pi Eta Cmmnctn 90-; Dns Lst; Intrn Univsn Spnsh Intl Ntwrk; IM Soccer/Sftbl/Bsktbl 89-90; AA Miami Dade Comm Coll 89; Cmmnctn; TV Prod.

**SANTACOLOMA, BIANCA S,** Fl International Univ, Miami, FL; SR; MA; BA; Elem Ed; Tchr.

**SANTAELLA, JUAN B,** Univ Of Miami, Coral Gables, FL; SR; BA; Bus Fin/Intl Fin; Bnkg.

**SANTAELLA, MARIA E,** Univ Of Miami, Coral Gables, FL; SO; Nrsng.

**SANTAGATO, CAROL,** Univ Of Pittsburgh At Bradford, Bradford, PA; SO; BS; Chrldng Capt 89-91; Alpha Lambda Delta 90-; Comp Sci.

**SANTAMARINA, LISA M,** Fl International Univ, Miami, FL; SR; BS; Future Edctrs Am 90-; Intrvrsty Chrstn Flwshp; Kappa Delta Pi 90-; Serv Awd 90; Outstndng Prtcptn Future Ed Am 90-; Outstndng Achvmnt Kappa Delta Pi 90-; Elem Ed; Dctrl Edctnl Ldrshp.

**SANTANA, BELKYS,** Miami Dade Comm Coll South, Miami, FL; SO; AA; Intrntl Scty Of Intr Dsgnrs; Tennis; Art; Intr Dsgn.**

**SANTANA, ILEANA,** Inter Amer Univ Pr Hato Rey, Hato Rey, PR; SR; BBA; Comp Assoc; Dsgnd Ofcl Logo Of Dept Of Bsns Admn Univ PR Mayaguez Campus 87; Comp Mgmt Inf Sys; Bsns Admn.

**SANTANA, IVIA,** Newbury Coll, Brookline, MA; SO; BA; Engl; Bus Mgmt.

**SANTANA, JOHN T,** Ny Institute Of Tech Ny City, New York, NY; BT; AOS Tech Careers Inst 85; Elect; Cmptr Sci.

**SANTANA, MARIBEL RIVERA,** Univ Of Pr Medical Sciences, San Juan, PR; SO; MD; Dns Hnr 86-; Cert Achvmnt 90-; Omicron Kappa Epsilon; BA Univ Puerto Rico 89; Dentistry.

**SANTANA, MARTHA S,** Fl International Univ, Miami, FL; SR; BED; Dns Lst 89-; AA MDCC North Capmus 86; Art Educ; Dctrl Dgree.

**SANTANA, MIGDALIA,** Univ Of Pr At Mayaguez, Mayaguez, PR; SO; Data Proc Mgmt Assn 90-; Cuadro De Hon-Univ De PR En Mayaguez 90-; Comp Info Syst; Syst Anlst.

**SANTANA, NORMA G,** Inter Amer Univ Pr San German, San German, PR; SO; Hon Pgm 89-; BA Pblc Admin/Pltcl Sci; Law.

**SANTANA, TERESA,** Barry Univ, Miami, FL; SR; BA; Natl Hnr 74-82; Guild Repet Musicans Classical Piano; Minister Music Of Justice 87-; Busn; Psychology.

**SANTANA, YANIRA E,** Inter Amer Univ Pr Hato Rey, Hato Rey, PR; FR; Asociacion De Estudiantes De Arte 90-.

**SANTANA-FERRER, VANESSA,** Univ Of Pr Cayey Univ Coll, Cayey, PR; FR; BBA; Future Bus Ldrs Of Am 87-88; Exec Sec.

**SANTANA-QUINONES, ALIDA I,** Univ Of Pr At Mayaguez, Mayaguez, PR; SR; BSEE; IEEE Actvs Org 89-; Hnr Rl 87-; Elec Engr.

**SANTANIELLO, JERRY,** Springfield Tech Comm Coll, Springfield, MA; SR; ASSC; Lady Mt Carmel Scty Clb 89-; Alpha Nu Omega 90-; Golf 89-; Bartender 88-; Science; Med.

**SANTANIELLO, PETER F,** Western New England Coll, Springfield, MA; SR; BA; Rvw Art Lit Tres 89-; Stglss Plyrs 89-90; Mngmnt Assn; Dean Lst 89-; BA; Bus Admn/Engl; Mgmnt.

**SANTAPAOLA, DAVID R,** Mount Saint Mary Coll, Newburgh, NY; JR; Bus Pres 89-; Pblc Rltns Clb Capt 89-; Actvts Cncl Sprts Co Edtr 88; Deans Lst 90; Bus Mgmt.

**SANTARELLI, DIANE M,** Indiana Univ Of Pa, Indiana, PA; SR; BS; PA St Ed Asoc 90; Bg Brthrs Sstrs 90; Deans Lst; Elem Ed; Tchng.

**SANTAROSA, ANTHONY,** Univ Of Rochester, Rochester, NY; SR; BS; Amer Soc Mech Eng; Sigma Phi Epsilon Alum Oper 90-; Mech Eng Intrnshp; Estmn Kodk Co; Rugby Ftbl 89-; Mech Eng; Phd Eng.

**SANTELLA, CHRISTINE J,** Univ Of Nh Plymouth St Coll, Plymouth, NH; SO; BED; Pres Schlr 89-; Elem/Early Chldhd Ed; Tchr.

**SANTERIAN, MICHAEL N,** Villanova Univ, Villanova, PA; JR; BA; Econ Socty; Econ Hnr Socty; Econ.

**SANTIAGO ARROYO, SONIA,** Inter Amer Univ Pr Hato Rey, Hato Rey, PR; GD; BA; SWA Pres; Rec Assn Vocal 90-; Soc Wrk.

**SANTIAGO CARABALLO, DANIEL,** Inter Amer Univ Pr Guayama, Guayama, PR; FR; AS; Natl Svc Corp City NY CVC 89-90; Overall Avg Engl Spnsh Math 90-; Trck Fld 89-90; Jehova Witness Arroya Frlgs 87; Cmptr Pgmg; Cmptr Pgmr Pvt Indstrl.

**SANTIAGO COLON, HILDA,** Inter Amer Univ Pr Hato Rey, Hato Rey, PR; GD; Psych Assn 90-; BA 90; Psych; Clncl Psych.

**SANTIAGO CRUZ, JOSE MIGUEL,** Inter Amer Univ Pr Guayama, Guayama, PR; FR; Hon Crtfct Gen 89-90; Cert Intr Amer Guayama 90; Engl; Law.

**SANTIAGO FELIX, ODDETTE M,** Univ Of Pr Cayey Univ Coll, Cayey, PR; FR; MBA; Mgmt.

**SANTIAGO FELIX, PRISCILLA,** Univ Of Pr At Mayaguez, Mayaguez, PR; JR; BA; Math; Acct.**

**SANTIAGO FRANCESCHI, LUDIAN I,** Catholic Univ Of Pr, Ponce, PR; SR; BS; ECOS; Athltc Leg Sec; UCPR 74-76; Elemntl Gnrl Edctn; Tchr.

**SANTIAGO IRIZARRY, ZULMA I,** Inter Amer Univ Pr San German, San German, PR; BA; BA 86-; Spnsh; Lingstc.

**SANTIAGO MALDONADO, JONAIDA,** Inter Amer Univ Pr Hato Rey, Hato Rey, PR; FR; Club Leo Ldr 86-89; Hnr In Math 87-88.

**SANTIAGO NAVEIRA, MIGUEL A,** Univ Politecnica De Pr, Hato Rey, PR; FR; Cvl Air Ptrl 84-; Mech Engr.

**SANTIAGO OCASIO, HECTOR LUIS,** Catholic Univ Of Pr, Ponce, PR; JR; BS; Cathlc Chrstn Grp Fndr 89-; Ed; Elem/Scndry Ed.

**SANTIAGO RAMOS, JANETTE,** Catholic Univ Of Pr, Ponce, PR; GD; Acctng Student Assoc 87-88; Hnr Dean List 86-90; US Achivmnt Acady Clgt 90; Dirty Vol V Pag 68/170; BBA UCPR 90; Acctng; CPA.

**SANTIAGO RIVERA, GRICEL,** Univ Of Pr At Mayaguez, Mayaguez, PR; BA; Drama Club 90-; Humanities Cir 90-; Comparative Lit; Law.

**SANTIAGO RIVERA, PEDRO,** Univ Of Pr At Mayaguez, Mayaguez, PR; SO; BA; Rotaraet Clb 89-; Ind Eng; Eng.**

**SANTIAGO TORRES, ANGEL E,** Inter Amer Univ Pr San German, San German, PR; FR; Nght Scd 90-.

**SANTIAGO VELEZ, IRIS A,** Inter Amer Univ Pr San German, San German, PR; JR; BA; Psych; Ph D.

**SANTIAGO, ANTHONY J,** Bunker Hill Comm Coll, Boston, MA; FR; AS; YMCA/ASSOC; Alumni Boys/Girls Club Am; IM Vlybl/Bsktbl/Flr Hockey; Alumni Roberts Comm Sch After Sch Pgm; Acctg/Finance; CPA.

**SANTIAGO, BENJAMIN,** Inter Amer Univ Pr Guayama, Guayama, PR; JR; Assn Rec Grdrya Pres 88-; Cnsj Padrs Ygstrs De Gdya Vp90-; Clb De Res Del Bo Grdrya Vcl 89-90; Assn De Wgbs De La Pol De Pr 87-; Fed De Pol De Pr 87-; Ofcl De La Zna De Gyma Pol De Pr88; Eqp Sftbl Gdya Ptls 88-90.

**SANTIAGO, CARLOS A,** Inter Amer Univ Pr San German, San German, PR; FR; Leones Clb Treas 88; MVP 89; Certif Ponce Clg 88; Math; Elctrnc Engr.

**SANTIAGO, CARLOS M,** Univ Of Pr At Mayaguez, Mayaguez, PR; SO; MS; Bell Cmnctns Rsrch; Lst Of Hon 89-90; Eng Awrd; Comp Eng; Sftwr/Comp Eng.**

**SANTIAGO, CARMEN,** Univ Del Turabo, Gurabo, PR; BED; Deans Lst 90-; Dschrg Plnng Offcr Hlth Dept; Elem Ed.

**SANTIAGO, CHERYL L,** Central Fl Comm Coll, Ocala, FL; FR; AS; Chld Care Mngmnt; Prschl Tchr/Schl Bd.

**SANTIAGO, DORIS,** Caribbean Univ, Bayamon, PR; GD; BA; Magna Cum Laude 90; Rcgntn Of Outstndng Acad Achievemnt 87-90; Bchlr Sec Sci/Exec Sec.

**SANTIAGO, HECTOR A,** Inter Amer Univ Pr San Juan, Hato Rey, PR; GD; JD; Am Bar Assn Law Stdnt Div/Crmnl Law Sec 88-; PR Ntl Law Stdnt Assn 88-; Dns Lst 89-; Law Rvw Edtr 89-; Cand Schls Bst Crim Law Stdnt; Bsktbl 90-; BA Univ PR 88; Law.

**SANTIAGO, IRIS A,** Antillian Adventist University, Mayaguez, PR; SR; BA; Psychlgy; Phd Psychlgry.

**SANTIAGO, JANET,** City Univ Of Ny La Guard Coll, Long Island Cty, NY; SO; AAS; Trvl/Trsm Clb 89-90; Phi Theta Kappa 90-; Bus Law Tutr 90-; Gnrl Psychlgy Tutr 90-; Walt Disney Wrld Clg Prog 90; Trvl/Trsm; Airln Mngmt.

**SANTIAGO, JEANETTE EVELINE,** Univ Of Pr Humacao Univ Coll, Humacao, PR; SO; BA; Acdmc Exclnc Awd; Acdmc Schlrshp; Bus Admnstrtn; Mgt.

**SANTIAGO, JOSE L,** Univ Politecnica De Pr, Hato Rey, PR; FR; BA; Vlybl 89; Cycling Sub Chmpn 89; Mech Engr.

**SANTIAGO, LINDA C,** Inter Amer Univ Pr Arecibo Un, Arecibo, PR; JR; BED; Ftr Tchrs Assn 88-; Hnr Prgrm 89-; Amrcn Red Crs Arecibo Chptr Vlntr 79-91; Slng Clb Aux Sec 86-88; Sccr Clb Tres 85-; Elem Schl; Clg Tchng.

**SANTIAGO, LIZ A,** Univ Of Pr At Mayaguez, Mayaguez, PR; SO; BA; Ai Che 89-; IQU 89-; Ntl Hnr Soc Psv 88-; Nacme Asstntshp; Chem; Engr.

**SANTIAGO, LIZBETH,** William Paterson Coll, Wayne, NJ; GD; BA; Spnsh Clb; Pell Grnts/Schlrshps 87-90; Dns Lst 90; Bst Top Slsprsn 88-; WPC 90; Spnsh; Ph D Spnsh.

**SANTIAGO, LOURDES S,** Univ Politecnica De Pr, Hato Rey, PR; SR; BS; SWE 88-90; CIAPR Voice 89-90; ASCE 88-90; Math; Civil Eng.

**SANTIAGO, MAURA,** Univ Of Pr At Mayaguez, Mayaguez, PR; SO; BA; Natl Hnr Soc 87-89; Cert Awd Rglrty/Pnctly 89; UPR Hnr Dplma 90; Hnry Awd; Fnce/Bsn Admn; Intl Bsn.

**SANTIAGO, NORZAIDA,** Univ Of Pr Cayey Univ Coll, Cayey, PR; GD; BBA; Cuadro De Hon 87-; BBA; Acctng/Bus Admn.

**SANTIAGO, ROBERT A,** Univ Politecnica De Pr, Hato Rey, PR; FR; BAME; Student Engineering Club 90-; Mathematics; Engineering.

**SANTIAGO, SECUNDINO A,** Inter Amer Univ Pr Guayama, Guayama, PR; FR; BA; US Army 84-89; Engrs Asst Hwy Authrty; Engl; Tchr.

**SANTIAGO-LOPEZ, JEANETTE,** Catholic Univ Of Pr, Ponce, PR; JR; BBA; APPED Cmptr Assn; Cmptr Mgtm; Prgrmng.

**SANTIAGO-RABRY, LYNETTE,** Inter Amer Univ Pr Guayama, Guayama, PR; JR; Dipl Hnr 89; Dpl Recog 89; Recog Excellence 89; Math; Bnk Admin.

**SANTILLI, FRANK A,** Bridgeport Engr Inst, Fairfield, CT; JR; BSEE; Aseme Nrwlk St Tech Coll 84; Elctrcl Engnrng.

**SANTILLI, JOSEPH E,** Bridgeport Engr Inst, Fairfield, CT; JR; BSME; AAS Wstchstr Comm Clg 78-81; Cert; Engr; Mech Engr.

**SANTILLI, LORETTA A,** Univ Of Rochester, Rochester, NY; JR; BA; Newman Cmmt Cthlc Cngrgtn 88-; Dorm Cncl 88-89; Ski Clb 88-; Deans List 90; Delta Gamma Fndtn Chrprsn 89-; Vol Admsns Ntwrk 88-; Dlion VP 89-90; Cross Cntry/Indr/Otdr Trck Crew Teams 88-; Clgy; Med Schl.

**SANTILLO, MICHAEL R,** Rochester Inst Of Tech, Rochester, NY; SO; BA; Engr Hse Pres 89-; Inst Elec Engrs 90-; Soc Mech Engrs 89-; NCAA Vars Bsbl Tm; AD Mech Engr; Mech Engr.**

**SANTINI, JEFFREY M,** Va St Univ, Petersburg, VA; JR; BS; Phys Ed Majs Clb 89-; Var Bsbl 88-; Phys Ed Tchr.

**SANTINO, JENNIFER,** Univ Of Miami, Coral Gables, FL; JR; BA; Cane Cmmr Org 89-; Gldn Key 90-; Psi Chi; TABS 90-; Mstr Tutor 90-; Psy; Schl Cnslr.

**SANTO, CHRISTINA M,** Marywood Coll, Scranton, PA; SO; Ski Clb Pblcty 89-; Phi Beta Lamba 89-; Bus Admin; Mrktg.

**SANTONATO, NICHOLAS,** Muskingum Coll, New Concord, OH; JR; Bacchus Sec 89-; Stdnt Life Ctr Brd Pblc Rltns 90-; Tour Guide; Tau Kappa Epsilon Chpln/VP 89-; YMCA Coach; Acdmc Schlrshp; IMS Capt 89-; Cmnctns; Law.

**SANTORA, JEANNETTE,** Montclair St Coll, Upr Montclair, NJ; SR; BS; Mngmt Clb; Phi Kappa Phi; Summa Cum Laude; Awd Fr Acad Exclnc/Outstndg Achvmnt; Bus Admin; Hmn Rsrcs.**

**SANTORELLA, PAUL T,** Schenectady County Comm Coll, Schenectady, NY; SO; Cook; Clnry Arts; Ownr Chf Of Rstrnt.

**SANTORI, GREG C,** Allegheny Coll, Meadville, PA; SR; BA; Stdnt Govt Dir Educ 90-; Dir Stdnt Actn Chf; Philosphcl Form 89-; MENS 90-; SAGE 88-; Sandra Doane Trk Prz 88-; Edw Hl Schlrshp 90-; Jons Hpkns Univ; Pol Theory.

**SANTORIELLO, PATRICIA A,** Indiana Univ Of Pa, Indiana, PA; SO; BED; Sci Educ; Tch.

**SANTORO, ALBERT J,** Mount Saint Mary Coll, Newburgh, NY; SO; Acctng; Lawyer.

**SANTORO, JOHN MICHAEL,** Georgetown Univ, Washington, DC; FR; BA; Varsity Tennis 90-; Finance/Mgt; Busn/Law/Profl Tennis.

**SANTORO, MARIA GABRIELLA,** Fl International Univ, Miami, FL; SO; BA; Mktg/Intl Bus; Law.

**SANTORO, SALVATORE,** S U N Y Coll Of Tech At Frmgdl, Farmingdale, NY; SR; Ftbl Capt 86-87; Lacrosse 86-87; Italian Hon Soc.

**SANTOS MARTINEZ, ELSA MELANIE,** Inter Amer Univ Pr Hato Rey, Hato Rey, PR; FR; MBA; US Nvl Sea Cdt Cprs Cdt 89-; Alphbt Clss Tchr; Upwrd Bnd Prgm 88-90; Rnng Athlt 88; Math.

**SANTOS MARTINEZ, JOSE A,** Univ Politecnica De Pr, Hato Rey, PR; SR; BSEE; ROTC Cadet Sgt 82-84; Soc Physics Stdnts 83-86; B S Physics U Of P R 87; Elect Engr; Engr.

**SANTOS, ANA T,** Univ Of Pr At Rio Piedras, Rio Piedras, PR; JR; BA; Pre Med Stdnts Assn; Chr Sec 90; Chmbr Chr 90; Msc Tchr Pr Comms 90; Cuadro De Hnr De La UPR 88-; Cdro De Hnr Del Depto De Ciencias Natrls; Blgy; Med.

**SANTOS, ARLENE P,** Univ Of Akron, Akron, OH; JR; BA; Gldn Ky; Phi Eta Sigma; Beta Gamma Sigma; Roush Schlrshp; Ernest Yng Schlrshp; Acctg; Pub Acctg.

**SANTOS, CHERYL A,** Southeastern Ma Univ, N Dartmouth, MA; JR; BA; Sigma Theta Tau; Nursing; Rn.

**SANTOS, DAVID W,** Hudson Valley Comm Coll, Troy, NY; SO; BS; Concrt Canoe Club Secy/Treas 90-; Albany Area Bldrs Assoc 89-; Assoc Genrl Crntrctrs 89-; Phi Theta Kappa 89-; Im Bsktbl 90-; Civil Engr.

**SANTOS, FLORENCE J,** Fl Atlantic Univ, Boca Raton, FL; SR; BBA; Acctg.

**SANTOS, GAYLENE F,** City Univ Of Ny City Coll, New York, NY; JR; BA; Phlppne Amer Orgnztn Of City Coll Pres; F Douglas Dbte Scty 90-; UFYC Sec; Stdnt Govt Of City Coll Sntr Of Hmnts; City Coll Lbrl Arts Hnrs Prog 88-; Blgy Tutor 89-; TASC; Schl Nwsppr; Fll Schlrshp Grgtwn Univ; Intrn; Wmns Fncng Tm; Engl Lit; Law Schl.

**SANTOS, IVANHOE M,** Univ Of Sc At Sumter, Sumter, SC; SO; ISO; CAB; Mov Familiar Cristian Juveni Sec 88-89; Cmnty Svcs San Vicente De Paul; Bsktbl Tm Hd-Coach 88-89.

**SANTOS, IVELISSE,** Pratt Inst, Brooklyn, NY; FR; BA; Art Dsgn; Indstrl Dsgn.

**SANTOS, JOSE J,** Catholic Univ Of Pr, Ponce, PR; GD; JD; Amer Bar Assoc 90-; Schls Judicial Review Leg Edtr; Phi Alpha Delta Clerk 90-; US Achvmnt All Amer Schlr Cllgt Awd; BBA Univ Hartford 89; Law.

**SANTOS, KATHERINE M,** Boston Coll, Chestnut Hill, MA; SO; BSN; Mass Stdnt Nrs Assn Comm Hlth/BTN Chrprsn 90-; Stdnt Nrs Assn Treas; Mass Stdnt Nrs Assn Co Edtr; Nrsng.

**SANTOS, KIMBERLY R,** Va St Univ, Petersburg, VA; SR; BS; Acctg Club Pres 90-; Natl Assoc Black Acntnts Inv V P 89-90; Stdnt Advsry Brd Advsr 90-; Deans List 90-; Philip Morris USA Intrnshp 90; Peat Marwick Main & Co Intrnshp 88; Tchn Instrmnts Corp Intrnshp 89; Acctg BIS.

**SANTOS, MARTHA E,** Saint Thomas Univ, Miami, FL; SO; BA; Acctng Assoc VP; Deans List 90; Acctng; CPA.

**SANTOS, MICHELLE A,** Colby Sawyer Coll, New London, NH; SO; BA; Yrbk Edtr 89-90; Phi Theta Kappa; AS Fisher Coll 90; Cmnctns; Wrtng.

**SANTOS, NELSON R,** Inter Amer Univ Pr Hato Rey, Hato Rey, PR; SR; BBA; Acctg; CPA.

**SANTOS JR, RODOLFO R,** A D Little Mgmt Educ Inst, Cambridge, MA; GD; Indstrl Mgmt Eng Scty 82; Phlppne Brd Of Advsrs 88; Sr Cnsltnt 90; Assn Of Mgmt And Indstrl Engs Of Phlppns Brd Mmbr 86-; MSM ADL MEI; BS IME De La Salle Univ Manila 82; Gen Mgmt Emphss In Fnnce.

**SANTOS, SHARON Y,** Univ Of Pr At Rio Piedras, Rio Piedras, PR; SO; BA; Sci; Med Tech.

**SANTOS-ARENAS, PEDRO,** City Univ Of Ny City Coll, New York, NY; JR; BARCH; RC Lfgrd; Asist Darkrm/Wdshp; Frshmn Mentor; IM Swim 90; Archtctre; Urban Dsgn.

**SANTROCK JR, DAVID A,** Univ Of Ky, Lexington, KY; SR; BS; Intervar Chrstn Fllwshp Pres 85-86; Ky Acad Pharm Stdnts 90-; Kappa Alpha Odr 84-87; Tchr Nlsn Co HS 87-89; BA Trsylvna Univ 87; Hosp/Comm Pharm.

**SANTUCCI, ROBIN E,** D Youville Coll, Buffalo, NY; JR; BSN; Prvncl Nrsg Admin Intrst Grp 83-; RN Assn 80-; Nrs Mgr Adult/Pediatric Intnsv Care; Med Ctr Hamilton; Nrse Prctnr Mcmaster Univ 80; Nrsng Unit Admin Ottawa Ontario 85; RN Honduk Clg Hamilton 76; Nrsg.

**SANTUS, KRISTINE E,** Duquesne Univ, Pittsburgh, PA; SO; BA; Union Prog Brd Prjct Dir 89-; Kappa Psi Soc Chair 90-; Vet Admin Phrmcy Intern; IM Sftbl/Ftbl/Vlybl; Phrmcy.

**SANUITA, LORIE M,** Methodist Coll, Fayetteville, NC; JR; BS; Psych Clb 88-; Fllwshp Chrstn Aths Stdnt Coord 89-; Phi Eta Sigma 89-; Chrstn Lf Cncl; Vllybl Capt 88-; Sftbl All Trnmnt All Conf 89-; Psych; Indstl Psych.

**SANUSI, ANNA,** Hillsborough Comm Coll, Tampa, FL; SO; AA; Mgmnt Dip IPPM Indonesia 89; Bus; Acctnt.

**SANYER, WOLFGANG F,** S U N Y Coll Of Tech At Frmgdl, Farmingdale, NY; FR; PHD; Mu Alpha Theta 90-; The Rosi Crucians 89-; Smithsonian Assoc 90-; Diplome De La Langue Et Civilizatioln Frangaise 80-81; Comp Sci; Software Engrng.

**SANZO, DAWN M,** Univ Of Pittsburgh, Pittsburgh, PA; FR; BSN; Hosp Aux Schlrshp; Nrsg; MSN Adm.

**SANZO, MICHELE,** Univ Of Med & Dentistry Of Nj, Newark, NJ; SR; AAS; SADHA Pres 87-; Dntl Hygn.

**SAO VICENTE, CARLOS MANUEL DE,** A D Little Mgmt Educ Inst, Cambridge, MA; GD; MSCM; Writers Union 89-; Institute Petroleum 88-; Scty Petroleum Engrs Assoc 86-; MCO M Adlmei Inc; B So Econ Agostinho Neto Univ 85; Mgt; Econ/Finance.

**SAOUD, JIHAD GHAZI,** Univ Of Southern Ms, Hattiesburg, MS; SR; BSBA; Intl Rltns Club 90-; Hnrs Stdnt Assn 90-; Fin Mgmt Assn; Gamma Beta Phi; Hnrs Clg Schlrshp 90-; Pres Lst 90; Hnrs Award Walsh Clg 90; Bnkng; Corp Fin.

**SAOUD, MARY LYNN A,** Seton Hall Univ, South Orange, NJ; FR; Spring Musical; Elem Ed/Math; Tchr.

**SAPANARA, NANCY L,** Univ Of Miami, Coral Gables, FL; SR; BS; Stu Alumni Ambssdrs VP 89-; Mstr Tutor Pro 89-; Pr Cnslr 88-89; Gldn Key; Sprtsfst 88-90; Biology; Med Sch.

**SAPERSTEIN, ERIK,** Russell Sage Coll At Troy, Troy, NY; SO; BS; Pep Band 89-; Symphnc Bnd 90-; Rnsslr Mdl 89-; Physcs And Phlsphy; Thrtcl Physcst.**

**SAPIR, FREDERICK S,** Univ Of Nc At Charlotte, Charlotte, NC; JR; BA; Coop Stdnt 90-; Mag; Engl Vsl Arts; Pblshng Grphc Arts.

**SAPONE, NADINE M,** Schenectady County Comm Coll, Schenectady, NY; SO; Lgl Prof Schndtdy Cnty Inc Sec 89-; Mcnamee Lochner Titus Williams; Engl; Law.

**SAPOVITS, PHILLIP A,** Widener Univ, Chester, PA; SR; BSEE; Institute Elctrcl Eltrnc Engr 89-; Tas Beta Pi 90-; Alpha Chi Rho 90-; Beta Phi Delta Pres 84-; BSBA Kutztown Univ Pa 88; Elctrcl Engr; Systems Engr.

**SAPP, JULIE M,** Saint John Fisher Coll, Rochester, NY; SO; BA; Lbrty Prtnrshps Fisher-Jefferson Pgm Tutorg 90-; NYS Grange 85-; Psychlgy; Schl Psychlgy.

**SAPP, KEVIN F,** Kent St Univ Kent Cmps, Kent, OH; SO; Cftrs 90-; Deans Lst 90; IM Bsktbl Trnmnt Vllybl 90-.

**SAPP, LISA D,** Medical Coll Of Ga, Augusta, GA; SR; RSN; Stdnt Govt Assoc Rep 89-90; Natl Stdnt Nrs Assoc 89-; GA Assoc Of Nrsng Stdnts 89-; Sigma Theta Tau; Natl Clgt Nrsng Award; AS Middle GA Clg 89; Nrsng.

**SAPRISTI, DONA,** Christopher Newport Coll, Newport News, VA; SR; BA; Phlsphy Clb 88-; Exec Stf Cptns Lg Stdnt Pr Phtgrphy Ed; Alpha Chi Natl Treas 90-91; Phi Sigma Tau; Phlsphy; Grdt Schl.

**SAPUTELLI, SHARON M,** Drexel Univ, Philadelphia, PA; FR; BA; Dance Ens Schlrshp 90; Deans Lst 90-; Phi Eta Sigma 90-; Arts/Sci Hnr Scty 90-; Deans Awd Outstndng Acad Achvmnt 90-; Science; Reg Dietician.

**SAPUTO, TODD R,** Univ Of Fl, Gainesville, FL; SR; Bus Admin Coll Cncl; Trnsfr Actvts Cncl 89-; Gtr Prde; FL Undrgrad Acad Schlr 88; Univ Of FL Coll Of Bus Dns Lst 89; IM Sccr Sftbl Vlybl Flg Ftbl 90; AA 89; BS; Bus Admin Fnnce; Mgmt.

**SARACENI, RAYMOND A,** Villanova Univ, Villanova, PA; SO; Acdmc Schlrshp; Hstry/Eng.

**SARACHAN, JEREMY H,** Univ Of Rochester, Rochester, NY; SR; BA; Univ Mag Mng Ed 87-; Flmkg Clb Bus Mgr 89-; Thtr Prdctn; Phi Beta Kappa; Psychlgy Tchg Asst 90; Flm Stds/Psychlgy; Tchg.

**SARACO, WENDY,** Univ Of Ma At Amherst, Amherst, MA; FR; Hs Cncl 90-; Area Govt 90-; Hnrs Prgm 90-; Mssprg 90-; Blgy; Psychtry.

**SARAGAS, TONY L,** Ky Wesleyan Coll, Owensboro, KY; SR; Stdnt Govt Assoc Chrmn Stdnt Lf Comm 88-; Flwshp Chrstn Athltcs 87-89; Plyrs Stg Hnd 90-; Dstngshd Schlr 87-; Govnrs Schlrs Pgm 86-; Pres Schlr; Phi Beta Lambda 87-89; Phi Alpha Theta 87-89; Sigma Nu Pldg Cls Pres 90-; Bsn Admin; Law.

**SARAHS, LAURA A,** Georgetown Univ, Washington, DC; SO; BA; Acctng; Law.

**SARANTOS, STACY A,** Daytona Beach Comm Coll, Daytona Beach, FL; SO; AS; Rdlgy; Rdlgc Tchnlgst.

**SARAO, CARRIE-ANN,** Newbury Coll, Brookline, MA; FR; ABTC; Radio Club Pres 90-; Clg Rando DJ 90-; Deans List 90-; Serv Schl Awd; Assitshp Lyx Rcrdng Assist; Studio Worcester Mass; Radio Brdctng; Radio Disc Jockey.

**SAREH, SAM,** Univ Of Miami, Coral Gables, FL; FR; BS; Mcrblgy Club; Blgy Club; Premed Hnrs Scty; Blgy Hnrs Scty 90-; Schlstc Hnrs Scty 90-; Hnrs Rsrch Jackson Mem Hosp 90-; Gnrl Hnrs Prgm 90-; Deans Lst 90-; Blgy; Med-Surg.

**SARGEANT, DEON LEE,** City Univ Of Ny City Coll, New York, NY; SO; BE; NSBE; ACM; Eng Retention Prog; Deans Lst 90; Elect Eng; Eng.**

**SARGENT, BRIAN R,** Univ Of Cincinnati-Clrmnt Coll, Batavia, OH; SO; BS; Dns Lst; Sci; Pharmcy.

**SARGENT, DEANNA JEAN,** Beckley Coll, Beckley, WV; FR; FBLA 87; Parlmntry Proc Pres 87; Medical; Resp Therp.

**SARGENT, DEBORAH DIANE,** Univ Of South Al, Mobile, AL; JR; BS; Tour De Force Ambsdr Goodwill Clge Of Ed Hstrn; Mobile Kosice Assoc 90-; Sister City Assoc Histrn; Czechoslovakia; Lesiure Services Tourism.

**SARGENT, JOSEPH M,** Univ Of Rochester, Rochester, NY; JR; BA; Psych Cncl Treas 90-; Music Floor Pres 89-; Pep Bnd Conductor 88-; Psi Chi; Reach Out Pres 89-; IM Soccer/Flr Hockey/Vlybl; Psych; Hmn Res Mgmt.

**SARGENT, TOMMIE D,** Bluefield Coll, Bluefield, VA; SO; BA; SGA; Alpha Phi Sigma; Gamma Phi Gamma; Bsktbl/Vllybll; Bsn; Acctnt.**

**SARGENT II, WILLIAM F,** Northeastern Christian Jr Coll, Villanova, PA; SO; AA; Delta Gamma Delta; Sccr 90-; Envrnmntl Sci; Mgmt Cnsrvtn.

**SARI, KIMBERLY K,** Univ Of Nc At Charlotte, Charlotte, NC; JR; BA; Phi Eta Sigma 90-; Golden Key; Psych; Ph D.

**SARIN, RAVINDER K,** Bunker Hill Comm Coll, Boston, MA; FR; IAGB; MCN; Advance Schlrshp 76-78; Htl Mgt/Cat Ntrtn Tech India/West Germany 73; Radiogrphy Tech.

**SARKAR, ANITA CHRISTINA,** Oh Wesleyan Univ, Delaware, OH; SR; MA; Envrnmnt/Wldlf Clb 90-; Alpha Kappa Delta; Psi Chi; Otstndng Clg Stdnts Of Amer; BA 90; Anthrplgy; Resrch/Tchr.

**SARKIS, MARGARET A,** Comm Coll Algny Co Algny Cmps, Pittsburgh, PA; SO.

**SARNO JR, ALFONSO,** Springfield Tech Comm Coll, Springfield, MA; SR; BA; Acctg; CPA.

**SARNO, GRAZIELLA M,** Duquesne Univ, Pittsburgh, PA; SO; BA; Intrntl Affrs Cncl Actvities VP 90; Italian Clb Treas 89; Pre-Law Scty 89; Ntl Mdl United Ntns Dlgte; Engl/Pol Sci; Intrntl Law.**

**SARNOSKI, CHAD K,** Pa St Univ Du Bois Cmps, Du Bois, PA; FR; ASB; ASSET Clb 90-; Stdnt Cncl 90-; Acctg.

**SARPONG, COMFORT A,** S U N Y Coll Of Tech At Frmgdl, Farmingdale, NY; FR; AAS; Mbr Hnrs Rsdnc Hl Cncl 90-; Ldr Rosevale Dorm 72-73; Dns Lst SUNY Coll Tech 90-; Hnr Rl Agric Coll Ghana 74-75; Grls Prfcta Agric Coll Ghana 74-75; Grls Perfecta; St Annes Anglcn Chrcn Ghana Lay Rdr 80-84; Gld Good Shprd St Ane Anglcn Ghana; Nrsng; RN.

**SARRO, PETER A,** Ny Institute Of Tech Ny City, New York, NY; JR; BA; NU Ypsilon Tau 90; ICDA Mbr 90-F AGO Mbr NY Chptr; Telef; Dipl Cret Engrg Instit Wash DC 81; Cert AT-T Corp Engrg Ctr 76-78; Elec Eng Techlgy; Techlgy/Busn.

**SARTAIN, CAROLYN D,** Middle Tn St Univ, Murfreesboro, TN; JR; BS; Kappa Delta Pi 90-; AS Motlow St Comm Coll 90; Elem Edn; Teach.

**SARTAIN, JEFFREY P,** Ga St Univ, Atlanta, GA; GD; MS; Mortar Brd 90; Sigma Nu 87-90; Head Ath Trnr 89-90; Ath Trng Pgm 90; W Chester U; Ntl Ath Trnrs Assn 88-; Sbs GA St U 90; Sprts Med.

**SARTAIN, SANDY C,** Univ Of Al At Birmingham, Birmingham, AL; JR; BA; Delta Gamma Rec Sec 90-; Compass Clb VP 89-90; Phi Theta Kappa 88-; Deans List 88-; Pres List 89-; Hmcmng Crt 88; Miss Walker Clg 89-90; Schlrshp Rot Clb ,8-; IM 89-; MS Walker Clg 90; Cmptr Scnc; Progrmmr.

**SARTEN, PATRICIA F,** Methodist Coll, Fayetteville, NC; FR; Sci; H S Educ.

**SARTIN, TRACEY A,** Schenectady County Comm Coll, Schenectady, NY; SR; AAS; Trvl/Trsm; Trvl/World.

**SARTORI, ANGELLA M,** Manhattanville Coll, Purchase, NY; SR; Deans Lst 89-; Fld Hcky; Bsktblle; Sftbll 87-; BA; Mgmt; Tchng.

**SARVER II, ERNEST M,** Liberty Univ, Lynchburg, VA; SO; BS; Lib Assoc Christian Tchrs V Pres 90-; Math Assoc Of Amer; Kappa Mu Epsilon V Pres; Kappa Delta Pi; Frshmn Math Awrd 89-90; Math; Educ.

**SARWAR, MUSHTAQ A,** Fl St Univ, Tallahassee, FL; SR; BS; Intl Assoc Pres 90-; Inst Elctrcl/Elctrncs Engrs; Golden Key Natl Hnr Soc; Engr Hnr Soc; Phi Theta Kappa; AA Tallahassee Comm Clg 88; Elec Engr.

**SASADU, JULIE A,** Univ Of Fl, Gainesville, FL; SR; BS; Career Expo Asst Dir 90-; Hnrs Pgm; Omcrn Delta Epsln; Alpha Omcrn Pi Chrmn 88-; Delta Tau Delta Ltl Sis 89-; AA Hnrs 90; Fnce.

**SASAKI, LARYCE M,** Oh Univ, Athens, OH; SR; BMUS; Msc Ed Natl Cnfrnc 87-; Trmpt Ensmbl; Brs Chr 87-; Wm Gl Clb/Chrl Un 90-; Pi Kappa Lambda; Alpha Lambda Delta 88-; Gldn Key 90-; Phi Kappa Phi 90-; B Mus; Msc Ed; Tchg.

**SASAKI, MAYUMI,** Andrew Coll, Cuthbert, GA; FR; AA; E/W Fndtn 90-; Deans Lst 90; Choraliers 90-.

**SASSE, LAURA J,** Seton Hall Univ, South Orange, NJ; FR; BSE; Field Exprnc/Stdnt Tchng Cmtee Stdnt Rep 90; Kappa Delta Pi 89; Magna Cum Laude 89; Acad Schlrshp 87-; E G Magnes Mem Schlrshp 8; Ele Ed/English; Tchng.

**SASSER, CATHERINE L,** Draughons Jr Coll Nashville, Nashville, TN; SO; AS; Emplyd Acct Clrk TN Dept Emplymnt Scrty 87-; Cmptr Pgmg.

**SASSER JR, JAMES B,** Univ Of Southern Ms, Hattiesburg, MS; SR; BS; Assoc Computing Machinery 90-; Soc Advcmnt Of Mgmnt 84-85; Upsilon Pi Epsilon Pres; Beta Gamma Sigma 84-85; Golden Key 84-; Pres List 84-; Hnrs Grad 85; Retail Mgmnt 85-90; BSBA 85; Computer Science; Software Engr.

**SASSER, KAREN E,** Univ Of Southern Ms, Hattiesburg, MS; SR; Assoc For Cmptng Mchnry 90; Phi Kappa Phi; Upsilon Phi Epsilon VP; Pres Lst 90; AS Santa Fe Cmmnty Clg 89; Applied Cmptr Sci; Sftwre Eng.

**SASSER, MICHAEL D,** Fl St Univ, Tallahassee, FL; SR; BS; Golden Key 90-; Engrng 90-; Civil Engrng.

**SASSER, TERRY L,** Union Univ, Jackson, TN; SR; BS; BSU 88-; Univ Sngrs 88-89; Un Stage Bnd 88-90; Alpha Chi 89-; Sigma Zeta 89-; Chem; Med.

**SASSO, ROBERT,** Bloomfield Coll, Bloomfield, NJ; SR; BS; Deans Lst 88-90; Bsbl All Cnfrnce Schlrshp 89-90; Bus Gnrl Mngmt; Fin Mngmt.

**SASSON, NICOLE L,** Univ Of Rochester, Rochester, NY; SO; BA; Jwsh Stdnt Union 90-; Hillel 90-; Frgn Lang Lvng-Frnch Flr; NY Rgnts Schlrshp; Nautilus; Psychlgy; Tchng Wrtng Bks.

**SASSONE, JOSEPH D,** S U N Y At Binghamton, Binghamton, NY; FR; BS; DJ Radio Sta 90-; Italian Clb 90-; Acctg/Mgmt Org 90-; Wnd Ensmbl 90-; Acctg; CPA.

**SASTRE, MARGARITA,** Saint Thomas Univ, Miami, FL; JR; BA; Write Stff Clb 89-; Chrch Serv Grp; Deans Lst 90-; AA Miami-Dade Comm Coll 89; Elem Ed; Tchng.

**SASZIK, ERIK A,** Cornell Univ Statutory College, Ithaca, NY; SR; BS; ASAE 90; Deans Lst 88; Frshmn/Vrsty Hvywght Crew 87-88; Ag Eng; Mngmnt Mfg.

**SATARIANO, ANDREA L,** Muskingum Coll, New Concord, OH; JR; BA; Tour Guide 90-; Acdmc Sr Hnry 90-; Acdmc Key Awrd 90-; Chi Alpha Nu 90-; Habitat Humnty 90-; SA 90-; Admsn Hs Mgr 90-; Campus Spch Cmptn 90; Var Bsktbl Chrldg Capt 90-; Bus; Admin.

**SATCHER, JAN K,** Abraham Baldwin Agri Coll, Tifton, GA; SO; BED; Deans List Dist Achvmnt Lst; Pres List Acad Schlrshp; Hnr Stdnt.

**SATO, AKEMI,** Faulkner Univ, Montgomery, AL; FR; MBS; Kirei Na A1 90-; Bio; Dietian.

**SATO, KEI,** Mount Aloysius Jr Coll, Cresson, PA; SO; Deans Lst 90-; Trvl/Trsm; Trvl Cndctr.

**SATO, SHINICHI,** Va Commonwealth Univ, Richmond, VA; FR; BS; Hnrs 90; Mdcl Clg VI Emrgncy Room Vlntr 90; Phi Eta Sigma 90; Rhoads Jhnsn Assc 90; Richmond Mtrpltn Blood Driver 90; New Stdnt Orntn Guide; Scrty Grd Residence Halls; IM Co/Cptn 90; Blgy/Premed; Medicine.

**SATO, TERUMI,** Comm Coll Algny Co Algny Cmps, Pittsburgh, PA; SO; Intl Stu Clb; Sec.

**SATTAR, KAZI M,** Bloomfield Coll, Bloomfield, NJ; FR; BS; Data Prcssng Mngmnt Assc Vp; Intrntl Stdnt Org 90; Cmptr Sci; Eng.

**SATTERFIELD, MICHAEL K,** Univ Of Nc At Charlotte, Charlotte, NC; SO; BA; Radical Thought Socty X Chckr 90-; Natl Coll Archtctr/Dsgn Awd; Archtctr.

**SATTERFIELD, RODNEY L,** Ga St Univ, Atlanta, GA; GD; MBA; I M Ftbl Bkbl; Ftbl GA Southwestern; BS 90; Spec Educ/L D; Tch/Admn.

**SATTERFIELD, TEKA R,** Middle Ga Coll, Cochran, GA; FR; AS; Btgrl; Stdnt Actvties Comm 90-; Gamma Beta Phi 90; Acctg; CPA.

**SATTERLEE, CHRISTEN D,** Memphis St Univ, Memphis, TN; SR; BS; Tiger Paws 88-; Cath Stdnt Ctr 88-; Gamma Beta Phi; Goldn Key 89-; Alpha Epsilon Delta Tr 90-; Pre Pharmcy.

**SATTERLY, MAUREEN B,** Spalding Univ, Louisville, KY; JR; BA; Human Resources.

**SATTIZAHN, BRIAN T,** Univ Of Pittsburgh, Pittsburgh, PA; JR; BS; Eng Mag Lyout Ed 89-; IEEE; Golden Key 90-; Eta Kappa Nu Treas 90-; Wstnghse Schlr 88-; IM Bsktbl 89-; Elec Eng.

**SATTLER, JEAN M,** Davis Coll, Toledo, OH; AD; Acctg; Finance.

**SAUBERAN, CLAYTON H,** Bowling Green St Univ, Bowling Green, OH; JR; BS; AGC VP 88-90; CMA 90-; Fire Dptmnt Vol 90-; AAS Suny Delhi 90-; Cnstrctn Mgmnt Tchnlgy; Cnstrctn.

**SAUCER, GELSUMINA C,** Methodist Coll, Fayetteville, NC; GD; Phi Sigma Iota 90-; Cmbrlnd Cnty Frnch Clb; Intrntnl Frgn Language; Hnr Scty; Ntnl Deans List 13th Edition; BS 90; Bsn Admin.

**SAUDER, JAY R,** Univ Of Al At Birmingham, Birmingham, AL; JR; BS; IM Sccr 89-; Alpha Lambda Delta 90-; Gldn Key 90-; Mennonite Brd Missions Prd Mngr; Mngmnt.

**SAUER, CHRISTEL R,** S U N Y Coll Of Tech At Alfred, Alfred, NY; FR; BS; MFA Sch Art 79; Lndscp Dev; Lndscp Dsgn.

**SAUER, DEVORAH,** Coppin St Coll, Baltimore, MD; GD; MS; BS; Spcl Edctn.

**SAUER, NANCY E,** Hillsborough Comm Coll, Tampa, FL; SO; AS; Dns Lst 79-80; Pres Lst 79-80; Word Prcssng Spec/Sec 80-; Law.

**SAUER, TIMOTHY D,** Westminster Coll, New Wilmingtn, PA; JR; BA; Radio Stn Prog Dir 90; TV Stn Flr Mgr; Chrstn Clg Sndy Dlvrd Srmn; Deans Lst 90; Indpndnt Hnrs Rsrch Stdnt Hnr Stdnt 90; Clg Rcgntn For Vol Serv Chldnrs Hosp 90; Cmmrcl/Flm Actor With Donna Belajac Agncy In Pgh Actor 88; Scuba Drvr 90; Telecmmnctns; Intractve TV Or Mtn Pctre.

**SAUERBREY, RICARDO A,** Univ Of Sc At Columbia, Columbia, SC; SO; BA; Mgmt; Bus Admin.

**SAUERS, BARBARA M,** Comm Coll Algny Co Algny Cmps, Pittsburgh, PA; FR; AS; Stdnt Actvts Advsry; Bsn; Bsn Mgr.

**SAUL, CHRISTINE M,** Johnson St Coll, Johnson, VT; FR; AD; Nursing; Midwife.

**SAUL, IRENE M,** Glassboro St Coll, Glassboro, NJ; SR; BA; Wmns Athltc Assc Pres 90-; Deans Lst 90; Fld Hcky/Lcrsse Vrsty 86-90; Math; Tchr.

**SAUL, MICHAEL A,** Univ Of Pa, Philadelphia, PA; FR; BA; New Student Orietn Prog; Pennlines; Math/Pre Medl.

**SAUL, MOISES,** Tn St Univ, Nashville, TN; SR; BA; Math Clb 89-; Spnsh Clb 89-; Alpha Mu Gamma; Sci Hnr Scty 89-; Otstndng Math Stdnt; Cert Otstndng Acdmc Excllnc Sci 90-; Math; Actrl Sci.

**SAUL, STACY M,** Memphis St Univ, Memphis, TN; SR; BA; Inds Orgnztn Psychlgy.

**SAULS, ANONA K,** Univ Of Cin R Walters Coll, Blue Ash, OH; JR; BA; Philosophy Soc 89-90; Phi Theta Kappa Plng Comm 90-; Phi Alpha Delta 90-; Stdnt Tutor 89-; Blood Drive Co Chrprsn 89-; Hist; Law.

**SAULS, ERIC R,** Glassboro St Coll, Glassboro, NJ; SO; BA; Econ; Econmst.

**SAULSBERRY, JANICE Y,** Fl A & M Univ, Tallahassee, FL; JR; BS; Alpha Sweetheart; Calif Club; Cmptr Infor Sys Club; Phi Eta Sigma; Cmptr Infor Sys; Cmptr/Database Mgmt.

**SAULSBERRY, JEAN P,** Christian Brothers Univ, Memphis, TN; JR; BS; Bus Adm; Mgmt.

**SAUNDERS CLARK, TONYA J,** Oh Univ-Southern Cmps, Ironton, OH; SO; BSED; Para Prof Dawson/Brynt Schl Syst; Coal Grv Little Leag Bd Dir 89-; Elem Educ/Math; Tchr.

**SAUNDERS, AKIRA R,** Norfolk St Univ, Norfolk, VA; FR; BA; Acctg/Bus.

**SAUNDERS, ANTOINETTE M,** City Univ Of Ny Baruch Coll, New York, NY; SO; BBA; Harlem Schl Arts Dance Asst 83-90; Dance Clb Instrctr; Bsns; Admnstrtv Asst.

**SAUNDERS, BRIAN C,** Univ Of Nc At Charlotte, Charlotte, NC; FR; BA; Engl; Wrtg/Edtng.

**SAUNDERS, CARRINGTON H,** Memphis St Univ, Memphis, TN; FR; Stu Gov Assn Sntr; Amb Bd 90-; Replctns 90-; Alpha Tau Omega 90-; Business.

**SAUNDERS, CHRISTY L,** Oh Univ-Southern Cmps, Ironton, OH; FR; BED; Math; Ed.

**SAUNDERS, CINDY S,** Patrick Henry Comm Coll, Martinsville, VA; FR; PTD Offcr Treas 89-; Schl Vol Coor Chrch Wrkr; Tchr Aide 90-; Educ Mjr; Tchr.

**SAUNDERS, ELIZABETH G,** Marshall University, Huntington, WV; GD; MBA; Kappa Delta Pi; Tchr Chptr I Mason Cnty Schls; BA Elem Ed 88; Rdng Spclst; Tchng.

**SAUNDERS, ERIKA V,** Wagner Coll, Staten Island, NY; SO; Sigma Gamma Rho; Thtr; Actng.**

**SAUNDERS, JAMIE S,** Univ Of Ky, Lexington, KY; FR; BS; Bat Conservation Intl 89-; Natl Geographic Scty 77-86; Geology/Geogralph; Seismology/Cartography.

**SAUNDERS, JENNIFER L,** Trinity Coll, Hartford, CT; SO; BA; Trinitones Bus Offcr 89-; Cncrt Choir 89-; Theatr Prod 89-; Comm Outrch 89-; Nghbrhd Posse 90-; Drama Clsscs Tchng Asst; Res Asst; Engl; Tchng.**

**SAUNDERS, JOHN R,** Memphis St Univ, Memphis, TN; SR; BA; E Memphis Sccr Assoc Coach 88-; Flm/Video Prod; Flmkng.**

**SAUNDERS, MATTHEW F,** Muskingum Coll, New Concord, OH; JR; BA; Stu Actv Org 88-90; Nwspr Stf Clmnst 88-90; Asso Cmptg Mchnry VP 89-90; Lambda Sigma 89-90; Omicron Delta Kappa Tres 89-; Sr Hnry; Phi Alpha Theta; Sigma Tan Delta; Kappa Sigma Tres 89-; John Glenn Schlrshp 88-; Engl; Prof Wrtr.

**SAUNDERS, MICHELLE A,** Comm Coll Algny Co Algny Cmps, Pittsburgh, PA; SO; AS; Med Asst.

**SAUNDERS, PATRICIA M,** Siena Coll, Loudonville, NY; FR; BS; Nwsppr 90-; Acctng.

**SAUNDERS, RORY T,** Norfolk St Univ, Norfolk, VA; JR; BS; NSBE 89-; IEEE 89-; NASA Langley Rsrch Ctr 90; Elect Engr.

**SAUNDERS, RUTH A,** Oh Univ-Southern Cmps, Ironton, OH; FR; BA; Deans Lst 90; Ironton Parade Cmmttee; Math; Eng.

**SAUNDERS, STEVEN J,** Clayton St Coll, Morrow, GA; JR; BS; ACM; Cmptr Science; Cmptr Prgrmmng.

**SAUNDERS, SYLVIA C,** Columbia Union Coll, Takoma Park, MD; GD; Natl Assn Fmale Exec; Laubach Lit Actn/Lit Cncl MC; Sr Propsl Spclst; BS; Mgmt.

**SAUNDERS, TAMMY L,** Wv Univ, Morgantown, WV; FR; BSAE; Gov Hnrs Acad Alumni Assn 90-; Phi Sigma Pi 90-; Aerospc Eng.

**SAUNDERS, TARA L,** Va St Univ, Petersburg, VA; FR; BA; Ntl Assoc Negro Bus/Prof Wmns Clb; Bus Admin; Stcks Anlyst.

**SAUNDERS, TINAMARIE,** Cheyney Univ Of Pa, Cheyney, PA; SR; BS; Rcrtn Mjr Clb Treas 89-; Rho Phi Lambda Chrprsn 90-; Sigma Gamma Rho VP 89-; March Dimes; Intrgrk Cncl; Tutor; Deans Lsts 90-; Intrnshp Thomas Jefferson Univ; Cross Cntry Capt 88-; Rcrtn/Psychlgy; Cntrct Lwyr.

**SAUNDERS, WALLACE M,** Univ Of Nc At Chapel Hill, Chapel Hill, NC; FR; IM Sccr Cptn 90; SEAC; Anglican Stdnt Flwshp; Deans Lst 90-; Env Engineering.

**SAURER, VALERIE E,** Fl St Univ, Tallahassee, FL; JR; BA; FSU Hon/Schlrs; Phi Theta Kappa 88-; Incntv Schlrshp 90-; Winthrop-King Schlrshp; FL Lgl Asst Inc 88-; Tallahassee Assn Lgl Asst 88-; Cert Lgl Asst; AA Tallahassee Comm Coll 90; Frnch/Spnsh; Prfssr.

**SAURO, ANGEL J,** Le Moyne Coll, Syracuse, NY; FR; Engl Lit.

**SAVAGE, DANIEL,** Tallahassee Comm Coll, Tallahassee, FL; JR; BS; AA; Soc Stds Ed; High Schl Tchr.

**SAVAGE, DERRICK J,** Ms St Univ, Miss State, MS; SO; BS; Univ Chrstn Stu Cntr Plng Comm Mbr 89-; IM Athltcs; Gamma Beta Phi 90-; Eta Kappa Nu 90-; IEEE; Elec Engr.

**SAVAGE, JODI LEIGH,** Univ Of Sc At Columbia, Columbia, SC; SR; BA; SAGE 89-90; VAA 87-88; Gamma Beta Phi 89-; Phi Beta Kappa; Sigma Iota Ro; Grad Asstntshp Mstrs Intl Bus; Rsrch Asstnt BA Intl Studies; Intl Studies; Bus.

**SAVAGE, KELA L,** Univ Of South Al, Mobile, AL; SR; BA; Elem Educ; Tchr.

**SAVAGE, KIMBERLY A,** Marywood Coll, Scranton, PA; FR; Cmmtr Clb 90-; Deans Lst 90-; Bus; Bus Admin/Mgmt.

**SAVAGE, PATIENCE D,** Univ Of West Fl, Pensacola, FL; JR; BS; Phi Beta Lambda; Busn Tchr Educ; Tchng.

**SAVALA, JOSEPH W,** Old Dominion Univ, Norfolk, VA; JR; BS; AAS Thomas Nelson Cmnty Clg 88; Mech Eng.

**SAVATTA, DOMENICO J,** Cooper Union, New York, NY; SO; BSE; Cncl Rep Actvts Cmtee 90-; FORZA 90-; Sftbl Co Capt I M; Engr; Med.

**SAVEL, BRIDGET A,** Radford Univ, Radford, VA; FR; Spec Educ; Tchng.

**SAVIDGE, KRISTY L,** Elizabethtown Coll, Elizabethtown, PA; FR; BA; Occuptnl Thrpy.

**SAVILLE, RONALD H,** Christopher Newport Coll, Newport News, VA; SR; BS; Assoc Of Psych Stdnts 87-90; Hillel 87-90; Yng Democrts 87-88; Alpha Chi Pres ,9; Psi Kappa Phi 90f Psi Chi 89; Golden Key 90; Grad Magna Cum Laude 90; BS Old Dominion U 90; Bio; Vet Med.

**SAVINELLI, DOMINIQUE,** Merrimack Coll, North Andover, MA; SO; BA; Benzene Ring Soc 89-90; CRC Press Frshmn Awrd 90; Chem; Research.

**SAVION, RABIN,** Fl International Univ, Miami, FL; SR; MBA; Srvd Stdnt Govt Actvts Bd Daytona Bch Comm Coll FL 89-90; Grad Hnrs Daytona Bch Comm Coll FL 90; Intrnshp Pannell Kerr Forster; CPA Hotel Indstry Mgmt Advsry Srvc Dept; AS Daytona Bch Comm Coll FL 90; Htl Mgmt; Bus.

**SAVITZ, GABRIELLA ANN,** Lesley Coll, Cambridge, MA; SR; BS Educ; Tchr.

**SAVITZ, MICHELLE LYNNE,** Temple Univ, Philadelphia, PA; SR; BS; Physcl Thrpy Clb 87-90; Bstn Athltc Assoc 90; Athltc Trnrs Clb 90-; Stdnt Athltc Trnr 90-; Athltc Trnng.

**SAVOLSKIS, DANIEL L,** Duquesne Univ, Pittsburgh, PA; SO; BM; Ski Clb 89-; Phi Mu Alpha VP 90-; Fndrs Schlrshp 89-; Music Performance.

**SAVORY, MICHELLE A,** Franklin Pierce Coll, Rindge, NH; FR; BA; Visl Arts; Adv.

**SAVVIDIS, IOANNA,** Bunker Hill Comm Coll, Boston, MA; FR; BS; Elem Ed; Tchng Chldrn.

**SAWH, VIDYA L,** Jersey City St Coll, Jersey City, NJ; JR; BSC; Natl Deans Compttn; Offc Mngr Albert Dureck Distrbtrs Inc; Dipl Schl Bus Machine 85-; Acctg-Bus Admin; CPA.

**SAWHNEY, VINNEY S,** City Univ Of Ny Baruch Coll, New York, NY; JR; BBA; Stdnt Mmbr Amer Acctng Assn 90; Brch Acctng Scty 90; Wrk Intrnshp Shrsn Lhmn Bros; Samuel And Irving Weinstein Schlrshp 89-; Dns Lst 90; Acctng Fnnce; Bus Cnsltng.

**SAWITZKI, LISA M,** Siena Coll, Loudonville, NY; SR; BS; Ski Clb 90-; Mth Clb 90-; Delta Epsilon Sigma; Sigma Xi; Perth Vol Fr Dept Lds Axlry Treas 87-; Amer Red Crs Dstr Srvc Vol 87-; Chmstry Achvmnt Awd 87-88; IM 90; Math; Cmptr Sci.

**SAWNEY, SANGEETA,** Fl International Univ, Miami, FL; JR; BS; Intrntl Cult Soc 87-89; Asian Stdnt Clb Sec 87-89; Alpha Gamma 87-89; Alpha Gamma Sigma 88; Alpha Gamma Sigma Schlrshp WVC CA 88; Valdctrn Grad 89; Acdmc Exclnc Schlrshp Dept Riology WVC CA 88; AS W Vly Coll 89; Clin Lab Sci; Med Tech/Rsrch Ch Lab.

**SAWTARI, AHMAD A,** Bethany Coll, Bethany, WV; SR; BS; Intrntl Stdnts Scty Offcr Sec; Phi Tau; Sigma Nu; Fllwshp Comp Sci Dept U Of KY; Sccr Clb; Math; Tchr.

**SAWTELLE, CAROLINA C,** Tri County Tech Coll, Pendleton, SC; FR; BA; Sec Sci.

**SAWYER, GINA J,** Unity Coll, Unity, ME; SO; BS; Nwsppr Asst Edit; Pr Cnclr Alpne Clb Gn Clb; SG; Bld Dnr Vol; Otdr Rcrtn.

**SAWYER, GLORIA J,** Erie Comm Coll, Buffalo, NY; FR; RN; Sisters Hosp Buffalo NY Employee; Nrsg; Phys Asstnt.

**SAWYER, JOSEPHINE L,** Thomas Nelson Comm Coll, Hampton, VA; FR; AAS; Offc Sys Tech; Exec Sec.

**SAWYER, KIMBERLY L,** Univ Of Sc At Columbia, Columbia, SC; JR; BA; Hnr Asc 90-; Kappa Tau Alpha; Gamma Beta Phi 90-; SPJ 90-; Tri Delta Chrmn 90-; Gamma Beta Phi 90-; Pharm Chem Labs Intrn; Dns Lst 88-; Adv/Pblc Rltns; Law.

**SAWYER, LISA A,** Liberty Univ, Lynchburg, VA; JR; Alpha Lambda Delta 88-.

**SAWYER, PAMELA C,** Asbury Theological Sem, Wilmore, KY; GD; MDIV; Married Stu Flwshp Sec 89-90; RN 63-; Lic Lcl Pstr UMC 90; Chrstn Bkstr Mgr 87; RN 63; BA 90; Religion; Mnstr.

**SAWYER, PATRICIA R,** Blue Mountain Coll, Blue Mountain, MS; SR; BS; Stdnt Educ Assn 70-72; Blue Mtn Commuters Clb 90-; Blue Mtn Coll Cls Of 1991 Alumni Sec; Phi Theta Kappa 70-72; Miss Assn Educ 90-; AS Northeast Miss Comm Coll 72; Elem Educ.

**SAWYER, SCOT M,** Univ Of New England, Biddeford, ME; FR; BS; Lic Phys Therapist.

**SAWYER, TIMOTHY M,** Atlantic Comm Coll, Mays Landing, NJ; FR; Bus Admin.

**SAWYER, TUSHINA S,** Coppin St Coll, Baltimore, MD; SO; BS; Stdnt Sntre Sntr 90-; Stdnt Rep Jdcl Brd; VP Of Soph; Alpha Phi Alpha; Pscyh; Psychlgst.

**SAWYERS, LA KAWANNA,** Marshall University, Huntington, WV; SR; AS; BA; Educ; Med.

**SAXON, EDWARD B,** Howard Univ, Washington, DC; JR; Cable Busnmn Awd 85; Alfreda Bunton Awd; Johnson Awd Exemplary Christian Conduct 86; NAACP 88-; Proj Self Sufficiency; BS Livingstone Clg 87; Theology; Ph D Teach Homiletics.

**SAXON, JEREMY R,** Saint Francis Coll, Loretto, PA; SO; BS; Hnrs Pgm 89-; Math/Cmptr Sci; Cmptr Pgmng.

**SAXONHOUSE, MATTHEW ADAM,** Emory Univ, Atlanta, GA; FR; BS; Spnsh Clb 87-90; Debate Tm 87; Tmpl Yth Grp 87-90; Dns Lst; JV Bsktbl/Fr Bsbll 86-; Hnrs Prgrm Advncd Plcmnt 87-90; Pi Kappa Alpha; Pkskll Hsptl Auxllry Schlrshp 90; Outstndng Hgh Schl Stdnt Awrd 90; Pres Awrd Acdmc/Physcl Ftnss 90; Vrsty Ftbl/Tnns; Bio; Med.**

**SAYASANE, PHONESAVANH,** Faulkner St Jr Coll, Bay Minette, AL; SO; BA; Phi Theta Kappa 89-; Hmcmng Md 89-90; Hmcmng Qn 90-; Mst Prmsng Frshmn Chrldr 89-90; Thrd Rnk Natl Chrldng Sqd Natl Chmpn Sqd 90-; Bkg/Fnce; Bnk Lnr.

**SAYBAN, CHAD A,** Gannon Univ, Erie, PA; FR; BS; Acctng Clb 90-; Scl Com 90-; Phi Eta Sigma; NCCCAA Div II Golf 90-; Acctng; Business.

**SAYDAH, JAYNE M,** Rensselaer Polytechnic Inst, Troy, NY; JR; BS; Panhel Pres 89; Prof Ldrshp Prog; Athletes Against Alcohol/Drug Abuse 89-90; Pi Beta Phi Membrshp Chr 89; Var Fld Hcky; Eng.

**SAYEED, SIRAJ A,** Univ Of Louisville, Louisville, KY; SR; BSEE; ROTC Asst Dpty Cmndr Oper; Alumni Assoc; Arnld Air Hnr Soc Dpty Cmndr 90-; IEEE; Engr Med/Bio Soc; Vets Admin Med Cntr Vol 87-; Elec Engr; Med.

**SAYER, ERIC S,** Methodist Coll, Fayetteville, NC; JR; BS; SGA Sntr 90; Stdnt Activities Cncl 89-90; Lambda Chi Alpha Rtlst 90; Smmr Intrnshps At Cntry Clb 89; Trck Tm 90; Bsnss Admin; Golf Prof/Mfg Rep.

**SAYERS II, CARL R,** S U N Y Coll Of Tech At Delhi, Delhi, NY; SR; AS; Automotive Tech; Auto Repair/Music.

**SAYERS, LASHAWN D,** Wilberforce Univ, Wilberforce, OH; JR; BA; Jr Cls Pres 90-; Sigma Omega; Kappa Theta Epsilon Pres; Pltcl Sci; Educ/Law.

**SAYESS, THOMAS W,** Me Maritime Academy, Castine, ME; JR; AS; Fire Brigade 90-; Castine Fire Dept 90-; Yacht Oprtns.

**SAYLES, CARLIN R,** Va St Univ, Petersburg, VA; SR; MA; Assn Intrntnl Stds Prsdnt; Hstry Clb 90-; CIAA Bnd Cymbls 89-90; Excptnl Bnd Mmbr 90-; Mrchng Bnd 88-; BA VA Unv; Intrntnl Stds Hstry Geogrphy; US Ambsdr.

**SAYLES, SALLY I,** Univ Of Fl, Gainesville, FL; JR; BA; Vol Girls Clb 89-; Asst Schlrshp Chrmn 90-; Sor Schlrshp Awrd 89-90; Gldn Ky 90-F; Sigma Tau Sigma 89-; Dean Lst; Alpha Omicron Pi; Mngmnt Intern Burdines; Fnnc; Invstmnt Bnkng.

**SAYLOR, ELIZABETH A,** Fl St Univ, Tallahassee, FL; JR; BED; Symphny Orchsta 90-; Kappa Kappa Gamma 90-; AA Polk Comm Coll 90; Msc Educ; Tch.

**SAYNE, DEBORAH J,** Univ Of Tn At Martin, Martin, TN; SO; BS; Stdnt Senate; Stdnt Pgmmng Com; MEA; ALA; Occptnl Therapy Clb; BBB; FCA; Bat Girl; BBB; ALA 89-; Mu Epsilon Delta 90-; Habitat Hmnty Amnsty Intl 89-; Acad Achvmnt Athletes 90; Tennis Tm/IM Vlybl/Sftbl/Bsktbl 89-; Occptnl Therapy.

**SAYOC, ROSEANN C,** Coll Of Charleston, Charleston, SC; FR; BS; Hons Progrm Stdnt Assoc; Hons Progrm; Copper River Bridge Run/Walk; Bio Pre Med; Psychtst.

**SAYRE, CHRISTINE L,** Univ Of Pittsburgh, Pittsburgh, PA; GD; MSN; Sigma Theta Tau 79-; NAACOG 90-; Kndrvlt Grp Erng Chldrn Hosp VP Lcl Chptr 90-; BSNRN 80; Nrsng.

**SAYRE, JENNIFER J,** Radford Univ, Radford, VA; SO; Canterbury; Cncl Excptl Chld 90-; Erly Ed Frnch; Tchng.

**SAYRE, NOEL D,** Oh Univ, Athens, OH; SO; BFA; OU Orch 3rd Chr Vln 89-; Qrtet Strng 1st Vln; Music Perf Vln.

**SBARRA, KRISTIN E,** West Liberty St Coll, West Liberty, WV; JR; BA; Crmnl Jstce Org VP/PRES 88-90; Intrned At Jvnle Dtntn Ctr Staff 89; Fremnshp I 90; Deans Lst 89; Estwd Vol Fre Dept Hd Of Arsn Invst Tm; Sears Optcl; Assoc In CJ WV U At Prkrsbrg 90; Crmnl Jstce; Law.

**SCAGLIONE, ANNEMARIE,** Univ Of Scranton, Scranton, PA; JR; BS; Bus Clb; Wmns Bus Hon Soc 90-; Pnsn Cnsltnt Merrill Lynch Inc 89-90; Mgmt; Hmn Rsrc Mgmt.

**SCAGLIONE, DOMENICK,** Dowling Coll, Oakdale Li, NY; SR; BA; Orphans Of Italy Bd 87-; OSIA 89-90; Ferrari Clb 88-; AAS St Univ NY 89; Mktng; Prfrmng Arts.

**SCALA, MARK M,** William Paterson Coll, Wayne, NJ; JR; BA; Humanities Clb 90; Chess Clb 90-; IM Billiards 87-; Engl.

**SCALABRINO, TINA M,** Univ Of New Haven, West Haven, CT; FR; BA; Deans Lst; Democratic Town Com Sec 90-; Hotel/Restaurant Mgmnt; Ownrshp.

**SCALERA, CHRISTOPHER R,** Villanova Univ, Villanova, PA; JR; BA; Delta Tau Delta Scl Chrmn 90; Specl Olympics 89; IMS 89-; English/Pol Sci.

**SCALESE, PATRICIA E,** Marywood Coll, Scranton, PA; JR; BM; Campus Mnstry Stdnt Ldr 88; St Cecelia Soc Treas 88; Vol In Actions 88; Delta Epsilon Sigma 90; Kappa Delta Pi 90; MENC 88; Presser Schlrshp; St Catherines Medal; Ntl Org Of Italian/Amer/Women Schol; Music; Music Ed.

**SCANLAN, JAMES B,** Merrimack Coll, North Andover, MA; SR; BA; Amer Scty Civil Engrs 87-; Civil Engrs; Envtl Engrg.

**SCANLAND, PAIGE C,** Christopher Newport Coll, Newport News, VA; JR; BA; Elem Ed.

**SCANLON, BRYAN K,** Johnson St Coll, Johnson, VT; JR; BFA; Stdnt Cngrs 89-; Stdnt Nwspr Edtr 89-90; Johnson Mandate Rvw Assnt Edtr 90-; Ltry Mag Edtrl Asst 88-89; Chesamore Pres 90-; Tutor 90-; Comnctns Intrn Ofc Pblc Afrs JSC 90; Merryl Lynch Schlrshp Acad Exclnc 90-; Wrtng/Lit; Grad Sch/Jrnlsm/Tchng.

**SCANLON, HEATHER J,** Edinboro Univ Of Pa, Edinboro, PA; SR; BA; WFSE FM Radio Spec Events Dir 89-90; Readers Theater 89-90; Debate Team 89; Pi Kappa Delta 89-; Nom Homecoming Queen Candidate 89; Awd Hnrs Schlrshp To China; Internship Taggart Moran Morehouse; Speech Comm/Pol Sci; Law.

**SCANLON, KELLY A,** Univ Of Ky, Lexington, KY; JR; BS; NSSLHA 90-; Serv Chldrns Hosp; St Elizbth Hosp; Cthdrl Chld Dvlpmnt Cntr; IM Soccr/Ftbl; Aerobics; Cmnctn Dsorders; Spch/Lang Pathlgy.

**SCANLON, SHANNA L,** Suffolk Comm Coll Eastern Cmps, Riverhead, NY; SO; BA; Phi Alpha Sigma; Deans Lst 90-; Crmnl Jstc; Law.

**SCANLON, SHELBY L,** Mount Aloysius Jr Coll, Cresson, PA; FR; AS; SADD 87-90; Frnch Clb 87-89; Trck/Fld 86-90; Nrsg; Ansthtst.

**SCARBER JR, PRESTON,** Univ Of Al At Birmingham, Birmingham, AL; JR; NSBE; TMS/ASM; Bspt Yth Instrctr; NASA Awrd; Chrch Finance Comm Pres; Yth Otrch; NASA Spc Flwshps 90-; Mtrl Sci Engr.**

**SCARBERRY, BARBARA N,** Ashland Comm Coll, Ashland, KY; GD; RN; Nursing.

**SCARBERRY, PAMELA,** Univ Of Ky, Lexington, KY; FR; BSN; Natl Clgt Nrsng Awd; Nursing.

**SCARBOROUGH, JANET W,** Anderson Coll, Anderson, SC; SO; BS; Gamma Beta Phi; Tcher.

**SCARBOROUGH, LAURA L,** Univ Of Sc At Columbia, Columbia, SC; SO; Deans Lst; Specl Olympics; Elem Educ; Elem Educ; Teaching.

**SCARBOROUGH, LEANNE M,** Salisbury St Univ, Salisbury, MD; SR; BED; SNEA 88-; Kappa Delta Pi 90-; Dean Lst; Elem Educ; Tchr.

**SCARBRO, BRENT J,** Univ Of Cincinnati-Clrmnt Coll, Batavia, OH; SO; BA; Bus Admin; Mktng.

**SCARBROUGH, CAROLYN,** City Univ Of Ny City Coll, New York, NY; SR; BS; Prnt Ldrshp Awd 83-84; Deans Lst 90-; PTA Sec 82-86; Educ Assc 86-; AA Hostos Cmnty Clg 79; Elem Educ.

**SCARBROUGH, JANINE F,** Southeastern Coll Of Hlth Sci, N Miami Beach, FL; JR; PHARM; Acdmy Stdnts Phrmcy 88-; Cls Treas 88-; Stdnt Liaison Com 89-; Rho Chi 90-; Phi Lambda Sigma 90-; Alpha Zeta Omega Pres 88-; BA Emory Univ 88; Clncl Phrmcy.

**SCARBROUGH, VALARIA S,** Alcorn St Univ, Lorman, MS; SR; BS; Inter Res Hl Cncl; Gspl Chr Treas 87-; Bio Clb; Beta Beta Beta; BS; Bio; Pharm.

**SCARCELLA, MARIA LINDA,** City Univ Of Ny Coll Staten Is, Staten Island, NY; SO; BA; Cmmnctns; Film Prdcr.**

**SCARCI, CELESTE M,** Duquesne Univ, Pittsburgh, PA; FR; BA; Residence Hall Assc 90; Orntn Staff; Phi Eta Sigma 90; Delta Zeta; Finance.

**SCARFONE, JOHN L,** Va Commonwealth Univ, Richmond, VA; JR; BS; Math Soc 90-; ACM Sec 90-; Gldn Key; Phi Eta Sigma 89-; Top Prcnt Rcgntn 90-; Cmptr Sci; Prgrmmr.

**SCARLINO, NICOLE A,** Wagner Coll, Staten Island, NY; SR; BS; Concert Bnd 89-; Dance Bnd 89-; Music Societies 89-; Dns Lst 89-; Arts Admin/Music; Law.

**SCARPELLI, SUSAN A,** S U N Y Coll Of Tech At Frmgdl, Farmingdale, NY; AS; Crmnl Just; Law Enfrcmnt.

**SCARPONE, PAUL,** City Univ Of Ny Baruch Coll, New York, NY; SO.

**SCATURRO, FRANK J,** Columbia Univ, New York, NY; FR; BA; Phi Eta Sigma 90-; Hstry; Law.

**SCAVO, ROSE MARIE A,** Dowling Coll, Oakdale Li, NY; GD; BBA; Stdnt Bus Assoc 88-90; Blood Dr Cmte 89-90; Orient Ldr For Incoming Frshmn 90.

**SCELFO, JACQUELINE M,** S U N Y Coll Of Tech At Frmgdl, Farmingdale, NY; JR; BSPLS; Assc Sprvsn Crclm Dvlpmnt 89-; Assc Chldhd Ed Intrntl 89-; Green Key 89-90; AS Suny Clg Tech Farmingdale 90; Elmntry Ed; Tchng.

**SCHAADE, JANE E,** Kent St Univ Kent Cmps, Kent, OH; SR; Brd Trustees 89-; Res Serv Advsr 89-; Eqstrn Tm Mgr 87-90; Gldn Key 89-; Alpha Lambda Delta 87-; Outstdng Clg Std Amer 87-; Ambssdr 89-; Cum Laude Hnrs; Std King Knndy Ctr 88-89; Outstdng Ldrshp Awd; Std Snt Ldrshp Awd 90; IM 90-; BBA; Bsn; Banking.

**SCHAAF, DAVID M,** Univ Of Louisville, Louisville, KY; GD; MENG; Amercn Soc Of Engrs 88-; Varsity Bsbl 85-88; Engr.

**SCHABER, BETHANN,** Long Island Univ C W Post Cntr, Greenvale, NY; SR; BS; Aesculapius Pre/Med Scty Pres 87-; Stdnt Crdntr Freshman Orntn 90; Sntr Stdnt Gov Assc 87-88; Beta Beta Beta Pres 88-; Phi Eta; Phi Eta Sigma 87-; Sigma Delta Omega Fndng Sis 89-; Univ Schlr Awrd Full Tuition Schrshp 87-; Blgy; Med.

**SCHABOWSKY, BARBARA J,** Central Fl Comm Coll, Ocala, FL; SO; AS; Heath Fair Glen Burnie MD; Medcl Asst; MA The Medix Sch 84; RN; Nrsng.

**SCHACHER, GARY M,** Schenectady County Comm Coll, Schenectady, NY; AAS; Reservist US Navy 83-; Certif Coach Spec Olymp 87-; Asst Dir Cmnty Res Dev Disabled Adults; Nrsg.

**SCHACHT, MELISSA A,** Univ Of Ky, Lexington, KY; FR; Team UK 90; Chancellors Schlrshp 90; English Ed; Scndry Ed.

**SCHACHTER, ALIZA R,** City Univ Of Ny Baruch Coll, New York, NY; JR; BA; Hillel VP 90-; Gldn Key; Baruch/Odess Schlr; NYS Rgnts Schlr; Merit Ltr Of Cmmndtn; Smr Intrn Mtrpltn Lifes Actrl Stdnt Prog; Math; Actrl Sci.

**SCHACHTSCHNEIDER, TRISHA A,** Western Piedmont Comm Coll, Morganton, NC; GD; MBA; AS; AA; Chem; Envrmntl Sci.

**SCHACKOW, CATHERINE,** Fl St Univ, Tallahassee, FL; JR; Lady Sclphntrs; Smnle Ambssdrs 90; Alumni Fndtn 88-89; Eta Sigma Delta 90; Zeta Tau Alpha Schlrshp Chr/Pres 88; GAMMA 90; Cmmnctns; Law.

**SCHAD, ALEXANDER N,** Univ Of Sc At Columbia, Columbia, SC; SO; BA; Dmncn Rpblc Dvs Cup Tnns Tm; Bsn/Mgmt/Fnce; Entprnr.

**SCHAEDEL, MARK W,** Univ Of Sc At Columbia, Columbia, SC; FR; BA; Sigma Phi Epsilon 90-; IM Sccr/Bsktbl/Ftbl; Bus; Finance.

**SCHAEFER, CATHY J,** Draughons Jr Coll Nashville, Nashville, TN; GD; AS; Prsnl Admin; AS; Bus.

**SCHAEFER, CHARLOTTE D,** Roane St Comm Coll, Harriman, TN; SO; BED; Gamma Beta Phi 85-; NSPI; Tstmstrs Clb; Adlt Educ; Trnng Indus.

**SCHAEFER, GLENDA M,** Defiance Coll, Defiance, OH; FR; AA; USDA 87-; Bus Admn.

**SCHAEFER, TERRI E,** Schenectady County Comm Coll, Schenectady, NY; AAS; Assisted Driver Field Trips/Other Schl Activites; Occupational Therapy Assist.

**SCHAEFER, WILLIAM M,** Univ Of Miami, Coral Gables, FL; FR; BA; Alpha Lambda Delta 90-; Marine Sci/Biology; Marine Biologist.

**SCHAEFER JR, WILLIAM M,** Hudson Valley Comm Coll, Troy, NY; JR; BA; Crmnl Jstce; Fed Law Enf.

**SCHAEFFER, HEIDI E,** Barry Univ, Miami, FL; SO; BS; Lit Vol 90; Hillel Membr 89; Greenpeace 87; Tri Beta 89; Psi Chi 89; Spec Olympics Vol Hugger 89-91; Pre-Med Psych; Physician.

**SCHAEFFER, KENNETH S,** Belmont Coll, Nashville, TN; JR; Stdnt Gov Assn Penn State VP 87-88; Berks Bus Soc Penn State Pres 87-88; Bapt Stdnt Union 90-; Stdnt Act Awd Penn State 88; MBA; Audio Eng/Prdcng.

**SCHAEFFER, SARA E,** Case Western Reserve Univ, Cleveland, OH; FR; BS; Mech Eng; Eng.

**SCHAEFFLER, CORI A,** S U N Y Coll Of Tech At Frmgdl, Farmingdale, NY; SO; AAS; Assoc For Legal Stdnts 89-; Legal Intrnshp; Schlrhsp; Crim Just.

**SCHAFER, CINDY A,** Univ Of Miami, Coral Gables, FL; SO; BA; Intervarsity Chrstn Flwshp Pres 89-; Prncpl Oboe Symphony Orch 90-; Pres Lst 89-; Singer Schlr Full Tuition 89-; Linda Mary Handleman Awd GPA 89-; Oboe Prfrmnce/Music Ind; Music/Chrstn Mnstry.

**SCHAFF, CHRISTINE P,** Clemson Univ, Clemson, SC; SR; BSN; Stdnt Liason Grp Nrsng 89-; Sigma Theta Tau; Hon Grad 86; Sigma Theta Tau; SPURS 87-88; Pres Lst 90; Deans Lst 89-; Grnvll Memrl Hosp Schlrshp 90-; Co-Ed Sftbl; Nrsng.

**SCHAFF, KAREN R,** Tn Temple Univ, Chattanooga, TN; SO; BA; Judson 89-90; Zeta Nu Rho 90-; Elem Ed; Telem Tchr.

**SCHAFFER, CHERYL L,** Univ Of South Al, Mobile, AL; SO; BA; Lsre Serv Asc 90-; Leisure Serv; Natl/State Park Serv.

**SCHAFFER, MICHAEL D,** Bowling Green St Univ At Huron, Huron, OH; SO; Bus; Accntng.

**SCHAFFER, STEPHANIE P,** Emory Univ, Atlanta, GA; JR; BBA; Deans Lst; Alpha Epsilon Phi Frml Chrmn 90; Fin; Bus.

**SCHAFFSTALL, ELIZABETH A,** S U N Y At Buffalo, Buffalo, NY; JR; MBA; U B Acctg Assoc; Wm Mgmt; Phi Eta Sigma 90-; Acctg.

**SCHAGER, MONICA M,** City Univ Of Ny Baruch Coll, New York, NY; SR; BBA; Acctg Scty; Beta Gamma Sigma; Gldn Key 90-; Incntv Awrd Schrlshp 87-; Prvst Schlrshp; Deans Lst 89-; Acctg.

**SCHALL, MICHELLE R,** Cornell Univ, Ithaca, NY; SR; BS; Htl Ezra Crnll 89-; Phi Kappa Phi; Rms Dvsn Intrnshp 88; Fd And Bvrge Intrnshp 89; Prprts Mgmt Asstnshp; Htl Rstrnt Admin; Prprts Mgmt.**

**SCHALLER, JENNIFER R,** Marywood Coll, Scranton, PA; FR; BS; Elem Ed/Erly Chldhd Ed; Tchng.

**SCHALM, KOENRAAD E,** Franklin And Marshall Coll, Lancaster, PA; SO; BA; Dgnhn Lit Soc Sec 90-; Physcs Clb VP 90-; Sigma Pi Sigma; Ph Kappa Sigma Rep 90-; Hackmn Rsch Schlp 90-; John L Kershner Awd; Thrtcl Physcs.

**SCHAMUS, ANITA,** City Univ Of Ny City Coll, New York, NY; SR; Exec Secy; Word Procsng; Data Entry Etc; AAS Borough Of Manhattan Cmnty Clg 87; Cert Nassau Cmnty Clg.

**SCHANDALL, WILLIAM J,** Glassboro St Coll, Glassboro, NJ; GD; Deans Lst; Aa Brkdl Comm Coll 87; Psychlgy; Bsns Mngmnt.

**SCHANDING, LORA G,** Lexington Comm Coll, Lexington, KY; SO; BS; Educ; Tchr.

**SCHANTZ, ERICA,** Fl St Univ, Tallahassee, FL; JR; BA; Stdnt Alumni Fndtn; Beta Kappa Alpha 91-; Dns Lst 90-; Kappa Delta Asst Mbrshp; Vol Chldrns Lghthse; Jr Olymps; Turner Brdcstng Sys Prod Asst; Tallahassee Chbr Comm Intrn; Comms.

**SCHANTZ, STEPHANIE E,** Davis & Elkins Coll, Elkins, WV; FR; BED; Phoeniz Allnc 90-; Wldrns Co-Op 90-; Dead Mjrs Soc 90-; People For The Ethical Trtmnt Of Anmls; All Amercn Schlr; Ed/Envrnmntl Sci; Tchng.

**SCHANZENBACHER, LISA A,** Saint John Fisher Coll, Rochester, NY; SR; BA; Spanisch Clb 90-; Mngmnt Clb 87-; Perk Dvlpmnt Corp 90-; Fin Mis Inter; Mngmnt Concentration Fin.

**SCHANZER, ROBERT J,** Yeshiva Univ, New York, NY; SR; AIPAC Exec Comm 88; SSSJ VP 89-; Pre-Med Hon Soc; Alpha Epsilon Delta VP 88-; Rsrch Asst NYU Med Cntr 90; Var Tns Tm Cpt 88-; Bio; Med Schl.

**SCHAPPACHER, CHARLES E,** Fayetteville St Univ, Fayetteville, NC; SR; Soc For Creative Anachronism Sceneschal 82-; USAR; BS 90; Educ.

**SCHARADIN, LORI E,** Central Pa Bus School, Summerdale, PA; FR; AS; Legal Assoc 90; Chrstn Flwshp Trvl Clb 90-; Chld Care Mgmt.

**SCHARDINE, NANCY A,** Lexington Comm Coll, Lexington, KY; SO; BA; Educ.

**SCHARDT, HEIDI L,** Univ Of Nc At Greensboro, Greensboro, NC; JR; BSC; Cmps Mnstrs Cncl Chrprsn 88-; Hnrs Prog Mbr 88-; Magzn Cnsltng Ed; Elem.

**SCHARF, DAVID,** Yeshiva Univ, New York, NY; SR; BA; Actry Clb Pres 89-; Phlnthrpy Scty 88-; Econ Scty 87-; Eta Beta Rho 89-; Univ Hm Hsptlty Prog 90-; Vrsty Trck Tm 87-88; Econ/Math; Bus.

**SCHARF, MICHAEL J,** Hillsborough Comm Coll, Tampa, FL; FR; BA; Otstdng Amer Hstry Stdnt 90-; Retl Mgr 79-89; Sheet Mtl Cont 89-; Cmptr Inf Syst; Cmptr Syst Analyst.

**SCHARF, MINDY G,** S U N Y Coll Of Tech At Frmgdl, Farmingdale, NY; SO; BA; Comp Inf Sys; Prog.

**SCHARFENBERG JR, THOMAS G,** Univ Of Al At Huntsville, Huntsville, AL; JR; BS; ASMC 89-; Soc Allied Weights Engrs; Pi Tau Sigma 90-; Co-Op Stdnt Boeing Intern 89-; Space Station Freedom Pgm; Mech Engr; Engr.

**SCHARFF, CHERYL L,** Neumann Coll, Aston, PA; JR; BA; Edtr Chf Stdnt Nws Pblctn Ed 90-; Wmns Vrsty Tnns Tm 88-; Delti Pi Chptr; Deans Lst; Rcgntn Schlrshp 88-89; Rcpnt Ptrc Mccrthy Urspmg Awrd Hnmts; Wmns Vrsty Tnns Tm 88; Engl.

**SCHATZ, MARK A,** Univ Of Pittsburgh, Pittsburgh, PA; JR; BS; IM Soccer 88-; Tau Beta Pi 90-; Golden Key 90-; Pi Tau Sigma V P; Gen Elect Intern 90; Univ Schlr 89-; Mech Engr; Engr.

**SCHATZMAN, ROSEMARY K,** Univ Of Cincinnati-Clrmnt Coll, Batavia, OH; SO; AA; Clrmnt Cnty Rpblcn Clb Nwslttr Edtr 82-; Clrmnt Cnty Wom Rpblcn Clb Sec 82-90; Exec Clrmnt Cnty Rpblcn Prty 82-; Deputy Auditor 89-; English; Mgmnt/Wrtng.

**SCHAUER, C RAE,** Milligan Coll, Milligan Clg, TN; SR; BA; Stdnt Hunger Comm 89-; Symphonic Ensmbl 88-90; Festival Of One Act Plays; Intrnshp At WJHL TV 90; Communications; Graphic Arts Or TV.

**SCHAUER, PEGGY SUE,** Indiana Univ Of Pa, Indiana, PA; FR; BA; Sign Lang Clb; Vstrs To The Aged 90; Elem Ed; Elem Schl Tchr.

**SCHEARER, JERRY W,** Salem-Teikyo Univ, Salem, WV; FR; BA; Stdnt Admin Fr Clss Rp Atty Gen 90-; By Scts Pres 90-; Drm Cncl Pres 90; Gamma Beta Phi 90-; Amer Hmnts Stdnt Assn Sec Elct 90-; Alpha Phi Omega Pres Elct 90; Rsdnce Lfe Stff RA; Chr Ldng 90-; Yth Hmn Srvcs; Prffsnl Sctng.

**SCHECTER, CHERYL B,** Fl International Univ, Miami, FL; GD; MS; Stdnt Dietetic Assoc; Ntl Hon Frat Phi Lambda Beta Chptr; Grad Asst In Utrtn Rsrch Lab; Marriott Hlth Care Svcs Clncl Intrnshp; BS; Dietetica/Nutrtn.

**SCHEETZ, FAITH R,** Kent St Univ Kent Cmps, Kent, OH; SO; BA; GAMMA; Inter-Grk Pgmg Bd VP Phlnthrpy; Hs Cncl Sec/Treas 89-; Psi Chi; Alpha Phi Phlnthrpy 90-; Orntn Instr; Tr Gd 90-; Outstndng Serv Awd; Amer Cncr Soc 90-; Crtfd Crisis Intrvntnst; Chld/Psychlgy.**

**SCHEFER, CHARLES W L,** George Mason Univ, Fairfax, VA; JR; BA; Co Fndr Stu Laptop Usrs Grp VP 90-; Dcsn Sci/Mis Clb 90-; FAA Prv Plts Lic; Blck Blt; Gldn Ky 90-; Mngmnt Infrm Syst; Bus Arspc Applctns Of MIS.**

**SCHEFF, ADAM S,** Columbus Coll Of Art & Design, Columbus, OH; FR; BA; Artist Rec Dept; Dsgn Logo Greater Cleveland Conf Athletic Lgue; Art/Illustration.

**SCHEFFLER, THEODORE M,** City Univ Of Ny Baruch Coll, New York, NY; SR; BA; Theatre-Tron 90-; Aids Cltn Unlsh Pwr 87-; Golden Key; GMHC; DIFFA 88-; Brdwy Cares 88-; Prof Dncr/Actor/Sngr 79-88; Engl Lit; Ed Scndry Lvl.

**SCHEHL, JOHN A,** Va Commonwealth Univ, Richmond, VA; SR; BA; Engl; Med.

**SCHEIBEL, JEANNE M,** Comm Coll Algny Co Algny Cmps, Pittsburgh, PA; SO; BA; Dean Lst 90-; Grcry Cshr 85-; Accntng; CPA.

**SCHEID, CARL G,** Dowling Coll, Oakdale Li, NY; SO; BA; IM Bsktbl 90; Arntcs/Mgmt; Comm Pilot.

**SCHEIMAN, MARY ELLEN,** Oh Univ, Athens, OH; SO; BFA; OUSUL Co-Fndr 89-90; Green Cncl 89-90; Delta Zeta Standards Chair 90-; Graphic Dsgn.

**SCHELBLE, NATHAN J,** Hilbert Coll, Hamburg, NY; SO; BA; Deans List; Kempo Martial Arts Black Belt 88; Psychlgy/Ed; Guidance Cnslng.

**SCHELL JR, RONALD T,** Hillsborough Comm Coll, Tampa, FL; FR; BA; Pre Med Scty; Hosp Axlry; Phi Beta Kappa; Bio Pre Med; Medcn.

**SCHELLENBACH, KEVIN J,** Savannah Coll Of Art & Design, Savannah, GA; SO; BA; Dns Lst; Arch.

**SCHELLINGER, SHIRLEY A,** Bridgewater Coll, Bridgewater, VA; FR; BS; Mu Epsilon Mu 90-; Aqua Aerobics 90-; Im Aerobics 90-; Home Ec; Interior Dsgn.

**SCHELLONG, STEVEN G,** Villanova Univ, Villanova, PA; SR; BA; Bxng Clb 89-90; Rugby Clb 89-90; Fireman 87-90; First Responder 87 89; Economics; Law/Envrnmntl.

**SCHENDEL, DONNA E,** Fl International Univ, Miami, FL; JR; BED; FHEA; Critical Care RN 78-; AS Miami-Dade Cmnty Clg 78; Hm Econ; Tch Voc Ed.

**SCHENK JR, LAWRENCE H,** Glassboro St Coll, Glassboro, NJ; SR; Cmptr Sci Clb 88-90; Lambda Chi Alpha 83-85; Masonville Vol Fire Co V P 87-; Assoc Cmptg Machinery 90-; Pgmr/Analyst Computer Sci Corp 89-; BS 90; Cmptr Sci; Pgmr.

**SCHENKEL, LINDA M,** Glassboro St Coll, Glassboro, NJ; SR; BA; SAB 87-89; Dns Lst; Fld Exp Psy; Psy; Wrk Hndcppd Chldrn.

**SCHENKER, ADAM E,** Univ Of South Fl, Tampa, FL; SO; BS; Natl Soc Prof Engrs; Engr Clg Cncl 90; Themis Hnr Soc; Admssns Dist 90; Univ Hnrs Pgm 90-; Dns Lst 90-; Engr.

**SCHENQUERMAN, SEBASTIAN,** Univ Of Pr At Rio Piedras, Rio Piedras, PR; SO; BS; Archtcte Dsgn Awrd 90; Archtcte.

**SCHEPER, PAMELA E,** Cornell Univ Statutory College, Ithaca, NY; JR; BS; Prtstnt Coop Mnstry Tres 89-; Mo Nun De Kah Ag Sch Hnr Soc Comm Chr 90-; Habitat Hmnty 89-; Old Wstbry Grdns Intrn 89; Yedowitz Mem Awrd Hrtcltr 89; Flrcltr; Plnt Pthlgy.

**SCHEPLER, VICKI L,** Niagara Univ, Niagara Univ, NY; JR; BBA; Delta Epsilon Sigma; Vol Income Tax Asst Prog 90; Acctg Intrnshp; Acctg.

**SCHEPPKE, KENNETH A,** S U N Y At Stony Brook, Stony Brook, NY; SR; MD; Stdnt Afrs Cmtee 88-; Amer Med Assn 90-; Amer Clg Emrgcy Physns; Alpha Omega Alpha; Amer Soc Clncl Pathlgsts Awd Acad Exclnc 90-; BS 88; Med; Phys.

**SCHERER, MICHELE D,** Anne Arundel Comm Coll, Arnold, MD; FR; AA; BS Towson State Univ 85; Comp Sci; Comp Sci/Psychlgy.

**SCHERER, NANCY,** S U N Y At Buffalo, Buffalo, NY; Phi Beta Kappa.

**SCHERER, RUSSELL L,** Univ Of Nc At Charlotte, Charlotte, NC; SR; BS; Soc Of Human Rsrc Mgt 9-; Scott Hall Cncl Ste Rep 87-88; Clg Schlrs Of Amer; Omicron Delta Kappa Nom; Im Sports/Referee Team Cptn 87-; Psychlgy/Bus; Human Rsrcs.

**SCHERER III, WILLIAM R,** Univ Of Miami, Coral Gables, FL; SR; BA; Sigma Chi Social Chrmn 89; Ski Clb; Eng; Law.

**SCHERIBEL, VICTORIA A,** Ma Inst Of Tech, Cambridge, MA; FR; BS; Muscl Theatre Gld; Res Asst Prof Wgh Lewin 90-; Physcs/Philo; Res.

**SCHERM, PAMELA W,** Owensboro Jr Coll Of Bus, Owensboro, KY; JR; AS; Emplyd Livingston Trvl Bkpr 90; Cmptr.

**SCHERMERHORN, CARA L,** Univ Of Rochester, Rochester, NY; JR; BABA; Edtr Logos 88-89; Rsdnt Advsr Frgn Lang Halls Smmr Intrnshp Brlnr Bnk Grmny 91-92; Blck Blt Tae Kwan Do 88-92; Grmn Pltcl Sci; Law.

**SCHERMERHORN, G BRIAN,** Embry Riddle Aeronautical Univ, Daytona Beach, FL; JR; BS; Nwspr Prod Mgr 89-90; Waterski Tm 90; Aeronautical Sci; Airline Pilot.**

**SCHERWINSKI, MELISSA A,** Tallahassee Comm Coll, Tallahassee, FL; SO; BA; AA Tallahassee Comm Coll 91; Psychlgy; Fmly/Mrrg Cnslr.

**SCHESNIAK, ROGER A,** Embry Riddle Aeronautical Univ, Daytona Beach, FL; FR; BS; Dns Lst 90-; Vlybl 90-; Eng.

**SCHEUERMAN, TRACY L,** Kent St Univ Kent Cmps, Kent, OH; SO; BA; Beta Alpha Psi; Acctg Assn; Outstndng Serv Awd; Acctg; Law.

**SCHEUFLER, KELLY S,** Bowling Green St Univ At Huron, Huron, OH; JR; BED; Milan Mthdst Church; Server Sandusky Brown Derby; Elem Ed; Tchr.

**SCHEUREN, SHANNON T,** Wilkes Univ, Wilkes-Barre, PA; FR; BS; Bio Clb; Univ Schlrs Soc; Bio; Optmtry.

**SCHEURING, MALISSA A,** Franciscan Univ/Steubenville, Steubenville, OH; FR; Natl Wldlfe Fed 90-; Dante Scty 90-; Lfegrd Instrctr 90-; Tnns; Gtr; La Salle Hnr Scty 90; Amblnce Vol 90-; Lmplghtrs; Tutor; Ntwrk Mrktng Intrnshp; Frdhm Univ Dns Schlrshp; Dscpls Of Christ Schlrshp; Trsts Schlrshp; Frsbee Ftbl; Bus Admin; Envir Law.

**SCHIAFFINO, SABRINA S,** Wagner Coll, Staten Island, NY; SO; BA; Schl Nwspr 89-; Pltcl Sci Clb 90; Yrbk; Alethea; Ctchst 88-; Pol Sci.

**SCHIAPPA, SUSAN M,** Providence Coll, Providence, RI; SR; BA; Wrtng Flw F89-; Pre Law Clb 90-; CCD Instrctr 88-89; Hon Pgm 89-; Phi Sgm Tau 90-; Intrn Dept Atty Gen; Engl; Law.

**SCHIAVONE, DYLAN L,** Univ Of Miami, Coral Gables, FL; SO; BA; Music.

**SCHICK, CRAIG M,** Fl A & M Univ, Tallahassee, FL; SR; BS; Elec Tech 82-; Elec; Naval Pilot.

**SCHICK, MARIAN L,** Marshall University, Huntington, WV; FR; BU; Campus Crusade Christ 90-; Bsns; Mgmnt.

**SCHICKRAM, DARLENE A,** Seton Hall Univ, South Orange, NJ; BS; N J Buddies Vol 89-; St Barnabas Med Ctr 86-; AS Harcum Jr Clg 85; Nrsg.

**SCHIELE, LORI M,** Coll Of Charleston, Charleston, SC; FR; BED; Mort Bnkng 6 Yrs Ln Offcr; Math Edctn; HS Tchr.

**SCHIFERLE, CAROL A,** S U N Y Coll At Fredonia, Fredonia, NY; JR; BS; Clg TV Sta Pgm Mgr 90-; Stdnt Assoc TV Pgm Prod; Clg Newspaper Stf Wrtr 90; Game Show Prod; Renaissance Color Guard 82-; Vars Vlybl 88-90; Cmnctns/Media; TV Prod.

**SCHIFF, JEFFREY C,** City Univ Of Ny Baruch Coll, New York, NY; GD; Arts Edtr For Nwspaper 89-90; Grad Magna Cum Laude; Sr Netwrk Admstrtr; Cert Weston Inc; BSX Univ Of NY State 90; Prsnl Comptr Applctns; Microtechnlgy/Cmnctns.

**SCHIFF, PATRICIA G,** Chattanooga St Tech Comm Coll, Chattanooga, TN; FR; AAS; PT Asst Clb VP 90-; Dept Mgr 75-89; Sci; Physcl Thrpst Asst.

**SCHIFFHAUER, KRISTIN L,** Allegheny Coll, Meadville, PA; SR; BA; Scty Fr Advncmnt Gndr Eqlty Co Pres 88-; Allegheny Stdnts Advctng Dvstmnt Pres 88-; Racl Issues Comm 88-; Lamba Sigma 88-89; Psi Chi; Tchng Asst 90-; Outstndng Cntrbtn Ldrshp 89-90; IMS 87-89; Psychlgy.

**SCHIFFMAN, RANDI ALLISON,** Cornell Univ, Ithaca, NY; SO; BS; Class Cncl 90-; Orntn; Consumer Econ & Hsng Advsng Frshmn Stdnt Advsr 90-; Blood Drive 90-; Chi Omega 90-; Econ; Law.**

**SCHIFFOUR, KATHLEEN G,** Comm Coll Algny Co Algny Cmps, Pittsburgh, PA; SR; Phi Theta Kappa 90-.

**SCHIFINO, MARIA,** Teikyo Post Univ, Waterbury, CT; JR; BA; AS Manchester Comm Coll 90; Fashion Mrchndsng; Fashion Industry.

**SCHILD, MARC A,** City Univ Of Ny Queensbrough, New York, NY; JR; AS; Accntng; Bus Admn.

**SCHILD, NANCY ZINK,** Univ Of Sc At Coastal Carolina, Conway, SC; SO; BA; Saddle Club/Own 40% Shrs Feed/Tack Shop; Asst Cntrllr 86-; Bkkpng/Mrktng; Bus; Cnsltnt.

**SCHILDMAN, HEIDI M,** Univ Of Cincinnati, Cincinnati, OH; JR; BA; Homecmng Comm 91; Social Comm Flr 89-90; Elmtry Ed/Hstry; Elmntry Tchr.

**SCHILLACI, CHRISTINE M,** Christopher Newport Coll, Newport News, VA; SR; Sigma Pi 88-; Prsnl Intrnshp; BA Communicadia Cert; Indl Org Psychlgy.

**SCHILLER, LAUREN R,** East Carolina Univ, Greenville, NC; SR; BFA; Prntmkng Gld 90-; Art Shows; Wilson Honorable Mention/3rd Pl Graphics; Art/Prntmkng; Grad Schl.

**SCHILLING, AMANDA M,** Univ Of Southern Ms, Hattiesburg, MS; JR; BA; Amer Soc Interior Dsgnrs Pres 89-; Inst Bsn Dsgnrs 90-; Stdnt Hme Econ Assn; Kappa Omicron Nu V P 89-; Chi Omega Rcptn Chrmn 88; Gamma Beta Phi 89-; Mst Outstndng Soph Interior Dsgn Stdnt 90; Betty Dukes Craft Schlrshp; Interior Dsgn; Cmrcl Interior Dsgnr.

**SCHILLING, CHRISTY L,** Saint Joseph Coll, West Hartford, CT; JR; BS; Bio Clb Treas; Stdnt Acad Affairs Com Stdnt Rep Natl Sci Div 90-; Sister Mary Theodore Awd 90; Bio; Ph D Molecular Bio Coll Prof.

**SCHILLING, EILEEN A,** Georgian Court Coll, Lakewood, NJ; SR; BA; Crt Sngrs 87; De La Salle 88; Psychlgy Clb 88-89; Psi Chi 88-; Pi Delta Phi 88-; Dean Schlr 87-90; Gertrude Truner Mahon Schlrshp 87-; Psych; Schl Psych.

**SCHILLING, JUNE M,** Neumann Coll, Aston, PA; SR; Sigma Theta Tau; Ntl Arthrts Fndtn; Sigma Theta Tau; BS; Nrsg; Tchg.

**SCHILLING, SANDRA L,** Univ Of Southern Ms, Hattiesburg, MS; SO; BA; Stdnt Alumnae Assoc 90-; Gamma Beta Phi; Pi Beta Phi Secy 89-; PACER 90-; Greek Acadmc Exclnc Award; Psychlgy; Clncl.

**SCHIMMOELLER, CHRISTINA E,** Georgetown Coll, Georgetown, KY; SR; BA; Envrnmntl Actn Grp Co Fndr 89-; Afro Amer Stdnt Fllwshp 90-; Stdnt Govt 88; Edtr Of Yrbk 90; Cpy Edtr Nwsppr 88; Sigma Tau Delta VP 89-; Phi Alpha Theta; Eta Delta Phi Mst Otstndng Mmbr 90-; Alpha Lambda Delta Pres 89; Adpt Grndprnt 87-; Engl; MA Wrtr Envrnmntl Actvst.

**SCHIMMOELLER, KATRINA K,** Georgetown Coll, Georgetown, KY; SR; BA; Envrnmntl Actn Grp Co Fndr 89-; Edtr 90; Nwsppr Cpy Edit 88; Sigma Tau Delta Pres; Phi Alpha Theta; Eta Delta Phi; Alpha Lambda Delta Edtr 89; Adpt Grndprnt 87; Rcylc Prog; Envrnmntl Spkr; USA Tdy All Str; GTE All Amer 90-; Engl Hnrs Prog; Engl; MA Poet Envrnmntl Actvst.

**SCHIMOLER, LORRAINE J,** City Univ Of Ny Grad School, New York, NY; JR; BA; Twnty Five Pls Clb VP 87; Phi Theta Kappa 88; Golden Key 90; Belle Zeller Schlr 88; Psych/Sclgy.

**SCHINDLER, LYDIA J,** Wv Univ At Parkersburg, Parkersburg, WV; SO; AAS; Riply Chrch Of Nazarene; Nrsng; RN.

**SCHIPF, JENNIFER M,** Va Commonwealth Univ, Richmond, VA; FR; BA; Lecture Cmmttee 90; AIESEC Mrktng Dir 90; Phi Eta Sigma 90; Ecnmc; Auction Hse Admin.

**SCHIRF, DENNIS J,** Mount Aloysius Jr Coll, Cresson, PA; FR; OTA; OT Clb Specl Olys Cmte 90-; Phi Thetta Cappa; Occuptnl Therapy.

**SCHIRMACHER, ERNESTO,** Univ Of Rochester, Rochester, NY; JR; BA; Mth Clb; Intrntnl Stdnt Assn Bsns Mngr 89-; Pew Mdwst Sci Fllwshp 90; Math; Rsrch.

**SCHIRMER, DAVID R,** Germanna Comm Coll, Locust Grove, VA.

**SCHIRMER, KAREN L,** Wv Univ At Parkersburg, Parkersburg, WV; SO; BA; Christian Educ Brd; Children Tchr; Elem Educ; Educator.

**SCHIUMO, JOANNA M,** Wagner Coll, Staten Island, NY; SR; Stdnt Govt Clss Pres 89-90; Cmps Hrng Brd Sngfst Cmmtt Kllstg Exctv Brd Sec 90-; Yrbk Stff; Msclr Dstrphy Sprdnc Cmmtt Cl Dvlpmntl Dir 90-; Althea 90-; Alpha Delta Pi Treas Rsh Char Hmcmng Chr; Deans Lst Awrd 90-; Sftbll 89-.

**SCHIVERS, KATHY A,** Ms Gulf Coast Comm Coll, Perkinston, MS; SO; BA; Elem Educ; Spec Educ.

**SCHJANG, HENRY E,** Livingstone Coll, Salisbury, NC; JR; BA; Blcks Against Drunk Driving; NAACP; Intl Stdnt Assn; Natl Deans Lst; Bus.

**SCHLACHTER, SANDRA LEE,** Defiance Coll, Defiance, OH; SR; Natl Athl Trnrs Assoc Stdnt Trnr; Trinity United Meth Church Choir Pres; Msc Commission Pres; Acad Dns Lst; Elizabeth Howsare Integrity Awd; Wellworks Intern Defiance Fire Dept; Dn Stdnts Ldrshp Recog; Natl Athl Trnrs Assoc; Wellness/ Sports Med; Trnr.

**SCHLANGER, CINDY T,** Yeshiva Univ, New York, NY; GD; JD; Std Cncl Pres 89-90; Pol Sci Soc VP 87-89; Class VP 87-88; Aishel Hnrs Soc 89; Dns Lst 86-90; Stf Wrtr Undgrad Nwspr 88-90; RA 89; NY Govt Schlr 89; Intrn Spkr NYS Assmbly 88; Exclnc Pol Sci Awd; Almni Asc Awd; BA 90; AA; Pol Sci; Law.

**SCHLARB, JENNIFER A,** Kent St Univ Kent Cmps, Kent, OH; SO; BA; Kappa Phi Clb Pldg Crdntr 90-; Acctg; Pblc Acctg.

**SCHLARMAN, TAMMY K,** Northern Ky Univ, Highland Hts, KY; FR; BA; Bsktbl Tm Schlrshp; Bus; Acctng.

**SCHLATMANN, ROSEANN ELIZABETH,** Cazenovia Coll, Cazenovia, NY; FR; BA; Ski Clb Yrbk Comm 90-; Scr 90-; AS; Eng/Algbr/Hstry/Comp I II; Fshn Mrchndsng.

**SCHLAUCH, DANIEL F,** Salisbury St Univ, Salisbury, MD; SR; BA; Dns Lst 90; ASS Arts Montgomery Clge Rockville 87; Hstry/Art/Grphc Dsgn; Tchg.

**SCHLAUPITZ JR, GERALD ALLEN,** Wv Northern Comm Coll, Wheeling, WV; FR; Hnrbl Dschr Vet Sp 4 E 4 87; Accntng; CPA.

**SCHLEGEL, JENNIFER S,** Univ Of Akron, Akron, OH; SR; BSED; Hall Gvrnmnt Prsdnt 87-90; Rsdnc Hall Cncl 89-90; Habitat Hmnty 88-89; Otstndng Clg Stdnts Amrca 90-; Rsdnc Hall Stf Rsdnt Asstnt 90-; IM Ftbl Vlybl Bsktbl Sftbl Coach 87-; Elem Edctn; Tchng.**

**SCHLEGEL, KURT D,** Carnegie Mellon Univ, Pittsburgh, PA; SO; BS; RA; Sigma Alpha Epsilon 89-; IM Sports; Indus Mgmnt.

**SCHLEICHER, DANIA M,** Teikyo Post Univ, Waterbury, CT; SR; BS; Interior Dsgn Clb Prsdnt 90-; Alpha Chi 90-; Interior Dsgn; Cmmrcl Intr Dsgn.

**SCHLEIDER, WENDI L,** Savannah Coll Of Art & Design, Savannah, GA; SO; BFA; Mary Rene Nelliings Whelan Schlrshp 89; Sid Richardson Memorial Fund Grant 89; Graphic Design.

**SCHLEMAN, JODEY H,** Central Fl Comm Coll, Ocala, FL; SO; AS; Archtctr; Eng.

**SCHLEMMER, FELICIA I,** Univ Of Louisville, Louisville, KY; SR; BS; Data Proc Mgmt Assn Pres 89-90; Bus/Prof Women River City; AAS City Coll Of Chicago 86; Info Sci/Data Proc.

**SCHLEMMER, MICHAEL P,** Pittsburgh Tech Inst, Pittsburgh, PA; GD.

**SCHLEMMER, TODD R,** Wv Univ, Morgantown, WV; SR; BS; Stdnt Admin Brd Gvrnrs; Rsdnt Asst; Chrstn Stdnt Flwshp; Acdmy Stdnts Phrmcy; Hnrs Pgm; Phi Kappa Phi; Chms; Mntn; Rho Chi; Mrtrbrd; Gldn Key; Kappa Psi; Sigma Chi; Natl Phrmctcl Cncl Indstry Intrn; W Va Univ Pres Schlrshp; Phrmcy; Phrmcy Mgmt.

**SCHLENKER, JASON JOHN,** Columbia Greene Comm Coll, Hudson, NY; FR; BA; Ski Clb; Photography Clb; Scuba Diving Clb; Tennis; Skiing; Bus Admin; Mktg.

**SCHLENKER, JENNIFER A,** Union Univ, Jackson, TN; JR; BA; Sngrs Pres 88-; Prclmtn Vcl Ensmbl 89-; Pnhlnc Cncl Sec 89-90; Alpha Chi 90-; Sigma Alpah Iota 90-; Kappa Delta Sec 88-; Wm Dorm Cncl 89; Rsdnt Life Brd 89; Stdnt Advsry Brd 89-; Music/Cmmnctns Arts; Clg Prof.

**SCHLEY, ROGER C,** Univ Of Akron, Akron, OH; SO; BS; Apostolic Chrstn Ch Yth Grp Chrmn; Lab Asst 89; Chem Engr; Rsrch.

**SCHLICHTING, MARK A,** Embry Riddle Aeronautical Univ, Daytona Beach, FL; JR; BS; Entertainment Com 89-; Naval Aviation Clb 88-89; Delta Airlines Co-Op; IM Ftbl/Wallyball; Aeronautical Sci; Pilot.

**SCHLICK, ROBERT T,** S U N Y Coll At Fredonia, Fredonia, NY; SR; BA; PAC 90-; Alpha Psi Omega; Lcuille Ball Lttl Thtr Brd/Ply Rdng Comm/Hist 90-; AA Jamestown Comm Clg 72; Theatre Arts; Director.

**SCHLINKERT, RENEE A,** Univ Of Cincinnati, Cincinnati, OH; SO; BED; Judicial Review Ct 89-; Elem Educ; Teaching.

**SCHLITTER, TANYA S,** Indiana Univ Of Pa, Indiana, PA; SO; BED; SADD 90; Activities Brd 89-91; Orient 90; Eqstrn Tm 89; Elem Ed; Tchr.**

**SCHLONSKY, ALLISON L,** Univ Of Miami, Coral Gables, FL; FR; BA; Vrsty Tnns Tm; Psi Chi; Pumpkin Prst; Pre Med/Sprts Thrpst.

**SCHLOSS, DANIEL,** Yeshiva Univ, New York, NY; JR; BA; Newspapr Cpy Edtr 89; Lit Jrnl Poetry Edtr 90; Drmtcs Scty 88; Engl Hnr Scty VP 90; Deans Lst 89-90; Wrtng Awd; Best Intrprtve Essay On Lit; Engl; MA JD.

**SCHLOSSER, DAWN E,** Coll Misericordia, Dallas, PA; JR; BS; Coll Hon Assn; Pi Theta Epsilon Rep 90; UPS Schlrshp; Occptnl Thrpy.

**SCHLOSSER, JONATHAN R,** S U N Y At Albany, Albany, NY; FR; BS; Vars Wrestlng 90-; Biol; Med.

**SCHLOTMAN, BRYAN T,** Va Commonwealth Univ, Richmond, VA; SO; BS; Phi Eta Sigma 90-; Sigma Pi Sigma; Physics; Engr.

**SCHLUETER, BELINDA J,** Northern Ky Univ, Highland Hts, KY; FR; BS; Info Systms.

**SCHLUETER, KELLY M,** Univ Of Akron, Akron, OH; JR; BSEE; IEEE; Natl Eagle Sct Assn; Eta Kappa Nu; Gldn Key; Alpha Lambda Delta; Phi Eta Sigma; Elect Eng.

**SCHLUSSEL, DANIELA,** James Madison University, Harrisonburg, VA; SR; BS; Bnai Brith Hillel Fndtn :Vp 87-; Crcqtbll Clb 88-; AEYC Sec 88-; Gldn Key 90-; Stdnt Advsry Cncl 89; Emrgng Ldrs Smnr 88; Erly Chldhd Ed.

**SCHMAC, DONALD P,** Univ Of Pittsburgh, Pittsburgh, PA; SR; BSEE; USAIR Simulator Engr; Elec Engr.

**SCHMADER, TANYA M,** Washington & Jefferson Coll, Washington, PA; FR; BA; Nwmn Clb 90-; Pi Beta Phi Pldg Cls VP; GIVE VP; Psych; Coll Prfsr.

**SCHMECKENBECHER, JANETTE R,** Elmira Coll, Elmira, NY; GD; Kappa Delta Phi 90-; Speech Hrng Tchr.

**SCHMEER, KAMMI K,** Allegheny Coll, Meadville, PA; SO; ALLIES 90-; Pn Hel 90-; Kappa Kappa Gamma 90-; Hbtat Hmnty 90-; Soup Ktchn 90-; Alden Schlr 90-; Doane Schlr 90-; Vars Sccr IM Sftbl/Bsktbl 89-.

**SCHMEHL, CORINNE C,** Univ Of Sc At Columbia, Columbia, SC; FR; BA; Pgm Union; Alpha Lambda Delta; Gamma Beta Phi; Engl.

**SCHMELZER, RUTH A,** Oh Dominican Coll, Columbus, OH; FR; BA; Cmps Mnstry 90-; AIM 90; Edtrl Stff; Cir K 90-; Acdmc Schlrshp 90-; Two Hnrs Courses 90-; Engl; Ed.

**SCHMERL, LAURYN T,** Cornell Univ Statutory College, Ithaca, NY; SR; PHD; Clss Cncl Cmncemnt Chrprsn 90-; Stdnt Serv Tutr 89; Goldn Key 90-; Gamma Sigma Delta 90-; Sigma Delta Tau 89-; Inst Chld Dvlpmnt Intrnshp 90; BS; Psychlgy.**

**SCHMID, ELSIE E,** Fayetteville St Univ, Fayetteville, NC; SO; BS; Engl; Tchr Scndry.

**SCHMID JR, G NICOLAS,** Central Pa Bus School, Summerdale, PA; FR; DPMA Treas; Steering Comm; Jdcry Comm; Phi Beta Lambda; Cmptr Sci; Prgrmr/Analyst.

**SCHMID, JULIE A,** Muskingum Coll, New Concord, OH; JR; BA; Phi Theta Beta; Asst Sndy Schl Tchr 89-; Admtnc Two Stdnt Juried Artshows 90-; Art Ed; Tchr.

**SCHMID, KATHRYN M,** Univ Of Cincinnati-Clrmnt Coll, Batavia, OH; FR; ASSOC; Pre-Scl Wrk; Scl Wrk.

**SCHMID, MATTHEW M,** Fl St Univ, Tallahassee, FL; FR; BA; Phi Eta Sigma; IM Ftbl Bsktbl Sftbl 90-.

**SCHMID, SHERI E,** Univ Of Miami, Coral Gables, FL; JR; BS; Res Asst 89-; Hmcmg Exec Comm 90-; Fndy Exec Comm 89-; Phi Kappa Phi 90-; Psy Chi 89-; Gldn Key 90-; Coll Arts/Sci Alumni Assoc Schlr 90-; Univ Miami Hnr Cncl 89-; IM Sccr 88-; Psychbio; Med.**

**SCHMID, URSULA E,** Cornell Univ Statutory College, Ithaca, NY; FR; BS; Ntv Amer Stu Crnl 90; Rcyclg Comm 90-; Res Advsr Slctn Comm; Bio; Rsrch.

**SCHMIDHAMMER, ROBIN D,** Saint Francis Coll, Loretto, PA; SR; BS; Educ Clb Pres 89-90; New Theatre 89-; Avante Guarde 89-; Delta Epsilon Sigma; Hon Soc; Elem Edn; Elem Tchr.

**SCHMIDLI, DOREEN M,** Niagara Univ, Niagara Univ, NY; SR; BA; National Assoc Accts 89; Niagara Univ Acct Society 89; VITA 90; Internship/DE Cubeuo CPA Firm; Internship/Batt Carroll CPA Firm 89; AS; Niagara County Comm Clg 89; Acct; CPA.

**SCHMIDLIN, AMY D,** Univ Of Cincinnati, Cincinnati, OH; SO; BSN; Untd Way; Almn; Grnpc; Fnd Rsrs; Deans Lsts Awards; Sctry Dubois Chmcl; Lgl Scrtry Santen Hughes; AAB 87; Sci; RN.

**SCHMIDT PREEST, P RENEE,** Oh Dominican Coll, Columbus, OH; SO; BA; Vlybl League Tm Cptn 86-; Deans List 88-90; Mary Matesich Gondola Schrlshp 90; Legal Secty/Assist; Comm/Law.

**SCHMIDT, ALAN E,** Univ Of New Haven, West Haven, CT; SO; Accntng Clb VP 90-; Schl Nwsppr 90-; Ornttn Ldr; Otstndng Achvmnt Awrd 90-; Fr Rsrch Ppr Awrd 90; IM Sftbl 90-; Accntng/Engl; Accntng.

**SCHMIDT, DORIS L,** Milligan Coll, Milligan Clg, TN; FR; BS; Wmns Ensmbl 90-; One Act Plays; Mrchng Bnd/Color Grd/ETSU 90; Delta Kappa 90; Marine Blgy.

**SCHMIDT, ELIZABETH M,** Providence Coll, Providence, RI; FR; BS; Prgrm Brd; Envrnmntl Clb 90-; Pstrl Cncl 90-; Math/Cmptr Sci.

**SCHMIDT, ERIC B,** Univ Of Fl, Gainesville, FL; SR; Grmn Tbl 90-; BSBA; Cmptr Infrmtn Sys; Cnsltng.

**SCHMIDT, GARY S,** Univ Of Cincinnati-Clrmnt Coll, Batavia, OH; SO; BA; Phi Beta Kappa 89-; Soc Wrk; MSW/CLNCL Soc Wrkr.

**SCHMIDT, HEATHER M,** Nyack Coll, Nyack, NY; SR; BS; Brklyn Gspl Tm Gen 89-; AA Nassau Comm Clg Garden Cty NY 89; Elem Educ; Tchr.

**SCHMIDT, HOLLY ANNE,** City Univ Of Ny Baruch Coll, New York, NY; SR; BA; Clg Radio Gen Mgr 90 Mus Dir 86; Psychology; Music Indus.

**SCHMIDT, JOSEPH D,** Embry Riddle Aeronautical Univ, Daytona Beach, FL; SR; BA; Soc Comm Aviatn Tech 90-; Deans Lst 89-90; Aviatn Maint Tech Lab Asst 89-; Assoc Aviatn Maint Tech; Aviatn Tech.

**SCHMIDT, JUAN R,** Barry Univ, Miami, FL; BA; Bus; Indus Engr.

**SCHMIDT, KEVIN E,** Le Moyne Coll, Syracuse, NY; FR; BA; Ski Clb; Radio Pres; Envrnmntl Coltn; Dean Lst; Pol Sci; Law.

**SCHMIDT, MARLA C,** Liberty Univ, Lynchburg, VA; JR; BA; Hlth Maj Cl Secy 89-; Dorm Prayer Ldr 89-; Alpha Lambda Delta 89-; Hlth 499 Intnshp Restorative Aide 90; Cmmnty Hlth Prmtn; Phys Therp.**

**SCHMIDT, MARTINA K,** Fl Atlantic Univ, Boca Raton, FL; SR; MBA; Phi Kappa Phi; Deans Lst 87-88; Tennis 89-; BA; Bus Admin; Intl Bus.

**SCHMIDT, MEGAN,** Comm Coll Algny Co Algny Cmps, Pittsburgh, PA; SR; Clnry Arts.

**SCHMIDT, NICOLE L,** Northern Ky Univ, Highland Hts, KY; SR; BA; Phi Theta Kappa 89; AS S St Comm Coll 89; Elem Ed; Tchr.

**SCHMIDT, PAULA S,** Catawba Valley Comm Coll, Hickory, NC; FR; Nrsng.

**SCHMIDT, PHYLLIS M,** Columbia Greene Comm Coll, Hudson, NY; FR; AS; Am Red Cross WSI 89-; Rcrtn Assc Brd Dir 88-; Nrsng.

**SCHMIDT, RAYMOND G,** Hudson Valley Comm Coll, Troy, NY; SO; BA; Amer History Sec Educ; Teacher.

**SCHMIDT, ROBYN P,** Marywood Coll, Scranton, PA; FR; Tchrs Tmrrw Clb VP 90-; Stu Gvt Soc Rep; Hnrs Prog 90-; Elem Educ; Educ.

**SCHMIDT, SARAH L,** Miami Jacobs Jr Coll Of Bus, Dayton, OH; FR; AABFM; Fashion Mchndsng; Buyer.

**SCHMIDT, STEPHANIE A,** Univ Of Akron, Akron, OH; SO; BS; ACES 90-; Tchr.

**SCHMIDTLING, SHELLY A,** Bishop St Comm Coll, Mobile, AL; SO; ADN; Daulphin Way Hstrcl Soc; Phi Theta Kappa; Cntrl Prsbytrn Church Ed Com; AS Drftng Dsgn Tech MS Gulfcoast Jr Clg Jefferson Davis Cmps 83; Nrsng RN.

**SCHMIEDER, GUYNELLE,** Saint Francis Coll, Loretto, PA; JR; BSN; Stdnt Nrsng Organ 88-; Tchng Asst Anatomy Phys 90-; Nrsng; Clncl Instrctr Nsrg.

**SCHMIEDER, LIZA L,** Va St Univ, Petersburg, VA; SO; BA; Science; Envrnmntl Sci.

**SCHMIEDER, LORI A,** Glassboro St Coll, Glassboro, NJ; SO; BA; Women In Cmmnctns; Public Rltns Stdnt Scty Amer; Natl Hnr Scty Secy 87-; Distngshd Schlr 87-; Cmmnctns Mjr Schlrshp 87-; Cmmunications; Law.

**SCHMIEDICKE, ERIC B,** Univ Of Tn At Knoxville, Knoxville, TN; FR; BA; Vlybl Tm Clb 90-; RUF 90-; Jr Inter Frat Cncl 90; Phi Eta Sigma; Alpha Lambda Chi; Phi Gamma Delta Pldg Pres 90-; Emrgng Ldrs Cnfrnce 90-; English/Business; Law.

**SCHMINK, SUZANNE MARIE,** Endicott Coll, Beverly, MA; JR; AS; Bsns Clb 89-; Phi Theta Kappa 90-; Intrnshp Kona Corp Gloucester MA 90-; Accntng; CPA.

**SCHMINKE, DARA C,** Pa St Univ Main Cmps, University Pk, PA; FR; BA; Art; Grphc Dsgn.

**SCHMIT, ANDREW D,** Embry Riddle Aeronautical Univ, Daytona Beach, FL; SO; BA; Soccr Clb 90-; Deans Lst 89-; Aerntcl Sci; Aviatn.

**SCHMITMEYER, KARLA J,** Wilmington Coll, Wilmington, OH; JR; BA; IM Vlybl Bsktbl 88-; Alpha Phi Kappa 89-; Dns Lst; Vrsty Vlybl 88-; Elem Educ; Tchr.

**SCHMITT, CAROL A,** Va Commonwealth Univ, Richmond, VA; GD; Tchr ESOL 89-; Phi Kappa Phi 90-; Sigma Sigma Sigma Alumni Advsr 73-79; Charlotte Newcomb Fndtn Awd Schlrshp 84; Outstanding Coed Contest 77; Smo Ketree Wmns Clb 89-90; PTA 88-; Sub Tchng; BBA 85; BA 77; Cmptr Sci/Bus Admin.

**SCHMITT, CHRISTIE A,** Liberty Univ, Lynchburg, VA; JR; BA; Engl; Ed.

**SCHMITT, DEANNA L,** Univ Of Nc At Chapel Hill, Chapel Hill, NC; GD; JD; Orient Cnslr Incoming Law Stdnts 90-; NC Law Review 90-; Phi Delta Phi 89-; Pblshd Law Review; IM Sftbl/Law Schl 90-; BA 89; Law.

**SCHMITT, DEANNE M,** Univ Of Rochester, Rochester, NY; JR; BS; Intern Strong Memorial Hosp; AS Comm Coll Finger Lakes 85; Molecular Gntcs; Rsrch Inhrtd Genetic Disease.

**SCHMITT, DENISE T,** Southeastern Coll Of Hlth Sci, N Miami Beach, FL; SR; PHARM; Cls Secr 89-; APHA 89-; NARD 90-; Dns Lst 89-; Pharmacy Intern 89-; Phrmcy.

**SCHMITT, JENNIFER A,** Spartanburg Technical Coll, Spartanburg, SC; SR; BA; Ltry Clb Pres 90-; Omicron Delta Kappa 90-; Herary Mag Edtr; Amer Yth Sccr Org Coach 89-; Engl; Pblctns/Advrtsng.

**SCHMITT, LAURA R,** Univ Of Akron, Akron, OH; JR; BA; Intrntl Bus Clb 90-; APICS Awds Dir; Golden Key 87-; Outstndg Coll Stdnts Amer 87-; Deans Lst 87-; Sigma Iota Epsilon 90-; Co-Op Ericsson GE 90; Bus Mgmt; Qlty Cntrl.

**SCHMITZ, BRIAN F,** Atlantic Comm Coll, Mays Landing, NJ; SO; AS; Law/Jstce; Law.

**SCHMITZ, JOELLE A,** Drew Univ, Madison, NJ; JR; BA; Frnch Clb Pres 88-; Coll Dem Pres Elect 88-; Dnc; Intrnatl Stdnts Assn Dorm Cncl 90; Fcath Stdnts Assn Smstr Abrd Mc Gill Univ Montreal Canada 90; Pi Sigma Alpha Sec; Dns Lst 88-; Intrnshp Montreal Bd Of Trade Spec Asst; Pol Sci.**

**SCHMITZ, TONY L,** Temple Univ, Philadelphia, PA; JR; BA; Deans Lst 89-; Acdmc Schlr Ftbl; Mchncl Engnrng.

**SCHMOLL, JERRON T,** Oh St Univ At Newark, Newark, OH; SO; BS; Hon Soc 89-90; Zoology; Envrnmntl Sci.

**SCHMOLT, JOHNATHAN P,** Northern Ky Univ, Highland Hts, KY; FR; BS; Amer Chem Soc Stdnt Afflt Pres; Cthlc Newman Cntr; Hon Clb; Chmstry.

**SCHMOOK, JEFFREY C,** Indiana Univ Of Pa, Indiana, PA; JR; BS; Kappa Mu Epsilon Vp 90; Ntl Clgte Math Awd Wnnr 90-91; IM 89-91; Math; Tchng.

**SCHMOYER, JASON S,** Temple Univ, Philadelphia, PA; JR; BS; Sigma Nu Soc Chmn 90-; Fuller Co; Mech Eng.

**SCHMUCKLER, AMIE R,** Ga St Univ, Atlanta, GA; SR; BED; Kappa Delta Pi; Delta Phi Epsilon; BA Univ Of GA 88; Early Chldhd Ed; Tchr.

**SCHNABEL, HERBERT H,** Columbus Coll Of Art & Design, Columbus, OH; JR; BFA; Illstrtn; Pblshng.

**SCHNARS, JOHN C L,** Univ Of Ga, Athens, GA; JR; BSPHR; Amer Stdnt Phrmcy Assn 90-; APHA GPHA 90-; Kappa Psi Phrmctcl 90-; Commnsity 88-89; Phrmcy Intrnshp 90-; Chem Tutr 89-90; IM Sprts 90-; Phrmcy; Med.

**SCHNATMEIER, ROBERT F,** Coll Of Charleston, Charleston, SC; SR; BS; Bata Gamma Sigma; Sigma Alpha Epsilon 90-; Cum Laude; Deans Lst 89-; Vrsty Bsktbl 87-; Bus; GA State Coll Law.

**SCHNATZ, AMY C,** Temple Univ, Philadelphia, PA; SO; BA; Phys Ed Undergrad Assn Sec 89-; Athltc Trnrs Clb 90-; Phys Ed; Athltc Trning.

**SCHNAUFER, JUDITH C,** S U N Y Coll At Fredonia, Fredonia, NY; JR; BS; Acctg Soc Sec 89-; Delta Mu Delta 90-; Acctg/Cmptr Sci; CPA.

**SCHNECK, MATTHEW J,** Villanova Univ, Villanova, PA; JR; BA; Villanova Stdnt Theater Savage Love/Wedding Eiffel Tower/Dr Tarr/Prof Fether 89-; Princeton Summer Theater Mousetrap/Much Ado About Nothing; Engl; Prfrmng Arts.

**SCHNEE, DIANE E,** Kent St Univ Kent Cmps, Kent, OH; SO; BS; Acctng.

**SCHNEIDER, DAVID E,** Barry Univ, Miami, FL; SO; BA; Crs Cntry Tm; MVP 89; Conf Runr Wk 89-90; Crs Cntry 89-; Sprts Med; Exer Physlgst.

**SCHNEIDER, DEBRA A,** Univ Of Akron, Akron, OH; JR; BSBA; Goldn Key; Delta Sigma Pi Sec; Coop Educ; Bus Mgmt.

**SCHNEIDER, DONNA S,** Radford Univ, Radford, VA; SO; BS; ASID 89-90; Gymnstcs Tm 89-90; Intr Dsgn; Archtctr.

**SCHNEIDER, ELISSA C,** Rivier Coll, Nashua, NH; JR; BA; Fine Arts Soc VP 90-; RA 90; Coll/Sunset Elem Buddy Pgm 89-; Studio Art; Art Admin.**

**SCHNEIDER, GLENN M,** Ramapo Coll Of Nj, Mahwah, NJ; SR; BA; Ski Club 88-; Church Youth Grp Ldr Asst Dir 88-; Phi Ro Pi Manhattan Clg 86-87; Vusual Arts Photogrphy; Photogrphr Stl/Video.

**SCHNEIDER, JEFFERY E,** Radford Univ, Radford, VA; SO; BA; Engl; Tchr.

**SCHNEIDER, JENNIFER,** Wagner Coll, Staten Island, NY; SR; BS; Sngfst Cmmttee; Hmcmng Cmmttee 90f Res Hall Guild Hall Treas 90; Alpha Kapa Delta; Alpha Delta Pi Treas 88; Campus Cmmnty Chest Frndrsr 88; Muscular Dystrophy Assoc Sprdnce 90; Im Sftbl 88-90; Econ/Bsnss Admin; Mngmnt In Bsnss Fld.

**SCHNEIDER, JEREL L,** Univ Of Ky, Lexington, KY; JR; BA; Engl/Creative Wrtng; Law.

**SCHNEIDER, LORI E,** Univ Of Akron, Akron, OH; SR; BED; Cncl Educ Stdnt 89-; Phi Theta Kappa 88-89; Gldn Key 89-; Rsdnt Asstnt; German Tutor; Elem Educ; Tchr.

**SCHNEIDER, MARK H,** Univ Of Akron, Akron, OH; SR; BA; Soc Stdnts Constr Active Mbr 87-88; Inter Clg Sftbl/Ftbl; ASC 89; Constr Tech; Engr.

**SCHNEIDER, MELISSA A,** Indiana Univ Of Pa, Indiana, PA; FR; Math; Elem Ed.

**SCHNEIDER, NANCY B,** Mount Saint Mary Coll, Newburgh, NY; JR; BA; Cmptr Prgrmr IBM 84-; AS Orange Cnty Comm Clg 84; Cmptr Sci; Prgrmmng.

**SCHNEIDER, NICHOLAS T,** Middle Tn St Univ, Murfreesboro, TN; SR; BBA; Fin Mgmt Assn Treas; Alpha Kappa Psi; Fin; Corp Anlst.

**SCHNEIDER, NOREEN M,** Newbury Coll, Brookline, MA.

**SCHNEIDER, PAUL,** S U N Y Coll Of Tech At Frmgdl, Farmingdale, NY; FR; BAS; Soc Of Mfg Engrs 90-; Mech Engrng Tech; Mech Engr.

**SCHNEIDER, ROBERT B,** Fl International Univ, Miami, FL; GD; Phi Kappa Phi 90-; Pblc Schls 90-.

**SCHNEIDER, ROSEMARY,** Notre Dame Coll, Cleveland, OH; FR; BA; Vp; Acctg Assc; Lambda Sigma Scty Treas; Intrclgte Vlybl/Bsktbl; Bus; Own Bus.

**SCHNEIDER, SHERRY,** Gallaudet Univ, Washington, DC; GD; MA; Pre Schlr Prog 89-; Acdmc Schlrshp 89-; Wmn Sobriety Inc 85-; Ratnl Rcvry Syst; BA City Univ (Y 75; Addctns Cnslng.

**SCHNEIDER, STEPHEN W,** Univ Of Cin R Walters Coll, Blue Ash, OH; SO; Ed; HS Engl Tchr.

**SCHNEIDER, TIMOTHY J,** Comm Coll Algny Co Algny Cmps, Pittsburgh, PA; FR; BA; Amer Water Wrks Assn 89-; Assoc Acctg 83; Sci; Eng.

**SCHNEIDER, VALERIE A,** Cornell Univ Statutory College, Ithaca, NY; FR; BS; Sage Chapel Choir; Red Carpet Hosting Soc 90-; Balch Hall Comm Outreach Com 90-; Bio; Genetic Rsrch.

**SCHNELLBACHER, ROBIN A,** Kent St Univ Kent Cmps, Kent, OH; SR; BA; Kent Cncl Fam Rels 90-; Kinder Care Lrng Ctr Intern; Indiv/Fam Stds; Day Care Adm.

**SCHNELLE, CHRISTINA A,** Wv Northern Comm Coll, Wheeling, WV; FR; AS; All St Church; Seszko Internal Tae Kwon Do 89; Wheeling Hostp LPN & CRTT 72-78; LPN Degree Bellaire Chl Practical Nsg 70; AA Degree Belmont Cnty Br Ohio Univ 77; Respiratory Care Technician.

**SCHNEPPLE, MICHELLE R,** Middle Tn St Univ, Murfreesboro, TN; SR; BS; STEA 88-; Elem Educ; Tchng/Spec Educ.

**SCHNESSEL, AMY L,** Fl International Univ, Miami, FL; JR; BA; HFTA 90-; Intrn Sonesta Intl Htls; Sir Sonesta Instnt Resrvtns; Hosp Mgmt; Food Bvrge Mgmt.

**SCHNIPPER, ALAN M,** Yeshiva Univ, New York, NY; JR; BA; Res Cncl 90-; Bk Sale Comm Mgr 89-; Deans Lst 89-90; Hist; Law.

**SCHNITTER, JANE T,** Univ Of Nc At Greensboro, Greensboro, NC; JR; BED; Author; Wrtrs Clb; Engl/Art/Educ; Wrt/Publsh/Tch.

**SCHNURR, EVELYN,** Ny Univ, New York, NY; SR; BA; Scl Sci.

**SCHNURR, SHERI S,** Gaston Coll, Dallas, NC; SO; AA; Outstndng Grdte Crmnl Justc; Oper Therapeutic Home 88-; Crmnl Justc; Law.

**SCHOCK, SANDY S,** Western Ky Univ, Bowling Green, KY; SR; BS; Chrch Choir; Bell Choir; Beta Gamma Sigma Vp; Phi Kappa Phi; Golden Key; Phi Beta Lambda; Prchsng Mgt Schlrshp; Bus Mngmnt; Mngmnt Cnsltg/Law.

**SCHOELEN, TERESA M,** Broward Comm Coll, Ft Lauderdale, FL; SO; BBA; Pres Lst OK Univ 89; Mgmt; Law.

**SCHOEN, STEPHANIE COOPER,** Smith Coll, Northampton, MA; Phi Beta Kappa; James T/Ellen M Mem Short Story Awd; Pres Discrtnry Fund Grant; Engl; Publshg.

**SCHOENBAECHLER, DAVID C,** Bellarmine Coll, Louisville, KY; SR; BS; Math Club 88-; Acctng 88-; Pres Ldrshp Soc 88-; Delta Epsilon Sigma 90-; Capital Holding Corp Intern 90-; Golf 88-89; Actuarial Sci; Acturial Acctng.

**SCHOENBERG, HEIDI S,** Temple Univ, Philadelphia, PA; JR; BA; Bsns Admn; Hotel/Rest Mgmt.

**SCHOENBORN, CARMEN L,** Christopher Newport Coll, Newport News, VA; JR; Lgl Sec 86-; Bsn Admn/Acctng; Lgl Sec.

**SCHOENEBERGER, MARLIES L,** Spalding Univ, Louisville, KY; SR; BA; Phi Theta Kappa 89; Delta Epsilon Sigma; Cert Merit Otstndng Achvmnt Soc 89; Cert Merit Hgh Distnctn Acdmc Achvmnt 89; AA Jefferson Comm Coll 89; Sociology/Psychology; Gerontology.

**SCHOENHERR, WILLIAM J,** Wright St Univ Lake Cmps, Celina, OH; SO; ADAS; Elec; Engr.

**SCHOENING, HELEN MATARAZZO,** Fl International Univ, Miami, FL; SR; BSN; Nrs; BA 78; Nrsg; RN.

**SCHOENLY, TARA M,** Pa St Univ York Cmps, York, PA; FR; BA; Aerbcs; IM Flr Hcky; Bsns; Airln Mgmt.

**SCHOENSTEIN, DOROTHY T,** Atlantic Comm Coll, Mays Landing, NJ; GD; BA; Jwsh Stdnts Assn VP 90; Prnt Advsry Com Helmbold Educ Cntr 89-90; Media Cntr Coord Rgnl Day Schl 87-89; Tchr Hndcppd.

**SCHOENSTRA, MARGARET A,** Ashland Comm Coll, Ashland, KY; FR; BA; History.

**SCHOEPFLIN, JONATHAN D,** Va Commonwealth Univ, Richmond, VA; FR; BA; Symphc Wnd Ensbl 90-; Intrcoll Bnd 90-; Brs Qnt 90-; Woodwnd Qnt 90-; Advsry Comm Rep 90-; Phi Eta Sigma; Asst Music Dept 90-; Music; Tchng/Prfrmng.

**SCHOETTMER, JASON M,** Univ Of Cincinnati, Cincinnati, OH; FR; BSBA; IM Bsktbl Hd Coach; Bsn/Mktg; Mktg.

**SCHOFIELD, KELLY A,** Lesley Coll, Cambridge, MA; SR; BS; Commuter Clb 89-; Blessed Scrmnt Wntrgrd Capt 89-90; Bus Mgt.

**SCHOFIELD, LORA L,** Univ Of West Fl, Pensacola, FL; JR; BA; AA Okaloosa Walton Cmmnty Clg 88-90; Elem Ed; Tchng.

**SCHOLLENBERGER, SCOTT R,** Univ Of Rochester, Rochester, NY; JR; BA; Undergrad Hstry Cncl Chrmn 90-; Intr Vrsty Chrstn Flwshp 88-; Hstry; Nvl Offcr.

**SCHOLZ, INGRID ANA WILHELMINA,** Saint Andrews Presbytrn Coll, Laurinburg, NC; SR; BA; Stdnt Lit Mag 90; Campus Paper Co Edtr 89-90; Alpha Chi 90-; St Andres 90-; Achvmnt Schlrshp 89-; SAAX Bradbury Flwshp 90-; Tchrs Asstshp Theatre Comm Dir; English Creative Wrtr; English.

**SCHOLZ, KEVIN E,** Hudson Valley Comm Coll, Troy, NY; FR; BA; Pres List & Deans List 90-; English; Film Writer.

**SCHOLZ, MICHAEL A,** Va Commonwealth Univ, Richmond, VA; SR; BA; Art Educ Soc Sec; Boys Club Of Richmond; AAS State Univ Of NY 83; Art Tchr.

**SCHON, LEIGH ANN,** S U N Y Coll Of Tech At Alfred, Alfred, NY; SO; AS; Actvts Cncl VP 90-; Stdnt Senate Acdmcs Chr 90-; Sigma Tau Epsilon 89-90; Srch Comm VP Stdnt Svc; Srch Comm Asst Dir Stdnt Actvts 90; Bus Adm; Mgmnt.

**SCHONTZ, MARK W,** West Liberty St Coll, West Liberty, WV; FR; BA; Engr/Pharmacy.

**SCHOOF, PATRICIA D,** Hudson Valley Comm Coll, Troy, NY; FR; AS; Ntry Pblc; Cmptrlr Employee Rltns Offc; Bsns Admnstrtn; Accntng.

**SCHOOLCRAFT, BRENT D,** Liberty Univ, Lynchburg, VA; SR; BS; Bus; Finance.

**SCHOOLCRAFT, GEORGE BERNARD,** Toccoa Falls Coll, Toccoa Falls, GA; SR; BS; Mssnry Flwshp Pres; Intclgt Rlgs Brdcstrs; Phi Delta Epsln; Cmmctns; Mssnry.

**SCHOOLER, LUCINDA J,** Univ Of Akron, Akron, OH; SR; ACES 90-; Goldn Key 89-90; Kappa Delta Pi 90-; Coll Of Ed Schlrshp 90-; Sec 87-; BED; Elem Ed; Tchng.

**SCHOOLEY, CRYSTAL L,** Daytona Beach Comm Coll, Daytona Beach, FL; SO; BS; Mdcl Rcrd Stdnt Assn Tres 90-; Prsdnts Lst 89-; Deans Lst 89-; AMRA Schlrshp 90-; ABWA Schlrshp 90-; PTA Offcr 84-88; Comm Chrwm 84-88; Wmns Sftbl Offcr 87-88; Mdcl Rcrd Tchnlgy; Accrdtd Rcrd Tchncn.

**SCHOOLEY, KARYN L,** Schenectady County Comm Coll, Schenectady, NY; SR; AA; Pres Lst 89-90; Dns Lst 90; Worked The Carl Company Dept Store Clifton Park NY; BA Virginia Intermont Clg 88; Travel/Tourism.

**SCHOOLEY, MARGARET ANN,** Univ Of South Al, Mobile, AL; SR; BS; Leisure Serv Assn Pres 90-; Ala Recrtn/Prks Assn 90; I M 90; Cmptr Prgrmr U S Marine Corp 83-90; BS Educ Media 75; Leisure Serv; Rcreatn Rsrc Mgmt.

**SCHOONE, DARLENE,** Chatfield Coll, Saint Martin, OH; SO; BS; Sclgy; Rehab Cnslr.

**SCHOONOVER, DARLENE S,** Columbia Union Coll, Takoma Park, MD; SO; BS; Campus Mnstries Tutrng Dir 90-; Alpha Sigma Beta 88-; Phi Eta Sigma 88-; Advntst Yth Serv Tchr 89-90; Bus; Admin.

**SCHOONOVER, SHEILA R,** Univ Of Tn At Martin, Martin, TN; SR; BS; Alpha Delta Pi Chpln 87-F Kappa Alpha Sthrn Blle 90-; Ordr Of Omega 90-; Phi Kappa Phi 89-F Phi Eta Sigma 88-; Scty Of Prfssnl Jrnlsts Pres 88-; Intrnshp Tnnssn 89-; Schl Nwsppr Exec Edit 88-; Hnrs Smnr Schlrshp 87-; Cmmnctns Jrnlsmf Jrnlsm Educ.

**SCHOORE, JEROLYN E,** Univ Of Tn At Martin, Martin, TN; SR; Beta Beta Beta; Phi Eta Sigma; Phi Kappa Phi; UTM Tchng Asst; Outstndng Stdnt Arts/Sci; Bio; Grad Schl.

**SCHOOTS, HARRIE P,** Western New England Coll, Springfield, MA; FR; Schl Nwspr; Photo Clb Treas; Chemstry.

**SCHORNAGEL, JAMES H,** Longwood Coll, Farmville, VA; SR; MS; Tutr 90-; Deans Lst; BS Physcs 86-; Envrnmntl Eng.

**SCHORY, DAVID H,** Allegheny Coll, Meadville, PA; JR; BA; Chemii Pres 91-; Beta Beta Beta; Alden Schlr 89-90; Natl Sci Fndtn; Track 88-89; Chem; Ph D Rsrch/Devlpmnt.

**SCHORZMAN, BRYAN G,** Univ Of Miami, Coral Gables, FL; SO; BS; Stu Govt Elctns Cmmssnr 90-; IFC Rep 89-; Tau Kappa Epsilon Hstrn 89-; Mstr Tutor; Biol Clb 89-90; Intern TX Utlts 90-; IM 89-; Chmcl Eng; Eng.

**SCHOSSLER JR, JOHN J,** Kent St Univ Kent Cmps, Kent, OH; SR; BA; Lambda Alpha Epsilon 90; Crmnl Jstce; MBA Drug Enfrcemnt Admin.

**SCHOTT, ELENA,** Cornell Univ Statutory College, Ithaca, NY; FR; BS; Ptry Wrkshp; Asst Entmlgy Lab; Blgy; Eclgy And Systmtcs.

**SCHOTTEL, DAVID MICHAEL,** Memphis St Univ, Memphis, TN; FR; BBA; Bus.

**SCHOTTNER, SUZANNE,** Univ Of Cincinnati, Cincinnati, OH; SR; Kappa Delta Pi; BED.

**SCHOU, THOMAS K,** Fl Atlantic Univ, Boca Raton, FL; JR; BA; Acctg Stdnts Assoc Bd Dir; Alpha Gamma Rho 88-90; Spcl Svc Teller; AAS Univ NH 89; Bsn/Acctg; CPA.

**SCHOULTIES, VICKI R,** Northern Ky Univ, Highland Hts, KY; SR; BA; Wesley Fndtn; SNEA Treas; Elem Ed K-4; Educ/Tchng.

**SCHRADER, S REBECCA,** Memphis St Univ, Memphis, TN; SR; BS; STEA 90-; Bsktbl Chrldng Co Capt 81-82; Jr Achvmnt Prog Instructor 89; Admin Asstnt 83-90; Elem Educ; Teach.

**SCHRAGE, LORINDA J,** Elmira Coll, Elmira, NY; SR; BA; Intrnshp Howell Advrtsng; Untd Way 89-; AS Corning Comm Clg 89; Bsns Admnstrtn; Mrktng.

**SCHRAM, SCOTT A,** Univ Of Akron, Akron, OH; FR; BS; Univ Hon Prog; Chem Engr.

**SCHRAMEK, KAREN E,** Hudson Valley Comm Coll, Troy, NY; FR; AAS; Erly Chldhd Club; Pres List 90; Erly Chldhd Edn; Elem Edn.

**SCHRAMM, C D BENEDIKT,** A D Little Mgmt Educ Inst, Cambridge, MA; GD; MSM; Genl Mgmt.

**SCHRANKEL, PETER,** Atlantic Union Coll, S Lancaster, MA; SR; BS; Dgtl Equip Corp 87-; Bus Admin; Law.

**SCHRANTZ, CYNTHIA A,** S U N Y Coll At Fredonia, Fredonia, NY; GD; BS; Grad Cum Laude 90; SPAS; Natl Stu Spch Hrng Assc; NY Tele Co 71-; Spch Thrpst; BS SUNY Fredonia 90; Spch Lng Pthlgy; Pthlgst.

**SCHRECK, WILLIAM E,** Bowling Green St Univ At Huron, Huron, OH; SO; BA; Soc Mfg Engrs Sec; Ski Clb 90-; Wght Lftng; Nvy Elctrcn 85-89; Elctrnc Engrg Tchnlgy; Engr.

**SCHRECKENGOST JR, RONALD D,** Pa St Univ Main Cmps, University Pk, PA; FR; BS; Cvl Engrg.

**SCHREFFLER, JEFFERY M,** Univ Of Akron, Akron, OH; JR; BA; Mu Kappa Tau; Alpha Tau Omega 89-; Vrsty Bsbl 89-90; Mktg; Mktg Mgr/Sales.

**SCHREIBER, AVRAHAM J,** Yeshiva Univ, New York, NY; GD; BA; SG Rep 88-90; Israeli Pblc Affrs Comm Infrmtn 90-; Deans Lst 89-90; Bio; Med.

**SCHREIBER, CAREY D,** Yeshiva Univ, New York, NY; SO; Coll Sen Sen 90-; Econ; Law.

**SCHREIBER, CHANI P,** Yeshiva Univ, New York, NY; GD; BA; Scl Wrk Yeshiva Univ; Hmn Svcs; Adm Scl Wrk.

**SCHREIBER III, EDWARD R,** Univ Of Richmond, Richmond, VA; FR; BS; Cmps Actvty Brd 90; Otng Clb 90; Phi Kappa Sigma Schlrshp Offcr 90.

**SCHREIBER, PATRICIA A,** Dowling Coll, Oakdale Li, NY; SR; BA; Bbl Enrchmnt Clb VP 90-; Assoc Sflk Co Comm Coll 89; Econmst.

**SCHREIBER, ROBERTA H,** Nova Univ, Ft Lauderdale, FL; GD; MBA; Var Acturties; Pi Lambda Theta Hon 68; Kappa Delta Pi Hon 65-; Alpha Delta Delta Treas 63-67; Tch Asstnshp; Rgnts Schlrshp; Grad Cum Laude; Amer Soc Trng/Dev V P Fin 85-; MENSA; Mgr Trng Docmntatn; MA; BA; AAM; Human Rsrs Dev/Trang.

**SCHREIBER, VALERIE L,** Samford Univ, Birmingham, AL; FR; JD; Cumberland Law Review; Pres Acad Schlrshp 90-; Jr Achvmnt Proj Bus 88-90; Sr Claim Rep 87-90; BA Auburn Univ 83-87; Law.

**SCHREINER, GEORGE M,** Memphis St Univ, Memphis, TN; SR; BA; Memphis Greens Fcltr 89-; Social Wrk/Philosophy.

**SCHREINER, SUSAN C,** Immaculata Coll, Immaculata, PA; GD; Sigma Alpha Iota Music Sor 69-71; Sing Natl Anthem New Eng Patriots Each Yr; Taught Choral Music Music Theory & Comp Music Hist Piano Lab I & Ii Voice Pedogogy; Dir Of Music Adult Edn Classes; Instr Grad Stdnts In Applied Voice Gov St Univ Ill; Music; Teach Music/Scndry Or Coll Level.

**SCHREMP, JULIE C,** Fl St Univ, Tallahassee, FL; SR; BS; Hl Govt Sec/Treas 88-89; Natl Res Hl Hnry 89; Ftr Educ Amer 90-; Natl Res Hl Hnry Treas 90-; Kappa Delta Pi; Elem Educ; Teach.

**SCHROADER, BARRY G,** Owensboro Comm Coll, Owensboro, KY; FR; BS; Eng; Med Psych.

**SCHROCK, BRANDIE J,** Daytona Beach Comm Coll, Daytona Beach, FL; FR; PHD; Stdnt Senate Assn Sntr Acad 90-; Phi Theta Kappa VP 90-; Publ Sch Tchrs Asst 90-; Outstndg Frnch I Stdnt 90-; Soc Psychlgy.

**SCHROEDER, BRENDA S,** Univ Of Akron, Akron, OH; JR; BED; Amnsty 88-89; Cmps Hbt Hmnty; Alph Lmbd Dlt 89; Deans List 88-90; Elem Educ Engl; Tchng.

**SCHROEDER, CHRISTOPHER P,** Oh St Univ, Columbus, OH; SR; BS; Math Clb Pres 90-; Phi Kappa Phi 90-; Pi Mu Epsln Pres 90-; Mgmt Spprt Intrn Chckfree Corp 90; Tchng Ast/Instctr Pre Clcls Math 90-; Math.

**SCHROEDER, CHRISTOPHER R,** Limestone Coll, Gaffney, SC; SO; LCP 89-; M C Wicht Mem Schlp 90-; Bsbl 89-; Bio/Bsn.

**SCHROEDER, CYNTHIA R,** Memphis St Univ, Memphis, TN; SR; Wmns Action Coaltion Treas 90; MSU Hnrs Assoc; Golden Key 88-; Chi Beta Phi; William C Addington Psy Awd; Psychology; Ph D Clinical Neuropsychology.

**SCHROEDER, DIANA CAROLINA,** Dowling Coll, Oakdale Li, NY; JR; BA; Alpha Chi 90-; Dns Lst 89-; Spec Educ; Tchg.

**SCHROEDER, JULIA M,** Villanova Univ, Villanova, PA; JR; BA; Vars Sftbl Capt 88-; Financial Serv Intern; Econ.

**SCHROEDER, KYLE J,** Savannah Coll Of Art & Design, Savannah, GA; SR; BA; Pblcty Coord Taylor Stdnt Orgnztn 90; Press Serv Coord Taylor Stdnt Orgnztn 90-; Taylor Alumni; Brothers Of Swallow Robin Hall; Univ Nursing Hm Vol; Summer Mission Tm Mission Mexico; Prodctn Artist Ram Graphics 89; Bike Race 89; Art; Missionary.

**SCHROEDER, LEANNE E,** Franklin And Marshall Coll, Lancaster, PA; SO; Theatre Costume Shop/Dsgn/Actng 89-; Deans List 90-; John K Evans Award For Study France 90; Crew 89; Econ/French.

**SCHROEDER, MATTHEW J,** Allegheny Coll, Meadville, PA; JR; BS; Chemii Clb 90-; Lambda Sigma 89-90; Alden Schlr 89-90; Chem/Physcs; Tchng.

**SCHROEDER, MONIQUE D,** Norfolk St Univ, Norfolk, VA; JR; BA; Art Gld 90-; Grace Lthrn Chrch Chr 89-; Fine Art; Grphc Dsgn.

**SCHROEDER, ROBERTA A,** D Youville Coll, Buffalo, NY; GD; BA; SOTA; Hnr Soc 89-90; Prsdntl Hnr Stdnt 86-90; Occptnl Thrpy.

**SCHROEDER, RONALD M,** Univ Of Cincinnati, Cincinnati, OH; JR; BA; Archtctrl Eng; Eng.

**SCHROFF, JENNIFER P,** George Mason Univ, Fairfax, VA; SO; BS; Stdnts Envir Action 90; Tae Kwon Do; Aerobics Clb; Dance Tm; Chi Omega Pldg Cls 90/Assist V P/Schlrsh Chrmn/Drkpr; Natl Blck Belt Assn 88-; Olympic Trng Camp 87-88; Natl USTU/AAU Tae Kwon Do Champ 86-87; Bus Mgmnt; Human Rsrcs.

**SCHROTH, CHRISTINE R,** Northern Ky Univ, Highland Hts, KY; SR; BA; Phi Alpha Theta 90-; Scl Stds/Hstry; Scndry Ed.**

**SCHROTH, KAREN L,** Canisius Coll, Buffalo, NY; FR; BA; Finance; Bus.

**SCHRUBY, RHONDA J,** Alcorn St Univ, Lorman, MS; SR; BS; Cmptr Sci Clb VP 88-89; Prayer Bnd Mnstry Sen 90-; Bapt Stdnt Un Pgm Coord 87-88; Alpha Kappa Mu; Alpha Mu Gamma 89-; Res Uc San Diego R Mc Naire Fellow 90; Natl Achvmnt Awd 89-90; Math/Cmptr Sci/App Math; Prof.

**SCHUBERT, AMY M,** Asbury Coll, Wilmore, KY; FR; BA; Flwshp Chrstn Athlts 90-; Chldrns Mnstry Schriener Hosp Pro Life Org 90-; Pres Schlrshp 90-; IM Vlybl 90-; Engl; Scndry Educ.

**SCHUBERT, RYAN K,** Fl International Univ, Miami, FL; SR; BS; Scuba Club 90; Sigma Alpha Mu Treas 89-90; AAS Middlesex Cnty Cmnty Clg 89; Hosplty Mgt; Hotel/Restrnt Mgt.

**SCHUBERT, SHERRI S,** Salisbury St Univ, Salisbury, MD; SR; Big Bro/Sis 88-; Deans Lst; Tau Kappa Epsilon Treas 87-; Seaford Hse Res Trtmnt Ctr Cnslr 90-; BSW; Clncl Soc Wrkr.

**SCHUCK, ANTONIO CARLOS,** Univ Of New Haven, West Haven, CT; SR; BS; AS; Avtn; Airline Plt.

**SCHUCK, JENNIFER L,** Univ Of Ga, Athens, GA; SO; BSW; IM Bsktbl/Sftbl 89-; Scl Wrk; Grntlgy.

**SCHUCKERS, ERIK J,** Allegheny Coll, Meadville, PA; JR; BA; Wnd Symphny 88-90; Coll Lit Mag Ed 89-90; Cmps Nwsppr Arts Lsr Ed 89-90; Aldn Schlr Dstngshd Aldn Schlr 89-; Dn Schlr 89-; Engl.

**SCHUECK II, DAVID P,** West Chester Univ, West Chester, PA; GD; CERT; Arthur E Jones Mem Schlrshp 90; Schlr Award Univ Salzburg 90; Opera Delaware; Chorale Delaware; Delaware Singers; BA 90; Music; Voice/Piano Perf/Tchng.

**SCHUELER III, ARTHUR M,** Univ Of North Fl, Jacksonville, FL; SO; BA; Psychlgy; Medcn.

**SCHUELER, CHLOE C,** Univ Of Sc At Columbia, Columbia, SC; SO; BA; Insurance/Finance.

**SCHUERER, DOUGLAS J E,** Allegheny Coll, Meadville, PA; SR; BS; Stdnt Govt Dir Voting 90-; Chemii 87-; Stdnt Orntn Advsr 89-90; Phi Beta Kappa 90-; Lambda Sigma Rituals Chair 88-89; Beta Beta Beta 88-; Doan Schlr; Chem Jr Mjr Awrd; Biology Jr Mjr Awrd; Chem Frshmn Stdnt Of Yr 87-; Chemistry/Biology; Medicine.

**SCHUERER, PAULA A,** Ms St Univ, Miss State, MS; SR; BS; Univ Chr 90-; Fnncl Mgt Assn; Phi Kappa Phi 90-; Gamma Beta Phi 89-; Alpha Lambda Delta 88-; Trck Fld 88-90; Anml Sci/Bus Admn/Vet Med; Vet Med Rsrch.

**SCHUERZINGER, STEFANIE E,** Saint John Fisher Coll, Rochester, NY; JR; BA; Campus Radio DJ 89-90; Alpha Gamma Mu 89-; Baden Street Stlmnt Vol Tutor 89-90; Tchrs Asst Allens Crk Sch Pittsford NY 90; Tchrs Asst Brooks Hl Sch Fairport NY; Psychlgy; Elem Edn.

**SCHUESSLER, JILL S,** Auburn Univ At Auburn, Auburn, AL; FR; Glomerata Yrbk Stf 90-; Intl Bus Clb 90-; Alpha Lambda Delta; Phi Eta Sigma; Intl Bus Corp Law.

**SCHUETTER, MICHELLE L,** Univ Of Louisville, Louisville, KY; JR; BS; Stdnt Cncl 90-; Soc Wmn Eng 89-; Gldn Ky 89-; Phi Eta Sigma 88-; Tau Beta Pi 90-; IM Vlybl 89-; Eng Comp Sci; Eng.

**SCHUH, JAMIE L,** Savannah Coll Of Art & Design, Savannah, GA; FR; Graphic Design/Illust; Commer Arts.

**SCHUHR JR, JOHN L,** Univ Of Southern Ms, Hattiesburg, MS; SR; BS; Gamma Beta Phi; Psychlgy; Optmtry.

**SCHUIT, AUDREY DORENE,** Univ Of Southern Ms, Hattiesburg, MS; SR; BS; Phi Beta Lambda Hstrn 81-83; Kappa Mu Epsilon 90-; Phi Kappa Phi 90-; Gldn Key 89-; Phi Theta Kappa Treas 82-83; Trnsfr Achvmnt Awd 88-90; Phi Theta Kappa Awd 88; B O Van Hook Math Schlrshp; William Winter Tchr Schlrshp 90-; AAS Ms Glf Cst Clge 83; Math; Ed.

**SCHULER, BRENDA J,** Philadelphia Coll Pharm & Sci, Philadelphia, PA; FR; BS; NJ Pharm Assoc 90-; Tutor 90-; Pharm.

**SCHULER, HEATHER L,** Glassboro St Coll, Glassboro, NJ; FR; BA; Comm; Brdcstng.

**SCHULER, LINDA C,** Judson Coll, Marion, AL; SR; BA; Eta Epsilon Gamma 90-; Sife; Intshp Henderson Mtl Hlth Ctr Ft Lauderdale FL; Psychology.

**SCHULER, PAULA J,** James Madison University, Harrisonburg, VA; SR; M ED; Grad Asstntshp; ; Athltc Schlrshp 87-; Vrsty Bsktbl 87-; Capt 89-; Phych; Gdnc Cnslng.

**SCHULLER, MARK A,** Oh St Univ, Columbus, OH; FR; BA; Schlr/Athlt Awrd 90-; Deans Lst 90-; Vrsty Bsbl Tm 90-; Bus; Law.

**SCHULMAN, AMA V,** Brown Univ, Providence, RI; FR; BA; Lit Mag Lit Ed 90-; African Stdnts Assoc 90-; Theatre 90-; Studio Art/Afro-Am; Art.

**SCHULMAN, AMY M,** Univ Of Miami, Coral Gables, FL; FR; BA; Hillel 90-; Ldrshp Trng Smnr; Fn Dy Spec Olymcs Cmte; Mstr Tutor; Aftr Schl Hse 90; Psychlgy/Elem Ed.

**SCHULMAN, HELAYNE A,** Univ Of Miami, Coral Gables, FL; JR; BS; Natl Press Phtgphrs Assoc 90-; Hillel Jwsh Stdnts Org 88-; Rho Lambda 90-; Phi Sigma Sigma Mbr At Lrg 89-; IM Vllybl Capt 89-; Photojrnlsm/Engl; Photojrnlsm.

**SCHULTE, KAREN M,** Univ Of Cincinnati-Clrmnt Coll, Batavia, OH; SO; BA; Assoc Apld Bsn Mgmt Univ Cincinnati Clermont Clge 90; Acctg; CPA.

**SCHULTE, MARY E,** Norfolk St Univ, Norfolk, VA; JR; BS; Alpha Kappa Mu 88-; Mc Daniel-Jones Mthmtcs Schlrshp Awd 88-; Applied Mthmtcs/Cmptr Sci.

**SCHULTE, PAULA S,** Livingston Univ, Livingston, AL; FR; Pgms Brd 90-; Stdnts Agnst Drvng Drnk Pres 90-; IM Sprts 90-; Mrn Blgy; Dlphn/Whl Spclst.

**SCHULTZ PAYNE, DEBORAH M,** Univ Of Sc At Aiken, Aiken, SC; SR; BA; Gamma Beta Phi 90-; Mu Rho Sgm 86-87; Gamma Sgm Sgm VP 82-83; Photos/Poetry Pblshd Un Ltry Mag; Engl/Studio Art; Librn.

**SCHULTZ, CATHERINE M,** Saint Elizabeth Hosp Sch Nurs, Utica, NY; FR; AAS; Mohawk Vly Comm Coll Elec Tech Clb 82-83; Cls Hist 90-; Dns Lst; Mohawk Vly Comm Coll VP Lst 81-82; AAS 85; Nrsng.

**SCHULTZ, ELENA RAE F,** Barry Univ, Miami, FL; GD; MS; Untd Hrng/Deaf Serv Asst Instrctr Sign Lang 86-; FL Assn Comp Educ 89-; IEEE; FRID 87-88; SEFRID 84-90; Admnstrtr-Ntnwd Scndry Mktg 86-89; VP-NTNWD Comp Serv 87-90; BS/CIS Barry Univ 90; Comp Sci; Comp Sci/Sftwr Eng.

**SCHULTZ, ERICA J,** Elms Coll, Chicopee, MA; JR; BA; Intrshp Hsng Dscrmntn Proj Inc; Sumner Ave Elem Sch Spngfld MA 90-; Cert; Paralegal; Envrnmntl Law.

**SCHULTZ, JACQUELYN KAY,** Univ Of Sc At Coastal Carolina, Conway, SC; SR; BS; Biology Clb 87-90; Psi Chi; Deans Lst 87-90; Biology/Psychology; Neuropsychology/Sprts.

**SCHULTZ, JENNIFER A,** Oh Wesleyan Univ, Delaware, OH; JR; BA; Democratic Mock Cnvtn Dir; Choice Pres 90-; Pi Alpha Sigma; Mortar Bd VP; OPK; Truman Schlrshp Fnlst; Intern Emilys Lst 90f Intern Atlantic/Pacific Exch Pgm; Politics/Govt/Sociology/Anthropology; Govt.

**SCHULTZ, JENNIFER L,** Otterbein Coll, Westerville, OH; FR; BS; Campus Pgm Bd 90; Sigma Alpha Tau; IM Sftbl; Chem; Resrch.

**SCHULTZ, JOHN P,** Kent St Univ Kent Cmps, Kent, OH; SR; BA; Amigos De Las Americas Rcrtng Dir 90-; Kent Cncl Fmly Rltns Sec 89-; Comm Actn Ntwrk; Fmly Studies; Cnslng.

**SCHULTZ, JOHN R,** West Liberty St Coll, West Liberty, WV; JR; BS; Auguatcs Inst YMCA 87-; Amer Heart Assn CPR Inst 89-; Red Crss Lifegrd Trnr 85-; YMCA 85-; Army Natl Grd WV 90-; Whg Pk Commssn Super 88-; Army Resrvs 80-; Crmnl Justc; Fed Govt.

**SCHULTZ, KIMBERLY A,** Northern Ky Univ, Highland Hts, KY; SO; BS; Psi/Chi; Spec Olympcs; Deans Lst; Psych.

**SCHULTZ, KIMBERLY R,** Cornell Univ Statutory College, Ithaca, NY; SO; BS; Hrsemns Asoc 89; Eqstrn Tm 89-90; Pre-Vet Scty 89-90; Amer Scty Of Anml Sci Schlrshp 90; Anml Sci; Vet Med.

**SCHULTZ, LAURIE A,** Univ Of Sc At Sumter, Sumter, SC; FR; BA; Nursing; Drug Rehab.

**SCHULTZ, LORETTA A,** The Kings Coll, Briarclf Mnr, NY; JR; BA; Missns Flwshp; Psi Chi 90-; Bibl Dept Tutr; Chrch Open Door Yth Dir 89-90; Psych; Yth Wrk.

**SCHULTZ, MARGARET B,** Oh Wesleyan Univ, Delaware, OH; FR; BA; Hbtt Hmnty 90-; Nwsppr Asst News Edtr; Phi Eta Sigma 90-; Delta Gamma Sng Ldr; Vrsty Tnns; Engl/Jrnlsm.

**SCHULTZ, PETER W,** Gallaudet Univ, Washington, DC; SO; BA; German Club Mbr 90-; EPOC Edctl Prog Off Campus Stdnt 90; Var Tennis 90-; TV Film Photography; Communications Media.

**SCHULTZ, SHERRI A,** Duquesne Univ, Pittsburgh, PA; SR; BSBA; Cmtr Cncl 87-; Orntn 88-90; Alph Sgm Tau Pres 88-; Acctg; Mktg/Cmnctns Fir.

**SCHULTZ, STACEY L,** Allegheny Coll, Meadville, PA; JR; Orchesis Dance Clb Pres; Pnhlnc Org VP 90-; Res Life Dir; Alden Schlr 88-; Kappa Kappa Gamma VP; Cmps Msntry; Diving Tm 88-89; Econ; Fncl Plng.

**SCHULTZ, STEVEN M,** Univ Of North Fl, Jacksonville, FL; JR; Frgn Lang Awd FCCJ 89-90; AA FL Comm Clg/Jacksonville 90; Math Educ; Teach Sec Math.

**SCHULTZ, WILLIAM G,** Le Moyne Coll, Syracuse, NY; JR; BS; Stdnt Sen 88-; Bio Club Secy; Beta Beta Beta 90-; Im Bsktbl 89-; Bo; Medcn.

**SCHULZ, ELMER C,** Oh St Univ At Marion, Marion, OH; SR; BSED; Giffin Soc 90-; Deans Stdnt Advsry Cncl Chrmn/Rep 89-; Psychlgy Clb 88-; Deans Ldrshp/Serv Rcgntn 89-90; Outstndng Stdnt Awd 90; AAS Eng Marion Tchncl Clg 81; Scndry Ed/Soc Sci; Tchng/Instrctn.

**SCHULZ, KELLY D,** Tn Temple Univ, Chattanooga, TN; GD; Yrbk 87-88; Scty Vlybl 87-88 90-; Alpha Kappa Rho Capt 90-; AS; Sec.**

**SCHUMACHER, KRISTIN A,** Villanova Univ, Villanova, PA; FR; BS; Proj Sunshn; Bio/Pre-Phys Ther; Phys Ther.

**SCHUMACHER, LINDA A,** Allegheny Coll, Meadville, PA; SR; Orientatn 89-90; Commnty Exchng Vol 88-89; Hall Cncl VP 87-88; Beta Beta Beta Hstrn 89-; Biolgy; Med.

**SCHUMACHER, MATTHEW S,** Syracuse Univ, Syracuse, NY; SR; BS; Beta Alpha Psi Pres 90-; Dean Advsry Brd 90-; Beta Gamma Sigma 89-; Phi Eta Sigma; Mngmnt Schlr; Frederick Killian Schlrshp 89-90; L Galloway Endwmnt Trst Schlrshp; Accntng; CPA.**

**SCHUMACHER, SANDRA E,** Bowling Green St Univ, Bowling Green, OH; SO; Sprt Mgmnt Alliance; Alpha Delta; Phi Eta Sigma; Red Cross Instrctr; Athltc Trnr; Athletic Trng; Sprts Med.

**SCHUMAN, CHARLES E,** Univ Of Rochester, Rochester, NY; SR; BA; Nvy ROTC Btln Exec Ofcr 87-; Resdnt Advsr 89-90; Stf Asst 90-; Im Soccer 87-88; Psychlgy; Ofcr In US Nvy/Nvy Pilot.

**SCHUMAN, DAVID A,** Fl International Univ, Miami, FL; SR; BS; Phi Kappa Phi 89-; Alpha Omega Chi Ctlgr 89-; NSPE 88-; ASCE 88-; FES 88-; ASCE Acdmc Exclnc Schlrshp 90; Flny Court Clrk 87-; AA MI Dade Cmmt Clg 81; Envrnmntl Engrng; MS Envrnmntl Engr.

**SCHUMANN III, RICHARD WILLIAM,** Embry Riddle Aeronautical Univ, Daytona Beach, FL; SR; BS; Arnld Ar Scty Cmptrllr Admn 88-90; Arntcl Sci.

**SCHUMANN, SHEILA J,** Duquesne Univ, Pittsburgh, PA; FR; BS; IM Sftbl; Acdmy Stu Phrmcy 90-; IM Ftbl 90-; Phi Eta Sigma; Deans Lst 90-; Dir Cir 90-; Phrmcy.

**SCHUMM, MICHAEL J,** Univ Of Akron, Akron, OH; JR; BSEE; Math Assn Amer Treas 90-; Gldn Ky 90-; Elec Eng; Eng.

**SCHUNK, RODNEY C,** Erie Comm Coll South Cmps, Orchard Park, NY; SR; AS; Crmnl Jstc.

**SCHUR, ANN MARIE R,** City Univ Of Ny Baruch Coll, New York, NY; SO; BA; Acctng.

**SCHURTZ, LISKA,** Univ Of Miami, Coral Gables, FL; FR; DA; Alpha Lambda Delta; Delta Phi Epsilon 90-; Mrn Sci.

**SCHUSTER, DEBORAH A,** Georgetown Univ, Washington, DC; JR; BS; Natl Nurses Stdnt Assoc Rep; Dorm Cncl Rep 88-89; Planned Parenthood 90-; Univ Womens Ctr; Sigma Theta Tau 90-; Nursing; MS.

**SCHUSTER, DIANNA L,** Univ Of Cincinnati-Clrmnt Coll, Batavia, OH; FR; BSN; Faith U M Ch Treas 89-; Nrsng; Med Emergency.

**SCHUSTER, JENNIFER C,** Muskingum Coll, New Concord, OH; SR; BA; Flwshp Chrstn Athlts Stdy Ldr 90-; Pblcty Co-Chr Prnts Wknd; Sigma Xi 90-; Omicron Delta Kappa Chrtr Pres 90-; Phi Alpha Theta 90-; Psi Chi 88-; Res Drctr 90-; Res Asst 89-90; Tr Gd 88-; Im Vlybl & Bsktbl 90-; Psychology; Coll Stdnt Prsnnl.

**SCHUSTER, MELANEY K,** Columbus Coll Of Art & Design, Columbus, OH; FR; BFA; Vlybl/Sftbl; Advrtsng Dsgn; Intr Dsgn.

**SCHUSTER JR, RUDOLPH M,** Castleton St Coll, Castleton, VT; SR; Castltn Geo Assn Pr/Tr 87-; Sci Assn 87-; Sigma Delta Chi Exec Brd 88-91; Fr Styl Ski Tm V P; Env Sci Geo/Chem; Geo/Chem; Grad/Phd/Env Sci.

**SCHUSTERMAN, ALLISON V,** Winthrop Coll, Rock Hill, SC; SR; BA; Theatre; Hotel Mngmnt.

**SCHUTT, DIANA B,** James Madison University, Harrisonburg, VA; SR; MS; Cncl Excptnl Chldrn 88-; Psychlgy Clb 90-; Outng Clb 87-89; Psi Chi 90-; Goldn Key 89-; Rcknghm Mem Hosp OT Dept 88-89; Cntr For Emtnlly Dstrbd 89-90; Altrntvs For Absd Adlts 90; BS; Psychlgy; MA Sci.

**SCHUTT, MARTHA C,** Fl St Univ, Tallahassee, FL; SO; BME; Bd Advrs Schl Music; Sigma Alkpha Iota V-P; Deans Lst 89-; Music; Tchr.

**SCHUTTE, CHARLES E,** Univ Of Sc At Columbia, Columbia, SC; SO; BA; USAF 81-; Comp Eng; Eng.

**SCHUTTEROP, MICHAEL R,** Clarkson Univ, Potsdam, NY; SR; BS; Clarkson Un Bd 88-89; Spectrumm 90-; Deans Lst 90-; Swim Tm 87-88; Mgmt Info Systms; Cnsltng.

**SCHUTZ, BRIAN A,** Univ Of Miami, Coral Gables, FL; JR; BS; Radio Producer 89-90; Tutor 89-; Alpha Epsilon Rho; Dns Lst 89-; Provosts Pres Hnr Rl 89; IM Bsktbl/Tennis 88-; Cmnctns; Crmnl Law.

**SCHUTZ, DONNA M,** The Kings Coll, Briarclf Mnr, NY; SO; BA; Msnry To Zaire Africa; Psychlgy; Cnslng.

**SCHUTZ, JEFFREY J,** The Kings Coll, Briarclf Mnr, NY; SO; BA; Drma Clb Actr Cnstr 89-90; Vllybll Clb 89-; Chrstn Serv Grgd; Natl Hnr Soc 87; Yth Chrst Stff 89-90; Proj SERVE 88-89; Acad All Amer; Pres Awrd 90-; Hstry; Educ.**

**SCHWAB, BARBARA J,** Glassboro St Coll, Glassboro, NJ; SR; BA; Stdnt Math Assc Soc Dir 90-; Math; Actry.

**SCHWAB, CHRISTINE A,** Daemen Coll, Amherst, NY; JR; BS; Deans Lst 88-90; Deans Schlrshp 88-; Phys Therpy.

**SCHWAB, JODI E,** Univ Of Ky, Lexington, KY; FR; BS; Athletic Drctrs Hnr Roll 90; Lttrd Swmmr 90-; Swmmr 90-; Biology; Sprts Med.

**SCHWAB, KAREN L,** Northern Ky Univ, Highland Hts, KY; JR; BED; SNEA; KEA; NEA; US Navy Ptty Offcr Mchnry Rprman 85-90; Mddle Grds Educ/Engl/Hstry; Tch.

**SCHWAB, TIMOTHY A,** S U N Y At Buffalo, Buffalo, NY; JR; BPS; AIAS 90-; Nwsppr 90; Phi Eta Sigma 89-; Gldn Key 90-; Hnrs Prog 88-; Archtct.

**SCHWALBERT, DAWN R,** Clemson Univ, Clemson, SC; JR; BS; SC Rec Prks Assoc 90-; Amer Therptc Rec Assoc; Rho Phi Lambda; Intrnshp VA Hosp Augusta GA; Clg Wk Sr Ctzns Clemsn Vol 90; Contiuum Of Cr Anderson Vol 90; IM Ftbl 88; Prks/Rec/Tourism Mgmt; Thrptc Rec.

**SCHWALM, SANDRA M,** Univ Of Sc At Columbia, Columbia, SC; SO; BS; Hnrs Assc 89-; Mrchng Bnd 89-; Pep Bnd 89-; Tau Beta Sigma Sec 90-; Resrch Apprntc Prog 90-; Marine Sci; Rsrch.

**SCHWARTING, ELIZABETH A,** Columbia Greene Comm Coll, Hudson, NY; SO; AS; Bus Admn; Acctg; Mrktng.

**SCHWARTZ, AMIT Y,** Yeshiva Univ, New York, NY; SR; BA; Chem Clb; Sigma Delta Rho; Phlnthrpy Soc; Rgnts Schlrshp; Blkn Schlrshp; Deans Lst; Bio; Med.

**SCHWARTZ, AMY L,** Oh Dominican Coll, Columbus, OH; JR; BA; Peer Cnsltnt 90-; Tau Pi Phi 90-; Chldrns Hosp Intrn 90; Hlth Bus Intrn; Bus Admnstrtn; MHA.

**SCHWARTZ, BETH K,** Fl Atlantic Univ, Boca Raton, FL; FR; BBA; Act Std Asc 90-; FICPA Atltc Chptr Schlp 90-; Brd Dir Vntn Terr Condo Asc Tr 90-; FL Inst CPA 90-; Act Supv/Prvt Ind/Self-Emp Pblc Act 80-; AS Cmdn Cty Clg 89; Act; CPA.

**SCHWARTZ, DANIEL J,** Providence Coll, Providence, RI; FR; BA; Bio Clb 90-; Rock Band 87-; Jazz Band 87-; Alpha Epsilon Delta; MA Battle Of Bands Awd 88; Berklee Clg Music Jazz Awd 90; Bio; Med.

**SCHWARTZ, ELIZABETH,** City Univ Of Ny Hunter Coll, New York, NY; GD; MS; Natl Stdnt Spch-Lang-Hrng Assn 89-; BA City Coll NY 71; Spch-Lang Pthlgy; Spch-Lang Pthlgst.

**SCHWARTZ, ERIC W,** Columbus Coll Of Art & Design, Columbus, OH; FR; BFA; Illustration; Art Career/Fr Lncng.

**SCHWARTZ, EYAL,** Radford Univ, Radford, VA; FR; BSCBA; Cmptr Sci/Math; Prgrmr/Sys Anlyst.

**SCHWARTZ, GARY S,** Boston Univ, Boston, MA; GD; MD; MA Med Soc Chr 88-; Amer Med Asc Dlgt 88-; Alpha Omega Alpha; Sigma Xi; Fght/Sght Std Flwshp; BA Brown Unv 87; Opthlmlgy.

**SCHWARTZ, JILL L,** Kent St Univ Kent Cmps, Kent, OH; SO; MBA; Hnr Clg 89-; Acct.

**SCHWARTZ, JOHN J,** Cornell Univ Statutory College, Ithaca, NY; SO; BS; Red Carpet Soc 89-90; Cornell Ski Clb 89-; E Sidney Lk Wtr Qlty Proj 90-; I M Soccr Vybl Sftbl 89-; Natl Rsrcs/Water Rsrcs; Grad Sch Envrnmntl.

**SCHWARTZ, KATHY L,** Duquesne Univ, Pittsburgh, PA; JR; BS; Amer Phrmctl Assoc 90-; Acad Stdnts Of Phrmcy 90-; Lambda Kappa Sigma; Phi Delta Chi Ltl Srs VP; Phrmcy Intrn Olean Gen Hosp; Dns Lst; IM Co-Ed Vllybl 90-; Phrmcy.

**SCHWARTZ, LYNDA M,** Radford Univ, Radford, VA; JR; BA; Crmnl Justc Club Pres; Lambda Alpha Epsilon; Intrnshp US Marshalls Svc; Crmnl Justc; Fdrl Invstgtns.

**SCHWARTZ, MICHELE G,** Castleton St Coll, Castleton, VT; SR; BSED; Phi Eta Sigma 89-90; Socl Sci; Elem Ed Tchr.

**SCHWARTZ, MICHELE M,** S U N Y Coll Of Tech At Delhi, Delhi, NY; SO; AA; RA 90; Deans Lst 89; Sclgy; Psychlgy/Wrtng.

**SCHWARTZ, PAUL F,** Manhattan School Of Music, New York, NY; SR; MM; Stdyng W/Sandra Davis/Peggy Neighbors Erwin; 1st Prize Grtr Miami Yth Symph 84-86; 1st Prize 1st Annual Broward Comm Coll Orch Cmptitn/Sr Concerto Div FL Fed Msc 86; Stdyng W/Paul Posnak Manhattan Schl Music W/Phillip Kawih; BM Mnhttn Schl Music 90-; Piano Perf; Cncrt Pnst.

**SCHWARTZ, RIVKA C,** Yeshiva Univ, New York, NY; GD; Grad Cum Laude; Asst Sys Mgr FOJP Serv Corp; BA 90.

**SCHWATKA, MELISSA L,** Merrimack Coll, North Andover, MA; FR; BA; Merrimack Mktg Assn 90-; Orntn Com 90-; Alpha Kappa Psi 90-; Deans Lst; Big Bro/Big Sis Grtr Lawerence Area; Mktg; Advrtsng.

**SCHWEDHELM, SANDRA M,** William Paterson Coll, Wayne, NJ; SR; BA; Engl Wrtng Intrnshp; Engl; Technel Wrtng.

**SCHWEERS, SHEILA N,** Coll Of Charleston, Charleston, SC; SO; BA; Alumni Assoc 90-; Tour Guide 89-; Cath Cmpus Clb 90-; I M Tennis Bkbl; English; Cmunctns/Pub Rltns.

**SCHWEICHLER, BETH M,** Le Moyne Coll, Syracuse, NY; SO; BA; CAN 90-; Sprngfld Tutor Pgm 90-; Se Moyne Wmns Lacrosse 89-; Psychlgy/Philosophy; Law/Wmns Studies.

**SCHWEICHLER, DAVID M,** Le Moyne Coll, Syracuse, NY; JR; BA; Rugby 88-; Psychlgy Clb 88-89; Envrmntl Coalition 88; Psi Chi 90-; Outstndg Coll Stdnts Am 89-; Chldrsn AIDS Netword; Wash Ctr Intern; IM Bsktbl/Ftbl 89-; Psychlgy/Philosophy.

**SCHWEIGER, ERIC A,** Cooper Union, New York, NY; SR; BE; Newspaper Editor In Chief 88-; Orientation 88-; Tau Beta Pi Pres 90-; Pi Tau Sigma Treas 90-; ASME 89-; Heart Lung Fndtn 85-; CU Schlrshp 87-; Dean Bakers Annual Canadian Ski Trip 90-; Mechanical Engrng; Auto Engrng.

**SCHWEIGER, TERESA A,** Univ Of Md Balt Cnty Campus, Catonsville, MD; SO; BS; Phrmcst.**

**SCHWEIKART, RICHARD C,** Univ Of Pittsburgh At Bradford, Bradford, PA; SR; MBA; Yng Dmcrts Clb 89-; Yrbk Assn Sr Edtr 87-89; Stu Gvt Assn Sen 87-89; Schlr 90-; Natl Merit Schlrshp; Bus Mngmng; Fnnc.

**SCHWEITZ, KRISTEN A,** Anderson Coll, Anderson, SC; GD; BS; Fash Merch Hon Club; Campus Minstrs; AA Anderson Clg 90; Fash Merchndsng; Merchnds Mgr/Buyer.**

**SCHWEITZER, JENNIFER L,** Northern Ky Univ, Highland Hts, KY; FR; BA; Comm Stdnts Assn 90-; SAM; Dns Lst; Exclnc Schlrshp; IM Sprts 90-; Mgmt.

**SCHWEITZER, TRACI L,** Mount Aloysius Jr Coll, Cresson, PA; SO; BS; BACCHUS VP 89-90; Phi Theta Kappa 89-90; AS 90; Acctg.

**SCHWEIZE, AMY K,** Univ Of Miami, Coral Gables, FL; GD; Trk 87-90; BS 90f; Psych; Erly Chldhd Spec Ed.

**SCHWEIZER, CAROL J,** Bob Jones Univ, Greenville, SC; FR; BED; Sigma Kappa Rho; Society Vllybll; Elmntry Ed; Tchr.

**SCHWEIZER, KAREN L,** Indiana Univ Of Pa, Indiana, PA; JR; BS; Act Brd Chr Flm/Video Comm 90-; Wmn Cmnctns Inc 90-; Amer Soc Trng/Dvlpmnt 88-89; Prgrmng Intrn WTXF Fox 29; Cmnctns Media; Corp Brdcstng.

**SCHWEIZER, SUSAN E,** Univ Of Southern Ms, Hattiesburg, MS; SR; BS; Rcrtn Mjr Assn V P 89-; BACCUS 89-; Thrptc Rcrtn Soc 89-; Chi Omega; Rcrtn Thrptc; CTRS.

**SCHWENDER, RUTH A,** Kent St Univ Stark Cmps, North Canton, OH; JR; BA; Vol Quest Rec Serv Drug/Alcohol Rehab 90; AD 90; Psychology; Researcher.

**SCHWER, KRISTI L,** Northern Ky Univ, Highland Hts, KY; SR; BM; Pep Bnd 87-; Alpha Chi Pres 89-; All-Clgt Bnd 88-; Music.

**SCHWIEBERT, PAMELA S,** Defiance Coll, Defiance, OH; SR; BA; Elem Ed; Teach.

**SCHWIEGER, DERK K,** U S Military Academy, West Point, NY; FR; BA; Flwshp Of Chrstn Athletes 90-; Var Bsktbl 90-; Political Science; Law/History Professor.

**SCHWIERZKE, MARIA D,** Andover Coll, Portland, ME; GD; AS; TA Cert 90; Immucell Corp Intrn 90-; Cmptr Sci; Prgrmng.

**SCHWINN, ADAM H,** City Univ Of Ny Queensbrough, New York, NY; SO; Deans Hnr Lst; US Air Force Rsrvs 89-; Oprtn Dsrt Shld Strm 90-; AF Otstndng Unit Awd; Ntnl Dfns Srvc Mdl; Mc Guire Air Force Aero Clb; Physcl Edctn; Aviation Pilot.

**SCHWITZGEBEL III, GREGORY F,** Univ Of Nc At Chapel Hill, Chapel Hill, NC; GD; JD; Jrnl Intl Law/Comm Rgltns Edtr 90-; Phi Beta Kappa 88-89; Pi Sigma Alpha 88-89; N C Crt Appls Intshp; Rsch Asst 90-; Amer Jrsprdnc Awd 90; GA Gvnrs Intn Pgm 88; Ntl Elks Fdn Schlr; Lvts Awd Pol Sci; Hrst Fdn Schlr; Cbl Nws Ntwrk Int; MA 89; BA; Law.

**SCHWOEPPE, DEBORAH KAY,** Owensboro Comm Coll, Owensboro, KY; GD; VICA 90-; Nrsg.

**SCIBELLI, CHRISTOPHER D,** Franklin And Marshall Coll, Lancaster, PA; SR; MD; Porter Scntfc Soc Exec Offcr 88-; Healing Art Clb 87-; Phi Beta Kappa; Dean Lst 88-; Hnrs Lst 87-88; BA; Biol; Med.

**SCIBETTA, GINA L,** Ocean County Coll, Toms River, NJ; FR; BS; Nrsg; Srgcl Nrs.

**SCIBETTA, MICHAEL P,** Univ Of Toledo, Toledo, OH; GD; JD; Eng Stdnt Assoc 89; Delta Theta Phi Tribune; Phi Kappa Theta Serv Chm 89; Univ Buffalo Lacrosse 88-89; BA SUNY Buffalo 89; Law.

**SCICUTELLA, VINCENT F,** Ny Chiropractic Coll, Glen Head, NY; GD; Phi Chi Omega; DC; Chiropractic; Private Practice.

**SCILLIA, JOANNE M,** Fl International Univ, Miami, FL; JR; BSN; Brwrd Gen Med Cntr Extrnshp; Nrsng; Crnry Crtcl Care.

**SCILLION, LESA D,** Univ Of Tn At Martin, Martin, TN; SR; BED; Deans Lst 89-; Phi Epsilon Mu VP 90-; Stdnt Tenn Educ Assoc 90-; Stdnt Asstnt Girls Bsktbl Coach 90-; Physcl Educ; Sci Teach Bsktbl Coach.

**SCIORTINO, DANIEL J,** S U N Y At Buffalo, Buffalo, NY; SR; MBA; Golden Key; Delta Sigma Pi 89-; Grad Asstshp 90-; Teach Asst 89; BS; Bus Mgmnt; Exec Position.

**SCIORTINO, MARIA G,** Saint Johns Univ, Jamaica, NY; SR; BS; Arbcs; IMS; Kappa Delta Pi 89-; Ed/Math; Ed.

**SCIPIO, ARLENE Y,** Sarah Lawrence Coll, Bronxville, NY; SO; BA; Hstry.**

**SCIULLI, DAVID R,** Univ Of Pittsburgh, Pittsburgh, PA; FR; BA; Engnrng; Elctrcl Engnr.

**SCLAFANI, LEE ANN,** Dowling Coll, Oakdale Li, NY; SR; BSPLS; Educ Clb 89-90; Kappa Delta Pi 90-; Flght Attndnt Tower Air 84-; AAS Rchstr Inst Tech 79-81; Educ; Tchng.

**SCLAFANI, MATTHEW C,** Siena Coll, Loudonville, NY; SR; BBA; Acctg Clb VP 88-; Alpha Kappa Alpha; Rgby Clb 88-; Acctg; CPA.

**SCLAFANI JR, PETER J,** S U N Y Coll Of Tech At Delhi, Delhi, NY; SR; MBA; Exec Clb 90-; Phi Theta Kappa; IM Vllybl 89-; Bus Admn/Fnnc; Fnnc.

**SCOBEL, PATRICIA L,** Allegheny Coll, Meadville, PA; JR; BA; Stdnt Exprmntl Theatr 88-; Alghny Choir 89-; Chmbr Choir/Chpl Choir 90-; Aldn Schlr; Engl; Tchng.

**SCOFFONE, DEBORAH M,** James Madison University, Harrisonburg, VA; SR; BS; Mrchng Bnd 87-; NAEYC 89-; SEA 89-; Tau Beta Sigma VP 88-; Cum Laude; Pres Lst; Dns Lst; Erly Chldhd Educ; Tchg.

**SCOFIELD, STEVEN M,** Coll Of Health Sci Stony Brook, Stony Brook, NY; GD; MD; Cncl For Excptnl Chldrn 80-; AMA 89-; AMSA 87-; Alpha Omega Alpha 90-; Spcl Eductr 80-86; BA Psychlgy SUNY Geneseo 78; MS Geneseo NY 81; Medcn.

**SCOGGINS, DARREN J,** Middle Tn St Univ, Murfreesboro, TN; SO; BA; Bapt Stdnt Un Cncl 89-; Pre-Law Soc Exec Cncl; Gamma Beta Phi Pres 90-; Hon Soc; IBM Customer Engr 89-; Columbia State Golf Tm Vrsty 89-90; Law.

**SCOGGINS, PAULA M,** Mobile Coll, Mobile, AL; SR; BS; SLATE 88-; Kappa Delta Epsilon 90-; Dns Lst 89-; Kappa Delta Epsilon 90-; Erly Chldhd Ed/Elem Ed; Tch.

**SCOGGINS, SONJA Y,** Southern Coll Of Tech, Marietta, GA; SR; NSBE Sec 89-90; SGA 88-89; ASQC; Orntn 87-89; Peer Cnslr 87-89; Diplmt Pres 89-; Dns Lst 88-90; Ind Eng Tech.

**SCOLLICK, KEITH A,** Villanova Univ, Villanova, PA; SR; PHD; Stdnt Theatre Publ Rels Ofcr 88-; Astronmcl Soc Publ Rels Ofcr 87-; Physic Clb Treas 88-; Phi Beta Kappa; Sigma Pi Sigma 88-; Campus Mnstry Singers 90-; NASA/JOVE Intern Univ GA 90; Fr Jenkins Schlrshp 89-; BS; Astronmy/Astrophy; Rsrch Planetary Astronmy.

**SCOMA, CHRISTINE M,** Villanova Univ, Villanova, PA; SO; BA; Cmnctn Arts; Law.

**SCOPA, JASON R,** Merrimack Coll, North Andover, MA; FR; Orntn Cmte; IM Sports/Actv; Ntnl Hon Soc V P 88-; Pol Sci.

**SCOPE, SAMANTHA L,** S U N Y Coll Of Tech At Frmgdl, Farmingdale, NY; SO; AS; )rly Chldhd Clb 89-; Elem Educ; Kndrgrdn Tchr.

**SCOPELLITI, JILL,** Univ Of Pittsburgh, Pittsburgh, PA; FR; BS; Pitt Dance Clb; Nutrition.

**SCOPES, ANGELA G,** Hillsborough Comm Coll, Tampa, FL; SO; BA; Accntng.

**SCORSOME, LISA L,** Nova Univ, Ft Lauderdale, FL; GD; MBA; Intrm Brd Of Dir Md-FL Mfg Assn; B/E Avioncs Plnt Mgr 81-; BA Syracuse Univ 89.

**SCOTLAND, ULRIC A,** Norfolk St Univ, Norfolk, VA; FR; BS; Intl Std Org VP 90-; Sprtn Alpha Tau 90-; Alpha Kappa Mu; Saad GA El-Fayoumy Schlp; IM Bsktbl/Bsbl/Vlybl; Fnce; Corp Law.

**SCOTT, AMIE R,** Thomas Nelson Comm Coll, Hampton, VA; FR; AS; Sci; Physcl Thrpy Drctr.

**SCOTT, AMY G,** Union Univ, Jackson, TN; JR; BS; SAC 90-; Lest We Forget 89-; Sigma Zeta 90-; Bio; Zoolgst.

**SCOTT, AMY L,** Union Univ, Jackson, TN; FR; BS; Sigma Alpha Epsilon Aux; Phy Thrpy; Bio; Phy Thrpy.

**SCOTT, ANDREW P,** City Univ Of Ny City Coll, New York, NY; SO; BA; Vllybl 90-; Engrng.

**SCOTT, ANTHONY L,** Alcorn St Univ, Lorman, MS; JR; BA; Comp Sci/Math Clb 88-; Hnr Org 88-; Alpha Kappa Mu 90-; Bell Comm Rsrch Intern 90-; Comp Sci; Comp Sftwr Dvlpng.

**SCOTT, ASHLEE J,** West Liberty St Coll, West Liberty, WV; SO; BS; Pro Life Grp 90-; Acad Tutor; Hnrs Prog 90-; Biol/Chem; Orthotics/Prosthetics.

**SCOTT, BART L,** Univ Of Al At Birmingham, Birmingham, AL; SR; Elctn Cmmsn; Intrfrtrnty Cncl 88; Greek Week Cmmtt 90; Omicron Delta Kappa 89-; Phi Kappa Phi 89-; Alpha Epsilon Delta 88-; Alpha Tau Omega Sec 88-; UAB Ambsdrs Pres 89-; Blazer Crew 90; Stdnt Rcrtrs 90; Hnrs Rsrch 90-; Bio; Med.

**SCOTT, BETH E,** Radford Univ, Radford, VA; SO; BA; IM Sftbl/Vlybl; Chem Tutor; Elem Tchr.

**SCOTT, BEVERLY T,** New England Coll Of Optometry, Boston, MA; GD; OD; VOSH 89-; Beta Sigma Kappa 90-; AOSA 89-; Tutor 90-; Neuromed Rn 82-; Icu Ophthlmlgy 90-; BSN Unv Ptsbrg 82; Optmtry.

**SCOTT, CARRIE E,** Queens Coll, Charlotte, NC; SO; BSN; Deans Lst 89-90; Tns Tm 89-90; Nrsg.

**SCOTT, CHARLOTTE E,** Ky St Univ, Frankfort, KY; FR; Scl Wrk Clb VP 90-; Chr; Drm Clb; Deans Lst; Otstndng Frshmn Ward Chr; Scl Wrk.

**SCOTT, CHRISTY J,** Temple Univ, Philadelphia, PA; GD; Cum Laude 90; Mktg; Hlth Admin.

**SCOTT, CLARE B,** Converse Coll, Spartanburg, SC; FR; BA; Coll Republicans; Alpha Lambda Delta; Boys/Girls Club Big Sis; Psychlgy/French.

**SCOTT, DANA J,** Davis & Elkins Coll, Elkins, WV; SO; BA; Educ; Tchr.

**SCOTT, DANIEL P,** City Univ Of Ny City Coll, New York, NY; SO; BA; Deans List; Engl; Novelist.

**SCOTT, DAPHNE A,** Univ Of Montevallo, Montevallo, AL; JR; BA; Alpha Lambda Delta 88-; Alpha Sigma Pi 90-; Kappa Delta Pi; Natl Spch Sgn Hrng Lang; Spch Hrng Assn Ala; Dean Lst; Pres Lst; Vldctrn Schlrshp 88-; Willena Peck Schlrshp 88-; Scottish Rite Schlrshp 88-; Spch Lang/Pthlgy.

**SCOTT, DAWN Y,** Univ Of Fl, Gainesville, FL; GD; Acad Of Stdnts Of Phrmcy 87-90; Rho Pi Phi Treas 88-90; Phrm D; Intrnshps Atkinsons Phrmcy Ornge Pk Fl 88-89; Care Plus Hm IV Infsn Spclsts 90; Hosp Phrmcy.

**SCOTT, DEBBIE M,** City Univ Of Ny City Coll, New York, NY; SO; BSN; Nrsng; Practitioner.

**SCOTT, DEIDRE ANN,** Univ Of Akron, Akron, OH; SR; BS; Pi Sigma Epsilon 90-; Gold Key 89-; Mu Kappa Tau; Pi Sigma Am Cncr Scty 87; Deans Lst 89-; Mrktng; Sales.

**SCOTT, DIONNE Y,** Tuskegee Univ, Tuskegee Inst, AL; SO; BS; FL Clb 89-; Gospel Ensmble 90-; NAACP 89-; Pres Schlrshp 89-90; Howard Hughes Med Inst Schlrshp; Bio; Med.

**SCOTT, DON W,** Univ Of Fl, Gainesville, FL; JR; BA; Archry Clb VP; Ftbl Sftbl Bsktbl Vlybl 89-; AA 90; Bus Mgmt; Corp Law.

**SCOTT, DONNA E,** Cheyney Univ Of Pa, Cheyney, PA; SR; BA; Ambssdrs 90-; Rcrd Nwspr 89-; Video Prod Clb Sec 89-; Alpha Phi Sigma 90-; Alpha Kappa Mu Acting Pres 90-; Natl Cncl Negro Wmn 89-; KYW-TV3 Intrnshp Edtrl/Pblc Serv Dept 90; Cmnctns; Brdcstng/Pblc Rltns.

**SCOTT, DUSTIN L,** Christopher Newport Coll, Newport News, VA; FR; BSA; Peninsula Mens Sccr League 90-; Deans Lst 90; Acctg; CPA.

**SCOTT, EDWARD D,** Beckley Coll, Beckley, WV; FR; AS; Gspl Chrch 86; Envrnmntl Cntrl Syst Spclst 77-89; Allied Hlth/Rsprtry Thrpy; BS Hlth Serv.

**SCOTT, ESTELLA A,** Univ Of Sc At Columbia, Columbia, SC; FR; BA; Alpha Swthrt 90-; Mnrty Asst Pgm Cnslr; Gamma Beta Phi 90-; Alpha Lambda Delta 90-; Phi Eta Sigma 90-; Pltcl Sci; Lawyr.

**SCOTT, FREDRICK M,** Brevard Coll, Brevard, NC; FR; AA; Stdnt Govt; Dorm Pres; Phi Theta Kappa VP/FINANCE; Music/Prcssn/Prfrmnce.

**SCOTT, GARTH I,** Univ Of Miami, Coral Gables, FL; JR; BA; AA Santa Fe Comm Clg 89; Psych/Prim Educ; Tchr.

**SCOTT, GARY M,** Middle Tn St Univ, Murfreesboro, TN; JR; BS; Educ; Teaching.

**SCOTT, GENA L,** Al A & M Univ, Normal, AL; SR; Afrcn Assc; Alpha Aux; Big Sister; Deans List 90; Hon Roll 90-; Dntst Ofc Intrn 89-; Zoology Chem; Med Schl.

**SCOTT JR, GEORGE E,** Morehouse Coll, Atlanta, GA; FR; BS; Gspl Chr 90-; STRIPES; Big Brthr Prgrm Drctr; Cora Cola Intrn Math GPA Awd; Cmptr Sci; Systm Analyst.

**SCOTT, GREGORY S,** Bristol Univ, Bristol, TN; GD; SAM; Univ TN Wtr Ski Tm; MBA 90; BS Univ TN 87; AS Roane St Comm Coll 83; Bus Mgt; Mgt.

**SCOTT, HOLLY F,** Nc Agri & Tech St Univ, Greensboro, NC; SO; Stdnt Actvty Cnsl 90-; Stdnt Govt Assn 90-; NAACP 90-; Acdmc Achvmnt.

**SCOTT, JACKIE A,** Wv Univ At Parkersburg, Parkersburg, WV; SO; BA; Scl Serv; Mntl Hlth Advcy.

**SCOTT, JACQUELYNE J,** Bennett Coll, Greensboro, NC; SO; BASIS; Nwspr Edtr 90-; Deans Lst 89; Rotary Schlrshp/Phillip M Thoman Schlrshp; Nursing Home Intrn; Engl Educ.

**SCOTT, JENNIFER D,** Middle Tn St Univ, Murfreesboro, TN; SR; BS; Kappa Delta Pi; Varsity Rifle Team; Elementary Education; Teaching.

**SCOTT, JENNIFER L,** Kent St Univ Kent Cmps, Kent, OH; FR; BA; Fltch Hl Hse Cncl Wng Repr 90-; Alpha Lambda Delta 90-; Chem/Predentistry.

**SCOTT, JERRI L,** Ms St Univ, Miss State, MS; SR; DPMA 88-90; Dns Lst; Pres Lst; AA NE MS Comm Clg 86; BBA MS St Univ 90; Bsns Inf Sys; Comp Prog/Anlyst.

**SCOTT, JOHN C,** Univ Of Louisville, Louisville, KY; SR; BSI; Ntl Egl Sct Assc 85-; Cmptr Sci; Cmptr Sys Eng.

**SCOTT, JOHN L,** West Chester Univ, West Chester, PA; JR; BS; Blck Grk Cncl VP; Blck Stdnt Union 90-; Iota Phi Theta Treas 90-; Mgmt Intrnshp At Penn Mtl Life Ins 90-; Bus Mgmt; Life Ins Mgr.**

**SCOTT, JULIE A,** Comm Coll Algny Co Algny Cmps, Pittsburgh, PA; FR; AS; Sci; Biochem.

**SCOTT, KAROLYN E,** D Youville Coll, Buffalo, NY; GD; ASSOC; Bio Clb Pres 88-89; Wrtrs Clb; The Poet Publshr 88-89; BS Bio 90; Vet Tech.

**SCOTT, KELLI N,** Jackson St Univ, Jackson, MS; FR; Bio; Pre Phy Thrpy.

**SCOTT, KIMBERLY D,** Middle Tn St Univ, Murfreesboro, TN; FR; NA; Gammba Beta Phi; Alpha Delta Pi; Rnld Mcdnld House; Grk Athltcs; Pre Dntl.

**SCOTT, LEANN,** Ms St Univ, Miss State, MS; JR; BA; BARK; Kappa Dlt Stnds Chrmn Pep Chrmn Pctr Chrmn; Chldrns Hosp; Natl Prvntn Chld Abs; Educ; Elem Educ.

**SCOTT, LISA A,** Allegheny Coll, Meadville, PA; SR; BS; Orchesis Chrgrphr 87-88; Alpha Delta Pi Actvts Chr 87-90; Lambda Sigma 88; PEW Intrnshp Univ Rchstr 90; Ledrshp Awd; Chrldng/Ftbl/Bsktbl 88-; Physics/Math; Teach/Rsrch/Eng.

**SCOTT, LISA G,** Midlands Tech Coll, Columbia, SC; SR; AS; Ambssdrs 90-; Hnr Rl 89-; Deans Lst; Phrmcy Tech; Med Degree.

**SCOTT, LISA N,** Morris Brown Coll, Atlanta, GA; SO; BABSN; Frgn Lng Clb VP 90-; Stdnt Nrsg Assoc 90-; Phi Sigma Iota Pres 90-; YWCA Pre Schl Pgm; Hnr Stdnt; Nrsg/Spnsh; Peds.

**SCOTT, MARK A,** Montgomery Comm Coll, Troy, NC; FR; Stu Govt Rep; Dean Lst; Automech.

**SCOTT, MARTIN F,** Coppin St Coll, Baltimore, MD; GD; Christian Council Inc VP 87-88; Project Deter Pres 88-; Chrmn Grad Commt Chrmn; MCL Social Sci Dept; Bible Studies Intr; Clg Algebra Tutor; MA Ed/Christian; BS; Social Sci; Ed.

**SCOTT, MEREDETH M,** King Coll, Bristol, TN; SR; BS; Health Sci Soc VP 88-; Track Club Pres 90-; Sympohnic Choir 87-; Katherine Stamper Awd 89; Samuel G Robinson Awd 90; Biology & Chem Lab Asst Tutor 87; Biology; Medicine.

**SCOTT, MICHELLE L,** Va Commonwealth Univ, Richmond, VA; FR; BA; Staff The Underground 90-; Mass Cmnctns; Pblc Rltns.

**SCOTT, NANCY M,** Va Commonwealth Univ, Richmond, VA; JR; BFA; Jr Board Sheltering Arms Hosp Sec 87-; Trustee Historic Richmond Foundation 87-; Fashion Merchandising.

**SCOTT, OLA P,** Talladega Coll, Talladega, AL; SO; Deans Lst; Eunice M Swift Trumbull Schlrshp Fnd; Soc Wrk; Prsn Cnslr.

**SCOTT, OMAR Y,** Mercer Univ Schl Of Pharm, Atlanta, GA; Cncl Stdnts 90-; Acdmy Stdnts Phrmcy 90-; Stdn Tnatl Phrmctcl Assoc 90-; Deans Lst 89deans Lst 90-; Phrmcy.

**SCOTT, PAMELA T,** Middle Tn St Univ, Murfreesboro, TN; SR; Clg Bowl 89; Phi Kappa Phi 90-; Phi Theta Kappa 87-89; Kappa Delta Pi 90-; Gamma Beta Phi Sec 87-89; BS; Elem Ed; Tchr.

**SCOTT, PETER B,** Hampton Univ, Hampton, VA; FR; BA; Radio Station DJ Asst Jazz Dir 90-; Radio Clb 90-; Announcer Mnth; Mass Media Arts; Radio/TV Prdctn.

**SCOTT, RICHARD D,** Middle Ga Coll, Cochran, GA; FR; BA; Pharmacy.

**SCOTT, ROBERT T,** Le Moyne Coll, Syracuse, NY; SR; BS; Unity Kitchen Chrty Socty Syracyse Cmps Coordn 89-; IM Bsktbl Co Capt 87-88; Bus/Fiance; Bus Admin.

**SCOTT, RODNEY L,** Al A & M Univ, Normal, AL; JR; BS; SGA Pres; Acctg Clb VP 90-; Assn Govt Actnts 90-; Phi Beta Lambda VP; Kappa Alpha Psi Exchqr; Natl Cllgt Stdnt Govt Awd; Acctg; CPA.

**SCOTT, RUTILIA M,** Albertus Magnus Coll, New Haven, CT; SR; BA; Pltcl Sci.

**SCOTT, SHERWAYNE L,** Ny Univ, New York, NY; FR; BA; Trust Co Accnt Co 90; Bsns; Accntng.

**SCOTT, SOMERA,** Williamsburg Tech Coll, Kingstree, SC; JR; Dns Lst 89-; Phi Theta Kappa; Bsn.

**SCOTT, STACEY M,** Capital Univ, Columbus, OH; FR; BA; Ftbl; PR Bus; PR.

**SCOTT, STEPHANIE,** City Univ Of Ny City Coll, New York, NY; SR; BA; Soc; Soc Serv.

**SCOTT, STEPHEN D,** Liberty Univ, Lynchburg, VA; SR; BS; Stdnt Govt Senate Del 90-; Univ Barbell Clb 88-; Sigma Tau Delta Pres 90-; Kappa Delta Pi 90-; Peer Tutor 89-; Dorm Ldr Pgm Grp Ldr 88-; IM Soccer 88-90; Engl Ed; Tchg/Med Sch.

**SCOTT, STEPHEN L,** Univ Of Southern Ms, Hattiesburg, MS; SR; BS; Gldn Ky; Upsilon Pi Epsilon 90-; US Air Frce 81-89; BS; Comp Sci; Engr.

**SCOTT, STEPHEN S,** Univ Of Sc At Columbia, Columbia, SC; SO; BS; Frtrnty Cncl Srvc Chrmn; Amer Chem Socty; Order Of Omega; Assn Hnr Stdnts 89-; Pi Kappa Alpha VP 89-; Med Extrnshp Sprtnbrg Rgnl Med Ctr 90; IM Ftbl/Soccer/Swmng/Trck; Biology; Medicine.

**SCOTT, SUSAN D,** Al St Univ, Montgomery, AL; FR; Math; Engr.

**SCOTT, SUSAN E,** Central St Univ, Wilberforce, OH; SR; BS; Bus Hnrs Clb 89/Pres 90; Alpha Kappa Alpha; Acctg; CPA.

**SCOTT, TAMMY LYNN,** Brevard Coll, Brevard, NC; FR; Brevard Clg Wmns Soccer; Soccer; Sci; Physical Therapy.

**SCOTT, TARA L,** Saint Johns Univ, Jamaica, NY; FR; BS; Crmnl Just; Law.

**SCOTT, THEMBA L,** Al A & M Univ, Normal, AL; SO; BA; Chr 89-; Amer Hm Ecnmcs Assc 89-; Stu Dietic Assc 89-; Kappa Omicrom Nu; Sci Olympc Guide 90; Yth Mtvtn Tsk Frc Guide 90; Wrkshp Ldr; Lab Asst Food Ntrtn 89-; ARA Serv 89-90; Food/Ntrtn; Hsptlty Htl Mngmnt.

**SCOTT, THOMAS E,** Jackson St Univ, Jackson, MS; JR; Pltcl Sci/Pre Law Clb SGA Rep 90-; Econ Clb Edtr; Yrbk Staff Edtr In Chf; Alpha Lambda Delta Edtr 89; Alpha Mu Gamma; Phi Kappa Phi; Hghst GPA Dixon Hall 88-90; Hghst GPA Pltcl Sci Dept 88-; Pltcl Sci; Music Indstry.

**SCOTT, TINA M,** Alfred Univ, Alfred, NY; JR; BS; Stdnt Athltc Mngr Hd Mngr 89-; NCWA Treas 90-; NAA; Alpha Iota Delta Pres; Pacioli Soc; Delta Mu Delta; Beta Gamma Sigma; Sigma Chi Nu Jdcl Rep 90-; Wmns Sftbl Clb; Bus; Acctg.

**SCOTT, TRACY M,** Norfolk St Univ, Norfolk, VA; SR; BS; Fresh/Soph Class Pblc Rltns 86-88; Jr Class Sec 88-89; Rsdnt Asst 87-89; Delta Sigma Theta Pntry Shwr Chrmn; Ambssdr VP 89-90; Ldrshp; Tchng Cert; Early Chldhd Ed; Tchng.

**SCOTT, TRACY M,** S U N Y Coll Of Tech At Alfred, Alfred, NY; FR; AS; Nrsng.

**SCOTT, VALERIE G,** Me Maritime Academy, Castine, ME; SO; BA; Naval ROTC Squad Ldr; Dns Lst; Navy Vet; Marine Eng Oper; Merchant Marine Eng.

**SCOTT, VICTORIA S,** Hillsborough Comm Coll, Tampa, FL; SO; AA; Education.

**SCOTT, VIOLET R,** Saint Josephs Coll New York, Brooklyn, NY; GD; BA; Mt Vrnn Nghbrhd Wtch 90; Nrss Fllwshp Pres 89; Prof Nrse Awrd 89; Crrbn Comm Grp Mt Vrnn Sec 89-; Dns Lst; NY Nrss Assn; Rgstrd Prof Nrse; AS BS New York Hosp; Psychtrc Nrsng Bellevue Hosp; Hlth Admin; MA.

**SCOTT, WALKEMMA J,** Tuskegee Univ, Tuskegee Inst, AL; SO; BS; Mrchng Bnd 89-; NSBE 90-; AICHE 90-; Ashlnd Oil Schlrshp 90-; Hon Rl 89-; Meth Schlrshp 89-; Chem; Chem Engr.

**SCOTT, WANDA C,** Clark Atlanta Univ, Atlanta, GA; SO; BA; Hstrcl Socty 90-; Grmn Clb VP 90-; Future Tchrs Of Amer VP 90-; FTA Sec 90-; Hnrs Prog 89-; Natl Coll Mnrty Ldrshp Awd 90-; Coll Schlrs Hstry Prog 90-; Hstry Educ; Edctr/Gdnc Cnslr.

**SCOTT, WILLIAM C,** Suffolk Comm Coll Western Cmps, Brentwood, NY; SO; Bus Clb V P; Stdnt Govt Sntr 89-90; African Amer Stdnts Assn 88; Former Postal Emplee; Cert 90; AAS; Bus Mgmt; Bus Law.

**SCOTT, WILLIAM E,** Saint Pauls Coll, Lawrenceville, VA; JR; BA; Alpha Kappa Mu Hnr Soc; Alpha Phi Alpha Frtrnty Inc; Bkstbl/Glf; Pol Sci; Law.

**SCOTT, YOLANDA R,** Meridian Comm Coll, Meridian, MS; FR; BA; Cmptr Sci; Anlyst/Prgmmr.

**SCOTT, YVETTE C,** Lincoln Univ, Lincoln Univ, PA; SR; BS; Natl Soc Blck Eng 88-; Natl Soc Physcs Stdnts 90-; PRIME 76-; Beta Kappa Chi; Alpha Chi; LASER Pgm Schlrshp Fllwshp 85-; BS; Physcs; Mech Eng.

**SCOTTO, KARA A,** Univ Of Ct, Storrs, CT; SR; BS; Animal Sci; Agribusiness.

**SCOTTON, KAREN L,** Salisbury St Univ, Salisbury, MD; JR.

**SCOTTON, TAMEKA M,** Tomlinson Coll, Cleveland, TN; FR; AA; Chorale Singing Mnstry; Frshmn Class Rep; Actvts Comm; Food Comm; Cert Of Rcgntn For Being On Pres List; Vlybl; Pwdrpff Ftbl; Eng; Cmmnctns.

**SCOUTEN, VICKI L,** Univ Of Tn At Chattanooga, Chattanooga, TN; JR; BSN; SNA 88-; Golden Key 84; Rho Lambda 84; Sigma Theta Tau; Chi Omega Alumnae; J Wheeler Mem Schlrshp; Ftns Trnr; BS 87; Nurs; OB RN.

**SCOZZAFAVA, MEGAN A,** Bay Path Coll, Longmeadow, MA; SO; AA; Glee Club/Chmbr Singers VP/CHOREGRPHR 89-; Stdnt Govt 90-; Maroon Key 90-; Resdnt Asst 90-; Stdnt Ambsdr 90-F Dorm Rep 89-90; Deans List 89-; Faculty Award; Arts/Sci.

**SCREWS, WILLIAM L,** Al A & M Univ, Normal, AL; JR; BA; Gd Hskpng Awrd 88-89; Dean Lst 88-; Elem Ed.

**SCRIBNER, DEBRA A,** Comm Coll Algny Co Algny Cmps, Pittsburgh, PA; GD; AS; Schlrs Awd 90; Deans Lst 88-; Wrd Prcsng Spclst; Cmptr Sci.

**SCRIVNER, JOSEPH F,** Crichton Coll, Memphis, TN; SO; BS; Assoc Bapt Mnstr; Hstry/Biblcl Stdes; Educ.

**SCROFANI, TRICIA A,** Univ Of Sc At Columbia, Columbia, SC; SO; BA; Hotel/Rstrnt/Trsm Admin; Mgmt.

**SCRONCE, JEFF S,** Western Piedmont Comm Coll, Morganton, NC; FR; Med Lab Tech; Med Lab Tech.

**SCRUGGS, LISA C,** Ms St Univ, Miss State, MS; JR; BA; Pltcl Sci; Law.

**SCRUGGS, MICHELLE D,** Univ Of Sc At Spartanburg, Spartanburg, SC; SO; Science Clb 89-; Math Clb 89-; Vlybl 89-; Pre Med.

**SCRUGGS, STEPHANIE C,** Al A & M Univ, Normal, AL; SR; BS; Stdnts Free Entrprs 89-; Lgstcs Clb 89-; Delta Mu Delta 90-; Acad Hnr Rl 89-90; Deans Lst 89-90; Bus/Lgstcs/Prcrmnt.

**SCUDDY, LISA J,** Fl International Univ, Miami, FL; GD; MPA; Jewish Fed Fndrsr 90; Richmond Elem Stdnt Tchr 90; Intrsnshp 89-90; BA FIU 88-90; AA Miami Dade Comm Clg 86-88; Pblc Admin; City Mgr.

**SCUDERI, MATTHEW G,** Cornell Univ Statutory College, Ithaca, NY; SO; Bio Bsnss; Med Schl Dr.

**SCULL, SHARON C,** Owensboro Jr Coll Of Bus, Owensboro, KY; SO; AS; SG 90-; Acad Hon Lst 90-; Comp Ofc; Acctnt.

**SCULLY, CHRISTINE H,** Boston Univ, Boston, MA; JR; BS; OT Clb; Wlk Hngr 88-90; Intn Lbrty Mtl Med Srvc; Intrn Lnrd Mrs Hsptl 90; Occptnl Thrpy.

**SCULLY, FERDINAND A,** Glassboro St Coll, Glassboro, NJ; JR; BA; Dept Hnrs Pol Sci 89; Drug/Alcohol Abse Thrpst Cnslr; AA Brlngtn Cnty Clg 89; Psychlgy; Clncl Psychlgy.

**SCUNGIO, LOUIS J,** Springfield Tech Comm Coll, Springfield, MA; SO; BA; Ntl Hon Soc 90-; Bnkg 86-87; Rtl Mgmt 87-; Acctg; CPA.

**SCURGGS, SHELBY L,** Volunteer St Comm Coll, Gallatin, TN; FR; BA; Eng; Sec Teacher.

**SCURLOCK, CYNTHIA A,** Nc Agri & Tech St Univ, Greensboro, NC; SR; AF ROTC Flght Cmmndr 90; Arnold Air Scty Pres; Sigma Tau Delta 89; AF Assoc 89; Hnr Stdnt 87; Grad As Cum Laude; BA; Prof Engl; Pblc Affrs Offcr USAF.

**SCURRY, ANN C,** Piedmont Tech Coll, Greenwood, SC; FR; BA; SGA; Indstrl Eng Grphcs Mech Drftng.

**SCUTCHALL, SUSAN R,** Mount Aloysius Jr Coll, Cresson, PA; FR; Spec Olympcs; Occptnl Thrpy.

**SCUTERI, SERGIO I,** Rutgers St Univ At Camden, Camden, NJ; JR; BA; Mktg Clb VP 90-; Stdnt Congress Rep; Dns Lst 88-; Mgmt/Mktg; Corp Law.

**SCZESNIAK, EDWARD J,** Marywood Coll, Scranton, PA; SO; BS; Scriblerus Clb; Orientn; Commuter Comm; Collgt Vol; IM Bsktbl Ftbl; Comm Disrdrs; Spch/Lang Pathlgy.

**SEAB, KELLY B,** Middle Tn St Univ, Murfreesboro, TN; JR; BS; Gamma Beta Phi 90; Chi Omega 89-; Pre-Med/Chem/Bio; Med/Dr.

**SEABERG, NICOLE S,** Barry Univ, Miami, FL; JR; BA; Engl Assoc 88-91; Alpha Mu Gamma 89-; Gldn Z Znt Srvc Clb 90-; Deans Lst 88-; Pres Lst 88-90; Brdcst Comm.

**SEABROOK, ERICA A,** Ky St Univ, Frankfort, KY; SO; BS; Pre Law 89-; Comp Sci 90-; NAACP 89-; Comp Sci; Law.

**SEACRIST, NOREEN B,** Daytona Beach Comm Coll, Daytona Beach, FL; SO; BA; Phi Theta Kappa Chrmn; Prsdnts Acdmc Lst; Deans Acdmc Lst; Extndd Fmly Adlt Dy Cr; Pht Jrnlst Clmnst Dytn News Jrnl; Psychlgy.

**SEAFORTH, GEORGE B,** Borough Of Manhattan Comm Coll, New York, NY; GD; AA; Lib Arts; Med.

**SEAGLE JR, HUBERT P,** Gaston Coll, Dallas, NC; FR; BS; US Army 86-90; Phrmcy.

**SEAGLE, SHERRY L,** Piedmont Tech Coll, Greenwood, SC; FR; ADN; BS Lander Coll 88; Nrsng.

**SEAGRAVES, CYNTHIA A,** Univ Of Ga, Athens, GA; SR; BED; Prfssnl Assn Of GA Edctrs 90-; Assn Fr Chldhd Educ Intrnatl 90-; Erly Chldhd Educ; Elem Educ.

**SEAGRAVES III, FRANK E,** Univ Of Ga, Athens, GA; SR; MED; Phys Educ Mjrs Clb 86-; GA Allnce Of Hlth Phys Educ Rcrtn And Dnce 88-; Spcl Olympics 86-; Univ Of GA Mtr Dev Clnc; Phys Educ Grad Asstnshp; IM Sftbl And Ftbl 88-; Bed; Phys Educ; Spclze In Spnl Crd Injrs.

**SEAL, SCOTT BRADLEY,** Univ Of Tn At Chattanooga, Chattanooga, TN; SR; BSE; Stdnt Alnc Chr Dvlpmnt 89-90; Stdnt Almn Cncl 88-90; Hnrs Cncl Pres 88-89; Gldn Key Pres 90-; Tau Beta Pi 89-; Phi Eta Rho 87-88; Univ Hnrs Flw 87-; Andrew D Holt Schlr; Engrg.

**SEALEY, RHONDA D,** Clayton St Coll, Morrow, GA; SO; SGA VP 90-; Early Childhood Ed/Spcl Ed; Elem Tchr.

**SEALS, ERIKA C,** Alcorn St Univ, Lorman, MS; JR; BS; Hon Org; Poetry Clb; Biolgy Clg; Alpha Kappa Mu; Chem/Biolgy; Pre-Med.

**SEALS, JANET G,** Mercer Univ Schl Of Pharm, Atlanta, GA; GD; PHARM; ASHP; BA Carson Newman Clg 85; Pharmacy.

**SEALS, LISA A,** Niagara Univ, Niagara Univ, NY; FR; BA; Biol; Vet Med.

**SEALS, SHELIA F,** Univ Of Ky, Lexington, KY; SR; BA; Stdnt Athl Cncl 90; Stdnt Athl Cncl 90; AAS Southeast Comm Coll 87; Socl Wrk.

**SEALY, EMMA S,** Birmingham Southern Coll, Birmingham, AL; FR; Stu Almn Assc; Phi Eta Sigma; Zeta Tau Alpha Scl Asst 90-; IM Ftbl Vllybl Bsktbl; Psychlgy; Clncl Psychlgsts.

**SEALY, MALYNDA P,** Univ Of South Al, Mobile, AL; SR; BA; Phi Theta Kappa 89-; Phi Kappa Phi; Elem Ed; Tch.

**SEAMAN, CLAUDIA L,** Univ Of Miami, Coral Gables, FL; SR; BS; ASCE; BS; Cvl Archtctrl Eng; Eng.

**SEAMAN, JEFFREY A,** Comm Coll Of Beaver County, Monaca, PA; SO; IM Tennis; CIS/TELE Commnctns; Cmptr Prgrmmng.**

**SEAMAN, LINDA J,** Hudson Valley Comm Coll, Troy, NY; FR; AS; Lbrl Arts; Psychlgy.

**SEAMAN, MICHAEL L,** Winthrop Coll, Rock Hill, SC; SO; BS; Pi Lambda Phi/Pa Beta Upsilon 82-85; Teddys Tavern Mgr 85-90; Intr Dsgn; Architecture.

**SEAMAN, TRACY ANN MARIE,** Univ Of Sc At Columbia, Columbia, SC; SO; Girl Scouts Of Am Asst Ldr; Elem Edn; Tchr.

**SEAMANS, JONATHAN D,** Clarkson Univ, Potsdam, NY; SR; BS; Amnesty Intrntl 87; Clrksn Intgrtr 89-90; Bstkbl 87-89; Ecnmcs/Pol Sci.

**SEAMON, JILL D,** Le Moyne Coll, Syracuse, NY; JR; BA; Inst Mgmt Acctnts Sec Elct; Acctg Soc 89-; Flk Grp 90-; Lemoyne Jesuit Schlrshp 88-; Coed Sftbl IMS; Acctg; CPA.

**SEAMSTER, PATRICIA D,** Longwood Coll, Farmville, VA; SR; MSW; Alpha Gamma Delta Rtl Chrprsn 89-90; Hosp Scl Wrk Intern; Probahm Parile Offcr InternBS; Slc Wrk; Clncl Scl Wrkr.

**SEAMSTER, SUSAN W,** Mary Baldwin Coll, Staunton, VA; JR; BA; Rsdnt Advsr 90-; Mrktng Comm.

**SEARCY, ANN MAXWELL,** Tallahassee Comm Coll, Tallahassee, FL; JR; BA; Fsu Bahai Club 90; AA 90; Engl Lit; Law.

**SEARCY, DOUGLAS,** Ny Univ, New York, NY; FR; Fnnc/Accntng; Law/Bus.

**SEARCY, LAURA F,** Emory Univ, Atlanta, GA; GD; MN; Sigma Theta Tau 90-; BSN Univ FL 76; Nrsng-Chld Hlth; Pdtrc.

**SEARCY, MARK W,** Univ Of North Fl, Jacksonville, FL; SR; AA FL Comm Clg 87; Bsn Admn; Hmn Rscs.

**SEARFOSS, ANJANETTE M,** Juniata Coll, Huntingdon, PA; SO; BS; JCAA 89-; Beta Beta Beta 90-; Swmmg Tm 89-; Mlclr-Blgy; Rsrch.

**SEARFOSS, MARK A,** Columbus Coll Of Art & Design, Columbus, OH; FR; BA; Advrstng Dsgn.

**SEARLE, PAMELA E,** Univ Of Sc At Columbia, Columbia, SC; JR; Eta Sigma Delta Sec; Chi Omega DWC Schlrshp Chrmn 88-; Htl Mngmnt; Trsm.

**SEARLS, MARY,** Hudson County Comm Coll, Jersey City, NJ; SR; AAS; Mdcl Rcrds Clb Pres 89-; Cum Laude; Mdcl Rcrds Tech.

**SEARS, ELLEN L,** Holyoke Comm Coll, Holyoke, MA; FR; AED; Edctn Clb Sec 90; Abner Gibbs Schl PTO 90-; Erly Chldhd Ed; Tchr.

**SEARS, ERIC N,** Marshall University, Huntington, WV; SR; BBA; Stdnt Govt Assoc Sgt At Arms 90; Stdnts For Christ 90-; Order Of Omega 89-; Scabbard/Blade 88-89; Sigma Phi Epsilon Cntrllr 87-; Amer Leg Awd ROTC; IM Wrstlng Chmpn 87-; Bus Mgmt; Law.

**SEARS, JAN M,** Commonwealth Coll, Virginia Beach, VA; FR; AS; Cert Excell Wrtng Tidewtr Comm Clg 88; Paralgl; Law.

**SEARS, MARK B,** Valdosta St Coll, Valdosta, GA; SO; BBA; Deans List 89-; John T Odum Schlrshp 89-; Bus Mgt; Bus Admnstrtn.

**SEARS, SHARON R,** Univ Of Cincinnati, Cincinnati, OH; SR; BS; Gldn Key 89-; Kappa Delta Pi 89-; Clg Std Amer 88-; Cum Laude 90; Cmptr Oprtr 71-77; Data Entry Clrk 85-86; Elem Ed; Tchr.

**SEASE, CYNTHIA J,** Coll Of Charleston, Charleston, SC; JR; BA; Educ; Tch Elem Schl.

**SEASE, P MICHELE,** Lenoir Rhyne Coll, Hickory, NC; FR; BA; Lutheran Student Mvt 90-; Flwshp Christ Athlet 90-; Campus Ministry Forum 90-; Phi Beta Lambda; Circle K Press Repres 90-; Nursingf Genealogy.

**SEATON, MELISSA G,** Brescia Coll, Owensboro, KY; JR; BA; NEA 90-; KEA 90-; Deans List 90-; AA Owensboro Comm Coll 90; Elem Edn; Teach.

**SEAVERS, BRANDON L,** Memphis St Univ, Memphis, TN; SO; BA; Full Schlrshp; Msc; Msc/Rcrdng.

**SEAWELL, SAM G,** Univ Of Nc At Greensboro, Greensboro, NC; SR; BM; Music/Percussion Perf; Music.

**SEAWRIGHT, ROBERT D,** Kent St Univ Kent Cmps, Kent, OH; SR; BBA; Rho Epsilon P 89-; FMA 89-91; Golden Key; Urban Land Inst; NACORE; Rl Estate/Sls/Cnstrctn/Dvlpmnt 86-; AA Cuyahoga Comm Coll 89; Real Estate/Fnc; Corp Real Estate Dvlpmnt.

**SEAY, JENNIFER N,** Germanna Comm Coll, Locust Grove, VA; FR; Engl; Elem Tchr.

**SEAY, JERRA L,** Ky Christian Coll, Grayson, KY; SR; BS; Class Secy 90-; Girl Sct Ldr 87-; Educ Bible; Tchng.

**SEAY, JO ANNE P,** Longwood Coll, Farmville, VA; SR; Trinty Presby Chrch Sch Tchr 86-; Comm Plysch Tchr; BS; Educ/Lib Sci; Elem Educ.

**SEAY, LISA G,** Averett Coll, Danville, VA; SR; BS; Sci Assoc VP 89; Alpha Chi 90; Phi Theta Kappa 86-87; Beta Beta Beta 90; Summa Cum Laude; AS Patrick Henry Cmmnty Clg 87; Bio Chmstry Mnr; Tchr.

**SEAY, STACY A,** Univ Of Al At Birmingham, Birmingham, AL; SR; BS; Natl Assn Scl Wrkrs 90-; Stdnt Rep Cncl Scl Wrk Educ 90-; Gldn Key 90-; Stdnt Scl Wrk Org Rprtr 89-; Meals Whls 90-; Scl Wrk Outstndng Stdnt Awd; Dept Yth Serv-Asstshp Pilot Pgm 90-; Dept Hmn Rsrcs-Scl Wrk Intrn 90-; Scl Wrk; Fmly Thrpst.

**SEBASTIAN, ANGELA L,** Univ Of South Al, Mobile, AL; SR; BS; Omicron Delta Kappa; Alpha Gamma Delta Corres Sec 88-90; IM Wtr Polo Sftbll; Elem Ed.

**SEBASTIAN, MARK J,** Univ Of South Al, Mobile, AL; SO; Engl.

**SEBASTIAN, RICHARD A,** Va Commonwealth Univ, Richmond, VA; SR; BA; Radio 87; Cable Radio 88-89; Commonwealth Times Folio Sect Stf Wrtr 89; Engl; Tchg/Wrtg/Film.

**SEBASTIEN, DEBRAH A,** Coppin St Coll, Baltimore, MD; JR; BA; Intl Std Asc Sec 88-; Alpha Kappa Alpha; Psy; Law.

**SEBES, STACY L,** Kent St Univ Kent Cmps, Kent, OH; SR; MBA; Natl Stdnt Nrs Assoc 88-; Stdnts Prof Nrsng 88-; Sigma Theta Tau Nrsng Hon Soc 90-; Sigma Theta Tau 90-; Pi Delta Inspnl Chrprsn 88-89; Dns Lst Kent St Univ 90-; KSU Schlrshp 90-; Lkwd Hosp Vol Schlrshp 90-; Wmns Sccr Tm 89-90; IM Sftbl 89-91; Nrsng.

**SECCHIARI, ALICE M,** Univ Of West Fl, Pensacola, FL; SR; BED; Elm Edn; Teach.

**SECH, CHRISTINE M,** Miami Univ, Oxford, OH; FR; BA; Hall Govt Comm Serv Chr 90-; Emrgng Ldrs 90-; Hstss 90-; Pres Lst 90-; Alpha Lambda Delta Bnqut Chr; Mktg; Bus.

**SECHLER, SCOTT D,** Univ Of Akron, Akron, OH; JR; Hnrs Pro; Phi Eta Sigma; Gldn Key; Pres Schlr 87-89; Altrntg Term Coop Dow Chem 90-; Chem Engr.

**SECHRIST, ERIKA L,** Savannah Coll Of Art & Design, Savannah, GA; SO; BFA; ISID 90-; ASID 90-; Interio Design; Residential.

**SECKBACH, KATHERINE D,** Snead St Jr Coll, Boaz, AL; FR; BS; LPN TN Voctnl Sch Of Nrsng 72; Pre Nrsng; Nrsng/Tchng.

**SECKEL, DEBRA J,** Cumberland Coll, Williamsburg, KY; JR; BS; Math Physcs Clb 89-F Bnd 90; Siler Awrd; Deans Lst 89; Math Physcs; Tchng.

**SECKMAN, CHAD A,** Marshall University, Huntington, WV; SR; BA; Hll Assoc 89-; RA 90-; Asstd Vslly Imprd Chldrn 90-; Elem Ed.

**SECKMAN, CHRISTOPHER V,** Marshall University, Huntington, WV; SR; BS; Assoc For Comp Mach Treas 90-; Upsilon Pi Epsilon Treas 90-; Comp Sci.

**SECNIK, MARTINA,** Cleveland St Univ, Cleveland, OH; SO; BA; Geolgy/Poli Sci; Envrnmntl Sci.**

**SECOLA-BIASCOECHER, ANTONIO F,** Univ Of Pr At Rio Piedras, Rio Piedras, PR; SO; BBA; Phi Sigma Alpha 90-; Acctg; Finance.

**SECORA, CHRISTOPHER M,** Youngstown St Univ, Youngstown, OH; SR; BE; IEEE 89-; Amer Nclr Soc 90-; Elctrcl Engrg.

**SECREST, SEAN S,** James Madison University, Harrisonburg, VA; FR; BS; Bapt Stdnt Un 90-; Biology; Dentist.

**SEDA SEDA, ELIZABETH,** Inter Amer Univ Pr San German, San German, PR; FR.

**SEDA TORO, LISSETTE,** Inter Amer Univ Pr San German, San German, PR; SR; Amer Mrktng Assn VP 90-; Harris Schlrshp 87-; Hnr Cert 87-; Medal Hghst Aver; Mrktng; Music Bus/Cmmnctns.

**SEDA, SANDRA LEE,** City Univ Of Ny Baruch Coll, New York, NY; GD; MBA; PRIDE 84-85; Fash 85; BBA Baruch Clg 90; Hlth Care Admin.

**SEDGWICK, JASON M,** S U N Y Coll Of Tech At Alfred, Alfred, NY; FR; MBA; Alfred Stdnt Activ Cncl Chrmn 90-; Alfred Karate Academy 90-; Bus Admin; Mktng.

**SEDKI, ASHLEY B,** Fl St Univ, Tallahassee, FL; FR; FSU Flying High Circus; Phi Eta Sigma; Kappa Delta.

**SEDLAK, ROBERT K,** Hudson Valley Comm Coll, Troy, NY; SR; AOS; Elctrcl Engnrng.

**SEE, CHIN S,** S U N Y At Buffalo, Buffalo, NY; SR; BS; Acctg/Fnc; Mgrl Acctnt.

**SEE, CHRISTINA M,** Fl St Univ, Tallahassee, FL; FR; BA; Phi Eta Sigma 90-; Cmnctns; Advrtsmnt.

**SEE, DANIEL A,** S U N Y Coll Of Tech At Delhi, Delhi, NY; FR; AOS Delhi Tech; Plmbng/Htng; Htng Vntltn Air Cond.

**SEE, MARK A,** Memphis St Univ, Memphis, TN; SR; BA; Stdnt Actvts Cncl 87-88; Gldn Ky 90-; Ord Omega 89-; Kappa Sigma Treas 87-; Acctg; CPA.

**SEE, SUSAN T,** Lexington Comm Coll, Lexington, KY; SO; BA; VP Amer Inst Bnkng 84-85; Natl Assc Bnk Wmn 85-86; Asst VP Bnk; Mtg Ln Offcr; Educ; Erly Elem Tchr.

**SEEBER, MATTHIAS R,** George Mason Univ, Fairfax, VA; SR; BS; Beta Gamma Sigma; MBA Assn; Mgmt; Intrnatl Bus Fnnce.**

**SEELEY, CATHY L,** Teikyo Post Univ, Waterbury, CT; JR; BA; Campus Fundraisers For Homeless 89-90; Deans Lst 89-; Jay Alix Schlrshp; Acctng; CPA.

**SEELEY, KIMBERLY A,** S U N Y Coll At Fredonia, Fredonia, NY; JR; BA; Tchr Edctn Clb Scl Chrmn 90-; Kappa Delta Pi; Deans Lst; Kappa Delta Pi; Thomas Mills Schlrshp 88-; Elem Edctn; Tchng.

**SEELHORST, LISA M,** Univ Of South Al, Mobile, AL; SR; BS; St Assoc For Hlth ASAHPERD 90-; SHAPE Clb 89-; Kappa Delta Pi 90-; IM 90-; Phys Educ; Tchr.

**SEELIG, MICHELLE D,** Wesleyan Univ, Middletown, CT; FR; BA; Red Crss Bld Dr 90-; IM Sftbl Sccr 90-.

**SEELY, JOAN E,** Newbury Coll, Brookline, MA; FR; BS; COBOL Cls Rep 90-; Acctng I Cls Rep 90-; Comptr Concepts 90-; Medicare B Appeals Blue Cross Blue Shield Of MASS Inc; Comptr Sci; Progrmng/Sys Anlyst.

**SEERS, BONNIE S,** Longwood Coll, Farmville, VA; JR; BFA; Art Works Inc Pres 88; Alpha Lambda Delta 88; Phi Kappa Phi; Art; Intr Dsgn.

**SEESE, KEVIN A,** Widener Univ, Chester, PA; JR; BA; RA 90-; Widener Vrsty Golf 89-; Coach Of St Albert Swm Tm Head Coach 87-90; Alpha Phi Omega 90-; Phi Delta Thea 90-; Vrsty Golf 89-; Acctng; Law.

**SEESE, VALERIE L,** Mount Aloysius Jr Coll, Cresson, PA; FR; BS; Erly Chldhd Edc; Tchng.

**SEEZOX, STACY A,** Indiana Univ Of Pa, Indiana, PA; JR; PA St Edctnl Assn 90-; Delta Zeta Rm Mngr 90; Prjct Stride; Elem Ed; Elem Tchr.

**SEGAL, ALAN B,** S U N Y At Stony Brook, Stony Brook, NY; GD; MD; Food/Hunger Concern Grp 82-84; Student Bk Coop 83-84; New York Comtyaction Ntwk 83-; Joel Robinson Schlrshp Comty Invlt 84; Deans List/Hunter Clg NY NY 90; United Edtn Tchrs 87-90; Amer Medl Assoc 90-; Med.

**SEGAL, PAMELA D,** Saint Thomas Univ, Miami, FL; JR; BA; Chrldrs 90-; Delta Epsilon Sigma 87-; Bsktbl Tm 86-88; AA 88; Scndry Educ; Prof.

**SEGALEN, YANN FRANCOIS,** Winthrop Coll, Rock Hill, SC; SR; BA; AMA 89-90; Mkrg; Intl Bus.

**SEGALL, SHANNON JILL,** Univ Of Ga, Athens, GA; SR; BSED; Sigma Delta Tau Pldg Trnr 87-; Ed Erly Chldhd; Tchr.

**SEGARRA NAVARRO, JOSE ANTONIO,** City Univ Of Ny City Coll, New York, NY; JR; Cmnty Hlth Educ Ctr Pres 89-; Cauducens Soc Pre Med 89-90; Aspira Of New York Brd Of Dir 87; Chldrns Aid Soc-Est Hrlm Cmnty Edctr 90-; City Clg Mntrs Mntr 90-; NY Hosp Cornell Med Ctr Intern 89; Educ/Med.

**SEGARRA, CESAR A,** Inter Amer Univ Pr Hato Rey, Hato Rey, PR; SR; BA; Biological Sci Assn Of Intewr Vocal 90; Am Univ Geo Assn 90; Natl Rifle Assn 90; Nu Sigma Beta 90; Biomed Sci; Med.**

**SEGARS, CHARLES E,** Embry Riddle Aeronautical Univ, Daytona Beach, FL; JR; BS; Chs Clb 89-90; Tr 89-90; Army ROTC Co Cmdr 88-; Cmptr Sci; Mltry.

**SEGER, JULIA L,** Univ Of Pittsburgh, Pittsburgh, PA; SO; BSN; Natl Stndt Nurses Assn 89-; Stdnt Nurses Assn Of PA 89-; Deans Lst 89-; Stdnt Nurses Assn Of Univ Of PA 89-; Alpha Tau Delta 90-; Childrens Hosp Vol 89-; Deans Lst 89-; CNA State Of PA; Cert Nursing Asst; Nursing.

**SEGER, KEVIN C,** Tn Temple Univ, Chattanooga, TN; SR; BS; Phi Beta Delta Pres 90-; Cls Sgt Arms 88-89; Chpln 89-90; Choir Vp 89-90; Deans Lst 90-; Moody Scty Vp 89-90; Sears Empl Of Mnth 89; Hghst Sales 90; Scty Ftbl/Bsktbl/Sccr/Vlybl/Sftbl 87-90; Assc Pstrl Stds; Assc Pstr/Yth Dir.

**SEGER, LORI D,** Kent St Univ Kent Cmps, Kent, OH; JR; BA; Std DPMA Sec 90-; Gldn Key 90-; Untd Chrch Chrst Vol 89-; Cmptr Sci/Bsn; Prgmmr/Anlys.

**SEGERS, AMANDA L,** Univ Of Ga, Athens, GA; SR; BSED; Wsly Fndtn 86-; Symphny 86-90; Army ROTC 88-90; Schlrshp Army ROTC 88-90; Dghtrs Armcn Rvltn Mtl Achvmnt 90; Scnd Ltnnt US Army 90; Engl.

**SEGERS, CAROLYN E,** Fl St Univ, Tallahassee, FL; SR; BS; AA Chipola Jr Clg 87; Elem Educ; Tchr.

**SEGO, ANTHONY R,** Commonwealth Coll, Virginia Beach, VA; FR; AS; Acctng Clb 90-; Alpha Beta Gamma; Boat Unit; 1st Cls Ctrkpr; US Navy 76-; Acctng; CPA.

**SEGOVIA, JAVIER,** Ma Inst Of Tech, Cambridge, MA; SO; BS; Assn Of PR Stdnts Athltc Chr 89-; Chss Clb 90-; Natl Hspnc Schlr 90; Inst Of Nclr Pwr Oprtns Schlr 89-; Natl Scty Of Prof Engs Schlrshp 90; Vsrty Vlybl Strtr 89-; Mech Eng; Eng Mgmt.**

**SEGREST, STEPHEN MARK,** Central Al Comm Coll, Alexander City, AL; FR; Bsbl Shrtstop; Acctng; Govt.

**SEGRO, DINA M,** Bloomfield Coll, Bloomfield, NJ; FR; Sftbl; Pre-Chiro Clb; Hnrs Lst; Sigma Phi Delta; Sftbl Tm; Pre-Chiro; Chiro.

**SEGUIN, JEANETTE R,** Univ Of Akron, Akron, OH; JR; Univ Akron Bsbl Tm Batgirl; Bus Admn; Matrls Mgmt.

**SEGUIN, LISA M,** Rivier Coll, Nashua, NH; FR; BS; HUG; Budd Prog 90-91; Chmstry; Phrmcy.

**SEHLMEYER, ELIZABETH J,** Saint Michaels Coll, Winooski, VT; FR; BA; Bsktbl Tm; Elem Ed.

**SEIBEL, MICHELLE L,** Carnegie Mellon Univ, Pittsburgh, PA; FR; BS; Lambda Sigma; Kappa Alpha Theta Hse Mngr 90-; Inf Syst/Ind Mngt; Art Intell.

**SEIBEL, NEIL D,** Northern Ky Univ, Highland Hts, KY; SO; BA; Theatr/Antrplgy; Prof Actr.

**SEIBERT, CRISTY R,** Savannah Coll Of Art & Design, Savannah, GA; GD; MFA; Asid 90; Chi-Omega 84-88; Ivan Allen Intrshp 90; Bernitas Intrnshp 91; Volleybll-Tennis 84-88; BFA; Marietta Clg 88; Interior Dsgn; Homebldr.

**SEIBERT, DEBORAH A,** Owensboro Jr Coll Of Bus, Owensboro, KY; GD; Indiana Dept Ins License 89-; Customer Svc; Cert 90; Word Proc Spec.

**SEIBERT, PAULA,** Point Park Coll, Pittsburgh, PA; SR; BS; Orient Guide; Alpha Sigma Lambda Pres 88-90; AS 88; Cert Bradford Schl 86; Bus Mgmt.

**SEIBT, BRIAN W,** Embry Riddle Aeronautical Univ, Daytona Beach, FL; JR; BS; SGA Avionics Degree Pgm Rep; Avionics Clb Pres 90-; Orntn Tm Ldr; Avionics Eng Tech Hon Soc 90-; Natl Eng Tech Hon Soc 90-; Natl Ldrshp Hon Soc 90-; Dive Blnd Serv Driver 90-; Eagle Flght Ctr 88; Avionics Eng Tech.

**SEICH, JENNIFER M,** Univ Of Akron, Akron, OH; SO; Commctv Disorders; Speech/Lang Path.

**SEIDEL, ALICE A,** Georgian Court Coll, Lakewood, NJ; SR; BA; AA Ocean Co Coll 85; Hstry; Sec Tchng.

**SEIDEL, KIMBERLY A,** Mount Saint Mary Coll, Newburgh, NY; SO; BS; Stdnt Govt 1st Asst To VP Of Inance 90-; Yrbk Edtr In Chf 90-; Ambsdr Clb 90-; Hnrs Allnc 90-; Ralph Schlr 90-; Girl Sct 76-; Psychlgy Elem/Spec Educ Cert; Tchr.

**SEIDEN, DEBORAH D,** Univ Of Nc At Asheville, Asheville, NC; FR; BA; Wrtng Awd; Democratic Party; Staff Acctnt/Recruiter Plcmnt Mgr; Cert Univ Of Paris 84; Lit/Philosophy; Law.

**SEIDEN, JERYL E,** Manhattanville Coll, Purchase, NY; SR; MBA; Mgmt Deprtmntl Hnrs; Mrktng.

**SEIDLE, PETER N,** Widener Univ, Chester, PA; FR; BS; Clg Republican Clb 90-; Newspaper Staff Photographer 90-; Phi Sigma Pi; Engrng.

**SEIFERT, DANA C,** Univ Of Southern Ms, Hattiesburg, MS; JR; BS; Chrldr Capt 87-89; Soc/Rehab Serv; Snclr.

**SEIFERT, MICHELLE M,** S U N Y Coll At Fredonia, Fredonia, NY; SO; BA; Bus Club Exec Secy 89-; Acctng Soc 89-90; Alumni Cncl 89-; All Amercn Schlr 90-; Bus; Acctng.

**SEIFERT, SONYA LORRAINE,** S U N Y Coll Of Tech At Alfred, Alfred, NY; SO; AS; Stdnts Inv Comm Actn VP 89-; Soc Behvrl Sci Clb Pres 89-; Otdr Rec Clb 89-; Hab Hmnties; Sigma Tau 89-90; Psi Beta 90-; Phi Theta Kappa Rec Sec 90-; Emnl Campus Mnstry Sonlf Sec 89-; Alfred St Clg Tour Gde Stdnt Ambsdr 89-; Humn Serv; Soc Wrk.

**SEIFERTH, CURTIS D,** S U N Y Coll Of Tech At Frmgdl, Farmingdale, NY; FR; BSN; SNA 90-; ARC Fndrsr; Nurs; Doc Med.

**SEIFRIED, JEFFREY A,** Univ Of Louisville, Louisville, KY; JR; MA; IEEE 90-; Gldn Ky 90-; Coop Intrnshp Metrpltn Swr Dstrct; General Elec Co; Elec Engr.

**SEIGH, DIANNE L,** Mount Aloysius Jr Coll, Cresson, PA; FR; AS; Mdcl Asstnt; Mdcl Fld.

**SEIPEL, KATHLEEN R,** Oh Dominican Coll, Columbus, OH; JR; BSED; Cmps Mnstry Pres 90; Circle K 90; Rsdnt Assoc 90; Peer Cnsltnt; Dns Lst; Anna Hayes Ruck Schlrshp; Elem Educ; Teach.

**SEIPLE, PENELOPE M,** Wilmington Coll, New Castle, DE; SR; Hd Nrs Med Ctr Delaware Christiana Hsp; BSN; Nrsg.

**SEITER, KELLY A,** Univ Of Ky, Lexington, KY; SR; BA; Eng; Ed/Wrtng.

**SEITER, TANYA A,** Univ Of South Al, Mobile, AL; SO; BS; Phi Eta Sigma; Bus.

**SEITZ, GREGORY K,** Univ Of North Al, Florence, AL; SR; BS; Sprts Info Stdnt Asst 88-; Jrnlsm.**

**SEITZ, JENNIFER B,** Univ Of Cin R Walters Coll, Blue Ash, OH; FR; BAMBA; Lbrl Arts; Mrktng Bus Admin.

**SEITZ, SHAWN E,** Gordon Conwell Theol Sem, S Hamilton, MA; GD; MDIV; Pre Vet Clb Pres 76-77; Amer Vet Med Assoc 85-; MI Vet Med Assoc 85-; BS MI State Univ 82; DVM MI State Univ 84; Theology; Tchr.**

**SEITZ, SHELLEY A,** Univ Of Nc At Greensboro, Greensboro, NC; Wsly/Lthr; Phi Mu Crrspndg Sec 88-90; Gamma Sigma Sigma Sec 87-88; IM Sftbl 87-89; BS UNG-GRNSBRO 90; Elem Educ.

**SEIZ, KRISTEN A,** Glassboro St Coll, Glassboro, NJ; FR; BA; Actvty Bd Advrtsng Comm 90-; Amer Mktg Assn Pres; Cmmnctns/Advrtsng.

**SEJOUR, JEANNETTE N,** Univ Of Fl, Gainesville, FL; JR; BA; Creole Clb; Beta Eta Sigma; Most Outstndg Cmnty Coll Grad 90; Deans Lst 90-; OMASP Hghst Hon Awd; AA 90; Psychlgy; Medicine.

**SEKOL, CHRISTOPHER P,** Youngstown St Univ, Youngstown, OH; SO; BED; Cvl Eng.

**SELBY, REGINA A,** Tn Tech Univ, Cookeville, TN; SO; BS; Psych.**

**SELDES, MARK A,** Va Commonwealth Univ, Richmond, VA; SO; BS; Hnrs Pgm; Air Frc Rsv SRA 86-90; Math; MS.

**SELDON, DARRELLE O,** Al St Univ, Montgomery, AL; SR; Bptst Cmps Mnstrs Pres 89-; Alpha Kappa Mu; Acdmc Schlrshp 87-; Math/Educ; Tchr.

**SELEKMAN, JEREMY B,** Villanova Univ, Villanova, PA; SR; BA; Vol Socl Actions Offc Crdntr Emer Actn Comm 87-; Hillel Pres 87-; Phi Beta Kappa; Phi Kappa Phi 90-; Omicron Delta Kappa 89-; Psi Chi 89-; Summa Cum Laude; Psychlgy Dept Medallion; Mentzer Awd Wnr; Psychlgy; Clin Psychlgy.

**SELFE, DONNA E,** Va Highlands Comm Coll, Abingdon, VA; FR; AAS; NANS 90-; VANS 90-; Deans Lst 90-; Leg Up Vol; PTA; Sub Tchr 85-; Cert VA Hghlnds Comm Clg 74-75; Nrsng; RN.

**SELIGMAN, LARRY S,** Univ Of Louisville, Louisville, KY; SR; MCS; Mensa 89-90; DPMA 89-90; BS 90; Comp Sci; Prfsrshp/Rsrch.

**SELKE, TAMALA SUE,** Columbia Coll, Columbia, SC; JR; BA; Dean Advsry Com 90-; Res Stdnt Cncl VC 90-; Library Co 90-; Omicron Delta Kappa; Deans Lst 89-; Res Stdnt Cncl Thank You Awd; Math; Engineering.**

**SELL, LINDA E,** Univ Of Sc At Coastal Carolina, Conway, SC; BED; SCEA; Cnslr/Therapist; ESL Tchr; BA Penn St 87; Secondary Ed; English Tchr.

**SELL, PATRICIA J,** Saint Francis Coll, Loretto, PA; JR; BS; Acctg Clb 88-; Orntn Asst 89-; Chors; Acctg; Publ Acctg.

**SELL, SHANNON M,** Wv Univ, Morgantown, WV; SR; BSN; Mrchg Bnd 87-88; Nrsg; Emrgncy Nrs.

**SELLARS, ANGELIA L,** Owensboro Jr Coll Of Bus, Owensboro, KY; GD; Pres List 90; Hnrs List 89; Perfect Attnd 89; Tutor Mdcl Trmnlgy 90; Dplm Mdcl; Off Asst; Medical; Lab Tech.

**SELLARS, SEAN P,** Tri County Tech Coll, Pendleton, SC; SO; BS; Accounting.

**SELLARS, SHERRIE L,** Draughons Jr Coll Nashville, Nashville, TN; SR; ASSOC 90; Sec Sci; Sec.

**SELLE, CHRISTOPHER R,** Middle Ga Coll, Cochran, GA; SO; Bapt Stdnt Union 88-90; Jyfl Mnstries 88-90; Gamma Beta Phi Rprtr 88-90; Elec Eng.

**SELLENTHIN, KATHLEEN M,** Le Moyne Coll, Syracuse, NY; JR; BS; Intl Hse 88-; Amnesty Intl 88-; Indstrl Rels-Pol Sci; Hmn Res Mgmt Adm.

**SELLEPACK III, JOSEPH D,** Asbury Theological Sem, Wilmore, KY; GD; MDIV; Habitat Humanity Treas; Hand Food Bank Coord Vol; Un Wesleyan Coll Hon Soc 89; Un Wesleyan Intercoll Bsktbl 87-89; BS Un Wesleyan Coll 89; Theology; Pastoral Mnstry.**

**SELLERS, DANA L,** Univ Of Southern Ms, Hattiesburg, MS; SO; Hnrs Std Asc Sec 89-; Plymr Sci Clb Treas 90-; Hl Cncl Sec 89-90; Gamma Beta Phi 90-; Delta Tau Delta Ltl Sis; Pres Schlr 89-; Hl Cncl Offcr Mnth 89; IM Sftbl; Plymr Sci; Indy.

**SELLERS, EDNA C,** Johnson C Smith Univ, Charlotte, NC; GD; BS; Cmptr Sci Clb 85-90; RW Spiritual Choir 85-89; Homecmng Comm 86; Cmptr Sci; Rsrch.

**SELLERS, HILDRED KAY,** Wv Univ At Parkersburg, Parkersburg, WV; SO; AAS; SS Tchr; Chrch Aux Pres; Dns Lst 88-90; Pennsboro Mfg 86-90; Bsns; Bureau Of Publ Dept.

**SELLERS, JOHN W,** Daytona Beach Comm Coll, Daytona Beach, FL; FR; BS; Cert Defense Lang Inst 87; Nurse; Intl Admin.

**SELLERS, KIMBERLY R,** Livingston Univ, Livingston, AL; SR; Natl Ed Assoc; AL Ed Assoc; Natl Bsn Ed Assoc; Livingston Univ Schlr Awd Bsn; BS; Bsn Ed; Tchg.

**SELLERS, LA SHELL,** Al St Univ, Montgomery, AL; FR; Math; Accntng.

**SELLERS, MIMI R,** Radford Univ, Radford, VA; SR; BBA; AMA 90-; Soc Advncmnt Mgt 90-; Schl Nwspr Staff Wrtr 90; Intrvrsty Flwshp 88-89; Aerbcs Clb 88-89; Vrsty Chrldng 87-88; Mrktng; Accnt Rep Sales.

**SELLERS, STACEY S,** Univ Of Cincinnati, Cincinnati, OH; JR; BA; Gold Key; Intshp WLM Radio; Media Arts; Brdcstng.

**SELLERS, STEPHANIE R,** Nc Agri & Tech St Univ, Greensboro, NC; JR; BS; Palmetto Aggie Clb 90-; NAACP 89-; Wmns Cncl 88-; Alpha Lambda Delta; Beta Alpha Psi 1st VP; ALOBEAEM 89-; US Dept Of Ed Smmr Enrchmnt Ed Prgrm Hampton Univ 90; Accntng; Crprte Law.**

**SELLERS, SUSAN E,** Mercer Univ, Macon, GA; FR; Sci; Med.

**SELLERS, TRAVELLA ANTOINETTE,** Lincoln Univ, Lincoln Univ, PA; FR; BA; Jpns Clb Pres 90-; Stdnt Govt Assc Rprtr 90-; Hon Pgm 90-; Pres Awrd 90-; Almn Merit Awrd 90-; Deans List 90-; Bio; Medcn.

**SELLEY, ELIZABETH A,** Univ Of South Al, Mobile, AL; JR; BSC; Tennis Schlrshp; Sprts Injry Mgmt; Athl Trnr.

**SELLIAH, NITHIANANDAN,** Univ Of Ky, Lexington, KY; SR; PHD; Csmpltan Clb; Golden Key; Acdmc Excell Schlrshp 90-; BE 90; Microbiology; Tchg.

**SELLINGER, MICHAEL R,** Springfield Coll, Springfield, MA; FR; Math; Eng.

**SELLS, SHIRLEY B,** Western Piedmont Comm Coll, Morganton, NC; FR; AA; Phi Theta Kappa; Cls Mrshl; Sthrn Bptst Lf Advsr; Bsn; Acctng.

**SELLS, TIMOTHY P,** Middle Tn St Univ, Murfreesboro, TN; JR; BS; Pi Kappa Alpha Pres 90-; Intr Frat Cncl Rush Chrmn 90-; Gamma Beta Phi; Pike Yr 90; Best Pldg 88; Dist Srvc Awrd 89; Aerospace; Cmrcl Pilot.

**SELNER, KRISTEN M,** Drexel Univ, Philadelphia, PA; FR; BS; Chorus 90-; Interiors Grp Rep 90-; Phi Eta Sigma; Interior Dsgn.

**SELSER JR, ALAN R,** Salisbury St Univ, Salisbury, MD; SR; BA; Yng Dmcrts 90-; Hnr Athlt 88; Accnts Rcvlb 88-; Tnns Tm 88; Bus Admn.

**SELTZER, SANDRA S,** Fl St Univ, Tallahassee, FL; SR; BS; AWS Sgt 87-89; Un Brd 87-88; UWS 90-; Kappa Delta Pi Sec 87-; Phi Eta Sigma Hstrn 87-89; Zeta Tau Alpha Hstrn 87-; Cir K 87-89; Suncst Area Tchr Trng Hnrs Pgm 89-90; Mst Act Pldg Awd 87-88; Acad Schlr 87-; Sci Educ; Sci Tchr/Pgm Evaltr.

**SELVA, KARIN A,** Univ Of Rochester, Rochester, NY; JR; Radiance Dance Thtr 89-; Mrdn Soc 88-; Stdnt Intrvwr; Rdr Omega 90-; Deans Lst 88-; Phi Sigma Sigma Pldg Mstrs 89-; Mt Hope Family Cntr Intrnshp; Buffalo Fndtn 88-; Erly Assrnc Prgrm Suny Buffalo Med Schl; Psychlgy; Hlth Soc; Medicine.

**SELVANATHAN, PADHMANATHAN,** City Univ Of Ny Lehman Coll, Bronx, NY; SR; BS; Multi Cltrl Cl 89-90; Lehman Pressure Brkrs; Lehman Schol; Deans List 90-; Pres Schol 90-; Peer Coun 89-90; Orntn 89-; Goto Cuny Hiroshima Colg/Japan; Cmptg/Mgmnt; Ph D Acctng.

**SELVEY-URBAS, CHRISTINA M,** Western Piedmont Comm Coll, Morganton, NC; FR; BFA; Gen Fine Arts; Prfssr.

**SEMAN, CHRISTINE,** Youngstown St Univ, Youngstown, OH; SR; Natl Std Nrs Asc 89-90; Std Nrs Asc Chrp 89-90; Steering Comm Sigma Theta Tau 90-; Phi Kappa Phi 90-; Nrs Hnr Soc; BSN; Nrsng.

**SEMANS, KIMBERLEY S,** Bapt Bible Coll & Seminary, Clarks Summit, PA; JR; BS; Bible/Educ; Mission Fld.

**SEMBER, REBECCA A,** Duquesne Univ, Pittsburgh, PA; SR; JD; Intrntl Afrs Cncl 89-; Natl Pol Sci Pres 90-; Hon Scty; Lmbd Sgm Hse Chrprsn 88-89; Dphi Eta Sgm 87-88; Intrnshp State Rep Thomas Muraphy 90-; State Lgsltr; BA; Intrntl Law.

**SEMBOKUYA, YUMI,** Middle Ga Coll, Cochran, GA; SO; BS; Vocal Ensmbl 89-90; Show Choir 90-; Minrty Advsng Prog Cnslr 90-; Acad Hon 90-; Actvty Hon 89-90; Var Tennis 90-; Aerospace Engr.

**SEMIAN, DOUGLAS D,** Allegheny Coll, Meadville, PA; SO; BS; Chemii Clb 89-; Soc For Free Exprssn 90-; Assn For Comptng Mchnry 90-; Phi Kappa Psi 89-; CRC Fr Chem Achvmnt Awrd 89-90; Alden Schlr 89-90; Ftbl 89; Chem; Med.

**SEMIDEI, DORLIZCA T IRIZARRY,** Univ Of Pr Medical Sciences, San Juan, PR; GD; GRAD; Coll Prsdnt Ethcl Cmmssn 87-; Schl Prhmcy 85; Grntlgy.

**SEMIDEY, MICHELLE M,** Univ Of Pr At Rio Piedras, Rio Piedras, PR; JR; BA; Hon Entrance 88; Humanities Awd 89-90; Deans Lst 88-; Frnch; Teach Trnsltng.**

**SEMLER, CHRISTOPHER L,** Southern Coll Of Tech, Marietta, GA; SR; BSCET; ASCE Treas 89-; Stu Govt Orgn Rep 89-90; Nwsppr Phtgrphy 87; Concrete Canoe 90-; ASCE Steel Brdg; C W Mathews Cnstrctn Schlrshp; EIT St GA; Cvl Eng; Mltry Eng.

**SEMONE, ETHAN B,** Lexington Comm Coll, Lexington, KY; SO; BA; Hist; Ed Coll Lvl.

**SEMPREVIO, STACEY M,** Hudson Valley Comm Coll, Troy, NY; FR; BA; Busn; Mktg.

**SEMUS JR, JOSEPH W,** Glassboro St Coll, Glassboro, NJ; SO; MBA; Stdnt Govt Assn Sntr 90-; Vlybl Clb 90-; Swmng Diving Tm 89-90; Econ; Prfsr.

**SENA, JENNY P,** Wagner Coll, Staten Island, NY; SR; BS; SGA 90-; Allied Hlth Sci Club 89-; Micr Medl Techlgy Scty Pres 90-; Omicron Delta Kappa 90-; Amer Scty Microbl 89-; Beta Beta Beta 87; Students Envir Vol Treas 89-; Hosp Vol; Deans List 89-; Acad Schlrshp 87-; Bacteriology/Hlth Sci; MS.

**SENA, MARGARET R,** Univ Of Cincinnati, Cincinnati, OH; JR; Wmn In Comm 86-88; Aid To Spec Peopl 86-88; CCM Prod Crew Membr 89-; Dns Lst 90-; Steppng Stns Vlntr 86; Tch Hndicp To Swim 86-88; Stdnt Bdy Serv Awrd 86; IM Vlybl/Sccr 86-88; Brdcstng; Comm Law.

**SENASI, DENEEN M,** Birmingham Southern Coll, Birmingham, AL; JR; Clscl Ballet 87-; Instr Balletl; English/Dance; Fine Arts Critic/Lit Jrnlsm.

**SENATI MARTINEZ, SANTIAGO,** Univ Politecnica De Pr, Hato Rey, PR; SO; BA; Intl Tae-Kown-Do Assn Blck Blt 80-; PR Natl Tae-Kwon-Do Tm Brnz Mdl 90; Elec Eng.

**SENDEZA, HENRY C,** Wilberforce Univ, Wilberforce, OH; FR; BSC; Bio; Med Dr.

**SENECAL, CRAIG P,** Univ Of Nh Plymouth St Coll, Plymouth, NH; FR.

**SENETHEP, SOUTHANOU,** Bridgeport Engr Inst, Fairfield, CT; JR; Dns Lst 88-90; Elec Engr.

**SENEY, SANDY A,** Hudson Valley Comm Coll, Troy, NY; FR; BSW; Fmly Cmnty Wrkr; Human Svc Degree; Soc Wrkr.

**SENG, KWAN KAM,** Univ Of Ky, Lexington, KY; SO; BS; Crct Anlyss; Elec Eng.

**SENGES, CHARLES A,** Clarkson Univ, Potsdam, NY; SR; BS; Amer Mktg Assn 89-; Alpha Kappa Psi Pldg Cls Pres 89-; Mktg/Mgmt; Mktg/Sls.

**SENHOUSE, ELBERT,** City Univ Of Ny Med Evers Coll, Brooklyn, NY; SO; BS; Acctg Clb; Natl Assoc Blck Accnt; Bsn Adm; Adm CPA.

**SENION, MELISSA A,** Univ Of Sc At Columbia, Columbia, SC; SO; Ski Clb 90-; Grk Serv Prjcts; Deans List 90-; Zeta Tau Alpha Soc Chrmn 90-; Career Ctr Vol 90; Harvest Hope Food Bank Vol 90; Bus Admin; Mgt.

**SENIOR, SCOTT D,** Pa St Univ Altoona Cmps, Altoona, PA; SO; MBA; Delta Phi Omega Pldg Ed 89-; Bsn; Acctg.**

**SENITZA, CHRISTINE ANNE-MARIE,** Gallaudet Univ, Washington, DC; JR; BS; SG 89-90; Class Treas 87-88; Fld Hcky 89-90; Bus Mgt.

**SENKO, CHRISTINA M,** Duquesne Univ, Pittsburgh, PA; SR; BA; Duquesne Duke Nws Rep 90-; Dns Lst 89-; Intrnshp KDKA TV; WDUQ Natl Pub Radio Nws Asst 90-; Comms; Brdcst Jrnlst.

**SENNETT, GREGORY J,** Erie Comm Coll, Buffalo, NY; SR; AAS; Bus Club 90; Alpha Beta Gamma 90; Phi Theta Kappa; Intern Buffalo Bd Of Edn MIS Dept; Deans List 89; Comp Inf Sys; Data Prcsng/Comp Prgmr.**

**SENNETT, PAULA J,** Indiana Univ Of Pa, Indiana, PA; JR; BSED; Kappa Delta Pi; Provost Schlr 89-; Elem Educ; Tchr.

**SENOFF, AMANDA E,** Atlantic Comm Coll, Mays Landing, NJ; SO; AAS; Tutorial Serv 90; AAS; Dip Ed Inst Amer Hotel Motel Assoc; Hotel Rstrnt Mgmt.

**SENRA, MYLENE M,** Fl International Univ, Miami, FL; JR; BS; Fut Educ Amer 90-; Deans Lst 90-; Encntros Jvnls Yth Cntr Nwspr Edtr ; AA 90; Elem Educ; Tchg.

**SENSABAUGH, DEBORAH K,** Oh St Univ At Newark, Newark, OH; SO; BS; Hnr Soc 89-; Alpha Lambda Delta 90-; Phi Eta Sigma 90-; Med; Phy Thrpy.

**SENSABAUGH, LA YVONNE C,** Lexington Comm Coll, Lexington, KY; SO; BASW; Soc Wrk; Law.

**SENSENEY, BRANDI K,** Ms Gulf Coast Comm Coll, Perkinston, MS; FR; Ftbl Chrldr 90-; Pltcl Sci; Law.

**SENSEVY LIRUSSO, MARIA G,** Univ Of Pr Medical Sciences, San Juan, PR; SR; MI; Argentine Sch Nrsg Assoc Secr 89; Univ Tchg Assoc Univ Rosario 88-89; Kellogg Intl Flwshp Pgm Schlrshp 90-; BA Nrsg Univ Rosario 84; Hlth.

**SENTER, KELLY M,** Merrimack Coll, North Andover, MA; SR; BS; Accntng.

**SENTMANAT, JOSE M,** Fl International Univ, Miami, FL; SR; Philsphy Clb Tr; Philsphy Disc Grp; Phi Sigma Tau Tr; Cert U S Mil Acad Prep Schl 87; Philsphy; Prof Philsphy/Wrtr.

**SENZARIN, KELLY L,** Youngstown St Univ, Youngstown, OH; JR; BS; Acdmc Snt Sntr 89-; Amer Soc Mtrls 90-; Soc Advncmnt Mtrls/Pro Engrs 90-; Cora E Emerson Memrl Schlrshp 88-89; Mtrls Eng; Eng.

**SENZON, CRAIG M,** Cornell Univ Statutory College, Ithaca, NY; SO; BS; Empthy Rfrrl Srvc Trn 89; Orttn Cnslr 90; Deans Lst; Zeta Beta Tau Cmmtt Chrmn 90; IMS Capt 89-90; Blgy; Med.

**SEPASY, NIMA M,** George Mason Univ, Fairfax, VA; SR; BS; Finance; Bnkng.

**SEPIC, CHRISTOPHER A,** Allegheny Coll, Meadville, PA; SO; BS; Stdnt Advsg Asst Ed Enhncmnt Pgm 90-; Alden Schlr 89-90; Bio; DDS Orthdntcs.

**SEPLIN, AMY MICHELLE,** Fl St Univ, Tallahassee, FL; SO; MA; Gay Lesbian Stdnt Un Sec 89-90; Acctg; CPA.

**SEPULVEDA ACOSTA, JULIO N,** Univ Of Pr At Mayaguez, Mayaguez, PR; JR; BS; KS St Univ Pre Vet Clb 90-; St Isidores Ltn Chr 90-; Alpha Zeta 89-; Snst Zoo Dcnt; Pre Vet Med; Vet Med.**

**SEPULVEDA, DAVID,** Borough Of Manhattan Comm Coll, New York, NY; JR; BS; Data Proc Clb 87-89; Talnt Rostr Otstdng Min Stdnts; Wrkg Data Proc Dept 87-90; AAS 90; Inf Mgmt; Busn Mgmt/Cmptrs.

**SEPULVEDA, MARIA,** Univ Of Pr Humacao Univ Coll, Humacao, PR; SO; BA; Camp Ldr 90; Tutor 89; Social Sci; Social Work.

**SERAFIN, ANNE MARIE,** Indiana Univ Of Pa, Indiana, PA; SR; PSEA 88-; NEA 88-; BED; Elem Educ; Tchg.

**SERAFIN, JOSEPH E,** Immaculata Coll, Immaculata, PA; SR; BS; AMA; Bus Admin/Econ; Bus/Fncl Mgmnt.

**SERAFINO, TERESA ROSE,** Schenectady County Comm Coll, Schenectady, NY; SO; AOS; Clnry Arts Clb 90-; Prsdnts Lst 90-; Clnry Htl Rstrnt Mngmnt; Chef.

**SERAMUR, SAMIAH E,** Broward Comm Coll, Ft Lauderdale, FL; SO; BA; Mid East Awrns Cmpgn Pres 90-; Amer Women Jeddah Actvts Cmt 89-90; Pres List; Inf Svc Saudi Arabian Embsy Lctr 90-; Phi Theta Kappa 90-; Pres List 90; Spckr Hon Broward Schls; JCS; Grl Scts Boys Scts 91; Crime Wtchrs Pompano; Intrntl Rltns; Dplmtc Core UN Cmt.

**SERAPHIN, NORMA C,** Mount Saint Mary Coll, Newburgh, NY; JR; BA; Admssns Clb 90-; Alpha Chi 90-; Beta Beta Beta; Chmstry Med.

**SEREN, ELIZABETH M,** Miami Dade Comm Coll South, Miami, FL; SO; AA; Elem Ed; Tchg.

**SERENO, MICHELLE A,** Barry Univ, Miami, FL; FR; BS; Campus Ministry 90-; Phi Alpha Theta 90-; Help Up Help Others 90-; Dns Lst 90; Pres Schlrshp 90-; Psych; Dr Clncl Psych.

**SERFASS, JENNIFER L,** Juniata Coll, Huntingdon, PA; JR; BA; Cntrbrd Chr; Fri Nite Live Chr; Hon Soc; Tau Pi Phi; Phi Chi Theta P 90-; Mrktg Oper Intrnshp Ntn Wide Insur 90-; Mktg Intnshp PA Rtlrs Assn; Mktg/Cmnctns; Mktg Mgmt.

**SERGEANT, BRIAN L,** Univ Of Fl, Gainesville, FL; SR; BA; FMA 90-; Univ Deans List 90; Finance.

**SERGI, DAWN M,** Univ Of Pittsburgh At Bradford, Bradford, PA; SR; BA; Chrldr Capt 88-89; Stdnt Govt Cmtee Rep 90-; Zeta Alpha Chi Pres 89-; Dickinson Mental Hlth Ctr Cnslr Intrn 90; Human Rltns; Spec Educ/Vsul/Hrng Imprd.

**SERGI, LAURA J,** Radford Univ, Radford, VA; SO; BS; Co Capt Wmns Gymnstcs Tm 89-91; Psychology; Sprts Psychlgst.

**SERIA, SAL N,** S U N Y Coll Of Tech At Frmgdl, Farmingdale, NY; JR; BAS; Schlrshp Grumman Aerospace; Outstanding Stdnt Achvmnt Awd 90; AAS 90; Mfg Engrng; Engrng.

**SERIG, VIRGINIA S,** Christopher Newport Coll, Newport News, VA; JR; BA; Leisure Studies; Recreation Director.

**SERIO, CHRISTINE B,** Fl International Univ, Miami, FL; JR; BA; Stdnt Hm Ecnmcs Assn Scy Tres 90-; HM Ecnmcs Advsry Brd 90-; Phi Kappa Phi 89-; Amrcn Hm Econ Assn 89-; Hm Ecnmcs Edctn Assn 90-; FL Hm Ecnmcs Assn Schlrshp 90-; La Leche Leg Intrntnl Ldr 86-; Intrntnl Lctatn Cnsltnt Assn 87-; Hm Ecnmcs Edctn; Tchr.

**SERKOSKY, MARY ANN,** Marywood Coll, Scranton, PA; FR; BS; Cub Scts Comm Sec 88-; Cert Reg Tech CMC Schl Radiology 73; Acctg; CPA.

**SERLETIC II, MATTHEW M,** Univ Of Miami, Coral Gables, FL; JR; BM; Mrchng Two Stp 88-; La Union Grande 90-; Hon Stdnt Assn 88-; Alpha Lambda Dleta 88-; Golden Key 90-; Henry King Stanford Schlrshp 88-; Music Schlrshp 88-; Music Perf; Tmbnst/Keybrdst.

**SERNA, JAVIER,** City Univ Of Ny Baruch Coll, New York, NY; GD; Acctg Soc 88-90; Acctncy; CPA MBA Fin.

**SERNIK, CRAIG F,** Allegheny Coll, Meadville, PA; SO; BA; Coll Rpblcns PA VP 89-; Clarke Schlrshp Wnnr 90-; Parson Schlrshp Wnnr 90-; Alden Schlr 89-; Pltcl Sci; Law.

**SERRA GARCIA, LIZBELLE,** Univ Metropolitano, Rio Piedras, PR; SR; BBA; Outstndg Acad Achvmnt Cert 89-90; Mgmnt.**

**SERRA, BRENDA L,** Villanova Univ, Villanova, PA; JR; BA; Nwspaper 89-; Cmnctns; Envrnmntl Lwyr.

**SERRA, ELIZABETH,** Miami Dade Comm Coll South, Miami, FL; SO; AA; YMCA Cmp Cnslr 90-; Outstndng Mnrty Stdnt Rster; Psych; BA.

**SERRA, MARIA T,** Barry Univ, Miami, FL; GD; BA; Tlcmmnctns; Mgr.

**SERRANO RODRIGUEZ, JORGE LUIS,** Univ Of Pr At Mayaguez, Mayaguez, PR; JR; IEEE 88-; Students Honor Pgor 88-; Engineering Math Science; Elec Engrng.**

**SERRANO SANTIAGO, WALDO,** Univ Of Pr Humacao Univ Coll, Humacao, PR; GD; BA; Bus Acctng.

**SERRANO, ALEJANDRO,** City Univ Of Ny La Guard Coll, Long Island Cty, NY; SO; AS; Cmptr Clb 90; Phi Theta Kappa 90-; Deans Lst 90-; Cmptr Scnc; Sftwr Dvlpmnt.

**SERRANO, ANGEL,** Univ Politecnica De Pr, Hato Rey, PR; FR; Mthmtcs; Elctrcl Engnr.

**SERRANO, JEANNETTE,** City Univ Of Ny Hostos Coll, Bronx, NY; SR; AAS; Nrsg Clb Secr 90-; Stdt Repr Nrsg Clb 89-90; Phi Theta Kappa 90; AAS; Nrsg.

**SERRANO, JOHN A,** Embry Riddle Aeronautical Univ, Daytona Beach, FL; GD; AS; IM Tnns 89-91; BS 90; Aerntcl Eng/Aviatn Maint Tech; Eng.

**SERRANO, MILAGROS,** Inter Amer Univ Pr Aquadilla, Aguadilla, PR; SR; Spnsh.

**SERRANO-HERNANDEZ, MAYRA I,** Univ Of Pr At Rio Piedras, Rio Piedras, PR; FR; Ornttn Grp Fr Fr 90-; Advncd Lvl Stdnt In Engl And Spnsh Clsses 90-; Cand Fr The Hnr Prog 90-; Blgy; Med Or Orthdncy.

**SERRATE, ELISABET,** Temple Univ, Philadelphia, PA; JR; BSN; SG Pres 90-; Gldn Key 90-; Phi Sigma Pi 90; Nrsng.

**SERRATO, JUAN C,** Fl International Univ, Miami, FL; SR; BS; IEEE Treas 90; Phi Eta Sigma; Sigma Phi Epsilon; Intrnshp Pan Amer World Arwys; NOAA; Elctrcl Engr; Engr.

**SERVATIUS, JENNIFER A,** S U N Y Coll At Fredonia, Fredonia, NY; SR; BS; Econ Clb Pres 90-; Ski Clb VP 89-; Undrgrad Alumni Cncl Ambass 90-; Omicron Delta Epsilon 90-; CPS Mgmt Trng Pgm 86-; Bus Admin Mgmt; Invntry Mgmt.

**SERVIS, JOSEPH G,** Longwood Coll, Farmville, VA; SO; BA; Longwood Players Pr 90-; Forensics Tm 89-90; Alpha Psi Omega VP; Undergrad Asst Hist Dept; Harold Annie Mae Cale Schlrshp 89-; Stdnt Involmnt Ldrshp Awrd; History.

**SERWATKA, NORA E,** Seton Hall Univ, South Orange, NJ; SR; Cmps Mnstry 87-; Kappa Delta Pi 90; Elzbth Ann Stn Hnrs Assoc 88-; Kappa Delta Pi 90; Cmps Mnstry 87-; BS; BA; El Ed Engl Tchr.

**SESHADRI, PRAKASH,** Univ Of Rochester, Rochester, NY; SO; BS; Dorm Coun 90-; Nautilaus 87-; Cmps Radio Stn 89-90; Cum Laude Soc 89; IM Flr Hcky 90-; Molecular Biology; Med/Gen Eng.

**SESSIONS, JESSICA C,** Univ Of Sc At Columbia, Columbia, SC; JR; BA; Campus Jdcl Brd 89-; Amoco Tchg Awrd Comm 90; Advsr Frshmn Cncl 90; Gamma Beta Phi; Gldn Key; Ordr Omega; Omicorn Delta Kappa; Mrtr Brd; Alpha Delta Pi Exec VP; Carolina Cares; Asstnt Trp Ldr GSA; IM; Chmstry; Medicine.

**SESSIONS, STEPHEN S,** Wallace St Comm Coll At Selma, Selma, AL; SO; BA; Info Sys.

**SESSLER, ANNA M,** Allegheny Coll, Meadville, PA; SO; BS; Im Bsktbl; Tenns 89-; Lambda Sigma 90-; Beta Beta Beta 90-; Aldn Schlr; Biochem; Resrch.

**SESSLER, RANDY S,** Fl A & M Univ, Tallahassee, FL; JR; BA; Phi Eta Sigma 89-; White/Gold; Purina Mills Inc Intrnshp Stf Acctnt 90; Loral Infrared/Imaging Sys Inc Intrnshp Stf Acctnt; British Petroleum Oil Inc Stf Acctnt; Acctg.

**SESTITO, DARCY MARIE,** Hudson Valley Comm Coll, Troy, NY; SO; BA; Chrldng 89-90; Theater Clb; SUNY Cntrl Admin Asst 90-; AAS; Publ Admin; Ph D.

**SESTITO, MARIO L,** Coll Of Insurance, New York, NY; SR; Sntr Stdnt Cncl Sntr 90-; Pres Msc Soc Pres 89-; AAS Hudson Vly Cmnty Clge 86-88.

**SETARO, NANCY R,** Teikyo Post Univ, Waterbury, CT; GD; MS ED; BS 90.

**SETHMAN, RICHARD G,** Mercyhurst Coll, Erie, PA; GD; Catholic Grad Hnr Soc; Frat Order Police 86-; James J Kinnane Grad Schlrshp 82-84; Grad Magna Cum Laude; PA State Police Cpl 86-; BA 80; Scl Wrk/Law Enfrcmnt; Crmnl Jstc.

**SETIONO, DEAN,** Univ Of Al At Huntsville, Huntsville, AL; FR; BSC; Karate Clb 90-; Amer Inst Of Chem Engr 90-; Chem Clb 90-; Alpha Tau Omega; Full Tuitn Hnr Schlrshp 90-; Chem Engr.

**SETLIFF, KIMBERLY D,** Univ Of Sc At Columbia, Columbia, SC; JR; BA; Kappa Kappa Gamma Asst Tr 90-; Engl.

**SETO, BENNY W,** City Univ Of Ny City Coll, New York, NY; SO; BS; Caduceus Scty 90-; Chrstn Fllwshp 90-; Chinese Assc 90-; Tutor 90; Deans List; Bchmstry; Med.

**SETTERS, SUSAN M,** Northern Ky Univ, Highland Hts, KY; FR; BA; Hair Stylst 82-; Elem Ed; Tchng.

**SETTINERI, JOHN E,** Bunker Hill Comm Coll, Boston, MA; SO; AS; Med Radgrphy; Dpt Mgr.

**SETTLE, ANGELA DAWN,** Univ Of Charleston, Charleston, WV; SO; BS; U Of Chas Acad Schlrshp 90; Capito Fnd For Nrsng Schlrshp 90; Deans Lst 89; St Francis Hosp Aux Schlrshp 90; Bach Of Sci In Nrsng; Nrsng.

**SETTLE, GLORIA J,** Wv Univ At Parkersburg, Parkersburg, WV; SO; AS; Phi Theta Kappa; Nrsng.

**SETTLE, TRACI A,** Univ Of Ky, Lexington, KY; SO; BS; FCA 89-90; SCEC 90-; Kappa Alpha Theta 90-; Cmmnctn Dsrdrs; Spch Pthlgy.

**SETTLE, WILLIAM S,** Johnson C Smith Univ, Charlotte, NC; SO; BA; Stdnt Spprt Pgm; Cls Pres; Hnr Stdnt Ath 89-; Dorm Hnr Tm 89; Natl Yth Sprts Pgm 89-90; FDY 89-90; Var Bsktbl 89-; Cmptr Sci; Consltnt.

**SETTLES, BRIAN K,** Radford Univ, Radford, VA; SR; BBA; Fnncl Mngmnt Assn; Dean Lst; AA Vir Wstrn Com Coll 90; Fnnc; Bnkng.

**SETTON, GAIL B,** Univ Of Miami, Coral Gables, FL; SO; BBA; Chmstry Clb 89-90; Hnr Stdnts Assn 89-; Sprtsfest 90; Acctng; CPA.

**SETZER, JENNIFER L,** Univ Of Sc At Columbia, Columbia, SC; FR; Wmns Choir; Kappa Alpha Theta Pres Pldg Cls 90; Jrnlsm; Advrtsg/Publ Rels.

**SEVERANCE, JENNY S,** Castleton St Coll, Castleton, VT; JR; BA; Athltc Trng Clb Sec 87-89; Res Hl Cncl 90-; RA; Twin-State Schlp; Dns Lst 87-; Trng Assgmnts; Tnns 88; Fld Hcky 88; Sftbl 89; Cmps Bsktbl; Exercise Tech; Med.

**SEVERANCE, MICHELE R,** Univ Of Cin R Walters Coll, Blue Ash, OH; SO; BA; Just Univ 3 Stdnt Ct 90-; Phi Theta Kappa 90-; Dns Lst 89-; Crisis Cnslng Pgm 90-; Psych/Econ.

**SEVERINO, AMY L,** Providence Coll, Providence, RI; SR; BA; Big Brother/Big Sis Org 90-; Spec Olympics 88-; Cum Laude; IMS 87-; Spec/Elem Educ.

**SEVERS, JEFF L,** Air Force Inst Of Tech, Wrt-Ptrsn Afb, OH; GD; MS; Sigma Iota Epsilon; BBA Univ GA 85; Acqstn Lgstcs; US Air Force.

**SEVERS, JILL ANN,** Christian Brothers Univ, Memphis, TN; JR; MBA; Natl Acctnts Assn 89-; Delta Sigma Pi 89-; Sigma Alpha Epsilon Lil Sis 90-; Acctg; CPA.

**SEWARD, CYNTHIA A,** Christopher Newport Coll, Newport News, VA; JR; BS; Newport News Shipyard 81-88; Marketing.

**SEWCHAND, FRANZ S,** Duke Univ, Durham, NC; SO; BS; Hdstrt 89-90; Gldn Key 90; Deans Lst 89-; IM Athltcs 89-; Psychlgy; Med.**

**SEWELL, BETTY D,** Wallace St Comm Coll At Selma, Selma, AL; JR; MBA; NEA AEA ESPO 88-; Bnd Boosters Sec 89-; Paraprofessional Spec Educ 88-; Cert Dentl Tech Career Academy 73; Spec Educ; Tch EMH.

**SEWELL, MARY E,** Carson Newman Coll, Jefferson City, TN; SO; BA; Brdcstrs Assoc Sec 90-; Bapt Un 89-; Crtv Mnstrs 89-; BSU; Gspl Chr 89-; TV Anchr; FCA; IM Sftbll; IM Vllybll 89-; Cmmnctns; Brdcstng.**

**SEWELL, STANLEY L,** Univ Of Tn At Knoxville, Knoxville, TN; SR; BS; Sprts Car Clb 90; Canoe/Hkng Clb 89-; Beta Alph Psi; IM Ftbl 89-; AA Valencia Comm Clg 89; Acctg; Corp Law.**

**SEWERT, RENEE E,** Bryant Stratton Bus Inst Roch, Rochester, NY; SR; AOS; Electrncs Tech Clb Pres; Intrshp W/Monroe Cnty; FCC Amtr Radio Lcns Tech; Elect Tech.

**SEXTON, BRYAN L,** Southern Coll Of Tech, Marietta, GA; SR; IEEE 89-; Tau Alpha Pi 89-; Brdcst Engr/Cable News Ntwrk 86-89; AS Elctrnc Dekalb Com Clg 86; Engr; Elctrcl Engr.

**SEXTON, DEBORAH E,** Tn Temple Univ, Chattanooga, TN; FR; BS; Theta Mu Rho; Elem Educ; Tchr.

**SEXTON, JENNIFER A,** Belmont Coll, Nashville, TN; SR; BBA; Gamma Beta Phi 82-84; Bsktbl 82-84; As 84; Finance; Fncl Plnr.

**SEXTON, JOHNA,** S U N Y Coll Of Tech At Alfred, Alfred, NY; FR; BSN; Med Asst Clb 88-89; Spec Olympics Coach Nordic Skng 88-89; Otsdng Stdnt Achvmnt Awd 89; Med Asst Merit Awd 89; G R Carader Schlrshp Awd 89; Med Asst Genesee Hosp 89-90; AAS 89; Nurs.

**SEXTON, LAUREEN A,** Mount Saint Mary Coll, Newburgh, NY; FR; BSN; Admssns Clb 90-; Gaelic 90-; Deans Lst 90-; Pres Schlrshp 90-; Nrsng.

**SEXTON, PERRY A,** Southern Coll Of Tech, Marietta, GA; SO; BS; Elect Eng; Eng.

**SEXTON, TRACIE K,** Winthrop Coll, Rock Hill, SC; SR; BS; Soc For Hum Res Mgmnt; Deans Lst; Beta Gamma Sigma 89-; Bus Basics Conslt; Amer Red Cross 89-; AAS York Tech Clg 87; Hum Res Mngmnt.

**SEYDA, AGNIESZKA,** Univ Of Sc At Columbia, Columbia, SC; FR; BS; Alpha Lambda Delta 90; Deans Lst 90; Phrmcy; Pharm Sci.

**SEYDI, ALY D,** City Univ Of Ny Med Evers Coll, Brooklyn, NY; JR; BSBE; ACM Pres; Afrcn Unty Clb Sec 89-; Ntrl Sci Clb; All-AM Clgt Awd 90-; Dns Lst Awd 89-; Comp Sci/Elctrcl Engr.**

**SEYFORS, TRACY L,** North Central Tech Coll, Mansfield, OH; SR; ADN; Natl Cllgt Nrsng Awd; LPN 81-; Nrsng.

**SEYMOUR ANDERSON, RAYMOND D,** Nova Univ, Ft Lauderdale, FL; GD; MBA; Chrstn Grad Thtre Co Chrmn 87; Scty Of Scis And Techs 87-; Fsh Frmrs Assn 89-; Htchry Mgr Aqcltre Jmca Ltd 87-; BSC University Of The West Indies 83; Mrktng Fnnce; Indstrl Eng.

**SEYMOUR, AMIR ROMAR,** Fl A & M Univ, Tallahassee, FL; FR; MBA; Genl Studies; Biology/Engrng.

**SEYMOUR, ANNE K,** Tallahassee Comm Coll, Tallahassee, FL; SO; Hsptlty Indstry; AA; Blgcl Sci; Vtrnry Schl.

**SEYMOUR, DAVID A,** Temple Univ, Philadelphia, PA; SR; Magna Cum Laude; Deans Lst; Rowley Lmbr Schlrshp 87; AAS St Univ NY 88; BS; Cvl/Cnstrctn Tech; Eng.

**SEYMOUR, DAYNA L,** Ga St Univ, Atlanta, GA; SR; BSED; Stdnt Govt Assoc Elections Comm Chr 88-89; Baptist Stdnt Un 87-; Resident Asstnt 88-89; Alpha Lambda; Phi Eta Sigma; Mortar Brd 90-; Blue Key; Golden Key; Rho Tau 89; Ldrshp Schlr 87-89; IM Chrldng Ftbl 87; Early Childhood Educ.**

**SEYMOUR, DEANNA J,** Univ Of North Fl, Jacksonville, FL; JR; BSN; FL Stdnt Nrss Assn Sec Co7 Chr 90-; Nrsng; Clncl Nrse Spclst Peds.

**SEYMOUR, JOHN F,** Memphis Academy Of The Arts, Memphis, TN; JR; BFA; Inhouse Agency Logo; Holliday Bazaar Poster Design; Library Logo Design; J R Hyde Schlrshp 90-; Deans Lst; Merit Schlrshp; VP List; Pres Lst; Dust Bonge Art Schlrshp 88-89; Aprentance Carpenter Painter; Graphic Dsgn Illustration; Graphic Dsgnr.

**SEYMOUR, JOY A,** Anne Arundel Comm Coll, Arnold, MD; FR; AA; Trnd Vol Rsc Old Wldlf 90-; Pre Ved; Mrn Mml Vet.

**SEYMOUR, KAREN R,** Duquesne Univ, Pittsburgh, PA; JR; BA; Dkts Dnc Tm; Res Hl Govt; Yrbk Phtgrphr; Natl Hnrs Soc; Delta Sigma Pi VP; Cmptv Schlp; Dns Lst; Acctg Schlp 90-; Std Yr; Bsn Intshp; Mgt Info Sys/Acctng; Cmptr Engr.

**SEYMOUR, RHONDA Y,** Thomas Nelson Comm Coll, Hampton, VA; FR; AA; Real Est Licns; Dietetics; Dietetic Tchncn.

**SEYMOUR, SCOTT CHRISTOPHER,** Schenectady County Comm Coll, Schenectady, NY; SR; SGA Treas 89-90; Mrt Awd 89-90; AAS; Bus Acctg.

**SEYMOUR, STEPHANIE L,** William Carey Coll, Hattiesburg, MS; SR; MBS; Natl Educ Assn; Miss Assn Edctrs; BS 90-; Counslng.

**SEYMOURIAN, ELIZABETH M,** Schenectady County Comm Coll, Schenectady, NY; FR; BA; Hon Grad Defense Info Schl Ft Harrison IN 88; Basic Jrnlsm Crse/Hon Grad; Basic Photo Grphc Spclst Crse Lowry AFB "CO 89-; US Coas Grd Pblc Affrs Spclst 2nd Clss E-5 86-90; Engl/Crmnl Just; Tech Prsn Sys.

**SEYS, STEPHEN M,** Memphis St Univ, Memphis, TN; FR; BA; Busn; Busn Owner/Mktng Exec.

**SEZOV JR, RICHARD L,** Glassboro St Coll, Glassboro, NJ; SO; BA; Chrstn Fllwshp VP 89-; Stdnt Bible Mnstry Pres Co Fndr; Intrnshp Kingsway Reg HS Tchrs Asst; Engl; Tchr/Prof Freelnce Wrtr.

**SFERRAZZA-CAPOBIANCO, DONNALEE,** Asnuntuck Comm Coll, Enfield, CT; SO; Sbrn Hsky Clb 88-; Mrn Cntr Of Hlyke 87-; Ptry Clb 90-; Phi Theta Kappa; Ltrcy Vol; St Ptrck Chrch Hly Fam Chrch; Natl Fnrl Dirs Exam; Bllt Nw Englnd Dnce Cnsrvtry; Dy Care Advsry; AS Asnuntuck; Bus Cert; Tght CCD.

**SGROI, SCOTT M,** S U N Y Coll Of Tech At Alfred, Alfred, NY; Wellsville Campus Honor Society VP 90-; Heavy Equip/Truck/Diesel Tech; Truck Tech.

**SHACK, WANDA K,** Alcorn St Univ, Lorman, MS; FR; BA; Bus Adm/Acctg; CPA.

**SHACKELFORD, CONNIE A,** Hillsborough Comm Coll, Tampa, FL; GD; AS; Radiation Thrpy Clb; Rad Thrpy Tech.

**SHACKELFORD, CRISTA L,** Wright St Univ Lake Cmps, Celina, OH; FR; BS; SHA 90-; Hnr Prog 90-; Alpha Lambda Delta 90-; Psychlgy; Chld Psychlgst.

**SHACKELFORD, DAVID G,** Southern Coll Of Tech, Marietta, GA; SR; BS; Tau Alpha Pi 89-; Comp Sci.

**SHACKELFORD, ERIN M,** Al A & M Univ, Normal, AL; SR; BS; Stdnt Dietetic Assn Stdnt Rep 89-90; BS CA Unv; Dietetics; Ntrtnst.

**SHACKELFORD, IRA C,** Univ Of Al At Birmingham, Birmingham, AL; SO; BS; Schl Hlth Rltd Prfssns Stdnt Assn Stdnt Affrs Comm 90; Amer Soc Radlgc Tchnlgsts; Stdnt Rep Radgrphy Cnvntn 89; Radlgy Stdnt Bowl Team 89; Cert 90; AS NW AL Comm Coll 88; Allied Hlth Sci; Mgmt.

**SHACKETT, CHERYL A,** Hudson Valley Comm Coll, Troy, NY; GD; MSW; Brittonkill PTA Pres 82-; Schl Bd VP 87-90; Renso Cty Task Frc Sec 78-85; Scty Radlgc Tech Cptl Dist Sec 70-; AAS 70; Scl Wk/Scl Wlfr; Cnslng.

**SHACREAW, LORI A,** Va Commonwealth Univ, Richmond, VA; SR; MED; Tutor J Sargeant Reynolds Comm Clg 86-89; Instr Of SS 85-89; Phi Theta Kappa 86-89; Univ Hons Prog Va Comm U 89; Deans Lst VCU 89; Deans Schlrshp 89-; C/P Tlphne Co 74-81; Engl; Tchr Sec Schl.

**SHADDIX, DONNA F,** Central Al Comm Coll, Alexander City, AL; SO; BA; Student Govt Assoc 89-; Marketing; Eingineering.

**SHADY, KATHRYN L,** Georgian Court Coll, Lakewood, NJ; SO; BA; Clionaes 89-; Clionaes Sec; Dns Schlr; Dns Lst 89-; Phi Alpha Theta 90-; Phi Alpha Theta; Delta Tau Kappa; Agenda Coord Sen J Russo Asmbly J P Doyle; Hstry/Sec Educ; Tchg.

**SHAFER, DOLORES JUNE,** Piedmont Va Comm Coll, Charlottesvl, VA; FR; A; Bptst Yth Grp; Schylr Yth Grp 90-; Sclgy/Elem Ed; Tchr/Nurse.

**SHAFER, ERICA L,** Cabrini Coll, Radnor, PA; FR; BA; Blgy Clb 90-; Phrmcy.

**SHAFER, KIMBERLY D,** Univ Of Ky, Lexington, KY; JR; Stdnts Agnst Violtn Envrnmnt 90-; Res Hall Assn Sec 90-; Alpha Lambda Delta 89-; Phi Mu 88-; Deans Lst 88/90-; Ed; Elem Ed.

**SHAFER, RHONDA L,** Radford Univ, Radford, VA; SR; BS; Bio Clb 90-; Bio; Hlth Sci.

**SHAFEY, JOE,** Univ Of Miami, Coral Gables, FL; JR; BA; Stdnts Scl Just Co-Fdr/Co-Chr 90-; Afrocentric Clb Fdr/Pres 90-; African Stdnt Union Hstry Spkr 90-; Rsrch Asst; IM Bsktbl; Hstry; Univ Prfsr.

**SHAFFER, CHRISTINA J,** Bridgewater Coll, Bridgewater, VA; FR; BS; Flwshp Of Christian Athletes 90-; Stdnt Cnslr 90-; Stdnt Ath Trnr 90-; Bio; Med.

**SHAFFER, CHRISTOPHER L,** Coll Of William & Mary, Williamsburg, VA; FR; BS; IM Sccr Bsktbl Sftbl 90-; Chem Pre Med; Med.

**SHAFFER, DEBRA S,** Muskingum Coll, New Concord, OH; SO; BA; Bus/Acctg; CPA.

**SHAFFER, JOHN A,** Old Dominion Univ, Norfolk, VA; JR; Deans List 89; Theta Chi Exec Cncl Sec 90-; Civil Eng Tchnlgy.

**SHAFFER, JULIE A,** Kent St Univ Kent Cmps, Kent, OH; SR; BS; Bnkng/Finance Exper 86-90; Finance.

**SHAFFER, LAURA JEAN,** Cornell Univ, Ithaca, NY; FR; BS; Biolgy Stdnt Advsry Comm; Cornell Trdtn 90-; Red Carpt Soc 90-; IM Vlybl/Sftbl 90-; Biolgy; Marine Biolgy.

**SHAFFER, LORI DE ANN,** Bowling Green St Univ, Bowling Green, OH; JR; BA; Air Natl Guard Heavy Equip Oprtr Stf Sgt 86; Lstd All Amer Schlr Clgte Dir 90-; Const/Engr; Constr Tech/Mgmt.**

**SHAFFER, ROBERT J,** Univ Of Akron, Akron, OH; SO; Alpha Lambda Delta 90-; Phi Eta Sigma 90-; Im Sftbl/Bsktbl/Fig Ftbl Cptn 89-; Chem Engr.

**SHAFFER, STEPHEN A,** Ga Inst Of Tech At Atlanta, Atlanta, GA; FR; Phi Kappa Tau 90-; Chem Engr.

**SHAFFER, STEVEN H,** Fl International Univ, Miami, FL; FR; BS; Fac Schlrs Prog 90-; Tau Epsilon Phi Hstrn 90-; IM Bkstbl Ftbl; Comms; Adv.

**SHAFFER, TAMMY R,** Indiana Univ Of Pa, Indiana, PA; JR.

**SHAFFER, TERRI S,** Pa St Univ Main Cmps, University Pk, PA; SO; Phi Eta Sigma 89-; Coed Wmns IM Vllybll 89-; Hstry; Tchng.**

**SHAFFER, TIMOTHY A,** Kent St Univ Kent Cmps, Kent, OH; SO; BED; Brs Choir 89-; Symph Bnd 89-; Mrchng Bnd 89-90; Hons Clg 89-; Music Educ; Tchr.

**SHAFFER, TINA R,** Broward Comm Coll, Ft Lauderdale, FL; SO; AS; Reqtbl Trnmnts; Acctg.

**SHAFFER, TRACEY L,** Univ Of Tn At Martin, Martin, TN; JR; BS; Stdnt Tenn Educ Assn 89-91; Sigma Pi 90-91; Educ; Tch Ele Grades.

**SHAFIQ, AMTUS SAMI,** Edison Comm Coll, Fort Myers, FL; SR; AA; SGA; Sceince; Doctor Phrmcy.

**SHAH, AMI A,** City Univ Of Ny City Coll, New York, NY; SR; MD; Amrcn Mdcl Stdnt Assn Prsdnt CCNT 87-; Amnsty Intrntnl Prsdnt 87-; Amrcn Acad Family Physicians Stdnt Rep Stdnts 88-; Stdnt Govt Acdmc Prgrs Comm Stdnt Rep 90-; Wmn Medicine 87-; Mack Lipkin Schlrshp; Bs; Med.

**SHAH, DIPTI A,** S U N Y At Stony Brook, Stony Brook, NY; JR; BS; SGA 90-; Acdmc Prgrss Cmmtt 87; Nwslttr Edtr 89-; Amer Mdcl Stu Assn 85-; Wmn Med 85-; Amer Acdmy Fmly Phys 90-; Guirati Samajot NY 80-; Bdmnt Tm; Sci; MD.

**SHAH, HARESH M,** City Univ Of Ny Baruch Coll, New York, NY; JR; BBA; Acctng Scty; Gldn Key; Acctng; Pblc Acctng.

**SHAH, HETAL A,** Fl A & M Univ, Tallahassee, FL; FR; BA; Spnsh Clb Treas 88-90; Brain Brawl 89-90; Future Nrs Amer; Hnr Rl 87-; Symposium Career Opportnts 90-; Certif Awd Achvmnt 90-; Chem; Phrmcy.

**SHAH, JAIBALA K,** Univ Of Med & Dentistry Of Nj, Newark, NJ; GD; ASMT; BA Rutgers NCAS 90; Med Tech.

**SHAH, KAMINI S,** Temple Univ, Philadelphia, PA; GD; Inst Elec Eng Ring 88-; Cty Phila Intrnshp 88; Brdg Srvy Dept.

**SHAH, MANAN D,** City Univ Of Ny City Coll, New York, NY; FR; BSE; Indian Cltr Clb VP 90-; Indo Pak Clb; English/Math; Elec Engr/Law.

**SHAH, MARYAM J,** George Mason Univ, Fairfax, VA; SR; BED; Muslim Yth Nrth Amer 87-89; Muslim Yth Cncl 89-; Islamic Yth Cncl 89-; Erly Chldhd Educ; Edctr.

**SHAH, MUNISH S,** Southern Coll Of Tech, Marietta, GA; JR; BS; ISKCON Tmpl; Mtrls; Engr.

**SHAH, NARESH,** Cooper Union, New York, NY; SO; BE; SG 90-; Actvts Comm 90-; Union Tae Kwon Do 89-; ASME 91; Citibank ICFD Citicorp Intrn; Skiing/Bowling/Tae Kwon Do 89-; Mech Engr; Aerospace/Astronautical Engr.

**SHAH, NIKHIL K,** Univ Of Med & Dentistry Of Nj, Newark, NJ; SR; BSMT; BSC Ahmedabad Sci Clg India 83; Clncl Lab Sci; Med Tchnlgst.

**SHAH, PRATICHI N,** Eckerd Coll, St Petersburg, FL; SR; BA; RA 89-; Nwspr 87-88; Acdmc Advsry Bd Sec 87-89; Omicron Delta Kappa 90-; Cir K 87-88; Meals Wheels Vol 90-; Wrtng Cnsltnt 88-; Psychlgy/Mgmt; Prsnnl Admin.

**SHAH, RAVIKUMAR A,** Fl St Univ, Tallahassee, FL; SR; BS; INSAT Treas 90-; Eng Hnr Soc 90-; AA Tallahassee Comm Coll 89; Elect Eng.

**SHAH, ROBERT HIDAYAT,** S U N Y At Buffalo, Buffalo, NY; SR; BS; Univ Buffalo Acctntng Assn 87-; Natl Accntng Assn 89-; Dns Lst; IM 89; Intrnshp Univ Hsng Prchsng Asst 89; Acctntng/Fin; Law Schl.

**SHAH, RONAK P,** Ashland Comm Coll, Ashland, KY; SO; BS; Phi Beta Lambda; Comp Sci; Sys Anlst.

**SHAH, SAPANA S,** Fl Atlantic Univ, Boca Raton, FL; SR; BA; Phi Beta Lambda 90-; Asian Cultural Orgztn 90-; Assoc Cmputr Mach; Phi Kappa Phi; Schlrshp Full Tuition 89-; I M Tennis 87-89; Cmptr Info; Sys; Cmptr Prgrmr Anlyst.

**SHAH, SHEFALI I,** Princeton Univ, Princeton, NJ; FR; BA; SG VP 90-; Asian Stdnt Assoc Cmnctns Chr 90-; Emrgncy Rm Vol 90-; Bio; Medcn.

**SHAH, SYED AFZAL A,** Franklin And Marshall Coll, Lancaster, PA; JR; BA; Intl Clb V P 90-; Math Clb Sec 90-; Res Asst 90-; Blk Pyramid Sr Hon Soc; Sigma Pi Sigma; Deans Off Dana Intrn 90-; Tch Ast Math Phys Dept 89-; C A Dana Schlr 90-; Math/Physics.

**SHAH, VIPUL B,** Bridgewater Coll, Bridgewater, VA; FR; BA; Intl Clb BCIC Tres; Ecnmcs Clb Mbr; All India Gujrati Samaj 87-90; Bus Admin; CPA.

**SHAH, VISHUL R,** City Univ Of Ny Baruch Coll, New York, NY; JR; BA; Actrl Sci Soc Sec 90-; Actrl Sci.

**SHAHAB, TAUHA,** Univ Of Ky, Lexington, KY; SR; BS; Muslm Stdnts Assn VP 90-; Pakstn Stdnts Assn VP 90-; Tau Beta Phi Mbr 90-; Dns Lst; Clg Eng Schlrshp; Ping Pong; Elec Eng; Syst Eng.

**SHAHAN, RACHELLE A,** Wv Univ, Morgantown, WV; FR; BS; IM Bsktbl 90-; Univ Hnrs Pgm 90-; Schlrs Pgm 90-; Pres Schlrshp 90-; Phrmcy.

**SHAHIN, MARWAN R,** Univ Of South Al, Mobile, AL; SR; MBA; Jordanian Eng Assoc 83; Archtct; BSC In Archtctre; BA U Of Jrdn 83; Archtctre.

**SHAHKOOHI, AFSHIN,** Yeshiva Univ, New York, NY; SR; BA; Sephadic Clb Mbr 88-; Chem Clb Mbr 88-; Physcs Clb Mbr 88-; Sigma Alpha Rho Mbr 88-; PARAS Jwsh Org Yth VP 89-; Irnian Educ Cultrl Soc Somid Mag Wtr 89-90; TLS Adv 89; Roth Schlr 90; Belkin Schlrshp 88-; Max Stern Schlr 88-; Biol/Soclgy; Med.

**SHAHRDAR, CAMBIZE,** Univ Of Miami, Coral Gables, FL; JR; BS; Itln Clb; Rsrch Asst Prknsns Disease 89-; Prvst Lst; Bio; Med.

**SHAIKH, SHIMA,** Univ Of Miami, Coral Gables, FL; JR; BS; India Stdnts Assn 89-; Hon Stdnt Assn 89-; Phi Eta Gisma 89-; Gldn Key 90-; Pre-Med Hon Soc 90-; Pres Hon Rl 89; Provosts Hon Rl 90 ; Blgy; Med.

**SHAIN, STACIE LYNN,** Bellarmine Coll, Louisville, KY; SR; BA; Scty Prfssnl Jrnlsts Pres 89-; Pres Schlrs 87-; Nwspr Stf Sprts Ed 88-89; Delta Epsilon Sigma 89-; Kappa Gamma Pi; Sigma Delta Chi 89-; Vol Soup Ktchn 89-; Vol Ntl Mltpl Sclrsis Scty 87-; Intrn Leader Charlestown IN 87-88; Mss Cmnctns; Sprts Wrtr.

**SHAIVITZ, GAIL COHEN,** Goucher Coll, Towson, MD; JR; BA; Bd Of Dir 85-89; Chrmn/Crdntr Grad Plcmnt Proc Yng Ldrshp Cndls 84-89; Pres Appointee 86-89; Wmns Div Advsr For Young Wmns Ldrshp Cncl 86-89; Chrmn Wmns Div Ldrshp Ints 85-86; Steering Comm Walk For Israel 85-86; Phlsophy/Pol Sci; Public Policy.

**SHAKED, ALON,** Univ Of Miami, Coral Gables, FL; JR; BA; Yng Judeae Yth Assoc Pres; Gold Coast Mac User Grp 89-; Golden Key; Phi Kappa Phi; Alpha Lambda Delta 89-; Beta Gamma Sigma; Pres Hnr Roll 88-; Provost Hnr Roll 88-; Dns Lst 88-; Fnce; Fncl Mgmt.

**SHAKFEH, SAMAR A,** Commonwealth Coll, Virginia Beach, VA; SO; Bed.

**SHAKIBI, ARYA G,** Middle Tn St Univ, Murfreesboro, TN; SO; Cmptr Sci.

**SHAKIR, AHMAR,** Wagner Coll, Staten Island, NY; SR; Bio; Med.

**SHALASH, AMINA A,** Univ Of Ky, Lexington, KY; FR; BS; Stdnts Agnst Drvng Drnk 90-; Mslm Stdnts Assn 90-; Hnrs Prog 90-; Alpha Epsilon Delta 90-; Coll Vols 90-; Blgy; Med.

**SHALAYDA, THOMAS SCOTT,** Univ Of Nh Plymouth St Coll, Plymouth, NH; SR; BS; Soc Advncmnt Mgmt Pres 88-; PACE 87-; Yrbk Stf 89-; Phi Kappa Phi; Pmgwst Ntl Bk Mgmt Schlrshp 90; IM 87-88; Mgmnt; Bus.

**SHALLO, DEBORAH A,** Comm Coll Algny Co Algny Cmps, Pittsburgh, PA; FR; BA; Sci; Nrsng.

**SHALOUM, JONATHAN,** Glassboro St Coll, Glassboro, NJ; SR; BA; Cnma Wrkshp 87-; Dns Lst 89-; NJ Cmmssn Fr Blnd Txtbk Rdr Blnd Stdnt 90; Flm Edtng Lab Sprvsn 90; Photos Dsplyd Photo Exhbt; 3 Flms Shwn Coll Flm Fstvl; Cmmnctns; Flmmkng.

**SHAMBLEN, JULIE L,** Davis & Elkins Coll, Elkins, WV; JR; BS; Fshn Clb Treas 90-; Yrbk Ed 90-; Stdnt Assmbly 90-; Fshn Mrchndsng.

**SHAMMA, NORA M,** Univ Of Cincinnati, Cincinnati, OH; FR; BA; Msln Stdnt Assc 90; Science Fiction Clb 90; Ed; Tch.

**SHANBROM, LESLIE S,** Albertus Magnus Coll, New Haven, CT; JR; BA; Hnrs Stu; Store Ownr; Humanities; Grad Schl.

**SHAND, JOHN D,** Meridian Comm Coll, Meridian, MS; FR; Bus Admin.

**SHAND, PAUL A,** Univ Of Md At Eastern Shore, Princess Anne, MD; SO; BA; Bus Admn; Entrepreneurshp.

**SHAND, SUSAN L,** George Mason Univ, Fairfax, VA; SO; BA; Deans Admssn Prog 89-; Dsbld Vol 90-; Erly Admssn Bus Prog; Bus; Acctg.

**SHANDOR, CAMILLE H,** Franklin And Marshall Coll, Lancaster, PA; FR; Chi Omega; Var Vlybl; Engl; Law.

**SHANDU, ROBERT S,** Jackson St Univ, Jackson, MS; FR; Math Clb 90; Alpha Lambda Delta 90; USYSA 89-90; Math Pre-Eng; Eng.

**SHANE, ERIK,** Univ Of Miami, Coral Gables, FL; SR; BA; Engl; Law.

**SHANE, LAWRENCE E,** Univ Of Miami, Coral Gables, FL; SR; BM; FL Clgte Music Ed Natl Conf 89-; Mrchg Bnd Drum Mjr 86-; Bsktbl Band Dir 87-; Golden Key 89-; Phi Mu Alpha Sinfonia Pres 86-; BM; Music Ed; Tchr.

**SHANER, SUSAN L,** Beaver Coll, Glenside, PA; BA Penn State Univ 77; M Ed 90; Ed; Tchg-Elem.

**SHANGE, THANDEKILE N,** Fl A & M Univ, Tallahassee, FL; SR; BA; Orchss Cntrmprry Dnce Thtre 89-; Engl Ltrry Gld 89-; Vols Inpctng Yth; Univ Of MI Smmr Rsrch 90; Opprtnts Prog Grad Lvl Prjct Dsgnd By Slf And Mntr; Engl; Essyst Prfssr Dncr.

**SHANK, CHRISTINE D,** Salisbury St Univ, Salisbury, MD; GD; MSW; Vol Life Crisis Ctr 87-88; Intrn Life Crisis Ctr Salisbury MD 88-89; Intrn Fmly Svcs Of Crest Cnty MD 90-; BSW 90; Clinical Soc Wrk.

**SHANKS, CHRISTY L,** Milligan Coll, Milligan Clg, TN; JR; BA; Delta Kappa Clb 89-90; Soc Affairs 90-; Stdnt Govt Assoc Rep 89-90; Drill Tm 88-90; Elem Edn.

**SHANKS, MICHAEL D,** Bethany Coll, Bethany, WV; JR; BA; Ba; Acct.

**SHANNON, DARCY L,** Daytona Beach Comm Coll, Daytona Beach, FL; SO; AS; Lgl Sec.

**SHANNON, ELIZABETH L,** Immaculata Coll, Immaculata, PA; SR; BS; Kappa Omicron Nu Pres 89-; Intrn QVC Network Inc 90-; Fashion Mrchdsng.

**SHANNON, GWEN A,** Villanova Univ, Villanova, PA; JR; Proj Sunshine 89-90; Pi Beta Phi 90-; Hosp 85-; Respite 90-; IM Spts; Soc; Clinical Psych.

**SHANNON, KATHLEEN LOUISE,** Spalding Univ, Louisville, KY; SR; BS; Phi Theta 85-; Pi Lambda Theta; Delta Epsilon Sigma; PTA 86-; Tchr 82-90; AA St Catharine Jr Colg 90; Elem Ed; Tchr.

**SHANNON, KEVIN RICHARD,** Salisbury St Univ, Salisbury, MD; SR; BA; Phi Alpha Theta; Pi Gamma Mu; MD Gen Assmbly Intern; Sgt USMC 82-89; Hstry; Law.

**SHANNON, KRISTINE E,** Providence Coll, Providence, RI; JR; BS; Vrsty Wmns Sccr 88-; Mrktng; Rsrch.

**SHANNON, MELODY ANN,** Fl International Univ, Miami, FL; SR; BA; Phi Kappa Phi; Brickell Christian Sch Dir; Flight Attendant Eastern Airlines; AA Bauder Fshn Clg 76; Elem Ed.

**SHANNON, SUSAN G,** Daytona Beach Comm Coll, Daytona Beach, FL; SO; BA; Greens Rcyclng Org Fndr Secy Treas; Org Erth Day 90; Pres Lstng Sessns Spkr; Pres Lst 89; Deans Lst USF; Hall Of Fme; Pres Cert Apprctn 90; AA Hiah Hnrs; Engl Lit; Clg Prfssr.

**SHANOWER, SUSAN M,** Kent St Univ Kent Cmps, Kent, OH; SR; Hse Cncl Kent Intrhl Cncl Flr Rep 88-89; Accntng Assoc Cmmttee Chr 89; ACM Treas 88-90; Golden Key 89; Pi Mu Epsilon Treas 88; Beta Gamma Sigma 90; Beta Alpha Psi Sec 89; UCM 88; Goodwill Stores 88; Hosp Vol 88-90; Im S 88; Accntng; CPA.

**SHAPIRA, TALI R,** Fl International Univ, Miami, FL; FR; Hillel 90-; Acctg; CPA.

**SHAPIRO, GAVRIEL Y,** Yeshiva Univ, New York, NY; SR; BA; Econ; Mktg.

**SHAPIRO, GLENN A,** Univ Of Fl, Gainesville, FL; JR; BA; Stdnt Govt Cmnty Affrs Cabinet Dir 89-90; Gator Growl Productions Asst Dir 90-; Amer Mktg Assoc 90-; Blue Key 90-; Golden Key 89-; Omicron Delta Kappa 90-; Pi Kappa Phi Asst Rsh Chrmn 88-; Acad Schlr 88-; US Sen Bob Graham Intern; Bsn Adm; Law/Politics.

**SHAPIRO, JEREMY A,** Rutgers St Un At New Brunswick, New Brunswick, NJ; FR; Coll Ave Plyrs Dir 90-; Opera 90-; Poltcl Sci Assn 90-; Phi Eta Sigma 90-; Hstry.

**SHAPIRO, LISA,** City Univ Of Ny Queensbrough, New York, NY; FR; SQUAW Pres; Massage Therapist 82-; Physical Therapy.

**SHAPIRO, NORMAN S,** Yeshiva Univ, New York, NY; JR; BA; Disc Jcky Clg Radio Sta/Clsscl Music Show 89-90; Wrtr Isaac Brewer Clg Nwspr 89-90; English; Educ.

**SHARAN, NIVEDITA,** Case Western Reserve Univ, Cleveland, OH; FR; UISA Frshmn Rep 90-; French Clb 90-; Alpha Chi Omega; Schl Hindi Lang/Cltr Tchr 90-; Indn Com Nwspr Wrtr; Camp India Vol/Inst; CWRU Biochem Dept Rsrch Asst; Frst Cls Dstnctn Hindi Crspndnc Cert Crse 90; Biochem; Medicine/Rsrch.

**SHARBAUGH, STEPHANIE A,** Radford Univ, Radford, VA; SO; MBA; Crmnl Juste; Law.

**SHARER, ANDREW E,** Univ Of South Al, Mobile, AL; JR; BBS; Acctng Clb 90-; Phi Theta Kappa 88-; Beta Alpha Psi; Deans List 90; VP List 88; IM; Acctng; CPA.

**SHARMA, KUMUD,** Univ Of Rochester, Rochester, NY; JR; BA; Wlsn Cmmns Prog Brd Entrtnmnt Coor 89-; Amnsty Intrntl 90; Mtstsis; Blgy Psych; Med.

**SHARMA, SHIVA P,** Inter Amer Univ Pr San Juan, Hato Rey, PR; SR; BSC; ACS Tres 90-; Hnrs Assn 90-; Hnrs Prgrm 89-; Chemistry; Medicine.

**SHARMAN, JILL R,** Univ Of North Fl, Jacksonville, FL; FR; Hstry.

**SHARP, BRAD C,** Univ Of Southern Ms, Hattiesburg, MS; SO; BM; Msc Indstry Stdnts Assn; Mrchng Bnd 89-90; Msc; Cmpsng/Audio Engrng.

**SHARP, DANIELLE K,** Tougaloo Coll, Tougaloo, MS; JR; BS; Alum Clb 88-89; Math/Cmptr Sci Clb 88-; Phy Sci Pre Eng Clb 88-89; Alpha Lambda Delta Sec 89-; Alpha Kalpa Pr 90-; NCNW 88-; Spec Servcs 89-; Pr Schlr 88-; CBS Schlr 90-; Sci Res Pgm 90; Math/Cmptr Sci.

**SHARP, ELLEN C,** Radford Univ, Radford, VA; SR; BS; Hse Cncl Treas/VP 87-88; Psychlgy Clb Pres 90-; Phi Beta Lambda Chrmprn 88/90; Indpndnt Rsrch Asst 89-90; Gst Spkr Grntlgy Intro Cls; Psychlgy/Sclgy/Grntlgy; Grntlgst.

**SHARP, EMILY S,** Lindsey Wilson Coll, Columbia, KY; FR; Deans Lst 90; Sec Sci.

**SHARP, KAREN M,** S U N Y Coll Of Tech At Alfred, Alfred, NY; JR; BET; Drm Cncl 89-; Krte Clb 90-; Tau Alpha Pi 89-; Paul B Orvis Awrd 90; Alfrd Wmns Rgby 89-; AAS 90; Elec Eng.

**SHARP, KATHLEEN T,** Atlantic Comm Coll, Mays Landing, NJ; SO; BS; Delta Phi Epsilon Rutgers Univ 88-; Bus Admin; Bus Law.

**SHARP, KEVIN J,** S U N Y Coll Of Tech At Alfred, Alfred, NY; FR; AOS; Wellsville Fitness Ctr; Deans Lst; Elec Serv Tech; Biomed Eng.

**SHARP, LINDA S,** Univ Of North Fl, Jacksonville, FL; SR; BBA; Res Hall Assoc Sunshine Comm 82-84; Alpha Lambda Delta; Deans Hnr Roll; Pres Hnr Roll; Early Recong Schlrshp 82; Le Cercle Francais Award; Res Hall Assoc Awd 82-84; US Navy Ofc Wives Club Pblcty Ofcr 86-; USDA/ASCS Club; Business; Mgmnt.

**SHARP, LINDA S,** Crichton Coll, Memphis, TN; GD; BS; Stndt Cncl Pblcty Chrmn 89-90; SACS 89; Gamma Beta Phi Scty 84; Phi Beta Lambda 83-84; All AM Schlr US Achvmnt Acdmy 88-89; Otstndng Stdnt Ecnmcs Eng Lit 84-85; Bsns Stdnt 90; PTA Pres 76-78; Assc Bsn; Bsn Admin.

**SHARP, MICHAEL B,** Univ Of North Fl, Jacksonville, FL; JR; BA; Stdnt Govt Assoc Sen; Pol Sci Soc 90-; Phi Theta Kappa 89-; Gldn Ky; Campus Cvtn Clb 90-; Dns Lst 90-; AA St Johns Rvr Comm Clg 90; Pol Sci; Law.

**SHARP, MICHAEL RAY,** Univ Of Sc At Coastal Carolina, Conway, SC; SO; BA; AA AZ Wstrn Clg 90; Physcl Edctn; Elem Physcl Edctn Instrctr.

**SHARP, PATRICIA GAIL,** Memphis St Univ, Memphis, TN; SR; BS; NAEYC 90-; SACUS 90-; TAYC 90-; Phi Kappa Phi; AS Shlby St Coll 90; Early Chldhd; Tchr.

**SHARP, SUSAN B,** Univ Of Tn At Martin, Martin, TN; SO; BS; Acctg.

**SHARP, TAMMY D,** Western Ky Univ, Bowling Green, KY; SR; MS; Natl Stdnt Spch Lang Hrng Assc 90; Gldn Key 90; Kappa Dlt Pi 90; AS Hopkinsville Comm Clg 87; Cmnctns Disorders; Pathlgst.

**SHARP JR, TERRENCE L,** Central Fl Comm Coll, Ocala, FL; JR; Phi Theta Kappa 90-; AA 90; Engrng; Computer.

**SHARP, TIM C,** Oh Univ, Athens, OH; JR; MBA; NORML 88-; Nauna Lani CC 88-; Deans Lst 90-; AGVA 87-; Grad Amer Acdmy Dramatic Arts 87-88; Theatre; Actg Coach.

**SHARP, WILLIE H,** East Tn St Univ, Johnson City, TN; SO; BBA; ROTC Army 89-; Gamma Beta Phi 90-; Bccnr Bttln Acad Excllnc Awd 90-91; Deans List 90-; Dghts Of Fndrs/Ptrts Of Amer Awd; Finances; USA.

**SHARPE, ANGELA D,** Univ Of Sc At Columbia, Columbia, SC; JR; BA; Pres List 90; Hotel Restauratn/Touresm.

**SHARPE, BRIAN F,** Univ Of Southern Ms, Hattiesburg, MS; FR; BA.

**SHARPE, CICELY,** Tn St Univ, Nashville, TN; SR; BS; Socialogy Club Secty 90-; Golden Key; Tutor 90-; NAACP 83-; Detroit Urban Leg; Socialogy; Social Res.

**SHARPE, COREY S,** John Wesley Coll, High Point, NC; SO; BA; Clg Plyrs; All Amer Schlr 90; Drama Music; History; Tchr.

**SHARPE, ELEANOR L,** Howard Univ, Washington, DC; JR; AIAS 90-; Carbbn Stdnts Assc 90-; Archtctrl Tech Clb Vp 87-90; Grl Gde; Stdnt Of Yr Bldg Dpt Clg Arts Sci/Tech Jamaica 88-89; Nom Stdnt Yr CAST 88-89; Bdmntn; Chss; Dip Arch Tech Clg Arts Sci/Tech 90; Hons CAST; Archtctr.

**SHARPE, KELLIE E,** Brevard Comm Coll, Cocoa, FL; FR; PHD; Cncrt Choir 90-; Madrgl Ensmbl 90-; Schlr Cntrm 90-; Deans List 90-; Hnrs List 90-; Local HS Eng Tutor 90-; Eng Educ.

**SHARPE, KERRI B,** Univ Of South Al, Mobile, AL; JR; BS; Acctng Clb 90-; T B Fdn Schlp 88-89; Acctng; CPA.

**SHARPE, KIMBERLY A,** Duquesne Univ, Pittsburgh, PA; SO; BA; Cmmtr Asst; Cmmtr Cncl; Prsdntl Awrd Schlrshp; Deans Lst; Bus.

**SHARPE, KRISTI,** Middle Tn St Univ, Murfreesboro, TN; SR; BS; Hypers Clb VP 88-; Gamma Beta Phi 88-; Kappa Delta Pi 89-; Tau Omicron 89-; Phi Epsilon Kappa 90-; Chi Omega IM Dir 88-89; Tommy Reynolds Awrd 89; Leona Drake Awrd 90-; OVC Cmsnrs Hon Rl 89-90; Vlybl 89-; Phys Educ Tchr.

**SHARPE, NARTARSHIA L,** Univ Of Nc At Charlotte, Charlotte, NC; SR; BA; Sanford Hl Cncl Pres 87-; Phi Beta Sigma Dove Ct Treas 88-89; Psych Clb Mbr 88-89; Psych; MA Cnslng.

**SHARPE, ROBERT H,** Barry Univ, Miami, FL; JR; BS; Software Engr NYMA Inc 89-; Mgmt Info Syst; Data Proc.

**SHARPE, SALLY A,** Univ Of Va, Charlottesville, VA; JR; BSN; Peer Lfstyle Eductrs; Phi Eta Sigma; Golden Key; Pi Beta Phi Pdg Trnr 90-; Intrmdte Hon 90-; Nurs Awd 89-; Nurs.**

**SHARPE, SHANDY,** Central Al Comm Coll, Alexander City, AL; SO; SGA Treas; Acctng Bus; Corp Lwyr.

**SHARPE, WILLIAM H,** Shaw Univ, Raleigh, NC; SR; MA; Univ Schlp; Tch Clg Math; Math; Math Rsch/Instctn.

**SHARPENBERG, GRACTIA A,** Bethany Coll, Bethany, WV; JR; BA; Cir K Intrntl 90-; Radio 90-; Gamma Sigma Kappa; Alpha Xi Delta VP 89-; Sr Flwshp Cmnctn; IM Sprts; Cmnctns; Law.

**SHARRETT, RENARD M,** Univ Of Cin R Walters Coll, Blue Ash, OH; SO; BA; Econ; Mktg/Law.

**SHARRON, GAIL L,** Hudson Valley Comm Coll, Troy, NY; FR; Erly Chldhd Clb 90-; Erly Chldhd Educ; Chld Psychlgy.

**SHARTZER, KATHY D,** Owensboro Comm Coll, Owensboro, KY; FR; AAS; Bus; Offc Admin.

**SHASHUA, MICHAL,** Fl International Univ, Miami, FL; FR; BA; Hillel Org 90-; FPIRG 90-; Sigma Sigma Sigma Music Chr; Bsn Adm.

**SHAT, DANIEL C,** Franklin And Marshall Coll, Lancaster, PA; FR; BS; Chinese Culture Clb 90-; Intervrsty 90-; Bus; Mktg.

**SHATTUCK, JAMES S,** Kent St Univ Kent Cmps, Kent, OH; SR; BA; USAF Tailgunner Strategic Air Command 83-89; AAS Resouce Mgmnt 86; Soviet/East European Studies; Foreign Studies.

**SHATTUCK, KRISTEN M,** Lesley Coll, Cambridge, MA; SO; BA; Educ Advsry Brd; Math/Sci Clb 90-; Tchr Martn Lthr King Schl 89; Newtn Day Si; Math/Sci; Tchr.

**SHAUGHNESSY, MICHAEL A,** Al A & M Univ, Normal, AL; GD; MBA; Magna Cum Laude; AS Calhoun Cmmnty Clg 87; Cmptr Sci; Prog.

**SHAUGHNESSY, TRACY,** Atlantic Union Coll, S Lancaster, MA; SO; BS; Amnesty Intrntl Pres 89-90; Stdnt Assn Sen 90-; Biology Clb; Hnrs Clb 89-; Pres Schlrshp 89-; Bsktbl 90-; Biology; Educ/Med.

**SHAUL, CHRISTINE,** Hudson Valley Comm Coll, Troy, NY; FR; Math/Phy Ed.

**SHAUL, JAMES A,** Cornell Univ Statutory College, Ithaca, NY; JR; BS; Entpnrs 88-; Std Advsr 90-; Orgnc Chem Tutor 90-; IM Bsktbl/Sftbl 88-; Trad Flw 90-; Mary Imgn Bsstt Hosp Rsch Asst; Sub Tchr 89-; Appld/Agri Ecnmcs; Med.

**SHAULIS, ALEXIS A,** Duquesne Univ, Pittsburgh, PA; SO; BS; Stdnt Affl Amer Chem Soc Sec 90-; Crew 89-; Chem.

**SHAURETTE, DEBORAH A,** Univ Of Sc At Columbia, Columbia, SC; SR; BS; Hall Govt Sec 87-90; Hall Assn 89; Golden Key 89; Natl Hall Hnry; RA 90-91; Acctg; CPA.

**SHAVER, DONNA LOUISE,** Winthrop Coll, Rock Hill, SC; FR; BS; Stdnt Ambssdrs 90-; Schlstc Hnr Soc; STEP; Aerobics 90; Math; Educ.

**SHAVER, DOUGLAS D,** Fairmont St Coll, Fairmont, WV; FR; BA; Comp Sci/Business Adm.

**SHAVER, ELIZABETH R,** Radford Univ, Radford, VA; JR; BSN; Nrsng.

**SHAVER, KIMBERLY D,** Marshall University, Huntington, WV; JR; BS; Majorette Capt 88-; Chorus Mbr 89; Hmcmng Attndnt 89; Order Of Omega; IM 89-; Delta Upsilon Pnhlnc Dele 89-; Gamma Beta Phi Hnr Soc Mbr 88-; Rd Crs Vol 89-91; Autism Ctr Vol 89-90; Dns Lst 88-; Educ; Tchng.

**SHAVER, LANCE D,** Middle Tn St Univ, Murfreesboro, TN; SR; BS; Soc Mfg Eng 90-; Mdl TN Ftbl 87-88; Team Co Op Ed 90-; Deans Lst; Co Op Educ; Mfg Eng Assist 90-; MTSU Ftbl; Eng/Mfg Tech; Eng Grad.

**SHAVER, REYNALDO,** Holyoke Comm Coll, Holyoke, MA; FR; ASSN; Med Rdlgst.

**SHAVER, STACEY A,** Chattanooga St Tech Comm Coll, Chattanooga, TN; SO; CS; IBM Collgt Rep 90-; DPMA; Comptr Sci; Anlyst.**

**SHAVERS, CARL,** Va Commonwealth Univ, Richmond, VA; JR; BS; Bro To Bro; Mnrty Stu Unn 88-90; Almn Assn 90-; US Achvmnt Acdmy Awrd 90; Gamma Of NJ Schlrshp 90; AA Burlington Co Coll 90; Accntng; CPA.

**SHAVERS, CONSWALLA U,** Cheyney Univ Of Pa, Cheyney, PA; FR; BA; Pom Poms Bnd 90-; Hostess Blck Clg Conv 90-; Bio Clb; Bio; Med.

**SHAW, CHASTA M,** Faulkner Univ, Montgomery, AL; FR; BA; Alpha Delta Psi 90; Dean Lst; Hstry; Law.

**SHAW, CHERYL LIANA,** Wilmington Coll, New Castle, DE; GD; BA; Lambda Alpha Omega Sec 81-82; Priv Invstgtr; AAS Del Tech Comm Coll 84; Crim Just; FBI/LAW Attny.

**SHAW, CHRISTINE D,** Niagara Univ, Niagara Univ, NY; JR; BA; Orientation 89-90; Mktg; Advdv.

**SHAW, CINDA G,** Hudson Valley Comm Coll, Troy, NY; FR; AS; Stdnt Affairs 90-; Albany Medl Clg; Deans Lst 90; Presidents Lst 90; AAPA Natl Conf; Hosp Medl Lab Tchnlgst 85-90; BA SUNY Binghamton 85; Physicians Asstnt Program.

**SHAW, COURTENAY R,** Lenoir Rhyne Coll, Hickory, NC; SR; BS; Vrsty Bsktbl 87-; Vrsty Sftbl; Mu Sigma Epsilon; Delta Zeta; Exrcs Physlgy; Phy Thrpy.

**SHAW, DAVID L,** Pearl River Jr Coll, Poplarville, MS; FR; BA; Cmptr Clb V Chrmn; Math; Space.

**SHAW, DAWN Q,** Medical Univ Of Sc, Charleston, SC; JR; BSN; Stdnt Nrs Assoc 90-; SGA 90-; Fllwshp; AA Trident Tech Clg 90; Nrsng.

**SHAW, DONNA E,** Radford Univ, Radford, VA; JR; BBA; Acctg.

**SHAW, ELIZABETH R,** Fayetteville St Univ, Fayetteville, NC; FR; BA; Chr Mbr 90-; Wllmsbrg Tech Clg Proj Upwrd Bnd Stdnt 86-89; Zeta Phi Beta Pr 89-90; Geotown Mem Hosp Cndy Strp 86-87; Chrch Flwshp Sec 88-90; BA; Bio; Phrmcst.

**SHAW, JOHN C,** Fl St Univ, Tallahassee, FL; SR; CMENA 90-; Dns Lst 90; Intrnshp Msc Educ E Lake High; BA; Bst Suprtng Actr Tallahassee Theatre 86-87.

**SHAW, KAREN B,** Va Commonwealth Univ, Richmond, VA; JR; BS; Golden Key; Alpha Sigma Alpha; Rsrch Asst Dr Jos Bush Psychology 90-; Psychology; Law.

**SHAW, KAREN K,** Univ Of Nc At Asheville, Asheville, NC; FR; BS; Stdnt Acctncy Assn; Chmbr Of Commerce Asheville NC; Acctng; CPA.

**SHAW, KENT M,** Lee Coll, Cleveland, TN; SR; BS; Afro Amer Cltrl Soc Pres 89; Stdnt Advsry Cncl 89; Pnrs Fr Christ 90; Mnstrl Intern Prog 88; Exhitrs Lic Church God 89; South Capitol Church God Pastor; State World Mission Rep; Distr Evang Div; Distr World Mission Rep; Biblical Studies; Pastor/Tchr.**

**SHAW, KONI A,** Al A & M Univ, Normal, AL; FR; BS; Mnrts Agri Natrl Rsrces/Rltd Sci 90-; USDA Apprntcshp 90; NC St Univ Intern; Plnt Sci/Chmstry; Gntc Eng.

**SHAW, LORI F,** Lesley Coll, Cambridge, MA; SO; BED; Hilel 89; Tchng Awd 90; Hon Roll 90; Elem Ed; Tch.

**SHAW, LOUENE K,** Oh St Univ At Newark, Newark, OH; FR; BS.

**SHAW, MARC D,** Pembroke St Univ, Pembroke, NC; JR; BA; Ftr Bsns Men America 90-; Hd Rsdnt Asst 90; Alpha Chi 90-; Phi Theta Kappa 90; All Amrcn Schlr Awd; Otstndng Stdnt Awd 90; Acdmc All Amrcn Bsbl 90-; AS S GA Clg 90; Bsns; Accntnt.**

**SHAW, MARGARET K,** Marywood Coll, Scranton, PA; JR; BS; Collegiate 89-; Vol In Action 89-; Delta Epsilon Sigma 90-; Alpha Mu Gamma; Phi Beta Lambda 88-; IHM Schlr 88-; Dns Lst 88-; Collegiate Schlr 90; Acctg; Law.

**SHAW, MARY BETH,** Lenoir Rhyne Coll, Hickory, NC; SO; BS; Phys Ed Mjr Club 89-; Delta Zeta Act Chr 89-; Lineberger Schlrshp 89-; Student Athletic Trnr LRC 89-; IM Cptn 89-; Exer Pshy/Sports Med; Medl Schl.

**SHAW, REUBEN J,** Cornell Univ Statutory College, Ithaca, NY; SO; BS; Lambda Chi Alpha Secr; Bio; Bio/Med Rsrch.

**SHAW, ROBERT H,** Clayton St Coll, Morrow, GA; SO; BS; Cmptr Sci.

**SHAW, ROBIN L,** Univ Of West Fl, Pensacola, FL; SR; BA; BA Early Chldhd/Elem Educ; Teacher.

**SHAW, TEKEIA MECHELLE,** Fl Memorial Coll, Miami, FL; JR; Acctg Clb Pres; NABA 90-; Dade Cnty Sch Bd Intern 90; Acctg; CPA.

**SHAW, TRICIA L,** Le Moyne Coll, Syracuse, NY; JR; BS; Bio Clb Tres 90-; Intl Hs Clb; Yrbk; Tri-Beta; PIC 89-; Indpndt Stdy Bio Rsrch; Bio; Med Rsrch.

**SHAW, WAYNE B,** Univ Of Ms Main Cmps, University, MS; FR; BA; Ambassadors; Hnrs Prgrm 90-; Gamma Beta Phi; Phi Kappa Psi 90-; Biology; Medicine.

**SHAWL, CYNTHIA A,** William Carey Coll, Hattiesburg, MS; JR; BS; Offcr Cndt Prior Srvc Hsptl Crpsmn 83-90; BS MS Clg Clntn MS 80; Nrsng.

**SHAWL, ERIC V,** Univ Of Southern Ms, Hattiesburg, MS; JR; BSN; Nrsng; BSN US Navy.

**SHAYREE, GEORGE,** City Univ Of Ny Baruch Coll, New York, NY; SR; BBA; Marketing Intl; Internatl Law.

**SHEA, CAPT JEFFRY W,** Air Force Inst Of Tech, Wrt-Ptrsn Afb, OH; GD; MS; Amer Socty Cvl Engrs Pres 83; Sigma Iota Epsilon; Phi Kappa Phi 82; Mrtr Bd 80; Chi Epsilon 81; Tau Beta Pi; Natl Rgstr Outstdng Coll Grad 83; BSCE SD State Univ 82; MBA Okla City Univ 90; Engr Mgmt.

**SHEA, COLLEEN,** Indiana Univ Of Pa, Indiana, PA; JR; BED; Cncl Exceptnl Chldrn; Mntl Retrdtn Div; Alpha Sigma Tau 90; Educ; Tchr.

**SHEA, DANIEL E,** Univ Of Al At Huntsville, Huntsville, AL; JR; BSCHE; Phi Kappa Phi 79-; Tao Beta Pi; Acad Achvmnt Biological Sci Awd 79; Grad Teach Asstntshp 79-81; Acad Achvmnt Civil Eng Awd 89; Water Poltn Cntrl Fed; Cert Hazardous Material Mgr 87-; Asst Dir Huntsville Dept Nat Res Env Mgt 90-; Bs; Chem Eng; Envrmntl Eng/Mgt.

**SHEA, DAVID M,** Castleton St Coll, Castleton, VT; JR; BA; Math Club 90; SG 90; Concert Band 88-90; Phi Eta Sigma 88; Dns Lst 88-90; Pres Schlrshp Math 91; Math Award 90; Math; Biostatistics.

**SHEA, DEBORAH J,** Elms Coll, Chicopee, MA; SO; BA; Stdnt Amb 89-90; Stdnt Act Cmte 90-; Campus Ministry 90-; Amer Studies/Elem Tchr.

**SHEA, JULIE A,** Marshall University, Huntington, WV; JR; BS; Mktg.

**SHEA, KATHLEEN A,** Fl International Univ, Miami, FL; SR; BA; Phi Theta Kappa; Phi Kappa Phi; Deans Lst; Outstndg Acad Achvment; Psychlgy.

**SHEA, KELLY M,** Lexington Comm Coll, Lexington, KY; FR.

**SHEA, LOUISA I,** Smith Coll, Northampton, MA; FR; BA; Clg Chr 90; Hrsbck Rdng 90; Intrvrsty Chrstn Flwshp 90-; Vol Old Age Hm; D; Arthur Ellis Hamm Prz; Comprtv Litr/Italian.

**SHEA, TODD M,** Salisbury St Univ, Salisbury, MD; SO; BA; Phi Eta Sigma 90-; Deans Lst 89-; Geo; Environ Cnslt.

**SHEAFFER, ELIZABETH A,** Lord Fairfax Comm Coll, Middletown, VA; SO; BA; Intrld Bsn/Sls Mgr 90-; SGA Hnr Cd Comm 89-90; Pr Tr 90-; Phi Theta Kappa Sec 89-; Ambsdrs VP 90-; VA Schlr; Pres Lst 89-; Phi Theta Kappa Assn Amer Comm/ Jr Cls; AA S Gen Stds; AA S Sci; Archtctr.**

**SHEAFFER, SUZANNE M,** Univ Of Fl, Gainesville, FL; SR; BA; Hmcmg Hnrd Guests Asst Dir; Hmcmg Alumni/Spcl Evnts Stf 90; Pnhlnc Prctr 90; Wmn/Mns Clndr Stf 89; COAR 89; Amer Soc Cvl Engr 90-; Delta Gamma Rcrdg Sec Exec Brd 89; Cvl Engr.

**SHEAHAN, LAURA C,** Oh Wesleyan Univ, Delaware, OH; SO; BA; Delta Zeta V P 90-; Nwspr Entrmtn Ed; Actvts Entrnmt Cmtee; Phi Soc; Deans Lst 90; Natl Cancedr Inst Intrn; Genetics; Rsrch Med.

**SHEALEY, ROXANNE E,** Abraham Baldwin Agri Coll, Tifton, GA; FR; AS; Phi Theta Kappa 90-; Hnr Stdnt 90-; Sftbl 90-; Sci; Phy Thrpy.

**SHEALY, ANDREW L,** Univ Of Sc At Aiken, Aiken, SC; FR; BA; Unbridled USCA Annual Photo; USCA Bsbl; Pltcl Sci; Photography.

**SHEALY, CARY R,** Univ Of Sc At Columbia, Columbia, SC; SO; BA; Theta Chi 89-90; Rugby Tm 90-; Business Adm.

**SHEALY, DEBORAH A,** Limestone Coll, Gaffney, SC; JR; BA; Cls Senate Treas 89-90; Stdnt Govt Rcrdr 90-; Kappa Delta Kappa 89-91; Jr Marshall 90-; RA 90-; Psychlgy; Cnslng.

**SHEALY, JANICE R,** Midlands Tech Coll, Columbia, SC; SR; AD; Deans List; AM Cancer Scty Vol; Sunday Schl Tchr; Hlth Science/Nrsng; Nrse.

**SHEALY, JILL MC FATHER,** Andrew Coll, Cuthbert, GA; SR; Dean Lst 90-; AA; Erly Chldhd Educ.

**SHEALY, KEVIN D,** Univ Of Sc At Columbia, Columbia, SC; FR; BS; Engr.

**SHEARD, TRACY V,** Bennett Coll, Greensboro, NC; SO; Trck Clb Pre-Almn Cncl 89-90; Pltcl Sci Clb Prss Sec 90-; NAACP Cls Corr Sec 90-; Trck Clb 89-90; Pltcl Sci; Law.

**SHEARER, ELIZABETH A,** The Johns Hopkins Univ, Baltimore, MD; SR; BSN; Hnr Soc; BS Chem Gettysburg Clg 90; Nrsg; Emerg Trauma Nrsg.

**SHEARER JR, JON D,** Salisbury St Univ, Salisbury, MD; GD; MD St Teachers Assoc 90-; Wicomico Cnty Brd Of Educ/Pinehrst Elem Schl 90-.

**SHEARER, LAURA A,** Univ Of Pittsburgh, Pittsburgh, PA; JR; BA; SWE 88-; Eng Wk Chrprsn 90; Phi Eta Sigma; Hosp Vol 90-; Rsrch Asst; Mtrls Sci Eng; Eng.

**SHEARER, LOU D,** Lexington Comm Coll, Lexington, KY; FR; BA; Deans Lst 90; Psychlgy/Poltcl Sci; Law Schl.

**SHEARER, MICHAEL J,** Ky St Univ, Frankfort, KY; JR; BS; Symphnc Bnd/Jz Ensmble 86-; Kappa Kappa Psi; Fdrl Hwy Admnstrtn Coop; Cmptr Sci; Systm Prgrmr/Anylst.

**SHEARIN III, HENRY B,** Vance Granville Comm Coll, Henderson, NC; GD; Fshng/Hntng/Swmmng/Bsktbl/Tnns Red Cross Cert Twn/Cntry Rec 83; Phi Theta Kappa; Usher Wood Bapt Chrch 86-; Comm Serv; Deans List 89-; AA; Bus Admin; Mrktng.**

**SHEARIN, MARY A,** Memphis St Univ, Memphis, TN; JR; BA; Gldn Key 90-; Deans Lst 88-; TN Ctzns Cncrnd Lf Sec 89-90; Josephine Cir Pres; Engl.

**SHEARN, KATHLEEN S,** Comm Coll Algny Co Algny Cmps, Pittsburgh, PA; FR; ASSOC; Nrsng.

**SHEATS II, JIMMY B,** Morehouse Coll, Atlanta, GA; SO; BS; Vrsty Dbte Tm 89-; Bus Assn 89-; Mrn Tgr Phtgrphr 90-; Hnr Rll 89-; Dns Lst 90-; GM Schlr; Strn Corp Intrn 90-; Bus Admin Mgmt; Exec.

**SHEBERT, GREGORY M,** Univ Of Miami, Coral Gables, FL; JR; BSEE; Radio; Eta Kappa Nu 90-; Tau Beta Pi; Elect/Comp Eng.

**SHEBLE, TERESA R,** Newbury Coll, Brookline, MA.

**SHEBOVSKY D C, JEFFREY N,** Ny Chiropractic Coll, Glen Head, NY; GD; DC; Phi Chi Omega 89-; Cert Prfcncy X-Ray Spclty Fld Spnl/Sktl Dsordrs 90; IM SUNY Albany 86-88; AA Kingsborough Comm Coll 86; BS U St NY 90; Chiro.

**SHEEDY, TRACEY A,** Wagner Coll, Staten Island, NY; JR; BED; Stdnt Govt Treas 90-; Comm Chest Chrprsn; Omicron Delta Kappa 90-; Alethea 90-; Kappa Delta Pi; Epsilon Delta Omicron V P 89-; RA 90-; Ldr Horizon Awd 90; Panhellenic Cncl Awd; Dean Stdnts Awd; Educ/Engl; Higher Educ.

**SHEEHAN, ANGELA L,** Univ Of Nh Plymouth St Coll, Plymouth, NH; FR; BA; Pres Lst 90; Engl; Scndry Educ.

**SHEEHAN, BRYAN M,** Pa St Univ Delaware Cty Cmps, Media, PA; JR; BS; Dsplnry Appeals Bd; Oper Rm Spclst; Phila/ Delaware Co Chmbr Of Comm; Med; Podiatric Surgery.

**SHEEHAN, CHARLES T,** Univ Of Miami, Coral Gables, FL; SO; BFA; Alpha Tau Omega 90-; Mtn Pctrs; Wrtng/Dir.

**SHEEHAN, JOHN J,** Western Piedmont Comm Coll, Morganton, NC; FR; BA; School Newspaper Mngr Reporter; Music Talent Schrlshp Award Brevard Clg; Music.

**SHEEHAN, KEVIN J,** Capitol Coll, Laurel, MD; SR; BS; Quill/ Anchor 90-; Alpha Chi 90-; Tau Alpha Pi; Golf Cl 89-; Chif Petty Offcr Asso 88; Coast Gd; AA S W Or Comm Colg 88; Cmptr Engrng Tech.

**SHEEHAN, KIMBERLY A,** Immaculata Coll, Immaculata, PA; SO; BA; Hnr Soc; Psi Chi 90-; Cmps Mnstry Stf 89-; Psy; Pstrl Cnslng/Mnstry.

**SHEEHAN, TERRI K,** Lexington Comm Coll, Lexington, KY; FR; ASN; LPN 85-; Nrsng.

**SHEEHY, KEVIN M,** Duquesne Univ, Pittsburgh, PA; SO; BS; Phi Chi Theta 89-; Zeta Beta Tau 90-; Acctng Clrk UPS 90-; Acctng; CPA.

**SHEEHY, MOLLY M,** Saint Vincents Coll & Seminary, Latrobe, PA; SO; BA; Stdnt Govt Sen 90-; Pre Law Soc Sec 89-; Orentn Comm Mbr 90-; Dns Lst 89-; Ldrshp Schlrshp 89-; Tutor Priv Ind Cncl 89-; Wrk For St Vincent Lib 89-; Wrk St Vincent Pol Sci Dept; Mbr Educ Pol Comm 90-; IM 89-; Pol Sci; Law.

**SHEEK JR, JAMES L,** East Carolina Univ, Greenville, NC; SR; BMED; Amer Chrl Dir Assn 87-; Music Ed Natl Cnfrnce Sec 90-; Opera Theatre 88-; Natl Collgt Schlr; Phi Mu Alpha Music Dir 89-; Deans Lst 89; Hon Roll 90-; Music Ed; Tchng Prfssn.

**SHEELY, DIANA IONE,** Fayetteville St Univ, Fayetteville, NC; SR; BA; NC Sclgcl Assc; Alpha Kappa Delta 89-90; Rtl Mngmnt 87-; Mtl Engrvr/Frntr Fnshr/Drct Whlsl Frntr Sls 71; Sclgy/Scl Wrk; HIV Cnslr.

**SHEELY, JO E,** Univ Of Southern Ms, Hattiesburg, MS; GD; MA; Golden Key 88-90; Gamma Beta Phi 89; Home Bldrs 89-90; Constr Specif Inst 88-90; Am Inst Bldg Designers 88-90; Sigma Lambda Chi 89-90; Dns Lst 87-90; Asstnshps Arch Wrkg Drwg II/ARCH Rndrg/Arch Grphcs/Rsdntl Dsgn/Plng; BS; Arch.

**SHEERAN, AMY M,** Stockton St Coll, Pomona, NJ; FR; BA; Math; Cmptr Sci.

**SHEERIN, KRISTA D,** Villanova Univ, Villanova, PA; SO; BA; Prjct Snshn 89-; Cmps Mnstry 90-; Spcl Olympcs 89-; Omicron Delta Kappa; Alpha Omicron Pi Scl Chr Schlrhsp Chr 90-; Cmmtt Hmles 90; Hnrs Prgm 89-; Prsdntl Schtchr; Hnrs Clsscl Stds; Edctn.

**SHEETS, KATHY L,** Oh St Univ At Marion, Marion, OH; SR; BA; Natl Educ Assn 87-; Stdnt Educ Assn 87-; Educ Scty 90-; AA 89; Elem Educ; Elem Tchr.

**SHEETS, KIMBERLY D,** Fl International Univ, Miami, FL; SR; BS; Natl Cncl Tchrs Of Math 90-; Deans Lst 90-; Ele Educ; Ele Tchr.

**SHEETS, NANCY A,** Univ Of Akron, Akron, OH; SR; BS; Univ Clg Ed Deans List 87-; Golden Key 89-; Elem Ed.**

**SHEETS, TROY A,** Fl International Univ, Miami, FL; SR; BS; Stage/Comm Actng; Intrnshp Sunst H Schl; Actrs Guld; AA Brwrd Comm Clg 87; Engl Educ; Tchg.

**SHEFFAR, MICHAEL P,** Kent St Univ Kent Cmps, Kent, OH; SR; BBA; Gldn Ky; Dns Lst 90-; Otstndng Stdnt Achvmnt Awrd 90-; AAB 90; Mrktng; Law.**

**SHEFFIELD, AMANDA I,** Southern Coll Of Seventh Day, Collegedale, TN; SO; BA; Intl Clb 89-90; Engl Clb Exec Cmmtt 89-; Astrnmy Clb 90-; Drm Clb 90-; Distnqshd Deans Lst 89-; Alpha Mu Gamma 89-; Stdnt Assoc 89-; AF Ruf Memorial Schlrshnrbl Mntn Trm Ppr Cntst 90-; Engl; Tchr Hgh Schl Engl.**

**SHEFFIELD III, ARTHUR,** Howard Univ, Washington, DC; SO; BA; AIAS 90-; Tstmstrs 89-; Trk/Fld 90; Archtct.

**SHEFFIELD, CHANNIE W,** Univ Of Sc At Columbia, Columbia, SC; FR; Elec Engrg.

**SHEFFIELD, CHRISTINE M,** Winthrop Coll, Rock Hill, SC; SR; BA; Lk Mchgn Jrnl Bus Mgr 85-86; Prsdntl Schlr 85; Prsdnts Lst 90-; Natl Hnr Scty 76; Spcl Nds Stdnts Ttr 85-86; Drk Bm Mrn Inc; Psychlgy.

**SHEFFIELD, CHRISTOPHER SCOTT,** Abraham Baldwin Agri Coll, Tifton, GA; SO; Engrng.

**SHEFFIELD, DE ANNA J,** Jackson St Univ, Jackson, MS; JR; BA; Les Exqst A La Mode Mdlng Sqd 89-; Dnc Ensmbl 90-; Assc Blck Jrnlst 90-; Alph Mu Gamma Pres 89-; Alph Lmbd Dlt Asst Sctry; NAACP 89-; INTRN Stn; Miss Alpha Phi Alpha 90-; Mass Cmnctns Brdcst Jrnlsm; TV Rprtr/Anchr.

**SHEFFIELD, DEBORAH L,** Itawamba Comm Coll, Fulton, MS; SO; BED; Chrldr Capt 89-; Indian Delegation 89-; Phi Theta Kappa 89-; Fitness Mgmt; Exer Phys.

**SHEFFIELD, WANDA LYNNE,** Livingston Univ, Livingston, AL; SR; BA; Erly Chldhd Ed; Tchr.

**SHEFFLER, KAREN M,** Indiana Univ Of Pa, Indiana, PA; SO; MBA; Natl Spch Hrng Lang Ass 89-; Sign Lang Clb 89-; Envrnmntly Cons Organ Fndr Pres 90-; Stdnt Advsry Coun Stdnt Comm Svcs; Provost Schlr; Dns Lst 89-; Spch Path Audiology.

**SHEHADEH, FATIMAH M,** City Univ Of Ny City Coll, New York, NY; JR; LAESA; Elctrcl Engr.

**SHEIKH, SAIMA R,** Univ Of Miami, Coral Gables, FL; JR; BS; Cncl Intl Stdnts/Org Cabinet 90-; Pres 100 First Aid Squad; Hnr Stdnt Assn; Alpha Lambda Delta; Phi Eta Sigma; Golden Key; Alpha Epsilon Delta; Vol Bapt Hosp; Bio; Med.

**SHEIKH, SILENA H,** Pellissippi St Tech Comm Coll, Knoxville, TN; SO; BSN; Nrsng; RN.

**SHEILDS, DESARAE L,** Va St Univ, Petersburg, VA; FR; BA; NAACP Chrprsn 90-; Sclgy; Drug Enfrcmnt Agnt.

**SHEILS, MAUREEN P,** City Univ Of Ny La Guard Coll, Long Island Cty, NY; SO; AS; Phi Theta Kappa 90-; Deans Lst 89-; Secy; Bus Admin; Bus Mgmnt.

**SHELBY, STANETT R,** Ky St Univ, Frankfort, KY; SR; BA; Tchr Educ Stdnt Rep 90-; FCA 88-; SNEA 90-; Grad Asstnshp Grad Asst 91-92; Bsbl Tm Capt 88-90; AS Enterprise St Jr Clg 88; Phy Educ; Tch.

**SHELDON, FRAN B,** City Univ Of Ny Queens Coll, Flushing, NY; SR; BA; Gldn Key 89-; Magna Cum Laude; Deans List; WINS ABC NBC Radio 90-; Cmnctns Arts/Media; Brdcst Jrnlsm.**

**SHELDON, HOLLY LYNN,** Daemen Coll, Amherst, NY; SO; BS; Phys Ther.

**SHELDON, PAUL L,** Univ Of Miami, Coral Gables, FL; JR; BBA; Tufts Univ Dns Lst 88-90; Acctg.

**SHELENBERGER, ANGELA D,** Kent St Univ Kent Cmps, Kent, OH; SR; BA; Gymnastics Clb 87-89; Lambda Alpha Epsilon 89-; Alpha Lambda Delta 87-; Golden Key 90-; Phi Beta Kappa; Prsdnts Lst 90; Rsrch Asstnt 89-90; Crmnl Jstc Psychology; Law.

**SHELESTOVICH, MARCI L,** Univ Of Akron, Akron, OH; SO; BS; Campus Focus; Alpha Lambda Delta 90; Phi Eta Sigma 90; Alpha Delta Pi Sec 89-; Hnrs Stdnt; Univ Chrldr Capt 89-; Elem Edn; Teach.

**SHELFORD, J MAXWELL,** Tn Temple Univ, Chattanooga, TN; JR; BS; Pi Kappa Dlt 90-; Bus Adm Intrnshp MBA Mktng 90-; Bus Admn; Sml Bus Mgr.

**SHELL, GLADYS MOORE,** Va St Univ, Petersburg, VA; SR; BS; Stdnt Ed Assn; Alpha Kappa Mu; Kappa Delta Pi Hstrn 90-; Deans Lst 87-90; Pres Lst 90-; Elem Ed; Tchr.

**SHELL, JAMES A,** Ms St Univ, Miss State, MS; GD; MA; Ftbl; Sr MVP Ftbl; SEC Ofnsv Plyr Wk; M-Club; Pres Schlr; Deans Lst; Acad All-Sec; Grad Asst Athletic Dept; BBA 90; Athletic Admin.

**SHELL, JENNIFER C,** Northeastern Christian Jr Coll, Villanova, PA; FR; Spring New England Tour NCJC Accapella Choir Soloist; Teen Missions Int; Vlntr Mission Work 8 Wks Summer Mexico Honduras 90-; Ldrshp Schlrshp Spring; Deans List Fall-Spring 90-; Bible/Missions Music; Missionary Of Cen Amer.

**SHELL, MICHELLE D,** Anderson Coll, Anderson, SC; FR; AA; Phi Theta Kappa; Soccer; Psych; Teach.

**SHELL, SUZAUN O,** Al A & M Univ, Normal, AL; SR; BED; Cncl For Exceptnl Chldrn 87-89; Bapt Stdtn Un 87-89; Specl Educ; Tchr.

**SHELLEY, BILLIE J,** Univ Of Cin R Walters Coll, Blue Ash, OH; SO; AAS; Alpha Beta Gamma; Prdctn Cntrl Spec 86-90; Sr Wrnty Admn; Bus; Bus/Pgm Mgmt.

**SHELLEY, CYNTHIA TURLEY,** Lexington Comm Coll, Lexington, KY; SO; AS; SMADHA; Schlp; Prctr/Gmble/ADHA Schlp 90-; Univ KY Dns Lst 90-; Brbn Cnty/Paris Grls Fnd 90-; Orthdntc Asst 81-; Appld Sci; Dntl Hygnst.

**SHELLEY, ELIZABETH A,** Coll Of New Rochelle, New Rochelle, NY; SO; BA; SADD Tres 89-; Actvts Cncl 89-; Wkndrs Clb 90-; Hnr Prog 89-; Psi Chi; Pres Schlrshp 89-; Psych/Pol Scif Clncl Psych.

**SHELLEY, HELENA T,** Univ Of Sc At Columbia, Columbia, SC; JR; BSN; SNA Pres; Nrsng.

**SHELLEY, JENNIFER L,** Univ Of Central Fl, Orlando, FL; FR; BA; Engl; Poltcs.

**SHELLITO, JULIE A,** Westminster Coll, New Wilmingtn, PA; JR; BA; Hnrs Pgm; Mortr Brd; VISA Serv Tms 89-; Pub Rel.

**SHELLS, TRACY J,** Alcorn St Univ, Lorman, MS; SR; BS; Hnr Stdnt Orgnztn 89-90; Intrfth Gspl Chr 88-89; Psychlgy Clb 90-; Alpha Kappa Mu 89-Dprtmnt Ed Awrd 90-; Psychlgy; Clncl Psychlgst.

**SHELLY, AKINS S,** Univ Of Tn At Martin, Martin, TN; JR; BA; Newspaper Staff 88-89; Nwsprgrm Schl Brd Cstng 88-89; AS Jcksn St Comm Clg 89; Scndry Ed Hstry; Tchr.

**SHELLY, ELIZABETH L,** Bethany Coll, Bethany, WV; SR; Frnch Clb 87-89; Psychlgy Clb Pres 89-; Alpha Beta Gamma 90-; Stdnt NEA 88-90; Alpha Xi Delta Treas 87-; Lab Prctr 88-; IM Sprts 89-90; BA; Psychlgy; Educ.

**SHELNUT, JENNIFER L,** Fl St Univ, Tallahassee, FL; FR; BACH; Circus Only Cllgte Circus 90f Batgrls 90; Phi Eta Sigma 90; Kappa Delta 90; Circus 90; Bsnss; Accntng.

**SHELNUTT, KIMBERLY A,** Ga St Univ, Atlanta, GA; SR; BED; Phi Kappa Phi 90-; Erly Chldhd; Tchng.

**SHELOMITH, ZACH B,** Univ Of Miami, Coral Gables, FL; FR; BBA; Stdnt Govt Cab Acad Affrs Comm 90-; Hillel Jewsh Stdnt Org 90-; Alpha Lambda Delta 90-; Hnrs Stdnt Assn 90-; Bacchus 90; Busn/Finc; Corp Law/Real Est.

**SHELTON, ANGELA D,** Coll Of Charleston, Charleston, SC; SO; BA; Intrnshp Schlstcs MUSC 91-; Nrsng; RN.

**SHELTON, APRIL D,** Union Univ School Of Nursing, Memphis, TN; FR; RN; Nrsng.

**SHELTON, BRONSON R,** East Tn St Univ, Johnson City, TN; JR; BA; Soc Mfg Engrs 89-; Epsilon Pi Tau; Glenwood Ruritan 88-; KY Military Acad 90; US Dept Energy Appt Sci/Engr Oak Ridge TN; US Army Reserves SP4 87-; Dispatcher Greeneville Light/Power 89-; Mfg/Math; Engr.

**SHELTON, CAROLYN FAYE,** Western Ky Univ, Bowling Green, KY; GD; Kappa Dlt Pi; BA; Mdl Grd Educ.

**SHELTON, CHRISTINA E,** King Coll, Bristol, TN; SO; Hlth Sci Soc 89-; Pre Phrmcy; Doctr Phrmcy.

**SHELTON, DAVIDA M,** Midlands Tech Coll, Columbia, SC; FR; Resp Thrpy Clb; Resp Thrpy.

**SHELTON, DEBORAH M,** Va St Univ, Petersburg, VA; JR; BA; Stdnt Edn Soc 89-; Yrbk Staff 89-; Kappa Delta Pi 90-; Alpha Kappa Alpha 90-; Eng Edn; Teach.

**SHELTON, DENISE M,** Univ Of Fl, Gainesville, FL; JR; BS; Amer Scty Ag Eng Tres 89-; Alph Epsln; Alpha Zeta 90-; Gamma Sgm Dlt 90-; FL Undrgrad Schlr 88-; Deans List 90-; Ag Eng; Eng Ph D Fclty Pos.

**SHELTON, JAMES S,** Pellissippi St Tech Comm Coll, Knoxville, TN; GD; Civil Eng; Eng.

**SHELTON, JANETTE L,** Ky St Univ, Frankfort, KY; FR; Deans Lst 90; Milwaukee Police Dept Aide 89-90; Sftbl; Pol Sci; Law.

**SHELTON, JENNIFER L,** Northeast State Tech Comm Coll, Blountville, TN; SO; AD; Office Sys Tech; Med Sec.

**SHELTON, JO E,** Marshall University, Huntington, WV; SO; BA; Acad Schlrshp 88-; Multi Sub; Tchr.

**SHELTON, JOHNNY M,** Ms St Univ, Miss State, MS; JR; BA; Eugene Butler Schlp Crtv Wrtng 90-; Pres Lst; Cub Scts; Coach; PTA; MSU Cmps Mail; Engl; Jrnlsm.

**SHELTON, JOYCE A,** Central Fl Comm Coll, Ocala, FL; JR; BA; Marion Citrus Mntl Hlth; AA 90; Crmnl Just; MA.

**SHELTON, JULIE L,** Bridgewater Coll, Bridgewater, VA; SO; BS; Home Econ; Day Care Mgmt.

**SHELTON, KAREN Y,** Univ Of Nc At Asheville, Asheville, NC; SO; BA; SNEA Actvts Chrmn 89-; RHA 89-90; Cmps Ambsdr 89-90; Phi Eta Sgm; Alph Dlt Pi Pldg Edctr 90-; Roy A Taylor Pblc Spkng Cntst 90-; Tchng Flw 89-; MA Hanna Schlrshp 89-; Ltr; Engl Educ.

**SHELTON, LAURA F,** Muskingum Coll, New Concord, OH; JR; BS; Flwshp Chrstn Athlts 88-; Chrch Chr Slst 88-; Prfsni Sngr 88-; Lambda Sigma Zeta 88-; Phi Alpha Theta 90-; Beta Beta Beta Hstrn 88-; Amer Chmcl Soc 88-; Rd Crs Bld Mbl 89-; Blgy Tr 90-; Bg Bro/Bg Sis Pgm 88-; Dns Lst 88-; Blgy; Med.**

**SHELTON, MARK T,** Western Carolina Univ, Cullowhee, NC; FR; BS; Electrncs; Engr.

**SHELTON, MELINDA K,** Mary Holmes Coll, West Point, MS; SO; Res Asst Awrd; Cert Merit; Dean Lst; Pres Awrd; Pres Schlr; AA; Elem Educ; Tchr.

**SHELTON II, PANNELL O,** Va Polytechnic Inst & St Univ, Blacksburg, VA; FR; BS; Coop Dupont Mrtnsvlle Vl; IM Bsktbl And Sftbl; Mech Eng Mchns Math Sci.

**SHELTON, PATRICIA L,** Limestone Coll, Gaffney, SC; SR; BA; Dns Lst; Sigma Kappa Sorority/Wstnr Carolina Univ 60-61; Wmn Chrch Prsbytrn Chrch; Prnt Edctr W/Pblc Schl; Cert Wstrn Carolina Univ 60-61; Cert Univ Missouri 89-; Elem Educ; Tchng.

**SHELTON, PATTI I,** North Ga Coll, Dahlonega, GA; FR; BS; Church Yth Grp 87-; Church Camp Cnslr 89-; Alpha Gamma Delta Pres 90-; Hwy Clean-Up Pgm; Juvenile Diabetes Fndtn; Powder Puff Ftbl; Sor Sftbl 90-; Pol Sci; Law.

**SHELTON, SANDRA J,** Georgetown Univ, Washington, DC; SO; Prog Brd; Crdt Union; Acctng Frm Intrn; Intrntl Bus; Acct.

**SHELTON, SHONNA L,** Bethany Coll, Bethany, WV; SR; BA; Grmn Clb Pres 89-; Rnnr Un Plnng Brd; Stdnt Lf Chrprsn 88-; Stdnt Brd Gvrnrs Rep 87-; Alpha Psi Omega VP 89-; Sigma Tau Epsilon 89-; Zeta Tau Alpha 89-; Rasias Lang Mthd Tchrs Asst 89; Leonora Cayard Prz Grmn; Grmn; Ed.

**SHELTON, TAMARA Y,** Va Commonwealth Univ, Richmond, VA; JR; BSN; Phi Theta Kappa; RN Stuart Circle Hosp; AAS 90; Nrsg.

**SHELTON, TERRANCE NATHANIEL,** Clark Atlanta Univ, Atlanta, GA; SR; BA; Stdnt Govt Assoc Mr Frshmn 87; Philharmonic Soc Pres 87-; Players Drama Clb 88-; Priv Indstry Cncl Summer Yth Empl Prog Cnslr 90-; Dns Lst 87-89; So So Def Prod Co-Prod 87-; Times Newspaper Gannett Affill Freelance Rep 88-89; Mass Cmnctns; Entertnmnt Cnsltg.**

**SHELTON, THOMAS W,** Medical Coll Of Ga, Augusta, GA; GD; DMD; Stdnt Gvrnmnt Pres 84-85; AM Stdnt Dntl Assc 90; Gamma Beta Phi 83; Bptst Stdnt Un 83-85; Mthdst Stdnt Un 85-87; Block/Bridle Clb 85-87; Stdnt Srv/Ldrshp Awrd 85; Sch Ag Schlrshp 85-86; Deans Lst 90; Tennis 83-85; AS; Science; Dntstry.

**SHELTON, VICKI L,** Tn St Univ, Nashville, TN; SR; MS; BS; Psych; Clncl.

**SHELTON, VICTORIA L,** Beckley Coll, Beckley, WV; SO; AA; Hons 90-; Scndry Ed; Ed Psych.

**SHEN, REBECCA C,** Harvard Univ, Cambridge, MA; FR; BA; Chrl Scty; Fncng; Physcs.

**SHENCAVITZ, SUSAN G,** Johnson St Coll, Johnson, VT; SR; BS; Chesamore Hnr Soc; VT Educ Media Assc 90-; Librn 89-90; AA Suffolk Co Comm Coll 76; Lbrry/Meda.

**SHENEFELT, RICHARD C,** Northern Ky Univ, Highland Hts, KY; FR; AD; Nrsng.

**SHENENBERGER, DONALD W,** Univ Of Sc At Columbia, Columbia, SC; SR; BS; ROTC 89; Alpha Epsilon Delta Pres 90-; Phi Eta Sigma 89-; Univ Schlr Schlrshp 90-; Jennie Z Schaver Pre Med Schlrshp 90-; Harry S Truman Mem Schlrshp; Trenholm Road Untd Meth Chrch Vstn Club 90; Bio Chem Rsrch; Dept Anatomy 90-; Chem; Med.

**SHENK, GREGORY C,** Bridgewater Coll, Bridgewater, VA; FR; BA; Phlsphy.

**SHENKUS, ERIC R,** Univ Of Rochester, Rochester, NY; SO; BA; Rsdnt Advsr; Cycling Team V P 89-; Poltcl Sci; Law.

**SHENTON, PAULA M,** Univ Of Ky, Lexington, KY; SO; Stdnt Adv Comm Phil Dept 90-; Phi Eta Sigma 89-; Zeta Tau Alpha 89-90; Singletary Schlrshp 89-; Phlsphy; Law.

**SHEOGOBIND, SHARMILLA T,** City Univ Of Ny Baruch Coll, New York, NY; SR; BA; Baaruch Psychlgy Soc 88-; Golden Key 88-; Psi Chi 89-; Deans List 88-; Varsty Fencing Team 88-; Psychlgy; Sch Psyclgst.

**SHEPARD, GLENN A,** Embry Riddle Aeronautical Univ, Daytona Beach, FL; SR; BS; Nvl Aviation Clb 87-; Am Assn Airport Exec 90-; Sr Class Cncl; Intrnshp Keene Municipal Airport Supvr Airport Op 90; Sftbl/Ftbl/Vlybl/Flr Hcky 87-; Aviation.

**SHEPARD, KAREN K,** Cornell Univ Statutory College, Ithaca, NY; SR; BS; Vars Crew 87-; Fd Sci; Fd Instry.

**SHEPARD, KRISTIN A,** Lesley Coll, Cambridge, MA; SO; BA; Educ/Natl Sci; Prof Educ.

**SHEPARDSON, TOBIN W,** Roane St Comm Coll, Harriman, TN; SO; AA; Excell Awd 90-; Drftsmn CAD Oper 89-; Librl Arts; Intl Busn.

**SHEPETUK, SHERRY A,** City Univ Of Ny La Guard Coll, Long Island Cty, NY; GD; Arnhold/Berri Schlrshp 90; Asst Chld Care Tchr 86-; AA 90; Erly Chldhd Ed; Tch.

**SHEPHERD, CAROL A,** Southern Coll Of Tech, Marietta, GA; GD; MS; ACM; Tau Alpha Pi; IBM Cooprtv Educ Intrn; Cmptr Sci Artfcl Intlgnc; Pgmr.

**SHEPHERD, CORDELIA M,** Univ Of The Dist Of Columbia, Washington, DC; SR; BPA; Odessa Starks Mem Schlrshp 87; Schlstic Achvmnt Awrd 89-; IRAC 85-; Pub Mngmnt.

**SHEPHERD III, JACK P,** Coll Of Charleston, Charleston, SC; SR; MD; Flwshp Chrstn Athlts Offcr Grp 88-89; Alpha Epsilon Delta; IM Water Polo; BS; Blgy; Med.

**SHEPHERD, KRIS R,** Oh Univ, Athens, OH; JR; BS; Soc Mech Engr 89; Golden Key; Tau Beta Pi; All Amer Schlr Award; Engr Dns Lst; Co-Op Gnrl Elctrc Intern; IM Vlybl/Sftbl/Flag Ftbl; Mech Engr.**

**SHEPHERD, KRISTA M,** Kent St Univ Stark Cmps, North Canton, OH; FR; BA; Harris/Day Archtcts Inc Drftsprsn; Intr Dsgn/Archtctr.

**SHEPHERD, LORRAINE E,** Wv Univ At Parkersburg, Parkersburg, WV; SO; BS; Phi Beta Lambda; Phi Theta Kappa; Dns Lst; Awrd Otstndng Svc 90-; Bus Admin Acctg.

**SHEPHERD, MICHAEL P,** Wilmington Coll, New Castle, DE; SO; Bsbl 89-; Crim Just; Law.

**SHEPHERD, TAMMY L,** Univ Of Tn At Martin, Martin, TN; FR; Alpha Gamma Delta Mbrshp Chrmn 90-; Ecnmcs; Intl Bus.

**SHEPHERD, TANYA H,** Andrew Coll, Cuthbert, GA; FR; AA; Lit Clb; Phi Theta Kappa; Phi Delta; Early Admn; Bsns; Corp Exec.

**SHEPHERD, VELEDA,** Sue Bennett Coll, London, KY; FR; Psych; Occup Thrpy.

**SHEPHERD, VIRGINIA E,** Eckerd Coll, St Petersburg, FL; SO; BS; Intrnshp Molecular Bio; Bio; Med.

**SHEPP JR, MICHAEL L,** Univ Of Fl, Gainesville, FL; SR; BA; FL Plyrs Sec 90-; Gldn Key 89-; Alpha Psi Omega 90-; Pres Hnr Rl; AA 89; Bsn Mgmt; Perf Arts.

**SHEPP, YAIMA E,** Cheyney Univ Of Pa, Cheyney, PA; FR; MBA; Choir 90-; Cmnctn Arts; Newcasting.

**SHEPPARD, CARLMETTA L,** Fl A & M Univ, Tallahassee, FL; SR; BA; CIS Clb 88-; Outstndng Coll Stdnts Amer 89-; Co-Op Gulf Pwr Co 90-; Comp; Anlyst.

**SHEPPARD, JACQUELINE A,** Birmingham Southern Coll, Birmingham, AL; SO; BA; Blck Stdnt Un 89-90; Blck Stdnt Un Secy 90-; Birmingham Sthrn Clg Partnrshp 89-90; Phi Eta Sigma 90; Alpha Lambda Delta 90; Triangle Club 90-; Actng.

**SHEPPARD, LORI L,** Howard Univ, Washington, DC; SO; AIAS 89-; Black Cngrssnl Caucus 89-; Schrlshp; Architecture.

**SHEPPARD, M BRANDON,** Southern Union St Jr Coll, Wadley, AL; FR; BA; Pre Phys Thrpy; Phys Thrpst.

**SHEPPARD, REBECCA L**, Slippery Rock Univ, Slippery Rock, PA; SO; BA; Spnsh Law.**

**SHEPPARD, ROBERT B**, Itawamba Comm Coll, Fulton, MS; SO.**

**SHEPPARD, SHAUNA R**, Longwood Coll, Farmville, VA; JR; BS; Stdnt Educ Assn 89-; Elem Ed; Elem Schl Tchr.

**SHEPPARD, TONY L**, Middle Tn St Univ, Murfreesboro, TN; SR; BS; Baptist Student Union Pres 87-; Gamma Beta Phi Sec 88-; Psychology; Adolescent Cnslng.

**SHEPPARD, VIVECA J**, James Madison University, Harrisonburg, VA; SO; BS; Psi Chi; Psychologist/Clinical.

**SHERARD, ANN CHEVES**, Univ Of Sc At Columbia, Columbia, SC; JR; BA; Alumni Assoc 90-; SG Asst Chf Stf 89-90; Mortar Bd; Omicron Delta Kappa; Kappa Delta Epsilon 90-; Delta Delta Delta Pres 88-; Rep David H Wilkins Page 89-; Gov Carroll A Campbell Jr Intern 90; Senator Strom Thurmond Intern; IM 88-; Early Chldhd Edn.

**SHERARD, TAWANA**, Jackson St Univ, Jackson, MS; FR; Yng Scientist Pgm 90-; Chemistry/Pre Med; Pediatrician.

**SHERBOURNE, JENNIFER L**, Univ Of Akron, Akron, OH; SR; BS; OH Bus Tchrs Assoc; Kappa Delta Pi 90-; Intrnshp Natl Cty Bnk; AAS 89; Scndry Ed Bus Tchng.

**SHERER, KANDIE J**, Life Coll, Marietta, GA; GD; DC; AL Clb Sec 90-; Thompson Technq Clb 90-; Motion Palpation Clb 89-90; Deans List 89-; Chrprctc.**

**SHERER, LINDA M**, Univ Of Al At Birmingham, Birmingham, AL; JR; BS; Pres Lst; Phi Theta Kappa; Deans Schlrshp.

**SHERF, DAVID E**, Univ Of Toledo, Toledo, OH; GD; JD; Sprt Law Assc VP; Moot Court Brd 90-; BBA Un MA 89; Corporate Law.

**SHERIDAN, BRENDA A**, Wv Univ, Morgantown, WV; GD; MST; Kappa Tau Alpha; Tchng Grad Asstnshp 90-; BA Penn St Univ 89; Jrnlsm/Brdcst; Tele Rprtr.

**SHERIDAN, DAVID A**, Fl St Univ, Tallahassee, FL; JR; BMED; Mrchng Chfs Sect Ldr 89-; Cmps Crd Chrst 89-90; Cllg Msc Edcts Ntal Conf 89-90; Kappa Kappa Psi 90-; Dean Lst 89-; Msc Educ; Grad Schl Coll Prfssr.

**SHERIDAN, KIMBERLY L**, Fl St Univ, Tallahassee, FL; SR; BS; Mrchng Chfs Bnd 87-89; Future Edctrs Of Amer 90-; Natl Assn Educ Yng Chldrn 89-90; Phi Mu 88-; Dns Lst 90-; Elem Educ; Tchr.

**SHERIDAN, LILLIAN M**, Asnuntuck Comm Coll, Enfield, CT; SR; Phi Theta Kappa 90-; Wmns Gld; Acctg; BA 52-; Acctg.

**SHERIFF, JEFFREY P**, Tri County Tech Coll, Pendleton, SC; FR; IETA; Alpha Zeta Beta; Indstrl Electrnc Tech; Electrnc Eng.

**SHERIFF, KIMBERLY E**, West Liberty St Coll, West Liberty, WV; SR; BS; Delta Mu Delta; Bus Admin; Acctg.

**SHERLIN, REGINA M**, Univ Of Nc At Asheville, Asheville, NC; JR; BA; Univ Ambassador 90-; Rsdnt Assist 89-; Stdnt Alcohol/Drug Educ Coord 89-; Alpha Kappa Delta; Hnr Stdnt 88-; Univ Rsrch Fllw 88-; Survival Drug Educ 88-89; Stdnt Ldrshp Svc Award 89-; Outstndng Rsdnt Assist 90-; Sclgy; Wrkng Adults W/Abuse Prblms.

**SHERMAN, ASHER B**, Univ Of Rochester, Rochester, NY; SR; YMCA Coor 90-; Rsdnt Advsr; Blck Stdnt Uni; Omicron Delta Epsilon; Hnrs; Natl Urbn Lgue Schlrshp; Inrds Bus Intrn; Grn Pce Actn; Econs; Law.

**SHERMAN, BONNIE G**, Brevard Coll, Brevard, NC; SO; BA; Amb 90-; AA; Soc/Crmnl Justice; Rehab Serv.

**SHERMAN, DEBORAH S**, Union Coll, Barbourville, KY; JR; BS; Cmmtr Cncl 90; Phi Theta Kappa 89-90; Elem Ed.**

**SHERMAN, GLENN F**, Samford Univ, Birmingham, AL; FR; JD; Chrstn Lgl Soc 90-; Cmbrlnd Law Rvw Membr; Ftbl Schlrshp 73-75; BBA GA Coll 90; Bus/Mdl Mgmt Bckgrnd; Law.

**SHERMAN, HOWARD J**, Fl International Univ, Miami, FL; JR; BA; Accntng; CPA.

**SHERMAN, JAMES**, Oh Univ-Southern Cmps, Ironton, OH; SO; BA; Chorus; Designated Stdnt Ldr; Minister For United Meth Church; Psych; Seminary.

**SHERMAN, JONATHAN S**, Ga Inst Of Tech At Atlanta, Atlanta, GA; JR; BS; Gamma Beta Phi 89-90; Eagle Sct 85; AS Phycs 90; Ind Engr.

**SHERMAN, KIMBERLY K**, Athens St Coll, Athens, AL; JR; Phi Theta Kappa 89; BSED Athens St Coll; Elem Educ; Mstrs Educ.**

**SHERMAN, LISA J**, Univ Of Pittsburgh, Pittsburgh, PA; JR; Chld Care; Elem Educ.

**SHERMAN, MONICA L**, S U N Y At Buffalo, Buffalo, NY; JR; BA; Amer Mrktng Assoc; Alpha Epsilon Phi; Golden Key; Alpha Epsilon Phi Fndrsr/Pblcty Chrmn 90-; Bus Admin/Mrktng Cnctrtn; Law.

**SHERMAN, RENE**, Oh St Univ At Marion, Marion, OH; SO; BSBA; EABS Pres; Alpha Lambda Delta 90-; Phi Eta Sigma 90-; Workshop Special 78-89; Mktg/Econ; Sales/Cust Serv.

**SHERMAN, ROBERT A**, Old Dominion Univ, Norfolk, VA; SO; BS; Cvl Eng; Eng Envrmntl.

**SHERMAN, ROGER F**, Univ Of Pittsburgh At Bradford, Bradford, PA; FR; BA; Chem Clb 90-; IM Bsktbl 90-; Phrmcy.

**SHERMAN, SHARON F**, Newbury Coll, Brookline, MA; GD; AA; Phi Theta Kappa 90; Deans Lst 88-90; World Tang Soo Do Assoc 87; Distr Mgr Bay Colony News; Admn Asst.

**SHERMAN, SHARON G**, Fl St Univ, Tallahassee, FL; SR; BA; DAR 87-; Sigma Alpha Epsilon Aux 90; AA Gulf Coast Comm Clg 89; Fshn Mrchndsng; Clthng Byr.

**SHERMAN, TRACY M**, Va St Univ, Petersburg, VA; JR; BA; Pi Omega Pres 90-; Bus; Tchr.

**SHERN, KATHERINE M**, Ga St Univ, Atlanta, GA; GD; Phi Kappa Phi 90-; Golden Key; Comm Advsry Cncl 87-; Atlanta Ski Clb 87-; Educ Dir Consumer Credit Cnslng Serv; BS 90; Scndry Educ/Bus.

**SHERON, JULIE A**, Union Univ, Jackson, TN; SO; BSN; Natl Stdnt Nrss Assn Of Unn Univ ASNA 90-; Csmtlgy Dgree; Fld Of Nrsng 85-; Cosmetology Degree Nestles Beauty School Paris TN 85; Nrsng Psychlgy; RN.

**SHEROUSE, TAMMY L**, Central Fl Comm Coll, Ocala, FL; AS; Wyomina Parr Bptst Chrch; Medcl Sec/Trnscrpt; Orvt MD Offcs.

**SHERRANGE, JAMES C**, S U N Y Coll Of Tech At Delhi, Delhi, NY; FR; AOS; Assn Genl Cntrctrs Am 90-; Marine Corps 84-88; Genl Cntrctrs; Eng.

**SHERRED, DAWN L**, Univ Of Sc At Spartanburg, Spartanburg, SC; SR; BSBA; Busns Club; Accntng Club; Gamma Beta Phi; Ntnl Collegiate Mnrty Ldrshp Awd; Best Write 88; Awd Of Merit 87-88; Pres List 87; Deans List; Accntng; CNA.**

**SHERRICK, TRISHA M**, Ny Univ, New York, NY; JR; BA; Natl Orgnztn Fr Wmn; Media Rfrm Com Coor Brd Of Dirs 89; Rprdctve Rghts Com Coor; Admin Sec 89-; Wmns Stds; Law.

**SHERRILL, DELAYNE W**, Western Piedmont Comm Coll, Morganton, NC; SO; AAS; MIM Cert; Bus Admn.

**SHERRILL, MARK D**, Johnson C Smith Univ, Charlotte, NC; JR; BS; Bsktbl Cpt; YMCA Cnslr; JCSU Mns Bsktbl Plyr Of Yr; NCAA; Sociolgy; Scrt Srvc Wrk.

**SHERRILL, MELISSA M**, Univ Of Montevallo, Montevallo, AL; JR; BMED; Wind Ensemble Prncpl 88-; Jazz Ensmbl Prncpl 88-; Music Ed Natl Conf 89-; Phi Alpha Mu 89-; Deans Lst; Music Edn.

**SHERROD, DENISE**, Norfolk St Univ, Norfolk, VA; JR; BS; U S Army Occupation Fd Svc Spec; Sociology; Mstrs Dgr.

**SHERROW, SANDRA K**, Hillsborough Comm Coll, Tampa, FL; FR; BA; Studio Arts; Artst/Desgnr.

**SHERRY, LYNN M**, Indiana Univ Of Pa, Indiana, PA; JR; BS; Pblc Rltns Clb VP 90-; IM Sftbl 90; Peer Advisor 90-; Provost Schlr 89-; Deans List 88-; Comm Media; Public Rltns.

**SHERSON, BRENDA L**, Fl Atlantic Univ, Boca Raton, FL; FR; BBA; Phi Eta Sigma Sec; Bus; Acctng/CPA.

**SHERTZER, D FAYE**, Manor Jr Coll, Jenkintown, PA; SR; AS; Real Est Invstrs Lancaster 86-; Bus Admin; Sales/Mktng.

**SHERWELL, STEPHANIE M**, Washington Coll, Chestertown, MD; FR; BA; Intl Rels Clb Pres 90-; Spnsh Clb Pres 90-; Dnce Clb 90-; Campus Chrstn Fllwshp 90-; Intl Rels; Diplomtc Serv.

**SHERWIN, SANDRA D**, Allegany Comm Coll, Cumberland, MD; FR; Phi Theta Kappa; Cert Asstng; Dntl Hygiene Asstng.

**SHERWOOD, KATHLEEN M**, Life Coll, Marietta, GA; SO; DC; Stdnt Govt Rep; Golden Key; BA Temple Univ 88; Chrprctc.

**SHERZEY, TERESA A**, Radford Univ, Radford, VA; SR.

**SHETH, SHIBANI Y**, Kent St Univ Kent Cmps, Kent, OH; SO; BA; Beta Alpha Psi 90-; Pres Lst 90; Dns Lst; India Assoc Yngstwn Sec/Treas 89-; Brbzn Shcl Mdlng Asst Tchr; Acctng/Bsn; CPA.

**SHETLER, BRIAN L**, Univ Of Akron, Akron, OH; JR; Cncrt Chr 90-; Schlrshps 88-; Mech Engr.

**SHETTLEMORE, MELISSA G**, Ms St Univ, Miss State, MS; FR; BS; Pre-Vet Clb 90-; Blgcl Eng Soc 90-; Soc Wmn Engrs 90-; Gamma Beta Phi 90-; Pres Lst 90-; Blgcl Eng; Eng Rsrch.

**SHETTY, SUJATHA**, Broward Comm Coll, Ft Lauderdale, FL; SO; AS; MRB Rao Mem Prz 79-; III Rank BA Eng Litt 80; BA Eng Litt Univ Madras India 80; Nurs.

**SHEVLIN, ANN MARIE**, Marywood Coll, Scranton, PA; JR; BS; Lang Clb 88-; Phi Beta Lambda 88-; Vol In Actn 88-; Via/Collgt Vol 88-; Deans Lst 89-90; Intl Bus; MBA.

**SHEWARD, AMY A**, Lesley Coll, Cambridge, MA; JR; BED; B Nai Brith Hiller 90-; RA 90-; Deans Lst 90-; Undergrad Schlrshp Acdmc Excellence; Early Chldhd Educ; Teach.

**SHIBILIA, DEBRA A**, Endicott Coll, Beverly, MA; FR; AS; Intrn District Atty Off; Paralegal; Law.

**SHIBLEY III, FREDERICK A**, Va Commonwealth Univ, Richmond, VA; SO; Phys Educ; Tchg.

**SHIDLOFSKY, CINDY M**, Broward Comm Coll, Ft Lauderdale, FL; SO; BA; Natl Hnr Roll 81-83; AA Broward Cmnty Clg; Acctg; CPA.

**SHIELDS, BOBBY L**, Univ Of Louisville, Louisville, KY; SR; MS; Stdnt Cncl Rep 89-90; Stdnt Org Almni Rltns 88-90; Amer Soc Mech Engrs 87-; Tau Beta Pi; Co-Op Stdnt GE Aircrft Engnes 89-90; BES; Mech Engrng; Eng/Bus.

**SHIELDS, DENA M**, Oh St Univ, Columbus, OH; FR; BA; Engl Pre Law; Law.

**SHIELDS, DERAK T**, Norfolk St Univ, Norfolk, VA; SR; BS; US Marine Corps Reservist Lance Cpl; Alpha Kappa Mu; Bsktbl/Sftbl/Vlybl; Math; MS Math.

**SHIELDS, DONNA M**, Coppin St Coll, Baltimore, MD; SR; Insprtn Clb V P 90-; Big Bros/Big Strs Tele Cmtee 90-; Stdnt Hon Assoc 89-; Intrnshp Univ Ill 90.

**SHIELDS, HEATHER K**, Lenoir Rhyne Coll, Hickory, NC; FR; AB; SGA Pres 90-; Pathway Rctr/Coord 90-; Debte Team 90-; Alpha Phi Omega 90-; Rotry Stdnt Of Mnth; Fr Medal; Hstry; Law.

**SHIELDS, JANETTE A**, Livingston Univ, Livingston, AL; JR; BA; I M Sftbl 89-90; Art Exhbtn 88-90; Chi Delphia 89-90; Fine Arts Cncl; Art Photo Exhib; Painting Prz; Hon Mntn Sculpture Mixed Media; Bus Admn/Art; Art Admn.

**SHIELDS, KELLIE A**, Univ Of Rochester, Rochester, NY; SR; BA; RA 89; Rsdntl Life Advsry Brd 89-90; Sftbl Capt 89-; Biology.

**SHIELDS, KEVIN J**, S U N Y Coll Of A & T Morrisvl, Morrisville, NY; SO; BS; Scl Wrkr 87-; Ins Examiner 89; BPS SUNY Clg Tech Utica/Rome 86; AS 90; Chem; MD.

**SHIELDS, KIMYLA G**, Univ Of South Al, Mobile, AL; JR; BS; Acctng Clb; Phi Eta Sigma 88-89; Phi Chi Theta VP; Beta Alpha Psi; Pres Schlp 88-; IM Sftbl 89-90; Pblc Acctnt.

**SHIELDS, LES LEE G**, Itawamba Comm Coll, Fulton, MS; SO; BA; SIFE 90-; Natl Acctg Ward; US Achvmnt Acad 90-; Acctg.

**SHIELDS, MELISSA T**, Valdosta St Coll, Valdosta, GA; SR; BS; Secty 87-; Early Childhood Ed; Elem Tchr.

**SHIELDS, NICOLE R**, Ms Univ For Women, Columbus, MS; SO; BA; Mass Cmnctn/Acctg; CPA/TV Brdcstr.

**SHIELDS, TRESSIA L**, Memphis St Univ, Memphis, TN; SR; BA; Blck Schlrs Unl 88-90; Alpha Kappa Delta 89-; Deans Lst 90; Sociology; Edn.

**SHIELDS, WILMA J**, Commonwealth Coll, Norfolk, VA; FR; AA; Alpha Beta Gamma; Cert Norfold Tech Voc Ctr 82; Bus; Law/Paralegal.

**SHIETS, STEVEN F**, Univ Of Akron, Akron, OH; FR; BA; Hon Clb 90-; Mrchng Bnd 90-; Cvl Eng.

**SHIFARRAW, TUTU**, Defiance Coll, Defiance, OH; SO; Intl Stdnts Assn; Cmptr Sci; Pgrmmr.

**SHIFFER, DANIEL T**, Norfolk St Univ, Norfolk, VA; SO; BA; Dwntwn Athl Clb Ath Inst; Sprtn Alpha Tau; Fld Eng Conc Const; Capt Jr Hcky; Pol Sci/Pre Law.

**SHIFLET, KELLY A**, Univ Of Sc At Columbia, Columbia, SC; SR; BAIS; Gamma Beta Phi 89-; Kappa Delta Epsilon 90-; Peabdy Schlrshp 90-; Carlina Schlr 90-; AA Andersn Jr Coll 89; Ed; Tch.

**SHIFMAN, DEBORAH H**, Fl International Univ, Miami, FL; JR; BED; Spcl Ed; Tchr/Cnslr.

**SHIH, GRACE**, Fl International Univ, Miami, FL; JR; BA; Acctng Asc; Intvars Chrstn Flwshp; Phi Kappa Phi; Acctng; Law.

**SHIH, JOHN Z**, Univ Of Md Baltimore Prof Schl, Baltimore, MD; SR; BA; Phi Kappa Phi 90-; Rho Chi 90-; Phrmcy.

**SHILLADY, LUCINDA L**, Va Commonwealth Univ, Richmond, VA; JR; BS; Orch 88-90; Ldrshp Cl 88-; Methodist Campus Minis 88-; Hon Prog 88-; Golden Key 90; Phi Eta Sigma 89; CRC Chem Awd 89; Top 1 Pct; Chmsty; Rsrch/Biochem; Molecular Biol.

**SHIMA, ANDREW V**, Bloomfield Coll, Bloomfield, NJ; SO; BS; PCA 90-; Peer Tutor 89-90; Chi Beta Theta Pledgemstr 90-; Bloomfield Clg Serv Awd Tutoring 90; Pre Chiroprtc; Chiroprtc Physcn.

**SHIMABUKURO, STACY N**, Radford Univ, Radford, VA; SR; BS; Aerobic Clb Instr 90-; Phys Edn Majors Clb 89-; Phys Edn/Cmrcl Fitness; Corp Fitness/Trnr.

**SHIMIZU, CRISTINA S**, Abraham Baldwin Agri Coll, Tifton, GA; FR; Engl; Ed.

**SHIMIZU, YUMIKO**, Comm Coll Algny Co Algny Cmps, Pittsburgh, PA; SO; ASSOC; Cmmnty Cllg Intl Clb Treas 90; Deans Lst 90; AS 89; Comp Info Systm.

**SHIMKO, JOSEPH J**, Eastern Nazarene Coll, Wollaston, MA; FR; Cls Cncl Tres 90-; Acpl Chr 90-; Bkstbl 90-; Hist; Law.

**SHIMKO, LISA M**, Univ Of The Arts, Philadelphia, PA; FR; BFA; Orntn Ldr; Pntng/Art Thrpy; Art Thrpst.

**SHIMOYAMA, MEHOSHI K**, Savannah St Coll, Savannah, GA; SO; BA; Hist; Prfssr.

**SHIMP, CHRISTINE E**, West Liberty St Coll, West Liberty, WV; SR; BS; Stdnt Govt Senator 90-; Chi Omega 89-90; Intrnshp WV State Pntntry; Intrnshp Brooke Cnty Sheriffs Dept; Miss Hilltopper 90-; Crmnl Jstce.

**SHIN, HEE YOUNG**, Georgetown Univ, Washington, DC; FR; BBA; Bsns; Prfsr.

**SHIN, HYUN B**, Carnegie Mellon Univ, Pittsburgh, PA; JR; BS; SG Pres 90-; Senate Campus Affr Cmte Chmn 90-; Asso/Indus Mgmnt/Econ Pres; Mortar Bd; Delta Tau Delta Alum Rltn Chmn 88-; A Carnegie Soc Pres Schol; Undergrad Rsrch Grant; Deans List; Indus Mgmnt/Econ.

**SHIN, JIN-UK**, Univ Of Louisville, Louisville, KY; JR; BES; Korean Stdnt Assn VP; Amer Intl Rltnshp Clb 89-90; Intl Bus Clb; Phi Eta Sigma; Gldn Key; Elec Engr; Professor/Rsrchr.

**SHIN, LINDA S**, Va Commonwealth Univ, Richmond, VA; GD; CERT; Koren-Am Stdnts Assn Edtr 85-89; East Asian Studies Clb 88-89; Beta Alpha Psi 90-; Cir K 85-86; Deans List 89-90; BA Clg William/Mary 89; Acctg; Pblc Acctg.

**SHIN, SARAH L**, Saint Josephs Coll, Windham, ME; FR; BA; SGA Tres; Frshmn Englsh Awd; Bsns Admnstrtn Accntng; CPA.

**SHIN, YOUNG H**, S U N Y At Buffalo, Buffalo, NY; GD; MA; BA 78; Archtct.

**SHINAULT, ANNETTE M,** Univ Of Nc At Charlotte, Charlotte, NC; SR; BS; Goldn Key 89-; Alpha Phi Sigma 89-; Intrnshp Surry Cnty Shrfs Dept 90; AA 89; AS; Crmnl Just/Comm Stds; Lab Evid Tech.

**SHINAULT, KAREN J,** Univ Of Sc At Spartanburg, Spartanburg, SC; SR; BA; Erly Chldhd Educ; Tchng.

**SHINDALA, CARMEN M,** Ms St Univ, Miss State, MS; SR; JD; Alpha Lambda Delta 87-88; Gamma Beta Phi 87-; Phi Mu 87-; Deans List Schlr 87; Pres List Schlr; BBA MS State Univ; Law; Law.

**SHINDE, SUNITA,** Oh Wesleyan Univ, Delaware, OH; JR; BA; Cir K Treas 89-; Envir Wldlf Clb 89; Pi Beta Phi Asst Pldg Ed 88-; History; Trnsltng/Intrprtg.

**SHING, CORINNE D,** Newbury Coll, Brookline, MA; SO; BA; Sr Acctng Coordntr At Codex Corp Manfield MA 83-; Acctng.

**SHINGLER, TIMOTHY J,** Bridgewater Coll, Bridgewater, VA; JR; BS; Econ Club Fndr/Pres 90-; Coll Rep 88-; Cath Campus Mnstry Exec Comm 90-; Physics Club Sec 90-; Phi Beta Lambda Pres 90-; Econ Club; Varsity Track Conf Champ 88-; Econ & Bus Ad.

**SHINKLE, CHRISTINA M,** Univ Of Miami, Coral Gables, FL; SR; Hon Cncl Rep 87-88; Bible Stds 70-; Chrstn Hsehlds Inc; Shprds Chr; Studio Msc/Jazz; Cmpsr/Tchr.

**SHINN, CARLA D,** Univ Of South Al, Mobile, AL; SR; BS; Erly Chldhd Ed; Edctr.

**SHINN, GABRIEL L,** Univ Of Southern Ms, Hattiesburg, MS; FR; BED; Mrchg Bnd 90-; Alpha Tau Omega 90-; Hnrs Coll Stu 90-; Elem Ed; Tchr.

**SHINN, JANIE S,** Cumberland Coll, Williamsburg, KY; JR; BS; Amer Chem Soc Treas 88-; Flwshp Chrstn Athls 89-; Bio Clb V P 88-90; Beta Beta Beta 90-; Full Acad Schlrshp 88-; Union Carbide Corp Intern 90; Vlybl 90-; Bio/Chem; Chem Ecologist.

**SHINSKEY, JEANNE L,** Providence Coll, Providence, RI; SO; BA; Otdr Clb 90-; Envrmntl Clb 90-; Pstrl Cncl 90-; Rsrch Asst; Psychlgy; Rsrch.

**SHIONARAIN, NAVINDRANAUTH,** City Univ Of Ny La Guard Coll, Long Island Cty, NY; JR; AAS; Accntng; CPA.

**SHIPE, SUZAN C,** Univ Of North Fl, Jacksonville, FL; SR; BAE; Sci Clb 90-; Gldn Ky 88-; Phi Kappa Phi 90-; Kappa Alpha Theta 85-; Biol; Phrmctcl Sales.

**SHIPLET, MICHELLE A,** North Central Tech Coll, Mansfield, OH; SR; AD; Campus Rght To Lf 87-; Assn Of Nrsng Stdnts 89-; Nrsng Stdnt Assn 90-; PTA 90-; Natl Collgt Nrsng Awrd 90; RN; Bs.

**SHIPLEY, DE ANNA MICHELLE,** Tusculum Coll, Greeneville, TN; SO; SGA Sec; Most Acdmc Athlt 90-; Chrldng Sqd 90-; Pre-Law; Lwyr.

**SHIPLEY, MILDRED V,** Coppin St Coll, Baltimore, MD; SR; BS; Scl Wrk Assn Treas 87-; SG 90; Lbrty Med Cntr Intrn 90-; Lbrry Aide 87-; Scl Sci Scl Wrk.

**SHIPMAN, ASHLEY E,** Fl A & M Univ, Tallahassee, FL; JR; BA; NABA 90-; Bus Wrtng Clb 90-; White Gld Hnr Soc; Delta Sigma Theta; Spcl Frnd Vl 90-; Dean Lst 88-; 3m Intern; Accntng; CPA.

**SHIPMAN, DAINA L,** Univ Of Fl, Gainesville, FL; JR; BA; Gldn Key 89-; Fnc.

**SHIPMAN, JOYCELYN ANNISE,** Al A & M Univ, Normal, AL; FR; BS; Early-Entrnce Fr 90; Zoolgy/Math; Orthdntst.

**SHIPMAN, YVETTE L,** Univ Of The Dist Of Columbia, Washington, DC; JR; BA; NATAS Stdnt Achvmnt Awrd; Mass Media; Wrtr Prdcr Dir.

**SHIPP, LAURA S,** Northern Ky Univ, Highland Hts, KY; SO; BA; Engl; Edtr.

**SHIPP, LAWRENCE L,** Free Will Baptist Bible Coll, Nashville, TN; JR; BS; Laymens Flwshp Pres 90-; Stdnt Body Prlmntrn 90-; Pi Gamma Chi 89-; Yrbk Staff Phtgrphr 89-; Chrstn Serv Grp Ldr 89-90; US Air Force 74-89; AAS Comm Clg Air Force 83; Scndry Ed/Engl; Tchng.

**SHIPP, TAMMI L,** Fisk Univ, Nashville, TN; JR; BA; FASE P 90-; Delta Mu Delta 90-; Beta Kappa Chi; Gold Key S; Delta Sigma Theta Corr S; Rsrch Asst Princeton U 90-; Rsrch Asst Mehavry Med Coll; Rsrch Asst Howard U; Bio; Pharmclgy.

**SHIRCLIFF, DAVID R,** George Mason Univ, Fairfax, VA; SR; BA; SEA 90-; AAS Nrthrn VA Comm Clg 90; Tech Educ; Law.

**SHIREY, JONATHAN W,** Duquesne Univ, Pittsburgh, PA; SO; BA; Zeta Beta Tau; Ftbl 89-; Bsns Mrktng.

**SHIRING, GARY J,** Point Park Coll, Pittsburgh, PA; JR; BS; Spprt Spec Blck Box Corp Tech Spprt Dpt 89; AS Penn Tech Inst 87; Elec Engr.

**SHIRLEY, ANGIE S,** Univ Of Southern Ms, Hattiesburg, MS; SR; BS; Amer Advrtsng Fdrtn Treas 89-; Dlgte Ad Fst 90; Kappa Tau Alpha; Phi Kappa Phi; Gldn Key; Donald M Dana Sr Advrtsng Awd; Advrtsng; Advrtsng Agncy.

**SHIRLEY, ANN D,** Ms St Univ, Miss State, MS; SO; Vet Med.

**SHIRLEY, DIANE M,** Valdosta St Coll, Valdosta, GA; SO; BSN; Nrsng.

**SHIRLEY, DONNA L,** Troy St Univ At Dothan, Dothan, AL; SR; BS ED; Stdnt Govt Assn Sntr 89-90; Gamma Beta Phi Sec 90-; Kappa Delta Pi 90-; Pres Schlrshp 88; Girl Scout Ldr 89-90; Socl Sci Educ; Tchr.

**SHIRLEY, ELEANORE LEIGH,** Comm Coll Algny Co Algny Cmps, Pittsburgh, PA; FR; BA; Show Choir 3 Credits 90; Vol Kane Hosp 87-; Private Voice Lessons Carlow Coll 87-; Deans List 90-; Discussion Grp 90-; Natl Hnrs Merit Finalist 90; Aerobics Dance; Liberal Arts; Psychiatrist/Teacher.

**SHIRLEY, JANET M,** Broward Comm Coll, Ft Lauderdale, FL; FR; Inst Canadian Bnkrs Asscte 85-; Schlrshp Clg Arts Sci/Tech Kingston Jamaica 76-79; Frst Plc Bus Strtgy Wth Inst Canadian Bnkrs; Prfssnl Bnkr 72-90; Cert Bnkg Clg Arts Sci/Tech 78; Dipl Bnkg Inst Canadian Bnkrs 88; Bus Admin; Corprte Lwyr.

**SHIRLEY, JOHN W,** Hillsborough Comm Coll, Tampa, FL; SO; AA; Phi Theta Kappa Treas 90-; Phys Dept Tchrs Asst 90-; Bst Phys Stdnt Awd; Solar Car Race 90; Math/Engr; Mech Engr.

**SHIRLEY, LISA A,** Fayetteville St Univ, Fayetteville, NC; FR; BS; Chancellors Schlrshp 90-; Acctg; CPA.

**SHIRLEY, REBECCA ANNE,** Univ Of Southern Ms, Hattiesburg, MS; JR; BMED; Marching Band; Symphonic Band; Pep Band; Phi Eta Sigma Treas 88-89; Alpha Lambda Delta 88-; Phi Delta Rho; Omicron Delta Kappa; Mu Phi Epsilon; Musicians Cncl 90; Tau Beta Sigma Pres 90-; Lambda Sigma; Band Cncl 90-; Music Educ.

**SHIRLEY, TAMARA J,** Piedmont Tech Coll, Greenwood, SC; FR; AAS; Phi Theta Kappa; Deans Lst 90-; S S Tchr 87-; Rad Tech.

**SHIRLEY, TERESA L,** Winthrop Coll, Rock Hill, SC; JR; BA; AAS Lord Fairfax Comm Coll 90; Nutrition; Dietetics.

**SHIRREL, DEA M,** Coll Of Charleston, Charleston, SC; JR; BED; Educ Clb 90-; Wmn ELCA Sec/VP; Elem Ed; Tchng.

**SHISLER, JAMES C,** Univ Of Akron, Akron, OH; SO; BS; Elec Engr.

**SHIVELY, STEPHANIE J,** Ky Wesleyan Coll, Owensboro, KY; JR; BA; Stdnt Govt Assn VP 88-; Un Meth Stdnt Flwshp Sec 88-; Res Asst 89-; Deans Lst 90-; Sigma Kappa Sor Pres 88-; Edn; Tchr.

**SHIVER, FELICIA A,** Univ Of Sc At Columbia, Columbia, SC; FR; Gspl Chr 90-; Rsdnc Hl Stdnt Govt 90-; Stdnt Chrstn Flwshp 90-; IM Bsktbl 90-; Phrmcy; Drg Rsrchr.

**SHIVER, LAURIE L,** Univ Of Ga, Athens, GA; SR; MED; Golden Key 89-; Phi Kappa Phi; Sigma Delta Pi 90-; Kappa Delta Pi 90-; Kappa Delta Epsilon 90-; Dns Lst 88-; Summer Study Spain 89; BS Ed; Spnsh; Tchg.**

**SHIVERS, SHERYL L,** Fl A & M Univ, Tallahassee, FL; JR; MBA; William C Smith Srvc Cntr Vol; Eastern Star; Boosting Alcohol Consciousness Cncrng Hlth Of Univ Stdnts; Econ Clb Schlrshp Rcvr; Prudential Ins Co 90; Merck Phrmctcl Co 90; AT/T Rsrch Asst; Bus Admin/Psychlgy; Indus Psychlgy.

**SHIVERS, SONJA D,** Morris Brown Coll, Atlanta, GA; SR; BS; Bio Mentor 89-; Beta Beta Beta; Beta Kappa 89-; Chi 90; Alpha Kappa Alpha Tr 87-; Hunger Vol 89-; Girls Clb Vol/Lit Actn Grp Vol 87-; Acad Schlr 86-89; #umarc Schlr 90-; Hon Rl 87-; Track/Chrldng Capt 88-90; Pre-Med; Bio.

**SHIVES, WILLIAM K,** Univ Of Sc At Columbia, Columbia, SC; FR; BA; WUSC FM Prmtns Dir 90-; Prtflo Ltry Mag Gnrl Stffr 90-; Stdnt Nwspr Advrtsng Exec 90-; SC Coll-Hon Coll USC 90-; SC Press Assn Offc Asstshp 90-; Jrnslm-Advrtsng/Pblc Rltns; Film Advrtsng Crt.

**SHLACKMAN, JED,** Univ Of Miami, Coral Gables, FL; FR; BA; WVUM Coll FM Radio Station DJ 90-; Sprtsfst Campus Sprts/Rec Sftbl Trnmnt; Psych.

**SHMIDMAN, ATARA R,** Yeshiva Univ, New York, NY; GD; Activities Cncl 85-89; Hall Cncl 88-89; Jewish Studies.

**SHOAF, LARRY A,** Oh St Univ At Marion, Marion, OH; JR; BA; AA 90; Crmnlgy; Fed Law Enfrcmnt.

**SHOCK, BEVERLEY J,** Salisbury St Univ, Salisbury, MD; SR; BS; Phi Theta Kappa 87-89; Asbury Chldhd Dvlp Ctr 88-89; Pres Schlrshp 87-89; Dlgts Schlrshp 88-89; Sntrl Schlrshp 89-; AA Wor-Wic Tech Comm Clg 89; Ed; Tchng.

**SHOCKLEY III, JOEL E,** Univ Of Sc At Columbia, Columbia, SC; FR; BS; Arete 90-; Prsdnts Lst 90-; Deans Lst 90-; Cmmcmnt Marshall; Phrmcy; Phrmcst.

**SHOCKLEY, JOHN J,** George Mason Univ, Fairfax, VA; JR; BS; Economics; Law Enfrcmnt.

**SHOCKLEY, KAY E,** Northeast State Tech Comm Coll, Blountville, TN; SR; 3rd In Prgrmng Cntstnt Pelassippi State Tenn; Cmptr Prgrmr.

**SHOCKLEY, SUSAN A,** Univ Of West Fl, Pensacola, FL; JR; BS; Phi Beta Lambda Hstrn; Natl FL/PENSACOLA Assn Lgl Sec; Beggs/Lane Attrnys Law 79-; AS Pensacola Jr Coll 90 79; Bus Tchr Educ; Tchng.

**SHOEMAKE, BOBBY S,** Mount Olive Coll, Mount Olive, NC; JR; BS; SIFE 89-90; Phi Theta Kappa 89-90; Phi Beta Lambda V Pres 89-90; Business Student Of Quarter 2 Times 89-90; Justice On Hnr Council 90; Golf Tm 88-89; AS Bus Admnstrn Wayne Cmnty Clge 90; AAS Mktg & Retailing 90; Bus Mgmnt; Govt Admnstrtn.

**SHOEMAKER, BRIAN D,** Univ Of Sc At Columbia, Columbia, SC; FR; BA; Bus; Acctnt.

**SHOEMAKER, KARL B,** Liberty Univ, Lynchburg, VA; SO; BA; Coll Rpblcns 89-; Natl Merit Schlr; Bsbl 89-; Bus.

**SHOEMAKER, SANDY M,** Goucher Coll, Towson, MD; JR; BA; Amnesty Intl Urgnt Actn Coord 89-; Prjct Hbt Cmnty Svc Pjct Exec Brd Mbr; Envir Cncrns Org 90; Natl Hnr Soc 88-89; Cmnty Axilary Svcs Pjct Coord; Part Mntrshp Pgm 90; Dns Schlr 89-90; Hstry; Museum Work.**

**SHOEN, THOMAS M,** Clarkson Univ, Potsdam, NY; SO; BS; Stdnt Sen; Bus Dir Integrator; Stdnt Orientation Svcs Chr 90-; Pre Law Soc VP 90-; Clarkson Soc Accntnts 89-; Dns Lst 89-; Trck Clb 89-; IM Rqtbl Clb Dir Officiating; Acctng Fin; Corp Tax Law.

**SHOFFEITT, MICHAEL B,** Palm Beach Comm Coll, Lake Worth, FL; SO; BA; Stdnt Yr; Comp Systms Eng.**

**SHOFFNER, KATHRYN P,** Guilford Tech Comm Coll, Jamestown, NC; SO; AA; Sngl Prnts Info Off 89-; Schl Nwsppr 90-; Ttr 88-; Tlnt Rst Otstndng Mnrty Stdnts 89; Ldrshp Rtrt 89; PTA Treas 80-; Bpbll Vol 89-; Drvr Bllngs Clrk Gate Trnsptn 85-; Comp Prgrmmng Coll Trnsfr Arts; Prgrmmr.

**SHOKRAVI, FAEGHEH,** Bunker Hill Comm Coll, Boston, MA; SO; ASSC; Deans List; Liberal Arts; Dsgn.

**SHOLA, JENNIFER M,** Merrimack Coll, North Andover, MA; FR; Big Brthr Big Sstr 90-; Alpha Kappa Psi 90-; Finance; Lawyer.

**SHOLAR JR, RAYMOND E,** Abraham Baldwin Agri Coll, Tifton, GA; SO; Valdosta St Gfl Tm; Hrtcltr Clb; Intern Golden Eagle Cntry Clb; AS Abraham Baldin; Glf Clb Mngmnt; Glf Crs Sprntnt.

**SHOLEYE, OLUFUNMIKEJI A,** Fl A & M Univ, Tallahassee, FL; SO; Nigeria Stdnt Union; NAACP; Phrmcy; Rsrch.

**SHOMO, PAMELA A,** Oh Univ, Athens, OH; SR; BFA; Ski Clb V P 87-; ACD 89-90; Pi Beta Phi 88-; Fine Arts/Studio Arts; Dsng/Advrtsng.

**SHOOK JR, ALAN C,** Anne Arundel Comm Coll, Arnold, MD; FR; BA; Gen Stdes.

**SHOOK, JULIE W,** Univ Of Nc At Charlotte, Charlotte, NC; SO; BA; Baptist Student Union Cncl Chrprsn 90-; Emerging Ldrs Mentor; Poplar Hall Cncl Sec 90-; Sigma Tau Delta Treas; Pi Sigma Epsilon Chrprsn; NC Teaching Fellow; English; Educ.

**SHOOK, STACEY L,** Wv Univ, Morgantown, WV; JR; BA; Psychlgy Clb 88-; Amnsty Intrntl 88-; Mrtrbrd/Sphnx Sr Hnr/Gldn Key 90-; Ordr Omega/Psi Chi Psych Hnr/Chimes Jr Hnr/Helvetia Frshmn Hnr 89-; Psi Chi 89-; Zeta Tau Alpha Schlstc Aschvmnt Chr 88-; Assoc Rtrd Ctzns 88-; Amnsty Intrntl 88-; Psychlgy; Chld Clncl Psychlgy.**

**SHOOP, MARVIN J,** Anne Arundel Comm Coll, Arnold, MD; SO; BA; LASA; CSA; Phi Theta Kappa; Dir Nghbrhd Wtch Prog 90-; EMT Comm Coll Allegheny 82; Pol Sci; Law/Govt.

**SHORE, KIRSTEN DE ANN,** Hillsborough Comm Coll, Tampa, FL; FR; BA; Phi Theta Kappa; Vol Wk Tampa Boys Clb.

**SHOREY, BONITA M,** Fayetteville St Univ, Fayetteville, NC; SO; BS; Scurlock PTA VP 89-; Scurlock Yrbk Stf Edtr In Chf 90-; Hoke Cnty Assoc Of Tchr Asstnts 89-; Tchr Asst Hoke Cnty 88-; Elem Ed; Tchr.

**SHORR, JANET C,** Hudson Valley Comm Coll, Troy, NY; SR; AAS; Hmn Srvcs Clb 89-; Phi Theta Kappa 90-; Scl Wrk; MSW.

**SHORT, AARON T,** Morehouse Coll, Atlanta, GA; FR; BA; Brntwds Blck Stdnt Un Treas 89-90; Graves Hl Drm Cncl Treas 90-; Spec Olymps; Bsns Admn; Mrktng.

**SHORT, CYNTHIA D,** Univ Of Va Clinch Valley Coll, Wise, VA; FR; Hstry.

**SHORT, DAWN R,** Wv Northern Comm Coll, Wheeling, WV; FR; BA; Elem Ed; Tch.

**SHORT, DENISE L,** Va St Univ, Petersburg, VA; FR; BAD; Bus Mgt.

**SHORT, JANICE L,** Morgan St Univ, Baltimore, MD; SR; BA; Ira Aldridge Plyrs Theatre Grp VP 87-90; Alpha Psi Omega; Alpha Kappa Alpha Mbrshp Chrprsn 89-; Telecomm; Theatre Arts.

**SHORT, JENNIFER L,** Savannah Coll Of Art & Design, Savannah, GA; JR; BFA; Painting; Fine Arts/Silk Screening.

**SHORT, KELLY R,** Middle Tn St Univ, Murfreesboro, TN; SR; BS; Hmcng Dir 89-; Ambsdr 87-; S G 87-; Gamma Beta Phi 87-; Tau Omicron 88-; Rho Lambda Hon 89-; Gamma Iota Sigma 88-; Pi Mu Epsilon 89-; Alpha Delta Pi Pres; Statistics/Actuarial Orgztn Sec 89-; Hon Rl; Deans Lst; MTSU Wrk Schlrshp; Math/Actuarial Sci; Actuary.

**SHORT, MARY F,** Manna Bible Inst, Philadelphia, PA; JR; BA; Stdnt Senate Pres 90-; Lesdix Mesdames Socl Chrty Sec 80-; Usher Mt Zion Bapt Chrch 89-; Bd Of Educ Phila 52-88; Retired Sec; Sci/Rlgn; Mnstr/Evnglst.

**SHORT, RACHAEL K,** Le Moyne Coll, Syracuse, NY; SO; Phi Alpha Theta.

**SHORT, RANDAL S,** Gaston Coll, Dallas, NC; FR; BA; Math; Tch.

**SHORT II, RONALD D,** Boston Univ, Boston, MA; SR; BS; Amer Phys Thrpy Assoc Msschstts Chptr; Amer Clg Sprts Med New Englnd Chptr 89-; Golden Key 90-; Masschstts Cltn Ctzns/Dsblts Rare Diseases Rsrch Inttrvwr; Var Bsbl Capt 88-; Phys Thrpy.

**SHORT, TERESA M,** East Tn St Univ, Johnson City, TN; SR; BS; Stdnt Govt Walters St Alt 88-89; Disc Brd 88-89; STEA-TEA-NEA-NBEA 90-; Grad Cum Laude 89; Deans Lst; IM Sftbl 90; AS Walters St Cmnty Clg 89; Bus Educ; Tchr.

**SHORT, TRISHA A,** Univ Of Louisville, Louisville, KY; SR; BES; Pr Admsns Cnslr 87-; Phi Eta Sigma 88-; Mrtr Brd 89; SWE 88; Spd Scntfc Schl Mntr 89-90; IEEE; Sigma Chi Ltl Sis Treas 88-89; Spd Schl Brd Trst Mnt 88-89; Coop Intrnshp GE Arcrft Engns 89-90; Elctrcl Engrg.

**SHORTEN, JOHN D,** Temple Univ, Philadelphia, PA; SR; BS; Rho Chi; Pharmacy.

**SHORTENCARRIER, LEA S,** Indiana Univ Of Pa, Indiana, PA; JR; BED; IM Bsktbl Vlybl Sftbl Capt 88-; Elem Educ Phys Educ.

**SHORTENCARRIER, RENEE L,** Indiana Univ Of Pa, Indiana, PA; SR; BS; ACS; PSEA/NEA; Red Crs; Prvst Schlr 89-90; Chem Awd 88-; Chem; Tch.

**SHORTER, DEBRA L,** Longwood Coll, Farmville, VA; SR; BS; Stdnt Soc Wrkrs V Chrmn 89-; Phi Kappa Phi; Jr Intrnshp Heritage Hall Nrsng Hm 90; Sr Internshp MVC Hosp; Deans Lst 88-; Social Work.

**SHORTER JR, JOSEPH CHARLES,** Univ Of Va Clinch Valley Coll, Wise, VA; SR; BA; Bptst Stu Unn; Cmptr Clb; Bethel Almn Pres; Camp Bethel Act Dir 90-; Red Crss 87; Magna Cum Laude 89-90; Army Achvmnt Mdl; Hnrbl Dschrg 90; US Army 87-90; Bbl Mssn S W VA Act Dir 90-; AS Tidewater Comm Coll 90; Hstry/Bus; Lgl Clnc Undprvldgd.

**SHORTIER, LYNN A,** Albertus Magnus Coll, New Haven, CT; JR; Yrbk Co Ed 89-; Jdcl Brd Sec 90-; Orntn Stf Cochrprsn 89-.

**SHOSHAN, ELANA Y,** Ny Univ, New York, NY; JR; Pub Rel Soc 90-91; ECA Eastern Comm Assoc; N Y Speech Soc Of Am; Deans List; United Jewish Appeal Fundrsng Campaign 89-90; Chabad 88-; Comm Studies; Speech Comm Cnsltng.

**SHOTSKY-CHARLES, JOHNA RAE,** Oh Univ-Southern Cmps, Ironton, OH; FR; BED; Women Of Wellness 90-; Red Cross 82-; Church Camp Cnslr 90-; Boy Scouts; Headstart Vol 89-; Tchrs Aid Vol; Dispatcher/Sec Day Care Tchr Fin Resrce Asst 83-90; Cert 83; Elem Tchr.

**SHOTWELL, JOHN O,** S U N Y At Buffalo, Buffalo, NY; SR; BS; Prod Our Town Sound Tech; Un Actvts Bd Prod Mgr 88-; IEEE 89-; Boy Scouts Amer Ast Sctmstr 87-; Eagle Scout 80-87; Elect Engr; MA Theater.

**SHOUDER, BARBARA A,** Union Univ, Jackson, TN; JR; BA; The Public Relations Soc 90-; Stdnt Foundtn; Phi Beta Lambda 89-90; Kappa Delta Asstnt Pledge Ed 90-; W TN Rgnl Blood Cntr Intern; Markham & Assoc Inc Elkhorn WI Apprentice; Communication Arts; Advertising/Pub Rel.

**SHOUKOOHI, MASOUD,** Medical Coll Of Ga, Augusta, GA; FR; Science; Dentistry.

**SHOUSE, MICHELLE M,** Lexington Comm Coll, Lexington, KY; SO; AS; Acctng; Bus/Econs.

**SHOVEY, ANNA M,** Central Fl Comm Coll, Ocala, FL; FR; AA; Vet Science; Equine Vet.

**SHOW, TIMOTHY E,** Mount Aloysius Jr Coll, Cresson, PA; GD; AS; Cmptr Sci.

**SHOWALTER, ANTHONY R,** Richard Bland Coll, Petersburg, VA; SO; BS; Wldlf Sci; Fshries/Wldlf Mgmt.

**SHOWALTER, LYNETTE M,** Bridgewater Coll, Bridgewater, VA; FR; BS; Math Clb 90-; Deans Lst 90-; Math; HS Tchr.

**SHOWALTER, TODD A,** Oh Wesleyan Univ, Delaware, OH; SR; BA; Intrfrat Cncl Treas 88-89; Intrfrat Jdcl Brd 90-; Coll Newspr Rprtr 90-; Deans Lst 90-; Greek Acad Hons 90-F Phi Kappa Psi Mst Oustndng Sr 90; Phi Kappa Psi Gov Brd 87-; Crstvw Proj Aid Innr Cty Chldrn 90-91; Intrntl Bus; Bnkng-Intrntl.

**SHOWALTER, WILLIAM E,** Va Commonwealth Univ, Richmond, VA; SR; BS; Chesterfield Cnty Plc Dept Intrnshp; Admin Just; Plc Ofcr.

**SHOWERS, KIMBERLY M,** Tougaloo Coll, Tougaloo, MS; SO; BS; Adult Reading Prog; Sociology Social Work; Law.

**SHOWSTEAD, JANET A,** Bunker Hill Comm Coll, Boston, MA; BED; Word Prcsng; Secretarial.

**SHRADER, GAYLON B,** Memphis St Univ, Memphis, TN; SR; Phi Theta Kappa 87-; Pi Tau Sigma Pres 90-; Distinguished Herff Engr Schlrshp 87-; AS Chem State Tech Memphis 88; EIT State TN; Mech Engr; Engr.

**SHRADER, JENNIFER L,** Hudson Valley Comm Coll, Troy, NY; GD; AS; Soc Wrk/Psychlgy; Child Or Sch Psychlgy.

**SHRADER, JOSEPH E,** Edinboro Univ Of Pa, Edinboro, PA; JR; BA; Earth Sci Clb 89-; Rfl Clb 90-; Phi Eta Sigma 89-; Alpha Chi; Sigma Gama Epsilon; Ednbr Univ Hon Stdnt 89-; Internshp Edinbr Pblc Rel Ofc; Rlng Scts Whlchr Athl 88-; Earth/Space Sci.

**SHRADER, TINA M,** Bethany Coll, Bethany, WV; JR; BA; Ltry Mag 90-; Lambda Iota Tau 90-; Kappa Delta Pnhllnc Rep 90-; Engl; Prfssr.

**SHREFFLER, PAMELA J,** Univ Of Nc At Asheville, Asheville, NC; FR; BA; Civic Ballet 87-; Concert Jazz Grp 87-; Phi Eta Sigma; Undrgrad Rsrch Flws; Lit; Doctorate/Wrtr.

**SHRESTHA, JALESHWAR,** Savannah St Coll, Savannah, GA; GD; MBA; Nepal Dmcrtc Assn Sec; Red Cross/Fmly Plng/Lion Clb; Schlrshp; Bdmntn/Ftbl; Hmn Right Assn 90; Admn Offcr Govt Nepal 83-90; MA Tribhuvan Univ Nepal 85; Bus.

**SHREVE, LORRAINE F,** Methodist Coll, Fayetteville, NC; SO; BS; Asst Buyer & Inv Control Asst 86-88; Bus; Mrktng-Buyer.

**SHREWSBERRY, RITA GAYLE,** Owensboro Comm Coll, Owensboro, KY; FR; Brescia Cllg Schlrshp; Oustndng Acadmc Achvmnt Ldrshp; Elem Edctn Emphsis Englsh; Tchr.

**SHREWSBURY, KEVIN C,** Marshall University, Huntington, WV; SR; BA; Alpha Kappa Psi 89-90; Fnce; Fncl Plnng/Cnsltng.

**SHRINER, JULIE L,** Mount Aloysius Jr Coll, Cresson, PA; FR; Crmnlgy; Crctns Cnslr.

**SHRIVER, LAURA M,** Davis & Elkins Coll, Elkins, WV; SR; BS; Alpha Chi 90-; Beta Alpha Beta 90-; NBEA 90-; NBEA Merit Award 90-; Meth Church Treas; Bsn Educ.

**SHROFF, GAUTAM,** Univ Of Rochester, Rochester, NY; SR; BS; Mech Eng.

**SHROFF, NINAD A,** Dartmouth Coll, Hanover, NH; FR; Stdnt Cncl; Nathan Smith Pre Hlth Scty; Squash Tm 90-; History.

**SHROPSHIRE, DAWN A,** Fayetteville St Univ, Fayetteville, NC; SR; Miss Fayettvl St Univ Queen 90; Senate Sec 90; Yng Dems Pr 87-89; SAAP 87-88; Dns Lst 88-90; Alpha Kappa Alpha Pr 89-90.

**SHRUM, VANISSA D,** Radford Univ, Radford, VA; JR; BBA; SGA; Bptst Stdnt Un VP 90-; Delta Mu Delta; Pi Omega Pi Sec 90-; Phi Beta Lambda; IM Sprts; Bus Admin; Tchng.

**SHTENDER, LYUBOV,** Bunker Hill Comm Coll, Boston, MA.

**SHU, FRED,** Cornell Univ Statutory College, Ithaca, NY; FR; BS; Aikido Clb 90-; IM Recr Fencing 90-; IM Recr Bsktbl 90-; Bio; Med.

**SHUBA, KENNETH E,** Comm Coll Algny Co Algny Cmps, Pittsburgh, PA; FR; BA; United Steel Wrks Amer; Blood Bk; Math; Engr.

**SHUCK, JAMES K,** Univ Of Nc At Asheville, Asheville, NC; SO; Zeta Alpha Sec 90-; Phi Eta Sigma 89-; Psychlgy; Tchr.

**SHUE, JENNIFER A,** James Madison University, Harrisonburg, VA; JR; SEA 90-; Gldn Ky 90-; Ordr Omega 90-; Kappa Delta Pi 90-; Delta Gamma VP 88-; Erly Chldhd Educ; Elem Schl Tchr.

**SHUERT, DELIA M,** Univ Of North Fl, Jacksonville, FL; JR; BS; Gldn Key; Fnc; Admn Mgmt.

**SHUEY, SYLVIA R,** James Sprunt Comm Coll, Kenansville, NC; JR; ADN; Nrsng.

**SHUFFETT, MICHELLE L,** Univ Of Ky, Lexington, KY; FR; BA; Phi Eta Sigma 90-; Deans List; Chem; Medcn.

**SHUFRAN, DONALD K,** Allegheny Coll, Meadville, PA; SR; BS; Chrstn Outrch Treas 88-; Chpl Dcns 89-; Coll Choir; Phi Beta Kappa 90-; Tennis 87-; Habitat For Hmnty 89-; Doane Schlr 88-; L W Blmr Eng Schlrshp 90-; Chem.

**SHUGART, ANGELA M,** Muskingum Coll, New Concord, OH; FR; BA; Cntr Brd 90; Deans Lst 90; History; Law.

**SHUGART, DEBORAH H,** Univ Of North Fl, Jacksonville, FL; JR; BA; AA St Johns River Cmuty Clg 90; Ele Educ; Tch.

**SHUGERT, CATRIONA L,** Radford Univ, Radford, VA; SR; Univ Ballet 88-90; Real Life 90-; Kappa Delta Pi 89-; Delta Zeta Sec 89-; Vol Wheatland Hills Ret Ctr 89-; Deans Lst 88-.

**SHUKAIR, YASMIN A,** Truett Mc Connell Coll, Cleveland, GA; FR; BS; Math; Anlyst CPA.

**SHUKLA, KIRANKUMAR J,** Univ Of Med & Dentistry Of Nj, Newark, NJ; GD; Best Stdnt Awd 89-90; MBBS MD S Gujarut Univ Surut India 82.

**SHULER, JULIE A,** Jacksonville Univ, Jacksonville, FL; JR; BA; Psych/Soc Clb; Hnr Stu Assc; Psi Chi; Alpha Epsilon Phi; Psych/Engl; Psychtry.**

**SHULER, RODDY M,** Cornell Univ Statutory College, Ithaca, NY; SR; MS; NY City Marathon 89; Ho-Nun-De-Kah 90-; Phi Kappa Phi 90-; Tchg Asst Stanford Univ; Dns Lst 87-; IM Tennis/Soccer 90; BS Cornell Univ; Elctrcl Engr; Rsrch/Tchg.

**SHULEVITZ, JAY,** City Univ Of Ny Baruch Coll, New York, NY; SO; BBA; Acctg.

**SHULL, GREG S,** Western Piedmont Comm Coll, Morganton, NC; SO.

**SHULMAN, KIMBERLY A,** Western New England Coll, Springfield, MA; SR; BA; Stdnt Snt 89-; Pre-Law Soc 88-; Stdnt Ambssdr 90-; Deans Lst 87-; Alpha Lambda Delta 89-; Alpha Lambda Delta Bk Awd; Excllnc Govt Awd; Govt; Law.

**SHULTS, JESSICA J,** Springfield Coll, Springfield, MA; FR; BA; Karate Clb; Jr Achvmnt 90-; Bus Mgt.

**SHULTZ, ADAM G,** Savannah Coll Of Art & Design, Savannah, GA; JR; BFA; Modl Sessn Coord 90-; Paintng Grp 89-; Mc Commn Schlrshp; Rousaks Trvl Schlrshp; Var Soccr 88-89; Paintng; Arts.

**SHULTZ, CONNIE J,** Indiana Univ Of Pa, Indiana, PA; FR; BS; Hist Clb Sec 90; Clg Rpblcns 90; Sec Soc Sci Ed; Hist Tchr.

**SHULTZ, JOHN R,** Univ Of Al At Huntsville, Huntsville, AL; SR; BS; Tau Beta Pi Ctlgr; Drury Coll Stdnt Sen Treas; Omicron Delta Kappa; Pi Tau Sigma; Tau Beta Pi; Outstdng Coll Stdnts Am 87; Alpha Sigma Lambda 86; Delta Chi; Res Adv Cncl; G Lindsay Endowed Schlrshp 90; Stdnt Afrs Ldrshp Schlrshp 88; Mech Engr.

**SHULTZ, TRAVIS R,** Wv Univ, Morgantown, WV; JR; Phi Kappa Phi; Gldn Key; Tau Beta Pi; Engr.

**SHUM, WILSON,** City Univ Of Ny Baruch Coll, New York, NY; JR; BBA; Day Stu Govt Pres 87-; Mns Var; Asian Amer Hghr Educ Cncl Brd Dir 90-; Brch Deans Lst 87-; Mns Var Archry Tm 87-; Hmn Rsrcs; Law.

**SHUMAKE, LAURA E,** Colby Sawyer Coll, New London, NH; FR; Band/Choir 90-; Biology.

**SHUMAKER, JEFFREY C,** Syracuse Univ, Syracuse, NY; SO; BA; Arch Stdnt Org; Peer Advng; Res Advsng Stf; Rag Arch Nwsltr; NYPIRG; Upper Div Hon; Lend A Hand/United Way; Arch.

**SHUMAKER, JENNIFER M,** Westminster Coll, New Wilmingtn, PA; SR; BA; Psych Clb; Res Lf Stf Asst Res Dir 88-; Psi Chi Sec 89-; Vol Srvv Actn 88-89; Intern Wstrn Pyschtrc Inst/Clnc 90; Intern Human Svc Ctr 91; Psych; Genetic Cnslng.

**SHUMAKER, STEPHAN K,** Columbus Coll Of Art & Design, Columbus, OH; JR; BFA; Illstrtn; Write Illstrtc Chldrns Bks.

**SHUMAKER, ZELLA C,** Northeast State Tech Comm Coll, Blountville, TN; SO; AD; OWLS VP 90; AD Bristol Unv 85; Bus Mngmt; BA.

**SHUMAN, CHEYENNE S,** West Liberty St Coll, West Liberty, WV; FR; BED; Sigma Tau Delta 90-; Thtre Stgmgng Intrnshp; Eng; Tchg Sec.

**SHUMANSKI, KERRY A,** Georgetown Univ, Washington, DC; JR; BSN; Natl Stdnt Nrs Assoc Sec 90-; Eldrly Outrch 90-; Nrsng.

**SHUMATE, ERIC J,** Northern Ky Univ, Highland Hts, KY; SO; BA; Acctng.

**SHUMER, DAVID M,** S U N Y Hlth Sci Cent Brooklyn, Brooklyn, NY; JR; BSN; Phi Theta Kappa 90; Smr Extern Pgm SUNY Downstate Hosp Clncl Asst II; Op Rm Nurse.

**SHUMOCK, GWENDOLYN E,** Bishop St Comm Coll, Mobile, AL; JR; Sr Citzns 89-; Phi Theta Kappa 88-90; Phys Sci; Nurs.

**SHUNNEY, KATE E,** Mary Baldwin Coll, Staunton, VA; SR; BA; Acvts Brd 88-; Amnsty Internatl Pres 89-90; Lit Mag Ed Brd 89-; Benn Schlrshp Awd Ptry 89-90; Sftbl 89-; Pol Sci; Tch.

**SHUPE, DIANA B,** Indiana Univ Of Pa, Indiana, PA; FR; BED; Eled Educ Math/Early Chldhd Dev; Cnslr.

**SHUPP, SANDRA M,** Teikyo Post Univ, Waterbury, CT; SR; BS; Cert Excell Meritorious 90; Achvmnt Connecticut Soc CPA; Unit Asst Univ Hosp; Acctg.

**SHUPPE, JULIE L,** Kent St Univ Kent Cmps, Kent, OH; SR; Sigma Theta Tau 89-; BSN; Nrs.

**SHURDEN, LORI A,** Ms St Univ, Miss State, MS; GD; MBA; Mtchmts 88-89; Untd Way Cbnt 89; Pgnt Comm 87; Phi Kappa Phi 88-; Gamma Beta Phi 86-; Gamma Alpha Epsilon 87-; Amer Mrktg Assoc 88; Kappa Delta Stndrds Chmn Asst Schlrshp Chmn 89-88; Grad Asst 90-; Mkt Mgt.

**SHURILLA, BARBARA M,** Univ Of Pittsburgh At Bradford, Bradford, PA; SR; BA; Sigma Alpha 89-; AS 80; Hmn Rltns/Educ; Tchng.

**SHURLEY, RHONDA K,** Ga St Univ, Atlanta, GA; SO; BSE; Erly Chldhd Educ; Tchng.

**SHUSTER, JOSEPH T,** Univ Of Akron, Akron, OH; JR; BS; Fin; Investment Banking.

**SHUSTER, MICHAEL P,** Fl St Univ, Tallahassee, FL; JR; BS; Phi Theta Kappa 89-90; Deans List 87-; AA Palm Beach Comm Clg 90; Mgt Info Sys; Bus Mgt.

**SHUTE, MICHAEL F,** Glassboro St Coll, Glassboro, NJ; SO; BA; Schl Radio Sta WGLS FM Pblc Srvc Dir 90-; Schl Radio Sta DJ 89-; Schl Radio Sta Sprts Dir; IM Sprts 90-; Cmmnctns; Sprts Brdcstng/Jrnlsm.

**SHUTT, MICHAEL A,** Muskingum Coll, New Concord, OH; JR; BA; OAC Acdmc Bsbll Team 89-90; Phi Alpha Theta 90-; Acct Hnry 90-; Schlrshp Day/Acdmc Achvmnt Awrd Top Five Prcnt Class 89-90; Rsdnt Asst 90-; Stdnt Asst Dept Ecnmcs 90-; Fra Luca Pciolo Acct Awrd 89-90; Bsbll 88-; Acct Bsn.

**SHUTTLESWORTH, ANNE L,** Univ Of Cincinnati, Cincinnati, OH; JR; BM; Accmpnst Mens Chrs 87-90; Accmnst Wmns Chrs 88; Delta Omicron Pres 90-; Dns Lst 87-; Voorheis Schlrshp 87-; Delta Omicron Schlrshp; Music; Musician.

**SHUTTLESWORTH, TRACI L,** Norfolk St Univ, Norfolk, VA; SO; BA; Pub Rltns Stdnt Soc Assoc; Spartan Alpha Tau; Tutor For Elem Stdnts; Jrnlsm; Pub Rltns.

**SIANIPAR, KONRAD T,** Oh Univ, Athens, OH; SO; BSEE; Natnl Soc Prfsnl Engnrng 90-; Elctrcl Engnrng; Cmptr Sci.

**SIBBLIES, MAUREEN A,** City Univ Of Ny Baruch Coll, New York, NY; JR; BBA; Full-Charge Bkkpr; Acctng; CPA.

**SIBILIA, HELEN,** Miami Dade Comm Coll North, Miami, FL; SO; BA; Asamblea Evangelica Sndy Sch Tchr 88-; Elem Sch Vol 90-; FEA 90-; AA Miami Dade Comm Coll; Elem Edn; Tchr.

**SIBILIO, PETER M,** Le Moyne Coll, Syracuse, NY; SR; Campus Mnstry; Cmmnty Proj; US Army ROTC Capt; Wm P Tolley Awd; Tae Kwon Do; Bshp Foery Awd; Rlgious Studies; Ed.

**SIBLEY, ANGELA R,** Univ Of Ky, Lexington, KY; SR; BA; Bapt Stdnt Un Sec 87-; Soc Work.

**SIBLEY, HEATHER A,** D Youville Coll, Buffalo, NY; FR; SOTA 90-; Cmps Mnstry 90-; Lambda Sigma Treas; Gospel Sensations Concert Pianist; Awd Dedicated Serv Cmps Mnstry 90-; Health Field; Occupational Therapy.

**SIBLEY, MARTHA N,** East Central Comm Coll, Decatur, MS; FR; AA; Phi Beta Lambda Sec; Phi Theta Kappa; Comp Prog.

**SIBLEY, SHEILA M,** Smith Coll, Northampton, MA; JR; BA; Wind Ensmbl 89-90; Newman Assoc 88-89; Hse Ofcr 89-90; Dns Lst 89-; First Grp Schlr 90-; Anthrplgy/Sclgy; Museum Studies.

**SICILIA, PENELOPE S,** Le Moyne Coll, Syracuse, NY; SR; BS; Bsns Clb Exec Brd; Sr Shw Lghtng Dir; Dns Lst 88-; Delta Mu Delta 90-; Dept Hons Stdy Dev Corp Limtd Liablty; Bsns Admn; Bnk Exmnr.

**SIDARI, GINA F,** Univ Of Akron, Akron, OH; JR; BS; RA 90-; Clss Sec; Alpha Lambda Delta 89-; Gldn Key 90-; Mu Kappa Tau; Advrstng.

**SIDEBOTTOM, WYNDELL R,** Tomlinson Coll, Cleveland, TN; SO; BA; AA; Thelgy; Mnstr/Cnslr.

**SIDES, MICHELLE M,** Univ Of Montevallo, Montevallo, AL; JR; Alpha Gamma Delta 87-; Delta Kappa Gamma Schlrshp; Early Chldhd/Elem Educ; Tchr.

**SIDHU, CHANDANJEET K,** Va Commonwealth Univ, Richmond, VA; SO; BS; Cvtn Intrntl 90-; Phi Eta Sigam 89-; Bio; Med.

**SIDNER, ALISON B,** Clark Atlanta Univ, Atlanta, GA; SR; BA; Phlhrmnc Soc 88; Intrnshp Zoo Atlanta Grphcs Dept 90; Magna Cum Laude; Art; Grphc Dsgn/Illstrtn.

**SIDNER, SCOTT M,** Muskingum Coll, New Concord, OH; SR; BA; Radio Stn Asst Prog Dir 89-; TV Stn Hdwrtr; Nwspr Stfwrtr 88-; Sr Hnry 90-; ODK; NFA Imprompto/Extemporaneous; Forensics VP 88-; Soccer Goalie 87; Tennis Singles 90; Speech Communication; Politics.

**SIDON, BABE N,** Oh St Univ, Columbus, OH; FR; BS; Med Park Vol 90; Athltc Schlrshp 90-; Wrstlng Wghtlftng; Phys Thrpst.

**SIDRAK, ROBERT J,** Univ Of Md At Eastern Shore, Princess Anne, MD; JR; BA; IFSEA; Sheraton Salisbury Intrnshp; Soccer Tm Co Capt 90; CFS Natl Sanitation Fndtn 90; Hotel/Rstrnt Mgmt.

**SIDWELL, BEVERLY ANN,** Univ Of Tn At Martin, Martin, TN; FR; BA; Hnrs Seminar Stdnts Soc 90-; Hnrs Seminar 90-; Merit Awd.

**SIEBEL, MATTHEW A,** Saint Francis Coll, Loretto, PA; FR; BS; Crs Cntry/Indr/Outdoor Trck 90-; Elem Educ; Tchng.

**SIEGEL, BRENDAN L F,** Niagara Univ, Niagara Univ, NY; GD; MA; IM Brmbl 90-; Delta Epsilon Sigma 88-90; Phi Sigma Iota Pres 88-90; Grad Tchng Asstshp; IM Brmbl; BA; Frnch; U S Govt.

**SIEGEL JR, CHARLES H,** Yale Univ, New Haven, CT; FR; BA; Hstry.

**SIEGEL, LARISSA M,** Univ Of Pr At Mayaguez, Mayaguez, PR; SR; BS; Inst Ind Engrs 88-; Natl Soc Pro Engrs 89-; Alpha Pi Mu 88-; Tau Beta Pi 88-; Phi Kappa Phi; Ind Eng; Eng.**

**SIEGFRIED, KIMBERLY DE ANNE,** S U N Y Coll At Fredonia, Fredonia, NY; SR; MBA; Inter Grk Cncl V P Schlrshp 90-; Panhellenic Assn Treas 88-89; Dorm Cncl 87-89; Ordr Omega Fndr; Sigma Kappa V P Pldg Educ 90-; Intrn White Pine Press; BA; English; Publshing.

**SIEGLER, ROBERT J,** Univ Of New Haven, West Haven, CT; SR; BA; Sdnt Art Show 89-; Deans Lst 89-; Pre Architecture.**

**SIEGMANN, HELENE M,** Birmingham Southern Coll, Birmingham, AL; SR; Southern Vol Srvcs 87-89; Kapa Delta Epsilon VP 89-; Psi Chi 90-; Alpha Chi Omega Property Team Mgr 87-; Dns Lst 89-; Dana Intrnshp 88-; IM Ftbl/Soccer/Bsktbl 87-; Elem Educ; Tchr.

**SIEJAK, JOELLE M,** D Youville Coll, Buffalo, NY; JR; BS; Spcl Ed Crtn Elem Educ.

**SIEMENSKI, STEPHEN J,** Merrimack Coll, North Andover, MA; FR; BS; Lib Arts.

**SIEMER, MATTHEW M,** Univ Of Cincinnati, Cincinnati, OH; JR; BS; AAS; Mech Engr.

**SIENERTH, SANDRA L,** Comm Coll Algny Co Algny Cmps, Pittsburgh, PA; FR; BA; Kaufmanns Este Lauder Counter Manager 85-; Teacher Ed; Teaching.

**SIEPEL, ADAM C,** Cornell Univ Statutory College, Ithaca, NY; FR; BS; Agri Engr.

**SIERPINSKI, MARY,** Middlesex County Coll, Edison, NJ; FR; AS; Concerns Comm; Clncl Dptmntl Comm; Alpha Delta Pi Sevl Ofcs 67-71; Ltr Commdtn 67; Rgnt Schlrshp 67-71; Advtsng 71-76; BA Brooklyn Coll Cuny 71; Radiography; X Ray/CT/ MRI.

**SIERRA, ANDRES F,** Ky Wesleyan Coll, Owensboro, KY; SO; BA; Deans Listf Ftbl; Mgt; Hosp Admin.

**SIERRA, ARSENIA,** Univ Of Sc At Sumter, Sumter, SC; JR; BA; Multicltrl Clb 87-89; AS Math Sci Jefferson Cmmnty Clg 89; Psych; Med.

**SIERRA, EILEEN Y,** Univ Politecnica De Pr, Hato Rey, PR; FR; BA; Cvl Engnrng.

**SIERRA, EITHEL M,** Miami Dade Comm Coll, Miami, FL; SO; BA; Phi Theta Kappa; Hnr Praise Exclnc Awd Math Wolfson Cmps; Hnr Stdnt Art Sci Fac Interamerican Ctr; Math; Cvl Eng.

**SIERRA, MARIA J,** Fl International Univ, Miami, FL; JR; BS; Amer Occptnl Thrpy Assoc Inc 89-; Occptnl Thrpy Clb 89-; Amer Amateur Rcqtbl Assoc; Pi Theta Epsilon Pres; Occptnl Thrpy.

**SIERRA, RAMON,** Miami Dade Comm Coll, Miami, FL; SO; BA; Math.

**SIERUK, ELAINE,** Bloomfield Coll, Bloomfield, NJ; SO; Bus Mngmnt; Bus.

**SIEVERS, ASHLEY L,** Univ Of Ky, Lexington, KY; FR; BS; Flag Crps 90-; Kappa Kappa Psi Band Frat 90-; Hnrs Pgm 90-; Dns Lst 90-; Chnclrs Schlp 90-; Dir Hnrs Pgm Acad Achvmnt Lst; Math; Tchr.

**SIEVERS JR, RAYMOND T,** Embry Riddle Aeronautical Univ, Daytona Beach, FL; SR; BS; Chf Plt Flght Oprtns Luth Gen Hosp 90; AA Oakton Comm Coll 83; Arntcs; Prfssnl Plt.

**SIFF, PHILIP S,** Winthrop Coll, Rock Hill, SC; SR; BA; PSC Pres 90-; Wght Lftng Clb Treas 88-89; Pi Sigma Alpha; Phi Alpha Theta; Pub Mngmnt Intrnshp 90-; Diplma Grnvl Tech Coll 87; Politcl Sci.

**SIGLER, CYNTHIA A,** Oh Wesleyan Univ, Delaware, OH; SR; BSN; Nrsng Bd 89; Nrsng Hnr Soc 90-; Florence Nightingale Soc; Pres Schlr 89-; William Hartnett Awd; Magna Cum Laud; St Thomas More Newman Ctr; Capital Area Humane Soc; BA Ohio State U 86; Nrsng.

**SIGLER, JOHN CURTIS,** Memphis St Univ, Memphis, TN; SR; BS; Assoc Mbr Amer Inst Archts 90-; Assoc State Techl Inst Memphis 89; Engrg; Architecture.

**SIGLER, SHERRI S,** Owensboro Comm Coll, Owensboro, KY; SO; Math Clb 90-; Anthrplgy Clb; Sci/Chmsry; Phrmcy.

**SIGMAN, JODI L,** Defiance Coll, Defiance, OH; FR; Fstptch Sftbl 90-; Athltc Trnr 90-; Theta Aux.

**SIGMAN, TERESA L,** Gallaudet Univ, Washington, DC; SR; BA; Chrldr Ftbl 87; Delta Phi Epsilon Scrtry; Accntng; CPA.

**SIGMON, CHRIS S,** Catawba Valley Comm Coll, Hickory, NC; FR; AAS; Bsns Comp Prog.

**SIGMON, DEBORAH A,** Catawba Valley Comm Coll, Hickory, NC; FR; AA; Acctg.

**SIGMON, JEFFERY M,** Catawba Valley Comm Coll, Hickory, NC; SR; AAS Comp Eng Tchnlgy.

**SIGMON JR, JIMMY L,** Catawba Valley Comm Coll, Hickory, NC; FR; AAS; Gamma Beta Phi; Rotaract Clb; Bsnss Admin/ Accntng; Bsnss Mngmnt.

**SIGURDARDOTTIR, KRISTIN,** Univ Of Sc At Columbia, Columbia, SC; SR; BS; Hotel Sls/Mktg Assn; Amer Mktng Assn; Eta Sigma Delta; Rest/Tourism Admin; Intl Bus.

**SIINO, SALVATORE G,** Georgetown Univ, Washington, DC; FR; Acctg/Am Govt; Law.

**SIKARSKIE, ANYA M,** Lesley Coll, Cambridge, MA; SR; BS; Educ Rep ED Comm 89-; Rsdnc Life Advsry Brd 89-; Cmtr Rep Stdt Gvt Assc 90-; Deans List 89-; Vol 89-; Assoc Degree Lansing Cmnty Cllg 89; History; Masters.

**SIKDAR, PIYALI,** City Univ Of Ny Baruch Coll, New York, NY; JR; Acctg; CPA.

**SIKES JR, DAVID GLENN,** Univ Of Ga, Athens, GA; GD; Track 85-90; BSED 90; Hlth/Phys Ed; Pilot.

**SIKES, ERIC J,** Middle Ga Coll, Cochran, GA; FR; BA; Bpt Student Union; Engrg Club; IM Sftbl; Elec Engrg; Engrg.

**SIKES, KAREN T,** S U N Y Coll Of Tech At Frmgdl, Farmingdale, NY; FR; BA; Bsn; Bsn Mgmt.

**SIKES, PHYLLIS L,** Chesterfield Marlboro Coll, Cheraw, SC; FR; AB; AAS Wayne Comm Coll 80; Bus; Accntg.

**SIKIC, SANJA,** Fl International Univ, Miami, FL; SR; Hsptlty Mgmt.

**SIKOPOULOS, ROULA JOSEPHINE,** Bloomfield Coll, Bloomfield, NJ; SR; BS; Sigma Phi Delta 90-; Acctg; CPA.

**SIKORA, MELODIE G,** Mount Aloysius Jr Coll, Cresson, PA; FR; BA; O T Clb 90-; AOTA 90-; Spec Oly 90-; Occup Thrpy.

**SIKORA, PAMELA E,** Comm Coll Algny Co Algny Cmps, Pittsburgh, PA; FR; BA; Biology; Rsrch.

**SIKULA, MICHELLE M,** Kent St Univ Kent Cmps, Kent, OH; SR; BA; Alpha Phi Sigma Chrg Tutrg 90-; Gldn Key; Alpha Phi Sigma Awd; Intrnshp Glynco GA-FLETC; Rsrch Asst Psych Dept; Psychlgy/Crmnl Juste; PhD Frnsc Psychlgy.

**SILAGYI, ADAM J,** Central Fl Comm Coll, Ocala, FL; SO; MASH 90-; Scncf Marine Biology.

**SILAS, ELIZABETH J,** Dutchess Comm Coll, Poughkeepsie, NY; FR; Univ Cinema; Deans List.

**SILBER, DANIEL J,** Yeshiva Univ, New York, NY; SR; BA; SGA Treas 89-90; Ec Soc Treas 89-90; Yrbk Editr In Chf 90-; Belkin Schlr 88-; Ec Hon Soc 88-; Deans Lst 88-; Hrvrd Natl Mdl UN Dlgate Comm 90; Tennis 88-; Econ; Law Schl.

**SILBERMINTZ-DANZER, ELANA L,** Yeshiva Univ, New York, NY; GD; JD; Photo Editor Yrbk; Poltcl Sci Soc Sec 87-88; Fin/Econ Soc Co-Fndr/V P 88-89; Dns Lst Stern Clg 86-89; Summa Cum Laude; David Bergand Fmly Schlrshp 89-; Vol Alyn Hosp For Hndcppd Chldrn 85-86; Tax Court Clinic; Harvard Univ/Univ PA 88; Fin/Tax-Corp Law; Law.

**SILBERT, JACK,** Carnegie Mellon Univ, Pittsburgh, PA; SR; Cmps Radio Statn Trng Dir 87-; Cmps Nwsppr Crtnst 88-; Cmps Ltrry Mgzn Ltrry Edtr 90-; Phi Eta Sigma 89-; Mrtr Brd 90-; Schlstc Mgzns Intern 90; BA; Engl; Publshg.

**SILCOX, CHERI L,** Glassboro St Coll, Glassboro, NJ; JR; BA; Stdnt Activ Bd 89; Res Stdnt Assn V P 89-90; Gamma Tau Sigma Sec; Phi Sigma Sigma 90-; Deans Lst 89-90; Sociology; Soc Wrk.

**SILEN, KARI L T,** Life Coll, Marietta, GA; FR; DC; Phys Thrpst Finland 86-89; PT Med Clg Tampere Finland 86; Chiropractic; Phys Thrpy.

**SILER, ANDREW F,** Wv Univ, Morgantown, WV; SO; Deans Lst 89-90; Pres Lst 90; Civil Eng.

**SILER, ARTINA A,** Saint Pauls Coll, Lawrenceville, VA; SO; BS; Alpha Kappa Mu; Sisters United In Non Phi Non 76-; Bsn Admin/Acctg; CPA.

**SILER, BECKY A,** Northern Ky Univ, Highland Hts, KY; SO; BA; Circuit Dsgn Assmblr 85-90; Weight Wtchrs Instr 90-; Elem Edn; Sch Tchr.

**SILER, CARLA J,** Univ Of Ky, Lexington, KY; JR; BSN; Amer Assoc Med Assts VP 88-; Natl Cert Amer Assoc Med Assts 87-; BS Ed Estern KY Univ 85; Med Asst Degree Indiana Voc Tech Clg 87; Nrsg; Surg Nrs.

**SILER, JAMES M,** Cumberland Coll, Williamsburg, KY; SO; BS; English; Education.

**SILER, JOHN S,** Cumberland Coll, Williamsburg, KY; SO; BS; Amrcn Chmcl Scty Pres Elect; Bptst Stdnt Un 90-; Chmstry; Indstrl Chmst.

**SILER, PATRICIA A,** Schenectady County Comm Coll, Schenectady, NY; Bkkpr Altair Audio 89-; Bsns Admnstrtn; Accntng.

**SILIPIGNI, KATHLEEN S P,** Bryant Stratton Bus Inst Roch, Rochester, NY; SO; AOS; Bus; Acctg.

**SILK, DANA K,** Duquesne Univ, Pittsburgh, PA; FR; BS; Phi Eta Sigma; Phrmcy.

**SILKEY, SHANNON L,** Syracuse Univ, Syracuse, NY; JR; BSW; Undergrad Socl Work Org V P; Hmn Concerns Cmte 88-89; Golden Key 90-; Undergrad Rsrch Asst/Dean 90-; Socl Work.

**SILLARO, STACY A,** Wagner Coll, Staten Island, NY; SR; BSN; Sigma Theta Tau; Deans List 90-; Amercn Nrs Assoc 88; NY State Nrs Assoc 88; Amercn Soc Of Post Anesthsa Nrs 90-; RN 88-; AAS Clg Of Staten Islnd NY 88; Nrsng; RN.

**SILLECK, DIANE L,** Oh St Univ At Marion, Marion, OH; SO; BA; Psychlgy Clb 90; Alph Lmbd Dlt 90; Psychlgy; Psychlgst.

**SILLS, AMY R,** Univ Of Ky, Lexington, KY; FR; BA; Res Hall Gov Rep 90-; Stdnt Actvts Cinema Comm 90-; Chrstn Stdnt Flshp 90-; Res Advsr; Chancellor 4 Yr Schlrshp; Blgy; Med.

**SILLS, LISA C,** Univ Of Tn At Martin, Martin, TN; SR; BFA; Bptst Std Un Edtr 88-89; Mrchng/Cncrt Bnd; Res Asst/Sr Res Asst; Chi Omega 87-88; Fresh Schlp; Snr Res Asst Year 89-90; Art.

**SILLS, RONALD E,** Nova Univ, Ft Lauderdale, FL; GD; MBA; Phi Sigma 82-83; Amrcn Mrktng Assoc Asst Plnng 88-90; BA 88; Bus.

**SILVA, ANTONIO E,** East Stroudsburg Univ, E Stroudsburg, PA; SR; BA; Intl Stdnts Organ S Chrprsn 89-; Polyglots Clb Sec 90-; Econ Mngmt Club 90-; Intl Econ Hnrs Soc; Brazilian Tele Intrnshp 86-87; Intl Inst Educ Schlrshp 89-; Intr Soccer 89-; Techn Univ Of Brasilea 88; Economics; Intl Bus.

**SILVA, ARTURO R,** Univ Of Md Univ Coll, College Park, MD; FR; BA; Govt Politics.

**SILVA, GINA M,** Merrimack Coll, North Andover, MA; SO; BA; Colg Repbl Treas 90-; Pol Sci Soc 90-; Pol Sci; Publ Admin.

**SILVA, JACQUELINE,** Miami Dade Comm Coll, Miami, FL; SO; BA; Accss Svc Dept 89-90; Outstndg Acdmc Achvmnt Awd 90-; Trtn Lqrs 87-90; Cert Inst Fin Educ 86; Spec Educ; Tchng.

**SILVA, KRISTINA A,** Univ Of Southern Ms, Hattiesburg, MS; SO; BFA; Natl Merit Schlr 89-; Theatre Exclnc Awd 90-; Acad Exclnc Awd 90-; Theatre/Dsgn Tech; Theatre Tech.

**SILVA, MARIA H,** Fl International Univ, Miami, FL; SO; BA; Engl Educ; HS Tchr.

**SILVA, MICHAEL L,** Hampton Univ, Hampton, VA; FR; BA; Litry Soc 90-; Pre Med Clb 90-; English Arts; Script Wrtr.

**SILVANAGE, LORI ANNE,** Coll Misericordia, Dallas, PA; SO; BS; Ocptnl Thrpy Assc; Peer Tutoring; Lector Mass; Amer Ocptnl Thrpy Assc; PA Ocptnl Thrpy Assc; Ocptnl Thrpy.

**SILVANIC, MONNA D,** Memphis St Univ, Memphis, TN; FR; BED; Elem Ed; Tchr.

**SILVANIO, DIANE M,** Rutgers St Univ At Camden, Camden, NJ; SR; BS; Hon Soc 90-; Intrnshp Intrn Dir Admin 89; Bus Mgmt; Admin.

**SILVAROLI, NICHOLAS J,** Niagara Univ, Niagara Univ, NY; FR; Econ & Fin Club 90; IM Flr Hockey 90; Econ.

**SILVER, BARBARA A,** Wv Northern Comm Coll, Wheeling, WV; GD; Bus Admin; Acctnt.

**SILVER, BRYAN J,** Va Commonwealth Univ, Richmond, VA; SR; BS; Phi Eta Sigma; Gldn Key; Kappa Tau Alpha; Sigma Zeta; Mss Cmmnctn; Advrtsng.

**SILVER, ELLIOT,** Univ Of Miami, Coral Gables, FL; SR; JD; Student Govt 87-90; Phi Eta Sigma 87-88; Lambda Chi Alpha Secty 87-91; Pres 100 87-; Communication Intern 90-; IM Soccer 87-89; Law.

**SILVER, GREGORY S,** Univ Of North Fl, Jacksonville, FL; SO; BS; Pi Mu Epsilon 90-; Elect Eng.

**SILVER, JOYCE J,** Memphis St Univ, Memphis, TN; BA; Acctncy Alumni Bd 89-; Chdrns Rehab Ctr 90-; Cert CPA Cert 86; AICPA 86-; TSCPA 86-; BBA 84; Sci; Med.

**SILVER, ROBIN T,** City Univ Of Ny Med Evers Coll, Brooklyn, NY; SO; Deans Lst 90; RMA; Flght Serv Mgr Trans Wrld Airlines 86-; RMA NY Sch Med/Dntl Asstnts 80; Psychlgy/Edn; Schl Psychlgy.

**SILVERMAN, GLENN A,** Comm Coll Algny Co Algny Cmps, Pittsburgh, PA; SO; AS; Slsprsn Plmbng Spplr; Cmptr Sci.

**SILVERMAN, KARIN M,** Wagner Coll, Staten Island, NY; JR; BE; Zeta Delta Alpha Rush Chrprsn; Elem Educ; Elem Eductr.

**SILVERS, CELESTE D,** Franklin And Marshall Coll, Lancaster, PA; JR; BS; Pre-Healing Arts Club V P 89-; Choral Soc/Chamber Singers 88-90; The Poor Richards 90-; One On One Tutoring 88-89; Lancaster Gen Hosp 89-90; John Carroll Assn Strn Comm 88-90; Hackman Hughes Schlrsph 89-; Dana Schlr 89-; Bio; Med.

**SILVERS, MARY LOU,** Mayland Comm Coll, Spruce Pine, NC; FR; AAS; H/R Blck Tax Preparer 90; Bus Cmptr Pgm; Cmptr Pgmr.

**SILVERSTEIN, DOUG N,** Nova Univ, Ft Lauderdale, FL; SR; MBA; Scuba Dvng Fshng Wtr/Snw Skiing 87-; Les Amis Du Vin 88-; Hadassah 87-; Dns Lst 87-; Sba Univ Miami 89; Henry King Stanford Schlrshp; OH Bd Regents Schrlshp; OH St Univ Schlrshp; IM 87-; Zeta Beta Tau 87-; Sommelier Gld 89-; Irn Hngr Sty 87-; Bus Admn; Law Schl.

**SILVEY, JEFFREY L,** Univ Of Cincinnati, Cincinnati, OH; SR; BSEET; AAS Univ Of KY 79; AAS S St Comm Clg 85; Elec Engr.

**SILVIS, JASON G,** Averett Coll, Danville, VA; FR; BS; Comp Sci; Comp Prog.

**SILVUS, MELANIE S,** Oh Univ, Athens, OH; JR; BA; Graphic Dsgn/Fine Arts.

**SIM, EUN J,** Ny Univ, New York, NY; SO; BA; Tutor For I Have A Dream Fndtn; SGA; KSA 90; Deans List 90; Poetry Publshd In West 4th Street Review; GSP Faculty Svc Award; AA; Anthroplgy; Rsrch/Tch.

**SIM, JOHN J,** Hudson Valley Comm Coll, Troy, NY; SO; MBA; Math/Econs Tutor; NYSMATYC Math Contst; AAS; Bus Admin; Law.

**SIM, LING L,** Va Commonwealth Univ, Richmond, VA; SR; BS; Sprt Team Capt 87; Malysn Assn/Chnse Assn/Intl Stdnt Un 88-; Decsn Sci Inst; Amer Statstcs Assn; Oprtns Rsrch/Statstcs; Anlyst.

**SIMAN, DEBORAH C,** Univ Of Miami, Coral Gables, FL; SR; BS; Bio; Med.

**SIMAO, KELLY J,** Rivier Coll, Nashua, NH; JR; BS; Paralegal Scty 88-; Paralegal Studies; Law/Law Enforcement.

**SIMAS, SUSAN L,** New England Inst Of Tech, Warwick, RI; ASSOC; ST Ar Rcdng Sec 89; Med; AMA.

**SIMBECK, DAWN A,** Memphis St Univ, Memphis, TN; SO; BSED; Hmphrys Soc 89-; Peer-Mntr Pgm Exec Cncl 89-; Sxul Asslt Tsk Frc; Alpha Lambda Delta P 90-; Phi Eta Sigma 90-; C C Humphrey Pres Schlrshp 89-; Ambass Brd; Hmn Lrng; Elem Tchr.

**SIMCOX, CHRISTINE L,** Youngstown St Univ, Youngstown, OH; SO; AAB; Natl Shrthnd Rprtrs Assc; Prfsnl Sec Intrntl Schrlshp 89; YSU Fndtn Schlrhsp 89-; Wstrn Rsrv Ofc Atmtn Prfsnls Schlrshp 89-; Stngrph Co Schrlshp; Crt/Conf Rprtng.

**SIMES, ROBERT G,** Mayland Comm Coll, Spruce Pine, NC; GD; Brnsvle Lit Theater VP 89; BSA Asst Dstrct Cmmssnr 84; Plce Offcr 72-85; Sales 90; BA Cal State U 76; AAT Balin Inst 87; Crmnl Jstce/Drftng.

**SIMINGTON, MICHELE R,** Univ Of Nc At Charlotte, Charlotte, NC; JR; Stdnt Ct Attny Gen 89-; Ambsdrs Treas; Alpha Kappa Alpha Parlmntrn; Dns Lst; Res Life Pgm Mnth 90; Pre-Law Soc 88-89; Hl Cncl 90-; Stdnt Legisltr 90; RA 90-; Pol Sci/Engl; Law.

**SIMKINS, CYNTHIA A,** Wilmington Coll, New Castle, DE; GD; BA; Del Clms Assn; Brd Dir Chldrns Hm Inc; Del Powr Lght Co; Assoc Sci Harcm Jr Clg 79; Busn Mgmt; Clms Rep.

**SIMMETH, THOMAS P,** Medaille Coll, Buffalo, NY; JR, BA, Phi Theta Kappa 87-88; AS Villa Maria Clg 88; Elem Educ; Elem Tchr Mstrs Rdng.

**SIMMONDS, GIOCONDA R,** S U N Y At Buffalo, Buffalo, NY; GD; MARCH; Gldn Ky; Deans Lst 88-90; Cum Laude 90; Minority Fllwshp; Natl Hispanic Schlrshp; BA City Clg New York 90; Arch.

**SIMMONDS, NORMA P,** Fl A & M Univ, Tallahassee, FL; JR; BA; Caribbean Stdnt Assn 88-90; Phi Eta Sigma 88-89; Mead Data Cntr; Cmptr Info Systs; Cmptr Prgrmr.**

**SIMMONS, ALAN J,** Western Ky Univ, Bowling Green, KY; SR; Goldn Key 89-; Assn Undrgrad Gntcsts 90-; Gene Tech/Chem; Med Schl.

**SIMMONS, ALBERTA M,** Central St Univ, Wilberforce, OH; GD; Wkly Radio Prog Child Dev Bermuda 63-64; Wkly Nwspr Reprtr Girl Gurde Assoc 63-64; Brownie Guide Advisor; Childrens Hme Auxlry Pres 79-82; Girl Guide Assoc Ldr; Tchrs Trng Schlrshp Canada 55-57; Ed; Mentor/Bermuda Schl Syst.

**SIMMONS, ANGEL A,** Voorhees Coll, Denmark, SC; SO; BA; Omega Swthrt Sec 90-; Hon Prog 90-; Comp Sci; Comp Prog.

**SIMMONS, ANNETTE,** Miles Coll, Birmingham, AL; SR; BS; Hnr Scty 90-; Dipl Sec Sci Southern Jr Clg Bos 86; Scndry Educ; Tchg.

**SIMMONS, BOBBY R,** Interdenominational Theo Ctr, Atlanta, GA; GD; M DIV; Theta Phi; BS Winston-Salem St Univ 85; AAS Surry Comm Coll 79; Thlgy; Tchng.

**SIMMONS, BRETT LEIGHTON,** Univ Of Sc At Columbia, Columbia, SC; JR; BA; Rfrmd Univ Fllwshp VP 89-90; Tchr Yr Com 90-; Dorm Govt 90-; TV Intrn 90-; Deans Lst 90-; Pres Hon Rl 90; Media Arts; TV Prdctn/Phtgrphy.

**SIMMONS, BRETT S,** Castleton St Coll, Castleton, VT; SR; BA; IM 87-; Athltc Crmns Com; Costa Rican Eclgcl Intrn 90-; Deans Lst 90; Wright Hs Hon Drm 88-89; Vrsty Bsbl Capt 87-; Cmbnd Ntrl Sci/Blgy/Glgy.

**SIMMONS, BRIAN K,** Alcorn St Univ, Lorman, MS; SR; NAACP 89; Tech Clb 90-; Alpha Phi Alpha Treas 88-; All Amer Schlr 90-; Coop Educ Fed Aviation Admn 90-.

**SIMMONS, BRIAN RUSSELL,** Central Al Comm Coll, Alexander City, AL; FR; Bapt Stdnt Union; Yng Adlt Ensmbl 90-; Chrch Mscls 90-; Biology/Voice; Phys Thrpy/Music Evnglsm.

**SIMMONS, BRIAN T,** Univ Of Va, Charlottesville, VA; FR; Skydvng Clb Tres 90-; Eng Cncl 90-; Systems Engineering.

**SIMMONS, CASSANDRA,** Johnson C Smith Univ, Charlotte, NC; FR.

**SIMMONS, CRYSTAL R,** Univ Of Sc At Columbia, Columbia, SC; SO; MBA; Bus; CPA.

**SIMMONS, CYNTHIA L,** Dyke Coll, Cleveland, OH; FR.

**SIMMONS, DAFFNEY K,** Central St Univ, Wilberforce, OH; SR; Alpha Angels; Delta Sigma Theta Pres 89; Ntl Coll Awrd 88; Bio; Oral Srgry.

**SIMMONS, DARLENE,** Johnson C Smith Univ, Charlotte, NC; SO; Jdcry Brd; Alpha Kappa Alpha; Engl/Cmmnctns.

**SIMMONS, DARRELL SCOTT,** Piedmont Tech Coll, Greenwood, SC; SO; AS; Hlth Sci; Radlogcl Tech.

**SIMMONS, DEBRA M,** Savannah St Coll, Savannah, GA; SR; BS; Stdnt Govt Sntr 80-81; Tri Beta Sec; Delta Sigma Pi Treas 82-83; Sigma Gamma Rho; Smmr Rsrch Prog Howard Univ 90; AS Middle Georgia Clg 90; Bus/Bio; Hlth Info Mgr.

**SIMMONS, DEIRDRA J,** Comm Coll Algny Co Algny Cmps, Pittsburgh, PA; ASN; PA Air National Guard SSGT 83-; Internship Allegheny Genrl & Divine Providence Hospital 90-; ASN; Nursing.

**SIMMONS, DENISE B,** City Univ Of Ny City Coll, New York, NY; SR; BA; Deans Lst 89; Jerry Lewis Tele 80-83; UNICEF 79; Carey Gdns Day Care Ctr 84-; AAS NY City Tech Clg 85; Art Tchr.

**SIMMONS, DWANDA L,** Mount Olive Coll, Mount Olive, NC; FR; BA; Business; Acctng.

**SIMMONS, ELIZABETH A,** Fl St Univ, Tallahassee, FL; JR; BA; Phi Eta Sgm 89-; Gldn Key 90; FL Acad Schlrs Schlrshp 88-; Engl.

**SIMMONS, EVELYN S,** Wv Univ At Parkersburg, Parkersburg, WV; FR; Phi Theta Kappa; Sndy Schl Tchr 62-; 4-H Ldr 87-89; Bible Schl Ldr 88-; Bus; Gnrl Bus.

**SIMMONS, HEATHER L,** Richard Bland Coll, Petersburg, VA; JR; BS; Phi Theta Kappa Treas 89-90; AS May 90; Bus Admin; Mktg.

**SIMMONS, HELEN J,** Central Fl Comm Coll, Ocala, FL; SO; BA; Phi Beta Lambda Chair-Ways/Means 89-90; Bsn Adm/Mgmt Advsry Bd Stdnt Rep 90; Phi Theta Kappa Treas 90; Ocala Hsg Auth Res Cncl; Citizens Crime Watch 90; AS 90; Ocala Pilot Clb Acad Schlrshp 90; Dns Lst 90; Pres Lst 88-90; Bsn Adm; Mgmt Consltnt.

**SIMMONS, JEANNETTE V,** Wv Univ, Morgantown, WV; FR; Hl Cncl RHA Ofcr 90-; Res Hl Assoc Rep 90-; St John Nwmn Chrch Grp; Aerospace; Engr.

**SIMMONS, JON P,** Medical Coll Of Ga, Augusta, GA; GD; DMD; Chmstry Cl 86-90; Grmn Clb 89; Tau Kappa Epsilon 84-85; Sr Yr Chmstry; BS Chmstry Ga Sthrn Univ 90; Dntstry.

**SIMMONS, JULIET Y,** Brevard Comm Coll, Cocoa, FL; SO; AA; Cncrt Bnd 89; Jz Bnd 89-90; Sigma Kappa Psi 89; Math/Sci; Elctrcl Engrg.**

**SIMMONS, KAREN,** City Univ Of Ny Baruch Coll, New York, NY; SR; MSW; ELITES Org Pres 88-; BBA Baruch Clg 90; Dns Lst Certif Baruch Clg 90; Sclgy; Hlth Care Scl Wrkr.

**SIMMONS, KARLA A,** Bridgewater Coll, Bridgewater, VA; SR; BS; Athltc Trnr 87-; Blgy.

**SIMMONS, KATHRYN L,** Univ Of Southern Ms, Hattiesburg, MS; FR; BS; Hons Stdnt Assoc 90-; Mbr Univ Hons Clg; Im Sports Team Mbr; Medcl Tech.

**SIMMONS, KATHRYN R,** William Carey Coll, Hattiesburg, MS; SR; BS; Hnrs Cls 87-90; Stdnt Tchr Of Yr; Pi Delta Kappa; Elem Educ; Tchr.

**SIMMONS, KIMBERLY C,** Fl A & M Univ, Tallahassee, FL; SO; Comp Info Syst; Comp Sci.

**SIMMONS, LA TONYA R,** Tn St Univ, Nashville, TN; GD; BS; NAACP CJO 86; Deans Lst 86; Delta Sigma Theta 87; Peer Cnslr 90; Intrnshp Pbl Dfndrs Offce; Mjrtte Square Co-Capt 86-89; BS Crmnl Jstce; Crmnl Jstce; Law.

**SIMMONS, LATONYA L,** Norfolk St Univ, Norfolk, VA; SO; BA; Ambassador Asst Rec Secr 90-; Phi Beta Lambda 90-; AAS Tidewater Cmnty Clg 90; Adm Syst Mgmt.

**SIMMONS, LAURA R,** Univ Of Ga, Athens, GA; JR; BA; Kappa Delta Pi; Pi Beta Phi 88-90; Lang; Arts.

**SIMMONS, MARY A,** Central St Univ, Wilberforce, OH; FR; BS; LPN Assoc 84-; LPN; LPN Dayton Sch Pract Nrsg 84; Psych; Psych Nrsg.

**SIMMONS, MARY J,** Fl International Univ, Miami, FL; JR; BS; ADA ASPEW; BS Nut Va Plytchnc Inst 82; Nrsng.

**SIMMONS, MARY J,** Lenoir Rhyne Coll, Hickory, NC; JR; BA; Lthrn Mvmnt Sec 88-; Sclgy/Psychlgy Clb 89-; Alpha Lambda Delta 90-; Mu Sigma Epsilon; Sclgy/Psychlgy.

**SIMMONS, MELISSA J,** City Univ Of Ny City Coll, New York, NY; SR; BA; Mntr 87-89; Ofc Ecnmc Fncl Opp Intrnshp.

**SIMMONS, MICHAEL E,** Univ Of West Fl, Pensacola, FL; SR; BA; AA Okaloosa Walton Cmmnty Clg 90; Erly Chldhd Elem Ed; Tchr.

**SIMMONS, PAMELA J,** Comm Coll Algny Co Algny Cmps, Pittsburgh, PA; FR; AS; AS Duffs Bsnss Inst 88; Crt Rprtng; Crt Stngrphr.

**SIMMONS, PHILLIPPIA A,** Al A & M Univ, Normal, AL; FR; Engr; Elctrcl Engr.

**SIMMONS JR, REYNOLD,** Univ Of Sc At Columbia, Columbia, SC; JR; BA; Cert USAF 89; Finance; Law Enfrcmnt.

**SIMMONS, ROBERT E,** Ky Mountain Bible Coll, Vancleve, KY; FR; BA; Stdnt Cncl Rep 90-; Frshmn Cls Pres 90-; Annual Stf Layout Dsgnr 90-; Youth Temprnc Cncl Treas 90-; B; Relgn; Church Mnstry.

**SIMMONS, SHANNON C,** Ga Southern Univ, Statesboro, GA; FR; BA; Afro Amer Gosp Chr 90-; Info Syst; Comp.

**SIMMONS, SHANNON L,** Lenoir Rhyne Coll, Hickory, NC; JR; BA; A Cappella Choir 88-; Clg Sngrs 89-; SNCAE; Mu Sigma Epsilon; Alpha Lambda Delta 89-; Marshall 88-90; H R Fwlr Schlrshp; Pres Schlrshp; N C Pros Tchr Schlrshp 90-; Educ; Tchr.

**SIMMONS, SHERYL J,** Middle Tn St Univ, Murfreesboro, TN; BA; SHEA 87-90; STEA 90-; Erly Chldhd Educ; Daycare Dir Tchr K-3.

**SIMMONS, TORY A,** Fl A & M Univ, Tallahassee, FL; FR; BA; Ethcs Inttve 90-; Dns Lst 90-; LL Boykin Awrd; Delta Sigma Theta Awrd 90-; Eta Phi Beta Awrd And Bggs Hsng Awrd 90-; Bus Admin.

**SIMMONS, VICKY D,** Southeastern Baptist Coll, Laurel, MS; SO; AA; Bapt Assn Sec 90; Hosp Vol; Nrsng Hme; Bus; Lgl Sec.

**SIMMONS, WENDY D,** Western Piedmont Comm Coll, Morganton, NC; FR; BS; Lab Clb Sec 90-; Phi Theta Kappa; Med Lab Tech; Microbiology.

**SIMMONS, YOLANDA T,** Lincoln Univ, Lincoln Univ, PA; SR; BS; Sclgy Clb 89-; Intl Clb 88-; Alpha Kappa Delta; Natl Adptn Cntr-Intrnshp 90-; Deans Lst 89-90; Hmn Serv; Scl Wrk.

**SIMMONS-DENBOW, LOUISE P,** Comm Coll Algny Co Algny Cmps, Pittsburgh, PA; FR; BSN; Nrsng; Pediatrician.

**SIMMS, ANITA K,** Fayetteville St Univ, Fayetteville, NC; SO; BS; US Army Mdcl Spec Sgt; Education.

**SIMMS, FRANCHESCA O,** Bennett Coll, Greensboro, NC; SO; BA; Busn Clb Fin Sec 89-; Afrcn Awrnss Assmbly Tr 89-90; Alumni Assn 90-; Dns Lst 90-; Tutr 89-90; NAACP Spkspersn 89-90; Westinghs Elec Co Int Comptrlr; Busn Admin; Fincl Mgr.

**SIMMS, KATRINA D,** Northeast State Tech Comm Coll, Blountville, TN; GD; Traffic Ct Jdg 90; AAS; Offc Sys Tech; Mngmnt.

**SIMMS, LEANNE,** Coll Misericordia, Dallas, PA; FR; Clg Msrcrd Std Occptnl Thrpy Asc 90-; Dns Lst; All Amer Schl Awd; Natl Bsn Mrt Awd; OT.

**SIMMS, ROIANNA L,** Daytona Beach Comm Coll, Daytona Beach, FL; FR; BA; Phi Theta Kappa Tutor 90-; Clg Pres Lstd 90-; Scndry Engl Educ; Tchr.

**SIMMS, SHANI M,** Jackson St Univ, Jackson, MS; JR; BS; Cls Sec; Asst Sec 90-; Dpsychlgy Clb Miss Psy Clb S Govt Rep 90-; Dpsi Chi VP 90-; Beta Kappa Chi; Mnrty Access Rsrch Careers; Soc Psychlgy.

**SIMMS-GREGG, KIMBERLEY JILL,** Spalding Univ, Louisville, KY; JR; BA; NEA Pblc Rltns Ofcr; Delta Delta Delta 89; Radio Intrn Asst Promo Coord 90; AA U FL 90; Cmnctns.

**SIMON, AMY M,** Northern Ky Univ, Highland Hts, KY; SR; BA; Elem Ed; Tchng.

**SIMON, DAVID P,** Univ Of Miami, Coral Gables, FL; SO; BAM; Wnd Ensmbl 89-; Alph Alamda Delta 90; Phi Eta Sigma 90-; Mdcl Schlrs Prgm; Music Schlrshp; FL Undrgrad Schlr; Music; Med.**

**SIMON, DEBBIE A,** Univ Of Scranton, Scranton, PA; JR; BA; Cls VP Stdnt Govt 89-90; Orntn Aid 89-; Bus Clb 88-; Omega Beta Sigma 89-; Delta Mu Delta 90-; Safety/Scrtny Cncl 89-90; Royal Ambsdr 89-; All Am Schlr Coll Awd 88-; Natl Coll Bus Merit Awd 88-; R C Hughs Meml Schlrshp; Mktg; Advrtsng.

**SIMON, GEORGE M,** Fl International Univ, Miami, FL; FR; BA; IM Bsktbl Capt; Math; Acctg.

**SIMON, JENNIFER L,** Kent St Univ Kent Cmps, Kent, OH; FR; Natl Acad Hon Soc 90-; Pre Med.

**SIMON, JONATHAN B,** Morehouse Coll, Atlanta, GA; SO; BS; Bus Assn 89-; Stdnt Govt Assn Co Chrmn Extrnl Affrs 90-; STRIPES Exec Sec 90-; Gldn Ky 90-; UNCF Ctcorp Fllws Prog 89-; Fnnce; Invstmnt Bnkng.

**SIMON, LOURDES,** Fl International Univ, Miami, FL; SR; BS; FEA 90-; Kappa Delta Pi Hstrn 89-; Phi Kappa Phi 90-; Tlnt Rstr Awd 88; Elem Schl Tchr Intrnshp 89-; Elem Ed; Law.

**SIMON, MARGARITA,** Central Ct St Univ, New Britain, CT; FR; BED; LASO 90; Art; Tchr.

**SIMON, PUSHPARANI,** Columbia Union Coll, Takoma Park, MD; SR; BA; Burnt Mills SDA Chrch; SAA Assn; Hot Line Teenagers; BA Org Mgmt; BA Spicer Mem Coll India 67; Org Mgmt.

**SIMON, ROBERT J,** Atlantic Comm Coll, Mays Landing, NJ; SO; IM Bsktbl Club 90-; Bsbl 87; Bsktbl 90-; Acctg; CPA.

**SIMON, SANDRA V**, Univ Of The Dist Of Columbia, Washington, DC; SR; BA; Caribbean Clb Tres 88-89; Antiqua/Berbuda Stdnt Asc 87-89; Acctg Clb; Deans List 90-; Deans List West Indies Clg 86-89; Assc Degree West Indies Clg Jamaica 89; Dipl Ofc Amdn Antigua State Clg Autigua 85; Acctg; CPA.

**SIMON, SCOTT T**, Univ Of Sc At Columbia, Columbia, SC; SO; BA; Hist Clb 90-; Phi Alpha Theta; Hist; Professor.

**SIMON, SCOTT T**, Univ Of Sc At Coastal Carolina, Conway, SC; SO; BA; History Clb; Phi Alpha Theta; Bchlr Arts Schlrshp; Hstry; Prfsr.

**SIMON, TRACEE L**, Coll Misericordia, Dallas, PA; FR; BA; Occptnl Thrpy.

**SIMONELLI, CHRISTOPHER**, City Univ Of Ny Queensbrough, New York, NY; SR; BS; CERTF 88; AAS; Bsns; Cmptr Prgrmmr.

**SIMONETTI, ALICIA M**, S U N Y Coll At Postdam, Potsdam, NY; JR; BM; Pi Kappa Lambda; Phi Eta Sigma; Prfrmnc Cert; Pres Hons 90; Msc Ed.

**SIMONETTI, NINA J**, Univ Of Nc At Charlotte, Charlotte, NC; JR; BA; Golden Key; Lacrosse Vybl 88-89; Arch.

**SIMONS, ETTA KATHERINE**, Coll Of Charleston, Charleston, SC; FR; BA; Law.

**SIMONS, MARY KATHERINE**, Juniata Coll, Huntingdon, PA; JR; BA; Amnesty Intl; Theatre 89-; Hon Soc; Circle K Intl 90-; Theatre Arts; Directing.

**SIMONSEN, SCOTT M**, Cooper Union, New York, NY; SO; BE; Elec Engr.

**SIMONTON, BRIAN E**, Univ Of Akron, Akron, OH; SR; BEE; IEEE 89-; IEEE Comp Soc VP 90-; Elect Eng; Eng.

**SIMONTON, TIMOTHY K**, Univ Of Cin R Walters Coll, Blue Ash, OH; FR; BA; Bus Admn.

**SIMPKINS, JOEY M**, East Tn St Univ, Johnson City, TN; SR; BS; Epsilon Pi Tau; Socty Mfg Engrs; IM 89-90; AAS New River Comm Coll 88; AAS New River Comm Coll 89; Elec.

**SIMPKINS, JOHN T**, Marshall University, Huntington, WV; JR; BA; Pi Kappa Alpha Comm Chrmn 89-90; IM 88-; Bsn Infor Sys; Sys Analyst.

**SIMPSON, ADRIAN H**, American Baptist Coll, Nashville, TN; JR; BA; Bapt Student Union; Biblical Theology; Paster/Tchr.

**SIMPSON, BRENT T**, Univ Of Sc At Columbia, Columbia, SC; FR; BA; Chldrns Grdn; Attend Other Natl Schls; Math; Prof.

**SIMPSON, BRIAN C**, Juniata Coll, Huntingdon, PA; SR; BA; Cathlc Cncl Jr Rep 89-90; Peace/Jstc Comm Chrmn 89-90; Amnsty Intrntl 90; Pi Sigma Alpha; Bailey Oratorcl Award 90; Leg Intrnshp; Im 87-89; Pol Sci; Govt.

**SIMPSON, CAROLYN E**, Fl St Univ, Tallahassee, FL; SO; BS; Blck Stdnt Unn; Du Bois Scty; Dns Lst; Incntve Schlr; Acctng Scty; AICPA Schlrshp; Acctng Fnnce; CPA.

**SIMPSON, CARRIE E**, Radford Univ, Radford, VA; JR; BS; Phi Sigma Sigma 90-; Intrnshp Wmns Rsrc Cntr 90-; Scl Wrk; Fmly Cnsnlg.

**SIMPSON, CHERYL AMY**, Northern Ky Univ, Highland Hts, KY; SR; BA; Bapt Stdnt Union Evng Coord/Fmly Coord/Cncl Sec 87-90; Deans Lst 89-90; Hons Lst 90; Charlotte Schmid Lapp Schlrshp/Loan 88; AAS 90; Mntl Hlth/Hmn Svcs; Scl Wrk.

**SIMPSON, CURTIS W**, James Sprunt Comm Coll, Kenansville, NC; SO; BA; Jrnlsm; News/Ed Jrnlst.

**SIMPSON, DIANNA R**, Tn Temple Univ, Chattanooga, TN; JR; BS; R A Torrey Soc 88-90f Eductnl Club 90-; Theta Kappa Rho 90-; Edtr Yrbk 90-; Secndry Ed/Hist; Tch.

**SIMPSON, ELIZABETH T**, Univ Of Southern Ms, Hattiesburg, MS; SR; BS; Cinema; Res Hall Assn Rep 89; Lambda Pi Eta Dnr Comm 90-; Lit Fstvl; Radio/TV/FLM; Prod.

**SIMPSON, GILBERTO D**, Amherst Coll, Amherst, MA; FR; BA; Blck Stdnts Un Pblcty Offcr; La Causa Stdnt Fnc Comtt Rep; Radio Stn DJ; Stdnts Edctnl Eqlty Ttr; Math; Prfssr.

**SIMPSON, GRETCHEN L**, Univ Of Tn At Knoxville, Knoxville, TN; GD; DVM; AAEP Clb Clss Rep 87-89; Equine Clb 87-; Gamma Sigma Delta 85-87; Gldn Ky 87-; Raptor Rehb 87-88; Pet Thrpy 87-88; Schlrshp Univ KY 85; Vet Med; Equine Prctnr.

**SIMPSON, HOLLY R**, Tn Wesleyan Coll, Athens, TN; JR; Chrldng 90-.

**SIMPSON, JAMES W**, Memphis St Univ, Memphis, TN; SR; BFA; AA Shelby State Cmnty Clg 82; Fine Arts; Art/Paintg.

**SIMPSON, JEFF R**, Shippensburg Univ, Shippensburg, PA; FR; BS; Math/Computer Sci.

**SIMPSON, JENNIFER D**, Univ Of Al At Birmingham, Birmingham, AL; SO; BSN; Blgy Clb 89-90; Gld Chrldr 90; Ms UAB Hmcmng Cmte Pblcty 90-; Alpha Delta Pi Phlnthrpy 89-90; Shelby Med Schlrshp 89-; Kiwanis Schlrshp 89-90; Nrsg.

**SIMPSON, JENNIFER K**, Lesley Coll, Cambridge, MA; SR; BS; Res Asst 89-; Res Life Advsry Bd 89-90; Math/Sci Clb 89-; Deans Lst 89-; Sociology Tchrs Asst; Elem Edn; Cnslng.

**SIMPSON III, JOHN R**, Univ Of Sc At Columbia, Columbia, SC; SO; BA; History; Law.

**SIMPSON, JOHN RAYMOND**, Memphis St Univ, Memphis, TN; JR; BA; Sigma Alpha Epsilon IFC 88-90; Yng Rpblcns 88-89; IM Ftbll Sftbll Vllybll 88-90; Mgmt Info Systms.

**SIMPSON, KACINDA D**, Washington & Jefferson Coll, Washington, PA; FR; BA; Drama Clb 90-; Pltcl Sci; Crprte Lwyr.

**SIMPSON, KATHERINE A**, Univ Of Tn At Martin, Martin, TN; SR; BS; SGA Elctn Cmsnr 88-; Phi Eta Sigma 88; Univ Schlr 87-; Mu Epsilon Delta Treas 87-89; Chi Omega Chptr Crspndnt 88-; Tchng Assist 90-91; Chem/Bio; Med Rsrch.

**SIMPSON, KEVIN A**, Univ Of Rochester, Rochester, NY; JR; BSEE; African/Caribbean Cultrl Club Pres; Natl Soc Of Blck Engrs 88-; Delco Prodcts Div GM Intrn 90-; Im Soccer 88-; Elec Engr.

**SIMPSON, KIMBERLY R**, Liberty Univ, Lynchburg, VA; JR; BS; Yth Quest Clb 88-89; Light Clb 88-89; Rsdnt Asst 90-; Acctng.

**SIMPSON, KOBOI M**, Morehouse Coll, Atlanta, GA; JR; Stdnt Govt Assoc Sen 89-; Sigma Tau Delta VP 90-F Gldn Key; KMT Frtrnty Inc VP 90; Mrhs Mntrng Prgm; Frdrc Dgls Ttrl Prgm; Ftbll; Trck; Engl; Law.

**SIMPSON, LUANNE J**, Bloomfield Coll, Bloomfield, NJ; SR; BS; Alpha Chi 90-; Bnkg/Credit/Finance Awd BCC 88; Schlstc Achvmnt Awd BCC 88; NACM 82-; Ciba-Geigy Corp Credit Adm 82-; AAS Bergen Cmnty Clg 88; Bsn Mgmt; Credit Mgmt.

**SIMPSON, NANCY A**, Hudson Valley Comm Coll, Troy, NY; FR; AAS; Hlth Sci; Nrsng.

**SIMPSON, PAMELA S**, Nyack Coll, Nyack, NY; SR; BA; Drama Ens Dir 88-; Yrbk Stf Edtr 89-90; Mnhttn Gspl Tm Dir 87-89; Alpha Chi 89-; Chrl 87-89; Clg Sngrs 87-89; Outstdng Serv Schl Awd 89-90; Engl; Prfmng Arts.

**SIMPSON III, ROBERT L**, Merrimack Coll, North Andover, MA; SR; BS; Yrbk Ed Chief 90-; Frntrs Hgh Cncllr 90-; Joseph P Daly Awrd Otstndng Chrctr; Crss Cntry 87-89; Chmstry; Grad Schl.

**SIMPSON, STEPHANIE L**, Univ Of Sc At Columbia, Columbia, SC; SO; BA; SGA Patterson Dorm Hall Rep 89-90; Alpha Lambda Delta 89-; Deans Lst 89-90; Blgy; Optmtry.

**SIMPSON, STEVEN S**, Univ Of Rochester, Rochester, NY; SR; PHD; Phi Theta Kappa 88-; BA; Poli Sci; Poli Cnsltng.

**SIMPSON, TERI L**, Hillsborough Comm Coll, Tampa, FL; SO; BA; TLC Moms Co-Fndr 87-; Hospice 90-; Military Exchng Comm Sys 80-89; Psychology; Cnslr.

**SIMPSON, TINA R**, Univ Of Tn At Martin, Martin, TN; FR; BS; Geology Environmental Sci.

**SIMPSON, TOD D**, Memphis St Univ, Memphis, TN; JR; BA; Fnc; Anlyst.

**SIMPSON, TONJA D**, Fl A & M Univ, Tallahassee, FL; SR; BA; FAMU Gspl Choir 89-; Golden Key; Urban League Tallahassee; AA Seminole Comm Clg 89; Agri-Bus; Tch Short Range.

**SIMPSON, WAYNE S**, Samford Univ, Birmingham, AL; SR; JD; Cumberland Schl Law Hnr Ct; Deans Lst 87-; Pres Hnr Roll 87-; Gldn Key 87-88; Alpha Lambda Delta; Phi Alpha Theta; Kapa Alpha Order Ofcr 87-; Pres Schlr 90-; Asaa Univ FL 88; BA Univ FL 89; Robert B Donwworth Frshmn Appellate Argmnt Comp; History/Bus; Law.

**SIMPSON, YOLANDA Y**, Alcorn St Univ, Lorman, MS; SR; BA; Engl Clb Tres 88-89; Cnnnctns Clb 90- Dean Lst 87-; Alpha Kappa Alpha 90-; Cum Laude; Engl Cmmnctns; Vdgrphy/Flm Mkr.

**SIMS WRIGHT, TOSHA R**, Middle Ga Coll, Cochran, GA; SO; BED; Educ.

**SIMS, ANDREA**, Alcorn St Univ, Lorman, MS; SR; BS; Comp Sci/Math Clb 87-; Phi Beta Lambda 90; NAACP 89; Alpha Kappa Alpha Prlmntrn 89-; Acdmc Schlrshp 87; Comp Sci/Appld Math; Prgrmmr.

**SIMS, BRYAN K**, Catawba Valley Comm Coll, Hickory, NC; SO; AAS; Furn Prod Mgmt; Indstl Engr.

**SIMS, CHERYL D**, Coll Of Charleston, Charleston, SC; SR; Phi Mu 88; BS Clg Of Chrlstn; Bio; Physcl Thrpst.

**SIMS, DEBRA G**, Vance Granville Comm Coll, Henderson, NC; SO; BA; Ambssdr Fr Vance Grnvlle Comm Coll; Phi Theta Kappa; Vance Grnvlle Coll Trnsfr Schlr; Acctng.

**SIMS, ERIC M**, Morehouse Coll, Atlanta, GA; FR; Sci; Eng Mech.

**SIMS, GREGORY J**, Clark Atlanta Univ, Atlanta, GA; SO; BS; Class Pr 89-; Spirit Booster Clb 90-; Hons Pgm 90-; Alpha Phi Alpha; United Church Nghbrhd Asst Ldr 85-90; Intern Exxon USA Houston TX; Deans Lst 89-; Hons Pgm Pr Schlr 89-; Comp Sci.

**SIMS, HENRY M**, Fl St Univ, Tallahassee, FL; SR; BS; AA Chipola Jr Clg 89; Econ; Law.

**SIMS, JODI M**, Wallace St Comm Coll At Selma, Selma, AL; FR; BA; Phi Theta Kappa Sec 90-; General.

**SIMS, JOHANNA C**, Ms St Univ, Miss State, MS; FR; BED; Hnrs Prog 90-; Phi Eta Sigma; Gamma Beta Phi; Phi Mu 90-; Pres Schlrs 90-F; Hstry; Law.

**SIMS, JOHN S**, Samford Univ, Birmingham, AL; GD; JD; Stdnt Bar Assn IL Rep 90-; Law Review; Nationa Moot Court Tm; BS Univ Alabama 90; Law.

**SIMS, JULIE A**, Univ Of North Fl, Jacksonville, FL; JR; BA; Elem Educ.

**SIMS, KATHRYN C**, Memphis St Univ, Memphis, TN; JR; BFA; Gldn Key 90-; Gamma Beta Phi 88-; Intrnshp-Connie Hendrix/Assoc-Advrtsng; Acdmc Excllnc Schlrshp 88-; Art; Dsgn.

**SIMS, KEITH L**, Al St Univ, Montgomery, AL; FR; Phi Eta Sigma; Cmptr Sci/Math; Ed.

**SIMS, KRISTIN E**, Univ Of Cincinnati, Cincinnati, OH; JR; BMA; Opera Wrshp; Opera Chrs; Cnsrvtry Chrl; Frnkln Bens Vc Cmptn; Lawson Vc Schlrshp; Vcl Prfrmnc; Opera.

**SIMS JR, LEE C**, Lexington Comm Coll, Lexington, KY; SO; Hist Tutor; US Army; Hist; Clg Profsr/Bsktbl Coach.

**SIMS, LISA L**, Central St Univ, Wilberforce, OH; SR; BS; Stdnt Govt Assn Chf Jstc 88-89; Mrchng Bnd 90-; Stdnt Ambssdr 89-90; Beta Beta Beta Secy 88-89; Drug/Alcohol Prvntv Prog 90-; Original Rsrch 87-88; Psychology; Ind Psychologist.

**SIMS, LYNDA L**, Union Univ, Jackson, TN; FR; Baptist Student Union 90-; IM Tennis Sftbl 90-; Pre-Phsical Therapy; Physical Therapy.

**SIMS, MICHAEL W**, Franklin And Marshall Coll, Lancaster, PA; SO; BA; Bessie Smith Soc Sec 89-; Award Excellence In Physics At F&M; Music & Pre-Med; Musical Comp Or Medicine.

**SIMS, RACHEL D**, Tougaloo Coll, Tougaloo, MS; FR; BA; Pltcl Scnc Clb; Pltcl Scnc; Law.

**SIMS, RITA N**, Central Al Comm Coll, Alexander City, AL; SO; BA; Phi Theta Kappa VP 90; Erly Chldhd/Elem Educ.

**SIMS, SAN PIER MARIA**, Central St Univ, Wilberforce, OH; FR; BA; Dorm Cncl Rep 90-; Math; Ph D/Math Tchr.

**SIMS, SCOTTY L**, Central St Univ, Wilberforce, OH; JR; BS; Acctng Clb PR 90-; AICPA Schlrshp 90-; Dns Lst 89-; Acctng; CPA.

**SIMS, SHERRY**, Washington State Comm Coll, Marietta, OH; SO; CERT; Phi Theta Kappa 90-; Tiger Cub Orgnzr Cub Sct Pk 222 Waterford OH 90-; AAB Washington Tech Clg 79; Tch Aid Elmntry Schl.

**SIMS, VICKIE J**, Alcorn St Univ, Lorman, MS; SO; BED; Elem Ed; Tch.

**SIMS, WILLIAM B**, Valdosta St Coll, Valdosta, GA; FR; Bio; Med.

**SIMSICK, JENNIE L**, Univ Of Fl, Gainesville, FL; GD; Amer Moo Duk Kwan Soc Tae Kwao Do Sec 86-90; Amer Mrktng Assoc Gtr Hnt Cmmttee 90; Golden Key 87-90; AA 89-90; BS; Bsnss Mrktng; Info Syst Mngmnt.

**SIMSICK, JENNIFER D**, S U N Y Coll At Fredonia, Fredonia, NY; SO; BS; Clge Events Comm Ast Lectur Chairprsn 90-; Math; Teaching.

**SIMUTYTE, JURATE**, Bunker Hill Comm Coll, Boston, MA; SO; MS; BS Physics 89; Computer Sci; Sftwr Engrng.

**SINACORE, NICOLE**, Radford Univ, Radford, VA; SR; BBA; Acctg Soc 89-; Delta Mu Delta 89-; Phi Kappa Phi; Partial Schlrshp Becker CPA Review Course; Acctg; Auditing.

**SINCLAIR, CAREN L**, Cornell Univ Statutory College, Ithaca, NY; SR; BS; Eating Disord Preventn Org Awareness Cnslr 89-90; Italian Clb 90-; Golden Key 89-; Gamma Sigma Delta 90-; Ho-Nun-De-Kah 90-; Alpha Epsilon Phi Asst Scl Chr 88; CIVITAS Vol Tutor 87-88; Dns Lst 87-; Mktg/Publ Rels Intern 90; Mktg.

**SINCLAIR, KELLY J**, Univ Of South Al, Mobile, AL; SR; BS; Prsdnts Lst 88-89; Deans Lst 91; Phi Theta Kappa; AS 90; Erly Chldhd Ed.

**SINCLAIR, KIM L**, Ms Valley St Univ, Itta Bena, MS; FR; BED; Mrchng Bnd Sax Sctn Ldr Drm Mjr; Jazz Bnd Pianist; Symph Bnd Obeist; Tau Beta Sigma; Pres Lst; Hons Coll Pgm; Music Edctrs Ntl Conf VP St Chptr; Yth Enhncmnt Success YES Tutr; Chrch Mscn; Music Ed; Bnd Dir/Choir Dir/Prdcr.

**SINCLAIR, KIMBERLY R**, Tuskegee Univ, Tuskegee Inst, AL; FR; EE; Natl Soc Blck Engrs 90-; Soc Wmn Engrs 90-; Swthrt Ct Alpha Phi Alpha Frat 90-; At/T Bell Labs Trainee Intern; Eng.

**SINCLAIR, LESLIE RUSSELL**, Univ Of Sc At Union, Union, SC; FR; BS; Stu Govt; Sftbl; Elec Engr.

**SINCLAIR, MARC W**, Fl Atlantic Univ, Boca Raton, FL; GD; MBA; Phi Theta Kappa 87-; Phi Beta Lambda 87-89; Pi Lambda Phi 89-; Certif Acad Achvmnt 89; AA Palm Bch Jr Clg 88; BA 90; Finance; Stckbrkr/Lawyer.**

**SINCLAIR, NICOLE A**, Columbia Union Coll, Takoma Park, MD; SR; BA; Phi Eta Sigma 87-; Hstry.

**SINCLAIR, ROBERT G**, Va St Univ, Petersburg, VA; FR; BA; Bus Admin.

**SINCLAIR, SONDRA L**, Univ Of Sc At Columbia, Columbia, SC; SR; BA; Psychlgy; Spch Pthlgy.

**SINCLAIR, TAYLOR JAMES**, George Mason Univ, Fairfax, VA; SO; BS; Bus; Govt/Law.

**SINCOCK, ANN P**, Elmira Coll, Elmira, NY; SR; BS; Elem Ed; Tchr.

**SINDELAR, CORY JOSEPH**, Georgetown Univ, Washington, DC; SR; Beta Gamma Sigma; Delta Phi Epsilon 88-90; BS; BA; Accntng.

**SINDHOJ, ERIK B**, Itawamba Comm Coll, Fulton, MS; BS; Engr; Envrmntl.

**SINE, LAUREN E**, Coll Of Charleston, Charleston, SC; FR; BS; Alpha Delta Pi; Dist 1st Team; Math.

**SINE, REXANNA T**, Patrick Henry Comm Coll, Martinsville, VA; FR; AA; Non-Trad Stdnts Org; Bassett-Walker Knitting 80-90; Dislocated Wrkr; Blue Ridge Nrsg Ctr 90-; Nrsg Sci; RN/ONCLGY.

**SINES, BRIAN JAMES**, Anne Arundel Comm Coll, Arnold, MD; JR; BE; Biomed Engr.

**SINES, LYNN A,** Air Force Inst Of Tech, Wrt-Ptrsn Afb, OH; GD; BS; SG Asst Sectn Ldr 90-; Sigma Iota Epsilon 90-; Bwlng/Sftbl; Air Force Assoc 84-; IEEE 80-; Cptn USAF; BS Purdue Univ 83; Sys Mgt; Prog Mgt.

**SINEY, JOHN A,** Salisbury St Univ, Salisbury, MD; SR; BS; AMA 90-; FMA 89-90; Phi Beta Lambda Fndrsng Chrm 87-89; Delta Mu Delta 89-; Sigma Alpha Epsilon VP 89-; Hnrs Prog 88-; Intern Dwntwn Salisbury Rvtlztn Offc 90-; IM Ftbl Vllybl Sftbl Bsketbl; Bus Mngmnt; Mngmnt Cnsltnt.

**SINGDAHLSEN, PAUL,** Ringling School Of Art, Sarasota, FL; JR; BFA; Pres Lst 90; Rnglng Awd Annl Juried Show 91; Fine Art.

**SINGER, AMY L,** Philadelphia Coll Pharm & Sci, Philadelphia, PA; SR; BS; Acad Stdnts Pharm Sec 87-; Intrnl Pharm Stdnts Fed Cntct US 89-; Kinsessing Sngrs 86-90; Rho Pi Phi Chplin 90-; Adpt Grndprnt 86-88f Tch Asst; Pharm.

**SINGER, DOROTHY,** Ny Univ, New York, NY; SR; BA; Scl Sci; Educ.

**SINGER, MELISSA C,** Univ Of Md Baltimore Prof Schl, Baltimore, MD; JR; BS; AA Villa Julie Coll 88; Med/Rsrch Tech; Lab Scientist.

**SINGFIEL, JEFFREY JAMES,** Toccoa Falls Coll, Toccoa Falls, GA; SR; Stdnt Govt Officers Pres 89-90; Sch Nwspar Staff Writer 88-90; Yrbk Phtgrphr 90; Delta Epsilon K 90-; Varsity Chrldng 89-; BA 87-; Missology; Career Missionary.

**SINGH, DEVADA,** Long Island Univ Brooklyn Cntr, Brooklyn, NY; FR; BS; Hon Vlybl Tm; Hon Pgm; Phrmcy The Sciences.

**SINGH, GURMEET,** City Univ Of Ny Queensbrough, New York, NY; FR; BSC; Cmptr Clb 90; Deans Lst 90; Indian Soc 90; Acctg.

**SINGH, HARRY P,** City Univ Of Ny City Coll, New York, NY; SR; BS; NYC Technlgy Ed Assoc; AAS Ofst Tech NYC Technel Clg 88; Technlgy Ed; Tchr.

**SINGH, JASPREET,** George Mason Univ, Fairfax, VA; JR; BS; Desc Mis; Systems Analyst.

**SINGH, MANJU,** S U N Y At Buffalo, Buffalo, NY; SO; BSN; Nrsng.

**SINGH, MICHAEL N,** Columbia Union Coll, Takoma Park, MD; SR; BA/BS; Pre-Med Soc 87-; Top Stdnt 90-; AA 89; Blgy/Mgmt; Med.

**SINGH, MOHANI D,** City Univ Of Ny Baruch Coll, New York, NY; SR; BBA; Beta Alpha Psi Intrntl Clb; Gldn Key; Beta Gamma Sigma; Beta Alpha Psi; Acctng; CPA MBA.

**SINGH, RAJINDER K,** Univ Of Cin R Walters Coll, Blue Ash, OH; SO; Rdtn Tech.

**SINGH, SARAH H,** East Carolina Univ, Greenville, NC; FR; BFA; Vsl Arts Comm 90-; E Carolina 90-; ECU Peace Grp; Exhbtr ECU Rebel Art Show; Exhbtr ECU Undrgrad Show; Exhbtr Stdnt Un Ninvtnl Show; Chnclrs List 90; Chncllrs Acad Excllnc Art List; Art.

**SINGH, SHARMILA,** City Univ Of Ny Baruch Coll, New York, NY; SR; BA; Soc Mgmt Acctnts ON; Ofc Coll Rltns Vol 88-90; Acctg.

**SINGH, VIPAN,** Univ Of Rochester, Rochester, NY; SR; BA; Dean Lst 88-; Pblc Dfnds Intern 90; Stu Intern Harris Evans Fox Chesworth; Cert Mngmnt Stu; Pol Sci; JD Law Schl.

**SINGHAS, CAMERON A,** Lenoir Rhyne Coll, Hickory, NC; SO; BA; Engrng Century Furniture Co; Comm; Pub Rltns.

**SINGLETARY, DESI A,** Johnson C Smith Univ, Charlotte, NC; SR; BS; Elctrnc/Cmptr Clb Pres 90-; Trck/Fld Crss Cntry Capt 86-90; Res Lf Jdcry Brd/Senator 88-90; US Dept Cmmrc 90; Trck/Fld Crop Walk NYSP; BS Johnson C Smith Univ; Cmptr Sftwr/Engr.

**SINGLETARY, SAM H,** Roane St Comm Coll, Harriman, TN; SO; BA; Deans Lst Roane St Comm Coll; Full-Tm Main Eng; Pre-Eng/Arch; Arch/Eng 2nd Degree.

**SINGLETERRY, JANET D,** Univ Of South Al, Mobile, AL; SR; BS; Ed/Erly Chldhd; Tchng.

**SINGLETON, ANGELA DENISE,** Univ Of Md Balt Cnty Campus, Catonsville, MD; FR; BS; Spnsh Clb 90-; Kappa Alpha Psi Aux; Biochmstry; Medicine.

**SINGLETON, BARBARA,** Cumberland County Coll, Vineland, NJ; SO; AAS; Afri/Amer Culture Clb Sec; Lorene Snider Schlrshp Fund Comm 90-; Blck Stdnts Un 90; Talent Roster Outstdndg Minority Grads 90-; Pres Lst 90; Deans Lst 90; Cmbrlnd Cnty Guidance Ctr Intrnshp 90; Spvsr Dvlpmntl Ctr 76-88; Comm Serv/Soc Wrk; Wrk/W Abused Victims.

**SINGLETON, BARRY J,** Univ Of Al At Birmingham, Birmingham, AL; JR; BA; Phi Sigma Kappa 87-88; Enlg; Prof.

**SINGLETON, BRIAN T,** Emory & Henry Coll, Emory, VA; FR; BA; Rcvd Frshmn E/H Chmstry Awd; Chmstry.

**SINGLETON, CANDICE E,** Christopher Newport Coll, Newport News, VA; SR; MBA; Krt Clb 85-87; SVEA 90-; Psychlgy Clb 86-87; Bg Brthr Bg Sstr 90-; BA; Erly Chldhd Ed; Tchng.

**SINGLETON, CHEREESE S,** City Univ Of Ny Baruch Coll, New York, NY; SR; BA; Stdnt Cntr Prgm Brd Chrprsn Cncrt Shwcs Srs 88-; J B Cmblnd Assoc Ja Acct Exec; Speech.

**SINGLETON, DEBBIE L,** Central Al Comm Coll, Alexander City, AL; FR; MBA; Pine Level Vol Fire Dept Fire Frfghtr 85-; Cert Vol Fire Fgtr AL State Fire Clg 89; Cert First Response SE AL Emrgncy Med Serv Inc 87; Psychlgy/Crmnl Justice; Crmnl Jstc/Prsn Systm.

**SINGLETON III, HARRY H,** Interdenominational Theo Ctr, Atlanta, GA; GD; MDIV; Stdnt Grvnc Comm Chrmn 87-88; Athltc Advsry Comm Stdnt Rep 87-88; Ntnl Assn Advncmnt Clrd People USC Brd Drctr 87-88; Otstndng Clg Stdnt Amrca 88; Kappa Alpha Psi 86-; Prsdnts Sprltv Lst; Deans Lst; BS Unvrsty 88; Theology; Tchr Lctr.

**SINGLETON, JAMES V,** Univ Of Southern Ms, Hattiesburg, MS; JR; BA; VCA 88-; Natl Hnrs Scty 90-; Pres Lst; Deans Lst; Ftbll 88-; Mchncl Eng Tch.

**SINGLETON, JULIE L,** Fl A & M Univ, Tallahassee, FL; SR; BS; Mrchng 100 Asst Sctn Ldr 88-90; Symphnc Bnd Prncpl Flutist 87-; Flute Choir 1st Flute 87-; Music Edctrs Natl Conf 88-90; Alpha Kappa Alpha 89; AA Prince Geo Comm Coll 87; Music Educ; Tchr.

**SINGLETON, KIMBERLY D,** Ms St Univ, Miss State, MS; SO; BPA; Gamma Beta Phi 90-; Deans Lst 90-; Acctg; CPA.

**SINGLETON, LAURA J,** Univ Of South Fl, Tampa, FL; FR; MBA; Litrry Magz Stff; Engl; Educ.

**SINGLETON, LEAH A,** Univ Of Nc At Asheville, Asheville, NC; JR; BA; Bsns; Accntng.

**SINGLETON, LEIGH A,** Le Moyne Coll, Syracuse, NY; SO; BA; Cmps Mnstry Stdnt Vol 90-; Cmps Vol Tr Gd 90-; Lctr Mss; Hstry; Bnkng Law Edctn.

**SINGLETON, MELANIE J,** Univ Of Al At Birmingham, Birmingham, AL; FR; BSN; Alpha Lambda Delta; Nrsng.

**SINGLETON, MICHAEL J,** Southern Coll Of Tech, Marietta, GA; FR; BA; Math; Cvl Engnrng.

**SINGLETON, PAMELA J,** Air Force Inst Of Tech, Wrt-Ptrsn Afb, OH; GD; Alpha Kappa Alpha 81-; Sigma Iota Epsilon 90; USAF Capt 83-; MS Univ SC 82; Anlys/MA; Air Frce.

**SINGLETON, PHYLLIS L,** Alcorn St Univ, Lorman, MS; SR; Biology; Physical Therapist.

**SINGLETON, RHONDA B,** Mobile Coll, Mobile, AL; GD; BA; Alpha Chi 90-; Kappa Delta Epsilon; Biology; Edctn.

**SINGLETON, SERVELL,** Univ Of Md At Eastern Shore, Princess Anne, MD; JR; BA; Bsn Mgmt; Sml Bsn.

**SINGLETON, STEVEN T,** Morehouse Coll, Atlanta, GA; SO; BA; Cltrl Asc Pres; Pre-Law Soc; Pol Sci Soc; Spnsh Clb; Clg Nwspr; Engl Clb; Sigma Tau Delta Sec; NAACP; Amnsty Intl; Boys Clb; Brailsford R Brazeal End Schlp; Hnr Lst; Engl; Law.

**SINGLETON JR, THOMAS J,** Catholic Univ Of America, Washington, DC; JR; BA; Phlsphy Clb Pres 90; Univ Ctr Brd 90; Clg Bwl 89; Phi Eta Sigma 88; Phi Sigma Tau Pres 90; Phlsphy; Clg Prof.

**SINGLETON, TIMOTHY D,** Univ Of Sc At Columbia, Columbia, SC; SO; BS; AS Univ SC-LANCSTR; Comp Sci.

**SINGLEY, AMY J,** Livingston Univ, Livingston, AL; SR; BS; Dance Line 88; Alpha Chi; Sigma Tau Delta 90-; Kelly Land Wrtng Schlrshp 88; Tucker Wrtng Awrd 90; English.

**SINGLEY, JULIE R,** Livingston Univ, Livingston, AL; SR; BA; IM Sftbl 90-; Delta Sigma Pi 90-; Busn Mktng.

**SINK, JOHN S,** Univ Of Nc At Charlotte, Charlotte, NC; JR; BA; Crtv Arts Leag 89-; By Scts Amer Asst Sct Mstr 87-88; Russell Agncy; Crss Cntry/Trck 88-; Vsl Arts; Grphc Artst.

**SINK JR, JOSEPH D,** Univ Of Tn At Knoxville, Knoxville, TN; SO; BSBA; Exec Undrgrdt Pgm; Bus Stdnts Advsry Cncl Deans 90-; Spcl Advsry Cncl Dean; Phi Eta Sigma; Alpha Lambda Delta; Alum Uppercls Schlrshp 90-; Acctng/Bus Law Schlrshp 90-; Acctng/German; Intl Tax.**

**SINKFIELD, RENEE S,** Va St Univ, Petersburg, VA; SR; BA; Jdcl Afrs Comm Chrprsn 87-; Yrbk Stf Edtr 87-; Chptr NAACP Cmt Chr 87-; Deans List 89-; Goddard Riverside Options Pgm 87-; Cncl Ec Priorities 90; Pblc Admn; Law Entrtnmnt/Corp.

**SINKLER, STEPHANIE,** Va St Univ, Petersburg, VA; JR; BS; Sr RA 90-; Dorm Cab Sec 88-89; Acctng Clb 88-89; Pr Acad Excel Pin 90-; Acctng; CPA.

**SINN, PAMELA R,** Univ Of Akron, Akron, OH; SO; BA; Hnrs Clb 89-; Symphny Orch 89-; Symphnc Wnd Ens 89-; Phi Eta Sigma 89-; Alpha Lambda Delta 89-; Hnrs Prog 89-; Music; Music Prfrmnc.**

**SINN, TIMOTHY G,** Defiance Coll, Defiance, OH; JR; BA; Stdnt Snte; Acctg/Fin Clb Pres 90-; Tau Pi Phi; Alpha Chi; Theta Xi; Kappa Nu Chapt Treas 90-; Pres Host; Acctg.

**SINNER, SCOTT W,** Franklin And Marshall Coll, Lancaster, PA; FR; BA; Premed Soc 90-; Amnsty Intl 90-; Hnrs Lst 90-; Fres Chem Achvmnt Awrd 90-; Flying Disc Soc 90-; Biol; Med.

**SINNETT, TANYA D,** Wv Univ At Parkersburg, Parkersburg, WV; SO; BED; Phi Eta Sigma 89-90; Elem Ed; Public Schl Edtr.

**SINSLEY, KATE GABRIELLE,** Hillsborough Comm Coll, Tampa, FL; SO; BA; Gratz Coll H S Bd 89-91; D A Elctn Cmpgn Jdg Cmpgn Asst 90; Pblc Accss TV Gldn Csstt Awds Hstss 90; Clthng/Toy Dntns St Josephs Hosp 90; Phone-A-Thon Tampa Jwsh Fdrtn 89; Chrty Symphny Clssc Run Maison Blnch 88; Brdcst Jrnlsm; Prdctn.

**SINT-JACOBS, LIONEL E,** Antillian Adventist University, Mayaguez, PR; BS; Mnstrl Clb Prchr 84-85; Clpltr Clb Treas 86; SDA Chrch Cher-Asile Treas 88-89; SDA Cnfrnc/Bkkpr 87; Advnt Bk/Hlth Cntr/Gnrl Mngr 88-89; AS/BUS Admin Advntst Univ Colombia 86; Acctg; CPA.

**SIOBERG, ANDREW W,** Radford Univ, Radford, VA; FR; BS; Concert Band 90-; Wind Ensemble 90-; Jazz Ensemble 90-; Combo 90-; Brass Quintet 90-; Nutcracker Orchestra/Virginia Intrcoll Bnd 90-; Pep Band 90-; Alpha Lambda Delta; Phi Mu Alpha Sinfonia; Otstndng Stdnt Awd Schlrshp Ldrshp Srvc 90-; Music; Coll Instrctr Prof Mscn.

**SIPE, LEE B,** Oh St Univ At Newark, Newark, OH; FR; BS; Phi Eta Sigma; Alpha Lambda Delta; IM 90; 1600 Communications Asn Inc 90-; Air Natl Gd 90-; Elec; Engr.

**SIPE, MELISSA A,** East Tn St Univ, Johnson City, TN; JR; BS; Stdnt Natl Envrnmntl Hlth Assoc VP 90-; Phi Kappa Phi; Gamma Beta Phi; Fclty Awd/Excllnc Env Hlth Dept; Costep Offcr/Ind Hlth Srvc; AS 90; Envrnmntl Hlth.

**SIPE, TARA-LEE M,** Shippensburg Univ, Shippensburg, PA; SO; BSED; Hon Pgm 90-; Phi Sgm Pi Almn Co Chr; Math; Tchng.**

**SIPES, STEPHANIE D,** Comm Coll Algny Co Algny Cmps, Pittsburgh, PA; FR; BA; Engl; Law.

**SIPOS, ADAM C,** Fl St Univ, Tallahassee, FL; FR; BMP; FL PIRG Prtcpts In Mtngs 90-; Sccr 90-; Wslyn Fndtn 90-; Clsscl Gtr; Msc Prfrmnce.

**SIPPERLY, HOLLY M,** Hudson Valley Comm Coll, Troy, NY; AAS; Erly Chldhd; Elem Tchr.

**SIPPLE, MARTHA CLARE,** Univ Of Ky, Lexington, KY; SR; BS; Amer Scty Lndscpe Archtcts Treas; Wbb Archlgcl Scty 87-; Gldn Ky 89-; Kappa Delta; Anthrplgy Lndscpe Archtctre; Lndscpe Archtcte.

**SIRAJ, SALAH M,** City Univ Of Ny Baruch Coll, New York, NY; GD; BBA 89; Comp Info Syst; Grad Schl.

**SIRBAUGH, ELIZABETH L,** Wv Univ, Morgantown, WV; JR; BSJ; Pblc Rltns Stdnt Scty Amrc Natl Lsn Offcr; Gldn Key; Kappa Tau Alpha; Pi Beta Phi; Pblc Rltns.

**SIREN, WILLIAM E,** Nova Univ, Ft Lauderdale, FL; GD; MBA; Natl Hnr Soc 90; FL Hosp Assoc 89-; Dir/Indstrl/Prvntv Med Cape Cnvrl Hosp 89-; BS Atlantic Chrstn Clg 85; MSS United States 86; Bus Admin; Hosp.

**SIRJU, ANJANIE R,** City Univ Of Ny Baruch Coll, New York, NY; SO; BBA; Stdnt Peer Ldr 89-; Deans List 89-90; Acctng; Taxatn.

**SIRMANS, MICHELE R,** Meredith Coll, Raleigh, NC; FR; BA; Spnsh Clb 90-; Mrdth Chrstn Asc 90-; Gvnr Mrhd Schl 90-; Phlrtn Soc; Spnsh; Educ.

**SIRN, ROBERT A,** Univ Of Akron, Akron, OH; GD; BEA; Schl Paper Ohio St Ed Chf 86-87; S Cmps Stdnt Assoc Treas 85-86; Amer Mktg Assoc 86-87; BSBA Ohio St Univ 87; Graphic Dsgn; Advrtsg.

**SIROIS, DENISE M,** Teikyo Post Univ, Waterbury, CT; JR; BS; Alpha Chi; CT Scty CPA Schlrshp Awrd; Excllnc Math Awrd; Max R Traurig Prz 90; Trsts Schlrshp 90; Acctg; CPA.**

**SIROTNAK, TANYA M,** Fairleigh Dickinson Univ, Teaneck, NJ; FR; BS; Interclgte Fld Hockey 90; IM Flr Hockey 90; Pres Schlrshp 90-; Bsn Mgmt; Bsn.

**SIROWITZ, ROBERT MARK,** Comm Coll Algny Co Algny Cmps, Pittsburgh, PA; SO; Chess Clb; Bus Mktg.

**SISCO, SANDRA K,** Univ Of Tn At Knoxville, Knoxville, TN; JR; BS; Beta Gamma Sigma; Dupont Schlrshp; Accntng Offcmngr 77-; AS Motlow St Comm Clg 76; Accntng Cmptr Sci; Tchr.

**SISK, CHARLES W,** Gaston Coll, Dallas, NC; AA; Bus; Bnkng Fnnc.

**SISK, MICKALA L,** Memphis St Univ, Memphis, TN; JR; BA; STEA; Kappa Delta Pi; Elem Ed; Tchg.

**SISK, PATRICIA H,** Cecils Coll, Asheville, NC; FR; AAS; Law.

**SISK, SUSAN J,** Union Univ, Jackson, TN; JR; BS; Flwshp Chrstn Athlts V P 89-90; Stdnts Fndtns; Bapt Stdnt Un; Alpha Chi; Prexy Club; Sigma Zeta; Chi Omega Prsnl Pres 89-90; Spec Olympcs; Hmcmng Ct; Deans List; Tennis; Bio; Phys Thrpst.

**SISKIND, STEVEN M,** Univ Of Rochester, Rochester, NY; SO; BA; Symph Orch 89-; Chi Phi 89-; Econ.

**SISLEY, LISA J,** Fl International Univ, Miami, FL; SO; BA; Phi Eta Sigma 90-; Delta Phi Epsilon 90-; Fclty Schlrshp 89-; FL Undergrad Schlrshp; Fclty Schlr Comp Lab Mntr 89-; Comp Sci.

**SISNEY, JENNIFER ROBIN,** Bob Jones Univ, Greenville, SC; FR; BED; Wrk Schlrshp Ldrshp Cncl 90-; Chi Epsilon Sigma Sec; Nursing Hm Ext 90-; Sftbl 90-; Educ; Missionary.

**SISODIA, TEERESA,** Univ Of Miami, Coral Gables, FL; JR; BS; Bdmntn Clb Pres 90-; Cncl Intl Stdnts Athltc Dir 88; Alpha Epsilon Delta; Gldn Key 90-; Hon Stdnts Assn 88; Deans Lst; Pres Lst 88; Blgy; Med.

**SISON, ANNA M,** Univ Of Nc At Charlotte, Charlotte, NC; JR; BA; Soc Hmn Res Mgnt Stdnt Chapt/Natl Mbr 90-; Psi Chi; IM Tennis; Psych.

**SISSON, DONNA J,** Meridian Comm Coll, Meridian, MS; SO; AA; Phi Theta Kappa; Chorus; Northrup Chpl Asst Pinst; 4-H Snlv Clb 90; Cert; Bus/Ofc Tech.

**SISSON, IRVIN C,** Embry Riddle Aeronautical Univ, Daytona Beach, FL; GD; BS; FCC Gen Rdio/Tele Oper Lscns/RETS Elec Schls/Prtcl Eletrncs Svcng 76; AS 81; Avncs/Arntcs; Comm Pilot.

**SISSON, LESLIE D,** Wv Univ, Morgantown, WV; JR; BS; Hlth Cr Opptnty Prog 88-; Ordr Grail 90-; Gldn Ky 90-; B Anderson Schlrshp 88-89; Pharm.

**SISTARE, JON F,** North Greenville Coll, Tigerville, SC; SO; BA; SGA; Nwspr Ed IM/BAND; Phi Theta Kappa/Pres Club/ Hnrs Prog; J Lacey Mc Lean Schlrshp; Pres Schlrshp; Gen Excllnc Awd; AA; Psych; Minister.

**SIT, SANNI,** City Univ Of Ny Baruch Coll, New York, NY; JR; BBA; Gldn Key 90-; Deans Lst 88-90; Mgmt; Oprtns Mgmt.

**SITAFALWALLA, SUHAIL,** S U N Y Coll Of Tech At Frmgdl, Farmingdale, NY; SO; AAS; IEEE; Cmptr Ad Dsgn; Physcs; Engrg.

**SITARAM, KRISHNA D,** City Univ Of Ny Queensbrough, New York, NY; SO; IEEE 90-; Tabl Tns 90-; Elctrncs; Engnrng.

**SITARAM, MAHENDRADAT,** City Univ Of Ny Queensbrough, New York, NY; SR; BA; Archt Clb Pres 89-90; AAS; Archt.

**SITAREK, PEGGY L,** Daemen Coll, Amherst, NY; SO; BS; Bus Clb 90-; Acctg; CPA.

**SITES, SANDRA S,** Davis & Elkins Coll, Elkins, WV; SR; BA; SEA 90-; PTO Treas 87-; Seneca Rks Presbytrn Chrch; Elem Ed; Tchr.

**SITHEBE, SIBONGILE,** City Univ Of Ny City Coll, New York, NY; GD; MA; So Afrcn Stdnt Org Treas 87-88; Fr Hon Soc; Psych Hon; Psych; Clncl Psychlgst.

**SITLER, STEFANIE DIANE,** Endicott Coll, Beverly, MA; SO; ASSOC; Clb Couture 90-; Vrsty Clb 90-; Phi Theta Kappa Treas 90-; Peer Tutor; Sftbl 90-; Splmntry Instrctr 90-; Co-Dsgnr Patrn Drftr New Unfrms Schl Chrs 90; Fashn Dsgn; 4 Yr Coll.

**SITTEL, CHRISTOPHER L,** Memphis Academy Of The Arts, Memphis, TN; SR; BFA; Painting.

**SITTERSON, KATHERINE E,** Univ Of North Fl, Jacksonville, FL; JR; BA; Hldy Hil Excl; Lv Grv Elem 89-90; AA FL Cmmnty Coll; Spcl Ed; Tchng.

**SITTINERI, ROBERT A,** Atlantic Comm Coll, Mays Landing, NJ; SO; BA; Bus Admin; Acctng.

**SITZMAN, PETER J,** Univ Of Rochester, Rochester, NY; SR; BA; Delta Sigma Phi Secy 87-; Studio Arts; MFA Wildlf Photogrphy.

**SIU, LAI MEI,** City Univ Of Ny Baruch Coll, New York, NY; JR; BBA; Acctng Soc 88-.

**SIUTA, MARK A,** S U N Y At Buffalo, Buffalo, NY; SR; BS; IEEE 89-; Dns Lst; Eagle Sct; WNY Indy Intshp; Elec/Cmptr Engr; Eleg Engr.

**SIVALI, VANVISA,** Univ Of Md Balt Cnty Campus, Catonsville, MD; FR; BS; Hon Stdnt Assn 90; Spkr Flr Comm Susquhnna Hall 90; Hstng Prspctv UMBC Stdnts; Rsrch Intrnshp Psychlgy Dept 90; Hon Coll Fllwshp 90-; Biolgcl Sci; Med/Pediatrcs.

**SIVANDZADEH, SHAHRZAD,** Hillsborough Comm Coll, Tampa, FL; JR; BS; Clinical Chem; Dctr.

**SIVAPRAKASAM, SANTHI,** Hillsborough Comm Coll, Tampa, FL; SO; BS; Med.

**SIVILLO, JOEL K,** Allegheny Coll, Meadville, PA; SO; BS; Lambda Sigma Hon Soc 90-; Delta Tau Delta Chptr Cnslr 90-; Alden Schlr 89-90; Schlstc Hnrs Initiate 90; Physcis/Eng; Eng.

**SIX, JANET M,** Marshall University, Huntington, WV; FR; BBA; Cmps Entrtnmnt Unlmntd; Res Hall Assc 90-; Management.

**SIX, JEFFREY M,** Univ Of Akron, Akron, OH; JR; BS; Acctg; Adtr.

**SIZEMORE, JORG F,** Ms St Univ, Miss State, MS; FR; BS; ASME 90-; Gamma Beta Phi 90-; Phi Eta Sigma 90-; Alpha Lambda Delta90-; Prsdnts Lst; Prsdnts Univ Schlrshp 90-; Chevron Schlrshp 90-; Eng; Mchncl Eng.

**SIZEMORE, MELISSA SUBLETT,** Univ Of Tn At Knoxville, Knoxville, TN; SR; BS; Exec Undgrdts 90-; Beta Gamma Sigma; Jr Lg Hstrn 87-90; Mktg.

**SIZEMORE, SHELLEY R,** Western Carolina Univ, Cullowhee, NC; JR; Mrchg Bnd 89-; Cncrt Chr 90-; Pep Bnd 89-; Symphny Bnd 90-; Sigma Tau Delta 90-; Tau Beta Sigma 89-; Engl; Ed.**

**SIZEMORE, TOM L,** Abraham Baldwin Agri Coll, Tifton, GA; SO; BA; FFA Cllgt 89-; Bptst Stdnt Union 90; Hon Stdnt 89-; Agri Major Awd; Agri; Agri Ecnmcs.

**SIZEMORE, VICKY L,** Central Fl Comm Coll, Ocala, FL; FR; AA; Cert Acct/Data Proc Webstr Clg 90; Acctg.

**SIZER, DEBRA LYNN,** Springfield Tech Comm Coll, Springfield, MA; SR; AAS; Alpha Nu Omega 89-; Wrd Prcssng; BS.

**SIZER, SUZANNE C,** Smith Coll, Northampton, MA; GD; JD; Wmns Law Coaltn Co-Chmn 90-; Cornell Law Outrch PR Dir 90-; Publ Interest Law Union 90-; Cum Laude 90; Displ Homekrs Lgl Adv 90-; Rape Crisis Coun 90-; Moot Ct Awd; Legal Aid Clin; St Repr Campgn 88; Hon Thesis; Law.

**SKAAR, ALICE D,** Converse Coll, Spartanburg, SC; FR; BMUS; Spartanburg Symphony 90-; Alpha Lambda Delta; Delta Omicron; Msc Comp; Msc.

**SKAGGS, CHRISTOPHER C,** Wv Univ, Morgantown, WV; SR; BA; ASP; Gold Key 89-; Phi Kappa Phi 89-; Rho Chi 90-; Phmcy; Med.

**SKAGGS, CYNTHIA M,** Marshall University, Huntington, WV; SR; BA; Acctg; CPA.

**SKAGGS, LEONDA L,** Oh Univ-Southern Cmps, Ironton, OH; JR; ASN; Nrsng; RN/HLTH Adminstrtr.

**SKAGGS JR, MICHAEL E,** Western Ky Univ, Bowling Green, KY; FR; BS; Blck Brdl Clb 90-; Rgnts Schlrshp 90-; Vet Med.

**SKAGGS, ROBERT D,** Shawnee St Univ, Portsmouth, OH; FR; BS; Phi Theta Kappa 90-; Math/Ntrl Sci.

**SKALECKI, MARGAUX A,** The Boston Conservatory, Boston, MA; SR; BFA; Dance; MA Dance/Healing.

**SKALL, ROBERT J,** Radford Univ, Radford, VA; SR; BS; Speech/Sprt.

**SKARUPSKI, MICHELE L,** Allegheny Coll, Meadville, PA; JR; BA; Lit Rvw Edtrl Brd 90-; Stdnt Orientatn Advsr 90-; Alpha Gamma Delta Rec Sec 89-; S D Turk Schlr 89-; Dstngshd Aldn Schlr 89-; Intrnshp Cngrssmn Offce 90-; Hstry; Tchr Coll Lvl.

**SKEATH, KATHRYN K,** Anne Arundel Comm Coll, Arnold, MD; JR; BA; SG V P 89-90; GAMMA 89-90; Delta Gamma 89-; Hstry.

**SKEEN, CYNTHIA L,** Toccoa Falls Coll, Toccoa Falls, GA; SR; Toccoa Lfe Htln 88-90; Good Nws Clb 88; Cmps Kds 87; Summa Cum Laude 90; Tchr 84-87; Sec Bkkpr 87-; AA Maranatha Bptst Bible Clge 79; BS 90; Tchg.

**SKEEN, JAMES W,** Toccoa Falls Coll, Toccoa Falls, GA; SR; Alto Prison Bible Stdy 87-90; Outstndg Yng Men Amer 88; Phlsphy/Rlgn Award 88; BA Summa Cum Laude 90; Wis Crrctnl Offcr Srgnt 79-87; BA 90; AA Milwaukee Area Tech Clg 79; Chrstn Cnslng.

**SKEEN, PAULINE M,** Wv Univ At Parkersburg, Parkersburg, WV; FR; AB; Nrsng.

**SKEENS, JOE G,** Univ Of Fl, Gainesville, FL; GD; JD; Spec Olymp 89-90; Nrsng Hom Vstn/Grdng Coord 90; Chrch Rcylng Pgm Coord; BSBA 90; AA Santa Fe Comm Coll 88; AS Abraham Baldwin Agri Coll 86; Mktg Ltgtn JD; Law.

**SKEENS JR, RICHARD W,** Radford Univ, Radford, VA; JR; BBA; Bus Mgmt; Hum Rsrc Mgt.

**SKEETE, DAVID N,** City Univ Of Ny Baruch Coll, New York, NY; SR; BBA; Beta Alpha Psi 89-; NABA 88-; Gldn Key 89-; BBA Baruch Clg; Acctg; CPA.

**SKEETE, KURT A,** City Univ Of Ny Baruch Coll, New York, NY; SR; BBA; Evening Stdnt Govt Pres 90-; BLACK; Gold Key; Sigma Alpha Delta Baruch Chapt; Econ; Law.

**SKEETERS, JAMES R,** Univ Of Louisville, Louisville, KY; JR; BS; DPMA Pres 90-; Nom Mrtr Bd; O Cooprtv Intrnshps; Dns Lst; IM; Info Sci/Data Prcsng; Cmptr Systs Engr Anlst.

**SKELL, LYNNE A,** Bloomfield Coll, Bloomfield, NJ; SR; BS; Alpha Chi 90-; Deans Lst Hgh Hon 88-; Gnrl Merch Coord/Asst Mngr Follett Coll Store; Bus Admin; Law.

**SKELLENGER, GRANT C,** Central Wesleyan Coll, Central, SC; SR; BA; Stdtn Mssns Fllwshp Pres 90-; Clss Offcr VP 89-; Alpha Chi 90; Chrstn Srvc Org 88-; Mjr Hnrs Englsh Rlgn 90; Bbl Stdnt Yr 90-; Engl Rlgn; Mssnry.

**SKELLY, TIMOTHY P,** Mount Saint Mary Coll, Newburgh, NY; SO; BA; Cls Pres; Ambsdrs Clb; Baachus; Prsdntl Schlrshp; Mth/Cmptr Sci; Engnrng/Prgrmr.

**SKELTON, CHRISTOPHER S,** Brewer St Jr Coll, Fayette, AL; SO; BE; Deans Lst; Prsdnt Lst; Elctrcl Engnrng.

**SKELTON, JILL N,** Itawamba Comm Coll, Fulton, MS; FR; BA; Phi Theta Kappa 90-; Paralegal Tchnlgy; Law.

**SKELTON, MARTA I,** Univ Of Al At Birmingham, Birmingham, AL; JR; BS; Amer Asc Crtcl Care Nrs 75-; Onclgy Nrs Soc 84-; Cpstn Nrs Soc 85-86; Sigma Theta Tau 81-; Key Clb Soc 86-; AL St Nrs Asc Dist 75-; Clncl Nrs Spec 86-; AL St Nrs Anstts Std; BSN Univ AL Tsclsa 82; MSN Trauma 86; Anesthesia; RN.

**SKELTON, THOMAS HENRY,** Northeast State Tech Comm Coll, Blountville, TN; GD; ADDA; Vol EMT IV Tchncn Church Hill EMS; Bd Mbr CHRS; AAS Nestcc 91; Cert EMT IV NESTCC 90; Drftng; Dsgn Tech.

**SKERRIT, MARIE E,** Castleton St Coll, Castleton, VT; SO; BSED; Drama Clb Treas 89-; Theater Arts Asst Stage Mgr 89-; Phi Eta Sigma; Orientation Coord 90-; Outstndg Fr Awd 89-; Fr Theater Awd 89-90; Deans Lst 89-90; Hon Hse 90-; Engl Lit/ Theater Arts; High Sch Tchr/Profr.

**SKIADAS, POTOULA,** Fl International Univ, Miami, FL; SR; BS; FL Pblc Intrst Rsrch Grp 89-90; Stdnt Assn Envrnmnt 89-90; Psi Chi; Phi Theta Kappa Pblctns Dir 88-89; IM Bsktbl Tm 88; AA Miami-Dade Comm Coll 89; Psych; Cnslr Ed Grad Pgm.

**SKIDMORE, BOBBIE D,** Immaculata Coll, Immaculata, PA; SO; Ed Clb 89-; Psychlgy Clb 89-; Intrclgte Tns 89-; BA Psychlgy; Elem Ed/Gdnc Cnslng.

**SKIDMORE, KAREN L,** Wv Univ, Morgantown, WV; SO; BA; Schlrs Pgm 89-90; Beta Beta Beta 90-; Frshmn Schlrshp 89-90; Ldrshp Hnrs 89-90; Lowell E Ball Sci Schlrshp 89-90; Blgy/Pre Med; Ped Med/Surg.**

**SKIDMORE, STEPHEN W,** Northeast State Tech Comm Coll, Blountville, TN; FR; AD; US Army Sgt 82-86; Auto Mechanic 86-90; Hlth Sci; Nrsng.

**SKIFF, WILLIAM O,** Hudson Valley Comm Coll, Troy, NY; FR; AAS; Cabinetmaker Shop Frmn MMC Custom Millwork; BM Crane Schl Music 77; Computer Info Syst; Programmer Syst Analyst.

**SKILES, KRISTEN J,** The Boston Conservatory, Boston, MA; JR; BFA; Stdnt Svc Office Asst Prgmr 90-; Cmnty Thtr Prdctns Ld Mscns 87/89; Educ Svc Assist Prgr 90-; Vocal Coaching 86-90; Dramatic Coaching 87-90; Schlrshp 90-; Assistantship 90-; Musical Thtr; Perf.

**SKIMDMORE, NANCY A,** Villanova Univ, Villanova, PA; SR; BA; Std Govt 87-88; Mntly Rtrd Fndrsrs 88-; Cystc Fbrs Fndrsrs 88-; Alpha Chi Omega 88-; Outstdng Clg Std Amer 87-; WCAU Intshp; IM Ftbl 88-89; Comm Arts; Tlvsn Brdcstng.

**SKINNELL, CORRIE L,** Winthrop Coll, Rock Hill, SC; FR; Cncl For Excptnl Chldrn 90-; Big Bro/Big Sis 90-; Alpha Lambda Delta 90-; Spec Olympics 90-; Spec Edn Teacher.

**SKINNER, DANIEL E,** S U N Y Coll At Fredonia, Fredonia, NY; SO; BA; Kung Fu Clb 90-; Undergrad Alumni Cncl 89-; Usher Corps; Hnrs Pgm 89-; Help Svc Steering Comm 90-; Engl/ Psych; Cnslg.

**SKINNER, DEIDRAH D,** Harford Comm Coll, Bel Air, MD; FR; AA; General; Lbry Sci.

**SKINNER, GREGORY PAUL,** Middle Tn St Univ, Murfreesboro, TN; JR; BS; Biology; Dentist.

**SKINNER, JASON T,** Univ Of Tn At Martin, Martin, TN; SO; BA; Stdnt Govt Stdnt Crt Jstc; Cngrssnl Rep Bus Dept; Otstndng Bus Stdnt Awrd; ATO Schlrshp Awrd; UTM Deans Lst; Alpha Tau Omega; Pre Law Clb; Univ Schlrs; Bus Fnc; Law.

**SKINNER, LAURA L,** Univ Of Nc At Charlotte, Charlotte, NC; JR; BS; Stdnt Crt Lt Chf Jstc 90-; 49 Rs Escrt Srvc Asst Drctr 90-; Pre Law Soc Wshngtn Trp Chrmn 89-90; Phi Heta Sigma; Gldn Key Sec 90-; Intrdscplnry Hnrs Prgrm 88-; Angl Flght Slvr Wings Cmmndr 90-; Crmnl Jstc; Prsctn.**

**SKINNER, LAURA S,** Anne Arundel Comm Coll, Arnold, MD; SO; BA; US Drssge Fed 88; Gm Drssge Fed Treas 90; Hosp Vol Phys Thrpy Dept; Otptnt Cntr Phys Thrpy And Rehab Vol; Sci; Phys Thrpy.

**SKINNER, MARGARET N,** Memphis St Univ, Memphis, TN; SR; BA; CO Clg Coalition For Homeless 87-88; Econs.

**SKINNER II, MELVIN W,** Saint Pauls Coll, Lawrenceville, VA; JR; BA; NAACP 90-; Mr Soph 90; Ntrl Sci And Math Dept Hnrs 89; Xerox Intrntl Cntr 90; Acad Schlrshp; Dns Lst 88-; St Pauls Bsbl Tm 88-; Bus Admin; Acctng CPA.

**SKINNER, MICHAEL A,** Univ Of Ga, Athens, GA; JR; BLA; GA Stu Lndscp Arch 89-; Stu Envrmntl Awrnss 90-; Sierra Clb 90-; Lndscp Arch; Envrmnntl Plnng.

**SKINNER, NANCY L,** West Liberty St Coll, West Liberty, WV; SR; BA; Crmnl Just Org Sec/Treas 87-88; Deans List 86-90; Pres List 90-; Intrnshp Wood Cty Prsctng Attrny 90; Scrtrl/Cnclng; AAS 89; Crmnl Just; Mstrs Clncl Psychlgy.

**SKINNER, SHIRLEY G,** East Central Comm Coll, Decatur, MS; FR; MED; Cmsnr Soil Cnsrvtn Serv; 4-H Ldr; Elem Ed.

**SKINNER, SUZANNE V,** Univ Of South Al, Mobile, AL; SR; BS; Fllwshp Chrstn Athlts 89-; Pbtst Chldrns Hm Vol 89-; Elem Educ; Adlt/Chld Psych.

**SKINNER, TRACIE A,** Palm Beach Atlantic Coll, W Palm Beach, FL; JR; BA; SGA VP 90-; CARE Coord 90-; Supper Hnrs Pgm 89-; Intern Pblc Defenders Ofc 90; Business/Mrktng; Law.**

**SKIPTON, CHARLES D,** Memphis St Univ, Memphis, TN; SR; BBA; SGA Chrmn Educ Comm 89-; Pres Stdng Comm Hmn Rel 90-; Progsv Party Pres/Campn Mgr; Hon Stdnt 88-; Gldn Key 90; Recycle Today Stdnt Ldr Com Chrmn 90; Deans Lst 90-; Carisle Award/Tn Intercoll St Legsltr 89; Intl Bus.

**SKIPWORTH JR, DAVID K,** Northwest Al Comm Coll, Phil Campbell, AL; GD; Stdnt Govt Assn Sen 89-90; Phi Theta Kappa; Mst Outstdng Tech Div 90; Pres/Deans Lst 89-90; Assoc Apld Sci 90; Assoc Apld Tech 90; Math; Engrng.

**SKIRPAN, CLEMENT A,** Marywood Coll, Scranton, PA; FR; BA; Deans List 90-; Teacher Choise/Art 90-; Talent Schlrshp/Art 90; Art; Graphic Designer.

**SKLENKA, JENNIFER M,** Wake Forest Univ, Winston-Salem, NC; FR; BA; Tutoring Undrpvldgd Chldrn 90-; Tennis Clb 90-; Ecnmcs; Bus Fld.

**SKLYAR, ADELINA M,** Ny Univ, New York, NY; SO; BA; Deans Lst 89-90; Englsh/Phlsphy; Law.

**SKOBLICKI, SUSAN E,** Dowling Coll, Oakdale Li, NY; JR; BBA; Acctng Soc 90-; Delta Mu Delta 90-; Deans Lst 90-; Intrnshp Mfg Hanover Trust 90-; Advncmnt Bus/Commerce Awd 88; Schlstc Aptitude Schlrshp 88-; Acctng; CPA.

**SKOKOWSKI, NICOLE E,** Duquesne Univ, Pittsburgh, PA; FR; BA; Campus Minstry Lector 90-; Phi Eta Sigma; Ed; Hist Tchr.

**SKOKOWSKI, RICHARD A,** Temple Univ, Philadelphia, PA; SR; BSEE; IEEE Stdnt Brnch Pres 88-; Am Nuclear Soc 90-; Eta Kappa Nu 89-; Gold Key 89-; Navy Achvmnt Medal 88; Natl Acad Nuclear Trng Schlrshp 90-; IEEE Vincent Bendix Awd 90-; Reactor Engr; Bradford N Clarke Awd NY Post Soc; Elec Eng.

**SKOLNY, VINCENT R,** West Liberty St Coll, West Liberty, WV; SO; BS; Comp Sci; Sftwr Eng.

**SKORA, ELIZABETH,** Western New England Coll, Springfield, MA; FR; Cmptr Info Systms/Bsn; Bsn.

**SKORICH, ELAINE L,** Kent St Univ Kent Cmps, Kent, OH; SR; BA; Kent St Univ Hnrs Clg 87-; Golden Key Treas 90-; Phi Alpha Delta 89-; Alpha Lambda Delta 88; Crmnl Jstc; Law.

**SKORVANEK, NANCY ANNE,** Providence Coll, Providence, RI; SR; BA; Educ Clb Pres 87-; CEC 87-; Pstrl Cncl 89-90; Elem Ed/Spec Ed; Tchr.

**SKOVENSKI, KIMBERLY R,** Indiana Univ Of Pa, Indiana, PA; JR; BA; Cmmnctns Media; Brdcstng.

**SKOVMAND, ANNELISE,** The Boston Conservatory, Boston, MA; FR; BM; Erevan Choral Soc 90-; Christian Fellowshp 90-; Vocal Perfrmnc; Opera Singer.

**SKOWRONSKI, JEFFREY D,** Neumann Coll, Aston, PA; FR; BS; Hnrs Prog 90-; Tutor 90-; Bsktbl 90-; Bio; Phys Thrpst.

**SKOWRONSKI, JOHN B,** Bloomfield Coll, Bloomfield, NJ; SR; S; Accntng; Law.

**SKRADA-KOROM, REBECCA R,** Univ Of Akron, Akron, OH; SR; BA; Alpha Gamma Delta 87-89; Tchng Assist; Crmnl Justice 90; Tech Educ; Law Enfrcmnt Fld.

**SKUCE, KRISTA S,** Univ Of Sc At Columbia, Columbia, SC; SR; BS; SC Natl Grd 86-; SCAPERD 90-; U S Army Lt 90-; ROTC 84-86; Dist Military Stdnt 84; Army Achvmnt Medal; SC Achvmnt Medal; Bsktbl/Vlybl 82-84; Phys Educ Tchr.

**SKUFCA, STEPHEN J,** Univ Of Nc At Asheville, Asheville, NC; FR; BA; Phi Theta Kappa 88-90; Hghst Hon RCC 90; Fresh Wrtng Awd; Hgh Cntry Hm Imprvmnt Ownr 90-; Fine/Crtv Wdwrkng Crpntry Exp 80-88; AAS Rcknghm Comm Coll 90; Ltrtr; Educ.

**SKULA, CHARLES R,** Atlantic Comm Coll, Mays Landing, NJ; FR; BA; Woodbridge Polc Dept Woodbridge N J Detect 71-86; Bus; Bus/Law.

**SKULL, LISA M,** Wv Univ, Morgantown, WV; SR; BS; Acad Stdnts Pharm 88-; Amer Chem Soc 87-88; Pharmacy.

**SKULLEY IV, JAMES MATTHEW,** Union Univ, Jackson, TN; FR; BA; Bapt Stdnt Unn; Unn Univ Pres Lst; Msc; Msc Bus.

**SKUTNIK, SAMANTHA C,** Oh St Univ, Columbus, OH; SR; BA; Hnrs Prog 87-; Arts & Sci Awd For Exclnc In Schlrshp; Eng; Lib Sci.

**SKVIRSKY, YELENA,** Columbia Union Coll, Takoma Park, MD; JR; BS; Assn Cmptng Mach Pres 81; Dns Lst 89-90; Cmptr Sci; Data Base Mgmt.

**SKYBERG, ALFRED E,** Roane St Comm Coll, Harriman, TN; AS; Planner Estimator; Hlth Physics; Plnr.

**SKYES, KATRINA L,** Fort Valley St Coll, Fort Valley, GA; SR; BA; Home Econ Club Treas 89; Amer Home Econ 89; Zeta Phi Beta 90-; Infant/Child Dvlpmnt; Educ.

**SKYPALA, DANIELLE J,** Gettysburg Coll, Gettysburg, PA; FR; Reach 90-; Actvts Cncl 90-; Hll Gvot Sec 90-; Alpha Delta Pi 90-; Bsktbl Vrsty 90-; Psych; Crmnl Psychlgst.

**SLAASTED, LESLIE A,** Radford Univ, Radford, VA; SO; BA; Camps Judcl Brd 90-; Newspr 90-; IRHC Pr Res Hall 89-90; Jrnlsm/Engl; Reprtng.

**SLACK, AMY L,** The Kings Coll, Briarclf Mnr, NY; JR; BA; Odyssey Engl Clb VP 88-; Drama Clb 88; Chapel Choir 88; Christian Svc Outrch 88; Engl Lit; Deaf Educ.

**SLACK, JO A,** Univ Of Ct, Storrs, CT; SR; BS; Pre-Vet Clb 90-; Alpha Zeta; Pathbio; Vet.

**SLACK, JOYCE E,** Fl International Univ, Miami, FL; SR; Tchrs Art Gld; Brwrd Art Gld; Brwrd Cnty Archlgcl Scty; Dns Lst Brwrd Comm Coll; Natl Art Educ Assn; BS; AA Broward Comm Coll 89.

**SLACK, KEVIN D,** Salisbury St Univ, Salisbury, MD; JR; BA; Natl Assoc Acctnts; Phi Kappa Phi; State Senatorial Schlrshp; Deans Lst; IM Sports; Acctng; Sales.**

**SLACK, LORA A,** Radford Univ, Radford, VA; SR; BS; Phi Theta Kappa 89-; Pi Gamma Mu 90-; Phi Kappa Phi; AA Crmnl Jstc VA Wstrn CC 89; Pol Sci; Law.**

**SLACK, MARILYN W,** Univ Of North Fl, Jacksonville, FL; JR; BBA; Stdnt Govt Assoc VP 86-88; Intrntl Stdnts Assoc VP 90-; Fin/Invstmnt Soc 90-; Phi Kappa Phi 90-; Golden Key 90-; Stdnt Appl Revw Comm Stdnt Rep 87-88; Provsts Advsry Cncl Stdnt Rep 87-88; UNF Campus Civitn; FCCJ Algebra Award 88; Mktg; Merchndsng Exec.

**SLADE, CELENA T,** Johnson C Smith Univ, Charlotte, NC; SO; BA; Poli Sci Clb Treas 89-; Pan-Afrcn Cncl Pres 90-; Bd Trsts SGA; ST Dept Intrnshp; Bsktbl 89-90; Poli Sci; Dplmt.

**SLADE, CRYSTAL O,** Howard Univ, Washington, DC; JR; BS; Alpha Swthrts 89-90; Gldn Key; Beta Kappa Chi; Phi Beta Kappa; Natl Cancer Inst Summer Pstn; Zoology; Physician.**

**SLADE, SHARON D,** Va Commonwealth Univ, Richmond, VA; JR; BSN; Pre Nurs Clb Pub Ofcr 87-89; Natl Stdnt Nurs Assn 89-90; Sentora Nurs Care Prtnr 90; Henrico Doctors Hosp Nurs Tech; Nurs; RN.

**SLAGENWEIT, BRIDGETTE M,** Indiana Univ Of Pa, Indiana, PA; JR; BED; Educ; Spec Educ Tchr.

**SLAGLE, JANA S,** Mayland Comm Coll, Spruce Pine, NC; FR; ADN; EMS Cncl Membr; BFA Austn Peuy St Univ 78; Nrsng; Emrgncy Nrsng.

**SLAGLE, TERRI D,** Tn Tech Univ, Cookeville, TN; SO; BS; Kappa Omicron Nu V P; Fashn Merchdsng; Retl Mgmt.

**SLAMPAK, FAITH D,** Duquesne Univ, Pittsburgh, PA; JR; Distr Stdnt Award 89; Trnsfr Schlrs Award 90; Intrnshp Data Scrty; Blue Cross/Blue Shield; AS Cmnty Clg Allegheny Cnty 90; Acctg/Cmptrs; Law/MBA.

**SLAN, STEVEN M,** Univ Of Sc At Columbia, Columbia, SC; FR; BA; Phi Theta Kappa; Deans Lst 90; Pres Lst 88-90; Grad Summa Cum Laude; AS 90; Phrmcy.

**SLAPER, KIMBERLY A,** Kent St Univ Kent Cmps, Kent, OH; SR; BA; Intrn Sf Lndng Yth Shltr Admn Supv; Indv/Fmly Stdies; Cnslng.

**SLAPPEY, LISA A,** Fl St Univ, Tallahassee, FL; SR; BA; Intl Stdnt Assn Sec 89-; Hnrs Schlrs Cncl Socl Chr Natl Mrt Rep 89-90; Phi Beta Kappa 89-; Phi Eta Sigma 88; Phi Kappa Phi; Lambda Iota Tau Pr 90-; Omicron Delta Kappa 90-; Mortr Brd 90-; Librl Stds Hnrs 87-89; Hnrs Major 89-; Engl; Univ Prof.

**SLATE, CHERYL A,** Allegheny Coll, Meadville, PA; JR; BS; Chemii Clb; Alden Schlr 88-; Doan Schlr 89-90; Bst Fresh Chem Stdnt 88-89; Chem; Rsrch.

**SLATE, KRISTEN J,** Smith Coll, Northampton, MA; GD; Synchionized Swim Clb 89-90; Dorm Cls 87-88; Eating Disorders Task Force Cnslr 88-; Head Residents Interviewer 90; Psi Chi; Cum Laude; First Grp Schlr; Deans Lst; Gymnastics; BA 90; Psychology; Human Resources.

**SLATER, ALYSSA K,** Univ Of Nc At Greensboro, Greensboro, NC; SR; BS; Inter-Vars Chrstn Flwshp 89-90; Cone Elem Sch Intern; Alpha Delta Kappa Schlrshp 90-; Univ Marshall; Elem Ed; Tchr.

**SLATER, CLIFTON L,** Ashland Comm Coll, Ashland, KY; SO; Asstnt Drctr Chrch Ppt Tm 88-; Chrch Mscn 87-; Mrch Of Dms 84-; Bsns Admn/Fnnc & Mrktng; Invstr.

**SLATER, KIMBERLY L,** Austin Peay St Univ, Clarksville, TN; FR; BS; Phys Thrpy; Phys Thrpst.

**SLATER, KRISTINE,** William Paterson Coll, Wayne, NJ; SR; BA; Spec Educ Clb 87-; Cncl Excptnl Chldrn 87-; Spec Olympcs 88-89; Comm Yth Grp 87-89; Spec Educ; Grad Schl.

**SLATER, MICHAEL L,** Morehouse Coll, Atlanta, GA; FR; BS; Mrhse Hlth Crrs Scty 90-; Stdnt Natl Med Assn Fr Rep 90-; Bylr Coll Of Med Crdgy Prcptrshp; Blgy; Crdlgy.

**SLATTER, KERRY C,** Morehouse Coll, Atlanta, GA; SR; BA; NAACP; Pol Sci Clb; GA Clb Assn; Forensics; Debate Tm; Frnch Clb; Civic Tutor Pgm; Un Negro Coll Fnd Vol; Elem Sch; Tutor Pgm; Dekalb Cnty Pretrial Intern Pgm; Pol Sci; Crmnl Law.

**SLATTERY, LISA A,** Fl St Univ, Tallahassee, FL; JR; BA; Nwspaper Asst Edtr 88-89; Golden Key 89-; Eta Sigma Phi 90-; Cultrl Exchng Soc 88-89; Dir Indivdl Study; Hons Thesis; Im Bsktbl 88-89; Visual Arts Fndtn 90-; AA 90; Soclgy/Classics; Rsrchr.

**SLATTERY, SUSAN M,** Winthrop Coll, Rock Hill, SC; SO; BA; Soc Wrk Clb Sec 89-; Cncl For Excptnl Chldrn 90-; Educ Puppet Shw 90-; Psychlgy; Chld Psychtrst.

**SLAUGENHAUPT, JANET M,** Davis & Elkins Coll, Elkins, WV; SO; BS; Phoenix Alliance Pres 90-; Psych Clb Treas 89; Stdnt Alumni Assn 90; Hon Assn Hstrn 89-; Zeta Tau Alpha Mstr Rituals 89; Acad Achvmnt Awds 90-; F J Daniels Cls Acad Achvmnt Awd 90-; L Newton Thomas Sr Schlr 90; Girls Sftbl; Psychology; Psychgst.

**SLAUGHTER, BARBARA E,** Ky St Univ, Frankfort, KY; SR; BS; Owen County Life Squad/Owen Rescue Squad; Natl Coll Busn Merit Awds 90; Current Emplyt Admin Spec Ky Dept Ed Frankfort Ky; Busn Admin; Purching Agent.

**SLAUGHTER, CARMANNA L,** Watterson Coll, Louisville, KY; SO; Deans Lst 90; Pres Lst; Cmptr Accntng; Accntnt.

**SLAUGHTER, CHRISTOPHER W,** Wv Univ, Morgantown, WV; SR; BSEE; WVU Mrchng Bnd 87; IEEE 88-; IEEE Cmptr Scty 89-; IM Sprts 87-; Elctrcl Engrg/Cmptr Engrg; Engr.

**SLAUGHTER, DELORES B,** Hampton Univ, Hampton, VA; SR; BSN; Alpha Kappa Mu 89-; Sigma Theta Tau; Chi Eta Phi 64-; Sdtnt Nrses Assn; Outstndng Achvmnt Nrsng 90-; RN 65-; Cert Freemens Hospt Schl Nrsg 65; Nrsng.

**SLAUGHTER, PAMELA G,** Univ Of Sc At Columbia, Columbia, SC; FR; BA; Mrchng Bnd; Symphonic Bnd; Symphony Orchestra; Music.

**SLAUGHTER, PASQUAL A,** Jackson St Univ, Jackson, MS; FR; BA; Finance; Law.

**SLAUGHTER, ROBERT A,** Thomas Nelson Comm Coll, Hampton, VA; SO; AS; Sci Biology; Med Dr.

**SLAUGHTER, ROBERT M,** Daytona Beach Comm Coll, Daytona Beach, FL; JR; Theta Kappo Epsilon 88-; Poli Sci; Law.

**SLAUGHTER, STACIE A,** Saint Thomas Univ, Miami, FL; FR; BA; Stdnt Govt Assn Sen 90-; Dns Lst 90-; Rsrchd Implmntd Hlth Tsk Frc Stdnts 90-; Pol Sci/Pub Admin; Law/Pol.

**SLAVEN, GRETA P,** Chattanooga St Tech Comm Coll, Chattanooga, TN; SO; AAS; Stdnt Ed Clb Treas 89-; Phi Tehta Kappa 90-; Psi Beta 90; Mrt Awrd Erly Chldhd Ed 91; AAS; Erly Chldhd Ed Elm Ed.

**SLAVGORODSKAIA, NINA TVANOVNA,** Coll Misericordia, Dallas, PA; GD; BS; Acctg Clb; Ph D Schlrshp Kiev State Union USSR; LLM USSR 73; Acctg; MAB/MS.

**SLAVICK, JOHN W,** Christian Brothers Univ, Memphis, TN; JR; CBU Chapter ACM Pres 90-; Memphis Pc Users Grp Inc Pres 90-; Assoc PC Users Grp Inc Advsry Brd.

**SLAVSKA, ALLYSON B,** Northeastern Christian Jr Coll, Villanova, PA; JR; BED; Snrd Gsplrs Perf Grps 87-89; Dns Lst 89; Sec Lazy Boy Wayne PA; John Wanamakers; AA 89; Msc Ed/Cmpstn; Tch.**

**SLAWSON, MICHAEL K,** Fl International Univ, Miami, FL; JR; BS; FEA 90-; Elem Ed.

**SLAYMON, ROZELLE L,** Savannah St Coll, Savannah, GA; JR; Pre Of Psychlgy Clb Pres 89; Rsdnt Assist 89; Peer Cnslr 90; Wesleyan Gspl Choir 88; Mass Cmmnctns Clb Treas 88-90; Sigma Gamma Rho; 4th Rnnr-Up Jr Women Of Excllnce 90; Intrnshp At Hrld Blk Newspapr; Mass Cmmnctns-Jrnlsm; Own/Pblsh Own Mag.

**SLAYTON, LINDA G,** Longwood Coll, Farmville, VA; SR; BS; Bio Clb 87-; Alpha Lambda Delta Pres 87-89; Beta Beta Beta 89-; Phi Kappa Phi 89-; Prof Womens Music Frat Chpln 90-; Nellie Ward Nance Schlrshp; Hull Schlrshp; CRC Press Fr Chem Achvmnt Awd; Sigma Alpha Iota Hon Cert; Bio/Music; Bio Rsrch.

**SLEDD, STACEY L,** Brevard Comm Coll, Cocoa, FL; FR; AA; Campus Cmpct Vol Parrish Med Ctr; English.

**SLEDGE, LANA D,** Faulkner Univ, Montgomery, AL; SR; BS; Alpha Alpha Alpha 89-; Comptr Bus Applctns.

**SLEDGE, LISA M,** Va St Univ, Petersburg, VA; SO; Natl Assn Blck Accntnts; Dean Lst 89-; Accntng; CPA.

**SLEEPER, ROBERT N,** Western New England Coll, Springfield, MA; SR; BSBA; By Scts Of Amer Adlt Ldr Asst Sctmstr 90; AS Springfield Tech Comm Coll 78; Bus Admin; Bus Mgmt.

**SLEET, MICHELE I,** Univ Of Ky, Lexington, KY; SO; BED; Engl; Ed.

**SLEIGH, MERRY J,** James Madison University, Harrisonburg, VA; JR; BA; Psych Clb 89-; Soph Class Ring Cmte 89-90; Hall Cncl Co-Adv 90-; Golden Key 89-; Psi Chi Treas 90-; Sigma Tau Delta/Engl Hon 90-; Compeer-Wrk With Mently Ill 89-; Vol Wrk-Blind Stdnts 88-89; R A 89-90; Asst Hall Dir 90-; IM 88-89; Psych; Engl.

**SLEIGHTER, JULIE A,** Duquesne Univ, Pittsburgh, PA; FR; BA; Duquesne Univ Cares 90-; Un Prog Brd 90-; Acctg; Law.

**SLICE, ALISON G,** Winthrop Coll, Rock Hill, SC; FR; BS; Ambsdr 90; Cassens Cup 90-; Alpha Lambda Delta; RA; Math; Scndry Edn/Inds.

**SLICE, ANGELA D,** Univ Of Sc At Columbia, Columbia, SC; FR; MBA; Theatre 90-; Theatre/Speech.

**SLICER, LORRAINE W,** Midlands Tech Coll, Columbia, SC; SO; AS; Stdnt Assn Of Surg Techs Pres Elect; Pres List 90-; Surg Tech; RN.

**SLIE, JO ANN L,** Wv Northern Comm Coll, Wheeling, WV; SO; AAS; Eng Cmpstn II Hnrs 89-90; Bwlg 89-90; RCT Pgm; Rsprtry Care Tchnlgy; Rsprtry Care/RN.

**SLIFKO, WILLIAM G,** Mount Aloysius Jr Coll, Cresson, PA; GD; AS; Microcmptr Sci.

**SLIGER, MELANIE S,** Univ Of Va Clinch Valley Coll, Wise, VA; FR; PHARM; Sci; Phrmcy.

**SLIGH, DARLA E,** Comm Coll Algny Co Algny Cmps, Pittsburgh, PA; Ntnl Actn Coun/Minorities/Engrng 83-; RC 83-; Beaver Vly Power Sta Nuc Info Svcs Grp 87-; Engrng/Busn.

**SLIGH III, JAMES E,** Piedmont Tech Coll, Greenwood, SC; FR; ASSOC; Phi Beta Lamda 90-; Assoc Piedmont Tech; BS Newberry; Acctng; CPA.

**SLIKE, JILL M,** Univ Of Pittsburgh At Bradford, Bradford, PA; SO; BS; Bio Clb Treas 89; Alpha Lambda Delta 90; Beta Beta Beta VP; Alpha Phi Omegao Sec 90; Bio/Chem; Med.

**SLIKSBIER, LORENE ANNA,** Univ Of Sc At Beaufort, Beaufort, SC; SO; BED; Amer Soc Of Prof Estimators Inc 79-81; Women In Const 78-79; Repub Party Vol; Admin Asst 89-; Structrl Steel Engr/Estimator Contracting Sls 78-; AS Manchester Cmnty Clg 73; Cert Morse Schl Of Bus 79; Math; Tchr.

**SLIMAN, ZORN T,** Salisbury St Univ, Salisbury, MD; GD; BS; Army ROTC Schlrshp Stdnt Cdt Mjr 89-90; Phi Eta Sigma 86-87; Delta Mu Delta 89-90; MD St Sntrl Schlrshp 87-90; ROTC Mltry Ordr Wrld Wars 88-89; Dghtrs Amer Rvltn ROTC Mdl 89-90; Mgmt; Lt US Army.

**SLINGHOFF, BETH J,** Wv Univ, Morgantown, WV; JR; BSW; Hospice 90-; In Touch Concrnd 90-; Socl Wrk Org Tr 90-; Chi Omega Rit Chrmn 88-; Cir K 89-; Socl Wrk.

**SLINKER, MARGARET H,** Univ Of Akron, Akron, OH; JR; BFA; Hnrs Prog; Disc Jockey & Bartender; Freelance Art; Art Edn/Thrpy; Art.

**SLIPKO, NATALIE M,** Niagara Univ, Niagara Univ, NY; SO; BA; Niagara U Theater Plyrs Corr Secy 90-; Prfrmng Ed Artsts Of NU Theatre 90-; Hons Prog 89-90; NU Chapel Choir 89-; Voice Schlrshp 90; Pres/Acadmc Schlrshps 89-; Deans List 89-90; Theater; Actress Or Law.

**SLISZ, ANGELA M,** Erie Comm Coll, Buffalo, NY; SR; BS; Phi Theta Kappa; Clerical Traffic Sfty Asst 85-; AS; Business; CPA.

**SLOAN, AMANDA L,** Tn Temple Univ, Chattanooga, TN; FR; AA; Stdnt Missions Flwshp 90-; Alpha Kappa Rho 90-; Df Ed-Sign Lang/Interpret.

**SLOAN, ANGELA M,** Phillips Jr Coll Spartanburg, Spartanburg, SC; AS; Comp Clb Treas; Comp Operator.

**SLOAN, CYNTHIA M,** Livingstone Coll, Salisbury, NC; JR; BA; Stdnt Gvrnmnt Tres 90-; Cmps Orgnztn Stdnts W Purpose Prsdnt 89-; Cncrt Chr; Peer Cnslr; Alpha Kappa Mu; Zeta Phi Beta; Stdnts Prps SWAP Prsdnt; Englsh; Edctn.

**SLOAN IV, DANIEL H,** Univ Of Fl, Gainesville, FL; SR; BS; FL Engnrng Soc 90-; AMRCN Inst Arnctcs Astrntcs 89-; Mrchng Bnd Sctn Ldr 87-; Tau Beta Pi; Gldn Key 89-; Alpha Lambda Delta 88-; FL Undrgrd Spc Grnt Cnsrtm; Aerospace Engnrng; Aerospace Dsgn Engnr.

**SLOAN, DONNA O,** Al A & M Univ, Normal, AL; SO; Univ Choir; Emtnl Cnflctd Chldrn Camp Vol 85-90; Mntl Hlth Assn Vol 85-90; Zlgy/Chem; Dntstry.

**SLOAN JR, GETER P,** Comm Coll Algny Co Algny Cmps, Pittsburgh, PA; FR; Law Edn; Admn.

**SLOAN, JENNIFER A,** Birmingham Southern Coll, Birmingham, AL; JR; BA; Rush Cnslr; Sigma Tau Delta; Phi Alpha Theta; Alpha Chi Omega Mrl Chrmn 90-; Engl/Hstry; Tchng H S.

**SLOAN, JOHN R,** Kent St Univ Kent Cmps, Kent, OH; SO; BA; IM Ftbl/Bsktbl/Bsbl 89-; Deans List 89-; Acdmc Schlrshp 89-; Bus Fin/Maths/Comp Sci; Fin Advsr/Agent.

**SLOAN, MARY C,** Western Ky Univ, Bowling Green, KY; SO; BA; Schlrs Pgrm 89-; Accntng.

**SLOAN, STEPHANIE R,** Comm Coll Algny Co Algny Cmps, Pittsburgh, PA; SO; AS; Pgh Goal Getters Disabled Sports Tm; US Disabled Sports Tm 90; Wmn Sports Challenged Athl Yr 90; Wmn Yr/Challenged Div Wmn Sports; Sports/Fitness/Recr; Sports Phys Ther.

**SLOBOD, MICHELE ILENE,** Cornell Univ Statutory College, Ithaca, NY; SR; BS; Stdnt Assmbly Coll Rep 88; Crnll Coll Rpblcns Sec 89; Coll Ambssdrs 90-; Alpha Omicron Pi Actvts 89; Gamma Sigma Delta; Phi Kappa Phi; Ho Nun De Kah 89-; Cngrssnl Intrnshp 88; Stdnt Exchnge To Korea 88; Eisenhower Intrnshp Natl Com 89; Ag Econs; Law Schl.

**SLOCUM, ALEXANDRA P,** Georgetown Univ, Washington, DC; SR; BSBA; Acad All Amer 89-90; Phi Lamda Phtrs 87; Intrnshp Ernst/Young Envir Cnsltns 89-90; Intern Smith Newcourt London UK 88-89; Vars Field Hcky 87-; Acctg.

**SLOCUM, JAY F,** The Kings Coll, Briarclf Mnr, NY; SR; BA; Packing Appeals Com Chmn 87-88; All Am Schlr Awd 90-; Campus Life Outrch Ldr 86-87; Lincoln Hall Outrch Ldr 87-89; Grtr NY Conf Soc Sci 89-90; Op Habilitation Trtmnt Ctr 89-; Prof Sociology.**

**SLONE, ANGLEA,** Univ Of Ky, Lexington, KY; SO; BS; Pre-Dntl Soc 89-; SMART 89-90; Dntl Schl Vol 89-90; Deans Lst; Acdmc Achvmnt; Dntl Asst; Dntstry.

**SLONE, KIMBERLY A,** Roane St Comm Coll, Harriman, TN; FR; ASSOC; Amer Assn Rsprtry Care; PTO 90-; Amer Hrt Assn 90-; Ntry Pblc At Lrg 89-; Med; Resp Thrpst.

**SLOOP, ANNE C,** Univ Of Ga, Athens, GA; JR; BSED; Ed Librarian 90-; Presbyterian Yth Ldr 88-89; Golden Key 90-; Kappa Delta Epsilon; Communiversity 89-90; Academic Schlrshp 86-87; Spcl Ed; Teach.

**SLOTNICK, ROBYN B,** S U N Y At Binghamton, Binghamton, NY; SO; BA; AMO 89-; Dean Lst 90; Vrsty Sftbl; IM Flr Hcky Sccr 89-; Bus Mngmnt Mrktng; Advrtsng.

**SLOYER, BRIAN P,** Duquesne Univ, Pittsburgh, PA; SO; BA; Rsdnc Cncl Of St Anns Flr Rep 89-90; SHARP Hsng 90; IM Ftbl/Hcky 89-; Srvcd Fnctn For Mntly/Physcly Hndcppd Chldrn 89; Indep Russian Tutor; Dns Lst 90-; Pol Sci; Govt Srvc.

**SLUCE, RAE L,** S U N Y At Buffalo, Buffalo, NY; JR; BS; Im Vlybl; League Outdr Vlybl Team Rec 88-; Bus Mgt; Fin/Mgt Info Sys.

**SLUGA, CAROL D,** Hillsborough Comm Coll, Tampa, FL; SO; ADN; Mbr Stdnt Nrs Org; Dns Lst; Ret Rad Tech; Nrsng.

**SLUGHER, DAWN D,** Anne Arundel Comm Coll, Arnold, MD; FR; BA; Omicron Theta; Phi Theta Kappa; Gen Stu/Bus; Accntng.

**SLUITER, REBECCA S,** Cornell Univ Statutory College, Ithaca, NY; FR; BS; Cmps Crsd Chrst 90-; Pre Vet Soc; Anml Sci; Vet Med.

**SLUMPFF, JONATHON G,** Alfred Univ, Alfred, NY; FR; Rescue Squad 90-; Jazz Ensemble Solo Trumpet 90-; Cmpting Serv Cmptr Cons 90-; Elec Eng; Entrepreneurship Eng.

**SLUNDER, BRADFORD S,** Ky Wesleyan Coll, Owensboro, KY; SR; BA; Phi Beta Lambda 90; Deans Lst 90; Bsebl 87; Accntng; CPA.

**SLUSARCZYK, DAWN M,** Kent St Univ Kent Cmps, Kent, OH; SR; Stu Prof Nrsng Fndrsng Chrmn 90-; ONSA 88-; NSNA 88-; Mrtr Brd Treas 90-; Sigma Theta Tau 90-; Heart Assn CPR Instr 89-; BSN Kent St Univ; Nrsng; RN.

**SLUSHER, NICOLE JEAN,** Goucher Coll, Towson, MD; JR; BA; Educ Clb; Study Skills Cnsltnt; Wrtng Ctr Tutor; Hist/Scndry Educ.

**SLUSHER, TERRY W,** Union Coll, Barbourville, KY; FR; BA; Cmptr Info Sys.

**SLUSSER, TEDDY D,** Memphis St Univ, Memphis, TN; FR; BS; Physcs; Pltcs.

**SLUZELE, JENNIFER V,** Pa St Univ Main Cmps, University Pk, PA; JR; BA; Amer Stds; Law.**

**SMALARZ, ANN M,** Broward Comm Coll, Ft Lauderdale, FL; AS; Irene Fischley Awd; Cert 90; Cert Lindsey Hopkins Tech Edctn 80; Med Sngrphy.

**SMALL, COREY A,** West Chester Univ, West Chester, PA; SO; BED; Music; Edctn.

**SMALL, DIANE L,** Univ Of Nc At Charlotte, Charlotte, NC; FR; BED; Elry Chldhd Ed; Elem Schl Tchr.

**SMALL, DONNA M,** Casco Bay Coll, Portland, ME; FR; AAS; Bus Admin; Law.

**SMALL, MICHELLE L,** Casco Bay Coll, Portland, ME; FR; AS; Secrtrl Sci; Law.

**SMALL, NANCY W,** Comm Coll Algny Co Algny Cmps, Pittsburgh, PA; FR; BA; Ptsbrgh Ltrcy Int Vol 89-90; Fndmntls Ltrcy Pgm Vol 89-90; Soc Wrk/Wmns Stds; Soc Wrk.

**SMALL, NICOLA-ANN S,** Fl International Univ, Miami, FL; SO; BA; Blck Stdnts Un 90-; Phi Eta Sigma 90-; Fnc Intl Bus; Bus.

**SMALLEY-HUNT, JENNIFER A,** Endicott Coll, Beverly, MA; SO; ASSOC; Endicott Clge Nwspr Staff; Intrnshp Caboots Inc Annapolis MD 90; Design Exchange Norwell MA 90; Commercial Art; Graphic Artist.

**SMALLS, LORI LEE,** Hillsborough Comm Coll, Tampa, FL; FR; Stdnt Sprt Serv Clb.

**SMALLS, MYLECHIA L,** Claflin Coll, Orangeburg, SC; SO; BS; Arspc Clb Exec Sec 90-; Hnrs Pgm 89-; Alpha Kappa Alpha; NAACP 89-; Natl Clgte Mnrty Ldrshp Awd 90-; All Amer Schlrs 90-; Vlybl Tm 90-; Elem Ed; Edctr/Prncpl.**

**SMALLWOOD, ANTOINETTE J,** Univ Of Md At Eastern Shore, Princess Anne, MD; SO; BA; Crmnl Justice Clb 90-; Ntnl Bsn League Sec 89-90; Kappa Sweetheart Ct Sec 89-; Boys/Girls Cmmnty Clb Sprvsr 88-; Cert Dept Treasury 89-90; Cert Barbizon Mdlng Schl 85; Crmnl Justice; Law.

**SMALLWOOD, CARLA J,** Univ Of Ky, Lexington, KY; JR; BA; AS Arts Elizabethtown Comm Coll 90; Elem Edn; Teach.

**SMALLWOOD, KRISTY G,** Truett Mc Connell Coll, Cleveland, GA; JR; BMUS; Phi Theta Kappa VP 88-90; SG 89-90; Cncrt Choir Sec 88-90; Trchbrs 88-90; Magna Cum Laude 3 In Cls 90; Fr/Soph Music Awd 88-90; Dir Awd 90; AS Truett Mc Connell Clg 90; Music Educ; Music Tchr.

**SMALLWOOD, STEVEN A,** Univ Of Nc At Charlotte, Charlotte, NC; SR; BS; Socty Of Physics Stdnts Pres 89-90; Sigma Pi Sigma; Stdnt Engr Rsrch Semester 90; Brookhaven Natl Lab Flwshp UNC Charlotte Optical Int Grp; Physics; Med Imaging.

**SMALTZ, ELIZABETH A,** Spartanburg Methodist Coll, Spartanburg, SC; JR; BA; Acad Appeals Comm 89-90; Phi Theta Kappa; Whos Who Amng Amer Jr Coll 90; Phi Beta Lambda 88-90; Highest Hnr Grad Career Trck Prog 90; Retail Mgmt Awd 88-90; Pres Hnr Lst 88-90; Chrldr Bsktbl Capt 88-90; Assn Retail Mgmt Spartanburg Meth Coll; Mktg.

**SMART, CLEVAN L,** Hillsborough Comm Coll, Tampa, FL; FR; BA; Chrs 90-; Chem; Eye Srgn.

**SMART, MARY STACEY,** Christopher Newport Coll, Newport News, VA; JR; BSBA; Psych Clb 90; Deans Lst; Pi Lambda Phi; York Lions Clb Variety Show; Finance/Econ.

**SMART, WILLIAM L,** S U N Y At Stony Brook, Stony Brook, NY; FR; BA; Stdnt Jdcry 90-; Pltcl Sci; Law.

**SMARZYNSKI, SHARON M,** Glassboro St Coll, Glassboro, NJ; JR; BA; Sld Rck Bptst Chrch Bus Mnstry 90-; AA Brlngtn Co Comm Coll 89; Hstry.

**SMATHERS, AMELIA LINDLER,** Univ Of Sc At Columbia, Columbia, SC; SO; BS; Bsn Admn; Acctng.

**SMATLAK, CONCORDIA R,** Cornell Univ, Ithaca, NY; SO; BS; Chimesmasters; Catholic Choir Pianist 90-; Cornell Tradition Acad Flwshp 90-; Bio/Chem; Envrnmntl Chem.**

**SMATTHERS, BETH A,** Indiana Univ Of Pa, Indiana, PA; SR; ACEI; Assn Chldhd Educ 88-90; Intl; Deans Lst 88-; BS 90; Elem Educ; Elem Tchr.

**SMAY, DIANNE,** Wilmington Coll, New Castle, DE; JR; BA; Stdnt Tutor Penn St Schl/Tech 86-87; Habilitation Asst/Mntlly Rtrd People; AAS Penn St Schl Of Tech 87; Bhvrl Sci; Case Mgmnt.

**SMAY, HEATHER A,** Cornell Univ Statutory College, Ithaca, NY; JR; BS; Cornell Ski Clb Jr Offcr 88-; Gornell Daily Sun Bus Bd 89-; Ho Nun De Kah; Alpha Omicron Pi Fndng Sis Asst Rush; Coll Of Ag/Life Sci Ambsdr 90-; Conrlel Eqstrn Tm 88-90; Bus Mgmt; Acctng.

**SMAYDA, JULIE ANN,** Lasell Coll, Newton, MA; FR; BA; Nwspr Ed 90-; Pres Hi Hon 90; COOL; Bsktbl 90; English.

**SMELSER, BETSY L,** Northwest Al Comm Coll, Phil Campbell, AL; SO; AAS; Phi Theta Kappa 90-; Tchg Chldrns Bible Cls Clg Church Christ 90-; LPN 90; LPN Oncology 88-89; LPN Santa Fe Cmnty Clg 88; Nrsg.

**SMELTZER, JENNIFER K,** Northeastern Christian Jr Coll, Villanova, PA; FR; BA; Bsktbl; Cmmnctns; Gdnce And Cnslng.

**SMELTZER, SHAUN A,** Fl International Univ, Miami, FL; JR; AOS Culinary Inst Amer 90; Hotel Restaurant Mngmnt.

**SMERAGE, BRADLEY D,** Fl St Univ, Tallahassee, FL; SR; BS; Symphony Orchstra 87-90; Fnnc Scty 90-; Beta Gamma Sigma; Gldn Key 89-; Phi Eta Sigma 88-; Alpha Kappa Psi 90-; IM Sprts 87-; Fnnc; Cnsltnt.

**SMERALDI, ALESSANDRO G,** Swarthmore Coll, Swarthmore, PA; FR; BA; Chstr Tutor 90-; Mlclr Bio Lab Tech Intshp; Bio; Med.

**SMIELECKI, LEANNE M,** D Youville Coll, Buffalo, NY; SR; Nrsg Supv Schofield Residence 88-; AAS Trocaire Clg 72; BSN; Nrsg.

**SMIETANA, STEPHANIE,** Indiana Univ Of Pa, Indiana, PA; SR; BED; Comm Vol W/Chldrn 87-; PSTA 90-; NEA/PSEA 89-; Kappa Delta Pi 89-; Provost Schlr 88; Elem Ed; Tchng/Grad Schl.

**SMIGELSKI, TERESA L,** Univ Of Fl, Gainesville, FL; SR; BS; Rho Chi 89-; IM Vllybl Ftbll Bsbll; Phrmcy; Cmm Phrmcy.

**SMILES, DANA D,** Radford Univ, Radford, VA; SR; BGS; Stdnt Educ Assn 90-; Phi Kappa Phi; Otstndng Stdnt Eductr Awrd; Educ K-8 Hrng Imprd Educ; Tch.

**SMILEY, KAY R,** Williamsburg Tech Coll, Kingstree, SC; FR; Deans Lst; Cook Off Clb; Prmnt Lcns Frtn Schl Rl Est 85; Wrd Prcsng.

**SMILEY, SARAH G,** Mary Baldwin Coll, Staunton, VA; JR; BA; SG 90-; Busn/Econ.

**SMILEY, WANDA H,** Gaston Coll, Dallas, NC; SO; AASD; Sec Lgl.

**SMILLIE, CATHY LEE,** Univ Of South Fl, Tampa, FL; GD; MSPH; H S Bio Tchr; BS Roosvlt Univ 65; Tropcl/Subtrop Comm Diseases; Phd.

**SMITH, ADAM BARRETT,** Ms St Univ, Miss State, MS; SR; Hnrs Prog Cnclmn; Phlsphy Clb; BS Univ S Miss 90; Phlsphy; Medicine.

**SMITH, ADAM J,** Ms St Univ, Miss State, MS; FR; BA; Prof Glf Mgmt Clb 90-; Dns Lst 90-; Bthsda Cntry Clb 90-; Intrn Dns Lst Awd 90-; Prof Glf Mgmt.

**SMITH, ADAM J,** Cornell Univ Statutory College, Ithaca, NY; FR; BA; Stf Wrtr Pub Access Chnl 13 T V Sta; Cmunctns; Publshng.

**SMITH, ADRIAN L,** Albany St Coll, Albany, GA; JR; BA; Alpha Kappa Mu; Golden Emb Marg Schlr; Pres Schlr; Chem; Bio-Chem Rsrch.

**SMITH, ADRIENE D,** Al St Univ, Montgomery, AL; SR; BS; Pr Alnc Career Cnslg/Awrns Tres 90-; Ntl Assoc Blck Acctnts 90-; Delta Mu Delta 89-; Alpha Kappa Psi VP Mbrshp 90-; Enrchmnt Educ Pro Hmptn Univ; Acctg; Auditor.

**SMITH, ADRIENNE C,** Ky St Univ, Frankfort, KY; JR; BA; Omega Pearl Club 89-; Alpha Kappa Mu 90-; Bus Admn/Mrktng; Mrktng Cnsltnt To Major Corp.

**SMITH, AIMEE E,** Savannah Coll Of Art & Design, Savannah, GA; SO; BFA; Res Asst 90-; Illstrn; Amntr.

**SMITH, ALAINA B,** Syracuse Univ, Syracuse, NY; FR; BS; Marching Bnd 90; SUFAR 90-; Hons Pgm 90-; Math; Prof.

**SMITH, ALAN C,** Tougaloo Coll, Tougaloo, MS; SO; BA; Math; Acctg.

**SMITH, ALAN J,** Univ Of Miami, Coral Gables, FL; SR; BFA; BS Univ Of London 55; Art; Painter.

**SMITH, ALISON J,** Mary Baldwin Coll, Staunton, VA; SO; BA; Amer Chem Soc 89-; Alpha Lambda Delta 90-; Beta Beta Beta 90-; Fncg 89-; Bio; Vet Med.

**SMITH, ALLISON R,** Livingston Univ, Livingston, AL; SO; Sigma Tau Delta; Delta Sigma Pi; Acct; CPA.

**SMITH, AMANDA H,** Ms St Univ, Miss State, MS; FR; DVM; Pre-Vet Clb 90-; Gamma Beta Phi 90-; Zeta Tau Alpha 90-; IM Blg Ftbl; Blgy; Vet.

**SMITH, AMBER M,** Valdosta St Coll, Valdosta, GA; SO; BED; Alpha Lambda Delta 89-90; Kappa Delta 90-; Spec Edn; Speech Thrpy.

**SMITH, AMY D,** Marshall University, Huntington, WV; SR; BBA; Accntg Clb 89-; Wv Soc Of Cpas 89-; Gamma Beta Phi 87-; All Amrcn Sclr 88-; Accntng; Cpa/Cma.**

**SMITH, AMY G,** James Madison University, Harrisonburg, VA; SR; BS; Educ Fr Yng Chldrn 90-; Gldn Ky 90-; Kappa Delta Pi 90-; Mrchng Ryl Djs Colr Grd 90; Educ; Elem Tchr.

**SMITH, AMY J,** Germanna Comm Coll, Locust Grove, VA; SO; ASBA; Lbrl Arts.

**SMITH, AMY K,** Univ Of Ky, Lexington, KY; JR; BME; MENC Pres 2 Yrs 88-; Sigma Alpha Iota VP 90-; Bnds 88-; Gldn Key 90-; Omicron Delta Kappa; Sigma Alpha Iota; Tau Beta Sigma 88-90; Stephen Foster Story Alt; Music Educ.**

**SMITH, AMY L,** Northeastern Christian Jr Coll, Villanova, PA; FR; MBA; Church Of Christ 90-; Bskbl Varsity 90-; Special Ed; Tchr.

**SMITH, AMY N,** Itawamba Comm Coll, Fulton, MS; SO; BA; Yrbk; Mdlng Sqd; Bty Pgnts Mst Btfl 90; All Amer Schlr Coll Awd; Deans Lst; Elem Ed; Tchng.

**SMITH, AMY R,** Miami Jacobs Jr Coll Of Bus, Dayton, OH; FR; BED; Career Clb 90-; Pres Lst 90; Deans Lst 90; Fashion Buying Trip; Fshn Merch; Buyer Major Dept Store.

**SMITH, ANDRA C,** Christopher Newport Coll, Newport News, VA; SR; BA; SVEA 89-90; Deans List 90; Stdnt Tchr Hampton Va 90; BA 90; Edn; Teach.

**SMITH, ANDRE L,** Jackson St Univ, Jackson, MS; FR; BA; Blgy; Med.

**SMITH, ANDREA D,** Lesley Coll, Cambridge, MA; SO; BA; Emrld Key Clb 89-; Schlr 89-; Acad Hons 89-; Soccer 89-; Elem Ed/Math/Sci; Tchr.

**SMITH, ANGELA D,** Norfolk St Univ, Norfolk, VA; SR; BS; DNIMAS; Stdnt Assn 87-; Bio Clb 87-90; ASLO 90-; Alpha Kappa Mu Rprtr 89-; Beta Kappa Chi Sec 90-F Sigma Xi 90-; Intrnshp VA Inst Marine Sci 90; Intrnshp Baruch Marine Lab 89; DNIMAS Schlrshp 87-; Bio; Marine Sci.

**SMITH, ANGELA L,** Univ Of North Fl, Jacksonville, FL; SR; BA; Phi Theta Kappa 88-; Gldn Key; Preinternships 90-; Ed; Tchr.

**SMITH, ANGELA M,** Tougaloo Coll, Tougaloo, MS; SO; BA; Pre Alumni Club 90-; Day Stdnt Union 89-; Alpha Kappa Alpha; Econ/Bsn Acctg; Prof Acct.

**SMITH, ANGELIQUE S H,** Lenoir Rhyne Coll, Hickory, NC; SO; BA; Intrvars Chrstn Fllwshp 89-90; Grl Scts 77-; Psych/Soc Clb 90-; Alpha Lambda Delta 90-; Alpha Phi Omega 89-; Broyhl Ldrshp Mntr Prog 90-; Dns Lst 89-; Pres Lst 89-; Psych; Quantitve Psych Res.

**SMITH, ANGIE D,** Gordon Coll, Barnesville, GA; SO; Grad HS As Salutorian June 4; Grad Coll W/4.0 June 8; First Time Ever Done At These Schls; AA Gordon Coll; Erly Elem Ed.

**SMITH, ANGIE J,** Piedmont Coll, Demorest, GA; JR; BA; SGAE 90-; Bstkbll 89-; Erly Chldhd Ed; Tch.

**SMITH, ANN M,** Clarkson Univ, Potsdam, NY; SO; BS; Scty Accntnts Treas 90-; Ambssdrs 90-; Acctg; CPA.

**SMITH, ANTHONY R,** S U N Y Coll Of Tech At Frmgdl, Farmingdale, NY; SR; Aircraft Maint; Aircraft Repair Shop.**

**SMITH, APRIL R,** Hillsborough Comm Coll, Tampa, FL; SO; AA; Vrsty Sftbl; Acdmc Athlt Awrds; Phi Theta Kappa; Lbrl Arts; Nvl Aviation.

**SMITH, ASPARSA M,** Alcorn St Univ, Lorman, MS; FR; BA; Hon Pgm; Bio; Nrsng.

**SMITH, AUDRA L,** Univ Of Al At Birmingham, Birmingham, AL; SR; BS; SOTA; Phi Theta Kapp; AS Snead St Jr Clg 88; Occup Thrpy.

**SMITH, BARBARA A,** Univ Of The Dist Of Columbia, Washington, DC; SR; AA Computer Opert Busn Clg Lear Siegler Inst 72; Busn Mgt; Prog Mgt Analyst.

**SMITH, BARBARA B,** James Sprunt Comm Coll, Kenansville, NC; SR; AAS; NC Asst Nsrg Stdnts; Nrsg.

**SMITH, BARBARA C,** Daytona Beach Comm Coll, Daytona Beach, FL; SO; AA; Pres Lst; Pub Sch Vol Wrtng Prsnl; Tch; English; Tch Cert/BA.

**SMITH, BARBARA O,** Tri County Tech Coll, Pendleton, SC; FR; ASSOC; Phi Theta Kappa; Avon Pres Club; St Andrew Untd Meth Chrch/Admin Brd Sec; News Route 87-; Bsn; Acctg.

**SMITH, BARRY W,** Patrick Henry Comm Coll, Martinsville, VA; FR; Math/Sci; Engr.

**SMITH, BELVIA B,** Fayetteville St Univ, Fayetteville, NC; SO; BED; Most Outstndg Imprvmnt Achvmnt Awd; Instrctnl Assist Howard Elem Schl.

**SMITH, BENNY SCOTT,** Fl Atlantic Univ, Boca Raton, FL; SO; BS; Auditor MHM Inc Deerfeild Beach FL 91; Accounting; CPA.

**SMITH, BETH N,** Liberty Univ, Lynchburg, VA; FR; IM Vlybl Capt 90; Psy; Cnslr.

**SMITH, BLAINE A,** S U N Y Coll At Fredonia, Fredonia, NY; JR; BS; ABATE 85-; AAS 83; AAS Jamestown Comm Coll 90; Geology; Envrnmntl Studies.

**SMITH, BONNIE J,** Beckley Coll, Beckley, WV; FR; BA; Nrsng; RN.

**SMITH, BRAD S,** Univ Of Southern Ms, Hattiesburg, MS; SR; BSBA; Stdnt Jdcl Cncl; Comm Fclty; Comm Stdnt Orgnztns; Envrnmntl Cncrs Comm; Bsns Stdnt Advsry Cncl; Englsh Clb; Bptst Un; Mrchng; Cncrt Bnds; Alpha Omega 87-88; Sigma Iota Epsilon 87-88; Ntnl Press Phtgrphrs Assn; Mrktng; Phrmctcl Sls Mgmnt.

**SMITH, BRADLEY S,** Bridgewater Coll, Bridgewater, VA; SR; BS; Wildlife Bio Asst U S Forest Svc; Microbio/Chem Lab Tech; Bio.

**SMITH, BRANDON K,** Univ Of Nc At Asheville, Asheville, NC; FR; BS; Church Youth Grp; Deans List; Schlrshp For Acadmcs; Acctng; CPA.

**SMITH, BRANDON W,** Western New England Coll, Springfield, MA; SO; Mktg; Advtsng.

**SMITH, BRENDA D,** James Sprunt Comm Coll, Kenansville, NC; FR; AAS; Elder Smith Presbyterian Church; Natl Soc Decorative Painters; Commercial Art; Teach.

**SMITH, BRENDA JO,** Hudson Valley Comm Coll, Troy, NY; AAS; Cmnctns/Engl; Pblc Rltns Wrtr.

**SMITH, BRENT A,** Northern Ky Univ, Highland Hts, KY; FR; BA; Hon List; Radio/TV/FILM; Broadcastng.

**SMITH, BRENT L,** Lenoir Rhyne Coll, Hickory, NC; JR; BA; Ntl Model United Nations 89-; Resdnt Advsr 89-; Pltcl Scie Clb Pres 88-; Mu Sigma Epsilon 90-; Pi Sigma Alpha VP 89-; Theta Xi Pres 89-; Business Admin/Political Scie; Law.

**SMITH, BRIAN D,** Duquesne Univ, Pittsburgh, PA; SO; BA; Dns Lst 89-; Vrsty Bsbl 90; Pol Sci Bus; Law.

**SMITH, BRIAN L,** Enterprise St Jr Coll, Enterprise, AL; FR; Bus; Acctg.

**SMITH, BRIAN P,** Glassboro St Coll, Glassboro, NJ; SR; BA; Info/Entrtnmnt Mag Wrtr/Prdctn Asst 90-; Nwspr Advrtsng Mngr 90-; Radio DJ 90-; AS Bergen Comm Coll 88; Advrtsng/Cmnctns; Advrtsng.

**SMITH, BRIDGET E,** Fl A & M Univ, Tallahassee, FL; SO; BSN; Dean Lst; Hnr Rll; Nrsng; RN/PRFSSR.

**SMITH, BYRON T,** Piedmont Tech Coll, Greenwood, SC; SO; AMTT; Machinist; Cert; Machine Tool Tech: AMTT/WORK As A-Machinist.

**SMITH, C ANNELIES,** Palm Beach Comm Coll, Lake Worth, FL; SO; USTA 89-; DAR 89-; AA; Intl Rltns; Intl Law.**

**SMITH, C WAYNE,** Univ Of Rochester, Rochester, NY; FR; BA; Cello Prfrmnc; Chamber Music.

**SMITH, CAMILLA,** Univ Of Rochester, Rochester, NY; JR; BA; Amnsty Intrntl Univ Of Rchstr Pblcst 88; Anmtn Intrst Grp 90-; Engl; Wrtr.

**SMITH, CANDACE L,** Fl A & M Univ, Tallahassee, FL; SO; BS; Pre-Phys Thrpy Club 90-; Phi Eta Sigma 89-; Phys Thrpy.

**SMITH, CANDACE V,** Univ Of Nc At Charlotte, Charlotte, NC; SO; BA; Hall Cncl Hse Pres 89-90; Delta Sigma Theta; Pol Sci; Law Or TV News Rprtr.

**SMITH, CANDIS S,** Lenoir Rhyne Coll, Hickory, NC; JR; BA; SNCAE; Elem Educ.

**SMITH, CARA L,** Queens Coll, Charlotte, NC; SO; BA; Stdnt Nwspr Edtr-Chf 89-; Pres Cncl 90-; Jstn Soc 90; Oasis 89-90; Intern C Mcklnbrg Pblc Dfndrs Ofc; T Srfrds Ntl Frm Pblc Opn 90; Poli Sci; Law.

**SMITH, CAROL A,** Bennett Coll, Greensboro, NC; SO; BS; Tennis; Cath Minis; Pres Schlr; Gymnstcs; Biology; Medicine Surgery.

**SMITH, CAROL J,** Univ Of Tn At Martin, Martin, TN; JR; BA; Socty Prof Jrnlsts Pres 85-86 90-; Alpha Epsilon Rho 90-91; Alpha Phi Omega 85-86; Univ Hnr Rl 90-; Hm Prnt Price Achvmnt Hm For Boys 89-90; Cmmnctns/Jrnlsm/Spnsh; Blngl Rprtr/Jrnlst.

**SMITH, CAROL J,** George Mason Univ, Fairfax, VA; FR.

**SMITH, CAROLINE L,** Tougaloo Coll, Tougaloo, MS; JR; BA; OUAP Brown Univ 88-89; A-APRP; NAACP Brown Univ 89-90; Urban League RI 89-90; Peer Sisters Pgm 89-90; Inroads Atlanta Intrn Assn 88-; J Walter Thompson Asst Media Plnr 88-; Clg Educ; Psych Resrch.

**SMITH, CAROLYN E,** Univ Of Sc At Columbia, Columbia, SC; SO; BA; Presbytrn Church Dcn; Acctng; Law.

**SMITH, CARRIE L,** Lesley Coll, Cambridge, MA; SO; BA; Hmn Servs Div Comm Rep 90-; SOAR Pblcty 89-90; Acdmc Hons 89-; Intrnshp Bosta Addescent Shltr 90; Intrnshp YWCA Daycare 89; Hmn Servs; Cnslng/Psychlgy.

**SMITH, CARRIE M,** Univ Of Nh Plymouth St Coll, Plymouth, NH; SR; BS; Eta Sigma Gamma 90-; Alpha Xi Delta 88-; Intrnshp Lttltn Reg Hosp Lttltn NH 90; Phys Educ; Nrusing/Medical.

**SMITH, CASEY N,** Univ Of Sc At Columbia, Columbia, SC; SR; BA; Assoc Hnrs Stdnts 89-; Phi Beta Kappa; Gamma Beta Phi 88-90; Sigma Iota Rho 89-; Phi Kappa Psi Secr 88-; Pol Sci; Law.

**SMITH, CASEY W,** Hartwick Coll, Oneonta, NY; FR; BA; Stdnt Senate 90-; Filed/Track Pole Vltng 90-; Nursing.

**SMITH, CATHLEEN D,** Liberty Univ, Lynchburg, VA; JR; BS; Bptst Stdnt Union Pres 90; Amer Mrktng Assoc; Clg Rpblcns; Hbtat For Hmnty; Bsnss Admin Mrktng; Cnsltng.

**SMITH, CATHRYN L,** S U N Y Coll At Fredonia, Fredonia, NY; SR; BA; AA Ricks Clg 89; Math; Sec Educ.

**SMITH, CECIL R,** Kent St Univ Stark Cmps, North Canton, OH; FR; ADN; Nrsng; CRNA.

**SMITH, CEDRICK L,** Jackson St Univ, Jackson, MS; JR; BS; ACM Bsnss Mgr 88; NSBE 89; Alpha Lambda Delta 89; Pi Mu Epsilon Bsnss Mgr 89; Beta Kappa Chi 89; Bellcore Smmr Intrnshp Rcpnt 89-90; Cmptr Sci; Grad Schl.

**SMITH, CHADD E,** Va Polytechnic Inst & St Univ, Blacksburg, VA; FR; BS; Cmps Rd 90-; Cmps Scts By Scts Amrc Asst Sctmstr 90-; Shaw Fndtn Treas 90-; Physcs; Prfssrshp Rsrch.

**SMITH, CHANDILYN D,** Fl St Univ, Tallahassee, FL; SO; BA; IM Vlybl 89; IM Sftbl 90; Hnrs Soc 89-90; Schlrs 89-90; Rep Jack Tobin Intern 90; Lady Seminole Bsktbl Mgr 90-; Psych/Crmnlgy; Victims Cnslg.

**SMITH, CHANDRA L,** Ms St Univ, Miss State, MS; SR; BS; Cmps Actvts Brd 88-89; Alph A Tau Omega Lttl Sstrs 90-; Alpha Lambda Delta 90-; Gamma Beta Phi 89-; Lambda Sigma 89-90; Phi Eta Sigma 89-90; Phi Kappa Phi; Natl Acctng Assoc 90-; Fncl Mgmt Assoc 90-; Fncl Mgmt Assoc Hnr Scty 90-; Crdnl Key; Bnkng.

**SMITH, CHANTEL D,** Alcorn St Univ, Lorman, MS; FR; BS; FFA Treas 90-; Ag Econ Clb 90-; Agriculture; Mngmnt Spclst.

**SMITH, CHARLENE M,** Kent St Univ Geauga Cmps, Burton Twp, OH; FR; BA; Crim Jstc.

**SMITH II, CHARLES G,** Univ Of Ga, Athens, GA; SR; BS; Middle Schl 90-; Soc Sci/Math; Educ.

**SMITH, CHARLES P,** Southern Coll Of Tech, Marietta, GA; JR; BA; Phi Eta Sigma 88; Natl Hon Soc Eng Tchnlgs Tau Alpha Pi Southern Tech; Rgstrtn Com Chrmn; Indl Eng.

**SMITH, CHARLOTTE G,** Memphis St Univ, Memphis, TN; SO; BA; Psychlgy.

**SMITH, CHARLOTTE M,** West Liberty St Coll, West Liberty, WV; JR; BA; Elem Ed; Tchng.

**SMITH, CHERI L,** Univ Of Sc At Sumter, Sumter, SC; FR; BED; Educ; Tchng.

**SMITH, CHERYL D,** Marshall University, Huntington, WV; GD; MA; Gamma Beta Phi; Big Bro/Big Sis; BA 89; Engl/Tchng; Tchr.

**SMITH, CHERYL J,** Johnson C Smith Univ, Charlotte, NC; SO; BS; Univ Marching Band 90-; Pep Band Univ 90-; Concert Band Univ 90-; Chem; Phrmctcl Rsrchr.

**SMITH, CHERYL R,** Thomas Nelson Comm Coll, Hampton, VA; SR; BSN; Hlth Care Advcts 89-; Cum Laude; RN John Hopkins Hosp; AAS; Nurs; Pediatrics.

**SMITH, CHERYL T,** Va Highlands Comm Coll, Abingdon, VA; SR; ADN; Nrsg Clb Treas 89-; Nrsg; RN.

**SMITH, CHRIS B,** Memphis St Univ, Memphis, TN; SR; BSET; Cmptr Eng Tech; Eng Tech.

**SMITH, CHRIS K,** Pellissippi St Tech Comm Coll, Knoxville, TN; SO; AAS; IEEE VP; Phi Theta Kappa; Tau Alpha Pi; Elec; Tchncn.

**SMITH, CHRISTINE M,** Univ Of Ky, Lexington, KY; JR; BS; IBM Pre Prof Prgrmmr 90-; Methodist Chr Fnncl Sec 89-; Cmptr Asst 84-90; Cmptr Sci; Systms Anlyst.

**SMITH, CHRISTOPHER E,** Fl A & M Univ, Tallahassee, FL; JR; BA; Graphic Arts Club 89-; Chi K Treas 90-; Stdnt Nwspr Design Edtr 89-; Hnr Roll 88-90; Graphic Artist Intrnshp At Ocala Star Banner Nwspr Ocala Fl 90; Graphic Design; Nwspr Or Adv Design.

**SMITH, CHRISTOPHER J,** Birmingham Southern Coll, Birmingham, AL; JR; Pres Stu Serv Orgn 90-; Natl Assc Accntnts; Phi Eta Sigma 89; Alpha Lambda Delta 89; Murry Arnold Schlr Athlt Awrd 90-; Vrsty Bsktbl Capt 88-; Accntng; Law.

**SMITH, CHRISTOPHER K,** Marshall University, Huntington, WV; SR; BA; All So Conf 89; Hon Rl 89-90; Trck/Fld 87-90; Soc Stdes Educ; Tchr/Coach.**

**SMITH, CHRISTOPHER L,** Johnson C Smith Univ, Charlotte, NC; JR; BA; Ssga Pres Elect; Stndt Judiciary Bd Univ Advoc 89-90; Charlotte Cnsrtn Blck Coll Stdnts Pres Elect; Hnrs Coll 89-90; Alpha Phi Alpha Dean Of Pldgs 90-; NAACP 88-; Pol Sci Clb/Yng Rep Clb VP 90-; Pol Sci; Atty At Law.**

**SMITH, CHRISTOPHER L,** Memphis St Univ, Memphis, TN; FR; BSE; Mech Engineering.

**SMITH, CHRISTOPHER M,** Ms St Univ, Miss State, MS; FR; BA; Miss St Famous Maroon Band 90; Stdnt Phy Soc 90-; Gamma Beta Phi 90-; Hnrs Prog 90-; Fed Jr Flwshp Prog 89-; Phys; Resrch Tchr.

**SMITH, CHRISTOPHER S,** Lurleen B Wallace St Jr Coll, Andalusia, AL; SO; BS; LBW Co-Op Prog 88-; Bus; Acctng.**

**SMITH, CLARISSA D,** Marshall University, Huntington, WV; SR; BBA; Acctg Clb Exec Advsry Com 89-; Buskirk Hall Advsry Cncl 87-89; WV Soc CPA 89-; Deans Lst 87/90-; IMS 87-89; Acctg.

**SMITH, CLAYTON ROBERT,** Al St Univ, Montgomery, AL; JR; BA; AAS Cntrl Ala Comm Clg 88; Music; Audio Engrng Film Scoring.

**SMITH, CLIFFORD A,** Le Moyne Owen Coll, Memphis, TN; SO; BA; Yth Dir Yth Minister Sprnghl Mssnry Bapt Chrch 89-; US Army 79-83; Bus Admin.

**SMITH JR, CLYDE E,** Limestone Coll, Gaffney, SC; SR; MBA; Amer Soc Quality Cntrl/Cert Quality Auditor 90-; Bsn Admin/Mgmt.

**SMITH, CONNIE L,** Central Al Comm Coll, Alexander City, AL; FR; BS; Hstry; Educ.

**SMITH, CONNIE L,** Wv Univ, Morgantown, WV; SR; BACH; Amer Soc Hsop Phrmcy 88-; Stdnt Govt V Pres 87-88; Sigma Phi Omega Hnr Soc V P 88-89; Kappa Psi 88-; Miss Teen Schlrshp For Clge Ed 86-87; Pharmacy.

**SMITH, CONNIE M,** Univ Of Sc At Columbia, Columbia, SC; SR; BS; Crmnl Jstc Assoc 89-; Wmn Bus 89-90; Lamda Chi Alpha 87-88; Intrnshp; IM Games; Crmnl Jstc; Fed Law Enfrcmnt.

**SMITH, COREY M,** Morehouse Coll, Atlanta, GA; SO; BA; Fla Clb 90-; Pre Law Soc 90-; Hnr Rl 90-; Pol Sci; Law.

**SMITH, CRAIG D,** Ms Coll, Clinton, MS; GD; JD; Moot Crt Brd 90-; Deans Stdnt Advsry Cmt 90-; Dlt Theta Phi Pres 90-; Herrin Hess Law Schlrshp 89-; Yng Lawyrs Div MS State Bar Assc 89-; Str Mgr Chldrns Palace Toy Stores 86-89; BS Un Sthrn MS 84; Law.

**SMITH, CRYSTAL S,** Marshall University, Huntington, WV; FR; BBA; Dean Lst Marshall 90-; Sigma Sigma Sigma; Marketing; Sales Mngmnt.

**SMITH, CYNTHIA A,** Wv Univ At Parkersburg, Parkersburg, WV; JR; BS; Chorale 89-90; Phi Theta Kappa 89; Art Ctr Rgnl Exhbtn 88-90; AS 90; Ophthlmc Tchncn To Dr R Johns 90; Ophthlmgy.**

**SMITH, CYNTHIA ANN,** Univ Of Nc At Greensboro, Greensboro, NC; SR; BED; Envrmntl Awrnss Fndtn 90-; Univ Mrshll 88-; Alpha Lamda Delta 88-; Mddl Grds Educ; Tchng.

**SMITH, CYNTHIA L,** Marshall University, Huntington, WV; SR; BBA; Am Mktg Assn 88-89; Awana Clbs Yth Ldr 89-; Deans Lst 89-; Shearson Lehman Bro Intrnshp Mktg Asst; Mktg; Retail Buyer.

**SMITH, CYNTHIA L,** Ga St Univ, Atlanta, GA; GD; SGAE Sec 88-90; GSU 88-90; Gldn Key 89-; Pi Lambda Theta; Mu Rho Sigma Sec 88-89; PTA GA Ntnl Pres VP 86-88; NAPM 75-77; NCTM 90-; NSTA 90-; BSE 90; Edctn Mddl Grds; Tchng.

**SMITH, CYNTHIA L,** Ky Wesleyan Coll, Owensboro, KY; SR; BA; Pltcl Sci Clb 90-; Alpha Phi Sigma 87-; Alpha Chi 90-; Crmnl Jstc Assoc 86-; Acdmy Crmnl Jstc Sci 90-; Sthrn Crmnl Jstc Assoc 90; Schrlshp 90; Hstrcl Scty; Kntckns Agnst Asslt Wpns; Scl Wrkr; Crmnl Jstc.

**SMITH, CYNTHIA R,** Geneva Coll, Beaver Falls, PA; FR; BS ED; Mrchng Band 90-; Cotton Candy Cnnctn; Ele Educ; Tch.

**SMITH, DANA E,** Christopher Newport Coll, Newport News, VA; SR; BSGA; Gamma Phi Beta 87-89; 7th Distr Juvenile/Domestic Rels Ct Vol Intern; Pol Sci; Crmnl Jstc.

**SMITH, DANA F,** Sue Bennett Coll, London, KY; SO; BAA; SNEA Pres 88-90; SGA 88-89; FCC 88-90; AA; Elem Ed.

**SMITH, DANA M,** Univ Of Sc At Columbia, Columbia, SC; FR; BA; Deans Lst; Sc Soc Prof Eng Schlrshp; Sci; Phy Thrpy.

**SMITH, DANA R,** Univ Of Sc At Columbia, Columbia, SC; JR; Bapt Yng Wmn 90-; Grnvlle Jycs 90-; Educ; Tchng.

**SMITH, DANIEL J,** Northeastern Christian Jr Coll, Villanova, PA; JR; BA; Bsktbll 88-90; Gama Delta Gama 89-; Scl Sci.

**SMITH, DANNY D,** Fayetteville St Univ, Fayetteville, NC; FR; BA; Math Edctn; Tchng.

**SMITH, DANNY E,** Univ Of South Al, Mobile, AL; GD; BA; Ed; Tch Emtnl Cnflctd Stdnts.

**SMITH, DARLENE M,** Hudson Valley Comm Coll, Troy, NY; SO; BA; Med Tech Virogenetics Corp Renss Tech Pk 86-; Math/Sci; Nursing.

**SMITH, DARLENE POWELL,** Wilmington Coll, New Castle, DE; SR; BSN; Head Nrs; Dipl Brandwine Hosp 78; Nrsng.

**SMITH, DAVID A,** Unity Coll, Unity, ME; SO; BEG; Emerg Response Tm Co-Dir 90-; Alpine Clb Advsr 89-; Forest Fire Prvntn Tm 90-; Mntr Pgm Prncpls Instr Ldrshp; Lacrosse Team 89-; AS Univ Coll; Forestry; Forest Tech.

**SMITH, DAVID E,** Va Commonwealth Univ, Richmond, VA; SR; BS; Stdnt Educ Assoc Pub Chr 90-; Elem Educ; Tchng.

**SMITH, DAVID RANDALL,** Univ Of Akron, Akron, OH; JR; BS; Future Physcns Cl 89-90; Alpha Lambda Delta 88-; Phi Etga Sigma 88-; Golden Key 90-; Tau Beta Pi; Phi Gamma Delta 89-; Acad Schlrshp 89-; AAS New Castle Schl/Tx 85; Chemcl Engrng; Med Schl; Biomed Engrng.

**SMITH, DAVID V,** Univ Of Md At Eastern Shore, Princess Anne, MD; SO; BA; Bus.

**SMITH, DAWN M,** Blue Mountain Coll, Blue Mountain, MS; SR; BS; BSU; MAE-SP; SGA Sr Atty 90-; Athl Cncl Modenian Athl Dir 89-90; Athl Cncl 90-; Dns Lst 90-; Modenian Socl Socty Athl Dir 89-90 Pres 90-; Athl Key Pin/Charm 88-89; Fld Day Maid; Swmng/Sftbl/Vlybl/Tns/Ping/Pong/Bsktbl/Trck All Star 87-; Elem Educ; Tchr.

**SMITH, DEBBIE A,** Mountain Empire Comm Coll, Big Stone Gap, VA; SO; AS EN; Envrnmntl Sci Clb VP 89-; PTA Norton Tres 89-; Intrnshp Big Stone Gap Water Plnt Oprtn Trng 88-90; MECC Stdnt Wrkr Dr Chuks Ogbonnaya Lab Asstnt 90; Sci; Water Works Oper.

**SMITH, DEBORAH C,** Mayland Comm Coll, Spruce Pine, NC; FR; AAS; Acctng.

**SMITH, DEBORAH D,** Tri County Tech Coll, Pendleton, SC; FR; BA; Alpha Zeta Beta; Prof Rctr Oprtr Soc 88; Amer Nclr Soc 89; Nclr Rctr Opr For Duke Pwr Co At Oconee Nclr Stn 86; Non-Licensed Opr 79-86; Electrical Eng.

**SMITH, DEBORAH H,** Belmont Coll, Nashville, TN; FR; BS; Psychlgy Clb; Gamma Beta Plhi; Bookkeeper.

**SMITH, DEBORAH L,** De Tech & Comm Coll At Dover, Dover, DE; GD; Nrsg Club Soc Coord 90; Dns Lst; Nrsg; RN.

**SMITH, DEBORAH L,** Glassboro St Coll, Glassboro, NJ; FR; Magazine 90-; Prod Asst; Certif Katharine Gibbs Sch 88; Sclgy; Ed.

**SMITH, DEBORAH L,** Univ Of Akron, Akron, OH; SR; BS; Math Clb 87-; Beta Gamma Sigma 90-; Golden Key 90-; Schlrshp Awds/Grnts; RIAA Gold Rcrd; Amer Fed Mscns H Fox Agncy; SHE Music BM P 78-; Moxie Music P 87-; Pro Mscn/Rcrdng Artist/Sng Wrtr 64-; Acctg; Law.

**SMITH, DEBORAH R,** Northeast Ms Cc, Booneville, MS; FR; AAS; Phi Theta Kappa; Phi Beta Lambda 90-; Micropcomputer Inf Prcsng.

**SMITH, DEBRA A,** Ky Wesleyan Coll, Owensboro, KY; SR; BS; Alpha Chi 89-; J G Brown Schlr; Sigma Kappa Choir 87-90; Math; Bus/Ins.

**SMITH, DEBRA JEAN,** Davis Coll, Toledo, OH; JR; AS; Acctng.

**SMITH, DEBRA W,** Univ Of Al At Birmingham, Birmingham, AL; SR; BS; AL Med Rec Assn 90-; Amer Med Rec Assn 90-; Stdnt Med Rec Clb 89-; Alpha Kappa Alpha Sec 87-; Yng Chrstn Wmn Assn 90-; Blck Stdnt Org 86-89; Deans Lst 90; Pres Hon Lst; Mnrty Schlrshp 89-; Med Rec Admin; Dir.

**SMITH, DEIRDRE M,** Western New England Coll, Springfield, MA; FR; BA; English; Law.

**SMITH, DELORES,** Middle Ga Coll, Cochran, GA; FR; AS; Bapt Union Camp Outrch Chr; SADD; Intrntl Rltns Clb Quiz Bwl; Deans Lst; GPA Awd Marshall; Bio; Med.

**SMITH, DENA L,** Clayton St Coll, Morrow, GA; GD; ASN; Ga Assoc Of Nrsng 89; Nrse Extrn At Clytn Gnrl Hosp 90; US Army 82-87; Nrsng; Nrsng Emer Rm.

**SMITH, DENISE A,** City Univ Of Ny Queensbrough, New York, NY; JR; AAS; C Stp; Orientn; Nrs Aide 88-; Nrsg.

**SMITH, DENISE M,** Atlantic Comm Coll, Mays Landing, NJ; GD; BA; Chrldng Capt 87; PTK Ntl Hnr Scty 89; Intrnshp At Lcl Law Offce Prlgl 89-90; Miss NJ; AAS 90; Cmmnctns; Crmnl Law.

**SMITH, DERRICK L,** Fl A & M Univ, Tallahassee, FL; SR; BS; Cmptr/Info Systs Clb Chpln; Caribbean Stdnt Assn; Gldn Key; IBM; Cmptr/Info Systs.

**SMITH, DESIREE L,** Univ Of Montevallo, Montevallo, AL; SR; Cir K Treas 87-88; Afro-Amer Soc Pres 87-89; SGA Sen; Omicron Delta Kappa 89-; Kappa Mu Epsilon Sec 89-; Kappa Delta Pi 90-; Zeta Phi Beta; AL Dlgt Ntl 4-H Cngrss 87; John A House Ldrshp Awd 89; Math; Ed.

**SMITH, DETRICE T,** Central St Univ, Wilberforce, OH; SR; BSED; Chrldr 88-; Miss SU 90-; NAACP; Alpha Kappa Alpha; Ohio Stdnt Educ Assoc; Adoptd Sch Prog; NATE; English.

**SMITH, DEXTREL J,** Morehouse Coll, Atlanta, GA; SR; BA; Bus Assn 89-; Ftbl Tm Co Capt 90-; Bus Mrktng.

**SMITH, DIANA A,** Univ Of North Fl, Jacksonville, FL; SR; BA; Phi Kappa Phi 89; Gldn Ky; Natl Hnr Soc Psych 90; Phi Theta Kappa 89; AA St Johns Rivert Comm Coll 89; Cert Soc Wlfr; Psych; Law.**

**SMITH, DIANA G,** Marshall University, Huntington, WV; FR; BA; Bus Mgmt; Htl/Rstrnt Mngr.

**SMITH, DIANA L,** Milligan Coll, Milligan Clg, TN; JR; BS; Acad Affrs Comm SGA Chrmn 90-; Cls Pres; IMS 88-; Acad Dns Lst 90; Delta Kappa VP 89-; Big Bro/Sis 88-89; ICU Bible Stdy Grp 89-90; RA 90-; Tnns 88-90; Bsn Admn/Psy.

**SMITH, DOLLY K,** Bristol Univ, Bristol, TN; SO; BA; Empl Bnfts Asst 88-; Bus Admn.

**SMITH, DONALD A,** Middle Tn St Univ, Murfreesboro, TN; FR; BS; Block/Brdl Clb; Pre Vet Socty; Sailor Of Qrtr Awd Navy 90; US Navy 88-90; USS Kalamazoo Adr 6 Gunners Mate Petty Offcr 3rd Cls; Anml Sci; Vet.

**SMITH II, DONALD C,** Ms St Univ, Miss State, MS; FR; BS; Greek Cncl For Christ; Campus Actvts Bd 90-; Refrmd Univ Flwshp 90-; Lambda Sigma; Gamma Beta Phi; Phi Gamms Delta 90-; Untd Way 90-; Giolgcl Sci; Medcn.

**SMITH, DONALD COLE,** Univ Of Akron, Akron, OH; SR; BED; Gilbert/Marguerite Dilly Hist Schlrshp 90-; Jr Vars Bsbl 71; Vol Coach 85-86; Crpntr; Assist Coach 71-91; Bsktbl Coach 90-; Assist Coach 87-; Soc Studies Cmprhnsv; Scndry Tchr.

**SMITH, DONNA DU VALL,** Comm Coll Algny Co Algny Cmps, Pittsburgh, PA; FR; AS; Gldn Trngle Dcrtve Pntrs Lbrrn 90-; Rsprty Thrpst.

**SMITH, DONNA K,** Radford Univ, Radford, VA; BGS; Phi Theta Kappa Pres 88-90; Wmns Rsrc Crisis Intrvntn Intrnshp 91-; Am Assn Univ Wmn Schlrshp 90-; Radfords Bus/Prfsnl Wmns Clb Schlrshp 90-; 4-H Ldr; Chrprsn Blacksburg Fun Day Horse Show; AAS New River Comm Clg 90; Psychlgy; Cnslng.

**SMITH, DONNA L,** Chattahoochee Vly St Comm Coll, Phenix City, AL; SO; BA; Loan Admin Dept 87-; AS; Fin.

**SMITH, DONNA L,** Univ Of Pittsburgh, Pittsburgh, PA; SR; MSW; Res Assc Pres 89-; Theta Chi Aux 89-; Chldrns Hosp Vol; RA 90-; Rehab Cntr Intern 90-; BSW; Soc Wrk; Hosp Soc Wrkr.

**SMITH, DONNA M,** Dyersburg St Comm Coll, Dyersburg, TN; FR; Phi Theta Kappa; Sci; Phrmcy.

**SMITH, DONNA MICHELLE,** Union Univ, Jackson, TN; JR; BS; Sigma Zeta 90-; Biology; Zoology.

**SMITH, DONNA R,** Univ Of Sc At Aiken, Aiken, SC; JR; BS; Gamma Beta Phi Sec 90-; Ed Mjrs Clb Chptr Rep 90-; GBP; Pres Hon Roll; Deans List; Awrd Alpha Dlt Kappa; Dlt Chptr Schlrshp; SCACUS; SACUS; AA Un SC 90; Erly Chldhd Ed; Tchng.

**SMITH, DORIS JULIE,** Univ Of South Al, Mobile, AL; SR; BS; Dns Lst; Pres Lst; Sprnghl Mem Hosp Sec 74-90; Lang Arts Cmpst; Tchng/Reading.

**SMITH, DWIGHT W,** Fl Atlantic Univ, Boca Raton, FL; JR; BA; DIP Clg Arts Science Tech 90; CERT Business Tech Ed Council London 86; Business Mngmnt; Finance.

**SMITH, EARNESTINE M,** Fayetteville St Univ, Fayetteville, NC; FR; BA; Psychlgy; Chld Cnslng.

**SMITH, EDITH I,** Vance Granville Comm Coll, Henderson, NC; SR; AA; Cmptr Clb VP 89-; Stdt Gvt Scl Comm 90-; Stdt Gvt Data Prcsng Rep 90-; Ambass 90-; Deans List 89-; Dept Schrlshp 90-; Alpha Sigma Chi Sec; Mbr Lsburg Un Meth Chur 69-; Data Processing; Bus Computer Prog.

**SMITH, ELAINE CLAIRE,** Ms St Univ, Miss State, MS; SR; BA; Mrchng Bnd Flg Corps 88 90; Drama Scty 88-; Scotch Guard 90-; Alpha Lambda Delta VP 89-; Alpha Psi Omega; Gamma Alpha Epsilon 90-; Sigma Tau Delta 90-; Alpha Gamma Delta VP 88-; Presidents Schlr 88-90; Deans Lst; English/Theatre; Professor.**

**SMITH, ELAINE M,** Hillsborough Comm Coll, Tampa, FL; SO; Bus; Interior Dsgn.

**SMITH, ELAINE M,** Univ Of South Al, Mobile, AL; JR; BS; Share Tm 89-; Alpha Gamma Delta Pldg Treas/Standards Chair 88-90; St Margarets Vol Grp 84-90; Edn Early Chldhd; Teach.

**SMITH, ELGIN K,** Morehouse Coll, Atlanta, GA; JR; BS; Intl Orgnztn 87-90; Bahamian Stdnts 87-88; Comp Sci Club 90-; Tstmstrs; Bnkng; Comp Sci; Prgmr Anlst.

**SMITH, ELIZABETH A,** Univ Of Tn At Martin, Martin, TN; SR; BA; Frst Bptst Chrch Chr VBS; Girls L L Sftbll; Carroll Co Brd Educ 79-90; AS Jackson St Jr Coll 87; Erly Chldhd/Elem Educ; Tchr.

**SMITH, ELIZABETH MARIE,** Univ Of Ga, Athens, GA; SR; BS; SHEA 90-; Stdnt Mrchndsg Assoc 90-; AATCC 90-; Alpha Zeta; Berry Clg Schlrshp 88-90; Txtl/Apprl Mngmnt; Mng Txtl Frm.

**SMITH, ELIZABETH VON TONYA,** Cheyney Univ Of Pa, Cheyney, PA; SR; BA; Natl Cncl Negro Womn 89-90; Dns Lst 87-; Acad Recog 89-; Socl Rel; Prob Offcr/Socl Wrkr.

**SMITH, ELSA LEE,** Middle Tn St Univ, Murfreesboro, TN; JR; BS; Kappa Delta Pi; Kappa Omicron Phi; Gamma Beta Phi; IM Sftbl/Vllybl 88-89; Early Chldhd Educ; Tchr.

**SMITH, ERIC P,** Univ Of New Haven, West Haven, CT; JR; BS; Mrktng; Law Schl.

**SMITH, ERIC S,** Oh Univ, Athens, OH; FR; BSME; Hall Cncl Res Rep 90-; Cmps Crsd Christ 90-; Ldrshp Dvlp Pgm 90-; IM Bsktbl/Sftbl 90-; Mech Engrng; Cnsltnt.

**SMITH, ERICA,** Springfield Tech Comm Coll, Springfield, MA; SO; BS; Blgy; Marine Blgy.

**SMITH, ERNEST L,** Norfolk St Univ, Norfolk, VA; SR; BS; Deans Lst 90-; Mngmnt Cmptr Infrmtn Systms; Prgrmr.

**SMITH, ETTA N,** Fl A & M Univ, Tallahassee, FL; SO; BA; Charge Nurse FSH Chatt Fl; Nursing; Surgical Nurse.

**SMITH JR, EUGENE,** Bowie St Univ, Bowie, MD; FR; BA; Bus/Mktg.

**SMITH, FAYE M,** Valdosta St Coll, Valdosta, GA; SR; BFA; Art Stdnts League 88; Art; Artst.

**SMITH, FLORINE,** Norfolk St Univ, Norfolk, VA; SR; BA; Spec Olympcs 89-90; Mkt Dys Comm 85-86; NAACP Pres 79-81; OES 80-82; Spec Educ Tchr Thms Hntr Schl; Cert Rappahanock Comm Clg 78; Spec Ed; Tchr.

**SMITH, FRANCINE M,** George Mason Univ, Fairfax, VA; JR; BA; Elem Educ; Tchng.

**SMITH II, FRANKLIN P,** Wv Univ At Parkersburg, Parkersburg, WV; SO; WTD.

**SMITH, FRANKLIN T,** Radford Univ, Radford, VA; SR; BBA; Ski Clb 87-88; People Undrstndg Svrly Hndcppd Ntl Phlnthrpy; Pi Kappa Phi Chr Ntl Phlnthrpy 88-; Bro Yr 90-; Bus Mgmt.

**SMITH, FRANKLYN N,** Univ Of Pittsburgh, Pittsburgh, PA; SR; MSW; Light Of Life Mission 90-; Res Advisor 87-; BSAW; Social Work; Counseling.

**SMITH, FREDREIKA W,** Columbia Union Coll, Takoma Park, MD; JR; BA; Lcl Govt Prsnl Asc 87-; Schlstc Achvmnt Awd 88; Dist 22-C Lns Clb Intl Coord; Lns Clb; Mamie D Lee Schl Vol; Crnthn Bptst Chrch Vol 85-; Lions Eye Bank Vol 85-; Columbia Lghthse Blind Vol 85-; Prsnnl Mgmt Spec 67-; AAS Univ DC 88; Org Dvlpmnt/Mgmt; Prsnnl Mgmt Cnsltnt.

**SMITH, GAYLE A,** Owensboro Comm Coll, Owensboro, KY; SO; AS; Nursing; RN.

**SMITH, GAYNA M,** Hampton Univ, Hampton, VA; SO; BA; Callipe Lit Soc 89-; Afrkn Stds Clustr 90-; Engl; Coll Tchr.

**SMITH, GEORGE A,** Al A & M Univ, Normal, AL; SR; BA; Stdt Govt Assctn Senate Ldr 87; Phi Beta Kappa 88-89; Sigma Tau Epsilon 88; Hstry; Tch/Law.

**SMITH, GERARD A,** Le Moyne Coll, Syracuse, NY; SO; BS; Intl Hse 89-; Proj Cmnty Vol Tutor; Vars Soccer 89-; IM Bsktbl 89-; Indstrl Rels.

**SMITH, GINA L,** Univ Of Sc At Spartanburg, Spartanburg, SC; FR; BS; Shriners Crippled/Burn Chldrn; Beauty Pageants; Modeling; Dancing; Karate; Mktg; Exec.

**SMITH II, GLENN E,** Daytona Beach Comm Coll, Daytona Beach, FL; FR; Deland Cltr Arts Grp; Stetson Chrl Unn 90-; Music; Educ.

**SMITH, GREGORY C,** Radford Univ, Radford, VA; FR.

**SMITH, GREGORY D,** Ny Univ, New York, NY; SR; BA; Alpha Sigma Lambda 89-; Intrnshp ABC Nws Nghtlne 90; Free Lnce Cpy Edit; Engl; Tchng.

**SMITH, GREGORY H,** Meridian Comm Coll, Meridian, MS; JR; BA; Bus Admin/Acctg.

**SMITH, GREGORY K,** Marshall University, Huntington, WV; JR; BA; Beta Phi; Acctg; Law.

**SMITH, GUY ALAN,** Coll Of Charleston, Charleston, SC; JR; BSEE; Otstndng Unit Awd One Oak Leaf Clstr; AF Good Conduct Mdl; AF Training Ribbon; US Air Force Srvcs Spclst Srgnt 86-89; ASSC Bsns Trident Tchncl Clg 85; Physics; Engnrng.

**SMITH, GUY R,** Southern Coll Of Tech, Marietta, GA; SR; BS; Tau Alpha Pi 89-; Gldn Ky 83-; Pi Kappa Lambda 83-; Acad Rcgntn; Otstndng Grad Sr Lckhd GA Mgmt Assn; BM Univ Of Georgia 83; Elec Eng.

**SMITH JR, HAROLD A,** Southern Coll Of Tech, Marietta, GA; SR; BS; ACM 90-; Tau Alpha Pi 89-90; BS Chem Univ GA 83; Cmptr Sci; Sftwre Dvlpmnt.

**SMITH, HEATHER,** Mary Baldwin Coll, Staunton, VA; SR; BA; Pre Law Soc Sec 89-; Actvts Bd Sec 89-90; Educ Plcy Cmtee 90-; Hon Lst; Deans Lst; Hon Schlr Soc 90-; Clert Intrn 90-; Ltcl Sci; Law.

**SMITH, HEATHER C,** Emory Univ, Atlanta, GA; JR; BA; Beta Gamma Sigma; Beta Alpha Psi Rec Secr 90-; Delta Delta Delta Asst Treas 89-; Emory Bsn Sch Schlrshp 88-; Dns Lst 88-; Acctg Intern 90-; Bsn/Acctg; Law.

**SMITH, HEATHER K,** Indiana Univ Of Pa, Indiana, PA; JR; Gymn 87-88; Diving 88-90; Elem Edn; Tchr/Coach.

**SMITH, HELEN D,** Tusculum Coll, Greeneville, TN; JR; BS; Phi Theta Kappa 90-; Otstndng Stu Educ Awrd 90; USS Greeneville Mmbrshp Cmmtt 90-; Prjct Choice Vol Ttr 90-; AS Walters St Comm Coll 90; Elem Educ; Educ.

**SMITH, HELEN E T,** Bloomfield Coll, Bloomfield, NJ; SR; BA; Hons Prog 89-; Blck Afrcn Amer Wmn Oral Hstries Asst; Natl Assoc Wmn Bnkng 88-; Mortg Bnkrs Assoc 87-; Engl Comms; Brdcst Jrnlsm.

**SMITH, HENRY W,** Howard Univ, Washington, DC; SR; B ARC; Iota Phi Theta Hstrn 87-; Arch; Arch.

**SMITH, HOLLY S,** Univ Of Sc At Coastal Carolina, Conway, SC; FR; BS; Business Clb; IM Sftbll; Marine Sci; Marine Biologist.

**SMITH, HOWARD D,** Chesterfield Marlboro Coll, Cheraw, SC; FR; Gen Bus.

**SMITH, HOWARD S,** George Mason Univ, Fairfax, VA; SO; BS; Hnr Admssn Prgrm; Chi Phi Zeta; IM Bsktbl Ftbl, Mgmt; Bsns.

**SMITH, IAN J,** Va St Univ, Petersburg, VA; SO; BS; Tidewater Pre Alumni Pres; Ddrftng Clb 90-; Seward Hall Exec Brd; Drftng; Archtctrl Eng.

**SMITH, INGRID T,** Wilberforce Univ, Wilberforce, OH; SR; Ntl Stdnt Bus Leag 88-; Alpha Kappa Mu 89-F Sigma Omega 90-; Alpha Kappa Alpha Sorty Inc Rcrdng Sec 89-; Hoyt Nrsng Hm Amind Intrn 90; F Isabel Askew Awd 90; Ldrshp Flw 90; BS; Hlth Care Admin.

**SMITH, JACKIE J,** East Stroudsburg Univ, E Stroudsburg, PA; SO; Vars Fld Hcky/Lcrs; Crmnl Jstc; Corrections.

**SMITH, JACQUELYN P,** Birmingham Southern Coll, Birmingham, AL; SO; BA; Human Resrcs.

**SMITH, JAMES A,** Tri County Tech Coll, Pendleton, SC; SO; AS; Alpha Beta Zeta 90-; VFW; Sr Master Sgt U S Air Force 66-90; Comp Sci.

**SMITH, JAMES B,** Wilmington Coll, Wilmington, OH; JR; SGA Bdgt Chrmn; Stdnt Free Entrprs Pres 89-; Grk Cncl Pres; Hon Scty; Gamma Phi Gamma Pres; Ec; Portfolio Mgmt.

**SMITH, JAMES L,** Daemen Coll, Amherst, NY; JR; BS; Stdnt Fclty Comm 90-; Fclty Srch 90-; Beta Beta Beta 90-; Vol Fire Dept 85-; Blgy; Rsrch.

**SMITH, JAMES R,** Duquesne Univ, Pittsburgh, PA; SR; Theta Chi Frtrnty Ctr 87-89; Mgmt Infor Sys; Pgmr/Analysis.

**SMITH, JAMIE L,** Fl International Univ, Miami, FL; SR; BS; Phi Kappa Phi; Sgm Phi Alph Edtr 90-; Otstndng Schlr FIU 89-90; Deans List 89-90; Ovrl Otstndng Prfrmc Sqd Ldr 85; Crctns Acad; Crmnl Jstc Inst; BS; Nghbrhd Crm Wtch Chrprsn; Mrch Dimes Wlk Amer Tm Capt 86; AA Miami Dade Comm Clg 88; Crmnl Jstc; Crmnl Law.

**SMITH, JANET L,** Trenton St Coll, Trenton, NJ; FR; BA; Pep Bnd; Sttstcs; Actry.

**SMITH, JANET L REED,** Ms St Univ, Miss State, MS; SR; BS; Deca Prsdnt 90-; Kappa Delta Pi; Deans Schlr 90; Prsdnts Schlr; Cmmnty Clg Rcgntn Schlrshp 90-; AA Meridian Cmmnty Cllg 88; Mrktng Edctn; Edctr Prfsr.

**SMITH, JANICE M,** Tri County Tech Coll, Pendleton, SC; SR; ASSOC; Phi Theta Kappa; Schlmbrgr Indstrs; Cert 87; Indstrl Elcntrncs.**

**SMITH, JASON P,** Richard Bland Coll, Petersburg, VA; SO; BA; IM Bsktbl 88; AS 91; Bus; CPA.

**SMITH, JAY D,** Northern Ky Univ, Highland Hts, KY; FR; BS; Bio Soc 90-; Am Chem Soc 90-; Physics Clb; William Greaves Schlrshp; Bio; Botany.

**SMITH, JEANETTE G,** Univ Of Akron, Akron, OH; JR; BFA; Stdnt Art League 89-; Cleveland Mag Intrnshp; Aurora Study Clb/Aurora Schls PTO 86-; Fundrsng Cmtes For Campfire Inc 88-90; Cleveland Ballet 90; AAS Corning Clg 72; BS Cortland Univ 76; Graphic Design; Adv.

**SMITH, JEANNA D,** Northern Ky Univ, Highland Hts, KY; FR; BA; Bsn; CPA.

**SMITH, JEANNIE J,** Univ Of Nc At Greensboro, Greensboro, NC; SR; BS; Amrcn Hm Ecnmcs Assn 90-; Kappa Omnicron Nu Tres 90-; Esther Segnr Schlrshp 89-; Schlr Awd 89-; Home Economics; Tchr.

**SMITH, JEFFREY,** Univ Of Southern Ms, Hattiesburg, MS; SR; BS; Afro Amer Stdnt Org 88; Hall Cncil Chrprsn 87-88; Cmptr Eng Tech.

**SMITH, JEFFREY H,** Univ Of Sc At Columbia, Columbia, SC; GD; SGA Rep 89; Unvrsty Bsns Soc Prsdnt 90; BS 90.

**SMITH, JEFFREY L,** Memphis St Univ, Memphis, TN; FR; BA; Graphcs Flm Assmblr 80-89; Lost Eyesgnt Voc Rehab Put Jeff Bck In Schl; Psych; Cnslng/Rehab Thrpy.

**SMITH, JEFFREY R,** S U N Y Coll Of A & T Morrisvl, Morrisville, NY; FR; Morrisville Strategy Gramers Guild Guildmstr; Scorekpr Wmns Vlybl Vrsty Tm 90; Hist Lib Arts Humanities; Edn Hist.

**SMITH, JENNIFER E,** Kent St Univ Kent Cmps, Kent, OH; FR; BSN; Aerobics 90-; Nrsng.

**SMITH, JENNIFER J,** Wright St Univ Lake Cmps, Celina, OH; SO; BA; Math; Edn.

**SMITH, JENNIFER L,** Oh St Univ At Marion, Marion, OH; SO; BA; Deans Lst; Scl Sci.

**SMITH, JENNIFER L,** Univ Of Southern Ms, Hattiesburg, MS; SR; BS; Home Ec Clb 87-; Kappa Omicron Nu 90-; Golden Key 90-; Ethel Summerhour Schlrshp 90; Johnmerl Tatum Schlrshp 90; IFCEA Schlrshp 90; AA Jones Cty Jr Clg 89; Nutrition; Clncl Dietitian.

**SMITH, JENNIFER L,** Georgetown Univ, Washington, DC; SO; BBA; Class Cmmttee 90; Admssns Ambssdrs Prog 89; Prtstnt Choir 90; Soup Ktchn; Sursum Corda Tutrng Prog Tutr 90; Accntng/Fnce.

**SMITH, JENNIFER L,** Kent St Univ Kent Cmps, Kent, OH; JR; BS; Campus Crusade 89-; IM Bsktbl 88-; Golden Key; Phi Epsilon Kappa; Mary Beth Ikerman Awd; IM Vlybl 88-; Phys Fitness Spec; Cardiac Rehab.

**SMITH, JENNIFER L,** Univ Of Cincinnati-Clrmnt Coll, Batavia, OH; SR; BED; Ed; Elmntry Ed.

**SMITH, JENNIFER M,** Belmont Coll, Nashville, TN; FR; Bapt Stdnt Union; IM Bwlng; BA; Msc Bus; Cpyrght Lwyr.

**SMITH, JERRY A,** Meridian Comm Coll, Meridian, MS; SO; MBA; Air Ntl Grd; E Cntrl Comm Schlp 89; Air Ntl Grd Schlp 89; ACT Schlp 89; Bsn Admn; Lwyr/Jdg Law.

**SMITH, JESSICA A,** Univ Of Med & Dentistry Of Nj, Newark, NJ; Amer Socty Cytotech 89-; Cytotechnlgst 90-.

**SMITH, JEWEL E,** Central St Univ, Wilberforce, OH; SR; BS; Math/Cmptr Sci Clb 90-; Math; Edctr.

**SMITH, JILL C,** Oh Wesleyan Univ, Delaware, OH; SO; BA; Delta Gamma VP Schlrshp 89-; Phi Eta Sigma; Vars Tnns 89-90; Intl Bsns/Spnsh.

**SMITH, JO ANN,** Fayetteville St Univ, Fayetteville, NC; GD; MBA; Kappa Delta Pi 89-; Activ Comm; Sndy Schl Tchr 83-89; ; Aa Fayetteville Tech Clg 88; Owner Private Erly Chldhd Schl.

**SMITH, JO-CAROLE L,** Univ Of Tn At Chattanooga, Chattanooga, TN; SO; Spnsh Clb; Q-Debs; Tri-Hi-Y; Explrng FCA; Chorus; Math Tutor; Natl Hon; Beta Clb; Pres Acdmc Awd; Deans Lst; Chem Eng.

**SMITH, JOANN M,** S U N Y Coll Of A & T Morrisvl, Morrisville, NY; SR; ASS; Dairy Clb Treas 89-; Agr Clb 89-; Phi Theta Kappa 90-; Agri Bus; Farm.

**SMITH, JOANNA L,** Oh Univ-Southern Cmps, Ironton, OH; SO; BBA; Gen Busn.

**SMITH, JODY L,** Lee Coll, Cleveland, TN; JR; BS; Vlybl Clb; Sci Clb; Covenant Discipleshp; IM Sftbl/Bstkbl/Ftbl; Hosp Vol; Tutor; Lab Asst; Alpha Phi Delta Sec/Treas; Alpha Chi VP; Upsilon Xi Pres; Epsilon Lambda Phi; Carl Colloms Schlrshp; March Dimes Schlrshp; Chem; Med Doc.**

**SMITH, JOHN D,** Univ Of Ga, Athens, GA; JR; BSED; UGA Pes Clb Chrmn 90-; Deans Lst; UGA Krt 88; Physcl Thrpy.

**SMITH, JOHN H,** Univ Of Nc At Asheville, Asheville, NC; SR; Hstry Assoc 89-; Lit Clb 87-; BA; Hstry/Lit; Wrting/Prof Res.

**SMITH, JOHN P,** Brescia Coll, Owensboro, KY; JR; BA; Ambassador 89-; Street Relief Prog 90-; Res Life Head R A 90-; Coaches Awd 90-; Noteworthy 90-; IM Soccer 88-; Graphic Dsgn.

**SMITH JR, JOSEPH E,** Oh Univ, Athens, OH; SO; BS; Stdnt Mentor 90; IM Bsketb; Math; Mechanical Engineering.

**SMITH JR, JOSEPH J,** Glassboro St Coll, Glassboro, NJ; SO; BA; Crmnl Justc; Law Enfcmnt.

**SMITH, JOSEPH NATHANIEL,** Va St Univ, Petersburg, VA; SO; BS; Acdmc Achvmnt Cert 89; Deans Lst; Mrchndsg; Rtl Buyer.

**SMITH, JOSIE PEARL,** Bethune Cookman Coll, Daytona Beach, FL; JR; AAS Indian Rvr Cmnty Clg 84; Certif Century Clg 86; Psych; Cnslg.

**SMITH, JUDITH E,** Univ Of Tn At Knoxville, Knoxville, TN; SR; Exec Undrgrad Cncl; Alpha Lambda Delta 88-; Phi Eta Sigma 88-; Golden Key 89-; Beta Gamma Sigma 90-; Phi Kappa Phi; Beta Alpha Psi; Alpha Gamma Dleta 88-89; Acctg; CPA.

**SMITH, JUDY E,** Univ Of Ga, Athens, GA; SR; BSED; Silver Stars Pres 87-90; ROTC Army Cadet Capt 87-90; Recon Co 88-90; Pershing Rifles 89-90; Reading For The Blind 89-90; IM Sprts 87-90; Erly Chldhd Ed; Tchr.

**SMITH, JULIA Y,** Univ Of Sc At Coastal Carolina, Conway, SC; JR; BS; Blgy Clb VP 90-; Fllwshp Chrstn Athlts Pres 89-90; Hmcmng Rep 88-90; Orttn Asstn 90; Upstg Cmpny 90-; Stdnt Govt Assn Sen 88-; Omicron Delta Kappa VP; Delta Iota Zeta 90erth Envrnmnlst Scty 9-; Acdmc Schlrshp 90-; FCA Hrry Cnty Adlt Chptr Sec 90; Blgy.

**SMITH, JULIE A,** Roane St Comm Coll, Harriman, TN; FR; BA; Hlth Physics; Hlth Phys Tech.

**SMITH, JULIE H,** Longwood Coll, Farmville, VA; SR; Ambssdrs VP 88-; Stdnt Educ Assn 87-; FM Radio 87-88; Natl Ordr Omega 90-; Geist Mdwy Co-Chrmn 90-; Sigma Kappa VP 89-; Invlvd Stdnt Awd; Cmmndtn Chi; BS; Elem Ed; Tch.

**SMITH, JULIE K,** Univ Of Cincinnati, Cincinnati, OH; SR; Sailng Clb Rear Cmmdr 89-90; Alpha Epsilon Rho; BA; Brdcstng; Flm/Phtgrphy.

**SMITH, JULIE K,** Daytona Beach Comm Coll, Daytona Beach, FL; SO; BA; Sigma Chi Lil Sis Pres Pldge Clss 89; AF ROTC 4 Yr Schlrshp Rcpnt 89-; Dytna Bch Prbtn Prle Intrn; IM Co Ed Vlybl 90-; AA; Crmnl Jstce; Law.

**SMITH, JULIE N,** Bellarmine Coll, Louisville, KY; JR; Psychlgy Club 89-; Ambsdrs 89-90; Tutoring 88-89; Pres Schlr 88-; Ldrshp Ed/Dev Co-Coordntr 90-; Delta Epsilon Sigma 90-; Recyclng Team 89-90; Retreat Team Ldr 88-; Trnbl Mntly Hndcpd Clsrm 88-90; Deans List 88-; Psychlgy; Cnslng/Org.**

**SMITH, KAREN,** Elmira Coll, Elmira, NY; SR; BA; Chrstn Fllwshp 89-90; Admin Asst Fincl Contrlr Bahamas Tele; AA Clg Bahamas 81; Mgmt; Fincl Mgmt.

**SMITH, KAREN E,** Merrimack Coll, North Andover, MA; JR; BA; MORE Retreat Prog Tm Ldr 90-; Orientation Com 89-; Merrimaction Serv Org 89-; Phi Alpha Theta 90-; Vrsty Soccer 88; Hist.

**SMITH, KAREN L M,** Davis Coll, Toledo, OH; FR; Self Emplyd; Acctg/Bus Mgmt; Acctg/Ofc Mgr.

**SMITH, KAREN M,** Marshall University, Huntington, WV; SR; Natl Mgmt Assn Treas 89-.

**SMITH, KAREN P,** Univ Of New Haven, West Haven, CT; SO; BS; Hall Cncl 89-; Club Mgrs Assn 90-; Htl/Rstrnt Mgmt Svcs 90; Marriotts Marco Islnd Rsrt 90-; Htl Rst/Mgmt Smnrs 90; Tennis 89-; Htl/Rstrnt Mgmt; Htl Indus Mgmt.

**SMITH, KAREN P,** Sue Bennett Coll, London, KY; FR; BA; Acctg.

**SMITH, KARLA D,** Columbus Coll Of Art & Design, Columbus, OH; SR; BFA; C M Tuttle Schlrshp 90; Art/Dsgn Exhbtn 90; Advsr; Licking Cty Art Assn Intrn; Dsgn Licking Cty Safety Pstr 90; Advtsng Dsgn.

**SMITH, KARON D,** Middle Tn St Univ, Murfreesboro, TN; JR; Fshn Mrchndsng.

**SMITH, KARYN A,** Memphis St Univ, Memphis, TN; FR; BA; Blck Stdnt Assn 90-; Orchstra Vlnst 90-; Peer Mntr Pgm 90-; Blck Schlrs 90-; Phi Eta Sigma 90-; Alpha Lambda Delta 90-; Jrnlsm; Rprtr/Jrnlst.

**SMITH, KATHERINE C,** Marshall University, Huntington, WV; SR; BBA; Buskirk Hall Advsry Cncl Gen 87-89; Alpha Kappa Psi Secy 90-; Co Rec Im Blybl/Soccer 87-; Mktg; Fedrl Govt.

**SMITH, KATHY D,** Middle Tn St Univ, Murfreesboro, TN; SR; BA; Biology,Environmental Tech; Envrnmntlst/Rsch.

**SMITH, KATHY F,** Univ Of Nc At Greensboro, Greensboro, NC; SR; BS; ESS Std Mjrs Asc 89-; Magna Cum Laude; Physcl Thrpy Intshp; AS Sand Hills Comm Clg 89; Exrcs/Sprts Sci; Physcl Thrpy.

**SMITH, KATHY S,** Midway Coll, Midway, KY; SO; ASN; Borden Comm Church Yng Adult Grp 90-; Stdnt Nrs Extern Bapt Hosp E Louisille Ky 90; Nrsg; RN.

**SMITH, KAY D,** Piedmont Tech Coll, Greenwood, SC; SO; AS; Machine Tool Tec; Eng.

**SMITH, KEISHA Y,** Al St Univ, Montgomery, AL; FR; BED; Spelman Coll Smnr Dance 87-; Art/Dance Asst; Dance Co 89-; Engl; Educ.

**SMITH, KEITH B,** Morehouse Coll, Atlanta, GA; SR; BS; Comp Sci; Comp Engr.

**SMITH, KEITH L,** Hampton Univ, Hampton, VA; SO; BA; Debate Tm Pres 89-; Afrcn Studies Clstr Gen Asmbly 89-; ROTC Crprl; Delta Sigma Roe; Afrcn Poetry Scty Khemetian Brthrhd; 113 Prcnct Yth Cncl 80-; ROTC Schlrshp; Hnrs 89-; IM Bsktbl; Business Ownrshp/Law.**

**SMITH, KELLI A,** Birmingham Southern Coll, Birmingham, AL; JR; BA; Capstone Hnrs Stdnt Univ Ala 80; MYF Ldr 89-; Jr Pioneers Amer 90-; Bus/Psychology; Human Resources Mngmt.

**SMITH, KELLI E,** Indiana Univ Of Pa, Indiana, PA; SR; BS; Sgn Lang Clb 88-90; CEC 88-90; Educ Of Excptnl; Tchng.

**SMITH, KELLI N,** Western Ky Univ, Bowling Green, KY; JR; BS; Crmnlgy Clb VP; Fresh Rep 88-89; Univ Hnrs Prog 88-; Univ Schlrs 88-; Phi Eta Sigma 89-; Coop Cntr Stdy Britain 90; Sthrn Rgnl Hnrs Conf 90-; Psych.

**SMITH, KELLI SUE,** Roane St Comm Coll, Harriman, TN; JR; AAS; Hlth Care; Phys Therapists Asst.

**SMITH, KELLY I,** Davis & Elkins Coll, Elkins, WV; SO; BA; Cmnctns Clb; Dead Mfrs Soc Sec 90-; Natl Fdrtn Blind Affil At Lrg VP 90-; Coll Hon Assn Soc Comm 90-; All Amer Schlrs Collgt Awrd 90-; Deans Lst 90-; Theatr Mk-Up Asstshp 90-; Advtsng Intrnshp; Creatv Advtsng.

**SMITH, KELLY J,** Slippery Rock Univ, Slippery Rock, PA; FR; BA; Dnce Thtre 90-; HPERD Clb 90-; Acad Exclince; Dnce; Prfrm Tch.

**SMITH, KELLY L,** Memphis St Univ, Memphis, TN; FR; BA; Phi Eta Sigma 90-; Soc Wrk.

**SMITH, KENDALL L,** Coll Of Charleston, Charleston, SC; SO; BS; Fllwshp Of Christian Athletes 89; Campus Crusade For Christ 89; Chrch Admin Cmmttee Chrmn 90; Elem Ed; Tchr.

**SMITH, KENNETH,** Comm Coll Algny Co Algny Cmps, Pittsburgh, PA; FR; Tennis/Bwlng; Deans List; Micro Sys Spclst; Micro Sys Spclst.

**SMITH, KENNETH R,** Western New England Coll, Springfield, MA; SR; Krte Clb Cch 90; Cmmnctns Nws Rprtr Pnto Jrnlst 86; Jwsh Wkly Nws; Assc Springfield Tech Comm Coll 87; Govt Hstry; Law.

**SMITH, KESHA A,** Johnson C Smith Univ, Charlotte, NC; FR; Bsktbl Tm Sftbl Tm 90-; Englsh; Law Tchr.

**SMITH, KEVIN,** Niagara Univ, Niagara Univ, NY; FR; ROTC Rfle Tm Mrksmn 90-; Stdnt Govt Rep 90-; Tau Kappa Epsilon VP 90-; Cmps Mnstry 90-; Pol Sci; Law Pols.

**SMITH, KEVIN A,** Christopher Newport Coll, Newport News, VA; FR; BA; English; Tch.

**SMITH, KEVIN D,** Va St Univ, Petersburg, VA; SR; BS; Acctg Clb 87-; ROTC 87-; Rsdnc Asst; Scabbard/Blade 89-; Phi Beta Lambda 90-; Acctg; Offcr US Army.

**SMITH, KEVIN T,** Univ Of Tn At Chattanooga, Chattanooga, TN; SO; BS; Engr.

**SMITH, KEVIN W,** Richard Bland Coll, Petersburg, VA; SO; BS; Rlgs Educ St Anns Chrch Lay Reader; AS; Bio; Bio Prfsr/Physcn.

**SMITH, KIM R,** Coppin St Coll, Baltimore, MD; JR; BS; Comp Sci; Fed Agnt.

**SMITH, KIM Y,** Kent St Univ Geauga Cmps, Burton Twp, OH; FR; BED; Chldrns Sndy Schl Prmry Pres 87-89; Elem Ed/Engl; Tchr.

**SMITH, KIMBERLY A,** Univ Of West Fl, Pensacola, FL; JR; BA; Alpha Sigma Lambda; AA 90; Elem Educ.

**SMITH, KIMBERLY A,** Coppin St Coll, Baltimore, MD; SR; Future Tchrs; Hons Pgm 86-88; Delta Sigma Theta Pr 89-; Track Clb 88; Specl Educ Tchr.

**SMITH, KIMBERLY A,** Edinboro Univ Of Pa, Edinboro, PA; SO; BS; Phi Eta Sigma 88-89; Acctg; CPA.

**SMITH, KIMBERLY A,** Univ Of Nc At Greensboro, Greensboro, NC; SR; Rcrtn Soc 90-; Bptst Union Cmmtr Chrprsn 89-90; Alpha Phi Omega VP Mbrshp 89-90; Kernersvl Rcrtn Intrnshp; BS UNCG 90; Rcrtn.

**SMITH, KIMBERLY C,** Univ Of Al At Huntsville, Huntsville, AL; JR; BS; Alpha Lambda Delta 87-88; Phi Eta Sigma 87-88; Tau Beta Pi 90-; Eta Kappa Nu 90-; Hon Schlr 88-90; Comp Eng.

**SMITH, KIMBERLY D,** Tuskegee Univ, Tuskegee Inst, AL; SR; BS; Miss Clb Pres 87-88; Stdnt Natl Educ Assn 88-90; Amer Psychlgcl Assn 90-; Alpha Kappa Alpha Prlmntrn 90-; Comm Boxing Food 90-; Psychlgy; Tchr.

**SMITH, KIMBERLY K,** Columbus Coll Of Art & Design, Columbus, OH; SR; BA; Owens IL Cmptn; Victorias Secret Comp; Advrtsng.

**SMITH, KIMBERLY L,** Liberty Univ, Lynchburg, VA; FR; BA; Light Clubh 90-; Chi Alpha 90-; Spiritual Life Dr; English; Tchng.

**SMITH, KIMBERLY L,** Christopher Newport Coll, Newport News, VA; FR; BA; Theatre; Hist/Theatre; Law/Tchng.

**SMITH, KIMBERLY P,** Univ Of Montevallo, Montevallo, AL; SR; MA; Stdnt Alabama Educ Assn 88-90; Alpha Delta Pi 87-90; Intrnshp Elem Schl; BS Cert St Of Alabama 90-; Cnslng/Guid; Tchr/Cnslr.

**SMITH, KIMBERLY P,** Va Commonwealth Univ, Richmond, VA; SR; Elem Educ; Undrwrtg/Tchg.

**SMITH, KIMBERLY T,** Lexington Comm Coll, Lexington, KY; SO; ASSOC; Bus Mgmnt.

**SMITH, KRISTIN L,** Ms St Univ, Miss State, MS; FR; United Way 90-; Compas Clb 90-; Alpha Lambda Delta; Gamma Beta Phi; Phi Eta Sigma; Delta Gamma 90-.

**SMITH, KRISTINA K,** Tallahassee Comm Coll, Tallahassee, FL; SO; BA; Flwshp Chrstn Athltc 88-89; Dns Lst 90-; AA; Art Hstry; Crtr/Glry Cir.

**SMITH, KYLE J,** Rutgers St Univ At Camden, Camden, NJ; SR; BS; Acctng Scty Treas 90; Mrktng Assn Treas 89; Dns Lst 89; Natl Assn Of Accts 89-; Acctng.

**SMITH, LA TALIA D MYTRYK,** Atlanta Metropolitan Coll, Atlanta, GA; SO; BS; Atlanta Metro Coll Sci Clb Pres; Deans Lst 89-; Atlanta Cluster 89-90; Atlanta Job Corps 89-; Gamma Chi; Jr Wmn Cmnty 89-; SFEP Med Coll GA Schlrshp; Invstgtv Trnsfr Pgm Agnes Scott Coll 90; AS; Dip Atlanta Job Corps; Phys Therapy Bio; Sports Med.**

**SMITH, LA WANDA K,** Fl A & M Univ, Tallahassee, FL; FR; BS; CIS Clb; Hmcmng Dcrtng Comm; Mcguinn Diamond Pgnt Comm; Prsdntl Schlrs Assn; Cmptr Sci Edctn; Prgrmr Analyst.

**SMITH, LAURA P,** Western Carolina Univ, Cullowhee, NC; JR; Acctg Assoc 90-; Beta Gamma Sigma; Mrtr Brd 90-; Mrshl 90-; Bus; Scl Law.

**SMITH, LAURI A,** Duquesne Univ, Pittsburgh, PA; FR; MBA; Dirs Cir; Phi Eta Sigma; Delta Sigma Pi; Bus; Acctng.

**SMITH, LAURIE A,** Marywood Coll, Scranton, PA; JR; BS; Bio Clb 88-; Delta Epsilon Sigma Pres 90-; Intrnshp Chesapeake Bay Fndtn 90; Intrnshp Dept Of Env Rsrcs 90; Intrnshp Lackawanna Cnty Cnsrvtn Dist; Var Vlybl 88-; Envrnmtl Sci; Rsrch.

**SMITH, LAVELLE L,** Clark Atlanta Univ, Atlanta, GA; SR; BA; Fin/Mktg/Mngmnt Clbs 88-90; Womens Res Ctr 88-90; Toastmasters Clb 88-90; UNUM Ins Sales Intrnshp 90; IM 89-90; Bus Admin; Mktg Mngmnt.

**SMITH, LEIGH A,** Christian Brothers Univ, Memphis, TN; SO; French Clb 89-; Honors Prog 89-; Tau Kappa Epsilon 89-; Stdt Ambassador 90-; Peer Counselor; English; Teaching.

**SMITH, LEIGH ANN,** Villanova Univ, Villanova, PA; SR; MS; Steering Com New Stdnt Orntn 89-90; Poms Squad Choreographer 87-89; Orntn Cnslr 89; Delta Gamma Asst Pledge Ed 89-90; Spcl Olympics 87-; Deans Lst 87-; Phys Therapy.

**SMITH, LELAND A,** Fl St Univ, Tallahassee, FL; SR; BS; ASCE 88; Golden Key 89; Eng Hnr Soc 88; Eng Awd 88; Acad All-Amer Awd 87; AA Tallahassee Cmmnty Clg 87; Civil Eng; Eng.**

**SMITH II, LENWOOD EARL,** Mount Olive Coll, Mount Olive, NC; JR; BS; Henderson Science Clb Prsdnt 88-; Freewill Bptst Fllwshp Tres 88-; Bptst Stdnt Un Cls VP 89-; Fclty Awd Otstndng Frshmn; Sci Awd 89-; Mrshl 89-; Mact Chrldng Tm 88-; Biology; Rsrch Rain Forest.

**SMITH JR, LEONARD CALVIN,** Univ Of Md At Eastern Shore, Princess Anne, MD; SR; BS; Stdnt Cnstrctrs Org 86-; NACP 90-; Pan Hellenic Cncl Chrtr 89-; Phi Beta Sigma Pres; Const Mgmt Tech; Proj Engr Mgr.

**SMITH, LINDA A,** Atlantic Comm Coll, Mays Landing, NJ; FR; AAS; Law; Prlgl.

**SMITH, LINDA L,** Norfolk St Univ, Norfolk, VA; JR; BSN; VA Beach Alumni Corres Secy 88-90; Assn Hlthcare Intrnl Auditors 88-; Natl Cncl Negro Wmn 88-; NAACP; PTA; RN 74-; AS 74; Nrsng; Mktng.

**SMITH, LINNIE U,** Va Commonwealth Univ, Richmond, VA; JR; BS; Blk Caucus 90-; Blk Stdnt Alnc 88-; Gldn Ky 91-; Delta Sigma Theta Treas 90-; Dns Lst 89-; Mass Comm; PR.

**SMITH, LISA A,** Univ Of Nc At Chapel Hill, Chapel Hill, NC; FR; BA; Carolina Choir 90-; Deans Lst; Intl Stdes/Poltcl Sci; Tch.

**SMITH, LISA A,** Howard Univ, Washington, DC; GD; MS; Sierra Clb 88-; HUGS Secr 90-; BS Univ Rochester 87; Human Genetics; Genetic Cnslng.

**SMITH, LISA H,** Longwood Coll, Farmville, VA; JR; BS; Elem Ed; Tchg.

**SMITH, LISA K,** Ramapo Coll Of Nj, Mahwah, NJ; SR; BA; Lit Clb 88-; Eng Lit; Edtr.

**SMITH, LISA M,** Univ Of Rochester, Rochester, NY; JR; BA; The View Cmmnctns Mgr 89-; Adlscnt Prgnncy Prntng Intrn; Dble Mjr Psych And Econs; Fam Plnng Cnslr.

**SMITH, LISA M,** Univ Of Nh Plymouth St Coll, Plymouth, NH; SO; BED; Space Sec 89; Music Prod Comm; Pres Lst 90; Elem Educ.

**SMITH, LORENE A,** Marshall University, Huntington, WV; SR; BA; Acctg Clb 88-; Cpa Soc 90-; Stdnt Spprt Svcs 87-; Hosp Acctg Clrk Intrn 90; Acctg/Busn; Acctg/Finance.

**SMITH, LORENZO M,** Johnson C Smith Univ, Charlotte, NC; FR; BS; Liston Hall Cncl Pres; Computer Sci.

**SMITH, LORETTA C,** Newbury Coll, Brookline, MA; SO; Stdnt Govt Cls Rep; Sunshine Comm For Ofc Functns 90-; Help In Functns For Hmls People; Wrk For New Englnd Telephn Test Lines; AS; Dale Carnegie 89; Bus Mgt; BS Bus Mgt.

**SMITH, LORI M,** Defiance Coll, Defiance, OH; JR; BA; Pres Host 89-90; Theta Xi Ltl Sis Treas 88-; Deans Lst 88-; Bsktbl Tm Tri-Capt 88-; Sftbl Tm 88-; Educ; Tchr.

**SMITH, LORI O,** Nc Agri & Tech St Univ, Greensboro, NC; FR; BS; Elem Educ; Tchr.

**SMITH, LU ANN B,** Elmira Coll, Elmira, NY; JR; BED; Kappa Delta Pi; Phi Beta Kappa Schlp 90; Fncl Sec 87-; Southport Vol Fire Dpt Aux Pres 74-; Sec 83-88; Elem Ed/Math; Tchr.

**SMITH, LUCILLE HUNT,** Alcorn St Univ, Lorman, MS; SR; BA; Assist Sec Church; Choir; Elem Educ; Tchr.

**SMITH, LYNN M,** Univ Of Sc At Columbia, Columbia, SC; SR; BS; Pi Epsilon Mu 87-; Var Vlybl MVP 91; Var Bsktbl MIP Co Capt 86-; Phys Educ; Tchr/Coach.

**SMITH, MAGGIE L,** Middle Tn St Univ, Murfreesboro, TN; MA; Stff Wrtr; Hnr Grd 89-90; BS 90; Clncl Psychlgy; Clncl Psy.

**SMITH, MARC H,** Westminster Coll, New Wilmingtn, PA; SO; BA; Habitat Humanity 89-90; Tau Pi Phi 89-; Trustees Schlrshp 89-; Gen Schlrshp 89-; Rev Hanley Spch Schlrshp; Acctg; Lawyer.

**SMITH, MARCIA G,** Miami Jacobs Jr Coll Of Bus, Dayton, OH; SO; AS.

**SMITH, MARIE J,** Howard Univ, Washington, DC; GD; MSW; Scl Wrkr; BA Morgan St Univ 67; Scl Wrk-Admstrtn.

**SMITH, MARIO D,** Central St Univ, Wilberforce, OH; FR; BS; Cross Cntry 88-90; Track 87-90; Acctng.

**SMITH, MARISSA R,** Inter Amer Univ Pr San Juan, Hato Rey, PR; SR; BA; Psych; Socl Wrk.

**SMITH, MARK A,** Youngstown St Univ, Youngstown, OH; JR; BE; Cvl Eng; Strctrl Eng.

**SMITH, MARK D,** Embry Riddle Aeronautical Univ, Daytona Beach, FL; JR; BS; Aerospc Scty 90-; Avtn; Pilot.

**SMITH, MARK E,** Marshall University, Huntington, WV; SR; BA; Stdnts Chrst Pr 88-; BACCHUS VP 90-; Amer Red Crs 90-; Intrnshp Time Out; Cnslng/Rehab; Minstr.

**SMITH, MARK W,** Univ Of Sc At Columbia, Columbia, SC; JR; BA; UVM Lawrence Debat Union Pres 87-90; Vrsty Debat Tm Pres 90-; DSR-TKA; Phi Eta Sigma 90; Phi Gamma Delta; Mst Outstndng Debatr Awrd 88-90; Navice Natl Debat Champ 88; Invstgatr/Pblc Dfndr Offc; Econ; Law/Econ.

**SMITH, MARK W,** Morehouse Coll, Atlanta, GA; SO; BA; Hon Roll 89-; IM Bsktbl 89-; Bnkg/Finance; Corp Finance.

**SMITH, MARLENE,** Sue Bennett Coll, London, KY; SO; MA; Sigma Nu; Phi Theta Kappa; Lrng/Bhvr Dsordrs; Spec Ed Tchr.

**SMITH, MARTHA A,** Lane Coll, Jackson, TN; SR; BA; Hnr Scty Amer 89-; Delta Sigma Theta 89-; Intrnshp Jackson Halfway House 90-; Hghst Acad Achvmt Awd 89-; Sociolgy; Dy Trtmnt Thrpst.

**SMITH, MARTHA JANE,** Western Ky Univ, Bowling Green, KY; SO; BA; Allen Cty Prnts Tchrs Org 86-; Mt Olive Untd Mthdst Church 73-; KY Rehab Assn Sec; KY Assn Rehab Sec Pres 90; Admnstrtv Sec Commonwealth KY Dept Vctnl Rehab 87-; Psychlgy/Bus; Cnslng.

**SMITH, MARTIN A,** Atlantic Comm Coll, Mays Landing, NJ; FR; AS; Fclty Stf Schlrshp; Pres Lst 90; Bus Adm; Fin.

**SMITH, MARTIN C,** City Univ Of Ny Med Evers Coll, Brooklyn, NY; JR; BS; SAM Treas 89-90; NABA Clg Chptr Pres 90-; Medgar Evers Clg Acad Hnrs Prog; CPA; AS Medgar Evers Clg; Acctg/Cmptr Mngmt Sys; CPA.

**SMITH, MARY G,** S U N Y Coll Of Tech At Alfred, Alfred, NY; FR; BA; ERGO Co Edit Pblcty 90-; Dns Lst; Cncrnd Ctzns Of Allghny Cnty Envir Grp Chrmn 90; Media Awrd 90-; Gst Spkr Erthdy 90; Allghny Brd Of Cnty Amer Cncr Scty Dirs; Engl; Jrnlsm.

**SMITH, MARY S,** Blue Mountain Coll, Blue Mountain, MS; SR; BS; MAESP 90-; Tippah Cnty Hrtg Scty 90-; Acctg/Pyrl Clrk Fr Sth Tippah Schl Dist 85-; Educ; Elem Tchr.

**SMITH, MARYANN,** Univ Of Nh Plymouth St Coll, Plymouth, NH; JR; BS; Blood Donor; CPA Employee; AS Nt Washussett Comm Clg 84; Acctg; CPA.

**SMITH, MATTHEW J,** West Liberty St Coll, West Liberty, WV; SO; BA; Stu Nwspr 90-; Stu Tutor 90-; SGA Rep 90; Jdg Frshmn Comp Cmptn; Moment Slnc Trp Sprtv Spkr; Jdg HS Frnsc Trnmnts; Engl; Wrtr.

**SMITH, MATTHEW L,** Bapt Bible Coll & Seminary, Clarks Summit, PA; JR; BS; Sccr Cpt 89-90; DPL Word Of Life Bible Inst 89; Bible; Pstrl Mnstry.

**SMITH, MATTHEW STEPHEN,** Univ Of Nc At Charlotte, Charlotte, NC; SO; BS; Criminal Justice; Law.

**SMITH, MAURA V,** Univ Of Ky, Lexington, KY; SR; BA; Tae Kwon Do; Spec Educ; Tch Mntlly Retarded.

**SMITH, MAUREEN A,** Saint John Fisher Coll, Rochester, NY; FR; BA; French Club; Intrntl Studies Assoc; Interntl Studies; Fin.

**SMITH, MAURICE T,** Va St Univ, Petersburg, VA; JR; BA; Athl Educ Club Educ Tutor 90-; Admissions Assist Advsr 90-; Ftbl/Track Starter 88-; Dns Lst 90-; Trojan Brothers Of Virginia State Outstndng Achvr 90-; Ftbl Fullback 90-; Track/Field Polevault 90-; BED Chowan Clg 90; Bsn/CPU Prmg; BIS/CMPTR Prmg.

**SMITH, MELAINE A,** Cheyney Univ Of Pa, Cheyney, PA; JR; Bsktbl 90-; Hlth/Physcl Educ/Rec.

**SMITH, MELANIE D,** Union Univ, Jackson, TN; JR; BA; Prexy Clb 90; Linguae Mundi Clb 90; Rsdnt Lfe Brd 90; Bapt Yng Women Mssn Stdy 88-90; New Drm Cncl Pres 90; Intrprtr For Med/Dntl Mssn Tm In Hndrs; Sigma Tau Delta; Spnsh; Tchr.

**SMITH, MELISSA A,** Birmingham Southern Coll, Birmingham, AL; SO; BA; Trngle Clb 90-; Pres Srvce Orgnztn; Circle K 90; Amnsty Intrntl; Tutor 90-; Lnks Up 90; RA; Chi Omega; Intrntl Bus; Govt.

**SMITH, MELISSA A,** Univ Of Tn At Martin, Martin, TN; FR; BS; Scty Hnrs Smnr 90-; Stdnts; Deans List; Nrsng; RN.

**SMITH, MELISSA G,** Saint Catharine Coll, St Catharine, KY; FR; AS; Stdnts Helping Admssns Recruting Prog Co-Pres 90; Phi Theta Kappa; History; Radiologist.

**SMITH, MELISSA I,** Fl Memorial Coll, Miami, FL; FR; BA; SGA Asst Chf Stff 90-; Acctg.

**SMITH, MELISSA L,** West Liberty St Coll, West Liberty, WV; FR; BA; Math; Elem Educ.

**SMITH, MICHAEL A,** Youngstown St Univ, Youngstown, OH; JR; BE; Crs/Cnty/Trck 87-; Amer Soc Mech Eng; Ben Scharsu Awd; Deans Lst 90-; Trck Letter 90; Mech Eng; Eng.

**SMITH, MICHAEL A,** Coker Coll, Hartsville, SC; JR; BA; Stdnt Govt Assc Rep Stndrds Comm 90-; Stdnt Invlvt Comm Sec 90-; Bio Clb 89-; Ambdsrds 89-; Cmsnrs 89-; Chrstms April; SGA Revsn Comm Cnstn 90-; Dean List 89-; Susan Coker Watson Sclrhsp Summer Abrd; Chem Hist.

**SMITH, MICHAEL D,** Tn Temple Univ, Chattanooga, TN; SR; AS; Zinzendorf Soc 85-87; Chrch Yth Ldr 84-85; Martco Lwn Care 90-; Irrgtn By Hntr Crw Ldr 86-89; Spch; Lndscpg.

**SMITH, MICHAEL G,** Livingston Univ, Livingston, AL; JR; BA; Tau Kappa Epsilon Edctr 90; Air Ntl Grd E-4 88-; Hnr Grad; Clncl Psych.

**SMITH, MICHAEL W,** Salisbury St Univ, Salisbury, MD; GD; BA; Amer Mktg Assn; Busn Admin/Mktg; Mktg/Res/Adv.

**SMITH, MICHELE L,** Savannah Coll Of Art & Design, Savannah, GA; SO; BA; S Fla Prntng Indstry Schlrshp 89-90; Dns Lst 89-90; S Miami Cntr Media Arts Intrn 89; Art; Illstrtn.

**SMITH, MICHELLE D,** Jackson St Univ, Jackson, MS; JR; BS; Dubois Hnrs Clg 88-; Alpha Kappa Mu; Alpha Chi; Meth/Epscpl Secy; Choir/Sndy Schl; Acad Schlrshp 88-; Herrin Hess Schlr; Mktng Awd; Mrktng; Sls.

**SMITH, MICHELLE E,** Central St Univ, Wilberforce, OH; FR; BS; Hnrs Pgm; Bsn Admn; Mgmt.

**SMITH, MICHELLE KIMBERLY,** Univ Of Nc At Asheville, Asheville, NC; JR; Feminst Collectv Co Fndr Pres 90-; Gullickson Award.

**SMITH, MICHELLE L,** Oh Wesleyan Univ, Delaware, OH; JR; BSN; Stdnt Y 88-89; Phi Eta Sigma 89-90; Phi Scty 90-; Hnr Scty Nrsng; IM Arbcs 90-; Nrsng.

**SMITH, MICHELLE L,** Neumann Coll, Aston, PA; SO; BA; Bus Clb 90-; Natl Assoc Accntnts 90-; Schlrshp Acdmc 89-93; Acctg Chmstry.

**SMITH, MICHELLE L,** Univ Of Tn At Martin, Martin, TN; FR; BSN; Clgte 4-H 90-; Martin Block Bridle Club 90; Nursing; Registered Nurse.

**SMITH, MICHELLE L,** Western Ky Univ, Bowling Green, KY; JR; BA; Pi Mu Epsilon Pres; Sigma Delta Pi Treas; Phi Kappa Phi; Gldn Key; Hugh P Johnson Math Dept Awd; Gvnrs Mrt Schlr; Prfsnl Ed Prprtn Pgm 88; Ogdon Schlrshp; Intrnshp Barren River Area Dev Dstrt; BA; Math/Spnsh; Actrl Sci.

**SMITH, MICHELLE L,** Itawamba Comm Coll, Fulton, MS; FR; Annual Staff 90-; Engl; Elem Ed.

**SMITH, MICHELLE W,** Fl International Univ, Miami, FL; JR; BSN; AA Brwrd Cmmnty Clg 89; Nrsng; Nrse Anshtst.

**SMITH, MICHEOLLE R,** Oh St Univ At Marion, Marion, OH; JR; BA; IM Dept 90-; Alpha Lambda Delta 88-; Phi Eta Sigma 88-; Phi Kappa Phi 88-; Hnrs Prog 88-; Vol At Alton Hall Elem Sch; Deans List 88-; IM Sftbl Vlybl 90-; Elem Edn-Math; Elem Teacher/Masters/Ph D.

**SMITH, MOLLY T,** Valdosta St Coll, Valdosta, GA; SR; BED; Stdnt Govt Assoc Sntr 89-90; Pnhllnc Rush Cnslr; Ornttn Insight Ldr; Stdnt GA Assoc Of Educ; Natl Educ Assoc; Chi Omega; Erly Chldhd Educ; Teaching.

**SMITH, MYRTLE P,** Wv Northern Comm Coll, Wheeling, WV; GD; AAS; Phi Theta Kappa 90-; Phi Beta Lambda Treas 90-; Pres Lst Outstndg Grad Awd 90-; Deans Lst Outstndng Stdnt Bus Div 90-; Co Op Sec Mobay Corp Intrnshp 90; Vol Amer Cancer Scty 80-; Sec State Farm Ins/Mobay Corp 89-90; Sec Sci; Bus.

**SMITH, N FAITH,** Va Commonwealth Univ, Richmond, VA; SR; Evangelical Assn For Prmtn Of Edtn 87-88; Golden Key 90; Phi Kappa Phi; BS; Bus Admn.

**SMITH, NANCY D,** Univ Of Sc At Columbia, Columbia, SC; SO; BSN; Natl Stdnt Nrs Assoc 89-; Nrsg.

**SMITH, NANCY GARDNER,** Memphis St Univ, Memphis, TN; SR; BSED; Phi Kappa Phi 90-; Bus Indstry; Adlt Ed.

**SMITH, NANCY L,** Univ Of Al At Birmingham, Birmingham, AL; SO; BS; Med Tech.

**SMITH, NANCY S,** Fl St Univ, Tallahassee, FL; SO; MBA; Fla Pblc Intrst Rsrch Grp 90; Habitat For Hmnty 90; Phi Eta Sigma; Bsnss; Accntng.

**SMITH, NANCY S,** Univ Of Nc At Asheville, Asheville, NC; SR; BA; SAM; Deans List 90; Mgt; Hlth Care Admnstrtr.

**SMITH, NATASHA N,** Va Union Univ, Richmond, VA; JR; SCEC 89-; SEA 89-; Commnty Schlrs 90-; Spec Educ; Tchr.

**SMITH, NOLAND G,** Clark Atlanta Univ, Atlanta, GA; SR; BA; Orientatn Gd Corp 87-89; Psychlgy Clb; Psi Chi; Alpha Phi Alpha Rec Sec/Hstrn 88-; Psychlgy; Doctrt.

**SMITH, NORA KAY,** Univ Of South Al, Mobile, AL; GD; BS; Beta Gamma Sigma; Staff Accountant 82-; EA Int Rev Svc 85; CEBS Intl Fdtn Empl Benefit Plns/Wharton Sch Univ PA 90; Acctg; CPA.

**SMITH, NORMAN J,** Hillsborough Comm Coll, Tampa, FL; SO; AS; Prcptr For Prmdc Prog; Outstndng Prmdc Of Yr Jaycees 87; Prmdc Instr/Coord; Fire Fghtr Prmdc; EMT-P Sarasota Cnty Vo-Tech 85; Nrsng; Med.

**SMITH, PAMELA A,** William Carey Coll, Hattiesburg, MS; SO; BSRN; Phi Theta Kappa JCJC; Schlrshp Dyess Ed Endowment Fund; Acteen Ldr Cedar Grove Baptist Church; Nursing; Surgery.

**SMITH, PAMELA C,** Tn St Univ, Nashville, TN; SO; Natl Hnr Soc 89-; Crim Just; Law.

**SMITH, PAMELA D,** Alcorn St Univ, Lorman, MS; JR; BA; Cmptr Sci/Apld Math Clb 88-; Dean Lst 88-; Frsty Srv Lakewood Co; Cmptr Sci; Cmptr Anlyst/Prgrmmr.

**SMITH, PAMELA D,** Western Piedmont Comm Coll, Morganton, NC; FR; AAS; Std Chrst; Med Asst Clb; Amer Asc Med Asst; Phi Theta Kappa; AS 88; Med Asstng; Cert Med Asst.

**SMITH, PAMELA D,** Union Coll, Barbourville, KY; SR; Iota Sigma Nu 88-; Grad Cum Laude; Dns Lst 87-; BA; Bus Ed/ Scndry Ed; Tchng.

**SMITH, PAMELA E,** East Tn St Univ, Johnson City, TN; JR; BA; Acctg Soc; Gamma Beta Phi; Acctg; CPA.

**SMITH, PATRICIA A,** Univ Of Rochester, Rochester, NY; SR; MA; Cinema Grp 90-; Cum Laude; Dean Lst 88-; Vllybl 87-88; BA; Spnsh/Lngstcs; Prfssr.

**SMITH, PATRICIA A,** Comm Coll Algny Co Algny Cmps, Pittsburgh, PA; SO; AS; Deans Lst 88-; Ltr Rcgntn Vol Income Tx Asst Prog; Tax Acctg.**

**SMITH, PATRICIA A,** Brewer St Jr Coll, Fayette, AL; SO; BS; Phi Theta Kappa; Study Clb Sec 88-90; Bank Vernon Loan Offcr 83-; Elem Ed.

**SMITH, PATRICIA A,** Univ Of Al At Huntsville, Huntsville, AL; JR; BS; Phi Theta Kappa 89-; Dns Lst Calhoun Clg UAH 88-; Calhoun Educ Soc 89-; Kds For Clg Chmpn Mntr 90-; Calhoun Clg Otstndng Stdnt Awd 91; Mst Otstndng Jr Clg Schlrshp Unv AL 90-; Soc Wmn Engrs UAH Chptr 90-; Engr/ Psych; Engr/Sls.

**SMITH, PATRICIA B,** Commonwealth Coll, Virginia Beach, VA; SO; AS; Opthlmc Tech Cataract/Laser Cntr; Med; Med Mgmt/RN.

**SMITH, PATRICIA C,** Univ Of Tn At Martin, Martin, TN; JR; BS; Undrgrd Almn Cncl VP 89-; Dpeer Enblng Pgm Grp Ldr; Pi Sgm Epsln 90-; Chi Omega Crspndnt 88-; IM Sprts Vlybl Bsktbl Sftbl 88-; Mktg Bus Admn; Sales.

**SMITH, PATRICIA E,** Univ Of Sc At Columbia, Columbia, SC; SO; BA; Alpha Chi Omega 90-; Bus Mgmt.

**SMITH, PATRICK J,** Air Force Inst Of Tech, Wrt-Ptrsn Afb, OH; GD; MSEM; Sigma Iota Epsilon 90-; Soc Amer Mltry Reg Sec 84-; Engineers; BSCE US Air Force Acad 84; Env Engr; Proj Mgmt.

**SMITH, PATRICK O,** Lexington Comm Coll, Lexington, KY; SO; BA; Acctg.

**SMITH, PATSY E,** Univ Of Ga, Athens, GA; JR; MSED; Golden Key 90; Alpha Delta Pi 88-; CSD; Crtfd Spch Lang Pthlgst.

**SMITH, PAUL E,** Univ Of Tn At Chattanooga, Chattanooga, TN; JR; BSCHE; AS Chattanooga St Tech Comm Coll 89; Chem Eng; Prof Engineer.

**SMITH, PAULETTE,** Columbia Union Coll, Takoma Park, MD; SR; MS; Rdlgc Tchnlgst Soc Pres; BS; Hlth Care Admin.

**SMITH, PENNI K,** Owensboro Comm Coll, Owensboro, KY; SO; CSI 90-; Bapt Ch Yth Cmtee Treas 90-; Capt Ch S Sch Sec 90-; Grad W Dstnctn; AAS; Off Admn; Bus Off.

**SMITH, PENNY LEE W,** Averett Coll, Danville, VA; JR; BA; Averett Sngrs; Bapt Union Msc Chrprsn 90-; Cmmtr Assn; Wycliffe Swain Msc Schlrshp; Music; Church Mnstrs.

**SMITH, PHILIP J,** Univ Of Sc At Columbia, Columbia, SC; SR; BA; NWL Control Systems Aerospace Contrctr Mfg Engr; AA 89; Mngmnt; Mfg.

**SMITH, PHYLLIS K,** Elmira Coll, Elmira, NY; SR; BS; Kappa Delta Pi; Christian Schl Tchr; AS Corning Comm Clg 89; Elem Educ; Tchr.

**SMITH, PORTIA ANN,** Commonwealth Coll, Virginia Beach, VA; SO.

**SMITH, PRICILLA J,** Fayetteville St Univ, Fayetteville, NC; SO; BS; Bsn.

**SMITH, RACHEL L,** Georgetown Univ, Washington, DC; JR; BS; Accntng Soc 90-; Stu Assn Trnsf Cmmtt; Trnsfr Stu Advsr; Accntng; CPA.

**SMITH, RALPH R,** Me Maritime Academy, Castine, ME; JR; BS; Varsity Sailing 88-; Nautical Sci.

**SMITH, REBECCA,** Univ Of Ms Medical Center, Jackson, MS; MS; DAR; UDC Ordr Eastern Star 85-; Dntl Cls Stdnt Ofcr V P 87-88; Deans Lst 89-; Alpha Delta Pi Prlmntrn 86-87; Gen Prctc Extrnshp; Quintessence Pub Co Avemnt Awd; J K Berdon Mem Awd Periodontology; Amer Dental Assn 87-; Miss Dental Assn 87; BA; Periodontics; Spec Dentl Clnc.

**SMITH, REBECCA A,** D Youville Coll, Buffalo, NY; JR; MBS; SOTA; Occup Thrpy.

**SMITH, REBECCA S,** Western Ky Univ, Bowling Green, KY; JR; BS; Phi Eta Sigma; Pres Schlr; Dns Schlr; Erth Sci; Tchr.

**SMITH, REGINA,** Sue Bennett Coll, London, KY; FR; Sigma Nu 90-; Math; Sec Educ.

**SMITH, REGINA C,** Univ Of Nc At Charlotte, Charlotte, NC; JR; BA; AIAS 90; Golden Key 90; Sigma Kappa; Ntl Cllgte Architecture/Dsgn Awd 90; Architecture.

**SMITH, REGINA MARIE,** Hillsborough Comm Coll, Tampa, FL; FR; AS; Donations 90- Police Ath League Frat Order Police; 84-88 Var Bnkg Pos; Paralegalism; Law.

**SMITH, REGINA T,** Davis Coll, Toledo, OH; FR; DIPLO; Swanton Fire Dept Aux Pres 85-87; Swanton Vol Rescue Squad EMT 89; Cert 4 Co Voc Sch 89; Med Asst; RN.

**SMITH, RHONDA ANNETTE,** Middle Tn St Univ, Murfreesboro, TN; SR; BED; Gamma Beta Phi 88-89; Deans Lst 88-89; AS Columbai State Comm Coll 90; Elem Ed; Tchr.**

**SMITH, RHONDA D,** Univ Of Al At Birmingham, Birmingham, AL; SO; BA; Engl/Hrsty; Tchng.

**SMITH, RHONDA N,** Johnson C Smith Univ, Charlotte, NC; BS; Un Prog Bd Pres/Treas 90-; Cls Ofcr Treas 89-90; Mst Outstndng Stdnt 90-; Intern GAO; Bus/Acctg; CPA.

**SMITH, RHONDA RENAE,** Univ Of Ga, Athens, GA; SR; Natl Std Spch Hrng Lang Asc; Gamma Sigma Sigma; BSED; Comm Sci/Disorders.

**SMITH, RICHARD B,** Point Park Coll, Pittsburgh, PA; SR; BS; Ast Penn Tech Inst 88; Elec Eng; Eng.

**SMITH JR, RICHARD J,** Middle Ga Coll, Cochran, GA; FR; BA; Baptist Stdnt Union 90-; Engineering Club; Assoc Old Crows 90-; Elec Engrng.

**SMITH JR, RICHARD L,** Waycross Coll, Waycross, GA; SO; MBA; Bsn Clb 90-; Big Bro/Big Sis Amer 87-; Bsn Adm; Finance-Invstmnts.

**SMITH, RICHARD NGUYEN,** Longwood Coll, Farmville, VA; JR; BME; MENC Secr 90-; Kappa Delta Phi Treas 89-90; Kiwanis Clb 89-; Karate Yr Awd 85; USAF 86-87; AS Richard Bland Clg 89; Msc Ed; Professor.

**SMITH, RICHARD T,** Univ Of West Fl, Pensacola, FL; SR; BS; Tennis Club 89-; Pres List 89-; Deans List 89-90; Grad Magna Cum Laude 91; AS Pensacola Jr Coll 89; Elect Engrng Tech; Cmmnctns Engrng.**

**SMITH, RICHEE L,** Hampton Univ, Hampton, VA; FR; BS; Accntng; Corp Law.

**SMITH, RICK A,** Southern Coll Of Tech, Marietta, GA; JR; BSCS; Comp Sci.

**SMITH, RITA J,** Western Ky Univ, Bowling Green, KY; JR; BA; Phi Theta Kappa 89-90; Phi Kappa Phi; Dairy Farm Ownr 78-; AA Elizabethtown Comm Col 89; Libr Media Educ; Libr Media.

**SMITH, ROBERT B,** Davis Coll, Toledo, OH; FR; AA; Frnc Instllr 90-92; MCA; Acctg.

**SMITH, ROBERT C,** Univ Of Md At Eastern Shore, Princess Anne, MD; JR; BA; Bus.

**SMITH, ROBERT D,** Univ Of Southern Ms, Hattiesburg, MS; JR; BS; Alumni Assn; Phi Theta Kappa; Gldn Key; IM Ftbl Bsktbl Sftbl Vlybl; Sci; Comp Sci.

**SMITH JR, ROBERT E,** Interdenominational Theo Ctr, Atlanta, GA; GD; MDIV; Stdnt Chrstn Leag Prlmntrn 90-; Stdnt Chrstn Leag Elctns Chr 90-; Thea Phi Chpln 90-; Cngrss Ntl Blck Chrchs Flw 90-; Church Of God In Christ Ordnd Eldr 83-; Prsh Mnstr; BA Moody Bible Inst 85; Pstrl Cnslng.

**SMITH, ROBERT J,** Radford Univ, Radford, VA; JR; BA; Pi Gamma Mu; Phi Sigma Pi; Crmnl Jstc; Law.

**SMITH III, ROBERT J B,** Univ Of Ga, Athens, GA; SR; BLA; Sigma Lambda Alpha 90-; Lndscp Archtctr; Dsgn Bld Fld.

**SMITH III, ROBERT LEE,** Univ Of Nc At Charlotte, Charlotte, NC; SO; BA; AIAS 90-; Act Fees Cmsn; Sem Symposium 90; Retail Mgmnt; Univ Of NC At Chapel Hill 86; Arch.

**SMITH, ROBERT S,** Tougaloo Coll, Tougaloo, MS; SO; Yng Dmcrts Rep 89-90; MS Yth Lgsltr Rep 88-89; Natl Hon Soc 87-89; Hall Of Fame 89; Mayrs Yth Cncl Rep 87-89; MS Dmcrtc Prty 89-; US Rep M Espy Intrnshp 90; Acctg; Law.

**SMITH, ROBIN J,** Faulkner St Jr Coll, Bay Minette, AL; SO; BA; Natl Hnr Soc; Phi Theta Kappa 90-; AA; Music.

**SMITH, ROGER D,** Univ Of Ky, Lexington, KY; FR; Tm 90; Epislon Delta; Lymn Gngr Schlrshp 90; Engl.

**SMITH, RONALD R,** Winthrop Coll, Rock Hill, SC; SO; BA; PACE; IM Capt 90-; Bsn Admn; Mktg Rsch.

**SMITH, ROSE M,** Bethel Coll, Mckenzie, TN; JR; BED; Barren Springs Cumberland Presbyterian Church; Elem Ed/Psy; Elem Tchr.

**SMITH, RUSSELL R,** Al A & M Univ, Normal, AL; FR; BA; Jdcl Brd Morris Hall VP 90-; Morris Hall Stdnt Cncl Prlmntrn 90-; Nasiha Roho Adinasi Frat Inc; IM Cptn 90-; Bsns Finance; Chf Exectv Offcr CEO.

**SMITH, RYAN P,** Univ Of Md At College Park, College Park, MD; FR; BS; Deans Lst; IM Sftbll; IM Ftbll; IM Bsktbll; Archtctr.

**SMITH, SADONNA L,** Middle Tn St Univ, Murfreesboro, TN; SR; Stdnt Tchr Educ Assn 87-; Chrch Ldrshp; Elem Ed; Tchr.

**SMITH, SANDEE J,** Univ Of Southern Ms, Hattiesburg, MS; SR; BS; Gamma Beta Phi 89-; Psi Chi 90-; Gldn Key 89-; Psychlgy.

**SMITH, SANDRA A,** Valdosta St Coll, Valdosta, GA; FR; BA; Intrntl Studies.

**SMITH, SANDRA L,** Elmira Coll, Elmira, NY; SO; BA; Phi Eta Sigma; English Lit; Mnstry.

**SMITH, SANDRA L,** Cincinnati Metropolitan Coll, Cincinnati, OH; GD; AS; PBL; Pres Lst 89-90; Intrnshp Dr Greg Woeste; Hired Full Time Bus Mngr; Comp Pgmg; Comp Sci.

**SMITH, SANDRA V,** Lexington Comm Coll, Lexington, KY; JR; BA; Beta Clb 85-; Tchr 3-7 Yr Olds Bryan Station Bptst Chrch 90-; Math Tutor; Deans Lst 88-90; Yth Salute 87-88; Math Biology; Scndry Math Edctn Biology Mnr.

**SMITH, SARAH B,** Castleton St Coll, Castleton, VT; JR; BSEDU; Stdnt Educ Assn Pres 89-; Acad Tutor; Phi Eta Sigma 90-; Kappa Delta Pi 90-; Elem Educ; Tch K-6.

**SMITH, SARAH J,** Endicott Coll, Beverly, MA; FR; Day Care Intrn; Educ; Tch.

**SMITH, SARAH Q,** Valdosta St Coll, Valdosta, GA; SO; PHD; Phi Mu Frat 90-; Engl; Prof.

**SMITH, SARITA D,** Beckley Coll, Beckley, WV; JR; BA; Accntng; CPA.

**SMITH, SCHALANDA E,** Va St Univ, Petersburg, VA; FR; Pre-Alumni 90; Mgr Bsktbl Tm 90; Bsnss Info Syst.

**SMITH, SCOTT E,** Morehouse Coll, Atlanta, GA; FR; BA; Hstry; Coll Prfssr.

**SMITH, SCOTT E,** Hudson County Comm Coll, Jersey City, NJ; SO; AAS; NY Fdshw/Cold Food Dsply 90; Almni Dnnrs 90-; Dns Lst Hnr 90-; Awd Acad Exclnc; Snttn Cert/Amer Htl/Mtl Asc Extrnshp Hltn Corp; AAS; Clnry Arts/Exec Chef.

**SMITH, SCOTT S,** Schenectady County Comm Coll, Schenectady, NY; GD; Ndt/Metelurgy.

**SMITH, SCOTT V,** S U N Y Coll Of Tech At Alfred, Alfred, NY; FR; Eng.

**SMITH, SHANE A,** East Tn St Univ, Johnson City, TN; SR; BS; Soc Mnfctrng Eng; St Franklin Trck Clb; Epsilon Pi Tau; John Deere Power Prod Intern; Inds/Eng Tech/Hstry/Fnnc.

**SMITH, SHANNON D,** Sue Bennett Coll, London, KY; FR; BA; Sci; Pharm.

**SMITH, SHANNON LEIGH,** Fl Coll, Temple Terrace, FL; SO; BA; Frshm Class Ofcr Treas 89-90; SGA Treas 90-; Chorus 89-; Hnr Roll 89-90; Deans List 90; Alpha Club 90-; Edctn/ Counseling.

**SMITH, SHARLENE H,** Fl International Univ, Miami, FL; SR; BSN; Phi Kappa Phi; Phi Lambda; Hon Mentor Pgm 90; Critical Care RN 80-; Cert Polk Voc Tech Ctr 79; ASN Miami-Dade Comm Coll 85; Nrsng; Med Rsrch.

**SMITH, SHARON A,** Norfolk St Univ, Norfolk, VA; SO; BS; Interdscplnry; Lnsd Clncl Soc Wrkr.

**SMITH, SHARON ANN,** Clayton St Coll, Morrow, GA; SO; BA; Music Club 89-; Phi Mu 72-74; Spivey Schlrshp 90-; GA Music Teachers Assoc 89-; GA Teching Cert Behavior Disorders 88-; Taught School 77-85; BE Elem Ed Tift Clge Mercer Univ 77; Med In Behvr Disordrs W GA Clge 79-80; Piano & Voice; Teach.

**SMITH, SHARON L,** Bowie St Univ, Bowie, MD; SR; BS; Kappa Delta Pi 89-; Suma Cum Laude; Educ; Tchng.

**SMITH, SHARON L,** Comm Coll Algny Co Algny Cmps, Pittsburgh, PA; SR; AS; Bus; Mgmnt.

**SMITH, SHAWNA M,** Univ Of Tn At Martin, Martin, TN; FR; MA; Mc Cord Hl Assoc 90-; Pep Grp; Alpha Phi Omega 90-; Pldg Cls Pres; Sec Ed-Engl/Spnsh; Ed.

**SMITH, SHEENA D,** Howard Univ, Washington, DC; JR; BA; Amer Inst Arch Stu Chptr Sec 90-; Exchng Arch Stu Budpst Hngry 89-90; Archtctr.

**SMITH, SHELIA,** Al St Univ, Montgomery, AL; SR; BS; Pre-Law Soc Treas 90-; Cmnty Ctr Vol 89-90; Brantwood Chldrn Hme Intern; Libr Asst Yr 88; Crim Just; Prob Ofcr/Lawyer.

**SMITH, SHELIA H,** Meridian Comm Coll, Meridian, MS; FR; BA; Phi Theta Kappa; Army Comm Svcs 86; Acctntng Asst; Accntng.

**SMITH, SHELLEY N,** Univ Of Southern Ms, Hattiesburg, MS; JR; BS; Phi Beta Lambda 89; Alpha Omega 90; Sexual Assault Crisis Center Vol; Spec Olympics 90; AS Copiah Lincoln Comm Clg 90; Psychology; Phd Clinical.

**SMITH, SHELLY J,** West Liberty St Coll, West Liberty, WV; GD; French Club Soc Org 87-88; Ifor Prsn For Stdnts/Visitors Clg 90; Mbr Chmpnshp WVIAC Tennis Team 86-87; BA 90; Engl/Sclgy.

**SMITH, SHEREE E,** Univ Of Al At Huntsville, Huntsville, AL; FR; BA; Alpha Lambda Delta 90-; Hnr Schlr 90-; Engrng.

**SMITH, SHERRY L,** Commonwealth Coll, Virginia Beach, VA; GD; ASSOC; Ofc Admin Clb; Commonwlth Clg Law Soc Day Rep; Collegian Sec Intl; Strawbridge Civic Leg VA Bch Sgt At Arms; Law; Clrk Of Cts.

**SMITH, SHERRY LYNN,** Oh St Univ At Marion, Marion, OH; SR; Show Choir 86 90; Corus Choir; AA 90; Elem Ed; Tchr.

**SMITH, SHERRY M,** Coker Coll, Hartsville, SC; SR; BA; Chstrfld Co Schl Dstrct 86-90; Elem Ed.

**SMITH, SHIRLEY A,** Middle Tn St Univ, Murfreesboro, TN; JR; BS; STEA Treas 90-; Hutton Prize Awd; Ext Hmkrs VP 90; BS Columbia St Comm Clg; Elem Educ; Teach.

**SMITH, SHIRLEY G,** Univ Of Southern Ms, Hattiesburg, MS; SR; Stdnt Educ Assn 90-.

**SMITH, SHONNA C,** Fl St Univ, Tallahassee, FL; SR; BME; Mrchng Chfs 87-; Brd Of Advsrs 89-90; Chrch Of Chrst Campus Mnstry 87-; Tau Beta Sigma 88-; All Amer Schlrs; IM Sftbl; AA 90; Instrmntl Music Ed; Bnd Dir.

**SMITH, SHONTELLE A,** Al St Univ, Montgomery, AL; JR; Yrbk Admnstrtv Asst 90-; Psi Chi; Deans List 89-; Hon Soc 90-; Child Psychlgst.

**SMITH, SIDNEY A,** Ms St Univ, Miss State, MS; FR; BS; Local 903 Intl Brthrhd Elec Wrkrs Jrnymn/Wireman 82-; Elec Engineering.

**SMITH, SISTER BEVERLY,** Mount Aloysius Jr Coll, Cresson, PA; SO; COTA; Occuptl Thpy Club 90-; Intcmm Retrmnt Commt Chrpsn 89-90; Pre-Schl Tchr 76-76 83-85; Activ Dr 76-83 86-90; BSE Carlow Clg 72; Occupt Therapy; Geriatric OT.

**SMITH, STACEY B,** Oh Univ, Athens, OH; FR; BSE; Deans Lst; Chrldng; Engr.

**SMITH, STACEY L,** Johnson C Smith Univ, Charlotte, NC; SR; BA; Yrbk Co Edtr 88-89; Soph Cls VP 88-89; Sclgy/Scl Wrk Clb VP 89-90; Deans Lst 88-; Stdnt Orient Ldr; Intern Adult Prbtn/ Prl Ofc 90-; Outstndng Jr; Sclgy; Grad Schl.

**SMITH, STACI L,** Carnegie Mellon Univ, Pittsburgh, PA; SO; BA; Graphic Cmnctn Clb 89-90; Amer Inst Arch Stdnts 90-; Lambda Sigma 90-; Engl; Writer.**

**SMITH, STACIA RAQUEL,** Ms St Univ, Miss State, MS; JR; BS; Clg Rpblcns 88-; Home Ec Clb 89-; Child Dvlpmnt Option Clb 90-; Phi Gamma Delta Ltl Sis Sec 89-; Dean Schlr 90-; Phi Mu Rcrdng Sec 88-; Proj HOPE 88-; Chldrns Miracle Ntwrk Telethon 88-; Adopt A Hwy Prog 90-; Home Ec/Child Life; Child Life Spclst Hosp.

**SMITH, STACIE A,** Univ Of Tn At Martin, Martin, TN; SO; Phi Eta Sigma 90; Pi Sigma Epsilon Rcdng Sec 89; Alpha Omicron Pi Crrspndng Sec 89; Phi Kappa Phi Otstndng Schrshp 90; Pom Pom Squad 90; Acct; CPA.

**SMITH, STACY R,** Northwest Al Comm Coll, Phil Campbell, AL; FR; AAS; Phi Theta Kappa 90-; Cmptr Sci; Cmptr Prgmmr.

**SMITH, STACY R,** Western Piedmont Comm Coll, Morganton, NC; SO; BS; Anthropology; Phys Anthrplgst.

**SMITH, STANLEY TODD,** Univ Of Sc At Lancaster, Lancaster, SC; FR; BA; Religion; Pastor.

**SMITH, STEFANIE J,** Univ Of Ga, Athens, GA; JR; BED; SGA Chr Publcty Cmtee; Pres Cncl; Phi Beta Kappa; Phi Theta Kappa 88; Delta Epsilon Chi 88; Totaract Serv Cmuty Proj Chrmn 90; Clg Stdnt Yr; Mktg Stdnt Yr; Delta Epsilon Chi Natl Conf Awd; Phi Beta Kappa Awd; Vybl I M; AD; Mktg; Pub Rltns/ Educ/Sls.

**SMITH, STEPHANIE E,** Al St Univ, Montgomery, AL; SO; BS; Phi Eta Sigma 89-90; Stdnt Of Yr 89-90; Pres Schlrshp; Bio; Phys Thrpy.

**SMITH, STEPHANIE L,** Middle Tn St Univ, Murfreesboro, TN; SO; BA; Chmbr Chr Sctn Ldr 90-; Opr Wrkshp Slst 90-; Msc Ed; Ed.

**SMITH, STEPHANIE M,** Albany St Coll, Albany, GA; JR; BA; Delta Sigma Theta Sec; GM Delco Intrn; Math Awd; Math; Professor.

**SMITH, STEPHEN J,** Univ Of Toledo, Toledo, OH; GD; Im Bsktbl/Sftbl; JD; Law.

**SMITH, STEPHEN K,** Ms St Univ, Miss State, MS; FR; BS; Bapt Stdnt Union 90; Phi Eta Sigma 90; Frmhse 90; Cir K; Chem Eng; Eng.

**SMITH, STEPHEN M,** Villanova Univ, Villanova, PA; JR; BA; Stdnt Cltn Agnst Aprthd And Rcsm Pres Co Coor 89-; Yr Of Dvrsty Strng Com 90-; Blck Cltrl Scty; Stdnts Agnst Sxl Strtyps; Cncrnd Abt Cntrl Amer 89-; Phi Alpha Phi; Phi Alpha Theta; Omicron Delta Kappa; Pce And Jstce Crrclm Com 90-; Hstry.

**SMITH, STEPHEN P,** Western New England Coll, Springfield, MA; SO; BS; IEEE; Lambda Delta Fr Hnr Scty 90; Alpha Lambda Delta; Ttrng 90-; Fr Acad Awrd 90; Soph Acad Awrd; Eng Scty Of Wstrn MA Schlrshp; Vrsty Bwlng 90; Bwlng Clb 89-; Math And Sci; Elec Eng.

**SMITH, STEVE W,** American Baptist Coll, Nashville, TN; SO; BA; Phi Beta Sigma; Bblcl Thlgcl Studies; Sociology.**

**SMITH, STEVEN,** Cornell Univ Statutory College, Ithaca, NY; JR; BS; Stdnt Advsr; Crnl Cthlc Comm 88-; KY Srvc Prjct 88-; Pi Kappa Phi Alumni Rltns Chrmn 90-; Habitat Hmnty 90; Intrnshp Irish Prlmnt 90; Pblc Rltns Intrn 90; IM Intra Frat Cncl 90-; Cmmnctn; Law Bsns.

**SMITH, STEVEN E,** Oh St Univ At Newark, Newark, OH; JR; MBA; Ski Club 90-; Alpha Lambda Delta 89-; Phi Eta Sigma 89-; Golden Key 90-; Acctg.

**SMITH, STEVEN E,** Wv Univ At Parkersburg, Parkersburg, WV; SR; BS; AA Parkersburg Comm Coll 88; Bus Admin/Mgt.

**SMITH, STEVEN G,** Univ Of Tn At Chattanooga, Chattanooga, TN; JR; BSE; Tau Beta Pi 90-; Pi Mu Epsilon 89-; Gold Key 89-; Chem Eng Soc 89-; Field Engr 87-88; Chem Eng; Naval Reactors.

**SMITH, STEVEN M,** Comm Coll Algny Co Algny Cmps, Pittsburgh, PA; SO; Phys Edn/Athletic Trng; Phys Ed Tchr.

**SMITH, STEVEN P,** Springfield Tech Comm Coll, Springfield, MA; JR; BA; Elec Eng.

**SMITH, SUSAN L,** Milligan Coll, Milligan Clg, TN; SR; BA; Cls Ofcr Pres 88-; Stdnt Govt Cls Rep 89-; Cncrt Choir Mbr 87-90; Dns Lst 87-; Sprtl Lf Comm Mbr 87-; Serv Seekrs Mbr 87-88; Drm Cncl Rep 87-89; Intrnshp Ofc Sen Al Gore Jr TN 90; Chrldng Co Capt 88-90; Psych; Cnslng/Hmn Rels.

**SMITH, SUSAN WIMBERLY,** Fl International Univ, Miami, FL; JR; BS; Elem Ed; Tch.

**SMITH, SUZANNE E,** Univ Of Southern Ms, Hattiesburg, MS; SR; BA; Var Bsktbl 87-89; Var Sftbl 87-88; Sci Ed; Tchr.

**SMITH, SUZANNE E,** Mercer Univ Schl Of Pharm, Atlanta, GA; GD; PHARM; Hnr Cncl Pres 90-; Rho Chi Sec; Acad Std Pharm Asc; BA Emory Univ 89; AA Oxford Clg 87; Clncl Pharm.

**SMITH, SYDNEY O,** Fl Memorial Coll, Miami, FL; GD; MPA; Natl Assoc Blck Accts 90-; Pianist/Organist Miami Gospel Chapel Choir 89-; AAS Boro Manhattan Cmnty Clg NY 85; AAS Clg Arts/Sci/Tech 80; Bsn Mgmt; CPA.

**SMITH JR, SYLVESTER S,** Al A & M Univ, Normal, AL; SO; Mrchg Bnd; Kappa Kappa Psi 90-; Engr.

**SMITH, SYLVIA J,** Indiana Univ Of Pa, Indiana, PA; JR; BA; Univ TV Prod 89-; Univ FM News Anchor 90; Ind Gazette Cntrbtng Wrtr; Deans Lst 88-; Natl Brdcstng Soc V P 90-; Zeta Tau Alpha Chrmn 90-; Bib Bros/Sis 90-; Spec Olympics 90; Proj Bundle Up Telethon 89-; Outstdng New Greek Awd 90-; Jrnlsm/ Comm; Pblc Rltns.

**SMITH, TABITHA F,** Savannah Coll Of Art & Design, Savannah, GA; FR; MFA; Deans List 90-; 4 Yr Schlrshp #10,000; Art.

**SMITH, TAMARA LEE,** Univ Of Sc At Columbia, Columbia, SC; SR; BA; Psychlgy Clb 90-; Yth Cnslr/Singles Dir/Sndy Sch Tchr Bel-Ridge Bapt Ch; Psychlgy.

**SMITH, TAMMY S,** Middle Tn St Univ, Murfreesboro, TN; JR; BS; Columbia State Comm Coll SGA Sntr 88-89; STEA 89-90; TN Assn FHA Cnvtn-Spkr; Plcd 2nd Rnnr-Up Miss Marshall Co Pgnt 90; Srvd Ldr 4-H Camp William P Ridley; AS Columbia State Comm Coll 90; Elem Educ; Tchng.

**SMITH, TANIA A,** Indiana Univ Of Pa, Indiana, PA; FR; Rec League Vlybl 90-; Math; Tchr.

**SMITH, TANIA D,** Yale Univ, New Haven, CT; FR; BA; Blk Stdnt Allnc 90-; Urban Imprvmnt Corps Math Tutor/Sat Wrkshp Ldr; Biology; Pediatrician.

**SMITH, TARA L,** Indiana Univ Of Pa, Indiana, PA; FR; Stdnt Cngrs Rep 90-; SADD Sec 90-; Sign Lang Clb 90-; Englsh; Tchng.

**SMITH, TAUNYA Y,** Alcorn St Univ, Lorman, MS; JR; BA; Deans Lst; Acctng; CPA.

**SMITH, TED D,** King Coll, Bristol, TN; SR; BA; Cmps Lfe Com 88; Athnn Ltrry Scty; Westrn Cvlztn Ttr 90-; Vrsty Tnns Sim Indr Sccr; Hstry; Govt Srvce.

**SMITH, TERESA ASKEW,** Averett Coll, Danville, VA; SR; BS; AAS Va Western Comm Clge 84; AAS Va Western Comm Clge 87; Hmn Rsrc Dvlpment.

**SMITH, TERESA K,** Union Coll, Barbourville, KY; FR; BA; Educ; Tchr.

**SMITH, TERONDA M,** Al A & M Univ, Normal, AL; SO; Acdmc Hnr Rll 89-; Dean Lst 90-; Kappa Delta Pi Sec; Elem Educ; Tchng.

**SMITH, TERRANCE C,** Fayetteville St Univ, Fayetteville, NC; JR; Ftbl 87-90; CIAA Dfnsv Plyr Of Yr 89-90; Kodak All Amer/ Blck Coll All Amer; Phys Ed/Psychlgy.

**SMITH, TERRENCE L,** Univ Of Tn At Chattanooga, Chattanooga, TN; JR; BSE; IEEE 88-; Ntl Soc Prof Engrs; Gldn Ky 90-; Alpha Lambda Delta89-; Phi Eta Sigma 89-; Ntl Coll Engr Awd 90-; Co-Op Stdnt Elec Pwr Bd Chttnga 89-; Elec Engr.

**SMITH, TERRY S,** Abraham Baldwin Agri Coll, Tifton, GA; FR; BA; Frstry-Wldlfe Clb Prog Chrprsn Elect; Wldlfe Tech; Cnsrvtn Rngr.

**SMITH, TESSA A,** Bridgewater Coll, Bridgewater, VA; SR; BS; Sheraton Bus Intrnshp 90-; Cum Laude; Deans Lst 89-; Bus Admin.

**SMITH II, THOMAS E,** Univ Of Nc At Charlotte, Charlotte, NC; JR; BABS; Hll Cncl Rep 89-; Assc Res Hll Del 89-90; Pre Law Soc 89-; Pi Sigma Alpha 90-; IM Sftbl Ump; Pol Sci/Crmnl Jus; Law.

**SMITH JR, THOMAS E,** Memphis St Univ, Memphis, TN; SR; BBA; ACM 88-90; Bapt Stdnt Union 85; Lambda Chi Alpha; Southern Fabricators Inc Dir Cmptr Svcs; Acctg; CPA.

**SMITH, TIFFANY A,** Va St Univ, Petersburg, VA; SO; BA; SAC; All-Amer Schlr; Outstndg Acad Achvmnt Awd 90; Outstndg Schlr Athl 90; VA Statesman Acad Achvmnt Awd 89-; Bsktbl 89-; Acctg; CPA.

**SMITH, TIFFANY L,** Va Commonwealth Univ, Richmond, VA; JR; BS; Nwsppr Ftr Ed 89-; Pblc Rltns Stdnt Scty Amr 89; Prjct Umoja 90; NAACP Sec 90-; Mass Cmmnctns; Pblc Rltns.

**SMITH, TIFFANY LYNETTE,** Coppin St Coll, Baltimore, MD; JR; BA; Sigma Gamma Rho Vp; Psychlgy.

**SMITH, TIGE D,** Howard Univ, Washington, DC; GD; JD; Mt Crt Sbstntv Brf Ed 90-; Hlp Scty Fndr Presdnt Pro Bono Admn 89-; Am Jur Awrd; Top 102 Clss; Lamda Chi Alpha Interfrtrnl Cncl Rep 84-88; HPILS Awrd 5 Stpnds 90-; Chrldr 85; BA Stetson Univ FL 88; Law.

**SMITH, TIMOTHY A,** Oh St Univ, Columbus, OH; JR; BSLA; Ohio Nrsrymns Assoc; Ntl Hnr Scty 83-87; Delta Tau Delta Cmmnty Serv Chrmn 88; Wrstlng 83-84; Pres Shwplce Lndscpng Inc 89; Lndscpe Archtctre; Dsgn/Bld.

**SMITH, TIMOTHY C,** Hudson Valley Comm Coll, Troy, NY; SO; MBA; Bus; Fnnc.

**SMITH, TIMOTHY L,** Marshall University, Huntington, WV; SR; BBA; Accntng Clb 89-; Wv Soc Of Cpas 89-; Gamma Beta Phi 88-; Accntng; Cpa.**

**SMITH, TIMOTHY M,** S U N Y Coll Of Tech At Frmgdl, Farmingdale, NY; SO; BA; Bsn Admn; Mgmt.

**SMITH, TINA F,** Middle Ga Coll, Cochran, GA; SR; BA; Natl Socty Prof Engrs 90-; Sftbl 90; Elec Engr Cmptr Sci.

**SMITH, TODD M,** Pearl River Jr Coll, Poplarville, MS; FR; Mech Eng.

**SMITH, TONI I,** Middle Tn St Univ, Murfreesboro, TN; SR; BS; Bio Clb 87-; Chem Clb 87-89; Beta Beta Beta 90-; Kappa Delta Pi 89-; Phi Mu Delta 89-; Gamma Beta Phi 89-; Chi Omega 87-; Bio; Physicians Asst.

**SMITH, TONYA A,** Va St Univ, Petersburg, VA; SR; BS; Gospel Choir 88-90; Phi Beta Lambda; Deans Lst 89-; Bus.

**SMITH, TRACEY,** Comm Coll Algny Co Algny Cmps, Pittsburgh, PA; FR; BA; Microbio Tech Prsbytrn Univ Hosp 89-; Bus; Law.

**SMITH, TRACEY M,** Univ Of Southern Ms, Hattiesburg, MS; JR; BS; Med Tchnlgy Clb Pblcty Chrprsn 90-; Phi Theta Kappa 89-90; Achvmnt Awd 90; Doris Barrett Med Tchnlgy Schlrshp; AA Jones Co Jr Clge 90; Med Tchnlgy.

**SMITH, TRACY B,** Union Coll, Barbourville, KY; JR; BA; Iota Sigma Nau 90-; Work Study Awd 90; Acctg/Bsn Mgmt; Acctg.

**SMITH, TRACY L,** Wv Univ, Morgantown, WV; SR; Pblc Rltns Stdnt Soc Am Sec 88-; Cmps Radio Station 88-; Golden Key; Order Omega Pres 90-; Rho Lambda 90-; Tau Kappa Alpha; Alpha Xi Dlta Corp Mgr 88-; Plnd Approach Comm Hlth 90; Stdnt Escort Sys; Arts/Sci Cert Merit 88; Advrtsng/Psychlgy; Dir Ad Agency/Cnslr.

**SMITH, TRAVIS E,** Southern Coll Of Tech, Marietta, GA; SO; BS; RHA 90-; IM Stfbl/Bsktbl 87-; Cvl Eng; Eng.

**SMITH, TRICIA L,** Thomas Nelson Comm Coll, Hampton, VA; FR; AAS; Bus/Office Tchnlgy; Info Prcsng Spclst.

**SMITH, TRISHA L,** Ms St Univ, Miss State, MS; SR; BS; Inst Indstrl Eng 90-; Scty Mft Eng Clb Rep Stdnt Cncl; Eng Stdnt Cncl Treas; Tau Beta Pi 90-; Alpha Pi Mu VP 90-; Eng.

**SMITH, VALERIE CLAIRE,** Univ Of Tn At Knoxville, Knoxville, TN; SO; MBA; Delta Sigma Pi 90-; Alpha Chi Omega Chpln 90-; Edward E Judy Schlrshps; Acctng; Law CPA.

**SMITH, VALERIE M,** Pellissippi St Tech Comm Coll, Knoxville, TN; FR; BA; Engr; Indstrl Engr.

**SMITH, VALINDA DENISE,** Va St Univ, Petersburg, VA; SO; BS; Gospel Choir Treas 89-; Track/Fld; Acctng; CPA.

**SMITH, VANESSA A,** Glassboro St Coll, Glassboro, NJ; JR; BA; RSA Tres 88-89; Campus Wide Rsdnt Stu Assoc Scl Dir 89-90; Ad Clb Phtgrphr; Intrnshp WHWH 1350 Am; Cmnctns; Ads.

**SMITH, VEDA A,** Tusculum Coll, Greeneville, TN; SO; BA; Amer Hrt Assc 89-; Elem Educ; Tchg.

**SMITH, VERA L,** Atlantic Comm Coll, Mays Landing, NJ; SO; AAS; Pediatric Nrs.

**SMITH, VERNICE A,** Central St Univ, Wilberforce, OH; SO; Psych; Chld Psych/Scl Wrk.

**SMITH, VICKI S,** Montgomery Comm Coll, Troy, NC; SR; BA; Alpha Chi 90-; Bs Of Amer; BA Gardner-Webb Clg Boiling Spgs NC 91; Elem Ed.

**SMITH, VICTORIA L,** Al A & M Univ, Normal, AL; SO; BA; Manars; Home Ec; Cooperative Extnsts.

**SMITH, VICTORIA L W,** Cecils Coll, Asheville, NC; FR; AAS; Clge Assoc Paralgls VP; Clge Mrshl; Dns Lst 90-; Prfsnl Lgl Asst Inc 90-; Rlgs Soc Fnds; BA Math Earlham Clge Richmond Ind 81; Paralegal Stds; Law.

**SMITH, WANDA E,** Mount Aloysius Jr Coll, Cresson, PA; SO; BA; Phi Theta Kappa 90-; Acctg.

**SMITH, WANDA R,** Walker Coll, Jasper, AL; FR; Pres Lst 90-; Spec Ed.

**SMITH, WENDY L,** S U N Y Coll At Fredonia, Fredonia, NY; SR; Hlth Admn Club 90-; Bus Club 89-90; Hlth Serv Admn Intern 90; Hlth Admn; Occptnl Thrpy.

**SMITH, WENDY LEE,** Lenoir Rhyne Coll, Hickory, NC; SR; BA; Stdnt Govt Assn 89-; Res Advsr 88-; Prog Bd Chrprsn 89; Stdnt Natl Educ Assn; Kappa Delta Edtr 88-; Habitate Hmntes 90-; Paint Heart Out 90-; Alumni Assn Ldrshp Awd; I M 87-88; Ele Educ; Tch/Cnslr.

**SMITH, WILLIAM C,** Al A & M Univ, Normal, AL; JR; AL A And M Bsbl 89.

**SMITH, WILLIAM MEL,** William Paterson Coll, Wayne, NJ; JR; BA; Big Band Jazz Ensmbl 87-89; Math Assn 90; Deans Lst 90; Math; Tchr.

**SMITH, WILLIAM S,** Roane St Comm Coll, Harriman, TN; SO; BS; Wrkd 2 Yrs Woods Metal Fabrctn Shop Nashvl TN; Comb Wldr St Area Voc/Tech Sch Harriman TN 86; Math/Engr; Engr.

**SMITH, WILLIAM T,** East Tn St Univ, Johnson City, TN; SR; BA; Epsilon Pi Tau 90-; Coprtv Ed Gen Electric Aplncs Columbia TN; AAS Elctrncs New River Cmnty Clge 89; AAS Instrmntn New River Cmnty Clge 90; Elctrncs; Engrg.

**SMITH, YOLANDA,** Rust Coll, Holly Springs, MS; SR; BS; Pre-Almn Cncl 89-; Ms Assn Educ/Stdnt Prg Sec 89-; Alpha Kappa Mu Sec 90-; Elem Educ; Edctr.

**SMITH, YOSHITA L,** City Univ Of Ny City Coll, New York, NY; SO; BA; Cmnctns; Advrtsng.

**SMITH, YVONNE H,** Western Piedmont Comm Coll, Morganton, NC; SO; Dem Party Lic Pract Fld Occuptn Thrpy N Car Brd Occup Thrpy 85; Occptnl Thrpy; AAS Caldwl Comm Coll 85; Nrsng; Med Surg/Telmtry Nrsng.

**SMITH-CHERRY, SANTE O,** Norfolk St Univ, Norfolk, VA; SR; BA; Hstry Clb Treas 90-; Miss Hstry/Geogrphy 90-; Advsr To Stdnt Crt 90-; C Gibson Schlrshp 90-; Hstry/Lbrl Arts; Prfssr Of Hstry.

**SMITH-HALL, OLIVE B L,** Al A & M Univ, Normal, AL; SO; BS; Erly Chldhd Ed; Ed.

**SMITH-MISNER, MICHELE L,** Kent St Univ Kent Cmps, Kent, OH; FR; BA; Alpha Lambda Delta 90-; NE Ohio Suzula Assoc 88-90; Music Educ; Teacher.

**SMITH-RANSOM, EVELYN C,** Jackson St Univ, Jackson, MS; JR; BA; Blue/White Flsh Entrtnmnt Edtr 89; Edtr In Chf 89-; Delta Sigma Theta 88-; The Clarion Ldgr Stf/Rprtr Intrnshp 89; Mass Cmnctns.**

**SMITH-TEETS, SHERRI L,** Davis & Elkins Coll, Elkins, WV; GD; AS; Beta Alpha Beta 90; AS 90; Bus; Admin Sec.**

**SMITH-ZAJKOWSKI, LINDA J,** William Paterson Coll, Wayne, NJ; GD; MA; Ortn Dyslx Soc 82-84; Brgn-Pssc Asc Educ Yng Chldrn 89-90; Cbmstr Pack 56 90-; Kappa Delta Pi 90; Rdng Tchr Alphbtc Phncs Thrpst 89-; Spec Ed/Admn.

**SMITHA, STEPHANIE S,** Oh Univ, Athens, OH; JR; BSE; AICHE 88-; IM Vlybl/Tnns; Tau Beta Pi; Smmr Intrn Prctr/Gmbl 90-; Deans Lst 90; Chem Eng.

**SMITHBOWER, BRENDA M,** Mount Aloysius Jr Coll, Cresson, PA; FR; BA; Bus Admn; Acctnt.

**SMITHER, CRAIG A,** Middle Tn St Univ, Murfreesboro, TN; SR; Assn Study Body Mem Hse Rep; Elect Cmn Elect Cmnsnr 89-90; Univ Rules Com; Kappa Alpha Order Ritualist 89-90; Stdnt Orntn Asst Tm Capt 89-90; BA; Mktg; Sls.

**SMITHERS OLIVER, CYNTHIA,** Memphis St Univ, Memphis, TN; SR; Grmn Clb Univ TN 85-87; Hon Stdnt Univ TN 83-87; Dnce Co 1st Co Univ TN 87-88; Perf/Chorgrphr/Dnce Instr Playhse On The Square Memphis TN 88-; Figure Sktng Instr Ice Capades Memphis 88-; BA Univ TN Knoxvl TN; Engl Lang/Lingstcs; Comms.

**SMITHEY, TARA L,** Meridian Comm Coll, Meridian, MS; FR; Bapt Stdnt Union; Clg Actvts Bd 90-; Ambassadors 90-; Phi Theta Kappa; Cmnty Svc Asst 90-.

**SMITHFIELD, WILLIAM J,** Univ Of Tn At Knoxville, Knoxville, TN; FR; BS; Fr Cncl 90-; Clg Rpblcns 90-; Sr Clsscl Leag 90-; Phi Eta Sigma Treas; Alpha Lambda Delta; Kappa Alpha Ordr Asst Hstrn 90-; Acctg; CPA.

**SMITHHART, JUDY K,** Univ Of Southern Ms, Hattiesburg, MS; SR; BS; Bptst Un 89-; Almni Assn Asst 89-; Gldn Ky 90-; Gamma Alpha Epsilon 89-; Psi Chi Pblc Rltns 90-; Alpha Sigma Alpha Schlrshp Chrmn 89-; Alpha Sigma Alpha Idl Pldg 89-; IM Sftbl 89-; Pre-Prof Psychlgy; Clncl Psychlgy.

**SMITHMEYER, KATHRYN L,** Fl St Univ, Tallahassee, FL; SR; BS; London Prog Res Cnslr 90; Recrtr 90; Fla Div Trsm Pub Rels Intrn; Bus Commctns; Pub Reltns.

**SMOAK, JOSEPH M,** Univ Of Sc At Columbia, Columbia, SC; SR; BS; Pi Mu Epsilon 90-; Pres Lst; Deans Lst; Rugby Clb; Marine Sci; Ocngrphy/Envrnmntl.

**SMOKE, JONATHAN P,** Rhodes Coll, Memphis, TN; SR; BA; Nwsppr Co Ed 87-; Stdnt Assmbly Cmmssnr 89-90; RA 89-; Phi Beta Kappa; Omicron Delta Kappa Sec Treas 90-; Mrtr Brd Dir Comm 90-; Omicron Delta Epsilon VP; Hll Fm; Phi Beta Peyton Nalle Rhodes Prz; Ralph C Hon Econ Awrd; JRHYDE Awrd Rlgs St; Eocn Rlgs Stds; Bus Wrting.**

**SMOKOWSKI, JAMES N,** Syracuse Univ, Syracuse, NY; JR; BARCH; Golden Key 89-; Arch.

**SMOLENSKI, MARK S,** Univ Of Ct, Storrs, CT; SR; BA; Mrchng Bnd 87-90; Ball Rm Dnc Clb 90-; Outing Clb 88; Kappa Kappa Psi; Asst Pldg Mstr 88-; Rsrch Asstnt 89-; Psychlgy/Sclgy.**

**SMOLINSKI, THOMAS J,** Hudson Valley Comm Coll, Troy, NY; FR; BA; Computer Infor Syst; Computer Prog.

**SMOLLER, JENNIFER H,** Fl International Univ, Miami, FL; SR; BA; Phi Kappa Phi; Dade Cnty Sch Vol; BA Swarthmore Coll 84; Chem; Med/Rsrch.

**SMOLYAK, REGINA,** Univ Of Rochester, Rochester, NY; SO; BS; Jwsh Cmmnty Cntr 90-; Bio Chmstry; Med.

**SMOOT, DONNA M,** Longwood Coll, Farmville, VA; JR; BS; Stdnt Advsry Commt Dprtmnt Ecnmcs Finance; Stdnt Excrsn Clb 90; Deans List 90; Bsn Admin; MBA Info Systms.

**SMOOT, KELLY M,** Va Commonwealth Univ, Richmond, VA; GD; MSN; NAACOG 90-; Sigma Theta Tau; BSN 90; Prnt Nrsng; Clncl Nrs Spec.

**SMOTHERMAN, SHERI L,** Middle Tn St Univ, Murfreesboro, TN; SR; BS; Tchr Edn Assn 90-; Natl Edn Assn 90-; Kappa Delta Pi; Elem Edn; Tchr.

**SMOTHERS, MARJORIE E,** Univ Of Tn At Martin, Martin, TN; SR; Phi Kappa Phi; Alpha Delta Mu; Intrn Infant Stmltn Pgm 90; Estnsn Hmmkrs Clb; BS.

**SMREKAR, BLAINE E,** Cincinnati Bible Coll & Sem, Cincinnati, OH; GD; MDIV; Ohio Army Ntl Grd 1st Lt 87; Chpln Cndte Oh Ntl Grd; BA Ohio State U 86; Thelgy; Mltry Chplncy Army.

**SMUCKER, JEANNE M,** Univ Of Pittsburgh, Pittsburgh, PA; GD; PH D; Amer Nrs Assn 86-; Sigma Theta Tau 68-; Prsn Fmlu Mnstry Bd 87-; Rch Out 81-84; Mrch Dimes Pro Advsry Bd 74-86; Chld Abs/Nglct Intrdscplnry Trng Grant 88-89; Pro Nrs Trneeshp 71-73; Pre-Nrsng Mnchstr Coll 63-65; Nrsng BSN Cornell Univ 68; Prnt-Chld Nrsng; Tch Nrsng.

**SNAPE, JASON J,** S U N Y At Buffalo, Buffalo, NY; SR; BA; Univ Dsgn Assc 89-; Scrty Grd UUDB 87-90; Ilstr Cmps Nwspr 90-; Dns List 89-; Gldn Key; Wrstlng 88; Grphc Dsgn/Ilstrtn.

**SNAPP, SCOTTIE L,** Va Highlands Comm Coll, Abingdon, VA; SO; BA; Law Enfrcmnt Clb Trea 89-; Deans List; Pres List; IM Sftbl; Assoc; Police Sci/Crmnl Justice; Law Enfrcmnt.

**SNAVELY, TRACY L,** George Mason Univ, Fairfax, VA; SR; BS; AMA 89-; Assoc Collegiate Entrepreneurs 89-; Golden Key 89-; Alpha Chi 89-; Beta Gamma Sigma; Marketing; Business.

**SNAY, CHERYL L,** Hudson Valley Comm Coll, Troy, NY; SO; BA; Stdnt Tchng 89-; AAS; Scl/Sci; Elem Ed.

**SNEAD, HELEN M,** Fort Valley St Coll, Fort Valley, GA; SR; BS; Vet Sci Clb V P 90-; Vet Tech; Vet Sci.

**SNEAD JR, JOHN S,** Piedmont Tech Coll, Greenwood, SC; GD; BS; Phi Beta Lambda 89-90; Bus; Mgmnt.

**SNEAD, KIMBERLY N,** Fayetteville St Univ, Fayetteville, NC; SO; Bio; Medcl/Pediatrcs.

**SNEAD, NIKKI G,** Wilberforce Univ, Wilberforce, OH; FR; Choir 90; Deans List; Mass Media Commn; TV News Anchor Woman.

**SNEAD JR, RICHARD M,** Va Commonwealth Univ, Richmond, VA; SO; BS; Phi Eta Sigma 90-; Acctng.

**SNEAD, SANDRA D,** Bethel Coll, Mckenzie, TN; SO; BS; Psyc Club VP 89-90; Wmn Isues Orgarf Nwspr Editor Chief 90-; Gamma Beta Phi P 90-; Scty Clg Jrl 89-; Iota Alpha Omega VP 90-; Amer Psych Assoc; Psy; Clinical Psy.

**SNEAD, TRACEY D,** Univ Of Nc At Charlotte, Charlotte, NC; JR; BA; Flr Pres 90-; Phi Eta Sigma 89-; IM Sprts Flg Ftbll Vllybll 89-; Psychlgy; Schl Cnslng.

**SNEED, BRAD V,** Christopher Newport Coll, Newport News, VA; SO; BS; ROTC 89-90; Math; Engr.

**SNEED, DAVID P,** Tn Temple Univ, Chattanooga, TN; SO; BA; Choir/Ensemble V P 90-; Forensics 90-; Dramatic Theatrical Prod 90-; Speech/Theatre; Educ/Tchng.

**SNEED, MONIQUE B,** Univ Of Md At Eastern Shore, Princess Anne, MD; JR; BA; Ifsea; Eta Sigma Delta 90-; Aa Prnc Grgs Comm Coll 89; Htl Rstrnt Mngmnt.

**SNEED, RAQUEL L,** Tn St Univ, Nashville, TN; SR; BA; Arstcrt Bnds 87-; Cncrt Bnd 88; Pep Bnd 87-; Phi Mu Alpha 87-; Alpha Phi Alpha Swthrt 87; Ntnl Assoc Advncmnt Clrd People 89-; Prod Asst WSIX 98FM Radio Sta 90; Prod Int TNN Nshvl Now TV Ntwrk; Spch/Theatre; Mass Cmmnctn/Prod.

**SNEED, SUSAN E,** Fl St Univ, Tallahassee, FL; SO; BA; Lib Stds Hnrs/Schlrs Prog 89-90; Alpha Gamma Delta 89-; Engl; Law.

**SNEED, TERRI L,** Tn St Univ, Nashville, TN; SO; BS; Agrnmy Clb Treas 89-; MANRRS; Intrnshp Soil Cnsrvtn Serv 89-; Ag Bus.

**SNEED, WHITNEY L,** Fl Coll, Temple Terrace, FL; SO; BA; Kappa Omicron 90-; Chorus 89-; Hon Rll; Deans Lst; Piano Schlrshp; Voice/Acad Schlrshps; Dr John Spencer Chuck Awd Outstndng Achiev Piano; AA; Bio; Phys Ther.

**SNEERINGER, REBECCA A,** Millersville Univ Of Pa, Millersville, PA; FR; BED; Res Hll Act Comm 90-; Hist Clb 90-; Res Asst 90-; Hist/Ed; Tchr.

**SNELL, JANIFER R,** Middle Tn St Univ, Murfreesboro, TN; SR; BS; HPER 88-90; Alpha Delta Pi 87; Red Cross 88-990; Spcl Olympcs 89; Bthsda Intrn In Cinn Oh; Im Ftbl Vllybl Bsktbl/Sftbl 87; Corp Fitness; Corp Fitness Or Physcl Thrpy.

**SNELL, JENNIFER L,** Indiana Univ Of Pa, Indiana, PA; SO; BED; Sign Lang Clb; CEC; Envir Clb Chr; Ed; Ed Hrg Imprd.

**SNELL, PAMELA C,** Va Commonwealth Univ, Richmond, VA; SR; BS; SEA 90-; Golden Key 90-; Phi Kappa Phi; AAS Rappahannock Cmnty Clg 89; Spec Ed-Mntl Retrdtn; Tchg.

**SNELL, PATRICIA J,** Le Moyne Coll, Syracuse, NY; JR; BA; LSPB Pblcty Chrprsn 89-; Rsdnt Advsr 90-; Folk Grp 89; Hnry Degree Com 90-; PIC 88-; Psychlgy Clb 90-; Art Clb 89-90; Alpha Sigma Nu; Math Tutor Math Ctr 90-; Myrtle Dershug Awd 89; Mary Mc Clusky Awd 90; Nominee Truman Schlrshp 90; Psychlgy; Psychlgy/Cnslng.

**SNELL, ROBERT,** Hillsborough Comm Coll, Tampa, FL; FR; BS; Nursing.

**SNIDER, CHRISTOPHER A,** Emory & Henry Coll, Emory, VA; SR; BA; Natl Assoc Of Accts 90-; Deans Lst 87-; Pi Gamma Mu 89-; Sigma Mu Pres 89-; Alpha Phi Omega 89-90; Intrnshp At E & H Bus Ofc 89-90; Tennis Tm 87-88; Acctng; CPA.

**SNIDER, CHRISTOPHER P,** Univ Of Cincinnati, Cincinnati, OH; JR; BA; Gldn Key; Tau Alpha Pi; Engr.

**SNIDER, JANINE R,** Bryant Stratton Bus Inst Roch, Rochester, NY; GD; Secr Clb 90; Secr-Typing/Cmptrs.

**SNIDER, NATHAN T,** John Wesley Coll, High Point, NC; SR; BA; Stdnt Govt Assoc VP 89-90; Sr Class Pres 90; Mr John Wesley Clg 89-90; Deans Lst 88-90; AAS New River Cmnty Clg 75; Bible/Theology.

**SNIDER, SUSAN Y,** Nova Univ, Ft Lauderdale, FL; GD; MBA; BS Univ Of MD 86.

**SNIDER, YON M,** Univ Of Al At Birmingham, Birmingham, AL; SR; EMT; Deans Lst 88-89; Prsdnts Lst 90-; Kappa Phi 88-; Lambda Chi Alpha 87-; Emrgng Artst; Excllnc Std Art Prntmkng 89; Sccr; IM Sprts 86-87; BFA 89; EMI Intrmdt 90; Alld Hlth.

**SNIPE, MARK D,** Cornell Univ Statutory College, Ithaca, NY; JR; BS; Minority Busn Students Assoc Edtr 89-; Democrats; Deans List; Finalist Busn Plan Competions; IM Sftbl; Applied Econ/Busn Mgmt; Finacial Mgt.

**SNIPES, JAMES C,** Abraham Baldwin Agri Coll, Tifton, GA; SO; AA; Fndtn Schlrshp 89-; STAR Stdnt Schlrshp 89-90; Psych; Fmly/Mrrg Cnslr.

**SNIPES, MIA H,** Catawba Valley Comm Coll, Hickory, NC; FR; AS; Gamma Beta Phi; Cert Sec Sci Kings Clg 83; Bsns; Bsns Admn.

**SNIPES JR, ROBERT C,** Va Commonwealth Univ, Richmond, VA; SR; BGS; Theatre/Cmctns.

**SNIPES, WAYNE B,** Univ Of Sc At Aiken, Aiken, SC; SR; BS; Mktg Awrd; Mrshl; Advtsng Dir/Cst Anlysis Corp Sec; AA Atlanta Schl Fshn/Dsgn 81; Bus Admn/Mktg.

**SNIVELY, SANDRA CHRISTINE,** Anne Arundel Comm Coll, Arnold, MD; FR; BA; Elem Ed; Tch.

**SNOCK, KELLEY A,** Univ Of Akron, Akron, OH; SR; BS; Gldn Key; Elem Ed.

**SNODGRASS, CHARLES E,** Ms St Univ, Miss State, MS; JR; BS; Psylgy Club; MS State Lacrosse Tm; Psy; Sport Psy Consulting.

**SNOW, ANGIE P,** Prince Georges Comm Coll, Largo, MD; SO; BS; Acctng; CPA.**

**SNOW, ARTHUR L,** Le Moyne Owen Coll, Memphis, TN; JR; BA; Nw Shlh MB Chrch Chrmn Dea Brd 85-; Edctnl Dir 80-; Area Mgr KY Frd Chckn; Bus Admn; Mddl Mgmt.

**SNOW, BARBARA E,** Univ Of Southern Ms, Hattiesburg, MS; JR; BA; Honors Stdnt Assoc 88-; Pre Law Scty 90-; Shotokan Karate Clb 90-; Phi Kappa Phi; Phi Eta Sigma 88-; Gamma Alpha Epsilon; Delta Zeta VP 89-; Southern Pltcl Sci Assoc 90-; Pltcl Sci Outstndng Stdnt Awrd 90; Politcal Sci; Law Foreing Plcy.

**SNOW, CANDACE M,** Oh Dominican Coll, Columbus, OH; SO; AA; Legal Asst Central OH 88; Board Mbr DANCE Dancers/Artsts Board 90; Ntwrkng Commt/Ed; Diploma Hnrs Orlando Clg Legal Asst Prgrm 88; Legal Studies/Social Sciences/Law Schl.

**SNOW, DEBORAH L,** Fl St Univ, Tallahassee, FL; SR; MS; Cncl Fr Excptnl Chldrn 90-; Spcl Educ; Tchr.

**SNOW, JAMIE,** Georgian Court Coll, Lakewood, NJ; SR; BED; Jr Chrch Dir; Tch Gftd/Tlntd Art Cls; AA Cum Laude Ocean Cty Clg Toms Rvr NJ 85; Art Educ.

**SNOW, JAMIE L,** Allegheny Coll, Meadville, PA; JR; BA; Nwspr Ed Edtrl Sec 90-; SG Dir Ed Affrs 90-; Tourgd 90-; Alden Schlr 88-90; Envrnmntl Crmnl Law Intrn; IM Sprts; Hist/Poly Sci; Envrnmntl Law.

**SNOW, JEN L,** Univ Of Tn At Martin, Martin, TN; GD; BA; BA Psychlgy 74; BA Scl Wrk 74; Elem Ed.

**SNOW, KAREN M,** Univ Of Sc At Spartanburg, Spartanburg, SC; SR; BA; Educ; Teacher.

**SNOW, KIMBERLEY D,** Univ Of Montevallo, Montevallo, AL; JR; BS; Erly Chldhd/Elem Educ; Tchr.

**SNOW, KYLE L,** Castleton St Coll, Castleton, VT; SR; BA; Stdntg Assoc Sen 88-90; Phi Eta Sigma 88-; N Eng Psych Assoc Undergrad Fellow 90-; Coll Serv Awd 90; Hnrs Psych; Coll Tchng.

**SNOW, LEE R,** Rivier Coll, Nashua, NH; JR; BS; Mktg Clb 89; Wstfrd Nrsng Hm Actv Vol 89; Oxford Mgmt Co Lsng Cnsltnt 88-89; Prlgl; Law.

**SNOW, MARK D,** Coll Of Charleston, Charleston, SC; JR; BA; Erly Msc Ensmble; Sngrs Gld; Chrlstn Comm Orchsta 88-; Omicron Delta Kappa Pres; Mdrgl Sngrs 89-; Pep Bnd 90; Fne Arts Schlr 88-; Dstngshd Hnrs 90; Msc Hstry; Ph D Msclgy Tch Rsrch.

**SNOW, MARY M,** Western Ky Univ, Bowling Green, KY; SO; BA; Phi Eta Sigma 90-; Incntve Awrd Schlrshp 90-; Phlsphy; Univ Prof.

**SNOW, PATRICK M,** Univ Of Tn At Knoxville, Knoxville, TN; FR; BS; Phi Eta Sigma; Alpha Lambda Delta; Executive Undrgrdte Prog; Accounting; International Business.

**SNOW, RICHARD K,** Western Ky Univ, Bowling Green, KY; SO; BS; Phi Eta Sigma 90-; Non Trad Schlrshp; Entrtnr/ Musician; Geography; Coll Tchr.

**SNOW, SONYA SIMPSON,** Northern Ky Univ, Highland Hts, KY; SR; BA; Pres Ambsdrs 87-90; Alpha Chi 88-; IM Flg Ftbl Vlybl; Psychlgy; Gdnc Cnslng.

**SNOW, TARA M,** Hudson Valley Comm Coll, Troy, NY; SO; BA; AAS; Marketing/Communicatins; Internatl Trade.

**SNOW, TRACI C,** Hillsborough Comm Coll, Tampa, FL; FR; Sci; Nrsg.

**SNOWDEN, BETH D,** Univ Of Tn At Knoxville, Knoxville, TN; FR; BA; Exec Bus Orgn 90-; Alpha Lambda Delta 90-; Bus; Fin.

**SNOWDEN, REGINA G,** Univ Of Ky, Lexington, KY; JR; BA; Social Wk Psy; Clinical Soc Wrk.

**SNOWDEN, SCOTT A,** Ga Inst Of Tech At Atlanta, Atlanta, GA; FR; BS; Amer Nclr Scty; AF Rsrve Offcr Trng Corp 90-; Nclr Eng; AR Cmmssnl Offcr.

**SNUGGS, KRISTY M,** Ms St Univ, Miss State, MS; FR; BS; Beta Beta Beta; IM Sports; Bio/Pre Phy Thrpy; Phy Thrpst.

**SNYDER, ADAM A,** Indiana Univ Of Pa, Indiana, PA; FR; BED; Eng; Tchr.

**SNYDER, ANGELA B,** Schenectady County Comm Coll, Schenectady, NY; JR; BS; Deacon Charlton Freehold Presb Church; German; Educ.

**SNYDER, BRAD M,** Oh St Univ, Columbus, OH; SR; BA; Alpha Lambda Delta 87-; Phi Eta Sigma 87-; Lower Lights Ministries 90-; Excellence Schlrshp Awrd 90; Computer Info Scie; Analyst.

**SNYDER JR, BRUCE D,** Nova Univ, Ft Lauderdale, FL; GD; MBA; Hnry Mrktg Assc 88; Sigma Phi Epsilon 85-88; BBA Stetson Univ 88; Mrktg/Bus Admin; Intrntl Bus.

**SNYDER, CAROL M,** Chattanooga St Tech Comm Coll, Chattanooga, TN; SO; AS; Chatt St Ambsdrs 90-; Phi Theta Kappa 90-; Allied Hlth; Nrsng.

**SNYDER, CASEY,** Univ Of Miami, Coral Gables, FL; FR; BS; Rathskeller Advsry Bd Com 90; AT/T Bell Lab 85-; Cnstrctn Mgmnt; Bldr/Cnstrctn Mgr.

**SNYDER, CHARLES D,** Hudson Valley Comm Coll, Troy, NY; SO; MBA; Pres List 89-; Bus Admin; Bus Owner.

**SNYDER, CHRISTOPHER A,** Oh Univ, Athens, OH; SO; WNWG DJ Elect Eng 89-; Sccr Clb 89-; Elect Cmptr Eng; Eng.

**SNYDER, DAWN C,** East Stroudsburg Univ, E Stroudsburg, PA; SR; BA; Spch Cmnctn Clb; Sgm Tau Dlt; Phi Sgm Sgm; Intrng Fall 91; IM Sftbl; Spch Cmnctns.

**SNYDER, ERIC D,** Wv Univ, Morgantown, WV; SR; BSEE; Bible Studies 89-; Bd Of Deacons Trinity Presbytrn Chrch Vice Chrmn 88; Musical Theater Guild 82-88; Tau Beta Pi 89-; Phi Theta Kappa 88; IEEE 90-; Schlstc All Amercn Awards 88; AA Butler Cmnty Clg 88; Elec Engr.

**SNYDER, GABRIELLE H,** Northern Ky Univ, Highland Hts, KY; FR; CERT; Deans Lst; All Amer Schlr; Travel/Tursm; Airlines.

**SNYDER, GLENDA G,** Greenville Tech Coll, Greenville, SC; GD; BSN; Psi Beta 88; RN Bapt Med Ctr; ADN Tri Cnty Tec 88; Nrsng.

**SNYDER, HOLLY K,** Anne Arundel Comm Coll, Arnold, MD; SO; AA; Law Enfrcemnt Clb Crmnl Jstce Sec; Prnts Anymous Vol; Cthlc Chrch CCD Tchr; Crmnl Jstce Law Enf; BA.

**SNYDER, JESSICA H,** Middle Tn St Univ, Murfreesboro, TN; FR; BA; Graphic Design; Cmmrcl Artist.

**SNYDER, JOANNE M,** Watterson Coll, Louisville, KY; GD; AA; Dns Lst Univ Toledo 89-; Pres Lst Univ Toledo Watterson Coll 88/90; Watterson Coll; Univ Of Toledo 87-89; Cmptr Prgrmg.

**SNYDER, JODIE J,** Davis & Elkins Coll, Elkins, WV; JR; BS; Phi Beta Lambda; Hnrs Assn 88-; Hnrs Prgrm 88-; Phi Beta Lambda 89-; Beta Alpha Beta 90-; Mngmnt Fshn Mrchndsng.

**SNYDER, JOHN L,** Kent St Univ Kent Cmps, Kent, OH; SR; BS; Geo Soc Pres 89-; Orntn Inst 88-89; Alpha Lambda Delta 87-88; Mortr Brd; Alpha Lambda Delta 87-88; Mortr Brd; Sigma Gamma Epsilon 90-; NORCUS Flwshp; N W Clg Univ Assn Sci; Geolgy.

**SNYDER, JOY L,** Memphis St Univ, Memphis, TN; GD; MS; ARHS Rep 88-90; Intrvrsty Sec/Treas 87-88; Delta Theta Pi 89-90; Cross Cntry 89; BA Trnty U 90; Accntnt CPA.

**SNYDER, JULIE A,** Coll Misericordia, Dallas, PA; SO; BA; Stdnt Hon Assn 89-; Jrnlsm; Wrtng.

**SNYDER, KAREN J,** Tallahassee Comm Coll, Tallahassee, FL; SO; MBA; Hlth/Rehab Svc Admn Asst 87-; Acctngf Cpa.

**SNYDER, KATHRINE H,** Georgian Court Coll, Lakewood, NJ; JR; BA; Crtcl Thnkng Sklls Tr 90-; Cncl Excptnl Stdnts 88-89; Rlgs Edctr 88; Spcl Edctn Stdnt Ambssdr NASTEC; Deans Schlr 89-90; Spcl Ed.

**SNYDER, KRISTY S,** Middle Tn St Univ, Murfreesboro, TN; FR; BA; Bus.

**SNYDER, MARY R,** Univ Of Sc At Columbia, Columbia, SC; SR; BS; Hillel At USC Pres 87-; Scuba Clb; Pi Mu Epsilon 89-; Tri Beta 89-; Marine Sci; Vet Schl.

**SNYDER, MEGAN E,** Univ Of Pittsburgh, Pittsburgh, PA; FR; BSN; Panther Pistol/Rifle Clb Senate Liason 90-; Panther Pocket Billiards Clb 90; Nrsng Stdnt Assn 90-; Phi Eta Sigma; Nrsng.

**SNYDER, MICHELLE L,** Clemson Univ, Clemson, SC; JR; BA; Elemntry Ed; Tchng.**

**SNYDER, RYAN G,** Norwich Univ, Northfield, VT; FR; BARCH; Hnr Cncl 90-; AIAS 90-; Archtctr; Lcnsd Archtct.

**SNYDER, SARAH A,** Schenectady County Comm Coll, Schenectady, NY; FR; AA; Cptl Phlhrmnc Orchestra 90; St Josephs Chmbr Orchstra 90-; Schuylerville Comm Theatr; Music; Tchng.

**SNYDER, TERRI L,** West Chester Univ, West Chester, PA; JR; BS; Mrchng Bnd 89; Symphnc Bnd Pres 90; Orchstra Treas 89-; Sigma Alpha Iota 89-; Msc Educ; Elem Msc.

**SNYDER, TIMOTHY M,** Philadelphia Coll Of Bible, Langhorne, PA; SO; AA; Brass Ensmbl 90-; Jr High Yth Grp Ldr; Bible; Cmptr Pgmng.

**SNYDER, WENDY I,** Western New England Coll, Springfield, MA; SR; BSW; Nwspr 88-90; Intnshp YWCA PAGE Prog Caseworker; Socl Work.

**SO, DAISY KWAN KWOK,** City Univ Of Ny La Guard Coll, Long Island Cty, NY; SO; AAS; Hong Kong Sec 84-88; Bus Admn; Hotel.

**SOARES, CACIA O,** Anderson Coll, Anderson, SC; FR; Blgy; Med.

**SOARES, KAREN ANNE,** Western New England Coll, Springfield, MA; JR; BA; Mgmt Assn 89-; Engl; Pub Rltns.

**SOARES, PETER J,** Providence Coll, Providence, RI; SR; BS; Sailing 87-90; Tau Pi Phi; Amer Red Cross Certif First Aid/First Responder; Amer Red Cross Certif CPR/ADVNCD Lfesvg/ Sailing Instr; R I Hosp Trust Natl Bnk Awd; Mktg; Phrmctcls.

**SOBALA, MALGORZATA,** Univ Of Fl, Gainesville, FL; SR; BM; Fl Flt Clb; Fl Flt Assoc; Gldn Key; Phi Kappa Phi; Tau Beta Sigma Msc Awd 89; Phi Mu Alpha Schlrshp Awd 90; M Reitz Schlrshp; Frnds Msc Schlrshp 89-; Msc Prfrmc/Flt; Msc.

**SOBCZAK, KELLY L,** Allegheny Coll, Meadville, PA; SR; BA; Yrbk 87-88; Lambda Sigma 88-89; Phi Sigma Iota 90-; Kappa Alpha Theta; Intrnshp Trst Bureau Carnac Franc 90; Alden Schlr 87-; Intrntnl Sts Frnch.

**SOBEL, MICHAEL P,** S U N Y At Binghamton, Binghamton, NY; JR; BS; Univ Prcsn Ensmbl 89-90; Pit Orchstr 89-; Accntng Mgmt Org 89-; Dns Lst 89-; Acctg; Internatl Bsn.

**SOBLESKIE, TAMMY A,** Univ Of Akron, Akron, OH; SR; BA; Hons Clb 86-; Hons Clg Full Schlrshp Rcpnt 86; Velma Hesselbart Mrktng Schlrshp 90-; Deans List 88-; Mrktng; Sales.

**SOBOCINSKA-FEINBAUM, YOANNA,** City Univ Of Ny La Guard Coll, Long Island Cty, NY; GD; AS; Occup Thrpy Clb Mbr 80-84; Qns Clg Choral Soc Mbr 88-; Amer Occup Thrpy Assoc Mbr; Belle Zeller Trst Fnd Schlrshp 80-81; Am Med Assoc Aux Inc Mbr 79-; Am Occup Thrpy Assoc Mbr; NY Stck Exch Acctg Sttlmnt 68-78; Music Tchr 69-80; Occup Thrpy; Mntly Dsbld Thrpst.**

**SOBOL, JOANN T,** Comm Coll Algny Co Algny Cmps, Pittsburgh, PA; FR.

**SOBOL, MICHAEL J,** Indiana Univ Of Pa, Indiana, PA; FR; BS; Supermkt Merch 76-; Elem Sch Tchr.

**SOCASH, KIM,** Coll Misericordia, Dallas, PA; JR; BA; Edn Club 90-; S S Sec 87-; Tchr; AS Luzerne Co Comm Coll 89; Elem Edn; Teach.

**SOCHA, FAITH A,** West Liberty St Coll, West Liberty, WV; SR; BS; Psychology; Cnslr.

**SOCORRO, RAUL E,** City Univ Of Ny City Coll, New York, NY; SR; PHD; Sch Hstry Soc Pres 88-; Phi Alpha Theta 89-; Golden Key 89-; BA Arts Magna Cum Laude; Dns Lst 89-; Archibald Bromsen Mem Schlrshp; Charles T Cromwell Awd; J Salwyn Schapiro Mem Schlrshp; BA; European Hstry; Ph D Hstry.

**SODANO JR, JERRY,** Johnson St Coll, Johnson, VT; SO; BS; JV Soccer 89-; Hockey Clb Pres/Capt 89-; Athletic Trng Clb 89-; Chesamore Hon Schlrshp 89-; Alumni Hon Schlrshp 90-; Deans/ Pres Lst 89-; Hlth Sci; Athletic Trnr/Phys Therapist.

**SODER, KARMI N,** Georgetown Univ, Washington, DC; JR; BSN; Nrsng; Pedtrc Nrs.

**SODT, CHRISTOPHER T,** Columbus Coll Of Art & Design, Columbus, OH; FR; MBA; IM Bsktbl; Art; Commrcl Art.

**SOEHREN, LAURA,** S U N Y Coll Of Tech At Frmgdl, Farmingdale, NY; FR; BS; Grphc Commnctns.

**SOFEN, LAURA B,** William Paterson Coll, Wayne, NJ; SR; BA; Beacon Nwspr Edtr Chf 89-90; Stdnt Govt Assc Exec VP 90-; Deans List; Ethcl Cltr Scty; Jrnlsm Intrnship; Engl; Ph D Wrtng.

**SOFIA, CAROL J,** City Univ Of Ny La Guard Coll, Long Island Cty, NY; SO; Exec Sec Tnns Crt Cnstrctn Co 77-; Engl; Tchng.

**SOFIA, LINDA J,** City Univ Of Ny La Guard Coll, Long Island Cty, NY; SR; AA; St Raphael CYO V P 89; Exec Board 87-89; Laguardia Cmnty Clg Assist 88-; Liberal Arts; Library Sci.

**SOFRANKO, CECILIA L,** Schenectady County Comm Coll, Schenectady, NY; SR; BA; Cul Arts Clb Pr 89-; Amer Culnry Fed Jr Mbr 89-; Dns Lst 89; Pres Lst 91; Elec Jr Chptr Mbr Yr Albny ACF; Sec Data Entry Oper 89; AOS; Nutrtn; Dietcn.

**SOFRANKO, RHONDA C,** Univ Of Cin R Walters Coll, Blue Ash, OH; FR; AS; Bsn.

**SOHN, DAVID H,** Harvard Univ, Cambridge, MA; FR; BA; Outing Clb 90; Newspaper Bsn Oper Mgr 90-; Koreans Athl Chrmn 90-; Newsltr Publshr 90-; Civics Svc Cnslr 90-; Cambridge Eco 90-; Peer Tutor; Appl Math; Envir Cnsltg.

**SOHN, DOUGLAS ANDREW,** Salisbury St Univ, Salisbury, MD; SR; BA; Intrnshp WMDT/TV Grphic Dsgnr; Deans List 90-; Pres Schlr 87-; Art; Grphc Dsgn.

**SOHN, JULIE E,** Johnson St Coll, Johnson, VT; JR; BA; Chesamore Hon Scty 89-; Msc/Art; Teach.

**SOHN, PAIGE J,** Duquesne Univ, Pittsburgh, PA; FR; BS; Univ Vol 90-; Stdnts Hlpng Admssn Recrtmnt Prog 90-; Pharm.

**SOKE, DUANE E,** Ms St Univ, Miss State, MS; SO; CHE; Chem; Eng.

**SOKOL, PAULA MARIE,** Wv Northern Comm Coll, Wheeling, WV; FR; BA; Phi Theta Kappa; Bus; Law.

**SOKOLICH, GIORDANA H,** Felician Coll, Lodi, NJ; SO; Educ Clb 89-; Educ/Hist; Tchr.

**SOKOLOWSKI, JULIE L,** Elmira Coll, Elmira, NY; SO; Sftbl Leag Coach; Phi Eta Sgm; Acctg; CPA.

**SOKOWOSKI, JANICE L,** Western Carolina Univ, Cullowhee, NC; FR; BS; Mrchng Band/Wind Ensemble/Symphony Band Clarinet Sec Ldr; Cmps Nwspr; Western Gold VP; Alpha Lambda Delta Sec; Sigma Nu; Fresh Math Awd; Coed Sftbl; Math; Actuary.

**SOLA, MARTIN R,** Fl St Univ, Tallahassee, FL; JR; BA; Univ Singers 89-; Univ Madrigals 89-; Univ Opera 90-; Music Schlrshp 89-; Burgin Schlrshp 90; NATS Comp Winner; Winter Fest Finalist 90; Music; Opera.

**SOLANO VAZQUEZ, FIDEL R,** Inter Amer Univ Pr Hato Rey, Hato Rey, PR; FR; Lbrry Clb Rfl Crdrr 87-88; Blgy Stdnt Assoc 88-89; Rcn Lst Hnr 90-; Ornttn Pdrc Asn; Prfct Asst 90-; Vlbl Clb 87-88; Math.

**SOLAR, MARY H,** Brewer St Jr Coll, Fayette, AL; FR; BA; GED U AL 74; Acctng; CPA.

**SOLARANA, ELIZABETH A,** Fl International Univ, Miami, FL; SR; Le Cercle Fran 88-90; French Ed; Guid Counselor.

**SOLBERG, PAAL T,** Univ Of Sc At Columbia, Columbia, SC; SR; BSBA; Delta Sigma Pi 88-; Pr Lst 89-90; Intl Stds; Bus Adm/Diplomacy.

**SOLDATI, SANDRA M,** Comm Coll Algny Co Algny Cmps, Pittsburgh, PA; FR; BA; Crossroads Religious Club 90; Single Mother Of 3 Chldrn; Sunday Schl Teacher 3rd & 4th Grades 83-; Life & Natural Sciences; Medcl Rec Admnstr.

**SOLE, KATHLEEN R,** Belmont Tech Coll, St Clairsvl, OH; SO; DPMA; Dns Lst 90-; AAB; Comp Prgmmng.**

**SOLE, ROBIN D,** Mount Saint Mary Coll, Newburgh, NY; JR; BA; Weekly Bible Study; Pi Beta Phi Alumna; Aquinas Schlr ; AA Walla Walla Cmnty Clg 84; Nursing.

**SOLER, CRISTINA M,** Univ Of South Al, Mobile, AL; SO; BA; Baptist Campus Ministries; Chi Omega Personnel; Elem Educ; Teacher.

**SOLER, PEDRO F,** Saint Thomas Univ, Miami, FL; SR; BA; Phi Sigma Alphs 85; Natl Assoc Hspnc Bus Ppl 90; Crncn Mgmt Grp 90; Mrktng.

**SOLER-ROIG, NICOLAS,** Ny Univ, New York, NY; SR; BA; Awrd For Excel 90; Deans Lst 90; Bank In Spain 85-88; Metal Ind Of Spain 83-85; Banking Cert EADA 87; Intl Bus/Fin; Bnkng.

**SOLIS, GINA S,** Pensacola Jr Coll, Pensacola, FL; SO; Otstndnt Mnrty; Comm Clg Grad; Art; Grphc Dsgn.

**SOLIS, SHIRLEY J,** Fl International Univ, Miami, FL; SO; BS; Archtctrl Stds; Archtctre.

**SOLLEY, WILLIAM,** Columbia Greene Comm Coll, Hudson, NY; FR; AA; Drama Clb; Phi Theta Kappa; Stnhl Thatr Prjct Intrn; Asst Stg Mngr; Waiter Brtndr; Hmnts; Edctn.

**SOLLIEN, TANYA G,** Univ Of Va Clinch Valley Coll, Wise, VA; JR; BA; Spanish; Tchng.**

**SOLOMON, JACQUELINE A,** City Univ Of Ny City Coll, New York, NY; SR; BS; Caduceus Soc 87-90; Mnrty Biomedical 87-90; Rsrch Sprt; Prgrm Asst; Certf 90; Biology; Medicine.

**SOLOMON, LESLIE J,** Univ Of Rochester, Rochester, NY; SR; BA; Study Abroad Peer Advsr 88-; Mock Trial Tm; Stdnt Admission Intervwrs; Dns Lst 88-; Kappa Delta Sr Events 88-; Vars Fld Hockey/Lacrosse 87-88; Philosophy; Law.

**SOLOMON, MARCHE L,** Central St Univ, Wilberforce, OH; FR; BA; Lady Diamonds Pres; Water Rsrc Mgmt; Eng.

**SOLOMON, MATTHEW H,** Cornell Univ Statutory College, Ithaca, NY; FR; BS; Clg Agitlife Sci Ambrs 90-; Natl Schlrs 90-; Natl Mentors 90-; Communication; Law/Govt.

**SOLOMON, MICHAEL S,** City Univ Of Ny Baruch Coll, New York, NY; JR; BBA; Am Mktg Assn Pres 89-; Advrtsng Intrnshp Furman Roth Advrtsng 89; Mktg Mgmnt; Publ Rel/Promo.

**SOLOMON, MICHELLE M,** Valdosta St Coll, Valdosta, GA; SR; BSED; Grad Cum Laude; Erly Chldhd Educ; Tch.

**SOLOMON, RANDALL P,** Southern Coll Of Tech, Marietta, GA; SO; BSIET; Natl Soc Blck Engrs 88-90; GA Tech Afro-Amer Assoc 88-90; Indstrl Engr Tech; Engr.

**SOLOMON, RENEE F,** Harvard Univ, Cambridge, MA; JR; Crmsn Key Scty Tour Guide 8; Harvard-Radcliffe Hillel Gabbai Serv Ldr; Sabbath Chr/Coord.

**SOLOMON, RUSSELL L,** Fashion Inst Of Tech, New York, NY; FR; BFA; Advtsng Dsgn Clb Pres 90-; AAS; Advtsng Dsgn/Graphic Dsgn; Grphc Dsgn Artist.

**SOLOMON, SHANA M,** Cornell Univ Statutory College, Ithaca, NY; JR; BS; Bio Advsr 90-; Agri/Life Sci Ambsdr 89-; NYS Assembly Intern; Sci/Tech/Publ Policy; Law/Academia.

**SOLOMON, TODD D,** Oh St Univ, Columbus, OH; SR; BS; Golden Key 90-; Phi Kappa Phi 90-; Arts/Sci Awd Schlrshp 90-; Hon Coll 88-; IM Sftbl/Flag Ftbl/Wrstlng 88-; Psychology; Medicine.

**SOLOMON, TRACY A,** Schenectady County Comm Coll, Schenectady, NY; SO; BA; Admin Aide 86-; Bus; Pblc Serv/Admin.

**SOLOMONOFF, GALIA,** City Univ Of Ny City Coll, New York, NY; SR; BARCH; Archtctl League Mbr 89-; Frgn Stu Schlrshp 88-; Best Stu 90; Dean Lst 88-; Archtctr.

**SOLOMONS, ANGELA R,** Univ Of Tn At Martin, Martin, TN; JR; BS; Pre Phys Thrpy Clb 88-; Lbry Stu Wrkr 88-; W Tenn Emmaus Comm 90-; Phi Eta Sigma 90-; Mu Epsilon Delta 89-; Kappa Alpha Ltl Sis 89-; Yth Cnslr 1st UMC 88-; Choir 90-; Deans Lst 88-; Schlrshps 88-; Phys Thrpy Tech 90; Psych; Phys Thrpy.

**SOLORZANO, PATTY,** City Univ Of Ny City Coll, New York, NY; SR; BS; Peer Advisor Of The Office Academic Advising 90-; CCAPP 89-; Golden Key 88; Steering Comm Presidents Commission On Pluvalism 90; School Of Medicine Summer; NY City Dept Of Health Resch Trng Prog; Sigmund Rebecca Mage Schlrshp; Biology; Medical School.

**SOLT, AUDREY L,** West Chester Univ, West Chester, PA; SR; BS; Marching Band; Pi Kappa Lambda; Sigma Alpha Iota Treas 89-; Music Education.

**SOLTANIAN, ALBA L,** City Univ Of Ny Baruch Coll, New York, NY; GD; BBA; Ntl Wstmnstr Bk USA Asst Tres 82-; AAS 83; Mgt; Intl Affrs.

**SOLTESZ, DAVID C,** West Liberty St Coll, West Liberty, WV; SO; BA; Sigma Nu Mgr 89-90; Nelle M Krise Crtv Wrtng Awd 90-; Math; Scndry Educ.

**SOLTESZ, SUSAN C,** Ursinus Coll, Collegeville, PA; SR; JD; Mstrsingrs 87-; Coll Chr 87-; Frnch Clb 87-; Chptr Schlr; Whtns; Phi Sigma Iota 88-; Tau Sigma Gammam Pldg Ldr 88-; Frnch Awrd; Robert Trucksess Awrd; Cum Laude; Frnch; Intl Law.

**SOLTYS, GARY M,** Western New England Coll, Springfield, MA; SO; Bsktbl 90-; Mgmt/Mktg; Bus.

**SOLTYSIAK, MARLY A,** Siena Coll, Loudonville, NY; JR; BA; Chrldr; AS 90; Mktg/Mgmt; Research.**

**SOMAIYA, MANISH A,** City Univ Of Ny Baruch Coll, New York, NY; JR; BS; Coll Assn Bd Dir 89-90; Fin Econ Soc Pres Mktng 88-90; Asian Bus Assn Mbr 90-; IBJ Schroder Bk Tr Co Asst Ln Admin 87-88; Badminton Racquetball 88-; Intrntl Smnr Jap Bus Mgmnt Sanno Coll Tokyo Japan Stdy Abrd; BS; Fin/Intrntl Bus; Fin Analyst.

**SOMARRIBA, ARISTIDES,** Ma Inst Of Tech, Cambridge, MA; FR; BS; MIT Central Amer Stdnt Assn 90-; Delta Upsilon Sec 90-; Jr Vrsty Tennis 90-; IM Soccer/Ftbl/Bsktbl; Elec Engr.

**SOMBRIC, THERESA L,** Colby Sawyer Coll, New London, NH; SR; BS; Ky Assn 88-90; Res Asst 88-89; Ntl Dn Lst; All-Am Schlr; Intern Inst Arbcs Rsch 90; Var Sccr 87-90; Sprts Sci/Exrc Physlgy; Physcl Thrpy.

**SOMCHANMAVONG, VIRASONE,** Strayer Coll, Washington, DC; Pres List; Deans List; Grad Hnr; Comp Prgmng; Bus.

**SOMERVILLE, HUBERT R,** Wv Univ At Parkersburg, Parkersburg, WV; JR; AAS; Phi Theta Kappa; Ind Mchncs; Indstrl Mchnc.

**SOMERVILLE, MOYA E,** Morgan St Univ, Baltimore, MD; FR; BS; Kappa Tau; Alpha Lambda Delta; Phi Eta Sigma; Bio; Med.

**SOMERVILLE, TAMMY RENEE,** Wv Univ At Parkersburg, Parkersburg, WV; FR; Bus.

**SOMMA, MITCHELL M,** Rutgers St Un At New Brunswick, New Brunswick, NJ; FR; BS; Tri Beta 90-; Rcqtbl Clb 90-; Trck Tm 86-; Hnr Rll 86-88; Microbio; Cytotech.

**SOMMA, TRACY ANN,** Georgian Court Coll, Lakewood, NJ; FR; Elem Ed; Tchr.

**SOMMER, DAVID G,** Salisbury St Univ, Salisbury, MD; SO; BA; Phi Eta Sigma; Maryland Army Natl Gd PFC 88-; Pol Sci; Educ.

**SOMMER, DEBRA A,** Wv Univ, Morgantown, WV; SR; BA; Rho Chi; Lambda Kappa Sigma; BA WV Univ 84; Pharmacy; Hospital Phrmcy.

**SOMMER, KIMBERLY A,** Univ Of Nc At Charlotte, Charlotte, NC; SR; Delta Zeta Actvts Chrmn; Sun Belt Hnr Roll; Tennis 87-90; BA; Sclgy; Art Gllry Dsgn/Exhbtn.

**SOMMER, VICKIE Z,** Owensboro Jr Coll Of Bus, Owensboro, KY; DIPL; PCMH Brkwlkrs Clb Fndr And Coor; Emplyee Rltns Com; Prry Cnty Mem Hosp Aux 89-; Frst Untd Meth Chrch Bible Schl Dir 90; Compoffce Prfssnl; Bus.

**SOMMERS, PATRICIA F,** Smith Coll, Northampton, MA; GD; BA; Clss Cbnt 87; Clss Hstrn 87; Cum Laude; Hgh Hnrs Engl 90; Dana Rsrch Grnt 89; Pianotech 77-86; Boston Chptr Piano Tech Gld 85-; Engl Lit/Lang; Prfssr.

**SOMMERS, TINA M,** Savannah Coll Of Art & Design, Savannah, GA; GD; Grphc Dsgn Clb VP 88; Magna Cum Laude 90-; Acad Awd 89.

**SOMOGYI, DAN M,** Yeshiva Univ, New York, NY; SR; BA; Club Canada VP 89-; Photogrphy Club Pres 88-89; Hacky Sak Club Pres 90-; Sigma Delta Rho Edtr Of Jrnl 89-90; Alpha Epsilon Phi; BAIS EZRA 89-; Camp Simcha Div Hd Of Chldrn W/Cander 89; NCSY Rgnl Advsr 88-90; Roth Schlrshp 90; Bio; Medcn.

**SOMOHANO, JAMES V,** Fl International Univ, Miami, FL; SR; BS; Phi Kappa Phi 90-; Alpha Phi Sigma 90-; Intrnshp Dade Cnty States Atty Offc 90-; Outstdng Achvmnt Awd 90-; Outstdng Undergrad Schlr 90-; Police Benevolent Assn 86-; Law Enfrcmnt Offcr 84; Hnrbl Dschrg USAF; Crmnl Jstc Admin; Juris Doctor Degree/Law.

**SOMRAH, DOWLATRAM,** City Univ Of Ny Queensbrough, New York, NY; SO; AS; Math Clb 90; Phi Theta Kappa; Tau Alpha Pi VP 90; Mech Eng; Eng.

**SONENFIELD, JONATHAN C,** Averett Coll, Danville, VA; SR; BSHRD.

**SONES, LINDIE D,** Alcorn St Univ, Lorman, MS; SO; ADN; SBO: MASN; St Francis Cabrini Hosp Intrnshp Schlrshp; Acad Schlrshp; Med; Nurs RN AD.

**SONES, PAULA T,** Saint Vincents Coll & Seminary, Latrobe, PA; JR; BA; Brdcst Clb Bus Mgr 90; Barnoffs Cntry Cabin Studio Fld Wrk 89-90; IM Ftbl 88-90; Courier Express Nwspr Advrtsng Intrnshp; Cmnctn; Pblc Rltns.

**SONG, GEORGE B,** Cornell Univ Statutory College, Ithaca, NY; SR; Vars Vlybl 87-88; Acad Ingrty Brd 90-; Std Advsr; Dns Lst 90-; Sigma Chi Sec 88-; Tchng Asst Oral Comm 90-; Indpdnt Study Prsnl Entprs Pgm; BS; Bsn Mgmt/Mktg; Bsn.

**SONG, IN Y,** Rensselaer Polytechnic Inst, Troy, NY; FR; BA; Wghtlftng Clb 90-; Korean Stdnt Assn 90-; Elec Eng.

**SONGCO, STACY L,** Salisbury St Univ, Salisbury, MD; JR; BS; Outdoor Clb; Alpha Omega; Phi Eta Sigma; Tri Beta; Omicron Delta Kappa Pres; Vol Salisbury Zoo; Rsdnt Asst; MD Dstngshd Schlr; Acad Key Awd; Biology; Animal Behavior.

**SONGER, MELISSA A,** Georgetown Coll, Georgetown, KY; JR; Vlybl/Sftbl 88-; Sigma Tau Delta 90-; Beta Beta Beta; Alpha Lambda Delta 88-89; Sigma Kappa 90-; Env Actn Grp 89-; Blgy Acad Hnr 90; Acad Athlete Awd; Coach Awd Sftbl; Env Sci.

**SONNELITTER, LESLIE L,** Niagara Univ, Niagara Univ, NY; JR; BA; Orntn Comm Capt 90-; Schlrshp; Intrnshp Micro Cmptr Tech Cnsltnts; Swmg Capt; Cmptr Sci; Sftwr Engr.

**SONNENBERG, BRIAN K,** Univ Of Akron, Akron, OH; SO; BS; Wghtlftng; Bdy Bldng; Church Chr; IM; Babcock/Wilcox Co Schlrshp; Dns Lst 89-; Electrical Eng.

**SONNEVELD, BETTINA,** Univ Of Miami, Coral Gables, FL; SO; BA; Tennis; Intl Finance/Mrktng; Bus/Law.

**SONNIER, YOLANDA F,** Norfolk St Univ, Norfolk, VA; FR; BS; Gspl Choir 90-; Praise Flwshp 90; Sclgy Crmnl Juste; Law.

**SONNY, NATASHA S,** Bloomfield Coll, Bloomfield, NJ; FR; Hstry; Professor.

**SONS, REBECCA J,** Univ Of Sc At Columbia, Columbia, SC; SR; BA; Golden Key 89-; BS Clemson Univ 85; AS Midlands Tech Clg 87; Interdiscplnry Studies/Elem Ed; Tchng.

**SOO, CHENG-LUN,** Univ Of Ky, Lexington, KY; SO; BS Natl Taiwan Univ Taipei Taiwan 80; MS 85; Med; MD.

**SOO, FOO K,** Sinclair Comm Coll, Dayton, OH; FR; AAS; Phi Theta Kappa 90-; Natl Alumni Assoc 90-; Clarion Nwspr 90-; Clarion Empl Yr 90-; Clarion Stf Awd 90-; Sinclair Appl Art Hnr Cmrcl/Cmptr Art 90-; Monarch Mrkg Syst Intern; ATS Assoc Tech Study Cmrcl Grphc 90; Cmptr Art; Cmptr Grphcs/Dsgn.

**SOOBRYAN, PAUL K,** City Univ Of Ny Bronx Comm Col, Bronx, NY; GD; BA; Phi Theta Kappa 89-; Accntng Awrd; AAS; Accntng; CPA.

**SOODEEN, REANN,** Broward Comm Coll, Ft Lauderdale, FL; JR; BSC; Ontrio Schlr 89; Eng Asst Agotec 90; AA Broward Comm Coll Of Ft Laud 90; Chem Eng.

**SOOHOO, LILLIAN K,** Newbury Coll, Brookline, MA; SO; AAS; Rtl Dept Mgr 88-89; Mchdse Dist 89-; BS Syracuse Univ 88; Fshn Dsgn; Fashion.

**SOOK, BRIDGET N,** Wv Univ At Parkersburg, Parkersburg, WV; SO; AAS; Phi Theta Kappa 90; Pres Schlr 90; Bsnss; Offce Admin.

**SOON, ISABELLA S,** City Univ Of Ny Baruch Coll, New York, NY; SR; Alpha Beta Psi 90-; Gldn Key 90-; VITA 90-; Tchr Cert Hong Kong Educ Dpt 86; Accntg.

**SOOS, MARK J,** Oh Univ, Athens, OH; FR; BSIT; Deans Lst 90-; Deans Schlrshp; Industrial Tchnlgy; Mfg Engr.

**SOOTS, KARI EGGLESTON,** Univ Of Nc At Greensboro, Greensboro, NC; SR; BS; Preschl Tchr 89-; Adult Cntr Enrchmt Vol; Child Dvlpmt; Preschl Tchr.

**SOPER, CATHERINE M,** Castleton St Coll, Castleton, VT; JR; BS; VT Assn Hlth/Phy Ed/Rec/Dance; DCC Stdnt Govt Sntr; CSC Athltc Trnrs Assn; Wegmans Schlrshp; Phy Ed; Sports Admnstrtn.

**SOPO, CHRISTINE A,** Univ Of Miami, Coral Gables, FL; FR; Alpha Lambda Delta 90-.

**SOPTELEAN, DALE L,** Univ Of Akron, Akron, OH; SO; BA; Bsn; Grd Schl.

**SORDS, KATHLEEN A,** Univ Of Cincinnati, Cincinnati, OH; SR; BS; Golden Key 87-; Alpha Lambda Delta 86; Kappa Delta Pi 87-; Mortar Bd 87-; Metro Cnfce Cmssnrs List 87-; Var Bsktbl 86-90/Co Capt 88-; BS Un/Cincinnatti; Elem Edctn; Tch.

**SORELLE, JACK D,** Clayton St Coll, Morrow, GA; SR; BBA; AA; CIS; Cmptr Systs Analyst.

**SORENSEN, ANGELIA M,** Abraham Baldwin Agri Coll, Tifton, GA; SO; AAS; Comuter Sci; Prgrmng.**

**SORENSEN, APRIL M,** Memphis St Univ, Memphis, TN; JR; BA; Stdnt Actvts Cncl Head Usher 89-; Tutor Core 89; Phi Eta Sigma Sec 90-; Alpha Lambda Delta 90-; Stdnt Hon Assn 89-90; Delta Gamma V P Frat Educ 89-; Peer Mentor Prog 89; Psychology; Mstrs Prog Psychology.

**SORENSEN, FRED,** Fl Atlantic Univ, Boca Raton, FL; SR; BS; Dive Clb Treas 90-; Rugby Clb Capt 90-; Frnkln Coll/Sprts Comm Chrmn 87; BS 90; Intl Bus/Mktg; Corp/Intl Bus.

**SORENSEN, KAREN M,** Southern Junior Coll, Birmingham, AL; FR; BSN; Nrsng; Hosp.

**SORENSEN, SHEILA Y,** Nova Univ, Ft Lauderdale, FL; GD; MBA; Prsnl Dvlpmnt Spclst Rockwell Intl; BA Miami Un 73; BS Un IA 80; Bus; Mgmt Sci.

**SORENSEN, TAMMY L,** Hudson Valley Comm Coll, Troy, NY; SO; MBA; Law.

**SORENSON, JAMES E,** Liberty Univ, Lynchburg, VA; JR; BS; Debate Team 89-; Pryr Ldr 90-; Econ; Law.

**SOREY, DORIS MICHELL,** Radford Univ, Radford, VA; FR; Pltcl Sci; Law.

**SORGE, BRADLEY E,** Bethany Coll, Bethany, WV; SO; BA; Phi Alpha Theta; Phi Kappa Tau; Big Bro/Big Sis OH Cnty; Pltcl Sci; Law.

**SORICHETTI, TONI M,** Saint Francis Coll, Loretto, PA; FR; BS; Scty Physcn Asst; Deans Lst; Physcn Asst; Med.

**SORIN, NATALIYA,** Univ Of Tn At Martin, Martin, TN; FR; BA; Assoc Trade Schl USSR 85-88; Bus; Acctg.

**SORNAT, GREGORY,** Pa St Univ York Cmps, York, PA; FR; BS; Engr.

**SOROKY, ROBERT M,** Univ Of Ky, Lexington, KY; SR; BA; Phi Kappa Tau 87; Deans Lst; Arch Dskn Book Awrd; AA Cyahoga Comm Coll 90; Arch.

**SORRELL, KELLY L,** Kent St Univ Kent Cmps, Kent, OH; JR; Mktg; Rsrch.

**SORRELL, KERRY K,** Ms St Univ, Miss State, MS; SR; BA; Roadrnr Stdnt Rcrtr 84-86; Intl Prtnrs Pgm 90; Scty Advncmnt Mgmt 90; Sigma Phi Episolon Pres 86; Pres Schlr 90; Deans Lst 90; Asst Mgr Rstrnt; First Pres Church Vstn Comm; Mgmt.

**SORRELL, KRISTINA JANINE,** Wallace St Comm Coll At Selma, Selma, AL; SO; BA; Erly Chldhd/Elem Educ; Tchng.

**SORRELL, RICHARD B,** Atlanta Christian Coll, East Point, GA; SO; BA; Roswell St Bapt Chrch 90-; PM Drv Anncr Prod 90-; Wftd Radio Atlanta Ga; "; Dipl Columbia Schl Brdcstng 86; Bible Prchng Mnstry; Mnstry.

**SORRELLS, FRANLEATA M,** Converse Coll, Spartanburg, SC; FR; BA; BSU Cnvrse Clg Chorale; Alpha Lambda Delta; Delta Omicron; Chrch Rltd; Daniel Music Schlr; Music/Engl; Cmnctns/Music.

**SORRENTINO, THERESA M,** Univ Of Fl, Gainesville, FL; SR; MHS; Comm Org Vol 90-; Pres Awd 90; AA 89; BHS; Rehab Cnslng.

**SORROW, JAMES R,** Piedmont Tech Coll, Greenwood, SC; FR; BA; AMT; Law Enfrcmnt.

**SORTINO, DAVID A,** Walker Coll, Jasper, AL; SO; BA; Phi Theta Kappa; Dean Lst 90-; US Army 9th Inf Div Spc 4/E-4 85-89; Fin Eco; Bnkng.

**SOSA MEDINA, MARIBEL,** Inter Amer Univ Pr San German, San German, PR; SR; BBA; Accntng.

**SOSA, DIANE M,** Liberty Univ, Lynchburg, VA; JR; BED; Kappa Delta Pi; Preschl Tchr; Elem Ed; Tchr.

**SOSA, LILLIAN ESTHER,** Bayamon Central Univ, Bayamon, PR; FR; BA; Cvl Air Ptrl Cadt Sgt 86-89; Merch.

**SOSLER, MICHAEL D,** Le Moyne Coll, Syracuse, NY; SO; BA; Sub-Com Stdnt Safety/Sec 89-90; Alpha Gamma Iota; Integral Hon Pgm 90-; IM Ftbl/Bsktbl 90-; Hist; Law Sch.

**SOSNOWSKY, GERRI L,** Glassboro St Coll, Glassboro, NJ; SR; BA; Stdnt Math Assoc Treas 90-; Math; Coll Prfssr.

**SOSNOWY, MICHAEL E,** Univ Of Nc At Charlotte, Charlotte, NC; SO; BA; Fin Mgt Assoc 90-; Hist/Econ; Money Mgt.

**SOSSAMAN, DIANA,** Univ Of Tn At Knoxville, Knoxville, TN; JR; BS; Bus Mgmnt.

**SOTO CARMENATTY, FELIX,** Inter Amer Univ Pr San German, San German, PR; SR; BA; Crclo Frtrnl Ctrjn Sc; Soc Ftr Edctrs PR VP; Physcl Ed; MBA Physcl Ed.

**SOTO CASTELLO, EVA S,** Inter Amer Univ Pr San Juan, Hato Rey, PR; GD; Hemapheresis Bld Dnr 90; Iglesia El Libano Inc 90-; Cum Laude Juris Dctr; Primer Premio Cert De Verano Devista Juridica 90; Fclty De Dereclio; Colegio De Abogados; Fiscal Espec Apto De Just Div Ofc Asu Monopolishios.

**SOTO CASTRO, CARMEN M,** Catholic Univ Of Pr, Ponce, PR; SO; Engl; Tchr.

**SOTO MORALES, BEATRIZ,** Univ Politecnica De Pr, Hato Rey, PR; JR; BA; Vlybl Clb 88-; Bausch/Lomb Mdl 89-90; Math/Hstry/Sci; Ind Eng.

**SOTO, ALFREDO J,** Goucher Coll, Towson, MD; SR; BA; Stdnt Actvts Prgrmmng Brd 88-89; Smmr Intrnshp Ntnl Inst Hlth 89-; Stimson Duvall Fllwshp; Leah Seidman Shaffer Prize Biology; Biology; Medicine.

**SOTO, ANTI NELLY,** Univ Of Pr At Rio Piedras, Rio Piedras, PR; SO; Dept Act Cult Ricardo Cobian 90-; Rnd Hls Clb Mauricio Van Den Brock 90-; Pgrm De Estudios De Hnr De La Univ Dr Carlos Ramos 90-; Biology; Med.

**SOTO, BISMARCK E,** Miami Dade Comm Coll South, Miami, FL; JR; BA; Comp Sci.

**SOTO, DAVID A,** Univ Of Pr At Rio Piedras, Rio Piedras, PR; JR; Un Bautista Estdntl VP 89-90; Gldn Key; Cuadro De Hnr UPR; Pre Med.

**SOTO, ELSIE M,** Univ Of Pr At Mayaguez, Mayaguez, PR; JR; FFA 88; Alphga Pi Mu 90; Amer Soc Quality Cntrl 90-; Natl Soc Prfsnl Engrs 90; Indus Engr Hon Rl; Indus Engr.**

**SOTO, GLORYUEE,** Inter Amer Univ Pr San German, San German, PR; FR; Cum Laude.

**SOTO, JUAN F,** Univ Of Miami, Coral Gables, FL; FR; BA.

**SOTO, JUAN J,** Inter Amer Univ Pr Aquadilla, Aguadilla, PR; JR; BS; Rotaract 81-82; Stdnt Bio Assoc UIA Aguadilla 83-84; Prog/Prdctn Dir WCXQ 87; Elctrnc Tchnlgy Elctrnc Clg/Cmptr Prog 81; Bio; Med.

**SOTO, OMAYRA,** Inter Amer Univ Pr Guayama, Guayama, PR; FR.

**SOTO, PEGGY,** Inter Amer Univ Pr San German, San German, PR; JR; BS; Astro Clb 88; Cath Dughtr Amer 88; Beta Beta Beta 90; Poly Natura 90; Leo Clb Sec 87; Ch Clb 88; Seton Hall Univ Exchng Stdnt; Allied Hlth Sci; Med Tech.

**SOTO, VIRGINIA I,** Fl International Univ, Miami, FL; JR; BA; Phi Lambda Beta; FPIRG; Elem Intrnshp 90-; Elem Educ; Tchr.

**SOTO-AGUILA, KAREN M,** Fl International Univ, Miami, FL; FR; BA; FPIRG; Elem Ed; Tchr.

**SOTO-FELICIANO, VICTOR L,** Inter Amer Univ Pr Hato Rey, Hato Rey, PR; FR; BA; USN Vet Avia; Tion Powerplants Mech E-4 86-90; Aviation; Airway Electronics.

**SOTO-HERNANDEZ, DENIS,** Evangelical Semimary Of P R, Hato Rey, PR; SR; M DIV; Theologcl Educ Schlrhsp 89-; Tremont Bapt Ch Schlrshp 90-; Ldrshp Awd; BA World Univ 83; Theology; Law.

**SOTO-TOLEDO, ROSALINDA,** Inter Amer Univ Pr Hato Rey, Hato Rey, PR; FR; BA; Cmptr Stdnts Assoc; Puerto Ricos Chess Fed Sec 85-; Cmptr Sci; Progrmr.

**SOTO-TORRES, BRENDA,** Univ Of Pr Medical Sciences, San Juan, PR; GD; MPHE; Pre Med Assc Prlmntrn 86-89; Stdnt Cncl Sec 89-; AFT 88-89; Beta Beta Beta 85-89; All Amer Schlr Cllgt Awd 90-; Research Asst 90-; BS 89; Public Health; Health Ed.

**SOTOMAYOR RAMIREZ, HECTOR R,** Inter Amer Univ Pr San German, San German, PR; JR; Band 1st Alto Saxophone 88; Yng Musician Asstnc Soc Sax Tutor 90-; Tae Know Do Karate Arecibo Clb Green Blt 84-88.

**SOTOMAYOR, JOHN V,** City Univ Of Ny Baruch Coll, New York, NY; GD; Bsbl; BBA 90; Mrktng.

**SOUBLO, GRETA RENEE,** Va Highlands Comm Coll, Abingdon, VA; AS; Sec Bkkpr; Nrsg.

**SOUCEK, SANDRA E,** Wilmington Coll, New Castle, DE; JR; BS; Otstndng Stdnt Erly Chldhd Stds 89-90; Erly Chld Advsry Brd 90-; Pres Mlfrd Dy Cr Assoc 88-; Dy Cr Prvdr; ECS Dplm 90; Elem Ed; Tchr.

**SOUCY, AMY L,** Providence Coll, Providence, RI; SR; BS; Pstrl Cncl 89; Spec Olympics Vol 89; Fnce Clb 90; Deans Lst 87; Tau Pi Phi; Hghst Acad Avrge In Fnce Dept; Im Sprts 90; Fnce; Fnce/Accntng.

**SOUCY, DAVID M,** Newbury Coll, Brookline, MA; FR; AS; Acdmc Achvmnt Awrd 90-; Clnry Arts.

**SOUCY, SHAY L,** Univ Of Me, Orono, ME; FR; BA; Drm Govt Brd; Alpha Lambda Delta; Erly Chldhd Devlpmnt; Tchr.

**SOUDAN, ADE T,** Morehouse Coll, Atlanta, GA; JR; BS; Morehouse Mntrng Pgm 89-90; Tchrs Aide 90; Psi Chi; Clg Monitor Supv 88-89; Psych; Cnslr.

**SOUDERS, VALERIE J,** Radford Univ, Radford, VA; JR; BBA; SAM 90-; FMA Tr; Alpha Lambda Delta; Phi Kappa Phi; Fin/Econs.

**SOUEIDAN, MAJED M,** Temple Univ, Philadelphia, PA; JR; In The Process Of Orgng An Invstmnt Club Off Campus; Golden Key 90-; Fin/Risk Mgt; Security.

**SOUILLIARD, NANCY,** Comm Coll Algny Co Algny Cmps, Pittsburgh, PA; SO; BA; Girl Scouts Ldr 87-90; ACC/CIS.

**SOULE, AMY R,** Georgetown Univ, Washington, DC; FR; MBA; Var Chrldng 90-; Hnr Rl; FOCI 90; Intl Bus/Japanese; Intl Bus.

**SOULE, SUZANNE R,** Univ Of Nc At Charlotte, Charlotte, NC; SR; BCA; Natl Art Educ Assoc Sec; Golden Key; Sales Binders Art Ctr Charlotte NC 87-; AFA Central Piedmont Cmnty Clg 84; Art; Educ.

**SOULES, JO-ANN,** Albertus Magnus Coll, New Haven, CT; SR; Tau Pi Phi; SNET Co 86-; BA 91; Bus Admin; Fin.

**SOULES, VERA,** Lexington Comm Coll, Lexington, KY; SO; BA; Unity 90-; Slctd Lst Outsndg Mnrty Comm Coll Grad/Tlnt Rstr; Brds The Mag 7/Montage; Cmptr Sci; Prgmng.

**SOURRAPAS, VASSILIS H,** City Univ Of Ny Baruch Coll, New York, NY; SR; BA; Westchester Athltc Clb 90; Assn Indpndnt Video/Flmkrs; Flm Prod; Dir/Prod.

**SOUSA, CHRISTOPHER L,** Southern Vt Coll, Bennington, VT; JR; BS; Crmnl Jstce Assn Pres 88-; Prvt Scrty Cmndtn; Deans Lst 88-; IM Ftbl/Bsktbl 90-; AS 90; Crmnl Jstce; Envrnmntl Enfrcemnt.

**SOUSA, MICHAEL D,** Broward Comm Coll, Ft Lauderdale, FL; SO; Phi Theta Kappa 90-; Pres Lst Broward Academic Schlrshp; Engl; Law.

**SOUSA, SHERRY D,** Adelphi Univ, Garden City, NY; SR; PH D; Psi Chi 90; Adelphi Trustee Achvmnt Awd 89; Stdnt Afflte Amer Psychlgd Assn 90-; Asst Traffic Mgr 84-88; AA Nassaw Cmuty Clg:; Clncl Psychology.

**SOUSA, STEFAN C,** City Univ Of Ny Baruch Coll, New York, NY; SO; BBA; Sccr Tm 89; Frnch Bcclrt Lycee De Lunel Frnc 88; Mktg/Adv.

**SOUTH, ANNA E,** Ms St Univ, Miss State, MS; JR; BS; Blckfrs Drama Soc 89; MENSA; Wsly Fndtn Clwn Troope 89-; Untd Meth Wmns Cir 90-; Sci; Mcrbio.

**SOUTH, GINA M,** Wilmington Coll, Wilmington, OH; SR; BA; Acctng Clb 90-; Green Key 90-; AA Chatfield Coll 89.

**SOUTH, MEGAN A,** Birmingham Southern Coll, Birmingham, AL; SR; BA; Alpha Lambda Delta 87-88; Phi Alpha Theta 90-; Pi Beta Phi Treas 87-89; TA 90; Hstry; Tch/Rsrch.

**SOUTHALL, ALYSIA D,** Wv Univ At Parkersburg, Parkersburg, WV; JR; AAS; Phi Theta Kappa; Cert A Moore JR Voc Tech Cntr 88; Cert A Moore JR Voc Tech Cntr 89; Offce Admin; Sec.

**SOUTHARD, BABETTE L,** Greenville Tech Coll, Greenville, SC; SR; AHS; SADHA Tr 89-; S Car Dntl Hygn Assn Schlrshp 90; Lw Ctry Dntl Hyg Assn Schlrshp 90; Dntl Hygiene.

**SOUTHARD, CHRISTINE M,** Roane St Comm Coll, Harriman, TN; SO; AAS; Cum Laude; Pol Sci Criminology; Law Enfrcmnt.

**SOUTHARD, JUDY M,** Univ Of Ga, Athens, GA; SR; Dns Lst; IM Sftbl 90; BSED UGA 90; Erly Chldhd Educ; Tch.

**SOUTHARD, STEPHANIE M,** Georgetown Univ, Washington, DC; SR; BSN; Glee Club 81-85; House Cncl Soc Chr 84-85; Nwspr Copy Edtr 82-83; Sigma Tau Delta 83-84; Sigma Theta Tau 89-; Planned Prnthd Exam Rm Aide 83-84; St Margarets Episcopal Ch Lay Rdr 89-; Evaluated Wrtn Essays 1st Yr Eng Cl 83-84; Nursing; Midwifery.

**SOUTHER, MICHAEL E,** Western Carolina Univ, Cullowhee, NC; JR; BS CS; Phi Theta Kappa 90; AS Wilkes Community College 90; AS Pre CS 90; Comp Sci.

**SOUTHERLAND, DANIEL S,** Middle Ga Coll, Cochran, GA; JR; BS; Batts Drugs; Deans List 89-; Phrmcy.

**SOUTHGATE, KENNETH L,** Asbury Theological Sem, Wilmore, KY; GD; MDIV; 13 Yrs TV Prod/Adv; BA Western KY Univ 81; Ministry; Clg Cmps.

**SOUTHWICK, JULIE M H,** Castleton St Coll, Castleton, VT; SR; BS; Mktg; Advrtsng Mgmt.

**SOUTHWOOD, DAWN R,** Univ Of Akron, Akron, OH; JR; BA; Natl Stdnt Spch/Lang/Hrng Assn 90-; Deans Lst 90-; Comm Disorders; Spch Pathology.

**SOUTHWORTH, ERIN M,** S U N Y Coll At Fredonia, Fredonia, NY; SO; BA; Tchr Ed Clb 90- Fnwmn Cntr 89-; IM Bsktbll; Hstry Scl Stds Sec Ed; Tchng Hstrcl Rsrch.

**SOUTHWORTH, LISA A,** Coll Of Charleston, Charleston, SC; SR; BS; Ed Clb 88-; Cncl Except Chldrn-Stdnt Org 88-; Natl Ed Assoc 89-; SC Ed Assoc 89-; Spec Ed; Tchg Chldrn W/Autism.

**SOUTO, FRANK J,** Univ Of Miami, Coral Gables, FL; SR; BA; Pre Law Soc 90-; Gldn Ky 90-; Phi Kappa Phi; Dean Lst 87-88; Prs Hnr Rll 90; Prvsts Hnr Rll; Sclgy Crmnl Jstc; Law.

**SOVIC, MATTHEW M,** Univ Of Fl, Gainesville, FL; SR; BA; Undergrad Economics Scty; IM Ftbl Sftbl Bsktbl Vlybl 87-; Economics.

**SOVINE, MELISSA A,** Marshall University, Huntington, WV; FR; BA; Phi Eta Sigma; Spcl Ed; Tch.

**SOW, MAIMOUNA,** Central St Univ, Wilberforce, OH; JR; Intl Stdnts Assn V P 90-; Finance/Invstmnt Soc; Ambassador 89-; Delta Sigma Theta Sgt At Arms 91-; Deans Lst 88-89; Hnr Stdnt 80-; Vllybl Mgr 89-90; Finance; Cmptr Info Sys.

**SOWDER, JENNIFER G,** Concord Coll, Athens, WV; SR; Kappa Delta Pi 89-; Cum Laude 89; AA Beckley Coll 89; BS 90; Elem Edn; Teach.**

**SOWDER, LOIS G,** Concord Coll, Athens, WV; SR; Kappa Delta Pi 88-; Summa Cum Laude 89; AA Beckley Coll 89; BS 90; Elem Edn; Teach.**

**SOWDERS JR, LARRY W,** Union Coll, Barbourville, KY; FR; BS; Flwshp Chrstn Athletes 90-; Bapt Stdnt Un 90-; Math/Sec Educ; Tch Math.

**SOWELL, ERIC A,** Polk Comm Coll, Winter Haven, FL; FR; BA; Chemistry; Medicine.

**SOWELL, STACY M,** Univ Of Ms Main Cmps, University, MS; FR; BS; Phi Eta Sigma 90-; Gamma Beta Phi 90-; Alpha Omcrn Pi 90-; Navy Spnsrs 90; Dns I st 90; Chnclrs Lst; Elem Ed; Tchr.

**SOWERS, BILLIE R,** Miami Jacobs Jr Coll Of Bus, Dayton, OH; FR; BA; Dayton Wmn Wrkng Coord 76-77; United Way Chr 86-87; Bus.

**SOWINSKI, ANTHONY,** Widener Univ, Chester, PA; JDMBA; Prsdnts Lst 88; Deans Lst 90; Cty Wlmngtn Smmr Intrnshp 87-88; Bsktbl Cptn 86-87; BA; AS 88; Mgmnt; Bsns Law.

**SOWLES, PAMELA C,** Univ Of Sc At Columbia, Columbia, SC; FR; Deans List; Bio; Secndry Ed.

**SOZA, JULIETA Y,** Barry Univ, Miami, FL; SO; BS; Respect Life Clb 90-; Econ Clb; Circle K Secr 90-; Chrldg 90-; Mgmt.

**SOZA, NORMA L,** Barry Univ, Miami, FL; SR; MSW; Rspct Life Clb Pres 88-; Circle K Pres 89-; Alpha Mu Gamma 88-; Pi Gamma Mu 90-; BS; Scl Wrk.**

**SOZA, RITA M,** Barry Univ, Miami, FL; JR; BS; Psych Clb 90-; Respect Life Clb 89-90; Hnrs Assoc 89-90; Circle K V P 89-; Psych; Child Psych.

**SPADA, LISA A,** Univ Of Fl, Gainesville, FL; SR; Bus Admin Coll Cncl Hmcmng Chr 90; US Vlybl Clb VP 90; Wado Kai Krte Clb; Gldn Ky; Omicron Delta Kappa; Beta Gamma Sigma; Delta Sigma Pi Scl Chr Srvce Chr 90; Delta Tau Delta Lil Sis; Crcle K 90; Swthrt Pgnt 90; Hmcmng Vlybl Trnmnt 90; BS; Bus Econs Fnnce; Ph D Phrmctcl Econs.

**SPADEA, JOHN,** Neumann Coll, Aston, PA; SO; BS; Mns Tennis 89-; Psych; Psychatry.

**SPADORCIA, STEPHANIE A,** Lesley Coll, Cambridge, MA; SO; BED; Emerald Key 90-; Acdmc Hons 89-90; Cnsltnt Plymouth North High Schl 90-; Hist; Spcl Ed.

**SPADY, BENEDICT Q,** Norfolk St Univ, Norfolk, VA; SR; BED; Voc Ind Clbs Of Amer Pres 90-; Ambssdr 90-; BSA Ast Sct Mstr 90-; Alpha Phi Alpha Dir; Mr C Hunt Mach Shop W/A 90-; Voc/Ind Educ; Teach.

**SPAGNUOLO, JOELLE M,** Wv Univ, Morgantown, WV; JR; BS; AIAA; Sigma Gamma Tau; Tau Beta Pi; Gldn Key; Tau Beta Pi; Mchncl Aerospace Dpt Schlrshp; Prsdnts Lst; Deans Lst; AFROTC Awd; DAC Awd; Aerospace Engnrng; Engnrng.

**SPAHN, SUZANNE C,** Philadelphia Coll Pharm & Sci, Philadelphia, PA; GD; BS; Stdnt Gov T-Sen T 88-90; Kingsessng Sngrs 89; Phys Ther Clb Chrty Comm Chr 86-88; Agape Chrstn Flwshp 89-; Adpt-A-Grndprnt/Join Hnds W/Elderly 86-88; Vlntr Tutr W Phldlphia Schls 87; Amer Phys Ther Assn 88-; Phys Ther.

**SPAIN, MELISHA A,** Brewer St Jr Coll, Fayette, AL; FR; BS; Black Union 90-; Phi Theta Kappa 90-; Math Chmstry; Chmcl Engnrng.

**SPAIN JR, STEVE RANDALL,** Longwood Coll, Farmville, VA; SR; MA; Lambda Iota Tau Pres 88-; Alpha Phi Omega PR 86-; BA 90; Engl.

**SPAIN, VICKI LYNETTE,** Univ Of Tn At Martin, Martin, TN; SR; BS; STEA 90-; NEA 90-; Phi Theta Kappa 89-90; Sigma Tau Delta 90-; English; Scndry Ed.

**SPAINHOWER, DEBRA L,** Ashland Comm Coll, Ashland, KY; JR; BS; Soc Wm Engrs; Amer Soc Mtlrgcl Engrs 90-; IM; AD 90; Mtrl Sci Engrg.

**SPAK, PAUL G,** Albertus Magnus Coll, New Haven, CT; JR; BA; NAIM 90-; Sikorsley Aircraft Div UTC Corp; Music Tchr; AA 90; Cert Music Shoreline Schl Art/Music 84; Bsn/Econ; Mgmt.

**SPAKES, DAVID S,** Roane St Comm Coll, Harriman, TN; SO; BS; Audio/Vsual Clb Pres 89-; Comp Clb Pres 90-; Pres Cncl 90-; Gamma Beta Phi Pres 90-; Outstndng Fr Awrd 90; Math Dept Awrd 90; Acdmc All Amer Nmnee 90-; Comp Sci; Prog/Anlyst.

**SPALVIERI, JEANNINE M,** Notre Dame Coll, Cleveland, OH; JR; BA; Class Secy 89-; Educ Cncl 89-; Ambassadors 88-; Pi Lambda Theta; Deans Lst 89-; Academic Serv Schlrshps 88-; English Achievement Awrd; IM Vlybl; Elem Educ.

**SPALVIERI, JENNIFER A,** Notre Dame Coll, Cleveland, OH; JR; BA; Literary Magazine Co Editor 89-; Resident Assoc VP 89-; Ambassadors 88-; Deans Lst 89-; Academic Serv Schlrshps 88-; IM Vlybl; Communications English.

**SPANG, ANDREW B,** The Boston Conservatory, Boston, MA; SR; BM; SGA Sec 90-; Pi Kappa Lambda; Phi Mu Alpha Sinfonia VP 88-; Boston Cnsrvtry Merit Schlrshp 88-; Music Performance.

**SPANGENBERG, AMY L,** Wilmington Coll, New Castle, DE; SR; BA; Rd Clb Hd Coll 88-89; Pr Cnslng 89-; Intrnshp Ttrng Hgh Rsk Chldrn 90; BA; Bhvrl Sci.

**SPANGLER, DAVID T,** Pellissippi St Tech Comm Coll, Knoxville, TN; SO; Student Ambassador 89-; Phi Theta Kappa 90-; Vision Vol 89-; Special Olympics Parent Vol 87-; Work With Trouble Adolescents Families; Social Work.

**SPANGLER, HEYWOOD B,** Univ Of Nc At Asheville, Asheville, NC; SO; Exec Asst Extrnl Affairs 90-; Dorm Rep RHA 90-; Delg NC Stdnt Leg; Phi Eta Sigma Pres 90-; Hon Pgm 89-; Circle K Intl; Weizenblatt Endwmnt Schlrshp; Intern Senator Terry Sanfords Wash Ofc; Jr Senator Stdnt Govt; Philosophy/Classics; Law/Divinity Sch.

**SPANGLER, KRISTI LEIGH,** Univ Of Sc At Columbia, Columbia, SC; SO; BA; USC Whitewater Raftng/Mntrng Clb; Jrnlsm Deans Lst; Jrnlsm Advrtsng; Media Law.

**SPANIK, KRISTEN L,** Indiana Univ Of Pa, Indiana, PA; JR; Radio; Alpha Epsilon Rho; Cmmnctns Media; Brdcstng.

**SPANIOL, STEVE D,** Old Dominion Univ, Norfolk, VA; SR; BBA; Dgnty/Intgrty Richmond 86-; Ntl Assoc Acctnts 89-; Beta Gamma Sigma/Gldn Key 90-; Phi Kappa Phi/Alpha Chi/Omicron Delta Epsilon 90-; Beta Alpha Psi; Ntry Pblc Cmnwlth Va 88-; Wmn Crisis Pro YWCA Vol 89-90; Stu Hlth Cntr DDU Vol; Mgmnt Info Sys/Acctg; Govt Dept Dfns.**

**SPANKO, JUSTIN R,** Slippery Rock Univ, Slippery Rock, PA; SO; BED; HPERD 90-; Phi Epsilon Kappa; Delta Psi Kappa; Hlth/Physcl Ed; Tchg.

**SPANN, LISA A,** Comm Coll Algny Co Algny Cmps, Pittsburgh, PA; FR; Usher At Hillcrest Seventh Day Adventist Church In Pgh PA Hd Usher 90-; Assoc Acct/Progrmng Comptr Sys Inst 84; Physcl Thrpy.

**SPANN, MARGARET D,** Univ Of Sc At Columbia, Columbia, SC; SO; BA; Advrtsng.

**SPANN, SUSANNA K,** Chattahoochee Vly St Comm Coll, Phenix City, AL; SO; BA; ASD; Crmnl Jstce; Law.

**SPANO, MELISSA A,** Manhattan Coll, Bronx, NY; JR; BSME; Plyrs/Sngrs 89-; Scty Wmn Eng Sec 88-; Cmps Mnstry 89-; Pi Tau Sigma 90-; Mech Eng.

**SPANOGLE, STEPHEN D,** Univ Of Al At Huntsville, Huntsville, AL; JR; BSE; Inst Indstl Engrs; Intl Soc Weighng/Measrmnt 85-; Empl Beowulf Corp Manuf Eng 85-90; AS Math Calhoun Comm Clg 85; Engr; Indstl Engr.

**SPARACINO, LESLIE A,** Univ Of Southern Ms, Hattiesburg, MS; JR; BA; Bnd 88-90; BSU P 89-90; RA 88-; Gmma Beta Phi; AA MS Gulf Coast Comm Coll 90; Elem Ed.

**SPARGER, JENNIFER A,** Emory & Henry Coll, Emory, VA; FR; BA; SPEC 90-; Schlr 90-; Engl.

**SPARGO, JANINE L,** Mount Aloysius Jr Coll, Cresson, PA; JR; BA; Big Bros/Big Strs; Nvy Rsrv Flt Hosp Unt; Med Lab Tchnlgy; Med Tchncn.

**SPARKMAN, WAYNE G,** Wv Northern Comm Coll, Wheeling, WV; FR; PHD; Spch; Vclst And Gtrst Rcrdng Artst 86-; Lbrl Arts; Msc Prdcr Pblshr.

**SPARKS, COURTNEY Y,** Watterson Coll, Louisville, KY; SR; AS.

**SPARKS, DANIEL RAYMUND,** Birmingham Southern Coll, Birmingham, AL; FR.

**SPARKS, DAVID T,** Western Ky Univ, Bowling Green, KY; SR; BCS; Phi Kappa Phi 90-; Omicron Delta Kappa 89-; Beta Gamma Sigma 90-; Univ Sclr Yr 88-; Phi Beta Lambda Pres Elect 87-; 1st Plc Nation Bus Prncpls Comp 90; Phi Beta Lambda Confrnc; Mngmnt; Law/Corp Mngmnt.

**SPARKS, GINA L,** Univ Of Al At Birmingham, Birmingham, AL; SR; BS; Homecoming Comm 88; Greek Week Comm 89; Order Of Omega 88-; Alpha Omicron Pi Pres 88; Presidential Hnrs; Deans List; Elem Ed; Teacher.

**SPARKS, GRACE B,** Allegheny Coll, Meadville, PA; BS; Outng Clb VP/EQUIP Mgr 89-; Soc Envrnmntl Awrnss 89-; Phtgrphr Nwspaper 89-90; Lambda Sigma 90-; J B Porter Prz; Doane Schlr/Dstngshd Alden Schlr; IM Vlybl/Soccr 89-90; Envrnmntl Sci; Fld Rsrch.

**SPARKS, GREGORY E,** Univ Of Sc At Aiken, Aiken, SC; FR; Math; Engrng.

**SPARKS, KIM A,** Univ Of Cin R Walters Coll, Blue Ash, OH; SO; BA; Communications/English; Chief Drtr Sales.

**SPARKS, MICHAEL J,** Owensboro Comm Coll, Owensboro, KY; FR; BS; Cmptr Sci; Prog.

**SPARKS, NICOLE S,** Fl A & M Univ, Tallahassee, FL; JR; BS; FELATE 89-; Wht/Gld; Gldn Ky; Dns Lst 89-; Hon Rl 89-; Elem Educ; Tchng.

**SPARKS, STACEY R,** Coll Of Charleston, Charleston, SC; JR; BS; Peer Mntr Assn 88; Cath Cmps Clb 90-; Alpha Phi Omega 87-; Psychlgy; Spec Educ Lrng Dsblts.

**SPARLING, KIMBERLY,** Guilford Coll, Greensboro, NC; FR; BA; Stdnt Orient Staff Grp Ldr; GGO Vol; Deans Lst; Pres Schlrshp; Political Science; Intl Relations.

**SPARNALL, BRIAN R,** Univ Of Cin R Walters Coll, Blue Ash, OH; SO; MBA; Stdnt Govt Rep 90-; The Grievance Comm Rep 90-; Acctg Tutor 89-; Peer Cnslr; Busn; Acctnt/Contrllr.

**SPARROW, SARAH J,** Univ Of Ky, Lexington, KY; SR; BS; Acad Of Stdnts Of Phrmcy 88-; Beta Beta Beta Sec 88; Phi Lambda Sigma 89-; Gldn Ky 89-; Kappa Delta Pres 87; Dns Awrd; BS Chem Georgetown Coll 88; Phrmcy.

**SPATARO, NANCY M,** Wagner Coll, Staten Island, NY; JR; BA; Soc Clb 90-; Tutrng Clb 90-; Pub Article Yng Adv S I; Omicron Delta Kappa; Kappa Delta Pi; Dns Lst Acad Schlrshp Wagner 88-; Teen Adv 90-; Rec Ldr 90-; Tchr/Asst Var Schools 88-; Seaman Soc Chldrn Cnslr 90-; Tchrs Asst 89-; Educ Concentrtn Social Wrk.

**SPATES, ANGELA M,** Va Commonwealth Univ, Richmond, VA; SR; BS; Physcl Thrpy Clb 89-; Afro Amrcn Schlrs Prgrm 90-; Rhbltatn Srvcs; Physcl Thrpst.

**SPATES, PATRICIA S,** Va Commonwealth Univ, Richmond, VA; SR; BS; Phi Kappa Phi; Hopewell Moose Ldg Schlrshp; VCU Schlrshp; AS Bus Richard Bland Coll Petersburg VP 89; Finance; Risk Mgr.

**SPATOLA, LISA J,** William Paterson Coll, Wayne, NJ; JR; BA; AA Co Coll Of Morris 89; Engl Lit.

**SPAULDING, BARBARA,** Ky St Univ, Frankfort, KY; FR; Nrsng; Nrse.

**SPAULDING, DEBBIE M,** Mount Saint Mary Coll, Newburgh, NY; SR; MS; NY State Nrses Assoc 87; Amer Nrses Assoc 87; Pblc Hlth Nrse; AS SUNY Canton 75; Nrsng; Nrse Pract.

**SPAULDING, MARKEITA M,** Savannah St Coll, Savannah, GA; JR; BA; Nwtnn Scty; Hnr Rll; Alpha Kappa Alpha Sec 90-; Grls Scts Ldr; Schlrshp Alpha Kappa; Chrldr 88-90; Math.

**SPAULDING, MICHAEL A,** Oh St Univ, Columbus, OH; JR; BA; Wldlf Mgmt; Phys Ther.

**SPAULDING, SCOTT K,** Southern Coll Of Tech, Marietta, GA; SR; BS; Tau Alpha Pi 89-; Alpha Tau Omega 81-83; Navy Achvmnt Medal 88; Hnr Grad 90-; USN 84-88; Elec Engr Tech.**

**SPAULDING-TOWNS, SHERRY A,** Waycross Coll, Waycross, GA; SO; BA; Phi Beta Lmbd 90-; Sgm 89-90; Phi Theta Kappa 90-; Amer Red Crs; AA 90; Am Ptry Assc Mrt Awrd 89; Awrd Dist Phi Beta Lmbd Conf Cmptr Cncpts; Cmptr Cncpt Cmptn State PBL Conf Atlnta; IM Bwlng Tm 88; Psychlgy; Rsrch/Cnslng.

**SPAWN-PAUL, BARBARA JENE,** Siena Coll, Loudonville, NY; SR; Hstry Clb 87-; Mrchg Band Instrctr 87-; Phi Alpha Theta 89-; BA; Hstry; Tchg.**

**SPAWTON JR, KENNETH D,** S U N Y At Buffalo, Buffalo, NY; SR; BS; Gldn Key 90; Banquet Cptn 88; Bnqt Mngr; Finance; Financial Anlyst Advisor.

**SPAZZARINI, JULIA T,** Birmingham Southern Coll, Birmingham, AL; JR; BA; Kappa Mu Epsilon Sec/Treas 90-; Phi Alpha Theta; Beta Beta Beta 89-; Alpha Chi Omega Pblc Rltns Offcr; Links-Up 90-; Habitat Fr Hmnty 89-; Fred B Joyner Schlrshp; Hstry; Clg Prfssr.

**SPEAKMAN, CHRISTINA LOUISE,** Va Commonwealth Univ, Richmond, VA; JR; BA; Natl Stdnt Ed Assoc 90-; Phi Kappa Phi; Phi Eta Sigma 88-89; Psi Chi; Wmns Bsktbll 88all Amrcn Schlr 89-90; Athltc Sn Blt Cnfrnc Hnr Rll 88-90; Psychlgy.

**SPEAKS, BRENDA M,** Jackson St Univ, Jackson, MS; SR; BBA; Acctng Scty 89-; Phi Beta Lambda 88-89; Delta Mu Delta 90-; Alpha Chi 89-; AICPA Schlrshp 90-; Acctng.

**SPEAKS, DWANA P,** Central Al Comm Coll, Alexander City, AL; FR; BS; Phi Theta Kappa 90-; Comp Sci; Prgrmmr.

**SPEAKS, ELLEN D,** Auburn Univ At Montgomery, Montgomery, AL; SO; BS; Phi Eta Sigma 89-; Alpha Phi Sigma 90-; Lamda Alpha Epsilon 90; Juste/Pub Sfty; Jvnl Juste.**

**SPEAKS, JUDITH L,** Tri County Tech Coll, Pendleton, SC; FR; Alpha Zeta Beta; Sci; Phrmcy.

**SPEAKS, PAULA K,** Central Al Comm Coll, Alexander City, AL; SR; BBA; Natl BETA Clb 79; Natl Schlrs Bwl Tm Tp Hnrs Al Cmptn 80-81; Dns Lst; Mt Zion Bptst Chrch; Cmptr Oprtr/Qlty Asrnc Tech 84-; Faulkner U; Bsn/Cmptr Sci; Sls/Mktg Cnsltnt.

**SPEAKS, SCOTT A,** Springfield Tech Comm Coll, Springfield, MA; JR; BS; Natl Scty Black Engrs 87-; Army Natl Guard Sgt 88-; United States Marine Corp 83-87; Elec Engrg; Engrg.

**SPEARMAN, CHRISTOPHER MARK,** Mount Olive Coll, Mount Olive, NC; SO; BS; Stdnt Govt Assoc 89-; Free Will Bptst Fllwshp 89-; Chapel Choir 89-; Pres List 89-; Fclty Awd 90-; Marshall 90-; Honors Schlrshp 89-; Intrmrl Bsktbl Vllybl 89-; Accntng; CPA.

**SPEARMAN, RUTH,** Fayetteville St Univ, Fayetteville, NC; SR; MA; Fyttvlln Ed 86-90; Pnhllncmss Zeta Sec 88-89; LEAP Prgm 88-89; SAAP 88-; Kappa Delta Pi 90; Zeta Phi Beta Pres VP 86-89 NEA Pres 88-90; Advsry Brd Sec 88-89zeta Pres 86-; Sen Comm 86-90; Ldrshp Comm 86-90; NCATE Comm 89; Tchr Awrd 89; Spcl Ed.

**SPEARS, CONNIE L,** Univ Of West Fl, Pensacola, FL; JR; AA; Elem Edn BA.

**SPEARS, DARLENE MARIE,** Univ Of The Dist Of Columbia, Washington, DC; JR; BA; Acctng Clb VP 90; Natl Assn Of Blck Accts 89-; Natl Assn Of Fmle Execs; Hnrs Prog 88-; Phi Sigma Pi 89-; Alpha Kappa Alpha Treas 90-; Acctng; CPA.

**SPEARS, DOLORES CHAVAE,** Fl A & M Univ, Tallahassee, FL; SR; BS; Allied Sci/Mdl Club 85-88; Rho Chi 90-; Alpha Lambda Delta 86-87; Alpha Epsilon Delta 8m-88; Pharmacy.

**SPEARS, ISAAC J,** Itawamba Comm Coll, Fulton, MS; FR; Ftbll 90; Res Asst; Industrial Tech.

**SPEARS, JEFFREY N,** Marshall University, Huntington, WV; SO; BA; Pi Kappa Alpha 90-; Intern CPA; Acctng; CPA.

**SPEARS, SUSAN C,** Univ Of Southern Ms, Hattiesburg, MS; SO; BS; Nwspr Stf Wrtr 90-; Alumni Assn Grp Chrmn 89-; Gldn Grls; Gamma Beta Phi; Chi Omega Asst Scl Chrmn 89-; PACERS 90-; Jrnlsm; Law.

**SPEARS, SUSAN D,** Truett Mc Connell Coll, Cleveland, GA; JR; BED; Hrt Co Comm Thtre; Mt Olvt Bapt Chrch; Phrmcy Tech; Erly Chldhd Educ; Elem Tchr.

**SPEARS, TONY K,** East Tn St Univ, Johnson City, TN; JR; BA; Mgmt.

**SPEARS, VELEKA S,** Alcorn St Univ, Lorman, MS; FR; BA; Inter-Faith Gospel Choir; Ms Soph Candidate; Alpha Kappa Alpha; Martin Temple Choir Dir 88-90; Asst Tylertown Nrsng Hm Candystriper 89; Schlstc Asst Alcorn Univ; Engl/Pre-Law; Lawyer.

**SPEARS, WENDI M,** Troy St Univ At Dothan, Dothan, AL; SR; MS; Compass Clb ESJC 88-89; Delta Zeta Chi 89-90; Gamma Beta Phi 90; Pres Lst 89-; Magna Cum Laude; AA 89; BS; Psychology/Soclgy.**

**SPEARS, YVETTE DAWN,** East Tn St Univ, Johnson City, TN; JR; MBA; TN Army Natl Grd SGT E5 85-; Mrktng.

**SPEAS, MARY ANN,** Univ Of Ky, Lexington, KY; SR; BA; SAC; BSU; Sigma Pi Little Sis; Metro Grp Home Gods Pantry; Elem Edn; Teach.

**SPECHT, TRACY L,** S U N Y Coll At Fredonia, Fredonia, NY; JR; BS; Inter-Vars Chrstn Flwshp Co-Pres; Yng World Singers Coord 88-; RA; Elem Ed/Cmptr Sci; Tchg Cmptrs.

**SPECIALE, VICTORIA E,** Univ Of Rochester, Rochester, NY; JR; Campus Judicial Cncl Assoc Chf Jus 90-; Meridian Scty 90-; Tae Kwon Do Purple Belt 88-90; English/Political Sci; Law.

**SPECK, BARBARA A,** Mount Aloysius Jr Coll, Cresson, PA; FR; AS; Deans Lst 90; Comp Sci.

**SPECKMANN, LAUREN M,** Casco Bay Coll, Portland, ME; FR; BA; Deans List 90-; Fashn Merch/Mgt; Fashn Byr/Entrepeneur.

**SPECKMANN, SHERYL R,** Hillsborough Comm Coll, Tampa, FL; SO; BA; Frgn Lng Awrd; Girl Sct Trp Ldr 85-; PTA Pres 85-; USAF Cvln Empl Prsnnl Mng 68-79; Educ; Tch.

**SPECTOR, HOWARD S,** Cumberland County Coll, Vineland, NJ; SO; BS; Stdnt Sen 90-; Coll Comp Clb Pres; Vol Fir Co 88-; AAS; Comp Sci; Prgrmmr Systms Anlyss.**

**SPEECH, LUCRETIA A,** Tougaloo Coll, Tougaloo, MS; FR; Stdnt Spprt Srvcs 90-; Math Comp Sci.

**SPEED, BILL N,** Fl A & M Univ, Tallahassee, FL; FR; BS; Phi Eta Sigma; Mechncl Engrng.

**SPEED, TRACI A,** Univ Of Al At Birmingham, Birmingham, AL; JR; BA; Spnsh Clb 89-90; Intl Stds; Frgn Srvc.

**SPEELER, NOIRA G,** Nova Univ, Ft Lauderdale, FL; GD; MBA; BS Profl Mgmnt 90; Bus Admin.

**SPEELER, ROBERT L,** Nova Univ, Ft Lauderdale, FL; GD; MBA; BS Profl Mgmnt 90; Bus Admin.

**SPEER, SUZANNE M,** Univ Of Cincinnati, Cincinnati, OH; FR; BA; Sci; Pediatric Nrsng.

**SPEES, SUZANNE M,** Univ Of Akron, Akron, OH; JR; BED; Gldn Key 90-; Kappa Delta Pi; Prtnrs In Excel Schlrshp 89-; IM Sprts 90-; Elem Educ; Tchr.

**SPEICHER, DAVID C,** Univ Of Sc At Columbia, Columbia, SC; SO; BA; Scuba Club Prsdnt; Sprts Clb Cncl Mmbr Lrg; Naval ROTC; Gamma Beta Phi; Delta Sigma Phi; Deans Lst; Advrtsng; Nvl Avtr.

**SPEICHER, KEVIN R,** Bridgewater Coll, Bridgewater, VA; SR; BS; Physics Club 89; Math Club 90; Lambda Soc 89; 2 Poems Pblshd 90; Ftbl 88; Math/Cmptr Sci/Physics; Engr.

**SPEIGHT III, CHARLES N,** Univ Of Sc At Aiken, Aiken, SC; FR; BS; German Clb; Gamma Beta Phi; USA Sgt E-5 85-89; Bio; Envrnmntl.

**SPEIGHT III, CHARLES N,** Univ Of Sc At Columbia, Columbia, SC; SO; BS; German Clb; Gama Beta Phi; U S Army Sergeant E5 85-89; Biology; Environmental.

**SPEIGHT JR, MAX,** Univ Of Tn At Martin, Martin, TN; SR; BS; Amer Rgstry Radiologial Tech 90-; Amer Acdmy Med Admins; Cert Med Xray Tech 90-; Gldn Key 89-; Beta Beta Beta 89-; Mu Epsilon Delta Sgt At Arms 89-; Amer Red Cross Crdiplumry Resus 86-; US Nvl Shlbck Soc 88; Magna Cum Laude; Biology; Hlth Care Admin.**

**SPEIGHTS, PAMELA V,** Craven Comm Coll, New Bern, NC; GD; BA; CCC Alumni; Intrnshp Nadep Cherry Pt NC 88-; AS; Math/Physics; Aerospace Engr.**

**SPEIGHTS, SHELDON D,** Univ Of Southern Ms, Hattiesburg, MS; JR; BA; Sigma Lambda Chi VP; Constr Engr Tech.

**SPEKHARDT, CHERYL A,** Rivier Coll, Nashua, NH; JR; BA; Stdnt Adm Comm 86; Tr Class 92 Tr 90-; Res Hall Cncl Tr 89-90; Cert ECE Rivier Clg 91; Comm; Publ Rel/Advrtsng

**SPELL, ALAN E,** Univ Of Sc At Columbia, Columbia, SC; SR; Army ROTC 89-; Rngr Clb 89-; Chi Delta Chi 90-; Ntl Grd Schlrshp 89-; IM Sftbl; BA; Ecnmcs; Envrmntl Law.

**SPELL, NANCY J,** Savannah Coll Of Art & Design, Savannah, GA; SR; BFA; Photo Grp 90-; Dean List; Phtgrphy; Cmmrcl Phtgrphy.

**SPELL, SHARON R,** Univ Of Southern Ms, Hattiesburg, MS; FR; BS; SADD 90-; Yrbk Stf Copy Asst 90-; Hnr Std Asc 90-; Cngrsm Gene Taylor Intrn; Bwlng Tm; Pol Sci; Govt Serv.

**SPELLER, MALCOLM N,** Al A & M Univ, Normal, AL; SO; BS; Food Sci Clb; Inst Parlmntrn; Food Tech; Afrcn Stdnts Assn Proj Dir 89-90; Northnrs Clb Parlmntrn; Hnr Roll; Dns Lst; MARC Fllwshp; Intrnshp Stdnt Res 90; Intrnshp Pillsbry Tech Ctr; IM Bsktbl; Food Sci/Tech; Food Eng/Res Dev.

**SPELLMAN, AMY L,** Kent St Univ Kent Cmps, Kent, OH; SO; BBA; Alpha Lambda Delta 89-90; Pres List 90; Ftbl Statstn 90-; Econ; Econ/Govt.

**SPELLMAN, JOHN J,** Univ Of Louisville, Louisville, KY; SO; Jr Achvmnt Pres 88-90; Jr Achvmnt Natl Alumni Assn; Phi Eta Sigma; Natl Hnr Soc 89-90; Phi Kappa Tau V P; Pres Schlrshp 90; Arthur Andersen Schlrshp 90; Deans Schlrshp; Chancellors Schlrshp; Elect Eng.

**SPELLMEYER, GREGORY A,** Franklin And Marshall Coll, Lancaster, PA; SO; Independent Newspaper Rep 90-; Tour Guide 90-; Bsktbl Mgr 90-; Natl Merit 89-; Phi Kappa Sigma; Vlybl 90-; Govt/Hstry; Diplomatic Svc.

**SPELLS, ADRIENNE N,** Tougaloo Coll, Tougaloo, MS; FR; Blgy.

**SPENCE, EMERSON A,** Univ Of North Fl, Jacksonville, FL; JR; BT; Intl Stu Assn 90-; Tlcmmntns Tech 83-90; AA Beliza Tech Coll 83; Elect Tech; Eng.

**SPENCE, JANA M,** Glassboro St Coll, Glassboro, NJ; SR; BA; Rsdnt Co Advsr 89; Cls Sec 89-90; Gamma Tau Sgm 90; Jvnl Dtntn Ofcr 90-; IM Sftbl 88-90; Psychlgy; Soc Wrk.

**SPENCE, KAREN C,** Catawba Valley Comm Coll, Hickory, NC; FR; BS; Yrbk Comm; Deans Lst; Nrsg; Tch.

**SPENCE, MICHELLE L,** Radford Univ, Radford, VA; JR; BBA; Dns Lst 88-; Acctng.

**SPENCE, RHONDA G,** Univ Of Sc At Columbia, Columbia, SC; FR; BA; Cmps Crsd; Hl Govt; Engl.

**SPENCE, RONDA L,** Univ Of Tn At Knoxville, Knoxville, TN; SO; BS; Chi Alpha 90-; People To People Ambsdr 88-89; Veterinarian.**

**SPENCE, THOMAS G,** Birmingham Southern Coll, Birmingham, AL; JR; BS; Amer Chem Scty Afflte 89-; Cnsrvncy 90-; Phi Eta Sigma 89-; Alpha Lambda Delta 89-; Hnrs Prog 88-; ACS Nclr Chem Fllwshp 90; Argnne Natl Lab Rsrch Asstshp; Chem; Rsrch.

**SPENCER, BECKY J,** Wright St Univ Lake Cmps, Celina, OH; SO; BS; MLT ASCP 85-; St Ritas Med Ctr Lima OH 82-85; CLA ASCP Lima Meml Sch Med Tech 82; Bio; Med Tech ASCP.

**SPENCER, BETH P,** Davis & Elkins Coll, Elkins, WV; SR; BS; Tcke Cnty EMS EMT 85-; AS Nrsng Davis Elkins Elkins WV 90; Nrsng.

**SPENCER JR, BRUCE E,** Wilmington Coll, New Castle, DE; SR; BA; USAF 82-; Avtn Mgmt; Mgmt.

**SPENCER, CATHERINE B,** Univ Of Sc At Columbia, Columbia, SC; SR; BA; Pacer Times Opinions Edtr 89-90; Summer Intrn Wstnghs; Savannah River Co 90; Jrnlsm/Graphic Art.

**SPENCER, CHARLES G,** Springfield Tech Comm Coll, Springfield, MA; SO; Am Wild Flwr Soc/Ntnl Wild Flwr Co Foun/V P 88-; Advocates/Safe Enf Co-Foun Dir 88-; Prod Cir/Wrtr/Host Gdn Wldflrs 88-; Ed Publ Radio Alamanc; Wtrt/Ed Ma Mutual Life Ins Co 86; Wilderness Outrch Prog Springfield Colg 83; TV Prod/Graphic Dsgn/Mrktg; Envnmtl Commctns.

**SPENCER, CYNTHIA G,** Asbury Theological Sem, Wilmore, KY; GD; Chrstns Biblical Eqlty; Alumni Falconettes Seattle Pac Univ 87-; BA Seattle Pacific Univ 87; M Div; Parish Mstry.

**SPENCER, DEIRDRE A,** Howard Univ, Washington, DC; JR; BA; SG Pres 88-89; NSBE 88-90; SWE 88-90; ASME 88-90; AIAS 90-; TX Clb 88-; Rcrt Vol 88-; Brdr Baby Vol 89-90; Tutor 89-; Shell Oil Co Intrnshp 88-90; Archtct.

**SPENCER, DONNA S,** Beckley Coll, Beckley, WV; SR; AS; Paralegal Intshp Attorney Larry Losch; Paralegal.

**SPENCER, JENNIFER L,** Hampton Univ, Hampton, VA; FR; BA; Afrcn Stds Clstr 90-; Pres Eminent Schlrshp; Hnrs Dy Rcgntn; Hnr Rll; Engl Arts; Law Schl.

**SPENCER, JENNIFER W,** Georgetown Univ, Washington, DC; JR; BS; Concert Bnd 88-; Intl Rltns Clb 88-; Pep Band 88-; Vol Marthas Table Soup Ktchn 89; U S Snte Intrn 89; Intl Mgmt; Academia.

**SPENCER, JESSICA R,** Savannah Coll Of Art & Design, Savannah, GA; FR; BFA; Drama Clb; Deans Lst 90; Intr Dsgn; Interior Dsgnr.

**SPENCER, JILL A,** Univ Of Tn At Knoxville, Knoxville, TN; JR; BS; Exectv Undrgrd 89-; Beta Gamma Sigma; Gldn Key; Gamma Beta Phi 90-; Deans Hnr Lst 88-89; Beta Alpha Psi; Accntng.**

**SPENCER, JILL E,** Comm Coll Algny Co Algny Cmps, Pittsburgh, PA; SO; BA; Legal Stds; Law.

**SPENCER, JULIA D,** Spartanburg Methodist Coll, Spartanburg, SC; JR; Pres Lst 90; Excell Engl Lit; Elem Ed; Elem Tchr.

**SPENCER, KAREN L,** Bridgewater Coll, Bridgewater, VA; FR; BS; Swinming Club 90-; Sftbl Tm; Busn; Acctng.

**SPENCER, LERRY T,** Commonwealth Coll, Norfolk, VA; SR; AAS; Alpha Beta Gamma 90-; Schl Assistance Awd 90; Cert Of Merit 90; Most Congenial Awd; Micro Computer Inf Sci.

**SPENCER, MARY A,** Marshall University, Huntington, WV; FR; BBA; Acctntng; CPA.

**SPENCER, MELINDA L,** Tn Temple Univ, Chattanooga, TN; JR; BA; Math/Spanish; Tch.

**SPENCER, NADINE LEEDS,** Atlantic Comm Coll, Mays Landing, NJ; SO; AS; Freshman Club Secty 87-88; Science Club Secty 90-; Continving Ed Toward Possible Vety Degree; Biology/Envtl; Ed Prog At Zoos.

**SPENCER, NOEL G,** Harford Comm Coll, Bel Air, MD; SO; BS; Blck Std Asc; Acctng; CPA CMA.

**SPENCER, SHERIA D,** Al A & M Univ, Normal, AL; SO; Finance.

**SPENCER, SHERIDAN H,** Emory Univ, Atlanta, GA; SR; Nl Hdgsn Sch Nrsg; NHWSN Sr Cls Stu Govt VP 90-; Stu Nrs Assoc 89-; Georgia Assoc Nrsg Stu 89-; Stu Govt 87-88; Sigma Theta Tau 90-; Omicron Delta Kappa 90-; Acdmc Dist 89-; Chi Phi Ltl Sis 87-89; Ordr Estrn Str 90; Nrsg.

**SPENCER, SHERNA G,** Nova Univ, Ft Lauderdale, FL; JD; Std Snt Cls Rep 79-80; Std Affrs 82-83; Mnrty Awrns 79-83; Big Bro/Sis 79-80; Cnsmr Affrs Div Bttr Bsn 81-82; Cmptr Prgmmr Anlyst 85-; BA Le Moyne Clg 83; Law; Intl Immgrtn.

**SPENCER, STACY L,** Univ Of Nc At Asheville, Asheville, NC; JR; BA; Chrldr Varsty 88-90; Justc On Stdnt Ct 88-89; Alpha Xi Delta VP 89-90; Soccer 89-90; Soclgy; PhD Soclgy.

**SPENCER, THOMAS K,** Wv Univ, Morgantown, WV; SR; IEEE; Golden Key; Tau Beta Pi; Elect Engr.

**SPENCER, TIMOTHY D,** Wv Northern Comm Coll, Wheeling, WV; FR; BA; Bus Admnstrn; Photography Studio.

**SPENCER, VALERIE L,** Christopher Newport Coll, Newport News, VA; JR; BA; Alpha Chi Pres 90-; Hnrs Schlrshp 88-89; Deans List 88-; Hist; Museum.**

**SPERA, CHRIS M,** Univ Of Al, Tuscaloosa, AL; FR; BA; IM Sprts Capt 90-; Phi Eta Sigma 90-; Alpha Lamda Delta 90-; All-Amer Schlr; Clncl Pscyh.

**SPERLING, SVETLANA,** Newbury Coll, Brookline, MA; SO; AD; Dipl Moscow Cvl Eng Inst 76; Mngmnt Htls.

**SPEROS, MICHELLE M,** Newbury Coll, Brookline, MA; SR; AAS; Interior Design Intshp Berkeley House; Interior Design.

**SPEZZANO, ELIZABETH A,** Lenoir Rhyne Coll, Hickory, NC; SR; BA; Sign Troupe VP 87-90; Nwmn Cath Club 89-90; Students NC Assoc Edtrs 87-88; Mu Sigma Epsilon 90-; Kappa Delta 89-; Truman Schlr Semi Finalist 88-89; Plyr Yr All Confer Pitcher 89-90; SAC Confer 1st Tm 90-; Sftlb Pitcher 89-; Deaf Ed; Tchng Counseling.

**SPICELAND, MICHELE R,** Fl St Univ, Tallahassee, FL; JR; BS; Lady Scalphunter 89-; Seminole Ambssdr 89-; Phi Eta Sigma 88; Alpha Delta Pi Corres Sec; Intrnshp Lewis Advertising; FLA Pblc Rltns Assn 80-; Pblc Rltns; Communications.

**SPICER, DARLENE M,** Gordon Conwell Theol Sem, S Hamilton, MA; SO; MDIV; Intervar 86-87; AOTA; Missions Cmte Sec 90; Alpha Epsilon Delta 86-87; Prison Flwshp 89; Byington Schlr 90-; BS Univ Of NH 87; Theology/Missions.

**SPICER, DENISE M,** Univ Of Tn At Martin, Martin, TN; SR; BS; AM Home Ecnmcs Assc 88-; Assc Stdnt Memeber Section 88-; Fashion Mrcndsng Assc 90-; Intrnshp Elder Beerman Paducah KY Retail Dept Store; Home Ecnmcs Fshn Mrchndsng; Dprtmnt Store Mng.

**SPICER, JOE D,** Dyersburg St Comm Coll, Dyersburg, TN; SO; AAS; Cprl 84-; Crmnl Jstc; Law.

**SPICER, KIRSTIE E J,** Lesley Coll, Cambridge, MA; SR; BSED; Class Exec Brd VP 89-; Emerald Key Tour Gd 89-; Stdnt Ldrshp Adv Brd 89-; Elem Tchr.

**SPICER, MARC,** Wagner Coll, Staten Island, NY; JR; BS; Amer Cncl Yng Pltcl Ldrs 89-; Cngrssnl Yth Ldrshp Cncl 89-; NCADD 89-; NY Pblc Intrst Rsrch Grp 87-; Rpblcn Party 88-; Partnrshp Imprvd Air Trvl 89-; Deans Hon Lst 89-90; Mayor Schlr 89-90; Wc Schlrshp 89; City Univ NY Grant 90-; Lbrl Arts/Sci; Entrprnr.

**SPICHER, JULIE A,** Indiana Univ Of Pa, Indiana, PA; JR; BED; PSEA 90-; NEA; Elem Ed; Tchg.

**SPICKARD, TODD S,** Univ Of Tn At Knoxville, Knoxville, TN; FR; BS; Pre-Law Scty VP 90; SGA Frshmn Cncl/Ugrd Acad Cncl 90-91; Bsnss Stdnts Advsry Cncl To Deans UAC Liason 90; Phi Eta Sigma; Alpha Kappa Psi 90; Exec Undrgrad Prog Ut Cllg Bus 90; Outstndng Invlvemnt In Alpha Kappa Psi 90; Gnrl Bsnss Pre-Law; Attrny.

**SPICKLER, THOMAS P,** Univ Of Pittsburgh, Pittsburgh, PA; JR; BA; Socl Wrk.

**SPIECH BAISDEN, DOROTHY A,** Marshall University, Huntington, WV; GD; Natl Educ Asc 85-; WV Educ Asc 85-; Lgn Cnty Educ Asc Ex Comm 90-; Gamma Beta Phi 85-86; Beta Sigma Phi VP 85-89; Jr Wmns Clb 81-83; Grl Scts 71-84; Mt Crml Altr Soc; Summa Cum Laude 85; Schlp 84; Ldrng Ctr Dir; AA 83; BA MA 85; Rdng Educ; EDD.

**SPIEGEL, DANIEL B,** Univ Of Miami, Coral Gables, FL; JR; BM; Stdnt Gvmt Prdctns Jazz Vcl Ens I Bus Mgr 90-; Stdnt Cncl 89-; Jazz Clb Pres 90-; Pres 100 Laison Scty 89-; Res Asst; Gldn Key 90-; Pi Kappa Lambda; Phi Kappa Phi; Alph Lambda Delta 88-; Phi Eta Sigma 88-; Presser Schlrsp; Ftbl; Bsbl; Bsktbl; Music; Bus.

**SPIERS, KRISTENA D,** Ms Gulf Coast Comm Coll, Perkinston, MS; SO; BS; Hnrs Pgm 89-; Phi Theta Kappa 90-; Pres Lst 89-; Hl Fm; Sci; Nrsg.

**SPIES, ROBERT K,** Embry Riddle Aeronautical Univ, Daytona Beach, FL; SR; BS; Sigma Nu; Deans Lst; Otstdng Grad Sr; BSBA Univ AR 88; Aerontcl Sci; Prof Pilot.

**SPIETH, GEORGE B,** Va Commonwealth Univ, Richmond, VA; SR; BS; BS Virginia Polytechnic Institute 86; Math Educ; Tch Hgh Schl.

**SPIETH, HEIDI D,** Va Commonwealth Univ, Richmond, VA; FR; BFA; Univ Hnrs Pgm 90-; Deans Schlrshp 90-; Deans Lst; Art Ed/Art History; Tchng/Writing/Illus.

**SPIEWAK, KEITH J,** Schenectady County Comm Coll, Schenectady, NY; FR; BS; Math/PC Users Clb VP 90-; Cmptr Sci; Pgrmmr/Engr.

**SPIGNER, CHARLENE D,** Bloomfield Coll, Bloomfield, NJ; SR; BS; Stdnt Gov Pres Soph Cls 88-90; Alpha Kappa Psi Chapln 89-; Sigma Gamma Rho 89-; Acctg.

**SPIKER, TODD D,** Shepherd Coll, Shepherdstown, WV; SO; BA; Catherine C Fix Essay Contest 90; English Journalism.**

**SPILEWSKI, MARLENE N,** Newbury Coll, Brookline, MA; AS; Stdnt Rep; Paralegal.

**SPILLER, ANGELA K,** Central Fl Comm Coll, Ocala, FL; SO; BS; Elem Educ.

**SPILLMAN, STEPHANIE S,** Norfolk St Univ, Norfolk, VA; JR; Delta Sigma Theta 89; Hnr Grad 90-; Occptnl Thrpy Assit; US Army 86; Psychology Ph D.

**SPILSBURY, THEODORE R,** Salisbury St Univ, Salisbury, MD; JR; BS; IM Sftbl Vlybl Rcktbl And Rnng; Phi Eta Sigma; Dns Lst; Phys Sci; Eng Elec.

**SPINELLA, TINA A,** S U N Y Coll At Fredonia, Fredonia, NY; JR; BA; Stdnt Assn Pres 90-; Pres Pro Temp 89; Stdnt Afrs Cmtee Bd 89-; Phi Alpha Theta; Donations Cmtee Superdance Musclr Dystpy 89; Chautauqua Cty Dist Atty Intrn; History/Pltcl Sci.

**SPINELLI, KAREN M,** Western New England Coll, Springfield, MA; SR; PHD; Bhvrl Scl Sci Clb 90-; Dns Lst 88-; BA; Bsn; Clncl Psy.

**SPINELLI, MICHAEL A,** Westchester Comm Coll, Valhalla, NY; SO; BA; Mercury Rcrds Intrnshp; Radio Statn Intrnshp; Pepsi-Co Cmnctns/Media Arts Awrd; AA; Jrnlsm/Mass Cmnctns; Pub Rltns/Brdcstng.**

**SPINK, LAURY A,** S U N Y Coll Of Tech At Alfred, Alfred, NY; FR; AAS; Pres Hons Schlrs Prog 90-; Acctng; Bus.

**SPINOSO, ALEXA A,** Univ Of Miami, Coral Gables, FL; FR; BFA; Film Assn; Wrkstdy Dsk Asst 90-; FL Undrgrad Schlrshp 90-; Sprts Fst; Motion Pic/Engl; Dir/Scrnwrtr.

**SPIRES, DAVID C,** Univ Of Akron, Akron, OH; SO; BS; Hnrs Prog 89-; Elec Eng.

**SPITALE, ANTHONY J,** Univ Of Akron, Akron, OH; SR; BA; Pblc Acctg.

**SPITLER, JOHN S,** Univ Of Akron, Akron, OH; JR; BS; Tau Kappa Epsilon; Acdmc Schlrshp; Chmcl Eng.

**SPITZ, BOAZ M,** City Univ Of Ny Baruch Coll, New York, NY; JR; BBA; Bnai Brith Hillel Pres 90-; Jwsh Cncl Treas 89-90; Cntr For Rtrn 89-; Goldn Key 90-; Deans Lst 89-; Supprt Awrd 89-90; Swm Team Coach 87-88; Intl Mktg; Intl Trdng.

**SPIVEY, ANDREA Y,** Bloomfield Coll, Bloomfield, NJ; JR; Jdcry Brd; Nwsppr Rprtr; Afrcn Amer Assn; Omega Essnc Swthrt; Chldrn Dycr Cnslr; Nrsng Hm; Acdmc Acvmnt; Dean Lst; Mngr Vllybl Tm; Med Soc Work.

**SPIVEY, DAVID S,** Temple Univ, Philadelphia, PA; GD; Hrtcltrl Almni Awrd; Fr Hnrs Awrd 90; Magna Cum Laude.

**SPIVEY, NATASHA L,** Norfolk St Univ, Norfolk, VA; SO; BA; Spartan Alpha Tau; Math; Corp Law.

**SPIVEY, SUSAN L,** Univ Of Tn At Knoxville, Knoxville, TN; FR; Engl; Envrnmntl Law.

**SPONAUGLE, IZETTA M,** Fairmont St Coll, Fairmont, WV; FR; AS; Std Med Rcrds Org; Fresh Cnslr; Pres Lst; Dns Lst; Med Rcrds Tech.

**SPONCHIADO, JODI A,** Shippensburg Univ, Shippensburg, PA; FR; BS; Rowland Elem Schl Vol 90-; Stu Hll Cncl 90-; IM Coed Vllybl Capt 90-; Engl/Sec Educ; Tchr.

**SPONHOLZ, ROBERTA A,** Daemen Coll, Amherst, NY; JR; BS; Delta Mu Delta 90-; Deans Lst 90-; Invntry Cstng Sls Adtr Accts Pybl 86-; AS Erie Comm Coll 85; Acctg; CPA.

**SPONSLER, LORI A,** Indiana Univ Of Pa, Indiana, PA; SR; BS; Natl Stdnts Spch/Lang/Hear Assoc VP 88-; Allied Hlth Profsns Org UPJ 87-88; Kappa Delta Pi 89-; Provost Schlr 88-; PA Spch/Lang/Hear Assoc 90-; Am Spch/Lang/Hear Assoc 90-; BS; Spch/Lang Pathology.

**SPOONER, HEATHER M,** The Johns Hopkins Univ, Baltimore, MD; SR; BSN; Stdnt Govt/Nsg Schl Pres 90-; Jr Clss Govt Socl Chr 89-90; NSNA-MANS 89-; Sigma Theta Tau 90-; Alpha Phi 89-; Univ Of Mich Extrn 90; Johns Hopkins Nurs Almni Assn Awrd; JHU NSNA Convntn Rep 90-; Nrsng; Burn Nrsng.

**SPOOR, CAROL D,** Emory Univ, Atlanta, GA; GD; MNMPH; Amer Coll Nrs-Mdwvs 90-; Sigma Theta Tau 86-; Rsrch Asst 90; BSN St Univ NY 87; BA St Univ NY 86; Nrsng/Pub Hlth; Nrs/Mdwfry.

**SPORER, KATHRYN S,** Fayetteville St Univ, Fayetteville, NC; SO; BA; Chancellors Lst 89-90; Spt Wrkr Cntact Fayetteville Contact USA; Acctg; CPA/LAW.

**SPOSITO, JAMES E,** Mount Aloysius Jr Coll, Cresson, PA; SO; AS; Jud Comm Officer 90-; Phi Theta Kappa 89-; Vol Lee Hosp Johnstown Pa; Comp Sci/Acctng; Electro-Mech Assembly; Comp Sci; Comp Bus.

**SPOTO, AMY E,** Le Moyne Coll, Syracuse, NY; FR; BS; Blgy; Med.

**SPOTORNO, ANNA MARIE,** Ny Univ, New York, NY; SO; BS; New York Univ Hosp; Word Processor; AAS Plaza Bus 88; Hlth Sci; Phys Therapy.

**SPOTTS, VINCENT J,** Univ Of Pittsburgh, Pittsburgh, PA; SR; MSE; Phi Eta Sigma 87-; Pi Tau Sigma 89-; Tau Beta Pi 89-; Big East Acadmc All East Team 90-; Schlr Athlete All Acadmc Team; Mech Engr Grad TA; Bsbl 89-; BSE; Math/Sci; Mech Engr.**

**SPRADLEY, SONIA D,** Univ Of Nc At Asheville, Asheville, NC; SR; Deans Lst 90-; Hon Lst; Chld Psychlgst.

**SPRADLIN, CAROLYN P,** Univ Of Sc At Columbia, Columbia, SC; SR; BA; Psychology Clb 90-; Gamma Beta Phi 90-; Honors Cls; Psychology; Counseling.

**SPRADLIN, STEWART R,** Univ Of Va Clinch Valley Coll, Wise, VA; SR; BS; CUC Golf Tm Most Vlbl Plyr; Bus Mgmt; Law.

**SPRADLING, DORA DENISE,** Union Univ, Jackson, TN; SO; BS; STEA 90-; SGA 90-; Zeta Tau Alpha Stnds/Enrchmnt Chrmn 89; Elem Educ; Tchr For The Deaf.

**SPRAGG, TINA M,** Bethany Coll, Bethany, WV; FR; BACH; Grmn Clb Sec And Rep 90-; Fr Actvts Cncl 90-; Cmps Chr Prctce Asst 90; Cmps TV Teleprmptr 90-; Rsdnce Asst; Hall Rep 90-; Frgn Lngge Cnfrnce; Grmn And Educ; Tchr.

**SPRAGGINS, WILLIAM R,** Central Al Comm Coll, Alexander City, AL; FR; BS; Bsn.

**SPRAGUE, BRUCE M,** Univ Of Rochester, Rochester, NY; SR; Pep Bnd Lbrn 87-; Outside Spkrs Comm Pblcty Chrmn 87-90; Bausch/Lomb Schlr 87-; BS Microbiology; Cert Biotech.

**SPRAGUE, ERIK M,** Hartwick Coll, Oneonta, NY; FR; BA; Stdnt Radio 90-; Rugby Ftbl Clb 90-; MIRROR 90-; Govt.

**SPRAGUE, JENNIFER L,** Atlantic Union Coll, S Lancaster, MA; SO; BS; Orchstra; Nrsng.

**SPRAGUE, KIMBERLY D,** Coll Of Charleston, Charleston, SC; FR; Alpha Delta Pi; Busn; Acctng.

**SPRAGUE, NANCY L,** Marist Coll, Poughkeepsie, NY; FR; BA; Crmnl Jstce; Law.

**SPRANCA, PAMELA J,** Univ Of Ga, Athens, GA; SO; BED; Greek Hnrs Clge; Alpha Lambda Delta 89-; Eta Sigma Gamma; Kappa Delta Hs Pres 89-; Deans List 89-; IM Ftbl 90-; Health Promo & Ed.

**SPRANKLE, JENNIFER F,** Mount Saint Mary Coll, Newburgh, NY; JR; Assoc Jstce Stdnt Judicial Bd 90-; Gaelic Soc 90-; Psychlgy; Cnslng.

**SPRATLIN, AMY R,** Northwest Ms Comm Coll, Senatobia, MS; SO; SGA V P; Stdnt Rectr 90-; Phi Theta Kappa 90-; Deans List 89-90; Engrng; Genetic Engr.**

**SPRATT, STEPHEN E,** Me Maritime Academy, Castine, ME; SO; BS; Cls Sec 90-; Propellar Clb; Fire/Damage Cntrl Crew T/V Ste Of Maine Lt 90-; MMA Fire Brig Lt 90-; Cmmdnts Lst 89; Dns Lst 90-; Rgmntl Post Offcr Lt; Alpha Phi Omega Pldg Cls Pres 89-; Eagle Scout Awd 86; Explr Sct Of Yr 89; Nautical Sci Engr; US Cst Grd/Mrchng Marine.

**SPRATT, STEPHEN MARCUS,** Univ Of Nc At Charlotte, Charlotte, NC; JR; BA; Nwspr 90-; Psychlgy Clb 90-; IM Swm Tm 90-; Psychlgy; Clin Psychlgy.

**SPRATT, SUSAN M,** Univ Of Akron, Akron, OH; JR; BS; Golden Key; Phi Eta Sigma; Alpha Lambda Delta; Dns Lst 88-90; Elem Educ; Tchng.

**SPRAYBERRY, JENNIFER A,** Central Al Comm Coll, Alexander City, AL; SO; AS; Bapt Campus Mnstries Pres 89; Phi Theta Kappa 89; Perf Arts Schlrshp 90; Music.**

**SPRAYBERRY, ROBBIE J,** Central Al Comm Coll, Alexander City, AL; AS; Sec Cert Alverson Draughon Bus Schl 62; Scrtrl.

**SPRIGGS, ADINA L,** Tuskegee Univ, Tuskegee Inst, AL; SO; BSN; NAACP Stdnt Nrs Assn 89-; Mrchng Bnd; New Eng Clb; Nrsng; Med Schl.

**SPRING, MELISSA J,** Oh Univ, Athens, OH; FR; BA; Ntl Soc For Prof Eng; Deans Lst; Chem Eng.

**SPRING, MICHELE R,** Coll Of Charleston, Charleston, SC; FR; BA; Eng; Law.

**SPRING, ROBERT G,** Schenectady County Comm Coll, Schenectady, NY; FR; AS; Stdnt Govt Assoc Frshmn Sntr 90-; Bdgt/Fnce Comm Sntr 90-; Hndcpd Awrns Comm Sntr 90-; Fl Tm Alchlsm Cncl Schenectady Co, Trvl/Trsm; Trvl Agt.

**SPRINGER, AIMEE J,** Oh St Univ At Marion, Marion, OH; SO; BA; Psychlgy Clb 89-; Alpha Lambda Delta 90-F Phi Eta Sigma 90-; Hnrs Bus Pgrm 90-; IM Vlybl 90; Psychlgy; Psychlgy/Bus.

**SPRINGER, ANTHONY,** Morehouse Coll, Atlanta, GA; JR; BA; Intshp Fedl Aviation Admin 89-; Ftbl Co Cptn 85-87; Political Sci/Pre Law; Law.

**SPRINGER, JOHN W,** Univ Of Sc At Columbia, Columbia, SC; SO; Mgmt.

**SPRINGER, JULIE E,** Kent St Univ Kent Cmps, Kent, OH; SR; BA; Accntng Assoc 90-; Beta Alpha Psi 90-; Gldn Key; Deans Lst 90-; Accntng.

**SPRINGER, LEAH S,** Univ Of Miami, Coral Gables, FL; FR; BA; Alpha Landa Pelta 90-; Music; Theatre Arts.

**SPRINGER, SCOTT C,** Radford Univ, Radford, VA; SR; BBA; Econ Clb; Hse Cncl Ingls Hl Pres 86-87; IRHC 86-87; Internshp Legg Msn Wd Wlkr Inc; Fin; Law.

**SPRINGFIELD, JASON M,** Snead St Jr Coll, Boaz, AL; SO; BA; SG Tres 90-; SAE 88-89; Eagle Scout Awrd 88; IM Actvts 90-; Psych; Chrstn Cnslr.

**SPRINGLE, DONNA A,** Univ Of Md Baltimore Prof Schl, Baltimore, MD; SR; BS; Sunday Sch Tchr 87-90; Reading Progrm Partcpnt 90; Phi Beta Kappa 89; Fairleigh Dickinson Univ Dntl Hygn Alumni Award 89; Pres Schlrshp FDU 87-89; Im Vlybl 89; Amercn Dntl Hugnsts Assoc 87-; Rgstrd Dentl Hyugnst 89-; BS; Dental Hygn; Rgstrd Dntl Hygnst.

**SPROWLS, KEVIN W,** Comm Coll Algny Co Algny Cmps, Pittsburgh, PA; SO; BA; Acctng; CPA.

**SPRUEIL, ROMANO A,** Embry Riddle Aeronautical Univ, Daytona Beach, FL; SO; BS; Sigma Chi; Medcl Fld/Doctr.

**SPRUELL, KYLE,** Tougaloo Coll, Tougaloo, MS; FR; Psych; Child Psychlgst.

**SPRUILL, JACKIE E,** Ms Gulf Coast Comm Coll, Perkinston, MS; SO; Delta Math Club 90-; Phi Theta Kappa 90-; Stone Cnty Rec Bd Bsbl/Ft Bl Coach 86-; Secndry Ed/Math; Tchr/Coach.

**SPRUILL, MARTHA ANN,** Queens Coll, Charlotte, NC; JR; BA; Peer Advsr 89-90; Intr Grk Cncl 90-; Panhellenic 89-90; Chi Omega Panhellenic 88-; Redd Schlrshp 88-; Spnsh/Art Hstry; Art.

**SPRUILL, ZANDRA G,** Vance Granville Comm Coll, Henderson, NC; SO; Locust Grv Bptst Chrch; NCHE Assoc; BA Teachers Assoc.

**SPRY, KELLY S,** Wv Northern Comm Coll, Wheeling, WV; FR; AAD; Deans Lst 90; Psychlgy-Hmn Serv; Psychlgst.

**SPURGEON, CHRISTOPHER T,** Oh Univ, Athens, OH; JR; BS; Alpha Lambda Badlwin Wallace; Golden Key OH U; Murray Stern Schlrshp; Art Hist Italy OU; Art Hist; Prof.

**SPURLIN, LISA K,** Tallahassee Comm Coll, Tallahassee, FL; SO; BA; Chrtr Membr Frnch Clb 90; Deans Lst 89-; IM Indr Soccer; US Navy Tchrs Aide 87-; Poltcl Sci; Law.

**SPURLOCK, ANGELA M,** Defiance Coll, Defiance, OH; SR; BS; Stdnt Senate Jr Cls Pres 89-90; Sorority 88-; Elem Educ; Tchr.

**SPURLOCK, ANITA J,** Pellissippi St Tech Comm Coll, Knoxville, TN; SO; AAS; Phi Theta Kappa; Computer Drafting/Design.

**SPURLOCK, LIA F,** Valdosta St Coll, Valdosta, GA; JR; Sec; Mddl Chldhd Educ; Tchr.

**SPURLOCK, PATRICIA S,** Mary Baldwin Coll, Staunton, VA; SR; BA; Stdnt Senate 88-; Hon Schlr Soc VP 87-; Math Assn Amer; Math; Hgh Schl Ed.

**SPYCHALSKI, JAMES N,** Kent St Univ Kent Cmps, Kent, OH; FR; Hnrs Clg 90-; High Hnrs Stdnt Harbour Hall 90-; Trck/Decathlon 90-; Medicine; Surgeon.

**SPYROPOULOS, BILL N,** Pa St Univ Delaware Cty Cmps, Media, PA; JR; BS; Opn Lvl Trnmnt Rcqtbl Div St Chmp; AHEPA; Clncl Psychlgy.

**SQUARE, FREDERICK J,** Al A & M Univ, Normal, AL; JR; BA; Pan Hellenic Coun 90-; Phi Beta Sigma Sec 90-; Pol Sci; Law.

**SQUARZINI, MICHAEL J,** Manhattan Coll, Bronx, NY; JR; BS; Amercn Soc Of Civil Engrs 90-; Soc Of Amercn Military Engrs 90-; Tau Beta Pi 90-; Chi Epsilon VP 90-; Offered Intrnshp At Univ Of ME; Manhattan Clg Engr Centennial Comm CE Rep; Civil Engr; Structural.

**SQUIBB, BARRY D,** Northeastern Univ, Boston, MA; JR; BSEE; IEEE 89-; Carl S Ell Pres Schlr 88-; Hnrs Prog 88-; Sci; Eng.**

**SQUIERS, WENDY E,** Portland School Of Art, Portland, ME; SR; BFA; Film Soc Staff 90-; Stdnt Gallery Dir 90-; Stdnt Govt Rep 90-; Eudolia Gross Awd Otsndg Cmuty Serv; Graphic Dsgn; Dsgn/Mktg.

**SQUIRE, GREER D,** Va Commonwealth Univ, Richmond, VA; SO; BS; USMC Musician/Drl Instrctr 85-; Admin Jstc; Law Enfrcmnt.

**SQUIRES, DAVID H,** Western New England Coll, Springfield, MA; JR; Engl; Tch.

**SQUIRES, STUART M,** Elizabeth City St Univ, Elizabeth City, NC; SR; MD; NAACP; Amer Chl Scty VP 90-; All Amer Schlr; US Achmt Acad; Bearer Of The Mace; Varsity Ftbl 87-; Bsbl 90; BS; Med.**

**SREDNI, MIRIAM B,** Barry Univ, Miami, FL; SR; Phtgrphy.

**SREENIVAS, MYTHELI,** Yale Univ, New Haven, CT; FR; BA; Clg Nwspr 90; Indn Clsscl Dance/Artst/Perf 75-; Yale Lit Prjct; Yale Hngr/Hmls Actn Prjct 90; Law.

**SRESHTHAPUTRA, NATTHAPAT,** Embry Riddle Aeronautical Univ, Daytona Beach, FL; JR; BS; AS Civil Aviation Traning Ctr Thailand 89; Aviation Tech; Aircraft Mech.

**SRINIVAS, CHRISTOPHER R,** Manhattan Coll, Bronx, NY; JR; BE; Tau Beta Pi 90-; Pi Tau Sigma 90-; Manhattan Coll Pres Schlrshp 88-; Mech Eng.

**ST AMANT, JOY DOWLING,** Fl St Univ, Tallahassee, FL; SR; BS; AA Gulf Coast Cmnty Clg 89; Sci; Engrng.

**ST CLAIR, ANDREW B,** Fl St Univ, Tallahassee, FL; JR; BS; Pre Law Scty 90-; Amer Criminal Justice Assoc 90-; Criminology; Law.

**ST CLAIR, BRANDON L,** Troy St Univ At Troy, Troy, AL; FR; BA; Evvrnmntl Sci; Indstrl State Envrnmnt Srvcs.

**ST CLAIR, FONDA L,** Comm Coll Algny Co Algny Cmps, Pittsburgh, PA; Sci; Nrsng.

**ST CLAIR, RICHARD D,** Oh St Univ At Newark, Newark, OH; SR; BSBA; Trans Logstcs Assn; Howrd/Cathrn Le Favre Schlrshp; IM Bsktbl/Glf/Tnns Tms; Trans Logstcs; Mgmt.

**ST DENIS, CHRISTINA M,** Western New England Coll, Springfield, MA; SR; Capt Chrldg; VP Sr Cls; VP Grad Comm Mgmnt Clb Yrbk Mbr; Stu Lit Vol; Intrn Frndly Ice Cream Corp; BSBA; Mgmnt; Hmn Rsrc Mgmnt.

**ST ESPRIT, ELIZABETH J,** Slippery Rock Univ, Slippery Rock, PA; SR; IM Sftbl/Sccr/Vlybl 87-; Hlth/Phy Ed/Rec/Dance 87-; Nea 87-; PSEA 87-; AAHPERD 87-; Acad Excellence Awd 87-; Schlr Athlete Awd; Outstanding Wmn In Sprt 87-; Vars Ftbl; Phy Ed/Hlth Tchr; Phy Ed/Hlth Coach.

**ST GEORGE, STACY L,** Fl St Univ, Tallahassee, FL; JR; AA; Thtr Vol 89; Advrtsng Clb 90-; Pres Hnr Rll 88-90; Dean Lst 88-; Advrtsng; BA.

**ST GERMAIN, PETER H,** Hudson Valley Comm Coll, Troy, NY; SO; BS; Mem Adirondack Three Style Wrestling Assn Athlete Partcpnt 89-90; Phi Theta Kappa 90-; Empire State Game Qualifer Wrstlng 89-90; Asst Wrstlng Coach 84-; Head Pee Wee Wrstlng Coach 88-90; Phys Edn/Phys Therapy.

**ST JACQUES, JODIE M,** Univ Of Tn At Martin, Martin, TN; JR; BS; Alpha Omicron Pi Chptr Rltns Chrmn 88-; Arthrts Rsrch Fndtn Coor; Cmnctns; Pub Rltns/Advrtsng.

**ST JOHN, MARJORIE,** Nova Univ, Ft Lauderdale, FL; GD; MBA.

**ST JOHN, TRACY L,** Southside Va Comm Coll, Alberta, VA; SO; BS; Fndtn Acad Schlrshp 90-; Pres Lst 89-; Psychlgy/Elem Edn; Tchr.

**ST LOUIS, JEAN D,** Morehouse Coll, Atlanta, GA; SR; SG 89-90; Pan Afrcn Allnc Pres 87-; Blck Pwr Serves Itslf Fndr 88-; Hlth Advsry 89-; Pres Awd Comm Serv 89-90; Vrsty Bsktbl 87-88; BA Trinity Coll; Sclgy; Med.

**ST LOUIS, MAGDALENE,** Central Fl Comm Coll, Ocala, FL; SO; AS; Volntr 89; Phi Theta Kappa 90; Coop Assoc Of States For Schlrshp 89; Indstrl Co-Op Ed At Microdyne Corp; In Poetry Geotwn U Wshngtn 90; Qlty Cntrl/Prdctn Mngmnt; BS Qlty Cntrl.

**ST PAUL, MATTHEW J,** Inter Amer Univ Pr San German, San German, PR; SR; BA; Internatl Org 88-90; Pblc Admin Assn VP 89-; Hnr Prgrm 89-; Bldg Comm; Prsnl Offc Intrn; Cncl Of Disabld Pres 84-85; Cert Sir Arthr Lewis Comm Coll 82; Pblc Admin; Pblc Serv.

**ST PETERY, JULIA E,** Fl St Univ, Tallahassee, FL; JR; BA; Tau Beta Sigma Pres 88-; Mrch Chfs 87-90; Phi Kappa Phi 89-; Ele Educ.

**ST PIERRE, MICHELLE C,** Boston Coll, Chestnut Hill, MA; FR; Frshmn Asst Prog; Nrsg Awd; Nrsg.

**ST VICTOR, KATHLEEN B,** City Univ Of Ny Baruch Coll, New York, NY; SO; BBA; NABA Asst Pblcty Dir; P Marwick Intern 90; Aggtg; CPA.

**ST VICTOR, SABINE,** City Univ Of Ny Baruch Coll, New York, NY; JR; BA; Golden Key; Oper Mgmnt.

**STAATS, ANGELA M,** Marshall University, Huntington, WV; SR; BBA; Cmps Crusade For Chrst 87-; Acctg Clb 90-; Twin Towers W Hall Advsry Cncl Sec 87-88; Gamma Beta Phi 88-89; Dns Lst; Acctg; CPA.

**STAATS, CONNIE S,** Kent St Univ Kent Cmps, Kent, OH; SO; BA; Air Force ROTC 89-90; Phi Alpha Delta Pre Law; KSU Schlrshp For Exclnc 90-; Dist Schlrs Awd 90-; Eng/Hist; Law.

**STAATS, JOY R,** Greenville Tech Coll, Greenville, SC; SO; BS; Anthropology; Native Amer Alaska.

**STAATS, MELISSA D,** Wv Univ At Parkersburg, Parkersburg, WV; SO; BA; Acctng; CPA.

**STAATS, THOMAS C,** Wv Univ, Morgantown, WV; JR; BS; ASME 90-; SAE 90-; Mchncl Engnrng.

**STABLER, BERT,** Oberlin Coll, Oberlin, OH; FR; BA; IM Bsktbl 90-; Aikido Clb 90-; Satire Nspr Stffwrtr Crtnst; Wrtng/Tchng/Fin.

**STABLER, DAVID R,** Univ Of Ga, Athens, GA; SR; BSED; Mrchng Band 85-90; Soc For Creative Anachronism 88-; Assoc For Comp Mchnry 87-89; Phi Eta Sigma 86; Phi Beta Lambda; Cir K 88-90; Athens Trombone Assoc Pres 88-90; St Champ Comp Applctns For Bus; Uga Rugby Club; Athens West Lions Club 90-; Bus Edn; User Support For Univ.

**STABY, JOANNE C,** S U N Y Coll At Fredonia, Fredonia, NY; JR; BA; Sclgy; Hlth Serv Admn.

**STACEY, CINDY D,** Livingston Univ, Livingston, AL; FR; BS; Bsnss; Accntng.

**STACEY, CRYSTAL D,** Middle Tn St Univ, Murfreesboro, TN; JR; BA; Chem; Rsrch Tchng.

**STACEY, DIANE L,** Northeastern Christian Jr Coll, Villanova, PA; JR; BA; Delta Psi Omega; Drama Clb; AA; Psychology; Technical Theatre.

**STACEY, KATHRYN M,** Fl Atlantic Univ, Boca Raton, FL; JR; BA; AA Palm Beach Comm Coll 90; Accntng; CPA.

**STACEY, VIOLA J,** Fayetteville St Univ, Fayetteville, NC; FR; Waitress 89-90; Crmnl Just; Lwyr.

**STACH, CONNIE L,** Anne Arundel Comm Coll, Arnold, MD; SO; Glen Burnie Vol Fire Dpt EMT; EMT Paramedic.

**STACH, TODD R,** Cedarville Coll, Cedarville, OH; FR; BA; Radio Statn Nght Sprts Dir; Nwsltr Sprtswrtr; IM Rqutbl/Soccr/Bsktbl/Sftbl 90-; Brdcst Mgmt.

**STACHLER, JENNIFER L,** Bluffton Coll, Bluffton, OH; SO; BA; Chmcl Rbbr Cmpny Awrd Bst Frshmn Chmst 89-90; Prsdntl Schlrshp 89-; Math; Scndry Ed.**

**STACHOWIAK, JENNIFER L,** Univ Of Akron, Akron, OH; SR; Gldn Key 88-; Kappa Delta Pi 89-; BS.

**STACHOWIAK, NICOLE M,** D Youville Coll, Buffalo, NY; FR; BSMS; Campus Ministry 90-; Adopt A Grandparent 90-; Friends Of The Night People 90-; Physical Therapy.

**STACHOWICZ, JOEL A,** Nyack Coll, Nyack, NY; SR; BA; Yrbk Asst Edtr 90-; SG Class Treas 89-90; Dept Asst 90-; Bible; Tchr/Ma.

**STACHOWICZ III, JOHN J,** Dartmouth Coll, Hanover, NH; Pres Rsrch Asst; Ultimate Frisbee; Biology/Envrmtl Studies.**

**STACHOWSKI, KEVIN C,** Ms Univ For Women, Columbus, MS; JR; BS; Bench Gavel VP 90-; Stdnt Advsry Comm 90-; Stdnt Alumni Ambsdr 89-; Delta Sigma Omega Pres 88-; Pres Coun 90-; Paralegal; Law.

**STACK, JOHN F,** Niagara Univ, Niagara Univ, NY; JR; BA; Ski Clb; Res Asst 90-; Lf Grd Stdnt Mgr Rec Ctr 90-; IM Spts; Bsns Mgmt; Fmly Bsns.**

**STACKHOUSE, GEORGIA L,** Wv Univ, Morgantown, WV; SR; Stdnt Nrs Assoc Lvl Repr Schl Nrsg 88-89; Stdnt Nrs Assoc Soph Repr 88-89; Dns Lst 89-; Nrsg Intrnshp Duke Univ Med Ctr 90; Lcrs 88-90; BSN; Nrsg; RN.

**STACKPOLE, BONNIE M,** Bunker Hill Comm Coll, Boston, MA; FR; AS; Lib Arts; Med Rdgrphy.

**STACKPOLE, DELILAH J,** Wv Univ At Parkersburg, Parkersburg, WV; FR; Acctg; Mgmnt.

**STACKPOLE, RICHARD C,** Saint Josephs Coll, Windham, ME; SO; BS; Hl Cncl Pres 89-; Inter Hl Cncl 89-90; Awds Slctn Comm; Dns Lst 89-; Crs Cntry 89-90; Mktg/Mgmt; Law.

**STACKS, SHANNON M,** Radford Univ, Radford, VA; JR; BA; Real Life Flwshp Pres 88-; Cmps Crusade For Christ 90-; Criminal Justice; Juvenile Justice.

**STACY, ANDREA V,** Univ Of Rochester, Rochester, NY; SO; BA; Gamma Phi Beta Rtl Chrmn; Hlth/Scty/Psychlgy; Bhvrl Med/Hlth Sci.

**STACY JR, JOSEPH E,** Norfolk St Univ, Norfolk, VA; SO; BA; DNIMAS Stdnt Assoc 90-; IEEE 90-; Spartan Alpha Tau 90-; DNIMAS Schlr 90-; Physics; Rsrch.

**STACY, KIMBERLY B,** Northern Ky Univ, Highland Hts, KY; JR; PHD; Spnsh Clb 90-; Iberian Trvl Schlrshp; Spnsh Achvmnt Awd; Spanish Interpretation.

**STACY, ROBERT G,** Bridgeport Engr Inst, Fairfield, CT; SR; BSEE; Martha K Rogers Mem Schlrshp Awd 90; Schlrshp Grnt Ntl Mchne Tool Bldrs Assoc 89; Stdnt Membr Of Audro Eng Scty 87; Hldr Of Gnrl Radio Tlphne Lcnse Fdrl Cmm Cmmssn 78; Emplyd As Elctrcl Eng By Trnstns Corp Of Dnbry Dsgng Mble Rbts; Dgtl Sgnl Prcssng Snsr Tchnlgy; Elctrnc Eng.

**STADLER, TIMOTHY G,** Univ Of Cincinnati, Cincinnati, OH; SR; BFA; Theta Alpha Phi Ohio Eta Chptr 85-86; Musical Thtr Perf.

**STADNICKI, JENNIFER L,** Univ Of Nc At Greensboro, Greensboro, NC; FR; BS; Alpha Lambda Delta 90-; Nrsng.

**STADNIK, MICHAEL,** Manhattan Coll, Bronx, NY; JR; BS; Amer Soc Mech Engrs; Pi Tau Sigma; Dns Lst; Mech Engr.**

**STADULIS, DANIEL J,** Kent St Univ Kent Cmps, Kent, OH; JR; Hl Cncl 90-; KIC 90-; Bus Mgt Sci.

**STAFF, MARGARET M,** S U N Y Coll At Fredonia, Fredonia, NY; JR; BS; Bus Club 90-; Delta Mu Delta 90; Tutoring 90-; Bus Admin.

**STAFFA, DENISE M,** East Stroudsburg Univ, E Stroudsburg, PA; FR; BS; Pocono Med Ctr Vol 90-; Deans Lst 90-; Wrk Stdy Pgm; Bio; Med Field.

**STAFFIN, ALLISON B,** Glassboro St Coll, Glassboro, NJ; SR; Phi Alpha Theta 90-; Hstry; Sec Tchg.

**STAFFORD, BEVERLY A,** Wilmington Coll, New Castle, DE; FR; BA; Elem Ed; Tchng.

**STAFFORD, DENISE D,** Hudson Valley Comm Coll, Troy, NY; SO; BA; Rlph Brn Award 90-; Trck Fld90; Bsktbll 90-; AAS; Rcrtn Ldrshp; Rcrtn Thrpst.

**STAFFORD, EDDIE R,** Mayland Comm Coll, Spruce Pine, NC; SO; BED; Crim Jstc; Dept Crctn Instrctr.

**STAFFORD, KEITH B,** Tn Tech Univ, Cookeville, TN; SO; DVM; Rodeo Clb VP 90-91; Msnry LDS Ch Zone Ldr 83-85; Qlty Cntrl Auditor Nielson Framing Co 87-; Agri; Vet Med.

**STAFFORD, KELLY J,** Schenectady County Comm Coll, Schenectady, NY; FR; ASSOC; Bus Clb Sec 90; Writing Tutor 90-; Acctng; CPA.

**STAFFORD, KEVIN J,** Chesterfield Marlboro Coll, Cheraw, SC; SO; AS; Phi Theta Kappa 89-; USN Rsrvs Ae3 88-; USN Actv Duty 86-88; Indstrl Mgmt.

**STAFFORD, MARY C,** Methodist Coll, Fayetteville, NC; SR; BA; Std Educ Asc 89-; Cncl Exptnl Chldrn 89-; Phi Eta Sigma 89-; Phi Sigma Iota 90-; Delta Phi Omega Tr 87-89; Elem Ed; Tch.

**STAFFORD, NA PRELL F,** Johnson C Smith Univ, Charlotte, NC; FR; Sprtl Chr; Stdnt Chrstn Assoc; Un Prgm Brd; Rgstrd Nrs; Med.

**STAFFORD, NOPPALADT,** Fayetteville St Univ, Fayetteville, NC; SR; BS; Army Comm Serv Vol 89-; ROB-NOP Corp VP 86-90; Bsn Admn/Mktg; Htl Mgmt.

**STAFFORD, ROBERT S,** Univ Of Ky, Lexington, KY; SR; Omicron Delta Epsilon 88-; Pi Gamma Mu 88-; MA; Ed/Scl Stdies; Tchng.

**STAFFORD, SUSAN M,** Ms Univ For Women, Columbus, MS; FR; BS; Acctng.

**STAFFORD, TAMARA N,** Ashland Comm Coll, Ashland, KY; SO; BS; Baptist Student Union 90-; Bellefonte Hosp Vol 90-; AS; Zoology; Medicine.

**STAFFORD II, THOMAS D,** Itawamba Comm Coll, Fulton, MS; FR; Dns Lst 90; Bsn; Insur Auto Claims Adjuster.

**STAGENHORST, KRISTIE L,** Colby Sawyer Coll, New London, NH; JR; BSN; Yrbk Edtr 88-90; Stdnt Nrs Assn VP 88-; NH Stdnt Nrs Assn Lgsltv Comm Chrmn 90-; Natl Collgt Nrsng Awrd 90-; Grl Scout Gold Awrd 78-89; All Amer Schlr 90-; Nrsng; RN.

**STAGGE, PEGGY L,** Univ Of Cin R Walters Coll, Blue Ash, OH; FR; Collegiate Sec Intrntl 89-; Ofc Admn; Admn Asstnt.

**STAGGS JR, DEAN,** Lake City Comm Coll, Lake City, FL; SO; AS; Jazz Attack Yth Minister Sunday Schl Tchr; Nursing.**

**STAGGS, PURSEFNEE K,** Univ Of Cincinnati-Clrmnt Coll, Batavia, OH; SO; AS; Phi Theta Kappa 89-; Acctg Asst OH-KY-IN Rgnl Cncl Govts 85-; Bus; Acctg/Fin.

**STAGGS, RONALD P,** Univ Of Tn At Martin, Martin, TN; SR; Phi Beta Sigma 87-; Scabbard/Blade 89-; ROTC Cadet/Major 87-; Bus; U S Army Officer.

**STAGNER, LAURA D,** Meridian Comm Coll, Meridian, MS; SO; AA; Phi Beta Lambda 90-; Schlrshp Profl Sects Inter; Busn/Office Techgy.

**STAHL, CHERYL M,** Md Coll Of Art & Design, Silver Spring, MD; JR; Cmnctn Dsgn/Art.

**STAHL, LISA K,** Mount Aloysius Jr Coll, Cresson, PA; FR; Occptnl Thrpy.

**STAHL, LORI M,** Liberty Univ, Lynchburg, VA; SO; BS; Yth Qust Clb 89-90; Engl Mjrs Clb; Drm Pryr Ldr; Dns Lst 89-; Engl; Librn.

**STAHL, SIMONE D,** Fl International Univ, Miami, FL; JR; BS; Stdnt Dietetics Assoc 89-; Amer Dietetics Assoc 89-; Health Serv & Sci; Public Health Nutrition.

**STAHMER, KATHLEEN G,** Univ Of South Al, Mobile, AL; JR; BS; Beta Sigma Phi 83-; Natl Assoc Of Ins Women 85-90; Soc Of Certfd Ins Cnslrs 87-90; Ins Exp Licnsd Agnt CIC/CPIW Profsnl Desgntns 81-; AA Northland Pioneer Clg 83; Elem Educ; Tchr.

**STAHURSKI, NEIL E,** Duquesne Univ, Pittsburgh, PA; SR; M; Amer Gld Of Orgnsts Sub Dn 90; Phi Kappa Phi; Asstshp Scrd Msc Dept; Andre Marchal Awrd; Prssr Schlr; BS Msc Educ; Msc; Tchr.

**STAINBROOK, TAD L,** Fl St Univ, Tallahassee, FL; SO; BA; FSU Hnrs Schlrs Cnl 84-; FSU Deans List 89-; IM Bstkbl 89-90; B1; AA/MRKTNG.

**STAINIO, GABRIELLE A,** Villanova Univ, Villanova, PA; SR; Special Olympcs Videogrphr 90; Asstshp Advanced TV Prod; BA; Cmmnctn; Television Prod.

**STALCUP, VICKI M,** Winthrop Coll, Rock Hill, SC; JR; BA; Cltn Hmlss Pres 89-; Chrl Scl Co-Chrmn 89-; Schl Ambssdr 89-; Psi Chi 90-; Alpha Lambda Delta 89-; Tau Alpha Kappa Ltl Sis 90-; Psychlgy; Stdnt Affrs.

**STALEY, ALISHA D,** Marshall University, Huntington, WV; FR; BA; Chorus; State Fed Of The Blind VP 89-; Educ/Mntlly Imprd; Teach.

**STALEY, ANGELA R,** Wilmington Coll, Wilmington, OH; JR; Stdnt Fndtn Sec 88-; Aggies 88-; Delta Tau Alpha 90-; WC Stdnt Fndtn Secy 88-; Hnr Schlrshp; Alumni Assoc Intern; Political Sci; Law.

**STALEY, JAMES A,** Middle Tn St Univ, Murfreesboro, TN; JR; BBA; Gamma Beta Phi 90-; Beta Gamma Sigma 90-; Phi Kappa Phi 90-; Beta Alpha Psi; Acctg; Mgr.

**STALEY, MICHELLE L,** Univ Of Tn At Martin, Martin, TN; JR; BA; AA 90; Spec Educ.

**STALEY, NICHOLE M,** Univ Of Pittsburgh, Pittsburgh, PA; FR; Cncl 90-; Govt Rltns Comm 90-; Phi Eta Sigma 90-; Pol Sci; Law.

**STALEY-BURLEY, GINA C,** Oh Northern Univ, Ada, OH; GD; JS; Bar Assc 89-; Deans List 90; Cnstnl Law Book Awrd 90; Mary S Wetherill Schlrshp 89-; Substitute Tchr 86-89; BS Bwlng Green State Univ 86; Law.

**STALLARD, DANIELLE S,** George Mason Univ, Fairfax, VA; SR; BS; Phys Educ; Thrpy.

**STALLING, TAWANA L,** Al A & M Univ, Normal, AL; FR; BA; NAACP; Natl Assn Female Exectrs; Eastern Star; Amer Lgn Awd; Cmptr Sci; Cmptr Engr.

**STALLINGS, ANN M,** Univ Of Ky, Lexington, KY; SR; BA; Gldn Ky 90-; Psych; Res.

**STALLINGS, DENISE H,** Univ Of Sc At Aiken, Aiken, SC; SR; ANN; Nrsng Cls Treas 90-; Deans List; Hgts Bptst Chrch; Stdnt Nrs St Jos Hosp; Med Asst 76-; MA Augusta Tech Schl; Nursing RN.

**STALLINGS, MARY P,** Birmingham Southern Coll, Birmingham, AL; SR; BS; AS Jeff St Comm Coll 82; Cmptr Info Sys; Cmptr Prgrmng.

**STALLWORTH, FRANOTIS R,** Fl A & M Univ, Tallahassee, FL; GD; BS; Kemetic Math Socty 90-; Urban League 89-; Orchesis 88-90; REU Rsrch Prog; Dnc Exch 89; Math; MS.

**STALLWORTH, LA TONYA M,** Fl A & M Univ, Tallahassee, FL; FR; PHARM; Flr Pres 90; Dow Chem Intrn 90; Hnr Roll; Phrmcy.

**STALSWORTH, TIMOTHY E,** Volunteer St Comm Coll, Gallatin, TN; SO; BA; AS; Bsn; Mktg.

**STAMATEDES, CHRIS W,** Widener Univ, Chester, PA; SR; BS; ASME 88-; Inter-Frat Cncl Treas; Alpha Chi 90-; Tau Beta Pi 89-; Theta Chi Pres 88-; Deans Lst 87; Natl Cllgt Eng Awd 89-90; IM Sftbl/Hcky; Mech Eng; Eng.

**STAMBER, KEVIN L,** Univ Of Pittsburgh, Pittsburgh, PA; JR; Eng Stdnt Cbnt 89-90; Golden Key 90; Tau Beta Pi 90; Alpha Pi Mu Pres 89; Prvst Schlr 88; Eng Hnrs Schlr 88-90; Lrd Corp Schlr 90; Indstrl Eng; Eng.

**STAMEY, DONNA L,** Univ Of Nc At Asheville, Asheville, NC; JR; BA; Hnr Scty 90-; Gamma Beta Phi 88; Engl Lit; Fctn Wrtr.

**STAMEY, JOY L,** North Greenville Coll, Tigerville, SC; FR; AS; Phi Theta Kappa; Acctg; CPA.

**STAMEY, KAREN A,** Brevard Coll, Brevard, NC; SO; AA; Office Mgmt.

**STAMPALIA, ANDREA M,** Univ Of Nh Plymouth St Coll, Plymouth, NH; SR; Natl Assn Accntnts V P 90-; VITA 90-; BS; Acctng; CPA.

**STAMPER, ALLEN,** Sue Bennett Coll, London, KY; FR; Yng Adults Christ Pres; Alum Welder; Elem Educ; Teach.

**STAMPER, CARRYL L,** Old Dominion Univ, Norfolk, VA; JR; Gldn Ky 90-; ADK Schlrshps 89-; Mech Eng.

**STAMPER, DAVID B,** Lees Coll, Jackson, KY; FR; BS; Biologyf Tchng HS.

**STAMPER, RICHARD B,** Lees Coll, Jackson, KY; SO; BS; Hnry King Stnfrd Schlp 89-90; Hrns Pgm 89-90; Bsbl 90-; Cmptr Sci.

**STAMPER, STEPHANIE A,** Medical Coll Of Ga, Augusta, GA; JR; BA; Natl Stdnt Nrs Assn 90-F; Nrsng.

**STAMPLEY, DONNA M,** Alcorn St Univ, Lorman, MS; JR; Stdnt Govt Pres 89-90; Phi Theta Kappa 89-90; Elem Educ; Tchr.

**STAMPLEY, TERRI E,** Univ Of South Al, Mobile, AL; SO; BA; Acctg.

**STAMPS, ERIC D,** Liberty Univ, Lynchburg, VA; SR; MBA; FMA 88-; Lacrosse Clb 88-; Acad Comm 88-89; Urban Outreach 90; Hnrs Pgm; BS; Bsn/Finance; Invest Bnkg/Corp Law.

**STAMPS, LISA A,** Brewer St Jr Coll, Fayette, AL; SO; BED; Mdrn Elite Clb 89-; Phi Theta Kappa; Gideons Aux Intl Pres 90-; Bptst Chrch Orgnst; Elem Educ; Tch.**

**STAMPS, SHARON L,** Univ Of Sc At Columbia, Columbia, SC; FR; BA; YABA 90-; Bus/Acctng; CPA.

**STAMPS, STACIE D,** Univ Of Southern Ms, Hattiesburg, MS; FR; BSBA; Stdnt Body Sen; Alum Assn; Alpha Lambda Delta; Phi Eta Sigma; Gamma Betas Phi; Delta Delta Delta Asst Pldg Edctr 90-; Acctng; CPA.

**STANA, CYNTHIA C,** Univ Of Fl, Gainesville, FL; SR; Brwrd Area Cncl Repr 87; Bus Admin Clg Cncl Pblcty Chr/Sprng Awds Bnqt 90; Career Expo Host 89-90; Phi Kappa Phi; Delta Sigma Pi Sec 89-; Golden Heart/Sigma Phi Epsilon 89-; Amer Red Cross/Tour De Hogtown Comm Mbr; Bus Admin/Mrktng; Educ.

**STANABACK, BRIAN KEITH,** Central Fl Comm Coll, Ocala, FL; SO; BA; Phi Theta Kappa; Deans Lst; Pres Lst; Collctns Admin Frst Fedrl Svngs/Loan; Math; Acctnt.

**STANBACH, SUSAN S,** Va Commonwealth Univ, Richmond, VA; SR; BA; Bsns Mrktng; Intrntnl Mrktng.

**STANCIL, DEBORAH A,** Salisbury St Univ, Salisbury, MD; SR; BS; Delta Mu Delta; Deans Lst 88-90; Inst Prprty Txtn; Sr Acctnt 85-; Acctg; Auditng.

**STANCIL, JANNIFER,** Ms Valley St Univ, Itta Bena, MS; JR; BA; Alpha Kappa Mu; Pres Schlr; IM Bsktbl Capt 89; Edn; Teach.

**STANCIL, JENNIFER L,** Coppin St Coll, Baltimore, MD; SO; BA; Vlybl; Bio/Math; Phy Thrpy.

**STANCIL, REX L,** Atlanta Christian Coll, East Point, GA; SO; BA; Bible Stdy Grp 90-; Chr 90-; All Am Schlr Awd 90-; Pres Schlrshp Awd 90-; Intrnshp Chrstn Chrch Stckbrdg; Theology/Msns; Chrch Grwth Conslt.

**STANCIL, YVONNE P,** Northwest Al Comm Coll, Phil Campbell, AL; SO; BA; AA Wallace St Cmmnty Clg; Mass Cmmnctns.

**STANDFIELD, FREDRICK L,** Birmingham Southern Coll, Birmingham, AL; SR; Stdnt Crt SGA Assc Jstc 88-89; Phi Theta Kappa 88-89; Alpha Kappa Psi; Deans Lst; CIGNA Corp Schlrshp J G H Morris Acctg Schlrshp; Jr Clg Trnsfr Schlrshp; AS Jefferson St Jr Clg 89; BS; Acctg.

**STANDLEY, HOWARD M,** Wv Univ, Morgantown, WV; JR; BSCPE; Tau Beta Pi; Elec Tech 82-88; Cmptr Engr/Elec Engr.

**STANEK, MARY F,** Saint Francis Coll, Loretto, PA; FR; BS; Lector At Masses Schl/Church; Dorothy Day Ctr Adopt A Grandparent Pgm; IM Vlybl; Math/Comps.

**STANFIELD, ERIC L,** Tallahassee Comm Coll, Tallahassee, FL; SO; AA; FJC SGA; SGA Pres; Rcyclng Task Frce; Phi Theta Kappa Treas; Fin; Invstmnt Bnkng.

**STANFIELD, KRISTINA M,** Univ Of Rochester, Rochester, NY; SR; MS; Wmns Ccs Bus Mgr 87-90; Rpdctv Physlgy; Rsrch Tchng.

**STANFIELD, PAMELA L,** Univ Of Ky, Lexington, KY; SR; Ballrm Dnc Soc 90-; Water Ski Clb 87; Gldn Key 89-; Mrtr Bd 90-; Lances 89-; Pi Mu Epsilon 89-; Cllgns Acdmc Excllnc 90-; Cmmnwlth Schlrshp 87; IM Ftbl 87; Bowman Schlrshp 90; Acdmc Excllnc Schlrshp 90; BS; Math.

**STANFIELD, SAMANTHA JILL,** Coll Of Charleston, Charleston, SC; SO; BS; Tri Delta; Pi Kappa Alpha Ltl Sis; Chrldr Univ Cntrl FL; Phy Thrpy.

**STANFIELD, SUSAN L,** Snead St Jr Coll, Boaz, AL; SO; BS; Phi Theta Kappa; Elem Ed; Tch.

**STANFILL, STACEY YVONNE,** Univ Of Tn At Martin, Martin, TN; FR; BSN; Sci; Nrsg.

**STANFORD, CHRISTINA B,** Ga St Univ, Atlanta, GA; SR; BED; Golden Key 90-; PAGE 89-; Early Chldhd; Tchg.

**STANFORD, GEORGIANNA M,** Middle Tn St Univ, Murfreesboro, TN; FR; BA; Gamma Beta Phi; Delta Zeta Pep Chrmn; MTSU Work Schlrshp 90-; Lucy Dye Home Econ Schlrshp 90-; Fashion Merchandising; Fashion Dsgn.

**STANFORD, JAMES L,** Livingston Univ, Livingston, AL; SR; BS; Lvngstn Histrcl Soc Pr; Dns Lst; Pres Lst; ASD Sheltn St Jr Clg 88; Hstry; Sls/Grad Schl.

**STANFORD, TOMIKO E,** Fisk Univ, Nashville, TN; SR; BS; SGA Yrbk Stf Sec 87-; Alabama Fish Clb Miss Alab 87-88; Delta Sigma Theta Rcrdng Sec 90-; Intrnshp Trvlrs 90; Bus Admin; Mgmt/Cmptr Sci.

**STANGE, DANIEL L,** Univ Of Akron, Akron, OH; JR; BS; ASME 90-; Univ Coop Pgrm; Mech Eng; Eng.

**STANGO, MARGARET R,** Elms Coll, Chicopee, MA; SO; BA; Cmmnctn Sciences Dsrdrs Clb 89-; Mnstry 90-; Actvts Clb Cls Rep 89-; Rsdnt Cncl Cls Rep 89-90; Cmmnctn Dsrdrs Sci; Spch Lang Pthlgy.

**STANIER, JULIE V,** Allegheny Coll, Meadville, PA; SO; BA; Wind Symph/Esmbl 89-; Stdnt Gov Assist Treas 89-; Lambda Sigma 90-; Kappa Alpha Theta Dpty Fnc 90-; Alden Schlor 89-90; PA Intrclgt Bnd; Dbl Econ Pltcl Sci Mjr; Corp Law.

**STANKIEWICZ, REBECCA L,** Univ Of Ct, Storrs, CT; SR; BS; Big Noise Presntns 89-90; Pre Vet Club 88-89; Indpndnt Rsrch In Genetics/Dev 89-90; Indpndnt Stdy In Devlpmntl Genetics 90; Indpndnt Stdy In Bovine Milk Genetic Selctn 89-90; Anml Sci.

**STANLEY, ARLENE G,** Catawba Valley Comm Coll, Hickory, NC; GD; AA Int Dsgn Randolph Cmnty Clg 88; Furn Dsgnr.

**STANLEY, CHERYL M,** Life Coll, Marietta, GA; GD; BS DC; Mtn Palpation Clb 87-88; Gonstead Clb/Thompson Clb 87-88; Upper Crvcl Clb VP 88-89; Alpha Delta Upsilon 88-90; Cls Sltrn Dec 90; BS 90; Intrnshp Adler Chrprctc Hlth Cntr 90-; Culpepper Chrprctc Cntr 89-90; DC 90; Chrprctc; Chrprctr.

**STANLEY, DANIELLE L,** S U N Y At Binghamton, Binghamton, NY; FR; Im Vlybl.

**STANLEY, DENISE R,** Univ Of Va Clinch Valley Coll, Wise, VA; JR; Engl; Comms.

**STANLEY, FAITH W,** Coppin St Coll, Baltimore, MD; SR; BS; Math Club 88-; Snr Class Schlrshp Comm Chrmn; Ronald E Mcnair Post Baccalaureate Pgm 90-; Math; Educ.

**STANLEY, KATHY,** Stillman Coll, Tuscaloosa, AL; FR; Ford Schlr Fndtn 90-.

**STANLEY, KIMBERLY D,** Patrick Henry Comm Coll, Martinsville, VA; SR; DPMA Pres 90-; Deans Lst 90.

**STANLEY, LISA G,** Univ Of Va Clinch Valley Coll, Wise, VA; SO; BS; Ttr Stdnt Spprt Srvcs 90-; Jfrshmn Math Awrd 89-90; Math; Indstry Tchng.

**STANLEY, MARIAN,** City Univ Of Ny Queensbrough, New York, NY; SR; BSN; Phi Theta Kappa 90; Ed Filmstrip Prod 74-; BFA Pratt Inst 74; Nrsg; Hm Hlth Care.

**STANLEY, MARK A,** Old Dominion Univ, Norfolk, VA; JR; BS; Phi Theta Kappa 90 ; Tau Alpha Pi 90-; Engrng Stdnt Of Yr 90; Granted By Intl Mngmnt Cncl; AAS VA Western Comm Clg 90; Electrcl Engrng Tchnlgy; Engrng Mngmnt.

**STANLEY, MONICA,** Univ Of Sc At Columbia, Columbia, SC; JR; BSN; Yrbk Edtr In Chf 88-; Stdnt Nrs Assn Sec 88-; Stdnt Govt Assn Org Rep 89-; Gamma Beta Phi 88-; Piedmont Soc 89-; Omicron Delta Kappa Nmnee; Fld Nrsng Schlr; Nrsng; Admin.

**STANLEY, PENNY S,** Endicott Coll, Beverly, MA; FR; BA; Shipmts Clb 90-; Peer Tutr; Intrnshp Wkfld Schl Dist; Psych; Erly Chldhd Educ.

**STANLEY, REGINA L,** Univ Of Tn At Martin, Martin, TN; JR; BA; STEA 90-; Alpha Omicron Pi Asst Treas/PR Chmn 90-; Early Chldhd Edn; Tchr.

**STANLEY JR, ROBERT R,** East Tn St Univ, Johnson City, TN; JR; BS; SME 90-; Deans Lst; Engr Dsgn Grphcs Tech; Proj Engr.

**STANLEY, SHA L,** Truett Mc Connell Coll, Cleveland, GA; SO; Bhvrl Sci Awrd; Dns Lst; Pres Clb; Sclgy Engl; Scl Wrkr Or Tchr.

**STANPHILL, JULIE N,** Univ Of South Fl, Tampa, FL; SR; BSN; Stu Govt Rec Sec 90-; Natl Sut Nrs Assn 90-; Sigma Theta Tau; Vol Judeo Chrstn Clnc; Frances Tumpklius Schlrshp 90-; Common Cse; Flght Attndt Pam Am; BA Univ Tampa 82; Nrsng.

**STANSBERRY, JANET H,** Univ Of Ky, Lexington, KY; SO; BS; Cath Wmns Altr Scty 87-; Lcnsd Rchrse And Jmpr Trnr 84-; Comp Sci Rssn; Comp Prgrmmng.

**STANSBURY, AUDREY J,** Univ Of Md Baltimore Prof Schl, Baltimore, MD; SR; BSN; Phi Kappa Phi 90; Sigma Theta Tau 90; Golden Key 88; Sigma Theta Tau Schlrshp 90; Whitehurst Hnr Schlrshp 89-90; Alumni Assn Award Hghest Schlstc Avrge; PTA 87; MD Assn Nrsg Stdnts 90; BS 77; Nrsg; Midwifery.

**STANSBURY III, JOSEPH E,** Univ Of Nc At Chapel Hill, Chapel Hill, NC; FR; BA; Pol Sci; Law.

**STANTON, AMY J,** Salisbury St Univ, Salisbury, MD; SR; BS; Physcl Educ Soc VP 87-; MAHPERD 87-; Dns Lst 89-; Athltc Hon Rl 89-; All-Am Schlr; All-Am Schlr 89; NCPEHA 89-; Wmns Lcrs 89; Crs Cntry Trck/Fld 90; Physcl Educ; Rcrtn Fld.

**STANTON, BEVERLY D,** Livingston Univ, Livingston, AL; SR; BS; Std Spprt Serv 87-; Educ; Elem Tchr.

**STANTON, KAREN L,** Piedmont Tech Coll, Greenwood, SC; GD; RRT; CRTT; Respiratory Therapy.

**STANTON, LEE E,** Livingston Univ, Livingston, AL; JR; BS; Sci And Math Clb Pres 89-; Stdnt Govt Assn Rep 90; Lvngstn Univ Hd Phtgrphr 89-; Delta Chi; Blgy; Eclgst.

**STANTON, MARCY A,** The Boston Conservatory, Boston, MA; FR; BFA; Dance; Nrsg Hme Asst; Dance.

**STANTON, MARY E,** Univ Of Ct, Storrs, CT; SR; DVM; Horse Prctcm; Pre-Vet Clb 89-; Horse Jdgng Tm; Zlpha Zeta VP 90-; Hgh Hopes 85-90; BS; Vet Med.

**STANTON, MYRA P,** Medical Univ Of Sc, Charleston, SC; JR; BS; Coll Actvs Brd; Stu Nrs Assoc Cmnty Hlth Comm Chrprsn 90-; Nrsg Flwshp Awrd Bon Secoursst Francis Hosp 90-; BS 89; Nrsg; Mdwf.

**STANTON, REBECCA L,** S U N Y Coll Of Tech At Alfred, Alfred, NY; FR; BA; Nrsng.

**STANTON, SCOTT T,** Univ Of Sc At Columbia, Columbia, SC; FR; BME; Mrchng Bnd 90-; Symphnc Bnd 90-; Presb Stdnt Ctr 90-; Phi Mu Alpha Sinfonia 90-; Msc Math Edctr.

**STANWOOD, WANDA F,** Alcorn St Univ, Lorman, MS; SR; BS; Prof Sec Intl Assist Treas; Dns Lst 87-; Cum Laude Hnrs; Sec Sci; Admin Sec.**

**STANZAK, LISA J,** Bethany Coll, Bethany, WV; JR; BA; Hd Rsdnt Assst; Res Asst 89-; TV 3 Bthcm 88-89; Coll Chr; Vc Lssns 88-; Alpha Psi Omega Pres 90-; Sigma Tau Epsilon Pres 90-; Alpha Beta Gamma; Delta Tau Delta Ll Sstr; Alha Xi Delta Phlnthrpy; Stdnts Offrng Spprt 90; Ed Pschlgy; Tchr.

**STANZIONE, DENISE R,** Bunker Hill Comm Coll, Boston, MA; SO; BA; Assoc Degree Liberal Arts BHCC 91; Hlth Field; Mdl Radiographer.

**STANZIONE, PAULA MARIE,** Seton Hall Univ, South Orange, NJ; SR; BS; Kappa Delta Pi 89-; Deans Lst 89-; Tchng Intern 90-; Acdmc Schlrshp 90; AA 89; Engl.

**STAPH, ROBERTA JEAN,** Comm Coll Algny Co Algny Cmps, Pittsburgh, PA; GD; BA; Pdlgy Clb 90-; Phi Theta Kappa 90-; Our Lady Grace Schl Vol Elem Schl Actvts 86-; Cub Sct Com Coord/Tiger Cubs/Rfrshmnt Chrprsn 89-; Sec/Advrtsng Agncy; AA Tchr Educ; Elem Ed Duquesne Univ.

**STAPLETON, BERNICE L,** City Univ Of Ny Baruch Coll, New York, NY; JR; BA; Admin Sec; Cmptr Sci.

**STAPLETON, DANIELLE L,** Emory & Henry Coll, Emory, VA; JR; BED; SVEA 90-; Emory Henry Schlr 90-; Pres Lst 89-90; Deans Lst 90-; Chick Fil A Schlrshp 89; Interdiscplnry English; Tch.

**STAPLETON, SHERRY L,** Radford Univ, Radford, VA; SR; BS; NSSLHA Chm Fund Rsng 89-; Plays & Shows Comm 90-; Intravarsity Chrstn 90-; Phi Sigma Pi 89-; Cmmnctn Disorders; Speech Lang Pthlgy.

**STAPLETON, TRACEY L,** Univ Of Rochester, Rochester, NY; JR; BA; Undergrad Cog Sci Cncl Pr 88-; Human Factors Soc 89-; Stdnt Un Pgm Brd 88-90; Deans Lst 88-; Meridian Soc Adm Vol; Adopt-A-Grandparent Pgm 88-; IM Vlybl/Ftbl 88-; Cog Sci/Psych; Human Factors Engr.

**STAPPAS, CHRISTOPHER G,** Emory Univ, Atlanta, GA; JR; BBA; Assn Collegiate Enterpreneurs Grad Liason; Order Of Omega; IM Spts; Phi Gamma Delta Pldg Edctr 89-; Bus/Fin Cncntrn.

**STAR, JODI E,** Univ Of Miami, Coral Gables, FL; SO; BS; Blgy Clb 90-; Alpha Lambda Delta; Hnr Stdnts Assn; Blgy; Med.

**STARCHER, JAMI D,** Wv Univ At Parkersburg, Parkersburg, WV.

**STARCHER, KEVIN D,** Wv Univ At Parkersburg, Parkersburg, WV; FR; Pres Schlr; Welding.

**STARCHER, SHERRI L,** Univ Of Akron, Akron, OH; SR; Hall Prgmmg Brd 86-88; IEEE 87-; Hl Hnry 88-; Pi Mu Epsln 88-; Alpha Lambda Delta 86-; Phi Eta Sigma 86-; Coop Educ Dpt Dfnse 89-; Pres Schlp 86-89; IM 86-90; BSEE; Elec Engr.

**STARCHOK, BRIGID M,** Mount Aloysius Jr Coll, Cresson, PA; FR; Occptnl Thrpy Clb 90-; Phi Theta Kappa 90-; Occptnl Thrpy Asst.

**STARCK, JOHN J,** Oh St Univ, Columbus, OH; SO; BS; Top Schlr 90; Natrl Rsrcs.

**STARK, BRIDGET M,** Mount Aloysius Jr Coll, Cresson, PA; SO; AA; Intrprtrs Clb Treas 89-; Nwslttr 90-; Intrprtr Trning; Intrprtng.

**STARK, DARRELL M,** Hudson Valley Comm Coll, Troy, NY; FR; AS; Schl/Bsnss Allnce Lbrty Prtnrshp Proj Cnsltnt 90; Bsnss; Ed.

**STARK, DEREK B,** Univ Of Al At Birmingham, Birmingham, AL; FR; BA; Crmnl Jstce; Law.

**STARK, JASON P,** Bapt Bible Coll & Seminary, Clarks Summit, PA; JR; BA; Class Pres; Bible; Missions.

**STARK, JEREMY D,** Northwest Tech Coll, Archbold, OH; FR; ASSOC; Deans Lst; Bus Mngmnt.

**STARK, MARIANNE E,** Middle Tn St Univ, Murfreesboro, TN; SO; BS; Spec Evnts Comm; Gamma Beta Phi; Kappa Delta Pi; MTSU Wrk Schlrshp 90-; Spec Educ; Tchr.

**STARK, NATHAN DANIEL W,** Central Al Comm Coll, Alexander City, AL; FR; Math; Cvl Engr.

**STARK, TIMOHTY B,** City Univ Of Ny Baruch Coll, New York, NY; JR; BBA; Amer Mktg Assn Pres; Goldn Key; Mayrs Off Oprtns-Dir Off 90-; Mktg; Vntr Cptlst.

**STARKER, CHRISTOPHER B,** Univ Of Sc At Columbia, Columbia, SC; FR; Math/Phys; Ed.

**STARKER, CHRISTOPHER B,** Univ Of Sc At Sumter, Sumter, SC; FR; Math/Phys; Ed.

**STARKEY, DAWN C,** Kent St Univ Kent Cmps, Kent, OH; BA; Psy Clb; Psi Chi; Gldn Key; Safer Futures; Nestle USA Schlp 88-; Psy; Cnslng Psy.

**STARKEY, KAREN L,** Wv Northern Comm Coll, Wheeling, WV; FR; AAS; Phi Theta Kappa; Dns Lst 90-; Phi Beta Lambda 90-; Sci/Math Awd 90; Acctng; Bkkpng.

**STARKEY, LAURA A,** James Madison University, Harrisonburg, VA; SR; BA; BSU Fd Coord 90-; Cl/91 Ring Cmte Sec 88-89; Early Chldhd Edctn; Tch.

**STARKS, LORETTA,** Alcorn St Univ, Lorman, MS; SO; BA; Bptst Chrch Sec 89-; FBLA 87; Jefferson Co Fd Serv Dept; AAS Utica Comm Clge 88; Pltcl Sci; Govt.

**STARKS, RAQUEL N,** Al St Univ, Montgomery, AL; FR; Busn Mgt; Administration.

**STARKS, TRACY M,** Alcorn St Univ, Lorman, MS; JR; BS; Ntl Hnr Scty; Ntl Hnr Rl; Smithland Mssnry Bptst Chrch; Cert Bkkppng Louisiana Bus Clg 89; Math Educ; Mathmtcn.**

**STARLING, CRYSTAL K,** Valdosta St Coll, Valdosta, GA; SO; BA; PAG; Sigma Alpha Chi 90-; Fresh Schlr 89-90; Erly Chldhd Educ; Tchr.

**STARLING, DARRICK K,** Univ Of Rochester, Rochester, NY; SR; BS; Soc Hispanic Prof Engrs V P 88-90; Spnsh/Latin Stdnt Assoc Publ Mgr 88-89; Undergrad Engr Cncl 89-90; Intl Lvng Ctr 88-90; Minority Stdnt Ambsdr Adm Vol 87-89; Tiernan Proj 87; Blue Light Escort 87-88; G Harold Hook Prize 89-90; Mech Engr; Mfg Supv Delco Prod.

**STARLING, DONNA M,** Univ Of Sc At Columbia, Columbia, SC; SO; BS; Alpha Kappa Alpha; Blgy; Med.

**STARLING, STEPHEN D,** Univ Of West Fl, Pensacola, FL; JR; BED; AA Comm Coll Air Force 90; Tech-Voc-Voc Tch Ed; Tchr.

**STARNES, CONNIE H,** Bristol Univ, Bristol, TN; GD; Paralegal Assn Upper East TN 88-90; Head Paralegal Herndon Coleman Brading & Mc Kee; AAS Bristol Univ 90; Paralegalism.

**STARNES, SUSAN K,** Lenoir Rhyne Coll, Hickory, NC; SR; BS; Mllrsvl Bptst Chrch 90; Bowman Gray Schl/Med Stdnt Med Tech 90-; Spnsh Frgn Lang 85-90; Amer Soc Clncl Path 90-; Med/Clncl Lab Tech/Sci 90; Med Tech; Medicine.

**STARNES, WAYNE SCOTT,** Univ Of Sc At Columbia, Columbia, SC; SR; BA; Std Dsgn 90; Gldn Key 90; Grphc Dsgn.

**STAROSCHUCK, SCOTT M,** Duquesne Univ, Pittsburgh, PA; JR; BA; Stu Accntng Assn 90-; Beta Alpha Phi 90-; Mellon Bank 90; Deloitte Touche; Accntng; Bus.

**STARR, ADREAL MICHELLE,** Al St Univ, Montgomery, AL; SO.

**STARR, ANDREW C,** Saint Marys Coll Of Md, St Marys Cy, MD; SR; BA; Psi Chi 90-; Dns Lst 89-; Cert Advncd Stdy Frnch; Psychlgy; Indstrl Psychlgy.**

**STARR, BARBARA J,** Wilmington Coll, New Castle, DE; SR; BSN; Amer Hrt Assoc BCLS Instr 88; NAACOG; Prnt Erly Ed Ctr Advsry Brd 90; YMCA Instr Vol 90; Beebe Schl Of Nrsng 76; Nrsng; Nrsng Grad Level.

**STARR, KARLA B,** Oh Univ, Athens, OH; FR; BFA; 1st Pl Stdnt Art Show; Art Educ; Educ H S Tchr.

**STARR, TIMOTHY J,** Castleton St Coll, Castleton, VT; SO; BS; Acctg; CPA.

**STARRETT, ROBERT C,** West Chester Univ, West Chester, PA; SR; BS; Assost Cndctr Wind Ensemble 89-90; Music Educ; Music Tchr.

**STARY, KRISTEN A,** Univ Of Akron, Akron, OH; JR; BS; ASCHE 88-; Ambssdrs; Phi Eta Sigma 87-; Alpha Lambda Delta 87-; Mrtr Brd; Delta Gamma 88-; Acdmc Schlrshp 87-89; Rho Lambda Schlrshp 89; Eng Coop 89-; IM 87-; Chmcl Eng; Eng.

**STAS, DONALD D,** Drexel Univ, Philadelphia, PA; FR; BS; Wrstlng 90-; Commerce/Eng; Bus/Eng.

**STASI, ANNMARIE,** Oh Univ, Athens, OH; SO; BA; Flyng Bobcats Capt; Alpha Eta Rho 89-; Big Bro/Big Sis; Airway Sci; Airln Polit-Engr.

**STASIK, MARK CARL,** Univ Of Pittsburgh, Pittsburgh, PA; SO; BS; Phi Eta Sigma 90-; Deans Lst 89-; Edward J Slack Endwd Schlrshp 90; Mat Sci Eng.

**STASIOWSKI, STACY L,** Comm Coll Algny Co Algny Cmps, Pittsburgh, PA; SO; Dns Lst; Nrsg.

**STASKEY, JERI L,** Wv Northern Comm Coll, Wheeling, WV; SO; AAS; Bakesale Clb 89-; ASMT; Phi Theta Kappa 90; Acad Achvmnt Awd 90; Allied Hlth; Med Lab Tech.

**STASSEN, ROBYN E,** Oh St Univ At Newark, Newark, OH; FR; BS; Lckng Hosp Vol; Phi Eta Sigma; Alpha Lambda Delta; Acad Exclnc Awd 90-; Biochem; Med.

**STASZ, STACIE A,** Kent St Univ Kent Cmps, Kent, OH; SR; BA; Amer Mktg Assn 90-; Camp Bus Clb 89-; Bus; Mktg/Bus Mgmt.

**STATES, MARK D,** Longwood Coll, Farmville, VA; JR; BS; Soc Physcs Stdnts Tres 90-; Alpha Chi Rho Tres 90-; IM Athletcis; Physcs/Pre Engr.

**STATES, SUSAN L,** Elmira Coll, Elmira, NY; FR; BS; Phi Eta Sigma 90-; Vol Wrk Vctms Asstnce Prog Spcl Ed Aide 90-; Psychlgy; Clncl Psychlgst.

**STATON, DEIRDRE A,** Va Commonwealth Univ, Richmond, VA; JR; BSW; Goldn Key; Richmnd AIDS Mnstry 90-; Chrtr Westbrk Hosp 90-; Soc Wrk; Mntl Hlth.

**STATON, PHAEDRA N,** Va St Univ, Petersburg, VA; JR; BS; Pblc Admn Clb 88-89; Stdnt Rsdnc Assoc Sec 89-90; Urbn Stds; Lwyr.

**STATTS, KIMBERLY D,** Savannah Coll Of Art & Design, Savannah, GA; MBA; PTO Sec 87; Prnt Advsry Bd/Bd Of Dir 89; Fine Arts Advsry Bd Chrprsn 88; Bd Of Dir/Presby Wmn Mbr 89-90; Grdn Clb Pres 89; Tchr/Elem Educ 70-72; Admin Ast/Emory Univ Hosp 72-74; BA GA State Univ 70; Illustration/Educ; Tchr.

**STATUCKI, LYNN M,** Niagara Univ, Niagara Univ, NY; GD; Ctzn Actn Pgm 86-88; Jr Wknd Comm 88-89; Orient Ldr 88; Natl Pltcl Sci Hnr Soc Pres 87; Dns Lst 87-90; Cert Merit Grdtn Cum Laude 90; IM Sftbl 90; Pltcl Sci; Law.

**STATUM, CONNIE G,** Middle Tn St Univ, Murfreesboro, TN; SR; BS; Sales Clerk; Spec Educ/Elem Ed; Teacher.

**STAUB, MICHAEL H,** Comm Coll Algny Co Algny Cmps, Pittsburgh, PA; GD; AS; BS Duquesne Univ 74; Computer Science.

**STAUD, DAWN L,** Northern Ky Univ, Highland Hts, KY; FR; BA; Bus; Mgmnt.

**STAUDIGEL, MARK W,** Northern Ky Univ, Highland Hts, KY; SR; BS; Hon Rl 4 Semesters; Indust Tech.

**STAUFFER, BRAD R,** Wagner Coll, Staten Island, NY; SO; BS; Winter Gd Intrntl 89-; Dns Lst 90-; Arts Admin; Theme Pk Mngmnt.

**STAUFFER, REBECCA A,** Indiana Univ Of Pa, Indiana, PA; JR; BA; Kappa Delta Pi; Psi Beta 89-; Hbtt Hmnty 90-; Prvst Schlr; Educ; Elem Educ.

**STAUFFER, SCOTT P,** Oh Univ, Athens, OH; FR; BS; Condor Aero Clb 88-; Phi Gamma Delta; Airway Sci; Aviatn.

**STAUFFER, SHERRY L,** Kent St Univ Kent Cmps, Kent, OH; SO; BBA; Bsn; Acctng/Cmptr Sci.

**STAUNCHES, KATHLEEN A,** Schenectady County Comm Coll, Schenectady, NY; SO; AS; Girl Scouts Of Niskayuna Dir 75-89; Travel/Tourism; Travel World.

**STAUNTON, JAMES F,** Merrimack Coll, North Andover, MA; JR; BS; ASCE 90-; Ftbll Clb 86-; Coop Ed Prgm 87-; IM Bsktbll; Cvl Eng.

**STAVRELLIS, LISA,** Georgian Court Coll, Lakewood, NJ; FR; BS; Blgy.

**STAVROPOULOS, PETER,** Oh Coll Of Podiatric Med, Cleveland, OH; SO; DPM; Class Pres 89-90; Pres Hockey Club 90; OCPM Srgry Club 90-; Ontario Soc Chiropodists V P 86-87; Ontario Gvrng Bd Rgnts Pdtry/Chrpdy 87-89; Dns Gold Medal Overall Acad Excel 83-84; Lux/Zwingenberger Award 83-84; Podiatric Med; Surgery.

**STAVROS, GEORGE S,** Hellenic Coll/Holy Cross, Brookline, MA; GD; MDIV; BS Purdue Univ 85; MS St Thomas Univ 86; Theology; Phd Stud Pastoral Psychology.

**STAVROS, SARA E,** Oh Univ-Southern Cmps, Ironton, OH; SR; BA; Goldn Key; Child Pschy.

**STAWARZ, KAREN A,** D Youville Coll, Buffalo, NY; SR; BA; DYCAA Pres; Bus Clb Sec 89; Eaton Deabold Awd Bryant/Stratton 89; Outstndng Stdnt Awd Bryant/Stratton 89; John T Kennedy Meml Awd 90; Kid Stuff Chrprsn 88; Rstrnt Mgt 73-85; AAS Bryant/Stratton 89; Acctg.

**STAYTON, CYNTHIA D,** Univ Of Cincinnati, Cincinnati, OH; SR; BS; Prfssnl Entrtnr 87-; Ntrtn; Ntrtn Educ And Srvcs.

**STEAD, BENET F,** Commonwealth Coll, Virginia Beach, VA; SO; AS; Med Clb Sec 90-; Stdnt Cncl 90-; Dsrt Strm Spprt Grp 91-; Med Sci; Med Asstnt.

**STEAD, MATTHEW A,** Ohio Valley Coll, Parkersburg, WV; JR; BA; Tmthy Clb 90-; Chi Pres 90; Bnk Tllr 89-; BS West Virginia Univ 90; Bible; Hghr Educ.

**STEAD, MICHAEL P,** Columbia Greene Comm Coll, Hudson, NY; FR; AS; Stdnt Snte Pres 90-; Ski Clb 90; Phi Theta Kappa; Vol Amer Rd Crss 90-; Bus; Invstmnt Bnkng Fnnce.

**STEAD, ROBERT E,** Bloomfield Coll, Bloomfield, NJ; Cert.

**STEAD, TRACI L,** Wv Univ At Parkersburg, Parkersburg, WV; JR; BA; Elem Educ; Tchng.

**STEADMAN JR, RONALD L,** Tn Temple Univ, Chattanooga, TN; SO; BS; Cai Sigma Delta Rep 90-; IM Bsktbl/Ftbl/Sftbl; Math; Eng/Educ.

**STEAGALD, SHANNON M,** Middle Tn St Univ, Murfreesboro, TN; SO; Nrsng.

**STEALEY, LORI A,** Wv Univ At Parkersburg, Parkersburg, WV; FR; BS; Trnty Chrch God 89-; St Josephs Hosp 82-; Cmptr Sci; Info Sys Anlyst.

**STEARN, DANIEL D,** Univ Of Miami, Coral Gables, FL; SO; Beta Beta Beta 90-; Rho Rho Rho 90-; IM Soccer 90-; Marine Science/Biology; Research.**

**STEARNS, ANGELA M,** S U N Y Coll At Fredonia, Fredonia, NY; JR; BA; Pblc Rltns Cert 87; Sls Cnsltnt 87-90; BA State Univ Buffalo 87; Ed; Elem Tchr.

**STEARNS, GRETA M,** Va Commonwealth Univ, Richmond, VA; SR; BA; Gallery Assist Curator Intern 88; Hnrs Schlrshp Guilford Clg 85-88; Munich Semester Guilford Clb 86; Art Hist; Lndscp Arch.

**STEARNS, JEFFREY T,** Samford Univ, Birmingham, AL; JR; MS; FL Stdnt Bar 89-90; Phi Delta Phi 89-; Grad Asst NE LA Univ; Pres Schlrshp Univ AL; BS Univ AL 87; Law.

**STEARNS, MARIDA A,** O'more School Of Design, Franklin, TN; GD; ASID Sec 90-; BID.

**STEARNS, MICHAEL S,** Auburn Univ At Auburn, Auburn, AL; FR; SGA 90-; Clg Repblcns 90-; Hall Cncl; Lambda Sigma; Phi Eta Sigma; Alpha Lambda Delta; Oper Tiger Storm PR; Deans List 90-; Men Of Auburn Calendar; Pre Law/Psychlgy; Law.

**STEARNS, PENNY J,** Clark State Comm Coll, Springfield, OH; FR; ASA; Piagets Proteges ECED Clb; Hndbell Grp; Ed; Erly Chldhd Ed.

**STEARNS, WARREN L,** S U N Y Coll Of A & T Morrisvl, Morrisville, NY; SO; BA; Phi Theta Kappa; Ed; Tchng.

**STEAVENS, ERIK H,** Middle Ga Coll, Cochran, GA; FR; BA; Boy Scouts Of Amer Asstnt Scoutmstr 85-; Profsnl Soc Of Engrs 89-; Deans List 90-; Civil Engrng; Envirnmntl Engrng.

**STEBBINGS, ERLEN A,** Albertus Magnus Coll, New Haven, CT; JR; BA; Chrl Clb; Nwspr Stf 90-; Cmps Mnstry 88-; Dns Lst 90; Blgy/Sclgy/Eng; Nrsg/Tchg.

**STEBBINS, BONNIE G,** Univ Of South Al, Mobile, AL; SR; BS; Sierra Clb Stdnt Gvmt 90-; Vol Spcl Olympics; Stdnt Bptst Ctr 89-; Schlrshp Univ So AL Acdmc Achvmnts; 20 Century Coll 86; Edctn; Tchng.

**STEBBINS, CHRISTINA L,** Bay Path Coll, Longmeadow, MA; SO; BS; Phi Beta Lambda 90-; Yrbk Comm 90-; Maroon Key 90-; Vlybl 90-; Bus Admin; Own My Own Business.

**STEBBINS, JULIA S,** Univ Of South Al, Mobile, AL; SR; BS; Sierra Clb Stdnt Govt 90-; Spec Olympcs Vol 90-; Stdnt Bapt Ctr 87-90; Sec 20th Century Clg 86; Educ; Tchr.

**STEBE, JULIA M,** City Univ Of Ny City Coll, New York, NY; SR; BA; Frnch Clb Assc Pres 81-85; Rssn Clb 86-88; Econ Soc 89-; Gldn Ky 89-; Thesbeen Soc 79-; Tau Epsilon Phi 84-86; DCPA Dnc Co 81-83; Acctnt Prec Mtls 87-; Psych; CPA.

**STECHER, MARIBETH T,** Univ Of Nh Plymouth St Coll, Plymouth, NH; SR; BS; Frgn Lang Soc Sec 88; Phi Sigma Iota; Photo Franklin Inst 80; Spanish Educ; Teach In HS.

**STECKEL, SHARI ELISE,** Dowling Coll, Oakdale Li, NY; SR; BA; NSSLHA 90-; Deans Lst; Trustee Achvmnt Awrd; Adelphi Univ 90-; Acdmc Awrd Schlrshp 88-; Cmnctv Dsordrs; Spch Educ.

**STECKLY, CHRISTINA M,** Jersey City St Coll, Jersey City, NJ; JR; BSN; Nrsg.

**STEED, CAROL E,** Memphis St Univ, Memphis, TN; SR; BA; Univ Prgms Assoc 81-82; Amrcn Home Econ Assoc 83-84; Kappa Omicron Phi 84-85; Pi Kappa Phi 82; Rtl 84-89; BS Univ TN Chattanooga 85; Art Hstry; Crtrl Tchr.

**STEED, CHAD L,** Coll Of Charleston, Charleston, SC; FR; BA; Hon Bd 90-; Swmmg Tm 90-; Bus; Law.

**STEEDLE, MARY A,** Comm Coll Algny Co Algny Cmps, Pittsburgh, PA; JR; AS; Sensor Lab Tech 81-; Pdlgy/Chld Dvlpmnt; Chld Dvlpmt Cntr.

**STEELE, ANDREW L,** Univ Of Miami, Coral Gables, FL; JR; BBA; Hon Stdnt Assoc 88-; Tau Beta Pi 90-; Alpha Pi Mu 90-; Lambda Chi Alpha 89-; Habitat Hmnty 90-; Alumni Mntr Prog; Intl Fin/Mrktng; Corp Fin.

**STEELE, CHARLES S,** Wv Univ, Morgantown, WV; FR; BA; Wildlife Wghtlftng 88-; Rep Soph Cls 88; Jr High Hnr 87; Hgh Schl Hnr 88-; Help Rotary Clb Crnvl 87-; Mu Alpha Theta 90-; Bsktbll/Ftbll/Trck/Wghtlftng 87-; Bsn.

**STEELE III, DAVID F,** Johnson C Smith Univ, Charlotte, NC; SR; BA; Spiritual Choir 89-; SCA; Jazz Band 86-; Omega Psi Phi Pres 89; Tennis Tm 88; Tele Cmnctns.

**STEELE, DONNA J,** Roane St Comm Coll, Harriman, TN; SO; BA; Cmpfr Inc Adlt Mbr 90-; AS 85; Psy.

**STEELE, GARY L,** Kent St Univ Kent Cmps, Kent, OH; JR; BBA; Hnrs Clg 88-; Golden Key; Dns Lst 89-; Pres Lst 90; IM Flg Ftbl Co-Capt 90; Finance; Fncl Plnr CFP.

**STEELE, GREGORY W,** Mount Aloysius Jr Coll, Cresson, PA; JR; BED; Phi Theta Kappa 89-90; Provosts Schlr Indiana Univ PA 90-; AS 90; Elem Ed; Elem Tchr.

**STEELE, JEANEANE D,** Ms Univ For Women, Columbus, MS; SR; BS; Sigma Theta Tau; Nrsng.

**STEELE, JILL P,** Univ Of Md At Eastern Shore, Princess Anne, MD; SO; Hon Prog 89-; Sociology; Law.

**STEELE, KATHERINE A,** Marshall University, Huntington, WV; FR; Hons Prog 90-.

**STEELE, LATANGA DEVELLA,** Roane St Comm Coll, Harriman, TN; SO; Certif Pillissippi State Tech Clg 90; Ofc Adm; Word Proc.

**STEELE, LATONDRA A,** Fl A & M Univ, Tallahassee, FL; FR; BA; Broadcast Jrnlsm.

**STEELE, MANIFA S,** Fl A & M Univ, Tallahassee, FL; JR; MBA; Phi Eta Sigma 89-; Arthr Andrsn Cmpny Intrnshp; Dscvr Crd Srvds Intrn 90; Acctg.

**STEELE, RHONDA L,** Truett Mc Connell Coll, Cleveland, GA; FR; BBA; Pres Clb; Bus; Acctng CPA.

**STEELE, SHARON K,** Univ Of Sc At Sumter, Sumter, SC; JR; BA; Stdnt Ed Assn Pblcty Chr 90-; BA Winthrop Coll 84; Elem Ed; Pblc Ed.

**STEELY, ELIZABETH S,** Middle Tn St Univ, Murfreesboro, TN; JR; Chem Asst 88-; Tutor 88-89; Ambassador 88-90; Wrk Schlrshp 88-; Pres Schlrshp 88; Schlstc All-Amer 90; IM Bsktbl 88-89; Elem Ed.

**STEELY, JEFFERY G,** Cumberland Coll, Williamsburg, KY; SR; Phi Alpha Theta 89-; BS; Hstry/Pltcl Sci.

**STEEMAN, KATHERYN M,** Radford Univ, Radford, VA; JR; BA; Natl Ed Assoc 90-; AA Wytheville Comm Clg 90; Erly Ed; Tch.

**STEEN, CAROL R,** Univ Of Southern Ms, Hattiesburg, MS; SR; BS; AASO; Metro Boy/Girls Clb; Lib Arts/Pol Sci; Law.

**STEEN, ROBYNN E,** Fl St Univ, Tallahassee, FL; SR; BS; Mrtr Brd 89-90; Gldn Key 88-; Intrnshp London; Ed; Pblc Srvc.

**STEENKEN, JANE M,** Northern Ky Univ, Highland Hts, KY; SR; Tutor Lrng Asst Ctr 89-90; Sigma Tau Delta 89-90; Cmps Rec Aerobic Ftns Prog 86-90; BA 90; Engl; Pblc Rltns/Law Schl.

**STEENSTRA, TIMOTHY,** Va Commonwealth Univ, Richmond, VA; SO; BFA; Graphic Art.

**STEERE, DEREK L,** Univ Of Cincinnati, Cincinnati, OH; SO; BS; ASME 90-; Tutor 90-; Cincnt Assc Blnd; USN 82-86; Eng/Math.

**STEEVER, CARLA L,** Christopher Newport Coll, Newport News, VA; JR; BA; Styron Schlrshp 89-90; Hstry; Educ.

**STEFAN, CHARLENE D,** Columbia Union Coll, Takoma Park, MD; JR; AA; Phi Eta Sigma; Cum Laude; AA; Acctg; CPA.

**STEFAN, DAVID R,** Asbury Theological Sem, Wilmore, KY; GD; MAMSW; World Otrch Nwsltr Edtr 89-90; Soccer Tm 89-; BA Miami U 88; Psychology; Cnslr.

**STEFAN, MICHAEL J,** Hilbert Coll, Hamburg, NY; SO; AA; Dairy Frmr; Educ; BA Jr Hgh Scl Stds.

**STEFANIC, NANETTE L,** Kent St Univ Geauga Cmps, Burton Twp, OH; FR; BED; Elem Educ.

**STEFANINI, MELISSA A,** Saint Francis Coll, Loretto, PA; JR; BS; Orchestra 87-88; Elem Educ; Tch.

**STEFANKIEWICZ, TABITHA A,** Wagner Coll, Staten Island, NY; SO; BA; Psych Clb 90-; Spec Olympcs 90-; Deans Lst 88-; Spnsh.

**STEFANO, VINCENT,** Embry Riddle Aeronautical Univ, Daytona Beach, FL; JR; BS; Stdnt Gvrnmnt Assn Prsdnt; Nvl Aviation Clb Prsdnt; Entrtnmnt Comm; Stdnt Ldrshp Dvlpmnt Prgrm Grad; Sftbl; S Hackensack Vlntr Amblnc Corps 87-89; Certf Prvt Pilot 89; Instrmnt Rtng; Arntcl Sci; Aviation.

**STEFANOVIC, NENAD B,** S U N Y At Buffalo, Buffalo, NY; GD; DDS; Dntl Med; Maxillo-Fcl Srgry.

**STEFANSKI, SANDRA M,** Wagner Coll, Staten Island, NY; SO; BS; Nrsng; Nrsng Instrctr.

**STEFANSSON, STEFAN TH,** Methodist Coll, Fayetteville, NC; FR; BS; Athltc Comm 88-89; Sccr; Mtrcltn Exam Cmmrcl Coll Iceland 89; Intrntnl Rltns; Bsns Frgn Affrs.

**STEFANY, KRISTIN L,** Fl St Univ, Tallahassee, FL; JR; Kappa Alpha Theta 88-; Intrnshp Spr Bwl XXV Tsk Frce 90-; Sprts Mrktng Cmmnctns.

**STEFANYAK, LISA J,** Duquesne Univ, Pittsburgh, PA; SR; BSBA; Commuter Cncl 87-88; Stdnts Acctg Assoc 88-90; Dns Lst 90-; Blue Cross Western Penn Acctg Intern 90-; ACCLAIM Proj Tm; Acctg; Law Sch.

**STEFFAN, NANCY M,** Coll Misericordia, Dallas, PA; JR; Campus Mnstry; SNAP; Peer Cnslr; Tutor Guyana Exp; Strategic Plng Com Instress; Lit Mag; Sigma Theta Tau; Campus Mnstry; Nrsng.

**STEFFAN, NORA M,** Le Moyne Coll, Syracuse, NY; JR; BS; Beta Beta Beta Pres; Dns Lst 88-; Integral Hnrs Pgm 88-; Tutor 88-; Bio Clb 88-; Intl Hse Secr 90-; Admissions Tour Guide 88-; Genencor Intl Intern 90; Bristol Myers-Squibb Intern; Barry M Goldwater Schlrshp 90; Bio/Chem; Biotech/Genetic Engr.

**STEFFENSEN, STEVEN H,** Oh Dominican Coll, Columbus, OH; SO; BA; Accnt Rep Eutech; Bsnss Admin.

**STEFFEY, BETH A,** Westminster Coll, New Wilmingtn, PA; SR; BA; Stdnt Alumni Assn; Tchng Assist Foreign Lang Dept; Pi Delta Phi; Omicron Delta Kappa; Sigma Kappa 90-; VISA Serv Tm; Intl Politics; Fed Govt.

**STEFFY, CHRISTINA J,** Ursinus Coll, Collegeville, PA; SR; BA; Meistersinger/Chmbr Singers 87-; PA State Collgt Choir 90; Clg Choir 87-; Pi Hu Epsilon; Sigma Tau Delta; Elizabeth Mc Kain Award 89; Engl; Tch Clg Lvl.

**STEFL, JANEEN M,** S U N Y Coll At Fredonia, Fredonia, NY; SO; BS; Music Thrpy Clb Treas; Music Thrpy/Music.

**STEGALL, DONALD K,** Itawamba Comm Coll, Fulton, MS; SO; MBA; Cert Nashville Auto Diesel Clg 88; Bus; Bus Admn.

**STEGALL, RENEE C,** Univ Of Nc At Charlotte, Charlotte, NC; SR; BA; Engl; Wrtg.

**STEGEMILLER, LAURIE L,** Ky Christian Coll, Grayson, KY; SR; BA; Stdnt Cncl VP 81-82; Tchr Ed Stdnt Assn Chpln; Chrldr 79-81; Chrch S 88-90; Pre-Schl Aide/Pre-Schl Tchr 86-88; BA Johnson Bible Coll 83; Ed; Tchr.

**STEGER, SHANNON M,** Univ Of Nc At Charlotte, Charlotte, NC; JR; BS; Epscpl Chrch 89-; Gldn Key; Biology; Medicine.

**STEHLEY, NANCY A,** Mount Aloysius Jr Coll, Cresson, PA; SO; AS; Occ Ther Clb; Awd Excell; Occ Ther Asst.

**STEHLIK, LIATE,** Oh Wesleyan Univ, Delaware, OH; SR; Panhllnc Cncl VP; Wmns Task Frce; Phi Beta Kappa; Phi Eta Sigma; Phi; Ord Of Omega; Delta Gamma VP; Vars Tnns 88-89; BA; Engl/Wmns Stdies.

**STEIDEL, SIGFRIDO,** Univ Of Pr At Rio Piedras, Rio Piedras, PR; JR; BA; Suicide Prvntn Brd 89-; Cltrl Cntr 87-; Pol Sci Stu Assn 89-90; Hnrs Stu Prog 89-; Gldn Ky; Natl Hispanic Schlrshp 88-90; Pol Sci; Law.

**STEIGER, DEBORAH GENE,** Spalding Univ, Louisville, KY; JR; BS; Natl Schlstc Hon Soc; Delta Epsilon Sigma; Spcl Olympics Event Coord; Data Trnsmsn Spclst 85-; AD Jefferson Comm Coll 89; Bus Admin; Employee Asstnce.

**STEIGER, JAMES A,** Saint John Fisher Coll, Rochester, NY; JR; BS; Phi Theta Kappa 90-; AAS Monroe Comm Coll 90; Fin/Bus; Anlyst.

**STEIGER, MATTHEW,** Univ Of Bridgeport, Bridgeport, CT; SR; BS; Clg Of Bus/Publc Mgt Sen 88-89; Stdnt Cncl Sentr Of CBPM 88-89; Stdnt Nwspaper Edtr 90-; Knight Sof The Rnd Tbl 88-; Intrntl Bus; Multintl Corp.**

**STEIGLEDER, LINDA A,** Broward Comm Coll, Ft Lauderdale, FL; SO; Asst Ofc Mgr 83-88; Ed; Tchng.

**STEIMAN, DORI E,** Ny Univ, New York, NY; FR; BFA; Actg/Sec Ed; Actor/Tchr.

**STEIMER, CHRISTINE B,** Embry Riddle Aeronautical Univ, Daytona Beach, FL; SR; BS; Stdnt Govt Assc Stdnt Fin Brd 88-; Orntn Tm Ldr 88-; Omicron Delta Kappa 90-; Mtrlgy Lab Stdnt Asst 89-; Chld Abse Vol 88-89; CARAL Vol 88-89; Univ Sxl Hrssmnt Comm Stdnt Rep 89-; Bicycle Clb 87-88; Tnns Tm 87-88; Arntcl Sci/Flght Sfty; Cmmrcl Airln Pilot.**

**STEIN, ABBY,** City Univ Of Ny Grad School, New York, NY; SR; BA; Psi Chi 87-; Lambda Alpha Epsilon; Bellevue Hosp Clncl Assmnt Trtmnt Vlnt Chldrn 90-; Frncs Psychlgy; Rsrch Nrpsychlgy Aggrssn.

**STEIN, BRUCE W,** Old Dominion Univ, Norfolk, VA; SR; BS; Mens Fllwshp V P/Deacon Abundant Life Tabernacle 85-; Electronics Tech 83-; Elect Eng Tech; Eng/Sys Analysts.

**STEIN, HARRIET S,** Comm Coll Algny Co Algny Cmps, Pittsburgh, PA; FR; BA; Deans List; Rtl Music; Rtl Clothing; Sls/Mktg; Video; Occuptnl Thrpy; Medcl.

**STEIN, IVY C,** Univ Of Rochester, Rochester, NY; SR; PH D; C Drew Pre Med Scty 89; Psi Chi; Cum Laude; BA; Psych Sclgy; Clncl Psych.

**STEIN, JEFFREY L,** Kent St Univ Kent Cmps, Kent, OH; GD; MBA; Fin Assoc 89-90; IM 86-90; Golden Key 89-90; Beta Gamma Sigma 89-90; BBA; Corp Fin.**

**STEIN, JOY B,** Univ Of Al At Birmingham, Birmingham, AL; SR; BA; Ambssdr Scl Chrmn 88-89; Debate Tm 88-89; Lctre Serv Cmmttee 90; Hnrs Prog 88; Omicron Delta Kappa Fstvl Of Trees Chrmn 89; Golden Key 89; Delta Gamma VP Schlrshp 90; Vol Bread/Roses Womens Shltr 89-90; GM Sprt Awd 88-89; Intrntl Studies; Law/Pblc Serv.

**STEIN, MARJORIE I,** Emory Univ, Atlanta, GA; JR; BBA; Delta Phi Epsilon Treas 90-; IM Ftbl/Hockey/Soccer Tm Capt 88-; Bus; Law.

**STEIN, RONALD D,** Liberty Univ, Lynchburg, VA; FR; BS; Shphrds Clb 90-; Alpha Lambda Delta 90-; Eng 77-90; Bbl Mnstry.

**STEIN-MARTIN, CLAUDIA L,** Fl Atlantic Univ, Boca Raton, FL; JR; BA; Phi Kappa Phi; Phi Theta Kappa 90; Otstdng Acad Achvmnt 89; Acad Excellnc Palm Bch Comm Clg 89; Dns Lst 87-; AA Miami Dade Comm Clg 90; Acctg.

**STEINBACH, RUSSELL P,** Anne Arundel Comm Coll, Arnold, MD; FR; AA; Syst Engrg Techlgy; Engrg.

**STEINBAUGH, DARLEEN J,** Comm Coll Algny Co Algny Cmps, Pittsburgh, PA; SO; ASSOC; Amer Water Ski Assoc 74-; Sandy Lake Water Ski Club 74-; Allied Health Field; Occupational Therapy.

**STEINBERG, ERIC L,** Fl International Univ, Miami, FL; SR; Invstgtns/Sprvsry Metro-Dade Cnty; Cert-Envrnmntl Studies; Admin Envrnmntl Studies; Trnsprtn Envrnmntl.

**STEINBERG, ERICA F,** Univ Of Miami, Coral Gables, FL; JR; BS; Stdnt Govt Comm Sen 89-90; Delta Phi Epsilon Pres; Intrn WPLG Ch 10 Miami 90-; Intrnshp Brockton Continental Cablevision News Dept 89-90; Rsrch Asst Psych; Brdcst Jrnlsm/Psych; T V.

**STEINBERG, JOHN S,** Central Fl Comm Coll, Ocala, FL; SO; DPM; Boy Scouts; Math/Sci Clb; Phi Theta Kappa 90-; AA; Med; Podiatry.

**STEINBERG, LARRY,** Kent St Univ Kent Cmps, Kent, OH; SR; BS; Var Ftbl 86-90; Pi Mu Epsilon 90-; Ftbl Schlrshp 86-; Math; Eng.

**STEINBOCK, SIGAL,** City Univ Of Ny Baruch Coll, New York, NY; SR; BBA; Golden Key 90; Beta Sigma 90; Bus/Mktg; Law.

**STEINER, CAROL A,** Comm Coll Algny Co Algny Cmps, Pittsburgh, PA; SO; Pre Hlth; Phy Thrpy.

**STEINER, CHARLES J,** Roane St Comm Coll, Harriman, TN; SO; BA; Psych; Yth Mnstr.

**STEINER, DEBORAH A,** Univ Of Akron, Akron, OH; SR; BS; ACES 90-; Phi Theta Kappa 77-; Brwnie Trp Ldr 88-; Cb Sct Den Ldr 87-90; Ownr Clsrm Crtns Fabrc Shp 83-; AD Akron Univ Wayne Clg 78; Elem Educ; Conc Math/Rdng.

**STEINER, LISA M,** Bridgewater Coll, Bridgewater, VA; SR; BA; Cncrt Bnd Pres 89-90; Stdnt VA Educ Assn Pres 90-; Cncrt Choir; Lambda Hon Soc; Elem Ed; Tchng.

**STEINER, ROBERT E,** Franklin And Marshall Coll, Lancaster, PA; JR; BA; ACS 90-; Porter Scientific 90-; Clg Repubs 90-; Dns Lst 90; Hnrs Lst; CRC Frshmn Chem Awd 90; Vlybl 90-; Chem; Indstrl Chem.

**STEINERT, DELORES G,** Christopher Newport Coll, Newport News, VA; JR; BS; Acctng.

**STEINERT, PETER N,** Hudson Valley Comm Coll, Troy, NY; SO; AA; German Clb Pr; Deans Lst 90-; Deans Lst 90-; Humanities.

**STEINHAUER, TERESA D,** Middle Tn St Univ, Murfreesboro, TN; FR; BS; ACM Assoc For Computational Machinery 90-; Math Actuarial/Stats Clb 90-; Gamma Beta Phi; Charles F Lewis Frshmn Math Awrd; Work Schlrshp 90-; Math; Actuary/Insurance.

**STEININGER, KATHERINE E,** Salisbury St Univ, Salisbury, MD; SR; BA; Psi Chi; Phi Alpha Theta; Pi Gamma Mu; Kappa Psi Kappa; Psychlgy/Hist; PhD In Psychlgy.**

**STEINKE, TRACY B,** Univ Of Cincinnati, Cincinnati, OH; JR; BA; Golden Key 90-; Kappa Delta Pi 89-; Alpha Lambda Delta 88; Respite Care Prgrm 89-; Spcl Edctn MH; Occptnl Rcrtnl Thrpy.

**STEINLY, DOUGLAS A,** Kent St Univ Kent Cmps, Kent, OH; SR; BBA; Gldn Key 90-; Acdmc All Amer 90-; Deans Lst 87-; Acdmc Cptn Gymnstcs 90-; Vrsty Gymnstcs 87-; Mrktngf Bus Mgt.

**STEINLY, RAE ANN,** Coll Of William & Mary, Williamsburg, VA; FR; BBA; Cathlc Stdnt Assoc 90-; Stdnts Assoc 90-; Recyclng Clb 90-; Bsns/Intl Stdies; Intl Fin.

**STEINMETZ, DAVID R,** Carnegie Mellon Univ, Pittsburgh, PA; SR; BS; Infrmtn Systms; Systms Analyst.

**STEINMETZ, DAWN V,** Bethany Coll, Bethany, WV; JR; BA; Art Clb 88-89; Yr Bk Artst 89-91; Gamma Sigma Kappa; Kappa Delta VP PR 89-; Renner Schlr 88-; Grphc Dsgn; Intrntnl Advrtsng.

**STEINMETZ, KAREN L,** Univ Of Tn At Martin, Martin, TN; FR; PHARM; Intrfth Cntr 90-; Prcssn Ensmble 90-; Hnrs Smnr Scty Clb 90-; Ldrs In Rsdnce 90-; Hnrs Smnr Wrkshp 90-; Pre Phrmcy; Phrmcsts.

**STEITIEH, EMAD N,** Al A & M Univ, Normal, AL; JR; BS; Elec Eng Tech.

**STEITLER, KELLY L,** Owensboro Comm Coll, Owensboro, KY; SO; BED; KY Educ Assn 89-; Natl Educ Assn 87-; Phi Theta Kappa; Pres Acdmc Awrd 90; Panther Exprss 81-; Bus World 76-90; Educ/Math; Mddl Schl Tchr.

**STEJSKAL, MARCELA,** Newbury Coll, Brookline, MA; GD; Med Asstng.

**STELIGA, STEPHANIE A,** Atlantic Comm Coll, Mays Landing, NJ; JR; Clnry Stdnt Assn Clss Rep 89-; Top Vine Wine Clb Ed 90-; Prof Chef Assn VP 89-; Deans Lst 90-; Gudnc Cnslr Peer Mntr 90-; ACF; Ntl Rest Assn Snitatn Cert 90; Clnry Arts; Pstry Chef/Tch.

**STELL, FREDERICK M,** Clemson Univ, Clemson, SC; SO; BA; Deans Lst 90; Entmlgy; Rsrch.

**STELL, MICHAEL J,** Bapt Bible Coll & Seminary, Clarks Summit, PA; SR; BS; Bapt Ch Apprntshp 90; Cert Empire State Bapt Sem 89; Bible; Tch/Clergy MS.

**STELLA, ANTHONY J,** Temple Univ, Philadelphia, PA; FR; Coachd Tmpls Wmns Sccr Clb Tm 90; Penn St Vars Sccr; Arch.

**STELLA, MICHAEL C,** Allegheny Coll, Meadville, PA; SR; BA; Jazz Lab Pres 87-; Wnd Sym/Esmbl 87-; SG Parl 87-90; Alden Schlr 89-90; Orntn Advsr 89-90; Psych; Cnslng.

**STELLATO, CAROLYN R,** Southern Ct St Univ, New Haven, CT; SR; BS; Natl Stdnt Nrs Assoc 87-; Wrk PCT Pgm Hosp St Raphael 90; Nrsg.

**STELLHORN, CHRISTINA L,** Defiance Coll, Defiance, OH; KEYS Sec 84-85; Delta Zeta Sec 81-85; Lambda Chi Alpha 81-82; Cntr For Cmmnty Invlvmnt 83-85; Tllr At State Bnk/Trst Co 82; BA Bsnss Cncntrtn In Mrktng Miami U 85; Elem Ed; Tchr/Readng Spclst.

**STELLMACH, LE ANNE M,** Edinboro Univ Of Pa, Edinboro, PA; FR; BS; Sim Vlybl; Blgy; Anml Sci.

**STELLRECHT, JULIE L,** Columbus Coll Of Art & Design, Columbus, OH; SR; BFA; Stdnt Bibl Stdy Strng Comm Mbr 90-; Xenos Chrstn Flwshp; Pres Lst 87-; Highst Achvmnt 88; Wilbr Kegg Mem Schlrshp 89; Vasa Canzani Schlrshp 90; Illstrtn Fine Arts.

**STELTER, SUSAN L,** Radford Univ, Radford, VA; FR; Wmns Choir 90-; Fashion Soc 90-; Phi Sigma Pi; Fshn Merch/Design; Buyer/Fshn Illustr.

**STELZER, RENEE A,** Yeshiva Univ, New York, NY; SR; Natl Conf Synagogue Yth Regl Advsr 89-90; Dns Lst 88-; AA; BA; Jwsh Erly Chldhd Assn Essay Awd Wnr 89; Elem Educ; Educ Admin.

**STEMANN, ELIZABETH C,** Va Commonwealth Univ, Richmond, VA; SO; BS; Nrsng Clb 90-; Nrsng; RN.

**STEMPFER, BRENDA S,** Comm Coll Algny Co Algny Cmps, Pittsburgh, PA; FR; BS; Receptionist Secr/Adm Asst 82-; Bsn; Mgmt.

**STENDAHL, PATRICIA L,** Univ Of Sc At Columbia, Columbia, SC; FR; Edctn; Tchr Cnslr.

**STENDER, SHARMAN H,** Univ Of Pittsburgh, Pittsburgh, PA; GD; MSN; Sigma Theta Tau; Trneeshp; Nrsng Admin; Grntlgy.

**STENGEL, DEBORAH A,** Univ Of Nc At Chapel Hill, Chapel Hill, NC; FR; AB; Nwspapr Phtgrphr 90-; Flm Comm 90-; Flm Fstvl Orgnzr; IM Fncng Trnmnt; Radio/TV/MTN Pctrs.

**STENGER, CHRISTINE M,** Kent St Univ Stark Cmps, North Canton, OH; FR; Preschl/Elem Educ; Tchng Birth Grad 3.

**STENGER, HEIDI M,** West Liberty St Coll, West Liberty, WV; JR; BA; Cls Sec 90-; Chi Beta Phi 89-; Sigma Phi Alpha 90-; AS; Dntl Hygn.

**STENHOUSE, KATY,** Portland School Of Art, Portland, ME; SR; BFA; BA Skidmore Coll 83; Graphic Dsgn.

**STENNETT, CHARMAINE F,** City Univ Of Ny Baruch Coll, New York, NY; JR; BBA; Sigma Alpha; Acctg.

**STENSON, LIBERATORE,** Va St Univ, Petersburg, VA; JR; BS; Phi Beta Lambda 90-; DPMA 90-; Systms Anlysts Prgmmr Info Rsrc Center; ALOA Schlrshp 90-91; Bus Info Systms.

**STENZEL, DUANE P,** Clarkson Univ, Potsdam, NY; JR; BS; Std Govt Asc 88-90; Vets Clb VP 88-90; Cmptr Clb VP 88-90; Phi Theta Kappa Rep 88-90; Phi Theta Kappa VP 90; Hrrngs Clg Schlr 90-; Clrksn Unv Trsts Schlr 90-; Amer Mktg Asc 90-; Amer Soc Mltry Cmptrlrs 78-; AAS 90; Mgmt Info Sys; Mgmt.

**STEPANEK, DONNA L,** Western New England Coll, Springfield, MA; SO; BS; Cmmttee On Prog/Entrtnmnt Chrprsn 90; Stdnt Snte Rep 90; Sprng Cncrt Cmmttee 90; Alpha Lambda Delta 90; Hlpng Hnds Scty 90; Stdnt Ambssdr; Stdnt Assoc Rcgntn Awd; Math Sci; Octuarial.

**STEPHAN, MARK A,** Fl International Univ, Miami, FL; SR; Amer Mktg Assoc; City Hamburg Support 90-; Univ Hamburg Dipl 90; Mktg; Advrtsg.

**STEPHEN, GARY R,** Univ Of Fl, Gainesville, FL; FR; IM Ftbl Sccr Bsktbl Sftbl Capt 90-; Jrnlsm; Advrtsng.

**STEPHEN, RUTH S,** Columbia Union Coll, Takoma Park, MD; SO; Drama Clb 89-; Phi Eta Sigma 89-90; Engl/Psychlgy; Psychlgst Cnslng.**

**STEPHENFIELD, TAMARA K,** Univ Of Fl, Gainesville, FL; SR; BS; SOTA 89-90; Golden Key 90-; Pres Lst 90; NE FL State Hosp Mac Clenny FL 90; Vet Amdin Ctr Gahesville FL 90; Morris Ctr Pdtrc Gainesville FL 90; AA Cntrl FL Comm Coll 87-89; Occ Ther.

**STEPHENS, ANGELA M,** Roane St Comm Coll, Harriman, TN; SO; Physcl Thrpst Asst Assn Pres 90-; Dns Lst 90-; Cum Laude Grad 90-; AAS; Physcl Thrpy.

**STEPHENS, ANN M,** Mount Aloysius Jr Coll, Cresson, PA; CVT; Cardvsclr/Hlth Fld; Cardvsclr Tech.

**STEPHENS, AUBREY L,** International Bible Coll, Florence, AL; FR; BA; Chrmn Sctn/Hsng Cmmsn 90-; Bible; Mnstr.

**STEPHENS, BARRY D,** Truett Mc Connell Coll, Cleveland, GA; SO; BA; Press Opr Sprvsr 79-89; Rlgn; Pstr.

**STEPHENS, BETTINA J,** Wv Northern Comm Coll, Wheeling, WV; FR; MBA; Psychlgy; Clncl Psychlgy.

**STEPHENS, BRADLEY C,** Le Moyne Coll, Syracuse, NY; SR; Mrktng Clb Pres Rsm Comm 90-; Delta Mu Delta; Fnnc.

**STEPHENS, CAROLYN S,** Univ Of West Fl, Pensacola, FL; JR; BED; Stdnt Govt Rep 89-90; Intrclb Cncl VP 89-90; Phi Beta Lmbd Pres 89-; AA Chipola Jr Clg 90; Bus; Ed.

**STEPHENS, CHERYL A,** Ky Christian Coll, Grayson, KY; SR; Deans Lst 87-; Hon Roll 87-; BS; Bus Admin; Bus Field.

**STEPHENS, CHRISTOPHER P,** Univ Of Ky, Lexington, KY; SR; BA; Big Bro/Big Sis 90-; Eucharistc Mnstr 86-90; BASW; Scl Wrk.

**STEPHENS, DONNA L,** Roane St Comm Coll, Harriman, TN; JR; BS; Elem Educ; Tchr.

**STEPHENS, DOTTIE M,** Wv Univ At Parkersburg, Parkersburg, WV; BA; Cert Mtn State Bsnss Clg Med Sec 89; Bsnss Admin.

**STEPHENS III, DOUGLAS,** Fayetteville St Univ, Fayetteville, NC; JR; BA; Sons Of Conf Vets 88-; Cumberland Co Cons Caucus Sec 88-; Avante Adv Inc 88-; History/Chem; Teach & Rsrch.

**STEPHENS, JAMES C,** Middle Tn St Univ, Murfreesboro, TN; JR; BA; Assoc Stdnt Bdy Cmmtt 90; Ftr Acctnts Assoc 90; Tau Kappa Epsilon Pres 90-; Vet Hosp 90-; Acctg; CPA.

**STEPHENS, JEFFREY D,** Marywood Coll, Scranton, PA; SR; BS; Kappa Mu Epsilon 89-; Delta Epsilon Sigma 88-; Tama Medal; BS; Math/Comp Sci; Tech Prgmng.

**STEPHENS, JOHN P,** Univ Of Sc At Columbia, Columbia, SC; FR; Physlgy; Phychtry.

**STEPHENS, LA TONYA,** Tuskegee Univ, Tuskegee Inst, AL; SR; Blgy/Chem Clb VP 90-; Delta Sigma Theta Srgnt Arms 90-; VA Hosp Vol; Blgy/Pre-Med; Medcl Schl.**

**STEPHENS, MARK L,** Morehouse Coll, Atlanta, GA; FR; IM Bsbl Ftbl; Ecnmcs; Intl Fnnc.

**STEPHENS, MARVIN D,** Al A & M Univ, Normal, AL; JR; MET; Bchtl Pwr Corp; AS Calhoun Comm Clg 87; Engnrng Tchnlgy.

**STEPHENS, MARY A,** Ms Univ For Women, Columbus, MS; SO; BS; Hnrs Prog; Torch; Highlander Soc Club Interclub Rep; Deans List 89-90; Pres List; Bus Admn.

**STEPHENS, MATTYNA L,** Johnson C Smith Univ, Charlotte, NC; JR; Alpha Sweetheart Aux 88-; Wmsn Bsktbl/Sftbl 90-; Phy Ed; Mortuary Sci.

**STEPHENS, MELANIE SUZANNE LEE,** Univ Of Southern Ms, Hattiesburg, MS; SR; BS; Hon Coll 86-87; ACT Schlrshp 86; GA Pacific Schlrshp 86; Cert Copiah-Lincoln Comm Coll 88-89; Engl; Tch Univ.

**STEPHENS, MELONIE L,** Univ Of Tn At Knoxville, Knoxville, TN; JR; BS; Fthls Ski Clb Soc Chrprsn 90; Gldn Key; Phi Eta Sgm 89-90; Beta Gamma Sgm; Beta Alpha Psi; Cmptr Systm Crdntr 86-88; Ofc Mgr 85-86; Assc Atlnt Sch Fshn/Dsgn 82; Acctg; Bus Cnsltng.

**STEPHENS, MICHAEL SCOTT,** Univ Of Sc At Columbia, Columbia, SC; JR; BS; IM Official 90-; Sigma Phi Epsilon 89-; Criminal Justice; Law.

**STEPHENS, NOLA M,** Middle Ga Coll, Cochran, GA; SO; BS; Intl Rels Clb VP 89-; Show Choir 89-; Clg Bowl 89-; SADD 90-; Early Invervention Pgm Mentor; RA 90-; Deans Lst 89-; AA; Med.

**STEPHENS, PAMELA B,** Lexington Comm Coll, Lexington, KY; SO; AAS; Comp Inf Sys; Prog.

**STEPHENS, PAMELA J,** Itawamba Comm Coll, Fulton, MS; SO; AD; SNA; Intrntl Pilot Clb; Yth Choir Dir; Untd Meth Yth Flwshp Ldr; Nrsng; RN.

**STEPHENS, ROLONDA A,** Fl A & M Univ, Tallahassee, FL; FR; Phi Eta Sigma; Bsns; Acctg.

**STEPHENS, SAMUEL DEAN,** Roane St Comm Coll, Harriman, TN; SO; BS; Isham United Bptst Church Deacon 75-; Crpntr Frmn Brdge Constctn 86-; Math; Engr Civil.

**STEPHENS, SCOTT E,** Appalachian St Univ, Boone, NC; FR; BS; Atmospheric Sci; Meteorology.**

**STEPHENS, SHANNON L,** Northern Ky Univ, Highland Hts, KY; SO; BA; CMENC Treas 90-; Msc Ed/Prfrmce; Orchstra.

**STEPHENS, SHONDA N,** Lincoln Univ, Lincoln Univ, PA; FR; BA; Sociology; Human Services.

**STEPHENS, STEPHANIE A,** Radford Univ, Radford, VA; SR; BBA; Fin Mgt Assoc 90-; Phi Beta Lambda 90-; Finf Bank Mgt.

**STEPHENS, STEVE A,** Union Univ, Jackson, TN; JR; BSBA; Bapt Stdnt Un 89-; Stdnt Fndtn 90-; Acctg Clb 89-; Schlrs Excell Rec 89-91; Acctg.

**STEPHENS, SUE N,** Va Commonwealth Univ, Richmond, VA; SR; BS; Biol; Tch.

**STEPHENS, SUSAN R,** Kent St Univ Kent Cmps, Kent, OH; SR; BS; Stdnt Dietetic Assn 87-; Wghtlftng Clb 86-; Golden Key; Delta Gamma 88-89; Schlrshp Awd Athltc Dept 86-87; Superior Schlrshp Awd; Intrnshp Mercy Med Ctr Baltimore MD; Vrsty Gym Tm 86-88; Am Assn Affiliate Mbr 90-; Nutrition; Rgstrd Dietitian.

**STEPHENS, TAMMY F,** James Madison University, Harrisonburg, VA; SR; Council Excptnl Chldren 89-; Stdnt Advsry Committee 90-; Very Specl Arts 90-; Golden Key 90-; Kappa Delta Pi; BS; Specl Educ/Mental Retardation; Grad Schl.

**STEPHENS, TERRANCE D,** Morehouse Coll, Atlanta, GA; SO; BA; Clg Paper Rep 90-; Spnsh Clb 90-; Pre-Alumni Assoc 90-; Mentoring Pgm 90-; Pol Sci/Spnsh; Law.

**STEPHENS, TIA W,** Fisk Univ, Nashville, TN; JR; BS; Choir Orientation Ldr 88-90; The KY Fisk Club Treas 88-89; Fisk Cmptr Club V P 90-; Stdnt Support Serv Tutor 89-; Metro Transit Authority Internship; The Travelers Ins Co Intrnshp; Cmptr Sco; Bus Mgr.

**STEPHENS, TRACY L,** Georgian Court Coll, Lakewood, NJ; JR; BA; Clionaes Soc Pres 89-; Crt Pg 90-; TLC Lrning Dsbld Prog Vol; Phi Alpha Theta Treas; Dean Schlr 89-90; Prclmtn Meritorious Serv; Hstry/Scndry Educ; Tchng/Admin.

**STEPHENS, WENDY S,** Univ Of Tn At Martin, Martin, TN; JR; BA; STEA 87-; US Achvmnt Acad All Amer Schr; Chi Omega Ldg Chrmn 87-; Tchng Intrnshp; Erly Chldhd Educ.

**STEPHENSON, CATHY K,** Auburn Univ At Auburn, Auburn, AL; SR; BS; Hmn Sci Stdnt Assoc Pres 90-; Hmn Sci Stdnt Cdr 89-; Amrcn Home Econ Assoc 89-; Kappa Omicron Nu 90-; Gamma Sigma Delta 90-; AS (E State Jnr Coll 80; Home Econ; Fmly Fncl Mgmt.

**STEPHENSON, DEBRA P,** Univ Of Central Fl, Orlando, FL; FR; BA; Orchestra; Mrtl Arts Tae Kwondo; NACME; Math; Engr.

**STEPHENSON, DWIGHT D,** Miami Univ, Oxford, OH; FR; BA; Brmbl; Cmps Crsd Chrst; Crew; Bsn Mgmt; Law.

**STEPHENSON, JAMES T,** Winthrop Coll, Rock Hill, SC; JR; Artery Treas 89; Pi Kappa Phi Pres 89; People Undrstndng Svrly Hndcppd 89; Graphic Svcs Intern; Graphic Dsgn.

**STEPHENSON, JENNIFER J,** Blue Mountain Coll, Blue Mountain, MS; SR; MAE-SP 90-; Commtr Club 90-; Deans List 90-; BA Ed; Elem Ed; Tchr.

**STEPHENSON III, JESSE H,** William Carey Coll, Hattiesburg, MS; SR; BS; Natl Mgmt Assoc Treas 87-; Pltcl Action Com 88-; Bdgt/Cost Analyst 82-; BS Univ Southern MS 82; MBA William Cargy Clg 86; Acctg; CPA.

**STEPHENSON, RAYMOND L,** Columbia Union Coll, Takoma Park, MD; SR; BS; ARRT 85-; Deans List 90-; Busn Admin; Hosp Admin.

**STEPHENSON, SANDRIA S,** Univ Of The Virgin Islands, St Thomas, VI; SR; BA; Sdtnt Govt Treas 90-; Acctng Assn; Pres Clb; Acctng Asssn; Outstanding Soph Acctng 90; Auditor/Accntnt 83-; Dip Duffs Bus Clg 87; Dip Prams Intl Trvl 87; Acctng; Auditor/Mgr.

**STEPHENSON, TINA L,** Univ Of Tn At Knoxville, Knoxville, TN; JR; BS; Gym Clb 88-; Gamma Beta Phi 90-; Golden Key; Chrldr 90-; Pom Pon Sqd 88-89; Trnsprtn/Lgstcs.

**STEPIC, MICHAEL J,** Univ Of Akron, Akron, OH; SO; BS; ASCE Soph Rep 90; Mrchng Bnd 89; Blue/Gold Brass 89; Kappa Kappa Psi 90; Hnrs Schlrshp 89; David H Timmerman Civil Eng Schlrshp 90; Deans Lst 89; Civil Eng; Cnsltng Eng.**

**STEPNOWSKI III, STANLEY V,** De Tech & Comm Coll At Dover, Dover, DE; FR; ARS; Dns Lst 90-; USN Nvl Nclr Pwr Prog; Elec Eng.

**STEPP, JAMES C,** Univ Of Sc At Columbia, Columbia, SC; SO.

**STEPP, JANICE G,** Central Fl Comm Coll, Ocala, FL; FR; ASN; Vlybl 90-; CNA Sheridan Voctnl 80; RN OB Nrs.

**STEPP, LA TOKA RENEE,** Al St Univ, Montgomery, AL; SO; Soc Wrk.

**STEPPE, ANITA F,** Liberty Univ, Lynchburg, VA; FR; BS; Ythqst Clb 90-; IM Vllybll 90-; Tech Drm.

**STERK, MICHELLE C,** Villanova Univ, Villanova, PA; SO; BA; Camps Mnstry Hosp Mnstr 89-; IM Flg Ftbl Capt 89-; Hse Cncl Wing Rep 89-; Delta Gamma; Habitat Humnty 90-; Comm Phila Homeless 89-90; Spec Oly 89-; IMS Capt 89-; Psych.

**STERLACCI, DEBRA LYNN,** S U N Y Coll Of Tech At Frmgdl, Farmingdale, NY; SO; AS; Eng Soc Adv Moblty 88-89; Busn; Automtv.

**STERLING, ALICIA A,** Coppin St Coll, Baltimore, MD; JR; BA; Usher Brd First Chrty Bptst Church 90-; Natl Assn Black Accnts Sec; Mgt Sci/Acctg.

**STERLING, HOWARD W,** Morehouse Coll, Atlanta, GA; SO; Bilogy; Medicine.

**STERLING, KENNETH W,** Bryant Stratton Bus Inst Roch, Rochester, NY; GD; CERTF; Bsns Clb; Trvl Clb; Tchncl Sprt Bryant Stratton Monroe Community Clg Smptrs; MS Unv MI 71; BS Unv Rochester 70; Cmptr Prgrmmng.

**STERLING, MARK P,** Hudson Valley Comm Coll, Troy, NY; SO; AAS; Data Proc Intrnshp N Y St Dept Crim Just; Cand Hudsn Vly Comm Clv Pres Mdl; Socr 88-90; Cmptr Inf Syst.

**STERN, LAURA M,** Carnegie Mellon Univ, Pittsburgh, PA; SR; BS; Ambssdrs 88-; Res Assist 88-90; Frshmn Orentation Cnslr 89-90; Detla Gamma V P 87-; Deans Lst 89-90; Valed/Salut Schlrshp 87-; Wmsn Clb Schlrshp 89-; Graphic Comm Mgmnt; Mktng.

**STERNER, DOUGLAS R,** Bloomsburg Univ Of Pa, Bloomsburg, PA; SO; BED; Schlrs Prog 89-; Am Chem Scty 90-; Chem Lab Asst 90-; Bowling VP 90-; Chem; Tchg.**

**STERNER, JENNIFER L,** Juniata Coll, Huntingdon, PA; SO; BS; Chemistry Clb 89-; Intrntnl Clb 89-; Mntn Day Hmcmng Comm 90-; Geisinger Intrnshp; Rugby 90-; Biochemistry; Frnsc Chmstry.

**STERZER, KENNETH M,** County Coll Of Morris, Randolph, NJ; FR; AS; Hsplty Mgmt.

**STETHERS, LORI S,** Widener Univ, Chester, PA; FR; BA; Ldrshp Inst; 4-H Club Pres 81; Big Friends 90; Tutoring 90; Vol Of The Week 90; Tennis/Mgr; Econ.

**STETTER, SALLY ANN,** S U N Y Coll Of Tech At Alfred, Alfred, NY; FR; AAS; Fr Nrsng Clb 90-; LPN; Nrsng; RN.

**STETTLER, DANA LEIGH,** Queens Coll, Charlotte, NC; JR; BA; Spcl Evnts Comm 88-89; Kappa Delta Sorty Rep 88-; Adlt Care/Share Vol 89; Bus Admn.

**STETTLER, LE ANNE LOUISE,** West Chester Univ, West Chester, PA; SR; Mrchg Bnd Wnd Ensmbl 87-; Symphnc Bnd Mstrwrks Chrs 87-; Clgm Mscm 90-; Hnr Roll; Sigma Alpha Iota Chpln 88-; Msc Ed Ntl Cnfrnc 87-; PA Msc Ed Assoc 90-; BS; Music; Tchg.

**STEUBER, JUDITH C,** Middle Tn St Univ, Murfreesboro, TN; SR; BS; Kappa Delta Pi 90-; Elem Educ; Tch.

**STEUERNAGEL, KELLY ANN,** Niagara Univ, Niagara Univ, NY; SR; BS; Delta Epsilon Sigma 89-; Intrnshp Ntl Fuel Gas 91; Sopho Awd Excell Comm 89; Ockerman Awd 91; Key Awd 91; Bus Mgmt; MBA Corp Fin.

**STEUERWALD, JAMES M,** Univ Of Southern Ms, Hattiesburg, MS; SR; BA; Comp Oprtr Prgrmmrs Assoc Pres 87-90; Phi Theta Kappa 87-; Otstndng Tchncl Stdnt 88-; AS 89; Appld Comp Sci; Sftwr Eng.

**STEVENS, ALLISON K,** Coll Of Charleston, Charleston, SC; SO; BA; Polt Sci.

**STEVENS, BRIAN S,** Memphis St Univ, Memphis, TN; FR; BS; Mrchng/Cncrt Bnd 90-; Gamma Beta Phi; ESP Tudor Core 90-; Electronics Tech.

**STEVENS, CHRISTOPHER ERIC,** Northern Ky Univ, Highland Hts, KY; SO; BA; Bsktbll 90; Bsn/Concentration Finance; Cnstrn Mngmnt.

**STEVENS, CHRISTY A,** Emory Univ, Atlanta, GA; GD; Emory Stdnt Nrs Assn 88-90; Amer Nrs Assn 88-89; Alpah Epsilon Upsilon 86-88; Sigma Theta Tau 90-; BSN Merit Schlrshp 88-90; BSN 90; Optomentry.

**STEVENS, CYNTHIA P,** Univ Of Montevallo, Montevallo, AL; SR; BS; Ntl Stdt Spch/Language/Hearing Assoc 90-; Spch/Hearing Assoc Al; ASALEX Jr Clg 88; Speech/Language Pathology.

**STEVENS, DEBORAH R,** Ashland Comm Coll, Ashland, KY; FR; MSPA; Chrprsn Cystc Fbrs Walk/Thon 90; Spch Pathlgy/Audlgy; Clncl Prctc.

**STEVENS, HEATHER M,** Kent St Univ Kent Cmps, Kent, OH; FR; BS; Dnc Ensmbl; Dnc Assoc VP; Alpha Lambda Delta; Stg Mgr Sprng Cncrt; Asst Stg Mgr Cncrt 90; Elem Ed.

**STEVENS, HEATHER M,** Kent St Univ Kent Cmps, Kent, OH; FR; BA; Kent Dnc Ensmbl; Kent Dnc Assoc VP; Alpha Lambda Delta; Dance; Tchr.

**STEVENS, ISMAY A E,** Al A & M Univ, Normal, AL; JR; BS; Elem Early Childhood Ed Club VP; Kappa Delta Pi; 9 Yrs Tchrs Aide 85-88; Certif Bermuda Clg 86; Elem Ed; Tchr Elem.

**STEVENS, JAMES E,** Mount Saint Mary Coll, Newburgh, NY; JR; BSN; Nrsng Stdnt Union; NLN Accrdtn Prep Comm; Lab Rep 90-; Beta Beta Beta; Sigma Theta Tau; Hnrs Allnc; Nom Clg Ldrshp Devlpmt Crse; Frst Army Enlstd Cmmssng Prog Nrsng 90-; Subst Tchr; Stf Sgt U S Army; LPN; Nrsng; Army Nrs.

**STEVENS, JASON M,** Brevard Coll, Brevard, NC; FR; Yrbk Photo 90-; Phi Thetta Kappa VP; City Logo Design; Art; Med.

**STEVENS, JEFFREY S,** S U N Y Coll Of Tech At Alfred, Alfred, NY; SR; AOS; Chr 89-; Tr Gd 90-; Dns Advsry Cncl 90-; Sigma Tai Epsilon 90-; Chrldr 89-; Cnstrctn/Mntnc Elctrcn; Elctrcl Fld.

**STEVENS II, JOEL R,** Cornell Univ Statutory College, Ithaca, NY; SR; Crnl Un Prsnl Entrprs Pgm Mbr 90-; Sm Sdbus Admn Incbtr Pgm 90; Sgm Nu Frat 88-; Bartener/Bncr Johnnys Big Red Bar/Grl; Dsgm Nu Frat Exec Cmt 88- Soc Chrmn 88-; BS 91; Cornell Frshmn Vrsty Ftbl IM Bwlng Trck/Sftbl Sqd; Cornell Frshmn; Bus Mgmt/Mktg; Sls Mgmt Fd/Fin/Hlgh Indstry.

**STEVENS, JULIE M,** Valdosta St Coll, Valdosta, GA; JR; BS; Tchr; AS Abraham Baldwin Agri Coll 87; Early Chldhd Edn; Teach.

**STEVENS, KATHERINE G,** Roane St Comm Coll, Harriman, TN; FR; BS; Gamma Beta Phi; Im Sftbl; Pre Med; Optmtry.

**STEVENS, LAURIE G,** Castleton St Coll, Castleton, VT; SR; BA; SEA 87-88; STEP Tutor 88-89; Yrbk Stf Phtgrphr 90-; Phi Eta Sigma 87-; Kappa Delta Pi 90-; Deans Lst 88-; Stdnt Teach 90-; Lit Sec Edn; Writer/Author.**

**STEVENS, LOUISE D,** Beaver Coll, Glenside, PA; GD; NCTM 84-; ATMOPAV 86; Theta Alph Awrd 58; BS Acad New Church 59; MEA; CEA Chldbrth Educ Assc Phila/Vinc Chr Nrsng Mthrs/Brd Dir 71-78; Wmn Guild 59-; Theta Alpha 59-; Chair Math Dept Acad New Chrch; Math.

**STEVENS, MICHAEL A,** Springfield Tech Comm Coll, Springfield, MA; FR; BA; Stdnt Govt VP 89-; All Coll Cncl Rep 90-; Fscl Affrs Comm Rep 90-; Tennis 90-; Telecmnctns; Early Chldhd Dvlpmnt.

**STEVENS, MICHELLE V,** Averett Coll, Danville, VA; JR; BS AC; Acctg; CPA.

**STEVENS, NICHOLE G,** Univ Of Southern Ms, Hattiesburg, MS; SR; Deaf Ed; Tchr.

**STEVENS, OLU A,** Morehouse Coll, Atlanta, GA; JR; BA; Psychology Assoc 89-; Golden Key; Psi Chi Pres; Hnr Roll & Deans Liost 90-; Psychology; Law.

**STEVENS, PAREASA R,** Greenville Tech Coll, Greenville, SC; FR; MBA; Natrl Hlpr 89-90; Natl Jr Hon Scty 83-; Hon Roll 82-87; Mnrty Schlrshp; Ntwrk Eng Schlrshp 90-; Ntwrk Admnstr; Cmptr Tech; Systms Anlyst.

**STEVENS, PENNY L,** Emory & Henry Coll, Emory, VA; FR; BA; Rdio DJ 90-; Alpha Psi Omega; Emory And Henry Fr Schlr 90-; Dns Lst 90-; Mss Cmmnctns Engl; Rprtng.

**STEVENS, RANDALL L,** Univ Of New Haven, West Haven, CT; JR; BS; Future Innkprs Amer Pres 90-; Stdnt Sen 90-; SHMAI; Alpha Beta Gamma 90-; Outstndng Sntr/Clb Ofcr 90-; Outstndng Ldrshp/Svc Awd 90-; Phlsphy Stdnt Yr Awd; AS Manchester Comm Coll; Bus Mgmt; Hotel Mgmt.

**STEVENS, ROSALIE A,** Cumberland County Coll, Vineland, NJ; SO; AAS; Phi Theta Kappa; Acctg.

**STEVENS, SHERRILYN A,** Va St Univ, Petersburg, VA; FR; BA; Academica Achvmnt Awd; Bus; Mngmnt.

**STEVENS, SYDNEY P,** Coll Of Charleston, Charleston, SC; SO; BS; Center Stage 89-; Chi Omega Song Chrmn 89-; IMS; Sociology; Broadcast Jrnlsm.

**STEVENS, TERRELL D,** Chattanooga St Tech Comm Coll, Chattanooga, TN; SO; Black Student Assoc Chrmn Acad Awareness 89-; Inner City Ministries 87-; Vol Parent Prog Henry L Barger Schl Chrmn 89-; Information Systems; Math Education.

**STEVENS, TIFFANY D,** Middle Tn St Univ, Murfreesboro, TN; SO; BS; Ed Clb 90-; Lit Clb 90-; Frst Bptst Chrch 86-; Phi Theta Kappa 90-; AS Motlow St Cmnty Clge; Math; Sec Ed.**

**STEVENS, TRACY N,** Univ Of Southern Ms, Hattiesburg, MS; JR; BS; Coll Rpblcns 2nd V Chrmn; Amer Mktg Assn; Lambda Sigma; Ordr Of Omega; Lambda Pi Eta; Chi Omega VP 90-; Advtsng/Mktg.

**STEVENS, VALERIE E,** Bloomfield Coll, Bloomfield, NJ; JR; BS; Pre Med Clb 88-89; Phi Sigma Sigma Asst Pldg Mstr 89-; Chrprcts.

**STEVENS, WENDY A,** Hudson Valley Comm Coll, Troy, NY; SO; AS; Lbrl Arts; Bus.

**STEVENS-STAHL, PAULA J,** Davis & Elkins Coll, Elkins, WV; SR; BA; Stdnt Cncl 87; Hnrs Assn 87-89; Alpha Chi 89-; W V Educ Assn 89-90; Natl Stdnt Tchrs 89-90; Acad Achvmnt Awds 88-90; Acad All Amer 90-; 4 H Cmp Inst 90; Beatucn; Frlnc Artst; Cpy Cam Oper; Cert Clrksbrg Bty Acad 77; Art Educ K 12; Educ/Fr Lance.

**STEVENSON, CELESTE,** Hilbert Coll, Hamburg, NY; GD; AAS; AA 82; Paralegal.

**STEVENSON, CHERYL A,** Saint Joseph Coll, West Hartford, CT; JR; BS; Choir VP 88-; Orntn Ldr; Big Sis 89-; PALS; Peer Tutor 88-; Elem Edn; Teach.**

**STEVENSON, CONIEKA J,** Nc Agri & Tech St Univ, Greensboro, NC; JR; BSW; Comm Cnnctns Vol Pres 90-; Sclgy/Scl Wrk Clb Treas 90-; Alpha Delta Mu; Hnrs Pgm 89-; Saford Frm Pblc Serv; Kellogg Fdn Grnt; Schl Scl Wrk/Bio; Cnslr.

**STEVENSON, DANIEL,** S U N Y Coll Of Tech At Frmgdl, Farmingdale, NY; GD; BA; AAS; Advrtsn Agncy.

**STEVENSON, GREGORY M,** Harding Grad School Of Relig, Memphis, TN; GD; MDIV; Stdnt Assn Rep 90-; Deans Lst; Grk Awd; BA 89; New Testament; Tchng.**

**STEVENSON, KIMBERLY T,** Glassboro St Coll, Glassboro, NJ; JR; BA; Radio 88-; Radio TV Assn; Radio Intrnshp; Comm; Radio/TV/FILM.

**STEVENSON, LARRY D,** Alcorn St Univ, Lorman, MS; JR; Phys Educ Club 89-; Dns Lst 90; AA Nrthwst Mississippi Cmnty Clg 89; Phys Educ; Tchng/Coaching.

**STEVENSON, MICHELLE D,** Univ Of Ky, Lexington, KY; SR; MSW; Deans Lst 88-; Otstdngn Acdmc Achvmnt Scl Wrk 90-; Min Schlrshp 87-; BASW; Med Scl Wrk; Mdcl Scl Wrkr.

**STEVENSON, REGINALD A,** Tuskegee Univ, Tuskegee Inst, AL; JR; BS; Natl Assoc Advcmnt Of Colored People 88-; Natl Sco Black Engrs 88-; Amer Soc Mechanical Engrs 88-; Omega Psi Phi Regnl Mbrshp Intake Team 90-; Pres Annual Hnr Roll 89; Dist Schlr 88-89; Deans List 88-; Mechanical Engineering.

**STEVENSON, ROBIN M,** West Liberty St Coll, West Liberty, WV; SO; BS; Trumpet Head Phtgrphr 89-; Cmmnctns; Pub Rel.

**STEVENSON, STACEY M,** Radford Univ, Radford, VA; SR; BBA; Amer Mrktng Assoc 89-; Intl Acad Mktg/Mgmnt 89-90; BBA; Mrktng; Sales.

**STEVENSON, WILLIAM C,** Memphis St Univ, Memphis, TN; GD; MBA; Metro Conf Commsnrs All Academic Tm 87-90; 2nd Tm All Conf Ftbl 89; Vrsty Ftbl 87-90; BBA 90; Mngmnt Lbr Rltns; Corp Lwyr.

**STEVERSON, TAMIKA D,** City Univ Of Ny Kingsborough, Brooklyn, NY; SO; BA; Alpha Epsilon Rho; Radio Nwscstr; Cert Achvmnt; Talent Rstr; Brdcstng; TV/ADVRTSNG.

**STEVERSON, TAVIA RAYE,** Univ Of Sc At Columbia, Columbia, SC; FR; BS; Pharmacy.

**STEWARD JR, GERALD EDWARD,** Central St Univ, Wilberforce, OH; GD; MBA; US Air Frc Career Cmptr Ops 76-; Aa Cmnty Clg Air Frc 90; BS Central St Univ 90; CIS; Cmptr Eng.

**STEWARD, JANET L,** Hudson Valley Comm Coll, Troy, NY; JR; AA; Bus Admin.

**STEWART, AMY JO,** Univ Of Bridgeport, Bridgeport, CT; SO; BS; Peer Cnslg 89-; Natural Highs 89-; Career Svcs Comm Co-Chrmn 89-; Dana Soc 90-; Italian Schlrshp Study Abroad; Bsktbl 89-; Sftbl 89-90; IM Flr Hockey 90-; Math/Intl Bsn.**

**STEWART, AMY K,** Me Maritime Academy, Castine, ME; FR; BA; Ycht Clb; Ntcl Sci; Lcnsd Oprtr In Mrne Indstry.

**STEWART, AMY L,** Blue Mountain Coll, Blue Mountain, MS; SR; BA; SGA 89-; Engl Clb Pres 90-; Euzealian Socty; Ms Assoc Of Educators; Engl Educ; Tchr.

**STEWART, ANDREA K,** Central St Univ, Wilberforce, OH; GD; Delta Sigma Theta 87-; BA Central State Univ 90; Pol Sci; Law Schl.

**STEWART, ANGELA A,** Converse Coll, Spartanburg, SC; FR; BA; SGA 90-; FCA 90-; Keyboard 90-; Deans Lst 90-; Sch Centnl Cmtee 90-; Alpha Lambda Delta 90-; Econ/Intl Bus; Intl Corp Law.

**STEWART, ANGELA L,** Univ Of Akron, Akron, OH; JR; BED; ACES; Zeta Tau Alpha Alumni Ritual Chr 88-89; Deans List 90; Mathf Tchng.**

**STEWART, ANGELA M,** Cheyney Univ Of Pa, Cheyney, PA; FR; BA; Mrchng Bnd; Crim Just; Law/Atty.

**STEWART, ANGELA S,** Alcorn St Univ, Lorman, MS; JR; BA; Scl Sci Dept/Soc 90-; Ecnmcs Clb Sntr 90-; Stdnt Snt 90-; Natl Scl Sci Awd 90-; Natl Mnrty Ldrshp Awd 90-; Ecnmcs; Coll Prfssr.

**STEWART, ANITA M,** Southern Union St Jr Coll, Wadley, AL; FR; Phi Theta Kappa.

**STEWART, ARLENE F K,** Univ Of The Dist Of Columbia, Washington, DC; SO; CATC; Yng Marines Montford Point Spprt Stff 90-; New Rose Sharon Bptst Chrch Treas 89-; Mtrpltn Plc Boys/Grls Clb Camp Cnslr 90-; US Lghths Soc; Pershing Angels Sor 77; J E Miller Chapman Schlrshp 90-; V Fulford Schlrshp; Awds/Cmmndtns 88-; Comp Acctg.

**STEWART, AUDREY M,** Clarkson Univ, Potsdam, NY; SR; BA; Soc Wmn Mgrs; Psychlgy Clb; Lacrosse Tm; AS Monroe Comm Clg 89; Mgt/Cmnctns; MBA Hlth Sys Admin.

**STEWART, BARBARA H,** Bryant Stratton Bus Inst Roch, Rochester, NY; SO; AOD; Trvl Clb 90-; Bus Clb; Assn Blind/Visually Impaired Prnt Chrprn 84-; Strong Memorial Chldrns Fnd Vol 90; Deans Lst 90-; Bus/Mktng Mgmnt; Bus/Advrtsng.

**STEWART, BEVERLY D,** Roane St Comm Coll, Harriman, TN; SO.

**STEWART, BRUCE KIFLE,** Morehouse Coll, Atlanta, GA; FR; BS; Psy Pre Med; Sprts Med.

**STEWART, CARLA R,** Jackson St Univ, Jackson, MS; JR; BS; Alpha Lambda Delta 88-; Hnrs Div 88-; Fll Acdmc Schlrshp 88-; Rsrchr Lawrence Berkeley Labs 90; Psych; Clncl Psychlgst.

**STEWART, CAROL E,** Winthrop Coll, Rock Hill, SC; SR; Baptist Student Un 87-; Campus Baptist Yng Wmn 87-; Lutheran Episcopal Mnstrs; Delta Psi Kappa; Specl Olympic Swm Tm Coach 87-89; IM Offcl 87-; BS; Physical Educ; State Supt Educ.

**STEWART, CATHY R,** Alcorn St Univ, Lorman, MS; FR; Ecnmcs; Invstmnt Bnkr.

**STEWART, CATINA MONIQUE,** Alcorn St Univ, Lorman, MS; FR; Vllybl 90-; Nrsng; RN.

**STEWART, CHARLENE H,** Univ Of Nc At Charlotte, Charlotte, NC; GD; Bapt Chrc Assc Mnstr 88-; Untd Bapt Assc Co Chrmn 89-90; Crss Asst Mnstrs 78-; NAACP 77-; Gldn Ky 90; Phi Kappa Phi 90; Benjamn E Mays Schlr; Chi Eta Phi 67-; BA 90; BSN 81; Rel Stu; Thlgn.

**STEWART, CHERYL G,** Univ Of South Al, Mobile, AL; JR; BS; Edn/Leisure Serv; Tourism & Comm Rcrtn.

**STEWART, CHRISTINA M,** Neumann Coll, Aston, PA; FR; BA; Nrsng.

**STEWART, CLAYTON R,** Howard Univ, Washington, DC; GD; MS; Amer Soc Cvl Engrs Pres 87; Asst Cvl Engr 90; Mentor 90; BS 89; Cvl Engr; Geotech Engr.

**STEWART, DAWN M,** Memphis St Univ, Memphis, TN; FR; BS; Phi Eta Sigma; Sigma Kappa Schlrshp Chrmn Exct Cncl Mbr; Psychlgy/Spch Pthlgy; Spch Pthlgst.

**STEWART, DEBORAH A,** Wv Univ, Morgantown, WV; JR; BS; ASP 90-; AS WVU Parkersburg 90; Phmcy.

**STEWART, DEIDRA M,** Al A & M Univ, Normal, AL; SO; BA; Medl Tchnlgy; Med Lab Techncn.

**STEWART, DONNA K,** William Carey Coll, Hattiesburg, MS; JR; BA; Nwspr Asstnt Edtr 90-; Cmps Bptst Yng Wmn Sec 90-; Bptst Stdnt Un 90-; Hnrs Prgrm; Englsh; Law.

**STEWART, EDWARD D,** Tn Temple Univ, Chattanooga, TN; SO.

**STEWART, ELYSE K,** Niagara Univ, Niagara Univ, NY; SR; BA; Tchng Asst Frshmn Smnr 88-90; Cmmnctns Englsh Pblc Rltns.**

**STEWART, ERIC R,** Eckerd Coll, St Petersburg, FL; SO; BA; SAM Bsn Clb; Econ; Prst Exclnc.

**STEWART, ERIN M,** Radford Univ, Radford, VA; SO; MBA; Spch Pthlgy; Spch Thrpy.

**STEWART, FELECIA A,** Jackson St Univ, Jackson, MS; FR; MBA; Alpha Lambda Delta; Miss Natl Guard; Active Military Trng Army; Acctng; Law.

**STEWART, FREDERIC M,** City Univ Of Ny Lehman Coll, Bronx, NY; GD; MAT; Gldn Key; Jos Delli Carri Mmrl Sclrshp; Fl Intrnshp Scnd Career Grad Prgrm Elmntry Edctn Mnhtnvl Coll; Ba-Music/Mat-Elmntry Ed; Tchr.

**STEWART, GARLINDA M,** Fayetteville St Univ, Fayetteville, NC; SR; BS; Prsdnt Stdnts Fr Entrprs Pres 89-; Mrktng Clb Mmbr; Capt Cmps Qz Bwl Cap 90-; Phi Beta Lambda 89-; Delta Sigma Theta; Intern Rsrch Evltn Assoc; Bus Admn Mrktng; Entrprnr.

**STEWART, GARY ALVIN,** Alcorn St Univ, Lorman, MS; JR; BS; Hon Pgm; ROTC Ldrshp Awd; Math; Offcr US Army.

**STEWART, GRANIS J,** Smith Coll, Northampton, MA; JR; AB; Ceramics Clb 90-; Dana Fndtn Grant Awrd For Study Intrnshp At FL Ctr Hum Dev 90; Novice Crew Tm Capt 88-89; RN St Lukes Hosp Schl Of Nursing 84; Anthropology.

**STEWART, HEATHER H,** Belmont Coll, Nashville, TN; FR; BBA; Rsdnce Hll Cncl; Bapt Stdnt Unn 90-; Acctng Assn 90-; Gamma Beta Phi 90-; IMS 90-; Acctng; CPA.

**STEWART, IDA GWEN,** Goldey Beacom Coll, Wilmington, DE; SR; Dns Lst 89-90; Stdnt Advsr Hgh Scl Cmte 90; Merit Schlrshp 89; Grdtd Caravel Acdmy Hnrs 89; Pres Ftns Awd 89; Caravel Stdnt Govt Srvc Awd 89; Caravels AFS Chptr Pres; Natl Stdnt Cncl Cnfrnc Dlgte 87; U S Achvmnt Acdmy 88; Ofc Mgmt; Ins Agnt.**

**STEWART, IONA M,** Cornell Univ Statutory College, Ithaca, NY; SO; Twnhse Cmuty Serv Clb 90-; Rsrch Asst Honey Bee Lab; Biology; Med.

**STEWART, JAMES L,** Cumberland Coll, Williamsburg, KY; JR; MBA; Bapt Stdnt Un Evnglsm Coord 89-90; Bapt Stdnt Un Mnstrl Assn Coor Pres 90-; Bapt Stdnt Un Discplshp Coor Chrprsn; Elderly Mstres Mbr 88-; Rlgn; Yth Mnstry/Tch.

**STEWART, JAMES N,** Piedmont Tech Coll, Greenwood, SC; FR; AA; Htng Vntltn Air Cond; Rfrgrtn Srvc.

**STEWART, JENNIER L,** Newbury Coll, Brookline, MA; FR; BA; Bsns Art.

**STEWART, JENNIFER M,** Oh Wesleyan Univ, Delaware, OH; FR; BA; Wesleyan Stdnt Fdn; Zoology Stdnt Brd; Phi Eta Sigma; Pi Beta Phi; Choosen To Go To COSEN Science & Math Convention; Zoology; Vet Med.

**STEWART, JOSEPH A,** Livingston Univ, Livingston, AL; FR; Univ Hstrcl Soc; Delta Chi; Math/Sci; Eng.

**STEWART, KARINA M,** Univ Of Miami, Coral Gables, FL; JR; BA; Hon Prog:; English/Phychology; Law/Psychology.

**STEWART, KEITH DE WAYNE,** Tusculum Coll, Greeneville, TN; SR; BA; Stdnt Govt Pres Candidate; Beta Theta Pi Sgt At Arms 88-90; Stdnt Amb 90-; Intern H Winstead & Assoc Law Firm Summer 91; Asst To Dean Of Bus Sch 90-; IM Sftbl Ftbl Tennis Rcqtbl 88-; Bus Mgmt; Law/Master Bus Admn.

**STEWART, KELLI L,** Marshall University, Huntington, WV; BA; Busn; Acctng.

**STEWART, KELLY A,** Seton Hall Univ, South Orange, NJ; JR; BSED; Lbrry Com; Kappa Delta Pi; Dns Lst; Dev Dsrdrs; Spcl Educ Tchr.

**STEWART, KERRIE A,** Ky St Univ, Frankfort, KY; JR; BA; Easter Seals Vlntr 90-; High Schl Crss Cntry Coach 90-; Part Time Employee/Full Time Mthr; Elem Ed.

**STEWART, KEVIN L,** Wv Univ, Morgantown, WV; SR; MSEE; WVU Hnrs Prog 87; Eta Kappa Nu 90-; IEEE 88-; Ky Clb 87; Tau Beta Pi 88-; Natl Mrt Schlrshp; Pres Schlr; Elec Eng.

**STEWART, KIMBERLEY NICOLE,** Johnson C Smith Univ, Charlotte, NC; FR; Myers Hall Cncl Flr Rep/Senator; Ladies At Blk/Gld; Psychology; Law.

**STEWART, LA SHONDA M,** Tougaloo Coll, Tougaloo, MS; FR; Outstndng Achvmnt Mssn Invlvmnt; Chrldr; Engl; Law.

**STEWART, LINDA M,** Univ Of Cin R Walters Coll, Blue Ash, OH; SO; BA; Dns Lst 90; Kndrvlt Bnfts Chldrns Hosp Chrprsn 90; Bus; Sales And Mrktng.

**STEWART, MARY C,** East Carolina Univ, Greenville, NC; SR; BFA; BA 90; Art Ed.

**STEWART, MELANIE R,** Tuskegee Univ, Tuskegee Inst, AL; SO; AS; Pre-Vet Med Assn 89-; Anml Sci; Vet Med.

**STEWART, MICHAEL TODD,** Memphis St Univ, Memphis, TN; SR; BS; Ambsdr Brd VP 89-; Esprit De Corps Alumni Brd; Intrfrat Cncl Schlrshp Chrmn 88-90; Alpha Epsilon Delta Pres 89-; Omiconr Delta Kappa 90-; Phi Kappa Phi 90-; Ordr Omega; Chi Beta Phi Pres 89-; Kappa Alpha Ordr Rcrdg Sec 87-; Pres Schlr 87-; Bio; Med.

**STEWART, MICHEAL W,** Norfolk St Univ, Norfolk, VA; FR; BA; Naval ROTC 90-; Spartan Alpha Tau 90-; Bio; Dr.

**STEWART, MICHELLE Y,** Univ Of The Dist Of Columbia, Washington, DC; JR; BA; Phi Sigma Pi Sec; Greenpeace 90-; Intshp Source Theatre Co; Natl Org Wmn; Dpt Cmmrc Hnr; Offc Prsnnl Mgmt Hnr; Theatre Arts; Acting/Dir/Tech Work.

**STEWART, MOLEENDO S,** Tougaloo Coll, Tougaloo, MS; FR; BA; Phi Beta Sigma Pres; Metro Miami Action Plan Comm Serv Org; Dept Crrctns Intern Psychlgcl Statistician; Hist/Psychlgy; Law.

**STEWART, NATALIE C,** Borough Of Manhattan Comm Coll, New York, NY; SR; AAS; Bus Adm; Mktg/Comp Pgr.

**STEWART, NELL THORNTON,** Union Univ, Jackson, TN; JR; BS; Elem Ed/Spcl Ed.

**STEWART, PAULA,** Comm Coll Algny Co Algny Cmps, Pittsburgh, PA; JR; SNAP 90; Nrsng.

**STEWART JR, RICHARD L,** Indiana Univ Of Pa, Indiana, PA; SR; BS; Chem Clb 88-89; Bio Clb 90-; Chrs 88-90; Deans List 90; Untd Meth Chr 87-; Lay Witness Untd Meth Spkr 89-; Natl Untd Meth Chr Erpn Tr 89; IM Bsktbl 87-; Bio Educ; Bio Grad Sch Tchng.

**STEWART, RICKEY DARNELL,** Fayetteville St Univ, Fayetteville, NC; SR; Criminal Justices Clb 90-; Asst Scoutmaster Boy Scouts; Substance Abuse Cnslr.

**STEWART, ROBERT C,** Fl St Univ, Tallahassee, FL; JR; BS; IM Ftbl Sftbl 88-89; Sci/Math; Mech Eng.

**STEWART, ROBERT L,** William Jennings Bryan Coll, Dayton, TN; FR; BS; Forensics Un 90-; FCA 89-; Bryan Coll Phonathon 90-; Alumni For Ldrshp 88-; Deans Lst 90-; Pres Schlr 90-; Acad Achvmnt Cert Awd 90-; Fresh Eng Trm Paper Awd 90; FCA Natl Mag Reviewer 90-; Comm Yng Adult Bible Stdy Co Ldr 88-; Math/Scndry Ed; Math Teacher.

**STEWART, SAMANTHA R,** Oh Univ-Southern Cmps, Ironton, OH; SR; Wrk Stdy 88-90; Deans Schlrshp 87-88; C E/J Peters Allen Schlrshp 87-; AS 89; BS Ed; Elem Ed; Tchr.

**STEWART, SARA L,** Eckerd Coll, St Petersburg, FL; SR; BA; Srch/Rscu 87-; Anthplgcl Soc 89-; Tour Guide 89-; Hnrs Pro 87-; Advct Shltr Achn/Pdg Emer Shltr Vol 90-; Anthrplgy; Archlgy.

**STEWART, SHAREN E,** Indiana Univ Of Pa, Indiana, PA; FR; BS; Elem Educ; Tchr.

**STEWART, SHARON S,** Central St Univ, Wilberforce, OH; SR; BED; IM Tennis 88; Gospel Choir; Delta Kappa Gamma Schlrshp 89-; Disabled Stdnt Sprts Assoc; Health Educ.

**STEWART, STEPHANIE R,** Univ Of Southern Ms, Hattiesburg, MS; FR; Gamma Beta Phi; Acctg; CPA.

**STEWART, SUSAN E,** Wilmington Coll, New Castle, DE; JR; BS; Deans Lst 89-90; Bsnss Mgt; Open Own Bsnss.

**STEWART, TERESA C,** Univ Of Montevallo, Montevallo, AL; SR; BA; SAEA VP 90-; Alabama Cncl Socl Stds 90-; Pres Lst 90; Dns Lst 89-; Educ Elem/Early Chldhd; Tchng.**

**STEWART, TERRI S,** Ms St Univ, Miss State, MS; JR; BPA; Roadrunner 90-; Fashion Board 89-; Omicron Delta Kappa 90; Mortar Brd Treas; Cardinal Key 90-; Beta Alpha Psi 90-; Kappa Delta Pres 88-; Acctg; CPA.

**STEWART, TIM D,** Ms St Univ, Miss State, MS; JR; BA; IM Sprts; Gamma Beta Phi 89-; Ntl Hnr Rl 90; Deans Lst 89-; Pres Schlr 90-; Finance.

**STEWART, TIMOTHY D,** Marshall University, Huntington, WV; SR; BA; Stdnt Govt Coll Of Bus Senator 90-; Ph Kappa Alpha Asstnt Pldg Edctr 88-89; Acctng & Fnnc; Cpa.

**STEWART, TRAVIS J,** Central Fl Comm Coll, Ocala, FL; SO; AA; Business Admin; Acctng.

**STEWART, TREVOR V,** Central Fl Comm Coll, Ocala, FL; SO; AA; Acctng.

**STEWART, WANDA D,** Alcorn St Univ, Lorman, MS; JR; BA; Sec Sci; Lgl Sec.

**STEWART, WILEY W,** Univ Of Nc At Charlotte, Charlotte, NC; JR; BA; Philosophy; Prfsr.

**STEWART-THOMAS, SONIA M,** Ny Univ, New York, NY; SO; BA; Admin Scrtry Human Rsrces Dept Of Brstl Myrs Squibb Co; Bsnss Admin Psychlgy Engl Math; Human Rsrce.

**STEYER, KAREN L,** Garrett Comm Coll, Mchenry, MD; SO.

**STICH, JANE M,** Mount Aloysius Jr Coll, Cresson, PA; FR; AS; Sci; Med Lab Technlgst.

**STICH, JOANNA L,** Longwood Coll, Farmville, VA; FR; Hall Cncl 90-; Dining Hall 90-; Stdnt Ldrshp Awd 90-; Deans Lst 90; Cmnctns; Media/Pblc Rltns.

**STICKER, THOMAS J,** Columbia Greene Comm Coll, Hudson, NY; FR; BS; Math/Sci; Engr.

**STICKLE JR, DAVID L,** Columbia Greene Comm Coll, Hudson, NY; SO; ASA; Crmnl Jstc; Law.

**STICKNEY, JEAN E,** Cornell Univ Statutory College, Ithaca, NY; SO; BS; Pre Vet Socty 89-90; Red Carpet Socty 89-; Sftbl 90; Anml Sci; Vet.

**STICKNEY, JENNIFER E,** Coll Of William & Mary, Williamsburg, VA; SO; BA; Psychlgy Clb 89-; Yearbook Staff 90-; Col Prtnshp Kids Schl Dir 90-; Psyc; Chld Clinical Psychlgst.**

**STICKNEY, SCOTT M,** Duquesne Univ, Pittsburgh, PA; JR; BA; Russian Clb Pres; Newspaper Sports Ed 89-; Lambda Sigma 90-; Soc Prof Jrnlsts Pres 89-; DUV 90-; Pittsburgh Penguins Ed Intern 90-; Tri-State Area Hockey Assoc Intern 90-; Amateur Hockey Mag Ed Intern 90-; Jrnlsm/Classics.

**STIDHAM, RHONDA L,** Catawba Valley Comm Coll, Hickory, NC; FR; AA; Dns GPA Awd; Bsn Adm; Rl Est Mgmt.

**STIDHAM, SHERRY L,** Ashland Comm Coll, Ashland, KY; SO; ADN; Nrsng.

**STIEB, SUSAN J,** Middle Tn St Univ, Murfreesboro, TN; FR; BA; Chi Omega 90-; Hosp Vol; Invtd To Hnrs Frat; Sci; Nrsng.

**STIFFLER, ALLAN P,** Univ Of Sc At Columbia, Columbia, SC; FR; BA; Karate Clb 90-; Discussion Grp 90-; ROTC 90-; Military Order Wrld Wars ROTC; Political Sicence; Foreign Svc/Intl Business.

**STIFFLER, KELLY W,** Mt Saint Marys Coll & Seminary, Emmitsburg, MD; SR; Srvd ARCC Advsry Com Rep Fr Clss 87; IM Vlybl Tm 89; Delta Mu Delta 90-; Pi Lambda Delta 90-; BS; Bus And Fnnce; Bus Arena.

**STIGALL, LISA M,** Ms St Univ, Miss State, MS; JR; Wesley Fndtn 88-; IM Ftbll Vllybll 90-; MI Assoc Chldrn Undr Sx 89-; Prsdnts Schlr; Deans Schlr 89-; Kappa Delta Pi 90-; Phi Mu 88-; Crscnt Sstr Tn Cnslng Prgm 89-; Elem Ed; Ech.

**STIGALL, MARY KATHERINE,** Univ Of Tn At Martin, Martin, TN; SO; BS; Future Tchrs Of Am; Hnr Roll 90; Phi Mu 87-; Spec Olympcs Org; Edn-Spec; Spec Edn Instr.

**STIGALL, STEPHEN GENE,** Univ Of Tn At Martin, Martin, TN; GD; BS; Alph Gamma Rho Chpln 88; FFA 89-90; Agrcltr Clb 86-; Yng Men Amrcn 90; Stdnt Drsdn Hgh Schl Ta 89-90; BS Hgh Schl Unv TN Mrtn 90-; Agcltr Edctn; Instrctr.

**STIGGERS, SHANNON A,** Al St Univ, Montgomery, AL; JR; BS; Baptist Campus Ministries Actvs Dir 89-90; Biomedical Sci Club Pres 90-; Toastmasters Internal 90-; Phi Eta Sigma 89-; Alpha Kappa Mu; Beta Kappa Chi; Biomedical Sci Prog 89; Biomedical Enrichment & Recruitment Prog 90-; Biology; Medicine.

**STIKELEATHER, LAURA C,** Toccoa Falls Coll, Toccoa Falls, GA; SR; Stdnt Msns Flwshp Sec 89-90; Dorm Cncl Sec 88-89; Cncrt Bnd 87-; Delta Epsilon Chi; Dns Lst 87-; BS; Mdl Grds Educ; Elem Elem Educ.

**STIKELEATHER, MARIA E,** Mount Saint Mary Coll, Newburgh, NY; SR; Ldrshp Development 90; Natural Sciences Council 90-; Amer Chem Soc Awd 90; Amer Inst Of Chemists Awd; Vincent J Gohring Chem Awd 90; Chem; Research & Development.

**STILES, DEBORAH L,** Saint Catharine Coll, St Catharine, KY; FR; AAS; Phi Theta Kappa VP; Offc Admin; Sec Wrk.

**STILES, KIM A,** S U N Y Coll Of Tech At Delhi, Delhi, NY; SR; BSN; Beta Blckrs Treas 89-; Blck/Brdl Clb Agric Stdnt Cncl Rep 79-83; Equestrian Tm Pblcty Chrmn 79-82; Phi Theta Kappa 90; Gldn Key 81; Phi Eta Sigma 80; Schlrs Prog 80-83; Coaly Socty 83; Delta Theta Sigma 82-83; Outstdng Jr Awd 82; Nrsng.

**STILES, TARA L,** Newbury Coll, Brookline, MA; SO; AAS; Clrgrd 89-90; Deans Lst 89-; Extrnshp Orchard Pk Cntry Clb NY 90; Crss Cntry Co-Cpt 90; Clnry Arts; Pstry Chf.**

**STILL, CAROLYN CHILTON,** Ga St Univ, Atlanta, GA; SR; BSE; Stdnt Georgia Assc Edctrs 90; Phi Kappa Phi; Phi Eta Sigma 86; Gldn Key Ntnl 90; Kappa Delta Pi; Phi Mu 86; Undergraduate Awrd Departmnt Curriculum Instr; Middle Chldhd Ed; Middle Schl Tchr.

**STILL, DAVID G T,** S U N Y Maritime Coll, Bronx, NY; FR; BS; Maritime Rescue 90-; NROTC 90-; Elec Eng.

**STILL, ELLIS R,** Al A & M Univ, Normal, AL; SO; BA; Bus; Fnnce.

**STILL, ETHEL R,** Selma Univ, Selma, AL; FR; Bsn Club Pres; Choir; Pre Med/Bio; Doctor.

**STILL, JAMES R,** Belmont Coll, Nashville, TN; JR; BA; SIFE Sec Treas 89-90; AES Sec 90-; Gamma Beta Phi 90-; Phi Theta Kappa 88-90; William G Hall Schlrshp Crtfd Fnlst; Asst Rcrdng Engr L Mc Auliff Studio 88-90; Music Bus; Entrprnr.

**STILL, REBECCA A,** Mary Baldwin Coll, Staunton, VA; JR; BA; Stdnt Advsr 89-90; Hnr Cncl Rep Soph 89-90; Sr Hnr Cncl; Alpha Lambda Delta 89-; Hnr Schlr 89-; Circle K 88-89; Cnslr Japanese Gov Schl Newport News VA 90; Dns Lst 89-90; Hnrs Lst 88-89; Japanese/Intl Rel; Tchr.

**STILL, SARA A,** Univ Of Sc At Columbia, Columbia, SC; JR; BA; Bapt Stdnt Un 88-; Wrkshp Theatre Actrss 88; Assoc Hons Stdnts 88-; Geo Shillito Schlrshp 88-; Engl; Librnshp.**

**STILLIO, HOLLY L,** Duquesne Univ, Pittsburgh, PA; FR; Phi Eta Sigma 90-.

**STILLIONS, JENNY R,** Frederick Comm Coll, Frederick, MD; SO; BS; Math Club 89-; Math Cmptitns 89-; AMATYC Cmptitns 90-; Bd Trustees Schlrshp 89; Hardees Schlrshp 90; AA Frederick Comm Coll; Math.**

**STILLO, LORRIE L,** Univ Of Akron, Akron, OH; JR; BS; Art; Tchr.

**STILLWELL, DAVID D,** Bethany Coll, Bethany, WV; SR; MFA; Oxford Exch Pgm 90-; Harbinger Lit Review 89-; Writers Forum Dir 90-; Tri Beta 87-88; Goodnight Hse Pres 89-; Vars Swim 87-89; Engl; Wrtr.

**STILWELL, MARY ICARD,** Catawba Valley Comm Coll, Hickory, NC; SO; Rockwell Int Prod Tech; Mchnst; Tool/Die Maker.

**STILWELL, PHILLIP C,** Limestone Coll, Gaffney, SC; JR; BA; Swim Clb Head Coach 90; Alpha Chi; Jr Mrshll At Grdtn; US Marine Corps Cpl 84-88; Cnsltng Bsnss; Bsnss Admin.

**STILWELL, RYAN A,** Ky Christian Coll, Grayson, KY; FR; BA; Stdnt Cncl Clss Rep; Sccr; Sci/Math; Scndry Ed.

**STIMAC, CHRISTOPHER R,** Eckerd Coll, St Petersburg, FL; SO; BS; Avant-Garde Cinema Chrmn 90-; Resrch; Comp Sci; Math.

**STIMELY, PAULA M,** Univ Of Akron, Akron, OH; SR; BS; Akron Cncl Edctn Stdnts Treas 90-; Deans List 89-; Elem Edn.

**STIMPSON, JOHN B,** Villanova Univ, Villanova, PA; JR; BA; Poltcl Sci; Law.

**STIMPSON, STEPHANIE C,** Georgetown Univ, Washington, DC; SR; BS; Stdnts Of Georgetown Asst Dir 87-89; Georgetown Mentors Pgm 90-; Study Abrd 89-90; Deans Lst 87-; Georgetown Childs Hosp 89-90; Washington Exec Svcs Intrn 90; Intl Mngmnt; Bus.

**STINE, KARI A,** Univ Of Miami, Coral Gables, FL; SR; BBA; Intl Bus Assoc Treas/V P 89-; UITA 90; Golden Key 90-; Beta Alpha Psi 90; Sigma Chi 87-; Deans List 87-; IM Sprts Tm Mgr 87-; Acctg; MBA Univ Of Del.

**STINE, KRISTA R,** Univ Of New Haven, West Haven, CT; JR; BA; Pol Sci Pre Law Soc 89-; Var Chrldg 89-; Soup Kitchen Asstnt 90-; Pol Sci; Govt Law.

**STINER, CIERRA S,** Davis Coll, Toledo, OH; GD; Illmntng Eng Scty 90-; Inst Bus Dsgnrs Spksmn 90-; Intern Assoc Lghtng Dsgnr 90.

**STINNER, THOMAS A,** Univ Of Tn At Knoxville, Knoxville, TN; GD; DVM; Golden Key 84-88; Phi Zeta; BS Penn State Univ; Vet Med.

**STINNETT, ANDREA B,** Va Commonwealth Univ, Richmond, VA; SR; Goldn Key 90-; Grad Magna Cum Laude; BS; Spec Ed; Tchr.

**STINNETT, MARIA L,** Shorter Coll, Rome, GA; FR; BS; Bptst Stdnt Un 90-; Nwsppr Stf 90; Chpl Chr 90-; Erly Chldhd Edctn; Mssnry.

**STINNETTE, PAMELA J,** Marshall University, Huntington, WV; JR; BBA; Gamma Beta Phi 90-; Acctg; CPA.**

**STINNETTE, PATRICIA L,** Marshall University, Huntington, WV; SR; BA; Hall Adv Cncl 85-88; Mrshl Mrchg Bnd 86-89; Dns Lst; Mgmt; Mgr.

**STINSON, CATHELENE J,** Hudson Valley Comm Coll, Troy, NY; GD; BA; Dns Lst 87-; Relg Tchr; Pryr Grp Core; Nrsry Sch Tchr; Cert Acct Albany Bsns Clg 59; Erly Chldhd; Tchr.

**STINSON, KATHRYN G,** Longwood Coll, Farmville, VA; SR; BA; Hist.

**STIPE, TARA A,** Oh Wesleyan Univ, Delaware, OH; SO; BA; Cir K Serv Chrmn 89-; Stdnt Hons Brd Sec 90-; Wmn In Sci 89-; Phi Eta Sigma 90; Phi Soc; Delta Zeta Sorority Rec Sec 89-; Dns Lst 89-; Chem/Zoolgy/Pre Med; Med.**

**STIPP, RONALD R,** S U N Y At Buffalo, Buffalo, NY; SR; BSEE; Alpha Sigma Lambda; Am Inst Plant Engs; Plant Eng; AAS Niagara Cty Comm Clg 85; Elec Eng.

**STIRLING, BRYAN P,** Univ Of Sc At Columbia, Columbia, SC; SR; BA; Inter-Frat Cncl J Bd Chf Jstc 88-; Alumni Assoc 90-; Order Omega 88-; Amoco Outstndg Tchr Awd Comm 88-; Alpha Tau Omega V P/Secr; Eisenhower Intern Rep Natl Comm 90; Sen J Strom Thurmond Intern 89; Pol Sci; Law.

**STITCHER, BARBARA J,** Salisbury St Univ, Salisbury, MD; SR; BFA; Yrbk Dsgnr 89-; Photo Clb Treas; 25 Stu Union 89-; Omicron Delta Kappa; Ocn Cty Mag Intrn Asstntshp; 2 Dmnsnl Dsgn 89; Bltmr Wtrclr Soc 86-; Art Inst Glry Slsbry Pres 89-90; FBC 85; Art.

**STITES, ANDREA D,** Madisonville Comm Coll, Madisonville, KY; SO; AS; Bus; Acctnt.

**STIVALETTA, LIA E,** Newbury Coll, Brookline, MA; SR; AS; Fashion Clb 89-90; Phi Theta Kappa; Vanson Leather Pattenmaker Intern; Fashion Dsng; Pattern Wrk.

**STIVES, ROBERT L,** Univ Of Pittsburgh At Bradford, Bradford, PA; SR; BS; Biology Clb 89-; Beta Beta Beta; AAS Jamestown Comm Clg 88; Envrnmntl Biologist.

**STIX, CRAIG A,** William Paterson Coll, Wayne, NJ; SR; Math Clb VP 88-; Tri-Co Ftbl Offcls Assn 87-; Elmwd Pk Jr Bsbl Lgue Umpr/Coach 87-; Deans Lst 87-90; N Jrsy Bld Drv Donr 87-; Acdmc Excllnce Schlrshp 90-; Almni Assn Schlrshp 87-; Elmwd Pk Mayrs Trphy 86; Applied Math.

**STOBBE, DEAN T,** Wv Univ, Morgantown, WV; SO; BS; Ski Club 89-90; Civil Engrg; Architecture.

**STOBINSKY, STACI J,** Fl International Univ, Miami, FL; SR; BA; Fut Educ Of Amer 90-; Phi Kappa Phi 90-; Phi Lambda Beta 90-; Top 10 Pct Clss 90-; Dns Lst; AA Broward Comm Clg 89; Elem Educ.

**STOCK, JENNIFER L,** Univ Of Akron, Akron, OH; JR; BA; Fncl Mgmt Asc 90-; Gldn Key 90-; Beta Gamma Sigma; Dns Lst 88-90; Acad Schlp 89-; Roush Schlp 90-; Mktg; Rsch.

**STOCK, MARGARET A,** Saint John Fisher Coll, Rochester, NY; SR; BA; Anthrplgy Clb VP 87-; Dlt Epsln Sgm 90-; Anthrplgy.

**STOCK, PETER M,** Albertus Magnus Coll, New Haven, CT; FR; BA; English/Comm; Jrnlsm.

**STOCKER, KAREN L,** Middle Tn St Univ, Murfreesboro, TN; SR; BBA; Bptst Stdnt Union; Gamma Beta Phi 86-; Offc Mgmt.

**STOCKI, TERESE M,** Univ Of Sc At Columbia, Columbia, SC; FR; MIB; Gamma Beta Phi 90-; Lambda Eta Sigma 90-; Spanish; Intrntnl Bsns.

**STOCKMAN, DENISE,** Va Commonwealth Univ, Richmond, VA; SR; Phi Eta Sigma 88; BFA; Paintg/Printmkg; Artist.

**STOCKMAN, L SUZANNE,** Ny Univ, New York, NY; JR; BA; Cntrbtng Edtr/Wrtr NYU Lit Mag 90-; Acad Achvmnt Awd; Dns Lst; Freelance Wrtr; ASSOC Endicott Coll Beverly Ma 85; Hmnts/Crtv Wrtng; Wrtr/Pblshng.

**STOCKS, SANDRA,** Univ Of Cin R Walters Coll, Blue Ash, OH; SO; BED; Stdnt Srvcs Tutor Peer Cnslr 90-; Elem Edctn; Edctn.

**STOCKSDALE, BRENT E,** Wright St Univ Lake Cmps, Celina, OH; SO; BED; WSU Lake Cmps Jr Schlstc Bowl Scorer; Soc Studies Cmprhnsv; Tchng.

**STOCKSDALE, ROBERT M,** Rochester-Hall-Crozer Dvty Sch, Rochester, NY; GD; Stdnt Cab Pres 90-; Bexley Soc 88-; Frat Order Of Police Treas 77-79; Supv Of Yr Law Enf 85; Inst Of Yr Law Enf 86-88; Otstndng Inst Natl Sfty Cncl 87; Natl Safty Cncl Inst 75-88; Law Enf Supv 67-88; MD Bexley Hl; Theol Stdies; Hosp Chpln.

**STOCKSLADER, ANNE M,** Elmira Coll, Elmira, NY; FR; BS; IM Sports Vlybl/Bwlng/Wllybl/Sftbl 90; Valedictorian Schlrshp 90; Class 1927 Prize; NCAA Division III Vlybl 90; Mathematic/Ed; Tch.

**STOCKSTAD, CHRISTINA BLANTON,** Medical Coll Of Ga, Augusta, GA; JR; DMD; SGA Sec/Treas 89-90; Omicron Kappa Upsilon 90; Stdnt Afrs Hnr Cde Violtn Comm 89-90; Tutr 88-; Hinman Schlr 90; Rcgntn Omicron Kappa Upsilon; Sftbl 88-; ASDA 88-; Dntl Hygnst 78-88; BS Old Dominion Univ 78; Dntstry.

**STOCKSTILL, GLENN F,** Univ Of Sc At Columbia, Columbia, SC; JR; BA; Gamma Beta Phi; Kappa Sigma 85-; Psychology; Clncl Psychlgst.

**STOCKTON, KAREN L,** Miami Univ, Oxford, OH; FR; MBA; Bus; Acctnt.

**STOCKTON, SCOT A,** Methodist Coll, Fayetteville, NC; FR; BS; Prks Rcrtn; Glf Prfssnl.

**STOCKWEATHER, JUDITH L,** S U N Y Coll At Fredonia, Fredonia, NY; JR; BS; Tchrs Edn Clb 89-; Deans Lst; Vol Tutor Elem Stdnts 88-; Fredonia State Ambsdr; Elem Edn; Teach.

**STODARD, MELANIE R,** Ms St Univ, Miss State, MS; FR; BS; Gamma Beta Phi; Alpha Lambda Delta; Phys Ther.

**STODDARD, ERIN,** Ny Univ, New York, NY; SO; BA; Wmns Clb 90-; Bus.**

**STODDARD, HEATHER L,** Castleton St Coll, Castleton, VT; JR; BSED; Stdnt Ed Assoc 90-; Spcl Olympcs; Deans Lst 90; Erly Chldhd.

**STODDARD, LATONYA A,** Univ Of Sc At Columbia, Columbia, SC; FR; BA; Deans List 90; Engl; Tch.

**STODDARD, LOUISE HAMILTON,** Coker Coll, Hartsville, SC; American Guild Of Organists/UNC Greensboro Pres 74/75; Dns Lst 90-; UNC-G Coker Clg; Orgnst/Dir Prtsnt Music 76-77; Orgnst/Choir Mstr 78-83; BM Salem Clg 73; MM Unc-G 75; Music; Tchr Elem Schl.

**STODDARD, SAMANTHA A,** Dartmouth Coll, Hanover, NH; FR; BA; Wind Symp/Mrchng Bnd; Coll Bwl; Camp TV Sta; Asian Org Collis Rep Stdnt Ctr Plng Brd; Hist/Clsscl Stds; Cmnctns.

**STODDARD, SCOTT T,** S U N Y Coll At Fredonia, Fredonia, NY; SO; BS; Coll Chr 89-; Opera Scns 89-90; Deans Lst 90-; IM Bsktbl 90-; Music Bus; Arts Admin.**

**STOECKER, DEBRA L,** Muskingum Coll, New Concord, OH; SR; BA; Wnd Ensmbl Pres 87-; Jz Ensmbl Pres 87-; Lambda Sigma 88-89; Omicron Delta Kappa; Sigma Alpha Iota Chptr Pres 90-; Oh Collgt Music Educ Assn Chptr Sec/Treas 87-; Awrd Acadmc Achvmnt 89-90; Acadmc/Music Schlrshp 87-; Music/Bus.

**STOESSNER, JEANNINE MARIE,** Oh St Univ, Columbus, OH; SR; BS; B Drke Schlrhsp Cncl 88; Grp Ldr Stdnt Pnl; Natl Mrt Schlr Rcrt Dy; Rmphs Soph; Hnrs Pr Spprt Prog 89; Undrgrad Chr OSU Com Acad Mscndct 90-; Phi Eta Sigma 88; Alpha Lambda Delta 88; Alpha Epsilon Delta 88-; Gldn Ky; Mrt Brd; Delta Zeta VP 90; Zlgy; Med.

**STOFA, JOHN M,** Schenectady County Comm Coll, Schenectady, NY; SR; BA; Fire Dept Frfghtr 87-; Rscue Sqd EMT 90-; Arson Invstgtn; Fire Marshall.

**STOFER, DEBBIE F,** Owensboro Comm Coll, Owensboro, KY; FR; BA; Schlrshp Green Rvr Ednl Fndtn Inc; KY Colonel; Boy Scout Ldr; Gallery Dir Ohio Co Lib Annex Gallery; Art/Hist/Edn; Art Gallery Dir/Teach.

**STOFFER, ROSS W,** Univ Of Akron, Akron, OH; SR; BS; Res Hall Govt 87-89; Clg Rpblcns 88-90; IM Sprts 87-; Gldn Ky 89-; Kappa Delta Pi 89-; Sdndry Educ; Admin.

**STOFFLET, KRISTINE M,** Indiana Univ Of Pa, Indiana, PA; SO; BED; Vrsty Sftbl 89-; Kappa Delta Pi; Alpha Xi Delta 90-; All Am Schlr; Stdnt-Athlete Awd 90; Vrsty Sftbl 89-; Elem Ed.**

**STOGDILL, CAROLINE N,** Coll Of Charleston, Charleston, SC; JR; BA; Sls Off Mngr 85-88; AA Plm Bch Comm Coll 85; Pol Sci.

**STOGNER, BELINDA B,** Univ Of Southern Ms, Hattiesburg, MS; SR; BS; Kappa Delta Pi; AA S W Ms Comm Clg 90; Elem Educ.

**STOGNER, MICHAEL J,** Ms St Univ, Miss State, MS; SR; BA; SMCC Ftbl 87-89; SMCC Stg Bnd Vclst 87-89; Engnrng Cncl; Phi Theta Kappa 87-; Omega Khi Epsilon 90-; AA SW MS Cmmnty Clg 89; Chmcl Engnr.

**STOHL, DAVID P,** Univ Of New Haven, West Haven, CT; FR.

**STOKER, JULIANNE,** Bapt Bible Coll & Seminary, Clarks Summit, PA; SR; BA; Chmbr Sngrs 86-88; Vlybl 87; Hstry; Spec Educ.

**STOKES, HARVEEN L,** Piedmont Tech Coll, Greenwood, SC; SO; BA; Phi Theta Kappa; Psi Beta Sec/Treas; Bkkpr Mgr; Psychlgy; Scl Wrk.

**STOKES, JENNIFER J,** Bethany Coll, Bethany, WV; FR; BS; Vars Vllybl 90-; Chem.

**STOKES III, JOSEPH BAILEY,** Samford Univ, Birmingham, AL; GD; JD; Amer Journal Of Trial Advcy 89-; Phi Delta Phi; Alpha Tau Omega; US States Attorneys Ofc Law Clerk 90-; BA Stetson Univ 88; Law; Attorney.

**STOKES, JULIE T,** Lenoir Rhyne Coll, Hickory, NC; JR; Dept Hrns Pltcl Sci; Intern Catawba Cty Mgr 90; Pltcl Sci; Law.

**STOKES, KARLA L,** Hampton Univ, Hampton, VA; SR; BA; Bio Clb 87-; Pre-Med Clb 87-; Beta Kappa Chi Sec 90-; Bio; Med.**

**STOKES, LEAH C,** Hinds Comm Coll, Raymond, MS; FR; BA; Pblc Rltns Grp; Tutor; Dorm Hl Cncl; Engl; Law.

**STOKES, LESLIE,** Ms Univ For Women, Columbus, MS; SR; EL/ED; Bapt Stdnt Union Missions Chmn 90; Drama Team 88-90; Beta Beta Beta 88-89; Laguna 87-90; Cheerleader 87-88; Tennis 89-90; Elem Educ; Tchr.

**STOKES, NICHOLE E,** Cheyney Univ Of Pa, Cheyney, PA; FR; BA; Cls Treas 86-90; Peer Cncl Prlmntrn 87-90; Natl Hon Soc 90-; In Effect 90-; Phi Beta Sigma Treas 90-; Tennage Neighbrhd Trpe 87-90; Stdnt Mo; Comm Serv Hon Awd; Cert Howard Career Ctr 90-; Bus Admn; Mktg Mgr.

**STOKES, QUINCY J,** Morehouse Coll, Atlanta, GA; FR; BS; Cmptr Sci; Cnsltnt/Sys Anlyst.

**STOKES, TAMI M,** Clark Atlanta Univ, Atlanta, GA; SR; BA; Fashion/Merchandising Clb 88-90; Yrbk Staff 86-87; Pep Clb 86-87; Deans Lst 88-90; Fashion Buying/Merchandising.

**STOKES, TERESA J,** Univ Of Al At Birmingham, Birmingham, AL; JR; BS; Jr League 90; Math.

**STOKES, TRACEY A,** Spartanburg Methodist Coll, Spartanburg, SC; FR; BA; Stdnt Govt Pres 90-; Annual Staff 90-; Hnr Code Comm Cl Rep 90-; Habitat For Hmnty 90-; Ldrshp Schlrshp 90-; Chrldr 90-; Pol Sci; Law.

**STOKLOSA, YVONNE M,** S U N Y At Buffalo, Buffalo, NY; GD; MARCH; Interior Dsgnr/Fclts Plnnr; AAS 81; BPS 90; Archtc.

**STOLARCYK, WENDY K,** Radford Univ, Radford, VA; SO; Kappa Mu Epsilon 90-; Spcl Kids Day Broome Cnty Fair Whitney Pt NY Vol 87-; Vrsty Field Hockey 89-90; Math; Tchr/Profr.**

**STOLER, JUAN PEDRO,** Fl Atlantic Univ, Boca Raton, FL; SR; BS; Fncl Mgmt Assoc; Fncl Mgmt Assoc; FAU Prsdnts Hrn Lst 90; Fnc.

**STOLL, SHERIDEEN S,** Univ Of Akron, Akron, OH; JR; BS; Golden Key 90-; Acctg; CPA.

**STOLL-STINCHCOMB, JENNIFER L,** Bethany Coll, Bethany, WV; SR; Yrbk Edtr 87; Theatre 87; TV-3 90; Alpha Psi Omega Pres 89; Sigma Tau Epsilon 90; Kappa Delta 88; Trmpt In Lnd Intrnshp In Prof Theatre 88-89; BA Bethany Clg; Fine/Applied Arts Sr Fllw Assistntshp 90; Fine Applied Arts Theatre; Perf.

**STOLLAR, LAUREL A,** West Liberty St Coll, West Liberty, WV; JR; BS; Hnrs Prgrm; Chi Beta Phi; Mcrblgcl Rsrch Prjct; Mdcl Tchnlgy.

**STOLLER, CHIP D,** Embry Riddle Aeronautical Univ, Daytona Beach, FL; SO; BS; Rising Young Amer 89; IM 90-; Aeronautical Sci; Profl Pilot.

**STOLLER, DANIEL G,** Cornell Univ Statutory College, Ithaca, NY; SO; BS; Natl Schlr; Alpha Tau Omega; Lightwgt Crew 89-90; Law/Med.

**STOLLER, PAMELA A,** Kent St Univ Stark Cmps, North Canton, OH; SO; BA; KSSEA Pr 90-; OSEA 90-; Ldrshp Recog Awd 90-; Mullen Awd Non-Trad Stdnts 90-; Dept Awd In Educ 90-; Sunday Schl Tchr 89-; YMCA T-Ball Coach 88-; Assoc Of Sci; Elem Tchr.

**STOLLINGS, VIDA L,** Defiance Coll, Defiance, OH; JR; BS; Scl Wrkrs Assoc 90; Habitat For Hmnty 90; Good Smrtn Prog 90; EMT Nrsry Chrch Wrkr 76; Firemens Aux Crisis Lne Vol 90; Head Strt 80-84; Park Lane Schl 84-89; Scl Wrk.

**STOLTZ, ELIZABETH MARIE,** Mount Aloysius Jr Coll, Cresson, PA; FR; Cmmty Farm Show Vol 87-; Acctng Bkkpr 87; Bsn; Acctnt.

**STOLTZ, GLENDA L,** Kent St Univ Kent Cmps, Kent, OH; JR; BA; Acad Achvmnt Awrd Kent Ashtabula 88-89; Anthropology.

**STOLTZ, ROBIN L,** Univ Of Sc At Columbia, Columbia, SC; SO; BSN; Gamma Beta Phi Hstrn 89-; Outstndng Stdnt Nat Sci Awd 90; AS; Science; Nurse.

**STOLTZFUS, SHERRY D,** Lenoir Rhyne Coll, Hickory, NC; SR; Alpha Lambda Delta 90-; Endwmnt Schlrshp 90-; Voigt R Cromr Awd Classcs 90; Chrch Pianst Hckry Chrst Fllwshp 81-; Stdnt NCAE; BA 90; Engl/Latin; Tchg H S.

**STOLZ, LESLIE E,** Villanova Univ, Villanova, PA; FR; BS; Bsktbll Clb 90-; Pi Beta Phi; Blgy.

**STOLZENBACH, CRAIG S,** Anne Arundel Comm Coll, Arnold, MD; FR.

**STOLZENBERG, SUZANNE J,** Univ Of Pittsburgh, Pittsburgh, PA; JR; BSN; Stdnt Hlth Advsry Brd Cmt Chrprsn 88-90; Rsdnt Stdnt Assc Flr Rep 88-89; Sgm Theta Tau 90-; Alpha Tau Dlt Pres 90-; Schlr 90; Intrnshp Hartford Hosp 90; Provost Schlr 88-; Nrsng.

**STONE, ANGELA C,** Christopher Newport Coll, Newport News, VA; SO; BS; C Nwprt Frch Clb Fndr/Pres 90-; SGA Sec 90-; Gamma Phi Beta 90-; Stdnt Ldrshp 90; Psych; Bus Cnsltng.

**STONE, BRENDA D,** Germanna Comm Coll, Locust Grove, VA; FR; BA; Bus Admin.

**STONE, BRONSON B,** Bloomsburg Univ Of Pa, Bloomsburg, PA; FR; BS; Trck/Fld; Sec Educ/Hstry; Tch.

**STONE, CATHERINE A,** Oh Coll Of Podiatric Med, Cleveland, OH; JR; DPM; Sprts Med Clb 89-; Amer Coll Ft Srgns Clb VP 90-; Alpha Gamma Kappa; Dean Lst; Merit Schlrshp 88-; Extern Cleveland Clnc Vsclr Srgry; BA Quinnipiac Coll 89; Podtrc Med; Podtrc Physcn.

**STONE, CHARLES A,** Oh St Univ At Marion, Marion, OH; JR; BED; Dns Stdnt Advsry Cncl 90-; Stdnt Alumni Cncl 90-; Ed Soc 90-; Psych Clb 90-; Joint Phys Plng Comm 90-; Griffin Hnr Soc Pres 90-; Buckeye Ambsdr 90-; Summa Awd 90-; Outstndg Stdnt Awd 90-; Dns Lst 88-; AA; Scl Sci; Elem Ed.

**STONE, CHRISTOPHER A,** Carnegie Mellon Univ, Pittsburgh, PA; FR; BSC; Mrchng Bnd 90-; Corroboree 90-; Pttsbrgh Supercomptr Cntr Smnr; Math; Comp Sci.

**STONE, DEIDRE G,** Valdosta St Coll, Valdosta, GA; SO; BSED; Hon Awd Rcgntn; Art; Teach.**

**STONE, ERIC W,** S U N Y Coll Of A & T Morrisvl, Morrisville, NY; GD; Bus Psychology; Mktg.

**STONE, HOWELL S,** Univ Of Ga, Athens, GA; JR; BLA; Lndscp Archtctr.

**STONE, IRENE E,** Tuskegee Univ, Tuskegee Inst, AL; JR; BA; Stdnt Natl Ed Assoc 90-; Kappa Delta Pi; Elem Ed; Tchg.

**STONE, J MICHELLE,** Judson Coll, Marion, AL; FR; BS; Judson Schlrs; J Jewett Hon Soc Awrd/Schlrshp; Ed; Tchr.

**STONE, JAMILA M,** George Mason Univ, Fairfax, VA; SR; BA; Stdt Educ Assoc 89-; Golden Key 89-; Deans List 89-; Kappa Delta Pi 89-; Spec Olympcs Vol 90; Va Educ Assoc 89-; Porter/Novelli Pblc Rltns Firm 82-; Middle Educ; Teaching/Counseling.**

**STONE, JEFFREY A,** Cincinnati Bible Coll & Sem, Cincinnati, OH; GD; MDV; Cncl Pres 87-89; Kenai Christian Church 90-; Bsktbl 86-90; Phila Chrstn Chrch 87-90; BS Cntrl Chrstn Coll Bbl 90; Chrch Hstry/Thlgy; Prch/Prof.**

**STONE, JENNIFER E,** James Madison University, Harrisonburg, VA; SO; BS; James Madison Dance Theatre Assoc Grp 90-; Pres Lst 89-; Univ Pgrm Bd 90-; Dunlop Schrshp; Karate Clb 89-90; Psychlgy/Erly Chlhd Educ; Tchng/Erly Chldhd.

**STONE, KAREN A,** Dowling Coll, Oakdale Li, NY; SR; BA; Trnsfr Schlrshp 87-89; AA Suffolk Comm Coll 89; Visual Arts; Art Tchr.

**STONE, KATHERINE S,** Smith Coll, Northampton, MA; SO; BA; Dysprng 89-; Int Vars Chrstn Flwshp 90-; Dns Lst 89-; Spnsh.

**STONE, KIMBERLY A,** Wilmington Coll, New Castle, DE; SR; BA; SG Treas 87-88; AS 90; Bhvrl Sci.

**STONE, LAKEISHA SARON,** Clark Atlanta Univ, Atlanta, GA; SO; Speech Arts; Spch Pathologist.

**STONE, LAURA M,** Daytona Beach Comm Coll, Daytona Beach, FL; FR; AS; Intr Dsgn Technlgy.

**STONE, MARY F,** Franklin And Marshall Coll, Lancaster, PA; SO; GOA Clb; Dana Schlr 91-; Tri Sigma 90-; Elderlink 90-; Spalding Flwshp Intrn; Cngrsmn Chandler Intern; Pltcl Sci; Foreign Serv/Rltns.

**STONE, MARY H,** Memphis St Univ, Memphis, TN; SR; BSW; Soc Wrkrs Clb; Deans Lst; Phi Kappa Phi; Church Choir; Unit Meth Wmn; Unit Meth Mnstr Alcohol/Drg Trtmnt; Soc Wrk; Meth Mstry.

**STONE, MELISSA GAIL,** Mount Aloysius Jr Coll, Cresson, PA; FR; BS; Entrtnmnt Comm Chrprsn 89-; Madrigal Dnr Spec Olympics 89-90; Chorus 89-; Orien Ldr 90-; Med Lab Techncn.

**STONE, MICHELE L,** Middle Ga Coll, Cochran, GA; FR; AS; Comp Sci; Systm Anlyss.

**STONE, NATHAN J,** Schenectady County Comm Coll, Schenectady, NY; FR; BA; Msc; Msc Educ/Perfmnc.

**STONE, NICOLE C,** Boston Univ, Boston, MA; SO; MSPT; Prog Cncl 89-; Orientatn Ldr 90; Big Sistr 90-; Deans Lst 89-; Phys Thrpy.

**STONE, NOONIE E,** Williamsburg Tech Coll, Kingstree, SC; SO; MED; Phi Theta Kappa Soc; Hd Grls Aux Ldr/Advsr 86-90; Wmns Aux Pres 71-74; Erly Chldhd Educ; Tchr.

**STONE, PAMELA L,** Abraham Baldwin Agri Coll, Tifton, GA; FR; BED; Ed; Tchng.

**STONE, PATRICIA A,** Newbury Coll, Brookline, MA; SO; AS; Sec; Legl Sec; Law.

**STONE, PAULA R,** Piedmont Tech Coll, Greenwood, SC; SR.

**STONE, RICHARD D,** Radford Univ, Radford, VA; SO; BA; Geology; Engineering.

**STONE, ROBIN L,** Kent St Univ Kent Cmps, Kent, OH; SO; BUS 89-; Peer Awareness 90-; King Kennedy Ctr; Oscar Ritchie Schlrshp 90-.

**STONE, SARA,** Univ Of Ky, Lexington, KY; SR; BS; KY Acdmy Stdnts Phrmcy Poison Prvntn Comm Chrprsn 89-; Rho Chi 90; Lambda Kappa Sigma 89-; Pharmacy.

**STONE, SCOTT D,** Le Moyne Coll, Syracuse, NY; JR; BS; Acctng Scty 90-; Mrktng Clb 90-; Syracuse Univ Intnl Audit Dept; Bond Schoeneck King Law Firm Acctnt Asstnt 89-90; IM Bsktbl Ftbl Coed Sccr Coed Vlybl; Acctng.

**STONE, SHANNON D,** Univ Of Sc At Columbia, Columbia, SC; FR; BA; Chmstry.

**STONE, SUSAN L,** Univ Of Montevallo, Montevallo, AL; FR; BFA; Art; Tchr.

**STONE, TAMMY M,** Jefferson Comm Coll, Watertown, NY; FR; BA; Off Mgr 86-90; Math Sci Engr; Envrnmntl Engr.

**STONE, TRACY J,** Univ Of Rochester, Rochester, NY; SR; BA; Chrldng Cptn 87-; Phi Beta Kappa 90-; Dstrct Attnry Intrn 90; Prvt Law Frm Intrn; Pltcl Sci; Law.

**STONECYPHER, TINA S,** Valdosta St Coll, Valdosta, GA; SR; BED; PAGE 88-; AED Abraham Baldwin Ag Clg 86; Mdl Grades Ed; Soc Stds Tchr.

**STONEHAM, ANNE E,** Cornell Univ Statutory College, Ithaca, NY; JR; DVM; Cornell Chorus Asst Fncl Mgr 89-; Cornell Pre Vet Socty Pub Rel Offcr 89-; Morrison Schlrshp $100 From Cornell; Anml Sci; Vet Med.

**STONEHOUSE, KAREN F,** Western New England Coll, Springfield, MA; SO; BS; Sociology; Human Resources.

**STONEKING, MICHELLE L,** Salem-Teikyo Univ, Salem, WV; JR; BA; Hmncs Assoc Fnc Chr; SG 90-; Psi Phi Sec; Delta Mu 90-; Untd Wy Intern; Deans Lst 90; Yth Hmn Srvcs.

**STONEMAN, CHERYL A,** S U N Y Coll Of Tech At Alfred, Alfred, NY; SR; AD; Nrsng Clb Alfrd St Coll 89-; Pr Ttr Nrsng; Hmn Blgy; Antmy Physlgy 89-; Dns Lst 88-; Sigma Tau 88-; Phi Theta Kappa; Zonta Awrd; Otstndng Achvmnt Awrd; Fam Vlnce Tsk Frce Brd Of Dirs VP 88-; Fam Vlnce Crss Htlne Vol 88-; Nrsng; Nrse Prcttnr.**

**STONER, ANITA M,** Kent St Univ Kent Cmps, Kent, OH; JR; BA; Acctg Assoc; Golden Key; Alpha Lambda Delta 89-; VITA; Pres List 89-90; Natl Clgt Bus Merit Awd; Acctg.

**STONER, SYLVIA F,** Skidmore Coll, Saratoga Spg, NY; FR; Chorus Lib 90-; Theater Co; Voice Awd; Highest Hnrs Acdmc I Hnrs; Win Concerto Comp; Music; Opera.

**STONESIFER, NICHOLAS E,** Comm Coll Algny Co Algny Cmps, Pittsburgh, PA; SO; BA; Carnegie Mellon Unvrsty Lacrosse Clb 89-; Cmmnctns; Jrnlsm Media.

**STONEWATER, JACQUE L,** Daytona Beach Comm Coll, Daytona Beach, FL; SO; BA; Phi Theta Kappa Treas 90-; Ed; Elem Ed.

**STONIER, JACQUELINE L,** Elmira Coll, Elmira, NY; SR; BA; Biology Tutor Basi Coll Courses 90-; Home Habilitation Asst Steuben ARC 90-; AAS Alfred State Coll 85; Biology; HS Biol/Chmstry Tchr.

**STONIKINIS, KERRYINGTON P,** Patrick Henry Comm Coll, Martinsville, VA; SO; AA; Alpha Psi Omega Pres 83-87; Delta Omicron Pi Pres 85-87; BA Emory Henry Coll 87; Appld Sci; Nrsng.

**STOOKEY, SHAWN L,** Union Univ, Jackson, TN; SR; Rutledge Hstry Clb 89-90; STEA 90; Phi Alpha Theta 90; IM Sftbl Bsktb Vllybl 89-90; BS 90; Hstry/Sec Educ; Mnstr Yth Actvts.

**STOOPS, SABRINA S,** Marshall University, Huntington, WV; SR; BS; Hall Advsry Cncl Treas 88-89; March Band 87-88; Kappa Delta Pi 90-; Good Will Assoc Awd 89-90; Elem Edn; Teach.

**STOREY, CLAYTON E,** Univ Of Sc At Columbia, Columbia, SC; FR; BA; Gamma Beta Phi; Deans Lst 90-; Edctn; Tch Coach.

**STOREY, FERNANDA L,** Al A & M Univ, Normal, AL; JR; BS; Bnd; Phi Beta Sigma Swthrt; Pi Delta Kappa; Mltry Hon Grad; Sigma Tau Epsilon; Army Rsrv Sclst 90-; Elem Ed; Tchr.

**STOREY, JANE B,** Univ Of New Haven, West Haven, CT; SO; BS; Hall Cncl Tres 90-; Amtr Fncng Assc Great Britain; Lmd Dlt; Vol Corps; Deans List; Acctg.

**STOREY, STEVEN C,** Tn Temple Univ, Chattanooga, TN; SO; BS; Tmple Advntrst Grtto VP 90-; Chi Sigma Delta IM Sccr Hlfbck 90-; Chi Sigma Delta IM Ftbl Dfnsve Line 90-; Chi Sigma Delta Actvts Dir 89-; Admin Mgmt; PR Plnng.

**STORIE, BILLY W,** Middle Tn St Univ, Murfreesboro, TN; SO; BA; Educ; Coach/Tchr.

**STORIE, ERIN C,** Ashland Comm Coll, Ashland, KY; SO; Assoc Sci; Biol; Med.

**STORM, BARBARA A,** Christopher Newport Coll, Newport News, VA; JR; BS; Wrld Taekwondo Fed; NASA Lngly Rsrch Cntr Scrty Serv Brnch Hmptn Va 90-; Assoc 82; Crmnl Jstc; Law Enfrcmnt.

**STORM, MARK G,** Embry Riddle Aeronautical Univ, Daytona Beach, FL; SR; BS; Ftbll Hcky; Arntcs.

**STORM, PAUL A,** Capital Bible Seminary, Lanham, MD; GD; MDIV; Stdnt Cncl Treas 90-; BA Appalachian Bible Clg 88; Theology; Minister.

**STORMES, CHRISTIAN T,** Immaculata Coll, Immaculata, PA; JR; BA; Engl; Sales.

**STORNIOLO, FRANK A,** Merrimack Coll, North Andover, MA; SR; BA; Acctg/Fin Soc; Co-Op Educ Prog; Deans Lst; Alpha Kappa Psi VP 90; Co-Op Educ Wrk Acctg; Var Ftbl IM Flg Ftbl/Bsktbl; Acctg/Bus; CPA.

**STORR, DION WALTON,** Fl A & M Univ, Tallahassee, FL; JR; BA; Stdnt Govt Elec Comm; Peer Fac Assn 88-90; Camps Allnc Lit; Phi Theta Kappa Pr 89-90; Phi Theta Kappa Alum Assn VP 90-; Univ Hnrs Awd; AA Miami Dade Comm Clg 90; Arch.

**STORR, KEVIN E,** Univ Of Southern Ms, Hattiesburg, MS; JR; BA; Gamma Beta Phi 90-; Gldn Key 90-; Kappa Alpha 88-89; Radio/Tlvsn/Film; Reporter.

**STORR, MEGHAN R,** Ramapo Coll Of Nj, Mahwah, NJ; JR; BA; Bcchs VP 90-; Ttr; Pltcl Sci.

**STORROD, SANDRA P,** Univ Of The Virgin Islands, St Thomas, VI; JR; BA; Phi Beta Lambda; Explrrs Clb; Bus Admin Comp Applctns; Systms Anlyst Acct.

**STORY, ALAN W,** Lenoir Rhyne Coll, Hickory, NC; JR; BS; Baptist Student Union VP 89-; Choir 89-90; Mu Sigma Epsilon; Alpha Beta Lamda 90-; Chi Beta Phi; Biology; Medical School.

**STORY, DAN W,** Savannah St Coll, Savannah, GA; SR; BA; Bus Mgmt; Fin.

**STORY, DEBORAH A,** Lenoir Rhyne Coll, Hickory, NC; FR; PHD; Baptist Student Union 90-; Stdnt Marshal Commencement Exercise; Chemistry; Pharmacy.

**STORY, GINA M,** Allegheny Coll, Meadville, PA; FR; BS; Lambda Sigma Pblcty Comm; Biochemistry; Neurochemical Rsrch.

**STORY, JENNIFER C,** Allegheny Coll, Meadville, PA; JR; BA; Choir Wonmens Ensemble 89; Resdnt Advisor 90; Civic Symphony Soloist; Lambda Sigma 89-90; Psi Chi 90; Alden Scholar 88; Lambda Sigma 89-90; Psi Chi 90; Alpha Gamma Delta VP 89; Loretta Strayer Awrd 89-90; Stdnt Orientn Advsr; Psych/Ed; Elem Teaching.

**STORY, JILL D,** Univ Of Ky, Lexington, KY; JR; BA; Pre Law Clb 90-; Cmnctns Comm SGA Elctn; Lambda Sigmasoc Chr 88-; Omicron Delta Kappa; Mrtr Bd Eltns Chm; Chi Omega Pres; Poli Sci; Law.

**STORY, MARY N,** Valdosta St Coll, Valdosta, GA; JR; BS; Phi Theta Kappa 87; Media Com A B Clark Elem Schl 88-; Trnr Co Yng Frmrs Wvs 87-; AS ABAC 87; Erly Chldhd Educ; Tchr.

**STORY, TINA R,** Univ Of Ga, Athens, GA; SR; BSHE; Vol GA Rtrdtn Cntr 88-89; Alpha Zeta Hon Chrnclr 89-; Phi Upsilon Omicron 90-; Gamma Sigma Sigma Pldg Treas 88-90; Chld/Fmly Dvlpmnt/Fmly Comm Spclst; Scl Wrk.

**STOSKUS, CARYN J,** Bucknell Univ, Lewisburg, PA; FR; BA; Cath Cmps Mnstry 90-; Orchestra 90-; Wind Ensmbl 90-; Delta Gamma 90-; Cath Cmps Mnstry 90-; IM Vlybl 90-; Intl Rltns/Music; Law.

**STOSS, KATHERINE P,** Univ Of Ky, Lexington, KY; SR; BA; Amnesty Intl 89-; Thtr Dept 87-; Golden Key 89-; Outstndg Fresh 88; Engl Educ; Teach.

**STOTHART, WENDY L,** Indiana Univ Of Pa, Indiana, PA; JR; BED; Circle K Mbrshp Chr 88-; Phi Sigma Pi 89-; Actvts Brd 89-90; Provost Schlr 90-; Mc Farland Acad/Comm Serv Schlrshp 90-; Elem Educ; Teacher.

**STOTKA, ANDREA M,** Duquesne Univ, Pittsburgh, PA; SO; BA; Zeta Tau Alpha 90-; Intern Sewickley Vlly Hosp; Schlr; Phrmcy.

**STOTLER, KIM M,** Duquesne Univ, Pittsburgh, PA; SR; BS; AA Tchr Ed Allegheny Cmnty Clg; Elem Ed; Tchng.

**STOTLER, MICHAEL B,** Memphis St Univ, Memphis, TN; JR; BA; Peer Mentor Progrm 88-F Tutor Core 89-; Psychlgy Club 90-; Phi Eta Sigma 89-; Alpha Epsilon Delta 90-; Deans List 88-; Psychlgy; Medcn.

**STOTT, DEBORAH A,** Fl International Univ, Miami, FL; GD; MPH; Natl Audubon Soc Stdnt Brd Mbr 88-89; Phi Kappa Phi; Soc Respiratory Therapy 86-; 2 Papers Publsh The Relationship Between Lung Cancer & Asbestus Exposure; Organizational Change In The Workplace; FSRT Crtt; BA FIU 88; Envirnmntl Health; Science.

**STOTT, JENNIFER A,** Univ Of Al At Birmingham, Birmingham, AL; SO; BS; Amer Chem Soc 90-; Alpha Lambda Delta 90-; All Amer Schlr 90-; Pr Lst 89-; Bio; Pediatrician.

**STOTTS, CARLA R,** Memphis St Univ, Memphis, TN; SO; BA; Phi Eta Sigma 90-; Hist.

**STOTZ, KAREN A,** Fl St Univ, Tallahassee, FL; SO; BS; Futr Eductrs Amer; Phi Eta Sigma; Fl Undergrad Schlrs Fnd; Engl Educ; Tchr.

**STOUDEMIRE III, CHARLES H,** Univ Of Sc At Columbia, Columbia, SC; JR; BA; Aiken Plyrs VP 88-; German Club 89-90; Best Stage Mgr 89-; Gold Mask Award 90-; Robert P Benjamin Mem Schlrshp 89-90; Theater; Stage Mgt.

**STOUDENMIRE, REBECCA S,** Univ Of Sc At Columbia, Columbia, SC; FR; BA; Sci/Math/Bio; Phys Thrpy.

**STOUFFER, AMY L,** Indiana Univ Of Pa, Indiana, PA; SO; BA; Oremus-Cont Christn Show Chr 89-; Coal Christian Outrch Ldrshp Tm 89-; Sign Lang Clb 89-90; Natl Cncl Excep Chldrn 90-; Deans Lst 89; Educ Excep Persns; Spec Educator.

**STOUFFER, STEPHANIE M,** Hagerstown Jr Coll, Hagerstown, MD; FR; Radlgy Clb; Phi Theta Kappa; Beard/Leila Miller Schlrshp; Deans Lst 90-; Cmptitv Admssn Rdlgy Pgm; Rdlgc Tech; Dgnstc Imgng.

**STOUGH, JONATHAN SCOTT,** Central Pa Bus School, Summerdale, PA; SR; Admin Mgmt Soc 90-; Untd Cmmrcl Trvlrs 87-; Holy Spirit Hosp 90-; St Johns Franklin Chrch Yth Grp Pres 86-88; Bsktbl-Tnns Tms 90-; ASB 89-; Bus Mgmt; Owner.

**STOUGHTON, MELANIE R,** Allegheny Coll, Meadville, PA; JR; BA; Alden Schlr 89-90; Biolgy; Vet Med.

**STOUP, JEANNE E,** Northern Ky Univ, Highland Hts, KY; JR; Rowing Clb Womens Capt 89-; Albright Hlth Cntr Wk Stdy Prog Lifegd 87-; IM Actvts Capt 87-.

**STOUT, CANDICE M,** Kent St Univ Ashtabula Cmps, Ashtabula, OH; FR; BA; Stdnt Snt 90-; Nwspr Bus Mgr 90-; Bus/Acctng Clb Sec/Tr 90-; Stdnt Ldrshp Awd 90-; Deans Lst 90-; Acctng; CPA.

**STOUT, CHARITY D,** Univ Of Tn At Martin, Martin, TN; FR; BA; Alpha Sweethearts 90; Biology; Medicine.

**STOUT, JANET E,** Livingston Univ, Livingston, AL; SR; Strs Of AL Dnce Tm Capt 89; Lvngstn Univ Envy 90; Pnhllnc Cncl Rep 90; Omicron Delta Kappa 90-; Phi Mu Pres 87-; Adpt A Mile Phi Mu Rep 90; IM Sprts 87-; Chldrns Mrcle Ntwrk 87-; BA Livingston Univ; Acctng; Acct.

**STOUT, NANCY F,** Marywood Coll, Scranton, PA; JR; BS; ESAC 2nd Dbls Tnns Chmpn 90; ESAC All-Star Tm 90; Tnns Tm 90-; Ordr Amrnth; Psychclgy; MSW/CNSLR.

**STOUT, PEGGY F,** Bristol Univ, Bristol, TN; SO; AAS; ALS 90-; Prlgl Assoc 90-; Glg Sec Assoc 90-; Prlgl; Law.

**STOUT, WESLEY C,** Comm Coll Algny Co Algny Cmps, Pittsburgh, PA; BA Univ Of Pitt 79; Urban Studies.

**STOVALL, CHARLES B,** Pasco Hernando Comm Coll, Dade City, FL; SO; AA; Stdnt Govt Prlmntrn 90-; Phi Theta Kappa Treas 88-89; Phi Theta Kappa Vp 89-90; Cmps Nwspr Rprtr/Crtc 88-; Cmnctns; Jrnlsm.**

**STOVALL, EILEENA R,** Memphis St Univ, Memphis, TN; FR; BA; Women Show Bus Cntry Music Assn Acdmy Cntry Music 87; Asst To Prdcr And Coordntr New Hllywd Sqres 86-90; Art Hstry; Tv.

**STOVALL, JOHNNIE B,** Univ Of Al At Huntsville, Huntsville, AL; JR; BS; Chrmn Mrt Promtn EEO 88; Geophysicist 80-88; BS Tenn Tech Univ 76; MS Univ Southern Miss 80; MS Univ Southern Miss 89; Cmptr Eng; Eng.

**STOVALL, LORI S,** Univ Of Southern Ms, Hattiesburg, MS; SR; MA; Stdnt Alumni Assn 90-; Stdnt Edctrs Assn 90-; BS; Engl; Educ Scndry.

**STOVARSKY, JENNIFER L,** Univ Of Akron, Akron, OH; SO; BA; Phi Eta Sigma 90-; Alpha Lambda Delta 90-; Elem Educ.

**STOVER, ELIZABETH C,** Georgetown Univ, Washington, DC; JR; BSBA; Bsn Day Steering Comm Chr/Mktg Subcomm 90-; Intl Rels Clb 88-; CHUMS 90-; Beta Gamma Sigma; Natl Symph Orch Vol Asst; Price Waterhouse Intern 90-; Eli Lilly Co Intern 90; Mktg; Publ Rels.

**STOVER, JO ANN,** Oh Dominican Coll, Columbus, OH; FR; BA; Lbry Sci; Media Spclst/Elem Ed.

**STOVER, JODI L,** Washington State Comm Coll, Marietta, OH; SO; AAB; Bus; Mktg.

**STOVER, PHILIP D,** Tidewater Comm Coll, Portsmouth, VA; FR; BA; Civil Eng.

**STOVER-CASSELL, LOU ANN,** Concord Coll, Athens, WV; SR; BS; Concord Clg Drama Soc 88; Tutor 89; Kappa Delta Pi Pres 89; Alpha Chi 89; Gamma Beta Phi 89; Cardinal Key 90; Tutor 89-90; EPPAC 90; Engl Mjr Award 90; Engl; WVU Clg Law.

**STOVER-TREADWAY, ALMETTA,** Wilmington Coll, New Castle, DE; GD; MBA; Advsry Cncl Membr Proj 70001 86-89; Chrch Orgnst 89-; Statstcl Admin Asst Cnsmr Mktg Rsrch.

**STOWERS, MAXINE,** Comm Coll Algny Co Algny Cmps, Pittsburgh, PA; SO; BA; Gen; Nrsg.

**STOWMAN, MARY N,** Chattanooga St Tech Comm Coll, Chattanooga, TN; GD; SA; Art Clb Pres 89-; Phi Theta Kappa Pres 90-; Grl Sct Smr Dy Cmp Ldr 90; Clvlnd St Art Shw 90; Nw Otstndnh Artst Crtfct 89; Hnrs Shw Mrt Awrd 90; End Of Yr Art Shw 89-; Soddy Untd Mthdst Chrch 88-; Art Education.

**STOY, THEODORE S,** Duquesne Univ, Pittsburgh, PA; JR; BA; Hstry Clb 90-; Phi Alpha Theta 90-; Hstry.

**STOYANOVSKI, LILY,** S U N Y At Buffalo, Buffalo, NY; SR; MBA; SHRM 89-; Women In Mngmnt 89-; Macedonian Youth Grp 84-; Golden Key 90-; Niagara Pr Schlrshp 87-88; BS 90; Bus Admin; Human Res Mngmnt.

**STRABLE, ELIZABETH A,** Defiance Coll, Defiance, OH; SR; BS; Alpha Chi 90-; Headstart 85-88; Tech Cert Chld Cre Tech IN Tech Coll 85; Elem Ed; Tchng.

**STRACHAN, DENISE A,** Savannah St Coll, Savannah, GA; SR; BA; Dlb Royl Bahamian 89-; Res Asst 90-; Delta Sigma Pi Pr 90-; Hstrn Wr 90; Mgmt; Persnl Mgmt.

**STRACK, ANN MARIE,** Glassboro St Coll, Glassboro, NJ; SR; Women In Cmmnctns Inc 89; Gamma Tau Sigma 90; Alpha Epsilon Phi Edctnl Chrprsn 90; Deans Lst 88; WPVI-TV Chnnl 6 Intrnshp 90; BA; Cmmnctns/Lbrl Arts.

**STRADER, JEANETTE L,** Corning Comm Coll, Corning, NY; SO; BA; Humanities Fclty Schlrshp; AA Corning Cmnty Clg; Infrmtn Stdys; Librarian.**

**STRAFACI, CHRISTINA M,** Le Moyne Coll, Syracuse, NY; JR; BA; Rsdnt Asst 90-; Lemoyne Stdnt Prgrmng Brd 88-90; Emmaus Retreat Prog 88-; Alpha Sigma Nu 90-; PIC 88-; Intl Studies Assn Schlrshp Summer Study France; Diploma Centre Intl D Etudes Francaises; French; Univ Ed.

**STRAGER, AMY L,** Oh St Univ At Newark, Newark, OH; SR; BS; Deans List 90; Elmntry Ed; Tch.

**STRAGER, MICHELLE HELENE,** Marshall University, Huntington, WV; FR; BS; Stdnt Orgnztn Alumni Stdnts 90-; Phi Eta Sigma Treas; Cross Cntry Indoor Outdoor Track 90-; Math/Computer Sci.

**STRAHAN, CAROLYN G,** Birmingham Southern Coll, Birmingham, AL; JR; BA; Rcrtng Comm 89; Mrtr Bd Cand; Omicron Delta Kappa; Alpha Kappa Psi; Cert Med Stf Crdntr/Carraway Meth Med Cntr 89-91; CMSC Natl Assn Med Stf Srvcs 89; Bus Admin/Mgmt; Law.**

**STRAIGHT, DARRYL S,** Hudson Valley Comm Coll, Troy, NY; SR; AAS; Theta Xi; Bus; Acctg.

**STRAIGHT, TIMOTHY M,** Wright St Univ, Dayton, OH; FR; BS; Pre Med Scty 90-; Blgy Clb 90-; Hnrs Assn 90-; Alpha Lambda Delta; Blgcl Scis; Med.

**STRAIT JR, FRANK D,** Univ Of Sc At Columbia, Columbia, SC; FR; BSBA; Arretc; Schlrshp; Atmosphrc Sci.

**STRALEY, SARAH J,** Emory & Henry Coll, Emory, VA; SR; BA; Concert Choir Section Head 88-; Res Advsr 88-; Blue Gold Soc 88-; Phi Sigma Iota 90-; Cardinal Key Hstrn 90-; Delta Rho Delta Pres 88; Alpha Phi Omega Pdgmstr; Winston Salem Jrnl Intrn 90; T V Intrnshp; Mass Cmunctns/Brdcstng; T V Reprtr Anchrng.

**STRAND, DEBORAH M,** Univ Of Miami, Coral Gables, FL; JR; BA; Flr Im Tm SCUM 88-90; Sigma Alpha Epsilon Ltl Sis 88-; After Sch House Vol 90; Deans List 90; Varsty Athlt Crew Tm 89-; Psychlgy; Educ/Cnslng.

**STRANDBERG, AMELIA K,** Northwest Al Comm Coll, Phil Campbell, AL; SO; BA; Pres Lst 90; Dns Lst; Ed; Tchg.

**STRANG, MICHELLE L,** Univ Of Sc At Columbia, Columbia, SC; FR; Acctg; Publ Accnt.

**STRANGE, CONNIE M,** Savannah St Coll, Savannah, GA; SO; MBA; Phi Beta Lambda Hstrn 90-; Hnrs Bnqt Deans Lst; Hnrs Rl 90-; Bus; Mngng.

**STRANGE, DANIEL R,** Spartanburg Methodist Coll, Spartanburg, SC; SO; Bio; Psychtry.

**STRANGE, JIMMY L,** Lenoir Comm Coll, Kinston, NC; FR; DAS; EDP Clb 90; Trbdrs 90; Cmptr Prog; Wrk IBM.

**STRANGE, NANCY M,** Truett Mc Connell Coll, Cleveland, GA; JR; BA; Med Rec Librn Nurs Aide; Paraprof; Nrsng.

**STRANZ, JAMES S,** Erie Comm Coll South Cmps, Orchard Park, NY; SR; BACH; Phi Theta Kappa 90-; Fed Cmmnctns Cmmssn Gen Radio Tlphne Lcnse Hldr; Elec Eng Tech.

**STRASSBURG, JILL A,** Niagara Univ, Niagara Univ, NY; SR; BSN; Niagara Adm Off Tour Guide 87-90; Delta Epsilon Sigma 90-; Natl Nurses Assoc 89-; Academ Schlrshp 87-; Pres Schlrshp 87-; Sftbl Cap 87-; Nursing.

**STRASSER, STEPHANIE S,** Anne Arundel Comm Coll, Arnold, MD; FR; Hmmkr 88-; BA Indiana Univ; Engl; Educ.

**STRATOS, MARIA,** Fl International Univ, Miami, FL; FR; BA; Cncl Excptnl Chldrn 90-; Secty; AA Miami Dade S Campus 90; Educ; Spec Educ.

**STRATTON, JENNIFER B,** Salisbury St Univ, Salisbury, MD; SR; BS; Med Crs Clb 88-; Alpha Omega Blgy Clb 89-; Peninsula Gen Hosp Vol 89-; IM Sprts 87-; Blgy; Med/Hlth.

**STRATTON, MARK S,** S U N Y Coll Of Tech At Alfred, Alfred, NY; FR; BA; Math/Physics; Electro Mech Eng.

**STRATTON, PAIGE C,** Marshall University, Huntington, WV; SO; Acctg; CPA.

**STRATTON, PIPER ISA,** Univ Of Rochester, Rochester, NY; SR; BA; D Lion Org 88-89; Reg Alumni Schlr 87-; Delta Gamma Rush Party Chrmn 87-; Intrnshp Priory Psychiatric Hosp 89; Natl Assn Andrexia Nervosa Intrnshp 90; Tchng Assist 90; Wmns Club Sftbl Pres/Fndr 88-; Psychology; Clinical Psychology.

**STRATTON, TIMOTHY,** Marshall University, Huntington, WV; SR; BA; Bus Mngmnt; Fnnc.

**STRAUB, ROBERT W,** Wv Northern Comm Coll, Wheeling, WV; SR; AAS; Acctg/Busn Admin.

**STRAUCH, MARC D,** Yeshiva Univ, New York, NY; SR; BA; Phlnthrpy Soc Chrmn 89-; Lbrary Comm 89-; Sigma Delta Rho 90-; Gds/Wlfr Comm 88-; Soviet Immgrnt Rstlmnt Aid 90-; Pre-Hlth/Sci; Med.

**STRAUM, MELODY H,** Bishop St Comm Coll, Mobile, AL; SO; ADN; Phi Theta Kappa Pres 90-; Stdnt Govt Assoc 89-; Pres Lst 89-; Phi Theta Kappa Pres 90-; Ldrshp Schlrshp 90-; AACJC Acad All Amer Tm Jr Clg 90-; Phi Theta Kappa 90-; Nrsng; RN.

**STRAUSS, DAVID A,** Univ Of Tn At Martin, Martin, TN; SO; BA; ROTC Rangers 90-; Political Sci Intrnshp; US Army; Political Sci/Spanish; Law/Army Cmmssn.

**STRAUSS, HOLLY L,** Fl International Univ, Miami, FL; SR; BS; Baptist Campus Ministries 89-; Hospitality Mgmt; Hotel Mgmt.

**STRAUSS, KEVIN E,** Cornell Univ Statutory College, Ithaca, NY; JR; BA; Entrprnr Clb; Pi Kappa Alpha VP 90; Study Abrd Australia; Frat Sports; Bus Mgt.

**STRAUSS, SUSAN E,** Liberty Univ, Lynchburg, VA; SR; BS; Kappa Delta Pi Sec 89-; Alpha Lambda Delta 88-; Elem Ed; Tchng.

**STRAUSS, W ROBERT,** S U N Y Coll At Fredonia, Fredonia, NY; SR; BABM; Chmbr Sngrs Asst Bus Mgr 87-; Opera Theatre VP 87-; Msc Edctrs Natl Cnfrnc 87-90; Am Chrl Dirs Assn Pblcty Co Chair 89-; Hillman Opera 89-; Phi Kappa Lambda 89-; Merit Schlrshp 87-88; Hillman Schlrshp 89-90; Hons Prog 87-88; Concerto Fnlst 90-; Msc Ed/Vcl Prfrmnc.

**STRAUTMANN, JAMES J,** Appalachian Bible Coll, Bradley, WV; FR; BA; Bibl/Yth Mnstries.

**STRAW, AUDRA RENEE,** Oh Univ-Southern Cmps, Ironton, OH; FR; BA; Educ; Spec Educ.

**STRAWBRIDGE, CAROLINE J,** Univ Of Al, Tuscaloosa, AL; FR; BA; Stdnt Almn Assoc Spkrs Br 90-; Phi Eta Sigma; Lambda Sigma; Delta Delta Delta; Pblc Rltns; Law.

**STRAWBRIDGE, ROBERT COLE,** Univ Of Tn At Knoxville, Knoxville, TN; SR; Ski Club Univ Auburn 85-87; Indstl Engrg Univ Ark 87-88; Gold Key; Ducks Unlimited Natl Wetland Prog 84-91; Student Mgt Prog 90-; Busn Mgnt/Industrial Eng; Industrial Mgnt.

**STRAYER, JASON P,** Ga Inst Of Tech At Atlanta, Atlanta, GA; FR; Cmptr Sci; Cybrspc Engr.

**STRAYHORN, HEATHER A,** Valdosta St Coll, Valdosta, GA; FR; BA; Alpha Lambda Delta 90-; Hstry; Educ.

**STRBIK, LISA M,** Univ Of Ky, Lexington, KY; SR; BS; AICHE; Grnpce; Doris Day Anml Lge; AS C S Mott Comm Clg 88; Chem Engr.

**STREAMS JR, MICHAEL L,** Fisk Univ, Nashville, TN; JR; BA; SGA VP 90-; Nwspr Ed Chf; Hons Pgm 89-; Gold Key Histrn; Alpha Phi Alpha Frat VP 90-; W E B Du Bois Prz Papr Awd 90; Alpha Phi Alpha GPA Awd 90; Princeton U Woodrow Wilson Fllw; Phlsphy; Intrntl Law.

**STREATER, ANN,** Bryant Stratton Bus Inst Roch, Rochester, NY; SO; AS; Bus Mgmt.

**STRECK, MARK W,** Bridgeport Engr Inst, Fairfield, CT; FR; BSEE; Deans Lst Hon; CT Sch Elec GPA Awd 85-87; Serv Tech Intl Mailing Sys 88-; Cert CT Sch Elec 87; Sftwre/Elect; Elec Eng.

**STRECKFUS, MICHELE L,** Goucher Coll, Towson, MD; SO; BA; Violinist 89-; Peer Wrtng Tutor 90-; Sec-Jeffrey Dorm 90-; Mgmnt/Econs Clb 90-; Cmctns Clb 89-90; IM Sftbl 89-; Engl/Mngmnt.

**STREDNEY, JULIANN M,** Oh St Univ At Newark, Newark, OH; SR; Dns Lst 89-; Elem Tutor; Whlchr Gms Vol 90; BS; Elem Ed; Tch.

**STREET, CHRISTI R,** East Tn St Univ, Johnson City, TN; JR; BS; Clg Repubs Sec/Treas 90-; Alpha Lambda Delta 88-; Upsilon Pi Epsilon; Cmte Of 1000 Schlrshp 88-; Comp Sci; Info Syst.

**STREET, JACQUELIN R,** East Tn St Univ, Johnson City, TN; JR; BA; Baptist Stdnt Union Frshmn Cncl Choir Cncl 88-89; Gamma Beta Phi; Beta Alpha Psi V P; Alpha Kappa Psi; 4 Yr Academic Schlrshp TTU; Outstanding Clge Stdnts Of Amer; Business; CPA.

**STREET, JEFFREY M,** Tn Temple Univ, Chattanooga, TN; SR; BS; John Wesley Scty; Alph Epsln Theta; Pi Kappa Dlt; Yth Mnstrs Dir 90; Word Of Life Ranch Summer Intrnshp; Word Of Life Camp Germany; Scndry Educ; Msnry.

**STREET, JENNIFER W,** Hillsborough Comm Coll, Tampa, FL; FR; AA; Teesn For Chrst Soc Stdies 87-90; Tchr Aid 90; SADD 89; Soc Sci; Tchng.

**STREET II, ROBERT E,** Temple Univ, Philadelphia, PA; SR; Puma 88-; Dns Lst 89-; Nom Otstndng Snr Awd; Stdnt Tchng Thomas Middle Schl; Ftbl Coaching Stf Geo Wshntngtn Hgh; Advntr Instrctr Camp America; Intrn Shriners Hosp Crpld Chldrn Phila Unit; Natl Strngth Cndtng Assn Psahperd; Tch Coach Run A Camp.

**STREETER, KAREN R,** Univ Of Tn At Martin, Martin, TN; GD; PHD; Stu Govt Exec Cbnt Sec Mnrty Affrs 89-90; Peer Prog Ldr 88-90; Almn Assc 88-90; Alpha Kappa Alpha Bslns 88-90; Mnrty Acdmc Schlrshp 86-90; Hnrs Smnr Schlrshp 86-87; Cum Laude 90; Blck Grad Fllwshp 90-; Blck Cltrl Cntr; Pacers 90; BS 90; Educ/Psychlgy; Schl Psychlgst.

**STREETER, KATHERINE M,** Morris Brown Coll, Atlanta, GA; SO; BA; Mass Cmmnctn; Brdcstng.

**STREETER, SONYA R,** Morris Brown Coll, Atlanta, GA; JR; BSN; SGA Sntr 86-87; Homecoming Court Fnlst 86-87; BSN Nrsg Class Officer Sec; Nrsg; PHD.

**STREETING, GARY D,** Anne Arundel Comm Coll, Arnold, MD; FR; AA; Business.

**STREETMAN, LEAH F,** Va Commonwealth Univ, Richmond, VA; JR; BFA; Amnsty Intl Pblcty Crdntr 89-; Stdt Envrnmntl Actn Cltn 90-; Shenandoah Hnr Scty 88-; Theatre; Acting.

**STREHLE, LISA F,** Memphis St Univ, Memphis, TN; FR; BBA; PTA Chmny Rck Elem Brd 90-; Bus; Sls Mgmt Mrktng.

**STREKAL, SHEILA A,** Univ Of Akron, Akron, OH; JR; BA; Gldn Ky 90-; Hnrs Prog 88-; Alpha Lambda Delta 89-; Phi Eta Sigma 89-; Beta Gamma Sigma 90-; Galen A Roush Mem Schlrshp; Bus Fnnce; Law.

**STRENG, JONATHAN D,** Univ Of Cin R Walters Coll, Blue Ash, OH; FR; Bowling Green S Univ Stdnt Exchng Pgm Univ Salzburg Austria 81-82; Cmptr Pgmng; Bsn Aplctns Pgmg.

**STRIBBLE, TOMMY J,** Univ Of Sc At Columbia, Columbia, SC; SR; BAIS; Crus Chrst 87-89; Gamma Beta Phi 88-; Golden Key 89-; Kappa Delta Epsilon; Outstng Clg Stdnts Amer 88; Res Trainnee 90; Elem Educ; Tchr.**

**STRIBLING, MICHAEL A,** Alcorn St Univ, Lorman, MS; FR; BA; Hnrs Clb 90-; Hnr Cert; Bus Admn.

**STRIBLING, STEPHANIE L,** Univ Of Southern Ms, Hattiesburg, MS; SO; BA; Nrsng; Ped Nrs.

**STRICK, LARA B,** Cornell Univ Statutory College, Ithaca, NY; FR; BS; Dns Lst 90-; Blgy; Blgst Or Psycho Pthlgst.

**STRICKER, ANGELA RENEE,** Univ Of Cincinnati, Cincinnati, OH; SO; BA; Stdnt Govt Actvty Aid 88-89; Nrsg; Med-Anesthslgy.

**STRICKER, KIMBERLY A,** Univ Of Ky, Lexington, KY; SR; BA; Act Brd Rep; Sarah Geurin Schlrshp; Delta Delta Delta; Rent A Greek; MASH Hlpr; Ed; Lwyr.

**STRICKLAND, ALISON D,** Auburn Univ At Auburn, Auburn, AL; SO; Auburn Tgrt 90-; Angl Flght 89-; Phi Eta Sigma 89-; Alpha Lambda Delta 89-; Dns Lst 90-; Law.

**STRICKLAND, BONITA B,** Univ Of Sc At Columbia, Columbia, SC; JR; BM; Music; Tchr.

**STRICKLAND, BRANTLEY A,** Univ Of Sc At Columbia, Columbia, SC; SR; ASP 90-; Beta Beta Beta 86-; Pres Lst 90; Deans Lst 85 90; BS U S C 87; Pharm; Med Sch.

**STRICKLAND, CASI R,** Univ Of Montevallo, Montevallo, AL; JR; BS; Kappa Delta Pi 90-; Lambda Sigma Pi; Phi Kapp Phi; Chi Omega 88-; Pres Lst; Deans Lst; Ldrshp Schlrshp; Elem Ed.

**STRICKLAND, CONNIE H,** Univ Of Al At Birmingham, Birmingham, AL; SR; BA; Sec Dcns Brd; Nrs Std Coord; Advsr Nrs Gld; AS Cert Med Asst; AS Lawson St 83; Cert 82; Alld Hlth Admn.

**STRICKLAND, CYNTHIA D,** Johnson C Smith Univ, Charlotte, NC; FR; BA; Bus; Hotel/Rstrnt Mgmt.

**STRICKLAND, DALLAS E,** Savannah Coll Of Art & Design, Savannah, GA; SO; BA; Art Hstry/Painting; Gallery Repr/Curator.

**STRICKLAND JR, DAVID M,** Vance Granville Comm Coll, Henderson, NC; SO; AA; Coll Trnsfr Prgm Schlr 90; Pnst Edgwd Bapt Chrch; Mchn Oprtr; Bus Admn.

**STRICKLAND, ERIC A,** Fl Atlantic Univ, Boca Raton, FL; SR; BBA; AA Palm Beach Comm Coll 88; Oprtns Mgmt; Mgmt Of Oprtns CEO COO.

**STRICKLAND, G DIANNE,** Univ Of Sc At Coastal Carolina, Conway, SC; SO; AD; Nrsng.

**STRICKLAND, JAMIE L,** Univ Of Nc At Charlotte, Charlotte, NC; GD; MA; Mmbr Amrcn Assn Geogrphrs; Sthestrn Div AAG; Sigma Gamma Epsilon Pres 89-; Gamma Thete Epsilon; Prsntr Sedaag Mttng 90; Prsntr Wmns Stds Cnfrnc; BS 90; Geography; Envrnmntl Plnng.

**STRICKLAND, JO R,** Vance Granville Comm Coll, Henderson, NC; SR; ADN; Tally Ho First Bapt Chrch; Nrsng.

**STRICKLAND, KENT V,** Long Island Univ C W Post Cntr, Greenvale, NY; BBA; Bsbl; Bus Admn/Mgmt.**

**STRICKLAND, KEVIN D,** Southern Coll Of Tech, Marietta, GA; SO; BS; Engr.

**STRICKLAND, KIMBERLY D,** Anderson Coll, Anderson, SC; SO; AD; Sftbl 89-; Elem Educ; Tchr.

**STRICKLAND, LYNN M,** Converse Coll, Spartanburg, SC; JR; BM; Dnce Tm Capt 88-; Alpha Lambda Delta 90; Mrtr Brd Natl Prjcts Chrmn; Delta Omicron Pres 88-; Mrshl 90-; Millikan Schlr 88-; Vce Prfrmnce; Opra Sngr.

**STRICKLAND, MARILARK,** Univ Of Ga, Athens, GA; SR; BED; SCEC 89-; Golden Key 90-; Sigma Delta Ch VP 87-89; A Ed Young Harris Coll 89; Mntl Rtrdtn; Edctr.

**STRICKLAND, MARY A,** Auburn Univ At Auburn, Auburn, AL; GD; MS; AACD; ASCA; ALACD 90-; AEA 89-; Auburn Bsebl Hostess Diamond Dolls Pres 88-; Phi Kappa Phi 90-; Pi Lambda Theta 89-; Sigma Nu Lil Sis 89-90; Miss A-Day Court 89; Grad/Admin Asst Auburn Univ Smng Tm 90-; Teach Intrnshp 90; Sch Cnslng Intrnshp; Elem Edn/Sch Cnslng K-12; Ed D Sch Cnslng.

**STRICKLAND, MARY CHRISTINA,** Abraham Baldwin Agri Coll, Tifton, GA; SO; BA; Alpha Beta Gamma 90-; Bus; Acctg.

**STRICKLAND, MAURI L,** Northeast Ms Cc, Booneville, MS; FR; DR; Physics.

**STRICKLAND, MICHAEL W,** Pellissippi St Tech Comm Coll, Knoxville, TN; SO; IEEE 89-; Tau Alpha Pi 89-; Elctrcl Engr.

**STRICKLAND, NICK,** Waycross Coll, Waycross, GA; FR; Tnns 90; Sci/Math Awd 90; Fresh Schlr 90; Mens Tnns; Royal Ambssdrs Chrch 90-; Math; Eng.

**STRICKLAND, RHONDA M,** Central Al Comm Coll, Alexander City, AL; SO; Phi Theta Kappa 90-; Comp Tchr At Day Care 89-.

**STRICKLAND, SUZETTE R,** Oh Univ-Southern Cmps, Ironton, OH.

**STRICKLEN, ELIZABETH A,** Marshall University, Huntington, WV; SO; BA; Gamma Beta Phi 90-; Kappa Delta Pi 90-; Educ; Tchng.

**STRICKLER, KEVIN L,** Wv Univ, Morgantown, WV; SR; BS; Acad Stdnts Pharm 88-; Golden Key 88-; Kappa Psi 88-89; Fcts/Cmprsns Awd; BA Chemistry 88; Pharm.

**STRICKLER, ROBERT A,** Tri County Tech Coll, Pendleton, SC; FR; AIT; Elctrncs; Engr.

**STRICKLER, WALTER M,** Univ Of Akron, Akron, OH; SR; IEEE 88-; Eta Kappa Nu 90-; BSEE; Elec/Elctrnc Engr.

**STRICKLIN JR, CHARLES VANCE,** Winthrop Coll, Rock Hill, SC; SR; Stdnt Gov Assc VP 87-; Dinkins Stdnt Union Chrmn 90-; Alumni Assc 88-; Phi Kappa Phi 89-; Phi Alpha Theta; Pi Sigma Alpha Pres 89-; Sigma Alpha Epsilon Pres 87-; Louis Rhone West Schlrshp 87-; Awrd Exl Stnt Gov 89-90; Potical Science/Phlsphy; Law Pblc Serv.

**STRICKLIN, DANIELA L,** Livingston Univ, Livingston, AL; SO; BS; Nwspaper Photo Editr 89-; Yrbk Photo Editr 89-90; Alpha Chi 90-; Cardnl Key 90-; Fr Chem Awrd 90-; Chem; Chem Engr.

**STRICKLIN, KIMBERLY L,** Univ Of Montevallo, Montevallo, AL; JR; BA; Montevallo Mstr 90-; Alpha Lambda Delta 88; Omicron Delta Kappa; Phi Chi Theta 89-90; Phi Mu Prsdnt Elct; Psychology; Cnslng.

**STRIDER, BRIGETTE M,** Western Carolina Univ, Cullowhee, NC; SO; BS; Crmnl Jstce Scty 90; Pi Kappa Phi Lit Sis 90; Hspce Of Rndlph Co; Spcl Serv 89; Pltcl Sci; Lgl Cnsltnt Law.**

**STRIDIRON, THOMAS J,** Dowling Coll, Oakdale Li, NY; SR; BA; Golf; Hcky; Sftbl; AA Suffolk Comm Coll Selden NY 89; Bus Mgmt; Corp CEO.

**STRIMIKE, DEBRA J,** Clark Univ, Worcester, MA; FR; BA; Alcohol Awns Grp 90-; Activ Brd 90-F Natl Hnrs Scty 89-; Schl Librn 90-F; Outplcmnt Assoc Intern 90-; Aerobics Track 90-; Sclgy/Spanish.

**STRIMPLE, ROBERT B,** Bowling Green St Univ At Huron, Huron, OH; SO; BA; Bus Clb 90-; Acctg.

**STRINE-RICHARDSON, MARY A,** Univ Of Md Baltimore Prof Schl, Baltimore, MD; GD; PHARM; Amrcn Scty Hosp Phrmcsts 89-; Amrcn Phrmctcl Assoc 87-89; Rho Chi Hstrn 89-; Lambda Kappa Sigma Corrs Sec 90-; Acdmc Excllnc Award 89-90; BA 87; Phrmcy.

**STRINGER, ANN C,** Atlantic Comm Coll, Mays Landing, NJ; JR; BS; Booth Cashier 86-; AS 90; Crmnl Juste; FBI/DEA.

**STRINGER, DAVID A,** Northern Ky Univ, Highland Hts, KY; JR; BA; Stdnt Govt Pres; Pres Ambssrs 90; Ordr Of Omega Pres; Pi Sigma Alpha; Sigma Phi Epsilon Pres 88; Pres Schlrshp 88; Key Awd 89; Deans/Hnrs Lst; Pol Sci; Law.

**STRINGER, JOHN M,** Univ Of Southern Ms, Hattiesburg, MS; JR; BS; Phi Beta Kappa 90-; Vrsty Bsktbl 88-89; Hstry.

**STRINGER, KAREN D,** Spalding Univ, Louisville, KY; SR; BS; Pi Lambda Theta; Delta Epsilon Sigma 90-; NEA SP 90-; Honrbl Order Of KY Colonels 88-; Elem Educ; Tchng.

**STRINGER, PAUL R,** Union Coll, Barbourville, KY; FR; BA; Engl; Tchr.

**STRINGFELLOW, VICKI A,** Univ Of Southern Ms, Hattiesburg, MS; JR; BA; Hon Coll Assn 89-90; Hon Coll 89-; Stdnt Almni Assn 89-; Lambda Sigma 90; Phi Eta Sigma 90; Alpha Lambda Delta 90; Delta Delta Delta 89- Treas 90; Rotoract 89-90; Miss Teen Of Amer 90; Miss Teen Of MS 89-90; Amer Stdies/Poltcl Sci; Educ.

**STRITE, SUZANNE D,** Middle Tn St Univ, Murfreesboro, TN; SR; BS; Ntl Stdnt Spch/Lang/Hrng Assn 88-; Spch/Hrng Clb T 88-; Gamma Beta Phi 88-; Kappa Delta Pi 88-; Tau Omicron 90-; Acad All-Amer Awd 89-90; All-Amer Schlr Awd 90-; Ntl Ed Awd 90-; Cmnctn Dsordrs; Spch-Lang Path.

**STRITTHOLT, JODI A,** Univ Of Cincinnati, Cincinnati, OH; SO; BA; Kappa Kappa Gamma Asst Mbrshp 89-; Edn.

**STROBEL, BERNARD C,** Coll Misericordia, Dallas, PA; JR; BS; Stdnt Occ Ther Assn 88-; AOTA 89-; POTA 89-; Phi Theta Epsilon 89-; Coach Tnrs Bsbl Tms Hd Coach 89-; Occ Ther; Occ Rehab.

**STROBEL, SHEILA A,** Liberty Univ, Lynchburg, VA; BS; Yrbk Stff 89-; Urbn Otrch 89-90; Inter Dscplnry Yth Mn Ed.

**STROCK, LOWELL L,** Wallace St Comm Coll At Selma, Selma, AL; JR; Fire Sci; Business.

**STRODE, BERNADINE,** Draughons Jr Coll Nashville, Nashville, TN; SO; DEGRE; Oustndng Data Processing Student Awd 90; Prof Career Admin; Certif Career Com Jr Clg 90; Busn Mgt.

**STRODE, NEKITA D,** Al A & M Univ, Normal, AL; FR; Bsns Mgmt; Bsns.

**STROEBELE, KIM M,** Coll Of Saint Rose, Albany, NY; JR; Chrle Sec 89-; MENC Sec 89-; Chmbr Sngrs; Bll Chr; Wnd Ensmbl; Fmly WE Crw 88-90; Orientn Bg Sstr 89-90; Lgsltv Rcgntn 90-; Amer Cncr Scty Vol; Wrkshp Hstss; Tippett Fstvl Hstess; HS Bnd Dy Hstss 90-; HS Jzz Ens Dy/HS Chr Dy Hstss; Musc Educ.**

**STROH, CAROLINE F,** D Youville Coll, Buffalo, NY; JR; BA; Bus Mngmnt; Bus.

**STROHMEYER, TODD S,** Samford Univ, Birmingham, AL; GD; Law Rvw 89-; IM Ftbl Sftbl Golf Tnns Rqtbl; Law.

**STROHSAHL, AMY L,** Memphis St Univ, Memphis, TN; SO; BFA; Grphc Dsgn/Art; Comp Grphcs.

**STROM, CYNTHIA V,** Ramapo Coll Of Nj, Mahwah, NJ; SR; BA; Grp Hm Vol; Tutor; Cert Outstndg Serv; Dept Spclzd Serv Tutor 88; Ofc Sprvsr; Bkpr; Comm Arts.

**STRONG, CARL A,** George Mason Univ, Fairfax, VA; SR; BED; Goldn Key 90; Phi Kappa Delta 90-; Dns Lst 90; Grad With Distnctn; Coll Soccer Plyr James Madison Univ 76-77; Prof Soccer Ply NASL 77-85; Tchr.

**STRONG, KATHY L,** Valdosta St Coll, Valdosta, GA; SR; MSN; Amrcn Nrsng Assoc 83-86; STEP 89; PET 86; Ortho Neruo RN; Unt Mgr Chld Unt; Chmcl Dpndncy Unt; Adlscnt Unt; Mntl Hlth Nursng Srs; Cs Mgmt; ADN Fayetteville Tch; Nrsng; Admn Nrsng.

**STRONG, SHEREE,** Southern Junior Coll, Birmingham, AL; FR; ASSOC; US Army 73; Swtchbrd Sprvsr 82.

**STRONG, TERESA K,** Chattahoochee Vly St Comm Coll, Phenix City, AL; SO; BED; Dns Lst 90; Pres Lst 90; Gamma Beta Phi 90; Acad/Geography; Homemaker/Sls Clerk 78; Soc Sci; Tch.

**STRONG, YOLANDA M,** Alcorn St Univ, Lorman, MS; SO; Tennis.

**STRONG-DORSEY, BARBARA,** Vance Granville Comm Coll, Henderson, NC; Cmptr Pgmmng; Word Perfect; Cosmetology; Bus Admin.

**STRONY, JENNIFER L,** Villanova Univ, Villanova, PA; SO; BS; Stdnt Prgrmng Cncl Co Chrmn 89-; Spcl Olympics Vol 90; Pi Beta Phi 90-; Summer Flwshp Awd To Aid Research Chemistry; CRC Press Frshmn Chem Awd 90; Chemistry; Chem Industry/Teaching.

**STROOP, ALISA M,** Bridgewater Coll, Bridgewater, VA; FR; BS; Deans List; Comptr Sci/Math; Bus Progrmr.

**STROSBERG, ROBERT T,** Univ Of Fl, Gainesville, FL; SR; BSBA; Clg Democrats Secy 88-; Financial Mngmnt Assoc 90-; Graham Area Cncl 88-89; Golden Key 90-; Phi Eta Sigma 89; Alpha Lambda Delta 89; Alpha Kappa Psi Treas 89-; Fla Undergrad Schlr 88-; Presidents Hnr Rl 88-; NCNB Internship; Finance; Banking Financial Analyst.

**STROSSMAN, CHRISTINE M,** Saint John Fisher Coll, Rochester, NY; SO; BA; Intl Stdes Assn Budgt Dir 90-; Cmpus Tour Gde 89-; Alpha Mu Gamma 89-; L; Econ/Intl Stdes; Intl Econ.

**STROTHER, ERIC S,** Marshall University, Huntington, WV; SO; BA; Baptist Campus Minstry Comm Chrmn; Stdnts For Christ 89; Delta Omicron; Music Ed K-12; Teacher.**

**STROUD, JEFFREY J,** S U N Y Coll Of Tech At Alfred, Alfred, NY; FR; AOS; Sigma Tau Epsilon; IM Sftbl Vlybl Flg Ftbl; BS Buffalo State Coll 90; AAS Erie Comm Coll 88; Fnnce Econs Bldng Cnstrctn; Bus Ownshp Cnstrc.

**STROUD, MARCIA T,** Bristol Univ, Bristol, TN; GD; MBA; Acctng W/Schlegel TN 90-; 7 Yrs Exper Ins Industry 82-89; BS Univ Of Tenn 80; Acctng.

**STROUD, SUZANNE L,** Winthrop Coll, Rock Hill, SC; SO; BA; Kappa Mu Epsilon; Math; Tchr.

**STROUD III, WILLIAM F,** Middle Tn St Univ, Murfreesboro, TN; SO; BBA; Hnrs Stdnt Assn 90; Gamma Beta Phi 90; Mktg; Bsn.

**STROUD, WILLIAM S,** East Carolina Univ, Greenville, NC; FR; BFA; Hon Org 90-; Phi Eta Sigma 90-; Cmnctn Arts; Advtsng.

**STROUSE, BONNIE J,** Comm Coll Algny Co Algny Cmps, Pittsburgh, PA; SO; BA; Dept Hon Acctg; Hi Hons 90; Assoc 90; Acctg; Own Bsns.

**STROUSE, KATHIE A,** Cumberland County Coll, Vineland, NJ; SO; AA; Coll Nwspaper Cntrbtng Editr 90-; Engl/Cmnctns; Photo Jrnlsm.

**STROUT, JOSEPH J,** Miami Univ, Oxford, OH; FR; AB; Japanese Cltr Clb 90-; Hons Pgm 90-; Psych; Cogntv Sci.

**STROUTH, JENNIFER L,** East Tn St Univ, Johnson City, TN; SO; BACCHUS 90-; Cllg Rpblcns 90-; Kappa Delta 89-; Comp Sci.

**STRUBEL, GARY F,** Hudson Valley Comm Coll, Troy, NY; SO; Hons; AA; Anthrplgy; Faclty.

**STRUBLE, DAVID L,** Middle Tn St Univ, Murfreesboro, TN; SR; BS; Undrgrad Chem Rsrch Pres; Chem Clb; Blgy Clb; Res Cncl; RA; Gama Beta Phi; Hon Stdnt Assn; Hon Cncl Sec; HSA Strng Com Sec; Phi Mu Delta Exec Com; Amer Chem Soc; Beta Beta Beta; Boy Scts; Goodlark Schlr; Rtry Schlrshp; Chem/Blgy; MD.

**STRUBLE, ELAINE,** William Paterson Coll, Wayne, NJ; JR; BA; Kappa Delta Pi; AAUW Schlrshp; Deans Lst; PTA Pres; Chrch Cnfrmtn Brd; TA Preschl Hndcpd 87-; Spec Ed; Tch.

**STRUBLE, MICHELLE L,** Central Fl Comm Coll, Ocala, FL; SO; AS; Phi Theta Kappa; CMT Sys Tech Inst 89; Electrn Engr.

**STRUEDER, DANIELA B,** Converse Coll, Spartanburg, SC; SR; BA; Stdnt Admsns Bd 88-89; Alcohol/Drug Abuse Tm 88-90; Phi Sigma Iota 88-; Phi Sigma Pi 89-; Co Ldr Jr Girl Scout Trp 88-90; Stdnt Vol Servs 87-; Hon Trustee Schlrshp 87; Deans Lst 88-; Ele/Early Chldhd Educ; Tch.**

**STRUFFOLINO JR, THOMAS J,** Bloomfield Coll, Bloomfield, NJ; SR; BS; Bus Mngmtn.

**STRUM, ERIC V,** Western Carolina Univ, Cullowhee, NC; SR; BA; Pi Gamma Mu; Phi Alpha Theta; Undrgrad Rsrch Cnfrnc; Grad Schl.

**STRUM, MATTHEW W,** East Central Comm Coll, Decatur, MS; FR; BA; VP Cls 88-89; Warrior Corps VP; Stu Bdy VP; Phi Theta Kappa Pres; All Amer Schlr; All Star 90; Miss Snt Page 87; Bsktbl Capt 89-90; Chrldr Capt; Math; Systms Anlyst.

**STRUNK, MELISSA D,** Oh Univ, Athens, OH; SO; BA; Cmps Crsd Christ 90-; Stdnt Dmcrts 90-; Engl Clb 90-; Alpha Lambda Delta 90-; Prtnrshp Pgm 90-; Chldcr Serv Plnnd Prnthd 90-; Deans Schlrshp 90-; Engl/Scl Wrk; Law.

**STRUNK, ROSE M,** Univ Of Cincinnati-Clrmnt Coll, Batavia, OH; SO; BA; Hmlt SDA Schl Brd Chrmn 88-90 Tchrs Aide 86-88; Ofc Admn Mgr 85-90; Bus; Hmn Rsrc Corp Mgmt.

**STRUVE, KIMBERLEY DAWN,** Asbury Theological Sem, Wilmore, KY; GD; M DIV; SGA Dorm Rep 90-; Fin/Acad Cmtee SGA 90-; Off Mgr ICHTHUS Mus Festvl 90-; Ch Assoc Pastor Intrn; I M Flag Ftbl Sftbl Frsbe Ftbl 90-; BFA 89; Yth Cmpus Msns Mnstry.

**STUARD, LORI W,** Univ Of Southern Ms, Hattiesburg, MS; SR; BS; Gamma Beta Phi 90; Golden Key; Kappa Delta Pi; Phi Kappa Phi; Frst Bptst Chrch; Simpson Co Sinfonia Musc Clb; Elem Educ; Tch.

**STUART, BRIAN I,** East Stroudsburg Univ, E Stroudsburg, PA; JR; BS; Pike Cnty Gypsy Moth Pgm Assist 90; Pike Cnty Cnsrvtn Distr Rsrce Cnsrvtnst 89; PA Rsrc Cncl; NE Pa Energy Comm; PA Septic Mgmt Assn; Pike Co Ctzns Advsry Comm; Pike Co Gnrl Authority; Pike Cnty Solid Waste/Recycling Coord; Envir Stds; Envir Cnsltnt.

**STUART, ROBERT A,** Fl St Univ, Tallahassee, FL; SR; MED; FL Eductrs Assoc 89-; Engl Intrn At Lincoln HS; Dir Of HS Musicls 89-; AA 89; BA; Engl; Engl/Drama/Spch Tchr.

**STUART, SHELLEY L,** Cornell Univ Statutory College, Ithaca, NY; SR; Strategic Simultns Soc V P 88-; Pew Schlr 90; BS; Biology; Rsrch.

**STUBBLEFIELD, LISA C,** J Sargeant Reynolds Comm Coll, Richmond, VA; SO; BA; Phi Theta Kappa 90-; Cmnctns; Media.

**STUBBLEFIELD JR, MICHAEL D,** Thomas Nelson Comm Coll, Hampton, VA; FR; BS; NASA Langley Co-Op Apprentice Prg 90; Mech Engr Tech.

**STUBBS, JENNIFER S,** Central Fl Comm Coll, Ocala, FL; SO; AA; Phi Theta Kappa; Bus.

**STUBBS, LISA D,** Salem-Teikyo Univ, Salem, WV; SR; BS; Elem Ed.

**STUBBS JR, ROBERT C,** Univ Of Sc At Coastal Carolina, Conway, SC; JR; BS; Alpha Mu Gamma VP; Comp Sci; Pgmr/Data Prcssr.

**STUBBS JR, ROBERT C,** Univ Of Sc At Columbia, Columbia, SC; JR; BS; Alpha Mu Gamma V P; Cmptr Sci; Prgmr/Data Proc.

**STUBENRAUCH, KIMBERLY A,** Univ Of Cincinnati, Cincinnati, OH; SO; BA; Ntl Merit Schlrshp Awd 89-; Deans Lst; Crmnl Just; Law.

**STUBNA JR, THOMAS L,** Comm Coll Algny Co Algny Cmps, Pittsburgh, PA; FR; BED; Sec Ed; H S Tchr.

**STUCKEY, CYNTHIA C,** Univ Of Southern Ms, Hattiesburg, MS; SO; B; Univ Sngrs 90-; Univ Chrl 90-; Hnr Stdnt Assoc 89; Gamma Beta Phi 90-; Gamma Beta Phi 89-; Hnr Scoll 89-; Acdmc Schlrshp 89-; Engl Scndry Ed; Hgh Schl Engl Tchr.

**STUCKEY, JANICE,** Volunteer St Comm Coll, Gallatin, TN; SO; AS; Gamma Beta Phi 90-; Psychology; Cnslng Scl Wrk.

**STUCKEY, JEFF W,** Immaculata Coll, Immaculata, PA; JR; BA; Rsdnc Hl Rep Bailey Hl UNC Greensboro 88-89; Psychlgy; Crmnl Psychlgy.

**STUCKEY, JON I,** Univ Of Akron, Akron, OH; FR; BA; Debate Tm 90-; IM Bsktbl/Sftbl/Rcqtbl/Ftbl 90-; Mech Eng.

**STUCKEY, JULIE A,** James Madison University, Harrisonburg, VA; SO; BS; Physchology Clb Hstrn 89-; Stdnt Educ Assn 90-; Natl Assn Ed Yng Chldrn 90-; Psi Chi; Alpha Phi Omega 90-; Acad Advsry Comm 89-90; Psychology/Erly Chldhd Ed; Cnslng.

**STUCKI, AMY,** William Paterson Coll, Wayne, NJ; SR; BA; Hon Prog; Humanities.

**STUCKY, DANIEL A,** Kent St Univ Stark Cmps, North Canton, OH; JR; BBA; Mst Outstndng Music Stdnt 89; Accntng.

**STUCKY, JON L,** Life Coll, Marietta, GA; JR; BS; Thompson Adjstng Technique; Actcvtr Adjstng Tchnq; Intl Chiropractic Assoc Rep; AA Brigham Young Univ; Nutrition; Chiropractor.**

**STUCZYNSKI, ADAM K,** Cooper Union, New York, NY; FR; BE; Mech Engr; Mgmt.

**STUCZYNSKI, KENNETH J P,** D Youville Coll, Buffalo, NY; SR; BA; Chrstns Actn Otrch Chrprsn 90-; Blk Stdnt Un Advrtsng Chrprsn 90-; Stdnt Assn Sen 87-89; Pres Hnrs Pgrm 87-; Dns Lst 87-; Philosophy; Tchng.

**STUDDARD, NAREATHA L,** Al A & M Univ, Normal, AL; SR; BS; Mrktng Clb Pres 87-; Mrktng.

**STUDEBAKER, CARLA A,** Valdosta St Coll, Valdosta, GA; SO; BA; Alpha Lambda Delta 90; Sigma Alpha Chi; Frshmn Scholar; Spanish.**

**STUDEBAKER, JENNIFER M,** Univ Of Southern Ms, Hattiesburg, MS; SO; BA; Actvts Cncl Sec 89-; Almn Assoc 90-; Acdmc Cncl 90-; Gamma Beta Phi 89-; Phi Eta Sigma 89-; Alpha Lambda Delta 89-; Pi Beta Phi Pnhllnc Dlgt 89-; Acdmc Excllnc Gamma Alpha Eislon 89- Deans Lst 89-; Mdl Pldg 90; Pltcl Sci.

**STUDER, DEBORAH R,** Northeast State Tech Comm Coll, Blountville, TN; FR; MBA; Bible Clb; Soc Wrk.

**STUELAND, SAMUEL J,** Gallaudet Univ, Washington, DC; SR; BA; Phi Alpha Pi; Prsdntl Schlr; Hstry; Rschr.

**STUERMAN, MICHAEL T,** Univ Of Fl, Gainesville, FL; JR; BS; Amer Ins Arntcs Astrntcs 89-; Lthrn Chrch Yth Cnslr 86-89; Grad Hnrs; AA St Petersburg Jr Coll 89; Aerospace Eng.

**STUFFLEBEAM, SHANNON K,** Univ Of Nc At Greensboro, Greensboro, NC; FR; Intrvrsty Chrstn Flwshp 90-; Dns Lst 90-; NC Tchng Flw 90-; Elem Educ.

**STUHLMAN, ANNE M,** Clarkson Univ, Potsdam, NY; SR; BS; Clarkson Socty Of Acctnts 89-; Alpha Beta Gamma; Pres Schlr; Dns Lst; Bsktbl/Sftbl Capt 87-; AAS Hilbert Coll Hamburg NY 89; Acctng.

**STUHR, PETER J,** S U N Y At Buffalo, Buffalo, NY; SR; BS; Jazz Ensemble; Big Band; IMS; Fin/Mngmnt; Hlth Cr Admin.

**STUKES, SYREATHA R,** Va St Univ, Petersburg, VA; SR; BA; Petersburg Dept Scl Svcs Chld Protect Svcs Intern 90-; Poplar Springs Hosp Vol 89; Outstndg Acad Achvmnt 89-90; Scl Wrk.

**STULER, LESLEY R,** Longwood Coll, Farmville, VA; SR; TRO 88-; VA Rec/Park Soc; Delta Psi Kappa 90-; Alpha Sigma Alpha VP 88-; Hl Cncl; Thrptc Rec Intshp; Vars Rdng Tm 87-89; BS; Thrptc Rec; Rec Thrpst.

**STULL, COREY W,** Univ Of Rochester, Rochester, NY; SO; BA; Optics Clb 90-; Soccer Tm 89-90; Optics; Engr.

**STULL, KATHRYN E,** Univ Of Sc At Columbia, Columbia, SC; FR; BA; Carolina Cares; Srty Cncl; Alpha Lambda Delta; Alpha Delta Pi Sprt Ofcr; IM Sprts; Bus; Acctng.

**STULL, MONICA L,** Saint Vincents Coll & Seminary, Latrobe, PA; SR; BA; Chem Clb 90-; Soc Clb 90; Physics Clb 90; IM Ftbl Sftbl Vlybl 88-; Soclgy.

**STULL, PATRICIA J,** Mount Aloysius Jr Coll, Cresson, PA; SO; Phi Theta Kappa; Ar Frc Mthrs Flght 42 Sgt Arms; Mncpl Plc Trng; Prvt Scrty; Crtfd Scb Dvr; Crtfd Lthl Wpns; Gld Blt Mrtnl Arts.

**STULTS, TAMMIE J,** Middle Tn St Univ, Murfreesboro, TN; SR; BS; Gamma Beta Phi 88; Spcl Evnts Cmmttee 88-90; Tau Omicron 89; Advrtsng Clb 88; WKRN Channel 2 Intrnshp; Mass Cmmnctns; Advrtsng Fld.

**STULTZ, RICHARD S,** Marshall University, Huntington, WV; JR; BBA; Acctg Cob 89-; Mrchn Gbnd 88-; Pp Bnd 88-; Gamma Beta Phi Scty Chrmn Wys Mns Cmmtt 88; Acctg.

**STULTZ, SHERRY J,** Ms St Univ, Miss State, MS; SO; BS; SCAPE Sec 90-; Univ Wldlf Soc 90-; Outdr Soc 90-; US Frst Serv Smmr Emplyee 90; MI Ins Cncl Schlr 89; SFR Undrgrad Awd Wldlf Mgmt; Wldlf Mgmt; Wtlnds Eclgst.

**STUMBAUGH, ROSEANNA M,** Columbia Union Coll, Takoma Park, MD; GD; BS; Phi Theta Kappa Mntgmmry Coll 89; A/P Sprvsr Hwltt-Pckrd Co 76-; Bus Admin; Mgmt.

**STUMP, ANGELA I,** Beckley Coll, Beckley, WV; SO; BS; Sci; Occ Ther.

**STUMP, PAUL E,** Birmingham Southern Coll, Birmingham, AL; SR; BS; Amer Mensa; Cntrl Bnk S Rcvry Dept; Bus Ad Finance.

**STUMPF, LAURA F,** Univ Of North Fl, Jacksonville, FL; JR; BA; Phi Theta Kappa 88-90; AA FL Cmnty Clg Jacksonville 90; Acctg.

**STUMPF, STACY J,** Indiana Univ Of Pa, Indiana, PA; SR; Two/Ten Schlrshp 86-90; Benz Schlrshp 89-90; BS 90; Educ Excptnl Prsns; Tchng.

**STUMPH, DEREK W,** Univ Of Tn At Martin, Martin, TN; JR; BS; Mu Epsilon Delta Pledge Master 89; Biology; Cytotechnology.

**STUMPH, JASON T,** Memphis St Univ, Memphis, TN; SR; BBA; Stdnt Govt Assoc Sen 88-89; Intr Frat Cncl AR St Treas 89; Delta Dorm Cncl AR St VP 87-88; Beta Alpha Psi; Pi Kappa Alpha AR St 87-89; Acctg Sls/Mrktg; Acctg.

**STUPAK, CYNTHIA K,** Long Island Univ C W Post Cntr, Greenvale, NY; JR; BS; Asian Clb Sec 89; Crmnl Jstc Assoc 89-; Deans Lst; Hnrs Rsdnc Hl; AS 90; Crmnl Jstc; Prbtn.

**STUPKA, KRISTY JO,** Fl A & M Univ, Tallahassee, FL; GD; MBA; Stdnt Govt Sntr 89-90; Seminole Ambssdrs; Stdnt Ldrshp Conf 86; Chi Omega Grk Wk Chrmn 90; Meals On Wheels; Yng Rpblcns; Summer Rep Theatre; IM Sccr 86-90; BA 90; Theatre.

**STURDEVANT, ROBERT WILLIAM,** Northern Ky Univ, Highland Hts, KY; GD; Sociology Clb; Stdnt Ntnl Edctn Assn; Speech Cmptn Jud; Wlcmng Comm Untd Ntns Offcr; Sollie Similone Aftcn Ntnl Cngrs; Ky Tchng Certf; Amrcn Hstry; Anthropology.

**STURDIVANT, MARION E,** Alcorn St Univ, Lorman, MS; FR; AD; MASN Sec 90; Nrsg.

**STURDIVANT, RYAN W,** Northern Ky Univ, Highland Hts, KY; SR; BS; Intrn At CBIS 90-; Flg Ftbl; Info Systms; Comp Proggrm Systm Anlyst.

**STURDIVANT, SUSAN M,** Volunteer St Comm Coll, Gallatin, TN; SO; BA; Deans Lst; Hnr Rll; Srr Clb ; Grnpc; Cmpssn Intl; Hlth Care.

**STURGEON, JOHN R,** Univ Of Southern Ms, Hattiesburg, MS; JR; BS; Cmptr Sci; Cmptr Sftwr Eng.

**STURGILL, FRAN A,** Ashland Comm Coll, Ashland, KY; SO; ASD; Deans List 90-; Com St Judes Church; Treas Lawrence Co Tip-Off Clb 88-; Spch/Lang Pthlgst 87-; Bus Admnstrtn/Med; Admnstrtn Med Fld.

**STURGIS, ANDREA DEON,** Morris Brown Coll, Atlanta, GA; JR; Mktg Club 88-; Vice Provist Dns Lst 90-; Mktg Rsrch Intrnshp 88-; Mktg; Rsrchr.

**STURM, CATHERINE M,** City Univ Of Ny Queensbrough, New York, NY; SO; BAMBA; Nutrition/Blgy; Tchr/Ntrtnst/ Entrepreneur.

**STURM, DEANNA M,** Univ Of Ga, Athens, GA; SO; BSFCS; Phi Upsilon Omicron 90-; Gene/Hazel Franklin Schlrshp 90-; Dietetics.

**STURM, MARY E,** Hillsborough Comm Coll, Tampa, FL; SO; BA; Hnr Roll 89; Crrllwd Prfssnl Bsnss Women Assoc 90; IBM Corp Opr Ntwrk Rgstrtn 87; AS Hllsbrgh Cmmnty Clg 90; Cmptr Sci; Cmmnctns.

**STURM, TRACY ANNE,** Univ Of Nc At Charlotte, Charlotte, NC; JR; BA; Law Soc; Hstry Clb; Amnsty Intl Dth Pnlty Coord 89-90; Goldn Key 90-; Pi Sigma Alpha 90-; Kappa Delta Schlrshp Chr 88-; Accsbl Lvng Vol 89; Deans Lst 89-90; Peer Advsr 89-90; Poltcl Sci/Hstry; JD/MBA/CORP Law.

**STUTHRIDGE, KEVIN A,** Tri County Tech Coll, Pendleton, SC; FR; Scl Sci Crmnl Law; Law Enfrcmnt.

**STUTLER, JOHN D,** Marshall University, Huntington, WV; JR; BA; Gamma Beta Phi 89-; Phi Eta Sigma Chartered Offcr Parliamentarian 90-; Sigma Tau Delta Secy 90-; English Spanish; Tchng.

**STUTLER, MICHAEL A,** Wv Univ At Parkersburg, Parkersburg, WV; JR; BA; Mktg; Indstrl Mktg.

**STUTSMAN, JANE L,** Univ Of South Al, Mobile, AL; SO; BS; PTA; Brownie Ldr; Mrktng; Univ Prfssr.

**STUTTS, JEANNINE W,** Univ Of Ky, Lexington, KY; SO; Phi Eta Sigma 90-; Speech/Communication Disorders; Education.

**STUTZ, ALAN R,** Catawba Valley Comm Coll, Hickory, NC; SR; VICA 85-87; Natl Hon Soc 82-; Kbldg Trds Cmptn 87; Bsbl Trck; Crpntr Wldng Uphlstry Painter; Bldg Trd 85-87; Air Cond 89-90; Bldg Trades; Engr.

**STUTZMAN, BRADLEY M,** S U N Y Coll Of Tech At Alfred, Alfred, NY; FR; AAS; Rotary Exchng Rotex Exchng Stdnt Brazil; Agri Bus; Intl Mktg.

**STUTZMAN, GREG E,** Univ Of Pittsburgh, Pittsburgh, PA; FR; BS; Elec Engr.

**STUYCK, PAMELA S,** Univ Of Sc At Columbia, Columbia, SC; SR; BSN; Stdnt Nrs Assn Commhlth Drctr 89-90; SC Stdnt Nrs Assn 88-90; Ntnl Stdnt Nrs Assn 88-90; Nrsng Alumni Fclty Schrshp 90-; Otstndng Undrgrd Stdnt Awd 90-; BA Converse Clg Sprtnbrg SC 81; Nrsng.

**STYLES, AUDREY D,** Caldwell Comm Coll & Tech Inst, Lenoir, NC; FR; Erly Chldhd Educ; Tchr.

**STYLES, DERRICK R,** Lenoir Rhyne Coll, Hickory, NC; JR; BA; Phi Beta Lambda 90-; Pi Kappa Phi; Bus Admn/Econ; Banker.

**STYLES, RITA,** Fayetteville St Univ, Fayetteville, NC; SO; BA; Chncllrs Acad Schlrshp; Bsnss; Accntng.

**STYRON, LAURA L,** Univ Of South Al, Mobile, AL; SO; BA; GPA Award Long Island Univ; Computer Scie/Educ; Teach.

**STYRON, REGINA,** City Univ Of Ny Baruch Coll, New York, NY; SR; Nwsppr 85; BBA 90; Mrktng Advrstng.

**SUARA, SAKA A,** Va St Univ, Petersburg, VA; SR; Econ Clb 90; BSC; Cmptr Pgm.

**SUARATO, JOSEPH A,** Wagner Coll, Staten Island, NY; SR; BA; Merrill Lynch Cnsmr Mrkts Intrnshp 90; Assistng Fncl Cnsltnt; Ecnmcs/Bsnss; Invstmnt Bnkng.

**SUAREZ ESCABI, SHARON L,** Inter Amer Univ Pr San German, San German, PR; SR; BA; Bilngl Eng Spnsh Org Pres 88-; Clg Sec Intl VP 90-; ULPR Sec Cmptns; Intermed Typing; Awrd In Spelling Shrthnd; Sec Sci.

**SUAREZ IGARTUA, GREGORIO MANUEL,** Inter Amer Univ Pr San Juan, Hato Rey, PR; GD; JD; Leo Dir 87-; Law Schl Scrty Comm 90-; Beta Beta Beta 87-89; Hnr Prog Jrnl-Edtr 87-88; Law Review Wrtr 90-; Brd Of Trustees; Cum Laude BS Biol 89; BS 89; Law.

**SUAREZ LOZADA, LINNETTE,** Inter Amer Univ Pr Hato Rey, Hato Rey, PR; FR; Bio; Phys Ther.

**SUAREZ, DIANA L,** Bloomfield Coll, Bloomfield, NJ; SO; BA; Acctg CPA.

**SUAREZ, EILEEN,** Univ Of Miami, Coral Gables, FL; SR; BS; Hosp Vol; Biolgy; Med.

**SUAREZ, ERNEST,** Seton Hall Univ, South Orange, NJ; FR; BA; Prsh/Comm Serv 90-; Bsn.

**SUAREZ, GEORGE B,** Fl International Univ, Miami, FL; JR; FMA 90-; Phi Kappa Phi 90-; IBM Latin Amer Crbbn Rgn Fnnce Intrn; USMC 87; AA Miami Dade Comm Coll 90; Fnnce; Mgmt.

**SUAREZ, IRENE M,** Fl International Univ, Miami, FL; SR; BA; FEA 89-; FPIRG 90; AA Broward Cmnty Clg 89; Elem Tchr.

**SUAREZ, KAREN,** Cornell Univ Statutory College, Ithaca, NY; SO; BS; Deans Lst 89; Marine Bio; Biolgcl Rsrch.

**SUAREZ, KAREN S,** Hillsborough Comm Coll, Tampa, FL; SO; Phi Theta Kappa; Engl Hon 90; Rpblcn Prty 86-87; Lone Plm Wmns Golf Assn Pres 82-; Palma Ceia Wmns Glf Assn 82-; Bus; Acctg/Acctg Law.

**SUAREZ, KIMBERLY N,** Midway Coll, Midway, KY; SO; AA; Std Govt Sntr 90-; Mdwy Mlrs Clb 100; Dns Lst 89-; Phi Theta Kappa 89-; Early Chldhd Educ; Chldcr Spec.**

**SUAREZ, LAURA C,** Univ Of Miami, Coral Gables, FL; FR; BA; Pblc Rltns Stdnt Soc Amer 90-; Yrbk Wrtr 90-; Orntn 90; Alpha Lambda Delta 90-; Deans Hon Rl 90-; Stanford Acdmc Schlrshp 90-; Chappie James Schlrshp 90-; Pblc Rltns/Mktg; Pblc Rltns Crprt.

**SUAREZ, MARCIA DIANE,** Union Univ, Jackson, TN; SR; BA; Stdnt TN Educ Assn 89-; Phi Theta Kappa 89; TN Army Natl Gard 86-; AS Jackson St Comm Coll 89; Elem Educ; Tchng.

**SUAREZ, MARY JANE,** Univ Of North Fl, Jacksonville, FL; JR; Stu Fclty Cmsn Rep 90; Mntr Pro 90-; Min Stu Assoc; Phi Theta Kappa Gldn Key 90-; Bus; Law.

**SUAREZ, SANDRA E,** Inter Amer Univ Pr San Juan, Hato Rey, PR; SO; BA; ROTC Cadet 89; Airway Sci Mgmnt; Air Traffic Cntrlr.**

**SUAREZ, SANDRA E,** Inter Amer Univ Pr Hato Rey, Hato Rey, PR; SO; BA; Air Frc ROTC Cadet 89; Airway Sci Mgmt; Air Trffc Cntrllr.

**SUAREZ, TERESA L,** Miami Dade Comm Coll, Miami, FL; AA; Acctg.

**SUAREZ-HERNANDEZ, SANDRA I,** Catholic Univ Of Pr, Ponce, PR; SR; JD; FBLA Advsr 76-; Nwsltr Wrtr 89-90; Delta Zeta Phi Trbne; Dvlpmnt Comm; Lcl Nwspapr Wrtr/Brd Of Dir; Bus Tchr; BS 76; MA 82; Law; St/Fed Law.

**SUAREZ-ROBLES, GERARDO A,** Catholic Univ Of Pr, Ponce, PR; GD; JD; Inst Hon Pgm 88-89; Stdnts Assn Sociology/ Crmnlgy Pres 86-89; Univ Stdnt Cncl VP 89; Hon Stdnts Assn 86-89; Catholic Univ Gym Clb 90-; Army Natl Guard Private 1st Cls 90; BA Crmnlgy 89; Soc Aesviation/Crmnl Conduct; Law.**

**SUBA, MICHAEL T,** Western New England Coll, Springfield, MA; FR; BS; Alpha Lambda Delta; Singular Acdmc Achvmnt Awd For Exclnc In Engrng Frshm Yr 90-; Mech Engrng.

**SUBA, RICHARD A,** Univ Of Akron, Akron, OH; SR; BA; ACES 90-; Big Bro; Sports Med/Elem Edn; Tchr Athletic Trnr.

**SUBER, PATRICK,** Spartanburg Methodist Coll, Spartanburg, SC; JR; BA; UBSA Pres; AA Spartanburg Mthdst Coll; Elem Ed; Tch.

**SUBIK, JEANNIE M,** Schenectady County Comm Coll, Schenectady, NY; SO; Jrsprdnc Clb Pres; Agr Mrks Yc Clb; Phi Theta Kappa; Otstndng Achvmnt Cntrbtn Awrd; St Cert WBE Ownr 90; Constrctn Bus; AAS Prlgl; Engl Tchng.

**SUBRAMANIAN, ASHA P,** S U N Y At Buffalo, Buffalo, NY; FR; BA; Ant Rp Tsk Frc 90-; Hnrs Cncl Asst Rep 90-; Hnrs Prgm Wlcmng Cmmtt Tr Gd Mgr Dcrtns; Univ Hnrs Prgm 90-; Cmmntyactn Crps Hosp Vol 90-; Frndshp Vol 90-; Natl Sci Fndtn Pscyphyslgy Rsrchpstn 90-; Deans Lst 90-; Blgy; Med.

**SUBRAMANIAN, KRUPA,** Coll Of Insurance, New York, NY; JR; BS; Stu Cncl Tres; Orgn Res Stu 90-; Actrl Sci; Actry.

**SUCEC, MARINA ROSE,** Daytona Beach Comm Coll, Daytona Beach, FL; FR; BA; Dns Lst 90-; Pres Lst 90-; Phi Theta Kappa; Osteen Civic Assn Pres 86-89; Amer Legion Aux Sec 89-; Engl; Admin.

**SUCHARSKI, NANCE E,** Daytona Beach Comm Coll, Daytona Beach, FL; SO; Phi Theta Kappa 90-; Educ; Spec Ed Tchr.

**SUCHCICKI, LORI A,** Rutgers St Un At New Brunswick, New Brunswick, NJ; FR; BA; Frnch Clb; SADD; Stdnt Cncl; Ed Yrbk; Coll Orttn Cmmtt; Frnch Natl Hnr Scty; Natl Hnr Scty; Sigma Kappa; Grdn St Schlr; Advrtsng Intern; Chrldr; Engl Psychlgy; Law.

**SUCHER, CARA M,** Univ Of Rochester, Rochester, NY; SO; BS; Sailing Clb Pblcty Ofcr 89-; COPA Rcrtng Ofcr 89-; Biomed Rsrch Flwshp; Chem Eng.

**SUCHER, LE ANN MC CAIG,** Medical Univ Of Sc, Charleston, SC; JR; BSN; Fllwshp St Frncs Hosp 90-; Schlrshp Amer Bus Wmns Assn 90-; Helen Fuld Fllwshp; Natl Ski Ptrl 87-; Cert Gstrntstnl Clncn 89; EKG Tech 89; BS Univ Of Wisconsin Milwaukee 85; Natl Cert Cert Gstrntstnl Clncn 87; RN; Crtcl Cre Nrsng.

**SUDANO, HYATT W,** Tallahassee Comm Coll, Tallahassee, FL; SO; AA; Pres Schlrs Clb 90; Civil Eng.

**SUDASASSI, DIANA L,** Fl International Univ, Miami, FL; FR; Hnrs Prgm 90-; Deans Lst 90-; Eng.

**SUDDEATH, LEE F,** Tn St Univ, Nashville, TN; SR; BS; Chmstry Clb Pres 90-; Gldn Ky 90-; Dean Lst 89-; US Navy 83-88; St Of TN Cmptr Oprtr I 89-; Chmstry; Grad Schl Chmcl Eng.

**SUDDETH II, CLIFFORD W,** Univ Of Tn At Chattanooga, Chattanooga, TN; FR; BA; Political Science; Law.

**SUDDUTH, DAUN R,** Univ Of Al At Birmingham, Birmingham, AL; JR; BA; Art; Journalism.

**SUDDUTH, SCOTT T,** Morehouse Coll, Atlanta, GA; SO; BA; Hon Roll 89-; Hist Hon Soc 89-; NAACP; Assemblyman Richard Polanco Intrnshp; Lorimar Prod; Pol Sci; Entertainment Law.

**SUDLOW, ALYSSA L,** Embry Riddle Aeronautical Univ, Daytona Beach, FL; JR; BS; 99s Sec 90-; Stdnt Govt Assn Repr; Yrbk 90-; Drama Clb 90-; Orientn Ldr; Deans Lst 89-90; Priv Pilots Lic; Aeronautical Sci; Pilot.

**SUDO, EMIKO S,** Univ Of Sc At Columbia, Columbia, SC; JR; BA; Engl; Educ.

**SUESS, CATHERINE I,** Syracuse Univ, Syracuse, NY; JR; BS; Syracuse Panhellenic Assc Co Rush Chrmn 90-; Orient Advsr Frshmn 89; Univ 100; Eta Pi Upsilon 90-; Phi Eta Sigma 89-90; Delta Delta Delta Panhellenic Rep 89-; Intern Sen Lombardi 90; Inter Dept Hlth/Human Svc; Nurturing Wrld Day Care Vol 90-; Mgmt Info Syst; Syst Analyst/Cnsltng/Trng.

**SUGARMAN, MARNE D,** Bucks County Comm Coll, Newtown, PA; FR; Gamma Sigma Sigma 90-; Am Inst/Blgcl Sci Secy 90-; IM Wise Gratz Colg 90; Libl Arts; Envmntl Sci/Prof.

**SUGGS, LEAH K,** Faulkner Univ, Montgomery, AL; JR; BS; SAEA VP 90-; Kirei Nai Ai; Chrs 90-; Art Clb Chrmn 90-; Appls Crt 89; FEA 89-90; Msc Awd 90-; Hrns Lst; AA Lake City Comm Clg 90; Elem Ed; Tchr.

**SUGIMOTO, IZUMI,** Comm Coll Algny Co Algny Cmps, Pittsburgh, PA; FR; Art; Interior Dsgnr.

**SUH, BYUNGHA,** Nyack Coll, Nyack, NY; SR; Chrch Nassau Yth Grp Dir 87-89; Dom Rep Gspl Tm Capt 90; Stdnt Tchng 90; Nu-Rocks 89-; Soc Sci; Mba.

**SUH, JEONG,** Fayetteville St Univ, Fayetteville, NC; JR; BS; Alpha Kappa Mu 90-; Comp Sci.

**SUH, JUNG,** Univ Of Nc At Charlotte, Charlotte, NC; FR; BA; Math; Prof.

**SUH, SOOJEE S,** Nyack Coll, Nyack, NY; JR; Readers Dig Schlrshp 90-; Pres Grant 89-90; Psychlgy; NS Acctng.

**SUHAR, KIMBERLY L,** Duquesne Univ, Pittsburgh, PA; FR; BS; Pharmcy.

**SUITER, CHRISTINE E,** Seton Hall Univ, South Orange, NJ; SR; BA; Spnsh Hnr Soc Sec; Educ Hm Soc; Spnsh Educ; Tchr.

**SUKENIK, THERESA E,** Duquesne Univ, Pittsburgh, PA; FR; Scndry Educ/Hstry; Educ/Tch.

**SUKENNIK, ILYA L,** Bunker Hill Comm Coll, Boston, MA.

**SUKOW, PATRICK R,** Salem-Teikyo Univ, Salem, WV; FR; BS; Gamma Beta Phi 90-; Sccr Capt 90-; Educ; Tchr.

**SULEK, JACQUELINE L,** Western Piedmont Comm Coll, Morganton, NC; FR; AAS; Prlgl Clb 90; Phi Thete Kappa 90; Natl Asc Govt Prchsng Offcrs 84-; AFL-CIO Comm Wrkrs Am Sec 80-82; DAV Adjtnt 70-90; Hntr Bld Ctr 71-81; Sggstn Awds Comm 85-88; US Navy Mdc 65-67; Prchsng Offcr 70-88; PPB Natl Inst Govt; Law/Bsn/Prchsng/Adlt Educ; Law/Prch Fed Govt.

**SULEMAN, SARA Y,** City Univ Of Ny City Coll, New York, NY; SO; AMSA 89-; Wmn In Med 89-; Lambda Alpha Mu Treas 90-; Trck 89-90; Bio; Med.

**SULESKI, JANET M,** Cornell Univ Statutory College, Ithaca, NY; SR; BA; Astrnmcl Scty; Rpblcns; Ag Econs; Bus Admin.

**SULICH, GREGORY,** Marywood Coll, Scranton, PA; JR; BS; Cmptr Info Systms; Clrgy.

**SULIVAN, JAY B,** Kent St Univ Kent Cmps, Kent, OH; SO; BA; Deans Lst 90-; IM Sprts; Bus.

**SULLENBERGER, LISA R,** Indiana Univ Of Pa, Indiana, PA; SR; BA; Chrldng 89-90; Delta Zeta 89-; Educ.

**SULLINS, RONALD W,** Strayer Coll, Washington, DC; SR; BS; AS 81; Bus Admin; Law Enfrcmnt.

**SULLIVAN, ALFRED J,** Niagara Univ, Niagara Univ, NY; JR; BFA; Stdnt Advsry Cncl Treas 87-89; Drma Club Pres 88-89; AFA Northern Essex Cmnty College 89; Theater Performance; Performance.

**SULLIVAN, ANNA C,** Coker Coll, Hartsville, SC; JR; BA; Elem Educ.

**SULLIVAN, BRIAN M,** Allegheny Coll, Meadville, PA; JR; BS; Mens Vllybl; SG; Lambda Sigma; Phi Delta Theta; Pew Smmr Flwshp Recip; Vllybl; Bio/Psych Major.

**SULLIVAN, BRIAN P,** Cornell Univ Statutory College, Ithaca, NY; FR; BS; Ntrl Rsrc Mngmnt; Grad Schl.

**SULLIVAN, BRUCE O,** Univ Of Southern Ms, Hattiesburg, MS; SR; BS; Summer Conf Tm Conf Mgr 90; Alpha Lambda Delta 88-89; Phi Eta Sigma 89-90; US Army 85-88; Psychlgy; Socl Wrk.

**SULLIVAN, CELIA A,** Univ Of Sc At Columbia, Columbia, SC; JR; BA; Deans Lst; R Roy Pearce; Schlrshp Dmnstrtng Otstndng; Vrbl Wrtn Sklls; Habitat Humanity; Cncl Chld Abs Nglct; Jrnlsm; Obtain MBA.

**SULLIVAN, CHARITY L,** Univ Of Cincinnati, Cincinnati, OH; FR; BUP; Circle K Family Chairman 90-; Alpha Lambda Delta 90-; Urban Planning.

**SULLIVAN, CHRISTINE E,** Glassboro St Coll, Glassboro, NJ; SR; BA; Okwd Smmr Thtr 87-; Ad Clb; Acme Mrkts Cshr/CSR 86-; Cmmnctns/Lib Arts; Advrtsng.

**SULLIVAN, CHRISTOPHER A,** Temple Univ, Philadelphia, PA; SO; BA; Cvl Eng.

**SULLIVAN, COLLEEN A,** City Univ Of Ny Baruch Coll, New York, NY; JR; BA; Mgmt Muscl Entrprs.

**SULLIVAN, CRISTIN L,** Allegheny Coll, Meadville, PA; SO; BA; Spnsh Tutr Elem Schls 90-; Allegheny Liaisons Ldrs Edctnl Spprt; Tourguide Admssns Offc; Lambda Sigma 90-; Psi Chi; Alpha Delta Pi Exec VP 90-; Alden Schlr 89-; Psychology.

**SULLIVAN, DANIEL R,** Hudson Valley Comm Coll, Troy, NY; FR; Indstrl; Automotive Tchnlgy.

**SULLIVAN, DAVID F,** Univ Of Sc At Columbia, Columbia, SC; SO; BA; Mrchg Bnd Cncrt 89-90; Chi Psi Pldg; Intnl Stdys; Intnl Law.

**SULLIVAN, DEBORAH H,** Coker Coll, Hartsville, SC; SO; BS; Blue Cross Blue Shield 85-; Bus.

**SULLIVAN, DELORIS M,** Piedmont Tech Coll, Greenwood, SC; FR; AS; Math; Engr.

**SULLIVAN, DONNA B,** Columbia Union Coll, Takoma Park, MD; SR; BS; AMTA; Educ Dir Potomac Massage Trnng Inst; Org Mngmnt.

**SULLIVAN, DONNA M,** Western Carolina Univ, Cullowhee, NC; FR; BA; Univ Plyrs 90-; Niggli Schlrshp 90-; Theatre Arts; Perf Theatre.

**SULLIVAN, EDWARD J,** Bloomfield Coll, Bloomfield, NJ; SR; BA; Pass Cnty Coll Alumn Assn Asst Dir 87; AA Pass Cnty Comm Coll 80; Psych; Cnslng.

**SULLIVAN, EDWARD T,** Glassboro St Coll, Glassboro, NJ; SR; BA; Stdnt Govt Assn Sntr 89-; Lit Forum Treas 90-; Clg Ctr Prog Bd Sec 88-89; Engl; Tchng.

**SULLIVAN, ELIZABETH M,** Clarkson Univ, Potsdam, NY; JR; BS; Soc Women Mgrs; Amer Mktng Assoc; Panhellenic Cnf; Res Advisor; Phi Mu 89-; Marketing; Sales.

**SULLIVAN, ERICA N,** Clark Atlanta Univ, Atlanta, GA; SO; BS; Chem Club 89-; Orientn Guide Coop 90-; Pre Profsnl Hlth Soc 89-90; Hon Progrm 89-; Howard Hughes Fellow 89-; Minrty Biomed Rsrch Supprt; Deans List 90; Chem; Medcn.

**SULLIVAN, ETHAN A,** Boston Coll, Chestnut Hill, MA; FR; BA; Hnrs Prog 90-; Busn/Law.

**SULLIVAN, JAMIE P,** Merrimack Coll, North Andover, MA; SR; Coaches Awd Var Hcky 88-89; Var Hcky Tm 87-90; Bus Mgmnt.

**SULLIVAN, JANET L,** Memphis St Univ, Memphis, TN; JR; BED; Chi Alpha Sec 89-; Spec Edn; Cnslng Or Speech Path.

**SULLIVAN, JAY B,** Kent St Univ Kent Cmps, Kent, OH; SO; BA; IM Sports; Business.

**SULLIVAN, JAYNE M,** Georgian Court Coll, Lakewood, NJ; SO; BSW; Re-Entry Wmn Pres 88-; Scl Wrk Clb 89-90; Sigma Phi Sigma 90-; TLC Pgm Notetaker 90; AAUW Schlrshp 90-; Toms Rvr Bus/Pro Wmns Schlrshp 89-90; Deans Schlr 90; Free-Lance Wrtr; Clwn Chrch Mnstry; Scl Wrk; MSW Psychthrpy.

**SULLIVAN, JENNIFER A,** Columbus Coll Of Art & Design, Columbus, OH; SR; BFA; Illstrtns/Cards Books.

**SULLIVAN, JENNIFER L,** Columbus Coll Of Art & Design, Columbus, OH; SO; BA; Chrch Wrk; Bible Stdy Grps; Fine Arts; Chld Art Psy/Tchng.

**SULLIVAN, JERRY L,** East Tn St Univ, Johnson City, TN; SR; BS; Tech Educ Coll Assn Pres 90-; TSA Advsr Gray Elem; Epsilon Pi Tau 90-; STEA; Ind Arts/Tech Edn; Indstrl Fields.

**SULLIVAN, JILL,** Endicott Coll, Beverly, MA; SR; AS; Phi Theta Kappa 89-; Delta Nu Chptr; Internshp Lndry Arcari Int Desgnrs 90; Stdnt Mbr Alld Brd Trade 86-; Frmrly Exec 78-85; Int Design.

**SULLIVAN, JOSEPH P,** Merrimack Coll, North Andover, MA; JR; Pltcl Scnc Soc 90-; Knights Of Columbus 88-; Poltcl Scnc; Law.

**SULLIVAN, JOYCE A,** Felician Coll, Lodi, NJ; SO; BA; SNJEA; Edn Clb; Deans Lst; Elem Edn/Art; Elem Sch Tchr/Prtnr Day Care.

**SULLIVAN, KANDICE R,** Univ Of Southern Ms, Hattiesburg, MS; SO; BA; Phi Eta Sigma 89-90; Gamma Alpha Epsilon 90-; Delta Gamma 90-; Gamma Beta Phi 89-; Psychology; Phy Thrpy.

**SULLIVAN, KAREN H,** Western New England Coll, Springfield, MA; JR; BS; Wmn Engrs Sec 88-; Sigma Beta Tau Sec; Coord Jr-High Bioeng; Std Tch Asst Fresh Engr 88-; Wstrn MA Engr Schlp Awd 90; Mgr Mns Vars Bsbl Tm 88-; Bioeng; Rehab Engr.

**SULLIVAN, KATHLEEN,** Glassboro St Coll, Glassboro, NJ; FR; BA; Stdnt Actvties Brd 90-; Poltcl Sci; Lawyer.

**SULLIVAN, KATHLEEN E,** Western New England Coll, Springfield, MA; SR; BSBA; Mktg Asc Sec 90-; Std Snt 88-90; Hmcmng Comm 90; Mktg Intshp; Wrstlng Tm Mgr 89-; Mktg; Fld Bsn.

**SULLIVAN, KATHLEEN E,** Villanova Univ, Villanova, PA; SR; BS; Stu NEA PSEA Mmbrshp Chr 90-; Kappa Delta Pi; Delta Delta Delta; Joseph Burn OSA Mdlln; Educ/Engl; Tchng.

**SULLIVAN, KATHLEEN M,** Univ Of Md Baltimore Prof Schl, Baltimore, MD; SR; BS; Stdnt Amer Dntl Hygnsts Assoc 89-; Dntl Hygn Recrtmnt Admssns Comm 90-; Phi Kappa Phi; Sen Schlrshp 87-; Dntl Hygne; Prvt Pract Dntl Hygnst.

**SULLIVAN, KEDRA Y,** Univ Of Sc At Columbia, Columbia, SC; FR; Gospel Chr 90-; Mnrty Asstnc Peer Prgrm 90-; Accntg; Law.

**SULLIVAN, KELLI A,** Eckerd Coll, St Petersburg, FL; SR; BA; Acdmc Afrs Comm 89-; Intl Bus Clb Tres 89-90; ASPEC Stu Liaison Tsk Frc 88-90; Cir K 87-88; Human Rsrc Inst Intrnshp 89-90; Cmprtv Cltr Coll Senate 89-; Intl Bus; Mgmt.

**SULLIVAN, KELLY A,** Univ Of Ky, Lexington, KY; SO; BA; Chi Omega 90-; Flwshp Chrstn Ath 89-; Phi Eta Sigma 90-; Lances Jr Hnry; Coll Schlrs Amer; IM Act Bsktbl Flg Ftbl 89-; Indust Psych.

**SULLIVAN, MARIA D,** Strayer Coll, Washington, DC; JR; BS; Acctg Clb 90-; Alpha Chi 90-; Wright Schlrshp 90-; AA In CIS 90; Acctg; CPA.

**SULLIVAN, MARY K,** Radford Univ, Radford, VA; FR; BS; Math; Teach.

**SULLIVAN, MAUREEN E,** William Paterson Coll, Wayne, NJ; JR; BA; Pi Lambda Theta 90-; Specl Educ Tchr.

**SULLIVAN, MELISSA J,** Univ Of Southern Ms, Hattiesburg, MS; FR; Std Almn Assc 90-; Std Eagle Clb 90-; Pi Beta Phi 90-; Gen Stds.

**SULLIVAN, MOLLY KATHLEEN,** Radford Univ, Radford, VA; JR; ASID; Wrk Stdy Prog; Schlrshp; Intr Dsgn.

**SULLIVAN, MONA L,** Univ Of Ky, Lexington, KY; SR; Epsilon Delta Publcty 89-; Lances 90-; Golden Key 90-; Alpha Gamma Delta 87-; Abuse Cnsl 90; Christn Flwshp Big Buddy 87; Livng Arts/Sci Ctr; Deans List 88-90; Alpha Gamma Delta Schlrshp Bowl 88-90; Alpha Gamma Fndrs Mem Schlrshp 89-90; Im; Erly Elem Ed; Tchr.

**SULLIVAN, NANCY A,** Newbury Coll, Brookline, MA; Intrr Dsgn.

**SULLIVAN, PATRICIA M,** Oh Coll Of Podiatric Med, Cleveland, OH; GD; DPM; OPMSA Dir Bsn Afrs 88-89; AAWP; Pi Delta Treas 89-90; BA Holy Cross Clge 87; Pdtry; Pdtrc Physcn.

**SULLIVAN, SEAN R,** Fl St Univ, Tallahassee, FL; SO; BA; Rsrv Offcrs Trng Cop U S Army 89-; Tau Kappa Epsilon VP 90-; AA St Leo Clg 88; Bus Mgmnt/Info Systems; Cmptr Analyst/Mgr.

**SULLIVAN, STEPHANY A,** George Mason Univ, Fairfax, VA; SR; BS; SEA VP 88-; AEYC 89-; Alpha Omega 86-87; IM 88-89; Early Edctn; Tchng.

**SULLIVAN, STEVEN W,** William Paterson Coll, Wayne, NJ; JR; BA; Intrvrsty Chrstn Flwshp Exec Bd Sec 90-; Grp Bbl Stdy Ldr 89-; Church Orch 87-; Intrvrsty Pblcty Co Ldr 90-; Trmbn Ens 90-; Jazz Bnd 86-; Chrch Chr87-; Envrnmntl Clb Advsr; Vol Wayne Schl Systm 90-; Sndy Schl Tchr/Chrch Snd Tech 89-90; Hstry; Tchng.

**SULLIVAN, THERESA M,** Ny Univ, New York, NY; FR; BA; Serv Org; Frnch; Intrprtr.

**SULLIVAN, TODD R,** Univ Of Ky, Lexington, KY; FR; BARCH; Hbtat Hmnty VP 90-; Arch.

**SULLIVAN, VICKI K,** Univ Of Fl, Gainesville, FL; GD; BS; Stdnt Dttc Assoc Pres 89-; Gnsvll Dttc Assoc 89-; Pblc Rltns Asst 83-84; Prgm Crdntr Lkm Scty 84-88; BA 83; Dttcs.

**SULLIVAN-NICHOLS, KATHLEEN D,** Cecils Coll, Asheville, NC; GD; Am Assn Med Asstnts Inc Buncombe Co NC 90-; United Prison Mnstrs WNC Conf; Div Prisons Vol Pgm Henderson Co Vol; Nrsng.

**SULLIVANT, ERIN E,** Western Ky Univ, Bowling Green, KY; SR; BFA; Western Players 88-; WKU Dance Co 89-; Univ Chorale 87-; Phi Kappa Phi 90-; Phi Eta Sigma 87-88; Alpha Psi Omega V P 90-; Russell H Miller Schlrshp 90-; Dr Mildred Howard Awd; Perf Art S; Prof Performer.

**SULLO, STEPHANIE,** Mount Saint Mary Coll, Newburgh, NY; FR; BA; Admssns Clb 90-; Engl; Elem Tchr.

**SULZER, JANICE MARIE,** Univ Of West Fl, Pensacola, FL; JR; BED; Alpha Chi Omega Rtls Advsr 90; Big Brthrs And Sistrs Amrca 89-.

**SUMLIN, CARMEN D,** Commonwealth Coll, Virginia Beach, VA; GD; BA; Med Clb; Pres Lst 90-; US Army Vet 80-81; Med/Fmly Prctc; Ofc Mgr.

**SUMMERFIELD, MARY B,** Univ Of North Fl, Jacksonville, FL; JR; BAE; Phi Theta Kappa; Upsilon Eta FL Cmnty College 89; Iota-UNF VP Pblcty Comm 90-; Pres List FL Cmnty Clge 90; Phi Theta Kappa Hall Of Hnr Outstanding Natl Alumni 91; Arts Asmbly Mbr/Vlntr; FL Jr Yacht Racing Assoc Vlntr 90-; AA FL Cmnty Clge 89; Art Education; Art Teacher Elem.

**SUMMERFIELD, MIKE S,** Christian Brothers Univ, Memphis, TN; JR; BA; Stdnt Gvrnmnt Assn VP 90-; Cool It Green Peace Fndr Prsdnt; Stdnt Sen Pres 90-; Soph Cls Pres 89-; Amrcn Mrktng Assn; Pi Kappa Phi Scl Chrmn 89-; Mifa Cllctng Fd Hmls Pr; Cmpgn Elct Hageyweyer Jdg Asstnt Vlntr 90; IMS 88-; Mrktng; Pblc Rltns Prdctn Mgmt.

**SUMMERFORD, TWYLA M,** Livingston Univ, Livingston, AL; SR; BED; Tau Kappa Epsilon Little Sister Pres 81-; Manager; Elementary Education; Teach.

**SUMMEROUR, KENYA N,** Tuskegee Univ, Tuskegee Inst, AL; SO; Ga Clb 89-; SAM 90-; USAF Schlrshp; Busn Admin; Exec.

**SUMMEROUR, MELANIE A,** Emory Univ, Atlanta, GA; GD; MA; Yng Lf Ldr 83-87; Arete Socty Pacific Luth Univ 85-87; Spurs 83-84; Bread For The World Treas 86-87; Dns Schlrshp 90-; Pres Schlrshp 82-88; Hnrs At Entrnc 82; RN Chldrns Hosp/Med Ctr 87-90; BSN Pacific Luth Univ 87; Chld Hlth Nrsng; Pediatric Nrs Prctntr.

**SUMMERS, DAWN M,** Liberty Univ, Lynchburg, VA; SO; BS; Yth Quest; Light; Yth Quest Gym; Alpha Lambda Delta; Psychology; Chlrns Cnslr.

**SUMMERS, JOY L,** Univ Of Tn At Martin, Martin, TN; GD; BA 90; Erl Chldhd Edctn.

**SUMMERS, KATHLEEN ANDERSON,** Mercyhurst Coll, Erie, PA; GD; MS; Stdnt Govt Assoc 78-79; Criminal Justice Clb 77-; Deans Lst 78-79; Internship Erie Cnty Juvenial Prob Ofc 78; Wrote 1 Annual Reprt Intsv Prbtn 77-78; Erie Ski Clb Past Mbr; BA Crminal Jstc 79; Admin Of Justice; Crim Just Prctnr.

**SUMMERS, KRISTY L,** Univ Of Ga, Athens, GA; JR; BED; Tch Armc 90-; Kappa Delta Epsilon 90-; Ttrl Prgm 90-; Erly Chldhd Spcl Ed; Tchng.

**SUMMERS, LESLIE C,** Hillsborough Comm Coll, Tampa, FL; FR; PHARM; Sci; Pharmaceuticals.

**SUMMERS, LISHA C,** Oh St Univ, Columbus, OH; SR; BS; Alpha Lamda Delta; Phi Eta Sigma; Phi Kappa Phi; Gldn Key; Excllnc Schlrsp Awrd; Dstngshd Schlrs Schlrshp; Chmstry Stdnt Instrctnl Ast; Chmstry.

**SUMMERS, MARGARET K,** Coll Of Charleston, Charleston, SC; JR; BA; Art Hstry.

**SUMMERS, STEPHEN J,** S U N Y At Buffalo, Buffalo, NY; JR; BA; Acctng Asc; Natl Asc Acctnts; Schssmstrs Ski Clb; Acctng.

**SUMMERS, TABITHA S,** Pellissippi St Tech Comm Coll, Knoxville, TN; GD; Radio/TV Clb Secr 88; Phi Theta Kappa Secr 90-; Phi Beta Gamma; AAS; Cmptr Acctg; Acctg/Job Mkt.**

**SUMMERS, TRACEY L,** Wv Univ, Morgantown, WV; SR; BS; Sigma Phi Omega 87-89; Rho Chi Sec Treas 90-; ASP 89-; Hsktt Schlr 87-89; Phrmcy Intern; AA 89; Phrmcy.

**SUMNER, CANDACE M,** Univ Of Ga, Athens, GA; SR; BED; Alph Omcrn Pi Ofcrs Cncl 90-; Adpt Grndprnt 88-89; Big Sis Pgm 90-; Mst Actv Sister; Erly Chldhd; Tchr.

**SUMNER, CAROL J,** Cumberland Coll, Williamsburg, KY; JR; BS; Cert Of Schlstc Achvmnt 90-; AA Somerset Comm Coll 73; Elem Edn.

**SUMNER, JANICE R,** Piedmont Tech Coll, Greenwood, SC; ASN; United Meth Chrch; Nrsg; RN.

**SUMNER, KAREN L,** Univ Of Central Fl, Orlando, FL; SR; BS; Accntng Soc 89-; Natl Soc Pblc Accts 89-; Bptst Chrch 82-; Phi Theta Kappa 88-89; Beta Gamma Sigma 90-; Gldn Ky 90-; Beta Alpha Psi Sec 90-; AA Polk Comm Coll 89; Bus Admn; Accntng.**

**SUMNER, MARGARET D,** Univ Of Sc At Columbia, Columbia, SC; SR; BA; Retired; Humanities.

**SUMNER, MELVETTA O,** Alice Lloyd Coll, Pippa Passes, KY; GD; MBA; Alpha Chi Sec 89-; Sr Elem Ed Awrd; BA; Elem Ed; Tchng.

**SUMNER, MILDRED ANN,** James Sprunt Comm Coll, Kenansville, NC; Bsn.

**SUMNER, RONALD A,** Univ Of Al At Birmingham, Birmingham, AL; AAS; Stdnt Phys Therapy Org 90-; Am Phys Therapy Org; Wilhoite Assoc RPT; AL Inst Deaf/Blind; Lakeshore Rehab Ctr Orthopedic Surgeons East; Acute Care Phys Therapy 77-; BS NS M Univ AL 86; BS Cmptr Sci 88; Bio/Cmptr Sci; Phys Therapy.

**SUMNER, TRACIE D,** Longwood Coll, Farmville, VA; JR; BS; Assn Blck Stdnts 88-; Hon Brd 90-F Fed Stdnt Scl Wrkrs 89-; Alpha Kappa Alpha Anti-Bsls 90-; Intrnshp Nottoway Corr Ctr; Scl Wrk.

**SUMPTER, KIM L,** Benedict Coll, Columbia, SC; GD; BA; Dns Lst 88-90; Alpha Kappa Alpha 89; Grnd Qn Islm Tmpl Shrnrs 90-; Mgr Trn; BA 90; Pblc Rltns/Mktg; Pblc Rltns Spec.

**SUMPTER, MARSHA L,** Comm Coll Algny Co Algny Cmps, Pittsburgh, PA; ASD; Soc Wrk Clb Corres Sec 90-; Dns Clb 90; Prnt Asst Chldrn Brd Educ Pre Sch Awd 86-87; Chrstms Prty Hom Aged 90; Soc Wrk Tech; Cnslr.

**SUMRALL, NORRIS D,** Fl A & M Univ, Tallahassee, FL; SR; Stdnt Govt Lbbyst 90-; Army ROTC B Co Cmmndr 90; Free And Accptd Msns 87-; Kappa Alpha Psi 87-; Intrnshp Bchtl Engs 90; Assct Gen Cntrctrs Of Amer; BS; Archtctrl And Cnstrctn Eng; Cntrctr.

**SUN, ALICE,** Syracuse Univ, Syracuse, NY; FR; BA; Asia Asn Stdnts Amer Clb 90-; Arch.

**SUN, JIMMY J,** Cornell Univ Statutory College, Ithaca, NY; FR; Radio Nwscstr; Blgy.

**SUN, SIEW PENG P,** Memphis St Univ, Memphis, TN; SR; BA; Intl Stdnt Assn Hd Pblc Rltns 89-90; Pblc Rltns Soc Amer; Gldn Key 91-; Mrtr Bd; Kappa Tau Alpha; C Thornton Jrnlsm Schlrshp 89-90; Pblc Rltns; MBA.

**SUNAMI, MAKI,** Brevard Coll, Brevard, NC; FR; BA; Phi Theta Kappa; Cmmnctn.

**SUNARA, INGRID S,** City Univ Of Ny Queensbrough, New York, NY; JR; ASN; SNA; Hnrs Cnvctn; Nrsng; RN.

**SUNASARA, KHURRAM M,** Oh Wesleyan Univ, Delaware, OH; FR; Phi Eta Sigma; Chmcl Eng.

**SUNDARAPURA, VORAANONG,** Christopher Newport Coll, Newport News, VA; SO; BS; Intl Stu Orgn 89-; Elec Eng; Eng.

**SUNDBERG, JANET L,** Ashland Comm Coll, Ashland, KY; SO; ADN; KANS 90; AACN 90; Hnrs Class 89; Phi Beta Lambda 90; Cub Mstr 83-85; Membr Fltwds Chrch Of Chrst 63; VBS Tchr; Bible Crrspndnce Crse Tchr/Dir; ACC Deans Lst 89-90; Nrsng; Mstrs In Nrsng.**

**SUNDERLAND, SIMON A,** Univ Of Miami, Coral Gables, FL; SR; BS; Rgby Clb Pres 87-89; Glgy Clb 90-; Lambda Chi Alpha 88-; Mrn Sci/Glgy; Hydrlgst/Envrnmntl Glgst.

**SUNDHEIMER, NICOLE C,** S U N Y Coll Of Tech At Frmgdl, Farmingdale, NY; FR.

**SUNDLAND, KAREN S,** Rochester-Hall-Crozer Dvty Sch, Rochester, NY; GD; MA; Bexley Soc 90-; Stdnt Rep Bibl Div Fac 87-90; Alpha Delta Mu 87-; Tch Engl 2nd Lang Vol; Refugee Resttlmnt Vol; Amer Acad Rel Soc Biblcl Lit 88-; Assoc Parishs; Dir Chrstn Educ; MD Bexley Hl 90; BA SWK Sioux Fls Clg 86-87; Rel/Biblcl Stdies; Mnstry/Educ.

**SUNDMAN, REBECCA J,** Smith Coll, Northampton, MA; SR; BA; Wstrn MI Gold Comp 88; Noetables 89-; Thtr Cstm Dsgnr 88-; Pro Life Allnc Smith; Cmps Crsd Chrst Ldrshp Role 90-; Intern Costume Shop 89; Intern Theatr Costume Shp; Dean Lst Wstrn MI 88; Dean Lst 89-; Frst Grp Schlr 89; Cum Laude; BA; Thtr; Chrstn Mnstry.

**SUNDSTROM, ALISA L,** Univ Of Southern Ms, Hattiesburg, MS; SO; BA; PRSSA Pres; Almn Assc 90-; Gamma Beta Phi 90-; Jrnlsm/Pblc Reltns; Crprt/Entrtnmnt PR.

**SUNG, CHIH-HSIUNG,** Georgetown Univ, Washington, DC; JR; BA; Accntng Math Ttr Foothill Clg Tutor 88-90; Chinese Stdnt Clb 89-90; Chnclrs Rcgntn Exclnc Prgrm UCSB 90-; Palo Alto Tennis Clb 88-90; Blck Vlntr Amrcn Hrt Assn 89-90; Blck Vlntr Amrcn Lng Assn 89-90; Accntng; Accntng Laws.

**SUNG, KAI LAM,** City Univ Of Ny La Guard Coll, Long Island Cty, NY; SO; BA; Computer Sci; Eng.

**SUNG, MARIA,** City Univ Of Ny Baruch Coll, New York, NY; JR; BBA; Acctg; Finance.

**SUNG, WAI-YAN,** City Univ Of Ny Baruch Coll, New York, NY; SR; BBA; Acctg Soc; Beta Gamma Sigma; Deans Lst 90; Acctg; CPA.

**SUPE, RONALD L,** Defiance Coll, Defiance, OH; JR; BS; Cmps Actvts Brd 89-; Crmnl Jstc Scty VP; Rsdnt Asst 90-; Sigma Phi Epsilon Pres; IM 88-; Crim Jstc/Pschlgy; Law Schl.

**SUPERCZYNSKI, CHRISTOPHER J,** Providence Coll, Providence, RI; SO; BS; Dns Lst; Alpha Delta Epsilon; Pre Med; Medicine.

**SUPKO, MICHAEL P,** Univ Of Sc At Columbia, Columbia, SC; FR; BA; Phi Eta Sigma; Engl; Clncl Psychlgy.

**SUPPLE, HEATHER R,** Castleton St Coll, Castleton, VT; JR; BA; Res Asst RA 89-; Stdnt Educ Assn Sec 89-; Deans Lst 90; Elem Ed; Tchng.

**SUPPLE, LEIGH A,** Marshall University, Huntington, WV; SR; Clg Repubs 88-89; Delta Zeta 88-; Cmctns Educ; Speech/Theatre/ Engl Tchr.

**SUPPLEE, JASON B,** Univ Of Cincinnati, Cincinnati, OH; JR; BM; Stdnt Artist Prog; HAM Radio Oper Clb; Cincinnati Cnsrvtry Of Music Hnrs Schlrshp; Music; Concert Artist.

**SURAGARN, USAR,** Fordham Univ, Bronx, NY; JR; BS; Acctg Stf 83-; Acctg.

**SURBER, DENISE,** Emory & Henry Coll, Emory, VA; JR; BS; Commtr Stdnt Org 88-; Pi Gamma Mu 90-; Intrnshp Bank Marion; Busn Mgmt/Soclgy.**

**SURBER, JOAN L,** Greenville Tech Coll, Greenville, SC; SO; ASSOC; Law.**

**SURBER, NATALIE K,** Bethel Coll, Mckenzie, TN; SO; BA; Stdnt Govt Assoc Sec Stdnt Affrs 90-; Psych Clb; Crestian Issues Org; Lambda Sigma VP 90-; Intrn Lakeside Hosp; Psych.

**SURBER, STEVEN J,** Middle Tn St Univ, Murfreesboro, TN; JR; BS; Computer Sci; Scientific Comp Field.

**SURBER, TONYA L,** Va Highlands Comm Coll, Abingdon, VA; GD; BS; Phi Theta Kappa; AAS; Bus Ed; Tchr/Ofc Mgr.

**SURI, HITESH,** S U N Y At Buffalo, Buffalo, NY; SR; Engr.

**SURIANO, JOSEPH P,** Kent St Univ Kent Cmps, Kent, OH; FR; BA; Theta Chi Secty; Pre Busn; Finance.

**SURIS-FERNANDEZ, RAMON,** Inter Amer Univ Pr San Juan, Hato Rey, PR; GD; LLM; BA Summa Cum Laude; Jrs Dctr Cum Laude; Mdl Mst Dstngshd Stndt Econ; JD 90; BA 86; Lrb Law.

**SURLES, BELINDA R,** Columbus Coll, Columbus, GA; JR; BA; Mdl Untd Ntns Chrmn 88; US Achvmnt Acad; Dns Lst 88-; Intrn Colmbs Msm Rsrchng Fr Exhbt 89; Intrn Orgnzng Actvts Vstng Artst 90; Art; Prdcr Fne Art Gllrs And Msms.

**SURLIS, CATHERINE M,** Coll Of Notre Dame Of Md, Baltimore, MD; FR; BA; Rstrctng Cmtee Stdnt Govt 90-; Emrgng Ldr Prog 90-; Campus Mnstry 90-; Cmuty Serv Orgztn Pres 90-; Stdnt Tm Admsn Rep 90-; Raquetball I M 90-; Lbr Arts.

**SURMAN, STEPHEN M,** Schenectady County Comm Coll, Schenectady, NY; FR; AS; Niskayunna Vol Fire Dept; Math/Sci; Med Physcn.

**SUROWIEZ JR, CHARLES M,** S U N Y At Buffalo, Buffalo, NY; SR; BA; Skydvrs Rchstr; Mbr PADI; Eta Kapap Nu VP 90-; Tau Beta Pi; IEEE; Mntr Ern Lrn Prsm Prgms; Smmr Intern Xerox Corp; Intern Calspan Corp; US Army ROTC Schlrshp; IM Ftbll; IM Sftbll; Elec Eng; Ptnt Law.

**SURPRENANT, DARCY L,** Clinton Comm Coll, Plattsburgh, NY; FR; AS; Phi Theta Kappa 90; Bus Admn; Htl/Rstrnt Mgmt.

**SURRENA, RENEA D,** Allegheny Coll, Meadville, PA; JR; BA; Alden Schlr 88-; Wilbur-Mayne Econ Schlrshp 90-; Vrsty Vlybl Co Cpt 88-; Econ; Corp Bnkng.

**SURTI, SULEMAN,** Oh Wesleyan Univ, Delaware, OH; FR; BA/BS; Univ Film Series VP; Assn Squash Plyrs Jnt Sec; Academic Cndct Rvw Bd Radio; Phi Eta Sigma; Florence Leas Prize; Math Physics; Eng.

**SURUN, MARIA D,** Hillsborough Comm Coll, Tampa, FL; FR; BA; SGA Sntr; Wrk VP Stdnt Serv Stdnt Asst; Bus Admin.

**SUSCA, TONILLA,** Saint Johns Univ, Jamaica, NY; JR; BS; Italian Clb 89; Golden Key 90; Kappa Delta Pi 90; Deans Lst 88; Math; Tchng.

**SUSKI, BOBBI J,** Middle Tn St Univ, Murfreesboro, TN; SR; BS; Outstndng Glgy Stdnt Murfreesboro Gem Mnrl Soc 90-; Glgy; Envrmntl Glgy.

**SUSKIE, MATTHEW R,** Hudson Valley Comm Coll, Troy, NY; FR; AOS; ECM Clb 90-; Elctrcl Sci.

**SUSKO, DAVID A,** Indiana Univ Of Pa, Indiana, PA; SR; Elem Educ.

**SUSLOW, ALEXANDRA F,** Immaculata Coll, Immaculata, PA; SR; BA; Cue/Crtn Plyrs Theater Stge Crew/Actng Treas 87-; Chem Clb 90-; Alpha Psi Omega 88; Immaculata 89; Delta Epsilon Sigma Kappa Gamma Pi; Sigma Zeta 89; Deans Lst 88; Bio/Chem Pre-Med; Med.

**SUSMAN, LAUREL ANN,** Univ Of Miami, Coral Gables, FL; SR; BA; TABS Advsr; Sigma Tau Delta; Sigma Delta Tau 87-; Crispin/Porter Advrtsng Agcy Intrnshp 88; Beber/Silverstein Advertsng Agcy Intrn 90; Eng; Advrtsng.

**SUSSER, THEODORE,** Fl International Univ, Miami, FL; SR; BS; Restaurant Mgr 86-; BA State Univ NY Albany 80; Hosptlty Mgmt; Corp Mgmt.

**SUSSMAN, KAREN S,** Manhattanville Coll, Purchase, NY; JR; BA; Stdnt Govt Pres 88-; Stdnt Govt Strg Comm 90; Orientn Brd Stdnt Advsr 89-; Sesqcntnnl Comm 90-; Rvw Brd Bdgt Comm Chrprsn 90-; Alchl Tsk Frc; Stdnt Acts Comm; Refrbshd Plygrnd Fr Undrprvlgd Chldrn; Ldrshp Schlr 88-; Poli Sci; Grad Schl.**

**SUSTAR, TAMARA R,** Univ Of Sc At Columbia, Columbia, SC; JR; BA; Baptst Stdnt Un 90-; Appt Babtst Stdnt Summer Missnry 90; Early Chldhd Educ; Tchr Elem.

**SUTAK, DAVID J,** West Liberty St Coll, West Liberty, WV; SO; BS; Kappa Delta Rho IM Chrmn 89-; Crmnl Jstce.

**SUTER, LAWRENCE C,** United States Naval Academy, Annapolis, MD; SR; MS; Airborne Trng Unit Prchtng Tm 89-; Mids/Kids Tutrl Pro Tchr 90-; Exec Ofcr 18th Co USN Acdmy 90-; AIAA 87-; Dstnctn; Mac Short Awrd; Capt Michael J Smith Awrd; Slg Tm 87-88; Astrospc Engr; Navy Pilot.

**SUTER, LORI L,** Oh Univ-Southern Cmps, Ironton, OH; JR; Elem Educ Social Studies; Instructor.

**SUTHERLAND, ALVIN C,** Owensboro Comm Coll, Owensboro, KY; FR; AD; Nrsng.

**SUTHERLAND, ANNA MAE,** Hudson Valley Comm Coll, Troy, NY; SO; AS; Deans List 89; Pres List 90; Watervliet Pop Warner 85-; St Brigid CYO 90-; Bus Admn; Acctng.

**SUTHERLAND, ANNE K,** Univ Of Rochester, Rochester, NY; SO; BS; Soc Phys Stdnts 90-; Tnns Tm 89-90; Phycs; Res/Dev Indstry.

**SUTHERLAND, DAVID C,** Birmingham Southern Coll, Birmingham, AL; JR; BA; Nwspr Ed 88-90; Judiciary Chmn 89-; Beta Beta Beta; Omicron Delta Kappa; Phi Sigma Iota; Phi Eta Sigma; Alpha Lambda Delta; Mortar Bd; Alpha Epsilon Delta; Sigma Nu VP 88-; Circl K Pres 90-; Amnesty Intl 89-; Carnegie Mellon; Rsrch Pgm; Bio/French; MD/PH D.

**SUTHERLAND, JOSEPH T,** Merrimack Coll, North Andover, MA; JR; BS; Elec Engr.

**SUTHERLAND, RACHEL E,** Radford Univ, Radford, VA; FR; BA; Intervar Chrstn Fllwshp Song Ldr; Madrgl Singrs; Psych.

**SUTHERLAND, ROBERT M,** Hudson Valley Comm Coll, Troy, NY; FR; Refrig/Htng/Air Cond Club 90-; Pre List; Refrig/ Air Cond/Htng.

**SUTHERLAND, SANDRA J,** Eckerd Coll, St Petersburg, FL; SO; BS; Choir 89-; Radio DJ 90-; Deans Lst 89-; Earth Soc 90-; Ford Pgm; Marine Sci; Rsrch.

**SUTHERLIN, WILLIAM E,** George Mason Univ, Fairfax, VA; SR; BS; Acctng.

**SUTIOSO, HENRI,** Carnegie Mellon Univ, Pittsburgh, PA; FR; BS; Indsn Stdnt Assoc 90-; Indstrl Mgmt.

**SUTLIFF, LECINDA L,** Kent St Univ Kent Cmps, Kent, OH; SR; BA; Midwstrn Crmnl Jstc Assn 90-; Gldn Key 90-; Lambda Alpha Epsilon 90-; Northeast Pre Release Cntr Intrnshp 90; Amer Corr Assn Cert 90; Crmnl Jstc/Corr; Prob/Parole Offcr.

**SUTLOVICH, MICHAEL A,** Bloomfield Coll, Bloomfield, NJ; FR; Bsbl Tm.

**SUTPHIN BUCK, DIANA R,** Volunteer St Comm Coll, Gallatin, TN; FR; GBA; Dns Lst; Madison Chrch Chrst; Parnt Tchr Assn; Cmptr Oper Mgr; Inf Syst Tech; Cmptr Sci.

**SUTPHIN, VIKI L,** Radford Univ, Radford, VA; FR; BS; Cmps Crsd For Chrst 90-; Real Life Mnstrs 90-; Alpha Lambda Delta 90-; Chmstry; Tchr.

**SUTTER, CHRISTINA M,** Case Western Reserve Univ, Cleveland, OH; SO; BA; Stdnt Assn; Sccr; Englsh Pltcl Sci; Tchng.**

**SUTTER, EDEN L,** Allegheny Coll, Meadville, PA; SO; Hbt Hmnty VP 90-; Kappa Kappa Gamma; Alden Schlr 89-; BA; Pol Sci/Clsscl Lang; Law.

**SUTTER, TIMOTHY P G,** Howard Univ, Washington, DC; GD; PHD; Chem Grad Stdnts Assn 88-; Gldn Key 86-; Grad Teach Asstntshp 88-; Sftbl 85-; BS 87; Chem; Acad.

**SUTTERLEY, REBECCA M,** Columbus Coll Of Art & Design, Columbus, OH; FR; BFA; Bsbl; Illstrtn Anmtn; Illstrtr Anmtr Dsny Stds.

**SUTTLE, LISA C,** Univ Of Montevallo, Montevallo, AL; JR; BME; Stdnt Govt Assn Sntr 90; Cncrt Chr; Phi Alpha Mu 90-; Pi Kappa Alpha Lil Sis 90; Phi Mu Rsh Chrmn 88-; Mntvllo Mstrs; Hnr Chr 89; Dns Lst 90-; Msc; Educ.

**SUTTLES, STEVEN D,** Univ Of Nc At Asheville, Asheville, NC; SR; BA; Sclgy Clb Pblctns Sec 89-90; ISAS Intrm Pres; Alpha Kappa Delta 90-; Sclgy/Psych; Prvt Prctc Cnslng.

**SUTTON, AMY L,** S U N Y Coll Of Tech At Delhi, Delhi, NY; SR; NY St Assn Vet Tech 90-; Phi Theta Kappa 90-; Humane Soc 90-; Mnfctrng Prcss Oper; Prsnnl Asst 87; Vet Etch 90; Lab Anml Tech; AAS Dutchess Comm Col 87; AAS; Vet Sci; Lab Anml Tech.

**SUTTON, CHARLES P,** Mount Olive Coll, Mount Olive, NC; JR; BS; AS Lenoir Comm Coll 90; Bus.

**SUTTON, CLAIRE E,** Elmira Coll, Elmira, NY; SR; Astrnmcl Soc 87-; Erpn Cltr/Cvlztn.

**SUTTON, DANIELL S,** Univ Of Sc At Columbia, Columbia, SC; FR; BS; Flwshp Chrstn Athl; Cmps Crsd For Chrsf; Phi Eta Sigma; Pres Lst; Elec/Cmptr Engr.

**SUTTON, DAVID S,** Ms Gulf Coast Comm Coll, Perkinston, MS; JR; BA; Kappa Sigma; Bsbl; AS 90; Brdcst/Jrnlsm; TV Sports Brdcstr.

**SUTTON, HEATHER A,** Univ Of Sc At Columbia, Columbia, SC; JR; BM; Symph Bnd 88-; Wnd Ensmbl 89-; Mrchng Bnd 88-; Golden Key 90-; Pi Kappa Lambda; MENC 89-; Music Schlrshp 88-; Music Ed; Tchng.

**SUTTON, JENNIFER K,** Gallaudet Univ, Washington, DC; FR; BA; Blue Nwspr 90-; Hon Stdnt Org Nwsltr Edtr 90-; SAB 90-; Pres Schlr 90-; Deans Lst 90; Frnch; Educ.

**SUTTON, LISA A,** Memphis St Univ, Memphis, TN; SR; BS; Schering Plough Grassrts Netwrk 89-; Vlybl/Sftbl; Lab Tech 88-; Bio; Micro-Med Tech.

**SUTTON, LONNA J,** Roane St Comm Coll, Harriman, TN; SO; Employed Fulltime/Go To Schl/Sngl Prnt Of 14 Yr Old Grl; Crmnl Jstc; Wrk W/Abuse Wmn.

**SUTTON, MARIETTA R,** S U N Y Coll Of Tech At Alfred, Alfred, NY; FR; Amer Orchd Assc; Flrcltr Mrchndsng/Prdctn; Whlsl Orchd Grwr.

**SUTTON, MICHAEL E,** Univ Of Tn At Chattanooga, Chattanooga, TN; JR; BSE; Amer Soc Cvl Engrs 87-; Alpha Lamba Delta 82; Phi Eta Sigma 82; Golden Key 87; BS 85; Engrg; Cvl Engr.

**SUTTON, SUSAN D,** Univ Of Fl, Gainesville, FL; JR; BFA; Florida Players 88; Isshinryu Karate Club; Golden Key 90; Alpha Psi Omega 89; Ann Der Flinger Mem Schlrshp Award 88-89; Undergraduate Schlrshp Award 88; Thtr Dept 90; Thtr; Educ/Dir.

**SUTTON, TERRI A,** Owensboro Jr Coll Of Bus, Owensboro, KY; FR; AS; Cmptr Ofc Prfsnl; Ofc Wrk.

**SUTTON, TRACI R,** Mount Aloysius Jr Coll, Cresson, PA; FR; ASSO; Inter Collgte Bsktbl/Vlybl Co-Capt; Deans List; Lgl Asst; Law.

**SUTTON, TYRESIA D,** Rutgers St Univ At Newark, Newark, NJ; FR; BS; Math; Elctrcl Engr.

**SUTTON, WAYNE M,** Capital Bible Seminary, Lanham, MD; SR; MDIV; Intrnshp-Carrubbers Chrstn Ctr Edinburgh Scotland 90; Eng; B Eng Stevens Inst Tech 83; Bible; Mssnry/Pstr Scotland.

**SUTTON-KARGER, SHARON P,** Duquesne Univ, Pittsburgh, PA; GD; MA; Lambda Fndtn Brd 84-; Cmmnty Advsry Brd 85-; Sigma Chi 87; Gay Lsbn Cmmnty Cntr 89-; Cum Laude Univ Pgh; Wmn Stu Cert Univ Pgh 87; BS Univ Pgh 87; Psych; Thrpst/ Cmmnty Mntl Hlth.

**SUTYAK, KATHERINE A,** Beckley Coll, Beckley, WV; SO; AS; Law.

**SUTYAK, SARA K,** Beckley Coll, Beckley, WV; SO; BED; Cub Scts Am Den Ldr 88-; Math/Lit; Tchng.

**SUVOSKI, JENNIFER L,** Marywood Coll, Scranton, PA; FR; BS; Tchrs Tomorrow 90-; Clgt Vltrs 90-; Prestl Schlrshp 90-; Elem Ed; Tchng.

**SUWALSKI, SANDRA L,** Comm Coll Algny Co Algny Cmps, Pittsburgh, PA; SO; RN.

**SUYES, KATHRYN R,** Richard Bland Coll, Petersburg, VA; FR; ASN; VA Nrsng Stdnts Assn Prsdnt; Yrbk Stf 90-; Nrsng.

**SUZARA, MYLENE M,** Univ Of Sc At Columbia, Columbia, SC; SO; BMUED; Mrchng/Concrt Band 89-; Delta Omicron 90-; Tau Beta Sigma 88-; Music Ed; Band Dir.

**SUZUKI, BENJAMIN K,** Syracuse Univ, Syracuse, NY; JR; Karate Clb Blck Blt 88-; Archtctr Stdnt Org 88-; Campus Crusd For Chrst 88-; Deans Lst 90; Habitat For Humnty 88-89; Archtctr.

**SUZUKI, KAZUFUMI,** Fl Atlantic Univ, Boca Raton, FL; SR; BBA; AA Broward Comm Coll 89; Bus Admin; Finance.**

**SUZUKI, REI,** Western New England Coll, Springfield, MA; SR; BSBA; Intl Stdnt Assoc 88-90; Mngmnt Assoc 89; Delta Mu Delta 90; Outstndng Stdnt; AA Nanzan Jr Clg Japan 87; Human Resources Mngmnt.

**SUZUKI, YASUYO,** Univ Of Miami, Coral Gables, FL; SR; BS; Alpha Lambda Delta 88; Psi Chi 89-; Dr Hurwirtz Lab Bhvrl Assmnt; Chem; Physlgcl Psy.

**SUZUKI, YOSHINORI,** Valdosta St Coll, Valdosta, GA; SO; BA; Soc Intl Stdnts 89-; Sigma Alpha Chi 90-; Otsdng Cntrbtn Intrcltrl Undrstdng 90-; Pltcl Sci; United Nations.

**SVENDSEN, KRISTEN M,** Providence Coll, Providence, RI; JR; BS; Lgue Vlybl; Gen Chem Lab Asst; Biolgy; Vet.

**SVENSEN, ERIK C,** Widener Univ, Chester, PA; SO; BS; Phi Delta Theta; Cvl Eng.

**SVERDLOV, ANYA,** Yale Univ, New Haven, CT; SR; BA; Mdl Untd Ntns Sec Gen 87-; Intrntl Rltns Assn Pres 87-; Stdnt Strggle Fr Svt Jwry 89; Qstns Of Jdsm Asst Coor 89; USSR Wntr Brk Sympsm Dir 89; Pol Union 89; Jwsh Appl; Sp Ktchn 88-; Govs Com Schlrshp 87-; Clb Of NJ Schlr Of The Yr 90-; BA; Econs And Pol Sci; Econs.**

**SVETZ, CAROLYN A,** Oh Wesleyan Univ, Delaware, OH; SO; BA; Circle K Serv Org VP 90-91; Wesleyan Stdnt Fndtn; Phi Eta Sigma 90-; Phi Soc; Pi Beta Phi Membrshp Chmn; Hist; Scndry Teach/Hist/Soc Studies.

**SVITAK, ANN E,** City Univ Of Ny Baruch Coll, New York, NY; SR; BBA; Soc Hmn Rsrcs Mgt 90-; Frshmn Orntn Ldr 90-; Golden Key 90-; Alpha Beta Gamma 88-89; Deans List Baruch/ Queensborough Comm Coll 88-; Deptmnl Awd Acdmc Exclnc Bus Admin; AS Queensborough Comm Clg 89; Mgt; Hmn Rsrcs Mgt.

**SVOBODA, TAMMY S,** Univ Of Cincinnati, Cincinnati, OH; JR; BA; Kappa Delta Pi; Golden Key; Bktbl Stanford Univ 87-89; Tns 90; Bsktbl Tm Stanford Univ/Univ Cincinati 87-; Hlth Ed/ Exrcs Physlgy; Physcl Thrpst.

**SVOR, SHANNON G,** Saint Josephs Coll, Windham, ME; FR; BA; IM Flr Hcky 90-; Hstry; Tch.

**SVOREN, DEREK A,** Allegheny Coll, Meadville, PA; SO; BS; Rugby Clb Pub Chrprsn 89-; Phi Kappa Psi Corr Sec; Lambda Sigma Pub Chr 90-; Comp Exam Schlrshp 89-; Whllr Mc Clntck Schlrshp 90-; Alden Schlr 90-; Econ; Busn.

**SWABE, JAMES L,** Hiwassee Coll, Madisonville, TN; SO; AA; Cmtr Clb 89-90; Coll Bowl Tm 89-90; Bapt Stdnt Un 89; Phi Theta Kappa Rptr 89-; Fr Hghst Grades Awd 89-90; Co-Valedictorian 90-; Outstndg Bus Awd 90-; Bus Admin; Acctg.

**SWABY, HELEN E,** Broward Comm Coll, Ft Lauderdale, FL; SO; PHARM; Afrcn Amer Stdnt Union 88-89; Intl Clb 88-89; Phi Theta Kappa Rcrdng Sec 89-; Hnrs Inst 88-; Hnrs Cncl 90-; AA; Phrmcy; Cnsltnt.

**SWAFFAR, CYNTHIA A,** Meridian Comm Coll, Meridian, MS; FR; MBA; Phi Theta Kappa Recrdng Secy; 4-H Advsr Lauderdale Cnty Ext Ofc 88-; Psychology; Cnslng.

**SWAFFORD, JEFFREY D,** Middle Tn St Univ, Murfreesboro, TN; JR; BS; Gamma Beta Phi Soc 89; Active In Clg Theatrical Prods; Broadcast Mngmnt; Producer.

**SWAGGER, LASHARA R,** Miami Dade Comm Coll North, Miami, FL; SO; AA; Phi Theta Kappa Hstrn 90-; Phi Beta Lambda 90-; Bus Admn; Cntrllr Acctnt.

**SWAIN, AYANNA N,** Clark Atlanta Univ, Atlanta, GA; SO; BA; NAACP 90-; Mrchg Bnd 90; Phi Beta Lambda VP 90-; Delta Sigma Theta Sor Inc; Intrnshp Pres Lines Ltd 89-; Mktg; Sls Rep.

**SWAIN, JENNIFER L,** Ms St Univ, Miss State, MS; SO; BA; Angel Flght Trnr 89-90; Hl Cncl Sec/Treas 90-; Std Cncrnd Prtctng Env 89-90; Pol Sci.

**SWAIN, MALINDA J,** Blue Mountain Coll, Blue Mountain, MS; SR; BED; Tchr Asst Prog BMC 84-; PTO Itwmba Co Schls 84-; Hnr Rll; Fltn Grmmr Schl PTO; Asst Tchr; Elem Educ; Cert In Spcl Educ.

**SWAIN, MARK C,** Radford Univ, Radford, VA; FR; MBA; Phi Sigma Pi 90-; Hnrs Prog 90-; Bus Acctg; CPA.

**SWAIN, RONTRILL D,** Fl A & M Univ, Tallahassee, FL; SO; BA; Math; Math Sci.

**SWAIN, SCOTT B,** Univ Of North Fl, Jacksonville, FL; FR; BA; SGA Senator; Political Sci; Law.

**SWAIN, THERESA P,** Newbury Coll, Brookline, MA; BA; Phi Theta Kappa Frat; Amer Lgn Aux Dist Dir 74; Eight/Frty Chapeau 74; Assoc Notre Dame Pres 85; Natl Cntrct Mgmt Assn; Exec Fml Assn; Corp Dir Cntrcts 86-; Master Cert George Washington Univ 89; Bus Mgmt; Govt/Cmmrcl Cntrcts.

**SWAINBANK, PAIGE M,** Mount Saint Mary Coll, Newburgh, NY; JR; BS; Hons Alliance 90-; Bus Assoc 90-F Alpha Chi; Soup Kitchen 89-; Bus Admn; Exec.

**SWAINSON, JOEY C,** Univ Of Tn At Knoxville, Knoxville, TN; SR; BS; Gldn Key 90-; Beta Gamma Sigma; Roddy Fndtn Acdmc Schlrshp 90-; Cdr Vly Bptst Chrch; Lfstcs/Trnsprttn; Shpng Mngr.

**SWALLOW, MICHELLE M,** Rivier Coll, Nashua, NH; FR; BS; Bsktbl 90-; Bio; Med.

**SWAMI, SANJAY MULESH,** Univ Of Sc At Columbia, Columbia, SC; SO; Amer Chem Soc; Gamma Beta Phi 89-; Phi Eta Sigma 89-; Gldn Ky 90-; Alpha Epsilon Delta 90-; Vol Dy Cr Ctr 90-; Biol; Med.

**SWAN, DENNIS DWAIN,** Methodist Coll, Fayetteville, NC; SO; BS; Beta Beta Beta 90-; Carpenter 80-90; Biology; Environment.

**SWANEY, DOREEN K,** Univ Of Akron, Akron, OH; JR; BA; Phi Eta Sigma 88-; Alpha Lambda Delta 88-; Gldn Ky 90-; Beta Gamma Sigma; Delta Sigma Pi; Dns Lst 88-; Fin; Bus/Bnkng.

**SWANGER, JEFFREY A,** Fayetteville St Univ, Fayetteville, NC; JR; BSW; Intl Sociology Hnr Scty 90; Chancellors Lst 90-; All American Track Field 79-80; Non Commissioned Ofcr USA 83-; ABA Campbell Univ 89; Social Work.

**SWANGO, BARBARA A,** Univ Of Ky, Lexington, KY; SR; NSSHLA; Golden Key; Cmnctn Dsordrs Spch Path.

**SWANIER, AARON L,** Air Force Inst Of Tech, Wrt-Ptrsn Afb, OH; GD; MS; Sigma Iota Epsilon; Prfsnl Dsgntn Cost Analysis 90; OH High Schl Bsktbl Offcl 88-; ASA Sftbl Umpire 86-; BS Jackson State Univ 82; Cost Analysis; Air Force Career.

**SWANK, DAVID R,** Univ Of Rochester, Rochester, NY; JR; BS; Ultmt Frsbee Clb Pres 89-; Bio Scty 89-; Envrmntl Grp 90-; Dekewiet Flwshp; Deans Lst 88-; IM Sccr/Vlybl 88-; Bio; Rsrch Ecology.

**SWANK, FREDERICK A,** Columbus St Comm Coll, Columbus, OH; JR; ASSOC; Bsnss Mngmnt.**

**SWANKLER, JENNIFER L,** Westmoreland County Comm Coll, Youngwood, PA; SO; BED; Hm Econ; Educ.**

**SWANN, ALICE M,** Converse Coll, Spartanburg, SC; FR; BS; Comp Sci/Math/Psych.

**SWANN, ALLISON J,** Fl St Univ, Tallahassee, FL; JR; BS; Seminole Ambassador 90-; Lady Scalp 89-; WVFS/NEWS Reporter 89-; Order Omega Sec; Gold Key; Pi Beta Phi Pres 90-; Gamma 90-; Intrnshp Cobb Co Superior Ct 89; Intrnshp WAGA Atlanta; Ftbl/Bsbl/Bsktbl 89-; Cmmunctns/Brdcst Jrnlsm; TV News Reporter.

**SWANN, PATRICIA JEAN,** Univ Of Nc At Charlotte, Charlotte, NC; SR; BAC; NAEA Pres Pres 90-; Gldn Key 89-; Phi Theta Kappa 85; CPCC Advrtsng Clb 83-85; AAS Cntrl Piedmont Comm Coll 85; BAC Univ NC 90; Chnclrs Lst 90-; Deans Lst 87-; US Scty Ed Art 90; Real Est Sls 75-80; Sub Tchr 86-88; Intl Scty Ed Art 88-; Art Ed; Tchr.

**SWANN, TONYA L,** Bowie St Univ, Bowie, MD; SO; BA; Nwsppr Orgnztn Cmps Edit 90-; Wmns Frm Fndrsng Com; Dns Lst; Otstndng Acad Excllnce In Jrnslm 90-; Cmmnctns; Jrnlsm.

**SWANSON, CAROLYN L,** Roane St Comm Coll, Harriman, TN; JR; BA; Gamma Beta Phi; Elem Educ; Tchr.

**SWANSON, JILL A,** S U N Y At Buffalo, Buffalo, NY; GD; MARC; Pella Schlrshp Awd 90; Int Designer 83-; BFA Univ Of Mich; Architecture.

**SWANSON, JODY D,** Univ Of Sc At Aiken, Aiken, SC; JR; BA; Educ Mjrs Clb 90-; Shoneys Restrnt; Erly Chldhd Educ; Tchng.

**SWANSON, JULIE A,** Oh Wesleyan Univ, Delaware, OH; FR; BA; Sftbl 90-; Cntrl OH Symphny Orchstra 90-; Phi Eta Sigma 90-; Mcrblgy; Brmdtn.

**SWANSON, LISA R,** Teikyo Post Univ, Waterbury, CT; SO; Acctng; CPA.

**SWANSON, NICHELLE M,** Univ Of Sc At Columbia, Columbia, SC; FR; Stdnt Govt 90-; Flwshp Chrstn Athlts 90-; Assn Hon Stdnts Hon Cncl 90-; Alpha Lambda Delta 90-; Phi Eta Sigma 90-; Gamma Beta Phi 90-; IM Sftbl; Poltcl Sci; Law/Poltcs.

**SWANSON, SANDRA J,** Univ Of Southern Ms, Hattiesburg, MS; SR; BSBA; Phi Kappa Phi 89-; Beta Alpha Psi 90-; Angl Flght 89-90; Res Asst 89-90; Acctng.

**SWANSON, SHANE E,** Univ Of Sc At Columbia, Columbia, SC; JR; BA; World Tae Kwon Do Club Fndr/Pres 88-; Phi Beta Kappa; World Tae Kwon Do Club Trnmnt Orgnzr 90; Wrting/ Classics; Latin Teacher.

**SWANSON, SHANNON C,** Univ Of Pittsburgh, Pittsburgh, PA; FR; BS; Lacrosse 90-; Touch Ftbl 90-; Phi Eta Sigma 90-; Lambda Sigma 90-; Engrs Wk 5 K Run; Engr.

**SWANSON, STACIE A,** Duquesne Univ, Pittsburgh, PA; JR; CEC Pres 90; Spec Ed Elem Ed; Tchr.

**SWANSON, TODD E,** Univ Of Nc At Asheville, Asheville, NC; JR; BS; Natl Acct Scty 89; Phi Eta Sigma 89; Big Bros Big Sis; Brkfst Try Schlrshp; Chncllrs Dns Lst 88-; Acctng; CPA.

**SWANSON, WARREN J,** Cornell Univ, Ithaca, NY; FR; BS; Res Hl Govt 90-; IM Comm 90-; Trad Svc/Faculty Rels Comm 90-; Dns Lst 90-; Red Carpet Hstg Soc 90-; Trad Schlrshp; IM Bsktbl/Vlybl 90-; Cvl/Envir Engr.

**SWANTON, JILL M,** Univ Of Cincinnati-Clrmnt Coll, Batavia, OH; SO; BBA; Retail Mgr; Acctng; CPA.

**SWAPP, JUDITH A,** Fl International Univ, Miami, FL; JR; BHSA; Greater Miami Scty Radiologic Technlgst; ARRT; AA Miami Dade Comm Clg 90; Radiographer ; Cat Scan; Technlgst Nclr Medcn Tchnlsts; HDCR TDCR DNM Clg Radgrphrs London Englnd 81; Hlth Svc Admn; Mgmt/Tchng.

**SWARTHOUT-HOWELLS, DIANE LYNN,** Hillsborough Comm Coll, Tampa, FL; FR; BA; Lib Arts; MA Soc.

**SWARTWOUT, EDWIN S,** S U N Y Coll Of Tech At Delhi, Delhi, NY; SO; BSED; Phys Educ Athltc Trng.

**SWARTWOUT, KAREN M,** Bapt Bible Coll & Seminary, Clarks Summit, PA; JR; BS; Bible Rlgn.

**SWARTZ, CYNTHIA S,** Atlantic Comm Coll, Mays Landing, NJ; SO; BA; Ed; Tchng Elem Ed.

**SWARTZ, DOUGLAS L,** Univ Of Pittsburgh, Pittsburgh, PA; SR; BA; Mech Engr.

**SWARTZ, IAN W,** Fl Atlantic Univ, Boca Raton, FL; SO; BS; Int Frat Cncl Dlgt 90-; Alpha Tau Omega Brthr 89-; IM Flr Hcky 90-; Acctng; CPA Law.

**SWARTZ, JOSEPH J,** S U N Y Coll Of Tech At Alfred, Alfred, NY; FR; BA; Sigma Tau Epsilon 90-; Wrstlng 90-; Drftng.

**SWARTZ, KAREN E,** Univ Of Cin R Walters Coll, Blue Ash, OH; SO; AAB; Prfsnl Sec Internatl 90-; Cmptr Lab Asst 90-; Dns Lst; Hnrs Stdnt; Asmbly God Chrch Wrshp Tm Ldr; Raymond Walters Col Hnr Stu Of Yr & Rep As A Marshall At Univ Of Cin 91; Raymond Walters Col Awd For Acad Excel; Med Ofc Admin; Ofc Admin.

**SWARTZ, NICOLE D,** Marywood Coll, Scranton, PA; SO; BFA; Art/Dsgn/Illstrtn.

**SWARTZWELDER, CHERYL LYNN,** Oh Univ-Southern Cmps, Ironton, OH; SO; BS; Nrsng Schl Stdnt Govt Treas 82-83; Girls Athltc Assn 80; Deans List; Hon Grad Sheppard Schl Hlth Sci 87; Alpha Lambda Delta 90; Vol Red Cross 83; Com Mbr Royal Air Force/USAF Air Show 87; USAF Sustained Superior Prfrmnc Awd 88; Allied Hlth Admnstrtr; Rgstrd Rcrds Admnstrv.

**SWASING, LORIE L,** Mount Aloysius Jr Coll, Cresson, PA; SO; ASSOC; OT Clb; Spcl Olympcs Vlntr Chrprsn; EEP Tutoring Prgrm; Phi Theta Kappa; Assoc Dubois Bsns Clg 89; Crtfd Occptnl Thrpy Asstnt; Occptnl Thrpy.

**SWATSON, ALICIA J,** Western New England Coll, Springfield, MA; SR; BA; Financial Mgt Assoc 90-; Peer Tutor 90; Finance.

**SWAYNGIM, ROBERT J,** Bowling Green St Univ At Huron, Huron, OH; JR; BA; Vrml Police Explrs 88-; Crmnl Jstc; Police Offcr.

**SWEARS, KATERI T,** Glassboro St Coll, Glassboro, NJ; SR; BA; Amer Assc Geogrphrs; Geo Clb; Troy St Univ Dothan Pres Lst 88-89; Marius Livingston Mem Acdmc Achvmnt Awd; Tomar Lgl Sec 90-; Geogrphy; Coll Prof.

**SWEAT, CAROLE K,** Lenoir Rhyne Coll, Hickory, NC; JR; BA; Phi Theta Kappa 90; Rufus Gwyn Meml Schlrshp CCC/TI 90; Vol Rdng Prog Valmead Elem Sch 90-; Acctg; CPA.

**SWEAT, PAMELA M,** City Univ Of Ny Baruch Coll, New York, NY; SO; MBA; CPR Rsrcr Red Crs 88-; Pblc Acctg.

**SWEAT, STEVEN M,** Fl St Univ, Tallahassee, FL; JR; Intrntl Affrs Soc; Pre-Law Sco; Phi Theta Kappa 90; Pi Gamma Mu VP; Fla Pbl Intrst Grp 90; Deans Lst 89-90; AA Polk Cmmnty Clg 90; Intrntl Affrs.

**SWEATMAN, TIMOTHY A,** Western Ky Univ, Bowling Green, KY; BS; Bptst Stdnt Union 90-; Prsdntl Schlr 90-; Finance; Bus.

**SWEELY, JOSEPH M,** Glassboro St Coll, Glassboro, NJ; SO; BA; Cmnctns; Radio/TV Prod.

**SWEEN, KAREN A,** Va Commonwealth Univ, Richmond, VA; JR; BSN; MCV Stdnt Nrs Assn 90-; Stdnt Nrs Assn; Ntl Stdt Nrs Assn 90-; Deans Lst 90-; Nrsng.

**SWEENEY, BRYAN J,** City Univ Of Ny Baruch Coll, New York, NY; SR; BBA; AIESEC-US 90; Gldn Key 90-; Beta Gamma Sigma Epsilon 90-; Coll Schlr Stipend; Mktg Mgmt; Advrtsng.

**SWEENEY, CHERYL A,** Univ Of Sc At Columbia, Columbia, SC; JR; BA; Symphny Orchstr 88-; Chmbr Orchstr 89-; Gamma Beta Phi 89-; Gldn Key 90-; Hon Clg; Deans List; Pres Hon Roll; Msc; Bus Admn Prsnl Mgmt.

**SWEENEY, CHERYL R,** Univ Of Toledo, Toledo, OH; GD; JD; Wmn Law Stdnt Assn Grad Stdnt 90-; Collgt Mktng Svcs Inc Sec Co Fndr 87-89; Spec Hnrs 87; Phillips Clscl Prz Comp Wnr 87; Univ Mich Hnrs Pgrm 85-87; Univ Mich Alumni Schlrshp 85-86; Lawn Alumni Recgntn Schlrshp 90-; Dns Lst 90; BA; Law/Engl.

**SWEENEY, DEBBIE-ANN,** Springfield Tech Comm Coll, Springfield, MA; SR; AS; PT Asst Clb VP 89-; Amer Physcl Thrpy Asc 90-; Alpha Mu Omega 90-; PT; Reg PT.

**SWEENEY, JAMES H,** City Univ Of Ny Queensbrough, New York, NY; GD; AA; Wheelchair Bsktbl Classics Org 80-; Homebound Stdnt Clb 86-; Alpha Beta Gamma 89-90; Dr Vera B Douthit Mem Awd; Bsn.

**SWEENEY, JAMES P,** Davis & Elkins Coll, Elkins, WV; FR; BS; Delta Clb; ACM; Statesmen VP; Trck Clb Treas; Hnrs Assn; Phi Beta Lambda; Dns Lst; Crs Cntry; Cmptr Sci; Cmptr Systs Analyst.

**SWEENEY, JAMES P,** Gordon Conwell Theol Sem, S Hamilton, MA; GD; MDIV; A J Gordon Schlr 89-90; Byngtn Schlr 90-; Lcnsd Mrnymn/Mstr Electrcn 78-; BA R Wesleyan Coll 89; Biblicl/Theolgcl Stdies; Tchng.

**SWEENEY, JEFFREY M,** Duquesne Univ, Pittsburgh, PA; JR; BS; Stdnt Acctg Assc 90-; Beta Alpha Phi Tres 90-; Dlt Sgm Pi VP Fnd Rsng 89; Cmptv Schlrshp 89-; Mc Donough Schlrshp 90-; Acctg/Bus Law; Tax Atty.

**SWEENEY, KATHLEEN,** Central Fl Comm Coll, Ocala, FL; SO; AS; Pre Nurs; RN.

**SWEENEY, MELISSA L,** Univ Of Sc At Columbia, Columbia, SC; JR; BA; Soc Prof Jrnlsts Pres 89-; PRSSA; Gamma Beta Phi 89; Phi Eta Sigma 89-; Golden Key; Kappa Delta Chap Hstrn 90; John C Kauthun Mem Schlrshp; Dns Lst 89-; Pres Lst 89; Carolina Classics 90; Jrnlsm/Hstry; Law/Pblc Rltns.

**SWEENEY, SCOTT H,** Fl International Univ, Miami, FL; SR; BA; Jr Amer Culinary Fed RI Pres 87-89; Hotel/Food/Trvl Assn 89-90; Phi Lambda Beta 90-; Summa Cum Laude 89; AS Johnson/Wales Univ 89; Hsptlty Mgmt; Rstrnt Mgmt.

**SWEENEY, SHARON A,** Newbury Coll, Brookline, MA; SO; AS; Food Serv Mgmt; Hosp Ind.

**SWEENEY, STEVEN C,** Univ Of Miami, Coral Gables, FL; FR; BS.

**SWEENEY, SUSAN H,** Savannah Coll Of Art & Design, Savannah, GA; GD; MFA; ISID Secty 90-; Deans List 90-; Lib Intern 90; Asst Desgr Intern; BS Skidmore Clg 87; Interior Design.

**SWEENY, GREGORY P,** Univ Of South Al, Mobile, AL; SO; Dstrct Crdntr Mayorial Cmpgn; VP Coop Sls Peppermill 90-; Sec Educ; H S Hstry Tchr/Coll Inst.

**SWEENY, MICHELLE S,** Wagner Coll, Staten Island, NY; SR; BS; Cmtr Clb 89-; Physcs Clb 90-; Metro Clgte Hcky Cnfrnc Tm Srvc Awd 90-; Ic Hcky Ststcn 87-; Physcs/Math; Arntcs/Arspc.

**SWEET, BARBARA A,** Ma Inst Of Tech, Cambridge, MA; JR; BS; Lectur Series Comm; Concert Bnd; Big Sisters; Tau Beta Pi; Scty Undrgard Material Sci; Matrl Sci/Engrg; Engrg.**

**SWEET, G ROBERT,** Hudson Valley Comm Coll, Troy, NY; SO; AAS; Mortuary Sci; Funeral Dir.

**SWEETAPPLE, AMY L,** Univ Of Ga, Athens, GA; SR; BED; Univ Chorus 87; Alpha Lambda Delta 87-; Gldn Key 89-; Kappa Delta Pi; Phi Kappa Phi; Hnrs Prog 90; Engl Educ; Scndry Tchr.**

**SWEETEN, RICHARD J,** Atlantic Comm Coll, Mays Landing, NJ; SO; BA; AS; Bsn Mgmt; Bsn.

**SWEETER, JOHN F,** Worcester Poly Inst, Worcester, MA; FR; BA; Glee Clb; Sci; Nuclear Eng.

**SWEETON, PATRICIA A,** Middle Tn St Univ, Murfreesboro, TN; JR; BSN; Tau Omicron; Amer Red Cross Vol; LPN; LPN TN Area Voc-Tech Sch 78; Nrsg.

**SWEITZER, ALMEDA B,** Garrett Comm Coll, Mchenry, MD; SO; AA; AWAY Sec 90; ILGWU Pres 73-89; Scl Bhvrl Sci.

**SWENSON, ANN M,** Fl St Univ, Tallahassee, FL; JR; BA; Caribbean Choir 89; Golden Key; Alpha Phi Omega 90-; Wellborn Mem Schlrshp 90; Intl Affairs/Spanish; Law.

**SWENSON, COREY M,** Univ Of Miami, Coral Gables, FL; FR; BS; Stdy Abrd Pgm U Of Wollngng Australia; Intl Finc/Mktg.

**SWENSON, SONJA E,** Univ Of North Fl, Jacksonville, FL; SR; BA; PRSSA VP 90-; Gldn Key 90-; Phi Kappa Phi; Engl Peer Tutor 87-89; Pblc Rltns Intshp; AA FL Comm Clg 89; Comm; Pblc Rltns.

**SWENTON, JEAN MARIE,** D Youville Coll, Buffalo, NY; SR; Ftr Tchr Cncl Pres 89-90; Dns Lst; Educ F/T Blind/Vsly Imprd; Vision Tchr.

**SWEPSON, CRYSTAL D,** Univ Of Nc At Greensboro, Greensboro, NC; SR; MM; Clgt Music Educ Natl Conf Treas 90 VP 89-90; Golden Chain 90-; Mu Phi Epsilon 89-; Teach Fellow Advsry Comm 87-; BM; Music; Educ.

**SWETZ, PHILIP J,** Saint Francis Coll, Loretto, PA; SR; BS; Std Actv Org Pres 90; Inv Clb Treas 90; Hnr Soc; Alpha Phi Delta; Std Act Intshp; IM 87-; Mgmt.

**SWEZEY, SCOTT W,** S U N Y Coll Of Envr Sci & For, Syracuse, NY; JR; BS; Sci; Mgmt.

**SWEZEY, WILLIAM A,** Widener Univ, Chester, PA; SR; BSEE; WANR DJ 87-88; IEEE 90-; Hon Cert Gen Educ; Elec Eng; Engrng.

**SWICEGOOD, ANGELA G,** Roane St Comm Coll, Harriman, TN; SO; BS; IM Vlybl; Acctg/Bus Law; CPA.

**SWIDERSI, KIMBERLY A,** Springfield Tech Comm Coll, Springfield, MA; SO; BA; Lbrl Arts; Psych.

**SWIDERSKI, BARBARA L,** S U N Y Coll At Oneonta, Oneonta, NY; JR; BS; Math Tutor Calculus 89-; Sko Clb 90-; Stu Tchg; Math Educ; Tchg.**

**SWIFT, MICHAEL R,** Memphis St Univ, Memphis, TN; SR; BS; RN; AAS Shlby St Comm Coll 84; AS 83; Phys Sci; Grad Schl.

**SWIFT, MICHELE L,** Bay Path Coll, Longmeadow, MA; FR; Aerobics Hlth Clb 90-; Dns Lst 90-; Law.

**SWIGER, LISA R,** Marshall University, Huntington, WV; SO; Gamma Beta Phi; Marshall Univ Hnr Soc; Elem Educ; Tchng.

**SWINDALL, REBECCA K,** Univ Of Va Clinch Valley Coll, Wise, VA; JR; Darden Scty; AA SE Comm Clg 90; Art; Teach Clg MFA.

**SWINDELL, KEVIN J,** Comm Coll Algny Co Algny Cmps, Pittsburgh, PA; SO; BS; Allegeny Gen Hosp Supv; Engr Tech; PE.

**SWINDLE, LA NELL M,** Blue Mountain Coll, Blue Mountain, MS; JR; BS; Phi Beta Lambda VP; SGA Rep; Chorale Tres 90-; All Amer Schlrs Assn; Evnmn Pres; Ed Yrbk; IM Bsktbll All Str 90-; Bus Admn; Sales Mrktng.

**SWINDLE, TARA D,** East Central Comm Coll, Decatur, MS; SO; BABED; Mrchg Cncrt Bnd 89-; Phi Theta Kappa 90-; Erly Chldhd Ed; Ed.

**SWINDLER, ANDREA Y,** Johnson C Smith Univ, Charlotte, NC; FR; BSWBS; Pan-African Cncl 90; NAACP 90; Schlstc Schlrshp; Scl Wrk Psyclgy.

**SWINEY, JONATHAN S,** Livingston Univ, Livingston, AL; JR; BA; Phys Ed/Bus; Ftnss Spas.

**SWING, GARY R,** Volunteer St Comm Coll, Gallatin, TN; GD; EMT; Firefighter 90-; BBA Harding Univ Searcy AR 88.

**SWING-LLENZA, MELISSA A,** Univ Of Nc At Greensboro, Greensboro, NC; SR; Intrnshp Stdnt Tchng 90-; Johnson St Elem Schl; BS Elem Educ; NC Class A Cert; Elem Tchr.

**SWINGLER JR, TIMOTHY D,** Wv Univ, Morgantown, WV; JR; BSEE; IEEE; Intrnshp PHH 89-; Eng.

**SWINSON, LILLIAN L,** Wright St Univ Lake Cmps, Celina, OH; JR; AS; Acctg.

**SWINSON, RELVA H,** James Sprunt Comm Coll, Kenansville, NC; SO; SGA Alt Sen 90-; James Sprunt Comm Choir Singer 88-89; Elem Sch Tchr.

**SWINT, LEESA C,** Eckerd Coll, St Petersburg, FL; JR; Ed Leisure Sect Triton Tribune Leisure Ed 89-90; Ed Chief Creations Indep Sec Same Paper 90; Am Studies; Law Prof Wmns Studies.

**SWITZER, CATHERINE P,** Union Univ, Jackson, TN; Yrbk Edtr 76-77; Intrsch Cncl Sec 76-77; Un Publ Comm; Nwspr Stf; Clg Brd Publ; Omicron Delta Kappa 75-77; Centnnl Hon Soc Pres 76-77; Crdnl Ky 76-77; Soc Clgt Jrnlsts Sec 75-77; Chi Omega 74-77; Hl Fme 77; Dyer Co Educ Plnng Com Sec; Comms; Tchr.

**SWITZER, ERIC A,** George Mason Univ, Fairfax, VA; SR; Gldn Key; BA Ed Northern VA Cmnty Clg 89; Phy Ed; Tch.**

**SWOPE, MICHAEL J,** Wv Univ, Morgantown, WV; SO; BSCHE; Amercn Inst Of Chem Engrs Nwsltr Edtr 89-; Tech Intrnshp Mobay Corp 88; Tech Intrnshp Union Carbide Corp; Tech Intrnshp Think Tank Resources Inc; Chem Engr.

**SWOPE, TERRY C,** Mount Aloysius Jr Coll, Cresson, PA; FR; AA; Webelos Den Ldr 88-; Prlgl; Law Schl.

**SWORDS, PATTI R,** Castleton St Coll, Castleton, VT; FR; MBA; Bus; Hmn Rsrcs.

**SWYGERT, KIMBERLY A,** Univ Of Sc At Columbia, Columbia, SC; SR; Stats Clb 89-90; March Band 86-88; Hon Coll 86-88; Psi Chi 89-; BS Psych Stats 90; Bhvrl Rsrch; Coll Prfsr Psych/Stats.

**SWYGERT, TRACIE B,** Johnson C Smith Univ, Charlotte, NC; FR; BA; Cmmnctns; Navy.

**SY, LAMINE MADEMBA,** Central St Univ, Wilberforce, OH; JR; BA; Poli Sci Assn 90-; Intrntl Assn 90-F Mulsin Assn; Mali Embassy 1st S/Fncl Ofcr 84-89; Treas Dept Bamako Mali W Africa 80-84; AS Ecica-Mali W Africa 79; Pltcl Sci Econ; Dplmt.

**SY, SEAV,** Middle Tn St Univ, Murfreesboro, TN; JR; BBA; Intl Stdnt Assoc 88-; Chinese Stdnt Assoc 88-; Gamma Beta Phi 89-; Fncl Mgmt Assoc 90-; Data Proc Mgmt Assoc 90-; Natl Hlth Corp Cert Nrs Asst 88-; Cmptr Lab Asst 89; 2 Yr Svc Pin Awd Mursfreesboro Hlth Care Ctr 90; Comp Inf Syst; P C Comp Spec.

**SYBERT, JOHN P,** Embry Riddle Aeronautical Univ, Daytona Beach, FL; SR; Stdnt Ldrshp Dvlpmnt Prog 90; La Crosse Tm 87; BS; Mngmnt; Law.

**SYED, ABDULLAH M,** Univ Of Sc At Salkehatchie, Allendale, SC; JR; BS; Stdnt Govt Sen 90-; Tennis 90-; Mktg; Bsn.

**SYED, AHMED R,** Old Dominion Univ, Norfolk, VA; SO; BS; IEEE 90-; Vol Spcl Engr 90-; Muslim Comm Tidewater 90-; Acdmc Hnrs Soc 90-91; Deans Lst 90; Acdmc Hnrs Pro Schlrshp 90-; Elec Engr.

**SYFRETT, DAVID A,** Fl St Univ, Tallahassee, FL; JR; BA; Phi Theta Kappa 89-90; Mu Alpha Theta 89-90; Psi Chi 90-; AA Chipola Jr Coll 89-90; Stdnt Advsry Comm/Dean Of Arts/Sci 90-; Psychlgy; Tchng/Fmly Therpy/Cnslng.

**SYGALL, PAUL B,** Univ Of Miami, Coral Gables, FL; JR; BSMD; Ambsdr 90-; Hon Stdnt Assc 89-; SGA Spec Asst Ombdsmn 90-; Alph Lmbd Dlt 90-; Paideia; Phi Eta Sgm 90-; Alpha Epsln Dlt 90; Lmbd Chi Alph Chrmn Cmt 89-; Orntn Stf Orntn Asst 90-; Tutoring Stf Mstr Tutor; Six Year Hon Pgm Medicine 89-; Bio; Medicine.

**SYKES, AUTUMN M,** Indian River Comm Coll, Fort Pierce, FL; SO; AA; Amer Bsn Wmns Assoc 90-; Learn-To-Read 90; Elem Ed, Tchg.

**SYKES, CHENOA A,** Univ Of Cincinnati, Cincinnati, OH; SO; BM; Alpha Lambda Delta 89-; Music; Music Ed/Perf.

**SYKES, DE ANNA R,** Univ Of Va Clinch Valley Coll, Wise, VA; SO; BA; Almn Assn 89-; Hnrs Prog 90-; Hstry/Govt; Crmnl Lwyr.

**SYKES, HEATHER L,** Univ Of Ga, Athens, GA; GD; BSW; Scl Wrk Clb Chrmn Publ Rels 84-90; Univ Union Variety Div Publ Rels Chrmn 85-88; IM Sftbl 85-88; Talking Book Ctr Vol 87; Dns Lst 90; Madison Co Yth Svcs Intern 89; Central State Hosp Long Term Care Div Intern 90; Scl Wrk; Priv Cnslg.

**SYKES, KATHERINE J,** Longwood Coll, Farmville, VA; SR; BFA; Vrsty Riding Tm 87-89; IM Pblcby Dir 87-; Kappa Pi Svp 89-; Artist Of Month 90; Jr/Sr Art Exhbt 90-; Visual Arts Perf Schlrshp 88; Fine Arts; Illstrtn/Grphc Dsgn.

**SYKES, LISA M THOMPSON,** Ms Coll, Clinton, MS; GD; JD; Clg Law Review Mgng Edtr 90-; Staff 89-90; Phi Alpha Delta Jstc 90/Clerk 89-; BS 88; Law; Atty.

**SYKES, LORI A,** Longwood Coll, Farmville, VA; SO; BA; Rsdnt Asstnt 90-; Orntn Ldr 90-; Hall Cncl Advsr 89-; Alpha Lmbd Dlt 90-; Phi Kappa Phi; Longwood Ambsdrs Fndrsng 90-; Pol Sci/ Mdrn Lang; Govt Wrk.

**SYKES, RANDAL H,** Catawba Valley Comm Coll, Hickory, NC; SR; BSN; Stdnt Nrsng Assn 88-; Fndtn Schlrshp 90; Natl Kdny Fndtn Awrd 88; AS; Ruritan Natl Expnsn Chrmn 90; Amer Hrt Assn Fclty 89-; Nrsng Dept; Stff RNA Crlns Med Cntr Chrltte NC; Nrsng.

**SYKES, SHAWNETTE D,** Norfolk St Univ, Norfolk, VA; SR; BA; Alpha Kappa Delta; Spartan Alpha Tau; Intrn Hunton YMCA; Daycare Ctr Asst Tchr; WEB Du Bois Citatn; I M Aerobics; Soclgy; Urban Rsrch.

**SYKES, STACEY M,** Ky St Univ, Frankfort, KY; SR; BS; Stdnt Govt Assn Sen 90-; Judcry Comm 90-; Symphnc Mrchng Bnd 89-; Delta Sigma Theta Corr Sec 89-; Dept Educ Intrnshp; Levr Bro Intrnshp 90; Busn Admin; Mgmt.

**SYKES, TERRANCE L,** Al A & M Univ, Normal, AL; SO; BA; Teen Oppor Prom Succ 88-89; Voctnl Indstrl Clb Amer VP 87-89; Educ Sec Hist.

**SYKES, WAYNE E,** Bowie St Univ, Bowie, MD; SR; BA; Mrktn Clb SGA Rep 87-88; Hll Cncl Pres 89-90; Delta Mu Delta 90; Alpha Phi Alpha Dn; Inrds Intern 89; Mrktng.

**SYLER, DONNA M,** Roane St Comm Coll, Harriman, TN; FR; BSN; Chrch Cncl Chrprsn 82-88; Red Crs Instrctr 82-88; Girl Sct Ldr 79-88; LPN 70-91; Nrsng.

**SYLER, JENNIFER L,** Roane St Comm Coll, Harriman, TN; SO; Stars Art Clb; Gamma Beta Phi Rcrdg Sec; Educ; Elem.

**SYLVESTER, DENAY A,** Albright Coll, Reading, PA; FR; BS; Beta Beta Beta 90-; Blgy Lab Asst; Admssns Offce Intrn; Fd Srvce Emplymnt; Dns Lst 90; Hnr Rll 90-; Blgy; Vet Med.

**SYLVIA, BETHANY A,** Endicott Coll, Beverly, MA; SO; AS; SGA 90; Orientation Ldr 90-; Phi Theta Kappa 90-; Deans Lst 89-; Interior Dsgn Scty 90-; Interior Design; BS.

**SYLVIA, SUZANNE R,** Univ Of Al At Huntsville, Huntsville, AL; FR; BS; Pre Med; Medical Field/Physician.

**SYMMES, ROBERT L,** Southern Coll Of Tech, Marietta, GA; SR; BSMET; GSPE Co-Chrmn 90-; ASME 90-; Sigma Alpha Epsilon; Mech Engr; Engr.

**SYMONDS, JACQUELYNE S,** Univ Of Sc At Columbia, Columbia, SC; FR; BA; Cmps Crsd 90-; Bptst Stu Unn 90-; Eta Phi Sigma; Cmps Arbcs 90-; Bus Admn Mngmnt; Hosp Admn.

**SYMONS, LORI S,** Nova Univ, Ft Lauderdale, FL; GD; MA; EDPAA 88-; Sr EDP Audtr 88-; BS Cal St Univ 85; Acctg.

**SYMS, JEAN A,** Blue Mountain Coll, Blue Mountain, MS; SR; BS; Elem Educ; Tchg.

**SYNDAB, RICKY V,** Morris Coll, Sumter, SC; SR; SGA Pres 90-; Vetrns Cl V P 87-88/Busn Mgr 89-90; Colg Chorale Pres 87-89; Phi Beta Lambda 1st V P 90-; Phi Beta Sigma Pres 88-; O R Reuben Schol; Deans List 88-; Outstndng Undergrad Sigma/Yr State/S C; Mayors Cert/Spch/Drugs; Pol Sci/History/Pre-Law; Prof/History/Lawyer.

**SYNNESTVEDT, CRAIG D,** Academy Of The New Church, Bryn Athyn, PA; BARCH; Deans Lst 88-90; Vrsty Lacrosse 88-90; AA 90; Archtctr.

**SYNNESTVEDT, MARA L,** Academy Of The New Church, Bryn Athyn, PA; SO; BED; SAC 89-90; Deans List 89-90; Cooperative Ed Prgrm Intern 90; Ed; Special Ed Tchr.

**SYNNOTT, PAMELA A,** Nova Univ, Ft Lauderdale, FL; GD; MHA; Alpha Chi 88-90; Am Reg Radlgc Tech 75-; Nuclear Med Tech Crtfct Bd 90-; Palm Bch Cty Soc Radlgc Tech Advsry Bd 90; Nuclear Med Spfsr; BS 90; AA Commnty Clg Denver 74; Hlth Svcs Admin.

**SYRACUSA, CHERI D,** S U N Y Coll At Fredonia, Fredonia, NY; SR; BA; Psychiatric Ctr Asst Rec Spvr 87; Spec Ed Tchrs Aide 88-89; AS Alfred Sta Univ 88; Sociology; Paralegal/Deaf Interprtr.

**SYTA, SUSAN B,** Catawba Valley Comm Coll, Hickory, NC; FR; BA; Gamma Beta Phi; Bus Admn Acctg; Bus.

**SYVERSEN, TOD L,** City Univ Of Ny Queensbrough, New York, NY; SO; BS; I Tappa Keg VP 90-; Elec Eng Tech.

**SZABO, LORI A,** Davis Coll, Toledo, OH; SR; ASSOC; Aviatn; Cmmrcl Pilot.

**SZABO, MICHELLE A,** Kent St Univ Kent Cmps, Kent, OH; SO; BA; Fin Assoc 90-; Intl Bus Clb 90-; Kent State Hons Assoc 89-; Kent State Hons Clg 89-; Beta Alpha Psi 90-; Delta Zeta Hist 89-; Red Cross 87-; Fin; Broker.

**SZALVA, WALTER L,** Broward Comm Coll, Ft Lauderdale, FL; FR; BA; Hkd Appalachian Trl GA ME 89 2139 Mi; Mass Comm/ Music; Brdcst Advrtsg.

**SZAROWICZ, DONNA L,** S U N Y Coll At Fredonia, Fredonia, NY; JR; BA; Math Clb V P 88-89; Cls Rep 88; Math; Sec Educ Math.

**SZCZECH, RADOSLAW,** Univ Of Sc At Columbia, Columbia, SC; SR; BA; Engl.

**SZCZERBOWICZ, KATHLEEN A,** Coll Misericordia, Dallas, PA; JR; BS; SOTA Treas 88-; Stdnt Govt 88-; Stdnt Ambsdr Msrcrdia 90-; Pi Theta Epsilon 90-; Orientatn Cnslr 89-; Campus Mnstry 88-; Euchrstc Mnstr 90-; Peer Cnslr 88-; Pottsvl Psychtry Intrnshp; Wilkes Barre Vtrns Admin Instrnshp; Intrmdiate Unit 90; Occptnl Therpy/Psychlgy.

**SZCZESNY, JONATHAN D,** S U N Y Coll At Fredonia, Fredonia, NY; JR; BA; Deans List ECC 88-89; AA Erie Comm Clg S Cmps 89; Elem Ed; Tchr.

**SZE, CHI KONG,** Fl A & M Univ, Tallahassee, FL; SR; BA; Knghts Columbus Cncl; Zeta Tau Beta Sec 88-; Cmptr Info Sys; Anlyst.

**SZEKELY, CHRISTOPHER G,** Saint Vincents Coll & Seminary, Latrobe, PA; FR; BA; Graphic Design.

**SZEKELY, JEFFREY P,** Univ Of Pittsburgh, Pittsburgh, PA; SR; MBA; Co-Op 88-90; Church Choir 89-90; Golden Key 88-; BSME 90.

**SZEKELY, ROBERT,** City Univ Of Ny Bronx Comm Col, Bronx, NY; SO; AAS; Dns Lst 89-; Phi Theta Kappa 89-; Hnr Soc 89-; Tutor Hgh Schl Stdnts 89; Prlgl; Law.

**SZETO, GREGORY C,** Univ Of Miami, Coral Gables, FL; FR; BM; Radio; Alpha Lambda Delta; Henry King Stanford Schlr; Msc Schlrshp; Msc Engnrng Tchnlgy; Rcrdng Tchncn.

**SZETO, JANSEN,** Old Dominion Univ, Norfolk, VA; SO; IEEE; Gldn Key; Elec Engr.

**SZLEGIER, RACHEL E,** Univ Of Miami, Coral Gables, FL; FR; BA; Hons Prog; Psych; Psychrst.

**SZMYR, ELLEN L,** Schenectady County Comm Coll, Schenectady, NY; AD; Sailing Clb; Cystic Fibrosis Fdn; Heart Assoc; Golf League; Word Proc/Offc Auto.

**SZNOL, RON,** Fl International Univ, Miami, FL; FR; MBA; Hillel 90-; Scuba Clb 90-; Jewish Awrns Clb Sch Advsr 88-89; Lions Clb 88-89; Math; Engr.

**SZTROIN, BETH M,** Indiana Univ Of Pa, Indiana, PA; SO; Deans Lst; Elem Ed; Tchr.

**SZULCZEWSKI, JENNIFER E,** Va Commonwealth Univ, Richmond, VA; JR; BS; Vlntr Wrk Bnbrdg Comm Mnstry 87-; Gldn Key 90-; Math; Engnrng.

**SZWARC, LESLIE KAREEN,** Indiana Univ Of Pa, Indiana, PA; SR; BED; Big Brothers/Sisters Day Care Ctr Proj Stride 86-90; Nursery Schl/PSEA; Alpha Phi Omega 89-90; Ed; Elem Ed.

**SZYDLOWSKI, ALAN J,** City Univ Of Ny Baruch Coll, New York, NY; JR; Golden Key V P Comm 90-; Bio-Med Soc; Beta Gamma Sigma; Baruch Schlrshp 88-; Dean Of Stdnts Schlrshp 88-; Fin.**

**SZYOLOWSKI, ALAN J,** City Univ Of Ny Baruch Coll, New York, NY; JR; BBA; Beta Gamma Sigma; Gldn Key Natl Hon Soc VP Cmnctns 90-91; Bio-Med Soc 90-; Baruch Schlrshp 88-; Dean Stdnts Schlrshp 89; Fin Crprt/Invstmnts; Invstmnt Bnkng.

# T

**TAAM, SZE WAI,** Broward Comm Coll, Ft Lauderdale, FL; SO; AA; Trnstnl Insight 90-; Eng.

**TABAK, MARK WILLIAM,** Univ Of Fl, Gainesville, FL; SR; MBA; Fncl Mgmt Assn Chrmn 88-89; Bus Admin Coll Cncl Chrmn 89; Jr Chmbr Of Comm Gainesvl Jaycees Chrmn 90; Dns Lst 90; Rho Epsilon 89-90; Intrnd W/Citadel Mtg Corp; IM Ftbl/Sftbl; BBA 90; Finance; Corp Finance.

**TABARES ALMEYDA, MARCIA I,** Inter Amer Univ Pr Hato Rey, Hato Rey, PR; FR; BA; Acctng; Cpa.

**TABB, BONNIE L,** Fayetteville St Univ, Fayetteville, NC; JR; BA; Super Achievers 90-; Phi Theta Kappa 84-85; US Army Soldier Of The Year 88; US Army Soldier Of The Northwest Region 88; US Army Hlth Sci Placed 3rd 88; Command Soldier Of The Year 88; AA Okaloosa-Walton Cmnty Clg 85; Bnkng/Fin/Acctg; Bnkng/Fin.

**TABBERER, AMY S,** Appalachian Bible Coll, Bradley, WV; SO; BA; Vlybl 90-; Educ; Tch.

**TABEI, YUKO,** Univ Of Tn At Martin, Martin, TN; SR; BS; Golf Clb 85-87; Japan Air Lines 87-89; Home Econ.

**TABER, ELIZABETH W,** Va Commonwealth Univ, Richmond, VA; SR; BS; Natl Athltc Trnrs Asc 88-; Physcl Thrpy Clb 87-89; Sprts Med Ctr 90-; Athltc Trnr 88-90; West End Orthpdc Clnc 88; Physcl Educ/Athltc Trng; Physcl Thrpy.

**TABER, KATHLEEN A,** S U N Y Coll At Fredonia, Fredonia, NY; JR; BA; Bsns Clb; Uppr Cls Bddy; Ambsdrs; Pol Sci Clb VP; Intl Bsns; Intl Trde.

**TABER, SCOTT,** Univ Of Pittsburgh At Bradford, Bradford, PA; SR; BS; Campus Radio Statn DJ 88; Comp Sci; Comp Indstry.

**TABLER, MARY E,** Broward Comm Coll, Ft Lauderdale, FL; FR; AS; Amer Payroll Assoc 86-; Payroll Mgr 82-90; Nursing; Nursing Admin.

**TABOR, BARBARA L,** Rust Coll, Holly Springs, MS; JR; Pre-Med Cncl VP; Pre-Alumni Cncl Treas; Alpha Kappa Mu; Crimson Schlr Assn; Deans Lst; Chi Beta Phi Treas; Delta Sigma Theta; G S Trp Ldr; Stdnt Of Wk; Bio/Pre-Med.

**TABOR, BRIAN L,** Tn St Univ, Nashville, TN; SO; BS; Ntl Soc Blck Engrs; NAACP; Pep Clb; Physics Clb; Big Bro/Big Sis Inc; Yth Flwshp; Pres Schlrshp; Deans Lst; Elec Engr.

**TABOR, JULIE L,** Roane St Comm Coll, Harriman, TN; FR; AD; LPN Prk W Hosp Knxvl Tn; Nrsg; RN.

**TABOR, MICHELE A,** Hudson Valley Comm Coll, Troy, NY; AAS; Mrtry Scnc Assoc Cntn NY 87-88; Mrtry Scnc Clb 90-; Peer Tutoring; Scnc; Funeral Directing.

**TABOR, STEPHANIE A,** Univ Of Sc At Aiken, Aiken, SC; SO; BA; Hnrs Coll Prgm; Gamma Beta Phi 90-; Gamma Beta Phi Schlrshp; Pltcl Sci; Law.

**TACHENKO, SHARON J,** Union Inst, Cincinnati, OH; SR; BED; Schl Bd; Indpndnt Dsktp Pblshr 86-; Elem Ed; Tchr.

**TACHIE-MENSON, URSULA M,** Howard Univ, Washington, DC; SR; BS; APHA 88-; Cls Sec 89-90; Rho Chi V P 90-; Phi Theta Kappa; Kappa Psi Sec 89-; AA Palm Beach Jr Clg 88; Phrmcy; Rsrch.

**TACK, KRISTY A,** Fordham Univ, Bronx, NY; SO; BS; Vrsty Tennis; USG United Stdnt Govt Sec; Orientn Advsr; Tennis; Acctng; CPA.

**TACKETT, BARBARA A,** Univ Of Sc At Columbia, Columbia, SC; SR; BAS; Elem Tchr.

**TACKETT, CRAIG,** Western Ky Univ, Bowling Green, KY; SR; BA; ROTC Exec Offcr 87-; Scbbrd/Blde Pres 88-; Sigma Nu Pldg Trnr 87-; Financl Exec Inst Awrd; Rsrv Offcrs Assn Awrd; Sr Frat Man Schlr Awrd; Finance; Anlyst.

**TACKETT, DANA L,** Va Commonwealth Univ, Richmond, VA; SO; BS; Kappa Tau Alpha; Gldn Key; Phi Eta Sigma 90; Pres Schlrshp 89; VCV Hnrs Prgrm 89; Mas Commnctn; Pblc Relations.

**TACKETT, LINDA F,** Ashland Comm Coll, Ashland, KY; FR; BA; Wrk With The Youth Of My Church Treas; Comptr Sci; Sys Engr.

**TACY, JOAN C,** Davis & Elkins Coll, Elkins, WV; SR; MA; Cum Laude; Spec Olymp Chrmn 86-89; Prnt-Tchr Assn State Sec 88-89; Plcy Advsry Comm Fdrl Pgms Chrmn 86-88; Spec Educ Tchr; BS; Educ; Tch.

**TADDEI, JOANN M,** Immaculata Coll, Immaculata, PA; SR; BMUS; MENC Pres 89-90; Pi Kappa Lambda; Intrnshp; Rittenhouse Care Cntr; Music Educ; Music Thrpy.

**TADDIE, TONYA M,** Univ Of Miami, Coral Gables, FL; SR; BA; Frgn Exchng Stdnt/Spain 89; Trnsft Advsr Bddy Systm 89-; Phi Theta Kappa 88-89; Pre Legal Soc Law Rvw Comm 89-; SADD 87-89; Deans List 87-; Intrnshp Law Firm 90; Bowman Ashe Schlrshp 89-; Bicentennial Schlrshp Geo Jenkings 88-89; AA Edison Comm; Sociology/Pltcl Sci/Spanish; Law.

**TADDY, TRINA S,** Ms St Univ, Miss State, MS; SO; BS; Cross Cntry Track 89-; Microbiology Pre Med; Medicine.

**TAGERT, STACEY D,** Univ Of Southern Ms, Hattiesburg, MS; SO; BA; Almn Assoc Grp Chrprsn 89-; Egl Clb 90-; Hnrs Stdnt Assoc 89-; Gamma Beta Phi Treas; Phi Eta Sigma 90; Alpha Lambda Sigma 90; Beta Gamma Sigma; Hnrs Clge 89-; IM Sprts 90-; Dmnd Drlngs 89-; Bsn; Acctg.

**TAGGART, DANIEL J,** Elmira Coll, Elmira, NY; FR; BA; Vars Bsktbl 90-; Fnc; Stck Brkr.

**TAGGART, HOLLY K,** Univ Of Rochester, Rochester, NY; JR; BA; Vol Park Hope Nrsg Home 90-; Outing Club 89-; Undrgrdte Anthrplgy Cncl Soc Chr 89-; IM Sports/Soccer; History; Museum Stds.

**TAGGART, JULIE A,** Columbus Coll Of Art & Design, Columbus, OH; SR; BFA; Otstndng Sr Fine Arts Div; Fine Art; Fine Artist/Tchng.

**TAGGART, JULIE KAY,** Oh St Univ, Columbus, OH; SR; BSLA; Stdnt Chptr Asla Sec 88-; Phi Kappa Phi 90-; Sigma Lambda Alpha Tres 90-; ASLA Mrt Awd; Landscape Archtctr Fclty Awd 90-; ASBA Frnkln Unvrsty 82; Landscape Archtctr.

**TAGGART, MARSHALL J,** Clark Atlanta Univ, Atlanta, GA; JR; BA; Jr Class Treas 90; Entrnrshp Clb Co-Fndr 88; Mrchng Bnd Bdgt Coord 88-89; Clrk Atlanta U Hnrs Prog Jr Class Lassigne 90; Phi Beta Lambda; Alpha Phi Alpha Pres 90; Orient Guide Corp Scl Cmmttee Chrmn 89-90; Frat Ims 89; Accntng; CPA Edctr.

**TAGGERT, JESSE A,** Smith Coll, Northampton, MA; JR; BA; People Org Wmns Rights 89-90; Tour Gd; Intrnshp Currier Gallery Of Art; Art Hstry; Tchng/Musuem Wrk.

**TAGLIARINI, SHEILA L,** Hillsborough Comm Coll, Tampa, FL; SO; BA; Hosp Vol 88-; AA Hillsborough Cmnty Clg 90; Amer Studies; Educ.

**TAGLIATERRA, LISA A,** Marywood Coll, Scranton, PA; JR; BA; Law Advsry Bd 90-; Stdnt Curr Cmtee 90-; Sem Plng Cmtee 90-; Pi Gamma Mu 90-; Sigma Pi Mu Pres 87-; Moosic Lks Wmn Clb 89; Deans Lst; M Cowley Esq Intrnshp; Vybl Tm Co Capt 88-; Legal Asst; Lawyr.**

**TAGLIERI, GINA D,** Clemson Univ, Clemson, SC; SO; BSN; Stdnt Nrs Assoc 90-; AS Harcum Jr Clg 88; Nrsng.

**TAGLIERI, JULIE A,** Merrimack Coll, North Andover, MA; FR; Pgm Brd 90-; Bsn Admn.

**TAGOE, CYNTHIA-CLARE,** Central St Univ, Wilberforce, OH; SO; BS; FCS Sec 89-; Intl Assn Sec 90-; Clg Hon 89; Otsdng Wmn Yr 90-; Water Rsrcs Mgmt; Civl Engr.

**TAHA, DARYOUSH,** Temple Univ, Philadelphia, PA; SO; Alpha Lambda Delta 89-90; Keystone Natl Hnrs Soc 90; Amer Cvl Lbrts Un; Lunchn Awd Outstdng Acad Perf Math/Sci/Engl/Law Schlp; Dir Lst; Dixon House 88-; S Phila Intrcl Intgnrtnl; Cmps Police 89-; Law/Pol Sci; Law/FBI/CIA.**

**TAHTINEN, TERRI L,** Univ Of Rochester, Rochester, NY; SO; BA; Undrgrad Psychlgy Cncl; Deans Lst 90-; Sftbl; Psychlgy.

**TAI, EDWARD R,** Cornell Univ Statutory College, Ithaca, NY; SO; BA; Amrcn Mtrlgcl Scty 89-; Crnll Wthr Phn; Mtrlgy.

**TAIT, EDWIN R,** Milligan Coll, Milligan Clg, TN; SO; BA; Humanities Awd 90-; English/History; Writer/Teacher.

**TAIT, GERTRUDE BEATRICE,** Milligan Coll, Milligan Clg, TN; JR; BA; Chrstn Pub; Emmanuel Bible Coll England 67; Engl; Tchng/Wrtng.

**TAITE, PHYLLIS CAROLE,** Fl A & M Univ, Tallahassee, FL; JR; BS; Stdnt Govt Assn Asst Atty Gen 90-; Army ROTC Platoon Srgnt 90-; Phi Eta Sigma 89-; Lambda Alpha Epsilon 89-; Col Hendricks Frshmn Achvmnt Awd 89; Schlstc Excel 90; Miss Army ROTC 91-92; Crmnl Jstc; Law.

**TAITE, SHIRLEY E,** Livingston Univ, Livingston, AL; JR; BS; Afrcn Am Cltrl Assn VP 89-; Natrl Sci/Math Soc VP 88-; Anglc Voices Of Faith 2nd VP 88-89; Omicron Delta Kappa; Alpha Kappa Alpha VP 89-; Alpha Kappa Alpha Sorority Inc VP 89-; IM 90; Math; Tchr.

**TAITE, TARA R,** Al St Univ, Montgomery, AL; FR; BS; Phi Eta Sigma; Hnr Cls 90-; Hnr Stu 90-; Sci; Engr.

**TAKABAYASHI, KEN,** Cooper Union, New York, NY; SO; BENG; Amer Scty Mech Eng 89-; Mech Eng.

**TAKACH, JANET M,** Western Ky Univ, Bowling Green, KY; SO; BS; TMC Of So Ky 89-; Cert Bowling Green St Voc Tech Sch 89; Bus; Acctng.

**TAKACS, TERESA A,** Univ Of Akron, Akron, OH; FR; BS; Res Hl Prog Brd Tech Cmmtt 90; Hnrs Clb 90-; Hnrs Schlrshp 90-; Hnrs Prog 90-; IM Vlybl/Sftbl/Asst Coach Ftbl 90-; Elctrcl Engr.

**TAKADA, TADASHI,** Univ Of Miami, Coral Gables, FL; SR; BA; Cane Cmmtr Orgnztn 90-; Japanese Stdnts Orgnztn 90-; Phi Kappa Phi; Prsdnts Hnr Roll; BA Konan Unvrsty 88; Art; Paintng Bsns.

**TAKAHASHI, KENICHI,** Barry Univ, Miami, FL; SO; BS; Rugby Ftbl Clb 90-; Pre Engnrng.

**TAKAHASHI, KOJI,** Saint Catharine Coll, St Catharine, KY; FR; AA; Phi Theta Kappa; Lib Arts; Jrnlsm.

**TAKAISHI, MASATO,** Brevard Coll, Brevard, NC; SO; AA; Vlybl Clb 90-; PTK 90-; Cmptr Sci; Cmptr Org.

**TAKEI, STEPHEN M,** Schenectady County Comm Coll, Schenectady, NY; FR; ELT Clb VP 90-; Drama Clb; Vocal Chmbr Ens; Elec Eng.

**TAKEUCHI, MOMOE,** Univ Of Sc At Spartanburg, Spartanburg, SC; JR; MA; Yth Hostel Club 87-90; Japanese African Am Soc 89-; Edctnl Exchg Prog Schlrshp 90-91; BA Gakushuin Univ 90; TJSL Edctnl Exch Prfog 90; Dvlpmnt Econ; UN Officer.

**TALARCZYK, MICHAEL J,** Ny Univ, New York, NY; FR; BA; Nwsltr Edtr 90-; Undrgrad Stdnt Orgztn 90-; Music Cmpsitn; Film Scoring.

**TALAREK, CHRISTOPHER A,** Univ Of Akron, Akron, OH; SO; BA; ASME 90-; Co-Op Pstn Brtsh Ptrlm 90; IM Frbl Bsktbl Sftbl Ping Pong 89-; Mchncl Engnrng; Engnrng.

**TALARICO JR, JOSEPH C,** Univ Of Rochester, Rochester, NY; JR; BA; Theta Delta Chi Secy/Treas 90-; Varsty Ftbl 88-89; Pol Sci; Law Sch.

**TALARO, NICOLE L,** City Univ Of Ny Baruch Coll, New York, NY; JR; BBA; Mktg Asst Intrnshp 90-; Euromny Inst Fin; Mktg/Advrtsng; Advrtsng.

**TALBOT, JOHN G,** Univ Of Sc At Columbia, Columbia, SC; JR; BS; Gamma Beta Phi 89-; Acctng/Finance; Law.

**TALBOT, JOSEPH S,** Univ Of Ga, Athens, GA; JR; BA; GSLA 89-; ASLA 89-; Gldn Key 90-; Lndscp Arch Natl Hnr Soc 90-; Std Env Awrns 89-90; Lndscp Arch.

**TALBOTT, BERYL MAY,** City Univ Of Ny City Coll, New York, NY; SR; BED; Sndy Schl Tchr Flatbush Cong; Cert Ed Bethlehem Tchrs Coll 71; Elem Ed Tchr.

**TALBOTT, JULIE A,** Univ Of Akron, Akron, OH; SO; BED; Elem Engl; Educ.

**TALBOTT-HILL, KARIN R,** Jefferson Comm Coll, Louisville, KY; SO; BA; Stdnt Snt Govt Sec Treas 90-; Sngl Prnt Clb VP 89-90; Mnrty Stdnt Un Mem 89-; Phlsphy Frm Psychlgy Tdy Clb Mem; PTA Hawthorne Elem 90; Jck Jll Amrc Inc; John T Smith Schlrshp 89; Tlnt Rst Otstndng Mnrty Cmmnty Coll Grad 90; KAEOPP 90-; Econ Mnr Engl; Law.

**TALEGHANI, CHRISTOPHER KELLY,** Georgetown Univ, Washington, DC; SR; BA; Accntng Soc Assoc VP 89; Ski Tm 89; U Of Md Pre-Med Soc 87-89; Delta Sigma Pi Sec 89; BA; Accntng; Med.

**TALIAFERRO, ALISA S,** Nc Agri & Tech St Univ, Greensboro, NC; SO; BS; Fndr Of The Spanish Club Pres 90-; Alpha Mu Gamma VP 90-; Delta Sigma Theta 90-; Deans List; Erly Chldhd Ed; Civil Law.

**TALIAFERRO, ELIZABETH W,** James Madison University, Harrisonburg, VA; SR; BSN; Bapt Stdnt Unn 88-; Nrss Chrstn Fllwshp 90-; Nrsng Stdnt Cncl 90-; Omicron Delta Kappa; JMU Nrsng Hnr Scty Pres 89-; Gldn Ky 88-; Alpha Phi Omega 90-; BSN; Nrsng.

**TALLENT, VANESSA G,** Tn Tech Univ, Cookeville, TN; FR; BA; Chld Psychlgst.

**TALLEY, CHRISTY L,** Memphis St Univ, Memphis, TN; GD; Fndr Crmnl Just Soc Pr 88-90; VP; Alpha Kappa Delta 90-; Memphis Mensa Schlrshp 89; Univ Coll Alumni Schlrshp 90; Univ Coll Allumni Assn Awd; BPS; Social Wrk.

**TALLEY, JACQUELINE S,** Union Coll, Barbourville, KY; SR; BA; Intnshp Comprhnsv Care Cen 90-; AA Catonsville Comm Colg 89; Psychlgy; Socl Work.

**TALLEY, LAURA C,** Bellarmine Coll, Louisville, KY; SR; BA; Soc For Human Resrcs Mngmnt 89-; Delta Epsilon Sigma 90-; Omicron Delta Epsilon; Deans Lst 87-; Bus Admin; Fin/Retl Mgmnt.

**TALLEY, MICHAEL D,** Tn Temple Univ, Chattanooga, TN; SR; BA; Sprvsr Sams Clb Mmbrs Only 90-; AAS Wallace State Cmmnty Coll 87; Bble; Mnstry.

**TALLEY, NATASHA Y,** Saint Pauls Coll, Lawrenceville, VA; FR; BA; Engl; Educ.

**TALLEY, TRACY J,** Univ Of Akron, Akron, OH; SR; BS; Amer Soc Chem Eng; Golden Key 89-; Tau Kappa Epsilon 86-; Eng Co-Op Prog 89-; Chem Eng.

**TALLEY-HORNE, JILL R,** East Tn St Univ, Johnson City, TN; SO; MD; Fmly Prac Intrst Grp 89-; Amer Med Soc Assn 88-; Sthrn Med Assn; IM Bsktbl/Ftbl 89-; BS 87; Med.

**TALLMADGE, RACHEL ANN,** Fl St Univ, Tallahassee, FL; JR; BA; Chrldg Capt 88-90; Stu Gov 89; Phi Theta Kappa VP 88-; Selby Schlrshp; Joe Fant Awrd; Dnc 89-; Ntrtn; Corp Ftns.

**TALLMAN, DEIDRA L,** Univ Of Tn At Martin, Martin, TN; FR; Mccord Hall Assc Senator 90-; Peer Enabling Prgrm PEP Stdnt Grp Ldrf; Hnrs Smnr 90-; Pi Sigma Epsilon Pldg Class Pres; Zeta Tau Alpha Pldg Clss Sec Trea; Deans List 90.

**TALLMAN, LEE A,** Fl St Univ, Tallahassee, FL; SR; Gldn Key 87-; Omicron Nu 88-; Chi Omega Comm Head 87-90; Intern WT Moore Elem Schl; BS; Educ; Tchng.

**TALLON, KATHLEENE M,** Coker Coll, Hartsville, SC; FR; BA; Criminology; Law Enforcement.

**TALLY, LINDA SUZANNE,** Northern Ky Univ, Highland Hts, KY; GD; JD; Phi Sigma Sigma Rush Chair 88-; Alpha Chi VP 90-; Pltcl Sci Clb; Xi Omega 89-; Chrstn Awkng Tm 87-; Outstndng Phlsphy Grad; Magna Cum Laude; Commonwealth KY Schlrshp Chase Law Schl; BA; Pltcl Sci/Phlsphy; Law.

**TALLY, LISA R,** Univ Of Nc At Greensboro, Greensboro, NC; JR; BS; Intervrsty 89-; Sgn Chr 89-90; Intrhsp Cone Elem Schl; Elem Ed; Schl Tchr.

**TALMADGE III, HARRY E,** Ms St Univ, Miss State, MS; SR; BS; MS St Univ Famous Maroon Bnd Pres 87-; Assoc Cmptng Mchnry VP 87-; Upsilon Pi Epsilon VP 89-; Gamma Beta Phi 90-; Phi Mu Alpha Sinfonia Pres 87-; Boy Scts Amer Asst Sctmstr 79-87; Eagle Sct; Comp Sci.

**TALON, DURWIN S,** Savannah Coll Of Art & Design, Savannah, GA; SR; Pres Cncl 90-; Clb Canada Prm Mnstr 90-; Deans Lst 88-; Summa Cum Laude; BFA; Illstrtn; Cmptr Grphc Dsgn.

**TALOTTA, SEBASTIAN N,** Saint Vincents Coll & Seminary, Latrobe, PA; SO; BS; Chem Clb 89-; Intrnshp Pittsburgh Energy Tchnlgy Ctr 90-; Chemistry; Medicine.

**TALTON, ELIZABETH P,** East Carolina Univ, Greenville, NC; SR; BS; SME 90; Gldn Key; Kappa Kappa Gamma; Coop Nrthrn Tlcm Crdmr NC Indstrl Engr Dept; Indstrl Tech; Archtct Dsgn.

**TALVACCHIO, DENISE M,** Widener Univ, Chester, PA; SR; Econ Clb 89-; Stdnt Govt Senator 90; Econ Tutor 89-90; Alpha Chi V P 90-; Omicron Delta Epsilon Treas 89-; Phi Kappa Phi; Charlotte W Newcombe Schlrshp 90; Widener Merit Schlrshp 88-90; Natl Dns Lst 88-; Keystone Auto Clb 74-87; Mgmt Mnr-Econ; Finance.

**TAM, KWOK HUNG,** Old Dominion Univ, Norfolk, VA; FR; BS; Scty Physcs Stdnts; Elec Eng; Rsrchr.

**TAM, ROLAND HOI-KIT,** Univ Of Ga, Athens, GA; JR; BS; Acad Std Pharm 90-; Amer Pharm Asc 90-; GA Soc Hosp Pharm 90-; Gldn Key 90-; Alpha Lambda Delta 89-; Gamma Beta Phi 89-90; Pharm.

**TAMAELA WATTIMENA, MICHA F,** Univ Of Miami, Coral Gables, FL; SR; BARCH; ISA Sec 90-; AIAS 90-; Pres 100 90-; Intrvrsty 90-; Grace Chrch Asst Msc Dir 89-; Archtctr.

**TAMAS, REBECCA L,** Univ Of Ky, Lexington, KY; SO; BA; SADD 89-; SAVE 90-; Cncrt Com 90; Lambda Sigma 90-; Alpha Lambda Delta 90-; Phi Eta Sigma 90-; Psi Chi 90-; Psych.

**TAMAYO, LUIS R,** Univ Of Fl, Gainesville, FL; FR; Phi Eta Sigma; Engrng/Mthmtcs.

**TAMBURELLO, KRISTIN,** City Univ Of Ny Baruch Coll, New York, NY; SR; BA; Hmn Rsrc Mgmt 90; Italian Soc 87; IM Vlybl/Bsktbl 87-88; Math Tutor; Dns Lst; Mgmt.

**TAMBURIN, VINCENT E,** Catawba Valley Comm Coll, Hickory, NC; FR; AAS; Accntng Clb VP 90-; Gamma Beta Phi Hstrn; Accntng; C&A.

**TAMBURRI, MARK L,** Carnegie Mellon Univ, Pittsburgh, PA; FR; BS; Invlvmnt Assoc 90-; Lambda Sigma Eta 90-; Trdtn Awrd 90-; Intrmrl Sftbll 90-; Pol Sci.

**TAMER, KERRY D,** Al A & M Univ, Normal, AL; SR; BS; Natl Stdnt Spch Lang Hrng Assoc Treas 88-89; Hmcmg Attndt 90; A/M Hon Rl 90; Kappa Delta Pi; Acad Schlrshps 89-; Huntsvl-Dwn Syndrm Assoc Brd Dir 87-; Comp Erly Intrvn Serv Cncl Prnt Rep 88-; AA Pasadena Cty Clg 75; Spch/Lang Path; Spch/Lang Thrpst.**

**TAN, CHIN-SOON,** Radford Univ, Radford, VA; SR; BBA; AAS VA Wstrn Comm Clg 89; Cert Mrktng Chartered Inst Mrktng UK 88; Finance; Fincl Analyst.

**TAN, CHIUNG F,** City Univ Of Ny Baruch Coll, New York, NY; JR; BBA; Untd Mlysn Stdnt Assn Tres 90; Gldn Key 90-; Deans Lst 90-; Prvst Schlrshp; BBA; Accntng; CPA.

**TAN, EDWARD L,** Bethany Coll, Bethany, WV; SO; Ski Clb VP 89; Kalon Ldrshp Awd; Kappa Mu Epsln; Sigma Nu Chpln; Sccr Treas 89-; Vol Fir Dpt 90-; NREMT A401374; Physcs; Env Sci.

**TAN, LEE-PENG PATSY,** Oh Univ, Athens, OH; JR; BMUS; Spec Tlnt Award 90; Music Theory/Cmpstn; Music Thrst.

**TAN, NYAN TUN,** City Univ Of Ny City Coll, New York, NY; SO; Elect Eng.

**TAN, SHYUE-CHANG,** Univ Of South Al, Mobile, AL; JR; BA; Asian Assn 90-; Mgmt; Bus.

**TAN, SIOK CHING,** Univ Of South Al, Mobile, AL; SO; BSC; Dip Bus Ngeeann Poly Tech Singapore 89; Hmn Rsrc Mgmt; Prsnnl Cmmnctn.

**TAN, SIOK-PENG,** Univ Of Cincinnati, Cincinnati, OH; FR; BM; Intl Stdnt Host Pgm Org Intl Visitors Ctr Inc 90-; Piano Accomp Suzuki Violin Cls CCM Prep Dept 90-; Choir CCM 90-; CCM Hnrs Awd 90-; Yamaha Piano Compet 88; Piano Perf; Music.

**TAN, SOKHAMA,** Bunker Hill Comm Coll, Boston, MA; FR; BA; Nrsng.

**TAN, THAI C,** Bunker Hill Comm Coll, Boston, MA; JR; Elec Technen Or Engr; Elec Tech; Engr.

**TAN, WAH WAI,** City Univ Of Ny City Coll, New York, NY; SR; BS; AS Kingsborough Comm Clg 84-86; Cmptr Sci; Cmptr Progmmr.

**TANACS, ANDREA M,** Emory Univ, Atlanta, GA; SR; BBA; Campus Tour Guide 90-; Emory Mktg Assn 90-; Emory Dance Co 87-88; Alpha Epsilon Upsilon; Kappa Alpha Theta Sor 87-; Vol Emory 87-88; Mktg Intrnshp; Mgmnt/Mktg; Human Resources Mgmnt.

**TANCULA, ALDONA,** City Univ Of Ny La Guard Coll, Long Island Cty, NY; SO; BS; Alpha Theta Phi 89-; Phi Theta Kappa 89-; Data Proc/Prog; Ed.

**TANDY, COLLEEN,** Niagara Univ, Niagara Univ, NY; JR; BS; Yng Entrprnrs VP 90-; Aviation Clb 90-; Exec Bd For Orientation Res Life; Prgrmg Bd Mbr; Sigma Alpha Sigma Outstdnt Soph 89-90; Stdnt Embsdrs 88-; Niag Univ Comm Actn Prog 88-; Socl Wrk Actn Comm 89-; RA 89-; Cmps Mnstry 89-; Mgmt; Bus.

**TANG, CHUN BONG,** Anne Arundel Comm Coll, Arnold, MD; FR; BA.

**TANG, CONNIE M,** Fl Atlantic Univ, Boca Raton, FL; SR; BA; Phi Kappa Phi 90-; Beta Gamma Sigma 90-; Epsilon Pi Epsilon 90-; Pres Lst 86-88; Deans Lst 87; Cmptr Info Sys; Cmptr Customer Sprt.

**TANG, CUONG KHANH,** Bunker Hill Comm Coll, Boston, MA; BS; Cmptr Prog.

**TANG, DAVID C,** Univ Of Pittsburgh, Pittsburgh, PA; SO; BA; Lambda Chi Alpha 89-; Mech Engr.

**TANG, FLORENCE W,** City Univ Of Ny Baruch Coll, New York, NY; SR; BBA; Chns Chrstn Fllwshp VP 90-; Chns Chrstn Fllwshp Treas 89-90; Dean Lst 89-90; Acctg.

**TANG, HINGMAN,** City Univ Of Ny Baruch Coll, New York, NY; SR; BBA; Hong Kong Assoc 90-; Golden Key; Cert Hong Kong Polytech 84; Acctg.

**TANG, HUE KHANH,** Bunker Hill Comm Coll, Boston, MA; BS; Cmptr Pro.

**TANG, KAR YEE,** S U N Y At Buffalo, Buffalo, NY; SR; BS; Fin Mgmt Assn Pblcty Offcr 90-; Amer Symphny Orchstra Leag Pro Afflt 90-; Gldn Key 90-; Intrnshp Fin Dept Buffalo Phlhrmnc Orchstra; Badmntn Clb Trvllng Tm 89-90; ATCL Trinity Coll Music London UK 88; Mgmt.

**TANG, LEI,** Univ Of Rochester, Rochester, NY; SO; BA; Schlrsch Univ Rchstr 90-; Econ.

**TANG, SHAN,** City Univ Of Ny La Guard Coll, Long Island Cty, NY; GD; AAS; Phi Theta Kappa 90-; BA 82; Phys Ther.

**TANG, WEI,** Jersey City St Coll, Jersey City, NJ; SR; BS; Chinese Stdnts Club V P; ISA 90; Writing Lab Tutor 90; Comp Sci; Comp Related Areas.

**TANG, WESLEY K,** City Univ Of Ny City Coll, New York, NY; GD; Marianne Cowan Mem Awd 87; Deans List 90; BS CUNY 90; Comp Sci.

**TANGORA, CHRISTINA M,** Univ Of Miami, Coral Gables, FL; FR; BBA; Jr Panhellenic Tres 90-; Hurricane Pgm Cncl; Sportsfest; Hnr Stdnt Assc 90-; Kappa Kappa Gamma Tres; Ldrshp Cert Pgm 90-; Bowman She Schlrshp; IM Vlybl/Sftbl 90-; Business; Sports Mgmt.

**TANGOREN, EMINE,** Mary Baldwin Coll, Staunton, VA; SR; BA; Var Bsktbl 87-88; Var Swmng 88; Camps Commnts Stf Wrtr 88; Phi Beta Kappa; Iota Sigma Pi 90; Hon Schlrs Soc 88; Muncpl Swm Tm 89; Georgetown Univ Hosp Vol Awd 87; Athl Schlr Awd 89; BA; Frnch/Chem.

**TANGREDI, LOUISE M,** Mount Saint Mary Coll, Newburgh, NY; SO; BS; Phoneathon 90; Special Olympcs 89; Tour Gldng 89; Beta Beta Beta; Nrsng; Nurse Practnr.

**TANGUAY, DONNA G,** Coll Misericordia, Dallas, PA; FR; BS; Biology Club 90-; US Marine Corps; Biology; Optometry Dr.

**TANI, JILL C,** Central Fl Comm Coll, Ocala, FL; SO; AA; ACRE Proj 90-; Peer Advsry Comm 90-; Phi Theta Kappa Asst Mrshl; Psychlgy; Chld Psychlgst.

**TANIS, PATRICIA J,** Georgian Court Coll, Lakewood, NJ; SR; BA; Stdnt Snt Ocean Cty Clg 88-89; Phi Theta Kappa Sec 88-89; Sgm Tau Dlt 90-; Cmncmnt Spkr Ocean Cty Clg 89; Laverne Weigold Mem Awrd 89; Deans List 87-; Soc Dir Sonata Bay Clb 90-91; AA Ocean Cnty Clg 89; Engl; Engl Tchr.

**TANKERSLEY, HOUSTON PAUL,** Tri County Tech Coll, Pendleton, SC; FR; AS; Phi Theta Kappa; Elec Eng Tech.

**TANKERSLEY, JULIA E,** Fl St Univ, Tallahassee, FL; JR; BA; Beta Gamma Sigma VP; Phi Kappa Phi; Phi Eta Sigma 88-; Mktg Resrch; Tchr.

**TANKSLEY, CHRISTIAN,** Jackson St Univ, Jackson, MS; FR; BS; Ed; Tch.

**TANN, TABITHA A,** Norfolk St Univ, Norfolk, VA; FR; BA; Engl Frgn Lnguage Clb 90; Sigma Tau Delta; Spartan Alpha Tau; Engl; Secondary Ed.

**TANNER, ANGELA T,** Greenville Tech Coll, Greenville, SC; SO; BS; Org Psychlgst.

**TANNER, ELIZABETH A,** Univ Of Tn At Martin, Martin, TN; SR; BED; Cllg Dmcrts VP 88-; Stdnt TN Edctn Assn 90-; Stdnt Gvrnmnt Comm 87-; Alpha Omicron Pi VP Pldg Edctr 87-; Theater Grp 90-; Unv Srvc Awd; Sister Smstr 90; IM Vllybl 89-; Elem Edctn; Law.

**TANNER, ELIZABETH A,** Abraham Baldwin Agri Coll, Tifton, GA; SO; BA; Hstry; Sec Educ.

**TANNER, GLENN R,** Univ Of Tn At Martin, Martin, TN; SR; BA; Phi Mu Alpha Sinfonia Pres 82-87; Cmnctns/Music; Wrtr/Mscn.

**TANNER, JOHN A,** S U N Y Coll Of Tech At Frmgdl, Farmingdale, NY; GD; AAS; Suprvsr Prodctn Cntrl Taytheon Electromagnetic Sys Div 83-; Bus Admn; Fin/Securities.

**TANNER, JULIE M,** Univ Of Ga, Athens, GA; JR; AB; Bapt Stdnt Union 88-90; Broad Acres Hsg Proj Chldrns Mnstry; Mission Trip Savannah 90; Easter Seals Vol 90; IM Ftbl/Sftbl/Vlybl; Engl; Cmnctns.

**TANNER, ROBIN J,** Univ Of Sc At Sumter, Sumter, SC; FR; BS; Pres Hnr Rl 90-; Dean Lst 90; Prdctn Bendix 87-; Accntng.

**TANNER, SABRINA K,** Alcorn St Univ, Lorman, MS; SO; Mrchng Band Gldn Girl Majorette 89-; Deans List 89-90; Engl Ed.

**TANNER, SARAH A,** Saint John Fisher Coll, Rochester, NY; SO; BA; Cmps Mnstry Intrnl Coord 89-; Spanish Clb 90-; Alpha Mu Gamma; Spanish; Scndry Educ.

**TANNER, STEVEN K,** Longwood Coll, Farmville, VA; SO; BA; Phi Beta Lambda 90-; Alpha Lambda Delta 90-; Bus.

**TANNER, STEVEN L,** Middle Tn St Univ, Murfreesboro, TN; JR; BA; Acctng Mgrl Acctng.

**TANNER, TOMEKA LA V,** Alcorn St Univ, Lorman, MS; FR; Acctg; CPA.

**TANNOUSE, EDWARD B,** Univ Of Rochester, Rochester, NY; JR; BA; Pre-Law Soc 89-90; Wrestling Clb 89-90; Radio 88-89; Delta Upsilon Pres 89-; Wash DC Intern Rep Eliot L Engel; Oxford England Ctr Medieval/Renaissance Studies 90; Pol Sci; Law.

**TANSEY, JEAN M,** Cornell Univ Statutory College, Ithaca, NY; SO; BS; Red Crpt Scty 90; Alpha Omicron Pi 90-; IMS 90; Ed; Acctg.

**TANSIL JR, THOMAS A,** Univ Of Tn At Martin, Martin, TN; JR; BS; Phi Alpha Delta 90-; Phi Theta Kappa 88-; Gvnrs Offc Intshp; Natl Almni Schlp 90-; Bsbl Capt 88-90; AS Dyersburg St Comm Clg 90; Crmnl Jstc; Law.

**TANSKI, TONIMARIE,** Wagner Coll, Staten Island, NY; JR; Pnhllnc Cncl; Alethea; Alpha Delta Pi Pldg Educ VP; Elem Ed; Edctr.

**TANTALO, MONICA L,** Duquesne Univ, Pittsburgh, PA; SR; Own Oper Maid To Ordr Entrp; Exec Sec Law Bradfrd Bsns Sch 80-81; Bsns/Mrktng.

**TANTLINGER, ANN,** Wv Univ, Morgantown, WV; JR; BS; Am Chem Soc 89-90; Am Pharm Assn 90-; Gldn Ky 89-; Hon Lst 88-90; Rho Chi Rcgntn Certf 90-; Pharm.

**TANTUM, STACY L,** Tufts Univ, Medford, MA; FR; BSE; Symph Bnd 90-; Engrg/Econ; Engrg.

**TAO, CHANG CHUN,** City Univ Of Ny Med Evers Coll, Brooklyn, NY; SR; Asian Clb Medgar Evers Clge Cuny 90-; Actvts Asian Cltrl Fstvl Mec/Cuny 90-; Hnrs Pgm Mec Hgh Acdmc Achvrs 90-; Acctng Clb 90-; Trng Pgm Srvng Tr Math/Actng/Fnce 89-90; Hnrs Grntd Mec Acdmc Exclnc 90-; Acctng; CPA.

**TAPLEY, HEATHER L,** Valdosta St Coll, Valdosta, GA; SR; MA; Wrtrs Blue 89-; Sigma Alpha Chi 87; Sigma Tau Delta 90-; Martha Mc Kay Awd; Grad Asstshp; Engl; Prof.

**TAPPLY, MELANIE J,** Smith Coll, Northampton, MA; FR; BA; Dance; Dance/Deaf Educ; Tch.

**TAPSCOTT, DONETTA R,** Morgan St Univ, Baltimore, MD; FR; BS; Tutoring 90; Teen Challenge Cnslng 89-90; Elegance Mdlng Club 89-90; Natl Hnr Soc 90; Grant-Brett Promethean Kappa Tau; Phi Eta Sigma; Alpha Lambda Delta; Clinton Teen Club 87; Acdmc Exclnc Awd 87-; Dist Schlr 90; Full Acdmc Schlrshp 90; Bus; Entreprenuer.

**TAPSCOTT, HUNTER HILTON,** Daytona Beach Comm Coll, Daytona Beach, FL; SR; AS; Pres Lst 89-; Deans Lst 89-; Phtgrphy; Phtgrphc Artst.

**TAR JR, PAUL,** Sacred Heart Univ, Fairfield, CT; FR; BA; Karate Clb; Chpl Sngrs; Yrbk Phtgrphr; Usher Schl Chpl; Math; Educ.

**TARAGIN, KEVIN E,** Yeshiva Univ, New York, NY; SR; BA; Class Rep; YUSSR; Engl Hnr Soc; Philos Soc; NCSY; Fencing Tm; Sci.

**TARANTINO, CYNTHIA A,** Bryant Stratton Bus Inst Roch, Rochester, NY; GD; Fash Mrchndsng Mgmt Clb VP 90-; Stdnt Govt; AOS; Fashion Merchndsng.

**TARANTINO, MARIA LUISA,** Fordham Univ, Bronx, NY; SR; BS; Psy Clb 89-; Psi Chi 88-; Rsrch Asst 90-; Albert Einstein Clg Intern 89-F; Psy; Psychometrician.**

**TARANTO, ALISA R,** Dowling Coll, Oakdale Li, NY; SR; BA; Spec Ed; Tchr.

**TARANTO, BRENDA K,** Univ Of Southern Ms, Hattiesburg, MS; JR; BS; Psy.

**TARASZKIEWICZ, TAMMARA A,** Le Moyne Coll, Syracuse, NY; FR; MBA; Radio Sta Prdctn 90-; Prjcts In Comm Intrntl Hse 90-; Spnsh Bus Admin; Law Mgmt.

**TARAVELLA, JENNIFER A,** Johnson St Coll, Johnson, VT; SO; BA; Dns Lst 89-90; Pres Lst; Art Ed; Phtgrphy Tchr.

**TARBET, TIMOTHY B,** Kent St Univ Kent Cmps, Kent, OH; SR; BBA; Natl Speleological Socty 90-; Kent State Alpine Ski Tm 88-; Cmptr Sci; Bus Info Systs.

**TARBOX, MARC A,** Me Maritime Academy, Castine, ME; JR; BS; Rcqtbl/Tnns Clb 88-; Wghtlftng 88-; Amer Soc Nvl Engrs; Cdt Shpng Awd 90; Rgmntl Cmmdnts Awd 88; Sys Engr.

**TARCZY, JANET M,** Edinboro Univ Of Pa, Edinboro, PA; GD; Phi Eta Sigma 86-87; Intern DA Ofc 89; Edinboro At Oxford Pgm/Schlrshp 89; Univ Hnrs Pgm 86-90; BA 90; Crmnl Justice; Law Schl.**

**TARDIF, ROBERT G,** Fl International Univ, Miami, FL; SR; MBA; Phi Lambda; Amer Mrktng Assn; Dean Lst; Grad Hnrs; Mrktng Bus; Prfssr Mrktng.

**TARGOS, PETER J,** Manhattan Coll, Bronx, NY; SO; BS; Coll Radio DJ 89-; MC Plyrs; ASME; Vygrs Clb; SAE 90-; De La Salle Hon Soc 89-; Cir K 89-; IMS 89-; Mech Eng.

**TARPLEY, REGINA D,** Truett Mc Connell Coll, Cleveland, GA; JR; MBS; Prod Coord Prsnnl 79-; AS Truett Mccnnll 90; AA; Educ/Bsn.

**TARR, GLEN C,** Hillsborough Comm Coll, Tampa, FL; SO; AS; Radiolgy Clb 89-; Hon Grad; US Air Force 80-88; Radilgc Technlgy.

**TARR, NATALIE A,** Allegheny Coll, Meadville, PA; SR; Amnesty Intl 88-89; Alden Schlr 89-; Alliance Francaise 87; First Aid CPR Am Red Cross; Medical Anthropology.

**TARRANCE, KAREN G,** Al A & M Univ, Normal, AL; SO; BA; Acctg; CPA.

**TARRANCE, KRISTI R,** Univ Of Ky, Lexington, KY; SR; BS; Lambda Kappa Sigma; Amer Phrmcsts Assoc; Phi Eta Sigma 88; Beta Beta Beta 89; Lambda Deans Lst 87-90; Pres Schlr 89-90; Phrmcy.

**TARRANT, TIMOTHY L,** Memphis St Univ, Memphis, TN; JR; BA; Intrntl Rel.

**TARTA, HEATHER A,** Radford Univ, Radford, VA; JR; BS; Intl Clb 89-90; Stdnt Ed Assc 90-; Early/Middle Ed; Tchng.

**TARTER, DAVID L,** Marshall University, Huntington, WV; SR; Acctg Clb W V Soc CPAS; Intrnshp Smart Grp; Acctg; CPA.

**TARTER, KENNETH W,** Abraham Baldwin Agri Coll, Tifton, GA; SO; AA; BS Troy State Univ 76; MED Valdosta State Clg 81; Turf Mgmt; Golf Sprntdnt.

**TARTERA, CHRISTINA T,** Villanova Univ, Villanova, PA; SO; BA; Special Olympcs 89-90; Prjct Sunshine 89-; Alpha Phi 89-; Pltcl Science; Law.

**TARTICK, JOHN M,** Hilbert Coll, Hamburg, NY; SR; ASA; Alpha Beta Gamma 90; Phi Beta Lmbd 90; ASA; Bus Admn; Mgmt.

**TARTT, DEXTER R,** Talladega Coll, Talladega, AL; SR; Pre Almni 87-; SGA Sntr 90-; Dns Lst; All Amer Schlr; Omega Psi Phi; NAACP; UNCF; Prmte Mnrty Enrllmnt In Grad Schl Ntre Dm Univ 90; Hrzns Abrn Univ; IM Ftbl; BA; Hstry; Law.

**TARTT, REBECCA C,** Ms St Univ, Miss State, MS; JR; BA; Gamma Beta Phi; Phi Theta Kappa; Pres Schlr 89-90; Educ Psych; Cnslng.

**TARVER, CANDY M,** Univ Of Southern Ms, Hattiesburg, MS; JR; MBA; Stdnt Govt VP 88-90; Yrbk Stff Edtr 87-; Stdnts Agnst Drnk Drvng Pres 90-; Phi Theta Kappa Pres 89-; Mu Alpha Theta Sntr 88-90; Delta Sigma Pi 90-; Alpha Beta Gamma VP 89-90; Golden Key Awd 89-90; Mst Otsdng Yng Wom/Amer 90-; Bus Admin/Mgmnt Info Syst.

**TARVER, CASSANDRA DENISE,** Al A & M Univ, Normal, AL; SO; BS; NAACP 90-; Drg Tsk Frce 90-; Deans Lst 89-; Comp Sci; Comp Prog.

**TARVER, CHAUN L,** Christopher Newport Coll, Newport News, VA; SO; BS; Dntl/Hygntst Asst; Dntl Hygn.

**TASCH, ELISA K,** William Carey Coll, Hattiesburg, MS; SR; BS; Stdnt Govt Chf Jstc 90-; Rsdnt Asst 90-; Athltc Comm Stdnt Repr 89-90; Omicron Delta Kappa 90-; Gamma Chi 89-; Schlr Athltc Awd; Tns 89-; Acctg/Bsn Mgmt; CPA.

**TASHLIK, SCOTT J,** Alfred Univ, Alfred, NY; SR; BS; AMA VP Cmnctns 88-; IM Sprts Capt 87-; Bus; Mktg.

**TASKER, MELANIE K,** Garrett Comm Coll, Mchenry, MD; FR; AA; Business Administration; Accounting.

**TASKER, ROBBIN A,** West Liberty St Coll, West Liberty, WV; SO; BA; Rep Schl Paper 90; Cmnctns; Pblc Rltns.

**TASSEY, AMY P,** Univ Of Tn At Martin, Martin, TN; SR; BS; Psych Clb; Drm Hl Assoc; Spcl Olympcs; Alpha Omicron Pi; Haury/Smith Adopt A Schlr Schlrshp; Chnclrs Hnr Rl; Deans Lst; Psych; Cnslg.

**TASSINARI, CAPRICE ANNA,** Fl International Univ, Miami, FL; GD; BA; Hosp Mgmnt.

**TATCH, MEREDITH N,** Valdosta St Coll, Valdosta, GA; SO; BSN; Prnts Anonymous Spnsr 84-85; Nrsng; Healing.

**TATE, BERNADETTE D,** Dekalb Coll, Decatur, GA; SO; BS; Gvt Assc Sec Treas 90-; Stu Crt Jstc 89-; Nwsppr Rprtr 89-90; Phi Theta Kappa 90-; Hstry Pol Sci Awrd 89-90; Psychlgy Awrd 90-; Otstndng Mnrty Stu Rstr 90-; AA Fshn Inst 86; Educ; Lbrrn/Lib Sci.

**TATE, DANA D,** Ga Southern Univ, Statesboro, GA; JR; BS; FHA 88-; Gamma Beta Phi 90-; Phi Theta Kappa 90-; Bapt Stdnt Un 88-; Top 15% Cls 90-; AS S Georgia Clg 90; Early Chldhd Educ; Tch.**

**TATE, DELOISE,** Alcorn St Univ, Lorman, MS; JR; BS; Econ Clb 89-90; Soc Sci Soc Pres 90-; Alpha Kappa Mu; Pres Schlr; Soc Sci Awrd; Econ; Hmn Rsrce Mgmt.

**TATE, ERROL H,** Univ Of Miami, Coral Gables, FL; FR; MBA; Fnce/Mktg; Cnsltnt.

**TATE, GRACE H I,** Jackson St Univ, Jackson, MS; FR; BA; Alpha Lambda Delta Pres; Acctg; Corp Law.

**TATE JR, JAMES D,** Univ Of West Fl, Pensacola, FL; GD; BS; Scuba Clb 90; Alpha Sigma Lambda; Otstndng Stu Elec Eng Tech; AS 87; Elect Eng Tech; Eng.

**TATE, JAMILA T,** Fl A & M Univ, Tallahassee, FL; FR; Engl Lit; Educ.

**TATE, JEFFREY W,** Univ Of Fl, Gainesville, FL; JR; BA; Phi Theta Kappa Pres 89-90; Tau Beta Pi; Bapt Cmpus Ministries; Stdnt Govt Assoc/Inter Varsity Senator 89-90; Tau Beta Pi; Phi Theta Kappa; Youth Agnst Cncr/Beta Clb/Amer Inst Chem Engrs; Summa Cum Laude; Schlrshp Awd; Chem Engr.

**TATE, JERONA N,** Univ Of Sc At Columbia, Columbia, SC; FR; BS; Chem Engr.

**TATE, LEE M,** Univ Of Nc At Greensboro, Greensboro, NC; SR; BS; Cmmtng Stdnts Assn 88-90; Cum Laude; AS Sandhills Comm Coll 88; Elem Educ; Tchr.

**TATE, MARTHA JANELL,** Mobile Coll, Mobile, AL; SR; BS; SLATE; Biol; Tchr.

**TATE, MARY KATHERINE,** Bridgewater Coll, Bridgewater, VA; JR; BS; Mu Epsilon Mu 90-; Stdnt Gov 90-; Lab Asst; Dns Lst 88-; Im Sprts; Elem/Sec Educ; Tch.

**TATE, MAYANNA L,** Rust Coll, Holly Springs, MS; SO; Pre Med Clb/Math/Sci 89-; Tennis 89-; Alpha Kappa Mu; Delta Sigma Theta; Chem; Sci Tchr.

**TATE, MELISSA A,** Univ Of Nc At Greensboro, Greensboro, NC; SO; BS; Aerobics 89; Elem Ed 2nd Mjr Cmmnctn; Tchr.

**TATE, SHERRI A,** East Tn St Univ, Johnson City, TN; SO; Hall Assn V P 90-; Clg Reps; Tau Kappa Epsilon Aux; IM Ftbl/Sftbl Capt 90-; Hstry; Profsr.

**TATE, TAMMY L,** Union Coll, Barbourville, KY; JR; BA; Gamma Beta Phi 84-86; Iota Sigma Nu 86-; Top 10 Prcnt Acas Schlrshp 83-84; Deans Lt 84-; Clrk-Typst 82-87; Bus Admin/Cmptr Sci Mktg; Advrtsng.

**TATE, TERRY L,** Livingston Univ, Livingston, AL; SR; BA; Bsbl Tm 89-; Pi Kappa Phi 89-; AA Patrick Henry Jr Clg 87-89; Soc Sci Cmprhnsve; Admn.

**TATEM, BARBARA E,** Commonwealth Coll, Virginia Beach, VA; SR; AS; Lgl Ofc Admn; Lgl Sec/Paralgl.

**TATEOSSIAN-ZORTIAN, BRUNO J,** Pellissippi St Tech Comm Coll, Knoxville, TN; FR; BS; Bptst Stdnt Un 90-; Chrmn Chrstn Grwth; Bus; Intl Bus.

**TATTERSON, KATHRYN A,** Mary Baldwin Coll, Staunton, VA; JR; BA; Otdr Prsts Cmmtt 90-; Ltrry Mag Art Ed; Hnrs Schlrs Scty 90-; Elzbth Nttnghm Hnr Sctyulyss Dsprts Awrd 90-; Tchng Asst; Artst.

**TATTO, MARC S,** Manhattan Coll, Bronx, NY; FR; BS; Elect Eng; Eng.

**TATUM, CANDICE C,** Polk Comm Coll, Winter Haven, FL; SO; PHD; CAVE Clb Fund Rsrs; Tubrial Serv; Entertainment 89-; Phi Theta Kappa 90-; Talent Roster Cert Achvmnt; Minerva Achvmt Awd Cert Merit; Phi Theta Kappa Cert; AA; Phrmcy.

**TATUM, KWAME I,** Lincoln Univ, Lincoln Univ, PA; SO; Big Bros/Str Org 90-; Educ Clb 89-; Speech/Japanese Clb 89-90; Gen Hnrs Prog 90-; Elem Schl Teacher.

**TATUM III, LUCIAN L,** Southern Coll Of Tech, Marietta, GA; FR; BARCH; Phi Kappa Phi 87-88; BA Georgia State Univ 87; AA Gordon Junior Clg 81; Architecture.

**TATUM, STEVEN D,** Radford Univ, Radford, VA; SO; MS; Stdnt Life 89-90; Hse Cncl 89-90; Psychlgy Clb 90-; Clin Psychlgy.

**TAUB, ERIC W,** Allegheny Coll, Meadville, PA; SR; Stdnt Arts Soc 89-; Ice Hockey Clb Tm 88-90; Delta Tau Delta Rush Chrmn 87-; Doane Prize Art Hstry Hnrbl Mntn; Aldn Schlr 89-90; Vrsty Tns 88-89; BA; Art Hstry; Advrtsng.

**TAULBEE, MICHELE A,** Oh Univ, Athens, OH; SO; AAS; Dmcrats 90-; Outstndng Grad Tchng Asst Awrd; Phi Sigma Sigma 90-; Bg Brthrs/Bg Sistrs 90-; Gymnstcs Instrctr 90-; Nrsng; RN.

**TAURMAN, RALPH L,** Syracuse Univ, Syracuse, NY; SO; BA; Delta Kappa Epsilon Pres 90; Acctg; CPA MBA Conslt.**

**TAURO, LORI ANN,** Univ Of Akron, Akron, OH; GD; JD; Pre Law Scty; Stdnt Bar Assn; Harry S Truman Schlrshp; Comp Achvmnt Awrd 87; Gldn Ky 89-; Clarence P Gould Hnr Scty 89-; Hnrs Dgree Prog; Hnrs Smnr Prog 86; Phi Kappa Phi 89-; Summa Cum Laude 90; Dns Lst; BA Youngstown St Univ 90; Law.

**TAUSON, CATHERINE J,** Providence Coll, Providence, RI; SR; RIC Ltrcy Prgrm 88-89; Intern Chldrns Friend Serv 89-90; Athltc Trnr Stu 87-; BA; Soc Wrk; Educ Hearing Imprd.

**TAVARES, GLYNIS A,** Univ Of Miami, Coral Gables, FL; SR; BA; Carbbn Stdnt Assc Vp 89-90; Org Fr Jmcn Unty; Mrktg Clb; Strctly Bus Prof Grp; Almn Mntr Prog; Bus Schl Fr Peer Cnslr; Strctly Bus Intrnshp Wth UM Bus Srvcs Dpt; Paine Webber Intrnshp; Intl Mkt.

**TAVARES, JOSE R,** City Univ Of Ny Hostos Coll, Bronx, NY; JR; AAS; Dominican Stdnt Assn 90-; Hostos Sftbl Clb 89-; Hostos Bsktbl Clb 90-; Cert Talent Roster Outstndg Mnrty Comm Coll Grad 90-; Sftbl/Bsktbl/Soccer/Ping Pong/Vlybl; Bus; Acctg.

**TAVAREZ, MARIA M,** City Univ Of Ny City Coll, New York, NY; GD; BA; WHCR Fm Nws Prgrm; Pckr Flm Fest Promo Dir 88-90; Lehbar-Friedman Inc Promo Asst 89; Cmmnctns; Ad/Brdcstng.

**TAVEL, CARMEN M,** Fl International Univ, Miami, FL; SR; BHSA; Bus; Admn.

**TAVIO, NOEL K,** Univ Of Miami, Coral Gables, FL; JR; BA; Radio Disc Jcky 89-; TABS Pgrm Trnsfr Advsr 89-; Dns Mstrs Tutor Pgrm Tutor 90-; Gldn Ky; Dns Lst 88-; Provost Hnr Rl 90-; Economics/Pol Sci/Ltn Amer Stud; Law.**

**TAYLOR REID, MARSHA LOUISE,** Oh Univ-Southern Cmps, Ironton, OH; JR; BED; Civic Club 89; Ironton African-Amer Hstry Comm 89; Tutor Mntr Pgm 90; Gamma Pi Delta 90; Golden Keys; Process/Utlities Oper 76-84; Cnctrtn Engl; Elem Educ.

**TAYLOR, ADAM F,** S U N Y Coll Of Tech At Alfred, Alfred, NY; FR; Sigma Tau Epsilon; O Vanderlinde Schlrhsp Awrd; Hvy Eqpmnt Trck And Dsl; Ownr Mgr.

**TAYLOR, ALAN A,** Fl International Univ, Miami, FL; SR; BA; Sntr Bob Grahams Off Intrn 90; Pltcl Sci.

**TAYLOR, ALLINIECE G,** Fl A & M Univ, Tallahassee, FL; FR; BA; Vlybl Clb 90; Tns Clb 90; Gannett Fndtn Schlrshp 90-92; Maya Angelou Awd 90-; Hostess Clb Sea Wa Schlrshp 90-; Radio Brdcstr WAMF 90-; Brdcst Jrnlsm.

**TAYLOR, ALVA DOUGLAS,** Eastern Ky Univ, Richmond, KY; FR; BED; Agri Bsns; Bsns Admn.

**TAYLOR, AMANDA A,** Saint John Fisher Coll, Rochester, NY; SO; BS; Chmstry Clb 90-; Circle K 90-; Biology/Psychlgy; Medicine.

**TAYLOR, AMY L,** Univ Of Southern Ms, Hattiesburg, MS; JR; BS; Prlgl Soc 90-; Achvmnt Awd Schlrshp; Prlgl Stds.

**TAYLOR, ANGELA D,** Univ Of Ky, Lexington, KY; SR; BA; Deans List 90-; Victory Chrstn Ch Diciples Of Christ Dir Of Edn; Deaconess 88-; Elem Ed; Tgeach.

**TAYLOR, ANGELA M,** Meridian Comm Coll, Meridian, MS; VICA 88-; Stdt Dental Hygienist Assoc 88-; Hu Friedy Golden Scaler Awd 90; Amer Dntl Hygienist Assoc 90-; Prctng Dntl Hygienist 90-; AA Meridian Comm Clg 90; Dental Hygiene; Education.

**TAYLOR, ANGELA P,** Univ Of Southern Ms, Hattiesburg, MS; FR; BA; Thertc Mnstry Schl; Nrsng.

**TAYLOR JR, BARNEY ANTONIO,** Norfolk St Univ, Norfolk, VA; SR; BSCS; ACM Team Capt; Math Assn Amer; Spartan Alpha Tau; Alpha Kappa Mu; Natl Tech Symposium Author; Acad Achvmnt Award; All Amer Schlr; Cmptr Sci; Grphcs Engr.

**TAYLOR, BRADMAN W,** Fl Atlantic Univ, Boca Raton, FL; SO; BA; Fencing Sec 90-; Frshmn Hnr Soc 89-90; Intl Bus; Bus.

**TAYLOR, BRENDA ROBERTS,** Ms Univ For Women, Columbus, MS; JR; BS; Bskbl Hosts Auburn Univ 86-87; Deans Lst 85-86; Pres Lst 90-; Kappa Delta Epsilon; Delta Zeta Sor 86-87; OWC Schlrshp; Harvest Bible Church Tchr; Flight Attndt 88-90; Elem Educ; Trhcr.

**TAYLOR, CARMEN J,** Wilberforce Univ, Wilberforce, OH; SO; Chldrns Choir-Dir; Scl Wrk-Sclgy.

**TAYLOR, CAROL L,** Averett Coll, Danville, VA; SR; BS; BACCHUS Pres 89-; Stdnt Fndtn Cmte Chrmn 90-; Singers Sec 87-; Alpha Chi; Intrnshp; Sftbl; Soc/Psych /Law; Crim Justice.

**TAYLOR, CHARLA J,** Dyersburg St Comm Coll, Dyersburg, TN; SO; ASSOC; Phi Theta Kappa; Delta Zeta Memphis St Univ Art Chrmn 88-89; Otstndng Econ Stdnt; Bsns Rel Tech/Mrktng; Bsns.

**TAYLOR, CHARLES D,** Univ Of Sc At Columbia, Columbia, SC; JR; BED; Elem Educ; Teacher.

**TAYLOR, CHENZIRA N,** Wilberforce Univ, Wilberforce, OH; FR; Busn Prof Amer Pres 87-90; Youth NAACP Secty 87-; Student Govt Assoc 90-; Natl Jr Hnr Soc 87-89; Kappa Alpha Psi Sweetheart 90-; Hnry Del Teen 88-; Busn Computer Infor Sys.

**TAYLOR, CHERYL L,** Georgetown Univ, Washington, DC; SR; Gospel Choir Dir 87-; Beta Gamma Sigma 90-; Beta Gamma Sigma Schlrshp 90-; Inroads Intrnshp 88-; Arthur Andersen Alumni Schlrshp 88-; Acctng.

**TAYLOR, CHRISTINA M,** Middle Tn St Univ, Murfreesboro, TN; JR; BA; Soc Crtv Anchrnsm UT Knoxville 75-78; Cir Plyrs Nashville TN 80-; Mddl TN Athro Soc; Gamma Phi Beta UT Knoxville Plg Chr 75-; Hmbldrs Assn Nashville TN 89-90; Amer Inst Bldg Dsgn 90-; Hm Dsgn 80-; Anthro-Arch Emphsis; Coll Prof.

**TAYLOR, CHRISTOPHER L,** Univ Of North Fl, Jacksonville, FL; JR; BS; Amer Assn Fr Rsprtry Care 76-; Peds Lng Com FL Lng Assn 85-; Advsry Brd FL Jr Coll Rsprty Thrpy 85-; AS Jefferson St Junior Coll 76; Hlth Admin.

**TAYLOR, CHRISTOPHER S,** Castleton St Coll, Castleton, VT; SO; BA; Stdnt Assc Senator; Phi Eta Sigma VP; Sherburne Vlntr Fire Depart 88; Haskell Hall Council 90; Mathematics; Bsn.

**TAYLOR, CHRISTYANNA JANE,** Northwest Al Comm Coll, Phil Campbell, AL; GD; AAT; Phi Theta Kappa; Comp Info Sys; Comp Pgrmr.

**TAYLOR, CINDY L,** Norfolk St Univ, Norfolk, VA; SR; BA; Sigma Tau Delta 90-; Hnr Rll 89-; Engl; Tchr.

**TAYLOR, CLAIRE D,** Hudson Valley Comm Coll, Troy, NY; FR; ASN; First Presby Chrch 90-; Nursing.

**TAYLOR IV, CLARENCE O,** Univ Of Ga, Athens, GA; SR; BSED; Mt Ordr Colombo 89-90; Tae Kwon Do Clb 90-; BSA 84-90; Indpdnt Rsrch Psychlgy; Educ Psychlgy; Envrnmtl Law.

**TAYLOR, DANIEL E,** Univ Of Fl, Gainesville, FL; SR; BM; Renaissance Ensmbl 87-; Phi Kappa Phi 90-; Alachua Co Schl Vol 85-; Artist Sch 90-; AA Santa Fe Comm Coll 88; Music Hist/Lit; Instrmnt Fabrication/Restor.

**TAYLOR, DANIELLE R,** S U N Y Coll Of A & T Morrisvl, Morrisville, NY; FR; BS; Cnsrvtn Clb 90-; Lbrl Arts.

**TAYLOR, DAVID M,** Old Dominion Univ, Norfolk, VA; SO; BS; Acdmc Hnrs Pro 89-; Mech Engr.

**TAYLOR, DAWN J,** Norfolk St Univ, Norfolk, VA; JR; BA; Pblc Rltns Stdnt Soc Amrca Vp 89-; Deans Lst 90-; Cln Cmnty Cmsn Vol 89-; Chldrns Hsptl Kngs Dghtrs Tlthn Vol 89-90; Sals Assit Mrl Lynch 81-86; Sub Tchr Va Bch Schl Dstrct 90-; Jrnlsm; Envrnmntl Pblc Rltns.

**TAYLOR, DAWN S,** Valdosta St Coll, Valdosta, GA; JR; BSN; Beta Beta Beta; Frrst St Untd Mthdst Chrch Trstee 90; Untd Mthdst Wmn Prsdnt 90-; AB Wslyn Clg 78; Nrsng.

**TAYLOR, DEBBIE J,** Anson Comm Coll, Ansonville, NC; SO; BED; NAACP Estrn Star 82-; Daughter Of Isis; Elem Eductnl Cnslr; Engl; Educ.

**TAYLOR, DEBORAH L,** Univ Of Ga, Athens, GA; SR; BSW; Soc Work Club 89-; Athens Comm Cncl On Aging Intrnshp Ctrl St Hosp; Soccer 86-88; Soc Work Gerontology.

**TAYLOR, DELPHIA,** Univ Of Sc At Salkehatchie, Allendale, SC; JR; BA; Psychlgy; Cnslr.

**TAYLOR, DEVERY L,** Univ Of Nc At Asheville, Asheville, NC; SR; BS; Data Proc Mngmnt Assoc 87-; Intl Stdnt Assoc VP 88-; Scty Advncmnt Mngmnt Sec 90-; Outstndng Ldrshp Achvmnts ISA 88-; Outstndng Work And Achievement 89-90; Baptist Stdnt Union Teacher Kids 89-; Big Prog Troubled Kids Teacher 89-90; Computer Sci; Systems Analyst.

**TAYLOR, DEXTER M,** Va Commonwealth Univ, Richmond, VA; JR; BS; Afro-Am Schol Prog Arts Cmte 90-; Newspr Graphic Asst 89-; Psi Chi 90-; Golden Key; Psychlgy; Indus Psychlgst.

**TAYLOR, DON T,** Nova Univ, Ft Lauderdale, FL; GD; MBA; Amer Mrktng Assoc; Mngr Prod Dev Serv Inc; BIA Genl Motors Inst 78; Mrktng.

**TAYLOR, DONNA C,** Univ Of Southern Ms, Hattiesburg, MS; JR; BS; Symp Wnd Ens 90; Phi Theta Kappa 89-90; Delta Psi Omega 89-90; Tau Beta Sigma 90; AA 90; Bio; Vet Med.

**TAYLOR, DONNA LEA,** Univ Of Sc At Columbia, Columbia, SC; SR; Hall Assoc 87-89; Towrs Cncl Pr 88-89; Hall Govt V P 89-90; Dns Lst 86; Otstdng Govt Offcr 89; Whitten Ctr Intrn 89-90; Yth Svcs Intrn 89; Batgirls 88; BAIS Univ S Car; Elem Educ; Tch.

**TAYLOR, DONNA S,** Spalding Univ, Louisville, KY; SR; NEA 90-; KEA 90-; Chrprsn-Boy Scts Amer 89-; Sub Tchr; BS Spalding Univ; Elem Ed K-4; Tch Pblc Schl Syst.

**TAYLOR, DOROTHY DENISE,** Faulkner Univ, Montgomery, AL; SR.

**TAYLOR, ELESIA R,** Univ Of Tn At Martin, Martin, TN; SO; Bus Admin/Admin Serv; Hosp Admnstrtr.

**TAYLOR, ELIZABETH L,** Univ Of Tn At Martin, Martin, TN; JR; BA; All American Schlrs; Stdnt TN Edctn Assn 90-; Alpha Omicron Pi 88-; Elem Educ; Grdte Schl.

**TAYLOR, ERIKA D,** Howard Univ, Washington, DC; FR; BS; Res Hl Adv Cncl 90-; Dorm Cncl Treas 90-; Res Hl Wk Schlstc Achvmnt 90-; Chld Psy.

**TAYLOR, EUNICE P,** Univ Of Miami, Coral Gables, FL; FR; BS; AFROTC GMC Advsr; Amer Scty Of Cvl Eng Treas; Eng Civil; AF Offcr Eng.

**TAYLOR, FELICIA C,** Univ Of Tn At Martin, Martin, TN; FR; BA; Econ/Fin; Fin Plnr.

**TAYLOR, FELICIA R,** Al A & M Univ, Normal, AL; FR; BED; Stdnt Drg Tsk Frc; Acctng.

**TAYLOR, GARRETT W,** Univ Of Cincinnati, Cincinnati, OH; SO; BA; Arch Engr.

**TAYLOR V, GEORGE P,** Univ Of Tn At Knoxville, Knoxville, TN; SO; BS; Waterski Clb; Exec Undergrads 90-; Alpha Lambda Delta 89-90; Gamma Reta Phi 90-; Laph Kappa Psi Rest Pldg; Hess Hl Repr 89-90; IM 89-; Finance; Planner.**

**TAYLOR, GERALD N,** Manhattan Coll, Bronx, NY; SR; BE; Soc Physics Stdnts Sec 89-; Eta Kappa Mu 89; Tau Beta Pi 90-; Epsilon Sigma Pi 89-; UFT Schlrshp Awd 87-; Elec Engr; Medicine.

**TAYLOR, GREGORY SCOT,** Milligan Coll, Milligan Clg, TN; JR; BSBA; Big Bro Ltl Bro Pgm 90-; Host 90-; Orntn Tm Ldr 90; Alph Omg 89-90; IM Bsktbl Sftbl Vlybl Ftbl 89-; Cmnctn Bus Cptr Sci.

**TAYLOR, HEATHER LANE,** Radford Univ, Radford, VA; SR; Stdt/Fclty Dvlpmt Com 90-; Sigma Theta Tau 90-; Vlntr Am Red Cross 88-.

**TAYLOR, J BRYCE,** Dartmouth Coll, Hanover, NH; FR; BA; Debate Tm; Fresh Crw Tm; Govt; Law.

**TAYLOR, JACQUELINE S,** James Sprunt Comm Coll, Kenansville, NC; FR; BA; Math; Tch.

**TAYLOR, JAMES D,** Univ Of Al At Birmingham, Birmingham, AL; SO; BA; Philosophy Clb Pres 90-; Philosophy; Ph D Teach Write.

**TAYLOR, JAMES J,** Barry Univ, Miami, FL; JR; BA; Ststcn Sprts Info Dept 90-; IM Ftbll; IM Bsktbll 88-; Cmmcntns; Pblc Rltns.

**TAYLOR JR, JAMES R,** Univ Of Sc At Columbia, Columbia, SC; SO; BA; Gamma Beta Phi; U S Marine Crps Corp 83-; Intl Affrs/Pol Sci; Forgn Serv.

**TAYLOR, JASON B,** Longwood Coll, Farmville, VA; SO; BS; Bio; Veterinarian.

**TAYLOR, JASON D,** Bowling Green St Univ At Huron, Huron, OH; FR; AS; Math.

**TAYLOR, JASON R,** Western Piedmont Comm Coll, Morganton, NC; FR; AS; Science; Nrsng.

**TAYLOR, JENNIFER A,** Southwest Va Comm Coll, Richlands, VA; SO; AAS; Sec Sci; Admin Asst.**

**TAYLOR, JENNIFER L,** Villanova Univ, Villanova, PA; JR; BA; Sailing Team 90-; French Club 88-; Pi Delta Phi 90-; Kappa Alpha Theta 90-; Political Science; Government.

**TAYLOR, JERRY L,** Fayetteville St Univ, Fayetteville, NC; SR; BS; Cumberland Hosp Of Fayetteville NC; Psychlgy; PH D Clin Psychlgy.

**TAYLOR, JESSICA D,** Tougaloo Coll, Tougaloo, MS; FR; BA; Alpha Lambda Delta Sec; Pol Sci; Law.

**TAYLOR, JOANN M,** Univ Of Cincinnati-Clrmnt Coll, Batavia, OH; SO; AAS; Natl Clg 90-; Bethel Tate Life Sqd; Police Explr 88; Crim Just/Pol Sci; Law Enfrcmnt.

**TAYLOR, JOANNE J,** Alcorn St Univ, Lorman, MS; SO; BA; Hon Stdnts Org 89-; Pre-Med/Bio; Pdtrcn.

**TAYLOR, JOHN B,** Auburn Univ At Montgomery, Montgomery, AL; JR; BS; Phi Theta Kappa 88-90 Mst Vlbl Mbr 90; Mu Alpha Theta 86; Sprts Rprtr Alexander City Outlook 89-90; AS Cntrl AL Comm Clg 90; Pre Law.**

**TAYLOR, JOHN P,** S U N Y Coll Of Tech At Alfred, Alfred, NY; JR; BT; Amer Soc Mech Engrs; AAS 90-; Mech Engr; Pilot Engr.**

**TAYLOR, JOHN W,** S U N Y At Buffalo, Buffalo, NY; SR; BS; Dean Lst; Elect Eng; Dsgn/Grad Schl.

**TAYLOR, JULIA G,** Roane St Comm Coll, Harriman, TN; FR; AAS; Bus Mgmnt Tech; Bnkng.

**TAYLOR, JULIA R,** Broward Comm Coll, Ft Lauderdale, FL; SO; AA; Liberal Arts; Pbl Serv.

**TAYLOR, JULIE R,** Lexington Comm Coll, Lexington, KY; FR; BED; Math; Elec Eng.

**TAYLOR, JULIE W,** Radford Univ, Radford, VA; JR; BA; Yearbook Staff 88-89; Stdnt Educ Assn 90-; Zeta Tau Alpha 2nd V P; IM Sorority 90-; Erly Educ; Tchng.

**TAYLOR, KARA B,** Wv Univ, Morgantown, WV; SO; BA; Amnsty Intl; Elder Care; Soc Wrk; MS Frnsc/Psych/Peace Crps.

**TAYLOR, KARA L,** Univ Of Sc At Columbia, Columbia, SC; JR; BFA; Italian Schlrshp 90-; Clairol Schlrshp Awd 90-; Prtcpnt In Mostra Exhib Cortona Italy 90-; Art Studio; Ceramist Artist.

**TAYLOR, KAREN M,** Christopher Newport Coll, Newport News, VA; SR; BS; Phi Theta Kappa 88-89; Alpha Chi 90-; Bus Dept Hnrs; Cum Laude; Summa Cum Laude 89; Brd Dirs Ltl League Plyr Agnt 88-; Fdrl Cvl Srvc GS 5 Trng Tech; AS Thomas Nelson Comm Clg 89; Mngmt; Govt Srvc.

**TAYLOR, KELLY L,** Univ Of Southern Ms, Hattiesburg, MS; JR; BS; Southern Christian Stdnt Ctr 89-; Stdnt Speech Hearing Assoc 90-; Stdnt Eagle Clb 90-; Speech Pathology.

**TAYLOR, KEVIN K,** Ms St Univ, Miss State, MS; JR; Natl Assoc Of Acctnts; Gamma Beta Phi 90-; Phi Eta Sigma 90-; Alpha Lambda Delta 90-; Acctng.

**TAYLOR, KEVIN T,** Univ Of Sc At Columbia, Columbia, SC; SR; MBA; Alpha Lambda Delta 87-; Phi Eta Sigma 87-; United Way Vol; BS; Business Administration; Professional.

**TAYLOR, KIMBERLY,** Al A & M Univ, Normal, AL; SR; BS; Univ Chr; Bapt Stdnt Un; Delta Mu Delta VP 90-; Alpha Kappa Alpha Phi 89-; Bus Mngmnt; Mngmnt.

**TAYLOR, KRISTIN D,** Marshall University, Huntington, WV; FR; BA; Lng/Spch Pthlgy.

**TAYLOR, LANCE A,** Univ Of Al At Huntsville, Huntsville, AL; JR; BS; Alpha Lmd Dlt 89; Huntsville Futlts Coop; Cvl Eng; Eng.

**TAYLOR, LANCE D,** Belmont Coll, Nashville, TN; JR; BS; Bapt Stdnt Un 88-; Gamma Beta Phi; Mngnl Intrnshp Super 88-; IM Bsktbllе; Hstry.

**TAYLOR, LAURA L,** Bowling Green St Univ At Huron, Huron, OH; SO; AS; Lib Stds/Art.

**TAYLOR, LEIGH A,** Hillsborough Comm Coll, Tampa, FL; SO; AA; Vlybl 90-; AA; Bsn Admin/Mgmt.

**TAYLOR, LEIGH A,** Livingston Univ, Livingston, AL; SR; BS; SG Sec 87-89; LU Envoy Hstss 87-89; Phi Eta Sigma 87-; Omicron Delta Kappa 89-; Alpha Sigma Tau Rsh Dir 90-; Res Asst 89-; Elem/Early Chldhd Ed; Educ MS.

**TAYLOR, LINDA G,** Univ Of Pittsburgh, Pittsburgh, PA; GD; MSN; Sigma Theta Tau; Grad Stdnt Asst Pitt 89-; Nrs Assc Sec/ Treas 86-; Amer Assc Crtcl Cre Nrs 84-; NRSG Dplma Sharon Gen Hsp Schl Nrsg 78; BSN Slippery Rock Univ 86; Nrsg Wth Educ Spclztn; Tch.

**TAYLOR, LINDA L,** Ringling School Of Art, Sarasota, FL; SR; BFA; Merit Award 90-; Soc Of Illustrtrs Show/Public Cation 90-; Best Of Artwrk 89-; Illustrtn.

**TAYLOR, LINDA M,** Mount Olive Coll, Mount Olive, NC; SR; BS; Phi Beta Lambda Treas 88-; Free Will Baptst Flwshp Pres 87-; Rsdnc Life Stf Resdnt Asst 89-; Clg Marshl 87-88; Ldr In Clg Hons Progrm 87-; Acctng; MS In Acctng/CPA.

**TAYLOR, LISA R,** Volunteer St Comm Coll, Gallatin, TN; SO; BS; CP 89; Elem Ed; Elem Schl Tchr.

**TAYLOR, LORI A,** Middle Tn St Univ, Murfreesboro, TN; SR; BA; Gamma Beta Phi; Bus; Bus Admin.

**TAYLOR, LUTAVIA A,** Livingston Univ, Livingston, AL; SO; BA; Stdnt Govt Frshmn Sntr 90-; Lvngstn Un Prog Bd 90-; Payrbk Asst Editor 90-; Panhellenic Cncl 90-; Phi Mu 90-; Orientation Ldr 90-; ; Im Sprts 90-; Acctng; CPA.

**TAYLOR, MABELINE,** Alcorn St Univ, Lorman, MS; SO; BA; Acctg Clb VP; NAACP 89-; Cmnty Vol Org Grp Ldr 89; Estrn Starlettes Matron 88-; Deans Lst Schlr 89-; Acctg/Bus; CPA.**

**TAYLOR, MALCOLM,** Fl A & M Univ, Tallahassee, FL; SR; BS; Grphc Dsgn Clb 89-90; Phi Theta Kappa Sec 87-89; Grphc Dsgn Intrn Nwspapr; US Marine Corps 82-86; AA Lake-Sumter Comm Coll 89; Grphc Dsgn; Art Dir/Art Ed.

**TAYLOR, MARCUS A,** Fl A & M Univ, Tallahassee, FL; SO; BA; Naval ROTC 89-; Naval Rifle/Pistol Tm; Semper Fl Soc 90; ROTC Awd Merit 90; Bsn Bronze Awd 89; Dns Lst 90; Econ; Bsn/Nvl Commission.

**TAYLOR, MARGARET E,** Univ Of Tn At Martin, Martin, TN; JR; PH D; SAACS 90-; SGA 88-89; Browning Hall Rsdnc Assn Pres 88-89; Alpha Gamma Rho Ltl Sis 90-; Alpha Omicron Pi Pldg Cls Socl Chrmn 88-; Arthritis Rsrch 88-; Vanager Nrsng Hm 88-90; Dns Lst 89-90; Ftbl Hostess 88-; Sci; Phrmcy.

**TAYLOR, MARIETTE F,** Nova Univ, Ft Lauderdale, FL; GD; DIBA; Swim Team; Ski Team; Fencing Team; Board Dir Chldrns Sci 86-; BS 85; Bs Physics Univ De Strasbourg; Intl Bsn; Mktg.

**TAYLOR, MARNIE LYNN,** Mary Baldwin Coll, Staunton, VA; SR; Baldwin Boosters 88-89; Lacrosse 87-88; Cross Cntry 89-90; House Pres 89-90; Natl Hnr Soc 87; Omicron Delta Epsilon 90; Wall Street Jrnl Bsn Award 90-; Mgmt/Trainee Intern JC Penney 90; Stdnt Assist Bsn Dept 88-; BA Acad Rl Est 91; Bsn Admin/ Mktg; Mktg/Cmnctns.

**TAYLOR, MARSHA L,** Fort Valley St Coll, Fort Valley, GA; JR; BS; Coop Dvlpmntl Energy Pgm 89-; Sci Clb VP 89-; Alpha Kappa Mu 90-; All Amer Schlr Clgt Awd; Zoology; Medicine.**

**TAYLOR, MARTHA L,** Univ Of Charleston, Charleston, WV; SO; ADN; LPN; Nursing; Oncology Nurse.

**TAYLOR, MARY K,** Middle Tn St Univ, Murfreesboro, TN; JR; BS; Tau Beta Pi 89-; Gldn Key 89-; Phi Eta Sigma 87-; Alpha Lambda Delta 87-; Inst Indstrl Eng 89-; Delta Gamma 87-; Coop Saturn Corp 90-; Almn Schlr 87-89; Indstrl Eng; Mfg Eng.

**TAYLOR, MAXINE B,** Abraham Baldwin Agri Coll, Tifton, GA; FR; ASN; Phi Theta Kappa; Pilot Clb Secr 89-; Cherokee Gdn Clb Pres 78-; Free-Lance Wrtr 74-79; Nrsg; RN Obstets.

**TAYLOR, MAXINE P,** Tn St Univ, Nashville, TN; SO; BA; Alpha Mu Gamma 89-; Tutor Nashville Vol Ltrcy Prog; Eng; Writing.

**TAYLOR, MELANIE J,** Daemen Coll, Amherst, NY; JR; BA; Hmn Svc Clb Sec 90; Crclm Slctn Cmt 90-; Deans List 90-; Bsktbl Tm 88-89; Soc Wrk.

**TAYLOR, MELISSA A,** Cumberland Coll, Williamsburg, KY; JR; BA; Yrbk Stf 90-; Frgn Lang Clb 90-; Phi Beta Lambda 90-; Phi Alpha Theta Sec 90-; Hstry/Poli Sci; Intrntl Rel.

**TAYLOR, MELISSA H,** Nc Central Univ, Durham, NC; GD; JD; Dns Lst 89-; Phi Delta Phi 89-; NC Dept Jstce Intrn 90; Bk Awrd 89; Law.

**TAYLOR, MELISSA L,** Hillsborough Comm Coll, Tampa, FL; FR; AA; Phi Theta Kappa; Mss Cmmnctns; Jrnlsm Brdcstng.

**TAYLOR, MERRITT K,** Univ Of Rochester, Rochester, NY; JR; BS; Soc Undergrd Bio Stdnts Bus Mgr 88-; Lit Mag Edtr 90-; Cmdy Mag Crtnst 90-; Frnds Strng Vol 89-90; Peace/Jstc Educ Comm 90-; Org W Afrcn Hlth 89-; Dekiewet Rsrch Flwshp; Nurosci; Med Clcl/Rscrch.

**TAYLOR, MICHAEL E,** Univ Of Sc At Columbia, Columbia, SC; JR; BS; Rugby Team 88-; Civil Engineering.

**TAYLOR, MICHELE D,** Howard Univ, Washington, DC; SR; JD; Charles Houston Pre-Law Soc 89-90; Stdnt Govt Soph Class Sec 88-90; Pltcl Sci Soc; Phi Beta Kappa 90; Golden Key Sec 90; Pi Sigma Alpha; Intrnshp Capitol Hill Cngrssmn Charles A Hayes 90; Schlrshp Phi Beta Kappa Hon Soc; Law.**

**TAYLOR, MICHELLE ANN,** Oh St Univ At Marion, Marion, OH; JR; BED; Phi Theta Kappa V P 89-90; Sub Tchr 84-90; Head Start Tchr 90-; AAS Cuyahoga Cmnty Clg 90; Elem Ed; Ph D.

**TAYLOR, MINDY S,** Salisbury St Univ, Salisbury, MD; SR; BS; NAA Pres 90-; VITA 89-; Phi Eta Sigma 88; Delta Mu Delta 90-; Phi Kappa Phi 90-; Perdue Schlrshp 87-; Salisbury Rotary Schlrshp 87-; INTRNL Rvnue Serv 90-; Acctg.

**TAYLOR, MONETTA R,** Univ Of South Al, Mobile, AL; SR; Elem Ed.

**TAYLOR, MONIQUE,** Al St Univ, Montgomery, AL; FR; Dns Lst; Sec Ed.

**TAYLOR, NANCY T,** Hillsborough Comm Coll, Tampa, FL; SO; HCC Vlybl Plyr Strtng Sttr 89-90; HCC Fdn USVBA Mbr 89-; Phi Theta Kappa 90-; Wrkd Meals On Wheels 89-; Kiwanettes 88-; Acad All Amer 90-; Wom Acad All FCCAA NJCAA Reg VIII Awd 0-; Vly Tm 89-; AA HCC; Math; Teacher.

**TAYLOR, NATALYE K,** Univ Of Ms Medical Center, Jackson, MS; JR; BS; BS Bio Belhaven Clg 89; Nrsng.

**TAYLOR, NICHELL J,** Clark Atlanta Univ, Atlanta, GA; SR; BA; Pnthrs Nwspr Rptr; Dns Lst; Soc Prof Jrnlst; Rprt Atlanta Jrnl Cnsttn Nwspr; AA Brwrd Comm Clg 89; Jrnlsm; Prnt Jrnlsm/Rptr.

**TAYLOR, NICHOLAS W,** Memphis St Univ, Memphis, TN; SO; BS; C C Humphreys Soc 89-; Alpha Lambda Delta; Comp Eng Tchnlgy.

**TAYLOR, NICOLE T,** Jackson St Univ, Jackson, MS; FR; BA; Alpha Lambda Delta 90-; Schlstc Awd Wmns Bsktbl 90-; Bsktbl 90-; Bio-Pre Phys Ther; Grad Schl Cert.

**TAYLOR, PAMELA L,** Johnson C Smith Univ, Charlotte, NC; SO; BA; Psychlgy Clb Crspdg 90-; Prt African Cncl Pres; Alpha Lambda Dlta 89-90; Mnrty Access Rsrch Greers MARC Prog; A O Steck Schlrshp Awd; Mnrty Biomdcl Rsrch Sprt MBRS Prog Stdnt Rep 89-; Psychlgy; Indstrl/Orgnztn Psychlgy.

**TAYLOR, PAMELA R,** Univ Of Nc At Asheville, Asheville, NC; SO; BA; Sociology/Crmnl Jstce; Juveniles Jstce.

**TAYLOR, PATRICK C,** Fl St Univ, Tallahassee, FL; SR; BA; Golden Key Pres 89-90; Ldrshp Hnry; Beta Kappa Alpha; Beta Gamma Sigma; Sigma Phi Epsilon V P 90; Mary D Scott Award; Fin; MBA.

**TAYLOR, PAUL E,** Anne Arundel Comm Coll, Arnold, MD; SO; BS; Amer Legn Judg Adv 88-; Vet Frgn Wars Pst Srgn 89-; U S Marine Corps 58-88; Pol Sci; Mil Intell.

**TAYLOR, RACHEL R,** Univ Of New England, Biddeford, ME; FR; BA; Stdnt Advcts 90-; Psych & Soc Rltns; Psychologist.

**TAYLOR, RACHELE D,** Cumberland Coll, Williamsburg, KY; FR; BA; Hnr Scty 90-; Mtn Otrch 90-; Lv In Actn 90; Engl; Scndry Ed.

**TAYLOR, REBECCA H,** Gaston Coll, Dallas, NC; GD; AAS; Cmptr Sci; Pgrmmr.

**TAYLOR, REBECCA L,** Radford Univ, Radford, VA; SO; Geo/Env.

**TAYLOR, REBECCA L,** Univ Of Ky, Lexington, KY; SR; PHARM; KY Assn Stdnts Pharm; Lambda Kappa Sigma; Kappa Psi Lil Sis; Pharm; Cncl Pharm.

**TAYLOR, REESHEMAH R,** North Fl Jr Coll, Madison, FL; FR; AA; SOAR; Blck Un; Mot Series Cert; Gen Stds; Military; Ba.

**TAYLOR, REGINA M,** Livingston Univ, Livingston, AL; SR; BS; Sigma Tau Delta Tr 90-; Cardinal Key; Phi Theta Kappa; Natl Educ Assn; Lang Arts/Sec; Tchg.

**TAYLOR, REGINA RENEE,** Thomas Nelson Comm Coll, Hampton, VA; FR; BSBA; Tutor 4th Grade Stdnt Hampton City Sch; Exec Sec; Bus; MBA Fin Mgmt.

**TAYLOR, RENA M,** Jackson St Univ, Jackson, MS; JR; BA; Phi Theta Kappa Photographer 90; SS Treas 90; Acad Schlrshp/Vldctrn Hinds Comm Clg 90; Music Schlrshp 88; AA Hinds Comm Clg 90; Acctg.

**TAYLOR, RHONDA K,** Tri County Tech Coll, Pendleton, SC; FR; BA; Housewives/Single Parents Club 90-; Assembly Line Optr Electric Meter Manuf 79-90; Psychlgy/Criminal Justice; Law.

**TAYLOR, RICHARD A,** Medical Coll Of Ga, Augusta, GA; GD; DMD; Coll Of Charleston Wghtlftng Club Sec/Treas 84-87; Pi Kappa Phi Alpha Chapter 84-87; Lab Tech 88-90; BS Coll Of Charleston 87; Chem/Dentistry.

**TAYLOR, RICHARD D,** Kent St Univ Kent Cmps, Kent, OH; JR; BBA; Hnrs Clg 90-; Golden Key; Alpha Lambda Delta Pres 90-; Beta Gamma Sigma; Delta Sigma Pi Chnclr; Pres Lst; Dns Lst; Econ; Envir Rsrch/Prof.

**TAYLOR, RISA H,** Northwest Al Comm Coll, Phil Campbell, AL; FR; ADAS; Phi Theta Kappa 90-; Draft/Dsgn; Mechncl Drftg.

**TAYLOR, SALLY B,** Abraham Baldwin Agri Coll, Tifton, GA; SO; BS; Phi Theta Kappa; Alapaha Preschool Tchr/Dir 90; Paraprofessional 2 Yrs 1st Grde & Specl Ed 87-89; Erly Chldhd Ed; Prmry Schl Tchr.

**TAYLOR, SANDRA R,** Wv Univ, Morgantown, WV; SR; BSN; Sigma Theta Tau; BSN; Nrsng; RN.

**TAYLOR, SAUNDRA A,** Bethune Cookman Coll, Daytona Beach, FL; SR; Acad Merit Award; Pres Schlr; Excep Stdnt Educ/Spec Lrnng Dsblts; Educ.**

**TAYLOR, SEAN P,** Georgetown Univ, Washington, DC; FR; BA; Chrldng 90-; Intl Bus; Bus.

**TAYLOR, SELENA R,** Greenville Tech Coll, Greenville, SC; CERT; BS Zoology Clemson Univ 81; Engr Drfng/Cad.

**TAYLOR, SHANA R,** Livingston Univ, Livingston, AL; SR; BS; Hstrcl Soc; Engl Clb; SGA Rep; Phi Theta Kappa; Cardinal Key; Phi Mu Secr 89-90; Res Life Staff RA; High GPA Among Res Life Staff 89-; Hstry; Law/Tchg Jr Clg.

**TAYLOR, SHANNON L,** Owensboro Comm Coll, Owensboro, KY; JR; AA 90; Ed; Tchr.

**TAYLOR, SHARON L,** Salisbury St Univ, Salisbury, MD; SR; BS; MD State Tchrs Assn; Natl Educ Assn; Phi Alpha Theta 89-90; Kappa Delta Phi 90-; Stdnt Tchr; Elem Educ.

**TAYLOR, SLATE B,** Gordon Coll, Barnesville, GA; JR; BBA; Russian Clb; Ins Soc; Bapt Stdnt Union 90-; Phi Theta Kappa 88-90; Phi Beta Lambda 88-90; Alumni Delegates 88-89; State Farm Ins Co Stf Asst 88-90; Summa Cum Laude Grad 90; Dns Lst 90-; AS 90; Risk Mgmt; Ins Underwrtg.

**TAYLOR, SPAMVETTA T,** Johnson C Smith Univ, Charlotte, NC; FR; Myers Hall Cncl Treas 90-; Alpha Lambda Delta; Acctg; CPA.

**TAYLOR, STEPHANIE A,** Fl A & M Univ, Tallahassee, FL; FR; MBA; Stdnt Govt 90; Pharm.

**TAYLOR, STEPHANIE G,** Univ Of Miami, Coral Gables, FL; SR; MA; Deans Mstr Tutor 88-90; Peer Cnslr Altrnt 88-89; Hon Stdnt Assc 88-90; Gldn Key 90-; Psi Chi 90-; Camillus Hse 90-; Fun Day 88-90; Bowman-Ashe Schlrshp 87-; BS 87-; Clncl Psychlgy.

**TAYLOR, SUE A,** Schenectady County Comm Coll, Schenectady, NY; Dr Who NE 87-; Schdy Nghbhd Wtch 88-; Lbry Assit; Elctrncs.

**TAYLOR, SUSAN DIANE,** Trenton St Coll, Trenton, NJ; FR; Edward J Bloustein Dist Schlrsh 90-; Early Chldhd Dvlpmnt/Psych/Education.

**TAYLOR, SUSAN T,** Coll Of Aeronautics, Flushing, NY; FR; AOS; Stu Aid Mo Undr Coll Wrk Stdy Pro 90; Sprt Spcl Olympcs; Chldrns Hosp; USN Phtgrphr 79-84; Audio Visual Spclst 85-89; USN Rsrvs Rcld Actv Duty Oper Dsrt Shld/Strm 89-; Avionics; Elctrnc Engr.

**TAYLOR, TAMARA D,** Savannah Coll Of Art & Design, Savannah, GA; JR; BFA; Graphic Arts Tech Fndtn; Graphic Dsgn; Dsgn Advrtsng Firm.

**TAYLOR, TAMMY A,** Radford Univ, Radford, VA; SR; BS; Rtrct Clb Treas 88-89; Kappa Delta Pi 90-; US Achvmnt Acdmy 87-88; Assoc In Ed SW VA Cmmnty Coll 89; BS; Erly Mddl Ed; Cert Tch Grds K8.**

**TAYLOR, TEENA Y,** Washington State Comm Coll, Marietta, OH; JR; AAB; Amer Lgn Aux Pblcty Edtr 77-78; New Matamoras Ltl League Tm Mthr 80-; Fmly Trad Perf Grp 87-; Phi Theta Kappa 89-; Ohio Dept Trans Sec 90-; Sec Sci; Med Trnscrptn Sec.

**TAYLOR, TIFFANY L,** Univ Of Central Fl, Orlando, FL; FR; BS; Miss UCF Pgnt Jdgs Chrmn 90-; Big Man Cmps Jdgs Chrmn 90-; Stdnt Tlnt Shwcs Jdgs Chrmn 90-; Zeta Tau Alpha Sis Cr Chr; Fresh Hon Cnvctn 90-; Acctg; CPA.

**TAYLOR, TONYA S,** Columbia St Comm Coll, Columbia, TN; FR; MBA; Nrsng; Anstst.

**TAYLOR, TRACY L,** Mount Saint Mary Coll, Newburgh, NY; SO; BA; Engl; Publishing.

**TAYLOR, TREINA A,** Mount Olive Coll, Mount Olive, NC; FR; BA; Acctng; CPA.

**TAYLOR, TRICIA L,** Radford Univ, Radford, VA; SO; BA; Radford Univ Assn Alumni Orgztn 90-91; Stdnt Govt Assn Sec 89-90; Radford Rdcts Equstrn Tm Sec 89-; Alpha Lambda Delta 90-; Anthropolgy; Archaeology.

**TAYLOR, TROY A,** Univ Of South Al, Mobile, AL; SR; BED; Beta Theta Pi 83-84; Birmingham Sthrn Coll Smmr Schlr 83; Cochng Stff USA Bsbl Smmr Camps; U AL Bham Bsbl Ptchr 86-88; Jefferson State Jr Coll Bsbl Pitcher 84-86; BS U Alabama Bham 88; AS Jefferson 86; Scndry Ed; Tch/Coach.

**TAYLOR, V JOYCE,** Chattanooga St Tech Comm Coll, Chattanooga, TN; SO; AAS; Med Rcrd Clb 89; Phi Theta Kappa; Amer Med Rcrd Assoc; Marion Co Tn Genealogical Hist Soc Treas 88; Med Rcrds Tech; Med Rcrd Techncn.

**TAYLOR, VERNA L,** Univ Of Cin R Walters Coll, Blue Ash, OH; FR; BA; U Amateur Radio Clb 78-80; Phi Theta Kappa 90; Emp Of Yr 89; Emp Of Mnth Nov 86; Accdnt Prvntn Cmmttee Scrtry 84-88; Marriott/Crtyrd By Marriott 83; Hstry; Tchr State Hst/Geogrphy.

**TAYLOR, VIRGINIA A,** Univ Of Ms Medical Center, Jackson, MS; JR; BS; MS Stdnt Nrs Assoc; Natl Stdnt Nrs Assoc; Natl Leag Of Nrsng Schlrshp 90; Nuclear Med Tech 87-90; BS Microbiol MS St Univ 85; Cert Nuclear Med Univ MS Med Ctr 87; Nrsng; Nrs Ansthlgy.

**TAYLOR, WANDA J,** Clark Atlanta Univ, Atlanta, GA; SO; BA; Insprtnl Voices Of Faith 89-; Readg Prog Cmbt Illtrcy 89-; Chldrn Prog Hlp Chldrn 89-; Hnrs Prog 89-; DST Intrnshp Rcptnst; Bus Fin.

**TAYLOR, WANDA Y,** Stillman Coll, Tuscaloosa, AL; JR; Cordell Wynn Hon Pgm; Stillman Schlr; Acctg.

**TAYLOR JR, WAYNE F,** Xavier Univ, Cincinnati, OH; JR; Delta Sigma Pi VP 90-; Pi Kappa Phi 86-87; ASSOC Univ Of Cincinnati 89; Bus Admin; Law.**

**TAYLOR, WILLIAM M,** Union Univ, Jackson, TN; FR; FCA 90; Vrsty Bsktbl NAIA 90; Eng.

**TAYLOR, YVONNE ELAINE,** Saint Pauls Coll, Lawrenceville, VA; JR; BS; Elem Educ; Tchng.

**TAYLOR, ZANE A,** Greenville Tech Coll, Greenville, SC; SO; AS; Chmstry/Physcs; Msn Spclst NASA/ASTRNT.

**TAYNOR, JULIA D,** Wilmington Coll, Wilmington, OH; SO; Stu Fndtns 90-; IM Stff 90-; All Conf Vllybl 90-; MVP Trck 89-90; Wilmington Hnrs Schlrshp 89-; Vrsty Vllybl Trck 89-; Sec Educ/Math/Phys Educ; Tch Coach.

**TCHOU, KATHLEEN,** City Univ Of Ny Baruch Coll, New York, NY; JR; Acctg Soc 90-; Asian Cultural Union 90-; Phi Chi Theta Asst V P Scl Affrs; Baruch Schlr 88-90; Acctg.

**TEAGARDEN REON, JULIA F,** Univ Of Miami, Coral Gables, FL; GD; MD; Hnr Cncl 86-87; Amer Med Assoc 87; Christian Med Dntl Soc 88; Alpha Omega Alpha 90; Phi Beta Kappa Jr VP 86; Omicron Delta Kappa 86; Vldctrn Clg Arts/Sci 87; Grad B S Gnrl Hnrs; Im Sprts 83; BS 87; MD; Med; Intrnl Med.

**TEAGARDEN, TRACY D,** Garrett Comm Coll, Mchenry, MD; FR; BS; Edctn; Sci Tchr Mdl Schl.

**TEAGUE, AUDREY E,** Commonwealth Coll, Virginia Beach, VA; GD; Coll Sec Intl 90; Offc Admin Clb 90; Cler Asst C/S Sovran Bnk Offc Pers Phar/Mar/Inc; BA; Offc Admin.

**TEAGUE, BRENDA J,** Jackson St Univ, Jackson, MS; SR; BS; Alpha Chi; Psi Chi; Incntv Pay Coord Deposit Guarnty Natl Bk; Psych; Tchr.

**TEAGUE, DALLAS A,** Univ Of South Al, Mobile, AL; JR; BS; Tour De Force Actvty Chrmn 89-; Lsr Srvc Assoc; AL Prk Rcrtn Assoc VP 90-; Mbl Hsc Assoc Brd Dir 90-; Natl Hnr Scty 87; Armcn Cncr Scty 87-89; Ed Dmcrcy 90; Lsr Srvcs; Mgmt.

**TEAGUE, DEBRA S,** Univ Of Tn At Knoxville, Knoxville, TN; SO; BS; Alpha Sigma Lambda; Acctg; CPA.

**TEAGUE, EVELYN F,** Al A & M Univ, Normal, AL; FR; Maroonette; Chrch Choir; Sci; Dntstry.

**TEAGUE, KELLEY S,** Univ Of Tn At Martin, Martin, TN; JR; BS; Frshmn Hall Monitor Mc Cord Hall Assoc 88-89; Stdnt Tn Edn Assoc 89-; Phi Eta Sigma; Phi Kappa Phi; Spec Olympcs Asstd 90-; Erly Chldhd Edn; Teach Lower Elem Grade.

**TEAGUE, SHERRY J,** Univ Of Al At Birmingham, Birmingham, AL; SR; BSN; ANS Chaplain/Hstrn 90-; Sigma Theta Tau; SGA Merit Awd; Red Cross; Blck Lung Clinic Vol; Nuclear Med Asst; Ward Sec; Lab/X Ray Tech; Nrsg.

**TEAHAN, DONALD M,** Fl A & M Univ, Tallahassee, FL; JR; BS; NATA; APTA; BA Univ South Florida 85; MSS Us Sports Acad 87; Phys Thrpy.

**TEAL, BONNIE J,** Middle Tn St Univ, Murfreesboro, TN; SO; BS; ACE 89-90; Phi Eta Sigma 89-90; Math; Acturl.

**TEAL, JOANN M,** Univ Of Sc At Columbia, Columbia, SC; JR; BS; Assoc Honor Stdts Sec 89-; Acad Planning Cmte Stdt Gvt; Economics Scty; Phi Beta Kappa; Gamma Beta Phi 90-; Golden Key 90-; Deans List; Legislative Internship SC Hs Reps; Fiance/Economics; Law School.

**TEASE, KELLIE M,** Johnson St Coll, Johnson, VT; SR; BA; Cheshamore 89-; Vars Sftbl 88-90; Elem Educ; Tchng.

**TEASLEY, JULIA A,** Univ Of Al At Huntsville, Huntsville, AL; JR; BS; SEDS Prncpl Invstgtr 90-; AIAA FL Inst Tchnlgy 86-87; NASA Co-Op Stdnt JSC Houston TX Eng Trnee 88-89; FL Inst Tchnlgy Crew Tm 86-87; Elect Eng; Spc Ind Eng.

**TEATOR, GLENNA L,** Columbia Greene Comm Coll, Hudson, NY; JR; BS; Clgte FFA; Alpha Zeta Rsh Co-Chr; AAS SUNY Cobleskill 80; Agri Econ; Law.

**TEBAY, BRENDA L,** Wv Univ At Parkersburg, Parkersburg, WV; FR; Jr Lgue Parkersburg Chrmn 86-89; Acctg/Tax Clrk 75; Bus/Pre Law/Pshch; Law/Psych.

**TEBAY, HARRY T,** Ringling School Of Art, Sarasota, FL; SO; BA; Fine Arts.

**TECTOR, LESLIE M,** Georgetown Univ, Washington, DC; SR; BSN; NSNA Mbr 87-; Sigma Theta Tau Mbr 89-; Track Runner 87-89; Nursing; Health Law.

**TEDDER, KRISTIN SUZANNE,** Central Fl Comm Coll, Ocala, FL; SO; BS; Fin; Invstmnt/Stock Brkr.

**TEDDER, NANCY H,** Univ Of Ga, Athens, GA; SR; Wesley Foundation; Golden Key; Alpha Chi Omega Sec 89-; Bis Sister Tutor; BS; Early Childhood Ed; Teach.

**TEDEKU, OBED K,** Central St Univ, Wilberforce, OH; FR; Flwshp Chrstn Stdnts 90-.

**TEDEROUS, ROSANN,** D Youville Coll, Buffalo, NY; JR; BSN; Stdnt Nrses Assoc D'youville Clg 90; Vrty Clb Tent 1 Co-Chr Nrsng Hm Div 88; NY State Stdnt Nrses Assoc Brkthrgh To Nrsng Dir; Deans Lst 90; Spirit Of Nrsng Awd; W Seneca Dvlpmntl Ctr Human Rltns Cmmttee Fnd Rsng Dir 88-90; Client Prog Coord; Nrsng; Nrsng Psychiatric.

**TEDESCHI, CARMEN A,** Atlantic Comm Coll, Mays Landing, NJ; SO; AAS; Co Op Educ 90-; Mobile Electrnc Equip Instlr 90-91; Electrn Tech; Electrnc Flds.

**TEDROW, CHRISTY S,** Tn Tech Univ, Cookeville, TN; SR; BS; Fncl Mgmt Assoc 90-; Scty Advncmnt Fnc Econ 90-; Jzz Bnd Sctn Ldr 87-90; Mrtr Brd 90-Kappa Mu Epsilon 88-; Phi Kappa Phi 90-; Chrstn Stdnt Cntr 87-; Mrtr Brd; Acdmc Schlrshp 87-; Grcrs Schlrshp 87-; Tch Eqstrn Tm Pres 89-; Intrmrl Bsktbll 88-; Fnc.

**TEE, ELAINE Y,** Hofstra Univ, Hempstead, NY; JR; Asian Amer Org VP 89-90; Org Intl Stdnts Treas 89-90; Acctg Soc; Tax Soc; Alpha Kappa Psi; Vol Incm Tx Asst; Fr/Soph Recog Awd 89-90; Dns Lst Mult Yr Awd 89-; Spec Olympc; Acctg; Law.**

**TEED, JULIA A,** Elmira Coll, Elmira, NY; SO; BS; Coll Radio DJ 90-; Stdnt Actvts Bd Big Event Vol 90-; Bsktbl 89-90; Elem Ed; Tchng.

**TEER, RICHARD J,** Fordham Univ, Bronx, NY; SO; Orntn Pro Advsr; Finance; Law.

**TEES, KRYSTA N,** Atlantic Comm Coll, Mays Landing, NJ; FR; AS; Bus Law; Law.

**TEETER, JAMES R,** Univ Of Sc At Columbia, Columbia, SC; SO; BS; Mrchng Band Sqd Ldr 89-90; Eagle Sct Boy Scts Am Ptrl Ldr 83-89; Acctg; Intl Bus.

**TEETER, JEFFREY A,** Snead St Jr Coll, Boaz, AL; SO; CERT; Mgr Dominos Pizza 90-; Electrnc; Bio Med Elect Eng.

**TEFFT, GREGORY R,** Ky Christian Coll, Grayson, KY; JR; BA; B C Hon Scty; Pi Zeta Nu; BS Bwlng Grn State Un 87; Chrstn Mnstry/Bible; Clg Prfsrshp.

**TEGANO, BRUNO J,** Univ Of Cincinnati, Cincinnati, OH; SO; BA; ASME; Mech Eng Jefferson Tech Inst 86-88; Mech Engr.

**TEGIACCHI, MICHAEL JOHN,** Hudson Valley Comm Coll, Troy, NY; SO; AA; Phi Theta Kappa; Spec Olmpcs; Army Ltr Aprctn; O V Gunther Schlrshp; Phi Theta Kappa; Achvmnt Awds; Hon Dschrge; Ltrs Cmndtn; Shiner Awd; Bsbl Ftbl Wrstlng Track; U S Army E4; X Ray Tech; English Educ; Tch/Wrtr.

**TEGTMEIER, JACK A,** Hudson Valley Comm Coll, Troy, NY; Auto Tech Srvcs 89-; ASEP Auto Serv Excllnc Prgrm 89-.

**TEH, AGNES Y,** Fl St Univ, Tallahassee, FL; SR; BA; Brd Advsr 89-; Dn Advsry Cncl 90-; Pr Tchg Comm; Phi Kappa Phi; Golden Key 90-; Sigma Alpha Iota Tr Pldg Clss 90-; Finc Mgmt Soc 90-; Atol Trnty Clg London 86; Ltol Trnty Clg London 89; Music; Tch.

**TEHFE, MAHMOUD H,** City Univ Of Ny La Guard Coll, Long Island Cty, NY; SO; BA; SGA; Arab Stdnts Org VP; Phrmcy.

**TEICHER, STACY A,** Smith Coll, Northampton, MA; SO; BA; House Cncl Acdmc Rep 90-; Coll Chr 89-90; 5-Coll Chrstn Sci Org Exec Brd Membr 90-; Womens Studs.

**TEICHMANN, LISA C,** Christopher Newport Coll, Newport News, VA; JR; Animal Aid Scty; Fnce; Law.

**TEICHMILLER, JASON W,** John C Calhoun St Comm Coll, Decatur, AL; JR; BS; Pi Theta Kappa 88-89; Theta Of AL 90-; Pres List 87; Deans List 89; Mech Engr.**

**TEIPER, MATTHEW S,** Hudson Valley Comm Coll, Troy, NY; SR; Pres Lst 89-90; Deans Lst; AA; Comp Sci.

**TEIS, MICHELLE A,** Wilmington Coll, Wilmington, OH; FR; BED; Actvts Progrmmng Vd Entertnmnt Chr; Cls Pres; Resdnc Hall Assn Actvts Chr; Ldr Schlr; Hons Schlr; Svc Award; Elem Ed/Math; Tchr.

**TEITSCH, DORRAINE F,** Hudson Valley Comm Coll, Troy, NY; SO; BA; Rprtr/Phtgrphr 90-; Stage Mgr Just A Sad Song; Tutor W Cvlztn Psych Math Eng 90-; Tutor Wrtng Lab ; Alpha Xi Sigma Pres 90-; Pub Rltns Intrnshp Capital Dist 90; A J Breton Mem Awd 91; Otto Von Guenther Schlrsphp Awd 91; AA; Eng Edn; Eng Prof.

**TEIXEIRA, DAMIAN O,** Univ Of Fl, Gainesville, FL; SR; BA; Amer Mktg Assoc; Gainesville Fire Rescue Assn 89-90; Acad Advsr Clg Bus Admn Advsr; Barnett Bk New Accts Rep Intrn 90; Intl Corp Serv Asst Accnt Exec Intrn 91; Bus Admn; Mktg.

**TEJADA, ANDRIA J,** Fl International Univ, Miami, FL; GD; MA; Sub Dade Cnty Pub Sch; Private Tutor; BS 90; Edn; Masters.

**TEJADA, CATHERINE V,** Cazenovia Coll, Cazenovia, NY; FR; BA; Ski Clb; Step Prog Mnrtes; Art; Cmrcl Illustrator.

**TEJEDA MERCADO, JOCELYN M,** Inter Amer Univ Pr San German, San German, PR; SR; BA; Cncl Res 89; Hnrs Prog; Asst Lamar Res 8-90; Tutor 89-90; Bus Cmmrcl Admn.**

**TEJUMOLA, OLADELE T,** Lincoln Univ, Lincoln Univ, PA; JR; BSC; Cmptr Sci Clb 90-; Intl Stdnts Assn 90-; Alpha Chi; Grad Asst Food Tech Univ Abeokuta Nigeria 88-89; Interned Delta Steel Co Aladja Nigeria 87-88; Soccer 90-; Bsc Univ Of Igadan 88; Cmptr Sci; Msc Engr/Phd Bus Admin.

**TEJUMOLA, ZAIDAT B,** Lincoln Univ, Lincoln Univ, PA; JR; Intrntl Stdnts Assoc Treas 90-; Acctng Club Sentr; Acctng; CPA.

**TEKIELI, TERESA A,** Wv Univ, Morgantown, WV; JR; BS; Jazz Dance Thtr 89-; Golden Key 90-; Pharmacy.

**TEKLEMARIAM, ANDEMESKEL,** Newbury Coll, Brookline, MA; SR; AA; Acctng; Mgmt.

**TELESCO, TONI L,** Teikyo Post Univ, Waterbury, CT; FR; BA; Acctng.

**TELFER, GENEVE R,** Asbury Theological Sem, Wilmore, KY; GD; MDIV; Intrntl Stdnt Assoc Pblshng Sec; Ichthus Brd Of Dir Sec 90; Kappa Kappa Gamma 80-84; Stdnt Govt Assoc-Mddl Class Sec; Yng Lfe Vol Ldr 80-82; Mssnry 84-89; STEP Prog Elem Schl Tutor 81-84; BA Vndrblt U 84; Engl Thlgy; Mssns Bible Trnsltn.

**TELLECHEA, MARK S,** Bloomfield Coll, Bloomfield, NJ; SR; BS; Stdnt Fcs Grps; All Star Tms; Deans Lst; Bsktbll; Bus Mgmt; Fnc.

**TELLER, R JEFFREY,** Wilmington Coll, New Castle, DE; SR; BA; Deans Lst 90-; Amer Inst Real Est Apprsrs; Natl Assn Realtrs; DE Dept Trnsprtn; AAS-BUS DE Tech/Comm Coll 81; Bus; Real Est Apprsr.

**TELLIS, LEVASSEUR,** Fl A & M Univ, Tallahassee, FL; FR; BAS; Pgm EXCEL; Natl Soc Blck Engrs; Dns Lst 90-; Natl Actn Cncl Mnrty Eng; Chem; Engr.

**TELLIS, TINA R,** City Univ Of Ny Baruch Coll, New York, NY; JR; BA; Intern Rprtr Phtgrphr Bronx Times; Gold Crwn Awrd; AAS Bronx Comm Coll 87; Engl/Jrnlsm.

**TELSTAD, MARY PAT,** Christopher Newport Coll, Newport News, VA; SR; BA; Captns Plyrs V P 89-; Fine Arts Soc Sec 90-; Intl Stdnts Assn 90-; Pens Fine Arts Ctr Tchr 89-; Artist Visls Mgr Nail Tech Int Desgnr 87-; Theatre; Museum Work.

**TEMPEST, ELISABETH F,** Univ Of South Al, Mobile, AL; SR; BS; Leisure Serv Assoc 88; Leisure Serv Assoc 88; Pres Schlrs; Erly Chldhd Educ; Tchr.

**TEMPESTA, MICHAEL C,** Univ Of Nh Plymouth St Coll, Plymouth, NH; SR; BA Plymouth St Coll.

**TEMPLE, DREAMA K,** Clark State Comm Coll, Springfield, OH; GD; Phi Theta Kappa 90-; Deans Lst 88-; Outstndng Stdnt Awrd Intrmdt Acctg Cls 90; AAB; Acctg.

**TEMPLE, JEFFREY S,** Univ Of Southern Ms, Hattiesburg, MS; JR; BS; Pre Med Awd 89-90; Mr/Mrs J D Lewis Schlrshp 89-90; Ethel Whetley Kroker Schlrshp; Chmstry/Biochmstry; Med.

**TEMPLE, MICHAEL W,** Oh Wesleyan Univ, Delaware, OH; JR; BA; Habitat For Humanity Pres 88-; Circle K VP 88-90; Stdnt Sfty Brd Treas 90-; Mortar Brd VP 90-; Omicron Delta Kappa 90-; Phi Eta Sigma 88-; Various Awrds Chemistry 88-; IM Vlybl Bsktbl 89-; Pre Medicine/Zoology; Physician Pediatrician.

**TEMPLETON, GLORIA P,** Eckerd Coll, St Petersburg, FL; SR; BA; Rotarace 87-88; Intl Stdnt Assn 87-; Catha Chrch 90-91; Citibank Summer; Hmn Rsrc Inst; Intl Bus; Mgmt.

**TEMPLETON, JAI J,** Union Univ, Jackson, TN; FR; Circle K 90-; Coll Republicans Sen 90-; Honors Clb.

**TEMPLETON, LISA D,** Ms St Univ, Miss State, MS; SR; ELED; Phi Kappa Phi 90-; Ed; Tchng.

**TENCH, CYNTHIA A,** Univ Of Ky, Lexington, KY; SR; BA; Arts/Sci Dns Schlrshp; N A Montessori Tchrs Assoc; Montessori Tchr; AA St Petersburg Jr Clge 65; Montessori Tchrs Dplm St Nicholas Clge 87; Erly Chldhd Ed; Tchg.

**TENER, CARMEN M,** Duquesne Univ, Pittsburgh, PA; FR; BA; Bus; Acctng.

**TENERALLI, CHRISTINE A,** Univ Of Sc At Columbia, Columbia, SC; SO; BA; Delta Gamma Frat 90-91; Carolina Cares 90-; Wings Of Columbia Vol 90-; Equestrian Tm/Clb 90-91; Niccolo/Co Ltd 87-89; Hstry/Engl; Hstry Prof.

**TENEROWICZ, SUZANNA J,** Columbia Greene Comm Coll, Hudson, NY; FR; AS; Nursing.

**TENN-YUK, SUZETTE A,** City Univ Of Ny Baruch Coll, New York, NY; JR; BBA; Intrntnl Stdnt Clb VP 90-; Accntng; CPA.

**TENNANT, EDWARD T,** Wv Univ At Parkersburg, Parkersburg, WV; JR; BA; US Army Vet; Bus-Mgmt Info Syst; Law/Bus.

**TENNANT, NOELLE,** Univ Of Med & Dentistry Of Nj, Newark, NJ; BS; Women In Trnstn 89-; Bsktbl 89-; Amer Assn Resp Care 90-; Phi Theta Kappa 89-; Biolgy; Resp Care.

**TENNENBERG, JOEL S,** Yeshiva Univ, New York, NY; JR; BA; SGA Pres 90-; Yeshiva Coll Stdnt Ct Assoc Justice 90-91; Deans List 88-; Samuel Belkin Schlr 88-; IM Bsktbl 88-; Pol Sci; Law.

**TENNER, SANDRA F,** Alcorn St Univ, Lorman, MS; FR; BA; Army Res Pfc 89-; Sci; Phys Ther.

**TENNEY, LISA A,** Hudson Valley Comm Coll, Troy, NY; FR; AS; Phi Theta Kappa V P 90-; Pres Lst 90-; Psych.

**TENNIS, JOSEPH BRAXTON,** Radford Univ, Radford, VA; JR; Soc Cllgt Jrnlsts 90-; Nwsppr Edtr 89-90; Tarton Stff 90-; Phi Theta Kappa 89; Intern Roanoke Times & World News; Virginian-Pilot Nwspprs Crrspndnt 90-; AAS Tidewater Comm Coll 90; Jrnlsm; Nwsppr Rprtr.

**TENNON, KEVIN C,** Central St Univ, Wilberforce, OH; FR; BA; Finance/Acctng; Corp Law.

**TENNY, RASHIDA,** Ny Univ, New York, NY; JR; BA; Intl Stds; Prfssnl Stff Untd Ntns.

**TENNYSON, CHARLENE J,** Anne Arundel Comm Coll, Arnold, MD; SO; AA; Gvrnrs Citation Awd; BS Glldt Univ 65; Human Serv; Cnslr For Sbstnce Abse.

**TENNYSON, SHERRY K,** Middle Tn St Univ, Murfreesboro, TN; SR; BS; STEA CSCC VP 90-; STEA CSCC Sec 88-89; Peer Cnslr CSCC Cnslr 88-89; Deans Lst 89-; AS Columbia Cmnty Clg 89; BS; Elem Tchr.

**TENPAS, JENNIFER L,** Liberty Univ, Lynchburg, VA; FR; BS; Psych; Human Serv/Cnslng.

**TENPENNY, PATRICIA S,** Middle Tn St Univ, Murfreesboro, TN; JR; BFA; Wrk Study Asstntshp Arwmnt Sch Arts/Crafts 90; AA Miss Wades Fshn Merch Coll 85; BS Middle TN State Univ; Art/Sculpture.

**TENSLEY JR, RICHARD L,** Mayland Comm Coll, Spruce Pine, NC; SO; AAS; SGA Pre 89-; Phi Theta Kappa Fnds Chrmn 89-; Sports Day Airball Cptn 90-; Gen; Law.

**TENSLEY, YOLANDA R,** Livingston Univ, Livingston, AL; FR; BS; Insprtnl Vcs Fth 90; Frshmn Md Nmn 90; Apll Tlnt Cntstnt 90; Elem Ed; Tchr.

**TEODORESCO, ADINA,** Univ Of North Fl, Jacksonville, FL; FR; BA; Pol Sci; Diplomacy.

**TEPE, NICOLE M,** Miami Univ, Oxford, OH; FR; BA; Vlybl Clb VP; Zoology.

**TEPLITZ, ROBERT F,** Franklin And Marshall Coll, Lancaster, PA; JR; BA; Res Hall Assn Pres 89-; Stdnt Actvts Advsry Bd Chrmn; Nwspr Nws Edtr 88-; Pi Gamma Mu; Pi Sigma Alpha; Blck Pyramid; C A Dana Intrn 89-90; K A Spalding Flw 90; T Gilmore Apple Prz 90; Govt; Law/Pltcs.

**TEPP, TARA L,** Hillsborough Comm Coll, Tampa, FL; FR; BA; Presidential Schlrshp 90-; Psychology.

**TEPPER, DAVID A,** Princeton Univ, Princeton, NJ; FR; AB; Princeton Tiger Stf Wrtr; Princeton Sentinel Sr Wrtr 90-; Hillel 90-; Molecular Blgy.

**TER WEEME, MAARTEN P,** Univ Of Louisville, Louisville, KY; SR; BS; Amer Inst Chem Eng 89-; Wght Clb 88-; Padi Naui 90-; Gldn Ky 90-; Tau Beta Pi 90-; Phi Eta Sigma V Pres 89-; Ord Of Omega 90-; Sigma Chi Treas 88-; Otstndg Frshmn; Hon Citzn; Speed Schl Wrk Stdy Schlrshp; Chem Eng.

**TERAN, GUILLERMO J,** Barry Univ, Miami, FL; FR; BA; Rugby Clb; Psychlgy.

**TERCYAK, CHERYL L,** Western New England Coll, Springfield, MA; JR; BA; Psi Chi; Dns Lst; Psychology; Soc Wk.

**TERESI BURCHAM, LISA M,** Savannah Coll Of Art & Design, Savannah, GA; GD; MS; Stdnt Prsrvtn Assoc Sec; Vldctrn 90; Summa Cum Laude; Scty Fr Cmrcl Archlgy 90-; Natl Trst Fr Hstrc Prsrvtn 85-; BFA 90; Hstrc Prsrvtn.

**TERHUNE, KIRA M,** Ky St Univ, Frankfort, KY; GD; BA; BS 90; Math; U S Army/Military Intell Officer.

**TERILLI, DAUNE MICHELLE,** Pa St Univ Delaware Cty Cmps, Media, PA; FR; BA; Law.

**TERLATO, NANCY G,** S U N Y Coll Of Tech At Frmgdl, Farmingdale, NY; SO; BED; Elem Ed; Teacher.

**TERLECKA, JOANNA M,** Univ Of Miami, Coral Gables, FL; JR; BSC; Acad Econ Poznan Poland Class Rep 89-90; Russian/German/Polish/English Lang; Beta Gamma Sigma; Poznan Food Dist Slsprsn; Plsh Natl Fair Asst Repr; Poznan Intl Fair Asst Sec; Trnsltr E Germ Tours; Polish Scts/Unit Ldr/Cmp Orgzr; Intl Bus/Economics.

**TERNEY, CAROL L,** Indiana Univ Of Pa, Indiana, PA; SR.

**TERRACIANO, JENNIFER,** Merrimack Coll, North Andover, MA; SO; IM Lacrosse 90; Law Scty; Deans Lst 90; Political Sci Economics; Law.

**TERRANA, JOSEPH C,** S U N Y At Binghamton, Binghamton, NY; FR; BA; Harpurs Ferry Amb Svc 90-; Mltpl Sclrsis Pblcty Chr 90-; Bio; Med.

**TERRANOVA, CARLEEN,** Cumberland County Coll, Vineland, NJ; JR; AAS; Grnpc Mbr; Audubon Soc Mbr; Aerobics; Ntry Pblc St NJ; CPR; Radiography; Med.

**TERRELL, JANA M,** Ky St Univ, Frankfort, KY; GD; CERT; Stdnt Ntl Educ Assc 90-; Fndtn Schlrshp; Pst Bchlr Stdnt Awd; Dir Montessoris Hse Of Chldrn 87-90; BS Estrn KY Univ 86; Erly Educ; Tch.

**TERRELL, JASON E,** Marshall University, Huntington, WV; FR; BA; Rsdnt Hll Assn 90-; IM Vlybl 90; Hnrs Prog 90-; Bus Admin; Bnkng Fnnce.

**TERRELL, KAREN L,** Univ Of Southern Ms, Hattiesburg, MS; SO; BA; Afrcn Amer Stdnt Orgnztn 90-; Hall Cncl Rep 89-90; Tres 90-; Gamma Beta Phi; US Geolgcl Srvy Chem Eng 89-; Chem; Law.

**TERRELL, PATRICE Y,** Fayetteville St Univ, Fayetteville, NC; JR; BS; Crmnl Jstc Clb 90-; Prsn Mnstry Ykflw Sec 90-; Jnr Honoree 90-; Crmnl Jstc/Sclgy; Corrections.

**TERRELL, TAMMY D,** Va St Univ, Petersburg, VA; FR; Gospel Choir; Social Wrk; Juvenile Probation Officer.

**TERRIO, FAY A,** Commonwealth Coll, Virginia Beach, VA; SR; AAS; Cmptr Oper; Cmptr Sci; Cmptr Prgmmng.

**TERRIZZI, ILONA E,** William Paterson Coll, Wayne, NJ; SR; MS; Sndy Sch Tchr 86-; Chrch Cncl 87-; BA; Spch Pthlgy.**

**TERRY, CHERYL A,** Roane St Comm Coll, Harriman, TN; SO; AAS; Bus Technlgy/Med Sec.

**TERRY, COTINA W,** Hampton Univ, Hampton, VA; JR; BS; SGA Senate; AL Pre/Alumni Treas; Bsn Clb; Alpha Kappa Mu; Bsn Mngmnt; Corp Law.

**TERRY, DEAN P,** Embry Riddle Aeronautical Univ, Daytona Beach, FL; FR; BA; Arntcl Sci; Cmrcl Plt.

**TERRY, DONYELLE R,** Va St Univ, Petersburg, VA; JR; BS; Nwspaper Stf Wrtr; Alpha Kappa Alpha; Mktg; Brdcstng.

**TERRY, G DIXON,** Ms St Univ, Miss State, MS; JR; BA; IM Sports 88-; Deans Lst Pres Lst 88-; Top 15 Cls 88; Vol Hosp Wrk 90-; Psychlgy Physcl Thrpy; Physcl Thrpst.

**TERRY, JANIS W,** Univ Of Sc At Salkehatchie, Allendale, SC; SO; AA; Busn Cl Secy 90-; Sctrl Intnshp 90; Voc Rehab 89-; Clerk M/M Variety/Greyhound.

**TERRY, JASON B,** Averett Coll, Danville, VA; FR; BS; BSU 90-; Phi Eta Sigma 90-; IM Spts 90-; Math.

**TERRY, JENNIFER LYNN,** Marshall University, Huntington, WV; SR; WV Assn CPA 90-; Bus/Acctng; CPA.

**TERRY, JULIA D,** Averett Coll, Danville, VA; JR; BS; Hmcmg Cmter 89-; Math/Mgmnt.

**TERRY, KIMBERELY R,** Roane St Comm Coll, Harriman, TN; SO; BA; Gamma Beta Phi 89-; Dean Lst 89-; Math/Elem Educ; Educ.

**TERRY, KIMBERLEE R,** Univ Of Miami, Coral Gables, FL; FR; Univ Miami Baseball Tm Sugarcares 90-; Univ Miani Hnrs Prog; Alpha Lambda Delta; Delta Gamma Assist Corr Secty; Univ Miami Hnr Prog; Stanford Acad Schlrshp; Novice Crew Coxswain 90; Med.

**TERRY, LAURA H,** East Carolina Univ, Greenville, NC; SO; BABS; Frnch Clb 90; Phi Sigma Iota; Chncllrs Lst 89-90; Deans Lst 89-90; Bio/French; Rsrch.

**TERRY, LISA S,** Roane St Comm Coll, Harriman, TN; FR; AS; Big South Fork Intrgncy Rscue Tm; Cert LPN Smrst Voc Schl 82; Cert SAC; Nrsng; Chem Dpndcy.

**TERRY, MARGARET F,** Beckley Coll, Beckley, WV; SO; BA; Rep Fndtn Indpndnt Clg; Amer Psychologcl Assn 90; Psychology; Clncl Psychlgst.

**TERRY, MATTHEW H,** Anne Arundel Comm Coll, Arnold, MD; SO; BA; Eng; Indstrl Dsgn.

**TERRY, MICHAEL S,** Middle Tn St Univ, Murfreesboro, TN; JR; Pol Sci; Law.

**TERRY, MICHELLE H,** Univ Of Cin R Walters Coll, Blue Ash, OH; FR; CERT; BA Purdue Univ 68; Lib/Media Tech.

**TERRY, NORNA L,** Duquesne Univ, Pittsburgh, PA; SO.

**TERRY, ONUWA D,** Univ Of Md At Eastern Shore, Princess Anne, MD; JR; BA; Pre Physcl Thrpy Clb 89-; Deans Lst; All Amrcn Schlr; Beta Kappa Chi 89-; Phi Kappa Phi 89-; NAACP 89-; NAM Hsptl 90; Tae Caun Doe Karate 89; Physcl Thrpy.

**TERRY, RANDALL B,** Columbia Union Coll, Takoma Park, MD; SR; BS; Alpha Sigma Beta V P Finc 89-90; Tr Sr Cls Tr 90-; Top Stdnt Acctg 89-90; BS 90; Acctg/Busn Admin.

**TERRY, ROSALYN A,** Howard Univ, Washington, DC; SR; BA; Cmps Crsd Chrst 89-; Tchr Sndy Schl; Scl Edctn Deans Lst; Otstndgn Yng Wmn Amrc 88; Elem Ed.

**TERRY, ROY A,** Ms St Univ, Miss State, MS; JR; BS; Phi Theta Kappa; Phi Alpha Theta; Kappa Delta Pi; Gamma Beta Phi; Pres List; Deans List; AA Holmes Cmnty Clg 88-90; Ed; Cnslng.

**TERRY-ANDERSON, CAROL R,** Univ Of Sc At Beaufort, Beaufort, SC; JR; BA; Gamma Beta Phi; AS Webber Coll 85; Intrdscplnry Stds Bus Mgmt; Mgmt Pstn Trvl In.

**TERRY-WINDELS, MARY E,** Dowling Coll, Oakdale Li, NY; SR; BA; Acad Partial Schlrshp; AAS Suffolk Comm Coll 87; BSPLS Elem Ed/Spcl Ed.

**TERSAK, CHRISTOPHER L,** Wagner Coll, Staten Island, NY; SO; BA; Deans List Wagner Clg 89-90; Delta Nu Frtrnty Rush Chrmn 90; Special Olympcs 89; Green Key 89; Pre/Optmty; Optmetrst.

**TERSHANA, DANIEL E,** Atlantic Comm Coll, Mays Landing, NJ; JR; Art Clb Sec 89-; Lit Mag; AA Atlantic Comm Clg 90; Sec Educ/Hstry; Tch.

**TERWILLIGER, CAROL L,** Univ Of Va Clinch Valley Coll, Wise, VA; JR; BS; Yrbk Asstnt Edtr Photographer & Editor 90-91; Outpost; AAS Education Deg 90; AAS Bus Admnstrn 90; Psychology/Sociology; Real Estate.

**TERZA, AMY L,** Indiana Univ Of Pa, Indiana, PA; JR; BA; Early Chldhd; Educ.

**TERZIAN, JULIET P,** Villanova Univ, Villanova, PA; SR; BFA; Envrnmntl Grp Pres 89-; Natnl Art Ed Assoc 90-; Intrnshp 90-; Fine Arts; Tchr.

**TERZIOGLU, ESIN,** Univ Of Rochester, Rochester, NY; SO; BS; Received Math Summer Camp Schlrshp 90; Deans List; IM Soccer; Ee/Optics; Engrng.

**TESCHKE, JEFFREY J,** Univ Of Rochester, Rochester, NY; SO; BA; Mrdn Scty Admssns Vol Ntwrk 90-; Mns Vlybl Clb Cpt 89-; Phi Kappa Tau Non Alchl Scl Chr 89-; Ntl Svngs Bnk Albany Intrnshp Prog; Econ; Fin/Bus.

**TESIK, MICHAEL A,** Manhattan Coll, Bronx, NY; JR; BS; Kappa Mu Epsilon; Alpha Chi; Eng/Math; Eng.

**TESORERO, DAWN MICHELLE,** Elms Coll, Chicopee, MA; JR; BA; Cmps Mnstry Cr Grp 88-; Ltrgcl Dnc 89-; Erth Clb 90-; Thtr Clb 90-; Appalachian Wrk Wk Coor 90-; Appalachian Outrch Wrk Wk 89-; Intrnshp Ed Dept Msm Sci; Scr 88-90; Cmnctns/Blgy Mnr; Envrnmnt/Pblc Rlts.

**TESSIER, DAVID A,** Nova Univ, Ft Lauderdale, FL; GD; Cntrlllr Yr Awd Marriott Corp 89; Adjnct Prfssr 89-; BA Bently Coll 80; City Laudrhl Plnng/Zoning Bd Bd 87-89; Cntrllr Marriotts Hrbr Bch Rsrt 87-; City Laudrhl Pllng/Zoning Cmmssn Cmmssnr 88-89; Fin/Acctg; Fin.

**TESSITORE, DONNA L,** Schenectady County Comm Coll, Schenectady, NY; FR; AAS; Pres Lst 90-; Schenectady Chmbr Cmmrc 90; Btfctn Cmmtt 90; Store Mgr 81-90; Accntng; Accntnt.

**TESSITORE, KEVIN M,** Univ Of Ct, Storrs, CT; FR; BS; Hrtcltr Clb; Hrtcltr; Garden Store Mgr.

**TESSLER, STEVEN,** Valdosta St Coll, Valdosta, GA; GD; BED; Tau Alpha Pi Treas 83-85; IEEE 83-85; NCO Assc 87-; Coop Educ Pgm 89-; Petty Offcr 1 Cls USN 79-; AS Grtr New Hvn St Tech Clg 85; Trade/Indl Educ; Voc Educ Instctr.

**TESSMANN II, PAUL J,** Univ Of South Al, Mobile, AL; JR; BA; Acctg Clb 90-; IM Ofcl 88-; Mortar Bd 90-; Kappa Sigma 88-; IM All-Star Bsktbl/Ftbl 90; Varsity Soccer 88-90; Acctg; CPA.

**TESSMER, JAY W,** Univ Of Miami, Coral Gables, FL; FR; Chem Dept Awrd; Dns Lst; Chem; Med Dr.

**TESSMER, ZACH P,** Oh Univ, Athens, OH; JR; BFA; Crmcs; Pttr Wrkng Artst.

**TESTANI, MATTHEW A,** Saint Bonaventure Univ, St Bonventure, NY; FR; BS; Pres Schlrshp; Gannett Schlrshp; Bsbl; Biol; Med.

**TESTER, CONNIE L,** Medaille Coll, Buffalo, NY; SR; BSED; Alpha Chi 90-; Tchg Asstnt 86-; Tchg.

**TESTERMAN, DONALD K,** Radford Univ, Radford, VA; FR; Med.

**TESTONE, ANDREA L,** Syracuse Univ, Syracuse, NY; SO; BS; Delta Phi Epsilon Asst Pldg Ed 90-; Info Studies; Mgmt Cnsltg.**

**TETER, DIANA L,** Salem-Teikyo Univ, Salem, WV; JR; Stdnt Admin Rep 89-; Gamma Beta Phi Treas Pres 90-; Dns Lst 90-.**

**TETER, JUANITA R,** Davis & Elkins Coll, Elkins, WV; FR; BA; Busn Mgt/Mktng/Fashion Merdng; Buyer Retl Crp.

**TETER, SETH W,** Wagner Coll, Staten Island, NY; FR; BA; Choir ; Theatre; Hnrs Pgm; Theatre; Education.

**TETLOW, DAVID C,** Va Commonwealth Univ, Richmond, VA; FR; BA; Hons Stdnt; Deans Lst; Mscn 77-; Music; Tchr/Prfrmr/Cmpsr.

**TETRAULT, PAUL T,** Villanova Univ, Villanova, PA; SR; MS; Psi Chi 90-; Phi Kappa Phi; Hons Pgm 87-; IM Capt 81-; Rugby Clb 87-89; Jrnlsm.

**TETZLAFF, KATHRYN L,** Columbus Coll Of Art & Design, Columbus, OH; JR; BFA; Fn Arts Schlrshp; Pres Lst 90-; Pntng Fn Arts.

**TEUTON, SUSAN E,** Daytona Beach Comm Coll, Daytona Beach, FL; FR; AS; Humn Svcx Para-Profsnl Club Liasn 90-; Save Our Soc Club Mbr 90-; Deans List 90-.

**TEW, CYNTHIA M,** Livingston Univ, Livingston, AL; SR; BS; Stdnt Govt Assn Rep 88; Cmps Assn Res Stdnts 89; Envir Educ Assn; Outstndng Yng Wmn Of Amer 90; Spec Olympics Vol 88-; Livingston Univ Cnsrvncy 90; Outstndng Elem Educ Lab Stdnt; Spec Educ; Tchr.

**TEW, HEIDI B,** Christopher Newport Coll, Newport News, VA; JR; BS; Larry Kng Schlrshp 90; Red Crs CPR Instrctr 86-89; Lebn Chrch Chrst 89-; Army Eye Tech Spc4 85-89; Bio/Chem; Env Eng.

**TEW, LAURA J,** Univ Of Sc At Columbia, Columbia, SC; SR; BA; Univ Chorus 88; Kappa Delta Pi 89-; Elem Ed; Tchng.

**TEW, SCOTT R,** Univ Of Fl, Gainesville, FL; SR; BA; Rho Epsilon; NXA 87-89; Finance; Appraisal MAI.

**TEWES, CAROL ANN,** City Univ Of Ny Queensbrough, New York, NY; JR; AAS; Phi Theta Kappa 90; Alpha Beta Gamma 90; Dns Lst 89-; New Apostolic Church Choir; New Apostolic Church Flower Arrang Comm; Sch Secr PS 221; Certif Word Proc QCC; Ofc Tech; Bsn.

**THACHER, JENNIFER K,** Univ Of Tn At Knoxville, Knoxville, TN; JR; BS; Phi Kappa Phi; Phi Eta Sigma 89; Alpha Lambda Delta 89; Delta Sigma Pi VP Pldg Ed 90-; Beta Alpha Psi; Clge Bsn Exec Undrgrdt 89-; Gen Elec Schlrshp; Acctg.

**THACKSTON, NANCY C,** Mary Baldwin Coll, Staunton, VA; JR; BA; Stu Gov VP; Hnr Cncl 90-; Stu Senate Co Chr 89-; Omicron Delta Kappa; Alpha Lambda Delta; Hnrs Lst 88-89; Intrnshp Tmbrlk Smith Thomas/Moses Law Frm 90; Var Vlybl Cocapt 88-; Bus Admin; Law.

**THAI, ANN M,** Duquesne Univ, Pittsburgh, PA; SO; BA; Pharmacy; Medicine.

**THAI, HIEN VAN,** Bunker Hill Comm Coll, Boston, MA.

**THAI, KWAN Y,** County Coll Of Morris, Randolph, NJ; SO; AAS; Phi Theta Kappa 90-; Talnt Rstr; Dns Lst 89-; Chem; Sci.

**THALER, CLIFFORD,** City Univ Of Ny Baruch Coll, New York, NY; FR; BBA; Advrtsng; Advrtsng Cpy Wrtr.

**THAMES, LYNN P,** Mount Olive Coll, Mount Olive, NC; SR; BS; Psychology Clb 89-; Psi Chi; Natl Cllgt Educ Awrds 90-; Marshall 90-; Bus Prof Wmns Assoc 90-; Psychology; Cnslng Teaching.

**THAMES, MICHELLE L,** Kent St Univ Kent Cmps, Kent, OH; FR; BSN; Alpha Lambda Delta 90-; Nrsng; Ansthtcs.

**THAMES, MICHELLE RENEE,** Barry Univ, Miami, FL; SR; BS; Mgmt Inf Sys; Prgmr/Anlst.

**THAMES, SCARLETTE Y CALCOTE,** Univ Of Southern Ms, Hattiesburg, MS; SR; BA; Gamma Lambda Sec 87-88; Humane Clb 87-88; Gamma Beta Phiu 90-; Vars Bsktbll 87-88; AA Copiah Lincoln Comm Clg 89; Bus Educ; Court Rprtng.

**THAMES, SHERI HOPE,** Tallahassee Comm Coll, Tallahassee, FL; FR; AS; Big Bend Soc Rdlgc Tech 83-; Cert Gnrl Rdgrphr 83-; Cert Rdgrphy St FL 83; Nrsng.

**THAMMAVONGXAY, SOMPHIL,** City Univ Of Ny Hostos Coll, Bronx, NY; SO; Talent Roster; CRS Press Frshmn Chem Achvmnt Awd 90; MLT; Dmi/Blgy/Chmstry; Medicine.

**THANAWALLA, RUTANG K,** Oh Wesleyan Univ, Delaware, OH; JR; BA; Univ Film Series VP 89-; Nwspr Mgr 89-; SG 89-; Omicron Delta Epsilon Editor 89-; Phi Eta Sigma 88; Phi Scty 89; Wesleyan Schlr; Philosphy/Economics; Wrtng Pblshng.

**THANGAVELU, ANURADHA,** Cornell Univ, Ithaca, NY; FR; BA; Bio Stdnt Adv Cmte 90-; Indian Stdnts Assn 90-; Biochem/German; Med.

**THARALDSON, KELLY L,** Univ Of Ct, Storrs, CT; JR; BS; Stdnt Ed Ntwrk Apprec Animals Pres/Fndr 90-; Swim Clb V P 89-; Alpha Zeta; Dairy Clb Publ Chr 89-; Block/Bridle Clb Publ Chr 89-; Agri Jrnlsm Intern 90-; Self-Dir Fitness Pgm 89; Animal Sci; Agri Jrnlsm.

**THARP, JIMMY R,** Wallace St Comm Coll At Selma, Selma, AL; FR; BS; Phi Theta Kappa 90-; Pres List; Deans List; Sci; Engrng.

**THARP, MARY J,** Fl St Univ, Tallahassee, FL; SR; BS; Compass Clb Pres 86-88; Phi Theta Kappa Pres 87-88/89-; Mortar Board; Otsdng Mbr 86-87; Otsdng Phi Theta Kappa Mbr 87-88; Pres Pilot Schlrshp Hs Tllhssee Deans List Pres 90-; AA Chipola Jr Clg 88f; Elem Educf Teacher Mstrs English.

**THARP, MARY J,** Saint Catharine Coll, St Catharine, KY; SO; Intl Clb 90-; Phi Theta Kappa 90-; Educ English.

**THARPE, ANGELA MICHELLE,** Birmingham Southern Coll, Birmingham, AL; SO; Pre Law Soc 89-; Sthrn Advntr Clb 89; Otrch Day 89-90; Phi Eta Sigma 89-; Alpha Lambda Delta 89-; Kappa Delta Pnhlnc Rep 89-; Peer Advsr 90-; Law Intrnshp 90-; Smmr Stdy France; Englsh Frnch; Intrntnl Law.

**THARPE, MARY E,** Fl A & M Univ, Tallahassee, FL; GD; Emplyd Dept Crrctns Prbtn Ofcr; AA Chipola Jr Clg Marianna 89; Scl Wrk; Cnslg.

**THARPE, TANGELA S,** Savannah St Coll, Savannah, GA; SO; BA; Beta Kappa Chi; Jr Wmn Excllnc; Deans Lst 90-; CNA Toomsboro Nrsng Cntr 90; Blgy; Occptnl Thrpy.

**THARPE, TIM D,** Lexington Comm Coll, Lexington, KY; FR; BA; Eng.

**THATCHER, SUSAN A,** Univ Of Southern Ms, Hattiesburg, MS; JR; BA; Sr Hon Clg 90-; AA Miss Gulf Coast Clg 90-; Soc Stdes/Sec Educ; Tch.

**THAXTON, DARI J,** Marshall University, Huntington, WV; FR; MBA; Hon Soc; Fnc/Bus; Bnkng.

**THAXTON, TINA M,** Northern Ky Univ, Highland Hts, KY; JR; Fashion Dsgng; Mrchndsng.**

**THAYER, ALISON J,** Coll Of Charleston, Charleston, SC; SR; Intl Stds Clb Sec 89-; Pol Sci Clb 89-90; Org Non Trad Stdnts 89-90; Phi Kappa Phi; Sigma Iota Rho 90-; Pi Sigma Alpha 90-; Dengate Schlrshp 90-; AA Cty; Clg Chgo 88; Pol Sci; Grad Schl Career Acad.

**THAYER, DANIEL T,** Cornell Univ Statutory College, Ithaca, NY; SR; Hortus Forum Treas 90-; Astrnmy Clb 90-.

**THAYER, DONNA M,** Le Moyne Coll, Syracuse, NY; FR; MBA; Accntng; CPA.

**THAYER, EMILY A,** Furman Univ, Greenville, SC; FR; BA; Colr Grd/Mrchng Bnd 90-; Fr Advsr; Collgt Ed Serv Corps 90-; IM Bsktbl/Sftbl 90-.

**THAYER, JOHN H,** Fl International Univ, Miami, FL; GD; EDP; Dctrl Stdnts Assoc 81-; EDS Nova Univ Miami 89; MS Miami FL 88; Ed.

**THAYER JR, SAM E,** Memphis St Univ, Memphis, TN; SO; BBA; Stdnt Cncl VP 88-89; Mu Alfa Theta Pres 88-89; Sci Club 87-89; Spanish Natl Hon Soc 87-88; Sewanee Award 88; Bsbl Cptn 82-89; Acctng.

**THCIKLIN, JONI D,** Al A & M Univ, Normal, AL; SO; BS; SDTF 90-; Zlgy; Med Rsrch.

**THEADO, NANCY T,** Kent St Univ Kent Cmps, Kent, OH; JR; BSN; Orientation Instr 90-; Stdnts Prfsnl Nrsg 88-90; Alpha Lambda Delta 88-90; Golden Key; Hnrs Clg 88-; Sigma Theta Tau; Vet Adm Hlth Prfsnl Schlrshp 90-; Columbus Chldrns Hosp Study Pgm 90-; Nrsg; MSN.

**THEAKSTON-MULVANIA, PATRICIA A,** Immaculata Coll, Immaculata, PA; SR; BSN; Emrgncy Nrs Assn; AD Bettendorf Comm Coll 84; Nrsng.

**THEIS, CHRISTINA M,** Univ Of Central Fl, Orlando, FL; SO; MBA; All Amer Schlr; Pres Lst Hon Rl; Soccer; Psychology; Clncl Psychlgst.**

**THEISEN, LORI A,** Bowling Green St Univ At Huron, Huron, OH; JR; Gldn Key 90-; Acctng.

**THELEN, AMY J,** Villanova Univ, Villanova, PA; JR; BA; Work Study Job 88-; Empire State Games Soccer Team 89-90; Campus Ministry 89-; Deans Lst 90-; Vars Sccr Capt 88-; IM Ftbl/Bsktbl/Sftbl 88-; Communications; Pblc Rltns.

**THELWELL, GILBERT A,** Borough Of Manhattan Comm Coll, New York, NY; GD; BS; Caribbean Clb 88-89; SG Vp 88-; Deans List 89; Hosp Vol 90-; Cert Of Achvmnt 90; Rsrch Opprtnts Prog 90; AA; Science; Phys Asst.**

**THEOBALD, MARIE D,** Clarkson Univ, Potsdam, NY; JR; BS; Scty Womens Mgrs Pres; Stdnt Admissions Rep 90-; Class Of 89 Alumni Rep; Deans Lst 89-90; Presidential Schlr; Xerox Xcel Prog Rochester NY; Genl Mngmnt; Human Resource Mngmnt.

**THEOBALD JR, RICHARD K,** Indiana Univ Of Pa, Indiana, PA; SR; BA; Grmn Clb 90-; AA 90; Ocmp Sci; Prgrmmng.

**THEODORE, MARYNICK,** City Univ Of Ny City Coll, New York, NY; GD.

**THEODORIDES, GREGG,** Mayland Comm Coll, Spruce Pine, NC; FR; BS; Part Co-Op Pgm; Acctng; CPA.

**THEODOSSAKOS, ANTOINETTE,** Fl Atlantic Univ, Boca Raton, FL; SR; BA; Yng Clg Dem 89; Phi Theta Kappa Treas 89-; Legalaid Scty Inter 89; Prestl Schlrshp Awd 89-; AA 90; Sociology; Law.**

**THEODOTOU, MARINA A,** Univ Of Sc At Columbia, Columbia, SC; JR; Greek Org Secr 90-; Econ Hnr Soc; Phi Eta Sigma; Econ; EEC.

**THERBER, JONATHAN W,** Volunteer St Comm Coll, Gallatin, TN; SO; BA; Bus Mgmnt.

**THERIAULT JR, DOUGLAS P,** Me Maritime Academy, Castine, ME; FR; BA; Power Plant Eng.

**THERMIDOR, MARJORIE M,** City Univ Of Ny City Coll, New York, NY; SR; BS; CADECUS 87-; Blgy Hnrs Scty; Bio Med Rsrch Asst 90-; Blgy; Med Dr.

**THERO, DANIEL P,** Siena Coll, Loudonville, NY; SR; BA; Siena Cmps Mnstry Pgm 86-; Bio Club 86-90; Stdnts Better World 90; Phi Sigma Tau V P 90; Delta Epsilon Sigma; Siena AIDS Peer Educ Comm 90; Siena KEX Cpysrc Prize Rsrch 90; Mjr Field Award Hghst Bio GPA 90; Phlsphy; Clg Tchng.

**THEROUX, KIMBERLY K,** Bay Path Coll, Longmeadow, MA; JR; BA; MADD 89-; AS; Bsn; Pblc Rltns.

**THERRIAULT, CHRISTOPHER D,** Embry Riddle Aeronautical Univ, Daytona Beach, FL; SO; Psi Upsilon Frat Treas 88-89; Aeronautical Sci Flght; Aviation Career.

**THERRIEN, JEAN PIERRE,** Barry Univ, Miami, FL; GD; MBA; Police Benevolent Assn Brd Dirs 90-; Frtrnl Order Police 90-; Law Enfrcmnt Ofcr; BA 90; Bus; Law.

**THERRIEN, ROBIN E,** Elms Coll, Chicopee, MA; SO; BSW; Hmpshr Hghts Tnt Asc Pres; BSA Coord; Amhrst Srvl Ctr Vol; Brd Cmmssnrs Hmpshr Cty Rgnl Hsng Auth 90-; Scl Wrk.

**THESING, TRACEY LYNN,** Univ Of Tn At Martin, Martin, TN; SR; SGA; Peer Enblng Pgm; Greekfest Com Chrmn; Phi Eta Sigma; Phi Kappa Phi; Hnrs Smnr; Occptnl Therapy Clb Pres/ Fndr; Alpha Omicron Pi; Comm Svc Awd; Stdnt Affairs Awd; Occptnl Therapy.

**THEW, STACEY L,** Bard Coll, Annandle-Hdsn, NY; FR; BS; COG 90-; Wash Cntrct Lgrs Assoc Schlrshp; IM Sftbl 90-; Envir Stds/Gntcs; Envir Gntcst.

**THEWES, AMELIA E,** Glassboro St Coll, Glassboro, NJ; SR; BA; Sigma Delta Upsilon Soc Chair; Acad Achvmnt Awd; Cmnctns; Music Inds.

**THEWSUVAT, PEERAPON,** Coppin St Coll, Baltimore, MD; SR; BS; BS 88; Cmptr Sci; Cmptr Prgmr.

**THIAGARAJAN, SHANTHINI L,** City Univ Of Ny Baruch Coll, New York, NY; JR; BA; Bus To Bus Mrktg Scty Prmtns Vp; AIMS Mntrs 88-89; Bus; Acctg.

**THIBAULT, KENNETH J,** Springfield Tech Comm Coll, Springfield, MA; GD; BSEET; Lasr/Electro Optcs; Engr/Lasr Stdy.

**THIBAULT, TINA M,** Rivier Coll, Nashua, NH; SO; BED; Stdnt Edn Assoc V P 90-; Elem Edn; Teach.

**THIBERT, GLENN A,** Western New England Coll, Springfield, MA; SR; BS; IEEE 88; Peer Tutor 90; Photo Clb 87-90; Sigma Beta Tau; Cmptr Eng; Eng.

**THIBODEAU, KRISTEN L,** Springfield Tech Comm Coll, Springfield, MA; GD; BA; Alpha Nu Omega; Resd Cnslr/ Providence Hosp Sys; EMT Holyoke Comm Colg 87; Socl Work; Hmn Svcs.

**THIBODEAU, LAURA L,** Endicott Coll, Beverly, MA; SR; BA; Bus Clb; SGA Senatr; Phi Theta Kappa; Bus Admin; Mktg/ Advtsng.

**THIEL, EMMA L,** Univ Of Med & Dentistry Of Nj, Newark, NJ; SR; BS; Stdnt Govt Phys Thrpy Clss Treas 89-; Phi Kappa Phi; Lambda Alpha Sigma 90-; Phys Thrpy.

**THIEL, MELISSA M,** Indiana Univ Of Pa, Indiana, PA; JR; BED; Assc Rehab Advcts 90-; Alpha Sigma Alpha Phlnthrpc Chrmn 89-; Deans Lst 89-90; Rehabltn; Occptnl Thrpy.

**THIEL, TRACY J,** Univ Of Southern Ms, Hattiesburg, MS; FR; BA; Hnrs Assn 90-; Hll Assn 90; Alpha Lambda Delta; Gamma Beta Phi; Sigma Pi Sigma Pr 90-; Angel Flight; Oliver Austin Schlr; Math Physcs; Math Edctn.

**THIELE, MICHELLE E,** Mount Saint Mary Coll, Newburgh, NY; JR; BED; AA Orange Co Comm Coll 90; Psych/Elem/Spec Ed; Tchr.

**THIESEN, CHADWICK L,** Fl St Univ, Tallahassee, FL; SO; BA; Golden Key; Alpha Tau Omega Jdcl Comm; Business; Investment Broker.

**THIGPEN, DEBRA W,** Western Carolina Univ, Cullowhee, NC; JR; BSW; Soc Wk Clb 90-; Pi Gamma Mu; Phi Alpha; Natl Assn Soc Wrkrs; Beta Sigma Phi 86-; Tom Uzabel Meml Schlrshp; First Bapt Chrch Intrnshp 78; AAS Tri Cnty Comm Coll 78; Smoky Mountain Ctr MH/DD/SAS Intrn; Exec Sec Smoky Mount Ctr MH/DD/SAS 87-; Soc Wk; Med Soc Wrkr.

**THIGPEN, PATRICK P,** Middle Ga Coll, Cochran, GA; SO; BA; Bus Adm; Finance.

**THIJM, DIANE C,** West Liberty St Coll, West Liberty, WV; SR; BS; Intl Stdnt Org; Grphc Dsng; Advrtsng Free Lnc Grphc Dsgn.

**THISDALE, KENNETH A,** Memphis St Univ, Memphis, TN; JR; BA; Gamma Beta Phi; Engl; Law.

**THISTLETHWAITE, ASHLEY D,** Central Al Comm Coll, Alexander City, AL; SO; BS; Stdnt Govt Assoc; Phi Theta Kappa Histrn; Fin/Econ; Fincl Anlyst.

**THOMA, MARTHA E,** Emory Univ, Atlanta, GA; GD; MN; Assoc Pedtrc Onclgy Nrs 90-; Onclgy Nrsng Scty 90-; Natl Schl Nrs Assoc 90-; Phi Theta Kappa 67; Nrs Edctnl Fnds Awrd; NAPNAP; Hosp Onclgy Nrs; AD Lake City Cmmnty Coll 67; M Ed Univ Tulsa 78; Nrsng; Clncl Nrs Spclst Pdctrc Nrs.

**THOMAE, TODD A,** Nyack Coll, Nyack, NY; JR; BS; Bsktbl 88-90; Bus; Hstry.**

**THOMAN II, BARRY E,** Univ Of Akron, Akron, OH; JR; BS; RA 90-; Acctng Asc 89-; Phi Eta Sigma; Alpha Lambda Delta; Gldn Key; Schlps; Acctng.

**THOMAN, JEFFREY B,** Nova Univ, Ft Lauderdale, FL; GD; MBA; BS Nova Univ 90; CDP Inst Cert Cmptr Prof 89; Bus; Data Prcsng.

**THOMAN, JOHN G,** Embry Riddle Aeronautical Univ, Daytona Beach, FL; SR; BA; Cmmrcl Pilot/Flght Instr 88-; Aeronautical Scnc; Pilot.

**THOMAS, AARON S,** Lynchburg Coll, Lynchburg, VA; FR; Stdnt Activities Bd 90-; Mc Wane Dorm Cncl Senator 90-; Phi Eta Sigma; Bus/Mgmnt/Mtkg; Tele Comm Mktng.

**THOMAS, ADRIAN S,** Anderson Coll, Anderson, SC; FR; BA; SGA Frshmn Pres 90-; Race Org Com 90-; Host Student Views Talk Show; Drama/Communications.

**THOMAS, ADRIANNE D,** Kent St Univ Kent Cmps, Kent, OH; SR; BA; Stdnt Nrse Orgnztn Cphga Comm Coll VP 87; RN Mt Snai Med Cntr Clvlnd OH 89-; AAS Nrsng Cuyahoga Comm Coll Cleveland OH 87; Clsscl Hmnts Mdvl Hstry; Law.

**THOMAS, ALAN E,** Univ Central Del Caribe, Cayey, PR; GD; MD; Stdnt Cncl 89-90; Dscplnry Comm Rep 89-90; Intrcomm Serv Effrt Adlt Ldr 87-; Collgt Ed Serv Corp Dvsn Head 83-87; BS Furman Univ 87; Med.

**THOMAS, ALEX W,** Univ Of Sc At Columbia, Columbia, SC; SR; Amer Mktg Assoc 90-; Delta Sigma Pi VP Prfsnl Act 90-; Mktg; Rtl Mgmt.

**THOMAS, ALFRED E,** Jackson St Univ, Jackson, MS; SO; BA; Prsdnts Lst; Pltcl Sci; Law.

**THOMAS, ALISA M,** Georgetown Coll, Georgetown, KY; JR; BA; Stdnt Fndtn Pres 90-; Panhellenic Coun Pres 90-; Sigma Tau Delta 90-; Phi Mu VP; Phi Alpha Theta; Eta Delta Phi; Dns Lst 90-; Engl/Amer Stud; Engl Prof.

**THOMAS, ALISON L,** Univ Of Louisville, Louisville, KY; SR; ME; IIE Pres 87-; SME V Chrmn 89-; Instr Dsgn/Mgmt Automation Syst Seminars 89; Instr Cmptr Integrtd Mfg Seminars 89; Gen Elect Appl Bd Overseers Mentors Pgm 89-90; Sigma Tau Alpha 87; Lambda Chi Alpha Ltl Sis 87-89; Intl Order Rainbow Girls 80-89; Indstrl Engr.

**THOMAS, AMY M,** Babson Coll, Babson Park, MA; FR; GIVE; Stdnt Govt Soc Cmte; Cmte Against Hunger/Homelessness.

**THOMAS, ANDRE L,** Howard Univ, Washington, DC; JR; BS; Chgo Clb 87-89; SNMA Pres 89-; Gldn Ky 89-; Beta Kappa Chi 89-; Dept Of Immnlgy Res Asst 88-89; Vars Ftbl 87-88; Zoolgy; Med.**

**THOMAS, ANGELA N,** Alcorn St Univ, Lorman, MS; FR; Biology; Phar.

**THOMAS, ANN M,** Clark Atlanta Univ, Atlanta, GA; JR; BA; Philharmonic Soc V P 90-; Orient Guide Corp 89-90; Kappa Delta Epsilon 90-; Delta Sigma Theta 89-; Erly Chldhd Educ; Tchng.

**THOMAS, ANTHONY J,** Atlantic Comm Coll, Mays Landing, NJ; SO; AS; Bus; Bus Admin.

**THOMAS, ANTHONY M,** Univ Of Southern Ms, Hattiesburg, MS; FR; BA; Sigma Phi Epsilon Almn Oprtns Dir; Gamma Beta Phi; U S Air Force 86-90; Crim Jstc; Law.

**THOMAS, ANTHONY S,** Univ Of Nc At Charlotte, Charlotte, NC; FR; BS; Baptist Stdnt Un 90-; Hall Cncl 90; Baptist Stdnt Un Missions Tm/Choir 90-; IM Bsktbl/Sftbl 90-; Bus Admin.

**THOMAS, ANTONIA I,** Johnson St Coll, Johnson, VT; SO; BA; Psych; Tchr.

**THOMAS, ARLETTE M,** Coppin St Coll, Baltimore, MD; SR; Stdnts Fr Entrprs Offcr 90-; Vc Chncllr Dbtng Clb Chncllr 90; Stdnt Govt Sen 88; Dept Hnr Scty Hnr Stdnt 90-; Ronald E Mc Nair Post B Mmbr 90-; Mgmt Sci Awrd Stdnt; Mgmt Sci; Law.**

**THOMAS, BERNIE J,** Christopher Newport Coll, Newport News, VA; JR; BA; Advsr Snt Comm; Psi Chi 90-; Alpha Chi 90-; Alpha Kappa Psi Pres 88-; Pnnsla Kiwanis Schlp 89-; Ecnmcs/ Mktg; Intl Bsn.

**THOMAS, BETH A,** Providence Coll, Providence, RI; SR; Res Bd Treas 88-89; IM Bsktbl Capt 87-; Bsn Adm Assoc 90-; Commencement Slideshow Comm 90-; BS; Bsn Adm; Mgmt MBA.

**THOMAS, BRENDA K,** Thomas Nelson Comm Coll, Hampton, VA; SO; AA; Pennisula Lit 90; Sociology.

**THOMAS, BRENT A,** Univ Of Sc At Columbia, Columbia, SC; SO; BS; The Navigators 89-; Soc Physics Stdnts; Sigma Pi Sigma; Habitat Fot Humanity 89-; Fres Yr Awd; Physics; Rsrch/ Teaching.

**THOMAS, BRIAN H,** Christopher Newport Coll, Newport News, VA; SO; BA; CNC Hnrs Prgm 90-; Hstry.

**THOMAS, BRYAN K,** Savannah Coll Of Art & Design, Savannah, GA; SR; BFA; Painting Clb Prsdnt 90-; Stdnt Gvrnmnt 90-; Prsdnt Cnsl 90-; Deans Lst; Phi Delta Kappa Awd Ldrshp; VA Calvin Kiah Schlrshp Hugh M Dorsey IL Schlrshp 89-; Painting; Edctn.

**THOMAS, CANDY N,** Univ Of Tn At Martin, Martin, TN; SR; BA, OSA 89-90, STEA 90-, Deans Lst, Jean Allfeld Cohen Mem Schlrshp 90; Elem Ed; Tchng.

**THOMAS, CECILE A P,** City Univ Of Ny City Coll, New York, NY; JR; BA; Peer Cnslg Coord 90-; Cmnctns; Advrtsg/Publ Rels.

**THOMAS, CHARLES P,** Methodist Coll, Fayetteville, NC; JR; BS; Sociology/Soc Wrk Clb Pblcty 89-; Democrats VP 89-90; Sigma Omega Chi Sec 89-90; Deans Lst 90-; Sociology/Soc Wrk; Cnslr.

**THOMAS, CHRISTA D,** Radford Univ, Radford, VA; SO; BA; Poltcl Sci; Law.

**THOMAS, CHRISTINE M,** Indiana Univ Of Pa, Indiana, PA; SR; BED; ACEI; PSEA; Kappa Delta Pi Histrn Reprtr 90-; Deans List 87-; Prvst Schlr 90-; Grad Magna Cum Laude; Elem Ed; Tchr.

**THOMAS, CLAUDIA A,** Univ Of Ky, Lexington, KY; JR; BA; Hon Pgm Stdnt Advsry Com Spec Com Chr 90-; Rtry Clb Schlrshp 90; Deans Lst 89-90; Sec/Edtrl Prdctn Asst Amer Bd Fmly Prctc 84-89; Scrtrl/Offc Admin; Assoc Lexington Comm Coll 84; Art Hstry/Engl; Museum Wrk.

**THOMAS, CLINTON W,** Liberty Univ, Lynchburg, VA; JR; BS; Lbrty Assoc Accntnts Tres; Stdnt Govt Dorm Snt 90-; Alpha Lambda Delta; Acctg; CPA.

**THOMAS, COREY I,** Richard Bland Coll, Petersburg, VA; SO; Stdnts Free Entrprs 90-; Bus; Acctg.

**THOMAS, CYNTHIA S,** Fl Atlantic Univ, Boca Raton, FL; GD; MBA; Beta Gamma Sigma 90-; Phi Kappa Phi 90-; Grad Assist 90-; BBA 90; Finance.

**THOMAS, DANA L,** Middle Ga Coll, Cochran, GA; JR; BA; SPAGE 90-; Gamma Beta Phi GSU 90-; Dean Lst 88-90; Dean Lst GSU 90-; Grad Hnrs 90; Phrmcy Clrk 88-; Art Wrk In Gllry 89-90; Pblshd MUSES 89-90; Mddl Grds Educ/Pre Phrmcy; Tchr Admn/Phrmst.

**THOMAS, DANIEL J,** Univ Of Akron, Akron, OH; JR; BA; Natl Stdnt Spch Lng Hrng Assoc 90-; Cmnctv Dsrdr; Adlgy.

**THOMAS, DAVID L,** Mount Olive Coll, Mount Olive, NC; SO; BA; USAF; Bus Mgmt.

**THOMAS, DAVID P,** Glassboro St Coll, Glassboro, NJ; JR; BA; Phi Sigma Alpha; Pol Sci; Second Educ.

**THOMAS, DEBRA,** Univ Of Pittsburgh, Pittsburgh, PA; JR; BA; Acad Excell Awd 88-89; PAACE 90; Intrnshp Agency Plng Chldrn Dvlpmntl Disabilites; AS PA State Univ 90; Soc Wrk.

**THOMAS, DIANNE L,** Newbury Coll, Brookline, MA; SO; BA; Cls Rep 90; Mktg/Fin.

**THOMAS, DONETH ELAINE,** City Univ Of Ny Baruch Coll, New York, NY; SR; BBA; Carbbn Clb 87-; Dns Lst 89-90; Acctg; Tax Law.

**THOMAS, DONNA L,** Volunteer St Comm Coll, Gallatin, TN; FR; Elem Educ; Tchr.

**THOMAS, DONNA M,** Atlantic Comm Coll, Mays Landing, NJ; FR; ASSOC; Spcl Edctn.

**THOMAS, ELONDA C,** Univ Of Sc At Columbia, Columbia, SC; JR; BA; Assoc Of Afrcn Amer Stdnts 89; NAACP 89; Alchl/ Drg Peer Edctr 89; Kappa Delta Epsilon; Mrtr Brd Ntl Hnr Scty; Ordr Of Omega; Alpha Kappa Alpha VP 89; Erly Chldhd Ed.

**THOMAS, GARY D,** Hudson Valley Comm Coll, Troy, NY; FR; AOS; AOS HVCC 89; Elec; Eng.

**THOMAS, GINA MARIE,** Oh Univ, Athens, OH; JR; IIE 88; Choral Union 89; Alpha Pi Mu; Indus/Sys Engr.

**THOMAS, HAZEL M,** Va Commonwealth Univ, Richmond, VA; SO; BS; Pre Phrmcy Clb 90-; Phi Eta Sigma 90-; Phrmcy.

**THOMAS, HEATHER A,** Allegheny Coll, Meadville, PA; SO; BA; SG 90-; Coll Chr/Chmbr Choir 89-; Orchss 90-; Lambda Sigma 90-; Kappa Kappa Gamma 89-; Doane Schlr 89-90; Alden Schlr 89-90; Cls Sec 89-; Engl/Hstry; Law/Jrnlsm.

**THOMAS, HENRY D,** Church Of God Sch Of Theology, Cleveland, TN; GD; MDIV; CPE Clinical Pastoral Educ; Erlanger Medl Ctr Chaplain; Ministers License Exhorter 87; Ministers License 89; Hospital Chaplain 90-; Residency Prog; BSBED Lee Clg 87; Bible; Pastoral Hospital Chaplain.

**THOMAS, HILARY L,** Univ Of Miami, Coral Gables, FL; SR; BA; Pol Sci; Law.

**THOMAS, HILDA S,** Marywood Coll, Scranton, PA; FR; BA; Engl; Tchng.

**THOMAS, HUGH,** Al A & M Univ, Normal, AL; FR; BA; Ftbl; Engr/Math; Elctrcl Engr.

**THOMAS, JACKIE D,** Bethel Coll, Mckenzie, TN; FR; AA; Nrsg.

**THOMAS, JAMES JEFFREY,** Ny Institute Of Tech Ny City, New York, NY; SR; BT; IEEE Treas 90-; Caribbean Assoc; Nu Epsilon Tau; Elctrcl/Elctrncs; Engrg Tchngly.

**THOMAS, JAMES R,** Pellissippi St Tech Comm Coll, Knoxville, TN; SO; AS; Otdrs Clb Tres 90-; Stdnt Govt Assc Sntr Lrg 89-; IEEE Tres 90-; Tau Alpha Pi 90-; Phi Theta Kappa 90-; Summa Cum Laude 90-; Pres Awrd 90-; Otstndng Stdnt Ldr 90-; Elect Eng Techcn; Cmptr Eng.

**THOMAS, JASTASIA T,** Clark Atlanta Univ, Atlanta, GA; SR; BS; Comptr Sci Club Treas 87-; NAACP 87-88 90-; Alpha Kappa Mu Pres 90-; Pi Mu Epsilon; Hons Progrm 88-; Greyhound Schlrshp 90-; James P Bronlay Schlr 90-; AT/T Bell Labs Intrnshp; Comptr Sci; Sys Anlyst.

**THOMAS, JEAN E,** The Johns Hopkins Univ, Baltimore, MD; SR; BSN; Grdt Tchg Asstntshp Indiana Univ Schl Med 80-82; Epscpl Chrch Vstry 87-90; Sr Bioprdts R D Prjct Mgr 85-90; BA Duke Univ 80; MS Indiana Univ 83; Nrsg.

**THOMAS, JENNIFER J,** Dowling Coll, Oakdale Li, NY; JR; BA; Alpha Chi 90-; Engl Honr Soc 90-; Elem Educ/Engl; Tchng.

**THOMAS, JENNIFER LYNAE,** Ms St Univ, Miss State, MS; JR; BA; Hnds Hi Stpprs Sprt Chrmn 88-90; Gamma Beta Phi; Phi Theta Kappa 89-; Alpha Beta Gamma Sec 89-; Cmmnty Coll Acdmc Schlrshp; Phi Theta Kappa Schlrshp; Deans Lst Prsdnts Lst 88-90; Cmmnctns; Pblc Rltns.

**THOMAS, JENNIFER REBECCA,** Wallace St Comm Coll At Hncvll, Hanceville, AL; FR; ADN; Natl Stdnt Nurs Assn; Nwspr 90-; United Way 89-; Vol Yr; Sci; R N.

**THOMAS, JERRY JERMAINE,** Al A & M Univ, Normal, AL; SO; ROTC 89-; IM Bsktbl 89-; Bus/Fnc; Fncl Mngr Anlyst.

**THOMAS, JILL S,** Faulkner St Jr Coll, Bay Minette, AL; BA; Waitress; Meat Cutter; Meat Wrapper; Paralegalism; Law.

**THOMAS, JOAN A,** Castleton St Coll, Castleton, VT; SR; BA; Bltmr Schl Brd 89-; BA; Rdng/Elem; Tch.

**THOMAS, JODI ANN,** Marshall University, Huntington, WV; JR; BA; The Parthenon Stf/Edtr 88-; Tutor Role Mdl Pgm 89-; Tutor Yr Awd Jvnl Jstc Role Mdl Pgm; Jrnlsm/Lbry Sci; Edctn.

**THOMAS JR, JOHN P,** Univ Of Miami, Coral Gables, FL; FR; BA; Waiter 86-90; Engl/Pol Sci; Law.

**THOMAS, JONEIS F,** Howard Univ, Washington, DC; JR; BS; Alpha Swthrt Ct Chpln 89-; Kwanzaa Clbrtn Com 88; Gldn Key; Beta Kappa Chi; Psi Chi; Phi Beta Kappa; Natl Sci Fndtn Awd Excllnce Psychlgy 90; Dns Hnr Roll 89-; Rsrch Ast Mnrty Access Rsrch Careers 89-; Rsrch Ast Mnrty Summer Rsrch 90; Psychology; Child Clncl Psychlgy.**

**THOMAS, JOY M,** Bob Jones Univ, Greenville, SC; FR; BS; ACT 90-; Univ Symphonic Band 90-; Univ Chorus 90-; Sigma Lambda Delta Chrstr 90-; Soccer Tm 90-; Vlybl 90-; Msc Ed; Tchng/Prfrmng.

**THOMAS, JUANITA G,** Wilmington Coll, New Castle, DE; FR; BED; Lab Tchncn For E I Du Pont 73; Ed; EDD.

**THOMAS, JULIANA V,** Coppin St Coll, Baltimore, MD; SO; BA; Big Bro/Sis 90-; Intl Std Asc 90-; Bsn Mgmt; Htl/Rest Mgmt.

**THOMAS, JULIE,** Northern Ky Univ, Highland Hts, KY; SR; BA; Alpha Chi 90-; Deans Lst 88-; Hon Lst 90-; Amer Red Crss Lfgrd/Instrctr 86-; Aqtc Exer Assoc Instrctr 90-; Intrnshp Exer Spclst Crdc Rehab; IM Sftbl Vlybl Mini Trthln Archry 87-; Rcrtnl Ftnss.

**THOMAS, KAREN D,** Va St Univ, Petersburg, VA; SR; BS; Scty Advncmnt Mgmt Treas 90-; Bsn Admin Clb 90-; Bsn Admin; Mgmt.

**THOMAS, KARIN R,** Cornell Univ, Ithaca, NY; FR; BA; Black Wmns Support Ntwk; Lacrosse Vrsty Tm; Sociology/ Anthropology; Law.

**THOMAS, KATHERINE B,** Atlantic Comm Coll, Mays Landing, NJ; FR; AA; Wms Clb; Lib Arts.

**THOMAS, KATHY L,** Wv Northern Comm Coll, Wheeling, WV; FR; ASSOC; Assoc 84; Cmptrs; Cmptr Prgrmmng.

**THOMAS, KATINA A,** Fisk Univ, Nashville, TN; FR; BA; Dns Lst 90-; Powder Puff Ftbl 90-; Bio/Pol Sci; Lawyer/Dr.

**THOMAS, KATRICE L,** Fisk Univ, Nashville, TN; JR; BS; NOBCCHE 90-; Hlth Careers Clb 89-; FASE 90; Beta Kappa Chi; Gold Key; Alpha Kappa Alpha 90-; Deans Hon Lst 90; Acad Schlrshp 88-; Chem; Med.

**THOMAS, KERINE A,** Univ Of The Dist Of Columbia, Washington, DC; SO; BBA; Acctg.

**THOMAS, KEVIN D,** Va St Univ, Petersburg, VA; JR; BA; NAACP 89; Class Offcr 88; Phldlphia Pre-Alumni Assoc 88; Ftbl/ Trck 88; Admin Jstce; FBI Agnt.

**THOMAS, KIM R,** Univ Of Al At Birmingham, Birmingham, AL; FR.

**THOMAS, KIMBERLEY M,** Central Al Comm Coll, Alexander City, AL; SO; Co Op 90-; Dean Lst 90-; Lib Arts; Elem Educ.

**THOMAS, KIMBERLY A,** Comm Coll Algny Co Algny Cmps, Pittsburgh, PA; JR; AAS; Comm Athletic Assn Sec; Lutheran Church Tchr; Acctnt.

**THOMAS, KIMBERLY L,** Al A & M Univ, Normal, AL; SO; BED; NAACP 90-; Omega Psi Phi 90-; Presdntl Hnrs Schlr 90-; Engl; Law.

**THOMAS, KRISTIE M,** Tougaloo Coll, Tougaloo, MS; FR; BS; PEPS; Pres Schlr 90-; Otstndng Stdnt Pre Cal II 90-; Physcs/ Math; Electrcl Eng.

**THOMAS, LA NISHA R,** Clark Atlanta Univ, Atlanta, GA; JR; BS; Math Club Pres 88-; Hons Prog 88-; Beta Kappa Chi Secy; Alpha Kappa Mu; Amoco Intrnshp; UNCF Mellon Fellow 90-; UNCF/GTE Schlr 90-; Math; PhD Math.

**THOMAS, LAVON D,** Roane St Comm Coll, Harriman, TN; FR; BA; English/Art; Elem Ed.

**THOMAS, LAY ONTRA S,** Univ Of Sc At Columbia, Columbia, SC; SR; BS; Car Pgm Un Contmpry Snds Comm 89-90; Video Corr Comm Edtr 89-90; Res Hall Govt Pub Comm Asst Hd 89-; Phi Beta Lambda 89-; Intrnshp Vol Bookstr; 3rd Pl Busn Law Econ; Phi Beta Lambda St Conf 90-; Min Stdnt Affrs Awd 87-; Retlng Fashn Merch; Fashn Desgnr.

**THOMAS, LEON C,** Jackson St Univ, Jackson, MS; SR; BS; Phi Theta Kappa 88-; Schlrshp Awd 89-; Acctg Awd 88; AA Copiah Lincoln Cmnty Clg 89; Bsn; Bsn Exec.

**THOMAS, LESLIE DIONE,** Al St Univ, Montgomery, AL; SO; BA; Univ Clg Hnr Roll 89-; Cmnctns; TV Prdcr/Wrtr.

**THOMAS, LESLIE L,** Slippery Rock Univ, Slippery Rock, PA; SR; BS; Phi Epsilon Kappa 90-; Phy Educ/Liftime Fitns; Card Rehab Spec.

**THOMAS, LINDA A,** Univ Of Miami, Coral Gables, FL; JR; BA; Phi Theta Kappa 88-90; Kphi Kappa Phi; Boys Towns Italy Inc Aide-P 88-; Grnd Jury Assn FL Inc Aide-P 88-; Hgst Hons/ Dstngctn 89; AA Miami-Dade Comm Coll S Camp 89; Hist/ Scndry Ed.

**THOMAS, LISCO D,** Univ Of Sc At Columbia, Columbia, SC; SR; BA; Outstndng Stdnt; Hon Grad; Deans Lst; AA Mdlnd Tech Coll 90; Soc Wrk; MA.

**THOMAS, LORETTA,** Alcorn St Univ, Lorman, MS; JR; BA; Bnd 89-; Sclgy/Scl Wrk Clbs 89-; Sclgy/Scl Wrk; Cnslng.**

**THOMAS, M LISA,** Radford Univ, Radford, VA; SO; BA; Hse Cncl; Bus Calculus Tutor; Bus Admin; Bus Mgmnt.

**THOMAS, MARIE H,** Univ Of Sc At Coastal Carolina, Conway, SC; FR; BS; Bio; Med Dr.

**THOMAS, MARILYN H,** Univ Of Sc At Columbia, Columbia, SC; SR; Stdnt Nwspr Rprtr Cpy Ed 90; Gamma Beta Phi 89-; Pres Hnr Roll 89-90; Dns Lst 88-90; BA 90; Eng; Wrtng Career/ Jrnlsm/Advtsg.

**THOMAS, MARITZEL O,** Saint Petersburg Jr Coll, St Petersburg, FL; SO; Intl Clb 89-; Phi Theta Kappa 87-; Outstndg Mnrty Stdnt; P T Kappa Art Awd; Spch Pthlgy/Psych.

**THOMAS, MARSHALL B,** Univ Of Pittsburgh, Pittsburgh, PA; JR; ASME; Theta Xi Hse Mgr; Mech Eng.

**THOMAS, MARY KAY,** Marshall University, Huntington, WV; GD; MA; Asst 88-; BA 82; Appld Soc/Anth.

**THOMAS, MATHEW,** Manhattan Coll, Bronx, NY; FR; BS; Elec Engr.

**THOMAS, MELANIE D,** Tuskegee Univ, Tuskegee Inst, AL; JR; BSN; Tuskagee Univ Stdnt Nrs Assn Pr 90-; Tuskagee Univ Chptr NAACP 89-; Dr T M Campbell Jr M D Awd; Nrsng.

**THOMAS, MELANIE L,** Fl St Univ, Tallahassee, FL; SR; BS; Cnslr 89-90; Phi Kappa Phi; Kappa Delta Pi; Delta Delta Delta 87-; Fut Educ Amer 90-; Educ; Tch.

**THOMAS, MELANIE R,** Georgetown Coll, Georgetown, KY; FR; Fllwshp Of Chrstn Athlts 90-; Cmps Actn Tm 90-; Sci; Dntstry.

**THOMAS, MICAH J C,** Central Fl Comm Coll, Ocala, FL; FR; BA; Variations 90-; Intervrsty Chrstn Flwshp 90-; IM Ftbl Vlybl; Music; Performance.

**THOMAS, MICHAEL ALLAN,** Salisbury St Univ, Salisbury, MD; SO; MAA; Young Life; Physcs/Eng.

**THOMAS, MICHAEL W,** Widener Univ, Chester, PA; SR; BS; IEEE Pres 90-; Army ROTC 87-; Army ROTC Schlrshp 89-; Rfle And Pstl Tm 87-; Elec Eng; Eng.

**THOMAS, MICKEY L,** Brevard Coll, Brevard, NC; FR; Art/ Bsn; Grphc Artst/Bsn.

**THOMAS, MONICA C,** Queens Coll, Charlotte, NC; SO; BA; Ntl Assc Acctnts Pres 90-; Admssns Core 90-; Union Brd Dirs; Janusian Ordr Vp 90-; Natl Assc Acctnts Schlr; Intrnshp Tinsley/ Terry; Pres Schlr 89-; Acctg.

**THOMAS, NADIA,** City Univ Of Ny City Coll, New York, NY; SR; BS; Caduceus Soc VP 89-90; Fresh Hnr Soc 86-; Gldn Ky 90-; Role Mdl Prog Part 90-; BS; Biol; Med.

**THOMAS, NANCY D,** Bristol Univ, Bristol, TN; GD; MBA; Env Eng Aide; BS Tusculm Clg 89; Cmptr Res Inf Mgmt; Mgmt Inf Syst.

**THOMAS, NANCY J,** Warren Wilson Coll, Swannanoa, NC; JR; BED; Warren Wilson Theatre 88-; Cmnty Choir; Soc Stdys; Tchng.**

**THOMAS, NATALIE H,** Meredith Coll, Raleigh, NC; FR; BS; SNCAE 90-; Alpha Lambda Delta; Phis; Deans Lst 90; NC Tchg Flws Schlrshp 90-; Chld Dvlpmnt; Elem Ed.

**THOMAS, NONET S,** Univ Of Md At Eastern Shore, Princess Anne, MD; JR; BS; Rehab Stdnt Assoc Pres 90-; Campus Pal Org VP 90-; Natl Rehab Assoc; Natl Assoc Advncmnt Colored People 90-; Rehab Serv; Occptnl Therapist.

**THOMAS, PEGGY E,** Mayland Comm Coll, Spruce Pine, NC; FR.

**THOMAS, PENNIE W,** Univ Of Southern Ms, Hattiesburg, MS; FR; Gamma Beta Phi; Sci; Pharmacy.

**THOMAS, PETER G,** Univ Of Al At Birmingham, Birmingham, AL; SR; BBA; Mrktng; Advrtsng Sls.

**THOMAS, PHAEDRA D,** Fl A & M Univ, Tallahassee, FL; FR; BS; Cmptr Inf Syst Clb Fr Rep 90-; Fla A/M Gospl Chr Muscn 90-; Pr Schlrs Assn 90-; Phi Eta Sigma; Tallahassee Urbn Lg; Exc Achvmnt Schlrshp Honywll 90-; Cmptr Inf Sys/Math; Syst Anlyst.

**THOMAS, REGINALD S,** Savannah St Coll, Savannah, GA; FR; BBA; Phi Beta Lamda; Future Business Ldrs Amer Hstrn 87-88; Natl Voc Techncl Hnr Scty; LIFE; Hnr Rl 90; Deans Lst; Disabled Employee Of Yr US Army Corps Engrn 90; AA 90; Acctng.

**THOMAS JR, REID S,** Asbury Theological Sem, Wilmore, KY; GD; MDIV; Cnslr Cntnry U M Yth Grp 90-; BA Houghton Coll 87; Thlgy; Pstrl Mntry.

**THOMAS, RICHARD R,** Ramapo Coll Of Nj, Mahwah, NJ; JR; BA; Model United Nations Clb; New Arts Alnce Bd Comm 90; Deans Lst 90-; Mahwah Yth Sprt Boosters; Jr H S Dir 8th Play; Sychology; Prctce/Tch.

**THOMAS, ROBERT L,** Castleton St Coll, Castleton, VT; FR; BA; IM; Sccr Asst Coach 89-; Cntrl VT Sccr Camp Stff; Cmbnd Scis Bio Geol; Wldlfe Fshry Tech.

**THOMAS, ROBIN KAY,** Kent St Univ Geauga Cmps, Burton Twp, OH; JR; BA; 4 H Clb Pres 84-87; Pny Clb Amrc Treas 86-88; Stdnt Snt VP 89-90; Acctg Assoc 90-; Deans Lst 87 90; Acctg.

**THOMAS, ROBIN L,** Dyke Coll, Cleveland, OH; FR; BA; Accntng; Law.

**THOMAS, RONNIE,** Ms St Univ, Miss State, MS; GD; MBA; Hl Cncl Tres 89-90; IFC; SAM; Phi Beta Sigma Prsdnt 89; Big Brthr; Adlt Lit; Habitat Hmnty; BBA MS 90; Bsns Admnstrtn; Mgmt.

**THOMAS, ROY A,** Miami Dade Comm Coll North, Miami, FL; SO; BA; AA Miami Dade Comm Clg; Finance; Law.

**THOMAS, SANDRA D,** Ga St Univ, Atlanta, GA; FR; BS; Bptst Stdnt Union Prgrm Coord; Alpha Lambda Delta; Phi Eta Sigma; Erly Chldhd Ed; Tchr.

**THOMAS, SEQWANA N,** Talladega Coll, Talladega, AL; JR; BA; Chem Club; Alumni Assn: SG Sntr 90-; RA; Alpha Chi; Beta Kappa Chi; Alpha Kappa Alpha; MIT Rsrch Intern 90; Pres Schlrshp; Ruben Sheares Schlrshp 89-; Hamilton-Weaver Award; Lucille Ish Walker Schlrshp; Chem; PHD.

**THOMAS, SHARLA R,** Va St Univ, Petersburg, VA; JR; BA; Admin Jstc Clb 90-; Admin Jstc; Law.

**THOMAS, SHAUN W,** Morehouse Coll, Atlanta, GA; SR; BA; Psych Assn 87-; Calif Club 87-; Hnr Roll 88-; Deans List 89-; Psych; Law.

**THOMAS, SHAYLA Y,** Alcorn St Univ, Lorman, MS; SO; BSN; Hon Stdnt Org Miss Hon 90-; Pre-Nrsng Clb 89-; NAACP 87-; Blackwatch; Deans Lst 89-; Cmps All-Star Chllng Natl All-Star Tm 89-90; Trck 89-90; Nrsng; Neontl Fld.

**THOMAS, SHERRI C,** Radford Univ, Radford, VA; JR; BS; Cncrt Com 90-; Early Ed; Tchr.

**THOMAS, STACEY L,** Stillman Coll, Tuscaloosa, AL; SO; BA; SGA Brd Trus 90-; Mdlng Trp 90-; Zeta Phi Beta Miss Zeta Phi Beta 90-; Dns Lst 89-; Tennis Bsktbl 89-; Math/Engl Educ; Pub Policy/Tch.

**THOMAS, STEVEN L,** Fayetteville St Univ, Fayetteville, NC; FR; BS; IM Tnns Trnmnt 90-; Chmstry.

**THOMAS, TAMMY C,** Piedmont Coll, Demorest, GA; FR; BA; Randall Schlrshp 90-; Engl; Tchr.

**THOMAS, TAMMY L,** Central Al Comm Coll, Alexander City, AL; FR; Bus Mgmt; Cert Acctnt.

**THOMAS, TERESA A,** Comm Coll Algny Co Algny Cmps, Pittsburgh, PA; SO; BFA; Art Assn Pres 88-; Arts Mag Art Edtr; Deans Lst 90-; Carngie 86-; Gllry Asst 90-; Natl Museum Wmn In Arts 90-; Art Hstry.

**THOMAS, TERRI D,** Gordon Coll, Barnesville, GA; FR; MBA; Phi Theta Kappa; Math; Tchr/Engr.

**THOMAS, TERRY-DAWN M,** Coll Of New Rochelle, New Rochelle, NY; SO; Madison Soc Tres 90-; Orntatn 90; Jdcl Brd 90; Hnr Roll Brd 89-; Hnr Cncl 90-; Deans Lst 90-; Pltcl Sci; Corp Lawyer.

**THOMAS, THOMAS W,** Liberty Univ, Lynchburg, VA; FR; BS; Acts 542 Clb Frshmn Pres 90-; Yth Qst Clb 90-; Lght Clb 90-; Blgy Pre Med; Mdcl Dctr.

**THOMAS, TIFFANY N,** Univ Of Tn At Knoxville, Knoxville, TN; FR; Exec Undergrad Prog 90-; Humes Hall Rsdnt Assn 90-; Phi Eta Sigma 90-; Vol Civitan Clb Bd Dir 90-; Tenn Hnrs Prog 90-; Bus Admin Frshmn Schlrshp 90-; Natl Alumni Assn Schlrshp 90-.

**THOMAS, TIM A,** Union Coll, Barbourville, KY; SR; BS; Natl Strength/Cndtning Assoc 89-90; Ftbl 87-90; Phys Educ/Hlth.

**THOMAS, TIMOTHY LEE,** Lincoln Tech Inst, Allentown, PA; SO; AS.**

**THOMAS, TRACEY L,** Memphis St Univ, Memphis, TN; FR; Phi Eta Sigma 90-; Alpha Lambda Delta 90-; Pom Pom Squad; Bsns Admnstrtn; Mrktng Mgmnt.

**THOMAS, TRACY L,** Birmingham Southern Coll, Birmingham, AL; SR; BS BA; Clg Publctns Bd Quad Art Edtr; Blck Stdnt Un V P Nwsltr Edtr Chf; Phi Eta Sigma; Alpha Lambda Delta; Southern Progress Corp Stdnt Intrn; Bus Adm/Mktg Art; Grphc Dsgn Advtsng Mag Pub.

**THOMAS, TRACY L,** Univ Of Cincinnati, Cincinnati, OH; SO; BS; Alpha Lambda Delta 90-; Dominos Pizza Incrprtd 86-; Elem Ed/Sci; Tchr.

**THOMAS, TRACY M,** Nc Agri & Tech St Univ, Greensboro, NC; SO; BS; Wmns Cncl 89-; Vol Cnntns VP; Spec Educ; Tchr/ Chld Psychlgst.

**THOMAS, TREVEAR A,** Clark Atlanta Univ, Atlanta, GA; SO; BS; Cmptr Sci Clb 89-; Cospl Chr 89-; Philhrmc Chr 89-; Hnrs Pgm 90-; Alpha Phi Alpha Fincl Sec; INROADS Intrn Shell Offshore Inc 89-; Cmptr Sci; Syst Analyst.

**THOMAS, TRICIA A,** Norfolk St Univ, Norfolk, VA; JR; BA; Stdngt Govt Assn Actvts Dir 90-; Engl/Foreign Lang Mjrs Clb Sec 90-; Jr Cls Sec; Sigma Tau Delta; Engl/Early Chldhd Educ; Tchng.

**THOMAS, URSULA CHARMAYNE,** Al St Univ, Montgomery, AL; FR; Alpha Phi Alpha 90-; Interdiscplnry Humanities Seqnc 90-; Erly Chldhd Ed/Psych; Erly Chldhd Dir/ Psych.

**THOMAS, VALERIE S,** Union Univ, Jackson, TN; FR; BS; Acctng Clb 90; Acctng.

**THOMAS, VICKI L,** Univ Of West Fl, Pensacola, FL; JR; AS Pensacola Jr Clge 80; Erly Chldhd Elem Ed; Elem Schl Tchr.

**THOMAS, VICTORIA A,** Wv Northern Comm Coll, Wheeling, WV; GD; BA; Humnties Award 89; OH Cnty Schls PTO 88-; Wheeling Pk HS Athltc Boosters 89-; Interior Dsgn/Decrtr; Chicago Sch Of Interior Dsgn 72; Bus/Human Rsrc Mgt.

**THOMAS, WESLEY M,** Univ Of Tn At Martin, Martin, TN; JR; BA; Natl Assn Of Acctnts Treas 90-; Phi Eta Sigma Treas 90-; Phi Kappa Phi 90-; Kappa Alpha 90-; Vrsty Glf 88-90; Bus Admin; Acctg.

**THOMAS, WILLIAM D,** Howard Univ, Washington, DC; SR; BSW; SG Treas 90; AFSW Scrtry 90; Hall Choir Chpln 90; Golden Key; All Amer Schlr; Scl Wrk; Edctr.

**THOMAS-PEARMAN, BERNARD C,** Fl A & M Univ, Tallahassee, FL; SR; BA; History; Law.

**THOMAS-ROMAN, FRANCES ESTEL,** Inter Amer Univ Pr Aquadilla, Aguadilla, PR; SR; MBA; Magna Cum Laude 87; Arnar Stone Inc Prod Engr Sec 79-81; Hwlt Pckrd PR QA Sec Assoc Sys Admin 81-84; 2001 Gfts Frm Arnd Wrld 86; Nuevo San Antonio Hsg Corp Admin 88; AA Bus Admin 87; AA Sec 79; Bus Admin; Prptrsho Rtl Mrktg.

**THOMASON, CONSTANCE R,** Voorhees Coll, Denmark, SC; SO; SGA Bd; Deans Lst 89-; Vybl Bkbl Sftbl Trck; Math; Math/ Cmptr Anlyst.

**THOMASON, PATRICK ALAN,** Univ Of West Fl, Pensacola, FL; SR; B ED; Phi Beta Lambda Prlmntrn 89-; Psncrt Hlth Rcqt Ftns Clb/Nght Mngr 87-; Bs Mrktng 87; Bsns Tchr; Tchng.

**THOMASON, SUSAN M,** Dyersburg St Comm Coll, Dyersburg, TN; SO; BA; AS 91; Educ; Elem Educ.

**THOMASSON, MARTHA A,** Ky Wesleyan Coll, Owensboro, KY; SR; BA; KY Educ Assn Stdnt Pgm 89-; KY Library Assn 90-; Phi Theta Kappa 88-89; Library Intrnshp 89-90; Fresh Writing Award 87-88; KEA-SP Edctnl Ldr Award 90-; Livermore Wmns Club 88-; Library/Audiovisual Svcs; Schl Media Ctr.

**THOMASTON, AMY M,** William Carey Coll, Hattiesburg, MS; JR; BS; SG 90-; Psyclgy Clb Treas 88-89; Bptst Union Fllwshp Chmn 89-90; Alpha Chi Vp 90-; Omicron Delta Kappa; Clg Hrns Prog 88-; Deans Lst 88-89; Pres Lst 89-90; Psychlgy.

**THOMISON, FELECIA D,** Middle Tn St Univ, Murfreesboro, TN; JR; BBA; Ldrshp/Perfrmnce Schlrshp 88-; Altruist Schlrshp 88; Alpha Kappa Psi Fnd Rsg Comm 89-90; Akpha Kappa Alpha Cmnty Svc Chr 90-; Nissan Motor Mfg Corp Purch-Trainee Intern 89-; INROADS 89-; IM Bsktbl Capt 88-90; Bsn Mgmt/Econ/Finance.**

**THOMPKINS, SHERRY L,** Meridian Comm Coll, Meridian, MS; FR; BA; MCC Pen Pal; Elem Ed K-8.

**THOMPSON, AMIE L,** Univ Of Sc At Columbia, Columbia, SC; FR; Emrgng Ldrshp Pgm 90-; Carolina Cares; Phi Eta Sigma Fresh Hon Soc 90-; Chi-Omega VP Pldg Cls 90-; Psychlgy; PhD Psychlgy.

**THOMPSON, AMY L,** Middle Tn St Univ, Murfreesboro, TN; FR; BA; Stdnt Ambssdr; Chi Omega; Engl; Tch.

**THOMPSON, AMY L,** Univ Of Sc At Columbia, Columbia, SC; SO; BA; Offc Admin.

**THOMPSON, ANDREA L,** Pa St Univ Main Cmps, University Pk, PA; FR; BA; Flg Ftbl 90; Bible Stdy Grp 90-; Pol Sci; Law.

**THOMPSON, ANDREA T,** Nc Agri & Tech St Univ, Greensboro, NC; SR; BS; Hall Cncl Prsdnt 88-89; NAACP Sec 88-; Cls Sec 90-; I Have A Dream Fndtn Intrn 90; SG Awrd 90; Math Edctn; Edctr Statistician.

**THOMPSON, ANGELA L,** Kent St Univ Kent Cmps, Kent, OH; FR; BS; Deans List 90-; Alpha Lambda Delta 90-; Pre-Med; Surgeon.

**THOMPSON, ANGELA M,** Middle Ga Coll, Cochran, GA; FR; BED; Speech Thrpy.

**THOMPSON, ANGELA R,** Tn Temple Univ, Chattanooga, TN; JR; BS; Stdnt Govt V Pres; Flwshp Chrstn Athletes VP 90; NC Assoc Of Educators; Pi Epsilon Rho; Dance Team At UNC Wilmington 89-90; Elem Ed; Teach.

**THOMPSON, ANN L,** Immaculata Coll, Immaculata, PA; FR; Phi Kappa Phi; BS Ithaca Clge 85; Ed; Tchr Elem.

**THOMPSON, APRIL M,** Valdosta St Coll, Valdosta, GA; SO; BSN; Wesley Fndtn Dele St Intrntl VP St Coun 89-; Georgia Assn Nrsng Stdnts 90-; Cmps Act Bd 89-; Frshmn Schlr 89-90; Elizabeth Wilmot Bull Schlrshp 90-; Dns Lst 89-; IM Vlybl,Sftbl Wesley BSU 90-; Nrsng.

**THOMPSON, APRIL M,** Salisbury St Univ, Salisbury, MD; SO; Alpha Sigma Tau Pres 90-; SUDS 89-; SNEA 89-; Phi Eta Sigma 90-; Seidel Edn Schlrshp; Pres Schlrshp; Senatorial Schlrshp; Elem Edn/Math; Admin/Bd Of Ed.

**THOMPSON, BARBARA F,** Itawamba Comm Coll, Fulton, MS; FR; BS; Schlrshp Bptst Mem Hosp 90-; Nrsg; Nrs Spclst.

**THOMPSON, BENJMAIN J,** Univ Of Nc At Charlotte, Charlotte, NC; SR; BA; Gldn Key 90-; Chncclrs Lst 90; IM Sccr; Engl; Bus Cr.

**THOMPSON, BERSHUAN T,** Univ Of Nc At Charlotte, Charlotte, NC; FR; Bsktbl Tm; Bus Fin.

**THOMPSON, BEVERLY A,** Wv Univ At Parkersburg, Parkersburg, WV; SO; BA; Ele Educ; Tch.

**THOMPSON, BEVERLY ANITA,** Norfolk St Univ, Norfolk, VA; SR; BS; AAS Manhattan Comm Coll 84; Emplyd Bkkpng; Accntng; Mss Cmmnctns; TV Prod.

**THOMPSON, BIBI S,** City Univ Of Ny Baruch Coll, New York, NY; GD; BA; Lit Vol; Edit Asst 87-90; Assoc Edtr 90-; Jrnlsm; Wrtng/Editing.

**THOMPSON, BRIAN R,** Cumberland County Coll, Vineland, NJ; SO; BA; Phi Theta Kappa; Cmptr Info Sys.

**THOMPSON, CANDACE L,** Univ Of Sc At Columbia, Columbia, SC; FR; BS; FCA; Bapt Stu Union; Phys Ed; Med Trnr.

**THOMPSON, CARLYLE VAN,** City Univ Of Ny City Coll, New York, NY; GD; PHD; Fclty Std Dscpln Comm Chrm 88-89; Alpha Sigma Lambda 88-90; Std Gov Pres 88-90; Gldn Key 88-90; Hnr Scty 86-87; Phi Beta Kappa 90-; Dia Fndtn 87-89; Orntn Gr Ldr 88; Heymann Schlshp 89; Ford Fllwshp 87-90; Val 90; Mellon Fllwshp 90-; MA Colmba Univ; English; Prof.

**THOMPSON, CARON J,** Central Fl Comm Coll, Ocala, FL; SO; AA; Elem Ed; Tchng.**

**THOMPSON, CATHERINE D,** Univ Of Charleston, Charleston, WV; JR; BA; Dbt Tm; Pi Gamma Mu; Psi Chi; Dvsn Cltr/Hstry Intrn; Prelaw/Psy; Law.

**THOMPSON, CHARLES A,** Saint Johns Univ, Jamaica, NY; FR; BA; Bus; Corp Exec.

**THOMPSON, CHARLES S,** Coker Coll, Hartsville, SC; FR; BA; Carnegie Hall Centennial Wrkshp; B; Music; Opera.

**THOMPSON, CHRISTIE L,** Univ Of Nc At Asheville, Asheville, NC; FR; BA; ICF 90-; Chrstn Action Flwshp 90-; Phi Eta Sigma VP 90-; Deans List 90-; Chnclrs List 90; Bio; Vet Med.

**THOMPSON, CHRISTINE E,** Elms Coll, Chicopee, MA; SR; BA; Phi Alpha Theta; Holyoke Comm Clg 90; Elem Hist Tchr; MA.

**THOMPSON, CHRISTOPHER A,** Saint Catharine Coll, St Catharine, KY; FR; AA; SG Secy 90-; Yrbk Editor 90-; Newspaper Editor 90-; Library Asvsry Comm; Cmptr Lab Assist 90-; Phi Theta Kappa; Phi Theta Kappa; April Stdnt Of Mnth; Bus Mgmnt; Bnkng.

**THOMPSON, CHRISTOPHER A,** Nc St Univ At Raleigh, Raleigh, NC; FR; BA; Economics; Cpa.

**THOMPSON, CHRISTY P,** Univ Of Sc At Columbia, Columbia, SC; FR; BA; March Band 90; Symphonic Band; Concert Band; Music Edn; Band Dir.

**THOMPSON, CRAIG A,** Univ Of Southern Ms, Hattiesburg, MS; SR; BS; Intrfrat Cncl Jdcl Bd 88; Coll Rpblcns/SAAD 89-90; Ordr Omega; Phi Eta Sigma; Alpha Lambda Delta; Alpha Epsilon Delta; Beta Beta Beta; Delta Tau Delta Pres 89; Omicron Delta Kappa Five Outstndng Fresh; Ftbl 87-88; Blgcl Sci; Med.

**THOMPSON II, CURTIS R,** Ms St Univ, Miss State, MS; JR; Presidents Lst Schlr; English; Writer Professor.

**THOMPSON, DANA N,** Lincoln Univ, Lincoln Univ, PA; FR; BS; Gspl Ensmble; Univ Plyrs; Rssn Clb; Hnrs Prog; Accntng/Pol Sci; Corp Law.

**THOMPSON, DAWN RENEE,** Methodist Coll, Fayetteville, NC; JR; BS; SGA Pres 90-; Stdnt Actvts Cncl V P 89-90; Stdnt Life RA 89-; Stdnt Senate Sen 89-90; Cafeteria Comm Chrprsn 90-; Tchr Ed Comm 90-; Natl Assoc Campus Actvts Repr 89-; Hl Fame Awd Campus Life 90-; Elem Ed; Rdg Spec.

**THOMPSON, DEBORAH L,** Cornell Univ Statutory College, Ithaca, NY; FR; BS; Stdnst Advctng Pstv Etng Sec 90-; Crw 90-; Bio Chmstry; Med.

**THOMPSON, DEBRA I,** Albany St Coll, Albany, GA; SR; Stdnt Govt 89-; Vol Fr Dghrty Cnty Schl Systms 89-; Awrds Rcvd Fr Vol Wrk Fr Schls; AS Darton Coll 89; Erly Chldhd Educ; Educ.

**THOMPSON, DEIDRA S,** Tougaloo Coll, Tougaloo, MS; FR; Support Svc; Econ; Bnkg/Finance.

**THOMPSON, DUSTIN T,** Ms Univ For Women, Columbus, MS; JR; BA; Stdnt Govt Assn Pres 88-; SGA Stdnt Senate Chpln 90-; Yrbk Staff Edtr 88-; Nwspr Staff Prdctn Mgr 89-; Dilletanti Lit Staff 90-; Union Advsry Cbnt 90-; Hottentots Ldrshp Hnry 90-; Troubadour Soc Clb Big Bro 90-; Bptst Stdnt Union VP; Jrnlsm/Pblc Rltns; Pltcs/Intl Law.**

**THOMPSON, EDDIE M,** Alcorn St Univ, Lorman, MS; SO; BS; Elem Educ; Tch Elem Lvl.

**THOMPSON, EILEEN HEGARTY,** Saint Thomas Univ, Miami, FL; SO; BED; Secy 89; Scndry Ed/Spnsh; Tch Spnsh Hgh Schl.

**THOMPSON, ELAINE M,** Univ Of Fl, Gainesville, FL; JR; BA; Gymnstcs Instrctr 89-; Bymnstcs Tm 88-89; Fnc; Fncl Plnng.

**THOMPSON, ELLEN E,** Columbia Greene Comm Coll, Hudson, NY; SO; BA; Phi Theta Kappa; Sigma Delt A Mu; Rape Crisis 89-; Hudson Corr Fclty 90-; AA; Crmnl Jstc; Law.

**THOMPSON, ERICA J,** Fisk Univ, Nashville, TN; JR; Treas Soph Cls 89-90; Beta Kappa Chi; Gold Key; Alpha Kappa Alpha 90-; Intrnshp At/T Bell Lab; Bsktbl Fr Yr 88-89; Physics; Med Examiner.

**THOMPSON, ERIKA Y,** Univ Of Md At Eastern Shore, Princess Anne, MD; FR; BA; Interclgte Vybl 90; English; Educator.

**THOMPSON, ERIN R,** Al A & M Univ, Normal, AL; SO; BS; Stdnt Govt Assoc 89-; Econ Clb 90-; Hwrd Hrrld Phi Beta 90-; Intrnshp Cnnt Bll; Econ.

**THOMPSON, FAY V,** City Univ Of Ny Med Evers Coll, Brooklyn, NY; JR; BSN; Svnth Day Advntst Chrch; Dean List Awrds 89-; NY State Nrs Assc 86-91; Invtn Sch Belle Zellar Schlrshp Hr Merit 89; RN Licnsr Jamaica W I 78; CGFNS ACLS Phildlph Amer Hrt Assc 82; Care Crtcly Ill Patnt Un Hosp Jamica W I 82; Nrsng; Med Sch Aftr Cmpltn BSN.

**THOMPSON, FRANK V,** Coll Of Charleston, Charleston, SC; JR; BA; Phi Alpha Theta VP; Intrnshp Patriots Point Naval/Maritime Museum; Hist.

**THOMPSON, GAIL R,** Savannah Coll Of Art & Design, Savannah, GA; SR; BFA; Intrior Dsgn/Art Hist; Tchr.

**THOMPSON, GARY D,** Univ Of Louisville, Louisville, KY; SR; BS; IEEE 89-; Engrng Club Trea 88; Mu Alpha Theta Trea 88; 2 Intrnshps At Brown-Forman Corp 90-; Elec Engrng.

**THOMPSON, HARRY,** Comm Coll Algny Co Algny Cmps, Pittsburgh, PA; Psychlgy Club Secy 89-90; Mech Engr; Now Like To Engage In Clncl/Rsrch Psychlgy; Psychlgy.

**THOMPSON, HEATHER S,** Smith Coll, Northampton, MA; JR; BA; Hs Pres Hs Cncl Pre S90-; Sngng Grp Mgr 88-90; Deans Lst 88-; Frst Grp Schlr 89-; Vol Emrgncy Rm 89; Spcl Stds 90-; Tchn Glab Asst 90-; Blgy.

**THOMPSON, HERMETHA CHANDLER,** Norfolk St Univ, Norfolk, VA; SO; BA; Spartan Alpha Tau 90-; Comp 86-; Oper Nvy/Fed Svc 74-; Clncl Psych.

**THOMPSON, HOLLY C,** Middle Tn St Univ, Murfreesboro, TN; FR; BA; Stdnt Hnrs Assn 90-; Gamma Beta Phi; Alpha Kappa Psi VP Pldge Clss Chrmn Of Srvce; Wrk Schlrshp 90-; Bus Acctng; Acctng CPA.

**THOMPSON, JACQUELYN M,** Univ Of Montevallo, Montevallo, AL; SR; MED; Phi Mu Pldg Dir 88-89; Kappa Delta Pi; Omicron Delta Kappa; Lambda Sigma Pi; Outstdng Undergrad; BS Ece/Elemeduc; Early Chldhd/Elem; Tchr.

**THOMPSON JR, JAMES A,** Univ Of Akron, Akron, OH; JR; BA; Frat Ord Eagles; Golden Key; Deans Lst 90; Fin; Bus Fin.

**THOMPSON, JANE L,** Radford Univ, Radford, VA; SR; Mofftt Hs Cncl Pr 88-; Stdnt Alum Assn Stdmt Educ Assn; Rush Cnslr; Kappa Delta Pi 90-; Zeta Tau Alpha 89-; Natl Res Hall Hnry 90-; BS; Educ; Tchr.

**THOMPSON, JANET C,** Savannah St Coll, Savannah, GA; FR; BBA; Gen Mdcl Corp Admn Asst 77-; Mrktng.

**THOMPSON, JENNIFER G,** Univ Of Tn At Martin, Martin, TN; FR.

**THOMPSON, JENNIFER L,** Western Ky Univ, Bowling Green, KY; SO; BS; Band 89; Flute Ensmbl 90-; Phi Eta Sigma; Fresh Chem Awd 90; Stdnt Lab Asst 90-; Intrn Argonne Natl Lab; Chem; Chemst.

**THOMPSON, JILL S,** Univ Of Nc At Greensboro, Greensboro, NC; FR; BM; Alpha Lambda Delta; Mu Phi Epsilon; Inst Music Educ; Middle H S Bnd Dir.

**THOMPSON, JOAN M,** Fl International Univ, Miami, FL; JR; BSW; AS Prospect Hl Clg 86; AA Miami Dade Cmnty Clg 90; Scl Wrk.

**THOMPSON, JOELY R,** Univ Of Cincinnati, Cincinnati, OH; FR; MED; Stdnt Cncl Excptnl Chldrn Pres 90-; Flwshp Chrstn Stdnts VP 90-; Alpha Lambda Delta 90-; Spcl Edn; Tchr.

**THOMPSON II, JOHN F,** Marshall University, Huntington, WV; JR; BBA; Marshall Univ Stdt Gvt Senate Assoc 90-; W Virg Scty CPA 90-; Accounting; CPA.

**THOMPSON, JOHN M,** Ms St Univ, Miss State, MS; SR; BS; Pi Delta Phi; French/Spansh/Gen Ag; Scriptrl Dscplshp.

**THOMPSON, JOHN MARCUS,** Ma Inst Of Tech, Cambridge, MA; SO; BS; Physcs; Rsrch Edctr.**

**THOMPSON, JOHN TYLER,** North Greenville Coll, Tigerville, SC; SO; Bus.

**THOMPSON JR, JORGE M,** Harford Comm Coll, Bel Air, MD; SO; BS; Phi Theta Kappa V P; Chem; Pharm.

**THOMPSON, JUDE C,** City Univ Of Ny City Coll, New York, NY; JR; BA; Tutor 90-; Gldn Key 90-; NYC Mayors Intrn Spec Asst Dir Hsng; Cmnctns; Law.

**THOMPSON, JUDITH R,** Fl International Univ, Miami, FL; JR; BS; AA Broward Cmnty Clg 89; Elem Ed; Tchng.

**THOMPSON, KATHRYN J,** Ferrum Coll, Ferrum, VA; JR; BA; Frt Trl Chrstn Chrch Asstnt Sndy Sch Supr; Acctg.**

**THOMPSON, KAYLA M,** Livingston Univ, Livingston, AL; JR; BS; Acctg Clb 90-; Intl Stu Assoc; Delta Sigma Pi VP 90-; Alpha Kappa Alpha; Deans Lst 89-; Acctg; CPA.

**THOMPSON, KELLY L,** Mary Washington Coll, Fredericksburg, VA; FR; BA; Intl Rltns Clb; ICF; Admssns Clb; Phone-A-Thon Vol; Coll Rpblcns; Kappa Gamma Sigma Pldg Comm Serv Ldr 90-; IM Vlybl; Hstry; Law.

**THOMPSON, KEVIN,** Gallaudet Univ, Washington, DC; JR; BA; Gamma Delta Iota; Intrmrl Sprts 88-; Psychlgy.

**THOMPSON, KEVIN J,** Va Polytechnic Inst & St Univ, Blacksburg, VA; SO; BA; Acdmc Deans Lst 90-; Mgmt Comp Sci.

**THOMPSON, KIM E,** Comm Coll Algny Co Algny Cmps, Pittsburgh, PA; FR; BS; Pitts Job Corps 90; Ass Spec Tech 86; Nurs; RN.

**THOMPSON, KIMBERLY A,** Colby Sawyer Coll, New London, NH; JR; BS; Key Assn 88-; Musicls 88-; Stdnt Athltc Trnr 88-; All Amer Schlr 89; A B Nickols Music Schlrshp 88-; Sprts Sci/Athltc Trng; Cert Athltc Trnr.

**THOMPSON, KIMBERLY DAWN,** Mary Baldwin Coll, Staunton, VA; SR; BA; Stdnt Govt Hse Pres 90; Mnrty Wmn In Unty Sec 90; Advsry Brd Of Vstrs Soph Jr Rep; M Bldwn Hnrs Scty Rep To Stdnt Actvts Brd 88; Phi Beta Kappa; Cir K Intrnatl 89; Big Bro Big Sis 88; Pple Agnst Rpe 89; Cltrl Immrsn Cnslr 90; Intrnshp 89; Intrnal Rltns Jpnse; Engl Tchr In Jpn.**

**THOMPSON, KIRK A,** Univ Of Al At Huntsville, Huntsville, AL; JR; BS; Alpha Beta Tau; Chmcl Engnrng.

**THOMPSON, KRISTIN N,** Ms St Univ, Miss State, MS; FR; Frtrnty Lttl Sstr 90-; Gamma Beta Phi 90-; Stwpt Hmlss; Med; Dctr.

**THOMPSON, LEAROY S,** City Univ Of Ny Kingsborough, Brooklyn, NY; SR; KCC Evng Cncl VP 90-; AAS; Bus; Hmn Rsrcs Mgmt.

**THOMPSON, LEIGH A,** Union Univ, Jackson, TN; JR; BS; Psychlgy Clb; Phi Beta Lambda; Kappa Delta Treas 89-90; Mgmt/Mktg; Law.

**THOMPSON, LISA A,** Univ Of Ky, Lexington, KY; JR; BA; Bnd 88-89; Stdnt Athl Cncl 90-; Phi Eta Sigma 89-; Natl Stdng Spch/Lang/Hrng Assn Pres 90-; Alpha Xi Delta 88-89; Speech/Lang Pathlgy.

**THOMPSON, LISA ANN,** Spalding Univ, Louisville, KY; JR; BA; Natl Edn Assoc Sntr 90-; Ambsdrs Clb; Deans Lst Jefferson Comm Coll 87-; Vlybl 90; Soc Studies/Elem Edn; Spnsh Minor/Teach.

**THOMPSON, LISA K,** Fl A & M Univ, Tallahassee, FL; JR; BS; Delta Sigma Theta; Crmnl Jstc; Law.

**THOMPSON, LISA MUNSON,** Albertus Magnus Coll, New Haven, CT; SR; BA; Spnsh Clb Sec 87-; Ntl Spnsh Hon Soc 90-; Ntl Frgn Lang Hon Soc 90-; Kappa Gamma Pt 90-; Tns Tm 87-88; Lgl/Exec Sec Ofc Mgr Marcus Law Frm 76-88; Soc/Spnsh; Soc Svcs.

**THOMPSON, LORA L,** Marshall University, Huntington, WV; FR; BA; Phi Eta Sigma 90-; Phi Beta Lambda Pres 89-90; File Clerk 1; MS Cert Steno/Word Proc/Accntg/Data Proc Garnet Career Cen 88-90; Cmptr Sci; Sftwr Anal.

**THOMPSON, MARLA KAE,** Roane St Comm Coll, Harriman, TN; JR; BS; DECA 87-88; Drama Clb 87-88; Crossties 87-88; Beta Clb 87-88; Stdnt Govt Sen 89-90; Traffic Ct Jstc 90-; Natl Yng Wmn Soc; Pres Comm Eval/Instr Dev 90-; Psych/Pol Sci; Law.

**THOMPSON, MARY A,** Lansdale School Of Bus, North Wales, PA; SO; Acctg; CPA.

**THOMPSON, MARY E,** Univ Of Al At Huntsville, Huntsville, AL; SR; BSEE; Coop Educ Prog 89-; Mgr Mcdonalds 88-; Elect Eng.

**THOMPSON, MARY H,** Hillsborough Comm Coll, Tampa, FL.

**THOMPSON, MARY LYNN,** Ky St Univ, Frankfort, KY; SR; BA; Math; Tchng.

**THOMPSON, MELANIE C,** Coll Of Charleston, Charleston, SC; JR; BA; Elem Ed; Teaching.

**THOMPSON, MELANIE G,** Ms Univ For Women, Columbus, MS; SR; BS; Natl Assoc Pblc Acctnts 90-; Natl Scty Pblc Acctnts 90-; Acctg Hnrry 90-; Snr Clss Dvsnl Schlr; Acctg.

**THOMPSON, MELANIE J,** Livingston Univ, Livingston, AL; JR; BA; Brewer 89-; State Jr Clg Sftbl Tm; Livingston Univ Sftbl Tm; AAS Brewer State Jr Clg 90; Phys Educ; Sftbl Coach.

**THOMPSON, MELISSA A,** Middle Tn St Univ, Murfreesboro, TN; FR; PHD; FFA St Pres 90-; Block/Bridle 90-; Voctnl Ed Prctnrs Comm; Outstndng Fr; Ag; Pre-Vet.

**THOMPSON, MELISSA A,** Univ Of Sc At Columbia, Columbia, SC; JR; BA; Alpha Phi Omega Admin Pres 90; Nvgtrs Chrstn Org; Humanities Erly Chldhd Ed; Tchr.

**THOMPSON, MICHAEL B,** Cumberland County Coll, Vineland, NJ; SO; BA; Comp Info Systems; Comp.

**THOMPSON, MICHAEL L,** Univ Of Ga, Athens, GA; JR; MBA; Rec Sprts Sprvsr; Beta Gamma Sigma; Beta Alpha Psi; IM Ftbl/Sftbl; Acctg; CPA.

**THOMPSON, MICHELLE L,** Duquesne Univ, Pittsburgh, PA; SO; BAS; Campus Ministry 89-; Theology Mjrs Committee 90-; Intgrd Hnrs Prog 89-; Lambda Sigma 90-; Resid Assist; Duqueshe Univ Vltr Awd 90-; Theology/Psy; Pastoral Ministry/Youth.

**THOMPSON, MIRIAM H,** Univ Of Sc At Spartanburg, Spartanburg, SC; JR; BED; Prfssnl Scrtrs 88-90; Admn Spclst Clemson Univ 85-90; AA Tri County Technicl Coll 90; Elem Ed; Tchr.

**THOMPSON, MONICA G,** Radford Univ, Radford, VA; JR; BBA; Stdtn Govt Assc Ldrshp Cnfrnc Coor 90-; Almn Assc 90-; Tour Gde 90-; Bonnie Hurlburt SGA Schlrshp 90-; SGA Exec Cncl Mbr Of Yr Awd 90-; Ambssdrs Rookie Of Yr Awd 90-; Mrktg.

**THOMPSON, MONIQUE L,** Univ Of Sc At Columbia, Columbia, SC; SO; BA; Freshman Marshall 90; English; Education.

**THOMPSON, NICHA MICHETTE,** Univ Of Southern Ms, Hattiesburg, MS; FR; Afro-Am Stdnt Org; Acdmcs Awd; Acctng; CPA.

**THOMPSON, NORMA A,** Univ Of The Dist Of Columbia, Washington, DC; JR; BA; Mgmt; MBA.

**THOMPSON, ODETTE V,** City Univ Of Ny Med Evers Coll, Brooklyn, NY; JR; BS; United Christian Flwshp Sec 90-; AS; Pub Admin; Family Cnslr.

**THOMPSON, PAMELA D,** Abraham Baldwin Agri Coll, Tifton, GA; FR; BA; FFA Sec 90-; Phi Theta Kappa; Ag Educ/Ag Mktg; H S Ag Eductr.

**THOMPSON, PATRICIA E,** Ashland Comm Coll, Ashland, KY; SO; Univ Louisville Intl Rel Clb Pres 84-85; U Of L Frnch Clb VP 83-84; U Of L Drm Cncl Rep 84-85; Pi Sigma Alpha; Mrtrbrd; BA Univ Louisville 85; Med.

**THOMPSON, PATRICIA HALL,** Emory & Henry Coll, Emory, VA; SR; BA; Stdnt VA Ed Assn; AA VA Highlands Comm Clg 90; Interdscplnry Engl; Elem Tchr.

**THOMPSON, PHILIP C,** Univ Of Sc At Columbia, Columbia, SC; SR; MBA; Sigma Na 79-80; Pres Chancellors Hnr List 90; S Cooper; Bsn Admnstrn.

**THOMPSON, PHYLLIS A,** Beckley Coll, Beckley, WV; SO; BA; Child Care Cntr; Mthdst Wmn Pres; Scl Wrk; Cnclng.

**THOMPSON JR, RALPH M,** The Kings Coll, Briarclf Mnr, NY; SR; BS; Untd Chrstn Cltn Co-Chrmn 90-; Crtv Mgmnt Concpts Clb 87-88; Chrstn Srvc Orgnztn 87-90; IM Bsktbl Ftbl; Accntng; Mnstry Entrprnr.**

**THOMPSON, RANDY M,** Oh Univ-Southern Cmps, Ironton, OH; SR; BGS; Vet Frgn Wars; Phi Kapp Phi; Deans Lst; Utd Meth Chrch; Pgm Crdntr Ironton/Lawrence CAO Head Start; AS Ohio Univ 89; CDA Cncl Erly Chldhd Prof Recog 90; Bhvrl Sci; Cnslng.

**THOMPSON, REBECCA L,** Univ Of Southern Ms, Hattiesburg, MS; SR; BS; SEA; Elem Educ; College Counselor.

**THOMPSON, ROBERT E,** Southern Coll Of Tech, Marietta, GA; GD; BS; Mech Engr.

**THOMPSON III, ROBERT R,** Univ Of Nc At Charlotte, Charlotte, NC; JR; BA; Boy Scts Amer Egl Sct 84-; Erth Sci; Env Sci.

**THOMPSON, ROBIN L,** Univ Of Nh Plymouth St Coll, Plymouth, NH; SR; Offc Admssns 89-; Jdcl Brd; Kappa Delta Pi Exec Brd 89-; Fllwshp 90-; Outstndg Stdnt; IM Bsktbl/Vlybl 87-90; BS Cum Laude; Educ/Art; Tchg/Admin.

**THOMPSON, ROSA F,** Helene Fuld Schl Of Nursing, New York, NY; GD; Blck Nurses Assn 89-; NLN 90-; Deans Lst 90; Clinical Recog Psychiatric Nrsng 90; Nrsg; Nrs Practitioner.

**THOMPSON, ROSARIO C,** Comm Coll Algny Co Algny Cmps, Pittsburgh, PA; FR; Clb Chr 90-; Sci.

**THOMPSON, ROSEMARY,** Tuskegee Univ, Tuskegee Inst, AL; SR; BA; Choir Treas 89-; Gspl Ensmbl 88-90; Soc Work Alliance Sec 87-; Pi Sigma Phi Treas 88-; Choir Schlrshp 88-; Soc Work; Child Welfare Soc Wrkr.

**THOMPSON, RUKEYSER S,** Alcorn St Univ, Lorman, MS; FR; BA; Pre-Med Clb Scrtry 90; Chem Clb; Queens Ct 90; Hnrs Org; Chem Bio Pre-Med; Ped Nrsrgn.

**THOMPSON, SALLY L,** Univ Of Al At Birmingham, Birmingham, AL; SR; BS; Intrnshp AL Dept Yth Svrces CPS Prgrm; Crmnl Jstice.

**THOMPSON, SAMUEL,** Glassboro St Coll, Glassboro, NJ; SR; BA; Stdnt Govt Assn Sntr 90-; Stdnt Cltrl Exch Bd Treas 89-; Geog Assn Treas 89-; Comm Outreach Grp 89-90; Stdnt Faculty Comm 90-; SCEB Ost Active Mbr 90-; Medallion Awd 90-; Geog; Lawd Econ/Urban Plng.

**THOMPSON, SHANE C,** Hartwick Coll, Oneonta, NY; FR; BA; College Chr 90-; Bowling Clb 90-; English; Pblshng/Tchng/Writing.

**THOMPSON, SHAWN P,** Daytona Beach Comm Coll, Daytona Beach, FL; SO; BS; Rcvd Awrd Otstndg Mrt/Accmplshmnt Physics 90-; IM Tns 89-90; Chem Engr.

**THOMPSON, SHAWNA R,** Portland School Of Art, Portland, ME; GD; Intrnshp Art Gallery 90; BFA 90; Phtgrphy.

**THOMPSON, SHAYNE R,** Univ Of Southern Ms, Hattiesburg, MS; FR; Alumni Assoc 90-; SADD 90-; Lambda Sigma 90; Alpha Lamdba Delta 90; Phi Eta Sigma 90; Delta Gamma 90-; Busn; Mgt.

**THOMPSON, SHEILA A,** Villanova Univ, Villanova, PA; SR; BA; Order Omega 90-; Omicron Delta Kappa 90-; Delta Gamma Pres 88-; Blue Key Camp Trs/P R 87-; Mdlln Awd; Gen Arts; Law.

**THOMPSON, SHEILA L,** Tougaloo Coll, Tougaloo, MS; SO; MBA; Pre Slumni Clb; Day Stdnt Un; Alpha Kappa Alpha; Intern Pat Gibson Electric 3 Mos; Ecnmcs/Acctg; Law Schl.

**THOMPSON, STEPHANIE L,** Western Ky Univ, Bowling Green, KY; SR; BS; Am Coll Of Hlthcare Execs Stdnt Assoc Treas 89-; Phi Kappa Phi; Eta Sigma Gamma; Golden Key; Alpha Omicron Pi Treas 90-; Girls Club; Sr Sor Women With Highest GPA; Deans Adv Comm; Hlth Care Admn; Nursing Admn.

**THOMPSON, STEVEN M,** Clarkson Univ, Potsdam, NY; JR; BS; Presidents Lst 90; Deans Lst 88-89; Newell Mfg Schlrshp 88-; IM Bsktbl 88-; Business; Acctng Mngmnt.

**THOMPSON, TAMMY L,** Walker Coll, Jasper, AL; SO; MBA; Phi Theta Kappa 90-; Acctnt; CPA.

**THOMPSON, TAMMY M,** North Greenville Coll, Tigerville, SC; FR; BA; Substitute Teacher 89-; English; Elem Educ.

**THOMPSON, TANDRA M,** Mitchell Comm Coll, Statesville, NC; SO; BA; Fne Arts 90-; Stdnt Govt Assn Rep 90-; Hnr Cncl 89-; Phi Theta Kappa VP 89-; Grad Hgh Hnrs; Mnd Lab Ttr At MCC; Assc Of Arts AA MCC; Bus Admin.**

**THOMPSON, TARA L,** Kent St Univ Stark Cmps, North Canton, OH; SO; BA; Hnrs Clg 89; Psych; Chld Psych.

**THOMPSON, TERESA M,** Lincoln Univ, Lincoln Univ, PA; JR; BS; Bus Club Histrn/Publc Rltns 89-; Acctng Club 89-90; NAACP 89-90; Alpha Kappa Alpha; Cert From Dean Of Admsns Youth Chrch Pres 85-88; Cert Ctr For Comprtv Stdy Of Humnts 90; Co-Op NJ Dept Of Ed Chld Nutrtn; Bus Admn; Mgt.

**THOMPSON, TERRI G,** East Carolina Univ, Greenville, NC; JR; BFA; Phi Theta Kappa 87; Chancellors Awd Hnr Ceremony; Art Educ.

**THOMPSON, TERRY L,** Boston Univ, Boston, MA; SR; BS; Deans Hst 90-; Occptnl Thrpy Clb Sec 87-; Stdnt Govt Cls Rep 88-; Univ CT Hlth Ctr Farmington CT; New Britain Meml Hsp; IM Brm Bl 90; Amer Occptnl Thrpy Assc 89; Occptnl Thrpy.

**THOMPSON, THOMAS L,** Univ Of Toledo, Toledo, OH; GD; JD; Law Almn Grnt 90-; Amer Jrsprdnc Awd 90-; Ntl Cncl Engl Tchrs 89-; Hgh Schl Tchr 87-90; BS Eastern MI Univ 86; Law.

**THOMPSON, TIMOTHY H,** Presbyterian Coll, Clinton, SC; FR; BS; Stdnt Cncl Frshmn Pres 90-; Fllshp Chrstn Athletes 90-; Deans Lst; IM Sports Capt 90-; Bus Admin; Law.

**THOMPSON, TODD M,** Barry Univ, Miami, FL; FR; BA; Rcrtnl Diving Mgt; Scuba Diving Related Bus.

**THOMPSON, TRACY D,** Morris Brown Coll, Atlanta, GA; SR; BA; SGA Bus Mgr 90-; Dstrbtv Educ Clbs Amer 87-; Sclgy Clb Prlmntrn 90-; Hnr Rll 89-; Alpha Kappa Alpha Asst Mbrshp Chrmn 90-; Girls Club 89-; Welcome House 90-; Dept Human Serv Intern 90-; Vlybl; Sociology; Social Worker.

**THOMPSON, TRACY R,** Ms Valley St Univ, Itta Bena, MS; SO; BS; Alpha Kappa Mu; Presidents Schlr 89-; Bus Admin; CPA.

**THOMPSON, TRESA K,** Roane St Comm Coll, Harriman, TN; SO; AS; Soc Sci; Hlth Admn.

**THOMPSON, TROY MAURICE,** Clark Atlanta Univ, Atlanta, GA; Cmptr Sci Clb Exec Chrmn Chrtr Comm 86-; Clark Coll Rcrtmnt Tm 86-87; SGA Rep 87-88; All Amer Schlr 87-; Alpha Kappa Mu 90; Kappa Alpha Psi VP 87-; Pan Hellenic Cncl Pres 89-90; NE Bcntnl Schlrshp Awrd 86; UN Wrld Peace Conf 88; Comp/Infrmtnl Sci.**

**THOMPSON, VICTORIA P,** Ga St Univ, Atlanta, GA; SR; AS; Innr Rlgs Cncl Pres 87-88; Outstndng Coll Stdnts Amer 89-90; Kappa Lambda Pi; Stdnt GA Assn Educ Hstrn 89-; Phi Kappa Phi; Gldn Key 90-; Blue Key Tm Ldr 89-; Alpha Xi Delta Asst Treas 89-; Undrgrad Awd Coll Educ; Deans Schlrshp Key; BS Educ; Math/Sci; Tchng.

**THOMPSON, VINSON F,** Univ Of Tn At Martin, Martin, TN; JR; BS; Clg Dem Prsdnt 89; SGA Cngrs 88-; Pre Law Clb Sec & Tres 89; Clg Dem Dbtng Tm 88; Pltcl Sci Hnr Soc; Deans Lst 90-; Phi Alpha Delta VP 90; Phi Alpha Delta Sec 89; Sigma Pi; Gvrnrs Stf; Pltcl Sci; Law.

**THOMPSON, VIVIAN S,** Tuskegee Univ, Tuskegee Inst, AL; SR; BS; Gospel Ens Pres 90-; Choir Chpln 89-; Occptnl Thrpy Clb VP 89-90; Alpha Kappa Mu 89-; Hnr Roll; Deans Lst ; Schlr; Occupational Thrpy.

**THOMPSON, WANDA L,** Northern Ky Univ, Highland Hts, KY; SO; BA; ASTRO; Srvc Repr Tele Co; Eng.

**THOMPSON, WENDY CHERYL,** Miami Jacobs Jr Coll Of Bus, Dayton, OH; SO; Stdnt Adv Comm Sec 89-; Deans List 89-; Coll Sec Intl Sec; AS Miami Jacobs Coll; Legal Sec; Law Office.

**THOMPSON, ZANDRA D,** Clark Atlanta Univ, Atlanta, GA; SO; BS; Natl Soc Blck Engrs 89-; Physcs Clb 89-; Tech Bnd Pgm; Cool Grls East Lake Cnslr; Engr Outstdng Soph 90-; Acad Exclnc Awd 90-; Math Acad Achvmnt Awd 90-; Math/Engr; Indl Engr.

**THOMSON, BLAKE T,** Wilmington Coll, New Castle, DE; GD; BS; USAF; AA CCAF 89; Hmn Rsrc Mngmnt; Bus.

**THOMSON, JACQUELYN LEE,** Bloomfield Coll, Bloomfield, NJ; JR; BSN; Hgh Hnrs 90-; AAS Co Clge Marris 89; Peds.

**THOMSON, JANICE K,** Columbia Union Coll, Takoma Park, MD; FR; BS; Busn Cl 90-; Phi Eta Sigma 90-; Alpha Sigma Beta 90-; Busn Admin; Own/Run Daycare Cen.

**THOMSON, MICHAEL J,** Lake City Comm Coll, Lake City, FL; FR; AA; Phi Theta Kappa Pres; Deans Lst 90-; Pre Med; Srgn.

**THOMSON, SHANA L,** Eckerd Coll, St Petersburg, FL; JR; BS BA; Rsdnt Advsr RA; Dorm Govt Pres 89-90; Campus Actvts Bd Spec Evnts Crdntr; Selected As Ford Schlr 89-90; Habitat For Humanity 89-; Vol Admsns Tour Guide 88-91; Selected As Ford Schlr 89-90; Admitted Into Tchr Educ Prog; IM Athl 89-; Psychlgy/Elem Educ; Tch Elem/Sec Lvl.

**THORBURN, LISA MURRAY,** Univ Of Nc At Greensboro, Greensboro, NC; SR; Alpha Lambda Delta 88-89; Otstdngn Colls Tdnts Amr 88-89; Kappa Omicron Nu 89-; Gldn Chan 90-; Hmn Envrnmntl Sci 89-; Intern Bernard Shepherd Clthing Str 90; Omicron Nu Awrd 87-88; Schlr 87-90; Otstndg Snr 90-; Cum Laude 87-; Chrch Yth Ldr; Clthn Txtls Fshn; Mgr Byr.

**THOREN, STEVEN C,** S U N Y At Buffalo, Buffalo, NY; GD; MA; Gldn Key 90; BA Cum Laude 90; Phlsphy; Scl Wrk.

**THORESON, TAMRA L,** Me Maritime Academy, Castine, ME; GD; Vrsty Slng Tm 86-90; Vrsty Chrldr Capt 86-90; Vrsty Bnd 86-90; Ycht Clb 87-; Alpha Phi Omega 86-; Alchl Drg Tsk Frcs 89-89; Amrcn Scty Nvl Eng 89-; Deans Lst; Mstrs Lst 89-; ASNE Natl Schlrshp; Chrng 86-90; Arbcs Instrctr 87-; BS 90; BS; Eng.

**THORISDOTTIR, PALA,** Univ Of Sc At Columbia, Columbia, SC; SO; BA; Htl Sales/Mktg Asc 90-; Jrnlsm.

**THORLEY, DALE G,** Univ Of Tn At Knoxville, Knoxville, TN; FR; BS; Alpha Lambda Delta; Phi Eta Sigma; Golf 90-; Bus; Mgmt.

**THORN, ANDREA M,** Ohio Valley Coll, Parkersburg, WV; FR; Sigma Epsilon Chi 90-; Acplla Sngrs Sec 90-; Exprssns Hstss 90-.

**THORN, MICHELLE E,** Oh Univ, Athens, OH; FR; BFA; Mrchng 110 90-; Bnd 90-; Tau Beta Sigma 90-; Deans Lst; Grphc Dsgn.

**THORN, PATRINA A,** Marshall University, Huntington, WV; JR; BA; Symphnc Bnd 89; Kappa Delta Pi; Rsdnc Schlrs 89-; Chpl Hll Untd Mthdst Chrch 87-; Elem Ed; Tchr.

**THORNBURG, GERALDINE E,** Gaston Coll, Dallas, NC; FR; SDN; Nurs; RN.

**THORNBURG, KAREN A,** De Tech & Comm Coll At Dover, Dover, DE; SO; AAS; SOSA; Alpha Beta Gamma; Acdmc Incntv Schlrshp; Deans Lst; Acctng.

**THORNBURG, MARY K,** Univ Of Southern Ms, Hattiesburg, MS; JR; BSN; Stdnt Nrs Assoc 90-; Mrchg Bnd 88-; Concert Bnd 88-89; Saxophone Ensmbl 88-89; Nrsg/Hlth-Hmn Svcs; Pediatric Nrsg.

**THORNE, ROBERT L,** Middle Tn St Univ, Murfreesboro, TN; SR; BA; MTSU Arspc Coop; AAS Ricks Clg 90; Arspc/ATC; Ar Trfc Cntrlr.

**THORNE, VIRGINIA L,** Faulkner St Jr Coll, Bay Minette, AL; JR; BS; Mu Alpha Theta Pres 89-90; Phi Theta Kappa 89-90; ABAS 90; Mktg.

**THORNHILL, CAROL F,** Univ Of Southern Ms, Hattiesburg, MS; SR; Sxl Asslt Crss Cntr Vol; BS 90; Psychlgy/Educ; Grad Schl MSW.

**THORNHILL, TANDY L,** Univ Of Southern Ms, Hattiesburg, MS; JR; BS; Engl Clb 89-90; FTA 89-90; Phi Theta Kappa 88-90; Pres Lst 88-90; Deans Lst 90-; AAD 90; Speech Pathology.

**THORNSBURY, G CAROLYN,** Va Commonwealth Univ, Richmond, VA; SR; BS; Phi Theta Kappa 77-; RN; ADN SW VA Comm Clg 79; Nursing; Masters Degree.

**THORNTON, BARBARA D,** Jackson St Univ, Jackson, MS; SR; BBA; Stdnt Advsry Cncl Sec 90-; Acctg Soc 87-90; Alpha Kappa Mu 90-91; Alpha Lambda Delta 88-91; Alpha Chi 89-; Delta Mu Delta 89-; Phi Kappa Phi; Zeta Phi Beta; Acctg; CPA.

**THORNTON, BRYON A,** Wallace St Comm Coll At Selma, Selma, AL; SO; ASSOC; Cedar Grove Meth Chrch Yth Dir; Hvy Equip Oper Gulf Farm Srvc; Crmnl Justc; Law.

**THORNTON, CHERYL L,** Roane St Comm Coll, Harriman, TN; FR; AS; Mthdst Mdct Cntr 86-; Rsprtry Thrpy; Hlth Cr Prfsnst.

**THORNTON, CHRISTINE M,** Atlantic Comm Coll, Mays Landing, NJ; SO; AAS; Ocean Bch Aux 90-; Howard Persina Schlrshp; Hsptlty Mngmnt.

**THORNTON, DAVID C,** Univ Of South Al, Mobile, AL; JR; BED; AD Tulsa Jr Coll 90; Spec Ed; Cnslng.

**THORNTON, DAWN Y,** Comm Coll Algny Co Algny Cmps, Pittsburgh, PA; FR; BA; Nrsng Recruitment Coalition 89-; File Clrk; Nrsng; RN.

**THORNTON, GAY L,** Univ Of Montevallo, Montevallo, AL; SR; BS; Phi Mu; Chldns Mrcl Ntwrk; Proj Hike Hope; Acdmc Trnsfr Schlrshp; Pres Ldrshp Schlrshp; Fine Arts Schlrshp Enterprise St Jr Coll; AS Enterprise St; Erly Chldhd/Elem Educ; Tchr.

**THORNTON, GLORIA A,** Morris Brown Coll, Atlanta, GA; SO; United Negor College Fund Schlrshp 89-; Nrsng; RN.

**THORNTON, HAROLD T,** Univ Of Louisville, Louisville, KY; FR; MBA; Incoming Porter Schlrs Advsr 90-; Woodford R Porter Schlr 90-; IM Bsktbl/Sftbl 90-; Cvl Engr; Engr.

**THORNTON, KIMBERLY A,** Saint Lawrence Univ, Canton, NY; FR; BA; SGA Sentr 90-; Acdmc Affrs Comm 90-; Govt/ Engl; Law.

**THORNTON, MARLA O,** Winthrop Coll, Rock Hill, SC; JR; BS; Wsley Cmps Mnstry 88-; Alpha Lambda Delta Pres 89-90; Omicron Delta Kappa; Phi Kappa Phi; Kappa Delta Pi; Winthrop Schlr 89-90; Engl Bostic Rogers Schlrshp; Jo Anne J Trow Asrd; Arbcs; Erly Chldhd Educ; Tch.

**THORNTON, MARY E,** Univ Of Tn At Knoxville, Knoxville, TN; JR; BS; SGA Leg Intrst Grp 89-; Chcllrs Com On Stdnt Pblctns 90; Gldn Ky 89-; Phi Kappa Phi 90-; Gamma Beta Phi 90-; Phi Eta Sigma 88-; Beta Alpha Psi 90-; Andy Holt Schlrshp 88-; Fred M Roddy Schlrshp 88-; TN Stdnt Of Dstnctn Schlrshp 89; Acctng; Law.

**THORNTON, MELANIE N,** Ms St Univ, Miss State, MS; JR; Ntl Assn Accts; Beta Alpha Psi; Phi Beta Lambda 89-; Phi Theta Kappa Pres 90-; Schl Accntncy Schlrshp; AA Jones Co Jr Coll 90; Acctg.

**THORNTON, MICHELE D,** Univ Of Dayton, Dayton, OH; Erth 90; La Crosse 90; Amnsty Intrntl 90; Ssclgy; Scl Wrk.

**THORNTON JR, NATHANIEL,** William Carey Coll, Hattiesburg, MS; JR; BS; Debate Team; St Johns Bapt Chrch Gulfport MS Pstr 84-; Chf Petty Offcr US Nvl Submarine Srvc 63-84; Psychlgy; Cnlsng.

**THORNTON, PAULA B,** Wallace St Comm Coll At Selma, Selma, AL; SO; BA; Math; Scndry Educ.

**THORNTON, REBECCA A,** Lee Coll, Cleveland, TN; SO; BA; Campus Choir 89-; Power Unlimited 89-; Music; Teacher.**

**THORNTON, REBECCA L,** Radford Univ, Radford, VA; FR; BA; Poltcl Sci Soc 90-; Coll Rpblcns Treas 90-; Alpha Lam Delta 90-; Poltcl Sci; Intl Law.

**THORNTON, RICHARD C,** Univ Of Nh Plymouth St Coll, Plymouth, NH; SR; BS; Phi Kappa Phi VP 90-; Pres Schlr 87-90; IM Athltcs 87-; Bus Admn.

**THORNTON JR, SAMUEL E,** Univ Of Southern Ms, Hattiesburg, MS; JR; BA; Cnslng Psychlgy; Cnslr.

**THORNTON, SCOTT R,** Alfred Univ, Alfred, NY; SR; BS; BS; Psychlgy.

**THORNTON, SUSAN DENIESE,** Univ Of Tn At Martin, Martin, TN; GD; BS; Stdnt Tchr Tn Educ Clb 89-; Ntl Tchr Clb; Dns Lst; Elem Educ; Tchr.

**THORNTON, TAMARA L,** Univ Of Ga, Athens, GA; JR; BSED; Yrbk 88-; Std Almni Cncl 90-; GA Rcrtmnt Tm 90-; Blck Affrs Cncl 90-; Tch Amer; GA Blck Educ Spprt Tm Ldr 90-; AASLAC; AACCPC; Delta Sigma Theta Schlr; UGA Cthlc Std Ctr; Cmps Life Stf Mbr/Yr 89; Asst Edtr/Yr 90; Erly Chldhd Ed; Tch.

**THORNTON, TOMMY S,** Al St Univ, Montgomery, AL; SO.

**THORNTON, TONY W,** Westminster Choir Coll, Princeton, NJ; GD; MM; Phi Mu Alpha 86-; Grad Asst Chrl Condtng La St U; Amer Chrl Dir Assn; Musc Tchrs Natl Assn 85-; BM Westmnstr Chr Coll 90; Music; Chrl Condctr.**

**THORNTON, TRENNA L,** Meridian Comm Coll, Meridian, MS; SO; BA; Phi Theta Kappa Pres 89-90; NOW; LPN; Engl; Law.

**THOROGOOD, MARK EDWARD,** Coker Coll, Hartsville, SC; JR; BS; USA Sgt; Noncmmssnd Offcr In Chge Crmnl Law Div Ft Jckson SC; A Gen Studies Central Tex Comm Clg 90; Bus Mgmnt.

**THORONKA, ZAMZAM M,** Atlantic Comm Coll, Mays Landing, NJ; SO; Alied Hlth; Nrsng.

**THOROUGHMAN, CYNTHIA E,** Oh Univ-Southern Cmps, Ironton, OH; JR; BA; Gus Admn; Acctng CPA.

**THORPE, ANDREW M,** N Va Comm Coll Woodbridge, Woodbridge, VA; SO; BA; Rcvd Clg Brd Tlnt Rstr Otstndg Mnrty Comm Clg Grad Awrd 90; Fin/Acctg Auditor; NCOA Non Cmsnd Ofcrs Assc 89; Yth Enhncmnt; Nrsng/Rsprtry Thrpy; Physcns Astnt/Resp Thrpy.

**THORPE, ANNE J,** Methodist Coll, Fayetteville, NC; SR; BS; Stdnt Govt Assoc Senator 88-89; Stdnt Judicial Sys Juror 88-; Omicron Delta Kappa 89-; Alpha Chi 89-; Stdnt Life Res Advsr 89-; All-Am Soccer 87-; Acad All-Am 88-; Varsity Soccer/Tennis Capt 88-90; Bio/Phys Edn; Phys Therapy.

**THORPE, ELLEN MA,** Springfield Tech Comm Coll, Springfield, MA; BSN; Natl Hon Soc CHS 87; Dns Lst 88-; Stdnt Nrs Assoc Prog Baystate Med Ctr 86-87; Reg Nrs 90; AS 90; Nrsng.

**THORPE, JENNIFER D,** Harcum Jr Coll, Bryn Mawr, PA; SO; BS; SG Pr 90-; WAA V P 90-; Hall Cncl Co Pr 90-; Harcum Clb 90-; Phi Theta Kappa Pr; TV Intrns; Pr Awd; Comm Awd; Badminton Sftbl Capt 90-; AS; Psych.**

**THORPE, LISA M,** Univ Of Pittsburgh At Bradford, Bradford, PA; FR; BA; Blgy Clb 90-; Actvts Cncl 90-; Alpha Lambda Delta 90-; IM Vllybll 90-; Arts Scis; Ocptnl Thrpy.

**THORPE, SANDRA D,** Morgan St Univ, Baltimore, MD; JR; BS; Chmstry Clb/Stdnt Tr/Amer Chmcl Soc 89-; Beta Kappa Chi Sec 90-; Phi Eta Sigma 90-; Alpha Lambda Delta 90-; NAACP 90-; Cs Wstrn Rsrv; Chmstry; Med.

**THORPE, SANDRA M,** Faulkner St Jr Coll, Bay Minette, AL; GD; BA; Phi Theta Kappa 90; Tchrs Aid-Swift Schl 88-; Assoc; Early Chldhd Educ; Tchng.

**THORSCHMIDT, CHANTEL M,** Univ Of South Fl, Tampa, FL; FR; BA; Coll Repblcns; Greekwk; Chi Omega 90-; FL Pblc Intrst Rsrch Grp Vtr Rgstrar; Crmnlgy; Law-Gov.

**THORTON, CHERYL A,** Auburn Univ At Auburn, Auburn, AL; GD; MED; Proj Uplft 87-88; Phi Kappa Phi 90; Kappa Delta Pi 89; Alpha Lambda Delta 88; Alpha Chi Omega Schlrshp 88; BED 90; Math; Scndry Schl Tchr.

**THOTTAKARA, SHAJAN S,** Temple Univ, Philadelphia, PA; SO; BS; Vllybl Clb 89-; Indn Cath Assoc 89-; Kevala Assoc 90-; Amer Soc Cvl Engrs 89-; Dip Govt Polytech Kerala India 85; Cvl Engr.

**THOUIN, SHARON A,** Hudson Valley Comm Coll, Troy, NY; FR; AS; Vol Vrs Chrch Rltd Fnctns; Comp Info Syst; Syst Anlyst.

**THRALL, DEBORAH K,** Wv Univ At Parkersburg, Parkersburg, WV; JR; BED; Assc Retarded Ctzns; Deans List; Fairlawn Bapt Chrch Mbr; Preschl Tchr 83-; Sthrn Assc Chldrn Under Six; Natl Assc For Ed Yng Chldrn 87-91; WV Assc Yng Chldrn; Dir Preschl Lrng Ctr 87-; Ed Multi/Subjct K-8 Pre K Math; Tch Pre K.

**THRASH, PAMELA D,** Univ Of Ms Medical Center, Jackson, MS; JR; BSN; MS Assoc Stdnt Nrs NSNA; Nrsng Stdnt Bdy VP 90-; Assoc Stdnt Bdy Rep 90-; Phi Theta Kappa 88-; Pres Cncl 90-; Schllng Schlr 90-; Yvonne Pressgrove Bertolet Awd; HEADWAE Rep Clarke Clg 89-90; Fuld Fllw; Nrs Of Yr; Nrsng.

**THRASH, TINA L,** Univ Of Southern Ms, Hattiesburg, MS; FR; BA; SADD 90-; Deans List 90-; Bio; Nrsng.

**THRASHER, KENNETH,** Old Dominion Univ, Norfolk, VA; SO; BS; Elec Engrg.

**THRASHER, MICHAEL D,** Roane St Comm Coll, Harriman, TN; SO; AAS; Musuc 84-; Drama 84-; AARC 84-; Circle K 84-; AMA 84-; FCA 84-; Resp Therpy Club; CSM 86-89; Phi Data Kapa 86-89; Choir; TV Progrms; Music Schlrshp; Respitherapst AA Hiwassee Clg; Deans List; Laude; AAS; Resprty Thrpy; BS Bus.

**THRASHER, REGINA,** Univ Of Al At Huntsville, Huntsville, AL; SO; IEEE 88-; SME 89-; Vol Adult Educ 87-89; Amer Dietetic Assn 82-87; DIETICIAN Univ TN 81; MS Univ TN 84; Elect Eng; Eng.

**THRASHER, TIMOTHY R,** Tri County Tech Coll, Pendleton, SC; FR; ASSOC; Cert Elec Mtr Rpr 79; Indstrl Mech; Maint.

**THREADGILL, NICHELLE L,** Fisk Univ, Nashville, TN; SO; BS; Hlth Careers Clb 89-; AL-FSK Clb 89-; NAACP 90-; Alpha Kappa Alpha; Biolgy; Physcn.

**THREET, KRISTIE L,** Univ Of Tn At Martin, Martin, TN; FR; BS; Nrsng.

**THROWE JR, EUGENE T,** Lenoir Rhyne Coll, Hickory, NC; SO; AB; NC Stdnt Lgsltr Vice Dlgtn Chrprsn 89-; Coll Dmcrts Pres 90-; Amnsty Sec/Treas 89-; Coll Radio 90-; Habitat Hmnty 89-; Intl Rltns; Pblc Srvnt.

**THRUSH, STEPHANIE M,** Univ Of Fl, Gainesville, FL; SR; BA; Mrchng Band 88-; Symph Band 88-; Golden Key 90-; Tau Beta Sigma 88-; Intrnshp Dillards Dept Store Gainesville; Mrktng.

**THUN, NOEL B,** Univ Of Nh Plymouth St Coll, Plymouth, NH; SR; BS; Phi Kappa Phi; Intrnshp United Ntns Disaster Preparedness Offce 88; Elem Ed; Tchr.

**THUNG, IANTHINA CARA,** Cornell Univ Statutory College, Ithaca, NY; SO; BS; Otdr Clb; Pub Rltns Stdnt Soc Amer; Amer Stdnt Assn Lanscape Arch; Planning Rsrcs Orgztn Systems Philipines Apprentice; Landscape Arch.

**THURAU, DONNA J,** Colby Sawyer Coll, New London, NH; FR; BA; SGA 90-; IM Sprts 90-; Athltc Trnng; Orthpdcs.

**THURDIN, ANNA J L,** Albertus Magnus Coll, New Haven, CT; JR; BA; Frnch Clb 90-; Swm Tm 90-; Intl Rels; Bsns/Educ.

**THURLOW, ANDREW C,** Syracuse Univ, Syracuse, NY; JR; BARCH; Proj TEME 89-90; Darkroom Monitor 89-90; Math Tutor 89-90; Deans Lst Greenfield Comm Coll 89-90; Greenfield Nwspr Adv Dept 89-90; Fred G Wells Schlrshp 88; Risky Case Schlrshp 89; Conway Fstvl Hills Schlrshp 87; Architecture.

**THURMAN, BIANCA D,** Savannah Coll Of Art & Design, Savannah, GA; GD; Stdnt Fnr Arts Assoc Co Fndr 86-90; Asst Fnr Arts Dept Chrprsn 87-89; Otstndng Achvmnt Fnr Arts Awrd 90; Awrd Hgh M Drsy Acdmc Schlrshp 86-90; BFA 90; Fnr Arts.

**THURMAN, CAROL L,** Memphis St Univ, Memphis, TN; SR; BA; Natl Asc Blck Jrnlst; Memphis Area Blck Jrnlsts; Wrtng Intshp; Jrnlsm; Brdcst News.

**THURMAN, CARRIE J,** The Kings Coll, Briarclf Mnr, NY; SO; BA; Jenny Clarkson Grls Hm; Uppr Rm City Mnstry; Jrnlsm; Wrtng.

**THURMAN, CHERYL E,** Univ Of Nc At Charlotte, Charlotte, NC; JR; BA; Frnds Ntl Zoo 87-; Wrld Wldlf Fund 88-; Chi Rho 90-; AA 89; Spnsh; UN Intrprtr.

**THURMAN, DEANNA M,** Columbia Union Coll, Takoma Park, MD; FR; MS; Phi Eta Sigma 90-; Sci; Phy Thrpy.

**THURMAN, ERIC T,** Cumberland Coll, Williamsburg, KY; FR; BA; Baptist Union 90-; Campus Ministry 90-; Philosphy Club 90-; Cumberland In China; Foreign Study Prog; IM Bsskbl 90-; History English; Teach.

**THURMAN, HORACE L,** Interdenominational Theo Ctr, Atlanta, GA; SR; MDIV; Trvl Smnr To India Chrmn Dcmntn Comm 90; Afrcn Rsrch Trvl Smnr Chrmn Docum Comm; Willie D Cusic/Mattie Turnman Nunnaly Awd; Bobby Brown Schlrshp Prog UNCF; Crance Schlrshp 90; Intrfth Chpl Of Trth Inc Fndr/ Pstr 85-88; Mid-Way Mssnry 88; BA; Thlgy/Pstrl Care; Prsh Mnstr.

**THURMAN JR, JAMES A,** Fl A & M Univ, Tallahassee, FL; JR; BS; AGC 90-; All-Amer Schlr; Tutor; Bond Comm Lbry; Pres Schlrs Assn 89; Burger King Awd 89; Bldg Cnstrctn Intrn/Polk Cnty Pblc Fac; Vrsty Ftbl 88-; Bldg Const/Eng Tchnlgy; Mgmt.

**THURMAN, LUCINDA ANN,** Univ Of Louisville, Louisville, KY; FR; BS; Dnc Acdmy 90-; Hnrs Pro 90-; Phi Eta Sigma 90-; Pr Admsns Cnslr Ofc Admsns Univ Lsvl 90-; Trustees Schlrshp 90-; GEMS Pro 90-; Ekstrom Lbry Stu Asst Univ Lsvl 90-; IM Sftbl Tm 90-; Biotechnlgy; Med.

**THURMAN, MARY C,** Coker Coll, Hartsville, SC; SR; BA; Tchr Educ Advsry Comm 90-; Natl Sci Tchrs Assn 90-; Natl Cncl Tchrs Of Math 89-; Phi Theta Kappa 89-; Alpha Beta Delta 88; AA Chstrfld/Mrlboro Tech Clg 89; Educ; Tchng.

**THURMAN, RALPH A,** Christopher Newport Coll, Newport News, VA; SO; BA; Bruton Parish Ch S Sch Bible Sch Vol 90-; Jamestown Yorktown Fndtn Vol; 53rd Va Inf Vol Admn Ofcr 88-; History; Tch.

**THURMOND, CHRISTOPHER J,** Old Dominion Univ, Norfolk, VA; SR; BS; Nvl Rsrv Ofcr Trnng Corps 87-; Soc Of Automtv Engrs 88-; Amercn Soc Of Htng/Refrgrtn/AC Engrs; Deans List; Mech Engr Tech; Navy Pilot.

**THURMOND, CRAIG R,** Univ Of Ga, Athens, GA; GD; Cmmnvrsty 88-90; Coll 4-H Clb 86-87; Asst Lndscp Arch Tom Fricks Assoc; Sftbl/Bsktbl/Ftbl Capt 86-90; Histrcl Sco; Lnd Plnr Eng/Lndscp Arch Lnd Tm Inc; BLA Lndscp Arch.

**THURMOND, REBECCA L,** Univ Of Ga, Athens, GA; GD; Natl Assoc Soc Wrkrs 90-; GA Juvnl Serv Assoc; Probtn Ofcr; BSW; Soc Wrk.

**THURSTON JR, JAMES R,** Averett Coll, Danville, VA; SR; BS; Mnfctrng Eng ITT EOPD; AAS Virginia Western Comm Coll 74; Hmn Rsrce And Dev; Eng Mnfctrng Mgr.

**THURSTON, MONICA M,** Norfolk St Univ, Norfolk, VA; JR; BS; Med Records Clb 90; Hlth Care Mgmt; Med Rcrds Admn.

**THWAITS, TERRY E,** Wright St Univ Lake Cmps, Celina, OH; JR; BS; Tutr 88-; Bsktbl 89; AS; Chem; U S Air Frc.

**TIAGAI, ILAN,** S U N Y At Buffalo, Buffalo, NY; JR; BS; Natl Soc Profl Engrs 90-; IEEE 90-; Robotics/Auto Soc 90-; Elec Eng.

**TIAN, JENNFIER WEI,** Bunker Hill Comm Coll, Boston, MA; FR; Accntng.

**TIBBETTS, CATHERINE M,** Newbury Coll, Brookline, MA; Sls Rep; Bus Mgmt.

**TICE, CHRISTY M,** The Boston Conservatory, Boston, MA; FR; BFA; Drama; Hl Comm 90-; Asstshps 90-; Intl Thespn Soc Clg Awd 90-; Muscl Thtr/Drama.

**TICE, MICHELLE M,** Kent St Univ Kent Cmps, Kent, OH; JR; BA; Hall Govt 90-; Acctng.

**TICEN, DENNIS L,** Asbury Theological Sem, Wilmore, KY; GD; MDIV; Methodist Pstrl Intern Stf; BS Ball St Univ 89; Biblical Stds/Thlgy; Meth Pstr.

**TICHES, NATALIA A,** Longwood Coll, Farmville, VA; SR; BS; FSSW 87-; Yth Serv Brd 90-; Alpha Sigma Alpha Treas 89-90; Dmstc Asst Intern; Yth Serv Intern; Soc Wrk; MSW.

**TICHINEL, DAWN E,** Garrett Comm Coll, Mchenry, MD; SO; AA; Intshp Potomac Vly Farm Credit ACA; Office Tchlgy.

**TIDWELL, CHERYL A,** Univ Of Akron, Akron, OH; JR; BED; IM Cpt 89; ACES 90; HD&L Ldr 90; IM Cpt 89; Elem Educ; Tchr.

**TIDWELL, DEBORAH R,** Strayer Coll, Washington, DC; SR; BS; Alpha Chi 84-; AS 76; Stst Mgr/Ntwrk Adm 86-; Lgl Sec 82-85; Bus Adm; Comp Syst Mgmt.

**TIDWELL, DUKE W,** Middle Tn St Univ, Murfreesboro, TN; FR; DVM; Horsemans Assoc 90-; Vet Med.

**TIDWELL, KATRINA F,** Central Fl Comm Coll, Ocala, FL; FR; BA; Sci Eclgy Blgy; Wildlife Eclgst Marine Blgst.

**TIDWELL, LAURIE L,** Jones County Jr Coll, Ellisville, MS; FR; BSN; Nrsg.

**TIDWELL, STACYE M,** Central Al Comm Coll, Alexander City, AL; FR; Phi Theta Kappa Dir Scl Actvts; Chrch Chrst; Scl Sci/Psychlgy.

**TIDWELL, STEPHANIE M,** Liberty Univ, Lynchburg, VA; SR; Rpblcns 86-88; Kappa Delta Pi 89-; Hnrs Prg 87-; Pryr Ldr 87-89; Sprtl Lfe Dir 89-90; Magna Cum Laude 90-; Hnrs Grad 90; IM Vlybl 87; BS 90; Elem Educ; Tchg.

**TIDWELL, TIMOTHY R,** Central St Univ, Wilberforce, OH; FR; Swmng Tm Co Capt 90; Debate Tm; Cmnty Ctr 88; Sci; NASA.

**TIEDEMANN, NICOLE M,** Cornell Univ Statutory College, Ithaca, NY; FR; Cthlc S S Tchr; Cmps Crsd Chrst; Appalachian Proj; Natural Rsrcs.

**TIEDGE JR, WILLIAM F,** Embry Riddle Aeronautical Univ, Daytona Beach, FL; FR; BS; Aircrft Ownrs Plts Assn 90-; Army Comm Medl Good Cond Mdl; Wrkng For Rest Corp 90-; Untd Prcl Serv Drvr 87-90; U S Army 84-87; Aerntcl Sci; Prof Airline Transprt Plt.

**TIEMAN, ANN M,** Northern Ky Univ, Highland Hts, KY; FR; BS; Employment At Robert T Longshore Md As Med Asst 88-; Nrsng.

**TIEMEYER, LA LENYA,** Hocking Tech Coll, Nelsonville, OH; SO; BA; Accntng Clb 90-; Amer Lgn Ld Aux Pres 86-87; Accntng; Bus.**

**TIEN, HUNG NICK,** Comm Coll Of Philadelphia, Philadelphia, PA; SR; MBA; Bus Mngmnt.

**TIERNAN, KAREN M,** Newbury Coll, Brookline, MA; FR; AAS; Fd Shw Nrthest Fd Srvc Ldgng Expstn Cnfrnc; Outstndng Frshmn Awd; Acdmc Awd Fl 90; BS Ed Univ Maine 79; Clnry Arts.

**TIERNAN, LIZA M,** Fl St Univ, Tallahassee, FL; SR; BSW; Assoc Student Social Wrks Treas 90-; Boosting Alcohol Conscious Hlth Univ Student 90-; Phi Alpha 91-; Intshp Disc Vlg; Social Wrkr; Durg/Alcohol Counselor.

**TIERNEY, DANALYN,** Anne Arundel Comm Coll, Arnold, MD; SO; Litry Magzn 2nd Prize Fictn 90; Stdnt Assoc Pres 80; Stdnt Sen Sentr 80; Tchng Asst American Univ French Lit 82; Bus; Comptr Engr.

**TIETTMEYER, DIANE E,** Northern Ky Univ, Highland Hts, KY; SO; BA; Human Serv Clb; Kappa Kappa Kappa 90; Mntl Hlth/Human Serv; Jvnle Cnslng.

**TIETZ, ERICA L,** Edinboro Univ Of Pa, Edinboro, PA; JR; BA; Scndry Ed Assoc 90-; Hnrs Prgm 88-; Phi Eta Sigam 89-; Alpha Chi 90-; Grmn.

**TIEU, LOC B,** S U N Y Coll Of Tech At Alfred, Alfred, NY; SR; AOS; Sigma Gau Epsilon 89-; Drftng; Mchncl Eng.

**TIFFANY, JOHN B,** Univ Of Sc At Aiken, Aiken, SC; GD; BS; Sci Clb Pres V Pres 89-; Alumni Ambsdr; Omicron Delta Kappa Pres 90-; Gamma Beta Phi; Amer Chem Soc; Stdnt Yr 90-; Otsdng Chem Mjr; Chem; Med Doctor.

**TIFFANY, SHERYL L,** S U N Y At Buffalo, Buffalo, NY; BS; Scty Hmn Rsrc Mgmt 90-; Bus Clb; Acctg Scty 89-; Delta Mu Delta 89-; Chi Delta Sigma; Mgmt; Hmn Rsrc Mgmt.

**TIFFNER, ANGELA L,** Univ Of Sc At Columbia, Columbia, SC; FR; BM; Mrchng/Symphnc/Jazz Bands 90-; Wnd Ens; Pres Hnr Rl; Dns Lst; Oakwood Bptst Chr 86-; Msc; Educ.

**TIFT, TONJA C,** Abraham Baldwin Agri Coll, Tifton, GA; SO; BED; Pres Lst; Dns Lst; Tstmstrs Intl 88-; AA; Spec Ed; Tch.

**TIGERT, SAM M,** Univ Of Cincinnati-Clrmnt Coll, Batavia, OH; FR; BA; Chemsty; Phmcy.

**TIGGETT, DENA PATRICE,** Wilberforce Univ, Wilberforce, OH; SR; BS; Natl Assn Blck Acctnts Stdnt Chptr Pres 88-; Natl Stdng Bus League Treas 90-; Finance Comm 90-; Stdnt Govt Assn 90-; Alpha Kappa Mu 89-; Sigma Hnr Socty Pres 88-; Delta Sigma Theta 90-; Natl Assn Acctnts; In Roads Northeast Ohio Inc 88-; Acctng; MBA.

**TIGNER, TRESA R,** Union Univ, Jackson, TN; JR; BS; STEA; Yth Twn Wkend Prnts; Fl Tm Stdnt; AS; BS; Elem Educ.

**TIGNOR, LAURA P,** Va Commonwealth Univ, Richmond, VA; JR; BS; Ntl Stdnt Nrses Assoc 90; Med Tech At Dialysis Ctr Tech; Nrsng; RN.**

**TIGNOR, TAMMY D,** Univ Of Va Clinch Valley Coll, Wise, VA; FR; BS; Phi Upsilon Omega Pres; Va Gov Sch Srvy Asst; Psych; Indstrl.

**TIKYANI, JAISHREE,** Univ Of Miami, Coral Gables, FL; SR; BS; Cane Cmmtr Orgnztn Hmcng Chrprsn 90-; Hnrs Stdnts Assc Orntn Orntn Asst 89; Gldn Key Crrspndng Sec 90-; ACM 90-; Vol Serv Social Issues Chr 89-90; Prsn Schlrshp 88-; Deans List Provosts List; Bdmntn Clb 90-; Cmptr Science; Prgrmmng/Sftw Engrng.

**TILEY, PAMELA A,** Babson Coll, Babson Park, MA; FR; Law Soc; Soc Org; Stdnt Life Com; Philanthrope Act Awd; Bus; Law.

**TILL, SHERYL C,** Livingston Univ, Livingston, AL; FR; AS; Stf Nurs Med Ctr Baton Rouge 89-; LPN Hammnd Area Voc Schl 89; Nrsng.

**TILLERY, BRANTLEY L,** Univ Of Tn At Martin, Martin, TN; JR; BS; Hstry Clb 90-; Phi Alpha Theta Pres; Upr Div Hstry Awrd; Deans Lst 90; Hstry.

**TILLERY, BRYAN R,** Memphis St Univ, Memphis, TN; FR; BA; Mid South Peace/Justice Cntr Comm 90-; Pol Scnc; Soc Wrk/Teaching/Admin.

**TILLERY, CLAUDIA B,** Wilberforce Univ, Wilberforce, OH; SR; BS; Natl Stdnt Bus Leag 89-; NAACP 87-; Kappa Swthrt Sec 88-; Comm Svc Sec Pres 88-89; Intrnshp Amer Mgmt Assc 87; Deans List 88-; Tuition USA Corps Eng 88-89; MS Psi 88; Mgmt/Mktg; Bus.

**TILLERY, LORETTA,** Cheyney Univ Of Pa, Cheyney, PA; JR; BA; Delta Epsilon Chi Sec 90; Rsdnc Hl Repr 88; Omega Psi Phi Pearl Ct VP 88-90; Bsn Admin; Fnce.

**TILLEY, ANGELA D,** Tn St Univ, Nashville, TN; SR; BS; Hs Cncl Treas 87-88; Rsdnc Cncl VP 87-88; Ornttn 88; RA 88-89; Asst Crdntr 89-90; Fdsrvc Admn.

**TILLEY, CATHY L,** Univ Of Tn At Martin, Martin, TN; JR; BS; Scl Wrk Clb; Scl Wrk.

**TILLEY, CHRISTOPHER E,** Univ Of Southern Ms, Hattiesburg, MS; SO; BA; Hall Cncl Stdnt Govt Treas 90; Gldn Eagle Stdnt Cntr Stdnt Assn VP 90-; Psychlgy; Cnslng Psychlgy.

**TILLEY, KENT D,** Duke Univ, Durham, NC; GD; MDIV; Auditor 86-89; BA 86; BA 90; Practical Ministry.

**TILLEY, LYNDE S,** Univ Of Nc At Charlotte, Charlotte, NC; SO; MA; Alpha Delta Pi Sunshine Girl; Psychology/C Jus.

**TILLEY, MICHAEL S,** Univ Of Al At Birmingham, Birmingham, AL; JR; BA; Bsbll Tm 89-; Deans Lst; Pres Lst; Hnr Roll; Commsnrs Awd; Psychology; Dentistry.

**TILLEY, RICKEY L,** Miles Coll, Birmingham, AL; SR; BA; Jud Cncl 90-; Cir K Intl 87; Phi Beta Sigma Pr 89-; Greyhound Dial Corp Schlrshp 90-; Frances B Gettman Schlrshp 89-90; Ftbl Tm Capt 87-; Bus Admin; Mngmnt/Law.

**TILLIS, GINA M,** Univ Of Fl, Gainesville, FL; FR; Envrnmntl Actn Grp 90-; Hnrs Org 90-; Tolbert Area Govt Repr 90-; Alpha Lambda Delta 90; Entmlgy Rsrch; Mudfest 90; Deans List; Engr/Envrnmntl.

**TILLIS, TRACI D,** Oh Univ-Southern Cmps, Ironton, OH; FR; BA; Cmnctns; Jrnlsm.

**TILLIS, VANESSA K,** Central Fl Comm Coll, Ocala, FL; FR; AA; Chrldr 90-; SGA Rep 90-; Stdnt Govt Assn V P; Phi Theta Kappa; Cmps Dplmnt; Chrldng; Pblc Rltns; Reg Dietician.

**TILLMAN, BETTY A,** Univ Of North Fl, Jacksonville, FL; JR; BA; Phi Theta Kappa 89-90; Phi Beta Lambda Hist/Rprtr 89-90; Cmptr Power Inc Prgmmr Trainee; AA St Johns Cmnty Coll Orange Park FL 90; Cmptr Info Sys; Cmptr Pgmng.

**TILLMAN, CEDRIC R,** Alcorn St Univ, Lorman, MS; JR; BA; Ntl Assn Blk Jrnlst 88-; Cmnctns Clb; Ntl Assn Blk Jrnlst Intrn Rprtr Ancr 90; Radio WPRL-FM Rprtr Ancr 88-90; IM Sftbl 89-90; Cmnctn; Brdcstng.

**TILLMAN, DENNIS K,** Livingstone Coll, Salisbury, NC; JR; BS; Wrstlng UNCF Ftbl 89-; Hon Role 89-; Lvngstone Coll; Fayetteville St U; Somar Incorprtd; Wrstlng/Ftbl 89-; Sing Church; Piano Chrch; Math; Avtnst.

**TILLMAN, EDWARD J,** Hillsborough Comm Coll, Tampa, FL; FR; BA; Pub Access T V 90-; Cable T V Instltn 88-90; Hon Dschg USMC 86; Cinematography/Art; Film Mkng.

**TILLMAN, ERIC A,** Fl International Univ, Miami, FL; SR; BS; Envrnmntl Clb Treas 90-; Envrnmntl Intrnshp; AA W/Hon Miami-Dade Comm Coll 88; Envrnmntl Stdies; MA Lndscp Archtctr.

**TILLMAN, IRA P,** Jackson St Univ, Jackson, MS; SO; Acctg Soc; Bapt Stdnt Un 89-90; Alpha Lambda Delta 90-; Dept Econ Cmnty Dvlp Intrnshp; Outstndg Stdnt Intermediate Acctg.

**TILLMAN, JEFFREY L,** Al A & M Univ, Normal, AL; SR; BS; Deans Lst; Hons Rl; Pol Sci; Law.

**TILLMAN, KIMYANA W,** Tn St Univ, Nashville, TN; JR; BS; AMRA; Sfty Clb; Med Rcrds Intrn; Prfrmnce Awrd; Med Rcrd Cdr LPN 87-; LPN Mississippi Delta Jr Coll 87; Med Rcrd Admin.

**TILLMAN, NICHOLE K,** Va St Univ, Petersburg, VA; FR; BA; Acad Excel Awrd 90-; Bus Info Syst.

**TILLMAN, STACEY L,** Chattanooga St Tech Comm Coll, Chattanooga, TN; SO; AAS; Chattanooga Soc Radlgc Tech 90-; TN Soc Radlgc Tech 90-; Phi Theta Kappa 89-; Dns Lst 88-; Info Syst Tech; Cmptr Oper/Ofc Mgr.

**TILLMON, CANDICE R,** Saint Pauls Coll, Lawrenceville, VA; JR; BA; NAACP 88-; Black Womens Coalition 88-; Outrch Progrm For Potntl HS 89-; Earth Team Salutes US Dept Of Ag Soil Consrvtn Svc Asstntshp 90-; Dance Troupe Grp Dancr 88-89; BA; Pol Sci; Law.

**TILLOTSON, MICHELLE M,** Vance Granville Comm Coll, Henderson, NC; SO; AAS; Phi Theta Kappa; Bus Computer Prgrmng.

**TILMONT, SCOTT D,** Clarkson Univ, Potsdam, NY; JR; BS; Phi Theta Kappa Sec 89-90; Indstrl Mgmnt; Bus.

**TILSON, CHRISTINE E,** Fl St Univ, Tallahassee, FL; SR; BA; SCALP 89-; RCRA 89-; FBPA 89-; Actn Stdnt Ptcl Prty Ofcr Fr Intrgrk Affrs 89-90; Kappa Delta Bg Evnts Ofcr 87-; Intrnshp Cry Spcl Evnts; Fld Wrk Eldrhstl Ast Dir 90; Rsrt/Cmrcl Stds; Htl/Rsrt Mngmnt.

**TIMBERLAKE, KRISTA,** Savannah Coll Of Art & Design, Savannah, GA; JR; BA; Cyclng Team 88-89; Intrnshp W/Pntr-Kldscpe Crftr 90; M Whelan Schlrshp 89-; Illstrtn/Art Hstry; Art Ed.

**TIMBROOK, KYLE W,** Strayer Coll, Washington, DC; SR; BS; U S Govt Wrkr 78-; AAS Nrthrn VA Cmnty Clg 82; 8333 Little Rvr Trnpk Annandale VA Summa Cum Laude; Cmptr Info Syst.

**TIMCHAK, JEANNINE M,** Colby Sawyer Coll, New London, NH; FR; BFA; Art League; Alumni Assn; Outing Clb; Deans Lst; Art Awd; Fine Arts; Art Rstrtn.

**TIMKO, DAVID A,** Oh St Univ, Columbus, OH; SR; BA; Phi Beta Kappa 90; Phi Kappa Phi; Hist; Grad Schl Hist Coll Tchng.

**TIMKO, KIMBERLY A,** Marshall University, Huntington, WV; SR; MED; Hl Advsry Cncl Secr 87-90; Res Hl Assoc; Campus Entertnmnt Unltd 87-; Alpha Kappa Psi V P 88-; Newman Assoc Pres 87-; Res Advsr 88-90; Res Hl Dir; BBA; Cnslr Ed; Adm/Stdnt Pers.

**TIMM, CHARLES G,** William Paterson Coll, Wayne, NJ; JR; BA; English.

**TIMM, TORSTEN,** George Mason Univ, Fairfax, VA; SR; BS; Amer Mktg Assoc 89-; Dcsn Sci/MIS Clb; Golden Key 89-; Alpha Chi; Beta Gamma Sigma; Intrnshp Cnvntnl Mntns Systms 90; Mgmt Info Syst; MBA.

**TIMMANY, JANELL M,** Hudson Valley Comm Coll, Troy, NY; SO; ASSOC; Guenther Schlrshp 89-; Assoc; Lib Arts; Elem Educ/Psychlgy.

**TIMMONS, DEBORAH I,** Univ Of Nc At Greensboro, Greensboro, NC; SR; BS; Mrshls 90-; Rsrch Tech 87-; Exrcs Sprts Sci.

**TIMMONS, ROBIN M,** Oh Wesleyan Univ, Delaware, OH; SO; BA; Phi Eta Sigma; Engl/Geology.

**TIMMONS, TIPPY M,** Univ Of Sc At Columbia, Columbia, SC; SR; BA; Univ Of SC Schlrshp 90; Geo A Wauchope Awd; Engl.

**TIMONEY, EUNICE A,** Immaculata Coll, Immaculata, PA; JR; BA; Stdt Assoc Treas 90-; Pres Cncl Stdt Rep 89-; Math Clb 89-; Sigma Zeta Pres 90-; Immaculata 90-; COOL 90-; Math; Bus.

**TIMONEY, OWEN,** Allentown Coll Of St Francis, Center Valley, PA; FR; Drama Club Pres 90; Arts Soc Assoc Mbr; Spice Williams Stunt Acad; Thtr.

**TIMORDJIAN, RITA A,** Hudson Valley Comm Coll, Troy, NY; SR; MBA; Assoc Sci; Bus Admn; Mrktng.

**TIMP, COURTNEY E,** Univ Of Rochester, Rochester, NY; JR; BA; PETA; Grnpce; Poltcl Sci; Poltcs.

**TIMPANARO, MARNI L,** Hudson Valley Comm Coll, Troy, NY; SO; BA; Pres List; Prof Cosmotologist 88-; Cert Austin Beauty Schl 88-89; Crim Just; Prob Ofcr.

**TIMS, SHERI E,** Univ Of Ms Medical Center, Jackson, MS; JR; BSN; Std Nrs Asc 90-; Dns Lst; Pi Beta Phi Pres 76-79; Univ MS Extern-Crtcl Care; Bsktbl; BS Univ Sthrn MS 79; CCN.

**TINCHER, DONNA F,** Blue Mountain Coll, Blue Mountain, MS; SR; BED; MAE-SP 90-; Como Bptst Chrch Chrprsn Of Cm 87; GS Asst Ldr 83; Tchr Ast Sntbia Cty Schls 90; Assoc Ed Northwest Mississippi Jr Coll 69; Elem Educ; Tchng.

**TINDAL, PEGGY G,** Univ Of Sc At Columbia, Columbia, SC; FR; BA; Emplyd Alld Sgnl; BADM; Bus.

**TINDLE, DEANNA J,** Watterson Coll, Louisville, KY; SR; AS; Presidents Lst; Stdnt Of Month May; Dipl Acctng Sullivan Jr Clg Bus 85; Medl Asstng; Nursing.

**TINE, LINDA M,** Dowling Coll, Oakdale Li, NY; JR; BA; Romnc Lang; Ed/Intrntl Bus.

**TINELLI, KELLY E,** Anne Arundel Comm Coll, Arnold, MD; SO; AA; Chem Club 90-; Nwsltr Stff Rcyclng Proj; Phi Theta Kappa 90-; Amer Chem Soc 90; Outsdng Achvmnt/Chem Awd; Chemistry; Pharmacy.

**TINEO, ERIC,** S U N Y Coll Of A & T Morrisvl, Morrisville, NY; SR; AS; Res Asst; IM Sprts; Rsprtry Thrpy.

**TINGLE, JIMMY M,** Saint Catharine Coll, St Catharine, KY; SO; BA; BA; Bsn Admin; Mgmt.

**TINGLE, SHARA D,** Midway Coll, Midway, KY; SO; BA; Amer Bus Wmns Assn 90-; Fshn Mrchndsng Stdnt Assn 90-; AA Midway Coll; Mgmt.

**TINGLER, MARISA S,** Marshall University, Huntington, WV; SR; BBA; IMS; Bus Mngmnt.

**TINGLING, TEJAN K,** Norfolk St Univ, Norfolk, VA; FR; BS; Dozoretz Natl Inst Minorities In Apld Sci; Stdnt Govt Org 90-; Spartan Alpha Tau 90-; IM Bsktbl 90-; Computer Science.

**TINKER, RICHARD,** Stillman Coll, Tuscaloosa, AL; JR; Citzens Partitn Org Tutor Prog 90-; Student Support Serv 89-; Plus Gor; Cordell Wynn Hnr Prog 90-; Math.

**TINKER, TAMARA A,** Castleton St Coll, Castleton, VT; SO; BA; Psychlgy.

**TINKHAM, ROBIN M,** Old Dominion Univ, Norfolk, VA; SR; BSBA; Mgmnt Inf Systms; Systms Analysis.**

**TINKLER, TRISHA L,** Kent St Univ Kent Cmps, Kent, OH; FR; BSN; Alpha Lambda Delta; Nrsng.

**TINNES, CHRISTY A,** Univ Of Sc At Columbia, Columbia, SC; JR; BS; Clg Repubs 88-89; Band 88; Concert Band 89; Omicron Delta Kappa V P 90-; Mortar Bd; Assoc Hnr Stdnts Rep 88-; Order Omega; Tau Beta Sigma Pldg Cls Pres 88-89; Kappa Alpha Theta V P-Finance 89-; Schlrshp Awd; Acctg.

**TINNEY, RENEE S,** Erie Comm Coll, Buffalo, NY; FR; AS; Antmy Physlgy Microbio Psych Engl Sclgy Nutr.

**TINO, MICHAEL J,** Cornell Univ Statutory College, Ithaca, NY; SO; BS; Results 88-; Lvg Lrng Cntr Chrmn Flr Cncl 89-; Stdnt Advsr 90-; Alpha Zeta Chrnclr 90-; Deans List 89-; Alpha Zeta Natl Schlrshp; IM Vlybl 90-; Bio Sci/Cell; Rsrch Scintst.

**TINSLEY, BARBARA L,** Univ Of Cincinnati, Cincinnati, OH; SO; BA; Paralegal Assn; Deans Lst 90-; Crmnl Jstc Crrctns; Law.

**TINSLEY, CHRISTOPHER S,** Western Carolina Univ, Cullowhee, NC; FR; BS; IM; Dept Arts Sci Awd; Math Awd; Eng; Naval Aviator.

**TIO, JOSE A,** Univ Of Pr Cayey Univ Coll, Cayey, PR; SO; BS; Deans Hon Lst 89-; Acctg; CPA.

**TIONG, ING C,** Univ Of Ky, Lexington, KY; SR; BS; Lxngtn Chns Chrstn Flwshp Chr; Mlysn Std Org 89-; Dns Lst 89-; Cmptr Sci; Sys Dsgnr.

**TIPPETT, GINA C,** Lexington Comm Coll, Lexington, KY; FR; AS; Nursing.

**TIPPETTE, SHANNON D,** Univ Of Nc At Charlotte, Charlotte, NC; JR; BA; Psychlgy/Engl.

**TIPPIE, TRACY N,** Allegheny Coll, Meadville, PA; JR; BS; Hon Com Chrmn 89-; Bd Trstes Stdnt Afrs Com 90-; Jazz Bnd 88-90; Sigma Alpha Epsilon 89-; Orntn Advsr; Alden Schlr 89-90; Chem; Pharm Rsrch.

**TIPPIN, MARTHA J,** Ringling School Of Art, Sarasota, FL; SR; Bst Of Rnglng Annl Stdnt Shw 89-; Pres Hnr Lst 90; BA Kansas St Emporia 69; Illstrtn.

**TIPPING, CHRISTOPHER A,** George Washington Univ, Washington, DC; JR; BA; G W Coll Rep Chrmn 90-; Geo Washington Stdnt Assn Sntr 90-; Gldn Key 90-; Pi Sigma Alpha 90-; Sigma Chi 89-; Cngrsmn Bob Mc Ewen R Ohio Intrnshp 90-; Geo Wash Univ Dns Lst 90-; Pol Sci; Law/Politics.**

**TIPTON, AUDREY P,** Mayland Comm Coll, Spruce Pine, NC; FR; AS; Dns Lst 90-; Gnrl Educ; Cmptr Prgmmr.

**TIPTON, BETH E,** Defiance Coll, Defiance, OH; JR; BA; Theta Xi Lil Sis Orgn Sec 90-; Gamma Omega Kappa; Alton J Kurtz Prz; Trck 89; Chrldng Sqd Capt 89-; Elem Educf Tchng Cnslng.

**TIPTON, CARRIE A,** Univ Of Ky, Lexington, KY; SR; JD; Hbtt Fr Hmnty 90-; Stdnt Govt Assn Admin Dir 88-; Grk Pol Actn Com Rep 88-; Mrtr Brd 90-; Pi Lambda Sigma 88-; Lncs 89-; Chi Omega Art Dir Rsh Cnsllr 87-; US Svt Stdnt Ldrshp Exchnge UK Dlgte 90; Pnhllnc Outstndng Acad Awrd; BA; Pol Sci Engl; Law Intrntl Dplmcy.

**TIPTON, HOLLY D,** Bridgewater Coll, Bridgewater, VA; SR; BA; Internatl Clb 88-; Spnsh Clb 88-90; Ortr Chr 87-; Internatl Stds.

**TIPTON, JOHN B,** Livingston Univ, Livingston, AL; JR; BA; Rgby Clb U AL 89-90; U AL IM Wrstlng Champ 87-; Dixie Yth Bsbl Coach 89-; Deans Lst 90-; Sigma Chi Pldg 87; Mktg.

**TIPTON, JUDY A,** Wv Univ At Parkersburg, Parkersburg, WV; FR; BA; Pri Art Bsnss.

**TIPTON, KELLY F,** Fl Coll, Temple Terrace, FL; FR; AA; Symphnc Bnd 90-; Alpha Clb; Phi Theta Kappa Treas; Arete 90-; Grdtn Mrshl; Math; Ed.

**TIPTON, MACHELLE R,** Mayland Comm Coll, Spruce Pine, NC; FR; Pres Lst; Dns Lst; Secr-Gen/Med Ofc.

**TIPTON, MARIE T,** East Tn St Univ, Johnson City, TN; JR; BBA; Gamma Beta Phi 89-; Alpha Lambda Delta 90-; Golden Poet Awd World Of Poetry 90; Acctg; Corp Acctg.

**TIPTON, MELANIE J,** Oh Univ, Athens, OH; FR; BBA; IM Bsktbl; Bsns Mgmt.

**TIPTON, MICHAEL F,** Bridgewater Coll, Bridgewater, VA; JR; BA; Jazz Bnd 89-; Econ Clb 90-; Concert Bnd 88-; Bus Admin; Real Est.

**TIPTON, REBECCA S,** S U N Y Coll At Fredonia, Fredonia, NY; SO; BA; Bacchus Sec 89-90; Tchng Asst; Acad Schlrshp 89-; Cmctns/Psych; Dramatic Film.

**TIPTON, ROBIN L,** Piedmont Coll, Demorest, GA; SR; MBA; Chapel Choir VP; Chmbr Singrs VP; Psychlgy Clb Pres; Alpha Chi Soc; Intrnshp Clarkesville Elem Cnslr 90; Intrnshp Lee Arrendale Corr Inst; AA Truett Mc Connel Coll 86; BA; Psychlgy; Cnslng.

**TIPTON, SUSAN A,** Mayland Comm Coll, Spruce Pine, NC; FR; Nrsng.

**TIRADO ORTIZ, BRENDA L,** Inter Amer Univ Pr Guayama, Guayama, PR; FR.

**TIRADO, MAYRA E,** Glassboro St Coll, Glassboro, NJ; SR; BA; Spnsh Clb 89-; ESL Clb 85; Glassboro St Coll Deans Lst 89-90; Edctnl Opp Fund 87; Spanish.

**TIRADO, RAFAEL D,** City Univ Of Ny Queensbrough, New York, NY; JR; BA; Dns Hnr Lst 90; Clg Bd 89-90; AAS; Bsn/Acctg; CPA.

**TIRADO-SANTIAGO, DAISY J,** Univ Of Pr At Rio Piedras, Rio Piedras, PR; SO; BA; Literature; Teach Prof.

**TIRADO-VALES, PABLO J,** Univ Of Sc At Columbia, Columbia, SC; JR; BS; Natl Stu Exch Assn 89-; Cvl Eng.**

**TIREY, ROBERT L,** Cumberland Coll, Williamsburg, KY; FR; BS; Hnrs Day 90; Math Physics; Eng.

**TIRINO, KRISTIN M,** Manhattanville Coll, Purchase, NY; JR; BA; Spplmntl Inst 90-; Portfolio Dist 90-; Dean Lst 89-; Ecnmcs; Law.

**TIRLONI, ROBERT P,** City Univ Of Ny Baruch Coll, New York, NY; JR; BBA; AMA 89-; Gldn Ky 90-; Bus; Mrktng.

**TIRPAK, BERNARD E,** Duquesne Univ, Pittsburgh, PA; SO; BS; Cmtr Cncl 89-; Cmtr Asst 90-; Dns Lst 89-; Phi Chi Theta 90-; YMCA 89-; St Robts Bsktbl Ch 7-8th Grd 90-; Acctng; Acctnt.

**TISCHER, HEIDI C,** Salisbury St Univ, Salisbury, MD; JR; BA; Liberal Studies/Psych.

**TISCHIO, DEBORAH A,** Georgian Court Coll, Lakewood, NJ; GD; Deans Schlr 89-90; Acctnt 88-; AS Ocean Cty Clg 87; BS 90; Acctg.

**TISCHLER, LINDA R,** Kent St Univ Kent Cmps, Kent, OH; SR; BGS; Sailng Team V Commadore 87-90; Gen Stdies; Physcl Thrpy.

**TISDALE, CARLA E,** Bloomfield Coll, Bloomfield, NJ; SO; BSW; BCA 89-; Stdnt Govt 90-; Highest Hnrs 89-90; Soc Work; Med Soc Work.

**TISDELL, CHARLES VONZIAH,** Tn St Univ, Nashville, TN; SO; BSC; Blck Stdnt Assoc 88-90; Comp Clb Pres 90; Phi Theta Kappa 89; Ftbll; Assoc 90; Appld Sci.

**TISON, SHIRLEY K,** Abraham Baldwin Agri Coll, Tifton, GA; SO; BED; DECA Prlmntrn 90; DECA Stdnt Of The Yr 90; Dvsnl Awrd Of Excllnce 89; Assoc 90; Spcl Educ Spch; Spch Pthlgst Elem.

**TISSANDIER, LISA A,** Wilmington Coll, Wilmington, OH; SO; BA; GAA 86-89; French Schlrshp Tm 85-86; English Schlrshp Tm 87-89; Natl Hon Soc Sec 87-; Var Schlr 87-89; Momair Schlrshp; Hon Schlrshp; Intrn G E Aircraft Engines; Media Rltns; Chrldr 85-89; French; Intl Mktg/Cmunctns.

**TISSANDIER, MICHAEL D,** Univ Of Dayton, Dayton, OH; SR; BS; Chem; Anlytcl Chmst.**

**TITARD, LAURA K,** Univ Of Southern Ms, Hattiesburg, MS; SR; BS; Singng Eagles 88-90; Newman Clb 87-90; Intl Adpt-A-Frnd 88; Phi Kappa Phi 90-; Gamma Beta Phi 88-89; Alpha Lambda Delta 87-88; Cnvntn Amer Instrctrs Deaf VP 88-; Hosp Vol 87-90; Chrch Orgnst 87-90; Pres Lst 87-; Deans Lst 87-; Outstndng Sr; Ed Of Deaf; Peace Corps Vol.

**TITKO, KRISTIN K,** Oh Coll Of Podiatric Med, Cleveland, OH; JR; DPM; Class Pres 89-90; AM Clg Foot Surgeons; Pdtrc Political Action Commt 89; Pi Delta Scientific Chrmn 90; Alpha Gamma Kappa Rush Chrmn 89; CPR Instrctr; Deans List 89-90; Podiatry.

**TITKOS, HENRIETTA,** City Univ Of Ny Queensbrough, New York, NY; SR; AAS; SNA 90-; Nursng Awd; Hosp Del Rm R N; Nrsng.

**TITON, ROSS L,** Univ Of Miami, Coral Gables, FL; FR; BS; Alpah Lambda Delta; Sigma Phi Epsilon; Biology.

**TITUS, DAVID H,** S U N Y Coll Of Tech At Delhi, Delhi, NY; SO; AS; Physics/Biology; Scientific Research.

**TITUS, JILL L,** Slippery Rock Univ, Slippery Rock, PA; JR; BA; HPERD; 89-; Deans Lst 90-; Phi Epsilon Kappa 90-; Phys Education; Phys Therapy.

**TITUS, KRISTI E,** Bridgewater Coll, Bridgewater, VA; FR; BA; Inter Vars 90; Engl; Elem Educ.

**TITUS, LYNN M,** Daemen Coll, Amherst, NY; SR; BS; Delta Mu Delta Sec 90-; Delta Mu Delta; Rd Crss; Amer Insttn Of Bnkng; Bus Admin; Anlyss Wrk.

**TITUS, PAUL A,** James Madison University, Harrisonburg, VA; JR; BA; Judicial Council; Clge Young Republicans 89-; Mortar Brd 90-; Phi Kappa Phi 90-; Golden Key 90-; Sigma Nu 90-; Presidents List 88-; Cross Cntry/Track 88-89; Political Science; Law.**

**TITUS, STACY A,** Kent St Univ Kent Cmps, Kent, OH; SR; BA; APA Mbr 90-; Psychlgy Dept Rsrch Asst; Townhall II 24 Hr Help Line Crisis Intrvntn; Dns Lst Hiram Coll 87; Dns Lst 88-; Pres Schlrshp Hiram Coll 87; Psychlgy; Cnslng.

**TIUTA, IOANA M,** City Univ Of Ny La Guard Coll, Long Island Cty, NY; SO; BA; MBA Univ Bucharest Romania 77-78; Acctntng.

**TIWARI, INDRA K,** Bloomfield Coll, Bloomfield, NJ; FR; CERT; Mtrls Mngmt/Bus.

**TJAHJANA, ANGELA PRIANI,** Saint Leo Coll, Saint Leo, FL; JR; BS; Mariae Legio Org Sec 89-90; Cmps Mnstry 90-; Legion Mary Org; Pre Nrsng; RN.**

**TJANDRA, LANNY,** Western New England Coll, Springfield, MA; FR; BSC; Ind Eng.

**TKACY, WALTER,** Columbia Greene Comm Coll, Hudson, NY; SO; BS; AAS; Crmnl Jstc; Law Schl.

**TKACZ, DOROTHY E,** Felician Coll, Lodi, NJ; SR.

**TKACZ, WILLIAM J,** Univ Of New Haven, West Haven, CT; SO; BS; Fire Sci Clb V P 89-; Res Assist 90-; Vol Firefighter 88-; Alpha Lambda Delta Treas 90-; Pres Schlrshp 89-; Trck/Fld 90; Fire Prot; Eng.

**TKATSCHOW, KATHRYN,** Le Moyne Coll, Syracuse, NY; SR; BS; Choir 87; Acctg Soc 87-; Acctg.

**TO, ANH HOANG,** Bunker Hill Comm Coll, Boston, MA; GD; Wrd Prcsg/Typg; AS.

**TO, DORIS H,** City Univ Of Ny City Coll, New York, NY; JR; BEE; IEEE 90-; Golden Key 90-; Tau Beta Pi; City Clge Schlr Awd 88-; Elctrcl Engrg.**

**TOADVINE JR, THEODORE A,** Salisbury St Univ, Salisbury, MD; GD; PHD; Scarab Lit Mag Editorial Bd 87-90; Chorus/Chmbr Choir 86-87; Tourguide 89-90; Phi Sigma Tau 88-90; Univ Hnrs Prog 86-90; Univ Philos 86-90; Sophanes 86-90; Hesse Awd Creataive Wrtng 89; Gen Hnrs Dipl 90; Grad Instrctshp 90-; Philosophy; Prof Of Philsophy.

**TOBEN, PETRA T,** Fl International Univ, Miami, FL; SR; BS; Soc Wmn Engrs 90; Amer Soc Mech Engrs; Phi Eta Sigma 89-; Alpha Omega Chi 90-; Phi Kappa Phi; Stdnt Hon Mentor Prog 89-; Fculty Schlrs 88-; Fla Undgrd Schlrs Awd 88; Engr Sci; Mech Engr.

**TOBER, SUSANNE B,** The Kings Coll, Briarclf Mnr, NY; JR; BA; Choir Pianist 88-; His Royalty Ensmbl Pianist 89-90; Sprng Musical Pianist 89-90; Natl Hnr Socty 86-; All Amer Schlr 90-; Fndrs Schlr 88-; Math; High Schl Tchr.

**TOBIAS, KAREN N,** Ms Univ For Women, Columbus, MS; SR; BS; Unn Advsry Cbnt 89-; Phi Kappa Phi; Mrtr Brd Treas 90-; Acctng Hnrry 90; AA Hinds Comm Coll 89; Bus; Mgmt.**

**TOBIAS, KENNETH F,** Springfield Tech Comm Coll, Springfield, MA; SR; BA; Busn Club Treas 89-90; Finance Acad Boston Clg; Joseph J Cooligan Awd 90; Alumni Schlrshp Awd 90; Busn Club Schlrshp Awd 90; Finance; Law.

**TOBIAS, REBECCA J,** Oh Wesleyan Univ, Delaware, OH; FR; BA; Bg Pal/Ltl Pal Prgrm 90-; Fllwshp Of Chrstn Athlts 90-; Phi Eta Sigma 90-; Crss Cntry/Indr/Outdr Trck 90-; Brdcstng Jrnlsm; Brdcstng Law.

**TOBIERRE, CHERYL M,** Inter Amer Univ Pr San German, San German, PR; FR; BA; Bus Admn; Acctg.

**TOBIN, JOHN P,** Embry Riddle Aeronautical Univ, Daytona Beach, FL; SO; BS; Aircraft Owners/Pilots Assoc 87-; Armed Forces Aero Clb 86-; Aerontcl Sci; Airline Pilot.

**TOBIN, KIMBERLY A,** Temple Univ, Philadelphia, PA; SR; BS; ASCE 90-; GBCA 90-; Natl Assoc Wmn Const Schlrshp 90-; Cvl/Const Engr Tech.

**TOBIN, KIRSTI N,** Duquesne Univ, Pittsburgh, PA; SR; SGA Sntr 90-; Pttsbrgh Soc Fncl Anlyst Inc 90-; Pnhlnc Cncl Sec 89-; Beta Alpha Phi 89-; Omcrn Delta Kappa 89-; Zeta Tau Alpha Brd 89-; Wntr Olympcs 90-; Fnce; Law Schl.

**TOBIN, PAUL J,** Manhattan Coll, Bronx, NY; SR; BSCE; NY Wtr Polltn Cntrl Assc Treas 90-; Amer Scty Cvl Eng 89-; Manhattan Clg Plyrs; Chi Epsilon 90-; Bro B Austin Barry Mdl Fr Cvl Eng; Cvl Eng; US Navy Eng.

**TOBISON, LINDA D,** Hudson Valley Comm Coll, Troy, NY; FR; Five Quad Vol Ambulance 78-79; Phi Theta Kappa; Vol Emerg Relief Sqd 79-85; Amer Red Crs CPR Instr 79; N Y Snte Cert Merit; Exec Sec Med Ctr Hosp 87-91; EMT N Y Dept Hlth 79; Nurs; RN/ANESTHETIST.

**TOBITT, TAMMIE R,** Univ Of Montevallo, Montevallo, AL; JR; BS; Bsktbl Schlrshp 88-; Elem Edn.

**TOBOLSKI, MICHELLE A,** Cumberland County Coll, Vineland, NJ; FR; Educ; Elem Educ Tchr.

**TOCCI, AMY M,** Elms Coll, Chicopee, MA; JR; Z Clb Elms Secr 90-; Elms Clg Equestrian Tm 90-; Acctg/Bsn Mgmt; CPA.

**TODD, AIMEE ELISE,** Univ Of Md Balt Cnty Campus, Catonsville, MD; FR; BA; Pre-Med; Dr.

**TODD, ALVIN A,** Al St Univ, Montgomery, AL; SO; MBA; Bsebl 90-; Ftbl; Math; Elctrcl Engr.

**TODD, AMY L,** Univ Of Pittsburgh At Bradford, Bradford, PA; FR; BS; Alpha Lambda Delta Editr; IM Vlybl/Sftbl; Human Rel; Conslng Educ.

**TODD, CHARLES J,** Univ Of Nc At Charlotte, Charlotte, NC; FR; BA; Intrvrsty Christian Flwshp 90-; Arch.

**TODD, DEBORAH M,** Middle Tn St Univ, Murfreesboro, TN; SR; BA; Phi Beta Lamda 90-; Beta Gamma Sigma; CPS 88-; Sls Asst Hitachi Metals Am LTD Nashville TN; Ofc Mgmt.

**TODD, ELAINE L,** Roane St Comm Coll, Harriman, TN; SR; BS; Sngrs 88-90; TN Tech Plyrs 90; Gamma Beta Phi 88-90; Home Demo Rptr 88-; AA 89; AA 90; Hstry; Govt.

**TODD, JANET LEE,** Memphis St Univ, Memphis, TN; SR; BFA; Dns Lst 87-; Priv Co Intrn 88; Grphc Dsgn; MFA.

**TODD, JOHN B,** Univ Of Tn At Knoxville, Knoxville, TN; FR; BS; Pep Club 90-; Phi Eta Sigma; Biochem; Profsr.

**TODD, KEVIN P,** Univ Of Md At Eastern Shore, Princess Anne, MD; SR; BA; BSU 87-88; FEA 90-; Odyssey Of The Mind; Kappa Delta Pi; Spec Educ; Pub Schl Rsrc Tchr.**

**TODD, KURT H,** Youngstown St Univ, Youngstown, OH; JR; BE; OSPE; Phi Eta Sigma 89-; Fire Dep Vol 88-; Civil Engrng.

**TODD, LINDA J,** Bethel Coll, Mckenzie, TN; JR; BS; Bsns Clb 89-; Henry Cnty Bnd Boostrs Tres 89-; Henry Cnty Food Bnk 88-; H & R Block 89-; Accntng Bsns; CPA.

**TODD, MARGARET J,** Middle Tn St Univ, Murfreesboro, TN; JR; BA; Amer Wmn Radio/T V 90-; Natl Assn Female Exec 87-; Kappa Delta Pi 90-; Tau Omicron 90-; Acctg; Mass Cmunctns; T V Mgmt.

**TODD, MELANIE E,** Univ Of Sc At Columbia, Columbia, SC; SR; BA; Cmps Crusade 89-; State Senate Intrn; Engl; Pblc Rltns.

**TODD, PAMELA H,** James Sprunt Comm Coll, Kenansville, NC; SR; ADN; Stdnt Govt Sr Sen 90-; Natl Acad Achvmnt Awd 90-; Nrsng; RN.

**TODD, SHERRILL L,** Va Commonwealth Univ, Richmond, VA; GD; MD; AMA 89-; AMSA 89; SFPA 89-; Zeta Tau Alpha 83-87; BS 87; Med.

**TODD, STEPHANIE A,** Union Univ, Jackson, TN; JR; BSBA; SGA Sen 90-; Acctg Clb 89-; Busn Clb 89-; Phi Bta Lambda 90-; Zeta Tau Alpha Tr 88-; Internshp 1st Natl Bnk Jacksn 90; Busn; Acctg.

**TODD, TAMMY L,** Univ Of Nc At Greensboro, Greensboro, NC; SR; Socl Wk Intrn Intrnshp Evergreens Inc 90-; BS Social Wk; Wocial Wk; Nrsng Hm Scl Wrkr.

**TODD, WATKING S,** Univ Of Southern Ms, Hattiesburg, MS; JR; Bnkg/Fin.

**TODD II, WOODROW L,** Wv Northern Comm Coll, Wheeling, WV; FR; BA; RLTCNA.

**TOEBBE, CAROLYN M,** Oh Univ, Athens, OH; FR; BA; Chem Eng.

**TOEBES, DANIEL B,** Univ Of Cin R Walters Coll, Blue Ash, OH; FR; Exec Chef; Engl.

**TOFFLING, KRISTEN W,** Va Polytechnic Inst & St Univ, Blacksburg, VA; FR; BS; Kappa Alpha Theta; Bus.

**TOH, KAI SIANG,** Univ Of Fl, Gainesville, FL; GD; Stdnt Hon Orgztn 87-88; Stdnt Art Lgue 89; Alpha Lambda Delta 88-90; Sigma Tau Sigma 88-90; Golden Key 89-90; Graphic Dsgn Awd 90; Cert Minrty Excnce 88; Fla Acad Schlr 88-; AA 88; BD 90; Graphic Dsgn.

**TOH, SIU Y,** Saint Andrews Presbytrn Coll, Laurinburg, NC; FR; BA; World Culture Soc; Model United Nations; ; Gce A Level Prime Clg Kuala Lumpur 90; Bus/Econs.

**TOKARCHIK III, THOMAS M,** Univ Of Vt & St Agri Coll, Burlington, VT; FR; BS; Dns Lst; Delta Psi; Vars Soccer; Mech Engr.

**TOKAYER, AMIEL Y,** Yeshiva Univ, New York, NY; SR; BA; Chem Clb 88-; Synag Yth 88-89; Act Ldr; Sigma Delta Rho 88-; Hosp Cell Bio Res 89; Var Trck 89; Var Soccr 88; Bio; Med.

**TOKOFSKY, BETH J,** Dowling Coll, Oakdale Li, NY; SR; BS; AAS Suffolk Comm Clg 89; Spec Educ; Teach.

**TOLA, DAISY J,** S U N Y Coll Of Tech At Frmgdl, Farmingdale, NY; FR; BA; Bsn Admin; Bsn Exec.

**TOLA, VICKY B,** City Univ Of Ny City Coll, New York, NY; SR; MD; Caduceus Soc Pre-Med Clb Treas 88-89; Caduceus Soc Pres 89-90; AMSA 88-; Golden Key; Peekskill Comm Vlntr Amblnc Corps EMT 87-; Holy Spirit Chrch Choir/Bnd Guitar 87-; Deans Lst; Daugh Amer Rvltn Awd 87; Bio; Med.

**TOLAND, ROBIN M,** Commonwealth Coll, Virginia Beach, VA; JR; AAS; Coll Sec Intl Sec 90-; Ofc Admin Clb Sec 90-; Sec 81-; Liberal Arts; Advrtsng.

**TOLAR, SHARON E,** Fayetteville St Univ, Fayetteville, NC; SO; BA; Agnts Asst Ntnwde Insrnce 81-; Bus; Insrnce.

**TOLBERT, ANGELA D,** Christopher Newport Coll, Newport News, VA; SO; BS; Chem; Env Chemist.

**TOLBERT, KAREN L,** Univ Of Southern Ms, Hattiesburg, MS; JR; BS; Sndy Schl Tchr Chrch Js Chrst Lttr Dy Snts; Scl Stds Sec Ed; Tchr.

**TOLBERT, KATRICE L,** Al A & M Univ, Normal, AL; SR; BS; Univ/Indust Clstr 90-; Alpha Kappa Mu Sec 89-; Soc Pres Schlrs 89-; Alpha Kappa Alpha Treas 89-; AICPA Schlrshp 89-; Acad Schlrshp 87-; Pres Cup 88-89; Acctg.

**TOLBERT, LEAH T,** Middle Tn St Univ, Murfreesboro, TN; FR; BA; English/French; Educ.

**TOLBERT, LILLIAN M,** Hampton Univ, Hampton, VA; SR; BS; Ed Club Pres 88-; Kappa Delta Pi 90-; Stdnt VA Ed Assoc Stdnt Rep 88-; Alpha Kappa Mu 90-; Grad Flwshp Asstncshp Univ Of Akron; Ed; Tchr.

**TOLBERT, LOVE J,** Union Inst, Cincinnati, OH; GD; Big Bro Prog; Coaches/Pros Anti-Drug Cmmttee; Cmmnty Alcohol Rehab Brd VP 89; BS.

**TOLBERT, SUSAN L,** Univ Of Ga, Athens, GA; SR; BSED; Kappa Delt Epsilon VP 89-; NTE 90-; PAGE; Hons Pgm 87-; Gamma Beta Phi 87-; Alpha Lambda Delta 87-; Kappa Delta Pi 90-; Kappa Delta Epsilon VP 89-; Harrish Schlrshp; KDE Schlrshp; Coll Ed Schlrshp; UGA Hons Achiev Cert; Engl Ed; Tchr.

**TOLBERT, TERESA L,** Radford Univ, Radford, VA; JR; BA; BS Wytheville Comm Clg 83; Acctg.

**TOLEDO GARCIA, AIXA E,** Univ Of Pr Cayey Univ Coll, Cayey, PR; FR; BA; Sci; Dentist.

**TOLEDO, ELISA G,** Fl International Univ, Miami, FL; JR; BS; FEA 90-; Kappa Delta Pi 90-; Chappie James Mst Prmsng Tchr Schlrshp 88-; AA Miami Dade Comm Coll 90; Elem Ed; Teacher.**

**TOLEDO, LICET A,** Saint Thomas Univ, Miami, FL; JR; BA; Bus Mgmnt; Bus.

**TOLEDO, SIMONE A,** Wagner Coll, Staten Island, NY; FR; Sprng Sngfst; Hmcmng 90; Deans List 90-; Alph Sgm Omega; Bio; Pedtrcs.

**TOLER, VIOLA L,** Concord Coll, Athens, WV; SR; CERT; Alpha Chi 90-; Kappa Delta Pi 90-; Med Tch 76-; BS W Va Univ 76; Chem/Sec Educ; Tch.

**TOLES, JANET L,** Southern Coll Of Tech, Marietta, GA; BIET; IIE 90-; Tau Alpha Pi 90-; Flwshp Chrstn Blvrs Alm Cmte Sec Soc Dir 89-; Engrg Tchnlgy; Indstrl Engrg.

**TOLLAND, MEGAN E,** Newbury Coll, Brookline, MA; FR; Culinary.

**TOLLE, NATALIE C,** Lexington Comm Coll, Lexington, KY; FR; Bus/Finance; Fincl Field/Acctg.

**TOLLEFSEN, ALBERT EARL,** Fort Valley St Coll, Fort Valley, GA; FR; AAS; Vtrnrn Clb VP; Deans List; BS Southern IL Univ 63; Vtrnrn Sciences; Exotic Anml Farm.

**TOLLESON, JANA M,** Univ Of Sc At Columbia, Columbia, SC; SO; BS; Phi Eta Sigma 89-; Psycology/Ed; Schl Psychology.

**TOLLEY, GREGORY T,** Middle Tn St Univ, Murfreesboro, TN; SO; BS; Bapt Stdnt Union 89-; Cmptr Sci.

**TOLLEY, JIMMY R,** Union Univ, Jackson, TN; SR; MS; U U Alchl/Drg Prvntn/Ed Comm 90-; Amer-Scandnvn Exchng Pgms 85-87; TN Yth Dvlpmnt Intrn 89; Psych Hosp Intern 90-; Cnslng Ctr Intrn Vlntr Ed Intern 90; SME 87-; Ntl Assn Alchl/Drg Abse Cnslrs 89-; Alchl/Drg TX Cnslr 89-; Scl Wrk; Alchl/Drg Scl Svcs.

**TOLLIS, ANNA L,** Saint Joseph Coll, West Hartford, CT; SR; BA; Dns Lst 88-; Itln Ttr Acad Rsrce Cntr 90; Pblshd Ptry In Coll Ltrry Mag 90; Pblshd Ptry Edtn Ptc Vcs Of Amer 90; Hnrble Mntrn In Wrld Of Ptry 90; Phlsphy; Tchng.**

**TOLLISON, MARK W,** Univ Of Sc At Columbia, Columbia, SC; GD; JD; Sr Plnnr Atlanta Rgnl Cmmssn 88-89; MRP Mstrs Rgnl Plnng Univ NC 88; BA Ecnmcs Clemson Univ; Law.

**TOLLISON, VERONICA L,** Univ Of Sc At Columbia, Columbia, SC; JR; BS; Alpha Chi Omega 88-; Retailing-Fshn Merch; Retail Mgmt.

**TOLLIVER, DARRYL C,** Morehouse Coll, Atlanta, GA; SR; BA; Bsnss Assoc 90; Stdnt Ntl Med Assoc 90; Deans Hnr Lst 87; Hnr Roll 90; Ntl Brdcstng Co Brbnk Ca Dist Srvs Clrk 85-88; Cert In Elctrnc Jour Video Tape Eng NBC-TV 87; Bsnss Admin Bnkng/Fin.**

**TOLMAN, DANIEL,** Coll Of The Holy Cross, Worcester, MA; FR; Vrsty Sccr; Blgy Scty; Blgy; Med Schl.

**TOLSON, LEIGH T,** James Madison University, Harrisonburg, VA; SR; BS; SEA 88-90; Ldrs Learning Pres 88-90; AEYC 88-90; Golden Key 90-; Kappa Delta Pi; Early Chldhd Ed; Tch.

**TOLTON, RICHELLE D,** Univ Of Sc At Columbia, Columbia, SC; FR; BS; Mrchng Band 90; Pep Band 90-; PALM 90-; Alpha Phi Omega; Acctng; Bus.

**TOM, DEBBIE A,** City Univ Of Ny City Coll, New York, NY; SR; BS; Rsrch Asst/Cnslr NY Foundling Hops Indpndnt Lvng Pgm 90-; Cmnty Hlth Ed Clb Chrprsn 89-; Pblc Hlth; Medicine.

**TOMA, EIKO,** Northeastern Christian Jr Coll, Villanova, PA; SO; Librl Arts.

**TOMALEWSKI, OPAL M,** Germanna Comm Coll, Locust Grove, VA; Assoc Germanna Cmmnty Coll; Blgy.

**TOMAN, SUE A,** Hillsborough Comm Coll, Tampa, FL; SO; BA; Phi Theta Kappa 89-; Beta Sigma Phi VP 88-91; Amer Stdies/Hstry; Tchr.

**TOMAS, ADRIANE M,** Fl Atlantic Univ, Boca Raton, FL; SR; Finance; Fncl Plnr.

**TOMASELLO, EDITH A,** Atlantic Comm Coll, Mays Landing, NJ; SO; BA; Gmng Suprvsr 89-; Bus Admn.

**TOMASSINI, JENNIFER K,** Providence Coll, Providence, RI; FR.

**TOMASZEWICZ, JAROSLAW T,** Temple Univ, Philadelphia, PA; SR; BS; Elect Engrng Tech.

**TOMASZEWSKI, JEFFREY D,** Univ Of Miami, Coral Gables, FL; BS; Eng Advsry Brd Chrmn 90; Inst Of Indstrl Engs Rcrdng Sec 89-; Army ROTC Rngr Chllnge Tm 88; Lambda Chi Alpha Hse Mgr 88-; Hcky Vlybl Trck Ftbl 87; Indstrl Eng; Eng.

**TOMBERLIN, JEFFERY K,** Middle Ga Coll, Cochran, GA; SO; BS; Rotarct Pr 90-; Dorm Cncl V P 90-; Busn Clb Pres Clb 90-; Otstdng Fr Chem Awd; AS; Bio; Bio Res.

**TOMBERLIN, MARTHA A,** Mobile Coll, Mobile, AL; FR; BS; Bsns Admnstrtn; Mrktng.

**TOMBLIN, GLORIA J,** Marshall University, Huntington, WV; JR; BA; Educ; Tchr.

**TOMCHIN, ERIC R,** Broward Comm Coll, Ft Lauderdale, FL; SO; AA; Pol Sci; Law.

**TOMCHO, LORI A,** Marywood Coll, Scranton, PA; SO; BRA; Nwspr Asst Grphcs Ed; St Luke Srt Soc; Anthrplgy Clb; Alpha Phi Omega; Adelphia Cable Comm Corp Intrn; Graphic Dsgn; Publctn Prod.

**TOMCSAK, STEPHEN L,** Kent St Univ Kent Cmps, Kent, OH; SR; BS; Golden Key Nhs 90-; Alpha Lambda Delta 88-; Beta Gamma Sigma 90-; Busn; Mktng/Mgt.

**TOMEI, JOHN P,** Providence Coll, Providence, RI; SR; BA; Pi Mu Epsilon Treas 90-; Lib Arts Hnrs Pgm 88-; Athltc Trng 89-; Summa Cum Laude 88-; Math; Apld Math.

**TOMENKO, ELVINA KONSTANTINOVNA,** Columbia Union Coll, Takoma Park, MD; JR; BA; Loaves/Fishes 90-; Thlgy/Rlgn Clb 90-; CUC Bnd 90-; Thela Alpha Beta 90-; Soup Ktchn 90-; Vol Trnsltr-Pblshng Hs R/H 90-; Lit/Lang USSR 88-89; Chf Lbrn Thlgcl Inst Instrctr/Prfssr Music 80-89; Thlgy; Prfssr Rlgn/Chpln/Author.

**TOMEU, HERMAN W,** Miami Dade Comm Coll, Miami, FL; FR; AA; Phi Theta Kappa; Amer Hispanic Edctrs Assoc Dade AHEAD Schlrshp; Cmptr Sci; Cmptr Syst Analysis.

**TOMINACK, DEBRA D,** Christopher Newport Coll, Newport News, VA; GD; BS Westrn Ky Univ 73; Bio; Tchng Mdl Schl.

**TOMISMAN, KATHRYN M,** Hudson Valley Comm Coll, Troy, NY; SO; AA; Bahamas Trip; Bsn.

**TOMKO, JENNIFER B,** Longwood Coll, Farmville, VA; SR; BS; Stu Educ Assn 89-; Kappa Delta Pi 90-; Phi Kappa Phi 90-; Elem Educ; Tchg.

**TOMKPINS, CHRISTINE M,** Western New England Coll, Springfield, MA; SR; BS; Deans Adv Cmte Rep 89-90; Soc Of Womens Engrs 88-90; Peer Tutor 89-; Sigma Beta Tau 90-; Stdnt Ath; Sftbl Capt 87-; Bio Engr.

**TOMLIN, RICHARD SCOTT,** Univ Of Ga, Athens, GA; SR; BS; Yrbk Phot 87-88; Foreign Lang Clb 87-88; Alpha Zeta Nomee; Yng Lfe Ldr 88-90; Yng Lfe Frntr Rnch Cook 89; Coca Colga Co Intrn 87-89; U Ga Chrldr 88-89; Ga Centenarian Study Intrvwr 90-91; Chld/Fam Dev; Sls Rep.

**TOMLINSON, CAROL S,** Wv Northern Comm Coll, Wheeling, WV; SO; AAS; Acctg.

**TOMLINSON, SHAWN M,** Kent St Univ Kent Cmps, Kent, OH; SO; BA; Bus; Acctng.

**TOMMASI, CAROL A,** Rutgers St Univ At Camden, Camden, NJ; SR; BS; Bsn Mgmt; Sales.

**TOMONTO, MELISSA A,** Fl St Univ, Tallahassee, FL; SR; BS; St Thomas Moore Campus Mnstry Rtrt Ldr 87-; Gldn Key 90-; Kappa Delta Pi 90-; Educ; Tchr.

**TOMPKINS, KARA G,** Univ Of Rochester, Rochester, NY; SO; BA; Symphny Orchstr 89-; ROAR 90-; Msc Intrst Flr Sec 89-; Dscty Wmn Eng 90-; Elect Eng.

**TOMPKINS, KEITH B,** Unity Coll, Unity, ME; SO; BSES; Atlantic Salmon Utopian Htchry Assist Mgr 90; Hockey; Aqcltre; Htchry/Fsh Pthlgy.

**TOMPKINS, KRISTI D,** Armstrong St Coll, Savannah, GA; FR; BSN; Nrsng; Med.

**TOMPKINS, SHEILA R,** Roane St Comm Coll, Harriman, TN; SO; Security Ptrl Cptn 80-; AS; Police Science/Security.

**TOMPKINS, STEPHANIE M,** Longwood Coll, Farmville, VA; SR; BS; Sclgy; Rsrch.

**TOMPKINS, VICTORIA M,** Columbia Union Coll, Takoma Park, MD; SR; BA; Bus Admin; Bnkng Finc.

**TOMS, BECKY G,** Univ Of Cincinnati, Cincinnati, OH; SO; SWE Pres 90-; Tau Alpha Pi VP 90-; Fclty Affrs Comm 90-; AAS Awd; AS Awd; Court 90; AAS; Chemistry.

**TOMS, JESSICA J,** Central Fl Comm Coll, Ocala, FL; SO; MA; Phi Theta Kappa; Marion Cnty Schl Vlntr; Deans Lst; AA; Scl Science; Tchr.

**TOMSOM, DONNA LEE,** Middle Tn St Univ, Murfreesboro, TN; SR; BS; Stdnt Advsry Com Rep 90-; Kappa Omicron Pi 90-; Kappa Delta Pi 90-; Brnch Mngr Credit Union 83-89; Early Chldhd Educ; MS Psychlgy.

**TONAHILL, KAREN D,** Memphis St Univ, Memphis, TN; FR; Vrsty Chrldng 90-; Phi Eta Sigma 90-; Alpha Lambda Delta 90-; Ed; Elem Tchr.

**TONARELLI, ALESSANDRO O,** Fl International Univ, Miami, FL; FR.

**TONEY, CHRISTINA N,** George Mason Univ, Fairfax, VA; JR; BA; Spec Olympics Gymnastics Coach; Marketing/Finance; Marketing Advertising.

**TONEY, LINDA B,** Va Commonwealth Univ, Richmond, VA; SR; BS; RN; ADN Muskegon Comm Coll 84; Nrsng; BSN.

**TONEY, TIMOTHY W,** Tuskegee Univ, Tuskegee Inst, AL; SR; BS; ASCAC 90-; Soc Maat 90-; Psychlgy; Prfssr.

**TONEY, TINA M,** Univ Of Cin R Walters Coll, Blue Ash, OH; SO; BA; Phi Theta Kappa 90-; Gentry Shps; Dttcs.

**TONG, XIN,** Univ Of North Fl, Jacksonville, FL; FR; BA; Math Assn Am; Eng/Comp Sci.

**TONG, YUEN YI,** City Univ Of Ny City Coll, New York, NY; SO; BS; Chrstn Flwshp; BS; Bio Chem; Hlth.

**TONG, YUI K,** City Univ Of Ny City Coll, New York, NY; SR; BS; Elec Engr Std Asn; Gldn Key; Elec Engr.

**TONKERY, LORI L,** Marshall University, Huntington, WV; JR; BBA; Intrnshp Inco Alloys Intnl Inc 89-; Mngmnt.

**TONKIN, VINCE N,** Indiana Univ Of Pa, Indiana, PA; SR; BS; Kappa Delta Pi; Pi Gamma Mu; Provosts Schlr 90; Scl Sci/Ed; Pblc Schl Tchr.

**TONN, JASON W,** Va Commonwealth Univ, Richmond, VA; FR; BS; Biol/Scdnry Educ; Scndry Tchng.

**TOOHEY, KIMBERLY K,** East Tn St Univ, Johnson City, TN; JR; BBA; Coca-Cola Schlrshp; Acad All Amer; Tnns Schlrshp; Mrktng; Advrtsng.

**TOOILL, ANGELA M,** Denison Univ, Granville, OH; FR; BA; Denison Cmnty Assoc 90; Wnd Ensmbl 90-; Host Perspective Stdnts 90; Frnch Clb Treas 90-; Hnrs Pgm 90-; Econ/Frnch; Intl Bsn.

**TOOLE, ELIZABETH R,** Colby Sawyer Coll, New London, NH; FR; BA; Singing Recitals 90-; Juried Stdnt Art Show; Cmps Actvty Brd; Art Educ; Teach Art.

**TOOLE, STEVEN M,** Syracuse Univ, Syracuse, NY; SO; BS; Govt 90-; Avtn Clb 90-; IM Flr Hcky 90-; Acctg; CPA.

**TOOMBS, CAROL LEANN,** Univ Of Ky, Lexington, KY; JR; BS; Soc Wmn Engrs 90-; Coop Educ Pgm-Eng 89-; Alpha Gamma Delta 88-; Elect Eng.

**TOOMBS, KATHLEEN M,** Schenectady County Comm Coll, Schenectady, NY; FR; AA; Ltrcy Vol Amer Tutor 90-; Lgl Exec Sec 85-; Hmnts/Tchr Cert; Sec Educ.

**TOOMBS, SHAWN M,** Al A & M Univ, Normal, AL; SO; BS; Alpha Phi Alpha; Hon Stdnt; Inrds Intrn Fleet Northstar Bnk Benefts Spclst; Pol Sci; Corp Law.

**TOOMBS, TARA M,** Middle Tn St Univ, Murfreesboro, TN; FR; BA; Assoc Stdnt Bdy Pblc Dfndr; Gamma Beta Phi; Pltcl Sci; Lwyr.

**TOOMER, TONYA MARIE,** Univ Of Sc At Salkehatchie, Allendale, SC; FR; BA; Comp Sci; Comp Anlyst.

**TOOMEY, CHRISTOPHER R,** Univ Of Miami, Coral Gables, FL; SR; IGFA; Blfsh Fndtn; Intl Ocngrphc Fndtn.

**TOOMEY, JOE R,** Univ Of South Al, Mobile, AL; SR; BS; Jaycees 90-; Omicron Zeta 90-; History; Teaching.

**TOOMEY, JOSEPH J,** Schenectady County Comm Coll, Schenectady, NY; SO; AAS; Albany Paid Profsnl Fire Fghtr Assoc 88-; Christian Bros Acad Fnd Dr Co Chrmn 87-; Centrl Babe Ruth VP 87-88; Fire Fghtr/EMT 88-; BS Clg Of St Rose 84; Fire Sci Tech.

**TOON, THOMAS H,** Univ Of Cin R Walters Coll, Blue Ash, OH; FR; ASN; Owner Dial One Cntmpry Dsgns Inc Cmcl Const Remodeling Co 80-88; Sci; Nrsng.

**TOOTHMAN III, JAMES R,** Univ Of Miami, Coral Gables, FL; FR; BBA; Alpha Lambda Delta; Lambda Chi Alpha 90-; Miami Prjct Walk Rep; Orientation Asst; IM Ftbl Bsktbl 90-; Bsns Mgmnt.

**TOPA, DENISE C,** Univ Of Scranton, Scranton, PA; JR; BS; Lctr St Anns Mnstry Prsh 84-; Lctr Madonna Chpl 88-89; Bishop Klonowski Bwlg League Capt 89-; Delta Mu Delta; All Amer Schlr 90; Ntl Coll Bus Merit Awrd 90; Acctg; CPA.**

**TOPAR, TAMMY L,** Valley Forge Christian Coll, Phoenixville, PA; JR; BSB; Band/Choir 88-; Ch Music.

**TOPIK, DEREK J,** Livingston Univ, Livingston, AL; SR; Jdcry Cncl Pres 89; Pres Lst 90-; Bsbl 85-89; BS; Hstry/Pol Sci; Mgmt.

**TOPLAK, DE ANN M,** Commonwealth Coll, Virginia Beach, VA; FR; Toastmstrs Internatl VP; US Navy; CNA State Of CA 85; Bus Mgmt; Law.

**TOPP, KALMAN S,** Yeshiva Univ, New York, NY; SO; BA; Belkin Schlrshp; Tennis Tm.

**TOPPIN, ABU H,** Morehouse Coll, Atlanta, GA; SO; BA; Pre Law Scty 89-; STRIPES Stdnt Tgrs Rcrtng Intrstd Prsns Enrllmnt Stblty 89-90; Hnr Rll; Pltcl Sci; Law.

**TOPPIN, STACY E,** Univ Of Southern Ms, Hattiesburg, MS; JR; Sprts Med; Athletic Trng/Tchng.

**TOPPS, DEMETRIA Y,** Alcorn St Univ, Lorman, MS; FR; BA; Bus Admin; Mgmt/Advtsng.

**TOPSHE, TRINA L,** Univ Of Sc At Columbia, Columbia, SC; JR; BS; Phrmcy.

**TORBA, MELISSA J,** Niagara Univ, Niagara Univ, NY; FR; BA; Choir 90; Intl Bus; Bus Mgmnt.

**TORBECK, STEVEN J,** Georgetown Univ, Washington, DC; SR; BS; Army ROTC Pltn Ldr 87-; FMA Hnr Scty; Finance; Eqty Rsrch.

**TORBERT, GLEN E,** Fl St Univ, Tallahassee, FL; FR; BA; Hnrs & Schlrs Cncl 90-; Phi Eta Sigma 90-; Philosophy; Coll Prof.

**TORBETT, JAMES A,** Embry Riddle Aeronautical Univ, Daytona Beach, FL; FR; BS; Aerospace Soc; Vet Clb; AS N E St Tech Comm Coll 90; Aviation.

**TOREN, TRINA MARIE,** Northern Ky Univ, Highland Hts, KY; JR; BED; Wmns Chrmn 89-90; Alpha Chi 90-; Deans Lst 89-90; Hnr Lst 90-; Elem Edctn; Tchr.

**TORGERSON, WILLIAM G,** Univ Of Al At Huntsville, Huntsville, AL; SR; BSE; IEEE Pres 89-; Dns Lst 89-; IM Ftbl 90-; Elec Engr.

**TORGGLER, DAVID J,** Oh Wesleyan Univ, Delaware, OH; SR; BA; IFC Judcl Brd 89-; Soccr Mgr 87-88; Omicron Delta Epsilon 90-; Tau Kappa Epsilon 88-; Dns Lst 89-; Var Lacrs 87-; Econ/Mgmt; Finc/Bnkg/Consltng.

**TORIAN, TIM,** Union Inst, Cincinnati, OH; SR; BS; ACM 89-; Cmptr Cnsltnt; AA Foothill Coll 87; Cmptr Sci.

**TORNABENE, PATRICIA A,** D Youville Coll, Buffalo, NY; FR; BS; SOTA 90-; Adpt/Grndprnt Cmps Mnstry 90-; Occptnl Thrpy; MS.

**TORNEY, DELLA TERESA,** Bowie St Univ, Bowie, MD; SR; Acctng/Finance Club Pres; Delta Mu Delta Treas 90-; Alpha Kappa Mu; All Amer Schlrs 89-; Deans List 87-; Auditor Dept Energy; BS; Acctng; Auditing.

**TORNICHIO, RENEE A,** Bethany Coll, Bethany, WV; FR; BA; Circle K; Amnsty Intl; Soc Wrk.

**TORNO, MICHAEL T,** Kent St Univ Kent Cmps, Kent, OH; FR; IM Sftbl/Ftbl/Bsktbl 90-; Wt Club; Alpha Lambda Delta; Austintown Hist Scty Schlrshp; Hist/Eng; Tchng.

**TORO RODRIGUEZ, KEILA M,** Inter Amer Univ Pr San German, San German, PR; JR; BA; Pltcl Sci Cir V Treas 90-; Hon Prog Stdnt Rep 89-; Rspnsblty Awd 89; Vybl 89-; Pltcl Sci; Law.

**TORO, ANA M,** Inter Amer Univ Pr Hato Rey, Hato Rey, PR; GD; BED; Hstry Clb 88-90; Hstry; Bus Admin.

**TORO, ANGEL A,** Univ Politecnica De Pr, Hato Rey, PR; SO; Engnrg.

**TORO, CLAUDIA J,** Embry Riddle Aeronautical Univ, Daytona Beach, FL; SO; BA; Hispanic Club Sec; Bros Of The Wind 90-; Ninety-Nines 90; Aeronautical Science; Pilot.

**TORO, EVELYN,** Univ Of Pr At Mayaguez, Mayaguez, PR; JR; Ordr Estrn Star; Ntl Hspnc Awrds 89-90; Sci; Cvl Engr.**

**TORO, LESLEY F,** Univ Of Pr Humacao Univ Coll, Humacao, PR; SO; BA; Engl; Tchr.**

**TORO, RADAMES,** Catholic Univ Of Pr, Ponce, PR; GD; BBA; APPED 89-; Natl Bsn Hnr Soc 90-; Mgmt/Cmptr; Mgmt/Cmptr Prgmmng.

**TORO-VELEZ, MARIA DEL C,** Catholic Univ Of Pr, Ponce, PR; SR; JD; Amer Bar Assn 87; Stdnt Govt 87; Puerto Rico Law Jrnl 88-90; Deans Lst 89-90; Delta Theta Phi Trbune 88-90; Hon Schlrshp 89-; Amnesty Intl 81; Sch Tchr 82; BA Univ P R 87; Pltcl Sci; Law.

**TOROCKIO, DANA L,** Indiana Univ Of Pa, Indiana, PA; SR; Big Bros Big Strs 88-90; Pa Sta Educ Assn 89-; Sigma Kappa Crspndg Sec 88-90; Proj Stride 89-90; BS; Ele Educ; Tch Ele Sch.

**TORODE, SARAH K,** Newbury Coll, Brookline, MA; SO; AD; Intrnshp Cambridge Stds; Allston MA Prdctn; Media Tchnlgy; Tlvsn Prdctn.

**TOROK, BONNIE L,** Kent St Univ Kent Cmps, Kent, OH; SR; BBA; Hmn Rsrc Mgmt.

**TORRALES, MENAH A,** Commonwealth Coll, Virginia Beach, VA; SO; AS; Amer Med Asst Assc 90-; Cert HHA NYC Spcl Touchhome Care Agcy 89; Cert Sna Magna Inst NYC 89; Mdcl Asstng; Phys Asstnt.

**TORRANS, BEVERLY A,** Mount Olive Coll, Mount Olive, NC; FR; BA; Bsn; Banking.

**TORRE, CHRISTOPHER C,** Mount Saint Mary Coll, Newburgh, NY; FR; BA; Busn Mgmt; Intl Mktg.

**TORRENCE, A ISHA NARFEEA,** City Univ Of Ny La Guard Coll, Long Island Cty, NY; SO.

**TORRENCE, JAMES S,** Fl International Univ, Miami, FL; SO; BA; Engl; Tchng Law.

**TORRENTE, JASON A,** Manhattan Coll, Bronx, NY; FR; BS; Bis Chmstry; Med.

**TORRES ADROVER, ROSA NEREIDA,** Bayamon Central Univ, Bayamon, PR; JR; BA; Cmptr Sci.

**TORRES COLON, ANA M,** Univ Of Pr At Mayaguez, Mayaguez, PR; JR; Amer Inst Chem Engrs 89-; Inst Electrnc/Elctrcl Engr Sec 90-; Deans Lst 87-; Chem Engr.

**TORRES COLON, CONCEPCION,** Catholic Univ Of Pr, Ponce, PR; JR; BBA; Asociacion De Futuros Asministradores De Oficina 90-; Office Admnstrtn.

**TORRES COLON, HILDA,** Catholic Univ Of Pr, Ponce, PR; SR; BBA; Acctg Stdnts Assoc 89-90; Acctg; CPA.

**TORRES DEL PINO, ENRIQUE P,** Univ Politecnica De Pr, Hato Rey, PR; SO; Indus Engr Soc 90; ROTC M S I; Hon Rl; Ftbl Semi Pro Plyr; Indus Engr; Engr.

**TORRES DELGADO, SHEILA J,** Univ Of Pr At Mayaguez, Mayaguez, PR; JR; BS; Amer Chem Soc 90-; Engr Std Hnr Soc 89-; Chem; Engr.**

**TORRES FRETTS, JOSE A,** Univ Of Pr At Mayaguez, Mayaguez, PR; SO; BA; String Orch 89-; Hon Bd 90-; Hon Dip Engr Fclty 90-; Elect; Engr.**

**TORRES GARCIA, DAINA J,** Univ Politecnica De Pr, Hato Rey, PR; SO; Ninas Esarchas; Coro Hgh Schl; Categoria Saliste 88-89; Vlybl Fergino Ponce P R; Canto Para Comparia De Jungles Com 90; Vlybl Sftbl Pista Y Campo 87-89; Tech Univ 89-90; Math; Eng.

**TORRES GARCIA, MARISOL,** Inter Amer Univ Pr San German, San German, PR; SR; Comp Sci; MA.

**TORRES GELPI, CAROL P,** Univ Of Pr Cayey Univ Coll, Cayey, PR; FR; BS; Chem Math Mktg; Pharm.

**TORRES MARTINEZ, EUNICE,** Inter Amer Univ Pr Arecibo Un, Arecibo, PR; FR; Cmptrs; Pgmmng.

**TORRES MARTINEZ, JESSY J,** Catholic Univ Of Pr, Ponce, PR; SO; Heraldos De Cristo 90-; Kairos 90-; Hon Lst Decano Art Dept 90-; Arts; Scl Trabajo.

**TORRES NEGRON, ARMANDO,** Inter Amer Univ Pr San German, San German, PR; FR; BA; Bsbll Tm; Blgy; Phrmcst.

**TORRES PEREZ, CHRISTINE D,** Inter Amer Univ Pr Hato Rey, Hato Rey, PR; JR; BBA; Assn De Estudiantes De Contabilidad 89-; Inst Mgmt Accntnts; Hnr Rl 88-; Acctg/Finc; Corp Tax Law.

**TORRES RIVERA, MARILYN,** Catholic Univ Of Pr, Ponce, PR; SO; BA; Hon Dns Lst 90; Acctg; CPA.

**TORRES ROMAN, ROSELINE,** Univ Politecnica De Pr, Hato Rey, PR; JR; BSIE; Inst Of Ind Engrs; Indstrl Eng; Mgmnt.

**TORRES VAZQUEZ, SENEN,** Univ Of Pr At Mayaguez, Mayaguez, PR; JR; BA; Air Frc ROTC Dir Admin 89-90; Amer Chem Scty Treas; Phi Eta Mu Vcl; Deans Lst 89-90; Chem; Anlytcl Chem.**

**TORRES VELEZ, WILFREDO,** Univ Politecnica De Pr, Hato Rey, PR; SR; BA; IEEE 89-; Assc Eng Bayamon Tech Clg 88; Elec Eng; Elect Pwr Sys.

**TORRES VINCENTY, DIEGO M,** Univ Politecnica De Pr, Hato Rey, PR; FR; BS; Cvl Eng.

**TORRES VINCENTY, LIGIA M,** Univ Politecnica De Pr, Hato Rey, PR; JR; BS; Elctrcl Eng.

**TORRES, ADA E,** Bunker Hill Comm Coll, Boston, MA; FR.

**TORRES, ANA L,** Univ Of Pr At Rio Piedras, Rio Piedras, PR; JR; 26th ACS Jr Tech Mtng; Amer Chem Soc 201st Ntl Mtng Act; Golden Key; MARC Hon Pgm 90-; Hon Brd Stdnts; Chem; Ph D.

**TORRES, CARLOS E,** Va Commonwealth Univ, Richmond, VA; SO; BA; Gldn Ndl Awrd; Fbrc Schlrshp; Fshn Dsgn.

**TORRES, CHRISTINE,** Fl International Univ, Miami, FL; JR; Emphasis Exclnc Awrd Schlrshps 88-90; AA; Bus; Mrktg.

**TORRES, DAISY,** Tn Temple Univ, Chattanooga, TN; SR; BS; Livingstone Soc Lds Athltc Dir 88-89; Intrnshp Ftns 101 Bdmnton 90; BS Phys Ed 90; Phys Ed; Arbcs Instrctr/Exrcs Physlgst.

**TORRES, DORA E,** Inter Amer Univ Pr Hato Rey, Hato Rey, PR; SR; BA; AIESEC; Labor Rltns.

**TORRES, ELIZABETH Y,** Cheyney Univ Of Pa, Cheyney, PA; SO; BS; Htl/Rstrnt/Inst Mgmt Clb Sec 90-; Radio Sta 89-; Spirit Ldr/Tour Guide 89-; Omega Treas 89-; Vrsty Tennis 90; Htl/Rstrnt/Instl Mgr.

**TORRES, EMILIO,** Saint Josephs Coll New York, Brooklyn, NY; SO; BS; NYC Polce Dept Hon Lgn 74-; NYC Polce Dept Lt; Cert 90; Bus Admin.

**TORRES, EUGENIO J,** Ma Inst Of Tech, Cambridge, MA; JR; BS; Assc Puerto Rican Stdnt VP 88-; Lvng Grp Soc Chrmn; Dorm Jdcl Cmt; IM Sprts Bsktbl Vlybl Sftbl Tnns Bsktbl Capt Vlybl Capt 89-; Envrnmntl/Cvl Eng; Law.**

**TORRES, GUILLERMO O,** Ny Univ, New York, NY; JR; BA; Sr Fld Eng Comp Mnfrms; AAS 89; Econ Intl Stds; Econ Dvlmpnt.

**TORRES, IVAN,** Univ Of Pr At Mayaguez, Mayaguez, PR; SO; BS; Mech Engr.

**TORRES, IVELISSE,** Univ Of Pr At Mayaguez, Mayaguez, PR; SO; BA; Psychlgy Stdnt Assn Sec; Psychlgy Stdnts Serv Orientation; Phi Alpha Delta; Mu Alpha Phi; Hon Diploma 89-90; IMMA; Clncl Psychlgst.

**TORRES JR, JOSE J,** Fl St Univ, Tallahassee, FL; JR; BS; Engr Hnr Soc; Elec Engr.

**TORRES, JUAN R,** Univ Politecnica De Pr, Hato Rey, PR; FR; Leo Clb 88-90; BSA Eagle Sct 77-; Cvl Engr; Law.

**TORRES, KEILA E,** Univ Of Pr At Rio Piedras, Rio Piedras, PR; SO; Hon Pgm 90-; Chrstn Yth Frat 89-; Yngr Scty Pres 89-90; Flwshp Abrhm Rosa Cooprtv 90; Chem; Bio Med Rsrch/Srgry.

**TORRES, LUIS A,** Bayamon Central Univ, Bayamon, PR; SO; MBA; Soc Cmrce Stdnts; Acctg; CPA.

**TORRES, MARIA I,** Inter Amer Univ Pr Arecibo Un, Arecibo, PR; SO; PHD; Promo Com Ed; Hon Pgm; Sigma Epsilon Alpha Pres 90-; Biomed Sci; Ophthalmology.

**TORRES, MARIA M,** Univ Of Pr At Rio Piedras, Rio Piedras, PR; SR; BA; Gldn Key 89-; Amer Chem Scty 88-89; Hon Role 89-90; Technlgia Medica; Medcn.**

**TORRES, MIRIAM DEL R,** Univ Of Pr Cayey Univ Coll, Cayey, PR; JR; MEPE Stdnt Org 89-90; Hnr Stdnt 89-; Invstgtn Biochmstry Ctr Sci Engrg PR; Blgy; Med.

**TORRES, NORAYMAR,** Univ Of Pr At Rio Piedras, Rio Piedras, PR; JR; Gldn Key; San Pedro Martir Chrch Catechist 84-; Hnr Stdnt Schl Natrl Sci 89-; Hnr Rgstrtn; MARC Pgm 90-; Aerobics/Aquaerobics 90-; Blgy; Phd.

**TORRES, OSCAR E,** Fl International Univ, Miami, FL; SR; BBA; Inst Mngmnt Accntnts 90-; Beta Alpha Psi 90-; Beta Gamma Sigma 90-; Phi Kappa Phi 90; Accntng; CPA.

**TORRES, REBECCA,** City Univ Of Ny Baruch Coll, New York, NY; JR; BBA; Acctg.

**TORRES, SARA G,** City Univ Of Ny Hostos Coll, Bronx, NY; SR.

**TORRES, VICTOR M BONILLA,** Catholic Univ Of Pr, Ponce, PR; FR; MBA; Blt Hspnc Assoc Mbr; Assoc Thtr PR; Jack Lalanne Ftns Ctr; Hghst Scr E D Dept 87-90; BFD 90; Fine Art; Crgrphr/Dnc Prf.

**TORRES, VIOLET D,** City Univ Of Ny City Coll, New York, NY; SR; BS; Amer Med Stdnt Assn 87-; Amer Famly Physn 87; Third World Orgztn 87-; Cmuty Hlth/Soc Med Soc Wrkr 88; Immunologcl Stdes; Queens Hosp Asst 87-88; Bio Med; Doc.

**TORRES, VIRGINIA B,** Thomas Nelson Comm Coll, Hampton, VA; SO; Phi Theta Kappa Phi Sigma 90-; OHA Hd Start Chld Dvlpmnt Ctr Aide 88-90; Frnds Hd Start; Seeking AAS Early Chld Ed; CC P Ed PTA Career Studies Pgm; Early Chldhd Edn; Tchr.

**TORRES, VIVIAN C,** Univ Of Miami, Coral Gables, FL; JR; BA; Runners Club 88-; Golden Key 90-; Beta Alpha Psi 90-; Vol Income Tax Asst Prog; Deans List 89-; Provost Hnr Roll; Acctng; MBA.

**TORRES, YAMID,** Univ Of Pr Medical Sciences, San Juan, PR; SR; BA; Rho Chi; Hnr Rl 86-89; Sci; Pharm.

**TORRES-COLON, EDUARDO L,** Univ Of Pr At Mayaguez, Mayaguez, PR; SR; BSEE; IEEE 88-; NASA Aerospace Tech Exhibtn Coor 90; Elec Engr Cls Secy 90-; Sch Of Engr Hon Roll 90-; Cume Laude 90; Engr.**

**TORRES-MORIN, MARIA L,** Univ Of Pr Medical Sciences, San Juan, PR; GD; MSN; Ntl League Of Nrsng 80-87; VHT U Of Puerto Rico 90; BSN Cthlc U Of PR 80; SJ Mncpl Hosp 80-84; Vtrns Admin Hosp PR Vol Wrk 87-88; Nrsng; Tchng.

**TORRES-PALACIOS, MARIA,** Univ Of Rochester, Rochester, NY; SR; BA; Spnsh/Latin Stdnt Assn 87-; Comm Oppression Latin Amer Countries 87-; Psychlgy Undergrad Cncl 90-; Delta Gamma Hnr Rlbk 88-; Delta Gamms Panhell Deleg 90; Newman Comm 87-; Rsrch Motivation Rsrch Asst 90-; Psychlgy; Dntstry.

**TORRES-SERRANO, JANET,** Inter Amer Univ Pr San German, San German, PR; SR; Clgt Sec Intl San German PR 90-; Deans List 87-.

**TORRES-SUSTAITA, JUAN A,** Univ Of Pr At Rio Piedras, Rio Piedras, PR; SO; MBA; AIAS 90; Hnr Awrd; AD Grphc Arts 88; Archtctr.

**TORRES-TERAN, VANESSA,** Inter Amer Univ Pr Hato Rey, Hato Rey, PR; SR; BBA; Accntng Stu Assn Cncl 90-; Dean Lst 89-; Accntng Ttr 90-; Accntng; CPA.

**TORREY, ANTHONY T,** Alcorn St Univ, Lorman, MS; JR; BA; Deans List; Masonic Ldg 485; USMC; Nvl Rsrv; Ofcr Candt Sch Marine Corp; Rcvd Schlrshp Frshmn; Schlrshp PN/CHS; Almns Assc; IM Ftbl Sftbl Bsktbl; Mass Cmnctns; TV Brdcstng Jrnlsm.

**TORREY, ELIZABETH J,** Ms St Univ, Miss State, MS; SR; BA; AICHE Secr 89-; Mortar Bd 90-; Omicron Delta Kappa 90-; Omega Chi Epsilon Pres 90-; Phi Kappa Phi 89-; Tau Kappa Pi 90-; Delta Gamma 87-; IM Ftbl Capt 88-89; Scotch Guard ROTC Aux V P 87-; Dow Outstndg Jr 90; Engr; Chem Engr-Envir.

**TORRUELLA-ORTIZ, MARTA I,** Ny Univ, New York, NY; SR; BA; Deans Lst 89-; Grants Mgmt Spclst NYU Med Cntr; AAS 88; BA; Ecnmcs Intl.

**TOTARO, DANA,** Neumann Coll, Aston, PA; SO; BSN; Stu Nrs Assoc 90-; Ntl Stu Nrs Assoc 90-; Pres Lst 88; Denas Lst 89; Nrsg.

**TOTE, SUSAN M,** Radford Univ, Radford, VA; SR; BA; Crmnl Jstc Clb Publ Rels Ofcr 89-; Pi Gamma Mu 90-; Telephone-A-Thon; Christmas Pgm Underpriv Chldrn 87-88; Crmnl Jstc; Invstgtn.

**TOTH, ARANKA,** Bunker Hill Comm Coll, Boston, MA; FR; ENGL; Intrntnl Stdnt Clb.

**TOTH, CANDACE M,** Duquesne Univ, Pittsburgh, PA; JR; Elem Educ; Teach Educ.

**TOTH, DAVID A,** Hudson Valley Comm Coll, Troy, NY; FR; ASSOC; Auto Body Repair; Eng.

**TOTH, ERIC P,** Univ Of Cincinnati, Cincinnati, OH; SO; BED; Metro Cnfrnc 89-90; Cmmssnrs Lst Rcgntn Outstndng Acdmc Achvmnt Athlt; Div I Tnns; Spnsh; Tchng.

**TOTH, JANET L,** Allegheny Coll, Meadville, PA; SR; BA; Swm Tm Capt 87-; Aldn Schlr 88-; Econs; Hmn Rsrcs.

**TOTH, ROBERT F,** Nova Univ, Ft Lauderdale, FL; GD; MIBA; Acdmy Intl Bus; BA 74; Intl Bus Admin; Multinational Enterprise Tch.

**TOTH, STEPHEN C,** Central Wesleyan Coll, Central, SC; SR; MA; Spring Prdctn Asst To Drctr 89-90; Spring Prdctn Drctr Cstmng 90-; Hstry Clb 88-89; Chrstn Svc Org 89-90/Sec 90-; Grad Hnrs Cum Laude; Library Asst 90-; BA; Christian Education.

**TOTH, TAMARA L,** Oh Univ, Athens, OH; FR; IM Bsktbl/ Vlybl; Aerospc Eng.

**TOTO, LORRAINE A,** Wagner Coll, Staten Island, NY; SO; BS; IMS; Peer Tutor; Sci; Tchr.

**TOTTEN, LA VIE GERMAINE,** Bennett Coll, Greensboro, NC; SR; BA; Bennett Schlrs 88-; Pres Lst 87-; Deans Lst 87-; Sigma Tau Delta; Alpha Kappa Alpha Prlmntrn 88-; Engl/ Interdisciplinary Studies; Law/Clg Tch.

**TOTTEN, RUTH K,** Univ Of Nc At Asheville, Asheville, NC; JR; BA; Biology; Rsrch Cell Biology.

**TOTTEN, TOMMY L,** Nc Agri & Tech St Univ, Greensboro, NC; FR; BS; Stdnt Govt Assoc Pres 87-90; Beta Clb VP 87-90; Beta Clb VP 89-90; Hlth Occptn Stdnts Of Amer VP 87-88; Jr Mrshll 88-89; US Census Bureau 90; Vac Bible Schl Tchr; Trk 87-89; Ed; Spec Ed.

**TOTTER, SUSAN E,** Univ Of Sc At Columbia, Columbia, SC; SO; BS; Crln Hsptlty Scty VP; Clnry Tm 90-; Clb Mgrs Assoc; Cncrt Chr 90; Crln Alv 90-; Wlt Dsny Wrld Intrn 88-; Appld Prfssnl Sci.

**TOUCHETTE, ALICE R,** Newbury Coll, Brookline, MA; SR; AA; N R Thtre Wrkshp 88-; Brd Rltrs 89; Beauty Cnsltnt Finelle Csmtcs 80; Fshn Dsgn Fshn Mrchndsng; Couture Fshn Dsgn.

**TOUCHTON, MICHELE L,** Memphis St Univ, Memphis, TN; FR; BA; Mariners NROTC 90-; Math.

**TOUCHTON SR, STEVEN E,** Norfolk St Univ, Norfolk, VA; SR; BS; Alpha Kappa Mu 90-; Chpln Assist 89-; USAR; Mgr Princess Anne Farmer Serv 89-; Psychology/Hmn Rltns; US Army Chaplain.

**TOUGHTON, DERIK A,** Central Fl Comm Coll, Ocala, FL; SO; Bus; CPA.

**TOUKMAJI, SAMEER YAKOB,** Univ Of Nc At Charlotte, Charlotte, NC; JR; BA; Allied Hlth Clb Treas 90-; Intl Club 89-; Beta Beta Beta 89-; Vol Univ Mem Hosp 90; Dean List UNC Charlotte 90; UNCC Excell Media Awd/Photographer 89-; Biology; Medical Technology.

**TOULSON, CECELIA S,** Coppin St Coll, Baltimore, MD; JR; BA; MA Math Stats; Math; Actrl Sci.

**TOUMA, MICHAEL E,** Univ Of Nc At Charlotte, Charlotte, NC; JR; BA; Model United Nations 90-; Commuter Assoc UNCC VP 87; Political Sci Repr; Pi Kappa Phi Social Comm Chair 89-90; Deans Lst; Soccer 87-88; Political Sci; PHD Tchng Clg.

**TOUMA, SIMON,** Univ Of Akron, Akron, OH; JR; BA; Tau Beta Pi; Eta Kappa Nu; Golden Key; Ldrshp Seminar Univ Akron; Engr; Elect Engr.

**TOUMANIDIS, MARIA,** S U N Y Coll Of Tech At Delhi, Delhi, NY; SO; BS; Stdnt Cncl Russell Hall Pres 89; Dns Lst 90; Hons Lst 91; AS St Univ Delni 89-91; Engr; Cvl Engr.

**TOURIAN, SHAHIN,** Broward Comm Coll, Ft Lauderdale, FL; SO; BS; Pres Lst 90-; N Lauderdl LSA Tr 89-90; Eng.

**TOURIAN, SHOHREH,** Broward Comm Coll, Ft Lauderdale, FL; SO; BS; Pres Lst 90-; N Lauderdl LSA 89-; Eng.

**TOURON, CHARLES F,** Elon Coll, Elon, NC; FR; BS; Eng.

**TOUROS, GEORGE D,** City Univ Of Ny La Guard Coll, Long Island Cty, NY; GD; AAS; Phi Theta Kappa; BS Long Island Univ 84; Phy Thrpst Assist; Sprts Med.

**TOUSSAINT, BRENDA J,** Al St Univ, Montgomery, AL; JR; BS; Frnch Clb 90-; Stu Ornttn Asst 89-; Phi Eta Sigma 89-; Pi Mu Epsilon Pres 90-; Alpha Kappa Mu; CASET; AME Tutor Prog 90; AL St Univ Pres Schlrshp 88-; Howard Univ Smmr Rsrch Prog; Pi Mu Epsilon Schlrshp 89; Eng/Math; MS/PHD/ RD Chmcl Eng.

**TOUSSAINT, HANIFF,** City Univ Of Ny Baruch Coll, New York, NY; GD; BBA; Stdnt Cntr Prgm Brd :Vp 88-89; Mrktng.

**TOUSSAINT, SHEILA,** City Univ Of Ny Baruch Coll, New York, NY; JR; BBA; Natl Assn Blck Accntnts Treas; Gldn Ky; Baruch Schlr; Inroads 88-; New York Telephone 88-; Acctng; CPA.

**TOUTAINT, MICHELLE L,** Thomas Nelson Comm Coll, Hampton, VA; SO; AAS; EMT Vol James City Cnty Rescue Squad; Vllybl 90; EMT Vol Yrk Cnty Rescue Squad; Plce Sci; Law Enf.

**TOVANI, KAREN T,** James Madison University, Harrisonburg, VA; JR; BS; Assn Edctnyng Chldrn 88-; Ntl Assn Edctn Yng Chldrn; Sthrn Asn Chldrn Undr Six; Gldn Key 90-; Kappa Delta Pi Sec 90-; Erly Chldhd Edctn; Tchr.

**TOVAR, ANDREA G,** George Mason Univ, Fairfax, VA; GD; NATA 87-; NVSMA 90-; Assist Athletic Trnr; Phy Thrpy Aide; Baseball 85-90; Phy Ed/Athltc Trng.

**TOVAR, YVONNE,** City Univ Of Ny Baruch Coll, New York, NY; JR; Std Gvt Cmpgn Mgr 88 VP Leg Affs 87-88; Yrbk Adm Mgr 88-89; Archy Vars Tm Capt 87; Acctng.

**TOVIN, CORY B,** Boston Univ, Boston, MA; SR; BS; Cls V P 87; Zeta Beta Tau Pldg Dir 88-; Stdnt Athl Trnr 87-88; IM Sftbl/ Ftbl 87-; Phys Ther; Sports Med-Phys Ther.

**TOW, RODNEY E,** Univ Of Sc At Columbia, Columbia, SC; SO; BA; Soc Prof Jrnlsts 90-; Assoc Hrns Stu 89-; IM Tennis 90f; Brdcst Jrnlsm; Sprtscstr.**

**TOWER, JEAN M,** Fl International Univ, Miami, FL; SR; BA; Les Amis Du Vin 90-; Hotel/Fd/Trvl Assn 90-; Stdnt Hon Mentor 90-; Essex Ag/Tech 88; Hosp Mgmnt; Rest Mgmnt.

**TOWER, JENNIFER E,** S U N Y Coll At Postdam, Potsdam, NY; JR; BME; Crane Stdnt Assc Pblc Rltns Sec 88-; Clg Stdnt Govt Assc Assmbly Prsn; Msc Edctrs Natl Conf/NY State Msc Edctrs Assc Edtr; Kappa Dlt Pi 90-; Pi Kappa Lmbd; Judith Tyra Mem Awrd 90; Msc Educ.

**TOWER, REBECCA L,** Vance Granville Comm Coll, Henderson, NC; SR; AAS; Med Clinc Cmptr Oprtr 88-; Bus Cmptr Pgrgmg.

**TOWERY, JAMES K,** Itawamba Comm Coll, Fulton, MS; FR; ICC All Am Band 90-; Msc Ed; Band Dir.

**TOWLER, REBECCA,** Emory Univ, Atlanta, GA; GD; MSN; Cls Pres 85-87; Natl Assoc Of Neonatal Nrs 88-; GA Assoc Of Neonatal Nrs 90-; Stf Chrg/Trnsprt Nrs Athens Regnl Med Ctr; BSN Medcl Clg Of GA 87; Nrsng; Neonatal.**

**TOWLES, CELIA A,** Liberty Univ, Lynchburg, VA; JR; BS; Liberty Assn Christian Tchrs Secy 90-; Kappa Delta Pi Pres; Reg Interpreters 85-; Engl; Tch.

**TOWLES, LA TONYA D,** Savannah Coll Of Art & Design, Savannah, GA; FR; BA; Deans List; Video/History Of Art; Cmnctns.

**TOWNER, CLIFFORD N,** Univ Of Cincinnati, Cincinnati, OH; SO; BED; U C Racquetbl Clb Treas 90-; OCMEA Music Educ Assoc; Alpha Tau Omega Song Chrmn 89; Phi Mu Alpha Asst Pldge Eductr 89; NESA Natl Eagle Scout Assn 89; I M 90-; Music; Educ/Prfrmnce.

**TOWNER, VALMADGE T,** Alcorn St Univ, Lorman, MS; SR; BS; SIFE Pres 88-; Stdt Gvt Rep 88-; Phi Theta Kappa; Phi Beta Lambda Sec 87-; Alpha Phi Alpha; NAACP Youth Sec; YMCA State Sec 86-; Ftbl/Bsbl/Track Capt 87-; AA Coahoma Comm Cllg 89; Mathematics; College Administrator.

**TOWNES, LATAVIA MONIQUE,** Coppin St Coll, Baltimore, MD; SO; BA; Mgmt Sci; Bsns Admnstrtn.

**TOWNLEY JR, MARSHTON K,** Oh St Univ, Columbus, OH; JR; BA; Dlwre Huf N Puf Sccr Leag 90-; Clmbs Bsch Sccr Leag; Golden Key; Phlsphy/Econ; Law.

**TOWNLEY, VICKI P,** Univ Of Md Baltimore Prof Schl, Baltimore, MD; SO; BSP; Envrnmntl Engr FMC Corp 78-88; BSCHE W Va Univ 77; Pharm.

**TOWNS, CHRISTINA G,** Polk Comm Coll, Winter Haven, FL; FR; MBA; Math; CPA.

**TOWNS, CYNTHIA J,** Middle Ga Coll, Cochran, GA; SO; BED; Mdl GA Plyrs Sec 89-; Stdnt Actvts Comm Co Chrmn 89-; Shw Chr 90-; AA Ed; Math; Ed.

**TOWNS, LAKISHA S,** Al A & M Univ, Normal, AL; FR; NAACP 90-; Elem Ed; Tchng.

**TOWNS, VICKYE TANYA,** Al A & M Univ, Normal, AL; SR; BA; Amer Mktg Assn 90-; Sigma Tau Delta 89-; Engl; Comm Fld.

**TOWNSEND, CLAYTON,** City Univ Of Ny Baruch Coll, New York, NY; GD; Gldn Key 89-90; Endwmnt Fnd Provosts Schlrshp 90; Chld Lf Pgm Intrnshp 90.

**TOWNSEND, DANIEL R,** Univ Of Nc At Charlotte, Charlotte, NC; GD; BA; Pre Law Soc 89-90; Anthrplgy Clb 89-90; Phi Alpha Theta 89-90; Chancllrs Lst 88-90; Dns Lst 89-90; Hstry; Law.

**TOWNSEND, DEBORAH S,** Jackson St Univ, Jackson, MS; JR; Phi Beta Lambda Edtr Nwsltr 87; Intrn Chldrns Advcy Ctr; Salutatrn 87; AS Utica Jr Clg 87; Bus Tech/Pltcl Sci; Law Sch.

**TOWNSEND, DEBRA M,** Tougaloo Coll, Tougaloo, MS; FR; BS; Pre Hlth Clb 90-; Alpha Lambda Delta 90-; Biology; Med.

**TOWNSEND, KAAREN M,** Hampton Univ, Hampton, VA; FR; BA; SGA; Amer Mktg Assn 90-; NJ Pre-Alumni 90; Inroads Intrnshp Prctr/Gmbl 90-; Pres Schlr 90-; Pres Lst 90-; Mktg; Advrtsng.

**TOWNSEND, KELLIE D,** Radford Univ, Radford, VA; SO; BS; Hous Council 89-90; Alpha Lambda Delta 89-90; 4-H Club Secty 80-81; United Meth Youth Flwshp Treas 80-82; Nurse Practr.

**TOWNSEND, LOREN B,** East Central Comm Coll, Decatur, MS; SO; AAS; VICA; IM Sports; Drftng; Engr.

**TOWNSEND, MERVICE M,** Al A & M Univ, Normal, AL; FR; Chrch Chr; Ltrcy Pgm; NAACP.

**TOWNSEND, MICHAEL A,** Piedmont Bible Coll, Winston-Salem, NC; JR; USAA All-Am Schlr 90-; Sccr 88-89; Theology; Missnry Aviation.

**TOWNSEND, NOEL V,** Broward Comm Coll, Ft Lauderdale, FL; SO; BA; Hon Inst 88-; Phi Theta Kappa 89-; Grad W/High Hon; Psychlgy; Rsrch.

**TOWNSEND, PATRICK W,** Salisbury St Univ, Salisbury, MD; SR; Alpha Omega; Beta Beta Beta 89-90; Phi Kappa Phi; BS 90.

**TOWNSEND, ROSA I,** Saint Pauls Coll, Lawrenceville, VA; JR; BA; Acdmc Schlrshp 90; Rdrs Dgst Awd; Math/Sci Awd; AAS Sthsd Comm Coll 90; Bus Educ; Tchr.

**TOWNSEND, SHEILA R,** Northeast State Tech Comm Coll, Blountville, TN; FR; AAS; Bus; Mgmt.

**TOWNSEND III, THOMAS R,** Univ Of Fl, Gainesville, FL; SR; BA; Surf Clb 88; Chi Phi Chrmn Fncl Comm 87-; Deans Lst 90; IM Ftbl/Sftbl 87-; AA 90; Mrtg; Bus Mgmt.

**TOWNSEND, TIFFANY B,** Samford Univ, Birmingham, AL; FR; BA; Mrchng Bnd/Symphnc Bnd Scrtry 90-; Yrbk Edtr 90-; Alpha Lambda Delta 90-; Delta Omicron; Sigma Delta Chi; Hnrs Dy Hghst Cls Hnrs; Schlstc Awrd; Jrnlsm/Ms Cmmnctns; Pblc Rltns.

**TOWNSEND, TIMOTHY G,** Wv Univ At Parkersburg, Parkersburg, WV; FR; BA; Phi Beta Lambda; Disabled/Job 87; Bsn.

**TOWNSEND, VALERIE R,** Univ Of Miami, Coral Gables, FL; SO; BBA; Alpha Lambda Delta 89-; Phi Eta Sigma 89-; Delta Sigma Pi 90-; Delta Gamma V P Rush 89-; Bsn; Law.

**TOWNSON, EDNA A,** Univ Of Nc At Asheville, Asheville, NC; SO; BA; Mathematics; Rsrch/Dvlpmnt In Industry.

**TOWSEY, TAMMY S,** Longwood Coll, Farmville, VA; JR; BS; Stdnt Athltc Trnrs Assn Pres 88-; Phys Educ Mjrs Clb Sec 88-; Alpha Lambda Delta 89; Intrvrsty Chrstn Fllwshp 88-; Phys Educ Mjr Hghst GPA 89-; Phys Educ; Physcl Thrpst.

**TOWSON, KENNETH M,** Valdosta St Coll, Valdosta, GA; SO; BBA; Mrchng Brigade Band 89-90; Exec Brd Miss Valdosta State Pgnts 89-; Pi Kappa Phi 89-; PUSH 89-; Acctg.

**TOY, MICHELLE L,** Univ Of Louisville, Louisville, KY; FR; MENG; Phi Eta Sigma; Mech Engr; Dsgn.

**TOYOS, RAMON V,** Fl International Univ, Miami, FL; JR; BS; Natl Hnr Soc 85-; AS Miami Dade Comm Clg 89; Cmptr Sci; Pgrmmr.

**TOZIER, LISBETH J,** Nyack Coll, Nyack, NY; SO; BA; Manhattan Gospel Tm 90-; Chorale 90; Psychology.

**TRABITS, JAMES ALAN,** Daytona Beach Comm Coll, Daytona Beach, FL; SO; BA; Engr; Sci.

**TRABUE, CATHY C,** Ky St Univ, Frankfort, KY; SO; BA; Hall VP 89-90; Cls Pres 90-; Leg Intrn Genl Assmbly; RA 90-; Mrchng Bnd 89-90; Pol Sci; Law/Pub Admin.

**TRABUE, SIMEYON C,** Central St Univ, Wilberforce, OH; SR; BA; Kapap Sweethearts Pblc Rltns 87-90; SCU Mrchng Mauraders Ci Capt 87-; Sociology 90-; Sociology; Pblc Rltns Mgr.

**TRACEWSKI, NICOLE K,** Indiana Univ Of Pa, Indiana, PA; SO; BS; Sgn Lang Clb 89-; Ntl Sp Lang Hrng Assn 90-; Kappa Delta Pi 90-; Spch Pthlgy; Rehab.

**TRACEY JR, JOSEPH P,** Merrimack Coll, North Andover, MA; SO; BA; Wrtng Tutor 90; Walt Disney World Pgm 90; IM Bsktbl 90-; Fnce; Ins Banking.

**TRACY, ANGELA R,** Livingston Univ, Livingston, AL; JR; BS; Stdnt Govt Assoc Senator 87-88; Univ Of S AL 88-89; AA Patrick Henry State Jr College 88; Elem Ed; Teach.

**TRACY, KEVIN P,** Univ Of Rochester, Rochester, NY; GD; Flr Pres 87-88; Dorm Cncl Tres 88-89; Arnold Air Soc 87-90; Dean Lst; IM Sprts; Tiernan Comm Serv Res Fclty 86-88; AFROTC Schlrshp; BS 90; Mech Eng; USAF.

**TRACY, MARITA L,** Fayetteville St Univ, Fayetteville, NC; FR; BS; Cvl Serv Sec 78-85; Animal Care Spclst 86-89; Biology; Vet Med.

**TRACY, MICHAEL C,** Union Univ, Jackson, TN; SO; BS; Yrbk Edtr 89-; Hnrs Stu Assoc 89-90; Kappa Mu Epsilon Hstrn Phtgrphr; Betty Foellinger Stu Pblctn Awrd 90-; Cmnctn Arts; TV.

**TRAEYE, MIRIAM R,** Fl A & M Univ, Tallahassee, FL; JR; BS; FFEA; Elem Edn; Tchr.

**TRAFFORD, CHRISTINE S,** James Madison University, Harrisonburg, VA; FR; Pre-Legal Soc 90-; Intrvrsty Chrstn Flwshp 90-; Lambda Alpha Epsilon 90-; Eng/Govt; Law.

**TRAFFORD, DEBORAH J,** Christopher Newport Coll, Newport News, VA; JR; BS; Brwni Ldr; Echrstc Mnstr 89-; US Nvy; Mth; Tchr.

**TRAFICANTI, BRYAN J,** S U N Y Coll Of A & T Morrisvl, Morrisville, NY; FR; BA; Hstry; Law.

**TRAFTON, PAULA B,** Western Ky Univ, Bowling Green, KY; SO; BA; Wmn In Trnsitn; Alpha Sigma Lambda; La Leche Lgue Intl Ldr 79-; Chldrn Americas Fstr Prnts 88-; History; Tch.

**TRAGER, SCOTT M,** Univ Of Tn At Knoxville, Knoxville, TN; FR; BA; Vol Pep Club 90-; IM Sprts 90-; Vol Comm 90-; Alpha Lambda Delta; Phi Eta Sigma; Alpha Epsilon Pi; Summa Cum Laude Fall 90; Exec Undrgrad Bus Prog 90-; IM Sprts; Bus Adm; Law.

**TRAGO, ANN M,** Marywood Coll, Scranton, PA; SR; BS; Psych Club 87-91; Newsletter 90-91; Psi Chi 90-91; Delta Epsilon Sigma 90-91; Cancer Soc 88-90; Hnr Pgm 87-; Psych; Elem Cnslng.

**TRAHANAS, PHILIP,** Cooper Union, New York, NY; JR.

**TRAHANAS, PHILIP P,** Cooper Union, New York, NY; JR; BE; IEEE Pres 90-; Zeta Psi; Schlp Cooper Un Rgnts Schlp Awd; Elec Engr.

**TRAIL, GEORGE JASON,** Middle Tn St Univ, Murfreesboro, TN; JR; BA; Intr Vrsty Chrstn Fllwshp Lrg Grp Crdr 90-; Chrstn Msc Scty 90-; Cmps Crsd 88-90; Mss Comm; Std Eng.

**TRAINA, LISA M,** S U N Y Coll Of Tech At Frmgdl, Farmingdale, NY; SO; AS; Bus; Bus Adm.

**TRAINOR, THOMAS P,** Univ Of New Haven, West Haven, CT; FR; BA; Aviation; Eng.

**TRAIT, DENISE M,** Le Moyne Coll, Syracuse, NY; SR; BS; AAS 87-89; Bus Admin.

**TRAMA, STEPHEN I,** Daemen Coll, Amherst, NY; SO; BS; B F Dvlpmnt Cntr 87; Mary Immclt Hosp Vol PT 90; Deans Lst 89; Deans List Daemen Coll 90-; IM Ftbl 89-; Physcl Thrpy.

**TRAMBLE, KATHY K,** Lenoir Rhyne Coll, Hickory, NC; GD; BA; Mu Sigma Epsilon 89-90; Tchr Assist Caldwell Cnty Schls; Ed; Tchng.

**TRAMMELL, SHANNON M,** George Mason Univ, Fairfax, VA; SO; BA; Alpha Lambda Delta 90-; Amer Mktg Assoc 90-; Cir K 90-; Dns Lst 89-90; Bsn Admin/Mktg; Mktg/Byr.**

**TRAMMELL, STEPHEN M,** Gainesville Coll, Gainesville, GA; JR; BA; Minrty Stdnt Assc 88-90; Deans List/Merit List 88-90; Otstndng Soph 89-90; AA 90; Bus Adm Fin.

**TRAMONTANA, CATHERINE J,** Villanova Univ, Villanova, PA; JR; BA; Chtqua Assc Edit 90-; USES Edit In Chf 90-; Wmns Stds Crrclm Com 90-; Phi Kappa Phi 90-; Omicron Delta Kappa; Stdnts Agnst Sxl Strtyping Chr 90; Pce And Jstce Ntwrk Mmbr 90-; Rpe Tsk Frce 90-; Elizabeth C Stanton Rsrch Awrd; Hnrs Engl; Grad Schl Univ Prof.

**TRAMONTOZZI, BECKY,** Becker Coll At Leicester, Leicester, MA; SO; AS; Phi Theta Kappa Secy; All Colonial/All New England Vlybll; Vllybl Intrcllgt Cptn; Trsm; Travel Agnt.

**TRAN, ANN T,** Univ Of Ky, Lexington, KY; JR; Envrnmntl Awareness Grp 89-90; Intrcltrl Awareness Grp 89-90; Boast Alchl Consciousness Concerning Hlth Unvrsty Stdnts 89-90; Phi Eta Sigma 89; Play Violin Flute Hsptl Nrsng Homnes Chrchs 88; Vol UK Vtrns Hosp Crdnl Hll Hsp 88; Blgy; Medicine.

**TRAN, BETH M,** Univ Of Tn At Knoxville, Knoxville, TN; SR; BS; Beta Gamma Sigma 90-; Beta Alpha Psi 90-; VITA 89-; Exec Undgrad Prog 90-; Stf Acctnt Law Firm 87-90; Acctg; Publ Acctg.

**TRAN, DIEU-THUY A,** Radford Univ, Radford, VA; SO; ACS 90-; Asn Assn 90; Kappa Mu Epsilon 90-; Dns Lst 89-; Chem; Dentstry.

**TRAN, DUNG HOANG,** Comm Coll Algny Co Algny Cmps, Pittsburgh, PA; FR; Engrng Science; Engineering.

**TRAN, HA-PHUONG T,** Univ Of Va, Charlottesville, VA; FR; BS; Yrbk Stf 90-; Vietnmse Stdnt Assoc 90-; Sigma Kappa; Recg Awd; IM Vllybl ASU Tnns Trnmnt 90-; Biol/Frnch; Med.

**TRAN, HIEN H,** Temple Univ, Philadelphia, PA; SR; BS; Gldnkey 88-89; Deans Lst 87-90; Elec Tech 87-; AAS Montgomery Cty Commcoll 86; Electronics/Electrical; Engineering.**

**TRAN, HIEP D,** Univ Of Sc At Columbia, Columbia, SC; SO; BS; Alpha Lambda Delta; Gamma Beta Phi; Phi Eta Sigma; Mech Eng.

**TRAN, HONG V,** Univ Of Vt & St Agri Coll, Burlington, VT; FR; BA; Intl Clb 90-; Dean Lst; Yth Grp 88-; La Asst; Biol; Dr.

**TRAN, HUY M,** City Univ Of Ny Baruch Coll, New York, NY; JR; BBA; Vietnamese Stdnt Assoc Pres 89; Chinese Culture Club; Vlybl; Acctng.

**TRAN, LINH,** Fl St Univ, Tallahassee, FL; JR; BA; Vietnamese Stdnt Assn Sec 90-; Collegiate Merch Assn; AA; Fashion Merch.

**TRAN, LY M,** Univ Of Rochester, Rochester, NY; SO; BA; Chns Stdnt Assoc Sec 90-; Econ.

**TRAN, MINH Q,** Va Commonwealth Univ, Richmond, VA; JR; VSA Vp 88-; Intrntl Clbs 89-; Pre Med Clbs 90-; Hnrs Prog 88-; Golden Key 90-; Phi Sigma 90-; Rsrch Flwshp NIH 88-; Vol MCV/EMRGNCY 87-; Dir Dnce Grp Vietnmse Buddist Assc 87-; Guartntd Admssn Med Clg VA 89-; Bio/Chem; Med Dctr.

**TRAN, QUAN T,** Coll Of Insurance, New York, NY; SO; BS; Dvrsty Awrns 90-; Bwlng Tm 90-; Hong Kong Stdnt Assn Syracuse U 89-90; IM Vlybl Syracuse U 89-90; Actrl Sci.

**TRAN, QUANG L,** Bunker Hill Comm Coll, Boston, MA; SO; Vietnamese Tester Lang 90-; Assmnt Ctr Boston Publ Sch; Cmptr Sci; Pgrmmr.

**TRAN, QUOC N,** Wv Univ, Morgantown, WV; FR; BA; BA; Civil Engr.

**TRAN, THONG BINH,** Capitol Coll, Laurel, MD; SR; Alumni Assn 87-88; Alpha Chi; Tau Alpha Pi 90.

**TRAN, TON V,** City Univ Of Ny City Coll, New York, NY; SO; Vtnms Std Asc CENY 89-; Intl Clb 90-; Optmtry Doctor.

**TRANCHITELLA, LYNDA L,** Wv Univ, Morgantown, WV; JR; BSN; Var Crew 87-90; Pgm Brd 89-90; Euch Mnstr 88-; Sigma Theta Tau; Nrnsg.

**TRANG, ANTHONY,** Widener Univ, Chester, PA; JR; BS; Jr Flwshp Pgm 87-; Elec Eng.

**TRANQUILLE, MAREE D,** S U N Y Coll Of Tech At Frmgdl, Farmingdale, NY; SO; AS; UBS Pres 88-; RA Ldr; Bsn Clb/Intl Std 88; AS BS; Bsn/Mgmt; Fnc/Invstmnt.

**TRANSIER, CHRISTINE M,** Univ Of Cincinnati, Cincinnati, OH; SO; BED; Elem Ed/Sclgy; Tchg/Adm.

**TRANUM, TRACI NANINE,** Southern Coll Of Tech, Marietta, GA; SO; BS; Schlrs Bowl Dltn Clg 87-88; Elec Eng Technlgy.

**TRAPNELL, CHERYL H,** Hillsborough Comm Coll, Tampa, FL; FR; AA; Elem Ed; Tch.

**TRAPNELL, SALLY S,** Univ Of Ga, Athens, GA; SR; BSED; Early Chlhd Ed; Tch.

**TRAPP, CHERYL L,** Georgian Court Coll, Lakewood, NJ; FR; BA; Schl Nwspr; Math; Tchr.

**TRAPP, CRYSTAL C,** Allen Univ, Columbia, SC; SR; Chrldng 87-89; Pan Helelnic Cncl Treas 89-; Alpha Kappa Alpha VP 90-; Natl Assn Univ Wmn Awd; SC Elec/Gas Co Intrnshp 89-.**

**TRASANDE, LEONARDO,** Harvard Univ, Cambridge, MA; FR; AB; Puerto Rican Stdnts Assn 90-; Democrats Clb 90-; Disabled Stdnts Asst 90-; Deans Lst 90-; IM 90-; Hist/Sci; Medicine.

**TRASK, GREGORY J,** Univ Of Miami, Coral Gables, FL; JR; BA; Stdnt Govt Sntr 90-; Hon Stdnts Assn S G Sntr 88-; Pre Legal Soc 88-; Golden Key 90; Alpha Lambda Delta 88-; Phi Eta Sigma 89-; Deans Lst 88-; All Amer Schlr 90-; Pltcl Sci; Intl Law.**

**TRASTER, KEITH ANDREW,** Kent St Univ Kent Cmps, Kent, OH; SR; BBA; AA Lorain County Comm Coll 89; Hmn Rsrce Mgmt; Bus Law.

**TRAUB, ANNE-MARIE,** Va Commonwealth Univ, Richmond, VA; JR; BA; VA Cmmnwlth U Hnrs Scty 89-; Actvtg Odds 88-; Stff Wrtr Cmmnwlth Tms; Deans Lst; Engl; Wrtg/Tchg.

**TRAUB, MICHELE D,** Widener Univ, Chester, PA; SR; Bus; Acctg.

**TRAUFFER, JOHN D,** S U N Y Coll At Postdam, Potsdam, NY; JR; BA; Intervar Chrstn Fllwshp 88-; Pi Kappa Lambda; Pi Mu Epsilon 89-; Phi Eta Sigma 88-; Music/Math; Edctn/Ministry

**TRAUGOTT, JENNIFER C,** Univ Of Rochester, Rochester, NY; SR; BA; Psychlgy Cncl Bus Mgr 89-; D Lions Dorm Rep 88-89; Trnsfr Advsrs 88-89; Psy Chi; Family Cntr Cnslr 90-; Rsrch Asst 88-90; Psychlgy; MA Academia Bus.

**TRAUTMAN, DAVID A,** Duquesne Univ, Pittsburgh, PA; JR; BS; Schl Bus Drvr 80-90; Chmstry; Indstry/Oil.

**TRAUTMAN, JASON P,** Comm Coll Algny Co Algny Cmps, Pittsburgh, PA; SR; ASSOC; Allghny Gnrl Hsptl; Chldrns Hsptl; Shadyside Hsptl; Prbstyrn Hsp 90-; Rsprtry Thrpy.

**TRAVERS, JEFFREY P,** Georgetown Univ, Washington, DC; JR; BSBA; Georgetown Univ Symphonic Bnd; Pep Bnd; Jazz Ensmble Sect Ldr 88-; Beta Gamma Sigma; Acctg; Law.

**TRAVERS, LYNN,** Newbury Coll, Brookline, MA; Class Rep 90-; Fash Desgn.

**TRAVERS, ROBERT B,** Comm Coll Algny Co Algny Cmps, Pittsburgh, PA; SO; BA; Scl Wrk Clb 90-; Psi Beta 90-; AARP 89-; Assn Rtrd Citizens 89-; Frmr Nrsnghm Aid; VA Vlntr; Deans Lst CCAC 88; Scl Wrk Psychlgy; Mntl Hlth Scl Wrk.

**TRAVERS, SHAWN M,** Jefferson Comm Coll, Watertown, NY; SO; BA; Eng 90-; Phi Theta Kappa 89-; Indoor Soccer; AS; Human Env/Dsgn Plnng; Architecture.**

**TRAVIESO, LIZETTE,** Fl International Univ, Miami, FL; SR; Ftr Edctrs Amer 88-89; Kappa Delta Pi Treas 88-; Almni Asc 90-; BS; Elem Educ; Tch.

**TRAVIS, CAMILLE D,** Wilberforce Univ, Wilberforce, OH; JR; BS; Student Govt Assoc Secty; Student Ambr Tour Guide 90-; Resd Assist 90-; Alpha Kappa Alpha Treas; Cargill Inc Acad Schlrshp Rece 90-; Deans List 90-; United Meth Acad/Religion Schlrshp Recip 86-88; IM Vlyb; Mktng; Corp Advisor.

**TRAVIS, CHRISTINE M,** Comm Coll Algny Co Algny Cmps, Pittsburgh, PA; FR; Acctg Spec; Priv Acct.

**TRAVIS, DARREN D,** Alcorn St Univ, Lorman, MS; FR; BA; Mrchng Bnd 90-; Hon Stdnt Orgztn 90-; Acctg.

**TRAVIS III, GLEN W,** Memphis St Univ, Memphis, TN; SO; BS; Hnrs Stu Pro 90-; Bkkpg Dept Hd 84-; Math Sci; Actry.

**TRAVIS, KELLY I,** Columbus Coll Of Art & Design, Columbus, OH; FR; BFA; Advrtsng.

**TRAVIS, KENDRA A,** Dyersburg St Comm Coll, Dyersburg, TN; FR; Ch Sec 89-; Stdnt Aflts ACS Awd Outstndg Fr Chem Stdnt 90-; Sci; Nrsng.

**TRAVIS, LINDA M,** Central Al Comm Coll, Alexander City, AL; FR; AA; Crctnl Ed Assoc Secr 89-90; Gospel Pearls Choir Dir 90-; S E Ingram Tech Clg 89; Cert; Bsn; Bsn Admnstrtr.

**TRAVIS, MICHEAL C,** Murray St Univ, Murray, KY; FR; BED; Pi Kappa Alpha 90-.

**TRAVIS, PATRICIA ANNE,** Coll Of Charleston, Charleston, SC; JR; BA; Early Chldhd Dvlpmnt Cntr 90-; Swim Tm 88-89; Anthrplgy.

**TRAVIS, THEODORE A,** Al St Univ, Montgomery, AL; SO; BA; Mrchng Bnd 90-; Hrnts Bnd Sctn Ldr; Free/Accepted Masons; Hnr Schlrshp Music; Achvmnt Awd; Music Educ.

**TRAVITT, KENNETH O,** Morehouse Coll, Atlanta, GA; SR; BA; NJ/NY Clb Sgt At Arms 87-; Bus Assoc 88-; Hnr Rl 87-; E B Williams Awrd; IM; Acctg; Finance.

**TRAWEEK, JULIE A,** Brewer St Jr Coll, Fayette, AL; SO; BSN; Phi Theta Kappa; Sci; Nrsng.

**TRAWICK, CHERYL A,** Fayetteville St Univ, Fayetteville, NC; JR.

**TRAXLER, LEAH J,** Jones County Jr Coll, Ellisville, MS; FR; BED; Letter J Awd 90-; Elem Educ; Teaching.

**TRAYER, KAREN A,** Niagara Univ, Niagara Univ, NY; SR; BS; Intshp Niagara Fls Intl Airprt; Amer Cncr Soc/Untd Way; AAS Niagara Cty Comm Clg 88; Bsn/Cmmrc; MBA.

**TRAYLOR, GEORGE T,** Point Park Coll, Pittsburgh, PA; SR; BS; Trng Ofcr Ntl Grd PA; Pblc Admin; Govt Srv.

**TRAYWICK, TINA F,** Univ Of Montevallo, Montevallo, AL; SR; Kappa Delta Pi; Lambda Sigma Pi VP; Stdnt Tchr Jemison Elem; Deans Lst 87-; Hnrs Certif 88-; BA; Early Chldhd Elem Educ; Teacher.

**TREADAWAY, DEBRA R,** Itawamba Comm Coll, Fulton, MS; FR; BA; Nrsng; RN.

**TREADWAY II, MAURICE D,** Univ Of Miami, Coral Gables, FL; SR; BS; Co Hst/Videogrphr Edtr TV 90-; Ae Rho 90-; Hst/Co Prod Ae Rho Ntl Awrd; Deans Lst Pvst/Hnr Rl 90-; Cbl Awrd Best Prod Sgmnt; Videogrphr Edtr WCNC 88-89; Prod Stf WCIX 90-; AA 86; Rec Studio Op 88; Motions Prod; Wrtr Dir Flm.

**TREADWAY, TOMARRA L,** Roane St Comm Coll, Harriman, TN; FR; Respiratory Care; Resp Therapist.

**TREANOR, SUSAN,** S U N Y Coll Of Tech At Frmgdl, Farmingdale, NY; GD; Phi Theta Kappa VP 89-90; Green Key 89-90.

**TREECE, AMY M,** Memphis Academy Of The Arts, Memphis, TN; SO; BFA; Colliervl Art Leag 88-; Smmr Arts Pgm Dir/Instrctr 86-; Grphc Dsgn.

**TREECE, SHEILA S,** Bristol Univ, Bristol, TN; GD; MBA; Blk Stdnts Cltrl Soc Pres 71-72; Amer Bus Wmsn Assn 80-; Natl Assn Accntnts 82-; Alpha Kappa Alpha 69-; Wmn/Ind Awd; Cmpt Lrng Ctr Advsry Cncl Trng 90-; BS Math Carson Newman Clg 72; Cmptr Info Rsrc Mgmt; CIR Mgr.

**TREFES, HARRY A,** Univ Of New Haven, West Haven, CT; SR; BS; Aviatn Clb VP 90-; Alpha Lambda Delta 90-; Prof Stdies; Aviatn/Pilot.

**TREGLIA, PAUL J,** S U N Y Coll Of Tech At Frmgdl, Farmingdale, NY; SR; BET; Grn Key 87-; Elec Eng Tchnlgy.

**TREHUB, LORNA B,** Springfield Tech Comm Coll, Springfield, MA; SR; AS; Retail Mgmnt 87-88; Sales 88-89; BA Univ MA Amherst 87; Court Reporting.

**TREIBITZ, CINDY ZOREN,** Univ Of Central Fl, Orlando, FL; FR; BS; Jewish Union 90-; Intrhll Cncl VP; Blgy; Dctr.

**TREILLE, MICHELLE,** Elmira Coll, Elmira, NY; SR; BA; Intl Clb 87-88; Dept Theatre Wrdrb Ms Trs 87-; Coll Brd Trustees Jr Awrd 89-90; Intrnshp Vntg Dnr Theatre Co 90-; Theatre; Thtrcl Dsgn.

**TREIS, JULIE A,** S U N Y Coll At Fredonia, Fredonia, NY; SR; BS; Dorm Cncl Treas 89; Invstmnt Clb 90; Acctng Scty 90; Bus Clb 90; FMA; Bus Admin.

**TREJOS-MURILLO, FERNANDO,** City Univ Of Ny City Coll, New York, NY; SR; BS; Assn Cmptng Mach 89-; Aspira Hispnc Clb 89-; Golden Key 90-; Cty Coll Deans Lst 89-90; Borough Mnhttn Comm Coll Deans Lst 86-87; Cmptr Sci; Sftwr Dvlpmnt.**

**TRELEASE, LISA M,** Salisbury St Univ, Salisbury, MD; JR; BA; Phi Eta Sigma 88-; Cmps Lfe Awd; Schlr Athl VA Wesleyan Clg 89; Tnns Cpt 88-; Scl Sci/Scndry Educ; Tchr.

**TRELLES, LYDIA M,** Fl International Univ, Miami, FL; FR; BA; Jr Orange Bowl Comm Brd Dirts; JOB Sports Ability Games Hosp Chrmn 87-; Intl Relations; Law.

**TRELLES, MERCEDES C,** Univ Of Pr At Rio Piedras, Rio Piedras, PR; SO; BA; Prgrma De Hnr Treas 90-; Comp Lit/Art Hstry; Tchr.

**TREMBLAY, LORI A,** Portland School Of Art, Portland, ME; SO; BFA; Fine Art.

**TREMENTOZZI, MARIA L,** Univ Of Md At College Park, College Park, MD; SR; BS; Immnls Sr Hgh Yth Grp Asst Ldr 90-; Drama Tm Ldr 90-; Agape Unlmtd 90-; Mary Pirg; Scndry Educ-Scl Studies; Tchng.

**TRENT JR, BAXTER ALTON,** Northeast State Tech Comm Coll, Blountville, TN; GD; Amer Dsgn/Drftng Assn Prlmntrn 90-; Deans Lst 89-; Grad W/Hghst Hon; AAS; Drftng.

**TRENT, NANCY E,** Univ Of Nc At Charlotte, Charlotte, NC; SR; BA; Golden Key 90; Intrn Cpywrtr 88; Chgo Cable Advrtsng; Im Tennis; AS Of Sci Mc Henry Cnty Clg 87; Engl; Advrtsng Pblc Rltn.

**TRENT, NANCY G,** James Madison University, Harrisonburg, VA; SO; BS; Natl Stdnt Nrs Assoc JMV Chptr 89-; Clg Rpblcns JMV Chptr 90-; Vol Serv Rcknghm Mem Hosp 90-; Natl Clgt Nrsng Awd 91; Nursing.**

**TRENT, PAMELA B,** Mountain Empire Comm Coll, Big Stone Gap, VA; JR; AAS; Envrmntl Sci Clb 90-; Intern DMLR; Cert 90; AAS 90; Envrnmntl Sci; Wldlf Rehab.

**TRENTHAM, LOUISE F,** Pellissippi St Tech Comm Coll, Knoxville, TN; FR; BS; Comp Sci.

**TREPICCIONE, KAREN A,** Dowling Coll, Oakdale Li, NY; SR; BA; Ed Clb 90; Pi Alpha Sigma 88-89; Magna Cum Laude 89-90; Deans Lst 88-90; Pres Acad Fitness Awd 89; Assoc In Lib Arts Suffolk Cmmnty Clg 89; Elem Ed/Hist Sec Ed; Tchr.

**TRESSLER, MELODY S,** Indiana Univ Of Pa, Indiana, PA; FR; BA; Spnsh; Tchr.

**TRESSLER, SHERI L,** Indiana Univ Of Pa, Indiana, PA; SR; BA; Res Hall Assn Tr 87-88; Sign Lang Clb 88-; Natl Stdnt Spch/Lang/Hrng/Assn 90; Phi Sigma Sigma 90-; Educ; Tchr Hrng Imprd.

**TRETTER, DENISE A,** Brescia Coll, Owensboro, KY; SR; BA; Cir K VP 90-; SGA 87-; Natl Ed Assn 90-; Alpha Chi 88-; Elem Ed; Tchr.

**TREVINO, ELENA MARITZA OJEDA,** Inter Amer Univ Pr San German, San German, PR; SR; BA; Poltcl Sci Assn; Phi Alpha Delta; Poltcl Sci; Law.

**TREVISAN, STEPHEN C,** Fordham Univ, Bronx, NY; JR; BS; Acctntg Soc 90-; Yng Rep Dorm Rep 88-; Alpha Beta Gamma 90-; Alpha Beta Psi 90-; Intrnshp Miller Tate & Co CPA Phila Pa; Varsity Golf 90-; Pub Acctng; Law.

**TRIAS, FERNANDO,** Univ Of Miami, Coral Gables, FL; FR; BBA; Chss Clb 90-; Hnrs Stdnt Assoc 90-; Comp Info Systms; Comp Cnsltng.

**TRIASSI, MICHAEL R,** Schenectady County Comm Coll, Schenectady, NY; SO; AAS; Htl Mgt.

**TRIBBLE, AHSHA N,** Fl A & M Univ, Tallahassee, FL; JR; BA; Kemetic Math Soc 90-; White Gold; Pres Schlrshp Awd 88-; AKA Schlrshp Awd 88-; Dns Lst 90-; Acctg/Act Sci; Audtr.

**TRIBETT, TAMMY R,** West Liberty St Coll, West Liberty, WV; FR; BA; Cross Country; Accounting; Cpa.

**TRIBOLET, SCOTT L,** Ms St Univ, Miss State, MS; FR; Bsbl; Bus.

**TRICARICO, AMI M,** Coll Misericordia, Dallas, PA; JR; BS; Clg Mis Stdnt Occptnl Thrpy Assn Sec 90-; Peer Tutrng Grp 88-; Pr Cnslng Grp 90-; Orntn Cnslr Grp 89-; Pi Theta Epsilon 90-; Occup Thrpy.

**TRIDICO, AMANDA L,** Univ Of Cincinnati, Cincinnati, OH; FR; BA; Math; Tchg.

**TRIEN, ELLEN M,** William Paterson Coll, Wayne, NJ; SR; BA; Spcl Olympcs; Costume Dsgnr Comm Theatre 86-; EDTA 87-; Ice Sktng Prfsnl 67-84; Spcl Ed; Tchr.

**TRIESKY, MICHAEL E,** Univ Of Pittsburgh At Bradford, Bradford, PA; BS; Engr Clb 90-; Arcrft Ownrs/Pilots Assoc 89-; Rdr Fld Serv Engr; Engr; Elec.

**TRIFARO, MICHAEL D,** Wagner Coll, Staten Island, NY; SR; BA; Wght Trng Cyclng Staten Islnd Bike Assn; St Vincents Hosp; Blgy; Physcl Thrpy.

**TRIGG, STEVEN M,** Tallahassee Comm Coll, Tallahassee, FL; SO; BS; Bus Cnsltnt.

**TRIGONIS, DEAN A,** Hellenic Coll/Holy Cross, Brookline, MA; GD; MDIV; Stdnt Rep 90-; Fclty Stdy Comm Reacredtn 89-; Byzantine Chr Yrbk Comm 91; Rl Est Inv Anlyst 86-88; Assc Prodcr T V 85; BS Univ Cal Rivrsd 84; Grk Orth Thlgy; Chrch Serv.**

**TRIMBLE, ANTHONY,** Livingston Univ, Livingston, AL; Flwshp Chrstn Athletes; Phi Beta Sigma Treas; Ftbl Ltrmn; Tch/Coach; BS 83; PE 90; Phys Educ; Tch/Coach.

**TRINDER, CATHERINE M,** Emory Univ, Atlanta, GA; JR; BBA; Rep Busn Scho Cncl; All Amer Schlr Coll Awd; Fla Acad Schlr; Dns Lst 89-; Busn/Mktg; Law Schl.

**TRINH, CHINH X,** Eckerd Coll, St Petersburg, FL; SO; BA; Dpty Chief Stf 73; Mnstry Frgn Afrs; S Vietnam; Spvlst Frgn Afrs 72-75; Pol Sci.

**TRINH, THUY T N,** George Mason Univ, Fairfax, VA; JR; BS; Acctg Clb; Acctg Hnr Scty 90-; MIS Clb; Vtnms Stdnt Assoc 89-90; Acctg Hnr Scty 90-; Coop Dept Dfns Bdgtng Asst 90-; Acctf; CPA.

**TRINIDAD, GLORIA I,** Univ Of Pr At Rio Piedras, Rio Piedras, PR; JR; ACS; Gldn Key; Hnr Rl 90-; Quimica; Indsrl.

**TRINIDAD, LOURDES S,** Princeton Univ, Princeton, NJ; FR; BA; DIA Undr Grdt Trng Asst Pgm; ROTC Army Sns Amer Rvltn Awd; Lng/Ltn Amer Stds; Tchg.

**TRINKALA, WALTER A,** Comm Coll Algny Co Algny Cmps, Pittsburgh, PA; FR; BS; BS Adm/Mgmnt La Roche Coll 87; Civil Eng.

**TRIPATHI, MEENAKSHI,** City Univ Of Ny Baruch Coll, New York, NY; SO; BBA; Clb Ind 89-91; Deans Lst 90; Bus.

**TRIPLETT, CHRISTINE A,** Duquesne Univ, Pittsburgh, PA; SO; BS; Phrmcy.

**TRIPLETT, GLORIA R,** Marshall University, Huntington, WV; SR; BA; Elem Educ; Tchng.

**TRIPLETT, SHERRY S,** Alcorn St Univ, Lorman, MS; FR; BA; Cmptr Sci Clb 90-; Hnrs Clb 90-; Dean Lst 90-; Cmptr Sci; Prgrmmn/Sys Anlys.

**TRIPODI, ROBERT J,** Hudson Valley Comm Coll, Troy, NY; SR; AAS; J N Mastrangelo/R Arnold Schlrshp 90-; O V Gunther Schlrshp 90-; Bus Admin; Mgmt.

**TRIPOLI, VALLYRE ROSE,** Univ Of Nc At Asheville, Asheville, NC; JR; BFA; Frnch Clb 88-89; Art Clb Commt Chm 90-; Alpha Delta Pi VP 89-90; Stdnt Show Accpt; Fine Art; Prfssr.

**TRIPP, CARY S,** Univ Of Sc At Columbia, Columbia, SC; FR; BS; Modl Untd Natns V Chr 90-; Grk Cncl 90-; Pi Kappa Phi Sec 90-; Dns Lst; Chrldr; Cmptr Sci.

**TRIPP, HEATHER L,** Newbury Coll, Brookline, MA; FR; BA; Girl Scouts; RI Military Miniatures; NAUI; Beach/Park Clean-Ups; Media Tech/Film.

**TRIPP, KIMBERLY J,** Cornell Univ Statutory College, Ithaca, NY; SR; MS; Civitas 89; Orntatn Cnslr 90-; Exprmntl Theater 90; Deans Lst; BS; Wildlife Biology.

**TRIPP, REGINA M,** Peace Coll, Raleigh, NC; SO; AA; Chrstn Assoc 89-; Tutor 89-; Phi Theta Kappa; Sigma Delta Mu; SEEK Intern; Cambridge Foreign Study Pgm 90; Hnrs Acad Schlrshp 89-; Chld Psych/Spec Ed.

**TRISCHLER, RONI SUE,** Comm Coll Algny Co Algny Cmps, Pittsburgh, PA; FR; BA; PCCA Cmpndng Cntr 90; Math/Sci; Phrmcy.

**TRISLER, JOANNE M,** Univ Of Cincinnati, Cincinnati, OH; SR; BS; Kappa Delta Pi; Kappa Omcrn Nu; Grr Cnnti Ntrtn Cncl Vol 90-; Amer Diet Asc 89-; Cinnti Diet Asc 89-; BS Ntrtn Cert Actv Dir 80; Nutrition; Reg Dietitian.

**TRITT, CAROL L,** Union Univ, Jackson, TN; SO; BA; Psych/Soc Clb; Rutldg Hnry Hist Clb; Kappa Delta Schlrshp Chmn 90-; Deans List; Psych/Soc; Grad Schl.

**TRIVELLI, JANET B,** Kent St Univ Kent Cmps, Kent, OH; SR; BA; Coll Rpblcns 90-; NCTE 90-; Rdng/Wrtng Fstvl 90-; Engl/Brit Lit; Tch.

**TRIVETTE, SHARON KAY,** Mount Olive Coll, Mount Olive, NC; SR; BS; Mt Olive Clg Secr-Acad Affairs 89-; AS 89; Cmptr Info Syst.

**TROESCHEL, DENISE T,** Bowie St Univ, Bowie, MD; SR; BS; Psychlgy.

**TROIANO, ANGELA M,** Oh St Univ At Marion, Marion, OH; SR; BS; Alumn Cncl Pres 88-; Deans Stu Advsrn Cncl 90-; Swing Choir 88-90; Griffin Soc 90-; Vlybl Tm 88; Soc Sci Educ; Intnl Tchng Peace Corps.

**TROIANO, DANIEL T,** Le Moyne Coll, Syracuse, NY; SO; BA; Pol Sci; Law.

**TROIANO, LAURIE,** Seton Hall Univ, South Orange, NJ; SR; BSE; Kappa Delta Pi; Elem Educ/Engl; Tchng.

**TROLIO, GLORIA A,** Western New England Coll, Springfield, MA; JR; BA; Acctg Assc 90-; Dlt Mu Dlt; Intrnshp WWLP TV 22; Acctg; CPA.

**TROLLINGER, GILMER DON,** Memphis St Univ, Memphis, TN; JR; BBA; Phi Theta Kappa VP 89-90; Beta Gamma Sigma VP; Prgmmr Anlyst PC Dvlpmnt 89-; AS IS St Tech Inst 90; Cmptr Op Cert Comm Clg AF 84; Data Prcssng; Mgmt Info Sys.

**TROMBLEY, AMANDA L,** Endicott Coll, Beverly, MA; FR; Shipmts; Peer Tutor; Intrnshp Marken Corp; Adv.

**TROMBLEY, ANITA M,** Albertus Magnus Coll, New Haven, CT; JR; BA; Peer Cnslng Prog 90-; Intrnshp Yale Child Life Prog; Womens Bsktbl Tm Co Capt 88-; Child Pscychologist.

**TROMBLEY, DAVID V,** Clarkson Univ, Potsdam, NY; SR; Var Hockey Capt 89; BSC; Mktg; Prfsnl Athlete.

**TROMBLEY, PAUL E,** Christian Brothers Univ, Memphis, TN; JR; BS; SGA Sentr 89-90; Nwspr Edtr 88-90; Alpha Chi; Scty Jour Treas 88-; Tri Beta 89-; Scty Clgt Treas 88-; Gamma Theta Phi Senator 89-; Alpha Chi 91-; Biology; Medicine.

**TROMZA, RANDY D,** Southern Coll Of Tech, Marietta, GA; GD; BSMET; ASME Chrmn 89-; SME 89-; Deans List 90-; BSMET; Mech Eng.

**TRONCO, TONYA M,** Univ Of Sc At Columbia, Columbia, SC; FR.

**TRONCOSO, JACQUELINE M,** Fordham Univ, Bronx, NY; SR; Amer Mktng Assoc 89-; Mktng Scty 88-; Fordham Commty Svce Prog 88; Commty Student Assoc 87-; Finance Scty; Alpha Mu Alpha; Fordham Commty Svc Prog 88; Deans Schlrshp 87-; Natl Hispanic Assoc Schlrshp 87; NYS Regents Schlrshp 87-; Marketing.

**TRONCOSO, JOHANNIE M,** Antillian Adventist University, Mayaguez, PR; SO; BA; Clb Interac Pres 87; Koinonia UAA Pres 90-; Schlrshp Seven Day Advntst Assn 86-90; Flores De Prinavera CAD UNAD Pres 87-88; UAA Gymnstcs Tm 88-; AS Dom Advntst Univ 88; Nrsng; MBA Nrsng.

**TROPEANO, MONICA A,** Univ Of Miami, Coral Gables, FL; SO; Sociolgy; Law.

**TROSMAN, HERNAN G,** Univ Of Fl, Gainesville, FL; JR; BSNE; Tau Beta Pi VP; Gldn Key; Ntnl Clgt Engnrng Awd; Prsdnts Hnr Rl; Deans Lst; IM Sccr; AA Miami Dade Comm Clg 87; Nclr Sci; Engnrng.

**TROSPER, STEPHANIE R,** Univ Of Ky, Lexington, KY; JR; BA; Pre-Law Clb 90; Alpha Lambda Delta 89; Lances 90; Lambda Sigma Soc 89; Sigma Tau Delta 90; Soc Pro Legibus 90; Alpha Delta Pi 88-; Dns Lst 89-; Engl Educ; Sec Educ.

**TROSS, DEBORAH J,** D Youville Coll, Buffalo, NY; SR; BED; Educ Clb 89-90; Tchng Intrns 89-; Spec Olympcs-Bwlng; Hm Schl Assn 87-; Sub Tchng; AAS Villa Maria Coll 79; Spec Ed/Elem Ed; Tchng Spec Ed MED Admin.

**TROST, STACY C,** Eckerd Coll, St Petersburg, FL; SR; BA; Eckerd Coll Hon Pgm 88-; Alfred Mckethan Schlr 88-; Ford Apprentise Schlr 90-; Sociology Rsrch Asstntshp 90-; Cmptr Sci/Sociology; Law.

**TROTMAN, ALVIN L,** City Univ Of Ny Med Evers Coll, Brooklyn, NY; FR; BS; Cmptr Lab/Bsn Div Cmptr Lab Tech; Anl Awds Crmny Hst; Cr Dy Asst; Grdtn Ushr; Cmptr Aplctns; Cmptr Anlyst.

**TROTTER, DAVID B,** Univ Of Sc At Columbia, Columbia, SC; SO; BA; Hstry; Law.

**TROTTER JR, GEORGE L,** Patrick Henry Comm Coll, Martinsville, VA; JR; AAS; Pdmnt Shrne Clb 80-; Kzm Shrnrs 81-; Msns AFAM 81-; Thi Beta Kappa 90-; Natl Assn Of Life Undrwrtrs 79-; Mlln Dllr Rnd Tble 85-; VA Pres Cncl 85-; Natl Qlty Awrd 80-; Jycs 79-; Acctng Bus Admin; Ins Sls Crr.

**TROTTER, HEATHER L,** Milligan Coll, Milligan Clg, TN; SR; BED; Intntl Awareness Clb 89-90; Buffalo Ramblers 90-; Sigma Tau Delta 90-; All Amer Schlr Collegiate Awd; Elem Educ; Tchng.

**TROTTER, LAURA L,** Univ Of Sc At Columbia, Columbia, SC; JR; BS; AMA VP Prfsnl Pgms 90-; CEO 89-; Mktg Schlrs Pgm 90-; Golden Key 89-; Mntr Pgm 90-; Internship IBM 89-; Bsn/Mktg; Law Schl.

**TROTTER, TUREKA A,** Univ Of Tn At Martin, Martin, TN; FR; BA; Pre Law Clb 90-; Bus Admin; Law Corp.

**TROTTER JR, WENDEL T,** Tri County Tech Coll, Pendleton, SC; SR; AIE; Phi Theta Kappa; Alpha Zeta Beta 90-; Stdnt Of Yr 90-; Clb Tnns 87; Tstle Mgmt.

**TROTTIER, KIMIKO,** Newbury Coll, Brookline, MA; FR; Wllsly Wmn Bus Awd 87; Acdmc Achvmnt 90-; Deans Lst 90-; Mngd Imprtd Laces Unlmtd/Bkkpr 85-90; Clnry Arts; Open Own Rstrnt.

**TROTZ, GARTH A,** City Univ Of Ny Baruch Coll, New York, NY; SR; BA; Pol Scnc; Law.

**TROUBLEFIELD, KIMBERLY A,** Univ Of Sc At Columbia, Columbia, SC; SR; Alpha Delta Pi 88-; BA; Early Chldhd Ed; Tch.

**TROUT, CAROLYN E,** Fl St Univ, Tallahassee, FL; SO; BA; Phi Eta Sigma 90-; AA FL St; Cmmnctns; Advrtsng.**

**TROUT, CERISE D,** Central Va Comm Coll, Lynchburg, VA; SO; BS; SG Treas 90-; Phi Theta Kappa 90-; AA/S; Bus Admin; Acctg.**

**TROUT, KATHY SUE,** Marshall University, Huntington, WV; JR; BA; Acctng Clb 90-; WV CPA Assoc 90-; Gamma Beta Phi 87-; Acctng Internship; Acctng; CPA.

**TROUTMAN, MASAI M,** Ky St Univ, Frankfort, KY; SO; BA; Bktbl/Trck Capt 89-; Acad All Amer 89-90; All Amer Div II Trck/Fld NCAA 90-; Alpha Phi Alpha 90-; Cmptr Eng; Eng.

**TROUTMAN, SHERRY L,** Elizabethtown Coll, Elizabethtown, PA; FR; BS; Concert Bnd 90-; Orch 90-; Alpha Lambda Delta 90-; Math; Tchg.

**TROVATO, LARA L,** Middle Tn St Univ, Murfreesboro, TN; SO; BS; Spec Evnts Comm 89; Gamma Beta Phi Soc; Mass Comms; Radio/T V Brdcstng.

**TROVINGER JR, KENNETH P,** Westminster Coll, New Wilmington, PA; SO; BM; Pep Bnd/Jazz Bnd/Cncrt Bnd/Brass Qntet/Cncrt Choir/Hndbll Chr Bnd Pres/Drm Mjr 89-90; MENC Mbr/Res Lif Staff RA; Deans List 89-; Harriett Boozel Abbott Schlrshp 89-; Turner Schlrshp; Mus Educ/Comp; Teacher/Composer.

**TROWBRIDGE, DIANE L,** Juniata Coll, Huntingdon, PA; SO; BSW; Hon Soc Schlrshp Fr Candidate 90-; Soc Casewrkr Intern; Soc Wrk; Med Soc Wrk/Elderly.

**TROWBRIDGE, KRISTI D,** Roane St Comm Coll, Harriman, TN; SO; BA; Cmptr Sci; Pgmr.

**TROWELL, CYNTHIA C,** Anne Arundel Comm Coll, Arnold, MD; SO; BA; Flight Atte US Air; Child Psych.

**TROWER, DELLA MARIA,** Bethany Coll, Bethany, WV; JR; BA; Stdnts Free Entrprs Chr 89-; Soc Bus Stdnts 90-; Vars Bsktbl 88-; Phi Gamma Mu; Phi Mu Treas 89-; Acctg/Econ Tutr; Intrnshp Bluett/Bluett Acctg Firm 89-90; Deans Lst 90; Ntl Coll Mnrty Ldrshp Awd; IM 88-; Acctg/Econ/Mgmt.

**TROWT, JEFFREY A,** Southern Vt Coll, Bennington, VT; SR; BS; Stu Govt Pres 90-; Crmnl Justc Assc VP 90-; Ftbll Hcky Capt 90-F; Crmnl Jstc; Prv Scrty Mgt.

**TROXEL JR, CHARLES E,** Nova Univ, Ft Lauderdale, FL; GD; MBA; Alpha Chi 88-; Dir 88-; BS 88; Bus Admn; Exec Mngmnt.

**TROXLER, LINDA D,** Univ Of Tn At Martin, Martin, TN; SO; Scty Hnrs Semnr Stdnts; Hnrs Semnr Prgm; Scndry Ed Engl.

**TROY, MELINDA E,** Providence Coll, Providence, RI; JR; BA; JRW Fndrsng Com 90-; PC Res Bd 88-90; PC Apt Cmplx Cncl 90-; Psi Chi 90-; Cncl Excptnl Chldrn 88-; Pastoral Cncl 89-; Chld Psychlgst.

**TROY, TERESA ANN,** Univ Of Med & Dentistry Of Nj, Newark, NJ; GD; MPT Rutgers Univ 90; Cert 90; Physician Thrpy.

**TROYER, KRISTINA L,** Univ Of Sc At Columbia, Columbia, SC; SO; BAIS; Frst Bptst Chrch Cncl 89- Choir 90-; Dns Lst 90; USC Mrchng Bnd 89; Elem Ed; Tchng.

**TROYER, TERESA K,** Oh Wesleyan Univ, Delaware, OH; FR; BA; Proj Hope 90-; Cir K 90-; Phi Eta Sigma 90-; IM Vlybl 90-; Engl/Spnsh/Ed; Tchng/Prof.

**TRUB, KARIN GISELA,** City Univ Of Ny City Coll, New York, NY; JR; BA; Art.

**TRUBY, KATHRYN E,** Case Western Reserve Univ, Cleveland, OH; FR; BS; Chmbr Orchstra 90-; Symphnc Wnds 90-; Jdg Sci Olympiad; Pres Schlrshp 90-; Acdmc Schlrshp 90-; Chem Eng; Matrls Rsrch/Dvlpmnt.

**TRUCHIO, KIMBERLY A,** Radford Univ, Radford, VA; SR; BS; Soc Wrk Clb; Phi Alpha; Intrnshp Hd Strt Prog 89; Psychtrc Hosp Intrn; Soc Wrk.

**TRUDELL, ERIC K,** Univ Of Sc At Columbia, Columbia, SC; JR; BS; FMA VP 90-; USC Econs Soc 90-; Gamma Iota Sigma 90-; Gamma Beta Phi 90-; Golden Key 90-; Delta Tau Delta 87-88; Pr Lst 90-; Deans Lst 89-; Risk/Insurance Schlrshp; AS 90; Fin.

**TRUDGEON, KRISTA R,** Roberts Wesleyan Coll, Rochester, NY; FR; Choir 90-; Chpl Pianist; Cntmpry Mnstry Cncntrtng Yth Mnstry/Music.

**TRUDO, MICHELLE J,** Portland School Of Art, Portland, ME; SO; BA; Graphic Dsgn; Artist.

**TRUEAX, PERRY G,** Columbia Union Coll, Takoma Park, MD; SR; BS; Accntng Sprvsr IEEE Cmptr Soc 89-; Bsns Admnstrtns Accntng; CPA.

**TRUEBA, JANINE M,** Saint Thomas Univ, Miami, FL; SR; BA; Fair Haven; Deans List; Psych; Cnslng.

**TRUESDALE, JONATHAN D,** Johnson C Smith Univ, Charlotte, NC; SR; BA; Yng Rep Clb Prlmntrn 89-; Rtrct Clb; Pnhllnc Exec Brd Sec 90-; Chr 89; Kappa Alpha Psi Sec 89-; Lbrry Srvce Awrd 88; Ctznshp Awrd 87; Mt Ct Tm Rep 90; Pol Sci; Corp Law.

**TRUESDALE, MELANIE E,** Univ Of Sc At Columbia, Columbia, SC; FR; BA; PALS Peer Advsmnt 90-; ARETE 90-; Hubbad Nrsng Schlrshp 90-; Nrsng.

**TRUESDALE, WALLACE J,** Morehouse Coll, Atlanta, GA; JR; BA; Mnbrng Pgm 89-; Bsn Asc 89-; Acctng Clb 90-; Hnr Rl 90; Anct Free/Acptd Msns Wrd 90-; Acctng; Corp Law.

**TRUESDELL, KENNETH F,** Columbia Greene Comm Coll, Hudson, NY; SO; AS; BS SUNY Albany 76; Nrsng; RN.

**TRUGLIO, DONNA F,** Georgetown Univ, Washington, DC; FR; BA; Cmnty Action Coalition Yth Svcs 90-; Hist; Tch/Rsrch/Wrtng.

**TRUIT, RICHARD J,** Salisbury St Univ, Salisbury, MD; GD; BA; Psi Chi 89-; Made Deans Lst 88; Psychology.

**TRUITT, HEATHER R,** Bethany Coll, Bethany, WV; FR; BS; Beta Beta Beta; Amer Chem Soc; Vlybl; Blgy; Fmly Physcn.

**TRUITT, JAMES BROOKS,** Salisbury St Univ, Salisbury, MD; FR; BA; Phylsphcl Scty 90; Thtr Clb 90-; Rdio Clb; Cmps Frthnkrs 90; Phi Eta Sigma 90-; Engl; Tchng Lit.

**TRUITT, LINDA T,** Norfolk St Univ, Norfolk, VA; GD; CERT; BA Temple Univ Phil Pa 89; Erly Chldhd Edn/Cmmnctns; Tchng/Media Cmmnctn.

**TRUITT, LISA A,** Univ Of Nc At Greensboro, Greensboro, NC; SR; BS; Educ; Tchg.

**TRUJILLO, ANGELICA M,** Univ Of Miami, Coral Gables, FL; FR; BA; Gen Hnrs Prog; Stdnt Alumni Ambssdr; Gen Hnr Soc; Pre Law Soc; Hnrs Prog In Law; History; Law.

**TRUJILLO, FLOR MARIA,** Fl International Univ, Miami, FL; GD; EDD; Clincl Tchr Prog 88-; Grad Stdnt Assn VP 83; SCEC Sec 82; Alpha Delta Kappa 89-; Kappa Delta Pi 82-; Tchr Year 89-90; Tchg Excep Stdnts Emersn Elem; BS 83; MS Univ Miami 85; Educ/Currclum.

**TRUJILLO, PEDRO J,** Nova Univ, Ft Lauderdale, FL; GD; MBA; Eta Kappa Nu 76; Assoc Mgr Bell South Corp 77-91; BSEE City Clg N Y 77; Bus Admn; Bus Mgmt.

**TRULUCK, BARBARA ANN,** Central Fl Comm Coll, Ocala, FL; SO; BA; Phi Theta Kappa 90-; Fla Pub Rltns Assn 89-90; Intl Conf Shpng Ctrs 88-90; Mktg Dir 88-90; AA 90-; Ele Educ; Tch.

**TRUMAN, VALERIE A,** Univ Of Sc At Columbia, Columbia, SC; JR; BFA; Intern Mary Clowney Antqs Interiors Inc; Std Art; Intrr Dsgn.

**TRUMP III, MARSHALL C,** Univ Of Sc At Beaufort, Beaufort, SC; SO; BS; Kappa Sigma Wffrd Coll Pldge Edctr 81; Hltn Hd Islnd Rgby Ftbl Clb; Sgt US Mrne Corps 83-; Econs Accntg; Bus Mngrl.

**TRUNDY, JENNY S,** Wv Univ, Morgantown, WV; FR; BSW; Phi Sigma Pi; Socl Wrk.

**TRUNNELL, ASHLEY B,** Liberty Univ, Lynchburg, VA; JR; BS; Light Clb Chrstn Mission Eastenr Europe 90; Alpha Lambda Delta 90-; Psychlgy; Cnslng.

**TRUNZO, JOSEPH J,** Marywood Coll, Scranton, PA; SO; BS; Psych Clb 89-90; Psych; Licensed Clncl Psych.

**TRUONG, DUNG M,** Univ Of Sc At Columbia, Columbia, SC; FR; Amer Asian Assn; Math; Tchng.

**TRUSSELL, DEBORAH L,** Christopher Newport Coll, Newport News, VA; FR; BA; Pol Sci; Law.

**TRUSSELL, GINA M,** Univ Of Sc At Columbia, Columbia, SC; SR; BA; Carolina Alive 89-; SPJ; Alpha Chi Omega 88-; Deans List 89; Pres Hnr Roll 90; Deans List 90; Brdcast/Jrnlsm; Television Mngmnt.

**TRUSTMAN, ROBIN L,** Daytona Beach Comm Coll, Daytona Beach, FL; FR; AA; Cmmnctns; Radio TV.

**TRYBUS, SHELBY R,** Mount Aloysius Jr Coll, Cresson, PA; SO; BA; Karate 90-; Phi Theta Kappa 90-; AA; Psych.

**TRYFONOS, NATALIE L,** Newbury Coll, Brookline, MA; SR; ASSOC; Phi Theta Kappa; Fash Dsgn.

**TRYON, MARLA J,** Albertus Magnus Coll, New Haven, CT; SO; BA; Risk Admin Pirelle Grp; Humanities.

**TSAHALIS, MICHAEL,** City Univ Of Ny Med Evers Coll, Brooklyn, NY; FR; BS; Bus; Mktg.

**TSAI, CHIN KWO,** Wagner Coll, Staten Island, NY; JR; Intl Stdnt Assoc Pres 90-; RA 90-; Omicron Delta Kappa; Biology.

**TSAI, DORIS Y,** S U N Y At Binghamton, Binghamton, NY; JR; BA; Badminton Clb 89-; Asian Stdnt Union 88-; Mktng/Psychology; Bus Fld.

**TSAI, JULIE HSUEH-PING,** S U N Y At Buffalo, Buffalo, NY; SO; BS; Chns Stdnts Assoc VP; Asian Amer Stdnts Union; Deans List 90-; Delta Sigma Pi; IM Vlybl Tm 89-90; Bus Admin; Fin Anlysis MIS.

**TSAI, KUHN-SHEN,** Harvard Univ, Cambridge, MA; FR; BA; Dudley House Orchestra 90-; Asian Am Assn 90-; High Hon 90-; Phillips Brooks Hse Assn 90-; Rsrch Apprentice Biochem Lab Princeton Univ 90; Rsrch Asst Bio Lab; IM 90-; Bio; Med.

**TSAKONAS, JUDITH A,** Georgian Court Coll, Lakewood, NJ; JR; BS; Deans Lst 88-; Intl Brthrhd Crpntrs Jnrs Amrc 85-; Unn Crpntr Lcnsd Rl Est Agnt 86-; AAB 84; Bus.

**TSALIK, SVETLANA,** Smith Coll, Northampton, MA; JR; BA; MASSPIRG Chrwmn 90; Stu Gvt Clss Rep 89-90; Phlsphcl Soc Cofndr 90; Dean Lst 88; Grp Schlr 89; Legal Intern 88; Rdng Lssns 89-90; Phlsphy; Pblshng.

**TSANG, WUN,** S U N Y At Buffalo, Buffalo, NY; SR; BS; IEEE; Golden Key; Eta Kappa; Phi Eta Sigma; Chinese Christian Church; Ronald Mc Nair Prog Awrd; Tennis; Electrcl/Cmptr Engrng.

**TSARFATI, JONATHAN H,** Fl Atlantic Univ, Boca Raton, FL; SR; BBA; Intl Bus; Bus.**

**TSCHANZ, GINA L,** Tn Temple Univ, Chattanooga, TN; SO; Zinzinduf Soc 89-; IM Bsktbl/Trck Tm 90-; Ba; Brdcstng/Jrnlsm; News Anchor/Reporter.

**TSCHEBOTARJEW, JORGE,** Cumberland County Coll, Vineland, NJ; SO; BA; Cert Temple Univ 89; F Lang/Soc Stdies; Educ.

**TSCHOPP JR, BARRY L,** Embry Riddle Aeronautical Univ, Daytona Beach, FL; JR; BS; IM Ftbl Sftbl 88-; Priv Pilot Cert; Aerntcl Sci; Fly Prof.

**TSCHOPP, NATALIE J,** Marywood Coll, Scranton, PA; SR; BA; PRSSA 89-; Nwspr Ent Edtr 89-; DJ Coll Statn 87-88; Eastr Seal Soc Nrthestrn PA Mini Intrnshp/Sr Wrkshp 89-; Cmnctn Arts; Pblc Rltns.

**TSE, KWONG MING V,** Univ Of Ky, Lexington, KY; JR; BS; Hong Kong Stdnt Assn P 90-; Intrnl Stdnt Cncl; Acad Excell Schlrshp 89-90; Cmptr Sci; Eng.

**TSE, PATRICK C,** Ga Inst Of Tech At Atlanta, Atlanta, GA; FR; BS; Aero Engr.

**TSEGGAI, BEREKET,** Queens Coll, Charlotte, NC; FR; BA; Intrntnl Clb Sccr Bost; Sccr; Cmptr Sci; Engnrng.

**TSENG, HSIEN-KUEI,** Fl International Univ, Miami, FL; JR; Mech Engr.

**TSERBOULE-CERBULE, EDITE,** Columbus Coll Of Art & Design, Columbus, OH; FR; Rtl Advrtsng; Fshn Dsgn.

**TSIAMIS, ARTHUR I,** George Mason Univ, Fairfax, VA; JR; BS; Gldn Key; Alpha Chi; Coop Edacctng; Acct; CPA.

**TSIOKOS, COSTA,** Eckerd Coll, St Petersburg, FL; SO; BS; Pub Mgr 90-; ECAS 89-; Campus Activ Bd; Alumni Assn Schlr 89-; House V P Leg Cncl 89-90; Cmpgn Wrkr; IM 90-; Pol Sci.

**TSIOUTSIAS, DIANE A,** Norfolk St Univ, Norfolk, VA; SR; Cncrt Choir; Alpha Kappa Mu; MENC; SVEA; 4-H Sec 87-; Ldrs Assn Chr Plng Com; Clean Comm Commission Rgl Forum 90-; PTA; Lgl Sec Comp Oprtr; BA; Msc Ed; Tchr.

**TSOI, KENNEDY,** City Univ Of Ny City Coll, New York, NY; SO; BE; Hong Kong Club 90; Sci/Engr Stdnt Assoc VICE Chrmn; Golden Key 90; Electrcl Engr; Police Ofcr.

**TSOI, KIN PING,** Long Island Univ C W Post Cntr, Greenvale, NY; BA; Econ Soc 89-; Lab Asst Chem Dept 89-; Amer Econ Assoc; Amer Heart Assoc BLS Rescuer 88-; Econ/Biol/Chem; Med.

**TSOUKATOS, DEMITRA DIMITRIOU,** Albertus Magnus Coll, New Haven, CT; JR; BA; Comm Corder 88-89; Dept Chldrn Yth Svc; Psychlgy; Cnslng.

**TSUI, GLORIA,** Cooper Union, New York, NY; SR; BE; Instt Elctrncs Elctrcl Eng Scty 88-; IEEE Comp Scty 89-; Scty Wmn Eng 88-; Tau Beta Pi Crrspndg Sec 89-; Eta Kappa Nu 89-; Delta Gamm Aepsilon Schlstc Chrprsn; Elec Eng.

**TSUI, SAU MEI,** City Univ Of Ny Baruch Coll, New York, NY; JR; HKCEE St Pls Sch 86; Acctg; CPA.

**TSUI, YEUKPING JASMIN,** City Univ Of Ny Baruch Coll, New York, NY; JR; BBA; AIESEC Pres 90; Helpline 90; United Malaysian Std Assoc 89-; Dns Lst 89-; Gldn Key 90-; Prvost Schlrshp; Alfred Iacuzzi Prize; Intrnshp 90; S C Johnson/Son; Mrktg Mgmt.

**TSUKERNIK, TANYA,** Bunker Hill Comm Coll, Boston, MA; FR; BED; Engr.

**TSUNG, ERIC F,** Univ Of Rochester, Rochester, NY; SO; BS; Univ Symp Orch 89-; Comp Intrst Flr 90; Chem Engr; Engrng.

**TSUNODA, ANDREA R,** Univ Of Rochester, Rochester, NY; JR; BA; Chmbr Sngrs Treas 88-; Vcl Pnt 89-; Dorm Cncl Rep 88-89; Psychlgy; Rsrch/Educ.

**TSUTSUMI, NAOMI,** Oh Univ, Athens, OH; SO; Chem Engr; Envrmnt/Marine Engr.

**TU, HUY D,** Bunker Hill Comm Coll, Boston, MA; SO; AA; Phi Theta Kappa 90-; Tutoring; Dns Lst 89-; Math And Phycs; Eng.

**TU, JENNY T,** City Univ Of Ny Baruch Coll, New York, NY; SR; BA; Acctg Clb 90; Acctg.

**TU, YU-WEN,** City Univ Of Ny City Coll, New York, NY; SO; BS; Cmptr Sci; Prgmmr.

**TUASON, MIGUEL A,** George Mason Univ, Fairfax, VA; FR; BS; Busn Admin/Mktg; Theatre/Prodctn.

**TUBB, ANGIE R,** Itawamba Comm Coll, Fulton, MS; SO; Frnch Clb 90-; Phi Beta Lambda 90-; Sci.

**TUBB, JULIE D,** Middle Tn St Univ, Murfreesboro, TN; JR; BS; Gamma Beta Phi 89-; Kappa Delta Pi 89-; Spcl Edctn; Tchr.

**TUBBS II, HERBERT O,** Wesley Coll, Florence, MS; JR; BS; Class Pr 90-; Stdnt Cncl 88-89; Alpha Chi Omega Hon Soc 87-; Ministerial Union Tr 89-90; Missionary Prayer Bnd 88-90; Yth Pastor 90-; Deans Lst 89-90; Bsktbl Asst Capt 88-; Tchr.

**TUBBS, KIMBERLY S,** Oh Univ, Athens, OH; SO; BA; STYLE Pblcty Dir 90-; Deans Lst; YMCA Hd Lfgrd/Mgmt 86-; Fine Arts/Art Hstry; Art Hstrn-Gllry.

**TUBBS, SHAUN C,** Wilmington Coll, Wilmington, OH; FR; BS; SMA 90-; Vrsty Ltr 90-; Chrch Yth Grp VP 90-; Stdnt Envrnmnt 90-; Deans List 90-; Hon Schlrshp Grades 90-; Bsktbl Vrsty Ltr 90-; Sprts Medcn/Pre Phys Thpry; Sprts Phys Thrpst.

**TUBERO, DANIELLE,** Univ Of Fl, Gainesville, FL; SR; BA; Stdnt Alumni Assoc 89; Bsnss Admin Peer Cnslr; Celebration Assist Dir Spec Evnts; Deans Lst 90; Delta Sigma Pi Spec Chr 89; JC Penney Mngmnt Trng Intrnshp 90; Jr Achievemnt Bsnss Basics Tchr 89; Bsnss Admin/Mrktng.

**TUBESING, A PAGE,** Northern Ky Univ, Highland Hts, KY; JR; BA; Cmnctns; Law.

**TUCCI, JOHN A,** S U N Y Coll Of Tech At Frmgdl, Farmingdale, NY; SO; BA; Penn State Barbell Clb 89-90; Pi Lambda Phi 89-; Lib Arts Achvmnt 90; IM Vllybl/Wrstlng/Sftbl 89-90; Pol Sci; Pol.

**TUCCI, NICHOLAS A,** Trenton St Coll, Trenton, NJ; FR; BS; TSC Alumni Schlrshp; Garden State Schlr Awd; Law/Jstc; Law Enfrcmnt.

**TUCCILLO, ANTHONY J,** Bridgeport Engr Inst, Fairfield, CT; BSEE; ISC Bunker Ramo 85-; Engr.

**TUCK, DERRICK D,** Gadsden St Comm Coll, Gadsden, AL; FR; BS; Math; Engrg.

**TUCK, MICHAEL S,** Univ Of Tn At Martin, Martin, TN; SR; BFA; Cmmrcl Artst.

**TUCKE, HEATHER C,** Mount Union Coll, Alliance, OH; FR; Mrchng Bnd 90-; Wind Ensmbl 90-; Brass Choir 90-; Kappa Kappa Psi Sec 90-; Aultman Hosp Co-Op 90-; Med/Bio.

**TUCKER, ANGELA K,** Memphis St Univ, Memphis, TN; JR; BSN; Pi Kappa Alpha; Alpha Delta Pi Exec Schrlshp Chrmn 89-; Ron Mc Donald Hs Vol; Womens Panhellenic Cncl Clb 90-; Nursing.

**TUCKER, ANN B,** Univ Of Nc At Greensboro, Greensboro, NC; GD; BS; Ele Educ; Tch Pub Sch.

**TUCKER, BONNIE C,** Univ Of Miami, Coral Gables, FL; SO; BS; Rho Rho Rho Treas; Alpha Lambda Delta 89-90; Summer Rsrch Flwshp Rosenstiel Schl Marine/Atmsphrc Sci; Marine Bio; Marine Bio/Rsrch.

**TUCKER, BRIAN W,** Coll Of William & Mary, Williamsburg, VA; FR; BS; Yng Amer For Freedom 90-; Rpblcns 90-; Math; Engr.

**TUCKER, CAROL J,** Univ Of Al, Tuscaloosa, AL; FR; BS; Mrchg Bnd 90-; Pep Bnd 90-; Phi Eta Sigma; Alpha Lambda Delta; Hnrs Pgm; Outstndg Chem Stdnt Awd; Aerosp Engr.

**TUCKER, CARRIE ANN,** Brewer St Jr Coll, Fayette, AL; FR; Nrsng.

**TUCKER, CHANDRA M,** Alcorn St Univ, Lorman, MS; JR; BSN; Alpha Phi Alpha Chpln 89-90; Blck Stdnt Org; Nrsng; RN.

**TUCKER, CHARLES K,** David Lipscomb Univ, Nashville, TN; SR; BA; French Clb 87-; Univ Dns Lst; Frnch; Busn.**

**TUCKER, CHESTER T,** Marshall University, Huntington, WV; SR; BA; MUSAC 88-; Gamma Beta Phi 89-; Educ; Tchr.**

**TUCKER, CYNTHIA H,** Richard Bland Coll, Petersburg, VA; FR; Bus Admin.

**TUCKER, DAVID L,** Univ Of Sc At Columbia, Columbia, SC; SO; BS; Dens List; US Navy E-6 90; Jaycees; Mecn Eng.

**TUCKER, GREGORY A,** Southern Coll Of Tech, Marietta, GA; SO; Elec/Cmptr; Engrng.

**TUCKER, JAMES E,** Hillsborough Comm Coll, Tampa, FL; FR; BA; Acctg; CPA.

**TUCKER, JAMES E,** Volunteer St Comm Coll, Gallatin, TN; SO; AA; US Air Frce 82-90; Phy Thrpy Asst.

**TUCKER, JANET L,** Kent St Univ Trumbull Cmps, Warren, OH; SO; BSN; Amer Red Cross SFAMM CPR Instrctr 86-; Nrsng; Psyc/Mntl Hlth Nrsng.

**TUCKER, JILL A,** Ashland Comm Coll, Ashland, KY; SO; AS; Res Ther Pgm.

**TUCKER, JODEE TEHANI,** Univ Of North Fl, Jacksonville, FL; JR; BS; Psi Chi 90-; Golden Key; Delta Sigma Pi VP Pldg Clss; Alpha Chi Omega VP 80-83; Deans Core/Alumni Affrs 90-; Big Str Org/Fres VP 81-82; Natl Assc Lfe Undrwrtrs 88-; Notary Pblc FL 86-; Mrktng Coord; Lic Agnt Dept Of Ins FL 87; Ind Psych/Bus Admin/Spanish; Human Rsrc Mgmnt.

**TUCKER, KENNETH M,** Coppin St Coll, Baltimore, MD; SR; BS; Psych Clb 90-; AA Essex Comm Coll 87-89; Psych; Clncl Psych.

**TUCKER, LAURIE A,** Univ Of Sc At Columbia, Columbia, SC; FR; Bus Admin; Acctg.

**TUCKER, LESLIE A,** Life Coll, Marietta, GA; SR; DC; BS High Pt Clg 85; Chiropractic.

**TUCKER JR, LEWIS L,** Va St Univ, Petersburg, VA; SO; BA; Hnrs Coll Bd Schlr 90-; So Reg Hnrs Conf 90-; Phi Theta Kappa 89-90; Bd Of Visitors Bd Schlr 90-; First Bd Schlr; Elect Engrng; Electronic Design.

**TUCKER, LISA A,** Univ Of Nc At Greensboro, Greensboro, NC; JR; BSN; Bapt Stdnt Union 88-; Assn Nrsng Stdnts 90-; Dns Lst 89-90; Natl Coll Nrsg Awds 90; IM Athl 89-; Nrsng.

**TUCKER, MICHAEL J,** Fl St Univ, Tallahassee, FL; SR; BA; AMA 90-; Phi Theta Kappa 89; AA St Petersburg Jr Clg 89; Mktg.

**TUCKER, MICHELLE L,** Columbus Coll Of Art & Design, Columbus, OH; SO; BA; Fshn Dsgn/Rtl Adv; Fshn Dsgnr/Merch.

**TUCKER, MONICA L,** Christian Brothers Univ, Memphis, TN; FR; Zeta Tau Alpha Schlstc Achvmnt; Intrn First TN Bnk 90-; Telecmctns; Info Syst Mngmnt.

**TUCKER, NESSA T,** Bethel Coll, Mckenzie, TN; FR; MBA; Vlybl 90-; Waitress/Bartender; Bsn Adm; CEO.

**TUCKER, PAMELA T,** Univ Of Southern Ms, Hattiesburg, MS; FR; MBA; Bus Admn/Bnkng Fnnc.

**TUCKER, PHILIP F,** Fl A & M Univ, Tallahassee, FL; GD; Gospel Choir 85-87; Stdnt Amer Pharm Assn 86-88; Keynote Piano Guild 86-87; Kappa Psi VP 88-89/Chapln 86-89; Ldrshp Awrd Pr 88; Robert S Scarbough Schlrshp; Deans Lst 87-90; BS; Pharm.

**TUCKER, RITA J,** Oh St Univ At Newark, Newark, OH; JR; BA; Deans Lst; Educ; Tchr.

**TUCKER, RODNEY S,** Fayetteville St Univ, Fayetteville, NC; JR; BA; Yng Dmcrts Clb 88-89; Arnld Air Soc 88-89; Res Asst 89-90; Kappa Delta Pi 90-; Alpha Kappa Mu 91; Geography; City/Rgnl Plnnr.

**TUCKER, SARA T,** Greenville Tech Coll, Greenville, SC; SO; BA; Acctg.**

**TUCKER, STERLING K,** Radford Univ, Radford, VA; SR; BS; Crmnl Juste Clb 90-; Deans Lst 89-; Summa Cum Laude; Crmnl Juste; Law Enfrcmnt.

**TUCKER, SUSAN E,** Union Coll, Barbourville, KY; JR; BA; Phi Theta Kappa 88; Hnrs; Assoc Arts/Hmnties Smrst Cmmnty Clg; Elem Ed.

**TUCKER, TAMARA L,** Fl A & M Univ, Tallahassee, FL; SO; BA; Pres Schlrs 89-; Alpha Phi Omega Pblc Rltns 90-; NAFEO Exchng Stdnt Awd/Schlrshp; Jrnlsm; Law.

**TUCKER, TANJI L,** Fl A & M Univ, Tallahassee, FL; FR; BS; NAACP 90-; Hmn Res Inc SBI 90-; Dns Lst 90-; Bsns Admn; Mgmt.

**TUCKER, TRACY L,** S U N Y Coll Of Tech At Alfred, Alfred, NY; SO; AAS; Accntng Clb 89-; Phi Theta Kappa Treas 90-; Sigma Tau Epsilon 89-90; Dns Lst 89-; William Mckensie Schlrshp 90-; Accntng; CPA BA.

**TUCKER, WARREN W,** Va St Univ, Petersburg, VA; JR; BED; Agri Sci Org Exec 90-; Iota Phi Theta; All Amer Wrster 90-; Most Outstndg/Dedicated Wrstlr 90-; Pres Lst 90-; Agri; Tchr.

**TUCKER II, WILLIAM J,** S U N Y Coll Of Tech At Alfred, Alfred, NY; SO; BS; CSM 90-; Math/Sci; Civil Eng.

**TUCKWILLER, JACK D,** Liberty Univ, Lynchburg, VA; JR; BS; Ythgst Clb 89-90; Alpha Lambda Delta 89-; Pryr Ldr 89-; Acctng; CPA.

**TUDOR, CHADWICK L,** Radford Univ, Radford, VA; JR; Outdrs 90-; Scuba Clb Pres 90-; Kappa Delta Rho Scl Chr 89-; Recrtn/Leisr Srvcs; Prks/Rec.

**TUELL, WILLIAM J,** Va Commonwealth Univ, Richmond, VA; SR; BS; RN Coor; AAS Wytheville Cmnty Clg 86; Cert Wytheville Cmnty Clg 81; Nrsg; Nrsg Admin.

**TUFANO, SYLVIA H,** Cornell Univ Statutory College, Ithaca, NY; FR; BS; Orientation Cnslr; Biology; Medicine.

**TUFFY, CHRISTINE M,** Providence Coll, Providence, RI; FR; BA; Ski Clb; IM Spts; Hstry; Nutrntst.

**TUFINO, ROGACIANO,** City Univ Of Ny City Coll, New York, NY; SO; BS; Taekown-Do Clb 90-; Cert Achvmnt 90-; Eng; E E.

**TUFTS, DONNA L,** Hudson Valley Comm Coll, Troy, NY; FR; RN; LPN Boces 81; Nrsng.

**TUIJNMAN, KAREN,** City Univ Of Ny City Coll, New York, NY; JR; BFA; Frnds Music 90-; Sy Peck Awrd 90; Victor Herbert Schlrshp Awrd; Music/Piano.

**TUK, KATHERINE L,** Marshall University, Huntington, WV; JR; BS; Gamma Beta Phi 88-; Kappa Omicron Nu 89-; Dietcs; Reg Dietcn.

**TULADHAR, SANJAY R,** Oh Wesleyan Univ, Delaware, OH; SR; BA; Hrzns Intl 88-; Omicron Delta Epsilon Exec Brd 89-; Sigma Pi Sigma 89-; Fclty Schlr; Oprtn Entrprs Amrcn Mgmt Assoc 89; Eng.

**TULL, JEFFREY D,** Christian Brothers Univ, Memphis, TN; JR; BA; Natl Assoc Of Acctnts; Alpha Chi Treas 90-; Pi Kappa Phi Treas 88-89; Natl Bus Merit Award; Ims; Acctng.

**TULPPO, TIMOTHY J,** Univ Of Tn At Martin, Martin, TN; JR; BA; Pre-Physcl Thrpy Clb 89-; Mu Epsilon Delta Sgt Arms 88-; Deans Lst 88-; Sigma Alpha Epsilon Comm Serv Chrmn 89-; Blgy; Pre-Physcl Thrpy.

**TUMARKIN, DANIEL P,** Univ Of Fl, Gainesville, FL; JR; BCHE; Ldrshp 87-88; Asst Parade Mrshl 88; Intrfrat Cncl Rep 88-89; Amer Inst Chem Engrs Corres Sec 90-; Alpha Epsilon Pi Chrmn Ltl Sr Prog 89; Dns Lst; Smmr Intrnshp Rhone-Poulenc; AA; Chem Engr.

**TUMBLESON, GREGORY L,** Oh Univ, Athens, OH; SR; BA; Reach Out 89-; Eta Kappa Nu 89-; Tau Beta Pi 89-; Alpha Lambda Delta 88-89; Elect Eng Awrd 90; IM Bsktbl Sftbl 88-; Elect Eng; Data Systms Eng.

**TUMBLESON, STEVE N,** Univ Of Cincinnati, Cincinnati, OH; JR; BMUSI; Ohio Clgte Music Edctrs Assn 88; Clg Tribunal Stdnt Repr 88; Phi Mu Alpha Hstrn 89; Dir Music/1st Bapt Chrch Amelia 89; 100 Div Army Reserve Bnd Spec 87-90; Music Educ; Tchng.

**TUMBLIN, LEONA S,** Fl St Univ, Tallahassee, FL; JR; BS; AA Pensacola Jr Clg 89; Crmnlgy; Crmnl Jstc.

**TUMMINIA, JULIE M,** Johnson St Coll, Johnson, VT; SR; BS; Lit Soc Sec 88-89; Nwspr 87-88; Wrtng Ctr Tr 89; Mgmt Intrnshp 90; Scr 87; Mgmt Info Systms; Cmptr Prgmr.

**TUMMLER, MARY L,** Univ Of Cincinnati, Cincinnati, OH; SO; BA; Spcl Ed; Tchg.

**TUMMOND, ANN B,** Univ Of North Fl, Jacksonville, FL; SR; BS; Phn Thn Rep; Phi Kappa Phi; Amrcn Lng Assoc Schlrsp; Otstndng Schlr Awrd Coll Hlth; Prfssnl Assoc; ASCP Rgstrd; Mdcl Tchnlgst; AS FL Cmmnty Coll 73; Hlth Sci; Wrk Grad Schl UNF.**

**TUNCA, DENIZ,** City Univ Of Ny Baruch Coll, New York, NY; GD; Soc Hmn Rsrc Mgt Pblc Rltns 89-90; Rtl Trade Soc 90; Dean Provosts Endwmnt Awd 89-90; Deans List 87-; BBA; Hmn Rsrc Mgt; Strtgc Plng.

**TUNG, CHRISTOPHER,** Oh Wesleyan Univ, Delaware, OH; SR; BA; Pres Clb Treas 87-89; Crs Cltrl Prog Cmtee 88-89; Illustr Pres Xmas Card; Phi Beta Kappa; Phi Eta Sigma 87-88; Omicron Delta Epsilon Pres 89; Mrtr Bd Sec 90-; Phi Soc Treas 88-89; Habitat Humty 88-90; Intrn Career Serv 90-; Econ Stdnt Bd; Econ; Bus.

**TUNG, SUSANNA K,** Radford Univ, Radford, VA; JR; BBA; Stdnt Govt Assoc Intrntl Stdnt Repr 90-; Asian Assoc Sec 90-; Internatl Wk Fd Cmte Chrprsn; Dns Lst 90-; Acctg/Info Systms.

**TUNG, TIMRA L,** The Kings Coll, Briarclf Mnr, NY; SR; BS; Sndy Schl Tchr 87-90; Soup Ktchn 88-90; Mc Auleys Wtr St Mission 85-87; Deans List; Summa Cum Laude; Wght Lftng Clb 88-89; Elem Ed.

**TUNING, MICHAEL J,** Savannah Coll Of Art & Design, Savannah, GA; SR; BFA; Fine Art/Photog; Photo-Imaging.

**TUNNELL, PAMELA W,** Ny Chiropractic Coll, Glen Head, NY; GD; DC; Phi Chi Omega; Pi Mu Epsilon 83; Pi Delta Phi 83; Amer Chiropractic Assn; Intl Chiropractors Assn; CT Chiropractic Assn; NY State Chiropractic Assn; Bristol-Myers Squibb Co/Pharm Rsrch/Dvlpmnt Div 84-87; BS Cornell Univ 83; Chiropractic; Rsrch.

**TUNON DE GRACIA, TANIA H,** Univ Politecnica De Pr, Hato Rey, PR; FR; BA; Vlybl Tm 86-87; Ch Wrk Fmlys Cntry Side Outside Panama; Indstrl Eng.

**TUNSTALL-EVANS, GIANNELI,** Vance Granville Comm Coll, Henderson, NC; CERIF; Ideal Club Pres; Friends Blk Children Org 84; NC Assoc Friends Blk Children Secty; Cosmetology.

**TUONG, PHUONG K,** Newbury Coll, Brookline, MA; SO; AS; AS; Fashin Dsgn; Fashion Dsgnr.

**TUONO, DONNA C,** Manor Jr Coll, Jenkintown, PA; SO; MBA; SUN 89-90; Joseph/Rose Wawriw Schlrshp 89-; Cert Excel 89-; Cert Clncl Prof 89-; Sci; Pthlgst Assist.

**TUPIS, LAURIE A,** Daemen Coll, Amherst, NY; JR; BA; Ishin-Ryu Karate Fdrtn Green Belt 85-88; Deans List 90; Intrn Cngrsmn Bill Paxon 90; Lgl Intrn Thomas Brinkworth 90; Pre Law/Pblc Rltns; Law.

**TURAN, BELINDA D,** Ms Gulf Coast Comm Coll, Perkinston, MS; FR; BA; Hnrs Prog 90-; Phi Theta Kappa 90-; Acctg; CPA.

**TURANO, DOROTHY C,** Marywood Coll, Scranton, PA; SO; BED; Elem Educ.

**TURANO, KELLI L,** Southeastern Ma Univ, N Dartmouth, MA; JR; BSN; Natl Stdnt Nurs Assn 89-; Sigma Theta Tau; Nurs Intrn 89-91; Hon Prog 88-91; Nurs; N Ped Nurs.

**TURBERVILLE, TRACY J,** Univ Of Al At Huntsville, Huntsville, AL; SR; BSIE; Amer Inst Indstrl Eng Treas 89-; Tau Beata Pi 90-; Tri Cities Grls Cotln Clb 87-90; Stdnt Eng Yr; Cand Alabama Soc Prof Eng Stdnt Eng Of Yr; Vrsty Tns Tm; Eng.

**TURCOTTE, LEAH E,** Ms St Univ, Miss State, MS; JR; Zeta Tau Alpha 88-.

**TUREK, KARLA J,** Columbia Greene Comm Coll, Hudson, NY; SO; BA; Chr 90-; Deans Lst 90; Sclgy; Scl Wrkr Gdnc.

**TURENNE, GILBERT,** City Univ Of Ny Baruch Coll, New York, NY; SR; MBA; Haitian Cltrl Soc; Clara Barton Mltcltrl Soc Coord; Alpha/Sigma/Delta 90-; Acctg Soc; Acctg; CPA/INTERNATL Bsn Law.

**TURGEON, RANDY S,** Univ Of Nh Plymouth St Coll, Plymouth, NH; SO; BA; Pres Lst 90; Cmptr Sci; Prgrmmg/Softwr.

**TURIANO-FINELLI, TERESSA LYNN L,** Fl International Univ, Miami, FL; SR; Natl Cncl For Social Studies 90-; Natl Geographic Soc 88-; 4-H Club 90-; BACUS; Ft Lauderdale Parks & Rec Dept; AA Broward Cmnty Clge 88; Social Studies; Education Recreation.

**TURK, ANTHONY J,** Al St Univ, Montgomery, AL; SO; Phi Eta Sigma 90-; 1st Plc Gladys Norris Piano Fstvl.

**TURK, KARI L,** Milligan Coll, Milligan Clg, TN; JR; BA; Fstvl One Act Plays 89-; Chldrns Theatre; OEDIPUS Under Milk Wood 89-; Deans Lst 89-; Alpha Psi Omega 90-; Communications.

**TURK, MARCUS T,** Morehouse Coll, Atlanta, GA; JR; BA; MBA 90-; NAACP 88-; Frncs/Debate Tm 88; Bnkg/Fin; Corp.

**TURK, MARK L,** Snead St Jr Coll, Boaz, AL; SO; BS; Phi Theta Kappa 90-; IM Bsktbl; Bio; Optmtry.

**TURK, MARY L,** Bloomfield Coll, Bloomfield, NJ; SO; Bus Mgmt; Edctnl Admn.

**TURK, THOMAS M T,** Va Commonwealth Univ, Richmond, VA; GD; MD; St Georges Stdnt Cancer Soc Pres 89-90; Alpha Omega Alpha; A H Robbins Schlrshp; Sidney B Barham Schlrshp; BS WA & Lee Univ 84; MS 88; Medicine.

**TURKAL, VICTORIA M,** Univ Of Akron, Akron, OH; SR; BS; NAA 89-; Alpha Sigma Lambda 89-; Magna Cum Laude; Med Asst 76-89; Acctg; CPA.

**TURKETT, ALISON L,** Univ Of Sc At Columbia, Columbia, SC; FR; BA; Crln Prgm Unn 90-; Phi Eta Sigma 90-; Phrmcy.

**TURKNETT, RUSSELL S,** Valdosta St Coll, Valdosta, GA; JR; BA; Stdnt Almni Assoc Actvies Chrmn 89-; Soc Intl Stdnts 89-90; Natl Mdl UN 90-; Phi Kappa Phi; Alpha Chi; Sigma Alpha Chi 90-; Alpha Lambda Delta 88-; Otstndng Clg Stdt Amer 88-; Mrchng Bnd 88-90; Cncrt Bnd 90; Sch Papr 90; Frch Awd; Frnch; Intl Publ Rel.

**TURLEY, DORIS A,** Gadsden St Comm Coll, Gadsden, AL; SO; BED; Baptist Cmps Ministries Comm Chrprsn 90-; A Capella Choir 89-; Band 89-; Music Educ; Music Theory Tchng.**

**TURLEY, NANCY J,** Marshall University, Huntington, WV; SO; BA; Phi Eta Sigma 90; Acctg; Accnt/CPA.

**TURMEL, TAMI A,** Teikyo Post Univ, Waterbury, CT; SR; AS Briarwood Clg 88; Acctng.

**TURNALI, M KAAN,** Widener Univ, Chester, PA; FR; BS; Widener Ldrshp Inst 90-; Modern Lang Cl; Hon Prog/Genl Ed; Schol/Mgmnt Hon Prog; Deans List 90-; Ambassador; RA; Undergrad Asst/Schl/Mgmnt; Soccer 90-; Pres Of Cls 1994; Natl Frshmn Scholastic Hnr Soc; Mngmnt; Fince.

**TURNBOW, FRANCES S,** Middle Tn St Univ, Murfreesboro, TN; SO; BA; Spcl Events Com 90-; Stdt Orientation 90-; Phi Mu Delta; Chi Omega Chptr Crspndc/Sec 90-; Vlntr Wrk Home Hlth 90-; There Care Cntr 90-; Sci; Physical Therapy.**

**TURNBULL, BETH A,** Portland School Of Art, Portland, ME; SR; BFA; BFA Portland Schl Of Art; Art.

**TURNBULL, THOMAS ANDREW,** Marshall University, Huntington, WV; JR; BA; Produce Clrk 85-; Mktg; Corp Adv.

**TURNER, ALTHEA L,** Radford Univ, Radford, VA; FR; BA; Fndtn Schlrshp 90-; P Douglas Tchr Schlrshp; Elem Ed; Tchng.

**TURNER, BOBBIE J,** Al A & M Univ, Normal, AL; SO; BS; Mrchng Bnd Asstnt Sect Ldr; Academic Awrd; Attendant Mass Buchanan Hall; Sclgy; Criminal Justice Law.

**TURNER, BONNIE E,** Univ Of Pittsburgh, Pittsburgh, PA; SO; BS; Ofc Mgr-Edtrs Aide Inc 90-; Indstrl Engr.

**TURNER, CAREY A,** Univ Of Ky, Lexington, KY; JR; BS; Kappa Delta; Nurs; RN.

**TURNER, CAROL R,** Va Commonwealth Univ, Richmond, VA; JR; BA; Golden Key; Pres Schlrshp In Internatl Educ; Pol Sci; Clg Lvl Tchng.

**TURNER, CAROLYN L,** Mary Holmes Coll, West Point, MS; FR; Bus Admin; Law.

**TURNER, CHARLES ASHLEY,** Middle Ga Coll, Cochran, GA; FR; BAS; Harris Hall Dorty VP 90-; Engrg Club 90-; Gamma Beta Phi 90-; IM Ftbl/Bskbl/Sftbl; Engrg; Industrial Engrg.

**TURNER, CHARLETTE V,** Pellissippi St Tech Comm Coll, Knoxville, TN; SO; AS; Cllgt Secretaries Intl Pres 90-; Phi Theta Kappa; Vision Vol Ntwrk 90-; Info Syst Tchnlgy; Ofc Mgr.

**TURNER, CHRISTOPHER S,** Unity Coll, Unity, ME; FR; BA; Wldng Cert EMTC 89; Cnsrvtn Law Enfrcmnt.

**TURNER, CLARICE J,** Salem-Teikyo Univ, Salem, WV; JR; BS; Stdnt Cndct Com; Alpha Eto Rho Sec 90; Natl Mnrty Ldrs Awrd; IM Sftbl 90; Eng Tech.

**TURNER, DAPHNE L,** Univ Of South Al, Mobile, AL; SO; BS; Hon Soc 89-90; Deans Lst 89; Ele Eductr.

**TURNER, DAVID ALAN,** Univ Of Ky, Lexington, KY; SR; Eng; Mining Eng.

**TURNER, DAVID J,** Oh St Univ, Columbus, OH; SR; BS; Rsdnc Halls Advsry Cncl VP 88-90; Phi Eta Sigma 87-; Alpha Lambda Delta 87-; Gldn Key 90-; Natl Rsdnc Hall 90-; Artsand Sci Awd 90; Mthmtcs; Economics.

**TURNER, DIANE D,** Old Dominion Univ, Norfolk, VA; JR; BS; Beta Gamma Sigma; Alph Chi; Phi Kappa Phi; Beta Alpha Psi; Accntng; CPA.

**TURNER, DONNA J,** Nc Agri & Tech St Univ, Greensboro, NC; SO; BED; Guilfrd Co Assoc Tchr Asst Schlrshp 89; NE Ath Assoc Chrldng Adv 83; Asst Sccr Coach; PTA; PTSA; Ath Bstrs; Clsfd Rep Madsn Elem Sch 88-89; Exec Brd GCATA Sec 88-; NCAE Spprt Stf; NCATA 88-; GCATA 85-; Tchr Asst; Elem Educ; Admn.

**TURNER, ELIZABETH A,** Indiana Univ Of Pa, Indiana, PA; SR; Engl Clb; PCTE; NCTE; Cncrt Dnc Co 88-; Deans Lst 89-; Engl Educ.**

**TURNER, GLORIA,** City Univ Of Ny Baruch Coll, New York, NY; SO; BBA; CPS Inst Prof Sec 86; Acctg; Law.

**TURNER, GWENDOLYN K,** Va Commonwealth Univ, Richmond, VA; SO; BA; Govnr Mrhd Schl Blnd 89-90; Hmls Prjct 90-; Chrch Nrsry; Clgt Schl Asst Cnslr; Psy/Educ; Tch ME.

**TURNER, HALEY J,** Memphis St Univ, Memphis, TN; SR; BA; Fshn Bd VP 87-; Pub Rltn Stdnt Soc Amer Cnvntn Hostess Coord 90-; Gamma Beta Phi 89-; Jrnlsm Hnr Soc 90-; Sigma Alpha Epsilon Ltl Sr 87-; Jrnlsm; Advtsng.

**TURNER, JACINTA B,** Alcorn St Univ, Lorman, MS; FR; BA; Music/Piano.

**TURNER, JAMES BRENT,** Bellarmine Coll, Louisville, KY; JR; BA; Acctg Assn 90-; IM Bsktbl; AAA Awd 89; Vrsty Bsbl 88-90; Acctg.

**TURNER, JAMES C,** Univ Of Akron, Akron, OH; SO; BSEE; IEEE; IM 89-; Elec Engr.

**TURNER JR, JAMES C,** Univ Of Southern Ms, Hattiesburg, MS; SR; BA; Guitar Ensemble 87-; Jcksn Clsscl Guitar Soc; Music Tchrs Natl Assn; Young Artist Awd 90; Guitar Comp 1st Pl; Guitar Perf Assist Masters; Music Educ; Tchng.

**TURNER, JAMIE A,** George Mason Univ, Fairfax, VA; SR; Cvc Assn 87-; BS; Bsns Mngmnt.

**TURNER, JANET ANN M,** Radford Univ, Radford, VA; JR; Thi Beta Lambda 90-; Alpha Kappa Alpha 90-; Deans Lst 90-; Bus Admn/Educ; Hosp Admnstr.

**TURNER, JANET C,** Univ Of North Fl, Jacksonville, FL; JR; BA; Golden Key; AA Fl Cmmnty Clg 90; Engl; Ed.

**TURNER, JEFFREY K,** Tougaloo Coll, Tougaloo, MS; FR; BA; Outstdng Achvmnt; Ecnmcs Bsn.

**TURNER, JENNIFER M,** Elms Coll, Chicopee, MA; SO; Stdnt Actvts Com 90-; Rsdnt Cncl 90-; Stdnt Ambssdr 89-90; Cmps Mnstry 90-; Eqstrn 89-90; Engl/Elem Ed; Educ.

**TURNER, JENNIFER M,** Univ Of Southern Ms, Hattiesburg, MS; SR; BS; Athltc Trnr Sprts Med Assn; Eagle Cnnctn Rcrtmnt Grp; Stdnt Alumni Assn; Phi Kappa Phi; Phi Delta Rho; Gldn Key; Omicron Delta Kappa; Gamma Beta Phi; Ntnl SE MS Athltc Trnrs Assn; Delta Delta Delta Tridnt Crrspndnt PR; Sprts Med; Athltc Trnr Physcl Thrpst.

**TURNER, JEREMY J,** Marshall University, Huntington, WV; SO; BA; Cnslng Rhblttn; Cnslng.

**TURNER, JOHN BRYAN,** Ashland Comm Coll, Ashland, KY; JR; BA; Transylvanian Pre Med Assoc Treas; Physics Club; Transylites Comm Ser Grp; Tennis Team; Chemistry/Biology; Medicine/Physician.

**TURNER, JONATHAN L,** Tomlinson Coll, Cleveland, TN; SO; BED; Chorale 89-; Phi Theta Kappa 90-; Bsbl 90; Phys Educ; Sec Schl Tchr.

**TURNER, JONI E,** Univ Of Cin R Walters Coll, Blue Ash, OH; SO; BA; Stdnt Court Justice; Tutor; Mcmicken School Of Honor; Natl Hnr Soc; Pres Hnr Soc; Crises Cnslr Court Advcte; Wmn Hlpng Wmn; Crises Cnslng Cert; Engl; Law.

**TURNER, JUSTICA LAKISHA,** Al St Univ, Montgomery, AL; JR; BA; Lambda Alpha Epsilon 90-; NAACP 88-; US Achvmnt Acad Clgte 88; Crmnl Jstc; Law.

**TURNER, JUSTIN T,** Tougaloo Coll, Tougaloo, MS; FR; BA; Outstndng Achvmnt Mission Invlvmnt; Comp; Eng.

**TURNER, KADEEJIA A,** Univ Of Md At Eastern Shore, Princess Anne, MD; SR; BS; Pre-Prof Hnr Soc 87-89; Hnrs Pgm 87-89; Phi Beta Sigma Secr/Ms Phi Beta/V P 88-; Mt Washington Ped Hosp SPT Intern; Univ MD Hosp SPT Intern; St Agnes Hosp SPT Intern 90; IM Sftbl 90; Phys Ther.

**TURNER, KAREN L,** Averett Coll, Danville, VA; FR; PHD; Nwspr Stf 90-; Phi Eta Sgm; Bischem; Pre Med/Psychlgy MD.

**TURNER, KIMBERLY L,** Univ Of Sc At Columbia, Columbia, SC; FR; BA; Assn Afrcn Amer Stdnts 90-; NAACP 90-; Mnrty Asst Peer Pgm; Dns Lst; Acctg.

**TURNER, LA SHANDA A,** Bethune Cookman Coll, Daytona Beach, FL; SO; BS; Dns Lst 89-; Elem Educ; Tchr.

**TURNER, LAURA K,** Univ Of Fl, Gainesville, FL; SR; BA; Stdnt Art Lg Cllctns Chrprsn 88-; Art Hstry Assoc 90-; Harn Msm Vol 90-; Art Hstry; Msm Crtrshp.

**TURNER, LEAH P,** Western Piedmont Comm Coll, Morganton, NC; SO; AAS; Paralegal Tech; Law.

**TURNER, LOUISE B,** Bethany Coll, Bethany, WV; SO; BA; Bethany Psych Clb 90-; Bethny Bsn Clb Bstrs 90-; Glf 90-; NSFRE 89-; CASE 87-; Dir Devel Dubuque Coord Major Gfts Bthny Clg 90-; Psych; Educ Psych.

**TURNER, MARY E,** Marshall University, Huntington, WV; SR; Hall Advsry Cncl 87-89; Deans List 87-; IM 87-; Home Ecnmcs/Nutrition; Dietitian.

**TURNER, MARY T,** Univ Of Akron, Akron, OH; JR; Spec Ed.

**TURNER, MELISSA R,** Univ Of Tn At Martin, Martin, TN; SO; BS; Recd Acdmc Awd From Sor 89-90; Math/Comp Sci.

**TURNER, MICHAEL C,** Al A & M Univ, Normal, AL; SO; BS; Fnnc; Bnkng.

**TURNER, MICHAEL K,** Piedmont Tech Coll, Greenwood, SC; FR; Cmptr Tech; Prgrmmng.

**TURNER, MICHELE A,** Univ Of Cincinnati, Cincinnati, OH; SR; BA; NAEYC; CCT Assoc 87; ASSOC 87; Early Chldhd Educ; Tchr.

**TURNER, MICHELLE,** Va St Univ, Petersburg, VA; SR; BA; Mktg Clb Pres; Pol Invlvmnt Comm; Assn Pol Scientist; Alpha Kappa Mu; Alpha Kappa Mu Hnr Socty; Rcpnt Pres Acad Pin; Pol Sci; Law.

**TURNER, MONICA E,** Hampton Univ, Hampton, VA; SO; BS; Bus Clb 90-; Deans Lst 89-; Intrnshp Equitable Financial Co 90; Intrnshp Mobil Corp; Fin; Hsp Admin.

**TURNER, NICOLE,** Saint Pauls Coll, Lawrenceville, VA; SR; BA; Stdnt Govt Enrlmnt Mgmt Socty 87-; Miss Sphinxmen 89; Hnr Socty 87-88; Alpha Kappa Alpha VP 89; Alpha Kappa Alpha Schlrshp 87; Bapt Schlrshp 89; Acad Schlrshp 87-; Pol Sci; Law.

**TURNER, PAMELA J,** Volunteer St Comm Coll, Gallatin, TN; SO; Nrsng; RN.

**TURNER, PATRICIA ANZELLA,** Norfolk St Univ, Norfolk, VA; SR; BS; Lpn; Math; Tch.

**TURNER, PATTI M,** Abraham Baldwin Agri Coll, Tifton, GA; SO; MBA; Assoc Educ Abraham Baldwin Ag Coll 90-; Engl/Math; Educ.

**TURNER, PAULE L,** Va Commonwealth Univ, Richmond, VA; SO; BFA; Actvtng Odds Prfrmng Arts Cncl Fndr Chr 89-; Amrcn Dnc Fstvl Full Schlrshp; Awrd Intern Ttn Schlr Awrd; VA Commonwealth Univ; Chrgrphy Prfrmnc.

**TURNER, REBECCA L,** S U N Y Coll Of Tech At Frmgdl, Farmingdale, NY; SO; BA; Circle K 88-89; Dns Lst 90-; Achvmnt Awd; Engl.

**TURNER, ROBERTNETTE,** Richard Bland Coll, Petersburg, VA; SO; AS; Crmnlgy; BA Fed Law Efrcr.

**TURNER, ROSEMARY F,** Nova Univ, Ft Lauderdale, FL; GD; MBA; Phi Beta Kappa; Data Proc Mgmt Assn Intl Dir 83-86; GTE Data Serv Inc 76-; Advsry Syst Engr; CDP Inst Cert Comp Pro 81; BA CUNY 72; Math/Comp Sci; Data Proc.

**TURNER, SHANE W,** Southern Coll Of Tech, Marietta, GA; JR; BA; Cnstrctrs Gld 90-; Amer Inst Cnstrctrs 90-; Sigma Lambda Chi 90-; Cnstrctn; Cntrtr.

**TURNER, SHANNON M,** Radford Univ, Radford, VA; JR; BED; Baptist Stdnt Un VP 88-; Kappa Delta Pi Sec; Stdnt VA Educ Assn; Tchr.

**TURNER, SHARON L,** Al A & M Univ, Normal, AL; SO; BS; Bapt Cmps Mnstrs Bapt Stdnt Unn Cncl Offcr 90-; Gspl Chr 90-; NAACP Chpln 90-; Mozelle Davis Awrd Apprl Merch Dsgn; Acad Hnr Rll 90; Dns Lst 90; Apprl Mrchndsng And Dsgn; Fshn.

**TURNER, SHERYL A,** Atlanta Christian Coll, East Point, GA; JR; BS; Mnstrl Assoc 88-90; Baptst Stdnt Un Chrmn Prayer Com 88-90; Fr Cncl 88; World Hunger Awareness Com 88-90; Christian Edn; Marriage Fmly Cnslng.

**TURNER, SHIRLEY,** Al St Univ, Montgomery, AL; JR; Natl Assoc For Blck Acctnts 90-; Acctnt; CPA.

**TURNER, STEPHANIE J,** Davis & Elkins Coll, Elkins, WV; SR; BS; Hons Assoc; Alpha Chi; Chi Beta Phi; Bsns Awd; Comp Sci Awd 90; Acctg/Comp Sci; CPA.**

**TURNER, TAMARA D,** Univ Of Nc At Greensboro, Greensboro, NC; JR; BS; Proj Chrprsn 89-; Bapt Stdnt Un Pres 88-; Golden Chain 90-; Intrnshp SW Elem Sch; Elem Educ; Teacher.

**TURNER, TAMERA J,** Tn Temple Univ, Chattanooga, TN; SR; BA; Choir Ensmbl Lbrn 88; Judson Soc Actvty Dir 88-89; Touring Music Ensmbl; English; Jrnlsm/Pubshng.

**TURNER, TAMMIE D,** Alcorn St Univ, Lorman, MS; SR; BS; Alcrn St Univ Mdlng Sqd; Alcrn St Univ Hstss Clb; Kappa Alpha Psi Swthrt Organ Treas; Natl Hnr Scty; Vol Incme Tax Asst Prog; Cert Of Mrt Awrd; Acctng Bus Admin; Acctng.**

**TURNER, TAMMY A,** Auburn Univ At Auburn, Auburn, AL; GD; MA; Drama Clb/Show Choir 87-88; Smmr Cncrt Choir 90; Bptst Stdnt Un 88-90; Phi Theta Kappa 88; Phi Kappa Phi 90-; Teacher 3rd Grd 91; Elem Educf Spec ECE.

**TURNER, TERRI D,** Stillman Coll, Tuscaloosa, AL; FR; BA; Stillman Schlr; Gamma Iota Sigma; Bus Admin; Accntnt.

**TURNER, TERRI M,** Western Piedmont Comm Coll, Morganton, NC; SO; BS; Phi Theta Kappa 90; Chemistry; Chemical Engineering.

**TURNER, TERRY L,** Volunteer St Comm Coll, Gallatin, TN; FR; BA; Clg Newspapr Staff Wrtr; Clg Radio Stn Anncr; Dean Lst; Hnr Roll; Ed; Tchng MBA.

**TURNER, TOY L,** Lees Coll, Jackson, KY; FR; BA; Mdcl Sec Cmptr Sci; Nrs Cmptr Prgrmr.

**TURNER, TRACEY C,** Ky St Univ, Frankfort, KY; JR; Frnch Clb 90-; Sigma Tau Delta 90-; Coop Cntr For Stdy In Brtn 89; Deans Schlr 90-; AA Ky St Univ 90; Engl; Law.

**TURNER, TRACIE P,** Piedmont Tech Coll, Greenwood, SC; FR; Deans Lst; Trinity United Meth Church Pr Of Womens Clb/Sunday Schl Tchr; 7 Yrs Senn Trucking Co; Med Asst Tech.

**TURNER, TRACY A,** Georgian Court Coll, Lakewood, NJ; JR; BA; Sccr Vrsty 88-90; Yrbk Com 90; Sigma Phi Sigma VP 89-; Epsilon Lambda Sec/Treas 90-; Jersey Nine Schlr 90; M A G Zarrelli Memrl Schlrshp 90; Deans Lst 88-; Spnsh/Elem Ed; ESL Tchr.

**TURNER, TRACY D,** Univ Of Nc At Greensboro, Greensboro, NC; FR; BS; Cmptrs; Mngmnt Info Systms.

**TURNER, TYNITA L,** Alcorn St Univ, Lorman, MS; SO; BA; Nrsng Club Treas 90-; Hon Stdnt Org; All Amercn Schlr; RN.

**TURNER, VIRGINIA L,** Vance Granville Comm Coll, Henderson, NC; SR; ASSO; Rdlgc Tech Pro Cls VP 89-; NC Soc Rdlgc Tech 89-; Acdmc Achvmnt Schlrshp; AS 81; Rdlgc Tech.

**TURNER, WENDY M,** Univ Of Southern Ms, Hattiesburg, MS; JR; BS; Gamma Beta Phi 90-; Elem Ed; Tchng.**

**TURNES, LAURA P,** Longwood Coll, Farmville, VA; FR; BS; Hnrs Prgrm 90; ASSET Stdnts 90; Alpha Lambda Delta 90; Bsn/Acct; CP Accnt.

**TURNEY, BROOKE H,** Univ Of Ky, Lexington, KY; SO; BA; Deans Lst; Pi Beta Phi; Psychology.

**TURNICK, KEVIN P,** Clarkson Univ, Potsdam, NY; JR; BA; Soc Acctnts; Deans Lst BCC 88-89; Deans Lst 90; Clrksn Trstees Schlrshp 90-; IM Bsktbl/Soccer; AS Broome Comm Coll 90; Acctg; Bus.

**TUROCZY, KATHRYN L,** Saint Vincents Coll & Seminary, Latrobe, PA; SR; MD; Frhsmn Orntn Cmt Co Chrprsn 90-; Stdnt Rsdnt Asst 89-; Bio Clb Nwsltr Edtr 87-90; Cmps Mnstry 87-; Sprt Frndship Day Rgstrtn Cmt Hd 87-; CRC Otstndng Frsh Chem 87; Intrnshp Diabetes Cmp Cnslr Chldns Hosp Pittsburgh 90; Bio Dept Awrd; BS; Bio/Pre Med; Medcn Fmly Prctc.

**TURPEL, MAUREEN E,** D Youville Coll, Buffalo, NY; SO; BSN; Women Of Moose; Ont Cert Of Competence; Nursing Conestoga Coll 75; Prenatal ICU Mohawk Coll 83; Nursing Sci; Continue Prof Nursing.

**TURPIN, C KAYE,** Univ Of Ky, Lexington, KY; SR; BA; Ntl Educ Assc; KY Educ Assc; Deans Lst; Alpha Gamma Delta 86-89; KY Athl Stdnt Comm 86-87; Elem Educ.

**TURPIN, JACQUELINE C,** City Univ Of Ny Baruch Coll, New York, NY; GD; AAS Kingsborough Comm Coll 85; BBA 90; Fin.

**TURPIN, KATHERINE M,** Birmingham Southern Coll, Birmingham, AL; SO; BSBA; Habitat Humnty 89-; Stdnt Judcry; Triangle Clb 90; Phi Eta Sigma 90-; Alpha Lambda Delta 90-; Psi Chi; Phi Sigma Iota; Alpha Chi Omega Hs Mgr 89-; Pres Stdnt Serv Org; Res Asst 90-; Pcych/Spnsh.

**TURRENTINE, CHRISTINE Y,** Univ Of Al At Huntsville, Huntsville, AL; JR; BSCE; Socty Wmn Engrs; SOTA; Cvl Engr Trainee 90-; BS S Benedictine Coll 78; AAS Calhoun Comm Coll 90; Cvl Engr.

**TURRENTINE, JEANA L,** John C Calhoun St Comm Coll, Decatur, AL; GD; AAS; Phi Theta Kappa; AAS J F Drake Tech Coll Elecs Tech 88; Cert Fundamentals Of Autocad From Huntsville Area 90; Drftng Dsgn Tech; Archtctrl Drftr Dsgnr.**

**TURSIC, STEPHANIE K,** Univ Of Akron, Akron, OH; SO; BFA; Hnrs Clb 89-; Hnrs Prog 89-; 4-H Advisor 89-; Graphic Desgn; Art Dir.

**TURTURRO, MICHAEL A,** S U N Y Coll Of Tech At Frmgdl, Farmingdale, NY; SO; Archtctrl Cvl Technlgies Clb Orgnzr 90-; Tchrs Asst 90-; IM Sftbl Tm ACT Clb 90-; Archtctr; Archtct/Prfsr.

**TURTZO, L CHRISTINE,** Swarthmore Coll, Swarthmore, PA; FR; BA; Stdnt Newspaper News Assc 90-; Wmns Vrsty Lacrosse; Biochemistry; Phd Biological Sci/Research.

**TURVAVILLE, KYNDEL,** Santa Fe Comm Coll, Gainesville, FL; FR; AA; AIDS Conf; Elem Edn.

**TURYAN, LINDA M,** Comm Coll Algny Co Algny Cmps, Pittsburgh, PA; AS; Assoc Mem Srgcl Technlgsts 84-; Surg Tech Eye/Ear Hosp; Cert Connelley Trade Schl 84; Nrsng.

**TUSING, DONELLE C,** Univ Of Nc At Greensboro, Greensboro, NC; JR; BS; AHEA Tres 90-; ASID 89-90; Chi Omega Asst Rush Chr 89-; Hm Ec.

**TUSSEY, SHIRLEY JEAN,** Maysville Comm Coll, Maysville, KY; SO; ADN; Dns Lst; Nrsg; BSN.

**TUSTAIN, MINDELYN H,** Univ Of Southern Ms, Hattiesburg, MS; FR; Stu Eagle Clb; BSU; SADD; SAA; Lambda Sigma; Gamma Beta Phi; Phi Mu Rtl Chrmn; IM Chmpns 4 Yrs; Bio; Med Sch.

**TUSTIN, WILLIAM M,** Comm Coll Algny Co Algny Cmps, Pittsburgh, PA; FR; BA; Rdtn Thrpy.

**TUSZYNSKA, BARBARA B,** S U N Y At Buffalo, Buffalo, NY; SR; BS; Beta Alpha Psi 90; Deans List 88-90; Acctg/Finance; Intl Corp Law.

**TUTAY, REBECCA C,** Duquesne Univ, Pittsburgh, PA; SO; Dns Lst Frshmn 88-90; Fld Site Assgnmnts Howe Elem Schl; Zonta Acad Schlrshp 90; Pacini Acad Schlrshp 90; Duquesne Educ/Pres Schlrshps 90-; Invlvd Chldrsn Hosp Diabetes Clinic 89-; PTA Mbr Peters Twnshp Schl 90-; Elem Educ.

**TUTEJA, CHARANJEET K,** Univ Of Al At Birmingham, Birmingham, AL; SR; BS; Amer Soc Clncl Pathlgst; Gold Silver Mdl Indore Univ India Stdnt 80-84; Dns Lst Stdnt 90; Natl Soc Svc Indore Univ India 80-85; Cytotechlgy Lab Stdnt 90-; Histtech Lab Intrnshp Stdnt 90-; Ntrtnl Sci Rsrch Asst 90-; BA 82; MA 84; Cytotechnolgist/Histchnlgst; Basic/Clin Sci.

**TUTON, TISHA L,** Merrimack Coll, North Andover, MA; FR; Pol Sci; Law.

**TUTOR, TINA M,** Blue Mountain Coll, Blue Mountain, MS; JR; BS; MAE-SP 90-; Phi Theta Kappa 89-90; Elem Educ; Tchng.

**TUTTAS, JENNIFER L,** Fl St Univ, Tallahassee, FL; JR; BA; Mrchng Band Row Ldr 89-; NSSLHA 90-; Spch/Lang Pthlgy; Pthlgst/Clncn.

**TUTTEROW, DIRK W,** Ky St Univ, Frankfort, KY; JR; BED; Hon Ordr Kentucky Colonels 89-; Chld Sprt Speclst Cabinet Human Rsrcs; History; Educ.

**TUTTEROW, LAURA S,** Southern Coll Of Tech, Marietta, GA; JR; BA; Indl Eng.

**TUTTLE, ANDREW C,** Tn Temple Univ, Chattanooga, TN; SR; BRE; Stdnt Missions Flwshp 85-; Alpha Eta Theta; ARRIBA Missionary 86-87; Summa Cum Laude; Bridgeport Bapt Church Pastor 88-; Ordained 90; BRE Summa Cum Laude; Missions.**

**TUTTLE JR, LYLES B,** Univ Of South Al, Mobile, AL; JR; BS; Propeller Clb US; Sigma Tau Theta; Marketing/Transportation; Logistics.

**TUZZOLO, JOSEPH J,** Univ Of Miami, Coral Gables, FL; SR; BA; Stu Gov 88-89; Frnch Clb 87-88; Omicron Delta Kappa 90-; Ordr Omega Tres 90-; Alpha Tau Omega VP 87-; Pol; Law.

**TWARK, LISA M,** Kent St Univ Kent Cmps, Kent, OH; SO; BS; Bio/Zoolgy; Hlth/Med Field.

**TWEDDLE, J CHRISTOPHER,** Oh Wesleyan Univ, Delaware, OH; FR; BA; Phi Eta Sigma; Sigma Phi Epsilon; Weslyan Schlr; Deans List; Club Rugby; Math; Profsr.

**TWEEDLIE, ISABELLA M,** Wv Northern Comm Coll, Wheeling, WV; SO; AAS; Phi Theta Kappa; Cmptr Prgrmmng.

**TWELKEMEIER, CYNTHIA K,** Union Univ, Jackson, TN; SR; BS; Rutledge Hnry Hstry Clb Pblc Rltns Offcr 89-; Psychology Sclby Clb 89-; STEA 88-; Acadmc Ldrshp Schlrshp 90-; Elem Edctn; Tchr.

**TWIFORD, JOHN SCOTT,** Richard Bland Coll, Petersburg, VA; JR; BA; Stdnt Free Entrps 89-90; Deans List 90; All Amer Schlrs 90; AS 90; Urban Stds; Envrnmntlst/Envrnmntl Plnr.

**TWIGG, STEVEN E,** Daytona Beach Comm Coll, Daytona Beach, FL; GD; AS; Otstndng Stdnt; 4.0 GPA; AS Elec Tech MS Gulf Coast Jr Coll 79; Drftng Mech; CAD Oprtr Drftr.

**TWILLEY, DANIELLE L,** Le Moyne Coll, Syracuse, NY; FR; BA; Wrk Stdy Prog 90-; Aerobics 90-; Bus Mktg.

**TWINE, JACQUELYN ANNE,** Bowling Green St Univ At Huron, Huron, OH; SO; ASSC; Res Care Clb Sec/Treas 90-; Firelnds Wght Clb Sec/Treas 90-; New Life Fitns Ctr 86-; Womns Intl Bwlng Assn 80-; Med; Res Thrpy Tech.

**TWITTY, JUNE L,** Coll Of Charleston, Charleston, SC; SR; BA; Pre Law Scty 90-; Phi Sigma Alpha 90-; Omicron Delta Kappa 90-; Pltcl Sci; Law.

**TWITTY, LISA L,** Univ Of Sc At Columbia, Columbia, SC; JR; BS; Cncl For Prvntn Of Chld Abuse; Golden Key 90; Pi Mu Epsilon 90; Camden Fire Dept Camden SC 88; Math Ed; Ed.

**TWOMEY, CHRISTINE A,** Lesley Coll, Cambridge, MA; JR; BSED; Commuter Clb 88-; Butler Sch Belmont Ma 88-89; Watertown Mid Sch 89-90; Math/Sci; Tchr.

**TWOREK, SUSAN T,** Embry Riddle Aeronautical Univ, Daytona Beach, FL; GD; BS; Ninety Nines Pres 90-; Amer Assn Airport Exec 89-; Future Prof Wmn In Aviation 89-90; Eastern Airlines Intrnshp 90-; AS Acctng Bus Admin 84-86; AAS Hotel Restrnt Mngmnt 86-88; Aeronautical Stds Mngmnt; Comml Pilot.

**TWORZYANSKI, JULIE B,** Univ Of Sc At Columbia, Columbia, SC; JR; BA; Legal Asst Stdnt Of Year Midlands Tech Coll 89-90; AA Midlands Tech Coll 90; Business/Criminal Justice; Law.

**TWYMAN, CAROL E,** Christian Brothers Univ, Memphis, TN; FR; BA; Socty Hmn Rsrcs Mgmt; Memphis Prsnl Assn; Dir Hmn Rsrcs 86-91; Bus/Hmn Rsrcs Mgmt.

**TYER, CHARLES T,** Univ Of Southern Ms, Hattiesburg, MS; SR; JD; Dns Lst; Pres Lst; RA BSU Stdnt Ctr Chm 88-90; Spch Cmptn; Steep Hls Hntng Clb CRJ VP 89-90; Fr Dept Vol; BSU Pgm Coord; Phi Theta Kappa Fnd Rsng Chm 88-90; Pblc Dfndrs Ofc Intrn; RA Yr; IM Ftbl/Sftbl; Law.

**TYER, MICHAEL J,** Western New England Coll, Springfield, MA; JR; BS; Elec Eng.

**TYERYAR, KAREN L,** Bridgewater Coll, Bridgewater, VA; SO; BA; Pinion Players 89-; Yrbk 90-; Hnr Cncl 90-; Lambda Scty 90-; English Dept Asstnt 90-; English; Teacher.

**TYGIER, MIRIAM,** Georgian Court Coll, Lakewood, NJ; SR; ACS 87-90; Mendel Soc 87-90; ACS Awd 90-; Sister M P Conkley Awd 90; BS 90; Biochem; Dental Sch.

**TYGREST JR, JAMES R,** Andrew Coll, Cuthbert, GA; SO; AS; SG 90-; Camps Plng Cncl 90-; Hnrs Comm; Phi Theta Kappa Pres 89-; Ga Hall Honr; Pres Lst; Busn Mgmt.

**TYL, JACQUELINE M,** Roane St Comm Coll, Harriman, TN; SO; BA; SGA VP 89-; Pres Cncl Chrmprn 90-; Bptst Stu Unn Ldr 90-; Gamma Beta Phi 90-; AS; Pol Sci; Law.

**TYLER, CARLA J,** Christopher Newport Coll, Newport News, VA; JR; BA; Alpha Chi 90-; First Aid CPR Cert; Rec/Concentration Pgmmng; Travel/Tourism.

**TYLER, ELISABETH M,** Memphis St Univ, Memphis, TN; FR; MBA; Sigma Alpha Iota Treas; Hstry; Tchg.

**TYLER, F KAYE,** Northern Ky Univ, Highland Hts, KY; SR; BA; Stdnt Alum Assn Ky Educ Assn; Natl Educ Assn; Stdnt Natl Educ Assn; Alphi Chi Hnr Soc 89-; Co Rec Vllybl 90-; Education.

**TYLER, JEANIE S,** Valdosta St Coll, Valdosta, GA; SR; BFA; Art Stdnts League; Art Stdnts League Abraham Baldwin Coll V P 87; Otstndng Coll Stdnts Of Am; Thomasville Art Guild 90-; Art.

**TYLER, LANCE A,** Univ Of Akron, Akron, OH; SO; BS; Fncl Mngmnt Assoc; Phi Eta Sigma; Alpha Lambda Delta; Bsnss Fnce; Fnce.

**TYLER, MAURICE A,** Nc Agri & Tech St Univ, Greensboro, NC; JR; BS; Stdnt Govt Assn Co Chr 89-90; ACM 89-; Digit Cir V P; Deans Lst 88-; Hnr Stdnt 88-; Intrnshp G E Aerospace 90-; Cmptr Sci; Sftwr Eng.

**TYLER, PAMELA G,** Georgetown Univ, Washington, DC; FR; MBA; Chrldr; Frst Hnrs; Bus.

**TYLER, RHONDA L,** Comm Coll Algny Co Algny Cmps, Pittsburgh, PA; JR; BS; Engrg; Biomedical Engr.

**TYLER, STEVEN D,** Tn St Univ, Nashville, TN; JR; BS; AAS Nashville State Tech 90; Architectural Eng.

**TYLER, TANYA M,** Comm Coll Algny Co Algny Cmps, Pittsburgh, PA; SO; ASSOC; Deans Lst 90-; Phlebotom Montefiore Hosp; Nurs; Nursing Career.

**TYLER, TENA S,** Memphis St Univ, Memphis, TN; SO; BA; Alpha Lambda Delta 90-; Phi Eta Sigma 90-; Jrnlsm; Advrtsng.

**TYLICKI, RICHARD B,** Ky St Univ, Frankfort, KY; SR; BA; Baptist Stdnt Union 87-88; ROTC 88-; SGA Sntr 87-; Alpha Kappa Mu VP 89-; Study Oxford Englnd 88; Study London Englnd 90-; ROTC Basic Camp 90; Engl/Lib Studies; Sports Admin.

**TYMESON, LYNDA S,** Hudson Valley Comm Coll, Troy, NY; SR; BA; Peer Edctnl Trng; Phi Thetta Kappa Treas 89-90; IM Vlybl; Hlth Edctn; Tch.

**TYNDALL, BRIAN L,** Ms Gulf Coast Comm Coll, Perkinston, MS; FR; BA; Bnd Gld; Sr MYF Vnclv UMC Pres 87-88; Hstry; Tchng.

**TYNDALL, LAWRENCE P,** Ms St Univ, Miss State, MS; SR; BA; Psychology Clb Sec 88-; Psi Chi Film Comm 90-; Gamma Beta Phi 90-; Phi Kappa Phi 89-; Pres Schlr 89; Clin Psychology.

**TYNDALL, MARGARET E,** Univ Of Nc At Greensboro, Greensboro, NC; JR; BS; Chld Dvlpmnnt Fmly Rltns; Prschl Edctn.

**TYNER, ANGELA I,** Faulkner St Jr Coll, Bay Minette, AL; SO; SG 89-; SPTO 90-; Faulkner Pow-Wow 89-90; Beta Sigma Phi; Phys Therapy.

**TYNER, FRED M,** Ms St Univ, Miss State, MS; JR; BS; Bapt Stdnt Un 87-; Amrcn Scty Cvl Eng 89-; Univ Hnrs Prgm; Chi Epsilon; Tau Beta Pi; Gamma Beta Phi; Phi Mu Alpha Sinfonia; 7I 4 H All Stars; Hnr Sprgm Schlrshp; Cook Coggin Eng Schlrshp; Robert E Wood Cvl Eng Schlrshp; IM Sprts; Cvl Eng.

**TYNER, SHEILA D,** Chesterfield Marlboro Coll, Cheraw, SC; SO; BED; Prsdnts Lst 90; History; Edctn.

**TYNER, TIFFANI S,** Univ Of Sc At Columbia, Columbia, SC; SO; BA; SG; Jdcry Cmte V Chrprsn; Hndcpd Advsry Cmte Chrprsn 90-; Gamma Beta Phi; Alpha; Dns Lst; Alpa Delta Pi Hsng Pres; Ronald Mc Donald Hse; Spec Olympcs; Eng Pgm Internatl; Pres Schlrshp; Almn Assoc Schlrshp; Alpha Delta Pi Bst Esy; Eng; Law.

**TYNES, NORMAN M,** Hampton Univ, Hampton, VA; BA; BA Mc Master Univ Canada 80; AS Mohawk Coll Canada 76; AIAS; Inst Bahamaian Arch; Mcmaster Univ Alum Assc; Physcl Plnr/Arch Asst; Architecture; Physcl Plnr/Dvlpr.

**TYRE, CHRIS J,** Central St Univ, Wilberforce, OH; FR; BA; SGA; DAPP; Hon Soc; Kappa Alpha Psi Aux; Indstrl Psychlgst.

**TYREE, AMY D,** Univ Of Tn At Martin, Martin, TN; JR; BMME; Phi Kappa Phi; Sigma Alpha Ioto Chpln 90-; Asstntshp; Allison Nelson Schlrshp; Music.

**TYRELL, JO-ELLEN,** Wagner Coll, Staten Island, NY; SO; Deans Lst; Elem Ed; Tch.

**TYRELL, MARY ELIZABETH,** Wagner Coll, Staten Island, NY; SR; BA; Soc Clb 90-; Deans Lst 90-; Natl Collegiate Soc Sci Awrd; Crim Just; Law.

**TYRELL, TERESA,** Wagner Coll, Staten Island, NY; SR; BA; Nwspr Writer 88-; Engl Clb 88-; Lit Mag; Engl Hon; Shpng Ctr Mktg Intern 90-; Engl; Writing/Pblshng.

**TYREN, AMELIA R,** Bowling Green St Univ At Huron, Huron, OH; JR; BA; Firelands Thtr; Phi Eta Sigma 89-; Alpha Lambda Delta 89-; Alpha Xi 90-; Intern May Co; Tutor 89-; Fshn Mrchndsng/Intl Bus; Law.

**TYRRELL CARDAMONE, SHARON ANN,** Marywood Coll, Scranton, PA; GD; Clg Litry Mag Staff Editr 90-; Clg Nwspr Wrtr 90-; Lambda Iota Tao VP 90-; Kappa Gamma Pi; Delta Epsilon Sigma; Pi Gamma Mu; Clg Wrtng Cntr Staff Editr 87-90; Peer Tutor Acad Spt Serv 87-90; Hospice St John Vol; Ldrshp Lackawanna; Engl; Clg Tchr.

**TYSON, AUDREY DELORIS,** Al A & M Univ, Normal, AL; JR; Baptst Stdnt Union Miss BSU 90-; Univ Choir 88-89; First Attendant Miss AL A&m Univ; Kappa Delta Pi; Delta Sigma Theta 90-; Adopt-A-Family Prog Tutor 89-; Upward Bound Prog Prog Asstnt 89-; Elem Ed; Teacher.

**TYSON, DAVID M,** Embry Riddle Aeronautical Univ, Daytona Beach, FL; SR; BS; Chess Club 88-89; Math Assoc Of Amer 90-; Deans List 90-; Intrnshp Fdrl Aviation Admnstrn ATCS 2199gs-3 88-89; ATCS 2199gs-4 89-90; Assistantship Aeronautical Univ 90; FAA Air Traffic Cntrl Spclst Trainee 89-; Aeronautical Studies/Mgmnt; Air Traffic Contr.

**TYSON, DIANE A,** Lancaster Bible Coll, Lancaster, PA; SR; BS; Yrbk Treas 90-F Chrstn Cnslng Flwshp Sec/Treas 90-F Sr Clss Treas 90-; Acctnt 80-89; AS Durham Tech Inst 77; Bible; Cnslng.

**TYSON, FREDA M,** S U N Y At Buffalo, Buffalo, NY; FR; Bsns; CPA.

**TYSON, IVY A,** Univ Of Nc At Charlotte, Charlotte, NC; FR; BS; NAACP Actvts Comm Chr 90-; Chldrn Of Son Cltrl Choir 90-; Blue Swthrt Ct Of Phi Beta Sigma Frat Inc 90-; Cmptr Sci; Systs Analyst.

**TYSON, LISA M,** S U N Y Coll Of Tech At Frmgdl, Farmingdale, NY; SO; AAS; Offc Mgmt Clb 90; Assoc Lgl Stdnts VP 90-; Deans Lst 90; Intern Law Frm; Cnty Lgl Sec Schlrshp; Offc Mgmt Lgl Spclztn.

**TYSON, MICHAEL C,** Lenoir Rhyne Coll, Hickory, NC; SR; BME; Choir Mgr 87-; K B Lee Music Clb Sec 87-; Fools/Christ 88 90; Srvnt Christ Awd 90; Hickory Musc Clb Schlrp 90; Mus Educ; Tch.

**TYSON, REBECCA L,** Mansfield Univ, Mansfield, PA; FR; BS; Stdnt Govt Assn 90; Phi Beta Lambda; Bsn; Hlth Admin.

**TYSON, STACY W,** Crichton Coll, Memphis, TN; SR; BA; Phi Theta Kappa 88-; Theology; Teaching.

**TYTKA, JULIE A,** S U N Y Coll At Fredonia, Fredonia, NY; JR; BS; Hlth Serv Admn Clb 90-; Hlth Serv Admn.

# U

**UBER, GARY P,** Asbury Theological Sem, Wilmore, KY; JR; MDIV; Unit Commndtn Mdl; Naval Rsrv Officer 90-; BA Hobe Sound Bible Clg 85; M Div MSW 89-; Religion/Social Wrk; Pstrl Ministries.

**UBER, MICHELLE L,** Volunteer St Comm Coll, Gallatin, TN; FR; BA; Art Clb 90-; Hnr Rl 90-; Fine Arts.

**UDANI, BELA H,** Univ Of The Virgin Islands, St Thomas, VI; SR; BA; Pr Clb 90-; 1st Fedl Svngs Bnk Intrn 90; Carribean Resrch Inst 90; BA Univ Of Bombay India 89; Bus Admin.

**UDEAHI, NIMESH V,** City Univ Of Ny Baruch Coll, New York, NY; SO; BA; Acctg Socty 89; Finc/Econ Socty 90; Dns Lst 89-90; CYO Yth Org 89-90; Rec Bsktbl 89-; Finc; Finc/Invstmnts.

**UDELL, DONNA,** Kent St Univ Geauga Cmps, Burton Twp, OH; SR; BA; Campus Animal Rts Exped; Network Ohio Animal Rts; Lake Cnty Humane Soc Vol 90-; People For Ethical Trtmnt Of Animals 88-; Spnsr Physicians Comm Resp Med 90-; Cmptr Lab Assist 89-90; Serv Rep GE 87-88; Cmptrs; Cmptr Prog.

**UDELL, DOROTHY,** Bloomfield Coll, Bloomfield, NJ; JR; BSN; Mdcl Srgcl Cert; Amrcn Nrs Assoc; RN John F Kennedy Mdcl Cntr; AAS Kingsborough Cmmnty Coll 76; Nrsng.

**UEHARA, SETSU,** Univ Of Nc At Charlotte, Charlotte, NC; SO; BA; Math; Engr.

**UEHARA, TAKAE,** Manor Jr Coll, Jenkintown, PA; SO; AA; Phi Theta Kappa 89-; Lbrl Art; Educ.

**UENO, HIROKO,** Abraham Baldwin Agri Coll, Tifton, GA; SO; Stdn Tun VP 90-; Stdnt Hm Econ Assoc; Intl Clb Sec 90-; Phi Theta Kappa; Home Econ; Intr Dsgn.**

**UHLHORN, MICHAEL C,** Univ Of Cincinnati, Cincinnati, OH; SR; BS; CSA 90; Golden Key 86; Grad Of Yr For Assoc Of Sci In Cnstrctn Sci Dept 89; AS 89; Sci; Cnstrctn Mngmnt.**

**UHRICH, HOLLY B,** Univ Of Fl, Gainesville, FL; SR; BS; Stu Dttc Assn VP 90-; Hlth Rltd Prof 89-90; Med/Ntrtn; Dttcs.

**UHRIG, KEITH A,** Westminster Coll, New Wilmingtn, PA; SR; BA; Radio Sports Dir 87-; Lambda Sigma 88-89; Theta Chi 88-; Pittsburgh Steelers Ftbl Cl Pblcty Intern 90; Cmmctns Intern 89-90; Var Bsbl 89; Track/Fld 88- 90; Telecmmctns; Publ Rltn.

**UKAWUILULU, JOHN O,** Howard Univ, Washington, DC; GD; PHD; Grad Stdnt Assmbly Pres/Coordntr 90-; Grad Stdnt Cncl Pres 89-90; Absalom Jones Stdnt Assc Pres 87-89; Golden Key; Alpha Kappa Delta; Tchg Fllwshp 88-; Trstee Schlrshp Awds 87-88; DC Pblc Dfndr Srvc Intrn Invstgtr 87; Med Soclgy/Gerntlgy; Tchg/Rsrch.

**UKEOMAH, PROTUS C,** Univ Of The Dist Of Columbia, Washington, DC; FR; BSC; Hon Pgm; Phi Sigma Pi; Phrmcy.

**ULAN, DONNA M,** Edinboro Univ Of Pa, Edinboro, PA; GD; BS; Orthdx Chrstn Flwshp VP 88-89; Bio Clb 88-; Alpha Chi 90-; Phi Eta Sigma 88-; Beta Beta Beta Hstrn 88-; K Barkhart Awd; G A Crowe Schlrshp; Pres Hon Schlrshp; Bio; Envrnmntl Sci.

**ULASEWICZ, KARA M,** Boston Univ, Boston, MA; FR; BA; Dnc Thtr Grp 90; DJ Intern; Lttl Brthrs Frnds Eldrly 90-; Frnch/PR; Entrtnmnt Law.

**ULBRICHT, ROBERTA R,** Fl International Univ, Miami, FL; JR; BED; PTA Coral Reef Elem Sec 86-89; PTSA Sthwd Mddl Schl Hsptlty 89-; AA Miami-Dade Comm Coll 89; Exrcs Physlgy; Hlth/Wllnss.

**ULDERICH, MARY M,** Univ Of Tn At Martin, Martin, TN; SR; BS; Stdnt Tn Educ Assn 89-; Elem Educ.**

**ULERY, AMY M,** Univ Of Ms Medical Center, Jackson, MS; SR; BSN; MS Natl Stu Nrs Assn 89-; Phi Theta Kappa 89-; Sigma Theta Tau; Stu Nrs Extern 90-; AA Hinds Comm Coll 89; Nrsng.

**ULERY, CHRISTOPHER J,** Kent St Univ Kent Cmps, Kent, OH; SO; BA; Grn Drgn Stdio Of Chnse Hlth And Fghtng Arts 90-; Pres Lst 90-; Pscyh Sclgy.

**ULERY, RENEE L,** Oh St Univ At Newark, Newark, OH; JR; BA; Educ; Elem Educ.

**ULFERS, SHAWN H,** Univ Of North Fl, Jacksonville, FL; SR; BBA; Phi Kappa Phi 90-; Deans List 90-; AA FL Comm Clg Jacksonville 89; Mrktng.

**ULISSE, CHRISTOPHER K,** Christopher Newport Coll, Newport News, VA; JR; BSA; Accntng; CPA.

**ULLE, RONALD C,** Univ Of Akron, Akron, OH; JR; BBA; Hnrs Pgm 88-; Golden Key; Phi Eta Sigma 89-; Alpha Lambda Delta 89-; Bsn Finance; Invstmnt Bnkr/Brkr.

**ULLMAN, ALBERT F,** George Mason Univ, Fairfax, VA; JR; BS; Co-Op Educ; Mgmt Info Sys; Cmptr Prgmmng/Anlyss.

**ULLOA, LEONARDO E,** Borough Of Manhattan Comm Coll, New York, NY; SO; AA; Swmmng Clb 87-88; Bsnss/Fnce Clb Pres 88-89; Bsnss Mngmnt; Clg Tchng.**

**ULLRICH, CAROL A,** Univ Of North Fl, Jacksonville, FL; SR; BSN; Swyr Coll Dorm VP 68; Delta Sigma Pi 82; NSNA 90-; Phi Kappa Phi 90-; Gldn Ky 90-; Hcky Skng La Crsse Plyr 69; Jggng 84; Delta Sigma Pi 80; Chrldng Coach 82; Sbrd Cstlne RR; AA Colby Sawyer Coll 69; Asst Mgr 86; Nrsng; Crtcl Cre Nrse.

**ULLRICH, CARRIE J,** Castleton St Coll, Castleton, VT; JR; Var Tns 88-89; IM Flr Hcky 90-; IM Sftbl 89-; Alpha Pi Omega Pres; Tns Var 88-89; Educ; Elme Tchr.

**ULLYETT, CLIVE B,** Univ Of South Al, Mobile, AL; FR; Deans Lst; Tennis.

**ULMER, MELANIE V,** Morgan St Univ, Baltimore, MD; SR; BA; AA Marygrove Coll 84; Spch Cmmnctn; Law.

**ULRICH, DIANA C,** Oh St Univ, Columbus, OH; SR; BS; Tau Beta Pi 90-; Eta Kappa 90-; Gldn Key 90-; Benjamin Lamme Schlshp Elec Engrng; NCR Awrd Of Exllnc; Big Ten Conf Medal Hnr Fnlst; Vrsty Synchrnzd Swim 87-; Elec Engrng.**

**ULRICH, JENNIFER L,** Ms St Univ, Miss State, MS; FR; BA; Black Friars Drama; Comm; Advtsng.

**ULRICH, JOSEPH M,** Kent St Univ Kent Cmps, Kent, OH; SR; BBA; Amer Mktg Assn 90-; Deans Lst 88-90; IM Golf/Sftbl 87-; Mktg.

**ULRICH, TONYA K,** Jacksonville St Univ, Jacksonville, AL; SR; BS; Natl Stdnt Nrsng Assn 89-; Assn Nrsng Stdnts 89-; Nrs Ambssdr 89-; Omicron Delta Kappa 90-; Sigma Theta Tau; AA Hobe Sound Bible Coll 88; Nrsng; RN.

**UMBRIACO, JACQUELINE M,** S U N Y Coll Of Tech At Alfred, Alfred, NY; FR; BA; Act Cncl Pr 89-90; Comedian Chr 88-89; Wellsville Stdnt Act Cncl 89-90; Sigma Tau Epsilon 90-; IM Var Sftbl Capt 88-90; Const/Carpentry.

**UMHOLTZ, HEATHER A,** Central Pa Bus School, Summerdale, PA; FR; AS; Busf Lgl Sec.

**UMSTED, ANGELA HIOTT,** Univ Of Sc At Aiken, Aiken, SC; SR; BA; Gamma Beta Phi 87-89; Acctng.**

**UN, WON K,** Methodist Coll, Fayetteville, NC; JR; BA; CLC 90-; FCA Organizer 90-; Comm; Mass Media.

**UNAR, INAMULLAH,** Manhattan Coll, Bronx, NY; JR; BE; Intl Stdnts Assoc 89-; Deans Lst 89-; Elec Eng.

**UNDERCOFFER, CHRISTINA I,** Univ Of Akron, Akron, OH; SO; BA; Western Res G S Ldr 84-88; Waitress 75-88; Elem Tchr.

**UNDERHILL, RAYMOND E,** Ny Univ, New York, NY; SO; BS; AS; Acctng/Finance; Portfolio/Mgr.

**UNDERHILL, TRACY G,** Univ Of Nc At Asheville, Asheville, NC; SR; BA; Indstrl/Orgnztnl Psychlgy.

**UNDERHILL, WILMA J,** Middle Tn St Univ, Murfreesboro, TN; SR; BS; Seidal VP 90; Business; Tchr.

**UNDERWOOD, GINA M,** Univ Of Ky, Lexington, KY; FR; BA; Psychology.

**UNDERWOOD, JAMES A,** Saint Petersburg Jr Coll, St Petersburg, FL; SO; BA; Intrnl Clb Mbr 88-90; AM Inst Archtcts Stdnt Chptr VP 90-; Talent Roster Otstndng Mnrty Stdnt 90-; Archtec Dsgn; Archtc.

**UNDERWOOD, JOHN R,** Ms St Univ, Miss State, MS; FR; BS; Mrchng Band/Symphnc Band MSU 90-; Anthrplgy Clb 90-; Phi Eta Sigma; Alpha Lambda Delta; Phi Mu Alpha Sinphonia 90-; Cobb Inst Archlgy Undergrad Rsrch Assntshp 90-; Anthrplgy.

**UNDERWOOD, JUDITH LYNN D,** Volunteer St Comm Coll, Gallatin, TN; SO; AS; Gamma Beta Phi 90-; Vital Margin Full Schlrshp 90-; Deans Lst/Hon Rl 90-; Bus/Cmmrce; Acctng.

**UNDERWOOD, LEE A,** Davis & Elkins Coll, Elkins, WV; SR; BS; Senator 89; Senatus 90-; Intl Clb 89-; Phys Ed Mjrs Clb 87-; Stdnt Tchr K-12 90; Vrsty Bsbl 87-89; Vrsty Tennis 89-; Phys Ed; Tchr/Coach.

**UNDERWOOD, PAULA L,** Middle Ga Coll, Cochran, GA; SO; Gamma Beta Phi Parlmntrn 89; Deans Lst; Bsnss Admin; CPA.

**UNDERWOOD, PAULETTE M,** Al St Univ, Montgomery, AL; SR; BA; SOS 89-; Alpha Kappa Mu 89-; ST AL Atty Genl Ofc Intrnshp 90; ST AL Dept Yth Serv CPS Pgm; Crmnl Jstce; Crmnl Invstgtr.

**UNDERWOOD, ROBERT J,** Univ Of Sc At Columbia, Columbia, SC; JR; MBA; Tres; Hist; Law.

**UNDERWOOD, RUSSELL B,** Univ Of Sc At Columbia, Columbia, SC; SR; Portfolio Lit Mag Asst Fctn Ed 88-; Gldn Key 90-; Gamma Beta Phi 90-; Laubach Lit Actn Tutor; BA; Englsh; Englsh Prfsr.

**UNDERWOOD, SIGRUNN L,** Jackson St Univ, Jackson, MS; SO; BA; Dunbar Drmtc Guild 90-; Mass Cmnctns; Radio Announcer.

**UNDERWOOD, SYLVIA J,** Memphis St Univ, Memphis, TN; SR; BBA; Omicron Delta Epsilon 90-; Gldn Ky 89-; Hnrs Stu Assn 87-88; Lambda Zeta Delta Pres 88-90; Bus Ecnmcs; Fnncl Anlyst.

**UNDERWOOD, TODD W,** Univ Of Sc At Coastal Carolina, Conway, SC; SO; BS; Flwshp Chrstn Athlts Sec 90; Mns Clb Vlybl 89-; Campus Crsde Chrst 89-; Phi Eta Sigma 90-; Alpha Mu Gamma; IM Vlybl/Sftbl 89-90; Marine Sci.

**UNDERWOOD, WAYNE S,** Roane St Comm Coll, Harriman, TN; SO; AAS; Natl Env Hlth Assoc 89-; AS 90; Envir Hlth.

**UNDERWOOD, WILLIAM H,** Roane St Comm Coll, Harriman, TN; SO; BS; Gamma Beta Phi 89-90; Chem Awd 89-90; AS 90; Mech Engrng.

**UNEMORI, MELISSA S,** Cornell Univ Statutory College, Ithaca, NY; FR; BS; WVBR-FM Ithaca Nws Rep Afrtn Clrnce 90-; Comm Affrs Dir; Rd Crpt Soc 90-; Radio Gld; Intrnshp Maui Inc Gld Mag; Dns Lst; Comms; Brdcstng.

**UNG, AY-KIM,** Univ Of Pittsburgh, Pittsburgh, PA; FR; Hlth Rltd Prfssns; Nrsng.

**UNG, BENG L,** City Univ Of Ny Baruch Coll, New York, NY; SR; BBA; Malaysian Assn Pub Rels 90; Comp/Quant Methods Soc; Golden Key; CIS.

**UNG, PADIWATH C,** Univ Of Rochester, Rochester, NY; JR; MD; Biochem Soc 90-; Sigma Nu Sentinel 90-; Early Selection 89-; Engr/Scientific/Tech Intern 89-; IM Vlybl/Soccer; Biochem/Philosophy; Med.

**UNGAR, CAROLE WILSON,** Univ Of Cincinnati, Cincinnati, OH; SR; BFA; Walter E Bartlett Awd Otstndng Wmn Stdnt In Brdcstng 89; Carole Wilson Publ Rels Inc Pres; Brdcstng; Publ Rels.

**UNGER, ADRIAN R,** Radford Univ, Radford, VA; JR; BA; Inter Res Hall Coun; Hall Coun Indiv Flr Rep/Pres 90-; RA; Sigma Nu Asst Pledge Mrshl 88-89; Engl; Proff/Engl.

**UNGER, BARBARA A,** Garrett Comm Coll, Mchenry, MD; SO; AA; Scl Sci; Hmn Svcs Wrkr.

**UNGER, BRENT M,** Univ Of Cincinnati, Cincinnati, OH; SR; BS; IM 89-; Kappa Delta Pi 90-; Pi Kappa Alpha 87-; Mgr Bsktbl Tm 90-; Crmnl Jstc/Spnsh; Fed Govt/Coaching.**

**UNGER, DAVID R,** Univ Of Rochester, Rochester, NY; SO; BS; Varsity Soccer 89-; Meridian Soc; Delta Upsilon Rush Comm; Chem Engrng.

**UNGRUHE, THERESA M,** Univ Of Cincinnati, Cincinnati, OH; SR; BS; Assn Ftnss Bus; Golden Key 90-F Eta Sigma Gamma 90-; Vlntr Hamilton Cnty Spec Olymps Trck/Fld/Bwlng/Ply Grw 87-; U Indy 2nd Hons 88-90; U Cincinnati Deans Lst 90-; Vars Crss Cntry/Trck 87-; Hlth Promo/Ed; Corp Ftnss/Cardc Rhbltn.

**UNTERBERG, DARA MICHELLE,** Yeshiva Univ, New York, NY; GD; Stdnt Struggle For Soviet Jewry Chrprsn 88; Div Of Youth Svcs 87-90; Tchr.

**UNTIEDT, THOMAS G,** Bristol Univ, Bristol, TN; SR; BS; Sndy Sch Suptndt/Elder Stone Meml Prsbytrn Ch; VP Atkins Comm Cncl; Pgm Coord Brunswick Defense; AS Wytheville Comm Coll; Bus Admin.

**UPCHURCH, JENNIFER D,** Ms St Univ, Miss State, MS; FR; GBA; Ldrshp Schlrshp 90-; Acctg.

**UPCHURCH, ROBERT L,** Univ Of Nc At Charlotte, Charlotte, NC; FR; BA; Architecture.

**UPCHURCH, SHANNON J,** Western Carolina Univ, Cullowhee, NC; SR; BA; Coll Dmcrts 88; Sigma Nu Aux 88-; IM Athltcs 86-; Spch Cmnctns; Culnry Advtsng.

**UPDIKE, DANIEL P,** S U N Y Coll At Fredonia, Fredonia, NY; SR; Radio Prod Dir 88-; Tch Asst 90; BS; Comm/Radio Prdctn.

**UPDIKE, KELLIE M,** Radford Univ, Radford, VA; JR; BS; Avec Mvemnt 88-89; Alpha Sigma Alpha Pres; Early Mddle Ed; Tchr.

**UPDIKE, SCOTT A,** Emory & Henry Coll, Emory, VA; JR; BA; Math Assoc Amer 90-; Appl Math; Law Sch.

**UPHAM, MELISSA J,** Southeastern Ma Univ, N Dartmouth, MA; FR; BA; Hon Pgm; Engl-Lit; Hgh Sch Educ.

**UPSHAW, BRIAN S,** Valdosta St Coll, Valdosta, GA; JR; BED; Bptst Stdnt Un Dscplshp Chrmn 89-90; Inttntnl Assn Jazz Edctrs VP 90-; Mrchng Bnd; Clg Msc Edctrs Ntnl Cnfrnc Prsdnt; Phi Beta Mu Otstndng Instrmntl Edctn; Msc Edctn; Mnstry.

**UPSHUR, DEVONNA L,** Morgan St Univ, Baltimore, MD; JR; BA; Mem Wmns Bsktbl Tm 90-; Stdnt Gov Assn 89-F Army Rsrvs 90-; Wmns Coll Bsktbl 90-; Bus Admin; Fncl Mgmt.

**UPSON, ALICIA L,** Tougaloo Coll, Tougaloo, MS; SO; BA; Gospel Choir 89-; Stdnt Support Services 89-; Stdnt Govt Assoc 90-; Political Sci; Law.

**UPTAIN, STEPHEN S,** Univ Of Al At Huntsville, Huntsville, AL; SO; BS; IEEE; Alpha Tau Omega Worthy Usher 89; Ntnl Collgte Engr Awd Winner; G D Johnston Schlrshp 89-; Engrng.

**UPTON JR, DONALD R,** Ga Inst Of Tech At Atlanta, Atlanta, GA; FR; BSE; Amer Scty Of Mech Engs 90-; Intrfrat Schlrshp Com; Intrfrat Phlnthrpy Com; Phi Eta Sigma 90-; Lambda Sigma 90-; Phi Gamma Delta 90-; Schl Chmpn Annl Wrstlng Trnmnt; Mech Eng; Eng.

**UPTON, J MICHELLE,** Liberty Univ, Lynchburg, VA; JR; BS; Yth Qst Clb 89-; Lght Clb 90-; Trvlng Strng Qrtt 89-; Alpha Lambda Delta 89-; Thomas Road Bptst Chrch Orch 89-; Mssns Wrk Argnt; Dns Lst 89-; Acctng; Pblc Acctng.

**UPTON, JAMIE L,** Kent St Univ Kent Cmps, Kent, OH; JR; BA; Equestrian Tm 89-90; Amer Soc Int Dsgnrs Stdnt Chptr 89-; Kappa Omicron Nu Treas 90-; Pi Delta Co-Chr; Collaborative Inc Intern 90-; Int Dsgn/Arch; Arch.

**UPTON, LAURIE L,** Providence Coll, Providence, RI; JR; BA; Big Strs 90-; Jr Ring Weeknd Semiformal 90; Deans List 89-.**

**UPTON, MARTHA S,** Univ Of Fl, Gainesville, FL; JR; BA; Alpha Lambda Delta 89-; Sigma Tau Sigma 90-; Gldn Key 90-; Sigma Alpha Iota Editr 90-; Music.

**UPTON, STEVEN T,** Oh Univ, Athens, OH; SR; BSIT; AAS Hocking Tech Coll 84; AAS Hocking Tech Coll 90; Ind Tchnlgy; Eng.

**URAND, RUTH F,** Univ Of Nc At Asheville, Asheville, NC; FR; BA; Intl Bus Machines S Africa-Syst Engr 78-87; Cert Comp Sci Cybernetics Inst Albany NY 71; Blgy; Med/Ntrpthy.

**URBAN JR, JAMES J,** Univ Of Pittsburgh, Pittsburgh, PA; SR; BS; Phi Beta Sigma Edinboro Univ 87; Alpha Chi 88-89; Alumni Assn Schlrshp 88-89; BA Edinboro Univ Of PA; Mech Eng.

**URBAN, RICHARD J,** Pa St Univ Delaware Cty Cmps, Media, PA; SO; BA; Camera Clb Sec 90; Hstry; Archives Mgmt.

**URBAN, WILLIAM J,** Saint John Fisher Coll, Rochester, NY; JR; BA; Omicron Delta Epsilon; Pi Gamma Mu; Economics; Govt.

**URBANSKI, NICHOLAS F,** Case Western Reserve Univ, Cleveland, OH; FR; BS; Mrrtt Fd Srvcs Drm Rep 90-; Sci Cntr Chem Stckrm Prjct Spclst 90-; Phi Kappa Theta Sgt At Arms; By Scts Asst Sctmstr; Prvst Schlrshp; Chem Eng Rssn; Rcyclng.

**URBANSKY, DAVID M,** Univ Of Nc At Charlotte, Charlotte, NC; JR; BA; Amercn Inst Of Arch 90-; Arch.

**URBANSKY, EDWARD T,** Allegheny Coll, Meadville, PA; SR; BS; Nwspr Edtr 89-90; SG Atty Gen 88-89; Soc Appld Spctrspy; Calgon Corp Anlytcl Rsrch Intrn Tech 88-; TA 87-90; Tutor/Lab Asst 89-; Chemistry; Teach/Rsrch.

**URCH, RALPH E,** Air Force Inst Of Tech, Wrt-Ptrsn Afb, OH; GD; MS; Tau Beta Pi 88-89; BS AAE Ohio State Univ 84; Aero Eng; Eng

**URDAZ, LORRAINE M,** Inter Amer Univ Pr Arecibo Un, Arecibo, PR; JR; Sociedad De Hon Estdnts Drvrsd Intrmrcn Reanto De Arecibo 90-; Mu Alpha Phi MAI 89-; Mktg; Bus Law.

**URENA, CARLOS J,** City Univ Of Ny Baruch Coll, New York, NY; JR; BA; US Postal Serv Carrier 87-; AAS Borough Manhattan Comm Clg 87; Mrktng; Fin.

**URICH, JENNIFER L,** Muskingum Coll, New Concord, OH; SO; BA; Dorm Cncl 89-90; Psych Clb Sec/Treas 90-; WMCO/COLL Radio Statn Wrkr; Lambda Sigma 90-; Psi Chi; Omnicron Delta Kappa; Theta Phi Alpha Hstrn; Crisis Htln Vol 90-; Dns Lst 89-; Intrcollgt Sccr 89-; Psych/Comm.

**URICK, BETSY M,** Oh Univ, Athens, OH; SO; BFA; Alpha Lambda Delta 89-; Fine Arts; Art Ed.

**URIELL, MARK WAYNE,** Univ Of Miami, Coral Gables, FL; JR; BSAE; Chi Epsilon Pres; Phi Alpha Epsilon Pres; NSAE Sec; Tau Beta Pi 90-; Golden Key 90-; Alpha Sigma Phi Sgt At Arms 89-; Am Soc Of Civil Engrs 89-; Natl Soc Of Arch Engrs 89-; Natl Soc Of Prof Engrs 89-; Schlrshp; Arch Engrng; Consulting/Cnstrctn.

**URION, MICHAEL S,** Glassboro St Coll, Glassboro, NJ; SR; BA; Cmtr Cncl Prsdnt 88-; Bureau Srvc Orgnztns Mmbr 90-; Alpha Kappa Delta 90-; US Army W Germany Battaln Sply Spclst 85-87; Sclgy; Indsrl Sfty Rsk Mgmt.

**URIZAR MENDEZ, BRENDA LIZETH,** Univ Of South Al, Mobile, AL; SR; BS; Latin Amer Stdnt Assn Treas Elect; Cncl Intl Stdnts V P Elect; U S Info Agcy Schlrshp 90; Soc Stdes; Sec Educ.

**URLAUB, ALLISON B,** Westminster Coll, New Wilmingtn, PA; SO; BA; Psych Clb Sec 89-; Hbt Hum; Bible Stdy Ldr 89-; Psi Chi; Sigma Kappa Chpln; Hdstrt 89; Yth Dev Cntr Tutor; Adpt Grndprnt Prg 89-; Wegmans Schlshp 89-; Westminster Schlrshp 89-; Psych; Cnslr.

**URQUIA, CELENA L,** Univ Of Sc At Columbia, Columbia, SC; FR; Bus Admin Fnnce; Fnnce.

**URRUTIA, JOHN-PAUL,** Univ Of Miami, Coral Gables, FL; SO; Meet Anchor Pgm; News-Edtrl Jrnlsm/Pol Sci; Law.

**URSO, MARIE A,** Seton Hall Univ, South Orange, NJ; JR; BSN; St Ns Assoc; Deans List 90-; Montclair St Alum 90-; BS Montclair St Coll 90; AAS Hostos Comm Coll 73; Nurse Prctntr.

**URWICK, PAULA W,** Univ Of Sc At Aiken, Aiken, SC; SR; BA; Educ Mjrs Clb 87-; Aiken Pnhlnc Schlrshp 89; Elem Educ; Tchr.

**USAVAKUL, NIPHON,** Kent St Univ Kent Cmps, Kent, OH; JR; Psy; Clncl Psy.

**USAVICH, DIANE M,** Schenectady County Comm Coll, Schenectady, NY; SO; AAS; NYS Div Parole Ct Rprtr; Bus Admin; Lgsltv.

**USHER, JAMES D CLINTON,** Samford Univ, Birmingham, AL; FR; BA; Rep Sprt Frdm Inc Ldrshp Cnsltnt 90-; Pblc Spkr Sprt Frdm Inc Spkr 90-; Ttr 87-; Blgcl Sci; Coll Ed.

**USHIO, AYAKO,** Lasell Coll, Newton, MA; FR; Lib Arts.

**USINSKI, JOSPEH F,** Hilbert Coll, Hamburg, NY; FR; AA; Crmnl Jstc; Law Enfrcmnt.

**USKO, SHERRI L,** Duquesne Univ, Pittsburgh, PA; SR; BS; Acad Std Pharm 89-; PA Pharm Asn 90-; Phi Eta Sigma 87-88; Lambda Delta Edtr; Tau Delta Tau Chrmn 88-; Sigma Nu 89-; Syncor Intl Corp Intshp; Vol Rcgtn Awd; Nclr Pharm.

**USSERY, GENEVA R,** Catawba Valley Comm Coll, Hickory, NC; FR; BED; Acctg.

**USTICKE, ALEXANDER E,** Mount Saint Mary Coll, Newburgh, NY; JR; BA; Stdnt Govt Assoc Pres 88-; Democrats Pres 89-; Nwspr Pltcl Scnc Ed 88-90; Delta Mu Delta; Alpha Chi 90-; Acctg; Politics.

**UTLEY, ELLEN M,** Lesley Coll, Cambridge, MA; JR; BED; Jr Cls Elctd Cls Ofcr 90-; Deans Advsry Cncl 90-; Stdnt Ldrshp Advsry Bd 90-; Edn/Sci; Tchr K-3.

**UTLEY, JULIE A,** Owensboro Comm Coll, Owensboro, KY; SO; ASSOC; Phi Theta Kappa; Nrsng RN; RN.

**UTRERA, RAFAEL M,** Temple Univ, Philadelphia, PA; JR; BARCH; Career Opprtnties/Info In Archtctre; Archtctre.

**UTSET, EDGAR R,** Seton Hall Univ, South Orange, NJ; SO; BA; Vrsty Bsbl 89-; Finance.**

**UTTER, ANGELA K,** Radford Univ, Radford, VA; SR; BS; Art Gld Pres 90-; Fshn Soc Mbr 89-; Vol Rdfrd Comm Hosp Mrktg/Pblctns Dept; IM Rcqtbl 90-; Art; Grphc Dsgn.

**UTTER, JAMES S,** Univ Of Nc At Charlotte, Charlotte, NC; SR; BA; Pre Law Socty Comm 89-; Univ Times Sr Stf Wrtr 90-; Coll Dem Treas 89-91; Phi Kappa Phi; Pi Sigma Alpha 90-; Dns Lst 90-; Chnclrs Lst 90; Stf Wrtr Of Wk 90-; Pol Sci; Law/Jrnlsm/Pub Admin.

**UTZ, KIRK A,** City Univ Of Ny La Guard Coll, Long Island Cty, NY; SO; AAS; Phi Theta Kappa; Dns Lst; Data Prcsng; Cmptr Prgm.

**UTZ, REGINA D,** George Mason Univ, Fairfax, VA; SO; BS; Alpha Lambda Delta 90-; Gamma Phi Beta Hstrn 90-; Circle K 89-90; Acctg.

**UUS, CHARLES R,** Univ Of Miami, Coral Gables, FL; JR; BBA; Mahoney Res In Clg Res Assist; Hnr Stdnts Assn; Golden Key; Alumni/Mentor Prog; Sprtsfst Tm Capt; Finance; Grad Bus Schl.

**UWALAKA, LILIAN C,** Tuskegee Univ, Tuskegee Inst, AL; GD; BS; African Stdnts Assn; Nigerian Stdnts Assn VP 89-90; Alpha Kappa Mu 89-90; Kappa Delta Pi 90; Fedl Schlrshp Awd Nigeran Govt 80-83; Hndbl IMO St Grshprs 76; Anl Hnr Rl Schlstc Achvmnt 89; Tchr Tech Trng Pgrm AID 88-90; TCII 78; NCE 83; Agribusiness Educ; Educ.

**UZELAC-FREIDHOFF, LINDA M,** Indiana Univ Of Pa, Indiana, PA; SR; Assoc Rehab Advocates Treas 88-90; Intern Hiram G Andrews Cntr Cambria Cnty Assoc; BSED 90; Rehab; Cnslor.

**UZZELL, CHRISTINE D,** Univ Of The Dist Of Columbia, Washington, DC; SR; BA; Toastmasters Intl Sec 86-; Accredited Union Cnslr 85-; Make/Wish Fond Vol; United Way Vol 89-; Office Mngr 88-; AS Johnson/Wales Cllg 80; Cmptr Inform Systems; Computer Consultant.

# V

**VACANTI, JULIE A,** Saint Bonaventure Univ, St Bonventure, NY; FR; BA; Yrbrk Writer 90-; Nwspr 90-; Public Relations Assoc 90-; Bridges Bunarenture 90-; Wmn Cummun Inc 90-; Public Relations Assoc 90-; Public Reltns Repres 90-; Rodester Genl Hospital Public Relations Dept Intern; Deans List 90-; Mass Comm; Public Reltns/Advtng.

**VACCA, DONNA R,** Univ Of South Al, Mobile, AL; SR; BS; Stdnt Cncl Excptnl Chldrn Pres; AL Fdrtn Scec Gvnr; Kappa Delta Pi; Natl Mgmt Assn 79-87; Spec Olympics 89; AA Sthwstrn Clg 78; Spec Educ; Tchr.

**VACCARO, JOHN F,** Cornell Univ Statutory College, Ithaca, NY; JR; BS; Daily Sun Asst Advrtsng Mgr 89-; Ambassadors 89-; Bus Opportunities Clb Treas 90-; Zeta Beta Tau 90-; Personal Enterprise Pgm Intrnshp Tompkins Cnty Trust Co; Bus Mgmnt.

**VACCARO, KRISTIN C,** Univ Of Miami, Coral Gables, FL; FR; Pizzazz Dnce Clb 90-; Campus Mnstry 90-; Alpha Lambda Delta 90-; Intrn Cath Chrch; Spts Fest; Comm/Soclgy.

**VACHON, CELESTE S,** Eastern Ky Univ, Richmond, KY; FR; BA; Neuman Cntr Ldrshp Tm; Wldlfe Assn; Explorers Clb; Estrn Kntcky Hnr Stdnts; Rcyclng Comm; Tae Kwon Do Yllw Blt; Blgy; Rcyclng.

**VACHON, KELLY J,** Johnson St Coll, Johnson, VT; JR; BA; Deans Lst; Prsdnt Lst; Stdnt Tchr 90; Elem Edctn; Edctr.

**VACHON, MARGARET L,** Framingham St Coll, Framingham, MA; SR; Exec Sec Prime Cmptr Inc Natick MA; Bus Mgmt.

**VACLAVIK, NICOLE E,** S U N Y Coll Of Tech At Alfred, Alfred, NY; FR; AS; Concert Choir Sec; Pres Hons Schlrshp 90-; Choir Schlrshp 90-; Lib Arts/Humanties; HS Tchr.

**VACULIK, TAMARA J,** Capital Univ, Columbus, OH; SR; BSN; Sigma Theta Tau; Theta Theta Chptr; Kappa Alpha Pi; Omega Phi Alpha Pldge Eductr 89-; Sigma Theta Tau; KL Heuerman Awrd 89; Nrsng; Nrsng Hosp Acte Care.

**VADALA, ANTHONY,** S U N Y Coll Of Tech At Frmgdl, Farmingdale, NY; SO.

**VADEN, LISA R,** Radford Univ, Radford, VA; SR; BBA; Hon Stdnt Assn Pres 89-90; Bsktbl Statstcn 86-; VCHC; SCHC; NCHC; Delta Mu Delta; Phi Kappa Phi; Alpha Lambda Delta Treas 87-88; St Rep Pub Inst VA Collgt Hon Cncl 89-90; Mktg; Mkt Rsrch.

**VADEN, SCOTT D,** Volunteer St Comm Coll, Gallatin, TN; FR; MA; BA Clear Crk Bapt Clg 85; Cmptr Sci/Inf Syst; Prgmr/Profsr.

**VADNAIS, ROBERT J,** Castleton St Coll, Castleton, VT; SO; BA; Diploma WY Tech Inst 83; Bus; Acctg.

**VAETH, VIRGINIA M,** City Univ Of Ny Baruch Coll, New York, NY; GD; BBA 90; Stats Mktng.

**VAGO, KIMBERLY A,** Wv Univ, Morgantown, WV; JR; BSN; Undrgrad Sch Scl Wrk Org 90-; NASW 90-; Deans Lst 89-; Rape/Dmstc Vlnc Info Cntr Shltr Wrkr Cnslr Cmpn 90-; Spcl Olympcs 87-88; Scl Wrk.

**VAHLENKAMP, HANS,** Trenton St Coll, Trenton, NJ; SO; BS; NJ St Schlrshp; Comp Sci.

**VAHLENKAMP, HENNING,** Trenton St Coll, Trenton, NJ; SO; BS; TSC Schlrshp 89-; Comp Sci Cmmndtn 90; Comp Sci.**

**VAIA, RENEE LYNN,** Cornell Univ Statutory College, Ithaca, NY; SO; Hl Senate Secr 89-90; Ambsdr 89-90; Fd Sci Clb 89-; Orientation Steering Comm 90-; Orientation 89-90; Rainbow 86-; Fd Sci Tech Schlrshp 89-90; Lab Tech; Sftbl 89-.

**VAIDYANATHAN, RANJANI S,** City Univ Of Ny La Guard Coll, Long Island Cty, NY; FR; AA; Comp.

**VAIL, JASON D,** Savannah Coll Of Art & Design, Savannah, GA; SO; BA; Deans List 90; Phogrphay; Cmmrcl.

**VAINA, BETH A,** Univ Of Miami, Coral Gables, FL; SR; BS; Hmcmng Exec Cmm Cmps Rel 90; Hnrs Stdnts Assoc Treas 89-90; Mrtr Brd 89-; Gldn Key 88omicron Delta Kappa 90-; Spcl Olmpcs Fndy Exec Cmmtt Chrprsn 90-; US Sen Intrnshp 90bshvs Sngr Schlrshp 87-; Jrnlsm.

**VAITI, VANESSA L,** Georgian Court Coll, Lakewood, NJ; JR; BS; Bus Clb 90; Deans Lst Tobe Coburn 87-; Intern Talbots 88-89; Intern George Green Assc Asst Pres Jean Greh 88; AOS Tobe Coburn Schl Fshn Careers 89; Acctng; Cpa.

**VAK, SUSAN L,** Allegheny Coll, Meadville, PA; JR; BA; Ldrs/Liasons Educ Support V P 90-; Nwscstr Radio 89-90; Greek Rush Cnslr; Alpha Delta Pi 90-; Alden Schlr 88-; Doane Schlr 88-89; Intrnshp Dist Office U S Cngrssmn Tom Ridge; Engl/Pol Sci; Law.

**VALADEZ, CYNTHIA L,** Barry Univ, Miami, FL; JR; BLS; Hmn Rsrc Mngmnt; Hmn Rsrc Dir.

**VALAIE, SARAH,** Tn St Univ, Nashville, TN; SR; Soc Work Clb 89-; Deans List; Alpha Delta Mu; BS; Soc Work; Emplymnt/Attend Grad Schl.

**VALCOURT, SCOTT A,** Saint Anselm Coll, Manchester, NH; JR; BA; Anselmian Abbey Players Gvrng Bd 88-; Boy Scts Of Amer OA Section Chf 88-90; Cmptr Socty Pres 89-; Dns Lst 88-; Assn Cmptng Mchnry 90-; K Of C Degree Tm Capt 88-; Cmptr Sci/Math; Sec Educ.**

**VALDES, DALIA R,** City Univ Of Ny Baruch Coll, New York, NY; SR; BSED; Teachers Of Tomorrow Club 90-; Phi Theta Kappa 87-; Golden Key 89-; Grace Baptist Church Pianist Choir Dir; AA LA NYC Tchncl Clge 88; Special Education; Teaching.

**VALDES, ELIZABETH,** Inter Amer Univ Pr Hato Rey, Hato Rey, PR; JR; BBA; Finance; Law.

**VALDES, FELIX H,** Fl International Univ, Miami, FL; JR; BS; AA Miami-Dade Cmnty Clg 89; Bus; MBA.

**VALDES, JANELLE L,** Hillsborough Comm Coll, Tampa, FL; FR; AA; Lil Sis Sigma Alpha Epsilon 90; Sci; Phrmcy.

**VALDES, MARISOL,** Fl International Univ, Miami, FL; FR; BA; Soc Studies/Scndry Edn; Tchr.

**VALDETERO, ELIZABETH B,** Univ Of Sc At Aiken, Aiken, SC; FR; BS; Gamma Beta Phi; Schlrshp; Dean Lst 90-; Cost Accntng.

**VALDIVIESO, KAREN S,** Univ Of Sc At Columbia, Columbia, SC; SO; BA; Educ; Spch Pthlgy.

**VALE, GEORGE W,** Kent St Univ Kent Cmps, Kent, OH; SR; BBA; IMS 87-; Amer Mktg Assoc 90-; Dns Lst 90-; Mktg; Mktg/Mgmt.

**VALEDON, ALEXIS D,** Catholic Univ Of Pr, Ponce, PR; SR; MBA; Acctg Stdnts Assoc 87-88; Amer Prod/Inv Contr Soc 90-; Hnrs Pgm 87-90; Alpha Chi 89-; Phi Beta Gamma Cancellor 89-; Dns Lst 87-88; US Achvmnt Acad 89; Inter-Dept Bsktbl 87-; Mgmt.

**VALENCIA, HENRY,** Atlantic Comm Coll, Mays Landing, NJ; GD; Elect Engr Univ Autonona Of Occidente 81; Sprmrkt Admn 81-89; Elect Engr.

**VALENCIA, HENRY,** Miami Dade Comm Coll, Miami, FL; SO; AA; Acess Dept Math Tutor 89-; Math Dept Tutor 89-; Hnrs Prog Schlrshp; Dean Lst 89-; Otstndng Achvmnt 90; Math; Thrtcl Math.**

**VALENCIA, JOSEPHINE,** City Univ Of Ny Baruch Coll, New York, NY; SO; BA; Auxlry Police Ofcr; Fencng Tm 89-; Publc Admn; Law.

**VALENCIA, SHERRI L,** Norfolk St Univ, Norfolk, VA; SR; BSW; Alpha Delta Nu V P 90-; Alpha Kappa Nu 90-; Qtrly Cntry Clb Schlrshp; Soc Wrk; MSW Ph D.

**VALENTA, MARCELLA A,** Holyoke Comm Coll, Holyoke, MA; FR; AS; Licensed Cosmotologist 72-; Compassionate Friends 86-; Ofc Mgr Integrating Computer Software 88-90; Computer Inf Systems; Programming.

**VALENTA, ROBIN A,** Midway Coll, Midway, KY; SO; AA; Intrnshp 90-; Equine Off Admn/Mgmt; Admn Wrk.

**VALENTE, ANGELA,** Saint Johns Univ, Jamaica, NY; SR; BED; Stdnt Govt; Inter Sor Cncl; Elec Cmte; Budget Cmte; Golden Key VP 90-; Kappa Delta Pi Sec 90; Sigma Chi Zeta Tr 89-90; Walk A Thon Starlight Fdtn; Blood Dr; Deans Lst 88-89; Stdnt Tchr; Speech; Own Day Care Ctr.**

**VALENTI, ANNETTE,** Duquesne Univ, Pittsburgh, PA; JR; BA; Italian Clb Pres 88; Rsdnt Assist 90; Chrl Grp 90; Phi Eta Sigma 88; Music Mnstry 88; Duquesne Univ Schlr 88; Amax Fndtn Schlrshp 88; Pbl Rltns Intrnshp; Pblc Rltns.

**VALENTI, FRANK,** Nova Univ, Ft Lauderdale, FL; SO; MBA; BS St Peters Coll 83; Bus Admin; Mktg Mgmt.

**VALENTI, MARIA P,** City Univ Of Ny Queensbrough, New York, NY; SR; AAS; Alpha Beta Gamma; Deans Lst Prfssnl Sec Intrntnl Dptmntl Awd; AAS Queensborough Comm Clg; Legal Asst NY City Tech Clg; Paralegal.

**VALENTI, RICHARD J,** Hudson Valley Comm Coll, Troy, NY; JR; AAS; Comp Oprtr NYS Hgr Ed Svc Corp 89-; Comp Info Syst; Comp Pgrmng.

**VALENTIN BON, IRIS ENID,** Inter Amer Univ Pr Hato Rey, Hato Rey, PR; JR; BA; Assn Geogrphrs In Actn 88; Assn Stdnt Biolgcl Sci 88-89; Chem Assn 88; Beta Beta Beta 88-; Rsrchr NIH-MBRS Prog 87-; Med Cntr Vol 90; F G Brooks Awrd; Biolgy; Mcrobiolgy.**

**VALENTIN FIGUEROA, FRANK EDGAR,** Univ Of Pr Cayey Univ Coll, Cayey, PR; SO; Cnfrntrndad Cristiana Univ De Cayey 89-; Sociedad De Hnr De Decano UPR; Skekina Chistian Musical Group; Blgy; MD.

**VALENTIN JUSINO, SHIRLEY,** Inter Amer Univ Pr San German, San German, PR; SO; BA; Pblc Rltns; Cmmnctns.

**VALENTIN RODRIGUEZ, RAFAEL,** Inter Amer Univ Pr Guayama, Guayama, PR; FR; Chinese Kunf Fu Assn 87; Bsktbl Team 88-90; Club Kaud 89-; Campana Cancer 88; Chrstms Club 87-; Hnr Cert; Table Tennis/Bsktbl 89; Acctblty; CPA.

**VALENTIN, DAVID O,** Columbia Union Coll, Takoma Park, MD; JR; BA; Elem/Secondary Ed; Tchng.

**VALENTIN, JANNETTE T,** Inter Amer Univ Pr San German, San German, PR; SO; Natl Exchng Clb 87-; Bio; Med Tech.

**VALENTIN, JEANNETTE,** Univ Of Pr At Mayaguez, Mayaguez, PR; SO; BBA; Natl Hispanic Schlrshp Fund Awards 90; Org Stds; Mgmt.

**VALENTIN, RAMON J,** Inter Amer Univ Pr Hato Rey, Hato Rey, PR; SO; BBA; Univ Intercoll Soccr Tm 90-; Acctg/Mktg.

**VALENTIN, WILSON M,** Univ Of Pr At Mayaguez, Mayaguez, PR; SR; BA; IEEE 89-90; Hon Cert Elec Eng Dept 87-; Elec Eng.

**VALENTIN-RIOS, JEANETTE,** Catholic Univ Of Pr, Ponce, PR; SR; MBA; Club De Futuros Maestros 88-90; Proyecto Palante 87-88; Ronald Mc Nair Prog 89-; Santiago Collazo Perez Elem Sch Juana Diaz 1st Gr Eng Tchr; Rainbow Sch Chgo Il Aide; Servicios Educativos UCPR Eng Ttr 90-; Natl Hispanic Schlrshp 90-91; BA Cum Laude; Eng Edn TESOL; Earn Doctoral Eng Edn.**

**VALENTINE, BARBARA L,** Liberty Univ, Lynchburg, VA; JR; BS; Lbrty Assoc Chrstn Tchrs; Kappa Delta Pi; Thomas Road Bapt Chrch Chldrns Mnstry 89-; Rdng Tutor TRBC Erly Lrng Cntr 90-; Bensalem Bapt Chrch Tchr 86-; Pdmnt Area Reading Cncl Jdg 90-; GPA Schlrshp 88-; Educ; Tchr.

**VALENTINE, BRENDA C,** Univ Of Montevallo, Montevallo, AL; SR; BS; Bio Clb 90-; Chorale 87; Bapt Campus Mnstry 87-; Kappa Mu Epsilon Tres 89-; Psi Chi; Psych; Phys Thrpy.

**VALENTINE, CHERYL K,** Dowling Coll, Oakdale Li, NY; SR; BBA; Sales Asst 89-; AAS Suffolk Cmmnty Clg 89; Bsn Mgmt; Law.

**VALENTINE, DEBORAH A,** Cumberland County Coll, Vineland, NJ; SO; BED; Cumberland Dist Awd Of Merit 88; Boy Scts Of Amer 88; Sctrs Key Awd Cbmstrs 87; B Scts Of Amer 87; Tenis Tm 68-69; Becker Coll 68069; Cub Scts/B Scts Ldrshp 84-91; Chldrns Gspl Play Dir 88-89; Tchng Preschl; AS Becker Coll MASS 70; Early Chldhd/Elem Educ; Tchg.

**VALENTINE, JUDITH L,** Livingston Univ, Livingston, AL; JR; BS; Singers 90-; Choir 90-; Alpha Chi; Cardinal Key; Jones Jr Clb Acad Ltr 89-90; Trustee Schlrshp 90-; Vocal Schlrshp 90-; Music; Tch Voice.

**VALENTINE, LINDA J,** Middle Tn St Univ, Murfreesboro, TN; SR; Ft Sanders Sch Nrsg Stdnt Cncl Pres 78-79; Ft Sanders Sch Nrsg Stdnt Body Pres 78-79; Psi Chi; In View 2nd Annual Awds; Domestic Violence Pgm Coord Elder Abuse Proj 90; RN; Certif Ft Sanders Sch Nrsg 79; RN State TN 79; CNOR Assoc Oper Rm Nrs 84; Psych; Clncl Cnslg-Victims Violent Crimes.

**VALENTINE, LORIANN T,** Marywood Coll, Scranton, PA; JR; BM; St Cecelia Music Soc Pres 90-; MENC Secr 89-; ACDA V P 90-; Wind Ensmbl Pblcty 88-; Chamber Choir Libr 88-; Campus Choir Treas 89-90; Crystal Bnd Scranton 87-; Meth Ch Choir 87-; Talent Schlrshp 88-; State Vars Bnd 90-; State Vars Chorus 88-; Music Ed; Tch MA.

**VALENTINE, MARY JOY,** S U N Y Coll Of Tech At Alfred, Alfred, NY; FR; AAS; Bus Admin; Hlth Ftns Bus.

**VALENTINE, SCOTT A,** S U N Y Coll Of Tech At Delhi, Delhi, NY; SR; BA; Bus Club; Small Fry Ftbl Coach 89-; Peer Tutoring 89-; AAS; Bus Admn.

**VALENTINE, STACY M,** Univ Of Hartford, West Hartford, CT; FR; BAMBA; African Am Stdnt Org 90-; Music Mgmt Assn 90-; Inter Varsity Chrstn Flwshp Gospel Choir 90; Talent Awd 90-; Deans List 90; Applied Music/Bus Mgmt; Music Mgmt/ Musician.

**VALENTINE-MURRELL, MARLENE F,** Univ Of Tn At Martin, Martin, TN; SR; BS; STEA 88-; Phi Kappa Phi 90-; Magna Cum Laude 90; A A 73; Elem Ed; Spcl Ed Tchr.

**VALENTINI, NICKY,** Hillsborough Comm Coll, Tampa, FL; SO; AS; Phi Theta Kappa Phi Chi Chaptr; Gloria Phillips Memrl Awrd 90; HCC Awrd Acad Achvmnt; USF CEU Mstr Cert Univ Of So Fla 79; Human Serv Tech; Soc Work.

**VALENTINO, MARIA C,** Marist Coll, Poughkeepsie, NY; SO; BS; Dns Lst 89-91; Bsns Admn; Publ.

**VALENTINO, MARIAELENA,** Nyack Coll, Nyack, NY; SO; BA; Sec 86-; Prlgl Amer Inst Prlgl Stds 86; Hist; Law.

**VALENZUELA JR, JOSE M,** Nova Univ, Ft Lauderdale, FL; GD; Catholic Yth Dir 89-90; NOVA Univ Deans Lst 89-90; Sr Engr Telecommunications 87-; BSEE Fla Atlantic Univ 85; Mngmnt Mrktng; Tchncl Sls/Engrng.

**VALERI, JODI L,** Univ Of Fl, Gainesville, FL; JR; BA; Chi Phi Ltl Sis; Golden Key; Alpha Lambda Delta; Phi Eta Sigma; Delta Gamma 89-; Finance; Law/Bsn.

**VALERI, PAMELA A,** Newbury Coll, Brookline, MA; SO; AAS; Cub Sct Den Mother 89-; Little League Tm Mother; Paralegal; Law.**

**VALERIANO, RICARDO C,** Va St Univ, Petersburg, VA; JR; BS; CT Clb Treas 89-90; Pub Admin Clb Treas 89-90; Econ Clb; Alpha Kappa Mu; Deans Lst; Chstrfld Co Schlrshp; Chase Mnhttn Bnk Mgmt Trning Prog; Econ; Financl Anlyst.

**VALERIO, EVELYN,** Catholic Univ Of Pr, Ponce, PR; JR; BA; Natl Assn Female Execs; Natl Assn Purchasing Mgrs; Purch Dir Ponce Schl Of Med; Gen Commerce; Masters In Purchasing.

**VALERO, STEPHEN N,** Wv Univ, Morgantown, WV; JR; ROTC Co Cmmndr; Rngr Co Exec Offcr; Chi Epsilon; Cvl Eng.

**VALERY, RAND S,** Western Ky Univ, Bowling Green, KY; FR; BED; Phi Eta Sigma; Psychology.

**VALIENTE ALVAREZ, LYANETTE M,** Inter Amer Univ Pr Hato Rey, Hato Rey, PR; FR; Vrsty 90-; Psychlg; Indtl Psychology.

**VALIENTE RIVERA, ERNESTO A,** Univ Of Pr Medical Sciences, San Juan, PR; SR; DMD; ASDA 87-; Dns Lst 87-; Omicron Kappa Upsilon; Phi Sigma Alta 87-; P Fauchard Awd; OMS Assn Awd; Dtl ASA Assn Awd; Odntlgy; OMS Res Prog.

**VALINOTI, DOMINIC J,** Manhattan Coll, Bronx, NY; JR; Fclty/Stdnt Cntnl Clbrtn Cmmttee EE Rep; Tau Beta Pi VP 90; Eta Kappa Nu Sec 90; Deans Lst 88; Elctrcl Eng.

**VALIQUETTE, DAVID M,** Hillsborough Comm Coll, Tampa, FL; SO; BA; Pharmacy.

**VALLA, DANIEL M,** Le Moyne Coll, Syracuse, NY; SR; BA; Cmunty Projcts Prog Coordr 90-; Folks Grp Singrs 89-; Psych Sec 90-; Sr Ctzns Dinners 89-; Hosp Intrn Chldrns Day Trtmnt 90-; AS Bus Admn Brcome Cmuty Clg 86-88; Psych.

**VALLANCE, KATHY A,** Marshall University, Huntington, WV; GD; MA; Chi Sigma Iota Pres 90-; BA Psychology 88; Cnslng Rehab.

**VALLARIAN, JOSEPH H,** Itawamba Comm Coll, Fulton, MS; SO; BA; Plbctns Clb 89-; Advrtsng Coord Stf Wrtr 89-; Nwspr; Intrnshp Prntng Bsns 90-; Cmmnctns; Pblc Rltns Advrtsng.**

**VALLARINO, JUAN C,** Fl International Univ, Miami, FL; SR; BS; ASCE Pres; PSA VP 90-; Alpha Omega Chi 90-; Swmng Schlrshp MDCC 88-89; Acdmc All Amer MDCC 89; AA MDCC 89; Engnrng; Phd Env Engnrng.**

**VALLARINO, ROBERTO E,** Fl International Univ, Miami, FL; SR; ASCE 89-; PSA 89-; Dns Lst; Sub Tchr MDCC/ALGEBRA 89-90; AA MDCC 88; Cvl Engr.

**VALLE, CHRISTINE N,** City Univ Of Ny Queensbrough, New York, NY; SO; AAS; Deans Hon Lst; Bus/Acctg; Corp Acctg.

**VALLE, ZULMA,** Univ Of Pr At Mayaguez, Mayaguez, PR; SO; BSIE; Math; Ind Eng.

**VALLEJO, NATALIA A,** Birmingham Southern Coll, Birmingham, AL; JR; BA; Stf Clmnst Coll Nwspr 90-; Cthlc Campus Mnstry Cthlc Cordntr 89-; Elem Sch Cnslr Links Up 89-90; Alpha Lambda Delta Tres 89-90; Phi Eta Sigma 89-; Alpha Kappa Psi; Arnold Air Soc Afrotc Serv Frat Pblc Afrs Ofcr 89-; Bus Admin; Law.

**VALLES, DAWN M,** Smith Coll, Northampton, MA; SO; BA; Nosotras 89; Hse Treas 90; CRC Chem Achievemnt Awd 90; Im Vllybl Flr Hcky 89; Chem/Ed; Tchr Admin.

**VALLON, MARIE J,** City Univ Of Ny Queensbrough, New York, NY; JR; BA; Microbio; Nrsng.

**VALLONE, MARY A,** Dowling Coll, Oakdale Li, NY; SR; Acctg Soc 88-; Delta Mu Delta 90-; Alpha Chi 90-.

**VALLORD, ALEXIA C L,** Inter Amer Univ Pr San German, San German, PR; JR; BA; Amer Psychlgl Assc; Escape Pgm Vol 90-; Psychlgy; Phd.

**VALMUS-JERNIGAN, MARIAN FAYE,** Univ Of West Fl, Pensacola, FL; SR; BA; Phi Theta Kappa 83-85; AA Pensacola Jr Clg 84; CASE Pensacola Jr Clg 84; Spl Ed; E H Tchr.

**VALOSIN, WILLIAM T,** Saint John Fisher Coll, Rochester, NY; JR; BA; Hstry Clb 89-; Taekwondo Clb 90-; Phi Alpha Theta; BSA Asst Sctmstr 88-; Eagle Sct; Dns Lst 89-90; Hstry; Educ.

**VALREE, ROOSEVELT,** Univ Of South Al, Mobile, AL; SR; EE; AOA Faulkner State Jr Clg 86; Elem Ed; Masters Ed Ldrshp.

**VALTRI, STEVEN A,** Widener Univ, Chester, PA; SR; BS; SGA Fin Char 86-88; Soc Advncmnt Mngt 90-; Intl Hnr Soc Economcs; Dns Lst 89-87; Pres Lst 87-88; Acad Hnrs 89-; Sup T-World Casino Entrnmnt Resort 85; Mngmt; Law Schl.

**VALUKEVICH, A THOMAS,** Teikyo Post Univ, Waterbury, CT; JR; BA; Post Drama Clb Pres 88-90; Coll Entrtnmnt Com 89-90; Rsdnt Asst 89-90; Mattatuck Dionysus Awd Best Spprtng Actor 87; AS 90; Cmnctn; TV/FLM Prod.

**VAMOSY, EILEEN M,** Daemen Coll, Amherst, NY; FR; Phys Therpy.

**VAN ABEL, KELLEY M,** Catawba Valley Comm Coll, Hickory, NC; FR; ABA; Acctg Bus Admn; Acctnt.

**VAN ALLEN, THODD G,** Syracuse Univ, Syracuse, NY; SR; BEA; Alpha Phi Omega Serv VP 89-90; Stu Mrshl; NYSATA 89-; NESA 80-; Anmtn Camera Oprtr 86-89; AST 84; Art Educ.

**VAN ALSTINE, CLARE A,** Univ Of Sc At Aiken, Aiken, SC; SR; MS; Science Clb Pres 87-; Gamma Beta Phi VP 88-; Omicron Scty 89-90; Amer Chem Scty 90-; BS Univ Of SC At Aiken; Chemistry; Teaching.

**VAN ARSDALE, CHRISTEL I,** Cornell Univ Statutory College, Ithaca, NY; FR; Crss Cntry 90-; Indr Otdr Trck 90-; Wldlf Biol; Endngred Species.

**VAN ARSDALE, ROSEMARY,** Hillsborough Comm Coll, Tampa, FL; FR; ADN; Phi Theta Kappa; Regstrd Real Est Brkr 64-; Nrsng; RN.

**VAN ASDLEN, MEREDITH L,** Longwood Coll, Farmville, VA; FR; BS; Natl Stu Spch Lang Hrng Assc 90-; Delta Zeta; Spch Pthlgy; MA.

**VAN AUKEN, KAY E,** Wilmington Coll, New Castle, DE; JR; BA; State DE Fmly Ct Georgetown DE 81-; Elem Ed/Erly Chldhd; Tchr.

**VAN BRUNT, JENNIFER L,** Davis & Elkins Coll, Elkins, WV; FR; BA; Dns Lst 90-; Busn; Law.

**VAN BUREN, BROOKE A,** Univ Of Ky, Lexington, KY; FR; CARE 90-; Little KY Drby 90-; Mrktg Com 90-; Hmcmg Com 90-; Chi Omega Career Dvlpmt Chr; Sftbl 90-.

**VAN BUREN, KAREN A,** Fayetteville St Univ, Fayetteville, NC; JR; BA; Political Sci Clb 90-; Cumberland Mills Elem PTA Pres; Deptmntl Awrd Pltcl Sci 90-; Medl Secy 89-; Data Entry Oper; Pltcl Sci Pblc Admin; Law.

**VAN BUREN, KATHLEEN A,** Western New England Coll, Springfield, MA; SR; BA; Bhvrl Soc Scncs Clb/Peer Tutor 87-; Hlpng Hnd Soc/Stdnt Teach Asst 90-; Peer Advsr/Yrbk Clb/ Grad Comm 90-; Psi Chi VP 89-; Vol Boys Clb 88; Vol Jr HS Tutor 89; Skookum Awd 90-; Intrnshp Forensic Servs Mntl Hlth Clnc 90-; Psych; Grad Schl PHD Psych.

**VAN BURIK, DENISE A,** Rutgers St Un At New Brunswick, New Brunswick, NJ; FR; BA; Emrgng Ldrs Pgm; Govt Asc Rep; Ornttn Comm; IM; Grmn/Pol Sci; Law.

**VAN BUSKIRK, RANDY A,** Nova Univ, Ft Lauderdale, FL; GD; MBA; BSEE Oakland Univ 79; Elec Engr.

**VAN BUSSUM, MARILYN R,** Owensboro Comm Coll, Owensboro, KY; SO; Hmn Srvcs; Scl Wrkr.

**VAN CAMP, CHRISTIE,** Mount Olive Coll, Mount Olive, NC; SO; BA; Psychology Clb 90-; Academic Schlr 89-; Marshall Highest GAA 89-90; Perritt Awd 90; Assoc; Biology; Phrmcy.

**VAN CAMP, WILLIAM E,** Va St Univ, Petersburg, VA; SR; BS; Phi Beta Lambda 90-; Admn Sys Mgmt; Data Prcssng Fld.

**VAN DALE, HEATHER L,** Muskingum Coll, New Concord, OH; JR; BA; Flwshp Chrstn Athlts Hd Advsr 90-; Sr Hnry; Phi Theta Beta; Chi Alpha Nu Clb Photo 90-; Hsp Vol 88-90; Mbr Tchr Advsry Comm; IM Vlybl 88-; Elem/Spcl Educ; Tchr.

**VAN DALEN, LAURA A,** D Youville Coll, Buffalo, NY; JR; BSMS; Phys Thrpy.

**VAN DALSEN, CHRISTINA,** Elmira Coll, Elmira, NY; SO; BS; Intrnatl Clb 90; Chrstn Fllwshp Clb 89-; Phi Eta Sigma Pres 90-; Beta Beta Beta 90-; Chem Awrd 90; Phi Eta Sigma Awrd; Yth Vol Of Yr 90; Pope AF Base; Blgy Chem; Med Pdtrcn.

**VAN DE WAL, BRIAN J,** Hudson Valley Comm Coll, Troy, NY; SO; BME; Vol Fire Co Frmn 87-; Otto V Guenther Schlrshp 90-; Engr; Structural.

**VAN DE WALLE, KENNETH J,** Univ Of Nc At Charlotte, Charlotte, NC; JR; BA; AIA 88-; Phi Eta Sigma 88-; SSGT USMC Actv Rsrvs Plt Sgt 84-; Archtctr Englsh; Archtctr Tchr.

**VAN DEN AKKER, WILLIAM J,** Liberty Univ, Lynchburg, VA; SR; BS; Cltrl Awrns/Comm Enrchmnt Comm Comm Mem 90-; Urban Outrch Clb 89-90; Coll Repblcn Clb 87-89; Lbrty Pnrs Kenya Mssnry Intrnshp 89; Urban Outrch Smmr Intrnshp Ldr 90; Crss-Cltrl Stds Relgn; Mssnry Chrch Plntng.

**VAN DER HEIDE, STELLA M,** Cornell Univ Statutory College, Ithaca, NY; JR; BS; Delta Delta Delta 88; Im Vllybl 89; Bsnss Pre-Med; Bsnss Or Med.

**VAN DER LOO, ERIC R,** Radford Univ, Radford, VA; SR; BS; Pi Gamma Mu 90-; Sociology/Anthropology; Human Services.

**VAN DERWARKER, WENDY A,** Castleton St Coll, Castleton, VT; JR; BA; SEA; AA Adirondack Comm Coll 90; Elem Ed/ Psychlgy; Tchng.

**VAN DEUSEN, MATHEW A,** Saint Francis Coll, Loretto, PA; FR; BS; Phi Kappa Theta; Vrsty Golf 90-; Chem; Pdtrc Med.

**VAN DEVENDER, DEBORAH K,** Marshall University, Huntington, WV; SO; BA; Bus; Acctng.

**VAN DEVENTER, BRIAN L,** Tomlinson Coll, Cleveland, TN; JR; Stu Govt Cls Pres 88-90; Sprtl Life Comm Chrprsn 90-; Phi Theta Cappa 88-; Alpha Chi 90-; Deans Lst 88-; Pres Lst 88-; Var Bsktbl 90-; AS 90; Mnstry; Tchg.

**VAN DINE, CLINT R,** West Liberty St Coll, West Liberty, WV; SR; Psychlgy Clb Pres 88-90; SGA 88-89; Am Pschlgcl Assn 87-; WLSC Acdmc Schlrshp 90; Cum Laude 90; BS 90; Psychlgy; Cnsmr Pshyclgy.

**VAN DROSS, RUKIYAH T,** Al St Univ, Montgomery, AL; JR; BS; Peer Alliance Coop Career Access 90-; Phi Eta Sigma 88-; Mnrty Access Careers Rsrch; Mnrty Biomed Rsrch Supt Pgm 90-; Alpha Kappa Mu; Delta Sigma Theta Sor VP 90-; Coop Experience Dntl Ofc 90; Wash State Univ Intern; Acad Schlrshp 88-; Chem; Pharmacology.

**VAN DUSEN, KATHLEEN,** Comm Coll Algny Co Algny Cmps, Pittsburgh, PA; SO; BS; Allghny Vw Ftrs Edtr/Wrtr 90-; Stdnts/ Hmn Life 90-; Rtntn Comm Stdnt Repr 90-; Acad Schlrshp Fin Awd 90-; Alpha Mu Theta; CCAC Comm Serv Proj Fnd Rsng 90-; CCAC Deans List Awd 89-; Pioneer Clubs Coord 90-; Cub Scts Ldr 89-; Wrk Stdy Exp 90; Elem Educ; Teacher.**

**VAN DUYNE, ELIZABETH A,** Cornell Univ Statutory College, Ithaca, NY; FR; BA; Northlake Hnr Stdnt 89-; ESL Tutor 90-; Legal Asst 87-89; Government; Law.

**VAN DYKE, CASSANDRA A,** Kent St Univ Kent Cmps, Kent, OH; FR; BFA; Dnc Ensmbl; Alpha Lambda Delta; Deans Lst 90-; Dnc Assoc Pblcty Coordntr; Dnc; Prfrmg Arts.

**VAN DYKE, KAREN M,** Memphis St Univ, Memphis, TN; FR; BA; Tutor Core 90-; Engl.

**VAN DYKE, POLLY A,** Univ Of Akron, Akron, OH; SR; BED; Gold Key 90-; Kappa Delta Pi; Deans Lst Stdnt 88-; Elem Educ; Educ.

**VAN ELLS, SUSAN L,** Colby Sawyer Coll, New London, NH; JR; BA; Art League; Juried Art Ex 90-; Deans Lst 90-; Psych; Art Therapy.

**VAN ETTEN, ERICA L,** Cornell Univ Statutory College, Ithaca, NY; SO; Cornell Grns 90-; Dont Waste NY; Ecol/Env Biol; Res.

**VAN ETTEN, JAMES P,** Indiana Univ Of Pa, Indiana, PA; SO; BA; Gamma Rho Tau 90-; Acctg.**

**VAN GESSEL, YVONNE A,** Cornell Univ Statutory College, Ithaca, NY; SR; DVM; Hll Govt Flr Rep 87-88; Pre Vet Soc VP 87-90; Amer Soc Amnl Sci Awrd 88-; Univ Edinburgh UK 89-90; Morrison Awrd 89-90; BS Hnrs; Anml Sci; Vet Med.

**VAN GULIK, MEGAN E,** Franklin And Marshall Coll, Lancaster, PA; FR; BA; Track Tm; Bus Admin/French; Intl Business.

**VAN GYSEL, KATIE C,** Univ Of Sc At Columbia, Columbia, SC; FR; BA; Carolina Cmp Cnslr; Dean Lst 90-; Tri Delta 90-; United Way 87-; Intern WAVY TV; IM Sprts 90-; Jrnlsm/Engl; Brdcstng.

**VAN HAITSMA, KARRI L,** Liberty Univ, Lynchburg, VA; SO; BS; Hlth Club 90-; Light Missons; Alpha Lambda Delta 90-; Fisher Kids Club 90-; Comm Hlth; Pub Hlth.

**VAN HASSEL, RACHEL L,** Ramapo Coll Of Nj, Mahwah, NJ; SO; BA; Psychlgy.

**VAN HEMEL, ELIZABETH A,** Univ Of Nc At Greensboro, Greensboro, NC; SO; BSN; Hlth Occup Stdnts Of Amer 89-90; Biology; Nrsng.

**VAN HOOK, RANDY M,** Wilberforce Univ, Wilberforce, OH; FR; BA; Eng.

**VAN HORN, AMY E,** Oh Univ, Athens, OH; SO; BA; Flyng Bobcts O U Flght Tm Capt 90-; Copeland Schlrs Bus 89-90; Alpha Eta Rho 89-; Arwy Sci; Avtn.

**VAN HORN, JAMES R,** Barry Univ, Miami, FL; JR; BS; Vol Camillus Hse/Ply Gtr At Nrsng Hms/Drg Rehab Cntr/Ron Mc Donald Hse 87-90; Jcksn Mem Chldrns Wing Santa 87-90; Phi Theta Kappa Acad Affrs/Fndrsr 87-90; Omicron Alumni 90-F Cmptr Scnc Assoc 87-; Delta Sigma Pi; Ambssdrs; Circle K Pres; Bus; Cmptr Info Systems.

**VAN HORN, LELA D,** Muskingum Area Tech Coll, Zanesville, OH; FR; BS; Acctg Clb 90-; Bus Prof Amer 90-; Deans List; Data Asst/Bus; Prof Of Amer State Comp 90-; Acctg.

**VAN HORNE, KATHERINE M,** Converse Coll, Spartanburg, SC; SR; BA; Bptst Stdnt Un Fllwshp Chr 88-; Nwsppr Rep 89-90; Mdrn Lng Clb 87-88; Mrtr Brd 90-; Phi Sigma Iota 89-; Jr Marshl Chf 89-90; Crscnt 88-89; Stdnt Vol Srvs Fnfst Chr 88-; Cmmnty Advsr 88-90; Cnvrs Schlrs 89-; Mllkn Schlr 87-; Mdrn Lang.

**VAN HOUSE, TANYA L,** Clarkson Univ, Potsdam, NY; JR; BS; Phi Mu Treas; Pep Bnd; Stdnt Wrkr; Deans Lst 89-90; Trsts Schlrshp; Acctg; CPA.

**VAN HOUTEN II, JOHN D,** Merrimack Coll, North Andover, MA; SR; BA; APIC V P; Japan Soc; AMA; Mgmt; Intl Bsn.

**VAN LANDINGHAM, KAREN L,** Va Commonwealth Univ, Richmond, VA; JR; BA; Hnrs Prog 89-; Golden Key; Kappa Tau Alpha; Fclty Stdnt Review Brd; Deans Lst; Mass Cmmnctns/Public Rltns; Corporate PR.

**VAN LANEN, JAMES C,** Oh Univ, Athens, OH; FR; BS; IM Ftbl/Sftbl 90-; US Army Lnce Mssle Crw Mbr Ft Sill OK 87-90; Chem Eng.

**VAN LOOSBROEK, ANTONIUS F,** Academy Of The New Church, Bryn Athyn, PA; SO; MBA; Dscplnry Cncl 90-; Bus.

**VAN LUVEN, W JAMES,** Embry Riddle Aeronautical Univ, Daytona Beach, FL; JR; BS; Arntcl Sci.

**VAN MATER, MARGARET R,** Anne Arundel Comm Coll, Arnold, MD; SO; AA; Bartender; Advtsng Dsgn; Promtn; Trvl Cert; AA; Comm Art Tech; Advtsng/Prmtns.

**VAN METER, JASON T,** Milligan Coll, Milligan Clg, TN; JR; BS; IM Staff Sport Chrmn 89-; Bsn/Mktg/Mgmt; Indstrl Sls.

**VAN METER, MARK W,** Mount Olive Coll, Mount Olive, NC; SR; BAS; Air Force Sergnts Assn 89-; AAS Comm Clg Air Forc 90; Busn Admin; Cons.

**VAN NAMEE, ELAINE D,** Immaculata Coll, Immaculata, PA; SO; BA; Prnts Gld Immclta Coll Pres; Pres Srch Com-Immaculata Coll; Lgl Sec; Psychlgy; Cnslng Psychlgst.

**VAN NESS, ROBERT A,** Memphis St Univ, Memphis, TN; GD; MBA; Staff Engr/Law Engrng 90; BS Vanderbilt Univ 89; Fin; Bus Fin/Bnkng.

**VAN NEST MULLINS, MELINDA L,** Marshall University, Huntington, WV; SR; BA; Rsdnt Hll Advsry Com 87; Alpha Chi Omega Treas 88; WV St Solo Twrlng Chmpn 88; WV St Mss Mjrtte 88; Elem Educ.

**VAN NESTE, RAY F,** Union Univ, Jackson, TN; JR; BS; Religion/Physics.

**VAN NETTE, JENNIFER K,** Indiana Univ Of Pa, Indiana, PA; JR; BED; Res Hsng Assc Sec 89-; Alpha Xi Delta Asst VP 89-90; Prjct Stride Intern 90-; Thames Plytchnc London Eng 90-; Bsktbl 90-; Early Chldhd/Elem Ed.**

**VAN NOOD, MONIQUE,** Univ Of Miami, Coral Gables, FL; SR; BA; Bapt Camps Mnstry 87; Rdrnrs Comm Org Nwsltr Comm 88-89; Swm Clb 87-; Goldn Key 89-; Elem Schl Intrnshp 90-; Dns Lst Prov Lst 88-; IM Swmng 87; Engl Lit; Tchng.

**VAN ORD, KEVIN T,** Oberlin Coll, Oberlin, OH; FR; BM; Orch 90-; Tappan Sngrs 90-; Cir K Intrntl 90-; Intrnshp Ntl Rprtry Orch; Music; Orch Prfrmng.

**VAN ORSDELL, HOLLY A,** S U N Y At Buffalo, Buffalo, NY; SO; Phi Eta Sigma; IM Sftbl; Bus Mgmnt.

**VAN PATTEN, JANINE M,** Merrimack Coll, North Andover, MA; JR; BA; Nwsppr Sbmssn Edtr 90-; Vol Clb Pres 89-90; Ttr 89-; Dean Lst 90-; Brdlf Wrtng Prog 89-; N Andover Yth Cntr Intern 90-; Wrtng Prog Inner Cty Kds Dir 90; Ptry Awrd 90; Engl/Sclgy.

**VAN PATTEN, RUSSELL A,** Univ Of Sc At Columbia, Columbia, SC; SR; BS; ASCE 90-; Cvl Engr.

**VAN PELT, JASON M,** Utica Coll Of Syracuse Univ, Utica, NY; FR; BS; Math.

**VAN RENSSELAER, KATE M,** Colby Sawyer Coll, New London, NH; FR; BA; Ski Tm; Art Ed; Tchr.

**VAN ROSSUM, MARTIN P,** Fl Atlantic Univ, Boca Raton, FL; JR; BS; Intl Bus Clb VP 90-; Deans Lst 89-90; Outstndg Coll Stdnts Am 89-90; Bus; Corp Trade.

**VAN RUITEN, CARRIE A,** Univ Of Ga, Athens, GA; SO; BED; Yrbk Stf 90-; Deans Lst 90-; Early Chldhd Dvlpmnt Educ; Teacher.

**VAN SCHAICK JR, WALTER H,** S U N Y Coll Of Tech At Frmgdl, Farmingdale, NY; SO; BA; Acctg; Accnt.

**VAN SCIVER, JENNIFER J,** Liberty Univ, Lynchburg, VA; SO; BS; Schl Psychlgst.

**VAN SUCH, STEPHEN C,** Westminster Coll, New Wilmingtn, PA; JR; BA; Fllwshp Chrstn Athletes 88-; Tau Pi Phi 90-; Rotary 87-; Holy Trinity Church Advsry Comm 89-; Bsebl League Financial Comm 90-; IM Ftbl/Trck/Bsktbl 88-; Acctng Firm; Acctng.

**VAN SYCKEL, GWENDOLYN L,** Midlands Tech Coll, Columbia, SC; SR; ADN; Sftbl Tm 90; Nrsng; Clincl Spec.

**VAN VICKLE, SHELLEY R,** Univ Of Tn At Martin, Martin, TN; SR; BS; Phi Eta Sigma 87-88; Beta Beta Beta 88; Biology; Medical Rsrch.

**VAN VLACK, ROBERT W,** Mount Saint Mary Coll, Newburgh, NY; SO; BS; Wrk CIBA Gegy Phrmctcls; Crdntr Clncl Pckgng Rsrch Dvlpmnt; Bus Admn Mgmt.

**VAN VOORHIS, KEVIN C,** Hillsborough Comm Coll, Tampa, FL; SO; AA; Acctg Smnr Univ S Fla; Bus Adm/Sci; Bus/Chrprctr.

**VAN VOORTHUIZEN-GOBEL, SYLVIA,** George Mason Univ, Fairfax, VA; GD; BIS; Intl Stdnt Org 90-; Golden Key 90-; Museum Guide Kenya Dir Anthroplgst 77-81; Art Tchr Publ Sch/Lewisvle Church 75-76; Coord Family/Emerg 86-; Welcoming Hostess; Phys Ther Netherlands 68; Gerontlgy/Art Psych; MA.

**VAN WAGENEN, ROBERT A,** Oh Univ, Athens, OH; FR; IEEE 90-; Tau Beta Pi 91-; Electrcn US Navy Nuclr Pwr Prog 84-90; Elec Eng.

**VAN WIE, JENNIFER H,** Univ Of Sc At Columbia, Columbia, SC; SO; BFA; Slf Emplyd Stained Glass Dsgnr Spinnys Studios Myrtle Bch SC 29577 79-87; Art/Studio.

**VAN WINKLE, AMY J,** Spartanburg Methodist Coll, Spartanburg, SC; SO; ASBS; Var Sftbl 89-; Phi Theta Kappa; Psi Beta 90-; Alpha Nu Gamma; Biology; Med.

**VAN WINKLE, CRAIG D,** Gallaudet Univ, Washington, DC; JR; BA; Hnrs Pgm; Wrkg Fndg Bsn Mgnt Clb; Kappa Sigma; IM Sprts/Ftbl/Wrstlg 90-; IM Flg Ftbl Coach 90-; Acctg; CPA/CNTRLR.

**VAN WORMER, TAMMY S,** Schenectady County Comm Coll, Schenectady, NY; SO; Sftbl VP 90-; Adpt A Fmly Xmas Prog 89-90; Ofc Of Mntl Hlth 85-.

**VAN WRIGHT, DEBORAH A,** Springfield Tech Comm Coll, Springfield, MA; FR; ME; BS Coll Of Charleston 86; Mech Engr.

**VAN WYK, DIANA M,** Fl International Univ, Miami, FL; FR; BA; Chappi James Mst Prmsng Tchr Schlrshp; Engl Ed; Scdnry Tchr.

**VAN ZUILEN, MARIA H,** Fl International Univ, Miami, FL; SR; BA; Sclgy/Anthrplgy Scty VP 90-; Sclgy/Anthrplgy Peoples Jrnl Edtr Chf 90-; Psi Chi; Phi Kappa Phi; Geriatric Nurse; AA Miami Dade Cmmty Clg 89; AS 89; Psychology/Sociology.

**VAN, VERONICA L,** Va Commonwealth Univ, Richmond, VA; SR; BA; Alpha Kappa Delta; AA Howard Coll 88; Rlgn/Anthrplgy; Tchng Univ Lvl.

**VAN-SLUYTERS, JILL E,** Hudson Valley Comm Coll, Troy, NY; SR; AAS; Sec Intern/Atty Henry F Zwack; Pres Lst 89-; Exec Office Assist.

**VANBEEK, KRISTIN P,** Western New England Coll, Springfield, MA; JR; BA; Fncl Mgmnt Assn Tres 88-; Data Prcsng Mgmnt Assn 88-; Mgmnt Assn 89-; Vita 89-; Rsdnt Advsr 88-; Resource Intrmdrs; Sftbl Mrthn 89-; Finance; Economics.

**VANCE, ANITA K,** Northwest Al Comm Coll, Phil Campbell, AL; SO; Nrsng.

**VANCE, JANIS L FRENCH,** Univ Of Southern Ms, Hattiesburg, MS; SR; Stdnt Ed Assc 88-; Phi Theta Kappa 88-89; Kappa Dlt Pi 90-; Pres List; Deans List; BPW Awrd; Phi Theta Kappa Schlrshp; Pres Awrd Jr Clg; Otstndng Stdnt Elem Ed; Jeanette Rankin Awrd; Kappa Kappa Iota Awrd; Dlt Kappa Gamma Awrd; GPA Schlrshp.

**VANCE JR, JESSE B,** Nova Univ, Ft Lauderdale, FL; GD; MBA; Rtry Intrnatl Clb Dir 90-; Brwrd Cnty Lbrry Spprt Grp 89-; Opra Gld 90-; MAI 90-; ASA 75-; SREA 81-; BA Earlham Coll 54; Rl Est Mgmt And Dev; Vltn.

**VANCE, KAREN L,** Georgetown Coll, Georgetown, KY; JR; BA; Diamond Clb 89-; Bapt Stdnt Un 88-; Wrtng Lab Tutor 89-; Alpha Lambda Delta 89-; Dns Lst 90-; Phi Alpha Theta; Phi Mu Treas 90-; IM Vlybl 89-; Hist.

**VANCE, LYNN S,** Oh St Univ At Marion, Marion, OH; JR; BA; Psych Clb Sec 90; Deans Stndt Adv Cncl; Griffin Soc Pres Elect 90; Alpha Lambda Delta; Phi Eta Sigma; Stdnt Alum Cncl VP 88-89; Prairie Tour Gde 89-90; Coop Educ Brd; Admin Asst II OH Acad Of Hist; AA 90; Psych; Research.

**VANCE, NADINE R,** Fl St Univ, Tallahassee, FL; SR; Res Hl Govt VP 87-89; IRHC Chrm Pgm 88-89; Pride-Stdnt Pol Party 88-89; Aids Task Force Rep Stdnt Body 88-89; Child Life Intrn 89-90; Tchrs Asst 89-90; Natl Assoc For The Educ Of Young Chldrn 88-; Assoc For Care Of Chlrns Hlth 89-; Child Dev; Psych.

**VANCE, QUINTON P,** Comm Coll Algny Co Boyce Cmps, Monroeville, PA; GD; BS; Jzz Ens Pres 89-90; Msc Clb Pres 89-90; Dns Lst 88-90; Msc Schlp 90-; Arts Fstvl Ent 90; Hnrs Bnqt Ent 90; AS 90; Jazz Cmpstn/Perf; Musician.

**VANCE, SARAH ELIZABETH,** Davis Coll, Toledo, OH; AS; Davis Dsgnrs; Interior Dsgn.

**VANCE, SHERRY L,** Comm Coll Algny Co Algny Cmps, Pittsburgh, PA; SO; AS; Prof Wmns Ntwrk Comm Invlvmnt Chrwmn 89-; Data Entry Prsnl 80-; Cert Schl Cmptr Tech 79-80; Cmptr Infrmtn Sys; Cust Acctg.

**VANCE, TRACI M,** Ms St Univ, Miss State, MS; FR; BS; Gamma Beta Phi; Phi Eta Sigma; Alpha Lambda Delta; Pre Phrmcy; Phrmcy.

**VANDALL, LAURA A,** Univ Of Charleston, Charleston, WV; SR; BS; Cptl Assoc Nrsng Students 88-; Natl Student Nrs Assoc 89-F Nrsng Hnr Scty; Helene Field Hlth Trust Flwshp 90; Deans List; Nrsng; Grad Nrs.

**VANDE PUTTE, CHANDRA J,** Univ Of Akron, Akron, OH; JR; Deans List 88-90; Spcl Ed SLD; Secondry Tchg.

**VANDE RYT, RICHARD C,** Univ Of Cincinnati, Cincinnati, OH; SR; Hamilton Cnty Police Explorer Prgrm Capt Prsdnt 87-; Deans Lst 89-; AS BA; Peace Offcr Certf; Crmnl Jstc; Law Law Enfrcmnt; Crmnl Jstc; Law Law Enfrcmnt.

**VANDE VEN, PATRICIA L,** Le Moyne Coll, Syracuse, NY; FR; BA; Pltcl Sci; Clg Prof.

**VANDEGRIFT, TRUDY A,** Germanna Comm Coll, Locust Grove, VA; FR; BA; Phi Theta Kappa; Psych; FBI.

**VANDEGRIFT, VIVIAN L,** Univ Of Sc At Columbia, Columbia, SC; SR; BMA; Media Fest Comm 90-; Alpha Psi Omega 84-; Intrnshp Media Arts WOLO TV 90; Asst Mgr Retail Str 86-; Stage Mgr Bristol Comm Thtre; Prod Sec Barter Thtre; BA Speech/Drama Winthrop Clg 85; Media Arts; Directing/Producing Entrtnmnt.

**VANDELL, MICHELE M,** Univ Of Med & Dentistry Of Nj, Newark, NJ; SR; BS; Amrcn Physcl Thrpy Assoc 89-; Lambda Alpha Sigma; Deans Lst 86-; Awrd Fr Acdmc Excllnc; Prvs Dymnstcs Dnc Prfsnl & Jdg 77-90; Prctc Physcl Thrpy.

**VANDER KOLK, JENNIFER L,** Endicott Coll, Beverly, MA; FR; BA; SG; Tchrs Assn Intrn; Early Chldhd Educ.

**VANDER LOOP, BARBARA A,** Middle Tn St Univ, Murfreesboro, TN; JR; BS; Hypers Clb 90-; Phi Epsilon Kappa; Dept Schlrshp; Dns Lst; Hnr Rl; AS Western Oklahoma St Coll 84; Wlns Ftns Phys Educ; Exercise Pysslgst.

**VANDER MEER, DAVID W,** Duquesne Univ, Pittsburgh, PA; SO; BA; Alpha Phi Omega 90-; Founders Awrd; Bus; Sprts Mgmt.

**VANDER STEEG, ANGELA R,** Union Univ School Of Nursing, Memphis, TN; JR; BSN; Christian Assn Pres 90-; SG 90-; Dir Lst 89-; Vlybl 89-; Sftbl 90-; Nrsng.

**VANDER WALL, KIMBERLY K,** The Boston Conservatory, Boston, MA; JR; BM; Mscl Thtr Accmpnst 89-90; Smms Clg Chrl 90-; Chmbr Msc 90-; Dns Lst 89-; Asstshp Mchl Lewin 89-; Piano Perf; Slst/Accmpnst/Tchr.

**VANDER WERT, CHAD D,** Memphis St Univ, Memphis, TN; FR; Tutr Care; Educ Spprt Pgm; Hnrs Pgm; Phi Eta Sigma; Engl; Law.

**VANDERLUGT, GODFRIED J H,** Fl International Univ, Miami, FL; GD; MS; Wine Clb Chrmn 87-88; Heerlen Hotel Ctrng Clg Netherlands; Cert Middelbare Hotelschl Heerlen 89; BS Fla Intl Univ 90; Hosptlty Mngmnt.

**VANDERVANDER, DEBRA A,** Mary Baldwin Coll, Staunton, VA; SR; BA; Ambssdrs Clb 88; Deans Lst 88-; Hosp Psych Unit Intern 88-; AAS Blue Ridge Comm Clg 89; Sosiology; Soc Wrk; Cnslng.

**VANDEVENDER, TINA R,** Davis & Elkins Coll, Elkins, WV; SO; BA; Elem Ed; Tchng.

**VANDIVER, RHONDA M,** Georgetown Coll, Georgetown, KY; JR; BS; Choir 88-89; Maskrafters 89-; Alpha Lambda Delta 89-; Eta Delta Phi; Phi Beta Lambda; Kappa Alpha Rose Clb; Sigma Kappa Sorority 91-92; Sprng Hvn Nrsng Hm 89-; Stdnt Envrnmntl Awrns Prgrm; Deans Lst 89-; Mrktng Finance; Fnncl Cnsltnt.

**VANDROSS-MONTGOMERY, CATRICE R,** Univ Of Md At Eastern Shore, Princess Anne, MD; SR; BS; St Ftr Tchrs MA VP 90-; Kappa Delta Pi; Acdmc Hnrs 88; Otstndng Stu Dept 87-88; Kappa Delta Pi; Sigma Dove Ct 89-90; NAACP Fnncl Sec 87-88; Cmps Pal Sec 88-90; U S Achvmnt Acdmy 90; Otrch Mnstry Vol 89-90; FEA 89-; Spec Educ.

**VANECEK, PENELOPE S,** Tn Tech Univ, Cookeville, TN; JR; BSN; Sigma Theta Taw 90-; Hnr Soc 89-; Schlrshp Bus Prof Women 90; Tenn Assoc Stdnt Nurses TTU Chptr Pres; Homespun Assoc Edtr 89-90; PTO Sec; Local Arts Organ Mbfr; LPN St Joseph Hosp 65; Nrsing; Obstet Emerg Dept.

**VANERSON, CAROLINE D,** Alcorn St Univ, Lorman, MS; SR; BS; ASU Wind Ensmbl; MENC; Concert Bnd; Mrchg Bnd; Saxophone Ensmbl; SNEA; Tau Beta Sigma Secr 89-; NCNW; Miss MENC 89-90; Msc Ed; Tch.

**VANG, KAO C,** Fayetteville St Univ, Fayetteville, NC; FR; BS; Sci Clb; Deans Lst; IM Vllybl; Arts; Architecture.

**VANGRIN, DAWN LYNN,** Juniata Coll, Huntingdon, PA; SR; Instrctrs Future Ed Clb Pres 90-; Spcl Friends Co-Dir 89-; Stdnt Rep Acdmc Plng Comm 89-90; Girl Sct Gld Awd 87; Instrctnl I Cert Elem Ed; BA; Mntn Day Comm; May Day Comm; Slctr 1991 Cls Gift; Elem Ed/Spcl Ed.

**VANHEIRSEELE, JULIE R,** Winthrop Coll, Rock Hill, SC; FR; BA; Amnesty Int Coor 88-90; Stdnts Peace; Deans Lst 90; Visual Arts/Photography.

**VANHOOK, DONNA M,** Alamance Comm Coll, Haw River, NC; SR; AAS; Crmnl Jstd Clb 88-; Ethnc Std Asc 89; Almnc Comm Ambsdr 90-; Phi Theta Kappa; NC St Govt Intshp Pgm 90; Outstdng Mnrty Std; Crmnl Jstc; Corrections.

**VANIM, MARCI Y,** George Washington Univ, Washington, DC; SO; BA; Vrsty Chrldr 89-90; Intl Affrs Socty 89-; Coll Rep 89-; Tau Kappa Epsilon 89-; Pres Hnr Schlrshp 89-; Dns Lst Rcpnt; Intl Affrs; For Rel.**

**VANKATACHALAM, NAVEEN,** S U N Y At Buffalo, Buffalo, NY; SO; BA; NE Mo St Univ Ntl Clb 89-90; Cir K 89-90; SUNY At Buffalo-Indian Stdnts Assoc 90; Deans Lst 89; Bsnss Admin; Mngmnt.

**VANLERBERG, SUSAN E,** Univ Of Akron, Akron, OH; JR; BSN; Deans Lst 89-; Cmnty Nrsng.

**VANN, WALTER D,** Va Commonwealth Univ, Richmond, VA; JR; BS; ACS; Physics Scty 90-; Gldn Key; Sigma Pi Sigma; Lab Asst; Chem; Rsrch.

**VANNATTER, MONA R,** Ashland Comm Coll, Ashland, KY; SO; AS; Phi Beta Lamda 89-90; Fndrsng/Socl Comm; Dns Lst 87/89-90; AS 90; Nrsng.

**VANNI, ANGELA M,** Tomlinson Coll, Cleveland, TN; SO; BA; Sldrs Undr Cnstrctn VP 89-; Spnsh Clb 88-89; In Touch Grp Ldr 90-; Ntnl Hnr Soc 88-89; Phi Theta Kappa 89-; Phi Theta Kappa 89-; Sprtl Life Comm 90-; Prsdnts Lst 89-; Bsktbl 89-; AA 89-; Mrktng Brdcstng; Cmmnctns.

**VANOVER, AMY L,** Western Ky Univ, Bowling Green, KY; FR; BA; Stdnt Rep 90-; Mrchng/Pep Bnd 90; Medical Tech; Rsrch.

**VANOVER, KAY L,** Univ Of Ky, Lexington, KY; JR; BA; Work Full Time Asst Cnslr LKLP Wmn/Chldrns Sfhs 87-; Psychlgy.

**VANTREASE, JENNIFER D,** Belmont Coll, Nashville, TN; FR; MBA; Baptist Stdnt Union 90-; Sec 91-92; TN Performing Arts Cntr; Historical Auxiliary; Gamma Beta Phi; Alumni Schlrshp; Glover Schlrshp 90-; Bus Admnstrn; Interior Design.

**VANTUNO, NICOLE E,** Cornell Univ Statutory College, Ithaca, NY; FR; BS; Symphnc Bnd 90-; Micrblgy; Med.

**VANZINI, MATTHEW F,** Westminster Choir Coll, Princeton, NJ; SR; MENC Treas 89-90; Dorm Cncl Pres 89-90; Cmpsrs Asc VP 89-90; BME; Prof Mscn.

**VARADY, RITA,** Newbury Coll, Brookline, MA; FR; AS; Optho Dspnsng; Optcn.

**VARAGIANNIS, VERONICA,** Manhattanville Coll, Purchase, NY; SO; BS; Pre Law Scty; Deans List; Pol Sci; Law.**

**VARALLI, GINA MARIE,** Lenoir Rhyne Coll, Hickory, NC; FR; MBA; Art Tchr.

**VARANO, MARCY A,** Newbury Coll, Brookline, MA; FR; Marco Polo Clb 90-; Travl/Toursm Mgmt; Trvl Agnt Res.

**VARANO, MARY T,** Pa St Univ Delaware Cty Cmps, Media, PA; SO; BSN; Stdnt Athletic Assoc Sec; Stdnt Govt Rep; Bsbl Clb Mgr 89-; Tutor 89-; Cath Chrtes Apl Dr 86-; Deans Lst 89-90; R Dlorio Schlr Athlete Prz; Otsdng Stdnt Achvmnt Acad 89-; Bkbl Tennis Vybl Bkbl Capt 89-; Nurs; MSN.

**VARANO, SEAN P,** Pa St Univ Delaware Cty Cmps, Media, PA; SO; BA; Juste Admn/Spanishf Fed Bur Invstgatn.

**VARELA MEJIAS, MYRTA N,** Univ Del Turabo, Gurabo, PR; SR; MBA; SGA 90-; Scl Serv Dept Coord Coord Eldrly Pgm 86-; BED/GRNTLGY Puerto Rico Jr Coll 89; Psychlgy.

**VARELA, TREABELE J,** Tusculum Coll, Greeneville, TN; JR; BA; Ambssdr; SG VP; Womens Bible Stdy; Alpha Chi; Pres Lst; Charles Oliver Gray Schlr; Psych; Chld Psychlgst.

**VARELLA, JAMES R,** Saint Thomas Univ, Miami, FL; SO; BA; Deans Lst 90-; Lnd/Wtr Olmpics Rookie Yr Awrd; IM All Star Sftbl/Vlybl/Ftbl/Bsktbl 90-; Sprts Admin; Mrktg.

**VARELLIS, ANGELIKI V,** City Univ Of Ny La Guard Coll, Long Island Cty, NY; SO; Law Clb Treas; Phi Theta Kappa; Bus Admin; Finance/Econ.

**VAREVICE, SUSAN,** Philadelphia Coll Pharm & Sci, Philadelphia, PA; SR; BS; AIBS Pres 89-; Pre Mdcl Scty VP 90-; Alpha Delta Theta Intrfrtrnty Cncl 89-90; Prsdntl Schlrshp 87-; IM Vllybll 89-; Blgy.

**VARGA, LILIAN,** Livingston Univ, Livingston, AL; JR; BA; Athltc Actvts 88-; Deans List 89; Tennis 88-; AA Jefferson Davis State J C 90; Bus Mgt/Mrktng; Bus.

**VARGA, LINDA M,** Georgian Court Coll, Lakewood, NJ; JR; BA; Hstry Clb 90-; Spnsh Hnr Soc; Phi Alpha Theta 90-; Natl Geographic Soc 90; Waitress 76-; Hmnts-Elem Ed-Hstry; Tch.

**VARGAS BEAUCHAMP, ENEIDA,** Inter Amer Univ Pr San German, San German, PR; GD; BBA; Natl Assoc Acctnts; Acctg.

**VARGAS DURAN, NATIVIDAD,** Caribbean Univ, Bayamon, PR; SO; BBA; Mgmt; Mngr.

**VARGAS GRANELL, GRICELLY,** Univ Of Pr Medical Sciences, San Juan, PR; JR; BS; APHA 90-; Orientation; Hnr Rl 89-90; Pharm Acad Excllnce Awd; Vllybl 90-; Phrmctcl Sci; Phrmcy.

**VARGAS GRANELL, MARICELLY,** Univ Of Pr Medical Sciences, San Juan, PR; JR; BS; APHA 90-; Orientn; Hnr Rl 88-90; Awd Nght GPA Awd 88-90; Vlybl 90-; Nat Sci; Phrmcy.

**VARGAS PEREZ, SOL M,** Inter Amer Univ Pr San German, San German, PR; FR; Busn Admin; Store Mgr.

**VARGAS, ARLINE,** City Univ Of Ny Bronx Comm Col, Bronx, NY; SR; AS; Phi Theta Kappa 90-; Dns Lst 88-; Church Of God Cncl Exhrtr Mnstr 90-; Sec 88-; Acctng; Educ.

**VARGAS, DIANA YANIRA,** Inter Amer Univ Pr San German, San German, PR; FR; BA; Mu Alpha Phi; Biol; Med.

**VARGAS, FRANCISCO J,** Univ Politecnica De Pr, Hato Rey, PR; FR; BS; Mech Engr.

**VARGAS, IVAN R,** Catholic Univ Of Pr, Ponce, PR; GD; BED; Deans Lst 86-; Tournaments Field Days Teacher Practice; Community Serv 89-; Tele Communications Specialist 80-; Physical Educ.

**VARGAS, MARISSA E,** Inter Amer Univ Pr San German, San German, PR; FR; BBA; Eta Gamma Delta; Mktg; Advrtsg Publshr.

**VARGAS, MAYRA I,** Inter Amer Univ Pr Aquadilla, Aguadilla, PR; FR; Math Acctg.

**VARGAS, PHILIP R,** S U N Y At Buffalo, Buffalo, NY; SR; BS; Amer Mktg Assn 90-; Soc Hmn Rsrcs Mgmt 90-; Mnrty Acdmc Achvmnt Pgm 88-; Mktg Intrn Ivoclar N A Inc; Hmn Rsrcs Intrn Crbrndm/Strctrl Crmcs Div; Bus Admin.

**VARGAS, RICARDO L,** Univ Of Pr At Rio Piedras, Rio Piedras, PR; SR; Psych Stdnt Assn; Peer Prjct/Aids Prvntn 90-; Lesbianism Panel; Golden Key; Aids Fndtn 90-; Hnr Tuition 88-; Natl Sci Fndtn Schlrshp 90; Phys Fitness Fair 90; Clinical Psych.

**VARGAS, RUBEN,** Inter Amer Univ Pr Aquadilla, Aguadilla, PR; SO; BS; Cvl Air Ptrl 84-90; Avtn; MBA.

**VARGAS, RUTH M,** Univ Of Pr At Rio Piedras, Rio Piedras, PR; FR; BS; Chem; Chem Eng.

**VARGAS, VIVIANNE MARIE,** Univ Of Pr Cayey Univ Coll, Cayey, PR; JR; BS; Math/Sci/Eng Prsnl Tchngs 88-; Hnr Stdnt 90-; Gen Sci; Indstrl Phrmcy.

**VARGAS, YVETTE,** Coll Of New Rochelle, New Rochelle, NY; SR; BS; Fin Aid Offcr Tchrs Aid Cashier Teller 83-; AAS Fshn Inst Tchnlgy 88; Art Educ; Tchng.

**VARGAS-COTO, ROSA M,** Miami Dade Comm Coll North, Miami, FL; JR; BA; Phi Theta Kappa Prvsnl Mmbr 90; Grad Hnrs Cum Laude; Otstndng Acd Achvmnt 90-; Talent Rstr; Cert Martin Tech Coll 88; Cmptr Sci; Rsrch Applctns.

**VARGHESE, SAM,** Berkeley Coll Of Westchester, White Plains, NY; SO; ASSOC; Phi Beta Lambda Treas Elect; Outstdng Bus Admin Stdnts; Acctng; CPA.

**VARGO, EDWARD J,** Indiana Univ Of Pa, Indiana, PA; JR; BA; WIUP Tv 88-89; Wiup Fm 90-; Deans Lst 90-; Cmmnctns; Phtgrphy.

**VARLEY, LORI A,** Univ Of Akron, Akron, OH; SO; Comm Dsrdrs; Spch Path.

**VARN, VALERIE O,** Valdosta St Coll, Valdosta, GA; JR; BA; Advsry Bd Valdosta Tech Inst 90-; Advsry Bd Riley Trng Inst 90-; Profl Sec Intl Pres 84-85; Cert Profl Sec 86; Corp Sec Ofc Mgr GA Gulf Sulfur Corp 89-; AS Valdosta Tech Inst 82; Human Resources; Corp Sec.

**VARNER, BARBARA A,** Wv Univ At Parkersburg, Parkersburg, WV; SO; AAS; Church; PTA; Athletic/Band Booster; Nrsng.

**VARNER, BARBARA J,** West Liberty St Coll, West Liberty, WV; SO; BED; Mltcltrl Fstvl Cmmtt; Elem Ed; Tchng.

**VARNER, REJEANA M,** Al A & M Univ, Normal, AL; SO; Hnr Stdnt 89-90; Nathan L Wilson Schlrshp 90; Alabama A-M Acad Schlrshp 89-90; Nrsg; RPN.

**VARNER, SHURRUN V,** Al St Univ, Montgomery, AL; SO; BS; Engl Ed; Law.

**VARNER, TRACI L,** Ohio Valley Coll, Parkersburg, WV; FR; BS; Pep Clb 90-; TIE 90-; Libry Confrnc Committee 90-; Sigma Epsilon Chi Pres 90-; IMS; Biology; Animal Pathology.

**VARNEY, CORY J,** Merrimack Coll, North Andover, MA; JR; BA; Mgmt.

**VARNEY, LISA M,** Univ Of Cin R Walters Coll, Blue Ash, OH; JR; ASN; Hon Stdnt Hon Soc; Sci; Nrsng.

**VARNEY, MATTHEW D,** Univ Of Ky, Lexington, KY; FR; BA; Mrchng Bnd 90-; Pep Bnd 90-; Kappa Kappa Psi 90-; Geology; Envrnmntl Geology.

**VARNEY, MELISSA K,** Univ Of Ky, Lexington, KY; FR; BA; Collgns For Acadmc Exclnc 90-; Baptst Stdnt Un 90-; Rsdnt Hsng Assoc ACES Chrprsn 90-; Alpha Lambda Delta; Phi Eta Sigma; Intrntl Rltns/French; Diplomcy.

**VARNUM, DIXIE A,** Hillsborough Comm Coll, Tampa, FL; SO; BA; Phi Theta Kappa 90-; Cmmnctns; Cmmnctns/Pub Rltns.

**VARNUM, PAMELA M,** Castleton St Coll, Castleton, VT; FR; BA; Motel Mngmnt; Hist.

**VARRASSO, KAREN,** Indiana Univ Of Pa, Indiana, PA; SR; P A State Ed Assn 87-90; P A Sci Tchrs Assn 88-90; Am Chldhd Educ Intl 89-90; Dns Lst; Stride Tutrng Intrnshp 88-89; BS 90; Elem Educ.

**VARRIS, PAMELA NANDI,** Bunker Hill Comm Coll, Boston, MA; SR; BS; Nwspr Rptr 90-; Lit Mag Wrtr 90-; Outstdng Mnrty Std Tlnt Rstr; Pres Ldrshp Awd; Hnrs; Bstn Nghbrhd Ntwrk Tv Rxbry Studio 88-; Drchstr Wmns Comm 85-; Blck Comm Info Ctr/Comm Kwanzaa Comm; AS; Mass Comm; Media/Prdcr/Dir.

**VARSEK, SUSAN RENEE,** Indiana Univ Of Pa, Indiana, PA; SR; BA; Kappa Delta Pi 90-; Provost Schlr 90; Elem Educ; Thcr.

**VASAN, INDU,** City Univ Of Ny La Guard Coll, Long Island Cty, NY; SO; BA; AS 90; Cmptr Info Systs; Cmptr Analyst.

**VASAN, PRIYA,** George Mason Univ, Fairfax, VA; SR; Amer Mrktng Assoc 89-; Yrbk Stf Sr Mag 89-90; Univ Sml Bsns Admn Proj Awd 90-; Bsns/Mrktng; Mrktng.

**VASCURA, DAVID J,** Muskingum Coll, New Concord, OH; FR; BA; Lambda Sigma; IM; Chem; Med.

**VASKO, MARY R,** Va Commonwealth Univ, Richmond, VA; SO; BFABS; Art Educ Scty 90-; Art Educ/Psychlgy; Art Thrpy.

**VASQUEZ, CARLOS R,** George Mason Univ, Fairfax, VA; FR; MBA; Bus Hons Admsns; Deans Admsns Prog 90-; Bus Hons; Soccer 90-; Bus Admnstrtn.

**VASQUEZ, ELKIN M,** Univ Of Miami, Coral Gables, FL; JR; BS; Blgy; Mdcl Schl.

**VASQUEZ, LOUIS A,** Newbury Coll, Brookline, MA; FR; AS; Bus; Law.

**VASQUEZ, MARIA M,** City Univ Of Ny Queensbrough, New York, NY; SO; AAS; Elctrncs; Engnrng.

**VASQUEZ, MICHELLE L,** Glassboro St Coll, Glassboro, NJ; JR; BS; 4 Yr Full Tuition Schlrshp 88-; Bsn Admin; Entrprnr.

**VASS, MATTHEW S,** Univ Of New Haven, West Haven, CT; FR; BS; Cmptr Sci; Eng/Syst Desgnr.

**VASSALLO, FRANCA,** Daemen Coll, Amherst, NY; FR; BA; Coll Tlnt Shw Sngr/Dncr; Biolgy; Med.

**VASSALLO, LIZZETTE M,** Bunker Hill Comm Coll, Boston, MA; FR; Cmptr Cert; Cumunctns.

**VASSENELLI, DAVID A,** Niagara Univ, Niagara Univ, NY; JR; BA; Varsity Bsebl 88-; Cmnctns.

**VASSILAS, GEORGE N,** Columbia Union Coll, Takoma Park, MD; GD; BS; Phi Eta Sigma 89; Alpha Chi; Summa Cum Laude; Chrch Of Jesus Chrst Of Lttr Dy; Mlln Dllr Agnt S Lchs Rl Est Co; BSBA; Bus Admin; Law Schl.

**VASSILIADES, MICHAEL E,** Kent St Univ Kent Cmps, Kent, OH; BBA; Mrktng.

**VATSALYA, VIJAY K,** Germanna Comm Coll, Locust Grove, VA; FR; Natl Soc Pblc Acctnts; Phi Theta Kappa 90-; Vlybl; Sls; Acctng; CPA.

**VAUCHER, SANDRA L,** Broward Comm Coll, Ft Lauderdale, FL; SO; AA; Phi Theta Kappa 90-; Amer Mktg Assoc Sec; Mktg/Bus Admin.

**VAUGHAN MORRIS, DAWN R,** Oh Univ-Southern Cmps, Ironton, OH; JR; BED; Deans Lst; SG Christmas Fund Drive 88; Sci/Math; Teach.

**VAUGHAN, CAMILLE A,** Georgetown Univ, Washington, DC; JR; BA; Inroads Org 88; Blk Dnce Mvmnts 89; Bsnss Mgr Blkbrd Jrnl Bsnss Mgr; Gospel Choir 89-90; Schlrshp Ntl Coaltn 100 Blk Women; Schlrshps Delta Sigma Theta/Alpha Kappa Alpha 88; Intrnshp W/Mrylnd Cslty Co 88; Bsnss Mngmnt; Human Rsrces.

**VAUGHAN, KENNETH M,** S U N Y Coll Of Tech At Frmgdl, Farmingdale, NY; SO; BA; Swimming Cptn 88; Amer Diabetes Assoc 87-; Natl Hnr Scty 88; Liberal Arts Hnr Scty; Amer Diabetes Assoc 87-; Swaimming; AA; Biology; Medl.

**VAUGHAN, LINWOOD S,** Richard Bland Coll, Petersburg, VA; FR; BA; Cmptr Sci; Tchr.

**VAUGHAN, MELANIE A,** Converse Coll, Spartanburg, SC; SO; BA; Delt Omicron Stdnt Gov Rep; Alpha Lambda Delta; Chem; Phrmcy.

**VAUGHAN, NICOLE L,** Union Univ, Jackson, TN; FR; BA; Drama; Tchr.

**VAUGHAN, PAMELA B,** Averett Coll, Danville, VA; GD; BS; Cablevision Ind Data Proc; AS Danville Comm Coll 83; Bus Mngmnt; Mgr/Dir.

**VAUGHAN, THOMAS F,** S U N Y Coll Of Tech At Frmgdl, Farmingdale, NY; SO; Lbl Arts/Sci 90-; Marine Corps Assoc 80-; Law.

**VAUGHAN, WENDI K,** Univ Of Al At Birmingham, Birmingham, AL; JR; BS; Amer Chem Scty; Alpha Lambda Delta 89-; Alpha Epsilon Delta 90-; Biology; Medicine.

**VAUGHAN-LOONEY, STEPHANNIE,** Univ Of Tn At Martin, Martin, TN; GD; Phi Chi Theta Corr Sec 89-; BS 90; Prsnnl/Hmn Res Mngmnt.

**VAUGHN, CAROL J,** Savannah Coll Of Art & Design, Savannah, GA; SO; BFA; M Whelan Schlrshp 88; Grphc Dsgn; Illstrtr.

**VAUGHN, DONYA D,** Northeast State Tech Comm Coll, Blountville, TN; SO; BSN; Kngsprt Lfsvng Crw 90-; Blntvl Emerg Resp/Resc; ER HUCH 90-; RN.

**VAUGHN, EMILY A,** Univ Of Tn At Martin, Martin, TN; FR; BA; March/Concert Band 1st Chair Frnch Horn 90-; Brass Ensmble; Ftbl Hostess; Sigma Alpha Iota; Alpha Omicron Pi Asst Pledge Ed 90-; IM; Hist/Music; Teach.

**VAUGHN, GAYELYNN,** Juniata Coll, Huntingdon, PA; SO; BA; Concrt Choir 89-; Clg Theater 89-; Deputation Club Staring Comm Mbr 89-; Elem Ed; Tchng.

**VAUGHN, HADRYAN H,** Al A & M Univ, Normal, AL; SR; BS; Pres Schlrs 88-; Alpha Kappa Mu 90-; Alpha Phi Alpha 90-; Pres Achvmnt Awrd; Med Rsrch Intrn; Zoology; Med.

**VAUGHN, JEWEL E,** Faulkner St Jr Coll, Bay Minette, AL; SO; BS; DPMA 89-; Deans Lst 90-; Cmptrs; Cnsltnt.

**VAUGHN, ROXANNE,** Norfolk St Univ, Norfolk, VA; SR; AB Psi 90-; Intrnshp Brambleton Comm Otrch Ctr 90-.

**VAUGHN, TAMMY M,** Ms St Univ, Miss State, MS; SR; Ag Econs Clb 89-; Blck And Brdle Clb 88-; Gamma Beta Phi 88-; Alpha Zeta Pres 89-; Coll Of Ag And Hme Econs Ambssdrs CAHE Ambssdrs 89-; Moorman Schlrshp 90-; MAEA Schlrshp 90; Paul T Blair Schlrshp 90-; BS; BBA; Ag Bus Mrktng; Fm HA Asst Cnty Super.

**VAUGHT, LOU ANN,** Memphis St Univ, Memphis, TN; JR; BS; Beta Sigma Phi Pres 82-; PTA V/TREAS; Phi Theta Kappa 89-; Broken Arrow OK Pblc Schls; Hmrm Mother; Shelby Cty Schls Germantown TN; Schlstc Schlrshp Tulsa Jr Clg; United Meth Wom Grp 82-; Assoc Lbrl Arts 90; Elem Educ.

**VAUGHT, SHERRY L,** Radford Univ, Radford, VA; SO; BA; Psych.

**VAUGHT, TAMMY L,** Univ Of Louisville, Louisville, KY; SR; BS; DPMA 90-; OWC Vicenight Tckt Chrprsn 85-; Cmptr Sci; Tch Cmptr Sci Hgh Sch Stdnt.

**VAUSE, DANITA A,** Fl St Univ, Tallahassee, FL; JR; BS; Golden Key 90-; State Univ Syst FL Empl; Grant Aid 90-; Exec Secr 86-; Scl Sci-Publ Admin/Hstry; Publ Admin.

**VAUZANGES, BERNARD P,** City Univ Of Ny City Coll, New York, NY; GD; BARCH; AIAS 89-; Extech Awrd 90; CSI Educ Awrd 90; BS 90; Architecture.

**VAVASOUR, DANIEL J,** Fl St Univ, Tallahassee, FL; FR; Phi Eta Sigma; Ims; Bio; Law.

**VAVRA, LESLIE L,** Bethany Coll, Bethany, WV; SR; BA; Ltry Mag 87-; Frnch Clb 89-; Yrbk Stf Fclty Admn Edtr 87-88; Gamma Sgm Kappa 90-; Lmbd Iota Tau Pres 90-; Kappa Dlt Chpln 87-; Renner Schlr 87-; Otstndng Jr Engl Mjr 90; Sr Flw Englsh Dept 90; Christine Burleson Awrd; Engl; Clg Prfsr.

**VAWTER, CHRISTY R,** Union Univ, Jackson, TN; JR; BS; Flwshp Chrstn Athlts 88-; Bptst Stdnt Un 88-; Cmnctns Clb; Stdnt Prod/Dir Awrd; Cmnctn Arts/Mgmt/Mktg; Brdcstng.

**VAZ, RENEE S,** Georgian Court Coll, Lakewood, NJ; SR; BS 90; Spcl Educ/Elem; Educ Tchr.

**VAZQUEZ BALLASTER JR, HECTOR,** Inter Amer Univ Pr San German, San German, PR; SO; Karate; Acacia 89-; Wrstlng/Ftbl/Karate 87-89; Eng Elec.

**VAZQUEZ BERRIOS, JUAN M,** Univ Of Pr At Mayaguez, Mayaguez, PR; SO; BA; Alpha Kappa Omcrn 89-; Doe Hnr Rsch Pgm BNL 89-; Engr Sq Hnr 90-; Cmptr Engr.**

**VAZQUEZ BURGOS, IVETTE,** Univ Of Pr At Rio Piedras, Rio Piedras, PR; SO; BA; Hnr Mtrcultn 90-; Natl Coll Merit Bus Awd 90-; Acctng; MBA/FINANCE.

**VAZQUEZ CINTRON, INES N,** Inter Amer Univ Pr San German, San German, PR; GD; BA; Soc Wrkr Stdnts Vcl 88-90; Hon Stdnt Univ 89-; BA; Soc Wrk; Law.**

**VAZQUEZ DE MIGUEL, BERTA T,** Fl International Univ, Miami, FL; SR; MBA; Metropolis Stff Wrtr 88; Centro Astrn De Miami 87-87; Phi Kappa Phi 90-; Phi Lambda Beta; Miami Dade Comm Coll Hon Schlrshp 87-89; AA Miami Dade Comm Coll 89; Pblc Admin; Fin.**

**VAZQUEZ LOPEZ, AIDA L,** Inter Amer Univ Pr Guayama, Guayama, PR; SO; BA; Advrtsng Clb 90-; High Hnrs Inst Eng 80; Inst Tech De Guayama 81; Acctng; Auditor.

**VAZQUEZ LOPEZ, TERESA,** Univ Of Pr Medical Sciences, San Juan, PR; GD; MBA; Stdnt Assn Tchng Prctces Chem Stdnts 90; Natl Sci Tchrs Assn 90; BA; Chem; Envrnmntl Hlth.

**VAZQUEZ NOVOA, MARIBEL,** Univ Politecnica De Pr, Hato Rey, PR; SO; Cvl Air Ptrl Mstr 87-; Hlp Oldr People; Hstry Sci; Engnrng.

**VAZQUEZ RIVERA, TANYA E,** Univ Of Pr Cayey Univ Coll, Cayey, PR; FR; Stu Cnslrs Grp 90-; Scl Sci; Law.

**VAZQUEZ SANTIAGO, IRANGELIE,** Univ Of Pr At Rio Piedras, Rio Piedras, PR; JR; Gldn Key; Accntng; CPA.

**VAZQUEZ URQUIA, RAFAEL A,** Inter Amer Univ Pr San German, San German, PR; JR; ACS; Beta Beta Beta; Hnr Rl; AJEC; B Ed Inst Biblico Mizpa 87.

**VAZQUEZ VAZQUEZ, MARIBEL,** Inter Amer Univ Pr Barranquita, Barranquitas, PR; GD; Orientatr Stdnt 88; Cert Of Hon Univ Intramercna 88-; Exec Sec; Sec.

**VAZQUEZ VAZQUEZ, NERY I,** Catholic Univ Of Pr, Ponce, PR; SR; Gerontology Assc; Hnrs Lst 89-90; Sci; Gerontology.

**VAZQUEZ VELEZ, MILDRED,** Univ Of Pr At Rio Piedras, Rio Piedras, PR; GD; BA; High Hnrs; Elem Educ.

**VAZQUEZ, ABIGAIL,** Univ Of Pr Medical Sciences, San Juan, PR; SR; MS; AAPS 89-90; MSD Awrd 85; BS 85; Inds Phrmcy.

**VAZQUEZ, ALICIA C,** Fl International Univ, Miami, FL; SR; BA; FEA 90-; Hnrs Cncl Repr 90-; Kappa Delta Pi Pres 89-; Chi Alpha Theta Pldg Pres 89-90; AA Miami Dade Cmnty Clg 88; Elem Ed; Tchr.

**VAZQUEZ, CARLOS RAFAEL,** Univ Central Del Caribe, Cayey, PR; JR; MD; Stdnt Govt Cls Pres 89-90; AMSA State Lgsltv Offcr 89-; OSR Stdnt Rep 90-; Acdmc Exclinc Amer Soc Clncl Pthlgst 90; Bsktbl Capt 88-; BA Chem Haverford Coll 87; BA Blgy Haverford Coll 87; Med; Rdlgst.

**VAZQUEZ, CARMEN L,** Touro Coll, New York, NY; SO; AA; Memories Yrbk Ed/Publshr 90-; Touro Voice Mag Ed/Publshr 90-; Stdnt Advsry Cncl Asst Treas 90-; Outstndg Acad Achvmnt Awd; Certif Center Media Arts 89; Lib Arts; Jrnlst.**

**VAZQUEZ, JENNY L,** Miami Dade Comm Coll North, Miami, FL; JR; AA; Bnkg/Fin; Bus.

**VAZQUEZ, JOSE R,** Univ Of Miami, Coral Gables, FL; SR; BA; Arch Club 90-; AA Miami Dade Comm Clg 86; Archt.

**VAZQUEZ, JOY E,** S U N Y At Albany, Albany, NY; FR; BA; Spellman Achvmnt Awrd; Math; Tchng/Actry.

**VAZQUEZ, LUIS,** Inter Amer Univ Pr Hato Rey, Hato Rey, PR; SR; Beta Beta Beta 90; Bdy Bldg Pwr Lft 86; Math Bio; Med Tchnlgy.

**VAZQUEZ, MARIA E,** Catholic Univ Of Pr, Ponce, PR; SO; BBA; Acctng Stdnt Assoc 90; Natl Bus Hon Soc; Eta Gamma Delta 90; Bus Admn Deans Award 90; NCBMA 90; Frshmns Stdnts Award 90; Secrtrl Sci; MBA.

**VAZQUEZ, MARIA L,** Inter Amer Univ Pr Aquadilla, Aguadilla, PR; JR; BA; Spnsh Clb 86-87; Fctry Wrkr 88-89; Rcptnst 90; Sec Edu; Hstry.

**VAZQUEZ, MARIA LOURDES ORTIZ,** Inter Amer Univ Pr San German, San German, PR; SO; BBA; BBSA BA; Accntng; CPA.

**VAZQUEZ, MARY L,** Dowling Coll, Oakdale Li, NY; SR; BA; Spec Edn; Teach.

**VAZQUEZ, MIGUEL IVAN,** Univ Of Pr At Mayaguez, Mayaguez, PR; JR; BSEE; SER 90-; Youthful Com; Hon Lst 89-; Table Tennis Varsity Capt 90-; Math/Sci; Elec Eng.

**VAZQUEZ, OLGA M,** Univ Of Miami, Coral Gables, FL; SR; BM; Symphonic Wind Ensemble Bass Clarinetist 90-; Sch Music Stdnt Cnl Treas 90-; Eaton Res Coll Cncl 89; Hon Stdnts Assoc 87-; St Augustine Cath Ctr Pianist 89-90; Eucharistic Mnstry; MSBS Sch Music Nwsltr Ed 90-; Choral Ofc Wrkstdy Pos 87-89; Music Inds; Grad Sch MM Concert Hall Mgt.

**VAZQUEZ, PAUL A,** International Bible Coll, Florence, AL; SO; BA; Mssn Clb Pres; Bible; Prchr.

**VAZQUEZ, VALARIE A,** Valdosta St Coll, Valdosta, GA; FR; Chi Omega Schlrshp Chrmn 90-; Nrsng.

**VAZQUEZ, VALERIE C,** Fl International Univ, Miami, FL; JR; BA; FEA 90-91; Instrctr Bk Clb ; Deans List 88-; Kappa Dlt Pi 91; Kappa Dlt Pi; Intrnd Dkey Largo Elm Sch/Miami Sprngs Elem Sch Intrnshp Rqrmnt; Assc Degree Arts Miami Dad Comm Clg 90; Elem Ed/Erly Chldhd; Cert Spec Ed/Erly Chldhd.

**VAZQUEZ-CINTRON, ANGEL RAFAEL,** Catholic Univ Of Pr, Ponce, PR; GD; JD; Law Rvw 90-; Phi Alpha Delta 89-; ANED 89-; Amer Bar Assoc 89-; Magna Cum Laude 89; BA 89; Law.

**VAZQUEZ-GONZALEZ, JOSE R,** Inter Amer Univ Pr San Juan, Hato Rey, PR; GD; JD; PR Chmbr Of Cmmrce 82; Amer Red Cross Rare Bld Dnr Rgstry; BA Inter-Amer U 77; Chief Fncl Offcr Michael Lith Of PR Inc 82; Law.

**VAZQUEZ-TIRADO, SARA S,** Univ Of Pr At Rio Piedras, Rio Piedras, PR; SO; BBA; Yng Leg Cncl 90-; Acctg Stdnt Assn 90-; Acctg; Law.**

**VEACH, CHERYL A,** Ashland Comm Coll, Ashland, KY; SR; BBA; Phi Beta Lambda Cvc Comm Chrmn 89; Kappa Delta Pi; AAS Ashland Comm Clg 89; AAS Ashland Comm Clg 90; Bus Admns; Sec Ed.

**VEACH, CHRISTIE R,** Ms St Univ, Miss State, MS; JR; BBA; The Reveille Sctn Edtr 89-; RA; Gamma Beta Phi 90-; Pi Sigma Epsilon; Utd Way Vol; Business; Mrktng.

**VEAHMAN, DIANE E,** Indiana Univ Of Pa, Indiana, PA; SO; BS; Phi Sigma Sigma 90-F; Educ; Tchng Elem Lvl.

**VEAL, ALANNA D,** Tougaloo Coll, Tougaloo, MS; SO; BS; Spprt Srvcs 89-; Blgy; Med.

**VEAL, ALISON L,** Univ Of Sc At Columbia, Columbia, SC; JR; BA; Delta Delta Delta 88-; Psychology; Guidance Cnslr.

**VEALS, VICKY R,** Jackson St Univ, Jackson, MS; FR; BA; Math; Engr.

**VEASLEY, MARY E,** Ms St Univ, Miss State, MS; SO; BS; GS Trp Ldr 85-90; Buffalo UMC SS Teacher 82-; Asst Teacher Kosciusko Lwr Elem 83-90; Elem Educ; Teacher.

**VEAZEY, DALINDA L,** Spartanburg Methodist Coll, Spartanburg, SC; FR; BA; Psi Beta 90-; BSU 90-; Glee Clb 90-; Phi Theta Kappa 90-; Pres Lst 90-; Elem Educ; Educ.

**VEAZEY, JENNIFER A,** S U N Y Coll Of Tech At Alfred, Alfred, NY; SR; BA; Karate Acdmy 89-; Otdr Clb 90-; Cncrt Chr 89-90; Dean Lst 90; AS; Mngmnt Sci; Bus.**

**VEAZEY JR, TERRELL L,** Southeastern Baptist Coll, Laurel, MS; SR; BA; Stu Govt Pres 90-; Choir Pres 88-; Stu Tchr 89-; Bsktbl; Mnstr Music Yth 87-; AA 90; Music; Mnstr.

**VECCHIO, CAROLYN B,** S U N Y Coll Of Tech At Frmgdl, Farmingdale, NY; SO; BA; Dns Lst 90-; Aitia Mag Intrn; AA; Hstry; Law.

**VECCHIONE, LISA J,** Univ Of Pittsburgh At Bradford, Bradford, PA; SR; BS; BA Rochester Inst Tchnlgy 89; Bio; Med.

**VECELLIO, MARK E,** Univ Of Pittsburgh At Bradford, Bradford, PA; SO; BA; Vol Bradford YMCA 89-; Acdmc Exclnc Athltcs Awd 89-90; Bsktbl 89-90; Hmn Rltns; Police Law Enfrcmnt.

**VEENEMAN, TERRY R,** Univ Of Cincinnati, Cincinnati, OH; SO; BA; Dean Lst 90-; Law.

**VEENMAN, DOROTHEA ESTHER,** Memphis St Univ, Memphis, TN; SR; MA; Leiden Stdnts Dvng Clb Comm Mbr 88-89; Hon Stdnt 90-; Scuba Dvg Cls Asst Instr 90; Frgn Lang/Philosopy; Crim Pol Invstgtn.

**VEGA DIAZ, WILMARIE,** Univ Of Pr Cayey Univ Coll, Cayey, PR; FR; BA; Cthlc Youth Grp Sec 86-; Chnclrs Hnr Rl; Vlybl; Human Rsrcs.

**VEGA DRANKUS, RONALD,** Inter Amer Univ Pr Hato Rey, Hato Rey, PR; FR; Math Hstry.

**VEGA MOJICA, MARYBEL,** Inter Amer Univ Pr San German, San German, PR; Hon Rl.

**VEGA MONTALVO, MIGDALIA,** Inter Amer Univ Pr San German, San German, PR; FR; Math; Adm.

**VEGA RIVERA, GERARDO M,** Univ Politecnica De Pr, Hato Rey, PR; GD; Mech Eng Inst 90-.

**VEGA RODRIGUEZ, ROBERTO,** Univ Politecnica De Pr, Hato Rey, PR; JR; Jehovah Witness Org.

**VEGA SUAREZ, CARLOS G,** Univ Politecnica De Pr, Hato Rey, PR; SR; BS; SG 86; Drama 85f Ntl Hnr Scty 84; Phi Eta Mu Treas 87-89; Mdl Hnr 86; Bskbl/Vlybl 85-86; Civil Engrg; Structure.

**VEGA, DEBORAH J,** Ms Univ For Women, Columbus, MS; JR; BS; Phi Beta Lambda Sec 88-; Phi Theta Kappa; Mortr Brd; AA Miss Gulf Cst Comm Clg 89; Busn Admin; Bnkg.

**VEGA, ERNESTY,** Inter Amer Univ Pr Hato Rey, Hato Rey, PR; SO; BA; Karate 90; Educ; Tchr.

**VEGA, FRANK,** Inter Amer Univ Pr Hato Rey, Hato Rey, PR; FR; Acctg; CPA.

**VEGA, LISA,** Thomas Nelson Comm Coll, Hampton, VA; JR; BA; Soc Clb Hamptn Univ 90; Dns Lst Hamptn Univ 90; Slng Tm Chrstphr Nwprt Coll 87-88; Soc; Crim Just.

**VEGA, LORINES,** Bloomfield Coll, Bloomfield, NJ; JR; BS; Deans Lst 89-; Wmns Bsktbl Pgm Capt 89-; Bus Gnrl Mgmt.

**VEGA, LUIS A,** City Univ Of Ny La Guard Coll, Long Island Cty, NY; SO; BA; Acctg-Comp; Eng.

**VEGA, SONIA R,** Univ Of Pr Medical Sciences, San Juan, PR; GD; MS; Biomedical Res 84-86; Biological Hnr Soc 85-; BS Univ Puerto Rico 86; Env Hlth; Spec.

**VEGA, WILLIE FRANCISCO,** Springfield Tech Comm Coll, Springfield, MA; SO; BA; VITA; ASSOC; Acctg; CPA.

**VEGA-ROSADO, LUZ L,** Univ Of Pr At Mayaguez, Mayaguez, PR; JR; BA; Cllgt Sec Intl Assn Rlgs Actvts; Hon Bd; Awd Dcmnt Admin Cmptncs PR APEC; Sec Sci; Exec Sec.

**VEINOT, JENNIFER,** Bay Path Coll, Longmeadow, MA; SO; AS; Stdnt Govt 90-; Internatl Frnds Pgm 90-; Rsdnt Asst 90-; Maroon Key 90-; Internshp Epirotiki Cruiselines 90-; Greece Hsts; Trvl Admin.

**VEITH, KEVIN R,** Elmira Coll, Elmira, NY; JR; BS; Big Evnts Com Pres 89-; Cmps Cntr Com 88-89; RA 89-; Psi-Chi 90-; Hon Schlr Athlt 88-; PAL 88-89; Smmr Rgstrtn Chrprsn; Orntn Ldr 89-; Mc Graw Wittesley Attnmnt Awd; Iris Ldrshp Schlrshp; NJ Alumni Schlrshp 90-; Psychlgy/Bus Admin/Mgmt; Bus Consltn.

**VEITINGER, ANN L,** Ramapo Coll Of Nj, Mahwah, NJ; SR; BS; RC Grl Sct Cncl Ldr 80; Alpha Beta Gamma; Delta Mu Delta; Phi Sigma Omcrn; Jrnl Nws Fml Bwlr/Yr; Std Snt Schlp; RN; AAS Lib Arts/Offc Tech Rcklnd Comm Clg 89; RN Bellevue Schl Nrsng 66; Pbl Admn/Mgmt; Bsn.

**VELA, ALEXANDRA J,** City Univ Of Ny La Guard Coll, Long Island Cty, NY; GD; AA; Deans Lst 90-; Hmn Serv; Scl Wrk.

**VELADO, PAMELA D,** Univ Of Tn At Knoxville, Knoxville, TN; FR; BA; Alpha Lambda Delta; Phi Eta Sigma; Env Ecology.

**VELARDO, ANTHONY M,** Merrimack Coll, North Andover, MA; SO; BA; SG Chrprsn Sprts Cmte 89-90; AMA VP 89-; Class Cncl 89-90; Delta Phi Kappa 90-; Bus; Fin.

**VELASCO, JULIAN,** Georgetown Univ, Washington, DC; SR; BSBA; Rpblcns 88-; Acdmc First Hnrs 88-; Finance; Law.

**VELASQUEZ, ALISON K,** Lexington Comm Coll, Lexington, KY; JR; BA; Hstry; Law.

**VELASQUEZ, ANA M,** Fl International Univ, Miami, FL; SO; BA; City Miami Bch Latin Am Adv Bd 90-; Hortcltrl Comm Chamb Of Comm; Alpha Epsilon Delta; Adopt A Father Prog Vets Hosp; Phi Lambda Beta; FIU 89-; Fla Pub Interest Rsrch Grp; PACE 90-; Natl Compnt Of ASPIRA Pub Policy Intrnshp 89; Ldrshp Parog; Math; Engrng.

**VELASQUEZ, BRYON S,** Central Fl Comm Coll, Ocala, FL; FR; Hspnc Clb 90-; Sccr; Indstl Mnt; Engr.

**VELASQUEZ, JOHN J,** Hudson County Comm Coll, Jersey City, NJ; SR; AAS; Accntng; Bus Admn.

**VELASQUEZ, ROGER A,** West Chester Univ, West Chester, PA; JR; BS; Phy Educ; Phy Educ Tchr.

**VELASQUEZ JR, VICTOR MEMEL,** Broward Comm Coll, Ft Lauderdale, FL; JR; BA; Dean Lst 90; Pres Lst 90; Mscn; AA 90; Accntng.

**VELAZQUEZ BULTED, RUTH K,** Caribbean Univ, Bayamon, PR; SO; Social Wrk; Law.

**VELAZQUEZ DIAZ, EDNA,** Univ Of Pr Cayey Univ Coll, Cayey, PR; SO; CADE 90-; Cuadro De Honor De La Rectora; 1st Prz Trio Prog Cntst 89; Acctng; Smba.

**VELAZQUEZ DIAZ, YANIRA,** Univ Of Pr Medical Sciences, San Juan, PR; JR; BSOT; Amer Occptnl Thrpy Asc 89-90; PROTA Rep 90-; Occptnl Thrpy.

**VELAZQUEZ MARRERO, LORNALIS,** Inter Amer Univ Pr San German, San German, PR; SO; Math; Med Tchnlgy.

**VELAZQUEZ MARRERO, ROSA YANIRA,** Inter Amer Univ Pr San German, San German, PR; SO; Clb Yng Chrch 87-88; Tchr; Math; Tech Rdlgy.

**VELAZQUEZ RIVERA, ROSARIO,** Inter Amer Univ Pr Guayama, Guayama, PR; SO; AD; BA Nrsng.

**VELAZQUEZ ROUSSET, RUBEN A,** Univ Of Pr At Mayaguez, Mayaguez, PR; SO; BA; Pre Med Cir 89-; Beta Beta Beta 90-; MN Rsch Intshp; CRCI Rsch Pgm 90; Med/PHD.

**VELAZQUEZ, ALINA,** Fl International Univ, Miami, FL; BA; Future Amer Eductrs; Stdnt Tch; BA; Educ; Tchr.

**VELAZQUEZ, DAVID,** Inter Amer Univ Pr Hato Rey, Hato Rey, PR; SO; BA; PR Natl Dvng Tm 87-88; Cert Metropolitan Schl Miguel Such PR 90; Acctg; CPA.

**VELAZQUEZ, LYNN,** City Univ Of Ny City Coll, New York, NY; SR; BED; Vol Work For Sal Army Core-Sunset Park 88-; Vol P T Sports Med Clinic 89; Phys Ed; Phys Thrpst.

**VELAZQUEZ, VICTORIA C ROSA,** Inter Amer Univ Pr Hato Rey, Hato Rey, PR; BA; Libr Clb Sec 89-; Yrbk Clb VP 90-; Educ Psych; Psych.

**VELEY, RONALD J,** Oh St Univ, Columbus, OH; SR; BS; Gamma Sigma Delta 90-; Ntrl Rscs; Env Comm/Educ.

**VELEZ MARI, ROSA M,** Inter Amer Univ Pr San German, San German, PR; FR; GA; Engl; Ciencias Sctrls.

**VELEZ MERCADO, EDGARDO,** Inter Amer Univ Pr San German, San German, PR; JR; BS; LEO Clubs 86-; Ismael Velez 89-; Caduceus 89-; Beta Beta Beta 89-; Biomed; Med.

**VELEZ MONTALVO, ROSA T,** Univ Of Pr Medical Sciences, San Juan, PR; GD; MBA; NSSLA; Beta Beta Beta; Mu Alpha Phi; BS Intr Amrcn Unvrsty PR 88; Mstr Adlgy.

**VELEZ RAMOS, JAIME D,** Catholic Univ Of Pr, Ponce, PR; SO; Lista De Honor Del Decano 90-; Bchlr Arts; Law.

**VELEZ RIVERA, CARLOS J,** Univ Of Pr At Mayaguez, Mayaguez, PR; SO; BES; Deans List 89-90; NC MLA 90-; Prog Compctition Bellcore 1st Place; Computer Engrg; Engrg.

**VELEZ VEGA, MARIELA,** Catholic Univ Of Pr, Ponce, PR; SO; BA; Cncrt Bnd 89; Lsta Del Dcno De La Univ Ctlica De PR 90; Natl Cllgte Bus Mrt Awrd; Math; Bus Admin.

**VELEZ VELEZ, ALEXIS B,** Inter Amer Univ Pr San German, San German, PR; GD; BA; Cmptr Sci; Prgmmr Anlyst.

**VELEZ VELEZ, LUIS A,** Inter Amer Univ Pr San German, San German, PR; FR; Cmptr Sci; Prgmg.

**VELEZ, ANGELA,** Univ Metropolitano, Rio Piedras, PR; SR; BA; Univ Hnr Scty 88-; Univ Achvmnt Awrd 90-; Hnr Stdnt 88-; Blgy; Med.

**VELEZ, JANET I,** Univ Of Pr At Rio Piedras, Rio Piedras, PR; JR; Pre-Med Assoc Secr 88-; Hnr Rl Awd 90-; Bio; Dr Med.

**VELEZ, JIMMY,** City Univ Of Ny City Coll, New York, NY; SO; BA; Econ; Mgmt.

**VELEZ, LARISSA I,** Univ Of Pr At Rio Piedras, Rio Piedras, PR; SO; BS; Pre-Med Assn 90-; All Am Schlrs; Bio; Med.

**VELEZ, LINA MARIA,** Fl International Univ, Miami, FL; FR; Pen/Sable 90; Quill/Scroll 90-.

**VELEZ, LISANNE M,** Williams Coll, Williamstown, MA; FR; BA; VISTA 90-; S Pcfc Mscl Prod; Asst Tchr Lang Prog; Biolgy; Rsrch Scintst.

**VELEZ, MARIA C,** Evangelical Semimary Of P R, Hato Rey, PR; GD; Evnglcl Smnry PR Lbry 88-90; Cnvtn Comm Dscpl Christ Chrch PR; Magna Cum Laude; BA Sclgy 68; M Div 90.

**VELEZ, MARIA F,** Univ Of Pr At Rio Piedras, Rio Piedras, PR; JR; BA; Assn Of Hstry Stdnts 90-; Gldn Ky; Hnr Tuitn 89-90; Hstry; Law.

**VELEZ, MICHAEL,** Univ Of Pr Medical Sciences, San Juan, PR; GD; MS; Codiplat Inc 90-; Musitrales Inc 87-88; BA 89; Demography; Tchr.

**VELEZ, MICHELLE,** Univ Of Pr At Mayaguez, Mayaguez, PR; JR; BED; Amer Inst Indtl Engrg 89-F Phi Kappa Phi; Alpha Pi Mu Secty 90-; Tau Beta Pi; Mu Alpha Phi Su Secty 88-90; Intsrl Engrg; Engrg.

**VELEZ, PABLO R,** Fl International Univ, Miami, FL; FR; BA; Hnrs Prgrm 90-; Fclty Schlrs 90-; Intl Rltns; Law.

**VELEZ, SONIA E,** Saint Thomas Univ, Miami, FL; SR; BA; AA Miami Dade Comm Coll 90; Psychlgy; Marriage/Fmly Thrpy.

**VELLECA, THOMAS J,** Cooper Union, New York, NY; JR; BE; ASCE 90-; Chi Epsilon VP; 2nd Pl Alumn Assoc Stdnt Arch Strctrl Dsgn Comp 90; IM Bwlng 88-; Cvl Engr.

**VELOX, SHELLY T,** City Univ Of Ny Baruch Coll, New York, NY; SO; BBA; Acctng.

**VELOZ, JENNIFER J,** Manhattan Coll, Bronx, NY; FR; BA; Tennis 90-; Engl/Hstry; Law.

**VELTEN, MARY JO,** Northern Ky Univ, Highland Hts, KY; SR; BS; Alpha Chi 90-; Kappa Mu Epsilon 88-89; Chi Omega Sorority 88-89; Dns Schlrshp 90-; Pres Schlrshp 87-89; Mrktng; Adv.

**VELTHEIM, PAULA R,** Hillsborough Comm Coll, Tampa, FL; FR; AS; Phi Theta Kappa; Nrsng; RN.

**VELTRI, LAURIE M,** S U N Y Coll Of Tech At Frmgdl, Farmingdale, NY; FR; AS; Acdmc Excllnc Awd Lbrl Arts/Sci; Lbrl Arts/Acctg; Acctg.

**VEMURI, SREEKANTH,** Boston Univ, Boston, MA; FR; BA; Premed Soc; IM Bsktbl/Soccr/Tennis; Pre-Med; MD.

**VENABLE, KATHY A V,** Va Highlands Comm Coll, Abingdon, VA; FR; ASN; Ret Home LPN 79-; LPN Smyth County Voc Schl 85; Nursing.

**VENCKUS, TANYA I,** Northern Ky Univ, Highland Hts, KY; JR; BA; Stdnt Dsgn 90-; Art; Grphc Dsgn.

**VENDIG, TAMARA L,** Univ Of Rochester, Rochester, NY; SR; BA; SG Chrmn 87-89; Phi Sigma Sigma 88-; Pol Sci/Psychlgy; Banking.

**VENDITTI, DEAN AUGUSTINE,** Fayetteville St Univ, Fayetteville, NC; JR; BS; USA; Deans List 90; EIED; Bus.

**VENDRELL, MARGARITA M,** Duquesne Univ, Pittsburgh, PA; JR; BS; Spnsl Clb 89-; Intrmrl Vllybll 88-; Blgy; Med.

**VENDRELL, PEDRO J,** Catholic Univ Of Pr, Ponce, PR; SR; BS; Honor Prog 89-; Ldrshp In Commnty 90-; Sciences; Medicine.

**VENDRELL, SUSIE,** Duquesne Univ, Pittsburgh, PA; JR; BS; Std Acctng Asc; Spnsh Clb Sec 90-; Beta Gamma Sigma; Lambda Sigma 90-; Phi Eta Sigma 89-90; Fndrs Awd 89-; Inctv Grnt 89-; Dns Lst 89-90; Acctng.

**VENEGAS-RIOS, LEOPOLDO J,** Univ Politecnica De Pr, Hato Rey, PR; SO; BA; Math; Eng.

**VENEY, JOHN E,** Univ Of Akron, Akron, OH; JR; BA; Goldn Key 90-; Acctg; CPA.

**VENEZIA, CHRISTOPHER G,** Dowling Coll, Oakdale Li, NY; SR; BS; Omcrn Delta Epsln; Dns Lst 88; AAS Suffolk Cty Comm Clg 89; Bsn/Math Educ; Tchr.

**VENEZIALE, MARY L,** Lansdale School Of Bus, North Wales, PA; SO; BA; DP Cert 90; Bus; Bus Mgmt.

**VENORD, JEAN M,** Bloomfield Coll, Bloomfield, NJ; SO; Gen Chem.

**VENTERS, NORMAN R,** Coker Coll, Hartsville, SC; SR; BS; U S Army; Bus.

**VENTEVOGEL, LISA K,** Fl International Univ, Miami, FL; SR; BS; Stdnt Dietc Assn 89-; Fla Dietc Assn 89-; Amer Dietc Assn; Chi Phi Little Sistr 84-87; Jaycees 88-; BS Busn Univ Fla 87; Diets Nutrtn; Busn/Pub Hlth.

**VENTRE, VICTORIA E,** Inter Amer Univ Pr Hato Rey, Hato Rey, PR; SR; BA.

**VENTRILLA, KERRI L,** Ga Coll, Milledgeville, GA; SO; Eta Sigma Alpha 89-; Gamma Beta Phi 90-; Erly Chldhd Educ; Tchr.**

**VENTRY, CHRISTOPHER J R,** Duke Univ, Durham, NC; FR; Ski Clb; Frshmn Advsry Cncl; Beta Theta Pi; CHANCE Big Brother; Frshmn Cls Scl Chr; Intl Relations; Business.

**VENTURA, JOAQUIN A,** Bunker Hill Comm Coll, Boston, MA; FR; BA; Math; Cmptr Sci.

**VENTURINO, ASSUNTA,** Broward Comm Coll, Ft Lauderdale, FL; SO; BA; Hnrs Inst 89-; Merit Schlrshp 89-; Fin; Planner.

**VENUS, JULIE M,** Jersey City St Coll, Jersey City, NJ; JR; BS; Byzantine Quartet 89-; Deans Lst 88-; Intrnshp Essex Co Prbtn Dept 90-; Crmnl Jstce/Law Enfrcmnt; Police Offcr.

**VENUTI, JENNIFER M,** S U N Y Coll Of Tech At Alfred, Alfred, NY; SR.

**VENUTI, STEVEN A,** Neumann Coll, Aston, PA; SO; BA; Theatr 90-; Alpha Lambda Delta Natl Hnr Soc 89-90; Temple Univ; NCCAA; Comm Arts; D J Brdcstng/Prod/Actng.

**VERA NEGRON, SANDRA,** Inter Amer Univ Pr Hato Rey, Hato Rey, PR; SR; BA; Assn Hist/Lit Stdnts 89-; Engl Lit; Tchng U Lvl.

**VERA, ANA A,** Catholic Univ Of Pr, Ponce, PR; SO; Acctng Std Asc; Sprt Asc; All-Amer Awd; Rtry Intl Awd; Acad Awd; Acctng; CPA.

**VERA, SANDRA J,** George Mason Univ, Fairfax, VA; SR; BS; Alpha Chi; Dean Lst 89-; Pblc Rltns Intern Inst Arts; Wmn Cmmnctns; Wrd Prcssng Bus Ownr 85-86-; Offc Mngr; AS Northern VA Comm Coll 80; Spch Cmmnctns/Thtr; Pblc Rltns/ Acting.**

**VERBIL, ANNA MARIE J,** Saint Josephs Coll New York, Brooklyn, NY; GD; BS; Deans Lst; Mmbr Nsg Dir Cltn Almn Assoc; Pstrl Afflitn; Rgstrd Nrs; Hlth Grntlgy.

**VERCANT, KERRIE A,** S U N Y Coll Of Tech At Alfred, Alfred, NY; SR; AAS; Pi Theta Kappa; Tau Alpha Pi; Sigma Tau Epsilon 90-; Crss Cntry 89; Acdmc All Amer; Trck 89; Digtil Equp Corp Mnrty Wmn Ttn Schl; Cmptr Grphs Eng Tech; Eng Tech.

**VERCHOT, JUNIUS B,** Birmingham Southern Coll, Birmingham, AL; SR; BS; Blue Blzr Pgm SW Corp 89-; Fnce; Fncl Plng.

**VERDARIS, NICHOLAS J,** Hellenic Coll/Holy Cross, Brookline, MA; SR; BA; Stdnt Gov Pres 89; Grdtn Commt 90; Acredidation Comm 90; Deans List 87; Outreach Prgrm 88-89; Young Adult League Greek Orthdx Chrch 87; Rev Efstrts Rghls Memorial Prize 89-90; Rev DR Sphcls M Sphcls Mrl Schlshp 89-90; Orthodox Theology; Greek Orthdx Prsthd.

**VERDUGO, ANTONIO,** Fl International Univ, Miami, FL; JR; BA; Soc Adv Mgmt 90-; Amer Mktg Asc VP 90-; Intvars 90-; Dns Lst; Grad Miami-Dade 89; Amer Mktg Asc; Sml Bsn Cnslr; Tchrs Asst Lctr; AA Miami-Dade 89; AMA; Mktg/Mgmt; Bsn.

**VERE, JARL C,** Fl International Univ, Miami, FL; SO; BA; Phi Eta Sigma; Cmptr Science; Prgrmmr.

**VEREEN, CALPRUNIA D,** Hillsborough Comm Coll, Tampa, FL; FR; AA; Sheperd Rd Bptst Church; Medicine; Obstetrician/ Gyn.

**VERES, GREGORY R,** Univ Of Sc At Columbia, Columbia, SC; FR; MBA; Dns Lst 90-; Alpha Lambda Delta 90-; Gamma Beta Phi 90-; Kappa Sigma 90-; Kappa Sigma Treas 90-; Bsn Adm; Intl Bsn.

**VERGARA, MAGALIE,** Caribbean Univ, Bayamon, PR; SR; BA; Acctg.

**VERGES, JUAN MANUEL,** Inter Amer Univ Pr San German, San German, PR; FR; BA; Cnslng Stdnts Assn Vocals 89-; Jrnlst Univ Rompiondo Barroras Vocals 90-; Psychlgy; PHD.

**VERGHESE, PHILIP K,** Norfolk St Univ, Norfolk, VA; SO; BS; Clg Rpblcns 88-89; Phi Dlt Theta 88-; Bio Chem Asst 90-; Crew 88-89; Bio; Medcn MS.

**VERHOFF, SUZANNE M,** Defiance Coll, Defiance, OH; FR; BA; Frnscs Tm 90-; Acrss Cmps 90-; Pi Kappa Delta 90-; Elem Educ; Tchng.

**VERLEY, ELIZABETH A,** Longwood Coll, Farmville, VA; SR; BA; Longwood Ambass Prom Mbrshp,Soc Chr 89-90; Peer Advisor 88; Phi Kappa Phi; Peer Tutor Elem Span 89-90; Sigma Delta Pi Pres 89-; Lambda Iota Tau 90-; Sem Abrd Merida Venezuela 89; Stdnt Tchg; Ambass Yr 89-90; Ambass Sen Hl Fame; Modern Lang/Cncntrtn Span Scndry Educ; Educ.

**VERMA, RAJAN K,** S U N Y At Buffalo, Buffalo, NY; SR; MS; Inst Elctrcl Elctrnc Engnrs Mmbr 89-; Engnrng Soc Buffolo Schlrshp 87-89; Buffalo Fndtn Cargl Schlrshp 8-; Top Schlsts Schlrshp 88; Mcs Grp India Asn Buffalo; Grad Indian Stdnt Assn 89-; Elctrcl Engnr Intrnshp; UB Badmntn Clb; Elctrcl Cmptr Engnrng; Engnr.

**VERMETTE, DENISE M,** Springfield Tech Comm Coll, Springfield, MA; SR; AS; Phys Therapy Asst Clb 89-; Phys Therapy Asst; BS.

**VERMEULEN, CHRISTOPHER N,** Hillsborough Comm Coll, Tampa, FL; SO; AA; Phi Theta Kappa 89-; Beta Phi Gamma; Intrnshp WTVT Community Rltns Newsroom 90-; AA; Mass Communications; Broadcast Jrnlsm.

**VERNA, LUKE J,** Indiana Univ Of Pa, Indiana, PA; FR; BED; Edctn; Tch.

**VERNACOTOLA, DEAN E,** Alfred Univ, Alfred, NY; SR; Amer Ceramic Soc Tr 89-; Var Soccr 87-88; Tau Beta Pi 90-; Phi Kappa Phi 90-; Keramos 89-.

**VERNACOTOLA, JOSEPH N,** Kent St Univ Kent Cmps, Kent, OH; SO; BED; Stdnt Instrctr; Scndry Ed; Tch High Schl Soc Sci.

**VERNE, SARA R,** Univ Of Sc At Columbia, Columbia, SC; JR; BA; Dinkins Stdnt Un Pgrm Bd Winthrop Coll Chr Prmtns Comm 88-90; Advrtsng Mjr/Psycho Mnr; Mass Comm.

**VERNER, LISA R,** Univ Of Sc At Columbia, Columbia, SC; SO; BA; Hotel Sls/Mktg Assoc 89-90; Kappa Delta Epsilon 90-; Tchr.

**VERNET, HILDEGARDE,** William Paterson Coll, Wayne, NJ; SR; BS; Stdnt Asst Blgy Dept 88-90; Stdnt Tchr; Blgy; Sci.

**VERNON, ANGELA M,** Bellarmine Coll, Louisville, KY; SR; BA; Acctg Clb 88-; Delta Epsilon Sigma 88-; Acctg; CPA.

**VERNON, DONNA M,** Mount Olive Coll, Mount Olive, NC; JR; BS; Marshall 90; Bus; Acctng.

**VERNON, SHANE F G,** Nova Univ, Ft Lauderdale, FL; GD; DIBA; FAU Fncng Club 89-; Phi Thesta Kappa 86-; Kiawanis Intl CLB Pompano Bch 84-; Hstrcl Soc 84-; Prof Phtgrphrs Of Fla Guild 83-; Chamber Of Comm 81-; Trinity U M Ch 70-; BPS Barry Univ 90; MIBA; Intl Bus Phd: Cnsltng.

**VERONESI, KAREN M,** Western New England Coll, Springfield, MA; SR; BA; Achvmnts Rep; Ski Clb Drctr Advrtsng 87-89; Gtwy Hl Cncl Rep 89-90; Deans Lst 89-; Hmn Rsrc Mngmnt.

**VERONIS, LUKE A,** Hellenic Coll/Holy Cross, Brookline, MA; GD; MDIV; Mssns Com Chrmn 90-; Natl Cncl Chrstns/Jews; Prsn Mnstry 89-; Deans Lst 89-; Bsktbl; BS PA St Univ 87; Thlgy; Prsthd-Mssnry.

**VERRENGIA, CYNTHIA S,** City Univ Of Ny Grad School, New York, NY; GD; BS; Wms Clb 89-90; Pltcl Sci Clb 89-90; Phi Beta Kappa 90; Dns Lst 88-90; NYPIRG Intrn 89; Dept St Ombdsmn 90; Med Tchncn 78-85; Hstry/Pltcl Sci; Law Schl.

**VERRET, EDDIE J,** Nova Univ, Ft Lauderdale, FL; GD; MBA; Phi Kappa Psi VP 86; Amrcn Exprs Trvl Rltd Srvcs; BSBA Unvrsty Swstrn LA 88; Bsns Mgmt.

**VERRET, THOMAS E,** Southern Coll Of Tech, Marietta, GA; SO; BS; Coop Stdnt Rsrch Tech GA Inst Tech 89-; Indust Eng.

**VERRICO, IVELISSE A,** Cornell Univ Statutory College, Ithaca, NY; FR; Donlon Hall Cncl Flr Rep 90-; Alpha Omicron Pi; Biology.

**VERRUSO, SHARIE MERCEDES,** Lesley Coll, Cambridge, MA; JR; BSED; LINC Sec 88-; Hon Rl 88-; Engl Tch Exchg; Stdnt Tchr Gleason Schl Medfrd MA; Stdnt Tchr Watertwn Sommorvl MA 88-90; Erly Chldhd/Elem Educ; Educ.

**VERSLUYS, GERALD J,** Univ Of Louisville, Louisville, KY; SR; MENG; BSE; Elec Eng.

**VERST, RANDALL WM,** Northern Ky Univ, Highland Hts, KY; JR; BA; Natl Pltcl Sci Hnr Scty 90-; Tmstrs 88-; Cthlc Ordr Frstrs 70-; Amrcn Coll Schlrs; Intrnshp Pol Sci 90; Deans Lst 90-; Pol Sci.

**VERTICHIO, ROBERT J,** Suffolk Comm Coll Eastern Cmps, Riverhead, NY; SR; BA; Hosptlty Club 90-; Cncl For The Advncmnt Of Standrd For Stdnt Svc Dev Prog; Phi Theta Kappa 90-; Deans List 90; Food/Bar Svc/Mgt 80-; AAS SUNY Farmingdale Landscp Dsgn 76; Hotel/Restrnt Mgt; Food/Vevrg Dir/MA/TCHNG.

**VERTREES, MATTHEW D,** Clarkson Univ, Potsdam, NY; JR; BS; Snr Clss VP 88-90; Clrksn Mns Rgby Clb 88-90; Dsc Jcky 88-90; Phi Kappa Sigma 89-; Frrnt Intl Coop Sls Accts 90-; Phlp Mrrs Schlrshp; Mgmt Fnc.

**VESCERA, DONNA A,** The Boston Conservatory, Boston, MA; FR; BFA; Music/Theater.

**VESPOINT, LORI L,** Kent St Univ Kent Cmps, Kent, OH; SR; BA; Knt Cncl On Fam Rltns 90; Chld Lfe Dept; Rnbw Babs And Chldrns Hosp OH; Indiv And Fam Stds; Chld Lfe.

**VESPOLI, ANNE K,** Duquesne Univ, Pittsburgh, PA; SR; BM; Piano Clb 87-88; Bible Study Grp 89-; Mortar Bd 90-; Pi Kappa Lambda 90-; Phi Kapp Phi; Mu Phi Epsilon Rcrdng/Corres/ Alumni Sec 88-; Tuition/Stipend Salutatorian Duquesne Univ Sch Music Cls; Suma Cum Laude; Music Perf; Higher Edn/Music.

**VESSELS, DAVID W,** Univ Of Louisville, Louisville, KY; SR; MENG; IEEE; Golden Key; All Am Schlr; Natl Coll Engrng Awd; Coop Intrnshp Dept Of Defense 90-; Elect Engrng.

**VEST, KIRSTEN M,** Radford Univ, Radford, VA; SO; BS; Hnrs Pgm; Dstngshd Hnr Grdt Prmry Ldrshp Dvlpmnt Crs Army Achvmnt Mdl 89; VA Army Natl Grd 87-; Flt/Pcl Plyr 29 Infntry Div Bnd Pres 88-; Clrcl Sprt Manpower Temp Srv 88-; Chld Dvlpmnt: Dycr Ctr Admin/Ownr.

**VEST, WANDA KAREN,** Beckley Coll, Beckley, WV; FR; AS; Sec; Lgl Sec; Resp Thrpy.

**VESTAL, DEREK A,** Memphis St Univ, Memphis, TN; FR; Sigma Alpha Epsilon Treas; Acctg; Investigative Law Enfrcmnt.

**VESTEVICH, KATHERINE CORDAHL,** Goucher Coll, Towson, MD; FR; BA; Cls Pres 89-90; Psychlgy Clb Pres 90-; Psi Chi Pres; APA 90-; Natl Inst Aging Rsrch Intern; Varsity Crs Cntry 89; Clncl Psychlgst.

**VETMAN, MICHAEL I,** Kent St Univ Kent Cmps, Kent, OH; JR; BA; Rssn Clb VP 89-; Pershing Rifles Corp Cdt 90-; Rangers ROTC Army Corp Rngr 90-; Pres Lst 88-90; Hons Deans Lst 90-; Golden Key; Golden Eagle Bttln Army ROTC 90-; Schlrshp Cdt; Stdnt Advsry Comm 90-; RTOC Schlrshp 90-; U Acad Schlrshp 89-; Mltry Sci/Rssn/Intr Ntl Bus; Mltry Ofcr.

**VETTER, MARCY M,** Dyersburg St Comm Coll, Dyersburg, TN; FR; BA; Bsns/Psych.

**VETTER, ROBERT W,** Kent St Univ Kent Cmps, Kent, OH; SO; BA; Cmps Bible Flwshp Pres 90-; Dns Lst 89-; Fnce.

**VEYTSMAN, NATASHA V,** Va Commonwealth Univ, Richmond, VA; SO; BA; Intl Un 89-; Newpspaper Folio Rprtr 89-90; Amer Soc Of Fashion 90; Fashion Merch; Intl Bus Affrs.

**VEZIROGLU, SAMIM K,** Univ Of Miami, Coral Gables, FL; FR; BS; Soccer Clb 90-; ASME 90-; Mech Engr; Engr.

**VIA, KAREN L,** Beckley Coll, Beckley, WV; SO; BA; Scndry Edn/Psychlgy Math.

**VIA, KELLI L,** James Madison University, Harrisonburg, VA; SR; MOT; Cncl Excptnl Chldrn Treas 87-; Psi Chi 90-; BS; Occptnl Thrpy.

**VIA III, WILLARD R,** Southern Coll Of Tech, Marietta, GA; JR; Deans Lst.

**VIANA, HUMBERTO CARLOS,** Univ Of Fl, Gainesville, FL; JR; BS; HSA 89-; ASCE 90-; Hon Stdnt Dept Of Civil Engr Univ Of FL; Im Soccer/Sftbl 88-; Sprachdiplm I/II Clg Lvl Grmn Lang Cert Colegio Aleman Barrangvilla Columbia 84 86; Civil Engr; Constrctn Mgt.

**VIANA, MERCEDES M,** Fl International Univ, Miami, FL; FR; BA; Phi Sigma Sigma Sec 90-; Peer Advsng 90-; Poltcl Sci; Law.

**VIAR, JUSTIN D,** Wv Inst Of Tech, Montgomery, WV; FR; BS; IM Ftbl 90-; IM Bsktbl Capt 90-; Bsebl 90-; Bsn/Drftg; Mgmt.

**VIATOR, ANGELA K,** Univ Of West Fl, Pensacola, FL; FR; Alpha Delta Pi 90-; Deans Lst; Hghst Pldg GPA 90.

**VIAU, JOHN F,** Johnson St Coll, Johnson, VT; SR; BS; Vlybl Clb 89-90; IM 87-; Phys Educ; Tchr/Admnstrtr.

**VIBBERT, JUDY D,** Hillsborough Comm Coll, Tampa, FL; SO; BA; Hnr Stdnt 88-; Prfsnl Secrtrs Intl 88; Natl Hnr Scty 83; Lrnd Lions 82-83; Ftr Bsns Ldrs Of Amrca 82-83; Cprtv Bsns Edctn 82-83; Acctng/Shrthnd Awrd Natl 82; Fbla Awrd Shrthnd Typng Accntng 82; Otstndng Stdnt Awrd Typng/Shrthnd 83; Bsns; Fnncl Anlyst.**

**VICARI, BRIAN K,** Atlantic Comm Coll, Mays Landing, NJ; JR; BS; Stdnt Govt Rep 88-89; Hotel Sls/Mktng Assn V P 89-90; Deans Lst 88-90; Adrian Phillips Schlrshp 89; IM Fotbl/Sftbl; AAS 90; Hotel/Rest Mgmnt; Hotel Sls.

**VICARI, MARY ANN,** S U N Y Coll At Fredonia, Fredonia, NY; JR; BA; SPAS; Kappa Delta Pi; Schlrshp Stdy Abroad Sadra Vatterbygdens Folkhog Skola; Cert Raphael Schl Beauty 86; Spch Pthlgy/Adlgy; Spch Pthlogy.

**VICARIA, JENINE C,** Barry Univ, Miami, FL; SR; BSN; Stdnt Nrse Assn; Sigma Theta Tau; Pres Lst; Deans Lst; Nrsng.

**VICARIO, BRETT A,** Fl St Univ, Tallahassee, FL; FR; AA; Peer Mentor; Phi Eta Sigma 90-; Campus Alliance For Literacy 90-; Im Tennis 90-; Engl; Law.

**VICE SR, CALVIN J,** Nova Univ, Ft Lauderdale, FL; GD; MBA; BA Carson Newman Clg 69; Mre Ed S W Bapt Sem 71-76.

**VICIC, MICHAEL A,** Univ Of Akron, Akron, OH; JR; AICHE; Hon Clb Pres 88-89/91; Hon Cncl Stdnt Rep; Phi Eta Sigma; Gldn Key; Tau Beta Pi; Rsrch Asst/Univ Akron; Co-Op Educ Stdnt-Dow Chem; IM Vlybl; Chem Eng.

**VICK, AMANDA C,** Livingston Univ, Livingston, AL; JR; BS; Acctng Club; Acctng.

**VICK, MICHAEL E,** Ms St Univ, Miss State, MS; JR; BPA; Inst Ind Engrs 90-; AA Meridian Comm Coll 90; Acctg; CPA.

**VICK, VIRGINIA M,** Middle Tn St Univ, Murfreesboro, TN; SR; MS; Middle TE State Univ Stdnt Prgrmmng Cmmt 88-; Columbia State Cmmty Clg Circle K Clb 87-89; Columbia State Cmmty Clg Peer Cnslr 86-89; AS Music Ed Columbia Cmmty Clg 89; Clncl Psyclgy; Clncl Psyclgst.

**VICK JR, WILLIAM W,** Old Dominion Univ, Norfolk, VA; JR; BS; Golden Key; IEEE 88-; Elec Coop Philip Morris USA; Elec Eng; Corp Law.

**VICKARYOUS, BRIAN K P,** Univ Of Miami, Coral Gables, FL; JR; BS; Army ROTC 89-91; Alpha Epsilon Delta 90-91; Phi Eta Sigma 89-91; Deans List 90; Alpha Epsilon Delta; Sigma Alpha Epsilon 90-91; Big Buddy Fresh 90-91; I M Ftbl 91; Sigma Alpha Epsilon Cmuty Serv Proj 90-91; Army Schlrshp 89-; Biology; Med.

**VICKERS, IRIS S,** Abraham Baldwin Agri Coll, Tifton, GA; SO; BED; Hnr Stdnts; Dns Lst; Educ; Tchr.

**VICKERS, SHANNON D,** Va Highlands Comm Coll, Abingdon, VA; SO; AAS; Cnvlsnt Hm Intrn; Human Serv; Psychology.

**VICKERY, KIER T,** Walker Coll, Jasper, AL; SO; BSW; Bptst Cmps Mnstrs; Phi Theta Kappa; Wal Mart Schlrshp; Walker Almni Schlrshp; Nearly New Schlrshp; Scl Wrk; Cnslng.

**VICKERY, MARGERY A,** Valdosta St Coll, Valdosta, GA; SO; BED; Mrchng Bnd 89-; Alph Lmbd 89-90; Sgm Alph Chi 90-; Pres Frshmn Schlr 90; Hon Pgm 89-; Erly Chldhd; Tchng.

**VICKERY, MELVIN S,** Roane St Comm Coll, Harriman, TN; SO; AS; Bus Admin; Bus.

**VICKMAIR, JULIE A,** Univ Of Southern Ms, Hattiesburg, MS; SO; BA; SGA 90-; Alumni Assn 89-; Eagle Clb 89-; Hnrs Colg 89-; Dance Team 89-; Lambda Sigma 90-; Gamma Beta Phi 90-; IM 90-; Psychology; Clinical Psychology.

**VICTOR, MONIQUE R,** Yeshiva Univ, New York, NY; GD; BA; Pre-Law Soc Treas 89-; Fine Arts Soc 88-; Hist Awd 90-; Judcl Intern 88-89; Hist; Law.

**VICTORIANO, CARMELA C,** Univ Of Sc At Columbia, Columbia, SC; FR; BSN; Deans Advsry Cmmtt 90-; Yng Lf 90-; Asn Amrcn Assoc 90-; Nrsng; Med.

**VICTORY, GEORGE L,** Oh Dominican Coll, Columbus, OH; JR; BS; Fed Mgrs Assn 89-; Fed Law Enfrcmnt Employee Of Yr 85; Vol Tutor Proj Plus Adult Lit Prog 87-88; USMC 65-67; Asst Dist Dir 88-; AA Southwest Coll 72; Bus; Fed Law Enfrcmnt.

**VIDA, MICHAEL J,** Kent St Univ Kent Cmps, Kent, OH; SR; BA; Rho Epsilon Pres 90-; IM Sftbl Hcky 88; IM Ftbl Capt 88; Fnnc; Cmmrcl Real Est.

**VIDA, VALERIE S,** Longwood Coll, Farmville, VA; SR; BS; Ambssdrs; Peer Hlprs; Psi Chi Pres 90-; Psych/Spc Educ.

**VIDAL, ELIZABETH A,** Barry Univ, Miami, FL; SO; BA; Econ Clb 90-; Drama Actvs; Dns Lst 89-; Pres Lst; Acctg/Bus; CPA/TAX Law.

**VIDAL, JAVIER A,** Oh Univ, Athens, OH; FR; BS; Airway Sci; Aviation.

**VIDAL, OSCAR LAINO,** Georgetown Univ, Washington, DC; FR; BSBA; Clb Filipino Treas 90-; Stdnt Fed Crdt Union Asst Cmptrlr 90-; Knights Columbus; Acdmc First Hons 90-; Acctg; CPA.

**VIDELA, ALEJANDRO,** City Univ Of Ny La Guard Coll, Long Island Cty, NY; SO; Acctng/Mngrl/Entrepenurial Clb Rep 90-; Phi Theta Kappa 90-; King Wallenberg Law Soc; Schls Nwspr Photog/Editor 90-; Amer Assn Higher Educ Pblc Rltns Coord; Cert Awd Outstndg Achvmnt Acctng Lab; Acctng; Finance.

**VIDETTI, ANNE L,** S U N Y Coll Of Tech At Delhi, Delhi, NY; SO; AS; Amer Dsgn/Drftng Assn V P 89-; Stdnt Govt Sntr 90-; Dorm Cncl Sntr 90-; Intrclgte Wmns Soccer 90-; Cert 90; Drftng; BS Engr.

**VIDOLI, RICHARD G,** Me Maritime Academy, Castine, ME; JR; Shiped With Arco Marine; V Football 90-; AA Edison Cmnty Clge 88; Nautical Science; Ocean Shipping.

**VIDONI, DIANE F,** Duquesne Univ, Pittsburgh, PA; SO; BA; Itlian Clb 89-91; DUV 89-91; Intl Bsns Mrktng.**

**VIDOUREK, SCOTT M,** Univ Of Cincinnati, Cincinnati, OH; FR; BS; Rcyclng Com; Archtctre Eng Tech; Archtctre.

**VIDOUREK, STEVEN J,** Univ Of Cincinnati, Cincinnati, OH; JR; BSN; Cntr Brd Chrmn Of Fclts And Oprtns 87-; Nrsng And Hlth Trbnl Treas 88-; Hnrs Stdnt Assn 89; Hnrs Prog 87-; Mrtr Brd; Natl Cllgte Nrsng Awrd 89-; Sigma Theta Tau; Alpha Lambda Delta 88; EMT-A Cert Scarlett Oaks Join Voc 89; Nrsng; Anstsia.

**VIECHNICKI, BETH A,** Muhlenberg Coll, Allentown, PA; FR; Hstry Spnsh; Scndry Educ.

**VIEHMAN, PATRICIA G,** Univ Of Ga, Athens, GA; SR; BS; Frnshng/Intrs; Intr Dsgnr.

**VIEIRA, DAVID P,** Newbury Coll, Brookline, MA; SO; AS; Pride Inc Supv 87-; Bsns Mgmt.

**VIEIRA JR, ORLANDO,** Commonwealth Coll, Virginia Beach, VA; GD; Rec Clb Motores Perkins SA Dir 71-76; S Bernards S P Brazil; Credit Union Pres 74-80; Clark Equip Trainee 69; Sngr Sewing Machines Trainee 70; Amer Mgmt Assn; Engrs/Archtcts Assn Brazil; MBA Mackenzie Univ SP Brazil 72; Mech Engr.

**VIEL, ANDREA M,** Tougaloo Coll, Tougaloo, MS; JR; BA; Engl Clb Sec 89-90; Tougaloo Coll Gospel Choir 88-90; Schl Nwspr Movie Critic Feature Ed 89-; Tougaloo Coll Comm Ctr Tutor Pgm 88-89; ROTC Advncd Ldrshp 3rd Cadet 90; Army Reserve Spec E-3 Hon Sldr 89; Engl/Jrnlsm; Jrnlst/Brdcst.

**VIENNA, JOHN D,** Alfred Univ, Alfred, NY; SR; MS; Amer Crmc Scty 89-; Ntl Inst Crmc Eng 89-; Keramos Vp 89-; US Army Instrctr 84-86; US Army Rsrv Evltr E6 86-; IM Cpt 88-; BS; Crmc Eng; Rsrch/Prdct Dvlpmnt.

**VIERA BARBOSA, YANIRA,** Inter Amer Univ Pr San Juan, Hato Rey, PR; GD; JD; Wmns Bowln Assoc Treas 88-89; Bwlrs Cnfdrtn Pres 85-88; Bwlng Fdrtn Dir 87-89; Cum Laude 77; Prss Info Offcr St Insrnc Fnd 82-; BA 77; Grad Stds 80; Law.

**VIERA, CLARIVEL,** Univ Of Pr At Mayaguez, Mayaguez, PR; SO; BS; Chem Eng; Biomed Eng.

**VIERA, DAN-EL,** Univ Of Pr At Rio Piedras, Rio Piedras, PR; SO; BA; AIAS 89-; Natl Hon Soc 86-89; Acdmc Awrds 90-; Deans Lst 90; NCADA 90; Ambntl Dsgn; Archtctr.

**VIERA, JOSE E,** Univ Of Rochester, Rochester, NY; JR; Spanish Flr Pres; Sigma Nu; Stdnt Emp Of Yr; Evnts Mngr; BA; Intl Brktng Analyst.**

**VIERA, MICHAEL ALBERTO,** Fl International Univ, Miami, FL; JR; Stdnt Gvmt 90-; AA Miami Dade Comm Coll 89; Pblc Adm; City Mgmt/Fed Gvmt.

**VIERS, DIANE M,** Defiance Coll, Defiance, OH; JR; BS; Natl Assoc Acctnts 88-; Tau Pi Phi 89-; Acctnt Cooper Inds 80-; AA 88; Bus; Acctg.

**VIETORISZ, JUAN A,** Gallaudet Univ, Washington, DC; SR; Englsh Dpt Tutor 90-; Amrcn Sign Language Nw Mvmnt 90; Stdnt Free Entrprs 88; Prsdnt Schlr 90; Fmly Srvc Fndtn Stf Vlntr; Dpt Linvistics Intrprtng ASL Pioneer 90; US Army Corps Engnrs Dpt Defense Cmptr Clrk 88; Englsh Psychology; Psychtrpy.

**VIETS, ROXIE J,** Western Piedmont Comm Coll, Morganton, NC; SO; AA; Art; Physcl Art Thrpy.

**VIFILSDOTTIR, HALLDORA,** Univ Of Nc At Charlotte, Charlotte, NC; SR; BA; Golden Key; Archtctr.

**VIG, MANISH,** Univ Of Rochester, Rochester, NY; SR; BA; Simga Nu 90-; Stdnt Assn 87-88; Viewpoint Mag Asst Ed 89-90; Order Omega Grk Hnry 89-; Rochester Plan Erly Med Schl Slctn 89-; Sigma Nu Cmndr 90-; Tiernan Soc 87-89; A L Jordan Condom Sense Pgm 90-; YMCA 88-89; BA Pltcl Sci/BS Mlclur Gntcs; Med.**

**VIGEANT JR, NORMAN P,** Saint Josephs Coll, Windham, ME; JR; BA; Hall Cncl Pres 89-; Radio Music Dir 88-; Newspr 90-; IM 88-; History; Law.

**VIGH, STEPHEN A,** Univ Of Akron, Akron, OH; SR; BED; Natl Cncl Tchrs Of Engl 90-; ACES; Vol Serv Sosl Wrkr Nrsng Hm Awds 88-; Cmprhnsv Cmmnctns; Sec Ed Engl Tchr.

**VIGIL, LORETTA E,** Ms St Univ, Miss State, MS; SO; PHARM; Cthlc Assoc Crdntr 89-; Angl Flght Scnd Lt 90-; Gamma Beta Phi 89-90; Hnrs Schlrshp; Phrmcy.

**VIGILANCE, DEON W,** Morehouse Coll, Atlanta, GA; FR; BS; NY/NJ Clb Dorm Repr 90-; John Hops Ctr Kids Vol 90-; Biochem; Med.

**VIGLAS, GEORGIA,** Boston Univ, Boston, MA; FR; BA; BV Hcky 90-; Blgy; Med.

**VIGLIOTTA, KAREN A,** Univ Of Miami, Coral Gables, FL; FR; BA; Hnrs Stdnts Assoc; Frshmn Hnr Soc; Sportsfest IM Sports Activities; Clinical Psych/Cnslng.

**VIGNA, BERNARD J,** Central Me Medical Center, Lewiston, ME; FR; ADN; SNA 90-; AACN 90-; Natl Ski Ptrl Ptrl Dir 83-; Nrsng; Cert Emr Nsg.

**VIGNONE, MARIA L,** Kent St Univ Kent Cmps, Kent, OH; JR; BS; Dance Assoc Pres; Dance Ensmbl 90-; Grievance Comm Chf Grvnce Ofcr 90-; Dns Lst 90-; Dance Marathon Alzheimers Fdtn Chrprsn 90-; Outstndg Dance Mjr Awd 90; Eugenia V Erdmann Awd; Dance.

**VIGORITO, MELISSA J,** Kent St Univ Kent Cmps, Kent, OH; JR; BA; Amnsty Intrntl Pres 88-; Hons Polcy Cncl Electd Rep 88-90; Hons Clg; Golden Key; Medtn Svc 90; HS Dir 90; Natl Inst For Disupte Resltn Intrn; Ldrshp Award 90; Vol Award 90; Pres Schlrshp 90; Pol Sci/Peace/Conflct Studies; MA Mgt.

**VIGUE, DAVID,** Southern Coll Of Tech, Marietta, GA; SO; BSMET; Inst Indstl Engrs 90-; Natl Soc Prof Engrs 90-; Amer Soc Mech Engrs; US Vet Wrkng In Engr Conslt 77-; Mech Engr/Physcs; Engr Res.

**VIK, KAREN M,** Univ Of Sc At Columbia, Columbia, SC; SO; BMUSI; US Army Rsrvs 108th Div Bnd 90-; Music; Tchr.

**VILA MALDONADO, GRISELLE,** Catholic Univ Of Pr, Ponce, PR; SR; Grntlgy Tchncn.

**VILA, LOUIS A,** Fl International Univ, Miami, FL; SR; MPA; Pblc Admn Scty 90-; ASPA; Phi Lmbd 90-; Soc Sec Admn Clms Rep Trainee 90; BPA; Pblc Admn; Gvmntl Svc.

**VILAIVANH, THONGSOUK,** Univ Of Sc At Columbia, Columbia, SC; FR; BA; Eng.

**VILANOVA, BRENDA I SANDOVAL,** Univ Of Pr Medical Sciences, San Juan, PR; GD; MS; NSSLHA Chptr PR V P 90-; Golden Key 87-89; Hnr Stdnts Soc Fclty Ed UPR 88-89; BA Univ PR 89; Spch/Lang Pthlgy.

**VILKAUSKAS, CYNTHIA A,** Marywood Coll, Scranton, PA; FR; Chr 90; Bsn; Acctng.

**VILLA, VIVIAN Y,** City Univ Of Ny La Guard Coll, Long Island Cty, NY; FR; Tutor; Phi Theta Kappa 90; Dental Assist/Rcptnst 81-; AS Queensborough Comm Clg 87; Nat/Applied Sci; Nrsng.

**VILLAFANE, IXIA E,** Univ Of Pr At Rio Piedras, Rio Piedras, PR; JR; BA; Deans Hon List; Assoc; Commerce/Sec Sci; Bus Ed.

**VILLAFANE-ONDER, DIANE L,** Evangelical Semimary Of P R, Hato Rey, PR; FR; MA; BA Magna Cum Laude Conservatory Of Music Of Puerto Rico 80; Rlgn.

**VILLALOBOS, BERTHA PATRICIA,** Western Ky Univ, Bowling Green, KY; JR; BS; Amer Scty Civil Engrs; Intl Student Org; Intl Wmn Club; Phi Kappa Phi; Golden Key Historian; Phi Eta Sigma; Pres Schlr/Latin Amer Awd Natl 88-; Clgt Engrg Awd/All Amer Schlr 89-; Golden Key Awd/Phi Kappa Phi Awd; Civil Engrg/Techlgy; Engrg.

**VILLALONA, IVETTE M,** Holyoke Comm Coll, Holyoke, MA; FR; Math; Accntng.

**VILLAMAR, MARCELA,** Univ Of Cincinnati, Cincinnati, OH; SO; BM; Mexcn Tele Mexcn Govt Piano Recitls; Cliburn Gorno Paino Schlrshp Comp 89-; Schlrshp Comp Three Arts Musc Clb; Tuitn Schlrshp 89-; Music.

**VILLANI, PETER L,** Univ Of New Haven, West Haven, CT; JR; BS; Day Std Govt 88-89; Delta Sigma Alpha Treas 90-; Cngrssnl Yth Ldrshp Awd 88; Mktg; Pblc Rltns.

**VILLANO, KEITH J,** S U N Y Coll Of Tech At Frmgdl, Farmingdale, NY; FR; BED; Crmnl Just; Law Enfrcmnt.

**VILLANUEVA, DAVID,** Embry Riddle Aeronautical Univ, Daytona Beach, FL; SR; BA; Racquet Ball Club 87; Bros Of The Wind 89-90; Hispanic Soc; Aircrft Engr Technlgy.

**VILLANUEVA JR, JAIME M,** Columbia Union Coll, Takoma Park, MD; FR; BA; Drama Prod 90-; Phi Eta Sigma 90-; Soccer; Med Tech/Engl; Surgery Cardio-Thoracic.

**VILLANUEVA, KIMBERLY C,** Catawba Valley Comm Coll, Hickory, NC; SR; BA; Acctg Clb Sec Treas 89-; Natl Scty Pblc Acctnts Stdnt Mbr 90-; Gamma Beta Phi Exec Cncl Schlrshp Chr 89-; Pi Lambda Phi Swthrt 87-; Sftbll; Swmmng; Assoc Acctg; Cert Bus Admn; Acctg; CPA.**

**VILLANUEVA, MIGUEL A,** Embry Riddle Aeronautical Univ, Daytona Beach, FL; SR; MBA; Clss Cncl; Indpndt Ordr Frstrs 89-; Air Force Assoc 86-; Patrick AFB Hspnc Hrtg Comm 88-; Oprtn Bootstrap Stf Sgt Cmmnd Pst Cntrllr; AAS Cmnty Clg Air Force 87; Aviation Mgmt; A F Comm.

**VILLANUEVA-VEGA, MARIA D,** Univ Of Pr At Rio Piedras, Rio Piedras, PR; JR; BA; Ballet Cncrto Dnc Co; Ballet Mncpl Dnc Co Pro Dncr; Hon Stdnt; Hmnts Fac Rep UPR 89-90; Exchng Stdnt Rio De Janeiro Fdrl Flmnnse Univ; Mdrn Lang Frnch Prtgs Grmn; Tchng.**

**VILLAR, MARINA M,** Fl International Univ, Miami, FL; FR; BA; Vlg Cncl Tamiami Cmplx 90-; EPIRG 90; Cmunctns; Pub Rltns.

**VILLARAN, MANUEL F,** Barry Univ, Miami, FL; SR; BA; Ecnmcs Clb 89-90; Amer Mrktng Assoc 90; Phi Kappa Tau 87-90; Tennis Tm 88-89; Assist Dept Of Sprts/Rcrtnl Sci 89; BA; Bsnss; Mrktng.

**VILLARREAL, CAMELINDA,** Univ Of Tn At Martin, Martin, TN; SR; BS; SGA VP 87-; Peer Enabling Pgm Ldr 88-; Univ Schlrs Org Treas 88-; Phi Eta Sigma 87-; Order Omega 89-; Phi Chi Theta; Alpha Delta Pi Serv Chmn 88-; Univ Schlr 88-; Econ/ Intl Bus; Law.

**VILLARRUBIA VEGA, JAVIER I,** Univ Of Pr At Mayaguez, Mayaguez, PR; JR; Amer Chcm Scty 90-; Chem.

**VILLAVER, JEFFREY L,** Univ Of Sc At Columbia, Columbia, SC; FR; BA; Finance; Law.

**VILLAVICENCIO-HERNANDEZ, LUISA,** City Univ Of Ny Lehman Coll, Bronx, NY; JR; AA; Yrbk Com Hostos Comm Coll; Utd Meth Chrch Sndy Schl Tchr 89-; Utd Meth Chrch Wrld Msn Pres 90-; Utd Meth Wmn Scty Chrstn Soc Conc 90-; Psychology; Elem Schl Tchr/Cnslr.

**VILLELLA, JANE R,** Comm Coll Algny Co Algny Cmps, Pittsburgh, PA; FR; BA; Admssns Rep Mercy Hosp; Gen Stds; Nrsng.

**VILLENA, ROBERTO A,** Fl International Univ, Miami, FL; GD; MBA; FMA 88-90; Phi Theta Kappa 87-88; Interamer Bus Assn Schlrshp; Bus Awd; IM Bsktbl; AA Miami Dade Comm Clg 88; BBA Fla Intl Univ 90; Finance; Corp Finance.**

**VILLERS, MELISSA J,** Wv Univ At Parkersburg, Parkersburg, WV; SO; AA; Prtcptd Cooprtv Educ Pro WVU-P Rcvd Coll Crdt Wrkg Rtl Str; Bus.

**VILLONE, JILL A,** Saint John Fisher Coll, Rochester, NY; SR; BA; Pre Law Clb 87-; Engl Clb 87-; Fisher Plyrs 88-89; Cmmtr Cncl Assc 87-; Amer Cncr Scty Intrnshp 90-; Mntrshp Prog Ad Cncl 90-; Deans Lst 87-; Summa Cum Laude; IM Sftbl 88-90; Wntr Olympcs 87-; Engl/Cmmnctns; Law.

**VILLORIA, BERTHA C,** Miami Dade Comm Coll North, Miami, FL; SR; AA; Psys Thrpy.

**VILORIA, ROSANA P,** Commonwealth Coll, Virginia Beach, VA; SO; MAA; Nightingales 90-; BSBA Holy Angel Univ Philippines 82.

**VINAS, JOAQUIN M,** Fl International Univ, Miami, FL; FR; BS; Cvl Engrg.

**VINCENT, BOBBY,** Va St Univ, Petersburg, VA; JR; BS; Engrg Techlgy Club 90-; Mechl Engrg Tchlgy; Engrg.

**VINCENT, CONNIE B,** Tn Wesleyan Coll, Athens, TN; SR; BS; Alpha Chi Hon Soc; Kiwns Academc Awrd 90; Elem Ed; Tch.

**VINCENT, DIANA L,** Belmont Coll, Nashville, TN; FR; BS; Bptst Stdnt Union; Math; Orthdntcs.

**VINCENT, EDDIE M,** City Univ Of Ny Brooklyn Coll, Brooklyn, NY; JR; BA; Tv/Radio; Tv Writer/Producer/ Director.**

**VINCENT, JACQUE K,** Middle Ga Coll, Cochran, GA; FR; AS; Hstry; Law.

**VINCENT, JASON H,** Savannah Coll Of Art & Design, Savannah, GA; SO; BFA; Hll Cncl Pres 89-90; Stu Ttrl Asst Rfrrl Prog 89-90; Video; Cmptr Anmtn Grphcs.

**VINCENT, JENNIFER L,** Univ Of Sc At Columbia, Columbia, SC; FR; BA; Bptst Std Un Dir 90-; Stdnt Govt Asc Sec; ARETE; Comm Plyhse; Engl Educ; Tchng.

**VINCENT, JOAN M,** Crichton Coll, Memphis, TN; SO; BA; Science; Nrsng.

**VINCENT, KRYSTAL A,** Tn St Univ, Nashville, TN; SR; BA; Stdnt Elctn Commssn Chrprsn 89-; Peer Cnslrs 88-90; NAACP; Alpha Mu Gamma; Alpha Kappa Alpha 90-; Smmr Rsrch Opprtnts Prog 90; Res Asst 89-; Engl; Law.

**VINCENT JR, LOWELL D,** Washington State Comm Coll, Marietta, OH; FR; AS; Brthrhd Of Elctrcl Tchnlgy Assoc 90; Deans Lst 90; Pres Lst; Elctrncs/Elctrcl; Eng.

**VINCENT, PATRICIA L,** Univ Of Nh Plymouth St Coll, Plymouth, NH; JR; BS; Vlntr Srvc; Prsdnts Lst 90-; Deans Lst 89-; Peer Tutor 90-; Chrldng 89-; Elem Edctn; Edctn.

**VINCENT, SUE R,** Commonwealth Coll, Virginia Beach, VA; FR; AAS; Wstwood Hll Bptst Chrch Membr; 3rd/4th Grdrs Snday Schl Tchr; Prvt Chrstn Schl Sec; Acctg; Bookkpr.

**VINCENT, SUSAN D,** Comm Coll Algny Co Algny Cmps, Pittsburgh, PA; SO; BA; AA Art Inst Pittsbrgh 88; Phlsphy; Law.

**VINCENT, TEENA D,** Volunteer St Comm Coll, Gallatin, TN; SO; BA; Retrng Women Org Pres 90-; Stdnt Govt Assoc Sen 90-; Gamma Beta Phi 89-; ASSOC Bus/Comrc; Bus; Law.

**VINCENT, VALERIE G,** Fl St Univ, Tallahassee, FL; JR; BA; Campus Alliance For Literacy; Gulf Winds Track Club; Landis Hall Govt Rep; Phi Eta Sigma 90-; Kappa Omnicron Nu Sec; F Mc Allister Schlrshp Dietitic Majors; Grad Lib Arts Hnrs Prog 90-; Soccer 90-; BA Nutrition/Fitness-Dietetics; Nutrition Fitness Dietitics; BA Dietitics.

**VINCENT, VICTORIA L,** S U N Y Coll At Fredonia, Fredonia, NY; JR; BA; Sclgy Clb 90-; Alph Kappa Dlt Deans List 90-; Ltrcy Vol AS Corning Comm Clg 88; Ltrcy Vol ESL Tutor Clwn Mnstry Prfsn Clwng Crng Phlhrmc; Soclgy Soc Wrk; Soclgy Prfsr Rsrch.

**VINCENTI-ORTIZ, MELISSA,** Inter Amer Univ Pr Hato Rey, Hato Rey, PR; FR; Yr Bk Club 89-90; Photghc Club 89-90; Sectl Sci.**

**VINES, CYNTHIA D,** Univ Of Montevallo, Montevallo, AL; JR; Hghst Hnrs; Pres Lst 89-; Kappa Delta Pi; Phi Kappa Phi; SNEA; Chi Omega Civic Chrmn 90-; Cvtn Clb Chrtr Mbr; Ed; Tchr.

**VINES, REBECCA W,** Univ Of South Al, Mobile, AL; SR; BED; Alpha Chi Omega 79-82; Span Ft Presby Ch; Legal Asst 82-; BS Bus Admn 82; Ele Educ; Tch.

**VINES, VIVIAN D,** Samford Univ, Birmingham, AL; GD; JD; Stdnt Bar Assn Cls Rep 89-; Amer Trial Lawyers Assn Stdnt Mbr 90-; Amer Jrnl Of Trial Advcy 90-; Psi Chi 87-88; Alpha Chi Omega Socl Chrmn 84-88; Chrldr 85-86; BS Birmingham Southern Coll 88; Law; Envrnmntl Law.

**VINGELIS, DANIELLE S,** Gallaudet Univ, Washington, DC; GD; MA; Crew Clb 87; Golden Key; Kappa Delta Pi 90; Assn Chldhd Edctrs Intrntl 90; Stdnt Ed Assn 90; BSED Geo Mason U 90; Deaf Ed-Prnt/Infnt Spclztn; Ed Deaf.

**VINGELIS, KRISTINA A,** Allegheny Coll, Meadville, PA; SO; BS; Alden Schlr 89-90; Alpha Chi Omega Phlnthrpy 90-; Soup Kitchen Vol 89-; Bio; Med.

**VINGLAS, ROBERTA J,** Saint Francis Coll, Loretto, PA; FR; BS; Act 101 Bnd; Accntng Clb; Red Key Clb; Accntng; Auditing.

**VINGLISH, PAULA E,** Mount Aloysius Jr Coll, Cresson, PA; SO; AS; Childrens Advocacy Assc Pres; Phi Thelta Kappa 90; Education; Early Childhood Ed.

**VINICKI, JON J,** Ms St Univ, Miss State, MS; SR; BA; Scty Prfssnl Jrnlst Treas 89-; Phi Kappa Phi; Gamma Beta Phi; Phi Eta Sigma; Sigma Mu Treas 87-; Cmmnctn.

**VINING, CAROL GRACE,** Univ Of Ga, Athens, GA; SO; BED; Alpha Lambda Delta; Phi Eta Sigma; Gamma Beta Phi; Educ; Spec Ed.

**VINING, SHARON D,** Bapt Bible Coll & Seminary, Clarks Summit, PA; JR; BS; Chmbr Sngrs Pnst 88-; Msc Intrst Fllwshp Sec 90-; Dns Lst; Bible; Tchr.

**VINOCUR, CATHERINE L,** Middle Tn St Univ, Murfreesboro, TN; SR; BS; Dance Clb; Guitar Ensemble; Danc Co; Crisis Intervention Cntr; Psycholgy; Grad Schl.

**VINROE, GWEN G,** Comm Coll Algny Co Algny Cmps, Pittsburgh, PA; GD; OD; Msc Sng Lng Mnstrs; Prsn Mnstry; GU Almn Assn; Tchr Deaf Sgn Lng Intrprtr; BA Univ Tulsa 79; AA Gallaudet Univ 83; Pre Optmtry; Dr Optmtry.

**VINSANT, MARY L,** Fl International Univ, Miami, FL; GD; MPH; Amer Med Assoc 90-; Amer Pub Hlth Assn 90-; Fla Pub Hlth Assn Stdnt Alumni 90 ; Phi Kappa Phi 76-; Alpha Epsilon Delta 76; Alpha Lambda Delta 76-; Bd Trustees Schlrshp 76-; Intrn Peds; Res Anesthesiology 81-; MD 80; BS 76; Epidemiology; Pub Hlth.

**VINSON, CAROLINE K,** Peace Coll, Raleigh, NC; FR; Ntl Assoc Of Accntnts 90; Peace Clg Tennis Tm 90; Phi Delta Kappa 90; Bsnss; Coop Lwyr.

**VINSON, JAMES R,** Northwest Al Comm Coll, Phil Campbell, AL; FR; Wildlife Sci; Wildlife Mgt.

**VINSON, KENNON L,** Cumberland Coll, Williamsburg, KY; JR; Acctg.

**VINSON, SHERRI R,** Univ Of Ga, Athens, GA; JR; BED; Cmnctn Sci/Disorders; Spch Pathology.

**VINSON JR, WILLIAM L,** Fl St Univ, Tallahassee, FL; SR; BS; Sigma Nu 86-89; Elec Eng/Soclgy.

**VIOLA, ELLA M,** City Univ Of Ny La Guard Coll, Long Island Cty, NY; GD; Anml Hlth Clb; Phei Theta Kappa 90-; Anml Hlth; Med.

**VIOLA, JENNIFER S,** Smith Coll, Northampton, MA; FR; BA; Choir Omega 90-; Soc Chair 90-; First Grp Schlr 90-; Spanish; Med.

**VIOLAND, JENNIFER L,** Slippery Rock Univ, Slippery Rock, PA; JR; BS; Campus Radio Stn Sec 90; Slppry Rck Mrchng Rckts Bnd Flg Lne 88; Phy Ed Sprts Mngmnt.

**VIRANYI, STEVEN E,** Univ Of Miami, Coral Gables, FL; SR; BM; AA William Rainey Harper Clg 84; Msc Eng; Audio Eng.

**VIRDI, AMANDEEP S,** Hamilton Coll, Clinton, NY; FR; BA; HAVOC Co-Chr 90-; Clinton Tutorial Tutor/Vol 90-; Blck Latin Stdnt Union 90-; Dale Carnegie Inst 87; Publ Policy-Sclgy; Govt.

**VIRDI, MANLOCHAN K,** Marymount Manhattan Coll, New York, NY; GD; MA; Alpha Chi 90-; BA; Intl Studies; Tchng.

**VIRGA, JO ANNE M,** Univ Of Nc At Greensboro, Greensboro, NC; SR; BED; Oak Hill Elem Schl Intern 90; TA; BSHE Unc Greensboro 87; Tch.

**VIRGIL, TRINA DIONNE,** Fl St Univ, Tallahassee, FL; FR; BA; Blck Std Un 90; Math; Cvl Engr.

**VIRGIN, MONICA D,** Coppin St Coll, Baltimore, MD; SR.

**VIRGOUS, CARLOS K,** Al St Univ, Montgomery, AL; SO; DVM; Vet Med.

**VIRICK, SANDI S,** Univ Of South Fl, Tampa, FL; GD; MPH; Hmn Soc 88-; People Ethcl Trtmnt Anmls 88-; BA St Francis Xavier Univ 88; BSW 89; Pblc Hlth Mtrnl/Chld Hlth; Hlth Cr Pro.

**VIRKLER, NOEL E,** Clarkson Univ, Potsdam, NY; SO; BS; Trustee Schlrshp; Acctg.

**VIRKLER, SARAH J,** Cornell Univ Statutory College, Ithaca, NY; SO; BA; RA; Natl Schlr 89-; Asst Tchr Ed 240; IM Sftbl; Comm; Jrnlsm.

**VIRTUE, CHRISTINE M,** Univ Of Sc At Columbia, Columbia, SC; SR; Soclgy Clb Vp 90-; Deans Lst; In Hse Arrst/Hm Cnfnmnt Intrn 90; Washington Ctr Hme/Hspce Intrn 90; Fld Hcky/Chrldng/Sftbl 87-88; Soclgy; Grad Schl PHD.

**VIRUET COLON, ZORAIDA,** Univ Politecnica De Pr, Hato Rey, PR; JR; Hist; Engr.

**VISALLI, MARIE ANN,** Barry Univ, Miami, FL; SR; BA; Dns Lst 89-90; Pres Lst 90; COA Miami Dade Med Campus 87; Lib Stds; MS Mental Hlth.

**VISALLI, ROSEMARIE A,** Glassboro St Coll, Glassboro, NJ; JR; BA; Psych Clb 90-F Cncl Exeptnl Chldrn 88-; Psi Chi Corr Sec; Hons Pgm Lbrl Arts/Sci; Wrt Jrnl Mnscrpt Mrtl Stsfctn W/ Prof Prsntd Estrn Psych Assn April; Child Psych.

**VISCO JR, DONALD P,** S U N Y At Buffalo, Buffalo, NY; JR; BS; Natl Soc Prof Engrs Ext VP 91-; AICE; IM Vllybl Capt 90-; Tau Beta Pi 90-; Chem Engr; Nvl Ofcr/Nuclr Engr.

**VISEL, MARESA E,** Smith Coll, Northampton, MA; FR; BS; Coll Lit Mag 90-; Deans Lst 90-; 1st Grp Schlrs 90-; Psychlgy/ Pre-Med; Rsrch Physiopsychlgy.

**VISHTON, PAIGE A,** Univ Of Sc At Columbia, Columbia, SC; SO; BA; Magzn Advtsng Dir 90-; Gamma Beta Phi 89-; Kappa Alpha Theta 89-; Deans Jrnlsm Schlrshp 90-; Advtsng; Mktg Exec.

**VISINSKY, JOSEPH W,** Saint Francis Coll, Loretto, PA; SO; BS; Naval Reserves Exec Ofcr 86-; Parish Confraternity Instructor Tchr 82-; Nursing; Anesthtist.

**VISNICH, VONNIE D,** Wv Northern Comm Coll, Wheeling, WV; FR; BSN; Nrsng.

**VITAL, GRISELLE EILEEN,** Fl International Univ, Miami, FL; JR; FEA 90-; AA Miami Dade Comm Clg 90.

**VITALE, CARLO BRUNO,** Ms St Univ, Miss State, MS; SR; DVM; Vet Med Brd 87-; Amer Assn Of Equine Practnrs 88; Kappa Delta Pi 84-85; Alpha Chi 85; Phi Kappa Phi 88-; Phi Zeta; Pet Ther 90; PA Vet Med Awd 88; Upjohn Small Animal Clin Prof Awd; Pr Scholar 87-89; IM Soccer 89-; Vet Med.

**VITALE, FAYE E,** Seton Hall Univ, South Orange, NJ; SO; BA; Hnr Rsch Pgm 90-; Cmps Mnstry Prsh Cncl 89-; Tae Kwon Do Blck Blt; Alpha Epsln Delta 90-; Bio; Med.**

**VITALE, JILL A,** Alfred Univ, Alfred, NY; JR; BS; Amer Mrktng Assn VP Cmmnctns; Dean Stu Advsry Cncl 90-; Sr Wk Cmmtt Pblc Rel; Delta Mu Delta; Alpha Iota Delta Sec; Pres Schlrshp 90 ; AS Monroe Comm Coll 90; Bus Admn; Mrktng.

**VITALE, TRACIE A,** Lasell Coll, Newton, MA; SO; BA; Wmn Bus Org 90-; Stdnt Gov Jr Clss Rep Elect; Merch Intrnsp Lmtd Express 90-; AS 91; Bus Admin; Mktg.

**VITALIS, SANDY B,** Coll Of Charleston, Charleston, SC; JR; BA; Alpha Lambda Delta Fresh Hon Soc 75-76; Squires Soph Hon Soc 76; Alpha Delta Pi 75-77; Fine Arts/Art Hstry; Grad Study Arch Hstry.

**VITASEK, KATE L,** Univ Of Tn At Knoxville, Knoxville, TN; JR; BA; Amer Mktg Assn Pres 90-; Gamma Beta Sigma; Phi Theta Kappa Sec 89-; Deans Lst-Hghst Hon 87-; Vol-March Dimes 89; Vol-MDA 88-90; Waters Schlrshp 90-; Rotary Clb Schlrshp 87-88; UT Bwlng Clb 90-; Mktg; Sls/Brand Mgmt.

**VITELLO, MICHELE T,** Saint Johns Univ, Jamaica, NY; SR; BS; Kappa Delta Pi 88-; CAUSE Exprnc Coll; AA; Early Chldhd Educ; Tchr.

**VITELLO, SHELLY E,** Daytona Beach Comm Coll, Daytona Beach, FL; FR; AS; Deans List 90-; Nrsng.

**VITELLO, VINCENT P,** Widener Univ, Chester, PA; JR; BS; APICS Treas; SAM; Wdnr Econs Clb; Phi Theta Kappa 90; Wdnrs Pres Trnsfr Schlrshp; Pres Lst DE Cnty Comm Coll 89-; WSLI; AS Delaware County Comm Coll; Bus Mgmt; Mgmt Mrktng.

**VITERETTO, TARA J,** Univ Of Rochester, Rochester, NY; SO; BA; Hill Crt Cncl Rep 90-; Kappa Delta Corres Sec 90-; Eqstrn Tm Co Capt 90-; Hstry/German; Law.

**VITO, JENNIFER B,** Merrimack Coll, North Andover, MA; SO; BA; Orientation Comm 89-90; Vol YMCA 88-90; Sum Pkwy Rentals Inc Inter 87-; Spanish Tutor Mid Schl Chldrn 89-; Aerobic Instr 89-; Internatl Bus; Law.

**VITTI, CYNTHIA L,** Univ Of New Haven, West Haven, CT; SR; BS; Fncl Acctng; CPA.

**VITTI, PATRIZIA E,** Fordham Univ, Bronx, NY; SR; JD; Frdhm Pre Law Scty Res 90-; Acctg Scty 89-; Brkfst Clb 89-90; Beta Alpha Psi 89-; Natl Jst Hnr Scty 89-; Beta Gamma Sigma 90-; Phi Kappa Phi 90-; Deans Lst 87-; Summa Cum Laude; Carmen Webster Kelly Schlrshp Awrd 90f BS; Acctg; Law.

**VITTITOW, JOHNA M,** Spalding Univ, Louisville, KY; JR; BA; SCN Rgnl Finance Comm; Yth Mnstr; Rel; Parish Mnstry.

**VITTORELLI, DANIELLE,** Rutgers St Univ At Camden, Camden, NJ; SR; Acctg Soc; Natl Assn Actnts; Deans Lst; Athaneum.

**VITUCCI, MARCIE M,** Kent St Univ Kent Cmps, Kent, OH; JR; BBA; IM Aerbcs Clb 88-; Golden Key; Beta Gamma Sigma; Hnrs Clg Schlrshp 88-; Acctng.

**VIVA, JOSEPH,** Schenectady County Comm Coll, Schenectady, NY; SR; AAS; Prsdnts Lst; Deans Lst; Natl Assoc Prchsng Mgrs; Amrcn Prdctn Invntry Cntrl Scty; Amrcn Scty Qlty Cntrl; Bus Admn.

**VIVENZIO, LAUREN MARIE,** Wagner Coll, Staten Island, NY; SR; BA; Alpha Delta Pi 88-; Theatr; Theatr Mgmt/Dir.

**VIVERETTE, WILLIAM T,** Ms St Univ, Miss State, MS; JR; BS; Deans Lst 82; IM Ftbl Bsktbl 82-84; MS Law Enfrcmnt Offcrs Assn 89-90; Cnstrctn Bsns MS 84; Scndry Edctn; MA.

**VIVIANO, TAMARA F,** Univ Of Central Fl, Orlando, FL; JR; BA; Jnr Achvmnt 90-; Rnbws 90-; Rsrch Asst 89-; Psi Chi 90-; Phi Eta Sigma 88-89; Gldn Key 90-; Prsdnts Lsts 88-; Deans Lst 88-; Fndrs Day Hnrs; Psychlgy; Chld Clncl Psychlgst.**

**VIVINO, JEANNINE V,** Indiana Univ Of Pa, Indiana, PA; SR; BS; CEC; Pace Schl Sec/Tchrs Asst; Spec Ed; Tchr.

**VIVONA, MARY H,** Western Piedmont Comm Coll, Morganton, NC; SO; AAS; Comptr Lab Asst; Best Comptr Stdnt 90-; Sngl Parent/Homemkr Of The Yr 90-; Schlrshps Breedens Bus/Potimist; Taught Own Dance Sch 90-; HRD 89; Comptr Prog; Dev Sftwr/Tch.

**VLAKANCIC, ALEX M,** Manhattan Coll, Bronx, NY; FR; BA; Dns Hnr Lst 90; Engr; Mech Engr.

**VO, NGUYET LE,** Univ Of Tn At Chattanooga, Chattanooga, TN; FR; BA; CHESS 90-; Soccer 91; Chem Engr; Engr.

**VO, THOMAS T,** Kent St Univ Kent Cmps, Kent, OH; SO; BS; IM 90; Softball; Medicine.

**VODOPALAS, VIDA I,** George Mason Univ, Fairfax, VA; SR; BA; Lith Amer Cath Yth Assoc VP 89-90; Gamma Phi Beta 89-90; Tennis Tm 86-; Phy Educ Sprts Mdcn; Physical Therapy.

**VOEGELI, RAYMOND T,** Nyack Coll, Nyack, NY; JR; Lyl Brthrhd Moseley Chrmn 90; Poetry Soc Pres 89-90; Coll Jrnl Copy Edtr; Deans Lst 89-; Ethcs/Pub Polcy Cntr Intrn; Nassau Chrstn Cntr Intrn; Engl/Psychlgy.

**VOELKEL, DIANE M,** Bloomfield Coll, Bloomfield, NJ; SO; BA; APICS; Mtrls Mgt; Mtrls Mgt; Mnfctrg.

**VOGEL, JOY G,** Ga St Univ, Atlanta, GA; SR; BSE; Bacchus 86-87; Yng Republicans 86-87; Alpha Omicron Pi Song Chrmn 86-88; Early Chldhd Edn; Tchr.

**VOGEL, JULIE M,** Fl Atlantic Univ, Boca Raton, FL; SR; BA; Prelaw Soc FL Atlantic Univ Broward Chptr Pres; Intrclb Cncl; Yth Mnstr 90-; Miami Dolphns Chrldr 84 86 90-; Paralgl For Becker/Poliakoff P A 87-; Engl; Law.

**VOGEL, KAREN A,** Franklin And Marshall Coll, Lancaster, PA; SO; BA; Hst/Hstss Prog 89-90; Stdnt Actvty Advsry Brd 89-90; Deans Lst 89; MAC Hnr Roll 90; Yrbk Staff/Phtgrphr Assist Edtr 89-90; CEC Cmmttee 89-90; Im Drctr 89-90; Lctr At Old Main Chrch 89-90; Vrsty Sftbl 89; Engl; Law.

**VOGEL, KAREN J,** Saint Francis Coll, Loretto, PA; SR; BS; Ed Clb 87-; SMILE Pgm 89-; Delta Phi Epsilon 90-; Tau Kappa Epsilon 89-90; Gamma Sigma Sigma Sec 87-; St Francis Chrldr Capt 87-; Elem Ed; Tchr.

**VOGEL, TAMMY A,** Va Commonwealth Univ, Richmond, VA; SR; Phi Kappa Phi; Golden Key 90-; Grad Magna Cum Laude; Hnrs Schlrshp; Provost Shlrshp; Legal Secty 84-87; BGS; Photghy Commtn; Writing.

**VOGELAAR, JOANNE S,** William Paterson Coll, Wayne, NJ; SO; BA; Spcl Ed Clb; Kappa Delta Pi Hstrn; Spcl Ed/Cnslng; Tchr.

**VOGELEY, KATHY,** Central Fl Comm Coll, Ocala, FL; JR; Citrus Mem Hosp Inverness Fl 87-; AA 90; Elem Edn; Tchng.

**VOGT, JENNIFER L,** Northern Ky Univ, Highland Hts, KY; SR; BED; Kappa Delta Pi 90; Alpha Chi 89; Phi Sigma Sigma V P 88; Elem Educ; Tchr.

**VOGT, JOHN D,** Kent St Univ Kent Cmps, Kent, OH; SR; BBA; Rho Epsilon 89-; Real Estates/Fin; Owng Real Estate Counltng.

**VOGT, JUDI L,** Chattanooga St Tech Comm Coll, Chattanooga, TN; SO; AS; Acctng Clb VP 90-; NAA 90-; Phi Theta Kappa 90-; VITA; STDNT Merit Awd Acctng 90-; Acctng; CPA.

**VOGT, WENDY F,** Ga St Univ, Atlanta, GA; SR; BED; Prof Assn Od GA Educ; Early Chldhd Educ; Schl Tchr.

**VOIGT, JODY L,** Gallaudet Univ, Washington, DC; SO; BA; SG Mssdf Fndrsng Asst Chrprsn 90-; Phi Kappa Zeta 90-; Mst Imprvd Wrkr Awrd; Univ Top Schlrs 89-90; Ed.**

**VOILES, SHERRI M,** Tusculum Coll, Greeneville, TN; SR; BA; SCEC 90-; George Oliver Grey Soc 90-; AS Walters St Comm Coll 85-89; Elem Spec Educ; Tchg.

**VOJTKO, ROBERT J,** Schenectady County Comm Coll, Schenectady, NY; SO; BS; AS; Bus Admn; Bus.

**VOJTUSH, DARYL L,** Univ Of Akron, Akron, OH; SR; BSIM; Mgmt/Prsnnl; Oper Mgmt.

**VOLCHECK, MARK J,** Oh St Univ, Columbus, OH; SR; BA; Undergrad Stdnt Govt 89-90; Alpha Lambda Delta; Phi Eta Sigma; Scarlet/Grey Schlrshp; Summa Awd; Acad Achvmnt Awd; Hist; Law Schl.

**VOLESHEN, LYDIA A,** Saint John Fisher Coll, Rochester, NY; SR; BA; Cmmtr Cncl Assoc VP 89; Wntr Olympic Plnng Cmmttee; Orient 89-90; Pi Gamma Mu 90; GS Co-Ldr 89-90; Wegmans Schlrshp 87; Emp Of Mnth 89; Im Sftbl 89; Psych; Elem Ed.

**VOLF, HEIDI S,** Columbia Union Coll, Takoma Park, MD; FR; BA; Hnr Soc Of Andrews Univ; Deans List; English/Computer Science.

**VOLHEIM, TODD A,** Southern Coll Of Tech, Marietta, GA; SR; BA; Sigma Lambda Chi 90-; Const Admin.

**VOLINO, ROBERT S,** Hudson Valley Comm Coll, Troy, NY; JR; MBA; Bus; Mgmnt.

**VOLK, DEAN F,** Savannah Coll Of Art & Design, Savannah, GA; FR; BFA; Ilstrtn; Anmtr.

**VOLK, JOANN,** Hudson Valley Comm Coll, Troy, NY; FR; BA; Bus Admin; Bus.

**VOLK, JOHN W,** Wilmington Coll, New Castle, DE; SR; BS; Spec Olympics Asst Chrmn; Police Explorers Post; Police Yth Bsktbl League 89-; Dns Lst 89-; Delaware State Troopers Assn 81-; Law Enfrcmnt; AA Delaware Tech/Comm Coll 84; Crmnl Jstc; Law.

**VOLL, DOROTHY A,** Northern Ky Univ, Highland Hts, KY; SO; BA; Advtsng Purch Coord 86-90; Crdit Spvr; Info Sys Acctg; Sys Anlyst/Accnt.

**VOLLET, TIMOTHY P,** Univ Of Cin R Walters Coll, Blue Ash, OH; SO; BA; Scndry Educ; Tchng.

**VOLLICK, SHAWN M,** Univ Of Nc At Charlotte, Charlotte, NC; FR; BS; Phi Eta Sgm 90-; Eng Mech; Eng.

**VOLOVICH, MARC C,** Saint Vincents Coll & Seminary, Latrobe, PA; SO; IM Ftbl 89-; IM Bsktbl 89-; Deans Lst 89-; Svc Olympcs; Hstry; Law.

**VOLPETTI, ANDREA M,** Marywood Coll, Scranton, PA; SO; Psychology Clb Corrspndg Sec 90-; Psychology.

**VOLPI, NICOLA M,** Georgetown Univ, Washington, DC; SO; BS BA; Chf Fin Ofcr 90-; Acctg/Fin; Cmrcl/Invstmnt Bkng.

**VOLPINI, STEFANO A,** Bethany Coll, Bethany, WV; JR; MBA; Offcl U S Soccer Ref; French Club 89-91; Bethany Vybl Clb; SBOG; Phi Delta Psi 89-91; Sigma Nu; Yth Soccr Coach/Swmng Instr; Var Soccer Trck; Phys Educ; Educ/Sprts Med.

**VOME, KATHLEEN P,** Univ Of Cincinnati-Clrmnt Coll, Batavia, OH; SO; BA; Bsns Mgmt Tchnlgy.

**VON AHNEN, CELESTE J,** Marywood Coll, Scranton, PA; JR; BFA; Art; Art Thrpy.

**VON BAMPUS, JENNY L,** Tallahassee Comm Coll, Tallahassee, FL; SO; AA; Kappa Alpha 90-; Engl; Law.

**VON BRIESEN, ELIZABETH M,** Springfield Tech Comm Coll, Springfield, MA; SO; MA; Alpha Nu Omega 90-; Joseph J Deliso Sr Schlrshp 90; Physics; Educ.

**VON BUELOW, ROBERT L,** Central Fl Comm Coll, Ocala, FL; AS; Phi Theta Kappa; Profsnl Fire Fghtr; AA FL Jr Clg 75; Fire Sci/Arson Invstgtn.

**VON DER LUFT, GRETA L,** Boston Univ, Boston, MA; SO; BS/MS; Lrng Dsblty Mntr Coord Big Str Clg 90-; Phy Thrpy.

**VON FLOTOW, T KATHLEEN,** Univ Of Rochester, Rochester, NY; SO; BS; Prtnrs In Readng; Wilson Soc 89-; Rchstr Crew Team 89-; Ecolgy/Evltnry Biolgy; Rsrch Scintst.

**VON FORELL, JENNIFER L,** George Mason Univ, Fairfax, VA; JR; BA; Oper Smile 90-; SEA 90-; Alpha Omicron Pi Phlthrpc Chrmn 89-; Elem Educ; Teaching.

**VON GOERRES, CINDY INGRAM,** Wilmington Coll, New Castle, DE; GD; BS; Magna Cum Laude Dlt Epsln Rho 89-90; AAS Delaware Technel Comm Clg 88; Crmnl Jstc; Prbtn/Parole/Vctm Svcs.

**VON GORSKI, REBECCA M,** Bethany Coll, Bethany, WV; SO; BA; Germn Clb 90-; Theatr 89-; Choir 89; Deans Lst 90-; Actvty Cncl 90-; Mxwls Cffee Hs Socl Soc Chrprsn 90-; Acdmc Schlrshp 89-; IM Sftbl; Commrcl Art/Art Mgmt; Advtsng/Grphc Dsgn.

**VON HAGEL, DONNA T,** Univ Of Al At Birmingham, Birmingham, AL; GD; BS; Assoc Of Stdnt Nrs Secy 83-84; Natl Stdnt Nrs Assoc; Sigma Theta Tau 84-; Amercn Nrs Assoc; Assoc Of Nrs Ansthtsts; Emr Dept; Cardic Srgry; Intnsv Care; Natl Inst Of Hlth Clncl Rsrch Progrm; Pharmctcl Sales Rep; BSN 84; RN; Nrs Anesthsia; MBA.

**VON IDERSTEIN, CINDIA A,** Lesley Coll, Cambridge, MA; SO; BA; Emrld Key Soc 89-; Aerbc Clb Instrctr Fclty 90-; Nw Englnd Kndrgrtn Cnfrnce 89-; Peer Tutrng; Aerbc Clb Instrctr; Early Chldhd/Daycare; Tchr.

**VON KAENEL, PETER A,** Univ Of Rochester, Rochester, NY; SO; BA; Tai Chi Chuan; Canoe/Kayak Clb 89-90; Deans Lst 90; Math/Cmptr Sci.

**VON KERCZEK, MATTHEW A,** Anne Arundel Comm Coll, Arnold, MD; FR; BA; Wrk Lndscpng Self Proprietor 85-; Golf 90-; Vol Elderly/Spec Olympics 90; Econ; US Govt.

**VON LUBBE, STEFAN K,** Ms St Univ, Miss State, MS; JR; DVM; Poultry Sci Clb; Dairy Sci Clb; Deans List 89-90; Vet Med/Sci.

**VON MEISTER, FREDERICK W,** George Mason Univ, Fairfax, VA; SR; Housing/Rsdntl Life Res Advsr 89-; Cherrydale Bptst Chrch/Cllg Sngls Dir 87-; Kappa Delta Pi 90-; BS ED George Mason Univ; Physical Educ/Health Science.

**VON REITZENSTEIN, CORNELIA B,** Eckerd Coll, St Petersburg, FL; SO; BA; Delta Phi Alpha 89-; Sigma Delta Pi 89-; Res Advsr ELS; Intl Studies; Law.

**VON RIMAN, KARIN,** William Paterson Coll, Wayne, NJ; SR; Phi Alpha Theta VP 89-; Hstry; Tchng.

**VON SCHWERDTNER, CHRISTINA M,** Anne Arundel Comm Coll, Arnold, MD; FR; BA; Stdnt Serv Clb 90-; Music; Msnry.

**VON STEIN, JEFFREY A,** Univ Of Fl, Gainesville, FL; SR; BS; Fncl Mgmt Asc 90-; Rho Epsln 90-; Fed Crstn Athlts; Merrill Lynch Intshp; Dns Lst; IM Ftbl; AA Hghlnd Comm Clg 87-88; Fnce; Comm Real Est.

**VON STEIN, LAURA E,** Univ Of Bridgeport, Bridgeport, CT; SO; BA; Drama Dept Stdnt Rep 90; Pres Lst 90; Theatre Arts; Acting.

**VONG, KEANG I,** City Univ Of Ny Baruch Coll, New York, NY; SO; Mlysn Clb 90-; Intl Trdng Scty 89-90; Intl Mrktng.

**VONG, NEVA,** Univ Of Rochester, Rochester, NY; SO; BS; Asn-Amer Assn 89-; Prt Tm Job 90-; Chem Eng.

**VORA, SONYA P,** Univ Of Rochester, Rochester, NY; JR; BS; D Lions Pblcty Cochr 89-90; Swngsht Bus Mgr 89-; Rsdnt Advsr 90-; IM Sccr 89-; Cell Dvlpmnt Bio; Medcn.

**VORE, AMY B,** Clarkson Univ, Potsdam, NY; JR; BS; SOS Org 89-; Phi Mu VP 89-; Cir K Tr 88-; Acctg/Finc; Cpa.

**VOREL, MICHAEL J,** S U N Y At Buffalo, Buffalo, NY; SR; BS; Geneseo Physcs Clb 86-89; Eta Kappa Nu 90-; Deans List Un Buffalos 90; BA Suny Geneseo; Elect Eng; Cntrl Systms Eng.

**VORGANG, DENISE M,** Dowling Coll, Oakdale Li, NY; SO; BBA; Bus; Acctng.

**VORHES, JONATHAN CLAY,** Barry Univ, Miami, FL; SO; BS; Stdnt Govt; Pol Sci; Law.

**VORHES, PAMELA C,** Nyack Coll, Nyack, NY; FR; BA; Var Vlybll 90-; Yrbk; Class Officer V Pres; Var Vlybl 90-91; Education; Elem Schl Tchr.

**VORIS, SHERRY E,** Gaston Coll, Dallas, NC; FR; BA; Causaulty Claims Law Assoc Am Edctl Inst; Charlotte Claims Assn Pres 85; Lcnsd Ins Adjstr Co-Owner; CCLA Am Edctnl Inst; Bus Adm; Ins.

**VORMBROCK, KAREN M,** Univ Of Louisville, Louisville, KY; SR; ME; Spd Scntfc Schl Stdnt Cncl P 87-; Stdnt Act Brd 86-88; Amer Soc Mech Eng ASME 88-; Tau Bet Pi 90-; Golden Key 89-; W S Spd Awd Svc; 4 Cooprtv Intrnshps Dow Chem Co USA 88-90; IM 86-88; BS 91; Mech Eng.

**VORONEC, IVAN D,** Fl St Univ, Tallahassee, FL; SR; BA; Intl Affiars Soc 90-; Intl Affairs; Law Sch.

**VORSE, CRAIG S,** Univ Of Pittsburgh, Pittsburgh, PA; JR; BSIE; IIE 90-; Tutor 90-; Tau Beta Pi Rec Sec 90-; Alpha Pi Mu Treas; IBM Charlotte Summer Intern 90; Procter & Gamble Hatboro Intern; Lord Corp Merit Schlrshp 90-; IM Bsktbl/Golf Club; Ind Engrng.

**VOSE, CAROLYN E,** Western New England Coll, Springfield, MA; JR; BA; Stdnt Tchg Asst; Child Advocacy Pgm Intern; Sftbl 87; Psych; Early Chld Dev.

**VOSE, DAVID SEARS,** Univ Of Nh Plymouth St Coll, Plymouth, NH; SR; BA; Assoc Of Non Trad Stdnts Sec 88-; Pi Gamma Mu 89-; Phi Kappa Phi 89-; Duane J Squires Hist Awrd 88; Hist Flwshp 88; Dist Sr In Hist 89-90; USAF 81-85; Hist; Educ.

**VOSE, HELEN J,** Belmont Coll, Nashville, TN; JR; BBA; Gamma Beta Phi; Tennis; Accntng; CPA.

**VOSICK, JOAN M,** D Youville Coll, Buffalo, NY; SO; BA; Future Tchrs Org Sec 89-; Artists & Writers Org 90-; Co-Edtr Campus Pblctn Poems 90-; Mbr Of Pres Hnrs Prog; Spec/Elem Edn; Spec Edn Tutor.

**VOSS, CATHERINE E,** Howard Univ, Washington, DC; GD; MSA; NASW Mbr; BA Xavier Univ 81; Soc Wrk.

**VOSS, LISA ROBERTS,** Union Univ, Jackson, TN; GD; MBA; Yng Rpblcns; Sci Clb; Ag Clb 87; Atrn Assn; Hnds Of Hpe Shre Grp Ldr 90; Chi Omega; Sigma Alpha Epsilon Lil Sis 86; Ctlln Clb; Arthrts Fndtn 90; CPR Cert 90; Stdnt Tchr Assn 90-; BS Biolgy Univ Of TN 86; Cert Of Educ Union Univ; Sci And Biology; Tchr.

**VOSTROVSKY, SUSAN D,** Seton Hall Univ, South Orange, NJ; JR; BSN; Stdnt Nrses Assoc 90; Fclted Hrzns Prog 90; SHU Campus Mnstry UMDNJ; Smmr Extrnshp At U Of Med/Dntstry NJ; Rutgers U Crew 87-88; Nrsng.

**VOTAVA, JAMES J,** Eckerd Coll, St Petersburg, FL; JR; BA; Intl Stu Assoc Tres/VP 90-; Crtv Art Stu Assoc Pres 89-; Eckerd Anthrplgcl Soc 90-; St Ptrbrgs Museum Fine Arts Intrnshp; Visual Arts; Museum Admin.

**VOUDOURIS, ANNA MARIA,** S U N Y Coll Of Tech At Frmgdl, Farmingdale, NY; FR; BA; Bus; Mktng Exec.

**VOUGHT, TRACEY A,** Roane St Comm Coll, Harriman, TN; FR; BA; Bus; Bnkng.

**VOUGHT, VICTORIA D,** Fl St Univ, Tallahassee, FL; JR; BSN; Phi Theta Kappa 88-89; Big Bend Hospice Vol 90; Mrchg Chiefs Flag Corps 89-90; Nrsg; Surg Nrs.

**VOWE, TED M,** Teikyo Post Univ, Waterbury, CT; JR; BA; Alpha Beta Gamma 89; AS Mattatuck Cmmnty Clg 90; Bsnss; Accntnt.

**VOWELL, CYNTHIA N,** Ms St Univ, Miss State, MS; SR; DVM; Otdr Scty Treas 90-; Alpha Zeta 90-; Gamma Beta Phi 90-; Phi Kappa Phi; Acdmc Schlrshp 88-; Vet Med; Wldlf Prcttnr.

**VOWELL, DENISE R,** Univ Of Va Clinch Valley Coll, Wise, VA; SR; BA; First Bapt Ch; Aerobics Inst 89-; Assoc Mountain Empire Comm Clg 82-84; Educ; Ele Tchr.

**VOWELL, KATHI T,** Roane St Comm Coll, Harriman, TN; FR; AS; Gamma Beta Phi 90-; Acctg.

**VOYLES, GREGORY A,** Valdosta St Coll, Valdosta, GA; SR; BA; Stu Govt Prlmntrn 87-90; Intrfrat Cncl Pres 89-90; Delta Chi Pres 87-; Ga St Spcl Olympcs Area Coordntr 89-90; Pol Sci; Law.

**VOYTEK, REBECCA A,** Endicott Coll, Beverly, MA; SO; ASSOC; Fitness Clb 90-; Phi Theta Kappa; Intrnshp D/L Strs 90; Scribbles; Mgmnt.

**VRICOS, JAMES H,** Fl St Univ, Tallahassee, FL; GD; MA; Tallahassee Zorbatic Co Fndr 90-; AA St Petersburg Jr Clg 89; BS/BA FL State Univ; Hist; Prof.

**VROMAN, DEBRA A,** Cornell Univ Statutory College, Ithaca, NY; SR; BS; ASAE Cmnty Svc Chrmn 90-; Sr Proj; Tchg Asst Cmptg Grphcs 89; Bio Engr.

**VRONICK, EFIMIA E,** Univ Of Akron, Akron, OH; SR; BS; ASME 88-; SAE VP 89-; Cls Bd 90-; Russian Brthrhd Orthodoxy 86-; Fed Rusn Orthdx Clbs Pres 81-; Delta Gamma Eta VP 86-; Gdyr Tire Rbr Co Coop 86-90; Biomed Eng Asstshp; Mech Eng; MS Biomed Eng.

**VROOM, DAVID SCHUYLER,** Fayetteville St Univ, Fayetteville, NC; FR; BS; Cpe Fr Cgd Brd Scty 89-; Scty Of Amer Mltry Engs 87-; Vets Of Frgn Wrs 89-; US Army Corps Of Engs 89; AA New York St Regents 74; BS Southern IL Univ School Of Engs And Tech 81; Chem; Envir Eng Chem.

**VROOMAN, DEIDRA E,** Univ Of Ga, Athens, GA; JR; Golden Key; Sigma Lambda Alpha.

**VRY, ALLISON K,** Winthrop Coll, Rock Hill, SC; SO; BME; Acdmy Arts 89-; Delta Omicron; Outstndg Delta Omicron Pldg; Sallie Claywell Hogan Awd 90; M Lewis Awd Univ KY; Music; Educ.

**VU NGUYEN, KHANHDUNG,** Univ Of Louisville, Louisville, KY; JR; SWE 89-; Amer Intl Rel Clb 89-; Gldn Ky 90-; Tau Beta Pi Natl; Vietnmse Assoc KY 84-; Engr Mth/Comp Sci; Engr.

**VU, ANH D,** Bunker Hill Comm Coll, Boston, MA; SO; BA; Stu Govt VP 90; Asian Clb; Dean Lst 89-90; Drama Clb 90; Tutor 89; Lttr Mrt 90; Holy Rdmr Prsh Ldr 89-; Psych; Cnslr.

**VU, GIAO D,** Bunker Hill Comm Coll, Boston, MA; FR; English/Elect Engr Tech.

**VU, HANH N,** N Va Comm Coll Woodbridge, Woodbridge, VA; JR; BA; Hope 90-; Acts 89-; Rstr Comm Clg 90-; Asoc; Englsh Pblc Rltns Indstry.

**VU, JOHN N T,** Villanova Univ, Villanova, PA; SO; BS; Stdt Prgrmg Cncl Sprg Brk Crdntr; Ski Clb; Karate Clb; Alpha Epsilon Delta; Dns Lst; Biology; Med.

**VU, THAO H,** Franklin And Marshall Coll, Lancaster, PA; FR; BSEBE; Blue/White Nwspr 90-; Amer Chem Soc 90-; Chem Rsrch Intrn 90-; Hackman Schlr 90-; Bioengr; Bio Tech Firm.

**VU, THU-HUONG T,** Howard Univ, Washington, DC; SR; Beta Sigma 89-; BS; Phrmcy.

**VUELTA, SHAORN R,** Univ Of Miami, Coral Gables, FL; FR; BA.

**VUKOVCAN, STACEY M,** Indiana Univ Of Pa, Indiana, PA; SO; BA; Orntn Ldr 90; Cmps Trgde 89-; Kappa Delta Pi; Fdn Dist Achvr Schlr 89-; Educ; Teacher.

**VULICH, DAVID A,** Kent St Univ Kent Cmps, Kent, OH; JR; Alpha Lambda Delta 88-89; Natl Gold Key; Human Resource Mgmt.

**VULIN, DONNA S,** Manhattan Coll, Bronx, NY; JR; BE; Dns Engr Cncl 90-; AFROTC Chf Info Mgmt Cadet Capt 88-90; St La Salle Hnr Soc 88; AFROTC Thunderbird Drl Tm 88-90; SAME 88-; SAME Pres 90-; ASME 88-; SAE 88-; SAME Schlrshp Engr 90; Sons Am Revol; Slvr ROTC Mdl 89; Kiwanis Clb Schlrshp 88-; Mech Engr; Aerosp Engr.**

**VULTAGGIO, ANNE M,** City Univ Of Ny Queensbrough, New York, NY; SR; AAS; Deans Hon List Queensborough Cmnty Clg 89-; Alpha Beta Gamma; Coop Ed In Bus Secrtrl; Admn Secy; Legal Secy.

**VUNCANNON, ARA M,** Ms St Univ, Miss State, MS; SR; Cath Stdnt Assoc 89-; Natl Assoc Indstrl Tech Sec 89-; IM Sprts 89-; Assoc Ml Gulf Coast Comm Jr Coll 89; Trd Tech Stds: Mrktng.

**VUONG, CUONG,** S U N Y Coll Of Tech At Delhi, Delhi, NY; FR; CERT; Cert 90-; Auto Tech; Eng.

**VUONG, KY,** Anne Arundel Comm Coll, Arnold, MD; FR; AA; Hlth/Phys Edn; Hlth Admn.

**VUONO, KATHLEEN J,** Comm Coll Algny Co Algny Cmps, Pittsburgh, PA; FR; BED; Deans Lst 83-85; Deans Lst Comm Clg Allg Cnty 91-; Mmbr Brd Rltrs; Rltr Admnstrtv Asst; AS Dffs Bsns Schl 85; Edctn; Elem Spcl Edctn.

# W

**WACASER, JEFFREY S,** Hillsborough Comm Coll, Tampa, FL; FR.

**WACCARD, JOHN L,** Cornell Univ, Ithaca, NY; FR; BS; Ski Club Officer 90-; Busn Mgt/Mktng; Law.

**WACHSMUTH, EVA M,** Livingston Univ, Livingston, AL; SO; BS; Yrbk 89-; SGA 90-; Engl Clb LU Envoy Hstss 90-; Alpha Psi Omega; Rcyclng Comm; Secndry Ed; Engl/Drama Tchr.

**WACHTER, AMY S,** Bridgewater Coll, Bridgewater, VA; SR; BS; Physics Club Sec 88-; Drama Club; Ski & Outdoor Club 87-; Yrbk 87-88; Math Club Pres; Lambda Soc 88-; Alpha Chi Hnr Soc 89-; Pres Schlrshp; Math.

**WACHTER, LESLIE A,** Univ Of Med & Dentistry Of Nj, Newark, NJ; SR; BS; APTA 89-; Lamba Alpha Sigma 90-; Keon Coll 87; Alumni Schlrshp; Betty Bacharach Rehab Hosp Intrn; Matheny Schl Intrn; St Peters Med Ctr Intrn; Vrsty Swm 89-90; Kean Coll NJ; Phys Thpry.

**WACHTER, REGINA T,** Seton Hall Univ, South Orange, NJ; FR; Engl/Elem Edn.

**WACK, GREGORY R,** Defiance Coll, Defiance, OH; JR; BA; Untd Mthdst Pstr 89-; Rlgn; Mnstry.

**WACKER, DIANA K,** Spalding Univ, Louisville, KY; SR; BS; Delta Epsilon Sigma 90-; Phi Theta Kappa 87-88; Accntng Analyst 90; AAS Jffrsn Cmmnty Clg 88; Bsns Admnstrtn; Accntng Hmn Rsrcs.

**WACTOR, PAMELA L,** Univ Of Sc At Columbia, Columbia, SC; FR; BS; Smmr Nrse Extrnshp 91; Nrsng.

**WACTOR, TAMMY L,** Univ Of Sc At Columbia, Columbia, SC; FR; BS; BSU 90-; Nurse Extern/Richland Meml Hosp; Biol.

**WADDELL, DANELLE,** Winthrop Coll, Rock Hill, SC; SO; Poli Sci Clb 87-89; Alpha Lambda Delta 90-; Vrsty Bsktbl 87-; Engl; Law.**

**WADDELL, JON M,** Marshall University, Huntington, WV; JR; BA; Acctg Clb; Acctg; CPA.

**WADDELL, KELLY J,** Univ Of Nc At Greensboro, Greensboro, NC; SO; BSN; Alpha Lambda Delta 89-90; Univ Mrshls 90-; Natl Collgt Nrsng Awrd 90; Coll Schlrs Of Amer 90; Nrsng; RN.

**WADDELL, LISA A,** Va Commonwealth Univ, Richmond, VA; FR; BA; Ladders/Succ 90-; Hon Soc; Bkpr 90-; Math.

**WADDELL, MARIANNE M,** Free Will Baptist Bible Coll, Nashville, TN; SR; BS; L M Alcott Soc; Bktbl Tm; Drama Tm 84-85; Bsktbl Tm; Mstrs Engl/Law Schl; BA Bible 88; BA Engl 88; Engl; Law.

**WADDELL JR, MICHAEL L,** Memphis St Univ, Memphis, TN; FR; Engl.

**WADDING, CORRENE A,** Westminster Coll, New Wilmingtn, PA; SR; BA; Asst Advsr Chrch Yth Grp 90-; Spcl Olympcs 89-; Orntn Stf; Kappa Delta Pi Slctn Chrprsn 90-; Deans Lst 90-; Acad All Amer 89; Kappa Delta Sec 90-; Habitat Fr Hmnty Fnd Rsng Comm 89-; Elem Edcn; Tchg/Coachg.

**WADDLES, RYAN D,** Univ Of Ky, Lexington, KY; JR; BA; Alpha Lambda Delta 89-90; Golden Key; Acad Excel Schlrshp 90-; Deans Lst 88-; Bio; Med.

**WADE, ADAM,** Ga Inst Of Tech At Atlanta, Atlanta, GA; FR; BEE; Elec Engr.

**WADE, ALISHA L,** Marshall University, Huntington, WV; JR; BBA; Gamma Beta Phi 90; COSIDA 90-; Intrnshp Mrshll Athltc Dept; Stdnt Asst Info Offce; Rsdnce Schlr 89; IM 88-; Bus Mgmt; Sprts Info.

**WADE, ANTHONY J,** Univ Of Tn At Martin, Martin, TN; FR; BED; Phi Mu Alpha 90-; Music.

**WADE, BARBARA L,** William Carey Coll, Hattiesburg, MS; SR; BS; Elem Educ.

**WADE, BETTY Y,** Benedict Coll, Columbia, SC; GD; Pre-Hlth Clb 85-86; Chrldr Sqd Cptn 84-86/87-; NAACP Sec 87; Vrsty Bsktbl; BS Benedict Coll 90; Blgy; Med.

**WADE, CHRISTY S,** Longwood Coll, Farmville, VA; SR; BS; ICF Grp Ldr; Baptist Union; Elem Educ; Tchng.

**WADE, CRAIG R,** Alfred Univ, Alfred, NY; SR; BS; Delta Mu Delta 90-; Phi Kappa Phi 90-; Alpha Lambda Delta 87-; Bus Tomorrow; IMS 87-; Bus Admin; Mgmnt.**

**WADE, GLADYS M,** Central St Univ, Wilberforce, OH; JR; Iota Phi Theta Pres 88-; Bnd Sctn Ldr 90-; Msc Acdmc Schlrshp 89-; Bnd Schlrshp 90-; Msc Ed; Clge Prfsr Msc.

**WADE, JASON F,** Memphis St Univ, Memphis, TN; FR; BA; Engr; Mech Engr.

**WADE, JOSEPH B,** Valdosta St Coll, Valdosta, GA; JR; BBA; Mgmt/Advrtsng; Bus; Mgmt/Mktg.

**WADE, JULEA,** Western Ky Univ, Bowling Green, KY; SR; BA; Psychol Clb 89-; Phi Eta Sigma 88-; Phi Kappa Phi; Psi Chi Treas 89-; Pres Schlr 89-; Psych; Fmly/Marriage Cnslng.

**WADE, KAREN M,** Univ Of Sc At Columbia, Columbia, SC; SR; BSN; IM Sports Soccer 88; Stdnt Nurses Assoc 90-; BSN; Nursing.

**WADE, LACHELLE C,** Lincoln Univ, Lincoln Univ, PA; FR; BA; Gospel Ens 90-; U B Kinsey Awd For Schlstc Achvmnt 90-; Psych.

**WADE, LORRI M,** Faulkner St Jr Coll, Bay Minette, AL; SO; AA; Schl Paper Stf Wrtr 90-; Spirit Team 90-; Res Assist 90-; Phi Theta Kappa Secy 90-; Interned Monsanto Chem Co 90; Video Lab 90-; Wkly Radio Brdcst 90-; Communications; Brdcst Jrnlsm.

**WADE, MICHAEL D,** Central St Univ, Wilberforce, OH; SR; BA; Intrntl Trmpt Gld 89-90; Ntl Symphny Fllwshp Prog 82; Hnrs Rctl 87; Phi Mu Alpha Pres; Bnd Schlrshp 87; Im Bsktbl 89; Music Ed; Prof Prfrmng Mscn.

**WADE, ROBERT L,** Univ Of Rochester, Rochester, NY; SO; BS; Drm Cncl Tres 90-; Sigma Nu; Mlclr Gntcs; Bsns.

**WADE JR, ROBERT L,** Boston Univ, Boston, MA; GD; MD; Stdnt Alumni Rltns Comm Pres 84-87; Res Assist Sr RA 85-; Alumni Schl Comm 87-89; Alpha Omega Alpha; Deans Lst 84-87; Cmmnwlth Schlr 85; Hery Bakst Schlrshp; BA 87; Med; Doctor.

**WADE, RONALD S,** Univ Of Sc At Columbia, Columbia, SC; FR; BS; Body Bldg Clb 90-; Exercise Sci; Sprts Med.

**WADE, SANDRA T,** S U N Y At Buffalo, Buffalo, NY; JR; Univ Of Bflo Acctg Assoc Chrprsn/Fndrsng 90-; Golden Key 89-; Beta Alpha Psi 90-; Deans List 89-; Natl Acct Assoc 90-; BS; Acctg; CPA.

**WADE, SHANNON K,** Liberty Univ, Lynchburg, VA; SO; BS; Ythqst 89-; Light 89-F Alpha Lamda Delta 90-; Prayer Groups Ldr 90-; Resid Assist; Psychology; Counseling Ministries.

**WADEMAN, RENEE G,** Marywood Coll, Scranton, PA; FR; BA; Psychlgy Clb 90-; Coll Vol 90-; Psych.

**WADKINS, HOLLY I M,** S U N Y Coll Of A & T Morrisvl, Morrisville, NY; SO; Res Asstnt Assoc 90-; Hl Cncl Rep 89-; Phi Theta Kappa 89-; AS; Psych; Law.

**WADSWORTH, BRUCE C,** Bryant Stratton Bus Inst Roch, Rochester, NY; GD; MBA; Elec Tech Club 89-90; Cert Rochester Career Stills Ctr 85; Electrncs; Engrng.

**WADSWORTH III, EDWIN T,** Fl St Univ, Tallahassee, FL; SR; BS; Lambda Pi Eta 90-; Intrnshp WTXL Chnnl 27-ABC; Media Cmnctns; TV.

**WADSWORTH, TRACY D,** Mount Olive Coll, Mount Olive, NC; SO; Hendrsn Sci Clb 90-; Natl Hnr Socty; Agrnmy; Ag.

**WAFFORD, CINDY A,** Univ Of Ky, Lexington, KY; FR; IM Sports; Cmps Crusade Christ; Alpha Lambda Delta; Chi Omega; Bus; Mrktng.

**WAGELEY JR, EDMUND L,** Fl International Univ, Miami, FL; SR; BS; Hotel/Fd/Travel Assoc; Intl Svcs Exec Assoc; Deans Lst; Advncd Intrnshp Marriott Harbor Bch Resrt; Sftbl/Bsktbl; Vol Home For Homeless; Hosp Mgmnt; Mktg.

**WAGENER, TRACEY A,** Univ Of Fl, Gainesville, FL; SR; BFA; Celebrtn Asst Dir 90-; Hmcmng Asst Dir 90; Art Hstry Assoc Sec 90-; Art Hstry Assoc Sec 90-; Gldn Ky 89-; Ord Of Omega 90-; Delta Gamma VP Schlrshp 87-; Pres Hon Rl 89; Dns Lst 88-; Art Hstry; Museum/Curatorl.

**WAGENHOFER, DIANA L,** Comm Coll Algny Co Algny Cmps, Pittsburgh, PA; FR; BA; Acctng/Bsn.

**WAGENSCHUTZ, EVA L,** Tn Temple Univ, Chattanooga, TN; FR; BA; Mscl Drm 90; Srty Bsktbl 90-; Cncrt Chr; Theta Kappo Rho 90-; Spch Cmnctns; Brdcstng.

**WAGES, VIRGINIA L,** Univ Of Ga, Athens, GA; JR; BSED; Engl Ed; Tchng.

**WAGGAMAN, MARY J,** Fl A & M Univ, Tallahassee, FL; JR; BS; FL Univ Geo Soc Treas 88-89; Amer Water Resrcs Assoc VP 89-; Golden Key 90-; Pharm.

**WAGGONER PARKER, KELLY M,** Oh Univ-Southern Cmps, Ironton, OH; SR; BSED; AS Ashland Cmnty Clg 88; Elem Educ.

**WAGGONER, SHARON A,** Wv Univ At Parkersburg, Parkersburg, WV; JR; BA; Alpha Beta Gamma 85-; Hons 87; Dir Data Proc Mt St BCBS; Supv Skls Cert 87; AAS 87; Mgmt.

**WAGNER, AMY S,** Radford Univ, Radford, VA; JR; BA; Pi Gamma Mi; Psychlgy.

**WAGNER, BRENT M,** Temple Univ, Philadelphia, PA; SO; BS; Sigma Tau Gamma; Envrnmntl Engr Tech.

**WAGNER, CATHLEEN M,** Comm Coll Algny Co Algny Cmps, Pittsburgh, PA; SO; BA; Nurs; Reg Nurs.

**WAGNER JR, CHARLES J,** William Carey Coll, Hattiesburg, MS; SO; BSN; AS LSU Dental Tech 83; Nrsng.

**WAGNER, CHRISTOPHER T,** Univ Of Rochester, Rochester, NY; SR; BS; AICHE Chapt Rep 90-; Biomed Engr Rsrch Intrn 89; S A Miller Dsgn Awd; Chem Engr; Engr Rsrch.

**WAGNER, CYNTHIA M,** Comm Coll Algny Co Algny Cmps, Pittsburgh, PA; GD; AS; Stdnt Med Record Assoc VP 90; WPMRA 90; PMRA 90; Phi Theta Kappa 90-90; Deans List 88-90; Medical Volunteer 90; Record Depart; Med Record Tech; Medical Record Tech.

**WAGNER, DEBBRA A,** Univ Of Cin R Walters Coll, Blue Ash, OH; SO; BA; City Of Hope Fndtn 89-; Bus/Comps; Mngmnt Info Syst.**

**WAGNER, DONNA S,** Oh Univ-Southern Cmps, Ironton, OH; FR; Englsh; Elem Edctn.

**WAGNER, EDWARD A,** Kent St Univ Kent Cmps, Kent, OH; SR; BBA; Acctng 89-; Im Sftbl; Beta Alpha Psi Treas 89-; Beta Gamma Sigma; Acctng Intrnshp 90; Acctng.

**WAGNER, ELENA P,** Univ Of Miami, Coral Gables, FL; FR; Diving Tm; Cert British Inst In Las Palmas 90; Psychlgy; Chld Psychlgst.

**WAGNER, ERIC M,** Duquesne Univ, Pittsburgh, PA; FR; BA; WDSR 90; Actng Grp 90; SHARP 90; Dir Cir 90; Cmmnctns; TV Radio/Law.

**WAGNER, HELEN O,** Utica Coll Of Syracuse Univ, Utica, NY; JR; FA; Fdrtn Hm Bureaus St Rsltn Chmn 71-75; Indpndnt Hmmkrs Tres 76-90; AA 84; AAS 89; Fine Art.

**WAGNER, JAMEY N,** Savannah Coll Of Art & Design, Savannah, GA; JR; BFA; Dns Lst 88-; Art Design Sympsm Schlrshp 88; Jos B Plumly Mem Schlrshp 88; Sean Moran Mem Schlrshp; Graphic Desgn/Art Hstry/Cmptr Art.

**WAGNER, JANET L,** Oh Univ-Southern Cmps, Ironton, OH; SR; BA; St Lawrence Otoole Cath Chrch Vol; Soc Work; AA SW; Soc Work.

**WAGNER II, JOSEPH E,** Richard Bland Coll, Petersburg, VA; SO; AS; Spnsh Clb; Phi Theta Kappa 90-; Fndtn Schlr 90-; Busn Awd; Bio; Med Resrch.

**WAGNER, JULIE J,** Columbia Greene Comm Coll, Hudson, NY; FR; BA; Stdnt Senate; Spanish Hnr Soc; Hnr Soc; Deans List; Individual Studies; Elem Educ.

**WAGNER, KAREN L,** Slippery Rock Univ, Slippery Rock, PA; JR; BA; AS Butler Cnty Comm Clg 90; Physcl Educ/Knsthrpy.

**WAGNER, KATHY M,** Northern Ky Univ, Highland Hts, KY; SR; BA; Cncl Fr Excptnl Chldrn 89-; IM Vlybl Sftbl; Elem Spcl Educ Tchr.

**WAGNER, LAURIE LYNN,** Univ Of Ct, Storrs, CT; SR; Nut Clb 90; CT Pub Int Res Grp 90; Stdnt Alumni Assoc 87; Womens Acapella Grp 90; Alpha Lambda Delta 87-; Coop Educ Nutritionist 89-; BS 90; Nutrition.

**WAGNER, MARTHA A,** Wright St Univ Lake Cmps, Celina, OH; FR; BA; Cmptr Sci; Ed.

**WAGNER, MARY E,** Defiance Coll, Defiance, OH; SO; BA; Golden Hammer Jrnlsm Awd; Hist/Eng; Museumolgy.

**WAGNER, MEGHAN R,** Univ Of Sc At Coastal Carolina, Conway, SC; FR; BA; Stdnt Govt Assoc Rep 90-; Delta Phi Omega Treas 90-; Marine Sciences; Marine Biologist.

**WAGNER, PRISCILLA L,** Univ Of Akron, Akron, OH; SR; BA; OH Dnce Assoc 90-; MI Dnce Assoc Mbr 85-88; Fac Dnce Dept 89-; Dnce; Univ Fac.

**WAGNER, RANDE K,** Miami Jacobs Jr Coll Of Bus, Dayton, OH; SO; AD; Miami Vly Lit Assn Tutr 88-90; Supervisor; Bus Admin.

**WAGNER, RONALD E,** Carnegie Mellon Univ, Pittsburgh, PA; SR; BS; Pnrs 90-; IM Vlybl 89-; Crngie Mlln Rcgntn Schlrhsp; Smll Undrgrad Rsrch Grnt; Indstrl Mgmt; Mrktng.

**WAGNER, RONALD K,** S U N Y Coll Of Tech At Frmgdl, Farmingdale, NY; SO; BA; Mktg; Adv.

**WAGNER, SANDRA L,** Salisbury St Univ, Salisbury, MD; GD; MS; Alpha Omega Blgcl Scty Pres 88-90f Beta Beta Beta; Blgy Fclty Awrd 90f Cmps Lf 90; Zlgy.

**WAGNER, SCOTT K,** U S Coast Guard Academy, New London, CT; JR; BS; Fxtrt Co Org Squad Ldr; Athltcs Ofcr; Amer Soc Cvl Engr; Ftbl/Rugby 88-; Cvl Engr; Cst Gurd Ofcr.

**WAGNER, SHARON L,** Univ Of Cincinnati-Clrmnt Coll, Batavia, OH; FR; BA; Psych; Psych Cnslr.

**WAGNER, STACIE S,** Juniata Coll, Huntingdon, PA; SR; BA; Admsns Assoc 89-; Internatl Club 89-; Barristers Club Secy 88-90; Hon Soc; Stdy Abrd At The Univ Of Strasburg France 89; Legal Intrn Keystone Legas Svcs Inc; Philsphy; Law.

**WAGNER, STEPHANIE LYNN,** Univ Of Ky, Lexington, KY; FR; BA; Water Ski Tm Sec 90-; Res Hall Govt 90-; Pi Beta Phi 90-; Fashion Merch.

**WAGNER, STEVEN J,** Univ Of Akron, Akron, OH; JR; BA; Brtndr 89-; Acctg.

**WAGNER, SUSAN L,** Salisbury St Univ, Salisbury, MD; SO; BA; Radio Sta DJ 90-; Plng Comm New Tutoring Prog 90-; Pres Schlrshp; Engl Creative Wrtng; Tchng/Wrtng Fctn/Poetry.

**WAGNER, THERESA S,** Wilmington Coll, New Castle, DE; SR; BS; Pres Jr Cls 85-86; Delta Epsilon Rho 90-; Formerly Bnkg Mgmnt; Bus Admin; Masters Edn.

**WAGNER, TRACY L,** S U N Y Coll At Fredonia, Fredonia, NY; SO; BA; Acctg Scty Mbr 90-; Drmtry Cncl Treas 90; Drmtry Cncl Advsr; Drmtry Rsdnt Asst; Fredonia Alumni Schlrshp; All American Schlar Awrd; Acctg Fnc; CPA.

**WAGNER, TRACY L,** Univ Of Cincinnati-Clrmnt Coll, Batavia, OH; SO; BA; Dns Lst 89-; Blgy Lab Asst 90; AA 90; Chem; Chem Eng.

**WAGNER, TRACY L,** Slippery Rock Univ, Slippery Rock, PA; FR; BED; Rocklettes Dance Team 90; Hlth Physcl Ed; Tchr.

**WAGNER, WENDY A,** Univ Of Akron, Akron, OH; JR; BA; Akron Coun Educ Stdnts 90-; Elem Educ; Tchng.

**WAGNER, WILLIAM S,** Temple Univ, Philadelphia, PA; JR; BS; Amer Phrmctcl Assoc 89-; Natl Assoc Rtl Drgsts 89-; Pa Soc Hosp Phrmcsts 89-; Rho Chi Soc Pres; Phrmcy.

**WAGNER, ZACHARY G,** Coll Of Charleston, Charleston, SC; FR; MBA; Hnrs Pgm 90-; Pi Kappa Phi 90-; Sailing 90-.

**WAGNER-STILES, PATRICIA D,** Al St Univ, Montgomery, AL; GD; BS Crmnl Just Auburn Univ Montgomery 82; MS Auburn Univ Montgomery 83; Early Chldhd Ed; Tchr Pblc Schl Sys.

**WAGUESPACK, DOROTHY E,** Southern Coll Of Tech, Marietta, GA; JR; BEE; Elec Engr.

**WAH, LEO C,** Univ Of Rochester, Rochester, NY; SO; BA; Statistics; MBA.

**WAHDAN, BASSAM ABID,** Al A & M Univ, Normal, AL; SR; BS; Mech Eng Tech; Mech Eng.

**WAHED, FARIDA,** Bunker Hill Comm Coll, Boston, MA; FR; ART; Wtrtwn Clb; MSRT; Instrctr Aerobic Cls 85-; Tchr 88-89; Dntstry.

**WAHL, JON A,** Middle Tn St Univ, Murfreesboro, TN; JR; BS; Physics; H S Tchr.

**WAHL, KATHLEEN M,** Comm Coll Algny Co Algny Cmps, Pittsburgh, PA; FR; ASN; Mngr Invstr Srvcs 86-90; Hlth Srvcs; Ansthlst Prgrm.

**WAHUS, ERIK D,** Wv Univ, Morgantown, WV; FR; BS; Newman Org 90-; Alpha Phi Omega 90-; Im Bowling 90; Engr.

**WAIBEL, DIANE M,** The Boston Conservatory, Boston, MA; SR; Music Edctrs Natl Cnfrnc Pres 87-; Boston Cnsrvtry Chrstn Fllwshp; Phi Kappa Lambda; BMED; Music Educ; Tch.

**WAIMALEONGORA-EK, VEERAWUT,** Ms Gulf Coast Comm Coll, Perkinston, MS; SO; BA; Indl Eng.

**WAIT, WILLIAM M,** Univ Of Sc At Columbia, Columbia, SC; JR; BA; Nvy Vet; Sclgy; MSW.

**WAITE, ANNE B,** Longwood Coll, Farmville, VA; SR; BS; Hall Cncl V P 88-89; Sr Ball Co Chrmn; Soc/Anthro Clb 88-; Sigma Kappa 90-; Nancy Ward Nance Acad Schlrshp 87-; IM 87-; Sociology/Psychology; Cnslng Dstrbd Adoles.

**WAITE, ELSA E,** Univ Of Miami, Coral Gables, FL; JR; BA; Prvst Lst; I Sands Edwd Schlrshp; B Ashe Schlrshp; Univ Miami Schlarshps; Lgl Stds; Law.

**WAITE, JACQUELINE M,** Johnson C Smith Univ, Charlotte, NC; SO; Psych Clb Sec 90-; NAACP 89-90; Alpha Lambda 89-90; Deans Lst 89-; Pres Lst 89-; Indust Org Psych.

**WAITE, JOHN B,** Ms St Univ, Miss State, MS; SR; BA; Mktg; Sales.

**WAITE, MARY,** Univ Of Cincinnati, Cincinnati, OH; JR; BM; Music Perf-French Horn; Orch Perf.

**WAITE, ROY G,** Memphis St Univ, Memphis, TN; JR; BBA; Accounting; CPA.

**WAITE, TIFFANY M,** Duquesne Univ, Pittsburgh, PA; JR; BSBA; Cmmtr Affrs Asst 90; Beta Alpha Phi 90-; Beta Gamma Sigma; VSX Corp Intrn 90-; Acctng; CPA.

**WAITES, CRYSTAL A,** Johnson C Smith Univ, Charlotte, NC; GD; MA; Spnsh Clb Pres 86-87; Nwsppr Rprtr 86-87; United Negro Schlrshp Fnd 89-90; WJZY TV Sta 87-88; Pub Rel Intrn Ken Koontz 89-90; Cmmnctns Arts/Pol Sci; Coll Prof/City Govt.

**WAITS, SUSAN B,** Univ Of Cincinnati-Clrmnt Coll, Batavia, OH; FR; BA; Phi Theta Kappa 83; Jr Achvmnt Adv 85-90; AS 85; Elec Eng.

**WAJCIECHOWSKI, TONYA A,** Radford Univ, Radford, VA; SO; BS; Radford Univ Cncrt Bnd 89; Prgrsve Stdnt Alnce 89-90; Psychology; Chld Psychlgst.

**WAKE, STEPHANIE E,** Fayetteville St Univ, Fayetteville, NC; SO; BA; AFAA Cert Aerobic Inst; Part Time Aerobic Inst; Engl; Tcher/Prof.

**WAKEFIELD, LARRY ALLEN,** Northwest Al Comm Coll, Phil Campbell, AL; SO; ADAS; Elec.

**WAKEMAN, REBECCA D,** Liberty Univ, Lynchburg, VA; JR; BS; Kappa Delta Pi 90; Educ.

**WALA, TOMASZ P,** Univ Of Ky, Lexington, KY; FR; BS; Chncllr Schlrshp 90-; Vlybl 90-; Mech Eng; Corp Or Bus Law.

**WALBORN, KIMBERLY M,** Liberty Univ, Lynchburg, VA; FR; BA; Hon Prog; Alpha Lambda Delta; Ch Chldrn Mnstry 90-; Chnclrs Schlrshp 90-; Deans Lst 90-; English; Educ.

**WALBURN, CARSON S,** Bridgewater Coll, Bridgewater, VA; JR; BA; Concrt Choir 89-; Chorale 89-; Hon Cncl 90-; Concrt Bank 88-; Cls Pres 88-; Lambda Soc 89-; Omicron Delta Kappa 90-; Intrntl Rltns; Intrntl Bus Law.

**WALCHAK, PATTY G,** Western Ky Univ, Bowling Green, KY; SO; BA; Chem Hon Soc Pres 90-; Alpha Epsilon Delta Histrn; Beta Beta Bets VP; Cio/Chem; Medcn.

**WALCK, TIMOTHY G,** S U N Y At Buffalo, Buffalo, NY; SR; BS; Amer Scty Cvl Eng Sec 87-; Tau Beta Pi 89-; Phi Eta Sgm 88-; Gldn Key 90-; Robert P Apmann Mem Awrd; Grace W Capen Mem Awrd 88; Cvl Eng.

**WALDBAUM, TAMARA,** Univ Of Rochester, Rochester, NY; SO; BA; Cmpr Vol Org 90-; Phi Sigma Sigma Pres 89-; Sp Ktchns 89-91; Psychlgy.

**WALDEN, ALICE M,** Univ Of Nc At Charlotte, Charlotte, NC; SO; BS; Nrsng.

**WALDEN, DAVID J,** Duquesne Univ, Pittsburgh, PA; GD; MBA; MBA Assoc 90-; Royal Crusaders Drum/Bugle Corps 75-77; MENC PMEA PSEA VEA 74-82; Cum Laude 78; Lgl Adm Asst/P C Coord/App Pgmr Caroselli Spagnolli Beachler 86-; BSME 78; Cert ABP Cmptr Tech 80; Pers Mgmt/Intl Bsn.

**WALDEN, DEIDRE L,** Valdosta St Coll, Valdosta, GA; JR; BS; Early Chldhd Educ; Tchr.

**WALDEN, LISA M,** Greenville Tech Coll, Greenville, SC; SO; AI; Elctrncs; Cmptr.

**WALDEN, LORI L,** Sue Bennett Coll, London, KY; FR; BA; Pep Clb; Acad Schlrshp/Chrldng Schlrshp; Mtn Laurel Prncss Rep 90; Deans Lst 90; Tennis 90; Chrldr Var Capt 90; Phrmst.

**WALDEN, PAMALA S,** Univ Of Al At Birmingham, Birmingham, AL; SR; BA; Bsns Clb; UAH Accntng Clb 90; Hnr Schlr 89-; Beta Alpha Psi; Uah Ndrgrd Crclm Advsry Brd 90; Inst Mgmnt Accntnts 90-; Assn Gvrnmnt Accntnts 90-; Accntng; Pblc Accntng.

**WALDEN, TIFFANY LYNNE,** Ms St Univ, Miss State, MS; SO; BA; Alpha Lambda Delta 89-; Phi Eta Sigma 89-; Gamma Beta Phi 89-; Math; Sec Educ.

**WALDEN, VICKI A,** Hillsborough Comm Coll, Tampa, FL; GD; BS; Elem Ed; Elem Schl Tchr.

**WALDERMAR, BERRIOS ANAYA,** Inter Amer Univ Pr Hato Rey, Hato Rey, PR; SR; BS; Assc Tchngy Engrng; Electnc; Tchlgy Engrng Eltrnc; Engrng.

**WALDERMO, JORGEN,** Univ Of Sc At Columbia, Columbia, SC; JR; BA; Pres Lst 90.

**WALDMILLER, MARK R,** S U N Y At Buffalo, Buffalo, NY; SR; BSEE; IEEE VP 89-; Tau Beta Pi 89-; Phi Eta Sigma 88-; Dns Lst 87-; Capen Mem Schlrshp; Eng Sr Fllwshp 90-; Elec Eng; MSEE.

**WALDON, HEATHER D,** Union Univ, Jackson, TN; FR; BS; Cmptr Clb Sec 90-; Rtldg Hnry Hstry Clb Astn Sec 90-; Hnr Stdnt Assn; Elem Ed; Tchng Elem.

**WALDRON, ANASTASIA H,** Fl A & M Univ, Tallahassee, FL; JR; BA; AA Lake City Comm Coll 88; Elem Educ; Tchr.

**WALDRON, DOUGLAS W,** Univ Of Louisville, Louisville, KY; FR; BS; Cinematic Arts Comm 90-; Cncrt Comm 90-; Hnts Prgrm; Chmcl Engnrng.

**WALDROP, ANNA MESHELLE,** Blue Mountain Coll, Blue Mountain, MS; SO; BA; Psych Clb Pres; Bapt Stdnt Union Chrmn; Modenian Soc 89-; Psych; Cnslr.

**WALDROP, BETHANY L,** Ms St Univ, Miss State, MS; SR; BS; Chrstn Stdnt Cntr 88-; Ag Cmmnctrs Of Tmrrw; Alpha Zeta 90-; Ag; Agrcmmnctn.

**WALDROP, GREGORY R,** Univ Of Al At Birmingham, Birmingham, AL; SR; BS; Pi Kappa Phi Schlrshp Chrmn 89-90; Intshp Burlington Northern RR 87-90; Mgt Infor Syst/Quantitative Mthds; Law.

**WALDROP, MICHAEL D,** Univ Of Sc At Columbia, Columbia, SC; SO; BS; Sprts Adm Clb 89-90; Hall Rep For Preston Dorm 90; Sprt Admin; Mngmnt.

**WALDROUP, HEATHER L,** Fl St Univ, Tallahassee, FL; JR; BA; Eng; Art Hist.

**WALDRUP, JANET DENISE,** Univ Of Nc At Asheville, Asheville, NC; SO; BS; Phi Eta Sigma 90-; Dns Lst 89-90; Bsn Mgmt; Ins Clm Repr.

**WALDRUP-WORSTER, CATHERINE A,** Univ Of Tn At Martin, Martin, TN; JR; AD; Kingwood Hm Schl Spprt Grp Pres 86-87; Volet Crook TN Nrs Assn Awd/Schlrshp 90; Ftts-Everett Schlrshp; Lay-Midwf 82-88; Nrsng; Crtfd Nrs Midwfry.

**WALESKA, ALFARO D,** Univ Of Pr At Rio Piedras, Rio Piedras, PR; JR; AEPM 90-; 100 Stu Grp Sci Fclty 88-; Gldn Key 90-; Sci/Math Hnr Cls 89-; Mu Alpha Phi 88-; Math/Sci Hnrs 89-; Ntrl Sci; Dntl Med.

**WALKER VON ELTEN, CLEONE M,** Converse Coll, Spartanburg, SC; SR; BFA; Theater; Converse II Assoc Rep Interior Design; Interior Design; Landscaping.

**WALKER, ALLISA M,** Memphis St Univ, Memphis, TN; FR; NROTC Schlrshp 90; Ed; Spec Ed.

**WALKER, ALMEDADA D,** Al A & M Univ, Normal, AL; JR; BA; Alpha Kappa Alpha 90-; Engl; Corprt Law.

**WALKER, AMY GUINN,** Roane St Comm Coll, Harriman, TN; FR; BED; Gamma Beta Phi; Bus Admn.

**WALKER, AMY P,** Univ Of Nc At Asheville, Asheville, NC; FR; BA; Intrntnl 90-; Englsh Lit; Jrnlsm Wrtng.

**WALKER, AMY S,** Lexington Comm Coll, Lexington, KY; JR; Church Bible Stdy; Kids; Christn Chldrns Fnd; Acctng.

**WALKER, ANDREA L,** Univ Of Montevallo, Montevallo, AL; SO; BS; NSSLHA 89-; SHAA; Gold Makeup Prod Comm 90; Orchesis Dance Co; Alpha Lambda Delta; Alpha Gamma Delta 90-; Walk A Thon Jvnl Diabetes Fndtn 90; Speech Pathology; Spec Ed.

**WALKER, ANNALISA,** Univ Of Nc At Charlotte, Charlotte, NC; JR; BA; IM Sports; Deans List; Soclgy/Ecnmcs; Rtlng/Prsnl.

**WALKER, BELINDA D,** New Comm Coll Of Baltimore, Baltimore, MD; SO; AA; Toastmstrs Intrntl 87-; Comptr Equip Anlyst; Acctng.

**WALKER, BILLY M,** East Central Comm Coll, Decatur, MS; SO; BS; Sigma Sigma Mu Tau 90-; Phi Theta Kappa 90-; AS 91; Sci; Nurse.

**WALKER, BRENT D,** Salisbury St Univ, Salisbury, MD; SR; BS; Geographic Treas 89-; Phi Eta Sigma 87-; Gamma Theta Upsilon 88-; Henson Schlr; Schl Sci; Geography; Meterology/Climatology.

**WALKER, BRONETTA P,** Bennett Coll, Greensboro, NC; JR; BS; Blgy Clb 88-; NAACP 90-; Beta Kappa Chi; Delta Sigma Theta Cstdn; Bnntt Coll Schlr; Mnrty Pre Mdcl Schlr 90-; Vllybll Sftbl; Blgy.**

**WALKER, CAROL R,** Vanderbilt Univ, Nashville, TN; FR; MBA; Econs.

**WALKER, CAROLINE L,** Univ Of Sc At Columbia, Columbia, SC; FR; MBA; Bus.

**WALKER JR, CEBERT L,** Belmont Coll, Nashville, TN; SR; BS; Wstvw Bapt Chrch Crtv Mnstrs Dir 90-; Musci Mnstry Asst Dir; Sndy Schl Tchr; Tri Betaassoc Oprtng Rm Nrs 9-; Cert Nrs Oprtng Rm Awrd Exmntn 90; Rgstrd Nrs 82-; AS 82; Blgy.

**WALKER, CHANTAY C,** Fisk Univ, Nashville, TN; SR; BA; Hlth Careers Clb 89-; Chrch Yth Advsr 87-; Yth Tsk Frce 89-90; Mrtr Brd Gld Key 90-; Pi Sigma Alpha 90-; Delta Sigma Theta Financl Sec 88-; Kdwtch Cnslr 87; Motivation Coord/Fndr 88-; Biolgy; Med Schl.

**WALKER, CHARLES JUDD,** Morehouse Coll, Atlanta, GA; SR; BA; Hnrs Pro; Hnrs Pro Clb Pres; Engl Clb; Sigma Tau Delta; Gldn Key; Frederick Douglass Tutrl Inst 89-90; Atlanta Univ Cntr Vol Task Frc 88-89; Flw Smn Min Inst Jrnlsm/Mass Cmnctn Kent St Univ Intrnshp; Blck Entrtnmnt Tv 90; Engl; Cmnctns.

**WALKER, CHARLES R,** Ms St Univ, Miss State, MS; SR; BS; ASLA 88-; ALCA Pres 87-; William J Locklin Ngtscpng Schlrshp 90; Bureau Land Mgt Design Awd 90; Chrldr 86; Ftbl 87; Lndscp Archt/Lndscp Contracting.

**WALKER, CHARLOTTE A,** Univ Of Ct, Storrs, CT; FR; BS; Pre-Vtrnry Clb 90-; Alpha Lambda Delta 90-; Anml Science; Veterinarian.

**WALKER, CHARLOTTE S,** Beckley Coll, Beckley, WV; SO; BA; Bus; CPA.

**WALKER, CRAIG W,** Springfield Tech Comm Coll, Springfield, MA; SO; ASEE; Eng Clb 88-; Alpha Nu Omega 90-; Elec Eng.

**WALKER, DANA S,** Univ Of Sc At Columbia, Columbia, SC; FR; BA; Frshmn Cncl 90-; Advrtsng Clb 90-; Gamma Beta Phi 90-; Alpha Delta Pi 90-; Sthrn Bls Dnc Tm; Jrnlsm; Advrtsng/Pblc Rltns.

**WALKER, DAPHNE M,** Spelman Coll, Atlanta, GA; FR; Frshmn Cls Cncl Stdnt Gvrmnmt Assn Frshmn Rep SGA 90-; Nwspr Stf Offc Mngr 90-; Pblc Rltns Trs 90-; Deans Lst Goth Smstrs 90-; Comm Srvc Awd 90-; Stdnt Gvrmnt Assn Awd 90-; Englsh Prelaw; Law Corp Dvl Rghts.

**WALKER, DAVID W,** Univ Of Va Clinch Valley Coll, Wise, VA; JR; BS; Dean Lst 88-; Awrd Merit 90; IM Bsktbl 90; Bus Admn; Mngmnt.

**WALKER, DAWN N,** Univ Of Ga, Athens, GA; JR; BS; Acad Stdnts Pharm 90-; Alpha Epsilon Delta 88-90; Alpha Lambda Delta 87-88; BS Bio Valdosta State Clg 90; Pharm.

**WALKER, DEBORAH D,** Stillman Coll, Tuscaloosa, AL; SO; BS; Unit Negro Clg Fund 89-; ROTORACT; Zeta Phi Beta 90-; Cmptr Sci; Cmptr Sys Anlyst.

**WALKER, DEBRA D,** Oh St Univ, Columbus, OH; JR; BSLA; Stdnt Lndscp Arch 90-; Lndscp Arch.

**WALKER, DENISE G,** Nova Univ, Ft Lauderdale, FL; GD; MBA; Cmptrllrs 74-; BS 88; Mngmt.

**WALKER, DERRICK C,** Central St Univ, Wilberforce, OH; SR; BS; Natnl Soc Blck Engnrs Pres 87-; Soc Mnfctrng Engnrs Pres 87-; Blck Prof Assoc 90-; Dytn P&l Cointrnshp Elec Engnr 88-89; Frto Lay Inc Intrnshp Proj Engnr 89-90; Gen Mtrs Corp Intrnshp Rbtcs Engnr 90-; Mnfctrng Engnrng; Engnrng.

**WALKER, DEXTER F,** Univ Of Sc At Columbia, Columbia, SC; JR; MBA; Pcsttrs; Bus; Mrktg.

**WALKER, DONNA F,** Alcorn St Univ, Lorman, MS; SR.

**WALKER, DOUGLAS E,** Wilmington Coll, Wilmington, OH; JR; BA; SIFE Treas 90-; Acctg Clb 89-90; Tau Kappa Beta Treas 89-; Econ Fnc Acctg Bus Mgmt.

**WALKER, ERICA N,** Birmingham Southern Coll, Birmingham, AL; SO; Trngl Clb 90-; Blck Stdnt Union VP 89-; Fresh Ldrshp Cls 89; Stff Clmnst Coll Nwspr; Kappa Mu Epsilon 90-; Mc Wane Hon Awd 89-; Deans Lst 90-; IM Vlybl 90-; Math.

**WALKER, ERNEST L,** Vance Granville Comm Coll, Henderson, NC; GD; Stdnt Quarter 90; Loyal Order Of Moose 90-; Wake Tech Automotive 76; Automotive Elctrncs/Elctrcl Engr.

**WALKER, FREDERICK EUCLID,** Morehouse Coll, Atlanta, GA; BS; Martin Luther King Chapel Assistant Publicity Chrmn 90-; Stdnt Concers Comm 90-; Dormitory Council Pres 90-; Banking Finance Re; RE Invstmnt Consultant.

**WALKER, GLENCIA M,** Tuskegee Univ, Tuskegee Inst, AL; SO; BS; Grl Sctg 90-; Choir 89-90; Hnr Schlrshp Cnvctn 90-; Bio/Pre-Med; Med Schl/Pract.**

**WALKER, GOLDIE V,** Hampton Univ, Hampton, VA; FR; Afrcn Clstr Mmbr 90-; Pltcl Sci Clb Mmbr 90-; Hnr Roll; Pltcl Sci; Law.

**WALKER, HEATHER J,** Carnegie Mellon Univ, Pittsburgh, PA; FR; BS; Tartan Magazine Wrtr/Law Club; Ind Mgmnt; Bus Admin.

**WALKER, HEATHER L,** Univ Of Nc At Charlotte, Charlotte, NC; SO; BA; Inter Soc Cncl 89-90; Sports 89-; Natl Stdnt Exchng 90-; Univ Times Stf Wrtr 90-; Zeta Tau Alpha Ritual Chr 89-; Spcl Olympcs Comm; YWCA Tutorng Progrm; Deans List 89-90; Engl/Pol Sci; Jrnlsm.

**WALKER, JACINTH R,** City Univ Of Ny City Coll, New York, NY; SR; BS; Ntl Assoc Fml Exec; Untd Fed Tchrs 89-; Alpha Sigma Lambda; Union Jamaica Alumni Assoc; Touro Deans Lst 88-89; Paraprof NYC Bd Educ 89-; AA 89; Educ; Tchg.

**WALKER JR, JAMES E,** Oh Univ, Athens, OH; SR; BA; Elec Engr.

**WALKER, JAMES F,** Bloomfield Coll, Bloomfield, NJ; SR; BS; Alpha Chi VP 89-90; Alpha Sigma Lambda; Alpha Kappa Psi; Accntng; CPA.

**WALKER, JAMES I,** Waycross Coll, Waycross, GA; FR; BA; Schl Nwspr Stff Wrtr; Phi Theta Kappa 90-; Music.

**WALKER, JANICE I,** City Univ Of Ny Med Evers Coll, Brooklyn, NY; GD; MBA; BS; Business /Finance; Fncl Analyst.

**WALKER, JANNA M,** Univ Of Montevallo, Montevallo, AL; SO; BS; Ed Hrg Imprd; Tchg.

**WALKER, JENNIFER,** Brewer St Jr Coll, Fayette, AL; FR; BS; Erly Chldhd Ed; Ed Admin.

**WALKER, JENNIFER D,** Roane St Comm Coll, Harriman, TN; FR; BA; Gamma Beta Phi 90-; Cont Dance Ens 90-; Arts Cncl 90-; Phys Ther.

**WALKER, JENNIFER L,** Eckerd Coll, St Petersburg, FL; SO; BA; AIDS Tsk Frc 90-; Chrldr Co Capt 89-; Stdnt Almn Cncl 90-; Trtn Sprt Wk Crntr; Intern Tlphn Cnslr; Coll Hnr Schlrshp 89-; Hmn Dvlpmnt Srvcs.

**WALKER, JENNIFER M,** Lexington Comm Coll, Lexington, KY; SO; BA; Bnd Ldsngr Prt Ownr 90-; Ctco Cnstrctn Bkkpng; CDA Cert Dntl Asst Central Kentucky Voc Tech School 86; Fnnce Econs; Bnkng.**

**WALKER, JONATHAN B,** Clayton St Coll, Morrow, GA; SO; AAS; AAS Aviation Maint Tech 90; Avionics; Aircraft Maint.

**WALKER, KAREN A,** Immaculata Coll, Immaculata, PA; SO; BA; Tchrs Aid 90-; Hnrs Prog 90-; Dns Lst 89-90; Sts Philip/James PTO 90-; Math; Sec Educ.

**WALKER, KAREN A,** Univ Of Scranton, Scranton, PA; SR; BS; Vita 89-90; Cmtr Ofcmps Assoc Ecxtv Brd 89-; Bsns Clb/Scty Accntng Stdnts 89-; Delta Mu Delta Vp 90-; Omega Beta Sigma; Scrntn Hl Nghbrhd Assoc 89-90; Intrnshp IPMG P Mrwck; Presnt III Schlrshp 87-; Gnstr Mmrl Schlrshp 87-; Accntng.

**WALKER, KAREN D,** Christopher Newport Coll, Newport News, VA; FR; BA; Scl Wrk Clb; Corrections Corr Ofcr/Intake Cnslr 87-; Licensure Priv Invest/Prov Sec Thomas Nelson Cmnty Clg 87; Crmnl Jstc/Scl Wrk; Corr/Foster Care/Scl Wrk.

**WALKER, KATHERYN R,** Central Fl Comm Coll, Ocala, FL; FR; AA; Educ; Tch.

**WALKER, KELSEY B,** Morehouse Coll, Atlanta, GA; SO; BA; GA Clb/Mass Cmnctns Clb 89-90; Stdnt Oprtd TV Show 90-; Mass Cmnctns; TV/FILM.

**WALKER, KENDRA L,** Tn St Univ, Nashville, TN; SR; BS; Amer Home Econ Assoc 89-; Fashion Guild/Modlng Troupe 89-; Kappa Omicron Mu Scty 92-; Zeta Phi Beta Pres 87-; Intshp Peach Tree Fashions 90; Tns Tm 88; Merchng; Display Merhdr/Buyer.

**WALKER, KEVIN B,** Southern Coll Of Tech, Marietta, GA; SR; BSEET; Lambda Chi Alpha 90-; IM 87-; Elec Engr Tech.

**WALKER, KIMBERLY DE SHONA,** Fl A & M Univ, Tallahassee, FL; FR; BA; Coll Choir 90-; Phi Eta Sigma; Engr; Mech.

**WALKER, KIMBERLY G,** Radford Univ, Radford, VA; SO; BS; Karate Clb 89-; Crmnl Jstce Clb 90-; Crmnl Jstce Sclgy; Law.

**WALKER, KIMBERLY L,** Al St Univ, Montgomery, AL; SO; BS; Ldrshp Schlrshp 90-; Hnr Rl 90-; Crmnl Jstc; Law.

**WALKER, KRISTIN S,** Univ Of Sc At Columbia, Columbia, SC; JR; BFA; Ntl Art Educ Assoc 90; Delta Delta Delta Campus Actvs Chr Scl Evnts Chr 90-; Kinney Shoe Corp Schlrshp 88-89; Art Educ; Tchr.

**WALKER, LARRY WAYNE,** Greenville Tech Coll, Greenville, SC; FR; AAS; PTA; S Spartanburg Athletic Assn; AAS York Tech Clg 80-; Indust Elect; Engr.

**WALKER JR, LAWRENCE A,** Morgan St Univ, Baltimore, MD; SR; BSBA; Ecsel Ambsdr; Bst Prfrmnc Calculus 88; Hnr Rcpnt; Elctrcl Engnrng; Rsrch Dvlpmnt Sld St Physics.

**WALKER, LEXINE D,** Univ Of Va, Charlottesville, VA; FR; BA; Stdnt Run Daily Paper Assoc Edtr 90-; Deans List 90-; Va St Hockey Club 90-; Eng; Law Or Jrnlsm.

**WALKER, LISA G,** Queens Coll, Charlotte, NC; SR; BA; Admsns Core 88-90; Natl Assn Accnts 87-88; Queens Clg Pres Schlrhsp 87-; Rotary Clb Columbia Schlrshp 87-; Eastover Reeritan Schlrshp 87-88; Bus Admn; Mktg Sls Advtsng.

**WALKER, LORA A,** Saint Josephs Coll, Windham, ME; SR; BS; Currier Busn Soc; Yrbook Phtgrphr 90-; Delta Epsilon Sigma; All Amer Schlr Coll Awd; Magna Cum Laude; Aerbcs Instrctr 89-; Busn Admin; Law/Cpa.

**WALKER, LYNN M,** Alice Lloyd Coll, Pippa Passes, KY; JR; Kappa Delta Epsilon.

**WALKER, MARGARET A,** Univ Of New Haven, West Haven, CT; SR; Clb Mgrs Asc Amer Treas 87-; Hl Cncl VP 88-; Htl/Rest Soc 89-90; Dns Lst; Htl/Rest Mgmt.

**WALKER, MARGARET R,** Wv Univ At Parkersburg, Parkersburg, WV; SO; Sci/Math; Engr.

**WALKER, MARJORIE V,** Univ Of Montevallo, Montevallo, AL; SO; BS; SGA Soph Sen 90-; Alpha Lambda Delta 90-; Alpha Gamma Delta VP Schlrshp 89-; Achieved Highest Hon 90; Fr Hon Schlrshp 89-; Stdnt Ed Hon Engl Class 90; Early Chldhd/Elem Edn; Teach.

**WALKER, MARK A,** Xavier Univ, Cincinnati, OH; SR; BA; Mrktng Clb 90-; Alfa Beta Gamma 89-; Dean Lst 87-; Mrktng; Law.**

**WALKER, MARK E,** S U N Y At Buffalo, Buffalo, NY; GD; DDS; Darien Lk Schlrshp 90; IM Hockey; AS Genesee Comm Coll 88; BA 90; Dntstry.

**WALKER, MELISSA L,** Ashland Comm Coll, Ashland, KY; SO; BA; Tutor Stdnt Supp Svcs 90-; Amer Qtr Hrse Assoc 90-; AA; Ed; Tchg.

**WALKER, MILLER W,** Longwood Coll, Farmville, VA; SO; BS; Intrnshp VA Power; Trained As Eng; Acctng/Mis; Accntnt/Prgmmr.

**WALKER, MINNIE ARLENE,** Owensboro Jr Coll Of Bus, Owensboro, KY; FR; AS; Std Govt Sec; Cmptr Sci; Cmptr Applctns.

**WALKER, NANCY JEANNE,** Central Fl Comm Coll, Ocala, FL; FR; AA; Nrsng; RN.

**WALKER, NATALIE A,** Middle Tn St Univ, Murfreesboro, TN; SR; BS; TV Nws Anchor 89-; Soc Brdcstng Stdnts 89-; Sigma Delta Chi 90-; TV Intrn 89-90; Brdcst Jrnlsm; TV News Reprtr Anchor.**

**WALKER, NICHOLE A,** Colby Sawyer Coll, New London, NH; JR; BA; Prgrmmng Comm 90; Rsdntl Educ Stf 90-; Intrnshp Butler Learfork Hstrcl Scty; Amer Stds; Musm Crtrshp.

**WALKER, NORALEE A,** Wellesley Coll, Wellesley, MA; SR; BA; Philharmonic Pres Asst Cndctr 87-; Chmbr Music Scty 87-; Aspen Music Fstvl; Yellow Barn Music Fstvl 88-89; Spoleto USA Music Fstvl 90; Music; Viola Performance.**

**WALKER, PAMELA J,** Ms St Univ, Miss State, MS; SR; Intr Rsdnce Hall Cncl Jdl Brd 89-90; Advrtsng Clb 88-90; Mtchmtes 88-89; Pres List Schlr; Delta Delta Delta Hstrn 88-89; Im Sftbl 89-90; BBA; Mrktng.

**WALKER, PATRICK R,** Al St Univ, Montgomery, AL; FR; Crmnl Jstce; Law.

**WALKER, RAHSAAN H,** Hampton Univ, Hampton, VA; FR; BA; Eng Dsgn Proj Tm; Univ Hon Lst; IM Bsktbl; Elec Eng; Ntl Dfnse Syst Dsgn.

**WALKER, RAYMOND S,** Central Al Comm Coll, Alexander City, AL; SO; Ftbl Miss Vly State Univ 87-88; Sociology; Law.

**WALKER, RAYMOND S,** Va Commonwealth Univ, Richmond, VA; SR; BA; WODU Radio ODU 85-86; ODU Mdl United Ntns Socty Pres/Intl Ct Of Jstc 87-88; Omicron Delta Kappa 88-89; Sigma Tau Delta 88-89; Gldn Key; Sigma Nu Lt Cmdr 86-89; Grad ODU Acad Hnrs Prog 85-89; BA Old Dominion Univ 89; Religious Stds; Univ Prfsr.

**WALKER, ROBERT D,** Va St Univ, Petersburg, VA; SR; Amer Socty Pub Admin 87-; Pub Admin Clb 87-; Pre Law Socty Pres 90-91; Trojans Rcrtmnt Univ Stdnts Clb 89-90; Natl Hnr Socty 88-; Acad Awrd Pin 89-; Undergrad Asst 87-; Systs Analyst US Army Fort Lee Smn Intrn 90; Pub Admin; Law/Pub Srvc.

**WALKER, ROLAND HAYES,** Morehouse Coll, Atlanta, GA; Hnrs Prog 89-; Biology; Med Dr.

**WALKER, RONALD,** Lexington Comm Coll, Lexington, KY; SO; BA; Blck Stdnt Union 89-; Dns Lst 89-; Blck Achvrs Mentor; KY Colonel 89; Disabled Vets Amer 84-; Marriott Htl/Resort Intern Mgr Front Ofc Trainee; John T Smith Awd 89-; Vietnam Vet Purple Hrt/Gallantry Cross/Bronze Stars 70; Htl/Rstrnt Mgmt; Bsn.

**WALKER, RONALD D,** Fayetteville St Univ, Fayetteville, NC; SR; BS; Blck Stdnt Movemnt Pres 89-90; Psychlgy Clb 89-; Alpha Kappa Mu Member; Dstngshd Mltry Grad Exec Offc 90-; Hnr Stdnt 89-; IM Ftbl/Bsktbl 89-; Fyttvll Urban Mnstry Big Bro 88; Greater Scnd Mt Olive Bptst Chrch Mbr 76; US Army; Psychlgy; Attnd Med Schl.

**WALKER, SCOTT A,** Birmingham Southern Coll, Birmingham, AL; FR; BA; Alpha Lambda Delta; Phi Eta Sigma; Alpha Tau Omega 90-; Conservancy 90-.

**WALKER, SHANNON A,** Stetson Univ, Deland, FL; FR; Alpha Xi Delta Fndrsng Chrmn 90-.

**WALKER, SHANNON N,** Wilberforce Univ, Wilberforce, OH; FR; Pre Law Clb 90-; Pltcl Sci; Law.

**WALKER, SHARON D,** Morris Brown Coll, Atlanta, GA; JR; BS; Comp Sci Clb 89-; Bio Clb 90; Golden Key; Hon Roll 88-90; Deans List 89; Comp Sci; Sys Analyst.

**WALKER, SHEILAH R,** S U N Y Coll Of Tech At Frmgdl, Farmingdale, NY; SO; AS; RA 89-; Gospel Choir 89-; Intrdorm Cncl 89-; Rsdnc Hl Cncl 89-; Alpha Beta Gamma 89-; Alpha Beta Gamma 89-; RA 90-; Grls Bsktbl Tm Scrkpr 90-; Bus Admin; Mktg/Advrtsng.

**WALKER, STEPHANIE G,** Norfolk St Univ, Norfolk, VA; SO; BA; Engl/Frgn Lang Clb 90-; Cmps Lit Mag Edtr; Chrch Assmltn Comm 90; Untd Meth Wmn 90; Janet Schaffer Cir VP 90; UMC; Engl; Educ.

**WALKER, STEPHANIE O,** Univ Of Ga, Athens, GA; SR; BSED; Bptst Stdnt Un 87-; Stdnt Cncl Excptnl Chldrn Pres 89-; Kappa Delta Epsilon 90-; Goldn Key 90-; IM Ftbl/Bsktbl/Sftbl 88-; Mntl Rtrdtn; Spec Ed Tchr.

**WALKER, STEVEN A,** Cornell Univ Statutory College, Ithaca, NY; JR; BS; Dairy Sci Clb Treas 88-; Phi Kappa Phi; Gldn Key; Alpha Zeta VP 89-; Farm Crdt Flws Intshp; Gamma Sigma Delta Awd Mrt Outstdng Schlp; Dairy Sci; Dairy Farm Mgmt/Owner.

**WALKER, TANYA D,** Central Fl Comm Coll, Ocala, FL; SO; BA; Afro Amer Stdnt Un VP; Campus Dip 90-; Vocal Ensmbl 89-; Talent Rstr Cert Achvmnt; Ollie Gary Plyrs; 3rd Rnnr Up Miss CFC Pagnt 90; 4th Rnnr Up Miss CFC Pagnt; Hmcmng Queen; Grl Sct Ldr 90; AA; Engl Educ; Law Sch.

**WALKER, TARIK D,** Morehouse Coll, Atlanta, GA; JR; BS; F Douglass Tutrl Prog 88-; Helth Career Soc 88-90; Fin Chrprsn 89-90; Mrshl M L King Jr Brthdy Parade; Lancaster Univ England; Merrill Schlr; French Clb; Golden Key; Clg Hon Prog; Hon Rl; Deans Lst; Amnesty Intl; Biology; Med/Law.**

**WALKER, TERESA M,** Muskingum Coll, New Concord, OH; FR; BA; Cntrbrd 90-; Prnts Wknd Comm 90-; Meta Phi Alpha; Lambda Sigma; Psychlgy.

**WALKER JR, THOMAS E,** Liberty Univ, Lynchburg, VA; SR; BS; Stdnt Govt Assn Sen 88-90; Debate Tm 87-; U S Sen Rep Pol Comm Leg Intrn; Pol Sci; Law.

**WALKER, THOMAS R,** Comm Coll Algny Co Algny Cmps, Pittsburgh, PA; FR; AS; Prtcptd In Grp Ldrshp Trng Actvts Tm Mmbr 89; Rcvd Awrd Outstndng Achvmnt Ldrshp 89; Natl Rpblcn Com; Comp Intrgrd Mfg Fld; Cert Center For Employment Training 81; Elec; Electro Mech Eng Tech.

**WALKER, TONJA E,** Univ Of Ga, Athens, GA; SR; Phi Kappa Phi; Georgia Wine/Spirits Schlrshp; Deans Lst; BSED; Erly Chldhd Educ; Tchr.

**WALKER, TRACI A,** Univ Of Nh Plymouth St Coll, Plymouth, NH; SR; BS; Admsns Rep 88-; Orient Ldr 89-; Mens Lacrosse Admin Asst 88-; Kappa Delta Pi VP 89-; Eta Sigma Gamma 89-; St Matthews Ch Hmels Proj 88-; Pres Schlr/Lil East Schlr Athlete Of Yr; PAT Schlrshp; Soccer 87-90; Elem Edn.

**WALKER, VICTORIA S,** Univ Of Sc At Columbia, Columbia, SC; FR; BA; NAACP 90-; AAAS 90-; Nrsng Dns Lst; Acad Excllnce Cert 90-; Nrsng.

**WALKER, WANDA A,** Va St Univ, Petersburg, VA; SR; BS; New Generation Cmps Mnstrs Pres 89-; Rsdnt Life Prog Res 89-90; Stdnt Sprt Srvcs 88-; Intrfaith Cncl 89-90; Intrnshp; Bus Admin; Financial Analyst.

**WALKER, WANDA N,** Oh Wesleyan Univ, Delaware, OH; JR; BA; Stdnt Union Blck Awrnss VP 88-89; Sis Untd P-VP 88-90; Wmns Tsk Frc 87-88; Delta Theta Sec 89-; Intrnshp Tchstn Grp Hm Inc; Deans Lst; Blk Alumni Ntwrk Schlrshp; Sclgy; Scl Wrk Admin.

**WALKER, WENDY L,** Le Moyne Coll, Syracuse, NY; SO; Yrbk Asst Editor; NAA; Acctng Scty; Big Brother Big Sister.

**WALKER JR, WILLIAM S,** Univ Of Ga, Athens, GA; JR; BS; Psych; Clinical.

**WALKER, YVONNE E,** Savannah St Coll, Savannah, GA; SO; MBA; Acctng Infor System; Bus Acct.

**WALKUP, SHERI M,** Beckley Coll, Beckley, WV; FR; BA; Educ.

**WALL, ANNE D,** Ny Univ, New York, NY; FR; AAS; Clinical Rsrch Mgmnt Dublin Ireland 84-90; Hlth Admin; Hlth Mgmnt.

**WALL, BESSIE S,** Daytona Beach Comm Coll, Daytona Beach, FL; FR; AA; Praise Assembly God 88-90; Head Nursery/Toddler; Hsptlty Mgmt.

**WALL, EILEEN M,** Univ Of Cincinnati, Cincinnati, OH; SR; BS; BS 91; Ed/Sclgy; Tchr.

**WALL, JENNIE N,** Livingston Univ, Livingston, AL; SR; Nwspr 87-88; Coll Jrnlsts 87-88; Delta Chi 87-; Trustee Schlrshp 87-88; Homer Schlrshp 87-88; Blue Key Pageant 88-89; Livingstns Loveliest 90; Bus Admin; Mktg/Advrtsng.

**WALL, JOHN D,** Longwood Coll, Farmville, VA; SR; BS; Rgby Clb 89-90; Phys Educ Mjrs Clb 89-90; Div IM Sprvsr 89-; AA Danville Comm Coll; Hlth Exrcs Sci; Phys Thrpy.

**WALL, KELLY M,** Bethany Coll, Bethany, WV; FR; BA; Cmps TV Sta Asst Prdcr 90-; Cmps Radio Sta Trng Dir; Soc Prof Jrnlsts 90-; Alpha Xi Delta; Commnctns; TV Brdcstng.

**WALL, KELLY S,** Ga St Univ, Atlanta, GA; SR; BA; Middle Chldhd Educ; Tchr.

**WALL, LINDA A,** Gallaudet Univ, Washington, DC; JR; BA; Phi Kappa Zeta 89-; Psychlgy.

**WALL, PATRICIA C,** Univ Of Sc At Columbia, Columbia, SC; JR; BA; Acctng Cl 90-; Grace Baptist Church Sec 83-; PTA Cmte 86-87; Busn Acctng.

**WALL, PATRICIA LYNN,** Univ Of Sc At Columbia, Columbia, SC; JR; BS; Stdnt Cncl Rep 90; S Car Ath Trnr Assn 90; Natl Ath Trnrs Assn 90; Phys Edn; Ath Trnr.

**WALL, RENEE V,** Central Al Comm Coll, Alexander City, AL; SR; BA; Manager Apparel Development/Atheltic Teamwear 88-; Management Business.

**WALL, SHELBY D,** Western Ky Univ, Bowling Green, KY; SR; BA; Christian Stdnt Fllwshp Ldrshp Fmly 87-; Fllwshp Christian Athletes 90-; Sigma Tau Delta Pres 87-; Phi Eta Sigma 88-; Phi Kappa Phi 89-; Summa Cum Laude; GM Communications Intrnshp Corvette Plnt; English Hnr Grad; Crss Cntry Track Tms; English/Allied Language Arts; Commnctns Publ.

**WALL, SUSAN M,** Villanova Univ, Villanova, PA; JR; BS; Omicron Delta Kappa Treas; Pi Mu Epsilon; Phi Kappa Phi; Delta Gamma Rcrdng Sec 89-; Cmps Mnstry Echrstc Mnstr; IM Flgftbl Sftbl Bsktbl 88-; Math; Tchng.

**WALL, TERESA MICHELLE,** Univ Of Sc At Columbia, Columbia, SC; SO; Science Club 89; Biology; Medicine/ Cardiology.

**WALL JR, TERRY W,** Univ Of Tn At Chattanooga, Chattanooga, TN; SR; Tau Beta Pi; BSE; Eng.

**WALLACE, AMBER A,** Fl International Univ, Miami, FL; SR; BHSA; Pblc Hlth.

**WALLACE, AMY C,** Univ Of Akron, Akron, OH; SR; BFA; Advrtsmnt Rep 88-89; Deans Lst 89-; Otstndng Clg Stdnts 88-; Fine Art Phtgrphy.

**WALLACE, ARIYAN S,** Broward Comm Coll, Ft Lauderdale, FL; SO; TS2 Tech/Sci Soc 89-90; Hnrs Inst 89-; Pre-Med; Radiology Med.

**WALLACE, BETH A,** Lexington Comm Coll, Lexington, KY; FR; AA; Creative Voices Lit Gld Treas 90-; Acctng Tech.

**WALLACE, BOBBI L,** Longwood Coll, Farmville, VA; JR; BS; Orientation Ldrs; Pol Sci/History Clb; Res Assist 90-; Alpha Lambda Delta 89-; Alpha Kappa Gamma Treas; Longwood Ambassadors Pres 89-; G Moss Schlrshp; Pol Sci/Pre Law; Law.

**WALLACE, CHRISTINA M,** Univ Of Cin R Walters Coll, Blue Ash, OH; FR; AAS; Phi Theta Kappa 90-; Nursing.

**WALLACE, CHRISTOPHER A,** Villanova Univ, Villanova, PA; JR; BS; Villanova Environmental Group 89-90; Phi Kappa Phi 90-; Phi Sigma 90-; Alpha Epsilon Delta 89-; IM Bsktbl Soccer 88-; Biology; Medicine.

**WALLACE, CRISTY A,** Brewer St Jr Coll, Fayette, AL; FR; Acctg.

**WALLACE, DARLENE D,** Daytona Beach Comm Coll, Daytona Beach, FL; FR; BA; Elem Ed; Missns/Tchng.

**WALLACE, DAWN E,** Wilmington Coll, New Castle, DE; JR; BA; Delta Epsilon Rho 90-; Nrsry Kndrgrtn Assoc 88-; Rd Ln Evnglcl Fr Chrch 88-; Tchr Crvl Acdmy Pre Kndrgrtn 88-; AS Ece 90; ECE Cert 88; Elem Ed.

**WALLACE, DI WELL,** Fl A & M Univ, Tallahassee, FL; SR; BS; Phi Theta Kappa 89-; Acdmc Excllnc Prgm 89-; AS Stdnt Yr 88-89; Prsdnts Awrd Exclln; All Armcn Schlr Coll Awrd 89-90-; AS FL Cmmnty Coll 89; AA FL Cmmnty Coll 89; Elec Eng; Eng.

**WALLACE, ELIZABETH L,** Coll Of Charleston, Charleston, SC; SO; BA; Chrlstn Pro Msc 89-; Clg Actv Brd Ptpri Comm 89-90; Phi Mu VP 89-; Engl; Tchng.

**WALLACE, GLORIA JEAN,** Roane St Comm Coll, Harriman, TN; SO; AS; Wmns Stdng Org; Bapt Stdnt Org; Gamma Beta Phi; Nrsng; RN.

**WALLACE, HATTIE L,** D Youville Coll, Buffalo, NY; SO; BNS; SWA; Nrsng; RN.

**WALLACE, HEATHER E,** Northern Ky Univ, Highland Hts, KY; SO; BA; Rep Stdnt Nwsppr 89-90; Jrnlsm; Jrnlst Rprtr.

**WALLACE, HERMAN L,** Alcorn St Univ, Lorman, MS; SO; BED; Mrchng Bnd; Cncrt Bnd; Jz Bnd; Cncrt Choir; Kappa Kappa Psi; Bpstst Chrch Ushr; IM Bsktbl/Bsbl; Music Ed; Tch/ Arrng/Cmps.

**WALLACE, JAY R,** Wv Univ, Morgantown, WV; JR; BS; Air Frce Assn 89-; Rsrv Offcrs Assn 89-90; AFROTC Trans Offcr 89-90; Chi Epsilon; Amer Lgn Mltry Excllnce Awrd 89; Amer Lgn Schlstc Exclnce Awrd 90; Airlft Assn Schlrshp Awrd 90; IM Flg Ftbl 89-90; Cvl Eng; Eng Cnsltnt.

**WALLACE, JEFFREY R,** Schenectady County Comm Coll, Schenectady, NY; FR; Dsny Wrld Intrnshp; Clntry Arts; Chef.

**WALLACE, JENNIFER A,** Univ Of Ky, Lexington, KY; FR; BS; Res Hall Gov VP 90-; Stu Recrtmnt 90-; Biology; Med Research.

**WALLACE, JESSE L,** Ashland Comm Coll, Ashland, KY; FR; Sci; Physcl Thrpy.

**WALLACE II, JOSEPH B,** Univ Of Sc At Columbia, Columbia, SC; SR; MBA; Res Hl Asc Treas 90-; Ame Mktg Asc 90-; Xerox Bsn Smnr Part; LEAD Conf Part 90; BS; Mgmt; Mktg/Pltcs.

**WALLACE, JOY L,** Cumberland Coll, Williamsburg, KY; JR; BME; Bapt Stdnt Union Sec 90-; Chorale Sec 90-; Music Stdnt Cncl 89-; Mu Phi Epsilon V P 90-; Outstndng Vocalist 89/91; All Clgte Choir 90; All Clgte Bnd 90; NATS 89; Music/Vocal/Instr; Educ.

**WALLACE, KAREN M,** Merrimack Coll, North Andover, MA; FR; BA; Sigma Phi Omega; Big Bro/Big Sistr Prog Undrprvldgd Chldrn; Engl/Scndry Educ; Hgh Schl Engl Tchr.

**WALLACE, MARCIA L,** Miami Dade Comm Coll South, Miami, FL; SO; AA; Phi Theta Kappa; Hstry CAD; Intr Dsgn.

**WALLACE, MARK A,** Columbia Greene Comm Coll, Hudson, NY; FR; BA; Phi Theta Kappa 90-; Crs Cntry Rng 90-; Prof Wldr/Stl Fbrctr 86-89; Acctg; Bus.

**WALLACE, MARTY A,** Univ Of Al At Huntsville, Huntsville, AL; SO; BS; Eng.

**WALLACE, MERITA J,** Miami Jacobs Jr Coll Of Bus, Dayton, OH; SO; Stdnt Advsry Comm; Otstndn Gstdnt Awrd; Bus; Trvl Agncy.

**WALLACE, MICHAEL A,** Old Dominion Univ, Norfolk, VA; SR; BS; Tau Beta Phi 90; IEEE 90-; Coop Educ Newprt 89-; Nws Shpbldng; U S Nav Res 89-; BS U S Navl Acad 80; Elec Eng.

**WALLACE, MICHELLE R,** Johnson C Smith Univ, Charlotte, NC; SO; BS; Stdsnt Chrstn Assoc Ms Stdnt Chrstn Assoc 90-; Choir; Natl Assoc Blk Accntnts; Acctng; CPA.**

**WALLACE, MONICA A,** Univ Of South Al, Mobile, AL; SR; BS; Coop Educ Prog 88-; Alpha Chi 90-; Beta Gamma Sigma 90-; Phi Chi Theta Corresponding Secy 90-; Presidents Lst 89-; Parallel Coop Student Of Yr 90-; Bus Mngmnt.

**WALLACE, OBDULIA E,** Univ Of The Dist Of Columbia, Washington, DC; FR; Spanish Math; RN.

**WALLACE, PATRICIA M,** Adelphi Univ, Garden City, NY; SR; BA; Pi Mu Epsilon; Math; Actrl.

**WALLACE, PAULA J,** Univ Of Al At Birmingham, Birmingham, AL; SR; CERT; SOTA 90-; AOTA 90-; ALOTA 90-; Pres Hon 90-; Florence Clnc Intrn; Medcl Cntr Intrn; Occptnl Thrpy Asst; BS Sclgy/Hlth Educ.

**WALLACE, REBECCA L,** Radford Univ, Radford, VA; SO; BBA; Acctg.

**WALLACE, REBEKAH L,** Fayetteville St Univ, Fayetteville, NC; SR; MS; Soclgy Clb Sec 89-90; Pembrk St Univ Blck Stdnt Org 87-88; FTCC Crim Just Clb; Alpha Kappa Delta; Alpha Kappa Alpha; Natl Forum On Publ Serv; BA 90; Soclgy; Socl Wrk.

**WALLACE, RICHARD H,** Springfield Tech Comm Coll, Springfield, MA; SR; AS; Electrnc Technlgy; BS.

**WALLACE III, RICHARD J,** Winthrop Coll, Rock Hill, SC; FR; Alpha Lambda Delta 90-; Sigma Alpha Epsilon E Rcrdr 90-; Var Tns; Poli Sci Hst; Law.

**WALLACE, SEAN A,** Spartanburg Methodist Coll, Spartanburg, SC; FR; BA; SMC Crmnl Just Clb; NAACP 90-; Wyatts Chpl Bapt Chrch Trst; Alpha Psi Beta; Spartanburg Meth Coll Deans Lst 90-; Sen Strom Thurmond Yth Law Awd 89; Crmnl Just; Law Enfrcmnt.

**WALLACE, STACY E,** Northern Ky Univ, Highland Hts, KY; SR; BA; NMTA 89-; Ky Inst European Stud 88; Phi Alpha Theta 90-; Dns Lst 90-; U S Army Rsrvs 86-; Army Commndtn Mdl 90; Msc Schlrshp 86-; Vrsty Crs Cntry 86-87; Cert Kathleen Wellman Mdlng Schl 89; Cert Basic Comm NBC 89; Music.

**WALLACE, STEVEN G,** Univ Of Ky, Lexington, KY; FR; Phi Eta Sigma; Alpha Lambda Delta; Deans Lst 90.

**WALLACE, STEVEN M,** Volunteer St Comm Coll, Gallatin, TN; FR; Amb Serv EMT 85-; EMT IV Dickson Vo-Tech 85; Paramedic; Emergency Care.

**WALLACE, SUSAN E,** Oh Univ-Southern Cmps, Ironton, OH; JR; BED; Trumbo Fam Schlrshp 90; Clifford E & Jean Peters Allen Schlrshp 90; Elem Edctn; Tchr.

**WALLACE, TAMARA L,** Clark Atlanta Univ, Atlanta, GA; SO; NAACP 90-; Ohio Clb Miss OH 90-; Gnrl Mtrs Schlrshp 90-.

**WALLACE, TAWANDA L,** Nc Agri & Tech St Univ, Greensboro, NC; JR; BS; Peer Advsr Prog 89-; Aggie Ambsdrs 90-; Pan Helenic Cncl Sec 90-; Alpha Kappa Alpha Fndrsng Chr 90-; NASA Schlr 89-; Duke Power Intrnshp 88-; Dns Lst 88-; Elec Engr.

**WALLACE, TERESA D,** Univ Of South Al, Mobile, AL; FR; BA; Educ.

**WALLACE, VANESSA L,** Averett Coll, Danville, VA; SR; BA; Sigma Lambda Epsilon; JR Hi Tchr Aide 90; High Schl Tchr Assist 90; AS Danville Cmnty Clg 89; Engl; Pblc Rltns/Advrtsg/ Tch.

**WALLACE, VERNA RENEE,** Central Al Comm Coll, Alexander City, AL; FR; BA; Computer Science; Business.

**WALLACE, VICTORIA EMMA A,** Hillsborough Comm Coll, Tampa, FL; SO; ASN; Phi Theta Kappa; Mt AME Church Yth Assoc Sec; Medl Assist Invty Clerk Phlebotomist 87-90; GED Adult Ed Ctr Richmond VA 86; Certif MBC Medl Ed Ctr FL 88; Nursing RN.

**WALLACE, WENDY L,** Christian Brothers Univ, Memphis, TN; JR; BA; WAMS Hstrn 89-; Nwspr; Yrbk Stf; Phi Theta Kappa; SCJ Sec; Sigma Alpha Epsilon Aux; Fed Exprs Pblc Intern; Comm Arts; Jrnlsm.

**WALLACE, WENDY Q,** Norfolk St Univ, Norfolk, VA; SO; BA; Spartan Alpha Tau 90-; Soclgy; Crmnl Jstc.

**WALLENFELSZ, JACQULYN I,** Kent St Univ Kent Cmps, Kent, OH; SR; BA; Empld Rbnsn Mmrl Hsptl Rvna Oh; Pre-Med/Psych/Soc; Hmn Srvcs.

**WALLER, ALLISON S,** Univ Of Sc At Columbia, Columbia, SC; JR; AD; Stu Nrs Assoc; Gamma Beta Phi; HCA Aiken Rgnl Med Cntrs; Diploma LPN 86; Nrsg.

**WALLER, DAWN P,** Univ Of South Al, Mobile, AL; SR; BS; Kappa Delta Phi; Alpha Chi 90-; Phi Eta Sigma 87-; Elem Ed; Prim Schl Trchr.

**WALLER, DEBORAH A,** Univ Of Sc At Columbia, Columbia, SC; JR; BA; Jrnlsm; Advrtsng Pblc Rel.

**WALLER, DENISE M,** Middle Tn St Univ, Murfreesboro, TN; SR; BS; Tau Omicron Hstrn 89-; Psi Chi 87-; Psych; Clncl Psych.

**WALLER, LISA M,** Auburn Univ At Auburn, Auburn, AL; JR; BSN; AF ROTC Capt; Auburn Univ Assoc Of Nrsng Stdnts; Arnold Air Soc Co-Comptrlr; Phi Eta Sigma; Alpha Lambda Delta; Arnold Air Soc 2nd Lt; Rep For Auburn Field Flwshp; IM Sftbl/Vlybl; Nursing; Air Force.

**WALLER, PAULA A,** Salisbury St Univ, Salisbury, MD; GD; MSW; Gospel Chr Pub Chrmn Pres 87-90; Dns Lst 89-; Kapa Alpha Psi Swthrt 87-; Church Chr 87-; Confirmation; IMS 87; BA SW; Social Wrk.**

**WALLER, TERESA F,** Radford Univ, Radford, VA; SR; BS; AAS Wythevl Comm Coll 89; Elem Ed; Tchr.

**WALLEY, ANGELA L,** Univ Of Southern Ms, Hattiesburg, MS; JR; Lamma Beta Phi; AA Jones Cnty Jr Coll 90; Acctng/Bus; Acctnt.

**WALLEY, BEVERLY M,** Univ Of Southern Ms, Hattiesburg, MS; SR; BA; Clg Bsn Admin Award 90; Bsn Admin.

**WALLEY, GLEASON E,** Cornell Univ Statutory College, Ithaca, NY; JR; BA; CUDS Rptr; Natl Jnr Clg Hnr Soc 89-90; Farm Crdt Flws; Dairy Sci Flws; Intshp; AAS SUNY Mrrsvl 90; Dairy Sci; Agri.

**WALLIN, CONSTANCE M,** Miami Dade Comm Coll, Miami, FL; SO; BA; Dns Lst; Otstndng Acad Achvmnt Awrd; William L Mc Knight Schlrshp 90; Hnrs Day Opn Coll Spcl Prog Rcpnt; AIB Gen Bkg Dipl 90; Rl Est Slsmn FREC DPR 89; Emplyd Bnk 88; FM Patricia Stevens Career Coll 86; Bus Admin; Bus Mgmt.

**WALLING, LEWIS G,** Univ Of Tn At Martin, Martin, TN; JR; BA; Unvrsty Sngrs Co VP 89-; New Pacer Singers Treas 89-90; Choral Soc 89-90; Piano Ensemble 90-; Phi Eta Sigma; Phi Mu Alpha Sec 89-; Harry Neal Mmrl Awd; Music Edctn; Msc Mnstry.

**WALLING, THOMAS K,** Middle Tn St Univ, Murfreesboro, TN; SR; BBA; Hon Rl Deans Lst; Prt-Tm Wrkr UPS; AS Vol St Comm Coll 88; Fin; Crprt Fin.

**WALLINGSFORD, SANDRA L,** Auburn Univ At Auburn, Auburn, AL; GD; MED; Natl Council Tchrs Math 90-; Phi Kappa Phi 90-; BS; Math Secondary Ed; H Schl Tchr.

**WALLIS, CHRISTOPHER P,** Liberty Univ, Lynchburg, VA; SO; BA; Stdnts Crtn Sci VP 89-90; Alpha Lambda Delta 90-; Hons Pgm 90-; Engl; Tchng/Wrtng.

**WALLIS, DELIA J,** Gallaudet Univ, Washington, DC; GD; PSY S; Schl Psych Advsry Bd Grad Rep 89-90; Stdnt Advsry Bd To Pres Grad Rep 89-90; Dean Of Stdnt Affairs Advsry Bd Grad Rep 89; MA 89; BA Mc Gill Univ 86; Pres Schlr 88-; Intl Stdnt Schlrshp 89-; Grad Tuition Schlrshp 86; Beatty Awd 86; Schl Psychology.

**WALLIS, DENISE D,** Univ Of Miami, Coral Gables, FL; SR; BS; AED Sec 90-; Biol Clb Sec 89-90; Latin Amer Stdnt Assoc Pres 89-90; Hons Stdnt Assoc 89-; Phi Theta Kappa 87-88; Vol Univ Miami Med Ctr 89-90; San Marco Cath Chrch Yth Coord 87-88; Dns Lst 87-88; Res Univ Miami Med Ctr; Biol/Microbiol; Med Sch/Physcn.

**WALLMARKER, CHRISTER P,** Univ Of Tn At Chattanooga, Chattanooga, TN; SR; Tau Beta Pi 88-; Golden Key 88-; Pi Mu Epsilon; NCEA; IEEE 87-; NSPE 87-; Sigma Chi Schlrshp Chrm 88-; IM Tnns/Rqtbl 88-89; BSEE; Elect Eng; Instmnt/Cntrls.

**WALLNER, BETTY J,** Western New England Coll, Springfield, MA; JR; BS; Soc Sci Clb; Stageless Players Clb Dir; Review Of Art/Lit; Psych; Mngmnt.

**WALLRATH, HEATHER B,** Oh Univ, Athens, OH; JR; BA; Hlth Careers Clb 89-; Univ Prog Cncl 90-; Natl Art Thrpy Org 90-; Pi Gamma Mu 90-; Psychology/Art; Art Thrpy/MS.

**WALLS, CALVIN H,** Ms St Univ, Miss State, MS; GD; Gamma Beta Phi; Deans Lst; Kappa Alpha Order; Mo Army Natl Grd; Bba Univ Of Mo 88; Sociology; Law.

**WALLS, CARLA D,** Alcorn St Univ, Lorman, MS; JR; BA; RIF Ldr 90-; Spcl Educ.

**WALLS, CAROLYN E,** Marshall University, Huntington, WV; GD; MA; BA 85; Educ; Preschl Handcpd Tchr.

**WALLS, DEBORAH M,** Univ Of North Fl, Jacksonville, FL; SR; MBA; FL Stdnt Ldrs Assc Tchr Ed FSLATE; NEA; Gldn Key; Phi Kappa Phi; Summa Cum Laude; Putnam Cnty Schrshp; Deans List; AA St Johns River Cmmnty Clg 89; BAE UNF; Reading Ed; Ed.**

**WALLS, GINGER E,** Wallace St Comm Coll At Dothan, Dothan, AL; FR; ADN; WANS 90-; Calender Girl; Nursing.

**WALLS, GREGORY A,** Ny Univ, New York, NY; FR; BA; Deans Lst 90-; Pltcl Sci/English; Law.

**WALLS, JAMES A,** Middle Tn St Univ, Murfreesboro, TN; SR; BBA; Beta Alpha Psi Pres 90-; VITA; Acctg; Publ Acctg.

**WALLS, JOAN A,** Central Fl Comm Coll, Ocala, FL; FR; AA; Drg Mnstry 87-; Dist Mgr Ocala Star Banner 90-; Elem Educ.

**WALLS, JONATHAN A,** Univ Of Southern Ms, Hattiesburg, MS; SR; BSMET; Eagle Connctn 90-; SME Vice Chrmn 87-; Amer Weldng Scty; AAS Itawamba Comm Cllg 89; Mech Engnrng Tech; Inspctn.

**WALLS, KATHERINE A,** Middle Tn St Univ, Murfreesboro, TN; FR; Nrsng.

**WALLS, LINDA D,** Cumberland Univ, Lebanon, TN; SO; BA; Hstry/Scl Sci; Law.**

**WALLS, MARION A,** Valdosta St Coll, Valdosta, GA; JR; BA; Msc; Tchr.

**WALLS, NICOLE A,** George Mason Univ, Fairfax, VA; FR; BS; Dnce Tm 90-; Hlth Educ Comm Hlth; Clncl Nutrnst.

**WALLS, PAULA J,** North Ga Coll, Dahlonega, GA; JR; BS; Phi Eta Sigma 89; Phi Kappa Phi; Pres List Hnr Roll 89-; Siler Awd; Erly Chldhd Edn; Teach.**

**WALLS, SALA K,** Ms St Univ, Miss State, MS; FR; Natl Soc Blck Engrs; Phi Eta Sigma; Gamma Beta Phi; Comp Eng.

**WALLS, STEVEN J,** Memphis St Univ, Memphis, TN; SO; BA; Cmps Crsd 89-90; Eng; Jrnlsm.

**WALLS, TARA L,** Pa St Univ Main Cmps, University Pk, PA; SO; BA; Ogontz Thtre Co VP 90; Cmmnctns.**

**WALLS, TRACEY N,** Cheyney Univ Of Pa, Cheyney, PA; JR; BED; Ed Clb VP; Hsptlty Commtt 90-; Stdnt Govt; Frshmn Orttn Ldr 90-; Acdmc Hnr Deans Lst; Erly Chldhd.

**WALLS, TRISAH V,** Alcorn St Univ, Lorman, MS; JR; Mrchng Bnd 88-; Tau Beta Sigma Srg Arms 90-; RIF Prog; Soc Sci Educ; Cnslng.

**WALMSLEY JR, JAMES D,** Middle Tn St Univ, Murfreesboro, TN; JR; BA; Im 88-91; Deans Lst 90-; Aa Hiwassee Coll 90; Blgy; Dntstry.

**WALMSLEY, TIMOTHY R,** Allegheny Coll, Meadville, PA; SR; BS; Allegheny Pre-Legal 89-; Tutor 88-; Alden Schlr 89-90; Phi Delta Theta 87-; Stdnt Orient Advsr 89-90; Varsity Soccer 87-89; Envrnmntl Studies; Law.

**WALORZ, ERIK T,** Newbury Coll, Brookline, MA; SO; ASSOC; Phi Theta Kappa; Cert Natl Rstrnt Assn 90; Cert Amer Hotel/ Motel Assn 90; Culnry Arts; Pastry Chef.**

**WALP, PRISCILLA M,** Elmira Coll, Elmira, NY; JR; BA; Othpdc Nrs Cert; Natl Assn Orthpdc Nrs; Asst Nrsng Mngr; RN; Nrsng.

**WALROND-CATO, SELMA M,** Bloomfield Coll, Bloomfield, NJ; GD; MSW; AAS Union Cnty Clge 87; BA 90; Social Work.

**WALSH, AMY B,** Rensselaer Polytechnic Inst, Troy, NY; FR; BS; Stdnt Govt VP 90-; Pre Med Scty 90-; Physcn.

**WALSH, AMY L,** Garrett Comm Coll, Mchenry, MD; SO; AA; Fine Prfrmng Arts.

**WALSH, BARBARA L,** Chesterfield Marlboro Coll, Cheraw, SC; SO; BED; Phi Theta Kappa Pres; AA; Engl; Educ.

**WALSH, BEVERLY J P,** Georgian Court Coll, Lakewood, NJ; SR; MBA; Coun Excptnl Chldrn 89-; Dns Lst 88-; Spec Educ Tchr 90-; BA 90; Spec Educ.

**WALSH, BRIAN D,** Kent St Univ Stark Cmps, North Canton, OH; SO; BS; Malone Players 87-; Campus Radio 89-90; Bill Denton Outrch Ctr Boxing; Psych; Cnslg/Tchg.

**WALSH, CHRISTINE A,** Indiana Univ Of Pa, Indiana, PA; SR; BED; Pi Gamma Mu 90-; Theta Phi Alpha Schlrshp Chrmn 89-; Sccr 89; Hstry; Scndry Educ.

**WALSH, COLLEEN M,** S U N Y Coll At Fredonia, Fredonia, NY; SR; BS; Bsn Clb VP Intrnl Affrs 89-90; Class Secy 88-89; AM Mrktng Assc; Delta Mu Delta Secy 89-; Wall Str Jrnl Awrd; Deha Mu Delta Secy 90-; Fanny A Hayward Mercy Hosp Admin Intrn 90; Bsn Hlth Admin; Hlth Care Admins.

**WALSH, CYNTHIA ANN,** George Mason Univ, Fairfax, VA; SR; Std Educ Asc 88-; Kappa Delta Pi 88-; Gldn Key 88-; Alpha Chi; Air Frght Agt 72-91; BS; Middle Educ; Tchr.**

**WALSH, DANIEL J,** Kent St Univ Kent Cmps, Kent, OH; SO; Accntng; CPA.

**WALSH, DEBORAH P,** Lenoir Rhyne Coll, Hickory, NC; JR; DBL; Tchr.

**WALSH II, DONALD E,** Youngstown St Univ, Youngstown, OH; JR; BE; Bicycle Mech/Slsprsn 84-; Elec Engr.

**WALSH, HEATHER M,** Marywood Coll, Scranton, PA; FR; BS; Clncl Psy.

**WALSH, JASON M,** Saint Francis Coll, Loretto, PA; SO; BA; Deans List 90-; Var Ftbl 89-90; Pol Scnc; Law.

**WALSH, JENNIFER K,** Univ Of Scranton, Scranton, PA; FR; BA; Stdnt Govt; Drm Pres 90-; Cmmnctns Clb; Yrbk; Cmps Mnstry Lctr; Crcle K; Hnd In Hnd; Spcl Jst Lbrl Arts Prog 90-; Dns Lst 90-; Cmmnctns; Advrtsng.

**WALSH, JUSTIN M,** Saint Francis Coll, Loretto, PA; FR; BA; Prsdntl Schlrshp Awd 90-; Deans Lst 90-; Ftbl 90-; Pltcl Sci; Law.

**WALSH, KATHLEEN M,** Middle Tn St Univ, Murfreesboro, TN; SR; BS; Psi Chi 87-88; Delta Gamma Sec Pldg Cls 87; Exprmntl Rsrch 87-90; Ind Psychlgst.

**WALSH, KELLEY L,** Catholic Univ Of America, Washington, DC; SR; BA; IM 87-; Pi Gamma Mu 90-; Deans Lst 90-; IM Water Polo Bsktbl Sftbl; Elem Ed; Elem Schl Tchr.

**WALSH, KELLY M,** Georgian Court Coll, Lakewood, NJ; JR; BA; Cncl Excp Chldrn 89-; Yrbk Stff 90-; NJ Educ Assc; Natl Mercy 90-; Spec Educ; Tchr.

**WALSH, KERRY A,** Providence Coll, Providence, RI; JR; BS; Mktg Clb 88-; Deans Lst; Comm Studies 90-; Mktg; Pblshng.**

**WALSH, KIMBERLY A,** Univ Of Southern Ms, Hattiesburg, MS; SO; Unn Brd Sec 90-; Nwsppr Stff 89-; Sigma Delta Chi; Jrnlsm; Jrnlst.

**WALSH, MARY C,** Bloomfield Coll, Bloomfield, NJ; FR; BS; Sec Work; Nrsng/Rsrch; Rsrch Pediatric Oncology.

**WALSH, MONICA E,** Coll Misericordia, Dallas, PA; SR; Cncl Excptnl Chldrn 88-; Cmps Mnstry 90-; Mdrgl Sngrs 87-; Hbt Hmnty 90; Wyoming Vly Santa 90; Stdnt Tchng Intrnshp; Oratorio Soc Wyoming Vly 88-89; Prsh Sngrs Cltrl Evnts 86-; Apld Msc; Mntsri Crtfctn.

**WALSH, PETER J,** Old Dominion Univ, Norfolk, VA; SO; BS; WTKR Ch 3 Weather Club 90-; Adcmc Hnrs Assn Od ODU; Mech Engrng.

**WALSH, ROSEMARY P,** Newbury Coll, Brookline, MA; FR; BA; Mngd Dpt Law Firm; Rtrnd Schl Aftr Layoff Ordr Sccsd Bsns Fld; Cmptr Sci; Opn.

**WALSH, SALLY J,** Newbury Coll, Brookline, MA; FR; Med Asst; Microbio/Pthlgy.

**WALSH, SUSAN E,** Atlantic Comm Coll, Mays Landing, NJ; FR; AAS; Secretary In Tropworld Casino; Nursing; Reg Nurse.

**WALSH, SUZANNE E,** Hudson Valley Comm Coll, Troy, NY; SR; BS; Intl Students Club 90-; Albany Acad Reunion Commt 90-; Hmn Serv Club Pres 90-; St Anne Inst Intern; Unity House Fmly Crisis Intern; Phi Theta Kappa Commty Serv Awd; State Univ NY Clg Techlgy; Social Wrk; Social Wk/Fmly Law.

**WALSH, THERESA M,** Central Fl Comm Coll, Ocala, FL; FR; MS; Phi Theta Kappa; Amer Lgn Aux 88-; Acctg; Acct.

**WALSH, WILLIAM P,** Glassboro St Coll, Glassboro, NJ; SO; BA; Hnrs Pgm 89-; Dns Lst 89-90; Cmnctns/Jrnlsm Spclztn; Prnt Media.

**WALSH-LAUDATI, MARIA S,** Univ Of Nc At Greensboro, Greensboro, NC; FR; BFA; Dance.

**WALSH-LEIBENGUTH, SARAH JANE,** Merrimack Coll, North Andover, MA; FR; MBA; Psychlgy Clb; Cmps Mnstry; Psychlgy; Psychlgst.

**WALSH-RENE, KATHLEEN L,** Coll Of Health Sci Stony Brook, Stony Brook, NY; GD; Alpha Omega Alpha 90-; Lambda Beta 86-; MD; BS; Itrnl Med.

**WALSHAW, BETH B,** Temple Univ, Philadelphia, PA; JR; BS; Stdnt Cnsl Rep 90-; Acad Stdnts Of Phrmcy 89-; Natl Assn Retail Drgsts 89-; Rho Chi VP 90-; AIDS Awareness Prog 90-; Stdnt Comm Drug Abuse Educ 89-; Clerk 3rd Party Dept 83-; Sprvsr/ Phmrcy Intrn; Retail Phrmcst.

**WALSIFER, DEBORAH L,** Bloomfield Coll, Bloomfield, NJ; SO; BS; Blvl Hs Msc Prnts Asc; Schering-Plough 90-; Bsn Admn/ Cmptr Info Sys; Bsn.

**WALTER BUCHKO, MARGARET ROSE,** Comm Coll Algny Co Algny Cmps, Pittsburgh, PA; JR; AS; Art Mag Asst Edtr 87-; Prtng 86-; AS Art Inst Pittsburgh 84; Bus Mgmt.

**WALTER, DANIEL J,** S U N Y Coll Of Tech At Alfred, Alfred, NY; FR; AOS; Rsdnce Hall Stdnt Staff Door Guard 90; Peer Tu 90; Auto Bdy Rpr; Ownr Of Own Bdy Shp.

**WALTER, DONALD J,** Univ Of Nc At Greensboro, Greensboro, NC; FR; BMED; NC Tchng Flws Prog 90-; Clgt Msc Edctrs Natl Cnfrnc 90-; St Marys Epscpl/Anglcn Ctr 90-; Phi Mu Alpha Sinfonia; Best Prbtnry Mbr Phi Mu Alpha; Instrmntl Msc Ed; Tchng Sr High Msc.

**WALTER, JAMES W,** Univ Of Miami, Coral Gables, FL; SR; Earth Alert 89-90; Deans Lst 87-90; Pi Kappa Alpha 86-90; Sub Tchr SAU 90; IMS 86-90; BA 90; Hist; Law.**

**WALTER, JANICE M,** Daemen Coll, Amherst, NY; SO; BS; Amer Dntl Hygnst Assn 84-90; St Joseph R C Chrch Prsh Cncl 89-; Dntl Hygnst 87-; AAS Erie CC 86; Physcl Thrpy; Pdtrc Physcl Thrpy.

**WALTER, JEFFREY J,** S U N Y Coll Of Tech At Alfred, Alfred, NY; SO; AS; Almn Assoc Brd Pres 89-; Outstndng Stdnt 90-; IM Rfr 89-; Frstry/Rsrc Mgmt; BS MS PHD.

**WALTER, KRISTINA M,** Coll Of Charleston, Charleston, SC; FR; BS; Hmcmng Queen Cand; Cougarettes Dnc Tm Sec 90-; Bus; Acctg.

**WALTER, PATRICIA DAWN,** Notre Dame Coll, Cleveland, OH; FR; BA; Commuter Bd V P 90-; NAA 90-; Acctng Assn Treas; Lambda Sigma V P; Acctng; CPA.

**WALTER, RICHARD D,** Central Fl Comm Coll, Ocala, FL; SO; AA; Phi Theta Kappa 89; Self Emplyd 90-; History; Law.

**WALTER, SHARON M,** Univ Of Cincinnati, Cincinnati, OH; JR; BA; NAEYC 90-; Gldn Key; R H Yngbld Schlp 90-; C/M Hntr Schlp 90-; Erly Chldhd Educ.

**WALTER, SUSAN J,** Mount Aloysius Jr Coll, Cresson, PA; SO; BA; Phi Theta Kappa 90-; St Pauls Chrch; Nrs 87-; Lgl Stds; Law.

**WALTER-SHAFER, MARY,** Belmont Coll, Nashville, TN; SR; BA; Amer Mktg Assn Pres; Lgsltv Cncl Rep; Pinnacle 90-; Gamma Beta Phi 90-; Jr Achvmnt Tchr; Tenn Recycling Coalition; Mktg; Non Profit Indstry.

**WALTERS JONES, JENNIFER V,** Spalding Univ, Louisville, KY; JR; BS; Ntl Ed Assn; AS Jefferson Comm Coll 89; Elem Ed K-4; Tch.

**WALTERS, AIMEY M,** Univ Of Tn At Martin, Martin, TN; SO; BA; Pre-Law Clb 90-; Zeta Tau Alpha VP 90-; Bsn; Law.

**WALTERS, ANNE M,** Saint Vincents Coll & Seminary, Latrobe, PA; JR; BA; Hstry Clb Sec 90-; In Tch Scl Awrns Clb Sec 89-; Cvl Wr Rndtbl Sec 90-; Phi Alpha Theta VP 90-; Adlt Ltrcy Trng Pgm 89-; Stdnt Asst St Vincent Pltcl Sci Dept 90-; Tchncl Asst Lib Carnegie Msm Ntrl Hstry 90; Hstry; Govt.

**WALTERS, CAROL L,** Georgian Court Coll, Lakewood, NJ; SR; All Amer 90-; Plyr Yr; Bsktbl Capt; Sftbl; BS; Bus; Mgmt.

**WALTERS, CHRISTIE L,** Indiana Univ Of Pa, Indiana, PA; SO; Delta Zeta Asst Rsh Chrmn; Elem Educ; Tchr.

**WALTERS, CHRISTINE M,** Cornell Univ Statutory College, Ithaca, NY; SO; BS; Orntn Strng Com Asst Trng Chr 90-; Mrchng Bnd Sec 89-; Ag Ambssdr 90-; Chi Omega Asst Hmne Rltns 90-; Intrnshp Nrrstwn Area Schl Dist 90-; Bus Admin; Hosp Admin.

**WALTERS, CHRISTINE M,** Wv Northern Comm Coll, Wheeling, WV; SR; Pres Lst; Dns Lst; AAS WV Nrthrn Comm Clg; Rsprty Thrpy.

**WALTERS, ELIZABETH J,** Univ Of Sc At Columbia, Columbia, SC; SR; BA; Coll Republicans 87-89; Phi Eta Sigma 88; Mothers Before Marriage Fndr 86-; Personal Growth Grp Ldr 89-; AA Midlands Tech Coll 90; Psychlgy; Cnslr Adolescents.

**WALTERS, HAMILTON S,** Ms St Univ, Miss State, MS; SR; BA; Blck Friars Wrkshp 201; Kappa Alpha; Phi Alpha Theta; Kappa Alpha; Hstry; Law Enfrcmnt.

**WALTERS, JANIE B,** Duquesne Univ, Pittsburgh, PA; FR; Phi Eta Sigma 90-; Lambda Sigma Treas; Vol Pgm; Arbcs Pgm/IM Ftbl 90-; Pharm.

**WALTERS, JENNIFER A,** Le Moyne Coll, Syracuse, NY; FR; BS; Blgy Clb 90-; Biology.

**WALTERS, JENNIFER L,** Indiana Univ Of Pa, Indiana, PA; JR; BED; WIUP Tv Tlthn Prdcr 90; WIUP Fm Nws Anchr 90; Alpha Epsilon Rho Co Chrprsn 88-; Intrnshp Wosd Tv Prod Asst; Fld Hcky 3 Yr Var Ltr 88-; Cmnctns Media; TV Prod.

**WALTERS, JOSEPH A,** International Bible Coll, Florence, AL; SO; BA; Missn Clb Tr 90; Missn Clb VP; Bible; Missnry.

**WALTERS, JUDY K,** Wv Univ At Parkersburg, Parkersburg, WV; SO; AD; Stdnt Nrs Assn Treas 90-; Nrsng.

**WALTERS, KATHRYN A,** Oh Univ-Southern Cmps, Ironton, OH; JR; AA; Gamma Pi Delta 89-; Clfford E Jn Ptrs Allen Schlrshp 90-; S Freewll Bapt Chrch Lad Aux Sec Nwsrprtr 85-; L Fed Sav/Loan Assn Teller 74-80; Sci; Cmptr Prgrmg.

**WALTERS, LAWRENCE A,** Oh St Univ At Newark, Newark, OH; FR; Voice Of Impared Stdnts 90-; Brd Dir Vietnam Vets Amer Chptr 55 87-90; Elem Tchr.

**WALTERS, LISA A,** Memphis St Univ, Memphis, TN; SR; BSN; Assoc Pediatric Oncology Nurses 90; #rn St Jos Hosp Sch Nurs 87; Nurs.

**WALTERS, MARILYN A,** Queens Coll, Charlotte, NC; SR; BA; New Dimensions Pres 90-; Phi Alpha Theta Pres 90-; Delta Gamma; New Dimensions Flwshp 88-; NC Cncl Social Studies Schlrshp; Mary Morrow Schlrshp 90-; Amer Inst Architects Aux; Sardis Presby Yth Advsr; History Educ; Sec Social Studies Educ.

**WALTERS, PAMELA D,** Univ Of Ga, Athens, GA; SR; BSCFS; Home Ec/Jrnlsm Clb 89-; Cmmnvrsty Big Sis 88-89; Yrbk Edtr 88-90; Gldn Key 90-; Alpha Omcrn Pi Sec 88-; Grace Hartley Schlp 90; Outstdng Clg Std Amer 88-; St Btncl Grdn Intrn 90-; Jrnlsm/Pblc Rltns.

**WALTERS, PAULA A,** Oh Univ-Southern Cmps, Ironton, OH; SR; Natl Dntl Hygnst Assc 84-86; Deans List 87-; Acad Tm Coach; PTA 90-; Rgstrd Dntl Hygnst 85-87; AAS Shawnee Ste Comm Clg 85.

**WALTERS, SCOT A,** Univ Of Ky, Lexington, KY; JR; BA; Amer Inst Arch Stdnts 89-; Stdnt Cncl 89-; Tau Sigma Delta; Arch.

**WALTERS, SHELIA A,** Radford Univ, Radford, VA; SR; BBA; Deans Lst 90; AAS Wythevl Comm Coll 89; Fin.**

**WALTERS, SUSAN R,** George Mason Univ, Fairfax, VA; SR; BS; Beta Gamma Sigma; Cmptr Sys Cnslnt 82-; Mgmt Info Sys; Sys Anlyst/Cnslnt.

**WALTERS, TAMMY L,** Livingston Univ, Livingston, AL; SO; BA; Lvngstn Hstrcl Soc 90-; IM Sftbl Tm 89-; Elem Ed.**

**WALTERS, TAMMY R,** Clemson Univ, Clemson, SC; SO; BSN; Stdnt Nrss Assn 90-; Coll Of Nrsng Stdnt Lsn Cncl Fr Rep 90-; Rsdnt Hll Cncl Bnt 90; Nrsng.

**WALTERS, THOMAS M,** Univ Of Al At Birmingham, Birmingham, AL; SR; BS; Amer Assoc Nrs Anesth 90-; Natl Guard Assoc 90-; Med Intensive Care Unit RN 88-90; BS Univ S MS 88; Nrs Anesth.

**WALTERS, WILLIAM W,** Meridian Comm Coll, Meridian, MS; JR; BA; Tennis Tm 88-90; Bus Admin; Mgmt.

**WALTHOUR, LA TONYA A,** Fl A & M Univ, Tallahassee, FL; SR; BA; FL Yng Dmcrts 87-; BACCHUS 87-; FSLATE 89-; NAACP 87-; Hnr Rll 87-; Leonard Wesson Elem Schl; Elem Ed; Grad Schl.

**WALTMAN, DEANA L,** Birmingham Southern Coll, Birmingham, AL; SR; BA; Lit Cncl Cntrl Al Tutor; Bus Admin; Mgt.

**WALTON, BRADLEY S,** Bridgewater Coll, Bridgewater, VA; FR; BA; Pinion Plyrs 90-; Coll Radio Sta 90-; Engl Mjr/Thtr Mnr; Wrt/Illstrt Comic Bks.

**WALTON, BRIAN D,** West Liberty St Coll, West Liberty, WV; GD; BS; Trck Clb Pres 89-90; Kappa Delta Kappa Treas 87-; Horns Wheeling Awrd 90; Vrsty Ftbl 87-89; Bus Admn/Mrktng; Sprts Mngmnt.**

**WALTON, CRYSTAL A,** Wilmington Coll, New Castle, DE; JR; BA; Hmn Srvcs Intrnshp 89; AAA DE Tech And Comm Coll 89; Bhvrl Sci; Cnslr.

**WALTON, HEATHER D,** Winthrop Coll, Rock Hill, SC; JR; BA; Nwspr 89; GED Tutor 90; Symph Band 88; Deans List 89-90; Watson Mem Schlrshp 88-; Winghrop Hnr Schlrshp 88-89; Psych; Cnslng.

**WALTON, JAY B,** Alcorn St Univ, Lorman, MS; FR; BA; Fr Clss Offcr Treas; DJ; Cmmnctns Clb; NAACP; Cmps All Str Chllng Tm; Tech Clb; Soph Clss Offcr VP; Hnrs Stu Orgn; Dean Lst; Tnns; Cvl Eng/Indstrl Tech; Eng.

**WALTON, JENNIFER A,** Univ Of Nc At Greensboro, Greensboro, NC; JR; BS; Stdnt Govt 89-90; Phi Theta Kappa Treas 89-90; Pres Lst 88-90; Girl Scouts; Outstndg Grad GTCC 90; AA Guilford Tech Cmnty Clg 90; Elem Ed; Tchg.**

**WALTON III, JOHN R,** Fl St Univ, Tallahassee, FL; JR; BA; Acctg Soc 90-; Phi Theta Kappa 88-90; I M Ftbl Bkbl Sftbl 90; AA Centrl Fla Comm Clg 90; Fin/Acctg.

**WALTON, KATHLEEN A,** Medical Coll Of Ga, Augusta, GA; SR; BSN; Kappa Alpha Theta 87-; UGA 87-; Nrsg.

**WALTON, KEVIN M,** Strayer Coll, Washington, DC; SR; BS; US Tbl Tnns Assoc Cert Coach; Phi Theta Kappa 89-; Gamma Beta Phi; Fllwshp Schlrshp 90-; Data Proc Dip 89; Comp Inf Sys; Anlyst/Prog.

**WALTON, KIMBERLY J,** Allegheny Coll, Meadville, PA; SR; Nwmn Fllwshp Plnng Grp 87-; Nwspr Stf Wrtr 88; Intl Stdnts Hl 90; Soup Ktchn 88-; KY Mssn; Intrnshp WGOT-TV 90-; Dept Grad Hons; Stdy Abrd Univ Shfld UK 89-90; BA Cum Laude; Pol Sci/Comm Arts.**

**WALTON, LYSA R,** Univ Of Cin R Walters Coll, Blue Ash, OH; SR; AAS; Crrclm Com Rep 90-; Phi Theta Kappa; Magna Cum Laude; Lcnsd Prctcl Nrs Assn; Nrsng.

**WALTON, MARK J,** Newbury Coll, Brookline, MA; FR; AA; Clnry Arts; Prof Chef.

**WALTON, ROBERT A,** Columbia Union Coll, Takoma Park, MD; SR; BS; Sys Engr 86-; AA Prince George Cmnty Clg 75; Bus Admn; Mgt.

**WALTON, VERONICA ELAINE,** Valdosta St Coll, Valdosta, GA; FR; BED; Educ.

**WALTON, VICTORIA A,** Al A & M Univ, Normal, AL; SO; BS; Mrchng Bnd 89-; Symph Bnd 89-; Kappa Delta Pi; MARC Flw; MBRS Stdnt 90-; Ruth Hindman Schlr 89-; Bio; Med.

**WALTON, YOLANDA V,** Hampton Univ, Hampton, VA; SR; BS; Bus Clb 89-; Ttrl Prog 90-; Amer Mrktng Assc 89-; J C Penney Intern; Bus Mngmnt.**

**WALTZ, JAMES J,** Salisbury St Univ, Salisbury, MD; SO; BA; Theatre 89-; Sophanes Thtr Clb 89-; Phi Eta Sigma; Psych; Ma.

**WALTZ JR, MARION P,** Bowling Green St Univ, Bowling Green, OH; SR; BA; LTCC Engineering Club V Pres 87-89; Math Tutor; Alpha Lambda Delta; Golden Key; All Amer Scholar Awd; Multiple Award; LTC Outstanding Acdmc Achvmnt Awd; Assoc Lima Tchncl Clge 89; Cert Apollo 87; Mfg Technology; Engineering/Education.**

**WALWYN, VAUGHN A,** Al St Univ, Montgomery, AL; SR; Alpha Kappa Mu Rprtr 90-; Alpha Phi Sigma; Intrmrl Bsktbll Ch; BSCRJ; Crmnl Jstc.

**WAMPLER, JOYCE K,** Thomas Nelson Comm Coll, Hampton, VA; FR; BA; Comm Bible Stdy Tchng Dir 86-90; Nwprt Nws Chrstn Wmns Clb Pres 83-84; Tchr.

**WAMPLER, MARIE D,** Loyola Coll In Md, Baltimore, MD; FR; IM Sccr; Dns Lst 90-; Eng Sci; Biomed Eng.

**WAMPLER, ROLANDA J,** Hillsborough Comm Coll, Tampa, FL; FR; BED; Musc; Musc Educ.

**WAMPLER, STEVEN E,** Ms St Univ, Miss State, MS; SO; BA; Bapt Stdnt Union; Phi Eta Sigma 90-; Gamma Beta Phi; Foreign Lang; Educ/Religious Voc.

**WAMSLEY, GINA S,** Milligan Coll, Milligan Clg, TN; SO; BED; Teacher Education Club Publicity 89-; Tutor For Learning Disabled 90-; Delta Kappa 89-; Deans List 90-; Elem/Special Education; Teacher.

**WAMSLEY, SHAWNA L,** Oh Wesleyan Univ, Delaware, OH; JR; BA; Wesleyan Stdnt Fndtn 90-; Pres Club 90-; Phi Eta Sigma Sr Adv 89-; Phi Soc 90-; Psi Chi; Crestview Proj Comm Serv 89-; Varsity Track 88-89; Child Psychologist.

**WANCATA, LINDA R,** Kent St Univ Kent Cmps, Kent, OH; FR; BA; Ameritech Inc 72-90; Int Dsgn.

**WANCOUR, PAULA R,** Central Pa Bus School, Summerdale, PA; FR; AA; Deans Lst 90-; Vlybl; Acctg.

**WANDS, DENISE M,** Endicott Coll, Beverly, MA; GD; AS; Haunted House 90-; Learn Cncl; Fashion Show Model; Sheraton Intern; Hotel/Restaurant Mgmt; Mgmt.

**WANG, ANN R,** Cornell Univ Statutory College, Ithaca, NY; SO; BS; Bus; Mgt.

**WANG, GREGORY,** Georgetown Univ, Washington, DC; SO; BS; Georgetown Stdnt Fedrl Crdt Un Hd Of Bnk Recncltns 90; DC Schls Projct Vol; Deans List 90-; DC Schlrs Vol Tutor For Immgrnts; Horizon Media Inc Fin Intrn; Acctng; Law.

**WANG, GUANGXI,** Univ Of Al At Birmingham, Birmingham, AL; FR; BS; Eng.

**WANG, HYUN JEONG,** Univ Of Cincinnati, Cincinnati, OH; SO; BA; Orch 89-; Symphony Bnd 89-; Music/Flute; Perf.

**WANG, ROSE S,** Smith Coll, Northampton, MA; SR; BA; Asian Stdnts Assn Treas; Handbell Chr; First Grp Schlr; Economics/Cmptr Sci; Actuarial Cnsltng.

**WANG, SONG CHYUAN,** Southern Coll Of Tech, Marietta, GA; SO; Elec Eng; Eng.

**WANG, STEVE C,** Cornell Univ Statutory College, Ithaca, NY; JR; BS; Clg Bowl Nationals; Ho Nun Da Kah Cmtee Chrm; Praxis Essy Awd; NASA Sp Grant Awd; Statstcs/Cmptr Sci Tchng Asstnshps; Statistics Hon Thesis; Statistics; Academia.

**WANG, TAN POR,** Savannah Coll Of Art & Design, Savannah, GA; JR; BFA; Photo Grp 89-; Grphx Grp 88-; Comp Math Class Asst 89-; Macintosh/Amiga Comp Lab Asst 89-; Grphc Dsgn.

**WANG, WENDY W,** Cornell Univ Statutory College, Ithaca, NY; FR; BA; Math/Pre Med; Doctor/Math Professor.

**WANG, YANG,** Coll Of Insurance, New York, NY; SR; BBA; Stndts Cncl Sen 87-89; ASA Chr 89-90; Dncng Clb Fndr 87-89; Deans Lst Coll Lawrence 89-; Bus/Rsk Mgmt; Intrntl Bus.**

**WANG, YIN KEI,** City Univ Of Ny City Coll, New York, NY; SR; BE; Inst Elec/Elect Engrs; Gold Key 89; Hon Soc 87; Deans Lst 87-; Math Lab Tutor 86-87; Math Awd 86; Track/Field 87; Elec Eng.

**WANG, ZHAN,** Univ Of Sc At Columbia, Columbia, SC; JR; BA; SC Philharmonic Orch 89-; SC Chmbr Orch 89-; Schleswig Holstein Music Fstvl Orch Schlrshp Aud In Germany; Mrng/Aftrn Clb Schlrsp; Yng Artist Clb Schlrshp Comp 6A 88; Yng Adlt Comp For Talented Musicians 88; Music/Violin; Musician.

**WANG-CHANG, XIA,** Saint Josephs Univ, Philadelphia, PA; GD; PHD; Cmptr Sci Awd; Tchg Asstshp 90-; 1st Prize Awd Shanghai Tech Assoc 88; Florida State Univ Panama Branch Tchg; BS Shanghai Univ Engr Sci 81-85; MS; Cmptr Sci.

**WANGARI, SUSAN,** Central St Univ, Wilberforce, OH; JR; FCS Pres 89-; ICOC; Acctg/Comp Info Syst Pres; Food Serv; Pres Lst; Vlybl; Acctg/Comp Info Syst; CPA Pgmmg.

**WANKO, STEPHANIE D,** Anne Arundel Comm Coll, Arnold, MD; FR; BA; Bus.

**WANNEMUEHLER, BRIAN J,** Ms St Univ, Miss State, MS; FR; BA; Hnrs Prog; Pres Schlr; Mktng; Golf Mgt.

**WANTLAND, LESLIE D,** Univ Of Ga, Athens, GA; SR; BED; Yrbk Asst Ed 89-90; Bng Invlvd GA Gd; Phi Kappa Phi; Gldn Key; Gamma Beta Phi; Kappa Delta Pi; Kappa Delta Epsilon Prlmntrn 90-; Eng Ed; Tchr.

**WARASSE, HERVE R,** Savannah Coll Of Art & Design, Savannah, GA; FR; BFA; Grphc Dsgn.

**WARBURTON, MARGARET J,** Tn Temple Univ, Chattanooga, TN; FR; BS; Intrdsplnry Stds; Tchr.

**WARCHOL, KATHLEEN ANNE,** Villanova Univ, Villanova, PA; SR; Stu Unn 87-89; Kappa Delta Pi; Cum Laude; Alpha Omicron Pi 89-; BS; Educ; Sec Tchr.

**WARD, ALICE E,** Marywood Coll, Scranton, PA; SO; BA; Math Club 89; Tchrs Of Tomorrow 89; Math; Educ.

**WARD, AMANDA M,** Middle Ga Coll, Cochran, GA; FR; BA; Gamma Beta Phi 90-; Early Intvtn Pgm; Batgirl Bsbl; Educ; Corp Law.

**WARD, AUBREY,** Morehouse Coll, Atlanta, GA; SO; BA; Am Aplnc Cinnaminson NJ Dlvrymn; Sursim Corda Day Care Ctr Cnslr; Cafe Capri Waiter; Capitol Hill Hsop Rcptnst; The Philadelphia Fndtn; Untd Ngr Clg Fund; UNCF Telthn; Engl; Law.

**WARD, AYANNA B,** Fl A & M Univ, Tallahassee, FL; FR; BA; FAMU Safe Team; SBI News; Phi Eta Sigma; Acctng.

**WARD, BEVERLEY J,** Univ Of Cincinnati-Clrmnt Coll, Batavia, OH; SR; BS; Amer Med Rcrd Assc 70-; OH Med Rcrd Assc 70-; Grtr Cincinnati Med Rcrd Assc 70-; Amer Assc Fr Med Trnscrptnsts 81-; Cincinnati Tech Clg Advsry Comm 86-; Univ Cinn Clermont Clg Advsry Comm 74-75; Locust Rdg Nrsg Hm Cnsltnt 77-78; Med Rcrd Admin.

**WARD, BRENDA LAVONNE,** Howard Univ, Washington, DC; SR; BS; Stdnt Natl Pharm Assoc Treas 90-; MWBB; Rho Chi 90-; Kappa Psi Regent-Pres 90-; Du Pont Summer Inter Pgm 90; Dns Hnr Rl 90-; Med Tech; AA Prince Georges Cmnty Clg 83; BS Univ MD 86; Pharm; Clncl Pharm.

**WARD, CARLA M,** Pellissippi St Tech Comm Coll, Knoxville, TN; FR; Vision Vlntr Thompson Cancer Survival Ctr; Schlrshp Pellissippi State 90-.

**WARD, CARY M,** Univ Of Nc At Greensboro, Greensboro, NC; JR; Tchng Intrnshp; BS; Ed; Tchng.

**WARD, CHRISTINE M,** Colby Sawyer Coll, New London, NH; FR; BS; Key Assn 90-; Trck 90-; Piano 90-; Adelaide Nichols Music Schlrshp 90-; Chld Psych.

**WARD, CHRISTOPHER E,** Morehouse Coll, Atlanta, GA; SO; BA; Kaiser-Permanente Acdmc Schlrshp 89; Sci Pgm 89; Hon Rl 90; Deans Lst 90; Intl Studies; Law.

**WARD, DARA A,** Hampton Univ, Hampton, VA; JR; BS; Am Mrktng Assoc V P 89-; Mich Area Pre Alum Assoc Rec Sec 88-; NAACP 88-89; Alpha Kappa Mu 90-; Alpha Kappa Alpha Dean Of Acdmcs 90-; Mrktng Intern Lotus Dev Corp; Mrktng.

**WARD, DAVID E,** Barry Univ, Miami, FL; FR; BS; Blgy; Med.

**WARD, DEIDRE L,** Al A & M Univ, Normal, AL; SO; BS; Mktg Clb 90-; Deans Lst 88-89; Pres Schlrs 89-90; Mktg.

**WARD, DONNA L,** Troy St Univ At Dothan, Dothan, AL; SO; BA; Data Prcssng Mngmnt Assc; Gamma Beta Phi 90-; Accntng Infr Sys; Accntng.

**WARD, DREAMA J,** Univ Of Ky, Lexington, KY; JR; BED; Phi Theta Kappa Sec 70-714; Phi Lambda; Phi Theta Kappa Sec 70-71; Valedictorian 71; Legal & Executive Sec; AA Midway College 71; Bus Ed; Teach.

**WARD, EILEEN C,** Univ Of Rochester, Rochester, NY; SO; D Lns Org; Eng; Flm Wrtng/Drctng.

**WARD, ENGA S,** Univ Of Sc At Columbia, Columbia, SC; FR; Hons Clg 90-; Cvl Engr.

**WARD, GINA K,** Univ Of Tn At Martin, Martin, TN; SO; PHARM; Phi Eta Sigma 90-; Pre Pharmacy.

**WARD JR, GREGORY F,** Youngstown St Univ, Youngstown, OH; SR; BE; ASM Pres 90-; SAMPE Pres 90-; ESSC; Natl Socty Prof Engrs; Amer Powder Mtlrgy Inst; Penn Ohio AIME Schlrshp 90-; Materials Engr Man Of The Year At Yngstwn State Univ; Materials Engr.

**WARD JR, JAMES P,** Church Of God Sch Of Theology, Cleveland, TN; GD; MDIV; Stdnt Govt Pres 89-90; Cls VP 87-88; Cls Pres 88-89; Annul Stf Layout Artst 87-88; Annul Stf Editr 88-89; N C A&T St Univ Alpha Lambda Delta; Fndrs Awrd 90; Off Campus Mnstries; BA Hlms Coll Of Bible 90; Theolgy; Educ/Theolgy.

**WARD, JAMES T,** Liberty Univ, Lynchburg, VA; SR; BS; Math Clb VP 89-; Kappa Mu Epsilon VP 89-; Hon Prog 89-; Peer Trng 90-; Sprtl Ldrshp Prgm 89-; Actrl Math Awd; Intern 1st Clny Lf Ins Co Actrl Dept 90; IM Glf 87; Math/Actrl Sci Cncntrtn; Actrl Sci.**

**WARD, JANET S,** Univ Of Akron, Akron, OH; SR; BS; SG Pres 87-89; Alpha Sigma Lambda 87; Phi Simga Alpha 88; Golden Key 88; Mgt 84-; Bus Mft/Technel Ed.

**WARD, JANINA N,** Coppin St Coll, Baltimore, MD; JR; Math; Engr.

**WARD, JEFFREY K,** Middle Tn St Univ, Murfreesboro, TN; SR; BS BS; Phi Kappa Phi; Gamma Beta Phi; Sigma Clb 90-; R A Vanderbilt Particle Acc Lab; Eagle Scout Assoc 82-; Navy Nuclear Sub Reactor Oprtr 82-88; Physics/Cmptr Engr.

**WARD, JESSICA A,** Memphis St Univ, Memphis, TN; SO; BSE; Rehabilitation Educ; Counseling.

**WARD, JOSEPH R,** S U N Y Coll Of Tech At Frmgdl, Farmingdale, NY; FR.

**WARD, JULIE B,** Univ Of Sc At Coastal Carolina, Conway, SC; SR; Hstry Clb; Flwshp Chrstn Athl; Omicron Delta Kappa; Phi Alpha Theta VP 90-; Dns Lst; Acad All Amer; All Amer Schlr; Hstry; Educ.

**WARD, JULIE BROOKE,** Univ Of Sc At Columbia, Columbia, SC; SR; BA; Hist Clb; Omcrn Dlt Kappa; Phi Alph Theta VP 90-; Acad All Amer; All Amer Schlr; SACS Cmt; Hist; Tchr.

**WARD, KIMBERLY A,** Merrimack Coll, North Andover, MA; JR; BA; Orientn Comm 90; Im Vlybl 88; Part Time Job 89-; Hist; Law.

**WARD, LA TONYA M,** Tn St Univ, Nashville, TN; SR; Fshn Gld Sect 88-90; Peer Cnslr; Alpha Kappa Alpha 89; NAACP 84; Intrnshp Dollar Gnrl Stores Assist Mgr 90; Clothing/Textiles; Visual Mrchndse Dsgnr.

**WARD, LINDA S,** Washington State Comm Coll, Marietta, OH; FR; AAB; Bus Lnch Clb; Sec.

**WARD, LORI A,** Univ Of Sc At Spartanburg, Spartanburg, SC; SR; BA; Acctg Clb 90-; Piedmont Soc 90-; Gamma Beta Phi 90-; Bptst Yng Wmn Pres 89-; Acctg Asst; Self Emplyd 83-; AA Okaloosa Walton Jr Coll 83; Bus Admin; Acctg/CPA.

**WARD, MELISSA L,** Catawba Valley Comm Coll, Hickory, NC; FR; BA; CVCC Rotaract Clb Sec 90-; Gamma Beta Phi 90-; CVCC Dns Lst 4.0 GPA; Acctng/Bus Educ; CPA/BUS Tchr.

**WARD, MIA A,** Alcorn St Univ, Lorman, MS; JR; BA; Nrsg Hms 89-90; Hnrs Rl 88-90; Palm Bch Cmnty Clg Bsktbl 88-90; Elem Ed.

**WARD, PATRICIA S,** Univ Of Sc At Aiken, Aiken, SC; JR; BS; SGA 89; Gamma Beta Phi State VP 88-; Pacesetter/Peer Cnslr; Wrtng Cntr Cnsltnt 89-; Exec Asst Mech Engr 82-88; Bus Admin; Exec Mgmt.

**WARD, PATTI J,** Blue Mountain Coll, Blue Mountain, MS; BS; Sci Club 89-; Psych Club 90-; MS Assoc Of Edctrs Stdnt Tchrs 90-; MS Sci Tchrs Assoc 90-; Un Meth Women 89-; Career Scndry Bio/Sci Tchr Planned; AS N E Ms Comm Coll 88; Bio; Scndry Tchr.

**WARD, PENNY L,** Ky Christian Coll, Grayson, KY; JR; BS; Priscilla Clb Pres 88-; VITA 90-; Bus.

**WARD, RACHEL A,** Villanova Univ, Villanova, PA; SO; BA; Pol Sci; Law.

**WARD, RONNIE C,** Winthrop Coll, Rock Hill, SC; JR; BME; Phi Mu Alpha Scl Chrmn; Performance Schlrshp; Music Ed.

**WARD, SARA D,** Peace Coll, Raleigh, NC; SO; BA; Times Rptr 89-; Yng Rpblcns 90-; Sigma Delta Mu; Peace Std Chrstn Asc 89-90; Cvtn Schlp 89-90; Hnrs Schlp 89-; George Chadwick Jr Mem Schlp 90-; Jazz Dance Co 89-90; AA; Cnslng Psy.

**WARD, SHELLY R,** Univ Of Tn At Martin, Martin, TN; FR; Mc Cord Hall Assoc 90-; Alpha Gamma Delta 90-; Edn; Teach.

**WARD, TERESA H,** Snead St Jr Coll, Boaz, AL; FR; BS; Pre Sch Tchr 84-; Early Chldhd Educ; Tch.

**WARD, THERESA A,** Houghton Coll, Houghton, NY; SO; BA; Spnsh Clb; Ed Clb; Ballet; Deans List; Empire State Chlngr Schlrshp; Paul Douglas Schlrshp; Houghton Clg Schlrshp; Ed N-9/ Spnsh; Tchr.**

**WARD, THOMAS F,** Beckley Coll, Beckley, WV; SO; ASSOC; Slf Emplyd; Atnd Nght Schl; Prlgl; Law.

**WARD, TODD,** Univ Of Sc At Coastal Carolina, Conway, SC; SR; BS; Soc Undersea World Secr 90-; Stdnt Govt Assoc Repr; Omicron Delta Kappa; Hnrs Cncl Treas 90-; Marine Sci; Research.

**WARD, TONYA D,** Western New England Coll, Springfield, MA; FR; BA; Pre Law Soc 90-; Untd/Mtlly Equal 90; Poltcl Sci Club 90; Alpha Lambda Delta 90-; Govt; Law.

**WARD, TRACY C,** Univ Of Nc At Greensboro, Greensboro, NC; JR; BA; Natl Hon Soc 86-90; Univ Marshall 90-; Engl/Hist Tchr.

**WARD, TRACY L,** S U N Y At Buffalo, Buffalo, NY; SR; BS; DPMA Pres 90-; Wmn Mgnt 89-; Golden Key 90-; Central Referral Svc Vol 89-90; M&t Bk Buffalo Intern; Bsn Adm; MIS.

**WARD, VIRGINIA D,** Univ Of Tn At Martin, Martin, TN; FR; Stdnt Govt Elec Comm; Mu Epsilion Delta 90-; Chi Omega 90-; Pre Phrmcy; Phrmcst.

**WARD, WENDY P,** Univ Of Ga, Athens, GA; JR; MBA; Natl Stdnt Speech/Lang/Hrng Assn Treas 90-; Yng Life Coll Ldr 90-; Wrldwide Dscplshp Assn 90-; Kappa Delta Pi 90-; Open Doors Hmls Shltr 89-90; St James Meth Chrch Chldrns 90-; Speech/ Lang Path.

**WARD, YVONNE V,** Fl St Univ, Tallahassee, FL; SO; BFA; Pres ADK Schlrshp Hse 90-; Interhse Cncl So Schlrshp Fnd; 90-; Phi Eta Sigma 90; IM Vlybl Tm Mem 90; AA; Motion Pic Prod; Film Producer.

**WARDE, HORTENSE A,** City Univ Of Ny Med Evers Coll, Brooklyn, NY; JR; BSN; Amer Nrss Assn; RN New York State 89; RM RN Guyana 79; Nrsng; Nrse Edctr.

**WARDEN, ANGIE R,** Univ Of Southern Ms, Hattiesburg, MS; SO; BA; Mrsng.

**WARDEN, CAROLYN B,** Alcorn St Univ, Lorman, MS; GD; AS; Univ Med Ctr Extrn R N 87; Riverland Med Ctr 88-; Nurs; RN.

**WARDEN, JANET R,** Fayetteville St Univ, Fayetteville, NC; SR; BS; Wrk At 1112th Sig Bn Ft Bragg 86; AA St Ptrsbrg Jr Clg 73; Math/Cmptr Sci.

**WARDRIP, SARA E,** Univ Of Sc At Columbia, Columbia, SC; FR; BS; Mrchng Band 90-; Cncrt Band 90-; Alpha Lambda Delta 90-; Phi Eta Sigma 90-; Bus.

**WARE, DANIELLE T,** Al St Univ, Montgomery, AL; FR; Chmstry.

**WARE, JEANETTA L,** Middle Tn St Univ, Murfreesboro, TN; FR; BS; Pre-Law Soc Info Ofcr; Pltcl Sci; Law Crmnl/Envrnmntl.

**WARE, JONATHAN A,** Univ Of Ky, Lexington, KY; SR; BARCH; AIAS; BFA Murray State Univ 88; Archtctre; Tchng.

**WARE, KAREN R,** Daytona Beach Comm Coll, Daytona Beach, FL; AS; Save Our Soc Clb 90-; Paraprof Clb 90-; Human Serv Awd; Pres Lst 90-; NAACP Fund Rsng Mbrshp Comm; Matrons Soc Pres 89-90; Nrsng Asst 84; Illstr US Army Denver CO Lowry 79; Yth Cnslng; Psych.

**WARE, LAWRENCE G,** Univ Of Sc At Spartanburg, Spartanburg, SC; JR; BA; Hstry Clb 90-; Gamma Beta Phi; Scndry Ed; Tch.

**WARE, LISA A,** Norfolk St Univ, Norfolk, VA; JR; BA; Mdcl Rcrds Clb Sec 90; Vlntr Nrflk Cmmn Hsptl 90; Intrn Hsptl 90; Mdcl Rcrds Admn Mdcl Rcrds Dcrctr.

**WARE, MONICA R,** Stillman Coll, Tuscaloosa, AL; SR; BA; Dean Lst; Alpha Kappa Alpha Grmmts; Stu Tchr Matthews Elem; Elem Educ; Tchr.

**WARE, REGINALD B,** Alcorn St Univ, Lorman, MS; JR; BS; Hon Stdnt Org 89-; Stdnt Govt Cls VP 90-; Alpha Kappa Mu 90-; Alpha Phi Omega Pres 89-; Intrnshp Hartford Grp; Acctg.

**WARE, RONALD K,** Alcorn St Univ, Lorman, MS; GD; Univ Choir; Intl Bskbl/Bsbl; Marching Concert Bnd; Alpha Phi Alpha; Kappa Kappa Psi; BS 90; Elec Telchlgy; Engrg.

**WARE, SUMIKO,** Morris Brown Coll, Atlanta, GA; SO; BA; Mck Trl Tm 90-; Hnrs Clb 90-; Prvsts Lst 89-; Prlgl Stds; Law.

**WARF, PHILLIP S,** Memphis St Univ, Memphis, TN; SR; BA; Poli Sci Soc 88-; Cmps Dmcrts; US Acad Poli Sci 89-; Gldn Ky 90-; J W Brrghs Awd; Erly Schlrs Schlrshp; Intl Rels; Frgn Svc/ Tchng.

**WARFEL, HEATHER A,** Va Commonwealth Univ, Richmond, VA; FR; BFA; Dnc Tm 90-; Dnc; Chrgrphy Prfrmnc.

**WARFIELD, NIMA A,** Morehouse Coll, Atlanta, GA; SO; BA; Hon Prog Club Parlmntrn 89-; Schlrs Prog 90-; SGA Acadmc Afrs Comm Vice Chrprsn 90-; Exxon Rsrch/Engr Intrnshp 89-; All Amercn Schlr Award 90-; Gloster Merit Schlrshp 89-90; Engl; Ed.

**WARFIELD JR, WILLIAM L,** Manhattan School Of Music, New York, NY; JR; BA; Amer Fdrtn Mscns; Natl Assn Jzz Edctrs; Mscns Brooklyn Initiatv; Jzz Ensmbl Dir Brklyn Cnsrvtry; Dir Jzz Studies Dalton Schl NYC 89-; Rcrdng Intrply Rcrds-Bill Warfld Big Bnd NY City Jzz; Jzz/Cmmrcl Music; Tchr/Rcrdng Artst.

**WARGO, KATHLEEN A,** Duquesne Univ, Pittsburgh, PA; SO; BS; DUV 90-; Amer Mrktg Assoc 89-90; Stu Hlpg Admsns/ Rcrtmnt Pro 89-; Lambda Sigma 90-; Alpha Gamma Delta Ofc Ritual; Deans Lst 89-; Mobay Job Grmny 89-; Fndrs Schlrshp; Ecnmcs; Intl Bus.

**WARGO, MAUREEN A,** Westminster Coll, New Wilmingtn, PA; SO; BA; Lambda Sigma Ritual Chrmn 90-; Alpha Gamma Delta; Stdnt Admissions Tm 90-; Tutor 89-90; Westminster/ Valedictorian Schlrshps; Thomas V Marsell Schlrshp; Bus Admin; Bnkng/Wrkng Corp Lvl.

**WARGO, MICHELE L,** Kent St Univ Kent Cmps, Kent, OH; JR; BA; ASID 90-; Gold Key; Interior Dsgn.

**WARING JR, THOMAS M,** Memphis St Univ, Memphis, TN; FR; Alpha Lambda Delta 90-; Phi Eta Sigma Sec 90-; Lambda Chi Alpah Rush Chr 90-; Bus; Finc.

**WARING, WILLIETTE D,** Univ Of Sc At Columbia, Columbia, SC; SO; BS; Criminal Justice; Law.

**WARMUTH, MATTHEW W,** Univ Of Rochester, Rochester, NY; JR; BS; Tau Beta Pi 90-; Elec Eng; PHD Elec Eng.

**WARNCKE, JULI A,** Defiance Coll, Defiance, OH; SO; BA; Elementary Ed/Special Ed; Teaching.

**WARNER, ANDREW J,** City Univ Of Ny Baruch Coll, New York, NY; SR; BBA; Frshmn Orientn Stdnt Ldr 90-; Stdnt Outrch Prog; Gldn Key; Beta Gamma Sigma; Marktng; Adv.

**WARNER, BETH A,** Muskingum Coll, New Concord, OH; SO; BA; Engl Tchr.

**WARNER, CINDY L,** Marshall University, Huntington, WV; JR; BBA; Ntnl Soc Pblc Acctnts Wv Soc Pblc Acctnts; Acctng Clb; Vita; Gamma Beta Phi Hnr Soc Vp; Gamma Beta Phi Hnr Soc Tres 90-; Accntng/Mnr Comp Sci; Cpa.

**WARNER, CLEOPHAS B,** Columbia Union Coll, Takoma Park, MD; BS; WA Hosp Cntr Unt Bsd Qlty Assrnce Com 88-; RN Nursing Council Of Trinidad WI 73; SRN RMN Nursing Council Of England And Wales 74-; Hlth Care Admin; Hlth Care.

**WARNER, DENISE L,** Georgetown Univ, Washington, DC; JR; BSBA; Natl Assoc Blck Acctnts Pres; Caribbean Cltre Cir 89-; Bsn Wkend Steering Comm 90; Delta Sigma Pi Chnclr; Love-In-Action 89-; Dns Lst; G U John Carroll Schlr; Natl Assoc Blck Accts Schlr; Coopers Lybrand Intern 90-; IM Vlybl 88-; Acctg.**

**WARNER, ERIK P,** S U N Y At Buffalo, Buffalo, NY; SR; BS; Eta Kappa Nu 90-; Gldn Key 89-; IEEE 89-; Eagle Sct 84-; Wegmans Schlrshp 88-; Rgnts Schlrshp 87-; Deans List 87-90; Elect Eng; Eng.

**WARNER, GREGORY R,** Univ Of Cincinnati, Cincinnati, OH; JR; BS; Am Inst Arch Stdnts Chapt Pres 90-; Am Inst Constructors Chapt Pres 89-90; Cincinnati Art Museum 88-; Miami Purchase Assoc 89-; U S Army 82-87; Assoc Arch Tech 90; 6; Arch Engrng; Masters Of Arch.

**WARNER, KIMBERLY J,** Univ Of Al At Huntsville, Huntsville, AL; FR; BA; Bapt Stdnt Un Ldrshp Cncl Mem 90-; Hnrs Frm 90-; Ed.

**WARNER, MARCIA L,** Davis Coll, Toledo, OH; JR; ASSOC; Credit Analyst Dana Corp 88-; Acctg.

**WARNER, PAMELA G,** Bennett Coll, Greensboro, NC; JR; BS; Blgy Clb 88-; NAACP 88-89; Bennett Schlrs 88-; Alpha Kappa Mu Deptmntl Rcgntn; Smmr Pgm Ftr Dctrs-E Carolina Univ 90; Medcl Educ Dvlpmnt Pgm-UNCH-CH; Bsktbl Co-Capt 88-; Blgy; Pdtrcs.

**WARNER, RICHARD L,** Univ Of Ky, Lexington, KY; SR; BSME; Tau Beta Pi 90-; Amer Soc Mech Eng 90-; Mech Eng; Eng.

**WARNER, ROSS,** Univ Of Rochester, Rochester, NY; SO; BA; Delta Sigma Phi VP; Hstry; Law.

**WARNER, SCOTT G,** Clarkson Univ, Potsdam, NY; SR; BS; Amer Prdctn/Invntry Cntrl Soc; Amer Soc Qlty Cntrl; Deans Lst; IM Hcky/Sftbl; Assn Canton Coll Tech 88; Indust Mgmt; Eng/ Qlty Cntrl.

**WARNER, TRACEY E,** Bethany Coll, Bethany, WV; SR; BS; Amer Chem Soc VP 88-; Hrtg Hse Mgr 88-; Gamma Sigma Kappa 90-; Gamma Sigma Epsln Sec 90-; Beta Beta Beta Treas 88-; Fns Flw Chem Dept 90-; Case Wstrn Rsv Env Hlth Sci Dept Intrn 90; Chem Awd 88; Chem; Biochem Rsch.

**WARNER, WENDY P,** Univ Of The Dist Of Columbia, Washington, DC; GD; Acad Achvmnt Awd 89-; Schlstc Achvmnt Awd 89-90; AA Montgomery Comm Coll 84; BA Univ DC 90; Instrmntl Wrkr Cmptr Pgmng.

**WARNICK, GLENN E,** Univ Of Fl, Gainesville, FL; JR; BA; Bus Admin Coll Cncl Comm Chr 90-; Fncl Mgmt Assn; Golden Key 90-; BACC Phlnthrpy Comm 90-; UF Bus Schls Deans Lst 90; Bus Admin Coll Cncl Svc Awd Outstdnng Stdnt Svc 90-; AA 90; Fnc; Frnchsd Rcyclng Bus.

**WARNOCK, MARK W,** Fl St Univ, Tallahassee, FL; SR; BME; Bptst Cmps Mnstry Prsdnt 89-; Msc Brd Advrsr 89; Pi Kappa Lambda; Gldn Key 90-; MENC 89-; Amrcn Chrl Drctrs Assn 90-; Chrl Msc; Msc Mnstry.

**WARNOCK, S ALANA,** Gaston Coll, Dallas, NC; SO; Deans List 90-; Pres List; Acctg.

**WARREN, AMY E,** Univ Of Miami, Coral Gables, FL; SO; BS; Eaton Coll Cncl; Alpha Lambda Delta 90-; Psi Chi; Dns Lst 89-90; Provosts Hnr Rl 90; IM Sftbl/Vlybl 89-; Sprtsfest 90-; Psychlgy/Chmstry; Medicine/Optometry.

**WARREN, ANDREA M,** Savannah St Coll, Savannah, GA; JR; BA; Layout Prsn Yrbk Stff; Betta Beta Beta; Betta Kappa Chi; Research Prog Howard Univ 90-; Research Prog Univ Of Missouri; Biology; Immunology Ph D.

**WARREN, ANTOINETTE SMITH,** Fayetteville St Univ, Fayetteville, NC; SR; BA; Student Ctr Advy Brd Pres 90-; Socilogy Club/Elec Brd; Nontraditional Club/BSWA; NABSW 90; Bapt Union 88-90; Sickle Cell Intshp; Certif Merit; Ldrshp Awd; Sociology/Social Wrk.

**WARREN, AUDRA G,** Va Commonwealth Univ, Richmond, VA; JR; BS; Phi Eta Sigma 89; 4-H Jr Ldr 88; Top 1% 90; Bio; Optometry.

**WARREN, BRETT K,** Emory Univ, Atlanta, GA; FR; BS; Bio; Biomed Engr.

**WARREN, CATHERINE E,** Ms St Univ, Miss State, MS; SR; BA; Choir; Blckfrs Drama Soc; Campus Pro Co Host; Phi Kappa Phi; Gamma Alpha Epsilon; Alpha Gamma Delta Pres 90-; Intrnshp TV Columbus MS; Cmnctn; Brdcst News.

**WARREN, CHRISTIAN E,** Morehouse Coll, Atlanta, GA; SR; BS; Natl Scty Black Engrs Ldrshp Conf Comm 86-; Engrng Scty Detroit 89-; Pi Mu Epsilon 90-; Genl Mtrs Co-Op Stdnt 88-; Genl Motors Schrlshp 89-; Physics; Mechanical Engrng.

**WARREN, DEBBIE J,** Columbus St Comm Coll, Columbus, OH; FR; Spcl Educ.

**WARREN, DEBRA J,** Itawamba Comm Coll, Fulton, MS; FR; BS; Forestry Clb; Forestry.

**WARREN, DIMITRI M,** Columbia Union Coll, Takoma Park, MD; SR; BS; Alpha Chi; Magna Cum Laude; Bus Admin/Mgmt; Law.

**WARREN, DONALD R,** Roane St Comm Coll, Harriman, TN.

**WARREN, GWENDOLYN K,** Univ Of Tn At Knoxville, Knoxville, TN; SO; BS; Vols Fr Christ 89-; Rsdnt Assn Flr Rep 90-; Exec Undrgrad Prog 89-; Gamma Beta Phi; Alpha Lambda Delta 89-; Mrktng; Bus.

**WARREN, JACQUELINE R,** Morgan St Univ, Baltimore, MD; SR; BA; Alpha Sigma Lambda 90; Alpha Delta Mu 90; Pi Gamma Mu; Scl Wrk; LSW Scl Wrkr.

**WARREN JR, JAMES W,** Valdosta St Coll, Valdosta, GA; FR; BS; Biology; Med.

**WARREN, JEFFREY W,** Limestone Coll, Gaffney, SC; FR; BS; Comp Sci; Anlysis.

**WARREN, JOHNISE Y,** Va St Univ, Petersburg, VA; JR; BS; Hotel/Rest Mgmnt Clb 88-; Intrnshp Pizza Hut; Hotel/Rest Mgmnt.

**WARREN, JUANNA L,** William Carey Coll, Hattiesburg, MS; JR; BS; Stdnt Natl Educ Assn 90-; Hon Pgm 89-; Bptst Yng Wmn 90-; Elem Ed; Tchr.

**WARREN, JUNE M,** Coll Of Charleston, Charleston, SC; SO; Rsdnt Hll Pr Cndct Brd 87-88; Rsdnt Pttrsn Hll Govt Pres 87-88; Opn Dr Hlth Org Inter; Acctg.

**WARREN, KELLY S,** Univ Of Akron, Akron, OH; FR; BS; Univ Concert Band 90; Phi Eta Sigma; Chem Eng.

**WARREN, KENNETH A,** Univ Of Sc At Columbia, Columbia, SC; SR; BS; Tau Kappa Epsilon 88-; Marine Sci; Research.

**WARREN, KENNETH S,** S U N Y Coll At Fredonia, Fredonia, NY; SR; MBA; Bus Clb Ed Chf 89-; Amrcn Mrkting Assoc 89-; Stdnts Stdnts Pblcty Asst 89-90; Richard O Lundquist Creativity Awrd; Mst Vlbl Gen Brd Mbr; Hnr Rll; AS Monroe Cmmnty Coll 89; Bus Admn; Mrktng Advrtsng Agncy.

**WARREN, LA SHAWN Y,** Savannah St Coll, Savannah, GA; SO; BA; Dbte Tm 90-; Poli Sci/Pre Law Scty Clb 90-; Alpha Kappa Alpha Lne Sec; Wmn Excllnc Awd; Poli Sci; Attrny.

**WARREN, LAURA L,** Ky Wesleyan Coll, Owensboro, KY; SO; BS; Pre-Profl Soc Sec 89-; KY Wesleyan Plyrs 89-90; Compass Clb Treas 89-; James Graham Brown Soc 89-; Sigma Zeta; Sigma Kappa Sor Rec Sec 89-; Richardson Meml Botany Awd 90; Writing Wrkshp Term Invstgtv Essay Hon Mntn; Bio/Chem; Genetic Rsrch.

**WARREN, LEAH A,** Univ Of Al At Birmingham, Birmingham, AL; JR; BA; Hmownrs Assn Sec/Brd Dir 90-; St Frm Ins Co; Cmnctn Arts.

**WARREN, LISA EVANS,** Middle Ga Coll, Cochran, GA; SO; BS; Para-Profl Laurens Cnty Bd Edn 85-; AA Edn; Edn; Tchr.

**WARREN, LUCINDY J,** Nc Agri & Tech St Univ, Greensboro, NC; GD; CERT; SNEA; New York Stck Exchng Series Seven License; Acct Exec 83-86; AS Elon Coll 83; Bus Admin Elon Coll Nc; Elem Educ; MA/TEACH.

**WARREN, MAXINE,** Middle Ga Coll, Cochran, GA; SO; AS; Eng Clb 89-90; Intercltrl Rel Clb Sec 90-; Stdnts Act Comm 90-; Otstdng Mnrty Stdnt Awd 90-; Coll Mnrty Ldrshp Awd 90-; Bio; Med Tech.

**WARREN, MELINDA R,** Central Fl Comm Coll, Ocala, FL; SO; Ed; Tchr/Anthrplgst.

**WARREN, PAUL A,** Pellissippi St Tech Comm Coll, Knoxville, TN; FR; BS; Phi Theta Kappa; Vltr Blounf Meml Hosp 87; Undwtr Instr 89-; Busn; Statistics.

**WARREN, REBECCA C,** Univ Of Tn At Chattanooga, Chattanooga, TN; JR; BSE; SGA Sntr; Golden Key; Tau Beta Pi; Phi Eta Sigma; Alpha Lambda Delta; Amer Soc Of Mech Sec; Amer Soc Of Civil Engrs Sec; Soc Of Women Engrs Sec; Univ Hons Fellow 88-; William E Brock Schlr 88-; Mech Engr.

**WARREN, ROBIN A,** Cornell Univ, Ithaca, NY; FR; BA; DJ At Rdio Sta; Delta Gamma; Psych And Spnsh Cnctrtn Wmns Stds; Law.

**WARREN, RONALD D,** Valdosta St Coll, Valdosta, GA; SO; BA; Prsntly Crrctnl Offcr Dept Crrctns 90-; US Marine Corps Vet 85-89; Crmnl Just; Law Enfrcmnt.

**WARREN, RONDA A,** Union Coll, Barbourville, KY; FR; BA; Ed; Tchng.

**WARREN, SANDRA LYNN,** Eckerd Coll, St Petersburg, FL; SR; BA; IM Sports 87-90; Straight Inc Sr I Peer Cnclr 88-90; YMCA Sr Ldr; Psychology; Education Field.

**WARREN, SHEILA M,** Middle Tn St Univ, Murfreesboro, TN; SO; BBA; Interclg Equestrian Tm 90-; Acctng; CPA.

**WARREN, SHERRI H,** Asheville Bunc Tech Comm Coll, Asheville, NC; FR; RDH; Allied Hlth; Dntl Hygienist.

**WARREN, SHIRLEY E,** Middle Ga Coll, Cochran, GA; SO; BSN; Academic Achvmnt Awd Annually Univ Sys Georgia Bd Regents 90-; Nrsng; Critical Care Nrsng/Pursue MSN.

**WARREN, TERESA L,** Al St Univ, Montgomery, AL; SO; BA; Bio; Doctr.

**WARREN, VALERIE B,** Miami Dade Comm Coll, Miami, FL; SO; BA; Ed; Tch.

**WARREN, VICTORIA,** Miami Dade Comm Coll North, Miami, FL; SO; BA; Wrtng Clb; Phi Theta Kappa; 2 Hon Tutrg Rdng/Wrtng; AA; News-Edtrl Jrnlsm; Talk Show Hstss.

**WARREN, WENDY J,** Fl St Univ, Tallahassee, FL; SO; BA; Poetry Ed Lit Mag; Deans Lst; AA 90; Bio; Med.

**WARREN-BROWN, JOAN E,** Atlantic Comm Coll, Mays Landing, NJ; SO; BA; Hstry/Govt Clb Stdtn Govt Rep 89-90; Tchrs Aide 90-; Pre Law; Law.

**WARRICK, AMY L,** Mount Olive Coll, Mount Olive, NC; FR; BA; Tennis Tm 90-; Spch Cmnctns; Pblc Rltns.

**WARRICK, MARGARET L,** Wv Northern Comm Coll, Wheeling, WV; FR; BA; Vlybl 90; Tennis 88; Hstry.

**WARRINER, LEIGH ANNE,** Middle Tn St Univ, Murfreesboro, TN; SR; BS; Spch Hrng Clb 89-90; TEA: NEA; Jugoju 85-86; Cmmnctn Dsrdrs; Pblc Schl Spch Thrpst.

**WARSAMA, AMINA N,** Univ Of New Haven, West Haven, CT; SO; BA; Pltcl Sci Clb 90-; David Humphrey Hnrs Pgm 89-; Alpha Lambda Delta 90-; Pltcl Sci; Law.

**WARSAW, WILLIAM F,** Univ Of Southern Ms, Hattiesburg, MS; JR; BSBA; Res Asst Advsry Brd Sec/Treas 90-; Res Lf Judcl Brd 89; Res Asst 89-; Hon Coll Stdnt 88; Bus Mgmt; Oprtns Mgmt.

**WARSHAVSKY, ALEX,** Christian Brothers Univ, Memphis, TN; FR; Jewish Stdnt Un; Eng; Bus.

**WARTHEN, MARY C,** The Johns Hopkins Univ, Baltimore, MD; JR; BSN; Phi Theta Kappa 89-; AA Catonsvl Comm Coll 90; Nrsng.

**WARTHEN, MICHAEL,** Johnson C Smith Univ, Charlotte, NC; JR; BA; Natl Assn Black Acctnts VP 89-; Tau Beta Chi Treas 90-; Bus; CPA.

**WARWELL, CRYSTAL T,** Fl A & M Univ, Tallahassee, FL; FR; BS; Stdnt Gov Stdnt Sen; Phi Eta Sigma; Jrnlsm; Pblc Rltns.

**WASH, KIMBERLY A,** Jackson St Univ, Jackson, MS; FR; MBA; Alpha Lambda Delta; Alpha Lambda Delta; Bsns Admnstrtn Pre Lar; Corp Law.

**WASHBURN, MARTHA L,** Patrick Henry Comm Coll, Martinsville, VA; SO; ABA; Phi Theta Kappa 89-; Bsn; Envir Sci.

**WASHBURN, MICHELLE M,** Methodist Coll, Fayetteville, NC; SO; BA; Yrbk 89-; Zoolgy; Vet.**

**WASHBURN, RACHEL H,** Tn St Univ, Nashville, TN; SR; BS; Comp Sci; Tchncn/Anlyst.

**WASHBURN, RONALD S,** Mount Saint Mary Coll, Newburgh, NY; JR; BA; Nwspr Nws Edtr; Actr 88-; L H Miller Schlrshp; Cert Marist Clg 90-; English/Hstry; Law.

**WASHINGTON, ADRIAN MAURICE,** Mercer Univ Schl Of Pharm, Atlanta, GA; SR; PHD; Stdnt Natl Pharm Assoc Pres 90-; Stdnt Natl Pharm Assoc V P 89-90; Amer Soc Hosp Pharm 87-; Stdnt Natl Pharm Assoc Cncl Stdnt Rep 88-89; Mercer Univ Sch Pharm Alumni; Phi Theta Kappa 84-86; Atlanta Soc Rad Tech 88-; Pharm; Clncl Pharm/Consultg.

**WASHINGTON, ANGELA R,** Wilberforce Univ, Wilberforce, OH; SR; BS; NSBL 90-; NAACP 90-; Deans Lst 88-; Red Cross Vol 89-; Big Sister 89-90; YMCA Yth Cnslr 90-; Alumni Schlrshp 88-; Hlth Care Mgmnt.

**WASHINGTON, ANGELA R,** Coahoma Comm Coll, Clarksdale, MS; SO; Math/Sci Clb Treas 90-; Phi Theta Kappa VP; 2nd Alternate Miss Coahoma Comm Clg; Delta Sigma Theta Schlrshp; Frank Grambrell Schlrshp; Bio; Nrs Prctnr.

**WASHINGTON, CERISE D,** Hampton Univ, Hampton, VA; FR; NAACP AICHE Sec; Inroads Inc; Hnr List 90-; Turning Pt Comm Serv Prj Orgnzr; 3m Co Intern 90-; Chem Engr Design.

**WASHINGTON, DARYL D,** Tougaloo Coll, Tougaloo, MS; SO; BA; SGA 90-; Gospel Choir 89-90; Law Club Pres Advsr 90-; Alpha Lambda Delta 90-; NAACP VP 89-90; Pre-Alumni 89-90; Pres Schlr 89-; GPA Awd 89-; Poltcl Sci; Crprte Lwyr.

**WASHINGTON, DE LOIS,** Fayetteville St Univ, Fayetteville, NC; SO; BA; Otstndng Chldhd Crrclm Stdnt 90; AA Robeson Comm Clg 90; Psych; Chld Psych.

**WASHINGTON, DEWAYNE A,** Norfolk St Univ, Norfolk, VA; SR; Brdcstr Schl Radio 88-; Alpha Kappa Mu 90-; Phi Chi; USMC Cmbt Corrspndt; Act Dty Marine Corps 74-; Psychlgy; TV Prod/Drctng.

**WASHINGTON, DOROTHY J,** Univ Of South Al, Mobile, AL; SR; Pres Lst; PAD 88-; MA Psychometry; BS; Spec Ed.

**WASHINGTON, FLETCHER V,** Norfolk St Univ, Norfolk, VA; JR; BA; Adv Army ROTC Plt Ldr 88-; Stdnt Ldrshp 90-; Poli Sci; Mltry Offcr.

**WASHINGTON, FREDA J,** Tuskegee Univ, Tuskegee Inst, AL; JR; BS; Natl Soc Blck Engrs 88-; Sr Cls VP; Alpha Kappa Mu; Elctrcl Engrg/Math; Engr.

**WASHINGTON, GARLANDA R,** Tougaloo Coll, Tougaloo, MS; FR; BA; Biology; Nursing.

**WASHINGTON, GERALD J,** Ky St Univ, Frankfort, KY; FR; BS; Deans Lst; Optometry.

**WASHINGTON, GINA L,** Hampton Univ, Hampton, VA; SO; BA; Mass Media Comm.

**WASHINGTON, GLENN L,** Comm Coll Algny Co Algny Cmps, Pittsburgh, PA; SO; Stdnt Govt Treas; AS; Cert Black Studies; Scl Scis; Corp Law.

**WASHINGTON, GRACE ROBERTA,** Interdenominational Theo Ctr, Atlanta, GA; GD; MDIV; UM Wmn; NAACP; YMCA; Pastor Flat Shoals UMC 85-; Cert 69; DE 90; Msslgy; Pastor.

**WASHINGTON, JAMES L,** Central St Univ, Wilberforce, OH; FR; BA; DAAP; KY Natl Gd US Army Cmbt Engr E-3 PFC; Ind Tchnlgy Engr.

**WASHINGTON, JASON K,** Southern Coll Of Tech, Marietta, GA; SO; BS; Elec Comp Eng.

**WASHINGTON, KEADRICK D,** Al A & M Univ, Normal, AL; FR; BA; Trck Phi Theta 90-; Mst Otstndng Frshmn Trck 90-; Acdmc Awd Certf 90-; Trck 90-91; Accntng; CPA Ecnmcs.

**WASHINGTON, KIM E,** Fort Valley St Coll, Fort Valley, GA; SR; BA; Stdnt Ga Assn Eductrs 89-; Kappa Delta Epsilon 90; Alpha Kappa Alpha; AA E Ga Clb 89; Educ; Early Chldhd Eductr.

**WASHINGTON, KRISSY N,** Alcorn St Univ, Lorman, MS; SO; HSO 89-; Elem Educ; Elem Tchr.

**WASHINGTON, LA DONNA M,** Jackson St Univ, Jackson, MS; SO; BA; Crmnl Jstc Clb Sec 90-; Pol Sci Clb Sec; Pres Lst Schlr Awd 90-; Dns Lst Schlr 89-; Engl; Cvl Atty.

**WASHINGTON, LASONYA SHERRIAL,** Johnson C Smith Univ, Charlotte, NC; SO; BS; Stu Govt Sec 90-; Ntl Educ Clb Tres 90-; Alpha Lambda Delta Sec 89-90; Soup Ktchn Vol; Tutrg Tsk Frc; Educ; Elem Tchr.

**WASHINGTON, LUTHER MARSHALL,** Oh Wesleyan Univ, Delaware, OH; SR; BA; Wesleyan Coun Stdnt Afrs 87-89; Stdnt Union Blck Awrns Pres 87-; Order Of Omega; Gospel Lyres Chr Pres 87-; Alpha Phi Alpha VP 88-; Ohio State Dept Educ Evltr; Univ Serv; WEB Dubois Talntd Tenth; Natl Ldrshp Srvc Awd; Elem Educ; Coll Prof.

**WASHINGTON, MARY ASHLEY,** Coll Of Charleston, Charleston, SC; SR; BS; SCEC Pres 89; AAMR 90; Educ Clb 89; Omicron Delta Kappa 90-; Alpha Delta Pi 88-; Dist Hnr Rll 90; Spec Educ; Tch.

**WASHINGTON, MEREDITH L,** Benedict Coll, Columbia, SC; JR; BS; Acctg Assn Sec 89-; Clg Hon Assn Edtr 89-; Alpha Kappa Mu; Alpha Chi; Phi Beta Lambda State Treas 90-; Acctg; Grad Sch.

**WASHINGTON, RHONDA L,** Alcorn St Univ, Lorman, MS; FR; BS; Bio; Phrmcy.

**WASHINGTON, RICHARD A,** Wilberforce Univ, Wilberforce, OH; SO; BS; Stdnt Gvrnmnt Stdnt Cncl Mmbr 89-; Chmstry; Phrmctcl Chmst.

**WASHINGTON, RUBY J,** Tallahassee Comm Coll, Tallahassee, FL; SR; AA; LPN Lvly Vctnl Schl 83; Hlth Care; RN.

**WASHINGTON, SABRINA Y,** Fisk Univ, Nashville, TN; SO; BED; AL Fsk Clb 89-90; Deans Lst 90-; Alpha Kappa Alpha; Stdnt Supprt Serv; Elem Ed.

**WASHINGTON, SENTA R,** Al St Univ, Montgomery, AL; SO; BA; Dorm Queen 90-; SC 89-90; Coll Engl Tutor 90-; Phi Eta Sigma 90-; Sweetheart Ltl Sis Alpha Phi Alpha VP 89-90; Recog Top Hnr Stdnt Alabama State Univ 90-; Dns Lst 89-; Sec Engl Educ; Engl Professor/TV Nws Anchr.

**WASHINGTON, SIRITA J,** Indiana Univ Of Pa, Indiana, PA; SR; BS; WIVP-TV WIVP 90.1 FM 90-; Alpha Kappa Alpha Pres 89-; Intrnshp WUSL 99 FM; Cmncnts/Media; Mgmt.

**WASHINGTON, TIFFANY D,** Comm Coll Algny Co Algny Cmps, Pittsburgh, PA; SO; ASSOC; Sftbl Tm; Engl; Law.

**WASHINGTON, TRACI B,** Jackson St Univ, Jackson, MS; FR; BS; NSBE 90-; Math/Pr Engr; Electrical Engr.

**WASHINGTON, WARREN WYDELL,** Howard Comm Coll, Columbia, MD; SO; BS; Stdnt Govt VP 90-; Intl Fstvl 90-; Maryland Sub Mass Choir 77-83; Baltimore City 4-H Clubs 75-77; AA; Finance; Hlth Care Admnstr.

**WASHINGTON-GILES, CHARLENE,** Howard Univ, Washington, DC; GD; Delta Sigma Theta; Am Cancer Soc Grant 90-; BS VA State Univ 84; MSW; Med Soc Wrk.

**WASIELESKY, MICHAEL J,** S U N Y Coll Of Tech At Delhi, Delhi, NY; FR; BA; Auto Mech; Auto Eng Dsgnr.

**WASILEWSKI, STEVEN G,** Averett Coll, Danville, VA; JR; BA; Stdnt Newspaper Editor In Chf 88-; Stdnt Judicial Brd Chrprsn 88-89; Stdnt Hndbk Comm 89-90; Pi Kappa Phi Vice Archon 88-; English Jrnlsm; Public Rltns.

**WASINGER, JOANNE L,** Daemen Coll, Amherst, NY; JR; BS; Bus Clb 90-; Delta Mu Delta; Beta Theta 90-; NY St Scty Of Cert Pblc Accts; JT Knndy Mem Awrd; Dns Lst Dmn Coll; AAS Niagara County Comm Coll Sanborn NY 85; Acctng; CPA.

**WASINGER, KEVIN S,** Longwood Coll, Farmville, VA; JR; BA; REACH Pres 89-; Acad Affairs Advsry 90-; VICTORS; Tau Kappa Epsilon Hstrn 90-; History; Tchr/Jrnlst.

**WASKI, MICHAEL J,** Kent St Univ Kent Cmps, Kent, OH; FR; Msc Ed; Ed.

**WASS, LAUREN M,** Fl International Univ, Miami, FL; SR; BS; Stdnt Govt Assn Sntr/Chrprsn Acad Comm 89-90; Peer Advsr 87-91; Ftr Educ Amer 90-91; Omicron Delta Kappa V P 90-91; Phi Kappa 90-; Kappa Delta Pi; Phi Sigma Sigma Phlnthrpy Chrprsn 87; Fclty Schlr 87-89; Elem Educ; Educ/Tchr.

**WASSEF, HEIDI R,** Ponce School Of Medicine, Ponce, PR; SO; MD; Biomed Engr Soc; Egypn Clb; AMSA; AMA; Wmn In Med; Alpha Epsilon Delta 87-; Mc Graw Hill Awd; Fllwshp Med Stdnts Chldns Hosp LA USC Sch Of Med 90; BS USC 89; Med.

**WASSER, SUSAN J,** Lansdale School Of Bus, North Wales, PA; MBA; Hatfield J C Sec 79; Adopt Hwy/Bucks Beautiful; Deans List 89-; Customer Service Specialist/Buyers Choice Ltd Chalford 90-; Cert Bus Word Proc 90; Business Administration.

**WASSON, LENORA L,** Univ Of Sc At Columbia, Columbia, SC; FR; Phi Eta Sigma; Bio.

**WASSON, MICHAEL C,** Me Maritime Academy, Castine, ME; FR; BS; Marine Engrng Tech.

**WASSON, ROBERT J,** Georgetown Coll, Georgetown, KY; SO; BS; Fllwshp Of Chrstn Athlts Co Pres; Bapt Stdnt Union 89-; Stnt Govt Assn Rep 90; Alpha Lambda Delta 90-; Amer Chem Scty Pres; Pres Hse Assn Co Athltc Chrmn 90-; Cmps Actn Tm Alchl Awrnss Grp 90-; Hlth Crs Oppor Prog Univ Of KY; Intrcllgte Ftbl; Blgy; Med.

**WASYLUK, MICHAEL W,** Rutgers St Univ At Camden, Camden, NJ; GD; Amer Mrktng Assoc 88-90; Intra Frat/Sor Cncl Pres 89-90; Kappa Sigma Upsilon Treas 87-90; Attnd Rank Of Eagle Sct BSA 86; BS 90; Mrktng Mgmt; Ret Mgmt.

**WATED, GUILLERMO C,** Univ Of Miami, Coral Gables, FL; JR; BA; Grmn Clb VP 90-; Pres 100 Intl; Fnnc Clb; Gldn Ky 90-; Vol Illtrcy Prog; Ornttn Asst 90; Focus Grp Asst 89-; Dean Lst; Fnnc; Intl Bus.

**WATERHOUSE, ANITA L,** Castleton St Coll, Castleton, VT; SO; BA; Scl Issues Clb Treas 90-; Phi Eta Sigma 90-; Bsktbl 90-; Scl Wrk; Law.

**WATERHOUSE, COLETTE M,** Medical Coll Of Ga, Augusta, GA; JR; BSN; GANS 90-; Gamma Beta Phi 88-89; Nrsng; RN.

**WATERMAN, ADONNA B,** Wells Coll, Aurora, NY; SO; BA; UWCA 89-; Bio; Dctr.**

**WATERMAN, CHARLES F,** Erie Comm Coll, Buffalo, NY; FR; AS; Cmptr Info Syst; Data Prcssng.

**WATERMAN, KIM S,** City Univ Of Ny Baruch Coll, New York, NY; JR; BA; Acctg.

**WATERMAN, SHANA CHRISTIE,** Yale Univ, New Haven, CT; FR; BA; Thtr Grp Pblcst/Actress 90-; Gospel Choir 90-; Herald Jrnlst 90-; Pontiac Post Jrnlst 88-; Amigos De Las Americas Pblct Hlth 90-; Poltcl Sci/Sclgy; Law/Pblc Police.

**WATERS PAYNE, MARCELL R,** Truett Mc Connell Coll, Cleveland, GA; FR; Bus Admin; Law.

**WATERS, CHRISTINE A,** Mt Saint Marys Coll & Seminary, Emmitsburg, MD; SO; BA; Admssns Stdnt Asst; Phtgrphr For Yrbk 90; Radio Statn DJ 90; Wmns Vrsty Sftbl 90-; IM 90-; N E Confrnce Stdnt Athlt 90-; Bus/Finance/Ecnmcs; Financl Anlyst.

**WATERS, COLLEEN L,** Hudson Valley Comm Coll, Troy, NY; SO; AS; Phi Theta Kappa 90-; Tutor 90-; Bus Admin; Acctnt CPA.

**WATERS, ERICA M,** Morgan St Univ, Baltimore, MD; SR; BS; Hl Cncl Chf Juste 89-90; Elem Ed Clb VP 89; Alpha Kappa Mu; Phi Eta Sigma Sr Advsr 90; Phi Delta Kappa VP 90-; Elem Ed.

**WATERS, JANICE E,** Univ Of Ky, Lexington, KY; SR; BS; Rho Chi 89-; Phrmcy; Clinical Phrmcst.

**WATERS, JHANSI C,** Va St Univ, Petersburg, VA; SO; BA; Dance Theater 89; Alpha Mu Gamma Pres; English/Mass Comm; T V Prod.

**WATERS, KAREN S,** Univ Of Miami, Coral Gables, FL; SR; BS; Pearson Pgm Cncl Chrprsn 88-90; Hmcmng Cmt 90; Miami Otrch 90-; Kappa Sgm Swthrt 87-88; Biology/Marine Sci; Envrnmntl Cnsrvtn.

**WATERS, KARYN M,** George Mason Univ, Fairfax, VA; SR; BSED; Zeta Tau Alpha Alumnai Chr 90-; Elem Ed; Tchg.

**WATERS, LA VERNE M,** Salisbury St Univ, Salisbury, MD; SO; BS; Stdnt Natl Edctnl Assn Sec; Union Afrcn Amer Stdnts 89-; Elem Ed; Tchng.

**WATERS, LISA A,** Bryant Stratton Bus Inst Roch, Rochester, NY; SO; AS; Cmptrs; Sys Analysis.

**WATERS, M SCOTT,** Central Fl Comm Coll, Ocala, FL; FR; Mns Sftbl League 86-; Phi Theta Kappa; Assoc Pstr Fth Asmbly Assoc Pstr 87-90; Mnstr; Hstry; Scndry Educ.

**WATERS, NATHANIEL,** Wilmington Coll, New Castle, DE; SR; BA; Non Com Ofcrs Assoc 87-; AA Cmnty Clg Of The Air Force 90; Human Resources Mngmnt.

**WATERS, NICOLE M,** Liberty Univ, Lynchburg, VA; FR; BA; Univ Chrl 90-; IM Bsktbll 90-; Hnrs Prgm 90-; Gd Smrtn Cntr 90-; Chncllr Schlrshp; Deans Lst 90-; Acctg Math; CPA.

**WATERS, SHEILA F,** Columbia Union Coll, Takoma Park, MD; SR; BS; Wash Ethical Soc Peace Comm 90-; Sexual Minority Yth Asst League; Child Welfare League Amer/Pub Policy; AS Uni State Of New York; Soc Psychlgy Mngmntf Human Resrcs/ Comm Cnsl.

**WATERS, STEPHANIE N,** Univ Of Sc At Columbia, Columbia, SC; FR; MBA; Greek Coun 90-; Spartanburg Steel Prod Inc Savg Bond 89; Acctng; CPA.

**WATERS, SUZANNE M,** Newbury Coll, Brookline, MA; SR; NE Broadcast Schl 87; Travel/Tourism.

**WATERSON, ALEX G,** Ms St Univ, Miss State, MS; FR; BS; Maroon Bnd 90; Cncrt Bnd; Gamma Beta Phi; Phi Eta Sigma; Phi Mu Alpha 90-; Pres Schlr 90; Chmstry; Chem Rsrch.

**WATERWORTH, WENDY S,** Univ Of Tn At Knoxville, Knoxville, TN; SR; BS; Beta Gamma Sigma 90-; Phi Kappa Phi 90-; Golden Key 89-; Beta Alpha Psi 90-; Acctng; CPA.

**WATFORD, DEBORAH D,** Livingston Univ, Livingston, AL; SO; Afro Amer Cultural Assoc 90-; Stdnt Support Serv 89-; Delta Sigma Theta Sor In V P 91-; Stdtns Support Serv Stdnt Awd 0-91; Business; Computer Science.

**WATFORD, JACQUELINE K,** Greenville Tech Coll, Greenville, SC; JR; AS; Phi Theta Kappa; Paralgl; Law.

**WATIA, TANYA L,** Georgetown Univ, Washington, DC; SO; BA; Intrnshp Japan Geos Publsh Inc 90; Mrktng; Intl Bsns.

**WATKINS, DEBORAH A,** West Liberty St Coll, West Liberty, WV; JR; BED; Resdnc Hall Cncl Rep 89-90; Hon Soc 88-89; Kappa Delta Pi VP 90-; Engl Ed; Tchng.

**WATKINS, DIANE B,** Univ Of Al At Birmingham, Birmingham, AL; GD; Stdnt Occptnl Thrpy Assn 89-90; AL Occptnl Thrpy Assn 89-; MS Occptnl Thrpy Assn; Sftbl Vlybl 89-90; Prnt/Tchr Assn 87-; Alld Hlth Admin; Assoc Shelton St Comm Coll 90-; Dplma Mckenzie Bus Coll 76; Occptnl Thrpy; Alld Hlth Admin.

**WATKINS JR, DONALD V,** Morehouse Coll, Atlanta, GA; FR; BA; Frshmn Fashion/Talent Show 90-; Ms Freshman Pageant 90-; Hmecmg Show 90-; Spelman Fashion Extravaganza 90-; Hnr Rl 90-; Dns Lst 90-; Bsn Adm; Priv Enterprise Bsn Exec.

**WATKINS, DONNA D,** Dowling Coll, Oakdale Li, NY; SR; BA; Psi Chi 90-; Vol Fld Wk Pilgrm St Psych Ctr 88; Dns Lst 90-; Psych; Mentl Hlth/Chldrn.

**WATKINS, EDMOND B,** Union Univ, Jackson, TN; SO; BS; Stdnt Fndtns; Sigma Zeta; Kappa Mu Epsilon; Lambda Chi Alpha Sec 89; Actvts Cncl; Blgy; Blgcl Research.

**WATKINS, ELAINE M,** Univ Of Tn At Martin, Martin, TN; SR; BS; Alpha Delta Pi Hstrn Stndrds Sr Mbr Lrg 87-; Stdt Tchr Educ Assoc 89-; Stdt Ambssdr 89-; Frshmn Stds Ldr PEP Ldr 90-; Phi Kappa Phi; Alpha Hnr Scty 89-; Kappa Alpha 89-; Order Omega 90-; Pnhllnc Sor Schlrshp 90; Snfrd Educ Schrlshp 90; Early Childhood Education; Teach.

**WATKINS, ERIC P,** East Stroudsburg Univ, E Stroudsburg, PA; SR; BS; Mgmnt/Econ Clb 89-90; Phi Beta Kappa; Cert Excptnl Acad Achvmnt 91; Vlybl 89-90; AA Harrisburg Area Comm Coll 89; Bus Mgmnt; Auto Ind.

**WATKINS, FLORETTA L,** Interdenominational Theo Ctr, Atlanta, GA; GD; MA; Justice Wmn Smnry Rep; Stdt Chrstn Lge VP; Black Presby Caucus Smnrn Rep; Kappa Delta Epsilon 84-; Phi Alpha Delta 85-; Delta Sigma Theta VP 85-; Sprltvs Lst 90-; Dns Lst 90-; Clrnc E Lnnon Awd; Cstmr Ser/Sls AT/T 87-; BA 86; Chrstn Educ/Wrshp/Hmltcs; Pstrng/Smnry Prssr.

**WATKINS, GLENN A,** Univ Of Ky, Lexington, KY; SO; BA; Bptst Stdnt Un Cncl 89-; Am Scty Ag Engrs 89-; FFA 85-; IM Bskbl/Sftbl/Vlybl 89-; Ag Eng.

**WATKINS, GREGORY J,** Univ Of Louisville, Louisville, KY; JR; MENG; Tau Beta Pi; Gldn Key 90-; Phi Eta Sigma 89-; 1st Co Op Rohm/Haas KY Inc; Chrch Choir; Play Guitar For Lcl Chrcn; USAF Rank E-5 83-88; Assoc Comm Coll Air Force 88; Veh Maintenance; Mech Engr; Slr Enrgy Applctns/Envrnmntl Eng.

**WATKINS, JENNIFER M,** Univ Of Tn At Knoxville, Knoxville, TN; JR; BS; Alpha Lambda Delta; Phi Eta Sigma; Beta Gamma Sigma; 1st Natl Bnk Loudon Co; AS Roane State Cmnty Clg 90; Fin; Bnkng.

**WATKINS, KATIE M,** Wv Univ At Parkersburg, Parkersburg, WV; SO; BA; Math; Tchng.

**WATKINS, KVONNE R,** Slippery Rock Univ, Slippery Rock, PA; JR; BED; HPERD Club 88/90-; Aerbcs Inst 89-; Stdnt Tour Gde 89-; Phi Eta Sigma 90-; Hlth/Phys Ed; Tchng.

**WATKINS, LANCE J,** Methodist Coll, Fayetteville, NC; JR; BS; All Dixie Conf Soccer 88-90; All South Region Soccer 90; Vars Soccer 88-90; Acctg; CPA.

**WATKINS, LEONTYNE,** Al A & M Univ, Normal, AL; SR; Stdnt Ind Cluster; Assn Cmptng Mach 90-; Inst Electronics/Elect Eng 90-; Alpha Kappa Mu 90-; Pres Schlrs Soc 88-90; Sigma Tau Epsilon V P 89-; State Farm Ins Co Intrnshp 90; At&t Ntwrk Sys Co Op Stdnt; Cmptr Sci/Math; Prgmr/Analyst.

**WATKINS, MONICA L,** Univ Of Tn At Knoxville, Knoxville, TN; SO; BS; EUBP; FMA; Alpha Lambda Delta; Phi Eta Sigma; Finance; Banking.

**WATKINS, MONICA P,** Savannah St Coll, Savannah, GA; FR; Acctg; CPA.

**WATKINS, NANCY G,** Vance Granville Comm Coll, Henderson, NC; SO; AAS; SGA 90; Beta Phi Upsilon 90-; Phi Theta Kappa; Bus; Admin Asst.

**WATKINS, PAMELA R,** Livingston Univ, Livingston, AL; SR; BS; SIFE 90-; Univ Hsts 88-; Omicron Delta Kappa VP 90-; Crdnl Key VP 90-; Scts Exlnt De Mercatus Lit Sec 90-; Phi Eta Sigma 88-; Delta Sigma Pi Pres 90-; Phi Mu VP 90-; Bsn Mgmt Dept Awd; Delta Sigma Pi Key Awd; Mst Prmsng Stdnt Bsn 90; Indstrl Engrg.

**WATKINS, PATRICIA L,** Christopher Newport Coll, Newport News, VA; SR; BA; Phi Theta Kappa 88-89; AS Paul D Camp Comm Coll 89; AS Ed Paul D Camp Comm Coll 89; Elem Ed; Tchr.

**WATKINS, SARAH B,** Univ Of Rochester, Rochester, NY; SR; Eng Cncl; BA; Psychlgy.

**WATKINS, STEPHANIE M,** Middle Ga Coll, Cochran, GA; FR; AS; Gamma Beta Phi 90-; Otstdng Chem Yr; Med Prfsns; Pre Pharm.

**WATKINS, STEPHEN T,** Lees Coll, Jackson, KY; SO; BA; Mdcl Alld Hlth Srvcs; Awrds Achvmnt Hmn Anatmy Physiology Rlgn; Mltry Adhvmnt Mdl; KY Army Ntnl Grd Wrk Cnstrctn; Mdcl; Nrsng.

**WATKINS, STEWART J,** Morehouse Coll, Atlanta, GA; JR; BA; Hnr Roll 88; Deans Lst 90-; Vrsty Bsktbl 88-; Urban Studies; Urban Plng/Dsgn.

**WATKINS, TERRY A,** Indiana Univ Of Pa, Indiana, PA; JR; BSED; Mrchng Bnd Chmbr Sngrs 88-89; Chorus 89-90; Concrt Danc Co 88-89; Inv Perfrm IUP Chorale Carn Hall 92; Bio; Sec Post Sec Educ.

**WATKINS JR, TERRY L,** Liberty Univ, Lynchburg, VA; SR; BS; Amer Choral Dir Assoc 89-; Msc Mnstry Clb Treas 90-; MENC 89-90; Alpha Lambda Delta 89-; Thomas Road Jr High Chrl Dir 90-; Univ Chrl Stdnt Dir 90-; Concert Choir 88-90; High Hnrs GPA Schlrshp 89-90; Hnrs GPA Schlrshp 90-; Msc Ed; Msc Bsn.**

**WATKINS, TIEKA M,** Univ Of Nc At Charlotte, Charlotte, NC; JR; BA; Engl.

**WATKINS, WILLIAM S P,** Johnson C Smith Univ, Charlotte, NC; FR; BA; Oratoricl Soc; Humanifest; Math; Math/Law.

**WATKINS-GIBSON, TERI A,** Univ Of South Fl, Tampa, FL; SO; BABSN; Alpha Lambda Delta 83; Phi Eta Sigma 83; Themis Hnr Soc; Sec Admnstrtv Asst Wrd Prcsr Phtgrphr Photo Prntr 82-; Fine Art Nrsng; Art Therapy.

**WATLEY, JEFRE R,** Fl St Univ, Tallahassee, FL; GD; IEEE 88-; Stdnt Govt Sntr 84-86; Eng Hon Scty 88-; Phi Theta Kappa 84-86; Natl Achvmnt Acad 88; Honrbl Dschrg USAF 80-84; BSEE FL State Un 90; Elect; Eng.

**WATLEY, REBEKAH V,** Union Coll, Barbourville, KY; JR; BA; Gamma Beta Phi; Iota Sigma Nu; Lit Awd; Short Story Rushton Awd; Pres Laureate Schlr 90-; Deans Lst 89-; Engl/Hist.

**WATLEY-JOHNSON, CARMALETHA M,** Oh Univ, Athens, OH; JR; BA; Music Thrpy Clb; Kappa Phi; Tau Beta Sigma; Sigma Alpha Iota; Wnd Enslbl; Sigma Alpha Iota Fndmntl Ed 89-90; Tau Beta Sigma Rcrdng Sec 90-; Kappa Phi; Music Thrpy.

**WATLINGTON, MARY J,** Bowie St Univ, Bowie, MD; SR; BS; Kappa Delta Pi; Cncl Excptnl Chldrn; PTA Pres 86-87; AA 73; Educ; Tchg.

**WATSKY, CARYN B,** Emory Univ, Atlanta, GA; JR; Beta Alpha Psi VP 90-; Delta Phi Epsilon; Sigma Chi; Lttle Sistr Sprt Chrmn 88-.

**WATSO, JAMES C,** Embry Riddle Aeronautical Univ, Daytona Beach, FL; FR; BS; Golf Clb 90-; Naval Avtn Clb 90-; Private Pilot; Aerospace Eng.

**WATSON, ALISA R,** Hillsborough Comm Coll, Tampa, FL; FR; AA; Stdnt Sppt Serv 90-; Better Un Stdnts 90-; Reg Phrmcst.

**WATSON, ANTHONY S,** Savannah Coll Of Art & Design, Savannah, GA; SR; BFA; AIGA; BS Univ West FL Pensacola 75; Graphic Dsgn/Art Hist; Coll Instr.

**WATSON, AVA H,** Nova Univ, Ft Lauderdale, FL; GD; Drctr Alachua Urgnt Care Cntr; AA Nrsng Santa Fe J C 68; AS Nrsng Albany J C 73; BSN Unv FL 85.

**WATSON, BEVERLY J,** Tallahassee Comm Coll, Tallahassee, FL; FR; Medical.

**WATSON, BRYAN W,** Piedmont Coll, Demorest, GA; SR; BA; Deans Lst 90-; Pres Lst; Bus Dept Awrd; Bsbll 88-89; Acctg; CPA.

**WATSON, CARL L,** Va St Univ, Petersburg, VA; SR; BA; Crmnl Jstc Clb 88; Crmnl Jstc; Law.

**WATSON, CAROL D,** Fl Memorial Coll, Miami, FL; FR; BA; Accntng.

**WATSON, CHRISTY L,** Univ Of Miami, Coral Gables, FL; SO; BA; Comm Serv Pro Dvrsty Cmmtt 90-; Intrvrsty 89-; Pres 100 90-; Intl Stu/Pltcs; Law/U S Frgn Srv.

**WATSON, COLLEEN B,** Comm Coll Algny Co Algny Cmps, Pittsburgh, PA; FR; BA; Math/Sci; Arch.

**WATSON, DALE LYNN,** Temple Univ, Philadelphia, PA; JR; BSN; SNAP 90-; Dscplnry Com; BS Kutztown Univ 76; Nrsng; Hosp Nrsng.

**WATSON, DANIEL J,** Saint Thomas Univ, Miami, FL; SR; WBFS-TV 33 Miami FL Prdctn Asst 90; Studio Cntr Video/Film Miami FL 90; BA 90; Cmnctn Arts; Filmmkg/TV/VIDEO.

**WATSON, DEBORAH A,** Univ Of Sc At Columbia, Columbia, SC; FR; ADN; Stdnt Nrss Assn 90-; Rdlgc Tech 72-; Cert RT Medical College Of GA 72; Nrsng.

**WATSON, DEBORAH R,** Memphis St Univ, Memphis, TN; SO; BS; Phi Eta Sigma 90-; Blck Schlrs Unlmtd 90-; PREP; US All Amer Schlr; Bio; Med/Pediatrics.

**WATSON, DONNA L,** Life Coll, Marietta, GA; SR; BS; Constead Clncl Stu Soc; FL Clb Chrprctc Stu VP; FL Chrprctc Soc; Phi Thetta Kappa 86-; Grad Hghst Hrs 88-; Rsrch Asst; Police Bevnlnt Assn 82-; Scrn Actrs Gld 78-; Police Offcr 82-; AA Browrand Comm Coll 86; BS Regents Coll; Chmstry/Pre Chrprct; Chrprctc Dctr.

**WATSON, DUHANE A,** City Univ Of Ny City Coll, New York, NY; GD; V P Assn Cmptng Mach V P 89-90; Soc Blck Eng 88-90; IEEE 89-90; Goldn Key; Assn Cmptng Mach V P 89-90; SBE 88-90; Pgm Ret Eng Stdnt Tutr 89-90; Sam Rudin Awd Eng Stdnt 89-90; BSC 90; Cmptr Sci; Prgmmr/Anlyst.

**WATSON, ERIK D,** Columbus Coll Of Art & Design, Columbus, OH; FR; BFA; Ebenezer M B Ch Yng Adult Gospel Ch 87-; Ebenezer M B Ch Band 87-; Columbus Coll Art/Dsgn Natl Schlrshp 90-; Illus Advrtsng; Cartooning Animation.

**WATSON III, ERNEST A,** Central Fl Comm Coll, Ocala, FL; FR; BA; Stdnt Govt Assc Pres 90-; Bnds 90-; Phi Theta Kappa; Ntl Clgte Stdnt Govt Awds; IM Coor 90-; Bus Admin; Bus.

**WATSON, FALESHA R,** Johnson C Smith Univ, Charlotte, NC; FR; BS; Bullfest Cmmtt Stdnt Govt; Alpha Lambda Delta; Prjct Vt; Bus Amdn; Acctg.

**WATSON, GARY J,** Univ Of Miami, Coral Gables, FL; FR; BA; Un Blck Stdnt 90-; Stanford Jazz Excell Grp 90-; Outstndg Blck Achiever 90-; Miami Crew Tm 90-; Architecture Dsgn.

**WATSON, GREGORY L,** Univ Of Pittsburgh At Bradford, Bradford, PA; FR; BA; Fine Arts; Art Edn/Theatrical Dsgn.

**WATSON, HEATHER R,** Blue Mountain Coll, Blue Mountain, MS; JR; BA; Psychlgy Clb Pres 88-; Athltc Assn Cncl 89; Modenian Soc Pres 88-; Koininea VP 88-; Mtn Breeze Edtr 88-90; Mtnr; Psychlgy.

**WATSON, JAMES C,** Univ Of Tn At Chattanooga, Chattanooga, TN; FR; BCE; Math/Science; Engr.

**WATSON, JANA M,** Eastern Ky Univ, Richmond, KY; SR; BS; Stdnt Natl Envrnmntl Hlth Assn Pres; Mbr Natl Envrnmntl Hlth Assn; Kappa Delta Srty Grd; Chem Awd Ashland Comm Coll; Envrnmntl Hlth Sci.

**WATSON, JOHN L,** Univ Of Sc At Columbia, Columbia, SC; SO; BS; AS Spartanburg Tech Coll 89; Mech Eng; Eng.

**WATSON, KANDACE,** Hampton Univ, Hampton, VA; FR; BA; Winona Hall Judiciary Comm Chrprsn 90-; Womens Sen Rep 90-; Fashn Show Extravgnza Mdl; Jet Proplsn Lab CA Inst Of Technlgy Techncl Intrn 90-; Math.

**WATSON, KAREN L,** Broward Comm Coll, Ft Lauderdale, FL; FR; BS; Phi Theta Kappa 90; Phi Beta Lambda V P Acting Pres 90; Wmns Coun/Realtors 89-90; Resp Ther 77-86; Realtor Asso Cmmcl Inv/R E 88-; RTI Miami Dade Comm Colg 77; Lgl Studies: Law.

**WATSON, KAREN T,** Fl St Univ, Tallahassee, FL; JR; BA; Phi Theta Kappa 89-; Pres Lst Talla Comm Coll 88-90; Wrk 5 Yrs Cmptr Optr 83-88; AA 89; Math; Tchr.

**WATSON, KEVIN M,** Bowling Green St Univ, Bowling Green, OH; GD; MS; Stu Athltc Trnr 87-90; Dean Lst 87-90; Acdmc Hnr Stu Athlt 87-; Natl Athltc Trnrs Assn; Intern Physcl Thrpy Wood Co Hosp 90; Cert Athltc Trnr; BS 90; Exrcs Physlgy; Athltc Trnr.

**WATSON, KIMBERLY R,** West Liberty St Coll, West Liberty, WV; SO; BS; Chi Omega 90; Acctng; CPA.

**WATSON, LAURIE L,** Va Commonwealth Univ, Richmond, VA; SR; BS; Ad 2 Club Of Richmond; Innovtv Images Publc Rltns Club 90-; George Crutchfield Adv Schlrshp 90; Adv; Art Dir.

**WATSON, LEE H,** Univ Of Rochester, Rochester, NY; JR; BS; Interclgte Vlybl Club Cap 88-; Res Advisor 89-; Admsisions Stdnt Interviewer 90-; Tiernan Project 89-; Stdnt Life Awd 90-; IBM Watson Schlr 88; Take Five Egypt; Optical Engrng; Business.

**WATSON, LISA M,** Millersville Univ Of Pa, Millersville, PA; FR; BSED; Erly Chldhd Educ Assn 90-; Cncl Fr Excptnl Chldrn 90-; Tchstne Yrbk Acads Edit 90-; Bwlng 90-; Elem And Spcl Educ; Tchr.

**WATSON, MICHAELE DAVID,** Univ Of Sc At Columbia, Columbia, SC; SR; BS; Fellowshp Of Christn Athlts 89-; Campus Crusade For Christ 88-; Im 87-; BS; Bus Admn/Mktg.

**WATSON, MICHELE J,** Jackson St Comm Coll, Jackson, TN; FR; AS; Offc Admn; Offc Wrk.

**WATSON, MONICA D,** Va St Univ, Petersburg, VA; JR; BA; Bus Admn Clb 89-90; Pres Lst 88; Deans Lst 88-; Acad Achvmnt Awd; Bus GPA Awd 89; Bus Fin.

**WATSON, PAMELA L,** Western New England Coll, Springfield, MA; SR; BSBA; Radio DJ 88-89; Mktg Clb 87-88; Wmns Vars Sccr 87-; Mktg.

**WATSON, PAMELA M,** Salisbury St Univ, Salisbury, MD; SR; BS; Stdnt Natl Educ Assc 89-; Kappa Dlt Pi 89-; Elem Educ.

**WATSON, PAULETTE L,** Cheyney Univ Of Pa, Cheyney, PA; FR; BA; Sub Comm Std Rttn 90; Bsn Admn; Acctng.

**WATSON, QUANDA N,** Clark Atlanta Univ, Atlanta, GA; JR; BA; Acctng Club 88-90; JBSU 88; BASTA Bro & Sis Taking Action; Read America 89-90; Outreach Big Sis 88-89; Intern Bureau Of Rclmtn; Campus Deans List 89; Miss Kappa Alpha Psi Frat 89; Bus Admn/Acctng; CPA.**

**WATSON, RICHARD M,** Jefferson Davis St Jr Coll, Brewton, AL; FR; Wrkng AA Degree; Psychlgy.

**WATSON, RONALD E,** Univ Of Sc At Columbia, Columbia, SC; SO; BA; Dir Pep Bnd Cstl Carolina Coll; Chrch Mnstry Music Asst/Pstr 88-89; Deans Lst; Mscn Ldr 90-; AA Prctcl Thlgy Christ Natn Dallas TX 85; Music; Music Edctr/Prfrmr.

**WATSON, SABRINA M,** Middle Tn St Univ, Murfreesboro, TN; SR; BS; Stdnt Hm Ec Assn V-Chr 87-; TN Hm Ec Assn 87-; Amer Hm Ec Assn 87-; Kappa Omicron Nu S 89-; Gamma Beta Phi 88-; Tau Omciron 89-; Phi Kappa Phi 90-; Deans Lst/Hon Rll 87-; Wrk Schlrshp 87-; Ko Nu Awd 88-89; Rita Davenport Schlrshp 89; Fash Merch; Store Mgmt/Entrprnrshp.

**WATSON, SABRINA R,** Fl A & M Univ, Tallahassee, FL; JR; BA; NABA; White/Gold; Intrnshp Motorola Inc Schaumburg Il 90; Cngrsnl Intrn Dept Of Urban Dev Wash DC; Acctng.

**WATSON, SHIRLEY J,** Abraham Baldwin Agri Coll, Tifton, GA; JR; AS; Phi Theta Kappa; Anml Sci Awd 90; Anml Sci; BS.

**WATSON, STEVEN P,** Univ Of Nc At Greensboro, Greensboro, NC; SR; MED; Exrcse And Sprt Sci; Mjrs Assn Sr Brd Mmbr 90-; Susan Stout Mem Schlrshp 90-; Spcl Educ Sndy Schl Tchr Frst Bapt Chrch NC; BS UNC Greensboro; Sprt Pdggy; Tchng.

**WATSON, SUSAN A,** Mount Olive Coll, Mount Olive, NC; FR; BS; Acdmc Schlrs 90-; Bus Mgmt.

**WATSON, TERWANNA E,** Al A & M Univ, Normal, AL; SO; BS; Gspl Choir 90-; Bptst Stdnt Union BSU Cncl; Amer Home Ec Assn Pres 90-; J F Drake Lrng Rsrc Cntr Asst 90; Fshn Mrchndsg; Fshn Cnsltnt/Entrprnr.

**WATSON, VALERIE M,** Wilmington Coll, New Castle, DE; SR; BS; Delta Epsilon Rho 90-; Bus/Pro Wmns Grp; Deans Lst 88-; AAS Comm Coll Air Frc; Crmnl Juste; Law.

**WATSON, WENDY R,** Univ Of Me, Orono, ME; FR; BA; Amer Inst Chem Engrs Sec; Alpha Lambda Delta; Chem Engr.

**WATSON, WILLIAM MARK,** Meridian Comm Coll, Meridian, MS; SO; BS; VICA 89-90; AA 89; Engrg/Busn; Engrg.

**WATT SHIPP, LINDA S,** Salisbury St Univ, Salisbury, MD; SO; BFA; Yrbk Phtgrphr Illstrtr 89-; 25 Stdnt Unn Hstrn 90; Phi Eta Sigma 90; Cmps Lte Awrd; Art; Phtgrphc Art.

**WATT, CHRISTOPHER BRIAN,** Univ Of Southern Ms, Hattiesburg, MS; FR; BA; Grk Wk Comm Phlntrpy Chrmn; Stdnt Aclumni Assoc; Hnr Stdnt Assoc; Assoc Stdnt Body Ambssdr Co Chr; Lambda Sigma Treas; Gamma Beta Phi; Golden Key; Phi Kappa Tau VP Alumni Affrs; Omicron Delta Kappa Outsdng Fres; IMS.

**WATT, CONSTANCE A,** Wilmington Coll, New Castle, DE; SR; BA; Human Resources Officer Core States Bank De Na 90; AA 90; Human Resource Management.

**WATT, KELLIE A,** Glassboro St Coll, Glassboro, NJ; JR; BA; Adv Club 89-; Am Adv Fed; Sigma Delta Upsilon Prlmntrn 90; Intern Krampf Cmmnctns Somerset N J; Cmmnctns/Advtsng.

**WATT, OLIVER M,** Univ Of Fl, Gainesville, FL; GD; MFA; Ky 90; VA Ahrens Pntng Schlrshp 88; Fll Art Hrvst Bst Stdnt Pntr 89; Prsnl Stdio Asst To Pntr W Schaaf; Kassel Art Acad West Germany; Fne Arts.

**WATTERS, JOHN A,** Wv Univ, Morgantown, WV; SR; RS; IEEE 88-; Intern AEP Martinka Mines; Ldrshp Schlrshp 87-; Elect/Comp Engrng.

**WATTERS, MONIQUE M,** Endicott Coll, Beverly, MA; JR; BA; Stdnt Govt Senate 90-; Class Sec; Psychlgy Clb; Mstr Peer Tutr 88-; Shpmts 90-; AS 90; Visual Cmnctns; Grphc Artst.

**WATTERSON, CHARLENE D,** Slippery Rock Univ, Slippery Rock, PA; JR; BS; Phi Sigma Pi; Phi Epsilon Kappa; Kinesiothearpy Phy Ed; Knsthrpst.

**WATTERSON, MARY L,** Univ Of North Fl, Jacksonville, FL; JR; BA; Gldn Ky 90-; AA Santa Fe Comm Coll 86; Cmmnctns; Brdcst Jrnlsm.

**WATTERSON, ROBERT B,** Univ Of Ky, Lexington, KY; FR; BS; Var Swmng 90-; Chem; Med.

**WATTLEWORTH, TIMOTHY S,** Univ Of Fl, Gainesville, FL; JR; BS; Soc Phys Stdnts 88-90; Amer Soc Cvl Engrs 90-; Fla Engr Soc 90-; Tau Beta Pi Vice Chrmn 90-; Sigma Phi Epsilon Fund Rsng Chrmn 88-; Habitat Humnty 90-; Electee Yr; Cvl Engr; Structrl Engr.

**WATTS, ANDREA T,** Commonwealth Coll, Virginia Beach, VA; SO; AS; Cmptr Clb 89-; Alpha Beta Gamma 89-; Pres Lst 89-; Prfct Atndnc 89-; Evnglst Nw Cmnty Chrch God Chrst 89-; Outrch/Wtnsng Ldr Pres; Mgmt Anlst 85-88; Admin Spec/Cmptr Oprtr 89-; Mstrs Tchrs Charles Harrison Mason Bible Clg 83; Cmptr Sci/Evnglsm; Pgmr/Anlst.

**WATTS, ARLEEN J,** Phillips Jr Coll Charlotte, Charlotte, NC; GD; SGA Pres; Prsdnts Lst; Phi Beta Lambda Pres; Prfct Attndnc; Exec Sec; Date Entry Cert 89; Exec Sec 90; Sectrl.

**WATTS, CASSANDRA L,** City Univ Of Ny Baruch Coll, New York, NY; SO; BA; Gspl Chrs 89-; Fntn Chrch Chrst Yth 81-; Cnslr Coordntr Chr Mmbr Ushr Sndy Schl; Deans Lst 90-; Accntng; CPA.

**WATTS, ELIZABETH K,** Birmingham Southern Coll, Birmingham, AL; JR; BS; Wind Ensmble 88; GS; Alpha Lambda Delta 89; Kappa Mu Epsilon 89; Zeta Tau Alpha; Physics.

**WATTS, FRANCIS E,** Coppin St Coll, Baltimore, MD; SO; BA; History.

**WATTS, GWEN E,** Emory Univ, Atlanta, GA; SR; MNMPH; Alpha Lambda Delta 62-64; Alpha Delta Pi 62-64; Univ GA Regents Schlrshp 61-64; Deans Schlrshp 90-; Natl Cnsrtm Chem Dpndncy Nrs 89-; GA Adctn Cnslrs Assc 89-; ADN Santa Barbara Cty Coll 77; Natl Assc Alchlsm/Drug Abuse Cnslrs 90-; Nursing.

**WATTS, JAMES C,** Univ Of Southern Ms, Hattiesburg, MS; FR; MBA; Mrchng Bnd 90-; Acctg; Law.

**WATTS, MICHAEL K,** Morehouse Coll, Atlanta, GA; JR; BA; Hon Prog Clb 88-; Schlr Prog 89-; Sch Nwspr Stf Wrtr 89-; Sigma Tau Delta; Golden Key; Atlanta Assn Blk Jrnlsts 90-; Kappa Alpha Psi; CNN Med Nws Intrn 90; Arsenio Hall Show Intrnsp; Hon Rl/Deans Lst Dstnctn 89-; English; T V Prodcr/Dir.

**WATTS, OZELL P,** Al St Univ, Montgomery, AL; SO; BS; Soc Work/Child Prtctn.

**WATTS, ROBERT V,** Columbia Union Coll, Takoma Park, MD; SR; BA; Stdnt Mmbr Brd Trustees Prince Georges Comm Clg 87-88; Deans Lst 86-88; Deans Lst 89-; Scout Ldr Boy Scouts America 72-; Cmmrcl Real Est Apprsr Glvr Asc 88-; AA Prince Georges Comm Clg 88-; Bsns Admnstrtn; Dsgntd Lcnsd Cmmrcl.

**WATTS, STEVEN A,** Univ Of Akron, Akron, OH; SR; BS; Elec Eng.

**WATTS, TAMMY S,** Lexington Comm Coll, Lexington, KY; FR; AAS; Red Crs/Lexington Comm Clg Ltrs Hm; Off Admn.

**WATTS, TRESA L,** Al A & M Univ, Normal, AL; SO; BS; Bsn Mgmt; Own Bsn.

**WATTS, VELVA F,** Queens Coll, Charlotte, NC; SR; BA; Deans Lst; Paul Douglas Tchr Schrlshp 89-; Tchr Asstnt Resrrctn Chrstn Schl; Professional Intrnshp Matthews Elem; Elem Educ; MED Reading Specialist.

**WATTS, YOLANDA L,** Al St Univ, Montgomery, AL; SO; Newspaper Sprts Wrtr; Engrng.

**WATY, MEGA,** Comm Coll Algny Co Algny Cmps, Pittsburgh, PA; FR; Mbr Comm Coll; Intl Club; Hotel Mgmt.

**WAUGH DICKENSON, MELODY,** Memphis St Univ, Memphis, TN; SO; BSN; Gamma Beta Phi; Nrsng.

**WAUGH, DEBRA L,** Columbia Union Coll, Takoma Park, MD; GD; BS; Emp At WUSA-TV In Wa DC 90-; Cert Wrtrs Digest Sch Fictn Wrtng 89; Bsns Mgmt; Entrprnrshp.

**WAUGH, DIANNA E,** Eckerd Coll, St Petersburg, FL; SR; BA; Psych Clb 89; Art Clb 89; Psych/Art.

**WAUGH, LAWRENCE W,** Anne Arundel Comm Coll, Arnold, MD; FR; Comp Info Srvcs.

**WAUGH, TONDA J,** Marshall University, Huntington, WV; SO; BA; Elem Ed; Elem Schl Tchr.

**WAUGH, TRANTINA E,** Howard Univ, Washington, DC; GD; MSW; Ntl Clgt Scl Sci Awd; All-Amer Schlr; Blck Scl Wrk Assc 90-; BA Univ DC 86; Scl Wrk.

**WAWRZYNIAK, JACALYN I,** S U N Y Coll Of Tech At Alfred, Alfred, NY; SR; BA; AS; Psy.

**WAY, AMANDA L,** Colby Sawyer Coll, New London, NH; SO; BS; Theater 90-; Assoc Alpha Chi 90-; Child Study; Spch Path/Spec Educ.

**WAY, AMY M,** S U N Y Coll At Fredonia, Fredonia, NY; SR; MBS; Stdnt Run Hlth Cntr Clnc Dir 89-90; Psychlgy Clb 89-90; Psi Chi 89-90; Theta Lambda Chi Treas 87-89; Intrnshp-Upward Bnd Pgm 90; Deans Lst 88-90; Indpndnt Study-Upward Bnd Pgm 90; BA 90; Psychlgy; Schl Psychlgst.

**WAY, CATHERINE A,** Anderson Coll, Anderson, SC; SO; AA; Gamma Beta Phi 90; Omicron Jota Kappa 89-; Salkehatchie Summer Srvc 86-90; Assistance Ctr Assist 89-; Chldrns Dept Buyer Intern 90; Fshn Merch; Fshn Boutique.

**WAY, DONNA D,** Columbia Greene Comm Coll, Hudson, NY; FR; AAS; Crmnl Juste; Law Enfrcmnt.

**WAY, HARRIETT G,** Wv Univ At Parkersburg, Parkersburg, WV; FR; Edn; Teach.

**WAY, KIRSTEN A,** Saint Francis Coll, Loretto, PA; FR; BS; Stdnt Nrs Org 90-; Gamma Sigma Sigma 90-; Crs Cntry Trck 90-; Nrsg.

**WAYDA, MICHELLE M,** Newbury Coll, Brookline, MA; SR; Ntnl Paralgl Assc; AS; Paralgl Stds; Legal Asst.

**WAYE, APRIL L,** Savannah St Coll, Savannah, GA; JR; BS; Natl Soc Blck Engrs 87-89; GA Tech Afro-Am Assn 88-89; Am Soc Mech Engrs 89-91; Beta Kappa Chi 90-; Alpha Kappa Alpha VP 90-; Girl Scouts Am Ldr 90-; Hon Roll; Deans Lst; Pres Lst 89-; Natl Coll Eng Awd; US Achvmnt Acad All-Am Schlr; Mech Eng Tech.

**WAYLAND, LISA D,** Oh Univ Chillicothe Branch, Chillicothe, OH; SR; Amer Cancer Soc; Myrl Shoemaker Schlrshp 89-90; Amer Assc Univ Wmn Shlrshp 90-; BS; Elem Educ.

**WAYMAN, LESLIE A,** Western Piedmont Comm Coll, Morganton, NC; FR; AAS; Dns Lst; Sx Eqty Stdnt Yr; Mech Drftng/Dsgn.

**WAYMAN, NICOLE C,** Wv Univ, Morgantown, WV; FR; BS; Vlybl/Soccer 90; Chem Eng.

**WAYNE, JACK,** City Univ Of Ny Baruch Coll, New York, NY; JR; BA; Amer Mktg Asc 89-; Dns Lst 90-; Pres Schlp 88-; Mktg; Adv Firm.

**WAYNE, KIM M,** Univ Of Pittsburgh At Bradford, Bradford, PA; FR; PPH; Phrmcy.

**WAYNE, MARIO J E,** Central St Univ, Wilberforce, OH; JR; BA; Deans List 88-; Kappa Alpha Psi Histn; Postive Peer Influence Counselor 89-; DAPP; E St Louis Il Big Brothers/Big Sisters 90; Acad Athelete Awd 88; Co-Op Intl Revenue Serv Intl Secty 90; Pre Law Political Sci; Practice Law.

**WAYNE, SANDSRA J,** Univ Of Md At Eastern Shore, Princess Anne, MD; SR; BS; AS Penn St Univ 85; Phycl Thrpy; Physcl Thrpst.

**WAYNICK, DENELLE J,** Howard Univ, Washington, DC; GD; JD; Stdnt Bar Assn 88-; Blck Law Stdnt Assn 88-90; Howard Law Jrnl Ld Artcls Edtr 89-; Merit Schlrshp 88-; BS Rutgers Univ 88; Law; Corp/Tax Law.

**WAZANEY III, NORMAN J,** Western New England Coll, Springfield, MA; SR; BA; Grdtn Cmte 90; Intrnshp Scrtry St Ofc Mass 90; Vrsty Krt Tm 86-89; Govt/Cmptr Sci.

**WEAKLAND, ANN M,** Mount Aloysius Jr Coll, Cresson, PA; SO; AS; Acctg; CPA.

**WEAKLAND, MICHELLE D,** Mount Aloysius Jr Coll, Cresson, PA; FR; Crmnlgy; Crmnl Invstgtns.

**WEAKS, ROY DE A,** Univ Of Tn At Martin, Martin, TN; JR; STEA 90-; Asst Ftbl Coach Martin Jr High 90-; Soc Studies; Scndry Edn Tchr/Coach.

**WEAKS, TRINA B,** Univ Of Tn At Martin, Martin, TN; JR; STEA 90-; Erly Chldhd Educ; Tchr.

**WEALAND, STACY L,** Central Pa Bus School, Summerdale, PA; FR; AS; Phys Thrpy Assts Hlpng Hnds Clb Sec 90-; Easter Seal Cmp; Phys Thrpst Asst.

**WEAN, JENNIFER K,** Kent St Univ Kent Cmps, Kent, OH; JR; BA; Ntl Golden Key; Psych.

**WEANT, SUSAN A,** Univ Of Tn At Martin, Martin, TN; SO; Alpha Delta Pi Pblc Rltns 90-; Elem Ed; Tchng.

**WEAR JR, JAMES C,** Methodist Coll, Fayetteville, NC; SR; BA; Cmptr Sci Clb; Hnrs Clb; Chrch Actv; MC Bsktbl All Conf/All Acad 89-; Cmptr Sci; Prgmmng.

**WEAR, MATTHEW E,** Marshall University, Huntington, WV; JR; BA; Inter Fraterwty Council VP Admin 90-; Gamma Beta Phi 89-; Order Of Omega; Phi Kappa Phi Treas 89-; Serve Cadet WV Natl Gaurd Cadet 90-; Accouting; CPA.

**WEAR, MICHAEL L,** Univ Of Akron, Akron, OH; SR; BS; Golden Key 90; Fncl Mgmt Assn Ntl Hon Soc; Delta Sigma Pi Chrmn Schlrshp Comm 89-; Bus Fnc; Corp Law.

**WEARE, HEATHER M,** Univ Of Sc At Columbia, Columbia, SC; FR; BA; Univ Wom On Cmps 90-; Fres Wrtng Awd 90-; Wmns Tennis Tm MVP 90-; English; Law.

**WEARS, JANET V,** N Va Comm Coll Woodbridge, Woodbridge, VA; SO; AA; Deans List 85-86; Hon Eng Comp II; Crrntly Lgl Sec US Dept Of Justice; Intrntnl Studies; Lnguage Spclst.

**WEARY, GERALDINE S,** Alcorn St Univ, Lorman, MS; SR; BS; Alpha Swthrt Orgnztn 89; Bsns Admnstrtn; Mngmnt/Accntng.

**WEATHERALL, JEFFREY S,** Memphis St Univ, Memphis, TN; FR; BS; Phi Eta Sigma 90-; Bio; Med.

**WEATHERALL, STEPHEN M,** Morehouse Coll, Atlanta, GA; JR; BA; Psychlgy Assn 90-; Pre-Law Soc 90-; Goldn Key 90-; Coll Hon Roll 88-; Prncetn Univ Smmr Rsrch Prog; Psychlgy; Frnsc Psychlgy.

**WEATHERBEE JR, FORREST R,** Univ Of Nh Plymouth St Coll, Plymouth, NH; SR; BS; Pi Gamma Mu 90-; Phi Kappa Phi; Prsdnts Lst 88-; Scl Science Edctn; Tchr.

**WEATHERBY, JEFFERY W,** Comm Coll Algny Co Algny Cmps, Pittsburgh, PA; SO; AD BS; Natl Rfle Assns; Natl Hnr Scty 76; Ex Stlwrkr 77-; Blgcl Sci; Rgstrd Rsprtry Thrpst.

**WEATHERFORD, KATHY L,** Union Univ, Jackson, TN; SR; BS; Phi Theta Kappa; Sigma Delta; Phys Educ/Hlth.

**WEATHERFORD, TIMOTHY W,** Univ Of Tn At Martin, Martin, TN; SO; BA; Golf Team Cptn; Bstkbl Team; Co Op Stdnt Forcum-Lannon Assoc; MVP Golf Team; Civil Engr.**

**WEATHERFORD, WILLIAM E,** Brewer St Jr Coll, Fayette, AL; SO; AS; Phi Theta Kappa 90-; Phrmcy.

**WEATHERMAN, MELISSA ANN,** Mayland Comm Coll, Spruce Pine, NC; GD; AAS; Elisha Honeycutt Schlrshp; Med Offc Tech; Med Fld.

**WEATHERSPOON, MELISSA J,** Central St Univ, Wilberforce, OH; SR; BA; Army Res E5 Sgt; Merck Shrp Dohme Res Asst Intrn; Prctr Gmble Res Asst Intrn; Res Army Achvmnt Mdl Oper Dsrt Strm; Chem; Physcn.

**WEATHERSPOON, TARSHA Y,** Jackson St Univ, Jackson, MS; FR; BA; Mass Cmnctns Clb; Blck PRIDE; Alpha Lambda Delta; Mass Cmnctns; Radio/TV Anchr/Rprtr.

**WEATHERWAX, RENEE HOPE,** Univ Of Sc At Coastal Carolina, Conway, SC; FR; Soclgy.

**WEAVER, ANTHONY B,** City Univ Of Ny City Coll, New York, NY; SO; BA; Ph D Math.

**WEAVER, BETTY M,** Wv Univ At Parkersburg, Parkersburg, WV; GD; Coldwell-Banker/Raleigh Real Estate Ctr Owner; BS 72; MA 78; Elem Ed/Rdg.

**WEAVER, BRETT H,** Memphis St Univ, Memphis, TN; SO; BSET; Crsd Chrst 89-; Mfg Eng Tchnlgy.

**WEAVER, BRUCE J,** Duquesne Univ, Pittsburgh, PA; FR; RPH; Phrmcy.

**WEAVER, CAMERON L,** Western Carolina Univ, Cullowhee, NC; SR; BS; Glgy Clb Pres 90; Alpha Lambda Delta 87-88; Phi Kappa Phi 90; Tble Tennis Vllybl 90; Wesley Fndtn Of Untd Mthdst Chrch Treas 89; Glgy; Scntfc Rsrch.

**WEAVER, COURTNAY A,** Univ Of Tn At Martin, Martin, TN; SR; Soc Prof Journlst Tr 89-90; Alpha Delta Pi Sec 87-88; Outsdng Grad Jrnlst 90.

**WEAVER, DAVID M,** Univ Of Akron, Akron, OH; SR; BS; Acctng Assoc 89-91; IM Spts 86-88; Golden Key 90-; Hnrs Prog 86-90; Coop Assignments With Ohio Edison 89-90; Public Pr Private Acctng.

**WEAVER, DERRICK SHANE,** Sue Bennett Coll, London, KY; JR; BED; Flwshp Chrstn Athltcs 88-90; Ofcl Ky Hgh Schl Athltc Assoc; Phi Theta Kappa 89-90; Intrnshp Ora Cliff Hyde CPA 90; Bsbl/Bsktbl 88-90; AA 90; Bsn Ed; Tch High Schl.

**WEAVER, DOUGLAS R,** Sue Bennett Coll, London, KY; FR; BS; FCA 90-; Bsbl Tm 90-; Stdnt-Athlt 90-; Sci; Phrmcy.

**WEAVER, EILEEN,** Coll Misericordia, Dallas, PA; SO; BS; Frndly Visitor Pro; Day Care Tchr 85; AS 90; Scl Wrk; Cnslg Adlscnts.

**WEAVER, ELIZABETH,** Oh Wesleyan Univ, Delaware, OH; FR; BA; Admsns; Tutor; Theatre 90; Phi Eta Sigma; English Spanish; Prfsr.

**WEAVER, GLENN R,** Temple Univ, Philadelphia, PA; SR; BSCCE; Amer Soc Cvl Engr 89-; Asc Gnrl Cntrctrs Amer 89-; Amer Cncrt Inst 90-; Dns Lst 89-; Jnr Engr 89-; ASEET Penn St Unv 81; El USAF 84; Engr; Prof Engr Lic.

**WEAVER, KAREN M,** Fayetteville St Univ, Fayetteville, NC; FR; BA; Pol Clb; Emer Med Tchncn NR Now Vol 88; Vet US Army Membr Of Actve Rsrves Army; Bio Mnr Spnsh; MD.

**WEAVER, KARYN A,** Bennett Coll, Greensboro, NC; JR; SGA Parliamentarian 90-; Bennett Schlrs 88-; Biology Clb Treas 88-; Sftbl 90-; Vlybl Co Capt 89-90; Biology; Pediatrician.

**WEAVER, KASEY D,** Methodist Coll, Fayetteville, NC; SO; BS; Elem Edctn; Tchr.

**WEAVER, KERRI K,** Livingston Univ, Livingston, AL; SO; RN; Nursing.

**WEAVER, KIM J,** Bapt Bible Coll & Seminary, Clarks Summit, PA; SO; BS; Stdnt Govt Sec 89-; Chrldr Capt 89-; Elem Ed; Tchr.

**WEAVER, KIMBERLY L,** Francis Marion Coll, Florence, SC; SO; BS; Pee Dee Firefghtrs Assn Sec 90-; Rural Vol Fire Dpt Statstcn 88-91; Chmstry; Arson Invstgtn.**

**WEAVER, KRISTIE A,** Tn St Univ, Nashville, TN; JR; BS; Thomas Edward Poag Plyrs Gld Treas 90-; Meter Wrtr; DJ Cmps TN St 90-; Gldn Key; Channel 5 Intshp Flr Dir; Pres Lst 89; Top GPA; Spch Comm/Theatre; Educ PR Radio-Tv Prod.

**WEAVER, LAURA L,** Oh Univ, Athens, OH; SR; BA; Crtve Arts/Phsophy Rlgn; Tch Phlosphy.

**WEAVER, MICHAEL J,** Duquesne Univ, Pittsburgh, PA; FR; BA; Phi Eta Sigma 90-; IM Ftbl Bsktbl Sftbl 90-; Bus Admin; Law.

**WEAVER, MITCHELL R,** Oh Wesleyan Univ, Delaware, OH; SO; Phi Scty; Delta Tau Delta; Chmstry Fclty Prz; Chmstry.

**WEAVER, PAMELA L,** Livingston Univ, Livingston, AL; SR; BS; Erly Chldhd/Elem Ed; Tchr.

**WEAVER, ROSE M,** Christopher Newport Coll, Newport News, VA; SO; BS; Computer Sci.

**WEAVER, STEFANIE V,** George Mason Univ, Fairfax, VA; FR; BS; Page Program; Frshmn Ctr 90-; Special Awrd Frshmn Ctr High GPA 90-; Pre Business; Acctng.

**WEAVER, SUSAN C,** Kent St Univ Stark Cmps, North Canton, OH; JR; BA; Stark Cnty Jvnl Ct Intrnshp; Crmnl Just; Lwyr.

**WEAVER, SUSAN M,** Univ Of Sc At Columbia, Columbia, SC; SR; BA; Gamma Beta Phi 89-; Phi Eta Sigma 88-; Kappa Delta Epsilon 89-; Dns Lst 88-; BA; Educ; Tchr.

**WEAVER, SUZANNE JOY,** Union Coll, Barbourville, KY; SR; BS; Gamma Beta Phi; Commuter Cncl; Deans Lst; Ldrshp Schlrshps; I M Vybl; Bus Admn; Finance.

**WEAVER, TAMARA A,** Hillsborough Comm Coll, Tampa, FL; FR; HCC Pres Schlrshp 90-; Med; Phys Therapy.

**WEAVER, TAMBRA ELIZABETH,** Univ Of Tn At Knoxville, Knoxville, TN; FR; BA; Univ Of TN Prde Of The Sthlnd Mrchng Bnd 90-; Sigma Alpha Iota 90-; Bnd Schlrshp 90-; Dns Lst 90-; Msc Educ; Bnd Dir.

**WEAVER, TRISCILLA B,** Ga St Univ, Atlanta, GA; SR; BS; NAE 90-; SGAE 90-; NCTM 89-; Phi Theta Phi; Crrclm-Instrctn Undrgrad Awd; Deans Schlrshp Key; Mddl Chldhd Educ; Tch.

**WEAVESR, DEBORAH DAWN,** Union Univ, Jackson, TN; SR; Psy Club Sentr Club 89-; Sociology Club 89-; Student Sent 89-; Rutilidge Hnry History Scty 89-; WRAP; Psy; Phd Psychology.

**WEAVILL, KATHRYN A,** Lesley Coll, Cambridge, MA; JR; BS; Jr Class Board 90-; Orientation Comm 90-; Deans List 88-; Tchr Plcmnts Asst 89-; Middle School Educ; Teaching.

**WEBB, AMY L,** Union Univ, Jackson, TN; JR; BSBA; Stdnt Fndtns; Alpha Chi; Chi Omega Rush Chrmn; Ecnmcs Finance Banking.

**WEBB, ANGELA S,** Washington State Comm Coll, Marietta, OH; SR; AAB; Intrnshp Oh Dept Trans 90; Pres Lst 89-; Rotry Stdnt Gst Of The Mnth; Bus Mngmnt; Mngmnt/Acctg.

**WEBB, BERNICE A,** Univ Of Ky, Lexington, KY; SR; BA; Gldn Key 90-; Epsilon Delta; Mdl Schl Assoc; Rltr Brkr/Slsmn; Math/Sci; Ed.

**WEBB, CARA L,** The Kings Coll, Briarclf Mnr, NY; FR; BS; Wind Ensemble 90-; Yrbk; Clg Wrk Stdy 90-; Vars Soccer 90-; Elem Educ; Tchng.

**WEBB, CARMEN A,** Inter Amer Univ Pr Hato Rey, Hato Rey, PR; FR; MBA; Acctg.

**WEBB, CAROLE R,** Univ Of Al At Birmingham, Birmingham, AL; SR; MS; Grad Asst Strtng; BA; Sclgy.

**WEBB, CARRIE E,** Memphis St Univ, Memphis, TN; JR; BED; Phi Kappa Phif Alpha Omicron Pi Chptr Rltns 88-90; Spec Ed; Tchr.

**WEBB, CATHERINE A,** Oh Univ-Southern Cmps, Ironton, OH; AS; Nursing; Rn.

**WEBB, DARCY L,** Memphis St Univ, Memphis, TN; SO; BA; Rssn Cltr Clb Pres; Mid-Wst Model UN; Pi Delta Phi; Intl Rltns; Intl Corp.

**WEBB, DAVID C,** Birmingham Southern Coll, Birmingham, AL; SR; BA; Kappa Alpha Scl Comm 90-; Chmbr Cmrc; Mrktg Intrn; Bus; Law.

**WEBB, DAVID L,** Union Univ, Jackson, TN; SR; BSBA; Rutlede Hon Hist Clb VP 90-; Alpha Chi; Intrnshp With Unions Ctr For Bus/Econ Svcs; IM Bsktbl/Sftbl; Econs; Law.

**WEBB, DAWN C,** Lincoln Univ, Lincoln Univ, PA; SR; BA; Soc Club Sentar 90-; Senate Comm; Internship Soc Agency Titled Families Murded Vict; Sociology; Psyclgt.

**WEBB, DAWN M,** Livingston Univ, Livingston, AL; SR; Res Asstnt Head RA 87-; Stu Gov Pres 87-; Phi Eta Sigma; Omicron Delta Kappa; Phi Mu Scl Serv Pnhlnc Rep 87-; Rainbow Grls Wrthy Advsr 86-; Trustee Schlrshp; Bio; Tchg.

**WEBB, DEBBIE A,** Livingstone Coll, Salisbury, NC; GD; BSW; Soc Welfare Action Grp VP 87-; March Band/Cncrt 88-90; Yrbk Ed 89-90; Rowan Helping Mnstrs 87-89; Brian Care Cntr 90-; Intern Brian Care Ctr; Vlybl 87-89; Soc Wrk; MBA.

**WEBB, DEREK J,** Wv Univ, Morgantown, WV; FR; BA; Debate 90-; IM Sccr/Tnns/Sftbl/Ftbl; Hnrs Prgrm; George Berry Schlr; Poli Sci/Phlsphy; Internatl Law.

**WEBB, DIANE L,** Wilmington Coll, New Castle, DE; JR; BSN; Acad Excllnc Awd Cecil Comm Clg 88; Reg Nurse/Union Hosp Of Cecil Cnty; AA Cecil Comm Clg 88; Nursing.

**WEBB, DIANNA J,** Oh Univ-Southern Cmps, Ironton, OH; JR; AA; Prnt Advsry Com 89-90; Pthwys MR/DD 90-; AA; Psychlgy; BA Rhbltn.

**WEBB, DOUGLAS M,** Univ Of Sc At Columbia, Columbia, SC; SO; BA; Acctg; Big G Acctg Firm.

**WEBB, EMERITUS L,** Marshall University, Huntington, WV; SO; BBA; Intrn Lever Brthrs Co; Mktg; Bsn.

**WEBB, ERIC D,** Eckerd Coll, St Petersburg, FL; SR; Vrsty Bsktbl 87-; RA 90-; SAM 90-; Bsns Mgmt; Mgmt Finance.

**WEBB, JAMES E,** Case Western Reserve Univ, Cleveland, OH; FR; Vrsty Bsbl 90-; Eng.

**WEBB, JANET L,** Ms Gulf Coast Comm Coll, Perkinston, MS; FR; BS; Physical Therapy.

**WEBB, JEANNE V,** Valdosta St Coll, Valdosta, GA; SR; BS; Ga Assoc Educ; Prof Assoc Ga Educ 89-; Alpha Chi; 4th Grd Tchr Mdsn Acdmy Mdsn Fl 87-89; BS 76; Erly Chldhd Educ; Tchr.

**WEBB, JENNIFER A,** Univ Of Tn At Knoxville, Knoxville, TN; SO; BA; Gamma Beta Phi 90-; Mohawk Ruritan Clb; Acctg.

**WEBB, JENNIFER A,** Ky St Univ, Frankfort, KY; SO; Deans List 88-90; Church Clowning 89-90; Mission Trips 87-; Nrsng Homes Vistor; Early Educ; Tchr.

**WEBB, JENNIFER M,** Univ Of Cincinnati, Cincinnati, OH; SR; Phi Theta Kappa 88-89; Sigma Theta Tau 90-; US Hosp 3 W Holmes Div Aids & Oncology; ADN UC Raymond Walters 90; BSN UC College Nursing & Health; Nursing Science; Nursing.

**WEBB, KIMBERLY A,** Coll Of Charleston, Charleston, SC; FR; Zeta Tau Alpha 90-; Harrison Randolph Schlrshp Natl Merit Commender Scholar; Harris-Teeter Schlrshp/Erskine Schlr; Coca-Cola Schlrshp Semi-Finlst Regnl; Faculty Hnrs; IM Ftbl Sftbl; Business & Computer Science.

**WEBB, LISA C,** Univ Of Tn At Knoxville, Knoxville, TN; FR; MBA; Phi Eta Sigma 90-; Alpha Chi Omega Pledge Class Asst VP Finance 90-; Finance/Pltcl Sci; Fincl Cnsltnt.

**WEBB, MELISSA D,** Itawamba Comm Coll, Fulton, MS; SO; BS; Fashion Tribe; Baptist Stdnt Union; Acad Schlrshp; Deas Lst; Occupational Thrpy.

**WEBB, MELLANIE V,** Wilberforce Univ, Wilberforce, OH; GD; BS; Mntl Hlth Awareness Com; Hlth Care Admin Clb; Ambassador; Phi Eta Psi Treas 90; Mt Ebenezer Bapt Ch; Deans Lst Cert; Cert Achvmnt; Coop Dept Hlth; Recgntn Prfrmnce; Nwspr; BS 90; Hlth Care Admin; Bus.

**WEBB, MISTY D,** Western Carolina Univ, Cullowhee, NC; FR; BS; Bapt Stdnt Un 90-; Chorus 90; Dns Lst 90-; Soc Wrk; Med Soc Wrk.

**WEBB, MONICA R,** Shaw Univ, Raleigh, NC; SR; MS; Sr Class VP 90-; SCA 90-; Sigma Dove Ct Tres Pres 87-88; Svc Awd Sr Class; Dvsn Hnr Outstndng Stdnt 90-; Bronze Medal Deans 88-; BS; Mgmt Info Systems; Syst Analysis/Prgrmr.**

**WEBB, MOUDA F,** Fayetteville St Univ, Fayetteville, NC; JR; BS; Criml Justice Club 89-; Hmcmng Repres Queen Miss CJ 90-; Air Force ROTC 89-90; Natl Yth Spts Prog Secty 90-; Crml Justice; Law.

**WEBB, NELDA A,** Northwest Al Comm Coll, Phil Campbell, AL; SR; Phi Theta Kappa 90-; Retirement Home Employee; Crmnl Justice; Soc Wrkr.

**WEBB, NICHOLE C,** Al St Univ, Montgomery, AL; SO; BA; Yrbk Bus Mgr 89-90; Schl Nwspr Assoc Ed 90-; Phi Eta Sigma 89-; Anchorwoman ASU; Journ; Law.

**WEBB, PAULA J,** Memphis St Univ, Memphis, TN; JR; BA; Black Stdnts Assn; Blck Schlrs Unlmtd Acad Cert 88-90; Acctg; Acct.

**WEBB, PIPER L,** Memphis St Univ, Memphis, TN; SR; BA; Kappa Delta Pldg Pres 87; Deans List; Psychologist.

**WEBB, REBECCA H,** Memphis St Univ, Memphis, TN; JR; Psychlgy; Grad Schl

**WEBB, ROBERT P,** Univ Of Southern Ms, Hattiesburg, MS; SR; BS; ACM; Comp Sci; Comp Prog.

**WEBB, SANDRA L,** Univ Of Southern Ms, Hattiesburg, MS; SR; BS; Eagle Clb Natl Assoc Undrwtr Div 89-; Stdnt Alumni Assoc; Lambda Pi Sec 90-; Speech Debate Assoc; Am Mktg Assoc 89-; Soc For Adv Mgmt 89-; So Style Deans Lst; Miss Meridian 87; Comp Awrd Winner Debate Tm 88-89; Scuba Diving 89-90; Speech Comm; Pub Rel.

**WEBB, SARAH W,** Birmingham Southern Coll, Birmingham, AL; FR; BS; Wind Ensmbl 90-; Alpha Lambda Delta; Phi Eta Sigma; Alpha Chi Omega Pldg Cls Treas 90-; Blgy; Med.

**WEBB, STEVE G,** Univ Of Tn At Martin, Martin, TN; SR; BSW; Scl Wrk Clb 87-; Phi Eta Sigma 87-; Alpha Delta Mu 89-; Phi Kappa Phi; Intrnshp Soc Wrk; Soc Wrk; Admin Soc Wrk.

**WEBB, SUSAN P,** Union Univ, Jackson, TN; GD; BS; Elem Ed.

**WEBB, TEAH D,** Univ Of Va Clinch Valley Coll, Wise, VA; SR; Intl Reading Assoc 89-; Va St Reading Assoc 89-; Ntl Educ Assoc 89-; Va Educ Assoc Bapt 89-; Stu Union 89-; AA 89; BA; Elem Ed; Tchr.

**WEBB, TONYA R,** Memphis St Univ, Memphis, TN; JR; Soc Wmn Engrs Treas 90-; Soc Optical Engr SPIE V P 90; Elect Engr; Engr.

**WEBB, VICKY L,** Ashland Comm Coll, Ashland, KY; JR; BBA; FBLA 90-; Acctng; CPA.

**WEBB, WILLIAM T,** Univ Of Sc At Columbia, Columbia, SC; SO; Stdnt Ath Trnr; Bio-Phy Ed; Sprts Med.

**WEBBE, HILARY T,** Univ Of The Virgin Islands, St Thomas, VI; SR; BA; Debatng Soc Treas 89-90; Pres Clb; Soc Sci/Econ.

**WEBBER, DAVID M,** Andover Coll, Portland, ME; SR; AD; Comp Sci; Comp Progrmg.

**WEBBER, DONALD J,** Nova Univ, Ft Lauderdale, FL; GD; MBA; Soc Plstcs Engrs Inc 89-; Amer Mgmt Assn 90-; Jr Achvmnt; Prdctn Sprvsr/Mnfctrng Engr 88-; AS Johnson Tech Inst 85; BS Ind Eng 88; Bus; Bus Law.

**WEBBER, EDITH E,** Central Fl Comm Coll, Ocala, FL; SO; BA; Phi Theta Kappa; AS Broward Cmnty Clg 78; Phys Ther.

**WEBBER, KRISTA LYNN,** Livingston Univ, Livingston, AL; FR; BA; Stars AL 90-; Marine Biol; Res.

**WEBBER, SANDRA L,** Bridgewater Coll, Bridgewater, VA; SO; BA; Pre-Med Soc 90-; Bio/Chem; Med.

**WEBBER-PARKER, CHERYL,** Comm Coll Algny Co Algny Cmps, Pittsburgh, PA; GD; MAT; Jr Chrch Instrctr 90-; Vactn Bible Schl Co Chrprsn 86-90; Sndy Schl Tchr 85-89; Deans Lst 90; BFA Carnegie Mellon Univ 80; Elem/Scndry Educ; Tchr.

**WEBBINK, MARK H,** Nc Central Univ, Durham, NC; GD; JD; Bd Of Dir Am Red Cross Chmn 86-; Bd Of Trustees Durham Tech Comm Coll 86-; Chf Admn Officer 89-; BA Purdue Univ 72; MPA Univ Of N C Chapel Hill 74; Law.

**WEBEL, HANSEN P,** Univ Of Akron, Akron, OH; FR; BA; Amrcn Soc Mchncl Engnrs 90-; Phi Eta Sigma 90-; Unvrsty Hnrs Prgrm 90-; Lakeside Pblcty Chrmn 90-91; OH Acdmc Schlrshp 90-; Lyle Wanda Ganyard Schlrshp 90-; Prsdntl Schlrshp 90-; Robert C Byrd Hnrs Schlrshp 90-; Deans Lst 90; Mchncl Engnrng.

**WEBER, ANITA M,** Kent St Univ Kent Cmps, Kent, OH; GD; MLS; Assoc Library Sci Stdnts Of Ohio V P 89-90; Amer Library Assn; Beta Phi Mu; Phi Alpha Theta; Soc Amer Archivists; Midwest Archives Conf; Rog Amer Hstrns; Assist Arch Librarian; BA N IL Univ 77; Library Sci.

**WEBER, CHERYL A,** Indiana Univ Of Pa, Indiana, PA; JR; BS; Univ TV Pgm Dir 90-; Natl Assn Coll Brdcstrs 88-; Wmn Cmnctns Inc 90-; Alpha Epsilon Rho Pres Elect; Intrn Videosmith Inc-Philadelphia; IVP Deans Lst 89-; Slph Yr-WIVP-TV 89-90; Mary Beth Liedman Schlrshp Awd; Cmnctns Media; TV/VIDEO Prdctn.**

**WEBER, COLLEEN M,** Univ Of Rochester, Rochester, NY; SO; BA; Dlion Org 90-; Rchstr Emrgncy Mdcl Rspns Tm 89-90; Delta Gamma Asst VP Pldg Edctn; Wmns Vrsty Bsktbll 89-; Engl Blgy; Dctr Med.

**WEBER, CONSTANCE H,** Queens Coll, Charlotte, NC; JR; BA; Comm Clb Pres 90-; Std Govt Asc Pres 90-; Nwspr Adv Mgr 90-; Mrtr Brd; Alpha Soc 90-; Ordr Omega; Alpha Delta Pi Chrmn 90-; Chrlt Obsvr Intrn 89; Pblc Dfndrs Intrn; Engl/Comm; Law.

**WEBER, DENISE M,** Univ Of Va, Charlottesville, VA; GD; MPT; Dsgnd T-Shirts; Alpha Delta Pi IM Chair 87-90; Hlth Sports/Rehab 87-88; BSED 90; Phys Therapy.

**WEBER, HEIDI A,** Upsala Coll, East Orange, NJ; FR; BA; Stdnt Gov Assn Clss Sen 90-; Pre-Law Clb Sec 90-; Choir VP 90-; Hons Pgm 90-; Alpha Kappa Psi; Coll Schlrshp Recpnt 90-; G Grindeland Schlrshp Recpnt 90-; Stdnt Abmass; Pltcl Sci; Law.

**WEBER, HEIDI D,** Univ Of Cincinnati-Clrmnt Coll, Batavia, OH; SO; BED; Phi Theta Kappa 90-; Acad Schlrshp 89-; Danahay Elem Edn Schlrshp 89-90; Mentoring Schlrshp 90-; Clermont Cnty Lit Cncl 90; Spcl Pgm Aid/Tchr Madeira Schls Latchkey Pgms 90-; Elem Edn; Tchr.

**WEBER, JOHN D,** Christopher Newport Coll, Newport News, VA; SR; BSGA; Dept Hon; Intrnsp Va Peninsula Econ Dev Cncl; Pres Barclay Woods Hmownrs Assn; Govt Admn; Local Govt Emplee.

**WEBER, KAREN L,** Comm Coll Algny Co Algny Cmps, Pittsburgh, PA; FR; BA; Allegheny Chmbr Cmrce 89-; Branch Mgr 84; Fin; Invstmnt Bnkg.

**WEBER, REBECCA C,** Univ Of Akron, Akron, OH; SR; BFA; Golden Key 90-; Juried Art Awrd 90; Art Schlrshp; LDSCHURCH Organist/Yth Ldr; Art.

**WEBER, STEPHANIE J,** Univ Of Tn At Martin, Martin, TN; SO; BS; Soc Hnrs Seminar Stu Treas 89-; Phi Eta Sigma; Phi Chi Theta Tres 90-; Bus; Law.

**WEBER, STEPHEN G,** Cornell Univ Statutory College, Ithaca, NY; SR; BS; Stdnt Un Cncl 87-89; Alpha Epsilon Delta 89-; Ho Nun De Kah Coll 90-; Deans Hon Lst 87-; Bio; Med.

**WEBER, SUSAN C,** Seton Hall Univ, South Orange, NJ; SR; BS; Kappa Deltqa Pi; Alpha Gamma Delta; Elem/Spec Ed; Tchr.

**WEBSTER, JUANITA V,** Salisbury St Univ, Salisbury, MD; SR; BA; Art.

**WEBSTER, KATHY A,** East Tn St Univ, Johnson City, TN; SR; BS; Sntrs Pgs Pres 88-89; Stdnt Tn Ed Assn VP 90-; Gamma Beta Phi; Phi Theta Kappa VP 88-89; Outstndng Stdnt; AS Walters State Comm Coll 89; Bus Ed/Acctg; Tchng.

**WEBSTER, KIMBERLY R,** Comm Coll Algny Co Algny Cmps, Pittsburgh, PA; FR; BSN; Ntnl Cncl Negro Wmn 87-; Nrsng/Blgy; Med.

**WEBSTER, LARA KAY,** Univ Of Sc At Columbia, Columbia, SC; SO; BA; Philharmonic Chorus 89-90; Carolina Cares 89-90; Gamma Beta Phi 89-; Sigma Lota Rho; Mortar Brd Undergrad Fllwshp; Stackhouse Meml Schlrshp 89; Intl Studies.

**WEBSTER, MARTHA H,** Fl Atlantic Univ, Boca Raton, FL; JR; BED; Plnnf/Zoning Commsn Vice Chrmn 87-; FAU Amercn Asmbly Facilitor 87; Mdl Sch Tchr; AA VA Intermont Clg Bristol BA 66; Ed; Mdle Sch Tchng.

**WEBSTER, MITCHELL E,** Memphis St Univ, Memphis, TN; SR; BBA; Act Cncl 87-88; Gamma Beta Phi 89-; Rho Epsilon 90-; Phi Mu Alpha Tr 87-89; St Brd Regnts Schlrshp 87-; Real Est; Devlpmnt/Invstmnt.

**WEBSTER, RICHARD INGERSOLL,** Univ Of Sc At Columbia, Columbia, SC; SR; BS; Math/Cmptr Sci; Prgmmr.

**WEBSTER, ROCKLYN D,** S U N Y Coll Of Tech At Frmgdl, Farmingdale, NY; SO; Caribbean Stdnt Org 90; Alpha Eta Rho 89; Deans Lst; Pri Pilot Cert; Outstndng Scholastic Achievemnt Awd; AAS; Aerospace Tchnlgy; Cmmrcl Pilot.

**WEBSTER, SEAN Y,** Roane St Comm Coll, Harriman, TN; FR; US Army SGT/E-5 Army Coll Fnd 87-90; ARMY Ntl Grd Sgt/E-5 90-; Bus; Acctg.

**WEBSTER, SHEILA A,** Univ Of Nc At Greensboro, Greensboro, NC; FR; BS; Elem Educ; Teaching.

**WEBSTER, TANYA,** Middle Tn St Univ, Murfreesboro, TN; JR; BA; Scl Wrkrs Org 89-91; Social Wrk; Cnslng Yng Adults.

**WEBSTER, WILLIAM BRET,** Atlantic Comm Coll, Mays Landing, NJ; FR; Bsn Adm.

**WEDDING, AGNES G,** Ky Wesleyan Coll, Owensboro, KY; SR; BA; Phi Beta Lambda VP 90; Acctg.

**WEDDLE, RACHEL A,** Merrimack Coll, North Andover, MA; JR; BA; Chrldng; Sccr; Pscyh Clb; Psi Chi; Dns Lst; Chrldng And Sccr; Asst Rsrchr Fr Hrvrd Prjct Undr Prof M Kanner-Mascolo; Pscyh Mjr Engl Mnr; Clncl Psych.

**WEDDLE, VAUGHN F,** Middle Tn St Univ, Murfreesboro, TN; SO; Audio Eng Scty 88-; Rcrdng Eng Snd Rnfrcmnt Eng 85-; Sci Educ; Tchng.

**WEDEMEYER, FRANK L,** Va Polytechnic Inst & St Univ, Blacksburg, VA; FR; BA; Vars Sccr 90-; Lee Jacksn Schlrshp 90-; Partl Sccr Schlrshp 90-; Sccr 90-; Engl; Tchg/Coachng Sccr.

**WEDGE, DIONNE M,** Univ Of Md At Eastern Shore, Princess Anne, MD; SO; BS; UMES Hnrs Pgm 89-; Humane Soc 88-; Thurgood Marshall Schlr 89; Pres Schlr 89; All-Amer Schlr 90; Animal Sci; Sml Animal Vet.

**WEE, GUAN-SENG,** East Tn St Univ, Johnson City, TN; SO; ITSU 90; Gamma Beta Phi; Lions Clb 88; Dipl Arch Malaysia 86; Bsn.

**WEED III, JOHN A,** Northern Ky Univ, Highland Hts, KY; SO; BA; Northern Ky Chptr Of Prof Eng Mbr; Hons Clb Treas 90; Physics; Eng.

**WEED, VIRIGNIA D,** Samford Univ, Birmingham, AL; FR; JD; Jursprdnc Book Awd; Cumberland Law Review; Deans Lst; BA U Of Ala; MS Univ Ak; Law.

**WEEDMAN, EDWARD B,** Western Ky Univ, Bowling Green, KY; SO; BA; Res Hl Asc VP 90-; Phi Alpha Theta 90-; Hstry; Sec Ed.

**WEEDMAN, LISA A,** Univ Of Nc At Charlotte, Charlotte, NC; JR; BA; Phi Eta Sigma 87-; Art Ed.

**WEEKES, BRIAN I,** Tuskegee Univ, Tuskegee Inst, AL; DVM; Intnl Stdnts Assoc 86-; Crbn Stdnts Assn 86-; Alpha Kappa Mu 88-; Phi-Zeta; Beta Kappa Chi/Gamma Sigma Delta 88-; Jycees 1st Vp 84-86; Mthdst Yth Assn 85-; Albma Vet Med Assn Awrd 88-89; Soccr 86-87; Vet Med; Vet Med Prvt Prctc.

**WEEKLEY, ANGELA C,** Faulkner St Jr Coll, Bay Minette, AL; SO; Phi Theta Kappa 90-; AAS; Elem Edn.

**WEEKLEY, KELLY N,** Marshall University, Huntington, WV; JR; BBA; Acctng Secy/Treas 89-; VITA Site Coord 90-; GE Plstcs Intrnshp 90; Acctng; CPA.

**WEEKLEY, SHARON D,** Wv Univ At Parkersburg, Parkersburg, WV; GD; BS; Big Tygrt Bapt Amer Bapt Womns Soc Pr 90-; St Jos Hosp R N 88-; Asso Nrsng Hckng Tech Clg Nelsnvl 88; Nrsng.

**WEEKS, AMY L,** Rivier Coll, Nashua, NH; SR; BA; Resident Asst 88-; Stdt Admsns Com 87-88; Stdt Ed Scty 89-; Acdmc Profile 90; Third Grade Stdt Tchr; Eulby Ldrshp Awd; Elem Ed; Tch.

**WEEKS, CHARLES M,** Gallaudet Univ, Washington, DC; JR; BA; Kappa Sigma Grnd Treas 91-; ATT Intern 90; Kngs By Nvy Sbmrn Intern; Bus Admn.

**WEEKS, EDSON GARY,** Brevard Coll, Brevard, NC; FR; BA; Nwspr Asst Sprts Ed 90-; Flwshp Chrstn Athl; Phi Theta Kappa; Beam Schlrshp; Jones Schlrshp; Ret Offcrs Assc Grnt; IM Bsktbl/Vlybl/Ftbl/Sccr; Cmmnctns; Brdcstng/Flm Mkg.

**WEEKS, LATASHA R,** Al A & M Univ, Normal, AL; FR; BA; Bus; Ins Sls.

**WEEKS, MELISSA D,** Memphis St Univ, Memphis, TN; JR; BS; Dns Lst; Elem Ed; Tch.

**WEEKS, NANCY,** Erie Comm Coll, Buffalo, NY; FR; AAS; Rbtcs Clb Treas; Phi Theta Kappa; Rbtcs Atmtd Mnfctrng; Eng.

**WEEKS, NANCY ANN,** Roane St Comm Coll, Harriman, TN; SO; AS; Roane State Sngrs 89-90; Oak Ridge Rowing Assn 87-89; Gamma Beta Phi; Anchor Clb Schlrshp; United Ch Schlrshp 89-90; Altrusa Schlrshp 89; Deans Lst 90-; Bus Admin; Cmptr Sci.

**WEEKS, STACEY N,** Univ Of Sc At Columbia, Columbia, SC; SR; BS; Englsh.

**WEEKS, SUSAN A,** Brewer St Jr Coll, Fayette, AL; SR; AA; Phi Theta Kappa 90-; Am Cncr Soc; Rch Rcvry Prog; Prchsng Clerk Am Olean Tile; Bus.

**WEEKS, TARA L,** Radford Univ, Radford, VA; FR; BBA; IM Tennis 90-; Mrktng; Cmptr/Grphc Arts.

**WEEMS, DANNY K,** East Tn St Univ, Johnson City, TN; JR; BS; ACM VP 90-; Kappa Mu Epsilon 90-; Comp Sci/Math; Syst Eng.

**WEEMS, HOPE L,** Ms St Univ, Miss State, MS; SO; BPA; Angl Flght Chf Prtcl Capt 90-; Gamma Beta Phi 90-; Phi Eta Sigma 90-; Alpha Lambda Delta; Prsdnts Lst 89-; Acctg.**

**WEENUM, SCOTT D,** Tn Temple Univ, Chattanooga, TN; SR; BA; Stdnt Govt Class Rep 79-82; Natl Hon Soc 80-82; USAF Reserve 88-90; USAF 83-87; AA Cmnctn Tech Comm Clg Air Force 87; Soc Sci; USAF Ofcr.

**WEERSMA, JEFF C,** Mount Olive Coll, Mount Olive, NC; FR; BED; Maintenance Professional Of Yr 83; AF Assoc; Veteran USAF; Business.

**WEESE, DOUGLAS K,** Davis & Elkins Coll, Elkins, WV; JR; BS; Beta Alpha Beta 89-; Alpha Chi Treas 90-; Phi Beta Lambda 89-; Town Cnclman 89-; Fire Dept 86-; BS Eagle 81-; Eagle Scout 88; All Amer Schlar; Natl Clgt Bus Merit Awrds; MBA West Virg Univ; Acctg; Bus.

**WEESE, LESLIE L,** Marshall University, Huntington, WV; SO; BA; Phi Theta Kappa Pres 90-; AAS; Law.**

**WEGENER, KATHRYN A,** Va Commonwealth Univ, Richmond, VA; JR; BFA; Spcl Olympcs; Amnsty; BA Virginia Tech 86; Art Edctn; Art Tchr.

**WEGRZYN, LISA M,** Niagara Univ, Niagara Univ, NY; JR; Pol Sci Frm VP 89-; Phi Alpha Delta Chrp 89-; Jdcl Brd 90-; Phi Sigma Alpha; Delta Epsln Sigma; Dpt Hnrs Pgm 90-; AEP Dns Adv Brd 88-; Cmps Mnstry 89-; Pol Sci; Law.

**WEHATLEY, MYRNA P,** Al A & M Univ, Normal, AL; SR; BS; Acctg Clb 87-; Intrntl Assn VP 88-90; Caribbean Assn VP 89-; Intrntl Frndshp Clb VP 89-; Delta Mu Delta 88-; Pres Schlrs 88-; Deans Lst 88; Hon Roll 88; Acctg Awd; Ldrshp Awd; Acctg.**

**WEHBE, DONNA LEBLANC,** Le Moyne Coll, Syracuse, NY; JR; BA; Law Clb 88-89; Alpha Lambda Delta 89-; Psi Eta Sigma 89-; Pol Sci; Law Schl.

**WEHNER, SEAN C,** Comm Coll Algny Co Algny Cmps, Pittsburgh, PA; FR; Phys Ther.

**WEHRLE, GARY R,** Northern Ky Univ, Highland Hts, KY; SO; BS; Planetary Scty 89-; Alumni Assoc; Prestl Ambrs 90-; Deans List 90-; Hmr List 90; IM Soccer 90-; Infor Syst; Data Base Mgt Syst.

**WEHUNT-OGRISSEG, RACHEAL L,** Kent St Univ Stark Cmps, North Canton, OH; SO; BS; Invrnmntl Awrns Clb VP 90-; Acad Of Life Scncs 90-; Canton Big/Bros/Strs 90-; Zoology; Curator/Profssr/Rsrchr.

**WEI, LISA L,** Univ Of Miami, Coral Gables, FL; JR; BS; Hnrs Stdnts Assn Exec Asst To Pres 90-; Biology Clb 90-; Mstr Tutor; Alpha Lambda Delta Pres; Phi Kappa Phi; CASAA Merit Schlrshp Nat Sci; Biology; Opthmlgy.

**WEIBLE, REBECCA L,** Allegheny Coll, Meadville, PA; JR; BS; Alden Schlr 88-90; Athltc Hnr Rl 90; Sftbl 88-90; Sccr 88-90; Math/Pre Eng; Mech Eng.

**WEIDEMANN, CYNTHIA S,** Liberty Univ, Lynchburg, VA; SO; BS; Youth Quest Club 89-; Elem Ed; Tch Engl.

**WEIDENBACHER, DREW,** City Univ Of Ny Baruch Coll, New York, NY; GD; BBA; Econ; Bus.

**WEIDLER, ERIKA H,** Univ Of Miami, Coral Gables, FL; SO; BSN; Provost Hnr Rll; Nrsng; Prfssr Nrsng.

**WEIDLER, WALTER W,** Univ Of Miami, Coral Gables, FL; SR; Univ Mm Fnc Scty 90-; Provost Hnr Rll; Deans Lst; BA; AA Mm Dd Cmmnty Coll 89; Fnc; Bnkng.

**WEIDNER, ERIC S,** Univ Of Louisville, Louisville, KY; SO; MENG; Speed Scntfc Schl Stdnt Cncl Prlmntrn 89-; Intl Ord Of De Molay Sr Cnclr 87-; Phi Eta Sigma; Golden Key; Louisville Gas/Elec Co Coop Intrnshp; Mech Engr.

**WEIDNER, KIERAN M,** City Univ Of Ny Bronx Comm Col, Bronx, NY; SO; BS; Lambda Nu VP 90; Lambda Nu Pres; Stdnt Evltn Rvw Cmmttee Chrprsn; Phi Theta Kappa; Mel Wntr Mem Awd; Giraffe Awd; AS; Bsnss Admin; Mrktng Mngmnt.

**WEIDNER, SHERI L,** Immaculata Coll, Immaculata, PA; SO; BA; Ecnmcs; Law.

**WEIGAND, RICHARD P,** Univ Of Cincinnati, Cincinnati, OH; JR; BSEET; Amateur Radio Clb; Process Mgr Lazarus Dept Store 72-88; Process Mgr Toys R Us Dstrbtn Ctr 89-90; ASEET 72; Elect; Eng.

**WEIGEL, DOUGLAS J,** Indiana Univ Of Pa, Indiana, PA; SR; BS; Amer Soc Trng/Dvlpmnt 90-; Intrnshp Mercy Hosp; IM Sfotbl; Communications; Advrtsng/Pblc Rltns.

**WEIKERT, SHANNON L,** Univ Of Pittsburgh At Bradford, Bradford, PA; FR; BS; Telemrktng 90-; Alpha Lambda Delta Sec; Res Asst; Comp Sci.

**WEIKLE, JULIA E,** Marshall University, Huntington, WV; JR; BBA; Hl Advsry Cncl Pers 89-90; Rsdnc Lf Rsdnt Advsr 90-; Stdnt Nwsppr Rprtr; Chf Jstc Yrbk Stf Lf Ed89-90; Gamma Beta Phi Hstrn 90-; Phi Eta Sigma; Alpha Kappa Psi Chpln 89-; Bsns; Mrktng/Advrtsng.

**WEIL, DONNA G,** Hillsborough Comm Coll, Tampa, FL; SO; AS; Nrsng/Hlth Prof.

**WEIL, WENDY A,** Ky Wesleyan Coll, Owensboro, KY; SO; BS; Ky Wesleyan Sngrs; Compass Clb Pres; Wesleyan Plyrs; James G Brown Schlrshp; Pre-Prof Scty; Sigma Kappa Ritual Chrmn; Mssngr Inquirer Wrtng Wrkshp Awd 2nd Pl; Bio; Vet Schl.

**WEILAND, JENNIFER K,** Auburn Univ At Auburn, Auburn, AL; GD; MBA; Orchstra 1st Oboist 88-90; Natl Stdnt Spch Lang Hrng Assn Fndrsng Cochrmn 90; Phi Kappa Phi 90-; Cmnctn Disordrs; Spch Lang Pthlgst.

**WEILER, WENDIE G,** Univ Of Cincinnati, Cincinnati, OH; JR; BM; Prncpia Rnnrs Clb Prncpia Outdr Clb Principia Coll 88-90; Chrstn Sci Org 88-; Anderson E Hs Bd Sec 89; Cnslr/Pere Marquette Dlnqnt Teens IL 88-90; Deans Lst 90-; Vrsty Trck Vrsty Crss Cntry Principia Coll 88-90; Clrnt Prfrmnc; Arts Admin.

**WEILHEIMER, SHEERA A,** Daytona Beach Comm Coll, Daytona Beach, FL; FR; BA; Phi Theta Kappa Mbrshp Chr 90-; Pr Lst 90-; Cable Adv Prod Intrn 90-; Comm; Tele Prod.

**WEIMER, DAVID,** Allegheny Coll, Meadville, PA; SR; RS; Aldn Schlr 89-; Phi Delta Theta Hs Mgr 87-; Intrnshp Mdvl Med Ctr 90; Var Bsbl All Conf Tm Capt 87-; Psych; Phy Thrpy.

**WEINBACH, JENNIFER D,** Univ Of Sc At Columbia, Columbia, SC; FR; BS; Alpha Lambda Delta/Phi Eta Sigma 90-; Schlrshps 90-; Bus Admin; Banking/Finance.

**WEINBAUM, DAWN R,** D Youville Coll, Buffalo, NY; JR; Vol Shea Buffalo Thtr 89-; Wrkd With Horses; BS Cornell Univ 88; AAS Suny 86; Dietetics; Reg Dttn.

**WEINBERG, JOSHUA D,** Univ Of Pa, Philadelphia, PA; FR; BA; Penn Singers; Benjamin Franklin Schlr; History; Law.

**WEINBRENNER, KIM M,** Rutgers St Univ At Camden, Camden, NJ; GD.

**WEINDORF, SALLY K,** Kent St Univ Kent Cmps, Kent, OH; SR; BA; Psychlgy.

**WEINER, ANDREW S,** Cornell Univ Statutory College, Ithaca, NY; SO; BS; Cncrt Cmsn 90-; Entrprnrs Clb 90-; IM Bsktbl/Sftbl 89-; Intrn Twn Ramapo Tx Assrs Ofc 90; Deans Lst 90-; Bus Mgt.

**WEINER, JACQUELINE K,** Univ Of Miami, Coral Gables, FL; SO; MED; Hillel 90-; Cure Aids Now 90-; FL PIRG 90-; Psychlgy/Spec Ed; Tchr.

**WEINER, JASON P,** Clarkson Univ, Potsdam, NY; SR; BS; Stdnt Org Sen; Fincl Mgmt Assn Pr; Dns Lst; Econ/Finc.

**WEINGARTH, DREW T,** Wagner Coll, Staten Island, NY; SR; BS; Blgy Clb VP 90-; Beta Beta Beta Pres 88-89; Omicron Delta Kappa Sec 90-; Excptnl Ldrshp Awrd; Mdcl Gntcs Intern; Blgy.

**WEINHOLTZ, SHARI L,** D Youville Coll, Buffalo, NY; SO; BA; Biol; Vet Med.

**WEINLE, DEBORAH A,** Univ Of Cin R Walters Coll, Blue Ash, OH; FR; BED; Stdnt Serv; Girl Scout Serv Tm/Ldr 86-; Ele Educ; Tch.

**WEINMAN, GREG M,** Univ Of Toledo, Toledo, OH; GD; JD; Stdnt Bar Assoc Pres 90-; Delta Theta Phi 88-; Jewish Law Stdnt Assoc Chrtr Mbr 88-; William Mc Daniel Meml Schlrshp 88-; BS Univ Cincinnati 88; Law.

**WEINREB, LAURIE A,** East Stroudsburg Univ, E Stroudsburg, PA; SO; Dlt Phi Epsln.

**WEINREB, YAAKOV Y,** Yeshiva Univ, New York, NY; SR; BA; Sigma Delta Rho Sci Rsrch 87-; Chem Clb VP 87-; Wrtg Cntr Tutor 87-; Max Stern Schlrshp 87-; Louis Werfel Awrd Hghst Rnkg Jr 90; Chem Awrd 88; Hstry; Med.

**WEINRICH, SUZANNE M,** Oh Univ, Athens, OH; GD; D O; Fmly Prctc Clb Chrstn Medcl Soc 89-; OUCOM Yrbk Com Ectr 89-; Phs/Cls Sec/Stdnt Cncl Sec 89; OUCOM Deans Lst; Sigma Sigma Phi 91; BS Bulter Univ 89; Ostpthc Med; Pdtrcs/Intrnl Med.

**WEINSTEIN, ELANA M,** Yeshiva Univ, New York, NY; GD; Hist Soc; Econ Soc; Deans Lst; Magna Cum Laude 87-90; BA; AA; Econ/Histy.

**WEINSTEIN, ELIZABETH A,** Univ Of Cincinnati-Clrmnt Coll, Batavia, OH; SO; Ambssdr 90-.

**WEINSTEIN, MICHAEL N,** Georgetown Univ, Washington, DC; JR; BSBA; Intl Mgmt.

**WEINSTEIN, SCOTT D,** Ny Univ, New York, NY; JR; BA; Econs; Stck Brkr.

**WEINSTEIN, WHITNEY-ANN,** Radford Univ, Radford, VA; SO; BA; SGA Rep; Pnhllnc Cncl Rep; Sigma Sigma Sigma 90-; Spch Cmnctns; Sec Ed.

**WEIPPERT, TROY A,** Embry Riddle Aeronautical Univ, Daytona Beach, FL; JR; BS; Math Assoc Of Am MAA 90-; Soc Comm Avtn Tech 90-; Avionics Club 90-; Hnr Roll 89; Deans List 89-; Wghtlftng/Pwrlftng Fitness Spvsr 89-; Daytona Bch Jet Ctr Parts Dept 89-; Elctrnc Tech 79-88; Diploma 84; CET 84; Avionics; Aerospace Tech.

**WEIR, CHARLES R,** Memphis St Univ, Memphis, TN; SO; MBA; Stdsnt Actvts Cncl; Spkrs Comm; Gamma Beta Phi; Intl Bus/Foreign Lang; Plans Restrain Potentl.

**WEIRI, KARIN C,** Daytona Beach Comm Coll, Daytona Beach, FL; FR; BA; Phi Theta Kappa; Hlfx Med Cntr 90-; Aerobic Instr 90; Phys Rcndtng Pro 90; Phys Therpy.

**WEIS, CONNIE L,** Mount Saint Mary Coll, Newburgh, NY; SR; BA; Ambsdr Clb 87-90; Hon Alliance 88-; Alpha Chi Sec/Treas 89-; Aquinas Schlr 90-; Ralph Sclr 89-90; Psychlgy; Teach Elem Sch.

**WEIS, ERIC J,** James Madison University, Harrisonburg, VA; JR; BS; ROTC Rngr Rgmnt Oper Offcr 88-; Rngr Chllng Tm 88-; Alpha Kappa Lambda Comm Serv Chrmn 89-; Army ROTC Schlrshp 88-; Advsry Brd 90-; IM Vlybl/Sccr/Sftbl 88-; Active Army Officer/Chld Psychologist.

**WEIS, ORVILLE G,** Ashland Comm Coll, Ashland, KY; SO; AS Ashland Bus Coll 75; Acctg Ashland KY; Cmptr Info Sys; Acctg.

**WEISENBECK, KELLIE S,** Longwood Coll, Farmville, VA; SR; Stdnt Educ 88; Alpha Sigma Tau 88-90; Lngwd Ambass 88-90; Prnc Edward Cnty Pub Library Strytlr 88; BED 90; Elem Tchr.

**WEISENFELD, SHARI G,** Cornell Univ Statutory College, Ithaca, NY; FR; BS; Alpha Epsilon Phi; Appl Econ/Bsn Mgmt; Law.

**WEISENSTEIN, DARREN G,** Wagner Coll, Staten Island, NY; JR; BA; Tri-Beta Pres 89; Allied-Hlth/Sci Org Pres 90; Deans Lst 88; Omicron Delta Kappa Scrtry 90; Feedor Eger Nrsng Hm 88; SI U Hosp; Schlrshp; Bio; MD.

**WEISGERBER, SHAWNA K,** Muskingum Coll, New Concord, OH; SO; BA; Msc Educ Assc Sec 89-; Cntr Brd 89-; Prnts Wknd Cmmtt Rcptn Co Chr 9-; Lambda Sigma; Omicron Delta Kappa; Sigma Alpha Iota VP Ritual; Chi Alpha Nu 90-; Msc Lctr 90-; Tour Guide 89-; Res Asst; Msc Ed Voice Kybrd Elem Ed; Instr.

**WEISMAN, ILANNA PATRICE,** Univ Of Sc At Columbia, Columbia, SC; FR; Cmps Rape Awrns; Wmns Stdnt Assn; Wmns Stdnt Assn; Cmps Rape Awrns; Deans Lst Clg Jrnlsm Intrn; Smmr 90 LT Gvrnr MI Martha Grffths; Aerobics; Jrnlsm; Law Degree.

**WEISNER, JODI E,** Comm Coll Algny Co Algny Cmps, Pittsburgh, PA; FR; Pharm Rsrch.

**WEISS, ANGELA R,** Univ Of Sc At Columbia, Columbia, SC; SO; BA; Bus Admin; Entrepreneur.

**WEISS, BRENDA L,** Fl International Univ, Miami, FL; BS; BA Psychlgy Univ PE 73; BS Elmntry Ed Univ TE 73; MS Rhbltn Cnslng BO Univ 75; Interior Dsgn; Instnl Dsgn/Hotel Dsgn.

**WEISS, DALIT,** Yeshiva Univ, New York, NY; SO; BBA; Pol Sci Jrnl Domestic Affairs Edtr 89-90; Acctng; CPA.

**WEISS, HOLLIE E,** Univ Of Tn At Knoxville, Knoxville, TN; FR; BS; Phi Eta Sigma; Bsn; Acctg.

**WEISS, JONATHAN M,** Univ Of Rochester, Rochester, NY; JR; BS; Skiing Club 88-; Univ Nwspr Reptr 88; Equestrian Club 88; NY Regents Schlrshp; Biology; Biology Research.

**WEISS, KAREN LYNNE,** Univ Of Miami, Coral Gables, FL; SR; MD; Amer Med Assn 87-; Amer Acad Fmly Physicians 87-; Alpha Omega Alpha 90-; Gldn Key 86-; BS 87; AA Edison Comm Coll 85; Med; Drmtlgy.

**WEISS, LORI A,** Hudson Valley Comm Coll, Troy, NY; GD; BA; Neslttr Pltsbrgh 87; St Clg Copy Edtr Crtv Cntrl; Prsdnts Lst 86-; Deans Lst 84-85-86-88; Intrnshp Wrtng Mtrlnd 89; Mag Albany NY; Artcl Pblshd Crazy Kat Msc Intrvw; AAS; Englsh Jrnlsm; Wrtr Mag Chldrns Bk.

**WEISS, MARGARET,** City Univ Of Ny City Coll, New York, NY; GD; Hillel 88-90; Gldn Key; Ward Medal; Menorah Awrd; Admin Asstnt; BA 90; Frnch.

**WEISS, MARTIN J,** Memphis St Univ, Memphis, TN; GD; Alpha Lambda Delta 86-; Gldn Ky; Beta Gamma Sigma; Phi Kappa Phi; Phi Eta Sigma; Reg Med Cntr; IM Tns/Bsktbl 87-88; BBA 89; Bus Fin; Med.

**WEISS, MARTIN N,** Cooper Union, New York, NY; SR; BE; Eta Kappa Nu; Tau Delta Phi 88-; Tae Kwon Do Clb 87-; Elec Eng.

**WEISS, MARY S,** Fl St Univ, Tallahassee, FL; SR; MS; Phi Eta Sigma 87-; Gldn Key 90-; Delta Zeta Phlnthrpy 88-; Sccr Tm 88; BS; Spch/Lang Pathlgy.

**WEISS, MELISSA LILLIAN,** Univ Of Ga, Athens, GA; SR; BS; Stdnt Org Fnd Rsng Comm 89-90; Communiv Chrprsn 87-; Bg Brthr/Bg Sistr Coord 87-; Stdnt Tchr; Early Chldhd Ed; Tchng.

**WEISS, OLIVER,** Merrimack Coll, North Andover, MA; FR; BS; Intcltrl Clb Treas 90; Intl Bsn; Intl Trnsprtn.

**WEISS, PATRICIA M,** Fl A & M Univ, Tallahassee, FL; JR; BA; Soc Prfssnl Jrnlst Pres 90-; Clb Hspnc De Famu 89-; Wmn Cmmnctns 89-; Gldn Ky; Intern FL Radio News; Stff Wrtr/Edtr; Hnr Rll; Dean Lst; Tallahassee Dmcrt Bus Nws; Prnt Jrnlsm; Nwsppr Mngmnt.

**WEISS JR, ROBERT A,** Ramapo Coll Of Nj, Mahwah, NJ; SO; BA; Oxfrd Hon Prog 89-; Econ; Bus.

**WEISS, RYAN N,** Wilmington Coll, New Castle, DE; GD; SGA Sec 89-90; Nwspr/Yrbk Entrnmnt Edtr 89-90; Cum Laude 89-90; Hertage Cblvsn Intrn 90-; AA Camden Cnty Clg 88; Video Prod Bus.

**WEISS, SCOTT A,** Cornell Univ Statutory College, Ithaca, NY; FR; Swmmng 90-; Alpha Epsilon Pi; Blgy; Dctr.

**WEISS, SUSAN L,** Atlantic Comm Coll, Mays Landing, NJ; SO; AAS; Phi Beta Lambda 90-; 1st Plc Acctng II; NJ Phi Beta Lambda St Ldrshp Cnfrnc; Fl Chrg Bkpr; Acctng; Acctng Sftwr Spclst.

**WEISS, TEDD J,** Wilmington Coll, New Castle, DE; SO; BA; Stdnt Govt Assoc VP; Mssn Gls Objctvs Cmm Sr Prtnr; Vygr Nwsppr Jr Edtr; Internn Wdl Rlty; Pscyhlgy; Clncl Psychlgst.

**WEISS, TIMOTHY J,** Grove City Coll, Grove City, PA; FR; BA; Warriors Chrst 90-; Chrstn Actn Tm 90-; Dramtc Prodctns; Habitat Humnty; Trck/Fld; Comm.

**WEISS, TRACI C,** Muskingum Coll, New Concord, OH; FR; BA; Sprt Bnd; Ctr Brd FCA; Cncrt Chr; Lmbd Sgm; FAD Soc Clb Sec; Presbytrn Chrch; Dstngshd Schlr Schlrshp; Musc/Drama; Tch Perform.

**WEISSBERG, AARON,** S U N Y At Albany, Albany, NY; FR; BA; Crtfd Scba Dvng; Skng; Mrtl Arts; Blck Blt; Bsn Fnce; Law.

**WEISSMAN, KAREN C,** Yeshiva Univ, New York, NY; SR; BA; Actvities Cncl Pres 89-; Chai Lifeline Vol 89-; Judaic Studies Ecnmcs; Law.

**WEISSMAN, LAURIE M,** Columbus Coll Of Art & Design, Columbus, OH; FR; BFA; Intrnshp Pratt; Schlrshp CCAD 90-; Illus; Art.

**WEISSMAN, STEVEN M,** Yeshiva Univ, New York, NY; SR; BA; Physics Clb; Chem Clb; YACHAD; Sigma Delta Rho; Deans Lst; Bio; Med.

**WEIST, ERIC S,** Moravian Coll, Bethlehem, PA; SO; BS; ACM 89-; Moravian Clg Gamming Clb V P 90-; The Comenian 90; Moravian Xmas Serv Sacristan 89-; Info Sys/Acctg; Accnt.**

**WEITZ, SARAH F,** James Madison University, Harrisonburg, VA; SR; Stdnt Gvrnmnt Assn 87-88; Sr Chlng Strng Comm; Psychology Club 88-; Hnrs Schlr Prgrm 90-; Psi Chi 90-; Mrtr Brd; Cntr Srvc Lrnng 87-88; Cnslng Cntr Prctcm 90-; Magna Cum Laude; Gloomsbrg Unv 90; Fncng Tm 89-90; Psychology; Hghr Edctn Admnstrtn.

**WEITZEL, CHRIS A,** Wright St Univ Lake Cmps, Celina, OH; JR; BSB; AS; ATS 90; Mngmnt Infor Sys; Database Software Dsgnr/Ana.

**WEIZMAN, MICHAEL S,** Univ Of Miami, Coral Gables, FL; JR; BS; Carni Gras Assoc Chrmn 89-; Progm Cncl Spcl Events Chair 90-; Pres 100 90-; Mortar Brd Spcl Evnts Chair; Oak Ldrshp Soc Phi Kappa Phi; Golden Key 90-; Research Asstnt 90; Biology; Physician.

**WELBORN, ROBYN B,** Univ Of Sc At Columbia, Columbia, SC; JR; BAIS; Kappa Delta Epsilon Rsng Pres; Intrdsplnry Study; Elem Sch Tchr.

**WELCH, BARBARA L,** Mary Baldwin Coll, Staunton, VA; SR; Stdnt Govt Asso Treas 90-; Pre-Law Soc V P 88-89; Yrbk Ed 90-; Omicron Delta Kappa V P 90-; Philsphy/Crmnl Jstce; Cmptr Info Sys.

**WELCH, BRIAN A,** Hudson Valley Comm Coll, Troy, NY; FR; AAS 89-90; Engr Optics; Engr R/D.

**WELCH, CAROLYN H,** Patrick Henry Comm Coll, Martinsville, VA; SR; AAS; Stu Nrs Assoc; Spire; PTK; Elks Ntl Fndtn Schlrshp; LPN 73-; Nrsg.

**WELCH, DEBRA D,** James Madison University, Harrisonburg, VA; JR; BA; Pnhllnc Cncl Pblc/Corr Sec 89-90; Pres Cbnt; Rho Chi; Alpha Sigma Tau Pnhllnc Chrmn; Dean Lst 90; Pres Lst; IM; Psych/Sclgy.

**WELCH, FRED H,** Wilmington Coll, New Castle, DE; JR; BA; Bsbl; BA West Chester Univ; Bus Mgmt.

**WELCH, HEATHER R,** Fl St Univ, Tallahassee, FL; JR; BA; WICI 90-; Wsly Fndtn 88-; Hnrs Schlrs Pgm 88-; Phi Eta Sigma 89-; Golden Key 90-; Beta Kappa Alpha 90-; Sigma Kappa VP 89-; Katherine Warren Panhellnc Schlrshp 90; Comm; Pub Rel/Non Prft Org.

**WELCH, JANE W,** Western Piedmont Comm Coll, Morganton, NC; FR; ADN; Nrsng Clb; NC Nrs Schlr 90-; Nrsng.

**WELCH, JODI L,** Hudson Valley Comm Coll, Troy, NY; AAS; SIFE Treas 89; Elem Ed; Tchr.

**WELCH, JOSHUA B,** Marshall University, Huntington, WV; SR; BBA; Alpha Kappa Psi; Bus/Fin/Bus Law; Invstmnt Bnkr.

**WELCH, KATHY V,** City Univ Of Ny Queensbrough, New York, NY; FR; AS; Humanities Clb; Alpha Beta Gamma; Bsnss Admin; Bsnss Law.

**WELCH, KIM R,** Marion Tech Coll, Marion, OH; FR; AS; Nrsng.

**WELCH, KIMBERLY S,** Union Univ, Jackson, TN; SR; BS; Var Bsktbl 87-; FCA 87-; Orntn Ldr 90-; Sigma Alpha Epsilon Aux 88-; STEA 90-; Chi Omega 89-; Tchng Intern 90-; Elem Educ; Tchr.

**WELCH, LEANNA JILL,** Tn Tech Univ, Cookeville, TN; JR; BS; Baptist Stdnt Union 90-; Phi Theta Kappa 89-90; Kappa Omicron Nu Sec 90-; Res Hall Schlrshp 90-; AS Walters State Cmnty Clg 90; Env Design; Arch.

**WELCH, LINN ANN,** Belmont Coll, Nashville, TN; SO; BS; Psych Clb; Gamma Beta Phi; Blgy Educ; Blgy Fld.

**WELCH, MICHAEL J,** Le Moyne Coll, Syracuse, NY; JR; BA; Pre-Law Soc 88-; Hstry Acad 88-; Phi Alpha Theta Pres 90-; Gaelic Soc 89-; Proj Cmnty 88-; Stdnt Sel Comm 90-; Integral Hnrs Pgm 88-; All-Amer Schlr 90-; Ice Hockey; IM Vlybl; Olympics Capt 88-; Hstry/Frnch; Law.

**WELCH, MICHELLE R,** Alcorn St Univ, Lorman, MS; BS; Stu Gov Org Sec 90-; Stu Ntl Educ Assoc VP 90-; GSA; Phi Theta Kappa 89-; Acdmc Achvmnt Awrd; Trck Tm Tm Capt 87-88; AA 90; Elem Educ.

**WELCH, PHYLLIS W,** Daytona Beach Comm Coll, Daytona Beach, FL; JR; BA; Pres Lst 90-; Ntl Hon Soc; Pres Lst; Career Advncmnt Schlrshp Nrthestrn U; Cert Hon Qunicy Jr Coll 77; AS Quincy Jr Coll Quincy MA 77; Cert S Shore Tech Inst Norwell MA 81; Unted Meth Wmns Chrstn Svc; Amer Ordnc Assn; Dsgn Tech; Grphc Arts.

**WELCH, REGINA L,** Garrett Comm Coll, Mchenry, MD; SO; AA; Wldlf Clb Sec/Treas 90-; Soc/Bhvrl Sci; Cnslr.

**WELCH JR, ROBERT F,** Atlantic Comm Coll, Mays Landing, NJ; SO; Prof Chfs Asc 89-; Culnry Arts/Htl Rest Mgmt; Chef.

**WELCH, ROBERTA R,** Newbury Coll, Brookline, MA; SO; AS; Coll Adminstrtr; Bus Mngmnt.

**WELCH, ROBIN L,** Univ Of Nc At Greensboro, Greensboro, NC; JR; BS; Yng Rep Peace Clg 87-89; Peace Clg Chr 87-89; Sigma Delta Mu Peace Clg 88-89; Hnr Stdnt 90-; Elem Ed Intrn 89; AA Peace Clg 89; Elem Educ; Tch.

**WELCH, SAMANTHA L,** Christopher Newport Coll, Newport News, VA; JR; BA; Indstrl/Orgnztnl Psychlgy.

**WELCH, SCOTLAND W,** Central Al Comm Coll, Alexander City, AL; GD; BED; Ag Econ Clb 90; Scty Advncd Mgmt 89-90; BS Auburn Univ 90; Math Sci Scl Stds; Tchr.

**WELCH, SHANNON J,** Univ Of Tn At Knoxville, Knoxville, TN; SO; BS; Phi Eta Sigma 90-; Alpha Lambda Delta 90-; Delta Sigma Pi 90-; Delta Gamma Pres 90-; Stdnt Dxtnctn 89-90; Clg Bus Admn Schlrshp 89-90; Alumni Assoc Schlrshp 89-90; Bus; Acctg.

**WELCH, SULE K,** Morehouse Coll, Atlanta, GA; FR; Math; Bus Mrktg/Eng.

**WELCH, VIRGINIA L,** Coll Of Charleston, Charleston, SC; SO; BA; Hnrs Pgm 90-; Engl; Law/Bsn.

**WELCH, WARRICK J A,** Academy Of The New Church, Bryn Athyn, PA; SR; BA; Relgn; Ministry.

**WELCH, ZINA V,** Univ Of Md At College Park, College Park, MD; FR; BS; Blk Stdnt Un; Alpha Lamda Delta; Bus/Span; Law.

**WELCOME, ANPHONETTA Y,** Al A & M Univ, Normal, AL; SR; BA; Acctg; CPA.

**WELCOME, JANET L,** City Univ Of Ny City Coll, New York, NY; SO; BA; Psy.

**WELDY, TERESA G,** Univ Of South Al, Mobile, AL; GD; MBA; Bay La Launch Comm Assoc Sec/Treas 89-; Dns Lst 84-85 89-90; Pres Lst 86-87; Loan Ofcr S AL Fed Cred Un; BA USA 90; Mgmt; Clg Prof.

**WELFORD, STEPHEN R,** Univ Of Al, Tuscaloosa, AL; FR; BS; AL Chess Clb Corr Ofcr 90-; Capstone Trvl Clb 90-; Clg Bowl Acad Tm 90; Mallet Assembly Male Hnrs Soc 90-; Cmptr-Bsd Hnrs Pgm 90-; Engr.

**WELKER, CHRISTA M,** Western Piedmont Comm Coll, Morganton, NC; FR; AA; Phi Theta Kappa; Psychology.

**WELKER, DAVID M,** Juniata Coll, Huntingdon, PA; JR; BS; Scapel/Probe 89-; Scuba Cl; DJ Radio Station 90-; Hon Soc; Beta Beta Beta 89-; Intern/Armed Forces Inst/Path; Bsktbl 88-; Biol; Med.

**WELLER, DWIGHT D,** Univ Of Nc At Charlotte, Charlotte, NC; SO; BA; Phi Eta Sigma 90-; Deans List 90-; Criminal Justice Psychology Pltcl Sci; Law.

**WELLER, JENNIFER L,** Alfred Univ, Alfred, NY; JR; BS; Socty Wmn Engrs VP 90-; Amer Ceramic Socty; Keramos; General Electric Co Intrn; Ceramic Engr.

**WELLER, STEVEN K,** Univ Of Nc At Charlotte, Charlotte, NC; JR; BS; Gamma Theta Upsilon 90-; Baptist Stdnt Union 90-; Geography; Cartography.

**WELLINGTON III, ROBERT C,** Bridgeport Engr Inst, Fairfield, CT; JR; BSME; APMI; A S Sciene Housatonic Comm Clg 86; Mech Eng.

**WELLMAN, DONNA K,** Meridian Comm Coll, Meridian, MS; SO; AA; Phi Beta Lambda Treas 89-; Phi Theta Kappa; Cert Rcgntn Outstndg Achvmnt; Bapt Ch; Yth Sftbl Coach; Cert Meridian Comm Coll 90; Bus Ofc Tech; Paralegal.

**WELLMAN, JEANINE,** Atlantic Union Coll, S Lancaster, MA; JR; BSC; Kappa Phi Gamma 90-; Kappa Nu Epsln 89-90; Med Tech/Pre-Med; Opthlmlgst.

**WELLMAN, PEGGY A,** William Carey Coll, Hattiesburg, MS; SR; BSN; Stdnt Nurs Assn 87-; Nurs.

**WELLS, AMANDA L,** Clemson Univ, Clemson, SC; SR; BS; Natl Wildlife Fed 89-; Natl Audubon Soc 89-90; Childrens Intrnshp; Park/Rec/Tourism Mngmnt.**

**WELLS, ANGELA D,** Univ Of Tn At Chattanooga, Chattanooga, TN; SR; BSE; Rowing Tm Capt 89-90; SG 88-; Tau Beta Pi Treas 89-; Golden Key 86-; Alpha Lambda Delta; Phi Eta Sigma 86-; ASME 88-; NSPE 88; ASHRAE 90-; Cath Stdnt Ctr Retrt Tm 86-; Deans Lst; Co Op Stdnt Saturn Corp; Ford Mtr Co Intrn; Mech Engr.

**WELLS, ANNA M,** Coll Of Charleston, Charleston, SC; FR; BA.

**WELLS, CHARLES F,** Old Dominion Univ, Norfolk, VA; SO; BS; SPS 90-; Gldn Key; Cntns Elctron Beam Acclrtr Intrn 90-; Inst Nclr Pwr Oprtns Schlrshp; US Navy Nclr Pwr Chmst Hlth Physcst; Mchncl Engnrng; Engnrng.

**WELLS, CHRISTINA W,** Abraham Baldwin Agri Coll, Tifton, GA; SO; MBA; Spch Frm; Hstry; Educ Cnslng.

**WELLS JR, CHRISTOPHER D,** Ms St Univ, Miss State, MS; FR; IM Sftbl/Bsktbl; Elec Eng.

**WELLS, CYNTHIA A,** Univ Of West Fl, Pensacola, FL; JR; BA; Acad Hon 89-90; Stdnt Fac Bsbl Gm 88-89; AA W/Hnrs Pnscla Jr Coll 90; Educ; Elem Tchr.

**WELLS, DARRELL A,** Longwood Coll, Farmville, VA; FR; MS; Longwood Ambsdrs; Alpha Lambda Delta; Herbert R Blackwell Schlr; Phi Kappa Phi; Math; Ecd.

**WELLS, DOROTHY M,** Va St Univ, Petersburg, VA; GD; MED; Stdnt Educ Assn 88-; Kappa Delta Pi 89-; Alpha Kappa Mu 89-; Natl Cllgte Educ Awrd; VA Educ Assn; BS C 90; AS C John Tyler Comm Coll 72; Elem Educ; Tchng.

**WELLS, FORREST S,** Birmingham Southern Coll, Birmingham, AL; SR; BS; Bio; Med.

**WELLS, HARRIET J,** Memphis St Univ, Memphis, TN; JR; BSN; Oncology Nrsng Soc Local/Natl 85-; Amer Cancer Soc Nrsng Sub Cmte 87-; Outstndng Young Women Of Amer 88; RN Staff Nurse; Staff Dev Educ; Nurse Mgr; Cert Oncology Nursing Soc 87-; Nursing.

**WELLS, JACQUELYNN M,** Howard Univ, Washington, DC; SR; BA; Archt Assn 87-; Hl Gsp Chr 89-; Wmn Archt 87-; Gldn Ky 88-; Tau Sigma Delta 89-; Big Sis Prog; P R Harris Intern; Bar Free Chrt; Arch; Arch Rnvtn.

**WELLS JR, JAMES E,** Piedmont Tech Coll, Greenwood, SC; SR; BA; Am Soc Of Radiologic Tech; Deans List; Field Day 90; Radiolgy/Hlth Sci; Admn.

**WELLS, JANE LEARCH,** Elmira Coll, Elmira, NY; SR; BS; Alpha Sigma Lambda 81; ASRT 77-81; Rdlgc Tech 76; Dpl St Josephs Hosp Schl Rdlgc Tech 74; Hmn Svcs/Psych; Wmns Hlth Advcy.

**WELLS, JANICE L,** D Youville Coll, Buffalo, NY; JR; BA; Scl Wrk Assoc 89-; Dns Lst Villa Maria Clg Buffalo 87-88; Dns Lst 89-90; Assoc Arts W/Hnrs Villa Maria Clg Buffalo 88; People Inc Aurora Hostel 90-; Central Referral Svc 90-; Niagara Frontier Aids Alliance 89; Scl Wrk; Wrkg Mntly Disabled.

**WELLS, JEFFREY D,** Embry Riddle Aeronautical Univ, Daytona Beach, FL; SO; MBA; Prvt Pilot; Aircrft Mech; Scuba Dvr; Frnt Dsk Clrk Resrt; Aviatn Maint Mgmt; Prof Aviatn.

**WELLS, JENNIFER J,** Longwood Coll, Farmville, VA; JR; BS; Va Bapt Stdnt Un Sec 90-; Bapt Stdnt Un Longwood/Hampden Sydney Soc V P 89-90; Inter Rel Cncl Pres 89-90; Kappa Delta Pi; Alpha Phi Omega; Heritage Bapt Ch Chldrns Mnstry Intern; Elem Edn; Amdn.

**WELLS, JERMAINE,** Central St Univ, Wilberforce, OH; FR; BS; Actvty Bd 90-; Chorus 90; Hon Dorm 90-; English Ed/Spch Com; English Tch/Pub Rltns.

**WELLS, JILL WARREN,** Blue Mountain Coll, Blue Mountain, MS; GD; BS; Baptist Stdnt Union 89-90; MS Assn Of Eductrs 89-90; Cmmutr Clb 89-90; Natl Educ Of Amer 89-; Euzelian Soc 89-90; 4-H Sponser; Pr Lst 90; Stdnt Tchr Of Mnth 90-; Annual Field Day 89-90; Rhythms I 89; BS Elem Educ; Elem Tchr.

**WELLS, JIMMY D,** Birmingham Southern Coll, Birmingham, AL; JR; BA; Phi Theta Kappa; State Of AL Court Systms; Acctg; Law.

**WELLS, JOEY R,** Univ Of Tn At Knoxville, Knoxville, TN; JR; BS; Amer Mkgt Assn Pro Liaisn 88-; Exec Undrgrad Bus Pgm 89-; Pnhllnc Rho Chi; Beta Gamma Sigma; Omicron Delta Kappa VP; Gldn Key 90-; Sigma Kappa VP 87-; Gamma Beta Phi Pblcty Chrmn 90-; Co-Op Educ Job Intl Paper 89-; Mktg; MBA.

**WELLS, JOHN B,** Univ Of Ky, Lexington, KY; SO; Acctg; CPA.

**WELLS, KAREN A,** Christopher Newport Coll, Newport News, VA; SR; BA; Data Prcssng Mgmt Assn DPMA Tdwtr Pres Schl Chptr 89; Bapt Stdnt Union Pres 89; Phi Theta Kappa 89; Alpha Beta Gamma 89; Slvr Fthr 5 Mst Otstndng Grads 89; Mst Otstndng DPMA Mmbr 89; Bst All Arnd Time Stdnt 89; AS Chowan Coll 89; Bus Admin Cncntrtn In Mgmt; Mgmt.

**WELLS, KENNEY H,** Bethel Coll, Mckenzie, TN; SO; BAS; TN Natl Grd Sgt 90-; Mcroblgy; Optmtry.

**WELLS, KEVIN T,** Fl St Univ, Tallahassee, FL; JR; BS; Lamda Alpha Episilon 90; Intrn State Attrny; AA Polk Cmnty Clg 90; Crmnlgy; Trial Lawyer.

**WELLS, KIMBERLY D,** Marshall University, Huntington, WV; SR; Kappa Delta Pi 89-; Tuition Wvr 88-; BA; Elem Educ; Tchr.

**WELLS, KIMBERLY K,** Wilmington Coll, New Castle, DE; SR; BSN; Bsc Trm Life Spprt Instctr; Phi Theta Kappa 82-83; BLS Instctr Amer Hrt Asc; ACLS Instctr 86-; PALS Instctr 89-; Cert Emer Nrs 86-; CEN; Clncl Radder CNIII; ENA 86; CARE 87; AAS DE Tech Comm Clg 83; Nrsng; Educ.

**WELLS, LEANNE M,** Salisbury St Univ, Salisbury, MD; SR; BS; Math Assoc Amer Pres 89-; Honors Prog 86-; Excell Physics 90; MCM Hnrbl Mntn Meritorious 90-; Deans List 88-; IM 90; Physics/Mathematics; Graduate School.**

**WELLS, LESLIE D,** Patrick Henry Comm Coll, Martinsville, VA; FR; BA; Deans Lst 90-; Horsepasture Chrstn Church 71-; Vol Wk Pharmacy Mem Hosp Martinsville; Sci; Pharmacy.

**WELLS, LISA J,** Saint Josephs Coll, Windham, ME; FR; Hl Cncl Treas 90-; Bodybldg 90-; Dns Lst 90-; Hstry; Law.

**WELLS, MARY E,** Mount Olive Coll, Mount Olive, NC; FR; BA; Bus; Acctnt.

**WELLS, MELISSA D,** James Sprunt Comm Coll, Kenansville, NC; SO; AAS; Bus Admin; Mgmt.

**WELLS, MICHAEL D,** Oh Univ, Athens, OH; GD; DO; SG Affrs Comm Chr 90-; Sigma Sigma Phi 90-; Delta Upsilon Chptr Rltns 87-88; BS OH Univ 84; Ostpthc Med; Fmly Prctc/Intrnl Med.

**WELLS, NANETTE Y,** Univ Of Al At Birmingham, Birmingham, AL; JR; CRNA; Emerg Nrses Assn 88-; SGA 85-88; Phi Kappa Phi 88-; Sigma Theta Tau 88-; Untd Prison Mnstries 85-; Crtcl Care Trnsprt Nrs; BS-RN 88; Med; Ansthtst.

**WELLS, REBBECCA L,** Univ Of West Fl, Pensacola, FL; JR; BA; SGA Faclty Sftbl 88-89; Acad Hnrs Awd 89-90; AA Pens Jr Clg 90; Educ; Erly Childhd Elem.

**WELLS, SHARON B,** Univ Of Sc At Spartanburg, Spartanburg, SC; SR; BA; Literary Club Pblcty Dir 90; Soc Free Thinkers 90; Tutor 90; Omicron Delta Kappa 90; Chi Omega 82-84; Thtr Schlrshp Intern; Prickly Pear Ltry Mag Fctn Editor; Outstndng Grmn Stdnt; Amnesty Intl 88; Greenville Ltrcy Assn 85-; Engl; PHD.

**WELLS, SHAWN J,** S U N Y Coll Of Tech At Canton, Canton, NY; FR; BA; Intr Vrsty Chrstn Clb; BACCHUS VP 90-; Crmnl Jstce Clb; Phi Theta Kappa; Crmnl Jstce; Law Enfrcmnt.

**WELLS, SHERRI D,** Wv Univ At Parkersburg, Parkersburg, WV; FR; BA; Deans Lst 89-; Phi Thata Kappa 90-; Hornsby Pod/Spas 89-; Physcl Thrpy; Physcl Thrpst.

**WELLS, SONJI J,** Tougaloo Coll, Tougaloo, MS; SO; BA; Pre Hlth Cl 90-; Stdnt Supp Svcs 89-; Biol; Med.

**WELLS, TERRI ANNETTE,** Univ Of Nc At Asheville, Asheville, NC; SO; BA; Poetry Pblshd American Anthology Of Poetry 90; Literature; Edn.

**WELLS, THOMAS E,** Gallaudet Univ, Washington, DC; SO; BA; Hons Org 89-; Deans Lst 90-; Schlr Ath Awrd 90-; Soccer Capt 89-; Track; Acctng; CPA.

**WELLS, TONYA M,** Univ Of Nc At Charlotte, Charlotte, NC; JR; BA; Phi Eta Sigma 88-; Beta Beta Beta; Bio; Rsch.

**WELLS, VICKI L,** Davis & Elkins Coll, Elkins, WV; SO; BS; Psychlgy Club; Phoenix Allnc; Deans List; Natl Deans List; Womnes Auxlry Elkins Mtn Sch; Psychlgy; Cnslng.

**WELLS, WILLIAM Q,** Fayetteville St Univ, Fayetteville, NC; FR; BA; Soc Creative Anachronism Marshall 80-; Chmbr Cmrce; US Army Spcl Forces 77-88; Indstrl Tech Comp Sci; Indstrl Eng.

**WELLS, WIRE K,** Benedict Coll, Columbia, SC; SR; Blck Alliance Clb Chpln 90; Gspl Choir Pres 90; Crmnl Jstc Clb 90; Ldrshp Awd 90; Assoc Sptbg Meth Coll 89; Crmnl Law.

**WELLS, YOLANDA L,** Alcorn St Univ, Lorman, MS; SO; BA; Pol Scnc; Law.

**WELSH, CHRISTINE E,** Immaculata Coll, Immaculata, PA; JR; BA; Engl.

**WELSH, EDWARD D,** Comm Coll Algny Co Algny Cmps, Pittsburgh, PA; SO; BA; Nrsng; Pschylgy.

**WELSH, JAMES S,** S U N Y At Stony Brook, Stony Brook, NY; GD; MD; NY Turtle & Tortoise Scty 88-; Phi Beta Kappa 84-; Grdtd Otstndng Acdmc Prfrmnc 84; Billiards 81; Tchr Resrch Scintst 85-90; MS Yale Univ 85; BA 84; Medicine; Dgnstc Imaging.

**WELSH, JENNIFER A,** Univ Of Akron, Akron, OH; JR; Peer Consltnt 90-; Chi Omega Pldg Treas 90-; Sndry Educ/Engl; Tchr.

**WELSH, JERALD R,** Columbia Union Coll, Takoma Park, MD; SR; BS; Sci Cl Pikes Peak Comm Colg; Mountaineering Cl; Alhpa Chi 90-; Am Soc/Q C; Surface Mount Tech Asso; Q A Assur Tech Asso; Busn Admin; Manuf Mgmnt.

**WELSH, JESSICA H,** Bethany Coll, Bethany, WV; FR; Bthny Tv 3 Assoc Prdcr/Entrtnmnt Anchrwmn 90-; IM Vlybl; Brdcst Cmmnctns; TV News.

**WELTY, JAMES D,** Westminster Coll, New Wilmingtn, PA; SR; BA; Eckrd Coll Org Stdnts Hs Pres 87-89; Swm Tm 89-; Mrtr Brd 90-; Omicron Delta Kappa 90pi Sigma Alpha Sec 90-; Theta Chi Prlmntrn 90-; Rtrct Clb 87; Smstr Lndn 89; Intern Pnnsylvn Chmbr Bus Indstry; Swm Tm 89-; Pltcl Sci.

**WELTZIN, RAYMOND A,** Inter Amer Univ Pr Hato Rey, Hato Rey, PR; FR; BA; Avtn; Plt.

**WELZ, ANTHONY W,** Glassboro St Coll, Glassboro, NJ; SO; BA; Natl Egl Sct Assoc 89-; Asst By Sct Ldr 88-; Theta Chi Pldg Mrshl 90-; Egl Sct By Scts Amer; Cmnctn; Pblc Rltns Wrtr.

**WEN, HSIU-TING TIANA,** Atlantic Comm Coll, Mays Landing, NJ; SO; Intrntl Clb Treas 90-; Bus Admin.

**WEN, KUANG-PING,** Radford Univ, Radford, VA; JR; BA; Intl Stdnt Sorg 90-; Assoc Comp Mchnry; BA Natl Taiwan Univ 82-86; Comp Sci; Sftwr Eng.

**WENBERG, KRISTINA J,** Lake City Comm Coll, Lake City, FL; SO; AA AS; Thtr Grp; Phi Theta Kappa; GOP Prcnct #10 Comm Wmn 88-90; Crmnlgy/Crmnl Jstc/Lgl Asst; Law.

**WENDEL, KARI M,** S U N Y Coll At Fredonia, Fredonia, NY; SR; Phi Alpha Theta 90-; Kappa Delta Pi; Deans Lst 89-; Wrtng/Engl Intern 90; Scndry Engl Educ; Library Sci.

**WENDELL, JESSAMYN B,** Rivier Coll, Nashua, NH; SO; BA; Images 91 Yrbk Layout Edtr 90-.

**WENDEROTH, CHRISTINA,** U S Coast Guard Academy, New London, CT; FR; BS; Vars Sailng Tm 90-; Elec Engr.

**WENDLAND, CATHY JO,** Suffolk Comm Coll Eastern Cmps, Riverhead, NY; SO; BS; Multi-Cultural Club 89-90; Biology; Medicine.

**WENDLER, SHIRLEY A,** City Univ Of Ny City Coll, New York, NY; SR; MBA; NY Hist Soc 89-; Smithsonian Assn 90-; Deans Lst 89-; Magna Cum Laude 90-; Alpha Sigma Lambda 90-; Natl Assn Postal Supvrs Delegate 84-; Publ Servant Mngrl Status; BA; Pol Sci; Publ Admin.

**WENGER, MELANI M,** Cumberland County Coll, Vineland, NJ; FR; BA; Phi Theta Kappa; Lbrl Arts Gnrl.

**WENGERT, WENDY S,** Juniata Coll, Huntingdon, PA; JR; BS; Stdnt Gov Sec 89-; P A Inst CPA Stdnt Affil 89-; Tau Pi Phi; Phi Chi Theta Cor Sec 90-; Acctg Intrn 90; Publ Acctg.

**WENGRYNIUK, JOSEPH J,** Southern Coll Of Tech, Marietta, GA; SR; BS; Tau Alpha Pi 90-; IEEE 88-; Elect Eng; Cmmnctns Eng.

**WENIG, CLARANN S,** Wv Northern Comm Coll, Wheeling, WV; FR; Sec Sci.

**WENIS, ERICH B,** S U N Y Coll Of Tech At Alfred, Alfred, NY; FR; AAS; Ergo Mag Edtr; Natl Computer Grphcs Assoc; Tor Echo Adv Comm; Dns Lst; Brian Maraschiello Schlrshp; Comm Awd Honree; Comp Grphcs Engr Tech; Comp Grphcs Oper.

**WENLOCK, AMY L,** Immaculata Coll, Immaculata, PA; SR; Psych Clb VP 90-; Big Sister 89-; Psi Chi VP 90-; Intrnshp CCIU 90-; BA; Psychology.

**WENNER, ANNAMARIA,** Univ Of Pittsburgh At Bradford, Bradford, PA; SR; Mnrty Stdnt Union Pres 89; Stdnt Actvty Cncl VP 90; Stdnt Govt Assn Chrprsn 90-; Stdnt Jdcl Brd; Rsdnt Asst Stff; Hmnts Schlrshp Cntst 87; Psych Coll Stdnt Prsnnl Wrk; Dean Of Stdnts.

**WENRICK, SHERRI J,** Bloomsburg Univ Of Pa, Bloomsburg, PA; FR; BED; Elem Ed/Erly Chld Dev; Tchr.

**WENTE, CHRISTOPHER T,** Univ Of Ky, Lexington, KY; FR; BA; Phlsphy.

**WENTLAND III, JACOB J,** Univ Of Scranton, Scranton, PA; JR; BS; Acctg Soc 90-; Bus Clb 90-; Sftbl/Street Hockey I M; Delta Mu Delta; Acctg.

**WENTWORTH, MELANIE SUSAN,** Fl International Univ, Miami, FL; JR; BA; Outstndg Acad Achvmnt Awd 88-89; Excell Awd 88-89; High Hnrs 89; Phys Ther Asst 89-; AA Miami Dade Cmnty Clg 89; Phys Ther.

**WENTWORTH, NANCY J,** Newbury Coll, Brookline, MA; SR.

**WENTWORTH, WENDY J,** Lesley Coll, Cambridge, MA; JR; BED; SGA Pub Ofcr 89-90; Sftbl Tm 88-89; Early Chlhd Educ.

**WENTZ JR, GARY L,** Univ Of Central Fl, Orlando, FL; SO; BS; Assist Syst Eng; Martin Marietta Electronic Syst; Aerospace Eng; Eng.**

**WENTZEL, CHARLES A,** Indiana Univ Of Pa, Indiana, PA; FR; Math Education; Teacher.

**WENTZEL, DUANE J,** Memphis St Univ, Memphis, TN; SR; BSEE; Black Stdnt Assn 86; Intrntnl Stdnt Assn 86; Karate Clb 89-; Intrntnl Soc Optcl Engnrng 90-; Navy ROTC Schlrshp 85-87; Hyoh B Wooten Schlrshp 90-; RA Dr Michael Dutey 89-; IM Bckgammon Chmpn 90-; Elctrcl Engnrng; Rsrch Elctro Optcs.

**WENZEL, ALSEN K,** Univ Of New Haven, West Haven, CT; SR; BS; Aviation 88-; Res Assist 89-; Alpha Lambda Delta Pres 89-; Crss Cntry/Trck Capt 88-; Aero; Pilot.

**WENZEL, LAUREN D,** Suffolk Comm Coll Eastern Cmps, Riverhead, NY; SO; BA; Pi Alpha Sigma 90-; Eastern Long Island Quilters Guild Schlrshp; Deans List 90-; Intrnshp Old Town Crossing South Hamptons 90-; Interior Dsgn.

**WENZEL, SHANNON A,** Juniata Coll, Huntingdon, PA; JR; BA; RHA VP 88-; Judicial Bd Sec 89-; Acad Affairs Trustee 89-; Amateur Radio Clb 90-; Cornwall Furnace Assoc Intern; Hist Latin Am Studies; Professor.

**WENZEL, STEPHANY M,** James Madison University, Harrisonburg, VA; SR; BS; Stdnt Ambassador Org 89-; Sports Cncl Bd; Assoc Edn Young Chldrn 87-; Kappa Delta Pi 90-; Zeta Tau Alpha Pledge Pres 89-; Center Service Learning 87-90; IM Hall Of Fame; Early Chldhd Edn; Teach.

**WENZLOFF, STEPHEN A,** Univ Of Ga, Athens, GA; SR; BLA; GA Stdnts Of Landscape Arch 89-; Amer Soc Landscape Arch 89-; Sigma Lambda Alpha; Landscape Arch.

**WERELUS, AMY M,** D Youville Coll, Buffalo, NY; SO; BS; Bio; Med/Pediatrics.

**WERLE, MELISSA A,** Oh Wesleyan Univ, Delaware, OH; FR; BA; Stdnt Adv Stdnt Jud Crts 90-; Stdnt Crts Justice; Mellon Socty 90-; Phi Eta Sigma 90-; Delta Zeta State Day Chr; Pres Schlrshp 90-; Dns Lst 90-; Vrsty Vlybl 90-; Hstry; Law.

**WERLEIN, E KENNETH,** Asbury Theological Sem, Wilmore, KY; SR; MDIV; Ichthus Festival Mnstrs Prog Dir 89-; Habitat For Humanity 89-; Evgcls For Soc Actn; Theta Phi; Lexington Comm Kitche Vol 90-; Intern Southern Hills UMC Lexington 90-; Intern M D Anderson Hosp Houston 90; Intern 1st UMC Houston 87-89; BS Vanderbilt U; Divinity; Ministerial.

**WERNE, TORY D,** Southern Coll Of Tech, Marietta, GA; SR; BS; IEEE V Chrmn 90-; Tau Alpha Pi 89-; Elctrncs Lab Instrctr 90-; Elctrcl Engrg Tech; Elctrcl Engr.**

**WERNER, BRIAN P,** Old Dominion Univ, Norfolk, VA; GD; MS; Kovner Achiev Schlrshp 90-; Outstndng EET Sr Awd; Alumni Ach Awd; AAS Northern Vl Commty Clg Elec Techlgy 85-88; BS Elec Eng Techlgy; Elec; Engr.

**WERNER, CATHY ANN,** Hillsborough Comm Coll, Tampa, FL; FR; AA; Otstndg Lit Stdnt 90-; Phi Theta Kappa; Sls Intr Dsgn 65-90; Educ/Engl; Inst.

**WERNER, DONNA M,** Univ Of Cincinnati, Cincinnati, OH; JR; BED; Gldn Ky; Ohio Phys Thrpst Asst Affnty Grp; Amer Phys Thrpy Assn 88-89; AA 89; Phys Thrpst Asst 89-; Hlth Educ/Comm Hlth; Ath Trng/Phy Thrpy.

**WERNER, EVELYN R,** Norwich Univ, Northfield, VT; FR; BARCH; Stdnt Govt Pres; Blue/Gold Key 90-; Amer Inst Of Arch Stdnts 90-; Wom Soccer 90; Architecture.

**WERNER, JANINE L,** Fl International Univ, Miami, FL; SR; BS; Hotl/Fd/Trvl Assn 90-; Delta Delta Phi 90-; Phi Kappa Phi 90-; Grad W/Hon; M Warner Schlrshp; Prsbytrn Chrch Choir; Tckt Mgr For Tennis Trnmnt; Airln Assoc; AA Miami-Dade Comm Coll 89; Hotel Mgmt; Grad Schl MBA.

**WERNER, LINDA L,** Univ Of Sc At Columbia, Columbia, SC; SR; BS; Psi Chi 89-; Otstndng Stdnt Awd In Psych; Worked For YMCA; Sch Psychlgst.**

**WERNER, NOEL D,** Westminster Choir Coll, Princeton, NJ; SR; M MUS; Pi Kappa Lambda 90; Organ Prfrmnc; Chrch Mscn.

**WERNER, PAMELA D,** Hillsborough Comm Coll, Tampa, FL; FR; BA; Mrne Blgy; Envir Sci.

**WERNER, SCOTT M,** Cornell Univ Statutory College, Ithaca, NY; SO; BS; Comm Access TV Prodcr 90-91; IM Ice Hcky 89-91; Communications; Film Making.

**WERNET, KATHLEEN M,** Dowling Coll, Oakdale Li, NY; JR; BS; Psych/Math/Bio; Doctor/Crdlgy.

**WERT, ANNE R,** Philadelphia Coll Pharm & Sci, Philadelphia, PA; JR; MPT; Pt Clb 88-; Chorus 88-; Nwspr Entrtmnt Co Edtr 88-; Kappa Epsilon Hstrn 89-; Adopt A Grndprnt 88-; Peer Cnslng 90-; Reading Hosp Intrn 89-; Phys Thrpy; Geriatric P T.**

**WERT, LORI A,** Central Pa Bus School, Summerdale, PA; SR; ASB; Clgte Secr Intl 89-; Big/Ltl Sis Pgm 89-; Judiciary Comm 90-; Adm Secr; Secr.

**WERT, MATTHEW P,** West Chester Univ, West Chester, PA; JR; BM; Symphny Orchstr; Flt Ensmbl; Msc/Instrmntl Prfrmc; Ensmbls/Instrctn.

**WERTHMAN, TODD F,** Southern Vt Coll, Bennington, VT; JR; BA; Phi Beta Lambda 87-88; URSA; Bsktbl 90; AAS Herkimer Cnty Comm Coll 89; Hlth; Admin Hlth Cr.

**WERTMAN, BECKY J,** Saint Francis Coll, Loretto, PA; FR; BS; Stdnt Soc Phys Assts 90-; Physcn Asst.

**WERTZ, JOAN M,** Allegheny Coll, Meadville, PA; SR; BS; Rsdnt Advsr 90; Rsdnt Dir 90-; Psi Chi 90-; Hbtt Fr Hmnty 90-; Frnds Of Yth Crwfrd Cnty PA 89; Tchng Asst; Psychlgy; Psychlgcl Rsrch.

**WERTZ, JOHN D,** Pa St Univ Delaware Cty Cmps, Media, PA; SO; BS; Rngr Clb 90-; Lions Grd Clb 89-; Army ROTC Exec Offcr Admn 89-; Vllybll Tm 90-; Math; Army Offcr Plt.**

**WERTZ, MICHELLE C,** Univ Of Rochester, Rochester, NY; SO; BA; Together Network Grads V P Rec 89-; D Lions Stdnt Intrvwr 90-; Actvts Bd 90-; Reach Out 89-; Psych German.

**WESBY, TUNYA D,** Alcorn St Univ, Lorman, MS; JR; BS; Kappa Alpha Psi 88-; Untd Way 90-; Chrstn Cncltn Srvc; Acctg.

**WESCH, DIANE L,** Nova Univ, Ft Lauderdale, FL; GD; MBA; Phi Kappa Phi 84-85; Deans Lst 84-85; Cntnty Cr Sec Treas 89-; BS 85; Bus Admn.

**WESCHE, COLLEEN P,** S U N Y Coll Of Tech At Alfred, Alfred, NY; FR; ASSOC; Cross Cntry/Alfred Univ 89; Lib Arts/Scl Sci; Ed.

**WESLEY, ANITA C,** Chatfield Coll, Saint Martin, OH; BA; Bus; Admn.

**WESLEY, ETHEL F,** Neumann Coll, Aston, PA; GD; Prfsnl Edctrs Clb; Phi Theta Kappa; Delta PA; Alpha Sigma Lambda; Dns Lst; DE Vly Assoc Ed Yng Chldrn; Diocesan Chrstn Ed Comm V-Chr 88; BA; Early Chldhd Elem Ed; Tchr.

**WESLEY JR, HAROLD J,** Al A & M Univ, Normal, AL; SR; BA; Choir; Thespian Soc; Alpha Kappa Mu; Soc Pres Schlr; Alpha Phi Alpha Ed 90-; Telecmnctns; MBA.

**WESLEY, JOHN W,** Columbia Union Coll, Takoma Park, MD; SR; BS; Data Prcssng Mgmt Assoc 88-; Phi Beta Lambda 78-80; Deans Lst 90-; Comp Spclst; Bus Admn.

**WESLEY, RICHARD T,** Merrimack Coll, North Andover, MA; SR; BA; Dns Lst; Co Op Stdnt Wrkng For IBM; Acad Schlrshp; Mktg.

**WESLEY, TRACIE L,** Savannah St Coll, Savannah, GA; SR; Comp Sci Clb Treas 90-; Nwtn Soc Sec 89-90; Beta Kappa Chi 90; Alpha Kappa Mu; SROP 89-90; Comp Sci/Math; Comp Prog/Tchr.

**WESLING, ERIN,** S U N Y At Buffalo, Buffalo, NY; JR; BS; FMA 89-; DPMA 90-; Women In Mgmnt Assoc 90-; Golden Key 89-; Phi Eta Sigma 89-; Chi Omega Sor 88-; Hosp Vol 90-; Cancer Soc 90-; Regents Schlrshp 88-; Mothers Clb Buffalo Schlrshps 89-; Tops Inc Schlrshp 89-; Mgmnt Finance MIS; Bus Mgmnt.

**WESOLOWSKI, PHILIP R,** Central Fl Comm Coll, Ocala, FL; FR; BA; Army Natl Guard 88-; Scndry Educ/Hstry.

**WESOLOWSKY, LUBA,** City Univ Of Ny Baruch Coll, New York, NY; SR; BBA; Bus Opers Mgmnt.

**WESS, BYRON P,** Oh Dominican Coll, Columbus, OH; SO; BA; Drug Intrvntn Crdntr; Bapt Chrch Media Mnstry Chf Rec Tech 66-; NAITI; Letter Carrier 84-; Theology; Mnstr/Professor.

**WESSANT, DAVID C,** Comm Coll Algny Co Algny Cmps, Pittsburgh, PA; FR; Resp Thrpy; Med.

**WESSEL, DEBORAH S,** Memphis St Univ, Memphis, TN; SR; BBA; Beta Alpha Psi Edtr Nwsltr 90-; Accountant 90-; Accounting.

**WESSELL, TRESSA RENEE,** Univ Of Sc At Columbia, Columbia, SC; SO; BA; Alpha Lambda Delta; Kappa Delta Stndrds Bd 90-; Bus Admin.

**WESSON, CATHERINE L,** Univ Of Al At Birmingham, Birmingham, AL; JR; BS; SOTA 90-; Alpha Lambda Delta 88-89; Gamma Beta Phi 88-89; Phi Eta Sigma 88-89; Delta Delta Delta 88-89; Cmnty Serv Comm Of SOTA 90-; Occupational Therapy.

**WESSON III, LAWRENCE MILTON,** Univ Of Southern Ms, Hattiesburg, MS; JR; BA; Leading RBI Httr 90-; Vrsty Bsbl 90-; Acctg/Bus-Fin; Acctg.

**WEST, ALLEN L,** Univ Of Sc At Columbia, Columbia, SC; SR; Stdnt Nwspr 89-; Stdnt Radio 89-; Kappa Tau Alpha 89-; Phi Beta Kappa 89-; Gamma Beta Phi 89-; Alpha Epsilon Rho 88-89; Sigma Delta Chi 88-; Stdnts Pstv Scl Chng; BA 91; Jrnlsm; Brdcstng.

**WEST, BARBARA C,** Univ Of Pittsburgh, Pittsburgh, PA; SR; BS; Assoc Pdlgy CCAC 80; Chld Dvlpmnt; Wrk W/Chldrn.

**WEST, BRIAN J,** Siena Coll, Loudonville, NY; SR; BS; Cls V P 87-88; Sibling Weekend Chr 89-90; Stdnt Affairs Advsry Comm Stdnt Rep 89-90; Delta Epsilon Sigma; Alpha Kappa Alpha; Pres Schlr 87-; Delta Sigma Pi Bro 87-; Big Bro 87-; Campus Mnstry Advsry Bd Lector 87-; Elderly Care Vol 89-90; Finance; Bsn.

**WEST, BRYAN C,** Kent St Univ Kent Cmps, Kent, OH; SR; Intl Fd Svc Execs Assoc Pres 89-90; BS; Hsptlty Fd Svc Mgmt; Bsn.

**WEST JR, BUDDY A,** Volunteer St Comm Coll, Gallatin, TN; SO; Acctg Clb 89-; Gamma Beta Phi 88-.

**WEST, CAROL L,** Va Polytechnic Inst & St Univ, Blacksburg, VA; SO; BS; Psych Club 90-; Psych Experiments 89-; Natl Hnr Soc In Psych 90-; Psych; Child Dvlpmnt Cnslng.**

**WEST, CHARLES L,** Mercer Univ Schl Of Pharm, Atlanta, GA; GD; PHARM; Hnr Coun 90-; Amer Soc Hosp Hrmcst 89-90; Rho Chi 90-; Phi Beta Sigma 78-82; BS Paine Coll Augusta Ga 81; Phrmcy.

**WEST, CHARLES V,** Univ Of Nc At Asheville, Asheville, NC; SO; BA; Phlsphy; Bsns Mgmnt.

**WEST, DAVID J,** City Univ Of Ny Baruch Coll, New York, NY; SO; Islamic Stds Club Sec; Fin/Econ Soc 90; Seventh House Pres 89-; Steven Bernstein Esq Admin Assist Intern 87-89; Fin/Phlsphy; Pblshng.

**WEST, DIANE M,** Hilbert Coll, Hamburg, NY; FR; AAS; Bus Admin.

**WEST, DONNA RAINES,** Memphis St Univ, Memphis, TN; SR; BPS; ASCP Am Soc For Clinical Path Med Tech Jackson Madison Co Gen Hosp 72-; AS Jackson St 72.

**WEST, DOUGLAS A,** Miami Dade Comm Coll North, Miami, FL; SO; BA; AA; Arch.

**WEST, GINA S,** Oh Univ, Athens, OH; FR; BS; Chem Eng; Eng.

**WEST, GINGER F,** Northeast State Tech Comm Coll, Blountville, TN; SO; CSI 90-; BS East TN State Univ 79; Ofc Sys Technlgy; Admnstrtv Secy.

**WEST, HARVEY L,** Ohio Valley Coll, Parkersburg, WV; JR; BA; Tmthy Clb Pres 88-; Assoc Mnstr Church Of Christ 90-; AA; Bible; Prchng And Chrstn Cnslng.

**WEST, JAMES A,** Appalachian Bible Coll, Bradley, WV; FR; BA; Yth Dir Glnvw Indpndnt Bapt Chrch 90-; Intr Coll Bsktbl Tm 90-; Theology; Educ.

**WEST JR, JAMES R,** Univ Of Ky, Lexington, KY; FR; BS; Physics.

**WEST, JENNIFER K,** Univ Of Tn At Knoxville, Knoxville, TN; FR; BA; Phi Eta Sigma; Alpha Lambda Delta; Clinical Psych.

**WEST, JENNIFER L,** Univ Of Montevallo, Montevallo, AL; FR; Biology Chem Phar; Optometry.

**WEST, JERRY L,** Spartanburg Methodist Coll, Spartanburg, SC; FR; Pioneer Basball 90; Physical Ed/Health; HS Coach.

**WEST, JOHN EDWARD,** Ms St Univ, Miss State, MS; SR; BS; IEEE; Phi Kappa Phi; Eta Kappa Nu; Tau Beta Pi Pres; Elec Eng; Eng.

**WEST, KAREN H,** James Sprunt Comm Coll, Kenansville, NC; SO; History.

**WEST, LYNN A,** Fl Atlantic Univ, Boca Raton, FL; JR; BA; Acctg Stdnts Assn 90-; Beta Alpha Psi Rprtg Sec; Arthur Andersen Ldrshp Confer; ADT Inc Jr Acct; AA Indian River Cmnty Clg 89; Acctg; CPA.

**WEST, MARCIA Y,** Alcorn St Univ, Lorman, MS; FR; BS; Nrsng; Pediatric.

**WEST, MARK R,** Old Dominion Univ, Norfolk, VA; JR; BA; AGC 90-; CSI 90-; Golden Key; Tutor 89; Grad DT/CC High Hnrs 2yrs Cum 88-90; Deans List 90-; AAS DE Techl/Commty Clg 90; Civil Engrg; Engrg.

**WEST, MICHAEL A,** Univ Of Nc At Asheville, Asheville, NC; SR; Coll Dmcrts 90-; Pi Sigma Alpha 90-; Pi Alpha Theta; Grad Dstnctn Pltcl Sci; NC State Dfns Militia 1st Lt; BA UNCA; Pltcl Sci/Hstry; Law.

**WEST, MICHAEL H,** Ms St Univ, Miss State, MS; JR; BSME; Amrcn Scty Mech Eng 88-; Phi Kappa Phi 90-; Tau Beta Phi 90-; Pi Tau Sigma 90-; Bell Rsrch Asstnt; US Navy Sbmrns 82-88; Mech Eng.

**WEST, MICHAEL S,** Austin Peay St Univ, Clarksville, TN; FR; Wesley Fndtn 90-; Gamma Beta Phi VP 90-; Alpha Lambda Delta 90-; Pres Emrgng Ldrs Pgm 90-; Chemistry; Medicine.

**WEST, MIKE J,** Univ Of Tn At Martin, Martin, TN; FR; BA; Church Of Christ Stdnt Ctr Treas 90-; IM Ftbl/Bsktbl/Vlybl/Sftbl; Acctg; CPA.

**WEST, NANCY L,** Univ Of South Al, Mobile, AL; SO; BS; Ofc Mgr Boja's Foods Inc 81-; Acctg; CMA.

**WEST, PAMELA JO,** Univ Of Ky, Lexington, KY; FR; BA; Tm Recruiting 90-; DEA; Student Develpmt Council Math Club; Alpha Lambda Delta 90-; Epsilon Delta; Phi Eta Sigma; Lambda Sigma; Deans List 90; Math/Secondary Ed; Tch High Schl Level.

**WEST, PETER L,** Lenoir Rhyne Coll, Hickory, NC; SR; BA; Intervrsty Chrstn Flwshp Pr 88-89; Litry Soc 88-; Engl; Minstr.

**WEST, RODERICK J,** Clark Atlanta Univ, Atlanta, GA; SO; BS/BS; Natl Soc Blck Engrs 89-; Physcs Clb Treas 89-; Math Clb 90-; Hon Pgm Treas 89-; Pi Mu Epsilon 90-; Phi Beta Sigma; J Robinson Fndtn Schlr 89-; Gnrl Mtrs Schlr/Intrnshp 90-; IM Bsktbl; Math/Ind Eng; Eng.

**WEST, SEANTE D,** Univ Of Md At Eastern Shore, Princess Anne, MD; SR; BA; Pom Squad Capt 88-89; Hon Roll 90-; Rehab Serv; Pub Serv.

**WEST, SHARON G,** Western Ky Univ, Bowling Green, KY; SR; BA; Engl; Tchr.

**WEST, SHARON M,** Wilmington Coll, Wilmington, OH; SO; BA; Fayette Cnty Wmns Sftbl Assn Pres 90-; Yth Comm Mbr 1st Bapt Chrch; Media Crdntr 85-; Staunton Parent Tchr Org Treas; Sec Engl Educ; Tchng.

**WEST, SHELLEY-ANN J,** Barry Univ, Miami, FL; FR; BS; Trinidad/Tobago Clb; Delta Phi Epsilon Tres; Cmptr Sci.

**WEST, STEPHANIE A,** Milligan Coll, Milligan Clg, TN; FR; BS; Sprtl Life Comm 90-; Cir K; Bio; Med.

**WEST, TARA V,** Univ Of Sc At Columbia, Columbia, SC; FR; BS; Deans List 90; Biology; Psychiatrist.

**WEST, TIFFANY A,** Univ Of Nc At Greensboro, Greensboro, NC; SO; Asc Educ Yng Chldrn 89-90; Alpha Lambda Delta 90-; Marshal 90-; Chld Dvlpmnt; Child Care.

**WEST, TONYA V,** City Univ Of Ny Baruch Coll, New York, NY; SR; BED; Educ; Tchr.

**WEST, VICTORIA M,** Salisbury St Univ, Salisbury, MD; JR; BA; Hist; Teach.

**WEST, YOLANDA L,** Tn St Univ, Nashville, TN; SR; SAYC VP 90-; Pep Clb 89-; NAYC 86-; Early Chldhd Educ; Tchr.

**WESTAWAY, SUSAN A,** Va Commonwealth Univ, Richmond, VA; SR; BFA; Cntmpry Crfts Socty 90-; Gldn Key; Crfts Txtls; Artist.

**WESTBERG, JANICE L,** Mount Olive Coll, Mount Olive, NC; JR; Acctng.

**WESTBERG, THOMAS C,** Univ Of Miami, Coral Gables, FL; SR; BA; Cinematic Arts Commission Spec Evnts Coord 90-; Stdnt Amer Inst Arch 87-; Surf Tm 87-88; Arch Stdnt Awd 89-90; IMS Capt 87-; Arch/Hstry; Arch.

**WESTBERRY, TANYA S,** Broward Comm Coll, Ft Lauderdale, FL; FR; BA; Singing Grp 88-; Bio; Marine Bio.

**WESTBROOK, ALANNA K,** Univ Of Southern Ms, Hattiesburg, MS; SR; Gamma Beta Phi 89-; BA W/Hnrs; Engl.

**WESTBROOK, JASON L,** Wv Univ At Parkersburg, Parkersburg, WV; FR; BA; Forgn Lang; Educ.

**WESTBURY JR, JAMES R,** Gordon Coll, Barnesville, GA; SR; BBA; Phi Theta Kappa 90-; Beta Gamma Sigma; Ga CPA Cert Exclnc 89-90; Fin Exec Inst Schlrshp; AS Gordon Clg 90; Fin; Law.

**WESTBURY, ROSE ELLEN,** Univ Of North Fl, Jacksonville, FL; SR; BA; Otstndng Achvmnt Awd Cmpstn FCCJ 89; Otstndng Achvmnt Awd Advncd Math 90; Spr Ratng Ntnl Paino Plyng Adtn FCCJ St Lvl 87-; Spsnsrd Amrcn Clg Mscns; Instrctr Douglass Andrsn Schl Prfrmng Arts Clscl Blt 88-90; Spnsh Ltn Amrcn Stds; Grad Wrk Lngstcs.

**WESTBURY, STEPHANIE JEAN,** Univ Of Sc At Columbia, Columbia, SC; FR; Phi Eta Sigma; Deans Lst; Engl.

**WESTBURY, STEPHEN L,** Univ Of Sc At Columbia, Columbia, SC; JR; BS; St George Jaycees; Bus Admin.

**WESTCOTT JR, BARRY L,** Pa St Univ Erie-Behrend Coll, Erie, PA; FR; BS; Jnt Rsdnt Cncl Cmte Chr 90-; Drm Clb Actr 90-; Schlrs Pgm 90-; Lambda Sigma Pres Elct; Irene Ryan Cndt Amer Clge Thtr Fstvl 90-; Bst Ftrd Actr Penn St Behrend 90-; Chmstry; Indstrl Chmst.

**WESTCOTT, JANICE M,** Comm Coll Algny Co Algny Cmps, Pittsburgh, PA; GD; BA; Phi Theta Kappa 90-; Prchsng Agnt 76-86; Elem Educ; Educ.

**WESTCOTT, JULIE A,** Boston Coll, Chestnut Hill, MA; SO; BA; Golden Eagle Dance Tm 90-; Nrsng; Nurse Pract.

**WESTENBERGER, TERRY LOU,** Atlantic Comm Coll, Mays Landing, NJ; FR; AA; Culinary Arts Assoc 90-; Culinary Arts; Pastry Chef.

**WESTENDORF, JULIEANNE,** Univ Of Cincinnati, Cincinnati, OH; JR; BSN; Nursing Stdnt Govt Rep 90-; Kappa Kappa Gamma Pub Relations 87-90; Composite Sportwear 90-; Rush Councilor 90; Nursing; RN.

**WESTENHAVER, KENNETH E,** Bristol Univ, Bristol, TN; GD; MBA; Knoxvl Chmbr Cmmrc 85-; Lions Clb Intl 81-; Rtry Clb 76-; Amer Coll Hlthcr Exec 83-; Bd Advsrs Coll Hlth Univ FL 82-83; Hlthcr Mgmt/Hosp Admin 63-; BBA Univ TX 72; Mgmt; Hlthcr Admin.

**WESTER, ANNA MARIA,** Univ Of Miami, Coral Gables, FL; SR; Ghg Schl Coll Under Grad Lvl Tchr Swdsh Hstry Rlgn Swdsh; MA Hstry Scl Sci Ed 89; Psychlgy; Tchng.

**WESTER, JANET S,** Hillsborough Comm Coll, Tampa, FL; JR; BA; Phi Theta Kappa 90-; SCATT; Spec Ed/Lrng Dsblts; Tchr.

**WESTERFIELD, PETER W,** Nova Univ, Ft Lauderdale, FL; GD; MBA; Mrktng.

**WESTERHOLM, JANETTA D,** Richard Bland Coll, Petersburg, VA; SO; AB; AS 90; Cmptrs; Acctnt.

**WESTERLING, DENISE,** Pa St Univ Delaware Cty Cmps, Media, PA; SO; BA; Psychlgy.

**WESTERMANN, ANN L,** Univ Of Cincinnati, Cincinnati, OH; SR; BED; Mscns Assn 73-; Amer Hrp Soc Treas 73-; Alliance Francaise; Kappa Delta Pi; Goldn Key; Magna Cum Laude Grad 77; Summa Cum Laude Grad; Schlrshps 90-; Tchr Ed Loan Prog Awrd 88-; Prfssnl Hrpst 77-; BM 77; Cert France 90; Frnch; Tch.

**WESTERVELT, KAREN E,** Allegheny Coll, Meadville, PA; JR; BA; Psi Chi Pres; Kappa Kappa Gamma VP; Alden Schlr 88-; Med Cntr Fmly Thrpy Intrn 90-; Psychlgy; Clncl Psychlgy.

**WESTERVELT, WAYNE A,** Le Moyne Coll, Syracuse, NY; JR; BA; Acdmc Tr HEPP; Tr Cnslr; Intrmrls; Engl; Pblc Rltns Wrtr.

**WESTFALL, CINDA K,** Marshall University, Huntington, WV; JR; BA; Accntng Clb Brd Of Dir 90-; Koinonia Cmps Chrstn Grp 88-; Gamma Beta Phi 89-; Vita 91-; Accntng Intrnshp; Accntng; Cpa.

**WESTHEIMER, RYAN N,** Univ Of Fl, Gainesville, FL; SO; BA; Sigma Phi Epsilon Alchl Awrnss Chr 90-; Jrnlsm/Telecmnctns; Film.

**WESTHOFEN, SUSANNE,** Manhattanville Coll, Purchase, NY; SR; Hon Schlrshp; Supr Prtflio Hon Final Rvw; E O'byrne Awd; Murdoch Magzns NYC Circltn Asst; BA Summa Cum Laude; Bus Mgmt; Pub/Advtsng.**

**WESTLAKE, DENNIS M,** Erie Comm Coll South Cmps, Orchard Park, NY; SR; BA; Phi Theta Kappa 90-; Cmptr Intnrshp Mark IV Indstrs Amhrst NY 90-; AS; Cmptr Sci; Prgrmr Mark IV Inds.

**WESTMARK, CHRISTINE M,** Univ Of Cincinnati, Cincinnati, OH; JR; BED; NAEYC 90; Soccer Team Coach; Bessie Allen Awrd; AS 90; Social Sciences; Erly Chldhd Ed.

**WESTMEIER, DAVID W,** Nyack Coll, Nyack, NY; SR; BM; Deans Lst 86; Clg Choir 87; Soccer 86-87; Cell Grp Ldr New Lfe Flllwshp Chrch 90; Music Ed; Grad Schl.

**WESTMORELAND, HOWARD,** Morehouse Coll, Atlanta, GA; JR; BA; Mass Comm Maj Clb 89; L B Johnson Intrnshp Flwshp Congrsm B J Cardin; Intntl Stu; Law; Educ.

**WESTON, BRADLEY A,** Univ Of Sc At Columbia, Columbia, SC; FR; Carolina Bnd/Carolina Alive 90-; Dscssn Grp 90-; Hon 90-; Macintosh Users Grp; Apple Comp Rep 90-.

**WESTON, CHERYL A,** Radford Univ, Radford, VA; JR; BA; Bptst Stdnt Un 89; Msc Thrpy Clb 90-; Phi Theta Kappa 88-89; AS Southern Seminary Clg 89; Music; Thrpy/Educ.

**WESTON, CHRISTINA L,** Old Dominion Univ, Norfolk, VA; FR; BSC; Stdnt Govt 87-89; Yrbk 87-88; Scty Wmn Eng 90-; Deans Schlr Pgm 90-; Clg N Career Mnstrs Bayview Bapt Chrch Nrflk VA Flwshp Dir; NASA Cooprtv Ed Trainee; Mech Deng; NASA Dsgn Prfsnl.

**WESTON, DAVID C,** Greenville Tech Coll, Greenville, SC; FR; AS; Univ Trnsfr Hnr Gd 90; Tch Ambssdr Prgm; Phi Theta Kappa Pres 90-; Deans Lst 90; Coop Stdnt Physcl Sci Dvsn Lab Ast 90-; Blgy.

**WESTON, MARY E,** Al A & M Univ, Normal, AL; SR; AEC; Jr League Huntsville 88-; Yng Frmr Fedtn; Reunion Commte; Agriculture; Ag Extension Agent.

**WESTON, RANIEKA D,** Fl A & M Univ, Tallahassee, FL; JR; BA; Karate Clb 89; NAACP 89; Hon Rl 88-; Intrnshp Pitney Bowes Stamford CT 90; Intrnshp Eastmn Kdk Rochester NY; Intrnshp Eastmn Kdk Oakbrook IL; Boys/Grls Clb Rochester; Bus Admin; Fin Plnng.

**WESTON, SHELLEY A,** Commonwealth Coll, Virginia Beach, VA; SR; AAS; Comp Clb; Stdnt Govt Rep; Alpha Beta Gamma; Phi Beta Lambda; Comp Sci; Nrs Ansthst.

**WESTPHAL, ROBBIN A,** Univ Of Akron, Akron, OH; SR; BS; CEC; Golden Key 90-; ABM Univ Md 88; Spec Edn.

**WESTWOOD, ANNA L,** Univ Of Sc At Columbia, Columbia, SC; SO; BS; Psychology Clb Treas Sec 90-; Chancellors Schlrshp 89-; Psychology.

**WESTWOOD, ANNA L,** Univ Of Sc At Aiken, Aiken, SC; SO; BA; Psylgy Clb Sec/Treas 90-; Psycholgy; Cnslng/Admn.

**WESTWOOD, MARGARET JOAN,** Catholic Univ Of Pr, Ponce, PR; SO; BA; Mrktng.

**WETHERALL, GRETCHEN C,** Villanova Univ, Villanova, PA; SR; MA; Stdnt Un Fstvls Comm Chrprsn 87-89; Alpha Phi Hstrn 88-; Spcl Olympcs 88; Prjct Sunshine Tutoring 88-89; Bsns Mnr Cmptv Slctn 88-; Deans Lst 90-; IM Flag Ftbl 88-89; BA; Englsh.

**WETHERBEE, LINDA L,** Emory Univ, Atlanta, GA; JR; BS; Std Nrs Asc VP 90-; Std Comm; Hnrs Cncl Altrnt 90-; Omcrn Delta Kappa; Sprt Nrs Awd 90; Arthrts Fdn 77-; BA OH St Univ 76; MS Univ Cinn 85; Nrs Prctnr.

**WETHINGTON, JOSEPH G,** Univ Of Ky, Lexington, KY; SR; SADD 90-; Middle Schl Asc 90-; BAACHUS 90-; Farmhouse VP 88-; Educ.

**WETMORE, JANET E,** Saint Vincents Coll & Seminary, Latrobe, PA; SR; BA; ACM 90-; Spcl Intrst Grp On Comptr Graphcs Of The ACM; Comptng/Info Sci; Comptr Sci.

**WETTIMUNY, SANNAKA A,** Alfred Univ, Alfred, NY; FR; BS; Alfrd Systms Grp; Alpha Labda Delta; Alpha Phi Omega; Bus Admn.

**WETZEL, CYNTHIA M,** Slippery Rock Univ, Slippery Rock, PA; SR; Nwspaper Advtsng Mgr 90-; Lambda Sigma 88-; Sigma Delta Pi 88-; Kappa Gamma 89-.

**WETZEL, DEBORAH L,** Kent St Univ Kent Cmps, Kent, OH; SO; BM; Ohio Collegiate Music Edctrs 90; Alpha Lambda Delta 90; Delta Upsilon Of Delta Omicron 90; Metcalf Awd Soph Music Mjr; Top Frshmn Female Music Mjr Awd 89-90; Sherri Jo Luft Mem Awd; Music Perf.

**WETZEL, KIMBERLY A,** Univ Of Akron, Akron, OH; SR; BS; Prsnnl Mgmt.

**WETZEL, LAWNI L,** Kent St Univ Kent Cmps, Kent, OH; SR; BBA; Ambassador 90-; Golden Key 90-; Hmn Rsce Intnhsp; Hmn Rsce Mgmnt; Busn.

**WETZEL, MARISSA H,** Providence Coll, Providence, RI; SR; BA; Pstrl Cncl MS Swmng Spec Olympcs/Adlt Ltrcy 88-; Ed Clb 88-; Jr Rng Dsgn Cmt 89-90; Cncl Excptnl Chldrn 89-; Pstrl Cncl 87-; Groden Ctr Prvdnc RI Intrnshp 90; Spec Ed/Elem Educ; Tchng.

**WETZEL, PAULA J,** Wv Northern Comm Coll, Wheeling, WV; SO; CAS; Bsn.

**WETZEL, TONY D,** Univ Of Al At Birmingham, Birmingham, AL; JR; BS; Stdnt Govt Assoc Lgsltr Vc Chrmn Srvcs Cmmtt 89-90; Coll Rep Treas 89-90; Tau Kappa Epsilon Fnd Rsng Chrmn 89-; S Richardson Hill Schlrshp 87-; Rl Est Fnc; Fnc.

**WETZELBERGER, CHARLES F,** Univ Of Louisville, Louisville, KY; FR; B; Data Proc Mngmnt Assoc; Computer Sci; Computer Prgrmng/Analyst.

**WETZONIS, WILLIAM K,** Howard Univ, Washington, DC; GD; JD; Howard Lw Jrnl 90-; Sigma Chi 84-87; Amer Jurisprdnce Awd 89-90; BA Univ MD Clg Pk 87; Law.

**WEXLER, KATHERINE A,** Columbus Coll Of Art & Design, Columbus, OH; SR; BFA; Art.

**WEYANDT, JENNIFER D,** Methodist Coll, Fayetteville, NC; SO; BABS; Frnch/Acctg; Intl Fin.

**WEYANDT, TERRY L,** Mount Aloysius Jr Coll, Cresson, PA; SO; ASN; Stdnt Nrsng Org Treas 90; Phi Theta Kappa 90; Nrsng.

**WEYE, PATRICIA A,** Elms Coll, Chicopee, MA; JR; BA; Grade 3 CCD Tchr 89-90; Bnk Teller SIS; Gymnastic Tchr; Assoc Spfld Tech Cmnty Clg; Elem Educ; Tchr.

**WEYER, ALEXANDRA,** Univ Of Miami, Coral Gables, FL; SR; BA; Cir K Pres 89-90; Psych; Tch.

**WEYMER JR, EDWIN L,** Mount Aloysius Jr Coll, Cresson, PA; SO; Bs Clb 90-; Bus Accntg; CPA.

**WHALEN, KATHLEEN L,** Clarkson Univ, Potsdam, NY; JR; BS; Natl Assoc Accntnts; Soc/Accntnts; AS Canton Clg 90; Acctg; Ind Bus.

**WHALEN, REBECCA S,** Castleton St Coll, Castleton, VT; JR; BSED; Phi Eta Sigma 88; Rgstr Rutland Rgnl Med Cntr 88-; Elmntry Ed/Reading; Tch.

**WHALEN, SCOTT F,** Fayetteville St Univ, Fayetteville, NC; FR; BA; Chanlellors Acdmc Schlrshp 90-; Med; Nrs.

**WHALEY, BONNIE A,** George Washington Univ, Washington, DC; SO; BA; Politics/Values Pgm 90-; Spanish Clb 90-; Phi Eta Sigma; Deans Lst 90-; Deaf Studies; Tchr.

**WHALEY, LORI B,** Univ Of Tn At Knoxville, Knoxville, TN; FR; BA; Alpha Lambda Delta 90-; Hnr Roll 90-; Bsn Admin; CPA.

**WHALEY, MARGARET B,** James Sprunt Comm Coll, Kenansville, NC; FR; BA; Sch Vol Sub Tchr; Ele Educ/Art; Tch.

**WHALEY, MARY C,** Coll Of Charleston, Charleston, SC; JR; BA; CAB Chrprsn 90-; Campus Amnesty Ntwrk 88-; Elem Ed; Tchr.**

**WHALEY, TRACY S,** Fayetteville St Univ, Fayetteville, NC; JR; BS; NTSO 89-; YMCA 90-; PTA 90-; Pharm Tech 84-89; AAS Fayetteville Tech Comm Coll 84; Math-Ed; Tch.

**WHALEY-BLAKER, WENDY,** Ms Gulf Coast Comm Coll, Perkinston, MS; JR; BS; Vars Bsktbl/Sftbl 88-90; SNA 90; Phi Theta Kappa Sec 88-90; Hnr Club 89-90; Hall Of Fame 89-90; Harrison/Hancock Sftbl; Bsktbl/Sftbl Vars 88-90; AD Sci Mgccc Perkinston Cmps 90; Nrsg.

**WHARTON, MARY H,** Fl St Univ, Tallahassee, FL; JR; BA; AA Tallahassee Cmmnty Coll; Cmmnctns; Flm Prdctn.

**WHATLEY, ANGEL J,** Ms St Univ, Miss State, MS; FR; BS; MSU Bnd; MSU Mjrt Ln; Bsn Prfsnl Wm; Phi Mu Srty; MSU Bnd Schlrshp; Bsbl Dmnd Grl; Cmptr Sci; Cmptr Anlyst.

**WHATLEY, CINDY A,** Univ Of Al At Birmingham, Birmingham, AL; SR; BS; Gods Hse Kindergarten; T/T Qlty Hms; Early Chldhd Edn; Masters.

**WHATLEY, LACY M,** Abraham Baldwin Agri Coll, Tifton, GA; FR; BA; Bptst Stdnt Un Prlmntrn; Phi Theta Kappa Treas; GA Jr Coll All Trnmnt Team; NJCAA Natl Trnmnt Team; NJCAA All Amer; Sftbl; Math; Eng.

**WHATLEY, SCOTT E,** Gordon Coll, Barnesville, GA; JR; BA; SGA Sec Treas 89-90; Driftwood Ltry Mag Sr Edtr 88-90; Phi Theta Kappa 89; Theatre G C Repertor Theatre 88-; Res Asst Dir 89-90; AA; English; Prfsnl Wrtr.

**WHATLEY, WILLIAM GARRARD,** Fl St Univ, Tallahassee, FL; SO; BFA; FOCUS 90-; Phi Eta Sigma 90-; Gldn Ky; Hnrs And Schlrs Prog; Schlstc Schlrshp; Flm Drctng.

**WHATLEY JR, WILLIAM THOMAS,** Piedmont Tech Coll, Greenwood, SC; SR; AAS; Elec/Elec Frmn Millwright/Millwright Frmn.

**WHATTS, TOMAS,** Univ Politecnica De Pr, Hato Rey, PR; FR; Engnrng.

**WHEALE, KERSTIN MARIE,** Davis & Elkins Coll, Elkins, WV; JR; BS; Wldrness Co Op V P 88-; Natl Psychology Clb 88-; Phi Mu Treas 88-; Wmsn Aid Crisis 90-; Preschl Dvlopmntly Impaired Chldrn 90-; Adolescent Cnslng 90-; Italy Semenster Abroad; Psychology; Child Psychlgst.

**WHEAT, RUSSELL G,** Univ Of Southern Ms, Hattiesburg, MS; SO; BS; U S Navy Pty Ofcr Pharm Tech 87-90; Hosp Corpsmn Cert 87; Pharm Tech Cert U S Naval Sch 87; Cmptr Sci; Prgrmr.

**WHEATLEY, CPT WILLIAM M,** Air Force Inst Of Tech, Wrt-Ptrsn Afb, OH; GD; MS; SGA 90-; Sgm Iota Epsln 90-; Army Schlrshp; APICS; Army Capt; BS Rider Clg 82; MS Un Cntrl TX 89; Logistics Mgmt; Natl Dfsns Us Army.

**WHEATLEY, JOANNE L,** Univ Of Akron, Akron, OH; JR; BS; Elem Ed; Tchr Engl.

**WHEATLEY, LE JEANNA D,** Univ Of Tn At Martin, Martin, TN; SR; BS; Chrch Of Chrst 86-; Stdnt Tchr Edctn Assoc 89-; Alpha Gamma Delta; Happy House Day Care 86-; Edctn-Scndry; Tchng.

**WHEELER, ALMA J,** Mayland Comm Coll, Spruce Pine, NC; SO; AAS; Accntg; Bus.

**WHEELER, ALVINA J,** Morris Brown Coll, Atlanta, GA; JR; BS; Acctg Clb Treas; Natl Assoc Blck Accntnts 90-; Phi Beta Lambda 90-; Stdnt Support Svcs 88-; Bsn Adm; Acctnt.

**WHEELER, ANDREA S,** Lenoir Rhyne Coll, Hickory, NC; SO; BA; Delta Zeta; Bsktbl Vlybl Tnns; Cmmnctns; TV Prod.

**WHEELER, ANITA L,** Daytona Beach Comm Coll, Daytona Beach, FL; AA; Fl Scty Rdlgc Tchnlgsts 90-; Rdlgc Tchnlgy.

**WHEELER, BENTLEY S,** Savannah Coll Of Art & Design, Savannah, GA; FR; BFA; Whelhan Schlrshp; Deans Lst; Intr Dsgn.

**WHEELER, BRUCE M,** Saint Francis Coll, Loretto, PA; SO; Pres Upprclsmn Schlrshp; Schlstc Prfrmnc Schlrshp; Pre Med; Med.

**WHEELER, CHER L,** Western Piedmont Comm Coll, Morganton, NC; SO; AAS; Accntng.

**WHEELER, DAWN M,** Univ Of Sc At Coastal Carolina, Conway, SC; SO; BA; Acctg.

**WHEELER, DONNA L,** Savannah Coll Of Art & Design, Savannah, GA; SO; BARCH; Art Stdnt Assoc Treas 89-90; Bio Clb Treas 89-90; Prtcpnt In Soph Art Show 90; Im 89-90; Archtctre.

**WHEELER, EVELYN DIANNE,** Roane St Comm Coll, Harriman, TN; FR; BS; Knox Area Families Actn VP; Vista Vol; Bkkpr; Sci; Nrsng.

**WHEELER, GWENDOLYN E,** Univ Of Akron, Akron, OH; JR; BFA; Dance Co 90-; Touring Ensmbl; Golden Key; Dance Schlrshp 90-; Dance.

**WHEELER, HILARY D,** Duquesne Univ, Pittsburgh, PA; SR; BA; Crew Tm 87-; RA 88-90; Wrtr DU Duke; Anncr WDSR 88-90; Omicron Delta Kappa 89-; Kappa Tau Alpha 90-; Zeta Beta Tau Lttr Sis 88-; PR Stu Soc Amer 90-; Cum Laude; Peoples Natl Gas Co Inter; IM Sprts 89-; Cmmnctns; PR/ADVRTSNG/MEDIA.

**WHEELER, JILL S,** Valdosta St Coll, Valdosta, GA; JR; MBA; GSHA 90-; NSSLHA 90-; AA Thomas Clg 90; Spch/Lang Pthlgy; Tchr.

**WHEELER, JULIE K,** Tn St Univ, Nashville, TN; SO; BS; Ntnl Hnr Soc; Biology; Tchng Scndry Ed.

**WHEELER, KATRINA M,** Le Moyne Coll, Syracuse, NY; JR; BA; Vol People Actn Prog 88-; Spnsh; Spnsh Tchr.

**WHEELER, KIMBERLY D,** Coll Of Charleston, Charleston, SC; JR; BS; Psych; Psych Research.

**WHEELER, MARY R,** East Central Comm Coll, Decatur, MS; SO; Phi Beta Lambda 89-; Phi Theta Kappa 89-; Mu Alpha Theta 89-; Cmptr Sci Awd; Cmptr Prgrmg.**

**WHEELER, SEAN T,** Univ Of Al At Birmingham, Birmingham, AL; JR; BS; Ldrshp Conf 90; Mentor Prog 90; Bldg Sci Coop Ed 89; Phi Kappa Phi; Gldn Ky; Phi Eta Sgima 88; Habitat For Humanity; Bldg Sci Bk Awd 89; Pres Lst 89-; Barbers Daries Schlrshp 90; Hugo L Black Sclrhsp; Finance; Law.

**WHEELER, SONYA M,** Stillman Coll, Tuscaloosa, AL; JR; BA; Deans Lst; Phi Beta; Bus Admin; Acctng.

**WHEELER, TERI L,** Univ Of Cin R Walters Coll, Blue Ash, OH; SR; Tchr Prnt Clb 90-; Evndl Gen Ele Mgmt Assn 89-; Gen Elec Emplyee Ath Assn 85-; Omicron Nu; St Clement Chrch 86-; Den Mthr 89-; Gen Elec 84-; BS U Cincinnati 79; Acctg; Fnc.

**WHEELER, WILLIAM A,** William Paterson Coll, Wayne, NJ; JR; BA; Math.

**WHEELEY, DONNA M,** Salisbury St Univ, Salisbury, MD; JR; BS; Amer Mrktng Assn 90-; Delta Mu Delta; Phi Beta Lambda Pres 90-; Intrn Prdue Frms 89-; Phi Beta Lambda Ldrshp Awrd; Dns Lst 89-; IM Vlybl 90; Bus Admin Mrktng; Prgrmmr.

**WHEELOCK, THOMAS C,** Me Maritime Academy, Castine, ME; FR; BA; Sci; Engnrg.

**WHELAN, DANITA D,** Univ Of Ky, Lexington, KY; FR; BS; Rock Climbing Clb Instr 90-; AVE 90-; Hon Pgm; Zoology; Rsrch Envrnmntl.

**WHELAN, SHARON E,** James Madison University, Harrisonburg, VA; JR; BS; Catholic Cmps Mnstry 88-; Southhold Twn Rcrtnl Pgm Dvlpmntly Dsbld 86-; Psi Chi 90-; Gldn Key 90-; Cmpr Pgm Mntly Il 90-; Ctr Srvc Lrng 88-; Southold Twn Prclmtn Cmnty Srvc 88; Prjct Yth Awd 88; Psychlgy; Conslng Psychlgy.

**WHELDON, HELEN LOUISE,** Univ Of South Fl, Tampa, FL; SR; BA; St Petes Fine Arts Museum Intrn 91; Amer Assoc Of Museums 90-; AA St Petes Jr Clg 82; Art Hist; Museum Wrk.

**WHERLEY, ELIZABETH A,** Kent St Univ Kent Cmps, Kent, OH; JR; BA; Acctn Assoc 90-; Golden Key; Alpha Lambda Delta 89; Phi Eta Sigma 89; Chi Omega 89-; CPA.

**WHETSELL, MARY ANN,** Univ Of Sc At Columbia, Columbia, SC; SO; Gamma Beta Phi 90-; Alpha Delta Pi 89-; USC Vldctrn Schlrshp 89-; Plough Schlrshp; Phrmcy Intrn; Phrmcy; Med Schl.

**WHETSTINE, COURTNEY M,** Univ Of Ga, Athens, GA; SO; Big Sis Prog 90-; Early Chldhd Educ; Tchr.

**WHETSTINE, MICHAEL A,** Western Piedmont Comm Coll, Morganton, NC; FR; BA; Stdnt Govt Assn Sntr 90-; Phi Theta Kappa 90-; Bus; Mktng/Advrtsng.

**WHETSTONE, CARRIE LYNN,** Univ Of Sc At Columbia, Columbia, SC; JR; BS; Deans Lst; Assn Degree/Gen Bsnss Orngebrg Calhoun Tech Clg 90; Cosmetolgy Cert/License Cope Area Voc Ctr 88; Info Syst; Bsnss/Sftwre Ed.

**WHETZEL, DENISE S,** Radford Univ, Radford, VA; JR; BS; VEA/NEA Va Edn Assn 90-; IM Sftbl Bsktbl Vlybl 90-; Cert Of Hnrs N Va Comm Coll Woodbridge Campus 88-90; Middle Edn Psych/Eng; Edn Guidance Cnslr.

**WHETZEL JR, JERRY W,** Va Commonwealth Univ, Richmond, VA; GD; MD; Am Med Assoc 89-; Family Pr Actice Assoc 89-; Alpha Chi 87-89; So Med Assoc Schlrshp 90-; Va Med Soc Schlrshp; BS George Mason Univ 89; Internal Med.

**WHETZEL, JOSEPH C,** Univ Of Sc At Columbia, Columbia, SC; SO; BA; Rugby Clb 89-; Jrnlsm; Advtsng.

**WHIDDON, STEFANE D,** Albany St Coll, Albany, GA; FR; BS; Crmnl Jstce; Lw Enfrcemnt Prle And Prbtn.

**WHILDEN, AMANDA S,** Spartanburg Methodist Coll, Spartanburg, SC; SO; Stats Mns Bsktbl 90-; Stats Wmns Bskbtbl 90-; Phi Theta Kappa 89-; Gen Excllnce 90; Acad All Amer 90-; Rsdnt Asst 90-; Ttr 90-; Sccr 89-; AA; Bus; Acct.

**WHINERY, DAVE W,** Brown Univ, Providence, RI; SR; MS; Amer Inst Aerontcs/Astrontcs 89-; Planetary Soc 87-; US Tennis Assoc 87-; Ski Tm 87; Tau Beta Pi Chptr Secr 90-; Sigma Xi; JV Bsebl 87-; IM Bsktbl 88-; Untd Telephone Syst Midwest Grp Merit Schlrshp 87-; Soc Exper Test Pilots Schlrshp; Aerontcs; Aerosp Engr.**

**WHIPKEY, TINA L,** Wv Northern Comm Coll, Wheeling, WV; FR; AS; Comp Pgm.

**WHISENANT, JUDY P,** Blue Mountain Coll, Blue Mountain, MS; SR; BS; Outstdng Coll Stdnts Of Amer 87; Elem Educ.

**WHISENANT, MICHAEL L,** Faulkner Univ, Montgomery, AL; SR; BA; SGA P 90-; Prchrs Clb 89-; Kappa Sigma Phi P 89-; Deans Lst; Ath Yr; Bible Bus Adm; Yth Mnstr/Corp Exec.

**WHISENHUNT, CONNIE R,** Birmingham Southern Coll, Birmingham, AL; SR; BS; Mortar Brd Treas 90-; Peer Advsr 89-; Clg Dmcrts 88-90; Alpha Lambda Delta 88-; Phi Eta Sigma 88-90; Phi Beta Kappa; Psi Chi Sec 88-; Alpha Chi Omega Crspndng Sec 87-; Triangle Clb 88-89; Pres Stdnt Serv Org 89-; Psychlgy.

**WHISLER, LAURA C,** Univ Of Rochester, Rochester, NY; SR; BA; Symphnc Bnd 88; Burton Schlrshp Stdy Germany; Crs Cntry Ski Tm Fnd Rsr 87-89; Biology; Med.

**WHISNANT, SHARON T,** Catawba Valley Comm Coll, Hickory, NC; SR; Gamma Beta Phi 90; NC Stdnt Nrses Assoc 89; Phrmcy Tchncn 88; Frye Reg Med Ctr; Assoc Of Applied Sci In Vet Tchnlgy; Lcnsed Vet Tech Cntrl Crlna Cmmnty Clg 81.

**WHITACRE, JENNIFER L,** Commonwealth Coll, Virginia Beach, VA; SO; AAS; Acctg Clb Sec 90-; Deans Lst 90-; Acctg.

**WHITAKER, JEANETTE L,** Univ Of Cin R Walters Coll, Blue Ash, OH; FR; Bsns Mjr; Legl Asst.

**WHITAKER, JENNIFER L,** Lexington Comm Coll, Lexington, KY; FR; AAS; Dntl Tech Lab.

**WHITAKER, JO DEE L,** Milligan Coll, Milligan Clg, TN; SO; BS; Dorm Cncl Treas 90-; Delta Kappa 89-; Deans Lst 90-; Elem Tchr.

**WHITAKER, JOHN MARTIN,** Eckerd Coll, St Petersburg, FL; JR; BA; Eckerd Coll Anthropology Clb 90-; Earth Soc 90-; Rotaract 89-90; Anthropology; Arch Cnsrvtn.

**WHITAKER, KAREN D,** Tusculum Coll, Greeneville, TN; SR; BA; Stdnt Cncl Excptnl Chldrn VP 88-; Old Oak Com Sec 89-90; Spcl Edn/Elem Edn; Deaf Educator.

**WHITAKER, KENYA LYVETTE,** Jackson St Univ, Jackson, MS; JR; BS; Acctg Soc 90-; Phi Beta Lambda 89-90; Vol Income Tax Asstnc; AS Coll Lake Cnty 90; Acctg; CPA.

**WHITAKER, PAMELA K,** Fl St Univ, Tallahassee, FL; JR; BA; Yrbk Fla Chrstn Coll 87-89; AA Fla Chrstn Coll 89; AA Tall Comm Coll 90; Elem Educ; Tchng Elem Schl.

**WHITAKER, SHAWN P,** Embry Riddle Aeronautical Univ, Daytona Beach, FL; SO; BA; Air Force ROTC 90; IM Sftbl 90; Cmptr Sci; Aviation.

**WHITAKER, SHAWN-MICHAEL,** Newbury Coll, Brookline, MA; FR; AAS; Radio Clb Treas 90-; Calde Accss TV Vol; Cmnctns; Video Prdctn.

**WHITAKER, SPARKLE A,** Middle Tn St Univ, Murfreesboro, TN; JR; BS; Band Blue; Symphonic Band 89-; Concert Choir 89-90; Theatrical Tech Crews 90-; Gamma Beta Phi; Cnslr High Sch Band Camps 90; Mass Cmnctns; Lighting Dsgnr.

**WHITAKER, STACY E,** Coll Of Charleston, Charleston, SC; FR; BABA; FCA; Hnrs Pgm Stdnt Assn; Med Univ S Car; Soccr 90; Theatre/Phy Educ; Sprts Med.

**WHITAKER, TINA G,** Coll Of Charleston, Charleston, SC; SO; BA; Sunday Sch Tchr Bapt Ch; Floral Dsgnr; Engl; Tchr.

**WHITAKER, WILLIAM M,** Snead St Jr Coll, Boaz, AL; JR; BS; Deans Lst; Biologcl Sci; Envrnmtlst.

**WHITBECK, STACEY M,** Old Dominion Univ, Norfolk, VA; SO; BA; Acctng/Bsn.**

**WHITCO, DANA M,** Oh Wesleyan Univ, Delaware, OH; JR; BA; Wslyn Stdnt Fndtn 89; Pres Clb 88-90; Womens Rsrce Ctr Tsk Frce 88; Alpha Kappa Delta; Delta Gamma VP 88; TA 90; Ldrshp For Tomorrow 89-90; Sclgy Anthrplgy/Womens Studies.

**WHITCOMB, AMY C,** Fl Coll, Temple Terrace, FL; SO; AS; Drma Clb 90-; Sci Clb 90-; Stdnt Dir Chrgrphr Fr Mscls 89-; Phi Theta Kappa 89-; ARETE 90-; IM Sprts 90-; Blgy; Med Tech Or Phrmcst.

**WHITE, A JILL,** Univ Of Southern Ms, Hattiesburg, MS; SO; BA; SG 90-; Alumni Assn 90-; Eagle Clb 90-; Lambda Sigma 90-; Alpha Lambda Delta 89-90; Phi Eta Sigma 89-90; Gamma Beta Phi 90-; Pi Beta Phi Rsh Chrmn 89-; Rcrtrs; Pi Beta Phi Pldg Schlrshp 89-90; Pres/Deans Lsts 89-; Hon Coll Schlrshp 89-; Bus Admin; Attrny.

**WHITE, ALLAN R,** Univ Of Nh Plymouth St Coll, Plymouth, NH; SO; BS; Dng Hl Cmte 90; Pres Lst 89-90; Dns Lst 90; Acctng; CPA.

**WHITE, ALLISON A,** Univ Of Nc At Charlotte, Charlotte, NC; JR; BA; Pi Sigma Alpha; AA Central Piedmont Comm Coll 90; Pol Sci; Jrnlsm.

**WHITE, AMY K,** Marshall University, Huntington, WV; SO; BA; Elem Educ; Tchg.

**WHITE, AMY M,** Univ Of Tn At Martin, Martin, TN; FR; Blck Brdl; Rodeo Clb; Rodeo.

**WHITE, ANGELA D,** Univ Of Nc At Greensboro, Greensboro, NC; SR; BS; Siler City Jaycees; Intrnshp Franklinville Sch 90; AS Sandhills Comm Coll 88; Edn; Teach.

**WHITE, ANGELA K,** Ms St Univ, Miss State, MS; JR; BED; AA Itawamba Cmnty Clg 90; Elem Ed/Sci; Tchr.

**WHITE, ANGELA L,** Tuskegee Univ, Tuskegee Inst, AL; SR; BS; Crspndg Sec Elec Engr Hnr Soc 90-; Eta Kappa Nu Sec 90-; Coop Educ Stu Ctrplr Inc Coop Stu 88-89; Deans Lst 86-87; Engr Elec; Tech Cmptnt.

**WHITE, ANGELA R,** Northern Ky Univ, Highland Hts, KY; JR; BA; Lalink English Clb 90-; Stdnt Rep Lit/Lang Dept; Thad Lindsey Book Awd 90-; English; Library Sci.

**WHITE, ANN M,** Savannah Coll Of Art & Design, Savannah, GA; JR; BFA; Baccus 89-90; ASID 88-89; Stdnt Of Yr 89-90; Acad Ath Awrd 90-; Tennis 89-; Vlybl Capt 90-; Int Design; Designer.

**WHITE, ANTHONY D,** J Sargeant Reynolds Comm Coll, Richmond, VA; SO; BA; Stdnt Govt Assoc Pres 90-; Phi Theta Kappa 90-; Hmn Srvcs Clb Treas Srgnt Arms 89-; Pblc Rltns; Jrnlsm.

**WHITE, ASHLEY JILL,** Univ Of Southern Ms, Hattiesburg, MS; SO; BA; SG 90-; Eagle Clb 90-; Alumni Assn 89-; Gamma Beta Phi 90-; Alpha Lambda Delta 90; Phi Eta Sigma 90; Lambda Sigma 90-; Pi Beta Phi Rsh Chrmn 89-; Recruters; Pr Deans Lst 89-; Hons Clg Schlrshp 89-; Acad Excel Schlrshp 89-; IM Ftbl 90; Bus Admin; Attrny.

**WHITE, AVA J,** Alcorn St Univ, Lorman, MS; FR; BA; Hnr Stdnts Org; Bio; Optmtry.

**WHITE, BENJAMIN A,** Ms St Univ, Miss State, MS; JR; BA; Gamma Beta Phi 90-; Phi Alpha Theta 90-; Deans Lst 90; IM Sports 88; Hstry; Law.

**WHITE, BENJAMIN J,** Univ Of Miami, Coral Gables, FL; SO; BA; Hon Prog 89-; I M Bkbl Vybl 90-; History; Bus/Diplomacy.

**WHITE, BERNADETTE S,** City Univ Of Ny City Coll, New York, NY; GD; Nursing Pinning Org Pres 88-90; Sigma Theta Tau 90-; BSN 90; Nursing; Cert Pediatric Prof Nurse.

**WHITE, BRENDA J,** Schenectady County Comm Coll, Schenectady, NY; SO; Wmn Trvl Svcs Schlrshp 90; NY State Trvl Schlrshp; Intrnshp Rotterdam Trvl; Trvl/Trsm.

**WHITE, BRIAN E,** Morehouse Coll, Atlanta, GA; SO; BA; STRIPES 89-; Hnr Roll 90-; Poltcl Sci; Bsn Law.

**WHITE, CAROL M,** Germanna Comm Coll, Locust Grove, VA; FR; U S Army Res 88-; Nrsng.

**WHITE, CATY B,** Univ Of South Al, Mobile, AL; JR; BA; Math; Edn.

**WHITE, CEIA R,** Clark Atlanta Univ, Atlanta, GA; SO; Spirit Booster Clb 90; Tutorial Pgm Oglethorpe 90; Dns Lst 90; Bsn Adm; CEO/ENTREPRENEURSHIP.

**WHITE, CHARLOTTE C,** Alcorn St Univ, Lorman, MS; JR; Intr Fth Gspl Choir; SNEA; NAACP; Deans Lst; Bio; Ntrtnst.

**WHITE, CHERI L,** Tuskegee Univ, Tuskegee Inst, AL; JR; BS; Blgy Clb 90-; Ga Clb 89-; NAACP 89-; Alpha Kappa Mu; Beta Kappa Chi; Dns Lst Tuskegee U 90-; Case Western Rsrv U Med Intrhsp Pgm 90; Blgy/Pre Med; Physcn Fld Orthpdc Srgy.

**WHITE, CHRISTINA L,** Wv Univ At Parkersburg, Parkersburg, WV; SR; BA; Bus; Mgmnt.

**WHITE, CHRISTINE T,** Unity Coll, Unity, ME; FR; Raido Clb; Otdr Extnsn Svcs 90; Frfghtr Unty Fire Dept Unity ME; Spec Olympcs; Otdr Rcrtn.

**WHITE, CHRISTOPHER W,** Northern Ky Univ, Highland Hts, KY; SR; BS; Ntnl Assn Accntns 89-; St Catherines Yth Grp Coord 85-; Alpha Xi; Nu Kappa Alpha Sec 88-; Pi Kappa Alpha Schlrshp Chrmn 89-90; Otstndng Stdnt 90; Accntng; CPA.

**WHITE, CONNIE M,** Univ Of Southern Ms, Hattiesburg, MS; SR; Vctnl Indstrl Clb America Prlmntrn 88-; Mngmnt Infrmtn Systm; AA Mrdn Cmm Clg 89; Bsns Admnstrtn; Mgmt Infrmtn Systm.

**WHITE, CONSTANCE A,** Univ Of Rochester, Rochester, NY; SR; BA; All Campus Jdcl Cncl 88-; Equestrian Tm 90-; Delta Gamma Asst Rituals 89; Arnold & Co Intrnshp 90; Promotions Dept London Royal Philharmonic Orch 90; Psychlgy; MBA Mktg Advrtsng.

**WHITE, CYNTHIA A,** Erie Comm Coll, Buffalo, NY; FR; MBA; Phi Theta Kappa; Bus Acctg; CPA.

**WHITE, DANIEL J,** Newbury Coll, Brookline, MA; FR; AS; Mrktng Rep 90-; Mrktng; Rsrch.

**WHITE, DARRIN J,** Cumberland County Coll, Vineland, NJ; SO; Delta Nu 90-; Wrstlng 88-; Finc; Invstmnt Bnkng.

**WHITE, DAVID C,** Elmira Coll, Elmira, NY; SR; BS; Hnrs Schlr 90; Dns Lst 90; Air Force 78-; AAS Comm Coll Air Force 85; Cmptr Infor Sys.

**WHITE, DAVID LLOYD,** Univ Of Ky, Lexington, KY; SO; BS; Zoology; Med.

**WHITE, DAVID R,** Va St Univ, Petersburg, VA; FR; Acad Achvmnt Awrd; Bus Info Syst.

**WHITE, DAVID R,** S U N Y Coll Of Tech At Alfred, Alfred, NY; FR; AD; Sigma Tie; Elect Serv Tech.

**WHITE, DAVID S,** Fl St Univ, Tallahassee, FL; SR; BA; Phi Theta Kappa; Golden Key; Ski Inst/Rest Mgr; AA Manattee Cmnty Clg 89; Music; Bus.

**WHITE, DAVID W,** Ms St Univ, Miss State, MS; SR; BSME; Amer Soc Mech Engrs 89-; Soc Auto Engrs 90-; Phi Beta Lambda 88; Phi Kappa Phi 89-; Gamma Beta Phi 89-; Phi Theta Kappa 87-88; Pi Tau Sigma 90-; Cum Laude; Pres Schlr; AA Copiah-Lincoln Comm Clg 88; Mech Engr.

**WHITE, DAWN M,** Univ Of Al At Birmingham, Birmingham, AL; SR; BS; Pre Law Clb 90-; Hnrs Schlrshp 87-; Crmnl Justice/Pysch; Law/Fed Gvmt.

**WHITE, DEBORAH MARIE,** Roane St Comm Coll, Harriman, TN; SO; BA; Chrldr 89-; Deans Lst 89-; Acctng Stdnt Hons Awd 90-; Archery Clb Chrldr 89-; BA Univ Of TN 88; Engr; CPA.

**WHITE, DEMOYNE V,** Norfolk St Univ, Norfolk, VA; FR; BS; Bus.

**WHITE, DENA L,** Piedmont Coll, Demorest, GA; FR; Educ; Erly Chldhd Educ.

**WHITE, DENISE L,** West Liberty St Coll, West Liberty, WV; SO; BS; Nurse.

**WHITE, DIANE KAY,** Davis & Elkins Coll, Elkins, WV; SO; BA; Honor Assn 89-; Busn Ed/Engl Lit Stds; Educ.

**WHITE, DWAYNE R,** Fl A & M Univ, Tallahassee, FL; SR; BS; Econ Clb; Econ Clb Oprtng Cmmtt 90-; Intrmrl Sccr; Phtgrphy Stff 90-; Mnrty Stdnt Un; Pi Gamma Gamma Pres 90-; Deans Lst 90; Hnrbl Srvc Awrd; Econ Clb 90; Cert Achvmnt Schl Bus IndstryFAMU 90; 1st Un Natl Bnk 86-; AA FL Cmmnty Coll 88; Econ; Invstmnt Bnkng.

**WHITE, ELIZABETH C,** Elmira Coll, Elmira, NY; SO; Outing Clb; Orchesis Sec 89-; Yr Abrd Scotlnd; Psychlgy.

**WHITE, ELIZABETH M,** Tn Temple Univ, Chattanooga, TN; SR; BS; Beta Bus Clb 89-; Univ Choir 88-89; Deans List TN Tmpl 88-; Mbr Lbty Bpst Chrch; Choir; Acctg.

**WHITE, ERICA K,** Cornell Univ Statutory College, Ithaca, NY; SO; BS; Bio Gntcs/Dvlpmnt; Rsrch.

**WHITE, G CHRISTOPHER,** Univ Of Sc At Columbia, Columbia, SC; SO; BA; Sailing Club Treas 89-; Yng Rep 90-; Phi Eta Sigma 90-; Sailing Tm 89-; Fin; Bnkng.

**WHITE, GARRETT D,** Kent St Univ Kent Cmps, Kent, OH; FR; BA; Clgt Bus Assc 90-; Korb Hall Tres; Alpha Phi Alpha 90-; Acctg; Acctnt.

**WHITE, GARY R,** Wagner Coll, Staten Island, NY; SO; BS; Allied Hlth Scnc Org VP 90-; Beta Beta Beta; Biology; Medicine.

**WHITE, GEOFFREY A,** Univ Of Nc At Greensboro, Greensboro, NC; FR; BM; Bapt Stdnt Union/Bible Stdy Grp 90-; Cncrt Bnd 90-; Alpha Lambda Delta 90-; Deans Lst 90-; Music Ed; Bnd Dir.

**WHITE, GEORGE M,** Commonwealth Coll, Virginia Beach, VA; SO; BS; Alpha Beta Gamma 89-; Comp Clb Pres 89-; Stdnt Cncl 90-; Alpha Beta Gamma 89-; Va Bch Cmps Bsktbl Tm 89; Thl Sta Condo Hmownr Assc Sec 87-; Comp Sci; Tchng.

**WHITE, GEORGIA M,** Ms Gulf Coast Comm Coll, Perkinston, MS; FR; BA; Chem; Eng.

**WHITE, GRACIELA L,** Middle Tn St Univ, Murfreesboro, TN; JR; BA; Vrsty Trck/Crs Cntry 90; Hlth Physcl Educ Rcrtn Dance Clb 89-; Gamam Beta Phi 90-; Phi Epsln Kappa; Stdnt TN Educ Assc Tres 90-; Kappa Delta Phi 90; Deans List 89-; OH Vly Conf Indr Trck Tm Chmpnshp; Natl Clgt Acad Awrd; Trck/Crs Cntry; Bio; Educ.

**WHITE, HEATHER C,** Univ Of South Fl, Tampa, FL; SR; BA; Stdnt Dnce Prod Brd Co-Chr 87-; Dnce Clb VP 87-; Goldn Key 88-; Ordr Of Omega 88-; Alpha Delta Pi Rec Sec 87-; Rsh Cnslr 89; H Parrish Schlrshp 89; Fclty Stff Schlrshp 89-90; Fn Arts Tlnt Awrd 90-; Cum Laude; BA; Dnce.**

**WHITE, IRENE L,** Garrett Comm Coll, Mchenry, MD; SO; BA; AA; Sociology; Soc Wrk.

**WHITE, JACK K,** Columbia Union Coll, Takoma Park, MD; SR; BA; Kiwanis Clb SWDC Prsdnt 85-87; Ntnl Assn Afrcn Amrcn Sfty Prfsnls 90-; Eastside Cmptv Tns Clb 90-; Tstmstrs Intrntnl Ogdn UT Sgt-At-Arms 67-68; Avtn Radio Spclst; US Mrn Crps Sgt 54-57; Attbry Job Crps Fdrl Crdt Un 66-68; Bsns Admn; Entrprnr.

**WHITE, JAMES A,** Univ Of Tn At Chattanooga, Chattanooga, TN; JR; BS; Engrng Soc Cncl 90-; Golden Key 89-; Am Soc Mech Engrng V Chm 90-; Natl Soc Prof Eng; Natl Coll Awd Winner Engrng; St Jude Cath Ch 89; Natl Guard Assoc; 10 Yrs Army Helicopter Pilot; Assoc Central Tx Coll 84; Mech Engrng.

**WHITE JR, JAMES F,** Clayton St Coll, Morrow, GA; SO; BS; Srvd Oper Spec US Navy 82-87; Physcs; Eng.

**WHITE JR, JAMES S,** Morehouse Coll, Atlanta, GA; JR; BS; Endvr Spc Clb 90-; Phi Beta Kappa; Pi Mu Epsln 90-; Gldn Key; Kappa Alpha Psi; NASA Mc Nair Eng Intrnshp 90-; UNCF/GTE Summer Sci Pgm; Deans List 89-; Math; Arspc Eng.

**WHITE, JANICE L,** Univ Of Md At Eastern Shore, Princess Anne, MD; SR; BS; Acad Hnrs 89-; Bus/Prof Wmns Clb 90; Baptist Church Youth Choir Dir 82-; Paralegal; Rehab; Crmnl Psychologist.

**WHITE, JASON C,** Juniata Coll, Huntingdon, PA; JR; BS; Explr Post 89-; Juniata Coll Secrty; Outwrd Bound Almni 87-; Tri-Beta; Ecology; Ecologist/Envrnmntl Scntst.

**WHITE, JASON P,** Anne Arundel Comm Coll, Arnold, MD; FR; BA; Gen Lbrl Educ; Law.

**WHITE, JENEEN PATRICE,** Va St Univ, Petersburg, VA; FR; PHD; Pre-Law Soc 90-; Asc Pol Sci Std 90-; Chrldr; Hnrs Clg 90-; VA St Univ Awd; Alpha Kappa Alpha Schlp; Sammy Young Jr Awd Pol Sci Dpt; Pol Sci/Hmnts/Scl Sci; Law.

**WHITE, JESSICA M,** Central Al Comm Coll, Alexander City, AL; SO; Bapt Campus Mnstry 89-; Phi Theta Kappa Pub Rltns Officer 90-; Nom For Most Otstndng Stdnt Cmpttn; Chem; Dentistry.

**WHITE, JOHN J,** Newbury Coll, Brookline, MA; SO; AB; Cls Rep; Ward Two Civic Assn Sec; U S Posta Service; U S Govt; Fmly Day Comm Career Conf Comm; Cert SMH Real Est Schl 86; Bus Admin; Govt.

**WHITE, JOHN W,** Pellissippi St Tech Comm Coll, Knoxville, TN; FR; MBA; Bus Mgmt/Mrktng; Dept Store Buyer.

**WHITE JR, JOHNNY E,** Univ Of Sc At Columbia, Columbia, SC; SR; BA; Stdnt Govt; Orientation Ldr; Peer Advsr; I Kappa Ph2; US Page; SC Senate Page; US Capitol Tour Guide; Strom Thurmond Fdtn Schlr; United Way Big Bro; BA USC 87; Scl Stds Edctn; Tchr.

**WHITE, JULIE A,** Fl International Univ, Miami, FL; SR; BS; Phi Theta Kappa Sec 87-89; Phi Kappa Phi 89-; Pres Lst 87-89; Dns Lst 89-; Exec Sec 72-84; AA Broward Comm Clg 89; Physc Thrpy.**

**WHITE, KARA A,** Va St Univ, Petersburg, VA; FR; BA; Law; Atty.

**WHITE, KAREN K,** Univ Of Sc At Lancaster, Lancaster, SC; SO; BA; Arete; Periodicals Tech Medofrd Library 82-; AA; Liberal Arts; Library Science.

**WHITE, KAREN M,** Univ Of Sc At Columbia, Columbia, SC; FR; BA; Carolina Cares 90-; Alpha Lambda Delta; Alpha Delta Pi 90-; Knghts Columbus Schrlshp; Poli Sci; Law.

**WHITE, KARL D,** Univ Of Md At Eastern Shore, Princess Anne, MD; JR; BS; SG Pres 90-; Cls 92 Exec Bd Pres 89-90; Stdnt Cnstrctrs 89-; Natl Assn Advncmnt Clr People 90-; Cmps Pals 89-; Ambssdrs Clb 89-; Cert Prtcptn Offc Res Lf/Res Asst 89-90; Cert Achnvng Acdmc Excllnc 90; IM Ftbl 88; Cnstrctn Mgmt Tchnlgy; Sccssfl Mnrty Gnrl.

**WHITE, KARLA L,** Univ Of Ga, Athens, GA; SO; MED; Clg Rep 89-; Tutor Athens Tutrl Serv 90-; Phy Ed Sprt Sci Clb IM 89-; Zeta Tau Alpha 89-; Athens Tutorial Serv 90-; UGA Clb Vlybl Tm 90-; Hlth Phys Educ; Tchr.

**WHITE, KATHY L,** Central Fl Comm Coll, Ocala, FL; SO; BA; African Am Stdnt Un Treas 89-; Psi Beta; Intern Marion Co Sch Bd Intern 90-; AA; Schl Psychlgst.

**WHITE, KAY,** Univ Of Miami, Coral Gables, FL; JR; BA; Untd Black Stdnts Pres 88-; Comm Outrch Prog 90-; Yellow Rose Soc 88-; Southern Bell Intrnshp 88-89; AT/T UCS Intrnshp 90; Finance; Analyst.

**WHITE, KELLE M,** Univ Of Sc At Columbia, Columbia, SC; JR; BA; Alpha Chi Omega Pldg Hstrn 90-; Faculty Choice Art Show; 2nd Pl State Fair Art Show 90; Studio Art; Illustration.

**WHITE, KELLI JO,** Wv Univ At Parkersburg, Parkersburg, WV; SR; BA; Amer Ad Fed 84-86; Amer Mrktg Assoc 85; Phi Theta Kappa; Delta Zeta 83-85; W Page Pitt Exclnc Media Plng Awrd 86; Ad Mrktg Rep 87-90; BA 86; Engl.

**WHITE, KELLY LYNN,** Middle Tn St Univ, Murfreesboro, TN; SR; BS; SHEA 88-; STEA 90-; Kappa Omicron Nu 90-; Pm Pm Capt 86; Erly Chldhd Ed.

**WHITE, KIM F,** Emory Univ, Atlanta, GA; GD; MSN; Sigma Theta Tau 90-; Kappa Kappa Gamma Phlnthrpy Chrmn 84-88; Deans Lst; Georgia Nrs Assc; BSN; Nrsg; Mdwfry/FNP.

**WHITE, KIMBERLY ANN,** Hillsborough Comm Coll, Tampa, FL; FR; AA; Schlrshp Tennis Pgm; Tnns Tm; Educ; Tchng.

**WHITE, KIMBERLY C,** Fl International Univ, Miami, FL; JR; BS; Geol Clb Actg VP 88-; Intrvars Chrstn Fllwshp 88-; Phi Kappa Phi 90-; Clg Arts Sci Awd Geol 89; Clg Arts Sci Awd Mnrlgy Geochem; Geol.

**WHITE, KIMBERLY I,** Central St Univ, Wilberforce, OH; SO; BS; United Way; Bowl For Kids Sake; Presidents Lst; Deans Lst; Tax Secy Arthur Andersen Co 90-; Political Sci; Law.

**WHITE, KRISTEN H,** Ga St Univ, Atlanta, GA; SR; BS; Stdnt Gov Sen 89-; Pgms Brd Assoc Dir 90-; Greek Wk Chr 90-; Omicron Delta Kappa 90-; Order Omega 90-; Mortar Brd; Zeta Tau Alpah VP 88-; Omicron Delta Kappa; Deans Key; Ed; Tchr.

**WHITE, KRISTIN LYNN,** Univ Of Miami, Coral Gables, FL; SO; BSBA; Sugarcrs Grls Org 90-; Stf Wrtr Sprts 90-; Panhllnc Jr Panhllnc 90-; Alpha Lambda Dleta; Rhi Eta Sigma 89-; Kappa Kappa Gamma Frat Educ Chrmn 90-; Sugrcns 90-; Prvsts Hnr Rl 89-90; Dns Lst 89-; Offc Asst; Var Swm Tm IMS 89-90; Brdcst Jrnlsm/Econ.

**WHITE, LAURIE L,** Univ Of South Al, Mobile, AL; SO; BS; Sigma Kappa 86-88; IM Ftbl 87-88; Circle Plyrs Community Theater 88-90; Mbl Infrmry Medl Ctr Admssns Registrar Schdlng 90-; Bus Admin Acctng.

**WHITE, LOUETTA J,** Bristol Univ, Bristol, TN; JR; BA; Bus Sci AS 89; Appld Sci AS 89; Bus Admin; Ofc Mgr.

**WHITE, LOUISE T,** Christopher Newport Coll, Newport News, VA; SR; BS; Vir Educ Assoc; Jr League Nrflk Va Bch Stnr; Nwprt News Rdg Cncl; St Rdg Assoc; Tdwtr Assoc Erly Chldhd Educ; Intl Rdg Assoc; AS 90; Elem Educ; Tch.

**WHITE, LUCRECER D,** Central St Univ, Wilberforce, OH; SO; BA; Academc Achvmnt Award; Adv Graphcs; Dsgnr.

**WHITE, MARCIA C,** Univ Of Sc At Columbia, Columbia, SC; JR; PHD; Acdmy Stdnts Phrmcy 90-; Deans List 90-; Pres Hon Roll 90-; Rsrch Analyst 84-87; Rsrch Assoc 87-90; BS Eastern KY Univ 80; Phrmcy.

**WHITE, MARK D,** Univ Of Nc At Charlotte, Charlotte, NC; SR; BA; SNEA 90-; Natl Cncl Soc Stds 90-; IM 88-; Golden Key 90-; Sanford V Davenport Schlrshp 90-; AAS Surry Comm Clg 88; History/Ed; Tchg.

**WHITE, MELISSA D,** Univ Of Akron, Akron, OH; SR; BS; Delta Sigma Pi; Bsn Admin/Mrktng.

**WHITE, MERLE C,** Univ Of New Haven, West Haven, CT; JR; BS; Criminal Justice 90-; IM Sftbl 89-; Criminal Justice; Law Schl.

**WHITE, MERRILL A,** Va Commonwealth Univ, Richmond, VA; FR; BA; Phi Eta Sigma; Hnrs Stu; Art; Illstrtn.

**WHITE, MICHAEL E,** Ms St Univ, Miss State, MS; JR; BS; M-Clb 90-; Alpha Lambda Delta; Phi Eta Sigma; Gamma Beta Phi; Critz Acdm Schlrshp; Pres Schlr 89-; Athltc Dept Hnr Rll 89-; Ftbl Mgr 89-; Bus Inf Sys; Cmptr Anlyst.

**WHITE, MICHAEL L,** Union Univ, Jackson, TN; SO; BSBA; Comp Sci; Pgmr.

**WHITE, MICHELLE A,** Univ Of Tn At Chattanooga, Chattanooga, TN; FR; BA; Chemistry; Medicine.

**WHITE, MIRIAM L,** Fl A & M Univ, Tallahassee, FL; SR; BA; Mrcs Garvey Clb 89; Eng Lit Gld 89-; Phi Theta Kappa; Eng; Edtng.

**WHITE, MONICA A,** Univ Of Ky, Lexington, KY; FR; BA; Stdnt Rcrtmnt 90-; Phi Eta Sigma; Deans Lst; IM 90; Blgy; Med.

**WHITE, MONICA L,** Univ Of Nc At Asheville, Asheville, NC; JR; BA; Alpha Kappa Delta; Big Sth Pres Hnr Roll; Vlybl/Sftbl 88-89; Deans Lst 90; Vlybl/Sftbl Schlrshp 88-89; Sclgy/Crmnl Jstc.

**WHITE, PAUL C,** Spartanburg Methodist Coll, Spartanburg, SC; JR; BA; Quill/Scrll Soc Pres 88-90; Nwspaper Edtr In Chf 88-90; Sigma Epsilon Alpha 88-90; Phi Theta Kappa VP 88-90; Alpha Mu Gamma 89-90; AA 90; Engl; Law.

**WHITE, PAULETTE R,** Marshall University, Huntington, WV; JR; BA; Hll Advsry Cncl 88-90; WV Scty Certfd Pblc Accts 90-; Phi Eta Sigma 89-; Alpha Kappa Psi Treas 89-; VITA; IMS; Bus Mgmt.

**WHITE, PERRY THOMAS,** Birmingham Southern Coll, Birmingham, AL; JR; BA; Hmcmng Com Chprsn; Greek Wk Chprsn; Urban Mnstries Tutor; Sigma Alpha Epsilon Treas; Acctg; Law.

**WHITE, PETITE O,** Piedmont Tech Coll, Greenwood, SC; SO; AD; NAA Dir Nwslttr 90; JR Acct Trnee; ASD; Acctg.

**WHITE, RAYNIA J,** Univ Of Nc At Asheville, Asheville, NC; BS; Mgmt.

**WHITE, REBECCA K,** Va Commonwealth Univ, Richmond, VA; SR; BS; Ram Reps Peer Admssns Cnslrs Pres 88; Ladder To Success 87; Alpha Phi Sigma 90; Lambda Alpha Epsilon 88; Intrnshp Offce Of Attrny Gen Medicaid Fnd Cntrl Unit 90; Admnstrtn Of Jstce; Crmnl Jstce.

**WHITE, ROBERT C,** Univ Of Montevallo, Montevallo, AL; FR; BA; Pi Kappa Phi Schlrshp Chrmn 90-; Engl.

**WHITE JR, ROBERT E,** Bloomfield Coll, Bloomfield, NJ; SR; MBA; Day Stdnt Govt Pres 88-90; Choir Dir 88-90; Afrcn Amer Assoc 87-90; Otsdng Ldrshp/Serv Awd 90-; AAS Mercer Cnty Comm Clg 87; BS 90; Mgmnt; Educ Admin.

**WHITE II, ROBERT S,** Morehouse Coll, Atlanta, GA; SO; BS; Mrchng Band 89-; Cncrt Band 90-; TN Clb Treas 90-; Bio; Med.

**WHITE, RONALD L,** Norfolk St Univ, Norfolk, VA; FR; BED; Stdnt Va Ed Assn VP 90-; Natl Soc Physcs Stdnts 90-; Spartan Alpha Tau; Natl Cncl Tchrs Of Math 90-; Natl Assn Math 90-; Tchr Asst Prog; Tchrs Aid 89-; Nrflks Outstndng Yth Awrd 89-90; Math Ed; Tchr.

**WHITE, RONALD P,** D Youville Coll, Buffalo, NY; SR; BSMS; Stdnt Phys Therpy Assn 89-; Amer Phys Therpy Assn 90-; Hosp Intrnshp; Phys Therpy.

**WHITE, SAKEISHA DAVIDA,** Univ Of Sc At Columbia, Columbia, SC; FR; BS; Ntl Soc Blck Engr 90-; Mnrty Asstnc Pr Grp 90-; Rsdnc Hl Govt; Deans Lst; Rsdnt Advsr; Intrn Drns Vet Hosp; Bio; Dntst.

**WHITE, SARAH A,** Saint John Fisher Coll, Rochester, NY; SO; BA; Yth ARC Sec 84-; Engl Hist; Publshng.

**WHITE, SHANNON A,** Ga Military Coll, Milledgeville, GA; FR; ABA; Stdnt Govt Cncl Pres 90-; Phi Theta Kappa/Alpha Omicron Epsilon V P 90-; Engl/Bsn; Law.

**WHITE, SHANNON E,** Pfeiffer Coll, Misenheimer, NC; SO; BA; Dns Lst 90; Big Sis Lil Sis; IM Sftbl 89-; Acctng; Intrntl Acctng.**

**WHITE, SHANNON P,** Ky St Univ, Frankfort, KY; SR; BS; Ntl Soc Blck Engr; Stu Gov Tres 88-; Jr Daughtrs Knghts Peter Clavee Tres 86-90; Bsktbl Capt 90-; Math; Engr.

**WHITE, SHAWYNE L,** Mohawk Valley Comm Coll, Utica, NY; SO; BA; SC 89-90; Mnrty Stdnt Un VP 89-90; ASBE 90-; Cncrt Dnc Clb 89-90; Finance Com 89-90; ADHOC II 89-90; Aux Svc Schlrshp 90; Mnrty Stdnt Schlrshp 89-; Gameroom Attndnt 90; AA; Psy/Soc; Human Svc.

**WHITE, SHEILA R,** Oh Univ-Southern Cmps, Ironton, OH; SR; BED.

**WHITE, SHELLEE A,** Univ Of Ky, Lexington, KY; JR; BA; Dnc Ensmbl 88-; Pnhlnc Cncl Pres 90-; Deans Lst; Order/Omega; Alpha Omicron Pi Pnhlnc 88-; SADD; Elem/Mdl Schls/Prctcm 89-; Ftbl Hmcmng Nmne 90; Spcl Olympcs 89; Dean Stdnts Srch Cmm; Elem Ed/Spcl Ed.

**WHITE, SHERRI E,** Morris Brown Coll, Atlanta, GA; JR; BS; Hlth Phys Educ Rcrtn Mjs Clb 88-; Glden Key; Morris Brown Hon Clb 90-; Pres List; Thrptc Rcrtn; Tchng Spec Educ Pblc Sch Systm.

**WHITE, SHERRY G,** Middle Tn St Univ, Murfreesboro, TN; FR; BS; Mass Cmnctns; Msc Ind.

**WHITE, SILENE B,** Teikyo Post Univ, Waterbury, CT; SO; BA; AS; Cert; Sci.

**WHITE, STEPHANIE Y,** Radford Univ, Radford, VA; FR; BS; Math; Educ.

**WHITE, STEVENSON MITCHELL,** Ms St Univ, Miss State, MS; SO; BED; Mc Cool Bsn Schlrshp 90-; Bsn/Mktg; Prfsnl Glf Mgmt.

**WHITE, STUART BRETT,** Faulkner Univ, Montgomery, AL; FR; Zeta Eta Theta 90-.

**WHITE, SUSANNE B,** Winthrop Coll, Rock Hill, SC; FR; BA; Big Bro/Sis Prog 90; Aerobics 90; Elem Ed; Tchr.

**WHITE, SUZANNE,** Univ Of Rochester, Rochester, NY; SO; Univ Chmbr Sngrs Wm Sctn Ldr Tr Mgr 89-; Grsrts Stdnt Untd Btr Envrnmnt 89-; Outng Clb 90-; Rigby Wile Prz Prfcncy Blgy; Slst Chmbr Sngrs Tr 90; N Y St Interclgte Bnd 89; Blgy/Glgy; Envrnmntl Ed.

**WHITE, SUZANNE D,** Univ Of Fl, Gainesville, FL; GD; UF Eqstrn Tm Clb 86-87; Alpha Kappa Psi 88; Deans Lst 90; BS 90.

**WHITE, SYLVIA J,** Saint Josephs Coll New York, Brooklyn, NY; GD; MPH; Stdnt Govt 89-90; Deans Lst 89-90; Comm Bd 17-Brklyn; Pres Trustee Bd Hyde Pk Chrstn Chrch Pres 90-; Coord Mngr Inst Pthlgy; BS St Josephs Coll 90; Pblc Hlth.

**WHITE, TAMARA J,** Univ Of Cincinnati-Clrmnt Coll, Batavia, OH; BNS; Mbr Lgue Animal Wlfre; R N Rehab Unit Stroke Trauma Vctms; Good Samaritan Hosp Sch Nurs 90-; Nurs; Masters Geriatrics.

**WHITE, TAMARA T,** Univ Of Sc At Columbia, Columbia, SC; SR; BS; Crmnl Jstce Assn 90-; Sistrcr Prog Vol 90; Crmnl Jstce; Rehabltv Cnslng.

**WHITE, TERESA A,** Fayetteville St Univ, Fayetteville, NC; SO; Gspl Chr 90; Afro Am Chr 87-89; Lvly Hl Gspl Chr Asst Sec 87-; Deans Lst 89-90; Univ Chnclrs Schlr 89-; Bus Educ; Educ.**

**WHITE, TERRI LYNN,** Stillman Coll, Tuscaloosa, AL; FR; BS; NAACP Pres; Sci Clb 90-; Untd Ngr Cll Fnd 90-; Gamma Iota Sigma 90-; Cordell Wynn Hnrs Soc 90-; Pres Hnrs Lst VP 90-; Rotaract Clb 90-; Pres Lst 90-; Dean Lst; Natl Sci Fndtn Rsrch Expr Intern; Biol/Engl; Optmtry.

**WHITE, THALIA E,** Alfred Univ, Alfred, NY; SR; BS; Zimoja Blck Stdnt Un Tres 88-; Ntnl Career Wmns Assn VP Fndrsng 88-; Amrcn Mrktng Assn 88-90; Fncl Mngrs Assn; Delta Mu Delta; Certf Acadmc Adhvmnt; Srvc Awd; All Amrcn Schlr Cllgt Awd; Bsns; Mgmnt.

**WHITE, TIMOTHY J,** Western New England Coll, Springfield, MA; JR; Boy Scts Order Of The Arrow Brthrhd; CT State Police Intern; Psychology; Law Enforcement.**

**WHITE, TISHA L,** Elmira Coll, Elmira, NY; JR; BA; Phi Eta Sigma; Vldctrn Hnrs Schlrshp 89-; Pltcl Sci.

**WHITE, TRACY,** Mattatuck Comm Coll, Waterbury, CT; SO; Alpha Betta Gamma; Tlnt Rstr Outstndng Comm Coll Stdnts 90; Tlnt Rstr Outstndng Mnrty Comm Coll Stdnts; Univ CT Waterbury Sec 88-; Cert Acctg-Mattatuck Comm Coll 90; Offc Admin; Acctg/Bus.

**WHITE, TYRONE J,** Al A & M Univ, Normal, AL; FR; BS; Sci Tchnlgy; Cvl Eng.

**WHITE, VALERIE E,** Bishop St Comm Coll, Mobile, AL; FR; ADN; Phi Theta Kapa Scty 90; Grls Scts Amer Trp Ldr 89-; Nrsng; Nrs.

**WHITE, VERNETTE C,** Fl Memorial Coll, Miami, FL; JR; BA; Acctng; CPA.

**WHITE, VERONICA Y,** Fl A & M Univ, Tallahassee, FL; SR; BA; Hon Rl 88-90; Deans Lst 90-; Magna Cum Laude; AA Edison Comm Coll 88; Comp/Info Syst; Pgmr/Anlyst.

**WHITE, WENDI L,** Converse Coll, Spartanburg, SC; SO; BM; Delta Omicron V P; Walter Montomgery Acad Schlrshp; Mjus Hnr Schlrshp; Music/Voice; Prof Singer/Music Tchr.

**WHITE, WENDY L,** Savannah Coll Of Art & Design, Savannah, GA; SO; BA; Fiber Arts Clb 89-; Fiber Arts; Srfc Dsgn.

**WHITE, WENDY M,** Bryant Stratton Bus Inst Roch, Rochester, NY; Acctg.

**WHITE, WENDY M,** James Madison University, Harrisonburg, VA; GD; U Prog Brd Pub Rel Chrmn 88-89; Wellness Nwsltr Ed 88-89; Admsns Ofc Std Astt 87-90; Phi Kappa Phi 90; Mortor Bd 89-90; Gldn Key 88-90; Order Omega 88-90; Delta Gamma Scl Chrmn 86-90; Std Ambssdrs VP 87-90; Cthlc Cmps Mnstry 87-90; Corp Communications.

**WHITE, WILLIAM B,** Fl St Univ, Tallahassee, FL; SR; BS; Inst Elctrcl Elctrncs Engnrs 89-; Mthmtcl Assn America 89-; IEEE Sgnl Prcsng Soc 89-; Gldn Key 90-; Tau Beta Pi 90-; Elctrcl Engnrng; Engnrng.

**WHITE III, WILLIAM C,** Va Commonwealth Univ, Richmond, VA; SO; BA; Lctr Cmmtt Sec 90-; Ltry Mgzn Asst Ed 90-; Mlt Cltrl Dvrsty Prjct 90-; Engl.

**WHITE, WILLIAM E,** Tri County Tech Coll, Pendleton, SC; AS; Hnr Rl; Wldng Cmptn; Indstrl Tchnlgy/Wldng.

**WHITE-NICHOLS, LAURA LYNN,** Savannah Coll Of Art & Design, Savannah, GA; GD; BFA; Grad Magna Cum Laude 90; Dns Lst 90; Otstndng Soph 89; Otstndng Sr 90; Mary Rene Whelans Schlrshp 90; Gordon Lewis Acad Schlrshp 89; Illstrtn Art Hstry; Illstrtr.

**WHITECAR, TAMMY L,** Univ Of Fl, Gainesville, FL; SO; BHS; Shands Tchng Hosp Schlrshp 90-; AA 89; Med Tech; Rsrch.

**WHITED, TAMMYE F,** Univ Of Al At Birmingham, Birmingham, AL; SR; BS; Phi Sigma Biological; Bio; Dentstry.

**WHITEFIELD, MARY A,** Middle Tn St Univ, Murfreesboro, TN; JR; BS; Kappa Delta Pi; Edn; Spcl Edn Tchr.

**WHITEHAIR, B CHRISTINE,** Anne Arundel Comm Coll, Arnold, MD; FR; Sclgy Cmps; Gnrl Studies; Drug/Alchl Cnslng.

**WHITEHAIR, ELIZABETH A,** Bridgewater Coll, Bridgewater, VA; SR; BS; Baptist Stdt Union Cncl 88-; Brethren Stdt Flwshp 87-; Concert Band 87-; Alpha Chi Sec 89-; Lambda 88-; Stdt Educ Assoc 88-; Pres Schlrshp 87-; Elementary Education; Teacher.

**WHITEHEAD, ADAM J M,** Saint Andrews Presbytrn Coll, Laurinburg, NC; SR; Busn Club Pres 90-; Intntl Prog Comm 89-; Student Nwspr Busn Mgr 90; Alpha Chi; Omnicron Delta Edsilon; Wall Street Jul Awd.

**WHITEHEAD, D ANTHONY,** Richard Bland Coll, Petersburg, VA; SO; BS; Stdnts Free Enterprise Sgt At Arms; Rotaract; IM Vlybl 90-; Biology; Dntstry.

**WHITEHEAD, DIANE M,** Schenectady County Comm Coll, Schenectady, NY; SO; AAS; Accntng.

**WHITEHEAD, DWIGHT A,** Richard Bland Coll, Petersburg, VA; SO; AS; Stdnts In Free Enterprise 90-; Rotoract 90-; Bio; Med.

**WHITEHEAD, GEOFFREY A,** Univ Of Tn At Knoxville, Knoxville, TN; SR; MACC; Exec Undrgrd; Beta Gamma Sigma; Golden Key; Phi Kappa Phi; Beta Alpha Psi; Top Grad/Clg Of Bus; Hilton Smith Grad Fllwshp; Cmmrcl Rl Est Brkr 86-89; BSDBA; Acctg/Tax/Finance; CPA.

**WHITEHEAD, JOHN G,** Fl Atlantic Univ, Boca Raton, FL; SR; MBA.

**WHITEHEAD, KAREN S,** Univ Of Ga, Athens, GA; SR; BSW; Dklb EOC/GWINNETT Co Offc; Alcv Yth Shltr; Gldn Key; Deans Lst 87-90; AS 88; Scl Wrk.

**WHITEHEAD, L SHANE,** Belmont Coll, Nashville, TN; FR; BBA; Bus/Finance Assn 90-; Clg Rpblcns 90-; Gamma Beta Phi 90-; Baseball 90-; Finance; Money Mgmnt.

**WHITEHEAD, STEVEN B,** Roane St Comm Coll, Harriman, TN; SO; Hlth Physics Soc; Martin Marietta Enrgy Sys; Hlth Physics; Chem Engr.

**WHITEHEAD, TRACY L,** Ms St Univ, Miss State, MS; FR; BS; Gamma Beta Phi; Alpha Lambda Delta; Phi Eta Sigma; Honors Prog 90-; Presidents Schlr; Physics; Aerospace Robotics.

**WHITEHEAD, URSULA O,** Univ Of Southern Ms, Hattiesburg, MS; JR; BA; Dixie Drlngs Hlftm Perfmnce Grp Capt 88-; Southern Style Hostess Orgnztn; Alumni Assoc; Stennis Space Cntr Coop 90-; Dixie Darling Of Yr; Sci Educ.

**WHITEHEAD, VICKI E,** Univ Of Al At Birmingham, Birmingham, AL; SR; AS; Pres Hnr Rl 90-; Amer Phys Ther Assoc; AS Gadsden State Cmnty Clg; Certif UAB; Phys Ther Asst.

**WHITEHEAD, WILMA F,** Pellissippi St Tech Comm Coll, Knoxville, TN; SO; BA; Phi Theta Kappa 88-; Turo Adult Basic Educ; Legal Assist Tech; Law.

**WHITEHORN, VIRGINIA P,** Memphis St Univ, Memphis, TN; SR; Bapt Stdnt Union 85-87; Beethover Clb 85-90; Gamma Beta Phi Chrprsn 85-90; Sigma Alpha Iota Pres 87-90; Pi Kappa Lambda 88-90; Natl Clgte Achvmnt Awd 88-90; Natl Clgte Ed Awd 89-90; BM 90; Music; Music-Percussion/Vcl Perf.

**WHITEHOUSE, BARBARA,** Comm Coll Algny Co Algny Cmps, Pittsburgh, PA; FR; Art Assoc 89-; Graphic Design.

**WHITEHURST, WILLIAM H,** Longwood Coll, Farmville, VA; SO; BA; Bsktbl Tm; Pi Kappa Phi; Phy Ed; Tchr.

**WHITELOCK, BENJAMIN ERIC,** Salisbury St Univ, Salisbury, MD; JR; BS; ROTC Outstndng Cadet Airborne Schl Pit Sgt 88-; Natl Hon Soc 88-90; Ftbl; Bus; Mltry Trnsprtn.

**WHITEMAN, AMY E,** Radford Univ, Radford, VA; SR; BBA; Intrntnl Acad Mgmt Mrktng 90-; SAM 90-; Amrcn Mrktng Assn 90-; Soc Mayflower Dscndnts St MO; Mrktng Psychology; Hess Co.

**WHITEMAN, RICHARD A,** Columbus Coll Of Art & Design, Columbus, OH; FR; BA; Deans Lst; Illstrtn; Advrtsng.

**WHITEN, LESLIE B,** Univ Of Sc At Spartanburg, Spartanburg, SC; JR; BA; Tennis 90; Chorus Schlrshp; Psych; Adlscnt Psych.

**WHITENER, JULIE A,** Univ Of Nc At Charlotte, Charlotte, NC; SO; BA; Elem Ed; Tchr.

**WHITESELL, NANCY L,** City Univ Of Ny Baruch Coll, New York, NY; SR; Finance/Econ Soc; Goldn Key 89-; Deans Lst 89-; Baruch Endwmnt Fnd Schlrshp 89-; BBA; Finance.

**WHITESIDE, CHERYL A,** Limestone Coll, Gaffney, SC; SR; BA; Sunshine Schl PTO V P 90-; Tri City Gym Booster Clb V P 90-; Elem Educ; Tchng.

**WHITESIDE JR, DANIEL L,** Univ Of Fl, Gainesville, FL; SR; BA; Sigma Tau Sigma 90-; Alpha Lambda Delta 88; Golden Key 90-; Phi Alpha Theta 90-; Dns Lst 89-90; Pres Lst 90; History.**

**WHITESIDE, RUSSELL E,** Univ Of Southern Ms, Hattiesburg, MS; JR; BS; Sigma Alpha Epsilon Treas; Acctng.

**WHITESIDE, TODD W,** Univ Of Pittsburgh, Pittsburgh, PA; FR; BSE; Elec Engr.

**WHITESIDES, DONNA L,** Univ Of Sc At Columbia, Columbia, SC; SR; BA; Rtrng Stdnts Assn VP 90-; Ed Clb 90-; SGA 90-; Socaster Elem PTA; Elem Ed; Tch.

**WHITESIDES, LEE M,** Medical Coll Of Ga, Augusta, GA; JR; DMD; Cls Pres EU 84-86; GSDA 88-; Omicron Kappa Upsilon 90-; GA Acad Gen Dntstry Schlrshp 90-; Vars Ftbl Davidson Clg 80-84; Acad Anesthslgsts Asst 86-88; Phys Asst Anesth; BS Davidson Clg 84; MMSC Emory 86; Dntstry; Oral Surg.

**WHITFIELD, ANGELA,** Tn St Univ, Nashville, TN; SR; Natl Panhlnc Cncl V P 90-; Phi Beta Lambda 88-89; Sigma Gamma Rho V P 90-; Frederick S Humphries Alumni Schlrshp 86-90; BS; Chem/Nat Sci; Hlth Svcs.

**WHITFIELD, ANISA L,** Nc Agri & Tech St Univ, Greensboro, NC; FR; BS; Ntl Soc Blck Engrs 90-; Flwshp Gspl Choir 90-; Elec Engr.

**WHITFIELD, ANTHONY G,** Ms Gulf Coast Comm Coll, Perkinston, MS; FR; Chaplins Awrd 90; Hll Fm 90; Bus Mgmt.

**WHITFIELD, DONNA F,** Tri County Tech Coll, Pendleton, SC; AB; Acctng.

**WHITFIELD, ERNEST M,** Mary Holmes Coll, West Point, MS; SO; BS; Stdnt Govt Assn Sec/Treas 89-90; NAACP Mbr; AS; Math/Sci; Engr.

**WHITFIELD, JENNIFER A,** Ga Southern Univ, Statesboro, GA; SO; Campus Otrch 90-91; Gamma Beta Phi 89-91; Kappa Kappa Gamma 91; Phillip Morris Acad Schlrshp 89-91; Med; Nrsng.**

**WHITFIELD, JOAN H,** Va Commonwealth Univ, Richmond, VA; GD; BS; Cthlc Yth Org Pres 76-77; Iretonettes 77-; Lttl Lge Coach 90-; Rlgs Cls Tchr 90-; Prschl Tchr 86-89; AAS Human Serv Mntl Hlth 80; Erly Chldhd Educ; Tch.

**WHITFIELD, JOSETTE C,** Norfolk St Univ, Norfolk, VA; SR; BS; Stdnt Ldrshp 90-; Miss NSU Pgnt Cntstnt 88; Assn Cmptng Mchnry 89-; Cmps All-Str Chllng Com; NTA Mnrty Sympsm Athr/Prsntr; Comp Sci; Info Syst Sftwr Eng.

**WHITFIELD, KESHIE L,** Norfolk St Univ, Norfolk, VA; FR; BA; Eng Foreign Lang Club 90-; Spanish Lit; Trnsltr/Intrptr.

**WHITFIELD, MARTHA M,** Ramapo Coll Of Nj, Mahwah, NJ; JR; Oxford Hon Pgm 90-; Hon Pgm 90-; Rgstrd Tchr Royal Acdmy Dncng; Assoc Imprl Soc Tchrs Dncng; Dnc Tchr 86-; DIP Nrthrn Ballet Schl Englnd 86; Bus Admin Mgmt; Arts Mgmt/Tchng.

**WHITFIELD, MICHELLE,** Comm Coll Algny Co Algny Cmps, Pittsburgh, PA; SR; VITA; Math; Acctnt/CPA.

**WHITFIELD, PRESELFANNIE E,** Jackson St Univ, Jackson, MS; JR; BA; Pierian Lit Soc 88-; Alpha Lambda Delta Secr 89-; Sigma Tau Delta Pres; Phi Kappa Phi; NAACP 89-; Bapt Stdnt Union Rep 88-; Rsrch Intern Univ MN 90-; Engl Lit.

**WHITFIELD, TAMMY J,** Morris Brown Coll, Atlanta, GA; SO; BA; Stdnt Spprt Srvcs 1st Att; Majorrette; Natl Hnr Soc; Chrch Chr Vol; Majorette; Nrsng; Ped Nurse.

**WHITFIELD, THOMASINA M,** Chesterfield Marlboro Coll, Cheraw, SC; FR; Sclgy; Soc Wrkr.

**WHITFIELD, WENDY L,** Enterprise St Jr Coll, Enterprise, AL; FR; Sci; Med.

**WHITFIELD, WES W,** Southern Coll Of Tech, Marietta, GA; JR; BS; Amer Cnrt Inst 90-; Amer Scty Cvl Eng 89-90; Lmbd Chi Alph Exec Cmt 88-; IM Ftbl Bsktbl Sftbl Sccr Hcky 87-; Cvl Eng; Eng.

**WHITFORD, JOSEPHINE M,** Cornell Univ Statutory College, Ithaca, NY; JR; BS; Advsr 89-; Ornttn Cnslr 89-; Jgglng Clb Pres 88-; Ho Nun De Kah; Fllwshp SUNY; Biol Sci; Rsrch.

**WHITFORD, SHARA L,** Univ Of Southern Ms, Hattiesburg, MS; JR; BA; Lbrl Stdnt Org; Drama Prdctn; Hnr Soc; Engl; Pblshng.

**WHITING, CYNTHIA A,** Univ Of Nc At Greensboro, Greensboro, NC; SO; BSN; BS Fds And Ntrtn 87; Nrsng.

**WHITING, IRIS R,** Salisbury St Univ, Salisbury, MD; Pol Sci Hon Soc 88-90; Intrnshp For Gen Asmbly Of St Leg For Delg Nathaniel Exum; BA 90; Pol Sci; Law.

**WHITING, PAULA A,** Fl A & M Univ, Tallahassee, FL; FR; BA; Cvl Eng.

**WHITING, SHARON S,** Al St Univ, Montgomery, AL; FR; BS; Yth Dept Chrch Org Sec 88-89; Yth Dept Chrch Org Asst Sec 89-90; Intrdscplnry Humants Seqnce Hnrs Prgrm 90-; Alpha Phi Alpha Actvts Asst Dir; Acdmc Dns Lst 90-; Hnrd In Schls Hnr Convctn; Bus; Mktg.

**WHITLATCH, SAMMY E,** Wv Univ At Parkersburg, Parkersburg, WV; FR; AAS; Wldg.

**WHITLEY JR, AUBREY R,** Memphis St Univ, Memphis, TN; SR; BS; DMPA 87-; ICCA 88-; AICCP 87-; Phi Theta Kappa 76-80; Comm Coll Trnsfr Schlrshp 90-; NROTC Schlrshp 71-73; Comp Cnsltnt 86-; AS St Tech Inst Memphis 81; AAS St Tech Inst Memphis 90; Comp/Info Syst; Comp Cnsltng.

**WHITLEY, JOHN C,** Southern Coll Of Tech, Marietta, GA; JR; BA; Civil Envrnmntl Eng; Envrnmntl Tchnlgst.

**WHITLEY, LORI C,** Bridgewater Coll, Bridgewater, VA; FR; BA; Intl Clb 90-; Sclgy.

**WHITLEY, MARY F,** Norfolk St Univ, Norfolk, VA; SR; AHEA Amer Home Ecom Assoc; Deans List 90-; Tabernacle Homeless; Ladies Clb Bus Mngr 89-; Prod Supervisor Gualtney Smithfield; AS Paul D Camp Comm Clg 76; Cert Southampton Hosp 76; BS Food/Nutrition; Nutritionist/Dietitian.

**WHITLEY, NIKI C,** Abraham Baldwin Agri Coll, Tifton, GA; SO; DOCT; Student Govt Senator 89-90f Raio Club DJ 89-90; Traffic Ct Mbr Judicianry 90-; Alpha Beta Gamma VP 89-; Delta Epsilon Chi 90-; Speech Forum 90-; Dorm Pres Pres 90; BA ABAC 90-; Animal Sci/Hlth; Vetry Med.

**WHITLEY, STACY LYNN,** Middle Tn St Univ, Murfreesboro, TN; BS; Bsn Adm; Mgmt.

**WHITLOCK, AMY K,** Anderson Coll, Anderson, SC; FR; BA; SGA 90-; Hons Pgm 90-; Spnsh Awd; Elem Ed; Tch.

**WHITLOCK, CHARLES CAMPEN,** Fl A & M Univ, Tallahassee, FL; SR; BARCH; AIAS Treas 90-; Alpha Sigma Phi; Archtctr.

**WHITLOCK, KARLA C,** Univ Of Sc At Columbia, Columbia, SC; SR; BA; SC Stdnt Lgstlt 89; USC Hnrs Clge 86-90; Trst Schlrshp 86; Warner Lambert Corp Schlrsp Frgn Exchng 84; Pltcl Sci; Law/Pltcs/Advrtsg.

**WHITLOCK, KEVIN M,** Va Commonwealth Univ, Richmond, VA; SR; Div I Sccr 87-; BS; Info Sys; Cmptrs.

**WHITLOCK, TRACEY J,** Piedmont Coll, Demorest, GA; SO; Early Chldhd Ed; Teach.

**WHITLOCK, WYMAN LEE,** Univ Of Sc At Columbia, Columbia, SC; FR; BS; Eng Math.

**WHITLOW, CHRISTIAN H,** Univ Of Nc At Charlotte, Charlotte, NC; JR; BA; Charlotte Psychlgy Clb Treas 88-; Psychlgy Enrichmnt Pgm Tutor; Phi Eta Sigma Treas 88-; Gold Key 90-; Psi Chi 90-; Coop Edn Pgm 89-; State Govt Intrnshp; Psychlgy; Cnslng.

**WHITLOW, CHRISTOPHER T,** East Carolina Univ, Greenville, NC; FR; BFA; Art Psycg; Doctorate Degree Clinical Psych.

**WHITLOW, TAMMI T,** Ky St Univ, Frankfort, KY; SO; Golden Girl 90-; Pres Schlrshp 89-; Deans List 90-; Cmptr Scnc; Prgrmmr.

**WHITMAN, ADAM E,** Cornell Univ Statutory College, Ithaca, NY; FR; BS; Dns Lst 90-; Phi Sigma Kappa; Biol; Med Dr.

**WHITMAN, RONALD E,** Tn St Univ, Nashville, TN; BS; AECOMP; Data Processing Award 85; AAS Data Procsng Columbia St Cmnty Clg 85; Comptr Sci; Progrmng.

**WHITMER, STEVEN D,** Univ Of Fl, Gainesville, FL; SR; BFA; Countryside Arts Festival Schlrshp 86; Amy Nicole De Grove Schlrshp; Sculptor.

**WHITMORE II, JOHN G,** Hudson Valley Comm Coll, Troy, NY; FR; ASSOC; Bus.

**WHITNER JR, EDWARD GRAY,** Univ Of Sc At Coastal Carolina, Conway, SC; SR; BS; Fllwshp Chrstn Athlts 87-; Psi Chi; Sy; Psychlgy; Psychtrst.

**WHITNER JR, EDWARD GRAY,** Univ Of Sc At Columbia, Columbia, SC; SR; BS; Flwshp Chrstn Ath 87-; Psi Chi 91-; Psych.

**WHITNEY, ANNETTE M,** Nyack Coll, Nyack, NY; SO; BA; St Agathas Gspl Tm; Elem Educ; Tchr.

**WHITNEY, BRIAN S,** Cornell Univ Statutory College, Ithaca, NY; SO; BA; Astrnmy Clb 90-; IM Sccr Capt 89; Econs Bus Mgmt; Bus Mgmt.

**WHITNEY, DOUGLAS,** Pamlico Comm Coll, Grantsboro, NC; SO; AAS; Phi Theta Kappa Alph Xi Omcrn; Elect Eng.

**WHITNEY, GERALDINE ALBEE,** Saint Josephs Coll, Windham, ME; SR; BS; Sr Cls Secr 90-; Orientation Comm 90; Delta Epsilon Sigma; All-Amer Schlr Clgte Awd; Natl Clgte Stdnt Govt Awd; IMS Vars Soccer 87-; Elem Ed; Elem Tchr.

**WHITNEY, KRISTI S,** Commonwealth Coll, Virginia Beach, VA; GD; Offc Admin Clb 89-90; Alpha Beta Gamma 89-90; AS Commonwealth Clg 90; Ofc Admin/Exec; Sec.

**WHITNEY, SHAWN M,** Northeastern Christian Jr Coll, Villanova, PA; FR; BA; Ambsdrs; Yr Bk Stf.

**WHITNEY, TARA E,** Va Commonwealth Univ, Richmond, VA; FR; BS; Phi Eta Sigma; Mass Comm; Mktg/Advrtsng.

**WHITSON, HOLLY J,** Pellissippi St Tech Comm Coll, Knoxville, TN; SO; BS; Phi Theta Kappa 89-; Cmptr Sci; Prgrmr.

**WHITSON, SANDRA L,** Cumberland County Coll, Vineland, NJ; JR; BS; Phi Theta Kappa; Admin Asst; Wrdprcssng 75-85; Instrctr/Dir Plcmnt; Typng/Shrthnd Instrctr; Cert Glassboro St Clg 77; Bus Admin; CPA.

**WHITT, ELIZABETH A,** Ms St Univ, Miss State, MS; JR; BA; Almni Dlgts VP 89-; Omcrn Delta Kappa; Mrtr Brd; Gamma Beta Phi Sec 88-; Phi Eta Sigma 88-; Lambda Sigma Treas 88-90; Fncl Mgmt Assc VP 88-; Pi Sigma Epsln; Phi Mu Sor Treas 88-90; Untd Way Cbnt; Stuart Vance Schlp; Ldrshp Schlp; IM Sprts; Banking/Finance; Invstmnt Anlys.

**WHITT, FREDERICK A,** Bryant Stratton Bus Inst Roch, Rochester, NY; Elctrnc Eng.

**WHITT, JACK D,** Marshall University, Huntington, WV; JR; BBA; Gamma Beta Phi 88-89; Alpha Kappa Psi VP 90-; Internship Anderson Matthews Attys At Law; Finance; Law.

**WHITT, JAMES M,** Emory & Henry Coll, Emory, VA; JR; BS; SGA Sec 87-88; Sigma Mu 90-; Hon Schlrshp 90-; TN Estmn Kodak Schlrshp; AAS VA Hghlnds Comm Coll 90; AAS 89; Physcs; Eng.

**WHITT, JAMES N,** Marshall University, Huntington, WV; SO; BA; SAGL 90; SADD 88-90; Army Acmdtn Mdl Oprtn Dsrt Strm; IM 89-90; Acctng; CPA.

**WHITT, JASON Y,** Ms St Univ, Miss State, MS; SR; BA; Gamma Beta Phi; Kappa Mu Epsilon; Delta Chi Treas 87-; Pres Schlr 90-; Deans Schlr 88-89; IMS Soccer/Bsktbl/Sftbll 87-; BBA 90; Mtmtcs; Clg Tchng.

**WHITT, LYDIA M,** Ms St Univ, Miss State, MS; JR; MA; Phi Alpha Theta; Phi Kappa Phi 90-; Gamma Beta Phi 90-; Alpha Lambda Delta 90-; Sigma Tau Delta; IM Wtrpl Bwlng; Mlln Bll 88-; Engl; Tchng Wrtng.

**WHITT, MELISSA C,** Va Commonwealth Univ, Richmond, VA; SO; BS; Pre Nrsng Clb Pres 90-; Nrsng; Nrss Anstsia.

**WHITT, REBECCA J,** Ohio Valley Coll, Parkersburg, WV; FR; BS; Stage Gnd 90-; Sigma Epsilon Chi 90-; Chrldng 90-; Psychology; Fmly Cnslng.

**WHITT, STEPHANIE,** Commonwealth Coll, Virginia Beach, VA; FR; BA; Med Clb Hstrn 90-; Med; Med Admn Asst.

**WHITTAKER, RUNAKO D,** Clark Atlanta Univ, Atlanta, GA; SO; BS; Pre Prof Hlth Soc 89-; Scnc Hntr Pblcty Chr; Gde Crps; Mnrty Med Educ Prog 90; Biology; Medicine.

**WHITTED, VALESIA M L,** Al A & M Univ, Normal, AL; SO; Hall Treas 90-; Dorm Cncl 90-; Alpha Kappa Alpha; Deans Lst 90-; Hnr Rl 90-; Sociology.

**WHITTEMORE, DAWN C,** Piedmont Tech Coll, Greenwood, SC; SO; AAS; Phi Theta Kappa 90-; Phi Beta Lambda 90-; Ttrng Cntr Pdmnt Tech 90-; Pr Advsr 90; Bus Acctng; Acctng.

**WHITTEMORE, EDDIE W,** Tn Tech Univ, Cookeville, TN; SR; MS; Cmptv Rock Clmbr Wrld Cup Evnts 90-; BS 87; Nutrition/Metabolism.

**WHITTEMORE, EDWARD SCOTT,** Southern Coll Of Tech, Marietta, GA; JR; BA; IIE 90-; Tau Kappa Epsilin VP; Adpt Hwy Red Cross; Deans Lst 89-90; Indstrl Engnrng.

**WHITTEN, CATHERINE B,** Univ Of Cincinnati, Cincinnati, OH; FR; BMUSI; Music/Math.

**WHITTEN, CHARLOTTE R,** Bethune Cookman Coll, Daytona Beach, FL; SO; BA; Rel Life 90-; Mc Knight Hnrs Soc 87-; Hnr Soc 90-; Alpha Kappa Alpha; Elem Edn 1st Grade Teacher.

**WHITTINGHAM, ANTOINETTE M E,** Fl International Univ, Miami, FL; JR; BA; Busn Admin/Persnl Mgmt/Mktg; Busn.

**WHITTINGHAM, JACQUELINE C,** Broward Comm Coll, Ft Lauderdale, FL; SO; BA; Intrntl Stdnt Clb 89; Priv Commcl Instrmnt Pilot Cert 90-; Phi Theta Kappa 89; Alpha Eta Rho 89; Merit Schlrshp 89-90; Aviation Bus Admin; Pilot.

**WHITTINGTON, LORI,** Meridian Comm Coll, Meridian, MS; SO; BA; Bptst Stdnt Union Pres 90; Drug/Alcohol Awareness Week/Red Ribbon Week Cmmt Pres 90; Adolescent Psychlgy.

**WHITTINGTON, RAENETTA L,** Wilberforce Univ, Wilberforce, OH; JR; BA; Choir Pres 90-; Sigma Omega Vp Elect; Music/Voice; Entrtnmnt/Law.

**WHITTINGTON JR, ROY M,** Tallahassee Comm Coll, Tallahassee, FL; SO; AA; Bus; Mgmt.

**WHITTINGTON, VICTORIA M,** Wittenberg Univ, Springfield, OH; FR; BA; Un Brd; Pre-Law Assoc; Bsns; Law.

**WHITTLE, CHRISTINE S,** Dowling Coll, Oakdale Li, NY; JR; BED; Educ Clb Sec 89; Alpha Chi; Elem Educ.

**WHITTON, BRADY S,** Atlantic Comm Coll, Mays Landing, NJ; FR; BA; Philosophy; Professor.

**WHITTON, KEVIN L,** Univ Of Cin R Walters Coll, Blue Ash, OH; SO; BA; Nrsng; RN.

**WHITTON, TERESA L,** Chattanooga St Tech Comm Coll, Chattanooga, TN; SO; AS; Ofc Syst Tchnlgy; Banking.

**WHITWORTH, MARIA N,** Thomas Nelson Comm Coll, Hampton, VA; BA; Pltcl Sci; Tchr.

**WHITWORTH, STEVEN M,** Tri County Tech Coll, Pendleton, SC; IET.

**WHOBREY, LORI M,** Livingston Univ, Livingston, AL; JR; MBA; Anchor Clb 86- Pres 87-88; Annual Stf Co Editor 86-88; Natl Hnr Scty 87-88; Academic All Amer Schlr 86-; Acctng; CPA.

**WHOOLEY, ELIZABETH A,** Merrimack Coll, North Andover, MA; FR; BA; IM Vlybl/Sftbl 90-; Biolgy; Med.

**WHOOLEY, MARY A,** Boston Univ, Boston, MA; GD; MD; Alpha Omega Alpha; BA Yale Univ 83; Med; Physician.

**WHORLEY, KIMBERLEY DAWN,** Western Ky Univ, Bowling Green, KY; JR; Psi Chi; Phi Eta Sigma; Pres Schlr; Phi Kappa Phi.

**WHYMAN, GARY J,** Elmira Coll, Elmira, NY; JR; BS; Deans List Hon Schlrs 89-90; Natl Assc Acctnts; 89-; Brd Assmnt Rvw 90-; Sprvsr Dmstc/Intrntl Invcng; AAS Suny Alfred 78; Bus Admn/Mgmt; Cntrlrshp.

**WHYNOTT, KATHLEEN ANN,** Oh Univ, Athens, OH; SR; BFA; Natl Assn Music Thrpy V P 90-; O V Symph Orch 87-; VFW 86-; Golden Key 90; Phi Kappa 89; Deans Lst 87-; ; Bfa; Music Thrpy.

**WHYTE, BRADLEY,** Atlantic Union Coll, S Lancaster, MA; SO; AS; Pr Ttr Antmty Physlgy 89-; Pr Cnslr Cncllr 90-; Asst Dean 89-; Nrsng.

**WHYTE, KATHERINE L,** Univ Of Sc At Columbia, Columbia, SC; JR; BA; Alpha Delta Kappa Schlrshp; Elem Educ; Tchr.

**WIAMER, CHRISTINE P,** Jersey City St Coll, Jersey City, NJ; JR; BS; Math Club 90-; Occup Schlrshp Pgm 90-; Amer Chem Soc 90-; Chem/Bio; Rsrch Scientist.

**WIANDT, KENNETH D,** Union Univ, Jackson, TN; SR; BSBA; Bsnss Clb 88-89; Alpha Chi 90; Phi Beta Lambda 89-90; Accntng; CPA.

**WIATROWSKI, LARA E,** Longwood Coll, Farmville, VA; JR; BS; Soc Anth Clb VP; Alpha Kappa Delta 90-; Zeta Tau Alpha Pr 89-; Rsrch Asst; Sociology.

**WIBRIGHT, AMY L,** Va Commonwealth Univ, Richmond, VA; FR; BA; Budget Cmmttee Stdnt Govt; Phi Eta Sigma; Accntng; Lawyer.

**WICHMANN, GREGORY A,** Wilmington Coll, Wilmington, OH; JR; BA; Gamma Phi Gamma Alumni Chrmn 89-; Mrktng Mgmnt.

**WICK, DAVID J,** Edinboro Univ Of Pa, Edinboro, PA; JR; BS; Physcs Engr Clb 87-90; Univ Hnrs Pgm 87-; Mgr Harley Davidson Erie; Physcs/Engr; Elec Engr.

**WICK, JANE E,** Coll Of Charleston, Charleston, SC; SO; BA; Hist; Tchng.

**WICKER, ROBIN L,** Univ Of Southern Ms, Hattiesburg, MS; SR; BS; MS Assoc Edctrs 90-; Phi Theta Kappa 90; AA SW MS Comm Coll 90; Elem Ed; Tchr.

**WICKHAM, MARY E,** Saint Francis Coll, Loretto, PA; JR; BS; Stdnt Actvts Org Pres; Stdnt Govt Org Sntr 89-; Orntn Stf 89-90; PLUSI 88-90; Bg Bro/Bg Sis 88-89; Undrcls Vol Awd 89; Natl Stdnt Govt Awd 90; Elem Ed; Tchg.

**WICKKISER, ELISABETH A,** Georgetown Univ, Washington, DC; JR; BSBA; Comm Actn Cltn 89-90; Asst Prof J T Garrity 89-; Dns Lst 90-; Bsn Mgmt.

**WICKLIFFE, DEBORAH F,** William Carey Coll, Hattiesburg, MS; SO; BSN; Jayne Gurtler MD Med Asst 85-90; Nrsng.

**WICKLUND, TIMOTHY B,** Strayer Coll, Washington, DC; SR; BS; Cmptr Info Sys; Cmptr Prgrmr.

**WICKS, DENISE L,** Univ Of Sc At Columbia, Columbia, SC; JR; BS; Rsdnt Hsng Assoc Sen 89-90; Hall Govt Sen 89-; Grk Strng Com Co Chrmn 90-; Delta Zeta Chrmn 90-; Rsdnt Advsr 90-; CPR Frst Ad Cert 89-; Marine Sci; Physcl Ocngrphy.

**WICKS, DONNA M,** Central Fl Comm Coll, Ocala, FL; FR; Probation Counselor Salvation Army; Criminal Justice; Probation/Parole.

**WICKS, JOHN C,** Oh Univ, Athens, OH; JR; BS; Natl Soc Prfsnl Engrs 88-; Amer Soc Cvl Engrs 90-; Intrn Ohio Dept Trnsprtn 89-; Rcktbl/Sftbl/Ftbl; Cvl Engrg.

**WICKS, MARIETTA,** Alcorn St Univ, Lorman, MS; SR; Cls Sntr 90-; Gspl Choir 88-90; Pan-Hllnc Cncl Sec 90-; Alpha Kappa Mu 89-; Alpha Kappa Alpha Pres 89-; US Dept Agri Intrn 90-; Chevron Schlrshp 89; ASU Tuition Schlrshp 87-; BS; Comp Sci/Appld Math; Syst Anlyst.

**WICKS, MARILYN A,** Middle Tn St Univ, Murfreesboro, TN; SR; BA; Early Chldhd Edn; Teach/Chld Care Ctr.

**WIDEN, STACEY J,** Pa St Univ Main Cmps, University Pk, PA; FR; BA; Dance Marthn Morale Comm; Pi Beta Phi 90-; Lib Arts; Busn.

**WIDENHOFER, SHAWN W,** Butler County Comm Coll, Butler, PA; SO; ASSOC; Comp Clb 90-; Peer Tutor 90-; Comp Sci Prctcm Butler Meml Hosp; Comp Prgrmng; Sys Analyst.**

**WIDER, FRANCISCA G,** Fl International Univ, Miami, FL; JR; Pres/Owner Dstnctv Dmstcs Inc 87-; Pedagogische Akademie Schyndel The Netherlands 82; BS Sknle Clg Schyndel 78; Hsptlty Mgt.

**WIDJAJA, JANTO,** City Univ Of Ny La Guard Coll, Long Island Cty, NY; SO; Phi Theta Kapha 90-; Alpha Theta Phi 90-; Legio Mariae 84-88; Vol Elctrncs Tchncn Rockefllr Univ; Comp Tchncn; Elect Eng.

**WIDMER, DAVID M,** Daytona Beach Comm Coll, Daytona Beach, FL; SO; AS; Highest Hnrs Mc Dowell Tchncl Comm Cllg; Certf Phtgrphy 89; Phtgrphy; Prfsnl Phtgrphy.

**WIDMYER, AMBER L,** James Madison University, Harrisonburg, VA; FR; BS; Marching Royal Dukes 90-; Inter Var Chrstn Flwshp 90-91; Psychology; Physical Therapy.

**WIEBER, AMY B,** S U N Y Coll At Fredonia, Fredonia, NY; SR; BA; Nwsppr Edit In Chf 90; Media Advsry Cncl Prnt Rep 89-; Assn Of Media Rep Chrprsn 90-; Dns Lst 88-; Tchng Asst 89-; Intrnshp Brdn Cmmnctns Mgmt York England 90; Engl Phlsphy; Prfssr Ph D.

**WIEBER, JOHN E,** Embry Riddle Aeronautical Univ, Daytona Beach, FL; SO; BS; Mgmt Clb Pres 90-; Skydvng Clb 90-; Amer Assn Arprt Exec; Fncng Clb; Aerntcl Sci; Cmmrcl Aviatn.

**WIEBOLDT, GUNNAR R,** Univ Of Rochester, Rochester, NY; JR; BA; Navy ROTC Marine Platoon Cmdr; Drill Tm; Military Excell; Engl Hon Pgm; Engl/Pol Sci; Military/Law/Govt.

**WIECZOREK, KENNETH B,** Temple Univ, Philadelphia, PA; SR; BS; PA Phrmctcl Assn 90-; Acad Stdnts Of Phrmcy 90-; Rho Chi; Phrmcy.

**WIEDE, YLJE J,** Univ Of Sc At Columbia, Columbia, SC; SO; BA; Asker Gymnstc Clb; Lndya Sprts Clb Rytmc Sprtgymnstc; Asker Ski Clb; Deans List; Stdnt Hsng Assc Tres; Jrnlst Awrd; Nrwgn Gymnstc Fdrtn; SOS Chldcr; D; Amer Fld Svc; Jr Chmbr; Gymnstc Coach; Cert Envrnmntl Stds Norwgn Envmntl Acad 90; Bus Admn; Ec.

**WIEDIGER, SUSAN D,** Univ Of Rochester, Rochester, NY; SR; BS; Fncng Clb VP 87-; Cmmtt Prfrmng Arts Chrmn 87-; Alpha Psi Omega 90-; NSF-REU Grant 90; Tchng Intern; Chmstry.

**WIEDMANN, JENNI R,** Lancaster Bible Coll, Lancaster, PA; SO; AS; Yearbk Lyout 90-; SGA Socl Comm 90-; Sec Intrnshp; Secrtrl; Bus.

**WIEGAND, FRANK R,** Radford Univ, Radford, VA; SR; BS; Phi Kappa Phi; Geog.

**WIEGERINK, KRISTINA R,** Brevard Coll, Brevard, NC; SO; BA; Environmental Club 89-; School Newspaper Photography Editor 89-90; Jrnslm Intrnshp Newspaper; Cross Cntry Track Field 89-; AA; Journalism; Photo.

**WIEGMAN, JOAN M,** Daytona Beach Comm Coll, Daytona Beach, FL; SO; BA; Acctng; CPA.

**WIELER, KENNETH M,** Bridgeport Engr Inst, Fairfield, CT; SR; BSME; ASME Grtr New Haven St Tech Clg 85-87.

**WIELT, JENNIFER,** Atlantic Union Coll, S Lancaster, MA; JR; BA; Engl; Sec Ed.

**WIEMS, MARY L,** Stillman Coll, Tuscaloosa, AL; SR; BS; Roteract Clb; Intl Intcltrl Assn; Pre Prof Sci 90-; Alpha Kapa Mu 91-; Beta Kappa Chi Pres 91-; Cordell Wynn Gamma Lota Sigma 89-; UNCF 21cntry Schlrshp; Eckerd Schlrshp 88-90; Univ S AL Biomdcl Enrchmnt Enrchmnt Rcrtment Prog 90; Biol; Med.

**WIENKE, JENNIFER A,** Univ Of Sc At Aiken, Aiken, SC; FR; Phi Mu Frat Soc Serv Chrmn 90-; Deans Lst; Calculus Lab Asst; Math; Educ.

**WIEPERT, SUSAN L,** Daemen Coll, Amherst, NY; SO; BS; Coop Educ In Pediatric Phys Therapy; Phys Ther.**

**WIERINGO, MICHAEL L,** Va Commonwealth Univ, Richmond, VA; SR; Comm Arts Assoc 89-; Phi Kappa Phi; Jill Drummond Awd Soph Achvmnt Sr Illstrtn Awd; BFA; Illustration; Freelance Illustration.

**WIERKS, KRISTIE A,** Coll Of Charleston, Charleston, SC; FR; BS; Bsn Econ.

**WIERNIK, DANIEL L,** Univ Of Miami, Coral Gables, FL; JR; BS; Pi Kappa Alpha Sec 88-; Deans Lst; Provists Lst; I M Ftbl Sftbl Soccer; Biology; Med.

**WIERZBICKI, MICHAEL A,** Muskingum Coll, New Concord, OH; SO; BA; Centerbd Stdnt Plng Org Co-Chair IM 90-; Deans Lst; Phi Alpha Theta; Ulster Soc Clb 90-; Pol Sci; Law.

**WIERZCHOWSKI, MATTHEW G,** Point Park Coll, Pittsburgh, PA; JR; BS; Boy Scts Amer Asst Cubmaster; Dir Elctrncs Inst 89-; AST Electronic Inst 75; Elctrcl Engnrng Tech; Edctn.

**WIESE, MONICA E,** Univ Of Sc At Columbia, Columbia, SC; JR; BA; Reprsntd Norway Intrntl Tnns 86-89; Deans Lst 89-90; Athl 89-90; Advrtsg.

**WIESE, VANCE M,** Univ Of Sc At Columbia, Columbia, SC; SO; BS; Gamma Beta Phi Treas; Exclnc Math/Cmptr Sci Awd; Marine Sci; Marine Blgst.

**WIESENHART JR, CHARLES,** City Univ Of Ny Baruch Coll, New York, NY; SO; BBA; Acctng Socty Treas 89-; Street Fair Comm; Vol Crdntr March Of Dimes Walk Amer; Rgnts Schlr 89-; Pres Schlr 89-; Acctng; CPA.

**WIESNIAK, LORI A,** Albertus Magnus Coll, New Haven, CT; SO; BA; Sftbl 89; Bsnss; Fnce.

**WIESTER, GARY K,** Point Park Coll, Pittsburgh, PA; SR; BS; Electronic Tech 82-; AS Westmoreland Cty Comm Coll 87; Electronics; Engineering.

**WIETHE, SCOTT A,** West Liberty St Coll, West Liberty, WV; SR; BA; Cmnctns.

**WIETMARSCHEN, JEANNE M,** Univ Of Cin R Walters Coll, Blue Ash, OH; FR; BED; Southwest Ohio Tumor Registrars Assn Pres 89-90 Sec 83; Med Rcrd Tech 74-; AS Cincinnati Tech Clg 74; Math; Scndry Educ.

**WIGDER, WENDY L,** Duquesne Univ, Pittsburgh, PA; SO; BA; Orientation 90-; Phi Delta Chi Aux; Tau Delta Tau Scl Chrmn 90-; SHARP 90-; RA; Bsn-Acctg; CPA.

**WIGFALL, ALMA L,** Morris Coll, Sumter, SC; FR.

**WIGFIELD, DENISE M,** Kent St Univ Geauga Cmps, Burton Twp, OH; SO; BA; Ele Educ; Tch.

**WIGGINS JR, BOBBY J,** Univ Of Southern Ms, Hattiesburg, MS; SR; BS; Intrfrtrnty Cncl Repr 88; Mrchng Bnd 86; IM Sprts Offcl 89; Sigma Delta Chi; Kappa Alpha VP 88-; Intrhsp WKRG TV Mobile AL; Province Cmndrs Ctns; Radio/TV/FLM; Nws.

**WIGGINS, JAMES L,** Central Al Comm Coll, Alexander City, AL; MBA; Ctrl AL Community Clg Chrmn; Debate Tm; Hnr Roll Intl; Deans List; Alexonde City Comm Clg; NOW Neighborhood Org; Wrks Prog Co Founderd 82-84; Persl Devep Rehab Tutor 89; Grad; Sociology; Communication.

**WIGGINS, JENNY L,** Fayetteville St Univ, Fayetteville, NC; JR; BS; AAS Johnston Comm Clg 90; Elem Educ; Teaching.

**WIGGINS JR, JESSIE L,** Fl A & M Univ, Tallahassee, FL; JR; BS; Bsns/Ofc Admn; Bsns Mgmt.**

**WIGGINS, KELLY A,** Middle Ga Coll, Cochran, GA; SO; BS; Criminal Justice Clb 90-; Deans Lst; Criminal Justice Awd; Grad W/Hnrs; AS; Soc Sci; Cnslr.

**WIGGINS, LAURA MARLENE,** Lurleen B Wallace St Jr Coll, Andalusia, AL; FR; BA; Pr Lst 90-; Deans Lst 90-; Engl/Spanish; Sec Educ.

**WIGGINS, LETITIA A,** Nc Agri & Tech St Univ, Greensboro, NC; JR; BS; Soph Clss Pblcty Comm Co-Chr 89-90; Stdnt Sen SGA/STDNT Jdcl Comm Chrprsn 90-; Network 90 Cmnctns Org S 90-; Cmnctns Brdcst News; Law Schl Stdy Cmnctns.

**WIGGINS, LISA M,** Volunteer St Comm Coll, Gallatin, TN; FR; AS; Honor Roll 90-; Deans List 90-; Radiologic Technologist; Medical.

**WIGGINS, LORI M,** Savannah Coll Of Art & Design, Savannah, GA; JR; BFA; Bacchus 89-; RA 89-; Hall Cncl 90-; Mary Nellings Whalen Schlrshp; Graphic Dsgn; Corp Identity.

**WIGGINS, MARTISSA L,** Univ Of Southern Ms, Hattiesburg, MS; SR; BA; Phi Alpha Theta 90-; J E Gonzales History Awd; History; Law.

**WIGGINS, RHONDA N,** Univ Of Southern Ms, Hattiesburg, MS; SR; BS; Dixie Darlngs Capt 85-86; Am Advtsng Fed 90-; Delta Delta Delta; Advertising.

**WIGGINS, RITA G,** Ms St Univ, Miss State, MS; JR; BS; Fshn Focus V P 90-; Home Economics; Fashion Mrchdsg.

**WIGGINS, SARA J,** Oh Univ, Athens, OH; JR; AA 90.**

**WIGGINS, TRACIE R,** Univ Of Sc At Columbia, Columbia, SC; SO; Pblc Rltns Std Soc Amer Chrmn 90-; Kappa Delta 89-90; Jrnlsm; Pharm Sales.

**WIGGINS, VIVIAN L,** Livingston Univ, Livingston, AL; SR; BS; New Horizon VP 88-89; Phi Theta Kappa 88-89; Chrch Chrst; Scl Sci; Tchng.

**WIGGINS, YOLANDA DENISE,** Central St Univ, Wilberforce, OH; SR; BS; Natl Stdnt Bsns League; Comp Inf Sys Clb Pres; St Frm Ins Co Intrnshp; Dns Lst; Natl Bsns League Awd; Vllybl; Comp Inf Sys/Mgmt.

**WIGGINTON, LEE ANN,** Univ Of Ky, Lexington, KY; SR; BS; Knty Acdmy Stdts Phrmcy 90-; Chrstn Phrmcy Flwshp Intl 90-; Bptst Stdt Union 88-; Stdt Alumni Assoc Mrry St Univ 89-; Gamma Beta Phi 89-; Phi Lambda Sigma; Lambda Kappa Sigma 90-; Kappa Psi Little Sister 90-; Alpha Phi Omega 89-; Pharmacy.

**WIGGLESWORTH, GARY LEWIS,** Atlantic Comm Coll, Mays Landing, NJ; FR; Electrncs; BA.

**WIGGLESWORTH, JAMAL E,** Va St Univ, Petersburg, VA; SR; Rsrv Ofcr Trng Corp ROTC Cmsned Officer 87-90; Big Bro/Big Str Orgztn 87-; Hall Cabinet Res Asst 89-; Kappa Alphaz Psi Fraternity Inc Pres 89-; Yth Choir 79-; Cmndtn Ft Lee Advtsng Dept Intrn; Deans Lst 87-; Lkappa Alpha Psi Pres; BA, Cmrcl Art/Dsgn; Graphic Engr.

**WIGHTMAN, KAREN S,** Fl International Univ, Miami, FL; JR; BA; Lions Clb 90-; Specl Educ; Professor.

**WIGLEY, GREGORY S,** Univ Of Southern Ms, Hattiesburg, MS; SO; BA; Indstrl Eng Tech; Engrng.

**WIGLEY, LONNIE E,** Southern Coll Of Tech, Marietta, GA; FR; IET; Bsbl; Ind Engr.

**WIKE, JAMES F,** Tomlinson Coll, Cleveland, TN; FR; BA; Coll Chrl; Coll Sngrs; Tnns Trnmnt; Food Lion Inc 86-; Bus Admn; Mngmnt/Sprvsn.

**WIKLE, TERESA J,** Univ Of Fl, Gainesville, FL; SR; BSN; Onclgy Nrsng Scty Natl SIG Com; Bone Mrrw Trnsplnt Spcl Intrst Grp Natl Coor 88-; Amer Cncr Scty St Nrsng Educ Com FL Com 89; Elglbe Sigma Theta Tau Indctn; Amer Cncr Scty 89; Dipl Deaconess Hosp School Of Nursing 81; Pblc Educ Vol 90-; Nrsng; Fam Nrse Prctnr.

**WIKTORCHIK JR, JONATHAN P,** Penn Coll Of Straight Chiro, Horsham, PA; GD; DC; Anatmy Clb Pr 90-; Kappa Delta Pi 76-79; New Jersey Educ Assn 78; Natl Educ Assn 79-; Penns St Educ Assn 79-; Rdng Spec Cert 78-; BA Lasalle Univ 73; MED Wstchstr Univ 79; Chrprctc.

**WIKTORSKI, AMY L,** Daemen Coll, Amherst, NY; SR; BS; Transprtn Trvl Clb 88-; Delta Mu Delta 89-; Trans Amer Custmhs Brkrg Frm; Trans Trvl Mgt.

**WILBANKS, CRISTIAN L,** Itawamba Comm Coll, Fulton, MS; JR; BA; Phi Theta Kappa 87; Gamma Beta Phi; Spcl Ed.

**WILBANKS, MARIA E,** Univ Of Sc At Columbia, Columbia, SC; JR; Alumni Assn 89; Food Serv Com 89; Bptst Stdnt Union 90-; Gamma Beta Phi Sec 89-; Phi Theta Kappa 89; Phi Eta Sigma; Marshall 89; Van Ray Kenny Harvey Schlrshp 89-90; Deans Lst 88-; Sclgy; Prsnnl Mgmt.

**WILBANKS, SHERI L,** Valdosta St Coll, Valdosta, GA; FR; BS; Odum Schlrshp 90-; Chmstry; Chmcl Eng.

**WILBER, LISA M,** Christopher Newport Coll, Newport News, VA; SR; BSBA; Fin Mngmt Assc 90-; Fndrs Hl Aerbcs 87-88; Deans Lst 88-90; Fin/Mgmnt.

**WILBERT, ANGELA Y,** Alcorn St Univ, Lorman, MS; FR; BS; Biology; Phys Thrpst.

**WILBORN, JENNIFER J,** Livingston Univ, Livingston, AL; FR; Phi Eta Sigma 90-; Bsn Admin; Mktng.

**WILBUR, DIANA L,** S U N Y Coll At Fredonia, Fredonia, NY; SO; BA; Intern Engl Dept Wilma E Watson Schlrshp 89-; Deans Lst 89-; Engl; Tchncl Wrtng.

**WILBURN, CARLIN S,** Ashland Comm Coll, Ashland, KY; FR; Offc Admn; Wrd Prcssr.

**WILBURN, DEVOUN ANTON,** Cheyney Univ Of Pa, Cheyney, PA; JR; BA; Tennis 88-; Outstanding Acdmc Achvmnt Awds 89-; Back Yark Bowl Awd; Communications Arts; Social Worker.

**WILBURN, MONICA M,** Al St Univ, Montgomery, AL; FR; BS; Cmptr/Info Sci; Prgrmmg.

**WILBURN, PAMELA J,** Garrett Comm Coll, Mchenry, MD; FR; BA; Stdnt Govt Treas Elect; Biolgy; Med Lab Tech/Bio Sci.

**WILBURN, RHONDA M,** Hiwassee Coll, Madisonville, TN; FR; BA; PTK Clb; Phi Theta Kappa; Indvdl Math Achvmnt Awrd; Fr Hghst Grds Awrd; Biolgy; Phrmcy.

**WILCHER, PATRICIA L,** Meridian Comm Coll, Meridian, MS; FR; BS; Nrsng.

**WILCOX, DAWNA L,** Elms Coll, Chicopee, MA; JR; BA; Art Thrpy Clb 90-; Actvts Cncl GCC 88-90; Natl Hon Scty 87-90; Vlybl 88-89; Hly Trnty Nrsry Sch 87; Dgrnfld Comm Chld Care Ctr 89; Holyoke Hosp Psychtrc Unt 90; Natl Assc Ed Yng Chldrn 90-; AS Greenfield Comm Clg 90-; AA Greenfield Comm Clg 90; Art Thrpy; Soc Svc.

**WILCOX, EDWARD GARRETT,** Clarkson Univ, Potsdam, NY; JR; BS; Sigma Delta 90-; Indstrl Mrktg; Sales.

**WILCOX, JENNETTA D,** Norfolk St Univ, Norfolk, VA; FR; IM Bsltbl; Acctng; CEO.

**WILCOX, JENNIFER L,** S U N Y Coll At Fredonia, Fredonia, NY; SO; BED; Orchesis Dnc Grp 89-; Elem Ed; Tchr.

**WILCOX, JOHN D,** Western New England Coll, Springfield, MA; SO; Tutor Math 111/Math 112 90-; Quantitative Methods.

**WILCOX, JULIE E,** Wv Univ At Parkersburg, Parkersburg, WV; FR; BED; Deans List 90-; Employed Citizens Natl Bank 84-89; Cert Bradford Bus Schl 84; Elem Ed; Teacher Jr High.

**WILCOX, LEANN,** Indiana Univ Of Pa, Indiana, PA; JR; BED; Sign Lang Clb 88-; Operation Uplift 88; Visiting Aged 88; Vrsty Chrldr 87; Parents Advocacy Grp; Edn Excptnl.

**WILCOX, LESLIE K,** Radford Univ, Radford, VA; SO; BS; Xmas Unprvlgd Kids 90; Psychlgy/Engl; Educ.

**WILCOX, PAMELA E,** Fisk Univ, Nashville, TN; JR; BS; Delta Mu Delta Treas 90-; Mrtr Brd; Alpha Kappa Alpha; Fncl Mgmt; Hlth Care Admn.

**WILCOX, SHARON A,** Saint Joseph Coll, West Hartford, CT; SR; BA; Ltrgcl Chr Pres 89-; Drm Pres 90-; Chr 89-90; Kappa Gamma Pi 90-; St Catherine Mdl 89-90; Tr Gds; RA 89-; Nwspr Intrn Ed Chf 90-; Arts Ctr Dvlpmnt Intrn 90-; Clrs Wrs 88-; Eng; Arts Mgmt.**

**WILCOX, SHAWN J,** S U N Y Coll At Fredonia, Fredonia, NY; JR; BS; Bio; Vet Med.

**WILCOX, SUSAN M,** Ashland Comm Coll, Ashland, KY; SO; BA; SGA Pres 89-; Drg Inf Unt Div Peer Edctr 90-; Deans List; Brdcst Jrnlsm; Law.

**WILCOX JR, WILLIAM R,** Castleton St Coll, Castleton, VT; JR; BA; Glgy Soc Castleton Pres 88-; Stdnt Assn Sntr/Fin Bd; Envrnmntl Grp 88-90; Phi Eta Sigma 88-89; Alpha Chi; Ricky Mezatta Awd 88-89; Coaches Awd-Athlt Yr 89-90; Mst Vlbl Skier Alpine Div I Ski Tm 88-89; Glgy; Envrnmntl Sci.

**WILCOXON, SHERRY L,** Spalding Univ, Louisville, KY; GD; BS; Bsns Orgnztn Spldng Stdnts Tres 90-; Phi Theta Kappa 87-; Delta Epsilon Sigma 90-; Ntnl Cngrs Prnts Tchr Assn 87-; Amnsty Intrntnl 90-; AA Jffrsn Comm Clg 88; BS; Bsns Admnstrtn; Hmn Rsrc Mgmnt.

**WILCZYNSKI, JOHN D,** Univ Of Akron, Akron, OH; JR; BS; AM Society Mchncl Eng; Varsity Basktbll Co-Captain 87; Mchnl Eng; Eng.

**WILDER, ANNETTE LAVELL,** Pellissippi St Tech Comm Coll, Knoxville, TN; SO; AS; Phi Theta Kappa 90-; Co/Op Pgm; Office Syst Tech; Med Office.

**WILDER, CAROLYN F,** Sue Bennett Coll, London, KY; FR; BA; Phi Theta Kappa; Nrsng; RN.

**WILDER, CHARLES P,** Southern Coll Of Tech, Marietta, GA; SO; BA; Mech Eng Tech; Eng In Trans.

**WILDER, ELYSIA L,** Univ Of Tn At Martin, Martin, TN; SO; BA; Nrsng Sci.

**WILDER, OLWYN D,** Ky St Univ, Frankfort, KY; JR; BA; Mrchng Thorobred Band Co-Capt 90-; Flag Corp; Hunter Hall Club Treas 90-; Intrnshp USDA Clerk 90; Dns Lst 90; Bsn Admin.

**WILDES, SIMONE S,** Barry Univ, Miami, FL; JR; BS; Sci Clb 90-; Jamaican Assoc 90-; Hnr Soc 90-; Beta Bet A Beta 90-; Phi Theta Kappa 88-90; Pathfinder Clb 89-; Miami Dade Cmnty Clg 89; Bio; MA Ph D.

**WILDFEVER, SUSAN M,** Boston Univ, Boston, MA; SR; Occptnl Thrpy Clb 89-; Stdnt Gvmt Sec 88-89; Binai Brith Hillel Hse 87-; BS; Occptnl Therapy.

**WILDING, MICHAEL A,** Methodist Coll, Fayetteville, NC; SO; BS; Res Offcr Trng Corp; Assoc U S Army; Pol Sci; Military.

**WILDMAN, GAIL A,** Neumann Coll, Aston, PA; SO; BSN; SNA 90-; Stdnt Adv Fac; Nrsng.

**WILDMAN, KENNETH R,** Kent St Univ Kent Cmps, Kent, OH; SR; BA; Soc Hmn Res Mgrs Natl Fnds Coord 90-; Soccer; AAS Bsn Mgmt Cazenovia Clg 88; AAS Indpndt Studies Cazenovia Clg 88; Hmn Res Mgmt; Indstrl Hmn Res.

**WILDMAN, WINSOME SANDRA,** S U N Y Hlth Sci Cent Brooklyn, Brooklyn, NY; SR; BSN; RN; RN Cerfit 78-; Sci; Nursing.

**WILDS, LAURINDA A,** Indiana Univ Of Pa, Indiana, PA; SR; BSEE; Proj Stride 89-90; Natl Dns Lst 89-90; Otstndng Stdnt Tchr 90-; Elem Educ.

**WILE, MERRIDETH A,** Columbia Union Coll, Takoma Park, MD; FR; BA; Pro Musica 90-; Phi Eta Sigma 90-; Theta Alpha Beta 90-; Psych/Theology; Cnslng/Pstrng.

**WILEN, DAWN E,** Glassboro St Coll, Glassboro, NJ; JR; BA; Std Actv Brd 89-; Std Tutor Cntr 90-; Play/Spprtng Role 88; Dns Lst 89-; Dns Lst 90; Law/Jstc.

**WILENSKY, DEBORAH,** Atlantic Union Coll, S Lancaster, MA; SO; BS; Vrsty Vlybl Atlantic Union Clg 89; Sci; Physcl Thrpst.

**WILES, ALLISON M,** Oh Univ, Athens, OH; SO; BA; Alpha Lambda Delta 90-; Phi Sigma Sigma VP; Kappa Phi Serv Chrmn 90-; Comm Vol Corps 89-; Psych; Psychlgst.

**WILES, JEFF L,** Belmont Coll, Nashville, TN; SO; BS; Tri Beta Tr 90-; BSU 89-; Cls Tr 90-; Vandrblt Res Trng Pgm; IM Bwlng Tm Capt 90-; Bio; Professr.

**WILES, JILL M,** Univ Of Cincinnati, Cincinnati, OH; SO; BA; Bus Tribunal/Chf Justice Of Jdcl Cmmssn 90-; Appeals Brd/ Advisor 90-; IM Vlybl/Track 90-; Acctg.

**WILES, KERRI L,** Defiance Coll, Defiance, OH; JR; BS; Alpha Chi 90-; Psi Chi; Gamma Omega Kappa Pres 89-; Indstrl Psychlogy.

**WILES, MARION M,** Univ Of Va Clinch Valley Coll, Wise, VA; SR; BS; Assoc Comp Mach Sec 90-; Marion Amy Wiles Mem Cir 88-; Comp Inf Sys; Prog.

**WILES, MARTIN W,** Fl Baptist Theological Coll, Graceville, FL; SR; HB; Theolby; Pastr/Tchr.

**WILES, MARY J,** Gaston Coll, Dallas, NC; FR; AA; PTO Chrryvll Grade Schls Chrmn Prjcts Com 85-89; Frst Untd Mthdst Chrch 84-; Bus Admin/Mgmt.

**WILEY, ANNA H,** New Comm Coll Of Baltimore, Baltimore, MD; SO; BA; Emplyee Mnth 85; Tchr Prnt Asc 89-90; Prsnnl Asst; Bsn Admn; Bsn/Hmn Rscs.

**WILEY, DONETTA M,** Belmont Coll, Nashville, TN; FR; BBA; Bapt Stdnt Unn 90-; Acctng And Comps; Acctng.

**WILEY, MERRY E,** Norfolk St Univ, Norfolk, VA; SR; BA; Spec Asst To Professor Mass Cmmnctns 88-; USAF 82-86; VA Air Natl Gd 88-; Hnr Rl 88-89; Dns Lst 90-; Mass Comm; Law.

**WILEY, ROBIN C,** Va St Univ, Petersburg, VA; FR; BA; Hnrs Coll; Awrd Hghst GPA; Scl Wrk.

**WILEY, SCOTT P,** Univ Of Ky, Lexington, KY; JR; BS; ADFPA 90-; Sigma Xi 88-; Rsrch Grnt Holcmb Rsrch Inst Butlr Univ 86-87; Trcks Field Lttrmn 87-88; Primry Lab Tech 90-; BS Butler Univ 88; Phrmcy; Grad Schl.

**WILEY, SHARON E,** Emory & Henry Coll, Emory, VA; FR; BA; Cmps Chrstn Fllwshp 90-; Stdnts Poole/Envrnmntl Cncrns Treas 90-; Emory/Henry Chapel Choir 90-91; Alpha Psi Omega; Alpha Phi Omega; Habitat For Humanity Treas 90-91; Hist.

**WILEY, SHERRY D,** Alcorn St Univ, Lorman, MS; SO; BS; Gspl Chr 89-90; Bptst Stdnt Un 90-; Prayer Bnd 90-; Unv Hnr Stdnts Orgnztn 89-; Biology Pre Optometry; Eye Care.

**WILEY, TROY L,** Norfolk St Univ, Norfolk, VA; SR; BS; YMCA 88-; USAF 81-87; VA Air Natl Grd 87-; Spartan Tau Mu 88-89; Hnr Roll 88-89; Alpha Kappa Mu 89-; Deans Lst 89-; Elec Tech; Elec Engnrng.

**WILFONG, KRISTIN L,** Western New England Coll, Springfield, MA; SR; BA; Sr Cls Ofcr Sec 90-; Grdtn Cmte Sec 90-; Yrbk Stf 90-; Hstry Intrnshp Chldrns Msm Holyoke Ma; Hstry.

**WILFONG, RHONDA D,** John C Calhoun St Comm Coll, Decatur, AL; FR; ASSOC; Prlgl.

**WILHAM JR, LARRY G,** Berea Coll, Berea, KY; SO; IMS 90-; Math; Tchr.**

**WILHAM, MELISSA A,** Berea Coll, Berea, KY; SR; BA; House Cncl Flr Rep 87-88; SGA Sntr 89; Vincit Qui Pititor; Bsktbl 87-88; Engl Educ; Tch Sec Engl.**

**WILHELM, DEBORAH L,** Comm Coll Algny Co Algny Cmps, Pittsburgh, PA; SR; AS; Mtn Vly Trail Riders 87-; AAS 86; AS; Nrsg.

**WILHELM, JEFFREY W,** Southeastern Coll Of Hlth Sci, N Miami Beach, FL; JR; BS; Phi Theta Kappa Hstrn 85-87; Deans Lst 90; AS 84; AA 87; Phrmcy.

**WILHELM, JONNI SUE,** Salisbury St Univ, Salisbury, MD; SR; BSW; Cmps Crusade For Christ Ldr 87-; Bible Study Ldr 90-; Soc Wrk 89-; Soc Wrk Hnr Soc 90-; Intrnshp Nrsg Home 90-; BS 88; Soc Wrk; Gerontology.

**WILHELM, KRISTINE M,** Cornell Univ Statutory College, Ithaca, NY; JR; BS; Stdnt Hrsmns Assoc VP 90-; Co Chair 90; Morrison Animal Sci Awd 89-; Deans List 89-91; Asst Plnt Path Rsrch Lab 89-; Animal Sci; Equine.

**WILHELM, MARIETTA L,** City Univ Of Ny City Coll, New York, NY; SR; BS; Amer Inst Arch 88-; Ntl Trst Hstrc Prsrvtn 77-; Arch League NY 88-; Gldn Key Jr Yr 89-; Deans Lst 89-; Amer Coll Schlrshp Fund 90; AIA/AAF Schrlshp 90; AIA Schlrshp 90; Gen Mtrs Schlrshp 90-; AIA 76-; Cert 76; Arch; Slr/ Envrnmnt Rsrch.

**WILHELM, NICOLE C,** Univ Of Nc At Asheville, Asheville, NC; FR; BA; Grmn/Intl Bus.

**WILHELM, RENEE A,** Univ Of Cincinnati, Cincinnati, OH; SO; Bnd; Alpha Lambda Delta; Orgnst Chrch 87-; Yng Lf Ldr; Trck; Spcl Educ; Tchg.

**WILK, JUDITH M,** Univ Of Cin R Walters Coll, Blue Ash, OH; AD; Rdlgc Tchnlgy; Med.

**WILKE, STACY A,** Univ Of South Fl, Tampa, FL; JR; BA; SGA 88-90; Bus Clb Pres 90-; Univ Pgm Stdnt Assc VP 90-; Phi Beta Lambda 88-; Gldn Gavel Awd 89; Future Bus Exec Scnd Pl; AA Manatee Comm Coll 90; Business Mgmt; Pre Schl Owner.**

**WILKENS, RALPH L,** New Comm Coll Of Baltimore, Baltimore, MD; SO; AA; Pres Recgntn Schlrshp Award 90; Distngshd Schlr Award 90-; Mntl Hlth Technlgy Curriclm Award; NAACP 89-; St Patricis Of Assisi 90-; US Pstl Polc Ofcr 88-; Mentl Hlth; Appld Psychlgy.

**WILKERSON, ANGELA L,** Concordia Coll, Selma, AL; FR; BA; Res Cross; Emerg Med Svc Bd; Emerg Mgmt Agcy Dir 88-; Psych; Cnslr.

**WILKERSON, GINA L,** Spalding Univ, Louisville, KY; JR; BA; Stdnt Govt Stdnt Actvts Bd 88-; AVANTI; Spldng Ambsdrs 88-; SADD 88-89; Vol Spec Olympc; Vol Spkr HS Stdnts; MAC Mrt Awd Wnr 89-90; IM Vlybl 89-; MAC Fnlst Acad Hon 89-; St Cthrns Mtl 90-; Art/Psych; Art Thrpy.

**WILKERSON, HEATHER E,** Catawba Valley Comm Coll, Hickory, NC; JR; Educ Assoc; Educ; Tchrs Asstnt.

**WILKERSON, KIMBERLY A,** Ky Wesleyan Coll, Owensboro, KY; JR; BS; Pltcl Sci Clb; FCA; Wesleyan Singers; Oak Ivy; Pre Prfsnl Soc Tres; Sigma Kappa Jr Rep; Ambsdr; Chem Biology; Pharmacy.

**WILKERSON, LORRAINE D,** Lincoln Univ, Lincoln Univ, PA; SO; BS; Acctng Clb; Alpha Kappa Alpha; Dns Lst; Acctng; CPA.

**WILKERSON, ROBERT CURTIS,** Meridian Comm Coll, Meridian, MS; FR; Phi Beta Lambda Prlmntrn 90-; Computer Tech; Programming.

**WILKERSON, SHANNON R,** Univ Of Tn At Martin, Martin, TN; FR; Chi Omega Chi Chr Chrmn; Dns Lst High Hnrs.

**WILKERSON, TAMMY L,** East Central Comm Coll, Decatur, MS; FR; Phi Theta Kappa.

**WILKES, DEBORAH S,** Duquesne Univ, Pittsburgh, PA; GD; MBA; Amer Instit Chemical Engrs 86-88; Natl Assoc MBA Wmn 90-; MBAA 90-; Grad Assisthp 90-; BS Che Pennsylvania Univ 88; Mgt MBA; Engrg.

**WILKES, LISA E,** Auburn Univ At Auburn, Auburn, AL; JR; BS; Kappa Omicron Nu; Crdnl Key; Prgnt Teens Vol Abuse Sfhs Shltr Vol 90-; East AL Mdcl Cntr Chld Lf Spclst 90-; Eglston Chldrns Hsptl Atlanta; Camp Smile A Mile Chldrn Cancer; Family Chld Dvlpmnt; Chld Lf Spclst.

**WILKES III, LUTHER M,** Ga Southern Univ, Statesboro, GA; JR; BSM; Math Assoc Of Amer 89-; Gamma Beta Phi 90-; Pi Sigma Epsilon 89-; Math.**

**WILKES, MICHELLE M,** East Stroudsburg Univ, E Stroudsburg, PA; JR; BA; Spch Comm Asc Pres 88-; Spch Comm Asc PA Rep 90-; Strd Crr Nwspr Stf Wrtr 89-; Natl Hnr Soc 90-; Natl Hnrs Frat VP 90-; Sigma Tau Delta 90-; Spec Oly Ski Cch 83-; Red Crs Instctr 89-; Choir 85-; Intshp 90; Bill Cerny Mem Schlp 90; Ornttn Ast; IM; Engl/Spch Comm; Pblc Rltns.

**WILKES, REGINA R,** Clayton St Coll, Morrow, GA; SO; BA; Deans List 88; Schlstc Achvmnt Awrd 90; Eng; Writer.

**WILKES, RICHARD L,** Univ Of Tn At Knoxville, Knoxville, TN; FR; BA; Stdnt Cncl 90-; Nwspr Staff Ed Clmnst 90-; Phi Beta Sigma Fash Show Model; Intrnshp APL Mgr Trnee 90-; IM Bsktbl 90; Gen Bus; Entrepreneur.

**WILKES, SHIRLEY W,** Middle Ga Coll, Cochran, GA; SO; MBA; AS 88 CCAF 88; Bus Admin; Mgmnt.

**WILKIE, LINDA M,** Johnson St Coll, Johnson, VT; SR; BS; AQHA 87-; VQHA 87-; MQHA 88-; Deans Lst 90; Pres Lst 90-; Sub Tchr 73-; Educ/Early Chldhd Crrclm; Tchr.

**WILKIE, RONALD S,** Piedmont Tech Coll, Greenwood, SC; GD; BS; Bsn.

**WILKIE, SHERRY J,** Isothermal Comm Coll, Spindale, NC; FR; Rdlgy Prgm Hndbk Rvsn Cmmtt; Deans Lst 90; Rdlgy; Rdlgc Tchnlgst.**

**WILKIE, SUSAN L,** Christopher Newport Coll, Newport News, VA; SR; BA; Psi Chi 90-; Dept Hons 90-; AS Thomas Nelson Comm Coll 88; Elem Ed; Tchr.

**WILKIN, PHILLIP T,** Univ Of Cincinnati, Cincinnati, OH; FR; Mountnrng Clb V P 88-; Mdl Ralrdng Clb Fndg Fathr; Inst Elec Elec Eng 90-; Gama Alpha; M Rowe Moore Adm Dist; Eagl Sct; Elec Eng Tech; Eng.

**WILKING, BART T,** Univ Of Pittsburgh, Pittsburgh, PA; SO; BS; Univ Hnrs Clg; Sigma Chi 89-; Mech Engr.

**WILKINS, BRYAN S,** Wallace St Comm Coll At Selma, Selma, AL; SO; BS; U S Achvmt Acdmy All-Am Schlr 90-; Agri; Farming.

**WILKINS, CAROLYN A,** Univ Of Sc At Columbia, Columbia, SC; JR; BA; Amer Mktg Assn 90-; Yng Rpblcns Clb 87-88; Acctg; Actnt.

**WILKINS, DONNA K,** Fl A & M Univ, Tallahassee, FL; FR; BS; Phi Eta Sigma Chrprsn Comm Svc Proj; Alpha Ldrshp Schlrshp 90-; Ruby Diamond Schlrshp; Cert Schlrshp FAMU Hsng Dept 90-; Phrmcy.

**WILKINS, DORNSWALO M,** Univ Of Nc At Charlotte, Charlotte, NC; SO; BA; Blck Stdnt Un 89-; Able Cmmtr Rep 89-90; Gspl Chr 89-90; Englsh; Jrnlst.

**WILKINS, DOUGLAS K,** Union Coll, Barbourville, KY; JR; BA; Iota Sigma; All Dstrct All Cnvrnc Vrsty Bsktbll; Athlts In Actn; Bus Admn; Bus Mgmt.

**WILKINS, HEATHER D,** Univ Of Tn At Martin, Martin, TN; SO; BS; Intrfth Cntr Scl Coord; RA; Phi Eta Sigma; Wildlife Biology; Biologist.

**WILKINS, KATHERINE E,** Comm Coll Of Beaver County, Monaca, PA; GD; AAS; Tau Pi Rho Bp 89-90; Stdnt Fclty Brd Rep 90-; Ntnl Colgt Nrsng Awrd 90-; Amrcn Rd Crs Vlntr 90-; Elwd Ctys Dysprng Pryr & Prs Chldrns Mnstry Chrprsn 89-; Nrsng; Nrs Prctnr.

**WILKINS, MARVA L,** City Univ Of Ny City Coll, New York, NY; SO; BA; Mnhtn Psych Cntr Soc Wrk Asst; Hmn Serv; Scl Wrk.

**WILKINS, MARY E,** Tidewater Comm Coll, Portsmouth, VA; SO; AS; PTA; Phone A Thon; Black Hist Mnth Coord; Career Day Spkr; Boys Club Cmptr Instrctr 88-; Rsrch Sys Analyst 82-; Cert Electronic Cmptr Prgmng Inst 88; Cmptr Sci.

**WILKINS, MICHAEL G,** Surry Comm Coll, Dobson, NC; FR; AS; Acctng Tech; Acctng.

**WILKINS, SCOTT M,** Bridgewater Coll, Bridgewater, VA; SO; BS; IM Sftbl 89-; Bus Admin.

**WILKINS, TAMMY R,** Patrick Henry Comm Coll, Martinsville, VA; FR; Nrsng.

**WILKINS, WENDY C,** Vance Granville Comm Coll, Henderson, NC; FR; BA; Bsns; CPA.

**WILKINSON, DAVID A,** Wv Northern Comm Coll, Wheeling, WV; SO; BA; Tmstrs Local 697; Bsn Admn.

**WILKINSON, GUYLA B,** Methodist Coll, Fayetteville, NC; JR; BS; Pvt Tutor 90-; Bus Drvr Pine Forest Sr Hgh 86-; Tchr Aide Summer Sch 89-; Elem Ed; Tchr.

**WILKINSON, JILL C,** Glassboro St Coll, Glassboro, NJ; JR; BA; Spnsh Clb Pres 89-; Deans Lst; Spnsh Tchr 90-; Co-Op Prog Tchr; Dominican Repl Nanny; Spnsh Tchr John H Glenn Elem Schl 90; Acctg 86-90; Spnsh; Govt/DEA/FBI.

**WILKINSON, KAREN J,** Roane St Comm Coll, Harriman, TN; JR; BS; Biology; Nursing.

**WILKINSON, KEVIN D,** Gaston Coll, Dallas, NC; SR; ASSOC; Auto Mchnc.

**WILKINSON, MARK A,** Emory & Henry Coll, Emory, VA; SO; BS; Pre Med Soc 89-; Emory/Henry Hnr Soc 89-90; Chem; Med.

**WILKOSZ, MARGARET Z,** Al A & M Univ, Normal, AL; FR; BS; Math Clb 89-90; Hlth Sci Clb 90; Deans Lst 90; Mnstry Clb 89-91; Ntrtn; Rgstrd Dietician.

**WILKS, CRYSTAL R,** New Comm Coll Of Baltimore, Baltimore, MD; SR; AABSN; Nursing.

**WILLARD, BETSY L,** Univ Of Rochester, Rochester, NY; SR; BS; Intervar Christian Fllwshp 87; Silvertones Flute Choir 87; Tau Beta Pi; Chem Eng; Eng.

**WILLARD, JENNIFER L,** Univ Of Miami, Coral Gables, FL; SR; BA; Goldn Key; Psi Chi; Phi Kapa Phi; AA Broward Comm Clg 89; Psych; Law.

**WILLAUER, ROBERT M,** Marshall University, Huntington, WV; SR; BA; Vllybll Clb; Alpha Sigma Pmi 87-; Sccr 87-; Fnc Mgmt.

**WILLCUTT, JUDY H,** Univ Of South Al, Mobile, AL; SR; BED; Alpha Chi; S S Tchr Turnerville Bapt Ch; Sub Tchr; Scndry Edn/Soc Sci Comp; Educator.

**WILLCUTT, LORITA R,** Brewer St Jr Coll, Fayette, AL; SO; BS; Elem Educ.

**WILLEMSEN, SUSAN M,** Univ Of Miami, Coral Gables, FL; SR; BSN; Phi Kappa Phi 90-; RN Mercy Hosp Infection Cntrl Miami FL; Rn Dip Norwalk Hosp School Of Nrsng 74; Nrsng.

**WILLENBORG, LAURA J,** Univ Of Sc At Columbia, Columbia, SC; SR; BS; Cath Org 89-90; Phi Beta Kappa 89-; Golden Key 89-; Gamma Beta Phi 88-; Beta Beta Beta Treas 88-; Delta Gamma Rtls Chr 88-; Angel Flight Treas 89-; Hmecmng Ct 90; Bio; Med.

**WILLENBROCK, TRICIA M,** Teikyo Post Univ, Waterbury, CT; SR; BS; Amer Mktg Assn 90-; Mktg.

**WILLETT, ANNA I,** Cornell Univ, Ithaca, NY; FR; BS; Red Carpet Soc 90-; Cornell Greens; Deans Lst 90-; Crew Tm 90-; Bio Engr.

**WILLETT, JOSEPH P,** Savannah Coll Of Art & Design, Savannah, GA; FR; BA; Archt; Lic Architect.

**WILLETT, MARY A,** Owensboro Comm Coll, Owensboro, KY; FR; BS; Elem Ed.

**WILLETT, WENDY A,** Georgetown Univ, Washington, DC; SR; BA; Invstmnt Allnce Pres 89; Admssns Cmmttee Vtng Mbr 90; Intrnshp W/Sntr Carl Levin Leg Asst Aide 90; Fnce/Intrntl Mngmnt.

**WILLETTE, GERALD J,** Albertus Magnus Coll, New Haven, CT; SR; MA; Deans List 90; Deans List Middlesex Comm Clg 80-83; Machnst/Free Lane Wrtr Loc Magz; AS Mddlesex Comm Clg 83; Comm; Motion Pictur Ind.

**WILLETTE, JENNIFER L,** Comm Coll Algny Co Algny Cmps, Pittsburgh, PA; SO; BA; Pittsburgh Action Against Rope Hotline Cnslr 90-; Anthropology; Paleoanthropology.

**WILLETTE, TIMOTHY D,** Univ Of Al At Huntsville, Huntsville, AL; JR; BSE; Co Op Gnrl Elctrc 89-; Vrsty Tnns NCAA Div 87-88; Mech Eng; Dsgn Engr.

**WILLEY, BETH-ANN,** Johnson St Coll, Johnson, VT; SR; BA; Msc Educ Ntl Conf Pres 87-88, 90; Intrvar Chrstn Flwshp VP 90-; Chesamore 88-; Outstdng Coll Stdnts Am 90-; All-Am Schlr; Fac/Stf Shclrshp 90-; Alumni Schlrshp 89-; Tlnt Schlrshp 87-; Msc Educ.

**WILLEY, CHARLENE D,** Kent St Univ Kent Cmps, Kent, OH; GD; MLS; Beta Phi Mu; Ohio Libr Assn; BS Ohio St Univ 67; MS Purdue Univ 72; Libr Sci; Info Spec.

**WILLEY, KATHERINE D,** Hudson Valley Comm Coll, Troy, NY; SO; AAS; Pres Lst 87-; Brd Mmbr Of NY St Tax 90-; Exmnrs Assn; Tx Tech Trnee; Acctng; Tax Adtng.

**WILLHIDE, ROBYN L,** Longwood Coll, Farmville, VA; FR; Res Hall Cncl Pblcty Chrprsn 90-; ASSET 90-; Frshman Hall Of Fame 90-; Alpha Gamma Delta Pldg Class Pres 90-; U S Achvmnt Academy Recog; IM Flag Ftbal/Aerobics; Psychology/Spec Educ; Spec Educ Tchr.

**WILLIAM, DANIEL R,** Le Moyne Coll, Syracuse, NY; JR; BA; Acctg Soc 88-; IM Referee 89-; Deans Lst 89-; Big Bro/Sis Pgm; Intrnshp Bennett Fndng Grp Inc 90-; IM Bsktbl/Soccer/Ftbl 88-; Publ Acctnt.

**WILLIAMS ANDERSON, ANGELICA Y,** Alcorn St Univ, Lorman, MS; FR; Chrldr; Mdlng Clb; Bapt Union; Engl Pre Law; Law Crmnl Atty.

**WILLIAMS, AARON S,** Morehouse Coll, Atlanta, GA; SR; BA; Clg Bsn Assoc 88; Engl Clb 89; Kappa Alpha Psi V P/Secr 87; Engl.

**WILLIAMS, ABRAM B,** Central Al Comm Coll, Alexander City, AL; FR; AD; Chrmn Drug Prog 90-; Soc; Drug Cnslr.

**WILLIAMS, ADRIENNE M,** Coll Of Charleston, Charleston, SC; SO; BA; Stu Almn Assn 90-; Hnrs Prog Stu Sec 89-; Hnrs Prog 89-; Hstry.

**WILLIAMS, ALI D,** Alcorn St Univ, Lorman, MS; SO; BA; Cmptr Sci Clb; Cmptr Sci; Prgrmr.

**WILLIAMS, ALYCE R,** Oh St Univ At Newark, Newark, OH; JR; BS; Cncl Tchrs Math 90-; OH Cncl Tchrs Math 90-; Math Educ; Tchng Scndry Math.

**WILLIAMS, AMY J,** Univ Of Fl, Gainesville, FL; SR; BS; Pi Beta Phi Fratl Exce Chrmn 89-90; Panhaellenic Delegate 89-90; Assist Rush Chrmn 89-90; Deans List; Amer Mktng Assoc 89-; Retail Intshp 90; Tchng Assist Principles Mktng 90-; IM Ftbl 88-; Mktng; Sales.

**WILLIAMS, AMY L,** Al A & M Univ, Normal, AL; FR; BA; Deans Lst; Biology; Med.

**WILLIAMS, AMY REBECCA,** Auburn Univ At Auburn, Auburn, AL; FR; Gymnstc Clb 90-; Sprt Cmmtt SGA 90-; Angl Flght Cmps Crsd 90-; Bld Drv Vol; Vol Wlk Amer; Educ; Tchr.

**WILLIAMS, ANDREA B,** Wilberforce Univ, Wilberforce, OH; FR; BA; Appld Sclgy; Scl Rsch.

**WILLIAMS, ANGELA CAROL,** Ms St Univ, Miss State, MS; SR; BA; Stu Assc Intrr Dsgnrs Mmbrshp Chrprsn 88-; Cmptr Sci Clb 87-88; Zeta Tau Alpha 87-; Nrsng Hm Mnstrs 87-88; Intrr Dsgn.

**WILLIAMS, ANGELA R,** Alcorn St Univ, Lorman, MS; FR; BA; Prayer Band 90-; Bapt Un 90-; Gospel Choir 90-; HSO 90-; Cmunctns; Jrnlsm.

**WILLIAMS, ANITA M,** Memphis St Univ, Memphis, TN; JR; BS; Act Cncl 88-90; Peer Mntr Pgm 88-89; Mnrty Schlrshp Awd 88-89; Bio; Dr.

**WILLIAMS, ANN L,** Juniata Coll, Huntingdon, PA; CERT; Delta Imicron Musc Sor 68; NEA PSEA 71; MENC 90; Elem Educ Tchr Bnd Dir; BED Ind Univ Penna 71; MED Penn St Univ 76; Erly Chldhd Educ; Mus Tchr.

**WILLIAMS, ANTHONY,** Norfolk St Univ, Norfolk, VA; SR; AGC 88; Kappa Alpha Psi 90; Inroads 87-89; Toyota Ldrshp Awd 90; Ftbl Capt 87.

**WILLIAMS, ANTHONY L,** Central St Univ, Wilberforce, OH; SR; BS; Bus Mgmnt; Hmn Rsrc Mgr.

**WILLIAMS, ANTOINETTE,** Thomas Nelson Comm Coll, Hampton, VA; FR; BA; SGA Vol; Phi Theta Kappa; Std Hlpng Std Pgm Vol; Cmptr Sci/Bsn Admn; Cmptr Anlyst.

**WILLIAMS, APRIL R,** Va St Univ, Petersburg, VA; SR; Hotel/Rest Mgmnt Clb 90-; NJ Pre-Alumni; Harrahs Marria Hotel Casino Intrnshp; Natl Rest Assoc Cert 90-; Outstndng First Yr Res Asst Awrd 88-; Hotel/Rest Mngmnt.

**WILLIAMS, ARETHA ANN,** Univ Of Southern Ms, Hattiesburg, MS; JR; BS; Resdnt Asst 89-; Gamma Beta Phi 90-; Schlstc Achvmnt Award From Afro Amercn Stdnt Org 90-; Psychlgy; Cnslr/Law Or Psychlgy.

**WILLIAMS, ARLEEN G,** City Univ Of Ny City Coll, New York, NY; JR; Newspapr Cpy Edtr; Brdcstng Intrnshp At WABC-TV; Cmmnctns; Brdcst Jrnlsm.

**WILLIAMS, ARNIE L,** Northern Ky Univ, Highland Hts, KY; SR; BS; ALC Legal Scty VP 87-88; Ec; Law.

**WILLIAMS, BECKY JO,** Beckley Coll, Beckley, WV; FR; BA; USN E5 84-88; Nvl Rsrve E5 89; Sailor Of Qtr; Annl Evltns Awd 86; Pol Sci/Paralegal; Law/Pltcl.

**WILLIAMS, BETTY B,** Norfolk St Univ, Norfolk, VA; BA; Art Educ.

**WILLIAMS, BOBBY L,** Crichton Coll, Memphis, TN; SR; BS; Ordained Minister 81-; Assoc 71-73; Psychology.

**WILLIAMS, BONITA T,** Coppin St Coll, Baltimore, MD; SO; BA; Acctg Sprvsr; Acctg; CPA.

**WILLIAMS, BRAD A,** Anne Arundel Comm Coll, Arnold, MD; SO; BA; Busn; Mngmt.

**WILLIAMS, BRIAN A,** Norfolk St Univ, Norfolk, VA; FR; BS; DNIMAS Assn 90-; Ist Of Elctrcl/Elctrnc Engr 90-; Pblcty Comm Of SGA 90-; Spartan Alpha Tau; Outstndng DNIMAS Stdnt; Dns Lst; IM Ftbl 90; Physcs; Ed/Engr.

**WILLIAMS, BRIDGETTE D,** Va Union Univ, Richmond, VA; JR; SSJ Sec 89-; NABSW 89-; Wmns Flwshp Pres 90-; Comm Schlrs 90-; Ldrshp Awd 89-; Mnrty Enrlmnt Grad Stds Prog Asstshp 90; Socl Wrk; Adlscnt/Fmly Cnslr.

**WILLIAMS, CASSANDRA B,** Faulkner Univ, Montgomery, AL; SO; SGA Tr 90-; Chrstn Womn Actn Pr 89-; SAEA 90-; Phi Lambda VP 89-; Ldrshp Tm 89-; Elem Educ; Tchr.

**WILLIAMS, CASSANDRA F,** Tougaloo Coll, Tougaloo, MS; SO; BS; Hnrs Stdnt 89-; Alpha Kappa Alpha 90-; Coop; Ecnmcs/Bsn Adm; Exec Mngmnt.

**WILLIAMS, CHADWICK B,** Univ Of Sc At Columbia, Columbia, SC; FR; BA; Alpha Lambda Delta; Sigma Alpha Epsilon 90-; IM Sports 90-; Marketing/Sports Admnstrtn; Sports Promotor.

**WILLIAMS, CHARLES R,** Norfolk St Univ, Norfolk, VA; JR; BA; Mmbr MCSA 90; IM Bsktbll 90-; Cert 89; Mss Cmmnctns.

**WILLIAMS, CHARLOTTE L,** Christian Brothers Univ, Memphis, TN; JR; BS; Brighton ARP Chrch Sndy Schl Tchr 87-; Wmns Org Church Sec; Syst Mngr 90-; Tlcmnctns.

**WILLIAMS, CHERYL A,** Norfolk St Univ, Norfolk, VA; SO; BA; NAACP 90-; Afrcn Amer Her; Sprtn Alpha Tau 89-; Carver Fed Svgs Bk Schlrshp 89-; Ldrshp Pgm Cert 90; Alum Assn Schlrshp; Pol Sci; Law.

**WILLIAMS, CHERYL D,** Fl A & M Univ, Tallahassee, FL; SO; BA; Math Clb; Beta Eta Sigma; Cir K; Math; Educ.

**WILLIAMS, CHERYL D,** Tn St Univ, Nashville, TN; SR; BS; Nashville Assn Yng Chldrn 89-; Stdnt Assn Yng Chldrn Chrprsn 90-; 3-W Clb; Deans List 87-; Zeta Phi Beta Sec 90-; I Have A Future Meharry Med Clg Vol; Home Ec; Tchr.

**WILLIAMS, CHERYL T,** Univ Of Tn At Martin, Martin, TN; SR; BED; Stu Tenn Educ Assoc 89-; Phi Kappa Phi; Elem Educ; Spec.**

**WILLIAMS, CHERYLYNN R,** Jackson St Univ, Jackson, MS; FR; Intern MS Dem Prty Hdqrtrs; Pltcl Sci; Law.

**WILLIAMS JR, CHESTER W,** Hillsborough Comm Coll, Tampa, FL; SO; BA; AA; Computer Engrng.

**WILLIAMS, CHRISTIE B,** Abraham Baldwin Agri Coll, Tifton, GA; SO; BS ED; Panther Crk Mtn Dncrs 91; Spch/Lang Path; Educ.

**WILLIAMS, CHRISTINE M,** Meridian Comm Coll, Meridian, MS; FR; CRTT; Sci; Resp Ther.

**WILLIAMS, CHRISTOPHER B,** Memphis St Univ, Memphis, TN; FR; BA; Phi Eta Sigma; Alpha Lambda Delta; Gamma Beta Phi; Business; Accountant.

**WILLIAMS, CHRISTOPHER L,** Va Commonwealth Univ, Richmond, VA; JR; BS; Str Tm; IM Flg Ftbl Sftbl Bsktbl 89-; Psychlgy; Ind Psychlgst/Prof.

**WILLIAMS, CHRISTOPHER M,** Manhattan Coll, Bronx, NY; FR; BA; Radio Sta Music Dir 90-; Amnesty Intl Asst Pub Dir 90-; Habitat For Hmnty Schl Crdntr 90-; Engl.

**WILLIAMS, CLINT D,** Sampson Comm Coll, Clinton, NC; FR; BA; Stdnt Govt 90-; Chorus 90-; SACS Comm 90-; Fruit/Veg Prod Awd Distr/Reg/State Wnr; Bsktbl Best Offense Awd 90-; Agri/Hortcltr; Tchr.

**WILLIAMS, CORINTHIA L,** Fl A & M Univ, Tallahassee, FL; SO; BA; Soph Cncl Parlmntrn 87; Sr Congr 89; Sci Clb 87; Key Clb 87-89; Circle K 90-; Pres Schlrs 89-; Falcon Awd 88-89; Spnsh Awd 89; Elem Ed; Tchr.

**WILLIAMS, COURTNEY M,** Jackson St Univ, Jackson, MS; SO; BA; Cmnctns Clb Treas 90-; NAACP 90-; Alpha Lambda Delta; Deans Lst 89-90; Pres Lst 90-; Mass Cmnctns; Media Law.

**WILLIAMS, DANIELLE E,** Clemson Univ, Clemson, SC; SR; BS; Cntrl Spirit Dir Sls 90-; Green Ldrshp Acad Oper Chr 90; Pres Intern; Alpha Chi Omega Grk Wk Chr 90; Conf Intrn 90; IM Sccr/Sftbl 87-; Mtng Plnnrs Intrntl 90-; Park/Rec/Trsm Mgmt; Hspltlty.

**WILLIAMS, DANTE D,** Hampton Univ, Hampton, VA; FR; BS; MI Clb Prlmntrn 90-; Hnrs Drm Clb; NSBE 90-; Hnrs Clb 90-; Prce Dorm Srvce Awrd 90; Cert Of Achvmnt 90-; Elec Eng.

**WILLIAMS, DAPHNE R,** Meridian Comm Coll, Meridian, MS; SO; BS; Ldrshp Effectvness/Dev Pgm 89-90; Dns Lst; Phi Theta Kappa 90-; Psych; Psych Resrch.

**WILLIAMS, DARNISHA R,** Univ Of Tn At Martin, Martin, TN; FR; DOCTO; Chem; Phrmcy.

**WILLIAMS, DARRELL L,** Rust Coll, Holly Springs, MS; FR; BA; Army Rsrv; Rev A Herd Ldg Ryl Arch; Omega Psi Phi; Elem Educ/ROTC; Tchr.

**WILLIAMS JR, DARRELL L,** Youngstown St Univ, Youngstown, OH; SR; Amer Inst Chem Eng Pres 88-; Eng Stdnts Soc Cncl Sec 90-; IM Sprts 87-; Omega Chi Epsln VP 90-; Gold Key 88-; Vlntr Yth Ftbl Coach Head Coach 88-; Eng Deans Awd 87-; Outstndng Jr Chem Eng 89-90; Amer Inst Chem Eng Reg Awd 90; Chem Eng; Ph D.

**WILLIAMS, DARRELL M,** Valdosta St Coll, Valdosta, GA; FR; BA; Clg Dns Lst; DAR Schlrshp; Telecomms; TV Brdcstr.

**WILLIAMS, DAVID A,** Univ Of Miami, Coral Gables, FL; JR; BA; Engl Lit; SED Tch.

**WILLIAMS, DAVID E,** Va St Univ, Petersburg, VA; JR; BS; Elec Engr.

**WILLIAMS, DAVINA C,** Syracuse Univ, Syracuse, NY; SO; NYPIRG; Archtctr.

**WILLIAMS, DAWN L,** Tn Wesleyan Coll, Athens, TN; SO; BS; Math Educ.**

**WILLIAMS, DAWN MARIE,** Univ Of Sc At Columbia, Columbia, SC; SO; Gamma Beta Phi 89-; Marion Pleacher Awd 90; Cmptr/Elec Eng.

**WILLIAMS, DAYNA C,** Univ Of Sc At Columbia, Columbia, SC; JR; BS; Delta Gamma PR 88-; Discovery Cntr Intern; IM; Cmnctns.

**WILLIAMS, DEBORAH E,** Al St Univ, Montgomery, AL; JR; BS; Pre Law Soc 90-; Lambda Alpha Epsilon; Crmnl Jstc; Law.

**WILLIAMS, DEBORAH KAY,** Fayetteville St Univ, Fayetteville, NC; FR; BED; Chncllrs Lst 90; Bwlng Champ; NC Assn Tchr Assist V P 84-90; PTA Sec/Treas 85-87; Tchr Assist 84-90; Elem Educ; Tchng.

**WILLIAMS, DEBORAH L,** Rivier Coll, Nashua, NH; JR; BA; Sexual Hrssmnt Cmmttee 88; Orient Ldr Cmmttee 89-90; Rcyclng Cmmttee 90; Bsktbl 89-90; Elem Ed Spcl Ed; Tchng.

**WILLIAMS, DEBRA A,** Al A & M Univ, Normal, AL; FR; BS; Army ROTC 90-; IM Girls Bsktbl 90-; Acctng; CPA.

**WILLIAMS, DEBRA S,** West Liberty St Coll, West Liberty, WV; SR; BS; Phi Theta Kappa; Hnrs Prgrm 90-; Acdmc Schlrshp WVNCC 88-90; Media Cntr Asstnt 90-; K-Mart 90-; Chldrns Hm Wheeling 88-89; Trckstps America 79-88; Psychology; Pblc Admnstrtn.

**WILLIAMS, DELVERT L,** American Baptist Coll, Nashville, TN; SO; BA; Yrbk Ed Chf 90-; Rcrtng Stff 90-; RA 90-; Chpl Attndnc Awrd 89-; Yrbk Srvc Awrd 89; Hlpln; Cert 67; Thlgy.

**WILLIAMS, DENISE Y,** Faulkner St Jr Coll, Bay Minette, AL; SO; Phi Theta Kappa; AL New South Coalition Tres 87-90; Educ; Instr.

**WILLIAMS, DENNIS C,** Abraham Baldwin Agri Coll, Tifton, GA; SO; AS; Hort Clb Pr 90-; Thesp Clb 90-; Deans Lst 90-; Pr List 90; Hon Stdnt 90-; Adopt-A-School Pgm 90-; Asst In FFA Comptns 89-; All Amer Schlr 90-; IM Sports 89-; ASSOC Of Sci; Orn Hort; Landscape Mngmnt.

**WILLIAMS, DENNIS M,** Castleton St Coll, Castleton, VT; SO; BED; Sigma Delta Chi Hd Comm Serv 90-; Vrsty Sccr 90-; Hstry Educ; Educ Fld.

**WILLIAMS, DEVERICK B,** Al A & M Univ, Normal, AL; SO; BA; Msnc Ldg 90-; SCLC Naacp 88-; Deans Lst; Inrds Tlnt Pl Atnt GA; Wlkr Wds Mn Yr 90; Hnry Lt Col Ad De Camp 90; Engl.

**WILLIAMS, DIANE P,** Bennett Coll, Greensboro, NC; FR; BA; Intrntnl Clb Bernett Clg; US Achvmnt Acdmy; Hrns Deans Lst; Cmptr Grphcs; Grphcs Dsgnr.

**WILLIAMS, DIETRICH G,** Fl A & M Univ, Tallahassee, FL; SR; BSN; Stdnt Nrs Assn Sec 89-; Stdnt Nrs Hon Soc Pres 90-; Wht/Gld 90-; Beta Kappa Chi; Clncl Execlnc; Pres Schlr Certf; Cthdrl Awd; Nrsng.

**WILLIAMS, DONALD EARL,** Stillman Coll, Tuscaloosa, AL; SR; BA; Hightown Church Of God Pres Usher Brd 87-; Sr Yth Treas 87-; Advsr To Yth Dept; Deans Lst; Bus Admin.

**WILLIAMS, DONALD R,** Univ Of Ky, Lexington, KY; SR; BASW; Acad Excllnce Schlrshp 90; AA Prestnbrg Cmmnty Clg 78; Soc Wrk; MSW Mntl Hlth.

**WILLIAMS, DONNA G,** Oh Univ-Southern Cmps, Ironton, OH; JR; BSED; Phi Kappa Phi 90; Gamma Pi Delta 89; SS Tchr Yth Ldr; Deans Lst; Ed; Tchr.**

**WILLIAMS, DONNA L,** Radford Univ, Radford, VA; SR; BS; Bptst Stdnt Un 89-; Cncrt Bnd 89; VA Stdnt Ed Assoc; Phi Kappa Phi 90-; Kappa Delta Pi 90-; Phi Theta Kappa Pres 88-89; AAS SW VA Comm Clge 89; Ed.

**WILLIAMS, DONNA L,** Univ Of Ga, Athens, GA; SR; BSED; Kappa Delta Epsilon 90-; Kappa Delta Pi; GA Cncl Tchrs Math 90-; Gldn Key 90-; AS Ed Gainesvl Coll 89; Educ; Early Chldhd.

**WILLIAMS, DONNA L,** Hudson Valley Comm Coll, Troy, NY; SR; AA; Head Cashier/Serv Clerk Fays Drug Co; Liberal Arts.

**WILLIAMS, DOUGLAS A,** Christopher Newport Coll, Newport News, VA; SR; JV Coach Bsbl; Bthl HS Hmptn Va; Spcl Olympcs; USGA 90-; AAHPERD 90-; Deans Lst 90-; Tchg Rvrsd/Plmr Elem/Dzr Mdl Sch; US Army 76-79; NCO Acdmy 79; Jmp Sch 80; Phys Educ; Tchr.

**WILLIAMS, DRODNEY L,** Fl A & M Univ, Tallahassee, FL; SR; BS; CIS Clb 89-; Cmptr Infrmtn Systm; Systm Analysis.

**WILLIAMS, ELIZABETH C,** Mary Washington Coll, Fredericksburg, VA; FR; BS; Natl Scty Physcs Stdt 90-; Radio Brdcstr 90-; COAR Asst 90-; COAR Cmnty Outrch Serv Asst Elderly Prog 90-; Coop Ed Prog Naval Surface Warfare Cntr Stdt Trainee; Mthmtcs/Cmptr Sci; Engr.

**WILLIAMS, ELIZABETH J,** Tn Wesleyan Coll, Athens, TN; SR; AS Clvlnd St Comm Clg 80; Humn Svcs; Soc Wrk/Aertrcs.

**WILLIAMS, ELIZABETH K,** Auburn Univ At Auburn, Auburn, AL; FR; BA; Gym Kana; Alpha Lambda Delta; Elem Ed; Tchng.

**WILLIAMS, ERNEST G,** Fl A & M Univ, Tallahassee, FL; FR; PHARM; Phi Eta Sigma; Phrmcy; Med Dr.

**WILLIAMS, ERNEST L,** Al St Univ, Montgomery, AL; SO; BS; SGA 89-; Phi Eta Sigma Chpln 90-; Elks Ortrcl Awd 89; Ordnd Bapt Mnstr 89; Pres Schlr 89-; Math; Tch.

**WILLIAMS, ETHEL B,** Le Moyne Owen Coll, Memphis, TN; JR; Stdnt Cncl Co Chrmn Constn Cmt 88-89; Boy Scts Am Chickasaw Cncl Den Ldr 75-77; Clg/Cummings Elem Liaison Prsn 87-; Stdnt Cncl Sec 89-90; Deans Schlr 90-; Memphis Pblc Sch Sec Assc Chpln 90-; Memphis Pblc Sch Sec Of Yr 90; Elem Ed W/Erly Chldhd Endrsmnt; Teach.

**WILLIAMS, EUDORA K,** Univ Of Ky, Lexington, KY; SR; Air Force ROTC Vice Commander 87-; 2901 Escrt Sqdrn Drll Tm Cmmndr 87-; Stdnt Orgnztn Assembly Dlgt 89-; Gldn Key 90-; Arnold Air Soc Vice Cmmndr 87-; Dghtrs Amrcn Rvltn Awd 90-; BA; Rssn; Nvl Flght Offcr.

**WILLIAMS, EVELYN G,** Memphis St Univ, Memphis, TN; SR; BS; Chors 70-71; Kappa Delta Pi 90-; Philmathns 69-71; AA Freed-Hardeman Coll 83; Elem Ed; Tchr.**

**WILLIAMS, FRANCIS E,** Coll Of Charleston, Charleston, SC; SR; BA; Husng Auth Intrn; Soc Wrk; Acad Success Ga Sta Univ; Tae Kuon Do Clb; Aikido Clb 87-90; Pltcl Sci; Intl Rltns/Asian Afrs.

**WILLIAMS, FRANK JASON,** Schenectady County Comm Coll, Schenectady, NY; FR; Culinary Arts.

**WILLIAMS, FRED B,** Alcorn St Univ, Lorman, MS; FR; BS; Alpha Pi Omega 90-; Mrchng Cncrt Bnd 90-; Math.

**WILLIAMS JR, GEORGE B,** Ms St Univ, Miss State, MS; JR; BS; Bptst Stdnt Un Stdnt Cntr Comm 90-; Univ Hnrs Prgrm Hnrs Cncl 89-; Hnrs Cncl Nwsltr Comm 89-; Alpha Lambda Delta 90-; Mthmtcs; Mthmtcs Prfsr.

**WILLIAMS, GEORJANNE P,** Univ Of Nc At Charlotte, Charlotte, NC; SR; Pre-Law Soc 89-90; Stdnt Advsrs Fr Exclnce 87-88; Orientatn Cnslr 88; Phi Eta Sigma; Pi Sigma Alpha; Phi Beta Sigma Pres 88-90; Lgsltv Intrn 89; BA 90; Poltcl Sci; Law.

**WILLIAMS, GLENN N,** The Kings Coll, Briarclf Mnr, NY; JR; BS; Physical Therapy Internship/Therafit Inc White Plains Ny; Soccer 88-; Cross Country 89-; Physical Educ; Sports Physical Therapy.

**WILLIAMS, GREGORY A,** Alcorn St Univ, Lorman, MS; SR; Hlth/Phys Ed Clb VP 87-; Mdlng Clb 88-; HBCU 90; Pres Lst 89-90; Deans Lst 87-; Vrsty Ftbl 88-90; Phys Ed/Rec; Coll Ftbl Coach.

**WILLIAMS, HEATHER K,** Union Univ, Jackson, TN; SO; BS; Hnrs Stdnt Assoc 89; Rprsntve For Miss Union 90; Aerobics Assist 90; Elem Ed; Elem Prncpl.

**WILLIAMS, HENRY A,** Mayland Comm Coll, Spruce Pine, NC; SO; AS; Phi Theta Kappa 90-; Pres List 90-; Tennis 90-; Skiing; US Air Force 85-89; Math.

**WILLIAMS, HILARY L,** City Univ Of Ny Baruch Coll, New York, NY; SR; BA; Psy Chi; St Lukes/Roosevelt Hosp Hm Vstr 90-; Athltc/Acdmc Awd; Bsktbl Capt 89-; Psychlgy; Law.

**WILLIAMS, HOLLY L,** Northern Ky Univ, Highland Hts, KY; JR; BS; Psi Chi; Phi Eta Sigma 88-; Altar Guild Episcopal Church 88-; Psychology; Soc Wrkr/Drug Abuse Cnslr.

**WILLIAMS, INDERRYA D,** Wesleyan Coll, Macon, GA; FR; Ga Spch Cmnctn Assoc 90-; Yrbk Stf 90-; Blck Stu Alnc 90; Sccr/Tns 90; Premed Biochem.

**WILLIAMS, JACQUES R,** Alcorn St Univ, Lorman, MS; SO; BA; Kappa Alpha Psi; NAACP; Urban Lea; Hon Roll 90-; Tennis Team; Pre-Pharmcy/Bio.

**WILLIAMS, JAMES A,** Kent St Univ Kent Cmps, Kent, OH; SR; BA; Rugby Clb 88; IM Ftbl; IM Sftbl 87; Assn Cr Chldrns Hlth 88-; Chld Lf Cncl 90-; Intrn-Rainbor Babies Chldrns Hosp; Prctcm St Lukes Hosp 90-; CCLS Chld Lf Cncl; Indvdl/Fmly Studies; Chld Lf Spclst.

**WILLIAMS, JAMES ANDREW,** Alcorn St Univ, Lorman, MS; SO; Hstry; Law.

**WILLIAMS, JAMES D,** Ms St Univ, Miss State, MS; JR; BA; SGA Cbnt Head; Rsdnt Asst Stdnt Hsng 89-; Air Force ROTC Grp Adjtn 89-90; DPMA 90-; Arnld Air VC 88-90; BARK Dir 90-; Pres List; Deans List; IMS Cptn 88-; Mngmnt Info Systms; Systms Anlyst Prgmmr.

**WILLIAMS II, JAMES KEMPER,** Pellissippi St Tech Comm Coll, Knoxville, TN; GD; AS; Vision Vol; Med.

**WILLIAMS, JAMES P,** Univ Of Cincinnati, Cincinnati, OH; JR; BS; Cnstrctn; Hvy Cnstrctn.

**WILLIAMS, JAMES THOMAS,** Al A & M Univ, Normal, AL; SO; BS; ROTC Cadet Lt; Masonic Clb; Hon Rl; Cvl Engr.

**WILLIAMS, JAMIE E,** Fayetteville St Univ, Fayetteville, NC; SR; BS; Kappa Delta Pi 88-; Alpha Kappa Mu VP 89-; Math/Ed; Tchng.

**WILLIAMS, JAMIE M,** Beckley Coll, Beckley, WV; SO; AS; Phi Beta Lambda; Bank Tlr; Bus; Legal Sec.

**WILLIAMS, JANICE L,** Miles Coll, Birmingham, AL; JR; Minister; Cnty Fmly Crt Bham Bd Of Educ 87-; Soc Sci; Soc Wrkr.

**WILLIAMS, JANICE M,** Western Piedmont Comm Coll, Morganton, NC; GD; AASC; Phi Beta Lambda 89-90; Phi Theta Kappa 89-; Dns Lst 89-; Ambsdr 90-; Marshall 89; Scmptr Oper Dip 90; Bus.

**WILLIAMS, JANICE P,** Miles Coll, Birmingham, AL; JR; BED; Elem Educ; Tchr.

**WILLIAMS, JEANETTE P,** Wallace St Comm Coll At Selma, Selma, AL; JR.

**WILLIAMS, JEANINE M,** Al St Univ, Montgomery, AL; FR; BA; Geog Tutor 90; Phi Eta Sigma; Hghst Ranking Fr 90-; Intrdscplnry Hons Prog 90-; Theatre; Prod/Dir.

**WILLIAMS, JENNIFER D,** Ms Gulf Coast Comm Coll, Perkinston, MS; FR; Bnd Mgr 90; Make A Fndtn MS Vlntr 86-; VP Lst 90; Wintr Guard 90; Elem Ed; Ed.

**WILLIAMS, JENNIFER J,** Bethany Coll, Bethany, WV; FR; BA; French Club 90; Track/Javelin 90.

**WILLIAMS, JENNIFER L,** Radford Univ, Radford, VA; SO; BA; Sftbl Tm 90-; Psych; Org/Ind Psych.

**WILLIAMS, JENNIFER L,** Merrimack Coll, North Andover, MA; SR; BA; History Club; Phi Alpha Theta; Sigma Phi Omega V Pres 90-; Intrnshp Resch Asstnt N Andover Historical Soc; History.

**WILLIAMS, JIM T,** Univ Of Southern Ms, Hattiesburg, MS; JR; BS; Exec Phys Club 90-; Student Alumni Assoc 90-; Dr Benjamin Schlrshp 90-; Ftbl 88-90; Exercise Phys; Physical Therapy.

**WILLIAMS, JIMMIE A,** Stillman Coll, Tuscaloosa, AL; SO; Chncllrs Scl Clb 89; Sclgy/Psychlgy; Cnslng.

**WILLIAMS JR, JOHN L,** Alcorn St Univ, Lorman, MS; JR; Bus Admin.

**WILLIAMS, JOHNNIE H,** Nova Univ, Ft Lauderdale, FL; GD; MBA; BS Nova Un 90; Bus Admn; Bus Mgmt.

**WILLIAMS, JOSEPH M,** Univ Of Sc At Columbia, Columbia, SC; FR; BA; Hist; Edn.

**WILLIAMS, JOY E,** Fl A & M Univ, Tallahassee, FL; SO; FAMU Caring Prjct 90-; Leon Cnty Schl Vol Tutor 90-; VIY Vol 90-; Hnr Soc 89-90; Hnr Stdnt 89-; Poltcl Sci; Law.

**WILLIAMS, JOYCE A,** Univ Of Sc At Columbia, Columbia, SC; SO; BSN; Nrsg.

**WILLIAMS, JUDY A,** Williamsburg Tech Coll, Kingstree, SC; Stdnt Govt Assc; Vol Dwilliams Mem Hosp Typst.

**WILLIAMS, JULIANNA M,** Univ Of Tn At Martin, Martin, TN; JR; BSN; Intrfth Stdnt Ctr Res Mgr/Pres 89-; Mu Epsilon Delta Pres/Pldg Trnr 89-; Nrsng.

**WILLIAMS, KARITA D,** Tougaloo Coll, Tougaloo, MS; FR; Pre Hlth Clb 90-; Stdnt Recrtmnt Tm 90-; Alpha Lambda Delta 90-; Bio; Pathlgst.

**WILLIAMS, KARLA A,** Central St Univ, Wilberforce, OH; JR; BED; Alpha Kappa Mu; Engl; Tch.

**WILLIAMS, KARLENE D,** City Univ Of Ny City Coll, New York, NY; FR; BA; Trintociti; Assist Sloan-Kettering Mem Hosp 90; Bio; Med.

**WILLIAMS, KARRY L,** John C Calhoun St Comm Coll, Decatur, AL; SO; AS 90; Bio; Athltc Trng.**

**WILLIAMS, KATINA A,** Al A & M Univ, Normal, AL; FR; BA; NAACP 90; AHEA 90-; Deans Lst; Hon Rl; Ch Choir; Lbrl Arts; Fshn Merch.

**WILLIAMS, KEINA M,** Shaw Univ, Raleigh, NC; JR; BA; Delta Sigma Theta Corr Sec 90-; Bus Mgmt; Hmn Rsrces.**

**WILLIAMS, KEITH A,** Neumann Coll, Aston, PA; SO; BS; Mtg Bus.

**WILLIAMS, KEITH A,** Univ Of Nc At Chapel Hill, Chapel Hill, NC; GD; JD; Chrstn Lgl Soc Pres; Ms Coll Stdnt Assn Pres 88-89; Sprng Brk Srvc Prjcts Chrprsn 88; Th Hrtg Fndtn Intrn 87; Th Rthfrd Inst Intrn; Ba Messiah Coll 89; Law.

**WILLIAMS, KEITH N,** Alcorn St Univ, Lorman, MS; JR; BS; Psych Clb; Bsebl; Psych.

**WILLIAMS, KELLEY E,** Univ Of South Al, Mobile, AL; SR; BA; Stdnt Govt Assn Sntr 90-; Chi Omega; Sigma Chi Lil Str Sec V P 87-90; Deans Lst; Pres Lst; I M Sftbl Tm; Erly Chldhd Educ; Tch.

**WILLIAMS, KELLEY L,** Livingston Univ, Livingston, AL; JR; BA; Stdnt Govt 87-; Educ Erly Chldhd; Tchng.

**WILLIAMS, KELLIE M,** Lasell Coll, Newton, MA; SR; AD; Spcl Olympcs Trck Flc Cch; Univ Hosp; Spldng Rhblttn Hosp; Chldrns Hosp Bstn; Physcl Thrpst Asst.

**WILLIAMS, KELLY D,** Lincoln Univ, Lincoln Univ, PA; SO; BA; French Clb 89-; Acctng Clb 89-; Hons Soc 90-; Mc Cormick/Co Intrn; Acctng.

**WILLIAMS, KENNETH J,** Fayetteville St Univ, Fayetteville, NC; SO; BS; Cmptr Sci.

**WILLIAMS, KERRI L,** Atlantic Comm Coll, Mays Landing, NJ; SO; AS; Art; Tchng Sllng Crfts.

**WILLIAMS, KESTER F,** Albertus Magnus Coll, New Haven, CT; SO; BA; Fren Ch Club Spanish Club 89-90; Peer Cnslr 90-; Edtr Sch Nwspr; Deans List 89-; Comm & Romance Lang-French/Spanish.

**WILLIAMS, KEVIN M,** Barry Univ, Miami, FL; SR; Phlsphy; Bus.

**WILLIAMS, KIMBERLY A,** Wilberforce Univ, Wilberforce, OH; SO; BA; Oh Pre Alum Sec 90-; Sigma Omega; Alpha Kappa Alpha Grammateus; Deans List 89-; Univ Schlrshp 89-; Clncl Psych; Dr Of Psych.

**WILLIAMS, KIMBERLY ANN,** Georgian Court Coll, Lakewood, NJ; JR; BS; Mendel Scty 88-; Sister Mary Grace Biology Awd 89; Biology; Hlth Related Field.

**WILLIAMS, KIMBERLY C,** Al St Univ, Montgomery, AL; SO; BS; Law Soc 90-; Bsns Admn Mgmt; Law.

**WILLIAMS, KIMBERLY J,** Itawamba Comm Coll, Fulton, MS; SO; MSRT; FRT; All Band; Appld Sci; Radiology.

**WILLIAMS, KIMBERLY L,** James Madison University, Harrisonburg, VA; SO; BA; BSA; Minorty Outrch; Contmpry Gospel Singers; Acadmc Athltc Achvmnt; Pres List; Intrclgt; Trck/Fld Team; Psychlgy.

**WILLIAMS, KIRT A,** Embry Riddle Aeronautical Univ, Daytona Beach, FL; SR; Natl Intrcllgt Flyng Assn Pres 89-90; Prcsn Flght Dmstrtn Tm Sfty Offcr 88-; Nvl Avtn Clb 87-; Delta Chi Treas-Srgnt Arms 88-; Pres Rl 90; BS; Spec Olymp Sftbl Mrthn 88; Aerntcl Sci.

**WILLIAMS, KISIA,** Al A & M Univ, Normal, AL; SO; BS; Amer Soc Cvl Engrs Secr 90-; Natl Soc Blck Engrs 90-; Cvl Engr; Engr.

**WILLIAMS, KRISTINE N,** S U N Y Coll Of Tech At Frmgdl, Farmingdale, NY; GD; Stdnt Nrs Assn 86-90; N Y State Nrs Assn 89-.

**WILLIAMS, KRISTOFFER J,** Cheyney Univ Of Pa, Cheyney, PA; FR; BS; Clg Mrchng/Cncrt/Jazz/Bsktbl Pep Bands; Music Ed; Professor.

**WILLIAMS, LALENA L,** Mount Saint Mary Coll, Newburgh, NY; SO; BA; Hnr Allnc 90-; Dns Lst 89-; Engl; Tch Elem Spec Ed.

**WILLIAMS, LASAUNDRA F,** Commonwealth Coll, Virginia Beach, VA; GD; Office Admin Clb 90-; Pres Lst 90-; Perfect Attendance Awd 90-; AAS; Secretarial Sci; Office Admin.

**WILLIAMS, LATRICA W,** Stillman Coll, Tuscaloosa, AL; SO; BA; Natl Assc Advncmnt Colored People Pres 89-; Drama Clb 90-; Phi Beta Lmbd VP; Cordell Wynn Hon Pgm 89-; Bus; Mktg.

**WILLIAMS, LAURIE L,** Univ Of Southern Ms, Hattiesburg, MS; FR; BS; Phi Eta Sigma; Med; Nrse.

**WILLIAMS, LE ANDREA L,** Central St Univ, Wilberforce, OH; FR; BA; Aux Bnd; Cmmnctns Clb; NAACP 90-; Radio TV Cmmnctns; NWS Brdcstng.

**WILLIAMS, LE ROY A,** Morehouse Coll, Atlanta, GA; SO; BA; Spnsh Clb Pres; PA Clb; Pol Sci; Law.

**WILLIAMS, LEE A,** Al St Univ, Montgomery, AL; FR.

**WILLIAMS, LEE A,** Memphis St Univ, Memphis, TN; SO; BA; Hnrs Stdnt Assoc 90-; Pltcl Scinc/Intl Rltns Org Sec/Treas 90-; Gamma Beta Phi 90; Pltcl Scnc/Intl Rltns; Govt Serv.

**WILLIAMS, LEOLA C,** Univ Of Ga, Athens, GA; SR; BSED; Angel Flight Of Robt W Long Flght Admin 89-F APWU Axlry Hist 87-; Hmwrk Hlpr Alps Rd Elem 87-88; Peer Cnslr Hillsman; Tutor E Athens Comm Cntr; Deans List 90-; Delta Sigma Theta Acad Excllnc 90-; Erly Chldhd Educ; Teach.

**WILLIAMS, LIANNA D,** Savannah St Coll, Savannah, GA; JR; BA; Res Hl Std Cncl SGA 89-; Theatre Prod; Nwspr Stf; Delta Sigma Theta Treas; Mrchng Bnd Capt 89-; Rec; Ftbl/Trck Coach.

**WILLIAMS, LIEN K,** Va St Univ, Petersburg, VA; JR; BA; Admin Jstr 89-; Scl Wrk.

**WILLIAMS, LISA D,** Catawba Valley Comm Coll, Hickory, NC; FR; Gamma Beta Phi; Bsn-Cmptr Pgm; BA.

**WILLIAMS, LISA J,** Providence Coll, Providence, RI; JR; BS; Ski Clb 90-; Wldlf Clb 90-; Accntng Clb 88-; Accntng; CPA.

**WILLIAMS, LISA M,** Wv Northern Comm Coll, Wheeling, WV; SO; BA; Bsnss Admin; Mngmnt.

**WILLIAMS, LISA M,** Univ Of The Dist Of Columbia, Washington, DC; SO; BS; Crim Just Assoc Sgt Arms; Schlrshp Natl Org Blck Law Enfrcmnt; Schlrshp Zonta Wmns Org; Crim Just; Forensic Pthlgst/Ballistics/Law.**

**WILLIAMS, LISA M,** Univ Of South Al, Mobile, AL; SR; MED; Trojan Hostess Troy State U 88-89; Sigma Chi Lil Sis 88-90; Alpha Gamma Delta Scl Chr 87-; Geo C Wallace Ldrshp Schlrshp 87-89; Pres Lst 90; Deans Lst 89-; BS; Specl Ed Gftd.

**WILLIAMS, LIZETTA B,** Fl A & M Univ, Tallahassee, FL; FR; BA; Elem Educ; Tchg.

**WILLIAMS, LYNN R,** Daytona Beach Comm Coll, Daytona Beach, FL; FR; AS; SRCA 90-; Pres List 90-; Phi Theta Kappa 88-89; Adult Ed Vlybl 90-; AARC; Resp Care Tchnlg/Therapy; Respiratory Therpy.**

**WILLIAMS, LYNNE L,** Edinboro Univ Of Pa, Edinboro, PA; SR; BS; Celbrtn Univ Chrstn Flwshp Pres 87-; Futr Edctrs Of Amer 87-; Alpha Chi 88-; Kappa Delta Pi 88-; Phi Eta Sigma 87-88; Summa Cum Laude; Cert Acad Excllnc 88-; Helen Sabin Reed Educ Schlrshp 90-; Elem Educ; Grad Stds/Psychlgy.

**WILLIAMS, MAHA H,** Schenectady County Comm Coll, Schenectady, NY; FR; Ofc Mgr For 4 Yrs.

**WILLIAMS, MANDEE L,** Univ Of Ga, Athens, GA; FR; BA; Drama Dangs; Theatre; Prfmnc/Edctn.

**WILLIAMS, MARGARET L,** Anne Arundel Comm Coll, Arnold, MD; FR; BA; Bus; Acct.

**WILLIAMS, MARIA A,** Univ Of Southern Ms, Hattiesburg, MS; FR; BA; Afro Amer Stdnt Org 90-; Choir 90-; Spec Ed; Tchng.

**WILLIAMS, MARIA A,** Univ Of New Haven, West Haven, CT; SR; BS; Trvl/Trsm Clb 88-90; Hotel/Rest Soc 88-89; Ski Club 89-90; Alpha Lambda Delta 90-; Eta Sigma Delta 89-; Deans List 89-; Tourism/Trvl Admin; Airline Mgmnt.

**WILLIAMS, MARIANNE E,** Nc Agri & Tech St Univ, Greensboro, NC; SR; BS; SNEA; NCAE; NCCTM; Choir Section Ldr 88-; Delta Sigma Theta Chpln; PRAISE Fndr/Pres 87-88; Bapt Yth Flwshp Pres 78-83; Mt Olivet Bapt Chrch Tchr 87-88; Chnclrs Exec Smnr; Elem Educ; Superintendent.

**WILLIAMS, MARK A,** Univ Of Sc At Columbia, Columbia, SC; SR; BA; Flwshp Christian Athletes Bapt Stdnt Un 87-; Stdnt Bsktbl Com 88-; Yrbk Sports Ed 89-; Res Hall Govt Hall Rep 89-; Phoenix Advrtsng Asstntshp; Vrsty Ftbl 88; Advrtsng.

**WILLIAMS, MARK E,** Ky Wesleyan Coll, Owensboro, KY; JR; BA; Untd Methdst Std Fllwshp Pres 88-; Actvts Prgrmmng Brd Cocordntr 89-; Alph Chi 90-; Sigma Alpha Mu Prior 88-; Chrldng Squad Co Capt 88-; Religion/History; Ministry.

**WILLIAMS, MARQUETTA Y,** Jackson St Univ, Jackson, MS; FR; PH D; Hist Clb 90; Alpha Lmbd Dlt 90; Hist; Prfsr.

**WILLIAMS, MARTHA A,** Union Univ, Jackson, TN; SR; BSBA; Phi Theta Kappa; Credit Prfssnls Pres 83-84; Bapt Church; Laubach Litcy Actn; D Wilhams Elec/Plbg Co Inc Sec Treas; AS Jackson St Comm Colg Summa Cum Laude 89; Busn.

**WILLIAMS, MARTHA L,** Stillman Coll, Tuscaloosa, AL; JR; SAEA Tr 89-; Ford Schlrs 89-; Eastrn Stars 76-; Chrstn Educ Dir 89-; Bio Prep Prnts Grp Pr 87-; Elem Educ; Tchr/Cnslr.

**WILLIAMS, MARULLUS A,** Fl A & M Univ, Tallahassee, FL; FR; Pres Schlrs Assoc 90-; CIS Clb 90-; IDS Fncl Intern 90; Dns Lst 90-; CIS; Pgm Syst Analysis.

**WILLIAMS, MARVA J,** Johnson C Smith Univ, Charlotte, NC; FR; Bio; Phrmcy.

**WILLIAMS, MARY ALICE,** Univ Of Sc At Columbia, Columbia, SC; FR; BA; Hnrs Prog; Hstry; Law.

**WILLIAMS, MARY E,** Northwest Al Comm Coll, Phil Campbell, AL; SO; AAS; Offce Admin/Sprvsn; Offce Mgmt.

**WILLIAMS, MARY JOYCE,** Chesterfield Marlboro Coll, Cheraw, SC; FR; AS; Bus.

**WILLIAMS, MARY K,** Cuyahoga Comm Coll, Cleveland, OH; JR; BA; Nwspr Wrtr 85-86; Crains Clvlnd Bus Rsrchr 89-; AA 86; Comnctns Pblc Rltns; Advrtsng.

**WILLIAMS, MARY L,** Coker Coll, Hartsville, SC; SR; BA; Stdnt Govt Assn Jdcl Chr 89-90; Educ Clb Pres; Sngrs 87-89; Commissioners 88-; Stdnt Tchr 90; Elem Educ; Tchr.

**WILLIAMS, MATHEW K,** Indiana Univ Of Pa, Indiana, PA; SR; BA; Intrhsp Cbl TV Stn KBL Sprtsbt Asst Prdcr; Bstbl Allegheny Cmnty Clg 86-87; Cmnctns Media.

**WILLIAMS, MEGAN E,** Longwood Coll, Farmville, VA; SO; BED; Sigma Kappa Chr 90-; Elem Ed; Tchr.

**WILLIAMS, MELANIE L,** Johnson C Smith Univ, Charlotte, NC; FR; BS; Hall Cncl VP 90-; Un Pgm Bd 90-; Alpha Lambda Delta 90-; Pres Awd 90; Bio; Optometry/Med.

**WILLIAMS, MELISSA K,** Indiana Univ Of Pa, Indiana, PA; JR; BS; Stdnt Cong Rep 90-; Chrl 88-90; Enlg Clb 89-90; Sigma Tau Delta 90-; Phi Sigma Simga; Engl Ed; Tch.

**WILLIAMS JR, MELVIN J,** Talladega Coll, Talladega, AL; SO; BS; NAACP 90-; HCOP 90-; Natl Hon Soc 90-; Alpha Phi Alpha 90-; All Amer Schlrs 89-90; Fresh Chem Awd 89-90; NCMLA 90-; IM Bsktbl 89-; Pre-Med Chem; Dctr/Med.

**WILLIAMS, MEREDITH E,** Birmingham Southern Coll, Birmingham, AL; FR; Tri Beta 90-; Bio/Chem; Med.

**WILLIAMS, MICHAEL A,** Bridgewater Coll, Bridgewater, VA; SO; Soph Class Pres Stnt Gov Pres 90; Bapt Stdnt Union 89; Cir K Clb Pblcty 89-90; Brdgewtr Chorale 90; Yrbk Staff 90f Stdnt Cncl Of Rlg Actvties Soc Com; Cir K Clb Pblcty 89-90; Engl; Tchng.

**WILLIAMS, MICHAEL A,** Ms St Univ, Miss State, MS; GD; Am Vet Med Assn 87-; Zoo/Avn Clb 87-; Wldlf Sprt Grp 88-; Gamma Beta Phi 85-87; Extrnshp Ntl Zlgcl Pk 90; Extrnshp Mrn Lf Ocnrm 90; IM Ftbl 85-88; DVM; Vet Med.

**WILLIAMS, MICHAEL J,** S U N Y Coll At Fredonia, Fredonia, NY; JR; BA; Prfrmng Arts Co 87-; Summer Theatre Ice Fire Perf Grp Vermont 90; Theatre/Cmmnctns; Film/TV Dir/Wrtng/Actng.

**WILLIAMS, MICHAEL LESLIE,** Tn St Univ, Nashville, TN; SR; BA; Cert Apprctn Gvnr TN; Intern TN Dept Yth Dvlpmnt; St Ftbl Sqd 86-89; BA; Crmnl Jstc; Law.

**WILLIAMS, MICHAEL P,** Atlantic Comm Coll, Mays Landing, NJ; FR; AAS; SCA 90-; JR Profl Chefs Assn; Sands Hotel/Casino Intern 90-; Culinary.

**WILLIAMS, MICHELE L,** Wilmington Coll, Wilmington, OH; SR; BS; Sports Medicine Assoc VP 89-; Natl Athletic Trainers Assoc 90-; Flwshp Christian Stdnts 89-; Faculty Hnr Schrlshp Recipient 87-; Var Sftbl 87-; Physcl Ed Sports Med; Teacher/Athltc Trainer.

**WILLIAMS, MICHELLE L,** Anne Arundel Comm Coll, Arnold, MD; SO; BA; Offc Tech; Educ.

**WILLIAMS, MICHELLE Y,** Tougaloo Coll, Tougaloo, MS; SO; BS; Pre Hlth Sec 89-90; Cltrl Connection Pres 90-; Alpha Lambda Delta 89-; MBRS 89-90; MHSRAP 90-; Chmstry/Pre Med; Physician.

**WILLIAMS, MONICA A,** Howard Univ, Washington, DC; GD; MSW; Luthern Soc Srvc Intrn Adptn Unt 90-; BSW; Soc Wrk; Fld/Fmly/Chld Srvc.

**WILLIAMS, MONICA R,** Stillman Coll, Tuscaloosa, AL; FR; Stillman Schlr Cordell; Wynns Hnrs Pgm; Chem/Chem Eng.

**WILLIAMS, MONICA V,** Central St Univ, Wilberforce, OH; JR; BS; Enlg/Acctg Tutr 88-; Deja Vu Mdlng P 88-; Acctg Clb VP 90-; Hons Clb; Delta Sigma Theta T 90-; BP Explrtn AK Inc Intrnshp 90-; Acctg.

**WILLIAMS, MONIQUE S,** Va St Univ, Petersburg, VA; FR; BA; Math; Math Eng.

**WILLIAMS, NANCY E,** Boston Univ, Boston, MA; SR; BS; NSSLHA Pres 87-; Deans Host; Peer Advsr; Big Sistr/Bro; Sargent Clg SGA Rep 87-90; Sargent Clg Deans List; Sargent Clg Hon Auxlry; Mortar Bd; Asstntshp Chldrns Hosp Boston Cmnctn Ctr 88-90; Aerbcs Instrctr Boston U Phy Ed 89-; Cmnctn Dsrdrs; Spch Pathlgy.**

**WILLIAMS, NANCY L,** Livingston Univ, Livingston, AL; SO; BA; IMS; Envrnmntl Sci.

**WILLIAMS, NATASHA H,** Johnson C Smith Univ, Charlotte, NC; FR; BS; Band 87-; Mrchg Symp Jazz/Concert 87-; Yth Competency Pgm Vol/Cler Aide/Tutor 89-90; Juvenile Restitution Pgm Cler Aide/Tutor; Tutor YCP 89-90; Engl/Psych; Crmnl Psych/Novelist.

**WILLIAMS, NELDA E,** Owensboro Comm Coll, Owensboro, KY; FR; AS; Grad Magna Cum Laude Brescia Clg 88; Hlth Careers Schlrshp 90-; Daviess Cnty Medl Scty Aux Schlrshp; First Bapt Chrch Adlt II SS Pianist; Acctng Materials Mngmnt 73-90; AA Bus Adm 85; BS Bus Adm 88; Nursing; Hospital Mngmnt.

**WILLIAMS, NICHOLAS J,** Al A & M Univ, Normal, AL; SO; BA; FBL Amer 88-89; Drama Clb 87-88; Spnsh Clb 86-89; Dns Lst 89-; Hnr Rl 89-; Natl Jnr Cvtns Amer 88-89; Acad Schlp 89-; Gnrl Serv Admn Intshp Prcrmnt Clrk; Trck Schlp 89-90; Track 89-90; Bsn Admn/Lgstcs/Prcrmnt; Cntrcts Spec.

**WILLIAMS, NINA M,** Fl St Univ, Tallahassee, FL; SO; BA; GAMMA Cmmnctn Dir 90-; Alum Fndtn; Delta Zeta V P Mbrshp; Church Choir Ens; Cmmnctns; Pub Rltns.

**WILLIAMS, OBBIE,** Univ Of Southern Ms, Hattiesburg, MS; FR; Cogic Clb Secy 90-; Math; Computer Sci.

**WILLIAMS, PAMELA A,** James Madison University, Harrisonburg, VA; FR; BS; J Mdsn Univ Ski Clb Com 90-; Zeta Tau Alpha 90-; Psych; Clncl Psychlgst.

**WILLIAMS, PAMELA B,** Syracuse Univ, Syracuse, NY; SR; Arch Stu Orgn 87-; Peer Advsng Prog 89-90; IM Vllybl Bsktbl Swmmng 86-87.

**WILLIAMS, PAMELA B,** Mount Saint Mary Coll, Newburgh, NY; JR; BA; Alpha Chi; AS Monroe Comm Clg 86; English; Special Educ.

**WILLIAMS, PAMELA L,** Saint Andrews Presbytrn Coll, Laurinburg, NC; SO; BA; Chpbk Comp Dir 90; Wrtrs Frm 89-; Ordr Msq 89-; Brkr Schlrshp; Eng Crtv Wrtng; Prof.

**WILLIAMS, PATRICIA E,** Coll Of Charleston, Charleston, SC; JR, Hnrs Pgm Exec Comm Rep 87-89; Cntbry Clb 87-88; Psi Chi VP 89-; Hnrs Pgm 87-; Omcrn Delta Kappa, Hrisn Rndlph Schlr 87-; AB; BS; Psy; Clncl Psy.

**WILLIAMS, PATRICIA Y,** Saint Thomas Univ, Miami, FL; JR; BA; Ordr Estrn Stars; Data Contrl Tech I 74; ASB Prospct Hall Clg 89; Hmn Rsrc; Admn Dept.

**WILLIAMS, PAULA R,** Univ Of Southern Ms, Hattiesburg, MS; JR; BA; Hillcrest Hall Cncl Sprt Chrmn 90-; Psychology.

**WILLIAMS, PEGGY J,** Ky St Univ, Frankfort, KY; SR; BA; Alpha Kappa Mu 90-; Pol Scnc Hnr Awd; Infnt/Preschl Hndcppd Chldrn; Blgrss Theatre Gld; Admin Asst/Spkr Pro Tem KY Gen Assmbly 88-F; Pol Scnc; Spkr Pro Tems Offc KY Gen Assmbly.

**WILLIAMS, PEGGY L,** Western Piedmont Comm Coll, Morganton, NC; FR; Phi Theta Kappa; Note Taker Handicap Stdnts 90-; Mktg/Advrtsng Bus; Sls Rep.

**WILLIAMS, PEGGY S,** Daytona Beach Comm Coll, Daytona Beach, FL; JR; AS; Fl Stu Nrs Assoc VP; Pres Lst 89-90; Pres Lst 90-; Deans Lst 90-; Amer Red Crs Vip Dnr 71-; Chsn Atnd Ntl Stu Nrs Assoc Srvd Fl Dlgt; Halifax Med Cntr Emply Mo 75; Volusia Cnty Sch Sys Vol 85-; GSA 86-; LPN 73-; Nrsg; RN.

**WILLIAMS, QUINTESSA,** Atlantic Union Coll, S Lancaster, MA; SR; MD; Lrng Res Com Stdnt Repr 90-; NAACP; Hlth/Temprnc Dept N E Conf Dist Cord 86-89; Sabbath Schl Dept Worcester SDA Chrch Super 90-; AD Nrsg; Lfestyle Ed/Cnslr 83-84; Veg Cuisine Instr/Cook 85-89; Cert Uchee Pines Inst 83-84; Cert Gen Conf 7 Adv 88; Nrsg/Pre-Med; Preventive Medicine.

**WILLIAMS, RACHAEL M,** Memphis St Univ, Memphis, TN; SR; Gooch Schlrshp; U S Navy 63-66; AA Shelby St Cmnty Clg 87; Romance Lang; Tch Latin/Spanish.

**WILLIAMS, RACHEL K,** Univ Of Southern Ms, Hattiesburg, MS; JR; BA; Sigma Swthrt Phi Beta Sigma 89-90; Wrkd Microbio Prep Lab 88-89; Microbio; Lab Wrk.

**WILLIAMS, RASHONDIA E,** Hampton Univ, Hampton, VA; FR; BS; Chem Clb 90-; FL Pre Alumni Clb 90-; IM Bsktbl 90-; Chem; Med Res.

**WILLIAMS, RAYMOND A,** Southern Coll Of Tech, Marietta, GA; GD; BS; ASCE Sec 90; Water Poll Cntrl Fed; Amer Concrete Inst; Engr.

**WILLIAMS, REBEKAH D,** Ms St Univ, Miss State, MS; JR; BFA; Yth Cnslr; Kappa Pi Pres 89-; Gamma Beta Phi 90-; Lambda Chi Alpha 89; Actvts Chrprsn 89; Mrt Awrd Art Comp 89-; Art; Grphc Dsgn.

**WILLIAMS, REGINA E,** Ny Theological Seminary, New York, NY; SR; US Pstl Srvc Clrcl Admnstrtv Dts; BA Clg New Rochelle NY Ts Campus; Sclgy; Scl Wrk Tchng Fld.

**WILLIAMS, RENELL A,** Central St Univ, Wilberforce, OH; GD; BA; Bus Admn.

**WILLIAMS, REWA C,** Fl A & M Univ, Tallahassee, FL; JR; BS; NAACP Fla Comm Assn 88-; Future FL Educ Of Amer Sec 90-; Baachus 88-; Mc Knight Achvr 86-; Alpha Kappa Alpha 90-; Natl Coll Educ Awds 90-; Elem Educ.

**WILLIAMS, RITA J,** Univ Of Tn At Martin, Martin, TN; SO; Stdnt Court SGA Sdnt Jstce 89-; Blck Stdnt Assn; Soc Hon Seminar Stdnts; Phi Chi Theta Beta Chi Chapt; Bapt Stdnt Un 90-; INROADS Memphis Light/Gas/Water/Utility Co 89-; Actg; Acctnt.

**WILLIAMS, ROBBIN R,** Central St Univ, Wilberforce, OH; FR; BA; Psychlgy; Lawyer.

**WILLIAMS, ROBERT DEMPSEY,** Univ Of Sc At Columbia, Columbia, SC; JR; BS; Math Cmptr Sci Clb VP 88-; Stdnt Gvrnmnt Assn Sntr 90-; Stdnt Alumni Ambsdr Ambsdr 90-; Gamma Beta Phi 88-; Coop Edctn Prgrm Wstnghse 90-; Stdnt Mnth USC Aiken; Rothfuss Opprntny Schlr 88-; Math Cmptr Sci; Cmptr Systm Analysis.

**WILLIAMS, ROBERT R,** Wv Univ, Morgantown, WV; FR; RESMG; Rsdnc Hll Jdcl Brd Brd Mmbr 90-; Coll FFA 4 H Clbs 90-; Ag Frstry Cncl Res Mgr Rep; Alpha Gamma Rho 90-; Pres Lst; Deans Lst 90-; Ag Econ; Ag Bus.

**WILLIAMS, ROBYN L M,** Ms St Univ, Miss State, MS; SR; BED; Rfrmd Univ Flwshp; Assn Dsbld Stdnts; Kappa Delta Pi; Educ Psychlgy.

**WILLIAMS, ROBYN R,** Fisk Univ, Nashville, TN; JR; BS; Jubilee Sngrs 89-; NABA 90-; Goldn Key; Mortr Brd; Bus Admin/Acctg.

**WILLIAMS, RODGER K,** Old Dominion Univ, Norfolk, VA; SR; BS; IEEE 85-; Bdybldng 85-; AS Richard Bland Clg 84; Comp Engr; Law.

**WILLIAMS, RODNEY S,** Lee Coll, Cleveland, TN; FR; BS; Acad Hnrs Schlrshp; Dns Lst W/Hnrs; IM Sftbl/Ftbl; Interclgte IM Bsktbl All Stars; Chem; Dentist.

**WILLIAMS, ROGER D,** Univ Of West Fl, Pensacola, FL; SR; BS; SME Chrmn; Deans Lst 83-86; AS Jefferson Davis Clg 86; Mfg Engr; Engr.**

**WILLIAMS JR, RUSS E,** Radford Univ, Radford, VA; JR; MBA; Sigma Phi Epsilon Exec Alumni Coor 89-; La Crosse 89; Mrktng; Bus.

**WILLIAMS, SAMANTHA G,** Al St Univ, Montgomery, AL; FR; BS; Phi Eta Sigma; Chem; Med.

**WILLIAMS, SANDRA I,** Saint Pauls Coll, Lawrenceville, VA; SR; BA; Wom Cncl Treas 88-; Intrfrtrnl Cncl Treas 90-; Alpha Kappa Mu; Sigma Gamma Rho Pres/Treas 89-; Trck Mngr 88-89; BA; Pltcl Scnc; Admin Of Justice.

**WILLIAMS, SANDRA K,** Univ Of Sc At Columbia, Columbia, SC; SR; BS; Schl Newspapr Phtgrphr 89; Awd For Best Phtgrphy In Schl Newspapis, Im Bsktbl 90; Bsnss Admin Mgmt; Phtgrphy Bsnss.

**WILLIAMS, SHANNON F,** Univ Of Sc At Columbia, Columbia, SC; SO; BA; Hist; Coll Prfssr.

**WILLIAMS, SHARON D,** Averett Coll, Danville, VA; SR; BS; Amer Bus Wmns Assn 88-; Jr Acct Fr Wd Fbr Indstrs VI 90-; Assoc Acctng Danville Comm Coll 84; Mgmt; Acctng.

**WILLIAMS, SHARON L,** S U N Y At Buffalo, Buffalo, NY; JR; BA; Alnc Wmn Tres 88-89; Pine Ridge Fmly Chrch Dir/Awn 88-90; Kenmore Alnc Chrch; Sngl Parent Sprt Grp Co Ldr; Tax Preparer 84-90; Acctg; Corp Acctnt.

**WILLIAMS, SHARON R,** Alcorn St Univ, Lorman, MS; SO; BS; Medcl Rcrds Admin.**

**WILLIAMS, SHARRON L,** Va Commonwealth Univ, Richmond, VA; SR; Pblc Rltns Stdnt Scty Amrc 89-; Stdn Talmn Ambssdrs Srvvl Kt Chrprsn 89-; Phi Eta Sigma 88; Omicron Delta Kappa 90-; Alpha Omicron Pi Rsh Chrprsn 87-; VCU Greek Councl Award Schlstc Achvmnt 88; BS; Mass Cmmnctns; Pblc Rltns.

**WILLIAMS, SHELIA D,** Alcorn St Univ, Lorman, MS; SO; BA; Phy Thrpy/Busn Admin; Exec Pres.

**WILLIAMS, SHERI L,** Alcorn St Univ, Lorman, MS; JR; BA; Englsh; Tchr.

**WILLIAMS, SHERLEE,** Gallaudet Univ, Washington, DC; GD; PSY S; Sign Language Clb Ball State Pres 86-88; Vice Chnclrs Lst Indiana Univ 79-83; Pres Schlr Gallaudet Univ 89-; Deaf Camp Cnslr 78-; Wrld Wldlf Fnd 90-; Greenpeace; Grad Asst 86-90; Schl Psychlgy Intrnshp 90-; NASP 88-; NAD 79-; Nrs Aide 77-85; Schl Psychlgy.

**WILLIAMS, SHERRI L,** Bluefield St Coll, Bluefield, WV; SO; BA; Rcmbnnt Gntcs; Med.**

**WILLIAMS, SHERRY L,** Lock Haven Univ, Lock Haven, PA; JR; BA; Kappa Delta Pi 90; Elem Ed; Tchng.**

**WILLIAMS, STACEE A,** Hillsborough Comm Coll, Tampa, FL; SO; MA; Phi Theta Kappa P 90-; AA; Cmnctn Dsrdrs; Spch Lang Path.

**WILLIAMS, STEFANIE L,** Alcorn St Univ, Lorman, MS; JR; BS; Bsn Admn.

**WILLIAMS, STEPHANIE K,** Middle Tn St Univ, Murfreesboro, TN; FR; BS; Felder Hall Sftbl Tm; Animal Sci; Bio.

**WILLIAMS, STEVE L,** Ms St Univ, Miss State, MS; FR; BS; Bapt Stdnt Union; IM Bsktbl; Engr; Cvl Engr.

**WILLIAMS, STEVEN D,** Savannah St Coll, Savannah, GA; SR; BS; Pre-Dental Study Clb 88-; Beta Beta Beta 90-; Ed Enrchmnt Pgm Med Clg GA 90; Bio; Dntstry.

**WILLIAMS, STUART A,** Univ Of Ky, Lexington, KY; JR; BS; Rsdnt Hall Govt 90; Im Bsktbl Tbletennis Sftbl; Im Ftbl Vllybl 90; Elctrcl Eng; Cmptr Eng Or Automtn.

**WILLIAMS, SUNNY M,** Ms Univ For Women, Columbus, MS; SR; BS; Lockheart Soc Club Prlmntrn 87-; SGA Treas 87-90; Stdnt Adv Comm Bus Div Pres 89-; Stdnt Alum Amb 88-90; Mortar Bd 90-; Hnrs Prog Sec 87-; Torch Sec 89-90; Otstndng Stdnt For Bus Admn; Bus Admn; Law.

**WILLIAMS, SUSAN,** East Central Comm Coll, Decatur, MS; FR; Phi Theta Kappa; Vrsty Bsktbl; Sci; Phys Thrpy.

**WILLIAMS, SUSAN DANIELLE,** Univ Of Southern Ms, Hattiesburg, MS; SR; BS; Stdnt Ed Assoc; Gamma Beta Phi; Amer Red Cross; BS; Elem Ed; Tchr.

**WILLIAMS, SUSAN J,** Ms Gulf Coast Comm Coll, Perkinston, MS; SO; Campus Beauty 90; Hmcmng Court 90-; Miss Perk; Perkette Dance Tm Cptn 90-; Ed; Clg Counselor.

**WILLIAMS, SUZANNE M,** Longwood Coll, Farmville, VA; SR; BS; Longwd Plyrs Tech Dir; Alpha Psi Omega; Delta Zeta Sec 90-; Rgby 88-89; Spec Educ; Tch.

**WILLIAMS, TAMMY J,** Fayetteville St Univ, Fayetteville, NC; JR; BA; SCC Crmnl Jstc Clb 88-90; SCC Stdnt Govt Assn VP 89-90; NCCC-SGA Rep 89-90; SCC Grad Mrshl 89; AA Smpsn Comm Coll 90; Crmnl Just; Prob Ofcr/Corrtnl Cnslng.

**WILLIAMS, TAMMY N,** Johnson C Smith Univ, Charlotte, NC; JR; Stdnt Govt/Shaki/Psych Clb/Yrbk Stff/Ms Kappa Alpha Psi; Alpha Kappa Alpha; We Beat The Odds; Prvt Indstry Cncl; Deans List; Marketing/Banking/Finance.

**WILLIAMS, TAMMY R,** Va St Univ, Petersburg, VA; BS 90; Bsnss Admin/Mngmnt; Proprietress Of Retail.

**WILLIAMS, TAMMY T,** Al A & M Univ, Normal, AL; FR; Elec Eng.

**WILLIAMS, TEKITA L,** Alcorn St Univ, Lorman, MS; FR; IRHC; Dean Lst; Miss Robinson Hll 90-; Pol Sci/Pre Law; Lwyr.

**WILLIAMS, TENSIE D,** Talladega Coll, Talladega, AL; SR; BA; Spnsh Clb Scl Wrk Clb; Phlctr; Big Sis/Big Bro Pro; Alpha Kappa Alpha 89-; Vlybl 89-; BA; Scl Wrk.

**WILLIAMS, TERESA,** Alcorn St Univ, Lorman, MS; SO; BA; SNEA 90-; Hnr Roll 89-90; Elem Edctn.

**WILLIAMS, TERESA F,** Saint Francis Coll, Loretto, PA; SR; BS; Stdnt Activ Org 87-88; Yrbk 88-89; Assn Clg Entrepeneurs 90-; NCAA Dvi I Wmns Sccr 87-89; Mgmnt; Financial Mgmnt.

**WILLIAMS, TERRENCE,** Sinclair Comm Coll, Dayton, OH; GD; BA; AF Srgnts Assn 89-; AFR Advsry Brd Cncl 88-; USAF Wrght Pat AFB OH Tech 78-; ABA Comm Clg Air Force 90; Mgmt; Law Bsns.

**WILLIAMS, THOMAS A,** Middle Tn St Univ, Murfreesboro, TN; SR.

**WILLIAMS, THOMAS D,** Univ Of Sc At Columbia, Columbia, SC; JR; BA; Bio; Recombinant DNA Tech.

**WILLIAMS II, THORNELL,** Morehouse Coll, Atlanta, GA; JR; BA; Prospctv Stdnts Smnr Vice Chrmn Pub Rel 90-; Bus Assn VP 89-; Actvts Crdntr 90-; Hnrs Prog 88-; Dns Lst 88-; Frederick Douglass Tutorial Inst 88-; Mntrng Prog; IBM Thomas J Watson Schlr 88-; E B Williams Bus Awds; Natl Achvmnt Schlr 88-; Bus Admin/Finance; Corp Admin.

**WILLIAMS, TIFFANY E,** Ky St Univ, Frankfort, KY; FR; Pep Clb 90-; Rec Amer Clg Assoc 90-; Bus; Acctng.

**WILLIAMS, TIFFANY Y,** Alcorn St Univ, Lorman, MS; SO; BA; Gospel Choir 89-; Nrsng; RN.

**WILLIAMS, TIMOTHY,** Univ Of Md At Eastern Shore, Princess Anne, MD; SO; BA; Bus; Marine Bio.

**WILLIAMS, TINIKA M,** Va St Univ, Petersburg, VA; SO; BA; Bus Admin Mgmnt; Real Estate/Bus.

**WILLIAMS, TONI M,** Tougaloo Coll, Tougaloo, MS; FR; BA; Natl Assn Advncmnt Colored People 90-; Ldr; Admn Recruiter; Engl/Jrnlsm; Law.

**WILLIAMS, TORI D,** Nc Agri & Tech St Univ, Greensboro, NC; SR; Am Chem Soc Pres 89-90; Alpha Chi; Alpha Lambda Delta Edtr 87-88; Beta Kappa Chi Treas 90; Mc Neil Cons Prod Coop Edn 88; Burroughs Wellcome Coop Edn 90-; BS 90; Chem; Ph D Biochem.

**WILLIAMS, TORRANCE,** Univ Of Sc At Columbia, Columbia, SC; FR; BA; NAACP 90-; Dean Lst 90; Frgn Exch Prog 90-; Bus Admn; Mrktng/MBA.

**WILLIAMS, TRACEY T,** Univ Of South Al, Mobile, AL; JR; Alpha Chi; Ed; Tch.

**WILLIAMS, TRACEY V,** Coppin St Coll, Baltimore, MD; JR; BS; SIFE Pres 90; Crmnl Jstc Clb 89-; Org/Unftnt Chldrn Cnslr/Grp Ldr 87-89; Crmnl Jstc; MA US Gov.

**WILLIAMS, TRACY L,** Duquesne Univ, Pittsburgh, PA; SR; BSBA; Beta Gamma Sigma; Phi Theta Kappa 89-; Mgmt Advsry Brd 90-; AS Nrthrn VA Comm Coll 89; Bus Admin/Mgmt.

**WILLIAMS, TRACY R,** Tn St Univ, Nashville, TN; JR; Peer Cnslr 89-; Alpha Kappa Alpha 90-.

**WILLIAMS, TRINA Y,** Alcorn St Univ, Lorman, MS; SO; BS; Alpha Kappa Alpha 90-; Acctg Bus Admn; CPA.

**WILLIAMS, TRISHA J,** Fl A & M Univ, Tallahassee, FL; SR; Grphc Arts Club V P; Acad Dscplne Comm 89-; Cum Laude; Intrnshp Atlanta Color Cncpts Grphc Tech 90; BS; Grphc Arts Prntng Prdctn Tech; Prdctn Mgr.

**WILLIAMS, TYSHELLY M,** Va St Univ, Petersburg, VA; SO; BS; Mrktg Clb 89-; NAACP 90-; Tide Wtr Pre Alumni 90-; Mrktg; Mngr.

**WILLIAMS, URSULA M,** Ohio Valley Coll, Parkersburg, WV; FR; BA; School Plays; Singers; Hnrs Pgm; Sigma Epsilon Chi; Weight Trng; Flg Ftbl; Appl/Msc Ed; Bnd Dir/Symph.

**WILLIAMS, VANESSA C,** Comm Coll Algny Co Algny Cmps, Pittsburgh, PA; SO; BA; Schlrs Awd; Drama Clb; Army Reserves; Assoc Deg Upholstery; Bus; Mgmnt.

**WILLIAMS, VERNA J,** Bishop St Comm Coll, Mobile, AL; SO; AD; Phi Theta Kappa; Ch Of God Mbr; AS N W Al Sta Jr Clg 77-79; Funeral Serv Educ; Lic Emblmr/Fun Dir.

**WILLIAMS, VICKIE E,** Univ Of Nc At Asheville, Asheville, NC; SR; BA; ISAS Treas 90-; Alpha Kappa Delta 89-; Phi Eta Sigma 87-; NC Dept Msng Persons Intern 90; Sociology Awd; Deans Lst 87-; Sociology/Crmnl Jstce.

**WILLIAMS, VICTORIA A,** Morris Coll, Sumter, SC; SO; Sociology.

**WILLIAMS, VIVIAN D,** Ny Univ, New York, NY; SO; BA; BDPA 85-; Beth Israel Hosp Vol; NYS Gov Sch Mentoring Prog Vol; Org Cmmnctns; Law.

**WILLIAMS, WARREN B,** Cumberland Coll, Williamsburg, KY; SR; BS; Yng Rpblcns Pres 87-88; Bptst Std Un 89-; Phi Alpha Theta VP 89-; AA Cntrl FL Comm Clg 88; Hstry; Clg Prfssr.

**WILLIAMS, WARREN M,** Manna Bible Inst, Philadelphia, PA; JR; Cumberaldn Coll; Moody Bible Inst; Lincoln Prep Coll; Phi Lambda Beta.

**WILLIAMS, WAYNE C,** Saint Pauls Coll, Lawrenceville, VA; SO; Cl Exec Cncl V P; Alpha Phi Alpha Asst Coord; Spec Pres Schlrshp 89-; Acctng; CPA.

**WILLIAMS, WILLIAM CHADWICK,** Waycross Coll, Waycross, GA; JR; BBA; Fnc.

**WILLIAMS IV, WILLIAM H,** Middle Tn St Univ, Murfreesboro, TN; JR; BA; Univ Thtr 88-; Thtr; Actor/Dir.

**WILLIAMS, WILLIAM K,** Univ Of Tn At Martin, Martin, TN; SR; BS; Coop Edn Prog 87-90; Phi Eta Sigma 83-; Phi Kappa Phi 90-; Comp Sci.

**WILLIAMS, WILMA E,** Beckley Coll, Beckley, WV; FR; BA; Elem Ed.

**WILLIAMS, WYVETTA G,** Tuskegee Univ, Tuskegee Inst, AL; SR; BS; SNEA 88-; Natl Coalition 100 Blck Wmn 90-; NAACP 89-; Kappa Delta Pi 90-; Alpha Kappa Mu; Schlrs Pgm Columbia Univ; Early Chldhd Edn; Tchr/Adminstr.

**WILLIAMS, YOLANDA A,** Columbia Union Coll, Takoma Park, MD; JR; BS; Afrcn Amrcn Wmn Assn; Amrcn Assn Blck Wmn Entrprnrs VP 84-86; Morris Clg Alumni Assn Corsp Sec 83-85; Ntnl Cncl Negro Wmn Inc BAAC Sectn Rcrdng Sec 81-84; Rosa Prks Awd Wmn Com Srvc 88; Orgnztnl Mgmnt; Pblc Rltns Comm.

**WILLIAMS, YOLANDE M,** Johnson C Smith Univ, Charlotte, NC; FR; Univ Choir 90-; Cmps All Star Chlng Tm 90-; Hnrs Coll Prog Frshmn 90-; Hstry/Pre Law; Corp Law/Prfsr.

**WILLIAMS, YVETTA L,** Tougaloo Coll, Tougaloo, MS; FR; BA; Ladies Blck Gold Sec 90-; Hall Pres 90-; NADSA 90-; VP Schlr 90-; Duo Drama Interprtn Awd 90-; Engl; Music/Movie/Tele/Prdcr/Wrtr.

**WILLIAMS, ZONDRAH L,** Memphis St Univ, Memphis, TN; SR; BA; Blck Stdnt Assn 90-; Phych Clb 90-; Gospel Choir; BSU Corres Sec 88-; Sigma Gamma Rho Sec 90-; Psych; MA Schl Psych.

**WILLIAMS-DAUGHERTY, KIMBERLEE,** Middle Tn St Univ, Murfreesboro, TN; SR; BS; STEA 89-; TEA 89; Tau Omicron 89-; Kappa Delta Pi 89-; Phi Kappa Phi; IM Sprts 87-90; Elem Educ; Prim Grd Sci Tchr.

**WILLIAMS-LESCAK, ANTHONY L,** Savannah Coll Of Art & Design, Savannah, GA; SR; BA; Illstrtn.

**WILLIAMS-ORAGE, CHARLESETTA L,** Savannah St Coll, Savannah, GA; BSW; Crvr Hghts Mssn Imprvemnt Cmmnty Org Asst Scrtry 90; AA Armstrong State Clg 72; Scl Wrk; Scl Wrk/Nrsng.

**WILLIAMSON, ANGELA L,** Johnson C Smith Univ, Charlotte, NC; JR; BS; Socty Opprtnts Sci SGAP Rep 90-; MSAC 90-; Alpha Chi 90-; Alpha Kappa Mu 90-; Hnrs Coll; Biology; Medicine.

**WILLIAMSON, BRENAE BETTRENA,** Stillman Coll, Tuscaloosa, AL; FR; BS; Hnrs Prgrm Gamma Iota Sigma 90-; Deans List 90-; Cllgt Awrd 90; Chmstry; Nrsrgn.

**WILLIAMSON, CHERYL A,** Snead St Jr Coll, Boaz, AL; SO; BA; Outstdng Biology Stdnt 90-; Phi Theta Kappa; Chmstry Lab Asst; Lola Tidwell Deeskiny Tidwell Strauss Schlrshp 89; Carl Roebuck Sci Schlrshp; Biology; Phys Thrpy.

**WILLIAMSON, CORINNE B,** Univ Of South Al, Mobile, AL; SR; BA; Phi Beta Kappa 85-86; Early Chldhd Edctn; Tchr.

**WILLIAMSON, DAVID A,** Univ Of Toledo, Toledo, OH; FR; BE; Sprts Med/Phys Therpy.

**WILLIAMSON, DEBBIE R,** Tn Temple Univ, Chattanooga, TN; SR; BS; Band 88-89; Choir VP 88-90; Univ Theatre 88-; Theta Kappa Rho Act Dir 90-; Wesley Soc Fml VP 88-89; Chrldng 88-90; Bible Degree Word Of Life Bible Inst 87-88; Speech Cmctns; Pub Rels/Church Drama.

**WILLIAMSON, DICK MURVIN,** Piedmont Comm Coll, Roxboro, NC; SO; BA; Gamma Beta Pai; AS; Human Resources Mngmnt; Social Serv Fld.

**WILLIAMSON, ELLEN M,** Univ Of Ri, Kingston, RI; SO; BS; Cert Katherine Gibbs Sch 82; Nrsng.

**WILLIAMSON JR, GARY W,** Guilford Coll, Greensboro, NC; FR; BA; IM Sftbl; Bio; Optmtry.

**WILLIAMSON, GINA R,** Lexington Comm Coll, Lexington, KY; FR; MBA; Nrsng.

**WILLIAMSON, HEATHER L,** Elon Coll, Elon, NC; JR; BA; Hon Pgm 88-; SNCAE; Zeta Tau Alpha Pgm Cncl 89-; IM Tennis 89; Elem Edn; Teach.**

**WILLIAMSON, HIRAM C,** Roane St Comm Coll, Harriman, TN; SO; BS; Gamma Beta Phi 90-; Cmptr Sci; Air Force Offcr.

**WILLIAMSON, HOLLY A,** Univ Of Cincinnati, Cincinnati, OH; SO; BSN; Natl Stdnt Nrs Assc; OH Stdnt Nrs Assc; Nrsng; Cont Ed Ph D Nrsng.

**WILLIAMSON, JASON R,** Univ Of Louisville, Louisville, KY; FR; Smile Clb; Ent Tech Crew; Cinemtc Arts Comm; Dns Schlr; Bld Donr.

**WILLIAMSON, JEFFREY D,** Univ Of Sc At Columbia, Columbia, SC; SO.

**WILLIAMSON, JESSICA L,** Cumberland Coll, Williamsburg, KY; SO; BA; SIFE; Phi Beta Lambda Sec 90-; Coats Cold Drv 90-; Bus Prncpls Evnt St; Accntng/Pol Sci; Corp Law/CPA.

**WILLIAMSON, JILL R,** Ms St Univ, Miss State, MS; JR; Mrchng Bnd 88-90; Symphnc Bnd 89; Stg Bnd 88-; Gamma Beta Phi 89-; Phi Eta Sigma 89-; Alpha Lambda Delta 89-; Sigma Alpha Iota Treas 9-; Delta Delta Delta Fndrsng Chrmn; Phrmcy.

**WILLIAMSON, JOANNA M,** Union Univ, Jackson, TN; FR; Hnrs Clb; Kappa Delta Asst Treas; BSBA; Accntng; Accntnt.

**WILLIAMSON, JULIE N,** Univ Of Nc At Charlotte, Charlotte, NC; SR; BA; Soc Hmn Rsr C Mgmnt 89-90; Blck Stdnt Un 88-89; NAACP 88-89; Psychology; Hmn Rsrc Mgmnt.

**WILLIAMSON, KATHLEEN M,** Wilmington Coll, New Castle, DE; JR; BSN; Amercn Heart Assoc 89-; DE Nrs Assoc; Sivic Assoc Breezewood I; Natl Assoc Of Hlth Care Recrtrs 90-; Phila Area Nrs Cruitr Assoc 90-; ADN VT Clg Of Norwich Univ 83; Nrsng.

**WILLIAMSON, KATRINA R,** Marshall University, Huntington, WV; SR; BBA; Ntnl Mngmnt Assc Soc Serv Chrmn Pres 90-; Panhellenic Cncl VP Enrchmnt 90-; Gamma Beta Phi Treas 90-; Sigma Sigma Sigma Model Pldg Sprt Chrmn 90-; Ashland Oil Inc Intrnshp 90-; Chrldr 89-; Mngmnt; Law.

**WILLIAMSON, KEVIN G,** East Tn St Univ, Johnson City, TN; SR; BS; Soc Of Mfg Engrs; Deans Lst 90; Elec Engr; Comp.

**WILLIAMSON, KONI J,** Watterson Coll, Louisville, KY; JR; Deans Lst 90-; Pres Lst 90-; Office Mgr 72-; Bus Mgmnt; Bus Admin.

**WILLIAMSON, LETHA,** Benedict Coll, Columbia, SC; GD; MA; Dns Lst 86-90; BA 90; Crmnl Jstc; Law.

**WILLIAMSON, MARLENE H,** Meridian Comm Coll, Meridian, MS; SO; BPA; Ambsdr 90-; Acctng Tutor 90-; Phi Theta Kappa VP 90-; Salute/Exclnc 90-; Cir Exclnc 90-; AA; Acctng; CPA Tchng.

**WILLIAMSON, MYRA A,** Comm Coll Algny Co Algny Cmps, Pittsburgh, PA; FR; ASSOC; Typing I II Acctng I; Cert CCAC Homewood B Branch 84; Pedology; Elem Sch Teacher.

**WILLIAMSON, NEIL A,** Miami Dade Comm Coll South, Miami, FL; SO; BA; Sci; Meteorology.

**WILLIAMSON, PAMELA J,** Winthrop Coll, Rock Hill, SC; FR; BS; Alpha Gamda Delta; Prsdnts Lst 90-; Dance Tm 90-; Elem Edctn; Tchr.

**WILLIAMSON, PATRICK A,** Voorhees Coll, Denmark, SC; JR; BS; Stdnt Gvmnt Assn Prlmntrn 88-89; Gnrl Bsns Clb Prsdnt 87-89; Nwspr Edtr Chf 90-; Alpha Chi 90-; Ntnl Tchncl Vctnl Hnr Soc 87-89; Alpha Phi Psi Chrmn 88-; Peer Cnslr 87-89; SIFE VP 88-89; AB Dnmrk Tchncl Clg 89; Bsns Admnstrtn; Mgmt.

**WILLIAMSON, RICHARD C,** Meridian Comm Coll, Meridian, MS; SO; Math; Mech Eng.

**WILLIAMSON, SHEILA W,** Union Univ, Jackson, TN; BA; Bpt Student Union 86-91; Sigma Tau Delta 91; Summer Foreign Missionary Hondaras Philippines/Mexico/Belize/Central Amer 87-91; Intern Jackson Psyht Hptl 89; Intern Rape Assist Prog 87; English Secdy Educ; Homemaking.

**WILLIAMSON, STACY L,** Georgetown Coll, Georgetown, KY; SO; BS; Envrmtl Action Clb 90-; Lambda Chi Alpha 90-; Biology.

**WILLIAMSON, STEPHEN M,** Fl Coll, Temple Terrace, FL; FR; AA; Forensics 90-; Play Prodctn The Sount Of Music; Soph Cls Orientn Comm; Phi Sigma Chi 90-; Pol Sci; Law/Medcn.

**WILLIAMSON, TODD D,** Univ Of Southern Ms, Hattiesburg, MS; SR; BSBS; Alpha Epsilon Delta; Sigma Chi Univ MS; BSBA 88; Zlgy; Med.

**WILLIAMSON, TONYA N,** Youngstown St Univ, Youngstown, OH; FR; BA; Comp Prgrmmng; Comp Prgrmmr.

**WILLIAMSON, TRACY A,** Wilmington Coll, Wilmington, OH; FR; AB; IM Bsktbl 90-; Vrsty Fst Ptch Sftbl Tm 90-; Acctng; CPA.

**WILLIAMSON-STAFF, JEAN,** Belmont Coll, Nashville, TN; SR; BS; Soc Work Clb 89-; Psi Chi VP; Tri Delta 78-79; Psychlgy; Clncl Soc Wrk.

**WILLIFORD, ELIZABETH L,** Wv Univ, Morgantown, WV; SR; Undrgrad Scho Of Soc Wrk Org 90-; Soc Wrk.

**WILLIFORD, JIPPER P,** William Carey Coll, Hattiesburg, MS; SO; BA; CRV 89-; Missions Biblical Studies; Pastor.

**WILLIFORD, REBECCA W,** Roane St Comm Coll, Harriman, TN; SO; Envrmntl Hlth Tech.

**WILLINGHAM, CRYSTAL N,** Howard Univ, Washington, DC; JR; BARCH; Amer Inst Of Archtctre Stdnts Hwrd Chap VP 88-; Hwrd Univ Bdmntn Clb Pres 89-; CA Clb 88-; Hstrc Amer Bldng Srvy Intrshp; Bdmntn Clb Pres 89-; Archtctre.

**WILLINGHAM, RANDY A,** Harding Grad School Of Relig, Memphis, TN; GD; MDIV; Dns Lst; NCAA All Amer Wrstlng Okla St; Olmpc Altrnt 84; BA 88; Cert 87; New Tstmnt; Tchg.

**WILLINGS, MICHAEL P,** Niagara Univ, Niagara Univ, NY; SO; BA; Hsty Clb 90; Bsbl 88-90; Hstry; Tchr.

**WILLIS, AMY L,** Truett Mc Connell Coll, Cleveland, GA; SO; Phi Theta Kappa Pr 90-; Class VP 90-; Bapt Union Exec Cncl 89-; Pr Clb 89-; Homecoming Crt 89-; Miss TMC 90-; Sftbl 89-; AS; Pharmacy.

**WILLIS, ANDREW S,** Georgetown Univ, Washington, DC; SR; BSBA; Std Actv Cmmssn 90-; Clg Rpblcns 87-; Grgtwn Invstmnt Allnc 87-; Beta Gamma Sigma 89-; Fncl Mgmt Asc 90-; Intrn Sntr Wm Cohen 90; Chs Mnhtn Bnk Intrn 90; ME Gvr Intrn 89; IM Sftbl/Ftbl/Bsktbl/Whfflbl 87-; Fnce/Govt; Invstmnt Bnkng MBA.

**WILLIS, ANGELA L,** Univ Of Cincinnati-Clrmnt Coll, Batavia, OH; FR; BA; Mntrng Schlrshp 90-; Vlybl; Bsn; Admin.

**WILLIS, CHRISTOPHER J,** Lincoln Univ, Lincoln Univ, PA; FR; Clss Pblc Rltns Commtt 90-; Engl; Law.

**WILLIS, DARLENE,** Univ Of Cin R Walters Coll, Blue Ash, OH; SO; BA; Phi Theta Kappa V P; NAR 86-; Bd/Rltrs 86-; CBR Lgstve Cmte; C/C 86-; Realtor Sls Mgr 86-; Busn Admin; R E Brkrge/Dvlp.

**WILLIS, EMILY BRANT,** Univ Of Sc At Columbia, Columbia, SC; SO; BA; Early Childhood Ed; Tchng.

**WILLIS, ERICA R,** Alcorn St Univ, Lorman, MS; JR; BA; Eastrn Star; Hon Stdnts Org; Alpha Kappa Mu; Deans Lst 88-; Acdmc Schlrshp; Bnd 88-; Bus Admin.

**WILLIS, GREGORY A,** Morehouse Coll, Atlanta, GA; FR; BA; Hnrs Prgm Clb 90-; Mrhse Mntrng Prgm 90-; Blgy.

**WILLIS, JENNIFER L,** Fl Coll, Temple Terrace, FL; SO; BA; Stdnt Body Govt V P 90-; Drama Clb V P 90-; Forensics; Phi Sigma Chi 89-90; Alpha Clb 90-; Hnr Rl 89-90; Deans Lst; AA; Elem Educ; Tchng.

**WILLIS, JENNIFER S,** Schenectady County Comm Coll, Schenectady, NY; FR; AS; Waitress; Acctg; Bk Keeper.

**WILLIS, JEWELL L,** Wv Northern Comm Coll, Wheeling, WV; FR; AS; Stdnt Nrs Assn; Phi Theta Kappa Campus Rep; Nrsng; RN.

**WILLIS, JOSEPH C,** Itawamba Comm Coll, Fulton, MS; BA; Med; Physcl Thrpst.

**WILLIS, KURT A,** Fl A & M Univ, Tallahassee, FL; SO; PHARM; Cir K Clb 90-; Cert Schlrshp Acad Exclnc 89-90; Phrmcst.

**WILLIS, LAUREN R,** Fl International Univ, Miami, FL; JR; BS; Stdnt Dietetic Assoc Secr 90-; Chi Phi Ltl Sis 86-88; AA Santa Fe Cmnty Clg 89; Dietetics/Nutr; Reg Dietitian.

**WILLIS, LE TRICA R,** Alcorn St Univ, Lorman, MS; SO; BS; Psych Clb; Chr; Educ Psych; Clncl Psych.

**WILLIS, LEONA D,** Howard Univ, Washington, DC; JR; BA; Schl Cmcntns Stdnt Cncl Grvnc Dir 90-; Univ Film Org Pres; Yrbk Video Dir 90-; Gldn Key; Zeta Phi Beta 1st Anti Basileus; Univ Trustee Schlrshp; Film Prdctn/Cmnctns; Film Dir.

**WILLIS, MARC D,** Central St Univ, Wilberforce, OH; GD; BS; Mngmnt Clb Pr 89-90; Fin/Inv Soc 90; Natl Bus League 89-90; Prin Schlrshp 86-87; Deans Lst 90; Prof Dev Cert 90; IM Bsktbl 86-89; Bus Mngmnt.

**WILLIS, MELISSA L,** Univ Of Ga, Athens, GA; SR; BSED; Stdnt Tchng Alps Rd Ele; IMS Gainesville Clg 87-89; Erly Chldhd Ed; Tchng.

**WILLIS, NANCY L,** Univ Of Nc At Greensboro, Greensboro, NC; SR; BSN; Sigma Theta Tau; Chrch Actvts Ltrcy Tutor; Hosp RN; ASN Rckngham Comm Clg 79; Nrsng; Hlth MS.

**WILLIS, RHONDA S,** Univ Of Va Clinch Valley Coll, Wise, VA; SR; BA; Appalachia PTA 89-; Elem Educ/Hstry; Elem Tchr.

**WILLIS, ROY T,** Fl St Univ, Tallahassee, FL; SR; MS; Eng Hnr Soc 90-; Amer Soc Cvl Eng 89-; FL Assc Cdstrl Mpprs 90-; BS; Cvl Eng.

**WILLIS, ROZETTER,** Alcorn St Univ, Lorman, MS; FR; BS; Pryr Bnd 90-; Bptst Stdnt Un 90-; Tennis 90-; Biolgy; Med.

**WILLIS, SEAN B,** Fl A & M Univ, Tallahassee, FL; FR; MBA; Cuong Nhu Martial Arts Slf Dfns Clb 90-; Music; Cmpstn/Prmnc.

**WILLIS, SHANNON K,** Bay Path Coll, Longmeadow, MA; FR; AS; Stdnt Govt 90-; Class Sec 90-; Goldn Z Clb Sec 90-; Bus.

**WILLIS, SHEILA L,** Daytona Beach Comm Coll, Daytona Beach, FL; FR; BA; Hglr Co Hmne Scty Brd Of Dirs 88-; Dytna Nrth Qdvsry Cncl Advsry Brd 90-; Jffrsn Co Anml Wlfre Lge Exec Brd 78; Prfssnl Flrl Dsgnr 88; Elem Educ Psych; Tch Whle Prsng M Div Psych.

**WILLIS, TAKEISHA,** Atlantic Comm Coll, Mays Landing, NJ; FR; AAS; Nrsg; RN.

**WILLIS, TAMMY J,** Commonwealth Coll, Virginia Beach, VA; SO; Acctg Clb 90; Alpha Beta Gamma 90; Phi Beta Lambda 89-90; AAS Bus Mgmt 90; AAS Acctg 90; Bus-Acctg; Mgmt.

**WILLIS, TEENICKIA R,** Ky St Univ, Frankfort, KY; FR; BA; Otsntng 90-; Whitney Yng Clg Outstndng 90-; Math; Profr.

**WILLIS, TINA M,** Fl St Univ, Tallahassee, FL; JR; BA; Pre-Law Soc VP 89-; Cmps Nwspr Wrtr 90; Amer Red Crs CPR Frst Aid Instctr 88-90; Phi Alpha Theta; Sigma Kappa 90-; Hstry; Law.

**WILLIS, TRACY D,** Stillman Coll, Tuscaloosa, AL; SO; BED; NAACP; Eckerd Schlrs; Elmntry Ed/Psychlgy; Principle.

**WILLIS, VALERIE M,** Fort Valley St Coll, Fort Valley, GA; FR; BA; Plyrs Guild 90-; Coop Dvlpmntl Energy Pgm 90-; Cmntr Banks Pierro Rutland Soc Sci Colloquium; Interpretation/Joseph Adkins Invtnl; Pol Sci; Law.

**WILLMORE, YOLANDA T,** Manhattanville Coll, Purchase, NY; SR; BA; Tchr Asst; Crdntd Mnhttnvll Stdnt Artst Cllbrtn; Ltn Amrcn Stdtn Org 87-; Pltcl Sci.

**WILLMOT, JACQUELINE M,** Univ Of Pittsburgh, Pittsburgh, PA; GD; MSN; Pnnsylvn Prntl Assoc; Natl Assoc Nntl Nrs; Sigma Theta Tau 88-; Hgh Hnrs; CPR Instr; Nntl Intsv Cr Lbr Dlvry RN; BSN 83; Prntl Nntl Nrsng.

**WILLMOTT III, ROBERT W,** Univ Of Ky, Lexington, KY; SR; BA; Sccr Clb 87-88; Clg Schlrs Amer 90-; Delta Tau Delta; Dns Lst 90; US Army; Anthrplgy; US Army.

**WILLOCK, EARDLEY G,** City Univ Of Ny Baruch Coll, New York, NY; SR; BBA; Nwspr Treas 89-; Golden Key Mbr 90-; Phi Theta Kappa 87-88; Beta Gamma Sigma Mbr 90-; AAS Borough Manhattan Comm Clg 88; Acctg; Bus.

**WILLOCK, GREGORY C,** City Univ Of Ny City Coll, New York, NY; JR; BSC; Antigua/Barbuda Stdnts Assn Treas 88-89; Frshmn Hnr Soc 88-; Gldn Ky 90-; T A Comm Arch Dept Tchrs Assist 90-; Architecture.

**WILLOCKS, BETTY GAIL,** Pellissippi St Tech Comm Coll, Knoxville, TN; SO; BSN; Beta Sigma Phi VP 78-87; Amer Red Cross Clinic Chrmn 88-89; Martha Washington Chptr 231 OES Past Matron 68-; Sci/Nursing.

**WILLOUGHBY, GREGORY L,** Western Ky Univ, Bowling Green, KY; JR; BS; Agronomy Clb Pres 89-; Assoc Stdnt Govt Sci Clg Rep 89; Ag Ed Clb Pres 88; Phi Eta Sigma Membr 88; Phi Kappa Phi; Golden Key Treas; Alpha Zeta Frat Chncllr; Gama Theta Upsilon Membr 90; Outstndg Sr Aer Scty Of Agrnmy; Outstndg Cmptnce; Ag/Grphy; Clg Prof.

**WILLOUGHBY, MARGARET E,** Ms St Univ, Miss State, MS; FR; BA; Fashion Brd/Refrmd Flwshp 90-; Gamma Beta Phi/Phi Eta Sigma 90-; Phi Mu Schlr Hd 90-; Childrens Miracle Netwrk TV United Way 90-; Pr Lst/Pr Schlr 90-; IM Tennis/Ftbl/Vlybl; Art; Comp Graphics.

**WILLOUGHBY, STEPHANIE JILL,** Memphis St Univ, Memphis, TN; JR; BS; Home Clb NMJC Regional Pres 87; Homecoming Queen NMJC 86-87; Class Favorite/Class Attractive NMJC 87; AS NE Mississippi JR Clg 87; Elmntry Ed.

**WILLS, ANGELA L,** Univ Of Sc At Columbia, Columbia, SC; SO; BS; Stdnt Govtmnt Class Senator 90-; Business Soc Stdnt Govt Rep 90; Natl Assoc Of Accntnts USCS Acctg Club; Piedmont Soc V Pres; Gama Beta Phi V Pres; Sigma Delta Psi Ed Dir 90; Rotaract Sec; Piedmont Scholar; Bus Admnstrn Acctg; Acctg.

**WILLS, CHERI J,** Mount Aloysius Jr Coll, Cresson, PA; FR; AA; Interpreters Clb 90-; Sign Lang Interpreting.

**WILLS, CLAYTON E,** Ashland Comm Coll, Ashland, KY; FR; ASN; ACC 21st Cntry Plnng Commsn Stdnt Rep; Nrsng.

**WILLS, ELIZABETH N,** Marshall University, Huntington, WV; JR; BA; Natl Stdnts Spch Lang Hrng Assn 89-; Phi Eta Sigma 89-; Spch Path/Audlgy; Spch Path.

**WILLS, JACQUELYN J,** Univ Of Southern Ms, Hattiesburg, MS; SO; BA; Shotokan Karate Clb V P 90-; Pol Sci; Law.

**WILLS, MELISSA A,** Indiana Univ Of Pa, Indiana, PA; JR.

**WILLS, REGINA A,** Central Al Comm Coll, Alexander City, AL; FR; BA; Ambassador; Phi Theta Kappa; Chem; Pharmacy.

**WILLS, SANDRA J,** Howard Univ, Washington, DC; GD; Spch Comm Assn 87-; Intl Assn Bus Cmnctns 82-; Estrn Comnctn Assn 87-; Grad Asst 88-90; Flw Grad Arts/Sci Schl 90-; MA Concordia U 87; BA Mt St Vincent U 81; Ph D; Org Cmnctns; Asst Prof.

**WILLS, STEPHANIE L,** Bridgewater Coll, Bridgewater, VA; SR; BS; Oratorio Chr; Cncrt Chr; Chrl; SEA VP 89-; Msn Educ Natl Cnfrnc Dorm Pres 90-; Rsdnc Hl Cncl; Acdmc Schlrshp 87-; Stdnt Tchng; Elem Ed; Tchng.

**WILLS, THOMAS A,** Ms St Univ, Miss State, MS; SR; BA; Trnsprttn; Physcl Dstrbtn.

**WILMOT, CHERYL A,** S U N Y At Binghamton, Binghamton, NY; JR; BS; Nalt Coll Bus Merit Awrd 90-; Bus Mngmnt; Hmn Rsrc Mngmnt.

**WILMOT, COREY L,** Atlantic Union Coll, S Lancaster, MA; JR; BS; Clss VP 90-; Slmndrs Pres 90-; Bus Admin; Lndscpng.

**WILMOTH, AMY R,** Marshall University, Huntington, WV; SR; BA; Mlti Sbjcts K-8; Tchr.

**WILMOTH, DANA M,** Va Commonwealth Univ, Richmond, VA; SO; BSN; Nrsng Clb 90-; Phi Eta Sigma; Dns Lst 89-; Nrsng.**

**WILMOTH, DEBORAH A,** Commonwealth Coll, Virginia Beach, VA; Pres Lst 90; Deans Lst 91; MAA.

**WILMS, JEREMY,** Brevard Coll, Brevard, NC; FR; BFA; Music; Perf/Educ.

**WILSHIRE, DEBRA A,** Patrick Henry Comm Coll, Martinsville, VA; SO; AD; SNAV 90-; ABWA 89-; Dns Lst; Hnrs Lst; Phi Thetta Kappa; Tutor Anatmy Phys; Nrsng.

**WILSON, ADAM J,** Cape Fear Comm Coll, Wilmington, NC; GD; ASSOC; Crmnl Jstc; Law Enfrcmnt.

**WILSON, ALICIA A,** Univ Of Southern Ms, Hattiesburg, MS; SR; BS; Bptst Stdnt Union; Stdnt Nrs Assn Sthrn MS; Nrsng; RN.

**WILSON, ALICIA S,** Shelton St Comm Coll, Tuscaloosa, AL; FR; BA; Full Tuition Acad Schlrshp; Acctng; CPA.

**WILSON, ALLEN L,** Mayland Comm Coll, Spruce Pine, NC; SO; AAS; Stdnt Govt Rep 90-; Cmptr Sci; Cmptr Prgrmr.

**WILSON, AMANDA T,** Univ Of Ga, Athens, GA; SR; BS; Bapt Stdnt Union; Early Chldhd Ed; Ed.

**WILSON, AMY R,** Memphis St Univ, Memphis, TN; SR; BBA; Bus/Acctng; CPA.

**WILSON, ANGEL S,** Owensboro Comm Coll, Owensboro, KY; SO; ASSOC; DPMA Pres 90-; Cmptr Info Systs; Prgrmr.

**WILSON, ANGELA M,** Central Al Comm Coll, Alexander City, AL; SO; BED; Phi Theta Kappa 90-; Engl; Tchr.

**WILSON, ANN M,** Alcorn St Univ, Lorman, MS; SR; BS; Prof Scrtries Pres 89-90; Var Bsktbl 87-88; Cert S Tchncl Clg; Offce Admin; Prlgl.

**WILSON, ANNA M,** Univ Of Tn At Martin, Martin, TN; SO; Pre Physcl Thrpy Clb 89-; Bnd Flg Capt 2 Yr 89-; Mu Epsilon Delta Lib 90-; Alpha Gamma Rho Ltl Sr Pldg Trnr 90-; IM Sftbl 90; Pre-Physcl Thrpy; Physcl Thrpst.

**WILSON, ANTHONY THOMAS,** Al A & M Univ, Normal, AL; FR; Chem; Chem Engr.

**WILSON, BARBARA A,** Memphis St Univ, Memphis, TN; SR; BA; Stdnt Govt Sntr; FLAGS; Sigma Chi; Amer Red Cross; Crim Just; Forensic Sci.

**WILSON, BARBARA J,** Davis & Elkins Coll, Elkins, WV; SO; BS; Nrsng Stdnt Assoc; DE Hnr Schlrhsp; Pyschtrc; OB; Nrs Anthtst; Nrsng.

**WILSON, BARRY A,** Univ Of Sc At Columbia, Columbia, SC; JR; Flwshp Christian Atheletes; ROTC; Crim Justice Assoc; Gama Beta Phi; Phi Eta Sigma; Natl Grd Assoc; IM; Criminal Justice; Law.

**WILSON, BEVERLEY R,** Fl International Univ, Miami, FL; GD; Stdnt Cncl VP 88-89; Htl Sls/Mktg Assn; Brtsh Cmmnwlth Schlrshp; Cert Merit-Wyndham Htl Chain Bahamas; Assoc Bahamas Htl Trng Coll 88; BS FL Intl Univ 90; Hotelier.

**WILSON, BEVERLY R,** Middle Tn St Univ, Murfreesboro, TN; SO; BS; Bsns; Bsns HS Tchr.

**WILSON, BRENDA JOY,** Univ Of Cincinnati-Clrmnt Coll, Batavia, OH; SO; BBA; Chrty Bapt Chrch; Bsnss; Info Syst.

**WILSON, BRETT E,** Radford Univ, Radford, VA; JR; BA; Deans Lst 90-; Tau Kappa Epsilon Advrtsng Com 89-; Acad All-Am Gymnastics 90-; Most Imprvd Gymnast 89-; Gymnastics Tm Capt 90-; Graphic Dsgn; Advrtsng Illustr.

**WILSON, BRETT M,** East Tn St Univ, Johnson City, TN; SO; BA; Alpha Lambda Delta 90-; Gamma Beta Phi; Delta Sigma Pi; Acctg Tutrg Srvc; Acctg.

**WILSON, BRIDGETTE E,** S U N Y Coll Of Tech At Alfred, Alfred, NY; SO; Bus Mktg Clb Alfred State Coll VP; Phi Theta Kappa; Stdnt Of Yr Bus Admin; Dns Lst; Bus Admin; Continue Educ.

**WILSON, CARISA M,** Univ Of Miami, Coral Gables, FL; FR; BMA; Stdnt Gvrnmnt Spcl Events 90-; Alpha Lambda Delta 90-; Msc Prfrmnc Scntfc Psychlgy; Orchstrl Prfrmr.

**WILSON, CARMICHAEL X,** Chesterfield Marlboro Coll, Cheraw, SC; FR.

**WILSON, CAROLYN A,** Bridgewater Coll, Bridgewater, VA; SR; BA; Ski Outdr Clb 90-; Brdgwtr Clg Intl Clb 90-; Math Clb 90-; Lambda Soc 88-; Alpha Chi 89-; Dns Lst 87-; Phi Beta Lambda Busn Clb V P 88-; Econ Clb 90-; Pres Schlrshp 87-; Schlrshp Excep Pot Mgmt 90-; Busn Admin/Econ; Law.

**WILSON, CAROLYN F,** Fl International Univ, Miami, FL; SR; BSW; Phi Lambda; Otstndng Schlr 90; Grdn Ad Litme 88-; Otstndng Srvc Grdns Ltm; Intern Grdn Ad Ltm; Tch Cordnt Deprmntl Exms; AA 88; Scl Wrk.

**WILSON, CASEY M,** Oh Wesleyan Univ, Delaware, OH; FR; BA; Wesleyan Stdnt Fdtn; Symph Wnd Ensmbl 90-; Circle K 90-; Phi Eta Sigma; Hnrs Stdnt 90-; Big Pal Little Pal 90-; Pres Schlrshp 90-; Psych/Frnch; Pstrl Cnslg.

**WILSON, CASSAUNDRA L,** Kent St Univ Kent Cmps, Kent, OH; FR; College Lf 90-; Hnrs Coll 90-; Psychology; Pediatrics.

**WILSON, CHAD E,** Piedmont Tech Coll, Greenwood, SC; FR; MBA; Deans Lst; Hvac Tech.

**WILSON, CHARLENE,** Bishop St Comm Coll, Mobile, AL; SO; BED; AS; Sec; Legal Office.

**WILSON, CHARLES T,** Daytona Beach Comm Coll, Daytona Beach, FL; SO; BSEE; Elctrcl Engnrng.

**WILSON, CHERIE N,** Memphis St Univ, Memphis, TN; JR; BFA; Wrkng Fed Express 5 Yrs; Art.

**WILSON, CHERYL A,** Northwest Al Comm Coll, Phil Campbell, AL; SR.

**WILSON, CHRIS L,** Univ Of Tn At Martin, Martin, TN; JR; BA; Phi Kappa Phi; Pi Sigma Epsilon; Alpha Delta Pi; Sthsd Bapt Chrch; Wm Bkr Schlrshp; Dlt Lf Ins Annty Schlrsh&; Econ.

**WILSON, CHRISTINA M,** Univ Of Akron, Akron, OH; SR; BA; Res Hall Pgm Bd 89-; Sr Cls Bd Pblc Rltns 90-; Natl Res Hall Hnry 90-; Sigma Delta Pi; ACES 90-; Tchr Ed Loan Pgm 89-; Natl Res Hl Hnry Schlrshp 90; Hmcmng Ct 90; Vrsty Track/IM 87-89; Scndry Ed/Spnsh/Phys Ed; Tchng.

**WILSON, CHRISTINE G,** Coll Of New Rochelle, New Rochelle, NY; JR; BA; Educ Advsry Bd 89-; CNR Big Sisters 88-89; Psi Chi Pres 90-; Deans Lst 88-89; Hnrs Stdnt 89-; Psychology/Elem/Spec Ed.

**WILSON, CHRISTOPHER W,** Univ Of Sc At Columbia, Columbia, SC; SO; BA; Campus Crusade For Christ 90-; Acctng; CPA.

**WILSON, CINDY R,** Tri County Tech Coll, Pendleton, SC; GD; IE; Fashion Merchndsng; Dsgnr.

**WILSON, CLAUDETTE M,** Gaston Coll, Dallas, NC; SO; AS; Wk Stdy Stdnt Offc Act 90-; Admin Offc Proc; Exec Sec.

**WILSON, CRYSTAL D,** Walker Coll, Jasper, AL; FR; BED; Early Chldhd Educ; Educ.

**WILSON, CURTISHA L,** Coppin St Coll, Baltimore, MD; JR; MSW; Bg Bro/Sis Lil Bro/Sis Grp 90-; Peer Cnslr 89-; Ron E Mcnair Cert; Peer Cnslng Cert; Socl Sci/Socl Wrk.**

**WILSON, DAMICA L,** Bennett Coll, Greensboro, NC; JR; BA; Acctg/Bus Clb Prlmntrn 90-; Engl Clb Pub Chr 90-; Sigma Tau Delta; Gspl Choir Chpln 90-; Stdnt Chrstn Flwshp Pres 90-; Alpha Kappa Alpha Pres; UNCF IN Univ/Prdue Univ Intrnshp; Engl/Acctg; Tax Attrny.

**WILSON, DANI M,** Clark Atlanta Univ, Atlanta, GA; SO; BS; Math Clb 90-; GTE/UNCF Summer Science Pgm; Ftbl/Trck Athletic Trnr 89-; Math; Actuarial Science.

**WILSON, DANITA A,** Middle Tn St Univ, Murfreesboro, TN; SO; MBA; Ftr Acctnts Amrc 89-; Kappa Delta 89-; Acctg.

**WILSON, DARLENE G,** Univ Of Va Clinch Valley Coll, Wise, VA; SO; BA; ECO P R Ofcr 90-; Commuting Stdnt Cncl 90-; Citizens Coal Cncl 90-; Bd Dir Client Ctrd Lgl Svcs SWVA Fin Cmte Chr/Policy Cmte Chr 89-; Publ TV; Non-Prof Agcy Mgmt; Grntsmnshp/Citizen Invlvmnt Envir Just Issues; Hstry/Philosophy; Grad Sch/Hstry/Law/Tch.

**WILSON, DARRAWN A,** Fl A & M Univ, Tallahassee, FL; JR; BA; Econ Clb V P; Stdnts Free Enterprise Pres 89-90; NAACP 90; Phi Beta Lambda 89-90; Methodist Campus Mnstry; All-Amer Schlr; Stdnts Free Enterprise Ldrshp Awd 90; IM Racquetbl 90; AA Hillsborough Cmnty Clg 90; Bsn Econ; Bnkg.

**WILSON, DARREN R,** Wv Univ At Parkersburg, Parkersburg, WV; FR; BS; Egl Sct By Scts Of Amer Asst Sctmstr 89-; Chem; Chem Engr.

**WILSON, DARREN T P,** Univ Of Tn At Chattanooga, Chattanooga, TN; SO; BS; Natl Clg Engr Awd Wnnr 90-; Cvl Engr.

**WILSON, DAVID ALAN,** Morehouse Coll, Atlanta, GA; SO; NROTC Pltn Ldr 89-; Psychlgy; Nvl Offcr.

**WILSON, DAVID K,** Lexington Comm Coll, Lexington, KY; SO; BHS; Radiological Hlth Sci; Hlth Physics.

**WILSON, DAVID L,** Roane St Comm Coll, Harriman, TN; SO; AS; IM Sftbl Bsktbl Ftbl 88-; AS; Crmnl Jstc; Law.

**WILSON, DAWN M,** Adelphi Univ, Garden City, NY; SR; BA; English.**

**WILSON, DEBBIE L,** Hillsborough Comm Coll, Tampa, FL; FR; BA; Bay Ntwrk Systm Drctr; Bsns.

**WILSON, DELANDRO C,** City Univ Of Ny Baruch Coll, New York, NY; SR; BBA; Tbl Tnns Clb Pres 88-89; Stu Govt Exec Sec 90-; Mrktng Mngmnt.

**WILSON, DEREK T,** Al St Univ, Montgomery, AL; SO; BA; Hstry; Law.

**WILSON, DIANE L,** De Tech & Comm Coll At Dover, Dover, DE; SR; AAS; Phi Theta Kappa 84-; Greenwood Vol Fire Co Aux 85-; Moose Aux 88-91; LPN 84-; Cert Delaware Tech/Comm Coll 84; Nrsng; RN BSN.

**WILSON, DONNA D,** Lenoir Rhyne Coll, Hickory, NC; SR; Tchr Asstnt Caldwell Cnty Schls; BA; Elem Edctn; Tchr.

**WILSON, EDDIE SIRENA,** Tougaloo Coll, Tougaloo, MS; FR; NAACP 90-; Day Stu Union 89-; Pol Sci/Pre Law Clb 90-; Pol Sci; Crmnl Law.

**WILSON JR, EDWARD E,** Samford Univ, Birmingham, AL; GD; JD; TN Stdnt Bar Assn 90-; Cmbrlnd Law Rvw; Beta Alpha Psi 89-90; Sigma Chi VP 87-90; BS/BA Univ TN Knxvl 90; Law.

**WILSON, ELAINE R,** Union Coll, Barbourville, KY; JR; BA; Gamma Beta Phi 90; Iota Sigma Nu 90; Engl Hstry; Ed.

**WILSON, ELIZABETH A,** Middle Tn St Univ, Murfreesboro, TN; GD; STEA 90-; AS Walters St Comm Coll 86; Elem Educ; Tchr.

**WILSON, EMILY N,** Winthrop Coll, Rock Hill, SC; FR; BA; Alpha Lambda Delta 90-; Prsdnts Lst 90-; Theatre; Alpha Lambda Delta 90-; Deans Mrtrs Schlrshp; Alpha Lambda Delta; Theatre Scndry Edctn; Actrs Tchr MS.

**WILSON, ERICA J,** Notre Dame Coll, Cleveland, OH; JR; BS; Biology Clb 88-; Women In Sci Wrkshp 90; Dns Lst 88-; Office Aide Vol 86-89; Walk Run Contest 88; Biology; Med.

**WILSON, ERIKA Y,** Central St Univ, Wilberforce, OH; FR; BA; Un Chorus 90-; Socl Work; Psychtrc Socl Wrkr.

**WILSON, FABIENNE M,** Fl St Univ, Tallahassee, FL; SR; BA; Conversation Grp Frnch 89-; Pi Delta Phi; Outstdng Undergrad Stdnt In Frnch; French; Univ Prfsr/Modern Lang/Lngstcs.

**WILSON, FRANCES C,** Richard Bland Coll, Petersburg, VA; FR; AA.

**WILSON II, G THOMAS,** Howard Univ, Washington, DC; GD; PHD; Afrcn/Othr Cltrl Pgms/Evnts Chr 71-84; Deans Lst 88; Prnc Hall Masons 79-87; Tuskegee Airmn 82-; AMVETS 84-; Amer Lgn 84-; OH U Deans Lst 88; VITA 64-; Air Frc 64-84; US Pres Fncl Mgmt Sprntdnt Worlwide Telecmnctns 81-84; Mass Cmnctn; Tlecmctn Plcy Dvlpmnt.

**WILSON, GILLIS L,** Christopher Newport Coll, Newport News, VA; GD; BS; Alpha Kappa Psi VP 89-; Mgmnt; Bus Admin.

**WILSON, GLENDA J,** Bethel Coll, Mckenzie, TN; FR; BA; Frshmn Math Awd; Elem Educ; Tchr.

**WILSON, GWENZETTA R,** Tougaloo Coll, Tougaloo, MS; FR; Math; Tchr.

**WILSON, HOLLIE B,** Tn Tech Univ, Cookeville, TN; JR; BS; Kappa Delta Sorty Alumni Rltns Chr; Deans Lst; Int Dsgn; Dcrtn.

**WILSON, HULDA A,** Interdenominational Theo Ctr, Atlanta, GA; GD; MDIV; Sigma Gamma Rho Pres 78-81; ALA; SELA; NAACP; Dpty Dir Woodruff Library 87-; MSLS Atlanta Univ 61; AB Spelman Clg 56; Chrstn Ed; Mnstry.

**WILSON, IRIS J,** Lane Coll, Jackson, TN; JR; BS; Blck Caucus Schlrshp Fnd 88-; UNCF 90-; Trck/Fld 89-90; Bus Admin.

**WILSON JR, JACK KIPLINGER,** Univ Of Pittsburgh At Bradford, Bradford, PA; JR; Wrld Fdrlst Assn 90-; Soc Sci; Law/Dplmcy.

**WILSON, JACQUELINE P,** Ms St Univ, Miss State, MS; JR; BBA; Deans Lst 90; Mktg.

**WILSON, JAMES R,** Owensboro Comm Coll, Owensboro, KY; SO; BS; Scl Srvcs Clb Prsdnt 88; Phi Theta Kapa 89-90; Intrntnl Clb; Stdnt Vlntr Yr Crisis Line; AAS; Psychology; Clinical Psychologist.

**WILSON, JANE H,** Faulkner Univ, Montgomery, AL; FR; BS; Bnkg/Trst Admin Asst 82-; Elem Educ; Tchr.

**WILSON, JANETTE M,** Norfolk St Univ, Norfolk, VA; SO; BA; Spartan Alpha Tau Hnr Soc Active; Pub Sch Vol Prog; Assoc Johnson & Wales Univ 88; Erly Chldhd Edn; Teach.

**WILSON, JARED K,** Cumberland Coll, Williamsburg, KY; SR; BS; Bio Clb 88; Amer Chem Scty 88-90; Med Careers Clb 88-90; Bio Awd; Hnrs Dstnctn 88; Bio; Med.**

**WILSON, JEANETTE N,** Univ Of Cincinnati, Cincinnati, OH; JR; BED; Brd Of Educ 85-; PTA Pres 84-; Sec And Exec Sec 64; Erly Chldhd Pre Schl Wth Hsty; Pre Schl Tchr.

**WILSON, JEFFREY J,** S U N Y Coll Of Tech At Alfred, Alfred, NY; SR; BA; Rock Bnd Gtr Plyr 90-; Own DJ Equipmnt Dj; Wrk Jones Mem Hosp 88-; Bus; MA In Music Bus.

**WILSON, JEFFREY W,** Milligan Coll, Milligan Clg, TN; SO; BA; Deans Lst Clayton Sta Clg 90; Deans Lst 90; Humanities.

**WILSON, JENNA TURNER,** Middle Tn St Univ, Murfreesboro, TN; SR; Math Orgn Pres 88; Kappa Delta Pi 89-; BS 90; Elem Educ; Tchg.

**WILSON, JENNI L,** Wv Univ, Morgantown, WV; FR; BA; FBLA 87; Stdnt Cncl Chrmn 89-90; Nwspr Stff Edtr Chf 88-90; Quill/Scrll Treas 88-90; 4-H Cllgt Pres 82-90; 4-H Jr Ldrs VP 87-90; 2 Dare You Ldrshp Awd 88; Jrnlsm; Pblc Rltns Spclst.

**WILSON, JENNIFER L,** Univ Of Ky, Lexington, KY; SR; BA; Elem Ed; Lrning/Bhvr Disordrs Tchr.

**WILSON, JERLAUNDA T,** Norfolk St Univ, Norfolk, VA; JR; BS; Hlth Srvcs Mgmnt Clb 87-; Alpha Kappa Mu; Hlth Srvcs Mgnt; Hlth Admnstrtn.

**WILSON, JILL K,** Bethany Coll, Bethany, WV; JR; BA; Nwsppr Ftrs Wrtr; TV Pblcty Coor; Admssn Offce Trgde; Scty Of Prof Jrnlsts; BISONS; PB Clb; Phi Mu PR Coor 90-; Intrnshp Ethyl Corp; Cmmnctns PR.

**WILSON, JO ANN L,** Rutgers St Un At New Brunswick, New Brunswick, NJ; FR; In Hs Cmmtt 90; Emrgng Ldrs; Martin Luther King Cmmtt Sec 90-; INROADS Intern; Econ; Bus.

**WILSON, JUAN E,** Va St Univ, Petersburg, VA; SO; Alpha Kappa Psi.

**WILSON, JULIE A,** Univ Of Montevallo, Montevallo, AL; JR; BA; Sigma Tau Delta 90-; Chi Omega 88-; Engl; Law.

**WILSON, KAREN A,** Atlantic Comm Coll, Mays Landing, NJ; SO; BA; Psych; Tchng Guidnc.

**WILSON, KAREN C,** Birmingham Southern Coll, Birmingham, AL; SR; BA; SGA Adlt Stdies Rep; Adlt Stdies Cncl 90-; Futr Tele Pionrs Of Amer; Bell South Serv 87-; Bsns Admn; Mgmt.

**WILSON, KASEY D,** Middle Tn St Univ, Murfreesboro, TN; SR; BS; Chrldr Col State; Comm Clg 88-; STEA 90-; Kappa Delta Pi 89-; Stdt Tchr Second Grade Spring Hill Elem Spring Hill Tn 88-; AS Colum State Comm Clg 89; Tchr Cert; Elem Educ; Elem Teacher.

**WILSON, KATHY L,** Kent St Univ Kent Cmps, Kent, OH; SR; BA; Alpha Lmbd Dlt 88; Gldn Key 89-; Dlt Zeta Sng Chrmn 88-; Deans List 88-; Indvdl/Fmly Stgds; Trvl/Htl Mgmt.**

**WILSON, KEITH D,** Alcorn St Univ, Lorman, MS; FR; BS; Cmps All Str Chllng Tm 90-; Biol; Med.

**WILSON, KELLI A,** Indiana Univ Of Pa, Indiana, PA; FR; BA; Crmnlgy Pre Law; Prlgl.

**WILSON, KENNETH B,** Savannah St Coll, Savannah, GA; SR; BS; Mrchng Bnd VP 87-; Cncrt Chr Pres 89-; Nwtnn Scty Comp Sci Clb VP 89-; Comp Sci Tech And Math; Math.

**WILSON, KENYAWN A,** Al A & M Univ, Normal, AL; FR; BA; Baptist Stdnt Union 90-; Deans List 90-; Honor Roll 90-; Computer Cience; Cmptr Engr/Analyst.

**WILSON, KETRA L,** Ms Univ For Women, Columbus, MS; SO; Blck Stdnt Cncl Pgm Chrprsn 90-; NAACP 85-; Yth Actvty Grp 85-; Pol Campaign Comm 85-; Zeta Deb Schlrshp 90; Cmptr Sci; Cmptr Pgmr.

**WILSON, KEVIN A,** Barry Univ, Miami, FL; SR; BPS; Air Trfc Cntrl Spclst; Stckbrkr/Ins Sales 88-90; US Marine Corp 84-88; Bus; Law.

**WILSON, KIM M,** Al St Univ, Montgomery, AL; SO; BA; Dome Bllt Corp 87; Gspl Choir 89; Kappa Swthrt 89; Dntl Asst 89; Bsktbl Grls Vars 88; Bio; Dntstry.

**WILSON, KIM Y,** Hillsborough Comm Coll, Tampa, FL; SO; PHARM; PTA 88; Boy Scouts; Sci; Cumm Pharm/Tech Wrtr.

**WILSON, KIMBERLY A,** Wilmington Coll, Wilmington, OH; FR; BA; I M Odzebl; Bio/Sci; Phys Thpry.

**WILSON, KIMBERLY L,** Salisbury St Univ, Salisbury, MD; JR; BA; FMA VP 90-; Delta Mu Delta; Phi Beta Lambda; Acctng/Fnce.

**WILSON, KIMBERLY M,** Coll Of Charleston, Charleston, SC; SR; Ind Sist Indpdnt Stdy 90; BA 90; Bus Admn; Pblc Serv.

**WILSON, KRISTI L,** Bridgewater Coll, Bridgewater, VA; JR; BS; Spec Olympcs Vol 89-; FCA 90-; Lcrs Tm Mgr 88-; Amer Alnc Hlth/Phy Ed Rcrtn Dnc 90-; Va Assoc Hlth/Phy Ed/Rcrtn/Dnc 90-; U S Olympc Acdmy XII/XIV Dlgte 88-90; Woodrow Wilson Rhbltn Ctr Cnslr 89-90; WAA 88-89; Dns Lst 90-; IM 88-; Hlth/Physcl Ed; Rcrtn.

**WILSON, L CORINNE,** Cincinnati Bible Coll & Sem, Cincinnati, OH; SR; BS; Tchng Sndy Schl 89-90; Tchng Engl Scnd Lang 90-; AA NE Chrstn Coll 77; Chrstn Ed; Cnslng.

**WILSON, LANA KAYE,** Univ Of Sc At Columbia, Columbia, SC; FR; Nrsg/Acctg.

**WILSON, LAURA A,** Univ Of Akron, Akron, OH; SO; BS; Hnrs Clb 89-; Hnrs Schlrshp 89-; Nrsng.

**WILSON, LAURA B,** Northern Ky Univ, Highland Hts, KY; JR; BA; Econ; Bus.

**WILSON, LAURALEE,** Western Ky Univ, Bowling Green, KY; SO; BS; Wmn Trstn; PTA W R Mcneill; Alpha Epsilon Delta Sec 90-; Beta Beta Beta 89-; Phi Kappa Phi; Phi Eta Sigma 90-; Schlrs Hnrs Pro 89-; Ogden Coll Found Schlrshp; Bio Dept Schlrshp; Dr D Hugh Puckett Schlrshp; RDA; Bio; Med.

**WILSON, LAURI R,** Ga Inst Of Tech At Atlanta, Atlanta, GA; FR; Civil Eng.

**WILSON, LAVONDA R,** Fisk Univ, Nashville, TN; GD; Oval Staff 86-90; Junior/Senior Class Sec 88-90; Pre Med Club V P 89-90; UNCF Pre Med Inst 89; Forensic Pathologist.

**WILSON, LEE R,** Univ Of Sc At Columbia, Columbia, SC; FR; BA; Englsh; Pblshng Indstry.

**WILSON, LESLIE K,** Univ Of Sc At Columbia, Columbia, SC; SO; BS; USC Sprky Wds Schlr 90; Pharm Intrn; Pharm.

**WILSON, LESLIE K,** Va St Univ, Petersburg, VA; JR; BS; Philadelphia Pre-Alumni 87-; NAACP Natl Tech Assoc 89-; Eng Tech Clb 90-; Mech Eng.

**WILSON, LESLIE L,** Alcorn St Univ, Lorman, MS; SR; BS; Chem Clb 87-; Ind Tech Clb 87-; NAACP 87-89; Hnrs Org 87-; So Reg Hnrs Cncl 87-89; Chem Eng.

**WILSON, LESLIE M,** Coll Of Charleston, Charleston, SC; JR; BA; Spnsh Clb 89-; Sigma Delta Pi 89-; Hon Soc; Spnsh; Tchng/Trnsltng.

**WILSON, LINDA L,** Georgian Court Coll, Lakewood, NJ; SR; BA; Lit Vols Of Amer; AS Humnties 89; Humnties/Elem Educ; Tchr.

**WILSON, LISA A,** Univ Of Al At Huntsville, Huntsville, AL; FR; Math/Sci; Civil Eng.

**WILSON, LISA C,** Gaston Coll, Dallas, NC; SO; Med Asstng Clb Sec 89-; Gastonia Surgical Assoc Intrnshp; Cherryville Primary Care PA Intrnshp; Med Asst.

**WILSON, LISA M,** Elms Coll, Chicopee, MA; SR; BA; Stdnt Tch Practicum 90; Elem Ed; Tch.

**WILSON, LORI A,** Springfield Tech Comm Coll, Springfield, MA; SR; AS; Deans Lst 90-; Bus Admin/Acctg; Acctnt.

**WILSON, LOUIS A,** Vance Granville Comm Coll, Henderson, NC; SO; AAS; SGA 90-; Cmptr Clb Treas 90-; Soc Clb Cmtee 90-; Phi Theta Kappa; Awd Acad Schlrshp 90-; Bus Cmptr Progmng; Artfcl Intlgnce Dev.

**WILSON, MARCUS L,** Ky St Univ, Frankfort, KY; FR; BA; Cmptrs Prgrmng; Cmptr Sci.

**WILSON, MARK A,** Univ Of Akron, Akron, OH; SO; BA; Engrng.

**WILSON, MARK D,** Gordon Conwell Theol Sem, S Hamilton, MA; FR; MDIV; VP Chorale Bstrs; Drama Coach Mdl Sch 90-; Mnstr Chrch Christ; BS 76; Prchg Cert 89; Theology; Prchg.

**WILSON, MARK R,** Fl International Univ, Miami, FL; FR; BS; Plus IV; Phi Kappa Phi; Psychlgy; PhD.

**WILSON, MARY JENNIFER,** Brevard Coll, Brevard, NC; SO; BMBFA; Vidoe Yrbk 90; Cllgate Sngrs; Hnr Rll 89-; Music; Thtr/Advrtsng/Sngwrtng/Cmpsng/Tchng.

**WILSON, MARY T,** Bunker Hill Comm Coll, Boston, MA; SO; BED; Choral Grp Orgnzr PR 87-; Alpha Kappa Mu 89-; Phi Theta Kappa 89-; Chldrns Museum Spc Ed Dept Asst Flr Mgr 87-; 2nd Pl Spch Comptn; Proj Outrch Asst Dir 88-90; Som Wildrns Prog Peer Cnslr 88-; AA; AS; Spcl Ed/Human Svcs; Tchr.

**WILSON, MATTHEW M,** Southern Coll Of Tech, Marietta, GA; SR; BSCET; Civil Eng; Eng.

**WILSON, MELISSA L,** Wv Univ At Parkersburg, Parkersburg, WV; FR; BA; Phi Theta Kappa 90-; Bus/Mgmt.

**WILSON, MICHAEL A,** Univ Of Cincinnati, Cincinnati, OH; JR; BS; Soc Manuf Engrs 87-; Stdnt Tribunal VP/TREAS 87-88; Heatherstone Hm Ownrs Assn Treas 89-90; Mgmnt Cons 88-; AS 90; Eng; Law.

**WILSON, MICHAEL B,** Univ Of Sc At Columbia, Columbia, SC; FR; BA; Gamma Beta Phi 90-; Pcr Bsbl 90-.

**WILSON, MICHELE L,** Longwood Coll, Farmville, VA; SR; BS; Earth Clb; Anthropology/Sociology Clb 90-; Art First Hand 90-; Natl Hon Soc 87-; Kappa Pi Natl Alumni Affairs Ofcr Fndrsng Chair 89-; Natl Hon Soc 87-; Hmls Shltr Aid W/Great Am Restaurants 88-90; Anthropology; Archaeology/Prehist Art.**

**WILSON, MICHELLE L,** Methodist Coll, Fayetteville, NC; FR; BS; Tennis 90-; Acctg; CPA.

**WILSON, MYRA L,** Brewer St Jr Coll, Fayette, AL; FR; AS; Corinth Bptst Chrch Pres WMA 74-78; Clrk Typst 74-78; Offr Mgr 78-90; Scif RN.

**WILSON, NANCY C,** Cumberland Coll, Williamsburg, KY; FR; BA; Elem Edn; Tchr.

**WILSON, NANCY M L,** Howard Univ, Washington, DC; FR; BA; Architecture.

**WILSON, NICOLE L,** Indiana Univ Of Pa, Indiana, PA; JR; BED; PA St Educ Assoc/Natl Educ Assoc 90-; Assoc Chldhd Ed Intl 90-; Cntr Imprvmnt 90-; Fmly Life/Chld Abuse Vol; Tutor Proj Stride 89-90; Elem Educ; Teach.

**WILSON, NIKI B,** Ms St Univ, Miss State, MS; JR; BED; Pres Schlr; Ed; Elem.

**WILSON, OTIS D,** Wilmington Coll, New Castle, DE; GD; BS; Base Advsry Cncl 88-; Bsktbl/Sftbl/Ftbl 87-; Blck Hertg Comm 89; Delta Epsilon Rho 89-; Dns Lst 88-; Pres Sprts Awd 88-89; J L Levtw Hnr Grad 89; Sftbl Coach 89-; Mrch Dimes Rep 89; U S Air Force; AAS Comm Clg Air Force; Busn Mgmt.

**WILSON, PAMELA J,** Univ Of Tn At Martin, Martin, TN; FR; BS; Mc Cord Hl Assoc 90-; Soc Hnrs Smnr Stdnts 90-; Deans List 90; Admin Serv.

**WILSON, PATRICIA A,** Univ Of Tn At Martin, Martin, TN; SR; BA; Chrldr 89; Pep Clb 89; Phi Theta Kappa 89; AS Dyersburg State 89; Psychlgy.

**WILSON, PAUL J,** Ohio Valley Coll, Parkersburg, WV; FR; Dns Lst 90-; Blgcl Scis.

**WILSON JR, PAUL L,** Norfolk St Univ, Norfolk, VA; SR; IEEE Pblcty/Prog Chrmn 87-; Engineering/Physics Scty Actvts Coord 87-; Ntl Collegiate Engnrng Awd Wnr 90; Outstanding Young Men Amer Awd 90; IM Bsktbl Schl Chmpns 90; BSEE 90; Electronics Engineering.

**WILSON, PAULETTE M,** Daytona Beach Comm Coll, Daytona Beach, FL; SO; AA; Spkr Ormond Bch Bapt Church 90; Spkr Coquina Pres Chrch 88; Collection Clrk 84; Spirtitual Life Chrprsn Prot Wm Chapel 87; Jr Hgh Schl Sndy Schl Tchr 80-87; Pool Dir 90; Collection Clrk 83; Ins Mgr 82; Liberal Stud; Bnkng.

**WILSON, PEGGY I,** Vance Granville Comm Coll, Henderson, NC; SO; AA; W Oxford Elem PTO; C G Credle PTO; Hstry Clb Treas 89-90; Phi Theta Kappa 90-; Pres Merit Awrd 90-; Coll Trnsfr Schlr 89-90; Coll Trnsfr; Intr Dsgnr.

**WILSON, PERCY R,** Old Dominion Univ, Norfolk, VA; JR; BS; Tau Beta Pi; Cmptr Sci Corp Schlrshp 88-; Dr M L King Jr Schlrshp 89-90; Cooprtv Educ Stu NASA 90-; Elect Eng.

**WILSON, POLLY A,** Union Univ, Jackson, TN; JR; BS; Acctg Clb 88-; Flwshp Chrstn Athletes 89-; Alpha Chi Natl Treas 90-; Phi Beta Lambda; Chi Omega Treas 89-; Acctg; CPA.

**WILSON, QUARDRALYNN D,** Al A & M Univ, Normal, AL; FR; BS; Lambda Sigma Pi; Drug Task Force 90-; Acadmc Schlrshp Award; Bio/Chem; Neurosurgeon.

**WILSON, REBECCA A,** Ashland Comm Coll, Ashland, KY; ASSOC; Nrsng.

**WILSON, RHONDA B,** Univ Of Sc At Columbia, Columbia, SC; SO; BA; Chrstn Flwshp V P 90-; Gamma Beta Phi; Early Chldhd Educ; Tch.

**WILSON IV, ROBERT C,** Richard Bland Coll, Petersburg, VA; FR; BA; SGA Rep; Deans Lst; Delta Tau Chi VP; Econ; Bsnss.

**WILSON, ROBERT DIRK,** Greenville Tech Coll, Greenville, SC; JR; Phi Theta Kappa; AS 88; Automotive Tech; Cmptr Tech.

**WILSON, ROBERT E,** Middle Tn St Univ, Murfreesboro, TN; SR; BBA; Intl Bus Assn VP; Dns Lst; Vtsty Ftbl At TENN Tehc Univ 84-85; Line Sprvsr 85-89; Bus Mgmt; MBA.

**WILSON JR, ROBERT P,** Univ Of Scranton, Scranton, PA; FR; BS; Phys Therapy Clb Fresh Rep 90-; Horizons/-Clgt Vol 90-; Campus Mnstrs 90-; Physical Therapy.

**WILSON, ROBERTA L,** Savannah Coll Of Art & Design, Savannah, GA; GD; MFA; C Probes Schlr; Intrnshp Eric Hogan; Mbr Irish Olypc Eqstrn Tm; Illstrtr 90; BPS Empire State Coll 84; Illstrtn/Art; Free Lnc Illstrtr.

**WILSON, ROSE M,** Fl St Univ, Tallahassee, FL; JR; BA; Hl Govt VP 88-89; Inter Res Hl Cncl 88-89; Intra Mural Sftbl 88-90; Acctg; CPA.

**WILSON, RYAN E,** Wv Univ, Morgantown, WV; FR; BS; IEEE; IEEE Cmptr Soc; Pres Schol 89; Am Philips Schlrshp 89; Hon Prog 89-; Elec/Cmptr Engrng.

**WILSON, SANDRA K,** Univ Of Cincinnati-Clrmnt Coll, Batavia, OH; ASSOC; Employeed By Scripps Howard For 9 Yrs As Media Svngs Spcst; Off Admin.

**WILSON, SCOTT T,** Univ Of Fl, Gainesville, FL; SR; 7BA; Coll Music Edctrs Natl Cnfrnc 88-; Amrcn Chrl Drctrs; Phi Eta Sigma 86-87; Phi Mu Alpha VP 87-; FL Cmmnty Jazz Orchstr 89; Mst Vlbl Chmbr Sngr Yr 87-; Internshp Mehane Mddle Schl Intern Bnd Dir; Internshp Lake Weir Hgh Schl Intern Chr; Music Ed; Jazz Stds.

**WILSON, SHARON Y,** Al A & M Univ, Normal, AL; SO; BSN; Pep Clb 89-90; Gospel Choir 89-; Bapt Stdnt Union 89-; Nursing.

**WILSON, SHERRON M,** Middle Tn St Univ, Murfreesboro, TN; SR; BS; Kappa Delta Pi 90-; Hon Rl/Deans Lst 90; Elem Ed; Tchr.

**WILSON, SHERRY LEE,** Gaston Coll, Dallas, NC; SR; High Hnrs Grad.

**WILSON, SHERRY M,** Univ Of Sc At Columbia, Columbia, SC; JR; BA; Adult Grp Edn 90-; ARETA Hon Pgm/Grp; Pres Lst 90; Deans Lst 90; Dick Richards Essay Cntst 89; Bd Dir Lancaster Cnty Rape Crisis Ctr 90-; Cert Profl Sec Intl 90-; Sec Plnt Mgr 77-; AA USC-L 89; Interdisciplinary Studies; Bus.

**WILSON, SHERYL L,** Schenectady County Comm Coll, Schenectady, NY; FR; AS; AD 90; Culnry Arts; Chef.

**WILSON, SHIRLEY A,** Lees Coll, Jackson, KY; FR; Phi Theta Kappa; Sci; Nrsg.

**WILSON, STACY R,** Clark Atlanta Univ, Atlanta, GA; SO; Rcvd 2 Cert For Making An I An Algebra; Speech Cmmnctn/Theatre; Pthlgst.**

**WILSON, STEPHANIE GENEVA,** Univ Of Sc At Columbia, Columbia, SC; FR; BA.

**WILSON, STEPHANIE M,** Fayetteville St Univ, Fayetteville, NC; FR; Concert Choir; Chamber Choir; Crmnl Justc; Law.

**WILSON, TAHN S,** Meridian Comm Coll, Meridian, MS; FR; LPN.

**WILSON, TAMARA L,** Bay Path Coll, Longmeadow, MA; SO; Pgm Comm 89; Tour Guide Prspctv Stdnts 90-; Intrn Clck Twr Trvl Agnt 90-; Hrsbck Rdng 89.

**WILSON, TAMMY C,** Abraham Baldwin Agri Coll, Tifton, GA; SO; BSED; Hon Stdnt 89-; Worked In Bnkng Prof 85-89; AS; Socl Stdies Tchr.

**WILSON, THALIA,** Tn St Univ, Nashville, TN; JR; BS; Pol Sci Clb; Indpndt League Vlybl; Deans Lst; Blck Chldrns Inst Intrnshp; Pol Sci; Law.

**WILSON, THERESA M,** Volunteer St Comm Coll, Gallatin, TN; SO; BA; Gamma Beta Phi 90-; Math Lab Practioner 90-; English Math; Law.

**WILSON, THOMASENA,** Univ Of Sc At Columbia, Columbia, SC; SR; BS; Theatr Bx Off Stf 86; Theatr Ushr 86; Theatr Hs Mgr 87; Deans Lst 86 90; Mnrty Stdnt Acdmc Awrd 86-; Indpndnt Ins Agnts SC Fndtn Awrd; Mgmt Sci/Ins; Ins Indstry.

**WILSON, TIMOTHY S,** Northeast State Tech Comm Coll, Blountville, TN; SO; AS; IEEE; Elctrncs; Eng.

**WILSON, TINA M,** Univ Of Southern Ms, Hattiesburg, MS; JR; BA; Math; Ed.

**WILSON, TONYA R,** East Tn St Univ, Johnson City, TN; SO; BA; Accntng.

**WILSON, TRACEY B,** Univ Of Fl, Gainesville, FL; SR; PHARM; Shnds Tstmstrs Intl Clb Pres 89-; Phrmcy; Clncl Phrmcst.

**WILSON, TRACEY JOHNSON,** Coppin St Coll, Baltimore, MD; SR; BS; Christa Mc Auliffe Tchr Schlrshp 89-; Tchng Pstn Balto Co Pblc Schl Spec Ed; BS 80; Spcl Ed; Tchng.

**WILSON, TRACI R,** Methodist Coll, Fayetteville, NC; JR; Stdnt Govt Assn Sntr 90-; Acdmc Advs Com 90; Fclty Cncrns Com Stdnt Rep 90; Fresh Ldrshp Assn Fclty Appt 88; Omicron Delta Kappa 90; Show You Care Com 88-; Spec Olympcs Vol 89-; All Rgn Wmns Sccr Tm-Hon Mntn 88; Phy Ed/Blgy; Alld Hlth/Coachg.

**WILSON, TRACIE A,** Elms Coll, Chicopee, MA; JR; BA; Stdnt Ambssdrs 88-90; Amer Cncr Soc; Vrsty Sccr 88-90; Scndry Educ/Math; Educ H S Math.

**WILSON, TRAVIS T,** Mayland Comm Coll, Spruce Pine, NC; FR; Gnrl Ed; Tchng.

**WILSON, VALERIA L,** Jackson St Univ, Jackson, MS; SO; BS; Alpha Lambda Delta; Delta Sigma Theta Treas; Hon Coll Stdnt; Acdmc Schlrshp; Comp Info Syst; Info Prcssr.

**WILSON, VALERIE A,** Stillman Coll, Tuscaloosa, AL; SR; BS; NAACP 90; Yrbk Stff 87-89; Clg Choir 87-89; Prgrm Beta Kappa Chi 89; Delta Signa Theta Treas 90-; Mthmtcs; Tch.

**WILSON, VIVIAN R,** Fl A & M Univ, Tallahassee, FL; SR; BS; Pi Omega Pi Pres 90-; FAMU Ntl Assn Ed Ofc Prsnl Pres 90-; USPS Grant In Aid Awd; AA Tallahassee Comm Coll 89; Bus Ed; Adlt Ed.

**WILSON, WENDY S,** Univ Of South Al, Mobile, AL; JR; BA; Deans List Fall 90; Edn; Erly Chldhd.

**WILSON, WENDY S,** Piedmont Coll, Demorest, GA; SR; BA; Stdnt Govt Area Rep 86; Drama Clb 89-90; Stdnt Ga Assn Educ/NEA 90-; Trch Clb; Easter Sls 89; Dns Lst 89-; Summa Cum Laude; IM Vlybl/Smng 88-89; AA Unv Fla 89; Mdl Grds Educ; Tchr.

**WILSON, WILLIAM C,** Savannah Coll Of Art & Design, Savannah, GA; FR; Art; Graphic Desgn.

**WILSON, WINIFRED K,** Eckerd Coll, St Petersburg, FL; JR; BA; Intl Stdnt Assn Pres 89-; Stdnt Govt Dorm Pres 89-; Intl Bus Clb 90-; Meals On Wheels Prog 90; Frshmn Orien Advsr 90; Foreign Stdnt Hsng Advsr 90; Intl Bus/Spnsh; Bus/Govt.

**WILSON, ZONDRA M,** City Univ Of Ny Baruch Coll, New York, NY; SR; BA; African Stdnt Assoc 89-90; Helpline 90; Highbridge Comm Ctr Tchrs Aid; Psych; Soc Work.

**WILSON-GREENE, JOAN M,** Univ Of Fl, Gainesville, FL; SR; MM; Mu Phi Epsilon So Meth Univ 87; Accpnst 89-; AA Pensacola Jr Clg 86; BB Univ Fla 90; Music; Prof Muscn.

**WILT, DARRELL L,** Columbus Coll Of Art & Design, Columbus, OH; FR; BA; SGA 90; Army; Art/Illust; Illustration.

**WILT, MELINDA K,** Garrett Comm Coll, Mchenry, MD; SO; BS; Erly Elem Educ; Tchng.

**WILTSE, CELESTE G,** Univ Of Sc At Columbia, Columbia, SC; SR; MD; Chrldng 86-; Spcl Olympics 86-87; Deans Lst; BS; Biology; Medicine.

**WILTSEY JR, THOMAS,** Monmouth Coll, W Long Branch, NJ; FR; BA; Phi Eta Sigma Treas; Trustee Schlrshp; IM Sftbl; Psych.

**WILTSHIRE, DIANE L,** Kent St Univ Kent Cmps, Kent, OH; SR; SKOPE Treas 88-89; Golden Key 89; Beta Gamma Sigma 90; Hnrs Clg 86; Canton Cty Schls PTA 86; Ernst/Young Accntng Excllnce Awd 90; Ohio Soc Of CPAS 90; Admin Sci Dept Awd 89; BS 90; Accntng; CPA.

**WIMBERLY, MELANIE C,** Bethel Coll, Mckenzie, TN; JR; BS; STEA 90-; Elem Educ; Teach.

**WIMBLE, SABRINA L,** Endicott Coll, Beverly, MA; SO; BS; ASID 90-; Dns Lst; GTM Elec Supply Intrn 90; House Crft Indstrs Intrn; Modern Jazz/Dnc Cls 89; AS; Intr Dsgn.

**WIMETTE, TODD A,** Castleton St Coll, Castleton, VT; JR; BA; Accntng; CPA.

**WIMMER, KIMBERLY M,** Birmingham Southern Coll, Birmingham, AL; SO; BA; Ofcl Hosts 90-; Tutoring Coordntr Urban Minstrs 90-; Alpha Omicron Pi Sngldr; Vol Svcs Coordntr 90-; 12 Theatrcl Prodctns; Muscl Theatre/Psychlgy; Entertnr.

**WIMMER, ROBERT JOHN,** Me Maritime Academy, Castine, ME; FR; BS; Rgmnt Of Mdshpmn; Marine Eng.

**WINANS, RACHEL E,** Villanova Univ, Villanova, PA; FR; BA; Stdnt Prgrmmng Comm; Englsh; Cmmctns.

**WINANS, THOMAS W,** Davis & Elkins Coll, Elkins, WV; JR; BS; Sigma Phi Epsilon 89-; Rec Mgt.

**WINANS, WENDY V,** Radford Univ, Radford, VA; JR; Crim Jstc Clb 90-; Psych Clb 90-; Pi Gamma Mu; RAFT Comm Htln.

**WINCHESTER, DIETRICH M,** Morehouse Coll, Atlanta, GA; SO; BA; AL Clb 90-; Acctng; CPA.

**WINCHESTER JR, ERIC R,** Ms St Univ, Miss State, MS; FR; BS; Scape 90; Biology; Veterinary Med.

**WINCHMAN, Y-VETTE M,** Wagner Coll, Staten Island, NY; FR; Choir; JCC Music Spclst 90; Tutoring Spnsh.

**WINDBIGLER, TRUDI M,** Univ Of Akron, Akron, OH; SR; BS; Golden Key 90-; Elem Ed.

**WINDER, CRAIG E,** Christopher Newport Coll, Newport News, VA; GD; BS; Bus Adm.

**WINDER, ROSALYN I,** Wilmington Coll, New Castle, DE; BS; Delta Epsilon Rho 90-; Dipl Gen Bus DE Tech Comm Coll 83; Hmn Rsrc Mngmnt; Prsnnl Mngmnt.

**WINDHAM, BEVERLY G,** Univ Of Southern Ms, Hattiesburg, MS; SR; BS; Alpha Of Miss 89; Gamma Beta Phi; AA Jones Cnty Jr Clg 89; Bio; Med.

**WINDHAM, DAVID L,** Univ Of Southern Ms, Hattiesburg, MS; JR; BS; Polymer Sci Clb 90; Scty Of Plastics Eng 90; Rsrch Assist For Dr Roger Hester USM; ASA Jones Cnty Jr Clg 90; Polymer Sci; Polymer Eng.

**WINDHAM JR, DOUGLAS M,** Fl St Univ, Tallahassee, FL; JR; Eng Hnr Soc; Phi Kappa Phi 90-; Golden Key 90-; Dobro Slovo 90-; IM Ftbl/Sftbl/Soccr; Cryptlgc Lingst U S Air Frc 84-88; Elec Eng/Russn; Eng/Highr Educ.

**WINDHAM, KATHY L,** Univ Of Akron, Akron, OH; JR; Yth Grp Spnsr 88-; Rdng/Math Tutor 90-; Golden Key 90-; Kappa Delta Pi; Acdmc Schlrshp; Litchfield Schlrshp; Psychlgy; Elem Ed.

**WINDHAM, MARIAH M,** Faulkner Univ, Montgomery, AL; FR; BA; SGA Treas 90-; Alpha Delta Psi 90-; Ed; Spcl Ed MA.

**WINDHAM, NANCY C,** Valdosta St Coll, Valdosta, GA; SR; BED; Alpha Chi; AD Fmly/Chld Dvlpmnt Abrhm Bldwn Agri Clg 85-; AD Gnrl Stds/Sci GA Mltry Clg 89-; Educ; Tchr.

**WINDHAM, STACEY L,** Coll Of Charleston, Charleston, SC; SO; Bio; Med/Radlgy.

**WINDHOLTZ, EMIL M,** Barry Univ, Miami, FL; SR; BS; AA Broward Comm Coll 89; Mngmnt Infor Sys; Pgrmr/Anaylst.

**WINDON, BRIANA V,** Marshall University, Huntington, WV; SR; BED; Hl Advsry Cncl 88-90; Rsdnt Advsr/MU Rsdnc Lf Offc 88-90; Vol Time Out Rnwy Cntr 90; Stdnt Asst/Upwrd Bnd Dept 90-; Stdnt Cnslr/Upwrd Bnd 90-; IM Sports 89-90; Cnslng/Rhbltn; Crisis Cnslr.

**WINDON II, DALE A,** Wv Univ, Morgantown, WV; FR; Ar Spc Eng.

**WINDROW, SHERYL LYNNE,** Middle Tn St Univ, Murfreesboro, TN; FR; Bsns.

**WINDS, CECILIA T,** Miami Dade Comm Coll North, Miami, FL; SO; AA; Phi Theta Kappa 90; Clg Brd Talnt Rostr 90-; Maimi Dade Clg Otstdng Acad 90-; Para Prof Of The Year; Para Prof; Elem Educ; Educ.

**WINDSOR, TAMRA M,** Md Coll Of Art & Design, Silver Spring, MD; GD; AA; Art/Phtgrhy; Photo Jrnlst.

**WINDSOR JR, WILLIAM D,** Broward Comm Coll, Ft Lauderdale, FL; FR; AS; Soc Prres Encrgmnt Barbrshp Qrt Sing Amer 81-; Irene Fishly Awd; Amer Assn Resp Care; Fla Soc Resp Care; Lcdr U S Navy 70-87; BSIM Ga Inst Tech 70; Resp Thrpy.

**WINDWER, MARK J,** City Univ Of Ny City Coll, New York, NY; SR; BS; Tech Educ Stdnt Assn Pres 90-; Golden Key; Dscplnry Comm; Tech Educ Exec Comm; AA Kingsborough Cmnty Clg 81; Tech Educ; Educ.

**WINE, MARCELLA O,** Benedict Coll, Columbia, SC; JR; BA; Eng Club; Stdnt Edn Assoc; Benedict Coll Hnr S Stdnts Assoc Sec 89-90; Alpha Kappa Mu; Alpha Chi Natl; Eng; Atty Spclzng In Domestics.

**WINEGAR, SUZANNE L,** Queens Coll, Charlotte, NC; SR; BSN; Assoc Nursing Stdnts Pres 90-; NC Assoc Nrsng Stdnts Dist Dir; Queens Wingate Hnr Scty By Laws Committee 90-; Gamma Beta Phi 85-87; Veterans Admin Hlth Prof Schrlshp 89-; Vail Schlrshp 89-; Dana Schlrsp 90-; LPN 79; Science; Nursing.

**WINFIELD, E ALAN,** Univ Of South Al, Mobile, AL; JR; BED; Phys Ed; Tchr.

**WINFREY, JOHNATHAN L,** Morehouse Coll, Atlanta, GA; FR; BS; Pre Alumni Sec; Hlth Careers Soc; Deans Lst; NAACP; IM Ftbl; Biology; Medicine.

**WING, JESSICA R,** Case Western Reserve Univ, Cleveland, OH; FR; BSN; Flm Scty; Dns Lst 90-; Nrsng.

**WING, KAREN L,** Brevard Coll, Brevard, NC; FR; BA; Elem Edn; Tchr.

**WING, LESLIE A,** Western Carolina Univ, Cullowhee, NC; JR; BFA; Art Stdnt League 90-; Stdnt Mrshal Clb 90-; Spec Olympics 84-86; Haywood Artists Coop; Art Graphic Dsgn; Illustration.

**WINGARD, GORDON G,** Univ Of Rochester, Rochester, NY; SO; BS; Res Advsr 90-; Sigma Chi Hist 90-; Rugby 89-90; Bio; Chiropractor.

**WINGARD, SANDRA V,** Truett Mc Connell Coll, Cleveland, GA; FR; AD; Fannin Co Resc; LPN 83-; Ped High Tech Nrsg 86-; LPN Pickens Tech Sch 83; Nrsg; RN.

**WINGARD, TRICIA A,** Edinboro Univ Of Pa, Edinboro, PA; FR; BS; Marine Blgst.

**WINGATE, ALEXIS J,** Georgetown Univ, Washington, DC; SR; BSBA; Sursum Corda Yth Tutrng Pgm Treas 88-; Deans Lst 90-; Rgby 87-89; Intl Bus; Bnkg/Real Est Dvlpmnt.

**WINGATE, CHARLES A,** City Univ Of Ny City Coll, New York, NY; BA; Golden Key 87-; Phi Theta Mappa 72; Borough Manhattan C C Music Awd 74-75; Faculty Mbr Gospel Music Wkrshp Amer 75-; Magna Cum Laude; Sr Intr 1150th United States Army Reserve Force Schl Ft Hamilton Br Ny; AAS 75; Liberal Arts; Clg Prof.

**WINGATE, SONYA L,** Lincoln Univ, Lincoln Univ, PA; SR; JD; Thurgood Marshall Law Soc Corr Sec 88-; Frnsc Soc/Spch Clb 90-; Tolson Soc 89-; Delta Sigma Theta VP 90-; BA; Engl; Corp Law.

**WINGATE, TRACY M,** Bowling Green St Univ At Huron, Huron, OH; JR; AS; Alpha Lambda Delta 88; Hlth Info Tech; Pharmacy.

**WINGET, SHARON E,** Howard Univ, Washington, DC; GD; MSW; Natl Assoc Soc Wrkrs 88-; Soc Wrkr 85-; BA Kalamazoo Clg 80; Soc Wrk; Mnthl Hlth.

**WINGFIELD, CHERIE D,** Belmont Coll, Nashville, TN; JR; BA; Stdnt Govt Assoc; Frnch Clb; Blue Key Pres; Gamma Beta Phi; AS Bus NA St Tech Inst; Engl; Grad Schl Engl.**

**WINGFIELD, JIMMY G,** East Tn St Univ, Johnson City, TN; JR; BSEH; Gamma Beta Phi 89-90; Intnshp ECOTEK; Bsbl Co-Capt 87-89; AAS Roane St Comm Colg 90; Envnmtl Hlth.

**WINGFIELD, RHONDA Y,** Morris Brown Coll, Atlanta, GA; SO; BA; Crim Just Clb 90-; Crim Just; Probtn/Parole.

**WINGLER, DAVID S,** Spartanburg Methodist Coll, Spartanburg, SC; FR.

**WINGO, AMANDA J,** East Stroudsburg Univ, E Stroudsburg, PA; SR; BA; Stdnt Senate Academic Afrs Comm 88-; Lutheran Stdnt Mvmnt NE OA Rep 89-; DARE 90-; Omicron Delta Kappa 90-; Phi Alpha Theta 90-; United Campus Minstry Cord; Hnrs Award; IM Sftbl 87-89; History; Geography.

**WINGO, TERESA M,** East Stroudsburg Univ, E Stroudsburg, PA; SR; BA; Stu Sen; MALSM; Phi Alpha Theta; Omicron Delta Kappa; IM Sftbl; Hstry Intl Stu; Ggrphy.

**WININGER, JILL M,** Church Of God Sch Of Theology, Cleveland, TN; GD; MA; World Chrstn Prayer Mvemnt Worship Ldr 90-; Big Bro/Big Sis; BA King Clg 89; Missions; Tch/Mission.

**WININGER, NANCY J,** Western Ky Univ, Bowling Green, KY; SO; AA; Bus/Bnkng; Bnkng Fld.

**WINITSKY, KIMBERLY O,** Fl International Univ, Miami, FL; SR; MBA; Hotel/Food/Trvl Assoc 90-; Fclty Schlr 87-; Phi Lambda 90-; Phi Eta Sigma 87-; Phi Kappa Phi 89-; Delta Delta Phi 89-; Intl Food Serv Exec Assoc 90-; Magna Cum Laude; Schlrshp 87-; Scholar; BS; Business; Food Service.

**WINK, LINDA I,** Central Pa Bus School, Summerdale, PA; JR; ASB; Phi Beta Lambda VP 89-; Coll Sec Intrntl 89-; Allied Hlth Clb Pres 89-; Extrnshp Good Hope Fmly Physcns; 4.0 GPA 89-; Sftbl 90; Allied Hlth-Med Sec; Trnscrptnst.

**WINKELMANN MARSH, RENATE A,** Hillsborough Comm Coll, Tampa, FL; JR; BA; Hnr Lst 88-; SW FL Bld Bnk Jb Pstn Atmtn Grphcs 90-; Tch Grmn Arts And Crfts; Combine Comp Sci With Arts And Crfts; BA Oberlin College Berlin-Dahlem Germany 61; Comp Sci; Comp Prgmmng Anlyze.

**WINKLEMAN, CHRIS A,** Mount Aloysius Jr Coll, Cresson, PA; FR; AS; Waitress Brtndr 81-90; RN; Med-Srgcl Nrs.

**WINKLEMAN, DIANA E,** Union Univ, Jackson, TN; JR; Prexy Club 90-; Literary Mag Sr Edtr 89-; Rutledge Hnry Hist Club Sntr 89-; Hnrs Stdnt Assoc Pres 88-; Alpha Chi 90-; Sigma Tau Delta 89-; Phi Kappa Delta 88-; Seta Tau Alpha 2nd V P 88-; Alpha Chi Schlrshp Paper Winner; English; Writing.

**WINKLER, LINDA A,** Memphis St Univ, Memphis, TN; SR; BS; Stdnt Govt Rep 87-88; Phi Kappa Phi 88-; Pnhllnc Clb 88-; Phi Theta Kappa 87-88; Gamma Beta Phi Rep 88-; Deans Lst 87-; Gldn Key 88-; Chi Beta Phi 89-; Lbrl Arts Hnr Scty 89-; Beta Beta Beta 89-; Alpha Gamma Delta 88-; Blgcl Sci; Vet Med.

**WINKLER, VERONICA LYNN,** Memphis St Univ, Memphis, TN; JR; BA; NBA Exhib Chrldr 88; NFL Exhib Chrldr 89; Memphis Rckrs Chrldr 90-; Main Attrctn Dance Tm; Cmmnctns.

**WINN, AMANDA J,** Endicott Coll, Beverly, MA; FR; BA; Fash Merch.

**WINN, CAITLIN,** Savannah Coll Of Art & Design, Savannah, GA; FR; Drama Clb; Phtgrphy.

**WINN, ERIN STACY,** Indiana Univ Of Pa, Indiana, PA; SR; BED; Sign Lang Clb 87-90; PA Stdnt Educ Assoc 90-; Phi Sigma Sigma Phil 90-; Tchr Hearing Imp.

**WINN, LORETHA R,** Univ Of Akron, Akron, OH; SR; BED; Golden Key 90-; Kappa Delta Pi 90-; AS Kent State 89; Elem Educ; Tchng.

**WINN, PETER S,** Eckerd Coll, St Petersburg, FL; JR; BA/BS; Psy Clb 90-; Earth Scty 90-; Nature Conservancy 86-; Psy/Pre-Med; Vtrnry Schl.

**WINN, SYBIL ANNIE,** Univ Of Southern Ms, Hattiesburg, MS; JR; BA; Crmnl Justc 90 Assn 90-; Crmnl Justc; Law.

**WINNEFELD, BRETT L,** Kent St Univ Kent Cmps, Kent, OH; BA; Yng Rpblcns Pres 88-; Accntng Assn 89-; Fnnc Clb; Beta Alpha Psi; Invstmnt Chllng Wnnr; Precinct Cmmtt 90-; Rpblcn Exec Cmmtt 90-; Fnnc Accntng.

**WINNIX, MAURICE S,** Piedmont Comm Coll, Roxboro, NC; FR; BS.

**WINRICH, ALICE M,** Savannah Coll Of Art & Design, Savannah, GA; SO; BFA; Graphic Dsgn.

**WINROW, NEVADA,** Lincoln Univ, Lincoln Univ, PA; BA; Bio Clb 90-; Psych Clb 90-; Psychneurmnlgy Rsrch Flwshp; Clncl Psych Intrn 90-; Psychobio; Ped Neurosurgy.

**WINSLOW, CHRISTOPHER J,** S U N Y Coll Of Tech At Frmgdl, Farmingdale, NY; FR; AS; Center Middle Lacrosse; Lib Arts; Elem Educ.

**WINSLOW, KEITH H,** Asbury Theological Sem, Wilmore, KY; GD; MDIV; Grnvl Clg Tnns Tm 86-89; Qtrt 86-89; Tri Beta Beta 87-89; St Louis Daisy Schlrshp St Louis Univ 88; Summa Cum Laude 86-89; Div Sr Schlr Awd; BA 89; Bibcl Stdies; Mssnry.

**WINSLOW, SHEREE L,** Vassar Coll, Poughkeepsie, NY; JR; BA; Class Sec/Stdnt Fellow 89-90; Stdnt Advsry Comm Soph Repr 89-90; Radio News Brdcstr 88-89; Poughkeepsie Prtnrshp/Intern 89; Margeotes/Fertitta/Weiss Intern; Psychology.

**WINSMAN, KATHRYN H,** Queens Coll, Charlotte, NC; SO; BA; Stdnt Govt Assn VP; Cls Pres 89-; Amer Mktg Assn; Marshl 90-; Chi Omega Asst Rsh; Comm Intrnshp; Comm; Sls/Mktg Mgmt.

**WINSTEAD, ANGELA T,** Vance Granville Comm Coll, Henderson, NC; AAS; Stdng Govt Assn Pres 91-92; Cmptr Clb 90-91; Phi Theta Kappa Mbrshp; Acad Achvmnt Schlrshp; Cmptr Prog/Acctg.

**WINSTEAD, LINDA S,** Watterson Coll, Louisville, KY; SO; AS; Bus Admn; Bus.

**WINSTEAD, MONIKA L,** Coll Of Charleston, Charleston, SC; SR; BA; Alumni Assn 89-90; Hostess/Rcrtng Pgm 88-89; Adopt A Troop Pgm 90-; Alpha Delta Pi Schlrshp 90; Engl; Govt.

**WINSTEAD, PATRICIA A,** Vance Granville Comm Coll, Henderson, NC; FR; AAS; Stdnt Govt Assn Sec Treas; Phi Theta Kappa VP; Beta Phi Upsilon Pres; Med Ofc Tech; Med Ofc Transcriptionist.

**WINSTEAD, SHERI L,** Commonwealth Coll, Virginia Beach, VA; JR; AS; Acctg Clb; Hon Roll 90-; Deans Lst 90-; Csmtlgst Apprntc; Acctg; Pres/Ownr Beauty Salon.

**WINSTEAD, TERRY M,** Univ Of Tn At Knoxville, Knoxville, TN; JR; BS; Beta Alpha Psi; Dean Exec Undrgrad Prog 89-; Cllgt 4-H Clb Rprtr 89-90; Phi Kappa Phi; Beta Gamma Sigma; Gldn Ky; Accntng; CPA.

**WINSTED, TINA A,** Athens St Coll, Athens, AL; JR; BA; Phi Theta Kappa 90-; Educ; Lrng Dsblts.

**WINSTEL, JOHN D,** Univ Of Cin R Walters Coll, Blue Ash, OH; SO; BA; Bus Law Tutor 90-; Nom Peer Cnslng; Univ Hnrs Schlrs 90-; Dns Lst 89-; Phi Theta Kappa; Raymond Walters Coll Hnr Stdnt; Pre Bus Hnr Grad Of Yr; Bus; Acctng.

**WINSTON, ALLYNDA S,** Al A & M Univ, Normal, AL; FR; Al A/M Univ Mrch Flg Corps 90-; Maroon/White Bnd; RN.

**WINSTON, ANITA D,** Morgan St Univ, Baltimore, MD; SR; BS; Acctg Clb 87-; Stu Chptr Ntl Assoc Blck Accntnts 87-; Pronethean Kappa Tau 87-88; Smr Intrshp Crwn Cntrl Petro Acct Pybl Clrk 88; Acctg; CPA.

**WINSTON, DENNIS D,** Al A & M Univ, Normal, AL; FR; Acdmc Schlrshp 90-; Pres Fresh Awrd 90; Elect Eng Tech; Eng.

**WINSTON, FREDDA J,** Lesley Coll, Cambridge, MA; SR; BS; Phtgrphy Fitness Dance; Mass Adptn Resource Exchng Intrnshp 89; Short Stop Rsdntl Trtmnt Shltr For At Risk Youth 89; CASPAR Drug Addctd Hmls Shltr 90; Human Serv Cnslng/Psych.

**WINSTON, KEVIN R,** Yale Univ, New Haven, CT; SR; BA; Stdnt Govt V P 90-; Art Journal Co Founder; Newspaper Rprtr 87-90; Comm Rep Security 90-; Bus & Econ Forum 90-; Invstmnt Grp; UCSD Rsrch Prog 90; Psych; Pub Hlth.**

**WINSTON, SABRINA,** Al St Univ, Montgomery, AL; SO; Bio; Tchr.

**WINSTON, WILLIAM B,** Columbia Union Coll, Takoma Park, MD; SR; BS; Deans Lst 88-; Employee Yr 90; Natl Assn Alcoholism/Drug Abuse Cnslrs 88; Hotline Cnslr WACADA 87-; Chldrens Hm Asst Pgm Coord 89-; AA Montgomery Coll 89; Orgnztnl Mgmnt; Trng Cons.

**WINTER, BARBARA L,** Daemen Coll, Amherst, NY; SO; BA; Psi Xi Omicron Sec 90-; Spec Olympics Bsktbl 90-; IM Vllybl/Bsktbl 90-; Nat Sci/Phy Thrpy.

**WINTER, KRISTIN M,** Univ Of North Fl, Jacksonville, FL; FR; MBA; Cvtn Clb Hstrn 90-; SGA Sen; Ftnss Prog; Stu Prgmmng Brd; Psych; Prv Prctc.

**WINTER, LORI A,** Davis & Elkins Coll, Elkins, WV; SO; BA; Stdnt Retntn Cmte; Hon Asso; All Am Schol; Deans List; Psych; Coun.

**WINTER, MICHELLE A,** Univ Of South Al, Mobile, AL; SR; BA; Leisure Serv Assn; Tour De Force Corres Sec; Natl Trsm Assn Schlrshp; Leisure Serv; Trsm & Cmmrcl Rcrtn.

**WINTERBOTTOM, LENA C,** Barry Univ, Miami, FL; SO; Sccr Tm Chmpns 89-; RHA 89-90; Chld Psy.

**WINTERHALTER, MICHAEL D,** Carnegie Mellon Univ, Pittsburgh, PA; JR; BS; Andrew Carnegie Soc Schlr; Indstrl Mgmnt; Intl Law.

**WINTERMANTEL, MARY F,** Duquesne Univ, Pittsburgh, PA; JR; BA; Stdnt Acctg Assn 90-; Beta Alpha Phi 90; Phi Kappa Phi 90; Beta Gamma Sigma V P 90-; Cmptvte Schlrshp; Acctg.

**WINTERODE, SUSAN L,** Villanova Univ, Villanova, PA; JR; Psy; Phd Psy.

**WINTERS, AMY,** Duquesne Univ, Pittsburgh, PA; SR; BA; Pi Sigma Epsilon; Intrn Pgh Hm Svgs Assoc Mrktg Assoc; Deans Lst 88-; Cmnctns; Copr Pblc Rltns Dir.

**WINTERS, ANGELA R,** Medical Coll Of Ga, Augusta, GA; JR; MSN; Bapt Stdnt Union 88-90; GA Assn Nrsng Stdnts 90-; Ntl Assn Nrsng Stdnts 90-; Phi Theta Kappa Sec 88-90; Coll Schlrs Amer 90-; Nrsng; Lbr/Dlvry Nrs.

**WINTERS, ANNETTE M,** S U N Y At Buffalo, Buffalo, NY; SR; BA; Intl Fac Mngmnt Assoc VP 89-; Design Clb 89-; Judo Clb 89-; Phi Eta Sigma 88; Golden Key 89-; Outstndng Acad Achvmnt Awrd Dept Of Planning/Design; Env Design; Fac Mngmnt.

**WINTERS, BLAKE A,** Nova Univ, Ft Lauderdale, FL; GD; MBA; Finance Socty; Alpha Tau Omega 85-88; Yng Repub; Securities Portfolio Intrn 89-; IM Ftbl/Sftbl; BS FLA State Univ 88; Finance.

**WINTERS, BRUCE C,** Southern Coll Of Tech, Marietta, GA; JR; BSACS; Proj Coord 85-; ASEET U Toledo Comm Tech Camp 18; Sftwr Eng.

**WINTERS, JULIE A,** Oh Univ-Southern Cmps, Ironton, OH; SO; BA; Psych.

**WINTERS, KIMBERLY H,** Fayetteville St Univ, Fayetteville, NC; SO; BA; S Eastern Hosp Sply Emplee; Ele Educ; Tch.

**WINTERS, MELISA A,** Univ Of Miami, Coral Gables, FL; FR; BS; Intrn 88-; Med Illstrtg/Photogrphy Montefrove Hosp; IM Tns 90; Biochem; Orthpdcs Sprts Med.

**WINTERS, ROY V,** Hudson Valley Comm Coll, Troy, NY; JR; AAS; Wells Comm Serv Inc 72-73; Newchnls Cable TV 74; Cty Troy Dept Publ Sfty 74; Cert De Vry Inst Tech 72; Elec Eng Tech; Asst Eng.

**WINTERS, SANDRA A,** Mayland Comm Coll, Spruce Pine, NC; FR; AAS; Phi Theta Kappa 91; Statstcs Clrk Hsptl 67-68; Mchn Oprtr 77-90; Mdcl; Offc Nrsng.

**WINTERS, SHARON A,** Capital Univ, Columbus, OH; SR; BSN; Nrsng; Pediatrics.

**WINTERS, STACEY A,** Univ Of Al At Birmingham, Birmingham, AL; JR; BA; Assoc Dgr Sci Southern Union St Jr Clge 89; Occptnl Thrpy.

**WINTERS, STACIE L,** Univ Of Sc At Columbia, Columbia, SC; SO; Natl Stdnt Exch Pres 90-; Columbia Hl Govt Repr 90-; Early Chldhd Ed; Tchg.

**WINTERSON, MICHELLE,** Western New England Coll, Springfield, MA; JR; Bank; Bsn; Finance.

**WINTON, MICHELLE A,** Fl International Univ, Miami, FL; SR; BA; Zeta Beta Tau Ltl Sis 84-87; BA 83-87; Elem Ed; Tchr.

**WINTON, ROBERT M,** Univ Of Rochester, Rochester, NY; SR; BA; Radio Sta DJ 87-90; Stu Drm Cncl 88-90; Omicron Delta Epsilon; Intern Mrkting Edicon Co; IM Hcky Sccr Bsktbl Vllybl Capt 87-; BA; Cert; Ecnncs; Accntng.

**WINZELER, JESSICA,** Columbus Coll Of Art & Design, Columbus, OH; SO; BFA; Fine Arts; Painting.

**WIPPMAN, MELISSA I,** Fl St Univ, Tallahassee, FL; JR; BA; Sclgy Clb Sec 89-90; Soc Bhvrl Sci Coun 89-90; Zeta Beta Tau Ltl Sr 88; Telephn Cnslng Rfrl Svcs; AA Univ S Fla 90; Psychlgy; Psychiatry.

**WIRE, CYNTHIA R,** Duquesne Univ, Pittsburgh, PA; SO; BED; Hallmark Store Clrk/Cashier; Kappa Delta Epsilon; Edn; Tchr.

**WIRES, KARI S,** Tri County Tech Coll, Pendleton, SC; SR; AS; NAVTA Sec 90-; Phi Theta Kappa 90-; NAVTA 89-; Deans Lst Mt San Antonio Coll 87-89; Deans Lst 89-; Hills Small Anml Diettn; Lgl Sec 79-87; Vtrnry Tchnlgy.**

**WIRICK, KIRSTIE D,** Pittsburgh Tech Inst, Pittsburgh, PA; GD.

**WIRKUS, ERICA L,** Fl St Univ, Tallahassee, FL; SO; BA; Alpha Gamma Delta Treas 90-; Lib Studies Hnrs Fnshr; Bsn; Bsn Adm.

**WIRT, ROGER A,** Washington State Comm Coll, Marietta, OH; GD; Dns Lst 90-; Pres Lst 90; AS; Auto/Dsl Tech; Trk Sls Rep.**

**WIRTH, COLLEEN M,** D Youville Coll, Buffalo, NY; JR; BSMS; Stdnt Phy Thrpy Assn Soc Chrmn; Alpha Omicron Pi Alum Corr Sec; St Stephns Parsh Ldr 90-; Retrt Conf Cand; Vol Buffalo Phy Thrpy Clnc; Stdnt Assn Schlrshp; Clincl Hosp Virg; Womns Bsktbl Tm 90-; Phy Thrpy.

**WIRTH, ERIC T,** S U N Y Coll Of Tech At Frmgdl, Farmingdale, NY; JR; BS; Pre-Med Soc 90-; AS SUNY Coll Tech 90; Bio; Med.

**WISBEY, TRICIA M,** Oh Univ, Athens, OH; FR; BA; Society Women Engr; Chi Omega; IM Water Polo; Chem Engr; Resrch Dev.

**WISBY, STEPHANIE L,** Univ Of Miami, Coral Gables, FL; JR; BA; Psi Chi; Pres Hnr Roll Fall; Provosts Hnr Roll; Psych/Soc; Ph D.

**WISCAVER, STEVE A,** Cumberland Coll, Williamsburg, KY; FR; MBA; Mtn Otrch 90-; All Armcn Schlr 90; Bus Psychlgy; Bus Admn.

**WISCHMEYER, JOHN D,** Savannah Coll Of Art & Design, Savannah, GA; SR; BA; Am Inst Of Archtctr Stdnts Envrnmntl Comm 87-; Natl Trst For Hstrc Prsrvtn; Am Inst Of Archtcts 87; Mary Whelan Schlrshp 87-; Archtctr; Hstrc Rstratn/Archtct.

**WISCOVITCH FERRER, SONIA V,** Inter Amer Univ Pr San German, San German, PR; JR; Beta Beta Beta; Mu Alpha Phi; Bio; Med Technlgy.

**WISDOM, JEFFREY F,** Austin Peay St Univ, Clarksville, TN; JR; BS; SGA Senator At Lrg; Coll Rep Pres 90-; Cmps Nwsppr Stf Wrtr; Alpha Kappa Psi 89-; Pi Sigma Alpha; Gov Ambsdr 89-; Dns Diplomat 88-90; Pol Sci; Grad Schl/Law Schl.**

**WISDOM, JEFFREY R,** Gordon Conwell Theol Sem, S Hamilton, MA; GD; MDIV; Phi Alpha Chi; Byington Schlrshl 90-; Greek Teaching Asstnt; New Testament; Professor.

**WISE, BIRUTE MARIJA,** Univ Of Sc At Columbia, Columbia, SC; JR; BS; Bio Clb 90-; Gamma Beta Phi Chrprsn Indctn Com 90-; Bio; Med.

**WISE, CARA R,** Ky St Univ, Frankfort, KY; SO; BA; Intl Clb 90-; Ownr Frmshp/Art Glry; Scndry Engl Ed; Educ.

**WISE III, DAVID M,** Saint Andrews Presbytrn Coll, Laurinburg, NC; JR; BS; Rgby Clb 90-; Drm Cncl 90-; Scb 90-; Tri Beta 90-; Bsbl 88-89; Blgy; Mrn Blgy.

**WISE, DENNIS DANIEL,** Coppin St Coll, Baltimore, MD; SR; BS; NAACP Pr 88-; Project Pub Rels 89-; Psych; Drug Rehab.

**WISE, GREG R,** Geneva Coll, Beaver Falls, PA; FR; BS; Mrchng Bnd; Cncrt Bnd; 2M Bsktbll; Bvr Cnty Wnd Symphny; Music Edctnrs Natl Cnfrnce; Deans Lst 90; Music Ed; Engl.

**WISE, JODIE L,** Juniata Coll, Huntingdon, PA; SO; Scalpel & Probe 90-; Sftbl 89-; Phys Thrpy.

**WISE, KAREN L,** Nc Agri & Tech St Univ, Greensboro, NC; FR; BED; Psych; Instr.

**WISE, MELANIE S,** Univ Of Cincinnati, Cincinnati, OH; FR; BSN; Stdnt Nrs Assc Mbrshp Chrmn 90-; Alpha Lmbd Dlt 90-; Hon Day; Acad Hon Schlrshp; IM Vlybl/Ftbl 90-; Nrsng; Pedtrc Nrs.

**WISE, RODNEY G,** Mayland Comm Coll, Spruce Pine, NC; FR; Tnns Clb 90-; Ski Clb; Dean Lst; Educ.

**WISE, SUSAN E,** Lenoir Rhyne Coll, Hickory, NC; FR; BS; Cmps Mnstrs Frm 90-; Fls Fr Chrst 90-; Pres Lst 90-; Blgy; Med.

**WISE, TRINA S,** Tougaloo Coll, Tougaloo, MS; SO; Ecnmcs/Bus Admin; Bus Exec/Stock Broker.

**WISEMAN, AMY L,** Bethel Coll, Mckenzie, TN; SO; BS; Math Clb; Natural Sci Soc Sec/Tres 90-; Clg Rltns Stdnt Wrtr; Gamma Beta Phi Rec Sec; Lambda Sigma VP; Diakonoi Rprtr 90-; Wrtng Cnsltnt Eng Tutor; Chrstn Issues Org Hist; Math/Chemistry/Humanities Awd; Biology/Chem; Rsrch/Teach.

**WISEMAN, FAITH A,** Brescia Coll, Owensboro, KY; JR; BS; SGA Jr Clss Senatr 90-; Sci Assn 89-; Res Lf Assn 88-; Sigma Alpha Mu; Deans Lst; Biolgy Ment Awrd; Natl Collgt Natrl Sci Awrd; Biolgy; Nrsng.

**WISEMAN, JOHN D,** Ashland Comm Coll, Ashland, KY; SO; BA; DKS Black Belt Club Assoc Davis Karate Studios/Amer Ftng Arts Fdtzn Ashland; March Of Dimes Vltr Wlkr; Deans List; Rose Hill Bpt Church; Acctng.

**WISEMAN, JOYCE E,** Watterson Coll, Louisville, KY; ASSOC; Womens Gld Treas; Accntnt.

**WISEMAN, KIMBERLEY K,** Fl International Univ, Miami, FL; SR; MFA; Clg Demo 90-; Phi Kappa Phi 89-; Hnry Arts/Sci Awd; BFA; Prof Artist/Teaching.

**WISEMAN, STEPHANIE J,** Univ Of Miami, Coral Gables, FL; SO; BFA; Alpha Lambda Delta 90; Theatre; Stage Mngmnt.

**WISHON, CONNIE F,** Western Carolina Univ, Cullowhee, NC; JR; BS; Gold 88-; Carolinian 89-; Bptst Stdnt Un 89-; Spch/Thtr Arts Hnr Cncl 90-; Hnr Pgm 88-; Alpha Epsilon Rho VP 90-; Ptrn Qlty Schlrshp 90-; Wstrn Comm Coalition Awd; Radio/Tv; Brdcst News/Prmtns.

**WISKEMAN, TAMI L,** Univ Of Pittsburgh, Pittsburgh, PA; JR; BA; Exec Cncl 90-; Deans Lst; NASW 90-; Psych Inst Vol 90-; Acad Schlrshp; Scl Wrk; MH/MR Adolscent Scl Wrk.

**WISKUP, LAURA A,** D Youville Coll, Buffalo, NY; JR; BSED; Future Tchrs Clb 90-; Vlybl Bsktbl Cptn 88-; Spcl Ed Elem Ed; Tchr.

**WISMILLER, TERESA A,** Memphis St Univ, Memphis, TN; SR; BA; Delta Sigma Pi Chrstn Brothers Univ; Psychlgy.

**WISNER, JANICE E,** Miami Dade Comm Coll, Miami, FL; SO; BS; Jste Sxly Absd Chldrn 90-; Ofc Adm Ntl Eng Frm 89-; Elec Eng.

**WISNIEWSKI, MARSI G,** Univ Of Nh Plymouth St Coll, Plymouth, NH; JR; Kappa Delta Pi 90-; Vol Wrk Snr Ctzns 89; Engl Ed; Tchng.

**WISNIEWSKI, TAMARA E,** Niagara Univ, Niagara Univ, NY; SR; MSN; Cls Sec 88-89; Psychlgy Clb Brd Mmbr 88-89; Cmps Radio DJ 87-; Radio Prmtns Drctr 88-90; Flms Comm 88-; Cir K VP 89-; NSNA Prgrm Drctr 89-90; Comm Actn Prgrm 87-; Unv Chpl Lctr 89-; Catholic Chrts 87-; Nrsng; Rhbltatn Nrsng.

**WISNISKI, VICTOR J,** Univ Of Miami, Coral Gables, FL; FR; BA; Hnrs Assn 90-; Alpha Lambda Delta 90-; Youth For Chrst 88-; Cmmnctns; Brdcst Jrnlsm.

**WISSINGER, JENNIFER J,** Nyack Coll, Nyack, NY; SR; St Agatha Gospel Tm Handcpd Chldrn 88-89; Hmcng Cmtee 88; Deans Lst 89; Deans St 90; Cert Exclnc Lrng Ctr Asst 91; Bkbl Chrldr Capt 88; BS Ele Educ 90; ACSI 90; Ele Educ; Ele Tchr.

**WISSMAN, KAREN B,** Univ Of Toledo, Toledo, OH; SR; BS; Cntrl Elem Prnts Clb Bd 89-; Prnts Clb 85-; Intrdscplnry Stds.

**WISSMANN, MARK J,** Christopher Newport Coll, Newport News, VA; FR; BS; Intvars Chrstn Flwshp Ldr; Cnts Elec Beam Acclrtr Fac Intshp 90-; USN Nclr Power Pgm 80-86; Math; Smnry/Mnstry.

**WISSOW, ELISSA,** Univ Of Fl, Gainesville, FL; JR; Fin Mgmt Assn 90-; Tchng Asst; Mt Olv Educ Ctr 90; Alpha Lambda Delta 89-; Alpha Chi Omega Asst Treas Pldg Schlrshp Chrmn 88-; Mtrls Nxt Gnrtn Acctg Intern; Fin.

**WITALEC, JOSEPH M,** Oh St Univ, Columbus, OH; SR; BSBA; Pre Law Club 90; Stdnt Jrnl Article Pblshd 90; Phi Sigma 90; Summa Award 90; Clg Bsn Pacesetter; Intern Pblc Utlts Cmsn 90; Dns Lst Laude; Tennis At Newark 89; Fin; Harvard Law Schl.

**WITCHER, CAROLYN DALE,** Coll Of Charleston, Charleston, SC; JR; BSN; Blgy Dept Wrk Stdy 88-; Zeta Tau Alpha Pgm Cncl 88-; Dstngshd Fclty Hon Lst; Nrsng.

**WITCHER, MALCOLM H,** Roanoke Bible Coll, Elizabeth Cy, NC; SO; BA; Spiritual Life Comm; Mission Awareness Comm; IM Sftbl; Bible/Theology; Chrstn Svc.

**WITCZAK, RISA J,** Oh Univ, Athens, OH; SO; BFA; Cath Coalition Art Chrprsn 90; Newman Cmnty 89; Cmps Crsde; Chrstns Engd Justc 90; Painting; Prof Artist.

**WITHAM, GEOFFREY D,** Vassar Coll, Poughkeepsie, NY; FR; BA; Vassar Spctatr Ed Assoc; I Won T Grow Up Day; Step Beyond Fest; IM Vlybl; Engl; Tch.

**WITHERINGTON JR, GORDON EDWARD,** Univ Of South Al, Mobile, AL; SR; BA; Natl Brd Rltr 88-91; Fin; Bus.

**WITHERITE, LISA A,** Oh Univ, Athens, OH; GD; DO; Undergrad Amer Acad Osteopathy 88-; Amer Coll Gen Prtctnrs 89-; Amer Ostpthc Assn Yrbk Edtr 88-90; Cls Offcr VP 88-89; Sigma Sigma Phi 90-; Gannon Univ Erie PA Dns Lst 82-86; TA Biology Prncpls Gannon Univ 84-86; Ostpthc Med; Fmly Prctc Physician.

**WITHEROW, DONALD SHANE,** Middle Tn St Univ, Murfreesboro, TN; SR; BS; Arnold Air Scty USAF 88; Kappa Alpha Order Schlrshp 90-; Aerospace; Arln Pilot.

**WITHEROW, LORI A,** Tn Tech Univ, Cookeville, TN; SR; BSBA; Scty Advncmnt Fnc Econ 90-; Stdnt Orttn Ldr; Beta Gamma Sigma; Mrtr Brd; Omicron Delta Epsilon Pres; Sigma Lota Epsilon; Phi Gamma Nu VP Ii 89; Tau Kappa Epsilon Lttl Sstr Pres 88-90; Fndtn Hnr Awrd 89; IM Sftbll Vllybll Bsktbll; Fnc.

**WITHERS, BARRY RYAN,** Univ Of Nc At Charlotte, Charlotte, NC; SO; BS; Dns Lst; Grphc Dsgn; Comm Artst.

**WITHERS, JACQUELINE R,** Christopher Newport Coll, Newport News, VA; SO; BA; Scl Wrk Clb 90-; Scl Wrk; LCSW.

**WITHERS, JENNIFER B,** Univ Of Fl, Gainesville, FL; JR; PA; Crtve Photo.

**WITHERS, MIRIAM L,** Univ Of Nh, Durham, NH; FR; BA; Univ Bkstre; Pol Sci; Tchr.

**WITHERSPOON, FELECIA S,** Alcorn St Univ, Lorman, MS; JR; BS; Intr Rsdntl Hll Cncl 90; Hnrs Stdnt Orgnztn 89; Zeta Phi Beta Sec 90-; Hnr Stdnt 88-; Ftbl Bsbl Bsktbl Stats 88-; Math; Tchr.

**WITHERSPOON, JONATHAN C,** Western Piedmont Comm Coll, Morganton, NC; SO; ASSOC; AA; Survyng Tech.

**WITHERSPOON, PHONECIA C,** Alcorn St Univ, Lorman, MS; JR; BA; Flg Capt ICC Bnd 89-90; Stdnt Crt ICC 88-89; Explrer Pst Prlmntrn 87-88; Math; Actury W/Ins Co.

**WITHROW, BILL,** Northern Ky Univ, Highland Hts, KY; SO; BA; Bus.

**WITHROW, MARY ANN,** Davis Coll, Toledo, OH; GD; BA; Riggles Fn Intrs As Intrn 90-; Int Dsgn; Arch.

**WITMER, JAMES C,** Univ Of Miami, Coral Gables, FL; JR; BS; Stdnt Govt 88-89; Golden Key 90-; Psychology; Med Sch.

**WITMER, WALTER D,** Greenville Tech Coll, Greenville, SC; SR; Data Procsng Mgt Assoc Treas 90; March Of Dimes Walk-A-Thon; Deans List; Im Ftbl/Sftbl; BS Clemson Univ 87; Comptr Progrmng; Comptr Indstry.

**WITNER, PAMELA E,** Univ Of Akron, Akron, OH; JR; BA; Kappa Delta Pi 90-; Ofc Mgr 86-; Scndry Educ/Engl; H S Tchng.

**WITT, ALISSA L,** Daemen Coll, Amherst, NY; SR; BA; Humn Svcs Clb V P 88-90; Pi Gamm Mu; Soc Wrk.

**WITT, ANNMARIE L,** Manhattan Coll, Bronx, NY; SR; BSCHE; Am Inst Chem Engr Sec 90-91; Soc Wmn Engrs 88-; NY Water Polltn Cntrl Assn 90-; Omega Chi Epsilon 89-; Deans Lst 87-89 90; Chem Engr; Engrng.

**WITT, BRADLEY K,** Memphis St Univ, Memphis, TN; JR; BED; Hlth Sfty Cncntrtn EMS; Nrsng.

**WITT, CHRISTOPHER S,** Pittsburgh Tech Inst, Pittsburgh, PA; SR; Acdmc Tutor 90-; Hon Rl 90-; IM Vlybl; AS; Comp Grphcs/Archtctrl Cadd; Archtct.

**WITT, COLLEEN M,** Methodist Coll, Fayetteville, NC; SR; BA; Nwspr Stff Wrtr 90-; Intrnshp TV Prod Studio; USAF Vet 83-87; Comm; Sls/Advrtsng.

**WITT, KEVIN L,** Univ Of Tn At Knoxville, Knoxville, TN; JR; BA; Phi Gamma Delta Rush Chrmn 88-; Stdnt Govt Assn-Fin Com 90-; Phi Eta Sigma; Gldn Key; Deans Lst 88-; Grt Amer Smkout 88-; Phi Gam Clothes Drive 88-; Helen Ross Mc Nabb Cntr 88-; Intrnshp St Marys Hosp Bdgt Aid; Acctg.

**WITT, LESLIE A,** Univ Of Fl, Gainesville, FL; GD; MED; Thtr Prfrmnc Awd 89; Thtr Schlrshp 86-87; BFA 90; Elem Ed; Tchr.

**WITTE, BRENDA L,** Defiance Coll, Defiance, OH; FR; BS; Crmnl Jstc.

**WITTE, HEIDI,** Memphis St Univ, Memphis, TN; SO; BA; Elem Ed; Tch.

**WITTE, KRISTINE M,** Defiance Coll, Defiance, OH; JR; BS; Alpha Chi; Deans Lst 88-; OH Acdmc Schlr; Math Actry.

**WITTENBERG, RACHEL,** Univ Of Ga, Athens, GA; SR; GSLA; Sigma Lamda Alpha; Gldn Key; Lndscp Arch.

**WITTLE, LINDA E,** Salisbury St Univ, Salisbury, MD; SO; BS; Perduc Schlrs Assoc 89-; Phi Eta Simga 89-; Franklin P Perdue Sch Of Bus Schlrshp 89-; Frederick R E Durrmem Schlrshp 89-; SICO Fndtn Schlrshp 89-; Bus Admn; Comptr Info Sys.

**WITTLER, DANA M,** Univ Of Ky, Lexington, KY; JR; BED; Emerging Ldrshp Inst 89; Epsilon Delta 89-90; Cmuty Rcrtn; Grad Sch Rcratn.

**WITTMAN, GREGORY A,** Univ Of Akron, Akron, OH; SR; BS; Phi Alpha Delta 90-; Amer Cunningham Brennan SPA Clrk Intern 89-90; Deans Lst 89-90; Tech Educ/Crmnl Just; Law/MS.

**WITTMAN, SANDRA M,** Univ Of Pittsburgh, Pittsburgh, PA; FR; BSN; Phi Theta Kappa 85-87; Nrsng.

**WITTMANN, JOHN F,** Youngstown St Univ, Youngstown, OH; JR; BE; IEEE; Deans Lst Wm Rayen Schl Eng; Eng Trng; State Brd Rgstrtn Prof Eng/Srvyrs State OH 89; BSAS EET 87; EIT State Brd Rgstrtn OH 89; Elec Eng; Prctc Eng PE.

**WITTMIER, CHRISTINE S,** Christopher Newport Coll, Newport News, VA; SR; BSBA; Bptst Std Un; Int Vars Chrstn Flwshp Pres 90-; Bsn; Mgmt.

**WITTSCHEN, SUSAN R,** Coll Of Charleston, Charleston, SC; JR; BED; Elem Edctn; Tch.

**WITUSZYNSKI, MARTIN W,** Air Force Inst Of Tech, Wrt-Ptrsn Afb, OH; GD; MASTE; Aero Clb 86-; Arcrft Ownrs Plts Assn 89-; Air Frc Assn 80-; Sigma Iota Epsilon 90-; Cert Acqustn Mgr 87-; BS Air Frc Acad 85; Syst Mgmt; Res/Devlpmnt.

**WITWICKI, DANUTA K,** Springfield Tech Comm Coll, Springfield, MA; GD; AS; Med Assist Assoc Clb 90; Alpha Nu Omega 90; Hosp Med Assist 90; AA 89; Med Assist; Nrsng.

**WITZIGREUTER, JOHN D,** Southern Coll Of Tech, Marietta, GA; FR; BS; Pi Kappa Hi Treas; Mechanical Engineering.

**WLAZIO, MARY JO,** Univ Of Miami, Coral Gables, FL; FR; BA; Pre Legal Soc 90-; Pizzazz Dance 90-; Alpha Lambda Delta 90-; Hon Prog 90-; Kappa Kappa Gamma Asst Treas 90-; Pres Hon Rl 90-; Deans Lst 90-; Panhellenic Pldg Schlrshp; Intl Rltns; Law.

**WLAZLO, MARY JO,** Univ Of Miami, Coral Gables, FL; FR; BA; Pre Lgl Scty 90-; Dnc Clb 90; Alpha Lambda Delta; Kappa Kappa Gamma Asst Treas; Prsdnts Hnr Rll; Deans Lst 90; Apol Plshng Awrd; Pnhllnc Pldg Schlrshp; Intl Rltns.

**WLEKLINSKI, ROBERT EDWARD,** Cornell Univ Statutory College, Ithaca, NY; SO; BS; Cornell Vrsty Ftbl 89-; Eng; MBA.

**WO, NGAI PAK,** City Univ Of Ny La Guard Coll, Long Island Cty, NY; SO; Accntng.

**WODENSCHECK, ROBERTA J,** Clarkson Univ, Potsdam, NY; SR; BS; POLIS Pres 88-90; Stdnt Govt Assn Constitution Com 90; Comp Users Clb Stdnt Govt Rep 89-90; Phi Theta Kappa 89-90; Hawes Prize; Phi Theta Kappa Schlrshp 90-; Nrthrn NY Comm Fndtn Schlrshp 90-; MIS; Sys Analyst Info Servs.

**WOERHEIDE, KATHRYN J,** Richard Bland Coll, Petersburg, VA; SO; Hon Ct Chrmn 90-; Stdnt Govt Assn 89-90; Hon Ct Sec 89-90; Cmps Notable 90-; Symphony Orchestra 90-; Sacred Heart Church Choir 90-; AS; Psychlgy; Fmly Thrpy.

**WOFFORD, JAMES A,** Snead St Jr Coll, Boaz, AL; SO; BS; Sci; Phrmcy.

**WOFFORD, JON M,** Union Univ, Jackson, TN; SR; BA; Yth Educ Music Missions Assn Pres 89-; Prexy Clb 89-; Sngrs 89-90; Baptist Stdnt Un 88-90; Yth Ldrshp Conf Co Chrmn 89-; Deans Lst 89-; Mus/Religion; Ministry.

**WOFFORD, MICHAEL R,** Univ Of Sc At Columbia, Columbia, SC; JR; BA; Acctg Clb 90-; Bus Affrs Offc On Cmps Asst; Ftbl Prsbytrn Coll 89; Bus/Acctg; CPA.

**WOFFORD, RICHARD W,** Valdosta St Coll, Valdosta, GA; FR; BFA; Art Stdnts League PR 90-; Alpha Lambda Delta Sec 90-; Appalachian Serv Proj 89-; Tammy Lee Fortner Art Schlrshp; Art; Advrtsng/Graphic Dsgn.

**WOFFORD, WENDY MICHELE,** Ms St Univ, Miss State, MS; SO; BA; Phi Beta Sigma 89-; Awd Schlrshp From Dept Of Psychlgy 90-; Psychlgy; Chld Psychlgst.

**WOGGON, STEPHEN ARTHUR,** Univ Of Nc At Asheville, Asheville, NC; SR; BA; Lit/Arts Jrnl Asst Edtr 86-87; Deans Lst 86-; Hons Pgm 86-; China Nanjing Univ Exchng; Philosophy; Prof.

**WOHLFORD, TERRY CLINTON,** Catawba Valley Comm Coll, Hickory, NC; FR; Fntr Wrkr; Elctrncs.

**WOHLGEMUTH, SUNG EUN K,** Duquesne Univ, Pittsburgh, PA; SR; BA; Music; Violnst.

**WOHLRAB, JULIETTE L,** Le Moyne Coll, Syracuse, NY; SR; MD; Biol Clb 87-; Amnsty Intl 88-90; Beta Beta Beta 89-; Hmn Srvs Assn 89-; Hosp; Indpndnt Rsrch Embryology 90; Magna Cum Laude; Vrsty Chrldng Capt 88-; BS; Biol; Med.

**WOIKE, LISA J,** Southeastern Ma Univ, N Dartmouth, MA; SO; BS; Clg Career Sec 90-; Bible Quizzing Coach 90-; Nrsng; Family Nrs Prctnr.

**WOJCIK, JULIE A,** Cornell Univ Statutory College, Ithaca, NY; SO; BA; Trck Tm 89-; Mrktg; Bus.

**WOJCIK, PAUL JOHN,** Methodist Coll, Fayetteville, NC; SO; BS; Stdnt Govt Assoc Senate; ROTC Color Guard Sergeant 90-; Sigma Omega Chi VP; Fellow Christian Athletes 90-; Reserve Offcrs Trng Course 90-; Sociology; FBI.

**WOLAK, JULIE M,** Lesley Coll, Cambridge, MA; SR; BS; Ritz-Carlton Sls/Mktg Intrn 89; New Englnd USA Intrn 90; Mgmt; Bus Admin.**

**WOLAN, LILA A,** Western New England Coll, Springfield, MA; JR; BA; Pol Clb Sec 90-; Radio Prog Rock Coord 88-; Model UN 90; Deans Lst 88-; Natl Yth Ldrs Cncl 90; Govt; Foreign Serv Ofcr.

**WOLBERT, KIMBERLY L,** Liberty Univ, Lynchburg, VA; JR; BS; Hlth Sci Clb 90-; Alpha Lambda Delta 89-; Voted Most Insprtnl Crs Cntry 89; Crs Cntry Tm/Track Tm; Comm Hlth Promo; Phys Therapy.

**WOLF, CAROLINE A,** Bellarmine Coll, Louisville, KY; SR; Delta Epsilon Sigma; BA Hstry; BA Elem Ed.

**WOLF, DEBRA C,** Roane St Comm Coll, Harriman, TN; FR; AAS; Hlth Sci; Lab Tech.

**WOLF, ERIC W,** Hampton Univ, Hampton, VA; SO; BS; NSNA 90-; VSNA 90-; AS George Washington Univ 85; Nrsng; Naval Ofcr.

**WOLF, J PHILIP,** Savannah Coll Of Art & Design, Savannah, GA; SR; BFA; Stdnt Art Pblctn; Photography; Fine Art.

**WOLF JR, JOHN H,** Polytechnic University, Farmingdale, NY; JR; BS; Assn For Computing Mach Pr; Deans Lst 88-; Tau Delta Phi 90-; U S Microsystems Intrnshp Head Pgmr 90-; Pr Schlrshp 88-; Perkin-Elmer Corp Schlrshp 90-; SRO Sftbl Trnmnt 90-; Comp Sci; Lan Mgr.**

**WOLF, KELLY M,** Fl St Univ, Tallahassee, FL; JR; BA; Dorm Im 88-89; Seminole Party 88-89; Panhlnc Line Dance 90; Deans List 89-; Phi Mu 88-; Phi Mu 89-90; Film/Cmnctns.

**WOLF, LINDA K,** Juniata Coll, Huntingdon, PA; SO; BS; Null Set 89-; Comp Soc 90-; Coll Hnr Soc; IM Vlybl 89-90; Math/Comp Sci.

**WOLF, MARLA A,** Muhlenberg Coll, Allentown, PA; FR; BA; English; Sec Educ.

**WOLF, MELINDA K,** Kent St Univ Trumbull Cmps, Warren, OH; SO; BA; Acctng; CPA.

**WOLF, ROSE M,** Selma Univ, Selma, AL; FR; Pltcl Sci Clb 90-; Bptst Stdnt Union 90-; Choir 90-; Hon Soc 90-; Elem Ed.

**WOLF-BERNADOS, ELLEN J,** Coll Of Charleston, Charleston, SC; SR; Educ Forum 90-; SC Educ Assn 88; Fclty Hnrs; Admin Asst; Assoc Bucks County Comm Coll 82; Elem Educ; Tchng.

**WOLFE, CATHERINE M,** Ms St Univ, Miss State, MS; FR; BS; Kappa Delta; Hm Ec/Chld Dvlpmnt; Nrsng.

**WOLFE, JAMES E,** U S Military Academy, West Point, NY; SO; Theatre Arts Guild 89-90; Math Fourm 89-90; Dmath Fourm; Dean List 89-; RAFA Rngrs Eng Dynmcs 90-.**

**WOLFE, JENNIFER D,** Fl St Univ, Tallahassee, FL; SO; BS; IM Bsktbl & Tennis; Sailing Club; Botany; Research.

**WOLFE, JOSEPH K,** Appalachian Bible Coll, Bradley, WV; SR; BA; Applchn Bible Coll Stdnt Cncl VP 89-90; Applchn Bible Coll Gspl Hrlds 89-90; Applchn Bible Coll Jblt Smmr Tm 90; Bible/Elem Ed; Tchng.

**WOLFE, KAMIE C,** Coll Of Charleston, Charleston, SC; JR; BED; Amer Assn Fr The Mntlly Rtrdd Sec; Stdnt Cncl Fr Excep Chldrn; Spec Educ; Tchng.

**WOLFE, KARIN L,** Univ Of Miami, Coral Gables, FL; JR; BSN; Natl Stdnt Nrs Assn 88-; Gldn Ky 90-; Phi Kappa Phi; Army Nrs Corps Sprt Nrsng Awd; AD Oakland Comm Coll 81; Nrsng.

**WOLFE, KATHLEEN A,** Hillsborough Comm Coll, Tampa, FL; FL Rl Estate Assoc 87-; Bsn Admin; Cmrcl Rl Estate Mgmt.

**WOLFE, KATHY E,** Phillips Jr Coll Spartanburg, Spartanburg, SC; SO; AAS; Cmptr Clb Sec; Crsds Christ 90-; Nwspr Ed 90-; Pres Lst 90-; Deans Lst 90; Brnz Achvr Pin 90-; Wrk Stdy 90-; Sec Sci; Tchng.

**WOLFE, KIRSTEN KAYE,** Union Univ, Jackson, TN; FR; BS; BSU Vocl Ensmbl 90-; Intrdscplnry Hons Soc 90-; Biol.

**WOLFE, LAURA C,** Memphis St Univ, Memphis, TN; SO; BA; SG Asst Pres 89; Pryr Grp 89-; Chrch Bnd 89-; Hnrs Assoc; Hnrs Pgm 89-; Hosp Vol 89; Hosp Spkrs Cmte 89-; ARC Cnslr 89-; Acdmc Exclnc Schlrshp 89-; Mrt Schlrshp Pepsi Co 89-; Psychlgy; PHD.

**WOLFE, MICHELLE E,** Marywood Coll, Scranton, PA; SO; BA; USPC Blck Dmnd Pony Clb Pres Jr Bd 87-; 4h Manes Tails Pres 87-89; Theta Epsilon Nu Peithisopmein 89; Centenary Intercoll Equestrian Tm 89; Legal Stud; Law.

**WOLFE, PATRICIA K,** Providence Coll, Providence, RI; SR; MS; Resid Life Resid Assist 89-; Pastoral Council Chrprsn 88-; Big Bros/Sisters 88-89; Council Exceplt Children Treas 88-90; Resid Life Progr Yr 90-; BA Providence Clg; Counseling/Clg Admin IN Univ; Ed.

**WOLFE, RAYMOND C,** Georgetown Univ, Washington, DC; SO; BS; Acctng.

**WOLFE, TRACIE M,** Hudson Valley Comm Coll, Troy, NY; FR; AAS; Erly Chldhd Clb 90-; Prsdnts Lst 90-; Stdnt Tchng 90-; Erly Chldhd Edctn; MED.

**WOLFE, VICTORIA S,** Univ Of Ms Main Cmps, University, MS; JR; BED; Phi Theta Kappa 89-90; Golden Key; French Awd 89; Acad Deans Awd 90; ED Young Harris Clg 90; Elem Educ; Teaching.**

**WOLFENBARGER, CARMEN M,** Pellissippi St Tech Comm Coll, Knoxville, TN; SO; AA; SGA VP 88-89; Lit Mag 90; Fclty Schlrshp 88-89; Art Schlrshp 90-; Carol Reece Museum Art Schlrshp 88-89; Studio Art; BFA.**

**WOLFENBARGER, SHONA C,** Roane St Comm Coll, Harriman, TN; SO; AS; Deans Lst 89-90; Intrnshp Oak Ridge Ntl Lab 90; Math; Tchr.

**WOLFF, DEBORAH M,** Temple Univ, Philadelphia, PA; JR; BA; Natl Stdnt Nurses Assn 90-; Alpha Lambda Delta 89-; Grad Hosp Nrs Extern Pgm 90-; Nrsng; Primary Fmly Hlth Care/Nrse Prctnr.

**WOLFF, DONNA L,** Lasell Coll, Newton, MA; SO; BS; Yrbk Co-Edtr Prod Mngr 89-; Sccr Tm 89-; Hon 89-; Deans Lst; On Cmps Fac The Barn Day Cr Cntr 89-; Asst Tchr-Appld Lrng Skills 90-; Bk Awd-Exclnc Early Chldhd Educ; Sccr 89-; AS; Early Chldhd Educ; Tchr/Dir Chld Cr Cntrs.

**WOLFF, KAREN ANITA,** Univ Of Tn At Chattanooga, Chattanooga, TN; JR; BS; Chem Engr Soc Secy 90-; Homecoming Cmte; Colg Bowl; Golden Key; Alpha Lambda Delta; Phi Eta Sigma; Mortar Bd; Tau Beta Phi V P; Hon Prog; Vlybl; Chem Engrng; Engrng.

**WOLFF, MARC STEVEN,** Univ Of Fl, Gainesville, FL; SR; BA; Gldn Key 88; Delt Atau Delta Pldg Trnr 90; IBM Srvc Spprt Rep 89-; AA 89; Bus Fnc; MBA.

**WOLFF, RANDELL L,** Bethel Coll, Mckenzie, TN; SO; BA; CWIL 90-; Nwsppr Edtr 90-; Gamma Beta Phi Pres 90-; Soc Cllgt Jrnlst; Bob Hope Hnr Schlrshp 89-; Prose Awrd; Engl Lit; Tch.

**WOLFGANG, HUGH E,** Okaloosa Walton Comm Coll, Niceville, FL; FR; AA; Equity Cmmttee; Phi Theta Kappa VP; Pres Lst 90; Cmptr Sic; Sftwre Eng.

**WOLFGONG, KEITH B,** Northeastern Christian Jr Coll, Villanova, PA; SO; Std Almni Asc VP; Bsktbl Capt 89-; Math Educ; Tchng/Coach.

**WOLFINGER, CAROL L,** Lansdale School Of Bus, North Wales, PA; SR; Mdcl Asst 89-; Mdcl Asst.

**WOLFORD, PAMELA K,** Westminster Coll, New Wilmingtn, PA; SR; BA; Theatre Wstmnstr Chrgrphr; Godspell First Voice Undr Mlk Wood; Pi Sigma Pi; Clara Cockerille Schlrshp; Theatre Elem Edctn; Tchng.

**WOLFORD, RONDA J,** Anne Arundel Comm Coll, Arnold, MD; FR; Gen Stdies.

**WOLFRIDGE, MARY M,** Ny Univ, New York, NY; BA; English; Grad Stdes.

**WOLFSOHN, MICHAEL D,** D Youville Coll, Buffalo, NY; GD; BS; SPTA Chrmn 88-; Hnr Soc Treas 88-89; Oldr Wsr Awrd; Hnrs Cnvctn Spker; APTA 90-; Hosp Rehab Tech 90-; Physcl Thrpst Asst 88-89; Sprts Prfrmnc Trnr 84-86; Ski Instr 78-81; Atpsy Asst 72-84; Hmdlyss Tech 72-84; Crnry Care Unt Tech 72-84; Physcl Thrpy; MS Prv Prctc.

**WOLFSON, ELLEN,** Broward Comm Coll, Ft Lauderdale, FL; JR; BA; Fla Intrl Univ Jrnlsm Prog; Wrkng Vet Supplies; Jrnlsm/Mass Comm.

**WOLGAMUTH, ANNA R,** Duquesne Univ, Pittsburgh, PA; FR; BS; Duquesne Univ Sch Of Pharmcy Cls Of 95 Secy 90-; Stdnt Intrn At York Hosp; Im Ftbl 90; Pharmcy.

**WOLIS, INGRID,** Fl International Univ, Miami, FL; SR; BA; Phi Theta Kappa 87-89; Phi Kappa Phi 89-; AA Broward Comm Coll 89; Elem Ed; Tchr.

**WOLLENWEBER, JODI C,** Palm Beach Comm Coll, Lake Worth, FL; SO; AA; Bsns; Trsm Htl Mgmt.**

**WOLOSEN, CHERYL A,** Georgian Court Coll, Lakewood, NJ; SO; BA; Vlybl Club 89-90; Delasalle Clyb Ed Commuter Coun Rep 89-91; Commuter Repre Student Govt 90-; Blybl Club 89-90; Special Ed; Remedial/Resource Tchng.

**WOLOSON, JOHN R,** Univ Of New England, Biddeford, ME; SO; BA; Stdnt Govt Dorm Rep 90-; Varsity Lacross; Pre Med; Orthopdc Surgn.

**WOLSEY, MICHAEL J,** Univ Of Southern Ms, Hattiesburg, MS; SO; BMED; Mst Prmsng Stdnt Gtrst 90; Yng Artst Awrd; Music Ed; Tchng/Prfrmnce.

**WOLSING, JENNIFER A,** Univ Of Ky, Lexington, KY; JR; BA; Tchrs Educ Prog; Very Spcl Arts Fstvl 90; Blue Grss Mrthn 90; Elem Educ.

**WOLSTENHOLME, PAIGE E,** Univ Of South Al, Mobile, AL; JR; Nrsng Hms Spcl Olympcs Vol 90-; Thrptc Rcrtn.**

**WOLTERS, RAYMOND W,** Thomas Nelson Comm Coll, Hampton, VA; FR; AS; Navy 84-; Eng; Cmmssn US Navy.

**WOLTHUIS, BETTY J,** Tn Temple Univ, Chattanooga, TN; JR; BS; Word Life Clbs 89-; Stdnt Mssns Fllwshp 89-; Delta Sigma Rho 90-; Hand Bell Chr 90-; Sftbl Tm/Soccr Tm 90-; Elem Educ; Tch.**

**WOLTJER, ULRIKE U,** Belmont Coll, Nashville, TN; SO; BSN; Stdnt Nrs Assn 90-; 25 Grp 90-; ISIS Tchng; Carver Intl Stdnt Awd; ISIS; BS Schl Of Engr Car Zeiss 87; Nrsng; MSN.

**WOLTZ, ANNE L,** Longwood Coll, Farmville, VA; SO; BA; Alpha Lambda Delta; Hstry; Elem Tchr.

**WOLVERTON, KEVIN D,** Marshall University, Huntington, WV; GD; BS; Ko Sotemi Seiei Kan Karate Org 1st Dgree Blk Blt; Pi Kappa Alpha Alumni; BBA 89; Cmptr Sci; Cmptr Prog.

**WOMACK, CHARLES E,** Western Carolina Univ, Cullowhee, NC; SR; BS; IM Sftbl 87; Ntrl Rsrce Mgmt Clb 88-; Rsdnce Hll Assn 89; Coop US Frst Srvce 90; Whtly Prdcts Inc 87; Ntrl Scis; Cnty Extnsn Srvce.

**WOMACK, CHRISTY A,** Univ Of Al At Huntsville, Huntsville, AL; SO; BSE; Baptist Campus Ministries Ldrshp Cncl 90-; Amer Soc Of Civil Engrs; Alpha Lambda Delta 90-; Outstndng Frshmn Ldrshp 90; Civil Engr.

**WOMACK, CONNIE J,** Middle Tn St Univ, Murfreesboro, TN; SR; BA; Intrntnl Reltns Clb Vice Pres 89; French Clb Sec 89; Frgn Lang Assc 88-; Model Un 89-90; Phi Sigma Iota 89-; Phi Kappa Phi 90-; Pi Sigma Alpha 90-; Gamma Rho 86-; Outstndng Stdnt French 90; Intrnshp W Sen Al Gore Jr; Frgn Lang; Frgn Serv.

**WOMACK, ELAINE S,** Defiance Coll, Defiance, OH; SO; BA; Hnrs Lst; Erwin Urch Awd 90-; Mgr Pizza Shop; Hstry; Libr Sci.

**WOMACK, RICHARD L,** Emmanuel Coll Schl Chrstn Min, Franklin Sprg, GA; SR; Stdnt Affairs Com 88; Emmanuel Plyrs 88-; Frnds Life 87-88; Phi Theta Kappa 87-88; Chrstn Serv Org 87-; Hon Grad; IM 87-; AA Emmanuel Coll 89; BA; Religion.

**WOMACKS, CATHERINE S,** Northern Ky Univ, Highland Hts, KY; JR; BS; Stdnts Natl Educ Assn 90-; Phi Beta Lambda 90-; Alpha Chi; Hnr Lst 90-; Prctr Gambl Cinc Oh Audtr 85-90; ABA Univ Cinc 81; Busn Educ/Sec Educ; Corp Trng Devlpmnt.

**WON, SUN-HEE D,** Ma Inst Of Tech, Cambridge, MA; FR; BA; Alpha Phi 90-; Mech Engrng/Mgmt; Corp Bus.

**WONG, ALICE C S,** The Kings Coll, Briarclf Mnr, NY; FR; BS; Deans Lst 90-; Acctg; BE Acctnt.

**WONG, ALICE Y,** Saint Thomas Univ, Miami, FL; FR; BA; Cmnctn Arts; Prdcr Flm.

**WONG, ANGELA,** Univ Of Sc At Columbia, Columbia, SC; SO; BS; Deans Lst 90; Erly Chldhd Educ; Day Care.

**WONG, ANTHONY Y,** Christian Brothers Univ, Memphis, TN; JR; BSEE; IEEE Pres 90-; Natl Socty Prof Engrs VP 90-; Intrcltrl Clb VP Clb Actvts 90-; CBU Chorale/Jazz Choir Piano Accmpnst/Std Dir 88-; Tau Beta Pi; CBU Acad Schlrshp 88-; CBU Prfrmng Arts Schl 88-; Memphis Beethoven Clb Yng Pnst; Elec Engr; Cmptr Sftwr/Hrdwr Dsgn.

**WONG, CHUEN HOONG,** City Univ Of Ny Baruch Coll, New York, NY; JR; BBA; United Malaysian Stdnts Assoc Pres 89; Asian Wk Plnng Cmmttee Co-Chrprsn; Cmptr Info Syst.

**WONG, DEBBIE A,** Coll Of Saint Elizabeth, Convent Sta, NJ; FR; BA; Bsn.

**WONG, EDDY,** Oh Wesleyan Univ, Delaware, OH; SR; Stdnt Chptr/Cmptng Mach Chrmn 88-; Cmptr Prog Tm 88-; Stdnt BBS Aix Syst Mngr 89-; Math Sci Dept Brd Clss Rep 89-; IEEE Cmptr Soc; Phi Eta Sigma 88; Phi 89; Pi Mu Epsilon 89; Omicron Delta Kappa; Phi Beta Kappa; Flbrght Iie Schlolar 88-89; Cmptr Scnc; Syst Prog/Rsrch.

**WONG, JOANNE,** City Univ Of Ny Baruch Coll, New York, NY; SO; BBA; C Step 88-; Intl Mrktng.

**WONG, JUDY S,** Newbury Coll, Brookline, MA; SR; Deans Lst.

**WONG, KAM T,** City Univ Of Ny Baruch Coll, New York, NY; SR; BBA; Hon Kong Stdnts Assoc Treas 89; Com Chinese Affairs 90; Gold Key 89-; Beta Gamma Sigma 89-; Baruch Helpline 90-; Math Ctr Rsrch 90-; Econ; Professor.

**WONG, KAREN ANN,** City Univ Of Ny Baruch Coll, New York, NY; SR; BBA; Bdy Bldng Clb VP 90-; Tae Kwon Do Treas 90; Beta Gamma Sigma; Magna Cum Laude; BBA; Mktg.

**WONG, KAREN S,** City Univ Of Ny Baruch Coll, New York, NY; SO; BA; Busn; Mgmnt/Mrktg.

**WONG, KIT M,** City Univ Of Ny Baruch Coll, New York, NY; JR; Chrstn Fllwshp 89-; Acctng.

**WONG, LAI NOOR,** Radford Univ, Radford, VA; FR; BA; Rgstrd Nrs; Cert 87; Psychlgy.

**WONG, LIH YUN,** City Univ Of Ny Queensbrough, New York, NY; SO; AAS; Phi Theta Kappa; Extrnl Educ Pgm Hmbnd Tutor 90-; Acctng.

**WONG, MAN HUNG,** City Univ Of Ny La Guard Coll, Long Island Cty, NY; SO; BA; Fitness Class 90; Librarian; Aerobic Cls; AD Laguardia Comm Coll; Bus Admin/Mktg; Mktg Analyst.

**WONG, MIRNA A,** City Univ Of Ny La Guard Coll, Long Island Cty, NY; SO; AAS; Office Tech; Cmptr Tech.

**WONG, PATRICK J,** Barry Univ, Miami, FL; SR; BS; Bahamain Clb 87-; Intl Stdnt Org 88-90; IM Sftbl 88-90; Bus; Mgmt.

**WONG, PAUL P,** Savannah Coll Of Art & Design, Savannah, GA; FR; Grphc Dsgn; Advrtsg.

**WONG, RAMA K,** Savannah Coll Of Art & Design, Savannah, GA; FR; BFA; Tnns Tm 90-; Grphc Dsgn/Comp Art; Advrtsng.

**WONG, SAMUEL C,** Cornell Univ Statutory College, Ithaca, NY; SR; MD; Chinese Bible Studey Grp 88-90; Hong Kong Student Assoc 90-; Hong Kong Christian Flwshp 90-; Golden Key 89-; Ho-Nun-De-Kah 90-; BS; Med; Physician.

**WONG, SHIRLEY W,** Va Commonwealth Univ, Richmond, VA; FR; Pre Phrmcy Clb 90-; Pre Med Clb 90-; Phi Eta Sigma 90-; Dns Lst 90-; Phrmcy.

**WONG, SHUI HEUNG,** City Univ Of Ny Baruch Coll, New York, NY; SR; BBA; Beta Gamma Sigma 90-; Deans Lst 89-; Full Time Mrchndsr; Finance.

**WONG, SIU SUN NELSON,** Bunker Hill Comm Coll, Boston, MA; FR; BA; Elctrcl Engr.

**WONG, WAI KUEN,** Miami Dade Comm Coll, Miami, FL; SO; Alpha Gamma Kappa Prvsnl Mbr; Vol Serv Victoria Hosp 90; Vol Serv Jcksn Mem Hosp; Calculus I/Ii Hnrs/Scl Envrnmnt Hnrs; Phrmcy.

**WONG, WAN BONG DOMINIC,** City Univ Of Ny Baruch Coll, New York, NY; SO; BBA; Chnse Chrstn Fllwshp Sec 88-89; Accntng.

**WONG, WINCY,** Western New England Coll, Springfield, MA; JR; BA; Intl Asc 89-; Alpha Kappa Psi 90-; Bsn Mgmt; Bsn.

**WONG-WYATT, CHERYL L,** Fayetteville St Univ, Fayetteville, NC; JR; BA; Englsh Clb Sec 87; All Amrcn Schlr; Vtrns Admnstrtn Ofc Asst; Englsh; Edctr.

**WOO, CHING-KIT A,** City Univ Of Ny Baruch Coll, New York, NY; SR; BBA; Goldn Key 89; Beta Gamma Sigma; Deans List 88; Mrktng; Law.

**WOO, HONG,** City Univ Of Ny La Guard Coll, Long Island Cty, NY; SO; AAS; Acctng.

**WOO, JI-SOO,** City Univ Of Ny City Coll, New York, NY; SO; BS; Physics.

**WOOD TERRY, PAMELA L,** Radford Univ, Radford, VA; JR; BS; VA Educ Asc NEA 90-; Natl Asc Ed Yng Chld 90-; Erly Chldhd Ed; Tchng.

**WOOD, ALUN D,** Lenoir Rhyne Coll, Hickory, NC; SR; BA; Alliance Health Physical Educ Recr Dance 90-; Physical Educ Majors Clb 90-; Presidents Hnr Lst 90; All American Sccr 89-; Soccer 89-; Sport Leisure Studies; Travel Tourism.

**WOOD, AMY L,** Fl Atlantic Univ, Boca Raton, FL; JR; BA; Phi Theta Kappa 90; Acctng; CPA.

**WOOD, ANGELA F,** Marshall University, Huntington, WV; JR; BBA; Flag Corp 88-89; Acctng Clb 90-; West Vl Scty CPAS 90-; Acctng; CPA.

**WOOD, ANGELA M,** Widener Univ, Chester, PA; JR; BA; Acctng Soc Offcr Adtr 89-90; Acctng; CPA.

**WOOD, ASHLI E,** Ga Southern Univ, Statesboro, GA; FR; BA; Kappa Delta Pldg Brd Scl Chrmn Awrd Schlrshp Chrmn; Bus; Ins.

**WOOD, BETH A,** Bridgewater Coll, Bridgewater, VA; SO; BS; Pinion Plyrs 89; Lambda Soc 90; Engl; Mdle Schl Educ.

**WOOD, CHRISTINA BETH,** East Carolina Univ, Greenville, NC; SR; BFA; Painting/Drawing; Gallery Work.

**WOOD, CHRISTINE K,** Niagara Univ, Niagara Univ, NY; SR; BSN; Natl Stdnt Nrs Assn Treas 89-; Univ Drmtry Cncl 87-88; Sigma Theta Tau 90-; Coll Nrsng Currclm Comm Stdnt Rep 90-; Delta Epsilon Sigma 90; All Amer Schlr 89-90; Nrsng Intrn; Natl Coll Nrsng Awrd 89-90; Wmns Swm Team Capt 87-; Nrsng; RN.

**WOOD, CORRENE L,** Western New England Coll, Springfield, MA; FR; BA; Alpha Lamda Delta; Bus; Acctnt.

**WOOD, DANA L,** Univ Of Louisville, Louisville, KY; JR; BS; Elctrnc Tech 79-; Assoc EE Tech 88; Elctrcl Engr.

**WOOD, DANIEL E,** Lexington Comm Coll, Lexington, KY; SO; AA; Cmptr Info Syst; MBA/CPA Accntng.

**WOOD, DANIEL W,** Univ Of Toledo, Toledo, OH; FR; BS; Stdnt Un Brd; Flms Cmmtt; Arts Scl Cmmtt; SUB Tch 90-; Actv Chrstns Tdys Grwth Grp; Phi Eta Sigma; IM 90; Blgy.

**WOOD, DAPHNE R,** Univ Of Al At Birmingham, Birmingham, AL; JR; BS; Gldn Key; Prsdnts Lst 88-; Deans Lst; Vrgna Anna Prytr Schlrshp; Psychlgy; Clncl Psychlgst.

**WOOD, DARA L,** Univ Of Cincinnati, Cincinnati, OH; SR; BS; Assn Fr Sprvsn Crrclm Dev 90-; Wmns Pnhllnc Assn Sec 88; Ordr Of Omega Archns 88; Gldn Ky; Kappa Delta Pi; Alpha Epsilon Phi Pres 88; Elem Educ; Tchr.

**WOOD, DAVID A,** Philadelphia Coll Pharm & Sci, Philadelphia, PA; SR; BS; Pre Med Soc 89-; ASP 88-; PA Phrmctcl Assn; Alpha Lambda Delta 87-; Rho Chi; Alpha Zeta Omega Sec 87-; Boy Scouts 87-; Eagle Scout Awd; God Cntry Rlgs Awd; Phrmcy; Medicine.

**WOOD, DAVID K,** Marshall University, Huntington, WV; SO; BA; Coll MENC; Delta Omicron; Delta Kappa Chptr; Music Educ.

**WOOD, GUADALUPE S,** Oh Univ-Southern Cmps, Ironton, OH; GD; BBA 90; AAS AS AAS Ashlnd Comm Clg 85 87 88 90; Bsns Admn; Purch.

**WOOD, HEATHER S,** Coll Of William & Mary, Williamsburg, VA; FR; BS; WATS 90-; Clge Prtnrshp Kds 90-; Cir K 90-; Blgy/Elem Ed; Elem Tchr.

**WOOD, JAMES L,** Middle Tn St Univ, Murfreesboro, TN; SO; BS; Husband/Father; Stones River Church Of Christ; Owned Landscape Bus; Elem Tchr.

**WOOD, JASON C,** Univ Of Tn At Martin, Martin, TN; FR; MBA; Hon Seminar Schlrshp Prog 90-; Busn; Acctng.

**WOOD, JENNIFER A,** Fl St Univ, Tallahassee, FL; FR; BA; Frnch Clb Pres 90-; Ballrm Dncng Clb 90-; Fr Hnr Soc 90-; Music Perf; Symph Orch.

**WOOD, JENNIFER J,** Averett Coll, Danville, VA; SR; BS; Sngrs 90-; AS 90; Math Comp Sci.

**WOOD, JENNIFER Y,** James Madison University, Harrisonburg, VA; JR; BS; Pres Lst 90; Deans Lst; Psych; Cnslg.

**WOOD, JILL E,** Tri County Tech Coll, Pendleton, SC; SO; AB; Amer Dntl Asst Assc 90-; Hlth Ed; Dntl Asst.

**WOOD JR, JOHN W,** Salisbury St Univ, Salisbury, MD; JR; BA; Psych Club 89; Surf Club 88; Ocean City Rcrtn Ctr Vol 89-; Sntrl Schlrshp 84-86; Gnrl State Schlrshp 89; Half Tide Board Riders 90-; Ocean City Tae Kwon DJ; Psych/Leisure Sci; MA.

**WOOD, KATHLEEN B,** Univ Of Miami, Coral Gables, FL; SO; BA; Earth Alert 89-; Spcl Olympc 89; Dns Lst 89-; Sports Fest; IMS 89-; Crmnl Jstc; Law Schl.**

**WOOD, KATHLEEN S,** Temple Univ, Philadelphia, PA; SR; BS; Rho Chi 89-; Phi Delta Chi 89-; Pharmacy.

**WOOD, KATHRYN R,** Saint Francis Coll, Loretto, PA; SR; BS; Hnr Soc 90-; Elem Educ; Tchg.

**WOOD III, LAWRENCE R,** Clemson Univ, Clemson, SC; JR; BA; Cntrl Sprt Dir 88-; Dns Lst; Nrsng.

**WOOD III, LEWIS O,** Radford Univ, Radford, VA; JR; BS; Jrnlsm Nws Edtrl.

**WOOD, LISA E,** Bryant Stratton Bus Inst Roch, Rochester, NY; AOS; Med Clb 90-; Deans Lst 90-; Tutor Engl Acctg Pharmacology 90-; Med Asst Pgm; Med Asst/Med Positions.

**WOOD, LORI A,** Univ Of Nc At Greensboro, Greensboro, NC; JR; BS; Stdnt Assn Edctrs 89-; Innrvrsty 88-89; Alpha Lambda Delta 88-; Unvrsty Mrshls 89-; Clg Schlrs America; All Amrcn Schlrs; Elem Edctn; Edctr.

**WOOD, LORNA E,** Saint Francis Coll, Loretto, PA; FR; BS; Educ Clb Sec; Elem Educ; Tchr.

**WOOD, MARION K,** Central Fl Comm Coll, Ocala, FL; GD; Phi Theta Kappa 77-79; Zoology Tutor 78; FL Cert Police Ofcr 87-; Vlntr EMT-FIREFIGHTER Derosa Vol Fire Dept 89-; Rural Letter Carrier US Postal Ser; AA 84; Pre-Med; USPS Law Enforcement.

**WOOD, MATTHEW Z,** Univ Of Nc At Greensboro, Greensboro, NC; FR; Res Clg Arts Comm 90-; R C Concerns Comm 90-; Hnrs Pgm 90-.

**WOOD, MICHAEL D,** Univ Of Akron, Akron, OH; FR; BSME; ASME 90-; AIAA Treas; Phi Eta Sigma; Hnrs Pgrm 90-; Dns Lst 90; Mech Eng.

**WOOD, MICHAEL L,** Memphis St Univ, Memphis, TN; SR; BBA; Deans List 90; IM Sftbl/Ftbl/Bsktbl 88-; Finance; Bnkng/Law.

**WOOD, NATALIA I,** Abraham Baldwin Agri Coll, Tifton, GA; FR; Intrntl Clb 90-; Cath Clb; Alpha Beta Gamma; Hon Assoc 88-90; Hon Stdnt 90-; Hon Stdnt U Panama Colon 89-90; Ofc Mgmt; Bus.

**WOOD, PAULA L,** Spalding Univ, Louisville, KY; JR; BA; Elem Educ; Engl.

**WOOD, RACHEL J,** Radford Univ, Radford, VA; SR; MS; Crmnl Just Clb Pres 90-; Crmnl Just Clb VP 89-90; Psych Clb Mem 90-; Intrnd Prbtn/Prle Dept Corr Dist 28 Lst Sem Sr Yr; Crmnl Just; Prbtn/Parole Corr.

**WOOD, REGINA M,** Middle Tn St Univ, Murfreesboro, TN; SR; BBA; Mktg; Mktg Res.

**WOOD JR, RICHARD H,** Western New England Coll, Springfield, MA; FR; BS; Bus.

**WOOD, ROBERT B,** Me Maritime Academy, Castine, ME; SR; BS; Ftbl Capt 90; Letterman; Mentorious Serv Awrd; Co Commander Chf 2 Asst Eng; BS; Marine Engrng.

**WOOD, SHARON O,** Dowling Coll, Oakdale Li, NY; SR; BS; Phi Theta Kappa 89; Pi Alpha Sigma 82; Kappa Delta Pi; Alpha Chi; Stdnt Ttrng; Natl Assn Of Accts 85-; Islp Arts Cncl Smthtwn Twnshp Arts Cncl 90-; AAS Suffolk County Comm Coll 85; LPN Cert Wilson Tech Schl Of Nrsng 71; Art And Bus; Educ Elem Scndry.

**WOOD, STEFANIE M,** Coll Of Charleston, Charleston, SC; SR; BS; Phi Kappa; Phi Eta Sigma 88-; Psi Chi 90-; Zeta Tau Alpha 87-88; Indpndnt Rsrch; Rsrch Asst 90; Scntfc Rsrch Pstr Ssn 91; Psychlgy.

**WOOD, STEPHANIE L,** Patrick Henry Comm Coll, Martinsville, VA; FR; AAS; Stdnt Nsrs Assc 90; VA Nrsng Stdnt Assc; Nrsng; Mntl Hlth Nrsng.

**WOOD, SUSAN EUGENIA,** Univ Of Ga, Athens, GA; JR; BS; Amer Stdnts Pharm; Zodiac; Phi Eta Sigma; Alpah Lambda Delta; Lamda Kappa Sigma; Alpha Omicron Pi Kpr Rtul 90-; K L Waters Pharm Schlrshp 4 Yr Schlrshp U GA; Cnsltnt Pharm.

**WOOD, TERESA A,** Piedmont Coll, Demorest, GA; SO; BA; Sftbl; RA; Acctg/Bus Admin; CPA.

**WOOD, TODD C,** Liberty Univ, Lynchburg, VA; FR; BS; Chorale 90-; Bio; Tch.

**WOOD, WILLIAM DAVID,** Univ Of Cin R Walters Coll, Blue Ash, OH; FR; BED; Hon Seminar/Gender Studies; Edctn; Engl; Tch Engl.

**WOODALL, JENNY R,** James Madison University, Harrisonburg, VA; SR; BS; Am Dbts Assn Natl Yth Actn Comm Natl Yth Adv 89-; Va St Yth Serv Comm Co Chm 89-; Big Bro Big Sis Vol 89-; Eddy Dalton Schlrshp In Emtnl Dstrbnc; Deans List 87-; Pres List 87-; Summa Cum Laude; Spec Edn Emot Dist; Teach.

**WOODALL, KELLY M,** Southern Coll Of Tech, Marietta, GA; SO; BA; Engineering Coop; Indstrl Engrng Tchnlgy; Engrng.

**WOODALL, MELANIE D,** Univ Of Montevallo, Montevallo, AL; SO; BA; SGA Soph En 90-; NSSULA 89-; Stdnt Wrkr Cmptr Svcs 89-; Chi Omega VP; Spch Pathlgy; Private Prac Spch Pathlgy.

**WOODALL, MELISSA G,** Mount Olive Coll, Mount Olive, NC; SO; BA; Psych Clb/Engl Soc Sec 89-; Peer Advsr 90; Hons Pgm 89-; Perret Awd 89-90; Marshal 89-; Engl; Cmnctns.

**WOODALL, STEVEN M,** Anne Arundel Comm Coll, Arnold, MD; FR; BA; D/D Wargame Clb DM 82-; Vlybl/Tennis; VFW; Star Trek Fam Assn; Applied Rdlgcl Cntrls; Toledo Scale; US Navy; Dcntmntn Spclst; Serv Tech; Elctrnc Tech Rx Oprtr; Cert Nucler Pwr Elctrncs A Schl Orlando FL 87; Elctrncs/Comp Sci; Prgrmr.

**WOODARD II, CARL L,** Morehouse Coll, Atlanta, GA; FR; BS; Mrchng/Cncrt/Jz Bnds 90-; TN Clb 90-; Gspl Choir 90-; Hon Roll 90-; Deans Lst 90-; Comp Sci; Law.

**WOODARD, EMILY SUZANNE,** Middle Tn St Univ, Murfreesboro, TN; SR; BS; Nwsppr Advrtsng Dept 89-; Intern WZEZ Asst Mrktng Dept; Radio Advrtsng Sales.

**WOODARD, JOANNE J,** Fayetteville St Univ, Fayetteville, NC; FR; BS; Bio; Rsrch.

**WOODARD, SANDRA A,** Central Fl Comm Coll, Ocala, FL; SO; BA; Phi Theta Kappa; Edn; Teach.

**WOODARD, TONYA M,** Coppin St Coll, Baltimore, MD; SR; BA; Crmnl Juste Clb V P 88; Acad Crmnl Juste Sci; Amer Soc Crmnlgy 89; Ohio Sta Univ Smmr Rsrch Prog 90-; Crmnl Juste/Soc; Crctnl Admn.

**WOODBERRY, ROBIN M,** Clark Atlanta Univ, Atlanta, GA; FR; BS; Pol Sci; Law.

**WOODBERY, SANDRA C,** Univ Of West Fl, Pensacola, FL; JR; Amer Hme Econ Assoc Pensacola Jr Clg Pres 88-90 Univ W Flr Pres 90- Natl lv Chr; Phi Theta Kappa Secty 89-90; Kappa Delta Pi 90-; PJC Schlrshp Awd 90; FL Hme Econ Assoc Student Yr 90; Ltheta Chi Tutoring Certif 90; Home Econ Ed; Ed.

**WOODBURY, CAROL,** Portland School Of Art, Portland, ME; JR; BFA; Auction Cmte 90; Phot Graphic Res Ctr 90-; Chartered Prop/Casualty Undrwrtr 85-; Photo; Art.

**WOODBURY, L LATOYA,** Univ Of The Dist Of Columbia, Washington, DC; SR; BA; Chptr NAACP Treas 87-88; Alpha Phi Psi; Hmcmng Steerng Comm 87; Delta Sigma Theta Prlmntrn/Proj Chr 89-; Chnl 9 Wash DL 89; Radio Atlntc Cty 89; Vtrns Admin Prod/PR 89-; Mass Media/TV Prod.

**WOODBURY, MICHELLE L,** Liberty Univ, Lynchburg, VA; JR; BS; Rsdnc Hll Ldrshp Tm SLC Elect; Deans Lst; AS Trn Tourism Mgmt Johnson Wals Univ 89; Bus Mrktg; Drct Sls Pblshng.

**WOODDELL, MICHELLE M,** Comm Coll Algny Co Algny Cmps, Pittsburgh, PA; SO; BSN; Awd Dedication/Commitment MH/MR D & A Bd; Assoc Retarded Citizens; Nrsng; RN.

**WOODEN, JODIE M,** Broward Comm Coll, Ft Lauderdale, FL; FR; AA; Phi Theta Kappa 90-; Sci/Math; BS Nurs.

**WOODEN, ROGER A,** Ny Univ, New York, NY; FR; AA; HBO Inc Tm AIDS Walk Cptn 89-; Home Box Ofc Inc 85-; Lbrl Arts.

**WOODEN-WITTY, DIANA S,** Western Ky Univ, Bowling Green, KY; JR; BS; Am Mrktng Assn; Rpblcn 89-; Hnrs Prog 88-90; Beta Gamma Sigma; Golden Key; Cong Yth Ldrshp Conf 90; Mrktng; Rsrch.

**WOODFIELD, LISA M,** Univ Of Sc At Columbia, Columbia, SC; SR; BS; Mrchng Bnd Bnd Cncl Rep 87-; Cncrt Bnd 87-; Tau Beta Sigma 89-; Alpha Lambda Delta; Pi Mu Epsilon 89-; Parsdnts Lst 88; Deans Slt 87-90; Math.

**WOODFIN, CLAYTON E,** Piedmont Coll, Demorest, GA; FR; BS; SGA Frshmn Rep 90-; Chem; Tchng.

**WOODFIN, KAREN S,** Central Fl Comm Coll, Ocala, FL; SO; Phi Theta Kappa.

**WOODFIN, KIMBERLY E,** Livingston Univ, Livingston, AL; JR; BA; Capt Of Chrldng Squad Capt; E Ms Cmmnty Clg; Music/Theatre Wrkshp Chrgrphr; Alpha Sigma Tau; Im Sftbl; Elem Ed; Tchr.

**WOODFORD, JOSEPH S,** Wv Univ, Morgantown, WV; JR; BS; C/N Prks/Swnsn Pltg 88-; Engr Asst/Qulty Cntrl; Cvl Engr; Envrmntl.

**WOODGEARD, BRETT A,** Oh Univ, Athens, OH; JR; BS; Alpha Eta Rho; Airway Sci; Aviation.

**WOODHAM JR, GARY E,** Univ Of South Al, Mobile, AL; SR; BS; Hnr Roll; Mrtl Arts Tchng Cert; Bsnss Mrktng; Sales.

**WOODLEY, MAUREEN P,** Univ Of The Virgin Islands, St Thomas, VI; BA; Deans List 87-; Pres List 90-; Acctg; Law.

**WOODMANSEE, MARLENA F,** Spalding Univ, Louisville, KY; SR; BA; Psych Bwl 87 Capt 88-89; Psi Chi 87-90; Delta Epsilon Sigma 90-; Brdwy Chrch Nzrne Treas 81-84; Acdmc All Amer Collgt Awrd 87; Admin Asst 73-76; Brd Membr Rnld Mcdnld Hs Hstrn 81-83; SE Chrstn Chrch 88-; Psychlgy; Marr/Fmly Therpy/Chld Psychlgy.

**WOODRING, JACQUELINE D,** Atlantic Comm Coll, Mays Landing, NJ; FR; ASSOC; Csmtlgst Gordon Phillips Bty Schl 89; Phy Thrpy Asst; BA PT Spclz PTA.

**WOODRING, WILLIAM M,** Fl St Univ, Tallahassee, FL; SR; Pre-Law Soc 90; Yng Coll Rpblcns 88; Gldn Key 90-; Phi Alpha Theta; Beta Theta Pi Alumni Chrmn 90-; BA; Hstry; Bus.

**WOODRUFF, DARREN S,** Univ Of North Fl, Jacksonville, FL; SR; BA; Stdnt Govt Sntr; Gldn Key; Pol Sci; Law.

**WOODRUFF, HEATHER L,** Univ Of Sc At Columbia, Columbia, SC; FR; MBA; Med; Dr.

**WOODRUFF, JEREMY W,** Columbia Union Coll, Takoma Park, MD; SO; BS; Natl Fresh Hnr Soc 89-; Ppt Mnstry 90-; Gymnstcs Co Capt 89-; Math Educ; Tchr.

**WOODRUFF, JOEL L,** Western Piedmont Comm Coll, Morganton, NC; FR; BS; Phlsphy/Crmnl Juste; US Mrshl/Prbtn Offcr.

**WOODRUFF, KIMBERLY J,** Va Commonwealth Univ, Richmond, VA; SO; BA; Pharm/Hmnts/Sci.

**WOODRUFF, NANCY A,** Univ Of Akron, Akron, OH; SO; BS; Sfty Twn Tchr 90-; Sndy Schl Tchr 87-; Spcfc Lrng Dsblts; Educ.

**WOODRUM, DAVID A,** Davidson Coll, Davidson, NC; FR; Var Soccer Tm; Phys; Med Doc.

**WOODRUM, MICHELE LYNN,** Marshall University, Huntington, WV; FR; Hnry Socty Frshmn 90-; Bus/Acctng; CPA.

**WOODS, AMELIA L,** Univ Of Tn At Martin, Martin, TN; JR; BS; Std Govt Asc Rep 90-; Std Crt 89-90; Psi Chi; Std Asc Amer Chem Soc 89-90; Phi Eta Sigma 89-; Tri Beta; Soc Hnrs Smnr 89-; Mu Epsln Delta 89-; SGA Acad Affrs Comm 90-; Trffc/Prkng Comm; Phlsphy Dpt Asst 90-; Bi/Psy; Optmtry.

**WOODS, CARRIE L,** Birmingham Southern Coll, Birmingham, AL; SO; BA; Chr 90-; Alpha Omicron Pi Kpr Of The Rtl 90-; Vol Srvcs Prjct Mgr 89-; Trngle Clb 90-; Pres Srvce Orgnztn; Admin Intrnshp Fr Admssns; Rsdnt Advsr; Mssn Trip To Zimbabwe; Engl Rlgn; Tchr Chrstn Educ.

**WOODS, CATHLEEN A,** S U N Y Coll At Fredonia, Fredonia, NY; JR; BS; Rcmbnt Gene Tech; Sci Rschr.

**WOODS, DEBRA M,** Abraham Baldwin Agri Coll, Tifton, GA; SO; BA; Phi Theta Kappa 90-; Sci; Educ.

**WOODS, DUSTY G,** Anderson Coll, Anderson, SC; FR; BA; Phi Theta Kappa; Gamma Beta Phi; Bsn; Admn Dir.

**WOODS, JACQUELYNN L,** Univ Of Al At Birmingham, Birmingham, AL; SR; Alpha Mu Alpha; Beta Gamma Sigma; Phi Kappa Phi; Bus; Mngmt.

**WOODS, KARL W,** Strayer Coll, Washington, DC; SR; BS; Presidents List 89-; US Nacy; Computer Inf Systems Diploma 90; AA 90; Cmptr Inf Systms; Engrng.

**WOODS, KATHRYN M,** Columbus Coll Of Art & Design, Columbus, OH; JR; Drm Clb 90-; Illstrtn Comp Anmtn.

**WOODS, KELVIN,** Tuskegee Univ, Tuskegee Inst, AL; SR; AKM HKN BKX; Dns Lst; Tnns; Elec Eng.

**WOODS, LAURA RENEE,** Univ Of Md At College Park, College Park, MD; SO; Crmnl Jstc Assoc 90-; Alpha Phi Omega Rec Sec; Acdmc Hnrs; Crmnl Jstc Sclgy; Law Govt.**

**WOODS, LISA K,** Longwood Coll, Farmville, VA; SO; BS; Natl Stdnt Spch Lang Hrng Assc 90-; Alpha Delta Pi Actvts/Hnrs 90-; Speech Path.

**WOODS, LYNETTE A,** Va St Univ, Petersburg, VA; SO; Art Clb 89-; Trahan Burden & Charles Advrtsng Agncy Trffc Crtv Prdctn; Cmmrcl Art/Dsgn; Cmmrcl Artst/Advrtsng.

**WOODS, MARCHELL L,** Central St Univ, Wilberforce, OH; JR; Hon Clb 90; Shprs Success Clb 90; Key Clb 88; Natl Hon Scty 88; All Amer Schlr 90; Bus Awrd; Ofc Admn; Bus.

**WOODS, MARY K,** Union Univ, Jackson, TN; SR; Scl Studies; HS Tchr.

**WOODS, MARYLYN JEAN,** Ms St Univ, Miss State, MS; SR; BA; CEC; Twn Plyrs 88-89; Cllgt Srvc Clb 87-89; Delta Psi Omega 88-89; BA; AA Holmes Jr 89; Spec Educ; Tch.

**WOODS, MELITHA L,** Fl St Univ, Tallahassee, FL; FR; Panhellenic Sec 90; Yng Repub 90-; Seminole Party Lady Sclphntrs 90-; Phi Eta Sigma; Alpha Chi Omega Dele 90; Pol Sci; Law Corp.

**WOODS, MICHELE J,** Coppin St Coll, Baltimore, MD; JR; BS; Ftre Tchrs Of MD Rec Sec 89-; Educ Crrclm Cncl; Estrwd Camp Cnslr; Prklne Bapt Chrch Ushr 89-; Dns Lst 90-; Chrldr 89; Elem Educ; Tchr.

**WOODS, RICHARD E,** Ky St Univ, Frankfort, KY; SR; BS; Cmptr Sci Clb 87-; Cum Laude; BS; Cmptr Sci.

**WOODS, SHARON L,** Lexington Comm Coll, Lexington, KY; JR; BBA; Bus Admin; Bus.

**WOODS, SUSAN ELIZABETH,** Univ Of Tn At Martin, Martin, TN; SO; BA; Zeta Tau Alpha; Crmnl Jstc Soc; All Amer Schlrs; Crmnl Jstc; Fed Prsctr.

**WOODS, SUSANN,** Al A & M Univ, Normal, AL; JR; Univ Choir Corrspndg Sec 89-; Thespian Soc Pres 88-; Kappa Delta Pi 90-; Mst Otsdng Thespian 88-89; Swim Tm 88-89; Sec Educ English/Psychology; H S Tch.

**WOODS, THOMAS R,** Oh Coll Of Podiatric Med, Cleveland, OH; SR; DPM; Amer Coll Foot Srgns 88-; Amer Coll Podopeds 88-; Oh Podiatric Med Stu Assoc 87-; Pi Delta VP 89-; Merit Schlrshp 90; BS 75; Podiatry; Physcn.

**WOODS, TRACEY L,** Duquesne Univ, Pittsburgh, PA; JR; BA; Sclgy Clb 89-; YMCA Vol 89-; Fmly Crisis Cntr; Shuman Jvnl Dtntn Cntr 89-90; Intern Cntr Vctms Vlnt Crime; Vol Recgntn Awrd 90; Psych/Crmnl Jstc; Soc Wrk/Soc Srvc.

**WOODS, VICKIE A,** Volunteer St Comm Coll, Gallatin, TN; SO; BNC; Bus; Cmaptr Sys Mngr.

**WOODSIDE, LA TANYA P,** Alcorn St Univ, Lorman, MS; FR; BS; Bus Admin; Sec Serv.

**WOODSON, DEMETRIA D,** Polk Comm Coll, Winter Haven, FL; SO; BBA; Phi Theta Kappa 89-; Dns Acdmc Hnrs 89-90; Bsn Admin; Bsn.**

**WOODSON, MARLA DIONE,** Bowie St Univ, Bowie, MD; JR; BS; Deans List 90; MD State Sentrl Schlrshp Award 90; Spcl Achvmnt Award 89; Affrmtv Actn Flwshp Award 88; Prince Georges Cmnty Clg Deans List 90; AA Prince Georges Cmnty Clg 90; Bus Admn/Mktg; Bus.

**WOODSTOCK, PETER A,** Embry Riddle Aeronautical Univ, Daytona Beach, FL; JR; BSC; Caribbn Assc Pres 90; Bdmntn Clb; Aerontcs; Avtr.

**WOODWARD, AMY R,** Clarion Univ Of Pa, Clarion, PA; JR; BSED; Koinonia Chrstn Flwshp 89-; WCCB 640 AM; Ambsdrs Pgm 90-; Phi Eta Sigma 90-; All Amer Schlr; Deans Lst/Pres Schlrshp 89-; Comp Sci Dept Stdnt Asst 90-; Tutor; IM Bwlng 90-; Apld Math/Scndry Ed; Tchng/Gvmnt Wk.**

**WOODWARD, CAREY L,** Christopher Newport Coll, Newport News, VA; SR; BA; SVEA 90; Elem Educ.

**WOODWARD, KARA L,** Univ Of Sc At Aiken, Aiken, SC; FR; Allied Sci; Physcl Thrpy.

**WOODWARD, KIMBERLY H,** Middle Tn St Univ, Murfreesboro, TN; SR; BA; Amnsty Intrntnl Prsdnt 89-; Greenpeace 90-; AS Columbia St Cmmnty Clg 88; Intrntnl Rltns; Tchng.

**WOODWARD, MICHAEL H,** Columbia Greene Comm Coll, Hudson, NY; FR; ASN; Nrsng; RN.

**WOODWARD, SUSAN C,** Savannah Coll Of Art & Design, Savannah, GA; GD; MFA; Deans Lst; BA Unvrsty Delaware 84; Phtgrphy; Phtgrphy Edctn.

**WOODWARD, TIMOTHY A,** Cedarville Coll, Cedarville, OH; FR; Soc Auto Engrs 90-; Elctrcl Engr.

**WOODWORTH, ROBERT W,** S U N Y Coll Of Tech At Alfred, Alfred, NY; FR; AOS; Sigma Tau Epsilon 90-; Coached Hornl Ltl Leag; Asst Cubmstr Sec Scts; Plmbng; Htng/Air Cond; Contrctr.

**WOODY, BIVIAN M,** Al A & M Univ, Normal, AL; SR; BA; Mktg Clb 89-90; Bus/Indstrl Cluster Assoc 90-; Free Enterprise 89-90; Alpha Kappa Treas 90-; NAACP; Co-Op Boeing 90-; Telecmnctns; Producer.

**WOODY, JANICE L,** Anne Arundel Comm Coll, Arnold, MD; SO; AA; Cmptr Oper 74-80; Data Proc; Cmptr Spclst/Prgmng.

**WOODY, MARIA A,** Va St Univ, Petersburg, VA; FR; MBA; Bus Info Syst; Engineering.

**WOODY, MARIA M,** Fl A & M Univ, Tallahassee, FL; FR; MBA; Hnr Rl 90-; Bsn; Entprnr.

**WOODY, MARY ELAINE,** Chattanooga St Tech Comm Coll, Chattanooga, TN; SO; AAS; CSI 88-; Deans Lst 89; Bus; Off Sys Tech.

**WOODY, PATRICK S,** Va St Univ, Petersburg, VA; SR; BA; Math Tutor; Prshng Rfls VP 87-; Coca Cola Schlp; BAD Awd Hgh Acad Achvmnt; Bsn Admn; Fncl Anlyst.

**WOODY, STACY A,** Roane St Comm Coll, Harriman, TN; SO; BA; Elem Teacher.

**WOODY, TRACEY D,** Univ Of Nc At Charlotte, Charlotte, NC; SO; BS; Phi Eta Sigma 90; Dns Lst 89-; Chnclrs Lst 90; Crmnl Jstce; Law.

**WOODYARD, JUSTINA D,** Al St Univ, Montgomery, AL; SR; Amer Mrktng Assoc VP 90-; Alpha Kappa Psi Hstrn 88-; Panhllnc Cncl Corres Sec 90-; Delta Sigma Theta Chrprsn Fnd Rsng 90-; Cust Excl Awd Coop Educ 90-; Ofcl Recmmnd Dept Army Rck Isl Arsnl 89-90; Mrktng; Mrktng Conslt.

**WOOLARD, JACKIE STYONS,** Roanoke Bible Coll, Elizabeth Cy, NC; GD; Chrl Clb 88; Mstrs Twlv 89-; Prdctn Trnr; AB 90; Bible.

**WOOLARD JR, MARK A,** Roanoke Bible Coll, Elizabeth Cy, NC; GD; Chrl Clb 88f Mstrs Twelve 88-; Delta Epsilon Chi 90; Cum Laude 90; Bsktbl 88; US Air Force 80-87; BA 90; Mnstry.

**WOOLDRIDGE, NGOC THI NGUYEN,** Univ Of Sc At Coastal Carolina, Conway, SC; SR; Math/Comp Sci Clb Pr 87-88; Campus Union/SGA 90-; Intl Clb; Kappa Delta Pi; Onicron Delta Kappa Sec/Treas 89-90; Pi Mu Epsilon Pr 87-88; Outstndng Stdnt 90-; Class Pr 90-; BS; Tchr.

**WOOLDRIDGE, SUSAN M,** Memphis St Univ, Memphis, TN; SR; BS; ANA TNA 87-; Sigma Theta Tau; Pi Epsilon Iota 84-85; F Nghtngl Awd; C E Trnr Awd-Mthdst Sn 84; Stf Nrs 85-89; Psychtrc Mntl Hlth Instr; Cert Mthdst Hosp Sch Nrsng 84; Nrsng.

**WOOLEDGE, STEVEN E,** Univ Of Akron, Akron, OH; FR; BS; Chem Clb 90-; Hnrs Stdt 90-; Deans List 90-; Chemical Engineering.

**WOOLEN, MICHAEL E,** Western Ky Univ, Bowling Green, KY; FR; BA; Emplyd Printers Inc 89-; Nrsng; MBA Nrsng.

**WOOLERY, MARY NELL V,** Meridian Comm Coll, Meridian, MS; FR; AS; Bptst Stdnt Union ECJC 86-88; AS E Cntrl Jr Clg Decatur MS 88; BA Mississippi Clg 90; Nrsg.

**WOOLEY, KAREN R,** Union Univ, Jackson, TN; JR; BA; Linguae Mundi 89; Stdnt Fndtn 90; Peer Cnslr 90; Zeta Tau Alpha Scholastics Chmn 89; Deans Lst 89; Psych/Spnsh; Mrrge/Fmly Thrpst.

**WOOLEY, LESLYE E,** Hood Coll, Frederick, MD; FR; BA; Stdnt Govt Bd Appeals Rep 90-; Circle K 90-; Hnrs Pgm; Pres Awd Schlrshp 90-; Pol Sci; Attny.

**WOOLEY, RYAN S,** Univ Of Akron, Akron, OH; FR; BA; Phi Eta Sigma; Alpha Lambda Delta Secr; Hnr Schlrshp 90-; IM Flg Ftbl 90; Engl; Law.

**WOOLLEY, S MARK,** Hudson Valley Comm Coll, Troy, NY; BA; Ind Studies; Engr.

**WOOLSLAYER, LORI A,** Saint Francis Coll, Loretto, PA; JR; BAPHD; Stdnt Govt Sntr; Rsdnt Asst 90-; Econ Clb 90-; Hstrns Rndtbl 88-; Phi Alpha Theta 90-; Pr Tutor 89-; Hstry/Sec Ed; Tchr/Prfsr.

**WOOLSON, DIANE C,** S U N Y At Buffalo, Buffalo, NY; JR; BA; Acctng Assn; Delta Sigma Pi VP; Beta Alpha Psi; Intrnshp; AAS Niagara County Comm Coll 90; Acctng.

**WOOLUMS, MICHELLE RENEE,** William Paterson Coll, Wayne, NJ; JR; BA; Cnsrvtn Clb 88-89; Poem Pub Whispers In The Wind 89; Engl/Wrtng; Photo/Jrnlst.

**WOOLWINE, MARK E,** Radford Univ, Radford, VA; JR; BA; Membrshp Clrk For Chrch 90-; Bsbl Team 88-90; Acctg.

**WOOSLEY, MELISSA RENEA,** Bellarmine Coll, Louisville, KY; SO; BED; Natl Educ Assn 89-; KY Educ Assn 89-; Stdnt Cncl Excep Chldrn Pres; Dorm Govt Flr Repr 90-; Ambassador 89-; St Robert Bellarmine Schlrshp 89-; Dns Lst 89-; Elem/Spec Educ; Tchng.**

**WOOTEN, ALLISON B,** Univ Of Nc At Wilmington, Wilmington, NC; SO; BA; Spnsh Clb; Elem Educ; Tchng.**

**WOOTEN, CENDA Q,** Univ Of Nc At Greensboro, Greensboro, NC; SR; BS; Elem Edn; Tchr.

**WOOTEN, DEBORAH E,** Valdosta St Coll, Valdosta, GA; SR; Deans Lst 90; Pridgen Bapt Chrch Lng Trm Plnng Cmmttee; Englsh Tchr Bcn Cnty HS; BSED; Assoc Of Arts S Ga Clg 89; Englsh; Tchr.

**WOOTEN, JANET B,** Tri County Tech Coll, Pendleton, SC; FR; AIT; Oolenoy Bptst Chrch; Holly Sprgs Elem Schl Vlntr; Textiles; Mgmt/Qulty Cntrl Tech.

**WOOTEN, RHONDA K,** Univ Of Sc At Aiken, Aiken, SC; FR; BA; Educ Mjrs Clb 90-; Cmps Crsd 90-; Pcsttrs 90-; Erly Chldhd Educ; Teacher.

**WOOTEN, RONALD SCOTT,** Coll Of Charleston, Charleston, SC; SR; BS; Cmps Crsd Christ 87-; Gamma Beta Phi 87-; Gamma Beta Phi 88-; Offcr Cmps Crsd/Christ USC/AIKEN; Stdnt Alumni Assoc; Who's Who Amng Amer Clg Stdts; Deans Listf; Phys Therapy.

**WOOTTON, DANA L,** Castleton St Coll, Castleton, VT; JR; BA; Stdnt Educ Assn 89-; Hall Cncl 90-; Stdnt Govt VP 89-90; Phi Eta Sigma 89-; Kappa Delta Pi 90-; Fresh Advsr Pgm 90-; Lit/Educ; Tchr/Prncpl.

**WORCESTER, PAMELA Y,** Manhattan School Of Music, New York, NY; SR; MM; BM; Music.

**WORD, BEVERLY A,** Ms St Univ, Miss State, MS; SR; BPA; Catholic Stdnt Assn 90-; Natl Assn Accntnts 90-; Soc Advncmnt Mngmnt 90-; Phi Eta Sigma 89-; Alpha Lambda Delta 89-; Beta Gamma Sigma 90-; Beta Alpha Psi 90-; Delta Sigma Pi 90-; Gamma Beta Phi 89-; Intrnshp Sullivan & Frey; Acad Schlrshp 88-; Acctng; CPA.

**WORD, TANIA R,** Middle Tn St Univ, Murfreesboro, TN; SO; BA; Erudite Emncptrs; Comp Info Syst; Anlyst.

**WORDEN, SHERON A,** Chattahoochee Vly St Comm Coll, Phenix City, AL; SO; AAS; Mag Prod Crew; News Intrn WRBL TV3; Radio TV Prod.

**WORDEN, SUSAN E,** S U N Y Coll Of Tech At Delhi, Delhi, NY; SR; BA; AS Suny Clg Of Tech At Delhi 91; Math; Tch.

**WORGHINGTON, KRISTA M,** Fayetteville St Univ, Fayetteville, NC; FR; BS; Elem Ed; Tchr.

**WORK, JAMES A,** Marshall University, Huntington, WV; JR; BA; Hall Advsry Cncl 87-89; Stdnt Govt Sntr 90; Stdnt Cndct/ Welfare Cmmttee Chrm 90; Omicron Delta Epsilon Sec-Treas; Alpha Kappa Psi 90; Lambda Chi Alpha 87-88; Outstndng Clg Stdnts Of Amer 88; Trck 87; Ecnmcs; Law.**

**WORKLEY, SUSAN M,** Univ Of Nc At Charlotte, Charlotte, NC; SR; BA; Acctg; CPA.

**WORKMAN, ANGELA SUSAN,** Ashland Comm Coll, Ashland, KY; SO; MBA; Cmnctn Dsrdrs; Spch Pthlgst/Adlgst.

**WORKMAN, BELINDA S,** Central Fl Comm Coll, Ocala, FL; FR; BA; CFCC Jzz Bnd Sctn Ldr 90-; Cncrt Bnd Sctn Ldr 90-; Cntrl Fshn; Acdmc Achvrs Awrd 90; Bus Admn; Bus Exec.

**WORKMAN, CHRISTINA M,** Emory & Henry Coll, Emory, VA; FR; Cmps Chrstn Flwshp 90-; Pre-Law Scty 90-; Concert Choir; Alpha Pi Omega; Hstry Ed.

**WORKMAN, DAWN R,** Univ Of Akron, Akron, OH; JR; Delta Gamma VP 90-; Dns Lst; Acctng; Acct.

**WORKMAN, WENDY M,** Univ Of Sc At Columbia, Columbia, SC; SO; BS; Stdnt Govt Assn Soph Class Pres 90; Fllwshp Chrstn Athl 89; Spartan Club 90-; Sports Editor Clg Paper 90; MS Soph 90; Athl Dir Hnr Roll 89; Dns Lst 90; Vlybl 89-; Crmnl Justc; Crmnl Invstgtns.

**WORKS, DEBORAH,** Miami Jacobs Jr Coll Of Bus, Dayton, OH; Pres Lst; Dns Lst; Data Entry; Cmptr Prgm Anlyst

**WORLDS, TAMIKA C,** Bloomfield Coll, Bloomfield, NJ; FR; BA; Yrbk Club & Colorlguard Underclass Edtr 87-90; Sigma Gamma Rho; Child Phych.

**WORLEY, ANGELA R,** Marywood Coll, Scranton, PA; SO; BS; Cmnctn Disorders Club 89; Tennis Chmpns; Tennis 89-90; Cmnctn Disorders; Speech Pthlgst.

**WORLEY, DANIEL L,** Southern Coll Of Tech, Marietta, GA; JR; BS; BBA Olgethorpe Univ 90-; Comp Eng; Eng.

**WORLEY, LISA M,** Vance Granville Comm Coll, Henderson, NC; FR; ADN; Cls Treas; Phi Theta Kappa; BA St Andrews Presby Clg 82; Nrsng; RN.

**WORLEY, RONALD C,** Averett Coll, Danville, VA; SR; BS; Clss Rep AACE 88-90; Rfrgrtng Eng Tchncns Assoc; Intl Scty Cert Elec Tchntns; AS 87; Cert 85; Bus Mgmt.

**WORLEY, RYAN K,** Roane St Comm Coll, Harriman, TN; JR; BA; Stdnt Govt Assn Stdnt Rep 89-90; Tenn Soc Med Tech Stdnt Rep 89-90; Cmps Chr 83; Amer Soc Med Tech 89-; Phi Theta Kappa Clb Ofcr 89-90; Natl Dns Lst 83-85; Psychlgy Clb 84-85; Bg Bros Bg Srs 89-90; Med Tech/Psychlgy; Med.**

**WORLOCK, ANDREA HELGA,** S U N Y Coll Of Tech At Alfred, Alfred, NY; SR; AAS; Mdcl Rcrd Tchnlgy.

**WORMLEY, MARILYNN YVONNE,** Columbia Union Coll, Takoma Park, MD; SR; BS; Citi-Stars Sftbl 87-; Washington Assoc Of Urban Bnkrs 89-; Not Pub 87-; Complnce Ofcr Citibank 78-; Dip Of Merit Inst Of Fin Educ 88; Bus Admin.

**WORMLEY, MARLA L,** Indiana Univ Of Pa, Indiana, PA; SR; BS; Alto Sctn Ldr 88-90; Lds Gntlmn Qlfd; Elem Edctn; Tchng.

**WORMUTH, NANCY A,** S U N Y Coll Of A & T Morrisvl, Morrisville, NY; FR; Phi Theta Kappa; Human Serv Intern; Individual Studies; Soc Wrkr.

**WOROBEY, THEA A,** Hudson Valley Comm Coll, Troy, NY; AAS; Acctng; Pnsn Admn.

**WORONIECKA, ANNA,** City Univ Of Ny Queensbrough, New York, NY; FR; AAS; Comp Prgrmmng; Bus.

**WORRELL, ALISON K,** Wallace St Comm Coll At Selma, Selma, AL; FR; Phi Theta Kappa.

**WORRELL, KATE E,** Univ Of Sc At Aiken, Aiken, SC; JR; BA; Acctng.**

**WORSHAM, MIRIAM M,** Univ Of Sc At Columbia, Columbia, SC; FR; BM; Womens Choir; Assoc Of Hons Stdnts 90-; Gamma Beta Phi 90-; Alpha Lambda Delta 90-; Delta Zeta 90-; Music/ Piano Pedagogy.

**WORSHAM, SUSAN V,** Va Commonwealth Univ, Richmond, VA; SO; BA; Awrd Rcpnt Art Fnd Shw; Awrd Rcpnt Juried Fine Arts Exhbtn; Sclptr Featured Rchmnd Arts Mag.

**WORSLEY, REBECCA A,** Univ Of Sc At Columbia, Columbia, SC; JR; BA; Stdnt Alumni Assn Sec 90-; Aglow Chrstn Wmns Clb Pres 91; Cmps Crsd Christ 89-; Mrtr Bd VP Clndr Edtr; Ordr Omega; Gldn Key 90-; Kappa Delta Epsilon Plnng 90-; Alpha Delta Pi Chpln 88-; Wmns Stdnt Serv Sor Dlgt 89-90; Alpha Hon Soc 88-; Early Chldhd Educ; Tchng/Grad Sch Spch Pthlgy.

**WORTHEM, KATHLEEN E,** Univ Of Ga, Athens, GA; JR; BA; Cntmpry Cncrts Univ Union 89-; Rsdnc Hall Assn RHA Rep 90-; IM Sftbl 90-; Telecmnctn Arts; Radio/Film/TV.

**WORTHEN, ROBERT J,** Ms St Univ, Miss State, MS; FR; BS; SAME Scrtry/Treas 90; ASME 90; Army ROTC 90; Gamma Beta Phi 90; Pres Schlr 90; Mchncl Eng; Eng.

**WORTHING, CHRISTINE M,** Kent St Univ Kent Cmps, Kent, OH; SR; Pi Kappa Lambda 90-; Gldn Key 88-; Delta Omicron Pres 88-; Crtv Arts Awd 87-90; Delta Omicron Grant/Schlrshps 89-; BM; Msc-French Horn; Pro Orchstrl Mscn.

**WORTHING, KARYN L,** Univ Of Akron, Akron, OH; SO; BFA; Repertory Dance Co 89-; Choreographers Wrkshp 90-; Phi Eta Sigma 90-; Alpha Lambda Delta 90-; Creative Artists Awd Kent State Univ 89; Dance Dept Schlrshp 89-; Acad Schlrshp; Dance; Profl Dncr/Tchr.

**WORTHINGTON, BRENDA J,** Loyola Coll In Md, Baltimore, MD; FR; B; Math Comp Sci; Comp Anlyst Math.

**WORTHINGTON, JULIE S,** Bristol Univ, Bristol, TN; FR; Pne Rdge Bapt Chrch Yth Chr; Admin Asst II Sprvsr Anlyss Corp; Cert Word Perfect Voc 89; Cert Lotus 1 2 3 Voc 90.

**WORTHY, DAVID L,** Univ Of Fl, Gainesville, FL; SR; BS; Beta Gamma Sigma; Gldn Key 90-; Pi Kappa Phi 90-; Omicron Delta Epsilon 90-; Fin Mgmt Assn 90-; Deans Lst 90-; Hon Grad; AA Palm Bch Jr Coll 87; Fin; Law.

**WORTHY, JEFFERY DEAN,** Duquesne Univ, Pittsburgh, PA; GD; MLS; INROADS 88-89; ESQUIRE Scl Clb V P 87-88; Amer Mktg Assoc 87-89; Kappa Alpha Pi Bd Dir 88-; Grad Asstntshp Ofc Res Life 90-; IM Bsktbl/Ftbl Capt 85-; Equibank Credit Analyst Intern 88-89; Corp Cmnctns; Corp Mktg.

**WOVCHKO, EDWARD A,** Saint Vincents Coll & Seminary, Latrobe, PA; JR; BS; St Vincent ACS Stdnt Afflte Chem Clb Sec 90-; Physics Clb 89-; Clg Prefect R A 90-; SACP Stdnt Exclnc Awd; Mens Clg Vybl 89-; I M Bkbl Vybl Ref 88-; Chem; Grad Study.

**WOWCZUK, YURIJ F,** Univ Of Pittsburgh, Pittsburgh, PA; FR; BA; Ukrainian Org Pres 90-; Coll Republicans 90-; Phi Eta Sigma; Ukrainian Schlrshp Awd; Deans Lst 90-; Econ; Indstrl Admin.

**WOZNIAK, CHAD C,** Me Maritime Academy, Castine, ME; FR; Asst Ed Yrbk Asst Ed; Vrsty Soccer; System Engr.

**WOZNIAK, KAREN J,** Mount Aloysius Jr Coll, Cresson, PA; GD; AS; Phi Theta Kappa 88-90; Micro Cmptr Scnc; Acctg.

**WOZNIAK, ROBERT J,** Univ Of Ct, Storrs, CT; SO; BA; Nwspr Wrtr 89-; Alpha Lambda Delta 90-; Chi Phi Pldg Pres; Engl; Jrnlsm.**

**WOZNIAK, TED R,** Central Fl Comm Coll, Ocala, FL; GD; BAMA; MENSA 72-; FL Mrt Schlr 74; US Army SSG 80-89; Rgstrd Rep 90-; BBA Unvrsty Miami Coral Gables FL 79; Grmn Math Edctn; Tchng.

**WRAGG, WENDY A,** Eckerd Coll, St Petersburg, FL; SR; BA; ECOS Legisl Council 90-; Sigma Delt Pi 88-; Student Assist Prof S Watson Wrtng Wkshp; Creative Wrtng; Wtng Edtng Translating.

**WRAY, CHERIE N,** Johnson C Smith Univ, Charlotte, NC; FR; Alpha Lambda Delta 90-; Pltcl Sci; Law.

**WRAY, LISA M,** Liberty Univ, Lynchburg, VA; SO; BS; LHEA; Alpha Lambda Delta Big Str; Human Eclgy; Int Dsgn.

**WRAY, RAY M,** Broward Comm Coll, Ft Lauderdale, FL; SO; BA; Chem; Med.

**WRAY, RHONDA G,** Univ Of Sc At Columbia, Columbia, SC; SR; BA; Varsity Tennis Tm 87-; BA USC Coastal; Erly Chldhd Edn; Teach.

**WRAY, TANYA J,** Kent St Univ Kent Cmps, Kent, OH; FR; BA; AIESEC; Intrntl Bus.

**WRAY, WENDE M,** Claflin Coll, Orangeburg, SC; FR; BS; Crr Clb 89-90; NAACP 90-; 4mrchng Bnd 87-88; Deans Lst 90-; Comp Sci.

**WREN, REBECCA S,** Saint Catharine Coll, St Catharine, KY; SO; BA; Phi Theta Kappa 90-; PTO: Cert/W Hon Sullivan Jr Colg 85; History; Tch K-4.

**WREN, ROBYNN E,** Washington State Comm Coll, Marietta, OH; SR; Capnet; Tchr 3 Yrs; Erly Chldhd Dvlpmnt; Tchr.

**WRENCH, KENNETH W,** Fl A & M Univ, Tallahassee, FL; FR; BA; Phy Thrpy Soc 90-; Phi Etta Sigma 90-; Pr Torreya Ltd Corp 86-90; Phy Thrpy.

**WRENN, DACIA M,** Univ Of Nc At Greensboro, Greensboro, NC; SR; BS; NCAE 89-; Hall Cncl Pres 90-; ICF 87-; Elem Educ; Tch.

**WRENN, EMMA J,** Winthrop Coll, Rock Hill, SC; SR; BS; Palmetto State Tchrs Assoc 90-; Phi Kappa Phi/Kappa Delta Pi 89-; Vol S C Corrs At Womens Corr Ctr Col SC; Christian Womens Clb; Mgr B F Kurtz Co Inc DBA Benjamins 84-89; Childhd Educ.

**WRENN, NANNIE JOANNA,** Piedmont Tech Coll, Greenwood, SC; SR; AS; Outstndng Mdcl Asst Grad; Deans Lst 90.

**WRIEDEN, GAIL D,** Life Coll, Marietta, GA; FR; CERT; Rn Lf Rd Mntr 89-90; Deans Lst; Otstndng Chrprct Tchncn Stdnt Awrd 91; Otstndng Clncn Awrd 91-; Vldctrn Grdtng Clss 91; Cert 85; Rdlgy.

**WRIGHT MORRIS, SUSAN RENEE,** Union Univ, Jackson, TN; SR; BS; Bus Clb 87-90; Acctg Clb 88-; Phi Beta Lambda 89-90; Intrnshp Acctg Firm 90-; Acctg.

**WRIGHT, ADRIENNE D,** Oh Univ, Athens, OH; SO; BFA; Photography; Commercial Photography.

**WRIGHT, AMY E,** Cornell Univ Statutory College, Ithaca, NY; SO; BS; Ag Ambsdr 90-; Div Ntrtnl Sci Cncl 90-; Stu Assmbly Cmnctns Comm 89-90; Stu Dng Serv Comm 89-90; Crnl Univ Wght Clb Bdybldg 89-; Ho Nun De Kah; Crnl Hlth Educ Dept Vol; Crnl Dng Emplye 90-; Cnsltg Dietitians Asst 90; Ntrtn; Med.**

**WRIGHT, AMY L,** Central Pa Bus School, Summerdale, PA; SR; AS; Trvl Clb Sec 89-; Trvl/Trsm; Trvl Agncy/Air Trffc Cntrl.

**WRIGHT, AMY M,** Univ Of Nc At Charlotte, Charlotte, NC; SR; BA; Nwspr 89-90; Intern Mercy Hosp; Eng; Pub Rltns.

**WRIGHT, ANDREW H,** Allegheny Coll, Meadville, PA; SR; BS; Outng Clb 87-88; USAA All Amer Schlr; Natl Strngth/ Cndtng Assn All Amer Athlt 90; Al Cnfrnce Athlt 87-; Trck/Fld Capt 87-; Aquatc Envrnmnts; MS.

**WRIGHT, ANGELA,** Savannah St Coll, Savannah, GA; SR; BS; Cmptr Sci Clb Sec 89-; Newtonian Soc Sec 89-; Jucry Brd 89-; Beta Kappa Chi VP 90-; Alph Kappa Mu; Delta Sigma Theta; USMC Offcr Candt US Navy 83-; Cmptr Sci Tchnlgy; Nvl Flght Offcr PHD.

**WRIGHT, ANGELA S,** Univ Of Sc At Lancaster, Lancaster, SC; SO; BA; ARETE 90-; Bptst Stdnt Union 89-; Scnd Pl Awd Richards Essay Cntst 89-90; Acad Schlrshp Charleston Sthrn Univ 90-; Psychlgy; Chld Psychlgst.

**WRIGHT, APRIL L,** Univ Of South Al, Mobile, AL; JR; Blck Stdnt Union Sntr 89-; Lsre Srvcs Assn; Alpha Area Cncl VP 90-; Stdnt Govt Assn Com Chrprsn; Yth Otrch Mnstry Co Fndr Treas 90-; Vcs Of Prse 90-; Educ; Thrptc Rcrtn Spclst.

**WRIGHT, AUDREY A,** Georgian Court Coll, Lakewood, NJ; JR; BA; Redeemer Lthrn Chrch VBS Tchr 87-; Grl Scouts Trp Ldr 88-; Humnties/Elem Ed; Tchr.

**WRIGHT, BARBARA A,** Daytona Beach Comm Coll, Daytona Beach, FL; SO; BS; Psychlgy.

**WRIGHT, BARBARA L,** James Madison University, Harrisonburg, VA; SR; BS; Clb Pckmstr; Kappa Delta Pi 90; Alpha Phi Omega Pres 89-; P S Douglas Schlrshp 88; Dickinson Awd 90-; Early Chldhd Educ; Ele Eductr.

**WRIGHT, BRETT D,** Univ Of Fl, Gainesville, FL; JR; BSFRL; Soc Amer Frstrs 88-; Wldlf Soc 90-; Frstry Clb Sec/Tres 90-; Frstry Stu Yr; Coop USDA Frst Serv 89; AA 90; Frstry; Rsrch.

**WRIGHT, BRIAN K,** Morehouse Coll, Atlanta, GA; JR; Clg Bus Assc 88-; Spnsh Clb 88-; MS Clb Organ Chrmn 89-90; Bus Mngmt.

**WRIGHT, CAFFEE S,** Beckley Coll, Beckley, WV; SO; BS; S Sch Tchr; Crmnl Juste; Law.

**WRIGHT, CAROL L,** Univ Of Sc At Columbia, Columbia, SC; SR; BS; ASME Sec 88-; Pi Tau Sigma 89-; Dean Lst 86-90; ASME Awrd; Mech Eng; Eng.

**WRIGHT, CASSANDRA KATHLEEN,** Alcorn St Univ, Lorman, MS; FR; BS; Chem Clb 90-; Pre-Med Clb 90- Hnrs Std Org 90-; Inroads GTE Intshp 90-; Dns Lst 90-; Chem; Drmtlgst/ Dntst.

**WRIGHT, CHAD P,** Univ Of Tn At Martin, Martin, TN; SR; BS; Soc Manuf Engrs V-Chrmn 90-; Soc Autmtv Engrs 90-; Coop Educ Stdnt 88-90; Crtfd Manuf Tchnlgsts 90-; Cert Soc Manuf Engrs 90; Mech Eng Tchnlgy; Eng.

**WRIGHT JR, CHARLES E,** Morehouse Coll, Atlanta, GA; JR; BA; Bus Assoc 90-; Honor Rl 89-; Mentoring Prog 89-90; Big Brother 90-; Onis Prog Co Chrprsn Food Comm 90-; Ameritrust Bank Intern Intl Audit 89-; Bus Admin Finance.**

**WRIGHT, CHRISTINE,** City Univ Of Ny Queensbrough, New York, NY; FR; AA; Ntl Bus Hnr Scty Cmnty/Jr Clgs; Acctg; CPA.

**WRIGHT, CLIFF O,** City Univ Of Ny Med Evers Coll, Brooklyn, NY; SO; BS; Crbbn Amer Std Asc 89-; Trck/Fld Tm 90-; Bsn/Cmptr Info Sys; Bsn Mgr.

**WRIGHT, DAVID C,** Atlantic Union Coll, S Lancaster, MA; SR; BS; Wmns Vrsty Vlybl Tm Asst Coach 89-; Mns Clb Vlybl Tm Cpt 88-; Choir/Schlrs Chpl Pres 87-; Bus Admin; Law.

**WRIGHT, DAVID L,** Middle Ga Coll, Cochran, GA; SO; BIE; Coop Grg Tch Rsrch Inst 89-; Natl Scty Prfssnl Eng; Indstrl Eng; Eng.

**WRIGHT, DAVID W,** Univ Of New Haven, West Haven, CT; SR; Air Force Natl Guard Sgt 87-; Flyng Clb 89-; Air Force Crw Mbr 84-87; Sftbl; Lght Cargo Plt 89; Flght Instrctr; Flght Instr Instrmnt; Avtn; Pilot.

**WRIGHT, DAWN S,** Middle Tn St Univ, Murfreesboro, TN; JR; BA; Tstmsts Yth Dvlpmnt Assc VP 88-89; Bptst Stdnt Union Gspl Choir 89-90; Nshvl AM Scty Qlty Cntrl; Inroads/Nshvll; Pi Sigma Epsilon 88; 4 Yr Intrnshp Mrktng Nrthrn Telecom Inc 88-; Mrktng.

**WRIGHT, ELISA D,** Univ Of Al At Birmingham, Birmingham, AL; FR; Dns Lst; Finance; Invstmnt Bnkr.

**WRIGHT, ELIZABETH B,** Athens St Coll, Athens, AL; SR; BS; Psi Chi; Psych; Clncl Psych.

**WRIGHT, ELIZABETH P,** Univ Of Sc At Columbia, Columbia, SC; FR; Frshmn Ldrshp Trng Prog; Deans List Frshmn Yr; Delta Delta Delta; Ldrslhp Trng; Frshmn Yr Worked With Homeless Chldrn; Jrnlsm Adv; Br Dcst Jrnlsm.

**WRIGHT, ERIKA M,** Univ Of Al At Birmingham, Birmingham, AL; SR; MPA; Internation Club 87-89; African Assn Sec 90; SGA; Golden Key; Dns Lst 90; Pres Lst; Youth Svcs Intern 90; BS; Pblc Admin; Law.

**WRIGHT, GARY,** Morehouse Coll, Atlanta, GA; SR; PHD; Psych Clb 90-; Psi Chi; Ford Schlr 90-; IM Bsktbl 88-90; BA; Psych; Clncl/Comm Psychlgst.

**WRIGHT, GREGORY C,** Morehouse Coll, Atlanta, GA; FR; BA; Pre Alumni Assn; Accntng; Prfrmng CPA.

**WRIGHT, HEATH D,** Livingston Univ, Livingston, AL; JR; BS; AS Shelton State Cmnty Clg 89; AA Shelton State Cmnty Clg 90; Tech Ed.

**WRIGHT, HENRIETTA L,** Fl A & M Univ, Tallahassee, FL; SR; BA; Famu Art Clb Pres; Ntl Deans Lst; Cosby Fine Arts Schlrshp; Art Educ; Grad Schl.**

**WRIGHT, J CHANCE,** Va Highlands Comm Coll, Abingdon, VA; SO; BAS; Phi Theta Kappa; All Amer Schlrs; IM Ftbl 89-90; Cmptr Sci; Rbtcs.

**WRIGHT, JACKQUELYN E,** Mount Saint Mary Coll, Newburgh, NY; JR; BA; Cmmtr Cncl 90-; Engl.

**WRIGHT, JAMES C,** Memphis St Univ, Memphis, TN; FR; BBA; Pi Kappa Alpha Rush Chrmn; Mktg; Sales Mgmt.

**WRIGHT, JAMES E,** Univ Of Nc At Charlotte, Charlotte, NC; SR; BA; AA Santa Fe Comm Clg 89; Soclgy.

**WRIGHT JR, JAMES E,** Copiah-Lincoln Comm Coll, Wesson, MS; FR; BS; Circkle K 90-; Phi Theta Kappa 90-; Physics Awd Outstndng Achvmnt; Electrical Engineering.

**WRIGHT, JAMES L,** Morehouse Coll, Atlanta, GA; FR; BA; Pre Alum Assn V P; Intl Affrs Ctr 90-; Stripes; Grav Hl Gee Phi S; Intrvrsty Chrstn Fllwshp 90-; Hnr Rl 90-; Busn; Mktg/Jap Lang.

**WRIGHT, JAMIE L,** Univ Of Ky, Lexington, KY; JR; BS; Chem Eng.

**WRIGHT, JAN S,** Univ Of Al At Birmingham, Birmingham, AL; SO; BA; Engl; MS Phys Thrpy.

**WRIGHT, JILLETTA,** Watterson Coll, Louisville, KY; SO; County Schls 88; Wrd Prcsng.

**WRIGHT, JOHN S,** Univ Of Tn At Martin, Martin, TN; FR; BA; Bus.

**WRIGHT, JUDITH E,** Univ Of Nh Plymouth St Coll, Plymouth, NH; SR; BA; Assn Non-Trdtnl Stdnts; Kappa Delta Pi Treas 89-; Undrgrad Flwshp 89-90; Gvrnrs Sccss Grant 88-89; Elem Ed; Tch.

**WRIGHT, KAMILLE E,** Norfolk St Univ, Norfolk, VA; SR; BA; SGA Assoc Justice 90-; Poli Sci Assoc 87-; Delta Sigma Theta; Voter Reg Vol 89-; Elem Tutor 90-; Charles S Robb Senate Intern; Pol Sci/Publ Admin; MPA.

**WRIGHT, KELLIE S,** Tn Temple Univ, Chattanooga, TN; SR; BS; Scndry Ed Sci; Ed.

**WRIGHT, KELLY J,** Oh St Univ At Newark, Newark, OH; SO; BS; Alpha Lambda Delta 90-; Phi Eta Sigma 90-; Math.

**WRIGHT, KELLY L,** Castleton St Coll, Castleton, VT; SO; BA; Jr Ski Pgm 90-; Killington Ski Patrol 89-90; Phys Ed; Exer Tech.

**WRIGHT, KENNETH J,** Wv Univ At Parkersburg, Parkersburg, WV; FR; BA; Comp Sci; Systms Anlyst And Prgrmmr.

**WRIGHT, KIM L,** Morris Brown Coll, Atlanta, GA; JR; BA; Engl Club Sec 90-; New Black Voices/Story Telling Drama Part 89-90; Hnrs Day Cnvctn 89-; Bsktbll Team 89-90; Engl; Corp Lawyer.

**WRIGHT, KIMBERLY,** Christian Brothers Univ, Memphis, TN; JR; BA; Wmns Flswhp Greater Imani Temple Chpln; Liberal Arts Assoc Outreach 90-; Psi Chi Treas; Psychgy; Clinical Psy.

**WRIGHT, KIMBERLY M,** Saint John Fisher Coll, Rochester, NY; SR; BS; Teddi Proj Prtcpnt 87-; Stdnt Orient Com 88; Sr Gift Com; Ford Rsrch Serv Intern; Mgmnt/Mktg.

**WRIGHT, LA WANDA L,** Al St Univ, Montgomery, AL; SO; BA; Humnts Fest 90-; Hnr Rll 90-; Crmnl Justc; Lawyr.

**WRIGHT, LANDA M,** Sue Bennett Coll, London, KY; FR; Phi Beta Lambda 90-; FCC 90-; Phi Theta Kappa; Bus.

**WRIGHT, LINDA E,** Va Commonwealth Univ, Richmond, VA; SO; BA; MEAD; Hon Stdnt; Engl; Jrnlsm.

**WRIGHT, LINDA S,** Gordon Conwell Theol Sem, S Hamilton, MA; GD; MA; Flwshp Chrstn Ath Pres 87-88; Omicron Delta Kappa Tr 88-89; Mortar Bd 88-89; Delta Mu Delta 88-89; Gamma Chi Chpln 87-88; Wall Str Jrnl Awd 89; BA 89; John S Courtney Awd 89; Vrsty Tns Capt 85-89; Old Testament; Tchng.

**WRIGHT, LYNETTE M,** Germanna Comm Coll, Locust Grove, VA; SO; BS; Dns Lst 89-; Pres Lst; Envrnmnt Sci; Envrnmtlst.

**WRIGHT, MARK A,** Univ Of Cin R Walters Coll, Blue Ash, OH; SO; AA; Univ Cincinnati Dns Lst 90; Raymond Walters Clge Dns Lst 90; Acctnt Gen Rev Corp; Acctg; Corp Acctg.

**WRIGHT, MARTHA L,** Athens St Coll, Athens, AL; SR; MSW; Psi Chi 90-; Grad W/Hnrs; BS; Psych/Sclgy Grad Sch Scl Wrk.

**WRIGHT, MELANIE L,** Ky Wesleyan Coll, Owensboro, KY; JR; BA; Rlgs Actvts Cmte Stdnt Govt Chrprsn 90-; Alpha Chi 90-; KY Ed Assoc Stdnt Pgm Pres 90-; Kappa Delta VP 88-; Untd Meth Stdnt Flwshp 90-; Elem Ed; Tchg.

**WRIGHT, MELANIE L,** Radford Univ, Radford, VA; JR; BS; Admn Jstc Clb 88-90; Crmnl Jstc Clb 90-; Phi Theta Kappa 89-90; Phi Sigma Pi 90-; IBM Coop 89-90; AA Northern VA Comm Coll 90; Crmnl Jstc; Law.

**WRIGHT, MELISSA A,** Coll Of Charleston, Charleston, SC; SR; Frnch Clb; Intrntl Clb; Phi Kappa Phi; Delta Mu Delta; Sftbl Aerobics.

**WRIGHT, MIRIAMM E,** Va St Univ, Petersburg, VA; SO; BS; Acctg Clb Treas 89-; NABA Corr Soc 90-; Big Bro Sistrs 90-; Alpha Kappa Alpha; NABA Intrnshp 90-; Cap Intrnshp Alcoa Schlrshp NABA Schlrshp 90-; Statsticn Bsktbl; Pub Acct.

**WRIGHT, MISTY LYNN,** Wv Univ At Parkersburg, Parkersburg, WV; JR; Univ Chrl 88-90; Optcn Royal Optcl; Ownr Mngr Fascination Baton Corp Natl Chmpns 89; AA 90; Spch/Engl; Cmnctn Dsrdrs Spclst.

**WRIGHT, MONICA L,** Middle Tn St Univ, Murfreesboro, TN; JR; BA; Frnch Clb 89-; Model UN; Theatre; Phi Sigma Iota; Wera Howard Frnch Awd 90-; Exchng Stdnt Univ Franche Conte; Fold Wrkshp 90; Frnch Lit/Culture; Univ Edn.

**WRIGHT, PAMELA J,** Winthrop Coll, Rock Hill, SC; SR; BA; Psychlgy Clb Pres 89-; Rfrmd Univ Flwshp 89-; Sr Gft Agnt 90-; Psi Chi Sec 89-; Delta Omicron Treas 89-; Alpha Xi Delta Almni Corrspndnt 87-; All Amer Schlr 87-88; Pres Lst 90-; Sftbl Mgr 87-89; Psychlgy.**

**WRIGHT, PATRICK L,** Univ Of Sc At Columbia, Columbia, SC; FR; BA; SEED; Mnrty Asstnc Peer MAP Tm; NAACP; Alpha Lambda Delta; Gamma Beta Phi; Phi Eta Sigma; Alpha Phi Alpha Dir Ed Actvts; SC Clg Hons Clg; Emrgng Ldrs Prog; Bus Admnstrtn; Law.

**WRIGHT, PAULETTE D,** Fl St Univ, Tallahassee, FL; SR; BS; Golden Key 90-; Phi Kappa Phi; Hnrs; Dns Lst 89-; IBM Boca Raton Fl; Sr Assoc Inf Devlpr 74-; Corp Comm.

**WRIGHT, PEGGY M,** Norfolk St Univ, Norfolk, VA; SR; CPR Instr 86-89; Alpha Kappa Mu 88-; Phi Theta Kappa 86-89; Greenpeace; Ntnl Pks; Cousteau Soc; Ntnl Arbor Day Foun; BASE ODU; History; Edctn; Tch.

**WRIGHT, R BRENT,** Univ Of Ky, Lexington, KY; JR; BS; Mrchng Bnd Treas 88-90; Prcssn Soc Sec 89-90f Emrgng Ldr Inst 90; Lances Jr Hnry 90-; Alpha Lambda Delta 89-; Prcssv Art Soc 87-; Kappa Kappa Psi 88-90; Hon Bndsmn Awds 90; Hlth Careers Opptnty Pgm; Bio; Med.

**WRIGHT, REBECCA ELIZABETH,** Univ Of Montevallo, Montevallo, AL; FR; BS; Alpha Lambda Delta 90-; Early Chldhd/Elem; Tchr.

**WRIGHT, REBECCA M,** Auburn Univ At Auburn, Auburn, AL; BS; SGA Sprt Comm 86-87; Assn/Chldhd Ed 88-90; Pi Lambda Theta 88-90; Phi Kappa Phi 90-; Kappa Delta 86-; Dns Lst 86-90; Magna Cum Laude 90; Elem Ed; Tchr.

**WRIGHT, RICHARD M,** Christian Brothers Univ, Memphis, TN; SO; BA; IM Bskbl Miss State Univ 89-90; Acctng; CPA.

**WRIGHT, ROBERT A,** Univ Of Rochester, Rochester, NY; SO; MBA; Rgby Clb 89-; FAC VP 90-; Tau Kappa Epsilon Asst Pldg Mstr 90-; Wlk Thn; Ecnmcs/Bus.

**WRIGHT, ROBIN D,** Roane St Comm Coll, Harriman, TN; SO; AS; Gamma Beta Phi Pres; Sec Or Sales Rep 77-91; English.

**WRIGHT, RONALD J,** Alfred Univ, Alfred, NY; SO; Alpha Lambda Delta; Ntnl Mrt Schlr Fnlst; Crmc Engnrng; Engnrng.

**WRIGHT, SCOTT T,** Springfield Tech Comm Coll, Springfield, MA; JR; BS; Alpha Nu Omega 90; Alpha Chi; Pres Schlrshp 90; Eng.

**WRIGHT, SEAN F,** Univ Of Nc At Charlotte, Charlotte, NC; JR; BS; Bapt Stdnt Union 90-; Ggrphy; Info Systms.

**WRIGHT, SHANA Q,** Middle Tn St Univ, Murfreesboro, TN; JR; BS; Bsktbl 88-; Pi Gamma Mu V P; Gamma Beta Phi; Tau Omicron; Pi Sigma Alpha; Delta Sigma Theta; Pre-Law; Law/Law Enfrcmnt.

**WRIGHT, SHANNON ELIZA,** Memphis St Univ, Memphis, TN; SR; PHARM; Hall Cncl Secy 90-; Kappa Alpha 90-; Phrmcy.

**WRIGHT, SHANTEL E,** Le Moyne Owen Coll, Memphis, TN; FR; Stdt Support Prog 90-.

**WRIGHT, SHAREE S,** Mobile Coll, Mobile, AL; SO; BS; SLATE Memb; Elem Educ.

**WRIGHT, SHARLENE,** Univ Of Miami, Coral Gables, FL; JR; BS; Church Yth Nwsltr Edtr 90-; Golden Key; Alpha Epsilon Delta; Bio; Med.

**WRIGHT, SHEDRICK T,** Jackson St Univ, Jackson, MS; FR; BA; Intern Math Dept Univ AZ; Cmptr Sci.

**WRIGHT, SHERI L,** Anne Arundel Comm Coll, Arnold, MD; SO; AA; Wrk Adlscnts Vlntr Dlng Bhvrl Addctns; Hmn Srvcs; Lcsw.

**WRIGHT, SHERRY S,** Catawba Valley Comm Coll, Hickory, NC; FR; AAS; Frmr Tchr Chld Dvlpmnt Cntr; Hrtcltrl Tchnlgy; Lndscpnt Grnhs Grwr.

**WRIGHT, STACY C,** Univ Of Sc At Columbia, Columbia, SC; SR; BA; Vars Swmmng/Dvng 87-; FCA; Crsd; Yng Life; Cllg Choir; Gldn Key 89-; Gamma Beta Phi 89-; Kappa Alpha Aux 88-89; Delta Gamma Cls Sec 89-; Fedrtn Blind 89-; Spcl Olympcs 89; Dvng Schlrshp 87-; Elem Ed/Fine Arts.

**WRIGHT, STEVEN J,** Wv Univ, Morgantown, WV; FR; Eng; Archtctrl.

**WRIGHT, SUSAN A,** Wv Univ At Parkersburg, Parkersburg, WV; JR; Deans Lst 89; Shell Chemical Co Internshp; Offc Admn; Scrtrl.

**WRIGHT, SUSAN D,** William Paterson Coll, Wayne, NJ; JR; BA; Hmnts Clb Treas 90-; Hstry Clb Fndr Pres 87-88; Nat Sci Clb; Hnrs Hmnts Prog; Cntr Acad Sprt Tutor 90-; Pol Sci; Envrnmntl Lawyer.

**WRIGHT, TARA B,** Stillman Coll, Tuscaloosa, AL; SO; BS; Cordell Wynn Hnrs Pgrm 90-; Gamma Iota Sigma 90-; U S Achvmnt Acdmy 90-; Dns Lst 89-; Cmptr Sci/Math; Cmptr Eng.

**WRIGHT, TERESA ANNE,** Middle Tn St Univ, Murfreesboro, TN; SR; BBA; Phi Beta Lambda 90-; Deans Lst 87-; Snr Hnr Stdnt Magna Cum Laude; Otstndng Stdnt Offc Mgmt; Otstndng Stdnt Spcl Bus Prgm; Bus Offc Mgmt.

**WRIGHT, TRACEY R,** Al St Univ, Montgomery, AL; SO; BA; Phi Eta Sigma 89-; Cmptr Infrmtn Systm; Analyst Prgrmmr.

**WRIGHT, TRULA M,** Va Highlands Comm Coll, Abingdon, VA; SR; Pres Lst 89; Deans Lst 89-; Intrnshp Cntr Indpndnt Lvng; Hmn Serv.

**WRIGHT, WAYNE A,** City Univ Of Ny Baruch Coll, New York, NY; SR; BBA; Cmptr Sci; Systms Analysis.

**WRIGHT, YOLANDA A,** Alcorn St Univ, Lorman, MS; SO; BA; Crmnl Jstc; Law.

**WRIGHT, YOLANDA S,** Nc Agri & Tech St Univ, Greensboro, NC; SR; BA; Stdnt Cncl Exceptnl Chldrn VP; Marching Bnd Capt/Maj Squad 90-; Band Cncl Capt Maj Squad 90-; Tau Beta Sigma Pr; Fldcrest Cannon Inc Schlrshp 90-; Greensboro Civitan Clb Schlrshp Rec 90-; Specl Educ.

**WRIGHT, ZANE G,** Western Carolina Univ, Cullowhee, NC; BSW; Phi Alpha 90-; Natl Chld Support Reform Policy; Vol Cnslr United Chrstn Mnstrs Facilitator Parent-Parent Drug Prevent; AA Gardner Webb Clg 65; BS Western Carolina Univ 71; Scl Wrk; Fam Ther/Pol Activist.

**WRIGHT-WILLIAMSON, SHEILA,** Union Univ, Jackson, TN; GD; CERT; Baptist Student Union 86-; Revival Tms Flwshp Ldr 86-89; Church Related Voc 86-89; Acdmc Excllnc Religion 90; Deans Lst; Pi Gamma Mu; Sigma Tau Delta; Sociology Psychology Clb 89-; Peer Cnslr 87-89; Intrnshp Social Wrkr 87-; BA 89; English Spanish Religion Educ; Secndry Educ.

**WRIGHTSMAN, AARON C,** Univ Of Sc At Columbia, Columbia, SC; FR.

**WRIGLEY, PATRICK A,** S U N Y Coll Of Tech At Alfred, Alfred, NY; SR; Photo Club Pres 89-90; Sigma Tau Epsi; Drafting.

**WRISTON, KELLIE J,** Beckley Coll, Beckley, WV; FR; AS; Social Wrk; Psychlgst.

**WROBEL, RAYMOND J,** Bapt Bible Coll & Seminary, Clarks Summit, PA; JR; BS; Ofc Stdnt Dvlpmnt RA 89-90; Alpha Gamma Epsilon 90-; Intern Grace Bptst Church 90; Intern Santiago Chile 89; Pre Seminary; Coll Prof/Pastor.

**WROBEL, ROBERT E,** S U N Y At Buffalo, Buffalo, NY; SO; BS; BSA Eagle Sct/Asst Sctmstr 87-; Flt/Norstar Serv Corp Intrn; Bsn Admn; Mgmt.

**WROBLEWSKI, MELANIE A,** Hilbert Coll, Hamburg, NY; SO; AAS; Phi Beta Lambda 90-; Pr Lgl Clb 90; Wstrn Ny Prlgl Assoc; Law.

**WROBLEWSKI, MICHAEL R,** Tuskegee Univ, Tuskegee Inst, AL; SR; BA; Amer Inst Of Architecture 89-; Frshmn Orentator Army ROTC; Tau Sigma Delta; ROTC Superior Cadet; W A Hazel Awd; Deans Lst 88; Architecture.

**WRONA, JAMES S,** Oh Northern Univ, Ada, OH; GD; JD; Intrfrtrnty Cncl Rep 87; All Amer Schls; Sigma Phi Epsilon VP 88-89; Leo Clb VP 88-89; Dns Lst 89; Dbck Awd 89; Ntnl Sclstc Awd; Vrsty Sccr Co Capt 89-90BA York Clg 90; Law.

**WRONSKI, CAROL J,** Erie Comm Coll, Buffalo, NY; FR; RN; Casset Clb 90-; Prkns Pgm 90-; Engl/Nrsng.

**WRUBEL, LISA C A,** Wilkes Univ, Wilkes-Barre, PA; FR; BA; Pre Med Soc 90-; Deans Lst 90-; Sftbl Tm 90-; Bio; Med.

**WTULICH, ANN M,** Pamlico Comm Coll, Grantsboro, NC; SO; AAS; Std Govt/Rep 89; Phi Theta Kappa; Alpha Xi Omcrn Treas 90-; MBA; Acct; CPA.

**WU, BAOWEN,** City Univ Of Ny City Coll, New York, NY; SO; BA; Eng.

**WU, CAROLYN S,** Georgetown Univ, Washington, DC; SO; BA; China Cir 89-; Amnsty Intrntl 89-; Choice 90-; Psych; Med.

**WU, CHENG LUNG,** Univ Of Tn At Martin, Martin, TN; FR; Acctg.

**WU, DEBRA C,** Univ Of Rochester, Rochester, NY; JR; BA; Omcrn Dlt Epsln; Ec; Bus.

**WU, DONGMEI,** Ms St Univ, Miss State, MS; JR; BA; Comp Sci.

**WU, EMILY T,** James Madison University, Harrisonburg, VA; SO; BS; Asian Amer Assoc Historian 90-; Asian Amer Student Conf Enter Chr 90-; Asian Christian Flwshp; Nrsng; Missionary Nurse.

**WU, FRED LEE CHONG,** City Univ Of Ny City Coll, New York, NY; GD; EMETS 89-90; Chnse Clb 87-88; AAS 85-88; Elec Tech.

**WU, GLENN L,** Rutgers St Un At New Brunswick, New Brunswick, NJ; FR; BS; Science/Engnrng.

**WU, HAI-XIN,** Manhattan School Of Music, New York, NY; SO; BM; Natl Orch Assoc Assocte Prin 90-; Seattle Yth Symph Co Concrtmstr 89090; N W Yng Artists Cmptetn Full Rctl Wnr 89; Manhattan Sch Music Comm Serv Prog 89; Waterloo Music Fest Flwshp 90; Music/Violin; Music.

**WU, JEANNIE,** Georgian Court Coll, Lakewood, NJ; SR; BS; Bus Clb 89-; Intl Clb 89-; Pre Law Soc 90-; Frnch Hnr Soc; Pi Delta Phi; Alnc De Francaise 90; Cert; Bus Admin; Law.

**WU, JOHN C,** Cornell Univ Statutory College, Ithaca, NY; JR; BS; Bsn Clb 90-; Entpnr Clb; Dns Lst; Phi Kappa Psi Comm 88-; Shrsn Lhmn Intrn; Fncl Frm Intrn 90; Lght Wght Ftbl/Bsbl IMS; Appld Ecnmcs; Fnce.

**WU, KAIPING,** Livingston Univ, Livingston, AL; JR; BS; Intl Stdnt Assn; Alpha Kappa; Asst Engr 88-89; BS Suzhou Voc Coll 82-85; Bus Admn Emphasis Comp Inf Sci; Comp.

**WU, LIJIA,** Barry Univ, Miami, FL; JR; Chinese Stdnts Assn 89-90; Tchr 85-89; BS Beijin Tchrs Clg 85; Cmptr Sci/Acctg; Syst Anlyst Acctnt.

**WU, QIANG,** City Univ Of Ny Baruch Coll, New York, NY; SR; BBA; Beta Alpha Psi 90-; Acctg.

**WU, SARA W,** Univ Of Rochester, Rochester, NY; JR; BA; Omicron Delta Epsilon; Econ/Religion; Bus.

**WU, SIMON ZHOU,** Belmont Coll, Nashville, TN; SO; BBA; Southern Bapt Cnvntn; Woodmont Bapt Ch Schlrshp; Carver Intl Schlrshp; Finance; Bus Bank.

**WU, XIANGHONG JOY,** Elms Coll, Chicopee, MA; JR; BA; Bus Clb Hstrn 90-; Intl Clb 89-; Self Evlutn Cmtee 90-; IFCSS; Gold Z Clb 90; Fashion Show Chicopee Bicntnl Clbrtn 90; Dinosaur Exhibit Sci Musem 89; I M Vybl Cptn 87-; AA Nanjing Univ 88-; Intl Stdes; Intl Bus.

**WU, XIAO J,** Univ Of Louisville, Louisville, KY; FR; BS; Drama Grp 90-; Phi Eta Sgm 90; Fclty/Stf Depndnts Schlrshp 90-; Badmntn Swmmng; Minerva Schlr 1 Yr Full Tuition Schlrshp; Maths/Cmptr; Eng.

**WUEBKER, RUTH C,** Wright St Univ Lake Cmps, Celina, OH; JR; BS; SME; PTA 89-; Parent Advsry Comm 88-; Dns Lst High Hnrs; Reynolds/Reynolds Celina OH 73-80; Mech Engr Tech; Engr.

**WUEBKER, TED J,** Wright St Univ Lake Cmps, Celina, OH; SO; BA; Alpha Lmbd Dlt 90-; Deans List 89-; Envrnmntl Hlth; Prtctn Envrnmnt.**

**WUENSCHEL, DANA M,** Saint Vincents Coll & Seminary, Latrobe, PA; SR; BS; Biolgy Clb Sec 87-; Orntn Comm Stdnt Govt Sntr 90-; Sprts Frndshp Day Comm Chr 87-; Grs Rts Plnng Comm 88-; Bio Nwsltr Co Ed 87-; Aerobics 87-; Natl Clgte Ntrl Sci Awd 90-; Edith Q Mollack Mem Schlrshp 90-; Biology; Med.

**WUERTZER, MICHAEL J,** Oh Univ, Athens, OH; JR; BSISE; Nastl Soc Of Prof Engrs 89-; Inst Of Ind Engrs 89-; Oh Soc Of Prof Engrs 89-; Engrng Coop Edn 89-; IM Mgr 90-; Ind Sys Engrng.**

**WUKOWITZ, BARBARA L,** Broward Comm Coll, Ft Lauderdale, FL; SO; BA; Phi Theta Kappa 90-; Cmptr Prog; Engr.

**WULLEN, DEBORAH A,** Husson Coll, Bangor, ME; SR; BSN; US Achvmnt Acdmy Awrd 90; Ntl Coll Nrsg Awrd 90; BS; Nrsg; Cardiac.

**WURST, KELLY M,** Glassboro St Coll, Glassboro, NJ; SO; BA; Law/Justc; Crmnl Justc/Crrctns.

**WURTS, ELIZABETH L,** Smith Coll, Northampton, MA; FR; BS; First Grp Schlr Smith Clg 90-; Economics; Business.

**WURTS, MICHELE D,** Oh Univ-Southern Cmps, Ironton, OH; SO; BA; SADD 88-; Deans List 89-; C E/J Peters Allen Schlrshp 89-90; Soclgy; Socl Wrkr.

**WURTS, SANDRA K,** Oh Univ-Southern Cmps, Ironton, OH; FR; Acctg Bsn Assoc.

**WYANT, BRADLEY T,** Gallaudet Univ, Washington, DC; SR; BA; Adv Dsgn.

**WYANT, JESSICA E,** Univ Of Md At Eastern Shore, Princess Anne, MD; JR; BS; Yrbk Stf 88-90; NAACP 90-; Cath Stdnt Assn 90-; Hnrs Prog 88-; REU Prog; Biology; Medicine.

**WYATT, BRYAN A,** Liberty Univ, Lynchburg, VA; SO; BS; Pre-Law Soc SGA; Hon Pgm Coll Rpblcn; Alpha Lambda Delta Pres 90-; Urban Outrch; Govt/Frgn Affrs; Law/Pltcs.

**WYATT, BRYAN L,** Wv Univ, Morgantown, WV; FR; BA; Eng.

**WYATT, DANIEL R,** Wv Univ At Parkersburg, Parkersburg, WV; BA; Profl Fighter; Jrnlsm; Graphic Artist.

**WYATT JR, DAVID R,** Old Dominion Univ, Norfolk, VA; SO; BSEE; IEEE 89-; Dns Lst 89; Co Op Ericsson GE Mobile Cmmnctns 90; Elec Engr.

**WYATT, HEATHER L,** Christopher Newport Coll, Newport News, VA; JR; BA; Pltcl Sci; Law.

**WYATT, JEAN D,** Al St Univ, Montgomery, AL; JR; BS; Phi Eta Sigma 89-; Alpha Kappa Mu; Edctnl Enrchmnt Prog Hampton Univ; Acctg; CPA.

**WYATT JR, KENNETH W,** Faulkner Univ, Montgomery, AL; JR; SGA Pres/Treas/VP 88-; Kappa Sigma Phi 89-; Prchrs Clb 89-; Spkr Hon Pgm; Edn; Mnstry.

**WYATT, LA FARINA G,** Stillman Coll, Tuscaloosa, AL; FR; MBA; Hstry Clb; Gamma Iota Sigma; Bsktbl 90-; Bus Admin; Htl Rstrnt Mgmt.

**WYATT, MICHAEL W,** Tri County Tech Coll, Pendleton, SC; SR; Alpha Zeta Beta 90-; Clemsn Chmbr Comm 83-; Citzns So Schlrshp 90-; AB 91; Acctg; Chrstn Finc Cnslng.

**WYATT, SAMUEL L,** Central Al Comm Coll, Alexander City, AL; FR; BA; Part Owner M&w Recycling V Pres 87-89; AS Gadsden State Jr Clg 83; Certif Bible/Cnslg/Chrstn Ed Gadsden State Jr Clg 79; Bsn.

**WYATT, TAMMY C,** Valdosta St Coll, Valdosta, GA; SR; BFA; Arts Advsry Cncl 90; Pi Sigma Alpha 85; Dist Attrnys Offce Intrn 85; AS S Ga Clg 83; BS Ga SW Clg 85; Theatre Telecmmnctns; TV Flms.

**WYATT, TERESA V,** Furman Univ, Greenville, SC; FR; BA; Sigma Nu Little Sis 90-; CESC Vol 90-; Deans Lst; Political Sicence; Law.

**WYCHE, ADRIANE D,** Va Commonwealth Univ, Richmond, VA; SO; BS; NABA Comm Chp 90-; African-Am Schlrs Prog 90-; Res Assoc Sec 90-; Phi Eta Sigma 90-; Project Umoja 90-; Bus; Acctng.

**WYCHE, ROQUELL E,** George Washington Univ, Washington, DC; FR; BS; Spkr Panel Mnrty Invlvmnt; Tchr Asst Summer Bio; Phi Eta Sigma 90-; Hnrs Pgm 90-; CRC Press Frshmn Chem Achvmnt Awd; Bio; Med.

**WYCHE, VANESSA S R,** Medical Coll Of Ga, Augusta, GA; SR; BSN; Army ROTC 88-; Blck Stdnt Mdcl Allnc 89-; Grg Stdnt Nrss Assoc 89-; Sigma Theta Tau; Chi Eta Phi Pres 89-; Nrsng.

**WYCHE, VIKKI ELIZABETH,** Tn Temple Univ, Chattanooga, TN; GD; BS; Dorm Rep Pres 89-90; Univ Choir 88-89; Alpha Epsilon Beta 89-; Wesley Soc; Biolgy; Med.

**WYCHERLY, HARRIETT P,** West Liberty St Coll, West Liberty, WV; JR; BA; Data Procsng Mgt Assoc Pres 89-90; Phi Theta Kappa Secy 90-; Deans List; Im Vlybl/Sftbl; Sftwr Applctns Spclst 90-; AAS WV Northrn Cmnty Clg 90; Bus Admn; Tchng.

**WYCKOFF, SAMUEL R,** Central Al Comm Coll, Alexander City, AL; SO; MA; Phi Theta Kappa 90-; Hstry; Post Sec Ed.

**WYDICK, MICHELLE M,** Ky Wesleyan Coll, Owensboro, KY; SR; BA; KY Ed Assoc Stdnt Prgm 89-; Pre Prfssnl Scty 88; Kappa Delta Corres Sec 86-; Deans Slt 89; Stdnt Ornttn Ldr 89; Mtn Lrl Cndt 89; Hmcmng Old Sth Rs Cndt 89-90; Chrldr Capt 86-90; Elem Ed.

**WYLIE, JAMES P,** Manhattan Coll, Bronx, NY; SO; BED; Sls Assc Banana Replbc 88-; BA Gettysburg Clg 86; Mech Eng; Dsgn/Robtcs Eng.

**WYLIE, JOHN R,** Univ Of Tn At Martin, Martin, TN; SO; BS; Block/Briddle Club V P; Agri/Anml Sci; Farmer.

**WYLIE, SCOTT W,** Rutgers St Un At New Brunswick, New Brunswick, NJ; FR; Mtrlgy Physcs; USAF.

**WYLLIE, DWIGHT F D,** Central Fl Comm Coll, Ocala, FL; FR; AS; Phi Theta Kappa; Induys Maint; Engr.

**WYMAN, BETTY A,** Birmingham Southern Coll, Birmingham, AL; SR; BS; Ntwrk Birmingham 88-; St Annes Home Inc Exec Brd 90-; Staff Mgr 66-; Bus Mgt; MA.

**WYMAN, MARK R,** S U N Y Coll Of Tech At Alfred, Alfred, NY; SR; AAS; Elect Eng.

**WYMS, FELICIA A,** Tn St Univ, Nashville, TN; SO; BS; KS State Univ Gspl Chr 88-90; Alpha Kappa Alpha Pres 89-; Mst Otstndng Trnsffrd Stdn; Archtctrl Eng; Epcnstrctn Mgmt.

**WYNDER, CHRISTOPHER V,** Fl A & M Univ, Tallahassee, FL; JR; Army ROTC Advanced Cmp Platoon Ldr 88-; NAACP Mbr 89-; Vrsty Bsbl Ltrmn Bsmn 88-89; Phi Eta Sigma 88-; Lamda Alpha Epsilon 88-; Pres Schlrshp; Big Brother; Criminal Justice; Law.

**WYNDER, LESLIE J,** Va St Univ, Petersburg, VA; JR; BS; Htl Rstrnt Mgmt Clb VP 90-; Fd Srvc Cmte 90-; Cr Explrs Htl Rstrnt Mgmt Vol 91-; Dns Lst 90; Cnfrnc Sls Srvc Dept Williamsburg Ldg Intrn 90; Fd Srv Dept Pa St U Intr; Apld Fd Srvc Sntn Crs Natl Rstrnt Assoc Cert Cmpltn 90; Htl/Rstrnt Mgmt; Cntng Ed.

**WYNDHAM, JACQUELINE ANNETTE,** Univ Of Md At Eastern Shore, Princess Anne, MD; SR; BS; Wellingborough Coll Stdnts Un Asst Soc Sec 87-88; NSBL; NAACP 90-; Cert Acad Achvmnt 90; Bus Admin; Fshn Mrchndsng.

**WYNENS, CHRISTOPHER P,** Ms St Univ, Miss State, MS; GD; SLAVMA 88-; Vet Med; Prvte Prctce.

**WYNER, ELFRIEDA B,** Univ Of North Fl, Jacksonville, FL; SR; BS; Jx Trck Clb Brd Mbr 83; Jx Trck Clb 80-; FL Assoc Pblc Hlth 71-73; FCCJ Aa Dgree; Grad Hgh Hnrs 88; UNF Deans Lst 90-; Lcnsd Mdcl Tchnlgst 66-; AS FCCJ 88; CLST Canadian Scty Lab Tchnlgst; Rgstrd Med Tchnlgst 69; Hlth Sci; Exrcs Spclst.

**WYNN, DONNA J,** Walker Coll, Jasper, AL; FR; ADN; Registered Nurse.

**WYNN, KEISHA N,** Fl A & M Univ, Tallahassee, FL; FR; BS; SBI Invstmnt Fund Inc Rsrch Anlyst 90-; Close Up Inc Asst P 90-; Pres Schlrs Assn 90-; Big Bro/Big Sis Phi Eta Sigma 90-; Deans Lst 90-; Smmr Intrn Pres Ofc Morehse Coll Invstmnt Fund Inc Spec Asst; Bus Admin; Cptl Mgmt.

**WYNN, KELLI A,** Hudson Valley Comm Coll, Troy, NY; SO; BA; Clerical Wrk; Indvdl Stdys-Human Serv.

**WYNN, PAIGE P,** Nova Univ, Ft Lauderdale, FL; GD; MBA; Econ/Finance 88; Fla Acctng Assn 90; Alpha Epsilon Alpha 89; IM Sprts 84-89; Assist Cntrlr; BBA Finance 88; BBA Acctng; Bus; Acctng.

**WYNN, PAMELA A,** Va St Univ, Petersburg, VA; JR; BA; Acctg Clb 90-; Voices Yth Chr Pres; Yth Usher Brd Sec; Msnry Wmn DAMET Chrch; Bus; Acctg.

**WYNN, TRACIE L,** Univ Of Southern Ms, Hattiesburg, MS; SO; AA; Social Wrk/Psychology.

**WYNN, WILLIAM H,** Vance Granville Comm Coll, Henderson, NC; FR; AA; Dns Lst 90-; HVAC Cert 90-; Engl; Jrnlsm.

**WYNNE, EMILY L,** Livingston Univ, Livingston, AL; SR; MED; Tau Kappa Epsilon Little Sis Pres 88-90; IM All Stars 88-90; AS Patrick Henry St Jr Coll 88; BS; Soc Sci; Teach.

**WYNNE, ERIN E,** Villanova Univ, Villanova, PA; JR; BA; Spec Olympcs Fl Fvstvl Chrprsn Fd Srv Mgmt Tm 90-; Dorm Pres 90-; Proj Snshn 89-; Gen Arts/Bus Jpnse.

**WYPY, CHRISTINE M,** Western New England Coll, Springfield, MA; SR; BSBA; Peer Rvw Brd Chrprsn 88-90; Comm Pgrmng/Entrtnmnt V Chr 89-90; Orient Grp Ldr 89; Alpha Lambda Delta 90-; Delta Mu Delta 90-; Stdnt Assn Awd 90; Alumni Assn Royal Skookum Awd 90; Bus; Mgmt.

**WYROSTEK, MICHAEL J,** Indiana Univ Of Pa, Indiana, PA; SR; BS; PSEA 90-; Hstry Clb 88-; IM Athletics Fed Wrk Stdy Prgrm 87-; Elem Edctn; Elem Schl Tchr.

**WYSOCKI, DENNIS T,** City Univ Of Ny Baruch Coll, New York, NY; SR; Finance Comm 89-; Archery 90; Gldn Ky 89-; Deans Lst; Serv Star Awd; Finance; Analyst.

**WYSOCKI, MARC P,** Colby Sawyer Coll, New London, NH; FR; BS; Orntn Ldr; Intrnshp Cntrl CT Phys Thrpy And Sprts Med Inc; Crss Cntry Skng Tm; Atltc Trng; ATC PT.

**WYSOCZANSKI, KIMBERLY A,** S U N Y At Binghamton, Binghamton, NY; FR; Kcklne Capt 90-; Sigma Delta Tau Clss Hstrn; Elec TA.

**WYSZKOWSKI, BRYAN P,** Univ Of Nc At Charlotte, Charlotte, NC; JR; BA; Amer Inst Of Arch Stdnts 89-; Golden Key; Zeta Beta Tau 87-; Dist Expert-NRA Jr Rifle Pgm 89; Deans Lst 90; Deans Lst Mercer Cmnty Clg 89-90; Arch.

**WYVILL, SUZEL,** Southern Coll Of Tech, Marietta, GA; JR; BA; Vol Srvcs Chldrn Brasil; Hnr Stdnt 77; Ind Engr Clg Brazil; Lang Spkn Portuguese,Italian/Spanish/English; Biochem Tech Colegio Sao Judas Tadeu Brazil 77; Appld Cmptr Sci/Math.

# X

**XIANG, HUI-XING,** City Univ Of Ny La Guard Coll, Long Island Cty, NY; SO; Phi Theta Kappa; Hosp Staff-China; Nursing.

**XU, JIANSHEN,** City Univ Of Ny Baruch Coll, New York, NY; JR; BA; Chnse Cltr Clb Baruch 89; Chns Stdnt Assc 89 ; Acctg; CPA.

**XU, JIREN,** City Univ Of Ny Baruch Coll, New York, NY; SR; BBA; Acctng Soc 90-; Deans List 87-; Beta Gamma Sigma 90-; Acctng; CPA.

**XU, QIUPING,** City Univ Of Ny Baruch Coll, New York, NY; JR; BBA; Acctg Soc Of Baruch 89-; China Intl Trvl Serv Shanghai Brnch 81-88; AA Shanghai Inst Of Tourism China 79-81; Acctg; CPA.

**XU, SAIJING,** Bunker Hill Comm Coll, Boston, MA; FR; ASSOC; Trnsltr Bus Ngtns 82-89; Intl Trvl Agncy Wuxi Of China Grmn Spkn Tr Org/Guide; Nrsg.

**XU, YUN C,** City Univ Of Ny Baruch Coll, New York, NY; SR; BBA; Beta Gamma Sigma; Fnce.

# Y

**YAAKOBI, EREZ,** Univ Of Rochester, Rochester, NY; SR; BS; Phi Beta Kappa; Physics.

**YABE, YOKO,** Univ Of Tn At Martin, Martin, TN; SR; BA; Phi Kappa Phi 90-; Alpha Kappa Psi; Gooch Hnrs 90-; Acctg; CPA.

**YACCARINO, ANNA M,** Eckerd Coll, St Petersburg, FL; SR; BS; Rprtr Nwspr 88-89; Phi Theta Kappa 87-89; YWCA Yng Wmns 88-90; Chrstn Assn; Intrnshp 620 AM WSUN Radio Prmtn Asst 89; Intrnshp Chnl 13; AA St Ptrsbrg Jr Clg 89; BS; Mgmnt Jrnlsm.

**YACHECHKO, LAURA M,** Va Commonwealth Univ, Richmond, VA; FR; BFA; Art; Cmrcl Art.

**YACHWAN, KEVIN G,** S U N Y At Buffalo, Buffalo, NY; GD; DDS; Amer Stdnt Dntl Soc; Acad Gen Dntstry; Delta Epsilon Sigma; Tucker Schlrshp 89/90; Rsdncy Genesee Hosp Dntl Clinic; Thomas H Morton Medal Excel 87; BS Bio Niagara Univ 87; Dental Medicine.

**YACKS, COLLIN TIMOTHY,** Northern Ky Univ, Highland Hts, KY; FR; BA; All Ath Academic Tm 90-; Cnsdrtn Northern Ky Univ Pres Ambass 90-; Vrsty Soccer 90-; Biology Premed; Radiology/MD.

**YACOUB, AMAL K,** Mary Baldwin Coll, Staunton, VA; SR; BA; Cosmos Intl Clb 89-; Mnrty Wmn Unty 89-; Hnr Schlrs Soc 89-; Phi Beta Kappa 90-; Frnch; Prof.

**YACOVINO, DONNA M,** City Univ Of Ny Lehman Coll, Bronx, NY; JR; BA; Psychlgy.

**YADAV, SANGITA,** Univ Of Miami, Coral Gables, FL; SR; BBA; COISO Sec 89-90; Pres 100 Ornttn Asst 89-90; Gldn Key 89-; Vol Serv; Hnrs Day Dpt Hnr; Tnns Clb; Intl Fnce/Mktg; Intl Bsn.

**YAEGER, ALLISON M,** Univ Of New Haven, West Haven, CT; SR; BS; Womns Fast Pitch Sftbl Tm Div II 88-; Travl/Toursm Admin; Trvl/Toursm.

**YAGER, JENNIFER A,** Schenectady County Comm Coll, Schenectady, NY; FR; AAS; Trvl/Toursm.

**YAKLEY, SHERRY R,** Central Al Comm Coll, Alexander City, AL; SO; BS; Bptst Cmps Mnstrs 89 ; 7th Day Fllwshp Assn 89-90; Phi Theta Kappa 89-; Mst Otstndng Mmbr; AS; Med; Physcl Thrpy.**

**YAKOOB, RUBINA Y,** Ny Univ, New York, NY; SO; BS; Islamic Ctr 90-F Muslm Pgrssv Allnc Cncl Mem 90-F Mock Trl Clb 90-; Bus; Law.

**YAKOUCHI, YASUE,** Lasell Coll, Newton, MA; SO; Lib Arts/Bsn; Acctg.

**YAKUBOVIC, JOHN R,** Univ Of Al At Birmingham, Birmingham, AL; SR; BS; IEEE 89-; Amer Mktg Assn 89-; Pi Sigma Epsilon 89-; Tau Beta Pi 89-; Phi Kappa Phi 90-; Gldn Key 90-; Alpha Mu Alpha; GTE Schlrshp 90-; NY State Rgnts Schlrshp 75; Sim Bsktbl; Mktg Indus Dstrbtn; Sls/Mgmt.**

**YALE, BRIAN J,** Univ Of Miami, Coral Gables, FL; JR; BM; Sngng Hrrcns 88-90; Sngrs Elctrc Bss Plyr 90-; Rck Ensmbl Elctrc Bss Plyr 90-; Music Md Indstry.

**YALIF, GUY U,** Princeton Univ, Princeton, NJ; FR; BSE; Crew Lacrosse; Aero Engr; Design.

**YALKUT, DENIS A,** Univ Of Ky, Lexington, KY; GD; Hang Gldng Clb Treas 90-; Pisgah Prsbytrn Church Yth Grp Dir 89-; Trnsylvnia Prsbytrn Yth Com; Kappa Alpha 87-90; Rugby Tm; BS 90; Bio; Med.

**YAMADA, WAKA,** Savannah Coll Of Art & Design, Savannah, GA; SO; Intl Stdnt Assn 89-; Sdwlk Fstvl 90; Grphc Dsgnr.

**YAMAMOTO, AKANE,** Brevard Coll, Brevard, NC; FR; BA; Spnsh Clb 90; Rho Tau Kappa; Art; Desgnr.

**YAMASHITA, JASON T,** Savannah Coll Of Art & Design, Savannah, GA; FR; BFA; Art; Intrr Dsgn.

**YAMASHITA, NORIKO,** Saint Thomas Univ, Miami, FL; SR; BA; English Non-Native Spkrs Outstndng Student Awd; Communt Arts; Journalism.

**YAMBO ARIAS, RAMON,** Inter Amer Univ Pr San German, San German, PR; JR; BS; Soc Natrl Hstry 90-; Biolgy; Med.

**YAMBOR, KIMBERLY J,** Univ Of Cincinnati, Cincinnati, OH; SO; BS; Deans List Winter/Sring Qtrs 90-; Crmnl Jstc; Law/Prvt Invstgtr.

**YAMIL, SANABRIA,** Univ Politecnica De Pr, Hato Rey, PR; FR; Lybrary Club Pres 88-89; Dale La Mano A P R Vocal 89.

**YAMRAJ, JASMATTIE,** Miami Dade Comm Coll, Miami, FL; JR; BA; Intrntl Stdnt Clb; Phi Theta Kappa; Hghst Hons W/Dist; Fdng Hmlss; AA 90; Med Sci; Bio; OB/GYN.**

**YAN, ANTONELLA K,** Georgetown Univ, Washington, DC.

**YAN, FRANCES YEEFEN,** City Univ Of Ny Baruch Coll, New York, NY; SR; BA; Sr Clss Bd Drctrs 90-; Glee Clb VP; Lbrl Art Scty 90-; New Apstlc Chrch Yth Grp Pres 90-; Finance; Import/Export.

**YAN, HOUDI,** City Univ Of Ny Baruch Coll, New York, NY; SR; BA; Beta Alpha Psi 90-; Acctg Hon Soc 89-; Hon Grad 88; Dens Lst 89-; Dns Lst SMC 86-88; I Weinstn Trst Fnd Schlrshp 90-; AA Santa Monica Coll 88; Acctg.

**YAN, LI,** City Univ Of Ny City Coll, New York, NY; SR; BE; Tau Beta Pai; Gldn Key; Elctcl Engrng; Engnrng.

**YAN, STELLA,** City Univ Of Ny Baruch Coll, New York, NY; SO; Asian Clb 89-; Hng Kng Assn 89-; Law.

**YANCEY, DEANNA,** Al St Univ, Montgomery, AL; SO; Psychlgy; Chld Psychlgst.

**YANCEY, DONNA S,** Beckley Coll, Beckley, WV; SO; BSN; Sci; Nurs.

**YANCEY, GEORGE A,** Hampton Univ, Hampton, VA; SR; BS; Bus Clb 88-; Yng Dem Clb 88-89; Mass Pre-Alm Clb Pblcty 87-; Alpha Kappa Mu 89-; Mgmt Awd 90; Bus Mgmt; Law.**

**YANCEY, MARCY L,** Winthrop Coll, Rock Hill, SC; JR; BS; Catrng Waitrs 90; Erly Chldhd Educ; Tchng K 4.

**YANCEY, MICHELLE L,** Fisk Univ, Nashville, TN; SO; BA; Psychlgy Clb Cmtee Dir 89-; Gospel Choir 89-90; MS Sga Clb 90; Hon Currclm 89-90; Psychlgy Educ Physchlgst.

**YANCEY, MICHELLE OWENS,** Univ Of Va Clinch Valley Coll, Wise, VA; SR; BS; AAS Southwest VA Cmnty Clg 89; Math; Tchg.

**YANCEY, TIMOTHY B,** Univ Of Ga, Athens, GA; BSED; Sports Wrtr; ABJ 86; Engl Tchr; Coach.

**YANCHIS, TINA L,** Western Carolina Univ, Cullowhee, NC; SR; Biology Clb Treas 90-; Stdnt Academic Advsry Comm; Schlrshp 87; Alpha Chi Omega Mystagogue Cultural Chrmn 87-; Rotary Clb Schlrshp 87; Sftbl Vlybl IMS 87-; BS; Biology; Rsrch Vet Med.

**YANCY, MARIO A,** Tn St Univ, Nashville, TN; SO; BS; PEP Clb 89-90; NSBE; Deans List 89-; Acdmc Awrd 89-; Track Clb 90-; Engrng/Math; Elctrcl Engrng.

**YANE, AUDREY C,** Oh Univ, Athens, OH; SR; BFA; Admttd Sr Show Undergrad Art Show; Fine Arts/Art Hstry.

**YANEZ, FRANCES E,** S U N Y Coll Of Tech At Frmgdl, Farmingdale, NY; FR; Prncpls Mngmnt Mrktng.

**YANG, GUANGXUE,** Fl International Univ, Miami, FL; GD; EDD; Taught Psychlgy/Ednl Rsrch China 82-87; MS Lamar Univ Beaumont TX 89; Excptnl Stdnt Edn; Rsrch.

**YANG, HORNG S,** Bloomfield Coll, Bloomfield, NJ; SR; BA; Swm Clb 88; Weiss Prz; Artst/So Ho Aprntceshp; Acctg; CPA.

**YANG, LIN JUN,** Bridgewater Coll, Bridgewater, VA; JR; BS; Intl Clb; China Intl Trvl Srvc; Ba Xia Men Univ China 82; Bsns Admnstrtn; Intl Bsns.

**YANG, TERESA,** Univ Of Pa, Philadelphia, PA; FR; Sub Rosa 90-; Intl Bsn Clb 90-; Env/Recycling Grp 90-; Ben Franklin Schlr 90-; Bsn; Law.

**YANG, TUE,** Western Piedmont Comm Coll, Morganton, NC; SO; AAAS; Tlnt Rstr Awrd; Tnns; Sci; Med.

**YANG, WOONG,** Oh St Univ, Columbus, OH; SO; BA; Archtctr Hnrs; Archtctr; Prof.

**YANG, YUHONG,** Coll Of Insurance, New York, NY; SO; BA; Insrnc.

**YANKLE, GLENN P,** Christian Brothers Univ, Memphis, TN; FR; BS; Inventory Planner 88-; Marketing.

**YANNELLO, LISA M,** Bryant Stratton Bus Inst Roch, Rochester, NY; FR; ASC; Certif Educ Opprtnty Ctr 89; Data Proc; Acctng.

**YANNI, ANTHONY J,** Hahnemann Univ, Philadelphia, PA; GD; AMA; AMSA; PMS; BS Univ Of Scranton 88; Medcn; Physcn.

**YANOSICK, JOSEPH A,** Comm Coll Algny Co Algny Cmps, Pittsburgh, PA; SR; BS; Grad W Hnrs 88; Syst Prgmr Pitts Natl Bnk 90-; AS Comm Clg Allghny Co 88; Cmptr Sci.

**YANOWITZ, BARRY S,** S U N Y At Buffalo, Buffalo, NY; JR; BS; Amer Mktng Assn 90-; Gldn Ky 90-; Mngmnt; Mktng.

**YANULAITIS, MARIANNE K,** Univ Of Scranton, Scranton, PA; JR; Soc Acctg Stdnts 90-; Delta Mu Delta; Dns Lst; Acctg; CPA.

**YAO, KAIYING,** Strayer Coll, Washington, DC; JR; CPR Instr 88-89; Acctg; Finance.

**YAO, KING-HAN,** Carnegie Mellon Univ, Pittsburgh, PA; SO; BS; Assoc For Ind Mgmnt/Ecnmncs Bos Chrman ; IM Ftbl Trnmnt Cpt 90; Mngmt Ecnomics; Corp Law.

**YAP, MEI-LENG,** Memphis St Univ, Memphis, TN; SR; BBA; Malaysian Stdnt Assoc 89-; Chinese Stdnt Assoc 89-; DPMA/DPSMA 90-; Golden Key 90-F Internatl Stdnt Org 89-; Mgmt Info Systms; Systms Anlyst/Pgmr.

**YARBOROUGH, GINGER D,** Vance Granville Comm Coll, Henderson, NC; SO; Sci Club Pres 88; Natl Hnr Soc 87; Lab Assist 88-89; Bio Sci Pgm; Engr.

**YARBOROUGH, KRISTY D,** Roane St Comm Coll, Harriman, TN; SO; Assoc Degree; Bus Mgmt; Lbr Relatns/Prsnnl.

**YARBOROUGH, RICHARD D,** Univ Of Sc At Columbia, Columbia, SC; FR; BA; Phi Eta Sigma; SC Phlhrmnc Chrs; Dns Lst 90-; Pres Hnr Roll 90-; Jrnlsm; Brdcstng.

**YARBROUGH, CHERYL D,** Nc Agri & Tech St Univ, Greensboro, NC; SO; BS; NAACP 90-; NC Tchng Fllw 90-; Aggie Ambsdr 90-; Elem Ed; Prfssr.

**YARBROUGH JR, HOUSTON A,** Al A & M Univ, Normal, AL; JR; BS; Kappa Delta Psi Accntng Clb Prlmntrn 88-; Tstmstrs Prsdnt 89-; Stdnt Clstr 89-; Soc Prsdntl Schlrs 88-; Alpha Kappa Mu Hnr Soc 90-; Ctrplr Intrnshp 90-; Accntng; Law.

**YARBROUGH, JAMES F,** Belmont Coll, Nashville, TN; FR; Class Officer President 90-; Environmental Alliance 90-; Internal Stdnt Comm 90-; Deans List 90-; Liberal Arts.

**YARBROUGH, JOSEPHINE C,** Vance Granville Comm Coll, Henderson, NC; SR; AAS; Phi Theta Kappa; Bus Admin/Acctng; Bus Acctng St Govt.

**YARBROUGH, JOSHUA L,** Memphis St Univ, Memphis, TN; JR; BSEE; Gamma Beta Phi; Phi Eta Sigma 90; Electrical Eng.

**YARGER, BRENDA J,** Daemen Coll, Amherst, NY; FR; BS; YMCA 90; Blgy; Mdcl.

**YARICK, DIANE L,** Coll Misericordia, Dallas, PA; FR; BA; Edctn Clb 90-; Deans Lst90-; Chld Dvlpmnt; Edctn.

**YARNELL, APRIL C,** Mount Aloysius Jr Coll, Cresson, PA; FR; BA; Deans Lst 90-; Cert; Cardiovascular Tech; Radiology/Nursing.

**YARNELL, CATHRYN R,** Univ Of Sc At Columbia, Columbia, SC; FR; BS; Asst Financial Analyst 90-; Math; Engrng.

**YARNS, FELISA IRIS,** Andrew Coll, Cuthbert, GA; SO; BA; Utilizing Freedom Org 90-; Phi Theta Kappa 89-; Natl Collegiate Miniority Ldrshp Awd; Acctng.

**YAROSH, BRIAN DENNIS,** East Tn St Univ, Johnson City, TN; FR; Aolpha Delta Lambda 90-; Dns Lst 90; Engr Dsgn Grphcs.

**YASKULSKI, ROBIN R,** S U N Y At Buffalo, Buffalo, NY; SR; MS; Tchng Asstnt; Alpha Pi Mu Prsdnt 90-91; Omega Rho Prsdnt 91-92; Tau Beta Pi 90-; Inst Indstrl Engnrs 89-; Amrcn Soc Qlty Cntrl 90-; Indstrl Engnrng Oprtns Rsrch; Engnrng.

**YATES, AMY E,** Wv Univ, Morgantown, WV; SO; BA; Aerospace Engr.

**YATES, CAROL E,** Univ Of Akron, Akron, OH; JR; BED; Lab Asst 65-90; Biolgy; Elem Ed.

**YATES, CASSANDRA A,** Salisbury St Univ, Salisbury, MD; JR; BA SW; Soc Wrk Hon Soc; Phi Eta Sigma 89-; Soc Wrk.

**YATES, CHRISTOPHER J,** Univ Of Miami, Coral Gables, FL; SO; BBA; Intfrnty Cncl Rep; Univ Hnrs Prog; Alpha Tau Omega Pres; Lacrosse Clb; Bus Law.

**YATES JR, JAMES N,** Univ Of Ky, Lexington, KY; JR; BA; IM Bsktbl 90; Cmmnctns; Brdcst Prdctn.

**YATES, JAMES R,** Nova Univ, Ft Lauderdale, FL; GD; MBA; Phi Kappa Phi 84-86; BSET 86; AA 84; Mgmt.

**YATES, JENNIFER L,** Univ Of Montevallo, Montevallo, AL; SO; BA; Sociology Club 90-; Carmichael Library Frshm Book Review Award 89; Sociology.

**YATES, KIMBERLY NICOLE,** Al A & M Univ, Normal, AL; SO; SG Prlmntrn 89-; Domm Cncl 89-; Kappa Delta Pi; Alpha Kappa Alpha; Top Teen Pres 88-; Girl Scouts; Ben Marcato Club 90-; Mcdonnell Douglas Intern 90-; Psychology; Corporate Psychology.

**YATES, LEAH DANIELLE,** Central Al Comm Coll, Alexander City, AL; FR; BS; Phi Theta Kappa; Mktg; Corp Law.

**YATES, LISA L,** Pellissippi St Tech Comm Coll, Knoxville, TN; FR; MBA; Phi Theta Kappa 90; Offc Mgr Fortune 500 Co 88-90; Psych.

**YATES, MARGARET S,** Roane St Comm Coll, Harriman, TN; SO; AS; Amer Dental Assist Assn; Amer Dental Hygienists Assn; Assist/Office Mgr Dntl; RDA Tn Dntl Assist Bd 78; CDA Dntl Assist Natl Bd 80; Hlth Sci/Dntl Hygiene; Reg Dntl Hygienist.

**YATES, PHILIP ANTHONY,** Univ Of Ky, Lexington, KY; SR; BS 90; Mech Engr.

**YATES, REBECCA J,** Oh St Univ At Newark, Newark, OH; SR; BA; SS Tchr 87-; Phi Sigma Schlstc 87-; Golden Key 89-90; Dogs Of Amer 89-90; Intl Bus Admin; Mrktng/Pub Rltns.

**YATES, SABRINA R,** Univ Of Md At Eastern Shore, Princess Anne, MD; SO; BA; Bus Admn; Bus Owner.

**YATES, TERESA A,** Comm Coll Algny Co Algny Cmps, Pittsburgh, PA; FR; AS; Amer Assn Rsprtry Cr 86-; St Margaret Memrl Hosp Rsprtry Cr Tchncn 81-; CRTT CA Coll Hlth Sci 85; Rsprtry Cr.

**YATES, TIFFANY M,** Valdosta St Coll, Valdosta, GA; SR; BS; Pi Gamma Mu Sec Tres 90-; Deans List; Psychlgy; Mntl Hndcpd Instr.

**YATTAW, DAVID J,** S U N Y At Buffalo, Buffalo, NY; SO; BS; Im Soccer Co-Capt 89; Phi Eta Sigma 90; Bsnss Admin.

**YAU, KAI WAI K,** Piedmont Coll, Demorest, GA; FR; BS; Schlrs Prog 90-; Trustee Schlrshp 90-; Phrmcy.

**YAU, SIEW CHOI,** Univ Of Miami, Coral Gables, FL; SO; BA; Hnrs Assoc 90-; Alpha Lambda Delta 90-; Phi Eta Sigma 90-; Pres Hnr Rl 90-; Jay F W Pearson Schlrshp 89-; Prvsts Hnr Rl 89-; Dns Lst 89-; Bsn; Systms Anlys.

**YAU, WAH LOK,** Clarkson Univ, Potsdam, NY; SR; BS; Intl Stdnt Org Comm 88-; Univ Bowling League 89-90; Fin Mgmt Assoc 90-; Phi Kappa Phi 89-; Beta Gamma Sigma 89-; Alpha Kappa Psi 88-; Pres Schlr 87-90; Hnry Schlrshp 88-; Deans List 90-; Mgmt/Fin; Intl Bus.

**YAVOSKI, BETH A,** S U N Y Coll Of Tech At Frmgdl, Farmingdale, NY; FR; BA; Acctng Soc; Bus Admin; Mngmnt.

**YAW, GARY F,** S U N Y Coll Of Tech At Alfred, Alfred, NY; FR; BA; Var Bsktbl 88-90; Jr Var Bsktbl 86-88; Smr Intrn Mcrotech Corp Elec Tech; Sci; Mech Engr.

**YAWBERG, JILL K,** Davis Coll, Toledo, OH; SR; ASSN; Cncrt Bnd 86-88; Trmbn Chr 86-88; Deans Lst 89-; Prsdnts Lst 89-; S Y Fabrications Intrn; Cmmrcl Art; Advrtsng Illstrtn.

**YAZAWA, ERIKO,** Savannah Coll Of Art & Design, Savannah, GA; FR; Bch Cln Up/Envrnmntl Grp 90-; Intl Stdnt Comm 90-; Amer Soc Intr Dsgnrs 90-; Tennis 90-; Intr Dsgn.

**YBAY, ALOYSIUS ANTHONY S,** Manhattan Coll, Bronx, NY; JR; Tau Beta Pi; Eta Kappa Nu.

**YEAGER, H TODD,** Pittsburgh Tech Inst, Pittsburgh, PA; GD; ASSOC; Mech Dsgn; Eng.

**YEAGER, JULI P,** William Carey Coll, Hattiesburg, MS; SR; BSN; Amer Hrt Assn Brd Dir; LPN Jefferson Prsh Hlth Occptns 81; RN ASN LA St Univ Med Cntr 89; Nrsng.

**YEAGER, KATHLEEN G,** Mount Aloysius Jr Coll, Cresson, PA; FR; AS; Science; Med Lbrtry Tchnlgy.

**YEAGER, LISA E,** Valencia Comm Coll, Orlando, FL; JR; BA; AA 90; Hlth/Prfsnl Stds; Crmnl Just.**

**YEAGER, MICHELLE A,** Anne Arundel Comm Coll, Arnold, MD; SO; Engl; Phys Thrpst.

**YEAGER, RAYE C,** Elmira Coll, Elmira, NY; SR; BS; AA Corning Cmnty Clg 71; Elem Educ; Tchng.

**YEAGER, SARAH L,** Wv Northern Comm Coll, Wheeling, WV; SO; AAS; Nrsng.

**YEAGLEY, KRISTI S,** Univ Of Akron, Akron, OH; SR; BED; Kappa Delta Pi 89-; Gldn Key 89-; Kappa Delta Pi 89-; Elem Ed; Tchng.

**YEARGIN, TERESA L,** Tri County Tech Coll, Pendleton, SC; Tri Co Tech Dntl Asst Cls Pres 90-; Amer Dntl Asst Assoc; Pndltn Jr Assmbly; Dntl Asstnt; Tchg.

**YEARTY, JAMES L,** Fl St Univ, Tallahassee, FL; SR; BS; Scalphunters Stdnt Booster Org 89-; Am Soc Civil Engrs 90-; Kappa Alpha Treas 90-; Deans List 89-90; Civil Engrng.

**YEARWOOD REAGAN, STACY D,** Tn Tech Univ, Cookeville, TN; JR; BA; Gamma Beta Phi Sec 89-90; AS Roane St Comm Clg; Sec Educ/Math; Tch.

**YEATMAN, AMY L,** Radford Univ, Radford, VA; SO; BS; Med Tech.

**YEBRA, MARIA E,** Fl A & M Univ, Tallahassee, FL; GD; BARCH; Vol Intl Stdnt Affrs 85-87; Arch Clb Tampa; Gargoyle Arch Hnr Soc 86-87; Alpha Lambda Delta 84-85; Amer Ins Arch Stdns 85-87; BA Design Univ Fla 87-; Archt.

**YEE, BECKY,** Chestnut Hill Coll, Philadelphia, PA; FR; BA; Chrs 90-; Fine Arts Clb 90-; Pro Lf Clb 90-; Business Adm.

**YEE, FLORA,** Columbus Coll Of Art & Design, Columbus, OH; SO; Illustration.

**YEE, MAN-CHING ANDY,** City Univ Of Ny City Coll, New York, NY; SR; BE; ASCE 89-; Cncrt Cne Clb 90-; Gldn Ky 89-; Chi Epsilon 89-; Tau Beta Pi 90-; Cvl Eng; Engrng.

**YEE, MARY,** Carnegie Mellon Univ, Pittsburgh, PA; JR; BS; AIESEC 89-90; Phi Eta Sigma 89-; Lambda Sigma 89-; Mrtr Brd; Indl Mgmt; Inv Bnkng/Intl Trade.

**YEE, MENG KAY,** S U N Y At Buffalo, Buffalo, NY; SR; MS; Malaysia Stdnt Assoc Spr Dir 89; Golden Key 90-; Tau Beta Pi; BS; Elect Engr.

**YELDELL, NICOLE L,** Howard Univ, Washington, DC; SR; BA; SG; NBCDI; NCNW; Elem Ed; Edctr.

**YELEY, GINA M,** Marshall University, Huntington, WV; FR; BS; Barth Co 4h Clb Pres 81-; Vllybll 90-; Bsn.

**YELTON, TODD A,** Western Carolina Univ, Cullowhee, NC; JR; BA; Pi Gamma Mu 90-; Dlt Chi Sgt Arms 90-; Pol Sci; Law.

**YELVERSTON, ROBERT F,** Norfolk St Univ, Norfolk, VA; SO; BA; Harrison B Wilson Awd; WTAR/WLTY Athl Schlrshp Awd; Norfolf St Ftbl Tm; Indstrl Mngmnt.

**YEMBA, ROSALIE A,** Bennett Coll, Greensboro, NC; SO; BS; Interntn Stdnts Assoc Sec 89-; Bennett Schlrs; Biolgy Clb; Chr; Mdl UN; Mrshl Brd; Dns Lst 89-; Hnr Roll 89-; Zeta Phi Beta; Blgy/Pre Med/Chmstry; Med Ped.

**YEN, EATON I,** City Univ Of Ny City Coll, New York, NY; SR; BS; Biopsychology; Medicine.

**YEN, MICHAEL T,** Univ Of Miami, Coral Gables, FL; JR; BS; Hnrs Assn 89-; Table Tennis Club 89-; Mstr Tutor Pgm 90-; Phi Kappa Phi; Golden Key; Phi Eta Sigma; Jay F Pearson Schlrshp 89-; Rsrch Grant 90; Bio; Med.

**YENDRICK, DAWN M,** Marywood Coll, Scranton, PA; FR; BA; Tchrs Of Tomorrow 90-; Elem Educ; Tchng.

**YEO, CHENG HOCK,** Broward Comm Coll, Ft Lauderdale, FL; SO; AS; Nursing.

**YEO, GREGORY L G,** Memphis Academy Of The Arts, Memphis, TN; JR; BFA; AA Saito Acad Graphic Dsgn 90; Graphic Dsgn.

**YEPEZ-CUVI, FERNANDO A,** Duquesne Univ, Pittsburgh, PA; FR; BA; Intl Stdnts Org Pblcy Offcr 90- V P; Lambda Sigma; Alpha Gamma; Bus/Admin; Econ.

**YERDON, ANGELA C,** D Youville Coll, Buffalo, NY; JR; BS; SPTA 88-90; Adopt/Grnd Prnt 89; Vrsty Vlybl 88-89; Phys Thrpy; MS.

**YERES, HERSCHEL W,** Yeshiva Univ, New York, NY; SR; MS; Coll Phys Clb Pres 89-; Cmpusci Cmptr Sci Soc Asst Oper 89-; Yavneh Olami Exec Brd Mem 89-90; Gov Citatn Schlstc Achiev 86-87; Sigma Delta Rho 88-90; NY State Rgnts Schlr 86-90; Deans Lst 88-90; Erly Admssns 86; Physcs; Elec Eng.

**YERIAN, BRENDAN L,** Va Commonwealth Univ, Richmond, VA; FR; Jazz Studies; Music.

**YERTY, GLENDA S,** Mount Aloysius Jr Coll, Cresson, PA; FR; BSN; Nrsng.

**YETKA, DENISE SUSAN,** Westminster Coll, New Wilmingtn, PA; SR; BA; Kappa Delta 89-90; VISA 89-; Elem Educ; Tchr.

**YETMAN, KEVIN R,** Merrimack Coll, North Andover, MA; JR; BS; Cmptr Sci; Cmptr Prof.

**YETTER, MARY L,** Trocaire Coll, Buffalo, NY; SO; AAS; Business Club VP 90-; Phi Theta Kappa Sec 90-; Scl Evnts/Scl Awrnss Comm Chrprsn 89-; Alpha Pi Eta Sec; Scl Awrnss Com Vol; Trocairing Awd 90; School Sirit Awd; Business; Marketing.

**YETZER, JILL E,** Duquesne Univ, Pittsburgh, PA; SR; BS; Amer Std Pharm 87-; SHARP Vol 87-89; Urges Chem Knwldg Comm 90-; Rho Chi; Cliffees/Rx Ctr Intrn 89; Elk Cnty Gnrl Hosp Intrn 90-; IM Ftbl/Vlybl/Bsktbl 87-; Pharm.

**YEUNG, ANGELA M,** Norfolk St Univ, Norfolk, VA; SO; BS; Assn Cmptng Mchnry; Gldn Key; Dns Lst 89-; Cmptr Sci; Cmptr Prgrmng.**

**YEUNG, KENNY,** Cooper Union, New York, NY; FR; Elect Eng.

**YEUNG, MAN-YAN,** Oh Dominican Coll, Columbus, OH; FR; Bus Admin.

**YEUNG, MEI Y,** City Univ Of Ny Baruch Coll, New York, NY; SR; BBA; Beta Alpha Psi VP; Ovrsee Chns Mssn Stff 90; Acctg.

**YEUNG, TIN FUK M,** Univ Of Ky, Lexington, KY; FR; BS; Cosmopolitan Clb Ofc Intl Affairs; Alpha Lambda Delta; Phi Eta Sigma; Emerging Ldr Inst Div Stdnt Affairs; Deans Lst Coll Arts/Sci 90-; Exper Edn; Cmptr Sci.

**YEWA, JULIA A,** Fl International Univ, Miami, FL; SR; BS; Flk Hotel Nairobi Intrnshp 84-86; Contntl Htl Nairobi Attchmnt 90; Lectrng Fd Svc Sales Mngmnt 87-; AS Kenya Utalii Coll 87; Cert Graffins Coll Nairobi 86; Hsptlty Mngmnt; Hotelier.

**YGLESIAS, CONCEPCION,** Miami Dade Comm Coll South, Miami, FL; SO; BA; Intrnshp Teacher Aide S Miami Elem 89-90; AA Elem Ed 90; AS Early Childhood Development 90; Elem Ed; Teacher.

**YI, EUNHUI,** Va Commonwealth Univ, Richmond, VA; JR; BS; MDIP; Mngd Rtl Store; Bank/Fncl Instn; Info Sys; Sys Prgmmr.

**YI, HO Y,** Univ Of Md At Eastern Shore, Princess Anne, MD; SO; Airway Comptr Sci.

**YI, LESLIE E,** Jersey City St Coll, Jersey City, NJ; SR; BA; Coop Ed Intrn; Deans Lst 87-; Art Advtsng Dsgn.

**YI, SANG H,** Univ Of The Dist Of Columbia, Washington, DC; SR; BBA; Delta Mu Delta; Cmptr Info Sci; Bsn.

**YI, YONHE,** City Univ Of Ny Baruch Coll, New York, NY; JR; BBA; Korean Stdnt Assoc V P 88-89; Korean Amer Govt 90-; Brooklyn Distr Attnys Law Intern 86-87; Pol Sci Intern Manhattanboro Pres Ofc; Intl Mktg/Pol Sci.

**YICK, KATHLEEN,** George Washington Univ, Washington, DC; FR; BSEE; Cmmndtn List 90; Deans List; Engrng; Elec Engrng.

**YIELDING, JANELLE L,** Hudson Valley Comm Coll, Troy, NY; SO; AAS; Alpha Xi Sigma; Phi Thetta Kappa 90-; Phi Beta Kappa; Cert Amer Inst Bkng 88; Publ Admin; Womns Issues.

**YIN, LE-MIN,** Univ Of Md At Eastern Shore, Princess Anne, MD; SR; BS; ACM; Upsilon Pi Epsilon Hnr Soc; UMES Chptr; Univ Hnr Lst Deans Lst 89-; Schlrshp Sch Arts/Sci 89; Cmptr Sci; Anlyst.**

**YIN, YI LE,** City Univ Of Ny City Coll, New York, NY; SR; Han Wave Intl 88-; Gldn Key 89-; Tau Beta Pi 90-; Eng.

**YINDRA, JONATHAN G,** Albertus Magnus Coll, New Haven, CT; SR; BA; Fd Comm Chr 89-90; Jdcl Brd Ch 90-; Stdnt Act Brd 90-; Brd Cnsltnts 90-; Nwspr; Stdnt Cmmncmnt Spkr; Cmnctns; Jrnlst.

**YINGLING, JEFFREY C,** Kent St Univ Kent Cmps, Kent, OH; SR; BA; Undrgrad Stu Snt Alctns Chr 89-; Intrhl Cncl Pres 85-; Choir; Mrtr Brd 88-89; Ntl Res Hl Hnry 87-88; Delta Upsilon Sng Ldr 90-; Untd Wy 86-87; Red Crs 87-88; Amer Cncr Soc 90-; Kent Intrhl Cncl Lf Tm Awrd 89; Delta Gamma Anchr Kng 90; Bus Mgmt; Hghr Educ Admin.

**YIP, HENRY C,** City Univ Of Ny Baruch Coll, New York, NY; SR; AMA; Hong Kong Clb; Malaysian Clb; BBA; Mrktng Mngmnt; Mngmnt.

**YIP, WENDY W,** Dowling Coll, Oakdale Li, NY; SO; BA; Intl Clb 89-; Acctng Scty 89-; Natl Scty Public Acctnts 90-; Acctng Internship 90-; Institutional Research Asstnt 90-; Acctng; CPA.

**YIU, KIN KIU,** Newbury Coll, Brookline, MA; FR; BA; Fr Awrds 90-; Comp Sci.

**YOAKUM, AGATHA M,** Hillsborough Comm Coll, Tampa, FL; JR; BA; Stdnt Govt 90; Phi Theta Kappa Pres 88-90; Girl Scts Amer Trp Ldr 88-90; AA 90; Hstry; Urban/Rgnl Plnng.

**YOAKUM, GINGER G,** Univ Of Al At Birmingham, Birmingham, AL; SR; BA; Stdnt Mdcl Rcd Club Pres 90-; Amer Mdcl Rcd Assoc 90-; Stdnt Sntrs Assoc Rep 89-90; Golden Key 90-; Omicron Delta 90-; Alphi Chi Delg 88-; Powell Vly Citizen Band Club 84-; Clinical Affiliation E TN Bptst Hosp; AS 88; Medical Record Administration; Admnstr.

**YOAKUM, STEFANIE L,** Dyersburg St Comm Coll, Dyersburg, TN; SO; BA; Phi Theta Kappa 89-; Fisher Maher Memorial Schlrshp; Psychlgy; Clncl Psychlgst.

**YOCHUM III, HENRY M,** Coll Of Charleston, Charleston, SC; FR; BS; Phys/Math; Engr.

**YODER, CHARLENE K,** Tri County Tech Coll, Pendleton, SC; FR; BSW; Scl Wrk.

**YODER, THOMAS L,** Univ Of Akron, Akron, OH; GD; Grk Prgrmmng Com Prsdnt 89-; Ordr Omega 89-; Vuckovich 90; Pi Sigma Epsilon Asst Edctr 88-; Phi Gamma Delta Crrspndng Sec 89-; Red Cross 88-; MDA; Cncr Soc; Big Bros Big Sstrs; Akros; IM Footbl; Mrktng.

**YOHE, BETHANY A,** Lebanon Valley Coll, Annville, PA; FR; BS; Std Educ Asc Sec; Mrchng Band; Elem Ed; Tchr.

**YOHO, EILEEN D,** Wv Northern Comm Coll, Wheeling, WV; FR; AS; Nrsng.

**YOKITIS, AMY M,** Saint Francis Coll, Loretto, PA; FR; Red Key Clb 90-; Sngrs 90-; Pre Law 90-; SAIL 90-; Cinema 90-; TEC Secular Franciscan Ord 90-; Hnrs Prog; Campus Ministry; Prolife; Hnrs Prog; Aerobics; Engl/Acctng; Law.

**YOKLEY, ELIZABETH B,** Univ Of Nc At Greensboro, Greensboro, NC; SR; MA; Phi Mu Exec Coun 89-90; Panhell Coun 89-90; Campus Crus 87-88; Tchr 90-; BS UNC Greensboro 90; Engl; Prof.

**YOKUM, PATRICIA A,** Va Highlands Comm Coll, Abingdon, VA; SO; AS; Pres Hon Rl 89-90; LPN; Brstl Vctnl Schl 78; Nrsng; RN.

**YOLANDA, ARZOLA,** Inter Amer Univ Pr Barranquita, Barranquitas, PR; JR; Asociacion De Estudiantes De Presidenta 90-; Adminstracion Comercial Interina; Senado Academico; Cuadro De Honor; Admn Cmrcl; Acctg.

**YONCE, KATHLEEN E,** Univ Of Sc At Columbia, Columbia, SC; SR; Gamma Beta Phi 88-; Delta Phi Alpha 90-; Gldn Ky 89-; Kappa Kappa Gamma 87-89; Goethe Inst Awrd; Mstrs Intrntn.

**YONCO, LAURA M,** Univ Of Bridgeport, Bridgeport, CT; JR; BS; Phi Kappa Phi; Outstndg Fr Awd 88-89; Pres Lst 90; Magna Cum Laude 90f AA 90; Fshn Merch/Retailing; Mgmnt.

**YONG, LEONARD T,** Univ Of Fl, Gainesville, FL; SR; BS; Sv Schlrshp Fdtn Chrmn 89-90; Prjct Grdtns; Phi Theta Kappa Treas; Shands Hosp Vol; Amer Cncr Soc 90-; Lkm Soc 88-89; Pres Ldr Intrnshp Lantana 89; U FL Pres Schlrshp 89; Sthrn Rotary Schlrshp UF 90; Army 85-; AA Bsn 89; Dcsn/Info Sci; Intlgnc Ofcr.**

**YONKERS, MARC E,** S U N Y At Buffalo, Buffalo, NY; JR; BS; Acctg Assn 90-; Local Band; Gold Key 90-; Beta Alpha Psi; Deans Lst Asst Scout Mstr 88-89; Eagle Scout; Acctg.

**YONKURA, RAYMOND C,** Kent St Univ Kent Cmps, Kent, OH; FR; BA; Clg Repubs Sec 90-; United Stdnts For Liberation 90-; Pol Sci.

**YONKUS, CHRISTINE T,** S U N Y Coll Of Tech At Frmgdl, Farmingdale, NY; SO; BA; Traffic Judge 90-; Asst Tchr BOCES Spec Ed 90; ASSOC; Pol Sci; Law.

**YONTS, JEANETTE T,** Univ Of Va Clinch Valley Coll, Wise, VA; JR; BA; AA Lees Clg 77; Early Ele Educ.

**YOO, DANIEL H,** Va Commonwealth Univ, Richmond, VA; JR; BA; Amrcn Cntr Dsgn 90-; Krn Assoc VP 89-; Gldn Key 90-; Cmmnctn Art; Grphc Dsgnr.

**YOON, LISA Y,** Saint Josephs Univ, Philadelphia, PA; FR; BS; Intl Stdnt Assn V P Pblcty; Asian Stdnt Assn Treas 90; Choir 90; Hnrs Pgm 90; Amnesty Intl 90; Chem; Med.

**YORK, BRIAN E,** Columbus Coll Of Art & Design, Columbus, OH; FR; BA; Stdnty Bible Stdy 90-; Illustrtn; Free Lance Art.

**YORK, JANICA L,** Birmingham Southern Coll, Birmingham, AL; JR; BA; Pblctns Brd Chr; Chf Ed Art Lit Mgzn Chf Ed 89-; Sthrn Acdmc Rvw Acdmc Jrnl Asst Ed 88-89; Mrtr Brd; Sigma Tau Delta; Alpha Lambda Delta 89-; Alpha Chi Omega Lyr Ed; Intrn EBSCO Md 90; Eng; Pblctns.

**YORK, KAY SELBY,** Univ Of Sc At Columbia, Columbia, SC; SR; BA; Gld Key Clb 89-; Engl; Law Grad Sch.

**YORK, KELLY C,** Catawba Valley Comm Coll, Hickory, NC; SO; AAS; Acctng.

**YORK, SHERRY B,** Western Piedmont Comm Coll, Morganton, NC; SO; TDD; Drafting Art; Design Furniture.

**YORK, STEPHANIE L,** Owensboro Comm Coll, Owensboro, KY; SO; AS; Ky Higher Educ Assoc; Natl Educ Assoc; Laubach Literacy Action Serv; Hnrs Vol Serv Tutoring; English/Communications; Tchng Schl Admin.

**YOSHIDA, SHINAKO,** Comm Coll Algny Co Algny Cmps, Pittsburgh, PA; FR; AS; Art Assn 91; Art; Indus Dsgn.

**YOSHII, TADASHI,** Wv Univ, Morgantown, WV; SR; BSIE; Alpha Phi Mu 90-; Dean Lst 89-; Indstrl Eng.

**YOSHIOKA, ERIKO,** Abraham Baldwin Agri Coll, Tifton, GA; SO; AS; Intl Clb 90-; Hnr Stdnts; Pres Lst; Muryl Yow Schlrshp; Mdl Sch Ed; Interpret/Tour Guide.

**YOST, KATHLEEN R,** Columbia Greene Comm Coll, Hudson, NY; SO; BA; Daycare Brd 89-90; Phi Theta Kappa 90-; Art Hist; Tchng Wrtng.

**YOST, KELLEY D G,** Midlands Tech Coll, Columbia, SC; GD; AS; Med Lab Tech Clb; Alpha Eta Kappa; Phi Theta Kappa; Med Lab Tech; Medicine.

**YOST, NINA S,** Radford Univ, Radford, VA; JR; BA; Phi Kappa Phi; Acctg; CPA.

**YOST, STACY R,** Beckley Coll, Beckley, WV; FR; AD; Law; Prlgl Asst.

**YOST, TONY E,** East Tn St Univ, Johnson City, TN; GD; MD; Chrstn Mdcl Dntl Scty 90-; Fmly Prctc Stdnt Intrst Grp Rep 90-; Fllwshp Chrstn Athltsgamma Beta Phi 85-86; Grdt Asst Dpt Hmn Dev Lrng 85-86; Sthrn Cnfrnc Acdmc Ftbll 83; Dbt Tm Capt 83; Intrcoll Ftbll 80-84; Lcnsd Psychlgcl Exmnr 87-89; BS 84; MED 86; Med.

**YOST, TRUDY L,** Draughons Jr Coll Nashville, Nashville, TN; SO; BA; Bus Mngmt/Acctng.

**YOU, SUNG YUL,** City Univ Of Ny Queensbrough, New York, NY; SO; BA; Krn Clb; Alpha Beta Gamma 90-; Deans Hnr Lst 90-; Bus Mgmt.

**YOUMANS, HENRIETTA,** Univ Of Sc At Columbia, Columbia, SC; SR; BA; SGA Exec Treas 87-89; Ed Majrs Clb 90-; Gamma Beta Phi Pres 88-89; AA USC 88; Erlyh Chldhd Ed; Tchr.

**YOUMANS III, WILLIAM H,** Fl A & M Univ, Tallahassee, FL; FR; BS; Cmptr Info Sys Clb 90-; Bacclrus Clb 90-; Stdnt Allnc Cltrl Dvlpmnt 90-; Phi Eta Sigma 90-; IBM Intrn 90; Cmptr/Info Sys/Math; Sftwr Eng/Math Pro.

**YOUNES, ABDULLAH F,** Savannah St Coll, Savannah, GA; JR; BS; Intl Student Assoc Pres 89-; Amer Scty Mechl Engrs Mbr 90-; Certif Distn Vltr Model Leag Arab States; Mechl Engrg; Engrg.

**YOUNG KONG, KEVIN F,** Fl International Univ, Miami, FL; SR; Crbbn Std Asc Exec Comm 86-87; Cir K Kiwanis 85-88; AA Miami-Dade Comm Clg 88; BSC FL Intl Univ 90; Hosp Mgmt.

**YOUNG ROBINSON, NANCY R,** Emory Univ, Atlanta, GA; GD; MNMPH; Phi Beta Kappa 84; Omicron Delta Kappa 85-; Sigma Theta Tau 85-; Robert W Woodruff Flwshp 89-; Maternal Child Hlth Schlrshp 89-; Amer Clg Nurse Midwives; BA 84; BSN 86; Nurse Midwafery Public Health.

**YOUNG, ADRIENNE M,** Central St Univ, Wilberforce, OH; JR; BA; Career Awrns Pgm 87; Natl Assn Negro Bus/Profl Wmn Clb VP; Natl Hon Soc 87; Bus; Mktg.

**YOUNG, ALLISON L,** Juniata Coll, Huntingdon, PA; SO; BS; Biology Clb 89-; Health Occupations Stdnt Amer; Concert Choir Choral Union 89-; Frshmn Steerign Comm 89-90; Admissions Assoc 90-; Stdnt Hlth Advsry Comm VP 89-; Peer Advsr 90-; Brumbaugh Ellis Schlrshp 89; Fndrs Awrd Music 89-90; Metr Fnd Awrd; Biology Pre Med; Physician.

**YOUNG, AMY E,** Middle Tn St Univ, Murfreesboro, TN; SR; BA; Gamma Beta Phi; Sigma Delta Pi; Hnrs Thesis Schlrshp; Psych; Clncl Psych.

**YOUNG, AMY M,** D Youville Coll, Buffalo, NY; JR; BA; Scl Wrk Assoc Prgrmmng Chr 88-; Lambda Sigma 89-90; Hosp Mdcl Scl Wrk.

**YOUNG, ANDRE M,** Morehouse Coll, Atlanta, GA; JR; BA; GIG I Lo 88; Ftbl 88; Trk/Fld 89; Gig Phi Lo 88; Bsnss; Bsnss Mngmnt.

**YOUNG, ANDREW FREDERICK,** Alfred Univ, Alfred, NY; SR; BS; Tae Kwon Do Clb Blck Blt Instrctr 86-; Amer Ceramic Scty 89-; Alph Chi Rho 87-; Rgnts Schlrshp 86-90; Ceramic Eng; Eng/Patent Law.

**YOUNG, ANGELA,** Muskingum Coll, New Concord, OH; FR; BA; Crisis Hotline Vol; Lambda Sigma; Math/Art; Tch Math/Engrng.

**YOUNG, ANGELA J,** Pellissippi St Tech Comm Coll, Knoxville, TN; FR; BA; Pellissippi State Ambassador; Phi Theta Kappa; Hist; Educator.

**YOUNG, ANGELA K,** Univ Of Tn At Knoxville, Knoxville, TN; JR; BA; Bsn Dns Advsry Cncl 90-F AMA 90-; Exec Undrgrdts 89-; Beta Gamma Sigma 9o-; Alpha Kappa Psi; Pi Beta Phi; Mktg; Law.

**YOUNG, ANGELA L,** Fl A & M Univ, Tallahassee, FL; SO; BS; NAACP VP 90-; Natl Assn Blck Jrnlsts; Pres Schlr; Cmnctns; TV Mgmt.

**YOUNG, ANGELA R,** Anderson Coll, Anderson, SC; FR; BS; Math/Sci; Biomed Engr.

**YOUNG, ANTHONY CARL,** Hillsborough Comm Coll, Tampa, FL; JR; BA; HELP 89-; 7IS Scty USF 903-; Data Prcssng Assoc; Phi Theta Kappa 90-; HCC; Achvmnt Acctg 89-90; Amrcn Lgn 89-; US Nvy Flt Rsrv 89-; US Nvy Chf Ptty Offc 69-89AA 90; Info Systms Mgmt.

**YOUNG, APRYL G,** Lincoln Univ, Lincoln Univ, PA; SR; Frnch Clb Pres 90-; Gospel Ensmbl 88-; Iota Eta Tau 90-; Alpha Mu Gamma 90-; Phi Sigma Iota 90-; Joseph J Rodgers Oral Lang Prfcncy Awrd; BA; French; Translation/Interpretation.**

**YOUNG, ATLISA M,** Univ Of Md At Eastern Shore, Princess Anne, MD; SR; BA; Campus Minstry VP 87-; Hons Progrm 88-; Alpha Kappa Alpha Histrn 89-; BA Univ Of MD; Soclgy; Law.

**YOUNG, AVA D,** Alcorn St Univ, Lorman, MS; FR; Bus Admin.

**YOUNG, BRENDA J,** Univ Of Nh Plymouth St Coll, Plymouth, NH; SR; BS; Rsdnce Hall Jdcl Brd 87-89; Kappa Delta Pi Cmnty Svc Comm 89-; Dns Lst; Pres Lst 90; Elem Educ; Tchng.

**YOUNG, BRIAN K,** Indiana Univ Of Pa, Indiana, PA; SR; BED; Alpha Chi Rho Rsh Chrmn 88-; Stnbro Vol Frfghtr 89; Math; Tchr Hgh Schl.

**YOUNG, BUDDY C,** Bristol Univ, Bristol, TN; JR; BS; Natl Assoc Accts 79-; Acctng Mgr/Sprvsr 76-; AAS Ulster Co Cmnty Clge 74; Acctg; CPA.

**YOUNG, CAROLYN R,** Tn St Univ, Nashville, TN; SR; BA; Lit Guild 90-; Lit Mag Edtr .0-; Sigma Tau Delta Exec Sec 90-; Golden Key; English; Clg Prof/Full Time Wrtr.

**YOUNG, CHARLES E,** Emory & Henry Coll, Emory, VA; SO; BA; Emory/Henry Coll Rpblcns Pres 89-; Pre-Law Soc Pres 90-; Appls Bd Assoc; Pol Sci; Law.

**YOUNG, CHARLES M,** Wv Northern Comm Coll, Wheeling, WV; FR; CAS; N Amer Huntng Clb; W V Shrfs Assn; Crctnl Ofcr I; Indus Maint Tech; Htng Air Cndtng Vntltn Tech.

**YOUNG, CHASITY N,** East Central Comm Coll, Decatur, MS; FR; BA; IM Sftbl; Phi Theta Kappa VP Fllwshp; Mu Alpha Theta; Elem Ed.

**YOUNG, CHRISTINE L,** Univ Of Akron, Akron, OH; JR; BED; ACES 90-; Kapp Mu Epsilon 89-; Deans Lst 89-; Elem Edctn; Tchr.

**YOUNG, CHRISTOPHER B,** Wallace St Comm Coll At Selma, Selma, AL; SO; BA; Math Tutor; Comp Info Syst; Comp Pgmr.

**YOUNG, CINDY D,** Valdosta St Coll, Valdosta, GA; JR; BSED; Schlr.

**YOUNG, DAVID E,** Oh Dominican Coll, Columbus, OH; SR; BA; Mst Val Assoc 90; Natl Assoc Cath Chplns 83-; Chpln Mt Carmel Med Ctr; Cert Diocese Columbus 83; Thelgy; Tchng.

**YOUNG, DAVID L,** Marshall University, Huntington, WV; JR; BA; Deans Lst 89-; Bapt Ch Lookout Mbr 85-; Ch Photogrphr Video Coord; Food Serv Mgmt; Catering Bus.**

**YOUNG, DEBBIE A,** Newbury Coll, Brookline, MA; FR; AD; Acctg; CPA.

**YOUNG, DEBRA L,** Indiana Univ Of Pa, Indiana, PA; SR; Elem Educ; Tchr.

**YOUNG, DEREK B,** Garrett Comm Coll, Mchenry, MD; SO; BA; Hnrs Lst 89-90; Dean Lst; Bsktbl 89-; AA; Bus Admn; CPA.

**YOUNG, DONNA L,** Wv Univ At Parkersburg, Parkersburg, WV; SO; BED; Phi Theta Kappa 90; Elem Ed.

**YOUNG, ELIZABETH D,** Univ Of Sc At Columbia, Columbia, SC; JR; AA; Hnrs Pgm; Cert York Tech Clg 89; Engl/Ed; Tchg/Ed.

**YOUNG, ELLEN C,** Cooper Union, New York, NY; FR; BS; SWE 90-; CSA 90-; Elec Engr.

**YOUNG III, ERNEST,** Williamsburg Tech Coll, Kingstree, SC; SO; AS; Sci; Engr.

**YOUNG, FELICE,** Univ Of South Al, Mobile, AL; SR; BA; ABENEEFOO Kuo 89-; Mbl Cnty Schl Brd; BS 87; Lang/Spnsh; Intrptr.

**YOUNG, FREDDIE E,** Al A & M Univ, Normal, AL; JR; BS; Food Sci Clb; Scty Pres Schlrs; All Amer Schlrs; Alpha Zeta; Fresh Pres Awd; Deans Lst; Hnr Roll; Chmpnshp Rng Ftbl; Univ MN Intern; Food Sci Tech/Chem.

**YOUNG, GRACE ELOISE,** Univ Of Richmond, Richmond, VA; FR; BA; Sccr; Sprt Sci/German; Athltc Trng.

**YOUNG, GREGORY EARL,** Livingston Univ, Livingston, AL; JR; BS; Phi Beta Sigma Frat; Mu Kappa Chptr Sgt Arms 90; Mbr SGA; Asst IM Dir; Tech Educ.

**YOUNG, HATTIE M,** Alcorn St Univ, Lorman, MS; SR; BSN; Adah Grand Chapt OES 88-; Zion Watch Bapt Ch Sec 90-; Clncl Mgr Hosp 91; ADN 80; Nurs; Nurs Mgmt.

**YOUNG, HEATHER S,** Univ Of Sc At Columbia, Columbia, SC; FR; BA; Marching/Concert Band 90-; Karate Club 90-; Tau Beta Sigma Pres 90-; Thtr/Tv Tech Work.

**YOUNG, IONA J,** Univ Of Nc At Asheville, Asheville, NC; SO; BSN; Chrch Nazarene Dir Wmns Mnstry 90-; Csmtlgy Inst Tchr 87-; Beauty Shop Ownr Stylst 88-; Cncr Ptnts/Fmls 81-; Schlrshp/Csmtlgy Sch Tchrs Cert 86; Tnns; US Air Frc Vet-Medcl Dschrg 79; Nrsng Asst Cert Csmtlgy Instr/Stylst; Nrsng.

**YOUNG III, JACK H,** Tougaloo Coll, Tougaloo, MS; FR; Poltcl Sci Clb 90-; Bsktbl 90-; English/Prelaw.

**YOUNG, JAMES T,** Coker Coll, Hartsville, SC; SR; BA; Lead Accntnt Sc Air Natl Grd 88-; Business; Real Estate/Imprt/Exprt.

**YOUNG, JANEL J,** Cheyney Univ Of Pa, Cheyney, PA; SR; Natl Cncl Negro Women Hist; ARS; Kappa Omicron Nu Pres; Dorm Cncl Pres; JACS Vol; Best Price Clothing; Clothing/Textiles; Fshn Merch Buyer.

**YOUNG, JAY A,** Middle Tn St Univ, Murfreesboro, TN; FR; BA; Pre Law Soc Intrntl Rltns 90; Gamma Beta Phi Hnrs Pgrm 90; Pol Sci,Engl,Hist; Law.

**YOUNG, JAY S,** Marshall University, Huntington, WV; FR; BS; Rugby Clb; HELP Prog; Math; Actuarial Sci.

**YOUNG, JENNIFER A,** Kent St Univ Kent Cmps, Kent, OH; SO; BA; Natl Acctg Assoc 90-; Deans List 90-; Acctg.

**YOUNG, JOAN M,** Lincoln Univ, Lincoln Univ, PA; SR; BS; Alpha Chi 90-; W Grove Free Library Bd Of Trustees; Real Estate Agnt 89-; Engl Educ; Tchr.

**YOUNG, JODI J,** Univ Of Nc At Greensboro, Greensboro, NC; FR; BFA; Costume Studion Asst 90-; Commnty Thtre; Tchncl Thtre.

**YOUNG, KAREN E,** Savannah Coll Of Art & Design, Savannah, GA; FR; Poetry; Sidewalk Arts Fstvl; Sculpture/Furn Dsgn; Fine Arts.

**YOUNG, KAREN RENEE,** Univ Of Sc At Lancaster, Lancaster, SC; JR; BS; AS 90; Bus Mngmnt; Air Traffic Controller.

**YOUNG, KAREN W,** Columbia Greene Comm Coll, Hudson, NY; SO; BS; Dance Club; Deans List 90-; AS Columbia-Greene Cmnty Clge; Art Education; Teacher.

**YOUNG, KATHERINE J,** Erie Comm Coll, Buffalo, NY; FR; DIPL; Mortar Bd; Alpha Gamma Delta; BS Troy St Univ 89; Nrsng; RN.

**YOUNG, KATHRYN D,** Univ Of Fl, Gainesville, FL; FR; Hnr Prgrm 90-; IM Flg Gtbl 90-; Pltcl Sci Rsn; Law.

**YOUNG, KEASHA N,** Fl A & M Univ, Tallahassee, FL; FR; Biol Pre-Med Soc 90-; Math.

**YOUNG, KEITH L,** Alcorn St Univ, Lorman, MS; SR; Phi Beta Lambda Pr 90-; Stdnts In Free Ent 89-; Alpha Kappa Mu 90-; Kappa Alpha Psi 90-; Pr Schlr 89-90; Greek Games 90-; BS; Bus Admin; Govt.

**YOUNG, KELLY ANNE,** Atlantic Comm Coll, Mays Landing, NJ; GD; MPT; Sigma Rho Delta; AAPHERD; NDA; Amercn Aerobic Assoc Cert; BA Glassboro State Clg 87; Physcl Thrpy; PT Hlth/Wellns.

**YOUNG, KELLY K,** Ms St Univ, Miss State, MS; FR; Coll Rpblcns; Rfrmd Univ Flwshp 90; Phi Eta Sigma; Chi Omega 90-; Untd Way Com 90; Phrmcy.

**YOUNG, KIMBERLY A,** Columbus Coll Of Art & Design, Columbus, OH; SO; Schlrshp 90-92; Fine Arts; Dsgn Hallmark Or Disney.

**YOUNG, KIMBERLY L,** Bethany Coll, Bethany, WV; JR; BS; Mc Diarmid Hse Hse Mgr; Vira Heinz Awd; Psych.

**YOUNG, KRISTIN Y,** Univ Of Southern Ms, Hattiesburg, MS; SR; BS; Psych; Occptnl Thrpy.

**YOUNG, LARAIN,** Mount Olive Coll, Mount Olive, NC; SR; BS; Psych Clb Pblcty Ofcr; Engl Soc; Pep Clb; AS; Clncl Psych; Grad Schl E Carolina Univ.

**YOUNG, LASHUN A,** Tougaloo Coll, Tougaloo, MS; FR; Business/Econ; Business Law.

**YOUNG, LAURIE S,** Birmingham Southern Coll, Birmingham, AL; SO; BS; Ornttn Stff; SGA Fr 90; Advsry Com 89; Alpha Phi Omega Pres 89-; Comp Sci; Sftwre Eng.

**YOUNG, LEA M,** Univ Of Southern Ms, Hattiesburg, MS; FR; BA; Staff Writer Nwspr; Gamma Beta Phi; Journalism; Enterinment Public Relations.

**YOUNG III, LESLIE K,** Univ Of Pittsburgh, Pittsburgh, PA; JR; BSME; Pi Tau Sigma; Coop Pratt Whitney CT; Mech Eng.

**YOUNG, LETTENIA M,** Piedmont Tech Coll, Greenwood, SC; SO; ASSOC; Phi Theta Kappa 90-; Acdmc Achvmnt Scty 90-; Legal Sec; Law.

**YOUNG, LINELLE C,** Fl A & M Univ, Tallahassee, FL; FR; BED; Gospel Choir 90; Ele Educ; Tch.

**YOUNG, LISA M,** Medical Coll Of Ga, Augusta, GA; GD; DMD; Dental.

**YOUNG, LISA M,** Al St Univ, Montgomery, AL; FR; BA; Acctg.

**YOUNG, MARK D,** Indiana Univ Of Pa, Indiana, PA; SR; NSA Pgrm 88-89; Phi Kappa Psi Sgt At Arms 89; IM; BS In Educ; Elem Educ; Tchr.

**YOUNG, MARYLOU,** Castleton St Coll, Castleton, VT; SR; BSN; Cncr Scty Brd Sec 83-; Nrsng.

**YOUNG, MASON P,** Univ Of Sc At Columbia, Columbia, SC; JR; BA; Palmetto Mmstrs Sngrs 90; SC Phlhrmnc Chorus 90-; USC Deans Lst 88-90; Fst Prsbtrn Choir; Co-Op Pgm 88; SC Educ Radio Spltto Fstvl Intrnshp 88; St Johns Epscpl Choir Sctn Ldr 90-; TV Prdctn Music; BMA 89; Music Vcl Prfrmnc; Prfrm Prfsnly Chrch/Opr Hs.

**YOUNG, MATTHEW W,** Indiana Univ Of Pa, Indiana, PA; FR; BS; Assist Lttl League Coach; US Army 86-90; Blgy Ed.

**YOUNG, MEL-CHRISTOPHER L,** Morehouse Coll, Atlanta, GA; FR; BA; Morehouse Bus Assc 90-; Morehouse Pre Law Scty 90-; Atlanta Univ Ctr Drama Clb 90-; Natl Urban Lge Essex Cty 89-90; City Natl Bank NJ Inter 90-; Morehouse Coll Acad Schlrshp; Econ/English; Law/Educationn.

**YOUNG, MELANIE J,** Indiana Univ Of Pa, Indiana, PA; JR; BA; PSEA/NEA 89-; Kappa Delta Pi 90-; Provost Schlr 90-; Educ; Elem Tchr.

**YOUNG, MELINDA E,** Union Univ, Jackson, TN; SR; BS; Stdnt Fndtn Rcrtrs 89-; Acctg Clb Sec 89-; Alpha Chi 89-; Chi Omega Treas 88-; Adtng Intrnshp 90; Acctg; CPA.

**YOUNG, MELISSA J,** Ashland Comm Coll, Ashland, KY; SO; Materials Sci/Engnrng.

**YOUNG, MICHAEL D,** Ms Gulf Coast Comm Coll, Perkinston, MS; SO; Vrsty Intrn; Clss Beau 90-; Bsbl 89-; AS; Bnkg/Fin/Law; Crprte Law.

**YOUNG, MICHAEL T,** Wv Univ, Morgantown, WV; SR; BS; Pharmacy.

**YOUNG, MICHELLE C,** Western Ky Univ, Bowling Green, KY; SO; BA; Assoc Res Assts 90-; Natl Org For Women; Res Hall Assoc; Phi Eta Sigma 89-90; Pres Schlr 89-; IM Flag Ftbl Sftbl 90-; Eng/Brdcstng; Brdsct Jrnlsm.

**YOUNG, NATASHA M,** Central St Univ, Wilberforce, OH; SO; BA; Cmnctns Clb S; Ntl Coll Blck Caucus 89-; NAACP 89-; Radio Ancr WCSU Radio 90-; IM Sftbl 90-; Cmnctns Radio/TV; Tchr/Indpndnt Flmmkr.

**YOUNG, PATRICIA A,** Hillsborough Comm Coll, Tampa, FL; SO; AA; Clg Brd Tlnt Rstr Otstndng Mnrty Comm Clg Grads 90-; Lib Arts; Educ.

**YOUNG, PATRICIA J,** Union Univ, Jackson, TN; JR; BS; Psychlgy/Sclgy Clb Pres 89-; Rutledge Hon Hstry Clb VP; SGA Sntr 89-; Prexy Clb 89-; Asst Co-Ord Natl Hstry Day 90-; Asst Co-Ord Hstry Cntst 90-; Psychlgy; Coll Prfssr/Clnc Cnslr.

**YOUNG, RALPH C,** Western Piedmont Comm Coll, Morganton, NC; SO; AA SC; Phi Theta Kappa; Drftng & Dsgn.

**YOUNG, RASHAUN JAMAL,** Alcorn St Univ, Lorman, MS; FR; MBA; Eng.

**YOUNG, RENEE G,** Univ Of Md At Eastern Shore, Princess Anne, MD; JR; BS; Jr Cls VP 90-; Cmps Pls Orgnztn Sec 89-; Pnhlnc Cncl Pan Rep 90-; Alpha Kappa Alpha Mmbrshp Chrprsn 89-90; Alpha Kappa Alpha Mmbrshp Chrprsn 89-90; Holy Cntr Intrnshp Tchrs Asst; Mst Otstndng Stdnt Schlrshp 88-89; Rhbltn Srvcs; Occptnl Thrpy.

**YOUNG, ROBERT,** Western Piedmont Comm Coll, Morganton, NC; SO; BA; Cooperative Educ; Bus Admin; Bus.

**YOUNG, ROLAND M,** Univ Of Tn At Martin, Martin, TN; JR; BA; Hons Semnr Schlrshp; Dns Lst; Acctg.

**YOUNG, SANDI L,** Anne Arundel Comm Coll, Arnold, MD; SO; AA; Sccr Sftbl; Gnrl; Info Systms.

**YOUNG, SANDRA KAY,** Oh St Univ At Marion, Marion, OH; SR; B EDU; Marion Educ Socty 90-; Ohio Educ Assn 87-; Natl Educ Assn 87-; Evelyn B Walter Schlrshp 88-89; Assoc Arts 90; Math; Tchg.

**YOUNG, SARAH L,** Univ Of Southern Ms, Hattiesburg, MS; SR; SEA 89-; Deans Lst-USM 87-; Pres Lst-USM 88-; BS Prjct Wld Cert Envrmntl-Tchng Cert 91; Elem Ed; Tchng.

**YOUNG, SHAVONNIE D,** Al A & M Univ, Normal, AL; SO; Bus Admn; Bus Ex.

**YOUNG, SHAWN D,** Univ Of Tn At Martin, Martin, TN; SO; BS; Kappa Alpha Ordr Pldg VP 90-; Ldrs Rsdnc Schlrshp 90-; IM Ftbl 90; Pblc Admnstrtn; Fdrl Law Enfrcmnt.

**YOUNG, STACEY J,** Salisbury St Univ, Salisbury, MD; SR.

**YOUNG, TERENCE S,** Morehouse Coll, Atlanta, GA; JR; BS; Hnrs Prgm Clb Treas 88-; Chmstry Clb VP 90-; SNMA Treas 88-; Gldn Key 90-; Univ Pittsburgh Rsrch 90-; Chmstry; Med.

**YOUNG, TERRI K,** Gaston Coll, Dallas, NC; SO; AAS; Gamma Beta Phi 90-; Bus Admn.

**YOUNG, THOMAS J,** Merrimack Coll, North Andover, MA; JR; BA; Sclgy Clb Pres; Amer Birding Assoc 88-; Natl Audubon Soc 86-; Sclgy; Prfsr Sclgy.

**YOUNG JR, THOMAS R,** Univ Of Sc At Columbia, Columbia, SC; SO; BA; Stdnt Govt Sen Chf Stf 89-; Clg Repbl 89-; Assoc Hon Stdnts Cls Rep 89-; Ord Omega; Sigma Iota Rho; Kappa Sigma Rsh Alumni Rel Chrmn 89-; St Sen Page John Courson 90-; US Sen Intrn Strom Thurmond 90; Campbell Gov Chr 90; Pol Sci/Engl; Law.

**YOUNG, TOBIE C,** Central St Univ, Wilberforce, OH; FR.

**YOUNG, TONI E,** Univ Of Rochester, Rochester, NY; SO; BA; SAB 90-; Deans Lst 89-; Delta Gamma Fndtn Asst 90-; Frnds Strong; Ganser Flwshp Meriter Hosp; Vrsty Sccr Vrsty Tnns 89-; Psychlgy Hlth/Soc.

**YOUNG, TRICIA A,** Univ Of Cincinnati, Cincinnati, OH; FR; BS; Coll Single Grp 90-; Hnrs Pgrm 90-; Elem Educ.

**YOUNG JR, WILLIAM SCOTT,** Univ Of Ky, Lexington, KY; JR; BA; Gldn Ky; Coll Schlrs Of Amer; Psych Hstry; Law.**

**YOUNGBERG, MELISSA C,** Univ Of Sc At Columbia, Columbia, SC; GD; DIPL; Educ Clb 89-; Pres Hon Rl 89-; Chncllrs Hon Rl 89-; Deans Hon Lst 82-83; BA MI State Univ 83; Educ; Tchr.

**YOUNGBLOOD, ANGELA M,** Tallahassee Comm Coll, Tallahassee, FL; SO; AA; Trstees Schlrshp 90-; Nrsng Mdwfry.

**YOUNGBLOOD, ESTHER M,** Univ Of Pittsburgh, Pittsburgh, PA; SR; MSW; Fcs Rnwl Comm Org Tutor 87-; OH Vly Gnrl Hosp Vol 84-; Escmb Cty Epsly Fdn 76-78; KC 76-78; Acad Schlp 88-89; Dns Lst; Magna Cum Laude; FOR Lit Tutor 87-; BASW; Social Work; Family Prct.**

**YOUNGBLOOD, JUDITH A,** Va Commonwealth Univ, Richmond, VA; SR; BS; Beta Sigma Phi 61-64; Art Cntst 65; Intrnshp; Bsktbl 65; Intl Flk Dnc Clb; Sprs/Prs Sqr Dnc Clb 85-; Med Sec 6364-; Meditechnlgst 67-; Med Sec Cert RPI 64; BSMT 67; Cert Bbl/Mssns Col Grad Schl Bbl/Mssns 79; The Nightingales Mcv-91; Nursing.

**YOUNGBLOOD, KEILA R,** Univ Of West Fl, Pensacola, FL; SR; BA; Alpha Sigma Lambda 90; Dns Hnr Rl 90-; Intrnshp Hdm Elec; Cum Laude; AA Pensacola Jr Coll 89; Elem Educ; Tchr.

**YOUNGBLOOD, KIMBERLY C,** Tn Temple Univ, Chattanooga, TN; GD; Zeta Tau Rho Pres 90-; Alpha Epsilon Theta; Dns Lst 88-; Primaries Christ Div Dir 88-90; BS; Elem Ed; MA Elem Ed.

**YOUNGBLOOD, MARGARET W,** Univ Of Fl, Gainesville, FL; GD; BSN; Amer Cancer Soc 88-; Roberta Pierce Scoffiedl Undergrad Schlrshp 90; FL Nurses Assn; Oncology Nrsng Soc 77-Pres 89-90; ASN FLA Jr Clg 73; AA Santa Fe Comm Clg 79; Oncology Nrsng.

**YOUNGBLOOD, SUE M,** Univ Of Sc At Columbia, Columbia, SC; SR; BA; Carolina Bnd Flag Corps Bnd Cncl Rep 87; Salsa Dnce Grp; Philharmonic Choir 89; Gamma Beta Phi 88; Phi Eta Sigma 88; Engl; Tchng.

**YOUNGBLOOD, SUSAN B,** Hillsborough Comm Coll, Tampa, FL; GD; BS; Rdlgy Clb; Rdlgy Srvc Awd; AA MCC 69; AS; Sci.

**YOUNGER, BARBARA J,** Salisbury St Univ, Salisbury, MD; SR; BSW; Soc Work Clb Pres 89-; Pi Gamma Mu 90-; Phi Alpha; Omicron Delta Kappa; Natl Assn Soc Wrkrs 90-; Soc Work; Clncl Cnslng.

**YOUNGER, REBECCA A,** Ms Univ For Women, Columbus, MS; JR; BA; Bench/Gavel 90-; Clg Rpblcns 88-89; Modeling Sqd 90-; Nu Epsilon Delta Treas 90-; Schlrshp Pageant; MUW Alumni Schlrshp 90-; Paralegal Studies/Pre Law; Law.

**YOUNGHANCE, STEVEN L,** Brewer St Jr Coll, Fayette, AL; SO; BS; Singers 89-; AS; Wldlf Mgmt; Biologist.

**YOUNGKIN, STEVEN K,** Kent St Univ Kent Cmps, Kent, OH; SR; BBA; Phi Alpha Delta 89-; Acctg Assn 89-; Coll Bwl 87-; Alpha Lambda Delta 88-; Goldn Key 90-; Jr Achvmnt Advsr 87-88; Acctg; Law.

**YOUNGPETERS, CHRISTINE M,** Univ Of Cincinnati, Cincinnati, OH; JR; BS; Nrsng; RN.

**YOUNGS, KELLY JEANNE,** Russell Sage Coll At Troy, Troy, NY; JR; BA; Flr VP 90; Res Asst 90-; Tutor; Amer Nrsg Assoc 90-; Nursing/Spanish Club VP 89-; Career Coach Mentor 90-; Deans List; Sftbl/Vlybl/Swmmng 89-; Nursing/Spanish; Neonatal ICU.**

**YOUNGS, TRACI L,** Watterson Coll, Louisville, KY; SO; Paralegal.

**YOUNKER, SUSAN R,** Central Pa Bus School, Summerdale, PA; SR; Travel Clb Pub 89-90; Anstos Xenia Tourisms; Travel/Tourism.

**YOUNKERS, STACY L,** Salisbury St Univ, Salisbury, MD; JR; BA; IM Flrhckcy Vlybl Wtrpolo; Cmmnctn Arts Mjr Engl Mnr; Tv Prdctn Edtng.

**YOUNT, AMY S,** Univ Of Ga, Athens, GA; JR; BFCS; Grg Grl 89-90; Jrnlsm Intern; Home Econ; Jrnlsm.

**YOUNT, JERRY W,** Ky St Univ, Frankfort, KY; SO; BA; Bsbl; Pro Bsbl; BA; Law.

**YOUNT, RAYMOND LAWRENCE,** Univ Of Montevallo, Montevallo, AL; SR; BS; Spch And Hrng Assn Of AL; Natl Stdnt Spch And Hrng Assn; Natl Hrng Aid Scty; AL Hrng Aid Dlr Assn; Cvtn Clb; Bltne Of Albrtvlle Ownr 89-; Spch Pthlgy Adlgy; Bltne Hrng Cntrs.

**YOUNT, WENDY A,** Appalachian St Univ, Boone, NC; FR; BA; NCAE 90-; Gamma Beta Phi; Phi Eta Sigma; Reich Clg Ed Hon Stdnt; Mud Vlybl; IM Vlybl/Bsktbl/Sftbl 90-; Math; Ed.

**YOURTCHI, MARYIA S,** Tallahassee Comm Coll, Tallahassee, FL; JR; BS; Out St Tuition Wvr 90-; Food Ntrtn Sci.

**YOUSTIC, KATHRYN S,** Duquesne Univ, Pittsburgh, PA; FR; BA; Hl Assoc; Radio Rcrd Lib DJ; Stdnt Aid Typst; Phi Eta Sigma; Lambda Sigma; Bnk Intrn Stdnt Trn; Internatl Bsn; Internatl Bsn Law.

**YOUTZ, JENNIFER L,** Denison Univ, Granville, OH; FR; Ad Rpe The Denisonian 90-; Nwscstr 90-; Soph Hon Soc; Hons Prog 90-; Cmnty Assoc 90-; French/Cmnctns.

**YOW, ARTHUR VAUGHN,** Memphis St Univ, Memphis, TN; SR; BA; Bus; Mgmt/Prsnnl.

**YOX, MARK D,** Univ Of Miami, Coral Gables, FL; SR; BSC; Golden Key 89-; Provost Hon Roll 89-90; Deans Lst 88-90; Video/Film/Psychlgy; Cmptr Info Sys.

**YSASAGA, ROSA MARIA MATA,** Defiance Coll, Defiance, OH; JR; BA; Defiance Cnty Bd Am Cancer Soc Bd Mem 88-; Dale Carnegie Course 89; Phi Theta Kappa Alumni 89-; Frozen Spclties Inc Acctnt; Defiance Hosp Inc Data Process Op; Cert Acct Asst NW Tech Coll 89; Acctg/Bus Admin/Data Process; Sr Acctnt.

**YU, ANN MARIE,** Colgate Univ, Hamilton, NY; JR; BA; Var Vlybl Team 88-90; Big Bros Big Sis Prog 88-90; Teaching Asstnt Orgn Chem Lab; Deans List; Beta Beta Beta; Lambda Alpha; Anthropology; OCSA; Kappa Kappa Gamma; Asst Pan Helenic Delg 89-; Sociology/Anthropology; Medicine.**

**YU, BIK-NOR,** City Univ Of Ny Baruch Coll, New York, NY; JR; BBA; Deans Lst 89-90; Baruch Endwmnt Fnd Prvsts Schlrshp 90; Accntncy; CPA.

**YU, BOLING,** City Univ Of Ny Baruch Coll, New York, NY; JR; Hong Kong Stdnt Assn VP 89-; Untd Coll Stdnt Assn 88-; Badminton Clb 89-; Gldn Ky 90-; Stat.

**YU, BONNIE B,** Ny Univ, New York, NY; GD; DDS; Dnstry.

**YU, CHUNG-YING S,** Univ Of Sc At Columbia, Columbia, SC; SO; BS; Intl Stdnt Assn-Hong Kong Stdnt Assn Treas 90-; Mgmt Sci Mgmt; Comp Info.**

**YU, ELISABETH H,** Univ Of Rochester, Rochester, NY; FR; BA; Korean Amer Stdnt Assc Sec; Chrstn Flwshp 90-; Korean Chrstn Flwshp 90-; Psychlgy/Bio; Medcn.

**YU, JAE H,** S U N Y At Buffalo, Buffalo, NY; JR; BS; Tau Eta Pi; Eta Kappa Nu; Prsbytrn Chrch Trea; IM Vllybl Co Capt 90-; Elect/Mech Eng; Eng/Tch.

**YU, JAIME P,** City Univ Of Ny Queensbrough, New York, NY; SO; AAS; B Arch Univ Santo Tomas Philippines 85; Dsgn Drftng Cmptr Grphcs; Archtctr.

**YU, JIHWAN,** Georgetown Univ, Washington, DC; FR.

**YU, NICHOLAS K,** Univ Of Sc At Columbia, Columbia, SC; JR; BS; Hong Kong Stdnt Assoc Sec 90-; Inst Of Electrical & Electronic Engrs 90-; Tau Beta Pi; Eta Kappa Nu 90-; Golden Key; Phi Beta Kappa; Gamma Beta Phi 90-; Phi Eta Sigma 89-; Electrical & Computer Engrng.

**YU, STEPHEN,** City Univ Of Ny Baruch Coll, New York, NY; SO; BBA; Acctg; CPA.

**YU, YU-PING,** Lasell Coll, Newton, MA; SO; BS; Intnl Clb 90-; Travel Clb 90-; Deans Lst 90-; Alumnae Assoc Phonathon 90-; AS; Hotel Travel/Tourism Adm.

**YUAN, PHILIP S,** Cornell Univ Statutory College, Ithaca, NY; SO; BS; Dorm Cncl 89-90; Chinese Stdnt Assoc 90-; Biochemistry; Medicine.

**YUE, MAN W,** Cooper Union, New York, NY; SO; BE; Full Tuition Schlrshp 90-; Elec Engr.

**YUEN, CHING M,** City Univ Of Ny Baruch Coll, New York, NY; SO; BA; Piano Rctl 89-; Aide Admssns Ofc Baruch 89-90; Bus; Hmn Rsrcs Mngmt.

**YUEN, MINDY M,** City Univ Of Ny Baruch Coll, New York, NY; JR; BBA; Golden Key 90; Mrktng; Mrktng Mngmnt.

**YUEN, PATTY,** City Univ Of Ny Baruch Coll, New York, NY; JR; BBA; Dlrs Sns Grphc Artst Lyt Stf 90-; Dns Lst 90-; Internatl Mktg.

**YUILL, MICHAEL J,** Western New England Coll, Springfield, MA; SR; BA; Cmptr Sci.

**YUN, JUNG HAN,** Univ Of Sc At Columbia, Columbia, SC; FR; BS; Baptst Std Union Publcty Off; Korean Asssc 90-; Korean Scintsts Engnrs Assc 90-; Comp Sci; Comp Prgrmmng.

**YUND, JOHN J,** Niagara Univ, Niagara Univ, NY; JR; BA; Kappa Mu Epsilon; Math; Actrl Sci.

**YUNG, CAMMY W K,** City Univ Of Ny Baruch Coll, New York, NY; JR; Gldn Key 90-; Acctg.

**YUNG, CHI KWOK,** Marshall University, Huntington, WV; JR; BBA; Intrntl Stdnts Assn 88-; Bus; Bus Mngmnt/Infor Sys.

**YUNG, HEIDI P,** City Univ Of Ny Baruch Coll, New York, NY; GD; MBA; Beta Gamma Sigma 90-; Gldn Ky 90-; BBA 90; Acct; CPA.

**YUNG, NITA,** Bunker Hill Comm Coll, Boston, MA; SR.

**YURECKA, KAREN C,** Univ Of Fl, Gainesville, FL; JR; BA; Amer Mrktng Assoc; Golden Key 90; Alpha Lambda Delta; Phi Eta Sigma; Chi Omega 89; Rtl Intrnshp The Gap; Tchng Assist-Excptnl People 90; Im Sprts 88; AA 89; Mrktng.

**YURESCKO, MICHAEL J,** Penn Coll Of Straight Chiro, Horsham, PA; GD; DC; Stu Govt Acdmc Cmmtt 90; Stu Book Str 90-; Temple Univ Nrsng Hnrs Soc VP 83-; FSCO 90-; Garden St Chrprctc Soc 90-; Dean Lst 90; Pres Lst 90-; RN Onclgy 83; Onclgy Nrsng Soc; Prsh Lay Cncl; Boy Scts; KC; BA Temple Univ 81; BS 83; Chrprctc; Dr Chrprctc.

**YURGANS JR, CHARLES W,** Schenectady County Comm Coll, Schenectady, NY; FR; AS; Jzz Ens; Wnd Ens; Brss Ens; Chrs; Plka Bnd; AS AAS Construction Tech; Prfrmng Arts Msc.

**YURGANS, GARY E,** Schenectady County Comm Coll, Schenectady, NY; SO; AS; Jzz Ens; Wnd Ens; Brss Ens; Chrs; Plka Bnd; 1st Yr Msc Achvmnt Awrd; AS; Prfrmng Arts Msc.

**YURKOVICH, CRAIG S,** West Liberty St Coll, West Liberty, WV; SR; BS; WVIAC Schlr Athltc Awd 90-; All Conf Ftbl 90; Acad All Amer Cptn 90; Sci Exercise/Bio; Physiology.

**YUROCHKO JR, DENNIS P,** Duquesne Univ, Pittsburgh, PA; JR; BS; Dns Advsry Comm; Admissions 88-89; Delta Sigma Pi Pres 90-; IM Ftbl 90; Acctg.

**YUSCAVAGE, MICHELE C,** Embry Riddle Aeronautical Univ, Daytona Beach, FL; SO; BA; Deans Lst; Aerntcl Studies/Mgmt; Avtn Mgmt/Flght.

**YUSKO, AMY M,** Univ Of Pittsburgh, Pittsburgh, PA; SO; BA; NSNA; Nursing; Admin.

**YUSOF, AMERUDDIN,** Widener Univ, Chester, PA; JR; BSC; Intl Stdnt Clb 90-; Natl Coll Acad Awd USA 90; Dns Lst 90-; AAD Indiana Univ Bloomington 88-90; Elec Engr.

**YUSUF, FAROOQ,** Va Commonwealth Univ, Richmond, VA; FR; BS; Pakistani Stdnt Assoc V Pres 90-; Biology; Medicine.

**YUTZY, LAURA M,** Univ Of Akron, Akron, OH; SR; BS; The Univ Sngrs 87-89; Gldn Key 89-; Phi Alpha Theta 89-; Kappa Deltapi 90-; Elem Ed; Tchr.

# Z

**ZAAL, ELGIN R,** Fayetteville St Univ, Fayetteville, NC; JR; Bsktbl; Bsns Adm/Mgmt.

**ZAATAR, WISSAM M,** Univ Of Nc At Asheville, Asheville, NC; JR; BA; Intrntnl Orgnztn Tres 89; Gnrl Un Palestinian Stdnts VP; Moslem Assn Sec; Dstngshd Lst 87-88; Elctrcl Engnrng; Engnrng.**

**ZABOHONSKI, SUSAN MARIE,** Univ Of Ct, Storrs, CT; SO; BS; Orientation Grp Ldr 90-; Pathobio; Vet Med.

**ZACCAGNINI, ROBERT M,** Saint Vincents Coll & Seminary, Latrobe, PA; SR; BS; Orientation Comm 88-; Fire Dept 88-; Biology Nwsltr Co Ed 88-; Phi Alpha Theta; All Amer Academic; IM Vlybl Co Capt 89-; Biology/Pre Med; Allopathic Med Schl.

**ZACHARIAS, ANDREA M,** Castleton St Coll, Castleton, VT; JR; BS; Stdnt Educ Assn 90-; Wmsn Vars 90-; Biathlon Clb 89-; Assist Vars Tennis Coach; Tennis 90-; Elem Educ/Reading; Tchr.

**ZACHARY, CHRISTINA LYNN,** Atlantic Comm Coll, Mays Landing, NJ; SO; Vrsty Clb; Emrgncy Med Tech; Chrldng Capt; EMT State Of NJ; CPR Amrcn Red Crss 90; Trama Nrs; Nrs EMT.

**ZACHARY, DAVE J,** Elizabethtown Coll, Elizabethtown, PA; FR; BA; Math Clb 90-; IM Vlybl 90-; Math/Comp Sci; Actuarial Sci.

**ZACHARY, DEREK W,** Univ Of Ky, Lexington, KY; SR; HPER Clb Chrmn 89-; Trck/Fld Tm Mngr 89-90; AA Maysville Comm Coll 88; Physcl/Hlth Educ; Educ Athltcs.

**ZACHARY, VIRGINIA C,** Middle Tn St Univ, Murfreesboro, TN; JR; BS; Stdnt Hm Ec Assn 89-; Amer Hm Ecnmcs Assn; Kappa Omicron Nu 90-; Albert L/Ethel Carver Smith Schlrshp; Kappa Omicron Nu Hon Soc Schlrshp; Ntrtn/Food Sci; Rgstrd Diettn.**

**ZACHER, KEVIN J,** Univ Of Rochester, Rochester, NY; SO; BS; Outside Spkrs Club 89-90; Clg Repblcns 89-90; Soc Mech Engrs 90-; Phi Kappa Tau Frat Athltc Chrmn 90-; Im Sports; Mech Engrng.

**ZACHMAN, DONNA M,** Broward Comm Coll, Ft Lauderdale, FL; FR; AS; Phi Theta Kappa 90-; Med; Physcl Thrpst Asst.

**ZACHMEIER, CAPT BRYAN K,** Air Force Inst Of Tech, Wrt-Ptrsn Afb, OH; GD; MS; Sigma Iota Epsilon; Sigma Alpha Epsilon 78-82; Socty Amer Mil Engrs 83-; Offcer USAF 82-; BS ND State Univ 82; Engr Mgmt; Offcr USAF.

**ZACHRICH, MARY D,** Defiance Coll, Defiance, OH; JR; BS; Tau Pi Phi Prgrm Chrmn; Defiance Hosp Auxiliary YMCA Defiance Clg Wmns Commission; Bsn Mngmnt.

**ZACHWIEJA, SHERRY M,** Marshall University, Huntington, WV; SR; BED; Natl AA Edctn Assoc 90-; Sigma Sigma Sigma Pldg Clss Pres Slt Chrmn 88-89; Rubby Page Memorial 88-; Art Ed; Art Thrpy.

**ZACKS, MICHELLE H,** Univ Of Nc At Asheville, Asheville, NC; SR; BA; Womens Studies Task Force Stdnt Mbr 89-; Womens Resource Ctr Co Founder 90; Arts Magazine Editor 90; Deans Lst 87-; Natl Hnr Scty 87-; All Amer Schlrs 90-; Gullickson Awrd 90; Carl Sandburg Prz Poetry Hnrbl Mention 88; Literature; Sea Turtle Conservation.

**ZACZKIEWICZ, MARION S,** Anne Arundel Comm Coll, Arnold, MD; FR; BA; Sec Educ Geog; Tch.

**ZAETZ, NISSAN M,** Comm Coll Algny Co Algny Cmps, Pittsburgh, PA; SO; Lubavitch Cen; Rabbi/Tchr/Funr Raiser/Yth Dir; Rabbincal Ordtn Rabbinical Colg/Canada Montreal 70; Acctng.

**ZAGARELL, MICHAEL,** City Univ Of Ny Lehman Coll, Bronx, NY; SR; BA; Gldn Key; Pi Sigma Alpha; Belle Zeller Awd-Kibee Schlr; Pres Schlrs Awd; Fndtn Schlrs Awd; Nwspr Edtr/Pblshr; Pltcl Sci; Tchng/Acdmc Rsrch.

**ZAGARELLA, DANIELLE,** D Youville Coll, Buffalo, NY; SR; BA; Philosphy; Law.

**ZAGARELLA, JOSEPH R,** Newbury Coll, Brookline, MA; JR; BA; Auctnrs Lic State N H Lic; Dns Lst Parlgl 90-; Amer Soc Hm Insp 86-; Natl Assn Home Bldrs 86-; Serv V P Insp V P 82-84; USA Corp; Pres Insp USA Corp; Ftbl; Wrstng; Trck; Wrstlng Co Cap 70-74; Appt Mayor Haverhl Constbl 89-90; Arch Eng; Law.

**ZAGLIN, SUSAN ALANNA,** Winthrop Coll, Rock Hill, SC; SO; BA; History Club 89-90; Dance Theatre 89-; Alpha Lambda Delta 89-90; Phi Alpha Theta 90-; Winthrop Coalition For Homeless Treas 89-; Deans List 89-; History; Archaeology.

**ZAGORSKI, KRISTEN M,** Lesley Coll, Cambridge, MA; JR; BS; England Exchange Program; Dns Lst 88-; Erly Chldhood Educ; Tchr.

**ZAGROBELNY, DIANE C,** Univ Of Miami, Coral Gables, FL; SR; BBA; Pres 100 87-; Hmcmg Exec Comm Ball Chr 90; Carni Gras Exec Comm Alum Chr; Mortor Brd 89-; Sigma Alpha Epsilon Ltl Sistr 87-; Muscular Dystrphy Assn; Stdnts Agnst Mltpl Sclerosis 87-; Chldrns Hm Soc 88-; Stdy Abrd Intrnshp 90; Human Res Mgmt; Hotel Admin.

**ZAGURSKIE, DONALD K,** Oh Northern Univ, Ada, OH; GD; Street Law Tchr 89-90; Ngtns 89-90; Phi Delta Phi 88-; Dns Awd Schlp 88-; Dns Lst; Buol Awd 90; Amer Jsprdnc Awd 88; BA Wynsbrg Clg 87; JD; Law.

**ZAGURSKY, MEREDITH CHRISTINE,** Christopher Newport Coll, Newport News, VA; JR; BA; Engl; Ed.

**ZAHED, CAMERON,** Oh Wesleyan Univ, Delaware, OH; SR; BA; Ice Hockey Chess Golf; ACM; Microbiology Board; Cum Laude NASDF; Michael Reese Medl Research; Anesthesia Research Chgo; Computer Sci Zoology; Medl Schl.

**ZAHIRUDDIN, MOIZ A,** Colgate Univ, Hamilton, NY; FR; BA; Philosophy/Rlgn Clb Pub Cmtee Ch 90-; Islamic Stdes Assn 90-; Chamberlain Soc 90-; Phi Eta Sigma 90-; Houston Read Cmsn Vol; Open Door Msn Hmls Vol; Rltcl Sci; Law.

**ZAHORCHAK, SCOTT M,** Kent St Univ Kent Cmps, Kent, OH; SO; BA; Cyclng Clb 89; IMS 89-90; Delta Sigma Pi Schlrshp; Bowmn Cup Rce 90; Bsns; Fin.

**ZAIDENWEBER, TAMARA D,** Univ Of Nc At Greensboro, Greensboro, NC; SR; BS; Dns Lst; Fd/Nutr; Fd Svc Mgmt.

**ZAIDI, SHOAIB H,** Univ Of Rochester, Rochester, NY; SR; MS; SGA Rep 86; Alpha Kappa Psi; Kappa Phi Sigma VP 87-88; BA Coll Wooster OH 89; BS 90; Elec Eng.

**ZAIGER, ADAM M,** Franklin And Marshall Coll, Lancaster, PA; SO; BA; Clg Entrtnmnt Comm Tech Dir 90-; Delta Sigma Phi 89-; Govt; Law.

**ZAINO, STACEY L,** Bunker Hill Comm Coll, Boston, MA; FR; Acctng; CPA.

**ZAJCHOWSKI, NANCY G,** Western New England Coll, Springfield, MA; SR; Delta Mu Delta 90; Summa Cum Laude; Cmpnstn Admn 71-; BSBA; Bus; Hmn Rsrcs.

**ZAK, SUZANNE M,** Philadelphia Coll Of Bible, Langhorne, PA; SR; BED; Chrl Treas 88-; All Clge Soc Clb 88; Chrch Orgnst 89-; Chrch Msc Comm 89-; Dns Lst 89-90; Msc Schlrshp 87-; Crs Cntry 88-89; Msc/Bible; Pn/Orgn/Vc.**

**ZAKAS, ILONA E,** Glassboro St Coll, Glassboro, NJ; SO; BA; Radio TV Assc; Wmn In Cmmnctns 90-; Res Assc Sec To VP 90-; Dean Lst; NJ Pirg 90; Cmmnctns Radio/TV/FILM; Dir Prod.

**ZAKES, DEANNA L,** Radford Univ, Radford, VA; SO; BS; Cmps Judcl Bd 90-; Lit Mag Edtr 89-; Alpha Sigma Tau 90-; Crim Just; Law.

**ZAKHARIA, YARA,** Univ Of Miami, Coral Gables, FL; SO; BS; Italian Clb 90-; Alpha Lambda Delta; Phi Eta Sigma; Pres Lst 90-; Provosts Lst 90-; Eng/Pblc Rltns; Paralegal/Pblc Rltns.

**ZALEWSKI, KRISTINE L,** Univ Of Sc At Coastal Carolina, Conway, SC; JR; BS; Psyclgy Club VP 89-90; Psychologyf Counseling Psy.

**ZALEWSKI, PATRICIA M,** Oh Univ, Athens, OH; JR; BFA; The Movement 90-; Ind Univ Dance Theater Stge Mgr 89-90; Golden Key Clb 91-; Alpha Lambda Delta 89-; Phi Eta Sigma 89-; Talent Schlrshp 90-; Ctzn Schlrshp 88-89; Asstshp Athens Factory St Studio Fculty 90-; Dance; Dance Educ.

**ZALFAS, CHERI R,** Univ Of South Al, Mobile, AL; SR; BED; SGA 88-89; Share Tm 89-90; Phi Mu 89-; Elem Ed; Tch.

**ZALLNICK, JOHN E,** Le Moyne Coll, Syracuse, NY; JR; BA; Im Soccor 90; Im Sftbl NE Univ Co-Cptn 89-90; Biology; Med MD.

**ZALOGA, GAIL P,** Schenectady County Comm Coll, Schenectady, NY; FR; Tvrn Ownrs Assn; Vet WW II; Rstrntr 72-; Fnrl Hms Csmtlgst 72-; Cert Royal Barber/Beauty Schl 72; Psychlgy/Bus Law.

**ZAMAN, MD AHASAMUZ,** Oh Univ, Athens, OH; SO; Engr.

**ZAMAN, NIKHAT,** Univ Of Central Fl, Orlando, FL; FR; MYNA 90-; MSA 90-; Islnc Soc; Mlclr Bio; Med.

**ZAMANIAN, AMIR,** Univ Of Pittsburgh, Pittsburgh, PA; SR; BA; Stdnt Govt Brd 90; Chi Epislon Treas 90; Amrcn Scty Cvl Eng 90; Deptcptl Prjcts IntrnAS 88; BA; Cvl Eng.

**ZAMBETTI, ANDREW R,** Southern Coll Of Tech, Marietta, GA; GD; BA Vndrblt Univ 88; Elctrcl Eng.

**ZAMBRANA, ELIVETTE,** Univ Of Pr At Rio Piedras, Rio Piedras, PR; JR; BA; Pre-Med Stdnts Assoc 88-; Beta Beta 89-; Golden Key 90-; Hnr Rl 90-; Bio; Med.

**ZAMBROWICZ, KEVIN A,** Catholic Univ Of America, Washington, DC; JR; BA; Truman Schlr; Phi Eta Sigma; Phi Sigma Tau; Philosphy; Law.**

**ZAMMARELLI, CHRISTOPHER M,** Roger Williams Coll Bristol, Bristol, RI; FR; Cmpus Radio Sta Pub Rltns Dir 90; Cmunctns; Syndicated Clumnst.

**ZAMMAS, TIMOTHY G,** Fl St Univ, Tallahassee, FL; GD; BS; FL Pblc Intrst Rsrch Grp Org Cmmtt 88-90; Schl Ppr Ed 90; Pre Law Scty 89-90; Otstdng Coll Stdnts Amrc; Gldn Key; Mrtr Brd; Omicron Delta Kappa; Phi Kappa Phi; Coll Law Intern 89; FL Hs Rep 90; James Madison Inst Intern 90; Cmmnctn Sclgy; Maritim Law.

**ZAMORA, LEDIA T,** Miami Dade Comm Coll, Miami, FL; SO; Business Adm; Mgmt.

**ZAMORA, MARIA C,** Miami Dade Comm Coll, Miami, FL; SO; AA; New Age Clb 90; Tlnt Rstr; Archtctr; Archtctr/Intr Dsgn.

**ZAMORA, NANCY V,** Univ Of Al At Birmingham, Birmingham, AL; SO; BA; Pres Hnrs 90-; Psychology; Ma/Phd.

**ZAMORA, PIEDAD M,** Fl International Univ, Miami, FL; FR; BSN; Nurs/Nutrition.

**ZAMPINI, GIOVANNI,** S U N Y Coll Of Tech At Frmgdl, Farmingdale, NY; SO; BA; AS; Busn.

**ZANAVICH, KRISTIN A,** Lesley Coll, Cambridge, MA; JR; BA; Stdnt Gov Act Coord 90-; Acad Schlrshp; Elem Ed; Tchr.

**ZANDERS, GELEAH N,** Hampton Univ, Hampton, VA; FR; BA; Hampton Plyrs/Co 90-; Deans Lst 90; Thtr Arts/Prfmnc; Actress/Dir.

**ZANE, VIRGINIA W,** Univ Of Al At Birmingham, Birmingham, AL; JR; BS; Amer Mktg Assn; Golden Key; Phoenicians Jefferson Sta Jr Clg 89-90; Wmns Serv Orgztn; Chmbr Cmrce Mbrshp Dr 90; Ala Power Co Mktg Dept; Bus Mktg.

**ZANELLI, SUSAN J,** City Univ Of Ny La Guard Coll, Long Island Cty, NY; GD; BA; Phi Theta Kappa 88-; AS; Food Serv; Reg Dietician.

**ZANFARDINO, KEVIN G,** Dowling Coll, Oakdale Li, NY; JR; BBA; Delta Mu Delta 89-; Fire Dept Vlnr Trustee 90-; Fireman Of The Year 90; Bus Admnstrn; Accntnt.

**ZANGOUI, KHATEREH,** Fl International Univ, Miami, FL; JR; BS; Tchrs Asst 89-; AA Miami Dade Cmnty Clg 89; Mngmt Info Sys; Prgrmmng.

**ZANIBONI, KATHLEEN M,** Lasell Coll, Newton, MA; SO; BA; Edctn; Tchr.

**ZANNINO, HELEN L,** Newbury Coll, Brookline, MA; SO; AS; Natl Acdmy Prlgl Stdies 86; Paralgl; Law.

**ZANNIS, IRENE L,** Fl International Univ, Miami, FL; SR; Phi Kappa Phi 89-.

**ZAPATA, CAROLINA M,** Univ Of Miami, Coral Gables, FL; SR; BBA; Bus Mgt/Org; Bus.

**ZAPATA, JORGE A,** Wilmington Coll, Wilmington, OH; SR; BA; Orion Ctr Rehab Intern; Sigma Delta Phi; Asst Coach Vlybl; Psych Spnsh.

**ZAPATA, LOURDES MARIE,** Inter Amer Univ Pr San German, San German, PR; SR; BS; Mu Alpha Phi Pres 90-; Hon Cert; Bio; Med Tchnlgy.

**ZAPATA, SOLA ANTONIO,** Caribbean Center For Adv Stds, San Juan, PR; GD; BA; AACD; AMHCA; Phi Sigma Alpha 85; BA 89; Psych; Indstrl.

**ZAPATOCHNY, REBECCA J,** Univ Of Pittsburgh, Pittsburgh, PA; SR; MSN; Amer Assoc Of Critical Care Nurses 85-; Cntrl PA Chptr Of Amer Assoc Of Care Nurses; Amer Truma Soc 90-; Soc Of Trauma Nurses 90-; Sigma Theta Tau 88-; Cert In Critical Care Nursing 87-; Lecturer; BSN 88; MSN Univ Of PA; Trauma Curical Nurse Spclst; Employed.**

**ZAPETIS III, ERNEST N,** Western Carolina Univ, Cullowhee, NC; SR; BSW; Scl Wrk Clb 89-; Cthlc Cmps Mnstry Mnstr 88-; Phi Alpha VP 90-; Pi Gamma Mu 89-; Deans Lst 88-; Knights Columbus Dpty Grnd Knight 82-; Patrons Qlty Schlrshp 89-; Otstndng Clg Stdnts America 89-; Ntry Pblc NC; Scl Sci; Cnslng.

**ZAPPIA, CONNIE J,** Georgian Court Coll, Lakewood, NJ; SO; BA; Deans List 90; Psych/Bus; Law.

**ZARETSKAYA, YEVGENIYA,** Bunker Hill Comm Coll, Boston, MA; FR; MS; Blgy; Tchr.

**ZARICKI, ADAM,** Univ Of Fl, Gainesville, FL; JR; BSE; Univ FL Eng Fr Chrmn; Bnds Sctn Ldr 88-; Amrcn Inst Arntcs Astrntcs; Kappa Kappa Psi VP 88-; Benton Eng Cncl; Mark Stoughton Mrl Band Schlrshp 90; FL Under Grad Schlrshp 88-89; Arspc Eng.

**ZARINCZUK, JAMES,** Univ Of South Fl, Tampa, FL; GD; MPH; Residency Aerospace Mdcn; Amer Med Assn ; Aerospce Med Assn; US Army Mdcl Crps 80-; Amer Assn Fmly Med; Assn Mltry Srgns US; BS Mcgill 68; MDCM 72; Envrmntl Occptn Mdcn; Aeropce Avtn Mdcn.

**ZARING, ROBERT A,** Bellarmine Coll, Louisville, KY; SR; Biology Club Sec 90-; Prsdntl Ldrshp Soc 90-; Amnsty Intrntnl 90; Kappa Gamma Pi; Delta Epsilon Sigma Pres 88-; Deans Lst 87-; BA 91; Biology Pre Med; Med Unv Lsvll Schl Med 91.

**ZARZAR, CLAUDIA M,** Queens Coll, Charlotte, NC; SR; BA; Art Clb 87-; Intl Clb 87-; Deans Lst 89-90; Art; Tchg.

**ZASTROW, MARY ANNE,** Niagara Univ, Niagara Univ, NY; BA; US Army Reserves E/4; Bio; Tchr.

**ZATORSKI, SHIRLEY JO,** Georgian Court Coll, Lakewood, NJ; JR; BA; Monsignor Donovan Alum Rep 88-; Pi Mu Epsilon; Math/Elem Tchr.

**ZAVACKY, MAUREEN A,** Philadelphia Coll Tex & Sci, Philadelphia, PA; FR; BS; Interior Dsgn Stdnt Cncl 90-; Stdnt Govt Flm Lctrs Cmt 90-; Interior Dsgn.

**ZAVALA, WALESKA M,** Fl International Univ, Miami, FL; SO; BED; Elem Ed; Tchng.

**ZAVETSKY, DAVID G,** Indiana Univ Of Pa, Indiana, PA; SR; BS; WIUP TV Trnsmssn/Edtng Sprv 90-; Alpha Epsilon Rho; Communications Media; Corp Video Prod.

**ZAVITZ, KAREN J,** S U N Y Coll At Fredonia, Fredonia, NY; SR; Kappa Delta Pi; Tchng Intrnshp 90-; Vrsty Vlybl 88-89; BS In Ed; Elem Ed; Clssrm Tchr.

**ZAWACKI, ELIZABETH,** Edison Comm Coll, Fort Myers, FL; JR; Sr Cust Serv Rep C/S Natl Bank 87-.

**ZAWACKI, KRISTIN L,** Georgetown Univ, Washington, DC; JR; BSN; NSNA VP 90-; Stdnts Georgetown Inc Purchaser/Prsnl 89-; New Stdnt Orntn 89-; Sigma Theta Tau; Stdnt Nurse Intern Univ MA Med Ctr 90-; Nrsng; Admin.

**ZAWADZKI, CHARLES R,** Univ Of Scranton, Scranton, PA; SR; Soc Acctng Stdnts; Delta Mu Delta 89-; Phi Alpha Theta 90-; Acctng; CPA.

**ZAWROTNY, DELANNE I,** S U N Y Coll Of Tech At Alfred, Alfred, NY; SO; RA 90-; Alpha Beta Chi 90-; Bsktbl/Sftbl Capt 90-.

**ZAYAS CLASS, GADRIAN,** Univ Politecnica De Pr, Hato Rey, PR; SO; Boy Scouts Of Amer Asst Sctmstr 85-; Physcs/Math; Eng.

**ZAYAS, JESSICA,** Univ Of Pr Medical Sciences, San Juan, PR; GD; MS; BS Univ Of PR Cayey Univ Clg 90; Occuptnl Hlth; Indstrl Hygnst.

**ZAYAS, MAYRA,** Univ Of Pr At Mayaguez, Mayaguez, PR; SO; Hon Lst Elec Eng Mayaguez Dept; Eng.

**ZAYAS, OVIDIO E,** Inter Amer Univ Pr Hato Rey, Hato Rey, PR; SO; BA; Ntnl Un Mrtl Arts 89-; Crmnl Jstc; Fbi.

**ZAYAS, YASMIN ORTIZ,** Catholic Univ Of Pr, Ponce, PR; JR; Clb Drtv De Pnc 89-; Instrctr Body Ftns 89-; Youth Soc 88-; Hnrs Deans Lst 90; Rnr/Swm 90-; Elem Educ; Tchr.

**ZAYAS-LYLE, JOSE F,** Univ Politecnica De Pr, Hato Rey, PR; JR; BA; Math/Nat Sci; Vet Dr.

**ZAYAT, SALOMON,** Miami Dade Comm Coll South, Miami, FL; SO; BA; Math Awd; AA; Sci; Engr.

**ZAYDA, SANCHEZ PEREZ,** Univ Of Pr At Rio Piedras, Rio Piedras, PR; JR; BA; Sube Pgm Asst 89; Ntrl Sci Hnr Rl 89-; Bio; Dntstry.

**ZAZZARA, JEFFREY B,** Temple Univ, Philadelphia, PA; SO; BSME; Private Pilot 86-; US Naval Reserve; Mech Engr.

**ZAZZARO, MICHAEL A,** Pasco Hernando Comm Coll, Dade City, FL; SO; ADN; Phi Theta Kappa 90-; Paramedic Firefighter Emrgncy Rm Paramedic 82-; AA 81; AS 82; Nursing.

**ZAZZERO, DIANE,** Mount Saint Mary Coll, Newburgh, NY; JR; BA; Hons Allnc 90-; Alpha Chi Sigma; Enlg; Spec/Elem Ed Tchr.

**ZBIERKOWSKA, AGATA,** Univ Of North Fl, Jacksonville, FL; FR; BA; Bsn Adm; Bsn Mgmt-Intl.

**ZBOZNY, JENNIFER A,** Duquesne Univ, Pittsburgh, PA; SR; Theater Co Costume Chair Sec VP 87-; Three-Rivers Arts Fstvl Poetry Coord 89; Magazine Asst Ed 87-90; Schlr Deans Lst 87-; BA; Clscl Civilization; Bus/Hist Museum Sci.

**ZDENEK, ROMANA E,** Anne Arundel Comm Coll, Arnold, MD; SO; Intl Std Asc 89-; Fnce; Intl Bsn.

**ZDIMAL, KEVIN P,** Le Moyne Coll, Syracuse, NY; JR; BS; Acctg Soc 88-; Bus Clb 88-; IM Cncl 90-; Testone/Marshall/ Discenza CPA Frm 90-; Smmr Intrn Agway; Acctg; Pblc.

**ZEALY, GRADY A,** Univ Of Ga, Athens, GA; SR; BLA; Hortcltr Clb 89-90; Stdnts Lndscp Arch 90-; US Coast Gd Rsrv 88-; Nrsrymn Assn 88-; Green Indstry Assn 90-; Owned Lndsap Cntrctng Co 84-89; Envrnmntl Desn; Indus Ecol Renov.

**ZEBEHAZY, SARAH A,** D Youville Coll, Buffalo, NY; JR; MS; SPTA 88-; Res Cncl 90-; Cmpus Mnstry 88-90; Lambda Sigma 89-90; CYO Advsr 90-; Rgnts Schlrshp 88-; Pres Hon Schlrsph 88-; Phys Thrpy; Sprts Med.

**ZEBROWSKI, ADRIANE J,** Daytona Beach Comm Coll, Daytona Beach, FL; SO; BA; Phi Theta Kappa; Tutor Awd 90; Intl Rltns; Jrnlst/U N Professor.

**ZECHER, BETHANY,** Academy Of The New Church, Bryn Athyn, PA; SO; BA; Hstry.

**ZECHMAN, HEATHER M,** Philadelphia Coll Pharm & Sci, Philadelphia, PA; FR; BA; Premed Scty; AIBS; SHAPE; Alpha Lambda Delta; Alpha Zeta Omega; Vrsty Vllybll; Blgy; Dctr.

**ZEDACK, KIMBERLY A,** Indiana Univ Of Pa, Indiana, PA; SR; BS; Provost Chlr; Deans List; PSEA-NEA 90-; NTE 90-; Eng Ed; Secondary English Teacher.

**ZEDEK, LYNN K,** Univ Of Sc At Columbia, Columbia, SC; FR; Carolina Cares; Gamma Beta Phi; Assoc Hnrs Stu.

**ZEDNIK, WILLIAM F,** Oh Univ, Athens, OH; JR; Intrmrl Sftbll; Alpha Lambda 88-; Tau Beta Pi 90-; Eta Kappa Nu; Frtz Dlrs Rss Schlr; Chrls Evlyn Mtthws Schlrshp 90; Elec Eng.

**ZEE, ENA,** City Univ Of Ny Baruch Coll, New York, NY; SO; BA; Math; Actrl Sci.

**ZEHAVI, YOSSEF,** Fl International Univ, Miami, FL; GD; Trnbry Clb; Cmptr Sci Hnrs; MIS Dir 87-; Mgmt Info Sys; Sys Anlys.

**ZEHNER, MARK J,** Univ Of Akron, Akron, OH; JR; BA; Gldn Key 90-; Pi Sigma Epsilon 90-; Mu Kappa Tau; Mrktg; Cmptr Elctrncs Prchsr.

**ZEHNGRAFF, TERRI L,** Savannah Coll Of Art & Design, Savannah, GA; SR; BFA; Wrk Exhbt 90-; Painting/Ills.

**ZEHRING JR, RICHARD C,** Univ Of Cincinnati, Cincinnati, OH; JR; BSCM; Const Assoc 90-; Rcyclg Com 90-; Const Engr Mgmt; Const Engr.

**ZEIGLER, BARBARA FAYE,** Northwest Al Comm Coll, Phil Campbell, AL; GD; IE; Csmtlgy.

**ZEIGLER, JACQUELINE B,** Fayetteville St Univ, Fayetteville, NC; SR; BS; FBLA Sec 79-80; FHA Frnch Clb Pres 77-78; Jr Beta Clb Pres 76-79; Sr Beta Clb 76-79; Sci Clb 76-79; Alpha Kappa 80-81; Phi Mu 90-; Model Co-Op Stdnt NC St Msm Ntrl Sci; Sftbl Tm 77-79; Blgy Educ; Ob-Gyn Dctr.

**ZEIGLER, NORMA E,** Coker Coll, Hartsville, SC; SR; BS; Flwshp Chrstn Athlts; Dorm Rep Stdnt Govt Dorm Rep 89-90; Dance & Video Club 88-; Jud Bd Mbr 88-; Sftbl 87-; Acctng; CPA.

**ZEIGLER, STANLEY T,** Norfolk St Univ, Norfolk, VA; GD; Student Athlete Award 86-; Presidents List 89-; Honor Roll 86-; Track/Cross Country Capt; BA Norfolk State Univ 90.

**ZEIGLER, SUZAN L,** Duquesne Univ, Pittsburgh, PA; SR; BA; Beta Lpha Phi 90-; Bus/Fin; Fin-Own Bus.

**ZEIN, MONICA C,** Univ Of Sc At Columbia, Columbia, SC; SR; BA; SC Tr Gd Assoc Pres 89-; Frshmn Otrch 89-; SAGE 90-; Phi Alpha Theta Pres 90-; Natl Key 90; Alpha Lambda 88-; Kappa Kappa Gamma Almn Actv Intrctn Offcr Schlrshp 89-Crln Crs 88-89; Abney Foundation Schlr Schlrshp 88-; Intern Cngrssmn Chris Shays; Hstry Bus; Law.

**ZEITZ, ROBIN G,** Widener Univ, Chester, PA; JR; BS; Acctng Scty; Widener Trnsfr Schlrshp 90-; Wall St Jrnl Awd 90; Alum Assc DE Cty Schlrshp 89-90; PA Inst CPA; Sec PA Stck Exchng Cstmr Svc Asst 85-88; Acctng.

**ZEKA, DWIGHT A,** Pa St Univ Delaware Cty Cmps, Media, PA; FR; BS; Prod Sprt Rep Unisys Corp; Elec Eng.

**ZELANAKAS, CHERYL ANN,** Manhattanville Coll, Purchase, NY; JR; BA; C R Crew Tr Gd Crdntr 90-; Stdnt Govt Scl Sci Rep; Stdnt Advsr; Frshmn Hnrs Schlr; Emrgng Ldrs Prgm; Mgmt; Coll Admssns.

**ZELENAK, FRANCIS P,** Pa St Univ Main Cmps, University Pk, PA; FR; BS; By Scts Of Amer Asst Sctmstr 90-; Egl Sct Awd; Lare Krause Awd; Arch Engr.

**ZELINSKI, JOHN J,** Univ Of Pittsburgh At Bradford, Bradford, PA; JR; BA; Bus Mgt Club VP 90-; SGA 89-; Im Asst Jdg Games 90-; Top 1 Pct In Natl AT/F Stck Chlng; Delta Omega Phi Sgt Of Arms 89-; Im Ftbl/Sftbl/Flrhcky/Vlybl/Air Band 88-; Bus Mgt.

**ZELIS, BRIAN D,** Kent St Univ Kent Cmps, Kent, OH; SO; BS; Natl Alpha Lambda Delta; Deans Lst 90; Hon Coll Schlrshp 90-; IM Sftbl 90; Intgrtd Lf Sci; Med.

**ZELL, RANDAL J,** Allegheny Coll, Meadville, PA; JR; BS; Mens Dining Assoc Pres; Resident Advsr 90-; Wind Symphony 90-; Lambda Sigma VP; Tchng Asstnt Physiological Psychlgy 90-; Alden Schlr 88-90; IM Capt 88-; Biology; Research Fld.

**ZELLER, BRENDA E,** Lansdale School Of Bus, North Wales, PA; GD.

**ZELLER, KIRSTEN A,** Albertus Magnus Coll, New Haven, CT; JR; BA; Internatl Bsn.

**ZELLER, MARY ANN,** Neumann Coll, Aston, PA; SR; BSN; Nrsg Dvlpmnt Comm Cls Rep 89-; Stu Nrs Assoc 90-; Pldg Dr Co Chrprsn 90-; Sigma Theta Tau; St George Crnvl/Wntrfst/ Chrstmas Bzr/Glnldn Fire Co Crnvl; Deans Lst 87-; Sr Margarella Oneill Awrd; Tns Tm; Nrsg; Pediatrics.

**ZELLER, SHERRIE L,** Morgan St Univ, Baltimore, MD; SR; BS; Hnr Stdnt; Hghbrhd Wtch Cptn; AA Dundalk Comm Clg 89; Scl Wrk.

**ZELLERS, TARA C,** Newbury Coll, Brookline, MA; SR; Htl/ Mtl Assc Hsptlty Law/Fd/Bvrg Cert.

**ZELLNER, ADAM J,** Glassboro St Coll, Glassboro, NJ; JR; BA; Econ; Mktng Cnsltng.

**ZELLO, CARLA,** Catawba Valley Comm Coll, Hickory, NC; SO; AS; Clrgrd 88; Pi Lambda Phi Lttl Sstr 89-90; Acctg; CPA.

**ZELLO, CHRISTOPHER G,** Univ Of Cincinnati, Cincinnati, OH; JR; BS; Clarinet Prfmn; Prfsnal/Free Lance Musician.

**ZELMAN, PAULA L,** Univ Of Miami, Coral Gables, FL; SO; BS; Vars Crew 89-; Athl Trng; Sports Sci.

**ZELTSMAN, MARAT,** Miami Dade Comm Coll, Miami, FL; SO; Mt Sinai Med Ctr Greater Miami Vol; Chemistry; Medicine.

**ZEMKE, CRAIG M,** Oh Wesleyan Univ, Delaware, OH; SO; BA; Amnesty Intl 90-; Habitat For Humanity 90-; Phi Soc; Intl Studies.

**ZENO, MONICA L,** Fl A & M Univ, Tallahassee, FL; FR; BS; Mktg Clb 90-; English Litcy Gld 90; Bus Admn; Mktg.

**ZENO-PIMENTEL, LUIS ARMANDO,** Inter Amer Univ Pr Hato Rey, Hato Rey, PR; JR; Yth Grp Untd Meth Chrch 87-; Kns Cty Univ Acad Achvmnt Ldrshp Schlrshp; Vrsty Bsktbl Tm 88-90; Athltc Trng; Sprt Medcn.

**ZENTZ, ROBERT L,** S U N Y Coll At Fredonia, Fredonia, NY; JR; MBA; Acctg Soc 88-90; VITA 89-90; IM Bsktbl 88-90; Acctg; CPA.

**ZEO, GEORGE A,** Temple Univ, Philadelphia, PA; JR; BA; Golden Key; Country Music Assn 89-; Natl Snd/Comm Soc 89; Gospel Music Assn 89-; Gen Mgr; AA Bucks Cnty Comm Clg 89; Psychology; Law.

**ZEOLI, MICHAEL D,** Albertus Magnus Coll, New Haven, CT; FR; BS; Acctg Clb 90-; Var Soccr 90-; Busn; Pre Law; Atty.

**ZEPEDA GUERRERO, ANGELA C,** Inter Amer Univ Pr Hato Rey, Hato Rey, PR.

**ZEPEDA, ZILMA E,** Miami Dade Comm Coll South, Miami, FL; SO; BA; Pre Med; Pediatrician/Medicine.

**ZEPHIRIN, PASCAL H,** City Univ Of Ny City Coll, New York, NY; SO; BS; Physcs Clb 89-; Ctr Anlys Strctrs/Intrfcs 90-; Physcs; Eng.

**ZEPP, AMY L,** Oh Wesleyan Univ, Delaware, OH; JR; BA; Stdnt Fndtn 89-; Kappa Delta Pi; Crestview Middle Sch Mentor Prog 89-; Diving Tm 88-90; Lacrosse Tm 88-89; Elem Edn; Teach.

**ZEPP II, RONALD E,** Southern Coll Of Tech, Marietta, GA; SR; BS; Eagle Mrtl Arts Acdmy Asst Instrctr 86-; NMHA 90-; Tau Alpha Phi 90-; Sftwr Eng Comp Sci; Rsrch/Dvlpmnt.

**ZEPP, WILLIAM A,** Capitol Coll, Laurel, MD; JR; BS; SGA Offcr 90-; Alpha Chi Pres; Tau Alpha Pi; Pres Schlrshp 88-; Glf Clb Vrsty Bsktbl 89-; Comp Eng Tchnlgy; Eng.

**ZEPPA, SCOTT L,** Coll Of Charleston, Charleston, SC; SR; BS; Tae Kwon Do Clb Pres 90-; Brds Soc Sec 90; Biolgy Clb 90-; Phi Kappa Phi; Hghly Dstngshd Hon Lst 90-; USAF Stf Sgt; AA Univ FL 83; AAS Comm Coll AF 89; Biochem; Nerosci Rsrch.

**ZERFOSS, PAULETTE R,** Coll Misericordia, Dallas, PA; SO; BS; Scl Wrk Clb Al-Anm Fmly Grps Rep 90-; Mothers Sprt Grp; Sec; Scl Wrk.

**ZERIA, BERHE,** Old Dominion Univ, Norfolk, VA; SR; SME Tres 89-90; Kovner Schlrshp 88-89; Tchrs Aide 89-90; Dsgn Eng AMF Bkry Systms; BMET Old Dominion Unv 90; AAS Blue Ridge Comm Clg 87; Mech Eng.

**ZERING, KELA,** Newbury Coll, Brookline, MA; FR; Fashion Clb 90-; Fashion Dsgnr; Dsgng.

**ZERMENO, OMAR R,** King Coll, Bristol, TN; SO; BA; Track Clb 90-; Tae Kwon Do Clb 89-90.

**ZERVOS, CHRISTINA,** Fl International Univ, Miami, FL; SO; BA; Phi Eta Sigma 89-; AA; Engl; Prfssr.

**ZETER, ROBERTA A,** Univ Of Cincinnati-Clrmnt Coll, Batavia, OH; SO; BA; Deans Lst 88-; AA; Liberal Arts.

**ZEWDU, MESERET,** Bunker Hill Comm Coll, Boston, MA; SO; BED.

**ZHANG, FEI YUE,** City Univ Of Ny La Guard Coll, Long Island Cty, NY; SO; BA; Phi Theta Kappa 90-; Pharm.

**ZHANG, JIANHUA,** Life Coll, Marietta, GA; FR; DC; Dctr Chns Mssg Mnpltn Inst Orthpdcs Trmtlgy Trdtnl Chns Med 84-90; MB Beijing Trdtnl Chinese Med 84; Chrprctc.

**ZHANG, LILY YI,** City Univ Of Ny La Guard Coll, Long Island Cty, NY; SO; AS; Asian Club 89-90; Hong Kong Club 90-F Alpha Theta Kappa Scty 90-; Laguardia Cmmty Clg Deans List 90; Laguardia Cmmty Clg Deans List; Swng Tns Self Defense 90-; Liberal Arts/Sci; Engrg.

**ZHANG, RANDY D Q,** City Univ Of Ny Baruch Coll, New York, NY; SR; MBA; Sigma Iota Epsilon; Alpha Iota Delta; Deans Lst 89-90; Deans Lst 85; BBA 90; Intl Bus.**

**ZHANG, SUIBIN,** City Univ Of Ny City Coll, New York, NY; JR; BE; Gldn Ky; Elect Eng; Eng.

**ZHANG, XUN NIAN,** Savannah Coll Of Art & Design, Savannah, GA; GD; MFA; Savannah Art Assoc 88-; Shanghai News Corr Assoc 81-88; Shanghai Illust Assoc 84-88; Shanghai Art Assoc 84-88; Monroe Curtis Propes Flwshp SCAD 88; Painting.

**ZHANG, YUAN,** Univ Of Ky, Lexington, KY; SR; MS; Gldn Key; Grad Dstnctn Dept Hon Math Sci; Tchng Asstshp UK Grad Sch; BS; Statstcs/Comp Sci.

**ZHANG, YUN AMY,** Manhattanville Coll, Purchase, NY; SO; BA; Interntl Club 90-; Econ/Mgt Club 90-; Hon Schlr 90-; Effron Entrprs Intrn; BS Armand Hammer Untd World Clg Of The Amercn West 90; Comptr Sci/Mgt; Progrmr/Fincl Anlyst.

**ZHAO, ANDREW XIAXI,** City Univ Of Ny Baruch Coll, New York, NY; SO; BBA; Mngmnt; Bsnss.

**ZHAO, FU-LIANG G,** City Univ Of Ny La Guard Coll, Long Island Cty, NY; SO; Comp Clb 89; Phi Theta Kappa 89-90; Amer Intl Corp Mail Clrk 85-; AAS; Cmptr; Comp Sci.

**ZHAO, GEORGE F,** City Univ Of Ny La Guard Coll, Long Island Cty, NY; SO; Comp Club 89; Phi Theta Kappa 89-90; Mail Clerk 85-; AAS Laguardia Comm Coll; Comp Sci.

**ZHAO, MEIHE,** Univ Of Tn At Martin, Martin, TN; SR; BS; Clthng Co Plng Sec 88-90; BS 88; Cmnctn.

**ZHAO, RUIZHEN,** Columbia Univ, New York, NY; FR; BS; Brdcstng Clb Prgrm Exec 90-; SWE 90-; Chinese Stu Clb 90-; H R Stu Schlrs Soc; Sci Math; Eng.

**ZHAO, XIAO-MEI,** Univ Of Rochester, Rochester, NY; SR; BA; Fllwshp Pkng Univ 88; Orgnc Chem.

**ZHAO, XIAOFANG,** Univ Of Rochester, Rochester, NY; JR; BA; Stdnt Govt Sctn Dir 88-89; Econ Assoc 87-89; Ppr Rep 87-89; Hghst Mrt Schlrshp 87-89; Schlrshp 90; Gns Schlrshp 90-; Econ.

**ZHAO, XIONG,** City Univ Of Ny Baruch Coll, New York, NY; GD; BBA; Finance/Invstmnt Club 89-90; ABL Law Sch Peoples Univ Of China 86; Finance/Invstmnt; Fncl Inst.

**ZHENG, KAI,** Indiana Univ Of Pa, Indiana, PA; JR; MBA; Bdmntn Assoc Chrmn Fclts 90-; Mgmnt Info Syst; Cmptr/Bus.

**ZHENG, YOUJIA,** City Univ Of Ny Baruch Coll, New York, NY; SR; BBA; Acctg Soc 90-; Acctncy.

**ZHONG, JANNIE L,** City Univ Of Ny Baruch Coll, New York, NY; SR; Chinese Culture Clb; Beta Alpha Psi; Acctg.

**ZHOU, HUAN SUE,** City Univ Of Ny City Coll, New York, NY; SO; Amrcn Mdcl Stdnts Assoc 89-; (Y State Acdmy Fmly Physcns 89-90; Asn Amrcn Cmmnctns Admn Asst; Tnns Tm; Bio Med; Mdcl Dctr.

**ZHOU, JINGSONG,** Ms St Univ, Miss State, MS; JR; BA; Chns Stdnts Assn MS State 89-; Amer Red Crs ; Asstshp Pres MS State Univ 89-; Acctncy.

**ZHOU, XUE-JING,** Atlantic Union Coll, S Lancaster, MA; JR; BS; Natl Scty Of Pblc Accts; Orntl Clb Treas 90-; Blain Richards Schlrshp; Rwai-Choi Lam Schlrshp 90-; Coll Acctng Offce 90-; Bkkpr Acct 79-; Acctng; CPA.

**ZHU, CHANGRONG,** Ms St Univ, Miss State, MS; SR; BS; Gamma Beta Phi; Nursing.

**ZHU, FONG,** Univ Of Ky, Lexington, KY; FR; BA; Frnch Clb; TV Com 90; Lil KY Derby 90-; Alpha Lambda Delta; Phi Eta Sigma; Tutor 90-; Deans Lst; Acad Excell Cert; Cmptr Sci/Frnch; Bus.

**ZHU, HONGTAO,** Univ Of Ky, Lexington, KY; SO; BA; Nucl Power Plant Guangdong Framatome/Spie Batijnolles Co Piping Erection Supv 88-90; Engr.

**ZHU, JUAO,** Bridgewater Coll, Bridgewater, VA; JR; BS; Comp Sci; Mgmt.

**ZHU, JULIANA,** S U N Y At Binghamton, Binghamton, NY; FR; BS; Exprssns Dcknsn Dnc Cmpny Treas 90-; Dcknsn Twn Cncl Rep 90-; Oconnor Hall Rep 90-; Blgy; Med.

**ZHU, JULU,** Bridgewater Coll, Bridgewater, VA; SR; BS; Soc Of Physics Stdnts 89-; Bridgewater Coll Intl Club P R Coord 88-; Coll Math Club; Coll Physics Club 89-; Intrnshp Comp Mgmt & Dvlpmnt Serv; Coll Tm On 90 Capital Region ACM Schlstc Prgmng Contest 90; Math Comp Sci/Physics; Prof.

**ZHU, KAI QI,** Manhattan School Of Music, New York, NY; SR; BA; Frst Prz Wnnr BA CA Piano 87; Elva Van Geldr Mem Schlrshp 89; Piano Perf; Tchr.

**ZHU, TAN-LU,** Oh Dominican Coll, Columbus, OH; FR; BS; American Intl 90; CRC Press Chem Award; Gen Chem Award; Cmptr Sci; Med.

**ZHU, XU,** Elms Coll, Chicopee, MA; JR; BA; Intl Clb VP 90-; Brdcst Sta China Anncr 87-90; Poetry Soc China 87-90; Lnrd Spch Awd 90-; Acad Awds/Schlp 87-90; Rhythmc Gym Tm China 87-90; Amer Stds.

**ZIADIE, SHARON L,** Barry Univ, Miami, FL; JR; BA; Jamcn Assoc; Frn Clb; Alpha Mu Gamma; Frnch Spnsh.**

**ZIAVALA, TANYA DEL ROCIO,** Univ Politecnica De Pr, Hato Rey, PR; SO; BSIE; IIE; Indstrl.

**ZIBBE, SUSAN E,** Georgian Court Coll, Lakewood, NJ; SO; BS; Cmps Mnstry 89; Psychlgy Clb 90; Deans Cnvctn 90; Jc Pny Acdmc Schlrshp 90-; Psychlgy; Chld Psychlgst/Abnrml Psych.

**ZICHETTELLA, MARLENE CERICOLA,** Dowling Coll, Oakdale Li, NY; SR; BA; Scl Sci.

**ZIDES, MELISSA J,** Merrimack Coll, North Andover, MA; JR; BA; SGA 90-; Psych Clb 90-; Law Soc; Psi Chi P 90-; Chld Psych.

**ZIEBER, CINDI A,** Defiance Coll, Defiance, OH; SR; BA; Inter-Var 87-; Campus Min Cncl Snt Rep 87-90; Stdnt Socl Wrk Assn 87-90; TORCH Cmnty Svc Org 87-89; Christian Eductr 90-; Pr Host 88-89; RA 88-89; Asst Res Dir 89-; Elem Tchr.

**ZIEGLER, ANDREA D,** Univ Of Ga, Athens, GA; JR; BSED; Big Bro Big Sis Area Coor 89-; Spcl Olympcs Hst 90; IM Sftbll 90; Dns Lst; Educ; Tchr.

**ZIEGLER, MECHELLE D,** Glassboro St Coll, Glassboro, NJ; JR; BS; Gamma Tau Sigma; Biolgcl Sci; Tchng.

**ZIEGLER, MICHELLE L,** Cumberland County Coll, Vineland, NJ; SO; AAS; Stdnt Senate 86-88; Phi Theta Kappa Secr 86-88; Dns Lst 86-; Basilian Schlrshp 86; Outstndg Achvmnt Awd-Paralegal Pgm 89; Certif Mainline Paralegal Inst 89; AS Manor Jr Clg 88; Lgl Asst; Law.

**ZIEGLER, ROBERT G,** Wilmington Coll, New Castle, DE; SO; Cmnctns Arts 89-; TV Prod 89-; Nwspr/Yrbk Stf 89-; Deans Lst 89-; Intrnshp Video Rcrt Tape; Wmns Bsktbl; Asstntshp Video Prod Cty W Chstr Unty Day; Cmnctns Arts; Jrnlst.

**ZIELONKA, RICHARD H,** Springfield Tech Comm Coll, Springfield, MA; SO; BS; Instltn Suprvsr For Pacific Bell Co San Francisco 79-88; Comptr Sci; Progrmr.

**ZIEMAN, JENNIFER Y,** Middle Tn St Univ, Murfreesboro, TN; FR; BA; Intrcoll Rdng Tm 90-; Gamma Beta Phi; Educ; Spec Educ/Tchng.

**ZIEMBICKI, JENNY A,** Duquesne Univ, Pittsburgh, PA; FR; Campus Mnstry 90-; Lambda Sigma Serv Chair 90-; Natl Hon Soc Serv Chair 90-; Fndrs Schlrshp 90-; Incentive Schlrshp 90-; Bio; Pre Med.

**ZIEMINICK, LISA R,** Hillsborough Comm Coll, Tampa, FL; FR; BA; Radiology; Radiologic Techgt.

**ZIERDEN, NEIL R,** Central Fl Comm Coll, Ocala, FL; SO; AS; Firefghtr NW Hernando Fire Dept 2nd Lt 89-; Fire Inspctr FL State Fire Clg; Fire Sci/Crmnl Justice; Arson/Crmnl Invstgtn.

**ZIERVOGEL, SHERI D,** Salisbury St Univ, Salisbury, MD; JR; BA; Psychlgy Club 90-; Phi Eta Simga 88-; Psi Chi; Vol Wrk Whlchr Gms MS Soc Plnnd Parnthd 90-; Rsrch Projct With Profsr; Ims Flr Hockey/Water Polo 89-; Psychlgy; Clincl Or Crmnl.

**ZIGMAN, JOHN I,** Kent St Univ Kent Cmps, Kent, OH; SR; Stdnt Dietetic Assoc Advrtsmnt Chrprsn; Undrgrad Stdnt Snte Hlth/Wlfre Cmmttee; Stdnt Intrn Cuyahoga Cnty WIC Prog; BS; Exrcse Physlgy; Dietetics/Exrcse Physlgy.

**ZIKOS, GEORGE,** Univ Of New Haven, West Haven, CT; FR; BA; GOYA; Accntng; Accntnt.

**ZILKA, JENNIFER L,** Saint Vincents Coll & Seminary, Latrobe, PA; SO; BA; Natl Assoc/Acctnts 89-90; Bus Forum 89-90; Deans List 89-90; Acctg Intrnshp 90; All Dist/Vlybl 90; IM Vlybl Co Cpt 89-; Bsktbl 89-; Math/Engr; Biomedical.

**ZILLA, RON C,** Univ Of Scranton, Scranton, PA; SR; BS; Socty Acctng Stdnts Assoc 89-; Bus Clb 89-; Bus Hnr Socty 89-; Delta Mu Delta 89-; Pa Socty Pub Acctnts Schlrshp 90; Father Gilbride Schlrshp 87-; Reddington Gen Schlrshp 87-; Rugby 89; Acctng; CPA.

**ZILLER, CAROLYN A,** Southern Vt Coll, Bennington, VT; SR; BS; Dns Lst 87-; Sthwstrn Vrmnt Cncl Aging Asst Adv 87-; Human Services; Offc Admin.

**ZIMBARDI, JILL M,** Kent St Univ Kent Cmps, Kent, OH; JR; BA; Gldn Key; Alpha Xi Delta Bwlng Grn 89; Ntrtn Dttcs.

**ZIMBARDI, JOANNA M,** Kent St Univ Kent Cmps, Kent, OH; SR; BA; Natl Hnr Soc; Gamma Phi Beta Chr 88; Mktg; Sales/Mgmt.

**ZIMMER, ERIK M,** Univ Of South Al, Mobile, AL; SO; BA; Phi Eta Sigma 89-90; Sigma Phi Epsilon Pldg Pres 89-90; IM Sprts 89-; Bus/Financ; Bnk Pres.

**ZIMMER, JILL S,** Lasell Coll, Newton, MA; JR; Big Sis Little Sis Pres 89-90; Intl Club 88-90; Tour Lguide 88-89; Gamma Delta Beta Pres 89-90; PC Lab Asst 89-90; Psych Tutor 90; Art Hist Tutor 90; AA Lasell Coll 90; Art Hist; Mgmt.**

**ZIMMERLE, DONALD P,** Daytona Beach Comm Coll, Daytona Beach, FL; FR; Engr.

**ZIMMERLE, SANDRA J,** Middle Tn St Univ, Murfreesboro, TN; JR; BS; Lord's Church 81-; Psychlgy; Clin Psychlgy.

**ZIMMERLY, DOUGLAS R,** Univ Of Akron, Akron, OH; SR; BA; Gldn Key 89-; Frmng; Physcl Ed.

**ZIMMERMAN, AMY L,** Garrett Comm Coll, Mchenry, MD; FR; BS; Elem Educ; Tch.

**ZIMMERMAN, BRIAN S,** Juniata Coll, Huntingdon, PA; FR; BS; Conservation Clb; Laughling Bush; Scalpal And Probe; Brumbaugh Ellis Schlrshp; IM Vlybl; Pre Med; Genl Practitioner.

**ZIMMERMAN, CAROLYN A,** Elmira Coll, Elmira, NY; SR; Perry Drm Cncl Treas 89-90; Orientatn Ldr 89; Coll Radio DJ; Ski Clb 89-; Hosp Intrnshp; BS 91; Math.

**ZIMMERMAN, DANA S,** Free Will Baptist Bible Coll, Nashville, TN; JR; BA; Choir 88-; Sngrs 89-90; Louise Mae Alcott Treas 89-90; Bilbe Mjr/Engl Mjr; Mstrs Enlg/Law.

**ZIMMERMAN, DANIEL M,** Univ Of Miami, Coral Gables, FL; JR; BS; Stdnt Govt Athltc Afrs Chrmn 88-90; Blrds Clb Two Time Chmpn 88-; Glf Clb 90-; Orntn Asstnt 89-90; Lmbd Chi Alph Hse Mgr 89-; Frat Phlnthrps 89-; Stdnt Govt Otstdng Mbr 89-90; IM Sftbl Rqtbl Sccr Ftbl 88-; Bio/Chem/Psychlgy; Medcn/Orthphdc/Pdtrc.

**ZIMMERMAN, DAVID C,** Kent St Univ Kent Cmps, Kent, OH; SR; BSN; Stdnts Prfssnl Nrs Chrmn Ed Cmm 90-; Bcclrt Crrclm Cmmtt Sph Stdnt Rep 88-89; Sigma Theta Tau 89-; Scty Nrsng; Gldn Key 90-; Med.

**ZIMMERMAN, DONYA TARRAINE,** Univ Of Md At Eastern Shore, Princess Anne, MD; SO; MA; Natl Hon Soc 90-; Sociology; Corp Lawyr.

**ZIMMERMAN, DWAYNE B,** Ky St Univ, Frankfort, KY; FR; BA; Ky Choir Accompnst 90-; Alpha Kappa; Delta Omicron; KSU Mst Otstdng Pianst Awd 90; Music Educ.

**ZIMMERMAN, ELIZABETH F,** Coll Of Charleston, Charleston, SC; JR; BA; Alliance For Planet Earth 89-; Cmps Amnesty 89-; Peace On Earth Coord 90-; Greenworld 89-; Hnrs Pgm 88-; Athl Acad Hnr; Equestrian Team MVP 88-; Philosophy; Prof.

**ZIMMERMAN, FRANKLIN HAWTHORNE,** Va Commonwealth Univ, Richmond, VA; JR; BS; REBOS Pres; Exec Dir Recovery House Sexually Abused; Facilitate Grp Relatives Friends Terminally Ill; Alcohol Drug Educ Rehbltn Prog; Cnslng.

**ZIMMERMAN II, G RICHARD,** Hahnemann Univ, Philadelphia, PA; GD; MD; Church Deacons 85-87; Masons 84-; Scottish Rite Syria Temple 89; Phi Sigma 87; Phi Beta Kappa 89-; Phi Kappa Sigma 87-; Deans Lst 85-89; Colportage Presbytrn Schlrshp 85-89; Cum Laude 89; W E Crane Schlrshp 89-90; Medicine; Physician.

**ZIMMERMAN, HEATHER M,** Univ Of Nc At Charlotte, Charlotte, NC; FR; BA.

**ZIMMERMAN, JANICE LEA,** Lincoln Univ, Lincoln Univ, PA; SR; BS; Educ Clb 89-; Alpha Chi 90-; Stdnt Tchr Yr Awd 90-; Art 101 Acdmc Adchvmnt Awd 90-; Educ; Tchng.

**ZIMMERMAN, JESSICA R,** Univ Of Ky, Lexington, KY; JR; BSN; Clg Of Nrsng Pres 89; Ntnl Cllgte Nrsng Awd; Nrsng.

**ZIMMERMAN, JOHN R,** Univ Of Louisville, Louisville, KY; JR; BSEE; IEEE 90-; Tau Beta Pi 90-; Golden Key; Phi Kappa Phi; Phi Eta Sigma 89; Samuel T Fife Awd; Elec Eng.

**ZIMMERMAN, KEITH M,** Clayton St Coll, Morrow, GA; JR; BA; Dns Lst; Acctg; CPA.

**ZIMMERMAN, KYRA C,** Commonwealth Coll, Virginia Beach, VA; SO.

**ZIMMERMAN, LARRY WILLIAM,** Ga St Univ, Atlanta, GA; SO; BA; Tchr Chld Dvlpmnt Ctr; Erly Chldhd Educ; Tch.

**ZIMMERMAN, LAURIE D,** Frederick Comm Coll, Frederick, MD; FR; BA; Ag Econ; Agribusiness.

**ZIMMERMAN, MARY C,** Merrimack Coll, North Andover, MA; JR; BS; Accntng Fin Soc 90-; Natl Assn Acctnts 90-; Accntng; CPA.

**ZIMMERMAN, MERRY L,** Ky St Univ, Frankfort, KY; FR; BA; Girl Scout Ldr 87-; Comp Sci.

**ZIMMERMAN, MONIQUE C,** Hillsborough Comm Coll, Tampa, FL; SO; AS; Nursing.

**ZIMMERMAN, NATALIE J,** Kent St Univ Kent Cmps, Kent, OH; JR; BA; Deans Lst; Pres Lst; Golden Key; Delta Gamma; Ambssdr; Smstr Geneva Switzerland; Intrnshp Untd Natns Geneva; Sailng Clb; Bus/Finance; Law.

**ZIMMERMAN, PAIGE A,** Providence Coll, Providence, RI; JR; BA; Pstrl Cncl 88-90; Phi Sigma Tau 90-; IM Frsbee/Wllyvl 90-; Math.

**ZIMMERMAN, ROBERT G,** Univ Of Tn At Martin, Martin, TN; GD; BS; Phi Kappa Phi; AS Milwaukee Inst Tech 67; Comm; Pub Rltns.

**ZIMMERMAN, ROGER S,** Oh Univ, Athens, OH; FR; BS; Ohio U Bnd 90; Math/Sci; Eng.

**ZIMMERMAN, TRACY L,** Cumberland County Coll, Vineland, NJ; SO; AAS; Prsnnl/Mgmt/Bus Admin.

**ZINGALI, JOHN T,** Georgetown Univ, Washington, DC; SO; BSBA; Mntr Pgm Area Coord 90-; Vars Chrldng 89-.

**ZINGARELLI, LAURA B,** Tallahassee Comm Coll, Tallahassee, FL; JR; BA; Pres Schlrs Clb 90; Deans Lst 90; Pres Lst 90; Whlsl Seafd Bus; AA 90; Intrdsclplnry Sco Sci; Educ.

**ZINGER, LANA,** Ny Univ, New York, NY; FR; Nutrition.

**ZINK, EMILIE R,** Univ Of Sc At Columbia, Columbia, SC; JR; BA; Eta Sigma Delta 90; IM Aerobics Pgm Weight Lifting 88-; Hotel/Restaurant/Tourism Admin; Hotel Mgmnt.

**ZINK, TRACIE L,** Commonwealth Coll, Virginia Beach, VA; SO; AAS; Med Clb Treas 90-; Amer Assn Med Asst; Alpha Beta Gamma 89; Extrnshp Licking Mem Hosp Fam Med Ctr; Licking Mem Hosp Co Care; Microbiology/Cytology.

**ZINN, DEDRA A,** Wv Univ, Morgantown, WV; SO; BS; NSNA 90-; WVSNA 90-; WVUSNA 90-; Hnrs Lst 89-; Nrsg; Neonatal/Oper Rm Nrsg.

**ZINN, DONNA M,** Duquesne Univ, Pittsburgh, PA; JR; BA; Intl Bus Mgmt.

**ZINN, MELANIE A,** Oh Dominican Coll, Columbus, OH; FR; BA; Margaret Gonda Matesich Schlrshp 90; Hnrs Engl Essay/Rsrch Class; Cmmnctns; Prof Wrtng.

**ZINSNER, RICHARD D,** Bowling Green St Univ, Bowling Green, OH; SR; BS; Flying Tm; Alpha Eta Rho; Pi Kappa Phi; IM Hockey; Aerotechnology; Cmrcl Airline Pilot.

**ZIOBRO, DEBRA A,** Univ Of Med & Dentistry Of Nj, Newark, NJ; GD; RD; Error Rtgrs Hm Ec Assoc 87-90; Rtgrs Tang Soo Do Karate Clb 89-90; Cook Coll Stu Advsr 86-87; Tri Beta 88-89; Omicron Nu 89-90; Dietetic Intrnshp Clrcl Exclnc Error Awrd 90-; Col Miriam Perry Goll Schlrshp 90-; Dietetics; Clncl Nutrtn.

**ZIOMKOWSKI, ROBERT M,** Siena Coll, Loudonville, NY; SR; BA; Fencing Club VP 87-90; History Club VP 90-; Phi Alpha Theta Pres 89-; History; Historian.

**ZIPLIN, KENNETH C,** Univ Of Nc At Charlotte, Charlotte, NC; JR; BA; Interdisciplinary Hon Pgm 89-; Pol Sci Hon; Tau Kappa Epsilon Pres 89-; Natl Essay; Pol Sci/Econ; Law/Govt.

**ZIRILLO, PHYLLIS,** S U N Y Coll Of Tech At Frmgdl, Farmingdale, NY; SO; BA; Accntng Soc 90; Foreign Lang Soc 89; VITA; Bsnss/Foreign Lang; Accntnt Foreign Lang Tchr.

**ZIRLOTT, SANDRA M,** Univ Of South Al, Mobile, AL; SR; BA; Sub Tchr 87-88; Early Chldhd Educ; Tchng.

**ZISK, LYNN C,** Springfield Tech Comm Coll, Springfield, MA; SR; AS; Alpha Nu Omega 90-; Cert Of Merit; Johnson Mem Hosp Stafford Spgs CT; Medcl Lab Techcn.

**ZITO, TONI A,** Richard Bland Coll, Petersburg, VA; FR; BA; Natl Stdnt Nrs Assoc 90-; SRMS Sch Nrsng Cert Hons Acad Achvmnt; Nrsng; RN.

**ZIVOJINOVIC, RADOVAN D,** Georgetown Univ, Washington, DC; JR; BSBA; We Care; Cntrl Amer Schlrshp Pgm Intrn 88; Intl Mgmt; Dir Forgn Inv.

**ZKAO, TIAN STUANG,** Oh Dominican Coll, Columbus, OH; JR; BA; Liter Cliko 87-90; IM Bsbkl 87-90; Spkng Awd; Scholastic Schlrshp 91; Huang He Univ 90; Busn Intl; Busn Mgt.

**ZMIJEWSKI, TINA M,** Le Moyne Coll, Syracuse, NY; SR; Mktg Clb; Bus Clb Sec 89; I M Bkbl; SADD V P 87; Folk Grp Stdnt Coord 88; Delta Mu Delta 89; Atty Gen Intrnshp 90; Dept Hon; I M Bkbl; Mktg/Orgztnl Bhvr; Fin Anlyst.

**ZMUDA, THOMAS J,** Univ Of Ct, Storrs, CT; SR; BS; Nutrition; Dietician.

**ZOBEL, DEANA M,** Univ Of Sc At Columbia, Columbia, SC; JR; BS; Gamma Beta Phi 90; Career Dvlpmnt INTER 90; Pres Hnr Roll 89; Mary Moody Schlrshp Scurry Schlrshp 89; Bsn; Mngmnt.

**ZOCHOWSKI, ROBIN L,** Univ Of Fl, Gainesville, FL; SR; BSN; Ntl Assoc Neonatal Nrs; Sigma Theta Tau; Phi Theta Kappa VP 82-84; Glvr Schlrshp; Adn Alumnus Rep 85-88; Stf RN Neontl Intnsv Care Unit Tchg Hosp; ADN 84; Nrsg; Educ Cnslg.

**ZOCK, LESLIE A,** Saint Francis Coll, Loretto, PA; SR; Stdnt Govt VP For Cmmnctns 89; Stdnt Activities Org 87-89; Bio Clb Pres 87; Beta Beta Beta; Hnr Soc; Delta Epsilon Sigma; Campus Mnstry 87-91; Big Bro/Sis 88-89; Plus-1 88; Elks Fndtn Schlrshp 87; Scholastic Perf Awd 87; Im 90; BS Bio 91; Bio; Grad Schl In Human Genetics.

**ZOCK, LORETTA T,** Saint Francis Coll, Loretto, PA; BS; Phi Theta Kappa; Cmps Mnstry; Intern; Sm Bus Dev Ctr; Mgmt.

**ZOELLNER, KAY L,** Central St Univ, Wilberforce, OH; SO; BA; Hll Cncl Rsdnc Hll Assoc Rep 90; Rsdnc Hll Assoc VP; Mdcl Tchnlgy.**

**ZOFFER, SHERYL D,** Atlantic Comm Coll, Mays Landing, NJ; SO; AAS; Jr Chefs Assn 89; Clnry Arts.

**ZOGLMANN, LAURIE A,** Indiana Univ Of Pa, Indiana, PA; JR; BA; Alpha Epsilon Rho Prmtns Chr 90-; Natl Assn Coll Brdcstrs 90-; Cmps TV Sgmnt Prdcr 88-; Cmnctns; Brdcstng.

**ZOHNI, MONA,** Univ Of Pittsburgh, Pittsburgh, PA; SR; BSA; Emerging Ldr 87-88; Amer Soc Mech Engr Comm Chr 87-; Natl Soc Prof Engr 87-90; Soc Wmn Engr 87-90; Hand In Hand Fstvl Comm; Engr Week; Kennedy Math Award 90; Gnrl Motors Schlrshp Award 89-; Merit Schlrshp 88-; Mech Engr; MBA.

**ZOKA, KATHERINE J,** Wilkes Univ, Wilkes-Barre, PA; FR; BA; Commtr Cncl VP 90-; Math/Comp Sci Clb 90-; Tutor 90-; Hon Soc 90-; Lector 89-; Bsktbl Statstcn 90-; Math Tchr.

**ZOLDAN, SHARON F,** Univ Of Rochester, Rochester, NY; JR; BA; Pnhlnc Jdcry Comm Repr 90-; Pnhlnc Extnsn Comm Repr 90-; Greek Week Awards Co Chrmn; Order Of Omega; Sigma Delta Tau Pres; Prtnrs In Rdng 89-90; Peer Assist Career Svcs/Plcmnt Ctr; Hstry/Cert Intl Rltns; Prsnnl Mgmt.

**ZOLDI, EVA L,** Kent St Univ Kent Cmps, Kent, OH; JR; BS; Golden Key; Phi Epsilon Kappa VP 90-; Pho Phi Lambda 90-; Leisure Studies; Mltry Rec.

**ZOLLER, DARRIN S,** Longwood Coll, Farmville, VA; SO; BS; Art Educ; Hgh Schl Art Tchr.

**ZOLLICOFFER, CARL D,** City Univ Of Ny City Coll, New York, NY; GD; MD; Day Stdnt Govt Sci Sntr 89-90; Caduceus Soc Pre-Med Clb Treas 88-89; Vol Emrgncy Sqd Advncd CPR Sqd Mbr 88-90; Gldn Key 89-; Mt Carmel Bptst Chrch Deacon 83-; Med; Physcn.

**ZOLLY, REGINA M,** Saint Francis Coll, Loretto, PA; SR; BS; Blgy Clb 87-; Yrbk Phtgrphr 87-89; Dorothy Day Ctr Pls Onco Bg Bro/Sb Sis 88; Mnr Psychlgy; Blgy; Fld Blgy/Eclgy.

**ZOMBEK, NANCY J,** Wv Northern Comm Coll, Wheeling, WV; SO; BHRM; Retreat Spkr Dir 89-; Evangelization Comm; After Obtaining My Degree I Want To Dedicate My Life In Serving People; Parish Work.

**ZONDERVAN, QUINTON Y,** Eckerd Coll, St Petersburg, FL; JR; BS; Earth Soc Pres 90-; Chss Clb Pres 88-; ACM Pres 88-; Rsrch Asst 90; Math Cmptr Sci; Tch.

**ZONTEK, SARAH J,** Wv Univ, Morgantown, WV; SR; BSN; Stdnt Nurs Orgztn 90-; Extrnshp Duke Univ Hosp 90; Spec Olympcs 90; Nurs.

**ZOPP, LESLIE A,** Marshall University, Huntington, WV; FR; BA; Phi Eta Sigma 90-; Merchdsr Amer Greetings 79-; Bus Mngmt.

**ZORAWOWICZ, EDWIN D,** Savannah Coll Of Art & Design, Savannah, GA; SO; BFA; Illustration; Free Lance.

**ZORN, ERIC J,** S U N Y Coll Of Tech At Frmgdl, Farmingdale, NY; GD; MS; Deans List; Lndscp Dsgn Show Recognition Plntng Flds Arbrtm Ldscp Cnst Cmpt Hrsy Pn; AAS 91; Lndscp Archtct; Lndscp Archtct.

**ZORN, PATRICIA B,** Abraham Baldwin Agri Coll, Tifton, GA; SO; Div Awd Scndry Edn 90-; Ch Secy Woodmen Wrld Treas; Beautician 20 Yrs; Engl; Scndry Edn Engl Tchr.

**ZORSKY, KAREN M,** Barry Univ, Miami, FL; SO; Vlybl Coach 90; Soccer Coach 90; Sftbl Coach 89-; Sftbl 89-; Crmnl Jstce; Law.**

**ZOTO, JASON S,** Georgetown Univ, Washington, DC; FR; BA; Stdnt Assc Soph Cls Com; Rugby Ftbl Clb 90-; Coll Rpblcns 90-; Lib Arts Smnrn 90-; American Studies; Law.

**ZOU, HAICHUAN,** Fl A & M Univ, Tallahassee, FL; FR; Soccer Champ Beijing Foreign Affairs Clg 88-90; Mech Engr; Engr.

**ZOU, QI R,** Bunker Hill Comm Coll, Boston, MA; FR; Engl.

**ZOULAS, PEGGY,** Schenectady County Comm Coll, Schenectady, NY; SO; BA; Bus Admin.

**ZOURIGUI, AZIZ,** City Univ Of Ny La Guard Coll, Long Island Cty, NY; JR; MBA; Moroccan Scr Clb 90; Iranian Jewish Ctr Wrkr 90; Gr Neck Jewish Syng 90; Comp Sci; Engr.

**ZRALLACK, DENISE M,** Barry Univ, Miami, FL; SO; BSN; Nrsng Stdnt Assn VP 90-; Cir K 89-90; Rspect Life 89-90; Hon Stdnt Assn 88-; Delta Phi Epsilon Rush Chrmn 88-; Cmps Mnstry 89-; Mover/Shaker Awd 89-90; Nrsng; Ansthtst.

**ZUAZAGA, GLORIA E,** Univ Politecnica De Pr, Hato Rey, PR; FR; Engineering.

**ZUBER, PATRICIA A,** S U N Y Coll Of Tech At Canton, Canton, NY; SR; AAS; Phi Theta Kappa 90-; VATA Sec 89-; Vet Tech; Vet Hlth Tech.

**ZUBERKO, MATTHEW J,** City Univ Of Ny Baruch Coll, New York, NY; JR; BBA; Roleplyrs Guild Pres 90-; Finance; Comp Prgrmng.

**ZUCCA, LOUISE E,** Westminster Choir Coll, Princeton, NJ; SR; Stdnt Govt VP 87-89/Sec 89-91; Dorm Cncl VP 89-90; Natl Music Hnr Soc; Fclty Wstmnst Cnsrvtry 89-; BM; Music; Piano Pedagogy.

**ZUCKERBERG, DINA,** Cornell Univ Statutory College, Ithaca, NY; JR; BS; Coll Ambssdr 88-; Deans Lst 88-; Alpha Omicron Pi 90-; Bus Mgmt; Fnc.

**ZUDE, RONALD S,** Univ Of Cincinnati, Cincinnati, OH; SO; BA; Dpty Shrff Hmltn Cnty OH Shrff; 2nd Clss Ptty Offcr US Nvy Rsrve Trnng Dept 89-; US Nvy USS FL; Bllstc Mssle Trdnt Sub; Nvgtn Asst 89; Crmnl Jstce; Fed Law Enfrcmnt Invstgtn.

**ZUENDEL, GLADYS ANNY,** Eckerd Coll, St Petersburg, FL; SO; MA; Assoc Des Lettres 89-90; Fed Des Assoc D Etudiants 89-90; Swiss Exchange Stdnt; Comitede Surveilliance Des Rest Univ 89-90; Coop Du Bevano Acct 88-; Intl Stdnt Exch Pgm Schlrshp; BA Univ Of Lausanne Switzerland 90; AA 89; AA 88; Engl; Tchr.

**ZUERCHER, KIMBERLY A,** Univ Of Sc At Columbia, Columbia, SC; JR; BA; Acctng.

**ZUGG, DONNA B,** Univ Of Southern Ms, Hattiesburg, MS; SR; BS; Jones Co Jr Coll 75; Spec Ed; Mastrs Cnslng Psych.

**ZUKIERSKI, DANA A,** Univ Of North Fl, Jacksonville, FL; SO; MACC; Chamber Singers 90-; Alpha Sigma Pi Sec 90-; Acad Deans Lst 89-; AA; Acctng.**

**ZULEGER, CANDY L,** Valdosta St Coll, Valdosta, GA; JR; Enlstd Wvs Clb Schlrshp; Biology; Medicine.

**ZULETA, JESSICA,** Univ Of Miami, Coral Gables, FL; SR; Mcrblgy; Phi Kappa Phi 89-; Gldn Key 90-; Phi Beta Kappa; Mcrblgy/Immnlgy; Med.

**ZULFIQAR, ASIM,** Nova Univ, Ft Lauderdale, FL; GD; MBA; Cmptr Prog 89-; BSE Univ Of Cntrl FL Orlando FL; Bus; Sftwr Prog.

**ZULINSKA, AGNES M,** City Univ Of Ny City Coll, New York, NY; SR; BECE; Emerg Med Squad; Soc Civil Engr; Concrete Canoe Club; Chi Epsilon V P; Tau Beta Pi Pres 90; Mjr Corps Engr 90; Civil Engr; MBA.

**ZULL, PETER N,** Kent St Univ Kent Cmps, Kent, OH; JR; BA; Gldn Key; Engl; Tech Wrtr.

**ZULLO, KARIN M,** Daemen Coll, Amherst, NY; SR; Cls Pres 90; Hmn Serv Clb 90; Trvl/Trsm Clb 90; Admssns Asst 89-90; Trvl Expo Buffalo; MS Walk 90; Hmlss Nwsltr 90; Intrnshp US Air Buffalo Intl Arprt; Intrnshp Stouroff/Taylor Trvl Agncy; BS; Trnsprtn/Tvl Mgmt; Mktg.

**ZULLO, PATRICIA J,** Univ Of Nc At Greensboro, Greensboro, NC; JR; BS; Prime Movers; Dance Ed.

**ZUMBRINK, SCOTT J,** Wright St Univ Lake Cmps, Celina, OH; SO; BA; Deans Lst 89-; Acctg/Finance; CPA.

**ZUMBRUNNEN, HEIDI JO,** West Liberty St Coll, West Liberty, WV; SO; BA; Std Ornttn Stf 90; Engl Ed; Clg Instctr.

**ZUNSKI, ROBERT J,** Duquesne Univ, Pittsburgh, PA; JR; BA; Elem Educ; Tchng.

**ZUR, KAREN B,** Yale Univ, New Haven, CT; FR; BS; Dncrs Pres; Spcl Olympcs; Holocaust Archives 90-; Neurosci Rsrch Cntr Intern/Rsch; Biology; Med/Neurosurgery.

**ZURAWEL, RUSSELL H,** Hudson Valley Comm Coll, Troy, NY; SO; BS; Phi Theta Kappa; Blgy; Med.

**ZURBUCH, JONATHAN M,** Kent St Univ Geauga Cmps, Burton Twp, OH; SO; BA; Bsn Admin; Acctng.

**ZURITA, GLENDA A,** Rutgers St Un At New Brunswick, New Brunswick, NJ; FR; BS; Union Hosp Vol; Fnc Pltcl Sci; Govt Wrk Law.

**ZURKO, SUSAN M,** S U N Y Coll Of A & T Morrisvl, Morrisville, NY; FR; AAS; Friars Drma Clb 90; Bsns; Infrmtn Prcsng.

**ZURNER, PATRICIA L,** Cornell Univ Statutory College, Ithaca, NY; BA; Cornell Chemists 90-; Golden Key 90-; IMS 90; Chem; Pharmctcls.**

**ZURZOLO, MARIA M,** Lasell Coll, Newton, MA; SO; Fshn Frm Oprtns Mngr 89-; Bsns Hnrs 89-; High Hnrs 90-; Exec Offcrs Intrn 90-; Flms Bsmnt Corp Hd Artrs Prsnl; Fshn Bsns Mrchndsng.

**ZUSHIN, JOY ANN,** Gallaudet Univ, Washington, DC; JR; Psychlgy Clb; Delta Phi Epsilon 89-; EPOC; Dns Lst; Psychlgy; Cnslr.

**ZWEIMAN, ARI J,** Yale Univ, New Haven, CT; FR; Yale Daily News; Independent Prty; SMART.

**ZWERSKI, SHERYL L,** Univ Of Fl, Gainesville, FL; GD; MSN; Phi Kappa Phi 90-; ADN Santa Fe Cmnty Clge 86; BSN Hgh Hnrs Univ FL 90; Nrsg; Ped Nrs Prctnr.

**ZWICKER, HUGH L,** Rochester-Hall-Crozer Dvty Sch, Rochester, NY; SR; MDIV; Wesley Scty Co-Cnvnr 88-; Wrshp Comm 88-; Phi Alpha Thetha 87-; Tchng Asst Thlgy 90; BA Bethany Bible Coll 85; BA Houghton Coll 87; Thlgy; Thlgcl Ed.

**ZWIENER, JOYCE V,** Univ Of Ky, Lexington, KY; FR; BS; Bio; Vet Med.

**ZWOLINSKI, BRIAN S,** Fl St Univ, Tallahassee, FL; JR; BS; Stdnt Afrs; USMC 83-86; AA FSU 90; Cmnctns Engl; Film Sch.

**ZWYGART, KIRA K,** Lenoir Rhyne Coll, Hickory, NC; SO; SG; Cmps Ministries; Lutheran Stdnt Mvmnt; Bnd; Orientation Ldr; Ldrshp Retreats; CROP Walk; Walk America; Alpha Lambda Delta 90-; Kappa Delta Secy 90; Alpha Phi Omega Secy; Frshmn Math Achvmnt Awd 90; Pre Med/Biol; Psychiatry.

**ZYGADLO, DOTTIE C,** Univ Of Sc At Columbia, Columbia, SC; FR; Walterboro Anl Art Shw 2nd Pl/3rd Pl/Hnrbl Mntn 88-90; Prsnl; Ed/Art; Elem Art Tchr.

**ZYGNERSKI, EVE,** Univ Of New Haven, West Haven, CT; JR; BA; Htl And Rest Scty 89-; Rsdnce Hll Cncl 90; Alpha Lambda Delta 90-; Coop Educ; Achvmnt Intrnatl Bus 90-; Univ Excllnce Awrd 89; Intrnatl Bus; Mrktng.

**ZYNE, NANCY J,** Kent St Univ Kent Cmps, Kent, OH; FR; BA; Vrsty Gymnstcs 90-; Phys Ftns Spclst; Physcl Thrpy.

**ZYNEL, CYNTHIA A,** Indiana Univ Of Pa, Indiana, PA; FR; BA; ROTC Commandos 90-; Cncl Excptnl Prsns; Vol Spec Olympcs Trck/Fld Evnts.

**ZYSK, ROBERT F,** S U N Y Coll At Geneseo, Geneseo, NY; FR; BA; Geneseo For Life Sec 90-; Model UN Club 90-; Hist Club 90-; Rpblcns .0-; Vol Emerg Squad 90-; GSTV 90; Harvard Natl Model Utd Ntns Comm Ldr; Mddl E Jeopardy Tm Chmpns; Hist/Pol Sci; US Frgn Serv.

**ZYSKOWSKI, JENNIFER M,** Clarkson Univ, Potsdam, NY; JR; BS; Soc Accntnts 88-; Soc Wmn Mgrs 88-; Alumni Phoneathon 88-; Phi Sigma Sigma Asstn Pldg Mstrss 89-; Stdnt Orient Serv 89-90; Pres Schlr 89; Acctng/Finance; Cert Mgmt Acctng/Corp Finance.

Ababio, Patricia K
Central St Univ
Wilberforce, OH

Abadia Munoz, Maressa
Inter Amer Univ Pr San Juan
Hato Rey, PR

Abadie, George A
Miami Dade Comm Coll
Miami, FL

Abbate, Steven M
Providence Coll
Providence, RI

Abbey, Judith L
Valdosta St Coll
Valdosta, GA

Abbot, Christy M
Univ Of Scranton
Scranton, PA

Abbott, Jennifer L
Univ Of Ky
Lexington, KY

Abbott, Terry L
Marshall University
Huntington, WV

Abdel Sater, Nina K
Bunker Hill Comm Coll
Boston, MA

Abdou, Fadi M
Wv Univ
Morgantown, WV

Abed-Rabbu, Yamilla Ivette
Miami Dade Comm Coll
Miami, FL

Abednego, David A
City Univ Of Ny John Jay Coll
New York, NY

Abeling, Christie A
Va Commonwealth Univ
Richmond, VA

Abella, Julie I
Fl International Univ
Miami, FL

Abernathy, Michele L
Middle Tn St Univ
Murfreesboro, TN

Abood, Paul H
Rutgers St Un At New Brunswick
New Brunswick, NJ

Abou Khalil, Ali K
Hillsborough Comm Coll
Tampa, FL

Abraham, Salome
Georgian Court Coll
Lakewood, NJ

Abramson, Stacy L
Wheaton Coll
Norton, MA

Abronson, Louis S
Ny Univ
New York, NY

Absher, Lisa R
Wilkes Comm Coll
Wilkesboro, NC

Abul Jobian, Ahmad N
Univ Of Miami
Coral Gables, FL

Accardo, Michelle I
Wv Univ
Morgantown, WV

Acevedo Rosa, Glorie A
Inter Amer Univ Pr Hato Rey
Hato Rey, PR

Acevedo Sosa, Alexis
Univ Politecnica De Pr
Hato Rey, PR

Acevedo, Ortencia
Univ Of Pr At Rio Piedras
Rio Piedras, PR

Acevedo-Cardona, Eileen
Bayamon Central Univ
Bayamon, PR

Acevedo-Marrero, Carlos A
Evangelical Semimary Of P R
Hato Rey, PR

Ackah, Samuel
Howard Univ
Washington, DC

Ackourey, Christine M
Western New England Coll
Springfield, MA

Acosta Acosta, Julmarie
Inter Amer Univ Pr San German
San German, PR

Acosta Floer, Juan B
Univ Politecnica De Pr
Hato Rey, PR

Acosta Ramirez, Deborah
Univ Of Pr At Mayaguez
Mayaguez, PR

Acosta, Ana C
Univ Of Miami
Coral Gables, FL

Acquaviva, Gina M
Villanova Univ
Villanova, PA

Acquaviva, Mary K
Anne Arundel Comm Coll
Arnold, MD

Adair, Matthew A
Embry Riddle Aeronautical Univ
Daytona Beach, FL

Adams, Alicia M
Al A & M Univ
Normal, AL

Adams, Erin A
Duquesne Univ
Pittsburgh, PA

Adams Jr, Gordon E
Mount Olive Coll
Mount Olive, NC

Adams, James J
Univ Of Va Clinch Valley Coll
Wise, VA

Adams, Jasper M
Denmark Tech Coll
Denmark, SC

Adams, Jennifer M
Howard Univ
Washington, DC

Adams, Lisa G
Marshall University
Huntington, WV

Adams, Luther Morris
Marshall University
Huntington, WV

Adams, Melissa D
Ashland Comm Coll
Ashland, KY

Adams, Robin R
Va St Univ
Petersburg, VA

Adams, Rodney Wayne
Columbia Union Coll
Takoma Park, MD

Adams, Shiryl J
Franklin Univ
Columbus, OH

Adams, Tonya R
Prestonburg Comm Coll
Prestonburg, KY

Adams, William J L
Stetson Univ
Deland, FL

Adamson, James M
Spartanburg Methodist Coll
Spartanburg, SC

Adamus, Marishka Brigida
Fl A & M Univ
Tallahassee, FL

Addeo, Maria E
Fl International Univ
Miami, FL

Addington, Debra L
Univ Of Va Clinch Valley Coll
Wise, VA

Addis, Angelia M
Spartanburg Methodist Coll
Spartanburg, SC

Adedun, Ebenezer A
Savannah St Coll
Savannah, GA

Adegoroye, Adeola O
Fl A & M Univ
Tallahassee, FL

Adekoya, Michael A
City Univ Of Ny La Guard Coll
Long Island Cty, NY

Adelman, Judd B
Univ Of Miami
Coral Gables, FL

Adepoju, Esther F
Fl A & M Univ
Tallahassee, FL

Adewunmi, Catherine S
Schenectady County Comm Coll
Schenectady, NY

Adewunmi, Felicia O
Univ Of The Dist Of Columbia
Washington, DC

Adeyemo, Mudasiru A
Southern Coll Of Tech
Marietta, GA

Adjei, Anthony Kwasi
City Univ Of Ny Baruch Coll
New York, NY

Adolph, Kimberly Ann
Fl St Univ
Tallahassee, FL

Agbenowosi, Newland K
Central St Univ
Wilberforce, OH

Agosto, Esther N
Inter Amer Univ Pr Hato Rey
Hato Rey, PR

Ahluwalia, Ish K
City Univ Of Ny City Coll
New York, NY

Ahmed, Rizwan
Univ Of Al At Huntsville
Huntsville, AL

Aikens, James E
Greenville Tech Coll
Greenville, SC

Akamune, Idomo Cynthia
Southeastern Coll Of Hlth Sci
N Miami Beach, FL

Akbar, Camile D
City Univ Of Ny Med Evers Coll
Brooklyn, NY

Aking, Marlene A M
Univ Of Miami
Coral Gables, FL

Akinpelu, Edward A
Worcester St Coll
Worcester, MA

Akouri, George
Fl International Univ
Miami, FL

Akrami, Ramin
Univ Of Louisville
Louisville, KY

Aksu, Yaman M
Franklin And Marshall Coll
Lancaster, PA

Al-Ammari, Khalid Salem
Daytona Beach Comm Coll
Daytona Beach, FL

Albaugh, Michael D
West Liberty St Coll
West Liberty, WV

Alberson, Lana P
Lake Sumter Comm Coll
Leesburg, FL

Albertorio, Edwin R
Inter Amer Univ Pr Guayama
Guayama, PR

Albino Figueroa, Janice
Inter Amer Univ Pr San German
San German, PR

Albino Rivera, Waleska
Inter Amer Univ Pr San German
San German, PR

Albinus, Nikolaj
Univ Of Miami
Coral Gables, FL

Albrecht, Joan T
East Stroudsburg Univ
E Stroudsburg, PA

Albright, James
Nova Univ
Ft Lauderdale, FL

Alcini, Brian D
Univ Of Akron
Akron, OH

Aldinger, Karla K E
Valdosta St Coll
Valdosta, GA

Aldous, Todd E
S U N Y Coll Of Tech
At Canton
Canton, NY

Aldridge, Carla J
Centre Coll
Danville, KY

Aldridge-Willis, Carol L
Cheyney Univ Of Pa
Cheyney, PA

Alduncin, Juan P
Univ Of Miami
Coral Gables, FL

Aleixo, Joao C
Univ Of New Haven
West Haven, CT

Alejandro Cisneros, Rogelio E
Inter Amer Univ Pr
Hato Rey
Hato Rey, PR

Alejandro Lora, Ramon
Univ Politecnica De Pr
Hato Rey, PR

Alejandro, Edwin
Univ Politecnica De Pr
Hato Rey, PR

Aleman, Harry E
Univ Of Pr Ponce Tech
Univ Col
Ponce, PR

Aletich, Kimberly A
Atlantic Comm Coll
Mays Landing, NJ

Alexander, Alton M
Al St Univ
Montgomery, AL

Alexander, David J
Univ Of Sc At
Columbia
Columbia, SC

Alexander, Grant S
Embry Riddle
Aeronautical Univ
Daytona Beach, FL

Alexander, Kathi J
James Madison
University
Harrisonburg, VA

Alexander, Phillip
Vernon
Al St Univ
Montgomery, AL

Alexander, Roslyn M
Walker Coll
Jasper, AL

Alexander, Shawna R
Johnson C Smith Univ
Charlotte, NC

Alexander, Tina M
Piedmont Tech Coll
Greenwood, SC

Alfonso, Carmen R
Miami Dade Comm Coll
Med Centr
Miami, FL

Alford, Christy Ann
Ms St Univ
Miss State, MS

Alford, Shanti E
Hampton Univ
Hampton, VA

Algeo, Donald W
Univ Of New England
Biddeford, ME

Ali, Alisha G
Broward Comm Coll
Ft Lauderdale, FL

Alicea Quiles, Melissa
Inter Amer Univ Pr
Hato Rey
Hato Rey, PR

Alicea, Sheila E
Univ Of Pr Medical
Sciences
San Juan, PR

Alkire, Sarah B
Univ Of
Cincinnati-Clrmnt Coll
Batavia, OH

Allen, Amber R
Va Union Univ
Richmond, VA

Allen, Arlonda Y
Livingston Univ
Livingston, AL

Allen, Deborah V S
Winthrop Coll
Rock Hill, SC

Allen, Johnetta
Tn St Univ
Nashville, TN

Allen, Jonathan K
Fl A & M Univ
Tallahassee, FL

Allen, Lagina M
Sue Bennett Coll
London, KY

Allen, Mary Elizabeth
Univ Of Rochester
Rochester, NY

Allen, Royce M
Tougaloo Coll
Tougaloo, MS

Allen, Tonya A
Bowie St Univ
Bowie, MD

Alleyne, George N
City Univ Of Ny Med
Evers Coll
Brooklyn, NY

Alleyne, Sharron D D
Inter Amer Univ Pr San
German
San German, PR

Allison, Christy L
Beckley Coll
Beckley, WV

Allison, Janet
Univ Of Cincinnati
Cincinnati, OH

Alloway, Matthew R
Miami Univ
Oxford, OH

Allwaters, Alvee O
Atlantic Union Coll
S Lancaster, MA

Almansa, Moises I
Univ Politecnica De Pr
Hato Rey, PR

Almeida, Jorge E
Nova Univ
Ft Lauderdale, FL

Almenas-Pabon, Brenda
Inter Amer Univ Pr
Hato Rey
Hato Rey, PR

Almonte, Gisela A
Hudson County Comm Coll
Jersey City, NJ

Alonso, Marlene E
Saint Thomas Univ
Miami, FL

Alston, Chrystal A
Norfolk St Univ
Norfolk, VA

Alston, Rebecca C
Lane Coll
Jackson, TN

Altman, Laurie B
William Paterson Coll
Wayne, NJ

Alvarado, Ivan
Univ Politecnica De Pr
Hato Rey, PR

Alvarez, Daniel
Glassboro St Coll
Glassboro, NJ

Alvarez, Leonides
Miami Dade Comm Coll South
Miami, FL

Alvarez, Liriana
Bunker Hill Comm Coll
Boston, MA

Alvarez, Santiago J
Barry Univ
Miami, FL

Alvarez, Susan M
Saint Thomas Univ
Miami, FL

Alvarez, Victor Javier
Univ Politecnica De Pr
Hato Rey, PR

Alvin, David A
Stetson Univ
Deland, FL

Amaratunge, Sadhana S
City Univ Of Ny La Guard Coll
Long Island Cty, NY

Amaro Jr, Elias
City Univ Of Ny City Coll
New York, NY

Amato, Joseph S
Worcester Poly Inst
Worcester, MA

Amendola, Lisa Antoinette
S U N Y Coll Of A & T Morrisvl
Morrisville, NY

Amir, Galit
Fl St Univ
Tallahassee, FL

Amlaw, Karen L
Univ Of Rochester
Rochester, NY

Amos, Evelyn L
Snead St Jr Coll
Boaz, AL

Anderson, Amy R
Union Inst
Cincinnati, OH

Anderson, Anne E
Middle Tn St Univ
Murfreesboro, TN

Anderson, Brian M
Washington State Comm Coll
Marietta, OH

Anderson, Crissy L
Shippensburg Univ
Shippensburg, PA

Anderson, Jason J
Fl A & M Univ
Tallahassee, FL

Anderson Jr, Jessie B
Tn Temple Univ
Chattanooga, TN

Anderson, Machelle P
Fl International Univ
Miami, FL

Anderson, Margaret Ann
Commonwealth Coll
Virginia Beach, VA

Anderson, Mary G
Georgetown Coll
Georgetown, KY

Anderson, Onya M
Tusculum Coll
Greeneville, TN

Anderson III, Randall Hudson
Univ Of Cincinnati-Clrmnt Coll
Batavia, OH

Anderson, Ronald H
S U N Y Coll Of Tech At Delhi
Delhi, NY

Anderson, Theophilus K
Interdenominational Theo Ctr
Atlanta, GA

Anderson, Travis B
Morgan St Univ
Baltimore, MD

Anderson, Trudy S
S U N Y Coll At Fredonia
Fredonia, NY

Anderson, Wayne A
City Univ Of Ny
Baruch Coll
New York, NY

Andollo, Aracely
Miami Dade Comm Coll
Miami, FL

Andonova, Monika L
Columbia Union Coll
Takoma Park, MD

Andrejack, Jessica L
Western New England
Coll
Springfield, MA

Andrus, Laura R
Radford Univ
Radford, VA

Angel Fontanills, Ennio
Inter Amer Univ Pr
Hato Rey
Hato Rey, PR

Angell, Shannon L
Anne Arundel Comm
Coll
Arnold, MD

Annese, Linda M
Merrimack Coll
North Andover, MA

Anthony, Michelle L
Catawba Valley Comm
Coll
Hickory, NC

Anthony, Patricia J
Univ Of Tn At
Knoxville
Knoxville, TN

Anthony IV, Raymond
Thomas Nelson Comm
Coll
Hampton, VA

Antonelli, Karen M
Univ Of Fl
Gainesville, FL

Apel, Christine E
Georgetown Coll
Georgetown, KY

Apel, Kristen L
Kent St Univ Kent
Cmps
Kent, OH

Apolonia, Maria M
Seton Hall Univ
South Orange, NJ

Aponte Figueora, Felix J
Univ Of Pr Cayey Univ
Coll
Cayey, PR

Aponte Osorio, Steven V
Bayamon Tech Univ
Coll
Bayamon, PR

Aponte Pagan, Jesinette
Inter Amer Univ Pr
Hato Rey
Hato Rey, PR

Aponte, Inalvis
Univ Of Pr Cayey Univ
Coll
Cayey, PR

Aponte, Martha P
Ny Institute Of Tech
Ny City
New York, NY

Appold, Wayne H
New Comm Coll Of
Baltimore
Baltimore, MD

Aquino, Marie J
Duquesne Univ
Pittsburgh, PA

Araminowicz, Hanna
Medical Univ Of Sc
Charleston, SC

Aratingi, Robert N
Villanova Univ
Villanova, PA

Arcaro, Gregory F
Mount Saint Mary Coll
Newburgh, NY

Arena, Nicholas J
Nova Univ
Ft Lauderdale, FL

Arenado, Edna M
Central Fl Comm Coll
Ocala, FL

Arent, Heather A
Newbury Coll
Brookline, MA

Aresta, Christine Lynn
Fl International Univ
Miami, FL

Argiro, Dominick P
Dowling Coll
Oakdale Li, NY

Arieta, Geraldine M
Inter Amer Univ Pr
Hato Rey
Hato Rey, PR

Arlotta, Christopher J
Teikyo Post Univ
Waterbury, CT

Armanini, David A
Cornell Univ
Ithaca, NY

Armitstead, Craig G
Bunker Hill Comm Coll
Boston, MA

Armstead III, Henry
Tuskegee Univ
Tuskegee Inst, AL

Armstrong, Dennis D
Stark Tech Coll
Canton, OH

Armstrong, Gregory K
Middle Tn St Univ
Murfreesboro, TN

Armstrong, Juan L
Univ Of Pr At Rio
Piedras
Rio Piedras, PR

Arnold, Andrea M
Clark Atlanta Univ
Atlanta, GA

Arnold, Mark W
Bethel Coll
Mckenzie, TN

Arnold, Penny L
Rider Coll
Lawrenceville, NJ

Arocho, Carlos A
Univ Politecnica De Pr
Hato Rey, PR

Arosemena, Jorge Federico
Old Dominion Univ
Norfolk, VA

Arrechea, Marisa Hawayek
Inter Amer Univ Pr Hato Rey
Hato Rey, PR

Arrington, David M
King Coll
Bristol, TN

Arrington, Tonya P
Chattahoochee Vly St Comm Coll
Phenix City, AL

Arroyo, Tara T
Hudson Valley Comm Coll
Troy, NY

Arroyo-Colomer, Jorge
Univ Of Pr Humacao Univ Coll
Humacao, PR

Arsenault, Jeanne M
Bunker Hill Comm Coll
Boston, MA

Arslan, Mazen
Tallahassee Comm Coll
Tallahassee, FL

Arthers, Cindy L
Univ Of South Al
Mobile, AL

Arufe, Jorge A
Miami Dade Comm Coll
Miami, FL

Asbrand, Kimberly D
Moravian Coll
Bethlehem, PA

Asetre, Steve B
Univ Of Al At Huntsville
Huntsville, AL

Ashe, Pamela R
Dartmouth Coll
Hanover, NH

Ashley, Robin M
Wv Wesleyan Coll
Buckhannon, WV

Ashraf, Mohammad Adnan
Cumberland County Coll
Vineland, NJ

Ashton, Shannon C
Middle Tn St Univ
Murfreesboro, TN

Askew, Juanita
Christian Brothers Univ
Memphis, TN

Assali, James B
Univ Of Miami
Coral Gables, FL

Astorelli, Nancy M
Newbury Coll
Brookline, MA

Asu, Aloysius M
Univ Of The Dist Of Columbia
Washington, DC

Asuncion, Van-John A
Embry Riddle Aeronautical Univ
Daytona Beach, FL

Atlas Jr, David Marlow
Salisbury St Univ
Salisbury, MD

Attipoe-Kploanyi, Evelyn S
City Univ Of Ny City Coll
New York, NY

Augustine, Kirk E
Univ Of Louisville
Louisville, KY

Augustine, Sandra E
Univ Of Scranton
Scranton, PA

Aulen, David B
Clarkson Univ
Potsdam, NY

Aulisio, Wendy M
Univ Of Scranton
Scranton, PA

Ausband, Elizabeth A
Univ Of Nc At Charlotte
Charlotte, NC

Austin, Antonio D
Hampton Univ
Hampton, VA

Austin, Archie R
Univ Of Tn At Martin
Martin, TN

Austin, Kimberly S
Draughons Jr Coll Nashville
Nashville, TN

Averill, Tod H
Univ Of Ct
Storrs, CT

Avery, Linda L
Owensboro Jr Coll Of Bus
Owensboro, KY

Avery, R Colleen
Western Piedmont Comm Coll
Morganton, NC

Avila, Carlos J
American Univ Of Pr
Bayamon, PR

Avila, Efrain
Univ Politecnica De Pr
Hato Rey, PR

Avis, Leigh A
Thomas Nelson Comm Coll
Hampton, VA

Avitabile, Gina M
Newbury Coll
Brookline, MA

Ayala Jr, Melvin
Univ Politecnica De Pr
Hato Rey, PR

Ayandipo, Abimbola Ibidunni
Tuskegee Univ
Tuskegee Inst, AL

Aycock, Melanie A
Jefferson St Comm Coll
Birmingham, AL

Ayers Hughes, Valerie
Meridian Comm Coll
Meridian, MS

Ayers, John M
Hocking Tech Coll
Nelsonville, OH

Ayers, Lawrence E
Southern Coll Of Tech
Marietta, GA

Ayres, Keith M
Va St Univ
Petersburg, VA

Ayres, Lisa S
Univ Of Akron
Akron, OH

Ayuk, Atem Didacus
Tri County Tech Coll
Pendleton, SC

Azi-Love, Emmanuel N
Cheyney Univ Of Pa
Cheyney, PA

Azpurua, Monica Medina
Barry Univ
Miami, FL

Azulay, Jone T
Nova Univ
Ft Lauderdale, FL

Baah, Sophia M
Hudson Valley Comm Coll
Troy, NY

Baase, Gretchen L
Bryant Stratton Bus Inst Roch
Rochester, NY

Babb Jr, Ralph E
Middle Ga Coll
Cochran, GA

Babiak, Natalie A
Medaille Coll
Buffalo, NY

Babik, Kathleen M
Indiana Univ Of Pa
Indiana, PA

Babin, Brian W
Saint Thomas Univ
Miami, FL

Babin, Tammi L
Bay Path Coll
Longmeadow, MA

Babwahsingh, Virginia
Jersey City St Coll
Jersey City, NJ

Bacher, James T
Jefferson Comm Coll
Louisville, KY

Backenstose, Heather N
Villanova Univ
Villanova, PA

Bacon, Candace R
Hillsborough Comm Coll
Tampa, FL

Baez, Caroline A
Columbia Univ
New York, NY

Bagga, Amit
Manhattanville Coll
Purchase, NY

Baggett, Gale E
Ky Mountain Bible Coll
Vancleve, KY

Bagley, Charles E
Fayetteville St Univ
Fayetteville, NC

Bagley, Jacqueline A
Bunker Hill Comm Coll
Boston, MA

Bagwell, Brad A
Central Fl Comm Coll
Ocala, FL

Bagwell, Tammy L
Piedmont Coll
Demorest, GA

Bailey, Adele
Bennett Coll
Greensboro, NC

Bailey, Lora Y
Univ Of Sc At Columbia
Columbia, SC

Bailey, Mark D
Southern Coll Of Tech
Marietta, GA

Bailey, Raymond D
Atlantic Comm Coll
Mays Landing, NJ

Bailey III, Samuel R
Tn Temple Univ
Chattanooga, TN

Bailey, Shawn
Western New England Coll
Springfield, MA

Bailey, Sylvia S
Longwood Coll
Farmville, VA

Bain, Mark E
Ms Gulf Coast Comm Coll
Perkinston, MS

Bain, Riselle
Daytona Beach Comm Coll
Daytona Beach, FL

Baker, Heidi L
Catawba Valley Comm Coll
Hickory, NC

Baker, Kimberly N
Western Piedmont Comm Coll
Morganton, NC

Baker, Kristin L
Old Dominion Univ
Norfolk, VA

Baker, Liam P
Bob Jones Univ
Greenville, SC

Baker, Melissa R
Miami Jacobs Jr Coll Of Bus
Dayton, OH

Baker, Nancy L
Oh Univ
Athens, OH

Baker, Peter S
Univ Of Cincinnati
Cincinnati, OH

Baker, Ramona
Ny Univ
New York, NY

Baker, Sherry J
Fayetteville St Univ
Fayetteville, NC

Baker, Wilton D
Morehouse Coll
Atlanta, GA

Bala, Priya
Colgate Univ
Hamilton, NY

Baldino, Denise
S U N Y Coll Of A & T Morrisvl
Morrisville, NY

Balducci, Ralph P
City Univ Of Ny Baruch Coll
New York, NY

Baldwin, Susan G
Glassboro St Coll
Glassboro, NJ

Baldwin, Tracy L
Tn Tech Univ
Cookeville, TN

Ball, John E
Ms St Univ
Miss State, MS

Ballard, Tosheia N
Bloomfield Coll
Bloomfield, NJ

Ballester, Brigitte
Univ Of Pr At Mayaguez
Mayaguez, PR

Balloveras, Gina C
Fl International Univ
Miami, FL

Ballow, Sarah
Cornell Univ Statutory College
Ithaca, NY

Balogh, Tina M
Walters St Comm Coll
Morristown, TN

Bandrich, Jorge L
Univ Of Miami
Coral Gables, FL

Bandy, Danna L
Anne Arundel Comm Coll
Arnold, MD

Bane, Amy Beth
Marshall University
Huntington, WV

Bane, Angela D
Roane St Comm Coll
Harriman, TN

Bangerter, Kurt D
Univ Of Miami
Coral Gables, FL

Bangura, Bernard Ansu
Clark Atlanta Univ
Atlanta, GA

Banister, Thelma
Bloomfield Coll
Bloomfield, NJ

Banks, Debra F
Mount Saint Mary Coll
Newburgh, NY

Banks, La Shandra Q
Al St Univ
Montgomery, AL

Banks, Lisa N
Bloomfield Coll
Bloomfield, NJ

Banks, Mary A
Miami Jacobs Jr Coll Of Bus
Dayton, OH

Banks, Rufus A
Nc Central Univ
Durham, NC

Banks, Samuel A
Western New England Coll
Springfield, MA

Bannister, Elizabeth Brooks
Converse Coll
Spartanburg, SC

Barba, Marlene S
City Univ Of Ny Baruch Coll
New York, NY

Barbee, Derrick B
Central St Univ
Wilberforce, OH

Barbee, Jennifer L
Kent St Univ Kent Cmps
Kent, OH

Barber, Clifford A
Ms St Univ
Miss State, MS

Bardales, Kimberly M
Univ Of North Fl
Jacksonville, FL

Bardeschewski, Lisa A
S U N Y Coll At Oswego
Oswego, NY

Bare, Susa E
Univ Of Pittsburgh
Pittsburgh, PA

Barefield, Myla D
Duke Univ
Durham, NC

Barfield, Rachel L
Alcorn St Univ
Lorman, MS

Bargallo, Hector S
City Univ Of Ny City Coll
New York, NY

Barile, Angela
Teikyo Post Univ
Waterbury, CT

Barkalow, M Kathleen
Mount Saint Mary Coll
Newburgh, NY

Barker, Jonda L
Wv Univ At Parkersburg
Parkersburg, WV

Barker, Melissa A
Univ Of Cincinnati
Cincinnati, OH

Barksdale, Larry A
Univ Of Al At
Birmingham
Birmingham, AL

Barnes, Allison R
Univ Of Sc At
Columbia
Columbia, SC

Barnes, Danielle S
Norfolk St Univ
Norfolk, VA

Barnes, Elizabeth R
Itawamba Comm Coll
Fulton, MS

Barnes, James T
Univ Of Al At
Birmingham
Birmingham, AL

Barnes, Shelly M
Hudson Valley Comm
Coll
Troy, NY

Barnett, Laura L
Univ Of Charleston
Charleston, WV

Barnwell, Janet L
Tusculum Coll
Greeneville, TN

Baron, Darlyse
Seton Hall Univ
South Orange, NJ

Baron, Kristin M
Elmira Coll
Elmira, NY

Barone, Paul F
Hampton Univ
Hampton, VA

Barousse, Phillip C
Saint Thomas Univ
Miami, FL

Barr II, Lesley H
Northeast State Tech
Comm Coll
Blountville, TN

Barranco Francois,
David G
Univ Politecnica De Pr
Hato Rey, PR

Barreras-Cifredo, Jorge
Univ Of Pr At Rio
Piedras
Rio Piedras, PR

Barreto Roman, Maria
Inter Amer Univ Pr
Arecibo Un
Arecibo, PR

Barreto Ybarra, Juan W
Univ Of Pr Medical
Sciences
San Juan, PR

Barrett, Benita D
Clark Atlanta Univ
Atlanta, GA

Barrett, Tracy D
Waycross Coll
Waycross, GA

Barringer, Daniel K
Cumberland County
Coll
Vineland, NJ

Barrios, Luis G
Miami Dade Comm Coll
Miami, FL

Barron, Robin Googe
Tallahassee Comm Coll
Tallahassee, FL

Barroso, Diana
Fl International Univ
Miami, FL

Barrow, Adrian G
City Univ Of Ny Ny
City Tech
Brooklyn, NY

Barry, Beth A
S U N Y At Buffalo
Buffalo, NY

Barry, John Hilary
Univ Of The Dist Of
Columbia
Washington, DC

Bart, Jennifer A
Draughons Jr Coll
Nashville
Nashville, TN

Barter, Nancy E
Oh Dominican Coll
Columbus, OH

Bartholomew, Bobbie
Riggs
Union Univ
Jackson, TN

Bartick, Tracy E
Ms St Univ
Miss State, MS

Bartley, Wanda E
Cumberland Coll
Williamsburg, KY

Barto, William W
S U N Y At Buffalo
Buffalo, NY

Basa, Alan A
Univ Of South Al
Mobile, AL

Basila, Jennifer A
Barry Univ
Miami, FL

Basinger, Lorrine R
Univ Of Miami
Coral Gables, FL

Baskerville, Franshon P
Va St Univ
Petersburg, VA

Basl, Bonnie L
Univ Of Pa
Philadelphia, PA

Basora-Cintron, Graciela
Inter Amer Univ Pr
Hato Rey
Hato Rey, PR

Basri, Ahmad Kamal
Hasan
Univ Of Rochester
Rochester, NY

Bastedo, Carleen Shawn
Atlantic Comm Coll
Mays Landing, NJ

Baswell, David C
Central Al Comm Coll
Alexander City, AL

Batista, Nancy A
Fl International Univ
Miami, FL

Batt, Christina M
Defiance Coll
Defiance, OH

Batt, Erik D
S U N Y At Buffalo
Buffalo, NY

Batten, Shirley J
Waycross Coll
Waycross, GA

Battista, Frances H
Bunker Hill Comm Coll
Boston, MA

Battle, Deana N
Va St Univ
Petersburg, VA

Bauer, Bonnie S
Northern Ky Univ
Highland Hts, KY

Bauer, Derek T
Brevard Coll
Brevard, NC

Bauerle, Dolores De Fanti
Univ Of Fl
Gainesville, FL

Baugess, Heather E
Oh Dominican Coll
Columbus, OH

Baumgartner, Wendy A
Univ Of Pittsburgh
Pittsburgh, PA

Baxa, Louise M
Valdosta St Coll
Valdosta, GA

Baxter, Ronald D
Nova Univ
Ft Lauderdale, FL

Bay, Kristin Kelli
Lasell Coll
Newton, MA

Baylosis, Anna Marie Ednaco
Old Dominion Univ
Norfolk, VA

Bayne, Robert E
Hillsborough Comm Coll
Tampa, FL

Bayron, Hector J
Inter Amer Univ Pr Hato Rey
Hato Rey, PR

Bazarov, Alex V
Cornell Univ Statutory College
Ithaca, NY

Bazylak, Gregory M
Duquesne Univ
Pittsburgh, PA

Beam II, James F
Nc St Univ At Raleigh
Raleigh, NC

Beaman, Rhonda M
City Univ Of Ny Baruch Coll
New York, NY

Bearden, Joan K
Owensboro Jr Coll Of Bus
Owensboro, KY

Beardslee, Peggy S
Lycoming Coll
Williamsport, PA

Beare, Anissa K
Memphis St Univ
Memphis, TN

Bearror, Danielle L
Fl St Univ
Tallahassee, FL

Beasley, Carlene A
The Johns Hopkins Univ
Baltimore, MD

Beaver, Frankie L
Norfolk St Univ
Norfolk, VA

Bechard, Bryan J
Le Moyne Coll
Syracuse, NY

Beck, Brian
Savannah Coll Of Art & Design
Savannah, GA

Becker, Carol J
Pa St Univ York Cmps
York, PA

Becker Jr, James R
Memphis St Univ
Memphis, TN

Becker, Stefan
George Mason Univ
Fairfax, VA

Beckett, Kelly C
Univ Of South Al
Mobile, AL

Becton, Belinda M
Duquesne Univ
Pittsburgh, PA

Bee, Lorinette R
Al St Univ
Montgomery, AL

Beggins, David Paul
Fl International Univ
Miami, FL

Begley, Susan J
Glassboro St Coll
Glassboro, NJ

Behar, Robert
Fl International Univ
Miami, FL

Behnken, Anna M
Longwood Coll
Farmville, VA

Belanger, Mary K
Univ Of South Al
Mobile, AL

Belcher, Amy L
Lock Haven Univ
Lock Haven, PA

Belcher, Joseph M
Oh Univ-Southern Cmps
Ironton, OH

Belcher, Michelle D
Middle Tn St Univ
Murfreesboro, TN

Beldarrain-Caputo, Yoany
Fl International Univ
Miami, FL

Belen, Uzziel E
Univ Politecnica De Pr
Hato Rey, PR

Belesovski, Rebecca
Daemen Coll
Amherst, NY

Belew, Gregory L
Univ Of North Fl
Jacksonville, FL

Bell, Andrea D
Univ Of Montevallo
Montevallo, AL

Bell, Bobbi A
York Coll Of Pa
York, PA

Bell, Gloria C
Lincoln Univ
Lincoln Univ, PA

Bell, Lea N
Kent St Univ Kent Cmps
Kent, OH

Bell, Nicholas R
Univ Of Nc At Asheville
Asheville, NC

Bell, Patricia L
Salisbury St Univ
Salisbury, MD

Bell, Sandra M
Univ Of Ga
Athens, GA

Bell, Tajuan N
Al St Univ
Montgomery, AL

Bell, Vicky L
Al St Univ
Montgomery, AL

Belton, David
Coppin St Coll
Baltimore, MD

Belton, Tammy L
Longwood Coll
Farmville, VA

Bencivenga, Mary Jo
Georgian Court Coll
Lakewood, NJ

Bencomo-Lara, Maria J
Inter Amer Univ Pr Hato Rey
Hato Rey, PR

Benedetti Diaz, Analissa
Fl International Univ
Miami, FL

Benharroch, Esther
Miami Dade Comm Coll
Miami, FL

Benjamin, Christina H
Norfolk St Univ
Norfolk, VA

Benner, Jay B
Widener Univ
Chester, PA

Bennett, Amy R
South Ga Coll
Douglas, GA

Bennett, Dara H
Waycross Coll
Waycross, GA

Bennett, Deborah A
S U N Y Coll Of Tech At Alfred
Alfred, NY

Bennett, Gerald L
Erie Comm Coll South Cmps
Orchard Park, NY

Bennett, Rachel L
Tn Tech Univ
Cookeville, TN

Bennett, Susan M
Univ Of Miami
Coral Gables, FL

Bennett, Timothy C
Tn Temple Univ
Chattanooga, TN

Bennett, Wynell M
Univ Of West Fl
Pensacola, FL

Benson, Dawn B
Univ Of Hartford
West Hartford, CT

Benson, Steven M
Hillsborough Comm Coll
Tampa, FL

Benzell, Kimberly B
Providence Coll
Providence, RI

Berardi, Jacquelyn G
James Madison University
Harrisonburg, VA

Berardino, Kathleen M
Seton Hall Univ
South Orange, NJ

Bergen, Robin M
Univ Of Va
Charlottesville, VA

Berger, Mary Ellen
Saint Francis Coll
Loretto, PA

Bergmann, Melissa A
Bloomfield Coll
Bloomfield, NJ

Berkovich, Evgeny
Ny Univ
New York, NY

Bermudez, David R
Univ Of Pr At Rio Piedras
Rio Piedras, PR

Bermudez-Carrasquillo, Alexis A
Inter Amer Univ Pr Hato Rey
Hato Rey, PR

Bermudez-Fresse, Maria
Univ Of Pr Cayey Univ Coll
Cayey, PR

Bernard, Alain M
Morehouse Coll
Atlanta, GA

Bernard, Christina M
Va Commonwealth Univ
Richmond, VA

Bernard, Rose C S
Columbia Union Coll
Takoma Park, MD

Berneburg, Scott W
Oh Coll Of Podiatric Med
Cleveland, OH

Bernier Jr, Paul D
Albertus Magnus Coll
New Haven, CT

Bernini-Schimpf, Nicole
Dowling Coll
Oakdale Li, NY

Berrios Diaz, Zoraya M
Univ Of Pr At Mayaguez
Mayaguez, PR

Berrios Mendez, Brenda
Inter Amer Univ Pr Hato Rey
Hato Rey, PR

Berrios, Edgardo
Univ Of Pa
Philadelphia, PA

Berrios, Joseph S
Inter Amer Univ Pr Hato Rey
Hato Rey, PR

Berrios, Maria
Inter Amer Univ Pr San Juan
Hato Rey, PR

Berry, Kristina M
Western Piedmont Comm Coll
Morganton, NC

Berry, Robert M
Comm Coll Algny Co Algny Cmps
Pittsburgh, PA

Berry, Shauna L
Ky St Univ
Frankfort, KY

Berry, Tammy M
Univ Of West Fl
Pensacola, FL

Berryann, Jill M
S U N Y Coll Of Tech At Delhi
Delhi, NY

Bersuder, Cynthia A
Miami Jacobs Jr Coll Of Bus
Dayton, OH

Berte, Lisa F
Neumann Coll
Aston, PA

Berthay White, Joyce Ann
Ms St Univ
Miss State, MS

Bertig, Jeannine L
Duquesne Univ
Pittsburgh, PA

Bertine, Deborah A
S U N Y Coll Of Tech At Frmgdl
Farmingdale, NY

Berton, Thomas S
Dowling Coll
Oakdale Li, NY

Berube, Nancy E
Univ Of New England
Biddeford, ME

Best, Esther Dunstene
Univ Of The Dist Of Columbia
Washington, DC

Bestrycki Jr, Chester M
Marywood Coll
Scranton, PA

Betancourt, Madeline
Duquesne Univ
Pittsburgh, PA

Betancourth, Edwin B A
Pace Univ At White Plains
White Plains, NY

Bethea, Tracey
Benedict Coll
Columbia, SC

Bettinger, April L
Ohio Valley Coll
Parkersburg, WV

Betzner, Rayna A
Univ Of Pittsburgh
Pittsburgh, PA

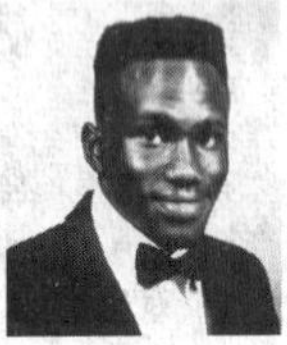
Bevelle Jr, Wesley
Al St Univ
Montgomery, AL

Beyer, Theodore M
Cornell Univ Statutory College
Ithaca, NY

Beyman, Brian J
Univ Of Toledo
Toledo, OH

Bezares Hernandez, Lianne
Inter Amer Univ Pr Hato Rey
Hato Rey, PR

Bhatia, Honey L
Duquesne Univ
Pittsburgh, PA

Bhattacharyya, Sudhir
City Univ Of Ny Baruch Coll
New York, NY

Bhojwani, Tina V
Georgetown Univ
Washington, DC

Biancardi, Kennth J
Daytona Beach Comm Coll
Daytona Beach, FL

Bianchini, Danielle M
Villanova Univ
Villanova, PA

Bias, Jennifer D
Marshall University
Huntington, WV

Biberica, Joyce D
Marymount Manhattan Coll
New York, NY

Bible III, Carl B
Univ Of Cin R Walters Coll
Blue Ash, OH

Bickelhaupt, Michael J
Central Fl Comm Coll
Ocala, FL

Biddle, Annie Kathryn
Christian Brothers Univ
Memphis, TN

Bidot, Maria E
Univ Of Pr Medical Sciences
San Juan, PR

Bienko, Mary C
S U N Y Coll At Fredonia
Fredonia, NY

Bigger, Teresa T
John C Calhoun St Comm Coll
Decatur, AL

Biggs, Catherine D
Hudson County Comm Coll
Jersey City, NJ

Bihler, Heather Erika
Bethany Coll
Bethany, WV

Biles, Charlie B
Univ Of Ga
Athens, GA

Bilker, Lawrence A
Univ Of Rochester
Rochester, NY

Billoch, Juan Carlos
Miami Dade Comm Coll South
Miami, FL

Bird, Marla L
Marshall University
Huntington, WV

Bird, Sandra J
Anne Arundel Comm Coll
Arnold, MD

Biro, Richard G
Univ Of Bridgeport
Bridgeport, CT

Birt, Carla C
Fl International Univ
Miami, FL

Bischoff, Julie L
Georgian Court Coll
Lakewood, NJ

Bishko, Timothy M
Becker Coll At Leicester
Leicester, MA

Bishop, Kimberly J
Memphis St Univ
Memphis, TN

Bishota, Furaha L
Widener Univ
Chester, PA

Black, Lisa J
Univ Of Tn At Martin
Martin, TN

Black, Melanie Elizabeth
Clemson Univ
Clemson, SC

Black, Shawtain M
Ky St Univ
Frankfort, KY

Blackledge, Jane E
Univ Of Southern Ms
Hattiesburg, MS

Blackledge, Joel L
Univ Of Southern Ms
Hattiesburg, MS

Blackwell, Melissa L
Greenville Tech Coll
Greenville, SC

Blackwell, Mitchell C
New Comm Coll Of Baltimore
Baltimore, MD

Blackwell, Monica L
Bennett Coll
Greensboro, NC

Blair, Joann L
Georgetown Coll
Georgetown, KY

Blair, Melissa D
Univ Of Ky
Lexington, KY

Blair, Sonja L
Middle Tn St Univ
Murfreesboro, TN

Blair, Tanya L
Andrew Coll
Cuthbert, GA

Blake, Michael S
Franklin And Marshall Coll
Lancaster, PA

Blanco, Barbara M
Saint Thomas Univ
Miami, FL

Blanco, Betty
Univ Of Miami
Coral Gables, FL

Blanco, Melanie Nishea
George Washington Univ
Washington, DC

Blanding, Donna S
Norfolk St Univ
Norfolk, VA

Blankenship, Carolyn
Union Coll
Barbourville, KY

Blankenship, Kelly M
Fl St Univ
Tallahassee, FL

Blankenship, Robert B
Old Dominion Univ
Norfolk, VA

Blanton, Kathryn Daisy
Univ Of Sc At Columbia
Columbia, SC

Blanton, Stanley B
Tri County Tech Coll
Pendleton, SC

Blass, Laura L
Fl International Univ
Miami, FL

Blauser, Michael J
Daemen Coll
Amherst, NY

Blay, Christina E
Coll Of New Rochelle
New Rochelle, NY

Blay, Emmanuel K
City Univ Of Ny
Baruch Coll
New York, NY

Bledsoe, Carole R
Central St Univ
Wilberforce, OH

Bledsoe, Mary Louise
Jacksonville St Univ
Jacksonville, AL

Blessing, Lisa A
Rutgers St Univ At
Camden
Camden, NJ

Blevins Watson, Suzie A
The Johns Hopkins Univ
Baltimore, MD

Bliamis, Christos
Hellenic Coll/Holy
Cross
Brookline, MA

Blomer, Ann M
Northern Ky Univ
Highland Hts, KY

Bloom, Brooke J
Cornell Univ Statutory
College
Ithaca, NY

Bloomfield, Marcy S
Oh Northern Univ
Ada, OH

Blount, David R
Univ Of Al At
Birmingham
Birmingham, AL

Bobo, Melissa G
Lexington Comm Coll
Lexington, KY

Bodiford, Felecia B
Univ Of Sc At
Columbia
Columbia, SC

Boel, Kathryn E
Le Moyne Coll
Syracuse, NY

Boenig, Doreen G
Saint Josephs Coll
Suffik Cmps
Patchogue, NY

Bogdon, Michele A
Univ Of Miami
Coral Gables, FL

Bogert, Susanne J
Georgian Court Coll
Lakewood, NJ

Bohusch, Therese A
Philadelphia Coll Pharm
& Sci
Philadelphia, PA

Bold, Sharon Lynn
Salisbury St Univ
Salisbury, MD

Bolden, Erica S
Jackson St Univ
Jackson, MS

Boling, Brian E
Univ Of Ky
Lexington, KY

Boling, Timothy A
Northeast State Tech
Comm Coll
Blountville, TN

Boltz, Mary F
Wagner Coll
Staten Island, NY

Bonanni, Judith D
Ramapo Coll Of Nj
Mahwah, NJ

Bonczek, Joseph V
Le Moyne Coll
Syracuse, NY

Bond, Sharon R
Tn St Univ
Nashville, TN

Bond, Tracey D
Radford Univ
Radford, VA

Bond, Trishun L
Hampton Univ
Hampton, VA

Bondy, Angie L
Oh Dominican Coll
Columbus, OH

Bongiorno, Christine L
Univ Of De
Newark, DE

Bonilla, Doris W
Medical Coll Of Ga
Augusta, GA

Bonilla, Zobeida E
Univ Of Pr Cayey Univ
Coll
Cayey, PR

Bonkowski, Holly A
William Paterson Coll
Wayne, NJ

Bonner, Kia M
Tuskegee Univ
Tuskegee Inst, AL

Bonney, Tammy H
Univ Of South Al
Mobile, AL

Bonney-Santucci,
Rebecca J
Old Dominion Univ
Norfolk, VA

Boodram, Dipnarine
Frankie
City Univ Of Ny
Queensbrough
New York, NY

Booker, Aletha L
Johnson C Smith Univ
Charlotte, NC

Booker, Gary A
Howard Comm Coll
Columbia, MD

Booker, Stacy M
Saint Pauls Coll
Lawrenceville, VA

Bookman, Debra M
Johnson C Smith Univ
Charlotte, NC

Books, Laurie C
Mount Aloysius Jr Coll
Cresson, PA

Boone, Christopher C
Univ Of Sc At
Columbia
Columbia, SC

Boone, Rhonda K
Christopher Newport Coll
Newport News, VA

Booth, Dennis L
Penn Coll Of Straight Chiro
Horsham, PA

Booth, Tracey D
Nc Agri & Tech St Univ
Greensboro, NC

Borge, Milind L
Columbia Union Coll
Takoma Park, MD

Borrero, Ana I
Catholic Univ Of Pr
Ponce, PR

Borrows, Janice R
Miami Dade Comm Coll
Miami, FL

Bos, Martha M
Suffolk Comm Coll Eastern Cmps
Riverhead, NY

Bosma, Mark A
Air Force Inst Of Tech
Wrt-Ptrsn Afb, OH

Bossard, T Dan-Xia
Smith Coll
Northampton, MA

Boston, David L
Chattanooga St Tech Comm Coll
Chattanooga, TN

Bostwick, Michele K
Central Fl Comm Coll
Ocala, FL

Boswell, Edmund O
Univ Of Sc At Columbia
Columbia, SC

Bosworth, Amelia Carol
Davis & Elkins Coll
Elkins, WV

Bothello, Deena B
Coll Of William & Mary
Williamsburg, VA

Bougrand, Nancy K
Bristol Univ
Bristol, TN

Bourgeois, Monique M
Auburn Univ At Auburn
Auburn, AL

Boutros, Geoffrey H
Fl Atlantic Univ
Boca Raton, FL

Bove, Denise E
Hudson County Comm Coll
Jersey City, NJ

Bowden, Alan G
Univ Of Nc At Charlotte
Charlotte, NC

Bowden, Mary T
Roane St Comm Coll
Harriman, TN

Bowen, Paul A
Morehouse Coll
Atlanta, GA

Bowen, Terra L
Fl A & M Univ
Tallahassee, FL

Bowens, Sylvia M
Columbia Union Coll
Takoma Park, MD

Bowers, Erin L
West Liberty St Coll
West Liberty, WV

Bowers, Vicki E
Univ Of Miami
Coral Gables, FL

Bowes, John E
Miami Dade Comm Coll
Miami, FL

Bowler, Michael W
Western New England Coll
Springfield, MA

Box, Anita C
Itawamba Comm Coll
Fulton, MS

Boyd, John T
Piedmont Tech Coll
Greenwood, SC

Boyd II, Robert A
Morehouse Coll
Atlanta, GA

Boyens, Lauren A
Schenectady County Comm Coll
Schenectady, NY

Boykin, Diane M
Ms St Univ
Miss State, MS

Boyle, Joanne M
Coll Misericordia
Dallas, PA

Bozeman, Jennifer L
Valdosta St Coll
Valdosta, GA

Bracamonte, Miriam A
Springfield Tech Comm Coll
Springfield, MA

Bracero, Mariel
Inter Amer Univ Pr Hato Rey
Hato Rey, PR

Brachmann, Claire R
Asnuntuck Comm Coll
Enfield, CT

Brackbill, Marlene L
Christopher Newport Coll
Newport News, VA

Bradley, Edith I
City Univ Of Ny Hunter Coll
New York, NY

Bradley, Mary V
Marymount Univ
Arlington, VA

Bradley, Nancy L
Atlantic Comm Coll
Mays Landing, NJ

Bradley, Troy
Truett Mc Connell Coll
Cleveland, GA

Bradley, Valerie A
Belmont Coll
Nashville, TN

Bradshaw, Billy R
Owensboro Comm Coll
Owensboro, KY

Brady, Frank Barco
Fl A & M Univ
Tallahassee, FL

Brady, Rosaleen A
Mount Saint Mary Coll
Newburgh, NY

Bragason, Atli Bjorn
Univ Of Sc At
Columbia
Columbia, SC

Brana, Marta
Univ Of Pr At Rio
Piedras
Rio Piedras, PR

Branch, Kevin W
Abraham Baldwin Agri
Coll
Tifton, GA

Branch, Tamara Y
Va St Univ
Petersburg, VA

Brank, Karen L
Johnson C Smith Univ
Charlotte, NC

Brannon III, Lee R
Al A & M Univ
Normal, AL

Branson, Ralph
Matthew
Oh St Univ At Newark
Newark, OH

Brasfield, Kinsley Todd
Fl St Univ
Tallahassee, FL

Brassard, Alison M
Western New England
Coll
Springfield, MA

Braswell, Sharon Y
City Univ Of Ny Med
Evers Coll
Brooklyn, NY

Bratcher, Beverly A
Duquesne Univ
Pittsburgh, PA

Bratkiv, Mark
Univ Of Miami
Coral Gables, FL

Braton, Tracey A
Kent St Univ Kent
Cmps
Kent, OH

Brau Sobrino, Alberto
Univ Politecnica De Pr
Hato Rey, PR

Braun, Beth Justine
Mount Saint Mary Coll
Newburgh, NY

Braxton, Aroneysa D
Alcorn St Univ
Lorman, MS

Brazzano, Lisa M
Dowling Coll
Oakdale Li, NY

Brea, Luis O
Fordham Univ
Bronx, NY

Bredine, David W
Ms St Univ
Miss State, MS

Breen, Anne E
Hudson Valley Comm
Coll
Troy, NY

Breidenbach, Julie G
Miami Jacobs Jr Coll
Of Bus
Dayton, OH

Breitmaier, Christine
Mount Saint Mary Coll
Newburgh, NY

Breland, Katy A
Auburn Univ At Auburn
Auburn, AL

Brenek, Laura M
Villanova Univ
Villanova, PA

Brenton, Richard M
City Univ Of Ny La
Guard Coll
Long Island Cty, NY

Brenzel, Seth A
Swarthmore Coll
Swarthmore, PA

Bresler, Kurt T
Central Fl Comm Coll
Ocala, FL

Brewer, Lynn A
Pasco Hernando Comm
Coll
Dade City, FL

Brewster, Tina D
Univ Of Louisville
Louisville, KY

Brice, Christian
Bunker Hill Comm Coll
Boston, MA

Brickner, Elizabeth H
Villanova Univ
Villanova, PA

Brickus, Joanna E
Cheyney Univ Of Pa
Cheyney, PA

Bridgeforth, Tony G
Lane Coll
Jackson, TN

Bridges, Cynthia A
Anne Arundel Comm
Coll
Arnold, MD

Bridges, Eddie
Nc St Univ At Raleigh
Raleigh, NC

Briggs, Dearn M
Immaculata Coll
Immaculata, PA

Briggs, Jonathan E
Ms St Univ
Miss State, MS

Briggs, Rawle R
City Univ Of Ny
Queensbrough
New York, NY

Brightwell-Schneider, Lisa C
Neumann Coll
Aston, PA

Brim, Frances Yvonne
Patrick Henry Comm Coll
Martinsville, VA

Brin, Nicole K
Univ Of Md At Eastern Shore
Princess Anne, MD

Bringas Castillo, Javier
Inter Amer Univ Pr Hato Rey
Hato Rey, PR

Brinson, Ivy D
Bryant Stratton Bus Inst Roch
Rochester, NY

Briones, Christine Hazel
City Univ Of Ny Baruch Coll
New York, NY

Briskman, Brian L
Ny Univ
New York, NY

Brister, Jo A
Univ Of Southern Ms
Hattiesburg, MS

Britnell, Patrick C
Embry Riddle Aeronautical Univ
Daytona Beach, FL

Britt, Errol W
Wilberforce Univ
Wilberforce, OH

Britt, Nancy L
Univ Of Sc At Columbia
Columbia, SC

Britt, Trulinda E
Nc Agri & Tech St Univ
Greensboro, NC

Britton, Robyn A
Central Al Comm Coll
Alexander City, AL

Brockelbank, Sandra L
Univ Of North Fl
Jacksonville, FL

Bromfield, Andrew W
Fl International Univ
Miami, FL

Broncato, Mianne L
Alfred Univ
Alfred, NY

Bronski, John E
City Univ Of Ny Baruch Coll
New York, NY

Bronson, Cheryl Y
S U N Y Coll Of Tech At Frmgdl
Farmingdale, NY

Bronson, Sharon L
Bennett Coll
Greensboro, NC

Brooks, Anthony T
Longwood Coll
Farmville, VA

Brooks, Bethany M
Wv Univ At Parkersburg
Parkersburg, WV

Brooks, Gerald Raymond
Nova Univ
Ft Lauderdale, FL

Brooks, Jennifer P
Va Polytechnic Inst & St Univ
Blacksburg, VA

Brooks, Lance H
Mercer Univ
Macon, GA

Brooks-Jones, Bernice
Barry Univ
Miami, FL

Broome, Joyce L
Piedmont Tech Coll
Greenwood, SC

Brouillard, Carol L
Mount Saint Mary Coll
Newburgh, NY

Brouillette, Kimberly B
Univ Of Nc At Charlotte
Charlotte, NC

Brown, Adrien Wesley
Daemen Coll
Amherst, NY

Brown, Angela Ranae
Univ Of Southern Ms
Hattiesburg, MS

Brown, Barry J
Marshall University
Huntington, WV

Brown, Bonnes Oneal
Alcorn St Univ
Lorman, MS

Brown, Byron A
Winthrop Coll
Rock Hill, SC

Brown, Calvin W
Limestone Coll
Gaffney, SC

Brown, Carol Joan
Newbury Coll
Brookline, MA

Brown, Chandra L
Wilberforce Univ
Wilberforce, OH

Brown, Christopher A
Univ Of Nc At Charlotte
Charlotte, NC

Brown, Christopher E
Clark Atlanta Univ
Atlanta, GA

Brown, Eric S
Enterprise St Jr Coll
Enterprise, AL

Brown, Evelyn Denise
Ashland Comm Coll
Ashland, KY

Brown, Geraldine Elliott
Oh Univ-Southern Cmps
Ironton, OH

Brown, Greta M
Abraham Baldwin Agri Coll
Tifton, GA

Brown, Heidi A
Casco Bay Coll
Portland, ME

Brown, Holly Christina
Smith Coll
Northampton, MA

Brown Jr, Hugh Oren
Univ Of Ga
Athens, GA

Brown Jr, James T C
Va St Univ
Petersburg, VA

Brown, Jeanne L
Lenoir Rhyne Coll
Hickory, NC

Brown, John P
Middle Tn St Univ
Murfreesboro, TN

Brown, Kenneth K
Fl A & M Univ
Tallahassee, FL

Brown, Kimberly F
Vance Granville Comm Coll
Henderson, NC

Brown, Kristie L
Central St Univ
Wilberforce, OH

Brown, Kristy L
Marywood Coll
Scranton, PA

Brown, Luanne
Oh Univ-Southern Cmps
Ironton, OH

Brown, Michael D
Morehouse Coll
Atlanta, GA

Brown, Mitzi I
Clayton St Coll
Morrow, GA

Brown, Patricia Y
Valdosta St Coll
Valdosta, GA

Brown, Penny L
Western Carolina Univ
Cullowhee, NC

Brown, Rebecca F
Oh St Univ
Columbus, OH

Brown, Sandra K
Beckley Coll
Beckley, WV

Brown, Shawn P
Newbury Coll
Brookline, MA

Brown, Sheila
Baldwin Wallace Coll
Berea, OH

Brown, Shermel A
Bloomfield Coll
Bloomfield, NJ

Brown, Stacie L
Mobile Coll
Mobile, AL

Brown, Susan R
Univ Of Cincinnati
Cincinnati, OH

Brown, Tanya S
Faulkner Univ
Montgomery, AL

Brown III, Thomas L
Univ Of Ct
Storrs, CT

Brown, Travis L
Albany St Coll
Albany, GA

Brown, William A
Tn Tech Univ
Cookeville, TN

Brownlow, Wanda F
Al A & M Univ
Normal, AL

Bruce, David C
Christopher Newport Coll
Newport News, VA

Brumfield, Melissa G
Univ Of Ga
Athens, GA

Brumley, Catherine L
De Tech & Comm Coll At Dover
Dover, DE

Brunner, Robin F
City Univ Of Ny Baruch Coll
New York, NY

Brunt, Steven T
Univ Of Akron
Akron, OH

Brusch, Wynette S
Tuskegee Univ
Tuskegee Inst, AL

Bryan III, James W
Union Univ
Jackson, TN

Bryant Workman, Leota
Oh Univ-Southern Cmps
Ironton, OH

Bryant, Sabrina M
Monroe Comm Coll
Rochester, NY

Bryant Jr, Thomas F
Univ Of Sc At Columbia
Columbia, SC

Bryk, Erica L
Kings Coll
Wilkes-Barre, PA

Bubb, Tracey J
Mary Washington Coll
Fredericksburg, VA

Bubb-Deane, Patricia
Ny Univ
New York, NY

Buccarelli, Rebecca J
City Univ Of Ny City Coll
New York, NY

Bucci, Michael P
Hartwick Coll
Oneonta, NY

Buchanan, Matthew A
Mayland Comm Coll
Spruce Pine, NC

Buchanan-Hill, Charlyn
Univ Of Cin R Walters
Coll
Blue Ash, OH

Buchanna, Reginald L
Al A & M Univ
Normal, AL

Bucheister, Kristi L
Commonwealth Coll
Virginia Beach, VA

Buckholts, Charles D
Middle Tn St Univ
Murfreesboro, TN

Buckland, Rebecca M
Beckley Coll
Beckley, WV

Buda, Melissa A
Dowling Coll
Oakdale Li, NY

Budhram, Arjune A
City Univ Of Ny
Baruch Coll
New York, NY

Bufalini, Helen A
Geneva Coll
Beaver Falls, PA

Buffin, Kelly A
Lexington Comm Coll
Lexington, KY

Bugash, Susan E
Lebanon Valley Coll
Annville, PA

Bui, Tram T
Columbus Coll Of Art
& Design
Columbus, OH

Bullock, Heidi L
Furman Univ
Greenville, SC

Bullock, Louisa M
Norfolk St Univ
Norfolk, VA

Bullock, Scott K
Wilmington Coll
Wilmington, OH

Bundy, Dan L
Atlanta Christian Coll
East Point, GA

Bundy, David W
Univ Of Sc At
Columbia
Columbia, SC

Bundy, Erica S
Glassboro St Coll
Glassboro, NJ

Burford, Cynthia A
Univ Of Tn At
Knoxville
Knoxville, TN

Burgard, Jesse F
Saint Petersburg Jr Coll
St Petersburg, FL

Burgess, Anissa
Spartanburg Methodist
Coll
Spartanburg, SC

Burgess, Barnard
Al A & M Univ
Normal, AL

Burgess, Wendy C
Univ Of Ga
Athens, GA

Burgo, Joao J M
Commonwealth Coll
Virginia Beach, VA

Burgos Sanchez, Hugo J
Univ Of Pr Humacao
Univ Coll
Humacao, PR

Burgos, Juan M
Bunker Hill Comm Coll
Boston, MA

Burgos, Lisie J
Inter Amer Univ Pr
Hato Rey
Hato Rey, PR

Burgos-Cotto, Javier R
Univ Of Pr Cayey Univ
Coll
Cayey, PR

Burgreen, Carl T
Univ Of Sc At
Columbia
Columbia, SC

Burkard, Karen L
Saint John Fisher Coll
Rochester, NY

Burke, Amy M
Walker Coll
Jasper, AL

Burke, Melissa A
Providence Coll
Providence, RI

Burke, Peggy D
Cumberland Coll
Williamsburg, KY

Burke, Sean D
Concordia Coll
Bronxville, NY

Burke, Shawn Patrick
Merrimack Coll
North Andover, MA

Burke, Susan A
Bunker Hill Comm Coll
Boston, MA

Burket, Michael C
Indiana Univ Of Pa
Indiana, PA

Burkett, Karen M
Christopher Newport
Coll
Newport News, VA

Burkhard, Rebecca F
Univ Of Ky
Lexington, KY

Burkhart, Jo Ann L
Univ Of Cin R Walters
Coll
Blue Ash, OH

Burks, Tabitha R
Wittenberg Univ
Springfield, OH

Burleson, Marsha L
Mayland Comm Coll
Spruce Pine, NC

Burnett, Melissa Dawn
Piedmont Tech Coll
Greenwood, SC

Burnett, Miguel G
City Univ Of Ny
Baruch Coll
New York, NY

Burns, Donna M
Pa St Univ York Cmps
York, PA

Burns, Jonathan D
Marshall University
Huntington, WV

Burns, Stephen W
Middle Tn St Univ
Murfreesboro, TN

Burr, Tracey M
Salem-Teikyo Univ
Salem, WV

Burrell, Sonya J
Fl A & M Univ
Tallahassee, FL

Burris, Roshunda R
Wilberforce Univ
Wilberforce, OH

Burroughs, Paula D
Christopher Newport Coll
Newport News, VA

Burroughs, Ronald W
Morehouse Coll
Atlanta, GA

Burrows, Lisa L
Casco Bay Coll
Portland, ME

Burton, Monica E
William Paterson Coll
Wayne, NJ

Burton, Nathan A
Tn Tech Univ
Cookeville, TN

Burton, Victoria J
Oh Dominican Coll
Columbus, OH

Buscemi, Vincent J N
Niagara Univ
Niagara Univ, NY

Bush, Jeffrey W A
Centenary Coll
Hackettstown, NJ

Bush, Kevin D
Alcorn St Univ
Lorman, MS

Butcher, Dionne R
City Univ Of Ny Bronx Comm Col
Bronx, NY

Butler, Christopher S
Wv Univ
Morgantown, WV

Butler, Earl D
City Univ Of Ny
Baruch Coll
New York, NY

Butler, Sherina M
Va St Univ
Petersburg, VA

Butler, Steven R
Tn Temple Univ
Chattanooga, TN

Butner, Julie E
High Point Coll
High Point, NC

Butt, Fauzia K
Ma Inst Of Tech
Cambridge, MA

Buttaro, Marissa L
Philadelphia Coll Pharm & Sci
Philadelphia, PA

Butterfield, O Renee
Bunker Hill Comm Coll
Boston, MA

Butterworth, Karen L
Bay Path Coll
Longmeadow, MA

Butts, David L
Al St Univ
Montgomery, AL

Byer, Fabian A
S U N Y At Buffalo
Buffalo, NY

Byers, Louise V
Univ Of Va
Charlottesville, VA

Byers, Michelle L
Va St Univ
Petersburg, VA

Bynum, Kesha Doreen
Bennett Coll
Greensboro, NC

Byrd, Ann M
Converse Coll
Spartanburg, SC

Cabeza Gonzalez, Carlos M
Univ Politecnica De Pr
Hato Rey, PR

Cable, Alana M
Oh St Univ At Newark
Newark, OH

Cable, Melissa L
Union Univ
Jackson, TN

Cabre, Adriana C
Duquesne Univ
Pittsburgh, PA

Cabrera Ramos, Antonio
Univ Politecnica De Pr
Hato Rey, PR

Cadeau, Katsia Marie
Saint Thomas Univ
Miami, FL

Cadet, Judith
Bunker Hill Comm Coll
Boston, MA

Cadman, Patricia A
Slippery Rock Univ
Slippery Rock, PA

Caetta, Gina M
Kent St Univ Kent Cmps
Kent, OH

Cagan, Holly B
Nova Univ
Ft Lauderdale, FL

Cage, Felicia E
Alcorn St Univ
Lorman, MS

Cagno, Joseph R
Rutgers St Un At New Brunswick
New Brunswick, NJ

Cahill, Marion K
Manhattanville Coll
Purchase, NY

Cairo, Adihelin
Fl International Univ
Miami, FL

Calderon, Brenda L
Inter Amer Univ Pr Hato Rey
Hato Rey, PR

Caldwell, Gary A
Fl A & M Univ
Tallahassee, FL

Caldwell, Margaret Elizabeth
Univ Of Nc At Greensboro
Greensboro, NC

Calero, Gisela
Fl International Univ
Miami, FL

Calero, Mirna
City Univ Of Ny La Guard Coll
Long Island Cty, NY

Calley, Daniel P
Boston Coll
Chestnut Hill, MA

Callwood, Cherisse M
Clark Atlanta Univ
Atlanta, GA

Calvert, Sheila W
Piedmont Tech Coll
Greenwood, SC

Calvo, Maria E
Fl International Univ
Miami, FL

Calzada Pagan, Ramon Luis
Univ Of Pr Medical Sciences
San Juan, PR

Camacho Conty, Mei Ling Z
Inter Amer Univ Pr Hato Rey
Hato Rey, PR

Camasto, Angela M
Cornell Univ Statutory College
Ithaca, NY

Cameron, Cheryl D
Johnson C Smith Univ
Charlotte, NC

Cameron, Karen J
Brown Univ
Providence, RI

Camino Torres, Jose R
Inter Amer Univ Pr San German
San German, PR

Camiola, Lisa M
William Carey Coll
Hattiesburg, MS

Camp, David R
Chattanooga St Tech Comm Coll
Chattanooga, TN

Campanaro, Christopher
Univ Of Fl
Gainesville, FL

Campbell, A Heather
Birmingham Southern Coll
Birmingham, AL

Campbell, Amy L
Roane St Comm Coll
Harriman, TN

Campbell, Andrea D
Jackson St Univ
Jackson, MS

Campbell, Cynthia Michelle
Univ Of Sc At Columbia
Columbia, SC

Campbell, Darlene G
Central St Univ
Wilberforce, OH

Campbell, David A
Wv Univ
Morgantown, WV

Campbell, Felina D
Univ Of Al At Birmingham
Birmingham, AL

Campbell, Hulian H
Alcorn St Univ
Lorman, MS

Campbell Jr, James R
Rutgers St Univ At Camden
Camden, NJ

Campbell, Jeffery G
Union Coll
Barbourville, KY

Campbell, Lisa A
Greenville Tech Coll
Greenville, SC

Campbell, Marcia J
City Univ Of Ny Queensbrough
New York, NY

Campbell, Robert B
Niagara Univ
Niagara Univ, NY

Campbell, Ruthanna J
Beckley Coll
Beckley, WV

Campbell, Tammy A
Fl International Univ
Miami, FL

Campero, Jennifer L
Gallaudet Univ
Washington, DC

Campion, Denise M
Central Pa Bus School
Summerdale, PA

Campo, Jairo
Saint Thomas Univ
Miami, FL

Campos, Joshua J
Daytona Beach Comm Coll
Daytona Beach, FL

Campos, Rosa A
Inter Amer Univ Pr San Juan
Hato Rey, PR

Canada, Broderick N
Al A & M Univ
Normal, AL

Canino, Michael J
Glassboro St Coll
Glassboro, NJ

Cannon, Judy P
Troy St Univ At Dothan
Dothan, AL

Cannon, Tracy L
Atlantic Comm Coll
Mays Landing, NJ

Cano-Alicea, Noemi
City Univ Of Ny Bronx Comm Col
Bronx, NY

Canonge, Hector A
City Univ Of Ny
Baruch Coll
New York, NY

Cantrell, Donna J
Central Al Comm Coll
Alexander City, AL

Cantrell, Mary E
Univ Of Ga
Athens, GA

Cape, Cynthia M
Anderson Coll
Anderson, SC

Capozzolo, Patrick E
Daytona Beach Comm Coll
Daytona Beach, FL

Cappel, Anita L
Univ Of Cincinnati
Cincinnati, OH

Caputo, Leonard S
City Univ Of Ny
Brooklyn Coll
Brooklyn, NY

Carabina, Matthew S
Univ Of New Haven
West Haven, CT

Caraway, John W
Lincoln Univ
Lincoln Univ, PA

Carbone, David G
Univ Of Miami
Coral Gables, FL

Carbonneau, Carol M
Central Me Medical Center
Lewiston, ME

Cardona, Andres
City Univ Of Ny
Baruch Coll
New York, NY

Cardonita, Donna L
Albertus Magnus Coll
New Haven, CT

Cardoso, Armando P
Saint Thomas Univ
Miami, FL

Cardwell, Joan B
Birmingham Southern Coll
Birmingham, AL

Care, D Desiree
Goucher Coll
Towson, MD

Careccia, Sharon L
Old Dominion Univ
Norfolk, VA

Carlberg, Charlene Marie
Pasco Hernando Comm Coll
Dade City, FL

Carlisle, Samantha A
Univ Of Al
Tuscaloosa, AL

Carlo Hernandez, Ileana
Inter Amer Univ Pr Fajardo
Fajardo, PR

Carlson, Kierstin K L
Cornell Univ Statutory College
Ithaca, NY

Carmen, Alicea L
Inter Amer Univ Pr Hato Rey
Hato Rey, PR

Carpenter, Alexandra C
Palm Beach Atlantic Coll
W Palm Beach, FL

Carpenter, Kristine A
Immaculata Coll
Immaculata, PA

Carpenter, Nevedia R
Blue Mountain Coll
Blue Mountain, MS

Carr, Cherell M
Spelman Coll
Atlanta, GA

Carr, Joel S
Univ Of Ga
Athens, GA

Carr, Valerie L
Alcorn St Univ
Lorman, MS

Carribon, Mahalia M
City Univ Of Ny City Coll
New York, NY

Carriles, Alfredo J
Miami Dade Comm Coll South
Miami, FL

Carrillo, Flavio
Univ Of Miami
Coral Gables, FL

Carrillo, Nivia Sara
Inter Amer Univ Pr Hato Rey
Hato Rey, PR

Carroll, Candace L
Clayton St Coll
Morrow, GA

Carroll, Florence Green
Univ Of The Dist Of Columbia
Washington, DC

Carroll, Harlan P
Kennesaw St Coll
Marietta, GA

Carroll, Lisa M
Oh Dominican Coll
Columbus, OH

Carroll, Sarah S
Greenville Tech Coll
Greenville, SC

Carson, Stephanie Dawn
Univ Of Tn At Martin
Martin, TN

Cartagena Villanueva, Enid M
Univ Of Pr Cayey Univ Coll
Cayey, PR

Carter, Brenda L
Univ Of Southern Ms
Hattiesburg, MS

Carter, Christopher M
Univ Of Akron
Akron, OH

Carter, De Wayne O
Al A & M Univ
Normal, AL

Carter, Gail A
Salisbury St Univ
Salisbury, MD

Carter, Janet L
Methodist Coll
Fayetteville, NC

Carter, Jennifer D
Valdosta St Coll
Valdosta, GA

Carter, Keita A
Strayer Coll
Washington, DC

Carter, Linda K
Watterson Coll
Louisville, KY

Carter, Marian V
Hampton Univ
Hampton, VA

Carter, Mary D
Western Piedmont Comm Coll
Morganton, NC

Carter, Melissa L
Univ Of Pittsburgh At Bradford
Bradford, PA

Cartwright, Amy B
Oh St Univ At Newark
Newark, OH

Carty, Patrick K
Glassboro St Coll
Glassboro, NJ

Caruso, Silvia L
Duquesne Univ
Pittsburgh, PA

Caruthers, Timothy N
Univ Of Fl
Gainesville, FL

Carver Jr, Jacky E
Roane St Comm Coll
Harriman, TN

Cary, Christopher D
Ky Wesleyan Coll
Owensboro, KY

Cary, Yvonne M
Vance Granville Comm Coll
Henderson, NC

Cascaddan Jr, Richard
Central Fl Comm Coll
Ocala, FL

Case, Paul C
S U N Y Coll Of Tech At Alfred
Alfred, NY

Cash, James D
Univ Of Ga
Athens, GA

Casher, David S
Widener Univ
Chester, PA

Casillas, David
Evangelical Semimary Of P R
Hato Rey, PR

Cassagnol, Hans P
Saint Johns Univ
Jamaica, NY

Cassiday II, John R
Univ Of Akron
Akron, OH

Castellano, John R
Fl Atlantic Univ
Boca Raton, FL

Castelli, Rosaria Maria
Barry Univ
Miami, FL

Castillo Vazquez, Maria
Univ Politecnica De Pr
Hato Rey, PR

Castle, Gerald S
Bristol Univ
Bristol, TN

Castle, Patricia D
Bristol Univ
Bristol, TN

Castler, Jeffrey D
Siena Coll
Loudonville, NY

Castro, Odalys
Fl International Univ
Miami, FL

Castro-Sanchez, Maria
Univ Of Pr Humacao Univ Coll
Humacao, PR

Castroman, Suzanne V
Fordham Univ
Bronx, NY

Catala, Adirenne M
Dowling Coll
Oakdale Li, NY

Catanzano, Tara M
Hofstra Univ
Hempstead, NY

Cate, Susan L
Le Moyne Coll
Syracuse, NY

Cates, Paula T
Voorhees Coll
Denmark, SC

Catledge, Andrea B
Kent St Univ Kent Cmps
Kent, OH

Catlett, Ramona I
Pellissippi St Tech
Comm Coll
Knoxville, TN

Cato, Patrick W
Spartanburg Methodist
Coll
Spartanburg, SC

Caudill, Deborah J
Univ Of Ky
Lexington, KY

Caullett, Alan B
Fl Atlantic Univ
Boca Raton, FL

Cavaggioni, Luigina
Marymount Manhattan
Coll
New York, NY

Cavagnaro, Augustine J
Univ Of Nc At
Asheville
Asheville, NC

Caviness, Elaine T
Memphis St Univ
Memphis, TN

Cebert, Marie Carmel
Al A & M Univ
Normal, AL

Cebula, Marc C
Hilbert Coll
Hamburg, NY

Cebular, Deanna V
Georgetown Univ
Washington, DC

Cecere, Christa A
Manhattan Coll
Bronx, NY

Censabella, Lisa M
Iona College
New Rochelle, NY

Center, Tracy D
Clemson Univ
Clemson, SC

Cerda, Elizabeth
Univ Of Miami
Coral Gables, FL

Cerja, Stacy L
Indiana Univ Of Pa
Indiana, PA

Cerritelli, E Gregory
Univ Of New Haven
West Haven, CT

Chach, Margaret M
Teikyo Post Univ
Waterbury, CT

Chahin, Roberto P
Fl International Univ
Miami, FL

Chakravarty, Arup
Tampa Coll
Tampa, FL

Chambers, Karlene T
Fl Memorial Coll
Miami, FL

Chambers, Teresa Kim
Greenville Tech Coll
Greenville, SC

Champ Jr, Richard C
Embry Riddle
Aeronautical Univ
Daytona Beach, FL

Chan, Kok Kuan A
City Univ Of Ny
Baruch Coll
New York, NY

Chan, Mai
City Univ Of Ny
Baruch Coll
New York, NY

Chan, Mei N
City Univ Of Ny
Baruch Coll
New York, NY

Chan, Steven Ho
Cooper Union
New York, NY

Chan, Susan C
City Univ Of Ny
Baruch Coll
New York, NY

Chandel, Leena K
Memphis St Univ
Memphis, TN

Chandler, Amy D
Middle Tn St Univ
Murfreesboro, TN

Chandler, Racheke A
Al A & M Univ
Normal, AL

Chandler, Sallie K
Lane Coll
Jackson, TN

Chandrasena, Bani
Western New England
Coll
Springfield, MA

Chang, Emily B
Colgate Univ
Hamilton, NY

Chang, John T
S U N Y At Buffalo
Buffalo, NY

Chang, Wei-Jen
Savannah Coll Of Art
& Design
Savannah, GA

Chansky, Neysa D
City Univ Of Ny
Queensbrough
New York, NY

Chao, Chun-Hsin
Manhattanville Coll
Purchase, NY

Chapman, Karen Lynn
Roane St Comm Coll
Harriman, TN

Chapman, Karen S
Marshall University
Huntington, WV

Chapman, Megan S
Univ Of Ct
Storrs, CT

Chapman, Melinda D
Columbia Union Coll
Takoma Park, MD

Chard, William I
Widener Univ
Chester, PA

Charles, Alfred
Miami Dade Comm Coll
Miami, FL

Charles, Alicia A
Middlesex County Coll
Edison, NJ

Charles, Carolyn G
Savannah St Coll
Savannah, GA

Charles, Rosa C
City Univ Of Ny
Baruch Coll
New York, NY

Charlesworth, Heather
Pa St Univ Altoona
Cmps
Altoona, PA

Charlot, Vera S
Univ Of Southern Ms
Hattiesburg, MS

Chase, Rebecca A
Bay Path Coll
Longmeadow, MA

Chase, Susan E
Univ Of New Haven
West Haven, CT

Chase, Todd P
Barry Univ
Miami, FL

Chason, Eric D
Brevard Coll
Brevard, NC

Chason, Kelly D
Brevard Coll
Brevard, NC

Chauhan, Jennifer D
Villanova Univ
Villanova, PA

Chauvin, Mary
Catherine
Univ Of Nc At
Greensboro
Greensboro, NC

Cheek, Kimberly A
Univ Of Nc At
Greensboro
Greensboro, NC

Cheever, Marvelle C
Barry Univ
Miami, FL

Chen, Carl C
Fl International Univ
Miami, FL

Chen, Evelyn I
Univ Of Miami
Coral Gables, FL

Chen, Fei
Univ Of Sc At Beaufort
Beaufort, SC

Chen, Huan X
Bunker Hill Comm Coll
Boston, MA

Chen, Soon Yik
Univ Of South Al
Mobile, AL

Chen, Wendy Fang
The Julliard School
New York, NY

Chen, Xiaobo
Savannah Coll Of Art
& Design
Savannah, GA

Chen, Yong Q
Bunker Hill Comm Coll
Boston, MA

Cheng, Su Ying
City Univ Of Ny
Baruch Coll
New York, NY

Cherian, Ann
Colby Sawyer Coll
New London, NH

Cherry, Wendi D
Va St Univ
Petersburg, VA

Cherry, William L
Savannah St Coll
Savannah, GA

Cheru, Fentaw
Mokonnen
Ny Institute Of Tech
Ny City
New York, NY

Chesen, Kathleen M
Savannah Coll Of Art
& Design
Savannah, GA

Chess, Karrie-Ann D
Central St Univ
Wilberforce, OH

Chess, Kimberly A
Va St Univ
Petersburg, VA

Chester, Karen L
Manatee Comm Coll
Bradenton, FL

Chew, Bee Sian
City Univ Of Ny
Baruch Coll
New York, NY

Chia, Cuong Q
City Univ Of Ny
Baruch Coll
New York, NY

Chiacchiaro, Maria
Georgian Court Coll
Lakewood, NJ

Chick, Martha M
Endicott Coll
Beverly, MA

Chicky, Ronald John
Worcester St Coll
Worcester, MA

Chidi, Paul Chukumalini
Norfolk St Univ
Norfolk, VA

Chikowore, Martha J
Marymount Manhattan
Coll
New York, NY

Childers, Gwen M
Western Piedmont
Comm Coll
Morganton, NC

Childers Jr, Terry O
Univ Of Ga
Athens, GA

Childress, Damali A
Fl A & M Univ
Tallahassee, FL

Childress, Donna Jill
Univ Of Tn At Martin
Martin, TN

Childs, Patrick Lee
Nova Univ
Ft Lauderdale, FL

Chin, Mava Y
Fl Atlantic Univ
Boca Raton, FL

Chin, Nicole A
Fl International Univ
Miami, FL

Chisholm, Tamara R
Longwood Coll
Farmville, VA

Chisler, Catharine Jewel
Alderson Broaddus Coll
Philippi, WV

Chisley, Karmilla V
Univ Of Md At Eastern Shore
Princess Anne, MD

Chiu, Susan A
Ma Inst Of Tech
Cambridge, MA

Choi, Annie H
City Univ Of Ny
Baruch Coll
New York, NY

Chojecki, Dobrochna M
William Paterson Coll
Wayne, NJ

Chong, Fee Ching
Univ Of Md At Eastern Shore
Princess Anne, MD

Chong, Hyunsoo
Radford Univ
Radford, VA

Chong, Jit Chee
Univ Of Al At Huntsville
Huntsville, AL

Chong, Yew-Keong
Ms St Univ
Miss State, MS

Chongsiriwatana, Songsdhit
Piedmont Coll
Demorest, GA

Choong, Vi-En
Allegheny Coll
Meadville, PA

Chot, Michael Lul
Interdenominational Theo Ctr
Atlanta, GA

Chow, Mei-Ling
Broward Comm Coll
Ft Lauderdale, FL

Chowdhary, Ajay K
Barry Univ
Miami, FL

Chrisco, P David
Tn Temple Univ
Chattanooga, TN

Christensen, Jarret R
James Madison University
Harrisonburg, VA

Christiansen, Cynthia L
Hudson Valley Comm Coll
Troy, NY

Christie, Lori A
Cumberland Coll
Williamsburg, KY

Christie, Lynn A
Drew Univ
Madison, NJ

Christoph, Jessica L
George Mason Univ
Fairfax, VA

Chromczak, Teresa M
Le Moyne Coll
Syracuse, NY

Chrsitopher, Dwayne L
Morehouse Coll
Atlanta, GA

Chrysostomou, Andreas Costa
City Univ Of Ny
Baruch Coll
New York, NY

Chu, Wan Tao Arvid
Univ Of Akron
Akron, OH

Church, David A
East Tn St Univ
Johnson City, TN

Ciafone, John Joseph
Ny Univ
New York, NY

Cibik, Erik C
Duquesne Univ
Pittsburgh, PA

Cicco, Tonina
Saint Johns Univ
Jamaica, NY

Cieszynski, Jeffrey E
Schenectady County Comm Coll
Schenectady, NY

Cihan, Nerkiz
City Univ Of Ny John Jay Coll
New York, NY

Cillan, Marcia L
Georgetown Univ
Washington, DC

Cisz, Mark Michael
Cornell Univ Statutory College
Ithaca, NY

Claggion, Linda Y
Norfolk St Univ
Norfolk, VA

Clancy, Theresa A
Duquesne Univ
Pittsburgh, PA

Clark, David M
Marshall University
Huntington, WV

Clark, Delnitta M
Wilberforce Univ
Wilberforce, OH

Clark, Jacqueline D
City Univ Of Ny Med Evers Coll
Brooklyn, NY

Clark, James P
Univ Of Louisville
Louisville, KY

Clark, Michael J
Bowling Green St Univ
At Huron
Huron, OH

Clark, Otelia S
Norfolk St Univ
Norfolk, VA

Clark, Peggy J
Life Coll
Marietta, GA

Clark, Peggy M
Norfolk St Univ
Norfolk, VA

Clark, Rose M
Middle Tn St Univ
Murfreesboro, TN

Clark, Ruth E
Al A & M Univ
Normal, AL

Clark, Ted J
Catawba Valley Comm
Coll
Hickory, NC

Clark Jr, William B
Cumberland Coll
Williamsburg, KY

Clarke, Anna M
Univ Of The Virgin
Islands
St Thomas, VI

Clarke, Sean
S U N Y Coll Of Tech
At Frmgdl
Farmingdale, NY

Clarke, Sharon N
Univ Of South Fl
Tampa, FL

Clary, Kimberly Fay
Univ Of Sc At
Columbia
Columbia, SC

Clay, Laura E
Marshall University
Huntington, WV

Claycomb, Leah M
Duquesne Univ
Pittsburgh, PA

Claypool, Lisa L
Univ Of
Cincinnati-Clrmnt Coll
Batavia, OH

Clayton, Catrenia N
Morehead St Univ
Morehead, KY

Clayton, Eric D
Bethune Cookman Coll
Daytona Beach, FL

Cleaver, Laura A
Dyke Coll
Cleveland, OH

Clegg, Melinda J
Univ Of Nc At
Greensboro
Greensboro, NC

Clem, Peter T
Daytona Beach Comm
Coll
Daytona Beach, FL

Clement, Jennifer A
S U N Y Coll Of Tech
At Frmgdl
Farmingdale, NY

Clements, Angel Y
Va St Univ
Petersburg, VA

Clements, Brian Jack
Chattahoochee Vly St
Comm Coll
Phenix City, AL

Clements, Jennifer L
S U N Y At Buffalo
Buffalo, NY

Clements, Wendell Kent
Saint Petersburg Jr Coll
St Petersburg, FL

Clemmer, Phillip A L
Beckley Coll
Beckley, WV

Clemons, Tene Tra N
Jackson St Univ
Jackson, MS

Cleveland, Darrell
Lanier
Morehouse Coll
Atlanta, GA

Cleveland, Denice D
Gordon Coll
Barnesville, GA

Clevenger, Nancy L
Comm Coll Algny Co
Algny Cmps
Pittsburgh, PA

Clevenger, Nicole Y
Tusculum Coll
Greeneville, TN

Clevinger, Anthony M
Broward Comm Coll
Ft Lauderdale, FL

Clevinger, Katherine J
Emory & Henry Coll
Emory, VA

Clifford, Jackie L
Endicott Coll
Beverly, MA

Clift, Freida
Lexington Comm Coll
Lexington, KY

Cline, Melissa A
Longwood Coll
Farmville, VA

Cline, William A
Oh Univ
Athens, OH

Clinton, Chantell
Lincoln Univ
Lincoln Univ, PA

Clive, Nicholas A
Georgetown Univ
Washington, DC

Cloud, Karen L
Georgian Court Coll
Lakewood, NJ

Clouden, Ynella N
Va St Univ
Petersburg, VA

Clouse, Dacy C
Roane St Comm Coll
Harriman, TN

Cobb, Allison A
Simmons Coll
Boston, MA

Cobb, Carolyn J
Bishop St Comm Coll
Mobile, AL

Cobb, Jacqueline A
Fl International Univ
Miami, FL

Cobbold, Ishmael F
City Univ Of Ny Bronx
Comm Col
Bronx, NY

Cobin, Marla R
Franklin And Marshall
Coll
Lancaster, PA

Coffinger, John J
S U N Y Coll Of Tech
At Delhi
Delhi, NY

Coggins, Allahna A
Univ Of Miami
Coral Gables, FL

Coghill, Glennis Wilson
Tri County Tech Coll
Pendleton, SC

Coghill, Penny D
Averett Coll
Danville, VA

Cohen, Martin D
Univ Of Al At
Birmingham
Birmingham, AL

Cohen, Seth A
Yeshiva Univ
New York, NY

Cohron, J George
Tn St Univ
Nashville, TN

Coker, Mytsi L
Converse Coll
Spartanburg, SC

Colantonio, Anthony J
Georgetown Univ
Washington, DC

Colbert, Timothy E
Ms St Univ
Miss State, MS

Colden, Colleen M
Neumann Coll
Aston, PA

Cole, Casaundra J
Columbus Coll Of Art
& Design
Columbus, OH

Cole, Jonathan H
Northwest Al Comm
Coll
Phil Campbell, AL

Cole, Michael G
Columbia Union Coll
Takoma Park, MD

Coleman, Tonya R
Valdosta St Coll
Valdosta, GA

Coleman, Tracy L
Middle Ga Coll
Cochran, GA

Colerangle, John B
Tuskegee Univ
Tuskegee Inst, AL

Collazo Gonzalez,
Melissa
Univ Politecnica De Pr
Hato Rey, PR

Collazo, Juan A
Inter Amer Univ Pr
Hato Rey
Hato Rey, PR

Collazo-Perez, Carlos E
Univ Of Pr At Rio
Piedras
Rio Piedras, PR

Collett, Danny J
Lexington Comm Coll
Lexington, KY

Collier, Betty R
Univ Of North Fl
Jacksonville, FL

Collier, Brekita T
Clark Atlanta Univ
Atlanta, GA

Collier, Charisse N
City Univ Of Ny
Baruch Coll
New York, NY

Collier, Laura E
Univ Of Southern Ms
Hattiesburg, MS

Collier, Shelia M
Tn St Univ
Nashville, TN

Collier, Tiffany L
Duquesne Univ
Pittsburgh, PA

Collins, Gloria G
Univ Of Southern Ms
Hattiesburg, MS

Collins, Janine Angelisa
Al St Univ
Montgomery, AL

Collins, Jennifer L
William Paterson Coll
Wayne, NJ

Collins II, Joseph O
Tuskegee Univ
Tuskegee Inst, AL

Collins, Mark
Embry Riddle
Aeronautical Univ
Daytona Beach, FL

Collins, Mary Dan
Univ Of Ky
Lexington, KY

Collins, Rebecca A
Beckley Coll
Beckley, WV

Collins, Susan L
Owensboro Comm Coll
Owensboro, KY

Collins, Yolanda N
Oh St Univ
Columbus, OH

Collum, Kevin L
Northwest Al Comm Coll
Phil Campbell, AL

Collum, Ricky D
Valdosta St Coll
Valdosta, GA

Colon Cortes, Magda J
Inter Amer Univ Pr Hato Rey
Hato Rey, PR

Colon, Gladys
Univ Of Pr Cayey Univ Coll
Cayey, PR

Colon, Lillian M
Univ Of Pr Cayey Univ Coll
Cayey, PR

Colon, Marcilyn
Univ Of Pr Medical Sciences
San Juan, PR

Colon, Marie Carmelite
Bunker Hill Comm Coll
Boston, MA

Colon, Rodrigo A
Georgian Court Coll
Lakewood, NJ

Colucci, Jamie M
Univ Of Rochester
Rochester, NY

Colwell, Matthew
Columbia Greene Comm Coll
Hudson, NY

Colwell, Rachel L
Georgian Court Coll
Lakewood, NJ

Combs, Melissa R
S U N Y Coll Of Tech At Frmgdl
Farmingdale, NY

Combs, Michael D
Wv Univ
Morgantown, WV

Comer, Alejandro J
Morehouse Coll
Atlanta, GA

Como, James A
Niagara Univ
Niagara Univ, NY

Compell, Christopher J
East Stroudsburg Univ
E Stroudsburg, PA

Compton, Gregg S
Central Al Comm Coll
Alexander City, AL

Conaway, Charissa E
Va St Univ
Petersburg, VA

Conaway, Cheryl L
Univ Of Miami
Coral Gables, FL

Concepcion Figueroa, Wanda I
Inter Amer Univ Pr Hato Rey
Hato Rey, PR

Concepcion Jimenez, Saul
Caribbean Univ
Bayamon, PR

Concepcion Marquez, Sheila E
Inter Amer Univ Pr Hato Rey
Hato Rey, PR

Condis, Myrna
Miami Dade Comm Coll South
Miami, FL

Condon, Cheri A
The Boston Conservatory
Boston, MA

Conerly, Elizabeth A
Ms St Univ
Miss State, MS

Coney, Mollie L
Fayetteville St Univ
Fayetteville, NC

Congdon, Melissa L
S U N Y Coll At Fredonia
Fredonia, NY

Conn, Kyle L
Vance Granville Comm Coll
Henderson, NC

Conner Jr, Dana H
Univ Of Sc At Columbia
Columbia, SC

Conner, Meredith L
Gaston Coll
Dallas, NC

Connolly, Loraine A
Villanova Univ
Villanova, PA

Conrad, Samantha N B
Schenectady County Comm Coll
Schenectady, NY

Consaga, Anthony J
Pace Univ At Pleasantville
Pleasantville, NY

Conserva, Cari A
Bentley Coll
Waltham, MA

Constable, Francine M
Coll Misericordia
Dallas, PA

Consul, Kevin C
Saint John Fisher Coll
Rochester, NY

Conway, Danielle M
Howard Univ
Washington, DC

Conway, Kendrick L
Univ Of Tn At Martin
Martin, TN

Conway, Terri L
Christopher Newport Coll
Newport News, VA

Conwell, Tess-Ella J
Univ Of Md At Eastern Shore
Princess Anne, MD

Cook Legge, Tammy R
Belmont Coll
Nashville, TN

Cook, James D
Memphis St Univ
Memphis, TN

Cook, Jennifer L
Wilmington Coll
Wilmington, OH

Cook, Michelle E
West Liberty St Coll
West Liberty, WV

Cook, Paul L
Fl A & M Univ
Tallahassee, FL

Cooke, Audra M
Roger Williams Coll
Bristol
Bristol, RI

Cooke Jr, Kevin R
Ky St Univ
Frankfort, KY

Cooper, Alison N
James Madison
University
Harrisonburg, VA

Cooper, Dana M
Tn St Univ
Nashville, TN

Cooper, Lori R
Livingston Univ
Livingston, AL

Cooper, Synae L
Lincoln Univ
Lincoln Univ, PA

Cooper, Tamara L
East Central Comm Coll
Decatur, MS

Coots, Alan F
S U N Y Coll Of Tech
At Alfred
Alfred, NY

Copeland, Carol A
Fl St Univ
Tallahassee, FL

Copeland, Courtney C
Duquesne Univ
Pittsburgh, PA

Copeland, Pamela R
Tn St Univ
Nashville, TN

Coppeto, Ellen K
Saint Joseph Coll
West Hartford, CT

Coppola, Martin R
Glassboro St Coll
Glassboro, NJ

Corbett, Jerry D
James Sprunt Comm
Coll
Kenansville, NC

Corcino Rivera, Jose H
Univ Politecnica De Pr
Hato Rey, PR

Corcoran, Candace M
James Madison
University
Harrisonburg, VA

Cordano, Jennifer B
Bloomfield Coll
Bloomfield, NJ

Cordero Luciano, Vivian
Inter Amer Univ Pr San
German
San German, PR

Cordova, Waldo G
Univ Politecnica De Pr
Hato Rey, PR

Corea, Sharmini D
Bloomfield Coll
Bloomfield, NJ

Corella, Christine
Univ Of Miami
Coral Gables, FL

Corley, Todd L
Le Moyne Coll
Syracuse, NY

Cornacchia, Christina
Franklin And Marshall
Coll
Lancaster, PA

Cornatzer, Jodi L
Univ Of Nc At
Charlotte
Charlotte, NC

Cornelius, Yolanda T
Allen Univ
Columbia, SC

Cornish, Michael A
S U N Y Coll Of Tech
At Delhi
Delhi, NY

Cornish, Sabrina Y
Fl A & M Univ
Tallahassee, FL

Cornwell, Michelle
Saint Josephs Coll
Windham, ME

Corprew, Talya T
Va St Univ
Petersburg, VA

Correa, Juliette D
Saint Marys Coll Of Md
St Marys Cy, MD

Correa, Larisa A
City Univ Of Ny La
Guard Coll
Long Island Cty, NY

Correia Santiago, Derek
Univ Politecnica De Pr
Hato Rey, PR

Corres, Vilma
Univ Of Pr Cayey Univ
Coll
Cayey, PR

Corriea, Kevin A
City Univ Of Ny
Baruch Coll
New York, NY

Corrigan, Kathleen M
Oh Univ
Athens, OH

Cortes, Aida I C
Inter Amer Univ Pr
Hato Rey
Hato Rey, PR

Cortes Jr, Jose H
Columbia Union Coll
Takoma Park, MD

Cosby, Gailien J
Lincoln Univ
Lincoln Univ, PA

Cosgrove, Dean W
Pasco Hernando Comm
Coll
Dade City, FL

Cosker Jr, Thomas
Worcester Poly Inst
Worcester, MA

Cosmo, Fredrik C
Va Commonwealth Univ
Richmond, VA

Costello, Jill C
Univ Of Ky
Lexington, KY

Cotter, Casey A
Wellesley Coll
Wellesley, MA

Couch-Goodman, Kendra B
Tomlinson Coll
Cleveland, TN

Coughlin, Dawn M
Bryant Stratton Bus Inst Roch
Rochester, NY

Courts, Melinda D
Alcorn St Univ
Lorman, MS

Cousins, Maria I
Tn Temple Univ
Chattanooga, TN

Covert, Tonya M
S U N Y Coll Of Tech At Alfred
Alfred, NY

Covington, Tony M
Middle Tn St Univ
Murfreesboro, TN

Cowan, Cynthia Diane
Wv Univ At Parkersburg
Parkersburg, WV

Cowan Jr, Fredrick H
Radford Univ
Radford, VA

Cowsert, Trent W
Univ Of Tn At Martin
Martin, TN

Cox III, Earl F
Elmira Coll
Elmira, NY

Cox, Gregory D
Oh Northern Univ
Ada, OH

Cox, Reginald Arnell
Fl A & M Univ
Tallahassee, FL

Cox, Robert J
Inter Amer Univ Pr Hato Rey
Hato Rey, PR

Coyne, Susan E
Univ Of Ga
Athens, GA

Craft, Antonio F
Ms Gulf Coast Comm Coll
Perkinston, MS

Craft, Elaine L
Univ Of Ky
Lexington, KY

Craft, Kimberly K
Univ Of Al
Tuscaloosa, AL

Craghead, Tonya M
Radford Univ
Radford, VA

Craig, Cathy L
Marshall University
Huntington, WV

Craig, Cathy L
Owensboro Comm Coll
Owensboro, KY

Crame, Maria-Elena Nacinopa
De Tech & Comm Coll At Dover
Dover, DE

Craney, Krisann
S U N Y Coll At Oswego
Oswego, NY

Cravatt, Ann M
Univ Of West Fl
Pensacola, FL

Crawford, Farley C
Central Fl Comm Coll
Ocala, FL

Crawford, Glynnis M
Fayetteville St Univ
Fayetteville, NC

Crawford, Meredith J
Coll Of Charleston
Charleston, SC

Crawford, Priscilla A
Atlantic Comm Coll
Mays Landing, NJ

Creamer, John W
Tallahassee Comm Coll
Tallahassee, FL

Creary, Pauline H A
Morgan St Univ
Baltimore, MD

Crespo La Salle, Daniel
Univ Politecnica De Pr
Hato Rey, PR

Criscuolo, David S
Neumann Coll
Aston, PA

Crispell, Valerie J
Nassau Comm Coll
Garden City, NY

Crivello, Frances M
City Univ Of Ny Baruch Coll
New York, NY

Croalgarraway, Eileen C
City Univ Of Ny Baruch Coll
New York, NY

Croft, Tammy R
Central Fl Comm Coll
Ocala, FL

Crosby, Faye E
Wagner Coll
Staten Island, NY

Cross, Deloris Mc Clam
Columbia Union Coll
Takoma Park, MD

Cross, Karen M
Christian Brothers Univ
Memphis, TN

Cross, Loren E
Univ Of Cincinnati
Cincinnati, OH

Crosswright, Deloris A
Central St Univ
Wilberforce, OH

Crouch, Connie E
Northeast State Tech Comm Coll
Blountville, TN

Crouch, Kathleen Fuller
Nova Univ
Ft Lauderdale, FL

Crowe, Elizabeth M
Western Piedmont Comm Coll
Morganton, NC

Crowell, Jeffrey A
Univ Of Cincinnati
Cincinnati, OH

Croy, Charlie J
Concord Coll
Athens, WV

Crum, Candace D
Ms St Univ
Miss State, MS

Crum, Robert J
Radford Univ
Radford, VA

Crumpton, Wendy L
Univ Of Al At Birmingham
Birmingham, AL

Crut, Felipe Castro
Inter Amer Univ Pr San Juan
Hato Rey, PR

Crutchfield, Stephen E
Emory & Henry Coll
Emory, VA

Crutchley, Julie A
Salisbury St Univ
Salisbury, MD

Cruz Narvaez, Carmen
Univ Of Pr Cayey Univ Coll
Cayey, PR

Cruz Roman, Rosa E
Inter Amer Univ Pr Hato Rey
Hato Rey, PR

Cruz Zeno, Edgardo M
Univ Of Pr At Mayaguez
Mayaguez, PR

Cruz Jr, Anthony
Univ Of South Fl
Tampa, FL

Cruz, Cynthia
Univ Of Pr Medical Sciences
San Juan, PR

Cruz, Kisha E
Western New England Coll
Springfield, MA

Cruz, Luz Idalia
Univ Of Pr Cayey Univ Coll
Cayey, PR

Cruz, Richard
Miami Dade Comm Coll North
Miami, FL

Cruz, Rocio
Caribbean Center For Adv Stds
San Juan, PR

Cruz, Vanessa
Univ Of Pr At Rio Piedras
Rio Piedras, PR

Cruzado, Pablo
Univ Of Pr Cayey Univ Coll
Cayey, PR

Cueto, Jose L
Univ Of Sc At Spartanburg
Spartanburg, SC

Cuevas Arvelo, Edgar
Univ Of Pr At Mayaguez
Mayaguez, PR

Cuevas, Cecilia
Inter Amer Univ Pr Hato Rey
Hato Rey, PR

Cuevas, Mary A
Fl International Univ
Miami, FL

Culbreath, Chandra D
Wilberforce Univ
Wilberforce, OH

Culton IV, Eugene
Univ Of Ky
Lexington, KY

Cumbo-Jones, Carolyn
Norfolk St Univ
Norfolk, VA

Cummings, Deborah L
Univ Of Sc At Columbia
Columbia, SC

Cummings, Jennifer E
Kent St Univ Kent Cmps
Kent, OH

Cunefare, Rick L
Limestone Coll
Gaffney, SC

Cunningham, Debbie F
Univ Of Al At Birmingham
Birmingham, AL

Cunningham, Gina
Barry Univ
Miami, FL

Cunningham, Pauler R
Miami Dade Comm Coll North
Miami, FL

Cupeles Matos, Israel
Inter Amer Univ Pr San German
San German, PR

Curcio, Kristine
Saint Francis Coll
Brooklyn, NY

Curlee, Tracey C
Tallahassee Comm Coll
Tallahassee, FL

Curley, Jacqueline Jerome
Saint John Fisher Coll
Rochester, NY

Curry, Alisha D
Fl A & M Univ
Tallahassee, FL

Curry, David W
Indiana Univ Of Pa
Indiana, PA

Curtin, Christian J
George Mason Univ
Fairfax, VA

Curtis, Christina A
Colby Sawyer Coll
New London, NH

Curtis-Attoh, Brenda
Coll Of New Rochelle
New Rochelle, NY

Cusack, Patrick P
American Univ
Washington, DC

Custodio, Cristina M
Harvard Univ
Cambridge, MA

Cutter, Margaret S
Cleveland Inst Of Art
Cleveland, OH

Cypher, Neal A
Liberty Univ
Lynchburg, VA

Cyphert, Kathleen M
Kent St Univ Kent
Cmps
Kent, OH

Cyr, Christy M
Central Fl Comm Coll
Ocala, FL

Cyrus-Charles, Rudolph
City Univ Of Ny Med
Evers Coll
Brooklyn, NY

D Amato, Deborah E
Univ Of Md Baltimore
Prof Schl
Baltimore, MD

D Ambrosio, Lisa M
Glassboro St Coll
Glassboro, NJ

Daetwyler, Ashley A
Va Commonwealth Univ
Richmond, VA

Dag, Mustafa
Tallahassee Comm Coll
Tallahassee, FL

Dagg, James M
Air Force Inst Of Tech
Wrt-Ptrsn Afb, OH

Dail, Melissa M
Palm Beach Atlantic
Coll
W Palm Beach, FL

Dale, Jason P
Western Piedmont
Comm Coll
Morganton, NC

Dalgado, Nympha G
Va Commonwealth Univ
Richmond, VA

Dallacqua, Kristen
Dowling Coll
Oakdale Li, NY

Dalton, Crystal L
Nc Agri & Tech St
Univ
Greensboro, NC

Dalton, Cyneva L
Peace Coll
Raleigh, NC

Damoudt, Sylma R
Univ Of Pr At
Mayaguez
Mayaguez, PR

Dandeneau, Nicole A
Southern Vt Coll
Bennington, VT

Daniel, Colette O
Va Union Univ
Richmond, VA

Daniel, Elena
Central St Univ
Wilberforce, OH

Daniel, Gregory C
Fl A & M Univ
Tallahassee, FL

Daniele, Carmela C
Springfield Tech Comm
Coll
Springfield, MA

Daniels, Andrew B
Dyersburg St Comm
Coll
Dyersburg, TN

Daniels, Oassie J
Livingston Univ
Livingston, AL

Daniels, Willie E
Fl International Univ
Miami, FL

Daniska, Kimberly L
Kent St Univ Kent
Cmps
Kent, OH

Danku, John M C
Central St Univ
Wilberforce, OH

Danner, Lolita Y
Gaston Coll
Dallas, NC

Danquah, Jubilant
Boakye
Interdenominational
Theo Ctr
Atlanta, GA

Dara, Kathleen M
Georgian Court Coll
Lakewood, NJ

Darby, Tina A
Broward Comm Coll
Ft Lauderdale, FL

Darden, Lornette D
Univ Of Southern Ms
Hattiesburg, MS

Darnell, K Lee
Catawba Valley Comm
Coll
Hickory, NC

Daroowalla, Farzana S
Kent St Univ Kent
Cmps
Kent, OH

Daubenspeck, Dawn M
Brevard Coll
Brevard, NC

Daugherty, Charles M
Ms St Univ
Miss State, MS

Daugherty, David Lee
Wittenberg Univ
Springfield, OH

Dauphinais, Kevin D
Temple Univ
Philadelphia, PA

Davenport, Cynthia L
Longwood Coll
Farmville, VA

David, Myrianthe S
City Univ Of Ny
Baruch Coll
New York, NY

Davidson, Augustine V
Germanna Comm Coll
Locust Grove, VA

Davidson, Michael W
Middle Tn St Univ
Murfreesboro, TN

Davie, Julianne J
Merrimack Coll
North Andover, MA

Davies, Angela L
Univ Of Nc At
Greensboro
Greensboro, NC

Davila Ayala, Maria V
Inter Amer Univ Pr
Hato Rey
Hato Rey, PR

Davis, Amy L
Emmanuel Coll
Franklin Spg, GA

Davis, Angela M
Cecils Coll
Asheville, NC

Davis, Anissa A
Fl A & M Univ
Tallahassee, FL

Davis, Christine Louise
Salisbury St Univ
Salisbury, MD

Davis, Colleen F
Lesley Coll
Cambridge, MA

Davis, Cora J
Saint Josephs Coll New
York
Brooklyn, NY

Davis, Cyndee M
Greenville Tech Coll
Greenville, SC

Davis, Daniel D
Ms Gulf Coast Comm
Coll
Perkinston, MS

Davis, David R
Morehouse Coll
Atlanta, GA

Davis, Glenroy L
Cheyney Univ Of Pa
Cheyney, PA

Davis, Hawanya S
Fl A & M Univ
Tallahassee, FL

Davis, Joy M
Univ Of New Haven
West Haven, CT

Davis, Lesli D
Greenville Tech Coll
Greenville, SC

Davis, Michelle R
Univ Of Nc At
Wilmington
Wilmington, NC

Davis, Shajuanda L
Univ Of Southern Ms
Hattiesburg, MS

Davis, Shawn L
Central St Univ
Wilberforce, OH

Davis, Stephanie M
Tuskegee Univ
Tuskegee Inst, AL

Davis Jr, William H
Vanderbilt Univ
Nashville, TN

Dawes, Linnea M
Norfolk St Univ
Norfolk, VA

Dawson, Joyce L
Widener Univ
Chester, PA

Dawson, Michael R D
Univ Of Miami
Coral Gables, FL

Dawson, Theresa F
George Mason Univ
Fairfax, VA

Day, Diane G
Georgetown Coll
Georgetown, KY

Day, Dover
Piedmont Tech Coll
Greenwood, SC

Day, Kimberly A
Teikyo Post Univ
Waterbury, CT

Dazen, Devon D
Wv Univ
Morgantown, WV

De Arment, Daniel W
Juniata Coll
Huntingdon, PA

De Boer, Barbara G
Queens Coll
Charlotte, NC

De Candido, Ann Marie
Md Coll Of Art &
Design
Silver Spring, MD

De Cracker, Daniel J
S U N Y Coll Of Tech
At Alfred
Alfred, NY

De Cunzo, Donna M
Fl International Univ
Miami, FL

De Golyer, Rosemary K
Catholic Univ Of Pr
Ponce, PR

De Jesus Casas, Gilberto
Univ Politecnica De Pr
Hato Rey, PR

De Jesus Seda, Jessica
Inter Amer Univ Pr San German
San German, PR

De Jesus, Elsa Milagros
Univ Of Pr Cayey Univ Coll
Cayey, PR

De Jesus, Tracy
City Univ Of Ny City Coll
New York, NY

De Jesus-Alicea, Dermis Edith
Univ Of Pr Medical Sciences
San Juan, PR

De Jesus-Perez, Jennie
Catholic Univ Of Pr
Ponce, PR

De La Cruz Santiago, Ysha M
Inter Amer Univ Pr Hato Rey
Hato Rey, PR

De La Cruz, Enrique M
Rutgers St Univ At Newark
Newark, NJ

De La Torre Davila, Sareida
Inter Amer Univ Pr Hato Rey
Hato Rey, PR

De La Torres Morales, Wilmarie
Inter Amer Univ Pr San German
San German, PR

De Lucca, Marcio R
Univ Of Southern Ms
Hattiesburg, MS

De Maio, Toni A
Dowling Coll
Oakdale Li, NY

De Martino, Lenore
Fl International Univ
Miami, FL

De Paoli, Gina Marie
The Boston Conservatory
Boston, MA

De Primo, Jimmy P
Tn Temple Univ
Chattanooga, TN

De Rodriguez, Janet Riefkohl
Inter Amer Univ Pr San Juan
Hato Rey, PR

De Santis, Marisa S
Dickinson Coll
Carlisle, PA

De Santo, Vanetta R
S U N Y Coll Of Tech At Frmgdl
Farmingdale, NY

De Sena, Michelle
Dowling Coll
Oakdale Li, NY

De Vellis, David M
Amherst Coll
Amherst, MA

De Vore, Myra C
Ms St Univ
Miss State, MS

De Witt Salvie, Christine M
Smith Coll
Northampton, MA

Dean, Andy A
Univ Of Al
Tuscaloosa, AL

Dean, Michelle T
Fl St Univ
Tallahassee, FL

Dean, Timothy A
Univ Of Al At Huntsville
Huntsville, AL

Deaton, Betty A
Union Univ
Jackson, TN

Deaton, Mark
Lees Coll
Jackson, KY

Decastro Carlo, Flor De Maria
Inter Amer Univ Pr San German
San German, PR

Decastro, Hector J
Inter Amer Univ Pr Hato Rey
Hato Rey, PR

Dechene, Traci Allen
Univ Of Nh Plymouth St Coll
Plymouth, NH

Deen, Sue-Ellen
Daytona Beach Comm Coll
Daytona Beach, FL

Deese, Jeanna L
Catawba Valley Comm Coll
Hickory, NC

Del Valle Mojica, Kiomarie
Univ Politecnica De Pr
Hato Rey, PR

Del Valle-Emmanuelli, Antonio L
Univ Of Pr At Rio Piedras
Rio Piedras, PR

Del-Valle-Lopez, Pedro
Univ Of Pr At Rio Piedras
Rio Piedras, PR

Dela Cruz, Liezl A
Columbia Coll
Columbia, SC

Delacotte, Stephane L
City Univ Of Ny Baruch Coll
New York, NY

Delesline, Charlene K
Wilberforce Univ
Wilberforce, OH

Delmanto, Janine R
Georgian Court Coll
Lakewood, NJ

Deluca, Claudine C
City Univ Of Ny Baruch Coll
New York, NY

Dempsey, Caroline C
Elms Coll
Chicopee, MA

Dendinger, Jenifer W
Univ Of Ms Medical Center
Jackson, MS

Dennis, Katie M
East Central Comm Coll
Decatur, MS

Densmore, Tara D
Shorter Coll
Rome, GA

Dent, La Sandra L
Central St Univ
Wilberforce, OH

Dent, Victoria Renee
Univ Of Sc At
Columbia
Columbia, SC

Deopersaud, Savitri A
City Univ Of Ny City
Coll
New York, NY

Derenburger, John A
Wv Univ
Morgantown, WV

Derickson, Christine
Lynn
Defiance Coll
Defiance, OH

Derilus, Osias
Tomlinson Coll
Cleveland, TN

Dermond, Andrea L
Widener Univ
Chester, PA

Desmarais, Lynne A
Univ Of North Fl
Jacksonville, FL

Despoth, Debra L
Univ Of Akron
Akron, OH

Desselle, Shawna D
Georgetown Univ
Washington, DC

Deszcz, Eric J
S U N Y Coll Of Tech
At Alfred
Alfred, NY

Dettweiler, Susan L
Longwood Coll
Farmville, VA

Dever, L Daniel
Bluefield Coll
Bluefield, VA

Devillier, John M
Fl St Univ
Tallahassee, FL

Devir, Ilan
City Univ Of Ny City
Coll
New York, NY

Devore, Deidra G
Oh Northern Univ
Ada, OH

Dhalwala, Ritu S
George Mason Univ
Fairfax, VA

Dhooge, Susan M
Savannah Coll Of Art
& Design
Savannah, GA

Di Bella, Ann M
Villanova Univ
Villanova, PA

Di Carlo, Diane F
Westchester Comm Coll
Valhalla, NY

Di Leo, Andrea
Univ Of Nh Plymouth
St Coll
Plymouth, NH

Di Loreto Jr, Romeo
Anthony
Savannah Coll Of Art
& Design
Savannah, GA

Di Santo, Danielle M
City Univ Of Ny
Queensbrough
New York, NY

Di Vincenzo, Joseph P
S U N Y At Buffalo
Buffalo, NY

Diacont, William D
Richard Bland Coll
Petersburg, VA

Diaconu, Alen S
Lenoir Rhyne Coll
Hickory, NC

Diaconu, Mirela
Lenoir Rhyne Coll
Hickory, NC

Dialectaki, Phivi
Atlantic Union Coll
S Lancaster, MA

Diamond, Robert H
S U N Y At Buffalo
Buffalo, NY

Diaz Rivera, Wanda S
Univ Of Pr Medical
Sciences
San Juan, PR

Diaz Valdes, Oscar L
Inter Amer Univ Pr
Guayama
Guayama, PR

Diaz, Barbara M
Fl International Univ
Miami, FL

Diaz, Juan Carlos
Saint Thomas Univ
Miami, FL

Diaz Jr, Ramon
Springfield Tech Comm
Coll
Springfield, MA

Diaz, Wendy D
Fl International Univ
Miami, FL

Dickens Jr, Frank T
City Univ Of Ny City
Coll
New York, NY

Dickerson, Christine L
Univ Of New Haven
West Haven, CT

Dickerson, Deanna K
Univ Of Nc At
Greensboro
Greensboro, NC

Dickert, Tanya J
Georgian Court Coll
Lakewood, NJ

Dickinson, Ginger Ann
Southern Vt Coll
Bennington, VT

Dicus, Jimmy P
Tampa Coll
Tampa, FL

Didier, David
Miami Dade Comm Coll
Miami, FL

Diehl, Lisa M
Shippensburg Univ
Shippensburg, PA

Dietrich, Denise A
Kent St Univ Stark Cmps
North Canton, OH

Dietrich, Jon D
Salisbury St Univ
Salisbury, MD

Dietz, Christine J
Tn Temple Univ
Chattanooga, TN

Diez-De-Onate, Beatriz
Fl International Univ
Miami, FL

Diez-De-Onate Jr, Jorge
Barry Univ
Miami, FL

Dillard, Christopher R
Roanoke Coll
Salem, VA

Dillman, Melissa G
Watterson Coll
Louisville, KY

Dillon, Claire M
Rutgers St Un At New Brunswick
New Brunswick, NJ

Dillon, Pamala J
Eckerd Coll
St Petersburg, FL

Ding, Hou-Wu
Univ Of South Al
Mobile, AL

Dingess, Kristy L
Marshall University
Huntington, WV

Dinh, Hong-Diem N
Univ Of Nc At Charlotte
Charlotte, NC

Dinkins, Michelle K
Central Fl Comm Coll
Ocala, FL

Diop, Seydina Issa Henry
Central St Univ
Wilberforce, OH

Dix, Martin T
Averett Coll
Danville, VA

Dixon, Angela L
Al A & M Univ
Normal, AL

Dixon, Antoine L
Al A & M Univ
Normal, AL

Dixon, Chandra E
Alice Lloyd Coll
Pippa Passes, KY

Dixon, Donna R
Mobile Coll
Mobile, AL

Dixon, Julie A
James Sprunt Comm Coll
Kenansville, NC

Dixon, Tracey L
Middle Tn St Univ
Murfreesboro, TN

Do, Long D
Harrisburg Area Comm Coll
Harrisburg, PA

Doaty, Sidney J
Birmingham Southern Coll
Birmingham, AL

Dodd, James E
Brevard Coll
Brevard, NC

Dodson, Kimberly J
Hagerstown Jr Coll
Hagerstown, MD

Dodson, Linda M
Wright St Univ Lake Cmps
Celina, OH

Dodson, Ralph Edward
Vance Granville Comm Coll
Henderson, NC

Doering, Cynthia L
Univ Of Akron
Akron, OH

Dolinger, Shayna G
Richard Bland Coll
Petersburg, VA

Dolly, Lindrell A
Hampton Univ
Hampton, VA

Domanski, Robynne Marie
Indiana Univ Of Pa
Indiana, PA

Domingo, Brenda E
Boston Univ
Boston, MA

Donahue, Katherine M
Nova Univ
Ft Lauderdale, FL

Donati, Matthew D
Wv Univ
Morgantown, WV

Dondelinger, Michael K
Chattahoochee Vly St Comm Coll
Phenix City, AL

Donnelly, Jeffrey J M
Bunker Hill Comm Coll
Boston, MA

Donohue, Julie A
Univ Of De
Newark, DE

Donovan, Jean D
Ny Univ
New York, NY

Dooley, Jennifer A
King Coll
Bristol, TN

Doras, Sharon B
City Univ Of Ny Med Evers Coll
Brooklyn, NY

Dorey, Deborah S
Liberty Univ
Lynchburg, VA

Dorman, Dawn E
Wilmington Coll
New Castle, DE

Dorn Jr, Allen A
Me Maritime Academy
Castine, ME

Dorsey, Laura B
Norfolk St Univ
Norfolk, VA

Dorta Martinez, Jose
Inter Amer Univ Pr
Hato Rey
Hato Rey, PR

Dortch, Schona S
Savannah St Coll
Savannah, GA

Dorton, John K
Ma Inst Of Tech
Cambridge, MA

Dos Santos, Aguinaldo J
City Univ Of Ny La
Guard Coll
Long Island Cty, NY

Dotson, Elizabeth J
Glenville St Coll
Glenville, WV

Dougherty, Regina M
Marywood Coll
Scranton, PA

Doughlin, Charles H
City Univ Of Ny
Baruch Coll
New York, NY

Doughty, Victoria L
Radford Univ
Radford, VA

Doughty, Wayne E
Me Maritime Academy
Castine, ME

Douglas, Aprile L
Fl A & M Univ
Tallahassee, FL

Douglas, Marquil D
Univ Of Sc At
Columbia
Columbia, SC

Douglas, Sandra L
Marshall University
Huntington, WV

Douglas, Tracy S
Thomas Nelson Comm
Coll
Hampton, VA

Douglas, Victoria J
Washington Coll
Chestertown, MD

Doward Jr, Oscar W
Al A & M Univ
Normal, AL

Dowd, John J
Boston Coll
Chestnut Hill, MA

Downard, Chrissondra D
Central Oh Tech Coll
Newark, OH

Doyle, Marilyn M
Atlantic Comm Coll
Mays Landing, NJ

Draheim, Timothy A
Livingston Univ
Livingston, AL

Drakeford, Kesha T
Va St Univ
Petersburg, VA

Draughn-Buttram, Gail
Denise
Roane St Comm Coll
Harriman, TN

Drayton, Toye S
Livingstone Coll
Salisbury, NC

Dreize, Livia Rebbeka
Catholic Univ Of Pr
Ponce, PR

Drenga, Craig
Springfield Tech Comm
Coll
Springfield, MA

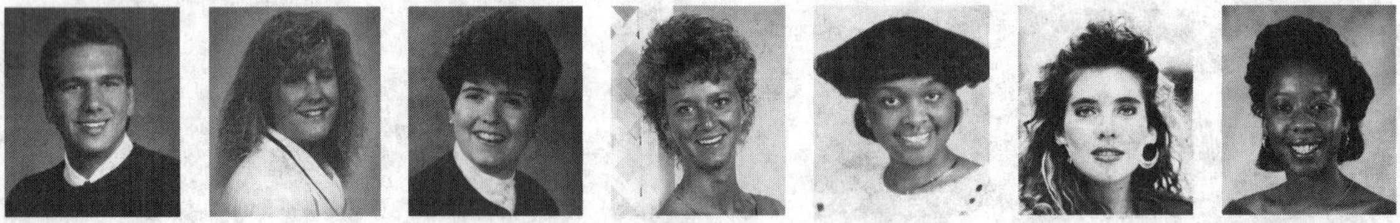

Drezek, Craig D
Teikyo Post Univ
Waterbury, CT

Driscoll, Leslie
Univ Of Fl
Gainesville, FL

Driscoll, Mary E
Assumption Coll
Worcester, MA

Driskill, Tonya Annette
Franklin Coll
Paducah, KY

Driver, Bridgette N
Memphis St Univ
Memphis, TN

Drpic, Ingrid G
Fl Atlantic Univ
Boca Raton, FL

Drummond, April M
Va St Univ
Petersburg, VA

Du Pree Jr, Louis S
Savannah Coll Of Art
& Design
Savannah, GA

Du Priest, Sonja L
Central Al Comm Coll
Alexander City, AL

Du Quette, Michael J
Cumberland County
Coll
Vineland, NJ

Du, Diem Chau D
Anne Arundel Comm
Coll
Arnold, MD

Dubose, Carrick M
Morehouse Coll
Atlanta, GA

Duca, Michelle E
Ms St Univ
Miss State, MS

Duckworth, Morie M
Meridian Comm Coll
Meridian, MS

Duda, Roger H
U S Military Academy
West Point, NY

Dudzinski, Kimberly A
Duquesne Univ
Pittsburgh, PA

Duffy, Peter R
Villanova Univ
Villanova, PA

Dugan, Mark W
Univ Of Rochester
Rochester, NY

Dugas, Moreau
Fl A & M Univ
Tallahassee, FL

Duggan, Joy Faith
Univ Of Sc At Coastal Carolina
Conway, SC

Duggan, Kelley D
Dowling Coll
Oakdale Li, NY

Duke, Anton L
Univ Of Tn At Martin
Martin, TN

Dukes, Donna D
Miles Coll
Birmingham, AL

Dumbroski, Lauren K
Univ Of Nc At Greensboro
Greensboro, NC

Dunac, Donald
Inter Amer Univ Pr San German
San German, PR

Dunaway, Eric K
Morehouse Coll
Atlanta, GA

Dunaway, Tammera S
Univ Of Ky
Lexington, KY

Duncan, Angela K
Emory & Henry Coll
Emory, VA

Duncan, Brian L
Middle Tn St Univ
Murfreesboro, TN

Duncan II, James R
Greenville Tech Coll
Greenville, SC

Duncan, Samantha J
Univ Of Ma At Amherst
Amherst, MA

Dungan, Christopher M
Free Will Baptist Bible Coll
Nashville, TN

Dunham, Cynthia J
Atlantic Comm Coll
Mays Landing, NJ

Dunlap, Charles Scot
Pellissippi St Tech Comm Coll
Knoxville, TN

Dunleavy, Kathleen T
City Univ Of Ny La Guard Coll
Long Island Cty, NY

Dunn, Catherine D
Central Al Comm Coll
Alexander City, AL

Dunn, Jami B
William Carey Coll
Hattiesburg, MS

Dunne, Martha F
Univ Of Cincinnati
Cincinnati, OH

Duppe, Katherine M
Duquesne Univ
Pittsburgh, PA

Durand, Gilbert Claude
Inter Amer Univ Pr San German
San German, PR

Durbin, Kelli E
Univ Of West Fl
Pensacola, FL

Durbin, Steven C
Clemson Univ
Clemson, SC

Durden, Ronald W
Univ Of South Al
Mobile, AL

Duren, Carla C
Hampton Univ
Hampton, VA

Durham, Disa N
Univ Of Sc At Columbia
Columbia, SC

Durkos, Elaine S
Hudson Valley Comm Coll
Troy, NY

Durlock, Debra L
Va Highlands Comm Coll
Abingdon, VA

Durnwald, Celeste P
Kent St Univ Kent Cmps
Kent, OH

Durr, Adrianne J
Clark Atlanta Univ
Atlanta, GA

Durr, Pasha O
Bowling Green St Univ
Bowling Green, OH

Durst, Rachael L
Widener Univ
Chester, PA

Dutey, Jennifer L
Marshall University
Huntington, WV

Dutton, Sandra Leigh
Dyersburg St Comm Coll
Dyersburg, TN

Dvorak, James K
City Univ Of Ny Baruch Coll
New York, NY

Dwyer, Jill M
Seton Hall Univ
South Orange, NJ

Dyke, Teresa S
Marshall University
Huntington, WV

Dykema, Kristen C
Univ Of Cincinnati
Cincinnati, OH

Dykema, Tamara D
Tallahassee Comm Coll
Tallahassee, FL

Dykeman, Kathy A
Univ Of Cincinnati
Cincinnati, OH

Dykes, Shannon P
Univ Of Md At Eastern Shore
Princess Anne, MD

Dykes, Wesley A
Univ Of Southern Ms
Hattiesburg, MS

Dysart, Charles Scott
Piedmont Tech Coll
Greenwood, SC

Dysart, Dennis A
Bridgewater Coll
Bridgewater, VA

Eagle III, Everett W
Radford Univ
Radford, VA

Eaker, Anthony D
Ms Gulf Coast Comm Coll
Perkinston, MS

Eargle, Carol D
Piedmont Tech Coll
Greenwood, SC

Earhart, Cynthia S
Gallaudet Univ
Washington, DC

Earnhardt III, William
East Tn St Univ
Johnson City, TN

Easley-Witcher, Terri L
Patrick Henry Comm Coll
Martinsville, VA

Easter, Angela C
Greensboro Coll
Greensboro, NC

Easterling, Jeffrey J
Univ Of Sc At Columbia
Columbia, SC

Eaton, Theresa M
Commonwealth Coll
Virginia Beach, VA

Eby, Elizabeth A
Philadelphia Coll Pharm & Sci
Philadelphia, PA

Eby, Kristin L
Univ Of The Arts
Philadelphia, PA

Eby, Valerie Denise
Univ Of Al
Tuscaloosa, AL

Eckhardt, Valerie Y
Liberty Univ
Lynchburg, VA

Economides, Constantine
Villanova Univ
Villanova, PA

Edens, Anita G
Middle Tn St Univ
Murfreesboro, TN

Edgar, Shelia R
Clemson Univ
Clemson, SC

Edgell, Dale R
Univ Of Miami
Coral Gables, FL

Edgson, Susan
Fl International Univ
Miami, FL

Edmondson, Edward O
Morehouse Coll
Atlanta, GA

Edwards, Amy L
Itawamba Comm Coll
Fulton, MS

Edwards, Carleen M
Nc Agri & Tech St Univ
Greensboro, NC

Edwards, Carolyn C
Vance Granville Comm Coll
Henderson, NC

Edwards, Darlene
Wilmington Coll
New Castle, DE

Edwards Jr, Donald W
Va St Univ
Petersburg, VA

Edwards, Judy C
Univ Of Sc At Coastal Carolina
Conway, SC

Edwards, Susan C
Belmont Coll
Nashville, TN

Edwards, Thomas C
S U N Y Coll Of Tech At Alfred
Alfred, NY

Edwards, Tina L
Wv Univ
Morgantown, WV

Egan, Michelle R
The Kings Coll
Briarclf Mnr, NY

Eger, Kim David
Christopher Newport Coll
Newport News, VA

Egner, John E
S U N Y Coll Of A & T Morrisvl
Morrisville, NY

Ehrlich, Stephen E
Hofstra Univ
Hempstead, NY

Eichenbaum, Dwayne S
Univ Of Miami
Coral Gables, FL

Eichhorst, Stephanie A
Southern Ct St Univ
New Haven, CT

Eichner, Robin C
Manor Jr Coll
Jenkintown, PA

Eicoff, Charmaine D
Central Fl Comm Coll
Ocala, FL

Eidelman, Jeffrey B
S U N Y Coll Of Tech
At Delhi
Delhi, NY

Eisberg, Christopher J
Cincinnati Bible Coll &
Sem
Cincinnati, OH

Eisner, Teri
City Univ Of Ny
Queensbrough
New York, NY

Ejekam, Michael C
Fl International Univ
Miami, FL

Ekpo, Ene Lazarus
Southern Coll Of Tech
Marietta, GA

Elam, Paula D
Alcorn St Univ
Lorman, MS

Elder, Carolyn H
Bloomfield Coll
Bloomfield, NJ

Elgin, Bruce Lane
Patrick Henry Comm
Coll
Martinsville, VA

Elias, Anthony A
U S Military Academy
West Point, NY

Elias, Lisette G
Western New England
Coll
Springfield, MA

Eller, Hanselena R
Central Wesleyan Coll
Central, SC

Eller, James J
Hillsborough Comm
Coll
Tampa, FL

Ellingboe, Patricia J
Atlantic Comm Coll
Mays Landing, NJ

Elliott, Avis A
Va St Univ
Petersburg, VA

Elliott, Johnathan V
Pfeiffer Coll
Misenheimer, NC

Elliott, Michael W
Univ Of Al
Tuscaloosa, AL

Elliott, Michelle D
Daytona Beach Comm
Coll
Daytona Beach, FL

Elliott, Tommy
Rust Coll
Holly Springs, MS

Ellis, Brian K
Mount Olive Coll
Mount Olive, NC

Ellis, Cathy Leanne
Pellissippi St Tech
Comm Coll
Knoxville, TN

Ellis, George
Bloomfield Coll
Bloomfield, NJ

Ellis, Kathy D
Univ Of Nc At
Charlotte
Charlotte, NC

Ellis, La Deidra A
Fl A & M Univ
Tallahassee, FL

Ellis, Todd D
Univ Of Sc At
Columbia
Columbia, SC

Ellish, Yaacov
Yeshiva Univ
New York, NY

Ellison, Jared K
Tuskegee Univ
Tuskegee Inst, AL

Ellsworth Pimentel,
Myriam
Inter Amer Univ Pr
Hato Rey
Hato Rey, PR

Elrod, Don B
Ky Wesleyan Coll
Owensboro, KY

Elsamouly, Abdelfattah
City Univ Of Ny
Queensbrough
New York, NY

Ely, Douglas J
Newbury Coll
Brookline, MA

Emrick, Virginia L
Glassboro St Coll
Glassboro, NJ

Endicott, Mareva L
Marshall University
Huntington, WV

Endres, Carrie L
Hudson Valley Comm
Coll
Troy, NY

Engel, Vicki L
Univ Of South Fl
Tampa, FL

Engelhardt, Andrea M
Univ Of Miami
Coral Gables, FL

Engelken, Lara H M
Univ Of The Dist Of
Columbia
Washington, DC

Englander, Sophia T
Univ Of Miami
Coral Gables, FL

Engle, Brian D
S U N Y Coll At
Oswego
Oswego, NY

Engle, Danny R
Sue Bennett Coll
London, KY

English, Allison C
Duke Univ
Durham, NC

English, Chantel M
Va Union Univ
Richmond, VA

English, Jennifer L
Duquesne Univ
Pittsburgh, PA

English, Leslie Monique
Va St Univ
Petersburg, VA

Ennis, Tracey E
Bloomfield Coll
Bloomfield, NJ

Enoki, Tomoko
Univ Of Sc At
Columbia
Columbia, SC

Epel, Nikki
Univ Of Central Fl
Orlando, FL

Epifanio, Iris M
Univ Of Miami
Coral Gables, FL

Epps, Justin N
Morehouse Coll
Atlanta, GA

Epstein, Wendy Jill
Cornell Univ Statutory
College
Ithaca, NY

Erickson, Courtney A
Cornell Univ Statutory
College
Ithaca, NY

Erique, Marisol Arceo
Miami Dade Comm Coll
Miami, FL

Erixton, Vicky G
Valdosta St Coll
Valdosta, GA

Ertac, Yusuf
S U N Y At Buffalo
Buffalo, NY

Ertwine Sr, Douglas M
New Comm Coll Of
Baltimore
Baltimore, MD

Ervin, Marcus
Stackhouse
Coll Of Charleston
Charleston, SC

Ervin, Sharon R
Union Univ
Jackson, TN

Escribano Sanchez,
Diana
Bayamon Tech Univ
Coll
Bayamon, PR

Espada-Miranda,
Amarilys
Caribbean Center For
Adv Stds
San Juan, PR

Espinosa, Corina J
George Mason Univ
Fairfax, VA

Esprit, Ulrec J
Tn St Univ
Nashville, TN

Esser, Tracy A
George Mason Univ
Fairfax, VA

Estabrook, Lezlie Hope
Lesley Coll
Cambridge, MA

Estela, Julio I
Inter Amer Univ Pr
Hato Rey
Hato Rey, PR

Estep, Jennifer A
Tn St Univ
Nashville, TN

Estes, Debra S
Brewer St Jr Coll
Fayette, AL

Estrada, Stephanie J
Univ Of Ga
Athens, GA

Etufugh, Alozie N
Manhattan Coll
Bronx, NY

Eubank, Thomas Kyle
Univ Of Southern Ms
Hattiesburg, MS

Eubanks, Stephen S
Castleton St Coll
Castleton, VT

Eui Hyang, Kim
Barry Univ
Miami, FL

Evakise, Lydia
Namondo
Howard Univ
Washington, DC

Evancho, Michael E
Saint Vincents Coll &
Seminary
Latrobe, PA

Evans, Felicia L
Comm Coll Algny Co
Algny Cmps
Pittsburgh, PA

Evans, Janet Lynne
Mount Vernon Coll
Washington, DC

Evans, Jean M
Univ Of Bridgeport
Bridgeport, CT

Evans, Kristi L
Ms Gulf Coast Comm
Coll
Perkinston, MS

Evans, Rhonda L
Kent St Univ Kent
Cmps
Kent, OH

Evans, Shari Elizabeth
D Youville Coll
Buffalo, NY

Evans, Shawn D
Fl A & M Univ
Tallahassee, FL

Everett, Alice E
Univ Of Miami
Coral Gables, FL

Everett, Gloria J
Meridian Comm Coll
Meridian, MS

Everetts, Anngina D
Middle Tn St Univ
Murfreesboro, TN

Exum, Brendan M
Hudson Valley Comm
Coll
Troy, NY

Eyink, Renee M
Wright St Univ Lake Cmps
Celina, OH

Eyob, Jerusalem
Selma Univ
Selma, AL

Ezekwe, Benjamin U
Va St Univ
Petersburg, VA

Ezzyk, Patricia G
Patrick Henry Comm Coll
Martinsville, VA

Fabelo, Michelle D
Univ Of Pr At Rio Piedras
Rio Piedras, PR

Faber, Kevin M
D Youville Coll
Buffalo, NY

Faber, Mark S
Methodist Coll
Fayetteville, NC

Fabiano, Tricia A
Le Moyne Coll
Syracuse, NY

Fabisch, Jason P
Trenton St Coll
Trenton, NJ

Failor, Angela K
Central Pa Bus School
Summerdale, PA

Fain, Christopher J
Morehouse Coll
Atlanta, GA

Fair, Donald A
Pa St Univ Berks Cmps
Reading, PA

Fair, Lori D
Piedmont Tech Coll
Greenwood, SC

Fairley, Deedee D
Al St Univ
Montgomery, AL

Fairley, Stephen G
Liberty Univ
Lynchburg, VA

Faisal, Mohammad Z
City Univ Of Ny La Guard Coll
Long Island Cty, NY

Fakhoury, Ruba A Ghani
Univ Of Nc At Asheville
Asheville, NC

Fakir, Ali Ahsan
S U N Y Coll Of Tech At Alfred
Alfred, NY

Falcone, Denise J
Atlantic Comm Coll
Mays Landing, NJ

Fales, Jody Allen
Univ Of Fl
Gainesville, FL

Falesto, Maria D
Daemen Coll
Amherst, NY

Falkenstein, Christy L
Eckerd Coll
St Petersburg, FL

Fallad, Mercedes C
Miami Dade Comm Coll North
Miami, FL

Famadas, Nelson E
Harvard Univ
Cambridge, MA

Fan, Qing
Old Dominion Univ
Norfolk, VA

Fan, Rick V
City Univ Of Ny Baruch Coll
New York, NY

Fanelli, Florence E
Georgian Court Coll
Lakewood, NJ

Fannin, Angela J
Morehead St Univ
Morehead, KY

Fantasia, Maria P
Saint Josephs Coll New York
Brooklyn, NY

Fantauzzi, John A
Siena Coll
Loudonville, NY

Farabaugh, Lisa A
Indiana Univ Of Pa
Indiana, PA

Faragalli, Craig M
Pa St Univ Delaware Cty Cmps
Media, PA

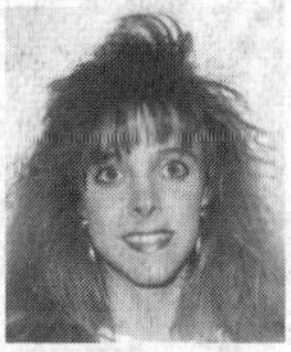
Farese, Michelle L
Ramapo Coll Of Nj
Mahwah, NJ

Farinas Exposito, Rossana L
Univ Of Miami
Coral Gables, FL

Farivar, Farhad F
Southern Coll Of Tech
Marietta, GA

Farkas, Robert J
George Washington Univ
Washington, DC

Farley, Rose T
Glassboro St Coll
Glassboro, NJ

Farmer, Linda Faye
Univ Of Sc At Aiken
Aiken, SC

Farmer, Paula D
Fl A & M Univ
Tallahassee, FL

Farrar, Sean E
U S Military Academy
West Point, NY

Farrow, David N
Cumberland County Coll
Vineland, NJ

Farrow, William Marshall
Columbia Union Coll
Takoma Park, MD

Faurot, Susan D
Auburn Univ At Auburn
Auburn, AL

Favaloro, Cristina E
Villanova Univ
Villanova, PA

Favaro, Gina Sue
Univ Of Sc At
Columbia
Columbia, SC

Faye, Rebecca J
Marywood Coll
Scranton, PA

Fazzari, Jennifer L
Cornell Univ Statutory
College
Ithaca, NY

Fazzino, Cristina M
Mount Saint Mary Coll
Newburgh, NY

Fazzino, Tabitha G
Fl St Univ
Tallahassee, FL

Febres-Cordero, Zulema
Univ Of Miami
Coral Gables, FL

Feder, Darrin M
William Paterson Coll
Wayne, NJ

Feeney, Brooke C
Salisbury St Univ
Salisbury, MD

Feigh Jr, John M
Christopher Newport
Coll
Newport News, VA

Feild Jr, John M
Valdosta St Coll
Valdosta, GA

Feldberg, Marnie A
Univ Of North Fl
Jacksonville, FL

Feliberty, Melba
Ny Univ
New York, NY

Feliciano, Yesenia
Inter Amer Univ Pr
Hato Rey
Hato Rey, PR

Felmet, Camilla H
Catawba Valley Comm
Coll
Hickory, NC

Feloso, Staci A
Indiana Univ Of Pa
Indiana, PA

Felton, Audrey Iris
Jackson St Univ
Jackson, MS

Fendelet, Quentin A
Merrimack Coll
North Andover, MA

Ferenc, Alana M
Saint Johns Univ
Jamaica, NY

Fergus, Cynthia
Williams
Strayer Coll
Washington, DC

Ferguson, Carol
Cuyahoga Comm Coll
Cleveland, OH

Ferguson, Cassandra
Tyiese
Memphis St Univ
Memphis, TN

Ferguson, Deborah J
Faulkner St Jr Coll
Bay Minette, AL

Ferguson, Donna J
Seton Hall Univ
South Orange, NJ

Ferguson, Jason S
Univ Of Tn At
Knoxville
Knoxville, TN

Ferguson, Lindsey N
Vanderbilt Univ
Nashville, TN

Ferguson, Porsetta A
Marshall University
Huntington, WV

Ferguson, Shannon R
Western New England
Coll
Springfield, MA

Fernander, Eloise M
Tuskegee Univ
Tuskegee Inst, AL

Fernander, Tieschka C
Clark Atlanta Univ
Atlanta, GA

Fernandez, Aida C
Fl International Univ
Miami, FL

Fernandez, Ramon Ruiz
Bayamon Central Univ
Bayamon, PR

Fernandez, Tara L
Univ Of Fl
Gainesville, FL

Ferran, Sarah C
Miami Dade Comm Coll
South
Miami, FL

Ferrari, Karen A
Univ Of Sc At
Columbia
Columbia, SC

Ferrari Jr, Richard J
Wv Univ
Morgantown, WV

Ferraro, Christine A
Endicott Coll
Beverly, MA

Ferreira, Custodio J S
Univ Of Rochester
Rochester, NY

Ferreira, Suzanne
Loureno
Gallaudet Univ
Washington, DC

Ferrer, Ernesto Juan
Univ Of Pr At Rio
Piedras
Rio Piedras, PR

Ferrer, Jacinto Robles
Caribbean Univ
Bayamon, PR

Ferrill, Julie D
Ms St Univ
Miss State, MS

Fery, Patricia A
Fl International Univ
Miami, FL

Fester, Traci E
Antonelli Inst Of Art & Photo
Cincinnati, OH

Fiacco, Kristin F
Eastern Nazarene Coll
Wollaston, MA

Field, Christopher R
Lehigh Univ
Bethlehem, PA

Field, Sherri A
Univ Of New England
Biddeford, ME

Fields, Kimberly M
Al A & M Univ
Normal, AL

Fields, Ritchie L
Tn Tech Univ
Cookeville, TN

Fields, Tarsha D
Johnson C Smith Univ
Charlotte, NC

Fields, Valerie K
Univ Of Nc At Chapel Hill
Chapel Hill, NC

Figueroa Lopez, Skarlet
Inter Amer Univ Pr San German
San German, PR

Figueroa Morales, Wilfredo
Bayamon Central Univ
Bayamon, PR

Figueroa Munoz, Angel
Catholic Univ Of Pr
Ponce, PR

Figueroa, Annette Marie
Univ Of Pr At Rio Piedras
Rio Piedras, PR

Files, Pamela L
Davis Coll
Toledo, OH

Filiano, Amy E
Immaculata Coll
Immaculata, PA

Filomia, Judith M
Fl International Univ
Miami, FL

Finch, Denise B
Northeastern Christian Jr Coll
Villanova, PA

Finch, Jeffery S
Northeastern Christian Jr Coll
Villanova, PA

Fink, Holly B
Lancaster Bible Coll
Lancaster, PA

Fink, Martin Jan
Middle Tn St Univ
Murfreesboro, TN

Finkelstein, Ariana D
Rutgers St Un At New Brunswick
New Brunswick, NJ

Finlay, Bobbie J
Nova Univ
Ft Lauderdale, FL

Finnerty, William Boone
Georgetown Univ
Washington, DC

Fiore, Daniel A
Carnegie Mellon Univ
Pittsburgh, PA

Fischer, Audrey A
Univ Of Cincinnati-Clrmnt Coll
Batavia, OH

Fischer, Daniel
Univ Of South Al
Mobile, AL

Fischer, Elizabeth A
Univ Of Sc At Columbia
Columbia, SC

Fisher, Alisia H
Memphis St Univ
Memphis, TN

Fisher Jr, David M
Univ Of Nc At Chapel Hill
Chapel Hill, NC

Fisher, Eric J
Morehouse Coll
Atlanta, GA

Fisher, Gina A
City Univ Of Ny Bronx Comm Col
Bronx, NY

Fisher, Maria P
Univ Of Akron
Akron, OH

Fisher, Scott Pearce
Radford Univ
Radford, VA

Fisher, Tobin J
Univ Of Al At Birmingham
Birmingham, AL

Fisher, Todd A
Slippery Rock Univ
Slippery Rock, PA

Fisher-Vines, Annette
Newbury Coll
Brookline, MA

Fitzgerald, Wayne H
Schenectady County Comm Coll
Schenectady, NY

Fiumara, Dino S
Duquesne Univ
Pittsburgh, PA

Fiutem, Stacey L
Western New England Coll
Springfield, MA

Fix, Melanie D
Radford Univ
Radford, VA

Fizer, Cecilia A
Concord Coll
Athens, WV

Flaherty, Thomas J
City Univ Of Ny
Queensbrough
New York, NY

Flanagan, Linda A
William Paterson Coll
Wayne, NJ

Flanigan, Kristie J
Salem-Teikyo Univ
Salem, WV

Flannery, Lee-Anne S
East Stroudsburg Univ
E Stroudsburg, PA

Fleitas, Ivonne M
Fl International Univ
Miami, FL

Fleming, Karen M
Columbus Coll Of Art
& Design
Columbus, OH

Flemming, Mauria A
Immaculata Coll
Immaculata, PA

Fleshman, Stephanie
Gray
Cumberland County
Coll
Vineland, NJ

Flickinger, Gregory L
Oh Univ
Athens, OH

Floden, Heather E
Georgian Court Coll
Lakewood, NJ

Flora Jr, William A
Old Dominion Univ
Norfolk, VA

Flores, Annabella
Valdosta St Coll
Valdosta, GA

Flores, Elsa R
Ma Inst Of Tech
Cambridge, MA

Floyd II, James Lee
Univ Of Sc At Coastal
Carolina
Conway, SC

Floyd, Tamara G
Middle Tn St Univ
Murfreesboro, TN

Fludd, Olivia V
Hampton Univ
Hampton, VA

Fodera, Rosalia
Lasell Coll
Newton, MA

Fogaros, John R
Western Ky Univ
Bowling Green, KY

Fogel, Alter S
City Univ Of Ny
Brooklyn Coll
Brooklyn, NY

Fogleman, Michael J
Univ Of Sc At
Columbia
Columbia, SC

Foley, Roger W
Le Moyne Coll
Syracuse, NY

Foley, Thomas P
Univ Of Al At
Birmingham
Birmingham, AL

Folland, Nora T
Webber Coll
Babson Park, FL

Fong, Amy Hsiao Ming
Georgetown Univ
Washington, DC

Fons, Benjamin A
Ga Inst Of Tech At
Atlanta
Atlanta, GA

Fonte, Jean-Nate
City Univ Of Ny
Kingsborough
Brooklyn, NY

Forbes, Rochelle N
Bethune Cookman Coll
Daytona Beach, FL

Ford Sr, Glenn J
Coppin St Coll
Baltimore, MD

Ford, Gurth A
Tuskegee Univ
Tuskegee Inst, AL

Ford III, James
Valdosta St Coll
Valdosta, GA

Ford, Juanakee
Vance Granville Comm
Coll
Henderson, NC

Ford, Lokitha T
Central St Univ
Wilberforce, OH

Forde, Everton D
Columbia Union Coll
Takoma Park, MD

Fordham, Michelle
Ms St Univ
Miss State, MS

Forlano, Bartholomew F
Cornell Univ Statutory
College
Ithaca, NY

Forman, Harriet E
Saint Josephs Coll New
York
Brooklyn, NY

Forrester, Pamela J
Roane St Comm Coll
Harriman, TN

Fortenberry, Tina M
Phillips Jr Coll
Spartanburg
Spartanburg, SC

Fortner, Douglas
Commodore
Catholic Univ Of
America
Washington, DC

Fortune, Lori A
Univ Of Tn At Martin
Martin, TN

Foster, April L
Coll Of William &
Mary
Williamsburg, VA

Foster, Cynthia D
Tn Temple Univ
Chattanooga, TN

Foster, Richard B
Nova Univ
Ft Lauderdale, FL

Fowler, Stephanie R
Birmingham Southern Coll
Birmingham, AL

Fowler, Teresa N
Saint Peters Coll
Jersey City, NJ

Fox, Darla R
Wallace St Comm Coll At Selma
Selma, AL

Fox, Debbie L
Univ Of Al At Huntsville
Huntsville, AL

Foy, Tammy L
Duquesne Univ
Pittsburgh, PA

Frack, Tricia L
Univ Of Pittsburgh
Pittsburgh, PA

Fraga, Ivonne
Univ Of Pr At Rio Piedras
Rio Piedras, PR

Fragoso, Ruben C
Princeton Univ
Princeton, NJ

Frame, Shannon A
East Tn St Univ
Johnson City, TN

Frances, Antonio C
Va St Univ
Petersburg, VA

Franceschini, Gilberto A
Univ Central Del Caribe
Cayey, PR

Francis, Brendan C
Barry Univ
Miami, FL

Francis, Elizabeth M
Fl St Univ
Tallahassee, FL

Francis, Monique M
Fisk Univ
Nashville, TN

Francisco, Pamela J
Ms St Univ
Miss State, MS

Franco Colon, Mayra Lee
Inter Amer Univ Pr Hato Rey
Hato Rey, PR

Franco, Alvaro
Univ Of Southern Ms
Hattiesburg, MS

Francois, Jacques Olcy
Miami Dade Comm Coll
Miami, FL

Francolino, Barbara R
Cabrini Coll
Radnor, PA

Franket, Dion D
Univ Of Sc At Columbia
Columbia, SC

Franklin, Charlene J
Dutchess Comm Coll
Poughkeepsie, NY

Franklin, Kimberly C
Gaston Coll
Dallas, NC

Franklin, Sandra A
S U N Y Coll Of Tech At Frmgdl
Farmingdale, NY

Franklin, Serena Y
Lincoln Univ
Lincoln Univ, PA

Franko, Carol M
Duquesne Univ
Pittsburgh, PA

Franks, Dawn E
Fl International Univ
Miami, FL

Frans, Kerenza T K
Webber Coll
Babson Park, FL

Franz, Joseph D
Univ Of Akron
Akron, OH

Franz, Lorraine M
City Univ Of Ny La Guard Coll
Long Island Cty, NY

Fraser, Charles H
Manhattan Coll
Bronx, NY

Fraterrigo, Robert
City Univ Of Ny City Coll
New York, NY

Frates, Laura L
Western New England Coll
Springfield, MA

Fratini, Colleen M
Univ Of New England
Biddeford, ME

Fratolill, April J
Univ Of Sc At Columbia
Columbia, SC

Frawley, Carolyn M
S U N Y Empire St Coll
Saratoga Spg, NY

Frazier, Bernice L
Central St Univ
Wilberforce, OH

Frazier, Jamie L
Univ Of Cin R Walters Coll
Blue Ash, OH

Frazier, Marjorie G
Emory Univ
Atlanta, GA

Frazier III, Robert E
Morehouse Coll
Atlanta, GA

Frazier, Scott A
Defiance Coll
Defiance, OH

Frechette, Mikell B
Savannah Coll Of Art & Design
Savannah, GA

Frederick, Kimberly J
Youngstown St Univ
Youngstown, OH

Fredreck, Jennifer L
Villanova Univ
Villanova, PA

Freeman Jr, Garry L
Univ Of Al At
Huntsville
Huntsville, AL

Freeman, Gina M
Union Univ School Of
Nursing
Memphis, TN

Freeman, Lettie L
Fl A & M Univ
Tallahassee, FL

Freeman, Mark M
Southern Coll Of Tech
Marietta, GA

Freeman, Patricia L
Christopher Newport
Coll
Newport News, VA

French, Frank E
Strayer Coll
Washington, DC

French, Jennifer A
Univ Of New England
Biddeford, ME

Frese, Glenn R
Univ Of Miami
Coral Gables, FL

Frett, Renard W
Christopher Newport
Coll
Newport News, VA

Freyre Cabrera, Militza
Inter Amer Univ Pr
Hato Rey
Hato Rey, PR

Friedline, Suzanne M
Fl St Univ
Tallahassee, FL

Frierman, Judith L
Fl Southern Coll
Lakeland, FL

Fritz Jr, John A
Jersey City St Coll
Jersey City, NJ

Frontera, Jose A
Univ Of Sc At
Columbia
Columbia, SC

Fuentes, Isha M
Inter Amer Univ Pr
Hato Rey
Hato Rey, PR

Fujioka, Misao
Methodist Coll
Fayetteville, NC

Fulkerson, Michael H
Ky Wesleyan Coll
Owensboro, KY

Fuller, Stacy L
Univ Of Nc At
Greensboro
Greensboro, NC

Fulton, Paula E
Bowie St Univ
Bowie, MD

Fulwider, Michelle R
The Johns Hopkins Univ
Baltimore, MD

Funches, Maurice O
Providence Coll
Providence, RI

Funchess, Chant Andrea
City Univ Of Ny City
Coll
New York, NY

Furcon, Therese C
Wilkes Univ
Wilkes-Barre, PA

Furey, Julie A
Univ Of Nh Plymouth
St Coll
Plymouth, NH

Furno, Laura A
Univ Of South Fl
Tampa, FL

Fury, Sherry S
Cumberland Coll
Williamsburg, KY

Fyfe, Susan E
Tuskegee Univ
Tuskegee Inst, AL

Gabriele, Linda M
Univ Of Ri
Kingston, RI

Gabriele, Rosella
Oh Coll Of Podiatric
Med
Cleveland, OH

Gadd, Marie A
Central St Univ
Wilberforce, OH

Gaddis, Christopher P
Alcorn St Univ
Lorman, MS

Gadi, Renu
Middlesex County Coll
Edison, NJ

Gadiare, Harold H
City Univ Of Ny
Baruch Coll
New York, NY

Gage, Adam F K
Berkshire Comm Coll
Pittsfield, MA

Gagliano, Jeffrey R
Cornell Univ Statutory
College
Ithaca, NY

Gailey Jr, Richard M
Waycross Coll
Waycross, GA

Gaiolini, Steven
Savannah Coll Of Art
& Design
Savannah, GA

Gaiter, Kathy F
Columbia Union Coll
Takoma Park, MD

Galanos, Konstantinos
Teikyo Post Univ
Waterbury, CT

Galarza, Nitza J
Inter Amer Univ Pr
Hato Rey
Hato Rey, PR

Gale, Gloria S
Va Highlands Comm Coll
Abingdon, VA

Gale, Nicole L
Univ Of Md At Eastern Shore
Princess Anne, MD

Galindo, Inocencio E
Georgetown Univ
Washington, DC

Gallegos, Clay W
Salisbury St Univ
Salisbury, MD

Gallimore, Kevin L
Univ Of Tn At Martin
Martin, TN

Gallop, Raecita A
Longwood Coll
Farmville, VA

Galloway, Aimee D
Coker Coll
Hartsville, SC

Galvam, Derek C
Bridgewater St Coll
Bridgewater, MA

Galvan, Walter
Bloomfield Coll
Bloomfield, NJ

Gamiles, Donald S
Bristol Univ
Bristol, TN

Gandy, James R
Wv Univ
Morgantown, WV

Ganeshan, Vinay S
Howard Univ
Washington, DC

Gangadhar, Narendra
Univ Of The Dist Of Columbia
Washington, DC

Ganguly, Samrat
Yale Univ
New Haven, CT

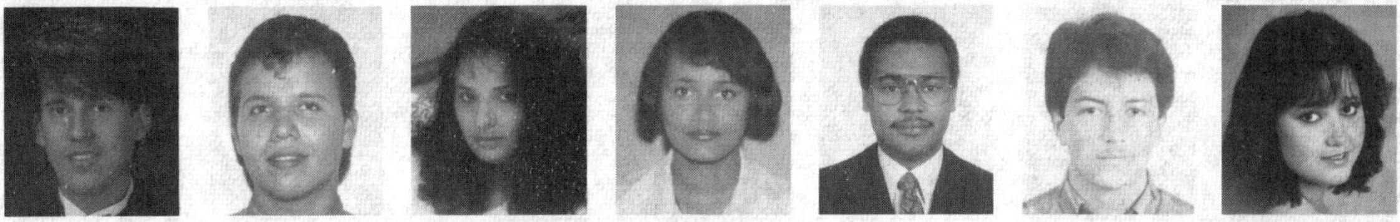

Garcia Espinosa, Filiberto
Inter Amer Univ Pr Hato Rey
Hato Rey, PR

Garcia Ramos, Ferdinand D
Univ Of Pr At Rio Piedras
Rio Piedras, PR

Garcia Rosario, Luz P
Univ Of Pr Medical Sciences
San Juan, PR

Garcia, Brenda M
Univ Of Pr At Rio Piedras
Rio Piedras, PR

Garcia, Felix
City Univ Of Ny Bronx Comm Col
Bronx, NY

Garcia, Luis H
City Univ Of Ny City Coll
New York, NY

Garcia, Maria P
Allegheny Coll
Meadville, PA

Garcia, Roxanne Kaye
City Univ Of Ny Baruch Coll
New York, NY

Garcia, Saudy E
Univ Politecnica De Pr
Hato Rey, PR

Garcia, Vivian P
Fl International Univ
Miami, FL

Gardenhour, Kelly A
Fl International Univ
Miami, FL

Gardiner, Birdette E
Smith Coll
Northampton, MA

Gardner, Carla D
Fisk Univ
Nashville, TN

Gardner, Charles A
Morehouse Coll
Atlanta, GA

Garfunkel, Steven F
Barry Univ
Miami, FL

Garland, Adam Lenear
Southern Coll Of Tech
Marietta, GA

Garner II, David T
Al A & M Univ
Normal, AL

Garner, Michele E
Middle Tn St Univ
Murfreesboro, TN

Garner-Richardson, Loretta Faye
Stillman Coll
Tuscaloosa, AL

Garrett, Lisa C
Univ Of Southern Ms
Hattiesburg, MS

Garris, Linda D
Fayetteville St Univ
Fayetteville, NC

Garrison, Jeff W
Univ Of Nc At Asheville
Asheville, NC

Garwood, Diane R
Glassboro St Coll
Glassboro, NJ

Gary, Kenneth A
Norfolk St Univ
Norfolk, VA

Gassman, Lisa J
S U N Y At Buffalo
Buffalo, NY

Gastel, Gary
Miami Dade Comm Coll North
Miami, FL

Gathings, Angela G
Wingate Coll
Wingate, NC

Gatlin, Tammy R
Univ Of South Al
Mobile, AL

Gavel, Kenneth Franklin
Asbury Theological Sem
Wilmore, KY

Gavin, Ellen M
Le Moyne Coll
Syracuse, NY

Gavin, Sarah A
Gallaudet Univ
Washington, DC

Gawin, Agnieszka M
Peabody Inst Of J
Hopkins Univ
Baltimore, MD

Gay, Sonia S
William Paterson Coll
Wayne, NJ

Gaynor, Shawna
Fl Atlantic Univ
Boca Raton, FL

Geagan, Peter
Becker Coll At Leicester
Leicester, MA

Gear-Stine, Sue N
Univ Of Cin R Walters
Coll
Blue Ash, OH

Gearhart, Sonya L
Duquesne Univ
Pittsburgh, PA

Geithmann, Suzanna L
Christopher Newport
Coll
Newport News, VA

Gelman, Natalya
Cooper Union
New York, NY

Generett Jr, William O
Morehouse Coll
Atlanta, GA

Genovese, Alexander V
Bloomfield Coll
Bloomfield, NJ

Gentile, Joseph A
S U N Y Coll At
Fredonia
Fredonia, NY

Gentle, Raymond
Patrick
Norwalk St Tech Coll
Norwalk, CT

George, Thomas A
Clayton St Coll
Morrow, GA

Georget, Rachel R
Coll Of Charleston
Charleston, SC

Gerchak, Roberta F
Wilmington Coll
Wilmington, OH

Gerdes, Stephan
City Univ Of Ny
Baruch Coll
New York, NY

Gerolimatos, Samantha
Clarkson Univ
Potsdam, NY

Gerometta, Dawn M
Palm Beach Comm Coll
Lake Worth, FL

Gerrell, Regina K
James Sprunt Comm
Coll
Kenansville, NC

Geswaldo, Andrea M
Le Moyne Coll
Syracuse, NY

Getson, Eileen C
Fl St Univ
Tallahassee, FL

Geyser, Sandra M
Duquesne Univ
Pittsburgh, PA

Ghansah, Agnes
Fisk Univ
Nashville, TN

Giangresso, Michele F
Bloomfield Coll
Bloomfield, NJ

Giardina, Toni-Anne
Ramapo Coll Of Nj
Mahwah, NJ

Gibbions Jr, James V
Nj Inst Of Tech
Newark, NJ

Gibbons, Kenneth M
Bloomfield Coll
Bloomfield, NJ

Gibbs Jr, Franklin G
Thomas Nelson Comm
Coll
Hampton, VA

Gibbs, James R
Interdenominational
Theo Ctr
Atlanta, GA

Gibson, Phillip A
Western Ky Univ
Bowling Green, KY

Giddings, Samia P
Morris Brown Coll
Atlanta, GA

Gikas, Christopher J
City Univ Of Ny City
Coll
New York, NY

Gil, Teresita
Fl International Univ
Miami, FL

Gilbert, Lynda Ruth
Bishop St Comm Coll
Mobile, AL

Giles, Amelia M
Winthrop Coll
Rock Hill, SC

Giles, Angela G
Greenville Tech Coll
Greenville, SC

Gilevich, Darlene J
West Liberty St Coll
West Liberty, WV

Gill, Dorothy M
Passaic County Comm
Coll
Paterson, NJ

Gill, Ginnie T
Tougaloo Coll
Tougaloo, MS

Gill, Mary E
Vanderbilt Univ
Nashville, TN

Gill, Scott T
Memphis St Univ
Memphis, TN

Gill, Stephanie L
Univ Of Pa
Philadelphia, PA

Gillenardo, Todd A
Univ Of Md At Eastern Shore
Princess Anne, MD

Gillespie, Michelle F
Broward Comm Coll
Ft Lauderdale, FL

Gilman, Caryn S
Teikyo Post Univ
Waterbury, CT

Gilmore, Andre A
Morehouse Coll
Atlanta, GA

Gilmore III, John
Sc St Coll
Orangeburg, SC

Gilroy, Bernard H P
Catholic Univ Of America
Washington, DC

Ginader, Jennifer L
Longwood Coll
Farmville, VA

Ginn, Catherine Maria
Univ Of Southern Ms
Hattiesburg, MS

Giordano, Guido L
Harvard Univ
Cambridge, MA

Giosi, Kenneth J
S U N Y Coll Of Tech At Frmgdl
Farmingdale, NY

Girard, J Andre
Univ Of Sc At Coastal Carolina
Conway, SC

Girard, Joseph M
Le Moyne Coll
Syracuse, NY

Gittens, Juliet M
Elmira Coll
Elmira, NY

Giunta, Jonathan P
S U N Y Coll Of Tech At Delhi
Delhi, NY

Giunta, Stephanie L
Villanova Univ
Villanova, PA

Given, Tonya G
Fairmont St Coll
Fairmont, WV

Gladwell, Jerrard M
Marshall University
Huntington, WV

Glasscock, Audrey Y
Longwood Coll
Farmville, VA

Glast, Veronica E
Va Union Univ
Richmond, VA

Glencer, Kathleen T
Birmingham Southern Coll
Birmingham, AL

Glenn, Roselyn Barton
Middle Ga Coll
Cochran, GA

Glenn, Scott A
Anderson Coll
Anderson, SC

Glenwright, Brian G
Bowling Green St Univ
Bowling Green, OH

Gloss, Kathleen L
Univ Of Pittsburgh At Bradford
Bradford, PA

Gluck, Karen E
Fl International Univ
Miami, FL

Goad, Delana R
Roane St Comm Coll
Harriman, TN

Gochakowski, Robin M
Bunker Hill Comm Coll
Boston, MA

Godoy, Bianca D
City Univ Of Ny La Guard Coll
Long Island Cty, NY

Godsey, Leah L
Univ Of Sc At Columbia
Columbia, SC

Godwin, Christie L
Univ Of South Al
Mobile, AL

Goff, Leslie B
Georgetown Coll
Georgetown, KY

Goff, Mary J
Madisonville Comm Coll
Madisonville, KY

Gohde, Kevin D
S U N Y Coll Of Tech At Delhi
Delhi, NY

Goins, Kathryn L
Johnson C Smith Univ
Charlotte, NC

Gold, Tracy L
Univ Of Sc At Columbia
Columbia, SC

Golden, Sabrina K
Abraham Baldwin Agri Coll
Tifton, GA

Golden, Travis L
Saint Pauls Coll
Lawrenceville, VA

Goldsmith, Michele E
Anne Arundel Comm Coll
Arnold, MD

Goldstein, Robert B
Univ Of Fl
Gainesville, FL

Goldstein, Stephanie L
Fl International Univ
Miami, FL

Goldwire, Lisa M
Savannah St Coll
Savannah, GA

Golub, Stacey H
Cornell Univ Statutory College
Ithaca, NY

Gomez, Adriana M
City Univ Of Ny La Guard Coll
Long Island Cty, NY

Gomez, Flor M
Univ Del Turabo
Gurabo, PR

Gomez, Mary C
Saint Thomas Univ
Miami, FL

Gomez, Oscar M
Va St Univ
Petersburg, VA

Gomez, Zachary A
Fl St Univ
Tallahassee, FL

Gongora, Michael C
Univ Of Miami
Coral Gables, FL

Gontkovsky, Samuel T
Kent St Univ Kent Cmps
Kent, OH

Gonzales, Francoise
Palm Beach Comm Coll
Lake Worth, FL

Gonzales, Patrick
Palm Beach Comm Coll
Lake Worth, FL

Gonzales, Sylveta A
Coll Of New Rochelle
New Rochelle, NY

Gonzalez Montes, Heriberto
Inter Amer Univ Pr San German
San German, PR

Gonzalez Moreno, Rosa
Inter Amer Univ Pr San German
San German, PR

Gonzalez Soto, Maribel
Univ Politecnica De Pr
Hato Rey, PR

Gonzalez, Adilia
Univ Del Turabo
Gurabo, PR

Gonzalez, Brenda
Univ Of Pr At Rio Piedras
Rio Piedras, PR

Gonzalez, Elvira M
Fl Atlantic Univ
Boca Raton, FL

Gonzalez, Iris M
Univ Politecnica De Pr
Hato Rey, PR

Gonzalez, Jesus C
Nova Univ
Ft Lauderdale, FL

Gonzalez, Leonor M
Inter Amer Univ Pr Fajardo
Fajardo, PR

Gonzalez, Luis E
Inter Amer Univ Pr Hato Rey
Hato Rey, PR

Gonzalez, Maritza Valerie
Fl International Univ
Miami, FL

Gonzalez, Nanette L
Univ Of Pr At Rio Piedras
Rio Piedras, PR

Gonzalez, Patricia D
Univ Of Miami
Coral Gables, FL

Gonzalez Jr, Ruben L
Fl International Univ
Miami, FL

Gonzalez-Quevedo, Belkys C
Fl International Univ
Miami, FL

Goode, Lelia C
Fayetteville St Univ
Fayetteville, NC

Goode, Melinda A
Radford Univ
Radford, VA

Gooden, Hazel G
Saint Josephs Coll New York
Brooklyn, NY

Gooden, Kelly L
Howard Univ
Washington, DC

Gooding, Karlene A
Borough Of Manhattan Comm Coll
New York, NY

Goodman Jr, Ronald L
Abraham Baldwin Agri Coll
Tifton, GA

Goodrich, Sarah J
Castleton St Coll
Castleton, VT

Goodson, Sheila A
Fl St Univ
Tallahassee, FL

Goodson, Wynn L
Fl A & M Univ
Tallahassee, FL

Goodwater, Torry F
Johnson C Smith Univ
Charlotte, NC

Goodwin, Jana L
Va Commonwealth Univ
Richmond, VA

Goodwin, Quentin W
Coll Of Charleston
Charleston, SC

Gordick, Robert A
Thomas Nelson Comm Coll
Hampton, VA

Gordon, Johnthan
Univ Of Sc At Columbia
Columbia, SC

Gordon, Karen M
Univ Of Sc At Columbia
Columbia, SC

Gordon, Kathy A
Edward Waters Coll
Jacksonville, FL

Gordon, Marleen K
Fl International Univ
Miami, FL

Gottesman, Beth C
Univ Of Miami
Coral Gables, FL

Gottsleben, Trevor Lee
Fl St Univ
Tallahassee, FL

Gould, Kimberly Lynn
Western New England Coll
Springfield, MA

Gourdine, Timothy
Norfolk St Univ
Norfolk, VA

Goyco Rodriguez, Osvaldo
Univ Of Pr At Mayaguez
Mayaguez, PR

Gradischek, Monica L
Ny Univ
New York, NY

Graf, Paul E
Providence Coll
Providence, RI

Gragg, Deanna E
Lenoir Rhyne Coll
Hickory, NC

Graham, Donna J
Comm Coll Algny Co Algny Cmps
Pittsburgh, PA

Graham, Jennifer
Fl A & M Univ
Tallahassee, FL

Graham, Meridith T
Univ Of Sc At Columbia
Columbia, SC

Graham, Susan L
Memphis St Univ
Memphis, TN

Graham, Troy A
Kent St Univ Kent Cmps
Kent, OH

Grajales Soto, Maribel
Inter Amer Univ Pr Hato Rey
Hato Rey, PR

Grammatico, Gary S
Univ Of New Haven
West Haven, CT

Grammatico Jr, Joseph
Quinnipiac Coll
Hamden, CT

Granderson, Kenneth E
Hampton Univ
Hampton, VA

Granitto, Matthew J
Cleveland St Univ
Cleveland, OH

Granizo, Diego E
Univ Of Pittsburgh
Pittsburgh, PA

Grannan, Elaine C
Ky Wesleyan Coll
Owensboro, KY

Grant, Betty J
Medaille Coll
Buffalo, NY

Grant, Camesha M
Va St Univ
Petersburg, VA

Grant, Edward A
Norfolk St Univ
Norfolk, VA

Grant, Jarrod K
Wilberforce Univ
Wilberforce, OH

Grant, Leone A
Univ Of The Dist Of Columbia
Washington, DC

Grant, Melissa A
Defiance Coll
Defiance, OH

Grant, Simone Y
Va St Univ
Petersburg, VA

Grappone, Rachele K
Le Moyne Coll
Syracuse, NY

Grasso, Molly A
Indiana Univ Of Pa
Indiana, PA

Gravish, Lori A
Pa St Univ Main Cmps
University Pk, PA

Grays, Ronda N
Tougaloo Coll
Tougaloo, MS

Graziano, Christina M
Philadelphia Coll Pharm & Sci
Philadelphia, PA

Graziano, Lisa J
Georgetown Univ
Washington, DC

Greaux, Christopher G
Univ Of Miami
Coral Gables, FL

Greaves, Sherry R
Ramapo Coll Of Nj
Mahwah, NJ

Greco, Jennifer J
S U N Y Coll Of Tech At Frmgdl
Farmingdale, NY

Greek, Cindy L
Rochester Bus Inst
Rochester, NY

Green, Michelle D
Dowling Coll
Oakdale Li, NY

Green, Sherri L
West Liberty St Coll
West Liberty, WV

Green, Shireen A
Fl A & M Univ
Tallahassee, FL

Greene, Daniel J
Marshall University
Huntington, WV

Greene, Delores J
Kent St Univ Kent Cmps
Kent, OH

Greene, Eric B
Claflin Coll
Orangeburg, SC

Greene, Gloria K
Norfolk St Univ
Norfolk, VA

Greene, Jamie J
Univ Of Akron
Akron, OH

Greene, John E
City Univ Of Ny La Guard Coll
Long Island Cty, NY

Greene, Kathryn
Savannah Coll Of Art & Design
Savannah, GA

Greenfield, Corey B
Bradford Coll
Bradford, MA

Greer Jr, Murphy R
Tougaloo Coll
Tougaloo, MS

Gregory, Charlotte A
Jackson St Univ
Jackson, MS

Gregory, Karen Y
Inter Amer Univ Pr San German
San German, PR

Greulich, Thomas G
Southern Coll Of Tech
Marietta, GA

Greve, Mark J
Oh St Univ Lima Campus
Lima, OH

Griffin, Dexter K
Jackson St Univ
Jackson, MS

Griffin, Jason E
Valdosta St Coll
Valdosta, GA

Griffin, Kristi L
Anderson Coll
Anderson, SC

Griffin, Lisa A
Univ Of Sc At Spartanburg
Spartanburg, SC

Griffin, Mary M
Auburn Univ At Auburn
Auburn, AL

Griffin, Ruby D
Univ Of North Fl
Jacksonville, FL

Griffin, Tammy L
Anne Arundel Comm Coll
Arnold, MD

Griffith, Gloria J
Nova Univ
Ft Lauderdale, FL

Griffiths, Sharronda L
Univ Of Sc At Columbia
Columbia, SC

Griggs, Barry Todd
Univ Of Tn At Martin
Martin, TN

Grim, Christopher J
Univ Of Miami
Coral Gables, FL

Grimaldi, Frances A
Le Moyne Coll
Syracuse, NY

Grinnell, Joseph N
Univ Of New Haven
West Haven, CT

Grinzayd, Alexander
City Univ Of Ny Baruch Coll
New York, NY

Grippo, Jacqueline M
Univ Of Med & Dentistry Of Nj
Newark, NJ

Groff, Kyla Lorelei
Samford Univ
Birmingham, AL

Gronau, Daphne Marie
Catholic Univ Of Pr
Ponce, PR

Grosner, David R
Providence Coll
Providence, RI

Grospe, Edwin B
Fordham Univ
Bronx, NY

Gross, Allen J
Davis & Elkins Coll
Elkins, WV

Gross, Pauline J
Fisk Univ
Nashville, TN

Gross, Ranelle D
Univ Of Md At Eastern Shore
Princess Anne, MD

Gross, Richard J
West Chester Univ
West Chester, PA

Grossman, Jordan P
Oh Coll Of Podiatric Med
Cleveland, OH

Grossnickle, Robert S
Univ Of Md At College Park
College Park, MD

Grove, Stephanie M
Duquesne Univ
Pittsburgh, PA

Groves, John Edward
Tn Temple Univ
Chattanooga, TN

Grubb, Rebecca G
East Tn St Univ
Johnson City, TN

Grubb, Stacey R
Spartanburg Methodist Coll
Spartanburg, SC

Grubbs, C Amy D
Radford Univ
Radford, VA

Grubbs, Denise A
Univ Of Al At Birmingham
Birmingham, AL

Gruber, Jodi
Nova Univ
Ft Lauderdale, FL

Grundy, Damon Lee
Univ Of New Haven
West Haven, CT

Guan, Chang-Qian
S U N Y Maritime Coll
Bronx, NY

Guarda, Michael E
Ny Univ
New York, NY

Guasp Fernandez, Liza
Inter Amer Univ Pr Guayama
Guayama, PR

Guba, Kurt V
The Boston Conservatory
Boston, MA

Gueh, Gbor Solomon
Interdenominational Theo Ctr
Atlanta, GA

Guerrios, Ricardo Matos
Caribbean Univ
Bayamon, PR

Guet, Sylvain B
Fl International Univ
Miami, FL

Guevara, Mirtha M
Fl International Univ
Miami, FL

Guffey, Teresa E
Western Piedmont Comm Coll
Morganton, NC

Guhse, Laura K
Anne Arundel Comm Coll
Arnold, MD

Guia, Barbara M
Saint Thomas Univ
Miami, FL

Guider, Kathy S
Benedict Coll
Columbia, SC

Guidry, Mona J
Thomas Nelson Comm Coll
Hampton, VA

Guilbaud, Stanley
Inter Amer Univ Pr Hato Rey
Hato Rey, PR

Gulam, Sandra D
Saint Johns Univ
Jamaica, NY

Gulla, Natalie M
Wv Northern Comm Coll
Wheeling, WV

Guma, Richard J
Ny Chiropractic Coll
Glen Head, NY

Gunasekara, Chanaka H
City Univ Of Ny City Coll
New York, NY

Gunasekara, Rukmal D
Strayer Coll
Washington, DC

Gunter, Jeana L
Judson Coll
Marion, AL

Gunter, Jerricka L
Univ Of Fl
Gainesville, FL

Gurevich, Yelena
City Univ Of Ny Baruch Coll
New York, NY

Gurley Jr, James R
Middle Ga Coll
Cochran, GA

Gurley, Steven N
Univ Of Tn At Martin
Martin, TN

Gutarra-Negron, Miguel
Bayamon Central Univ
Bayamon, PR

Guthrie, Beverly D
Walker Coll
Jasper, AL

Guthrie, Lynne J
Greenville Tech Coll
Greenville, SC

Gutierrez, Maria L
Inter Amer Univ Pr Hato Rey
Hato Rey, PR

Gutierrez, Ramiro L
Cornell Univ
Ithaca, NY

Gutzmer, Justin E
Morehouse Coll
Atlanta, GA

Guy, Cheryl A
Univ Of Ky
Lexington, KY

Guynes, Sharon V
Univ Of South Al
Mobile, AL

Guyton, Russell B
Brewer St Jr Coll
Fayette, AL

Guzman, Claudia P
Fl International Univ
Miami, FL

Gygax, Jeffrey S
Castleton St Coll
Castleton, VT

Haas, Patricia J
Kent St Univ Kent Cmps
Kent, OH

Hackett, Harry L
Hamilton Coll
Clinton, NY

Haddad, Raedah S
Worcester Poly Inst
Worcester, MA

Haddox, Stacie Aline
Univ Of Ms Medical Center
Jackson, MS

Haffner, Andrea M
Fordham Univ
Bronx, NY

Hagel Sr, Richard L
Wilmington Coll
New Castle, DE

Hager, Teresa J
Univ Of Charleston
Charleston, WV

Haggard, Stephania L
Troy St Univ At Dothan
Dothan, AL

Haggerty, Shanon A
Berkeley Coll Of Westchester
White Plains, NY

Haile, Lemlem
Clark Atlanta Univ
Atlanta, GA

Hakes, Christopher F
S U N Y Coll Of Tech At Alfred
Alfred, NY

Hakes, Jahn K
Univ Of Fl
Gainesville, FL

Hakim, Kabir S
Howard Univ
Washington, DC

Hale, Darrell R
Capitol Coll
Laurel, MD

Hale, Gloria C
Le Moyne Coll
Syracuse, NY

Hale, Jacqueline Tracy
Centenary Coll
Hackettstown, NJ

Haley, Robert James
Life Coll
Marietta, GA

Hall, Courtney L
Paine Coll
Augusta, GA

Hall, David E
Memphis St Univ
Memphis, TN

Hall, Dorothy E
Central Fl Comm Coll
Ocala, FL

Hall, Ingrid C
Ny Univ
New York, NY

Hall, Jenna R
Anne Arundel Comm Coll
Arnold, MD

Hall, John C
Univ Of Ga
Athens, GA

Hall, Laura L
Midlands Tech Coll
Columbia, SC

Hall, Lisa Ann
Ky St Univ
Frankfort, KY

Hall, Lynn M
Southern Vt Coll
Bennington, VT

Hall, Michelle T
Univ Of Nc At Chapel Hill
Chapel Hill, NC

Hall, Nailah O
Temple Univ
Philadelphia, PA

Hall, Phyllis P
Pellissippi St Tech Comm Coll
Knoxville, TN

Hall, Rebekah D
Univ Of Montevallo
Montevallo, AL

Hall, Robin M
Lincoln Univ
Lincoln Univ, PA

Hall, Teresa Gail
Univ Of Sc At Columbia
Columbia, SC

Hall, Terry R
Univ Of Tn At Knoxville
Knoxville, TN

Hallowell, Thomas Ace
Bloomfield Coll
Bloomfield, NJ

Halper, Lisa M
Syracuse Univ
Syracuse, NY

Halpin, Nancy C
The Kings Coll
Briarclf Mnr, NY

Halsey II, Paul D
Eastern Ky Univ
Richmond, KY

Halthon, Meredith N
Talladega Coll
Talladega, AL

Ham, German
Univ Of Miami
Coral Gables, FL

Hamann, Theresa M
Adelphi Univ
Garden City, NY

Hamblen, H Dean
Southside Va Comm Coll
Alberta, VA

Hamblen, Tasha L
Greenville Tech Coll
Greenville, SC

Hamby, Betty C
Roane St Comm Coll
Harriman, TN

Hamilton Jr, Eugene R
Manhattan Coll
Bronx, NY

Hamilton, Heather D
Miami Univ
Oxford, OH

Hamilton Jr, Ronald N
Northeastern Univ
Boston, MA

Hamilton, Thomas B
William Carey Coll
Hattiesburg, MS

Hamlin, Jon H
Valdosta St Coll
Valdosta, GA

Hammell, Tara L
Talladega Coll
Talladega, AL

Hammer, Ann M
Villanova Univ
Villanova, PA

Hammond, Andrea L
Colby Sawyer Coll
New London, NH

Hammond, Michelle L
Univ Of Southern Ms
Hattiesburg, MS

Hammond, Nina S
Barry Univ
Miami, FL

Hammond, Sharon Ann
Providence Coll
Providence, RI

Hammonds, Jeanine C
Univ Of Cin R Walters Coll
Blue Ash, OH

Hammons, Linda A
Brewer St Jr Coll
Fayette, AL

Hampe Jr, Charles R
Comm Coll Algny Co Algny Cmps
Pittsburgh, PA

Hampton, Judy A
Livingston Univ
Livingston, AL

Hams, Mary Kay K
Fayetteville St Univ
Fayetteville, NC

Hance Colon, Carmen Iris
Catholic Univ Of Pr
Ponce, PR

Hancock, Denae H
Defiance Coll
Defiance, OH

Handel, Susan B
Wagner Coll
Staten Island, NY

Handley, Misty L
Walker Coll
Jasper, AL

Hanna, George N
Wv Univ
Morgantown, WV

Hannah, Carolyn B
Vance Granville Comm Coll
Henderson, NC

Hannibal, Neaver L
Ny Univ
New York, NY

Hanning, Julie L
Hocking Tech Coll
Nelsonville, OH

Hannon, John M
Oh Univ
Athens, OH

Hansen, Clare M
Ithaca Coll
Ithaca, NY

Hansen Jr, Harold James
Bridgeport Engr Inst
Fairfield, CT

Hansen, Michael R
Glassboro St Coll
Glassboro, NJ

Hanson, Shannon M
Univ Of Sc At Beaufort
Beaufort, SC

Hanson-Beckles, Carol
S U N Y Hlth Sci Cent Brooklyn
Brooklyn, NY

Harbin, Jeryl L
Alcorn St Univ
Lorman, MS

Harbouri, Diana L
Defiance Coll
Defiance, OH

Harden, Gregory M
Alcorn St Univ
Lorman, MS

Harden, Tania Driver
Middle Tn St Univ
Murfreesboro, TN

Harder, Natasha M
Univ Of Tn At Martin
Martin, TN

Hardick, David J
Philadelphia Coll Pharm & Sci
Philadelphia, PA

Hardie, G Ellen
Patrick Henry Comm Coll
Martinsville, VA

Hardin, Marty R
Univ Of Tn At Knoxville
Knoxville, TN

Hardison, Jay-Chris
Savannah Coll Of Art & Design
Savannah, GA

Hardison, Joseph E
Morris Brown Coll
Atlanta, GA

Hardwick, Sherron F
Miles Coll
Birmingham, AL

Hardy, Bianca Juselle
Tn St Univ
Nashville, TN

Hargis, Mark W
Lindsey Wilson Coll
Columbia, KY

Hargrove, Melinda F
Middle Tn St Univ
Murfreesboro, TN

Harless, Roger Eugene
Wv Univ At
Parkersburg
Parkersburg, WV

Harmon, Keisha M
Va St Univ
Petersburg, VA

Harp, Devona N
Middle Ga Coll
Cochran, GA

Harper, Darlene Y
Fayetteville St Univ
Fayetteville, NC

Harper, Janice C
Alcorn St Univ
Lorman, MS

Harrell, Carter B
Christopher Newport
Coll
Newport News, VA

Harrell, Deborah L
Univ Of Ga
Athens, GA

Harrell, Eric A
Norfolk St Univ
Norfolk, VA

Harrell, Laura E
Greenville Tech Coll
Greenville, SC

Harrington, Lisa H
Catawba Valley Comm
Coll
Hickory, NC

Harris, Andrea M
Cuyahoga Comm Coll
Cleveland, OH

Harris, Annette S
Cheyney Univ Of Pa
Cheyney, PA

Harris, April E
Johnson And Wales
Univ
Providence, RI

Harris, Christine R
Western Piedmont
Comm Coll
Morganton, NC

Harris, Dana L
Coll Of Charleston
Charleston, SC

Harris, James R
Wv Univ
Morgantown, WV

Harris Jr, James R
Abraham Baldwin Agri
Coll
Tifton, GA

Harris, Lizette A
Hofstra Univ
Hempstead, NY

Harris, Patsy J
East Central Comm Coll
Decatur, MS

Harris, Philip T
Southern Coll Of Tech
Marietta, GA

Harris, Ramona Hines
Phillips Jr Coll
Charlotte
Charlotte, NC

Harris Sr, Richard J
Mount Olive Coll
Mount Olive, NC

Harris, Shonda Lynn
Walker Coll
Jasper, AL

Harris, Stephenie G
Univ Of Sc At
Spartanburg
Spartanburg, SC

Harris, William R
David Lipscomb Univ
Nashville, TN

Harris-Coleman, Judith
Atlantic Comm Coll
Mays Landing, NJ

Harrison, Amy M
Wv Univ At
Parkersburg
Parkersburg, WV

Harrison, Betty S
Mayland Comm Coll
Spruce Pine, NC

Harrison, Clarissa C
Volunteer St Comm Coll
Gallatin, TN

Harrison, Clifton
City Univ Of Ny
Baruch Coll
New York, NY

Harrison, Franklin R
Central St Univ
Wilberforce, OH

Harrison, In-Hyang P
Va Commonwealth Univ
Richmond, VA

Harrison, Rebecca G
Univ Of Va Clinch
Valley Coll
Wise, VA

Hart, David P
Northeast State Tech
Comm Coll
Blountville, TN

Hart, Rahmon S
Slippery Rock Univ
Slippery Rock, PA

Hart, Tamara M
Central Fl Comm Coll
Ocala, FL

Hart, Tonya F
Savannah St Coll
Savannah, GA

Hartleb, Mary Beth
Upsala Coll
East Orange, NJ

Hartman Jr, Randall L
Nova Univ
Ft Lauderdale, FL

Hartzfeld, Anita E
Nyack Coll
Nyack, NY

Harvey, Gillian R
Fl Coll
Temple Terrace, FL

Harwood, Russell B
Cleveland St Univ
Cleveland, OH

Hashim, Sadia
Bloomfield Coll
Bloomfield, NJ

Haslett, Krista
Mount Saint Mary Coll
Newburgh, NY

Hassa Jr, George C
Rensselaer Polytechnic Inst
Troy, NY

Hastie, James A
Le Moyne Coll
Syracuse, NY

Hastie, Maronda Lizette
Savannah St Coll
Savannah, GA

Hatcher, Lisa M
Radford Univ
Radford, VA

Hathcock, Elizabeth Dennise
Union Univ
Jackson, TN

Hattaway, Shannon G
Ashland Comm Coll
Ashland, KY

Hatten, Jurine D
Spelman Coll
Atlanta, GA

Hauser, Lisa A
Cedar Crest Coll
Allentown, PA

Hawa, Grace A
Marymount Manhattan Coll
New York, NY

Hawari, Majid M
Univ Of Southern Ms
Hattiesburg, MS

Hawkins, Constance A
Oh Dominican Coll
Columbus, OH

Hawkins, Leigh K
Tougaloo Coll
Tougaloo, MS

Hawkins, Steven B
Broward Comm Coll
Ft Lauderdale, FL

Hawkins, Tasha D
Hillsborough Comm Coll
Tampa, FL

Hay, Angela R
Middle Tn St Univ
Murfreesboro, TN

Hayashi, Naoko
D Youville Coll
Buffalo, NY

Hayes, Carol Ann
Coppin St Coll
Baltimore, MD

Hayes, Christa E
Coker Coll
Hartsville, SC

Hayes Jr, Clifford David
Central St Univ
Wilberforce, OH

Hayes, Cynthia D
Edinboro Univ Of Pa
Edinboro, PA

Hayes, Cynthia M
Glassboro St Coll
Glassboro, NJ

Hayes, Shannon L
Fl A & M Univ
Tallahassee, FL

Haygood, Carlton L
Livingston Univ
Livingston, AL

Haynes, Artyce M
Clark Atlanta Univ
Atlanta, GA

Haynes III, George W
Middle Tn St Univ
Murfreesboro, TN

Haynes, Krista D
Gaston Coll
Dallas, NC

Haynes, Sheila A
Univ Of Tn At Knoxville
Knoxville, TN

Hays, Anna-Maria A
Emory & Henry Coll
Emory, VA

Hayward, Ronda C
Benedict Coll
Columbia, SC

Haywood, Barbara S
Alcorn St Univ
Lorman, MS

Hazelrigs, Kristie A
Spartanburg Methodist Coll
Spartanburg, SC

Hazlewood, Julie M
Hinds Comm Coll
Raymond, MS

He, Katherine Yihua
Savannah Coll Of Art & Design
Savannah, GA

Headrick, Wilma D
Pellissippi St Tech Comm Coll
Knoxville, TN

Heald, Benjamin F
Milligan Coll
Milligan Clg, TN

Healey, Theresa V
Georgian Court Coll
Lakewood, NJ

Healy, Jennifer M
Western New England Coll
Springfield, MA

Heard, Davita L
Al A & M Univ
Normal, AL

Heard, William T
Southern Coll Of Tech
Marietta, GA

Heckman, Christine D
Shippensburg Univ
Shippensburg, PA

Heckmann, Natascha
Miami Dade Comm Coll
Miami, FL

Hector, Ron E
Oh Univ
Athens, OH

Hedin, Diane Marie
George Mason Univ
Fairfax, VA

Hedrick, Kimberly A
Gaston Coll
Dallas, NC

Heger, Allyson R
Univ Of Cin R Walters Coll
Blue Ash, OH

Hegwood, Barbara L
Univ Of Ga
Athens, GA

Heidenreich, Beth E
Anderson Coll
Anderson, SC

Heigh, Irene M
Coppin St Coll
Baltimore, MD

Heinemann, Mark G
S U N Y Coll Of Tech At Alfred
Alfred, NY

Heleman, Beth S
Rutgers St Un At New Brunswick
New Brunswick, NJ

Helf, Janice D
Borough Of Manhattan Comm Coll
New York, NY

Helfer, Wendy
Ursinus Coll
Collegeville, PA

Helfgott, Batsheva
Yeshiva Univ
New York, NY

Heller, David M
Univ Of Nc At Greensboro
Greensboro, NC

Hemby Jr, William E
Va St Univ
Petersburg, VA

Hemsley, Bonnie J
Ms St Univ
Miss State, MS

Henderson, Douglas A
Embry Riddle Aeronautical Univ
Daytona Beach, FL

Henderson, Evalyn H
Spelman Coll
Atlanta, GA

Henderson, Nhyere Lynn
Central St Univ
Wilberforce, OH

Henderson, Paula Evette
Central St Univ
Wilberforce, OH

Hendrick, Sureya Z
Al St Univ
Montgomery, AL

Hendrix, Dustin D
Middle Tn St Univ
Murfreesboro, TN

Henke, David Thaddeus
Duquesne Univ
Pittsburgh, PA

Henke, Stephanie J
Univ Of Southern Ms
Hattiesburg, MS

Henriques, Christina T
Univ Of Miami
Coral Gables, FL

Henriquez, Carlos H
Atlantic Union Coll
S Lancaster, MA

Henry Andino, George Mc D
Univ Politecnica De Pr
Hato Rey, PR

Henry, Janet Lynn
Millersville Univ Of Pa
Millersville, PA

Henry, Melinda S
Univ Of Sc At Columbia
Columbia, SC

Henry, Ronald A
City Univ Of Ny Lehman Coll
Bronx, NY

Henry, Viva C
Fl A & M Univ
Tallahassee, FL

Henry-Forde, Vanessa A
City Univ Of Ny Med Evers Coll
Brooklyn, NY

Hensley, Jamie Luanne
Mercer Univ Schl Of Pharm
Atlanta, GA

Hensley, Mary Helen
Coker Coll
Hartsville, SC

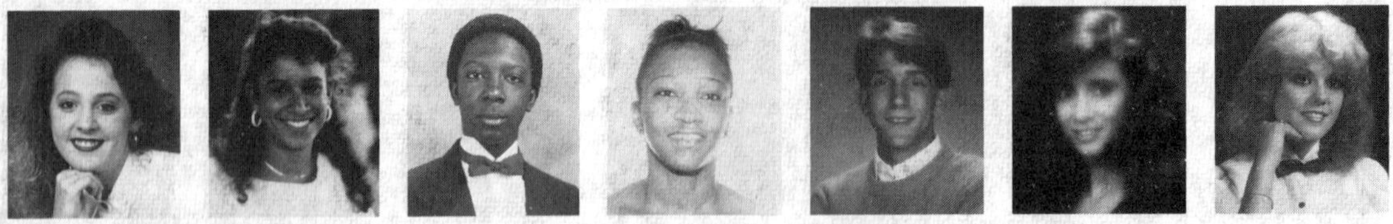

Henson, Cristina L
Livingston Univ
Livingston, AL

Henson, Natalie S
Howard Univ
Washington, DC

Henton, Eulando D
Bethel Coll
Mckenzie, TN

Hepburn, Inga A
Barry Univ
Miami, FL

Herchenhahn, Jay D
Tn Temple Univ
Chattanooga, TN

Heredia, Yolanda
Univ Of Pr At Rio Piedras
Rio Piedras, PR

Herman, Gail L
D Youville Coll
Buffalo, NY

Herman, Kenneth Steven
Broward Comm Coll
Ft Lauderdale, FL

Hermida, Teresa E
Smith Coll
Northampton, MA

Hernandez Carlo, Marangelli
Inter Amer Univ Pr San German
San German, PR

Hernandez Reyes, Miguel A
Univ Politecnica De Pr
Hato Rey, PR

Hernandez Rivera, Janette
Inter Amer Univ Pr Hato Rey
Hato Rey, PR

Hernandez Rodriguez, Maria I
Univ Of Pr At Mayaguez
Mayaguez, PR

Hernandez, Alyna L
Va St Univ
Petersburg, VA

Hernandez, Aura V
Howard Univ
Washington, DC

Hernandez, Danessa
Caribbean Univ
Bayamon, PR

Hernandez, David A
Barry Univ
Miami, FL

Hernandez, Gilbert N
Northern Va Comm Coll
Annandale, VA

Hernandez, Jose I
Univ Of Pr Medical Sciences
San Juan, PR

Hernandez Jr, Juan
Valley Forge Christian Coll
Phoenixville, PA

Hernandez, Karitzma
Inter Amer Univ Pr San German
San German, PR

Hernandez, Leanel A
Univ Of Pr Medical Sciences
San Juan, PR

Hernandez, Rafael A
Rutgers St Univ At Newark
Newark, NJ

Hernandez, Roger I
Columbia Union Coll
Takoma Park, MD

Hernandez, Rosanne P
Fl Atlantic Univ
Boca Raton, FL

Hernandez, Silvia M
Univ Of Miami
Coral Gables, FL

Herod, Christal L
Clark Atlanta Univ
Atlanta, GA

Herrera, Annette M
Fl International Univ
Miami, FL

Herrera, Sharon M
Dowling Coll
Oakdale Li, NY

Herrero Roman, Glorimar
Inter Amer Univ Pr Hato Rey
Hato Rey, PR

Herrero, Vivian E
Univ Of Pr At Mayaguez
Mayaguez, PR

Herring, Tiria E
Middle Tn St Univ
Murfreesboro, TN

Herrington, Alexia Y
Morris Brown Coll
Atlanta, GA

Herrman, John E
Athens St Coll
Athens, AL

Herron, Angela D
Coker Coll
Hartsville, SC

Herzog, Michelle S
Flagler Coll
St Augustine, FL

Hesse, Jennifer M
Univ Of Cincinnati
Cincinnati, OH

Hetrick, Georgia A
Pa St Univ Altoona Cmps
Altoona, PA

Hettiarachchi, Lawrence Pradeep
Saint Thomas Univ
Miami, FL

Hewins, Kelly L
Clemson Univ
Clemson, SC

Hewitt, Susan L
Univ Of Southern Ms
Hattiesburg, MS

Heyner, Matthew G
Va Commonwealth Univ
Richmond, VA

Hickey, Michele D
Columbia Greene Comm Coll
Hudson, NY

Hickman, Georgia E
Cedarville Coll
Cedarville, OH

Hickman, Sherri D
Atlantic Comm Coll
Mays Landing, NJ

Hicks, Anterria L
Fl A & M Univ
Tallahassee, FL

Hicks, Christy L
Middle Tn St Univ
Murfreesboro, TN

Hicks, Kelley F
Becker Coll At Leicester
Leicester, MA

Hicks, Vincent T
Western Ky Univ
Bowling Green, KY

Hicks, Willene A
Georgetown Univ
Washington, DC

Hidalgo, Carmen C
City Univ Of Ny La
Guard Coll
Long Island Cty, NY

Hidalgo, Myriam C
Univ Of Miami
Coral Gables, FL

Hiebler, Charlotte M
Univ Of Md Baltimore
Prof Schl
Baltimore, MD

Hiers, Yvonne M
Piedmont Tech Coll
Greenwood, SC

Higby, Ralph F
S U N Y Coll Of Tech
At Alfred
Alfred, NY

Higginbotham, James W
Marshall University
Huntington, WV

Higgins, Mary Ellen
Pa St Univ Delaware
Cty Cmps
Media, PA

Higgins, Susan L
Radford Univ
Radford, VA

High, Kristen L
Fl St Univ
Tallahassee, FL

Hightower, Maria A
Fl A & M Univ
Tallahassee, FL

Higuera, Evelyn Lucy
Hilbert Coll
Hamburg, NY

Hilal, Frederic
Goucher Coll
Towson, MD

Hilderbrand, Charlotte
Univ Of Southern Ms
Hattiesburg, MS

Hill III, Charles E
Georgetown Univ
Washington, DC

Hill, Donovan L
Al A & M Univ
Normal, AL

Hill, Francis M
Univ Of Montevallo
Montevallo, AL

Hill, Helen Louise
Roane St Comm Coll
Harriman, TN

Hill, Jean E
Coppin St Coll
Baltimore, MD

Hill, Jessica G
Tn St Univ
Nashville, TN

Hill, Kimberly R
Ms St Univ
Miss State, MS

Hill, Lisa L
Univ Of Southern Ms
Hattiesburg, MS

Hill, Tiffani A
Brewer St Jr Coll
Fayette, AL

Hill, Tonia D
Central Al Comm Coll
Alexander City, AL

Hill, Vida M
Savannah St Coll
Savannah, GA

Hillman, Kimberly J
Va Commonwealth Univ
Richmond, VA

Hills-Johnson, Sharon L
Bloomfield Coll
Bloomfield, NJ

Hilton, Candie J
East Tn St Univ
Johnson City, TN

Hinkle, Cheryel
Fayetteville St Univ
Fayetteville, NC

Hinman, Kathy L
Va Commonwealth Univ
Richmond, VA

Hinson, Nicole A
Univ Of Md At Eastern
Shore
Princess Anne, MD

Hinson, Robert H
Spartanburg Methodist
Coll
Spartanburg, SC

Hinson, Tanya S
Ga St Univ
Atlanta, GA

Hinton, David A
Univ Of Southern Ms
Hattiesburg, MS

Hinton Jr, Garry L
Va St Univ
Petersburg, VA

Hinton, Vernetta L
Va St Univ
Petersburg, VA

Hiraldo Hiraldo, Olga I
Caribbean Univ
Bayamon, PR

Ho, Kah Kin
S U N Y At Buffalo
Buffalo, NY

Hobbs, Heather L
Livingston Univ
Livingston, AL

Hocker, Jonathan E
Univ Of Ky
Lexington, KY

Hodge, Consuela A
Fayetteville St Univ
Fayetteville, NC

Hodge, David B
Kent St Univ Kent
Cmps
Kent, OH

Hodges, Philip D
Lancaster Bible Coll
Lancaster, PA

Hoffman, Diana K
Endicott Coll
Beverly, MA

Hoffman, Hilary S
S U N Y Coll At New Paltz
New Paltz, NY

Hoffman, Jodi I
Dowling Coll
Oakdale Li, NY

Hoffmeier, Brent L
Univ Of Louisville
Louisville, KY

Holbrook, Vickie L
Univ Of Tn At Memphis
Memphis, TN

Holder, Cathy M
Midlands Tech Coll
Columbia, SC

Holder, Tessa O
City Univ Of Ny City Coll
New York, NY

Holihan, Michael P
Bryant Stratton Bus Inst Roch
Rochester, NY

Holland, Karen M
Georgian Court Coll
Lakewood, NJ

Holland, Sacha B
Fl Atlantic Univ
Boca Raton, FL

Holland, Sia L
Morris Brown Coll
Atlanta, GA

Holley, La Shaunn
Tuskegee Univ
Tuskegee Inst, AL

Holley, Nichole R
Va St Univ
Petersburg, VA

Holliman, Christma Y
Auburn Univ At Auburn
Auburn, AL

Hollingsworth, Brenda B
Fayetteville St Univ
Fayetteville, NC

Hollingsworth Jr, Garl L
Al A & M Univ
Normal, AL

Hollis, Robb A
California Univ Of Pa
California, PA

Holloway, Anne E
Bridgewater Coll
Bridgewater, VA

Holmes, Gussie R
Memphis St Univ
Memphis, TN

Holmes, Patrick J
Youngstown St Univ
Youngstown, OH

Holmes, Samantha K
Middle Tn St Univ
Murfreesboro, TN

Holmes, Stacey L
Lincoln Univ
Lincoln Univ, PA

Holsclaw, Sharon L
Univ Of Nc At Chapel Hill
Chapel Hill, NC

Holt, Patsy M
Sue Bennett Coll
London, KY

Holt, Robert F
Queens Coll
Charlotte, NC

Holtby, Krista Anne
Niagara Univ
Niagara Univ, NY

Holterman, Denise Ellen Stewart
Georgian Court Coll
Lakewood, NJ

Holynski, Debora Ann
Hilbert Coll
Hamburg, NY

Homberg, Kimberly A
Anne Arundel Comm Coll
Arnold, MD

Homick Jr, Paul S
Saint Vincents Coll & Seminary
Latrobe, PA

Honan, Kim L
Methodist Coll
Fayetteville, NC

Hood, Gina R
Pellissippi St Tech Comm Coll
Knoxville, TN

Hood, Nicole R
Va St Univ
Petersburg, VA

Hooker, Thomas F
Villanova Univ
Villanova, PA

Hooper-Gulley, Le Vonne L
Middle Tn St Univ
Murfreesboro, TN

Hooten, Chris A
Univ Of Al At Birmingham
Birmingham, AL

Hoover, Carla L
Hillsborough Comm Coll
Tampa, FL

Hopkins, Angelia M
Bluefield St Coll
Bluefield, WV

Hopkins, Tricia L
Northern Ky Univ
Highland Hts, KY

Hoppe, Susan K
Bethany Coll
Bethany, WV

Hopper, Candis D
Volunteer St Comm Coll
Gallatin, TN

Hopper, Catherine L
Tri County Tech Coll
Pendleton, SC

Hopper, Diane S
Bishop St Comm Coll
Mobile, AL

Hopper, Ronald
Pasco Hernando Comm Coll
Dade City, FL

Hord, Michelle D
Howard Univ
Washington, DC

Horn, Shelia D
Al A & M Univ
Normal, AL

Hornberger, Rita L
Glassboro St Coll
Glassboro, NJ

Horne, Michelle L
Univ Of Nc At Charlotte
Charlotte, NC

Horner, Gregory W
Old Dominion Univ
Norfolk, VA

Hornyak, Debra A
Univ Of Pittsburgh
Pittsburgh, PA

Horst, James N
Fl International Univ
Miami, FL

Horvat, Keri Lynda
Univ Of Miami
Coral Gables, FL

Horvath, Star M
Salisbury St Univ
Salisbury, MD

Hosmer, David P
D Youville Coll
Buffalo, NY

Hotaling, Scott C
Mohawk Valley Comm Coll
Utica, NY

House, Kerry C
Univ Of Sc At Columbia
Columbia, SC

House, S Dwane
Sue Bennett Coll
London, KY

Housenbold, Jeffrey T
Carnegie Mellon Univ
Pittsburgh, PA

Houser, Bryan G
Hampton Univ
Hampton, VA

Howard, Arneida C
Central St Univ
Wilberforce, OH

Howard, Cynthia A
Ms St Univ
Miss State, MS

Howard, Denise A
Converse Coll
Spartanburg, SC

Howard, Ethan D
Youngstown St Univ
Youngstown, OH

Howard, Glen N
Barry Univ
Miami, FL

Howard, Jacqueline P
Mount Olive Coll
Mount Olive, NC

Howard Jr, James B
Thomas Nelson Comm Coll
Hampton, VA

Howard, John M
Western Carolina Univ
Cullowhee, NC

Howard, Linda J
Savannah St Coll
Savannah, GA

Howard, Michael H
S U N Y Coll Of Tech At Alfred
Alfred, NY

Howard, Tara J
Norfolk St Univ
Norfolk, VA

Howard, Trina R
Newbury Coll
Brookline, MA

Howe, Megan E
Gaston Coll
Dallas, NC

Howell Jr, Walter L
Morehouse Coll
Atlanta, GA

Hoyos, Orlando
Miami Dade Comm Coll
Miami, FL

Hoyt, Denise I
City Univ Of Ny Bronx Comm Col
Bronx, NY

Huang, Yuhui
Howard Univ
Washington, DC

Hubbard, Randy D
Georgetown Coll
Georgetown, KY

Huber, Matthew J
Providence Coll
Providence, RI

Huckaby, Donna Gail
Tri County Tech Coll
Pendleton, SC

Hudak, Daniel M
Columbus Coll Of Art & Design
Columbus, OH

Huddleston III, Edward
Univ Of Southern Ms
Hattiesburg, MS

Huddleston, Tjuana P
Clark Atlanta Univ
Atlanta, GA

Hudgins, Angela E
Western Piedmont Comm Coll
Morganton, NC

Hudson, Charlette Y
Va St Univ
Petersburg, VA

Hudson, Dedric L
Pa St Univ Gt Valley
Grad Cntr
Malvern, PA

Hudson, Michele R
Morgan St Univ
Baltimore, MD

Hudson, Patricia E
Davis & Elkins Coll
Elkins, WV

Hudson, Tina M
Volunteer St Comm Coll
Gallatin, TN

Huffman, Lisa M
Indiana Univ Of Pa
Indiana, PA

Huffstutler, Vincent E
Univ Of Al At
Birmingham
Birmingham, AL

Hughes, Lisa Marie
Kennesaw St Coll
Marietta, GA

Hughes, Pattye L
Jackson St Univ
Jackson, MS

Hughes, Thomas A
Univ Of Rochester
Rochester, NY

Hughes, Wendy P
Barry Univ
Miami, FL

Hulan, Christy A
Univ Of Tn At Martin
Martin, TN

Hull, Amy E
Nc Agri & Tech St
Univ
Greensboro, NC

Humber, Toni Cheryl
Howard Univ
Washington, DC

Humphries, Gregory S
Bridgeport Engr Inst
Fairfield, CT

Hunt, Margaret M
D Youville Coll
Buffalo, NY

Hunt, Rita R
Univ Of Sc At
Spartanburg
Spartanburg, SC

Hunt, Stacey E
Tuskegee Univ
Tuskegee Inst, AL

Hunt III, Willie G
Fayetteville St Univ
Fayetteville, NC

Hunter, Chaunsey Z
Morehouse Coll
Atlanta, GA

Hunter, Tracey L
Al A & M Univ
Normal, AL

Huntley, James A
Al A & M Univ
Normal, AL

Hurley, Bryan R
Salisbury St Univ
Salisbury, MD

Hurley, Kim M
Le Moyne Coll
Syracuse, NY

Hurst, Derrick A
Univ Of Nc At
Asheville
Asheville, NC

Husein, Imad F
S U N Y At Buffalo
Buffalo, NY

Hussain, Zeenat A
Univ Of Miami
Coral Gables, FL

Huston, Mary E
Allegheny Coll
Meadville, PA

Hutcherson, Pamela D
Union Univ
Jackson, TN

Hutchinson, Dawn B
Nova Univ
Ft Lauderdale, FL

Hutchinson, Lisa A
Univ Of Southern Ms
Hattiesburg, MS

Hutchinson, Pamela S
Wv Univ
Morgantown, WV

Hutchinson, Tonya M
Casco Bay Coll
Portland, ME

Hutchison, James S
Beckley Coll
Beckley, WV

Hutmaker, Christopher
Columbia Univ
New York, NY

Hutton Jr, Doyle G
Middle Tn St Univ
Murfreesboro, TN

Hutton, Lisa A
Neumann Coll
Aston, PA

Hwang, Edward
Univ Of Al At
Birmingham
Birmingham, AL

Hwang, Richard F
Univ Of Al At
Birmingham
Birmingham, AL

Hwang, Sunha
Kent St Univ Kent
Cmps
Kent, OH

Hyera, Asteria B
Howard Univ
Washington, DC

Hyman, Denise R
Wv Northern Comm
Coll
Wheeling, WV

Hynes, Teresa M
City Univ Of Ny
Queensbrough
New York, NY

Hyora, Jennifer K
Colby Sawyer Coll
New London, NH

Hysong, Sylvia J
Univ Of Rochester
Rochester, NY

Iacobucci, Steven O
Univ Of Cin R Walters
Coll
Blue Ash, OH

Iacona, Leigh M
Saint Andrews Presbytrn
Coll
Laurinburg, NC

Iacovangelo, Anthony B
Niagara Univ
Niagara Univ, NY

Ifkovich, Patricia M
Erie Comm Coll South
Cmps
Orchard Park, NY

Iglesias, Cindy A
Nova Univ
Ft Lauderdale, FL

Igwebuike, Adaeze R
Kent St Univ Kent
Cmps
Kent, OH

Ikpoh, Vincent A
Springfield Tech Comm
Coll
Springfield, MA

Iles, Roger D
Crichton Coll
Memphis, TN

Imburgia, Karen Eileen
Atlantic Comm Coll
Mays Landing, NJ

Imparato, Dawn M
Centenary Coll
Hackettstown, NJ

Indriolo, Joseph
Ny Univ
New York, NY

Infantino, Daniel P
Saint Andrews Presbytrn
Coll
Laurinburg, NC

Ingold, Eric A
Va Commonwealth Univ
Richmond, VA

Ingram, Reba D
Alcorn St Univ
Lorman, MS

Ingram, Robert R
Chattahoochee Vly St
Comm Coll
Phenix City, AL

Inman, Susan M
Le Moyne Coll
Syracuse, NY

Inthapannha, Somnet
Bridgeport Engr Inst
Fairfield, CT

Ippolito, Danny A
Seton Hall Univ
South Orange, NJ

Iranipour, Afsaneh
Hillsborough Comm
Coll
Tampa, FL

Irene-Colon, Omayra
Bayamon Central Univ
Bayamon, PR

Irizarry, Waleska I
Inter Amer Univ Pr San
German
San German, PR

Irvine, Holly E
Colby Sawyer Coll
New London, NH

Irving, Valorie J
Bennett Coll
Greensboro, NC

Irwin, Kimberlee L
Howard Univ
Washington, DC

Isabell, Lee J
Norfolk St Univ
Norfolk, VA

Iseman, Stephanie A
Rutgers St Univ At
Camden
Camden, NJ

Islam, Farhana
Saint Francis Coll
Loretto, PA

Islam, Mahbubul
City Univ Of Ny City
Coll
New York, NY

Isley, Carol M
Univ Of Al At
Birmingham
Birmingham, AL

Ito, Mari
Savannah Coll Of Art
& Design
Savannah, GA

Itro, Margaret A
Glassboro St Coll
Glassboro, NJ

Jablonski, Nancy C
Glassboro St Coll
Glassboro, NJ

Jack, Hopeton L
City Univ Of Ny City
Coll
New York, NY

Jackson, Akiba N
Miami Dade Comm Coll
North
Miami, FL

Jackson, Ayanna M
Bowie St Univ
Bowie, MD

Jackson, Christine
Allen Univ
Columbia, SC

Jackson, Danielle P
Fl A & M Univ
Tallahassee, FL

Jackson, Debra L
Ms St Univ
Miss State, MS

Jackson, Donna W
Blue Mountain Coll
Blue Mountain, MS

Jackson, Kelly A
Northeast Ms Cc
Booneville, MS

Jackson, Linda J
Univ Of West Fl
Pensacola, FL

Jackson, Malikka N
Clark Atlanta Univ
Atlanta, GA

Jackson, Michael A
Tri County Tech Coll
Pendleton, SC

Jackson, Monica I
Univ Of Ga
Athens, GA

Jackson, Roderick D
Jackson St Univ
Jackson, MS

Jackson, Rodney Bernard
Interdenominational Theo Ctr
Atlanta, GA

Jackson, Rosalind L
Al A & M Univ
Normal, AL

Jackson, Sheree J
Al St Univ
Montgomery, AL

Jackson, Staci M
Roane St Comm Coll
Harriman, TN

Jackson, Stacy R
Okaloosa Walton Comm Coll
Niceville, FL

Jackson, Tamara D
Roane St Comm Coll
Harriman, TN

Jackson III, Tellis X
Cheyney Univ Of Pa
Cheyney, PA

Jackson, Valerie B
Va Commonwealth Univ
Richmond, VA

Jackson, Verna M
Southern Junior Coll
Birmingham, AL

Jacob, Jacqueline Renee
Univ Of Southern Ms
Hattiesburg, MS

Jacob, Stephanie M
Univ Of Ga
Athens, GA

Jacobs, Kristalean R
Univ Of Ky
Lexington, KY

Jacobs, Susan E
Duquesne Univ
Pittsburgh, PA

Jacquot, Amy J
Univ Of Bridgeport
Bridgeport, CT

Jadavji, Shafiq
S U N Y At Buffalo
Buffalo, NY

Jaffar, Muhammed Amin
Fl International Univ
Miami, FL

Jagan, Judy N
Barry Univ
Miami, FL

Jain, Kalpana
Univ Of Al At Birmingham
Birmingham, AL

Jalowitz-Thom, Edwina
Cumberland County Coll
Vineland, NJ

James, Barbie R
Thomas Nelson Comm Coll
Hampton, VA

James, David Berlin
Middle Ga Coll
Cochran, GA

James, Edward J
City Univ Of Ny Med Evers Coll
Brooklyn, NY

James, Jennifer J
Fl International Univ
Miami, FL

James, Joycelyn T
Columbia Union Coll
Takoma Park, MD

James, Teresa L
Univ Of Sc At Columbia
Columbia, SC

James, Vanderius L
Morehouse Coll
Atlanta, GA

James, Won-Yau
City Univ Of Ny City Coll
New York, NY

Jamrog, Diane C
Smith Coll
Northampton, MA

Janco, Julie A
Case Western Reserve Univ
Cleveland, OH

Jang, Tammy J
Ms St Univ
Miss State, MS

Janney, Joel Owen
Anne Arundel Comm Coll
Arnold, MD

Jardines, Elizabeth A
City Univ Of Ny Queensbrough
New York, NY

Jaroll, Michelle Lynn
Univ Of Sc At Columbia
Columbia, SC

Jarrett, Karen A
Albany St Coll
Albany, GA

Jarvis, Deborah L
D Youville Coll
Buffalo, NY

Jarvis, Ulric S
Embry Riddle Aeronautical Univ
Daytona Beach, FL

Jary, Frank J
Cornell Univ
Ithaca, NY

Jasinski, Joseph M
Univ Of De
Newark, DE

Java, Joelle Anne
Niagara Univ
Niagara Univ, NY

Jayakody, Uditha D
Univ Of Sc At
Columbia
Columbia, SC

Jean-Baptiste,
Charlygore
City Univ Of Ny
Kingsborough
Brooklyn, NY

Jean-Louis, Marie Josee
Barry Univ
Miami, FL

Jefferson, Sheilah M
Howard Univ
Washington, DC

Jeffords, Pearl F
Coker Coll
Hartsville, SC

Jellie, Casey J
Longwood Coll
Farmville, VA

Jendrisak, David J
Kent St Univ Kent
Cmps
Kent, OH

Jenerette, Collette R
Benedict Coll
Columbia, SC

Jenifer, Shade L
Hampton Univ
Hampton, VA

Jenkins, Jacqueline
Darling
Nova Univ
Ft Lauderdale, FL

Jenkins, Lisa J
James Madison
University
Harrisonburg, VA

Jenkins, Shawn L
Bluefield Coll
Bluefield, VA

Jenkins, Treva G
Spartanburg Methodist
Coll
Spartanburg, SC

Jenkins, Tyra D
Johnson C Smith Univ
Charlotte, NC

Jennings, Rodney D
Norfolk St Univ
Norfolk, VA

Jensen, Kristin Nelda
Univ Of Nc At
Greensboro
Greensboro, NC

Jeremie, Danielle
Bunker Hill Comm Coll
Boston, MA

Jernigan, Grace E
Auburn Univ At Auburn
Auburn, AL

Jernigan, Richard Craig
Fayetteville St Univ
Fayetteville, NC

Jeter, Tamara L
Univ Of Akron
Akron, OH

Jewell, Edward A
Ky St Univ
Frankfort, KY

Jimenez Cardona,
Madeline
Inter Amer Univ Pr
Hato Rey
Hato Rey, PR

Jimenez, Carlos
Univ Of Pr At Rio
Piedras
Rio Piedras, PR

Jimenez, Edwin
Univ Politecnica De Pr
Hato Rey, PR

Jimenez, Frances
Va St Univ
Petersburg, VA

Jimenez, Joseph Alberto
Miami Dade Comm Coll
Miami, FL

Jimenez, Sandra P
Miami Dade Comm Coll
Miami, FL

Jimenez-Calderin,
Edgardo R
Inter Amer Univ Pr San
Juan
Hato Rey, PR

Jindal, Asha R
Vanderbilt Univ
Nashville, TN

Jirau, Inoel
Temple Univ
Philadelphia, PA

Johannesen, Janet L
S U N Y Coll At
Plattsburgh
Plattsburgh, NY

John, Deborah K
Tusculum Coll
Greeneville, TN

Johns, Jennifer A
Longwood Coll
Farmville, VA

Johnson, Angela D
Hampton Univ
Hampton, VA

Johnson, Basil D
Univ Of The Virgin
Islands
St Thomas, VI

Johnson, Cassandra D
Al St Univ
Montgomery, AL

Johnson, Cheryl A
Lurleen B Wallace St Jr
Coll
Andalusia, AL

Johnson, Christine A
Marywood Coll
Scranton, PA

Johnson, Denise S
Catawba Valley Comm
Coll
Hickory, NC

Johnson, Earline
Central St Univ
Wilberforce, OH

Johnson, Edward K
Hofstra Univ
Hempstead, NY

Johnson, Eugene M
Savannah St Coll
Savannah, GA

Johnson, Haroldeen
Morris Brown Coll
Atlanta, GA

Johnson, Inga Jo Anne
Embry Riddle
Aeronautical Univ
Daytona Beach, FL

Johnson, James W
Ms St Univ
Miss State, MS

Johnson, Jessie L
Union Univ
Jackson, TN

Johnson, Katrina B
Howard Univ
Washington, DC

Johnson, Katrina L
Alcorn St Univ
Lorman, MS

Johnson II, Kenneth M
Catawba Coll
Salisbury, NC

Johnson, Kerry S
Univ Of Al At
Birmingham
Birmingham, AL

Johnson, Kimberly
Dawn
Wilkes Comm Coll
Wilkesboro, NC

Johnson, Kimberly F
Owensboro Comm Coll
Owensboro, KY

Johnson, Kimberly J
Univ Of Nc At
Greensboro
Greensboro, NC

Johnson, L Tanya
Norfolk St Univ
Norfolk, VA

Johnson, Letitia D
Alcorn St Univ
Lorman, MS

Johnson, Marcia P
Univ Of The Dist Of
Columbia
Washington, DC

Johnson, Marilyn P
Univ Of The Virgin
Islands
St Thomas, VI

Johnson, Marlo D
Alcorn St Univ
Lorman, MS

Johnson, Michael T
Al St Univ
Montgomery, AL

Johnson, Michelle D
Univ Of Al At
Birmingham
Birmingham, AL

Johnson, Monique La
Shawn
Lane Coll
Jackson, TN

Johnson, Nathan
Atlantic Union Coll
S Lancaster, MA

Johnson, Olivia N
Ma Inst Of Tech
Cambridge, MA

Johnson, Paul B
Morehouse Coll
Atlanta, GA

Johnson, Pleshette G
Va St Univ
Petersburg, VA

Johnson, Reginald
Jackson St Univ
Jackson, MS

Johnson, Renee S
City Univ Of Ny City
Coll
New York, NY

Johnson, Rosalind J
Savannah St Coll
Savannah, GA

Johnson IV, Samuel
Quinton
Salisbury St Univ
Salisbury, MD

Johnson, Sean K
Morehouse Coll
Atlanta, GA

Johnson, Sheryline Y
Bloomfield Coll
Bloomfield, NJ

Johnson, Sonja M
Univ Of Md At Eastern
Shore
Princess Anne, MD

Johnson, Sonya L
Bloomfield Coll
Bloomfield, NJ

Johnson, Stephanie M
Univ Of Md At Eastern
Shore
Princess Anne, MD

Johnson, Terrell G
Univ Of Md At Eastern
Shore
Princess Anne, MD

Johnson, Toya J
Hampton Univ
Hampton, VA

Johnson, Tracy L
Marshall University
Huntington, WV

Johnson, Vance A
Spartanburg Methodist
Coll
Spartanburg, SC

Johnson Jr, Vaughn G
Central Al Comm Coll
Alexander City, AL

Johnston Albert, Susan
Marie
Cheyney Univ Of Pa
Cheyney, PA

Johnston, Wendy L
Winthrop Coll
Rock Hill, SC

Joho, Brian C
Upsala Coll
East Orange, NJ

Joiner, Lottie L
Jackson St Univ
Jackson, MS

Jolivette, Vincent D
Oh Univ
Athens, OH

Jones, Angela B
Al St Univ
Montgomery, AL

Jones, Charlene W
Tougaloo Coll
Tougaloo, MS

Jones, Christopher E
Georgetown Univ
Washington, DC

Jones, Daliah N
Va St Univ
Petersburg, VA

Jones, Deborah K
Elon Coll
Elon, NC

Jones, Donna J
Wilmington Coll
New Castle, DE

Jones, Ethel Simpson
Ny Theological
Seminary
New York, NY

Jones Jr, Frank Weston
Md Inst Coll Of Art
Baltimore, MD

Jones, Gillian Camille
Univ Of Miami
Coral Gables, FL

Jones, Glenda L
Chipola Jr Coll
Marianna, FL

Jones, James D
Davis & Elkins Coll
Elkins, WV

Jones, James V
Union Univ
Jackson, TN

Jones, Jeffory Vincent
Coppin St Coll
Baltimore, MD

Jones, Jerry Allen
Wallace St Comm Coll
At Dothan
Dothan, AL

Jones Jr, Jodie W
Troy St Univ At Troy
Troy, AL

Jones, Joyce E
Comm Coll Algny Co
Algny Cmps
Pittsburgh, PA

Jones, Karen
Va St Univ
Petersburg, VA

Jones, Leslie D
Univ Of Ga
Athens, GA

Jones, Lisa M
De Tech & Comm Coll
At Dover
Dover, DE

Jones, Lori R
Hillsborough Comm
Coll
Tampa, FL

Jones, Mark T
Northeast State Tech
Comm Coll
Blountville, TN

Jones, Melva E
Central St Univ
Wilberforce, OH

Jones, Melva O
Univ Of Southern Ms
Hattiesburg, MS

Jones, Michael E
Barry Univ
Miami, FL

Jones, Michael E
Samford Univ
Birmingham, AL

Jones, Michele L
Southern Coll Of Tech
Marietta, GA

Jones, Michele L
Northern Ky Univ
Highland Hts, KY

Jones, Priscilla M
Memphis St Univ
Memphis, TN

Jones, Robin D
Va St Univ
Petersburg, VA

Jones, Sharen J
Fl International Univ
Miami, FL

Jones, Shawndelle L
Central St Univ
Wilberforce, OH

Jones, Sophia C
Bennett Coll
Greensboro, NC

Jones, Susan S
Gaston Coll
Dallas, NC

Jones, Wendy S
City Univ Of Ny City
Coll
New York, NY

Jonsson, Eva B
Broward Comm Coll
Ft Lauderdale, FL

Jordan, Edith R
Univ Of South Al
Mobile, AL

Jordan, Erica R
Seton Hall Univ
South Orange, NJ

Jordan, Jane Marie
Miami Univ
Oxford, OH

Jordan, Jennifer S
Va Polytechnic Inst &
St Univ
Blacksburg, VA

Jordan, Sandra R
Univ Of Sc At
Spartanburg
Spartanburg, SC

Jorgensen, Kimberly E
Dowling Coll
Oakdale Li, NY

Jose, Patricia L
Endicott Coll
Beverly, MA

Jose, Rivera Torres
Arnaldo
Bayamon Central Univ
Bayamon, PR

Joseph, David E
Morehouse Coll
Atlanta, GA

Joseph, Glennis-Ann L
City Univ Of Ny Bronx
Comm Col
Bronx, NY

Joseph, Mercy K
Southeastern Coll Of
Hlth Sci
N Miami Beach, FL

Joseph, Molvie E L
Univ Of The Virgin
Islands
St Thomas, VI

Jovings, Nick A
Univ Of Al At
Birmingham
Birmingham, AL

Joy, Jennifer L
Univ Of Akron
Akron, OH

Joy, Sirretha
Southern Coll Of Tech
Marietta, GA

Joyce, Sharon G
Thomas Nelson Comm
Coll
Hampton, VA

Juan-Juan, Pedro E
Inter Amer Univ Pr San
German
San German, PR

Judd, Beverly C
Johnson St Coll
Johnson, VT

Jules, Albert L
City Univ Of Ny
Baruch Coll
New York, NY

Jules, Julienne
Ramapo Coll Of Nj
Mahwah, NJ

Junkin, Mary Ann
Univ Of Al
Tuscaloosa, AL

Jusino, Ismael E
Catholic Univ Of Pr
Ponce, PR

Justice, Colette G
Hillsborough Comm
Coll
Tampa, FL

Justiniano Jr, Jorge
Daniel
Univ Of Southern Ms
Hattiesburg, MS

Jutson, Daniel J
Fayetteville St Univ
Fayetteville, NC

Kachanovsky, Asya
Berkeley School-New
York
New York, NY

Kagel, Geoffrey A
Case Western Reserve
Univ
Cleveland, OH

Kale, Elaine D
Catawba Valley Comm
Coll
Hickory, NC

Kale, Vijay K
Al A & M Univ
Normal, AL

Kaloudelis, Ioanna
Clark Univ
Worcester, MA

Kalter, Stewart M
Widener Univ
Chester, PA

Kameh, Darian S
Univ Of Va
Charlottesville, VA

Kamentz, Diane M
Univ Of Miami
Coral Gables, FL

Kamholz, Jennifer L
Syracuse Univ
Syracuse, NY

Kan, Yu-Hsiang
Univ Of Al At
Huntsville
Huntsville, AL

Kane, Kathleen P
City Univ Of Ny
Baruch Coll
New York, NY

Kapetanakis, Karen
Georgian Court Coll
Lakewood, NJ

Kapoor, Rosy
City Univ Of Ny
Baruch Coll
New York, NY

Kapoor, Shaiwal
City Univ Of Ny
Queensbrough
New York, NY

Karadimas, Ioannis
City Univ Of Ny
Baruch Coll
New York, NY

Karagiannis, Evangelos
Duquesne Univ
Pittsburgh, PA

Karelis Jr, Thomas E
Univ Of Ky
Lexington, KY

Karkos, Melanie
Univ Of Miami
Coral Gables, FL

Karr, Betty J
Sue Bennett Coll
London, KY

Karr, Kim L
Univ Of Akron
Akron, OH

Karr, Michael E
Kent St Univ Kent
Cmps
Kent, OH

Karst, Lucy P
Miami Univ
Oxford, OH

Kasam, Nassem I
Union Univ School Of Nursing
Memphis, TN

Kasarda, Lee A
Univ Of Akron
Akron, OH

Kasparek, Dorigen K
Univ Of Sc At Columbia
Columbia, SC

Kasza, Kristen A
S U N Y Coll Of Tech At Delhi
Delhi, NY

Katholi, Constance D
Snead St Jr Coll
Boaz, AL

Katsikas, Epaminontas
Strayer Coll
Washington, DC

Katz, Stacey A
Fl St Univ
Tallahassee, FL

Kaufman, Margot A
Goucher Coll
Towson, MD

Kavic, Stephen M
Univ Of Pa
Philadelphia, PA

Kawabata, Nobuko
Endicott Coll
Beverly, MA

Kawarabayashi, Theresse K
Georgetown Univ
Washington, DC

Kayne, Manuel A
Yale Univ
New Haven, CT

Kazouris Jr, Nikitas
Emory Univ
Atlanta, GA

Kearney, Jennifer L
Duquesne Univ
Pittsburgh, PA

Kearns, Brian P
Va Commonwealth Univ
Richmond, VA

Kearns, Edwina H
Univ Of Nc At Charlotte
Charlotte, NC

Keating, James A
Saint Vincents Coll & Seminary
Latrobe, PA

Keefe, Alison M
Univ Of West Fl
Pensacola, FL

Keeley, Karen M
Wagner Coll
Staten Island, NY

Keis, Abdallah A
Univ Of Cin R Walters Coll
Blue Ash, OH

Keisler, Richard Berlin
Johnson C Smith Univ
Charlotte, NC

Keith, Richard B
Vance Granville Comm Coll
Henderson, NC

Kellem, Paula J
Owensboro Jr Coll Of Bus
Owensboro, KY

Keller, Keven B
Capitol Coll
Laurel, MD

Keller, William B
Ms St Univ
Miss State, MS

Kelley, Rowena Y
De St Coll
Dover, DE

Kelley, Sharon B
Asbury Theological Sem
Wilmore, KY

Kelley, Tara Lea
Liberty Univ
Lynchburg, VA

Kelley, Teresa L
Pikeville Coll
Pikeville, KY

Kelley, Wayne Daniel
Bryant Stratton Bus Inst Roch
Rochester, NY

Kellum, Michael David
Samford Univ
Birmingham, AL

Kelly, Charlana M
Central Fl Comm Coll
Ocala, FL

Kelly, Colleen J
Fayetteville St Univ
Fayetteville, NC

Kelly, Heather A
James Madison University
Harrisonburg, VA

Kelly Jr, James R
Univ Of Southern Ms
Hattiesburg, MS

Kelly, Katherine E
Winthrop Coll
Rock Hill, SC

Kelly, Kristine M
Fl Atlantic Univ
Boca Raton, FL

Kelly, Lori J
Univ Of Pittsburgh
Pittsburgh, PA

Kelly, Michael J
Hudson Valley Comm Coll
Troy, NY

Kelly, Selah D
Methodist Coll
Fayetteville, NC

Kelner, Sarah E
Bay Path Coll
Longmeadow, MA

Kelsey, Maureen E
Georgian Court Coll
Lakewood, NJ

Kendall, Arteka D
Tn St Univ
Nashville, TN

Kendall, Cathy L
Univ Of Tn At Martin
Martin, TN

Kendra, Rachel A
Neumann Coll
Aston, PA

Kenia, Karen L
Marywood Coll
Scranton, PA

Kennedy, Heather L
Hudson Valley Comm Coll
Troy, NY

Kennedy, Kyle R
Univ Of Rochester
Rochester, NY

Kennedy, Laura S
Univ Of Cin R Walters Coll
Blue Ash, OH

Kennedy, Michael K
Old Dominion Univ
Norfolk, VA

Kennedy, Michelle L
Union Univ
Jackson, TN

Kennedy, Miranda L
James Sprunt Comm Coll
Kenansville, NC

Kenney, John M
Bloomfield Coll
Bloomfield, NJ

Kenny, Alison M
Seton Hall Univ
South Orange, NJ

Kenny, Linda J
Saint Johns Univ
Jamaica, NY

Kenny, Ranier L
Va St Univ
Petersburg, VA

Keown Jr, Larry E
Chattanooga St Tech Comm Coll
Chattanooga, TN

Kerfoot, Lynn A
Seton Hall Univ
South Orange, NJ

Kern, Tracy E
Davis Coll
Toledo, OH

Kerton, Cora L
Va St Univ
Petersburg, VA

Kesterson, Kyle L
Savannah Coll Of Art & Design
Savannah, GA

Key, Valerie M
Tuskegee Univ
Tuskegee Inst, AL

Keyhani, Roya Amanda
Oh St Univ
Columbus, OH

Keyser, Nancy L
Hillsborough Comm Coll
Tampa, FL

Keyton, Elizabeth G
Univ Of Al At Birmingham
Birmingham, AL

Khaldi, Omar R
Schenectady County Comm Coll
Schenectady, NY

Khalil, Mehnoor M
Univ Of Sc At Aiken
Aiken, SC

Khalil, Wesam N
Al A & M Univ
Normal, AL

Khan, Mahsiul I
City Univ Of Ny La Guard Coll
Long Island Cty, NY

Khan, Mohammad Ali
Univ Of The Dist Of Columbia
Washington, DC

Khayat, Victor Rudolph
Washington & Lee Univ
Lexington, VA

Kidd, Ronald P
Hillsborough Comm Coll
Tampa, FL

Kiefer, Celia S
Ky Christian Coll
Grayson, KY

Kiehl, Sandra M
Univ Of Akron
Akron, OH

Kielczynski, Elizabeth C
Seton Hall Univ
South Orange, NJ

Kihali, Elekiah Andago
Hellenic Coll/Holy Cross
Brookline, MA

Kiider, Melissa M
S U N Y Coll Of Tech At Frmgdl
Farmingdale, NY

Kildow, Barbara A
Wv Northern Comm Coll
Wheeling, WV

Kilfeather, Lisa M
City Univ Of Ny La Guard Coll
Long Island Cty, NY

Kilgore, C Denise
Univ Of Ga
Athens, GA

Kilian, Karin Alison
Walters St Comm Coll
Morristown, TN

Kilpatrick, Ashley D
Ms Univ For Women
Columbus, MS

Kilpatrick, Brian M
Univ Of Al At Birmingham
Birmingham, AL

Kim, Eun-Mi
Manhattan School Of Music
New York, NY

Kim, George J
Ny Univ
New York, NY

Kim, Jiyoung
Va Commonwealth Univ
Richmond, VA

Kimble, Frederick A
Glassboro St Coll
Glassboro, NJ

Kincaid, Rabecca Ann
Bluefield Coll
Bluefield, VA

King, Angela P
Piedmont Coll
Demorest, GA

King, Antoinette
Univ Of Md At Eastern Shore
Princess Anne, MD

King, Janice N
Jackson St Univ
Jackson, MS

King, Jonathan E
Bryant Stratton Bus Inst Roch
Rochester, NY

King, Keith A
Wv Univ
Morgantown, WV

King, Marvin L
Talladega Coll
Talladega, AL

King, Nichole M
East Tn St Univ
Johnson City, TN

King, Nicole Maria
Wilberforce Univ
Wilberforce, OH

King, Sophia Lafrance
Al A & M Univ
Normal, AL

Kingsley, Ursula R
D Youville Coll
Buffalo, NY

Kinnon, Alfreda L
Fl A & M Univ
Tallahassee, FL

Kinsinger, Jacqueline C
Prince Georges Comm Coll
Largo, MD

Kinsley, Kathleen
S U N Y At Binghamton
Binghamton, NY

Kipple, Dwayne W
Me Maritime Academy
Castine, ME

Kirby, Jeremy P
Ma Inst Of Tech
Cambridge, MA

Kirk, Loretta L
Central Al Comm Coll
Alexander City, AL

Kirkman, Tracey L
Univ Of Va
Charlottesville, VA

Kirkwood, Larry J
Jackson St Univ
Jackson, MS

Kirkwood, Yvette R
Fl A & M Univ
Tallahassee, FL

Kirnes, Andre C
Middle Tn St Univ
Murfreesboro, TN

Kirschstein, Margaret A
City Univ Of Ny Baruch Coll
New York, NY

Kishi, Kouichiro
Salem-Teikyo Univ
Salem, WV

Kite, Sally L A
Middle Tn St Univ
Murfreesboro, TN

Kiyaga, Michael
Stockton St Coll
Pomona, NJ

Kizelnik, Yosefa D
Yeshiva Univ
New York, NY

Kizer, Brian S
Univ Of Sc At Columbia
Columbia, SC

Kizzire, Michael D
Central Al Comm Coll
Alexander City, AL

Klasmeyer Jr, Ronald M
Anne Arundel Comm Coll
Arnold, MD

Klein, Christina L
Wagner Coll
Staten Island, NY

Klemic, George G
Case Western Reserve Univ
Cleveland, OH

Klingelsmith, Shelley L
Oh Univ
Athens, OH

Klodzinski, Kristi Michelle
Memphis St Univ
Memphis, TN

Klug, Christie M
Seton Hall Univ
South Orange, NJ

Klymok, Theodore W B
Tomlinson Coll
Cleveland, TN

Knepper, Kirby S
Duquesne Univ
Pittsburgh, PA

Knight, Amanda S
Hillsborough Comm Coll
Tampa, FL

Ko, Joeson Cho-Shun
Newbury Coll
Brookline, MA

Koch, Richard A
Univ Of Md Baltimore
Prof Schl
Baltimore, MD

Kocianic, Michael A
Univ Of Akron
Akron, OH

Kocimski, Maribeth C
Savannah Coll Of Art
& Design
Savannah, GA

Koepfinger Jr, Leroy R
West Liberty St Coll
West Liberty, WV

Kogen, Zeev M
Yeshiva Univ
New York, NY

Kohn, Deena R
Yeshiva Univ
New York, NY

Koide, Kana
Tougaloo Coll
Tougaloo, MS

Kolawole, Kehinde
Hiwassee Coll
Madisonville, TN

Kolcharno, Maria
Marywood Coll
Scranton, PA

Kong, Kelly
City Univ Of Ny
Baruch Coll
New York, NY

Koon, Georgina C
Carnegie Mellon Univ
Pittsburgh, PA

Kordonsky, Alexander
Ny Univ
New York, NY

Korogi, Todd M
Univ Of Akron
Akron, OH

Kosowski, Kristina M
Georgian Court Coll
Lakewood, NJ

Koury, Louis Elias
Hudson Valley Comm
Coll
Troy, NY

Koutrakos, Mary G
Mount Saint Mary Coll
Newburgh, NY

Kovach, Kimberly A
Wagner Coll
Staten Island, NY

Kozak, Renata K
Saint Joseph Coll
West Hartford, CT

Kozak, W Mike
Clarkson Univ
Potsdam, NY

Kratzer, Vincent X
Glassboro St Coll
Glassboro, NJ

Krebs, Jeannie M
Northern Ky Univ
Highland Hts, KY

Kreizman, Isaac J
Yeshiva Univ
New York, NY

Krentz, Tamara S
Auburn Univ At Auburn
Auburn, AL

Krescanko, Cynthia A
Univ Of Pittsburgh
Pittsburgh, PA

Kreutz, Matthew P
Cornell Univ
Ithaca, NY

Kromer, Jeffery L
Savannah Coll Of Art
& Design
Savannah, GA

Kronfle, Henry F
Univ Of Miami
Coral Gables, FL

Kruse, Susan J
D Youville Coll
Buffalo, NY

Kruzelnick, Linda M
William Paterson Coll
Wayne, NJ

Krznaric, Snezana
Stockton St Coll
Pomona, NJ

Ku, Yan Yan
Fl International Univ
Miami, FL

Kuder, Karen M
Wagner Coll
Staten Island, NY

Kuderer, Lisa M
Univ Of Cincinnati
Cincinnati, OH

Kuhn, Sheri R
Mt Saint Marys Coll &
Seminary
Emmitsburg, MD

Kula, Theodore J
Bethany Coll
Bethany, WV

Kumaraditya,
Vijayaditya P
City Univ Of Ny
Baruch Coll
New York, NY

Kumbatovic, John L
Saint Johns Univ
Jamaica, NY

Kumbatovic, Robert J
Ny Univ
New York, NY

Kunselman, Cheryl A
Indiana Univ Of Pa
Indiana, PA

Kupiszewski, Joseph
Andrew
Fl St Univ
Tallahassee, FL

Kuri, Yamil G
Fl International Univ
Miami, FL

Kurland, Michael D
Pa St Univ Delaware
Cty Cmps
Media, PA

Kurtz, Arthur Louis
Longwood Coll
Farmville, VA

Kurtz, Robert D
Broward Comm Coll
Ft Lauderdale, FL

Kuruc, David J
East Stroudsburg Univ
E Stroudsburg, PA

Kuss, John Kenneth
Daemen Coll
Amherst, NY

Kutter, Angelia M
Miami Jacobs Jr Coll
Of Bus
Dayton, OH

Kutz III, William A
Furman Univ
Greenville, SC

Kuwamura, Manami
Ny Univ
New York, NY

Kvyat, Busya
Bunker Hill Comm Coll
Boston, MA

Kyriakides, Lakis C
City Univ Of Ny City
Coll
New York, NY

La Bue, Brad A
Life Coll
Marietta, GA

La Casse, Tina M
Springfield Tech Comm
Coll
Springfield, MA

La Coe, Jean A
Univ Of Pittsburgh At
Bradford
Bradford, PA

La Forest, Robbie M
Chattanooga St Tech
Comm Coll
Chattanooga, TN

La Lande, Gwendolyn
Louise
Interdenominational
Theo Ctr
Atlanta, GA

La Rosa, Bridget
Ny Univ
New York, NY

La Rose, Sherry L
Castleton St Coll
Castleton, VT

La Sala, Deana M
Saint Johns Univ
Jamaica, NY

La Torre, Keziah L
Pa St Univ Hazleton
Cmps
Hazleton, PA

La Vallee, Michelle A
Columbia Greene Comm
Coll
Hudson, NY

La Zarou, Georgios Y
City Univ Of Ny City
Coll
New York, NY

Labrada, Luidmila
Miami Dade Comm Coll
Miami, FL

Lacayo, Eduardo Rafael
Miami Dade Comm Coll
Miami, FL

Lachman-Militello,
Holly F
Saint Thomas Univ
Miami, FL

Lachnicht, Dana M
Bloomfield Coll
Bloomfield, NJ

Lacoma, Nathalie A
Manhattan Coll
Bronx, NY

Lacy, Walter M
Al A & M Univ
Normal, AL

Ladas II, Ludwig
Nicholas
Barry Univ
Miami, FL

Ladewig, Ragna I
Bergen Comm Coll
Paramus, NJ

Lafon, Stephane
Christian
Fl International Univ
Miami, FL

Laguerre, Grace D
Univ Politecnica De Pr
Hato Rey, PR

Lai, Chi-Wang Albert
Univ Of Miami
Coral Gables, FL

Lajewski, Sandra J
Western New England
Coll
Springfield, MA

Lakomy, Renee A
Duquesne Univ
Pittsburgh, PA

Lam, Anmay
Ny Univ
New York, NY

Lam, Stephen W
Univ Of Va Clinch
Valley Coll
Wise, VA

Lamarche, Rosemarie N
Fl International Univ
Miami, FL

Lambert, Lionel
City Univ Of Ny
Queensbrough
New York, NY

Lambert, Michael J
Glassboro St Coll
Glassboro, NJ

Lambiase, Christina M
Dowling Coll
Oakdale Li, NY

Lambo, Allyson M
Radford Univ
Radford, VA

Lamme, Jennifer A
Albertus Magnus Coll
New Haven, CT

Lampo, Valerie J
Comm Coll Algny Co
Algny Cmps
Pittsburgh, PA

Lancaster, Laurielyn
Tn St Univ
Nashville, TN

Lance, Phoebie E
Cumberland Coll
Williamsburg, KY

Landin, Paul A
Ny Univ
New York, NY

Landrum, Melinda K
Christian Brothers Univ
Memphis, TN

Lang, Jennifer Christian
Endicott Coll
Beverly, MA

Lang, Lori A
Comm Coll Algny Co
Algny Cmps
Pittsburgh, PA

Lang-Thorbs, Kathi D
Bishop St Comm Coll
Mobile, AL

Lange, Barbara J
Brunswick Coll
Brunswick, GA

Langham, Carvine
Stillman Coll
Tuscaloosa, AL

Langley, Joyce D
Widener Univ
Chester, PA

Langley, Rahna M
Kent St Univ Kent
Cmps
Kent, OH

Langston, Diane K
Univ Of Sc At
Columbia
Columbia, SC

Lanier, Julie A
Fl A & M Univ
Tallahassee, FL

Lankford Jr, Robert L
Western Ky Univ
Bowling Green, KY

Lanotte, Janine
Manhattanville Coll
Purchase, NY

Lao, Lixing
Univ Of Md Baltimore
Prof Schl
Baltimore, MD

Larkin, Colleen R
Hillsborough Comm
Coll
Tampa, FL

Larkin, Veronia R
Central St Univ
Wilberforce, OH

Larsen, Lonni L
Elmira Coll
Elmira, NY

Larson, Julie N
Ms St Univ
Miss State, MS

Laster, Jonathan E
Cumberland Coll
Williamsburg, KY

Lauber, Jordana
Univ Of Toledo
Toledo, OH

Laufman, Darma
Miami Dade Comm Coll
North
Miami, FL

Laurino, Juan C
Hillsborough Comm
Coll
Tampa, FL

Laury, Aqualyn Y
Spelman Coll
Atlanta, GA

Laux, Steven A
Saint Johns Univ
Jamaica, NY

Lauzurique, Elizabeth A
Univ Politecnica De Pr
Hato Rey, PR

Lavas, Michele
City Univ Of Ny Coll
Staten Is
Staten Island, NY

Lavelle, Brian C
Providence Coll
Providence, RI

Law, Cassandra M
Clark Atlanta Univ
Atlanta, GA

Lawhorn, Glenda F
Central Fl Comm Coll
Ocala, FL

Lawrence, Levonie Z
City Univ Of Ny
Lehman Coll
Bronx, NY

Lawrie, Jodi L
Hilbert Coll
Hamburg, NY

Laws, Gary Scott
Brevard Coll
Brevard, NC

Lawson, Kevin W
Radford Univ
Radford, VA

Lawson, Mollie C
Tusculum Coll
Greeneville, TN

Lawver, Kimberly D
Univ Of Akron
Akron, OH

Layne, Paul J
Univ Of Miami
Coral Gables, FL

Lazarides, Anastassis A
City Univ Of Ny City
Coll
New York, NY

Le Beau, Carole M
Univ Of Akron
Akron, OH

Le Blanc, Jennifer E
Lasell Coll
Newton, MA

Le Boulch, Thierry R
Strayer Coll
Washington, DC

Le Clair, Christine May
Univ Of Nh Plymouth
St Coll
Plymouth, NH

Le Mire, Janice L
Endicott Coll
Beverly, MA

Le Vardi, Lisa A
Western New England
Coll
Springfield, MA

Le Vien, Douglas A
La Salle Univ
Philadelphia, PA

Le, Tam H
Hillsborough Comm
Coll
Tampa, FL

Leabo, Kim E
Anne Arundel Comm
Coll
Arnold, MD

Leak, Tanya Christina
Univ Of Med &
Dentistry Of Nj
Newark, NJ

Leaks, Tracey D
Jackson St Univ
Jackson, MS

Lebkicher, Eliza A
Juniata Coll
Huntingdon, PA

Ledford, Michelle E
Niagara Univ
Niagara Univ, NY

Ledford, Richard S
Central Al Comm Coll
Alexander City, AL

Lee, Cha Hwa
City Univ Of Ny Bronx
Comm Col
Bronx, NY

Lee, Christopher Yung
Ling
Belmont Coll
Nashville, TN

Lee, Daphne P
Va St Univ
Petersburg, VA

Lee, Elizabeth M
Dutchess Comm Coll
Poughkeepsie, NY

Lee, Kyung Muk
Univ Of North Fl
Jacksonville, FL

Lee, Michael D
Univ Of Sc At
Columbia
Columbia, SC

Lee, Shannon M
Northern Ky Univ
Highland Hts, KY

Lee, Voncelle L
Tuskegee Univ
Tuskegee Inst, AL

Lee, William Barry
Univ Of Ky
Lexington, KY

Lee, Yonghwa
City Univ Of Ny
Queensbrough
New York, NY

Leedy, Marvin R
Radford Univ
Radford, VA

Leflore, Amy E
Ms St Univ
Miss State, MS

Lehman Jr, Harold
Hans
Daytona Beach Comm
Coll
Daytona Beach, FL

Lehmann, Patricia A
Univ Of Akron
Akron, OH

Leigers, Gidget A
Bridgewater Coll
Bridgewater, VA

Leighton, Ernestine S
Andover Coll
Portland, ME

Leister, Michelle L
Susquehanna Univ
Selinsgrove, PA

Leister, Scott B
Temple Univ
Philadelphia, PA

Lemaire, Nancy S
Christopher Newport
Coll
Newport News, VA

Lemanski, Janet M
Howard Comm Coll
Columbia, MD

Lembo, Diana S
William Paterson Coll
Wayne, NJ

Lemon, Marvetta
Wilmington Coll
New Castle, DE

Lenahan, Jeffery M
Brewer St Jr Coll
Fayette, AL

Lenhardt, Gary A
Hudson Valley Comm
Coll
Troy, NY

Lenox, Kimberly J
Widener Univ
Chester, PA

Lentini, Gregory J
Boston Univ
Boston, MA

Lentz, Charles W
Indiana Univ Of Pa
Indiana, PA

Leocani, Letizia M
Eckerd Coll
St Petersburg, FL

Leon, Barbara C
Univ Of Miami
Coral Gables, FL

Leon, Ernesto Gabriel
Univ Of Miami
Coral Gables, FL

Leon, Frances R
Univ Of Pr Cayey Univ
Coll
Cayey, PR

Leon, Sonia M
City Univ Of Ny La Guard Coll
Long Island Cty, NY

Leon, Yesenia
Fl International Univ
Miami, FL

Leonard, Alma M
Nc Central Univ
Durham, NC

Leonard, Joan E
Va Highlands Comm Coll
Abingdon, VA

Leonard, Ron Matthew
Univ Of Nc At Greensboro
Greensboro, NC

Leonard, Susan Wenrick
Glassboro St Coll
Glassboro, NJ

Leonardo, Monica
City Univ Of Ny City Coll
New York, NY

Leonardo, Robert
Georgetown Univ
Washington, DC

Leone, Dennis D
Univ Of Miami
Coral Gables, FL

Lescalleet, Scott F
Bridgewater Coll
Bridgewater, VA

Lesicki, Robert J
Temple Univ
Philadelphia, PA

Leslie, Michael A
Bethel Coll
Mckenzie, TN

Leslie, Neville M
Univ Of Miami
Coral Gables, FL

Lestardo, Melissa A
Neumann Coll
Aston, PA

Lester, Donna M
North Ga Coll
Dahlonega, GA

Lester, Jeannie L
Owensboro Jr Coll Of Bus
Owensboro, KY

Leventhal, Danielle M
Oh Univ
Athens, OH

Leverett, Hazel G
Bristol Univ
Bristol, TN

Levin, Jill R
Temple Univ
Philadelphia, PA

Levy, Kimberly
Norfolk St Univ
Norfolk, VA

Levy, Lynette
Barry Univ
Miami, FL

Lewandowski, Denise A
Va Commonwealth Univ
Richmond, VA

Lewis IV, Albert M
Fl St Univ
Tallahassee, FL

Lewis, Antoinette D
Coppin St Coll
Baltimore, MD

Lewis, Caya B
Spelman Coll
Atlanta, GA

Lewis, Deena N
Va St Univ
Petersburg, VA

Lewis, Deirdre M
Fl A & M Univ
Tallahassee, FL

Lewis, Earlean D
Clark Atlanta Univ
Atlanta, GA

Lewis, Eric J
Memphis St Univ
Memphis, TN

Lewis, Garnet A
City Univ Of Ny City Coll
New York, NY

Lewis Jr, George E
Norfolk St Univ
Norfolk, VA

Lewis, Harold D
Interdenominational Theo Ctr
Atlanta, GA

Lewis, James R
Vance Granville Comm Coll
Henderson, NC

Lewis, Jonathan G
Memphis St Univ
Memphis, TN

Lewis, Kathryn M
Univ Of Ky
Lexington, KY

Lewis, Kelli A
Univ Of Miami
Coral Gables, FL

Lewis, Kristin M
Kent St Univ Kent Cmps
Kent, OH

Lewis, Leslie R
Clark Atlanta Univ
Atlanta, GA

Lewis, Lori D
Southeast Comm Coll
Cumberland, KY

Lewis, Monique Y
Va St Univ
Petersburg, VA

Lewis III, Oliver J
Morehouse Coll
Atlanta, GA

Lewis, Phillip R
Beckley Coll
Beckley, WV

Lewis, Roseline Kagonya
Univ Of Ms Medical Center
Jackson, MS

Lewis, Teresa A
Dyersburg St Comm Coll
Dyersburg, TN

Lewis, Tonya R
Alcorn St Univ
Lorman, MS

Lewis, Victoria A
Cumberland County Coll
Vineland, NJ

Li, Shao J
Cooper Union
New York, NY

Li, Ying-Shi
City Univ Of Ny La Guard Coll
Long Island Cty, NY

Liber, Liza L
Fl International Univ
Miami, FL

Liberatore, Adrian J
Duquesne Univ
Pittsburgh, PA

Liberti, Tricia
S U N Y Coll At Oneonta
Oneonta, NY

Liddle, Sarah L
Anne Arundel Comm Coll
Arnold, MD

Lieb, Justin G
George Mason Univ
Fairfax, VA

Lien, Chiung Y
Univ Of Nc At Charlotte
Charlotte, NC

Liff, Joe A
Washington State Comm Coll
Marietta, OH

Lightford, Willie P
Al A & M Univ
Normal, AL

Likin Jr, Richard O
Bridgewater Coll
Bridgewater, VA

Lilly, Tamara Y
Beckley Coll
Beckley, WV

Lim, Geok Lian
Memphis St Univ
Memphis, TN

Lim, Kwai Fatt
City Univ Of Ny La Guard Coll
Long Island Cty, NY

Lim, Lois
Nyack Coll
Nyack, NY

Lima, Avelino F
Wv Univ At Parkersburg
Parkersburg, WV

Linaugh, Philip J
Univ Of Sc At Columbia
Columbia, SC

Lindley, Angela S
Walker Coll
Jasper, AL

Lindor Jackson, Marie
Inter Amer Univ Pr San German
San German, PR

Lindsey, Pamela M
Phillips Jr Coll Charlotte
Charlotte, NC

Link, Teresa G
Radford Univ
Radford, VA

Linkous, Michelle Nicolle
New River Comm Coll
Dublin, VA

Lins, Jennifer C
Salisbury St Univ
Salisbury, MD

Linster, Shaun M
Thomas Nelson Comm Coll
Hampton, VA

Lipps, Daniel R
Univ Of Cin R Walters Coll
Blue Ash, OH

Lipscomb, Christine E
Univ Of Nc At Charlotte
Charlotte, NC

Lipscomb, Tiffany C
Spelman Coll
Atlanta, GA

Lipton, Mark Drew
Barry Univ
Miami, FL

Lirag, Manolito R
Bloomfield Coll
Bloomfield, NJ

Lisenby, Rod S
City Univ Of Ny City Coll
New York, NY

Lishinsky Jr, David M
Univ Of Pittsburgh
Pittsburgh, PA

Lister, Donna M
North Greenville Coll
Tigerville, SC

Lister, Nathan A
Thomas Nelson Comm Coll
Hampton, VA

Little, Betty S
Liberty Univ
Lynchburg, VA

Little, Tyra J
City Univ Of Ny La Guard Coll
Long Island Cty, NY

Littman, Eva D
Duke Univ
Durham, NC

Liu, Ching-Hsiu M
William Paterson Coll
Wayne, NJ

Liu, Hsueh M
City Univ Of Ny Baruch Coll
New York, NY

Liu, Su Hua Woo
City Univ Of Ny La Guard Coll
Long Island Cty, NY

Liu, Yiming
Savannah Coll Of Art & Design
Savannah, GA

Liversedge, Kelly-Ann
Mount Olive Coll
Mount Olive, NC

Livesey, Sarah T
Boston Univ
Boston, MA

Livingston, Franklin M
Ky St Univ
Frankfort, KY

Livingston, Jeffrey O
Wilmington Coll
New Castle, DE

Livstone, Michael S
Yale Univ
New Haven, CT

Lizotte, Linda M
Teikyo Post Univ
Waterbury, CT

Llanos-Quintero, Edgar
City Univ Of Ny La Guard Coll
Long Island Cty, NY

Lleonart, Gilberto R
Fl International Univ
Miami, FL

Llewellyn, Deobrah A
S U N Y Coll Of Tech At Frmgdl
Farmingdale, NY

Llinas, Isabel
Nova Univ
Ft Lauderdale, FL

Llobera, Jeanette
Fl International Univ
Miami, FL

Lluveras-Garcia, Iris I
Evangelical Semimary Of P R
Hato Rey, PR

Lobato Jr, Flavio A
Univ Of Miami
Coral Gables, FL

Lobo, Lygia Bruno
Miami Dade Comm Coll
Miami, FL

Lockard, Melissa K
Campbell Univ
Buies Creek, NC

Loeb, Susan B
Beaver Coll
Glenside, PA

Loffreda, Renato
Univ Of Pittsburgh
Pittsburgh, PA

Lofton Jr, Lionel S
Univ Of Sc At Columbia
Columbia, SC

Lohberg, Birgit
Fl Atlantic Univ
Boca Raton, FL

Lohmeyer, David C
Fl Atlantic Univ
Boca Raton, FL

Lomastro, Jennifer L
Univ Of Ct
Storrs, CT

Lombardi, Carol A
Berkeley Coll Of Westchester
White Plains, NY

Lonetto, Sherry G
Dowling Coll
Oakdale Li, NY

Loney, Christopher G
Atlantic Comm Coll
Mays Landing, NJ

Long, Angel R
Northern Ky Univ
Highland Hts, KY

Long, Bettye Lee
Athens St Coll
Athens, AL

Long, Jennifer L
De St Coll
Dover, DE

Long, Jerod F
Wv Univ
Morgantown, WV

Long, Linda A
Univ Of Ga
Athens, GA

Long, Matrecia S
Fl A & M Univ
Tallahassee, FL

Long, Steven Ray
Pellissippi St Tech Comm Coll
Knoxville, TN

Long, Tricia A
Loyola Coll In Md
Baltimore, MD

Longo, Lisa Marie
William Paterson Coll
Wayne, NJ

Longstreet, Yolanda D
Fayetteville St Univ
Fayetteville, NC

Looney, Melanie L
Birmingham Southern Coll
Birmingham, AL

Lopez Arroyo, Emilio Jose
Inter Amer Univ Pr San German
San German, PR

Lopez Echegaray, Alex
Inter Amer Univ Pr San German
San German, PR

Lopez Lopez, Milagros
Inter Amer Univ Pr Barranquita
Barranquitas, PR

Lopez Roche, Laura Lis
Univ Of Pr At Rio Piedras
Rio Piedras, PR

Lopez, Alejandro Paul
Miami Dade Comm Coll
Miami, FL

Lopez, Carlos R
Nova Univ
Ft Lauderdale, FL

Lopez, Hector J
Univ Of Miami
Coral Gables, FL

Lopez, Norayma
Univ Politecnica De Pr
Hato Rey, PR

Lopez, Richard A
S U N Y Coll Of Tech
At Frmgdl
Farmingdale, NY

Lopez, Sandra L
Univ Of Miami
Coral Gables, FL

Lopez-Cando, Anthony J
Barry Univ
Miami, FL

Lopez-Jimenez, Carlos J
Inter Amer Univ Pr San
Juan
Hato Rey, PR

Lopez-Rosado, Nilsa H
Univ Of Pr Medical
Sciences
San Juan, PR

Lopresto, Margaret A
Saint Johns Univ
Jamaica, NY

Lorenzo, Lourdes M
Univ Of Pr At Rio
Piedras
Rio Piedras, PR

Lorusso, Nicole A
Teikyo Post Univ
Waterbury, CT

Lossi, Jeanine M
Castleton St Coll
Castleton, VT

Lotito, Elizabeth-Anne
Villanova Univ
Villanova, PA

Lotito, Joseph G
Fl Atlantic Univ
Boca Raton, FL

Lough, Daniel L
Va Polytechnic Inst &
St Univ
Blacksburg, VA

Loughran, Jennifer A
Merrimack Coll
North Andover, MA

Louis, Jean Bernard
Hudson County Comm
Coll
Jersey City, NJ

Loukedis, Alexander L
Villanova Univ
Villanova, PA

Love, Jeffrey I
Cornell Univ Statutory
College
Ithaca, NY

Lovelace III, Glen C
Univ Of De
Newark, DE

Lovell, Amy B
Western New England
Coll
Springfield, MA

Lovell, Jackie A
Southern Junior Coll
Birmingham, AL

Loverin, Robert Alfred
Univ Of Sc At
Columbia
Columbia, SC

Lovett, W Niguel
Vance Granville Comm
Coll
Henderson, NC

Lovio, Jessica B
Fl International Univ
Miami, FL

Lowe, Michael A
Univ Of Southern Ms
Hattiesburg, MS

Lowe, Tien S
Univ Of Miami
Coral Gables, FL

Lowe, Tonia J
Roane St Comm Coll
Harriman, TN

Lowery, April A
Glassboro St Coll
Glassboro, NJ

Lowther, Gayla L
Washington State
Comm Coll
Marietta, OH

Lowy, Kenneth M
City Univ Of Ny John
Jay Coll
New York, NY

Loy, Connie G
Roane St Comm Coll
Harriman, TN

Lubiniecki, Gregory M
Ma Inst Of Tech
Cambridge, MA

Lucas, Robert D
Manhattan Coll
Bronx, NY

Luccani, Luis D
Columbia Union Coll
Takoma Park, MD

Ludolf, Tammy J
Itawamba Comm Coll
Fulton, MS

Lue Fook Sang, Andre S
City Univ Of Ny City
Coll
New York, NY

Lugo, Jamie V C
Rutgers St Un At New
Brunswick
New Brunswick, NJ

Lugo, Loimar G
Inter Amer Univ Pr San
German
San German, PR

Lugo, Pedro A
Univ Politecnica De Pr
Hato Rey, PR

Lugovoy, Tamar M
Neumann Coll
Aston, PA

Luke, Kathy R
Abraham Baldwin Agri
Coll
Tifton, GA

Luna, June Annette
John C Calhoun St
Comm Coll
Decatur, AL

Lunder, Terje A
Fl International Univ
Miami, FL

Lungarini, David G
Providence Coll
Providence, RI

Lunstrum, Maj-Stina N
Cornell Univ Statutory
College
Ithaca, NY

Lusan, Monique D
Univ Of Miami
Coral Gables, FL

Lusardi, Luca H
Univ Of Miami
Coral Gables, FL

Luster, Elizabeth M
Salisbury St Univ
Salisbury, MD

Lutz, Mark M
Pittsburgh Tech Inst
Pittsburgh, PA

Lutz, Melissa W
Lexington Comm Coll
Lexington, KY

Lutz, Nancy J
S U N Y Coll Of Tech
At Delhi
Delhi, NY

Lutz, Rachel Y
Northwest Ms Comm
Coll
Senatobia, MS

Luu, Sydney D
Widener Univ
Chester, PA

Ly, Cu
Bunker Hill Comm Coll
Boston, MA

Lynah, Angela L
Claflin Coll
Orangeburg, SC

Lyons, Christopher D
Va Commonwealth Univ
Richmond, VA

Lysiuk, Lance C
Embry Riddle
Aeronautical Univ
Daytona Beach, FL

Lyttle, Deborah R
Roane St Comm Coll
Harriman, TN

Ma Mbemba, Mahungu
Jeff
Shaw Univ
Raleigh, NC

Maas, Pierre F
Miami Dade Comm Coll
Miami, FL

Maastricht, Kari L
Coll Of Charleston
Charleston, SC

Mabe, Kimberly D
Va Polytechnic Inst &
St Univ
Blacksburg, VA

Mabinuori, Kehinde Ola
City Univ Of Ny
Baruch Coll
New York, NY

Mabry, Corey V
Greenville Tech Coll
Greenville, SC

Mabry, Heather L
Central St Univ
Wilberforce, OH

Mabry, Otha E
Univ Of Tn At Martin
Martin, TN

Mac Donald, Melanie L
Nc Agri & Tech St
Univ
Greensboro, NC

Mac Donnell, Margaret
Loyola Coll In Md
Baltimore, MD

Mac Eachron, Sonya A
Radford Univ
Radford, VA

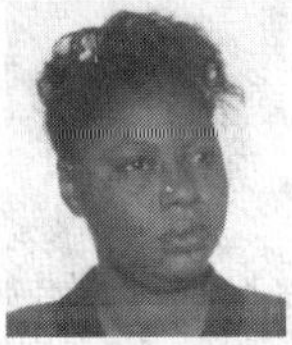
Macaulay, Henrietta O
City Univ Of Ny City
Coll
New York, NY

Machobane, Noliwe B
Jackson St Univ
Jackson, MS

Machuga, Shelly L
Erie Comm Coll South
Cmps
Orchard Park, NY

Maciaszek, Andrew S
New England Coll Of
Optometry
Boston, MA

Mack, Joanne A
Miami Dade Comm Coll
North
Miami, FL

Mack, La Juane D
Fl Memorial Coll
Miami, FL

Mackel, Yvette D
Tougaloo Coll
Tougaloo, MS

Mackie, Jennifer S
Wilmington Coll
New Castle, DE

Mackie, Tonja L
Univ Of Nh Plymouth
St Coll
Plymouth, NH

Maddox, Aaron L
Univ Of Tn At
Knoxville
Knoxville, TN

Madera, Merilee
Duquesne Univ
Pittsburgh, PA

Madison, Eric D
Univ Of Nc At
Asheville
Asheville, NC

Madrigal, Enrique A
Univ Of Sc At Sumter
Sumter, SC

Maestre, Osmel R
Nova Univ
Ft Lauderdale, FL

Magalhaes, Paulo T
Manhattan Coll
Bronx, NY

Magee, Clayton C
Univ Of Southern Ms
Hattiesburg, MS

Magee, Jamie G
Alcorn St Univ
Lorman, MS

Magid, Michelle
Ny Univ
New York, NY

Magnet, Marcus
City Univ Of Ny City Coll
New York, NY

Magoon, Indu
Georgetown Univ
Washington, DC

Magoon, Sanjeev
Georgetown Univ
Washington, DC

Magos, Zeny C
Glassboro St Coll
Glassboro, NJ

Maguire, Kevin C
Belmont Coll
Nashville, TN

Mahadeo, Harnarine
De Tech & Comm Coll At Dover
Dover, DE

Mahadevan, Karthikeyan
Univ Of Ms Main Cmps
University, MS

Mahaffey, Russell K
Univ Of Sc At Spartanburg
Spartanburg, SC

Maheswari, Sunita
Fl Atlantic Univ
Boca Raton, FL

Mahmood, Akhtar H
Edinboro Univ Of Pa
Edinboro, PA

Maholmes, Mavis Y
Paine Coll
Augusta, GA

Mahon, Carrie J
Western New England Coll
Springfield, MA

Maier Jr, Robert Willard
Wv Univ
Morgantown, WV

Main, Tina M
Univ Of Southern Ms
Hattiesburg, MS

Mainville, Tamara E
Longwood Coll
Farmville, VA

Majors, Susan L
Univ Of Cin R Walters Coll
Blue Ash, OH

Mak, Po H
S U N Y Coll Of Tech At Frmgdl
Farmingdale, NY

Mak, So Han
Fl International Univ
Miami, FL

Makar, Tamala S
Georgian Court Coll
Lakewood, NJ

Makay, Cherie D
Univ Of Nc At Charlotte
Charlotte, NC

Makupson Jr, Lemuel B
Central St Univ
Wilberforce, OH

Malave, Maria G
Inter Amer Univ Pr Barranquita
Barranquitas, PR

Malcolm, Lisa E
Limestone Coll
Gaffney, SC

Maldonado Sanchez, Reinaldo
Univ Politecnica De Pr
Hato Rey, PR

Maldonado Vega, Mirna
Univ Of Pr Medical Sciences
San Juan, PR

Maldonado, Luis A
Univ Politecnica De Pr
Hato Rey, PR

Maldonado, Roberto E
Inter Amer Univ Pr Hato Rey
Hato Rey, PR

Maldonado, Vivian B
Catholic Univ Of Pr
Ponce, PR

Maldonado-Serrano, Maria A
Univ Of Pr At Rio Piedras
Rio Piedras, PR

Maldony, Christopher M
Andrew Coll
Cuthbert, GA

Maleki, Soheila J
Univ Of Tn At Martin
Martin, TN

Maley II, Jimie G
Embry Riddle Aeronautical Univ
Daytona Beach, FL

Mallard, Todd S
Saint Pauls Coll
Lawrenceville, VA

Mallet, Marie A
Anne Arundel Comm Coll
Arnold, MD

Malloy, Kelly A
Villanova Univ
Villanova, PA

Malone, Kimberly
Georgian Court Coll
Lakewood, NJ

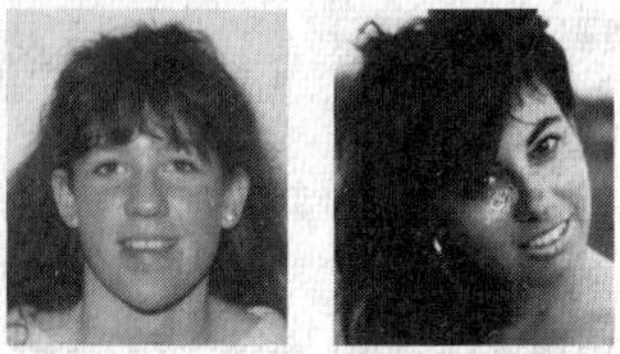
Maloney, Jean M
Bucknell Univ
Lewisburg, PA

Maloof, Cynthia A
William Paterson Coll
Wayne, NJ

Maloof, Linda E
Western New England Coll
Springfield, MA

Maltes, Claudia M
Fl International Univ
Miami, FL

Malveira, Darlene J
Newbury Coll
Brookline, MA

Mamela, Jonathan C
Bethany Coll
Bethany, WV

Mamma, Constance M
Norfolk St Univ
Norfolk, VA

Mamun, Shahriar A
Coppin St Coll
Baltimore, MD

Mancuso, Anthony J
Appalachian St Univ
Boone, NC

Mancuso, Michael
Dickinson School Of Law
Carlisle, PA

Manente, Cara A
Niagara Univ
Niagara Univ, NY

Mangels, James R
Lenoir Rhyne Coll
Hickory, NC

Manigauit, Lorraine Yvonne
Coll Of New Rochelle
New Rochelle, NY

Mann, Joyce A
Clark Atlanta Univ
Atlanta, GA

Mann, Victoria L
Saint Francis Coll
Loretto, PA

Manning Jr, Paul R
Ashland Comm Coll
Ashland, KY

Mano, Samuel A
Marshall University
Huntington, WV

Manolakes, Lucinda A
S U N Y At Stony Brook
Stony Brook, NY

Mantas, Angeliki
Univ Of South Fl
Tampa, FL

Mantello, Melinda A
Salisbury St Univ
Salisbury, MD

Manu, Samuel O
Asbury Theological Sem
Wilmore, KY

Manuel, Christopher N
Tn St Univ
Nashville, TN

Manzano, Helen S
West Chester Univ
West Chester, PA

Marando, Rosanna
Univ Of Miami
Coral Gables, FL

Marbuary, La Tonia A
Clark Atlanta Univ
Atlanta, GA

Marca, Myrna Y
Univ Of Ky
Lexington, KY

March, Kelly J
Fl International Univ
Miami, FL

Marchionda, Cynthia J
Univ Of Cincinnati
Cincinnati, OH

Marciniak, Sheila J
D Youville Coll
Buffalo, NY

Marcos, Glenn
Fl International Univ
Miami, FL

Mardales Escanellas, Maria M
Univ Politecnica De Pr
Hato Rey, PR

Marderian, Richard V
Broome Comm Coll
Binghamton, NY

Mariani, Theresa M
Hilbert Coll
Hamburg, NY

Mariea, Cherise R
Bowling Green St Univ
Bowling Green, OH

Marien, Angela Noelle
Ramapo Coll Of Nj
Mahwah, NJ

Marina, Victor G
Fl International Univ
Miami, FL

Marinas, Brian C
Liberty Univ
Lynchburg, VA

Marino, Louis A
Glassboro St Coll
Glassboro, NJ

Markland, Stacy R
James Madison University
Harrisonburg, VA

Marlin, Melinda Jo
Univ Of Ga
Athens, GA

Marlowe, Debra A
Wv Univ
Morgantown, WV

Marlowe, Lisa A
Broward Comm Coll
Ft Lauderdale, FL

Maroni, Bobbie J
Oh Dominican Coll
Columbus, OH

Maronski, Vincent P
S U N Y Coll Of A & T Morrisvl
Morrisville, NY

Marquez-Morales, Alfredo
Inter Amer Univ Pr San Juan
Hato Rey, PR

Marquez-Scott, Emma
Methodist Coll
Fayetteville, NC

Marrelli, Marietta F
Univ Of Nc At Asheville
Asheville, NC

Marrero-Ortiz, Sandra Enid
Univ Central Del Caribe
Cayey, PR

Marsch, Lisa A
Univ Of Md Baltimore Prof Schl
Baltimore, MD

Marsh, Heather D
Duquesne Univ
Pittsburgh, PA

Marsh, Ricaldo F
City Univ Of Ny City Coll
New York, NY

Marsh, Sheila M
Central St Univ
Wilberforce, OH

Marshall, David T
Benedict Coll
Columbia, SC

Marshall, Eric C
Morehouse Coll
Atlanta, GA

Marshall, Kent S
Ms St Univ
Miss State, MS

Marshall, Sophia S L
Jackson St Univ
Jackson, MS

Marston, Lorraine
Wilmington Coll
New Castle, DE

Martel, Sylvia S
Miami Dade Comm Coll North
Miami, FL

Martens, Jill E
Univ Of Miami
Coral Gables, FL

Marti, Marla C
Inter Amer Univ Pr San Juan
Hato Rey, PR

Martin, Andrea L
Ga Southern Univ
Statesboro, GA

Martin, Calvin R
Morehouse Coll
Atlanta, GA

Martin, Deborah S
Tri County Tech Coll
Pendleton, SC

Martin, Douglas J
Coker Coll
Hartsville, SC

Martin, Gregory A
Utica Coll Of Syracuse Univ
Utica, NY

Martin, Laura L
Faulkner Univ
Montgomery, AL

Martin, Terry L
Phillips Jr Coll Spartanburg
Spartanburg, SC

Martin-Duarte, Ignacio
Univ Of Miami
Coral Gables, FL

Martinelli, Linda A
Centenary Coll
Hackettstown, NJ

Martinez, David
City Univ Of Ny La Guard Coll
Long Island Cty, NY

Martinez, Doris M
Inter Amer Univ Pr Hato Rey
Hato Rey, PR

Martinez, Eileen
Temple Univ
Philadelphia, PA

Martinez, Jose S
Univ Of Med & Dentistry Of Nj
Newark, NJ

Martinez, Marilu
Inter Amer Univ Pr Hato Rey
Hato Rey, PR

Martinez-Velky, Deborah J
Dutchess Comm Coll
Poughkeepsie, NY

Martynick, Vera C
City Univ Of Ny La Guard Coll
Long Island Cty, NY

Marucci, Joseph P
Glassboro St Coll
Glassboro, NJ

Marx, Lisa G
Fl International Univ
Miami, FL

Marx, Margaret A
Central Fl Comm Coll
Ocala, FL

Marzilli, Deneane
Univ Of Ri
Kingston, RI

Masadeh, Lana B
Univ Of Cincinnati-Clrmnt Coll
Batavia, OH

Massee, Judith H
Piedmont Coll
Demorest, GA

Massengale, Tim A
Faulkner Univ
Montgomery, AL

Massi, Giuliana M
Bryant Coll Of Bus Admin
Smithfield, RI

Massie, Ethelia C
Comm Coll Algny Co Algny Cmps
Pittsburgh, PA

Massing, Catherine Ann
Glassboro St Coll
Glassboro, NJ

Mast, Darcy A
S U N Y Coll At
Fredonia
Fredonia, NY

Masters, Karie M
Columbus Coll Of Art
& Design
Columbus, OH

Masukawa, Masako
Savannah Coll Of Art
& Design
Savannah, GA

Matheny, Jerrie J
Univ Of Tn At Martin
Martin, TN

Matheus, Jean D
City Univ Of Ny
Queensbrough
New York, NY

Mathews, Tracy L
Savannah Coll Of Art
& Design
Savannah, GA

Mathis, Sandra L
Middle Tn St Univ
Murfreesboro, TN

Matos Caceres, Silvia
Univ Del Turabo
Gurabo, PR

Matsutani, Tomoko
Endicott Coll
Beverly, MA

Mattes, Raymond Alan
Duquesne Univ
Pittsburgh, PA

Matthew, Lett R
Univ Of The Virgin
Islands
St Thomas, VI

Matthew, Myrna G
City Univ Of Ny Bronx
Comm Col
Bronx, NY

Matthews, Kizzie A
Ga St Univ
Atlanta, GA

Matthews, Robin G
East Central Comm Coll
Decatur, MS

Matthews, Tammy A
Gordon Coll
Barnesville, GA

Mattison, Eddie B
Hampton Univ
Hampton, VA

Mattos, John L
Univ Of Rochester
Rochester, NY

Mattox, Robbie R
Draughons Jr Coll
Nashville
Nashville, TN

Matura, Amy L
S U N Y Coll Of Tech
At Delhi
Delhi, NY

Matuskey, Michael G
Central Fl Comm Coll
Ocala, FL

Matveyeva, Polina
Yeshiva Univ
New York, NY

Mawilmada, Nayana N
Hampton Univ
Hampton, VA

Maxwell, Susannah F
Truett Mc Connell Coll
Cleveland, GA

May, Kimberly A
Hudson Valley Comm
Coll
Troy, NY

May, Laura M
Coker Coll
Hartsville, SC

Maybury, Melanie E
Wilmington Coll
Wilmington, OH

Maye, April
Al St Univ
Montgomery, AL

Maye, Warrick E
Al St Univ
Montgomery, AL

Mayer, Keira L
Mercer Univ Schl Of
Pharm
Atlanta, GA

Mayes, Ernest M
Morehouse Coll
Atlanta, GA

Maynard, Bobbi Jo
Univ Of New England
Biddeford, ME

Maynard, Prisca
Univ Of The Virgin
Islands
St Thomas, VI

Mayo, Bethany L
Univ Of Tn At Martin
Martin, TN

Mayo, Corina A
Univ Of Cincinnati
Cincinnati, OH

Mayo, Kerri L
Alfred Univ
Alfred, NY

Mayor, Stephanie A
Wv Univ
Morgantown, WV

Mays, Kennetha Marie
Tuskegee Univ
Tuskegee Inst, AL

Mays, Michael E
Tn Temple Univ
Chattanooga, TN

Maze, Brian L
Univ Of Al At
Huntsville
Huntsville, AL

Mazinani, Ali
Fl International Univ
Miami, FL

Mazyck, Warren
Claflin Coll
Orangeburg, SC

Mbuakoto, Namanga C
Univ Of Med &
Dentistry Of Nj
Newark, NJ

Mc Afee, Tanya R
Memphis St Univ
Memphis, TN

Mc Alexander, Mary A
Patrick Henry Comm Coll
Martinsville, VA

Mc Allister, Dawn L
Katherine Gibbs School
Providence, RI

Mc Allister, Diana A
Univ Of Southern Ms
Hattiesburg, MS

Mc Atee, Brian W
Univ Of Sc At Columbia
Columbia, SC

Mc Atee, Chrystal G
Univ Of Akron
Akron, OH

Mc Bee, Norwood M
Clemson Univ
Clemson, SC

Mc Bride, David A
Kent St Univ Kent Cmps
Kent, OH

Mc Bride, Ronald J
Fayetteville St Univ
Fayetteville, NC

Mc Cabe, Christopher J
Hudson Valley Comm Coll
Troy, NY

Mc Caffery, Michael H
Bloomfield Coll
Bloomfield, NJ

Mc Call, Lisa L
Univ Of Sc At Columbia
Columbia, SC

Mc Callum Jr, Rodney
Tusculum Coll
Greeneville, TN

Mc Cants, Kimberly M
Va St Univ
Petersburg, VA

Mc Cants, La Shawn M
Lincoln Univ
Lincoln Univ, PA

Mc Carthy, Blane G
Stetson Univ
Deland, FL

Mc Carthy, John Francis
Middle Tn St Univ
Murfreesboro, TN

Mc Carthy, Linda J
Niagara Univ
Niagara Univ, NY

Mc Caskill, Luther D
Jackson St Univ
Jackson, MS

Mc Caughey, Anne F
City Univ Of Ny Baruch Coll
New York, NY

Mc Chesney Jr, David C
Cedarville Coll
Cedarville, OH

Mc Clanahan, Brent M
Marshall University
Huntington, WV

Mc Clinton, Malana R
Bloomfield Coll
Bloomfield, NJ

Mc Closkey, Robert T
Bloomfield Coll
Bloomfield, NJ

Mc Clure, Phyllis G
Saint Josephs Coll New York
Brooklyn, NY

Mc Colley Jr, Joseph V
Villanova Univ
Villanova, PA

Mc Common, Sandra B
Memphis St Univ
Memphis, TN

Mc Connell, Debra A
Central Fl Comm Coll
Ocala, FL

Mc Cormack, Charlotte
Itawamba Comm Coll
Fulton, MS

Mc Coy, Susie Y
Johnson St Coll
Johnson, VT

Mc Creary, Arlinda L
Wilberforce Univ
Wilberforce, OH

Mc Crory, Ricky L
William Carey Coll
Hattiesburg, MS

Mc Cullagh, Eileen M
Temple Univ
Philadelphia, PA

Mc Cune III, Frank B
Tougaloo Coll
Tougaloo, MS

Mc David, Cary Nicholas
Valdosta St Coll
Valdosta, GA

Mc Dermott, Lisa M
Elmira Coll
Elmira, NY

Mc Donald, Anna H
Daytona Beach Comm Coll
Daytona Beach, FL

Mc Donald, Deborah D
Lincoln Univ
Lincoln Univ, PA

Mc Donald Jr, Thomas
Ga Southern Univ
Statesboro, GA

Mc Donough, John B
Thomas Nelson Comm Coll
Hampton, VA

Mc Evoy, Sharon A
Teikyo Post Univ
Waterbury, CT

Mc Fall, Carol Renee
Memphis St Univ
Memphis, TN

Mc Fall, Patricia A
Glassboro St Coll
Glassboro, NJ

Mc Garry, Andrya M
Embry Riddle
Aeronautical Univ
Daytona Beach, FL

Mc Gee, Deborah A
Broome Comm Coll
Binghamton, NY

Mc Ghee, Steven W
Roane St Comm Coll
Harriman, TN

Mc Glone, Eileen R
Radford Univ
Radford, VA

Mc Griff, Russell O
Morehouse Coll
Atlanta, GA

Mc Gruder, Jonathan
City Univ Of Ny
Queensbrough
New York, NY

Mc Guigan, Christine
Ann
William Paterson Coll
Wayne, NJ

Mc Hayle, Mark M
Cumberland County
Coll
Vineland, NJ

Mc Inerney Jr, John J
Duquesne Univ
Pittsburgh, PA

Mc Innis, Lisa J
City Univ Of Ny
Baruch Coll
New York, NY

Mc Intire, Sherri L
Univ Of Akron
Akron, OH

Mc Intosh, Clara
Cumberland Coll
Williamsburg, KY

Mc Intosh, J Randall
Mayland Comm Coll
Spruce Pine, NC

Mc Inturff, Natalie F
East Tn St Univ
Johnson City, TN

Mc Jilton Jr, Robert R
Coppin St Coll
Baltimore, MD

Mc Kahan, Robert C
Fl A & M Univ
Tallahassee, FL

Mc Kee, David R
Bristol Univ
Bristol, TN

Mc Kee, Sheila S
Univ Of South Al
Mobile, AL

Mc Kellar, Dianna L
Christopher Newport
Coll
Newport News, VA

Mc Kellar, Preston L
Christopher Newport
Coll
Newport News, VA

Mc Kenna, Patricia J
Daemen Coll
Amherst, NY

Mc Kenzie, Carie J
Atlanta Christian Coll
East Point, GA

Mc Kenzie, Lori A
Univ Of Tn At Martin
Martin, TN

Mc Keon, Bernadette M
S U N Y Coll Of Tech
At Frmgdl
Farmingdale, NY

Mc Kibben, Bobbie L
Fl International Univ
Miami, FL

Mc Kinley, Elnore M
Al A & M Univ
Normal, AL

Mc Kinney, Harold L
Duquesne Univ
Pittsburgh, PA

Mc Kinney Jr, Howard
Middle Tn St Univ
Murfreesboro, TN

Mc Kinney, Pamela M
Bloomfield Coll
Bloomfield, NJ

Mc Kinstry, Barry L
Brewer St Jr Coll
Fayette, AL

Mc Kinzie, Monique
Shaw Univ
Raleigh, NC

Mc Kitrick, Kristin L
Anderson Coll
Anderson, SC

Mc Kitrick Jr, Robert
Christopher Newport
Coll
Newport News, VA

Mc Knight, Joi M
Bethune Cookman Coll
Daytona Beach, FL

Mc Laughlin, Timothy
Catawba Valley Comm
Coll
Hickory, NC

Mc Laughlin, Tracy J
Palm Beach Comm Coll
Lake Worth, FL

Mc Laurin, Tanya T
Johnson C Smith Univ
Charlotte, NC

Mc Lean, Carolyn H
Gaston Coll
Dallas, NC

Mc Lean, Jennifer L
Bethany Coll
Bethany, WV

Mc Lendon, Sylvia C
Morris Brown Coll
Atlanta, GA

Mc Leod, Veronica P
Bloomfield Coll
Bloomfield, NJ

Mc Millan, Deborah E
Univ Of Pittsburgh
Pittsburgh, PA

Mc Millan, Shelly Christine
Gaston Coll
Dallas, NC

Mc Millan, Susan D
Univ Of Nc At Greensboro
Greensboro, NC

Mc Miller Jr, Love V
Al A & M Univ
Normal, AL

Mc Minn, Melinda B
S U N Y Coll At Fredonia
Fredonia, NY

Mc Minn, Varsha B
Union Univ
Jackson, TN

Mc Mullen, Erin M
S U N Y Coll At Fredonia
Fredonia, NY

Mc Murphy, Matthew
Villanova Univ
Villanova, PA

Mc Nair, Rebecca
William Carey Coll
Hattiesburg, MS

Mc Neal, Kenneth A
Ms St Univ
Miss State, MS

Mc Neal, Michelyn Rae
Valdosta St Coll
Valdosta, GA

Mc Neil, Mary L
Univ Of Ga
Athens, GA

Mc Neil, Nicolie M
Temple Univ
Philadelphia, PA

Mc Phee, Presleith Y
Nova Univ
Ft Lauderdale, FL

Mc Queen, Michael S
Draughons Jr Coll Nashville
Nashville, TN

Mc Queen-Goss, Sharon Kay
Kent St Univ Stark Cmps
North Canton, OH

Mc Querrey, Sandra L
George Mason Univ
Fairfax, VA

Mc Rae, Alexis N
Lincoln Univ
Lincoln Univ, PA

Mc Reed, Wendy L
Al St Univ
Montgomery, AL

Mc Reynolds Jr, John T
Ms St Univ
Miss State, MS

Mc Tighe, Mary Anne
Saint Vincents Coll & Seminary
Latrobe, PA

Mc Whorter, Darren E
Union Coll
Barbourville, KY

Mdigos-Mulli, Samuel
Hudson Valley Comm Coll
Troy, NY

Meade, Michele L
Ga Southern Univ
Statesboro, GA

Meade, Michelle A
Loyola Coll In Md
Baltimore, MD

Meadows, Lynecia A
Alderson Broaddus Coll
Philippi, WV

Mearns, Melissa M
Methodist Coll
Fayetteville, NC

Mears, Monifa D
Bloomfield Coll
Bloomfield, NJ

Meau, Amelia Man Chu
Univ Of Nh Plymouth St Coll
Plymouth, NH

Mechas, Anthony M
Davis & Elkins Coll
Elkins, WV

Medina, Brian F
Teikyo Post Univ
Waterbury, CT

Medina, Zenaides A
City Univ Of Ny Coll Staten Is
Staten Island, NY

Medlock, Celeste V M
Cheyney Univ Of Pa
Cheyney, PA

Medwynter, Clive G
Nova Univ
Ft Lauderdale, FL

Mee, Christopher A
Nyack Coll
Nyack, NY

Meeks, Patty L
Hocking Tech Coll
Nelsonville, OH

Meeler, Jennifer A
Longwood Coll
Farmville, VA

Meenan, Katherine E
Le Moyne Coll
Syracuse, NY

Mehta, Heeta
Beckley Coll
Beckley, WV

Mei, Hong
City Univ Of Ny La Guard Coll
Long Island Cty, NY

Meister, Erin S
Anne Arundel Comm Coll
Arnold, MD

Melba, Ortiz Archilla
Caribbean Univ
Bayamon, PR

Melchiorre Jr, Louis P
Philadelphia Coll Pharm
& Sci
Philadelphia, PA

Melei, Steven Edward
Fl St Univ
Tallahassee, FL

Melendez Rodriguez,
Ileana
Univ Politecnica De Pr
Hato Rey, PR

Melendez, Raphael J
City Univ Of Ny
Baruch Coll
New York, NY

Meliski, Mary C
Hudson Valley Comm
Coll
Troy, NY

Mello, Brooke
Univ Of Ma At
Amherst
Amherst, MA

Melovitz, Cheryl A
Univ Of Med &
Dentistry Of Nj
Newark, NJ

Melson, Melissa A
Wilmington Coll
New Castle, DE

Melton, Cynthia L
Volunteer St Comm Coll
Gallatin, TN

Melton, Gabriele
Fl St Univ
Tallahassee, FL

Melvin, Bobby E
Alcorn St Univ
Lorman, MS

Melvin, Christopher M
Johnson C Smith Univ
Charlotte, NC

Menarchick, Catherine
S U N Y Coll Of Tech
At Alfred
Alfred, NY

Menard, Karen S
Elms Coll
Chicopee, MA

Mencarelli, Victor A
D Youville Coll
Buffalo, NY

Mendez Rivera, Bibiana
Inter Amer Univ Pr
Hato Rey
Hato Rey, PR

Mendez, Alvaro F
Univ Of Miami
Coral Gables, FL

Mendez, Marisol
Inter Amer Univ Pr San
German
San German, PR

Mendez-Rivera, Carmen
Catholic Univ Of Pr
Ponce, PR

Mendoza, Bernice M
Univ Of Pr Cayey Univ
Coll
Cayey, PR

Mendoza, Carmen F
Radford Univ
Radford, VA

Mendoza, Evelyn
Univ Politecnica De Pr
Hato Rey, PR

Mendoza, Mayra I
Univ Politecnica De Pr
Hato Rey, PR

Menedez, Daniel
Fl International Univ
Miami, FL

Mentgen, Patricia J
Memphis St Univ
Memphis, TN

Mercado Toro, Pablo E
Inter Amer Univ Pr San
German
San German, PR

Mercado, Awdelyn
Univ Of Pr At
Mayaguez
Mayaguez, PR

Mercado, Doris E
Inter Amer Univ Pr
Hato Rey
Hato Rey, PR

Mercado, Hilsa E
Inter Amer Univ Pr San
German
San German, PR

Merced Ramos, Mayra
Univ Of Pr Cayey Univ
Coll
Cayey, PR

Mercer, Terry B
Christopher Newport
Coll
Newport News, VA

Merena, Ann P
Villanova Univ
Villanova, PA

Mergl, Michele L
Suffolk Comm Coll
Eastern Cmps
Riverhead, NY

Meriwether, Candi R
Howard Univ
Washington, DC

Merk, Holly J
Holy Family Coll
Philadelphia, PA

Merkle, Melissa L
Univ Of Sc At
Columbia
Columbia, SC

Merritt, Tanya L
Mount Olive Coll
Mount Olive, NC

Mersman, Elizabeth N
Univ Of Sc At
Columbia
Columbia, SC

Meshotto, Kimberly R
Middle Tn St Univ
Murfreesboro, TN

Messenger, Thomas J
Springfield Tech Comm
Coll
Springfield, MA

Messer, Rayford D
Western Piedmont
Comm Coll
Morganton, NC

Messer, Rhonda M
Univ Of Nc At Chapel
Hill
Chapel Hill, NC

Messick, Scott M
Bowie St Univ
Bowie, MD

Messina, Diane M
Lesley Coll
Cambridge, MA

Messmer, Michele C
Ga St Univ
Atlanta, GA

Mestre, Adelaida S
Hillsborough Comm
Coll
Tampa, FL

Metz, Michael T
Oberlin Coll
Oberlin, OH

Meyers, Corey
Life Coll
Marietta, GA

Mezquida, Armando
Luis
Saint Thomas Univ
Miami, FL

Miceri, Diana
Pa St Univ Delaware
Cty Cmps
Media, PA

Michael, Danyel J
Defiance Coll
Defiance, OH

Michel, Edward
City Univ Of Ny
Baruch Coll
New York, NY

Mickler Jr, Johnny M
Al A & M Univ
Normal, AL

Middleton, Elaine M
Union Inst
Cincinnati, OH

Middleton, Juanice G
Fl A & M Univ
Tallahassee, FL

Midgley, Diana L
Ringling School Of Art
Sarasota, FL

Miga, Mike A
S U N Y Coll Of Tech
At Alfred
Alfred, NY

Miglino, Kelly J
Dowling Coll
Oakdale Li, NY

Milburn, Debora L
Univ Of Miami
Coral Gables, FL

Miles, Deirdre U
Duquesne Univ
Pittsburgh, PA

Miller, Amy S
Bridgewater Coll
Bridgewater, VA

Miller, Anna G
Interdenominational
Theo Ctr
Atlanta, GA

Miller, Chantel E
Miami Jacobs Jr Coll
Of Bus
Dayton, OH

Miller, Christy G
Univ Of West Fl
Pensacola, FL

Miller, Connie Walton
Univ Of Al At
Birmingham
Birmingham, AL

Miller, David P
Garrett Comm Coll
Mchenry, MD

Miller, Elizabeth A
Pa St Univ Main Cmps
University Pk, PA

Miller, Herbert A
Northeast State Tech
Comm Coll
Blountville, TN

Miller, Ingrid N
Wagner Coll
Staten Island, NY

Miller, Jacquie M
Middle Tn St Univ
Murfreesboro, TN

Miller, Jewel V
Glassboro St Coll
Glassboro, NJ

Miller, Julieanne L
Atlantic Comm Coll
Mays Landing, NJ

Miller, Kim A
Univ Of Med &
Dentistry Of Nj
Newark, NJ

Miller, Kristin M
Univ Of Akron
Akron, OH

Miller, Melissa A
Lindsey Wilson Coll
Columbia, KY

Miller, Melissa L
Radford Univ
Radford, VA

Miller, Nancy K
Catawba Valley Comm
Coll
Hickory, NC

Miller, Nicholas M
Union Coll
Barbourville, KY

Miller, Paul J
Univ Of Med &
Dentistry Of Nj
Newark, NJ

Miller Jr, Ronald Lee
Columbia Union Coll
Takoma Park, MD

Miller, S Ayanna
Fl A & M Univ
Tallahassee, FL

Miller, Sheryl Lynn
Va Commonwealth Univ
Richmond, VA

Miller, Tammy M
Western Ky Univ
Bowling Green, KY

Miller, Timothy E
Ms St Univ
Miss State, MS

Miller, Tonya A
Hampton Univ
Hampton, VA

Milley, Tammy M
Univ Of Nh Plymouth St Coll
Plymouth, NH

Millington, Liesa P
City Univ Of Ny City Coll
New York, NY

Mills, Anna M
Anne Arundel Comm Coll
Arnold, MD

Mills, Jennifer L
Univ Of Southern Ms
Hattiesburg, MS

Mills, Tammy R
Beckley Coll
Beckley, WV

Milner, Kelly A
Saint Leo Coll
Saint Leo, FL

Mims, Jacqueline L
Univ Of Md At Eastern Shore
Princess Anne, MD

Mincavage, Karen M
Univ Of Nc At Chapel Hill
Chapel Hill, NC

Minguel, Tino F
Fl A & M Univ
Tallahassee, FL

Minor, Patricia L
Norfolk St Univ
Norfolk, VA

Minott, Mark L
Duquesne Univ
Pittsburgh, PA

Minson, Holly A
Richard Bland Coll
Petersburg, VA

Minter, Crystal A
Middle Tn St Univ
Murfreesboro, TN

Minton, Jeffrey C
East Carolina Univ
Greenville, NC

Mirabal, Alejandro J
Fl International Univ
Miami, FL

Miranda, Dorys D
Univ Of Pr At Rio Piedras
Rio Piedras, PR

Miranda, Evelyn
Fl International Univ
Miami, FL

Mirante, Audra M
Clarkson Univ
Potsdam, NY

Mirolli, Karen T
Va Commonwealth Univ
Richmond, VA

Misunas, Anissa L
Providence Coll
Providence, RI

Mitchell, Bayyinah M
Strayer Coll
Washington, DC

Mitchell, Crystal A
Longwood Coll
Farmville, VA

Mitchell, Dawn Victoria
Wv Wesleyan Coll
Buckhannon, WV

Mitchell, Emerson W
Univ Of Rochester
Rochester, NY

Mitchell, Faith C
City Univ Of Ny Queensbrough
New York, NY

Mitchell, James J
Univ Of West Fl
Pensacola, FL

Mitchell, Tracie D
Univ Of Nc At Charlotte
Charlotte, NC

Miyajima, Hiroshige
Valdosta St Coll
Valdosta, GA

Mjorndal, Lena C
Univ Of Al At Birmingham
Birmingham, AL

Mobley, Janet L
Univ Of Southern Ms
Hattiesburg, MS

Moderski, Mark M
Univ Of New Haven
West Haven, CT

Modzelewski, Linda A
Glassboro St Coll
Glassboro, NJ

Mohabir, Usha
City Univ Of Ny La Guard Coll
Long Island Cty, NY

Mohammed, Mohammed Yusuf
Howard Univ
Washington, DC

Mohammed, Nikki N
Fl St Univ
Tallahassee, FL

Mohammed, Shaliza
Embry Riddle Aeronautical Univ
Daytona Beach, FL

Mohd Ali, Ismail
Memphis St Univ
Memphis, TN

Mohd-Razalli, Ahmad-Albakree
Univ Of Miami
Coral Gables, FL

Mohseni, Majid
Southern Coll Of Tech
Marietta, GA

Moise, May C
Inter Amer Univ Pr San German
San German, PR

Mojica Morales, Zoe M
Inter Amer Univ Pr Hato Rey
Hato Rey, PR

Mojica-Flores, Elizabeth
Univ Of Pr Medical Sciences
San Juan, PR

Molenda, Sally M
George Washington Univ
Washington, DC

Molfetta, Frank S
Carnegie Mellon Univ
Pittsburgh, PA

Molina Roque, Lynnette
Inter Amer Univ Pr Hato Rey
Hato Rey, PR

Molina, Maritza
Univ Of Pr At Rio Piedras
Rio Piedras, PR

Molina, Michelle
Inter Amer Univ Pr San Juan
Hato Rey, PR

Monaco, Jennifer L
Duquesne Univ
Pittsburgh, PA

Monaco, Steven J
Carnegie Mellon Univ
Pittsburgh, PA

Monahan, Susan A
Mount Aloysius Jr Coll
Cresson, PA

Monell Cruz, Javier
Inter Amer Univ Pr Hato Rey
Hato Rey, PR

Moneypenny, Donna Lee
Beckley Coll
Beckley, WV

Moniruzzaman, A B M
S U N Y At Stony Brook
Stony Brook, NY

Moniz, Lisa A
Suffolk Univ
Boston, MA

Monks, Joseph C
Slippery Rock Univ
Slippery Rock, PA

Monroe, Jennifer
Wilberforce Univ
Wilberforce, OH

Monroe, Meredith Lee
Univ Of Nc At Charlotte
Charlotte, NC

Monroy, Marta R
Miami Dade Comm Coll North
Miami, FL

Monserrate Morera, Marisol
Univ Of Pr At Mayaguez
Mayaguez, PR

Montalbano III, Carmine
Bloomfield Coll
Bloomfield, NJ

Montalvo Castro, Ivelisse
Caribbean Univ
Bayamon, PR

Montalvo Toledo, Helvia
Inter Amer Univ Pr San German
San German, PR

Montalvo, Michele
Inter Amer Univ Pr Hato Rey
Hato Rey, PR

Montana, Melissa T
Saint Johns Univ
Jamaica, NY

Montes Aviles, Roberto
Univ Politecnica De Pr
Hato Rey, PR

Montes Colon, Monica
Inter Amer Univ Pr Hato Rey
Hato Rey, PR

Montes Vivar, Dora M
Inter Amer Univ Pr San German
San German, PR

Montes, Danielle K
Fl International Univ
Miami, FL

Montgomery, Albertnetta R
Univ Of South Al
Mobile, AL

Montgomery, Monique
Hillsborough Comm Coll
Tampa, FL

Montilla, Maria Elena
Georgetown Univ
Washington, DC

Moody Jr, James Stephen
City Univ Of Ny Baruch Coll
New York, NY

Moody, Tricia J
Shaw Univ
Raleigh, NC

Moore, Able A
Savannah St Coll
Savannah, GA

Moore, Cecilia A
Univ Of Sc At Columbia
Columbia, SC

Moore, Christina L
Commonwealth Coll
Norfolk, VA

Moore, Heather S
Univ Of Ga
Athens, GA

Moore, Kathy C
Anson Comm Coll
Ansonville, NC

Moore, Kayla M
Marshall University
Huntington, WV

Moore, Laquita M
Univ Of Rochester
Rochester, NY

Moore Jr, Leonard Daniel
Spartanburg Methodist Coll
Spartanburg, SC

Moore, M Ashley
Barry Univ
Miami, FL

Moore, Mae W
Fayetteville St Univ
Fayetteville, NC

Moore, Melissa K
Univ Of North Fl
Jacksonville, FL

Moore, Patricia A
Livingston Univ
Livingston, AL

Moore, Peggy J
Jersey City St Coll
Jersey City, NJ

Moore, Robin M
Xavier Univ
Cincinnati, OH

Moore, Shannon V
Clemson Univ
Clemson, SC

Moore, Tina L
Central Al Comm Coll
Alexander City, AL

Moore, Tracy D
Columbia Greene Comm Coll
Hudson, NY

Moore, Trevan C
Al A & M Univ
Normal, AL

Moore, Verita R
Savannah St Coll
Savannah, GA

Moore, Zachary D
Univ Of Sc At Columbia
Columbia, SC

Moosa, Shavzab J
Ny Institute Of Tech
Ny City
New York, NY

Moraitis Jr, George R
United States Naval Academy
Annapolis, MD

Morales, Cardona Jose Ivan
Univ Politecnica De Pr
Hato Rey, PR

Morales, Gricel
Univ Politecnica De Pr
Hato Rey, PR

Morales, Marcia
S U N Y Coll Of Tech At Frmgdl
Farmingdale, NY

Morales, Mario J
Miami Dade Comm Coll South
Miami, FL

Morales, Patricia E
Fl International Univ
Miami, FL

Morales Jr, Robert D
Mount Saint Mary Coll
Newburgh, NY

Morano, Michael W
City Univ Of Ny Grad School
New York, NY

Moratelli, Jacqueline S
Cumberland County Coll
Vineland, NJ

Moravitz, Carla D
Va Polytechnic Inst & St Univ
Blacksburg, VA

Moreira, Maria E
Saint Thomas Univ
Miami, FL

Morel, Judith
Univ Of Miami
Coral Gables, FL

Morelock, Linda A
Univ Of Sc At Columbia
Columbia, SC

Moreno, Michael C
Univ Of Al At Birmingham
Birmingham, AL

Morgan, Deborah A
Germanna Comm Coll
Locust Grove, VA

Morgan, Felicia D
Alcorn St Univ
Lorman, MS

Morgan, Glenda A
Savannah St Coll
Savannah, GA

Morgan, Jeffrey D
Univ Of Sc At Columbia
Columbia, SC

Morgan, Lisa L
Indiana Univ Of Pa
Indiana, PA

Morgan, Michele R
Marshall University
Huntington, WV

Morgan, Roni L
Union Univ School Of Nursing
Memphis, TN

Morgan, Shawn A
Northeastern Christian Jr Coll
Villanova, PA

Morgan, Troy C
Auburn Univ At Montgomery
Montgomery, AL

Morgison, Tchula L
Va Polytechnic Inst & St Univ
Blacksburg, VA

Morin, Mary T
Wagner Coll
Staten Island, NY

Morrill, Mary E
Utica Coll Of Syracuse Univ
Utica, NY

Morris, Jean
Owensboro Jr Coll Of Bus
Owensboro, KY

Morris, Shirlette R
Albany St Coll
Albany, GA

Morris, Susan L
Glassboro St Coll
Glassboro, NJ

Morris, Timothy S
Univ Of Sc At Columbia
Columbia, SC

Morrison, Julia L
Middle Tn St Univ
Murfreesboro, TN

Morse, Carlin P
Al A & M Univ
Normal, AL

Morton, Jonathan Lee
Birmingham Southern Coll
Birmingham, AL

Moseley, Donald
Norfolk St Univ
Norfolk, VA

Moses, Ari H
Ramapo Coll Of Nj
Mahwah, NJ

Moshtaghi, Mahsa
Univ Of Al At Birmingham
Birmingham, AL

Mosley, Rhonda L
Univ Of Miami
Coral Gables, FL

Mosley, Tammy R
Univ Of Southern Ms
Hattiesburg, MS

Moss, Racquel M
Hampton Univ
Hampton, VA

Moss, Tracy L
Al St Univ
Montgomery, AL

Mostafavi, Armaghan Amy
Boston Univ
Boston, MA

Motley III, Albert E
Old Dominion Univ
Norfolk, VA

Motley, Byron M
Middle Tn St Univ
Murfreesboro, TN

Mourad, David Lawrence
Univ Of New Haven
West Haven, CT

Moyka, Ana S
Rensselaer Polytechnic Inst
Troy, NY

Mozee, Thomacina F
Alcorn St Univ
Lorman, MS

Mpinga, Peter
Allen Univ
Columbia, SC

Mueck, Andrew G
S U N Y Coll Of Tech At Frmgdl
Farmingdale, NY

Mughal, Shazia P
Edison Comm Coll
Fort Myers, FL

Mulanax, Tina L
Cedarville Coll
Cedarville, OH

Mularz, Mary
Atlantic Comm Coll
Mays Landing, NJ

Mulholland, Daniel J
City Univ Of Ny Baruch Coll
New York, NY

Mulkey, Lora L
Oh Univ-Southern Cmps
Ironton, OH

Mullarkey, J Scott
S U N Y Coll Of Tech At Delhi
Delhi, NY

Mullings, Melinda J
Savannah St Coll
Savannah, GA

Mullins, B Irene
Univ Of Va Clinch Valley Coll
Wise, VA

Mullins, Rebecca A
Lees Coll
Jackson, KY

Mullins, Robert S
Univ Of Al At Huntsville
Huntsville, AL

Mullins, Stuart R
Univ Of Va Clinch Valley Coll
Wise, VA

Mullray, William T
Merrimack Coll
North Andover, MA

Mulvany, Cristine J
Univ Of North Fl
Jacksonville, FL

Mulzac, Dianna M
Howard Univ
Washington, DC

Mumpower, Amy N
Patrick Henry Comm Coll
Martinsville, VA

Mundahl, Merrilee M
Eckerd Coll
St Petersburg, FL

Muniz, Adelaida M
Univ Of Miami
Coral Gables, FL

Muniz, Alicia
Fl International Univ
Miami, FL

Munnerlyn, Ginger R
Univ Of Sc At Columbia
Columbia, SC

Munnings, Monique M
City Univ Of Ny City Coll
New York, NY

Munoz, Sandra E
City Univ Of Ny La Guard Coll
Long Island Cty, NY

Murchie, Carolyn
Providence Coll
Providence, RI

Murdock, Melissa A
Alcorn St Univ
Lorman, MS

Murkis, Paul A
City Univ Of Ny Baruch Coll
New York, NY

Murphy, Charlotte W
Univ Of Al At Birmingham
Birmingham, AL

Murphy, Dana S
Union Univ
Jackson, TN

Murphy, Deannia J
Roane St Comm Coll
Harriman, TN

Murphy, Ethel I
Wilmington Coll
New Castle, DE

Murphy, Heather M
Hillsborough Comm Coll
Tampa, FL

Murphy, Jennifer E
Georgian Court Coll
Lakewood, NJ

Murphy, John Charles
Villanova Univ
Villanova, PA

Murphy, Karla E
Va St Univ
Petersburg, VA

Murphy, Marlo M
Le Moyne Coll
Syracuse, NY

Murphy, Patricia E
City Univ Of Ny Baruch Coll
New York, NY

Murphy Jr, Ronald L
Comm Coll Algny Co Algny Cmps
Pittsburgh, PA

Murphy, Torrii Alonza
Nc Agri & Tech St Univ
Greensboro, NC

Murphy, Xavier A D
Miami Dade Comm Coll North
Miami, FL

Murray, Kelly C
Ashland Comm Coll
Ashland, KY

Murray, Lori J
Memphis St Univ
Memphis, TN

Murray, Melvia M
Coppin St Coll
Baltimore, MD

Murray, Uwada M
City Univ Of Ny City Coll
New York, NY

Murry, Debra Yvette
Lane Coll
Jackson, TN

Musharraf, Bilal
Univ Of Miami
Coral Gables, FL

Musolino, Antoinette
City Univ Of Ny Baruch Coll
New York, NY

Musselman, Robin A
George Mason Univ
Fairfax, VA

Musser, Marilee A
Fl St Univ
Tallahassee, FL

Mustafic, Nezir
Fordham Univ
Bronx, NY

Mutzfeld, Christe L
Daytona Beach Comm Coll
Daytona Beach, FL

Myer, Dina F
Ms Univ For Women
Columbus, MS

Myers, Erin N
Oh Univ
Athens, OH

Myers, Stephen C
Oh Univ-Southern Cmps
Ironton, OH

Myers, Vonda K
Ashland Comm Coll
Ashland, KY

Myles, Victoria E
Marywood Coll
Scranton, PA

Myrick, Tina N
Central St Univ
Wilberforce, OH

Mzwakhe Msimanga, Frans
Teikyo Post Univ
Waterbury, CT

Naaman, Marwan G
Univ Of Miami
Coral Gables, FL

Nabutete, Marjorie F
Bergen Comm Coll
Paramus, NJ

Nails, Stephanie R
Lincoln Memorial Univ
Harrogate, TN

Nakagami, Kyoko
Univ Of Nc At Charlotte
Charlotte, NC

Nakamura, Kazuyo
Univ Of New Haven
West Haven, CT

Nakonechny, Walter S
Univ Of Ct
Storrs, CT

Nalbone, Leslie J
Allegheny Coll
Meadville, PA

Nalbone, Sherry
Northeast State Tech Comm Coll
Blountville, TN

Nance, David K
Univ Of Al At Birmingham
Birmingham, AL

Nangle, Kevin M
Temple Univ
Philadelphia, PA

Naragon, Molly L
Tn Temple Univ
Chattanooga, TN

Narese, Nicole
Saint Peters Coll
Jersey City, NJ

Nary, Sean J
Castleton St Coll
Castleton, VT

Nash, Toyia G
Clark Atlanta Univ
Atlanta, GA

Nason, Keith
Nc Agri & Tech St
Univ
Greensboro, NC

Natalini, Michele Marie
City Univ Of Ny
Baruch Coll
New York, NY

Nater Nater, Margarita
Inter Amer Univ Pr
Hato Rey
Hato Rey, PR

Nation, Heather L M
Fl International Univ
Miami, FL

Nattiline Dunstan, Cheryl-Ann
Barry Univ
Miami, FL

Naugle, Amy M
Radford Univ
Radford, VA

Navarre, Lenell Q
Jackson St Univ
Jackson, MS

Navarro, Gladys C
Georgetown Univ
Washington, DC

Navarro, Yayleene
Calzada
Univ Of P R Bayamon
Tech Univ
Bayamon, PR

Navin, Terence F
Villanova Univ
Villanova, PA

Nayak, Laxmeesh D
Yale Univ
New Haven, CT

Naylor, Michele L
Methodist Coll
Fayetteville, NC

Naylor, Nan W
Union Univ
Jackson, TN

Nazareno, Ann
Strayer Coll
Washington, DC

Nazareno, Darren R
Old Dominion Univ
Norfolk, VA

Nazario Detres, Dario
Inter Amer Univ Pr San
German
San German, PR

Nazario, May-Ling Del
Inter Amer Univ Pr San
German
San German, PR

Ndoye, Makhtar
Ny Univ
New York, NY

Neal, Linda A
Norfolk St Univ
Norfolk, VA

Neal, Sheila R
Radford Univ
Radford, VA

Neal, Wendy M
Tn Temple Univ
Chattanooga, TN

Nealy, Lisa N
Jackson St Univ
Jackson, MS

Nebot-Marin, Carlos
Alberto
Miami Dade Comm Coll
Miami, FL

Nedoma, Timothy K
Univ Of Sc At Aiken
Aiken, SC

Neel, John F
Anderson Coll
Anderson, SC

Neeley Jr, Frank
Patrick Henry Comm
Coll
Martinsville, VA

Neely, Edward M
Washington & Jefferson
Coll
Washington, PA

Negron, Luis O
Univ Of Pr Medical
Sciences
San Juan, PR

Negron-Aponte, Jose A
Univ Of Pr At Rio
Piedras
Rio Piedras, PR

Negron-Gonzalez, Marie
Del C
Bayamon Central Univ
Bayamon, PR

Nelson, Audrey E
City Univ Of Ny
Queensbrough
New York, NY

Nelson, Jack D
Saint Thomas Univ
Miami, FL

Nelson, Kelvin W
Morehouse Coll
Atlanta, GA

Nelson, Patty S
Southern W V Comm
Coll
Logan, WV

Nelson, Samartian M
Faulkner St Jr Coll
Bay Minette, AL

Nelson Jr, Thomas Boye
Strayer Coll
Washington, DC

Nelson, Tracy D
Norfolk St Univ
Norfolk, VA

Nelson, William J
Univ Of Southern Ms
Hattiesburg, MS

Neptune Rivera, Vivian
Univ Of Pr At Rio
Piedras
Rio Piedras, PR

Nester, Michael B
Univ Of Nc At
Charlotte
Charlotte, NC

Nestor, Nestor B
Lycoming Coll
Williamsport, PA

Neubeck, Tamatha J
Oh Univ-Southern Cmps
Ironton, OH

Nevel, Michael A
Bloomsburg Univ Of Pa
Bloomsburg, PA

Neville, Diane S
Clayton St Coll
Morrow, GA

Newby, Sharon L
Alcorn St Univ
Lorman, MS

Newcombe, Richard E
Ny Inst Tech Old
Westbury
Old Westbury, NY

Newell, Peter T
Univ Of Miami
Coral Gables, FL

Newkirk, Deseree
Saint Josephs Coll New
York
Brooklyn, NY

Newman, Cynthia L
Union Univ
Jackson, TN

Newman, Kelcey L
Norfolk St Univ
Norfolk, VA

Newman, Melissa S
Webber Coll
Babson Park, FL

Newman, Michele L
Mount Saint Mary Coll
Newburgh, NY

Newsome, Gloria R
Norfolk St Univ
Norfolk, VA

Ng, Huey Lin
Oh Wesleyan Univ
Delaware, OH

Ng, Kwai-Fong Raina
Muskingum Coll
New Concord, OH

Ng, Rigoberto
Fl International Univ
Miami, FL

Ng, Siu H
Univ Of The Dist Of
Columbia
Washington, DC

Nguyen, Han D
Norwalk St Tech Coll
Norwalk, CT

Nguyen, Huyenlinh
Truc
George Mason Univ
Fairfax, VA

Nguyen, Jay Phuong L
Ny Univ
New York, NY

Nguyen, Minhcuong C
Univ Of Louisville
Louisville, KY

Nguyen, Minhtam C
Univ Of Louisville
Louisville, KY

Nguyen, Trucmai C
Univ Of Louisville
Louisville, KY

Niboh, Martin
Mbangtang
Kent St Univ Kent
Cmps
Kent, OH

Nichols, Ann B
Coker Coll
Hartsville, SC

Nichols, Connie F
Middle Tn St Univ
Murfreesboro, TN

Nichols, Katrina M
Alcorn St Univ
Lorman, MS

Nichols, Sharon L
Bob Jones Univ
Greenville, SC

Nichols, Tiffany A
Belmont Abbey Coll
Belmont, NC

Nicholson, David A
Truett Mc Connell Coll
Cleveland, GA

Nicholson, Heather R
Univ Of Southern Ms
Hattiesburg, MS

Nicolay, Kathleen H
Univ Of Md Baltimore
Prof Schl
Baltimore, MD

Nicome, Patricia
City Univ Of Ny City
Coll
New York, NY

Nida, Lesa L
Marshall University
Huntington, WV

Nido, Rafael J
Emory Univ
Atlanta, GA

Nielsen, Jeffrey A
Albertus Magnus Coll
New Haven, CT

Nieman, James
Univ Of Nc At
Charlotte
Charlotte, NC

Nieves, Jose S
Univ Of Pr At Rio
Piedras
Rio Piedras, PR

Nieves, Karen
Daytona Beach Comm
Coll
Daytona Beach, FL

Niklas, Christian E
Kent St Univ Kent
Cmps
Kent, OH

Niles, Lynn E
Ma Inst Of Tech
Cambridge, MA

Nischan, Melissa L
Franklin And Marshall
Coll
Lancaster, PA

Nix, Raleshia L
Univ Of Montevallo
Montevallo, AL

Nixon, Alisa L
Al A & M Univ
Normal, AL

Nkosi, Mandla M
Univ Of The Dist Of Columbia
Washington, DC

Nnadi, Michael C
Howard Univ
Washington, DC

Noah, Jennifer R
The Johns Hopkins Univ
Baltimore, MD

Nobles, Toni R
Beaufort County Comm Coll
Washington, NC

Noblin, Tammy R
Richard Bland Coll
Petersburg, VA

Nobrega, William K
Providence Coll
Providence, RI

Nocentino, Stefanie
Drexel Univ
Philadelphia, PA

Nocera, Kristi
Glassboro St Coll
Glassboro, NJ

Nohara, Michiko
Brevard Coll
Brevard, NC

Nomi, Aki
Converse Coll
Spartanburg, SC

Nordan, Eric C
William Carey Coll
Hattiesburg, MS

Nordberg, Carrie Lynn
Atlantic Comm Coll
Mays Landing, NJ

Nordby, Karena S
Radford Univ
Radford, VA

Nordin, Gamal Adlan
Univ Of Miami
Coral Gables, FL

Nordland, Heather L
S U N Y Coll Of Tech At Alfred
Alfred, NY

Noriega-Pagan, Carol I
City Univ Of Ny La Guard Coll
Long Island Cty, NY

Norman, Mark A
De Vry Inst Of Tech
Columbus, OH

Norman, Terri E
Western Carolina Univ
Cullowhee, NC

Norris, Corey L
Morris Brown Coll
Atlanta, GA

Northrop, Christy
Auburn Univ At Auburn
Auburn, AL

Norton, Kevin S
Southern Coll Of Tech
Marietta, GA

Norton, Richard B
Glassboro St Coll
Glassboro, NJ

Norton-Coke, Ethlyn M Mc K
Nova Univ
Ft Lauderdale, FL

Norwood, Candra M
Tougaloo Coll
Tougaloo, MS

Norwood, Doris A
Univ Of Nc At Charlotte
Charlotte, NC

Nuel, Craig E
Cornell Univ Statutory College
Ithaca, NY

Nunez, Rodolfo P
Barry Univ
Miami, FL

Nunley, Jeanetta
Al St Univ
Montgomery, AL

Nuovo, Krista J
S U N Y Coll Of Tech At Frmgdl
Farmingdale, NY

Nusbaum, Lisa C
Md Coll Of Art & Design
Silver Spring, MD

Nutter, Cynthia M
Northeast State Tech Comm Coll
Blountville, TN

Nutting, Rebecca L
Endicott Coll
Beverly, MA

Nwokeafor, Cosmas U
Howard Univ
Washington, DC

Nyarko, Yaw O
Central St Univ
Wilberforce, OH

O Banion, Joy L
Ashland Comm Coll
Ashland, KY

O Brien, Aimee L
Endicott Coll
Beverly, MA

O Brien, Catherine E
Wilmington Coll
New Castle, DE

O Brien, Justin
Inter Amer Univ Pr San German
San German, PR

O Brien, Paulina M
Coll Of The Holy Cross
Worcester, MA

O Connell, Karen J
Duke Univ
Durham, NC

O Connor, Catherine P
Manhattan Coll
Bronx, NY

O Connor, Margaret M
Iona College
New Rochelle, NY

O Connor, Sean P
Iona College
New Rochelle, NY

O Donald III, Arthur J
Holyoke Comm Coll
Holyoke, MA

O Donnell, Sheryl L
D Youville Coll
Buffalo, NY

O Donoghue, Diana L
Providence Coll
Providence, RI

O Hara, Heather M
Cornell Univ Statutory College
Ithaca, NY

O Mara, Patrick J
Manhattan Coll
Bronx, NY

O Neal, Lorry Sunshine
Univ Of Nc At Wilmington
Wilmington, NC

O Neill, Kelly M
Bryant Stratton Bus Inst Roch
Rochester, NY

O Shea, Harmony D
Central Me Medical Center
Lewiston, ME

O Shea, Lisa A
Albertus Magnus Coll
New Haven, CT

O-Saka, Linda B
Univ Of Toledo
Toledo, OH

Oats, La Tonya T
Central Fl Comm Coll
Ocala, FL

Oberholtzer-Meza, E Katrina
Barry Univ
Miami, FL

Ocana-Castillo, Rose M
Caribbean Center For Adv Stds
San Juan, PR

Ocasio, Elvyn D
Inter Amer Univ Pr San German
San German, PR

Odom, Billy G
Spartanburg Methodist Coll
Spartanburg, SC

Odom, Frankie B
Coker Coll
Hartsville, SC

Odom, Sharon R
Roane St Comm Coll
Harriman, TN

Odum, Irene R
Midlands Tech Coll
Columbia, SC

Ogino, Ryoko
Hilbert Coll
Hamburg, NY

Ogueri, Udo Peace
Daytona Beach Comm Coll
Daytona Beach, FL

Ohms, Marshae L
Oh Univ
Athens, OH

Ohtsuka, Yuka
Endicott Coll
Beverly, MA

Okhravi, Simindokht J
Strayer Coll
Washington, DC

Okuyama, Kazuko
Elms Coll
Chicopee, MA

Olaya, Nayibe
City Univ Of Ny La Guard Coll
Long Island Cty, NY

Old III, Ephriam M
Univ Of Tn At Martin
Martin, TN

Oldaker, Jeffrey S
Wv Univ
Morgantown, WV

Olds, Tawana T
Va Union Univ
Richmond, VA

Olesiewicz, Timothy W
Fl International Univ
Miami, FL

Olivencia Petiton, Carmen I
Catholic Univ Of Pr
Ponce, PR

Oliver, Kyle M
Univ Of Fl
Gainesville, FL

Oliver, Linda S
Memphis St Univ
Memphis, TN

Oliver, Lisa D
Bethel Coll
Mckenzie, TN

Oliver, Michelle R
Savannah St Coll
Savannah, GA

Oliver, Shawynne M
Savannah St Coll
Savannah, GA

Oliver, Yvette T
Tn St Univ
Nashville, TN

Olivera, Charles H
Ponce School Of Medicine
Ponce, PR

Oliveros, Yesenia
Saint Thomas Univ
Miami, FL

Ollis, Cindy Y
Western Piedmont Comm Coll
Morganton, NC

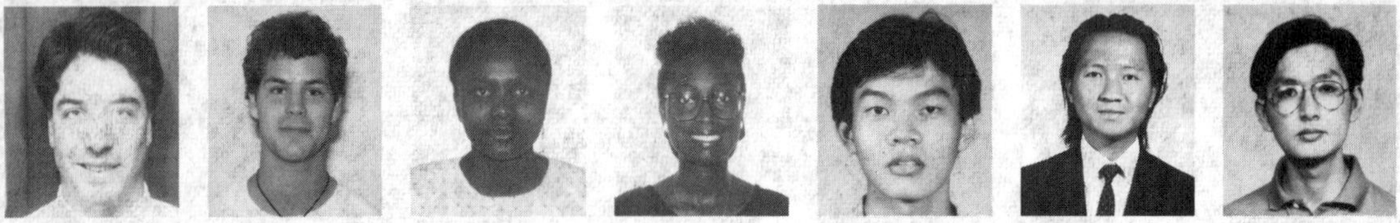

Olsen, Clifford S
S U N Y Coll Of Tech
At Frmgdl
Farmingdale, NY

Olsen, Gregory J
Hudson Valley Comm
Coll
Troy, NY

Olugbodi, Lydia O
Gallaudet Univ
Washington, DC

Omene, Coral O
City Univ Of Ny City
Coll
New York, NY

Ong, Daryl Gim Loo
Columbus Coll Of Art
& Design
Columbus, OH

Ong, Jonathan A
Embry Riddle
Aeronautical Univ
Daytona Beach, FL

Ong, Julian
City Univ Of Ny
Baruch Coll
New York, NY

Ono, Noriko
Univ Of South Al
Mobile, AL

Onufrey, Nicole S
Oh Wesleyan Univ
Delaware, OH

Onuoha, Augustina A
Al A & M Univ
Normal, AL

Onyeuka, Angela A
Cheyney Univ Of Pa
Cheyney, PA

Oppenheimer, Michael
Univ Of Akron
Akron, OH

Oquendo, Aida M
Univ Of Pr At Rio
Piedras
Rio Piedras, PR

Orehgo-Rodriguez,
Nestor
Univ Politecnica De Pr
Hato Rey, PR

Ormsby, Heather E
De Tech & Comm Coll
At Dover
Dover, DE

Orner, Lisa E
Pa St Univ Mont Alto
Cmps
Mont Alto, PA

Orobitg, Marielsa
Inter Amer Univ Pr
Hato Rey
Hato Rey, PR

Orr, Tami L
De Tech & Comm Coll
At Dover
Dover, DE

Orrico Jr, Donald A
Old Dominion Univ
Norfolk, VA

Ortega, Lee Corbin
Newbury Coll
Brookline, MA

Ortega, Maria
Inter Amer Univ Pr San
German
San German, PR

Ortiz Collado, Carlos E
Inter Amer Univ Pr
Hato Rey
Hato Rey, PR

Ortiz Rivera, Eileen
Inter Amer Univ Pr San
German
San German, PR

Ortiz Rosario, Edgardo
Univ Politecnica De Pr
Hato Rey, PR

Ortiz Silva, Lisandra
Inter Amer Univ Pr
Hato Rey
Hato Rey, PR

Ortiz, Annie E
Univ Of Pr Medical
Sciences
San Juan, PR

Ortiz, Carlos E
Inter Amer Univ Pr San
Juan
Hato Rey, PR

Ortiz, Cira D
Hudson County Comm
Coll
Jersey City, NJ

Ortiz, Grisel
Univ Of Pr Cayey Univ
Coll
Cayey, PR

Ortiz, Luis F
Univ Of Pr Medical
Sciences
San Juan, PR

Ortiz, Miguel R
Univ Of Pr At
Mayaguez
Mayaguez, PR

Ortiz, Wanda I
Dowling Coll
Oakdale Li, NY

Ortiz-Ortiz, Sonia M
Bayamon Central Univ
Bayamon, PR

Osakwe, Lucy V
Howard Univ
Washington, DC

Osamor, Eva J
Saint Thomas Univ
Miami, FL

Osborne, J A Terry
Va Commonwealth Univ
Richmond, VA

Osborne, Shawn V
Wallace St Comm Coll
At Selma
Selma, AL

Osegueda, Mauricio E
Fl International Univ
Miami, FL

Osian, Nellie W
Univ Of Nc At
Charlotte
Charlotte, NC

Ote, Yoshino
Elmira Coll
Elmira, NY

Otero Caraballo, Grisel
Univ Politecnica De Pr
Hato Rey, PR

Otero, Lydia E
Bayamon Central Univ
Bayamon, PR

Ott, Jennifier Michelle
Univ Of Sc At
Columbia
Columbia, SC

Ott, Jodi B
Va Commonwealth Univ
Richmond, VA

Ottey, Sandra A
City Univ Of Ny Med
Evers Coll
Brooklyn, NY

Overton, Cheryl A
Longwood Coll
Farmville, VA

Overton, Jean K
Vance Granville Comm
Coll
Henderson, NC

Owen, Laura M
Vance Granville Comm
Coll
Henderson, NC

Owens, Angie
Southwest Va Comm
Coll
Richlands, VA

Owens, Kelly A
Salisbury St Univ
Salisbury, MD

Owens, Pamela
Fort Valley St Coll
Fort Valley, GA

Owens, Rebecca S
Lexington Comm Coll
Lexington, KY

Owens, Tammy R
Rust Coll
Holly Springs, MS

Owoso, Taiwo F
Tuskegee Univ
Tuskegee Inst, AL

Oxendine, Jennifer L
Neumann Coll
Aston, PA

Ozdamar, Ayse C
Southeastern Coll Of
Hlth Sci
N Miami Beach, FL

Paar, Nadine
Glassboro St Coll
Glassboro, NJ

Pabon, Aida I
Univ Of P R Bayamon
Tech Univ
Bayamon, PR

Pace Howard, Sherrie
Lynn
Univ Of Nc At
Greensboro
Greensboro, NC

Pace, Patricia E
Judson Coll
Marion, AL

Pacheco, Josue
Univ Of Pr Medical
Sciences
San Juan, PR

Pacheco, Ramona
Catholic Univ Of Pr
Ponce, PR

Pacheco-Roman, Sonia
Inter Amer Univ Pr San
Juan
Hato Rey, PR

Padamadan, Sarry M
Univ Of Akron
Akron, OH

Padgett, David L
Truett Mc Connell Coll
Cleveland, GA

Padgett Jr, Edward E
Univ Of Sc At
Columbia
Columbia, SC

Padilla, Lymaries
Univ Of Pr At Rio
Piedras
Rio Piedras, PR

Padilla, Mariel
Bayamon Tech Univ
Coll
Bayamon, PR

Padovani, Julio C
Inter Amer Univ Pr San
German
San German, PR

Padron, Otto M
Univ Of Miami
Coral Gables, FL

Padula, Kathleen
Middlesex County Coll
Edison, NJ

Paez, Carlos M
Univ Politecnica De Pr
Hato Rey, PR

Pagan Gonzalez, Ramon
Antonio
Catholic Univ Of Pr
Ponce, PR

Pagan, Angel R
Inter Amer Univ Pr
Hato Rey
Hato Rey, PR

Pagan, Edward M
Boricua Coll
New York, NY

Pagan, Gilberto
Ny Univ
New York, NY

Pagan, Mayra
Univ Of Pr Cayey Univ
Coll
Cayey, PR

Page, Eric John
Schenectady County
Comm Coll
Schenectady, NY

Pagliuca, Domingo A
Univ Of Miami
Coral Gables, FL

Paige, Mark A
Stonehill Coll
North Easton, MA

Palachi, Hilel Ilan
Fl International Univ
Miami, FL

Palacino, Christine
City Univ Of Ny
Queensbrough
New York, NY

Palacio, Marlene
City Univ Of Ny La
Guard Coll
Long Island Cty, NY

Palacios Frau, Aleida M
Inter Amer Univ Pr
Hato Rey
Hato Rey, PR

Palmer, Brian S
S U N Y Coll Of A &
T Morrisvl
Morrisville, NY

Palmer, Julie W
Union Univ
Jackson, TN

Palmer, Karen A
City Univ Of Ny City
Coll
New York, NY

Palsson, Magnus
Fl International Univ
Miami, FL

Pamon Jr, Stephen R
Morehouse Coll
Atlanta, GA

Panagiotopoulos,
Constantina
Montgomery Coll At
Rockville
Rockville, MD

Pandeya, Vandana
King Coll
Bristol, TN

Panfil, Katherine
Kent St Univ Kent
Cmps
Kent, OH

Panno, Tina M
Univ Of Cincinnati
Cincinnati, OH

Paoli, Giovanni A
Univ Of New Haven
West Haven, CT

Papadopoulou, Corinna
Univ Of Miami
Coral Gables, FL

Papadopulos, Miguel F
Ms St Univ
Miss State, MS

Papas, Elaine D
Barry Univ
Miami, FL

Papas, Wassilli
Georgetown Univ
Washington, DC

Paradies, Jennifer
Newbury Coll
Brookline, MA

Paradis, Adrienne E
Columbia Union Coll
Takoma Park, MD

Paranal, Rowena R
Univ Of Sc At
Columbia
Columbia, SC

Paredes Velez, Sara A
Inter Amer Univ Pr
Aquadilla
Aguadilla, PR

Parel, Amethel A
Western Ky Univ
Bowling Green, KY

Parent, Tamara A
Comm Coll Of
Philadelphia
Philadelphia, PA

Pares Agosto, Gilmartin
Inter Amer Univ Pr
Hato Rey
Hato Rey, PR

Parham, Rovanda L
Commonwealth Coll
Norfolk, VA

Parigian, Bonnie Lynn
Radford Univ
Radford, VA

Parise, Donna M
Fl International Univ
Miami, FL

Park, Ji-Ah
Eckerd Coll
St Petersburg, FL

Park, John C
Univ Of Ky
Lexington, KY

Park, Johnny L
Middle Tn St Univ
Murfreesboro, TN

Park, So Young
City Univ Of Ny
Baruch Coll
New York, NY

Parker, Bernadette
Elmira Coll
Elmira, NY

Parker, Ellen L
Andover Coll
Portland, ME

Parker, Jeffery B
Pellissippi St Tech
Comm Coll
Knoxville, TN

Parker, Patricia A
Ms Univ For Women
Columbus, MS

Parker, Samantha J
Endicott Coll
Beverly, MA

Parker, Stephanie E
Morgan St Univ
Baltimore, MD

Parker, Suzanne H
Univ Of Sc At
Columbia
Columbia, SC

Parkhill, Gregory J
Oh St Univ
Columbus, OH

Parks, Christian Hunter
Fl Atlantic Univ
Boca Raton, FL

Parks, Rochelle Eve
Central St Univ
Wilberforce, OH

Parler, Penny I
Univ Of Sc At
Columbia
Columbia, SC

Parmegiani, Anthony C
Saint Johns Univ
Jamaica, NY

Parmelee, Heidi A
S U N Y Coll Of Tech
At Delhi
Delhi, NY

Parnell, Traci D
Birmingham Southern
Coll
Birmingham, AL

Parong, Fil A
Old Dominion Univ
Norfolk, VA

Parreira, Anabela S
Ct Coll
New London, CT

Parrish, Lisa M
Univ Of Ms Medical Center
Jackson, MS

Partlow, Kevin E
Itawamba Comm Coll
Fulton, MS

Partlow, Tammy C
Saint Josephs Coll Sufflk Cmps
Patchogue, NY

Pasquale, Cesare
Manhattan Coll
Bronx, NY

Passalaqua, Kim
S U N Y Coll Of Tech At Frmgdl
Farmingdale, NY

Pastor, Irmina Bosch
Saint Thomas Univ
Miami, FL

Patane, Bryan M
S U N Y Coll Of Tech At Delhi
Delhi, NY

Patel, Alpesh K
Salisbury St Univ
Salisbury, MD

Patel, Lina I
Middlesex County Coll
Edison, NJ

Patel, Navin K
Univ Of Pittsburgh
Pittsburgh, PA

Paterson, Sharyn M
Georgian Court Coll
Lakewood, NJ

Patnode, Kimberly L
Schenectady County Comm Coll
Schenectady, NY

Patriarca, Daniela
Georgian Court Coll
Lakewood, NJ

Patrick, Bryan W
Fl Coll
Temple Terrace, FL

Patrick, Cindy R
Ms Univ For Women
Columbus, MS

Patrikus, Paul J
Pellissippi St Tech Comm Coll
Knoxville, TN

Patten, Susan
Ursinus Coll
Collegeville, PA

Patterson, Darvin Okera
Morehouse Coll
Atlanta, GA

Patterson, Joyce A
Hillsborough Comm Coll
Tampa, FL

Patton, Bradley G
Kings Coll
Wilkes-Barre, PA

Patton, Sean A
Fl A & M Univ
Tallahassee, FL

Patton, Susan T
Radford Univ
Radford, VA

Paul, Michael A
Georgetown Univ
Washington, DC

Paul, Natashia R
Va Union Univ
Richmond, VA

Pavlock, Mary E
Hillsborough Comm Coll
Tampa, FL

Pawlikowski, Scott M
Univ Of Akron
Akron, OH

Pawlowski Jr, James R
S U N Y Coll At Fredonia
Fredonia, NY

Paxton, Robert G
Tn Tech Univ
Cookeville, TN

Payne, Jennifer L
Ms St Univ
Miss State, MS

Payne, Morganna C
Albertus Magnus Coll
New Haven, CT

Payne, R Steven
Ga Southern Univ
Statesboro, GA

Payne, Ronald D
Northeast State Tech Comm Coll
Blountville, TN

Payson, Andrianne S
City Univ Of Ny Med Evers Coll
Brooklyn, NY

Pearce, Gary L
Ashland Comm Coll
Ashland, KY

Pearson, Melissa L
Central Al Comm Coll
Alexander City, AL

Pearson, Nancy L
Univ Of Al At Birmingham
Birmingham, AL

Pearson, Richard E
Lincoln Univ
Lincoln Univ, PA

Pearson, Sara J
Benedict Coll
Columbia, SC

Peatross, Vonda K
Longwood Coll
Farmville, VA

Peck, Andrew C
Villanova Univ
Villanova, PA

Peck, Jill L
Beckley Coll
Beckley, WV

Pedigo, Mark A
Middle Tn St Univ
Murfreesboro, TN

Pedraza Santiago, I
Elsie
Inter Amer Univ Pr
Hato Rey
Hato Rey, PR

Pedrosa, Sheila D
Hillsborough Comm
Coll
Tampa, FL

Peebles, Gaylin L
Ky St Univ
Frankfort, KY

Peery, Starla G
Univ Of Tn At Martin
Martin, TN

Peixinho, Scott A
Providence Coll
Providence, RI

Pelcyger, Lisa R
City Univ Of Ny
Brooklyn Coll
Brooklyn, NY

Pellard, Bridget L
Springfield Tech Comm
Coll
Springfield, MA

Pellegrinelli, Lara V
Univ Of Rochester
Rochester, NY

Peltier, Marlene B
Univ Of Sc At
Columbia
Columbia, SC

Pemberton, Victoria
Univ Of The Virgin
Islands
St Thomas, VI

Penn, Arthur W
Western Ky Univ
Bowling Green, KY

Penn, Richelyn E
East Stroudsburg Univ
E Stroudsburg, PA

Pennisi, Linda A
Centenary Coll
Hackettstown, NJ

Pepe, Deanna A
Glassboro St Coll
Glassboro, NJ

Peragine, John N
Fl St Univ
Tallahassee, FL

Peraza, Javier
Saint Thomas Univ
Miami, FL

Perdomo, Nestor A
Univ Of Sc At Sumter
Sumter, SC

Pereira, John S
Univ Of Sc At
Columbia
Columbia, SC

Perello, Mayte D
Univ Of Pr At Rio
Piedras
Rio Piedras, PR

Perez Albertorio,
Vanessa
Univ Of Pr Medical
Sciences
San Juan, PR

Perez Castillo, Esther M
Univ Of Pr At
Mayaguez
Mayaguez, PR

Perez Colon, Eddie
Inter Amer Univ Pr
Hato Rey
Hato Rey, PR

Perez Ortiz, Maria P
Inter Amer Univ Pr San
German
San German, PR

Perez Ortiz, Ricardo
Inter Amer Univ Pr
Hato Rey
Hato Rey, PR

Perez Ramos, Elisamuel
Inter Amer Univ Pr
Hato Rey
Hato Rey, PR

Perez Rodriiguez,
Carmen
Inter Amer Univ Pr
Hato Rey
Hato Rey, PR

Perez Vazquez, Sara N
Inter Amer Univ Pr
Hato Rey
Hato Rey, PR

Perez, Alba I
Univ Of Pr Medical
Sciences
San Juan, PR

Perez, Alfredo J
Saint Thomas Univ
Miami, FL

Perez, Dianne
Miami Dade Comm Coll
South
Miami, FL

Perez, Donna Lee
Fl International Univ
Miami, FL

Perez, Francisco J
Univ Politecnica De Pr
Hato Rey, PR

Perez, Griselda C
Fl International Univ
Miami, FL

Perez, Iris D
Tn Temple Univ
Chattanooga, TN

Perez, Jerry F
Fayetteville St Univ
Fayetteville, NC

Perez, Maria I
Caribbean Univ
Bayamon, PR

Perez, Mariliz
Univ Of Pr At
Mayaguez
Mayaguez, PR

Perez-Llana, Mercedes
Catholic Univ Of Pr
Ponce, PR

Perez-Rivera, Eidan
Maria
Tuskegee Univ
Tuskegee Inst, AL

Perkins, Irene E
Western New England
Coll
Springfield, MA

Perkins, Kassandra F
Wesley Coll
Florence, MS

Perkins, Raquel C
Jackson St Univ
Jackson, MS

Perna, Kevin A
Wilmington Coll
New Castle, DE

Perng-Fussell, Hwey-Fen
Tallahassee Comm Coll
Tallahassee, FL

Perozich, John P
Lebanon Valley Coll
Annville, PA

Perri, Giovanna
Teikyo Post Univ
Waterbury, CT

Perrino, Janet M
Le Moyne Coll
Syracuse, NY

Perry, Diane M
Univ Of South Al
Mobile, AL

Perry, Mark W
Marshall University
Huntington, WV

Perry, Twyla D
Univ Of Al
Tuscaloosa, AL

Persaud Sr, Narayan D
Catawba Valley Comm Coll
Hickory, NC

Pertl, Franz Andreas Johannes
Wv Univ
Morgantown, WV

Pesantes, Eileen R
Univ Of Pr At Mayaguez
Mayaguez, PR

Pestana, Julia Esther
Fl International Univ
Miami, FL

Peterman, Istvan
City Univ Of Ny City Coll
New York, NY

Peters, Alexandra C
Marymount Manhattan Coll
New York, NY

Peters, Douglas E
Nc Agri & Tech St Univ
Greensboro, NC

Peters, Michael W
Union Coll
Barbourville, KY

Peterson, Dean T
Brevard Coll
Brevard, NC

Peterson, Gerald P
Fayetteville St Univ
Fayetteville, NC

Peterson, Scott J
Fl International Univ
Miami, FL

Peterson, Scott J
S U N Y Coll Of Tech At Delhi
Delhi, NY

Petrazzi, Antoinette R
Duquesne Univ
Pittsburgh, PA

Petrin, Susan M
Newbury Coll
Brookline, MA

Petrosky, William T
Ga Inst Of Tech At Atlanta
Atlanta, GA

Pettit, Mark L
Ga St Univ
Atlanta, GA

Pettko, Theodore M
Saint Vincents Coll & Seminary
Latrobe, PA

Phan, Khanh Thi Hong
Univ Of Louisville
Louisville, KY

Phelan, Cathy M
Glassboro St Coll
Glassboro, NJ

Phelps, Gloria M
Valdosta St Coll
Valdosta, GA

Phelps, Tonya J
Eastern Ky Univ
Richmond, KY

Philbrick, Faustena L
Longwood Coll
Farmville, VA

Philemon, Danny R
Central Fl Comm Coll
Ocala, FL

Philippi, Bruce M
Univ Of Al At Birmingham
Birmingham, AL

Phillippi, Amy J
Seton Hill Coll
Greensburg, PA

Phillips, David J
S U N Y At Buffalo
Buffalo, NY

Phillips, Debra L
George Mason Univ
Fairfax, VA

Phillips Jr, James G
Bunker Hill Comm Coll
Boston, MA

Phillips, Julie A
Valdosta St Coll
Valdosta, GA

Phillips, Kevin A
Morehouse Coll
Atlanta, GA

Phillips, Michelle D
Va St Univ
Petersburg, VA

Phillips II, Ronald W
Western Carolina Univ
Cullowhee, NC

Phillips, Sabine L
Northern Va Comm Coll
Annandale, VA

Phillips, Scott A
Piedmont Tech Coll
Greenwood, SC

Phillips, Tonya L
Beckley Coll
Beckley, WV

Phinney, Jennifer L
Andover Coll
Portland, ME

Phipps, Linda O
Univ Of Sc At Columbia
Columbia, SC

Phister, David T
Univ Of Akron
Akron, OH

Piacentini, Lisa A
Providence Coll
Providence, RI

Piazza, Jennifer R
Glassboro St Coll
Glassboro, NJ

Piazza, Michael J
S U N Y Coll Of Tech At Alfred
Alfred, NY

Piccirillo, Angelo A
Adelphi Univ
Garden City, NY

Pick, Tracy Martin
Nova Univ
Ft Lauderdale, FL

Pickens, John C
Univ Of Ga
Athens, GA

Pickett, Paul A
Ms St Univ
Miss State, MS

Piedrahita, Jairo
Nova Univ
Ft Lauderdale, FL

Pierce, Elizabeth G
Univ Of Sc At Aiken
Aiken, SC

Pierce, Kristy L
Wv Univ
Morgantown, WV

Pierce, M Therese
Gallaudet Univ
Washington, DC

Pierce, Shannon D
Rutgers St Un At New Brunswick
New Brunswick, NJ

Pierre, Kevin
American Baptist Coll
Nashville, TN

Pierre, Sandra Marie
City Univ Of Ny City Coll
New York, NY

Pierson, Debra M
Defiance Coll
Defiance, OH

Pifer, Richard G
Temple Univ
Philadelphia, PA

Pilate, Marcenia S
Jackson St Univ
Jackson, MS

Pilgrim, Marlon D
Morehouse Coll
Atlanta, GA

Pilgrim, Steven S
S U N Y Coll Of Tech At Alfred
Alfred, NY

Pimentel, Flerida M
City Univ Of Ny Hostos Coll
Bronx, NY

Pimentel, Loida V
Bunker Hill Comm Coll
Boston, MA

Pineda, Albino Ariel
Univ Politecnica De Pr
Hato Rey, PR

Pineiro Santiago, Luis A
Univ Of Pr At Mayaguez
Mayaguez, PR

Pinho, Anabela A
Saint Joseph Coll
West Hartford, CT

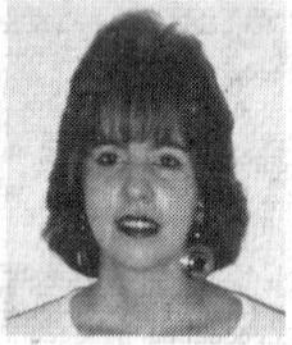
Pino, Maria Del Carmen
Inter Amer Univ Pr Hato Rey
Hato Rey, PR

Piper, Tony L
Middle Ga Coll
Cochran, GA

Pipersburgh, Olivia H
Saint Josephs Coll New York
Brooklyn, NY

Pippin, James A
Tallahassee Comm Coll
Tallahassee, FL

Pirmohamed, Rosemin
Mercer Univ Schl Of Pharm
Atlanta, GA

Pisaris, John B
Oh Northern Univ
Ada, OH

Pistacchio, Ugo Salvatore
Strayer Coll
Washington, DC

Pitsenbarger, Lisa M
Bridgewater Coll
Bridgewater, VA

Pittman, Latonya Y
Alcorn St Univ
Lorman, MS

Pitts, Amber E
Atlantic Comm Coll
Mays Landing, NJ

Pitts, Bianca M
Cleveland St Univ
Cleveland, OH

Pitts III, David M
Morehouse Coll
Atlanta, GA

Pizem, Richard D
Bowling Green St Univ
Bowling Green, OH

Plankers, James M
Univ Of Tn At
Knoxville
Knoxville, TN

Plasencia, Mireya
Fl Atlantic Univ
Boca Raton, FL

Platkin, Steven A
City Univ Of Ny
Baruch Coll
New York, NY

Plebaniak, Anita B
Fl International Univ
Miami, FL

Plichta, Anjanette L
Coll Of William &
Mary
Williamsburg, VA

Pochas, Eric M
Marywood Coll
Scranton, PA

Podkowka, Lisa A
Western New England
Coll
Springfield, MA

Poe, Laura E
Longwood Coll
Farmville, VA

Pogue, David D
Central St Univ
Wilberforce, OH

Pola, Martalina
Oh Univ
Athens, OH

Polcyn, Donna M
Hilbert Coll
Hamburg, NY

Polidoro, Jennifer A
Marywood Coll
Scranton, PA

Polite, Sandra J
Saint Johns Univ
Jamaica, NY

Polk, Laura E
Capital Univ
Columbus, OH

Pollock, Carole Sumner
Blue Mountain Coll
Blue Mountain, MS

Pollock, Gary M
S U N Y Coll Of Tech
At Alfred
Alfred, NY

Pomerleau, Tammy M
Newbury Coll
Brookline, MA

Ponger, Robert L
City Univ Of Ny
Baruch Coll
New York, NY

Poole, Cindy S
Radford Univ
Radford, VA

Poole, Jennifer L
Rivier Coll
Nashua, NH

Poole, Stephanie M
Va Commonwealth Univ
Richmond, VA

Pooler, Jason C
Univ Of Tn At
Knoxville
Knoxville, TN

Pope, Ohridia A
Emory Univ
Atlanta, GA

Porelle, Susan M
Merrimack Coll
North Andover, MA

Porras, Jesus
Saint Thomas Univ
Miami, FL

Porrata Vega, Carlos A
Inter Amer Univ Pr
Guayama
Guayama, PR

Posada, Baldemar
Bunker Hill Comm Coll
Boston, MA

Poss, Alissa M
Middle Tn St Univ
Murfreesboro, TN

Potkovic, Troy M
Stetson Univ
Deland, FL

Pou, Javier A
Bridgewater Coll
Bridgewater, VA

Pouget, Lawrence A
Va Commonwealth Univ
Richmond, VA

Pournaras, Vasiliki C
Univ Of Sc At
Columbia
Columbia, SC

Pourrostamian, Mahnaz
Yeshiva Univ
New York, NY

Powell, Andrea D
James Madison
University
Harrisonburg, VA

Powell, Francine P
Saint Thomas Univ
Miami, FL

Powell, Geraldine S A
Coppin St Coll
Baltimore, MD

Powell, Richard M
Birmingham Southern
Coll
Birmingham, AL

Powell, Shalisa D
Fl A & M Univ
Tallahassee, FL

Power, Bertina Marian
Hampton Univ
Hampton, VA

Powers, Faith A
Dickinson Coll
Carlisle, PA

Powers II, Robert P
Fordham Univ
Bronx, NY

Powers, Scott W
Rochester Inst Of Tech
Rochester, NY

Powers, Stacey R
East Central Comm Coll
Decatur, MS

Powledge, Patrick W
Bayamon Central Univ
Bayamon, PR

Poynor, Karen E
Nyack Coll
Nyack, NY

Pozniak, Laurie E
Univ Of Md At College Park
College Park, MD

Pratt, Dona Chimene
Bennett Coll
Greensboro, NC

Pratt, Louis L
Broome Comm Coll
Binghamton, NY

Presley, Trent J
Union Univ
Jackson, TN

Pressley, Jannie J
Comm Coll Algny Co South Cmps
West Mifflin, PA

Preston, Edwin H
Morehouse Coll
Atlanta, GA

Preston III, George E
Bishop St Comm Coll
Mobile, AL

Pretty, Christina M
Newbury Coll
Brookline, MA

Prezzano, Denise Ann
S U N Y Coll Of Tech At Frmgdl
Farmingdale, NY

Price, Gabrielle M
Fl St Univ
Tallahassee, FL

Price, Glynn E
Central Al Comm Coll
Alexander City, AL

Price II, Johnny T
Germanna Comm Coll
Locust Grove, VA

Price, Stephanie K
Piedmont Tech Coll
Greenwood, SC

Price, Zoana O
Clark Atlanta Univ
Atlanta, GA

Priddle, Kristina M
Schenectady County Comm Coll
Schenectady, NY

Priddy, Gary W
Ms St Univ
Miss State, MS

Priest Jr, James A
Coppin St Coll
Baltimore, MD

Prieto, Miguel A
Catholic Univ Of Pr
Ponce, PR

Prince, Dia D
Ky St Univ
Frankfort, KY

Prince, Natasha A
Alcorn St Univ
Lorman, MS

Prince, Terra L
Central Al Comm Coll
Alexander City, AL

Prince, Tony D
Univ Of Sc At Columbia
Columbia, SC

Pritchard, David K
Middle Ga Coll
Cochran, GA

Proctor, Stephen P
Univ Of Sc At Coastal Carolina
Conway, SC

Proni, Frederick P
Utica Coll Of Syracuse Univ
Utica, NY

Propp, Alison L
Savannah Coll Of Art & Design
Savannah, GA

Prosperie, Desiree A
Fl St Univ
Tallahassee, FL

Prue, Linda M
Southern Vt Coll
Bennington, VT

Pruett, Elisa A
Univ Of North Fl
Jacksonville, FL

Pruitt, Darlene
Bunker Hill Comm Coll
Boston, MA

Pruitt, Nancy L
Univ Of Ga
Athens, GA

Pryor, Marsha R
Fl A & M Univ
Tallahassee, FL

Prytherch, Tamera D
Kent St Univ Kent Cmps
Kent, OH

Puckett, Dale C
Middle Ga Coll
Cochran, GA

Puckett, Gerald C
Fayetteville St Univ
Fayetteville, NC

Puebla, Margaret G
Fl International Univ
Miami, FL

Puga, Fernando Gabriel
Inter Amer Univ Pr Hato Rey
Hato Rey, PR

Pugh Mack, N Beth
Ky Christian Coll
Grayson, KY

Pugh, Keith W
Savannah Coll Of Art & Design
Savannah, GA

Pugh, Kimberly Renee
Norfolk St Univ
Norfolk, VA

Puharic, Erin M
Glassboro St Coll
Glassboro, NJ

Puig Medina, Marines
Univ Of Pr At Mayaguez
Mayaguez, PR

Pulley, Camille A
Va St Univ
Petersburg, VA

Pullin, Kenneth B
Hillsborough Comm Coll
Tampa, FL

Punj, Guarav
Duquesne Univ
Pittsburgh, PA

Purdham, Penny L
Tomlinson Coll
Cleveland, TN

Purdy, Violet Rolen
Roane St Comm Coll
Harriman, TN

Puryear Jr, Samuel Gibson
Tn St Univ
Nashville, TN

Pusch, Gabriela S
Kent St Univ Kent Cmps
Kent, OH

Pusey, Daniel L
Bapt Bible Coll & Seminary
Clarks Summit, PA

Putnam, Cristi G
Belmont Abbey Coll
Belmont, NC

Putnam Jr, Paul David
North Greenville Coll
Tigerville, SC

Pyle, Jill M
Clarion Univ Of Pa
Clarion, PA

Quan, Lupita T
Fl International Univ
Miami, FL

Quarles, Glenda J
Valdosta St Coll
Valdosta, GA

Quasney Jr, Robert S
Anne Arundel Comm Coll
Arnold, MD

Questel, Allison P
City Univ Of Ny Baruch Coll
New York, NY

Quiles, Lisa
Univ Of Miami
Coral Gables, FL

Quinn, Frederick Douglas
Tougaloo Coll
Tougaloo, MS

Quinn II, Luther J
Eckerd Coll
St Petersburg, FL

Quinn, Sherry P
Oh Univ-Southern Cmps
Ironton, OH

Quinones Alicea, Louise Marie
Inter Amer Univ Pr Hato Rey
Hato Rey, PR

Quinones Aquino, Jacqueline
Inter Amer Univ Pr Hato Rey
Hato Rey, PR

Quinones Belazquez, Javier E
Inter Amer Univ Pr Aquadilla
Aguadilla, PR

Quisenberry, Annette
Radford Univ
Radford, VA

Qureshi, Mohammad M
Univ Of Rochester
Rochester, NY

Raddalgoda, Lalith S
Anne Arundel Comm Coll
Arnold, MD

Rafalski, Stephen P
Utica Coll Of Syracuse Univ
Utica, NY

Ragiab, Ali T
Al A & M Univ
Normal, AL

Rahgozar, Mohamad
Bunker Hill Comm Coll
Boston, MA

Rahming, Jason D
Morehouse Coll
Atlanta, GA

Rai, Sanjiv
Old Dominion Univ
Norfolk, VA

Raines, Lorrie A
Univ Of Sc At Spartanburg
Spartanburg, SC

Rainey, Mary E
Coll Of Charleston
Charleston, SC

Rainey, Perry C
City Univ Of Ny Baruch Coll
New York, NY

Rainey, William D
Univ Of Tn At Martin
Martin, TN

Raja, Jamil M
Strayer Coll
Washington, DC

Rajan, Rallis M
Columbia Union Coll
Takoma Park, MD

Raley Jr, Robert C
Pellissippi St Tech Comm Coll
Knoxville, TN

Ramadan, Basma F
Wagner Coll
Staten Island, NY

Ramey, Donald G
Univ Of Va Clinch
Valley Coll
Wise, VA

Ramezanian, Mitra
Youngstown St Univ
Youngstown, OH

Ramirez Lugo, Angel L
Univ Of Pr At
Mayaguez
Mayaguez, PR

Ramirez Vilela, Jose E
Bayamon Central Univ
Bayamon, PR

Ramirez, Ana M
Univ Of Sc At
Columbia
Columbia, SC

Ramirez, Wanda J
Inter Amer Univ Pr San
German
San German, PR

Ramjohn, Stephanie I
Wilberforce Univ
Wilberforce, OH

Ramos, Francisco J
Miami Dade Comm Coll
Miami, FL

Ramos, Jose Gabriel
Saint Thomas Univ
Miami, FL

Ramos, Juan D
Ma Inst Of Tech
Cambridge, MA

Ramos, Karen L
Inter Amer Univ Pr
Hato Rey
Hato Rey, PR

Ramos, Luis R
Inter Amer Univ Pr
Aquadilla
Aguadilla, PR

Ramos, Maria A
Univ Of Pr At Rio
Piedras
Rio Piedras, PR

Ramos, Maria M
Bloomfield Coll
Bloomfield, NJ

Ramsby, Shannon G
Va Commonwealth Univ
Richmond, VA

Ramsey Jr, Robert C
Emory & Henry Coll
Emory, VA

Rand, Renata
Saint Johns Univ
Jamaica, NY

Randall, Matthew M
Univ Of Cin R Walters
Coll
Blue Ash, OH

Randle, Katherine M
Itawamba Comm Coll
Fulton, MS

Randolph, Doris D
City Univ Of Ny City
Coll
New York, NY

Randolph, Kimberly A
Limestone Coll
Gaffney, SC

Randolph, Stephanie S
Univ Of Ga
Athens, GA

Rangel, Carlos A
Univ Politecnica De Pr
Hato Rey, PR

Rankins, James L
Central St Univ
Wilberforce, OH

Ransom, Sandra C
Hillsborough Comm
Coll
Tampa, FL

Ranta, Margaret E
Bristol Univ
Bristol, TN

Rao-Kathi, Prasanth
Burri
Georgetown Univ
Washington, DC

Rapaport, Aimee J
Univ Of Miami
Coral Gables, FL

Rappold, James A
Carnegie Mellon Univ
Pittsburgh, PA

Ratliff, Chris A
Univ Of Ky
Lexington, KY

Rauls, Valerie D
Alcorn St Univ
Lorman, MS

Rawls, Angelique
Jackson St Univ
Jackson, MS

Rawls, Rhonda L
Univ Of Southern Ms
Hattiesburg, MS

Ray, Janice A
Al A & M Univ
Normal, AL

Ray, Kimberly L
Vanderbilt Univ
Nashville, TN

Raymond, Kim M
Tallahassee Comm Coll
Tallahassee, FL

Reagan, Erin C
Atlantic Comm Coll
Mays Landing, NJ

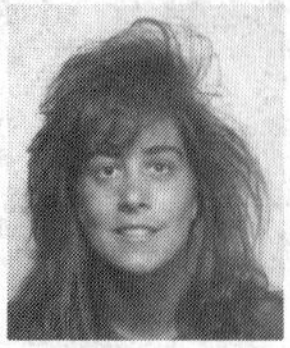
Rebecca, Marie
Ny Univ
New York, NY

Reda, Christine
Coll Of New Rochelle
New Rochelle, NY

Redcross, Kenneth E
Va Commonwealth Univ
Richmond, VA

Redd, Harry H
Morehouse Coll
Atlanta, GA

Reddick, Linda L
Columbia Union Coll
Takoma Park, MD

Reddy, Venkata Nb
Memphis St Univ
Memphis, TN

Redfern, Jennifer L
Hilbert Coll
Hamburg, NY

Redmon, Kimberly Beth
Fl A & M Univ
Tallahassee, FL

Redmond, Idella L
Tougaloo Coll
Tougaloo, MS

Redner, Debra E
Ramapo Coll Of Nj
Mahwah, NJ

Redrick, P Lamont
Morehouse Coll
Atlanta, GA

Reed, Dianna L
Glassboro St Coll
Glassboro, NJ

Reed Jr, James B
Roane St Comm Coll
Harriman, TN

Reed, John W
Southern Coll Of Tech
Marietta, GA

Reed, Michael S
Univ Of Richmond
Richmond, VA

Reed, Pamela L
S U N Y Coll Of A & T Morrisvl
Morrisville, NY

Reents, Mark J
Embry Riddle Aeronautical Univ
Daytona Beach, FL

Reeve, Jonathan T
Univ Of Ky
Lexington, KY

Reeves, Sandra D
Memphis St Univ
Memphis, TN

Regan, Jennifer A
Miami Univ
Oxford, OH

Register, Dianna L
Univ Of West Fl
Pensacola, FL

Rego Rios, Hilda L
Univ Of Pr At Mayaguez
Mayaguez, PR

Rehberg, Delbert John
Columbia Greene Comm Coll
Hudson, NY

Rehm, Patrick G
Univ Of South Al
Mobile, AL

Reiber, Gina M
Columbus Coll Of Art & Design
Columbus, OH

Reid, Aseem B
Atlantic Comm Coll
Mays Landing, NJ

Reid, Charmaine A
City Univ Of Ny Bronx Comm Col
Bronx, NY

Reid, Stephanie N
Univ Of Al
Tuscaloosa, AL

Reinhardt, Jennifer L
Glassboro St Coll
Glassboro, NJ

Reist, Jessica A
Glassboro St Coll
Glassboro, NJ

Remillard, Kristine M
Univ Of Ma At Amherst
Amherst, MA

Remington, Laura J
Immaculata Coll
Immaculata, PA

Remington, Sharon L
Castleton St Coll
Castleton, VT

Renner, Jennifer D
Saint Francis Coll
Loretto, PA

Renner, Robert A
Charles County Comm Coll
La Plata, MD

Reott, Suzanne M
Univ Of North Fl
Jacksonville, FL

Rephan, Dina
Yeshiva Univ
New York, NY

Repko, Robert T
Coll Misericordia
Dallas, PA

Replogle, Pamela S
Saint Francis Coll
Loretto, PA

Retell, Kevin R
Hudson Valley Comm Coll
Troy, NY

Rethwilm, Craig R
Univ Of Tn At Chattanooga
Chattanooga, TN

Retman, Deborah J
Miami Jacobs Jr Coll Of Bus
Dayton, OH

Reus, Juan L
Fl International Univ
Miami, FL

Reuscher, Tracey L
D Youville Coll
Buffalo, NY

Reuss, Vicki A
Univ Of Cincinnati-Clrmnt Coll
Batavia, OH

Revah, Albert
Georgetown Univ
Washington, DC

Revel, Mark C
Campbell Univ
Buies Creek, NC

Revell, Arethlia B
Norfolk St Univ
Norfolk, VA

Reyes Agosto, Pedro N
Univ Of Pr Humacao
Univ Coll
Humacao, PR

Reyes, Alexander
Broward Comm Coll
Ft Lauderdale, FL

Reyes, Alexandria
William Paterson Coll
Wayne, NJ

Reyes, Carlos Aviles
Inter Amer Univ Pr San
Juan
Hato Rey, PR

Reyes Jr, Efrain
Univ Politecnica De Pr
Hato Rey, PR

Reyes, George
Harvard Univ
Cambridge, MA

Reyes, Henry
Univ Of Ct
Storrs, CT

Reyes, Ivette
Univ Of Sc At
Columbia
Columbia, SC

Reyes-Medina, Selena
Evangelical Semimary
Of P R
Hato Rey, PR

Reynolds, Kathy S
Pellissippi St Tech
Comm Coll
Knoxville, TN

Reynolds, Sherrie L
Univ Of Nc At
Greensboro
Greensboro, NC

Rezazadeh, Hassan
Erie Comm Coll
Buffalo, NY

Rhee, John S
Coll Of Health Sci
Stony Brook
Stony Brook, NY

Rhinehart, Scott C
Emmanuel Coll Schl
Chrstn Min
Franklin Sprg, GA

Rhoads, Gerald W
Christopher Newport
Coll
Newport News, VA

Rhodes, Benae L
Univ Of Nc At
Charlotte
Charlotte, NC

Rhodes, Charise R
Fl A & M Univ
Tallahassee, FL

Rhodes, Lou Ann
Kent St Univ Kent
Cmps
Kent, OH

Rhodus, Samuel L
Univ Of Ky
Lexington, KY

Ribaudo, Rebecca T
Bloomfield Coll
Bloomfield, NJ

Ribavaro, Ruthann
Widener Univ
Chester, PA

Rice, Conserverina Y
Univ Of Sc At
Columbia
Columbia, SC

Rice, David M
Northern Ky Univ
Highland Hts, KY

Rice, Tiffany A
Murray St Univ
Murray, KY

Richard, David W
Univ Of Southern Ms
Hattiesburg, MS

Richard, Gwendolyn D
Jackson St Univ
Jackson, MS

Richards, Betty J
Univ Of Rochester
Rochester, NY

Richards, Judy A
Borough Of Manhattan
Comm Coll
New York, NY

Richardson Soto,
Patricia L
Univ Of Pr Cayey Univ
Coll
Cayey, PR

Richardson, Barbara A
Fl A & M Univ
Tallahassee, FL

Richardson, Da Meta J
Tougaloo Coll
Tougaloo, MS

Richardson, Dana F
City Univ Of Ny
Baruch Coll
New York, NY

Richardson, Dwayne A
Fl A & M Univ
Tallahassee, FL

Richardson, Eric A
Bethune Cookman Coll
Daytona Beach, FL

Richardson, Jacqueline
Alcorn St Univ
Lorman, MS

Richardson, Joseph
Tulloss
John C Calhoun St
Comm Coll
Decatur, AL

Richardson, Melissa A
Spartanburg Methodist
Coll
Spartanburg, SC

Richardson, Paul D
Air Force Inst Of Tech
Wrt-Ptrsn Afb, OH

Richardson, Sharlyn
Bloomfield Coll
Bloomfield, NJ

Richardson, William E
Coker Coll
Hartsville, SC

Richbourg, Brenda L
Univ Of West Fl
Pensacola, FL

Richeme, Maurice F
Teikyo Post Univ
Waterbury, CT

Richert, Candace S
Eastern Coll
Saint Davids, PA

Richmond, Ronald E
Wv Northern Comm Coll
Wheeling, WV

Rickels, Lisa A
Univ Of Al At Birmingham
Birmingham, AL

Rickles, Angela
Brewer St Jr Coll
Fayette, AL

Rico, Martha L
City Univ Of Ny City Coll
New York, NY

Ridenhour, David E
Southern Coll Of Tech
Marietta, GA

Riebe, Theresa E
Lehigh Univ
Bethlehem, PA

Riedel, Barbara E
Kent St Univ Geauga Cmps
Burton Twp, OH

Rieder, Jill Lynette
Sue Bennett Coll
London, KY

Ries, Melissa J
Ky Christian Coll
Grayson, KY

Riggins, Lana A
Fisk Univ
Nashville, TN

Riggs, Kenneth J
Univ Of Sc At Sumter
Sumter, SC

Rightmire, April L
High Point Coll
High Point, NC

Rigsbee, Jackie A
Longwood Coll
Farmville, VA

Riley, Tracy L
Voorhees Coll
Denmark, SC

Rinaldi, Elza M
Univ Of Miami
Coral Gables, FL

Rinehart, Christopher A
Wittenberg Univ
Springfield, OH

Rines, Barbara A
Andover Coll
Portland, ME

Rini, Sylvia M
Univ Of Miami
Coral Gables, FL

Rios, Melva N
Univ Of Pr At Rio Piedras
Rio Piedras, PR

Rios, Vivian A
Univ Of Pr At Rio Piedras
Rio Piedras, PR

Rios-Lyle, Leandro V
Inter Amer Univ Pr Hato Rey
Hato Rey, PR

Rissmiller, Lisa L
S U N Y Coll Of Tech At Frmgdl
Farmingdale, NY

Ritchey, Emily M
Kent St Univ Kent Cmps
Kent, OH

Rivenburg, Timothy J
Columbia Greene Comm Coll
Hudson, NY

Rivera Bonet, Sheila L
Univ Of Pr At Mayaguez
Mayaguez, PR

Rivera Cruz, Teresa
Inter Amer Univ Pr Hato Rey
Hato Rey, PR

Rivera Isaac, Emily
Univ Politecnica De Pr
Hato Rey, PR

Rivera Malave, Laura
Inter Amer Univ Pr Hato Rey
Hato Rey, PR

Rivera Miranda, Carlos
Inter Amer Univ Pr Arecibo Un
Arecibo, PR

Rivera Morales, Ivonne Yanira
Inter Amer Univ Pr San German
San German, PR

Rivera Perez, Edith J
Inter Amer Univ Pr Hato Rey
Hato Rey, PR

Rivera Reyes, Richard
Univ Politecnica De Pr
Hato Rey, PR

Rivera Rodriguez, Maralexi
Univ Of Pr At Mayaguez
Mayaguez, PR

Rivera, Artemio
Inter Amer Univ Pr San Juan
Hato Rey, PR

Rivera, Daniel
Coll Of New Rochelle
New Rochelle, NY

Rivera, Genaro L
Inter Amer Univ Pr Hato Rey
Hato Rey, PR

Rivera, Hector C
Bayamon Tech Univ Coll
Bayamon, PR

Rivera, Ivette R
Long Island Univ C W Post Cntr
Greenvale, NY

Rivera, Ivia G
Inter Amer Univ Pr Hato Rey
Hato Rey, PR

Rivera, Militza
Univ Of Pr Humacao Univ Coll
Humacao, PR

Rivera, William
Brown Univ
Providence, RI

Rivera, Zaida E
Univ Of Pr Medical Sciences
San Juan, PR

Rivera-Collazo, Carmen Iris
Caribbean Univ
Bayamon, PR

Rivera-Rivera, Diana G
Univ Of Pr At Rio Piedras
Rio Piedras, PR

Rivlin, Dan G
Fl International Univ
Miami, FL

Rizvi, Syed Shaukat Abbas
City Univ Of Ny Med Evers Coll
Brooklyn, NY

Roach, Kerry J
Villanova Univ
Villanova, PA

Roadcap, Patricia M
James Madison University
Harrisonburg, VA

Roadman, Charles W
Ms St Univ
Miss State, MS

Roadman, Samuel E
Univ Of Pittsburgh
Pittsburgh, PA

Roark, Sandra R
Fl International Univ
Miami, FL

Robaina, Teresa I
Fl International Univ
Miami, FL

Robbins, Julia E
Univ Of Ky
Lexington, KY

Robbins, Mark A
Univ Central Del Caribe
Cayey, PR

Robbins II, Richard E
Univ Of Sc At Columbia
Columbia, SC

Roberts, Derrick L
Northeast Ms Cc
Booneville, MS

Roberts, Harriett E
Central Carolina Comm Coll
Sanford, NC

Roberts, Kenneth D
Univ Of Southern Ms
Hattiesburg, MS

Roberts, Kerry L
Duquesne Univ
Pittsburgh, PA

Roberts, Melanie M
Va St Univ
Petersburg, VA

Roberts, Nicole Y
Saint Pauls Coll
Lawrenceville, VA

Roberts, Rosalie N
Univ Of Miami
Coral Gables, FL

Roberts, Tamara L
Univ Of West Fl
Pensacola, FL

Roberts, Tammy M
West Liberty St Coll
West Liberty, WV

Robertson, Craig Francis
Niagara Univ
Niagara Univ, NY

Robertson, Jermaine A
Old Dominion Univ
Norfolk, VA

Robertson, Suzette D
Winthrop Coll
Rock Hill, SC

Robertson, Tommie L
Union Inst
Cincinnati, OH

Robillard, Denise A
Newbury Coll
Brookline, MA

Robinette, Melinda F
Univ Of West Fl
Pensacola, FL

Robinson, Andrea
City Univ Of Ny Baruch Coll
New York, NY

Robinson, Antoinette
Al St Univ
Montgomery, AL

Robinson, Brent D
Fl International Univ
Miami, FL

Robinson, Cynthia L
Univ Of Sc At Aiken
Aiken, SC

Robinson, Derrick E
Morehouse Coll
Atlanta, GA

Robinson, Donna Lee
Southern Coll Of Tech
Marietta, GA

Robinson, E Raynette
Columbia Union Coll
Takoma Park, MD

Robinson, Elliott S
Norfolk St Univ
Norfolk, VA

Robinson, Helja I
Univ Of Ms Main Cmps
University, MS

Robinson, Jeffrey A
Univ Of Akron
Akron, OH

Robinson, Jennifer S
West Chester Univ
West Chester, PA

Robinson, L C
Alcorn St Univ
Lorman, MS

Robinson, Lisa R
Sinclair Comm Coll
Dayton, OH

Robinson, Melone A
City Univ Of Ny Med
Evers Coll
Brooklyn, NY

Robinson, Micakl
Central St Univ
Wilberforce, OH

Robinson, Nikki H
Hampton Univ
Hampton, VA

Robinson, Peter C
The Kings Coll
Briarclf Mnr, NY

Robinson, Robyn M
Fl A & M Univ
Tallahassee, FL

Robinson, Shana L
Univ Of Sc At
Columbia
Columbia, SC

Robinson, Todd T
Va St Univ
Petersburg, VA

Robinson, Vivian L
Benedict Coll
Columbia, SC

Robinson-Gato, Susan L
Bergen Comm Coll
Paramus, NJ

Robison, Sherry E
Univ Of Sc At
Spartanburg
Spartanburg, SC

Robles Rivera, Dory
Jean
Inter Amer Univ Pr San
Juan
Hato Rey, PR

Robles Jr, David A
Western New England
Coll
Springfield, MA

Roby, Robert J
Oh Univ
Athens, OH

Roca, Amparo
Miami Dade Comm Coll
South
Miami, FL

Roch, Denise L
Dowling Coll
Oakdale Li, NY

Rocha, Andrew G
Univ Of Rochester
Rochester, NY

Roche, Daniel E
Oh Dominican Coll
Columbus, OH

Rock, Darlene K
Fl A & M Univ
Tallahassee, FL

Roda, Cheryl J
Columbia Union Coll
Takoma Park, MD

Roderick, Stacey A
Norfolk St Univ
Norfolk, VA

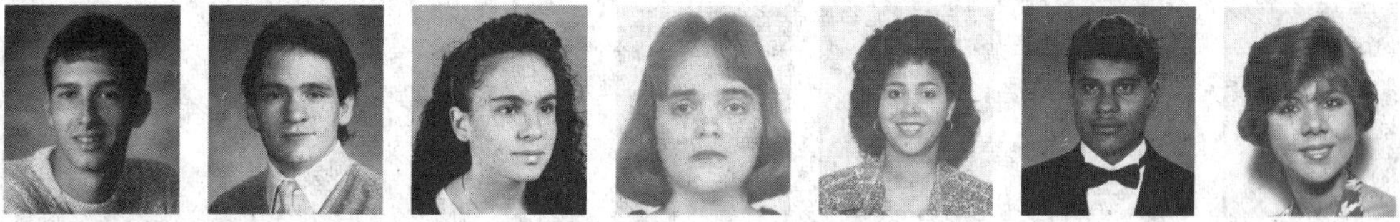

Rodgers, James A
Univ Of Sc At
Columbia
Columbia, SC

Rodgers, John B
Univ Of Med &
Dentistry Of Nj
Newark, NJ

Rodil, Carla M
Georgetown Univ
Washington, DC

Rodriguez Diaz,
Milagros
Inter Amer Univ Pr San
Juan
Hato Rey, PR

Rodriguez Matos, Maria
Del C
Bayamon Central Univ
Bayamon, PR

Rodriguez Ocasio,
Ruben
Inter Amer Univ Pr
Hato Rey
Hato Rey, PR

Rodriguez Perez, Nancy
Univ Of Pr Medical
Sciences
San Juan, PR

Rodriguez Rosa, Gladys
Inter Amer Univ Pr
Arecibo Un
Arecibo, PR

Rodriguez Vazquez,
Juan F
Inter Amer Univ Pr
Hato Rey
Hato Rey, PR

Rodriguez, Alejandro A
Broward Comm Coll
Ft Lauderdale, FL

Rodriguez, Beatriz
Rodriguez
Caribbean Univ
Bayamon, PR

Rodriguez, Carmen H
Univ Of Pr At Rio
Piedras
Rio Piedras, PR

Rodriguez, G Patricia
Ny Univ
New York, NY

Rodriguez, Heriberto
Univ Politecnica De Pr
Hato Rey, PR

Rodriguez, Ivan
Saint Thomas Univ
Miami, FL

Rodriguez, Julia E
Nova Univ
Ft Lauderdale, FL

Rodriguez, Liza I
Univ Of Pr At Rio
Piedras
Rio Piedras, PR

Rodriguez, Maria
Michelle
Inter Amer Univ Pr
Hato Rey
Hato Rey, PR

Rodriguez, Raquel E
Teikyo Post Univ
Waterbury, CT

Rodriguez, Sandra E
Univ Of Pr At Rio
Piedras
Rio Piedras, PR

Rodriguez, Zoe M
Univ Politecnica De Pr
Hato Rey, PR

Rodriguez-Duran, David
Catholic Univ Of Pr
Ponce, PR

Rodriguez-Paraja, M
Cristina
Strayer Coll
Washington, DC

Rodriguez-Perez, Juana
Univ Of Pr Medical
Sciences
San Juan, PR

Rogers, De Anna L
Univ Of Tn At Martin
Martin, TN

Rogers, Evans M
Tuskegee Univ
Tuskegee Inst, AL

Rogers, Kimberly S
Univ Of Sc At
Columbia
Columbia, SC

Rogers, Kristen Lynn
Anderson Coll
Anderson, SC

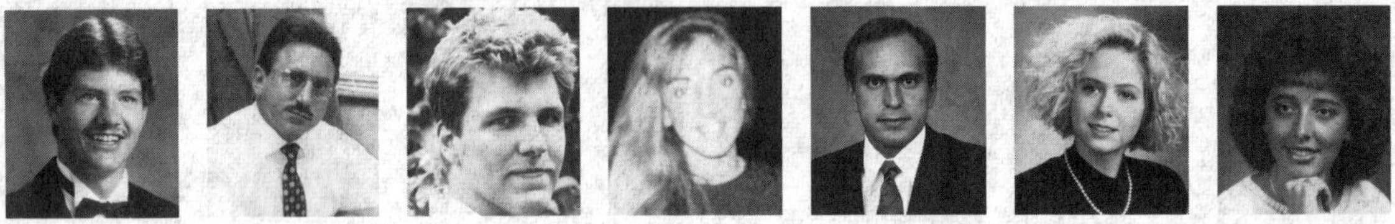

Rogers, Neil D
Univ Of Sc At Aiken
Aiken, SC

Rogers, William M
Nova Univ
Ft Lauderdale, FL

Rohr, Michael L
Fayetteville St Univ
Fayetteville, NC

Roig, Anna Patricia
Fl International Univ
Miami, FL

Rojas Andraca, Maximo
Univ Politecnica De Pr
Hato Rey, PR

Rolland, Sandra C
Endicott Coll
Beverly, MA

Rollins, Rachelle R
Northern Ky Univ
Highland Hts, KY

Roman, Alberto
Saint Thomas Univ
Miami, FL

Roman, Jossie I
Inter Amer Univ Pr San
Juan
Hato Rey, PR

Roman Jr, Roman
Miami Dade Comm Coll
Miami, FL

Romans, H Jordan
Univ Of Al At
Huntsville
Huntsville, AL

Romer, Rhonda K
Hudson Valley Comm
Coll
Troy, NY

Romero, Jose A
Univ Politecnica De Pr
Hato Rey, PR

Romero, Romulo H
Fl International Univ
Miami, FL

Romero-Pineiro, Antonio
Inter Amer Univ Pr
Hato Rey
Hato Rey, PR

Roney, Edith Ann
Clayton St Coll
Morrow, GA

Roney, Scott M
Pa St Univ Delaware
Cty Cmps
Media, PA

Rooker, Margie Elaine
Univ Of Sc At Aiken
Aiken, SC

Rooks, Amy T
Norfolk St Univ
Norfolk, VA

Roos, Michelle L
Ms St Univ
Miss State, MS

Root, Chad M
Oh St Univ
Columbus, OH

Roque Falcon, Brian A
Bayamon Central Univ
Bayamon, PR

Roque-Nieves, Pedro
Jose
Bayamon Central Univ
Bayamon, PR

Roques, Annie
Fl International Univ
Miami, FL

Rorie, Ivey
Univ Of Sc At
Spartanburg
Spartanburg, SC

Rosa, Bryan P
Southern Vt Coll
Bennington, VT

Rosa, Cuevas Cesar
Inter Amer Univ Pr San
Juan
Hato Rey, PR

Rosa, Hector Wm Colon
Univ Of Pr Cayey Univ
Coll
Cayey, PR

Rosado Santiago, Luis E
Caribbean Univ
Bayamon, PR

Rosario Morales, Eneida
Univ Of Pr At
Mayaguez
Mayaguez, PR

Rosario Rivera, Sonia M
Univ Of Pr Humacao
Univ Coll
Humacao, PR

Rosario, Caroline
Bayamon Central Univ
Bayamon, PR

Rosario, Michaelangelo
Inter Amer Univ Pr
Hato Rey
Hato Rey, PR

Rosas, Angel L
Univ Of Pr At
Mayaguez
Mayaguez, PR

Rose, Anthony
Indiana Univ Of Pa
Indiana, PA

Rose, Maureen
S U N Y Coll Of Tech
At Frmgdl
Farmingdale, NY

Rose, Michael A
Lexington Comm Coll
Lexington, KY

Rose, Roger E
Tallahassee Comm Coll
Tallahassee, FL

Roseberry, Trevor D
Fl A & M Univ
Tallahassee, FL

Roselli, Anthony T
S U N Y Coll Of Tech
At Alfred
Alfred, NY

Rosen, Rosa Ines
City Univ Of Ny City
Coll
New York, NY

Rosenbalm Jr, Larry F
Roane St Comm Coll
Harriman, TN

Rosenhaus, Jason C
Univ Of Miami
Coral Gables, FL

Rosman, Deanna Lyn
Univ Of Miami
Coral Gables, FL

Ross, Amanda K
Bluefield St Coll
Bluefield, WV

Ross, Brian A
United States Naval
Academy
Annapolis, MD

Ross, Gerrit D
Morehouse Coll
Atlanta, GA

Ross, Jennifer M
Oh Univ
Athens, OH

Ross, Kimberly M
Univ Of Sc At
Columbia
Columbia, SC

Ross, Nicolla R
Oh St Univ
Columbus, OH

Ross, Robin L
Glassboro St Coll
Glassboro, NJ

Ross, Theresa K
Prince Georges Comm
Coll
Largo, MD

Ross-Wade, Kim
City Univ Of Ny
Baruch Coll
New York, NY

Rossini, Dan J
Bridgeport Engr Inst
Fairfield, CT

Roth, Edit
Ny Univ
New York, NY

Roth, Michael J
Univ Of Ct
Storrs, CT

Roth, Rachel D
Ursinus Coll
Collegeville, PA

Rothermel, Stacy L
Savannah Coll Of Art
& Design
Savannah, GA

Rothrock, Donna L
Va Commonwealth Univ
Richmond, VA

Rothrock, Edward K
Pa St Univ Main Cmps
University Pk, PA

Rottenberg, Jason L
Georgetown Univ
Washington, DC

Rotzko, Vicki Lynn
Univ Of Pa
Philadelphia, PA

Rountree, Zeloma C
Vance Granville Comm
Coll
Henderson, NC

Rouse, Scott L
Univ Of Southern Ms
Hattiesburg, MS

Rowan, Roslyn
Marywood Coll
Scranton, PA

Rowe, Angela E
S U N Y Coll Of Tech
At Delhi
Delhi, NY

Rowe, Kirstin T
Mary Baldwin Coll
Staunton, VA

Rowe, Melanie Leigh
Ga Southwestern Coll
Americus, GA

Rowe, Michael M
Duquesne Univ
Pittsburgh, PA

Rowe, Olivia M
Bennett Coll
Greensboro, NC

Roxbury, Linda F
Commonwealth Coll
Virginia Beach, VA

Roy, Anjana
City Univ Of Ny
Kingsborough
Brooklyn, NY

Rozenshteyn, Gary
City Univ Of Ny
Baruch Coll
New York, NY

Rozenveld, Jan
Fl International Univ
Miami, FL

Rozewski, Tricia A
Oh Wesleyan Univ
Delaware, OH

Ruane, John G
Embry Riddle
Aeronautical Univ
Daytona Beach, FL

Rubin, Susan R
Lesley Coll
Cambridge, MA

Rubinstein, Reena D
Univ Of Sc At
Columbia
Columbia, SC

Rubio, Nancy V
Bunker Hill Comm Coll
Boston, MA

Rucci, Sergio
Univ Of Rochester
Rochester, NY

Rudder, Gail J
Long Island Coll Hosp
Of Nrsng
Brooklyn, NY

Rudolph, Timothy B
Al A & M Univ
Normal, AL

Rudolph-Thompson,
Marilyn J
Bowie St Univ
Bowie, MD

Rudy, Stacey R
Northampton County
Area Coll
Bethlehem, PA

Ruffin, Jeffrey D
Ms St Univ
Miss State, MS

Ruggeri, Gina M
Univ Of Ct
Storrs, CT

Ruiz Tomassini, Maritza
Inter Amer Univ Pr
Aquadilla
Aguadilla, PR

Ruiz, John L
Inter Amer Univ Pr
Hato Rey
Hato Rey, PR

Ruiz, Joy
Univ Of Pr At Rio
Piedras
Rio Piedras, PR

Ruiz, Maria B
Inter Amer Univ Pr San
German
San German, PR

Runnels, Michael S
Fl St Univ
Tallahassee, FL

Ruppel, Kim B
Kent St Univ Kent
Cmps
Kent, OH

Rushing, Daniel Harry
Univ Of South Fl
Tampa, FL

Russell, Chad S
Northeastern Univ
Boston, MA

Russell, Dannielle L
Paine Coll
Augusta, GA

Russell, David C
Union Coll
Barbourville, KY

Russell, Dolan L
Savannah St Coll
Savannah, GA

Russell, Evelyn H
Vance Granville Comm
Coll
Henderson, NC

Russell Jr, Gary
Fl Memorial Coll
Miami, FL

Russell, Kimberley F
Coll Of William &
Mary
Williamsburg, VA

Russell, Macresia L
Al A & M Univ
Normal, AL

Russell, Mary H
Western Ky Univ
Bowling Green, KY

Russell, Michelle A
Elmira Coll
Elmira, NY

Russell, Wilma V
Coll Of New Rochelle
New Rochelle, NY

Russo, Anna Nicole
Birmingham Southern
Coll
Birmingham, AL

Russo, Lucille G
Seton Hall Univ
South Orange, NJ

Russo, Rick J
Wagner Coll
Staten Island, NY

Russo, Susie M
Newbury Coll
Brookline, MA

Rutner, Heather W
Yeshiva Univ
New York, NY

Rutty, Sophia A
Cheyney Univ Of Pa
Cheyney, PA

Ryan, Melissa A
Le Moyne Coll
Syracuse, NY

Ryan, Patricia L
S U N Y Coll At
Fredonia
Fredonia, NY

Rybak, Kevin R
Niagara Univ
Niagara Univ, NY

Rycraw, Ramsey G
Georgetown Univ
Washington, DC

Rylke, Patrice L
Saint Francis Coll
Loretto, PA

Ryon, David B
Central St Univ
Wilberforce, OH

Rzeznikiewicz, Nancy E
Western New England
Coll
Springfield, MA

Sabella, Terri-Marie E
The Boston
Conservatory
Boston, MA

Sabine, Naropa
Memphis Academy Of
The Arts
Memphis, TN

Sabree, Rachel
Claflin Coll
Orangeburg, SC

Sadeghi, Abbas Ali
Miami Dade Comm Coll
Miami, FL

Sadlon, Amy M
Schenectady County
Comm Coll
Schenectady, NY

Sadock, Dr Jennifer B
Life Coll
Marietta, GA

Saether, Debra L
Dowling Coll
Oakdale Li, NY

Safeek, Abraham
Tn St Univ
Nashville, TN

Saini, Tina K
Univ Of Pa
Philadelphia, PA

Saint-Aime, Pascale
Coll Of Insurance
New York, NY

Saitowitz, Hadley N
New England Coll Of
Optometry
Boston, MA

Sak, Gilbert
Manhattan School Of
Music
New York, NY

Sakaya, Helio S
Nova Univ
Ft Lauderdale, FL

Sakkab, Dalia H
Le Moyne Coll
Syracuse, NY

Sal, Natalie J
Wv Univ
Morgantown, WV

Salaam, Al-Nisa
Benedict Coll
Columbia, SC

Salam, Basilio
Central Fl Comm Coll
Ocala, FL

Saldana, Javier A
Methodist Coll
Fayetteville, NC

Saleem, Fazana S
Bryn Mawr Coll
Bryn Mawr, PA

Salerni, Christine M
Saint Joseph Coll
West Hartford, CT

Sales, Susan A
Univ Of Nc At
Asheville
Asheville, NC

Salinas Ramirez,
Francisco J
Univ Politecnica De Pr
Hato Rey, PR

Salinas, Rosa D
Saint Lawrence Univ
Canton, NY

Salinsky, Heather L
Indiana Univ Of Pa
Indiana, PA

Saller, Timothy R
Fl International Univ
Miami, FL

Salley, Laguamna M
Norfolk St Univ
Norfolk, VA

Salmon, Cynthia H
Fl International Univ
Miami, FL

Salter, Jennifer J
Ms St Univ
Miss State, MS

Saltzman, James M
Glassboro St Coll
Glassboro, NJ

Salus, Lori A
Marywood Coll
Scranton, PA

Salva Figueroa, Luis
Raul
Inter Amer Univ Pr
Hato Rey
Hato Rey, PR

Salva, Catherine E
Univ Of Pr At Rio
Piedras
Rio Piedras, PR

Salva, Eric W
Edinboro Univ Of Pa
Edinboro, PA

Samarasinghe, Deepthi J
Eckerd Coll
St Petersburg, FL

Samaroo, Marlyn S D
City Univ Of Ny La
Guard Coll
Long Island Cty, NY

Samms, Donovan A
Nova Univ
Ft Lauderdale, FL

Sample II, Byron
Rensselaer Polytechnic
Inst
Troy, NY

Sampson, Michelle K
Daytona Beach Comm
Coll
Daytona Beach, FL

Sams, Gregory B
Morehouse Coll
Atlanta, GA

Samuel, Modestine J
Coker Coll
Hartsville, SC

Samuels, Jennifer L
Univ Of Sc At
Columbia
Columbia, SC

San Severino, Anita R
Bunker Hill Comm Coll
Boston, MA

Sanan, Abhay
Boston Univ
Boston, MA

Sanchez, David
Univ Of Pr Medical
Sciences
San Juan, PR

Sanchez, Eldaliz
Inter Amer Univ Pr
Guayama
Guayama, PR

Sanchez, Giovanny F
City Univ Of Ny City
Coll
New York, NY

Sanchez, Marlon
Mikhail
Morehouse Coll
Atlanta, GA

Sanchez, Pedro L
Inter Amer Univ Pr San
German
San German, PR

Sanchez, Rosemary
Fl International Univ
Miami, FL

Sanchez, Roxanna N
Coastal Carolina Comm
Coll
Jacksonville, NC

Sandelin, Levi D
Tn Temple Univ
Chattanooga, TN

Sander, Douglas W
Union Univ
Jackson, TN

Sanders, Carole L
East Tn St Univ
Johnson City, TN

Sanders, Cynthia Joy
Ga St Univ
Atlanta, GA

Sanders, David J
Chattahoochee Vly St
Comm Coll
Phenix City, AL

Sanders, Jeannette
Mattatuck Comm Coll
Waterbury, CT

Sanders, Jennifer L
Clark Atlanta Univ
Atlanta, GA

Sanders, Kaz G
Morehouse Coll
Atlanta, GA

Sanders, Keevin C
Al St Univ
Montgomery, AL

Sanders, Margaret C
Allen Univ
Columbia, SC

Sanders, S Darryl
Brewer St Jr Coll
Fayette, AL

Sanders, Tanya M
Middle Ga Coll
Cochran, GA

Sang, Shiwei
City Univ Of Ny City
Coll
New York, NY

Sankowski, Alex J
Univ Of Sc At
Columbia
Columbia, SC

Sano, Laura K
Saint Bonaventure Univ
St Bonventure, NY

Santa Maria, Rafael P
Fl Memorial Coll
Miami, FL

Santana, Belkys
Miami Dade Comm Coll
South
Miami, FL

Santana, Ileana
Inter Amer Univ Pr
Hato Rey
Hato Rey, PR

Santana-Ferrer, Vanessa
Univ Of Pr Cayey Univ
Coll
Cayey, PR

Santiago Felix, Priscilla
Univ Of Pr At
Mayaguez
Mayaguez, PR

Santiago Maldonado,
Jonaida
Inter Amer Univ Pr
Hato Rey
Hato Rey, PR

Santiago, Carmen
Univ Del Turabo
Gurabo, PR

Santiago, Doris
Caribbean Univ
Bayamon, PR

Santiago, Janet
City Univ Of Ny La
Guard Coll
Long Island Cty, NY

Santiago, Jose L
Univ Politecnica De Pr
Hato Rey, PR

Santiago, Lourdes S
Univ Politecnica De Pr
Hato Rey, PR

Santiago, Robert A
Univ Politecnica De Pr
Hato Rey, PR

Santiago, Secundino A
Inter Amer Univ Pr
Guayama
Guayama, PR

Santiago-Lopez, Jeanette
Catholic Univ Of Pr
Ponce, PR

Santilli, Loretta A
Univ Of Rochester
Rochester, NY

Santillo, Michael R
Rochester Inst Of Tech
Rochester, NY

Santini, Jeffrey M
Va St Univ
Petersburg, VA

Santo, Christina M
Marywood Coll
Scranton, PA

Santora, Jeannette
Montclair St Coll
Upr Montclair, NJ

Santoro, John Michael
Georgetown Univ
Washington, DC

Santos Martinez, Elsa
Melanie
Inter Amer Univ Pr
Hato Rey
Hato Rey, PR

Santos, Ana T
Univ Of Pr At Rio Piedras
Rio Piedras, PR

Santos, Gaylene F
City Univ Of Ny City Coll
New York, NY

Santos, Ivelisse
Pratt Inst
Brooklyn, NY

Santos Jr, Rodolfo R
A D Little Mgmt Educ Inst
Cambridge, MA

Santos, Sharon Y
Univ Of Pr At Rio Piedras
Rio Piedras, PR

Sanyer, Wolfgang F
S U N Y Coll Of Tech At Frmgdl
Farmingdale, NY

Sao Vicente, Carlos Manuel De
A D Little Mgmt Educ Inst
Cambridge, MA

Saoud, Jihad Ghazi
Univ Of Southern Ms
Hattiesburg, MS

Saperstein, Erik
Russell Sage Coll At Troy
Troy, NY

Sapp, Julie M
Saint John Fisher Coll
Rochester, NY

Saputelli, Sharon M
Drexel Univ
Philadelphia, PA

Saraceni, Raymond A
Villanova Univ
Villanova, PA

Sargeant, Deon Lee
City Univ Of Ny City Coll
New York, NY

Sargent, Deanna Jean
Beckley Coll
Beckley, WV

Sargent, Tommie D
Bluefield Coll
Bluefield, VA

Sarno, Graziella M
Duquesne Univ
Pittsburgh, PA

Sarpong, Comfort A
S U N Y Coll Of Tech At Frmgdl
Farmingdale, NY

Sartin, Tracey A
Schenectady County Comm Coll
Schenectady, NY

Sarwar, Mushtaq A
Fl St Univ
Tallahassee, FL

Sasser, Catherine L
Draughons Jr Coll Nashville
Nashville, TN

Sasso, Robert
Bloomfield Coll
Bloomfield, NJ

Sasson, Nicole L
Univ Of Rochester
Rochester, NY

Satterfield, Michael K
Univ Of Nc At Charlotte
Charlotte, NC

Saunders, Christy L
Oh Univ-Southern Cmps
Ironton, OH

Saunders, Rory T
Norfolk St Univ
Norfolk, VA

Saunders, Steven J
Clayton St Coll
Morrow, GA

Sawyer, Kimberly L
Univ Of Sc At Columbia
Columbia, SC

Sawyer, Patricia R
Blue Mountain Coll
Blue Mountain, MS

Sawyer, Timothy M
Atlantic Comm Coll
Mays Landing, NJ

Sawyer, Tushina S
Coppin St Coll
Baltimore, MD

Saxon, Edward B
Howard Univ
Washington, DC

Sayban, Chad A
Gannon Univ
Erie, PA

Sayeed, Siraj A
Univ Of Louisville
Louisville, KY

Saylor, Elizabeth A
Fl St Univ
Tallahassee, FL

Scaglione, Domenick
Dowling Coll
Oakdale Li, NY

Scarber Jr, Preston
Univ Of Al At Birmingham
Birmingham, AL

Scarbrough, Carolyn
City Univ Of Ny City Coll
New York, NY

Scavo, Rose Marie A
Dowling Coll
Oakdale Li, NY

Scelfo, Jacqueline M
S U N Y Coll Of Tech At Frmgdl
Farmingdale, NY

Schacht, Melissa A
Univ Of Ky
Lexington, KY

Schaefer Jr, William M
Hudson Valley Comm Coll
Troy, NY

Schanzenbacher, Lisa A
Saint John Fisher Coll
Rochester, NY

Scharadin, Lori E
Central Pa Bus School
Summerdale, PA

Schenker, Adam E
Univ Of South Fl
Tampa, FL

Schenquerman, Sebastian
Univ Of Pr At Rio Piedras
Rio Piedras, PR

Schermerhorn, Cara L
Univ Of Rochester
Rochester, NY

Scheuerman, Tracy L
Kent St Univ Kent Cmps
Kent, OH

Scheuren, Shannon T
Wilkes Univ
Wilkes-Barre, PA

Scheuring, Malissa A
Franciscin Univ/ Steubenville
Steubenville, OH

Schiffman, Randi Allison
Cornell Univ
Ithaca, NY

Schlatmann, Roseann Elizabeth
Cazenovia Coll
Cazenovia, NY

Schlemmer, Todd R
Wv Univ
Morgantown, WV

Schmid, Sheri E
Univ Of Miami
Coral Gables, FL

Schmidt, Juan R
Barry Univ
Miami, FL

Schmidt, Sarah L
Miami Jacobs Jr Coll Of Bus
Dayton, OH

Schmink, Suzanne Marie
Endicott Coll
Beverly, MA

Schmitz, Tony L
Temple Univ
Philadelphia, PA

Schneider, Donna S
Radford Univ
Radford, VA

Schoeneberger, Marlies
Spalding Univ
Louisville, KY

Schoepflin, Jonathan D
Va Commonwealth Univ
Richmond, VA

Schoettmer, Jason M
Univ Of Cincinnati
Cincinnati, OH

Schoots, Harrie P
Western New England Coll
Springfield, MA

Schreiner, Susan C
Immaculata Coll
Immaculata, PA

Schrock, Brandie J
Daytona Beach Comm Coll
Daytona Beach, FL

Schroeder, Christopher
Limestone Coll
Gaffney, SC

Schroeder, Diana Carolina
Dowling Coll
Oakdale Li, NY

Schuler, Brenda J
Philadelphia Coll Pharm & Sci
Philadelphia, PA

Schuler, Linda C
Judson Coll
Marion, AL

Schultz, Elena Rae F
Barry Univ
Miami, FL

Schultz, Kimberly A
Northern Ky Univ
Highland Hts, KY

Schultz, Kimberly R
Cornell Univ Statutory College
Ithaca, NY

Schultz, Loretta A
The Kings Coll
Briarclf Mnr, NY

Schultz, Sherri A
Duquesne Univ
Pittsburgh, PA

Schultz, Steven M
Univ Of North Fl
Jacksonville, FL

Schuman, David A
Fl International Univ
Miami, FL

Schutterop, Michael R
Clarkson Univ
Potsdam, NY

Schwab, Jodi E
Univ Of Ky
Lexington, KY

Schwartz, Eric W
Columbus Coll Of Art & Design
Columbus, OH

Schweers, Sheila N
Coll Of Charleston
Charleston, SC

Schweitzer, Jennifer L
Northern Ky Univ
Highland Hts, KY

Schweize, Amy K
Univ Of Miami
Coral Gables, FL

Schwierzke, Maria D
Andover Coll
Portland, ME

Sciulli, David R
Univ Of Pittsburgh
Pittsburgh, PA

Scoggins, Darren J
Middle Tn St Univ
Murfreesboro, TN

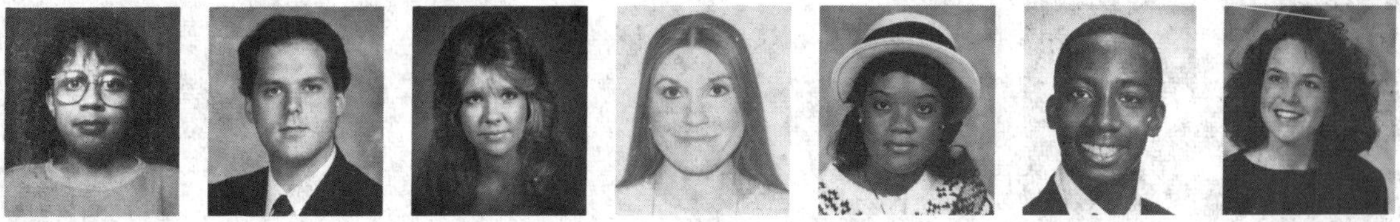

Scoggins, Sonja Y
Southern Coll Of Tech
Marietta, GA

Scollick, Keith A
Villanova Univ
Villanova, PA

Scott, Amie R
Thomas Nelson Comm Coll
Hampton, VA

Scott, Beverly T
New England Coll Of Optometry
Boston, MA

Scott, Estella A
Univ Of Sc At Columbia
Columbia, SC

Scott, John L
West Chester Univ
West Chester, PA

Scott, Leann
Ms St Univ
Miss State, MS

Scott, Lisa N
Morris Brown Coll
Atlanta, GA

Scott, Tammy Lynn
Brevard Coll
Brevard, NC

Scott, Violet R
Saint Josephs Coll New York
Brooklyn, NY

Scotton, Tameka M
Tomlinson Coll
Cleveland, TN

Scrivner, Joseph F
Crichton Coll
Memphis, TN

Scurlock, Cynthia A
Nc Agri & Tech St Univ
Greensboro, NC

Scutchall, Susan R
Mount Aloysius Jr Coll
Cresson, PA

Seals, Lisa A
Niagara Univ
Niagara Univ, NY

Sears, Jan M
Commonwealth Coll
Virginia Beach, VA

Secnik, Martina
Cleveland St Univ
Cleveland, OH

Secora, Christopher M
Youngstown St Univ
Youngstown, OH

Seda, Sandra Lee
City Univ Of Ny Baruch Coll
New York, NY

Segal, Pamela D
Saint Thomas Univ
Miami, FL

Segalen, Yann Francois
Winthrop Coll
Rock Hill, SC

Segarra, Cesar A
Inter Amer Univ Pr Hato Rey
Hato Rey, PR

Seger, Julia L
Univ Of Pittsburgh
Pittsburgh, PA

Segovia, Javier
Ma Inst Of Tech
Cambridge, MA

Seifert, Dana C
Univ Of Southern Ms
Hattiesburg, MS

Seiferth, Curtis D
S U N Y Coll Of Tech At Frmgdl
Farmingdale, NY

Seitz, Gregory K
Univ Of North Al
Florence, AL

Seiz, Kristen A
Glassboro St Coll
Glassboro, NJ

Sejour, Jeannette N
Univ Of Fl
Gainesville, FL

Selby, Regina A
Tn Tech Univ
Cookeville, TN

Selke, Tamala Sue
Columbia Coll
Columbia, SC

Sellers, Kimberly R
Livingston Univ
Livingston, AL

Selvanathan, Padhmanathan
City Univ Of Ny Lehman Coll
Bronx, NY

Semian, Douglas D
Allegheny Coll
Meadville, PA

Semprevio, Stacey M
Hudson Valley Comm Coll
Troy, NY

Sena, Jenny P
Wagner Coll
Staten Island, NY

Senati Martinez, Santiago
Univ Politecnica De Pr
Hato Rey, PR

Sendeza, Henry C
Wilberforce Univ
Wilberforce, OH

Senhouse, Elbert
City Univ Of Ny Med Evers Coll
Brooklyn, NY

Senior, Scott D
Pa St Univ Altoona Cmps
Altoona, PA

Sennett, Paula J
Indiana Univ Of Pa
Indiana, PA

Sensevy Lirusso, Maria
Univ Of Pr Medical Sciences
San Juan, PR

Sepic, Christopher A
Allegheny Coll
Meadville, PA

Serfass, Jennifer L
Juniata Coll
Huntingdon, PA

Serna, Javier
City Univ Of Ny
Baruch Coll
New York, NY

Seshadri, Prakash
Univ Of Rochester
Rochester, NY

Seto, Benny W
City Univ Of Ny City
Coll
New York, NY

Setzer, Jennifer L
Univ Of Sc At
Columbia
Columbia, SC

Severance, Michele R
Univ Of Cin R Walters
Coll
Blue Ash, OH

Sewell, Betty D
Wallace St Comm Coll
At Selma
Selma, AL

Seydi, Aly D
City Univ Of Ny Med
Evers Coll
Brooklyn, NY

Seymour Anderson,
Raymond D
Nova Univ
Ft Lauderdale, FL

Sferrazza-Capobianco,
Donnalee
Asnuntuck Comm Coll
Enfield, CT

Shaffer, Stephen A
Ga Inst Of Tech At
Atlanta
Atlanta, GA

Shafiq, Amtus Sami
Edison Comm Coll
Fort Myers, FL

Shah, Jaibala K
Univ Of Med &
Dentistry Of Nj
Newark, NJ

Shahin, Marwan R
Univ Of South Al
Mobile, AL

Shand, John D
Meridian Comm Coll
Meridian, MS

Shane, Lawrence E
Univ Of Miami
Coral Gables, FL

Shannon, Gwen A
Villanova Univ
Villanova, PA

Sharan, Nivedita
Case Western Reserve
Univ
Cleveland, OH

Sharer, Andrew E
Univ Of South Al
Mobile, AL

Sharp, Emily S
Lindsey Wilson Coll
Columbia, KY

Sharp, Michael Ray
Univ Of Sc At Coastal
Carolina
Conway, SC

Sharp, Willie H
East Tn St Univ
Johnson City, TN

Sharpe, Cicely
Tn St Univ
Nashville, TN

Sharpe, Robert H
Barry Univ
Miami, FL

Shashua, Michal
Fl International Univ
Miami, FL

Shattuck, James S
Kent St Univ Kent
Cmps
Kent, OH

Shattuck, Kristen M
Lesley Coll
Cambridge, MA

Shaw, Marc D
Pembroke St Univ
Pembroke, NC

Shaw, Reuben J
Cornell Univ Statutory
College
Ithaca, NY

Shea, Todd M
Salisbury St Univ
Salisbury, MD

Sheaffer, Elizabeth A
Lord Fairfax Comm
Coll
Middletown, VA

Sheaffer, Suzanne M
Univ Of Fl
Gainesville, FL

Shealey, Roxanne E
Abraham Baldwin Agri
Coll
Tifton, GA

Shealy, Cary R
Univ Of Sc At
Columbia
Columbia, SC

Shearin III, Henry B
Vance Granville Comm
Coll
Henderson, NC

Sheffar, Michael P
Kent St Univ Kent
Cmps
Kent, OH

Sheffield, Amanda I
Southern Coll Of
Seventh Day
Collegedale, TN

Sheffield III, Arthur
Howard Univ
Washington, DC

Shelton, April D
Union Univ School Of
Nursing
Memphis, TN

Shelton, Laura F
Muskingum Coll
New Concord, OH

Shelton, Patti I
North Ga Coll
Dahlonega, GA

Shenk, Gregory C
Bridgewater Coll
Bridgewater, VA

Sheriff, Jeffrey P
Tri County Tech Coll
Pendleton, SC

Sherrow, Sandra K
Hillsborough Comm Coll
Tampa, FL

Sherson, Brenda L
Fl Atlantic Univ
Boca Raton, FL

Shevlin, Ann Marie
Marywood Coll
Scranton, PA

Shifarraw, Tutu
Defiance Coll
Defiance, OH

Shin, Hee Young
Georgetown Univ
Washington, DC

Shipley, Mildred V
Coppin St Coll
Baltimore, MD

Shirley, Tamara J
Piedmont Tech Coll
Greenwood, SC

Shiver, Laurie L
Univ Of Ga
Athens, GA

Shivers, Sonja D
Morris Brown Coll
Atlanta, GA

Shola, Jennifer M
Merrimack Coll
North Andover, MA

Shook, Stacey L
Wv Univ
Morgantown, WV

Short, Cynthia D
Univ Of Va Clinch Valley Coll
Wise, VA

Short, Denise L
Va St Univ
Petersburg, VA

Shorten, John D
Temple Univ
Philadelphia, PA

Shoukoohi, Masoud
Medical Coll Of Ga
Augusta, GA

Showstead, Janet A
Bunker Hill Comm Coll
Boston, MA

Shroff, Ninad A
Dartmouth Coll
Hanover, NH

Shtender, Lyubov
Bunker Hill Comm Coll
Boston, MA

Shu, Fred
Cornell Univ Statutory College
Ithaca, NY

Shultz, John R
Univ Of Al At Huntsville
Huntsville, AL

Shuttlesworth, Traci L
Norfolk St Univ
Norfolk, VA

Sianipar, Konrad T
Oh Univ
Athens, OH

Sidon, Babe N
Oh St Univ
Columbus, OH

Sidrak, Robert J
Univ Of Md At Eastern Shore
Princess Anne, MD

Sierra, Eileen Y
Univ Politecnica De Pr
Hato Rey, PR

Sierra, Maria J
Fl International Univ
Miami, FL

Sierra, Ramon
Miami Dade Comm Coll
Miami, FL

Sievers Jr, Raymond T
Embry Riddle Aeronautical Univ
Daytona Beach, FL

Sigler, Sherri S
Owensboro Comm Coll
Owensboro, KY

Sigmon, Deborah A
Catawba Valley Comm Coll
Hickory, NC

Sigurdardottir, Kristin
Univ Of Sc At Columbia
Columbia, SC

Sikes Jr, David Glenn
Univ Of Ga
Athens, GA

Sikopoulos, Roula Josephine
Bloomfield Coll
Bloomfield, NJ

Siler, Artina A
Saint Pauls Coll
Lawrenceville, VA

Silvaroli, Nicholas J
Niagara Univ
Niagara Univ, NY

Silvers, Celeste D
Franklin And Marshall Coll
Lancaster, PA

Silverstein, Doug N
Nova Univ
Ft Lauderdale, FL

Sim, Ling L
Va Commonwealth Univ
Richmond, VA

Simas, Susan L
New England Inst Of Tech
Warwick, RI

Simmonds, Gioconda R
S U N Y At Buffalo
Buffalo, NY

Simmons, Alberta M
Central St Univ
Wilberforce, OH

Simmons, Brian T
Univ Of Va
Charlottesville, VA

Simmons, Helen J
Central Fl Comm Coll
Ocala, FL

Simmons, Karen
City Univ Of Ny
Baruch Coll
New York, NY

Simmons, Latonya L
Norfolk St Univ
Norfolk, VA

Simmons, Mary A
Central St Univ
Wilberforce, OH

Simmons, Pamela J
Comm Coll Algny Co
Algny Cmps
Pittsburgh, PA

Simmons, Tory A
Fl A & M Univ
Tallahassee, FL

Simmons, Wendy D
Western Piedmont
Comm Coll
Morganton, NC

Simms, Anita K
Fayetteville St Univ
Fayetteville, NC

Simms, Franchesca O
Bennett Coll
Greensboro, NC

Simms, Roianna L
Daytona Beach Comm
Coll
Daytona Beach, FL

Simon, Amy M
Northern Ky Univ
Highland Hts, KY

Simon, Sandra V
Univ Of The Dist Of
Columbia
Washington, DC

Simpson, Carolyn E
Fl St Univ
Tallahassee, FL

Sims, Henry M
Fl St Univ
Tallahassee, FL

Sims, Scotty L
Central St Univ
Wilberforce, OH

Sinclair, Kelly J
Univ Of South Al
Mobile, AL

Sinclair, Leslie Russell
Univ Of Sc At Union
Union, SC

Sines, Brian James
Anne Arundel Comm
Coll
Arnold, MD

Singer, Melissa C
Univ Of Md Baltimore
Prof Schl
Baltimore, MD

Singh, Mohani D
City Univ Of Ny
Baruch Coll
New York, NY

Singhas, Cameron A
Lenoir Rhyne Coll
Hickory, NC

Singleton, Barry J
Univ Of Al At
Birmingham
Birmingham, AL

Singleton, Brian T
Emory & Henry Coll
Emory, VA

Singleton, Michael J
Southern Coll Of Tech
Marietta, GA

Singleton, Timothy D
Univ Of Sc At
Columbia
Columbia, SC

Sistare, Jon F
North Greenville Coll
Tigerville, SC

Sitafalwalla, Suhail
S U N Y Coll Of Tech
At Frmgdl
Farmingdale, NY

Sitler, Stefanie Diane
Endicott Coll
Beverly, MA

Siu, Lai Mei
City Univ Of Ny
Baruch Coll
New York, NY

Six, Janet M
Marshall University
Huntington, WV

Skaggs, Robert D
Shawnee St Univ
Portsmouth, OH

Skidmore, Bobbie D
Immaculata Coll
Immaculata, PA

Skinner, Deidrah D
Harford Comm Coll
Bel Air, MD

Skinner II, Melvin W
Saint Pauls Coll
Lawrenceville, VA

Skinner, Tracie A
Palm Beach Atlantic
Coll
W Palm Beach, FL

Slaughter, Carmanna L
Watterson Coll
Louisville, KY

Slaughter, Christopher
Wv Univ
Morgantown, WV

Slaughter, Delores B
Hampton Univ
Hampton, VA

Slaughter, Robert A
Thomas Nelson Comm
Coll
Hampton, VA

Slaughter, Stacie A
Saint Thomas Univ
Miami, FL

Sliger, Melanie S
Univ Of Va Clinch Valley Coll
Wise, VA

Sliman, Zorn T
Salisbury St Univ
Salisbury, MD

Sloan, Amanda L
Tn Temple Univ
Chattanooga, TN

Sloan, Stephanie R
Comm Coll Algny Co Algny Cmps
Pittsburgh, PA

Sluzele, Jennifer V
Pa St Univ Main Cmps
University Pk, PA

Small, Michelle L
Casco Bay Coll
Portland, ME

Smalls, Lori Lee
Hillsborough Comm Coll
Tampa, FL

Smallwood, Antoinette J
Univ Of Md At Eastern Shore
Princess Anne, MD

Smart, Clevan L
Hillsborough Comm Coll
Tampa, FL

Smith, Adam J
Cornell Univ Statutory College
Ithaca, NY

Smith, Adrian L
Albany St Coll
Albany, GA

Smith, Amy J
Germanna Comm Coll
Locust Grove, VA

Smith, Amy N
Itawamba Comm Coll
Fulton, MS

Smith, Anthony R
S U N Y Coll Of Tech At Frmgdl
Farmingdale, NY

Smith, Bonnie J
Beckley Coll
Beckley, WV

Smith, Caroline L
Tougaloo Coll
Tougaloo, MS

Smith, Casey W
Hartwick Coll
Oneonta, NY

Smith, Chandilyn D
Fl St Univ
Tallahassee, FL

Smith, Chandra L
Ms St Univ
Miss State, MS

Smith, Charlene M
Kent St Univ Geauga Cmps
Burton Twp, OH

Smith II, Charles G
Univ Of Ga
Athens, GA

Smith, Cheryl J
Johnson C Smith Univ
Charlotte, NC

Smith, Christopher L
Johnson C Smith Univ
Charlotte, NC

Smith, Christopher S
Lurleen B Wallace St Jr Coll
Andalusia, AL

Smith, Cynthia A
Wv Univ At Parkersburg
Parkersburg, WV

Smith, Dana E
Christopher Newport Coll
Newport News, VA

Smith, Deborah D
Tri County Tech Coll
Pendleton, SC

Smith, Deborah R
Northeast Ms Cc
Booneville, MS

Smith, Denise A
City Univ Of Ny Queensbrough
New York, NY

Smith, Florine
Norfolk St Univ
Norfolk, VA

Smith, Fredreika W
Columbia Union Coll
Takoma Park, MD

Smith, Gayle A
Owensboro Comm Coll
Owensboro, KY

Smith, Gina L
Univ Of Sc At Spartanburg
Spartanburg, SC

Smith, Guy Alan
Coll Of Charleston
Charleston, SC

Smith, Helen E T
Bloomfield Coll
Bloomfield, NJ

Smith, Henry W
Howard Univ
Washington, DC

Smith, Holly S
Univ Of Sc At Coastal Carolina
Conway, SC

Smith, Ingrid T
Wilberforce Univ
Wilberforce, OH

Smith, Jamie L
Fl International Univ
Miami, FL

Smith, Jay D
Northern Ky Univ
Highland Hts, KY

Smith, Jennifer M
Belmont Coll
Nashville, TN

Smith, Jerry A
Meridian Comm Coll
Meridian, MS

Smith, Jo-Carole L
Univ Of Tn At
Chattanooga
Chattanooga, TN

Smith, Joanna L
Oh Univ-Southern Cmps
Ironton, OH

Smith, John H
Univ Of Nc At
Asheville
Asheville, NC

Smith, John P
Brescia Coll
Owensboro, KY

Smith, Joseph Nathaniel
Va St Univ
Petersburg, VA

Smith, Julie A
Roane St Comm Coll
Harriman, TN

Smith, Karen P
Univ Of New Haven
West Haven, CT

Smith, Karyn A
Memphis St Univ
Memphis, TN

Smith, Keith L
Hampton Univ
Hampton, VA

Smith, Kelly J
Slippery Rock Univ
Slippery Rock, PA

Smith, Kevin A
Christopher Newport
Coll
Newport News, VA

Smith, Kimberly L
Christopher Newport
Coll
Newport News, VA

Smith, Kimberly P
Va Commonwealth Univ
Richmond, VA

Smith, La Talia D
Mytryk
Atlanta Metropolitan
Coll
Atlanta, GA

Smith, Leigh Ann
Villanova Univ
Villanova, PA

Smith Jr, Leonard
Calvin
Univ Of Md At Eastern
Shore
Princess Anne, MD

Smith, Lorene A
Marshall University
Huntington, WV

Smith, Mark W
Morehouse Coll
Atlanta, GA

Smith, Martha Jane
Western Ky Univ
Bowling Green, KY

Smith, Martin C
City Univ Of Ny Med
Evers Coll
Brooklyn, NY

Smith, Michael A
Coker Coll
Hartsville, SC

Smith, Michael W
Salisbury St Univ
Salisbury, MD

Smith, Michelle D
Jackson St Univ
Jackson, MS

Smith, N Faith
Va Commonwealth Univ
Richmond, VA

Smith, Pamela D
Western Piedmont
Comm Coll
Morganton, NC

Smith, Rhonda N
Johnson C Smith Univ
Charlotte, NC

Smith, Richard Nguyen
Longwood Coll
Farmville, VA

Smith, Richard T
Univ Of West Fl
Pensacola, FL

Smith, Shawna M
Univ Of Tn At Martin
Martin, TN

Smith, Sherry Lynn
Oh St Univ At Marion
Marion, OH

Smith, Tania D
Yale Univ
New Haven, CT

Smith, Tara L
Indiana Univ Of Pa
Indiana, PA

Smith Jr, Thomas E
Memphis St Univ
Memphis, TN

Smith, Tiffany A
Va St Univ
Petersburg, VA

Smith, Timothy A
Oh St Univ
Columbus, OH

Smith, Travis E
Southern Coll Of Tech
Marietta, GA

Smith-Hall, Olive B L
Al A & M Univ
Normal, AL

Smolenski, Mark S
Univ Of Ct
Storrs, CT

Snay, Cheryl L
Hudson Valley Comm
Coll
Troy, NY

Sneed, Monique B
Univ Of Md At Eastern
Shore
Princess Anne, MD

Snipe, Mark D
Cornell Univ Statutory
College
Ithaca, NY

Snowden, Regina G
Univ Of Ky
Lexington, KY

Snowden, Scott A
Ga Inst Of Tech At Atlanta
Atlanta, GA

Snyder, Angela B
Schenectady County Comm Coll
Schenectady, NY

Snyder, Ryan G
Norwich Univ
Northfield, VT

Snyder, Terri L
West Chester Univ
West Chester, PA

Soares, Cacia O
Anderson Coll
Anderson, SC

Sobala, Malgorzata
Univ Of Fl
Gainesville, FL

Socorro, Raul E
City Univ Of Ny City Coll
New York, NY

Sohn, David H
Harvard Univ
Cambridge, MA

Sole, Kathleen R
Belmont Tech Coll
St Clairsvl, OH

Sollien, Tanya G
Univ Of Va Clinch Valley Coll
Wise, VA

Solomon, Russell L
Fashion Inst Of Tech
New York, NY

Soltysiak, Marly A
Siena Coll
Loudonville, NY

Somaiya, Manish A
City Univ Of Ny Baruch Coll
New York, NY

Somarriba, Aristides
Ma Inst Of Tech
Cambridge, MA

Somerville, Moya E
Morgan St Univ
Baltimore, MD

Sommer, Kimberly A
Univ Of Nc At Charlotte
Charlotte, NC

Sonneveld, Bettina
Univ Of Miami
Coral Gables, FL

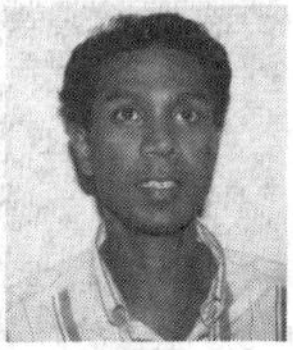
Soobryan, Paul K
City Univ Of Ny Bronx Comm Col
Bronx, NY

Soodeen, Reann
Broward Comm Coll
Ft Lauderdale, FL

Sorensen, Angelia M
Abraham Baldwin Agri Coll
Tifton, GA

Sorin, Nataliya
Univ Of Tn At Martin
Martin, TN

Sorrentino, Theresa M
Univ Of Fl
Gainesville, FL

Sosa, Lillian Esther
Bayamon Central Univ
Bayamon, PR

Soto Carmenatty, Felix
Inter Amer Univ Pr San German
San German, PR

Soto, Alfredo J
Goucher Coll
Towson, MD

Soto, Anti Nelly
Univ Of Pr At Rio Piedras
Rio Piedras, PR

Soto, Virginia I
Fl International Univ
Miami, FL

Soto-Hernandez, Denis
Evangelical Semimary Of P R
Hato Rey, PR

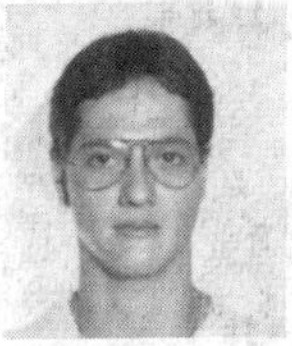
Sotomayor Ramirez, Hector R
Inter Amer Univ Pr San German
San German, PR

Sousa, Stefan C
City Univ Of Ny Baruch Coll
New York, NY

Southall, Alysia D
Wv Univ At Parkersburg
Parkersburg, WV

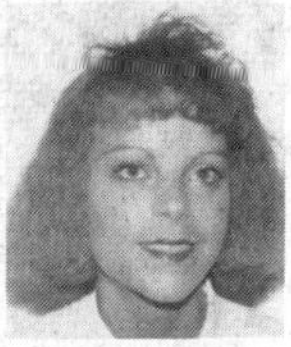
Southard, Babette L
Greenville Tech Coll
Greenville, SC

Southard, Christine M
Roane St Comm Coll
Harriman, TN

Southerland, Daniel S
Middle Ga Coll
Cochran, GA

Sow, Maimouna
Central St Univ
Wilberforce, OH

Sowell, Stacy M
Univ Of Ms Main Cmps
University, MS

Spady, Benedict Q
Norfolk St Univ
Norfolk, VA

Spahn, Suzanne C
Philadelphia Coll Pharm & Sci
Philadelphia, PA

Spawn-Paul, Barbara Jene
Siena Coll
Loudonville, NY

Speaks, Ellen D
Auburn Univ At Montgomery
Montgomery, AL

Speckmann, Lauren M
Casco Bay Coll
Portland, ME

Speights, Pamela V
Craven Comm Coll
New Bern, NC

Spells, Adrienne N
Tougaloo Coll
Tougaloo, MS

Spencer, Deirdre A
Howard Univ
Washington, DC

Spencer, Mary A
Marshall University
Huntington, WV

Spicer, Darlene M
Gordon Conwell Theol Sem
S Hamilton, MA

Spicer, Kirstie E J
Lesley Coll
Cambridge, MA

Spilsbury, Theodore R
Salisbury St Univ
Salisbury, MD

Spivey, Natasha L
Norfolk St Univ
Norfolk, VA

Spotorno, Anna Marie
Ny Univ
New York, NY

Spotts, Vincent J
Univ Of Pittsburgh
Pittsburgh, PA

Sprayberry, Jennifer A
Central Al Comm Coll
Alexander City, AL

Squires, Stuart M
Elizabeth City St Univ
Elizabeth City, NC

Sreenivas, Mytheli
Yale Univ
New Haven, CT

Srinivas, Christopher R
Manhattan Coll
Bronx, NY

St Louis, Magdalene
Central Fl Comm Coll
Ocala, FL

St Victor, Sabine
City Univ Of Ny Baruch Coll
New York, NY

Stachowicz III, John J
Dartmouth Coll
Hanover, NH

Staffin, Allison B
Glassboro St Coll
Glassboro, NJ

Stafford, Susan M
Ms Univ For Women
Columbus, MS

Stafford II, Thomas D
Itawamba Comm Coll
Fulton, MS

Stagenhorst, Kristie L
Colby Sawyer Coll
New London, NH

Staggs Jr, Dean
Lake City Comm Coll
Lake City, FL

Stainio, Gabrielle A
Villanova Univ
Villanova, PA

Staley, Nichole M
Univ Of Pittsburgh
Pittsburgh, PA

Stamps, Sharon L
Univ Of Sc At Columbia
Columbia, SC

Stamps, Stacie D
Univ Of Southern Ms
Hattiesburg, MS

Stanfield, Eric L
Tallahassee Comm Coll
Tallahassee, FL

Stanley, Regina L
Univ Of Tn At Martin
Martin, TN

Stanzione, Paula Marie
Seton Hall Univ
South Orange, NJ

Stark, Nathan Daniel W
Central Al Comm Coll
Alexander City, AL

Starks, Loretta
Alcorn St Univ
Lorman, MS

Starks, Raquel N
Al St Univ
Montgomery, AL

Stebbins, Bonnie G
Univ Of South Al
Mobile, AL

Stebbins, Julia S
Univ Of South Al
Mobile, AL

Steckly, Christina M
Jersey City St Coll
Jersey City, NJ

Stefanic, Nanette L
Kent St Univ Geauga Cmps
Burton Twp, OH

Stefano, Vincent
Embry Riddle Aeronautical Univ
Daytona Beach, FL

Stefanski, Sandra M
Wagner Coll
Staten Island, NY

Stefansson, Stefan Th
Methodist Coll
Fayetteville, NC

Steiman, Dori E
Ny Univ
New York, NY

Stein, Ronald D
Liberty Univ
Lynchburg, VA

Stein-Martin, Claudia L
Fl Atlantic Univ
Boca Raton, FL

Steiner, Charles J
Roane St Comm Coll
Harriman, TN

Stejskal, Marcela
Newbury Coll
Brookline, MA

Steliga, Stephanie A
Atlantic Comm Coll
Mays Landing, NJ

Stella, Michael C
Allegheny Coll
Meadville, PA

Stelter, Susan L
Radford Univ
Radford, VA

Stelzer, Renee A
Yeshiva Univ
New York, NY

Stenger, Christine M
Kent St Univ Stark Cmps
North Canton, OH

Stephens, Rolonda A
Fl A & M Univ
Tallahassee, FL

Stephens, Scott E
Appalachian St Univ
Boone, NC

Stephens, Terrance D
Morehouse Coll
Atlanta, GA

Stephenson, Sandria S
Univ Of The Virgin Islands
St Thomas, VI

Sterling, Kenneth W
Bryant Stratton Bus Inst Roch
Rochester, NY

Stevens, Ismay A E
Al A & M Univ
Normal, AL

Stevens, Jason M
Brevard Coll
Brevard, NC

Stevens II, Joel R
Cornell Univ Statutory College
Ithaca, NY

Stevens, Katherine G
Roane St Comm Coll
Harriman, TN

Stevens, Laurie G
Castleton St Coll
Castleton, VT

Stevens, Tiffany D
Middle Tn St Univ
Murfreesboro, TN

Stevens, Valerie E
Bloomfield Coll
Bloomfield, NJ

Stevenson, Cheryl A
Saint Joseph Coll
West Hartford, CT

Stewart, Cheryl G
Univ Of South Al
Mobile, AL

Stewart, Christina M
Neumann Coll
Aston, PA

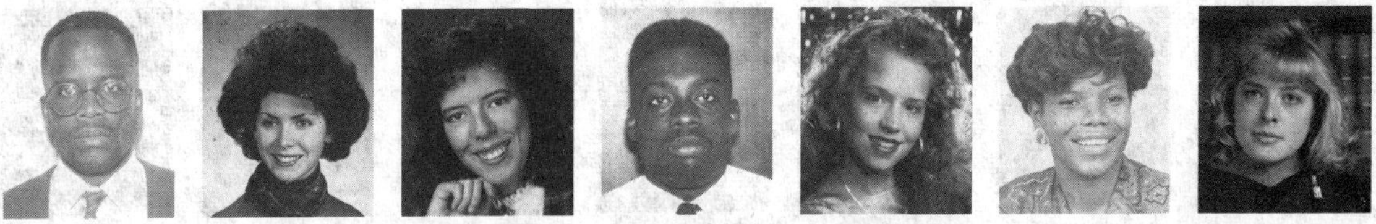

Stewart, Clayton R
Howard Univ
Washington, DC

Stewart, Elyse K
Niagara Univ
Niagara Univ, NY

Stewart, Ida Gwen
Goldey Beacom Coll
Wilmington, DE

Stewart, Moleendo S
Tougaloo Coll
Tougaloo, MS

Stewart, Sharen E
Indiana Univ Of Pa
Indiana, PA

Stewart-Thomas, Sonia
Ny Univ
New York, NY

Stiffler, Kelly W
Mt Saint Marys Coll & Seminary
Emmitsburg, MD

Still, Ethel R
Selma Univ
Selma, AL

Stilwell, Phillip C
Limestone Coll
Gaffney, SC

Stilwell, Ryan A
Ky Christian Coll
Grayson, KY

Stimpson, Stephanie C
Georgetown Univ
Washington, DC

Stinnette, Pamela J
Marshall University
Huntington, WV

Stinnette, Patricia L
Marshall University
Huntington, WV

Stoessner, Jeannine Marie
Oh St Univ
Columbus, OH

Stohl, David P
Univ Of New Haven
West Haven, CT

Stokes, Karla L
Hampton Univ
Hampton, VA

Stoler, Juan Pedro
Fl Atlantic Univ
Boca Raton, FL

Stoltz, Elizabeth Marie
Mount Aloysius Jr Coll
Cresson, PA

Stone, Bronson B
Bloomsburg Univ Of Pa
Bloomsburg, PA

Stone, Deidre G
Valdosta St Coll
Valdosta, GA

Stone, Jennifer E
James Madison University
Harrisonburg, VA

Stone, Pamela L
Abraham Baldwin Agri Coll
Tifton, GA

Stoneman, Cheryl A
S U N Y Coll Of Tech At Alfred
Alfred, NY

Storey, Jane B
Univ Of New Haven
West Haven, CT

Storrod, Sandra P
Univ Of The Virgin Islands
St Thomas, VI

Stoskus, Caryn J
Bucknell Univ
Lewisburg, PA

Stough, Jonathan Scott
Central Pa Bus School
Summerdale, PA

Stover, Philip D
Tidewater Comm Coll
Portsmouth, VA

Stover-Treadway, Almetta
Wilmington Coll
New Castle, DE

Strang, Michelle L
Univ Of Sc At Columbia
Columbia, SC

Straw, Audra Renee
Oh Univ-Southern Cmps
Ironton, OH

Streck, Mark W
Bridgeport Engr Inst
Fairfield, CT

Strickland, Alison D
Auburn Univ At Auburn
Auburn, AL

Strickland Jr, David M
Vance Granville Comm Coll
Henderson, NC

Strickland, Kent V
Long Island Univ C W Post Cntr
Greenvale, NY

Strickland, Kimberly D
Anderson Coll
Anderson, SC

Strickland, Mary A
Auburn Univ At Auburn
Auburn, AL

Stricklin, Kimberly L
Univ Of Montevallo
Montevallo, AL

Strider, Brigette M
Western Carolina Univ
Cullowhee, NC

Stridiron, Thomas J
Dowling Coll
Oakdale Li, NY

Strimike, Debra J
Clark Univ
Worcester, MA

Stringer, John M
Univ Of Southern Ms
Hattiesburg, MS

Stringfellow, Vicki A
Univ Of Southern Ms
Hattiesburg, MS

Strouth, Jennifer L
East Tn St Univ
Johnson City, TN

Struffolino Jr, Thomas J
Bloomfield Coll
Bloomfield, NJ

Stuard, Lori W
Univ Of Southern Ms
Hattiesburg, MS

Stubblefield, Lisa C
J Sargeant Reynolds Comm Coll
Richmond, VA

Stubblefield Jr, Michael
Thomas Nelson Comm Coll
Hampton, VA

Stubna Jr, Thomas L
Comm Coll Algny Co Algny Cmps
Pittsburgh, PA

Stuckey, Julie A
James Madison University
Harrisonburg, VA

Stucki, Amy
William Paterson Coll
Wayne, NJ

Studebaker, Jennifer M
Univ Of Southern Ms
Hattiesburg, MS

Sturgis, Andrea Deon
Morris Brown Coll
Atlanta, GA

Sturm, Mary E
Hillsborough Comm Coll
Tampa, FL

Stutts, Jeannine W
Univ Of Ky
Lexington, KY

Stutzman, Greg E
Univ Of Pittsburgh
Pittsburgh, PA

Styles, Derrick R
Lenoir Rhyne Coll
Hickory, NC

Styron, Laura L
Univ Of South Al
Mobile, AL

Suarato, Joseph A
Wagner Coll
Staten Island, NY

Suarez Escabi, Sharon L
Inter Amer Univ Pr San German
San German, PR

Suarez Igartua, Gregorio Manuel
Inter Amer Univ Pr San Juan
Hato Rey, PR

Suarez, Diana L
Bloomfield Coll
Bloomfield, NJ

Suber, Patrick
Spartanburg Methodist Coll
Spartanburg, SC

Sucher, Le Ann Mc
Caig
Medical Univ Of Sc
Charleston, SC

Sudo, Emiko S
Univ Of Sc At
Columbia
Columbia, SC

Sulek, Jacqueline L
Western Piedmont
Comm Coll
Morganton, NC

Sullivan, Colleen A
City Univ Of Ny
Baruch Coll
New York, NY

Sullivan, Jayne M
Georgian Court Coll
Lakewood, NJ

Sullivan, Steven W
William Paterson Coll
Wayne, NJ

Sullivan-Nichols,
Kathleen D
Cecils Coll
Asheville, NC

Summerour, Kenya N
Tuskegee Univ
Tuskegee Inst, AL

Summers, Leslie C
Hillsborough Comm
Coll
Tampa, FL

Summers, Tracey L
Wv Univ
Morgantown, WV

Sumner, Tracie D
Longwood Coll
Farmville, VA

Sumpter, Kim L
Benedict Coll
Columbia, SC

Sunara, Ingrid S
City Univ Of Ny
Queensbrough
New York, NY

Sunderland, Simon A
Univ Of Miami
Coral Gables, FL

Sung, Chih-Hsiung
Georgetown Univ
Washington, DC

Supko, Michael P
Univ Of Sc At
Columbia
Columbia, SC

Suri, Hitesh
S U N Y At Buffalo
Buffalo, NY

Suriano, Joseph P
Kent St Univ Kent
Cmps
Kent, OH

Suris-Fernandez, Ramon
Inter Amer Univ Pr San
Juan
Hato Rey, PR

Surti, Suleman
Oh Wesleyan Univ
Delaware, OH

Suski, Bobbi J
Middle Tn St Univ
Murfreesboro, TN

Sutherland, Anna Mae
Hudson Valley Comm
Coll
Troy, NY

Suttles, Steven D
Univ Of Nc At
Asheville
Asheville, NC

Sutton, Claire E
Elmira Coll
Elmira, NY

Suzuki, Benjamin K
Syracuse Univ
Syracuse, NY

Suzuki, Kazufumi
Fl Atlantic Univ
Boca Raton, FL

Swain, Malinda J
Blue Mountain Coll
Blue Mountain, MS

Swann, Tonya L
Bowie St Univ
Bowie, MD

Swanson, Warren J
Cornell Univ
Ithaca, NY

Swartz, Karen E
Univ Of Cin R Walters
Coll
Blue Ash, OH

Sweeney, Cheryl R
Univ Of Toledo
Toledo, OH

Sweeney, James P
Davis & Elkins Coll
Elkins, WV

Sweeny, Michelle S
Wagner Coll
Staten Island, NY

Sweet, Barbara A
Ma Inst Of Tech
Cambridge, MA

Sweeten, Richard J
Atlantic Comm Coll
Mays Landing, NJ

Swift, Michele L
Bay Path Coll
Longmeadow, MA

Swiger, Lisa R
Marshall University
Huntington, WV

Swindler, Andrea Y
Johnson C Smith Univ
Charlotte, NC

Switzer, Eric A
George Mason Univ
Fairfax, VA

Sy, Lamine Mademba
Central St Univ
Wilberforce, OH

Syed, Ahmed R
Old Dominion Univ
Norfolk, VA

Sykes, Autumn M
Indian River Comm Coll
Fort Pierce, FL

Sykes, Chenoa A
Univ Of Cincinnati
Cincinnati, OH

Sykes, Heather L
Univ Of Ga
Athens, GA

Sylvester, Denay A
Albright Coll
Reading, PA

Sylvia, Suzanne R
Univ Of Al At
Huntsville
Huntsville, AL

Tabor, Michele A
Hudson Valley Comm
Coll
Troy, NY

Tai, Edward R
Cornell Univ Statutory
College
Ithaca, NY

Takacs, Teresa A
Univ Of Akron
Akron, OH

Takada, Tadashi
Univ Of Miami
Coral Gables, FL

Takei, Stephen M
Schenectady County
Comm Coll
Schenectady, NY

Takeuchi, Momoe
Univ Of Sc At
Spartanburg
Spartanburg, SC

Tallent, Vanessa G
Tn Tech Univ
Cookeville, TN

Talley, Tracy J
Univ Of Akron
Akron, OH

Tallman, Deidra L
Univ Of Tn At Martin
Martin, TN

Tamburello, Kristin
City Univ Of Ny
Baruch Coll
New York, NY

Tang, Lei
Univ Of Rochester
Rochester, NY

Tang, Wei
Jersey City St Coll
Jersey City, NJ

Tangora, Christina M
Univ Of Miami
Coral Gables, FL

Tanner, Sabrina K
Alcorn St Univ
Lorman, MS

Tannouse, Edward B
Univ Of Rochester
Rochester, NY

Tanski, Tonimarie
Wagner Coll
Staten Island, NY

Tantum, Stacy L
Tufts Univ
Medford, MA

Tao, Chang Chun
City Univ Of Ny Med
Evers Coll
Brooklyn, NY

Tapscott, Donetta R
Morgan St Univ
Baltimore, MD

Tar Jr, Paul
Sacred Heart Univ
Fairfield, CT

Tarczy, Janet M
Edinboro Univ Of Pa
Edinboro, PA

Tate, Jerona N
Univ Of Sc At
Columbia
Columbia, SC

Tatum, Kwame I
Lincoln Univ
Lincoln Univ, PA

Tatum, Steven D
Radford Univ
Radford, VA

Taurman, Ralph L
Syracuse Univ
Syracuse, NY

Tauro, Lori Ann
Univ Of Akron
Akron, OH

Tavares, Glynis A
Univ Of Miami
Coral Gables, FL

Tavares, Jose R
City Univ Of Ny Hostos
Coll
Bronx, NY

Taylor, Alliniece G
Fl A & M Univ
Tallahassee, FL

Taylor, Alva Douglas
Eastern Ky Univ
Richmond, KY

Taylor, Angela D
Univ Of Ky
Lexington, KY

Taylor IV, Clarence O
Univ Of Ga
Athens, GA

Taylor, Danielle R
S U N Y Coll Of A &
T Morrisvl
Morrisville, NY

Taylor, Delphia
Univ Of Sc At
Salkehatchie
Allendale, SC

Taylor, Donna Lea
Univ Of Sc At
Columbia
Columbia, SC

Taylor V, George P
Univ Of Tn At
Knoxville
Knoxville, TN

Taylor, Gregory Scot
Milligan Coll
Milligan Clg, TN

Taylor, James J
Barry Univ
Miami, FL

Taylor Jr, James R
Univ Of Sc At
Columbia
Columbia, SC

Taylor, Jason D
Bowling Green St Univ
At Huron
Huron, OH

Taylor, Jennifer A
Southwest Va Comm
Coll
Richlands, VA

Taylor, Joann M
Univ Of
Cincinnati-Clrmnt Coll
Batavia, OH

Taylor, Julia G
Roane St Comm Coll
Harriman, TN

Taylor, Kara L
Univ Of Sc At
Columbia
Columbia, SC

Taylor, Lance D
Belmont Coll
Nashville, TN

Taylor, Margaret E
Univ Of Tn At Martin
Martin, TN

Taylor, Mariette F
Nova Univ
Ft Lauderdale, FL

Taylor, Nichell J
Clark Atlanta Univ
Atlanta, GA

Taylor, Spamvetta T
Johnson C Smith Univ
Charlotte, NC

Taylor, Stephanie G
Univ Of Miami
Coral Gables, FL

Taylor, Tammy A
Radford Univ
Radford, VA

Taylor, Teena Y
Washington State
Comm Coll
Marietta, OH

Taylor, Tiffany L
Univ Of Central Fl
Orlando, FL

Taylor, Zane A
Greenville Tech Coll
Greenville, SC

Teague, Evelyn F
Al A & M Univ
Normal, AL

Tee, Elaine Y
Hofstra Univ
Hempstead, NY

Tejeda Mercado, Jocelyn
Inter Amer Univ Pr San
German
San German, PR

Teller, R Jeffrey
Wilmington Coll
New Castle, DE

Teneralli, Christine A
Univ Of Sc At
Columbia
Columbia, SC

Tenney, Lisa A
Hudson Valley Comm
Coll
Troy, NY

Tenny, Rashida
Ny Univ
New York, NY

Tepper, David A
Princeton Univ
Princeton, NJ

Terry, Donyelle R
Va St Univ
Petersburg, VA

Tershana, Daniel E
Atlantic Comm Coll
Mays Landing, NJ

Tesik, Michael A
Manhattan Coll
Bronx, NY

Tessmer, Zach P
Oh Univ
Athens, OH

Testone, Andrea L
Syracuse Univ
Syracuse, NY

Teter, Juanita R
Davis & Elkins Coll
Elkins, WV

Thai, Kwan Y
County Coll Of Morris
Randolph, NJ

Thaler, Clifford
City Univ Of Ny
Baruch Coll
New York, NY

Thames, Michelle Renee
Barry Univ
Miami, FL

Thames, Scarlette Y
Calcote
Univ Of Southern Ms
Hattiesburg, MS

Thayer, John H
Fl International Univ
Miami, FL

Theis, Christina M
Univ Of Central Fl
Orlando, FL

Theodossakos,
Antoinette
Fl Atlantic Univ
Boca Raton, FL

Theroux, Kimberly K
Bay Path Coll
Longmeadow, MA

Therrien, Robin E
Elms Coll
Chicopee, MA

Thew, Stacey L
Bard Coll
Annandle-Hdsn, NY

Thiel, Emma L
Univ Of Med &
Dentistry Of Nj
Newark, NJ

Thomas, Aaron S
Lynchburg Coll
Lynchburg, VA

Thomas, Adrian S
Anderson Coll
Anderson, SC

Thomas, Alison L
Univ Of Louisville
Louisville, KY

Thomas, Gary D
Hudson Valley Comm Coll
Troy, NY

Thomas, Joy M
Bob Jones Univ
Greenville, SC

Thomas, Kevin D
Va St Univ
Petersburg, VA

Thomas, Kimberly L
Al A & M Univ
Normal, AL

Thomas, Leslie Dione
Al St Univ
Montgomery, AL

Thomas, Maritzel O
Saint Petersburg Jr Coll
St Petersburg, FL

Thomas, Mickey L
Brevard Coll
Brevard, NC

Thomas, Nancy D
Bristol Univ
Bristol, TN

Thomas, Robert L
Castleton St Coll
Castleton, VT

Thomas, Roy A
Miami Dade Comm Coll North
Miami, FL

Thomas, Sharla R
Va St Univ
Petersburg, VA

Thomas, Tammy L
Central Al Comm Coll
Alexander City, AL

Thomas, Tracy L
Univ Of Cincinnati
Cincinnati, OH

Thomas, Tricia A
Norfolk St Univ
Norfolk, VA

Thomas-Roman, Frances Estel
Inter Amer Univ Pr Aquadilla
Aguadilla, PR

Thomison, Felecia D
Middle Tn St Univ
Murfreesboro, TN

Thompson, Andrea L
Pa St Univ Main Cmps
University Pk, PA

Thompson, Carlyle Van
City Univ Of Ny City Coll
New York, NY

Thompson, Caron J
Central Fl Comm Coll
Ocala, FL

Thompson, Christopher
Saint Catharine Coll
St Catharine, KY

Thompson, Craig A
Univ Of Southern Ms
Hattiesburg, MS

Thompson, Dana N
Lincoln Univ
Lincoln Univ, PA

Thompson, Dawn Renee
Methodist Coll
Fayetteville, NC

Thompson, Eileen Hegarty
Saint Thomas Univ
Miami, FL

Thompson, Fay V
City Univ Of Ny Med Evers Coll
Brooklyn, NY

Thompson, Gail R
Savannah Coll Of Art & Design
Savannah, GA

Thompson Jr, James A
Univ Of Akron
Akron, OH

Thompson, John Marcus
Ma Inst Of Tech
Cambridge, MA

Thompson, John Tyler
North Greenville Coll
Tigerville, SC

Thompson, Kelly L
Mary Washington Coll
Fredericksburg, VA

Thompson, Kevin
Gallaudet Univ
Washington, DC

Thompson, Kim E
Comm Coll Algny Co Algny Cmps
Pittsburgh, PA

Thompson, Victoria P
Ga St Univ
Atlanta, GA

Thorisdottir, Pala
Univ Of Sc At Columbia
Columbia, SC

Thornburg, Mary K
Univ Of Southern Ms
Hattiesburg, MS

Thorpe, Jennifer D
Harcum Jr Coll
Bryn Mawr, PA

Thorpe, Lisa M
Univ Of Pittsburgh At Bradford
Bradford, PA

Thrash, Pamela D
Univ Of Ms Medical Center
Jackson, MS

Thurman, Horace L
Interdenominational Theo Ctr
Atlanta, GA

Thurman, Lucinda Ann
Univ Of Louisville
Louisville, KY

Thurman, Ralph A
Christopher Newport Coll
Newport News, VA

Tidwell, Deborah R
Strayer Coll
Washington, DC

Tidwell, Stephanie M
Liberty Univ
Lynchburg, VA

Tiernan, Karen M
Newbury Coll
Brookline, MA

Tiffany, Sheryl L
S U N Y At Buffalo
Buffalo, NY

Tignor, Tammy D
Univ Of Va Clinch Valley Coll
Wise, VA

Tillery, Loretta
Cheyney Univ Of Pa
Cheyney, PA

Tilley, Michael S
Univ Of Al At Birmingham
Birmingham, AL

Tillman, Nichole K
Va St Univ
Petersburg, VA

Timko, Kimberly A
Marshall University
Huntington, WV

Tingle, Shara D
Midway Coll
Midway, KY

Tinsley, Barbara L
Univ Of Cincinnati
Cincinnati, OH

Tio, Jose A
Univ Of Pr Cayey Univ Coll
Cayey, PR

Tirado, Mayra E
Glassboro St Coll
Glassboro, NJ

Tischer, Heidi C
Salisbury St Univ
Salisbury, MD

Tissandier, Michael D
Univ Of Dayton
Dayton, OH

Titkos, Henrietta
City Univ Of Ny Queensbrough
New York, NY

To, Doris H
City Univ Of Ny City Coll
New York, NY

Tobierre, Cheryl M
Inter Amer Univ Pr San German
San German, PR

Tobin, Kimberly A
Temple Univ
Philadelphia, PA

Todd, Deborah M
Middle Tn St Univ
Murfreesboro, TN

Tokayer, Amiel Y
Yeshiva Univ
New York, NY

Tola, Daisy J
S U N Y Coll Of Tech At Frmgdl
Farmingdale, NY

Toledo Garcia, Aixa E
Univ Of Pr Cayey Univ Coll
Cayey, PR

Toledo, Elisa G
Fl International Univ
Miami, FL

Tollison, Veronica L
Univ Of Sc At Columbia
Columbia, SC

Tolliver, Darryl C
Morehouse Coll
Atlanta, GA

Tonarelli, Alessandro O
Fl International Univ
Miami, FL

Toney, Christina N
George Mason Univ
Fairfax, VA

Tong, Yuen Yi
City Univ Of Ny City Coll
New York, NY

Toppin, Stacy E
Univ Of Southern Ms
Hattiesburg, MS

Tornabene, Patricia A
D Youville Coll
Buffalo, NY

Torney, Della Teresa
Bowie St Univ
Bowie, MD

Toro, Evelyn
Univ Of Pr At Mayaguez
Mayaguez, PR

Torres Garcia, Daina J
Univ Politecnica De Pr
Hato Rey, PR

Torres Garcia, Marisol
Inter Amer Univ Pr San German
San German, PR

Torres Gelpi, Carol P
Univ Of Pr Cayey Univ Coll
Cayey, PR

Torres Perez, Christine
Inter Amer Univ Pr Hato Rey
Hato Rey, PR

Torres Vazquez, Senen
Univ Of Pr At Mayaguez
Mayaguez, PR

Torres, Ana L
Univ Of Pr At Rio Piedras
Rio Piedras, PR

Torres, Daisy
Tn Temple Univ
Chattanooga, TN

Torres, Ivelisse
Univ Of Pr At Mayaguez
Mayaguez, PR

Torres, Juan R
Univ Politecnica De Pr
Hato Rey, PR

Torres, Keila E
Univ Of Pr At Rio
Piedras
Rio Piedras, PR

Torres, Noraymar
Univ Of Pr At Rio
Piedras
Rio Piedras, PR

Torres, Victor M Bonilla
Catholic Univ Of Pr
Ponce, PR

Torres-Morin, Maria L
Univ Of Pr Medical
Sciences
San Juan, PR

Totaro, Dana
Neumann Coll
Aston, PA

Toth, Candace M
Duquesne Univ
Pittsburgh, PA

Touchette, Alice R
Newbury Coll
Brookline, MA

Toukmaji, Sameer
Yakob
Univ Of Nc At
Charlotte
Charlotte, NC

Toumanidis, Maria
S U N Y Coll Of Tech
At Delhi
Delhi, NY

Toutaint, Michelle L
Thomas Nelson Comm
Coll
Hampton, VA

Tovar, Yvonne
City Univ Of Ny
Baruch Coll
New York, NY

Tower, Jean M
Fl International Univ
Miami, FL

Townsend, Loren B
East Central Comm Coll
Decatur, MS

Townsend, Mervice M
Al A & M Univ
Normal, AL

Trabue, Cathy C
Ky St Univ
Frankfort, KY

Trabue, Simeyon C
Central St Univ
Wilberforce, OH

Tran, Ha-Phuong T
Univ Of Va
Charlottesville, VA

Tran, Hien H
Temple Univ
Philadelphia, PA

Tranum, Traci Nanine
Southern Coll Of Tech
Marietta, GA

Trapp, Crystal C
Allen Univ
Columbia, SC

Trasande, Leonardo
Harvard Univ
Cambridge, MA

Travis, Theodore A
Al St Univ
Montgomery, AL

Travitt, Kenneth O
Morehouse Coll
Atlanta, GA

Traylor, George T
Point Park Coll
Pittsburgh, PA

Trelease, Lisa M
Salisbury St Univ
Salisbury, MD

Trias, Fernando
Univ Of Miami
Coral Gables, FL

Tribble, Ahsha N
Fl A & M Univ
Tallahassee, FL

Trien, Ellen M
William Paterson Coll
Wayne, NJ

Tripathi, Meenakshi
City Univ Of Ny
Baruch Coll
New York, NY

Tripoli, Vallyre Rose
Univ Of Nc At
Asheville
Asheville, NC

Tromza, Randy D
Southern Coll Of Tech
Marietta, GA

Trotman, Alvin L
City Univ Of Ny Med
Evers Coll
Brooklyn, NY

Trovinger Jr, Kenneth P
Westminster Coll
New Wilmingtn, PA

Troxler, Linda D
Univ Of Tn At Martin
Martin, TN

Trudgeon, Krista R
Roberts Wesleyan Coll
Rochester, NY

Trueba, Janine M
Saint Thomas Univ
Miami, FL

Trundy, Jenny S
Wv Univ
Morgantown, WV

Tsahalis, Michael
City Univ Of Ny Med
Evers Coll
Brooklyn, NY

Tsai, Kuhn-Shen
Harvard Univ
Cambridge, MA

Tsarfati, Jonathan H
Fl Atlantic Univ
Boca Raton, FL

Tse, Patrick C
Ga Inst Of Tech At
Atlanta
Atlanta, GA

Tsung, Eric F
Univ Of Rochester
Rochester, NY

Tubb, Julie D
Middle Tn St Univ
Murfreesboro, TN

Tuck, Derrick D
Gadsden St Comm Coll
Gadsden, AL

Tucker, Cynthia H
Richard Bland Coll
Petersburg, VA

Tucker, Jodee Tehani
Univ Of North Fl
Jacksonville, FL

Tucker, Leslie A
Life Coll
Marietta, GA

Tucker, Pamela T
Univ Of Southern Ms
Hattiesburg, MS

Tucker, Philip F
Fl A & M Univ
Tallahassee, FL

Tucker, Susan E
Union Coll
Barbourville, KY

Tumminia, Julie M
Johnson St Coll
Johnson, VT

Tummler, Mary L
Univ Of Cincinnati
Cincinnati, OH

Tunnell, Pamela W
Ny Chiropractic Coll
Glen Head, NY

Tunon De Gracia, Tania
Univ Politecnica De Pr
Hato Rey, PR

Tunstall-Evans, Gianneli
Vance Granville Comm Coll
Henderson, NC

Turcotte, Leah E
Ms St Univ
Miss State, MS

Turnali, M Kaan
Widener Univ
Chester, PA

Turner, Gloria
City Univ Of Ny
Baruch Coll
New York, NY

Turner, Janet Ann M
Radford Univ
Radford, VA

Turner, John Bryan
Ashland Comm Coll
Ashland, KY

Turner, Joni E
Univ Of Cin R Walters Coll
Blue Ash, OH

Turner, Justica Lakisha
Al St Univ
Montgomery, AL

Turner, Kadeejia A
Univ Of Md At Eastern Shore
Princess Anne, MD

Turner, Patricia Anzella
Norfolk St Univ
Norfolk, VA

Turner, Sharon L
Al A & M Univ
Normal, AL

Turner, Tammy A
Auburn Univ At Auburn
Auburn, AL

Turner, Terri M
Western Piedmont Comm Coll
Morganton, NC

Turpel, Maureen E
D Youville Coll
Buffalo, NY

Turpin, C Kaye
Univ Of Ky
Lexington, KY

Tustin, William M
Comm Coll Algny Co Algny Cmps
Pittsburgh, PA

Tuszynska, Barbara B
S U N Y At Buffalo
Buffalo, NY

Tuteja, Charanjeet K
Univ Of Al At Birmingham
Birmingham, AL

Tuttle, Andrew C
Tn Temple Univ
Chattanooga, TN

Tyndall, Lawrence P
Ms St Univ
Miss State, MS

Tynes, Norman M
Hampton Univ
Hampton, VA

Tyre, Chris J
Central St Univ
Wilberforce, OH

Tyrell, Teresa
Wagner Coll
Staten Island, NY

Tyson, Ivy A
Univ Of Nc At Charlotte
Charlotte, NC

Uehara, Takae
Manor Jr Coll
Jenkintown, PA

Ulisse, Christopher K
Christopher Newport Coll
Newport News, VA

Ulloa, Leonardo E
Borough Of Manhattan Comm Coll
New York, NY

Underwood, John R
Ms St Univ
Miss State, MS

Underwood, Judith Lynn
Volunteer St Comm Coll
Gallatin, TN

Unger, Adrian R
Radford Univ
Radford, VA

Upton Jr, Donald R
Ga Inst Of Tech At
Atlanta
Atlanta, GA

Urand, Ruth F
Univ Of Nc At
Asheville
Asheville, NC

Urbansky, Edward T
Allegheny Coll
Meadville, PA

Urlaub, Allison B
Westminster Coll
New Wilmingtn, PA

Usko, Sherri L
Duquesne Univ
Pittsburgh, PA

Uus, Charles R
Univ Of Miami
Coral Gables, FL

Uwalaka, Lilian C
Tuskegee Univ
Tuskegee Inst, AL

Vadala, Anthony
S U N Y Coll Of Tech
At Frmgdl
Farmingdale, NY

Vago, Kimberly A
Wv Univ
Morgantown, WV

Vahlenkamp, Hans
Trenton St Coll
Trenton, NJ

Vahlenkamp, Henning
Trenton St Coll
Trenton, NJ

Valcourt, Scott A
Saint Anselm Coll
Manchester, NH

Valedon, Alexis D
Catholic Univ Of Pr
Ponce, PR

Valencia, Henry
Atlantic Comm Coll
Mays Landing, NJ

Valentin Figueroa,
Frank Edgar
Univ Of Pr Cayey Univ
Coll
Cayey, PR

Valentin-Rios, Jeanette
Catholic Univ Of Pr
Ponce, PR

Valentine, Loriann T
Marywood Coll
Scranton, PA

Valentine, Scott A
S U N Y Coll Of Tech
At Delhi
Delhi, NY

Valiente Alvarez,
Lyanette M
Inter Amer Univ Pr
Hato Rey
Hato Rey, PR

Vallarino, Juan C
Fl International Univ
Miami, FL

Vallarino, Roberto E
Fl International Univ
Miami, FL

Vallon, Marie J
City Univ Of Ny
Queensbrough
New York, NY

Van Abel, Kelley M
Catawba Valley Comm
Coll
Hickory, NC

Van Brunt, Jennifer L
Davis & Elkins Coll
Elkins, WV

Van De Wal, Brian J
Hudson Valley Comm
Coll
Troy, NY

Van Mater, Margaret R
Anne Arundel Comm
Coll
Arnold, MD

Van Voorthuizen-Gobel,
Sylvia
George Mason Univ
Fairfax, VA

Vance Jr, Jesse B
Nova Univ
Ft Lauderdale, FL

Vance, Sherry L
Comm Coll Algny Co
Algny Cmps
Pittsburgh, PA

Vandell, Michele M
Univ Of Med &
Dentistry Of Nj
Newark, NJ

Vanderlugt, Godfried J
Fl International Univ
Miami, FL

Vanover, Amy L
Western Ky Univ
Bowling Green, KY

Varagiannis, Veronica
Manhattanville Coll
Purchase, NY

Varevice, Susan
Philadelphia Coll Pharm
& Sci
Philadelphia, PA

Vargas Perez, Sol M
Inter Amer Univ Pr San
German
San German, PR

Vargas, Diana Yanira
Inter Amer Univ Pr San
German
San German, PR

Vargas, Francisco J
Univ Politecnica De Pr
Hato Rey, PR

Vargas, Marissa E
Inter Amer Univ Pr San
German
San German, PR

Vargas, Ruth M
Univ Of Pr At Rio
Piedras
Rio Piedras, PR

Vargas, Vivianne Marie
Univ Of Pr Cayey Univ
Coll
Cayey, PR

Varghese, Sam
Berkeley Coll Of
Westchester
White Plains, NY

Varney, Lisa M
Univ Of Cin R Walters Coll
Blue Ash, OH

Vasquez, Carlos R
George Mason Univ
Fairfax, VA

Vasquez, Michelle L
Glassboro St Coll
Glassboro, NJ

Vassilas, George N
Columbia Union Coll
Takoma Park, MD

Vaughan, Wendi K
Univ Of Al At Birmingham
Birmingham, AL

Vawter, Christy R
Union Univ
Jackson, TN

Vazquez Lopez, Aida L
Inter Amer Univ Pr Guayama
Guayama, PR

Vazquez Lopez, Teresa
Univ Of Pr Medical Sciences
San Juan, PR

Vazquez Urquia, Rafael
Inter Amer Univ Pr San German
San German, PR

Vazquez Velez, Mildred
Univ Of Pr At Rio Piedras
Rio Piedras, PR

Vazquez, Carlos Rafael
Univ Central Del Caribe
Cayey, PR

Vazquez, Carmen L
Touro Coll
New York, NY

Vazquez, Jose R
Univ Of Miami
Coral Gables, FL

Vazquez, Olga M
Univ Of Miami
Coral Gables, FL

Vazquez, Valerie C
Fl International Univ
Miami, FL

Veach, Cheryl A
Ashland Comm Coll
Ashland, KY

Veazey, Dalinda L
Spartanburg Methodist Coll
Spartanburg, SC

Vega Rivera, Gerardo
Univ Politecnica De Pr
Hato Rey, PR

Vega Suarez, Carlos G
Univ Politecnica De Pr
Hato Rey, PR

Vega, Ernesty
Inter Amer Univ Pr Hato Rey
Hato Rey, PR

Vega, Frank
Inter Amer Univ Pr Hato Rey
Hato Rey, PR

Vega, Sonia R
Univ Of Pr Medical Sciences
San Juan, PR

Velasquez, John J
Hudson County Comm Coll
Jersey City, NJ

Velazquez Bulted, Ruth
Caribbean Univ
Bayamon, PR

Velazquez, Victoria C Rosa
Inter Amer Univ Pr Hato Rey
Hato Rey, PR

Velez Mari, Rosa M
Inter Amer Univ Pr San German
San German, PR

Velez, Janet I
Univ Of Pr At Rio Piedras
Rio Piedras, PR

Velez, Pablo R
Fl International Univ
Miami, FL

Venditti, Dean Augustine
Fayetteville St Univ
Fayetteville, NC

Vendrell, Susie
Duquesne Univ
Pittsburgh, PA

Venezia, Christopher G
Dowling Coll
Oakdale Li, NY

Venord, Jean M
Bloomfield Coll
Bloomfield, NJ

Venters, Norman R
Coker Coll
Hartsville, SC

Ventura, Joaquin A
Bunker Hill Comm Coll
Boston, MA

Vera, Ana A
Catholic Univ Of Pr
Ponce, PR

Verbil, Anna Marie J
Saint Josephs Coll New York
Brooklyn, NY

Verdugo, Antonio
Fl International Univ
Miami, FL

Vereen, Calprunia D
Hillsborough Comm Coll
Tampa, FL

Vernon, Shane F G
Nova Univ
Ft Lauderdale, FL

Verrengia, Cynthia S
City Univ Of Ny Grad School
New York, NY

Verruso, Sharie Mercedes
Lesley Coll
Cambridge, MA

Vessels, David W
Univ Of Louisville
Louisville, KY

Vest, Kirsten M
Radford Univ
Radford, VA

Vetman, Michael I
Kent St Univ Kent
Cmps
Kent, OH

Veytsman, Natasha V
Va Commonwealth Univ
Richmond, VA

Viar, Justin D
Wv Inst Of Tech
Montgomery, WV

Vibbert, Judy D
Hillsborough Comm
Coll
Tampa, FL

Viera Barbosa, Yanira
Inter Amer Univ Pr San
Juan
Hato Rey, PR

Vig, Manish
Univ Of Rochester
Rochester, NY

Vigeant Jr, Norman P
Saint Josephs Coll
Windham, ME

Viglas, Georgia
Boston Univ
Boston, MA

Villalobos, Bertha
Patricia
Western Ky Univ
Bowling Green, KY

Villanueva, Miguel A
Embry Riddle
Aeronautical Univ
Daytona Beach, FL

Villar, Marina M
Fl International Univ
Miami, FL

Vinas, Joaquin M
Fl International Univ
Miami, FL

Vincenti-Ortiz, Melissa
Inter Amer Univ Pr
Hato Rey
Hato Rey, PR

Vingelis, Danielle S
Gallaudet Univ
Washington, DC

Vinglas, Roberta J
Saint Francis Coll
Loretto, PA

Virdi, Amandeep S
Hamilton Coll
Clinton, NY

Virick, Sandi S
Univ Of South Fl
Tampa, FL

Vishton, Paige A
Univ Of Sc At
Columbia
Columbia, SC

Vitale, Tracie A
Lasell Coll
Newton, MA

Vitello, Vincent P
Widener Univ
Chester, PA

Vitti, Cynthia L
Univ Of New Haven
West Haven, CT

Vo, Nguyet Le
Univ Of Tn At
Chattanooga
Chattanooga, TN

Vogel, Julie M
Fl Atlantic Univ
Boca Raton, FL

Vogel, Karen A
Franklin And Marshall
Coll
Lancaster, PA

Voiles, Sherri M
Tusculum Coll
Greeneville, TN

Von Goerres, Cindy
Ingram
Wilmington Coll
New Castle, DE

Von Stein, Jeffrey A
Univ Of Fl
Gainesville, FL

Voris, Sherry E
Gaston Coll
Dallas, NC

Vowell, Denise R
Univ Of Va Clinch
Valley Coll
Wise, VA

Vronick, Efimia E
Univ Of Akron
Akron, OH

Vu, Thu-Huong T
Howard Univ
Washington, DC

Vuelta, Shaorn R
Univ Of Miami
Coral Gables, FL

Vulin, Donna S
Manhattan Coll
Bronx, NY

Vuong, Cuong
S U N Y Coll Of Tech
At Delhi
Delhi, NY

Waddell Jr, Michael L
Memphis St Univ
Memphis, TN

Wade, Adam
Ga Inst Of Tech At
Atlanta
Atlanta, GA

Wade, Ronald S
Univ Of Sc At
Columbia
Columbia, SC

Wadsworth III, Edwin T
Fl St Univ
Tallahassee, FL

Wagner, Brent M
Temple Univ
Philadelphia, PA

Walden, Lori L
Sue Bennett Coll
London, KY

Waldermar, Berrios
Anaya
Inter Amer Univ Pr
Hato Rey
Hato Rey, PR

Walker, Amy Guinn
Roane St Comm Coll
Harriman, TN

Walker, Carol R
Vanderbilt Univ
Nashville, TN

Walker, Chantay C
Fisk Univ
Nashville, TN

Walker, Charles R
Ms St Univ
Miss State, MS

Walker, Dana S
Univ Of Sc At Columbia
Columbia, SC

Walker, Daphne M
Spelman Coll
Atlanta, GA

Walker, Ernest L
Vance Granville Comm Coll
Henderson, NC

Walker, Jacinth R
City Univ Of Ny City Coll
New York, NY

Walker, Janice I
City Univ Of Ny Med Evers Coll
Brooklyn, NY

Walker, Jennifer D
Roane St Comm Coll
Harriman, TN

Walker, Karen D
Christopher Newport Coll
Newport News, VA

Walker, Kimberly G
Radford Univ
Radford, VA

Walker, Melissa L
Ashland Comm Coll
Ashland, KY

Walker, Natalie A
Middle Tn St Univ
Murfreesboro, TN

Walker, Noralee A
Wellesley Coll
Wellesley, MA

Walker, Robert D
Va St Univ
Petersburg, VA

Walker, Ronald
Lexington Comm Coll
Lexington, KY

Walker, Shannon A
Stetson Univ
Deland, FL

Walker, Thomas R
Comm Coll Algny Co Algny Cmps
Pittsburgh, PA

Wall, Bessie S
Daytona Beach Comm Coll
Daytona Beach, FL

Wallace, Ariyan S
Broward Comm Coll
Ft Lauderdale, FL

Wallace, Bobbi L
Longwood Coll
Farmville, VA

Wallace, Cristy A
Brewer St Jr Coll
Fayette, AL

Wallace, Dawn E
Wilmington Coll
New Castle, DE

Wallace, Mark A
Columbia Greene Comm Coll
Hudson, NY

Wallace, Tawanda L
Nc Agri & Tech St Univ
Greensboro, NC

Wallace, Wendy L
Christian Brothers Univ
Memphis, TN

Walls, Deborah M
Univ Of North Fl
Jacksonville, FL

Walls, Ginger E
Wallace St Comm Coll At Dothan
Dothan, AL

Walorz, Erik T
Newbury Coll
Brookline, MA

Walsh, Jason M
Saint Francis Coll
Loretto, PA

Walsh, Justin M
Saint Francis Coll
Loretto, PA

Walsh, Suzanne E
Hudson Valley Comm Coll
Troy, NY

Walter, Daniel J
S U N Y Coll Of Tech At Alfred
Alfred, NY

Walter, Kristina M
Coll Of Charleston
Charleston, SC

Walters, Susan R
George Mason Univ
Fairfax, VA

Walthour, La Tonya A
Fl A & M Univ
Tallahassee, FL

Walton III, John R
Fl St Univ
Tallahassee, FL

Walton, Kimberly J
Allegheny Coll
Meadville, PA

Wang, Guangxi
Univ Of Al At Birmingham
Birmingham, AL

Wang, Yang
Coll Of Insurance
New York, NY

Wang, Yin Kei
City Univ Of Ny City Coll
New York, NY

Ward, Beverley J
Univ Of
Cincinnati-Clrmnt Coll
Batavia, OH

Ward, Mia A
Alcorn St Univ
Lorman, MS

Ward, Theresa A
Houghton Coll
Houghton, NY

Warde, Hortense A
City Univ Of Ny Med
Evers Coll
Brooklyn, NY

Warden, Angie R
Univ Of Southern Ms
Hattiesburg, MS

Ware, Karen R
Daytona Beach Comm
Coll
Daytona Beach, FL

Warner, Cleophas B
Columbia Union Coll
Takoma Park, MD

Warner, Denise L
Georgetown Univ
Washington, DC

Warner, Wendy P
Univ Of The Dist Of
Columbia
Washington, DC

Warren, Antoinette
Smith
Fayetteville St Univ
Fayetteville, NC

Warren, Jeffrey W
Limestone Coll
Gaffney, SC

Warren, Kenneth S
S U N Y Coll At
Fredonia
Fredonia, NY

Warren, Sherri H
Asheville Bunc Tech
Comm Coll
Asheville, NC

Warren, Teresa L
Al St Univ
Montgomery, AL

Warsama, Amina N
Univ Of New Haven
West Haven, CT

Washburn, Rachel H
Tn St Univ
Nashville, TN

Washington, Angela R
Coahoma Comm Coll
Clarksdale, MS

Washington, Cerise D
Hampton Univ
Hampton, VA

Washington, De Lois
Fayetteville St Univ
Fayetteville, NC

Washington, Dewayne A
Norfolk St Univ
Norfolk, VA

Washington, Grace
Roberta
Interdenominational
Theo Ctr
Atlanta, GA

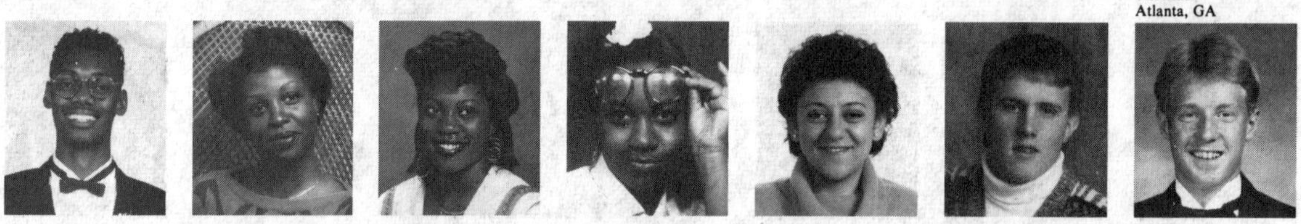

Washington, Keadrick D
Al A & M Univ
Normal, AL

Washington, Ruby J
Tallahassee Comm Coll
Tallahassee, FL

Washington, Senta R
Al St Univ
Montgomery, AL

Washington, Tiffany D
Comm Coll Algny Co
Algny Cmps
Pittsburgh, PA

Wassef, Heidi R
Ponce School Of
Medicine
Ponce, PR

Wasson, Michael C
Me Maritime Academy
Castine, ME

Wasson, Robert J
Georgetown Coll
Georgetown, KY

Waterman, Adonna B
Wells Coll
Aurora, NY

Waters, Karyn M
George Mason Univ
Fairfax, VA

Waters, M Scott
Central Fl Comm Coll
Ocala, FL

Waters, Nicole M
Liberty Univ
Lynchburg, VA

Watkins, Donna D
Dowling Coll
Oakdale Li, NY

Watkins, Stewart J
Morehouse Coll
Atlanta, GA

Watkins Jr, Terry L
Liberty Univ
Lynchburg, VA

Watkins, William S P
Johnson C Smith Univ
Charlotte, NC

Watkins-Gibson, Teri A
Univ Of South Fl
Tampa, FL

Watley, Jefre R
Fl St Univ
Tallahassee, FL

Watson, Carol D
Fl Memorial Coll
Miami, FL

Watson, Donna L
Life Coll
Marietta, GA

Watson, Karen L
Broward Comm Coll
Ft Lauderdale, FL

Watson, Lisa M
Millersville Univ Of Pa
Millersville, PA

Watson, Monica D
Va St Univ
Petersburg, VA

Watson, Pamela L
Western New England Coll
Springfield, MA

Watson, Quanda N
Clark Atlanta Univ
Atlanta, GA

Watts, Andrea T
Commonwealth Coll
Virginia Beach, VA

Watts, Cassandra L
City Univ Of Ny Baruch Coll
New York, NY

Watts, Tresa L
Al A & M Univ
Normal, AL

Waugh, Debra L
Columbia Union Coll
Takoma Park, MD

Waugh, Trantina E
Howard Univ
Washington, DC

Waynick, Denelle J
Howard Univ
Washington, DC

Wear, Matthew E
Marshall University
Huntington, WV

Weare, Heather M
Univ Of Sc At Columbia
Columbia, SC

Weatherspoon, Melissa J
Central St Univ
Wilberforce, OH

Webb, David C
Birmingham Southern Coll
Birmingham, AL

Webb, Janet L
Ms Gulf Coast Comm Coll
Perkinston, MS

Webb, Jennifer A
Univ Of Tn At Knoxville
Knoxville, TN

Webb, Mellanie V
Wilberforce Univ
Wilberforce, OH

Webb, Monica R
Shaw Univ
Raleigh, NC

Webb, Mouda F
Fayetteville St Univ
Fayetteville, NC

Webb, Robert P
Univ Of Southern Ms
Hattiesburg, MS

Webbe, Hilary T
Univ Of The Virgin Islands
St Thomas, VI

Weber, Heidi A
Upsala Coll
East Orange, NJ

Webster, Mitchell E
Memphis St Univ
Memphis, TN

Webster, Tanya
Middle Tn St Univ
Murfreesboro, TN

Wedge, Dionne M
Univ Of Md At Eastern Shore
Princess Anne, MD

Wee, Guan-Seng
East Tn St Univ
Johnson City, TN

Weekley, Kelly N
Marshall University
Huntington, WV

Weeks, Edson Gary
Brevard Coll
Brevard, NC

Weeks, Melissa D
Memphis St Univ
Memphis, TN

Weeks, Nancy Ann
Roane St Comm Coll
Harriman, TN

Wehbe, Donna Leblanc
Le Moyne Coll
Syracuse, NY

Wehner, Sean C
Comm Coll Algny Co Algny Cmps
Pittsburgh, PA

Weinberg, Joshua D
Univ Of Pa
Philadelphia, PA

Weinbrenner, Kim M
Rutgers St Univ At Camden
Camden, NJ

Weindorf, Sally K
Kent St Univ Kent Cmps
Kent, OH

Weiner, Andrew S
Cornell Univ Statutory College
Ithaca, NY

Weinstein, Elana M
Yeshiva Univ
New York, NY

Weippert, Troy A
Embry Riddle Aeronautical Univ
Daytona Beach, FL

Weisman, Ilanna Patrice
Univ Of Sc At Columbia
Columbia, SC

Weiss, Karen Lynne
Univ Of Miami
Coral Gables, FL

Weissberg, Aaron
S U N Y At Albany
Albany, NY

Welch, Jodi L
Hudson Valley Comm Coll
Troy, NY

Welch, Kimberly S
Union Univ
Jackson, TN

Welch, Roberta R
Newbury Coll
Brookline, MA

Welch, Robin L
Univ Of Nc At Greensboro
Greensboro, NC

Welker, Christa M
Western Piedmont Comm Coll
Morganton, NC

Wellman, Donna K
Meridian Comm Coll
Meridian, MS

Wellman, Jeanine
Atlantic Union Coll
S Lancaster, MA

Wells, Cynthia A
Univ Of West Fl
Pensacola, FL

Wells, Darrell A
Longwood Coll
Farmville, VA

Wells, Jill Warren
Blue Mountain Coll
Blue Mountain, MS

Wells, Jimmy D
Birmingham Southern Coll
Birmingham, AL

Wells, Rebbecca L
Univ Of West Fl
Pensacola, FL

Wells, Shawn J
S U N Y Coll Of Tech At Canton
Canton, NY

Wells, Sonji J
Tougaloo Coll
Tougaloo, MS

Welty, James D
Westminster Coll
New Wilmingtn, PA

Weltzin, Raymond A
Inter Amer Univ Pr Hato Rey
Hato Rey, PR

Wen, Hsiu-Ting Tiana
Atlantic Comm Coll
Mays Landing, NJ

Wenzel, Lauren D
Suffolk Comm Coll Eastern Cmps
Riverhead, NY

Werner, Brian P
Old Dominion Univ
Norfolk, VA

Werner, Linda L
Univ Of Sc At Columbia
Columbia, SC

Wert, Lori A
Central Pa Bus School
Summerdale, PA

Wert, Matthew P
West Chester Univ
West Chester, PA

Wesby, Tunya D
Alcorn St Univ
Lorman, MS

West, Carol L
Va Polytechnic Inst & St Univ
Blacksburg, VA

West, Donna Raines
Memphis St Univ
Memphis, TN

West, Mike J
Univ Of Tn At Martin
Martin, TN

West, Pamela Jo
Univ Of Ky
Lexington, KY

West, Seante D
Univ Of Md At Eastern Shore
Princess Anne, MD

West, Tara V
Univ Of Sc At Columbia
Columbia, SC

Westenberger, Terry Lou
Atlantic Comm Coll
Mays Landing, NJ

Westerfield, Peter W
Nova Univ
Ft Lauderdale, FL

Weston, Cheryl A
Radford Univ
Radford, VA

Wetzel, Paula J
Wv Northern Comm Coll
Wheeling, WV

Whalen, Rebecca S
Castleton St Coll
Castleton, VT

Whaley, Bonnie A
George Washington Univ
Washington, DC

Whatley, Angel J
Ms St Univ
Miss State, MS

Wheatley, Le Jeanna D
Univ Of Tn At Martin
Martin, TN

Wheeler, Alvina J
Morris Brown Coll
Atlanta, GA

Wheeler, Dawn M
Univ Of Sc At Coastal Carolina
Conway, SC

Whetzel, Denise S
Radford Univ
Radford, VA

Whetzel Jr, Jerry W
Va Commonwealth Univ
Richmond, VA

Whinery, Dave W
Brown Univ
Providence, RI

Whisenant, Michael L
Faulkner Univ
Montgomery, AL

Whitaker, Stacy E
Coll Of Charleston
Charleston, SC

Williams, Shannon F
Univ Of Sc At Columbia
Columbia, SC

Williams, Sheri L
Alcorn St Univ
Lorman, MS

Williams, Stuart A
Univ Of Ky
Lexington, KY

Williams, Tinika M
Va St Univ
Petersburg, VA

Williams, Tracey V
Coppin St Coll
Baltimore, MD

Williams, Yolande M
Johnson C Smith Univ
Charlotte, NC

Williams, Yvetta L
Tougaloo Coll
Tougaloo, MS

Williams, Zondrah L
Memphis St Univ
Memphis, TN

Williamson, Julie N
Univ Of Nc At Charlotte
Charlotte, NC

Williamson, Koni J
Watterson Coll
Louisville, KY

Williamson, Tonya N
Youngstown St Univ
Youngstown, OH

Williamson, Tracy A
Wilmington Coll
Wilmington, OH

Willis, Andrew S
Georgetown Univ
Washington, DC

Willis, Darlene
Univ Of Cin R Walters Coll
Blue Ash, OH

Willis, Gregory A
Morehouse Coll
Atlanta, GA

Willis, Leona D
Howard Univ
Washington, DC

Willis, Marc D
Central St Univ
Wilberforce, OH

Willis, Valerie M
Fort Valley St Coll
Fort Valley, GA

Wilmot, Corey L
Atlantic Union Coll
S Lancaster, MA

Wilson, Alicia S
Shelton St Comm Coll
Tuscaloosa, AL

Wilson, Beverley R
Fl International Univ
Miami, FL

Wilson, Brenda Joy
Univ Of Cincinnati-Clrmnt Coll
Batavia, OH

Wilson, Brett E
Radford Univ
Radford, VA

Wilson, Curtisha L
Coppin St Coll
Baltimore, MD

Wilson, Darrawn A
Fl A & M Univ
Tallahassee, FL

Wilson, David Alan
Morehouse Coll
Atlanta, GA

Wilson, Eddie Sirena
Tougaloo Coll
Tougaloo, MS

Wilson, Elizabeth A
Middle Tn St Univ
Murfreesboro, TN

Wilson II, G Thomas
Howard Univ
Washington, DC

Wilson, James R
Owensboro Comm Coll
Owensboro, KY

Wilson, Kenneth B
Savannah St Coll
Savannah, GA

Wilson, Ketra L
Ms Univ For Women
Columbus, MS

Wilson, Kevin A
Barry Univ
Miami, FL

Wilson, Kristi L
Bridgewater Coll
Bridgewater, VA

Wilson, Lauri R
Ga Inst Of Tech At Atlanta
Atlanta, GA

Wilson, Lisa A
Univ Of Al At Huntsville
Huntsville, AL

Wilson, Louis A
Vance Granville Comm Coll
Henderson, NC

Wilson, Otis D
Wilmington Coll
New Castle, DE

Wilson, Robert Dirk
Greenville Tech Coll
Greenville, SC

Wilson, Scott T
Univ Of Fl
Gainesville, FL

Wilson, Tamara L
Bay Path Coll
Longmeadow, MA

Wilson, Zondra M
City Univ Of Ny Baruch Coll
New York, NY

Wiltsey Jr, Thomas
Monmouth Coll
W Long Branch, NJ

Winchester, Dietrich M
Morehouse Coll
Atlanta, GA

Windwer, Mark J
City Univ Of Ny City Coll
New York, NY

Wing, Leslie A
Western Carolina Univ
Cullowhee, NC

Wingate, Charles A
City Univ Of Ny City Coll
New York, NY

Wingate, Sonya L
Lincoln Univ
Lincoln Univ, PA

Wingfield, Rhonda Y
Morris Brown Coll
Atlanta, GA

Winkelmann Marsh, Renate A
Hillsborough Comm Coll
Tampa, FL

Winkler, Veronica Lynn
Memphis St Univ
Memphis, TN

Winstel, John D
Univ Of Cin R Walters Coll
Blue Ash, OH

Winston, Dennis D
Al A & M Univ
Normal, AL

Winston, Kevin R
Yale Univ
New Haven, CT

Winston, William B
Columbia Union Coll
Takoma Park, MD

Winter, Michelle A
Univ Of South Al
Mobile, AL

Winters, Blake A
Nova Univ
Ft Lauderdale, FL

Winters, Roy V
Hudson Valley Comm Coll
Troy, NY

Winters, Sandra A
Mayland Comm Coll
Spruce Pine, NC

Wirth, Colleen M
D Youville Coll
Buffalo, NY

Wirth, Eric T
S U N Y Coll Of Tech At Frmgdl
Farmingdale, NY

Wisdom, Jeffrey F
Austin Peay St Univ
Clarksville, TN

Wise, Cara R
Ky St Univ
Frankfort, KY

Wise, Greg R
Geneva Coll
Beaver Falls, PA

Wise, Jodie L
Juniata Coll
Huntingdon, PA

Wiseman, John D
Ashland Comm Coll
Ashland, KY

Wisniewski, Tamara E
Niagara Univ
Niagara Univ, NY

Witherington Jr, Gordon Edward
Univ Of South Al
Mobile, AL

Withers, Jacqueline R
Christopher Newport Coll
Newport News, VA

Wittman, Sandra M
Univ Of Pittsburgh
Pittsburgh, PA

Wolf, Kelly M
Fl St Univ
Tallahassee, FL

Wolfe, James E
U S Military Academy
West Point, NY

Wolfe, Michelle E
Marywood Coll
Scranton, PA

Wolfe, Tracie M
Hudson Valley Comm Coll
Troy, NY

Wolverton, Kevin D
Marshall University
Huntington, WV

Womack, Richard L
Emmanuel Coll Schl Chrstn Min
Franklin Sprg, GA

Won, Sun-Hee D
Ma Inst Of Tech
Cambridge, MA

Wong, Alice C S
The Kings Coll
Briarclf Mnr, NY

Wong, Debbie A
Coll Of Saint Elizabeth
Convent Sta, NJ

Wong-Wyatt, Cheryl L
Fayetteville St Univ
Fayetteville, NC

Woo, Hong
City Univ Of Ny La Guard Coll
Long Island Cty, NY

Wood, Angela F
Marshall University
Huntington, WV

Wood, Christina Beth
East Carolina Univ
Greenville, NC

Wood, Daniel E
Lexington Comm Coll
Lexington, KY

Wood, Daniel W
Univ Of Toledo
Toledo, OH

Wood, Heather S
Coll Of William & Mary
Williamsburg, VA

Wood, Sharon O
Dowling Coll
Oakdale Li, NY

Wood, Stefanie M
Coll Of Charleston
Charleston, SC

Wood, William David
Univ Of Cin R Walters Coll
Blue Ash, OH

Woodard, Sandra A
Central Fl Comm Coll
Ocala, FL

Wooden, Jodie M
Broward Comm Coll
Ft Lauderdale, FL

Woodrum, David A
Davidson Coll
Davidson, NC

Woods, Amelia L
Univ Of Tn At Martin
Martin, TN

Woods, Dusty G
Anderson Coll
Anderson, SC

Woods, Lynette A
Va St Univ
Petersburg, VA

Woods, Marchell L
Central St Univ
Wilberforce, OH

Woods, Melitha L
Fl St Univ
Tallahassee, FL

Woods, Richard E
Ky St Univ
Frankfort, KY

Wooledge, Steven E
Univ Of Akron
Akron, OH

Wooley, Leslye E
Hood Coll
Frederick, MD

Woolums, Michelle Renee
William Paterson Coll
Wayne, NJ

Workman, Dawn R
Univ Of Akron
Akron, OH

Worlds, Tamika C
Bloomfield Coll
Bloomfield, NJ

Worley, Ryan K
Roane St Comm Coll
Harriman, TN

Worthington, Julie S
Bristol Univ
Bristol, TN

Wray, Tanya J
Kent St Univ Kent Cmps
Kent, OH

Wright, Angela S
Univ Of Sc At Lancaster
Lancaster, SC

Wright, Audrey A
Georgian Court Coll
Lakewood, NJ

Wright, Elizabeth P
Univ Of Sc At Columbia
Columbia, SC

Wright, Pamela J
Winthrop Coll
Rock Hill, SC

Wright, Patrick L
Univ Of Sc At Columbia
Columbia, SC

Wright, Shantel E
Le Moyne Owen Coll
Memphis, TN

Wright, Tara B
Stillman Coll
Tuscaloosa, AL

Wright, Yolanda S
Nc Agri & Tech St Univ
Greensboro, NC

Wrona, James S
Oh Northern Univ
Ada, OH

Wu, Simon Zhou
Belmont Coll
Nashville, TN

Wyatt, Bryan L
Wv Univ
Morgantown, WV

Wyatt Jr, David R
Old Dominion Univ
Norfolk, VA

Wyatt, Heather L
Christopher Newport Coll
Newport News, VA

Wyatt, Samuel L
Central Al Comm Coll
Alexander City, AL

Wyche, Vanessa S R
Medical Coll Of Ga
Augusta, GA

Wyndham, Jacqueline Annette
Univ Of Md At Eastern Shore
Princess Anne, MD

Wyvill, Suzel
Southern Coll Of Tech
Marietta, GA

Yachwan, Kevin G
S U N Y At Buffalo
Buffalo, NY

Yamashita, Noriko
Saint Thomas Univ
Miami, FL

Yambor, Kimberly J
Univ Of Cincinnati
Cincinnati, OH

Yan, Frances Yeefen
City Univ Of Ny
Baruch Coll
New York, NY

Yan, Houdi
City Univ Of Ny
Baruch Coll
New York, NY

Yancey, George A
Hampton Univ
Hampton, VA

Yanez, Frances E
S U N Y Coll Of Tech
At Frmgdl
Farmingdale, NY

Yang, Woong
Oh St Univ
Columbus, OH

Yates, Kimberly Nicole
Al A & M Univ
Normal, AL

Yau, Kai Wai K
Piedmont Coll
Demorest, GA

Yau, Siew Choi
Univ Of Miami
Coral Gables, FL

Yau, Wah Lok
Clarkson Univ
Potsdam, NY

Yeager, H Todd
Pittsburgh Tech Inst
Pittsburgh, PA

Yee, Becky
Chestnut Hill Coll
Philadelphia, PA

Yee, Man-Ching Andy
City Univ Of Ny City
Coll
New York, NY

Yemba, Rosalie A
Bennett Coll
Greensboro, NC

Yen, Michael T
Univ Of Miami
Coral Gables, FL

Yeo, Gregory L G
Memphis Academy Of
The Arts
Memphis, TN

Yielding, Janelle L
Hudson Valley Comm
Coll
Troy, NY

Yokitis, Amy M
Saint Francis Coll
Loretto, PA

Yolanda, Arzola
Inter Amer Univ Pr
Barranquita
Barranquitas, PR

Yonco, Laura M
Univ Of Bridgeport
Bridgeport, CT

Yong, Leonard T
Univ Of Fl
Gainesville, FL

Yoshioka, Eriko
Abraham Baldwin Agri
Coll
Tifton, GA

Youmans III, William
Fl A & M Univ
Tallahassee, FL

Young, Andre M
Morehouse Coll
Atlanta, GA

Young, Apryl G
Lincoln Univ
Lincoln Univ, PA

Young, Brenda J
Univ Of Nh Plymouth
St Coll
Plymouth, NH

Young, David E
Oh Dominican Coll
Columbus, OH

Young, David L
Marshall University
Huntington, WV

Young, Michael D
Ms Gulf Coast Comm
Coll
Perkinston, MS

Young, Ralph C
Western Piedmont
Comm Coll
Morganton, NC

Young Jr, William Scott
Univ Of Ky
Lexington, KY

Yu, Chung-Ying S
Univ Of Sc At
Columbia
Columbia, SC

Yu, Jaime P
City Univ Of Ny
Queensbrough
New York, NY

Yu, Jihwan
Georgetown Univ
Washington, DC

Yuill, Michael J
Western New England
Coll
Springfield, MA

Zaccagnini, Robert M
Saint Vincents Coll &
Seminary
Latrobe, PA

Zagarella, Joseph R
Newbury Coll
Brookline, MA

Zagrobelny, Diane C
Univ Of Miami
Coral Gables, FL

Zak, Suzanne M
Philadelphia Coll Of
Bible
Langhorne, PA

Zakes, Deanna L
Radford Univ
Radford, VA

Zambrana, Elivette
Univ Of Pr At Rio
Piedras
Rio Piedras, PR

Zamora, Ledia T
Miami Dade Comm Coll
Miami, FL

Zamora, Maria C
Miami Dade Comm Coll
Miami, FL

Zangoui, Khatereh
Fl International Univ
Miami, FL

Zapata, Carolina M
Univ Of Miami
Coral Gables, FL

Zapata, Lourdes Marie
Inter Amer Univ Pr San German
San German, PR

Zatorski, Shirley Jo
Georgian Court Coll
Lakewood, NJ

Zayas-Lyle, Jose F
Univ Politecnica De Pr
Hato Rey, PR

Zayat, Salomon
Miami Dade Comm Coll South
Miami, FL

Zazzara, Jeffrey B
Temple Univ
Philadelphia, PA

Zbierkowska, Agata
Univ Of North Fl
Jacksonville, FL

Zebrowski, Adriane J
Daytona Beach Comm Coll
Daytona Beach, FL

Zee, Ena
City Univ Of Ny Baruch Coll
New York, NY

Zemke, Craig M
Oh Wesleyan Univ
Delaware, OH

Zeno-Pimentel, Luis Armando
Inter Amer Univ Pr Hato Rey
Hato Rey, PR

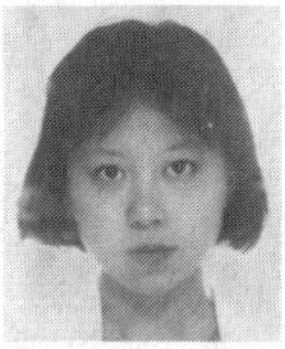
Zhang, Yun Amy
Manhattanville Coll
Purchase, NY

Zhao, Xiaofang
Univ Of Rochester
Rochester, NY

Zhou, Xue-Jing
Atlantic Union Coll
S Lancaster, MA

Zhu, Fong
Univ Of Ky
Lexington, KY

Zhu, Kai Qi
Manhattan School Of Music
New York, NY

Zibbe, Susan E
Georgian Court Coll
Lakewood, NJ

Zimmerle, Donald P
Daytona Beach Comm Coll
Daytona Beach, FL

Zimmerman, Amy L
Garrett Comm Coll
Mchenry, MD

Zimmerman, Laurie D
Frederick Comm Coll
Frederick, MD

Zito, Toni A
Richard Bland Coll
Petersburg, VA

Zivojinovic, Radovan D
Georgetown Univ
Washington, DC

Zolly, Regina M
Saint Francis Coll
Loretto, PA

Zoto, Jason S
Georgetown Univ
Washington, DC

Zuendel, Gladys Anny
Eckerd Coll
St Petersburg, FL

Zulfiqar, Asim
Nova Univ
Ft Lauderdale, FL

Zunski, Robert J
Duquesne Univ
Pittsburgh, PA

Zurko, Susan M
S U N Y Coll Of A & T Morrisvl
Morrisville, NY